NORTH CAROLINA CRIMINAL AND TRAFFIC LAW MANUAL

2021–2022 EDITION

Current through Session Laws 2021-162 of the 2021 Regular Session of the General Assembly, except for Chapter 17E of the General Statutes, as amended by Session Laws 2021-107 and 2021-136 through 2021-138, and does not reflect possible future codification directives relating to Session Laws 2020-95 through 2020-97 and 2021-1 through 2021-162 from the Revisor of Statutes pursuant to G.S. 164-10

Blue360°
Media

This publication is dedicated to the hard-working law enforcement officers who risk their lives every day to protect and serve the community.

www.blue360media.com

To contact Blue360° Media, LLC, please call: **1-844-599-2887**

ISBN: 978-1-63729-242-6

Blue360° Media, LLC
2750 Rasmussen Rd., Suite 107
Park City, Utah 84098
1-844-599-2887
www.blue360media.com

(Pub. 30547)

PREFACE

We are pleased to offer to the law enforcement community the 2021-2022 edition of **North Carolina Criminal and Traffic Law Manual.** Current through Session Laws 2021-162 of the 2021 Regular Session of the General Assembly, except for Chapter 17E of the General Statutes, as amended by Session Laws 2021-107 and 2021-136 through 2021-138, and does not reflect possible future codification directives relating to Session Laws 2020-95 through 2020-97 and 2021-1 through 2021-162 from the Revisor of Statutes pursuant to G.S. 164-10. We continue to carry a listing of Sections Affected by 2021 Legislation.

We are committed to providing law enforcement professionals with the most comprehensive, current, and useful publications possible. If you have comments and suggestions please call the Blue360° Media Publisher, 1-844-599-2887; email us at *support @blue360media.com*; or visit our website at *www.blue360media.com*. Your valuable comments help keep this publication handy and more useful every year.

Visit the Blue360° Media home page at *www.blue360media.com* for an online bookstore, technical support, customer service, and other company information.

December 2021

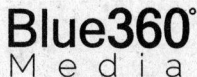

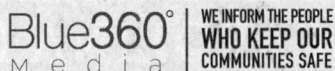

Blue360° Media — WE INFORM THE PEOPLE WHO KEEP OUR COMMUNITIES SAFE

Active Shooter Response Checklist for Patrol Officers

Since the Columbine High School (Colorado) shooting in 1999, response tactics by police to an active shooter incident have evolved. There is an ever-increasing number of active shooter events which calls for quick, effective response by police. (Complete this form and email completed version to yourself for your log or to facilitate reporting.)

Email address: _____

Case Number: _____

1. Development of an Action Plan
check all that apply

- ☐ Be aware of potential targets in your jurisdiction.
- ☐ Create a repository and access to floor plans for schools and other structures such as malls, etc.
- ☐ Conduct frequent tabletop exercises that include SWAT and all first responders such as the fire department, EMS etc.

Blue360° Media Officer Series 2020 EDITION

Preparing for an Active Shooter Threat
The Law Enforcement Response Guide

Ken Wallentine   Chris Walden

Buy Now From Blue360Media.com

2. Immediate Deployment

- ☐ Respond in emergency mode with lights and siren.
- ☐ All available officers in the area will be dispatched to the scene and should be en-route immediately advising dispatch.
- ☐ First responders will expect the school or other facility to be in a "lockdown" when they arrive.
- ☐ If any students or other bystanders are outside, move them to a safe area quickly.
- ☐ GO IMMEDIATELY AND DIRECTLY toward the sound of the gunshots or threat; DO NOT WAIT for back-up or SWAT to arrive before you enter; follow your training and agency's policies and procedures.
- ☐ Ideally, at least two officers should enter at the same time, but current training emphasizes going directly to the threat even if you are alone---follow your agency's training and protocol!
- ☐ Dispatch will follow protocol by requesting other first responders and notifying surrounding schools or other public sites of the incident to accomplish lockdown of the sites, restricting exterior access.
- ☐ Perimeters and traffic control should be set up as soon as possible.

3. Locate and Engage the Active Shooter

- ☐ Move quickly and directly toward the sound of gunshots.
- ☐ Do not stop to help injured students or others.
- ☐ If you must enter a closed room, enter quickly announcing yourself.
- ☐ Always use cover and concealment as you move through the building, move as quickly as possible—it may take only a few minutes for casualties to happen.
- ☐ Keep in mind that there may be more than one shooter in one or more different locations.
- ☐ Maintain radio contact with dispatch as much as possible but try to keep your radio at a lower volume than normal.
- ☐ When you locate the suspect, use the necessary level of force to stop the shooter, which may include deadly force to protect your life or the life of others.
- ☐ After the encounter is made with the shooter, advise of your actions and the need for the type of assistance based on your actions and on the observations you made as you came through the building.

4. Command Posts

- ☐ An initial secure, safe area should be set up as soon as possible after the responding officers are inside to stop the shooting or threat.
- ☐ Immediate and special consideration for parents who respond to the scene must be in place.
- ☐ Parents and other non-tactical personnel should be moved away from the command post to a safe venue, such as a neighboring church, school, etc. with adequate manpower to secure the area.
- ☐ Remember to have enough officers at the scene to direct traffic and maintain a perimeter.
- ☐ The process of responding to the shooter, providing emergency medical assistance, rendering the scene safe and collecting evidence may take hours. Lockdown will remain in effect during this time.
- ☐ All of these elements are normally contained in an Incident Command System (ICS) where all first responders have been trained to follow specific protocol and training. Again, rely on your training and agency protocol.

Add any other comments, information, or details for this incident.

_____
_____
_____
_____
_____

Mistakes for Active Shooter Incident

⊘ **Lack of Action Plan and Floor Plans to Potential Targets**
-No awareness and information on targets in your jurisdiction.
-No floor plans for schools, other structures, malls etc. to refer to.
-Lack of joint training with first responders from within your agency, such as specialty units, and others such as the fire department, EMS.

⊘ **Deployment**
-Lack of or miscommunication of exact direction, location, and emergency response.
-Not dispatching all available manpower and resources to the scene.
-If you are the first officer at the scene, *NOT ENTERING IMMEDIATELY* and going directly to the active shooter or other threat.
-Not setting up a perimeter, when possible, after entry to locate the threat or active shooter.

⊘ **Locating and Engaging the Active Shooter**
-Waiting for back-up officers.
-Not entering immediately.
-Stopping to help injured students or others.
-Not using "cover and concealment" as you move through the building.
-Lack of "situational awareness;" there may be more than one shooter.
-Not keeping dispatch and supervisory staff updated of the incident.

⊘ **Command Post**
- Not expediting a secure, safe area to set up a command post (ICS-Incident Command Center) with sufficient supervisors or command staff in place to coordinate emergency resources such as EMS, fire department, etc.
- Not keeping non-essential personnel away from the scene, especially concerned parents or others.

KEY U.S. SUPREME COURT CASES FOR LAW ENFORCEMENT

Jurisdictions may be more restrictive than US Supreme Court

US Constitution *Preamble*	*"We the people of the United States, in order to form a more perfect union, establish justice, insure domestic tranquility, provide for the common defense, promote the general welfare and secure the blessings of liberty to ourselves and our posterity, do ordain and establish this Constitution for the United States of America."*

	1st Amendment	Religion, Speech, Press, Public Assembly
Bill of Rights Selected Amendments	2nd Amendment	To Keep and Bear Arms
	4th Amendment	Search & Seizure
	5th Amendment	Due Process, Eminent Domain, Self-Incrimination, Grand Jury, Double Jeopardy
	6th Amendment	Speedy Trial, Informed of Accusations, Confront Accuser, Obtain Witnesses
	8th Amendment	No Excessive Bail, or Cruel & Unusual Punishment
	14th Amendment	Citizenship, Civil Rights, Due Process

1st Amendment	Religion, Speech, Press, Public Assembly
Freedom of Speech	**Political Speech - NAACP v. Claiborne Hardware Co.**, 458 U.S. 886 (1982): Nonviolent political speech is entitled to the protection of the 1st Amendment.
	Public Figures - Hustler Magazine v. Falwell, 485 U.S. 46 (1988): Parodies of public figures, including those intended to cause emotional distress, are protected by the 1st Amendment.
	Fighting Words - Chaplinsky v. New Hampshire, 315 U.S. 568 (1942): Words to inflict injury, or incite a breach of the peace, are not protected by the 1st Amendment. **Snyder v. Phelps**, 562 U.S. 443 (2011): Updates this stance, and while **Chaplinsky** is cited often, its rule has not been enforced by a government action since its decision. **Snyder** holds that "speech cannot be restricted simply because it is upsetting or arouses contempt."
	Flag Burning - Texas v. Johnson, 491 U.S. 397 (1989): Flag burning as political protest symbolic speech is protected by the 1st Amendment.
	Symbolic Speech - Tinker v. Des Moines Independent Community School District, 393 U.S. 503 (1969): Public school students may wear armbands in protest at school as a form of protected symbolic speech.
	School Speech - Bethel School District v. Fraser, 478 U.S. 675 (1986): Students do not have a 1st Amendment right to make obscene speeches in school.
	Obscenity - Miller v. California, 413 U.S. 15 (1973): Obscene material is not protected by the 1st Amendment. Obscene works fail the Miller test, which determines if it has any "serious literary, artistic, political, or scientific value."
	Child Pornography - New York v. Ferber, 458 U.S. 747 (1982): Laws that prohibit child pornography are constitutional even if the content is not "obscene."
	Restraint Must Be Narrowly Tailored - Reno v. American Civil Liberties Union, 521 U.S. 844 (1997): Overbroad regulation of certain content on the internet is an unconstitutional restraint on the 1st Amendment.
Freedom of Peaceful Assembly, Expression	**Peaceful Protests - Edwards v. South Carolina**, 372 U.S. 229 (1963): 1st Amendment Free Protest Clause extends to the states.
	Prohibition of Inciting Others - Brandenburg v. Ohio, 395 U.S. 444 (1969): The mere advocacy of the use of force or of violation of the law is protected by the 1st Amendment. Only inciting others to take direct and immediate unlawful action is without constitutional protection. Overruled **Schenck v. United States**, 249 U.S. 47 (1919), which previously allowed speech limits during wartime when there was "clear and present danger."
	Public Demonstration May Exclude Groups - Hurley v. Irish-American Gay, Lesbian, and Bisexual Group of Boston, 515 U.S. 557 (1995): Private citizens organizing a public demonstration have the right to exclude groups whose message they disagree with from participating.
Freedom of Religion	**Establishment Clause - Town of Greece v. Galloway**, 572 U.S. 565 (2014): A town council's practice of opening its sessions with a sectarian prayer does not violate the Establishment Clause. **Free Exercise + Establishment Clause = Freedom of Religion**
	Religious Belief is no Defense - Reynolds v. United States, 98 U.S. 145 (1879): Religious belief or duty cannot be used as a defense against a criminal indictment.

2nd Amendment	To Keep and Bear Arms
18 U.S.C. § 921 et seq. **18 U.S.C. § 845**	**The Gun Control Act (1968)** US federal law that regulates the firearms industry and firearms owners. It primarily focuses on regulating interstate commerce in firearms by generally prohibiting interstate firearms transfers except among licensed manufacturers, dealers and importers. **The Firearm Owners Protection Act of 1986 (FOPA)** is a United States federal law that revised many provisions of the Gun Control Act of 1968
Gun Ownership Lawful Purposes	**District of Columbia v. Heller**, 554 U.S. 570: The 2nd Amendment protects an individual's right to keep and bear arms for lawful purposes, such as self-defense within the home, and that the DC's handgun ban and requirement that lawfully owned rifles and shotguns be kept "unloaded and disassembled or bound by a trigger lock" violated this guarantee. The right to bear arms is not unlimited and it will continue to be regulated. Check your jurisdiction for relevant restrictions. **McDonald v. City of Chicago**, 561 U.S. 742 (2010): Protections of the 2nd Amendment are incorporated by the Due Process Clause of the 14th Amendment to states. **Nunn v. Georgia**, 1 Ga. (1 Kel.) 243 (1846): This was the first gun control measure to be overturned on 2nd Amendment grounds; a GA law ban on handguns was ruled a violation of the 2nd Amendment. **Presser v. Illinois**, 116 U.S. 252 (1886): No 2nd Amendment violation for law prohibiting citizens from forming personal military organizations and activities as it does not limit the personal right to keep and bear arms. **United States v. Miller**, 307 U.S. 174 (1939): The federal government and the states can limit access to all weapons that do not have "some reasonable relationship to the preservation or efficiency of a well regulated militia." Here, sawed-off shotgun did not have any reasonable relationship.
Stun Gun	**Caetano v. Massachusetts**, 577 U.S. 411 (2016): 2nd Amendment extends to all types of bearable arms, including stun guns; however, the 2nd Amendment does not protect weapons not typically possessed by law-abiding citizens for lawful purposes. (Remember that state and local laws can be more restrictive).
"Castle Doctrine"	The castle doctrine and **"stand-your-ground"** laws provide legal defenses to persons who have been charged with various use of force crimes when they reasonably believe it to be necessary to defend against deadly force, great bodily harm, kidnapping, rape, or (in some jurisdictions) robbery or some other serious crime in their home or places they legally occupy (such as a vehicle). This doctrine has many variations and has been controversial. Check your jurisdiction.
4th Amendment	Searches are Presumed Unreasonable Unless There is a Warrant or Recognized Exception
Search	**Secure in Persons, Houses, Papers & Effects - Search** happens when government makes 1) a physical trespass into a constitutionally protected area (i.e., persons, houses, papers, and effects); and 2) with the purpose of obtaining information. **Expectation of Privacy - Katz v. United States**, 389 U.S. 347, 353 (1967): A reasonable expectation of privacy will be violated if: 1) the person exhibited an actual (subjective) expectation of privacy; and 2) his expectation is one that society is prepared to recognize as reasonable (objective). Under the 4th Amendment a warrant issued by a "neutral and detached magistrate" must be obtained before police officers may lawfully search personal property, absent an exception. Superseded by statute in CA and NY; check your jurisdiction.
No Arbitrary Arrests or Unreasonable Searches	**4th Amendment Protections - Payton v. New York**, 445 U.S. 573 (1980): Protect against arbitrary arrests as well as against unreasonable searches
	Reasonableness **U.S. v. Jacobsen**, 503 U.S. 540 (1992): "An otherwise lawful seizure can violate the 4th Amendment if it is executed in an unreasonable manner. **U.S. v. Rohrig**, 98 F.3d 1506 (6th Cir. 1996): The 4th Amendment "does not mandate that police officers act flawlessly, but only that they act reasonably." **U.S. v. Goddard**, 312 F.3d 1360 (11th Cir. 2002): The "reasonable person" test asks, "not … what the defendant himself … thought, but what a reasonable man, innocent of any crime, would have thought had he been in the defendant's shoes."
	Government Searches - The 4th Amendment controls government officials, not private actors. If search directed by government and undertaken with intent to help police discover evidence, a private search may be turned into a government search so long as scope is not exceeded making it unreasonable. **Coolidge v. New Hampshire**, 403 U.S. 443 (1971): No government search evidence simply handed over.
	Warrantless Arrest in Public - **United States v. Watson**, 423 U.S. 411 (1976): Warrantless arrests in public are allowed. **United States v. Santana**, 427 U.S. 38 (1976): Warrantless arrest in suspect's home when she was initially approached in her doorway and then retreated into house was reasonable. **Atwater v. Lago Vista**, 532 U.S. 318 (2001): In most states, the misdemeanor must occur "in the officer's presence" to arrest without a warrant (needed for probable cause).

Hunches	**Request to Exit Vehicle** - **Driver - Pennsylvania v. Mimms**, 434 U.S. 106 (1977): A police officer may order the driver of a lawfully stopped car to exit his vehicle. - **Passenger - Maryland v. Wilson**, 519 U.S. 408 (1997): Extends Pennsylvania v. Mimms, 434 U.S. 106 (1977) to allow officers to request passengers of a lawfully stopped car may also be asked to exit the vehicle. The officer may more than a hunch but less than reasonable suspicion -- check your jurisdiction as application varies. **Demeanor - I.N.S. v. Delgado**, 466 U.S. 210, 216 (1984): Being uncooperative is a hunch, not reasonable suspicion
4th Amendment	**Reasonable Suspicion**
Terry Stop & Frisk	**Terry v. Ohio**, 392 U.S. 1 (1968): A "stop and frisk" is a "search and seizure" and does not violate the 4th Amendment when police have reasonable suspicion that 1) suspects may be (or have, or are about to) commiting a crime, and 2) may be armed and dangerous. Note: states differ, with about half of the states believing that suspects who are armed are dangerous. Seized items may be used as evidence.
Stop & Frisk - Vehicle Passenger	**Arizona v. Johnson**, 555 U.S. 323 (2009): Police may conduct a pat down search of a passenger in an automobile that has been lawfully stopped for a minor traffic violation, if the police reasonably suspect the passenger is armed and dangerous.
Stop & Identify	**Hiibel v. Sixth Judicial District Court of Nevada**, 542 U.S. 177 (2004): Laws requiring suspects to provide their names during a valid Terry stop by law enforcement officers do not violate the 4th Amendment, nor necessarily the 5th Amendment. Officers in Nevada must have a reasonable and articulable suspicion of criminal involvement to request that the person detained "identify himself", but the law there does not compel the person to answer any other questions. About half of the states have a stop & identify law for motorists, and several versions of stop & identify laws have been challenged. Generally to compel ID you need reasonable suspicion of a crime (plain view, plain smell, or commission of an offense), even though a suspect's refusal to identify coupled with surrounding events may give rise to probable cause in certain instances and jurisdictions. Be aware that some detainees ditch their ID if they anticipate police questioning so that they may confuse matters by providing someone else's name.
Reasonable Inference	**Kansas v. Glover**, 589 U.S. ___ (2019): When an officer runs a license plate and learns that the owner has a violation—absent knowledge of any contradictory facts—it is reasonable for the officer to infer that the driver is also the owner of the vehicle, and the traffic stop is justified.
Confidential Informant	**Adams v. Williams**, 407 U.S. 143 (1972): Confidential informant may be used to build reasonable suspicion.
Warrantless Vehicle Stop	**United States v. Cortez**, 499 U.S. 411 (1981): Reasonable suspicion means a suspicion particularized for a given person or persons. The 1) objective facts and 2) circumstantial evidence together justified the investigative stop of the vehicle.
4th Amendment	**Probable Cause**
Traffic Offense	**Whren v. United States,** 517 U.S. 806 (1996): Any traffic offense committed by a driver is a legitimate legal basis for a traffic stop. A concern with this holding is that police may controversially racially profile through traffic stops.
Totality of the Circumstances	**Draper v. U.S.**, 358 U.S. 307 (1959): Probable cause to arrest exists "where 'the facts and circumstances' known to be reasonably trustworthy information warrant the belief that an offense has been or is being committed."
Search Warrant Requirements	**Groh v. Ramirez**, 540 U.S. 551 (2004): A search warrant is a court order that a magistrate or judge issues to authorize law enforcement officers to conduct a search of a person, location, or vehicle for evidence of a crime and to confiscate evidence they find. An incorrectly written search warrant could result in any evidence obtained being excluded from trial. Here, the particularity of items sought repeated the address description in error, rather than drugs. The result was a narrowing of the mistake justification for qualified immunity.
Knock-and-Announce	**Wilson v. Arkansas**, 514 U.S. 927 (1995): "Reasonable entry" considers whether knock-and-announce (wait) was adhered to as a factor. Should law enforcement fail to knock and announce, then the search may violate the 4th Amendment. **Hudson v. Michigan**, 547 U.S. 586 (2006): When the police violate the knock-and-announce rule, the appropriate remedy is not generally suppression of the evidence.
No-Knock Warrant	**United States v. Ramirez**, 523 U.S. 65 (1998): A no-knock warrant is a warrant issued by a judge that allows law enforcement to enter a property without immediate prior notification of the residents, such as by knocking or ringing a doorbell. A no-knock entry is justified if police have a reasonable suspicion that knocking and announcing their presence before entering would be dangerous or futile, or inhibit the effective investigation of the crime. There have been some high profile media about no-knock warrants, so make sure you know your jurisdiction, are compliant and watch out for any changes.
Search Warrants to Third Parties	**Zurcher v. Stanford Daily**, 436 U.S. 547 (1978): the 4th Amendment does not prevent issuing a warrant against a third party not suspected of committing a crime. Preconditions for the issuance of a search warrant must be applied with "particular exactitude" if the materials being searched are protected by the 1st Amendment. Be aware some legislation such as the Privacy Protection Act of 1980 has tried to codify sections from this decision to supersede it; however, this case is still cited for reasonable cause and specificity for a warrant.
Vehicle Search	**Carroll v. U.S.**, 267 U.S. 132 (1925): Police may conduct a warrantless search of a vehicle stopped in traffic if there is probable cause to believe that the vehicle contains contraband or evidence.

Confidential Informant	**Aguilar–Spinelli test**: former test for the validity of a search warrant or a warrantless arrest based on a confidential informant or an anonymous tip which was abandoned in favor of the **"totality of the circumstances"** evaluation per **Illinois v. Gates**, 462 U.S. 213 (1983); however, a few states (AK, HI, MA, NY, VT, OR, WA) retain the Aguilar-Spinelli test under their state constitutions. This former two-prong test based on **Aguilar v. Tex.**, 378 U.S. 108 (1964) (overruled) and **Spinelli v. United States**, 393 U.S. 410 (1969) required the issuing magistrate to be informed 1) why the informant is reliable and credible, and 2) underlying circumstances relied on by the CI.
Balloons / Drugs	**Texas v. Brown**, 460 U.S. 730 (1983): Probable cause that balloons contained drugs based on officer's experience.

4th Amendment	Exceptions to Search Warrant
C Consent	**Schneckloth vs. Bustamonte**, 412 U.S. 218 (1973): The consent given police to search the car of a driver stopped for a traffic violation is valid even if the driver was unaware he had the right to refuse. Usually the police have no duty to warn a person that he has a right to refuse consent to a warrantless search. **Illinois v. Rodriguez**, 497 U.S. 177 (1990): If consent is given by a person reasonably believed by an officer to have authority to give such consent, no warrant is required for a search or seizure.
A Arrest	**Chimel v. California**, 395 U.S. 752 (1969): A search incident to lawful arrest does not require issuance of a warrant. If someone is lawfully arrested, the police may search her person and any area surrounding the person that is within reach (within his or her "wingspan") as a protective measure for police and to secure evidence that might be destroyed. However, the arrest of a person in his home does not allow the warrantless search of the whole house incident to arrest. **United States v. Robinson**, 414 U.S. 218 (1973): In the case of a lawful custodial arrest, a full search of the person is reasonable. **United States v. Leon**, 468 U.S. 897 (1984): Evidence will be admitted when it was seized in reasonable, good-faith reliance on a search warrant, even if the warrant was subsequently found to be defective. **Arizona v. Gant**, 556 U.S. 332 (2009): During a lawful investigative traffic stop, with reasonable suspicion and clear facts that permit officer to conclude that the person is, has been, or will be engaged in criminal activity, police may conduct search. Police may search a vehicle of the arrestee only if the arrestee is within reaching distance (e.g., weapon) or if it is reasonable to believe that crime-related evidence will be found/disposed of in the vehicle.
P Plain View	- **PLAIN VIEW** - **Arizona v. Hicks**, 480 U.S. 321 (1987): Requires the police to have probable cause to seize items in plain view; **Horton v. California**, 496 U.S. 128 (1990): Warrantless seizure of evidence which is in plain view does not violate 4th Amendment; **Coolidge v. New Hampshire**, 403 U.S. 443 (1971): Police may not rely on the plain view doctrine when conducting a warrantless search of an automobile if the police expected in advance to find evidence and failed to secure a warrant. - **PLAIN FEEL / SMELL** - **Minnesota v. Dickerson**, 508 U.S. 366 (1993): The 4th Amendment permits the seizure of contraband detected through a police officer's sense of touch during a protective pat down search. - **HEAR/SOUND** - **United States v. Hairston**, 402 F. App'x 84, 88 (6th Cir. 2010): Extends Terry Stop of individual near sound of recent gunshots fired; **Katz v. United States**, 389 U.S. 347, 353 (1967): Warrantless use of listening and recording device placed on outside of phone booth violates 4th Amendment. Superseded by statute in CA and NY, check your jurisdiction. - **FLASHLIGHT/ILLUMINATE** - **United States v. Dunn**, 480 U.S. 294 (1987): Officer may use flashlight to illuminate barn interior; **Texas v. Brown**, 460 U.S. 730 (1983): Officer allowed to shine flashlight in interior of car; **United States v. Lee**, 274 U.S. 559 (1927): A search light may be used by police; **Kyllo v. United States**, 533 U.S. 27 (2001): Thermal imaging device to detect activity within a building by measuring heat outside the home is unreasonable absent a warrant or exception.
E Exigent	**Carroll v. U.S.**, 267 U.S. 132 (1925): Police may conduct a warrantless search of a vehicle stopped in traffic if there is probable cause to believe that the vehicle contains contraband or evidence. **Chambers v. Maroney**, 90 S. Ct. 1975 (1970): Applied the Carroll doctrine the warrantless search of the suspects' car, although at the police station (rather than during exigent traffic stop), after Chambers and the other occupants were arrested for robbery did not violate the 4th Amendment. **Cady v. Dombrowski**, 413 U.S. 433 (1973): Police have a community caretaking imperative to ensure that impounded automobiles do not contain revolvers or other dangerous items. **Kentucky v. King**, 563 U.S. 452 (2011): Warrantless searches conducted in exigent circumstances do not violate the 4th Amendment so long as the police did not create the exigency by violating or threatening to violate the 4th amendment. **Warden v. Hayden**, 387 U.S. 294 (1967): "Mere evidence" may be seized and held as evidence in a trial. **Schmerber v. California**, 384 U.S. 757 (1966): The 4th Amendment's protection against warrantless searches that intrude into the human body means that police may not conduct warrantless blood testing on suspects absent an emergency that justifies acting without a warrant. A state may draw blood for the purpose of determining intoxication in a drunken driving case without a warrant. The withdrawal of blood does not equate to giving a statement and therefore is not a 5th Amendment violation nor does it invoke the 6th Amendment right to counsel.
R Roadside	**United States v. Martinez-Fuerte**, 428 U.S. 543 (1976): Allows a brief, warrantless seizure at fixed roadside checkpoints aimed at intercepting illegal aliens to protect the nation's border (narrowly tailored reason). **Mich. Dep't of State Police v. Sitz**, 496 U.S. 444 (1990): sobriety checkpoint program to ensure roadway safety does not violate 4th Amendment. **Indianapolis v. Edmond**, 531 U.S. 32 (2000): When detecting ordinary criminal activity is the primary purpose of a checkpoint, it violates the 4th Amendment.

4th Amendment	Seizure
Of a Person	**Brower v. County of Inyo**, 489 U.S. 593 (1989): A seizure of a person occurs under the 4th Amendment when force is used with the intent to seize. **California v. Hodari**, 499 U.S. 621 (1991): Person seized when there is a sufficient show of authority that would lead a reasonable person to believe he was not free to leave.
Of Property	A **seizure** of property occurs under the **4th Amendment** when there is meaningful interference with someone's possessory interest in his property.
Consent	**United States v. Mendenhall**, 446 U.S. 544 (1980); **Fla. v. Bostick**, 501 U.S. 429 (1991): No seizure if there is consent. The test for a consensual encounter is not only the ability to leave, but also the ability to terminate the encounter.
Exclusionary Rule	**Mapp v. Ohio**, 367 U.S. 643 (1961): Evidence seized unlawfully, without a search warrant, and derivative evidence cannot be used. "Fruit of the Poisonous Tree."
Break in Chain	**Wong Sun v. United States**, 371 U.S. 471 (1963): verbal evidence and recovered narcotics where they were both fruits of an illegal entry are inadmissible in court except where there is a break in chain of evidence.
Unlawful Seizure	**Soldal v. Cook County**, 506 U.S. 56 (1992): Officers that "kept the peace" liable for unlawful seizure of property.
PC Hearing After Arrest	**Gerstein v. Pugh**, 420 U.S. 103 (1975): to keep arrestee in custody following a warrantless arrest, a "prompt" "administratively convenient" hearing to determine probable cause is needed. **County of Riverside v. McLaughlin**, 500 U.S. 44, 56 (1991): detention for up to 48 hours without a probable-cause hearing shifts the burden to the government to demonstrate extraordinary circumstances justifying further detention.
4th Amendment	Use of Force
Breaking Doors & Windows	**8 U.S.C. § 3109** governs breaking doors and windows if law enforcement is refused entrance.
Use of Force	**Graham v. Connor**, 490 U.S. 386 (1989): An objective reasonableness standard should apply to a free citizen's claim that law enforcement officials used excessive force in the course of making an arrest, investigatory stop, or other "seizure" of his person.
Fleeing Felon	**Tennessee v. Garner**, 471 U.S. 1 (1985): Deadly force OK if necessary to stop a fleeing felon from escaping, and the suspect poses a significant threat of death or serious physical injury to the officer or others.
Lesser Force	**Plakas v. Drinski**, 19 F.3d 1143 (7th Cir. 1994): When deadly force is authorized, there is no constitutional duty to use a lesser force.
Failure to Train	**City of Canton, Ohio v. Harris,** 489 US 378 (1989): Inadequacy of police training and § 1983 liability where failure to train was "deliberate indifference" to the rights of persons with whom the police came into contact.
5th Amendment	Due Process, Eminent Domain, Self-Incrimination, Grand Jury, Double Jeopardy
Due Process Equal Liberty	**United States v. Windsor**, 570 U.S. 744 (2013): The federal government cannot define the terms "marriage" and "spouse" in a way that excludes married same-sex couples from the benefits and protections that married opposite-sex couples receive.
Felonies are Infamous Crimes	**United States v. Moreland**, 258 U.S. 433 (1922): incarceration in a prison or penitentiary, as opposed to a correction or reformation house, attaches infamy to a crime. **Green v. United States**, 356 U.S. 165 (1957): "imprisonment in a penitentiary can be imposed only if a crime is subject to imprisonment exceeding one year."
Coercion/Duress	**Chambers v. Florida**, 309 U.S. 227 (1940): Confessions compelled by police through duress are inadmissible at trial.
Double Jeopardy	**Blockburger v United States** (1932): Double jeopardy is not absolute. Established the "Same elements test" whereby defendant could be convicted of two crimes arising from one fact situation so long as there is a unique element to each crime making them separate charges vs. lesser included offenses.
5th / 6th Amendments	**Miranda** Rights 1. You have the right to remain silent 2. Anything you say can be used against you 3. You have the right to an attorney 4. If you cannot afford an attorney, one will be appointed for you 5. This means you can choose not to answer an officer's questions and may request an attorney. Understand? Proceed?
Miranda Warning	**Miranda v. Arizona**, 384 U.S. 436 (1966): Presumption that a statement is involuntary if made during a custodial interrogation without the "Miranda Warnings" given. Not only must the statement not be coerced, the suspect must know their rights when being interrogated and in custody (arrest, or when freedom is significantly deprived). "Interrogation" is the use of words or actions to elicit an incriminating response from an average person. Some exceptions to the Miranda Warnings have been carved out either by statute or case law (questioning when necessary for public safety is permitted, see **New York v. Quarles**, 467 U.S. 649 (1984); statute and case law regarding criteria for "voluntariness" of confession have been discussed for various fact situations and jurisdictions).
Questioning: Right to Counsel	**Edwards v. Arizona**, 451 U.S. 477 (1981): Once a defendant invokes his 6th Amendment right to counsel, police must cease interrogation until defendant's counsel has been made available to him, or he himself initiates further communication, exchanges, or conversations with the police. Statements obtained in violation of this rule are a violation of a defendant's 5th Amendment rights.

Re-Questioning	**Maryland v. Shatzer**, 559 U.S. 98 (2010): Police may re-open questioning of a suspect who has asked for counsel after there has been at least a 14-day break since Miranda custody.
Inmates	**Illinois v. Perkins**, 496 US 292 (1990): The Miranda Warnings are not required when an incarcerated person speaks freely to another inmate who is actually an undercover officer.
Juvenile	**Kaupp v. Texas**, 538 U. S. 1 (2003): The removal of an adolescent from his home in handcuffs and improperly clothed taken for interrogation about a murder without probable cause resulted in the exclusion of the confession because the officers violated his 4th Amendment rights. The reading of the Miranda warnings did not overcome the illegal actions of the officers.
Law Enforcement "Garrity Warning"	**Garrity v. New Jersey**, 385 U.S. 493 (1967): Law enforcement officers and other public employees have the right to be free from compulsory self-incrimination. The "Garrity Warning," is administered to suspects in internal and administrative investigations in a similar manner as the Miranda warning is administered to suspects in criminal investigation.

6th Amendment	Speedy Trial, Informed of Accusations, Confront Accuser, Obtain Witnesses
Unanimous Verdict	**Ramos v. Louisiana**, 590 U.S. ___ (2020): The 6th Amendment right to a jury trial requires a unanimous verdict to convict a defendant of a serious offense.
Right to counsel	**Texas v. Cobb**, 532 U.S. 162 (2001): The right to counsel attaches only to charged offenses, and there is no exception for crimes that are uncharged, yet "factually related" to a charged offense. Cobb burglarized a home, then he murdered to conceal the burglary. Cobb was charged with the burglary and obtained counsel. He was later Mirandized and questioned about the murders for which he had not been charged. These related crimes are separate crimes. The confession to the murders was properly obtained.
	Powell v. Alabama, 287 U.S. 45 (1932: that indigent or illiterate defendants charged with a capital crime must be given competent counsel at the expense of the public.
	United States v. Ash, 413 U.S. 300 (1973): The accused does not have a right to have counsel present when the Government conducts a post-indictment photographic display, containing a picture of the accused, for the purpose of allowing a witness to attempt an identification of the offender.

8th Amendment	No Excessive Bail, or Cruel & Unusual Punishment
Punishment Must be Proportional	**Kennedy v. Louisiana**, 554 U.S. 407 (2008): The 8th Amendment bars the execution of a child rapist where the crime did not result, and was not intended to result, in the victim's death. The punishment must be proportional to the seriousness of the crime. There are many cases with various fact patterns regarding the principle of proportionality introduced in **Weems v. United States**, 217 U.S. 349 (1910). Note: less than half of the states authorize capital punishment for any offense as states may be more restrictive than federal laws.
Juvenile Sentence	**Roper v. Simmons**, 543 U.S. 551 (2005): A death sentence may not be imposed on juvenile offenders. **Graham v. Florida**, 560 U.S. 48 (2012): Juvenile offenders cannot be sentenced to life imprisonment without parole for non-homicide offenses.
Intellectually Disabled cannot be executed	**Madison v Alabama**, 586 U.S. ___ (2019): Executing a person currently suffering from dementia would be cruel and unusual punishment; however, the 8th Amendment may permit executing a prisoner with psychotic delusions or no memory of committing the crime. **Atkins v. Virginia**, 536 U.S. 304 (2002): death sentence may not be imposed on intellectually disabled defendants, but the states can define what it means to have an intellectual disability.
Addiction is a Condition	**Robinson v. California**, 370 U.S. 660 (1962): 1) The cruel and unusual punishment clause applies to the states, and 2) punishing a person for a medical condition is a violation of the 8th Amendment ban on cruel and unusual punishment. Addiction to narcotics is a "condition."
No Excessive Bail	**United States v. Salerno**, 481 U.S. 739 (1987): The Bail Reform Act's authorization of pretrial preventive detention on the ground of future dangerousness was not facially unconstitutional, and violated neither the due process clause of the 5th Amendment nor the excessive bail language of the 8th Amendment.

14th Amendment	Citizenship, Civil Rights, Due Process
Due Process	**Gitlow v. New York**, 268 U.S. 652 (1925): 1st Amendment freedoms apply to states via 14th Amendment due process.
Civil Rights	Color of Law - Criminal Civil Rights Violations (**18 U.S.C. § 242**): It a crime for government officials to deprive any person of federally protected rights or to impose different punishments based on a person's race. The DOJ must prove the defendant: (1) acted "under color of" law; (2) acted "willfully"; and (3) deprived the victim of rights or was subjected to different punishments on account of the victim's race, color, or alien status. **Hernandez v. Texas**, 347 U.S. 475 (1954): The **equal protection** of the laws guaranteed by the 14th Amendment covers any racial, national, and ethnic groups against whom discrimination can be proved.
	No Sexual Harassment - **Meritor Savings Bank v. Vinson**, 477 U.S. 57 (1986): sexual harassment is unlawful discrimination too; **Oncale v. Sundowner Offshore Services, Inc.**, 523 U.S. 75 (1998): no same-sex harassment.
	Gender Identity or Sexual Orientation - **Bostock v. Clayton County**, 590 U.S. ___ (2020): Title VII protects employees against discrimination due to their sexual orientation or gender identity.
	Right to Liberty - **O'Connor v. Donaldson**, 422 U.S. 563 (1975): The states cannot involuntarily commit individuals unless they are a danger to themselves or others.

TABLE OF CONTENTS

CHAPTER 163A. ELECTIONS AND ETHICS ENFORCEMENT ACT... 2316

CHAPTER 166A. NORTH CAROLINA EMERGENCY MANAGEMENT ACT 2318

CONSTITUTION OF NORTH CAROLINA..................... 2323

INDEX.. I-1

SECTIONS AFFECTED BY 2021 LEGISLATION

CITATION	EFFECT	S.L.	BILL	BILL SECTION
7A-27	Amended	18	S113	1
7A-38.1	Amended	47	S255	12(a)
7A-38.2	Amended	47	S255	4(a)
7A-38.3B	Amended	47	S255	12(b)
7A-47.3	Amended	47	S255	1(b)
7A-49.6	Added	47	S255	9(a)
7A-98	Added	47	S255	17(a)
7A-133	Amended	148	H476	1
7A-180	Amended	47	S255	7(b)
7A-271	Amended	123	S207	3(a)
7A-273	Amended	78	S605	2(a)
7B-101	Amended	123	S207	5(a)
7B-101	Amended	132	S693	1(a)
7B-101	Amended	100	H132	1(a)
7B-302	Amended	100	H132	2
7B-302	Amended	132	S693	1(c)
7B-320	Amended	132	S693	2(a)
7B-505	Amended	100	H132	3
7B-505	Amended	132	S693	1(d)
7B-602	Amended	100	H132	4
7B-901	Amended	100	H132	5
7B-903	Amended	132	S693	1(e)
7B-903.1	Amended	132	S693	1(f)
7B-903.1	Amended	100	H132	6
7B-903.2	Added	132	S693	5(b)
7B-904	Amended	100	H132	7
7B-905	Amended	100	H132	8
7B-905	Amended	132	S693	1(j)
7B-905.1	Amended	100	H132	9
7B-905.1	Amended	132	S693	1(g)
7B-906.1	Amended	100	H132	10
7B-906.1	Amended	132	S693	1(h)

CITATION	EFFECT	S.L.	BILL	BILL SECTION
7B-906.2	Amended	100	H132	11
7B-906.2	Amended	132	S693	1(k)
7B-908	Amended	100	H132	12
7B-910.1	Amended	100	H132	13
7B-912	Amended	100	H132	14
7B-1000	Amended	100	H132	16
7B-1000	Amended	18	S113	2
7B-1001	Amended	18	S113	2
7B-1001	Amended	100	H132	1(b)
7B-1001	Amended	132	S693	1(b)
7B-1101.1	Amended	100	H132	17
7B-1103	Amended	132	S693	1(l)
7B-1501	Amended	123	S207	5(b)
7B-1601	Amended	123	S207	1(b)
7B-1602	Amended	123	S207	1(c)
Art. 17	Amended	123	S207	5(c)
7B-1700	Amended	123	S207	5(c)
7B-1701	Amended	123	S207	5(c)
7B-1702	Amended	123	S207	5(c)
7B-1703	Amended	123	S207	5(c)
7B-1706	Amended	123	S207	5(c)
7B-1706.1	Added	123	S207	5(c)
7B-1902	Amended	123	S207	3(b)
7B-1906	Amended	123	S207	3(c)
7B-1906	Amended	47	S255	10(a)
7B-2102	Amended	123	S207	5(d)
7B-2200.5	Amended	123	S207	4
7B-2204	Amended	123	S207	2
7B-2502	Amended	123	S207	8(b)
7B-2513	Amended	123	S207	1(a)
7B-2514	Amended	123	S207	1(d)
7B-2516	Amended	123	S207	1(e)
7B-2600	Amended	123	S207	1(f)
Art. 27A	Added			
7B-2710*	Added	123	S207	5(e)
7B-2711	Added	123	S207	5(e)

* Session Laws 2021-123, s. 5(e), designated the sections in this Article as G.S. 7B-2710 through 7B-2713. The sections have been renumbered as G.S. 7B-2715 through 7B-2718 at the direction of the Revisor of Statutes.

CITATION	EFFECT	S.L.	BILL	BILL SECTION
7B-2712	Added	123	S207	5(e)
7B-2713	Added	123	S207	5(e)
7B-2901	Amended	100	H132	18
7B-3100	Amended	123	S207	5(f)
7B-3807	Repealed	100	H132	19
8-53.14	Added	22	S103	3
14-4	Amended	138	S300	13(c)
14-56*	Amended	167	HB761	1
14-72.8	Amended	154	S99	1
14-72.9*	Added	167	HB761	2
14-86.1	Amended	134	H650	1.2(b)
14-113.8	Amended	68	H238	1
14-113.9	Amended	88	H67	2
14-113.9	Amended	68	H238	2
14-135	Amended	78	S605	5(a)
14-135.1	Added	78	S605	6(a)
14-160.1	Amended	36	H743	1
14-208.6	Amended	138	S300	18(b)
14-208.16	Amended	115	H84	3
14-208.18	Amended	115	H84	1
14-208.39	Added	138	S300	18(a)
14-208.40	Amended	138	S300	18(c)
14-208.40A	Amended	138	S300	18(d)
14-208.40B	Amended	138	S300	18(e)
14-208.41	Amended	138	S300	18(f)
14-208.42	Amended	138	S300	18(g)
14-208.43	Amended	138	S300	18(h)
14-208.46	Added	138	S300	18(i)
14-209	Amended	47	S255	17(b)
14-223	Amended	138	S300	19(a)
14-234	Amended	117	H366	1(a)
14-309.26	Amended	150	H890	32.1
14-309.27	Amended	150	H890	32.1
14-309.28	Amended	150	H890	32.1
14-309.35	Amended	150	H890	32.1
14-309.36	Amended	150	H890	32.1
14-401.4	Amended	36	H743	2

* See Session Law 2021-167, included in frontmatter of this book, for 2021 amendment details.

CITATION	EFFECT	S.L.	BILL	BILL SECTION
14-415.4	Amended	116	H481	1.2(a)
15A-101.1	Amended	47	S255	10(b)
15A-145	Amended	115	H84	2
15A-145.4	Amended	107	H312	7(b)
15A-145.5	Amended	118	S301	1
15A-145.5	Amended	107	H312	7(c)
15A-145.5*	Amended	167	HB761	2.3.(a)
15A-145.6	Amended	107	H312	7(d)
15A-145.8A	Amended	118	S301	2
15A-150	Amended	47	S255	15
15A-151	Amended	107	H312	6
15A-151	Amended	118	S301	3
15A-151.5	Amended	88	H67	3
15A-151.5	Amended	118	S301	4
15A-153	Amended	107	H312	7(a)
15A-245	Amended	47	S255	10(c)
15A-304	Amended	47	S255	10(d)
15A-305	Amended	47	S255	6(a)
15A-401	Amended	138	S300	16(a)
15A-401	Amended	137	H536	1(a)
15A-511	Amended	47	S255	10(e)
15A-532	Amended	47	S255	10(f)
15A-601	Amended	138	S300	14(a)
15A-601	Amended	47	S255	10(g)
15A-941	Amended	47	S255	10(h)
15A-951	Amended	47	S255	16(a)
15A-1011	Amended	47	S255	7(a)
15A-1215	Amended	94	H522	1
15A-1221	Amended	94	H522	2
15A-1340.16	Amended	94	H522	3
15A-1343	Amended	138	S300	18(j)
15A-1343.2	Amended	138	S300	18(k)
15A-1344	Amended	138	S300	18(l)
15A-1368.4	Amended	138	S300	18(m)
15A-1374	Amended	138	S300	18(n)
17C-2	Amended	138	S300	3(a)
17C-6	Amended	136	H436	1(a)

* See Session Law 2021-167, included in frontmatter of this book, for 2021 amendment details.

CITATION	EFFECT	S.L.	BILL	BILL SECTION
17C-6	Amended	138	S300	15(a)
17C-6	Amended	137	H536	2(a)
17C-10	Amended	138	S300	7(c)
17C-10	Amended	136	H436	1(c)
17C-14	Added	138	S300	1(a)
17C-15	Added	138	S300	3(b)
17C-16	Added	138	S300	4(a)
17C-16	Added	137	H536	3(a)
Chapter 17E, Article 1	Added	107	H312	3(a)
Chapter 17E, Article 2	Added	107	H312	3(b)
17E-2	Amended	138	S300	3(c)
17E-4	Amended	138	S300	7(b), 11(b), 15(b)
17E-4	Amended	136	H436	1(b)
17E-4	Amended	137	H536	2(b)
17E-7	Amended	138	S300	7(d)
17E-7	Amended	136	H436	1(d)
17E-7	Amended	34	H203	1
17E-11	Amended	107	H312	4
17E-14	Added	138	S300	1(b)
17E-15	Added	138	S300	3(d)
17E-16	Added	138	S300	4(b)
17E-16	Added	137	H536	3(b)
Chapter 17E, Article 3	Added	107	H312	5
17E-20*	Added	107	H312	5
17E-21 through 17E-24*	Added	107	H312	5
17E-25*	Added	107	H312	5
17E-26 through 17E-29*	Added	107	H312	5
17E-30*	Added	107	H312	5
17F-10	Added	138	S300	8(a)
18B-101	Amended	150	H890	27.1
18B-103	Amended	150	H890	23.1
18B-302	Amended	88	H67	4(a)

* See Session Law 2021-107, included in frontmatter of this book.

CITATION	EFFECT	S.L.	BILL	BILL SECTION
18B-302	Amended	150	H890	10.1(a)
18B-401	Amended	150	H890	28.3
18B-404	Amended	150	H890	30.1
18B-502	Amended	150	H890	22.1
18B-800	Amended	150	H890	1.1, 2.1, 1.2, 15.1
18B-800	Amended	117	H366	12(a)
18B-1000	Amended	150	H890	17.1
18B-1001	Amended	117	H366	12(b)
18B-1001	Amended	150	H890	9.2(a), 19.1, 28.1
18B-1001.4	Amended	150	H890	26.1
18B-1004	Amended	150	H890	12.1
18B-1006	Amended	150	H890	3.1, 31.1
18B-1010	Amended	150	H890	11(a)
18B-1011	Added	150	H890	19.4
20-4.01	Amended	33	S241	1
20-7	Amended	78	S605	12(a)
20-7	Amended	89	H297	1
20-11	Amended	24	S69	1
20-11	Amended	134	H650	12
20-16.2	Amended	134	H650	9(a)
20-17	Amended	128	H692	2
20-17.8	Amended	134	H650	9(b)
20-19	Amended	128	H692	3
20-19	Amended	134	H650	9(c)
20-30	Amended	134	H650	3
20-35	Amended	89	H297	2(a)
20-52.2	Added	126	S379	1
20-58	Amended	134	H650	7(a)
20-58.3A	Amended	134	H650	6.2
20-58.4	Amended	134	H650	6.3
20-58.4A	Amended	134	H650	8(a)
20-79	Amended	134	H650	4
20-79.4	Amended	134	H650	4.5(a)
20-88.03	Amended	89	H297	3
20-109.1A	Added	126	S379	2
20-109.2	Amended	134	H650	6.1
20-121.1	Amended	33	S241	2
20-135.4	Amended	128	H692	1

CITATION	EFFECT	S.L.	BILL	BILL SECTION
20-179	Amended	94	H522	4
20-183.4C	Amended	147	H403	14
20-183.4C	Amended	134	H650	10
20-187.2	Amended	116	H481	1.3
20-286	Amended	33	S241	2.3
20-286	Amended	147	H403	2(c), 10
20-287	Amended	134	H650	1.1
20-292	Amended	147	H403	15
20-294	Amended	134	H650	1.2(a)
20-295	Amended	134	H650	5
20-299	Amended	134	H650	1.3
20-305	Amended	147	H403	1(a),2(a),1(b),2(b), 3(a),4,6,1(c),11, 3(b),5,7,8,12,13
20-305.1	Amended	147	H403	9
20-305.4	Repealed	90	S126	16(a)
20-305.5	Amended	90	S126	16(b)
20-398	Amended	23	H217	1
50B-2	Amended	47	S255	10(i)
66-421	Amended	154	S99	2
66-424	Amended	154	S99	4
66-429	Amended	154	S99	3
66-430	Amended	154	S99	5
74C-17	Amended	84	H68	3
84-4.1	Amended	60	S277	1.1
90-87	Amended	155	S321	1
90-89	Amended	155	S321	2
90-90	Amended	155	S321	3
90-90	Amended	155	S321	4
90-91	Amended	155	S321	5
90-92	Amended	155	S321	6
90-93	Amended	155	S321	8.5
90-95	Amended	155	S321	7
90-95	Amended	155	S321	8
90-288	Amended	84	S8	8
106-950	Amended	78	S605	3(a)
122C-3	Amended	77	H734	1
122C-28	Amended	77	H734	7.2(a)

CITATION	EFFECT	S.L.	BILL	BILL SECTION
122C-28.1	Added	77	H734	7.1(a)
122C-251	Amended	138	S300	6(a)
122C-255	Amended	77	H734	5
122C-263	Amended	77	H734	6(a)
122C-266	Amended	77	H734	6(b)
122C-268	Amended	47	S255	10(l)
122C-283	Amended	77	H734	6(c)
122C-285	Amended	77	H734	6(d)
132-1.4A	Amended	138	S300	21(a)
143B-805	Amended	123	S207	6(a)
143B-806	Amended	123	S207	6(b)
143B-811	Amended	123	S207	6(c)
143B-831	Amended	123	S207	6(d)
143B-853	Amended	123	S207	6(e)
143B-919	Amended	138	S300	10(a)
143B-925	Amended	90	S126	8(c)
143B-963	Amended	23	H217	22
143B-972.1	Added	138	S300	2(a)
143B-974	Added	107	H312	9
153A-123	Amended	138	S300	13(a)
153A-145.9	Added	150	H890	20.1
153A-145.10	Added	150	H890	21.1
153A-221	Amended	143	H608	3(b)
Chapter 153A, Article 10, Part 2B	Added			
153A-229.1	Added	143	H608	3(a)
153A-229.2	Added	143	H608	3(a)
153A-229.3	Added	143	H608	3(a)
153A-229.4	Added	143	H608	3(a)
160A-175	Amended	138	S300	13(b)
160A-205.4	Added	150	H890	20.2
160A-205.5	Added	150	H890	21.2
162-2	Amended	107	H312	1
162-5	Amended	107	H312	8(a)
162-5.1	Amended	107	H312	8(b)
162-5.1	Amended	141	H143	1
162-18	Amended	47	S255	14(d)
163-302	Amended	56	S722	1.5(c)

NORTH CAROLINA 2021 SESSION LAWS

The below statutes were amended or added by the 2021 Session but were not officially added to the North Carolina General Statutes when this publication went to press. Please check the State website at https://www.ncleg.gov/Laws/GeneralStatutes for further updates.

SESSION LAW 2021-107

SECTION 5. Chapter 17E of the General Statutes is amended by adding a new Article to read:

"ARTICLE 3.
"SHERIFFS.

"§ 17E-20. Disclosure of convictions and expungements for the office of sheriff.

(a) Each individual filing, or intending to file, a notice of candidacy for election or any individual prior to appointment to fill a vacancy to the office of sheriff shall request the Commission to prepare a disclosure statement verifying that individual has no prior felony convictions or expungements of felony convictions. The individual shall provide such information as required by the Commission for the completion of the disclosure statement, including any evidence that the individual has been granted an unconditional pardon of innocence for a felony crime in this State, any other state, or the United States.

(b) Upon the request of an individual filing, or intending to file, a notice of candidacy for election as sheriff or any individual prior to appointment to fill a vacancy to the office of sheriff, the Commission shall prepare a disclosure statement verifying that the individual has no prior felony convictions or expungements for felony convictions. The disclosure statement shall be in a format as determined by the Commission but shall include at least all of the following:

(1) Name of the individual.

(2) Date the disclosure statement was prepared.

(3) County of residence of the individual.

(4) A statement that the individual has no prior felony convictions or expungements for felony convictions, if in fact the individual has no prior felony convictions or expungements for felony convictions.

(c) In preparing the disclosure statement, the Commission shall do at least all of the following:

(a) Conduct a criminal history record check of State and national databases to determine if the individual has a record of a felony conviction.

(b) Contact the Administrative Office of the Courts and request confirmation of whether or not the individual has previously received an expunction of a felony record.

(c) Determine if the individual has ever been convicted of a felony in violation of Section 2 of Article VII of the North Carolina Constitution.

(d) Any request for a disclosure statement, any supporting documentation used in the preparation of any disclosure statement, and any disclosure statement prepared by the Commission in accordance with this section is confidential and not a public record under Chapter 132 of the General Statutes.

"§§ 17E-21 through 17E-24.

Reserved for future codification purposes.

"§ 17E-25. Expunction records access.

Notwithstanding G.S. 15A-145.4 or G.S. 15A-145.5, the Commission may gain access to an individual's felony conviction records, including those maintained by the Administrative Office of the Courts in its confidential files containing the names of persons granted expunctions for the purposes of this Article.

"§§ 17E-26 through 17E-29.

Reserved for future codification purposes.

"§ 17E-30. Expiration of disclosure of convictions and expungements for the office of sheriff.

Any disclosure statement prepared by the Commission shall be valid for the purpose of filing in accordance with G.S. 163-106, 162-5, or 162-5.1 for 90 days after issuance."
****

SECTION 10. This act becomes effective October 1, 2021, and applies to elections and appointments to the office of sheriff on or after that date.

SESSION LAW 2021-167

SECTION 1. G.S. 14-56 reads as rewritten:

"§ 14-56. Breaking or entering into or breaking out of railroad cars, motor vehicles, trailers, aircraft, boats, or other watercraft.

(d) If any person, with intent to commit any felony or larceny therein, breaks or enters any railroad car, motor vehicle, trailer, aircraft, boat, or other watercraft of any kind, containing any goods, wares, freight, or other thing of value, or, after having committed any felony or larceny therein, breaks out of any railroad car, motor vehicle, trailer, aircraft, boat, or other watercraft of any kind containing any goods, wares, freight, or other thing of value, that person is guilty of a Class I felony. It is prima facie evidence that a person entered in violation of this section if he is found unlawfully in such a railroad car, motor vehicle, trailer, aircraft, boat, or other watercraft.

(a1) If any person violates subsection (a) of this section, that person is guilty of a Class H felony if both of the following conditions are met:

(1) The railroad car, motor vehicle, trailer, aircraft, boat, or other watercraft of any kind is owned or operated by any law enforcement agency, the North Carolina National Guard, or any branch of the Armed Forces of the United States.

(2) The person knows or reasonably should know that the railroad car, motor vehicle, trailer, aircraft, boat, or other watercraft of any kind is owned or operated by any law enforcement agency, the North Carolina National Guard, or any branch of the Armed Forces of the United States.

(e) It shall not be a violation of this section for any person to break or enter any railroad car, motor vehicle, trailer, aircraft, boat, or other watercraft of any kind to provide assistance to a person inside the railroad car, motor vehicle, trailer, aircraft, boat, or watercraft of any kind if one or more of the following circumstances exist:

(1) The person acts in good faith to access the person inside the railroad car, motor vehicle, trailer, aircraft, boat, or watercraft of any kind in order to provide first aid or emergency health care treatment or because the person inside is, or is in imminent danger of becoming unconscious, ill, or injured.

(2) It is reasonably apparent that the circumstances require prompt decisions and actions in medical, other health care, or other assistance for the person inside the railroad car, motor vehicle, trailer, aircraft, boat, or watercraft of any kind.

(3) The necessity of immediate health care treatment or removal of the person from the railroad car, motor vehicle, trailer, aircraft, boat, or other watercraft of any kind is so reasonably apparent that any delay in the rendering of treatment or removal would seriously worsen the physical condition or endanger the life of the person."

SECTION 2. Article 16 of Chapter 14 of the General Statutes is amended by adding a new section to read:

"§ 14-72.9. Larceny of law enforcement equipment.

(d) Definitions.—

(1) "Law enforcement equipment" means any equipment owned or operated by a law enforcement agency and used by law enforcement agencies to conduct law enforcement operations, including firearms and any other type of weapon, ammunition, radios, computers, handcuffs and other restraints, phones, cell site simulators, light bars, and sirens.

(2) "Law enforcement vehicle" means any railroad car, motor vehicle, trailer, aircraft, boat, or other watercraft of any kind owned or operated by any law enforcement agency, the North Carolina National Guard, or any branch of the Armed Forces of the United States.

(e) Offense.— A person is guilty of a Class H felony if the person commits larceny of law enforcement equipment from a law enforcement vehicle and the person knows, or reasonably should know, that the vehicle was a law enforcement vehicle and that the property was law enforcement equipment.

(f) Additional Offense.– A person is guilty of a Class G felony if the person violated subsection (b) of this section and the law enforcement equipment is valued in excess of one thousand dollars ($1,000)."

SECTION 2.3.(a) G.S. 15A-145.5(c1)(1), as amended by Section 1 of S.L. 2021-118, reads as rewritten:

"(1) An affidavit by the petitioner that the petitioner is of good moral character and <u>one of the following statements:</u>

 a. If the petition is for the expunction of one or more nonviolent misdemeanors, <u>that the petitioner</u> has not been convicted of any other felony or misdemeanor, other than a traffic violation, under the laws of the United States or the laws of this State or any other state during the applicable <u>five-year, seven-year, 10-year, or 20-year</u> five-year or seven-year waiting period set forth in subsection (c) of this section.

 <u>b. If the petition is for the expunction of one or up to three nonviolent felonies, that the petitioner has not been convicted under the laws of the United States or the laws of this State or any other state of any misdemeanor, other than a traffic violation, in the five years preceding the petition, or any felony during the applicable 10-year or 20-year waiting period set forth in subsection (c) of this section.</u>"

SECTION 2.3.(b) This section becomes effective December 1, 2021, and applies to petitions filed on or after that date.

SECTION 2.4.(a) Section 7 of S.L. 2021-123 reads as rewritten:

"**SECTION 7.** The Juvenile Justice Section of the Division of Adult Correction and Juvenile Justice of the Department of Public Safety shall report to the Joint Legislative Oversight Committee on Justice and Public Safety no later than March 1, 2023, and annually thereafter, on all complaints filed <u>received</u> against a juvenile less than 10 years of age, but at least 6 years of age. The report shall include the following information about the complaints and the juveniles against whom the complaints were made:

 (1) A summary containing the following information about all complaints filed since the last report:

  <u>a.</u> The total number of complaints.

  <u>b.</u> The offenses alleged in the complaints, organized by class of offense.

  <u>c.</u> The age of the juveniles at the time of the offense.

  <u>d.</u> The number of complaints that resulted in a juvenile consultation. <u>e.</u> The number of complaints that resulted in juvenile court jurisdiction for delinquency, including a breakdown of the number of those complaints that were handled through diversion and the number that led to the filing of a delinquency petition.

  <u>f.</u> The number of juveniles receiving a juvenile consultation that have previously received juvenile consultation services.

 (2) A detailed listing of all complaints filed since the last report, with any identifying information removed, containing the following information for each complaint:

  <u>a.</u> The age of the juvenile.

b. The offenses, including class of offense, allegedly committed by the juvenile.

c. The initial determination by the juvenile court counselor to treat the complaint as a vulnerable juvenile complaint or a delinquent juvenile complaint.

d. If the juvenile is a vulnerable juvenile, whether the juvenile received juvenile consultation services.

e. If the juvenile is a vulnerable juvenile, whether the juvenile has received juvenile consultation services for a previous complaint.

f. If the juvenile is alleged delinquent, whether the juvenile was diverted or a petition alleging delinquency was filed."

SECTION 2.4.(b) This section becomes effective December 1, 2021, and applies to offenses committed on or after that date.

SECTION 3. Sections 1 and 2 of this act become effective December 1, 2021, and apply to offenses committed on or after that date. Except as otherwise provided, the remainder of this act is effective when it becomes law.

In the General Assembly read three times and ratified this the 7th day of October, 2021.

HIGHLIGHTS OF THE 2021 NORTH CAROLINA LEGISLATIVE SESSION

HIGHLIGHTS OF THE 2021 NORTH CAROLINA LEGISLATIVE SESSION

concerning legally accurate information stops and other thod auth...

USE OF FORCE

New law requires a law enforcement officer who observes another law enforcement officer use excessive force to intervene. The officer must also report that excessive force
within 72 hours.

DATABASE OF SUSPENSIONS

New law requires creation and maintenance of public database of law enforcement officer certification suspensions and revocations.

EARLY WARNING SYSTEM

"Development of law enforcement early warning system" requires every agency in the
State that employs personnel certified by the North Carolina Criminal Justice Education
and Training Standards Commission or the North Carolina Sheriffs' Education and Training Standards Commission to develop and implement an early warning system to document and track the actions and behaviors of law enforcement officers for the purpose of
intervening and improving performance.

PSYCHOLOGICAL SCREENINGS

New law requires psychological screenings of law enforcement officers prior to certification or employment.

SHERIFF CANDIDATES MUST DISCLOSE FELONIES

Candidates or appointees for the office of sheriff must disclose all felony convictions,
including any expunged convictions.

SOCIAL MEDIA

In order to raise public awareness about resisting, delaying, and obstructing law enforcement officers and encourage North Carolina residents to interact with law enforcement
officers safely, the Department of Public Safety shall create a targeted social media campaign and television commercials that address the concerns of not resisting arrest and
raising public awareness about resisting, delaying, and obstructing law enforcement officers. DPS shall also make available on its internet website a public service announcement

containing legally accurate information regarding the public's responsibilities during traffic stops and other interactions with law enforcement.

USE OF FORCE

New law requires a law enforcement officer who observes another law enforcement officer use excessive force to intervene. The officer must also report that excessive force within 72 hours.

ABOUT THE AUTHOR OF THE SEARCH & SEIZURE SURVIVAL GUIDE

Anthony Bandiero, JD, ALM, is an attorney and retired law enforcement officer with experience as both a municipal police officer and sergeant with a state police agency. Anthony has studied constitutional law for over twenty years and has trained countless police officers in advanced search and seizure.

View his bio at BlueToGold.com/about

SEARCH & SEIZURE SURVIVAL GUIDE*

---

* In addition to this National version of the Search & Seizure Survival Guide, Anthony Bandiero, JD, ALM, has authored several state-specific guides which highlight deviations in state statutes and case law. Please visit Blue360Media.com for details.

14. LAW ENFORCEMENT LIABILITY 186

15. LEGAL CHECKLISTS 201

Chapter 1
Let's Start with the Basics

1.1 Fourth Amendment

Out of all of the Bill of Rights, the Fourth Amendment is the most litigated. It is also the most important when it comes to your job as a police officer. At the core of every police action is the Fourth Amendment and you need to understand case law in order to do your job effectively and lawfully. That is what this book is all about.

⭐ LEGAL STANDARD

The Fourth Amendment is best understood in two separate parts:

Search and seizure clause:
1. The right of the people to be secure in their;
2. persons, houses, papers, and effects;
3. against unreasonable searches and seizures
4. shall not be violated; and

Search warrant clause:
1. no warrants shall issue, but upon probable cause;
2. supported by oath or affirmation;
3. and particularly describing the place to be searched;
4. and the persons or things to be seized.

1.2 Fifth Amendment

The Fifth Amendment is the most famous. Because of Hollywood, everyone seems to know their rights. Yet, the Fifth Amendment is extremely complex. For example, how many times has a suspect complained that you did not read them his Miranda rights after an arrest, even though you did not interrogate him? Better yet, what if you forget to read someone his rights and he confesses? How do you fix that mistake? This book gives you these answers (Interview and Interrogation section).

⭐ LEGAL STANDARD

There are a lot of subsections to the Fifth Amendment, and you probably won't deal directly with any of them except #4, the right against self-incrimination (*i.e.*, Miranda):

1. No person shall be held to answer for a capital, or otherwise infamous crime;
2. unless on a presentment or indictment of a grand jury, except in cases arising in the land or naval forces, or in the militia, when in actual service in time of war or public danger;
3. nor shall any person be subject for the same offense to be twice put in jeopardy of life or limb;
4. nor shall be compelled in any criminal case to be a witness against himself;
5. nor be deprived of life, liberty, or property, without due process of law;
6. nor shall private property be taken for public use, without just compensation.

1.3 The Right 'To be Left Alone'

The Supreme Court has recognized another "right," though it is not solely defined in the Bill of Rights, and that is the right "to be left alone." (The original phrase is the right "to be let alone." Modern English prefers "left alone.")

Whatever its source, whether common law, civil tort law, or the Bill of Rights, professional law enforcement officers must realize, and accept, that citizens have the right to be left alone. This is especially true today because more and more citizens are refusing police consensual encounters. I witnessed this firsthand when subjects, who I wanted to talk with, in order to develop intel, would bluntly ask me if they were free to go. When I replied yes, a few would immediately leave (usually on their bicycle or moped). However, this country was founded on an unwavering respect for individual liberties. It's just one of many reasons why this country is the best.

As Justice Brandies wrote in a dissenting opinion that was later endorsed by courts around the country:

> The makers of our Constitution undertook to secure conditions favorable to the pursuit of happiness. They recognized the significance of man's spiritual nature, of his feelings and of his intellect. They knew that only a part of the pain, pleasure and satisfactions of life are to be found in material things. They sought to protect Americans in their beliefs, their thoughts, their emotions and their sensations. They conferred, as against the Government, the right to be let alone—the most comprehensive of rights and the right most valued by civilized men. To protect that right, every unjustifiable intrusion by the Government upon the privacy of the individual, whatever the means employed, must be deemed a violation of the Fourth Amendment.[1]

1.4 Decision Sequencing

Every search and seizure decision you make must be constitutional. If not, the evidence seized later will be "tainted" by the unconstitutional decision and the evidence may be suppressed. More importantly, an unconstitutional decision may have violated someone's constitutional rights. If true, you may be successfully sued even if the suspect suffered no real harm. For example, if you illegally searched a backpack and found cocaine. The suspect may be able to recover damages and

---

[1] *Olmstead v. U.S.*, 277 U.S. 438 (1928).

attorney's fees even though they were never allowed to possess the cocaine in the first place.

A great way to conceptualize how this works is to think of constitutional decisions as upright dominos, each stacked next to each other.[2] Remember doing that as a kid . . . or last week? You line them up and when one falls, the rest fall after that one. In other words, if you just flicked the domino in the middle, only half the dominos would fall. Fourth Amendment decisions work the same way. For example, you make a lawful traffic stop (domino #1). You lawfully question the occupants about unrelated matters but it does not measurably extend the stop (domino #2). Eventually, you gain consent to search the trunk, but exceed the scope of search by searching inside the vehicle. This would violate the constitution and therefore that domino falls . . . and so do the decisions and evidence that come after it. Here, if you found drugs in the car, made an arrest, and found more drugs from a search incident to an arrest (another domino), that domino falls over too and that evidence is suppressed because it was tainted by a domino that fell over before.

Finally, remember everything that you found before the first domino that fell is constitutional. Any evidence discovered during that period would not be suppressed.

🛡 LEGAL STANDARD

Constitutional decisions are like upright dominos—an unconstitutional decision will cause the domino to fall over, knocking over (*i.e.*, "tainting") all the dominos that come later.

1.5 C.R.E.W.

The Supreme Court stated that all Fourth Amendment searches are presumed unreasonable unless there is a warrant or recognized exception. There are several exceptions, including "consent." C.R.E.W. is an acronym to help you remember this important limitation.

The "C" stands for consent. "R.E." stands for recognized exceptions. "W" stands for—yep, you guessed it—warrant.

🛡 LEGAL STANDARD

Whenever you conduct a search or seizure you need one of the following:

1. Consent
2. Recognized Exceptions, examples include:
   ✓ Exigency
   ✓ Community caretaking
   ✓ Reasonable suspicion
   ✓ Probable cause arrest in public place

---

[2] This concept came from Bruce-Alan Barnard, JD.

    ✓ Mobile conveyance exception
    ✓ Plain view (or smell, feel, hear)
    ✓ Emergency searches
    ✓ Hot/fresh pursuit
3. Warrant

1.6 Fourth Amendment Reasonableness

The ultimate touchstone of the Fourth Amendment is reasonableness.[3] In particular, the Fourth prohibits "unreasonable searches and seizures." In other words, if a search or seizure is reasonable, it's probably lawful.

Yet, how do we define what's reasonable? Most of our definitions come from case law. What we can, and cannot, do is usually spelled out by judges. But remember, courts do not expect you to do your job perfectly—cops are humans and make mistakes. But you must be able to articulate why you are doing something. If you cannot then it's probably unreasonable.

⭐ LEGAL STANDARD

The "reasonable person" test asks, "not ... what the defendant himself ... thought, but what a reasonable man, innocent of any crime, would have thought had he been in the defendant's shoes."[4]

"An otherwise lawful seizure can violate the Fourth Amendment if it is executed in an unreasonable manner."[5]

Finally, the "Fourth Amendment does not mandate that police officers act flawlessly, but only that they act reasonably."[6]

1.7 Private Searches

The Fourth Amendment controls government officials, not private actors. Therefore, there's generally no restriction on using information gained from a private citizen's search as long as he was not acting as a government agent. This is true even when the private search was conducted in a highly offensive, unreasonable, or illegal manner.[7]

Remember, you may not exceed the scope of the original private search. The point here is that the suspect loses any reasonable expectation of privacy in those areas searched by the private person, so police can view the same evidence. But that does not mean the suspect lost his expectation of privacy in other, non-searched areas.

---

[3] *Riley v. California*, 134 S. Ct. 2473 (2014).
[4] *U.S. v. Goddard*, 312 F.3d 1360 (11th Cir. 2002).
[5] *U.S. v. Jacobsen*, 503 U.S. 540 (1992).
[6] *U.S. v. Rohrig*, 98 F.3d 1506 (6th Cir. 1996).
[7] *Skinner v. Railway Labor Executives' Ass'n*, 489 U.S. 602 (1989).

An agent is anyone who conducts the search or seizure on your behalf. Government agents must abide by the same rules you do, otherwise agents become a way to violate the Fourth Amendment. Again, as long as the person is not your agent, you can use any evidence they bring to you.

🛡 LEGAL STANDARD

Whether a private search becomes a government search depends on three factors:

- Did you direct or participate in the search or seizure? And,
- Did the private person conduct the search with the intent to help police or discover evidence? If so,
- Did you exceed the scope of the private search?

The first two factors must both be present for a private search to turn into a government search. The third factor will turn a private search into an unreasonable government search.

🏛 CASE EXAMPLES

Government did not exceed private search by opening another box on the same pallet

Private carrier's employee opened one of thirteen boxes on a pallet and discovered marijuana. Police later searched the other boxes without a warrant. Typically, this would have exceeded the "scope" of the original private search. However, the government effectively argued that the additional boxes on the same pallet was essentially a "single" box. The court agreed and the search was upheld.[8]

No government search where wife simply handed over evidence

Officers went to the defendant's home and questioned his wife. Officers asked if husband owned any guns and what clothes he had worn on the night of the crime. Wife then grabbed the items and gave them to police. This was a private search—no evidence police told her to do it, she did it on her own to clear her husband's name.[9] That last part backfired!

Hotel manager was government agent while searching room for drugs

Hotel manager called police and asked that police protect him while he searched a suspected drug dealer's room. The officers stood guard at the door and listened to the manager describe the drug evidence found. This was a government search because police participated in (*i.e.*, stood guard) and the manager was motivated to help police (*i.e.*, look at what I just found boys!).[10]

---

8 *U.S. v. Garcia-Bercovich*, 582 F.3d 1234 (11th Cir. 2009).
9 *Coolidge v. N.H.*, 403 U.S. 443 (1971).
10 *U.S. v. Reed*, 15 F.3d 928 (9th Cir. 1994).

FedEx employee not agent despite wanting to find evidence for police

A FedEx employee who previously found drugs in eight packages, and testified in court two times, not government agent simply because he wanted to find evidence to turn over to the government.[11]

Private search exceeded after laboratory tests performed

Where a previous private search was limited to visual inspection of pills but the government subsequently had a series of tests performed on the material at a toxicology laboratory that revealed its precise molecular structure, the action was a search because of the danger that private facts about the items could be revealed and because the search exceeded the scope of the private search. The court distinguished a field test that would reveal only whether or not the pills were a particular contraband substance but would not otherwise reveal exactly what they were.[12]

No violation where police viewed same child pornography wife viewed

Police officers who examined defendant's child pornography obtained and brought to the officers by defendant's wife did not violate defendant's privacy expectations, where defendant's wife had performed a private search of the materials, and the police officers only viewed those materials that had already been viewed by defendant's wife.[13] Still, officers are highly encouraged to get a search warrant for electronic devices, especially those suspected of containing child pornography.

1.8 "Hunches" Defined

You cannot make a stop or detention based "on mere curiosity, rumor, or hunch . . . even though the [you] may be acting in complete good faith."[14] The solution is to work on converting those hunches into reasonable suspicion so they can make investigatory detentions. As the Court said:

> The officer, of course, must be able to articulate something more than an "inchoate and unparticularized suspicion or 'hunch.'" The Fourth Amendment requires "some minimal level of objective justification" for making the stop. That level of suspicion is considerably less than proof of wrongdoing by a preponderance of the evidence. We have held that probable cause means "a fair probability that contraband or evidence of a crime will be found," and the level of suspicion required for a Terry stop is obviously less demanding than that for probable cause.[15]

---

[11] *U.S. v. Koenig*, 856 F.2d 843 (7th Cir. 1988).
[12] *U.S. v. Mulder*, 808 F.2d 1346 (9th Cir. 1987).
[13] *U.S. v. Starr*, 533 F.3d 985 (8th Cir. 2008).
[14] *In re Tony C.*, 21 Cal. 3d 888 (1978).
[15] *U.S. v. Sokolow*, 490 U.S. 1 (1989).

🛡 LEGAL STANDARD

You cannot seize a person or property based merely on a hunch. Instead, you may make a consensual encounter or pursue other investigative techniques that are not prohibited by the Fourth Amendment.

🏛 CASE EXAMPLES

Hunches cannot support a stop, but are nevertheless valuable

"A hunch may provide the basis for solid police work; it may trigger an investigation that uncovers facts that establish reasonable suspicion, probable cause, or even grounds for a conviction."[16]

Criminal history alone is a hunch, not reasonable suspicion

During a traffic stop, the facts that a computer check reveals that driver had once been involved in a hit-and-run incident and had once been arrested on a drug charge did not provide reasonable suspicion for further detention. Officer was impermissibly acting on a hunch that defendant might presently be involved in criminal activity.[17]

1.9 Reasonable Suspicion Defined

You may conduct an investigative detention (*i.e.*, Terry Stop) when you can "point to specific and articulable facts which, taken together with rational inferences from those facts, reasonably warrant" you to detain the suspect for further investigation.[18]

Like probable cause, reasonable suspicion is fact specific. Each situation is different. Therefore, the key is to articulate why this particular person appears engaged in criminal activity.

🛡 LEGAL STANDARD

Reasonable suspicion exists when:

- You can articulate facts and circumstances that would lead a reasonable officer to believe the suspect is, or is about to be involved in criminal activity;
- If your suspicions are dispelled, the person must be immediately released or the stop converted into a consensual encounter.

---

[16] *U.S. v. Thomas*, 211 F.3d 1186, 1191 (9th Cir. 2000).
[17] *U.S. v. Sandoval*, 29 F.3d 537, 543 (10th Cir. 1994).
[18] *Terry v. Ohio*, 392 U.S. 1 (1968).

🏛 CASE EXAMPLES

Confidential informant may be used to build reasonable suspicion

An informant known to the officer who had provided him information in the past told him that a person seated in a car nearby was dealing drugs and was armed. Reasonable suspicion for an investigative stop was present.[19]

Being uncooperative is a hunch, not reasonable suspicion.

The mere fact that a suspect refuses to cooperate with police when the suspect has no duty to do so, is insufficient to support reasonable suspicion.[20]

Fact that car is parked in front of fugitives house not enough for stop

"That on one occasion a car is parked on a street in front of a house where a fugitive resides is insufficient to create reasonable suspicion that the car's occupants had been or are about to engage in criminal activity."[21]

1.10 Probable Cause Defined

Articulating precisely the definition of "probable cause" or "reasonable cause" is not possible. P.C. is a fluid concept and whether you had P.C. to arrest or conduct a search will be evaluated on a case-by-case basis. "On many occasions, we have reiterated that the probable-cause standard is a 'practical, nontechnical conception' that deals with the factual and practical considerations of everyday life on which reasonable and prudent men, not legal technicians, act."[22]

Remember, evidence found after a search cannot be used retroactively to establish probable cause.[23] It may be tempting to try to cure an unlawful search by telling the prosecutor, "But I found 100 kilos of cocaine! There must have been probable cause!" That's a great argument, but it is legally flawed. Similarly, just because the evidence sought was not found does not mean that there was no probable cause at the beginning.[24]

🛡 LEGAL STANDARD

Probable cause to arrest:

Probable cause to arrest exists "where 'the facts and circumstances within [the arresting officer's] knowledge and of which he had reasonably trustworthy information [are] sufficient in themselves to warrant a man of reasonable

---

[19] *Adams v. Williams*, 407 U.S. 143 (1972).
[20] *I.N.S. v. Delgado*, 466 U.S. 210, 216 (1984).
[21] *U.S. v. Green*, 111 F.3d 515 (7th Cir. 1997).
[22] *Illinois v. Gates*, 462 U.S. 213 (1983).
[23] *Maryland v. Garrison*, 480 U.S. 79 (1987).
[24] *U.S. v. Gaschler*, 2009 U.S. Dist. LEXIS 48449 (N.D. W. Va. June 3, 2009).

caution in the belief that an offense has been or is being committed,"[25] and that the defendant is the perpetrator.[26]

Probable cause to search:

Probable cause to search, on the other hand, arises when there are reasonable grounds to believe, "not that the owner of the property is suspected of a crime, but that there is reasonable cause to believe that the specific 'things' to be searched for and seized are located on the property to which entry is sought,"[27] and there is probable cause to believe the things sought are evidence of a crime.[28] In fact, the identity of the offender need not be known.[29]

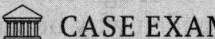 CASE EXAMPLES

Officer had probable cause to search vehicle

"There was probable cause to search a vehicle where police knew that a "blue compact station wagon" with four men in it had been circling a service station shortly before it was robbed by two men and sped away from an area near the scene shortly thereafter, that one occupant wore a green sweater as did one of the robbers, [and] that there was a trench coat in the auto similar to that worn by another of the robbers."[30]

Officer had probable cause that tied-off balloon contained narcotics

Where an officer observed a tied-off, uninflated opaque party balloon in a vehicle together with additional balloons, small plastic vials, and white powder in the glove compartment, and when the officer knew from his experience that such balloons were often used to deal drugs, probable cause existed to believe that the balloon contained narcotics.[31]

Probable cause existed to arrest party goers in near-empty house

A reasonable officer could have concluded that there was probable cause to believe the partygoers knew they did not have permission to be in the house, and the officers had probable cause to arrest the partygoers because the officers found a group of people who claimed to be having a bachelor party with no bachelor, in a near-empty house, with strippers in the living room and sexual activity in the bedroom, and who fled at the first sign of police.[32]

---

[25] *Draper v. U.S.*, 358 U.S. 307 (1959).
[26] *U.S. v. Watson*, 423 U.S. 411 (1976).
[27] *Zurcher v. Stanford Daily*, 436 U.S. 547 (1978).
[28] *State v. Tamer*, 475 So. 2d 918 (Fla. Dist. Ct. App. 3d Dist. 1985).
[29] *State v. Warren*, 301 S.E.2d 126 (N.C. Ct. App. 1983).
[30] *Chambers v. Maroney*, 90 S. Ct. 1975 (1970).
[31] *Tex. v. Brown*, 103 S. Ct. 1535 (1983).
[32] *District of Columbia v. Wesby*, 138 S. Ct. 577 (2018).

Probable cause defines the scope of search

Smelling the odor of drugs can give probable cause to search for drugs. Scope is always an issue with probable cause. For example, the odor of burnt marijuana may give probable cause to search the passenger compartment while a powerful smell of unburnt marijuana may give probable cause to search the vehicle's trunk.[33]

1.11 Collective Knowledge Doctrine

The collective knowledge doctrine is one of the most powerful and important doctrines in law enforcement. It allows a single police officer to benefit from the collective knowledge of all officers working on a case. For example, if a detective asks another officer to search a vehicle for drugs, the search would be valid even if the officer conducting the search had no idea why he was authorized to search the vehicle, as long as the detective had probable cause.

The key with the collective knowledge doctrine is that officers communicate with each other. This does not mean officers have to know everything about the case, but they at least have to be working together.

⬟ LEGAL STANDARD

The collective knowledge doctrine has two requirements:

- The officers must be involved in the same investigation, but may be from different departments (*i.e.*, task forces); and
- Officers must be in communication with each other related to the investigation.

🏛 CASE EXAMPLES

Collective knowledge doctrine applied to officer who stopped vehicle

A narcotics task force requested that an officer stop a vehicle for any observed traffic violation. Though the arresting officer only observed a traffic offense, the collective knowledge of the task force permitted the later arrest and warrantless search of the vehicle for drugs.[34]

Officer may wholly rely on the probable cause of a fellow officer

A police officer relied on the instruction of a fellow officer, who had probable that drugs were in a vehicle. The police officer stopped the vehicle and searched it under the automobile exception. Even though the initiating officer did not have probable cause, because he was in communication with a fellow officer that did, the stop and search were lawful.[35]

---

[33] *U.S. v. Downs*, 151 F.3d 1301 (10th Cir. 1998).
[34] *U.S. v. Thompson*, 533 F.3d 964 (8th Cir. Mo. 2008).
[35] *U.S. v. Chavez*, 534 F.3d 1338 (10th Cir. 2008).

Intel from confidential information contributed to collective knowledge

Officers who stopped defendant for a traffic violation had probable cause to arrest him for drug trafficking; at the time of the stop, law enforcement collectively knew that a confidential informant made a controlled drug purchase from defendant five days earlier, the informant made a controlled drug payment of $5,000 to defendant on the day of the stop, and defendant engaged in what appeared to be other drug transactions shortly before the stop.[36]

Collective knowledge doctrine controls even when agent told officer to develop his own probable cause

A DEA agent had probable cause that the defendant was is possession of drugs. He told a local officer to watch out for the defendant, and to develop his own probable cause and stop the vehicle, but the officer had no knowledge of the facts underlying the DEA's probable cause. The officer stopped the vehicle and searched it. The court held the officer had probable cause under the collection knowledge doctrine.[37]

Collective knowledge doctrine can also be used for investigatory detentions

Officer worked in a fast-paced, dynamic situation in an area known for drug sales, in which the officers worked together as a unified and tight-knit team. One officer developed reasonable suspicion to stop the defendant. A fellow officer, unaware of the officer's reasonable suspicion, stopped the defendant without his own individualized suspicion. The court upheld the stop under the collective knowledge doctrine.[38]

Supervisor's knowledge, not on scene, was too remote for collective knowledge doctrine

Knowledge of all officers on the scene is imputed to each officer in determining whether "collective knowledge" provided probable cause but knowledge of a supervisor not on the scene cannot be imputed when the information was not communicated to those on the scene.[39]

1.12   What is a "Search" Under the Fourth Amendment?

It is important to understand that the term "search," as used in this book at least, refers to conduct that invokes the protections of the Fourth Amendment. Police may engage in hundreds of "searches" every day, and yet invoke the Fourth Amendment only a few times.

For example, when police look into a stopped vehicle, they may be searching for weapons or contraband, but that conduct is not protected by the Fourth Amendment. In other words, just using your senses while lawfully positioned somewhere is not a Fourth Amendment search. On the other hand, opening the trunk of that

---

[36] *U.S. v. Nicksion*, 628 F.3d 368 (7th Cir. 2010).
[37] *U.S. v. Williams*, 627 F.3d 247 (7th Cir. 2010).
[38] *U.S. v. Whitfield*, 634 F.3d 741 (3d Cir. 2010).
[39] *U.S. v. Edwards*, 885 F.2d 377 (7th Cir. 1989).

same vehicle and looking around for contraband would be a protected search because that area is protected as a closed container.

There are two constitutional searches, a "physical intrusion" search or a search where a person has a "reasonable expectation of privacy."

⭐ LEGAL STANDARD

Physical Intrusion

A physical intrusion will be a search under the Fourth Amendment if:

- You make a physical trespass into a constitutionally protected area (*i.e.*, persons, houses, papers, and effects); and
- You did it for the purpose of obtaining evidence.

Reasonable Expectation of Privacy

A reasonable expectation of privacy will be violated if:

- The person exhibited an actual (subjective) expectation of privacy; and
- His expectation is one that society is prepared to recognize as reasonable (objective).

1.13   What is a "Seizure" Under the Fourth Amendment?

A seizure of a person occurs when a reasonable person would believe that he or she is not free to leave, even if for a brief period of time.

> The test is necessarily imprecise because it is designed to assess the coercive effect of police conduct, taken as a whole, rather than to focus on particular details of that conduct in isolation. Moreover, what constitutes a restraint on liberty prompting a person to conclude that he is not free to "leave" will vary, not only with the particular police conduct at issue, but also with the setting in which the conduct occurs. . . . [40]

There are two ways to seize a person. First, and most obviously, you may use physical force to make the seizure. For example, intentionally grabbing a person's shoulder or more drastically shooting him are both seizures. Alternatively, and more commonly, police may seize a person when there is a show of authority sufficient enough to lead a reasonable person to believe he was not free to avoid the officer without legal consequences and the person submits (*i.e.*, does not run away).

A Fourth Amendment seizure of property occurs whenever you intentionally interfere with an individual's possessory interest in his property. The most important element here is intent. For example, if you blow a red light and run into another person's car, you have unintentionally interfered with his property and will be subject to tort liability, not a constitutional violation.

---

[40] *Mich. v. Chesternut*, 486 U.S. 567 (1988).

Remember you can be held vicariously liable if you "keep the peace" while someone takes another person's property. For example, if you are called to a civil standby while a subject removes property from a residence, it may be unwise to allow any disputed property to leave the residence.

🛡️ LEGAL STANDARD

A seizure of a person occurs under the Fourth Amendment when:

- You use force on a person with the intent to restrain,[41] even with minimal force.
- Additionally, a seizure occurs even if the suspect is trying to escape (submission is not required);[42] or
- There is a sufficient show of authority that would lead a reasonable person to believe he was not free to leave or avoid you without legal consequences and submits.[43]

A seizure of property occurs under the Fourth Amendment when:
- You intend some meaningful interference with someone's possessory interest in his property.

🏛️ CASE EXAMPLES

No seizure by DEA agents at airport

The defendant was not seized under the Fourth Amendment when she was asked by airport DEA agents if she would accompany them back to their office to discuss some discrepancies with her plane ticket. Once there, they asked for consent to search and she was informed of her right to refuse. She agreed and a female officer asked her to partially disrobe, after which bundles of heroin were discovered. The whole encounter was consensual.[44]

Consensual contacts on a bus

Narcotics agents boarded a Greyhound bus and without any reasonable suspicion asked various passengers for consent to search their luggage. Arrested smuggler later argued that he was not free to leave because he was stuck on the bus in order to complete his journey and therefore consent was tainted. The Supreme Court disagreed and stated that the test for a consensual encounter is not only the ability to leave, but also the ability to terminate the encounter while staying on the bus (*e.g.*, "Leave me alone officer").[45]

---

[41] *Brower v. County of Inyo*, 489 U.S. 593 (1989).
[42] *Torres v. Madrid*, 141 S. Ct. 989, 209 L. Ed. 2d 190 (2021).
[43] *California v. Hodari*, 499 U.S. 621 (1991).
[44] *U.S. v. Mendenhall*, 446 U.S. 544 (1980).
[45] *Fla. v. Bostick*, 501 U.S. 429 (1991).

Officers that "kept the peace" liable for unlawful seizure of property

Police were called to "keep the peace" while a trailer park manager illegally removed a mobile home for non-payment. The trailer was removed and the homeowner was told by police to not interfere with the park manager. The Court said police transformed the situation into a government seizure.[46]

---

[46] *Soldal v. Cook County*, 506 U.S. 56 (1992).

Chapter 2
Consensual Encounters

2.1 Consensual Encounters

The most common police encounter is the consensual one. You do not need a specific reason to speak with people and consensual encounters are a great way to continue an investigation when you have neither reasonable suspicion nor probable cause. As the Supreme Court said, "Police officers act in full accord with the law when they ask citizens for consent."

Start a consensual encounter by asking a question: "Can I talk to you?" Not, "Come talk to me." Also, your conduct during the encounter must be reasonable. Lengthy encounters full of accusatory questioning will likely be deemed an investigative detention, not a consensual encounter.

Finally, your un-communicated state of mind has zero bearing on whether the person would feel free to leave. Therefore, even if you had probable cause to arrest this factor will not be considered as long as the suspect did not know you intended to arrest him.

🛡 LEGAL STANDARD

A consensual encounter does not violate the Fourth Amendment when:

- A reasonable person would believe he was free to leave or otherwise terminate the encounter.[1] In other words, a reasonable person would have believed he was not detained.

🏛 CASE EXAMPLES

Order to come over and talk is not consensual

Suspect was observed walking in mall parking lot after stores were closed. Officer said, "Come over here, I want to talk to you." Court held officer gave command to suspect and therefore needed reasonable suspicion. Evidence suppressed.[2]

Suspect fit drug courier profile and police conduct was not a consensual encounter

A suspect who fit the so-called "drug-courier profile" was approached at an airport by two detectives. Upon request, but without oral consent, the suspect produced for the detectives his airline ticket and his driver's license. The detectives, without returning the airline ticket and license, asked the suspect to accompany them to a

---

[1] *Fla. v. Bostick*, 501 U.S. 429 (1991).
[2] *People v. Roth*, 219 Cal. App. 3d 211 (Cal. App. 4th Dist. 1990).

small room approximately 40 feet away, and the suspect went with them. Without the suspect's consent, a detective retrieved the suspect's luggage from the airline and brought it to the room. When the suspect was asked if he would consent to a search of his suitcases, the suspect produced a key and unlocked one of the suitcases, in which drugs were found. Court found this was not a consensual encounter and suppressed the evidence.[3]

Even if police have probable cause, they can still seek a consensual encounter with the suspect

"Therefore, even assuming that probable cause existed at some earlier time, there was no violation of the Fourth Amendment...No Fourth Amendment privacy interests are invaded when an officer seeks a consensual interview with a suspect."[4]

Consensual encounter and search valid after officer released driver following a traffic stop

Where officer stopped vehicle to issue traffic citation, concluded traffic stop, indicated to the driver he was free to leave, but then asked whether driver had drugs and whether officer could search vehicle, consent to search was voluntary.[5] Many cops call this move the "two step." After releasing the offender, the officer will turn around towards his patrol car, stop, turn around, and in a Columbo- manner say, "Sir, can I ask one more question before you leave...." It's a solid way to separate the stop from the consensual encounter.

Violation of a state law does not equal automatic Fourth Amendment violation

Although the officers may have violated state law requirements in not informing the person answering the door during "knock and talk" investigation that he had a right to terminate the encounter, that circumstance did not render the consent to talk involuntary under the Fourth Amendment.[6]

2.2 Knock and Talks

There is no Fourth Amendment violation if you try to consensually contact a person at his home. The key to knock and talks is to comply with social norms. Think about it this way, if the Girl Scouts could do it, you can too.

You must be reasonable when you contact the subject. Constant pounding on the door, for example, would likely turn the encounter into a detention if the subject knows that it's the police knocking (an objectively reasonable person would believe that police are commanding him to open the door). Additionally, waking a subject up at 4 a.m. was viewed as a detention requiring reasonable suspicion (see below). In other words, if the Girl Scouts would not do then it's probably unreasonable.

---

[3] *Fla. v. Royer*, 460 U.S. 491 (1983).
[4] *People v. Coddington*, 23 Cal. 4th 529 (2000), as modified on denial of reh'g (Sep 27, 2000).
[5] *U.S. v. Rivera*, 906 F.2d 319 (7th Cir. 1990).
[6] *U.S. v. Cormier*, 220 F.3d 1103 (9th Cir. 2000).

What about "No Trespass" signs? You can usually ignore them because trying to have a consensual conversation with someone is not typically considered trespassing. Same goes with "no soliciting" signs.

🛡 LEGAL STANDARD

Knock and talks are lawful when:

- The path used to reach the door does not violate curtilage and appears available for uninvited guests to use;
- If the house has multiple doors, you chose the door reasonably believed to be available for uninvited guests to make contact with an occupant;
- You used typical, non-intrusive methods to contact the occupant, including making contact during a socially acceptable time;
- Your conversation with the occupant remained consensual; and
- When the conversation ended or was terminated, you immediately left and did not snoop around.

🏛 CASE EXAMPLES

Knock and talk at 4 a.m. held invalid

Officers went to suspect's residence at 4 a.m. with the sole purpose to arrest him. There was no on-going crime and the probable cause was based on an offense that occurred the previous night. Violation of knock and talk because officers exceeded social norms.[7]

Command to open door was not a consensual encounter

"Officers were stationed at both doors of the duplex and (an officer) had commanded (the defendant) to open the door. A reasonable person in (defendant's) situation would have concluded that he had no choice but to acquiesce and open the door."[8]

Constant pressure to consent to search held unlawful

During knock and talk officers continued to press defendant for permission to enter and search. Later consent-to-search was product of illegal detention.[9]

Officer's statement that he did not need a warrant to talk with occupant found to have tainted consent to enter

Officers made contact with a suspected alien at his apartment. The officers asked to enter the apartment, and the occupant asked whether they needed a warrant for that. The officers said they "did not need a warrant to talk to him." Based on the totality of

---

[7] *U.S. v. Lundin*, 47 F. Supp. 3d 1003 (N.D. Cal. 2014).
[8] *U.S. v. Poe*, 462 F.3d 997 (8th Cir. Mo. 2006).
[9] *U.S. v. Washington*, 387 F.3d 1060 (9th Cir. Nev. 2004).

the circumstances, the consent was involuntary since a reasonable occupant would have thought police did not need a warrant to enter and talk.[10]

Unless there is an express order otherwise, officers have the same right to knock and talk as a pollster or salesman

"Consensual encounters may also take place at the doorway of a home. In a frequently cited opinion, one federal appeals court stated more than forty years ago: 'Absent express orders from the person in possession against any possible trespass, there is no rule of private or public conduct which makes it illegal per se, or a condemned invasion of the person's right of privacy, for anyone openly and peaceably, at high noon, to walk up the steps and knock on the front door of any man's 'castle' with the honest intent of asking questions of the occupant thereof—whether the questioner be a pollster, a salesman, or an officer of the law.'"[11]

2.3 Investigative Activities During Consensual Encounter

Just because you are engaged in a consensual encounter does not mean you cannot investigate. However, be careful about how you go about it. Be cool, low key, and relaxed. Make small talk and just present yourself as a curious cop versus someone looking to make an arrest (though that may be your goal).

During a consensual encounter, there are really three investigative activities you can engage in; questioning, asking for ID, and seeking consent to search.

"(L)aw enforcement officers do not violate the Fourth Amendment by merely approaching an individual on the street or in another public place, by asking him if he is willing to answer some questions, (or) by putting questions to him if the person is willing to listen."[12]

Asking for ID and running a subject for warrants does not automatically convert encounter into a detention.[13] Hint, return ID as soon as possible so a reasonable person would still "feel free to leave."[14]

🛡 LEGAL STANDARD

Questioning

Questioning a person does not convert a consensual encounter into an investigative detention as long as:

- Your questions are not overly accusatory in a manner that would make a reasonable person believe they were being detained for criminal activity.

---

[10] *Orhorgaghe v. I.N.S.*, 38 F.3d 488 (9th Cir. 1994).
[11] *People v. Rivera*, 41 Cal. 4th 304 (2007).
[12] *Fla. v. Royer*, 460 U.S. 491 (1983).
[13] *People v. Bouser*, 26 Cal. App. 4th 1280 (Cal. App. 4th Dist. 1994).
[14] *U.S. v. Chan-Jimenez*, 125 F.3d 1324 (9th Cir. Ariz. 1997).

Identification

Asking a person for identification does not convert a consensual encounter into an investigative detention as long as:

- The identification is requested, not demanded; and
- You returned the identification as soon as practicable, otherwise a reasonable person may no longer feel free to leave.

Consent to search

Asking a person for consent to search does not convert the encounter into an investigative detention as long as:

- The person's consent was freely and voluntarily given;
- He has apparent authority to give consent to search the area or item; and
- You did not exceed the scope provided, express or implied.

🏛 CASE EXAMPLES

Child illegally questioned at school while officer was present

A child was illegally seized and questioned by a caseworker and police officer when they escorted the child off private school property and interrogated the child for 20 minutes about intimate details of his family life and whether he was being abused. The government argued this was a consensual encounter, but no reasonable child in that position would have believed they were free to leave.[15]

Note: This case may have come out differently if they did not remove the child from school grounds. Involuntary transportation usually converts an encounter into an arrest.

Consent to search was involuntary after arrest-like behavior

Suspect did not voluntarily consent to the search of his person, and suppression of a handgun discovered was warranted, where the suspect was in a bus shelter, was surrounded by three patrol cars and five uniformed officers, an officer's initial, accusatory question, combined with the police-dominated atmosphere, clearly communicated to the suspect that he was not free to leave or to refuse the officer's request to conduct the search, the officer never informed the suspect that he had the right to refuse the search, and the suspect never gave verbal or written consent, but instead merely surrendered to an officer's command.[16]

2.4   Asking for Identification

If you make a consensual encounter, you can always request that the subject identify themselves. But remember, there is no requirement that he do so.

---

[15] *Doe v. Heck*, 327 F.3d 492 (7th Cir. 2003).
[16] *U.S. v. Robertson*, 736 F.3d 677 (4th Cir. 2013).

Additionally, there is likely no crime if the subject lied about his identity during a consensual encounter (however, possession of a fraudulent ID may be a crime).

I know a lot of officers do not understand how a person can lie about his identity and get away with it. But think about it, what law requires a person to identify himself during a consensual encounter? There may be a requirement the suspect identify himself during an investigative detention, but not a consensual one.

On the other hand, lying about ones' identity may help develop reasonable suspicion the person is engaged in criminal activity, but this cannot be the sole reason to detain or arrest the person.

🛡 LEGAL STANDARD

Asking a person for identification does not convert a consensual encounter into an investigative detention as long as:

- The identification is requested, not demanded; and
- You return the identification as soon as practicable, otherwise a reasonable person may no longer feel free to leave.

🏛 CASE EXAMPLES

Detaining a subject for identification requires reasonable suspicion

"When the officers detained [suspect] for the purpose of requiring him to identify himself, they performed a seizure of his person subject to the requirements of the Fourth Amendment.[17]

Providing a false name not a crime unless lawfully detained or arrested

Defendant's arrest was premised on his giving a false name. The state statute criminalizes a person's false representation or identification of himself or herself to a peace officer "upon a lawful detention or arrest of [that] person...." The law applies only where the false identification is given in connection with lawful detention or arrest and does not apply to consensual encounters with police. Since defendant's subsequent arrest was based upon an unlawful detention, and the search incident to the arrest was likewise unlawful suppression is required of contraband seized after search incident to unlawful arrest.[18]

Asking for identification, among other activities, held to be consensual

Where a narcotics officer approached the defendant after she deplaned, identified himself and asked to speak with her; asked for her ticket, which she gave to him;

---

[17] *Brown v. Tex.*, 99 S. Ct. 2637 (1979).
[18] *People v. Walker*, 210 Cal. App. 4th 165 (Cal. App. 6th Dist. 2012).

asked for identification, which was produced; asked for permission to search her purse, which she allowed; and asked whether a female officer could pat her down for drugs to which she agreed; all consents were voluntary even though the defendant was visibly nervous and became more so as the interview progressed.[19]

Consent to search for identification valid

Following a pat down of defendant, and after defendant was not "immediately forthright" about his identity, giving only his first name and providing several false dates of birth, the officer asked defendant if he had any identification. Defendant indicated that it could be found in his back pocket. The officer asked for, and was granted, consent to retrieve the identification from defendant's back pocket, but the pocket turned out to be empty. When asked if the identification might be located elsewhere, defendant suggested that it might be in his left front pocket, where the officer found not only an identification card, but what appeared to be cocaine.[20] Double prizes!

Holding passenger's identification while seeking consent to search from driver held be an unlawful detention

After stopping a car, the trooper obtained the driver's license and the passenger's identification card. After writing the citation, the trooper spoke to the driver outside the car. He handed the driver a citation and his license but held onto the passenger's identification. The trooper sought and obtained consent to search. The court held that since the passenger's ID was still being held, the driver was not truly free to leave, and the search was suppressed.[21]

2.5 Removing Hands from Pockets

Generally, you may ask a subject to remove his hands from his pockets without worrying about converting the encounter into a detention. Courts understand the importance of officer safety.[22] What if the subject refuses to comply? If you can articulate a legitimate officer safety issue, then ordering a suspect to show his hands may be deemed reasonable.

Moreover, an order to show hands may not even implicate the Fourth Amendment, because the interference with a person's freedom is so minimal it may fall under the "minimal intrusion doctrine."

What if the suspect still refuses to show his hands and tries to leave? Remember, this is a consensual encounter and if you decided to detain the subject you would need reasonable suspicion. An order to show hands may be a minimal intrusion, but a detention is not.

---

[19] *U.S. v. Galberth*, 846 F.2d 983 (5th Cir. 1988).
[20] *U.S. v. Chaney*, 647 F.3d 401 (1st Cir. 2011).
[21] *U.S. v. Macias*, 658 F.3d 509, 524 (5th Cir. 2011).
[22] *People v. Franklin*, 192 Cal. App. 3d 935 (Cal. App. 5th Dist. 1987).

🛡 LEGAL STANDARD

Asking a person to remove his hands from his pockets does not convert a consensual encounter into an investigative detention as long as:

- You requested that he remove his hands from his pockets; and
- You did it for officer safety purposes.

Ordering a person to remove his hands from his pockets may not convert a consensual encounter into an investigative detention if:

- You had a legitimate safety reason for ordering it; and
- You articulate that ordering the person to remove his hands was a minimal intrusion of his freedom.[23]

2.6 Transporting to Police Station

There is no Fourth Amendment violation if you consensually transport a subject to the police station for a consensual interview or to a crime scene. The key is that the subject's consent must be freely and voluntarily given.

🛡 LEGAL STANDARD

You may voluntarily transport a person in a police vehicle. However, if the person is a suspect to a crime and you are transporting the person for an interview, remember:

- Make it clear to the person that he is not under arrest;
- Seek consent to patdown the suspect for weapons, if the patdown is denied, do not patdown and you probably should not transport.

🏛 CASE EXAMPLES

No violation when a person agrees to accompany police

Appellate courts have held that when a person agrees to accompany the police to a station for an interrogation or some other purpose, the Fourth Amendment is not violated.[24]

No seizure after agreeing to accompany police to station and stay for five hours

No seizure where defendant went with police to station and stayed there five hours before probable cause developed for his arrest.[25]

---

[23] *U.S. v. Enslin*, 327 F.3d 788 (9th Cir. Cal. 2003).
[24] *In re Gilbert R.*, 25 Cal. App. 4th 1121 (Cal. App. 2d Dist. 1994).
[25] *Craig v. Singletary*, 27 F.3d 1030 (11th Cir.1997).

Detention ended when suspect consented to go to police station

Law enforcement officer's Terry stop of automobile ended when defendant, who was riding in automobile, agreed to go to police station, rather than when defendant was arrested several hours later.[26]

2.7 Consent to Search

Absent good reason, you should routinely seek consent to search a person or his property even if you have reasonable suspicion or probable cause. Why? Because this will add an extra layer of protection to your case. For example, let's imagine you have probable cause to search a vehicle for drugs but still receive consent to search, the prosecution essentially needs to prove that consent was freely and voluntarily given.[27] If that fails, the prosecutor can fall back on your probable cause.

Without consent your case depends entirely on articulating P.C. Why not have both? Plus, juries like to see officers asking for consent. Either way, do your prosecutor a solid and write a complete and articulate report.

⭐ LEGAL STANDARD

Asking a person for consent to search does not convert the encounter into an investigative detention as long as:

- The person's consent was freely and voluntarily given;
- He had apparent authority to give consent to search the area or item; and
- You did not exceed the scope provided, express or implied. Courts may look at four factors when evaluating whether or not the scope of search was exceeded: time, duration, area, and intensity. See case examples below.

🏛 CASE EXAMPLES

"I do not care"

Suspect was stopped for speeding. He was suspected of drug possession and officer asked for consent to search. Suspect responded, "I do not care." Search revealed crack cocaine. Suspect's statement implied consent to search.[28] Note: this type of consent is not ideal and officers should try to get unambiguous consent to search.

Patdown of suspect who wanted to get out of vehicle upheld

Vehicle was stopped for an equipment violation. Driver wanted to get out and see proof that his taillight was broken. Officer said only on the condition that he

---

[26] *U.S. v. Kimball*, 25 F.3d 1 (1st Cir. 1994).
[27] *Bumper v. North Carolina*, 391 U.S. 543 (1968).
[28] *U.S. v. Polly*, 630 F.3d 991 (10th Cir. Okla. 2011).

be subject to a patdown. Suspect said, "that was fine" and stepped out. Patdown revealed drugs. Suspect voluntarily consented to patdown.[29]

Time: Search of van two days after written consent received was upheld as reasonable

In-custody suspect gave written consent to search van for forensic evidence of a rape. Van was searched two days later by different agents. Under these particular circumstances, the time of the search was reasonable.[30] Note: Ideally, the suspect would have been told the search would be executed two days later. But since he was in custody and never revoked consent, the court upheld it.

Duration: Request for a "real quick" search exceeded after 15 minutes and unscrewing speaker box

With defendant agreeing to the officer's request to "check (defendant's car) real quick and get you on your way," the scope of that consent was exceeded at some point before the search had continued for fifteen minutes without finding anything, and certainly when the officer later pulled a box from the trunk and removed the back panel to the box by unscrewing some screws.[31]

Area: Directly "touching" genitals outside implied consent

Officer got consent to search for drugs and "within seconds" reached down the defendant's crotch and felt the suspect's genital area searching for drugs. This area was not included in the consent to search. Note, searching "near" genital area is often upheld.[32]

Intensity: Damaging property requires "express consent"

Officer got consent to search for drugs and opened a "tamales in gravy" can, drugs were found inside. Since the officer "rendered the can useless" express permission was required.[33]

2.8 Third-Party Consent

You may seek consent to search a residence from co-occupants. However, the situation changes when there is a present non- consenting co-occupant. If one occupant tells you to "Come on in and bring your friends!" and another yells "Get the hell out, I'm watching Netflix!" Well, you must stay out.

What about areas under the exclusive control of the consenter? For example, the "cooperative" tenant says you can still search his bedroom? Or a shed he has exclusive control over in the backyard? There is no case that deals directly with this issue, but if the area is truly under the exclusive control of the consenting party, and you can articulate that the non-consenting party has no reasonable expectation of privacy in that area, It would likely be reasonable to search just

---

[29] *State v. Cunningham*, 26 N.E.3d 21 (Ind. 2015).
[30] *U.S. v. White*, 617 F.2d 1131 (5th Cir. 1989).
[31] *People v. Cantor*, 149 Cal. App. 4th 961 (2007).
[32] *U.S. v. Blake*, 888 F.2d 795 (11th Cir. 1989).
[33] *U.S. v. Osage*, 235 F.3d 518 (10th Cir. 2000).

that area. But one thing is certain, you still may not be able to access the area under the cooperative tenant's control without walking through common areas— common areas would still be off limits.

The best practice is to wait until the non-consenting occupant left the residence and then seek consent from the cooperative occupant. In other words, if the non-consenting occupant goes to work, store, or is lawfully arrested, the remaining occupant can consent to search. Still, do not search areas under the exclusive control of the non-consenting party. This may include file cabinets, "man-caves," purses, backpacks, and so forth.

Finally, if the consenting party has greater authority over the residence, then police may rely on that consent. For example, if a casual visitor or babysitter objected to police entry, it may be overruled by the homeowner. Remember, you may not search personal property under the exclusive control of the visitor or babysitter.

🛡 LEGAL STANDARD

Spouses and Co-Occupants:

Spouses or co-occupants may consent to search inside a home if:

- The person has apparent authority;
- Consent is only given for common areas, areas under his exclusive control, or areas or things the person has authorized access to; and
- A non-consenting spouse or co-occupant with the same or greater authority is not present.

Articulating Greater Authority:

An occupant with greater authority over the premises may consent to search over areas either under his exclusive control or common areas if:

- The co-occupant had greater authority over the area searched;
- You did not enter or walk through any area where the non- consenting occupant had equal or greater authority;
- You did not search any property under the exclusive control of the non-consenting occupant; and
- Your search did not exceed the scope provided by the consenting occupant.

🏛 CASE EXAMPLES

If non-consenting occupant is arrested or leaves, remaining occupant may consent to search despite prior objection

Police could conduct warrantless search of defendant's apartment following defendant's arrest based on consent to the search by a woman who also occupied the apartment, although defendant had objected to the search prior to his arrest and was absent at the time of the woman's consent because of his arrest.[34]

---

[34] *Fernandez v. California*, 571 U.S. 292 (2014).

Consent of wife valid after non-consenting husband left residence

"The consent of one who possesses common authority over premises or effects" generally "is valid as against the absent, non- consenting person with whom that authority is shared."[35]

If an occupant invites police inside, police may assume other occupants would not object

"[S]hared tenancy is understood to include an 'assumption of risk,' on which police officers are entitled to rely, and although some group living together might make an exceptional arrangement that no one could admit a guest without the agreement of all, police need not assume that's the case"[36]

2.9 Mistaken Authority to Consent

If you are a prudent officer you normally ask for consent to search, even if you have P.C.. Why? Because valid consent adds an extra layer of protection for your criminal case.

But sometimes you may think you are dealing with an occupant who has the authority to consent, but later find out you were wrong. For example, the consent was received from a guest, not homeowner. Here, courts will look to see if your mistake was reasonable.

⚜ LEGAL STANDARD

If you mistakenly receive consent from a person who had "apparent authority," courts will employ a three-part analysis to determine if your mistake was reasonable:

- Did you believe some untrue fact;
- Was it objectively reasonable for you to believe that the fact was true under the circumstances at the time; and
- If it was true would the consent giver have had actual authority.

🏛 CASE EXAMPLES

Police may assume the adult that answered door had authority

Police were trying to locate a robbery suspect and knocked on his door. A visitor answered and consented to their request to enter. "Police may assume, without further inquiry, that [an adult] person who answers the door in response to their knock has the authority to let them enter."[37]

---

[35] *U.S. v. Cordero-Rosario*, 786 F.3d 64 (1st Cir. P.R. 2015).
[36] *Georgia v. Randolph*, 547 U.S. 103 (2006).
[37] *People v. Ledesma*, 39 Cal. 4th 641 (Cal. 2006).

Simply claiming to live at home may not be enough without more info

Even if person claims to live at home, "the surrounding circumstances could conceivably be such that a reasonable person would doubt its truth and not act upon it without further inquiry."[38]

---

[38] *Ill. v. Rodriguez*, 497 U.S. 177 (1990).

Chapter 3
Investigative Detentions

3.1 Specific Factors to Consider

In determining whether you have reasonable suspicion, consider the following factors. If one or more of these factors exist, articulate them in your report.

Remember that courts use the "totality of the circumstances" test when determining whether you had reasonable suspicion to detain a person. Therefore, it is in your best interest to articulate as many factors as possible in your report. That way, courts have enough information to rule in your favor.

⭐ LEGAL STANDARD

Specific factors you should consider include:

- **Nighttime**: Activity late at night, especially in residential areas, is often more suspicious than in daytime;[1]
- **High-crime area**: An areas reputation for criminal activity is an appropriate factor is assessing R.S.;[2]
- **Identity profiling**: Race, age, religion, etc. may only be used to support R.S. if you have specific suspect attributes;
- **Unprovoked flight**: Flight is a significant factor in assessing R.S., and combined with another factor, like a high-crime area, may justify a detention;[3]
- **Training and experience**: Your training and experience is possibly one of the most important factors is assessing reasonable suspicion. For example, if you believe a suspect is lying, this can help establish R.S. or P.C.[4] Still, the key is to translate these experiences in your report. The court needs to know what you know. Otherwise, what separates you from John Q Citizen? Articulate, articulate, articulate.
- **Criminal profiles**: Courts are cautious about giving cops authority to detain a person simply because he fit a "criminal profile." Therefore, use "criminal profiles" only in connection to contemporaneous facts and circumstances that would lead a reasonable officer to believe criminal activity is afoot, and do not rely on race or ethnicity characteristics unless you have intel that a specific suspect possesses those traits;[5]
- **Information from reliable sources**: You can use information from reliable sources. Reliable sources include fellow police officers, citizen informers not involved in criminal conduct, confidential informants if proved reliable, and so forth;[6]

---

[1] *See People v. Souza*, 9 Cal.4th 224 (1994).
[2] *See People v. Souza*, 9 Cal.4th 224 (1994).
[3] *See Illinois v. Wardlow*, 528 U.S. 119 (2000).
[4] *See Devenpeck v. Alford*, 543 U.S. 146 (2004).
[5] *See U.S. v. Sokolow*, 490 U.S. 1 (1989).
[6] *See People v. Stanley*, 18 Cal. App. 5th 398 (2017).

- **Anonymous tips**: If a reliable source provides information, but they do not want to get involved or be known, they are not truly "anonymous" since you know who they are. A true anonymous tip is from someone who's identity is unknown. Before acting on anonymous tips, you need to prove the information is reliable through an independent investigation;[7]
- **9-1-1 calls**: The Supreme Court has held that 9-1-1 callers are rarely "anonymous" because dispatch can trace the call and tipsters can be charged with a false report.[8] Still, whether or not you can make the stop depends on the totality of the circumstances.

3.2 Detaining a Suspect

If you have an articulable reasonable suspicion that a suspect is involved in criminal activity, you may briefly detain him in order to "maintain the status quo" and investigate.[9] Courts use the "status quo" language because it implies that you are not really doing anything to the suspect, besides taking some of his time. This distinction is important because all Fourth Amendment intrusions must be reasonable. If all you are doing is temporarily detaining a suspect, versus conducting a full search or other arrest-like behavior, then it's more likely to be considered reasonable.

🛡 LEGAL STANDARD

A suspect may be detained when:

- You can articulate facts and circumstances that would lead a reasonable officer to believe the suspect has, is, or is about to be involved in criminal activity;
- You use the minimal amount of force necessary to detain a cooperative suspect;
- Once the stop is made, you must diligently pursue a means of investigation that will confirm or dispel your suspicions;
- If your suspicions are dispelled, the person must be immediately released or the stop converted into a consensual encounter.

🏛 CASE EXAMPLES

Long wait for K9 held reasonable under the circumstances

A 31-minute wait for drug dog was not an unreasonable after trooper developed R.S. for narcotics, was denied consent, and acted diligently in pursuit of his investigation.[10]

---

[7] *See Alabama v. White*, 496 U.S. 325 (1990).
[8] *See Navarette v. California*, 134 S. Ct. 1683 (2014).
[9] *Terry v. Ohio*, 392 U.S. 1 (1968).
[10] *U.S. v. Lyons*, 486 F.3d 367 (8th Cir. 2007).

Detention of man with axe at 3 a.m. reasonable

Cops had R.S. to stop man with axe at 3 a.m., though no "axe crimes" were reported. "Some activity is so unusual ... that it cries out for investigation."[11]

3.3   Officer Safety Detentions

The vast majority of investigative detentions occur because you believe the person detained is involved in criminal activity. However, a detention based on officer safety concerns is also lawful "when an individual's actions give the appearance of potential danger to the officer."[12] These detentions are often for people connected to the target suspect, such as lookouts.

⭐ LEGAL STANDARD

A subject may be detained for officer safety when:

- You can articulate facts and circumstances that would lead a reasonable officer to believe the subject is a potential danger;
- You use the minimal amount of force necessary to detain the subject; and
- Once a patdown is conducted and no weapons are discovered, the subject should be released or converted to a consensual encounter unless the subject poses another risk, such as wanting to physically attack the officers.

🏛 CASE EXAMPLES

Detention based on legitimate officer safety upheld

"A consensual encounter may turn into a lawful detention when an individual's actions give the appearance of potential danger to the officer ... There is no question that 'a perfectly reasonable apprehension of danger may arise long before the officer is possessed of adequate information to justify taking a person into custody for the purpose of prosecuting him for a crime.'"[13]

3.4   How Long Can Detentions Last?

Whenever you detain someone for reasonable suspicion, you must diligently pursue a means of investigation that is likely to confirm or dispel the suspicion quickly.[14] Once your suspicion has been dispelled, the person must be allowed to go on his way.[15] At the same time, the Supreme Court has never provided a maxi-

---

[11] *People v. Forensic*, 64 Cal. App. 4th 186 (1998).
[12] *People v. Mendoza*, 52 Cal.4th 1056 (2011).
[13] *People v. Mendoza*, 52 Cal. 4th 1056 (2011).
[14] *U.S. v. Sharpe*, 470 U.S. 675 (1985).
[15] *Terry v. Ohio*, 392 U.S. 1 (1968).

mum duration for investigative detentions.[16] Rather, as long as you are diligently pursuing the investigation, it should not matter that the stop took ten minutes or, in an extreme case, two hours. Each investigation is unique and different. What's more, no violation occurs simply because a least intrusive investigation could have been utilized. Instead, the means chosen must be reasonable.

Finally, if you have dispelled your suspicions but still have a "hunch" you want to pursue, convert the stop into a consensual encounter or release the suspect. Failure to do so is a Fourth Amendment violation.

⭐ LEGAL STANDARD

The duration of an investigative detention is determined by these factors:

- Once the stop is made, you must diligently pursue a means of investigation that will confirm or dispel your suspicions;
- If your suspicions are dispelled, the person must be immediately released or the stop converted into a consensual encounter.

🏛 CASE EXAMPLES

Extending stop for 25 minutes was reasonable

Original stop was for erratic driving but was appropriately extended for 25 minutes to investigate trafficking due to conflicting answers, masking odor, and other circumstances.[17]

3.5 Investigative Techniques During a Stop

If you make a stop based on reasonable suspicion, you may perform various investigative techniques as long as they are reasonably related to why you stopped the person and are minimally intrusive. The techniques may also be used to continue your investigation after the person is released, not just to build probable cause to arrest. For example, you may take the suspect's picture, or quickly take in-field fingerprints, and then release the suspect and use the photo and prints to continue your investigation.

⭐ LEGAL STANDARD

You may conduct investigative techniques in the field when:

- The suspect is still lawfully detained; and
- The technique employed is minimally intrusive.

---

[16] *U.S. v. Sharpe*, 470 U.S. 675 (1985).
[17] *People v. Russell*, 81 Cal. App. 4th 96 (101).

You may demand identification if:

- The suspect is still lawfully detained;
- You need the identification to pursue your investigation;

You may capture a suspects fingerprints in the field when:

- You have reason to believe fingerprints may have been left at the scene;
- Minimally intrusive means were used to recover the suspect's fingerprints; and
- The fingerprints will aid your investigation after the suspect is released.

🏛 CASE EXAMPLES

Police may obtain fingerprints with reasonable suspicion

"There is support...that the Fourth Amendment would permit seizures for the purpose of fingerprinting, if there is a reasonable basis for believing that fingerprinting will establish or negate the suspect's connection with that crime."[18]

Officers may open door if they cannot see through tinted windows

During a lawful traffic stop, where the vehicle's windows were so heavily tinted that the officer could not see inside, it is reasonable to open the vehicle's door in order to be able to observe the interior. The court adopted this proposition as a "bright-line" rule.[19]

Collective knowledge doctrine applies to Terry Stops

An Illinois state police officer had reasonable suspicion that a suspect was transporting drugs in his airplane. He passed this information onto Federal Homeland Security...who passed it onto a Wyoming officer who stopped the suspect at the airport. The court found that there was significant communication between all of the officers and that they functioned as a team. Therefore, the collective knowledge doctrine applies and the stop was lawful.[20]

Statute requiring people stopped to supply "credible and reliable" ID struck down as vague and gave police too much discretion

A California statute required persons who loiter or wander on the streets to provide a "credible and reliable" identification and to account for their presence when requested by a peace officer. The statute was struck down, among other reasons, because it vested virtually complete discretion in the hands of the police to determine whether the suspect had supplied "credible and reliable" identification.[21]

---

[18] *Hayes v. Florida*, 105 S. Ct. 1643 (1985).
[19] *U.S. v. Stanfield*, 109 F.3d 976, 981 (4th Cir. 1997).
[20] *U.S. v. Latorre*, 893 F.3d 744 (10th Cir. 2018).
[21] *Kolender v. Lawson*, 461 U.S. 352 (1983).

3.6   Identifications - in the Field

Courts are scrutinizing police identification procedures more than they have in the past. One reason is because research has shown that eyewitnesses are easily swayed by suggestive practices. For example, if police make an investigative detention on an armed robbery suspect, it would be improper to say to the victim, "We have the perpetrator, but we still need you to ID him."

You may also conduct a "show-up" between the suspect and witness under a few circumstances. Usually, these show-ups are conducted soon after the crime has occurred when police have detained a suspect (on-scene or in the vicinity).

Remember, it is vital that you stay as neutral and detached as possible when it comes to identification procedures.

🛡 LEGAL STANDARD

A suspect may be required to participate in solo in-field "show-up" if:

- The procedure is not overly suggestive of guilt (*e.g.*, not surrounding suspect with cops, if safe, removing handcuffs, and not telling the witness that the suspect is the perpetrator).

🏛 CASE EXAMPLES

In field show-up was not overly suggestive

Where victim was around assailant for about 30 minutes, and could see him under artificial lighting, described him before show- up, said "I do not think I could ever forget" his unique appearance, and so forth, the following in field show-up was not overly suggestive.[22]

3.7   Unprovoked Flight Upon Seeing an Officer

If you are patrolling a "high crime" area and a person suddenly, and without provocation, runs upon seeing you, then these may be sufficient conditions to conduct an investigative detention in order to determine whether he is involved in criminal activity. Unprovoked flight, by itself, does not provide sufficient reason to conduct a pat- down. You need to articulate something more, such as a known gang member, history of violence, or possible drug dealer (not just drug user).

Finally, this rule may also include wealthy areas where a rash of recent burglaries have occurred, or a business district when all the stores are closed. Articulate, articulate, articulate.

---

[22] *Neil v. Biggers*, 409 U.S. 188 (1972).

⬟ LEGAL STANDARD

A suspect that flees upon seeing you may be detained if:

- You are patrolling a high crime area;
- Upon seeing you or a readily apparent police vehicle, the suspect suddenly, and without provocation;
- Engages in a headlong flight commensurate with evasion; and
- You use a reasonable amount of force necessary to detain the suspect.

Note: Unprovoked flight alone does not justify a patdown.

🏛 CASE EXAMPLES

Unprovoked flight away from police may be suspicious evasive behavior

"Refusal to cooperate, without more, does not furnish reasonable suspicion. But unprovoked flight is simply not a mere refusal to cooperate. Flight by its very nature, is not 'going about one's business'; in fact, it is just the opposite."[23]

3.8 Detentions Based on an Anonymous Tip

You may make an investigative detention based on an anonymous tip if the information has some indicia of reliability and, where appropriate, the information is independently corroborated. The courts will use the totality of the circumstances test and it's vital you articulate all pertinent facts and circumstances in your report.

One of the best methods to corroborate information is to determine whether the tipster shared something unknown to the general public and therefore represents "inside" knowledge. For example, if a tipster shared that a red Chevy truck was going to buy drugs at a particular gas station at 1 p.m., this information is easily corroborated. If the truck shows up at the time and place stated, that is not something the general public would know.

On the other hand, if the tipster said the red Chevy truck in the Walmart parking lot is dealing drugs, you would need to know more. Any member of the public could see the truck. It does not predict any future conduct.[24]

⬟ LEGAL STANDARD

A suspect may be detained based an anonymous tip if:

- The tip had an indicia of reliability;[25] and

---

[23] *Illinois v. Wardlow*, 528 U.S. 119 (2000).
[24] *Florida v. J.L.*, 529 U.S. 266 (2000).
[25] *Navarette v. California*, 134 S. Ct. 1683 (2014).

- The tip was sufficiently corroborated[26] to show that the caller had information not readily available to the general public.

🏛 CASE EXAMPLES

Anonymous report that 25 people were being loud and displaying handguns justified Terry Stop, despite group being smaller and quieter

An anonymous 911 call, reporting that a group of 25 people were being loud and displaying handguns in a parking lot at a location where violent crime and drug activity were regularly reported, supported a reasonable suspicion that a crime was in progress or about to be committed and justified a Terry Stop. Even though the group at the scene was smaller and quieter than reported, and was not brandishing weapons, nature of call required a lower level of corroboration. Additionally, five-minute response time could have accounted for the change in the number of people present and their activities.[27]

Reality that some facts could not be corroborated due to dark tinted windows was considered in whether stop was reasonable

Reasonable suspicion existed when an anonymous tip stated that three black males, one of whom had a gun and wore a hooded sweater, would be found in a four-door gray Cadillac in the parking lot of a particular fast food restaurant. The officers corroborated the presence of the vehicle at that location, but could not corroborate more due to the vehicle's darkly tinted windows and its unusual location in a distant area of the parking lot.[28]

Generalized tip was not enough for reasonable suspicion stop

Police officers did not have a reasonable, articulable, and individualized suspicion that the suspect was engaged in criminal activity, where they only had an anonymous tip that a male matching the suspect's description was in possession of a gun. The suspect was located in a high-crime neighborhood in which a shooting had occurred over one hour earlier, and it was late at night; the suspect's failure to comply with the order to show his hands could not be considered because it occurred after the moment of the seizure, and his few steps backward were entirely consistent with a surprised reaction and even acquiescence.[29]

3.9 Handcuffing and Use of Force

Generally, if you handcuff a suspect, point a firearm, or use force during an investigative detention, it will likely be deemed an arrest requiring probable cause. Exceptions exist, but you need to have legitimate reasons. If you make a reasonable suspicion stop on a suspect you believe is about to pull a gun on you, then of course

---

[26] *Alabama v. White*, 496 U.S. 325 (1990).
[27] *U.S. v. Williams*, 731 F.3d 678 (7th Cir. 2013).
[28] *U.S. v. Bold*, 19 F.3d 99 (2d Cir. 1994).
[29] *U.S. v. Lowe*, 791 F.3d 424 (3d Cir. 2015).

you get point your firearm on them and conduct a patdown! Your safety comes first but articulate that in your report. Similarly, if you believe a suspect is about to run, then handcuff him. Again, articulate why in your report.

🛡 LEGAL STANDARD

If a suspect fights or flees during an investigative detention, then:

- You may use a reasonable amount of force to detain the suspect;
- The suspect's flight upon a lawful order to stop, or a battery upon an officer, may be probable cause to arrest; and
- Deadly force cannot be used to detain a suspect, unless the suspect poses a deadly force threat to you or others.

Handcuffing a suspect is appropriate when:

- The suspect appears to be a flight risk; or
- The suspect appears to be a danger to himself or others.

🏛 CASE EXAMPLES

Frisk may still be reasonable, even if suspect is handcuffed

Where there is reasonable suspicion that a suspect is armed (thus justifying a frisk under Terry) and where the facts make it reasonable to handcuff the suspect during the investigative seizure, the fact that the suspect is handcuffed does not negate the right of the officer to conduct the frisk.[30]

Mere handcuffing does not always indicate an arrest

The court stated that, "handcuffing a suspect does not necessarily dictate a finding of custody." The use of handcuffs "does not necessarily convert a Terry stop into an arrest."[31]

3.10 Detaining Victims or Witnesses

Generally, you cannot force a victim or witness to cooperate with your investigation. It is a "settled principle that while the police have the right to request citizens to answer voluntarily questions concerning unsolved crimes they have no right to compel them to answer."[32]

If you have located an uncooperative witness, and they are vital for your investigation, then identify them. Give his information to the prosecutor and let him decide whether or not the witness should be subpoenaed.

---

[30] *U.S. v. Sanders*, 994 F.2d 200 (5th Cir. 1993).
[31] *U.S. v. Bravo*, 295 F.3d 1002 (9th Cir. 2002).
[32] *Davis v. Mississippi*, 394 U.S. 721 (1969).

⭐ LEGAL STANDARD

A witness may be detained if:

- He is a material witness for your investigation;
- The detention should last no longer than necessary to determine his identification and whether he's willing to cooperate with your investigation;
- If the witness is uncooperative, identify and release. Contact your prosecutor and get advice on how to proceed.

🏛 CASE EXAMPLES

Detaining victim in order to continue investigation unreasonable

It would be an unreasonable detention for an officer, after investigating and determining that a person was an injured victim rather than a suspect, to continue to detain him and to prevent him from being taken to a hospital. The officer required that he wait for an ambulance and would not allow others who had been trying to take him to a hospital to do so.[33]

3.11 Patdown for Weapons

A pat-down (or "Terry frisk") is a limited search of a suspect's outer clothing for weapons. You must articulate two things before you can conduct a patdown. First, the investigative stop itself must be lawful (based on individualized reasonable suspicion). Second, you must articulate that the person is armed and dangerous.

Additionally, if you feel an object that may be a weapon, but you are not positive, you may retrieve and inspect it.

⭐ LEGAL STANDARD

A suspect may be frisked for weapons under the following circumstances:

- If the suspect is lawfully or unlawfully armed with a weapon, the weapon may be secured and a patdown of outer clothing conducted for additional weapons;
- If no weapon is visible, and you believe the suspect is armed and dangerous, a patdown of outer clothing may be conducted; or
- If the suspect was stopped for a violent crime or one involving weapons, an automatic patdown may be conducted.

---

[33] *Eubanks v. Lawson*, 122 F.3d 639 (8th Cir. 1997).

 **CASE EXAMPLES**

Officer does not need to be certain

"The officer need not be absolutely certain that the individual is armed; the issue is whether a reasonably prudent man in the circumstances would be warranted in the belief that his safety or that of others was in danger."[34]

Relevant considerations

Relevant considerations may include: observing a visible bulge in a person's clothing that could indicate the presence of a weapon; seeing a weapon in an area the suspect controls, such as a car; "sudden movements" suggesting a potential assault or "attempts to reach for an object that was not immediately visible;" "evasive and deceptive responses" to an officer's questions about what an individual was up to; unnatural hand postures that suggest an effort to conceal a firearm; and whether the officer observes anything during an encounter with the suspect that would dispel the officer's suspicions regarding the suspect's potential involvement in a crime or likelihood of being armed.[35]

Refusal to remove hands is a factor justifying frisk

"The officers, after initiating the stop, twice ordered that [defendant] remove his hands from his pockets, which he refused to do. The report of an assault in progress, the matching description, and the additional factors that supported the stop provided the officers with reason to believe that [defendant] was armed and dangerous, and that the refusal to remove his hands was an effort to conceal a weapon."[36]

Stop in gang-ridden area helped justify patdown

"[T]the area in which the incident occurred gave police officers particular reason to be concerned about the possibility of gun- related violence. The neighborhood was known as a high-crime area of the city; but more importantly, there were indications of gang activity, recent reports of shots fired, and the occurrence of a drive-by shooting with two victims two days earlier and one block away from the location where the men were discovered drinking. These specific and recent indicia of violence, including gun-related violence, increased the odds that an individual detained at this location for apparent criminal activity (even a petty offense like the one at issue here) might be armed."[37]

"Tap" by officer to open hand was a frisk requiring justification

Police officer's "tap" of the defendant's wrist to open closed-hand was a frisk that constituted a search subject to the protections of the Fourth Amendment.[38]

---

[34] *Terry v. Ohio*, 392 U.S. 1 (1968).
[35] *Thomas v. Dillard*, 818 F.3d 864 (9th Cir. Cal. 2016)
[36] *U.S. v. Simmons*, 560 F.3d 98 (2d Cir. 2009).
[37] *U.S. v. Patton*, 705 F.3d 734 (7th Cir. Ill. 2013).
[38] *U.S. v. Camacho*, 661 F.3d 718 (1st Cir. 2011).

> **Drug dealing and weapons go hand-in-hand**
>
> "Illegal drugs and guns are a lot like sharks and remoras. And just as a diver who spots a remora is well-advised to be on the lookout for sharks, an officer investigating cocaine and marijuana sales would be foolish not to worry about weapons."[39]

3.12 Patdown Based on Anonymous Tips

A patdown (or "Terry frisk") is a limited search for weapons. If you receive an anonymous tip that someone is illegally carrying a weapon, you must prove that the tip is reliable.[40] Typically, this means that the tipster has an indicia of reliability and the information is independently corroborated. See previous sections on how to do this.

Here's what to watch out for in this area: citizens boldly claiming that someone illegally possesses a weapon, without evidence, cannot be acted upon. Otherwise, a person could easily harass someone he did not like by claiming, without proof, that someone is illegally carrying a gun. This does not mean the tipster has to see the gun with his own eyes. But he would need to provide you with inside information, information that the general public would not know.

For example, a tipster tells you that he overheard that John Doe is going to burglarize ABC jewelry store at two p.m., and he is armed with a gun. You look up John Doe and he's on parole for robbery. You then see John Doe walking up to ABC jewelry store at 3:30 (criminals have horrible time management). You could lawfully detain and frisk Doe based on this tip, even though the tipster never saw the gun and remained anonymous.

🛡 LEGAL STANDARD

A suspect may be frisked based an anonymous tip if:

- The call states or implies that the suspect is engaged in criminal activity;
- The tip indicates the suspect is armed and dangerous;
- The tip had an indicia of reliability; and
- The tip was sufficiently corroborated to show that the caller had information not readily available to the general public.

3.13 Plain Touch Doctrine

Under the plain touch (or "feel") doctrine, you can seize any item that is immediately apparent as contraband or evidence if you are conducting a lawful patdown for weapons.[41]

---

[39] *People v. Simpson*, 65 Cal. App. 4th 854 (1998).
[40] *Fla. v. J.L.*, 529 U.S. 266 (2000).
[41] *Horton v. California*, 496 U.S. 128 (1990).

✪ LEGAL STANDARD

Evidence or contraband discovered during a frisk is admissible if:

- Your frisk was lawfully conducted and limited to weapons;
- When you felt the item, it was immediately apparent that the item was contraband or evidence of a crime; and
- You did not build probable cause by manipulating the item.

🏛 CASE EXAMPLES

Suspect has no reasonable expectation of privacy in item immediately apparent as contraband during patdown

"The rationale of the plain-view doctrine is that if contraband is left in open view and is observed by a police officer from a lawful vantage point, there has been no invasion of a legitimate expectation of privacy and thus no "search" within the meaning of the Fourth Amendment...The same can be said of tactile discoveries of contraband. If a police officer lawfully pats down a suspect's outer clothing and feels an object whose contour or mass makes its identity immediately apparent, there has been no invasion of the suspect's privacy beyond that already authorized by the officer's search for weapons; if the object is contraband, its warrantless seizure would be justified by the same practical considerations that inhere in the plain-view context."[42]

Officer reasonably believed "cylindrical-shaped" object was crack pipe

During a patdown, "the officer felt an object which, based on its contour and mass and based on his experience with such contraband, he correctly believed to be a crack pipe."[43]

3.14 Involuntary Transportation

Typically, involuntarily transportation of a suspect back to the crime scene for identification[44] will be considered a formal arrest requiring probable cause.[45] But like all good rules, there are exceptions.

During some particularly serious investigations you may have no choice but to transport the suspect. Just like the use of firearms or handcuffs will not always convert an investigative detention into an arrest, transporting a suspect against his will does not always equal arrest (though it usually does, so be careful here).

In practice, involuntary transportation occurs with some frequency. Sometimes a suspect is found a couple of blocks from the crime scene and then (involuntarily) transported back for an interview or witness identification.

---

[42] *Minnesota v. Dickerson*, 508 U.S. 366 (1993).
[43] *Ingram v. City of Los Angeles*, 418 F. Supp. 2d 1182 (C.D. Cal. 2006).
[44] *Hayes v. Florida*, 470 U.S. 811 (1985).
[45] *Dunaway v. N.Y.*, 442 U.S. 200 (1979).

Remember, without consent, probable cause, or exigency, this is an arrest. If this happens, one doctrine may save the day—the collective knowledge doctrine (in this book). If another officer on- scene developed probable cause before the transportation took place, the transportation is lawful even though the transporting officer did not have his own P.C. You may still have a Miranda issue.[46] But at least you would not have an illegal arrest.

⭐ LEGAL STANDARD

Police may not involuntarily transport a suspect away from the location where he was stopped unless:

- You have legitimate exigent circumstances (rare). Involuntary transportation without exigency is an arrest, requiring probable cause.

🏛 CASE EXAMPLES

Transport away from "hostile crowd" upheld

A hostile crowd, in a high-crime area, gathered around detention stop. Officer's involuntary movement away from scene upheld.[47]

Valid transportation to find out what happened to children

A female walked into the police station and said that she had "done something very bad" to her children. An officer then told her she was not under arrest, but that he would drive her home to find out what happened. Officer discovered three of the six children were shot and killed. This was a lawful detention, not an arrest.[48]

Transport to ID suspect upheld in gang rape

An officer investigating a brutal gang rape stopped two suspects. They did not speak English and the officer handcuffed them and transported them to the hospital for identification. The involuntary transport was reasonable under the circumstances and evidence was not suppressed.[49]

Involuntary transportation for questioning unlawful

Officers picked up suspect, took him downtown for questioning, and eventually obtained a confession. The officers contended that the suspect was just being "detained" for questioning, but the Supreme Court disagreed, ruling that the movement resulted in the arrest of the defendant—Confession suppressed.[50]

---

[46] *Kaupp v. Texas*, 538 U.S. 626 (2003).
[47] *People v. Courtney*, 11 Cal. App. 3d 1185 (Cal. App. 1st Dist. 1970).
[48] *U.S. v. Charley*, 396 F.3d 1074 (9th Cir. Cal. 2005).
[49] *In re Carlos M.*, 220 Cal. App. 3d 372 (1990).
[50] *Dunaway v. N.Y.*, 442 U.S. 200 (1979).

Moving high-level trafficking suspect from sidewalk into surveillance house was justified for safety concerns

"The most compelling factor supporting a finding that Medina was arrested was the agents' transport of Medina from the street to the surveillance residence for questioning...Even so, an officer may move a suspect or use greater force against a suspect, without probable cause, if safety concerns justify such precautions."[51]

Transportation reasonable where lack of officers and desire to not leave patrol vehicles unattended

Police acted reasonably in transporting suspect brief distance to scene of reported burglary in patrol car as part of Terry stop, where it was reasonable to believe that victim might be able to identify perpetrator, and, although officers could have walked witness to scene, doing so would have required more officers, and might have required leaving patrol car unattended in high-crime area.[52]

3.15   Detaining People Who Publicly Record Police Officers

Generally, you have no right to stop a person from recording your public activities. Do not detain the person unless you have specific articulable reasonable suspicion he is engaged in criminal activity. This is rarely the case and 99% of the time these people want to catch you doing something stupid and have it go viral on YouTube. Don't fall for it.

Additionally, if you lawfully detain a person who is recording you, and you have R.S. that he is dangerous, you can order him to put his phone away for officer safety purposes. But do not order him to stop recording unless you can articulate legitimate officer safety reason or distraction (*e.g.*, Facebook live).

If a non-detained person is interfering with your investigation, like yelling or too close to the scene, give him orders to quiet down or move back. But be professional and explain what you want done and why.

🛡 LEGAL STANDARD

A person may video or audio record if:

- He is recording a public officer;
- In a public place;
- Doing his public duties; but
- A lawfully stopped person may be ordered to put the device away or stop recording for legitimate safety or investigative purposes.

---

[51] *U.S. v. Lopez-Medina*, 461 F.3d 724, 740 (6th Cir. 2006).
[52] *U.S. v. McCargo*, 464 F.3d 192 (2d Cir. 2006).

🏛 CASE EXAMPLES

Filming a public officer, doing a public act, in a public place, is protected

Filming or videotaping of government officials engaged in their duties in a public place, including police officers performing their responsibilities, is protected by First Amendment.[53]

---

[53] *Glik v. Cunniffe*, 655 F.3d 78 (1st Cir. Mass. 2011).

Chapter 4
Arrests

4.1 Lawful Arrest

Officers make millions of warrantless arrests every year. Though there may be additional state laws in play (*e.g.*, cannot arrest for misdemeanor not committed in your presence), the Fourth Amendment is not violated as long as you have probable cause, authority to make the arrest, and lawful access to the suspect.[1]

You are not required to obtain an arrest warrant when the suspect is located in a public place.[2] A public place would be described as any place where you have a lawful right to be.[3]

Additionally, the arrest is lawful even if the charged offense is dropped for lack of probable cause as long as there was probable cause for another offense, even if uncharged.[4]

⬢ LEGAL STANDARD

A lawful arrest has three elements:

- You must have probable cause that a crime has been committed;
- You need legal authority to make the arrest; and
- You must have lawful access to the suspect.

There are two ways to effectuate an arrest:

- You may use any physical force with the intent to arrest; or
- You may make a show of authority sufficient enough to make a reasonable person believe he was under arrest.

🏛 CASE EXAMPLES

If the arrest is based on any probable cause, arrest is constitutional

"The standard of probable cause applies to all arrests, without the need to 'balance' the interests and circumstances involved in particular situations. If an officer has probable cause to believe that an individual has committed even a very minor criminal offense in his presence, he may, without violating the Fourth Amendment, arrest the offender." Note, still abide by your agency/state rules.[5]

---

[1] *Virginia v. Moore*, 553 U.S.164 (2008).
[2] *U.S. v. Watson*, 423 U.S. 411 (1976).
[3] *People v. Patterson*, 156 Cal. Rptr. 518 (Cal. App. 2d Dist. 1979).
[4] *Devenpeck v. Alford*, 543 U.S. 146 (2004).
[5] *Atwater v. City of Lago Vista*, 532 U.S. 318 (2001).

Warrantless arrest inside private office unlawful

It was illegal for police, without consent, exigent circumstances, or a warrant, to go past a receptionist and enter the locked office of an attorney to arrest him for selling cocaine.[6]

Probable cause existed to search based on belief that spare tire contained drugs

A police officer had probable cause to lower the spare tire on defendant's vehicle and cut it open, where the tire was hanging lower than normal, it was clean while the rim was salty and dirty, the tire had fingerprints and tool marks where the rim and tire met, the tire was a different brand and larger than the other four tires on the vehicle, the results of the "echo test" performed on the spare tire were consistent with the presence of contraband hidden therein, there were four cans of Fix-A-Flat Tire in the vehicle, which was unusual considering the vehicle was a rental, the tire was extraordinarily heavy, and the officer had experience with drugs being transported in spare tires.[7]

Probable cause existed based on smelling "burnt" marijuana even though only "fresh" marijuana was discovered

A police officer's testimony that he smelled the odor of burning marijuana and saw smoke coming out of the truck parked in defendant's driveway was not required to be corroborated by physical evidence of burnt marijuana from inside the truck in order to show that the officer had probable cause to conduct the warrantless search of the truck, where the officer's failure to locate ash or burnt marijuana cigarettes inside the truck did not render his testimony inherently incredible, since officers did find over 350 grams of non-burnt marijuana inside the truck.[8]

Suspect must be physically touched or submit to your authority

"There can be no arrest without either touching or submission." Therefore, is suspect runs away he is not arrested until you catch him.[9]

4.2   Entry into Home with Arrest Warrant

An arrest warrant allows an officer to not only arrest the suspect in a public place, but inside his home as well. In essence, the arrest warrant is really two warrants: a warrant to arrest the suspect and a warrant to search for the suspect at his home. However, before entering a suspect's home you must have reason to believe he is presently home and knock and announce before entering. Of course, the warrant does not authorize a search for evidence, but plain view seizures are permissible.

Make no mistake, arrest warrants are powerful tools for law enforcement officers to arrest wanted suspects. Finally, these rules apply equally to all criminal arrest warrants, whether for a misdemeanor or felony.

---

[6] *People v. Lee*, 186 Cal. App. 3d 743 (Cal. App. 4th Dist. 1986).
[7] *U.S. v. Lyons*, 510 F.3d 1225 (10th Cir. 2007).
[8] *Gilliam v. U.S.*, 46 A.3d 360 (D.C. 2012).
[9] *California v. Hodari D.*, 499 U.S. 621 (1991).

⬟ LEGAL STANDARD

Entry into a home based on an arrest warrant is lawful when:

- You have probable cause that this is the suspect's home, and not a third-party's home (get a search warrant for third- party homes);
- You have reason to believe the suspect is home;
- You knock and announce;
- If appropriate, protective sweeps are permissible; and
- You may look for the suspect in people-sized places, but not search for evidence, but plain view seizure applies.

🏛 CASE EXAMPLES

Arrest warrant allows entry into suspect's home, not third- party's

"Thus, for Fourth Amendment purposes, an arrest warrant founded on probable cause implicitly carries with it the limited authority to enter a dwelling in which the suspect lives when there is reason to believe the suspect is within ... [but] is plainly inapplicable when the police seek to use an arrest warrant as legal authority to enter the home of a third party to conduct a search.[10]

4.3 Warrantless Entry to Make Arrest

You cannot make a warrantless entry into a home to make an arrest without consent or exigency.[11] Even if the arrest was for a violent triple-murder, you would have to articulate consent or exigency before entering.

⬟ LEGAL STANDARD

A warrantless entry into a home to make an arrest may be made under five circumstances:

Consent:
- You may enter if you have consent from an occupant with apparent authority over the premises and you make known your intention to arrest the suspect.

Hot Pursuit:
- You are in hot pursuit of a suspect believed to have committed an arrestable offense and he runs into a home (a surround and call-out may also be done for officer safety purposes).

Fresh Pursuit:
- You are in fresh pursuit of the suspect after investigating a serious violent crime and quickly trace the suspect back to his home.

---

[10] *Steagald v. U.S.*, 451 U.S. 204 (1981).
[11] *Payton v. N.Y.*, 445 U.S. 573 (1980).

Suspect will Escape:
- You have probable cause that the suspect committed a serious violent crime, and you reasonably believe he will escape before obtaining a warrant.

Undercover Officer - Immediate Reentry with Arrest Team:
- You are an undercover officer and conduct a narcotics transaction inside the home, you may leave and immediately reenter with an arrest team when two conditions are met: First, there must be a legitimate officer safety reason why you had to leave first, instead of summoning the arrest team into the home and you must articulate that an exigency exists, such as destruction or loss of evidence.

Remember for all Uninvited Entries:
- Knock and announce rules apply; and
- You cannot search for evidence, but may make a plain view seizure.

🏛 CASE EXAMPLES

Entry to make any arrest, even for murder, requires consent, exigency, or a warrant

"To be arrested in the home involves not only the invasion attendant to all arrests but also an invasion of the sanctity of the home. This is simply too substantial an invasion to allow without a warrant, at least in the absence of exigent circumstances, even when it is accomplished under statutory authority and when probable cause is clearly present."[12]

Additional officers may enter if undercover officer is inside the residence

An informant and undercover police officer went to defendant's residence to arrange a drug transaction. Defendant showed the pair a bag containing cocaine. The pair left the residence and returned with another agent, who was the purported purchaser. The door had been left ajar, so police officers entered the residence and arrested defendant.[13]

Delayed entry unlawful without exigency

"In a prosecution arising out of the purchase of stolen weapons from an undercover police officer in defendants' home. Although the undercover officer had been voluntarily admitted into the home, he had walked outside of the house to signal uniformed officers to arrest defendants. The officers then arrested defendants within the house without first obtaining an arrest warrant, seized the weapons sold, and uncovered a rifle in their subsequent search of the house. The court held that despite the legality of the officer's initial entry, his reentry without consent and in the absence of exigent circumstances rendered the arrest and the search incident thereto unlawful."[14]

---

[12] *U.S. v. Reed*, 572 F.2d 412, 423 (1978).
[13] *Toubus v. Superior Court*, 114 Cal. App. 3d 378 (Cal. App. 1st Dist. 1981).
[14] *People v. Garcia*, 139 Cal. App. 3d Supp. 1 (Cal. App. Dep't Super. Ct. 1982).

Immediate reentry lawful

Warrantless arrest of defendant in his residence upheld when defendant had consented to initial entry by police officer, during which time defendant committed crime in officer's presence, after which officer left and immediately reentered with other officers to arrest defendant.[15]

4.4   Private Searches

The Fourth Amendment controls government officials, not private actors. Therefore, there's generally no restriction on using information gained from a private citizen's search as long as he was not acting as a government agent. This is true even when the private search was conducted in a highly offensive, unreasonable, or illegal manner.[16]

Remember, you may not exceed the scope of the original private search. The point here is that the suspect loses any reasonable expectation of privacy in those areas searched by the private person, so police can view the same evidence. But that does not mean the suspect lost his expectation of privacy in other, non-searched areas.

An agent is anyone who conducts the search or seizure on your behalf. Government agents must abide by the same rules you do, otherwise agents become a way to violate the Fourth Amendment. Again, as long as the person is not your agent, you may use any evidence they bring to you.

🛡 LEGAL STANDARD

Whether a private search becomes a government search depends on three factors:

- Did you direct or participate in the search or seizure? And,
- Did the private person conduct the search with the intent to help police or discover evidence? If so,
- Did you exceed the scope of the private search?

The first two factors must both be present for a private search to turn into a government search. The third factor will turn a private search into an unreasonable government search.

🏛 CASE EXAMPLES

Government did not exceed private search by opening another box on the same pallet

Private carrier's employee opened one of thirteen boxes on a pallet and discovered marijuana. Police later searched the other boxes without a warrant. Typically, this

---

[15] *People v. Cespedes*, 191 Cal. App. 3d 768 (Cal. App. 1st Dist. 1987).
[16] *Skinner v. Railway Labor Executives' Ass'n*, 489 U.S. 602 (1989).

would have exceeded the "scope" of the original private search. However, the government effectively argued that the additional boxes on the same pallet was essentially a "single" box. The court agreed and the search was upheld.[17]

No government search where wife simply handed over evidence

Officers went to the defendant's home and questioned his wife. Officers asked if husband owned any guns and what clothes he had worn on the night of the crime. Wife then grabbed the items and gave them to police. This was a private search—no evidence police told her to do it, she did it on her own to clear her husband's name.[18] That last part backfired!

Hotel manager was government agent while searching room for drugs

Hotel manager called police and asked that police to protect him while he searched a suspected drug dealer's room. The officers stood guard at the door and listened to the manager describe the drug evidence found. This was a government search because police participated in (*i.e.,* stood guard) and the manager was motivated to help police (*i.e.,* look at what I just found boys!).[19]

FedEx employee not agent despite wanting to find evidence for police

A FedEx employee who previously found drugs in eight packages, and testified in court two times, not government agent simply because he wanted to find evidence to turn over to the government.[20]

Private search exceeded after laboratory tests performed

Where a previous private search was limited to visual inspection of pills but the government subsequently had a series of tests performed on the material at a toxicology laboratory that revealed its precise molecular structure, the action was a search because of the danger that private facts about the items could be revealed and because the search exceeded the scope of the private search. The court distinguished a field test that would reveal only whether or not the pills were a particular contraband substance but would not otherwise reveal exactly what they were.[21]

No violation where police viewed same child pornography wife looked at

Police officers who examined defendant's child pornography obtained and brought to the officers by defendant's wife did not violate defendant's privacy expectations, where defendant's wife had performed a private search of the materials, and the police officers only viewed those materials that had already been viewed by defendant's wife.[22]

---

[17] *U.S. v. Garcia-Bercovich*, 582 F.3d 1234 (11th Cir. 2009).
[18] *Coolidge v. New Hampshire*, 403 U.S. 443 (1971).
[19] *U.S. v. Reed*, 15 F.3d 928 (9th Cir. 1994).
[20] *U.S. v. Koenig*, 856 F.2d 843 (7th Cir. 1988).
[21] *U.S. v. Mulder*, 808 F.2d 1346 (9th Cir. 1987).
[22] *U.S. v. Starr*, 533 F.3d 985 (8th Cir. 2008).

4.5   Collective Knowledge Doctrine

The collective knowledge doctrine is one of the most powerful and important doctrines in law enforcement. It allows a single police officer to benefit from the collective knowledge of all officers working on a case. For example, if a detective asks another officer to search a vehicle for drugs, the search would be valid even if the officer conducting the search had no idea why he was authorized to search the vehicle, as long as the detective had probable cause.

The key with the collective knowledge doctrine is that officers communicate with each other. This does not mean officers have to know everything about the case, but they at least have to be working together.

⬢ LEGAL STANDARD

The collective knowledge has two requirements:

- The officers must be involved in the same investigation, but may be from different departments (*i.e.*, task forces); and
- Officers must be in communication with each other related to the investigation.

🏛 CASE EXAMPLES

Collective knowledge doctrine applied to officer who stopped vehicle

A narcotics task force requested that an officer stop a vehicle for any observed traffic violation. Though the arresting officer only observed a traffic offense, the collective knowledge of the task force permitted the later arrest and warrantless search of the vehicle for drugs.[23]

Officer may wholly rely on the probable cause of a fellow officer

A police officer relied on the instruction of a fellow officer, who had probable that drugs were in a vehicle. The police officer stopped the vehicle and searched it under the automobile exception. Even though the initiating officer did not have probable cause, because he was in communication with a fellow officer that did, the stop and search were lawful.[24]

Intel from confidential information contributed to collective knowledge

Officers who stopped defendant for a traffic violation had probable cause to arrest him for drug trafficking; at the time of the stop, law enforcement collectively knew that a confidential informant made a controlled drug purchase from defendant five days earlier, the informant made a controlled drug payment of $5,000 to defendant on the day of the stop, and defendant engaged in what appeared to be other drug transactions shortly before the stop.[25]

---

[23] *U.S. v. Thompson*, 533 F.3d 964 (8th Cir. Mo. 2008).
[24] *U.S. v. Chavez*, 534 F.3d 1338 (10th Cir. 2008).
[25] *U.S. v. Nickson*, 628 F.3d 368 (7th Cir. 2010).

Collective knowledge doctrine controls even when agent told officer to develop his own probable cause

A DEA agent had probable cause that the defendant was in possession of drugs. He told a local officer to watch out for the defendant, and to develop his own probable cause and stop the vehicle, but the officer had no knowledge of the facts underlying the DEA's probable cause. The officer stopped the vehicle and searched it. The court held the officer had probable cause under the collection knowledge doctrine.[26]

Collective knowledge doctrine can also be used for investigatory detentions

Officer worked in a fast-paced, dynamic situation in an area known for drug sales, in which the officers worked together as a unified and tight-knit team. One officer developed reasonable suspicion to stop the defendant. A fellow officer, unaware of the officer's reasonable suspicion, stopped the defendant without his own individualized suspicion. The court upheld the stop under the collective knowledge doctrine.[27]

Supervisor's knowledge, not on scene, was too remote for collective knowledge doctrine

Knowledge of all officers on the scene is imputed to each officer in determining whether "collective knowledge" provided probable cause, but knowledge of a supervisor not on the scene cannot be imputed when the information was not communicated to those on the scene.[28]

4.6 Meaning of "Committed in the Officer's Presence?"

If you have probable cause to believe that a person has committed even a very minor criminal offense in your presence, you may arrest the offender without violating the Fourth Amendment.[29] Still, adhere to state law when making any arrest.

Additionally, most states require that misdemeanor crimes be committed "in the officer's presence." Under this requirement, you must perceive the acts or events which constitute the offense while they are taking place, and not just learn of them later or simply see evidence of the crime.

⭐ LEGAL STANDARD

An offense is committed within the officer's presence when:

- You observed or experienced an essential element of the crime through one of your senses, namely sight, smell, hearing, or touch.

---

[26] *U.S. v. Williams*, 627 F.3d 247 (7th Cir. 2010).
[27] *U.S. v. Whitfield*, 634 F.3d 741 (3d Cir. 2010).
[28] *U.S. v. Edwards*, 885 F.2d 377 (7th Cir. 1989).
[29] *Atwater v. City of Lago Vista*, 532 U.S. 318 (2001).

🏛 CASE EXAMPLES

Watching shoplifting incident on video did not satisfy "within the officer's presence" requirement

An officer watched a video which clearly showed the suspect shoplifting. However, this did not satisfy the state's requirement that misdemeanors be committed within the officer's presence.[30]

Driver's failure to produce license, registration, and insurance was a misdemeanor committed in the officer' presence

When the officer asked the driver for her license, she said that she did not have one and that the constitution did not require one. Her subsequent arrest was lawful as a misdemeanor committed in the officer's presence.[31]

4.7 Line-Ups

Courts are scrutinizing police identification procedures more than they have in the past. One reason is because research has shown that eyewitnesses are easily swayed by suggestive practices. For example, if police make an investigative detention on a potential armed robbery suspect, it would be improper to say to the victim, "We have the perpetrator, but we still need you to ID him."

It's vital that police stay as neutral and detached as possible when it comes to identification procedures.[32]

Police may also conduct a "show-up" between the suspect and witness under a few circumstances. Usually, these show-ups are conducted soon after the crime has occurred when police have detained a suspect (on-scene or in the vicinity).

Overall, when you conduct any kind of identification procedure it's important that you do not use words or conduct that's overly suggestive.

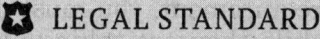

🛡 LEGAL STANDARD

Photo Arrays:

A photo array (*e.g.*, "six pack") may be done at any time, without probable cause, and without notifying a suspect's court-appointed counsel if:

• You minimized suggestive influences.

Physical Line-Ups:

A suspect may be required to participate in a physical line-up if:

• You minimized suggestive influences;
• The suspect consents to the line-up or is lawfully arrested; and

---

[30] *Forgie-Buccioni v. Hannaford Bros., Inc.*, 413 F.3d 175 (1st Cir. 2005).
[31] *Hallstrom v. City of Garden City, Idaho*, 811 F. Supp. 1443, 1448 (D. Idaho 1991).
[32] *Neil v. Biggers*, 409 U.S. 188 (1972).

- If the suspect has been arraigned, indicted, or appointed counsel, the attorney must be notified and allowed to attend, but not control, the line-up.

In-Field Show-Up:

A suspect may be required to participate in solo in-field "show-up" if:

- You minimized suggestive influences (*e.g.,* not surrounding suspect with cops, if safe, removing handcuffs, and not telling the witness that the suspect is the culprit).

🏛 CASE EXAMPLES

A person has no expectation of privacy in a photograph of his or her face

A person has no expectation of privacy in a photograph of his or her face. Thus, a probation officer's conduct in taking a photograph of a defendant, allegedly at the request of law enforcement agents, which was later used by the agents in a photographic lineup during which the defendant was identified by two witnesses as the perpetrator of a bank robbery, did not violate the defendant's Fourth Amendment rights.[33]

Unzipping suspect's jacket during show-up was a search

Partial unzipping and opening of suspect's jacket so that a robbery complainant could see the sweatshirt underneath the suspect's jacket during a show-up identification procedure was a non-protective evidentiary search that violated the Fourth Amendment.[34] However, it is possible that this search may have been justified under the minimal intrusion doctrine. But that was not argued in this case.

4.8 Protective Sweeps

If you make a lawful arrest inside a home, you are allowed to conduct a protective sweep.[35] There are three zones, or areas, you may search depending on the circumstances.

🛡 LEGAL STANDARD

A protective sweep may be made inside a home during an arrest under the following conditions:

- **Zone 1**: You may automatically search areas under the immediate control of the suspect for weapons, evidence, or means of escape;

---

[33] *U.S. v. Emmett*, 321 F.3d 669 (7th Cir. 2003).
[34] *U.S. v. Askew*, 529 F.3d 1119 (D.C. Cir. 2008).
[35] *Maryland v. Buie*, 494 U.S. 325 (1990).

- **Zone 2**: You may automatically search for people in people-sized places in adjacent areas (*e.g.* closets); and
- **Zone 3**: If you have reasonable suspicion that dangerous confederates are in the house, you may search for people in people-sized places and detain the confederates until the arrest is completed.

Remember: Zone 2 and 3 sweeps may never be used to search for "evidence"; only people in people-sized places.

 ## CASE EXAMPLES

Severity of crime committed can help justify protective sweep

"(T)he type of criminal conduct underlying the arrest or search is significant in determining if a protective sweep is justified."[36] Generalized safety concerns are not enough.[37]

Protective sweep of other rooms must be justified

Protective sweeps of the areas of the home beyond the adjacent area (*i.e.*, any adjoining rooms) of the arrest will not be upheld absent an articulable reason for believing someone in the home is present who constitutes a potential danger to the officers.[38]

Warrantlessly entering home and seizing a domestic violence suspect's guns is not permitted under community caretaking

"Decades ago, this Court held that a warrantless search of an impounded vehicle for an unsecured firearm did not violate the Fourth Amendment. In reaching this conclusion, the Court observed that police officers who patrol the 'public highways' are often called to discharge noncriminal 'community caretaking functions,' such as responding to disabled vehicles or investigating accidents. The question today is whether... these 'caretaking' duties creates a standalone doctrine that justifies warrantless searches and seizures in the home. It does not."

Justice Alito went on to say, "This case also implicates another body of law that petitioner glossed over: the so-called 'red flag' laws that some states are now enacting. These laws enable the police to seize guns pursuant to a court order to prevent their use for suicide or the infliction of harm on innocent persons. They typically specify the standard that must be met and the procedures that must be followed before firearms may be seized. Provisions of red flag laws may be challenged under the Fourth Amendment, and those cases may come before us. Our decision today does not address those issues."[39]

---

[36] *People v. Ledesma*, 106 Cal. App. 4th 857 (Cal. App. 1st Dist. 2003).
[37] *People v. Werner*, 207 Cal. App. 4th 1195 (Cal. App. 6th Dist. 2012).
[38] *U.S. v. Furrow*, 229 F.3d 805 (9th Cir. Idaho 2000).
[39] *Caniglia v. Strom*, 141 S. Ct. 1596, 1598 (2021).

4.9   When to "Unarrest" a Suspect

There are two situations where you should unarrest a suspect. The first scenario occurs when you arrest a suspect with probable cause, but later determine they are innocent. Constitutionally, you must unarrest the suspect without unreasonable delay. The second scenario occurs when you (or supervisor) decide that continued arrest is not the best outcome for a case. This usually occurs before transportation to jail. As long as the initial arrest had P.C. and you acted reasonably (*i.e.*, did not arrest the person just to conduct a warrantless search or to embarrass the suspect), then it's permitted.

Either way make sure your report is rock solid and fully explain what you did and why you did it.

🛡 LEGAL STANDARD

An in-custody suspect must be released:

- If you discover new evidence that clearly eliminates probable cause the suspect must be released; or
- If you already booked the suspect, you must notify the prosecutor in writing.

An in-custody suspect may be release when:

- You made the arrest with the intent to book the suspect; and
- You learned of new facts or circumstances that warrant releasing the suspect with a citation or warning.
- Remember, you may not use an arrest-and-release as loophole to search the suspect without consent, exigency, or a search warrant.

🏛 CASE EXAMPLES

Initial arrest of burglary suspect lawful, but additional evidence showed that suspect lived at apartment, and therefore did not commit burglary

After police arrested defendant for attempted burglary of apartment based on a complaint from the alleged tenants, the landlord approached police and said that the defendant was the actual tenant, not the alleged tenants. Additionally, police found no evidence of a burglary or forced break-in. The court held, at that point police should have immediately released the defendant, since police no longer had probable cause to believe he had committed the offense of attempted burglary.[40] Remember, the original arrest here was lawful and police made the right call based on the information they had at the time. Therefore, there was no constitutional violation. But once the case falls apart and police realize they arrested the wrong person, there is no longer probable cause to maintain an arrest and release is required...if nothing else transform the encounter to an investigative detention in needed.

---

[40] *People v. Quarles*, 88 Ill. App. 3d 340 (1980).

Reasonable suspicion to stop car dissipated once police realized it was a different color with different suspects

Officers on the roadside at night were notified that a blue car with three black males had just robbed the victim. Police immediately saw a car matching the description and stopped it. However, once police walked up to vehicle, it was green, not blue. And instead of having three suspects, it only had two. Finally, the occupants were not black, but Hispanic. The court held at that point there was no reason to continue to detain the vehicle.[41]

Probable cause existed to field test bag, but once multiple tests came back negative probable cause was eliminated

Search of defendant's bag on consent revealed white powder, the defendant then terminated consent. Since the white powder was believed to be illegal substance police field tested it three or four times, but all were negative, thus there was no longer probable cause to continue searching the bag.[42]

Court dismissal of information against defendant

Here, the court dismissed the information found against the defendant because, first, the patdown "search of his pant's pocket was over broad as a patdown." In addition, the officer "did not believe that defendant had drugs," and thus the search was unjustifiable since the defendant "could have been released after his initial arrest."[43]

4.10 "Contempt of Cop" Arrests

Do not make an arrest for "disorderly conduct" or "obstruction" primarily because a person criticizes, insults or challenges your authority. The Supreme Court has made it very clear that they expect law enforcement officers to rise above these insults. They also hold you to a higher standard when it comes to "fighting words."

"The freedom of individuals to verbally oppose or challenge police action without risking arrest is one of the principal characteristics by which we distinguish a free nation from a police state."[44]

Additionally, you may be liable even if you had probable cause to arrest, but were primarily motivated to suppress free speech. The point is do not mess with people's free speech rights.[45]

---

[41] *Castellano v. State*, 585 P.2d 361 (Okl. Crim. App. 1978).

[42] *Berg v. State*, 384 So. 2d 292 (Fla. App. 1980).

[43] *People v. West*, 31 Cal. App. 3d 175 (1973).

[44] *Houston v. Hill*, 482 U.S. 451 (1987).

[45] *Lozman v. City of Riviera Beach*, 138 S. Ct. 1945 (2018). *But see Nieves v. Bartlett*, 139 S. Ct. 1715 (2019) (need obj. evidence of retaliatory motive).

> ### ⭐ LEGAL STANDARD
>
> A person may not be arrested because:
>
> - A person criticized, insulted or challenged you; or
> - The arrest is primarily motivated to suppress a person's First Amendment rights (plaintiff would need to show objective evidence that arrest was primarily motivated for retaliatory reasons if P.C. also existed).

> ### 🏛 CASE EXAMPLES
>
> **Officer criminalized First Amendment speech**
>
> Suspect yelled "Why do not you pick on somebody your own size?" while his friend was getting arrested. When officer asked if he was interfering with his duties, suspected yelled, "Why do not you pick on someone my size!" Suspect was arrested for obstruction. Court held the arrest was unlawful and police cannot criminalize First Amendment speech.[46]

4.11 Arrests at Public Protests

Generally, be very hesitant before you take any enforcement action against a person or group who appears to be exercising their rights under the First Amendment. Courts are very quick to come down on officers who violate a person's freedom of speech.

You usually cannot regulate the content of a person's speech, just the time, place and manner. For example, if a group was loudly protesting in a residential neighborhood at two in the morning, it would be permissible to order that they move their protest to the main city park, away from sleeping residents.

However, these rules must be content neutral and apply equally to all groups. "Content neutral" means police cannot regulate "what" a person says, but "how" they say it (*e.g.*, "say whatever you want, just not with a bullhorn inside city hall"). If police need to regulate a protest they should first seek consent, if that fails, and there's no immediate breach of the peace, consult with legal counsel.

> ### ⭐ LEGAL STANDARD
>
> When dealing with public protests, you may:
>
> - Only regulate the time, place and manner of protests;
> - Generally, you may not take enforcement action based on "what" someone says, only how, when, and where they say it. Tread lightly here!

---

[46] *Houston v. Hill*, 482 U.S. 451 (1987).

🏛 CASE EXAMPLES

Protestors at deceased soldier's funeral protected by First Amendment

Protester's message was vile to solder's father (*e.g.*, "God loves dead soldiers"). But they did not actively disturb the funeral. Therefore, their message was protected by First Amendment.[47]

4.12 Search Incident to Arrest

You have automatic authority to conduct full searches (except strip or cavity searches) once a person has been lawfully arrested.[48] You may also search any items the person is going to bring with them to jail.

If you are going to take other property and store it for safekeeping, you may conduct an inventory.

⭐ LEGAL STANDARD

An arrested suspect and belongings within his "immediate control" may be searched under the following conditions:

- You are looking for weapons, evidence, contraband, or means of escape;
- The search occurs substantially at the same time and within the immediate vicinity of the arrest;
- If the search occurs later or at a different location, articulate a reason why (*e.g.*, dangerous scene, severe weather, etc.).

🏛 CASE EXAMPLES

A citation and release, no matter how serious the crime, will not justify a search

Only full custodial arrest gives right to conduct search incident to arrest. Being placed in a patrol car does not automatically mean the person is arrested. Therefore, you cannot search the person, though a patdown may be allowed if you articulate the person may be armed and dangerous.[49]

Probable cause to arrest must come before the search

Where the search provided probable cause for the arrest, the search could not be justified as incident to a lawful arrest.[50]

---

[47] *Snyder v. Phelps*, 562 U.S. 443 (2011).
[48] *Chimel v. Cal.*, 395 U.S. 752 (1969).
[49] *U.S. v. Parr*, 843 F.2d 1228 (9th Cir. 1988).
[50] *U.S. v. Rivera*, 867 F.2d 1261 (10th Cir. 1989).

> **Search of property within "immediate control" lawful despite no possibility of access**
>
> These searches are lawful "without requiring the arresting officer to calculate the probability" the suspect will access the items.[51]

4.13 Search Prior to Formal Arrest

Generally, there is no prohibition in making a pre-arrest "patsearch" of a subject right before you formally arrest them (compare to "patdown," which is only for weapons). The Supreme Court requires that a search incident to lawful arrest be conducted "contemporaneously."[52] This means the search may occur before the formal arrest (though uncommon).

A pre-arrest "patsearch" often occurs when police see a hand-to- hand transaction and go over to the suspect and pull the drugs out of the suspect's pocket. This is obviously not a patdown for weapons, and therefore requires probable cause. Remember, once you start looking in a suspect's pockets for evidence, that's instantly an arrest—requiring Miranda if you plan to interrogate. Therefore, if you plan to talk to the suspect consider leaving the evidence in his pocket and begin the encounter as an investigative detention.

> ### ⭐ LEGAL STANDARD
>
> A pre-arrest search of the suspect may be made when:
>
> - You have probable cause to arrest before the search;
> - You intend to make a formal arrest; and
> - Your search occurs contemporaneously before the arrest.

> ### 🏛 CASE EXAMPLES
>
> **Searches should be "contemporaneous" with the arrest**
>
> "The fact defendant is not formally arrested until after the search does not invalidate the search if probable cause to arrest exists prior to the search and the search is substantially contemporaneous with the arrest."[53]
>
> **If officer develops P.C. during patdown, he may conduct full search**
>
> When an officer finds contraband, "the patdown may be expanded to a full search permitted incident to arrest."[54]

---

[51] *U.S. v. Chadwick*, 433 U.S. 1 (1977).
[52] *Chimel v. Cal.*, 395 U.S. 752 (1969).
[53] *People v. Adams*, 175 Cal. App. 3d 855 (Cal. App. 2d Dist. 1985).
[54] *People v. Collins*, 2011 Cal. App. Unpub. LEXIS 5863 (Cal. App. 3d Dist. Aug. 4, 2011).

4.14   Search Incident to a "Temporary" Arrest

Sometimes you'll make an arrest with the intention to later "release" the suspect at another location. For example, you may arrest a juvenile with the intent to release him to his parents. Or you may take a person into civil custody for public intoxication with the intent to transport him for a "civil hold." Even under these conditions you may make a full search incident to arrest for officer safety reasons.

⭐ LEGAL STANDARD

A suspect taken into custody for a lawful reason, such as truancy or public intoxication, but not booked into jail, may be searched when:

- You had lawful authority to take the suspect into custody; and
- You transported the suspect.

Note: No search if a suspect is "cited and released" on-scene.[55]

🏛 CASE EXAMPLES

Transporting truant juvenile back to school was an arrest

An officer stopped a truant juvenile several miles from school. After determining that the student was indeed skipping class, the officer searched the teen before transporting him back to school. A dagger was found and the teen argued it was an unlawful search. The court disagreed, and said that the teen was technically arrested, even though the result was school, not jail. Therefore, the search was incident to a lawful arrest. Note, a key point in this case was the way California law classified this law. Some states may not classify truancy as an "arrestable offense."[56]

Arrest must be likely, not just possible, before search

Officer stopped bicyclist for traffic violation and searched his cell phone and discovered child porn. Evidence suppressed since there were no facts that suspect would have been arrested prior to search.[57]

4.15   Attempt to Swallow Drugs

Sometimes a suspect will try to swallow drugs before you arrest him. "A suspect has no constitutional right to destroy or dispose of evidence by swallowing, consequently he cannot consider the mouth a 'sacred orifice' in which contraband may be irretrievably concealed from the police."[58]

---

[55] *Knowles v. Iowa*, 525 U.S. 113 (1998).
[56] *In re Humberto O.*, 80 Cal. App. 4th 237 (Cal. App. 2d Dist. 2000).
[57] *People v. Macabeo*, 1 Cal. 5th 1206 (2016).
[58] *State v. Williams*, 16 Wn. App. 868 (Wash. Ct. App. 1977).

If possible, you should prevent the drugs from going inside his mouth, but if that does not work I suggest you do not place your hands around the subject's throat to prevent swallowing. Some courts have held this practice per se deadly force. You are under no legal obligation to retrieve drugs that the suspect tries to swallow.

Let the medical professionals figure it out. Remember, it's worth losing a case then catching the Alphabet Soup (HIV/Hep). Is that worth preventing a "victimless crime?"

⭐ LEGAL STANDARD

Treat a suspect attempting to swallow drugs in the following manner:

- If safe, use a reasonable amount of force to prevent him from putting the drugs in his mouth;
- If swallowed, order him to spit it out and call medical; and
- Inform medical what occurred and allow them to make all medical decisions, do not ask or order medical to help retrieve the drugs unless you have a search warrant.

🏛 CASE EXAMPLES

Ordering a suspect to spit out drugs reasonable

Officers were presented with exigency and were permitted to order him to spit out the drugs. Note, the officers did not grab the suspect's neck.[59]

Applying hands to a suspect's throat is the equivalent of choking

"An application of force to the throat sufficient to prevent swallowing is, in our opinion, the equivalent of choking."[60]

4.16 DUI Breath Tests

The courts do not view DUI breath tests and blood tests the same. A blood test, because it is naturally more invasive, usually requires a search warrant absent exigent circumstances. As the Supreme Court pointed out in Birchfield;

A breath test does not 'implicat[e] significant privacy concerns.' Blood tests are a different matter. . . . Blood tests are significantly more intrusive, and their reasonableness must be judged in light of the availability of the less invasive alternative of a breath test. . . . Breath tests have been in common use for many years. Their results are admissible in court and are widely credited by juries, and respondents do not dispute their accuracy or utility. . . .

---

[59] *State v. Alverez*, 111 P.3d 808 (Utah Ct. App. 2005).
[60] *People v. Trevino*, 72 Cal. App. 3d 686 (Cal. App. 2d Dist. 1977).

Nothing prevents the police from seeking a warrant for a blood test when there is sufficient time to do so in the particular circumstances or from relying on the exigent circumstances exception to the warrant requirement when there is not.[61]

⭐ LEGAL STANDARD

If a suspect is arrested for DUI, you may:

- You may order the suspect to produce a breath sample, unless a state statute states otherwise; and
- If he refuses, you may use his refusal as additional evidence of DUI and it may be admitted against him in court.

🏛 CASE EXAMPLES

Officer may order a suspect submit to breath test after an arrest

"Because breath tests are significantly less intrusive than blood tests and in most cases, amply serve law enforcement interests, we conclude that a breath test, but not a blood test, may be administered as a search incident to a lawful arrest for drunk driving. As in all cases involving reasonable searches incident to arrest, a warrant is not needed in this situation."[62]

4.17 DUI Blood Tests

If you have consent, exigent circumstances, or a search warrant you may conduct a blood draw in a medically approved manner. If you have exigent circumstances or a search warrant, you may use reasonable force to hold down the suspect while medical personnel obtains the blood sample.[63]

⭐ LEGAL STANDARD

If a suspect is arrested for DUI, a blood draw may be conducted if:

- You obtain the suspect's consent;
- You have legitimate exigent circumstances; or
- You obtain a search warrant for a blood sample.

---

[61] *Birchfield v. N.D.*, 136 S. Ct. 2160 (2016).
[62] *Birchfield v. N.D.*, 136 S. Ct. 2160 (2016).
[63] *Missouri v. McNeely*, 133 S. Ct. 1552 (2013).

🏛 CASE EXAMPLES

Blood draws invoke the Fourth Amendment

"Intrusions into the human body, including the taking of blood, are searches subject to the restrictions of the Fourth Amendment."[64]

Miranda not required while administering field sobriety tests

A driver is not "in-custody" for Miranda purposes when they are performing field sobriety tests.[65]

Even when officer knows he will arrest, Miranda is not required until the arrest is made

If the driver has not been advised he is under arrest (or a reasonable driver would feel they have not been arrested), Miranda is not required even if the officer decided the driver would be arrested no matter how he performed during the field sobriety tests.[66]

Warrantless blood draw from unconscious driver permitted

Unconsciousness of the arrestee will "almost always" permit a warrantless blood draw in that unconsciousness itself is an exigent circumstance.[67]

4.18   Searching Vehicle Incident to Arrest

If you arrest any vehicle occupant, you may search the vehicle incident to arrest if the suspect is within the lunge distance from the vehicle and unsecured (rare situation).[68] Here, you are mainly looking for weapons or a means to escape. Once the suspect is secured you may no longer automatically search the vehicle incident to arrest.[69]

You may also search a vehicle if you have reason to believe evidence of the crime is inside the vehicle. No warrant is required. Two things should be noted. First, "reason to believe" evidence is inside the vehicle is a slightly lower standard than probable cause. And second, it does not matter if the suspect has immediate access to the vehicle. Still, this type of search must be conducted contemporaneously (around same time) with arrest.

🛡 LEGAL STANDARD

When a suspect is arrested and unsecured, his vehicle may be searched if:

• The suspect is within the lunge distance of the vehicle;

---

[64] *U.S. v. Wright*, 215 F.3d 1020 (9th Cir. Cal. 2000).
[65] *Pennsylvania v. Bruder*, 488 U.S. 9 (1988).
[66] *Berkemer v. McCarty*, 468 U.S. 420 (1984).
[67] *Mitchell v. Wisconsin*, 139 S. Ct. 2525 (2019).
[68] *N.Y. v. Belton*, 453 U.S. 454 (1981).
[69] *Arizona v. Gant*, 556 U.S. 332 (2009).

- The suspect is unsecured; and
- You may search for weapons, evidence, and a means of escape.

When a suspect is arrested and secured, his vehicle may be searched if:

- You have reason to believe[70] evidence of the crime for which he was arrested may be inside the vehicle;
- You do not exceed the scope of search necessary to find the evidence; and
- When you no longer have reason to believe evidence of the crime is inside the vehicle, the search must end unless you develop additional probable cause to search for something else.

🏛 CASE EXAMPLES

Officer can search vehicle if reasonable to believe evidence in vehicle

An officer is permitted to conduct a vehicle search when an arrestee is within reaching distance of the vehicle or it is reasonable to believe the vehicle contains evidence of the offense of arrest.[71] Note, you may still conduct a probable cause or inventory search if appropriate.

Search after issuing speeding ticket unlawful

Defendant was stopped by a police officer for speeding and was issued a citation rather than arrested. The officer then conducted a full search of defendant's car, incident to the citation. The officer found a bag of marijuana and pipe. Defendant was then arrested and charged with violation of Iowa state laws dealing with controlled substances. The Supreme Court held the search unlawful, since the officer did not arrest the defendant before the search or gain consent.[72]

Reason to believe marijuana is inside car does not allow search of credit cards

Police had probable cause to search the car for marijuana, because the defendant had been smoking marijuana in his car. However, there was no showing that the officer observed any device that could be used in credit card fraud, or that, when the officer looked in the bag and saw multiple cards, he actually knew that they were credit cards, as opposed to gift cards, insurance cards, membership cards, or library cards, and that they did not belong to the defendant, as required to support probable cause for inspection of the cards.[73]

Police search a "container within a container" permissible as long as probable cause exists for each container

A container within a container is within the scope of the vehicle search so long as the second container is a place which could hold the item for which there is probable cause to search.[74]

---

[70] *U.S. v. Vinton*, 594 F.3d 14 (2010).
[71] *Arizona v. Gant*, 556 U.S. 332 (2009).
[72] *Knowles v. Iowa*, 525 U.S. 113 (1998).
[73] *U.S. v. Saulsberry*, 878 F.3d 946 (10th Cir. 2017).
[74] *U.S. v. Ford*, 88 F.3d 1350, 45 Fed. R. Evid. Serv. 174 (4th Cir. 1996)

Chapter 5
Vehicles

5.1 General Rule

You may stop a vehicle if you have reasonable suspicion or probable cause that an offense has been, or will be, committed. It does not matter what you subjectively thought about the driver or passengers (unless racial profiling). What matters is objective reasonableness. However, it would be unlawful to unreasonably extend the stop while you pursued a hunch. If you develop reasonable suspicion that the occupants are involved in criminal activity, then you may diligently pursue a means of investigation that will confirm or dispel those suspicions.

🛡 LEGAL STANDARD

A vehicle may be lawfully stopped if:

- There is a community caretaking purpose;
- You have reasonable suspicion for any occupant, or
- You have probable cause for any occupant.

Note: The scope of a traffic stop is similar to an investigative detention. Therefore, the officer must diligently pursue the reason for the stop and not measurably extend the stop for reasons unrelated to the original reason for the stop unless additional reasonable suspicion or probable cause develops.

🏛 CASE EXAMPLES

Stop by undercover narcotics officers for minor violation upheld

D.C. detectives in an unmarked vehicle had a hunch that two suspects were dealing narcotics. The only violation they observed was failure to use a turn signal. The stop violated a policy that unmarked vehicles could only make stops for serious crimes. Drugs were observed in plain view. The Supreme Court held that the subjective mindset of the officers was irreverent as long as the initial stop was legal.[1] And a violation of a department policy does not affect Fourth Amendment analysis.

---

[1] *Whren v. U.S.*, 517 U.S. 806 (1996).

5.2 Scope of Stop Similar to an Investigative Detention

The scope of a routine traffic stop is similar to an investigative detention. As one court stated, this is because "the usual traffic stop is more analogous to a so-called 'Terry stop' than to a formal arrest."[2]

It also makes sense that a DUI stop will take longer than an equipment violation. And a traffic stop will last longer if you are writing a ticket than just giving a verbal warning. Remember, as long as you are diligently working on the original reason for the stop you should be fine. However, once that reason of the stop is over, the driver must be allowed to leave.[3]

Finally, you may ask miscellaneous questions without additional reasonable suspicion, but those inquires must not measurably extend the stop.

🛡 LEGAL STANDARD

The duration of a traffic stop is determined by these factors:

- Once the stop is made, you must diligently pursue the reason for the traffic stop;
- Unrelated questioning must not measurably extend the stop unless additional reasonable suspicion or probable cause develops.

🏛 CASE EXAMPLES

Stop was not measurably extended by asking about drug possession

Officer did not exceed the scope of the stop by inquiring if defendant had drugs or weapons in his possession even though the reasonable suspicion leading to the stop concerned a robbery. Based on the driver's answers, reasonable suspicion developed for drug possession.[4]

5.3 Community Caretaking Stops

You may make a traffic stop on a vehicle if you believe any of the occupant's safety or welfare is at risk. If you determine that the occupant does not need assistance, you must terminate the stop or transition the stop into a consensual encounter. Otherwise, you would need to articulate reasonable suspicion (*e.g.,* DUI) or other criminal involvement (*e.g.,* domestic violence).

Stranded motorists fall under this rule. It's not illegal for a vehicle to break down. So, you cannot demand ID, or otherwise involuntarily detain stranded motorists unless you can articulate they are involved in criminal activity.

Remember, these are essentially "implied" consensual encounters unless you have a reasonable suspicion of criminal activity. In other words, if someone needs help there's a reason to believe they would have impliedly consented to police assistance. Once there's no more consent, the occupants must be left alone.

---

[2] *Berkemer v. McCarty*, 468 U.S. 420 (1984).
[3] *U.S. v. Salzano*, 1998 U.S. App. LEXIS 17140 (10th Cir. Kan. 1998).
[4] *Medrano v. State*, 914 P.2d 804 (Wyo. 1996)

⊛ LEGAL STANDARD

A vehicle may be stopped if:

- You have a reason to believe one of the occupants needs police or medical assistance; and
- Once you determine that no further assistance is required, the occupant must be left alone.

🏛 CASE EXAMPLES

Community caretaking stop unreasonable based on passenger who appeared extremely drunk

An officer observed a staggering suspect get into the passenger seat of a car. The officer wanted to make sure he was not in need of medical attention. The court held the stop unreasonable, since he was not the driver and did not appear in medical distress.[5]

5.4 Reasonable Suspicion Stops

You may stop a vehicle if you have individualized reasonable suspicion that any occupant may be involved in criminal activity. Probable cause is not required.

⊛ LEGAL STANDARD

A vehicle and its occupants may be detained if:

- You can articulate facts and circumstances that would lead a reasonable officer to believe that one of the occupants has, is, or is about to be involved in criminal activity;
- Once the stop is made, you must diligently pursue a means of investigation that will confirm or dispel your suspicions;
- If your suspicions are dispelled, the occupants must be immediately released or the stop converted into a consensual encounter.

🏛 CASE EXAMPLES

Stop of possible stolen truck, even with different plates, reasonable

Observation of a truck that matched the description of one that had just been stolen in a carjacking, but with a different license plate that appeared to be recently

---

[5] *People v. Madrid*, 168 Cal. App. 4th 1050 (Cal. App. 1st Dist. 2008)

attached, and with two occupants who generally matched the suspects' description, constituted the necessary reasonable suspicion to justify the defendant's detention.[6]

Terry stop conducted after officer told driver, "sit tight"

Suspect was subjected to a Terry stop at the time the police car parked behind the car in which he sat, where three officers shined their flashlights into the car, and one officer told the suspect to "sit tight."[7]

5.5 Stops to Verify Temporary Registration

You cannot stop a vehicle solely to verify that a temporary registration is valid or not fraudulent. Even if you have a "hunch" that the registration is fake, you still need articulate individualized articulable suspicion that a vehicle may have fraudulent registration. It is irrelevant that based on your "training and experience" temporary permits are often forged.[8]

🛡 LEGAL STANDARD

A vehicle with temporary registration may be stopped if:

- You can articulate facts and circumstances that would lead a reasonable officer to believe that the temporary registration may be fraudulent, altered, expired, or belongs to another vehicle; and
- Once the stop occurs, you must diligently pursue whether the registration is legitimate. If it is, you no longer have reason to detain the vehicle and you must immediately allow it to leave, unless the stop is converted to a consensual encounter or you develop reasonable suspicion for a different crime.

🏛 CASE EXAMPLES

Stop to verify temporary tag held unlawful

In November, a deputy stopped a vehicle with expired license plates. The deputy confirmed through dispatch that the registration had expired two months earlier but the renewal was "in process." The deputy also observed that a temporary operating permit with the number "11" (*i.e.,* November) had been taped to the window. Court held the stop unlawful and evidence was suppressed.[9]

---

[6] *U.S. v. Hartz*, 458 F.3d 1011 (9th Cir. Wash. 2006).
[7] *U.S. v. Young*, 707 F.3d 598 (6th Cir. 2012).
[8] *People v. Hernandez*, 45 Cal. 4th 295 (Cal. 2008).
[9] *People v. Brendlin*, 45 Cal. 4th 262 (Cal. 2008).

5.6 DUI Checkpoints

The Supreme Court has upheld DUI checkpoints because the state's interest in preventing drunk driving accidents is outweighed by the minimal intrusion upon driver's who are temporarily stopped.[10] Nevertheless, some states have outlawed DUI checkpoints and some prosecutors refuse to take these cases. Check before setting up a checkpoint.

Also, do not get sucked-in by drivers who record you at checkpoints. Often these drivers roll down their window a few inches and refuse to answer any questions. If you think they're sober and just playing games, let them go! The purpose of a DUI checkpoint is to get drunk drivers off the road, not teach people to stop being jackasses. On the other hand, if you cannot reasonably determine that the driver is not intoxicated, then keep your cool, take your time, follow protocol, and investigate.

⭐ LEGAL STANDARD

A vehicle may be stopped at a DUI checkpoint if:

- The checkpoint furthers a legitimate state interest and is established by a high-ranking police official;
- There is a plan in place that minimizes police discretion on who may be stopped absent reasonable suspicion;
- Based on that plan, vehicles are stopped in a systematic method;
- The means used to determine whether a driver is under the influence are minimally intrusive; and
- Driver wait time does not become unreasonable.

🏛 CASE EXAMPLES

Evasive driving away from roadblock is reasonable suspicion

"Evasive behavior in response to a roadblock" may contribute to reasonable suspicion that the driver is possibly DUI."[11]

5.7 Information Gathering Checkpoints

Police are permitted to setup checkpoints in order to gather information concerning a serious crime that has been recently committed. An example would be asking motorists if they witnessed a fatal accident that occurred a week ago.

---

[10] *Mich. Dep't of State Police v. Sitz*, 496 U.S. 444 (1990).
[11] *U.S. v. Smith*, 396 F.3d 579 (4th Cir. N.C. 2005).

⭐ LEGAL STANDARD

A vehicle may be stopped at an information-gathering checkpoint if:

- There was a serious crime recently committed;
- The means used to determine whether an occupant was a witness to the crime are minimally intrusive; and
- Driver wait time does not become unreasonable.

🏛 CASE EXAMPLES

Information checkpoint upheld after fatal hit-and-run

About a week after a hit-and-run driver killed a bicyclist, local police set up a checkpoint, to obtain information from motorists about the accident. Officers asked motorists whether they had seen anything and handed out flyers. As one driver approached, his van swerved, nearly hitting an officer. The officer smelled alcohol, administered a sobriety test and then arrested the driver. The Supreme Court upheld the checkpoint as reasonable.[12]

Fake "Drug Checkpoint Ahead" ruse not unlawful as long as stop based on reasonable suspicion or probable cause

Posting a sign for a fictitious drug checkpoint, to create opportunity for law enforcement officers to observe motorists' suspicious behavior of taking exit after signs, was not illegal police activity, and officer's search and seizure of package voluntarily abandoned by motorist at top of exit ramp therefore did not violate Fourth Amendment.[13]

5.8 Legal Considerations for Any Checkpoint

Police supervisors should address the following factors in any checkpoint operations plan.

⭐ LEGAL STANDARD

If police setup a checkpoint, keep these considerations in mind:

- The decision to establish a sobriety checkpoint, the selection of the site, and the procedures for the operation of the checkpoint, are made and established by supervisory law enforcement personnel;
- Motorists are stopped according to a neutral formula, such as every third, fifth or tenth driver;

---

[12] *Illinois v. Lidster*, 540 U.S. 419 (2004).
[13] *U.S. v. Flynn*, 309 F.3d 736 (10th Cir. 2002).

- Adequate safety precautions are taken, such as proper lighting, warning signs, and signals, and clearly identifiable official vehicles and personnel;
- The location of the checkpoint was determined by a policy-making official, and was reasonable, *i.e.*, on a road having a high incidence of alcohol-related accidents or arrests;
- The time the checkpoint was conducted and its duration reflect "good judgment" on the part of law enforcement officials;
- The checkpoint exhibits indicia of its official nature (to reassure the public of the authorized nature of the stop);
- The average length and nature of the detention is minimized; and finally,
- The checkpoint is preceded by publicity.

5.9   Ordering Passengers to Stay in, or Exit Vehicle

The Supreme Court has stated that passengers are seized under the Fourth Amendment during traffic stops. This means that they may challenge the constitutionality of the stop if they are later charged with a crime.[14]

You are allowed to order passengers out of a vehicle,[15] or alternatively, order them to stay in the vehicle if they demand to leave, even if they haven't committed an offense. The courts understand the risks associated with traffic stops, and the intrusion upon controlling passengers is minimal.

🛡 LEGAL STANDARD

Any occupant inside a vehicle may be ordered to stay, or exit vehicle if:

- The stop was based on reasonable suspicion or probable cause; and
- You can articulate any legitimate reason (*i.e.*, officer safety or need to interview separately).

🏛 CASE EXAMPLES

Officer can order occupant out of vehicle for any legitimate reason

"[O]nce a motor vehicle has been lawfully detained for a traffic violation, the police officers may order the driver to get out of the vehicle … and may order passengers to get out of the car pending completion of the stop as well."[16]

Passengers may challenge stop under Fourth Amendment

"A traffic stop necessarily curtails the travel a passenger has chosen just as much as it halts the driver." Therefore, they may challenge the reason for the stop.[17]

---

[14] *Brendlin v. California*, 551 U.S. 249 (2007).
[15] *Md. v. Wilson*, 519 U.S. 408 (1997).
[16] *Arizona v. Johnson*, 129 S. Ct. 781 (2009).
[17] *Brendlin v. California*, 551 U.S. 249 (2007).

5.10 Detaining a Recent Vehicle Occupant

An occupant is any person inside the vehicle when the stop is made, or any person who was inside the vehicle moments before the stop.[18] Why is this important? Because if a person qualifies as an occupant of a vehicle, and is near that vehicle when they are arrested, you may conduct a warrantless search if you have reason to believe evidence of the crime is inside the vehicle.

⭐ LEGAL STANDARD

A suspect may be treated like an occupant of a vehicle if:

- You observed or had probable cause that the suspect was an occupant in the vehicle;
- You stopped the suspect within the vicinity of the vehicle;
- The stop occurred almost immediately after the occupant exited the vehicle; and
- You had reason to believe evidence of the crime charged is inside the vehicle.

🏛 CASE EXAMPLES

Driver, who exited vehicle before police pulled up, was a "recent occupant"

An officer observed the defendant make an unsafe left-hand turn, which caused oncoming traffic to slam on their brakes. By the time the officer caught up to the vehicle the driver had exited and was walking away. The driver was later arrested and the search incident to arrest of vehicle was lawful.[19]

5.11 Consent to Search a Vehicle

There is no Fourth Amendment violation if you seek consent to search a vehicle from a lawfully stopped driver.[20] Whether consent was voluntarily given will be judged by the totality of the circumstances. Finally. if consent to search is obtained, it will not be considered an unreasonable extension of the traffic stop.

⭐ LEGAL STANDARD

A person may consent to search a vehicle if:

- It is reasonable to believe the driver or occupant has authority to consent to the search;
- The consent is freely and voluntarily given; and

---

[18] *Thornton v. U.S.*, 541 U.S. 615 (2004).
[19] *U.S. v. Mapp*, 476 F.3d 1012 (D.C. Cir. 2007).
[20] *Schneckloth v. Bustamonte*, 412 U.S. 218 (1973).

- Your search did not exceed the scope of the consent provided, whether express or implied.

🏛 CASE EXAMPLES

The scope of consent to search is normally defined by the object of the search

The officer informed the driver that he believed drugs were in the car, and that he would be looking for narcotics in the car. "We think that it was objectively reasonable for the police to conclude that the ... consent to search [driver's] car included consent to search containers within that car which might bear drugs. A reasonable person may be expected to know that ... contraband goods rarely are strewn across the trunk or floor of a car. The authorization to search in this case, therefore, extended beyond the surfaces of the car's interior to the paper bag lying on the car's floor."[21]

5.12 Frisking Vehicle and Occupants for Weapons

If you can reasonably articulate that any occupant is armed and dangerous, you may conduct a patdown for weapons. This applies even if the occupant is not suspected of any crime.[22] Courts recognize the inherent danger of traffic stops and provide officers wide discretion when it comes to officer safety.

★ LEGAL STANDARD

Any occupant may be frisked for weapons if:

- You can articulate that the occupant is armed and dangerous;
- You may only pat down the suspect's outer clothing; and
- A frisk may include inside the passenger compartment, including containers, where a weapon may be retrieved, if the person can access the vehicle.[23]

🏛 CASE EXAMPLES

Protective sweep upheld despite stopping wrong suspects

"Based on information obtained during the investigation of a series of armed robberies of drug dealers, law enforcement officers used 'felony stop' tactics to stop a vehicle under the belief that it carried armed and dangerous suspects for whom

---

[21] *Florida v. Jimeno*, 500 U.S. 248 (1991).
[22] *Arizona v. Johnson*, 555 U.S. 323 (2009).
[23] *Mich. v. Long*, 463 U.S. 1032 (1983).

arrest warrants had been issued." Based on the totality of the circumstances protective search was reasonable.[24]

Traffic stops are inherently dangerous

"Every traffic stop is a confrontation....That expectation becomes even more real when the motorist or a passenger knows there are outstanding arrest warrants or current criminal activity that may be discovered during the course of the stop."[25]

5.13 Frisking People Who Ride in Police Vehicle

Whether you may patdown a person depends on why he is in your patrol vehicle. If you are being nice and giving someone a ride home (*e.g.*, mom and kids on freezing day) then you must seek consent. If, on the other hand, you had no choice but to transport them (*e.g.*, take driver off highway after accident) then you may conduct a patdown for weapons.

🛡 LEGAL STANDARD

A person receiving a courtesy ride may be frisked for weapons if:

- You have received consent to patdown the suspect;[26]
- If consent is denied, a compulsory patdown is likely unlawful (maybe no ride should be offered).

A person being transported under a legal or policy obligation may be frisked for weapons if:

- You first ask for consent (recommended);
- If consent is denied, a patdown for weapons will likely be considered reasonable if you were legally required to transport the person, or agency policy allows patdowns under the circumstances.[27]

🏛 CASE EXAMPLES

Policy requiring patdown of all lawfully transported suspects lawful

In cases where the police may lawfully transport a suspect to the scene of the crime in the rear of a police car, the police may carry out a departmental policy, imposed for reasons of officer safety, by patting down that person.[28]

---

[24] *U.S. v. Holmes*, 376 F.3d 270 (4th Cir. S.C. 2004).
[25] *U.S. v. Dennison*, 410 F.3d 1203 (10th Cir. Colo. 2005).
[26] *People v. Scott*, 16 Cal. 3d 242 (Cal. 1976).
[27] *People v. Tobin*, 219 Cal. App. 3d 634 (Cal. App. 1st Dist. 1990).
[28] *U.S. v. McCargo*, 464 F.3d 192 (2d Cir. N.Y. 2006).

5.14 K9 Sniff Around Vehicle

Generally, there's no Fourth Amendment protection of the air around a vehicle.[29] Therefore, you may run a drug detection canine around a vehicle during a traffic stop or when the vehicle is left in a place that you are lawfully allowed to be, like a parking lot. Canine alerts give you probable cause to either search it under the mobile conveyance exception or to apply for a warrant.

Keep in mind two important restrictions. First, do not intentionally command the canine to touch, climb or jump onto a vehicle as this would be a trespass in violation of *U.S. v. Jones*.[30] Second, a canine sniff cannot extend the traffic stop unless you had reasonable suspicion for a drug offense.

🛡 LEGAL STANDARD

If no reasonable suspicion exists that drug evidence is inside the vehicle, then:

- You may conduct a free-air sniff around the vehicle as long as there is no break in the investigation that led to the stop; and
- The free-air sniff must not extend the stop.

If reasonable suspicion exists that drug evidence is inside the vehicle, then:

- You may continue to detain the vehicle for a reasonable amount of time for a drug canine to arrive on scene; and
- You may conduct a free-air sniff around the vehicle but may not make a physical intrusion in or on the vehicle without probable cause.

🏛 CASE EXAMPLES

Use of K9 during a stop is reasonable
No violation where one officer wrote ticket while another ran drug dog.[31]

5.15 Searching Vehicle Incident to Arrest

If you arrest any vehicle occupant, you may search the vehicle incident to arrest if the suspect is within the lunge distance from the vehicle.[32] Here, you are mainly looking for weapons or a means to escape. Once the suspect is secured you may no longer automatically search the vehicle incident to arrest.[33]

You may also search a vehicle if you have reason to believe evidence of the crime is inside the vehicle. No warrant is required. Two things should be noted. First, "reason to believe" evidence is inside the vehicle is a lower standard than probable

---

[29] *U.S. v. Place*, 462 U.S. 696 (1983).
[30] *U.S. v. Jones*, 565 U.S. 400 (2012).
[31] *U.S. v. Hernandez-Mendoza*, 600 F.3d 971 (8th Cir. S.D. 2010).
[32] *N.Y. v. Belton*, 453 U.S. 454 (1981).
[33] *Arizona v. Gant*, 556 U.S. 332 (2009).

cause. And second, it does not matter if the suspect does not have immediate access to the vehicle. Still, this type of search must be conducted contemporaneously (*i.e.*, soon after) with arrest.

⭐ LEGAL STANDARD

When a suspect is arrested and unsecured, his vehicle may be searched if:

- The suspect is within the lunge distance of the vehicle;
- You reasonably believe the suspect may gain access to inside the vehicle; and
- You may search for weapons, evidence, and a means of escape.

When a suspect is arrested and secured, his vehicle may be searched if:

- You have reason to believe[34] evidence of the crime for which he was arrested may be inside the vehicle;
- You do not exceed the scope of search necessary to find the evidence; and
- When you no longer have reason to believe evidence of the crime is inside the vehicle, the search must end unless you develop additional probable cause to search for something else.

🏛 CASE EXAMPLES

Officer can search vehicle if reasonable to believe evidence in vehicle

An officer is permitted to conduct a vehicle search when an arrestee is within reaching distance of the vehicle or it is reasonable to believe the vehicle contains evidence of the offense of arrest.[35] Note, you can still conduct a probable cause or inventory search if appropriate.

Search after issuing speeding ticket unlawful

Defendant was stopped by a police officer for speeding and was issued a citation rather than arrested. The officer then conducted a full search of defendant's car, incident to the citation. The officer found a bag of marijuana and a "pot pipe." Defendant was then arrested and charged with violation of Iowa state laws dealing with controlled substances. The Supreme Court held the search unlawful, since the officer did not arrest the defendant or gain consent.[36]

Arrest of an occupant does not permit search of fellow occupant

Officers arrested an occupant for possession of fraudulent government documents. This search permitted the search of the vehicle, but not a fellow passenger absent consent or a lawful arrest.[37]

---

[34] *U.S. v. Vinton*, 594 F.3d 14 (2010).
[35] *Arizona v. Gant*, 556 U.S. 332 (2009).
[36] *Knowles v. Iowa*, 525 U.S. 113 (1998).
[37] *U.S. v. Di Re*, 332 U.S. 581 (1948).

Search of coin box upheld for ammunition

A search of the coin box and bank bag, found within the vehicle, was upheld, but only because they could have contained "ammunition and paperwork related to the firearms investigation."[38]

Search of car lawful after wanted suspect threw drugs under it

Though officers initially approached the suspect to execute an outstanding bench warrant for failure to appear, search of vehicle was lawful after suspect threw a bindle of cocaine under the car and had $1,010 on his person.[39]

5.16   Searching Vehicle with Probable Cause

If you have probable cause that a vehicle contains evidence or contraband, you can usually conduct a warrantless search.[40]

There are two reasons why the Supreme Court allows these searches:

1. Ready mobility of the vehicle means evidence could leave the jurisdiction before obtaining a warrant; and
2. Vehicles have a lowered reasonable expectation of privacy because they are heavily regulated.

★ LEGAL STANDARD

A vehicle may be searched without a warrant if:

- You have probable cause that contraband or evidence is inside the vehicle;
- You have lawful access to the vehicle (*i.e.*, not within curtilage or in a backyard);
- The vehicle appears to be readily mobile (*e.g.*, needs no more than gas, tires, or battery to become mobile); and
- Your search does not exceed the scope of the probable cause.

🏛 CASE EXAMPLES

If probable cause exists to search a vehicle, police may search all containers, including those of a non-arrested occupant

"If probable cause justifies the search of a lawfully stopped vehicle, it justifies the search of every part of the vehicle and its contents that may conceal the object of the search." This applies "broadly to all containers within a car, without qualification as to ownership."[41]

---

[38] *U.S. v. Casteel*, 717 F.3d 635 (8th Cir. 2013).
[39] *Robbins v. Commonwealth*, 336 S.W.3d 60 (Ky. 2011).
[40] *Md. v. Dyson*, 527 U.S. 465 (1999).
[41] *Wyoming v. Houghton*, 526 U.S. 295 (1999).

5.17 Dangerous Items Left in Vehicle

If you have reason to believe a dangerous item was left inside a vehicle, which may endanger public safety if left unattended, you may secure the item for safekeeping.

🛡 LEGAL STANDARD

A vehicle may be entered without a warrant if:

- You have reason to believe a dangerous item is left unattended inside a vehicle; and
- Leaving the item inside the vehicle unattended would pose a risk to the community.

🏛 CASE EXAMPLES

Warrantless search for gun upheld

Chester Dombrowski was a Chicago officer who was drunk and involved in a one-car traffic accident while driving a rental car in Wisconsin. He identified himself as a Chicago officer to the investigating officers, who understood that Chicago police officers were supposed to carry their weapons at all times. Dombrowski had no weapon on him, and none were found in the passenger compartment. They had the car towed to a private garage several miles from the police station. Dombrowski was arrested for drunk driving and then taken to the hospital. One of the officers returned to the car to retrieve Dombrowski's service revolver. While looking for it, the officer found evidence which strongly suggested that Dombrowski was involved in a crime of violence. When confronted with the evidence, he gave the location of a body. He was ultimately convicted of first degree murder.[42]

5.18 Inventories

You may conduct an inventory search whenever you impound a vehicle. The main purpose of the inventory is specific—to protect your agency from false allegations about stolen or damaged property and protect the owner from theft or damage caused by tow companies. These inventories are searches, but they are not for evidence. Of course, plain view applies.

You cannot use vehicle inventories as a pretext to search a vehicle for contraband. This behavior is unlawful and can result in the suppression of evidence and 1983 lawsuits. In other words, officers cannot use inventories as a loophole to the probable cause requirement.[43] Additionally, some states require police to give

---

[42] *Cady v. Dombrowski*, 413 U.S. 433 (1973).
[43] *Colorado v. Bertine*, 479 U.S. 367 (1987).

on-scene owners the opportunity to take possession of their vehicle, if feasible, instead of towing it.[44]

Finally, if you want to inventory a locked container, develop probable cause or get consent. I would not break it open under your inventory policy.

⭐ LEGAL STANDARD

A vehicle may be inventoried when:

- Your agency has a written inventory policy which minimizes your discretion;
- The policy describes what may be searched and inventoried; and
- You must articulate a legitimate community caretaking rationale.

🏛 CASE EXAMPLES

Officer admitted that inventory was a ruse to search—not good

The narcotics team wanted Defendant stopped on a traffic offense, and deputies stopped him for failing to signal a turn. Upon determining that Torres was an unlicensed driver, they impounded his truck. The lead deputy testified that he was "basically using the inventory search as the means to go look for whatever "community caretaking function warranting the impoundment." The court suppressed three pounds of methamphetamine, cocaine, a rifle, and over $113,000 in cash found in defendant's home.[45]

Lawful inventory when officer looked under ripped carpet

The inventory search, including search under the floor carpeting, was within the department's policy, which authorized the search of all interior areas. Here, the carpet was "ripped up," which drew the officer's attention, the officer simply lifted an already loose flap of carpet that appeared to have been tampered with based on his reasonable belief that it might be concealing a hiding place for items, and the officer did not search under all of the carpeting, but just the portion that appeared to have been disturbed.[46]

Officer opened locked suitcase during inventory

During an inventory search an officer forced open a locked suitcase and found drugs. Evidence suppressed because the agency's written policy did not tell officers that they could break open locked containers.[47]

---

44 *Commonwealth v. Naughton*, 2003 Mass. Super. LEXIS 65 (Mass. Super. Ct. 2003).
45 *People v. Torres*, 188 Cal. App. 4th 775 (Cal. App. 4th Dist. 2010).
46 *U.S. v. Jackson*, 682 F.3d 448 (6th Cir. 2012)
47 *Florida v. Wells*, 495 U.S. 1 (1990)

Officer had tow driver unlock door

An officer towed a car that had been illegally parked. He asked the tow driver to open the car and the officer continued his inventory. Drugs were found in the glovebox and the owner was charged.[48]

Tow of suspected mobile PCP lab valid

Officers responded to house fire and observed a vehicle with suspected PCP lab inside. Tow reasonable because vehicle was unregistered, appeared abandoned, and owner could not be identified.[49] Note, this vehicle could also have been searched under the mobile conveyance exception.

Statutory authority to tow a vehicle is not enough, you must also articulate a community caretaking rationale

Generally, the Community Caretaking Doctrine has been held to apply (allowing for the impoundment of a vehicle) only when the vehicle, if left at the scene, is parked illegally, blocks traffic or passage, or stands at risk of theft or vandalism.[50]

5.19   Identifying Passengers

There is no constitutional violation by requesting a passenger identify himself.[51] However, you may not demand identification when you have no reasonable suspicion the passenger was involved in criminal activity.

My advice is to not push the issue unless you have developed reasonable suspicion that the passenger may be involved in criminal activity.

🛡 LEGAL STANDARD

If you want to identify a passenger, then:

- You may request identification, without reasonable suspicion;
- If you have reasonable suspicion that the passenger was involved in criminal activity, you may demand identification. Failure to identify may be an arrestable offense under state law.

🏛 CASE EXAMPLES

Officers may ask passenger for identification

A traffic stop "may include asking a passenger for identification and running a computer check if the passenger consents to the request for identification."[52]

---

[48] *South Dakota v. Opperman*, 428 U.S. 364 (1976)
[49] *U.S. v. Bullette*, 854 F.3d 261 (4th Cir. 2017)
[50] *People v. Lee*, 40 Cal. App. 5th 853 (2019).
[51] *People v. Vibanco*, 151 Cal. App. 4th 1 (Cal. App. 6th Dist. 2007).
[52] *U.S. v. Cloud*, 594 F.3d 1042 (8th Cir. Minn. 2010).

Asking for identification does not implicate the Fourth Amendment

Asking passenger for identification while he was lawfully detained did not implicate the Fourth Amendment because the police did not need to have reasonable suspicion in order to ask questions or request identification.[53]

5.20 Unrelated Questioning

The Supreme Court stated, "An officer's inquiries into matters unrelated to the justification for the traffic stop . . . do not convert the encounter into something other than a lawful seizure, so long as those inquires do not measurably extend the duration of the stop."[54]

Officers may ask various questions, such as where the driver is coming from, going to, where they work, *etc*. If you develop additional reasonable suspicion, then articulate those facts and circumstances in your report.

⭐ LEGAL STANDARD

Inquires into matters unrelated to the reason for the stop are permissible if:

- Your inquires do not measurably extend the traffic stop; and
- The unrelated inquires should resemble a consensual encounter, otherwise a court may view it as an investigative detention requiring reasonable suspicion.

🏛 CASE EXAMPLES

Unrelated inquires cannot measurably extend stop

"An officer's inquiries into matters unrelated to the justification for the traffic stop ... do not convert the encounter into something other than a lawful seizure, so long as those inquiries do not measurably extend the duration of the stop."[55]

An officer may further detain occupant with additional reasonable suspicion

"[T]he officer may detain the driver for questioning unrelated to the initial stop if he has an objectively reasonable and articulable suspicion illegal activity has occurred or is occurring....A variety of factors may contribute to the formation of an objectively reasonable suspicion of illegal activity."[56]

---

[53] *People v. Vibanco*, 151 Cal. App. 4th 1 (Cal. App. 6th Dist. 2007).
[54] *Arizona v. Johnson*, 555 U.S. 323 (2009).
[55] *Arizona v. Johnson*, 555 U.S. 323 (2009).
[56] *U.S. v. Hunnicutt*, 135 F.3d 1345 (10th Cir. Okla. 1998).

5.21　Constructive Possession

If you discover contraband inside a vehicle with multiple occupants and no one wants to claim ownership, you may charge all occupants with constructive possession.[57] However, it's not enough that the contraband was simply in the vehicle. You also need to articulate why the arrested occupants likely knew the contraband was inside the vehicle. For example, if burglary tools were found in the trunk that would not permit you to arrest passengers without articulating that the passengers probably knew the tools were there.

Alternatively, you could choose which occupant is the most culpable (usually the driver) and only charge him. Nothing requires you to arrest everyone under constructive possession. If you could arrest all, you may arrest one.

★ LEGAL STANDARD

Multiple occupants may be charged for constructively possessing contraband when:

- You articulate that there was at least a fair probability that the arrested occupant knew contraband was inside the vehicle; and
- The occupant could have possessed the contraband if he wanted to.

🏛 CASE EXAMPLES

All suspects involved in a hand-to-hand transaction were lawfully arrested

Two officers observed three suspects, in two vehicles, exchanging objects between their vehicles. Based on reasonable suspicion that they witnessed a hand-to-hand transaction, they made a stop. Drugs were eventually located and the court upheld the arrest of all suspects based on constructive possession, even though the drugs were only found in one vehicle.[58]

Associate can be arrested when he willfully and knowingly exercises control

It is well-established that one need not actually possess the controlled dangerous substance to violate the prohibition against possession thereof, as constructive possession is sufficient. The mere presence in an area where drugs are located or the mere association with one possessing drugs does not constitute constructive possession, a person may be deemed to be in joint possession of a drug which is in the physical custody of a companion, if he willfully and knowingly shares with the other the right to control it.[59]

---

[57] *Maryland v. Pringle*, 540 U.S. 366 (2003).
[58] *U.S. v. Lopez*, 441 Fed. Appx. 910 (3d Cir. Pa. 2011).
[59] *Eyer v. Evans*, 2004 U.S. Dist. LEXIS 1266 (E.D. La. Jan. 28, 2004).

Boyfriend who stayed with girlfriend had constructive possession of full-auto AK-47

Defendant argues that the officer did not have probable cause to believe that he actually or constructively possessed the firearm. He asserts that the bedroom where the AK-47 was found belonged to his girlfriend, and there was no evidence at the time of the arrest that he had knowledge of its existence. The court disagreed because defendant stayed at apartment, and suspiciously sat on bed when asked about the firearm.[60]

Passenger was in constructive possession of large amount of narcotics

There was probable cause to arrest the only passenger in a vehicle in which 37 pounds of marijuana were discovered by border control agents as the vehicle attempted to cross from Tijuana, Mexico into the United States. Here, the facts and circumstances support a fair probability that the passenger was linked to the crime of drug trafficking. He was a passenger in a car loaded with a commercial quantity of marijuana, the car belonged to neither occupant, and the car was procured under suspicious circumstances. Given these facts, a prudent and experienced police officer might reasonably suspect that the passenger is involved in drug smuggling.[61]

---

[60] *U.S. v. Brooks*, 270 Fed. Appx. 382 (6th Cir. Ohio 2008).
[61] *U.S. v. Buckner*, 179 F.3d 834 (9th Cir. 1999).

Chapter 6
Homes

6.1 Warrant Requirement

A person's home is the most protected area under the Fourth Amendment. Therefore, tread lightly whenever you make a warrantless search or seizure inside a home.

Whether a particular place is deemed a "home" will depend upon whether the place provides a person with a reasonable expectation of privacy, such that he would be justified in believing that he could retreat there, and be secure against government intrusion. In simple terms, where a person sleeps is usually his home.

⭐ LEGAL STANDARD

When an unlawful search and seizure occurs, only persons with "standing" may take advantage of the exclusionary rule. Generally, standing exists based on the following factors:

- The defendant has a property interest in the thing seized or the place searched;
- He has a right to exclude others from the thing seized or the place searched;
- He exhibited a subjective expectation that the item would remain free from governmental intrusion; and
- He took normal precautions to maintain privacy in the item.

🏛 CASE EXAMPLES

Hotel rooms have the same protections as homes

The rule that a warrantless entry by police into a residence is presumptively unreasonable applies whether the entry is made to search for evidence or to seize a person. It applies no less when the dwelling entered is a motel.[1]

A lawfully erected tent is equivalent to a home

"The thin walls of a tent are notice of its occupant's claim to privacy unless consent to enter be asked and given. One should be free to depart a campsite for the day's adventure without fear of his expectation of privacy being violated. Whether of short- or longer-term duration, one's occupation of a tent is entitled to equivalent protection from unreasonable government intrusion as that afforded to homes or hotel rooms."[2]

---

[1] *People v. Williams*, 45 Cal. 3d 1268 (Cal. 1988).
[2] *People v. Hughston*, 168 Cal. App. 4th 1062 (Cal. App. 1st Dist. 2008).

Subject had no reasonable expectation of privacy in his campsite

"Defendant had no authorization to camp within or otherwise occupy the public land. On at least four or five recent occasions he had been cited by officers for 'illegal camping' and evicted from other campsites in the preserve. Thus, both the illegality, and defendant's awareness that he was illicitly occupying the premises without consent or permission, are undisputed. "Legitimation of expectations of privacy by law must have a source outside of the Fourth Amendment, either by reference to concepts of real or personal property law or to understandings that are recognized and permitted by society."[3]

Tent over vehicle at music festival was a home

Suspect went to a music festival and pitched a '10x30' tent-like structure over his SUV. Suspect was later arrested for dealing drugs. Police conducted warrantless search on vehicle. Court held it was an illegal search inside "home." Tent was similar to a garage.[4]

Frequent visitor may have privacy inside friend's home

A frequent visitor, with free reign of the house despite the fact that he did not stay overnight, might also have standing to contest an allegedly illegal entry of a third person's home.[5]

Officer could not crouch under home's window and listen to conversation

An officer, unable to see inside the home from the sidewalk, crossed a ten-foot strip of grass and crouched under a window. He then heard a telephone conversation about a narcotics transaction. The court suppressed the evidence and said the officer's behavior was similar that of a "police state."[6]

6.2 Hotel Rooms, Tents, RVs, and so Forth

Generally, hotel rooms receive full Fourth Amendment protections. You cannot enter a room without consent, recognized exception, or a warrant (C.R.E.W.).

Additionally, a hotel manager may not give authorization to search a room while the occupants are gone. Again, the room is treated like a temporary home. However, once the room has been vacated, police may search anything abandoned, like trash containers.

Finally, if a person is lawfully evicted by hotel management (police should not be involved in this decision), usually due to non-payment or consuming drugs inside the room, police may assist in evicting the occupants. Remember, you cannot instantly enter the room or search for evidence. Under normal circumstances, let management provide the occupants with a reasonable amount of time to pack-up and leave.

---

[3] *People v. Nishi*, 207 Cal. App. 4th 954 (Cal. App. 1st Dist. 2012).
[4] *People v. Hughston*, 168 Cal. App. 4th 1062 (Cal. App. 1st Dist. 2008).
[5] *People v. Stewart*, 113 Cal. App. 4th 242 (Cal. App. 1st Dist. 2003).
[6] *Lorenzana v. Superior Court*, 9 Cal. 3d 626 (Cal. Sup. Ct. 1973).

The exception is if there is legitimate exigency to immediately remove the occupants, such on damage to the premises or a violent act between the remaining occupants. Either way, tread lightly here and if you are unsure ask a supervisor.

⭐ LEGAL STANDARD

Hotel rooms, tents, overnight guests, and so forth are protected by Fourth Amendment when:

- Hotel rooms are considered a home for the person who rented the room and invited overnight guests;
- Tents are considered a home when lawfully erected, or if unlawfully erected, in an area where a person would have a reasonable expectation of privacy, such as an area frequented by transients;
- Recreational Vehicles are considered homes whenever they are hooked up to a utility, setup in a camping configuration, or not readily mobile (*e.g.*, side skirts, no tires, etc.).

🏛 CASE EXAMPLES

Police may assist in evicting occupants

"A defendant, justifiably evicted from his hotel room, has no reasonable expectation of privacy in the room under the Fourth Amendment and police may justifiably enter the room to assist the hotel manager in expelling the individuals in an orderly fashion."[7]

Hotel manager may not authorize search of occupant's room

Defendant was a suspect in an armed robbery. After police officers obtained information where defendant was staying, they went to the hotel and received permission from a hotel clerk to enter defendant's room, where they seized evidence without a warrant. Search held to be a violation of the Fourth Amendment.[8]

Blocking front door with foot considered a warrantless entry

It has also been found that police blocking door of home with foot constituted entry. Further that lack of warrant, probable cause and exigent circumstances or consent rendered seizure unlawful.[9]

Guest did not inform hotel he was extending room, therefore abandoned

The defendant rented a motel room for a single night, paid only for one night, and never informed the desk that he wished to stay beyond that time. After check-out

---

[7] *U.S. v. Molsbarger*, 551 F.3d 809 (8th Cir. N.D. 2009).
[8] *Stoner v. California*, 376 U.S. 483 (1964).
[9] *State v. Larson*, 266 Wis. 2d 236 (Ct. App. 2003).

time the following day, the manager entered the room, saw a weapon, and summoned the police. In upholding the police entry of that room, the court reasoned: "[W]hen the term of a guest's occupancy of a room expires, the guest loses his exclusive right to privacy in the room. The manager of a motel then has the right to enter the room and may consent to a search of the room and the seizure of the items there found."[10]

No abandonment where hotel did not strictly enforce checkout time

Where hotel did not strictly enforce noon checkout and defendant indicated he would stay until 12:30, abandonment occurred only after later time and therefore police search of the room held unlawful.[11]

6.3 Knock and Talks

There is no Fourth Amendment violation if you try to consensually contact a person at their home. The key to knock and talks is to comply with social norms. Think about it this way, if the Girl Scouts could do it, so could you.

You must be reasonable when you contact the subject. Incessant pounding on the door, for example, would likely turn the encounter into a detention if the subject knows that it's the police knocking (an objectively reasonable person would believe that police are commanding him to open the door). Additionally, waking a subject up at 4 a.m. was viewed as a detention requiring reasonable suspicion (see below). Again, if the Girl Scouts would not do then it's probably unreasonable.

What about "No Trespass" signs? You can usually ignore them because trying to have a consensual conversation with someone is not what is typically meant by trespassing. Same goes with "no soliciting" signs.

⭐ LEGAL STANDARD

Knock and talks are lawful when:

- The path used to reach the door does not violate curtilage and appears available for uninvited guests to use;
- If the house has multiple doors, you chose the door reasonably believed to be available for uninvited guests to make contact with an occupant;
- You did not employ extraordinary efforts to contact the occupant, including making contact during a socially acceptable time;
- Your conversation with the occupant remained consensual; and
- When the conversation ended or was terminated, you immediately left and did not snoop around.

---

[10] *U.S. v. Parizo*, 514 F.2d 52 (2d Cir.1975).
[11] *U.S. v. Dorais*, 241 F.3d 1124 (9th Cir. 2001).

🏛 CASE EXAMPLES

Knock and talk at 4 a.m. held invalid

Officers went to suspect's residence at 4 a.m. with the sole purpose to arrest him. There was no on-going crime and the probable cause was based on an offense that occurred the previous night. Violation of knock and talk because officers exceeded social norms.[12]

Persistent knock in the middle of the night not consensual

Officers knocked on motel room door in middle of night for a full three minutes in order to make the occupant answer. Conduct constitutes investigative detention, not consent.[13]

Command to open door was not a consensual encounter

"Officers were stationed at both doors of the duplex and (an officer) had commanded (the defendant) to open the door. A reasonable person in (defendant's) situation would have concluded that he had no choice but to acquiesce and open the door."[14]

Officer's statement that he did not need a warrant to talk with occupant found to have tainted consent to enter

Officers made contact with a suspected alien at his apartment. The officers asked to enter the apartment, and the occupant asked whether they needed a warrant for that. The officers said they "did not need a warrant to talk to him." Based on the totality of the circumstances, the consent was involuntary since a reasonable occupant would have thought police did not need a warrant to enter and talk.[15]

Warrantless entry to secure gun during knock and talk reasonable

While conducting a knock and talk, it was reasonable for the sheriff's deputy to believe a gun may have been within reach of defendant in his camper and to fear for his safety, and exigent circumstances justified the sheriff's deputy's warrantless entry into defendant's camper to complete the arrest of defendant and subdue the security risk, where the underlying incident that brought the deputies to defendant's property to question him involved a firearm, defendant was uncooperative, angry, and made a threat toward another person, and defendant resisted arrest and attempted to retreat behind a hanging blanket and out of view, escalating a tense situation.[16]

6.4 Open Fields

Open fields are those areas that do not receive any Fourth Amendment protections. Typically, these areas are literally "open fields," and there are no structures

---

[12] *U.S. v. Lundin*, 47 F. Supp. 3d 1003 (N.D. Cal. 2014).
[13] *U.S. v. Jerez*, 108 F.3d 684 (7th Cir. Wis. 1997).
[14] *U.S. v. Poe*, 462 F.3d 997 (8th Cir. Mo. 2006).
[15] *Orhorgaghe v. I.N.S.*, 38 F.3d 488 (9th Cir. 1994).
[16] *U.S. v. Council*, 860 F.3d 604 (8th Cir. 2017).

on them (like sheds). Sometimes police will commit a technical trespass in order to reach open fields and view evidence (*e.g.*, marijuana grows). The Supreme Court has held that there is no constitutional violation because the open field itself is not a "house" or "effect" or an area where a person has a reasonable expectation of privacy.[17]

If you want to inspect something that is on private property, you may do so without a warrant as long as the property is not within the curtilage of a home. Also, just because there is a physical structure on the open field does not mean it's curtilage (*e.g.*, tool shed 300 feet away from home). You cannot enter any structure unless it was abandoned, even on open fields.

⭐ LEGAL STANDARD

An area is considered an "open field" not protected by the Fourth Amendment when:

- The area is not enclosed by a building or other structure (unless the building is abandoned); and
- The area is not curtilage (discussed next).

🏛 CASE EXAMPLES

The Fourth Amendment does not protect open fields

"[T]he special protection accorded by the Fourth Amendment to the people in their persons, houses, papers, and effects, is not extended to the open fields. The distinction between the latter and the house is as old as the common law."[18]

6.5 Curtilage

The home is the most protected area of the Fourth Amendment. The space around the home, called curtilage, is also offered this high level of protection.

Whenever you run into a curtilage issue, the first question is whether or not the space is actually curtilage. If not, the area is considered an open-field and not protected by the Fourth Amendment.

If a space is deemed curtilage, then the question becomes whether the area may be used by "uninvited guests" to make contact with an occupant.[19] Usually, this area is the pathway up to the front door.

---

[17] *Oliver v. U.S.*, 466 U.S. 170 (1984).
[18] *Hester v. U.S.*, 44 S. Ct. 445 (1924).
[19] *Florida v. Jardines*, 133 S. Ct. 1409 (2013).

✪ LEGAL STANDARD

Whether an area around a home is curtilage, protected by the Fourth Amendment, depends on weighing four factors:[20]

- The proximity of the area to the home itself (closer the better);
- Whether the area is included within a single enclosure, natural or artificial, surrounding the home;
- The use of the area (*e.g.,* BBQ pit, pool, kid's toys, etc.);
- Steps taken by the resident to protect the area from observations by people passing by (built high wooden fence, guard dog, etc.).

🏛 CASE EXAMPLES

Area around unoccupied trailer was not curtilage

A suspect had an uninhabited trailer on his property. Police looked around and saw a meth lab inside. Suspect argued the area immediately surrounding the trailer was curtilage. Court held area around trailer was not curtilage.[21]

Private boat dock not curtilage

Police entered a private dock area, passing a "No Trespass" sign, and looked around. The area was used by boaters who docked their boats there. Area was not curtilage or protected by the Fourth amendment.[22]

Installing an electric meter on pole in backyard did not violate curtilage

An electric meter installed on a utility police in the suspect's backyard by PG&E at police request to monitor theft of electricity did not violate curtilage. PG&E had lawful access to pole and the meter did not reveal anything private, such as what devices were powered by the electricity.[23]

Observation from side yard of apartment lawful

"In sum, although the defendants could easily have shielded their activities from public view, they failed to take the simple and obvious steps necessary to do so. By exposing their illicit cocaine activities to the side yard—a place where they should have anticipated that other persons might have a right to be—defendants failed to exhibit a subjective expectation that they intended their dealings in the bedroom to be private." Hence, police observations lawful."[24]

---

[20] *U.S. v. Dunn*, 480 U.S. 294 (1987).
[21] *Olson v. State*, 166 Ga. App. 104 (Ga. Ct. App. 1983).
[22] *U.S. v. Edmonds*, 611 F.2d 1386 (5th Cir. Ga. 1980).
[23] *People v. Stanley*, 72 Cal. App. 4th 1547 (1999).
[24] *U.S. v. Fields*, 113 F.3d 313 (2d Cir. Conn. 1997).

Apartment lobby not curtilage

"[T]he only issue before us is whether tenants in a large, high-rise apartment building, the front door of which has an undependable lock that was inoperable on the day in question, have a reasonable expectation of privacy in the common areas of their building. Our answer is no. There was nothing to prevent anyone and everyone who wanted to do so from walking in the unlocked door and wandering freely about the premises."[25]

Whatever the Girl Scouts may do, police may do

The authority of police to conduct a knock and talk "typically permits the [officer] to approach the home by the front path, knock promptly, wait briefly to be received, and then (absent invitation to linger longer) leave." In other words, whatever the "Girl Scouts" or "trick- or-treaters" would feel lawfully permitted to do, so may police.[26]

Automobile exception does not apply when vehicle parked inside curtilage

Warrant required when vehicle is parked under carport next to home.[27]

6.6 Plain View Seizure

Under the Plain View Doctrine, you may seize any item, that is immediately apparent as contraband or evidence, where you have lawful access.[28]

The rationale of the plain view doctrine is that if contraband is left in open view and is observed by a police officer from a lawful vantage point, there has been no invasion of a legitimate expectation of privacy and thus no search within the meaning of the Fourth Amendment—or at least no search independent of the initial intrusion that gave the officers their vantage point.[29]

Again, you need lawful access. For example, as you make a knock and talk you glance over and see a stolen motorcycle behind a fence, in the backyard. Can you open the gate and seize the motorcycle? Nope, you cannot invade curtilage without consent, exigency, or a warrant.

⬟ LEGAL STANDARD

Evidence may be seized if:

- Your protective sweep was lawful;
- The item was immediately apparent as evidence or contraband; and
- You had lawful access to the item.

---

[25] *U.S. v. Miravalles*, 280 F.3d 1328 (11th Cir. Fla. 2002).
[26] *Florida v. Jardines*, 133 S. Ct. 1409 (2013).
[27] *Collins v. Virginia*, 138 S. Ct. 1663 (2018).
[28] *Horton v. California*, 496 U.S. 128 (1990).
[29] *Minn. v. Dickerson*, 508 U.S. 366 (1993).

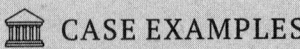 CASE EXAMPLES

Plain view seizure inside home is reasonable

"The seizure of property in plain view involves no invasion of privacy and is presumptively reasonable, assuming that there is probable cause to associate the property with criminal activity."[30]

6.7 Trash Searches

It has been clearly established by the Supreme Court that a suspect has no reasonable expectation of privacy in trash that has been left out, in order to be collected by the garbage company (*i.e.*, trash has been "abandoned").

The key here is that the trash has been put out for collection. If the trash is within the curtilage, and the trash company does not pick-up trash from that location, it has not been abandoned . . . yet.

⭐ LEGAL STANDARD

Evidence seized from a "trash pull" is lawful when:
- The person put his trash out for collection; and
- The trash was seized around a time and at a location where normal collection occurs.

🏛 CASE EXAMPLES

Seizing trash for twelve days straight considered lawful

Police seized an apartment dweller's trash for 12 days straight. Court held trash was abandoned.[31]

Garbage not protected on commercial property unless effort made to keep people out

No reasonable expectation of privacy in garbage left in dumpster[32] near commercial premises, on private property, where no reasonable effort has been made to keep people out. Remember, commercial property is typically not curtilage, so it is treated as an "open field."

---

[30] *Payton v. N.Y.*, 445 U.S.573 (1980).
[31] *Smith v. State*, 510 P.2d 793 (Alaska 1973).
[32] *U.S. v. Dunkel*, 90-1 U.S. Tax Cas. (CCH) P 50243 (7th Cir. 1990).

6.8   Consent to Search by Co-Occupants

You may seek consent to search a residence from co-occupants. However, the situation changes when there is a present non-consenting co-occupant. If one occupant tells you to, "Come on in and bring your friends!" and another yells, "Get the hell out, I'm watching Netflix," then you must stay out.

What about areas under the exclusive control of the consenter? For example, the "cooperative" tenant says you can still search his bedroom? Or a shed they have exclusive control over in the backyard? There is no case that deals directly with this issue, but if the area is truly under the exclusive control of the consenting party, and you can articulate that the non-consenting party has no reasonable expectation of privacy in that area, it would likely be reasonable to search just that area. But one issue remains, you still may not be able to access the area under the cooperative tenant's control without walking through common areas—evidence found in common areas may still be off limits.

The best practice is to wait until the non-consenting occupant left the residence and then seek consent from the cooperative occupant. In other words, if the non-consenting occupant goes to work, store, or is lawfully arrested, the remaining occupant can consent to search. Still, do not search areas under the exclusive control of the non-consenting party. This could include file cabinets, "man-caves," purses, backpacks, and so forth.

Finally, if the consenting party has greater authority over the residence, then police may rely on that consent. For example, if a casual visitor or babysitter objected to police entry, it could be overruled by a homeowner. Remember, you may not search personal property under the exclusive control of the visitor or babysitter.

⬥ LEGAL STANDARD

Spouses and Co-Occupants

Spouses or co-occupants may consent to search inside a home if:

- The person has apparent authority;
- Consent is only given for common areas, areas under his exclusive control, or areas or things the person has authorized access to; and
- A non-consenting spouse or co-occupant with the same or greater authority is not present.

---

[33] *People v. Superior Court*, 23 Cal. App. 3d 1004 (1972).

Articulating Greater Authority

An occupant with greater authority over the premises may consent to search areas either under his exclusive control or common areas if:

- The co-occupant had greater authority over the area searched;
- You did not enter or walk through any area where the non-consenting occupant had equal or greater authority;
- You did not search any property under the exclusive control of the non-consenting occupant; and
- Your search did not exceed the scope provided by the consenting occupant.

🏛 CASE EXAMPLES

If non-consenting occupant leaves, remaining occupant may consent

"[A] co-tenant's consent to a search can prevail over a defendant's refusal to consent when the defendant has left the scene, where there is "no evidence that the police have removed the potentially objecting tenant from the entrance for the sake of avoiding a possible objection."[34]

Consent of wife valid after non-consenting husband left residence

The consent of one who possesses common authority over premises or effects" generally "is valid as against the absent, non-consenting person with whom that authority is shared.[35]

If an occupant invites police inside, police may assume other occupants would not object

"[S]hared tenancy is understood to include an "assumption of risk," on which police officers are entitled to rely, and although some group living together might make an exceptional arrangement that no one could admit a guest without the agreement of all, police need not assume that's the case."[36]

6.9 Parental Consent to Search Child's Room

Generally, a parent can grant consent to search a child's room, particularly a minor child, even if the child objects to the search.

🛡 LEGAL STANDARD

A child's room may be searched, even when the child denies consent, under the following circumstances:

---

[34] *People v. Strimple*, 267 P.3d 1219 (Colo. 2012).
[35] *Fernandez v. California*, 571 U.S. 292 (2014).
[36] *Georgia v. Randolph*, 547 U.S. 103 (2006).

Minor children:

- A parent may consent for you to search a child's belongings and living areas; unless
- The child possesses an item which the parents have no right to access (like a friend's backpack).

Adult children:

- Courts will look at whether the child pays rent, if so, it is likely a landlord/tenant relationship and parents may not consent to search; or
- Has the child taken steps to deny his parents access to the property or living area in question, if so, then child may have a reasonable expectation of privacy.

🏛 CASE EXAMPLES

Parents may consent to search over a child's objection

"While there is no question minors are entitled to the protection of the Fourth Amendment, adults and minors are not necessarily entitled to the same degree of constitutional protection...To fulfill their duty of supervision, parents must be empowered to authorize police to search the family home, even over the objection of their minor children."[37]

6.10 Mistaken Authority to Consent

If you are a prudent officer you normally ask for consent to search, even if you have P.C. Why? Because valid consent adds an extra layer of protection for your criminal case.

But sometimes you'll think you are dealing with an occupant who has the authority to consent, but later find out you were wrong. For example, the consent was received from a guest, not homeowner. Here, courts will look to see if your mistake was reasonable.

⭐ LEGAL STANDARD

If you mistakenly receive consent from a person who had "apparent authority," courts will employ a three-part analysis to determine if your mistake was reasonable:

- Did you believe some untrue fact;
- Was it objectively reasonable for you to believe that the fact was true under the circumstances at the time; and
- If it was true would the consent giver have had actual authority.

---

[37] *In re D.C.*, 188 Cal. App. 4th 978 (Cal. App. 1st Dist. 2010).

🏛 CASE EXAMPLES

Police may assume adult that answered door had authority

Police were trying to locate a robbery suspect and knocked on his door. A visitor answered and consented to their request to enter. "Police may assume, without further inquiry, that [an adult] person who answers the door in response to their knock has the authority to let them enter."[38]

Simply claiming to live at home may not be enough without more info

Even if person claims to live at a home, "the surrounding circumstances could conceivably be such that a reasonable person would doubt its truth and not act upon it without further inquiry."[39]

6.11 Protective Sweeps

If you make a lawful arrest inside a home, you are allowed to conduct a protective sweep.[40] There are three zones, or areas, you may search depending on the circumstances.

🛡 LEGAL STANDARD

A protective sweep may be made inside a home during an arrest under the following conditions:

- **Zone 1**: You may automatically search areas under the immediate control of the suspect for weapons, evidence, or means of escape;
- **Zone 2**: You may automatically search for people in people-sized places in adjacent areas (*e.g.*, closets); and
- **Zone 3**: If you have reasonable suspicion that dangerous confederates are in the house, you may search for people in people-sized places and detain the confederates until the arrest is completed.

Remember: Zone 2 and 3 sweeps may never be used to search for "evidence," only people in people-sized places.

🏛 CASE EXAMPLES

Severity of crime committed can help justify protective sweep

"(T)he type of criminal conduct underlying the arrest or search is significant in determining if a protective sweep is justified."[41] Generalized safety concerns are not enough.[42]

---

[38] *People v. Ledesma*, 39 Cal. 4th 641 (Cal. 2006).
[39] *Ill. v. Rodriguez*, 497 U.S. 177 (U.S. 1990).
[40] *Maryland v. Buie*, 494 U.S. 325 (1990).
[41] *People v. Ledesma*, 106 Cal. App. 4th 857 (Cal. App. 1st Dist. 2003).
[42] *People v. Werner*, 207 Cal. App. 4th 1195 (Cal. App. 6th Dist. 2012).

Protective sweep of other rooms must be justified

Protective sweeps of the areas of the home beyond the immediate area (*i.e.*, other rooms) of the arrest will not be upheld absent an articulable reason for believing someone in the home is present who constitutes a potential danger to the officers.[43]

6.12   Hot Pursuit and Fresh Pursuit

There's a difference between "hot pursuit" and "fresh pursuit." Hot pursuit is when you are literally chasing a suspect who is trying to flee. You can follow him anywhere he goes, but you will need some form of exigency (see below). Fresh pursuit, on the other hand, is where you have identified a suspect in a serious violent felony and are actively tracking him down. If you quickly track down where he's hiding you may make a warrantless entry and arrest him if there's exigency (see below). In two recent U.S. Supreme case, the Court has severely restricted law enforcement ability to enter a home without a warrant and exigency.

Here's the bottom line, if you don't have some form of exigency, get a warrant.

⭐ LEGAL STANDARD

You may make a warrantless entry into a residence to arrest a suspect if:

Hot Pursuit:[44]

- You have probable cause to arrest the person (if the original stop was for reasonable suspicion, his flight transforms into obstruction; check state law);
- You are actively chasing the person and do not lose sight of him for an unreasonable amount of time (+/-15 minutes);
- The suspect knows you're trying to stop him before he flees into his home;
- Knock and announce rules apply (if you're right on the suspect's tail you don't need to stop and knock. Instead, this refers to losing the suspect briefly and then tracking him down into his house. Depending on the circumstances, you may have to knock and announce before entering);
- The crime is a felony or misdemeanor with exigency:
  - Prevent the destruction of evidence;
  - Prevent the suspect's escape;
  - There is a safety risk to the officer or public;
  - Need to render aid to an occupant;
  - Need to protect an occupant from imminent harm;
  - Any other situation where there is a compelling need for official action and no time to get a warrant; and
- You cannot search for evidence, but may make a plain view seizure.

---

[43] *U.S. v. Furrow*, 229 F.3d 805 (9th Cir. Idaho 2000).
[44] *People v. Lloyd*, 216 Cal. App. 3d 1425 (Cal. App. 2d Dist. 1989).

Fresh Pursuit:[45]

- You have probable cause that the person committed a serious violent felony;
- You develop probable cause that the suspect has fled inside his home;
- You are fresh on the suspect's trail since the crime was committed (elapse of more than three hours is pushing it);
- Knock and announce rules apply; and
- You have exigency:
  - Prevent the destruction of evidence;
  - Prevent the suspect's escape;
  - There is a safety risk to the officer or public;
  - Need to render aid to an occupant;
  - Need to protect an occupant from imminent harm;
  - Any other situation where there is a compelling need for official action and no time to get a warrant; and
- You cannot search for evidence, but may make a plain view seizure.

 CASE EXAMPLES

Officers were in fresh pursuit of murder suspect 2 ½ hours later

Where there was a two and a half hour investigation between a robbery-murder and the location of the defendant's home, the officers were found to be in "fresh pursuit," justifying a warrantless entry to arrest the suspect.[46]

Police were not in fresh pursuit of suspected get-away driver in convenience store robbery-murder

Exigent circumstances did not justify warrantless entry into upstairs duplex for purpose of arrest of overnight guest; police knew that suspect was in upstairs duplex with no suggestion of danger to other occupants of duplex and it was evident that suspect was going nowhere. Additionally, the crime occurred the previous day.[47]

Attempting to arrest DUI suspect who makes it home before police arrival does not automatically allow entry to make warrantless arrest

An officer informed an occupant that she could be charged for interfering with the investigation if he was not allowed to come in and arrest the driver, at which point she let the police in. The driver was in a locked bedroom and refused to come out. However, when the officer threatened to break down the door, she opened it and was arrested. The court found no exigency and suppressed the evidence (blood draw).[48]

Following fresh snow prints after rape fell under fresh pursuit

When an officer began following the suspect's footprints 30 to 45 minutes after the rape was committed, it was reasonable to assume that the suspect, who left the

---

[45] *Minnesota v. Olson*, 495 U.S. 91 (1990).
[46] *People v. Gilbert*, 63 Cal. 2d 690 (Cal. 1965).
[47] *Minnesota v. Olson*, 495 U.S. 91 (1990).
[48] *State v. Lovig*, 675 N.W.2d 557 (Iowa 2004).

scene on foot, might still be in flight and therefore entering his hotel room to make the arrest was lawful fresh pursuit (the court called this "hot pursuit").[49]

Misdemeanor hot pursuit does not automatically equal entry

"In misdemeanor cases, flight does not always supply the exigency that this Court has demanded for a warrantless home entry."[50]

6.13 Warrantless Arrest at Doorway

Normally, you cannot enter a person's home to make a warrantless arrest. There are two exceptions: 1) "exigency" and, 2) the "threshold doctrine." If a person is standing "in" his doorframe (*i.e.*, threshold) you may physically take him into custody because the court views the threshold as quasi-public. Same logic applies to any area where the public has access, like porches. If the suspect runs you may chase him based upon hot pursuit.[51] However, under a recent Supreme Court ruling, entering the home requires exigency.[52]

Tread lightly here because if the suspect successfully argues that he was a few inches inside his house, and not within the "threshold," it would be an unconstitutional entry and arrest.

⭐ LEGAL STANDARD

A suspect may be arrested if:
- You are conducting a lawful knock and talk;
- He is standing "in" or "outside" his doorway; and
- You have probable cause.

If the suspect flees into his home, exigency will likely be required before you can enter and arrest him. Courts typically look at these factors:

- Felony offense;
- Prevent the destruction of evidence;
- Prevent the suspect's escape;
- There is a safety risk to the officer or public;
- Need to render aid to an occupant;
- Need to protect an occupant from imminent harm;
- Any other situation where there is a compelling need for official action and no time to get a warrant.

---

[49] *State v. Campbell*, 104 Idaho 705 (Idaho App.1983).
[50] *Lange v. California*, No. 20-18, 2021 WL 2557068, at *7 (U.S. June 23, 2021).
[51] *People v. Hampton*, 164 Cal. App. 3d 27 (Cal. App. 1st Dist. 1985).
[52] *See Lange v. California*, No. 20-18, 2021 WL 2557068 (U.S. June 23, 2021).

🏛 CASE EXAMPLES

Suspect standing in doorway was lawfully chased in hot pursuit

Standing in the doorway is a public place for arrest purposes.[53] Therefore, when the suspect ran back inside his home it was a lawful hot pursuit.

Courts generally do not permit "body snatching" suspects out of their home without exigency

Officers decided that they had probable cause to arrest a suspect for aggravated stalking. Though they had no warrant or exigent circumstances, the officers went to his home to arrest him. In response to the officers' knock, the suspect opened his front door. One of the officers immediately reached into his home and arrested him. The officers violated the suspect's Fourth Amendment right to be free from unreasonable seizure.[54]

6.14   Warrantless Entry to Make Arrest

You cannot make a warrantless entry into a home to make an arrest without consent or exigency.[55] Even if the arrest was for a violent triple murder, you would have to articulate consent or exigency before entering. Also, the entry should be "peaceful," if possible.

★ LEGAL STANDARD

A warrantless entry to make an arrest may be made with:

Consent:

- You may enter if you have consent from an occupant with apparent authority over the premises and you make known your intention to arrest the suspect.

Hot Pursuit:

- You are in hot pursuit of a suspect believed to have committed an arrestable offense and they run into a home (a surround and call-out may also be done for officer safety purposes);
- You will also need some form of exigency. Flight alone is not enough.

Fresh Pursuit:

- You are in fresh pursuit of the suspect after investigating a serious violent crime and diligently track the suspect back to his home (anything over three hours is pushing it).

---

[53] *U.S. v. Santana*, 427 U.S. 38 (1976).
[54] *Moore v. Pederson*, 806 F.3d 1036, 1045 (11th Cir. 2015).
[55] *Payton v. N.Y.*, 445 U.S. 573 (1980).

Suspect will Escape:

- You have probable cause that the suspect committed a serious violent crime, and you reasonably believe he will escape before obtaining a warrant.

Undercover Officer - Immediate Reentry with Arrest Team:

- You are an undercover officer and conduct a narcotics transaction inside the home, you may leave and immediately reenter with an arrest team when two conditions are met: First, there must be a legitimate officer safety reason why you had to leave first, instead of summoning the arrest team into the home and you must articulate that an exigency exists, such as destruction or loss of evidence (not hard to do).

Remember for all Uninvited Entries:

- Knock and announce rules apply; and
- You cannot search for evidence, but may make a plain view seizure.

 CASE EXAMPLES

Entry to make any arrest, even for murder, requires consent, exigency, or a warrant

"To be arrested in the home involves not only the invasion attendant to all arrests but also an invasion of the sanctity of the home. This is simply too substantial an invasion to allow without a warrant, at least in the absence of exigent circumstances, even when it is accomplished under statutory authority and when probable cause is clearly present."[56]

Additional officers may enter if officer is inside the residence

An informant and undercover police officer went to defendant's residence to arrange a drug transaction. Defendant showed the pair a bag containing cocaine. The pair left the residence and returned with another agent, who was the purported purchaser. The door had been left ajar, so police officers entered the residence and arrested defendant.[57]

Delayed entry unlawful without exigency

"In a prosecution arising out of the purchase of stolen weapons from an undercover police officer in defendants' home. Although the undercover officer had been voluntarily admitted into the home, he had walked outside of the house to signal uniformed officers to arrest defendants. The officers then arrested defendants within the house without first obtaining an arrest warrant, seized the weapons sold, and uncovered a rifle in their subsequent search of the house. The court held that despite the legality of the officer's initial entry, his reentry without consent and in the absence of exigent circumstances rendered the arrest and the search incident thereto unlawful."[58]

---

[56] *U.S. v. Reed*, 572 F.2d 412, 423 (1978).
[57] *Toubus v. Superior Court*, 114 Cal. App. 3d 378 (Cal. App. 1st Dist. 1981).
[58] *People v. Garcia*, 139 Cal. App. 3d Supp. 1 (Cal. App. Dep't Super. Ct. 1982).

Immediate reentry lawful

Warrantless arrest of defendant in his residence upheld when defendant had consented to initial entry by police officer, during which time defendant committed crime in officer's presence, after which officer left and immediately reentered with other officers to arrest defendant.[59]

6.15 Warrantless Entry for an Emergency

You may make a warrantless home entry if you have an objective reasonable basis for believing that an occupant requires emergency assistance,[60] or an occupant is threatened with imminent injury.

Remember, the scope of your entry is limited and you must leave, if demanded, once the emergency is over.

⭐ LEGAL STANDARD

A warrantless entry into a home may be made when:[61]

- You have reason to believe an immediate need exists for the protection of human life;
- The search or entry is motivated by the emergency, rather than by an intent to arrest or secure evidence;
- There is a reasonable connection between the emergency and the area in question;
- Knock and announce rules apply; and
- You cannot search for evidence, but may make a plain view seizure.

🏛 CASE EXAMPLES

Warrantless entry for serious injury or threatened injury reasonable

A warrant is not required when there is a "need to assist persons who are seriously injured or threatened with such injury. 'The need to protect or preserve life or avoid serious injury is justification for what would be otherwise illegal absent an exigency or emergency.'"[62]

Warrantless entry justified to protect domestic violence victim

"Officers' decisions to enter a home to ensure the safety of those believed to be at risk of domestic violence have been found reasonable" by most courts.[63]

---

[59] *People v. Cespedes*, 191 Cal. App. 3d 768 (Cal. App. 1st Dist. 1987).
[60] *Michigan v. Fisher*, 558 U.S. 45 (2009).
[61] *State v. Bookheimer*, 221 W. Va. 720, 656 S.E.2d 471 (2007).
[62] *Brigham City v. Stuart*, 547 U.S. 398 (2006).
[63] *Fletcher v. Town of Clinton*, 196 F.3d 41 (1st Cir. Me. 1999).

Warrantless entry into home and seizing a domestic violence suspect's guns is not permitted under community caretaking

"Decades ago, this Court held that a warrantless search of an impounded vehicle for an unsecured firearm did not violate the Fourth Amendment. In reaching this conclusion, the Court observed that police officers who patrol the 'public highways' are often called to discharge noncriminal 'community caretaking functions,' such as responding to disabled vehicles or investigating accidents. The question today is whether...these 'caretaking' duties creates a standalone doctrine that justifies warrantless searches and seizures in the home. It does not."[64]

6.16   Warrantless Entry for Officer Safety

Generally, you may make a warrantless entry when you have reason to believe violence is imminent upon officers.

Courts have recognized two situations where this can occur. First, if you are making an arrest outside of a person's home (*i.e.*, front yard) and you have an objective reasonable basis to believe that someone inside the home is about to attack you, police may make entry and conduct a protective sweep.

Second, if you are interviewing a suspect outside his home and he suddenly flees back into the home, you can follow him if you have an objective reasonable belief that he was going to get a weapon.

⭐ LEGAL STANDARD

An warrantless entry into a home may be made if:
- You have reason to believe that someone inside the home possesses a serious threat to an officer's safety;
- Once there is no longer a threat, you must leave unless you receive consent or a warrant;
- Knock and announce rules apply; and
- You cannot search for evidence, but may make a plain view seizure.

🏛 CASE EXAMPLES

Judges should be cautious about second guessing officer safety

Officers in Burbank were investigating reports that a student was going to "shoot up" the school. They went to his house and spoke to his mother, who acted oddly and when asked about whether there were guns in the house quickly turned around and went into the house. Officers followed in case she was going to get a gun....an officer may enter if he had a reasonable basis for concluding that there is an imminent threat of violence ...Judges should be cautious about second-guessing a police

---

[64] *Caniglia v. Strom*, 141 S. Ct. 1596, 1598 (2021).

officer's assessment, made on the scene, of the danger presented by a particular situation.[65]

6.17 Warrantless Entry to Investigate Child Abuse

If you have an objective reasonable basis to believe that a child needs protection or aid you may make a warrantless entry to render aid.[66]

🛡 LEGAL STANDARD

An warrantless entry into a home may be made if:

- You have a reason to believe that a child inside the home is in immediate need for protection or aid;
- Knock and announce rules apply;
- If the child is determined to be safe, you must leave unless you receive consent or a warrant; and
- You cannot search for evidence, but may make a plain view seizure.

🏛 CASE EXAMPLES

Exigency existed for caseworker to enter home and remove child

Exigent circumstances permit a social services caseworker to seize a child without a warrant if the caseworker has reasonable cause to believe that the child is likely to experience serious bodily harm in the time that would be required to obtain a warrant.[67]

However, if police and caseworker work as team, probable cause and exigency required, not lower "reasonable cause" standard

Exigent circumstances did not justify an officer's warrantless entry into the parents' home while accompanying social workers following up on a child abuse referral.[68]

6.18 Warrantless Entry to Protect Property

If you have an objective reasonable basis to believe that a warrantless entry will help protect property from damage, such as theft or vandalism, you may enter the property in order to help secure it or to contact the owner.

---

[65] *Ryburn v. Huff*, 565 U.S. 469 (2012).
[66] *People v. Brown*, 6 Cal. App. 3d 619 (Cal. App. 4th Dist. 1970).
[67] *Gates v. Texas Dept. of Protective and Regulatory Services*, 537 F.3d 404 (5th Cir. 2008).
[68] *Andrews v. Hickman County, Tenn.*, 700 F.3d 845 (6th Cir. 2012).

🛡 LEGAL STANDARD

An warrantless entry into a building may be made if:

- You have a reason to believe that the property is in immediate need of protection (*e.g.,* on fire, gas leak, *etc.*);
- Once the property is secured or the owner notified, you must leave unless you receive consent or a warrant;
- Knock and announce rules apply; and
- You cannot search for evidence, but may make a plain view seizure.

🏛 CASE EXAMPLES

Warrantless entry upheld in search of starving horses

Animal control officer determined that a horse on defendant's farm had died of starvation. A warrantless search of the barn for other horses was justified under "state policy to render aid to relatively vulnerable and helpless animals when faced with people willing or even anxious to mistreat them."[69]

Lawful entry when investigating a burglary and television was outside of window

While investigating a possible home burglary, the officer noticed a television set outside the window of a house, entered the residence without a warrant, and came upon a methamphetamine lab. The court held the entry as valid, "as the television set outside the window was substantial evidence indicating the burglars could still be inside."[70]

6.19 Warrantless Entry to Investigate Homicide Crime

Generally, you cannot make a warrantless entry into a home unless you have consent, recognized exception or a warrant (C.R.E.W.). There's a recognized exception to make a warrantless entry to render emergency aid to a shooting victim. However, it would be a violation to fully process the crime scene without first obtaining consent or a search warrant. There is no "crime scene exception" to the warrant requirement, even for a violent murder.

🛡 LEGAL STANDARD

An warrantless entry into a home may be made if:

- You have a reason to believe that a serious crime has occurred inside the property and police need to check for additional victims or secure the scene for a warrant;

---

[69] *State v. Bauer*, 127 Wis.2d 401 (1985).
[70] *People v. Duncan*, 42 Cal.3d 91 (1986)

- Once the property is secured, you must receive consent or a warrant;
- Knock and announce rules apply; and
- You cannot search for evidence, but may make a plain view seizure.

🏛 CASE EXAMPLES

There is no "murder scene exception" to warrant requirement

The United States Supreme Court rejected the contention that there is a "murder scene exception" to the Warrant Clause of the Fourth Amendment. Police may make warrantless entries onto premises if they reasonably believe a person is in need of immediate aid and may make prompt warrantless searches of a homicide scene for possible other victims or a killer on the premises, but searching for evidence requires a warrant.[71]

6.20   Warrantless Entry to Prevent Destruction of Evidence

Generally, you cannot make a warrantless entry into a home unless you have consent, recognized exception or a warrant (C.R.E.W.). One of the recognized exceptions is the warrantless entry to prevent the destruction of evidence.[72] Remember, you cannot create the exigency. But simply knocking on the door does not count.

🛡 LEGAL STANDARD

A warrantless entry into a home or business may be made if:

- You have probable cause that an occupant is or is about to destroy evidence or contraband;
- You did not create the exigency;
- Once the home is secured, you must get a warrant; Knock and announce rules apply; and
- You cannot search for evidence, but may make a plain view seizure (or quickly photograph, leave it, and attach photo to affidavit).

🏛 CASE EXAMPLES

Knocking on door and saying "police" did not create the exigency

Officers smelled marijuana coming from apartment. After knocking on the door and saying "police" they heard suspects destroying evidence. Warrantless entry was lawful to preserve evidence.[73]

---

[71] *Mincey v. Arizona*, 437 U.S. 385 (1978).
[72] *Minnesota v. Olson*, 495 U.S. 91 (1990).
[73] *Kentucky v. King*, 563 U.S. 452 (2011).

6.21 Warrantless Entry Based on "Ruse" or Lie

Generally, courts do not like "ruses." A ruse is where someone is tricked. Still, it's okay to "lie" about your identity, but not your purpose. For example, as an undercover cop you couldn't sneak around a suspect's home during a drug buy, that would be a lie about purpose (*i.e.*, there to buy drugs, not snoop around).

Additionally, it's inappropriate to use a ruse in order to gain entry into someone's home in order to arrest him. For example, if you planned to arrest a suspect (without arrest warrant) it would not be okay to conduct a knock and talk and lie to the subject that you wanted to come in, "just to talk." On the other hand, if your intention was to talk and during the conversation you developed P.C. to arrest, you could make the warrantless arrest since you were lawfully inside the home. Do you see the subtle difference?

Alternatively, the majority of cases hold that you may use a ruse to get the subject to voluntarily exit the residence if you had P.C. For example, you could tell a wanted suspect that his car was illegally parked and to move it even if not true since that tactic does not invade the sanctity of the home.

⭐ LEGAL STANDARD

A ruse or lie may not be used to enter a home and search for evidence unless:

- You possessed a search warrant; and
- You had exigency which justified not announcing your purpose to enter the home under "knock and announce."

🏛 CASE EXAMPLES

Unlawful ruse by ATF agent who portrayed himself as state LEO

ATF tagged along with a CA DOJ agent to perform a licensing inspection. ATF was actually conducting a different investigation. Court held the entry was an unlawful ruse.[74]

6.22 Convincing Suspect to Exit Based on "Ruse" or Lie

Generally, you may use a ruse to get a suspect to come out of his house if you have R.S. or P.C.[75] Once the suspect is outside, you may arrest or detain him. "Outside" the home includes the front porch and anywhere the general public has lawful access. These areas usually include walkways to the front door and driveways.

Be cautious whenever you use a ruse or trick. Keep in mind:

---

[74] *U.S. v. Bosse*, 898 F.2d 113 (9th Cir. Cal. 1990).
[75] *U.S. v. Rengifo*, 858 F.2d 800 (1st Cir. R.I. 1988).

- If you have probable cause to arrest, it's best to come up with a ruse that includes identifying yourself as a police officer. For example, if true, you can tell the suspect that if they do not come outside and talk to you then you'll apply for a warrant which could result in the SWAT team serving an arrest warrant.
- If you have exigent circumstances to enter the home and arrest the suspect (*e.g.*, hot/fresh pursuit) then it would also be lawful to surround and call out for officer safety purposes. Best practice: Do not use ruses. They are heavily scrutinized.

⭐ LEGAL STANDARD

You may use a ruse or lie to get a suspect to exit his home if:

- You have an arrest warrant; or
- You have probable cause and exigent circumstances to make the arrest.

🏛 CASE EXAMPLES

Unlawful ruse where plainclothes cop told citizen he just hit his car

Where subject came out to inspect damage on car, court held that ruse was unreasonable since even innocent people would leave their residence. Evidence from consent to search suppressed.[76] Here, there was no probable cause and exigent circumstances.

6.23   Detaining a Home in Anticipation of a Warrant

Generally, you may "freeze" or "detain" a residence if there's probable cause to believe there's evidence inside, and exigent circumstances exist to believe the evidence will be gone before receiving a search warrant.[77]

If you are inside the home to exclude occupants and see evidence in plain view, you may make a warrantless seizure of the evidence. But often the best practice is to leave the evidence inside the residence, exclude the occupants, and obtain judicial approval with a warrant.

Remember, knock and announce rules apply.

---

[76] *People v. Reyes*, 83 Cal. App. 4th 7 (Cal. App. 4th Dist. 2000).
[77] *Illinois v. McArthur*, 531 U.S. 326 (2001).

🛡 LEGAL STANDARD

A residence may be detained in anticipation of a search warrant when:

- You have clear probable cause to get a search warrant;
- You have additional probable cause that the evidence or contraband will be destroyed or moved prior to executing the search warrant;
- You may not enter the residence unless you have a reason to believe the home is currently occupied;
- You must diligently apply for the warrant; knock and announce rules apply; and
- You cannot search for evidence, but may make a plain view seizure.

Note: I strongly suggest you do not include evidence observed during the detention of the home in your search warrant. First, you shouldn't need it because you needed probable cause before the entry. Second, the defendant may argue that you only got the warrant because of the evidence observed during the warrantless entry and therefore your pre-detention probable cause was insufficient. Save yourself the headache and leave it out.

6.24 Surround and Call-Out

A barricaded suspect is one who poses a danger to himself or others and refuses to leave his residence. Often, police will surround the house and try to convince the suspect to come out peacefully. Surrounding a home is a seizure under the Fourth Amendment and must be justified by exigency (usually not an issue in these cases).

If the subject is suicidal, the recognized exception is the "community caretaking doctrine." Often there's no crime committed by the subject (attempting suicide is generally not a "crime") and police are trying to take the suspect into custody for a mental evaluation.

🛡 LEGAL STANDARD

A surround and call-out is lawful when:

- You have probable cause and authority to enter the home to make the arrest or a civil commitment; and
- You have reason to believe that the suspect poses a threat to officers;
- Additionally, a surround and call-out is lawful under the community caretaking doctrine when the subject is a danger to himself or others (usually suicidal with weapon);
- If entry is made you cannot search for evidence, but may make a plain view seizure.

🏛 CASE EXAMPLES

No warrant needed during a surround and callout

During an armed standoff, once exigent circumstances justify the warrantless seizure of the suspect in his home, and so long as the police are actively engaged in completing his arrest, the police need not obtain an arrest warrant before taking the suspect into full physical custody.[78]

---

[78] *Fisher v. City of San Jose*, 558 F.3d 1069 (9th Cir. Cal. 2009).

Chapter 7
Businesses & Schools

7.1 Warrantless Arrest Inside Business

Generally, you may enter "public areas" of a business to make an arrest. However, you do not have an automatic right, even when you possess an arrest warrant, to enter business offices and other private areas where there is a reasonable and legitimate expectation of privacy.[1] These areas are typically private offices where the public does not have access.

🛡 LEGAL STANDARD

A warrantless arrest inside a business is lawful when:

- You make the arrest in a public area of the business; or
- If the suspect is in a private area where he has a reasonable expectation of privacy, consent to enter is given by someone with apparent authority and the suspect does not object before entry.

🏛 CASE EXAMPLES

Entry into closed portion of business unlawful

Officers entered a casino bingo hall that was presently closed to the public. Officers saw evidence of illegal gambling. Since bingo hall was not presently accessible to the public, the court suppressed the evidence.[2]

Forced entry into private area of dental office unlawful

Police officers, who were investigating claim that dentist had sexually assaulted his receptionist, could not make unannounced forcible entry into private area of the business without exigency.[3]

Entry into public areas does not require a warrant

Warrant not necessary to enter reception area through unlocked door during business hours, as there was "no reasonable expectations of privacy there."[4]

---

[1] *Steagald v. U.S.*, 451 U.S. 204 (1981).
[2] *State v. Foreman*, 662 N.E.2d 929 (Ind. 1996).
[3] *People v. Polito*, 42 Ill.App.3d 372, 355 N.E.2d 725 (1976).
[4] *U.S. v. Little*, 753 F.2d 1420 (9th Cir. 1984).

7.2 Customer Business Records

Generally, a customer has no reasonable expectation of privacy in information kept by a third party.[5] Therefore, you may request access to business records. However, if access is denied then a court order, subpoena, or search warrant is required. You cannot demand a business hand over its records.

🛡 LEGAL STANDARD

Police may request or subpoena customer records without a warrant if:

- The company consents to provide the records; or
- You receive a subpoena for the records; and
- If the records are digital tracking data, such as cell phone location records, which would violate the suspect's reasonable expectation of privacy in his movements or activities, a search warrant is required.

🏛 CASE EXAMPLES

Customer has no reasonable expectation of privacy in banking records

"The Fourth Amendment protects against intrusions into an individual's zone of privacy. In general, a depositor has no reasonable expectation of privacy in bank records, such as checks, deposit slips, and financial statements maintained by the bank. Where an individual's Fourth Amendment rights are not implicated, obtaining the documents does not violate his or her rights, even if the documents lead to indictment."[6]

Tracking suspect through cell-site records requires a warrant or exigency

The Government's acquisition of the cell-site records was a search within the meaning of the Fourth Amendment.[7]

7.3 Heavily Regulated Businesses

In general, businesses enjoy Fourth Amendment protections. One notable exception is when you conduct warrantless administrative inspections of heavily regulated businesses. These often include bars, gun stores, and junk yards.

🛡 LEGAL STANDARD

The following is required to conduct warrantless administrative searches:

---

[5] *Smith v. Md.*, 442 U.S. 735 (1979); *U.S. v. Miller*, 425 U.S. 435 (1976).
[6] *Marsoner v. U.S. (In re Grand Jury Proceedings)*, 40 F.3d 959 (9th Cir. Ariz. 1994).
[7] *Carpenter v. U.S.*, 138 U.S. 2206 (2018).

- A statutory scheme must be in place so that the business is on notice that a warrantless administrative search may be conducted; and
- The scope of the search must comply with the statute.

🏛 CASE EXAMPLES

Owners of heavily regulated businesses are on notice for warrantless searches

"Certain industries have such a history of government oversight that no reasonable expectation of privacy could exist for a proprietor over the stock of such an enterprise. Liquor…and firearms…are industries of this type; when an entrepreneur embarks upon such a business, he has voluntarily chosen to subject himself to a full arsenal of governmental regulation."[8]

Fishing business is heavily regulated industry in Massachusetts

Fishing industry is heavily regulated industry in Massachusetts and statute authorizing random document checks was constitutional.[9]

Warrantless safety inspection of commercial vehicles upheld

Texas statute authorizing stop and safety inspection of trucks without individualized suspicion is constitutional administrative search because trucking is a pervasively regulated industry.[10]

7.4 Fire, Health, and Safety Inspections

Generally, businesses enjoy Fourth Amendment protections. One notable exception is "fire, health and safety" inspections.

🛡 LEGAL STANDARD

The following is required to conduct warrantless safety searches:

- A statutory scheme must be in place so that the business is on notice that a warrantless administrative search may be conducted;
- The scope of the search must comply with the statute;
- However, unlike heavily regulated businesses, if you are denied entry, an administrative warrant is required based on the statute.

---

[8] *Marshall v. Barlow's, Inc.*, 98 S. Ct. 1816 (1978).
[9] *Tart v. Com. of Mass.*, 949 F.2d 490 (1st Cir. 1991).
[10] *U.S. v. Fort*, 248 F.3d 475 (5th Cir. 2001).

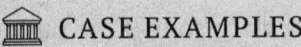 CASE EXAMPLES

OSHA inspections require a warrant without consent

OSHA attempted to make a safety inspection on a plumbing business. The owner denied OSHA entry, and demanded a warrant. The Court held that it was not overly burdensome for OSHA to get a warrant if consent was denied.[11]

Warrantless health inspection of rabbits upheld

Warrantless inspection, by the Animal and Plant Health Inspection Service, of breeder of rabbits for research, pursuant to Animal Welfare Act, met constitutional requirements.[12]

Officer may not use admin search as loophole to seize evidence

"[W]hen a law enforcement officer intends to seize a particular piece of criminal evidence from the premises of a pawnshop, the seizure may not be substantiated by relying on the pretense of an administrative search coupled with the plain view doctrine. In such a situation, the officer must obtain a warrant."[13]

7.5 Government Workplace Searches

The Fourth Amendment applies to all government searches and seizures, including government workplace searches and drug tests. However, the Supreme Court has significantly lowered the bar for these searches and they are generally upheld if conducted for a legitimate purpose and carried out in a reasonable manner. A government supervisor may search an employee's desk, filing cabinets, or other areas without a warrant or probable cause so long as the search is reasonable at its inception and reasonable in scope. As the Supreme Court noted:

In our view, requiring an employer to obtain a warrant whenever the employer wished to enter an employee's office, desk, or file cabinets for a work-related purpose would seriously disrupt the routine conduct of business and would be unduly burdensome.[14]

LEGAL STANDARD

You may search a government employee's work area if:

- The search is justified by a legitimate workplace need;
- The search is carried out in a reasonable manner;
- The search is not excessively intrusive in light of the circumstances given rise to the search; and

---

[11] *Marshall v. Barlow's, Inc.*, 436 U.S. 307 (1978)
[12] *Lesser v. Espy*, 34 F.3d 1301 (7th Cir. 1994)
[13] *Winters v. Bd. of Cty. Comm'rs*, 4 F.3d 848, 854 (10th Cir. 1993).
[14] *O'Connor v. Ortega*, 107 S. Ct. 1492 (1987).

- The employee does not enjoy a reasonable expectation of privacy in the particular area or thing searched.

🏛 CASE EXAMPLES

The Fourth Amendment applies to government workplace searches

"The Amendment guarantees the privacy, dignity, and security of persons against certain arbitrary and invasive acts by officers of the Government," without regard to whether the government actor is investigating crime or performing another function. The Fourth Amendment applies as well when the Government acts in its capacity as an employer."[15]

7.6 School Searches

The Fourth Amendment applies to public schools. However, school administrators may search under the reasonable suspicion standard instead of the typical probable cause standard.

On the other hand, the Fourth Amendment does not apply to private school searches, even if the school receives most of its operating funds from public revenue. Therefore, any search conducted by a private school is admissible as evidence and not subject to the exclusionary rule.

Finally, police officers must apply regular Fourth Amendment protections.

🛡 LEGAL STANDARD

Lockers

Students have little reasonable expectation of privacy in their lockers. Some factors courts may consider are whether the student was informed that lockers could be searched at any time, whether the school provided the lock, and whether the locker contents could be viewed without opening it (*e.g.*, mesh door). Locker searches based on general or individualized suspicion will be upheld. Random and suspicionless locker searches will be judged on a case by case basis and officials should articulate the need to maintain a safe campus, and why students would not have a reasonable expectation of privacy in their locker.

Desks and work areas

Students and staff members have no reasonable expectation of privacy in areas that are shared with others. Additionally, this applies to hallways, classrooms, and school computers.

---

[15] *City of Ontario v. Quon*, 560 U.S. 746 (2010).

Vehicles on School Grounds

School officials may run a drug K9 on the outside of vehicles without reasonable suspicion. However, officials need individualized suspicion in order to conduct a warrantless search for drugs, firearms, or evidence of school policy violations.[16]

Metal Detectors and Bag Searches

Metal detectors and student bag searches upon entry to a school is considered a special needs search and will be upheld without reasonable suspicion.[17]

Searches of Student Social Media Accounts and Cell Phones

Officials may surf the internet and view publicly available information. However, compelling a student to provide a Facebook password likely violates the First and Fourth Amendments. Officials cannot search a student's confiscated cell phone absent reasonable suspicion that a violation of school policy would be found.[18]

Strip Searches

Strip searches are highly intrusive and should only be done if absolutely necessary. If possible, arrest the juvenile and have the detention center conduct the search. If that is not an option, and it is imperative that the evidence be recovered, conduct the search in the most delicate and professional manner possible. Same sex searcher, private, and use professional language at all times. Consider recording the encounter with a body cam but hold hand over camera to block any view of private areas (*i.e.*, keep recording audio).

Field Trips

The lowered standard applies to off-campus field trips.

🏛 CASE EXAMPLES

School searches only require a "moderate chance" of finding evidence

The lesser standard for school searches could as readily be described as a moderate chance of finding evidence of wrongdoing.[19]

Purse Search

A teacher at a New Jersey high school found a 14-year-old freshman smoking cigarettes in a school lavatory in violation of a school rule, and took them to the Vice Principal's office. The student denied that she had been smoking and claimed that she did not smoke at all. The Vice Principal demanded to see her purse. Upon opening the purse, he found cigarettes and rolling papers that are commonly associated with the use of marijuana. He then proceeded to search the purse and found some

---

[16] *Myers v. State*, 806 N.E.2d 350 (Ind. Ct. App. 2004).
[17] *People v. Pruitt*, 278 Ill. App. 3d 194 (Ill. App. Ct. 1st Dist. 1996).
[18] *G.C. v. Owensboro Pub. Sch.*, 711 F.3d 623 (6th Cir. Ky. 2013).
[19] *Safford Unified Sch. Dist. #1 v. Redding*, 129 S. Ct. 2633 (U.S. 2009).

marijuana, a pipe, plastic bags, a fairly substantial amount of money, an index card containing a list of students who owed the student money, and two letters that implicated her in marijuana dealing. The search was constitutional.[20]

Strip Search for Prescription Ibuprofen Illegal

A school principal made a warrantless search of a student's belongings because she apparently possessed over the counter ibuprofen. The search included telling the student to pull out the elastic on her underwear in order to release any contraband that may have been hidden there. The Supreme Court found this "strip search" unreasonable and a violation of the Fourth Amendment.[21]

Search of Shoes Not Strip Search

A search of socks and shoes for stolen money was not a strip search.[22]

Private school search not bound by the Fourth Amendment

Defendant went on a private school-sponsored ski trip. He and the other trip participants stayed at a resort hotel. Defendant and other students were aware that they were subject to certain rules, including the seizure of contraband either at school or on school trips. A chaperone learned that some students had been to their room unsupervised and investigated. He found marijuana and cocaine. The Defendant was arrested and argued that the school violated his rights. The court held that the school was not a government actor.[23]

Video surveillance inside locker room violated Fourth Amendment

The videotaping by school officials of middle school students while they changed their clothes in school locker rooms, using video surveillance cameras installed in the locker rooms, was an unreasonable search.[24]

Viewing student's text messages unreasonable search

School officials' knowledge that, a year and a half earlier, a public high school student had expressed suicidal thoughts and had admitted that he smoked marijuana, combined with the student's violation of school policy barring use of cell phones in classrooms, did not provide reasonable grounds for school officials, upon seizing the phone based on a violation of the policy, to search the phone by reading the student's text messages.[25]

7.7 Student Drug Testing

Schools are allowed to conduct random, suspicionless, urinalysis of public school students who participate in extracurricular activities (primarily athletic).

---

[20] *New Jersey v. T.L.O.*, 105 S. Ct. 733 (1985).
[21] *Safford Unified Sch. Dist. #1 v. Redding*, 129 S. Ct. 2633 (2009).
[22] *Wynn v. Board of Education*, 508 So. 2d 1170 (Ala. 1987).
[23] *Commonwealth v. Considine*, 448 Mass. 295 (Mass. 2007).
[24] *Brannum v. Overton County School Bd.*, 516 F.3d 489 (6th Cir. 2008).
[25] *G.C. v. Owensboro Public Schools*, 711 F.3d 623 (6th Cir. 2013).

However, schools cannot conduct random drug testing of the entire student body. Additionally, a school may require a student to submit to drug testing if it has reasonable suspicion of illegal drug use.

⭐ LEGAL STANDARD

Schools may conduct random drug testing on students if:

- Student participates in extracurricular activities;
- School has legitimate concern of illegal drug use;
- The manner of the testing is the least-intrusive; and
- The results are shared on a need-to-know basis.

It is imperative that school officials coordinate drug testing with their attorneys. This is an area that could generate expensive lawsuits.

🏛 CASE EXAMPLES

Random urinalysis drug testing upheld as reasonable

Public school district's student athlete drug policy, which authorized random urinalysis drug testing of students who participated in its athletic programs, did not violate student's federal or state constitutional right to be free from unreasonable searches; school district had immediate, legitimate concern in preventing student athletes from using drugs, invasion of student privacy interest was negligible, and district was not required to come up with "least intrusive" search.[26]

7.8 SROs, Security Guards, and Administrators

When the Supreme Court issued its opinion in T.L.O.,[27] which authorized warrantless searches based on reasonable suspicion instead of probable cause, school resource officers were rare. In fact, the Court noted that the official's search of the students purse for cigarettes may have been different if the search was conducted by a police officer.

Today SROs are common and the question is whether or not the lower Fourth Amendment standard applicable to school searches applies to SROs. The short answer appears to be no—SROs are held to the higher probable cause standard. But things get a little more complicated when the SRO and school official work together. Which standard applies? Read guidelines below, that should help.

---

[26] *Vernonia Sch. Dist. 47J v. Acton*, 515 U.S. 646 (1995).
[27] *New Jersey v. T.L.O.*, 105 S. Ct. 733 (1985).

🛡 LEGAL STANDARD

Police give information to school officials:

- If you learn of criminal activity, and relay that information to school officials, the reasonable suspicion standard applies.

Police act as school's agent:

- If school officials learn of criminal activity and call police for assistance, and ask officers to conduct the search on the school's behalf, then the reasonable suspicion standard applies. The key here is that the police are acting as the school's agent. If the police "take over" the investigation, then probable cause is required.

Police conduct a criminal investigation:

- If police take over the investigation, or the SRO intends to file criminal charges based on his investigation, then apply regular police rules. At the end of the day, try to use common sense. If the search is primarily a school search, then T.L.O. applies. If the search is primarily a criminal investigation, full Fourth Amendment protections apply.

🏛 CASE EXAMPLES

Officers can perform patdown, but not full search on truant student

Two police officers came into contact with the juvenile at a government housing project behind a high school. The officers believed she was truant, so they stopped her. She appeared to be 16 or 17-years old and wore a polo shirt bearing the high school emblem. After confirming she should be in school, they told her they were going to transport her back. Before placing her in the police car, one of the officers, searched all of her pockets and found a small bag of marijuana. Court held that officers were permitted to conduct a patdown, but not a full search.[28] However, if this state classified truancy as a "crime" then a full search would be authorized as a search incident to arrest, even if transported back to school, not jail. Check your state laws.

Officer who searched student at dance required probable cause

An officer at a school dance required probable cause before searching a student who smelled of alcohol (my kind of high school!). The lower reasonable suspicion standard did not apply because the officer was acting in a criminal investigation capacity.[29]

Reasonable suspicion standard applied to SRO

A SRO helped school officials investigate a fight. The SRO was acting as a school official at the time of the school search because "[h]e was on duty as an SRO and

---

[28] *L.C. v. State*, 23 So. 3d 1215 (Fla. Dist. Ct. App. 3d Dist. 2009).
[29] *State v. Tywayne H.*, 123 N.M. 42 (N.M. Ct. App. 1997).

acting under his authority as an SRO when he personally observed the activity that formed the basis for his search."[30]

Probable cause not required merely because police are involved

School official's reasonable suspicion standard for search is not elevated to probable cause merely because the school official asks a police officer to help conduct the search.[31]

7.9 Use of Force Against Students

You must be very cautious and hesitant whenever force is used against a child. If you use any force, make sure that it's absolutely necessary under the circumstances. Kids are not adults. And many times, it may be wise to allow the kid to yell and scream without restraining them if he is not a danger. You make the call, but remember that if you use force be able to articulate why.

⭐ LEGAL STANDARD

Only use force against a child if:

- It is necessary under the circumstances;
- It is not done for punitive reasons; and
- Deescalation techniques are employed.

🏛 CASE EXAMPLES

Taping kid's head to tree unreasonable punishment (real case!)

A teacher told a student to stand against a tree and stay there as punishment for fighting. The student did not stay still and the teacher taped the student's head to the tree. A fact finder could find that the official's conduct was objectively unreasonable because there was no indication that the student posed a danger to others, he was only eight years old, and the conduct was so intrusive that another fifth grader said it was inappropriate.[32]

Handcuffing is not reasonable punishment

A SRO witnessed a child refusing to do jumping jacks and talking back to the coach. The deputy told her, "this is what it feels like to be in jail" and handcuffed her. The court held that the deputy's action was excessive force.[33] Note: I cannot make this stuff up.

---

[30] *In re J.F.M.*, 168 N.C. App. 143 (N.C. Ct. App. 2005).

[31] *J.A.R. v. State*, 689 So. 2d 1242 (Fla. Dist. Ct. App. 2d Dist. 1997).

[32] *Doe v. Haw. Dep't of Educ.*, 334 F.3d 906 (9th Cir. Haw. 2003).

[33] *Gray v. Bostic*, 458 F.3d 1295 (11th Cir. Ala. 2006).

Chapter 8
Personal Property

8.1 Searching Containers

If you develop probable cause that a container (package, luggage, etc.) contains evidence or contraband, you may seize it in order to apply for a search warrant.[1] Remember, the length of the detention must be reasonable and the more "intimate" the container, the more courts will scrutinize the detention.

For example, detaining a woman's purse is more intimate than seizing an undelivered UPS parcel. A nine-hour detention on the purse may be struck down as unreasonable, where a two-day detention on the parcel may not. Either way, diligently seek the warrant unless you are relying on a recognized exception to the warrant requirement.

> ## 🛡 LEGAL STANDARD
>
> A container seized with probable cause that it contains contraband or evidence may not be searched without a warrant unless:
>
> - Someone with apparent authority gave you consent to search; or
> - The container was seized from a vehicle; or
> - The container's contents were obvious under the single purpose container doctrine; or
> - The container was in the suspect's possession and searched incident to arrest; or
> - You conducted a legitimate inventory; or
> - The container was searched under the community caretaking doctrine; or
> - You had exigent circumstances.
>
> Remember, container plus probable cause does not equal warrantless search. You need C.R.E.W—consent, recognized exception, or a warrant (C.R.E.W. is explained in first section of book).

8.2 Single Purpose Container Doctrine

The single purpose container doctrine is an extension of the plain view doctrine. Here, an officer that sees a container and knows instantly what is inside—a gun case, or a balloon containing heroin, or kilos of packaged cocaine. If officers see these items in plain view, and have lawful access, they can seize it as evidence and search the because there is no expectation of privacy in the container.

---

[1] *U.S. v. Hernandez*, 314 F.3d 430 (9th Cir. Cal. 2002).

✪ LEGAL STANDARD

A container may be seized and searched without a warrant if:

- You were lawfully present when you observed the container;
- Even though the container's contents were not visible, based on the shape, weight, size, material, and so forth, the contents were obvious (*i.e.*, drugs);
- These observations gave you probable cause; and
- You had lawful access to the container when it was seized.

🏛 CASE EXAMPLES

Convicted felon had no privacy in container labeled "gun case"

Defendant had no reasonable expectation of privacy in contents of case located in his residence and labeled as "gun case." Thus, police officers' warrantless search of the case after officers' valid entry into residence did not violate the Fourth Amendment, where officers knew that defendant was convicted felon prohibited from possessing guns.[2]

A "drug bindle" is a single-purpose container

Because it was immediately apparent to experienced officers that paper bindle viewed in defendant's identification folder contained contraband, defendant did not have reasonable expectation of privacy which would have prevented opening of bindle or field testing of it.[3]

8.3 Searching Abandoned or Lost Property

A person has no reasonable expectation of privacy in abandoned, lost, or stolen property. The courts have defined abandonment broadly for search and seizure purposes. Abandonment occurs whenever a person leaves an item where the general public (or police) would feel free to access it. It can also occur whenever a person disowns property.

When it comes to abandonment, traditional property rights do not matter (*i.e.*, a person could legally own an item, but still "abandon" it).[4] If abandonment occurs after an illegal detention, the evidence would be tainted and inadmissible.[5]

Additionally, if the defendant stole the item, like a purse or vehicle, he would not have a reasonable expectation of privacy in that item (but may have privacy in his own containers).

---

[2] *U.S. v. Meada*, 408 F.3d 14 (1st Cir. Mass. 2005).
[3] *State v. Courcy*, 48 Wash. App. 326, 739 P.2d 98 (1987).
[4] *Stoner v. California*, 376 U.S. 483 (1964).
[5] *People v. Verin*, 220 Cal. App. 3d 551 (Cal. App. 1st Dist. 1990).

⚜ LEGAL STANDARD

A container is considered abandoned when:

- Based on the totality of the circumstances, a reasonable person would believe that it was intentionally abandoned; or
- Based on the totality of the circumstances, it appears the container was inadvertently abandoned, but the container's owner would not have a reasonable expectation of privacy that a member of the general public, including a police officer, would not search it; and
- If the container was inadvertently abandoned (*e.g.*, accidentally left at the crime scene), your scope of search was similar to what a member of the public could have done (*e.g.*, no forensic analysis).

🏛 CASE EXAMPLES

No privacy in stolen property

"The Fourth Amendment does not protect a defendant from a warrantless search of property that he stole, because regardless of whether he expects to maintain privacy in the contents of the stolen property, such an expectation is not one that 'society is prepared to accept as reasonable.'"[6]

Dropping paper bag and running equals abandonment

Police got a tip that the defendant was selling drugs and patrolled the area. They saw defendant leaning into a car, so the officers pulled over and walked in a "semi-quick" pace towards the defendant. In response, the defendant dropped the bag full of drugs and ran. The bag was abandoned and could be searched without a warrant.[7]

Search of burglar's cell phone six days after crime committed was reasonable

The suspect forgot his cell phone at the crime scene. Police later searched it without a warrant, finding evidence. The court held the phone was abandoned because the "idea that a burglar may leave his cell phone at the scene of his crime, do nothing to recover the phone for six days, cancel cellular service to the phone, and then expect that law enforcement officers will not attempt to access the contents of the phone to determine who committed the burglary is not an idea that society will accept as reasonable."[8]

Abandonment is clearer when it occurs before the suspect was seized by police

When the officer entered the bar, defendant dropped a crumpled cigarette package on the floor, under the table, and turned away. The officer retrieved the package, which contained illegal drugs, and arrested defendant.[9]

---

[6] *U.S. v. Caymen*, 404 F.3d 1196 (9th Cir. Alaska 2005).
[7] *In re Kemonte*, 223 Cal. App. 3d 1507 (1990).
[8] *State v. Brown*, Opinion No. 27814 (S.C. 2018).
[9] *Cooper v. State*, 806 P.2d 1136 (1991).

> **Reclaiming ownership revokes abandonment**
>
> Although defendant initially vacillated on whether he owned the bag or not, by the time the search was conducted he had claimed ownership, which police knew and therefore, had not abandoned the bag.[10]

8.4 Searching Mail or Packages

You cannot search any first-class mail or package(s) without a warrant. However, if you have lawful access you may read any writing on the outside of mail and packages.[11]

⬟ LEGAL STANDARD

The outside of first-class mail or packages may be observed if:

- You had lawful access to the item;
- You did not manipulate or open the item;
- You observations were in plain view or free-air canine sniff; and
- The duration of the detention was reasonable.

🏛 CASE EXAMPLES

No reasonable expectation of privacy in mail addressed to "alias"

Agents with the USPS became suspicious of a package. Inspectors found that both the sender and receiver's names did not match mail records. The investigation revealed that the actual intended recipient had the package sent to a friend's house under a fake name. The friend consented to allow police to search the package and narcotics were discovered. The intended recipient was arrested. The court found that since the recipient used a fake name and sent it to a friend's house, he did not have a reasonable expectation of privacy.[12]

Police may seize mail and apply for a warrant

Officers who have probable cause may seize a package and apply for a warrant.[13]

---

[10] *U.S. v. Grant*, 920 F.2d 376 (6th Cir. 1990).
[11] *U.S. v. Burnette*, 375 F.3d 10 (1st Cir. N.H. 2004).
[12] *State v. Williams*, 184 So. 3d 1205 (Fla. Dist. Ct. App. 1st Dist. 2016).
[13] *Garmon v. Foust*, 741 F.2d 1069 (8th Cir. Iowa 1984).

Chapter 9
Electronic Searches

9.1 Sensory Enhancements

Generally, you may use sensory enhancements if they are in general public use (like binoculars and flashlights). But you must be reasonable, especially when you use sensory enhancements to observe inside protected areas, like a home. If not, your actions may be classified as a warrantless search requiring exigent circumstances.

⬢ LEGAL STANDARD

If sensory enhancements are used to view public areas, then:

- There are essentially no restrictions unless the enhancement captures information where a person would have a reasonable expectation of privacy (*e.g.*, microphone that can detect two people whispering in a park).

If sensory enhancements are used to observe inside a home, then:

- The technology used must be in general public use; and
- Only enhance that which was seen with the naked eye or heard with the naked ear (*e.g.*, binoculars used to confirm motorcycle in garage is similar to stolen motorcycle).

🏛 CASE EXAMPLES

Use of a thermal imaging device against home unreasonable search

"We think that obtaining by sense enhancing technology any information regarding the interior of the home that could not otherwise have been obtained without physical "'intrusion into a constitutionally protected area,'" constitutes a search-at least where (as here) the technology in question is not in general public use."[1]

9.2 Flashlights

Generally, you may use flashlights to enhance your vision. There are two good reasons for this: First, something visible during the day should not get additional protections simply because it was concealed by darkness. Second, flashlights are in "general public use" and the public expects police officers to use them, wherever a police officer has a lawful right to be.

---

[1] *Kyllo v. U.S.*, 533 U.S. 27 (2001).

Still, flashlights can violate a person's reasonable expectation of privacy if the flashlight is used in an unreasonable manner. Take, for example, a police officer who is conducting a knock and talk. It would be unlawful to shine a high-powered LED flashlight through closed blinds in order to illuminate inside the home. On the other hand, if the blinds were open, then a person would lose his reasonable expectation of privacy and enhancing your view with a flashlight would be lawful.

🛡 LEGAL STANDARD

If a flashlight is used to view public areas, then:

- There are no restrictions.

If a flashlight is used to observe inside a home, then:

- You may use the flashlight to observe that which would have been observable in broad daylight. In other words, if you use a flashlight to observe something inside the home which would not have been visible in full daylight, then it likely violated an occupants reasonable expectation of privacy; but
- This restriction does not apply when conducting an investigation with exigency (burglary, shots fired, etc.).

🏛 CASE EXAMPLES

Typical use of flashlight does not violate Fourth Amendment

Officers use of a flashlight to illuminate interior of driver's car, "trenched upon no right secured ... by [the] Fourth Amendment."[2]

9.3 Binoculars

You may use binoculars to enhance your vision to view items or people if they are in a public place, such as parks, sidewalks or streets.[3] You may not, however, use binoculars to view items or people inside private areas that would otherwise be completely indistinguishable by the naked eye. For example, if you were investigating a jewelry heist and you saw a "gold glint" coming through the suspect's open apartment window, you may lawfully use binoculars to confirm what you saw.[4]

On the other hand, it would be unlawful to use binoculars to peer into a suspect's apartment window from 200-300 yards away to determine whether he was viewing child pornography. In this case, there was no way an officer could see any incriminating evidence with the naked eye and therefore the suspect does not lose his reasonable expectation of privacy.[5]

[2] *Texas v. Brown*, 460 U.S. 730 (1983).
[3] *U.S. v. Shepard*, 1995 U.S. App. LEXIS 23118 (9th Cir. Ariz. 1995).
[4] *Cooper v. Superior Court*, 118 Cal. App. 3d 499 (Cal. App. 1st Dist. 1981).
[5] *People v. Arno*, 90 Cal. App. 3d 505 (Cal. App. 2d Dist. 1979).

🛡 LEGAL STANDARD

If binoculars are used to view public areas, then:

- There are no restrictions.

If binoculars are used to observe inside a home, then:

- You may use binoculars to observe that which would have been observable with the naked eye. You only need to be able to see the item, not necessarily know what it is. However, if the item is completely hidden from view, using binoculars to view the item likely violates an occupants reasonable expectation of privacy; but
- This restriction does not apply when conducting an investigation with exigency (hot pursuit, fresh pursuit, surround and call-out, etc.).

🏛 CASE EXAMPLES

Use of binoculars from open field not a Fourth Amendment search

"At the trial, Special Investigator Griffith testified that through binoculars, he observed the appellant, a known liquor violator, placing two large cardboard boxes (each of which contained six gallons of untaxed whiskey), in a 1961 Buick. The observations were made from a field belonging to another, about 50 yards from the appellant's house. This did not constitute an illegal search."[6]

Use of high-power telescope to see inside a hotel room an unlawful search

Police made a binocular search of a hotel room through the uncurtained window by means of a powerful telescope on a hilltop a quarter of a mile from the hotel. There were no buildings or other locations closer to the hotel from which anyone could see into the hotel room. By using the telescope, the police observed a well-known gambling sheet. The court held the defendant had a reasonable expectation that no one could see into his room under these circumstances: "[I]t is inconceivable that the government can intrude so far into an individual's home that it can detect the material he is reading and still not be considered to have engaged in a search."[7]

Viewing marijuana grow in backyard from street not a search

While standing in the roadway, officers used a 60-power scope to view a marijuana grow in the suspect's backyard. The court held that this was not a Fourth Amendment search.[8]

Use of binoculars to see something in suspect's hand not a search

The police officer became suspicious that a drug transaction was underway. He parked his vehicle, walked back to the alleyway and, with the aid of binoculars, saw

---

[6] *U.S. v. Grimes*, 426 F.2d 706 (5th Cir. Ga. 1970).
[7] *U.S. v. Kim*, 415 F. Supp. 1252 (D. Haw. 1976).
[8] *State v. Bennett*, 205 Mont. 117, 666 P.2d 747 (1983).

Barr display metal slugs to his companion in his upturned hand. The officer was no more than seventy-five feet from Barr when he saw the slugs. Barr then entered a casino abutting the alleyway. The officer followed him, and Barr was arrested for possession of a cheating device.[9]

Climbing on fellow officer's shoulders to see in backyard was a search

Where an officer on neighboring property climbed three-quarters of way up fence and braced himself on fellow officer's shoulder, and then, using a 60-power telescope, was able to see marijuana plants in defendant's back yard, this was a search.[10]

9.4   Night Vision Goggles

There is no particular restriction if you use night vision goggles. They fall under the same rules as flashlights. However, some prosecutors and judges may not understand this technology and may equate it with thermal imaging, which is very restricted. Therefore, articulate that night vision goggles simply amplify the ambient light and do not detect any heat signatures.

⭐ LEGAL STANDARD

If night vision goggles are used to view public areas, then:

- There are no restrictions.

If night vision goggles are used to observe inside a home, then:

- You may use the night vision goggles to observe that which would have been observable in broad daylight. In other words, if you use night vision goggles to observe something inside the home which would not have been visible in full daylight, then it likely violated an occupant's reasonable expectation of privacy; but
- This restriction does not apply when conducting an investigation with exigency (hot pursuit, fresh pursuit, surround and call-out, *etc.*).

🏛 CASE EXAMPLES

Night vision goggles the same as a flashlight

"It was dark the entire time he was there. While he did not use a flashlight, the deputy wore "night vision" goggles during both this visit and a subsequent visit. The goggles enhanced the available light by magnifying it, allowing him to see better in the dark. The goggles merely amplify ambient light to enable one to see something that is already exposed to public view."[11]

---

[9] *State v. Barr*, 98 Nev. 428, 651 P.2d 649 (1982).
[10] *State v. Kender*, 60 Haw. 301, 588 P.2d 447 (1978).
[11] *People v. Lieng*, 190 Cal. App. 4th 1213 (Cal. App. 1st Dist. 2010).

9.5 Thermal Imaging

Generally, you may not use thermal imaging to look at homes. You may use thermal imaging in public areas, like open fields or parks. If you want to use thermal imaging on a house you need consent, exigent circumstances, or a warrant.

⭐ LEGAL STANDARD

If a thermal imaging device is used to view public areas, then:
- There are essentially no restrictions unless a person would have a reasonable expectation of privacy (*e.g.*, tent located on public land).

If a thermal imaging device is used to observe a home, then:
- You need consent, exigency or a warrant. An example of exigency may include use by a SWAT team to ascertain where a suspect is located.

🏛 CASE EXAMPLES

Cannot use a thermal imager against a home, without warrant

When the police use a thermal imager to gain any information regarding the interior of the home that could not otherwise have been obtained without physical intrusion, that constitutes a search.[12]

Police may use thermal imager in open fields

"[T]he officers in this case were entitled to observe the steel building either by air or on foot because the building, like the barn in Pace, stood in an open field. And, as we have already discussed, the fact that the officers enhanced their observations with a thermal imager does not require a different conclusion."[13]

9.6 Cell Phones, Laptops, and Tablets

You may not search cell phones without consent, exigency or a search warrant. This includes searches incident to arrest, even where you have probable cause that evidence of the crime is contained on the device. The Supreme Court no longer includes cell phones as part of the "search incident to arrest" exception. This rule applies to all devices that can contain "vast amounts of personal data," like laptops and tablets.

Valid exigency would include looking in an active shooter's cell phone to determine if there were undiscovered accomplices. Or looking in a kidnapper's cell phone if the victim has not been found. However, the possibility of a remote wipe, standing alone, does not justify exigency.

---

[12] *Kyllo v. U.S.*, 533 U.S. 27 (2001).
[13] *U.S. v. Ishmael*, 48 F.3d 850 (5th Cir. Tex. 1995).

⭐ **LEGAL STANDARD**

A cell phone may be searched if:

- You have a search warrant; or
- Legitimate exigency (*e.g.*, such as searching cell phone immediately after terrorist incident to determine whether other confederates are on the loose).

🏛 **CASE EXAMPLES**

Search of cell phone after arrest unlawful

Defendant was stopped for a traffic violation, which eventually led to his arrest on weapons charges. An officer searching incident to the arrest seized a cell phone from defendant's pants pocket. The officer accessed information on the phone and discovered evidence of gang activity, which led to evidence of a shooting a few weeks earlier. The Court found the warrantless search unreasonable since mobile devices hold a vast amount of personal data.[14]

9.7   Cell Phone Location Records

Electronic surveillance is a search or seizure protected under the Fourth Amendment if it occurred in protected areas (*i.e.*, house or car) or where a person has a reasonable expectation of privacy (*i.e.*, cell phone location records).

The Supreme Court has struggled to keep up with technological advancements. However, the Court is beginning to see just how intrusive modern technology can become and is limiting the use of technology searches in investigations. The Court's latest position is that obtaining cell phone location records, even from a third-party, is a Fourth Amendment search when those records are combined to recreate a person's activities over a period of time.[15] This is especially important because cell phone companies typically retain location information for five years. Therefore, it is possible for police to retrace a person's steps for the last five years if he kept his cell phone with him.

Therefore, if you want cell location information, you need a search warrant.

⭐ **LEGAL STANDARD**

Cell phone location information may obtained if:

- You have a search warrant; or
- Legitimate exigency (*e.g.*, such as requesting a tower dump immediately after a child has been kidnapped).

---

[14] *Riley v. California*, 134 S. Ct. 2473 (2014).
[15] *Carpenter v. U.S.*, 138 S. Ct 2206 (2018).

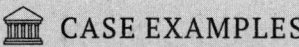
CASE EXAMPLES

Use of Cell Site Location Information violated Fourth Amendment

Mapping a cell phone's location over the course of 127 days provides an all-encompassing record of the holder's whereabouts. As with GPS information, the time-stamped data provides an intimate window into a person's life, revealing not only his particular movements, but through them his "familial, political, professional, religious, and sexual associations." Therefore, a search warrant is required.[16]

9.8 Aerial Surveillance

Generally, police are not prohibited from flying an aircraft over protected areas, like a person's home and backyard.[17] Anything observed falls under plain view and may be used in a search warrant.

There are three notable guidelines: First, police should not violate FAA rules unless there are exigent circumstances, such as tracking a fleeing suspect. Second, the manner of flight shouldn't be highly intrusive, like a loud helicopter hovering directly over the home, or multiple passes over the home, otherwise the manner of the surveillance may become unreasonable.[18] Third, police are permitted to use "moderate enhancement" to view the protected area. It may help to review the guidelines on flashlights, binoculars, and thermal imaging. Overall, if your conduct is reasonable, then it is likely lawful.

⬡ LEGAL STANDARD

Aerial surveillance is permissible when:

- You obey FAA regulations;
- The flight is not conducted in a highly intrusive manner; and
- You do not utilize unreasonable sensory enhancements.

CASE EXAMPLES

Available technology helps determine what is reasonable

"It would be foolish to contend that the degree of privacy secured to citizens by the Fourth Amendment has been entirely unaffected by the advance of technology. For example,...the technology enabling human flight has exposed to public view (and hence, we have said, to official observation) uncovered portions of the house and its curtilage that once were private."[19]

---

[16] *Carpenter v. U.S.*, 138 S. Ct 2206 (2018).
[17] *Cal. v. Ciraolo*, 476 U.S. 207 (1986).
[18] *People v. Mayoff*, 42 Cal. 3d 1302 (Cal. 1986).
[19] *Kyllo v. U.S.*, 121 S. Ct. 2038 (2001).

9.9 GPS Devices

You may not attach a GPS tracker to a vehicle without consent, exigency, or warrant. An example of exigency is if you found a kidnapper's vehicle in a parking lot and needed to immediately track it back to the victim's location.

☆ LEGAL STANDARD

A GPS may be placed on a vehicle if:

- You have a search warrant; or
- Legitimate exigency.

🏛 CASE EXAMPLES

Warrantless attachment of GPS to vehicle unlawful

Agents installed a GPS tracking device on the undercarriage of a vehicle registered to defendant's wife while it was parked in a public parking lot. Over the next 28 days, the Government used the device to track the vehicle's movements. The U.S. Supreme Court determined that the Government's installation of the GPS device on defendant's vehicle, and its use of that device to monitor the vehicle's movements, constituted a "search."[20]

Tracking suspect through their cellphone GPS is a Fourth Amendment search

Warrantless GPS tracking constitutes a search even in the absence of a trespass, because a Fourth Amendment search occurs when the government violates a subjective expectation of privacy that society recognizes as reasonable.[21]

9.10 Obtaining Passwords

If you need a defendant's digital password after he asserts his Fifth Amendment rights, good luck. If the password is in the defendant's head, then courts will likely refuse to compel the defendant to provide the password because it would be viewed as testimony, and therefore protected.[22] Some courts recognize an exception where police know with certainty what information is inside the device and therefore its contents are a "forgone conclusion." If so, courts may order the defendant to produce his password.

On the other hand (pun intended), if the phone can be opened with a fingerprint, then get a court order. Fingerprints are physical evidence unprotected by the Fifth Amendment.

---

[20] *U.S. v. Jones*, 132 S. Ct. 945 (2012).
[21] *State v. Brereton*, 2013 WI 17 (Wis. 2013).
[22] *U.S. v. Kirschner*, 823 F. Supp. 2d 665 (E.D. Mich. 2010).

⭐ LEGAL STANDARD

Passwords are protected as follows:

- Passwords inside a suspect's head are protected by Miranda;
- If the contents are a foregone conclusion, a court may order the defendant to provide his password;
- If the password is physical, like a fingerprint, get a search warrant.

🏛 CASE EXAMPLES

Cannot compel suspect to provide password to computer

Compelled testimony that communicates information that may "lead to incriminating evidence" is privileged even if the information itself is not inculpatory.[23]

Suspect may be compelled to unlock device with fingerprint

Defendant cannot be compelled to produce his passcode to access his smartphone, but he can be compelled to produce his fingerprint to do the same.[24]

---

[23] *Doe v. U.S.*, 487 U.S. 201 (1988).
[24] *Commonwealth v. Baust*, 89 Va. Cir. 267 (Va. Cir. Ct. 2014).

Chapter 10
Miscellaneous Searches & Seizures

10.1 Cause-of-Injury Searches

You're allowed to conduct a limited "medical search" of an unconscious person or someone in serious medical distress in order to determine the cause of injury (if unknown) and to ascertain his identification to help render aid.

Your search should be objectively reasonable under the circumstances. An example of a lawful search would be a victim who was found unconscious and there were no clear signs why. It would be lawful to look for a medical alert bracelet, identification, medicines, or even illegal drugs he may have overdosed on in order to provide that information to medical. Any contraband or evidence found in plain view could be admitted into evidence.

⬛ LEGAL STANDARD

A limited search of a suspect's backpack or purse may occur if:

- You have a reason to believe that the person is in medical distress;
- Finding medications, medical-alert bracelet, or reason for overdose will assist in the medical response;
- Search of belongings is limited in scope and terminates once items are found or are not present.

🏛 CASE EXAMPLES

Search of purse while driver getting x-rays unreasonable

A driver was transported to the hospital after an accident. The officer took her purse to the hospital and looked inside for ID in order to finish his report. He found drug paraphernalia. The court found the search was not needed and suppressed the evidence.[1]

Search of locked briefcase was reasonable

Driver was found passed out, foaming at the mouth. Officers opened two locked briefcases to look for ID or medicines. Instead, they found money from a recent bank robbery. Court upheld search as reasonable.[2]

---

[1] *People v. Wright*, 804 P.2d 866 (Colo.1991)
[2] *U.S. v. Dunavan*, 485 F.2d 201 (6th Cir.1973)

10.2 Medical Procedures

If you have probable cause that a suspect has swallowed evidence, or has contraband in their anal or vaginal cavities, you'll need to consult with medical personnel to retrieve it. Rarely will you have exigent circumstances to retrieve it yourself (why would you want to?). For example, if a corrections officer discovered partially concealed contraband during a visual strip search, it may be unlawful to pull it. The officer would either have to request the inmate remove it himself (if it was safe to do so), or contact medical.

If an arrestee swallowed evidence (like drugs) and it created a medical emergency, no search warrant would be required as long as medical personnel made all decisions, including not retrieving the evidence and allowing the drugs to metabolize or pass.

If no medical emergency exists, and you want to retrieve the evidence, you must seek a search warrant and it's very unlikely a court will issue it. The evidence must be vital for your case and you must convince a judge the medical procedure is safe for the suspect.

⭐ LEGAL STANDARD

Medical procedures may be done if:

- They are conducted by medical personnel without police influence or direction; or
- With a search warrant that describes the necessity of the evidence and the relative risks of the procedure; and
- If time allows, the defendant should have an opportunity to challenge the search warrant in an adversarial hearing.

🏛 CASE EXAMPLES

If police request medical staff to recover evidence, then Fourth Amendment applies

"When a medical procedure is performed at the instigation of law enforcement for the purpose of obtaining evidence, the fact that the search is executed by a medical professional does not insulate it from Fourth Amendment scrutiny."[3]

Surgical intrusions for evidence will rarely be approved

"A compelled surgical intrusion into an individual's body for evidence implicates expectations of privacy and security of such magnitude that the intrusion may be unreasonable even if likely to produce evidence of a crime."[4]

---

[3] *Sanchez v. Pereira-Castillo*, 590 F.3d 31 (1st Cir. P.R. 2009).
[4] *Winston v. Lee*, 105 S. Ct. 1611 (1985).

Unless there's legitimate exigency, you must seek a warrant

"Search warrants are ordinarily required for searches of homes, and, absent an emergency, no less could be required where intrusions into the human body are concerned. The importance of informed, detached and deliberate determinations of the issue whether or not to invade another's body in search of evidence of guilt is indisputable and great."[5]

Removal of bullet upheld as reasonable

The suspect sustained two gunshot wounds during a robbery-turned-murder inside a doctor's office. The prosecutor wanted one of the bullets lodged in the suspect. The court held an adversarial hearing and thereafter issued the search warrant. "As the skilled and experienced surgeon who performed the operation testified 'maximum precautions' were taken when the bullet was removed, 'we bent over backwards'. The bullet, which was small, close to the skin and easily felt, was extracted by gentle squeezing after an incision an inch long had been made. Less than five cc.'s of blood were lost, an amount smaller than may be taken in a premarital examination. The entire operation took ten minutes. In the opinion of the surgeon the risk was 'negligible' and in fact there were no complications."[6]

Search warrant denied where there was a fatal risk to suspect

The bullet was close to the suspect's spinal cord and there was a risk that the surgery would have caused the suspect's death. Therefore, the search warrant was properly denied.[7]

Medical search warrants require higher showing of P.C.

The more intense, unusual, prolonged, uncomfortable, unsafe or undignified the procedure contemplated, or the more it intrudes on essential standards of privacy, the greater must be the showing for the procedure's necessity.[8]

10.3   Discarded DNA

A person has no reasonable expectation of privacy in an item that has his DNA which he later discards. For example, if a suspect drinks from a cup and throws it away, you can test it for DNA as long as you had lawful access to the cup (for example, restaurant trash). Since the suspect has no privacy in the cup there's no Fourth Amendment search.

---

[5] *Schmerber v. Cal.*, 86 S. Ct. 1826 (1966).
[6] *U.S. v. Crowder*, 543 F.2d 312 (D.C. Cir. 1976).
[7] *Bowden v. State*, 256 Ark. 820, 510 S.W.2d 879 (1974).
[8] *People v. Scott*, 21 Cal.3d 284 (1978).

⭐ LEGAL STANDARD

An item may be searched for DNA if:

- The item was abandoned or discarded; or
- The suspect has no reasonable expectation of privacy in the DNA sample (*i.e.*, CODIS database).

🏛 CASE EXAMPLES

Abandoned cigarette butt

There was not Fourth Amendment violation when defendant voluntarily discarded his cigarette butt by tossing it onto a public sidewalk and left it in a place particularly suited for public inspection. He thus abandoned the cigarette butt in a public place and had no reasonable expectation of privacy concerning the DNA testing of it to identify him as a suspect in a murder.[9]

Suspect abandoned DNA in letter sent to undercover officer

Undercover officer sent letter to suspect with the intent of testing reply letter for his DNA. The court held that the suspect "abandoned" his DNA when he sent his letter.[10]

10.4 Fingernail Scrapes

If you have probable cause to believe a suspect committed a crime, and currently has evidence underneath his fingernails, you may conduct a warrantless "scrape" and retrieve any evidence such as dirt, blood, DNA, and so forth. You are allowed to use the minimal force necessary to recover the evidence. Moreover, no arrest is required—you may test the evidence and make the arrest later.

⭐ LEGAL STANDARD

You may conduct a fingernail scrape in the field when:

- You have probable cause evidence of the crime may be under the suspect's fingernails;
- Minimally intrusive means were used to recover the evidence; and
- Due to the evanescent nature of the evidence exigency existed.

---

[9] *People v. Gallego*, 190 Cal. App. 4th 388 (Cal. App. 3d Dist. 2010).
[10] *State v. Athan*, 160 Wash.2d 354, 158 P.3d 27 (2007).

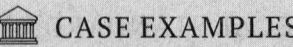 CASE EXAMPLES

Officer permitted to conduct fingernail scrape during arrest

Where there is probable cause, a very limited intrusion undertaken incident to a station house detention, and a ready destructibility of evidence, a warrantless search of a defendant's fingernails does not violate the Fourth Amendment.[11]

10.5 Arson Investigations

Generally, warrants are required when investigators search for evidence in a protected area. However, firefighters are allowed to search for the "origin of a fire," in order to prevent a fire from restarting.

⚜ LEGAL STANDARD

A warrantless search may be made when:

- A fire occurred inside a home;
- Firefighters remain in the home to discover the origin of the fire, in order to prevent it from restarting;
- After the fire is out and no risk of restarting is present, a search warrant or consent is required to stay or reenter the home and look for evidence.

🏛 CASE EXAMPLES

Firefighters permitted to search house after waterbed broke

The defendant accidentally caught his waterbed on fire (how?), which in turn caused the waterbed to leak into the basement. Firefighters entered the basement in order to ascertain whether there was an electrical fire hazard (due to water leak). Firefighters found explosives in the basement and these observations were upheld as lawful.[12]

Search warrants apply to arson investigators

"Evidence of arson discovered in the course of such [origin of fire] investigations is admissible at trial, but if the investigating officials find probable cause to believe that arson has occurred and require further access to gather evidence for a possible prosecution, they may obtain a warrant only upon a traditional showing of probable cause applicable to searches for evidence of crime."[13]

---

[11] *Cupp v. Murphy*, 412 U.S. 291 (1973).
[12] *U.S. v. Buckmaster*, 485 F.3d 873 (6th Cir. Ohio 2007).
[13] *Michigan v. Tyler*, 436 U.S. 499, 98 S. Ct. 1942, 56 L. Ed. 2d 486 (1978).

10.6 Airport & Other Administrative Checkpoints

A person has a reduced expectation of privacy if he is attempting to access a secure area of an airport or government building. Additionally, a person who has started the screening process cannot "opt-out" and leave.

🛡 LEGAL STANDARD

Government administrative searches must follow these rules:

- The search is made in good faith for weapons or explosives;
- The search must have a legitimate, non-criminal goal;
- People may avoid the search by electing not to fly, which must be done before placing luggage on x-ray conveyor belt.

🏛 CASE EXAMPLES

Passengers that enter screening area impliedly consented to search

The passenger was subjected to a random search, at an airport security checkpoint, of a carry-on bag that passed through an x-ray scan without arousing suspicion. Nothing was found in his bag and he proceeded to board the airplane. The passenger argued that random post-x-ray searches were unconstitutional, unless the x-ray scan aroused suspicion. The court held that the passenger impliedly consented to the random search by placing his bag on the x-ray conveyor belt.[14]

Social Security Security checkpoint was reasonable

Hand searches conducted of visitor defendants' possessions at the entrance of a Social Security Administration (SSA) office, which revealed evidence of methamphetamine possession in their purses, were reasonable and no more intrusive than necessary as required for the searches to qualify for the administrative search exception.[15]

10.7 Border Searches

An exception to the warrant requirement developed for searches at the border or its functional equivalent because of the specific difficulties and governmental interests involved in border crossings and the problem of smuggling contraband, dutiable goods, and illegal aliens.

Under the border search exception, neither probable cause, reasonable suspicion, nor a search warrant are required for a Customs or immigration search of persons, personal effects, belongings, or vehicles at the border or its functional equivalent.

---

[14] *Torbet v. United Airlines, Inc.*, 298 F.3d 1087 (9th Cir. Cal. 2002).
[15] *U.S. v. Kerr*, 300 F. Supp. 3d 1226 (E.D. Wash. 2018).

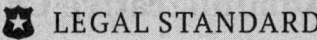

⬟ LEGAL STANDARD

Who may conduct a border search?

Customs agents, Coast Guard officers, immigration officers, agriculture officers, and Border Patrol officers are all Customs officials capable of conducting a border search. FBI agents and local police officers are not included. However, local officers are permitted to be present and assist a border search (See case below).

When may a border search be conducted?

Merely presenting oneself for entry is "gaining entry," and is sufficient to warrant a border search, and one cannot attempt to decline entry to avoid it.[16] Additionally, a suspect who was turned around by Canadian border officials was found to be crossing the border, and subject to search.[17]

What is the scope of a border search?

Border searches may be as intense as the situation permits.[18] Officers may search persons, papers, computers, vessels, luggage, airplanes, mail, and packages. Strip searches are not authorized unless justified with articulable facts. Body cavity searches are only authorized in officers who have a "clear indication" of smuggling (basically you can see it visually or via x-ray).

🏛 CASE EXAMPLES

State police trooper allowed to help with border search

Customs officials and a state trooper patrolled the Louisiana coast. Without any suspicion of criminal activity, they boarded a boat and conducted an inspection where they found bales of marijuana. The court found the search lawful under Fourth Amendment.[19]

Municipal guardsman not authorized to make border search

A suspect ran from a border search and was caught by a municipal guardsman. The guardsman conducted a search and found cocaine which they handed over to an arriving custom's agent. The court found the guardsman was not allowed to make searches on behalf of the customs agent. Still, the evidence was admitted under inevitable discovery doctrine.[20]

Miranda warnings not required

Miranda warnings are not required because it is considered a "routine administrative interview."[21]

---

[16] *U.S. v. Cascante-Bernitta*, 711 F.2d 36 (5th Cir. La. 1983).
[17] *U.S. v. Serhan*, 2015 U.S. Dist. LEXIS 72899 (E.D. Mich. June 5, 2015).
[18] 2-35 Search and Seizure § 35.10 (2015).
[19] *U.S. v. Villamonte-Marquez*, 462 U.S. 579 (U.S. 1983).
[20] *U.S. v. Brown*, 858 F. Supp. 297 (D.P.R. 1994).
[21] *U.S. v. Miller*, 2009 U.S. Dist. LEXIS 62396 (E.D.N.Y. July 21, 2009).

Strip search must be justified

"[A]lthough anyone entering or leaving the country may expect to have his luggage and personal effects examined, he does not expect that his entry or departure, standing alone, will cause him to be subjected to a strip search. Before a border official may insist upon such an extensive invasion of privacy, he should have a suspicion of illegal concealment that is based upon something more than the border crossing, and the suspicion should be substantial enough to make the search a reasonable exercise of authority."[22]

10.8 Probationer & Parolee Searches

Most probationers/parolees have a "search clause" or "Fourth Amendment waiver" that authorizes warrantless searches of their person, residence, car, and any property under their control at any time of day.

Additionally, police officers may conduct the search on behalf of the probation officer if the search is related to the probationer's status. These rules are general and differ by state.

🛡 LEGAL STANDARD

If the probation officer is not present and the search is done by police, the warrantless search is constitutional if:

- Authorized by a probation officer or release condition; and
- Related to the suspect's probationary status.
- The probation officer should not become an "agent" of police

🏛 CASE EXAMPLES

Arrest of probationer inside doctor's office held unconstitutional

"The evidence, interpreted in the light most favorable to [plaintiff medical office manager], is sufficient for a jury to conclude that her Fourth Amendment rights were violated [by probation officer's unwarranted entry into medical office in search of probationer for whom arrest warrant had been issued]. Though physical entry of the home is the chief evil against which the wording of the Fourth Amendment is directed, its protection extends to any area in which an individual has a reasonable expectation of privacy. Offices and other workplaces are among the areas in which individuals may enjoy such a reasonable expectation of privacy."[23]

---

[22] *U.S. v. Asbury*, 586 F.2d 973 (2d Cir. N.Y. 1978).
[23] *O'Rourke v. Hayes*, 378 F.3d 1201 (11th Cir. Fla. 2004).

Warrantless search of cellphone was upheld

A warrantless search of a cellphone was upheld, because "a probationer consents to the waiver of his or her Fourth Amendment rights in exchange for the opportunity to avoid service of a state prison, except insofar as a search might be undertaken for harassment or for arbitrary or capricious reasons."[24]

---

[24] *People v. Sandee*, 16 Cal. App. 5th 294 (2017).

Chapter 11
Search Warrants

11.1 Overview

There are four core requirements of a search warrant. If any of these elements are later found to be missing the evidence discovered may be suppressed.

⭐ LEGAL STANDARD

The four requirements of a search warrant are:

- You must establish probable cause within the affidavit, cannot add information later;
- The warrant must be supported by oath or affirmation;
- You must particularly describe the people or places to be searched; and
- You must particularly describe the things to be seized.

🏛 CASE EXAMPLES

Warrantless searches of home are presumptively unreasonable

No reasonable officer could claim to be unaware of the basic rule, well established by our cases, that, absent consent or exigency, a warrantless search of the home is presumptively unconstitutional.[1]

Courts grant search warrants great deference

An officer got a warrant to search a suspected gang member's house for firearms. The trial court later found that the warrant was defective. However, the Supreme Court held that because the officer acted in good faith and was not "plainly incompetent" the exclusionary rule did not apply.[2]

11.2 Why Get a Warrant, Even if You Don't Need to?

A search warrant is given significant deferential treatment by the courts. In other words, if you take the time to obtain pre- authorization from a neutral and detached magistrate before conducting a search or seizure, the defendant will have a hard time proving that the warrant was invalid.

This is no easy task. The defendant would usually have to prove that the officer was plainly incompetent or reckless with his facts, and that an objectively

---

[1] *Groh v. Ramirez*, 540 U.S. 551 (2004).
[2] *Messerschmidt v. Millender*, 132 S. Ct. 570 (2011).

reasonable officer would know that the warrant did not establish the necessary probable cause.

⬢ LEGAL STANDARD

For a search warrant to be invalid, the defendant would need to prove:

- The magistrate was not neutral or detached; or
- The search warrant did not particularly describe the place to be searched or the things to be seized; or
- The officer was plainly incompetent or reckless with his facts; and
- An objectively reasonable officer would know that the warrant did not establish the necessary probable cause.

🏛 CASE EXAMPLES

Courts grant search warrants great deference

An officer got a warrant to search a suspected gang member's house for firearms. The trial court later found that the warrant was defective. However, the Supreme Court held that because the officer acted in good faith and was not "plainly incompetent" the exclusionary rule did not apply.[3]

11.3   Particularity Requirement

All search warrants must describe with particularity the places to be searched and things or people to be seized. This ensures that officers executing the warrant know where to go, where to look, and what to seize. Otherwise, the warrant becomes more like a "general search warrant" which is forbidden by the Fourth Amendment.

⬢ LEGAL STANDARD

All search warrants must:

- Particularly describe the people or places to be searched; and
- Particularly describe the things to be seized.

---

[3] *Messerschmidt v. Millender*, 132 S. Ct. 570 (2011).

CASE EXAMPLES

Warrant must be described with particularity

The uniformly applied rule is that a search conducted pursuant to a warrant that fails to conform to the particularity requirement of the Fourth Amendment is unconstitutional. That rule is in keeping with the well-established principle that except in certain carefully defined classes of cases, a search of private property without proper consent is unreasonable unless it has been authorized by a valid search warrant.[4]

Facially invalid warrant will not be saved by Good Faith reliance

The officer "contends that the search in this case was the product, at worst, of a lack of due care, and that our case law requires more than negligent behavior before depriving an official of qualified immunity." But "a warrant may be so facially deficient—*i.e.*, in failing to particularize the place to be searched or the things to be seized—that the executing officers cannot reasonably presume it to be valid. This is such a case."[5]

11.4 Anticipatory Search Warrant

An anticipatory search warrant is where probable cause will be established once a "triggering event" occurs. For example, the triggering event could be whenever an occupant, unknown at the time, receives a parcel known to contain narcotics.

LEGAL STANDARD

A search warrant may be received on prospective probable cause when:

- There is reason to believe that contraband or evidence will be delivered at a particular residence;
- The warrant may be executed upon probable cause that a triggering event has occurred, such as observing package being accepted for delivery.

CASE EXAMPLES

Supreme Court upheld anticipatory warrants

"When an anticipatory warrant is issued, the fact that the contraband is not presently located at the place described in the warrant is immaterial, so long as there is probable cause to believe that it will be there when the search warrant is executed."[6]

---

[4] *Groh v. Ramirez*, 540 U.S. 551 (2004).
[5] *Groh v. Ramirez*, 540 U.S. 551 (2004).
[6] *U.S. v. Grubbs*, 547 U.S. 90 (2006).

Anticipatory warrants are not authorized in every state

"While the anticipatory search warrant issued in this case does not run afoul of either the United States Constitution or the Oklahoma Constitution, it was not authorized by the plain language of our statute which specifically sets forth the requisites for when a search warrant may be issued."[7]

11.5   Confidential Informants

If you use a confidential informant (C.I.) to establish reasonable suspicion or probable cause, you need to articulate he was trustworthy. Do this by articulating how the C.I. was "credible" and how he obtained his "basis of knowledge."[8]

Credible means that the C.I. was telling the truth. Basis of knowledge means that the information shared by the C.I. was accurate, usually because of first-hand observations.[9]

⭐ LEGAL STANDARD

A C.I. may be used to develop probable cause when:

- There is reason to believe the C.I. is credible;
- The C.I. has a basis of knowledge;
- Both factors are judged under the totality of the circumstances.

🏛 CASE EXAMPLES

Judge has discretion to meet C.I. in person to confirm he actually exists

If there is doubt as to the credibility of a C.I., or if one even exists, a judge may order the prosecution to produce the C.I. in court for a non-public hearing (in chambers) without the defendant's attorney being present. As one court put it, "in proper cases, such a hearing can avoid an otherwise irreconcilable conflict between the legitimate need for informant anonymity and the right of the defendant to be free of unfounded infringements of his privacy and liberty."[10]

Confidential informant allowed to use video recorder inside apartment

A confidential informant's use of visual recording equipment when conducting a controlled drug purchase, in defendant's apartment, did not exceed the scope of the informant's license to be in the apartment and was admissible in court.[11]

---

[7] *Dodson v. State*, 150 P.3d 1054, 1055-59 (Okla. Crim. App. 2006).
[8] *Aguilar v. Tex.*, 378 U.S. 108 (1964).
[9] *Illinois v. Gates*, 462 U.S. 213 (1983).
[10] *People v. Dailey*, 639 P.2d 1068, 1077 n.11 (Colo. 1982).
[11] *U.S. v. Thompson*, 811 F.3d 944 (7th Cir. 2016).

11.6   Sealing Affidavits

Typically, you are supposed to leave a copy of the search warrant, including affidavit, during the search warrant execution. Unfortunately, leaving the affidavit may compromise your investigation. You are allowed to seal a search warrant affidavit for "good cause." You can seal the affidavit for a specific number of days, or until the court authorizes the release.

★ LEGAL STANDARD

An affidavit may be sealed if:

- You have a compelling need, such as protecting an on-going investigation or protecting informant's safety;
- The search warrant particularly describes what is sought and where to search, without the affidavit; and
- There is a continuing need to maintain seal.

🏛 CASE EXAMPLES

Federal courts have inherent discretion to seal affidavits

The district court has the inherent power to seal affidavits filed with the court in appropriate circumstances. "The government contends that the materials should be sealed to protect the informant and to keep confidential ongoing investigations. We find that, on this basis, the district court did not abuse its discretion."[12]

Police may maintain seal if disclosure would endanger safety of informant

"In our view, a sealed search warrant affidavit, like search warrant affidavits generally, should ordinarily be part of the court record ... However, a sealed search warrant affidavit may be retained by the law enforcement agency upon a showing that disclosure of the information would impair further investigation of criminal conduct or endanger the safety of the confidential informant."[13]

11.7   Knock and Announce

Whenever you enter a person's home without his consent, you must meet the requirements of knock and announce.[14] This applies whether you enter with a warrant or under a recognized exception. For example, even if you plan to enter a home because of a medical emergency, you are required to knock and announce before making a non-consensual entry unless an exception to knock and announce applies.

---

[12] *U.S. v. Mann*, 829 F.2d 849 (9th Cir. Or. 1987).
[13] *People v. Galland*, 45 Cal.4th 354 (2008).
[14] *Wilson v. Ark.*, 514 U.S. 927 (1995).

Reasons for knock and announce:

- The protection of the privacy of the individual in his home;
- The protection of innocent persons who may also be present on the premises where an arrest is made;
- The prevention of situations which are conducive to violent confrontations between the occupant and individuals who enter his home without proper notice;
- The protection of police who might be injured by a startled and fearful home-owner;[15] and
- To avoid the unnecessary "destruction or breaking of any house."[16]

⭐ LEGAL STANDARD

Elements of knock and announce:

- Police must notify the occupants of their presence. This is usually done by knocking but includes door bell, telephone, bullhorn, *etc.*
- Police must announce their "authority" and "purpose." This is usually done by yelling, "Police, search warrant!"
- Police must wait a reasonable time before making forced entry. Reasonable time is often based on how long it would take to destroy the evidence.

Violations of knock and announce:

- Evidence found after a knock and announce violation may not be suppressed during trial (unless the violation was particularly shocking). However, violations may result in discipline and § 1983 lawsuits.

Exceptions to knock and announce (must articulate):

- The officer's presence is already known to the occupant;
- The suspect is armed and will use his weapon;
- Delay would allow suspect to escape;
- During hot pursuit; or
- Delay may cause the evidence to be destroyed.

🏛 CASE EXAMPLES

Opening screen door, before announcement, was a knock and announce violation

Officers walked up to the residence to serve a search warrant and observed that the front door was open, along with a closed screen door. The lead officer knocked several times but did not announce his identity and purpose. He then opened the screen door and walked into the home, while announcing their identity and purpose.

---

[15] *People v. Peterson*, 9 Cal. 3d 717 (Cal. 1973).
[16] *Wilson v. Ark.*, 514 U.S. 927 (1995).

The court found this to be a violation of knock and announce. Still, the evidence was not subject to suppression.[17]

Knock and announce applies to all uninvited entries, including warrantless entries into the home

"Whatever the circumstances under which breaking a door to arrest for felony might be lawful, however, the breaking was unlawful where the officer failed first to state his authority and purpose for demanding admission."[18]

Delay of 15-20 seconds held reasonable for drug warrant

"[T]he court ruled that a delay of only 15 or 20 seconds from the point in time at which police officers knocked on the defendant's door and announced that they were there to execute a search warrant for illegal narcotics was reasonable because of the exigent circumstance of possible destruction of evidence." On the other hand, police looking for a stolen piano "may be able to spend more time to make sure they really need the battering ram."[19]

11.8 Detaining Occupants Inside and in Immediate Vicinity

Generally, you may detain individuals who are on-scene for the duration of the search warrant. Courts recognize the officer safety concerns during a warrant execution, and why it is important to maintain absolute control over the residence.

If a suspect came to the residence during the execution of a search warrant, he may be detained if he appears involved in the crime at issue (*e.g.*, there to purchase drugs).

The best practice would be to detain only the following individuals:

- The home's occupants so they may open locked containers or otherwise assist in an orderly search of the residence;
- Any individual who will likely be arrested as a result of the search;
- Any individual who would present an officer safety issue if released (gang members or other hostile people);
- Any other individual for good cause.

I strongly recommend that you do not needlessly detain uninvolved individuals not listed above, especially children. This is a best practice and makes law enforcement appear more professional and reasonable.

---

[17] *People v. Peterson*, 9 Cal. 3d 717 (Cal. 1973).
[18] *Miller v. U.S.*, 357 U.S. 301 (1958).
[19] *U.S. v. Banks*, 540 U.S. 31 (2003).

⭐ LEGAL STANDARD

Occupants present at the execution of a search warrant may be detained if:[20]

- They are in the immediate vicinity of the premises to be searched;
- The manner of detention is reasonable.

🏛 CASE EXAMPLES

Whether someone is within the immediate vicinity depends on several facts

These factors include the lawful limits of the premises, whether the occupant was within a line of sight of the premises being searched, the ease of reentry from the occupant's location, and other relevant factors (undefined by Court).[21]

Visitors may be detained briefly during probation/parole search

A probation officer may lawfully "briefly" detain a visitor in a house who is present in the house of a juvenile probationer during a Fourth Amendment waiver search long enough to determine whether he is a resident of the house or is otherwise connected to illegal activity.[22]

14-hour detention/interrogation of party-goers unreasonable

A sheriff's investigator was held not to be protected by qualified immunity when sued for detaining partygoers for as long as 14 hours after a warrant search for evidence of illegal gaming was executed. Interrogating the participants is not part and parcel of executing a warrant. Also, the detentions could not be justified as Terry stops because individualized suspicion was not established by the partygoers' mere presence in the same large mansion where some limited drug and gaming contraband was discovered, and because detentions as long as 14 hours did not remotely resemble the brief detention authorized by *Terry v. Ohio*.[23]

Note: this search warrant was executed by SWAT and yielded two non-functioning slot machines and three grams of pot! Whoops.

Authority to detain is categorical

An officer's authority to detain incident to a search is categorical; it does not depend on the quantum of proof justifying detention or the extent of the intrusion to be imposed by the seizure. Note, the Supreme Court still requires that the duration of detention be reasonable. Over-detention is still unreasonable.[24]

---

[20] *Michigan v. Summers*, 452 U.S. 692 (1981).
[21] *Bailey v. United States*, 568 U.S. 186 (2013).
[22] *People v. Rios*, 193 Cal. App. 4th 584 (Cal. App. 5th Dist. 2011).
[23] *Guillory v. Hill*, 233 Cal. App. 4th 240 (Cal. App. 4th Dist. 2015).
[24] *Muehler v. Mena*, 544 U.S. 93 (2005).

> **Lawful detention of subject who arrived on-scene of large marijuana grow operation**
>
> Subject likely knew about grow operation and used a code to enter the facility.[25]

11.9 Frisking Occupants

You cannot automatically patdown every occupant present during the execution of a search warrant. The standard for a patdown remains the same: individualized reasonable suspicion that a person is armed and dangerous.

Fortunately, this standard is not difficult to meet, especially because search warrants can be inherently dangerous in the sense that occupants know exactly where the weapons are inside the residence and no officer would be able to watch the occupant 100% of the time. This "home court advantage" may help justify conducting a patdown.

The purpose of the warrant itself can also be a significant factor. Naturally there's different officer safety considerations if you are looking for a handgun versus tax records. But remember that mere presence at the scene of the warrant may not be sufficient, the occupant should be directly connected with the location. For example, if you were executing a search warrant at a bar known for selling drugs, this would not provide independent justification for patting down (for weapons or drugs) of every patron that happens to be there.[26]

🛡 LEGAL STANDARD

An occupant may be frisked for weapons when:

- The occupant is connected to the residence and the search warrant is inherently dangerous; or
- Reasonable suspicion is developed that an occupant is armed and dangerous.

🏛 CASE EXAMPLES

Police cannot search people simply because they are at the house

Persons detained during a search for evidence cannot be searched simply because they are there. Accordingly, those officers who conducted indiscriminate searches of all persons present at the family residence failed to act in an objectively reasonable manner, and are not entitled to qualified immunity.[27]

---

[25] *U.S. v. Davis*, 530 F.3d 1069 (9th Cir. Or. 2008).
[26] *Ybarra v. Ill.*, 444 U.S. 85 (1979).
[27] *Marks v. Clarke*, 102 F.3d 1012 (9th Cir. Wash. 1997).

Patdown usually authorized of narcotics dealers

Courts tend to recognize the likelihood that narcotics suspects are often armed and may allow a patdown with no more than the conclusory opinion that the "need for officer safety" dictated the need for a patdown.[28]

Cannot conduct patdown because it is "the safe thing to do"

During a probation search an officer cannot patdown a present known associate, even when there's evidence of drug abuse occurring at the house, just because it is "the safe thing to do." Officers still need individualized suspicion that a particular person is armed or dangerous.[29]

Frisk lawful of person arriving at house the same time as police executed the warrant

Officer did not violate defendant's Fourth Amendment rights in performing patdown frisk of his outer clothing, where defendant arrived contemporaneously with officers at location where valid narcotics search warrant was about to be executed; frisk was not motivated by anything other than need to secure immediate vicinity of ongoing judicially-approved police operation.[30]

11.10   Handcuffing Occupants

You cannot automatically handcuff people present during the execution of a search warrant. Like patdowns, you must have an articulable reason before applying any restraints. Remember, courts consider handcuffs a use of force and the mere presence during the execution of a search warrant may not call for using force. Naturally, you may use handcuffs whenever you execute a dangerous search warrant.[31] Best practices require that if prolonged restraints are required (*e.g.*, more than an hour or so) then other accommodations should be considered so that restraint-based injuries do not occur.

Further, prolonged detentions may require bathroom breaks and access to water. Courts may find the initial detention reasonable, but the method (prolonged handcuffing) unreasonable. You should constantly re-evaluate whether or not restraints are still necessary.

⭐ LEGAL STANDARD

Factors to consider if occupants are handcuffed:

- Occupants may be handcuffed during the execution of a dangerous search warrant;
- If reasonable, occupants may remain in handcuffs until search is completed;

---

[28] *People v. Samples*, 48 Cal. App. 4th 1197 (Cal. App. 1st Dist. 1996).
[29] *People v. Sandoval*, 163 Cal. App. 4th 205 (Cal. App. 3d Dist. 2008).
[30] *U.S. v. Banks*, 628 F. Supp. 2d 811, 817-18 (N.D. Ill. 2009).
[31] *Muehler v. Mena*, 544 U.S. 93 (2005).

- If continuous handcuffing may cause injuries, alternatives should be considered;
- If it is readily apparent an occupant poses no danger, restraints should be removed.

11.11 Serving Arrest Warrant at Residence

An arrest warrant not only authorizes the suspect's arrest in public, but also authorizes you to enter the suspect's home if he is home to make the arrest. This is an extremely helpful option for arresting wanted suspects.

On the other hand, if the suspect is at a third-party's home, like a friend's house, you must apply for a search warrant.

Finally, the arrest warrant can be a bench warrant, misdemeanor traffic warrant, and of course, a felony warrant.

⭐ LEGAL STANDARD

An arrest warrant may be served at a residence if:

- You possess a valid arrest warrant;
- You have probable cause the person lives at the home;
- You have reason to believe the suspect is currently home;
- You knock and announce;
- You may conduct a protective sweep if justified; and
- You may not search for evidence, but plain view seizure applies.

🏛 CASE EXAMPLES

An arrest warrant authorizes entry into the suspect's home

"For Fourth Amendment purposes, an arrest warrant founded on probable cause implicitly carries with it the limited authority to enter a dwelling in which the suspect lives when there is reason to believe the suspect is within."[32]

11.12 Wrong Address Liability

Whenever police execute a search warrant at the wrong house there will likely to be a lawsuit. How much is paid usually depends on three factors:

1. Lack of pre-warrant due diligence;
2. Amount of damage to residence or injuries to occupants; and
3. Police conduct once they knew, or should have known, they were at the wrong address.

---

[32] *Payton v. N.Y.*, 445 U.S. 573 (1980).

It is vital that before you seek a search warrant, especially one involving SWAT, you conduct a quality investigation and verify the address. Most mistakes can be corrected before the warrant is executed.

It is also vital that once police realize they hit the wrong house they immediately begin to correct or diminish the injury caused.

✪ LEGAL STANDARD

If a search warrant is served on the wrong residence, liability will depend on three factors:

1. Reasonableness of pre-warrant investigation;
2. Reasonableness of warrant execution; and
3. Remedial measures taken once mistake was known.

🏛 CASE EXAMPLES

No automatic Fourth Amendment violation when warrant unknowingly served on new tenants

"Officers executing search warrants on occasion enter a house when residents are engaged in [lawful] activity; and the resulting frustration, embarrassment, and humiliation may be real, as was true here. When officers execute a valid warrant and act in a reasonable manner to protect themselves from harm, however, the Fourth Amendment is not violated."[33]

11.13   Receipt, Return, and Inventory

You are required to leave a copy of the search warrant with an occupant or at the residence. Additionally, you must leave a receipt for the items you seized and file a return and inventory with the issuing court. Finally, many courts require that the return be filed promptly, often within 48 hours.

✪ LEGAL STANDARD

After executing a search warrant, you must:

- Leave a copy of the warrant, along with a receipt of what was seized, with an occupant or at the residence; and
- File a return, along with an inventory of what was seized, with the issuing court within the specified time.

---

[33] *L.A. County v. Rettele*, 550 U.S. 609 (2007).

🏛 CASE EXAMPLES

Leaving a copy of the warrant and a receipt is a constitutional requirement

"[W]hen law enforcement agents seize property pursuant to a warrant, due process requires them to take reasonable steps to give notice that the property has been taken so the owner can pursue available remedies for its return."[34]

Actual notice not required, simply good faith effort to notify is required

Police served a search warrant at a suspect's home who was incarcerated. Police mailed him a copy of the warrant and receipt and he claimed he never received it. The Supreme Court held that this effort satisfied due process.[35]

---

[34] *City of West Covina v. Perkins*, 525 U.S. 234, 240 (1999).
[35] *Dusenbery v. U.S.*, 534 U.S. 161 (2002).

Chapter 12
Use of Force

12.1 Non-Deadly Force

Whenever police use non-deadly force it must be objectively reasonable. The key is to articulate every material fact in the report. Police should not add important details later, otherwise it loses credibility.

> ### 🛡 LEGAL STANDARD
>
> Factors to consider whether non-deadly force was reasonable include:[1]
>
> - How serious was the offense you suspected had been committed?
> - Did the suspect pose a physical threat to you or some other person present at the scene?
> - Was the suspect actively resisting or attempting to evade arrest?
> - Reasonable force will be judged by the totality of the circumstances.
> - Courts must step into the shoes of the officer and not use 20/20 hindsight.

> ### 🏛 CASE EXAMPLES
>
> **Trooper liable after using pepper spray on handcuffed suspect**
>
> When the trooper "maced" the motorist, she was handcuffed and standing beside his cruiser. He admitted he had no fear for his own safety at that time. There was no indication that the motorist actively resisted or attempted to flee, or that she was physically aggressive. Thus, there was no stressful and dangerous condition forcing the trooper to make a split-second judgment on what to do.[2]

12.2 Use of Force to Prevent Escape

You may use deadly force in order to protect yourself or others from imminent or immediate serious bodily harm or death. Additionally, you may use deadly force to "arrest" a violent fleeing felon who would pose a significant risk to others if not captured immediately. Finally, you must give a warning, if feasible, before using deadly force.

---

[1] *Graham v. Connor*, 490 U.S. 386 (1989).
[2] *Martinez v. New Mexico Dept. of Public Safety*, 47 Fed. Appx. 513 (10th Cir. 2002).

🛡 LEGAL STANDARD

Deadly force to prevent an escape may be reasonable, if:

- The suspect poses an imminent threat of serious bodily harm or death; or
- You have probable cause that the suspect has committed a violent felony; and
- If the suspect escapes he will pose an imminent threat of serious bodily harm or death to others; and
- A warning, if feasible, is given before deadly force is used.

🏛 CASE EXAMPLES

It is better that a non-violent felony suspect get away then be shot dead

"The use of deadly force to prevent the escape of all felony suspects, whatever the circumstances, is constitutionally unreasonable. It is not better that all felony suspects die than that they escape. Where the suspect poses no immediate threat to the officer and no threat to others, the harm resulting from failing to apprehend him does not justify the use of deadly force to do so. It is no doubt unfortunate when a suspect who is in sight escapes, but the fact that the police arrive a little late or are a little slower afoot does not always justify killing the suspect. A police officer may not seize an unarmed, nondangerous suspect by shooting him dead."[3]

12.3 Deadly Force During Vehicle Pursuit

Police may use reasonable force to end a dangerous pursuit. This may include deadly force if the fleeing suspect poses an imminent threat of serious bodily harm or death to innocent people. Still, this area of the law is not completely settled.[4]

Therefore, best police practices must be considered. The Supreme Court cannot prevent suspects and innocent people suing you and your agency. These lawsuits could easily drain your agency of hundreds of thousands of dollars in legal fees. Therefore, only use deadly force when necessary.

🛡 LEGAL STANDARD

Deadly force may be reasonable against a fleeing motorist where:

- The fleeing suspect poses an imminent threat of serious bodily harm or death to others outside his vehicle;
- A warning, if feasible, is given before deadly force is used (probably not feasible while chasing a suspect, but it's required by *Tenn. v. Garner*).

---

[3] *Tennessee v. Garner*, 471 U.S. 1 (1985).
[4] *Plumhoff v. Rickard*, 134 S. Ct. 2012 (2014).

🏛 CASE EXAMPLES

No violation after using deadly force to end dangerous pursuit

"[W]e are loath to lay down a rule requiring the police to allow fleeing suspects to get away whenever they drive so recklessly that they put other people's lives in danger. It is obvious the perverse incentives such a rule would create: Every fleeing motorist would know that escape is within his grasp, if only he accelerates to 90 miles per hour, crosses the double-yellow line a few times, and runs a few red lights.... Instead, we lay down a more sensible rule: A police officer's attempt to terminate a dangerous high-speed car chase that threatens the lives of innocent bystanders does not violate the Fourth Amendment, even when it places the fleeing motorist at risk of serious injury or death."[5]

12.4 Improper Handcuffing

Handcuffing is a use of force and therefore must meet the reasonableness requirements under *Graham v. Connor*. You may be held liable for excessive force if you improperly handcuff a suspect. Additionally, liability can be incurred if you fail to remove handcuffs when no longer necessary. Remember, handcuffs are temporary restraints.

⭐ LEGAL STANDARD

Handcuffing is proper when:

- They are used when reasonably necessary;
- They are not over-tightened;
- They are double-locked to prevent over-tightening (no liability if not double-locked and no injury occurs); and
- If a suspect complains about handcuffs, and the situation permits it, they should be checked to confirm proper fit.

🏛 CASE EXAMPLES

Suspect may go to trial over excessive force claim

The suspect complained that his handcuffs were on too tight. They remained on for an additional 15 minutes while being booked. He sued and the court held that claim could go to trial.[6]

---

[5] *Scott v. Harris*, 550 U.S. 372 (2007).
[6] *Martin v. Heideman*, 106 F.3d 1308 (6th Cir. Ky. 1997).

The law against over-tightened handcuffing is clearly established

"The law was clearly established that the overly tight application of handcuffs was a violation of an arrestee's constitutional right not to have excessive force applied during an arrest."[7]

Involuntary consent to search due to unnecessary handcuffing

The court found a lack of reasoning for the officer's handcuffing of the subject in question. Since there was no establishment that "the detention was lawful," and the officer did not have probable cause to search the subject, then the consent to search, given by the subject, was involuntary.[8]

12.5 Pointing Gun at Suspect

Officers should never point their firearm at anyone unless justified by a serious threat. First, an officer could have a negligent discharge (never good). Second, pointing guns during an investigative detention could result in a de facto arrest, requiring probable cause. Finally, courts have found that needlessly pointing guns at suspects may result in excessive force. Nothing good can come from needlessly pointing your firearm.

Naturally, un-holstering your firearm at the low ready position is much different and usually does not result in liability if you can articulate a valid reason.

⭐ LEGAL STANDARD

Pointing a gun at a suspect is appropriate if:

- You can articulate a serious officer safety reason.

🏛 CASE EXAMPLES

Holding children at gunpoint unreasonable

"While the SWAT Team's initial show of force may have been reasonable ... continuing to hold the children directly at gunpoint after the officers had gained complete control of the situation outside the residence was not justified under the circumstances at that point. This rendered the seizure of the children unreasonable, violating their Fourth Amendment rights."[9]

---

[7] *Baskin v. Smith*, 50 Fed. Appx. 731 (6th Cir. 2002).
[8] *People v. Stier*, 168 Cal. App. 4th 21 (2008).
[9] *Holland v. Harrington*, 268 F.3d 1179 (10th Cir. Colo. 2001).

Pointing firearm at unarmed and cooperative suspect unlawful

Under ordinary circumstances, when the police have only reasonable suspicion to make an investigatory stop, drawing weapons and using handcuffs and other restraints will violate the Fourth Amendment.[10]

12.6 Using Patrol (*i.e.*, Bite) Dogs

Generally, patrol canines are not considered deadly force, even if a suspect dies as a result of its deployment. However, a jury may find its use objectively unreasonable if a suspect was not given a warning and an opportunity to peacefully surrender before deploying a canine trained in the bite-and-hold method.

If no warning was given articulate why it was unreasonable, unsafe, or impractical under the circumstances.

⭐ LEGAL STANDARD

A patrol "bite dog" may be deployed if:

- The suspect is armed and dangerous or was involved in violent serious felony;
- If he's escaping, you first give a warning and an opportunity to surrender peacefully; and
- If no warning was given, articulate why.

🏛 CASE EXAMPLES

A warning should be given, if feasible, before releasing a bite dog

A jury can properly find that the failure to give a verbal warning before using a police dog trained to bite and hold is objectively unreasonable.[11]

Use of trained police dog is not deadly force

The court stated that, "there was no basis to instruct the jury regarding the use of deadly force because the use of a trained police dog does not constitute deadly force."[12]

12.7 Hog/Hobble Tie

Only use a hog-tie as a last resort and if you obtained the proper training,[13] otherwise you may be liable for excessive force. Additionally, avoid using these restraints on suspects who have a diminished capacity.

---

[10] *Robinson v. Solano County*, 278 F.3d 1007 (9th Cir. 2002).
[11] *Kuha v. City of Minnetonka*, 176 F. Supp. 2d 926 (D. Minn. 2001).
[12] *Thompson v. County of Los Angeles*, 142 Cal. App. 4th 154 (2006).
[13] *Garrett v. Unified Government of Athens-Clarke County*, 246 F. Supp.1262 (M.D. GA. 2003).

⭐ LEGAL STANDARD

A hobble tie may be used as a last resort to control a suspect, unless he is under the influence of:

- Severe intoxication;
- Under the influence of a controlled substance;
- Severe mental disability, like excited delirium;
- Any other condition that would lead an officer to believe a hobble tie would cause a significant risk to the suspect's health.

Note: Many people that require a hog-tie experience excited delirium, and therefore are highly susceptible to in-custody death. Get medical in-route ASAP and have them evaluate the suspect and monitor him constantly

🏛 CASE EXAMPLES

Hobble tie restraints may be used unless diminished capacity is apparent

"We do not reach the question whether all hog-tie restraints constitute a constitutional violation per se, but hold that officers may not apply this technique when an individual's diminished capacity is apparent. This diminished capacity might result from severe intoxication, the influence of controlled substances, a discernible mental condition, or any other condition, apparent to the officers at the time, which would make the application of a hog-tie restraint likely to result in any significant risk to the individual's health or well- being."[14]

---

[14] *Cruz v. Laramie*, 239 F.3d 1183 (10th Cir. 2001).

Chapter 13
Interview and Interrogation

13.1   When Miranda is Required

Two requirements must be met before you are required tell a suspect his Miranda rights. The requirements are the suspect must be "in-custody" and "interrogation" must be imminent.[1] Additionally, these requirements must be present at the same time. Otherwise, Miranda is not required.

Remember that you do not need to formally tell a suspect they are under arrest for him to be in-custody. Instead, courts look at whether an objectively reasonable person would have believed he was under arrest based on the totality of the circumstances, even if you never intended to arrest him (referred to as a de facto arrest).

Miranda also requires that you interrogate the suspect. In other words, when you are seeking "testimony" from the suspect. Testimony means a statement which tend to prove, or disprove, the crime in question. This is why booking-type questions are not normally considered interrogation, because they seek inmate information and not particular information related to his crime.

Note: a suspect cannot pre-invoke Miranda. For example, if you arrest a suspect and he says, "I want my lawyer!," but you haven't even started to interrogate him, then it's not a valid Miranda invocation because he's not in-custody at the same time he's interrogated.

⬟ LEGAL STANDARD

Miranda rights are required when:

- A person is in-custody (*i.e.*, arrested); and
- You are interrogating him (*i.e.*, "Tell me why you committed this crime").

🏛 CASE EXAMPLES

Miranda not necessarily required after detaining a suspect with handcuffs

"Handcuffing a suspect during an investigative detention does not automatically make it (a) custodial interrogation for purposes of Miranda."[2]

---

[1] *Miranda v. Ariz.*, 384 U.S. 436 (1966).
[2] *People v. Davidson*, 221 Cal. App. 4th 966 (Cal. App. 2d Dist. 2013).

Temporarily placing suspect in patrol car not an arrest

Handcuffing and putting an uncooperative suspect in the backseat of a patrol car while the officer checked the vehicle for weapons held not to be an arrest. "A brief, although complete, restriction of liberty, such as handcuffing (and, in this case, putting into a patrol car), during a Terry stop is not a de facto arrest, if not excessive under the circumstances."[3] Still, this confinement is usually an arrest.

Police may use a suspect's awkward silence during questioning if he is not in custody

Officers interviewed the suspect who was not in custody. He answered most questions but when asked about the gun used in the crime, he became suspiciously silent, as if he knew about it (because he did!). His silence was properly used against him at trial because he wasn't in custody and under these circumstances there was no attempt to invoke his Fifth Amendment rights.[4]

No violation where suspect invoked right to counsel but subsequently made incriminating statements to his wife

The suspect was accused of murder and child abuse. He was arrested and read Miranda. He subsequently invoked his right to counsel and all questioning ceased. The suspect asked to speak with his wife, and police agreed. An officer remained in the room while the couple spoke and openly tape recorded the conversation. The Supreme Court held there was no violation since police did not ask the wife to speak with the suspect, they simply agreed to allow it.[5]

Prohibited interrogation also refers to its "functional equivalent"

"For purposes of the Miranda rules, the term 'interrogation' refers not only to express questioning but also to any words or actions on the part of the police, other than those normally attendant upon arrest and custody [booking questions], that the police should know are reasonably likely to elicit an incriminating response from the suspect; the latter portion of this definition focuses primarily on the perceptions of the suspect, rather than on the intent of the police.[6]

13.2 Miranda Elements

The following Miranda warnings are required when you interrogate an in-custody suspect.[7] Additionally, you must read a suspect his entire Miranda rights, even if they cut you off and tell you he already knows his rights.[8] This is true even if you arrest a judge! All warnings must be given. Period.

Keep in mind that courts do not require these rights to be read verbatim. But police must inform the suspect of all four and articulate the fifth. It is highly

---

[3] *Haynie v. County of L.A.*, 339 F.3d 1071 (9th Cir. Cal. 2003).
[4] *Salinas v. Texas*, 133 S. Ct. 2174 (2013).
[5] *Arizona v. Mauro*, 481 U.S. 520 (1987).
[6] *Rhode Island v. Innis*, 446 U.S. 291 (1980).
[7] *Miranda v. Ariz.*, 384 U.S. 436 (1966).
[8] *U.S. v. Patane*, 542 U.S. 630 (2004).

suggested that you read Miranda from a pre-printed pocket card, otherwise be prepared to be slammed in court by a decent defense attorney, because you do not know exactly what you said to the defendant.

🛡 LEGAL STANDARD

Miranda requires the suspect to understand the following rights:

- He has the right to remain silent;
- That any statements made may be used against him in court;
- That he has the right to consult with an attorney and to have that attorney present during questioning;
- That if he cannot afford an attorney, one will be appointed to represent him prior to questioning; and
- The suspect must knowingly and intelligently waive rights.

🏛 CASE EXAMPLES

The Miranda decision does not require precise words

"The four warnings Miranda requires are invariable [plus articulating the waiver], but this Court has not dictated the words in which the essential information must be conveyed…The inquiry is simply whether the warnings reasonably 'conve[y] to [a suspect] his rights as required by Miranda.'"[9]

13.3   Coercive Influences and De Facto Arrests

You may unintentionally create a coercive environment when you detain a suspect. For example, you may need to draw your firearm or use handcuffs for safety purposes. If you intend to obtain a voluntary statement you should minimize those coercive influences and articulate your actions in your report.

Remember, an arrest occurs when a reasonable person would believe he was "in-custody." It does not matter what you "believed." Instead, courts will focus on the environment, what you did, what you said, and how you said it. If courts decide a "de-facto" arrest occurred Miranda would be required.

For example, if police made a highly intrusive detention based on legitimate safety concerns, *e.g.*, pointing a firearm to detain a violent-crime suspect, then police should try to minimize those coercive activities before they conduct an interview.

---

[9] *Powell v. Florida*, 130 S. Ct. 1195 (2010).

> ### 🛡 LEGAL STANDARD
>
> A person's statement is admissible in court if:
>
> - It was voluntary and not coerced; and
> - If under arrest, he waived his Miranda rights.

> ### 🏛 CASE EXAMPLES
>
> **Subjective intentions do not matter**
>
> An individual is deemed "in custody" where there has been a formal arrest, or where there has been a restraint on freedom of movement, of the degree associated with a formal arrest so that a reasonable person would not feel free to leave. A suspect's or the police's subjective view of the circumstances does not determine whether the suspect is in custody.[10]
>
> **Lying about purpose of interview not per se coercive**
>
> The Court has held that failing to tell a suspect what it is they intend to question him about is irrelevant to the issue of the voluntariness of a Miranda waiver. Still, be careful here ... honesty is often better.[11]

13.4   Miranda Inside Jail and Prison

Interviewing a suspect in jail or prison about an unrelated crime does not necessarily mean they are in custody for Miranda purposes. Courts will look at several factors. Still, a good rule of thumb is to read Miranda for jail inmates and optionally for prison inmates. This is because jail is not a person's "home" and therefore jail inmates are in "in-custody" for Miranda purposes. However, courts typically view prisons as quasi-homes for inmates, and therefore are not "per se" in-custody. But your actions should not be more "restrictive or coercive" than typical for the prison environment. For example, if a locked interview room is used tell him he is free to leave at any time (after getting the guard to take him back to his cell).[12]

> ### 🛡 LEGAL STANDARD
>
> Jail inmates:
>
> - You should read pre-convicted jail inmates their Miranda rights.
>
> Prison inmates:
>
> - You are not required to read a prison inmate his Miranda rights because he is not typically considered "in-custody" because the prison is his "home."

---

[10] *Stansbury v. Cal.*, 511 U.S. 318 (1994).
[11] *Colorado v. Spring*, 479 U.S. 564 (1987).
[12] *Miranda v. Ariz.*, 384 U.S. 436 (1966).

🏛 CASE EXAMPLES

Prisoner was not in custody during interview with investigators

Defendant was not in-custody for Miranda purposes when he was escorted into a conference room and questioned by sheriff's deputies about allegations that he had sexual contact with a minor before prison. The defendant was told he could leave and return to cell whenever he wanted to, he was not physically restrained or threatened, he was interviewed in well-lit, average-sized conference room in which he was not uncomfortable, he was offered food and water, and door to conference room was sometimes left open.[13]

13.5 Miranda for Juveniles

Miranda rules that apply to adults equally apply to juveniles. In schools, Miranda is not required if the school is investigating a violation of school policy. However, if a police officer is present, Miranda will be required if there is a criminal investigation.

🛡 LEGAL STANDARD

Keep in mind the following issues regarding Miranda and juveniles:

- Miranda rules that apply to adults apply to juveniles;
- Police should be aware that due to the child's immaturity, courts will scrutinize whether the waiver was knowing and voluntarily provided;
- States often have additional requirements, such as parental notification.

🏛 CASE EXAMPLES

Miranda not required when interviewed by principal

A vice-principle interrogating an "in-custody" student about drug possession was not required to Mirandize the student before police had arrived.[14]

Dean not required to give Miranda before ordering student to empty pockets

A dean received information that a student possessed drugs and confronted the student and ordered him to empty his pockets, which revealed narcotics.[15]

Age must be a factor in whether to Mirandize

"It is beyond dispute that children will often feel bound to submit to police questioning when an adult in the same circumstances would feel free to leave."[16]

---

[13] *Howes v. Fields*, 132 S. Ct. 1181 (2012).
[14] *People v. Pankhurst*, 365 Ill. App. 3d 248 (Ill. App. Ct. 2d Dist. 2006).
[15] *People v. Stewart*, 63 Misc. 2d 601 (N.Y. City Crim. Ct. 1970).
[16] *J.D.B. v. North Carolina*, 564 U.S. 261 (2011).

13.6 Witnesses and Victims

Often when you investigate a crime, you will talk to various witnesses and victims. Courts have held that uninvolved witnesses or victims are presumed to be reliable, unlike a criminal confidential informant.

Obviously, this does not relieve you of conducting a quality investigation that seeks the truth.

🛡 LEGAL STANDARD

Citizen witnesses and victims are presumptively reliable; therefore, you do not need to corroborate their basis of knowledge.

🏛 CASE EXAMPLES

Police do not need to be skeptical about ordinary citizen witnesses

"We begin by noting that when examining informant evidence used to support a claim of probable cause for a warrant, or a warrantless arrest, the skepticism and careful scrutiny usually found in cases involving informants, sometimes anonymous, from the criminal milieu, is appropriately relaxed if the informant is an identified victim or ordinary citizen witness."[17]

Witness not unreliable just because he was intoxicated

"Although it is possible that an angry and intoxicated person may be less reliable than a detached uninterested observer who is sober, it is equally possible that those same factors can make a witness more inclined to be truthful than they otherwise might."[18]

Defendant has a right to cross examine witness who provided "testimony"

Domestic battery victim's written statements in affidavit given to police officer were testimonial, and therefore, defendant had a right to cross exam victim before statement could be used in court.[19]

13.7 Invocation Prior to Interrogation

The law is clear that a person may invoke his Fifth Amendment right against self-incrimination, whether or not he is in-custody. At the same time, he cannot invoke his "Miranda" rights prior to being in- custody and before interrogation is imminent.

---

[17] *Easton v. Boulder*, 776 F.2d 1441 (10th Cir. Colo. 1985).

[18] *Hale v. Kart*, 396 F.3d 721 (6th Cir. Mich. 2005).

[19] *Davis v. Washington*, 547 U.S. 813 (2006).

What does this mean in practice? It means that you must respect a person's desire to not incriminate himself, and if a person does not want to talk you must respect it. However, if you later arrest him and want to interrogate, then his previous "invocation" does not apply to Miranda. Therefore, you may Mirandize him and seek a waiver. If he waives, then it is a valid waiver and you may use what he says against him.

Finally, what if the suspect invokes his right to counsel, instead of his right against self-incrimination? First, remember, there is no right to counsel when a suspect has not been charged with a crime—so there is no invocation. Still, it may be a sign that the suspect may also want to invoke his right against self-incrimination, which exists 24/7.

⭐ LEGAL STANDARD

If the suspect invokes his right to remain silent before arrest, then:

- If the invocation is unambiguous,
- Scrupulously honor the request; and
- If he's still not in-custody, you may later try to interview him.

If the suspect invokes his right to counsel, then:

- Inform the suspect that he is free to hire a lawyer;
- Be aware that you cannot coerce the suspect to speak with you.

🏛 CASE EXAMPLES

Suspect pre-arrest invocation did not apply to arrest interrogation.
Suspect's request for lawyer prior to arrest was not a Miranda invocation.[20]

13.8 Ambiguous Invocations

If a suspect intends to invoke his rights, he must do so clearly, directly, and unambiguously (You're not a mind reader for God sakes!). Suspects that merely mention abstract ideas about their rights will not be viewed as actually invoking them. For example, if a suspect says, "Maybe I should get a lawyer." That's ambiguous and a reasonable person would not take that to mean the suspect wants a lawyer, but is merely thinking about getting one. Therefore, you may keep asking questions. As I side note, never respond with a phrase such as, "If I were you, I would not get a lawyer." If anything, tell him, "Look that's totally up to you, I cannot make that decision for you."

---

[20] *Bobby v. Dixon*, 132 S. Ct. 26 (2011).

🛡 LEGAL STANDARD

A Miranda invocation is valid if:

- A suspect invoked his right to silence or counsel in an unambiguous manner;
- In other words, the suspect must say, write, or do something that an objectively reasonable person would clearly know was intended as an invocation, not merely a question or verbalized inner-thoughts.

🏛 CASE EXAMPLES

Suspect must clearly invoke his rights

"The suspect must unambiguously request counsel. A statement either is such an assertion of the right to counsel or it is not...he must articulate his desire to have counsel present sufficiently clearly that a reasonable police officer in the circumstances would understand the statement to be a request for an attorney."[21]

Silence alone may not be enough to invoke Miranda

The fact that defendant was silent during first two hours and 45 minutes of three hour interview was insufficient to invoke his right to remain silent under Miranda.[22] Note: This could have gone either way, articulation is the key.

13.9   Suspect Invoked, Now What?

If you begin the interrogation process, and the suspect tells you he does not want to talk, you must not question him further. The only exception would be public safety questions and routine booking questions. However, the Supreme Court said that after a "significant period of time" you may reengage the suspect and seek a knowing and intelligent waiver as long as you "scrupulously honored" the suspect's prior invocation (left him alone).

On the other hand, if a suspect invokes his right to counsel, the interrogation must stop and there is no "cooling off" period while in custody. You are done. The only two exceptions are if he independently restarted the interrogation or you waited at least fourteen days after he was released from custody.

🛡 LEGAL STANDARD

If a suspect invokes his right to remain silent:

- All questioning must immediately cease;
- You may try to question him after an appropriate "cooling off" period. In one case, the Supreme Court found a two-hour period sufficient.[23]

---

[21] *Davis v. U.S.*, 114 S. Ct. 2350 (1994).
[22] *Berghuis v. Thompkins*, 130 S. Ct. 2250 (2010).
[23] *Michigan v. Mosley*, 423 U.S. 96 (1975).

If a suspect invokes his right to counsel:

- All questioning must immediately cease;
- There is no "cooling off" period and counsel must be present before further questioning;
- If suspect is released from jail, then his previous invocation is valid for fourteen days from the day he is released. This right is not "crime" specific—all questioning must cease.

 CASE EXAMPLES

Two-hour break, along with Miranda waiver, found to be sufficient

"After an interval of more than two hours, Mosley was questioned by another police officer at another location about an unrelated holdup murder. He was given full and complete Miranda warnings at the outset of the second interrogation. He was thus reminded again that he could remain silent and could consult with a lawyer and was carefully given a full and fair opportunity to exercise these options." Suspect gave a valid waiver.[24]

All questioning must cease if a suspect invokes right to counsel

"When an accused has invoked his right to have counsel present during a custodial interrogation, a valid waiver of that right cannot be established by showing only that he responded to further police- initiated custodial interrogation even if he has been advised of his rights. An accused, having expressed his desire to deal with the police only through counsel, is not subject to further interrogation by the authorities until counsel has been made available to him, unless the accused himself initiates further communication, exchanges, or conversations with the police."[25]

Request for counsel means that counsel be present during questioning

"When counsel is requested, interrogation must cease, and officials may not reinitiate interrogation without counsel present, whether or not the accused has consulted with his attorney. In context, the requirement that counsel be 'made available' to the accused refers not to the opportunity to consult with an attorney outside the interrogation room, but to the right to have the attorney present during custodial interrogation."[26]

Even if a suspect has a lawyer, police may seek a waiver

"Our precedents also place beyond doubt that the Sixth Amendment right to counsel may be waived by a defendant, so long as relinquishment of the right is voluntary, knowing, and intelligent. The defendant may waive the right whether or not he is already represented by counsel; the decision to waive need not itself be counseled."[27]

---

[24] *Michigan v. Mosley*, 423 U.S. 96 (1975).
[25] *Edwards v. Ariz.*, 451 U.S. 477 (1981).
[26] *Minnick v. Mississippi*, 498 U.S. 146 (1990).
[27] *Montejo v. Louisiana*, 556 U.S. 778 (2009).

13.10 Suspect Invoked, Now Wants to Talk

If a suspect unambiguously invokes his Miranda rights, questioning must cease. However, it's possible for a suspect to change his mind after invocation if you keep the below guidelines in mind.[28]

🛡 LEGAL STANDARD

A suspect is allowed to revoke his previous invocation if:

- The decision to revoke the invocation was made freely by the suspect and not because of undue police influence;
- The suspect wanted to open up a general discussion about the crime, as opposed to merely asking questions about routine matters regarding his custody; and
- You reread Miranda and obtained an express waiver.

🏛 CASE EXAMPLES

Suspect must initiate further communication with police

"An accused who requests an attorney, having expressed his desire to deal with the police only through counsel, is not subject to further interrogation by the authorities until counsel has been made available to him, unless the accused himself initiates further communication, exchanges, or conversations with the police.[29]

Question, "Well, what is going to happen to me now?" was general dialogue about crime

Suspect invoked his right to counsel. Later, he asked "Well, what is going to happen to me now?" Police spoke to him and he made incriminating statements. The courts held there was "no doubt in this case that in asking, "Well, what is going to happen to me now?", respondent "initiated" further conversation in the ordinary dictionary sense of that word."[30]

13.11 Intentional Versus Accidental Miranda Violations

Sometimes you will mistakenly interrogate a suspect without Miranda. If this happens then naturally that testimony may not be used. Courts separate the violations into two categories: intentional and unintentional. Depending on which rule you violated, you may still be able to obtain a valid Miranda waiver.

If you intentionally interrogate a suspect without Miranda as a tactic to gain a confession, or coerce the suspect, it will not matter that you later obtained a waiver, both confessions will be suppressed.

---

[28] *People v. Davis*, 46 Cal. 4th 539 (Cal. 2009).
[29] *Minnick v. Mississippi*, 498 U.S. 146 (1990).
[30] *Oregon v. Bradshaw*, 462 U.S. 1039 (1983).

If you accidentally fail to Mirandize you may be able to obtain a valid waiver later.[31] Courts will want to see that you "cleansed" the invalid interrogation. For example, by telling the suspect his previous answers will not be used and obtaining a new express waiver.

⭐ LEGAL STANDARD

If you intentionally interrogate a suspect without Miranda, then:

- It will not matter that you later obtained a waiver, both confessions will be suppressed.

If you unintentionally interrogate a suspect without Miranda, then:

- You may be able to obtain a valid waiver later if you "cleansed" the invalid interrogation (*e.g.*, tell him previous statement won't be used).

🏛 CASE EXAMPLES

Intentional interrogation without Miranda, in order to "soften up" suspect, is prohibited

Officers intentionally violated Miranda, so that later interrogation after Miranda would be easier. Such tactics violate Due Process and are prohibited.[32]

13.12 When to Provide Miranda Again

Generally, you do not have to "remind" a suspect of his Miranda rights during interrogation. If the suspect gave a knowing and intelligent waiver once, you are usually fine. However, during some complicated investigations the waiver may become "stale" and therefore courts may want to see follow-up waivers.

⭐ LEGAL STANDARD

A Miranda re-advisement may be appropriate when considering:

- A lot of time has passed between the waiver and suspect's statement;
- Significant interruptions in the continuity of investigation;
- Change in locations;
- Different officers interview the suspect; and
- Whether the suspect has later changed his testimony.

Note: Re-advisements are usually not needed unless multiple factors are present.

---

[31] *Or. v. Elstad*, 470 U.S. 298 (1985).
[32] *Missouri v. Seibert*, 542 U.S. 600 (2004).

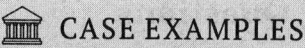 CASE EXAMPLES

Asking suspect if he remembered Miranda upheld

"Where defendant voluntarily appeared at police station to inquire of shooting and...led officer to believe that defendant's involvement was more than casual curiosity and thereupon officer read defendant's rights from a "Miranda card" after which defendant was questioned briefly and remained in station until investigation shifted to him as a prime suspect approximately two hours later and defendant was asked again if he had been advised of his rights and he answered in the affirmative, renewal of Miranda warnings was sufficient under the circumstances."[33]

13.13 Public Safety Exception

Miranda warnings are not required if you are asking legitimate public safety questions. The safety concern must be something that is pressing and will likely cause substantial bodily harm or death.

Stay away from "why" type questions since that has to do with motive, not public safety. "Why" questions usually violate Miranda. Also, remember that a suspect's answers to public safety questions may be used against him in court.

🛡 LEGAL STANDARD

An in-custody suspect may be interrogated without Miranda if:

- You ask about legitimate public safety concerns (*e.g.,* Where did you toss the gun near the school?);
- You do not ask "why" type questions, but instead focus on pressing public safety concerns;
- Once the public safety questions have been handled, Miranda will be required for further questioning.

🏛 CASE EXAMPLES

Police lawfully asked suspect where he ditched the gun

The Supreme Court crafted an exception to Miranda for situations where a suspect's silence may imminently endanger the public or police. After cornering a rape suspect in a supermarket, police found that the suspect, reported to be armed, was wearing an empty holster. Without first giving him Miranda warnings, police asked him where he had ditched the gun. He responded, "the gun is over there," and gestured toward a stack of empty cartons. Behind the cartons, police found a loaded revolver and his admission was admitted against him at trial.[34]

---

[33] *State v. Dixon*, 107 Ariz. 415 (Ariz. 1971).
[34] *N.Y. v. Quarles*, 467 U.S. 649 (1984).

13.14 Routine Booking Questions

Police may ask routine biological information in order to complete booking and pre-trial services. However, if the information is not needed for booking, and would likely produce an incriminating response, it is considered interrogation.[35]

🛡 LEGAL STANDARD

An in-custody suspect may be asked questions during the booking process without Miranda if:

- The questions seek routine biological information in order to complete booking and pre-trial services;
- If the information is not needed for booking, and would likely produce an incriminating response, it is considered interrogation.

🏛 CASE EXAMPLES

Questions about where suspect worked not proper booking question

The suspect was arrested after he solicited sex from an underage teenager on the internet. During an interrogation, he invoked his right to counsel twice. Subsequently, the detective asked him various questions from the booking sheet, including where he worked. This information was used at trial. The court of appeals found this was a Miranda violation, and suppressed the evidence.[36]

A request for basic information is not interrogation

"A request for routine information necessary for basic identification purposes is not interrogation under Miranda, even if the information turns out to be incriminating. Only if the government agent should reasonably be aware that the information sought … is directly relevant to the offense charged, will the question be subject to scrutiny."[37]

13.15 Evidence Discovered after Miranda Violation

The Exclusionary rule applies to Fourth Amendment violations, and Miranda is a Fifth Amendment right. Therefore, if a police officer interrogates a suspect without obtaining a Miranda waiver then only the testimony cannot be used. Any evidence found as a result of the testimony may be admitted at trial.

Remember, the seizure of any evidence must be done legally and this type of conduct is highly discouraged. In fact, in one extreme case the 9th Circuit has allowed lawsuits against police officers who intentional violate Miranda.[38]

---

[35] *Pa. v. Muniz*, 496 U.S. 582 (1990).
[36] *U.S. v. Hart*, 2009 U.S. Dist. LEXIS 72473 (W.D. Ky. Aug. 17, 2009).
[37] *U.S. v. Johnson*, 2008 U.S. Dist. LEXIS 110421 (D.S.D. July 10, 2008).
[38] *Cooper v. Dupnik*, 963 F.2d 1220 (9th Cir. Ariz. 1992).

Additionally, flagrant conduct by officers may be seen as a Due Process violation, subject to a civil rights lawsuit and suppression of evidence. Do not use this as evidence-gathering tactic.

⭐ LEGAL STANDARD

Evidence discovered from an un-Mirandized interrogation will not be suppressed if:

- The suspect was not coerced or compelled to speak; and
- There were no other flagrant police conduct that would violate Due Process.

🏛 CASE EXAMPLES

Miranda violation does not apply to physical evidence

The Fifth Amendment is not violated by introduction of physical evidence obtained as result of voluntary statements; thus, failure to give suspect Miranda warnings does not require suppression of evidence found after suspect's unwarned but voluntary statements.[39]

---

[39] *U.S. v. Patane*, 542 U.S. 630 (2004).

Chapter 14
Law Enforcement Liability

14.1 Exclusionary Rule

The exclusionary rule states that evidence obtained in violation of the Fourth Amendment (and in extreme circumstances, Due Process) is inadmissible in a criminal trial. The purpose of the rule "is to deter future unlawful police conduct and thereby effectuate the guarantee of the Fourth Amendment against unreasonable searches and seizures."[1]

The Fourth Amendment also seeks to "safeguard the privacy and security of individuals against arbitrary invasions by government officials."

Before a suspect may rely on the exclusionary rule, they must have "standing" to object. In other words, the suspect must have a legitimate privacy interest in the place or thing searched or seized. Without this "skin in the game" the suspect lacks standing, and the exclusionary rule will provide no relief.

Finally, even when police violate the Fourth Amendment, and the suspect has standing to object to using the evidence, there are many exclusionary rule exceptions that may come into play. If so, the evidence may still be used against the suspect. But remember, since using an exception typically means that a Fourth Amendment violation occurred, the suspect may still be able to sue you in a 1983 lawsuit. You do not need that stress. Use this book, get additional training, and comply with the Constitution.

⬟ LEGAL STANDARD

Evidence obtained by police may be excluded if:

- You obtained the evidence illegally, particularly in violation of the Fourth Amendment;
- Excluding evidence will serve a deterrent effect for future unlawful police conduct; and
- The evidence is primarily introduced as evidence in a criminal trial against the defendant.

🏛 CASE EXAMPLES

Despite unlawful detention, evidence of assault on LEO will not be suppressed as fruit of poisonous tree

"There are limitations to the exclusionary rule which are largely based on common sense. One such limitation is that the rule does not immunize crimes of violence

---

[1] *U.S. v. Calandra*, 414 U.S. 338 (1974).

committed on a peace officer, even if they are preceded by a Fourth Amendment violation.[2]

Fact that evidence is vital for a prosecution does not weigh on the exclusionary rule

Federal prosecutors argued that if evidence was suppressed under the exclusionary rule, they would not be able to prosecute the case. The court dismissed this "necessity" argument. If there is a violation, the exclusionary rule applies no matter the consequences.[3]

Exclusionary rule does not apply if police rely on binding legal authority

If police search or seize in an objectively reasonable reliance on binding court authority, which is later overruled, the exclusionary rule does not apply because there is no need to deter unlawful police activity.[4]

For example, where police placed a GPS-tracker on a vehicle without a warrant in reliance of then Supreme Court precedent involving "homing beacons," tracking data should not be suppressed even though the Court later held warrantless GPS tracking offended the Fourth Amendment.[5]

The exclusionary rule does not apply to violations of state or federal statutes unless the state legislature or congress specifically required exclusion

The Fourth Amendment is controlled the Constitution, not by statutes. Therefore, even when police violate a statute the result is not automatic exclusion of evidence unless the legislature intended that result.[6] Additionally, even if a violation of state law requires suppression, that same law has no effect on federal court proceedings.[7]

14.2 Exceptions to the Exclusionary Rule

The exclusionary rule states that evidence obtained as a result of an illegal search and/or seizure is inadmissible in a criminal trial. This rule is meant to deter police misconduct.[8] But there are several exceptions.

---

[2] *In re Richard G.*, 173 Cal. App. 4th 1252 (2009), as modified (May 20, 2009).
[3] *U.S. v. Marts*, 986 F.2d 1216 (8th Cir. 1993).
[4] *Davis v. U.S.*, 564 U.S. 229 (2011).
[5] *U.S. v. Aguiar*, 737 F.3d 251 (2d Cir. 2013).
[6] *Penn. Steel Foundary and Mach. Co. v. Sec. of Labor*, 831 F.2d 1211 (3d Cir. 1987).
[7] *U.S. v. McMurray*, 34 F.3d 1405 (8th Cir. 1994).
[8] *U.S. v. Janis*, 428 U.S. 433 (1976).

> ### ⭐ LEGAL STANDARD
>
> Some of the exceptions to the exclusionary rule, include:
>
> - The defendant has no standing to object;
> - Evidence can be used to impeach a defendant;
> - Good faith exception;[9]
> - Foreign searches;
> - Forfeiture proceedings;[10]
> - Inevitable discovery;
> - Deportation proceedings;
> - Grand juries;[11]
> - Civil tax proceedings.

14.3   Fruit of the Poisonous Tree

The exclusionary rule forbids the admission of illegally obtained evidence. The "fruit of the poisonous tree" doctrine says that any evidence found as a consequence of the first illegal search or seizure will also be suppressed.

This can get a little confusing but remember this, all illegally obtained evidence will usually be suppressed.

> ### ⭐ LEGAL STANDARD
>
> Derivative evidence will be excluded as evidence if:
>
> - You discovered evidence subject to the exclusionary rule;
> - That evidence led you to discover additional (*i.e.,* derivative) evidence; and
> - There are no applicable exceptions.

> ### 🏛 CASE EXAMPLES
>
> **Observations after unlawful entry cannot be used**
>
> Observations made after an unlawful, warrantless entry into a structure cannot be used to establish probable cause for later obtaining a search warrant.[12]
>
> **All evidence tainted after unlawful arrest**
>
> Where defendant was unlawfully arrested, evidence recovered from his person, incriminating statements, and the products of a search warrant that used all the above as part of its probable cause, were subject to being suppressed.[13]

---

[9] *U.S. v. Leon*, 468 U.S. 897 (1984).
[10] *One 1958 Plymouth Sedan v. Pennsylvania*, 380 U.S. 693 (1965).
[11] *U.S. v. Calandra*, 414 U.S. 338 (1974).
[12] *Murray v. U.S.*, 487 U.S. 533 (1988).
[13] *U.S. v. Nora*, 765 F.3d 1049 (9th Cir. Cal. 2014).

14.4 Standing to Object

In order for a defendant to challenge the constitutionality of a search or seizure he must show that he had some "skin in the game." In other words, the actual search and seizure must have intruded into area where he had a legitimate expectation of privacy.

It is helpful to the prosecution to ask ownership questions in the field. If someone denies ownership of a bag, backpack, car, *etc.*, that may help show he did not have standing to object to the search or seizure (even if he legally owned the item).

★ LEGAL STANDARD

When an unlawful search and seizure occurs, only people with "standing" may take advantage of the exclusionary rule. Generally, standing exists based on the following factors:[14]

- The defendant has a property interest in the thing seized or the place searched;
- He has a right to exclude others from the thing seized or the place searched;
- He exhibited a subjective expectation that the item would remain free from governmental intrusion; and
- He took normal precautions to maintain privacy in the item; Whether he was legitimately on the premises.

🏛 CASE EXAMPLES

Defendant that visited apartment to conduct drug transaction had no reasonable expectation of privacy in premises

Defendants "were obviously not overnight guests, but were essentially present for a business transaction [drugs] and were only in the home a matter of hours. There is no suggestion that they had a previous relationship with [the apartment occupants], or that there was any other purpose to their visit.[15]

14.5 Good Faith Exception

The Supreme Court outlined a "good faith exception" to the exclusionary rule.[16] For example, when police, in good faith, relied upon a warrant that was later found to be defective (*e.g.*, lacked probable cause) any evidence found may be admitted during the trial.

The good faith exception also applies when police rely upon an existing law that is later found to be unconstitutional. It would serve no useful purpose to exclude evidence under these circumstances since there is no police misconduct.

---

[14] *People v. Roybal*, 19 Cal. 4th 481 (Cal. 1998).
[15] *Minnesota v. Carter*, 525 U.S. 83 (1998).
[16] *United States v. Leon*, 468 U.S. 897 (1984).

⭐ **LEGAL STANDARD**

The "good faith" exception typically applies to warrants and has three requirements:

- You exhibited good faith in your actions, and were objectively reasonable in those beliefs;
- The warrant was issued by a neutral and detached magistrate; and
- The warrant must not have been so lacking in probable cause that a reasonable officer would have known that the existence of probable cause was unreasonable.

🏛 **CASE EXAMPLES**

"Good faith" is based on objective reasonableness

In evaluating a "good faith" claim, the courts will look to whether a "reasonably well trained officer would have known that the search was illegal" in light of all the circumstances. The officer's subjective belief is not a consideration. The inquiry looks to the objective facts only, which can include a particular officer's knowledge and experience but not the officer's subjective intent or belief.[17]

14.6 Attenuation

A court may admit evidence discovered after an illegal police search or seizure if the prosecution can show that there was no significant relationship between the unlawful conduct and the discovery of the evidence. This is known as attenuation or an "intervening circumstance."[18]

⭐ **LEGAL STANDARD**

The attenuation doctrine may save evidence from the exclusionary rule based on a review of the following factors:

- How much time was there between your unlawful search and seizure and the discovery of the evidence? The more time the better;
- Was there intervening circumstances having nothing to do with the unlawful conduct? If so, that's good; and
- What was the purpose and flagrancy of your misconduct? Honest mistakes are better than sloppy police practices.

---

[17] *Herring v. U.S.*, 555 U.S. 135 (2009).
[18] *U.S. v. Ceccolini*, 435 U.S. 268 (1978).

CASE EXAMPLES

Arrest warrant attenuated illegal detention

"While Officer Fackrell's decision to initiate the stop was mistaken, his conduct thereafter was lawful ... Moreover, there is no indication that this unlawful stop was part of any systemic or recurrent police misconduct. To the contrary, all the evidence suggests that the stop was an isolated instance of negligence that occurred in connection with a bona fide investigation of a suspected drug house ... Applying these factors, we hold that the evidence discovered on Strieff's person was admissible because the unlawful stop was sufficiently attenuated by the pre-existing arrest warrant."[19]

Arrest warrant attenuated unlawful stop of passenger

Unlawful stop of passenger did not require the suppression of evidence found on his person after he was arrested for an outstanding warrant. The evidence was found because of the warrant, not the illegal stop.[20]

14.7 Inevitable or Independent Discovery

The exclusionary rule forbids the admission of illegally obtained evidence. However, if the prosecution can show that the evidence would have been discovered irrespective of the illegal conduct, the evidence will not be suppressed.[21]

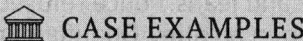

LEGAL STANDARD

The inevitable discovery doctrine may save evidence from the exclusionary rule if:

- There was a standard procedure (*e.g.*, vehicle inventory) in effect that would have inevitably discovered the same evidence.

The independent discovery doctrine may save evidence from the exclusionary rule if:

- At the time of the misconduct, there was an independent line of police investigation underway which developed facts which would have led to the discovery of the evidence.

CASE EXAMPLES

Police search party would have discovered tainted evidence

Police violated Miranda rights and suspect eventually identified child's buried location. Evidence not suppressed because police had a search party in the area and

---

[19] *Utah v. Strieff*, 136 S. Ct. 2056 (2016).
[20] *People v. Brendlin*, 45 Cal.4th 262 (2008).
[21] *See People v. Weiss*, 20 Cal. 4th 1073 (1999).

would have likely discovered the remains anyway. Of course, suspect's admission where body was buried was suppressed.[22]

Evidence admissible if police show they would have gotten a warrant

"The doctrine may even apply where the subsequent search that inevitably would have uncovered the disputed evidence required a warrant and the police had probable cause to obtain this warrant...if the government produces evidence that the police would have obtained the necessary warrant absent the illegal search."[23]

14.8   Duty to Protect

You have no legal or constitutional obligation to protect people from harm caused by third-party, non-governmental actors.[24] This is true even if the injury was caused in your presence and you "could have done something." It is only at the point that you actually get involved, or somehow placed the third-party in harm, that you may be held liable. Though, of course, I am not advocating not doing your job—just pointing out a liability principle.

🛡 LEGAL STANDARD

There may be a duty to protect a person from harm if:

- A special relationship exists because you seized the person; or
- You created or enhanced the danger suffered by the person.

🏛 CASE EXAMPLES

Police not liable for death of TPO victim

A suspect violated a TPO and fled before police arrived. The suspect returned later and killed the applicant, even though police did not look for the suspect. Police had no special relationship with victim, and therefore were not liable.[25]

Police liable for ejected bar patron that froze to death

Police were called about a drunk patron at a bar. Police ejected the patron into freezing weather in only a t-shirt and jeans. Police refused to give him his jacket. He was found dead the next morning in an alley. Qualified immunity denied.[26]

---

[22] *Nix v. Williams*, 467 U.S. 431 (1984).
[23] *U.S. v. Jones*, 2016 U.S. Dist. LEXIS 71181 (W.D. Pa. June 1, 2016).
[24] *Deshaney v. Winnebago County Dep't of Social Services*, 489 U.S. 189 (1989).
[25] *Town of Castle Rock v. Gonzales*, 545 U.S. 748 (2005).
[26] *Munger v. City of Glasgow Police Dep't*, 227 F.3d 1082 (9th Cir. Mont. 2000).

Police liable after returning naked and beaten minor back to assailant

In a bizarre case in the extreme, police detained a naked and beaten minor during an investigation, then released him to his assailant, Jeffrey Dahmer (before police knew who he really was). After police left, victim was killed. Court found special relationship existed and parents could sue police.[27] Whoops.

14.9 Duty to Intervene

You must intervene on behalf of a person whose constitutional rights are being violated by another law enforcement officer (including outside agencies). If not, you may be held vicariously liable and sued. This topic is a touchy one and no cop wants to be put in this situation. But remember, if you have to get involved it's not you that caused it, it's the other officer who failed to follow the rules. At the end of the day it's your career, your family, and your agency you need to protect.

⭐ LEGAL STANDARD

You may be liable for failure to intervene if:

1. You witness a **clear violation** of a civil or federal right;
2. You had an **opportunity** to intervene;
3. The person violating the rights is **law enforcement**; and
4. You fail to make a **reasonable intervention**.

🏛 CASE EXAMPLES

An officer must intervene, if they have an opportunity

A police officer "has a duty under § 1983 'to intervene to prevent a false arrest or the use of excessive force if the officer is informed of the facts that establish a constitutional violation and has the ability to prevent it.' Thus, in an excessive force case, a police officer who is present and does not intervene to stop other officers from infringing the constitutional rights of citizens is liable under § 1983 if the officer had reason to know "that excessive force was being used,...and the officer had a realistic opportunity to intervene to prevent the harm from occurring."[28]

The law requiring intervention is clearly established

"It is not necessary that a police officer actually participate in the use of excessive force in order to be held liable under section 1983. Rather, an officer who is present at the scene and who fails to take reasonable steps to protect the victim of

---

[27] *Sinthasomphone v. Milwaukee*, 785 F. Supp. 1343 (W.D. Wis. 1992).
[28] *Smith v. Hunt*, 2010 U.S. Dist. LEXIS 101526 (N.D. Ill. Sept. 27, 2010).

another officer's use of excessive force, can be held liable for his nonfeasance [*i.e.*, just standing there and watching]."[29]

14.10 Supervisor Liability

Supervisors must supervise. If you fail to document misconduct or take corrective actions against a subordinate, you may be held liable for similar future misconduct even if you weren't directly involved.[30]

★ LEGAL STANDARD

Supervisors may be liable for a subordinate's actions if:

- You had actual or constructive knowledge that a subordinate was engaged in conduct that posed a pervasive or unreasonable risk of constitutional violations;
- Your lack of response showed a deliberate indifference or tacit approval of the subordinate's conduct; and
- There was a causal link between your inaction and the injury.

🏛 CASE EXAMPLES

Supervisor may be liable for failure to supervise

A supervisor may be held liable for the alleged unconstitutional acts of his subordinates if plaintiffs demonstrate an "affirmative link" that he actively participated or acquiesced in the constitutional violation. That "affirmative link" can be shown through the supervisor's personal participation, his exercise of control or direction, or his failure to supervise.[31]

Not liable for mere negligent supervision

"Supervisors who are merely negligent in failing to detect and prevent subordinates' misconduct are not liable."[32]

14.11 Unequal Enforcement of the Law

You will sometimes be criticized because you are not enforcing a law on everyone. For example, if you pull a subject over for speeding a common defense is that another person was speeding faster. This attack on your discretion is usually not a Fourth Amendment violation. In order to succeed, the suspect would have to prove

---

[29] *Fundiller v. City of Cooper City*, 777 F.2d 1436, 1441-42 (11th Cir. 1985).
[30] *Shaw v. Stroud*, 13 F.3d 791 (4th Cir. N.C. 1994).
[31] *Holland v. Harrington*, 268 F.3d 1179 (10th Cir. Colo. 2001).
[32] *Morfin v. City of E. Chicago*, 349 F.3d 989 (7th Cir. Ind. 2003).

you had no rational basis for choosing him over another suspect. In reality, this is a very difficult thing to prove.

⬟ LEGAL STANDARD

A claim that a law was unequally enforced against a person in violation of the Equal Protection Clause must prove:

- The plaintiff was treated differently from others similarly situated; and
- There was no rational basis for the different treatment (rational basis is an easy test to satisfy).

Note: A "rational basis" could simply be that you can only enforce the law on one person at a time.

🏛 CASE EXAMPLES

Towing just one car is not unequal enforcement

Noble argues that the Mayor did not like him and that's why he ordered his car towed. As it stands, "[a]ll it takes to defeat [Noble's] claim is a conceivable rational basis for the difference in treatment ... If we can come up with a rational basis for the challenged action, that will be the end of the matter ... a rational basis for the difference in treatment is that the Village cannot be expected to tow every inoperable vehicle at once."[33]

14.12 Behavior that "Shocks the Conscious"

You may be liable if you had an intent and purpose to cause harm unrelated to the legitimate object of the arrest, or use of force. This standard is much higher than gross negligence or deliberate indifference and is difficult for a plaintiff to meet.

⬟ LEGAL STANDARD

Some police behavior is so appalling that it will violate the Due Process Clause, even without a specific Fourth Amendment violation.[34] Here, the standard is:

- You had an intent and purpose to cause harm; and
- This purpose was unrelated to the legitimate object of arrest.

---

[33] *Noble v. Vill. of Elliott*, 605 Fed. Appx. 572 (7th Cir. Ill. 2015).
[34] *County of Sacramento v. Lewis*, 523 U.S. 833 (1998).

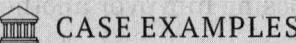

CASE EXAMPLES

Illegal home entry and stomach pumping shocked the conscious

"This is conduct that shocks the conscience: Illegally breaking into the privacy of a petitioner, the struggle to open his mouth and remove what was there, the forcible extraction of his stomach's contents—this course of proceeding by agents of government to obtain evidence is bound to offend even hardened sensibilities."[35]

Digital rectum searches on prisoners shocked the conscious

"Under the facts as alleged by Vaughan, a reasonable prison official in 1984 would have understood that the [rectum] searches were conducted in a brutal fashion that was not justified by a need for force. The extent of possible injury was great, and at least one inmate suffered significant injury. The joking and insults directed at the inmates support an inference that the force was maliciously and sadistically applied."[36]

14.13   Deliberate Indifference

A police agency may be liable for a constitutional violation where the officer's actions were deliberately indifferent to the plaintiff. In plain English, this means that the agency had a policy or custom that deprived the plaintiff of a constitutional or federally protected right.

LEGAL STANDARD

An agency has been deliberately indifferent to the plaintiff if:

- The agency had a policy or custom, or lack of policy;
- which denied the plaintiff a constitutional or federally protected right;
- This right was foreseeable; and
- That deprivation must have caused the plaintiff's injury.

CASE EXAMPLES

Whether an agency is deliberately indifferent depends on what tasks employees are expected to perform

"We hold today that the inadequacy of police training may serve as the basis for §1983 liability only where the failure to train amounts to deliberate indifference to the rights of persons with whom the police come into contact ... In resolving the issue of a city's liability, the focus must be on adequacy of the training program in relation to the tasks the particular officers must perform"[37]

---

[35] *Rochin v. California*, 342 U.S. 165 (1952).
[36] *Vaughan v. Ricketts*, 859 F.2d 736 (9th Cir. Ariz. 1988).
[37] *Monell v. Department of Social Services*, 436 U.S. 658 (1978).

Mere negligence, or isolated deprivations, will not result in agency liability

"That a particular officer may be unsatisfactorily trained will not alone suffice to fasten liability on the city, for the officer's shortcomings may have resulted from factors other than a faulty training program...Neither will it suffice to prove that an injury or accident could have been avoided if an officer had had better or more training."[38]

14.14 Sharing Crime Scene Photos on Social Media

You may be held civilly liable for taking pictures of crime scenes and sharing them with friends or other outsiders, when not in the course of official business. Additionally, the defense may subpoena your personal cell phone for inspection.

Do not take pictures of any crime scene with your phone, it is unprofessional and may get you fired and/or sued.

★ LEGAL STANDARD

A lawsuit may be commenced if offensive investigation photos are shared with friends or on social media. The elements are:

- The photos end up shared on a public platform, like Facebook;
- The photos contain information not generally available to the public;
- The information is offensive or objectionable to a reasonable person; and
- There are no applicable First Amendment protections.

🏛 CASE EXAMPLES

CHP officer liable for sharing accident scene photos with friends

Once photographic evidence is collected, it is not the role of the CHP...to distribute that evidence to friends and family members. [And] it is not the role of the CHP to put the parents and siblings of the decedent at risk of harm of seeing the grotesque death images of their deceased loved one made the subject of Internet spectacle.[39]

14.15 Section 1983 Civil Rights Violations

"1983" civil lawsuits are based on Federal code 42 U.S.C. § 1983. It is a common lawsuit and provides citizens with a remedy for violations of constitutionally protected rights.

---

[38] *Monell v. Department of Social Services*, 436 U.S. 658 (1978).
[39] *Catsouras v. Department of CHP*, 181 Cal. App. 4th 856 (2010).

Even if there is no real "damage" you may still be sued. For example, during a knock and talk you notice the garage door is open and without consent you enter and knock on the garage's interior door. This is a clear violation of the Fourth Amendment (warrantless entry), yet a court may award $1 in nominal damages. But his attorney may get "reasonable attorney's fees" and that could cost your agency tens of thousands of dollars.

⭐ LEGAL STANDARD

A § 1983 civil rights suit may be commenced if:

- You violated a constitutionally or federally protected right; and
- You were acting under the color of law (*i.e.*, you were on duty).

🏛 CASE EXAMPLES

Probable cause is absolute defense for false arrest

Probable cause is an absolute defense to any claim under § 1983 for wrongful arrest or false imprisonment.[40]

A violation of the law may still be actionable under § 1983

Thirteen police officer made a warrantless entry into suspects home in the middle of the night, ransacked his house, and took him to the station house for questioning. Even though this violated state law, the officers were still held liable for a constitutional rights violation.[41]

14.16   Section 242 Criminal Charges

If you intentionally violate a person's constitutionally or federally protected rights, you may be charged criminally under 18 U.S.C. § 242. Under a § 1983 suit, the plaintiff does not need to prove intent, here, he does. That's why the DOJ reserves these actions for the most egregious bad actors.

Remember Rodney King? Initially the LAPD cops were charged under state criminal statutes and were acquitted. That's when the DOJ came in and convicted the officers under § 242. Not good.

---

[40] *Bailey v. City of Chicago*, 779 F.3d 689 (7th Cir. Ill. 2015).
[41] *Monroe v. Pape*, 365 U.S. 167 (1961).

🛡 LEGAL STANDARD

The federal government may file a criminal charge if:

- You intentionally violate a person's constitutionally or federally protected rights; and
- You were acting under the color of law (*i.e.*, you were on duty).

🏛 CASE EXAMPLES

Koon v. United States

"On August 4, 1992, a federal grand jury indicted the four officers under 18 U.S.C. § 242, charging them with violating King's constitutional rights under color of law. Powell, Briseno, and Wind were charged with willful use of unreasonable force in arresting King. Koon was charged with willfully permitting the other officers to use unreasonable force during the arrest. After a trial in United States District Court for the Central District of California, the jury convicted Koon and Powell but acquitted Wind and Briseno."[42]

14.17 Bringing Non-Essential Personnel Into the Home

Generally, you may not take non-essential personnel into an area protected by the Fourth Amendment, particularly a home.

🛡 LEGAL STANDARD

It is a constitutional violation if:

- You entered a constitutional protected area (*e.g.*, home); and
- You invited non-essential personnel (*e.g.*, media) without consent.

🏛 CASE EXAMPLES

Bringing media into the home is a violation

"It is a violation of [Fourth Amendment] for police to bring members of the media or other third parties into a home" while police perform their duties.[43]

Evidence will not be excluded if media violate this rule

A Guam Police Department search warrant resulted in one of the largest busts of stolen items in Guam's history. The "woefully inadequate" management of the search

---

[42] *Koon v. U.S.*, 518 U.S. 81 (1996).
[43] *Wilson v. Layne*, 526 U.S. 603 (1999).

of the residence attracted members of the media and victims who came to claim their property while the two-day execution of the warrant was ongoing.

Although the conduct of the search was highly questionable, given the participation of the public and the media, the district court did not err by deciding not to exclude the stolen items, drugs, and other paraphernalia found in the compound.[44]

14.18 Qualified Immunity

You work in a dynamic and unpredictable environment. Therefore, you encounter situations where you are tasked to solve unique problems despite no direct training or case law to guide them. Qualified immunity protects you whenever you venture into constitutionally unchartered territories.

⭐ LEGAL STANDARD

Even if a constitutional violation occurred and evidence is suppressed under the exclusionary rule, there is no § 1983 violation when:

- You violated a constitutionally or federally right; but
- That right was not clearly established at the time of the violation.

🏛 CASE EXAMPLES

Officer that attempted knock and talk on side door, versus front door, entitled to qualified immunity

It is an open, undecided issue, with authority going both ways, as to whether it is lawful for an officer to conduct a "knock and talk" at other than the front door. A trooper was sued by homeowners because he knocked on a side door, instead of the front door. The Supreme Court determined that the officer was entitled to qualified immunity in that the issue is the subject of conflicting authority.[45]

No qualified immunity for prison guard who obviously violated rights

Guard who handcuffed shirtless prisoner to hitching post as punishment not eligible for qualified immunity since it obviously violated the Fourth Amendment.[46]

---

[44] *U.S. v. Duenas*, 691 F.3d 1070 (9th Cir. Guam 2012).
[45] *Carroll v. Carman*, 135 S. Ct. 348 (2014).
[46] *Hope v. Pelzer*, 536 U.S. 730 (2002).

Chapter 15
Legal Checklists

15.1 Consensual Encounters

15.1.1 Generally

A consensual encounter does not violate the Fourth Amendment when:

✓ A reasonable person would believe he was free to leave or otherwise terminate the encounter. In other words, a reasonable person would have believed he was not detained.

15.1.2 Knock and Talks

Knock and talks are lawful when:

✓ The path used to reach the door does not violate curtilage and appears available for uninvited guests to use;
✓ If the house has multiple doors, you chose the door reasonably believed to be available for uninvited guests to make contact with an occupant;
✓ You used typical, non-intrusive methods to contact the occupant, including making contact during a socially acceptable time;
✓ Your conversation with the occupant remained consensual; and
✓ When the conversation ended or was terminated, you immediately left and did not snoop around.

15.1.3 Investigative Activities During Consensual Encounter

Questioning

Questioning a person does not convert a consensual encounter into an investigative detention as long as:

✓ Your questions are not overly accusatory in a manner that would make a reasonable person believe they were being detained for criminal activity.

Identification

Asking a person for identification does not convert a consensual encounter into an investigative detention as long as:

✓ The identification is requested, not demanded; and
✓ You returned the identification as soon as practicable, otherwise a reasonable person may no longer feel free to leave.

Consent to search

Asking a person for consent to search does not convert the encounter into an investigative detention as long as:

✓ The person's consent was freely and voluntarily given;
✓ He has apparent authority to give consent to search the area or item; and
✓ You did not exceed the scope provided, express or implied.

15.1.4 Asking for Identification

Asking a person for identification does not convert a consensual encounter into an investigative detention as long as:

✓ The identification is requested, not demanded; and
✓ You return the identification as soon as practicable, otherwise a reasonable person may no longer feel free to leave.

15.1.5 Removing Hands from Pockets

Asking a person to remove his hands from his pockets does not convert a consensual encounter into an investigative detention as long as:

✓ You requested that he remove his hands from his pockets; and
✓ You did it for officer safety purposes.

Ordering a person to remove his hands from his pockets may not convert a consensual encounter into an investigative detention if:

✓ You had a legitimate safety reason for ordering it; and
✓ You articulate that ordering the person to remove his hands was a minimal intrusion of his freedom.

15.1.6 Transporting to Police Station

You may voluntarily transport a person in a police vehicle. However, if the person is a suspect to a crime and you are transporting the person for an interview, remember:

✓ Make it clear to the person that he is not under arrest;
✓ Seek consent to patdown the suspect for weapons, if the patdown is denied, do not patdown and you probably should not transport.

15.1.7 Consent to Search

Asking a person for consent to search does not convert the encounter into an investigative detention as long as:

✓ The person's consent was freely and voluntarily given;
✓ He had apparent authority to give consent to search the area or item; and
✓ You did not exceed the scope provided, express or implied.

15.1.8 Third-Party Consent

Spouses and Co-Occupants:
Spouses or co-occupants may consent to search inside a home if:

✓ The person has apparent authority;

✓ Consent is only given for common areas, areas under his exclusive control, or areas or things the person has authorized access to; and

✓ A non-consenting spouse or co-occupant with the same or greater authority is not present.

15.1.9 Articulating Greater Authority

An occupant with greater authority over the premises may consent to search over areas either under his exclusive control or common areas if:

✓ The co-occupant had greater authority over the area searched;

✓ You did not enter or walk through any area where the non-consenting occupant had equal or greater authority;

✓ You did not search any property under the exclusive control of the non-consenting occupant; and

✓ Your search did not exceed the scope provided by the consenting occupant.

15.1.10 Mistaken Authority to Consent

If you mistakenly receive consent from a person who had "apparent authority," courts will employ a three-part analysis to determine if your mistake was reasonable:

✓ Did you believe some untrue fact;

✓ Was it objectively reasonable for you to believe that the fact was true under the circumstances at the time; and

✓ If it was true would the consent giver have had actual authority.

15.2 Investigative Detentions

15.2.1 Reasonable Suspicion Defined

Reasonable suspicion exists when:

✓ You can articulate facts and circumstances that would lead a reasonable officer to believe the suspect is, or is about to be involved in criminal activity;

✓ If your suspicions are dispelled, the person must be immediately released or the stop converted into a consensual encounter.

15.2.2 Detaining a Suspect

A suspect may be detained when:

✓ You can articulate facts and circumstances that would lead a reasonable officer to believe the suspect has, is, or is about to be involved in criminal activity;

✓ You use the minimal amount of force necessary to detain a cooperative suspect;

✓ Once the stop is made, you must diligently pursue a means of investigation that will confirm or dispel your suspicions;

✓ If your suspicions are dispelled, the person must be immediately released or the stop converted into a consensual encounter.

15.2.3 Duration of Detentions

The duration of an investigative detention is determined by these factors:

✓ Once the stop is made, you must diligently pursue a means of investigation that will confirm or dispel your suspicions;
✓ If your suspicions are dispelled, the person must be immediately released or the stop converted into a consensual encounter.

15.2.4 Investigative Techniques

You may conduct investigative techniques in the field when:

✓ The suspect is still lawfully detained; and
✓ The technique employed is minimally intrusive.

You may demand identification if:

✓ The suspect is still lawfully detained;
✓ You need the identification to pursue your investigation; and
✓ And failure to identify is an arrestable offense under applicable state law.

You may capture a suspects fingerprints in the field when:

✓ You have reason to believe fingerprints may have been left at the scene;
✓ Minimally intrusive means were used to recover the suspect's fingerprints; and
✓ The fingerprints will aid your investigation after the suspect is released.

15.2.5 Identifications in the Field

A suspect may be required to participate in solo in-field "show-up" if:

✓ The procedure is not overly suggestive of guilt (*e.g.*, not surrounding suspect with cops, if safe, removing handcuffs, and not telling the witness that the suspect is the perpetrator).

15.2.6 Unprovoked Flight

A suspect that flees upon seeing you may be detained if:

✓ You are patrolling a high-crime area;
✓ Upon seeing you or a readily-apparent police vehicle, the suspect suddenly, and without provocation;
✓ Engages in a headlong flight commensurate with evasion; and
✓ You use a reasonable amount of force necessary to detain the suspect.

15.2.7 Detentions Based on Anonymous Tip

A suspect may be detained based an anonymous tip if:

✓ The tip had an indicia of reliability; and
✓ The tip was sufficiently corroborated to show that the caller had information not readily available to the general public.

15.2.8 Handcuffing and Use of Force

If a suspect fights or flees during an investigative detention, then:

- ✓ You may use a reasonable amount of force to detain the suspect;
- ✓ The suspect's flight upon a lawful order to stop, or a battery upon an officer, may be probable cause to arrest; and
- ✓ Deadly force cannot be used to detain a suspect, unless the suspect poses a deadly force threat to you or others.

Handcuffing a suspect is appropriate when:

- ✓ The suspect appears to be a flight risk; or
- ✓ The suspect appears to be a danger to himself or others.

15.2.9 Detaining Victims or Witnesses

A witness may be detained if:

- ✓ He is a material witness for your investigation;
- ✓ The detention should last no longer than necessary to determine his identification and whether he's willing to cooperate with your investigation;
- ✓ If the witness is uncooperative, identify and release. Contact your prosecutor and get advice on how to proceed.

15.2.10 Patdown for Weapons

A suspect may be frisked for weapons under the following circumstances:

- ✓ If the suspect is lawfully or unlawfully armed with a weapon, the weapon may be secured and a patdown of outer clothing conducted for additional weapons;
- ✓ If no weapon is visible, and you believe the suspect is armed and dangerous, a patdown of outer clothing may be conducted; or
- ✓ If the suspect was stopped for a violent crime or one involving weapons, an automatic patdown may be conducted.

15.2.11 Patdown Based on Anonymous Tip

A suspect may be frisked based an anonymous tip if:

- ✓ The call states or implies that the suspect is engaged in criminal activity;
- ✓ The tip indicates the suspect is armed and dangerous;
- ✓ The tip had an indicia of reliability; and
- ✓ The tip was sufficiently corroborated to show that the caller had information not readily available to the general public.

15.2.12 Plain Touch Doctrine

Evidence or contraband discovered during a frisk is admissible if:

- ✓ Your frisk was lawfully conducted and limited to weapons;
- ✓ When you felt the item, it was immediately apparent that the item was contraband or evidence of a crime; and
- ✓ You did not build probable cause by manipulating the item.

15.2.13   Involuntary Transportation

Police may not involuntarily transport a suspect away from the location where he was stopped unless:

✓ You have legitimate exigent circumstances (rare). Involuntary transportation without exigency is an arrest, requiring probable cause.

15.3   Arrests

15.3.1   Entry into Home with Arrest Warrant

Entry into a home based on an arrest warrant is lawful when:

✓ You have probable cause that this is the suspect's home, and not a third-party's home (get a search warrant for third-party homes);
✓ You have reason to believe the suspect is home;
✓ You knock and announce;
✓ If appropriate, protective sweeps are permissible; and
✓ You may look for the suspect in people-sized places, but not search for evidence, but plain view seizure applies.

15.3.2   Warrantless Entry to Make Arrest

A warrantless entry into a home to make an arrest may be made under five circumstances:

Consent:

✓ You may enter if you have consent from an occupant with apparent authority over the premises and you make known your intention to arrest the suspect.

Hot Pursuit:

✓ You are in hot pursuit of a suspect believed to have committed an arrestable offense and he runs into a home (a surround and call-out may also be done for officer safety purposes).

Fresh Pursuit:

✓ You are in fresh pursuit of the suspect after investigating a serious violent crime and quickly trace the suspect back to his home.

Suspect will Escape:

✓ You have probable cause that the suspect committed a serious violent crime, and you reasonably believe he will escape before obtaining a warrant.

Undercover Officer - Immediate Reentry with Arrest Team

✓ You are an undercover officer and conduct a narcotics transaction inside the home, you may leave and immediately reenter with an arrest team when two conditions are met: First, there must be a legitimate officer safety reason why you had to leave first, instead of summoning the arrest team into the home and you must articulate that an exigency exists, such as destruction or loss of evidence.

Remember for all Uninvited Entries:

- ✓ Knock and announce rules apply; and
- ✓ You cannot search for evidence, but may make a plain view seizure.

15.3.3 Private Searches

Whether a private search becomes a government search depends on three factors:

- ✓ Did you direct or participate in the search or seizure? And,
- ✓ Did the private person conduct the search with the intent to help police or discover evidence? If so,
- ✓ Did you exceed the scope of the private search?

The first two factors must both be present for a private search to turn into a government search. The third factor will turn a private search into an unreasonable government search.

15.3.4 Collective Knowledge Doctrine

The collective knowledge has two requirements:

- ✓ The officers must be involved in the same investigation, but may be from different departments (*i.e.,* task forces); and
- ✓ Officers must be in communication with each other related to the investigation.

15.3.5 Meaning of "Committed in the Officer's Presence?"

An offense is committed within the officer's presence when:

- ✓ You observed or experienced an essential element of the crime through one of your senses, namely sight, smell, hearing, or touch.

15.3.6 Identifications

Photo Arrays

A photo array (*e.g.,* "six pack") may be done at any time, without probable cause, and without notifying a suspect's court-appointed counsel if:

- ✓ You minimized suggestive influences.

Physical Line-Ups

A suspect may be required to participate in a physical line-up if:

- ✓ You minimized suggestive influences;
- ✓ The suspect consents to the line-up or is lawfully arrested; and
- ✓ If the suspect has been arraigned, indicted, or appointed counsel, the attorney must be notified and allowed to attend, but not control, the line-up.

In-Field Show-Up

A suspect may be required to participate in solo in-field "show-up" if:

✓ You minimized suggestive influences (*e.g.*, not surrounding suspect with cops, if safe, removing handcuffs, and not telling the witness that the suspect is the culprit).

15.3.7 Protective Sweeps

A protective sweep may be made inside a home during an arrest under the following conditions:

✓ Zone 1: You may search the immediate vicinity where the suspect has access to weapons, evidence, or means of escape;
✓ Zone 2: You may search for people in people-sized places in the same area where the arrest occurs; and
✓ Zone 3: If you have reasonable suspicion that dangerous confederates are in the house, you may search for people in people-sized places and detain the confederates until the arrest is completed.

15.3.8 When to Unarrest a Suspect

An in-custody suspect must be released:

✓ If you discover new evidence that clearly eliminates probable cause the suspect must be released; or
✓ If you already booked the suspect, you must notify the prosecutor in writing.

An in-custody suspect may be release when:

✓ You made the arrest with the intent to book the suspect; and
✓ You learned of new facts or circumstances that warrant releasing the suspect with a citation or warning.
✓ Remember, you may not use an arrest-and-release as loophole to search the suspect without consent, exigency, or a search warrant.

15.3.9 Attempt to Swallow Drugs

When a suspect is arrested and unsecured, his vehicle may be searched if:

✓ The suspect is within the lunge distance of the vehicle;
✓ You reasonably believe the suspect may gain access to inside the vehicle; and
✓ You may search for weapons, evidence, and a means of escape.

When a suspect is arrested and secured, his vehicle may be searched if:

✓ You have reason to believe evidence of the crime for which he was arrested may be inside the vehicle;
✓ You do not exceed the scope of search necessary to find the evidence; and
✓ When you no longer have reason to believe evidence of the crime is inside the vehicle, the search must end unless you develop additional probable cause to search for something else.

15.4 Vehicles

15.4.1 Community Caretaking Stops

A vehicle may be stopped if:

✓ You have a reason to believe one of the occupants needs police or medical assistance; and
✓ Once you determine that no further assistance is required, the occupant must be left alone.

15.4.2 Reasonable Suspicion Stops

A vehicle and its occupants may be detained if:

✓ You can articulate facts and circumstances that would lead a reasonable officer to believe that one of the occupants has, is, or is about to be involved in criminal activity;
✓ Once the stop is made, you must diligently pursue a means of investigation that will confirm or dispel your suspicions;
✓ If your suspicions are dispelled, the occupants must be immediately released or the stop converted into a consensual encounter.

15.4.3 Controlling Passengers

Any occupant inside a vehicle may be ordered to stay, or exit vehicle if:

✓ The stop was based on reasonable suspicion or probable cause; and
✓ You can articulate any legitimate reason (*i.e.,* officer safety or need to interview separately).

15.4.4 Consent to Search Vehicle

A person may consent to search a vehicle if:

✓ It is reasonable to believe the driver or occupant has authority to consent to the search;
✓ The consent is freely and voluntarily given; and
✓ Your search did not exceed the scope of the consent provided, whether express or implied.

15.4.5 Frisking Vehicle and Occupants for Weapons

Any occupant may be frisked for weapons if:

✓ You can articulate that the occupant is armed and dangerous;
✓ You may only pat down the suspect's outer clothing; and
✓ A frisk may include inside the passenger compartment, including containers, where a weapon may be retrieved.

15.4.6 K9 Sniff Around Vehicle

If no reasonable suspicion exists that drug evidence is inside the vehicle, then:

✓ You may conduct a free-air sniff around the vehicle as long as there is no break in the investigation that led to the stop; and

✓ The free-air sniff must not extend the stop.

If reasonable suspicion exists that drug evidence is inside the vehicle, then:

✓ You may continue to detain the vehicle for a reasonable amount of time for a drug canine to arrive on scene; and

✓ You may conduct a free-air sniff around the vehicle, but may not make a physical intrusion in or on the vehicle without probable cause.

15.4.7 Searching Vehicle Incident to Arrest

When a suspect is arrested and unsecured, his vehicle may be searched if:

✓ The suspect is within the lunge distance of the vehicle;

✓ You reasonably believe the suspect may gain access to inside the vehicle; and

✓ You may search for weapons, evidence, and a means of escape.

When a suspect is arrested and secured, his vehicle may be searched if:

✓ You have reason to believe evidence of the crime for which he was arrested may be inside the vehicle;

✓ You do not exceed the scope of search necessary to find the evidence; and

✓ When you no longer have reason to believe evidence of the crime is inside the vehicle, the search must end unless you develop additional probable cause to search for something else.

15.4.8 Searching Vehicle with Probable Cause

A vehicle may be searched without a warrant if:

✓ You have probable cause that contraband or evidence is inside the vehicle;

✓ You have lawful access to the vehicle (i.e., not within curtilage or in a backyard);

✓ The vehicle appears to be readily mobile (e.g., needs no more than gas, tires, or battery to become mobile); and

✓ Your search does not exceed the scope of the probable cause.

15.4.9 Inventories

A vehicle may be inventoried when:

✓ Your agency has a written inventory policy which minimizes your discretion;

✓ The policy describes what may be searched and inventoried; and

✓ If you have discretion to tow a particular vehicle, the inventory should not be primarily motivated by an intent to search for evidence instead of community caretaking.

15.4.10 Constructive Possession

Multiple occupants may be charged for constructively possessing contraband when:

✓ You articulate that there was at least a fair probability that the arrested occupant knew contraband was inside the vehicle; and

✓ The occupant could have possessed the contraband if he wanted to.

15.5 Homes

15.5.1 Knock and Talks

Knock and talks are lawful when:

✓ The path used to reach the door does not violate curtilage and appears available for uninvited guests to use;

✓ If the house has multiple doors, you chose the door reasonably believed to be available for uninvited guests to make contact with an occupant;

✓ You used typical, non-intrusive methods to contact the occupant, including making contact during a socially-acceptable time;

✓ Your conversation with the occupant remained consensual; and

✓ When the conversation ended or was terminated, you immediately left and did not snoop around.

15.5.2 Curtilage

Whether an area around a home is curtilage, protected by the Fourth Amendment, depends on weighing four factors:

✓ The proximity of the area to the home itself (closer the better);

✓ Whether the area is included within a single enclosure, natural or artificial, surrounding the home;

✓ The use of the area (e.g., BBQ pit, pool, kid's toys, etc.);

✓ Steps taken by the resident to protect the area from observations by people passing by (built high wooden fence, guard dog, etc.).

15.5.3 Plain View Seizure

Evidence may be seized if:

✓ Your protective sweep was lawful;

✓ The item was immediately apparent as evidence or contraband; and

✓ You had lawful access to the item.

15.5.4 Consent to Search by Co-Occupants

Spouses and Co-Occupants

Spouses or co-occupants may consent to search inside a home if:

✓ The person has apparent authority;

✓ Consent is only given for common areas, areas under his exclusive control, or areas or things the person has authorized access to; and

✓ A non-consenting spouse or co-occupant with the same of greater authority is not present.

Articulating Greater Authority

An occupant with greater authority over the premises may consent to search over areas either under his exclusive control or common areas if:

✓ The co-occupant had greater authority over the area searched;

✓ You did not enter or walk through any area where the non-consenting occupant had equal or greater authority;

✓ You did not search any property under the exclusive control of the non-consenting occupant; and

✓ Your search did not exceed the scope provided by the consenting occupant.

15.5.5   Protective Sweeps

A protective sweep may be made inside a home during an arrest under the following conditions:

✓ Zone 1: You may search the immediate vicinity where the suspect has access to weapons, evidence, or means of escape;

✓ Zone 2: You may search for people in people-sized places in the same area where the arrest occurs; and

✓ Zone 3: If you have reasonable suspicion that dangerous confederates are in the house, you may search for people in people-sized places and detain the confederates until the arrest is completed.

15.5.6   Warrantless Entry for Emergency

A warrantless entry into a home may be made when:

✓ You have reason to believe that any occupant is in immediate need of medical assistance or is threatened with imminent injury;

✓ Once the emergency is over, you must leave unless you receive consent or a warrant;

✓ Knock and announce rules apply; and

✓ You cannot search for evidence, but may make a plain view seizure.

15.5.7   Warrantless Entry to Prevent the Destruction of Evidence

A warrantless entry into a home or business may be made if:

✓ You have probable cause that an occupant is or is about to destroy evidence or contraband;

✓ You did not create the exigency;

✓ Once the home is secured, you must get a warrant;

✓ Knock and announce rules apply; and

✓ You cannot search for evidence, but may make a plain view seizure (or quickly photograph, leave it, and attach photo to affidavit).

15.5.8   Detaining a Home in Anticipation of Warrant

A residence may be detained in anticipation of a search warrant when:

✓ You have clear probable cause to get a search warrant;

✓ You have additional probable cause that the evidence or contraband will be destroyed or moved prior to executing the search warrant;

✓ You may not enter the residence unless you have a reason to believe the home is currently occupied;

✓ You must diligently apply for the warrant;

✓ Knock and announce rules apply; and

✓ You cannot search for evidence, but may make a plain view seizure.

15.6 Personal Property

15.6.1 Searching Containers

A container seized with probable cause that it contains contraband or evidence may not be searched without a warrant unless:

✓ Someone with apparent authority gave you consent to search; or

✓ The container was seized from a vehicle; or

✓ The container's contents were obvious under the single purpose container doctrine; or

✓ The container was in the suspect's possession and searched incident to arrest; or

✓ You conducted a legitimate inventory; or

✓ The container was searched under the community caretaking doctrine; or

✓ You had exigent circumstances.

15.6.2 Searching Abandoned or Lost Property

A container is considered abandoned when:

✓ Based on the totality of the circumstances, a reasonable person would believe that it was intentionally abandoned; or

✓ Based on the totality of the circumstances, it appears the container was inadvertently abandoned, but the container's owner would not have a reasonable expectation of privacy that a member of the general public, including a police officer, would not search it; and

✓ If the container was inadvertently abandoned (e.g., accidentally left at the crime scene), your scope of search was similar to what a member of the public could have done (e.g., no forensic analysis).

15.7 Interview & Interrogation

15.7.1 When Miranda is Required

Miranda rights are required when:

✓ A person is in-custody (i.e., arrested); and

✓ You are interrogating him (i.e., "Tell me why you committed this crime").

15.7.2 Miranda Elements

Miranda requires the suspect to understand the following rights:

- ✓ He has the right to remain silent;
- ✓ That any statements made may be used against him in court;
- ✓ That he has the right to consult with an attorney and to have that attorney present during questioning;
- ✓ That if he cannot afford an attorney, one will be appointed to represent him prior to questioning; and
- ✓ The suspect must knowingly and intelligently waive rights.

15.7.3   Miranda inside Jail and Prison

Jail inmates:

- ✓ You should read pre-convicted jail inmates their Miranda rights.

Prison inmates:

- ✓ You are not required to read a prison inmate his Miranda rights because he is not typically considered "in-custody" because the prison is his "home."

15.7.4   Ambiguous Invocations

A Miranda invocation is valid if:

- ✓ A suspect invoked his right to silence or counsel in an unambiguous manner;
- ✓ In other words, the suspect must say, write, or do something that an objectively reasonable person would clearly know was intended as an invocation, not merely a question or verbalized inner-thoughts.

15.7.5   Suspect Invoked, Now What?

If a suspect invokes his right to remain silent:

- ✓ All questioning must immediately cease;
- ✓ You may try to question him after an appropriate "cooling off" period. In one case, the Supreme Court found a two-hour period sufficient.

If a suspect invokes his right to counsel:

- ✓ All questioning must immediately cease;
- ✓ There is no "cooling off" period and counsel must be present before further questioning;
- ✓ If suspect is released from jail, then his previous invocation is valid for fourteen days from the day he's released. This right is not "crime" specific—all questioning must cease.

15.7.6   Suspect Invoked, Now Wants to Talk

A suspect is allowed to revoke his previous invocation if:

- ✓ The decision to revoke the invocation was made freely by the suspect and not because of undue police influence;

✓ The suspect wanted to open up a general discussion about the crime, as opposed to merely asking questions about routine matters regarding his custody; and

✓ You reread Miranda and obtained an express waiver.

15.7.7 Public Safety Exception

An in-custody suspect may be interrogated without Miranda if:

✓ You ask about legitimate public safety concerns (*e.g.*, Where did you toss the gun near the school?);

✓ You do not ask "why" type questions, but instead focus on pressing public safety concerns;

✓ Once the public safety questions have been handled, Miranda will be required for further questioning.

NORTH CAROLINA CRIMINAL AND TRAFFIC LAW MANUAL

TABLE OF CONTENTS

TABLE OF CONTENTS

TABLE OF CONTENTS

Table of Contents

TABLE OF CONTENTS

TABLE OF CONTENTS

239

Table of Contents

TABLE OF CONTENTS

TABLE OF CONTENTS

Table of Contents

Table of Contents

Table of Contents

TABLE OF CONTENTS

Table of Contents

TABLE OF CONTENTS

CHAPTER 1
CIVIL PROCEDURE

SUBCHAPTER 01.
DEFINITIONS AND
GENERAL PROVISIONS

ARTICLE 1
DEFINITIONS

§ 1-1. Remedies

Remedies in the courts of justice are divided into --
    (1) Actions.
    (2) Special proceedings.

History.
C.C.P., s. 1; Code, s. 125; Rev., s. 346; C.S., s. 391

§ 1-2. Actions

An action is an ordinary proceeding in a court of justice, by which a party prosecutes another party for the enforcement or protection of a right, the redress or prevention of a wrong, or the punishment or prevention of a public offense.

History.
C.C.P., s. 2; 1868-9, c. 277, s. 2; Code, s. 126; Rev., s. 347; C.S., s. 392

§ 1-3. Special proceedings

Every other remedy is a special proceeding.

History.
C.C.P., s. 3; Code, s. 127; Rev., s. 348; C.S., s. 393

§ 1-4. Kinds of actions

Actions are of two kinds --
    (1) Civil.
    (2) Criminal.

History.
C.C.P., s. 4; Code, s. 128; Rev., s. 349; C.S., s. 394

§ 1-5. Criminal action

A criminal action is --
    (1) An action prosecuted by the State as a party, against a person charged with a public offense, for the punishment thereof.

    (2) An action prosecuted by the State, at the instance of an individual, to prevent an apprehended crime against his person or property.

History.
Const., art. 4, s. 1; C.C.P., s. 5; Code, s. 129; Rev., s. 350; C.S., s. 395

§ 1-6. Civil action

Every other is a civil action.

History.
C.C.P., s. 6; Code, s. 130; Rev., s. 351; C.S., s. 396

§ 1-7. When court means clerk

In the following sections which confer jurisdiction or power, or impose duties, where the words "superior court," or "court," in reference to a superior court are used, they mean the clerk of the superior court, unless otherwise specially stated, or unless reference is made to a regular session of the court, in which cases the judge of the court alone is meant.

History.
C.C.P., s. 9; Code, s. 132; Rev., s. 352; C.S., s. 397; 1971, c. 381, s. 12

SUBCHAPTER 05.
COMMENCEMENT
OF ACTIONS

ARTICLE 8
SUMMONS

§ 1-105. Service upon nonresident drivers of motor vehicles and upon the personal representatives of deceased nonresident drivers of motor vehicles

The acceptance by a nonresident of the rights and privileges conferred by the laws now or hereafter in force in this State permitting the operation of motor vehicles, as evidenced by the operation of a motor vehicle by such nonresident on the public highways of this State, or at any other place in this State, or the operation by such nonresident of a motor vehicle on the public highways of this State or at any other place in this State, other than as so permitted or regulated, shall be deemed equivalent to the appointment by such nonresident of the Commissioner of Motor Vehicles, or his successor in

277

office, to be his true and lawful attorney and the attorney of his executor or administrator, upon whom may be served all summonses or other lawful process in any action or proceeding against him or his executor or administrator, growing out of any accident or collision in which said nonresident may be involved by reason of the operation by him, for him, or under his control or direction, express or implied, of a motor vehicle on such public highways of this State, or at any other place in this State, and said acceptance or operation shall be a signification of his agreement that any such process against him or his executor or administrator shall be of the same legal force and validity as if served on him personally, or on his executor or administrator.

Service of such process shall be made in the following manner:

(1) By leaving a copy thereof, with a fee of ten dollars ($ 10.00), in the hands of the Commissioner of Motor Vehicles, or in his office. Such service, upon compliance with the other provisions of this section, shall be sufficient service upon the said nonresident.

(2) Notice of such service of process and copy thereof must be forthwith sent by certified or registered mail by plaintiff or the Commissioner of Motor Vehicles to the defendant, and the entries on the defendant's return receipt shall be sufficient evidence of the date on which notice of service upon the Commissioner of Motor Vehicles and copy of process were delivered to the defendant, on which date service on said defendant shall be deemed completed. If the defendant refuses to accept the certified or registered letter, service on the defendant shall be deemed completed on the date of such refusal to accept as determined by notations by the postal authorities on the original envelope, and if such date cannot be so determined, then service shall be deemed completed on the date that the certified or registered letter is returned to the plaintiff or Commissioner of Motor Vehicles, as determined by postal marks on the original envelope. If the certified or registered letter is not delivered to the defendant because it is unclaimed, or because he has removed himself from his last known address and has left no forwarding address or is unknown at his last known address, service on the defendant shall be deemed completed on the date that the certified or registered letter is returned to the plaintiff or Commissioner of Motor Vehicles.

(3) The defendant's return receipt, or the original envelope bearing a notation by the postal authorities that receipt was refused, and an affidavit by the plaintiff that notice of mailing the registered letter and refusal to accept was forthwith sent to the defendant by ordinary mail, together with the plaintiff's affidavit of compliance with the provisions of this section, must be appended to the summons or other process and filed with said summons, complaint and other papers in the cause.

Provided, that where the nonresident motorist has died prior to the commencement of an action brought pursuant to this section, service of process shall be made on the executor or administrator of such nonresident motorist in the same manner and on the same notice as is provided in the case of a nonresident motorist.

The court in which the action is pending shall order such continuance as may be necessary to afford the defendant reasonable opportunity to defend the action.

History.
1929, c. 75, s. 1; 1941, c. 36, s. 4; 1951, c. 646; 1953, c. 796; 1955, c. 1022; 1961, c. 1191; 1963, c. 491; 1967, c. 954, s. 4; 1971, c. 420, ss. 1, 2; 1975, c. 294; 1989, c. 645, s. 1

§ 1-105.1. Service on residents who establish residence outside the State and on residents who depart from the State

The provisions of G.S. 1-105 of this Chapter shall also apply to a resident of the State at the time of the accident or collision who establishes residence outside the State subsequent to the accident or collision and to a resident of the State at the time of the accident or collision who departs from the State subsequent to the accident or collision and remains absent therefrom for 60 days or more, continuously whether such absence is intended to be temporary or permanent.

History.
1955, c. 232; 1967, c. 954, s. 4; 1971, c. 420, ss. 1, 2

SUBCHAPTER 07.
PRETRIAL HEARINGS; TRIAL AND ITS INCIDENTS

ARTICLE 19
TRIAL

§ 1-180.1. Judge not to comment on verdict

In criminal actions the presiding judge shall make no comment in open court in the presence or hearing of all, or any member or members, of the panel of jurors drawn or summoned for jury duty at any session of court, upon any verdict rendered at such session of court, and if any presiding judge shall make any comment as herein prohibited, or shall praise or criticize any jury on account of its verdict, whether such comment, praise or criticism be made inadvertently or intentionally, such praise, criticism or comment by the judge shall constitute valid grounds as a matter of right, for the continuance for the session of any action remaining to be tried during that week at such session of court, upon motion of a defendant or upon motion of the State. The provisions of this section shall not be applicable upon the hearing of motions for a new trial, motions to set aside the verdict of a jury, or a motion made in arrest of judgment.

History.

1955, c. 200; 1967, c. 954, s. 3; 1971, c. 381, s. 12

CHAPTER 1A
RULES OF CIVIL
PROCEDURE

§ 1A-1 RULES OF CIVIL PROCEDURE

ARTICLE 6
TRIALS

Rule 45. Subpoena

(a) **Form; Issuance. --**

(1) Every subpoena shall state all of the following:

a. The title of the action, the name of the court in which the action is pending, the number of the civil action, and the name of the party at whose instance the witness is summoned.

b. A command to each person to whom it is directed to attend and give testimony or to produce and permit inspection and copying of designated records, books, papers, documents, electronically stored information, or tangible things in the possession, custody, or control of that person therein specified.

c. The protections of persons subject to subpoenas under subsection (c) of this rule.

d. The requirements for responses to subpoenas under subsection (d) of this rule.

(2) A command to produce records, books, papers, electronically stored information, or tangible things may be joined with a command to appear at trial or hearing or at a deposition, or any subpoena may be issued separately. A subpoena may specify the form or forms in which electronically stored information is to be produced.

(3) A subpoena shall issue from the court in which the action is pending.

(4) The clerk of court in which the action is pending shall issue a subpoena, signed but otherwise blank, to a party requesting it, who shall complete it before service. Any judge of the superior court, judge of the district court, magistrate, or attorney, as officer of the court, may also issue and sign a subpoena.

(b) **Service. --**

(1) **Manner. --** Any subpoena may be served by the sheriff, by the sheriff's deputy, by a coroner, or by any person who is not a party and is not less than 18 years of age. Service of a subpoena upon a person named therein shall be made by delivering a copy thereof to that person or by registered or certified mail, return receipt requested. Service of a subpoena for the attendance of a witness only may also be made by telephone communication with the person named therein only by a sheriff, the sheriff's designee who is not less than 18 years of age and is not a party, or a coroner.

(2) **Service of copy. --** A copy of the subpoena served under subdivision (b)(1) of this subsection shall also be served upon each party in the manner prescribed by Rule 5(b).

(3) Subdivision (b)(2) of this subsection does not apply to subpoenas issued under G.S. 15A-801 or G.S. 15A-802.

(c) **Protection of Persons Subject to Subpoena. --**

(1) **Avoid undue burden or expense. --** A party or an attorney responsible for the issuance and service of a subpoena shall take reasonable steps to avoid imposing an undue burden or expense on a person subject to the subpoena. The court shall enforce this subdivision and impose upon the party or attorney in violation of this requirement an appropriate sanction that may include compensating the person unduly burdened for lost earnings and for reasonable attorney's fees.

(2) **For production of public records or hospital medical records. --** Where the subpoena commands any custodian of public records or any custodian of hospital medical records, as defined in G.S. 8-44.1, to appear for the sole purpose of producing certain records in the custodian's custody, the custodian subpoenaed may, in lieu of personal appearance, tender to the court in which the action is pending by registered or certified mail or by personal delivery, on or before the time specified in the subpoena, certified copies of the records requested together with a copy of the subpoena and an affidavit by the custodian testifying that the copies are true and correct copies and that the records were made and kept in the regular course of business, or if no such records are in the custodian's custody, an affidavit to that effect. When the copies of records are personally delivered under this subdivision, a receipt shall be obtained from the person receiving the records. Any original or certified copy of records or an affidavit delivered according to the provisions of this subdivision, unless otherwise objectionable, shall be admissible in any action or proceeding without further

certification or authentication. Copies of hospital medical records tendered under this subdivision shall not be open to inspection or copied by any person, except to the parties to the case or proceedings and their attorneys in depositions, until ordered published by the judge at the time of the hearing or trial. Nothing contained herein shall be construed to waive the physician-patient privilege or to require any privileged communication under law to be disclosed.

(3) **Written objection to subpoenas.** -- Subject to subsection (d) of this rule, a person commanded to appear at a deposition or to produce and permit the inspection and copying of records, books, papers, documents, electronically stored information, or tangible things may, within 10 days after service of the subpoena or before the time specified for compliance if the time is less than 10 days after service, serve upon the party or the attorney designated in the subpoena written objection to the subpoena, setting forth the specific grounds for the objection. The written objection shall comply with the requirements of Rule 11. Each of the following grounds may be sufficient for objecting to a subpoena:

a. The subpoena fails to allow reasonable time for compliance.

b. The subpoena requires disclosure of privileged or other protected matter and no exception or waiver applies to the privilege or protection.

c. The subpoena subjects a person to an undue burden or expense.

d. The subpoena is otherwise unreasonable or oppressive.

e. The subpoena is procedurally defective.

(4) **Order of court required to override objection.** -- If objection is made under subdivision (3) of this subsection, the party serving the subpoena shall not be entitled to compel the subpoenaed person's appearance at a deposition or to inspect and copy materials to which an objection has been made except pursuant to an order of the court. If objection is made, the party serving the subpoena may, upon notice to the subpoenaed person, move at any time for an order to compel the subpoenaed person's appearance at the deposition or the production of the materials designated in the subpoena. The motion shall be filed in the court in the county in which the deposition or production of materials is to occur.

(5) **Motion to quash or modify subpoena.** -- A person commanded to appear at a trial, hearing, deposition, or to produce and permit the inspection and copying of records, books, papers, documents, electronically stored information, or other tangible things, within 10 days after service of the subpoena or before the time specified for compliance if the time is less than 10 days after service, may file a motion to quash or modify the subpoena. The court shall quash or modify the subpoena if the subpoenaed person demonstrates the existence of any of the reasons set forth in subdivision (3) of this subsection. The motion shall be filed in the court in the county in which the trial, hearing, deposition, or production of materials is to occur.

(6) **Order to compel; expenses to comply with subpoena.** -- When a court enters an order compelling a deposition or the production of records, books, papers, documents, electronically stored information, or other tangible things, the order shall protect any person who is not a party or an agent of a party from significant expense resulting from complying with the subpoena. The court may order that the person to whom the subpoena is addressed will be reasonably compensated for the cost of producing the records, books, papers, documents, electronically stored information, or tangible things specified in the subpoena.

(7) **Trade secrets; confidential information.** -- When a subpoena requires disclosure of a trade secret or other confidential research, development, or commercial information, a court may, to protect a person subject to or affected by the subpoena, quash or modify the subpoena, or when the party on whose behalf the subpoena is issued shows a substantial need for the testimony or material that cannot otherwise be met without undue hardship, the court may order a person to make an appearance or produce the materials only on specified conditions stated in the order.

(8) **Order to quash; expenses.** -- When a court enters an order quashing or modifying the subpoena, the court may order the party on whose behalf the subpoena is issued to pay all or part of the subpoenaed person's reasonable expenses including attorney's fees.

(d) **Duties in Responding to Subpoenas.** --
(1) **Form of response.** -- A person responding to a subpoena to produce records, books, documents, electronically stored information, or tangible things shall produce them as they are kept in the usual course of business or shall organize and label them to correspond with the categories in the request.

(2) **Form of producing electronically stored information not specified.** -- If a subpoena does not specify a form for

producing electronically stored information, the person responding must produce it in a form or forms in which it ordinarily is maintained or in a reasonably useable form or forms.

(3) **Electronically stored information in only one form.** -- The person responding need not produce the same electronically stored information in more than one form.

(4) **Inaccessible electronically stored information.** -- The person responding need not provide discovery of electronically stored information from sources that the person identifies as not reasonably accessible because of undue burden or cost. On motion to compel discovery or for a protective order, the person responding must show that the information is not reasonably accessible because of undue burden or cost. If that showing is made, the court may nonetheless order discovery from such sources if the requesting party shows good cause, after considering the limitations of Rule 26(b)(1a). The court may specify conditions for discovery, including requiring the party that seeks discovery from a nonparty to bear the costs of locating, preserving, collecting, and producing the electronically stored information involved.

(5) **Specificity of objection.** -- When information subject to a subpoena is withheld on the objection that it is subject to protection as trial preparation materials, or that it is otherwise privileged, the objection shall be made with specificity and shall be supported by a description of the nature of the communications, records, books, papers, documents, electronically stored information, or other tangible things not produced, sufficient for the requesting party to contest the objection.

(d1) **Opportunity for Inspection of Subpoenaed Material.** -- A party or attorney responsible for the issuance and service of a subpoena shall, within five business days after the receipt of material produced in compliance with the subpoena, serve all other parties with notice of receipt of the material produced in compliance with the subpoena and, upon request, shall provide all other parties a reasonable opportunity to copy and inspect such material at the expense of the inspecting party.

(e) **Contempt; Expenses to Force Compliance With Subpoena.** --

(1) Failure by any person without adequate excuse to obey a subpoena served upon the person may be deemed a contempt of court. Failure by any party without adequate cause to obey a subpoena served upon the party shall also subject the party to the sanctions provided in Rule 37(d).

(2) The court may award costs and attorney's fees to the party who issued a subpoena if the court determines that a person objected to the subpoena or filed a motion to quash or modify the subpoena, and the objection or motion was unreasonable or was made for improper purposes such as unnecessary delay.

(f) **Discovery From Persons Residing Outside the State.** --

(1) Any party may obtain discovery from a person residing in another state of the United States or a territory or an insular possession subject to its jurisdiction in any one or more of the following forms: (i) oral depositions, (ii) depositions upon written questions, or (iii) requests for production of documents and tangible things. In doing so, the party shall use and follow any applicable process and procedures required and available under the laws of the state, territory, or insular possession where the discovery is to be obtained. If required by the process or procedure of the state, territory, or insular possession where the discovery is to be obtained, a commission may issue from the court in which the action is pending in accordance with the procedures set forth in subdivision (2) of this subsection.

(2) **Obtaining a commission.** --

a. The party desiring a commission to obtain discovery outside the State shall prepare and file a motion indicating the party's intent to obtain a commission and requesting that the commission be issued.

b. The motion shall indicate that the moving party has conferred, or describe fully the moving party's good faith attempts to confer, with counsel for all other parties regarding the request and shall indicate whether the motion is unopposed. The motion shall also attach a copy of any proposed subpoena, notice of deposition, or other papers to be served on the person from whom the moving party is seeking to obtain discovery.

c. The motion shall indicate that counsel for the moving party has read the applicable rules and procedures of the foreign state and that the moving party will comply with those rules and procedures in obtaining the requested discovery.

d. If the motion reflects that it is unopposed or indicates that the moving party has made reasonable, good faith efforts to confer with all other parties and that no other party has indicated that it opposes the motion, the motion shall immediately be placed on the calendar for a hearing within 20 days before the court in which the action is pending where the commission shall be issued. However, if the court determines, in its discretion, that the moving party has failed to make reasonable, good faith efforts to confer with all other parties prior to filing the motion, the court shall refuse to issue the commission, and the motion shall be denied.

e. If the motion does not reflect that it is unopposed or that the moving party has made reasonable, good faith efforts to confer with all other parties and that no other party has indicated that it opposes the motion, any party wishing to oppose the motion shall file written objections to issuance of the commission within 10 days of being served with the motion, and the motion shall immediately be placed on the calendar for a hearing to be held within 20 days before the court in which the action is pending. The hearing may be held by telephone in the court's discretion. The court may refuse to issue the commission only upon a showing of substantial good cause to deny the motion.

f. If the court, in its discretion, determines that any party opposing the motion did so without good cause, the court shall require the party opposing the motion to pay the moving party the reasonable costs and expenses incurred in obtaining the order, including attorneys' fees, unless circumstances exist which make an award of expenses unjust.

(3) In addition to any terms required by the foreign jurisdiction to initiate the process of obtaining the requested discovery, the commission shall:

a. State the time and place at which the requested discovery is to occur;

b. State the name and address of the person from whom the discovery is sought, if known, and, if unknown, a general description sufficient to identify the person or the particular class or group to which he or she belongs; and

c. Attach a copy of any case management order, discovery order, local rule, or other rule or order establishing any discovery deadlines in the North Carolina action.

History.
1967, c. 954, s. 1; 1969, c. 886, s. 1; 1971, c. 159; 1975, c. 762, s. 3; 1983, c. 665, s. 1; c. 722; 1989, c. 262, s. 1; 2003-276, s. 1; 2007-514, s. 1; 2011-199, s. 6; 2011-247, s. 3

CHAPTER 1D
PUNITIVE DAMAGES

§ 1D-1. Purpose of punitive damages

Punitive damages may be awarded, in an appropriate case and subject to the provisions of this Chapter, to punish a defendant for egregiously wrongful acts and to deter the defendant and others from committing similar wrongful acts.

History.
1995, c. 514, s. 1

§ 1D-5. Definitions

As used in this Chapter:

(1) "Claimant" means a party, including a plaintiff, counterclaimant, cross-claimant, or third-party plaintiff, seeking recovery of punitive damages. In a claim for relief in which a party seeks recovery of punitive damages related to injury to another person, damage to the property of another person, death of another person, or other harm to another person, "claimant" includes any party seeking recovery of punitive damages.

(2) "Compensatory damages" includes nominal damages.

(3) "Defendant" means a party, including a counterdefendant, cross-defendant, or third-party defendant, from whom a claimant seeks relief with respect to punitive damages.

(4) "Fraud" does not include constructive fraud unless an element of intent is present.

(5) "Malice" means a sense of personal ill will toward the claimant that activated or incited the defendant to perform the act or undertake the conduct that resulted in harm to the claimant.

(6) "Punitive damages" means extracompensatory damages awarded for the purposes set forth in G.S. 1D-1.

(7) "Willful or wanton conduct" means the conscious and intentional disregard of and indifference to the rights and safety of others, which the defendant knows or should know is reasonably likely to result in injury, damage, or other harm. "Willful or wanton conduct" means more than gross negligence.

History.
1995, c. 514, s. 1

§ 1D-10. Scope of the Chapter

This Chapter applies to every claim for punitive damages, regardless of whether the claim for relief is based on a statutory or a common-law right of action or based in equity. In an action subject to this Chapter, in whole or in part, the provisions of this Chapter prevail over any other law to the contrary.

History.
1995, c. 514, s. 1

§ 1D-15. Standards for recovery of punitive damages

(a) Punitive damages may be awarded only if the claimant proves that the defendant is liable for compensatory damages and that one of the following aggravating factors was present and was related to the injury for which compensatory damages were awarded:

(1) Fraud.

(2) Malice.

(3) Willful or wanton conduct.

(b) The claimant must prove the existence of an aggravating factor by clear and convincing evidence.

(c) Punitive damages shall not be awarded against a person solely on the basis of vicarious liability for the acts or omissions of another. Punitive damages may be awarded against a person only if that person participated in the conduct constituting the aggravating factor giving rise to the punitive damages, or if, in the case of a corporation, the officers, directors, or managers of the corporation participated in or condoned the conduct constituting the aggravating factor giving rise to punitive damages.

(d) Punitive damages shall not be awarded against a person solely for breach of contract.

History.
1995, c. 514, s. 1

§ 1D-20. Election of extracompensatory remedies

A claimant must elect, prior to judgment, between punitive damages and any other remedy pursuant to another statute that provides for multiple damages.

History.
1995, c. 514, s. 1

§ 1D-25. Limitation of amount of recovery

(a) In all actions seeking an award of punitive damages, the trier of fact shall determine the amount of punitive damages separately from the amount of compensation for all other damages.

(b) Punitive damages awarded against a defendant shall not exceed three times the amount of compensatory damages or two hundred fifty thousand dollars ($ 250,000), whichever is greater. If a trier of fact returns a verdict for punitive damages in excess of the maximum amount specified under this subsection, the trial court shall reduce the award and enter judgment for punitive damages in the maximum amount.

(c) The provisions of subsection (b) of this section shall not be made known to the trier of fact through any means, including voir dire, the introduction into evidence, argument, or instructions to the jury.

History.
1995, c. 514, s. 1

§ 1D-26. Driving while impaired; exemption from cap

G.S. 1D-25(b) shall not apply to a claim for punitive damages for injury or harm arising from a defendant's operation of a motor vehicle if the actions of the defendant in operating the motor vehicle would give rise to an offense of driving while impaired under G.S. 20-138.1, 20-138.2, or 20-138.5.

History.
1995, c. 514, s. 1

§ 1D-30. Bifurcated trial

Upon the motion of a defendant, the issues of liability for compensatory damages and the amount of compensatory damages, if any, shall be tried separately from the issues of liability for punitive damages and the amount of punitive damages, if any. Evidence relating solely to punitive damages shall not be admissible until the trier of fact has determined that the defendant is liable for compensatory damages and has determined the amount of compensatory damages. The same trier of fact that tried the issues relating to compensatory damages shall try the issues relating to punitive damages.

History.
1995, c. 514, s. 1

§ 1D-35. Punitive damages awards

In determining the amount of punitive damages, if any, to be awarded, the trier of fact:

(1) Shall consider the purposes of punitive damages set forth in G.S. 1D-1; and

(2) May consider only that evidence that relates to the following:

   a. The reprehensibility of the defendant's motives and conduct.

   b. The likelihood, at the relevant time, of serious harm.

c. The degree of the defendant's awareness of the probable consequences of its conduct.

d. The duration of the defendant's conduct.

e. The actual damages suffered by the claimant.

f. Any concealment by the defendant of the facts or consequences of its conduct.

g. The existence and frequency of any similar past conduct by the defendant.

h. Whether the defendant profited from the conduct.

i. The defendant's ability to pay punitive damages, as evidenced by its revenues or net worth.

History.
1995, c. 514, s. 1

§ 1D-40. Jury instructions

In a jury trial, the court shall instruct the jury with regard to subdivisions (1) and (2) of G.S. 1D-35.

History.
1995, c. 514, s. 1

§ 1D-45. Frivolous or malicious actions; attorneys' fees

The court shall award reasonable attorneys' fees, resulting from the defense against the punitive damages claim, against a claimant who files a claim for punitive damages that the claimant knows or should have known to be frivolous or malicious. The court shall award reasonable attorney fees against a defendant who asserts a defense in a punitive damages claim that the defendant knows or should have known to be frivolous or malicious.

History.
1995, c. 514, s. 1

§ 1D-50. Judicial review of award

When reviewing the evidence regarding a finding by the trier of fact concerning liability for punitive damages in accordance with G.S. 1D-15(a), or regarding the amount of punitive damages awarded, the trial court shall state in a written opinion its reasons for upholding or disturbing the finding or award. In doing so, the court shall address with specificity the evidence, or lack thereof, as it bears on the liability for or the amount of punitive damages, in light of the requirements of this Chapter.

History.
1995, c. 514, s. 1

CHAPTER 1E
EASTERN BAND OF CHEROKEE INDIANS

ARTICLE 1
FULL FAITH AND CREDIT

§ 1E-1. Full faith and credit

(a) The courts of this State shall give full faith and credit to a judgment, decree, or order signed by a judicial officer of the Eastern Band of Cherokee Indians and filed in the Cherokee Tribal Courts to the same extent as is given a judgment, decree, or order of another state, subject to the provisions of subsections (b) and (c) of this section; provided that the judgments, decrees, and orders of the courts of this State are given full faith and credit by the Tribal Courts of the Eastern Band of Cherokee Indians.

(b) Judgments, decrees, and orders specified in subsection (a) of this section shall be given full faith and credit subject to the provisions of G.S. 1C-1705 and G.S. 1C-1708 and shall be considered a foreign judgment for purposes of these statutes.

(c) Any limited driving privilege signed and issued by a Judge or Justice of the Cherokee Tribal Courts in accordance with the applicable provisions of Chapter 20 of the General Statutes and filed in the Cherokee Tribal Courts Clerk's Office shall be valid and given full faith and credit as specified in subsection (a) of this section. For purposes of this subsection, any reference to the issuing "judge" or "court" in the applicable provisions of Chapter 20 of the General Statutes shall be construed to mean the appropriate Judge or Justice in the Cherokee Tribal Courts or the appropriate Cherokee Tribal Court.

History.
2001-456, s. 1; 2015-287, s. 1

§ 1E-2. County services

A county is not compelled to provide services on lands held in trust by the United States for the Eastern Band of Cherokee Indians, except for public health or human services traditionally provided by county agencies and not otherwise assumed by the Eastern Band of Cherokee Indians, unless there is an agreement between the Eastern Band of Cherokee Indians and the county describing each party's responsibilities. The agreement must be approved and signed by the Principal Chief of the Eastern Band of Cherokee Indians on behalf of the Eastern Band

of Cherokee Indians and must be signed by the county manager or delegated department head. The agreement may be effective for a definite period of time or an indefinite period of time, as specified in the agreement.

History.
2015-262, s. 1(b); 2016-123, s. 2.4(a)

§§ 1E-3 through 1E-9

Reserved for future codification purposes.

ARTICLE 2
TRIBAL LAW ENFORCEMENT AUTHORITY

§ 1E-10. Tribal law enforcement

(a) Except for the sections listed in subsection (b) of this section, Article 13 of Chapter 160A of the General Statutes is applicable to the Eastern Band of Cherokee Indians.

(b) The following provisions of Article 13 of Chapter 160A of the General Statutes shall not apply to the Eastern Band of Cherokee Indians:

(1) G.S. 160A-283.
(2) G.S. 160A-286.
(3) G.S. 160A-287.
(4) G.S. 160A-289.1.

History.
2015-287, s. 1

§ 1E-11. Application and meaning of terms

For purposes of the application of the applicable provisions of Article 13 of Chapter 160A of the General Statutes, the following terms contained in Article 13 of Chapter 160A of the General Statutes shall be construed as follows:

(1) **City.** -- To mean the Eastern Band of Cherokee Indians.

(2) **Council or governing body.** -- To mean the Tribal Council of the Eastern Band of Cherokee Indians.

(3) **City clerk.** -- To mean the clerk of the Tribal Council of the Eastern Band of the Cherokee Indians.

(4) **Corporate limits of the city.** -- To mean the boundaries of the trust lands of the Eastern Band of the Cherokee Indians wherever located within the State of North Carolina.

(5) **Law enforcement agency or local law enforcement agency.** -- To include the Cherokee Police Department, the Cherokee Marshals Service, the Tribal Alcohol

Law Enforcement Division of the Eastern Band of the Cherokee Indians, and the Natural Resources Enforcement Agency of the Eastern Band of Cherokee Indians.

History.
2015-287, s. 1

§ 1E-12. Qualification of law enforcement officers; limitations of authority

(a) For purposes of this section, "law enforcement officer" means any person appointed or employed as (i) Chief of Police of the Cherokee Police Department, Chief of the Cherokee Marshals Service, Chief of the Tribal Alcohol Law Enforcement Division of the Eastern Band of the Cherokee Indians, or Chief of the Natural Resources Enforcement Agency of the Eastern Band of the Cherokee Indians or (ii) a police officer, auxiliary police officer, marshal, alcohol law enforcement agent, reserve alcohol law enforcement agent, or resources officer with the Cherokee Police Department, the Cherokee Marshals Service, the Tribal Alcohol Law Enforcement Division of the Eastern Band of the Cherokee Indians, or the Natural Resources Enforcement Agency of the Eastern Band of the Cherokee Indians.

(b) A law enforcement officer shall, prior to the exercise of the officer's authority pursuant to Article 13 of Chapter 160A of the General Statutes, comply with the provisions of Article 1 of Chapter 17C of the General Statutes and any rules or regulations adopted pursuant to the authority of Article 1 of Chapter 17C of the General Statutes. The courts of this State shall have the jurisdiction pursuant to G.S. 17C-11 to enjoin the Cherokee Police Department, the Cherokee Marshals Service, the Tribal Alcohol Law Enforcement Division of the Eastern Band of Cherokee Indians, the Natural Resources Enforcement Agency of the Eastern Band of the Cherokee Indians, or any law enforcement officer or agent employed or appointed by the department, agency, or division from exercising any or all of the authority under color of State law conferred by Article 13 of Chapter 160A of the General Statutes if any law enforcement officer or agent of the department, agency, or division fails to meet the required standards established pursuant to Article 1 of Chapter 17C of the General Statutes.

(c) The jurisdiction of a law enforcement officer shall be (i) on all property owned by or leased to the Eastern Band of Cherokee Indians located within the trust lands of the Eastern Band of the Cherokee Indians and (ii) during the immediate and continuous flight of an offender in accordance with G.S. 15A-402(d).

(d) Service as a law enforcement officer shall constitute service as (i) a "criminal justice officer" as defined in G.S. 17C-2(c) and (ii) a "law enforcement officer" for purposes of Article 12E of Chapter 143 of the General Statutes. For purposes of Article 12E of Chapter 143 of the General Statutes, the term "employer," as defined in G.S. 143-166.50, shall be construed to include the Eastern Band of Cherokee Indians with respect to law enforcement officers.

(e) A law enforcement officer may be enjoined from exercising his authority under color of State law pursuant to Article 13 of Chapter 160A of the General Statutes for the reasons set forth in G.S. 128-16 and pursuant to the provisions of Article 2 of Chapter 128 of the General Statutes.

(f) Nothing contained in this Chapter or in Article 13 of Chapter 160A of the General Statutes shall be construed as doing any of the following:

(1) Limiting or revoking the authority of the Eastern Band of Cherokee Indians, the Cherokee Police Department, the Cherokee Marshals Service, the Tribal Alcohol Law Enforcement Division of the Eastern Band of the Cherokee Indians, the Natural Resources Enforcement Agency of the Eastern Band of the Cherokee Indians, or any law enforcement officers or other persons appointed or employed by those entities, in the exercise of their inherent powers of self-government, or exercise of authority conferred by federal law, regulation, or common law.

(2) Modifying, either by way of enlargement or limitation, the jurisdiction of the Cherokee Tribal Courts.

(3) Waiving any sovereign immunity that may otherwise apply.

(g) Nothing contained in this Chapter shall be construed as modifying, either by way of enlargement or limitation, the jurisdiction or authority of any federal, State, or local law enforcement agency, governmental entity, or any of their officers or employees, except the Eastern Band of Cherokee Indians, the Cherokee Police Department, the Cherokee Marshals Service, the Tribal Alcohol Law Enforcement Division of the Eastern Band of the Cherokee Indians, the Natural Resources Enforcement Agency of the Eastern Band of the Cherokee Indians, and their law enforcement officers, agents, and employees to the extent set forth in this Chapter.

History.
2015-287, s. 1

§§ 1E-13 through 1E-19

Reserved for future codification purposes.

ARTICLE 3
PROBATION AND PAROLE

§ 1E-20. Cherokee Marshals Service

(a) The Supreme Court of the Eastern Band of Cherokee Indians is authorized to establish a probation and parole agency known as the "Cherokee Marshals Service."

(b) Marshals of the Cherokee Marshals Service shall (i) be required to meet the standards set forth in G.S. 1E-12 for law enforcement officers and (ii) have the same territorial jurisdiction, powers, and immunities as a law enforcement officer under G.S. 1E-12.

(c) Notwithstanding any other provision of law, marshals of the Cherokee Marshals Service shall have access to all probation and parole records of the North Carolina Department of Public Safety to the same extent as a probation or post-release supervision officer of the Department for any person over which the Cherokee Tribal Courts have jurisdiction to proceed in a criminal case and impose a sentence, including a fine, community service, or imprisonment. The Department may enter into a memorandum of understanding addressing the specifics of transferring information to the Cherokee Tribal Courts.

History.
2015-287, s. 1

CHAPTER 4
COMMON LAW

§ 4-1. Common law declared to be in force

All such parts of the common law as were heretofore in force and use within this State, or so much of the common law as is not destructive of, or repugnant to, or inconsistent with, the freedom and independence of this State and the form of government therein established, and which has not been otherwise provided for in whole or in part, not abrogated, repealed, or become obsolete, are hereby declared to be in full force within this State.

History.
1715, c. 5, ss. 2, 3, P.R.; 1778, c. 133, P.R.; R.C., c. 22; Code, s. 641; Rev., s. 932; C.S., s. 970

CHAPTER 5A
CONTEMPT

ARTICLE 1
CRIMINAL CONTEMPT

§ 5A-11. Criminal contempt

(a) Except as provided in subsection (b), each of the following is criminal contempt:

(1) Willful behavior committed during the sitting of a court and directly tending to interrupt its proceedings.

(2) Willful behavior committed during the sitting of a court in its immediate view and presence and directly tending to impair the respect due its authority.

(3) Willful disobedience of, resistance to, or interference with a court's lawful process, order, directive, or instruction or its execution.

(4) Willful refusal to be sworn or affirmed as a witness, or, when so sworn or affirmed, willful refusal to answer any legal and proper question when the refusal is not legally justified.

(5) Willful publication of a report of the proceedings in a court that is grossly inaccurate and presents a clear and present danger of imminent and serious threat to the administration of justice, made with knowledge that it was false or with reckless disregard of whether it was false. No person, however, may be punished for publishing a truthful report of proceedings in a court.

(6) Willful or grossly negligent failure by an officer of the court to perform his duties in an official transaction.

(7) Willful or grossly negligent failure to comply with schedules and practices of the court resulting in substantial interference with the business of the court.

(8) Willful refusal to testify or produce other information upon the order of a judge acting pursuant to Article 61 of Chapter 15A, Granting of Immunity to Witnesses.

(9) Willful communication with a juror in an improper attempt to influence his deliberations.

(9a) Willful refusal by a defendant to comply with a condition of probation.

(9b) Willful refusal to accept post-release supervision or to comply with the terms of post-release supervision by a prisoner whose offense requiring post-release supervision is a reportable conviction subject to the registration requirement of Article 27A of Chapter 14 of the General Statutes. For purposes of this subdivision, "willful refusal to accept post-release supervision or to comply with the terms of post-release supervision" includes, but is not limited to, knowingly violating the terms of post-release supervision in order to be returned to prison to serve out the remainder of the supervisee's sentence.

(10) Any other act or omission specified elsewhere in the General Statutes of North Carolina as grounds for criminal contempt.

The grounds for criminal contempt specified here are exclusive, regardless of any other grounds for criminal contempt which existed at common law.

(b) No person may be held in contempt under this section on the basis of the content of any broadcast, publication, or other communication unless it presents a clear and present danger of an imminent and serious threat to the administration of criminal justice.

(c) This section is subject to the provisions of G.S. 7A-276.1, Court orders prohibiting publication or broadcast of reports of open court proceedings or reports of public records banned.

History.

1977, c. 711, s. 3; 1994, Ex. Sess., c. 19, s. 1; 2011-307, s. 6

§ 5A-12. Punishment; circumstances for fine or imprisonment; reduction of punishment; other measures

(a) A person who commits criminal contempt, whether direct or indirect, is subject to censure, imprisonment up to 30 days, fine not to exceed five hundred dollars ($ 500.00), or any combination of the three, except that:

(1) A person who commits a contempt described in G.S. 5A-11(8) is subject to censure, imprisonment not to exceed 6 months, fine not to exceed five hundred dollars ($ 500.00), or any combination of the three;

(2) A person who has not been arrested who fails to comply with a nontestimonial identification order, issued pursuant to Article 14 of Chapter 15A of the General Statutes is subject to censure, imprisonment not to exceed 90 days, fine not to exceed five hundred dollars ($ 500.00), or any combination of the three; and

(3) A person who commits criminal contempt by failing to comply with an order to pay child support is subject to censure, imprisonment up to 30 days, fine not to exceed five hundred dollars ($ 500.00), or any combination of the three. However, a sentence of imprisonment up to 120 days

may be imposed for a single act of criminal contempt resulting from the failure to pay child support, provided the sentence is suspended upon conditions reasonably related to the contemnor's payment of child support.

(b) Except for contempt under G.S. 5A-11(5) or 5A-11(9), fine or imprisonment may not be imposed for criminal contempt, whether direct or indirect, unless:

(1) The act or omission was willfully contemptuous; or

(2) The act or omission was preceded by a clear warning by the court that the conduct is improper.

(c) The judicial official who finds a person in contempt may at any time withdraw a censure, terminate or reduce a sentence of imprisonment, or remit or reduce a fine imposed as punishment for contempt if warranted by the conduct of the contemnor and the ends of justice.

(d) A person held in criminal contempt under this Article shall not, for the same conduct, be found in civil contempt under Article 2 of this Chapter, Civil Contempt.

(e) A person held in criminal contempt under G.S. 5A-11(9) may nevertheless, for the same conduct, be found guilty of a violation of G.S. 14-225.1, but he must be given credit for any imprisonment resulting from the contempt.

History.
1977, c. 711, s. 3; 1985 (Reg. Sess., 1986), c. 843, s. 1; 1987 (Reg. Sess., 1988), c. 1040, ss. 2, 4; 1989 (Reg. Sess., 1990), c. 1039, s. 4; 1991, c. 686, s. 3; 1999-361, s. 3; 2009-335, s. 1

§ 5A-13. Direct and indirect criminal contempt; proceedings required

(a) Criminal contempt is direct criminal contempt when the act:

(1) Is committed within the sight or hearing of a presiding judicial official; and

(2) Is committed in, or in immediate proximity to, the room where proceedings are being held before the court; and

(3) Is likely to interrupt or interfere with matters then before the court.

The presiding judicial official may punish summarily for direct criminal contempt according to the requirements of G.S. 5A-14 or may defer adjudication and sentencing as provided in G.S. 5A-15. If proceedings for direct criminal contempt are deferred, the judicial official must, immediately following the conduct, inform the person of his intention to institute contempt proceedings.

(b) Any criminal contempt other than direct criminal contempt is indirect criminal contempt and is punishable only after proceedings in accordance with the procedure required by G.S. 5A-15.

History.
1977, c. 711, s. 3

§ 5A-14. Summary proceedings for contempt

(a) The presiding judicial official may summarily impose measures in response to direct criminal contempt when necessary to restore order or maintain the dignity and authority of the court and when the measures are imposed substantially contemporaneously with the contempt.

(b) Before imposing measures under this section, the judicial official must give the person charged with contempt summary notice of the charges and a summary opportunity to respond and must find facts supporting the summary imposition of measures in response to contempt. The facts must be established beyond a reasonable doubt.

History.
1977, c. 711, s. 3

§ 5A-15. Plenary proceedings for contempt

(a) When a judicial official chooses not to proceed summarily against a person charged with direct criminal contempt or when he may not proceed summarily, he may proceed by an order directing the person to appear before a judge at a reasonable time specified in the order and show cause why he should not be held in contempt of court. A copy of the order must be furnished to the person charged. If the criminal contempt is based upon acts before a judge which so involve him that his objectivity may reasonably be questioned, the order must be returned before a different judge.

(b) Proceedings under this section are before a district court judge unless a court superior to the district court issued the order, in which case the proceedings are before that court. Venue lies throughout the district court district as defined in G.S. 7A-133 or superior court district or set of districts as defined in G.S. 7A-41.1, as the case may be, where the order was issued.

(c) The person ordered to show cause may move to dismiss the order.

(d) The judge is the trier of facts at the show cause hearing.

(e) The person charged with contempt may not be compelled to be a witness against himself in the hearing.

(f) At the conclusion of the hearing, the judge must enter a finding of guilty or not guilty. If the person is found to be in contempt, the judge must make findings of fact and enter judgment. The facts must be established beyond a reasonable doubt.

(g) The judge presiding over the hearing may appoint a prosecutor or, in the event of an apparent conflict of interest, some other member of the bar to represent the court in hearings for criminal contempt.

History.

1977, c. 711, s. 3; 1987 (Reg. Sess., 1988), c. 1037, s. 44

§ 5A-16. Custody of person charged with criminal contempt

(a) A judicial official may orally order that a person he is charging with direct criminal contempt be taken into custody and restrained to the extent necessary to assure his presence for summary proceedings or notice of plenary proceedings.

(b) If a judicial official who initiates plenary proceedings for contempt under G.S. 5A-15 finds, based on sworn statement or affidavit, probable cause to believe the person ordered to appear will not appear in response to the order, he may issue an order for arrest of the person, pursuant to G.S. 15A-305. A person arrested under this subsection is entitled to release under the provisions of Article 26, Bail, of Chapter 15A of the General Statutes.

History.

1977, c. 711, s. 3

§ 5A-17. Appeals; bail proceedings

(a) A person found in criminal contempt may appeal in the manner provided for appeals in criminal actions, except appeal from a finding of contempt by a judicial official inferior to a superior court judge is by hearing de novo before a superior court judge.

(b) Upon appeal in a case where the judicial official imposes confinement, a bail hearing shall be held within a reasonable time period after imposition of the confinement. The judicial official holding the bail hearing shall be:

(1) A district court judge if the confinement is imposed by a clerk or magistrate.

(2) A superior court judge if the confinement is imposed by a district court judge.

(3) A superior court judge other than the superior court judge that imposed the confinement.

(c) A person found in contempt and who has given notice of appeal may be retained in custody not more than 24 hours from the time of imposition of confinement without a bail determination being made by a judicial official as designated under subdivisions (1) through (3) of subsection (b) of this section. If a designated judicial official has not acted within 24 hours of the imposition of confinement, any judicial official shall act under the provisions of subsection (b) of this section and hold the bail hearing.

History.

1977, c. 711, s. 3; 2013-303, s. 1

CHAPTER 6
LIABILITY FOR COURT COSTS

ARTICLE 5
LIABILITY OF COUNTIES IN CRIMINAL ACTIONS

§ 6-40. Liability of counties, where trial removed from one county to another

When a prisoner is sent from one county to another to be held for trial, or for any other cause or purpose, the county from which he is sent shall pay his jail expenses, unless they are collected from the prisoner.

History.
1889, c. 354; 1901, c. 718; Rev., s. 1285; C.S., s. 1263; 1971, c. 269, s. 8

ARTICLE 6
LIABILITY OF DEFENDANT IN CRIMINAL ACTIONS

§ 6-47. Judgment confessed; bond given to secure fine and costs

In cases where a court permits a defendant convicted of any criminal offense to give bond or confess judgment, with sureties to secure the fine and costs which may be imposed, the acceptance of such security shall be upon the condition that it shall not operate as a discharge of the original judgment against the defendant nor as a discharge of his person from the custody of the law until the fine and costs are paid.

History.
1879, c. 264; Code, s. 749; 1885, c. 364; Rev., s. 1293; C.S., s. 1269; 1971, c. 269, s. 9

§ 6-48. Arrest for nonpayment of fine and costs

In default of payment of such fine and costs, it is the duty of the court at any subsequent term thereof, on motion of the solicitor of the State, to order a capias to issue to the end that such defendant may be again arrested and held for the fine and costs until discharged according to law.

History.
1879, c. 264; Code, s. 750; 1885, c. 364; Rev., s. 1294; C.S., s. 1270; 1971, c. 269, s. 10

ARTICLE 7
LIABILITY OF PROSECUTING WITNESS FOR COSTS

§ 6-49. Prosecuting witness liable for costs in certain cases; court determines prosecuting witness

In all criminal actions in any court, if the defendant is acquitted, nolle prosequi entered, or judgment against him is arrested, or if the defendant is discharged from arrest for want of probable cause, the costs, including the fees of all witnesses whom the judge before whom the trial took place shall certify to have been proper for the defense and prosecution, shall be paid by the prosecuting witness, whether marked on the bill or warrant or not, whenever the judge is of the opinion that there was not reasonable ground for the prosecution, or that it was not required by the public interest. If a greater number of witnesses have been summoned than were, in the opinion of the court, necessary to support the charge, the court may, even though it is of the opinion that there was reasonable ground for the prosecution, order the prosecuting witness to pay the attendance fees of such witnesses, if it appear that they were summoned at the prosecuting witness's special request.

Every judge is authorized to determine who the prosecuting witness is at any stage of a criminal proceeding, whether before or after the bill of indictment has been found, or the defendant acquitted: Provided, that no person shall be made a prosecuting witness after the finding of the bill, unless he shall have been notified to show cause why he should not be made the prosecuting witness of record.

History.
1799, c. 4, s. 19, P.R.; 1880, c. 558, P.R.; R.C., c. 35, s. 37; 1868-9, c. 277; 1874-5, c. 151; 1879, c. 49; Code, s. 737; 1889, c. 34; Rev., s. 1295; C.S., s. 1271; 1947, c. 781; 1953, c. 675, s. 1; 1971, c. 269, s. 11

§ 6-50. Imprisonment of prosecuting witness for willful nonpayment of costs if prosecution frivolous

Every such prosecuting witness may be adjudged not only to pay the costs, but he shall also be imprisoned for the willful nonpayment thereof, when the judge before whom the case was tried shall adjudge that the prosecution was frivolous or malicious.

History.
1800, c. 558; R.C., c. 35, s. 37; 1879, c. 49; 1881, c. 176; Code, s. 738; Rev., s. 1297; C.S., s. 1272; 1971, c. 269, s. 11.1

CHAPTER 7A
JUDICIAL DEPARTMENT

SUBCHAPTER 01.
GENERAL COURT OF JUSTICE

ARTICLE 1
JUDICIAL POWER AND ORGANIZATION

§ 7A-1. Short title

This Chapter shall be known and may be cited as the "Judicial Department Act of 1965."

History.
1965, c. 310, s. 1

§ 7A-2. Purpose of Chapter

This Chapter is intended to implement Article IV of the Constitution of North Carolina and promote the just and prompt disposition of litigation by:

(1) Providing a new chapter in the General Statutes into which, at a time not later than January 1, 1971, when the General Court of Justice is fully operational in all counties of the State, all statutes concerning the organization, jurisdiction and administration of each division of the General Court of Justice may be placed;

(2) Amending certain laws with respect to the superior court division to conform them to the laws set forth in this Chapter, to the end that each trial division may be a harmonious part of the General Court of Justice;

(3) Creating the district court division of the General Court of Justice, and the Administrative Office of the Courts;

(4) Establishing in accordance with a fixed schedule the various district courts of the district court division;

(5) Providing for the organization, jurisdiction and procedures necessary for the operation of the district court division;

(6) Providing for the financial support of the judicial department, and for uniform costs and fees in the trial divisions of the General Court of Justice;

(7) Providing for an orderly transition from the present system of courts to a uniform system completely operational in all counties of the State not later than January 1, 1971;

(8) Repealing certain laws inconsistent with the foregoing purposes; and

(9) Effectuating other purposes incidental and supplemental to the foregoing enumerated purposes.

History.
1965, c. 310, s. 1

§ 7A-3. Judicial power; transition provisions

Except for the judicial power vested in the court for the trial of impeachments, and except for such judicial power as may from time to time be vested by the General Assembly in administrative agencies, the judicial power of the State is vested exclusively in the General Court of Justice. Provided, that all existing courts of the State inferior to the superior courts, including justice of the peace courts and mayor's courts, shall continue to exist and to exercise the judicial powers vested in them by law until specifically abolished by law, or until the establishment within the county of their situs of a district court, or until January 1, 1971, whichever event shall first occur. Judgments of inferior courts which cease to exist under the provisions of this section continue in force and effect as though the issuing court continued to exist, and the General Court of Justice is hereby vested with jurisdiction to enforce such judgments.

History.
1965, c. 310, s. 1

§ 7A-4. Composition and organization

The General Court of Justice constitutes a unified judicial system for purposes of jurisdiction, operation and administration, and consists of an appellate division, a superior court division, and a district court division.

History.
1965, c. 310, s. 1

SUBCHAPTER 02.
APPELLATE DIVISION OF THE GENERAL COURT OF JUSTICE

ARTICLE 2
APPELLATE DIVISION ORGANIZATION

§ 7A-5. Organization

The appellate division of the General Court of Justice consists of the Supreme Court and the Court of Appeals.

History.
1965, c. 310, s. 1; 1967, c. 108, s. 1

ARTICLE 3
THE SUPREME COURT

§ 7A-10. Organization; compensation of justices

(a) The Supreme Court shall consist of a Chief Justice and six associate justices, elected by the qualified voters of the State for terms of eight years. Such election shall be under Article 25 of Chapter 163 of the General Statutes or Article 1A of this Chapter. Before entering upon the duties of the office, each justice shall take an oath of office. Four justices shall constitute a quorum for the transaction of the business of the court. Except as otherwise provided in this subsection, sessions of the court shall be held in the city of Raleigh, and scheduled by rule of court so as to discharge expeditiously the court's business. The court may by rule hold sessions not more than twice annually in the Old Chowan County Courthouse (1767) in the Town of Edenton, which is a State-owned court facility that is designated as a National Historic Landmark by the United States Department of the Interior. The court may by rule hold sessions not more than twice annually in the City of Morganton; unless a more suitable site is identified by the court, the court shall meet in the Old Burke County Courthouse, the location of summer sessions of the Supreme Court from 1847-1862.

(b) The Chief Justice and each of the associate justices shall receive the annual salary provided in Current Operations Appropriations Act. Each justice is entitled to reimbursement for travel and subsistence expenses at the rate allowed State employees generally.

(b1) In addition to the reimbursement for travel and subsistence expenses authorized by subsection (b) of this section, and notwithstanding G.S. 138-6, each justice whose permanent residence is at least 50 miles from the City of Raleigh shall also be reimbursed for the mileage the justice travels each week to the City of Raleigh from the justice's home for business of the court. The reimbursement authorized by this subsection shall be calculated for each justice by multiplying the actual round-trip mileage from that justice's home to the City of Raleigh by a rate-per-mile established by the Director of the Administrative Office of the Courts, but not to exceed the business standard mileage rate set by the Internal Revenue Service.

(c) In lieu of merit and other increment raises paid to regular State employees, the Chief Justice and each of the Associate Justices shall receive as longevity pay an annual amount equal to four and eight-tenths percent (4.8%) of the annual salary set forth in the Current Operations Appropriations Act payable monthly after five years of service, nine and six-tenths percent (9.6%) after 10 years of service, fourteen and four-tenths percent (14.4%) after 15 years of service, nineteen and two-tenths percent (19.2%) after 20 years of service, and twenty-four percent (24%) after 25 years of service. "Service" means service as a justice or judge of the General Court of Justice, as a member of the Utilities Commission, or as an administrative law judge. Service shall also mean service as a district attorney or as a clerk of superior court.

History.
1967, c. 108, s. 1; 1983, c. 761, s. 242; 1983 (Reg. Sess., 1984), c. 1034, s. 165; c. 1109, ss. 11, 13.1; 1985, c. 698, s. 10(a); 1997-56, s. 1; 2007-323, ss. 14.21(a), 28.18A(a); 2015-66, s. 2; 2015-89, s. 1; 2017-57, s. 35.4(d)

§ 7A-10.1. Authority to prescribe standards of judicial conduct

The Supreme Court is authorized, by rule, to prescribe standards of judicial conduct for the guidance of all justices and judges of the General Court of Justice.

History.
1973, c. 89

§ 7A-11. Clerk of the Supreme Court; salary; bond; fees; oath

The clerk of the Supreme Court shall be appointed by the Supreme Court to serve at its pleasure. The annual salary of the clerk shall be fixed by the Administrative Officer of the Courts, subject to the approval of the Supreme Court. The clerk may appoint assistants in the number and at the salaries fixed by the Administrative Officer of the Courts. The clerk shall perform such duties as the Supreme Court may assign, and shall be bonded to the State, for faithful performance of duty, in the same manner as the clerk of the superior court, and in such amount as the Administrative Officer of the Courts shall determine. The clerk shall adopt a seal of office, to be approved by the Supreme Court. A fee bill for services rendered by the clerk shall be fixed by rules of the Supreme Court, and all such fees shall be remitted to the State treasury. Charges to litigants for the reproduction of appellate records and briefs shall be fixed by rule of the Supreme Court and remitted to the Appellate Courts Printing and Computer Operations Fund established in G.S. 7A-343.3. The operations of the Clerk of the Supreme Court shall be subject to the oversight of the State Auditor pursuant to Article 5A of Chapter 147 of the General Statutes. Before entering upon the duties of his office, the clerk shall take the oath of office prescribed by law.

History.
1967, c. 108, s. 1; 1969, c. 1190, s. 2; 1973, c. 750; 1983, c. 913, s. 3; 2002-126, s. 2.2(j); 2019-243, s. 19(a)

§ 7A-12. Supreme Court marshal

The Supreme Court may appoint a marshal to serve at its pleasure, and to perform such duties as it may assign. The marshal shall have the criminal and civil powers of a sheriff, and any additional powers necessary to execute the orders of the appellate division in any county of the State. His salary shall be fixed by the Administrative Officer, subject to the approval of the Supreme Court. The marshal may appoint such assistants, and at such salaries, as may be authorized by the Administrative Officer of the Courts. The Supreme Court, in its discretion, may appoint the Supreme Court librarian, or some other suitable employee of the court, to serve in the additional capacity of marshal.

History.
1967, c. 108, s. 1

§ 7A-13. Supreme Court library; functions; librarian; library committee; seal of office

(a) The Supreme Court shall appoint a librarian of the Supreme Court library, to serve at the pleasure of the court. The annual salary of the librarian shall be fixed by the Administrative Officer of the Courts, subject to the approval of the Supreme Court. The librarian may appoint assistants in numbers and at salaries to be fixed by the Administrative Officer of the Courts.

(b) The primary function of the Supreme Court library is to serve the appellate division of the General Court of Justice, but it may render service to the trial divisions of the General Court of Justice, to State agencies, and to the general public, under such regulations as the librarian, subject to the approval of the library committee, may promulgate.

(c) The library shall be maintained in the city of Raleigh, except that if the Court of Appeals sits regularly in locations other than the city of Raleigh, branch libraries may be established at such locations for the use of the Court of Appeals.

(d) The librarian shall promulgate rules and regulations for the use of the library, subject to the approval of a library committee, to be composed of two justices of the Supreme Court appointed by the Chief Justice, and one judge of the Court of Appeals appointed by the Chief Judge.

(e) The librarian may adopt a seal of office.

(f) The librarian may operate a copying service by means of which he may furnish certified or uncertified copies of all or portions of any document, paper, book, or other writing in the library that legally may be copied. When a certificate is made under his hand and attested by his official seal, it shall be received as prima facie evidence of the correctness of the matter therein contained, and as such shall receive full faith and credit. The fees for copies shall be approved by the library committee, and the fees so collected shall be administered in the same manner as the charges to litigants for the reproduction of appellate records and briefs.

History.
1967, c. 108, s. 1

§ 7A-14. Reprints of Supreme Court Reports

The Supreme Court is authorized to have such of the Reports of the Supreme Court of the State of North Carolina as are not on hand for sale, republished and numbered consecutively, retaining the present numbers and names of the reporters and by means of star pages in the margin retaining the original numbering of the pages. The Supreme Court is authorized to have such Reports reprinted without any alteration from the original edition thereof, except as may be directed by the Supreme Court. The contract for such reprinting and republishing shall be made by the Administrative Office of the Courts in the manner prescribed in G.S. 7A-6. Such republication shall thus continue until the State shall have for sale all of such Reports; and hereafter when the editions of any number or volume of the Supreme Court Reports shall be exhausted, it shall be the duty of the Supreme Court to have the same reprinted under the provisions of this section and G.S. 7A-6. In reprinting the Reports that have already been annotated, the annotations and the additional indexes therein shall be retained.

History.
Code, s. 3634; 1885, c. 309; 1889, c. 473, ss. 1-4, 6; Rev., s. 5361; 1907, c. 503; 1917, cc. 201, 292; C.S., s. 7671; 1923, c. 176; 1929, c. 39, s. 2; 1975, c. 328

ARTICLE 4
COURT OF APPEALS

§ 7A-16. Creation and organization

The Court of Appeals is created effective January 1, 1967. It shall consist initially of six judges, elected by the qualified voters of the State for terms of eight years. The Chief Justice of the Supreme Court shall designate one of the judges as Chief Judge, to serve in such capacity at the pleasure of the Chief Justice. Before entering upon the duties of his office, a judge of the Court of Appeals shall take the oath of office prescribed for a judge of the General Court of Justice.

The Governor on or after July 1, 1967, shall make temporary appointments to the six initial judgeships. The appointees shall serve until January 1, 1969. Their successors shall be elected at the general election for members of the General Assembly in November, 1968, and shall take office on January 1, 1969, to serve for the remainder of the unexpired term which began on January 1, 1967.

Upon the appointment of at least five judges, and the designation of a Chief Judge, the court is authorized to convene, organize, and promulgate, subject to the approval of the Supreme Court, such supplementary rules as it deems necessary and appropriate for the discharge of the judicial business lawfully assigned to it.

Effective January 1, 1969, the number of judges is increased to nine, and the Governor, on or after March 1, 1969, shall make temporary appointments to the additional judgeships thus created. The appointees shall serve until January 1, 1971. Their successors shall be elected at the general election for members of the General Assembly in November, 1970, and shall take office on January 1, 1971, to serve for the remainder of the unexpired term which began on January 1, 1969.

Effective January 1, 1977, the number of judges is increased to 12; and the Governor, on or after July 1, 1977, shall make temporary appointments to the additional judgeships thus created. The appointees shall serve until January 1, 1979. Their successors shall be elected at the general election for members of the General Assembly in November, 1978, and shall take office on January 1, 1979, to serve the remainder of the unexpired term which began on January 1, 1977.

On or after December 15, 2000, the Governor shall appoint three additional judges to increase the number of judges to 15.

The Court of Appeals shall sit in panels of three judges each and may also sit en banc to hear or rehear any cause upon a vote of the majority of the judges of the court. The Chief Judge insofar as practicable shall assign the members to panels in such fashion that each member sits a substantially equal number of times with each other member, shall preside when a member of a panel, and shall designate the presiding judge of the other panel or panels.

Except as may be provided in G.S. 7A-32, three judges shall constitute a quorum for the transaction of the business of the court when sitting in panels of three judges, and a majority of the then sitting judges on the Court of Appeals shall constitute a quorum for the transaction of the business of the court when sitting en banc.

In the event the Chief Judge is unable, on account of absence or temporary incapacity, to perform the duties placed upon him as Chief Judge, the Chief Justice shall appoint an acting Chief Judge from the other judges of the Court, to temporarily discharge the duties of Chief Judge.

History.
1967, c. 108, s. 1; 1969, c. 1190, s. 3; 1973, c. 301; 1977, c. 1047; 2000-67, s. 15.5(a); 2004-203, s. 16; 2016-125, 4th Ex. Sess., s. 22(a); 2017-7, s. 1; 2019-2, s. 1

N.C. Gen. Stat. § 7A-17

Repealed by Session Laws 1969, c. 1190, s. 57.

§ 7A-18. Compensation of judges

(a) The Chief Judge and each associate judge of the Court of Appeals shall receive the annual salary provided in the Current Operations Appropriations Act. Each judge is entitled to reimbursement for travel and subsistence expenses at the rate allowed State employees generally.

(a1) In addition to the reimbursement for travel and subsistence expenses authorized by subsection (a) of this section, and notwithstanding G.S. 138-6, each judge whose permanent residence is at least 50 miles from the City of Raleigh shall also be reimbursed for the mileage the judge travels each week to the City of Raleigh from the judge's home for business of the court. The reimbursement authorized by this subsection shall be calculated for each judge by multiplying the actual round-trip mileage from that judge's home to the City of Raleigh by a rate-per-mile established by the Director of the Administrative Office of the Courts, but not to exceed the business standard mileage rate set by the Internal Revenue Service.

(b) In lieu of merit and other increment raises paid to regular State employees, a judge of the Court of Appeals shall receive as longevity pay an annual amount equal to four and eight-tenths percent (4.8%) of the annual salary set forth in the Current Operations Appropriations Act payable monthly after five years of service, nine and six-tenths percent (9.6%) after 10 years of service, fourteen and four-tenths percent (14.4%) after 15 years of service, nineteen and two-tenths percent (19.2%) after 20 years of service, and twenty-four percent (24%) after 25 years of service. "Service" means service as a justice or judge of the General Court of Justice, as a member of the Utilities Commission, as an administrative law judge, or as the Director of the Administrative Office of the Courts. Service shall also mean service as a district attorney or as a clerk of superior court.

History.
1967, c. 108, s. 1; 1983, c. 761, s. 243; 1983 (Reg. Sess., 1984), c. 1034, s. 165; c. 1109, ss. 11, 13.1; 1985, c. 698, s. 10(a); 2007-323, ss. 14.21(b), 28.18A(b); 2015-241, s. 30.3(e); 2017-57, s. 35.4(e)

§ 7A-19. Seats and sessions of court

(a) The Court of Appeals shall sit in Raleigh, and at such other locations within the State as the Supreme Court may designate.

(b) The Department of Administration shall provide adequate quarters for the Court of Appeals.

(c) The Chief Judge shall schedule sessions of the court as required to discharge expeditiously the court's business.

History.
1967, c. 108, s. 1

§ 7A-20. Clerk; oath; bond; salary; assistants; fees

(a) The Court of Appeals shall appoint a clerk to serve at its pleasure. Before entering upon the clerk's duties, the clerk shall take the oath of office prescribed for the clerk of the Supreme Court, conformed to the office of clerk of the Court of Appeals, and shall be bonded, in the same manner as the clerk of superior court, in an amount prescribed by the Administrative Officer of the Courts, payable to the State, for the faithful performance of the clerk's duties. The salary of the clerk shall be fixed by the Administrative Officer of the Courts, subject to the approval of the Court of Appeals. The number and salaries of the clerk's assistants, and their bonds, if required, shall be fixed by the Administrative Officer of the Courts. The clerk shall adopt a seal of office, to be approved by the Court of Appeals.

(b) Subject to approval of the Supreme Court, the Court of Appeals shall promulgate from time to time a fee bill for services rendered by the clerk, and such fees shall be remitted to the State Treasurer. Charges to litigants for the reproduction of appellate records and briefs shall be fixed by rule of the Supreme Court and remitted to the Appellate Courts Printing and Computer Operations Fund established in G.S. 7A-343.3. The operations of the Court of Appeals shall be subject to the oversight of the

State Auditor pursuant to Article 5A of Chapter 147 of the General Statutes.

History.
1967, c. 108, s. 1; 1983, c. 913, s. 4; 2002-126, s. 2.2(k); 2019-243, s. 19(b)

§ 7A-21. Marshal; powers; salary

The Court of Appeals may appoint a marshal to serve at its pleasure and to perform such duties as it may assign. The marshal shall have the criminal and civil powers of a sheriff and any additional powers necessary to execute the orders of the appellate division in any county of the State. His salary shall be fixed by the Administrative Officer, subject to the approval of the Court of Appeals.

History.
1981, c. 485

ARTICLE 5
JURISDICTION

§ 7A-25. Original jurisdiction of the Supreme Court

The Supreme Court has original jurisdiction to hear claims against the State, but its decisions shall be merely recommendatory; no process in the nature of execution shall issue thereon; the decisions shall be reported to the next session of the General Assembly for its action. The court shall by rule prescribe the procedures to be followed in the proper exercise of the jurisdiction conferred by this section.

History.
1967, c. 108, s. 1

§ 7A-26. Appellate jurisdiction of the Supreme Court and the Court of Appeals

The Supreme Court and the Court of Appeals respectively have jurisdiction to review upon appeal decisions of the several courts of the General Court of Justice and of administrative agencies, upon matters of law or legal inference, in accordance with the system of appeals provided in this Article.

History.
1967, c. 108, s. 1

§ 7A-27. Appeals of right from the courts of the trial divisions

(a) Appeal lies of right directly to the Supreme Court in any of the following cases:

(1) All cases in which the defendant is convicted of murder in the first degree and the judgment of the superior court includes a sentence of death.

(2) From any final judgment in a case designated as a mandatory complex business case pursuant to G.S. 7A-45.4 or designated as a discretionary complex business case pursuant to Rule 2.1 of the General Rules of Practice for the Superior and District Courts.

(3) From any interlocutory order of a Business Court Judge that does any of the following:

     a. Affects a substantial right.

     b. In effect determines the action and prevents a judgment from which an appeal might be taken.

     c. Discontinues the action.

     d. Grants or refuses a new trial.

(4) Any trial court's decision regarding class action certification under G.S. 1A-1, Rule 23.

(5) Repealed by Session Laws 2021-18, s. 1, effective July 1, 2021, and applicable to appeals filed on or after that date.

(a1) Repealed by Session Laws 2016-125, s. 22(b), 4th Ex. Sess., effective December 1, 2016.

(b) Except as provided in subsection (a) of this section, appeal lies of right directly to the Court of Appeals in any of the following cases:

(1) From any final judgment of a superior court, other than one based on a plea of guilty or nolo contendere, including any final judgment entered upon review of a decision of an administrative agency, except for a final judgment entered upon review of a court martial under G.S. 127A-62.

(2) From any final judgment of a district court in a civil action.

(3) From any interlocutory order or judgment of a superior court or district court in a civil action or proceeding that does any of the following:

     a. Affects a substantial right.

     b. In effect determines the action and prevents a judgment from which an appeal might be taken.

     c. Discontinues the action.

     d. Grants or refuses a new trial.

     e. Determines a claim prosecuted under G.S. 50-19.1.

     f. Grants temporary injunctive relief restraining the State or a political subdivision of the State from enforcing the operation or execution of an act of the General Assembly. This sub-subdivision only applies where the State or a political subdivision of the State is a party in the civil action.

(4) From any other order or judgment of the superior court from which an appeal is authorized by statute.

(c) through (e) Repealed by Session Laws 2013-411, s. 1, effective August 23, 2013.

History.
1967, c. 108, s. 1; 1971, c. 377, s. 3; 1973, c. 704; 1977, c. 711, s. 4; 1987, c. 679; 1995, c. 204, s. 1; 2010-193, s. 17; 2013-411, s. 1; 2014-100, s. 18B.16(e); 2014-102, s. 1; 2015-264, s. 1(b); 2016-125, 4th Ex. Sess., s. 22(b); 2017-7, s. 2; 2021-18, s. 1

§ 7A-28. Decisions of Court of Appeals on post-trial motions for appropriate relief, valuation of exempt property, or courts-martial are final

(a) Decisions of the Court of Appeals upon review of motions for appropriate relief listed in G.S. 15A-1415(b) are final and not subject to further review in the Supreme Court by appeal, motion, certification, writ, or otherwise.

(b) Decisions of the Court of Appeals upon review of valuation of exempt property under G.S. 1C are final and not subject to further review in the Supreme Court by appeal, motion, certification, writ, or otherwise.

(c) Decisions of the Court of Appeals upon review of courts-martial under G.S. 127A-62 are final and not subject to further review in the Supreme Court by appeal, motion, certification, writ, or otherwise.

History.
1981, c. 470, s. 1; 1981 (Reg. Sess., 1982), c. 1224, s. 16.; 2010-193, s. 18

§ 7A-29. Appeals of right from certain administrative agencies

(a) From any final order or decision of the North Carolina Utilities Commission not governed by subsection (b) of this section, the Department of Health and Human Services under G.S. 131E-188(b), the North Carolina Industrial Commission, the North Carolina State Bar under G.S. 84-28, the Property Tax Commission under G.S. 105-290 and G.S. 105-342, the Commissioner of Insurance under G.S. 58-2-80, the State Board of Elections under G.S. 163-127.6, the Office of Administrative Hearings under G.S. 126-34.02, or the Secretary of Environmental Quality under G.S. 104E-6.2 or G.S. 130A-293, appeal as of right lies directly to the Court of Appeals.

(b) From any final order or decision of the Utilities Commission in a general rate case, appeal as of right lies directly to the Supreme Court.

History.
1967, c. 108, s. 1; 1971, c. 703, s. 5; 1975, c. 582, s. 12; 1979, c. 584, s. 1; 1981, c. 704, s. 28; 1983, c. 526, s. 1; c. 761, s. 188; 1983 (Reg. Sess., 1984), c. 1000, s. 2;

c. 1087, s. 2; c. 1113, s. 2; 1985, c. 462, s. 3; 1987, c. 850, s. 2; 1991, c. 546, s. 2; c. 679, s. 2; 1993, c. 501, s. 2; 1995, c. 115, s. 1; c. 504, s. 2; c. 509, s. 2; 1997-443, ss. 11A.118(a), 11A.119(a); 2003-63, s. 1; 2006-155, s. 1.1; 2013-382, s. 6.4; 2015-241, s. 14.30(v); 2017-6, s. 3; 2018-146, ss. 3.1(a), (b), 6.1

§ 7A-30. Appeals of right from certain decisions of the Court of Appeals

Except as provided in G.S. 7A-28, an appeal lies of right to the Supreme Court from any decision of the Court of Appeals rendered in a case:

(1) Which directly involves a substantial question arising under the Constitution of the United States or of this State, or

(2) In which there is a dissent when the Court of Appeals is sitting in a panel of three judges. An appeal of right pursuant to this subdivision is not effective until after the Court of Appeals sitting en banc has rendered a decision in the case, if the Court of Appeals hears the case en banc, or until after the time for filing a motion for rehearing of the cause by the Court of Appeals has expired or the Court of Appeals has denied the motion for rehearing.

History.
1967, c. 108, s. 1; 1983, c. 526, s. 2; 2016-125, 4th Ex. Sess., s. 22(c)

§ 7A-31. Discretionary review by the Supreme Court

(a) In any cause in which appeal is taken to the Court of Appeals, including any cause heard while the Court of Appeals was sitting en banc, except a cause appealed from the North Carolina Industrial Commission, the North Carolina State Bar pursuant to G.S. 84-28, the Property Tax Commission pursuant to G.S. 105-345, the Board of State Contract Appeals pursuant to G.S. 143-135.9, the Commissioner of Insurance pursuant to G.S. 58-2-80 or G.S. 58-65-131(c), a court-martial pursuant to G.S. 127A-62, a motion for appropriate relief, or valuation of exempt property pursuant to G.S. 7A-28, the Supreme Court may, in its discretion, on motion of any party to the cause or on its own motion, certify the cause for review by the Supreme Court, either before or after it has been determined by the Court of Appeals. A cause appealed to the Court of Appeals from any of the administrative bodies listed in the preceding sentence may be certified in similar fashion, but only after determination of the cause in the Court of Appeals. The effect of such certification is to transfer the cause from the Court of Appeals to the Supreme Court for review by the Supreme Court. If the cause is certified for transfer to the Supreme Court before its determination in the Court of Appeals, review is not had in the Court of Appeals but the cause is forthwith transferred for review in the first instance by the Supreme Court. If the cause is certified for transfer to the Supreme Court after its determination by the Court of Appeals, the Supreme Court reviews the decision of the Court of Appeals.

Except in courts-martial and motions within the purview of G.S. 7A-28, the State may move for certification for review of any criminal cause, but only after determination of the cause by the Court of Appeals.

(b) In causes subject to certification under subsection (a) of this section, certification may be made by the Supreme Court before determination of the cause by the Court of Appeals when in the opinion of the Supreme Court any of the following apply:

(1) The subject matter of the appeal has significant public interest.

(2) The cause involves legal principles of major significance to the jurisprudence of the State.

(3) Delay in final adjudication is likely to result from failure to certify and thereby cause substantial harm.

(4) The work load of the courts of the appellate division is such that the expeditious administration of justice requires certification.

(5) The subject matter of the appeal is important in overseeing the jurisdiction and integrity of the court system.

(c) In causes subject to certification under subsection (a) of this section, certification may be made by the Supreme Court after determination of the cause by the Court of Appeals when in the opinion of the Supreme Court any of the following apply:

(1) The subject matter of the appeal has significant public interest.

(2) The cause involves legal principles of major significance to the jurisprudence of the State.

(3) The decision of the Court of Appeals appears likely to be in conflict with a decision of the Supreme Court.

Interlocutory determinations by the Court of Appeals, including orders remanding the cause for a new trial or for other proceedings, shall be certified for review by the Supreme Court only upon a determination by the Supreme Court that failure to certify would cause a delay in final adjudication which would probably result in substantial harm.

(d) The procedure for certification by the Supreme Court on its own motion, or upon petition of a party, shall be prescribed by rule of the Supreme Court.

History.
1967, c. 108, s. 1; 1969, c. 1044; 1975, c. 555; 1977, c. 711, s. 5; 1981, c. 470, s. 2; 1981 (Reg. Sess., 1982), c. 1224, s. 17; c. 1253, s. 1; 1983, c. 526, s. 3; c. 761, s. 189; 2010-193, s. 19; 2016-125, 4th Ex. Sess., s. 22(d); 2017-7, s. 3

§ 7A-31.1. Discretionary Review by the Court of Appeals

(a) In the case of a court-martial in which appeal is taken to the Wake County Superior Court under G.S. 127A-62, the Court of Appeals may, in its discretion, on motion of any party to the cause or on its own motion, certify the cause for review by the Court of Appeals after it has been reviewed by the Wake County Superior Court. The effect of such certification is to transfer the cause from the Wake County Superior Court to the Court of Appeals, and the Court of Appeals reviews the decision by the Wake County Superior Court.

(b) In causes subject to certification under subsection (a) of this section, certification may be made by the Court of Appeals after determination of the cause by the Wake County Superior Court when in the opinion of the Court of Appeals:

(1) The subject matter of the appeal has significant public interest, or

(2) The cause involves legal principles of major significance to the jurisprudence of the State, or

(3) The decision of the Wake County Superior Court appears likely to be in conflict with a decision of the United States Court of Appeals for the Armed Forces.

Interlocutory determinations by the Wake County Superior Court, including orders remanding the cause for a new trial or for other proceedings, shall be certified for review by the Court of Appeals only upon a determination by the Court of Appeals that failure to certify would cause a delay in final adjudication which would probably result in substantial harm.

(c) Any rules for practice and procedure for review of courts-martial that may be required shall be prescribed pursuant to G.S. 7A-33.

History.
2010-193, s. 20

§ 7A-32. Power of Supreme Court and Court of Appeals to issue remedial writs

(a) The Supreme Court and the Court of Appeals have jurisdiction, exercisable by any one of the justices or judges of the respective courts, to issue the writ of habeas corpus upon the application of any person described in G.S. 17-3, according to the practice and procedure provided therefor in chapter 17 of the General Statutes, and to rule of the Supreme Court.

(b) The Supreme Court has jurisdiction, exercisable by one justice or by such number of justices as the court may by rule provide, to issue the prerogative writs, including mandamus, prohibition, certiorari, and supersedeas, in aid of its own jurisdiction or in exercise of its general power to supervise and control the proceedings of any of the other courts of the General Court of Justice. The practice and procedure shall be as provided by statute or rule of the Supreme Court, or, in the absence of statute or rule, according to the practice and procedure of the common law.

(c) The Court of Appeals has jurisdiction, exercisable by one judge or by such number of judges as the Supreme Court may by rule provide, to issue the prerogative writs, including mandamus, prohibition, certiorari, and supersedeas, in aid of its own jurisdiction, or to supervise and control the proceedings of any of the trial courts of the General Court of Justice, and of the Utilities Commission and the Industrial Commission. The practice and procedure shall be as provided by statute or rule of the Supreme Court, or, in the absence of statute or rule, according to the practice and procedure of the common law.

History.
1967, c. 108, s. 1

§ 7A-33. Supreme Court to prescribe appellate division rules of practice and procedure

The Supreme Court shall prescribe rules of practice and procedure designed to procure the expeditious and inexpensive disposition of all litigation in the appellate division.

History.
1967, c. 108, s. 1

§ 7A-34. Rules of practice and procedure in trial courts

The Supreme Court is hereby authorized to prescribe rules of practice and procedure for the superior and district courts supplementary to, and not inconsistent with, acts of the General Assembly.

History.
1967, c. 108, s. 1

N.C. Gen. Stat. § 7A-34.1

Repealed by Session Laws 2011-145, s. 31.23(f), effective July 1, 2011.

History.
2001-388, s. 2

N.C. Gen. Stat. § 7A-35

Repealed by Session Laws 1971, c. 377, s. 32.

N.C. Gen. Stat. § 7A-36

Repealed by Session Laws 1969, c. 1190, s. 57.

N.C. Gen. Stat. § 7A-37

Repealed by Session Laws 1993, c. 553.

§ 7A-37.1. Statewide court-ordered, nonbinding arbitration in certain civil actions

(a) The General Assembly finds that court-ordered, nonbinding arbitration may be a more economical, efficient and satisfactory procedure to resolve certain civil actions than by traditional civil litigation and therefore authorizes court-ordered nonbinding arbitration as an alternative civil procedure, subject to these provisions.

(b) The Supreme Court of North Carolina may adopt rules governing this procedure and may supervise its implementation and operation through the Administrative Office of the Courts. These rules shall ensure that no party is deprived of the right to jury trial and that any party dissatisfied with an arbitration award may have trial de novo.

(c) Except as otherwise provided in rules promulgated by the Supreme Court of North Carolina pursuant to subsection (b) of this section, this procedure shall be employed in all civil actions in district court, unless all parties to the action waive arbitration under this section.

(c1) Except as provided in subsection (c2) of this section, in cases referred to nonbinding arbitration as provided in this section, a fee of one hundred dollars ($ 100.00) shall be assessed per arbitration, to be divided equally among the parties, to cover the cost of providing arbitrators. Fees assessed under this section shall be paid to the clerk of superior court in the county where the case was filed and remitted by the clerk to the State Treasurer.

(c2) In appeals in small claims actions under Article 19 of Chapter 7A of the General Statutes, if (i) the arbitrator finds in favor of the appellee, (ii) the arbitrator's decision is appealed for trial de novo under G.S. 7A-229, and (iii) the arbitrator's decision is affirmed on appeal, then the court shall consider the fact that the arbitrator's decision was affirmed as a significant factor in favor of assessing all court costs and attorneys' fees associated with the case in both the original action and the two appeals,

including the arbitration fee assessed under subsection (c1) of this section, against the appellant.

(d) This procedure may be implemented in a judicial district, in selected counties within a district, or in any court within a district, if the Director of the Administrative Office of the Courts, and the cognizant Senior Resident Superior Court Judge or the Chief District Court Judge of any court selected for this procedure, determine that use of this procedure may assist in the administration of justice toward achieving objectives stated in subsection (a) of this section in a judicial district, county, or court. The Director of the Administrative Office of the Courts, acting upon the recommendation of the cognizant Senior Resident Superior Court Judge or Chief District Court Judge of any court selected for this procedure, may terminate this procedure in any judicial district, county, or court upon a determination that its use has not accomplished objectives stated in subsection (a) of this section.

(e) Arbitrators in this procedure shall have the same immunity as judges from civil liability for their official conduct.

History.
1989, c. 301, s. 1; 2002-126, s. 14.3(a); 2003-284, s. 36A.1; 2013-159, s. 3; 2013-225, s. 1

N.C. Gen. Stat. § 7A-38

Repealed by Session Laws 1995, c. 500, s. 3 .

§ 7A-38.1. Mediated settlement conferences in superior court civil actions

(a) **Purpose.** -- The General Assembly finds that a system of court-ordered mediated settlement conferences should be established to facilitate the settlement of superior court civil actions and to make civil litigation more economical, efficient, and satisfactory to litigants and the State. Therefore, this section is enacted to require parties to superior court civil actions and their representatives to attend a pretrial, mediated settlement conference conducted pursuant to this section and pursuant to rules of the Supreme Court adopted to implement this section.

(b) **Definitions.** -- As used in this section:

(1) "Mediated settlement conference" means a pretrial, court-ordered conference of the parties to a civil action and their representatives conducted by a mediator.

(2) "Mediation" means an informal process conducted by a mediator with the objective of helping parties voluntarily settle their dispute.

(3) "Mediator" means a neutral person who acts to encourage and facilitate a

resolution of a pending civil action. A mediator does not make an award or render a judgment as to the merits of the action.

(c) **Rules of procedure.** -- The Supreme Court may adopt rules to implement this section.

(d) **Statewide implementation.** -- Mediated settlement conferences authorized by this section shall be implemented in all judicial districts as soon as practicable, as determined by the Director of the Administrative Office of the Courts.

(e) **Cases selected for mediated settlement conferences.** -- The senior resident superior court judge of any participating district may order a mediated settlement conference for any superior court civil action pending in the district. The senior resident superior court judge may by local rule order all cases, not otherwise exempted by the Supreme Court rule, to mediated settlement conference.

(f) **Attendance of parties.** -- The parties to a superior court civil action in which a mediated settlement conference is ordered, their attorneys and other persons or entities with authority, by law or by contract, to settle the parties' claims shall attend the mediated settlement conference unless excused by rules of the Supreme Court or by order of the senior resident superior court judge. Nothing in this section shall require any party or other participant in the conference to make a settlement offer or demand which it deems is contrary to its best interests.

(g) **Sanctions.** -- Any person required to attend a mediated settlement conference or other settlement procedure under this section who, without good cause, fails to attend or fails to pay any or all of the mediator's or other neutral's fee in compliance with this section and the rules promulgated by the Supreme Court to implement this section is subject to the contempt powers of the court and monetary sanctions imposed by a resident or presiding superior court judge. The monetary sanctions may include the payment of fines, attorneys' fees, mediator and neutral fees, and the expenses and loss of earnings incurred by persons attending the procedure. A party seeking sanctions against another party or person shall do so in a written motion stating the grounds for the motion and the relief sought. The motion shall be served upon all parties and upon any person against whom the sanctions are being sought. The court may initiate sanction proceedings upon its own motion by the entry of a show cause order. If the court imposes sanctions, it shall do so, after notice and a hearing, in a written order, making findings of fact and conclusions of law. An order imposing sanctions shall be reviewable upon appeal where the entire record as submitted shall be reviewed to determine whether the order is supported by substantial evidence.

(h) **Selection of mediator.** -- The parties to a superior court civil action in which a mediated settlement conference is to be held pursuant to this section shall have the right to designate a mediator. Upon failure of the parties to designate a mediator within the time established by the rules of the Supreme Court, a mediator shall be appointed by the senior resident superior court judge.

(i) **Promotion of other settlement procedures.** -- Nothing in this section is intended to preclude the use of other dispute resolution methods within the superior court. Parties to a superior court civil action are encouraged to select other available dispute resolution methods. The senior resident superior court judge, at the request of and with the consent of the parties, may order the parties to attend and participate in any other settlement procedure authorized by rules of the Supreme Court or by the local superior court rules, in lieu of attending a mediated settlement conference. Neutral third parties acting pursuant to this section shall be selected and compensated in accordance with such rules or pursuant to agreement of the parties. Nothing in this section shall prohibit the parties from participating in, or the court from ordering, other dispute resolution procedures, including arbitration to the extent authorized under State or federal law.

(j) **Immunity.** -- Mediator and other neutrals acting pursuant to this section shall have judicial immunity in the same manner and to the same extent as a judge of the General Court of Justice, except that mediators and other neutrals may be disciplined in accordance with enforcement procedures adopted by the Supreme Court pursuant to G.S. 7A-38.2.

(k) **Costs of mediated settlement conference.** -- Costs of mediated settlement conferences shall be borne by the parties. Unless otherwise ordered by the court or agreed to by the parties, the mediator's fees shall be paid in equal shares by the parties. For purposes of this section, multiple parties shall be considered one party when they are represented by the same counsel. The rules adopted by the Supreme Court implementing this section shall set out a method whereby parties found by the court to be unable to pay the costs of the mediated settlement conference are afforded an opportunity to participate without cost. The rules adopted by the Supreme Court shall set the fees to be paid a mediator appointed by a judge upon the failure of the parties to designate a mediator.

(*l*) **Inadmissibility of negotiations.** -- Evidence of statements made and conduct occurring in a mediated settlement conference or other settlement proceeding conducted under this section, whether attributable to a party, the mediator, other neutral, or a neutral observer present at the settlement proceeding, shall not be subject to discovery and shall be inadmissible in any proceeding in the action or other civil actions on the same claim, except:

(1) In proceedings for sanctions under this section;

(2) In proceedings to enforce or rescind a settlement of the action;

(3) In disciplinary hearings before the State Bar or the Dispute Resolution Commission; or

(4) In proceedings to enforce laws concerning juvenile or elder abuse.

As used in this section, the term "neutral observer" includes persons seeking mediator certification, persons studying dispute resolution processes, and persons acting as interpreters.

No settlement agreement to resolve any or all issues reached at the proceeding conducted under this subsection or during its recesses shall be enforceable unless it has been reduced to writing and signed by the parties against whom enforcement is sought or signed by their designees. No evidence otherwise discoverable shall be inadmissible merely because it is presented or discussed in a mediated settlement conference or other settlement proceeding.

No mediator, other neutral, or neutral observer present at a settlement proceeding shall be compelled to testify or produce evidence concerning statements made and conduct occurring in anticipation of, during, or as a follow-up to a mediated settlement conference or other settlement proceeding pursuant to this section in any civil proceeding for any purpose, including proceedings to enforce or rescind a settlement of the action, except to attest to the signing of any agreements, and except proceedings for sanctions under this section, disciplinary hearings before the State Bar or the Dispute Resolution Commission, and proceedings to enforce laws concerning juvenile or elder abuse.

(m) **Right to jury trial.** -- Nothing in this section or the rules adopted by the Supreme Court implementing this section shall restrict the right to jury trial.

History.
1995, c. 500, s. 1; 1999-354, s. 5; 2005-167, s. 1; 2008-194, s. 8(a); 2015-57, s. 1; 2017-158, s. 26.7(a); 2021-47, s. 12(a).

§ 7A-38.2. Regulation of mediators and other neutrals

(a) The Supreme Court may adopt standards of conduct for mediators and other neutrals who are certified or otherwise qualified pursuant to G.S. 7A-38.1, 7A-38.3, 7A-38.3B, 7A-38.3D,

7A-38.3E, and 7A-38.4A, or who participate in proceedings conducted pursuant to those sections. The standards may also regulate mediator and other neutral training programs. The Supreme Court may adopt procedures for the enforcement of those standards.

(b) The administration of the certification and qualification of mediators and other neutrals, and mediator and other neutral training programs shall be conducted through the Dispute Resolution Commission, established under the Judicial Department. The Supreme Court shall adopt rules and regulations governing the operation of the Commission. The Commission shall exercise all of its duties independently of the Director of the Administrative Office of the Courts, except that the Commission shall consult with the Director regarding personnel and budgeting matters.

(c) The Dispute Resolution Commission shall consist of 18 members: five judges appointed by the Chief Justice of the Supreme Court, at least two of whom shall be active superior court judges, and at least two of whom shall be active district court judges; one clerk of superior court appointed by the Chief Justice of the Supreme Court; two mediators certified to conduct superior court mediated settlement conferences and two mediators certified to conduct equitable distribution mediated settlement conferences appointed by the Chief Justice of the Supreme Court; one certified district criminal court mediator who is a representative of a community mediation center appointed by the Chief Justice of the Supreme Court; a district attorney appointed by the Chief Justice of the Supreme Court; a court management staff member appointed by the Chief Justice of the Supreme Court; two practicing attorneys who are not certified as mediators appointed by the President of the North Carolina State Bar, one of whom shall be a family law specialist; and three citizens knowledgeable about mediation, one of whom shall be appointed by the Governor, one by the General Assembly upon the recommendation of the Speaker of the House of Representatives in accordance with G.S. 120-121, and one by the General Assembly upon the recommendation of the President Pro Tempore of the Senate in accordance with G.S. 120-121. Commission members shall serve three-year terms and shall be ineligible to serve more than two consecutive terms. Members appointed to fill unexpired terms shall be eligible to serve two consecutive terms upon the expiration of the unexpired term. The Chief Justice shall designate one of the members to serve as chair for a two-year term. Members of the Commission shall be compensated pursuant to G.S. 138-5.

Vacancies shall be filled for unexpired terms and full terms in the same manner as incumbents were appointed. Appointing authorities may receive and consider suggestions and recommendations of persons for appointment from the Dispute Resolution Commission, the Family Law, Litigation, and Dispute Resolution Sections of the North Carolina Bar Association, the North Carolina Association of Professional Family Mediators, the North Carolina Conference of Clerks of Superior Court, the North Carolina Conference of Court Administrators, the Mediation Network of North Carolina, the Dispute Resolution Committee of the Supreme Court, the Conference of Chief District Court Judges, the Conference of Superior Court Judges, the Director of the Administrative Office of the Courts, and the Child Custody Mediation Advisory Committee of the Administrative Office of the Courts.

(d) An administrative fee, not to exceed two hundred dollars ($ 200.00) per certification, may be charged by the Dispute Resolution Commission to applicants for certification and annual renewal of certification for mediators and mediation training programs operating under this Article. The fees collected shall be deposited in a Dispute Resolution Fund. The Fund shall be established within the Judicial Department as a nonreverting, interest-bearing special revenue account. Accordingly, interest and other investment income earned by the Fund shall be credited to it. All moneys collected through the fees authorized and assessed under this statute shall be remitted to the Fund. Moneys in the Fund shall be used to support the operations of the Commission and used at the direction of the Commission.

(e) The chair of the Commission may employ an executive director and other staff as necessary to assist the Commission in carrying out its duties. The chair may also employ special counsel or call upon the Attorney General to furnish counsel to assist the Commission in conducting hearings pursuant to its certification or qualification and regulatory responsibilities. Special counsel or counsel furnished by the Attorney General may present the evidence in support of a denial or revocation of certification or qualification or a complaint against a mediator, other neutral, training program, or trainers or staff affiliated with a program. Special counsel or counsel furnished by the Attorney General may also represent the Commission when its final determinations are the subject of an appeal.

(f) In connection with any investigation or hearing conducted pursuant to an application for certification or qualification of any mediator, other neutral, or training program, or conducted pursuant to any disciplinary matter, the chair of the Dispute Resolution Commission or the chair's designee, may do any of the following:

(1) Administer oaths and affirmations.

(2) Sign and issue subpoenas in the name of the Dispute Resolution Commission or direct its executive director to issue such subpoenas on its behalf requiring attendance and the giving of testimony by witnesses and the production of books, papers, and other documentary evidence.

(3) Apply to the General Court of Justice, Superior Court Division, for any order necessary to enforce the powers conferred in this section, including an order for injunctive relief pursuant to G.S. 1A-1, Rule 65, when a certified mediator's conduct necessitates prompt action.

(4) Assess and collect an administrative fee from any person who appeals an adverse determination to the full Commission for a hearing and fails to attend the hearing without good cause as determined by the chair of the Commission. The fee assessed shall be the lesser of the Commission's actual expenses for the hearing or two thousand five hundred dollars ($ 2,500). The fees collected shall be deposited in the Dispute Resolution Fund established pursuant to subsection (d) of this section.

(g) The General Court of Justice, Superior Court Division, may enforce subpoenas issued in the name of the Dispute Resolution Commission and requiring attendance and the giving of testimony by witnesses and the production of books, papers, and other documentary evidence.

(h) The Commission shall keep confidential all information in its files pertaining to the initial and renewal applications for certification of mediators, the qualification of other neutrals, and the initial and renewal applications for certification or qualification of training programs for mediators or other neutrals, except that in the case of an initial or renewal application for certification in the District Criminal Court Mediation Program, Commission staff shall notify the Executive Director of the Mediation Network of North Carolina, Inc., and the Executive Director of the community mediation center that is sponsoring the application of any matter regarding the qualifications, character, conduct, or fitness to practice of the applicant. The Commission shall also keep confidential the identity of those persons requesting informal guidance or the issuance of formal advisory opinions from the Commission or its staff.

All information in the Commission's disciplinary files pertaining to a complaint regarding the moral character, conduct, or fitness to practice of a mediator, other neutral, trainer, or other training program personnel shall remain confidential, unless the subject of the complaint requests otherwise, until such time as all of the following conditions are met:

(1) A preliminary investigation is completed.

(2) A determination is made that probable cause exists to believe that the words

or actions of the mediator, neutral, trainer, or other training program personnel:

a. Violate standards for the conduct of mediators or other neutrals;

b. Violate other standards of professional conduct to which the mediator, neutral, trainer, or other training program personnel is subject;

c. Violate program rules or applicable governing law; or

d. Consist of conduct or actions that are inconsistent with good moral character or reflect a lack of fitness to serve as a mediator, other neutral, trainer, or other training program personnel.

(3) One of the following events has occurred:

a. The respondent does not appeal the determination before the time permitted for an appeal has expired.

b. Upon a timely filed appeal, the Commission holds a hearing and issues a decision affirming the determination.

Upon a finding of probable cause under this subsection against a mediator arising out of a mediated settlement conference, Commission staff shall provide notice of the finding of probable cause to any mediation program or agency under whose auspices the mediated settlement conference was conducted. Commission shall also make reasonable efforts to notify any such agency or program of any public sanction imposed by the Commission pursuant to Supreme Court rules governing the operation of the Commission against a certified mediator who serves as a mediator for any such agency or program. Commission staff and members of the Grievance and Disciplinary Committee of the Commission may share information with other committee chairs or committees of the Commission when relevant to a review of any matter before such other committee.

The Commission may publish names, contact information, and biographical information for mediators, neutrals, and training programs that have been certified or qualified.

(i) All appeals from denials of initial applications for mediator certification and initial applications for mediator training program certification shall be held in private, unless the applicant requests a public hearing. Appeals from a denial of a mediator or mediator training program application for certification renewal or reinstatement that relate to moral character, conduct, or fitness to practice shall be open to the public, except that for good cause shown, the presiding officer may exclude from the hearing room all persons except the parties, counsel, and those engaged in the hearing. All other appeals from denials of a mediator training program's application for certification renewal shall be held in private, unless the applicant requests a public hearing.

(j) Appeals from the Commission's initial determination after review and investigation of a complaint that probable cause exists to believe that the conduct of a mediator, neutral, trainer, or other training program personnel violated a provision set out in subdivision (2) of subsection (h) of this section shall be open to the public, except that for good cause shown, the presiding officer may exclude from the hearing room all persons except the parties, counsel, and those engaged in the hearing. No hearing shall be closed to the public over the objection of the mediator, neutral, trainer, or training program personnel that is the subject of the complaint.

(k) Appeals of final determinations by the Commission to deny certification or renewal of certification, to revoke certification, or to discipline a mediator, trainer, or other training program personnel shall be filed in the General Court of Justice, Wake County Superior Court Division. Notice of appeal shall be filed within 30 days of the date of the Commission's decision.

(*l*) The Commission may issue a cease and desist letter to any individual who falsely represents himself or herself to the public as certified or as eligible to be certified pursuant to this section, or who uses any words, letters, titles, signs, cards, Web site postings, or advertisements that expressly or implicitly convey such misrepresentation to the public. If the individual continues to make such false representations after receipt of the cease and desist letter, the Commission, through its Chair, may petition the Superior Court of Wake County for an injunction restraining the individual's conduct and for any other relief that the court deems appropriate.

(m) Members of the Commission and its employees are immune from civil suit for all conduct undertaken in the course of their official duties.

History.
1995, c. 500, s. 1; 1998-212, s. 16.19(b), (c); 2005-167, ss. 2, 4; 2007-387, ss. 2, 3; 2010-169, s. 21(b); 2011-145, s. 15.5; 2011-411, s. 5; 2017-158, s. 26.8; 2019-243, s. 2(a); 2021-47, s. 4(a)

§ 7A-38.3. Prelitigation mediation of farm nuisance disputes

(a) **Definitions.** -- As used in this section:

(1) "Farm nuisance dispute" means a claim that the farming activity of a farm resident constitutes a nuisance.

(2) "Farm resident" means a person holding an interest in fee, under a real estate contract, or under a lease, in land used for farming activity when that person manages the operations on the land.

(3) "Farming activity" means the cultivation of farmland for the production of crops, fruits, vegetables, ornamental and flowering plants, and the utilization of farmland for the production of dairy, livestock, poultry, and all other forms of agricultural products having a domestic or foreign market.

(4) "Mediator" means a neutral person who acts to encourage and facilitate a resolution of a farm nuisance dispute.

(5) "Nuisance" means an action that is injurious to health, indecent, offensive to the senses, or an obstruction to the free use of property.

(6) "Party" means any person having a dispute with a farm resident.

(7) "Person" means a natural person, or any corporation, trust, or limited partnership as defined in G.S. 59-102.

(b) **Voluntary Mediation.** -- The parties to a farm nuisance dispute may agree at any time to mediation of the dispute under the provisions of this section.

(c) **Mandatory Mediation.** -- Prior to bringing a civil action involving a farm nuisance dispute, a farm resident or any other party shall initiate mediation pursuant to this section. If a farm resident or any other party brings an action involving a farm nuisance dispute, this action shall, upon the motion of any party prior to trial, be dismissed without prejudice by the court unless any one or more of the following apply:

(1) The dispute involves a claim that has been brought as a class action.

(2) The nonmoving party has satisfied the requirements of this section and such is indicated in a mediator's certification issued under subsection (g) of this section.

(3) The court finds that a mediator improperly failed to issue a certification indicating that the nonmoving party satisfied the requirements of this section.

(4) The court finds good cause for a failure to attempt mediation. Good cause includes, but is not limited to, a determination that the time delay required for mediation would likely result in irreparable harm or that injunctive relief is otherwise warranted.

(d) **Initiation of Mediation.** -- Prelitigation mediation of a farm nuisance dispute shall be initiated by filing a request for mediation with the clerk of superior court in a county in which the action may be brought. The Administrative Office of the Courts shall prescribe a request for mediation form. The party filing the request for mediation also shall mail a copy of the request by certified mail, return receipt requested, to each party to the dispute. The clerk shall provide each party with a list of mediators certified by the Dispute Resolution Commission. If the parties agree in writing to the selection of a mediator from that list, the clerk shall appoint that mediator selected by the parties. If the parties do not agree on the selection of a mediator, the party filing the request for mediation shall bring the matter to the attention of the clerk, and a mediator shall be appointed by the senior resident superior court judge. The clerk shall notify the mediator and the parties of the appointment of the mediator.

(e) **Mediation Procedure.** -- Except as otherwise expressly provided in this section, mediation under this section shall be conducted in accordance with the provisions for mediated settlement of civil cases in G.S. 7A-38.1 and G.S. 7A-38.2 and rules and standards adopted pursuant to those sections. The Supreme Court may adopt additional rules and standards to implement this section, including an exemption from the provisions of G.S. 7A-38.1 for cases in which mediation was attempted under this section.

(f) **Waiver of Mediation.** -- The parties to the dispute may waive the mediation required by this section by informing the mediator of their waiver in writing. No costs shall be assessed to any party if all parties waive mediation prior to the occurrence of an initial mediation meeting.

(g) **Certification That Mediation Concluded.** -- Immediately upon a waiver of mediation under subsection (f) of this section or upon the conclusion of mediation, the mediator shall prepare a certification stating the date on which the mediation was concluded and the general results of the mediation, including, as applicable, that the parties waived the mediation, that an agreement was reached, that mediation was attempted but an agreement was not reached, or that one or more parties, to be specified in the certification, failed or refused without good cause to attend one or more mediation meetings or otherwise participate in the mediation. The mediator shall file the original of the certification with the clerk and provide a copy to each party. Each party to the mediation has satisfied the requirements of this section upon the filing of the certification, except any party specified in the certification as having failed or refused to attend one or more mediation meetings or otherwise participate. The sanctions in G.S. 7A-38.1(g) do not apply to prelitigation mediation conducted under this section.

(h) **Time Periods Tolled.** -- Any applicable statutes of limitations relating to a farm nuisance dispute shall be tolled upon the filing of a request for mediation under this section, until

30 days after the date on which the mediation is concluded as set forth in the mediator's certification, or if the mediator fails to set forth such date, until 30 days after the filing of the certification under subsection (g) of this section. The filing of a request for prelitigation mediation under subsection (d) of this section does not constitute the commencement or the bringing of an action involving a farm nuisance dispute.

History.
1995, c. 500, s. 1; 2013-314, s. 2

§ 7A-38.3A. Prelitigation mediation of insurance claims

(a) **Initiation of Mediation.** -- Prelitigation mediation of an insurance claim may be initiated by an insurer that has provided the policy limits in accordance with G.S. 58-3-33 by filing a request for mediation with the clerk of superior court in a county in which the action may be brought. The insurer also shall mail a copy of the request by certified mail, return receipt requested, to the person who requested the information under G.S. 58-3-33.

(b) **Costs of Mediation.** -- Costs of mediation, including the mediator's fees, shall be borne by the insurer and claimant equally. When an attorney represents a party to the mediation, that party shall pay his or her attorneys' fees.

(c) **Mediation Procedure.** -- Except as otherwise expressly provided in this section, mediation under this section shall be conducted in accordance with the provisions for mediated settlement of civil cases in G.S. 7A-38.1 and G.S. 7A-38.2, and rules and standards adopted pursuant to those sections. The Supreme Court may adopt additional rules and standards to implement this section, including an exemption from the provisions of G.S. 7A-38.1 for cases in which mediation was attempted under this section.

(d) **Certification That Mediation Concluded.** -- Upon the conclusion of mediation, the mediator shall prepare a certification stating the date on which the mediation was concluded and the general results of the mediation, including, as applicable, that an agreement was reached, that mediation was attempted but an agreement was not reached, or that one or more parties, to be specified in the certification, failed or refused without good cause to attend one or more mediation meetings or otherwise participate in the mediation. The mediator shall file the original of the certification with the clerk and provide a copy to each party. Each party to the mediation has satisfied the requirements of this section upon the filing of the certification, except any party specified in the certification as having failed or refused to attend one or more

mediation meetings or otherwise participate. The sanctions in G.S. 7A-38.1(g) do not apply to prelitigation mediation conducted under this section.

(e) **Time Periods Tolled.** -- Time periods relating to the filing of a claim or the taking of other action with respect to an insurance claim, including any applicable statutes of limitations, shall be tolled upon the filing of a request for mediation under this section, until 30 days after the date on which the mediation is concluded as set forth in the mediator's certification or, if the mediator fails to set forth such date, until 30 days after the filing of the certification under subsection (d) of this section.

(f) **Medical Malpractice Claims Excluded.** -- This section does not apply to claims seeking recovery for medical malpractice.

History.
2003-307, s. 2

§ 7A-38.3B. Mediation in matters within the jurisdiction of the clerk of superior court

(a) **Purpose.** -- The General Assembly finds that the clerk of superior court in the General Court of Justice should have the discretion and authority to order that mediation be conducted in matters within the clerk's jurisdiction in order to facilitate a more economical, efficient, and satisfactory resolution of those matters.

(b) **Enabling Authority.** -- The clerk of superior court may order that mediation be conducted in any matter in which the clerk has exclusive or original jurisdiction, except for matters under Chapters 45 and 48 of the General Statutes and except in matters in which the jurisdiction of the clerk is ancillary. The Supreme Court may adopt rules to implement this section. Such mediations shall be conducted pursuant to this section and the Supreme Court rules as adopted.

(c) **Attendance.** -- In those matters ordered to mediation pursuant to this section, the following persons or entities, along with their attorneys, may be ordered by the clerk to attend the mediation:

(1) Named parties.
(2) Interested persons, meaning persons or entities who have a right, interest, or claim in the matter; heirs or devisees in matters under Chapter 28A of the General Statutes, next of kin under Chapter 35A of the General Statutes, and other persons or entities as the clerk deems necessary for the adjudication of the matter. The meaning of "interested person" may vary according to the issues involved in the matter.
(3) Nonparty participants, meaning any other person or entity identified by the

clerk as possessing useful information about the matter and whose attendance would be beneficial to the mediation.

(4) Fiduciaries, meaning persons or entities who serve as fiduciaries, as that term is defined by G.S. 36A-22.1, of named parties, interested persons, or nonparty participants.

Any person or entity ordered to attend a mediation shall be notified of its date, time, and location and shall attend unless excused by rules of the Supreme Court or by order of the clerk. No one attending the mediation shall be required to make a settlement offer or demand that it deems contrary to its best interests.

(d) **Selection of Mediator.** -- Persons ordered to mediation pursuant to this section have the right to designate a mediator in accordance with rules promulgated by the Supreme Court implementing this section. Upon failure of those persons to agree upon a designation within the time established by rules of the Supreme Court, a mediator certified by the Dispute Resolution Commission pursuant to those rules shall be appointed by the clerk.

(e) **Immunity.** -- Mediators acting pursuant to this section shall have judicial immunity in the same manner and to the same extent as a judge of the General Court of Justice, except that mediators may be disciplined in accordance with procedures adopted by the Supreme Court pursuant to G.S. 7A-38.2.

(f) **Costs of Mediation.** -- Costs of mediation under this section shall be borne by the named parties, interested persons, and fiduciaries ordered to attend the mediation. The rules adopted by the Supreme Court implementing this section shall set out the manner in which costs shall be paid and a method by which an opportunity to participate without cost shall be afforded to persons found by the clerk to be unable to pay their share of the costs of mediation. Costs may only be assessed against the estate of a decedent, the estate of an adjudicated or alleged incompetent, a trust corpus, or against a fiduciary upon the entry of a written order making specific findings of fact justifying the taxing of costs.

(g) **Inadmissibility of Negotiations.** -- Evidence of statements made or conduct occurring during a mediation conducted pursuant to this section, whether attributable to any participant, mediator, expert, or neutral observer, shall not be subject to discovery and shall be inadmissible in any proceeding in the matter or other civil actions on the same claim, except in:

(1) Proceedings for sanctions pursuant to this section;

(2) Proceedings to enforce or rescind a written and signed settlement agreement;

(3) Incompetency, guardianship, or estate proceedings in which a mediated agreement is presented to the clerk;

(4) Disciplinary hearings before the State Bar or the Dispute Resolution Commission; or

(5) Proceedings for abuse, neglect, or dependency of a juvenile, or for abuse, neglect, or exploitation of an adult, for which there is a duty to report under G.S. 7B-301 and Article 6 of Chapter 108A of the General Statutes, respectively.

No evidence otherwise discoverable shall be inadmissible merely because it is presented or discussed in mediation.

As used in this section, the term "neutral observer" includes persons seeking mediator certification, persons studying dispute resolution processes, and persons acting as interpreters.

(h) **Testimony.** -- No mediator or neutral observer shall be compelled to testify or produce evidence concerning statements made and conduct occurring in anticipation of, during, or as a follow-up to the mediation in any civil proceeding for any purpose, including proceedings to enforce or rescind a settlement of the matter except to attest to the signing of any agreements reached in mediation, and except in:

(1) Proceedings for sanctions pursuant to this section;

(2) Disciplinary hearings before the State Bar or the Dispute Resolution Commission; or

(3) Proceedings for abuse, neglect, or dependency of a juvenile, or for abuse, neglect, or exploitation of an adult, for which there is a duty to report under G.S. 7B-301 and Article 6 of Chapter 108A of the General Statutes, respectively.

(i) **Agreements.** -- In matters before the clerk in which agreements are reached in a mediation conducted pursuant to this section, or during one of its recesses, those agreements shall be treated as follows:

(1) Where as a matter of law, a matter may be resolved by agreement of the parties, a settlement is enforceable only if it has been reduced to writing and signed by the parties against whom enforcement is sought or signed by their designees.

(2) In all other matters before the clerk, including guardianship and estate matters, all agreements shall be delivered to the clerk for consideration in deciding the matter.

(j) **Sanctions.** -- Any person ordered to attend a mediation conducted pursuant to this section and rules of the Supreme Court who, without good cause, fails to attend the mediation or fails to pay any or all of the mediator's fee in compliance with this section and the rules promulgated by the Supreme Court to implement this section, is subject to the contempt powers of the clerk and monetary sanctions. The monetary sanctions may include the payment of fines, attorneys' fees, mediator fees, and the expenses and loss of earnings incurred by persons attending the mediation. If the clerk imposes sanctions, the clerk shall do so, after notice and a hearing, in a written order, making findings of fact and conclusions of law. An order imposing sanctions is reviewable by the superior court in accordance with G.S. 1-301.2 and G.S. 1-301.3, as applicable, and thereafter by the appellate courts in accordance with G.S. 7A-38.1(g).

(k) **Authority to Supplement Procedural Details.** -- The clerk of superior court shall make all those orders just and necessary to safeguard the interests of all persons and may supplement all necessary procedural details not inconsistent with rules adopted by the Supreme Court implementing this section.

History.
2005-67, s. 1; 2008-194, s. 8(b); 2015-57, s. 2; 2017-158, s. 26.7(c); 2021-47, s. 12(b)

N.C. Gen. Stat. § 7A-38.3C

Repealed by Session Laws 2007-419, s. 4, effective August 21, 2007.

§ 7A-38.3D. Mediation in matters within the jurisdiction of the district criminal courts

(a) **Purpose.** -- The General Assembly finds that it is in the public interest to promote high standards for persons who mediate matters in district criminal court. To that end, a program of certification for these mediators shall be established in judicial districts designated by the Dispute Resolution Commission and the Director of the Administrative Office of the Courts and in which the chief district court judge, the district attorney, and the community mediation center agree to participate. This section does not supersede G.S. 7A-38.5.

(b) **Enabling Authority.** -- In each district, the court may encourage mediation for any criminal district court action pending in the district, and the district attorney may delay prosecution of those actions so that the mediation may take place.

(c) **Program Administration.** -- A community mediation center established under G.S. 7A-38.5 and located in a district designated under subsection (a) of this section shall assist the court in administering a program providing mediation services in district criminal court cases. A community mediation center may assist in the screening and scheduling of cases

for mediation and provide certified volunteer or staff mediators to conduct district criminal court mediations.

(d) **Rules of Procedure.** -- The Supreme Court shall adopt rules to implement this section. Each mediation shall be conducted pursuant to this section and the Supreme Court Rules as adopted.

(e) **Mediator Authority.** -- In the mediator's discretion, any person whose presence and participation may assist in resolving the dispute or addressing any issues underlying the mediation may be permitted to attend and participate. The mediator shall have discretion to exclude any individual who seeks to attend the mediation but whose participation the mediator deems would be counterproductive. Lawyers for the participants may attend and participate in the mediation.

(f) **Mediator Qualification.** -- The Supreme Court shall establish requirements for the certification or qualification of mediators serving under this section. The Court shall also establish requirements for the qualification of training programs and trainers, including community mediation center staff, that train these mediators. The Court shall also adopt rules regulating the conduct of these mediators and trainers.

(g) **Oversight and Evaluation.** -- The Supreme Court may require community mediation centers and their volunteer or staff mediators to collect and report caseload statistics, referral sources, fees collected, and any other information deemed essential for program oversight and evaluation purposes.

(h) **Immunity.** -- A mediator under this section has judicial immunity in the same manner and to the same extent as a judge of the General Court of Justice, except that a mediator may be disciplined in accordance with procedures adopted by the Supreme Court. A community mediation center and its staff involved in supplying volunteer or staff mediators or other personnel to schedule cases or perform other duties under this section are immune from suit in any civil action, except in any case of willful or wanton misconduct.

(i) **Confidentiality.** -- Any memorandum, work note, or product of the mediator and any case file maintained by a community mediation center acting under this section and any mediator certification application are confidential.

(j) **Inadmissibility of Negotiations.** -- Evidence of any statement made and conduct occurring during a mediation under this section shall not be subject to discovery and shall be inadmissible in any proceeding in the action from which the mediation arises. Any participant in a mediation conducted under this section, including the mediator, may report to law enforcement personnel any statement made or conduct occurring during the mediation process that threatens or threatened the safety of any person or property. A mediator has discretion to warn a person whose safety or property has been threatened. No evidence otherwise discoverable is inadmissible for the reason it is presented or discussed in a mediated settlement conference or other settlement proceeding under this section.

(k) **Testimony.** -- No mediator or neutral observer present at the mediation shall be compelled to testify or produce evidence concerning statements made and conduct occurring in or related to a mediation conducted under this section in any proceeding in the same action for any purpose, except in:

(1) Proceedings for abuse, neglect, or dependency of a juvenile, or for abuse, neglect, or exploitation of an adult, for which there is a duty to report under G.S. 7B-301 and Article 6 of Chapter 108A of the General Statutes, respectively.

(2) Disciplinary hearings before the State Bar or the Dispute Resolution Commission.

(3) Proceedings in which the mediator acts as a witness pursuant to subsection (j) of this section.

(4) Trials of a felony, during which a presiding judge may compel the disclosure of any evidence arising out of the mediation, excluding a statement made by the defendant in the action under mediation, if it is to be introduced in the trial or disposition of the felony and the judge determines that the introduction of the evidence is necessary to the proper administration of justice and the evidence cannot be obtained from any other source.

(*l*) **Written Agreements.** -- Any agreement reached in mediation is enforceable only if it has been reduced to writing and signed by the parties against whom enforcement is sought. A non-attorney mediator may assist parties in reducing the agreement to writing.

(m) **Dispute Resolution Fee.** -- A dispute resolution fee shall be assessed and paid to the clerk in advance of mediation as set forth in G.S. 7A-38.7. By agreement, all or any portion of the fee may be paid by a person other than the defendant.

(n) **Definitions.** -- As used in this section, the following definitions apply:

(1) **Court.** -- A district court judge, a district attorney, or the designee of a district court judge or district attorney.

(2) **Neutral observer.** -- Includes any person seeking mediator certification, any person studying any dispute resolution process, and any person acting as an interpreter.

History.
2007-387, s. 1; 2012-194, s. 63.3(b); 2015-57, s. 3; 2016-107, s. 7; 2017-158, s. 26.7(d)

§ 7A-38.3E. Mediation of public records disputes

(a) **Voluntary Mediation.** -- The parties to a public records dispute under Chapter 132 of the General Statutes may agree at any time prior to filing a civil action under Chapter 132 of the General Statutes to mediation of the dispute under the provisions of this section. Mediation of a public records dispute shall be initiated by filing a request for mediation with the clerk of superior court in a county in which the action may be brought.

(b) **Mandatory Mediation.** -- Subsequent to filing a civil action under Chapter 132 of the General Statutes, a person shall initiate mediation pursuant to this section. Such mediation shall be initiated no later than 30 days from the filing of responsive pleadings with the clerk in the county where the action is filed.

(c) **Initiation of Mediation.** -- The Administrative Office of the Courts shall prescribe a request for mediation form. The party filing the request for mediation shall mail a copy of the request by certified mail, return receipt requested, to each party to the dispute. The clerk shall provide each party with a list of mediators certified by the Dispute Resolution Commission. If the parties agree in writing to the selection of a mediator from that list, the clerk shall appoint that mediator selected by the parties. If the parties do not agree on the selection of a mediator, the party filing the request for mediation shall bring the matter to the attention of the clerk, and a mediator shall be appointed by the senior resident superior court judge. The clerk shall notify the mediator and the parties of the appointment of the mediator.

(d) **Mediation Procedure.** -- Except as otherwise expressly provided in this section, mediation under this section shall be conducted in accordance with the provisions for mediated settlement of civil cases in G.S. 7A-38.1 and G.S. 7A-38.2 and rules and standards adopted pursuant to those sections. The Supreme Court may adopt additional rules and standards to implement this section, including an exemption from the provisions of G.S. 7A-38.1 for cases in which mediation was attempted under this section.

(e) **Waiver of Mediation.** -- The parties to the dispute may waive the mediation required by this section by informing the mediator of the parties' waiver in writing. No costs shall be assessed to any party if all parties waive mediation prior to the occurrence of an initial mediation meeting.

(f) **Certification That Mediation Concluded.** -- Immediately upon a waiver of mediation under subsection (e) of this section or upon the conclusion of mediation, the mediator shall prepare a certification stating the date on which the mediation was concluded and the general results of the mediation, including, as applicable, that the parties waived the mediation, that an agreement was reached, that mediation was attempted but an agreement was not reached, or that one or more parties, to be specified in the certification, failed or refused without good cause to attend one or more mediation meetings or otherwise participate in the mediation. The mediator shall file the original of the certification with the clerk and provide a copy to each party.

(g) **Time Periods Tolled.** -- Time periods relating to the filing of a claim or the taking of other action with respect to a public records dispute, including any applicable statutes of limitations, shall be tolled upon the filing of a request for mediation under this section, until 30 days after the date on which the mediation is concluded as set forth in the mediator's certification, or if the mediator fails to set forth such date, until 30 days after the filing of the certification under subsection (f) of this section.

(h) [Other Remedies Not Affected.] -- Nothing in this section shall prevent a party seeking production of public records from seeking injunctive or other relief, including production of public records prior to any scheduled mediation.

History.
2010-169, s. 21(a)

§ 7A-38.3F. Prelitigation mediation of condominium and homeowners association disputes

(a) **Definitions.** -- The following definitions apply in this section:

(1) **Association.** -- An association of unit or lot owners organized as allowed under North Carolina law, including G.S. 47C-3-101 and G.S. 47F-3-101.

(2) **Dispute.** -- Any matter relating to real estate under the jurisdiction of an association about which the member and association cannot agree. The term "dispute" does not include matters expressly exempted in subsection (b) of this section.

(3) **Executive board.** -- The body, regardless of name, designated in the declaration to act on behalf of an association.

(4) **Mediator.** -- A neutral person who acts to encourage and facilitate a resolution of a dispute between an association and a member.

(5) **Member.** -- A person who is a member of an association of unit or lot owners organized as allowed under North Carolina law, including G.S. 47C-3-101 and G.S. 47F-3-101.

(6) **Party or parties.** -- An association or member who is involved in a dispute, as

that term is defined in subdivision (2) of this subsection.

(b) **Voluntary Prelitigation Mediation.** -- Prior to filing a civil action, the parties to a dispute arising under Chapter 47C of the General Statutes (North Carolina Condominium Act), Chapter 47F of the General Statutes (North Carolina Planned Community Act), or an association's declaration, bylaws, or rules and regulations are encouraged to initiate mediation pursuant to this section. However, disputes related solely to a member's failure to timely pay an association assessment or any fines or fees associated with the levying or collection of an association assessment are not covered under this section.

(c) **Initiation of Mediation.** -- Either an association or a member may contact the North Carolina Dispute Resolution Commission or the Mediation Network of North Carolina for the name of a mediator or community mediation center. Upon contacting a mediator, either the association or member may supply to the mediator the physical address of the other party, or the party's representative, and the party's telephone number and e-mail address, if known. The mediator shall contact the party, or the party's representative, to notify him or her of the request to mediate. If the parties agree to mediate, they shall request in writing that the mediator schedule the mediation. The mediator shall then notify the parties in writing of the date, time, and location of the mediation, which shall be scheduled not later than 25 days after the mediator receives the written request from the parties.

(d) **Mediation Procedure.** -- The following procedures shall apply to mediation under this section:

(1) **Attendance.** -- The mediator shall determine who may attend mediation. The mediator may require the executive board or a large group of members to designate one or more persons to serve as their representatives in the mediation.

(2) All parties are expected to attend mediation. The mediator may allow a party to participate in mediation by telephone or other electronic means if the mediator determines that the party has a compelling reason to do so.

(3) If the parties cannot reach a final agreement in mediation because to do so would require the approval of the full executive board or the approval of a majority or some other percentage of the members of the association, the mediator may recess the mediation meeting to allow the executive board or members to review and vote on the agreement.

(e) **Decline Mediation.** -- Either party to a dispute may decline mediation under this section. If either party declines mediation after mediation has been initiated under subsection (c) of this section but mediation has not been held, the party declining mediation shall inform the mediator and the other party in writing of his or her decision to decline mediation. No costs shall be assessed to any party if either party declines mediation prior to the occurrence of an initial mediation meeting.

(f) **Costs of Mediation.** -- The costs of mediation, including the mediator's fees, shall be shared equally by the parties unless otherwise agreed to by the parties. Fees shall be due and payable at the end of each mediation meeting. When an attorney represents a party to the mediation, that party shall pay his or her attorneys' fees.

(g) **Certification That Mediation Concluded.** -- Upon the conclusion of mediation, the mediator shall prepare a certification stating the date on which the mediation was concluded and a statement that an agreement was reached or that mediation was attempted but an agreement was not reached. If both parties participate in mediation and a cause of action involving the dispute mediated is later filed, either party may file the certificate with the clerk of court, and the parties shall not be required to mediate again under any provision of law.

(h) **Inadmissibility of Evidence.** -- Evidence of statements made and conduct occurring during mediation under this section shall not be subject to discovery and shall be inadmissible in any proceeding in a civil action arising from the dispute which was the subject of that mediation; except proceedings to enforce or rescind a settlement agreement reached at that mediation, disciplinary proceedings before the State Bar or Dispute Resolution Commission, or proceedings to enforce laws concerning juvenile or elder abuse. No evidence otherwise discoverable shall be inadmissible merely because it is presented or discussed in a mediation under this section.

No mediator shall be compelled to testify or produce evidence concerning statements made and conduct occurring in anticipation of, during, or as a follow-up to a mediation pursuant to this section in any civil proceeding for any purpose, including proceedings to enforce or rescind the settlement agreement; except in disciplinary hearings before the State Bar or Dispute Resolution Commission and proceedings to enforce laws concerning juvenile or elder abuse, and except in proceedings to enforce or rescind an agreement reached in a mediation under this section, but only to attest to the signing of the agreement.

(i) **Time Periods Tolled.** -- Time periods relating to the filing of a civil action, including any applicable statutes of limitations or statutes of repose, with respect to a dispute described in subsection (a) of this section, shall be tolled upon the initiation of mediation under this section until 30 days after the date on which the mediation is concluded as set forth in the mediator's certification. For purposes of this section, "initiation of mediation" shall be defined as the date upon which both parties have signed the written request to schedule the mediation.

(j) **Association Duty to Notify.** -- Each association shall, in writing, notify the members of the association each year that they may initiate mediation under this section to try to resolve a dispute with the association. The association shall publish the notice required in this subsection on the association's Web site; but if the association does not have a Web site, the association shall publish the notice at the same time and in the same manner as the names and addresses of all officers and board members of the association are published as provided in G.S. 47C-3-103 and G.S. 47F-3-103.

History.
2013-127, s. 1

N.C. Gen. Stat. § 7A-38.4

Repealed by Session Laws 2001-320, s. 1, effective October 1, 2001.

§ 7A-38.4A. Settlement procedures in district court actions

(a) The General Assembly finds that a system of settlement events should be established to facilitate the settlement of district court actions involving equitable distribution, alimony, or support and to make that litigation more economical, efficient, and satisfactory to the parties, their representatives, and the State. District courts should be able to require parties to those actions and their representatives to attend a pretrial mediated settlement conference or other settlement procedure conducted under this section and rules adopted by the Supreme Court to implement this section.

(b) The definitions in G.S. 7A-38.1(b)(2) and (b)(3) apply in this section.

(c) Any chief district court judge in a judicial district may order a mediated settlement conference or another settlement procedure, as provided under subsection (g) of this section, for any action pending in that district involving issues of equitable distribution, alimony, child or post separation support, or claims arising out of contracts between the parties under G.S. 52-10, G.S. 52-10.1, or Chapter 52B of the General Statutes. The chief district court judge may adopt local rules that order settlement procedures in all of the foregoing actions and designate other district court judges or administrative personnel to issue orders implementing those settlement procedures. However, local rules adopted by a chief district court judge shall not be inconsistent with any rules adopted by the Supreme Court.

(d) The parties to a district court action where a mediated settlement conference or other settlement procedure is ordered, their attorneys, and other persons or entities with authority, by law or contract, to settle a party's claim, shall attend the mediated settlement conference or other settlement procedure, unless the rules ordering the settlement procedure provide otherwise. No party or other participant in a mediated settlement conference or other settlement procedure is required to make a settlement offer or demand that the party or participant deems contrary to that party's or participant's best interests. Parties who have been victims of domestic violence may be excused from physically attending or participating in a mediated settlement conference or other settlement procedure.

(e) Any person required to attend a mediated settlement conference or other settlement procedure under this section who, without good cause fails to attend or fails to pay any or all of the mediator or other neutral's fee in compliance with this section is subject to the contempt powers of the court and monetary sanctions imposed by a district court judge. A party seeking sanctions against another party or person shall do so in a written motion stating the grounds for the motion and the relief sought. The motion shall be served upon all parties and upon any person against whom sanctions are being sought. The court may initiate sanction proceedings upon its own motion by the entry of a show cause order. If the court imposes sanctions, it shall do so, after notice and hearing, in a written order making findings of fact and conclusions of law. An order imposing sanctions is reviewable upon appeal, and the entire record shall be reviewed to determine whether the order is supported by substantial evidence.

(f) The parties to a district court action in which a mediated settlement conference is to be held under this section shall have the right to designate a mediator. Upon failure of the parties to designate within the time established by the rules adopted by the Supreme Court, a mediator shall be appointed by a district court judge.

(g) A chief district court judge or that judge's designee, at the request of a party and with the consent of all parties, may order the parties to attend and participate in any other settlement procedure authorized by rules adopted by the Supreme Court or adopted by local district court rules, in lieu of attending a mediated settlement conference. Neutrals acting under this section shall be selected and compensated in accordance with rules adopted by the Supreme

Court. Nothing herein shall prohibit the parties from participating in other dispute resolution procedures, including arbitration, to the extent authorized under State or federal law. Nothing herein shall prohibit the parties from participating in mediation at a community mediation center operating under G.S. 7A-38.5.

(h) Mediators and other neutrals acting under this section shall have judicial immunity in the same manner and to the same extent as a judge of the General Court of Justice, except that mediators and other neutrals may be disciplined in accordance with enforcement procedures adopted by the Supreme Court under G.S. 7A-38.2.

(i) Costs of mediated settlement conferences and other settlement procedures shall be borne by the parties. Unless otherwise ordered by the court or agreed to by the parties, the mediator's fees shall be paid in equal shares by the parties. The rules adopted by the Supreme Court shall set out a method whereby a party found by the court to be unable to pay the costs of settlement procedures is afforded an opportunity to participate without cost to that party and without expenditure of State funds.

(j) Evidence of statements made and conduct occurring in a mediated settlement conference or other settlement proceeding conducted under this section, whether attributable to a party, the mediator, other neutral, or a neutral observer present at the settlement proceeding, shall not be subject to discovery and shall be inadmissible in any proceeding in the action or other civil actions on the same claim, except:

(1) In proceedings for sanctions under this section;

(2) In proceedings to enforce or rescind a settlement of the action;

(3) In disciplinary proceedings before the State Bar or the Dispute Resolution Commission; or

(4) In proceedings to enforce laws concerning juvenile or elder abuse.

As used in this subsection, the term "neutral observer" includes persons seeking mediator certification, persons studying dispute resolution processes, and persons acting as interpreters.

No settlement agreement to resolve any or all issues reached at the proceeding conducted under this section or during its recesses shall be enforceable unless it has been reduced to writing and signed by the parties against whom enforcement is sought and in all other respects complies with the requirements of Chapter 50 of the General Statutes. No evidence otherwise discoverable shall be inadmissible merely because it is presented or discussed in a settlement proceeding.

No mediator, other neutral, or neutral observer present at a settlement proceeding under this section, shall be compelled to testify or produce evidence concerning statements made and conduct occurring in anticipation of, during, or as a follow-up to a mediated settlement conference or other settlement proceeding pursuant to this section in any civil proceeding for any purpose, including proceedings to enforce or rescind a settlement of the action, except to attest to the signing of any agreements, and except proceedings for sanctions under this section, disciplinary hearings before the State Bar or the Dispute Resolution Commission, and proceedings to enforce laws concerning juvenile or elder abuse.

(k) The Supreme Court may adopt standards for the certification and conduct of mediators and other neutrals who participate in settlement procedures conducted under this section. The standards may also regulate mediator training programs. The Supreme Court may adopt procedures for the enforcement of those standards. The administration of mediator certification, regulation of mediator conduct, and decertification shall be conducted through the Dispute Resolution Commission.

(*l*) An administrative fee not to exceed two hundred dollars ($ 200.00) may be charged by the Administrative Office of the Courts to applicants for certification and annual renewal of certification for mediators and mediator training programs operating under this section. The fees collected may be used by the Director of the Administrative Office of the Courts to establish and maintain the operations of the Commission and its staff. The administrative fee shall be set by the Director of the Administrative Office of the Courts in consultation with the Dispute Resolution Commission.

(m) The Administrative Office of the Courts, in consultation with the Dispute Resolution Commission, may require the chief district court judge of any district to report statistical data about settlement procedures conducted under this section for administrative purposes.

(n) Nothing in this section or in rules adopted by the Supreme Court implementing this section shall restrict a party's right to a trial by jury.

(o) The Supreme Court may adopt rules to implement this section.

History.
1997-229, s. 1; 1998-212, s. 16.19(a); 1999-354, s. 6; 2000-140, s. 1; 2001-320, s. 2; 2001-487, s. 39; 2005-167, s. 3; 2008-194, s. 8(c); 2015-57, s. 4; 2017-158, s. 26.7(b)

§ 7A-38.5. Community mediation centers

(a) The General Assembly finds that it is in the public interest to encourage the establishment of community mediation centers, also known as dispute settlement centers or dispute resolution centers, to support the work of these centers in facilitating communication, understanding, reconciliation, and settlement of conflicts in communities, courts, and schools, and to promote the widest possible use of these centers by the courts and law enforcement officials across the State. A center may establish and charge fees for its services other than for criminal court mediations. Fees for criminal court mediation are set forth in G.S. 7A-38.7, and centers and mediators shall not charge any other fees in such cases.

(b) Community mediation centers, functioning as or within nonprofit organizations and local governmental entities, may receive referrals from courts, law enforcement agencies, and other public entities for the purpose of facilitating communication, understanding, reconciliation, and settlement of conflicts.

(c) Each chief district court judge and district attorney shall encourage mediation for any criminal district court action pending in the district when the judge and district attorney determine that mediation is an appropriate alternative.

(d) Each chief district court judge shall encourage mediation for any civil district court action pending in the district when the judge determines that mediation is an appropriate alternative.

(e) Except as provided in this subsection and subsection (f) of this section, each chief district court judge and district attorney shall refer any misdemeanor criminal action in district court that is generated by a citizen-initiated arrest warrant or criminal summons to the local mediation center for resolution, except for (i) any case involving domestic violence; (ii) any case in which the judge or the district attorney determine that mediation would be inappropriate; or (iii) any case being tried in a county in which mediation services are not available. The mediation center shall have 45 days to resolve each case and report back to the court with a resolution. The district attorney shall delay prosecution in order for the mediation to occur. If the case is not resolved through mediation within 45 days of referral, or if any party declines to enter into mediation, the court may proceed with the case as a criminal action. For purposes of this section, the term "citizen-initiated arrest warrant or criminal summons" means a warrant or summons issued pursuant to G.S. 15A-303 or G.S. 15A-304 by a magistrate or other judicial official based upon information supplied through the oath or affirmation of a private citizen.

(f) Any prosecutorial district may opt out of the mandatory mediation under subsection (e) of this section if the district attorney files a statement with the chief district court judge declaring that subsection shall not apply within the prosecutorial district.

(g) Nothing in this section is intended to prohibit or delay the appointment or engagement of an attorney for a defendant in a criminal case.

History.
1999-354, s. 1; 2011-145, s. 31.24(b); 2012-194, s. 63.3(a); 2016-107, s. 8

N.C. Gen. Stat. § 7A-38.6

Repealed by Session Laws 2014-100, s. 18B.1(g), effective July 1, 2014.

History.
2001-424, s. 22.2; 2003-284, s. 13.15(c); 2006-66, s. 14.12; 2006-203, s. 10; 2009-570, s. 28; 2011-145, s. 31.24(c); repealed by 2014-100, s. 18B.1(g), effective July 1, 2014

§ 7A-38.7. Dispute resolution fee for cases referred to mediation

(a) In each criminal case filed in the General Court of Justice that is referred to a community mediation center, a dispute resolution fee shall be assessed in the sum of sixty dollars ($ 60.00) per mediation of that criminal case, in accordance with subsection (c) of this section, to support the services provided by the community mediation centers and the Mediation Network of North Carolina. Prior to mediation, the court shall cause the mediation participants to be informed that the dispute resolution fee shall be paid as part of any mediation of a criminal case. The fee shall be paid to the clerk in advance of the mediation. Fees assessed under this section shall be paid to the clerk of superior court in the county where the case was filed and remitted by the clerk to the Mediation Network of North Carolina. The Mediation Network may retain up to three dollars ($ 3.00) of this amount as an allowance for its administrative expenses. The Mediation Network must remit the remainder of this amount to the community mediation center that mediated the case. The court may waive or reduce a fee assessed under this section only upon entry of a written order, supported by findings of fact and conclusions of law, determining there is just cause to grant the waiver or reduction.

(b) Before providing the district attorney with a dismissal form, the community mediation center shall require proof that the defendant has paid the dispute resolution fee as required by subsection (a) of this section and shall attach the receipt to the dismissal form.

(c) All related criminal charges per defendant that are subject to mediation shall be treated as a single criminal case for the purpose of calculating the sixty-dollar ($ 60.00) dispute resolution fee. In advance of the mediation, the participants, including all complainants, defendants, and other parties to the mediation, shall discuss whether the dispute resolution fee shall be allocated between them. If the participants do not reach agreement on an allocation of the dispute resolution fee, then the fee shall be the responsibility of the defendant, unless the court waives or reduces the fee upon entry of a written order, supported by findings of fact and conclusions of law, determining there is just cause to waive or reduce the fee. In connection with any mediation subject to this section, no mediator or any other community mediation center volunteer or employee shall receive any payment directly from any participant in the mediation, regardless of whether the payment is a dispute resolution fee, cost of court, restitution, or any other fee required by law or court order. No mediator or community mediation center shall charge or collect any fees for mediating criminal cases other than the dispute resolution fee assessed pursuant to subsection (a) of this section.

History.
2002-126, s. 29A.11(a); 2003-284, s. 13.13; 2011-145, s. 31.24(d); 2012-142, s. 16.6(a); 2016-107, s. 9

§ 7A-39. Cancellation of court sessions and closing court offices; extension of statutes of limitations and other emergency orders in catastrophic conditions

(a) *Cancellation of Court Sessions, Closing Court Offices.* -- In response to adverse weather or other emergency situations, including catastrophic conditions, any session of any court of the General Court of Justice may be cancelled, postponed, or altered by judicial officials, and court offices may be closed by judicial branch hiring authorities, pursuant to uniform statewide guidelines prescribed by the Director of the Administrative Office of the Courts. As used in this section, "catastrophic conditions" means any set of circumstances that makes it impossible or extremely hazardous for judicial officials, employees, parties, witnesses, or other persons with business before the courts to reach a courthouse, or that creates a significant risk of physical harm to persons in a courthouse, or that would otherwise convince a reasonable person to avoid traveling to or being in a courthouse.

(b) *Authority of Chief Justice.* -- When the Chief Justice of the North Carolina Supreme Court determines and declares that catastrophic conditions exist or have existed in one or more counties of the State, the Chief Justice may by order entered pursuant to this subsection:

(1) Extend, to a date certain no fewer than 10 days after the effective date of the order, the time or period of limitation within which pleadings, motions, notices, and other documents and papers may be

timely filed and other acts may be timely done in civil actions, criminal actions, estates, and special proceedings in each county named in the order. The Chief Justice may enter an order under this subsection during the catastrophic conditions or at any time after such conditions have ceased to exist. The order shall be in writing and shall become effective for each affected county upon the date set forth in the order, and if no date is set forth in the order, then upon the date the order is signed by the Chief Justice.

(2) Issue any emergency directives that, notwithstanding any other provision of law, are necessary to ensure the continuing operation of essential trial or appellate court functions, including the designation or assignment of judicial officials who may be authorized to act in the general or specific matters stated in the emergency order, and the designation of the county or counties and specific locations within the State where such matters may be heard, conducted, or otherwise transacted. The Chief Justice may enter such emergency orders under this subsection in response to existing or impending catastrophic conditions or their consequences. An emergency order under this subsection shall expire the sooner of the date stated in the order, or 30 days from issuance of the order, but the order may be extended in whole or in part by the Chief Justice for additional 30-day periods if the Chief Justice determines that the directives remain necessary.

(c) *In Chambers Jurisdiction Not Affected.* -- Nothing in this section prohibits a judge or other judicial officer from exercising, during adverse weather or other emergency situations, including catastrophic conditions, any in chambers or ex parte jurisdiction conferred by law upon that judge or judicial officer, as provided by law. The effectiveness of any such exercise shall not be affected by a determination by the Chief Justice that catastrophic conditions existed at the time it was exercised.

(d) Nothing in this section shall be construed to abrogate or diminish the inherent judicial powers of the Chief Justice or the Judicial Branch.

History.
2000-166, s. 1; 2006-187, s. 6; 2009-516, s. 11

SUBCHAPTER 03. SUPERIOR COURT DIVISION OF THE GENERAL COURT OF JUSTICE

ARTICLE 7 ORGANIZATION

§ 7A-40. Composition; judicial powers of clerk

The Superior Court Division of the General Court of Justice consists of the several superior courts of the State. The clerk of superior court in the exercise of the judicial power conferred upon him as ex officio judge of probate, and in the exercise of other judicial powers conferred upon him by law in respect of special proceedings and the administration of guardianships and trusts, is a judicial officer of the Superior Court Division, and not a separate court.

History.
1965, c. 310, s. 1; 1967, c. 691, s. 1; 1969, c. 1190, s. 4; 1971, c. 377, s. 4

§ 7A-41. Superior court divisions and districts; judges

(a) The counties of the State are organized into judicial divisions and superior court districts, and each superior court district has the counties, and the number of regular resident superior court judges set forth in the following table, and for districts of less than a whole county, as set out in subsection (b) of this section:

Judicial Division	Superior Court District	Counties	No. of Resident Judges
First	1	Camden, Chowan, Currituck, Dare, Gates, Pasquotank, Perquimans	2
First	2	Beaufort, Hyde, Martin, Tyrrell, Washington	1
First	3A	Pitt	2
Second	3B	Carteret, Craven, Pamlico	3
Second	4	Duplin, Jones, Onslow, Sampson	2
Second	5A	(part of New Hanover, Pender see subsection (b))	1
	5B	(part of New Hanover, see subsection (b))	1
	5C	(part of New Hanover, see subsection (b))	1

Judicial Division	Superior Court District	Counties	No. of Resident Judges
First	6A	Halifax	1
First	6B	Bertie, Hertford, Northampton	1
First	7A	Nash	1
First	7B	(part of Wilson, part of Edgecombe, see subsection (b))	1
First	7C	(part of Wilson, part of Edgecombe, see subsection (b))	1
Second	8A	Lenoir and Greene	1
Second	8B	Wayne	1
First	9	Franklin, Granville, Person, Vance, Warren	2
Third	10A	(part of Wake, see subsection (b))	1
Third	10B	(part of Wake, see subsection (b))	1
Third	10C	(part of Wake, see subsection (b))	1
Third	10D	(part of Wake, see subsection (b))	1
Third	10E	(part of Wake, see subsection (b))	1
Third	10F	(part of Wake, see subsection (b))	1
Third	11A	Harnett, Lee	1
Third	11B	Johnston	1
Third	12A	(part of Cumberland, see subsection (b))	1
Third	12B	(part of Cumberland, see subsection (b))	1
Third	12C	(part of Cumberland, see subsection (b))	2
Second	13A	Bladen, Columbus	1
Second	13B	Brunswick	1
First	14A	(part of Durham, see subsection (b))	1
First	14B	(part of Durham, see subsection (b))	3
Third	15A	Alamance	2
Fourth	15B	Orange, Chatham	2
Third	16A	Anson, Richmond, Scotland	2
Second	16B	Robeson	2
Fourth	17A	Caswell, Rockingham	2
Fourth	17B	Stokes, Surry	1
Fourth	18A	(part of Guilford, see subsection (b))	1
Fourth	18B	(part of Guilford, see subsection (b))	1
Fourth	18C	(part of Guilford, see subsection (b))	1
Fourth	18D	(part of Guilford, see subsection (b))	1
Fourth	18E	(part of Guilford, see subsection (b))	1
Fourth	19A	Cabarrus	1
Third	19B	Randolph	2
Fourth	19C	Rowan	1
Third	19D	Hoke, Moore	2
Third	20A	Montgomery, Stanly	2
Third	20B	Union	2
Fourth	21A	(part of Forsyth, see subsection (b))	1
Fourth	21B	(part of Forsyth, see subsection (b))	1
Fourth	21C	(part of Forsyth, see subsection (b))	1
Fourth	21D	(part of Forsyth, see subsection (b))	1
Fourth	22A	Alexander, Iredell	2
Fourth	22B	Davidson, Davie	2
Fourth	23	Alleghany, Ashe, Wilkes, Yadkin	1
Fifth	24	Avery, Madison, Mitchell, Watauga, Yancey	2
Fifth	25A	Burke, Caldwell	2
Fifth	25B	Catawba	2
Fifth	26A	(part of Mecklenburg, see subsection (b))	1
Fifth	26B	(part of Mecklenburg, see subsection (b))	1
Fifth	26C	(part of Mecklenburg, see subsection (b))	1
	26D	(part of Mecklenburg, see subsection (b))	1
	26E	(part of Mecklenburg, see subsection (b))	1
	26F	(part of Mecklenburg, see subsection (b))	1
	26G	(part of Mecklenburg, see subsection (b))	1
	26H	(part of Mecklenburg, see subsection (b))	1
Fifth	27A	Gaston	2

Judicial Division	Superior Court District	Counties	No. of Resident Judges
Fifth	27B	Cleveland, Lincoln	2
Fifth	28	Buncombe	2
Fifth	29A	McDowell, Rutherford	1
Fifth	29B	Henderson, Polk, Transylvania	1
Fifth	30A	Cherokee, Clay, Graham, Macon, Swain	1
Fifth	30B	Haywood, Jackson	1.

(b) For superior court districts of less than a whole county, or with part of one county with part of another, the composition of the district and the number of judges is as follows:

(1) District 5A: New Hanover County: VTD CF01, VTD CF02, VTD CF03, VTD H01, VTD W25, VTD W27; Pender County. It has one judge.

(2) District 5B: New Hanover County: VTD H02, VTD H03, VTD H04, VTD H05, VTD H06, VTD H07, VTD H08, VTD H09, VTD M02, VTD M05, VTD W13, VTD W18, VTD W24, VTD W28, VTD WB. It has one judge.

(3) District 5C: New Hanover County: VTD FP01, VTD FP02, VTD FP03, VTD FP04, VTD FP05, VTD M03, VTD M04, VTD W03, VTD W08, VTD W12, VTD W15, VTD W16, VTD W17, VTD W21, VTD W26, VTD W29, VTD W30, VTD W31. It has one judge.

(4) District 7B: Edgecombe County: VTD: 1101: Block(s) 0650213001035; VTD: 1201, VTD: 1202, VTD: 1203, VTD: 1204, VTD: 1205: Block(s) 0650203001005, 0650203001006, 0650203001007, 0650203001008, 0650203001009, 0650203001010, 0650203001011, 0650203001012, 0650203001013, 0650203001014, 0650203001015, 0650203001016, 0650203001017, 0650204001000, 0650204001001, 0650204001002, 0650204001003, 0650204001004, 0650204001005, 0650204001006, 0650204001007, 0650204001008, 0650204001009, 0650204001010, 0650204001011, 0650204001012, 0650204001013, 0650204001014, 0650204001015, 0650204001016, 0650204001017, 0650204001018, 0650204001019, 0650204001020, 0650204001021, 0650204001022, 0650204001023, 0650204001024, 0650204001025, 0650204001026, 0650204001027, 0650204001028, 0650204001029, 0650204001030, 0650204001031, 0650204001032, 0650204001033, 0650204001034, 0650204001035, 0650204001036, 0650204001037, 0650204001038, 0650204001039, 0650204001040, 0650204001041, 0650204001042, 0650204001043, 0650204001044, 0650204001045, 0650204001046, 0650204001047, 0650204001048, 0650204001049, 0650204002000, 0650204002001, 0650204002002, 0650204002003, 0650204002004, 0650204002005, 0650204002006, 0650204002007, 0650204002008, 0650204002009, 0650204002010, 0650204002011, 0650204002012, 0650204002013, 0650204002014, 0650204002015, 0650204002016, 0650204002017, 0650204002018, 0650204002019, 0650204002020, 0650204002021, 0650204002022, 0650204002023, 0650204002024, 0650204002025; VTD: 1301: 0650214002017; VTD: 1401; Wilson County: VTD: PRBL: Block(s) 1950009001045, 1950009001046; VTD: PRGA: 1950007001065, 1950007001066, 1950007001067, 1950012001000, 1950012001001, 1950012001002, 1950012001003, 1950012001012, 1950012001013, 1950012001014, 1950012001015, 1950012001016, 1950012001017, 1950012001018, 1950012001019, 1950012001020, 1950012001021, 1950012001022, 1950012001023, 1950012001025, 1950012001026, 1950012001031, 1950012001032, 1950012001033, 1950012001034, 1950012001035, 1950012001036, 1950012001038, 1950012002000, 1950012002001, 1950012002002, 1950012002003, 1950012002004, 1950012002005, 1950012002006, 1950012002007, 1950012002008, 1950012002009, 1950012002010, 1950012002011, 1950012002012, 1950012002013, 1950012002014, 1950012002016, 1950012003000, 1950012003001, 1950012003002, 1950012003003, 1950012003004, 1950012003005, 1950012003006, 1950012003007, 1950012003008, 1950012003009, 1950012003010, 1950012003011, 1950012003012, 1950012003013, 1950012003014, 1950012003015, 1950012003016, 1950012003017, 1950012003018, 1950012003019, 1950012003020, 1950012003021; VTD: PRSA: 1950011001025, 1950011001028, 1950011001030, 1950011002000; VTD: PRST: 1950008022045, 1950008022047, 1950008022055, 1950008022059, 1950008022060, 1950008022061, 1950008022063, 1950008023031, 1950008023032, 1950008023033, 1950008023034, 1950008023035, 1950008023039; VTD: PRTO: 1950012001004, 1950012001005, 1950012001006, 1950012001007, 1950012001008, 1950012001009, 1950012001010, 1950012001011, 1950012001024, 1950013001000, 1950013001001, 1950013001002, 1950013001003, 1950013001004, 1950013001005, 1950013001006, 1950013001007, 1950013001008, 1950013001009, 1950013001010, 1950013001011, 1950013001012, 1950013001013, 1950013001014, 1950013001015,

1950013001016, 1950013001017, 1950013001018, 1950013001019, 1950013001020, 1950013001021, 1950013001022, 1950013001023, 1950013001024, 1950013001025, 1950013001026, 1950013001027, 1950013001028, 1950013001029, 1950013001030, 1950013001031, 1950013001032, 1950013001033, 1950013001034, 1950013001035, 1950013001036, 1950013001037, 1950013001038, 1950013001039, 1950013001040, 1950013001041, 1950013001042, 1950013001043, 1950013001044, 1950013001045, 1950013002000, 1950013002001, 1950013002002, 1950013002003, 1950013002004, 1950013002005, 1950013002006, 1950013002007, 1950013002008, 1950013002009, 1950013002010, 1950013002011, 1950013002012, 1950013002013, 1950013002014, 1950013002015, 1950013002016, 1950013002017, 1950013002018, 1950013002019, 1950013002020, 1950013002021, 1950013002022, 1950013002023, 1950013002024, 1950013002025, 1950013002026, 1950013002027, 1950013002028, 1950013002029, 1950013002030, 1950013002031, 1950013002032, 1950013002033, 1950013002034, 1950013002035, 1950013002036, 1950013002037, 1950013002038, 1950013002039, 1950013002040, 1950013002041, 1950013002042, 1950013002043, 1950013002044, 1950013002045, 1950013002046, 1950013002047, 1950013002048, 1950013002049, 1950013002050, 1950013002051, 1950013002052, 1950013002053, 1950013002054, 1950013002055, 1950013002056, 1950013002057, 1950013002058, 1950013002059, 1950013002060, 1950013002061, 1950013002062, 1950013002063, 1950013002064, 1950013002065, 1950013002066, 1950013002067, 1950013002068, 1950013002069, 1950013002070, 1950013002074, 1950013002075, 1950013002078, 1950013002079, 1950013002080, 1950013002081, 1950013002082, 1950013002083, 1950013002084, 1950013002087, 1950013002088; VTD: PRWA, VTD: PRWB: Block(s) 1950002001000, 1950002001001, 1950002001002, 1950002001003, 1950002001004, 1950002001005, 1950002001006, 1950002001007, 1950002001008, 1950002001009, 1950002001010, 1950002001011, 1950002001012, 1950002001013, 1950002001014, 1950002001015, 1950002001016, 1950002001017, 1950002001018, 1950002001019, 1950002001020, 1950002001021, 1950002001022, 1950002001023, 1950002001024, 1950002001025, 1950002001026, 1950002001027, 1950002001028, 1950002001029, 1950002001030, 1950002001031, 1950002001032, 1950002001033, 1950002001034, 1950002001035, 1950002001036, 1950002001037, 1950002001038, 1950002001039, 1950002001040, 1950002001041, 1950002001042, 1950002001043, 1950002001044, 1950002001045, 1950002001046, 1950002001052, 1950002001053, 1950002001054, 1950002001055, 1950002001056, 1950002001057, 1950002001058, 1950002001059, 1950002001060, 1950002001062, 1950002001063, 1950002001064, 1950002001065, 1950003002000, 1950003002001, 1950003002002, 1950003002003, 1950003002004, 1950003002005, 1950003002006, 1950003002013, 1950003002017, 1950003002018, 1950003002019, 1950003002020, 1950003002021, 1950003002022, 1950003002023, 1950003002025, 1950003002026, 1950003002027, 1950003002028, 1950003002029, 1950003002030, 1950003002031, 1950003002032, 1950003002033, 1950003002034, 1950003002035, 1950003002036, 1950003002037, 1950003002038, 1950003002039, 1950008011000, 1950008011001, 1950008012000, 1950008012001, 1950008012002, 1950008012003; VTD: PRWC: 1950001003004, 1950001003005, 1950001003006, 1950001003007, 1950001003008, 1950001003015, 1950001003020, 1950001003021, 1950001004005, 1950001004006, 1950001004007, 1950001004008, 1950001004009, 1950001004017, 1950001004019, 1950001004021, 1950001004022, 1950001004023, 1950001004024, 1950001004025, 1950001004026;VTD:PRWE:1950001002003,1950001002004,1950001002005,1950001002024, 1950001002025; VTD: PRWH, VTD: PRWN, VTD: PRWQ, VTD: PRWR. It has one judge.

(5) District 7C: Edgecombe County: VTD: 0101, VTD: 0102, VTD: 0103, VTD: 0104, VTD: 0201, VTD: 0301, VTD: 0401, VTD: 0501, VTD: 0601, VTD: 0701, VTD: 0801, VTD: 0901, VTD: 1001, VTD: 1101: Block(s) 0650213001009, 0650213001034, 0650213002000, 0650213002001, 0650213002002, 0650213002003, 0650213002004, 0650213002005, 0650213002006, 0650213002007, 0650213002008, 0650213002009, 0650213002010, 0650213002011, 0650213002012, 0650213002013, 0650213002014, 0650213002015, 0650213002016, 0650213002017, 0650213002018, 0650213002019, 0650213002022, 0650213002025, 0650213002026, 0650213002027, 0650213002028, 0650213002029, 0650213002035, 0650213002036, 0650213002037, 0650213002038, 0650213002039, 0650213002040, 0650213002041, 0650213002042, 0650213002043, 0650213002044, 0650213002045, 0650213002046, 0650213002048, 0650213002049, 0650213002050, 0650213002051, 0650213002052, 0650213002053, 0650213002054, 0650213002055, 0650213002056, 0650213002057, 0650213002058, 0650213002059, 0650213002060, 0650213002061, 0650213002062, 0650213002063, 0650213002064, 0650213002065, 0650213002066,

0650213002067,   0650213002068,   0650213002069,   0650213002070,   0650213002071,
0650213002072,   0650213002073,   0650213002074,   0650213002075,   0650213002076,
0650213002077,   0650213002078,   0650213002079,   0650213002080,   0650213002081,
0650213002082, 0650213002087, 0650213002088; VTD: 1205: 0650206001083, 0650206001084,
0650206001085,   0650206001086,   0650206001087,   0650206001089,   0650206001090,
0650206001091, 0650206001092; VTD: 1301: 0650214002000, 0650214002001, 0650214002002,
0650214002003,   0650214002004,   0650214002005,   0650214002006,   0650214002007,
0650214002008,   0650214002009,   0650214002010,   0650214002011,   0650214002012,
0650214002013,   0650214002014,   0650214002015,   0650214002016,   0650214002018,
0650214002019,   0650214002020,   0650214002021,   0650214002022,   0650214002023,
0650214002025,   0650214002026,   0650214002027,   0650214002028,   0650214002029,
0650214002030,   0650214002031,   0650214002032,   0650214002033,   0650214002034,
0650214002035,   0650214002036,   0650214002037,   0650214002038,   0650214002039,
0650214002040, 0650214002041, 0650214002042, 0650214002043; Wilson County: VTD: PRBL:
Block(s) 1950009001000, 1950009001001, 1950009001002, 1950009001003, 1950009001004,
1950009001005,   1950009001006,   1950009001007,   1950009001008,   1950009001009,
1950009001010,   1950009001011,   1950009001012,   1950009001013,   1950009001014,
1950009001015,   1950009001016,   1950009001017,   1950009001018,   1950009001019,
1950009001020,   1950009001021,   1950009001022,   1950009001023,   1950009001024,
1950009001025,   1950009001026,   1950009001027,   1950009001028,   1950009001029,
1950009001030,   1950009001031,   1950009001032,   1950009001033,   1950009001034,
1950009001035,   1950009001036,   1950009001037,   1950009001038,   1950009001039,
1950009001040,   1950009001041,   1950009001042,   1950009001043,   1950009001044,
1950009001047,   1950009001048,   1950009001049,   1950009001050,   1950009001051,
1950009001052,   1950009001053,   1950009001054,   1950009001055,   1950009001056,
1950009001057,   1950009001058,   1950009001059,   1950009001060,   1950009001061,
1950009001062,   1950009001063,   1950009001064,   1950009001065,   1950009001066,
1950009001067,   1950009001068,   1950009001069,   1950009001070,   1950009001071,
1950009001072,   1950009001073,   1950009001074,   1950009001075,   1950009002000,
1950009002001,   1950009002002,   1950009002003,   1950009002004,   1950009002005,
1950009002006,   1950009002007,   1950009002008,   1950009002009,   1950009002010,
1950009002011,   1950009002012,   1950009002013,   1950009002014,   1950009002015,
1950009002016,   1950009002017,   1950009002018,   1950009002019,   1950009002020,
1950009002021,   1950009002022,   1950009002023,   1950009002024,   1950009002025,
1950009002026,   1950009002027,   1950009002028,   1950009002029,   1950009002030,
1950009002031,   1950009002032,   1950009002033,   1950009002034,   1950009002035,
1950009002036,   1950009002037,   1950009002038,   1950009002039,   1950009002040,
1950009002041,   1950009002042,   1950009002043,   1950009002044,   1950009002045,
1950009002046,   1950009002047,   1950009002048,   1950009002049,   1950009002050,
1950009002051,   1950009002052,   1950009002053,   1950009002054,   1950009003000,
1950009003001,   1950009003002,   1950009003003,   1950009003004,   1950009003006,
1950009003007,   1950009003008,   1950009003009,   1950009003010,   1950009003011,
1950009003013,   1950009003014,   1950009003015,   1950009003016,   1950009003017,
1950009003018,   1950009003019,   1950009003020,   1950009003021,   1950009003022,
1950009003023,   1950009003024,   1950009003025,   1950009003026,   1950009003027,
1950009003028,   1950009003029,   1950009003030,   1950009003031,   1950009003032,
1950009003033,   1950009003034,   1950009003035,   1950009003036,   1950009003037,
1950009003038,   1950009003039,   1950009003040,   1950009003041,   1950010001023,
1950017001000,   1950017001001,   1950017001002,   1950017002021,   1950017002022,
1950017003004,   1950017003005,   1950017003006,   1950017003007,   1950017003008,
1950017003009, 1950017003010, 1950017003035, 1950017003036; VTD: PRCR, VTD: PRGA:
Block(s) 1950012002015; VTD: PROL, VTD: PRSA: Block(s) 1950011001000, 1950011001001,
1950011001002,   1950011001003,   1950011001004,   1950011001005,   1950011001006,
1950011001007,   1950011001008,   1950011001009,   1950011001010,   1950011001011,
1950011001012,   1950011001013,   1950011001014,   1950011001015,   1950011001016,
1950011001017,   1950011001018,   1950011001019,   1950011001020,   1950011001021,
1950011001022,   1950011001023,   1950011001024,   1950011001026,   1950011001027,
1950011001029,   1950011001031,   1950011001032,   1950011001033,   1950011001034,
1950011001035,   1950011001036,   1950011001037,   1950011001038,   1950011001039,
1950011001040,   1950011001041,   1950011001042,   1950011001043,   1950011001044,
1950011001045,   1950011001046,   1950011001047,   1950011001048,   1950011001049,
1950011001050,   1950011002001,   1950011002002,   1950011002003,   1950011002004,

1950011002005, 1950011002006, 1950011002007, 1950011002008, 1950011002009, 1950011002010, 1950011002011, 1950011002012, 1950011002013, 1950011002014, 1950011002015, 1950011002016, 1950011002017, 1950011002018, 1950011002019, 1950011002020, 1950011002021, 1950011002022, 1950011002023, 1950011002024, 1950011002025, 1950011002026, 1950011002027, 1950011002028, 1950011002029, 1950011002030, 1950011002031, 1950011002032, 1950011002033, 1950011002034, 1950011002035; VTD: PRSP, VTD: PRST: Block(s) 1950008022062, 1950008022064, 1950008022065, 1950008023036, 1950008023037, 1950008023038, 1950009003005, 1950010001000, 1950010001001, 1950010001002, 1950010001003, 1950010001004, 1950010001005, 1950010001006, 1950010001007, 1950010001008, 1950010001009, 1950010001010, 1950010001011, 1950010001012, 1950010001013, 1950010001014, 1950010001015, 1950010001016, 1950010001017, 1950010001018, 1950010001019, 1950010001020, 1950010001021, 1950010001022, 1950010001024, 1950010001025, 1950010001026, 1950010001027, 1950010001028, 1950010001029, 1950010001030, 1950010001031, 1950010001032, 1950010001033, 1950010001034, 1950010001035, 1950010001036, 1950010001037, 1950010001038, 1950010001039, 1950010001040, 1950010001041, 1950010001042, 1950010001043, 1950010001044, 1950010001045, 1950010001046, 1950010001047, 1950010001048, 1950010001049, 1950010001050, 1950010001051, 1950010001052, 1950010001053, 1950010001054, 1950010001055, 1950010001056, 1950010001057, 1950010001058, 1950010001059, 1950010001060, 1950010001061, 1950010001062, 1950010001063, 1950010001064, 1950010001065, 1950010001066, 1950010001067, 1950010001068, 1950010001069, 1950010001070, 1950010001071, 1950010001072, 1950010001073, 1950010001074, 1950010001075, 1950010001076, 1950010001077, 1950010001078; VTD: PRTA, VTD: PRTO: Block(s) 1950013003000, 1950013003001, 1950013003002, 1950013003003, 1950013003004, 1950013003005, 1950013003006, 1950013003007, 1950013003008, 1950013003009, 1950013003010, 1950013003011, 1950013003012, 1950013003013, 1950013003014, 1950013003015, 1950013003016, 1950013003017, 1950013003018, 1950013003019, 1950013003020, 1950013004000, 1950013004001, 1950013004002, 1950013004003, 1950013004004, 1950013004005, 1950013004006, 1950013004007, 1950013004008, 1950013004009, 1950013004010, 1950013004011, 1950013004012, 1950013004013, 1950013004014, 1950013004015, 1950013004016, 1950013004017, 1950013004018, 1950013004019, 1950013004020, 1950013004021, 1950013004022, 1950013004023, 1950013004024, 1950013004025, 1950013004026, 1950013004027, 1950013004028, 1950013004029, 1950013004030, 1950013004031, 1950013004032, 1950013004033, 1950013004034, 1950013004035, 1950013004036, 1950013004037, 1950013004038, 1950013004039, 1950013004040, 1950013004041, 1950013004042, 1950013004043, 1950013004044, 1950013004045, 1950013004046, 1950013004047, 1950013004048, 1950013004049, 1950013004050, 1950013004051, 1950013004052, 1950013004053, 1950013004054, 1950013004055; VTD: PRWB: 1950002001047, 1950002001048, 1950002001049, 1950002001050, 1950002001051, 1950002001061; VTD: PRWC: 1950004002000, 1950004002001, 1950004002010, 1950004002011, 1950004002012, 1950004003000, 1950004003001, 1950004003002, 1950004003003, 1950004003004, 1950004003005, 1950004003006, 1950004003007, 1950004003008, 1950004003009, 1950004003010, 1950004003011, 1950004003012, 1950004003013, 1950004003014, 1950004003015, 1950004003016, 1950004003017, 1950004003018, 1950004003019, 1950004003020, 1950004003021, 1950004003022, 1950004003023, 1950004003024, 1950004003025; VTD: PRWD, VTD: PRWE: Block(s) 1950001001000, 1950001001001, 1950001001002, 1950001001003, 1950001001010, 1950001001011, 1950001001013, 1950001001014, 1950001001015, 1950001002000, 1950001002001, 1950001002002, 1950001002011, 1950001002012, 1950001002013, 1950006002000, 1950006002001, 1950006002004, 1950006002005, 1950006002006, 1950006002007, 1950006002008, 1950006002009, 1950006002010, 1950006002011, 1950006002012, 1950006002013, 1950006002014, 1950006002015, 1950006002016, 1950006003000, 1950006003001, 1950006003002, 1950006003003, 1950006003004, 1950006003005, 1950006003006, 1950006003007, 1950006003008, 1950006003009, 1950006003010, 1950006003011, 1950006003012, 1950006003013, 1950006003014, 1950006003015, 1950006003016, 1950006003017, 1950006003018, 1950006003019, 1950006003020, 1950006005019, 1950006005020, 1950006005021, 1950006005022, 1950006005023, 1950006005075, 1950013003021, 1950013003022; VTD: PRWI, VTD: PRWJ, VTD: PRWK, VTD: PRWL, VTD: PRWM, VTD: PRWP. It has one judge.

(6) Superior Court District 10A consists of Wake County Precincts: VTD: 01-01, VTD: 01-02, VTD: 01-06, VTD: 01-07, VTD: 01-14, VTD: 01-16, VTD: 01-23, VTD: 01-29, VTD: 01-31, VTD:

01-32, VTD: 01-33, VTD: 01-41, VTD: 01-48, VTD: 01-49, VTD: 04-01, VTD: 04-02, VTD: 04-03, VTD: 04-04, VTD: 04-06, VTD: 04-07, VTD: 04-10, VTD: 04-11, VTD: 04-12, VTD: 04-13, VTD: 04-14, VTD: 04-15, VTD: 04-16, VTD: 04-19, VTD: 04-20, VTD: 04-21, VTD: 11-02, VTD: 18-01, VTD: 18-04, VTD: 18-06, VTD: 18-08. It has one judge.

(7) Superior Court District 10B consists of Wake County Precincts: VTD: 01-12, VTD: 01-13, VTD: 01-18, VTD: 01-19, VTD: 01-20, VTD: 01-21, VTD: 01-22, VTD: 01-25, VTD: 01-26, VTD: 01-27, VTD: 01-34, VTD: 01-35, VTD: 01-38, VTD: 01-40, VTD: 01-46, VTD: 01-50, VTD: 13-01: Block(s) 1830527043000, 1830527043023, 1830527043024, 1830540081000, 1830540081001, 1830540081002, 1830540081003, 1830540081004, 1830540081005, 1830540081006, 1830540081007, 1830540081008, 1830540081009, 1830540081010, 1830540081011, 1830540081012, 1830540081013, 1830540081014, 1830540081015, 1830540082000, 1830540082001, 1830540082002, 1830540082003, 1830540082004, 1830540082005, 1830540082006, 1830540082007, 1830540082008, 1830540082009, 1830540082010, 1830540082011, 1830540082012, 1830540082013, 1830540082014, 1830540082015, 1830540082016, 1830540083000, 1830540083001, 1830540083002, 1830540083003, 1830540083004, 1830540083005, 1830540083006, 1830540083007, 1830540083008, 1830540083009, 1830540084000, 1830540084001, 1830540084002, 1830540181012, 1830540181013, 1830540181014, 1830540181015, 1830540181016, 1830540181017, 1830540181018, 1830540181027, 1830540181033, 1830540181034, 1830541041022, 1830541041023, 1830541041024, 1830541041025, 1830541041026, 1830541041028, 1830541041030, 1830541041031, 1830541041032, 1830541041033, 1830541041039, 1830541041040, 1830541041041, 1830541041042, 1830541041043, 1830541041044, 1830541041045, 1830541041046, 1830541041047, 1830541041048, 1830541041049, 1830541041050, 1830541042000, 1830541042002, 1830541042010, 1830541042023, 1830541042024, 1830541042025, 1830541042026, 1830541042027, 1830541042029, 1830541042030, 1830541043014, 1830541043015, 1830541043016, 1830541043017, 1830541043018, 1830541043019, 1830541043045; VTD: 13-05, VTD: 13-07, VTD: 16-02, VTD: 16-03, VTD: 16-06, VTD: 16-08, VTD: 17-06, VTD: 17-07, VTD: 17-08, VTD: 17-09, VTD: 17-10, VTD: 17-11. It has one judge.

(8) Superior Court District 10C consists of Wake County Precincts: VTD: 02-01, VTD: 02-02, VTD: 02-03, VTD: 02-04, VTD: 02-05, VTD: 02-06, VTD: 07-02, VTD: 07-06, VTD: 07-07, VTD: 07-11, VTD: 07-12, VTD: 08-02, VTD: 08-03, VTD: 08-04, VTD: 08-05, VTD: 08-06, VTD: 08-07, VTD: 08-08, VTD: 08-09, VTD: 08-10, VTD: 08-11, VTD: 13-10, VTD: 13-11, VTD: 14-01, VTD: 14-02, VTD: 19-03, VTD: 19-04, VTD: 19-05, VTD: 19-06, VTD: 19-07, VTD: 19-09, VTD: 19-10, VTD: 19-11, VTD: 19-12. It has one judge.

(9) Superior Court District 10D consists of Wake County Precincts: VTD: 01-03, VTD: 01-04, VTD: 01-05, VTD: 01-09, VTD: 01-10, VTD: 01-11, VTD: 01-15, VTD: 01-17, VTD: 01-30, VTD: 01-36, VTD: 01-37, VTD: 01-39, VTD: 01-43, VTD: 01-45, VTD: 01-51, VTD: 04-05, VTD: 04-08, VTD: 04-09, VTD: 04-17, VTD: 04-18, VTD: 05-01, VTD: 05-03, VTD: 05-04, VTD: 05-05, VTD: 05-06, VTD: 07-01, VTD: 07-03, VTD: 07-04, VTD: 07-05, VTD: 07-09, VTD: 07-10, VTD: 07-13, VTD: 11-01, VTD: 20-02, VTD: 20-04, VTD: 20-10. It has one judge.

(10) Superior Court District 10E consists of Wake County Precincts: VTD: 01-28, VTD: 01-42, VTD: 01-44, VTD: 01-47, VTD: 09-01, VTD: 09-02, VTD: 09-03, VTD: 10-01, VTD: 10-02, VTD: 10-03, VTD: 10-04, VTD: 13-01: Block(s) 1830541041000, 1830541041001, 1830541041002, 1830541041003, 1830541041004, 1830541041005, 1830541041006, 1830541041007, 1830541041008, 1830541041009, 1830541041010, 1830541041011, 1830541041012, 1830541041013, 1830541041014, 1830541041015, 1830541041016, 1830541041017, 1830541041018, 1830541041019, 1830541041020, 1830541041021, 1830541042028; VTD: 13-02, VTD: 13-06, VTD: 13-08, VTD: 13-09, VTD: 15-01, VTD: 15-03, VTD: 15-04, VTD: 16-01, VTD: 16-04, VTD: 16-05, VTD: 16-07, VTD: 16-09, VTD: 17-01, VTD: 17-02, VTD: 17-03, VTD: 17-04, VTD: 17-05, VTD: 19-16, VTD: 19-17. It has one judge.

(11) Superior Court District 10F consists of Wake County Precincts: VTD: 03-00, VTD: 06-01, VTD: 06-04, VTD: 06-05, VTD: 06-06, VTD: 06-07, VTD: 12-01, VTD: 12-02, VTD: 12-04, VTD: 12-05, VTD: 12-06, VTD: 12-07, VTD: 12-08, VTD: 12-09, VTD: 15-02, VTD: 18-02, VTD: 18-03, VTD: 18-05, VTD: 18-07, VTD: 20-01, VTD: 20-03, VTD: 20-05, VTD: 20-06, VTD: 20-08, VTD: 20-09, VTD: 20-11, VTD: 20-12. It has one judge.

(12) District 12A: Cumberland County: VTD: AH49, VTD: CC18: Block(s) 0510007011012, 0510007011013, 0510007011014, 0510007011015, 0510007011016, 0510007011021, 0510007011034, 0510007011035, 0510007013011, 0510007013012, 0510007013013, 0510007013014, 0510007013015, 0510007013016, 0510007013017, 0510007013018, 0510007013019, 0510007013020, 0510007013021, 0510007013022, 0510007013023, 0510007013024, 0510007013025, 0510007013026, 0510007013027, 0510007013028,

0510007013029, 0510007013030, 0510007013031, 0510007013032, 0510007022007, 0510007022008; VTD: CC24: 0510020011058, 0510020021002, 0510033022004; VTD: CC25, VTD: CC27, VTD: CC29, VTD: CC31, VTD: CC32, VTD: CC33, VTD: CC34, VTD: CU02, VTD: G10: Block(s) 0510016011001, 0510016011002, 0510016011004, 0510016011005, 0510016011006, 0510016011007, 0510016011009, 0510016011010, 0510016011011, 0510016011012, 0510016011013, 0510016011014, 0510016011015, 0510016011016, 0510016011017, 0510016011018, 0510016011019, 0510016011020, 0510016011021, 0510016011022, 0510016011023, 0510016011024, 0510016011025, 0510016011026, 0510016011027, 0510016011032, 0510016011041, 0510016012041, 0510031021000, 0510031021001, 0510031021002, 0510031021003, 0510031021004, 0510031021005, 0510031021006, 0510031021007, 0510031021008, 0510031021009, 0510031021010, 0510031021011, 0510031021012, 0510031021013, 0510031021014, 0510031021015, 0510031021016, 0510031021017, 0510031021018, 0510031021019, 0510031021020, 0510031021021, 0510031021022, 0510031021023, 0510031021024, 0510031021025, 0510031021026, 0510031021027, 0510031021028, 0510031021029, 0510031021030, 0510031021031, 0510031021032, 0510031021033, 0510031021034, 0510031021035, 0510031021036, 0510031021037, 0510031021038, 0510031021039, 0510031021040, 0510031021041, 0510031021042, 0510031021043, 0510031021044, 0510031021045, 0510031021046, 0510031021047, 0510031021048, 0510031021049, 0510031021050, 0510031021051, 0510031021052, 0510031021053, 0510031021054, 0510031021055, 0510031021056, 0510031021057, 0510031021058, 0510031021059, 0510031021060, 0510031021061, 0510031021062, 0510031031001, 0510031031002, 0510031031003, 0510031031004, 0510031031005, 0510031031006, 0510031031007, 0510031031008, 0510031031009, 0510031031010, 0510031031016, 0510031032004, 0510031032005, 0510031032006, 0510031032007, 0510031032008, 0510031032009, 0510031032010, 0510031032011, 0510031032012, 0510031032013, 0510031032014, 0510031032015, 0510031032017, 0510031032018, 0510031032019, 0510031032020, 0510031032021, 0510031032023, 0510031032024, 0510031032026, 0510031032027, 0510031032028, 0510031032029, 0510031032034, 0510031032036, 0510031032041, 0510031032042, 0510031032043, 0510031032044, 0510031032046, 0510031032047, 0510031032048, 0510031032049, 0510031032052, 0510031032053, 0510031032054, 0510031033000, 0510031033001, 0510031033009, 0510031033010, 0510031033011, 0510031033013, 0510031033015, 0510031033016, 0510031033030, 0510031033036, 0510032012000, 0510032012001, 0510032012002, 0510032012003, 0510032012004, 0510032012005, 0510032012006, 0510032012007, 0510032012008, 0510032012009, 0510032012010, 0510032012011, 0510032012012, 0510032012013, 0510032012014, 0510032012015, 0510032012016, 0510032012017, 0510032012018, 0510032012019, 0510032012020, 0510032012021, 0510032012022, 0510032012023, 0510032012024, 0510032012025, 0510032012026, 0510032012027, 0510032012028, 0510032012029, 0510032013000, 0510032013001, 0510032013002, 0510032013003, 0510032013004, 0510032013005, 0510032013006, 0510032013007, 0510032013008, 0510032013009, 0510032013010, 0510032013011, 0510032013012, 0510032013013, 0510032013014, 0510032013015, 0510032013016, 0510032013017, 0510032013018, 0510032013019, 0510032013020, 0510032013021, 0510032013022, 0510032013023, 0510032013024, 0510032013025, 0510032013026, 0510032013027, 0510032013028, 0510032013029, 0510032013030, 0510032013031, 0510032013032, 0510032013033, 0510032013034, 0510032013035, 0510032013036, 0510032013037, 0510032013038, 0510032013039, 0510032013040, 0510032013041, 0510032013042, 0510032013043, 0510032013044, 0510032013045, 0510032013046, 0510032014026, 0510032014027, 0510032014028, 0510032014029, 0510032014030, 0510032014031, 0510032014032, 0510032014033, 0510032014034, 0510032014040, 0510032014041, 0510032014042, 0510032014045, 0510032014046, 0510032014047, 0510032014048, 0510032014049, 0510032014050, 0510032014051, 0510032014057; VTD: G5, VTD: G8: Block(s) 0510016011003, 0510016011008, 0510017001035, 0510017003011, 0510017003013, 0510017003014, 0510017004022, 0510017004023, 0510017004024, 0510017004025, 0510017004026, 0510017004027, 0510017004028, 0510017004029, 0510017004030, 0510017004031, 0510017004032, 0510017004033, 0510017004034, 0510017004035, 0510017004036, 0510017004037, 0510017004038, 0510017004039, 0510017004040, 0510017004041, 0510017004042, 0510017004043, 0510017004046, 0510017004047, 0510017004048, 0510019011000, 0510019011001, 0510019011002, 0510019011003, 0510019011004, 0510019011005, 0510019011008, 0510019011009, 0510019011010, 0510019011011, 0510019011012, 0510019011013, 0510019011014, 0510019011015, 0510019011016, 0510019011017, 0510019011018, 0510019011020,

0510019011021, 0510019011022, 0510019011023, 0510019011024, 0510019011025, 0510019011026, 0510019011028, 0510019011029, 0510019011030, 0510019011031, 0510019011032, 0510019011033, 0510019011034, 0510019011035, 0510019011036, 0510019011037, 0510019011038, 0510019011039, 0510019011041, 0510019011042, 0510019022014, 0510019022015, 0510019022018, 0510019022022, 0510019022023, 0510019022024, 0510019022025, 0510019022026, 0510019022027, 0510019022028, 0510019022029, 0510019022030, 0510019022031, 0510019022032, 0510019022033, 0510019022034, 0510019022035, 0510019022036, 0510019022037, 0510019022038, 0510019022039, 0510019022040, 0510019022041, 0510019022044, 0510019022045, 0510019022046, 0510019031003, 0510019031004, 0510019031005, 0510019031006, 0510019031007, 0510019031008, 0510019031009, 0510019031010, 0510019031011, 0510019031012, 0510019031015, 0510019031016, 0510019031017, 0510019031018, 0510032014000, 0510032014001, 0510032014002, 0510032014003, 0510032014004, 0510032014005, 0510032014006, 0510032014007, 0510032014008, 0510032014009, 0510032014010, 0510032014011, 0510032014012, 0510032014013, 0510032014014, 0510032014015, 0510032014016, 0510032014017, 0510032014018, 0510032014019, 0510032014020, 0510032014021, 0510032014022, 0510032014023, 0510032014024, 0510032014025, 0510032014035, 0510032014036, 0510032014037, 0510032014038, 0510032014039, 0510032014043, 0510032014044, 0510032014055, 0510032014056, 0510032033016, 0510032033017, 0510032033019, 0510032033020, 0510032033021, 0510032033022, 0510032033023, 0510032044002, 0510032044003, 0510032044004, 0510032044005, 0510032044006, 0510032044007, 0510032044008, 0510032044009, 0510032044010, 0510032044011, 0510032044012, 0510032044013, 0510032044014, 0510032044015, 0510032044016, 0510032044017, 0510032045003, 0510032045004, 0510032045005, 0510032045006, 0510032045007, 0510032045008, 0510032045009, 0510032045011, 0510032045013, 0510032045014, 0510032045015, 0510032045016, 0510032045017, 0510032045018, 0510032045019, 0510032045020, 0510032045021, 0510032045022, 0510032045023, 0510032045024, 0510032045025, 0510032045026, 0510032045027; VTD: MB62: 0510033104011, 0510033111015; VTD: MR02. It has one judge.

(13) District 12B: Cumberland County: VTD: CC01, VTD: CC03, VTD: CC05, VTD: CC13: Block(s) 0510008001000, 0510008001002, 0510008001003, 0510008001004, 0510008001018, 0510008001019, 0510010001001, 0510010001002, 0510010001003, 0510010001004, 0510010001005, 0510010001006, 0510010001007, 0510010002000, 0510010002001, 0510010002002, 0510010002003, 0510010002010, 0510010002014, 0510010002015, 0510010002016, 0510010002017, 0510010002018, 0510010002019, 0510010002020, 0510010002021, 0510010002022, 0510010002023, 0510010002024, 0510010002025, 0510010002026, 0510010002027, 0510010002028, 0510010002029, 0510010002030, 0510010002031, 0510010002032, 0510010002033, 0510010002034, 0510011003017, 0510011003018, 0510011003019, 0510011003020, 0510011003021, 0510011003022, 0510011003023, 0510011003024, 0510011003025, 0510011003026; VTD: CC15: 0510006003000, 0510006003001, 0510006003002, 0510006003003, 0510006003004, 0510006003005, 0510006003006, 0510006003007, 0510006003008, 0510006003013, 0510006005000, 0510006005001, 0510006005002, 0510006005003, 0510006005004, 0510006005005, 0510006005006, 0510006005007, 0510006005008, 0510006005009, 0510006005010, 0510006005011, 0510006005012, 0510006005013, 0510006005014, 0510006005015, 0510006005016, 0510006005018, 0510006005019, 0510006005020, 0510006005021, 0510006005022, 0510006005023, 0510038003033, 0510038003034, 0510038003060, 0510038003061; VTD: CC16, VTD: CC17, VTD: CC19, VTD: CL57, VTD: G11: Block(s) 0510025041000, 0510033132008; 0510034011000, 0510034011001, 0510034011002, 0510034011003, 0510034011004, 0510034011005, 0510034011006, 0510034011007, 0510034011008, 0510034011009, 0510034011010, 0510034011011, 0510034011012, 0510034011013, 0510034011014, 0510034011015, 0510034011016, 0510034011017, 0510034011018, 0510034011019, 0510034011020, 0510034011021, 0510034011022, 0510034011023, 0510034011024, 0510034011025, 0510034011026, 0510034011027, 0510034011028, 0510034011029, 0510034011030, 0510034011031, 0510034011032, 0510034011033, 0510034011034, 0510034011035, 0510034011036, 0510034011037, 0510034011038, 0510034011039, 0510034011040, 0510034011041, 0510034011042, 0510034011043, 0510034012000, 0510034012001, 0510034012002, 0510034012003, 0510034012004, 0510034012005, 0510034012006, 0510034012007, 0510034012008, 0510034012009, 0510034012010, 0510034012011, 0510034012012, 0510034012013, 0510034012014, 0510034012015, 0510034012016, 0510034012017, 0510034012018, 0510034012019, 0510034012020, 0510034012021, 0510034012022, 0510034012023,

0510034012024, 0510034012025, 0510034012026, 0510034012027, 0510034012028,
0510034012029, 0510034012030, 0510034012031, 0510034012032, 0510034012033,
0510034012034, 0510034012035, 0510034012036, 0510034012037, 0510034012038,
0510034012039, 0510034012040, 0510034012041, 0510034012042, 0510034012043,
0510034012044, 0510034012045, 0510034012046, 0510034012047, 0510034012048,
0510034012049, 0510034012050, 0510034012051, 0510034012052, 0510034012053,
0510034012054, 0510034012055, 0510034012056, 0510034012057, 0510034012058,
0510034012059, 0510034012060, 0510034012061, 0510034012062, 0510034012063,
0510034012064, 0510034012065, 0510034012066, 0510034012067, 0510034012068,
0510034012069, 0510034021000, 0510034021001, 0510034021002, 0510034021003,
0510034021004, 0510034021005, 0510034021006, 0510034021007, 0510034021008,
0510034021009, 0510034021010, 0510034021011, 0510034021012, 0510034021013,
0510034021014, 0510034021015, 0510034021016, 0510034021017, 0510034021018,
0510034021019, 0510034021020, 0510034021021, 0510034021022, 0510034021023,
0510034021024, 0510034021025, 0510034021026, 0510034021027, 0510034021028,
0510034021029, 0510034021030, 0510034021031, 0510034022000, 0510034022001,
0510034022002, 0510034022003, 0510034031000, 0510034031001, 0510034031002,
0510034031003, 0510034031004, 0510034031005, 0510034031006, 0510034031007,
0510034031008, 0510034031009, 0510034031010, 0510034031011, 0510034031012,
0510034031013, 0510034032000, 0510034032001, 0510034032002, 0510034032003,
0510034032004, 0510034032005, 0510034032006, 0510034032007, 0510034032008,
0510034032009, 0510034032010, 0510034032011, 0510034032012, 0510034032013,
0510034032014, 0510034032015, 0510034041000, 0510034041001, 0510034041002,
0510034041003, 0510034041004, 0510034041005, 0510034041006, 0510034041007,
0510034041008, 0510034041009, 0510034042000, 0510034042001, 0510034042002,
0510034042003, 0510034042004, 0510034042005, 0510034042006, 0510034042007,
0510034042008, 0510034042009, 0510034042010, 0510034042011, 0510034042012,
0510034042013, 0510034042014, 0510034042015, 0510034042016, 0510034042017,
0510034042018, 0510034042019, 0510034051000, 0510034051001, 0510034051002,
0510034051003, 0510034051004, 0510034051005, 0510034051006, 0510034051007,
0510034051008, 0510034051009, 0510034051010, 0510034051011, 0510034051012,
0510034051013, 0510034051014, 0510034051015, 0510034051016, 0510034051017,
0510034051018, 0510034051019, 0510034051020, 0510034051021, 0510034051022,
0510034051023, 0510034051024, 0510034051025, 0510034051026, 0510034051027,
0510034051028, 0510034051029, 0510034051030, 0510034051031, 0510034051032,
0510034061000, 0510034061001, 0510034061002, 0510034061003, 0510034061004,
0510034061005, 0510034061006, 0510034061007, 0510034061008, 0510034061009,
0510034061010, 0510034061011, 0510034061012, 0510034061013, 0510034061014,
0510034061015, 0510034061016, 0510034061017, 0510034061018, 0510034061019,
0510034061020, 0510034061021, 0510034061022, 0510034061023, 0510034061024,
0510034061025, 0510034061026, 0510034061027, 0510034061028, 0510034061029,
0510034061030, 0510034061031, 0510034061032, 0510034061033, 0510034061034,
0510034061035, 0510034061036, 0510034061037, 0510034061038, 0510034061039,
0510034061040, 0510034061041, 0510034061042, 0510034061043, 0510034061044,
0510034061045, 0510034061046, 0510034061047, 0510034061048, 0510034061049,
0510034061050, 0510034061051, 0510034061052, 0510034061053, 0510034061054,
0510034061055, 0510034061056, 0510034061057, 0510034061058, 0510034061059,
0510034061060, 0510034061061, 0510034061062, 0510034061063, 0510034061064,
0510034061065, 0510034061066, 0510034061067, 0510034061068, 0510034061069,
0510034061070, 0510034061071, 0510034061072, 0510034061073, 0510034061074,
0510034061075, 0510034061076, 0510034061077, 0510034061078, 0510034061079,
0510034061080, 0510034061081, 0510034061082, 0510034061083, 0510034061084,
0510034061085, 0510034061086, 0510034061087, 0510034061088, 0510034061089,
0510034061090, 0510034061091, 0510034061092, 0510034061093, 0510034061094,
0510034061095, 0510034061096, 0510034061097, 0510034061098, 0510034061099,
0510034061100, 0510034061101, 0510034061102, 0510034061103, 0510034061104,
0510034061105, 0510034061106, 0510034061107, 0510034061108, 0510034061109,
0510034071000, 0510034071001, 0510034071002, 0510034071003, 0510034071004,
0510034071005, 0510034071006, 0510034071007, 0510034071008, 0510034071009,
0510034071010, 0510034071011, 0510034071012, 0510034071013, 0510034071014,
0510034071015, 0510034071016, 0510034071017, 0510034071018, 0510034072000,
0510034072001, 0510034072002, 0510034072003, 0510034072004, 0510034072005,

0510034072006,	0510034072007,	0510034072008,	0510034072009,	0510034072010,
0510034072011,	0510034081000,	0510034081001,	0510034081002,	0510034081003,
0510034081004,	0510034081005,	0510034081006,	0510034081007,	0510034081008,
0510034081009,	0510034081010,	0510034081011,	0510034081012,	0510034081013,
0510034081014,	0510034081015,	0510034081016,	0510034081017,	0510034081018,
0510034081019,	0510034081020,	0510034081021,	0510034081022,	0510034081023,
0510034081024,	0510034081025,	0510034081026,	0510034081027,	0510034081028,
0510034081029,	0510034081030,	0510034081031,	0510034081032,	0510034081033,
0510034081034,	0510034081035,	0510034081036,	0510034081037,	0510034081038,
0510034081039,	0510034081040,	0510034081041,	0510034081042,	0510034081043,
0510034081044,	0510034081045,	0510034081046,	0510034082000,	0510034082001,
0510034082002,	0510034082003,	0510034082004,	0510034082005,	0510034082006,
0510034082007,	0510034082008,	0510034082009,	0510034082010,	0510034082011,
0510034082012,	0510034082013,	0510034082014,	0510034082015,	0510034082016,
0510034082017,	0510034082018,	0510034082019,	0510034082020,	0510034082021,
0510034082022,	0510034082023,	0510034082024,	0510034082025,	0510034082026,
0510034082027,	0510034082028,	0510034082029,	0510034082030,	0510034082031,
0510034082032,	0510034082033,	0510034082034,	0510034082035,	0510034082036,
0510034082037,	0510034082038,	0510034082039,	0510034082040,	0510034082041,
0510034082042,	0510034082043,	0510034082044,	0510034082045,	0510034082046,
0510034082047,	0510034082048,	0510034082049,	0510034082050,	0510034082051,
0510034082052,	0510034082053,	0510034082054,	0510034082055,	0510034082056,
0510034082057,	0510034082058,	0510034082059,	0510034082060,	0510034082061,
0510034082062,	0510034082063,	0510034082064,	0510034082065,	0510034082066,
0510034082067,	0510034082068,	0510034082069,	0510034082070,	0510034082071,
0510034082072,	0510034082073,	0510034082074,	0510035001000,	0510035001001,
0510035001002,	0510035001003,	0510035001004,	0510035001005,	0510035001006,
0510035001007,	0510035001008,	0510035001009,	0510035001010,	0510035001011,
0510035001012,	0510035001013,	0510035001014,	0510035001015,	0510035001016,
0510035001017,	0510035001018,	0510035001019,	0510035001020,	0510035001021,
0510035001022,	0510035001023,	0510035001024,	0510035001025,	0510035001026,
0510035001027,	0510035001028,	0510035001029,	0510035001030,	0510035002000,
0510035002001,	0510035002002,	0510035002003,	0510035002004,	0510035002005,
0510035002006,	0510035002007,	0510035002008,	0510035002009,	0510035002010,
0510035002011,	0510035002012,	0510035002013,	0510035002014,	0510035002015,
0510035002016,	0510035002017,	0510035002018,	0510035002019,	0510035002020,
0510035002021,	0510035002022,	0510035002023,	0510035002024,	0510035002025,
0510035002026,	0510035002027,	0510035002028,	0510035002029,	0510035003000,
0510035003001,	0510035003002,	0510035003003,	0510035003004,	0510035003005,
0510035003006,	0510035003007,	0510035003008,	0510035003009,	0510035003010,
0510035003011,	0510035003012,	0510035003013,	0510035003014,	0510035003015,
0510035003016,	0510035003017,	0510035003018,	0510035003019,	0510035003020,
0510035003021,	0510035003022,	0510035003023,	0510035003024,	0510035003025,
0510035003026,	0510035003027,	0510035003028,	0510035003029,	0510035003030,
0510035003031,	0510035003032,	0510035003033,	0510035003034,	0510035003035,
0510035003036,	0510035003037,	0510035004000,	0510035004001,	0510035004002,
0510035004003,	0510035004004,	0510035004005,	0510035004006,	0510035004007,
0510035004008,	0510035004009,	0510035004010,	0510035004011,	0510035004012,
0510035004013,	0510035004014,	0510035004015,	0510035004016,	0510035004017,
0510035004018,	0510035004019,	0510035004020,	0510035004021,	0510035004022,
0510035004023,	0510035004024,	0510035004025,	0510035004026,	0510035004027,
0510035004028,	0510035004029,	0510036001011,	0510036001018,	0510036001020,
0510036001023,	0510036001024,	0510036001025,	0510036001026,	0510036001027,
0510036001028,	0510036001029,	0510036001030,	0510036001031,	0510036001032,
0510036001033,	0510036001034,	0510036001035,	0510036001036,	0510036001037,
0510036001038,	0510036001043,	0510036001044,	0510036001045,	0510036001046,
0510036001047,	0510036001048,	0510036001049,	0510036001050,	0510036001051,
0510036001052,	0510036001053,	0510036001054,	0510036001055,	0510036001056,
0510036001057,	0510036001058,	0510036001059,	0510036001060,	0510036002000,
0510036002001,	0510036002002,	0510036002003,	0510036002004,	0510036002005,
0510036002006,	0510036002007,	0510036002008,	0510036002009,	0510036002010,
0510036002011,	0510036002012,	0510036003013,	0510036003034,	0510036003036,

0510036004002, 0510036004003, 0510036004004, 0510036004005, 0510036004006, 0510036004007, 0510036004008, 0510036004009, 0510036004010, 0510036004011, 0510036004012, 0510036004013, 0510036004014, 0510036004015, 0510036004016, 0510036004017, 0510036004018, 0510036004019, 0510036004020, 0510036004021, 0510036004022, 0510036004023, 0510036004024, 0510036004025, 0510036004026, 0510036004027, 0510036004028, 0510036004029, 0510036004030, 0510036004031, 0510036004032, 0510036004033, 0510036004034, 0510036004035, 0510036004036, 0510036004037, 0510036004038, 0510036004039, 0510036004040, 0510036004041, 0510036004042, 0510036004043, 0510036004044, 0510036004045, 0510036004046, 0510036004047, 510036004049, 0510036004050, 0510036004051, 0510036004052, 0510036004053, 0510036004054, 0510036004055, 0510036004056, 0510036004057, 0510036004058, 0510036004059, 0510037001003, 0510037001023, 0510037001024, 0519801001005, 0519801001006, 0519801001009, 0519801001017, 0519801001018, 0519801001019, 0519801001020, 0519801001021, 0519801001022, 0519801001023, 0519801001024, 0519801001025, 0519801001026, 0519801001027, 0519801001028, 0519801001029, 0519801001030, 0519801001031, 0519801001032, 0519801001033, 0519801001034, 0519801001035, 0519801001036, 0519801001037, 0519801001038, 0519801001039, 0519801001040, 0519801001041, 0519801001042, 0519801001043, 0519801001044, 0519801001045, 0519801001046, 0519801001047, 0519801001048, 0519801001049, 0519801001051, 0519801001052, 0519801001053, 0519801001054, 0519801001055, 0519801001056, 0519801001057, 0519801001058, 0519801001059, 0519801001060, 0519801001061, 0519801001062, 0519801001063, 0519801001064, 0519801001065, 0519801001066, 0519801001067, 0519801001068, 0519802001000, 0519802001001, 0519802001002, 0519802001003, 0519802001004, 0519802001005, 0519802001006, 0519802001007, 0519802001008, 0519802001009, 0519802001010, 0519802001011, 0519802001012, 0519802001013, 0519802001014, 0519802001015, 0519802001016, 0519802001017, 0519802001018, 0519802001019, 0519802001020, 0519802001021, 0519802001022, 0519802001023, 0519802001024, 0519802001025, 0519802001026, 0519802001028, 0519802001029, 0519802001030, 0519802001031, 0519802001032, 0519802001033, 0519802001034, 0519802001035, 0519802001036, 0519802001037, 0519802001038, 0519802001039, 0519802001040, 0519802001041, 0519802001042, 0519802001043, 0519802001044, 0519802001045; VTD: G2: 0510012001000, 0510012001001, 0510012001002, 0510012001003, 0510012001004, 0510012001005, 0510012001006, 0510012001007, 0510012001008, 0510012001009, 0510012001010, 0510024022002, 0510024022003, 0510024022005, 0510024022006, 0510024023000, 0510024023001, 0510024023002, 0510024023003, 0510024023004, 0510024023005, 0510024023006, 0510024023007, 0510024023008, 0510024023009, 0510024023011, 0510024023012, 0510024023013, 0510025013009, 0510025013010, 0510025013011, 0510025013012, 0510025013013, 0510025013018, 0510025013019, 0510025013021, 0510025013022, 0510025013024, 0510025013025, 0510025013026, 0510025013027, 0510025013028, 0510025013029, 0510025013030, 0510025013032, 0510025013034, 0510025013035, 0510025013036, 0510025013041, 0510025013042, 0510025013043, 0510025013044, 0510025013045, 0510025013046, 0510025013047, 0510025013048, 0510025013049, 0510025013050, 0510025013051, 0510025013052, 0510025013063, 0510025013064, 0510025013065, 0510025013068, 0510025013071, 0510025013072, 0510025013073, 0510025013074, 0510025013075, 0510025013076; VTD: LR63, VTD: MB62: Block(s) 0510033071009, 0510033071010, 0510033072000, 0510033072001, 0510033072002, 0510033072003, 0510033072004, 0510033072005, 0510033072006, 0510033072007, 0510033072008, 0510033072029, 0510033141000, 0510033141001, 0510033141002, 0510033141003, 0510033141004, 0510033141005, 0510033141006, 0510033141007, 0510033141008, 0510033141009, 0510033141010, 0510033141011, 0510033141012, 0510033141013, 0510033141014, 0510033141015, 0510033141016, 0510033141017, 0510033141018, 0510033141019, 0510033141020, 0510033141021, 0510033141022, 0510033141023, 0510033141024, 0510033141025, 0510033143000, 0510033143001, 0510033143002, 0510033143003, 0510033143009, 0510033143010, 0510033143011, 0510033143012, 0510033143013, 0510033143014. It has one judge.

(14) District 12C: Cumberland County: VTD: AL51, VTD: CC04, VTD: CC06, VTD: CC07, VTD: CC08, VTD: CC10, VTD: CC12, VTD: CC13: Block(s) 0510009004000, 0510009004020; VTD: CC14, VTD: CC15: Block(s) 0510006001000, 0510006001001, 0510006001002, 0510006001003, 0510006001004, 0510006001005, 0510006001006, 0510006001007, 0510006001008, 0510006001009, 0510006001010, 0510006001011, 0510006001012, 0510006001013, 0510006001014, 0510006001015, 0510006001016, 0510006002000, 0510006002001,

0510006002002, 0510006002003, 0510006002004, 0510006002005, 0510006002006, 0510006002007, 0510006002008, 0510006002009, 0510018001000, 0510018001001, 0510018001002, 0510018001003, 0510018001004, 0510018001005, 0510018001006, 0510018001007, 0510018001008, 0510018001009, 0510018002000, 0510018002001, 0510018002002, 0510038003035; VTD: CC18: 0510007022006, 0510007022010, 0510007022011, 0510007022013, 0510007022014, 0510007022015, 0510007022016, 0510007022017, 0510007022018, 0510007022019, 0510007022020, 0510007022021, 0510007022022, 0510007022023, 0510007022024, 0510007022025, 0510007022026, 0510038003030, 0510038003031, 0510038003032, 0510038003055; VTD: CC21, VTD: CC24: Block(s) 0510020011006, 0510020011007, 0510020011008, 0510020011010, 0510020011011, 0510020011012, 0510020011013, 0510020011014, 0510020011015, 0510020011016, 0510020011025, 0510020011026, 0510020011030, 0510020011031, 0510020011032, 0510020011033, 0510020011034, 0510020011035, 0510020011036, 0510020011037, 0510020011038, 0510020011039, 0510020011040, 0510020011041, 0510020011042, 0510020011043, 0510020011044, 0510020011045, 0510020011046, 0510020011047, 0510020011048, 0510020011049, 0510020011050, 0510020011051, 0510020011052, 0510020011053, 0510020011055, 0510020011056, 0510020012000, 0510020012001, 0510020012002, 0510020012003, 0510020012006, 0510020012007, 0510020012008, 0510020012009, 0510020012010, 0510020012011, 0510020012012, 0510020012013, 0510020012014, 0510020012015, 0510020012016, 0510020012017, 0510020012018, 0510020012019, 0510020012021, 0510020012022, 0510020012023, 0510020012024, 0510020021001; VTD: CC26, VTD: EO61-1, VTD: EO61-2, VTD: G1, VTD: G10: Block(s) 0510031031000, 0510031031011, 0510031031012, 0510031031013, 0510031031014, 0510031031015, 0510031031017, 0510031031018, 0510031031019, 0510031031020, 0510031031021, 0510031031022, 0510031032000, 0510031032001, 0510031032002, 0510031032003, 0510031032016, 0510031032022, 0510031032025, 0510031032030, 0510031032031, 0510031032032, 0510031032033, 0510031032035, 0510031032037, 0510031032038, 0510031032039, 0510031032040, 0510031032045, 0510031032050, 0510031032051; VTD: G11: 0510036001000, 0510036001001, 0510036001002, 0510036001003, 0510036001004, 0510036001005, 0510036001006, 0510036001007, 0510036001008, 0510036001009, 0510036001010, 0510036001012, 0510036001013, 0510036001014, 0510036001015, 0510036001016, 0510036001017, 0510036001019, 0510036001021, 0510036001022, 0510036001039, 0510036001040, 0510036001041, 0510036001042, 0510036003000, 0510036003001, 0510036003002, 0510036003003, 0510036003004, 0510036003005, 0510036003006, 0510036003007, 0510036003008, 0510036003009, 0510036003010, 0510036003011, 0510036003012, 0510036003014, 0510036003015, 0510036003016, 0510036003017, 0510036003018, 0510036003019, 0510036003020, 0510036003021, 0510036003022, 0510036003023, 0510036003024, 0510036003025, 0510036003026, 0510036003027, 0510036003028, 0510036003029, 0510036003030, 0510036003031, 0510036003032, 0510036003033, 0510036003035, 0510036003037, 0510036003038, 0510036003039, 0510036003040, 0510036003041, 0510036003042, 0510036003043, 0510036003044, 0510036003045, 0510036003046, 0510036003047, 0510036003048, 0510036003049, 0510036003050, 0510036003051, 0510036004000, 0510036004001, 0510036004048, 0510037001007, 0510037001008, 0510037001009, 0519801001000, 0519801001001, 0519801001002, 0519801001003, 0519801001004, 0519801001007, 0519801001008, 0519801001010, 0519801001011, 0519801001012, 0519801001013, 0519801001014, 0519801001015, 0519801001016; VTD: G2: 0510012004001, 0510012004002, 0510012004003, 0510012004004, 0510012004021, 0510012004022, 0510012004023, 0510012004024, 0510012004025, 0510012004026, 0510012004027, 0510012004028, 0510024011000, 0510024011001, 0510024011002, 0510024011003, 0510024011004, 0510024011005, 0510024011006, 0510024011007, 0510024011008, 0510024011009, 0510024011010, 0510024011011, 0510024011013, 0510024011014, 0510024011015, 0510024011016, 0510024011017, 0510024011018, 0510024011019, 0510024011022, 0510024011024, 0510024011025, 0510024011026, 0510024011027, 0510024011028, 0510024011029, 0510024011030, 0510024011034, 0510024011035, 0510024011036, 0510024011038, 0510024011041, 0510024011042, 0510024011043, 0510024012004, 0510024012007, 0510024012025, 0510024021000, 0510024021005, 0510024022000, 0510024022001, 0510024022004, 0510024022007, 0510025011000, 0510025011001, 0510025011002, 0510025011003, 0510025011004, 0510025011005, 0510025011006, 0510025011007, 0510025011008, 0510025011009, 0510025011010, 0510025011011, 0510025011012, 0510025011013, 0510025011014, 0510025011015, 0510025011016, 0510025011017, 0510025011018, 0510025011019, 0510025011020,

0510025011021, 0510025011022, 0510025011023, 0510025012000, 0510025012001,
0510025012002, 0510025012003, 0510025012004, 0510025012005, 0510025012006,
0510025012007, 0510025012008, 0510025012009, 0510025012010, 0510025012011,
0510025012012, 0510025012013, 0510025012014, 0510025013000, 0510025013001,
0510025013002, 0510025013003, 0510025013004, 0510025013005, 0510025013006,
0510025013007, 0510025013008, 0510025013014, 0510025013015, 0510025013016,
0510025013017, 0510025013020, 0510025013023, 0510025013031, 0510025013033,
0510025013037, 0510025013038, 0510025013039, 0510025013040, 0510025013053,
0510025013054, 0510025013055, 0510025013056, 0510025013057, 0510025013058,
0510025013059, 0510025013060, 0510025013061, 0510025013062, 0510025013066,
0510025013067, 0510025013069, 0510025013070, 0510025013077, 0510025013078,
0510025013079, 0510025013080, 0510025013081, 0510025021000, 0510025021001,
0510025021002, 0510025021003, 0510025021004, 0510025021005, 0510025021006,
0510025021007, 0510025021008, 0510025021009, 0510025021010, 0510025021011,
0510025021012, 0510025021013, 0510025021014, 0510025021015, 0510025021016,
0510025021017, 0510025021018, 0510025021019, 0510025021020, 0510025021021,
0510025021022, 0510025021023, 0510025021024, 0510025021025, 0510025021026,
0510025021027, 0510025021028, 0510025021029, 0510025021030, 0510025021031,
0510025021032, 0510025021033, 0510025021034, 0510025021035, 0510025021036,
0510025021037, 0510025021038, 0510025021039, 0510025021040, 0510025021041,
0510025021042, 0510025021043, 0510025021044, 0510025021045, 0510025021046,
0510025021047, 0510025021048, 0510025021049, 0510025021050, 0510025021051,
0510025021052, 0510025021053, 0510025021054, 0510025021055, 0510025021056,
0510025021057, 0510025021058, 0510025021059, 0510025021060, 0510025021061,
0510025021062, 0510025021063, 0510025021064, 0510025021065, 0510025021066,
0510025021067, 0510025022000, 0510025022001, 0510025022002, 0510025022003,
0510025022004, 0510025022005, 0510025022006, 0510025022007, 0510025022008,
0510025022009, 0510025022010, 0510025022011, 0510025022012, 0510025022013,
0510025022014, 0510025022015, 0510025022016, 0510025022017, 0510025022018,
0510025022019, 0510025022020, 0510025022021, 0510025022022, 0510025022023,
0510025022024, 0510025022025, 0510025022026, 0510025022027, 0510025022028,
0510025022029, 0510025022030, 0510025022031, 0510025022032, 0510025022033,
0510025022034, 0510025022035, 0510025022036, 0510025022037, 0510025022038,
0510025022039, 0510025022040, 0510025022041, 0510025022042, 0510025022043,
0510025022044, 0510025022045, 0510025022046, 0510025022047, 0510025022048,
0510025022049, 0510025022050, 0510025022051, 0510025022052, 0510025022053,
0510025022054, 0510025022055, 0510025022056, 0510025022057, 0510025022058,
0510025022059, 0510025022060, 0510025022061, 0510025022062, 0510025022063,
0510025022064, 0510025022065, 0510025022066, 0510025022067, 0510025022068,
0510025022069, 0510025022070, 0510025022071, 0510025022072, 0510025022073,
0510025022074, 0510025022075, 0510025022076, 0510025022077, 0510025022078,
0510025022079, 0510025022080, 0510025022081, 0510025022082, 0510025022083,
0510025022084, 0510025023000, 0510025023001, 0510025023002, 0510025023003,
0510025023004, 0510025023005, 0510025023006, 0510025023007, 0510025023008,
0510025023009, 0510025023010, 0510025023011, 0510025023012, 0510025023013,
0510025023014, 0510025023015, 0510025023016, 0510025023017, 0510025023018,
0510025023019, 0510025023020, 0510025023021, 0510025023022, 0510025023023,
0510025023024, 0510025023025, 0510025023026, 0510025023027, 0510025023028,
0510025023029, 0510025023030, 0510025023031, 0510025023032, 0510025023033,
0510025023034, 0510025023035, 0510025023036, 0510025031000, 0510025031001,
0510025031002, 0510025031003, 0510025031004, 0510025031005, 0510025031006,
0510025031007, 0510025031008, 0510025031009, 0510025031010, 0510025031011,
0510025031012, 0510025031013, 0510025031014, 0510025031015, 0510025031016,
0510025031017, 0510025031018, 0510025031019, 0510025031020, 0510025031021,
0510025031022, 0510025031023, 0510025031024, 0510025031025, 0510025032000,
0510025032001, 0510025032002, 0510025032003, 0510025032004, 0510025032005,
0510025032006, 0510025032007, 0510025032008, 0510025032009, 0510025033000,
0510025033001, 0510025033002, 0510025033003, 0510025033004, 0510025033005,
0510025033006, 0510025033007, 0510025033008, 0510025033009, 0510025033010,
0510025033011, 0510025033012, 0510025033013, 0510025033014, 0510025033015,
0510025033016, 0510025033017, 0510025033018, 0510025033019, 0510025033020,
0510025033021, 0510025033022, 0510025033023, 0510025033024, 0510025033025,

0510025033026, 0510025033027, 0510025033028, 0510025033029, 0510025033030,
0510025033031, 0510025033032, 0510025033033, 0510025033034, 0510025033035,
0510025041001, 0510025041002, 0510025041003, 0510025041004, 0510025041005,
0510025041006, 0510025041007, 0510025041008, 0510025041009, 0510025041010,
0510025041011, 0510025041012, 0510025041013, 0510025041014, 0510025041015,
0510025041016, 0510025041017, 0510025041018, 0510025041019, 0510025041020,
0510025041021, 0510025041022, 0510025041023, 0510025041024, 0510025041025,
0510025041026, 0510025041027, 0510025041028, 0510025041029, 0510025041030,
0510025042000, 0510025042001, 0510025042002, 0510025042003, 0510025042004,
0510025042005, 0510025042006, 0510025042007, 0510025042008, 0510025042009,
0510025042010, 0510025042011, 0510025042012, 0510025042013, 0510025042014,
0510025042015, 0510025042016, 0510025042017, 0510025042018, 0510025042019,
0510025042020, 0510025042021, 0510025042022, 0510025042023, 0510025042024,
0510025042025, 0510025042026, 0510025042027, 0510025042028, 0510025042029,
0510025042030, 0510025042031, 0510025042032, 0510025042033, 0510025042034,
0510025042035, 0510025042036, 0510025042037, 0510025042038, 0510025042039,
0510025042040, 0510025042041, 0510025042042, 0510025042043, 0510025042044,
0510025042045, 0510025042046, 0510025042047, 0510025043000, 0510025043001,
0510025043002, 0510025043003, 0510025043004, 0510025043005, 0510025043006,
0510025043007, 0510025043008, 0510025043009, 0510025043010, 0510025043011,
0510025043012, 0510025043013, 0510025043014, 0510025043015, 0510025043016,
0510025043017, 0510025043018, 0510025043019, 0510025043020, 0510025043021,
0510025043022, 0510025043023, 0510025043024, 0510025043025, 0510025043026,
0510025043027, 0510025043028, 0510025043029, 0510025043030, 0510025043031,
0510025043032, 0510025043033, 0510025043034, 0510025043035, 0510025043036,
0510025043037, 0510025043038, 0510026002016, 0510037001001, 0510037001002,
0510037001004, 0510037001005, 0510037001006, 0510037001010, 0510037001011,
0510037001012, 0510037001013, 0510037001014, 0510037001015, 0510037001016,
0510037001017, 0510037001018, 0510037001019, 0510037001020, 0510037001021,
0510037001022, 0510037001025, 0510037001026, 0510037003088, 0510037003089,
0510037003090, 0510037003098, 0510037003099, 0510037003100, 0510037003101,
0510037003103, 0510037003104, 0510037003105, 0510037003106, 0510037003107,
0510037003110, 0510037003111, 0510037003112, 0510037003113, 0510037003114,
0519802001027; VTD: G3, VTD: G4, VTD: G6, VTD: G7, VTD: G8: Block(s) 0510016011000,
0510016011028, 0510016011029, 0510016011030, 0510016011031, 0510016011033,
0510016011034, 0510016011035, 0510016011036, 0510016011037, 0510016011038,
0510016011039, 0510016011040, 0510016011042, 0510016012003, 0510016012004,
0510016012005, 0510016012006, 0510016012007, 0510016012008, 0510016012009,
0510016012012, 0510016012013, 0510016012014, 0510016012016, 0510016012017,
0510016012018, 0510016012019, 0510016012020, 0510016012021, 0510016012022,
0510016012023, 0510016012024, 0510016012025, 0510016012026, 0510016012027,
0510016012028, 0510016012029, 0510016012030, 0510016012032, 0510016012033,
0510016012034, 0510016012035, 0510016012036, 0510016012037, 0510016012038,
0510016012039, 0510016012040, 0510016012042, 0510016012043, 0510016012044,
0510016012045, 0510016012046, 0510016012047, 0510016012048, 0510016012049,
0510016012050, 0510016012051, 0510016012052, 0510016012053, 0510016032017,
0510016032018, 0510016032019, 0510016032020, 0510016032022, 0510016032023,
0510016032028, 0510016032029, 0510016032030, 0510016032031, 0510016032032,
0510016032044, 0510019011006, 0510019011007, 0510019011019, 0510019011027,
0510019011040, 0510019031013, 0510019031014, 0510031033002, 0510031033003,
0510031033004, 0510031033005, 0510031033006, 0510031041002, 0510031041003,
0510031041004, 0510031041005, 0510031041006, 0510031041007, 0510031041008,
0510031041009, 0510031041010, 0510031041011, 0510031041012, 0510031041013,
0510031041014, 0510031041015, 0510031042011, 0510032014052, 0510032014053,
0510032014054; VTD: G9, VTD: LI65, VTD: SH77. It has two judges.

(15) District 14A: Durham County: VTD: 09, VTD: 12, VTD: 13, VTD: 14, VTD: 15, VTD: 18, VTD: 31: Block(s) 0630010013033, 0630018024009; VTD: 34, VTD: 35: Block(s) 0630020211023, 0630020212002, 0630020212003, 0630020212004, 0630020212005, 0630020212006, 0630020212007, 0630020212008, 0630020212009, 0630020212010, 0630020212013, 0630020212015, 0630020212016, 0630020212018, 0630020212020, 0630020212021, 0630020272052; VTD: 40, VTD: 41, VTD: 42, VTD: 48, VTD: 53-1, VTD: 54, VTD: 55. It has one judge.

(16) District 14B: Durham County: VTD: 01, VTD: 02, VTD: 03, VTD: 04, VTD: 05, VTD: 06, VTD: 07, VTD: 08, VTD: 10, VTD: 16, VTD: 17, VTD: 19, VTD: 20, VTD: 21, VTD: 22, VTD: 23, VTD: 24, VTD: 25, VTD: 26, VTD: 27, VTD: 28, VTD: 29, VTD: 30-1, VTD: 30-2, VTD: 31: Block(s) 0630010013034, 0630010013038, 0630010013039, 0630010013040, 0630010013043, 0630018071037, 0630018071038, 0630018091000, 0630018091001, 0630018091002, 0630018091003, 0630018091004, 0630018091005, 0630018091006, 0630018091007, 0630018091008, 0630018091009, 0630018091010, 0630018091011, 0630018091012, 0630018091013, 0630018091014, 0630018091015, 0630018091016, 0630018091017, 0630018091018, 0630018091019, 0630018091020, 0630018091021, 0630018091022, 0630018091023, 0630018091024, 0630018091025, 0630018091026, 0630018091027, 0630018091028, 0630018091029, 0630018091030, 0630018091031, 0630018091032, 0630018091033, 0630018091034, 0630018091035, 0630018091036, 0630018091037, 0630018091038, 0630018091041, 0630018091042, 0630018091043, 0630018091044, 0630018091045, 0630018091046, 0630018091062, 0630018091063, 0630018091064, 0630018091065, 0630018091066, 0630018091067, 0630018091071, 0630018091072, 0630018091073, 0630018091074, 0630018091077, 0630018091079, 0630018091080, 0630018092000, 0630018092001, 0630018092002, 0630018092003, 0630018092004, 0630018092005, 0630018092006, 0630018092007, 0630018092008, 0630018092009, 0630018092010, 0630018092011, 0630018092012, 0630018092013, 0630018092014, 0630018092015, 0630018092016, 0630018092017, 0630018092018, 0630018092019, 0630018092020, 0630018092021, 0630018092022, 0630018092023, 0630018092024, 0630018092027, 0630018092028, 0630018092029, 0630018092030, 0630018092031, 0630018092032, 0630018092033, 0630020271000, 0630020271001, 0630020271002, 0630020271003, 0630020271004, 0630020271005, 0630020271006, 0630020271007, 0630020271008, 0630020271009, 0630020271010, 0630020271011, 0630020271012, 0630020271013, 0630020271014, 0630020271015, 0630020271016, 0630020271017, 0630020271018, 0630020271019, 0630020271020, 0630020271021, 0630020271022, 0630020271023, 0630020271024, 0630020271025, 0630020271054, 0630020271055, 0630020271063, 0630020271064, 0630020271065, 0630020271067, 0630020271070, 0630020271071, 0639801001012, 0639801001013; VTD: 32, VTD: 33, VTD: 35: Block(s) 0630020131000, 0630020131001, 0630020131002, 0630020131003, 0630020131004, 0630020131005, 0630020131006, 0630020131007, 0630020131008, 0630020131009, 0630020131010, 0630020131011, 0630020131012, 0630020131013, 0630020131014, 0630020132000, 0630020132001, 0630020132002, 0630020132003, 0630020132004, 0630020132005, 0630020132006, 0630020132007, 0630020132008, 0630020132009, 0630020132010, 0630020132011, 0630020132012, 0630020132013, 0630020132014, 0630020132015, 0630020133000, 0630020133001, 0630020133002, 0630020133003, 0630020133004, 0630020133005, 0630020133006, 0630020133007, 0630020133008, 0630020133009, 0630020133010, 0630020133011, 0630020133012, 0630020133013, 0630020133014, 0630020133015, 0630020133016, 0630020133017, 0630020133018, 0630020133019, 0630020202000, 0630020202001, 0630020202002, 0630020202003, 0630020202004, 0630020202005, 0630020202006, 0630020202007, 0630020202008, 0630020202009, 0630020202010, 0630020202011, 0630020202012, 0630020202013, 0630020202014, 0630020202015, 0630020202016, 0630020202017, 0630020202018, 0630020202019, 0630020202020, 0630020202021, 0630020202022, 0630020202023, 0630020202024, 0630020202025, 0630020202026, 0630020202027, 0630020202028, 0630020202029, 0630020202030, 0630020202031, 0630020202032, 0630020202033, 0630020202034, 0630020202035, 0630020202036, 0630020202037, 0630020202038, 0630020202039, 0630020202040, 0630020202041, 0630020202042, 0630020202043, 0630020202044, 0630020202045, 0630020202046, 0630020202047, 0630020202048, 0630020202049, 0630020202050, 0630020202051, 0630020202052, 0630020202053, 0630020202054, 0630020202055, 0630020202056, 0630020202057, 0630020202058, 0630020211021, 0630020211022, 0630020211024, 0630020211049, 0630020211050, 0630020212011, 0630020212014, 0630020212017, 0630020212019, 0630020272070, 0630020272071, 0630020272072, 0630020272073, 0630020272074, 0630020272075; VTD: 36, VTD: 37, VTD: 38, VTD: 39, VTD: 43, VTD: 44, VTD: 45, VTD: 46, VTD: 47, VTD: 50, VTD: 51, VTD: 52, VTD: 53-2. It has three judges.

(17) District 18A: Guilford County: VTD: FEN1, VTD: FEN2, VTD: G04, VTD: G05, VTD: G06, VTD: G46, VTD: G52, VTD: G67, VTD: G68, VTD: G69, VTD: G70, VTD: G71, VTD: G72, VTD: G73, VTD: G74, VTD: G75, VTD: NCLAY1, VTD: NCLAY2, VTD: PG1, VTD: PG2, VTD: SCLAY. It has one judge.

(18) District 18B: Guilford County: VTD: H01, VTD: H02, VTD: H03, VTD: H04, VTD: H05, VTD: H06, VTD: H07, VTD: H08, VTD: H09, VTD: H10, VTD: H11, VTD: H12, VTD: H13, VTD: H14, VTD: H15, VTD: H16, VTD: H17, VTD: H18, VTD: H19A, VTD: H19B, VTD: H20A, VTD: H20B, VTD: H21, VTD: H22, VTD: H23, VTD: H24, VTD: H25, VTD: H26, VTD: H27, VTD: HP, VTD: JAM1, VTD: JAM5, VTD: NDRI, VTD: SDRI. It has one judge.

(19) District 18C: Guilford County: VTD: CG1, VTD: CG2, VTD: CG3A, VTD: CG3B, VTD: FR1, VTD: FR2, VTD: FR3, VTD: FR4, VTD: FR5, VTD: G17, VTD: G30, VTD: G31, VTD: G32, VTD: G33, VTD: G34, VTD: G36, VTD: G37, VTD: G38, VTD: G39, VTD: G40A1, VTD: G40A2, VTD: G40B, VTD: G41, VTD: G42, VTD: G43, VTD: G64, VTD: G65, VTD: G66, VTD: JAM2, VTD: JAM3, VTD: JAM4, VTD: MON3, VTD: NCGR1, VTD: NCGR2, VTD: OR1, VTD: OR2, VTD: SF1, VTD: SF2, VTD: SF3, VTD: SF4, VTD: STOK. It has one judge.

(20) District 18D: Guilford County: VTD: G01, VTD: G11, VTD: G12, VTD: G13, VTD: G14, VTD: G15, VTD: G16, VTD: G19, VTD: G35, VTD: G44, VTD: G45, VTD: G47, VTD: G48, VTD: G49, VTD: G50, VTD: G51, VTD: G53, VTD: G54, VTD: G55, VTD: G56, VTD: G57, VTD: G58, VTD: G59, VTD: G60, VTD: G61, VTD: G62, VTD: G63, VTD: SUM1, VTD: SUM2, VTD: SUM3, VTD: SUM4. It has one judge.

(21) District 18E: Guilford County: VTD: G02, VTD: G03, VTD: G07, VTD: G08, VTD: G09, VTD: G10, VTD: G18, VTD: G20, VTD: G21, VTD: G22, VTD: G23, VTD: G24, VTD: G25, VTD: G26, VTD: G27, VTD: G28, VTD: G29, VTD: GIB, VTD: GR, VTD: JEF1, VTD: JEF2, VTD: JEF3, VTD: JEF4, VTD: MON1, VTD: MON2, VTD: NMAD, VTD: NWASH, VTD: RC1, VTD: RC2, VTD: SMAD, VTD: SWASH. It has one judge.

(22) District 21A: Forsyth County: VTD: 051, VTD: 052, VTD: 053, VTD: 054, VTD: 055, VTD: 071, VTD: 072, VTD: 073, VTD: 074, VTD: 075, VTD: 091, VTD: 092, VTD: 122, VTD: 123, VTD: 131, VTD: 132, VTD: 133, VTD: 701, VTD: 702, VTD: 703, VTD: 704, VTD: 705, VTD: 706, VTD: 707, VTD: 708, VTD: 709, VTD: 806, VTD: 807, VTD: 808. It has one judge.

(23) District 21B: Forsyth County: VTD: 042, VTD: 043, VTD: 501, VTD: 502, VTD: 503, VTD: 504, VTD: 505, VTD: 506, VTD: 507, VTD: 601, VTD: 602, VTD: 603, VTD: 604, VTD: 605, VTD: 606, VTD: 607, VTD: 901, VTD: 902, VTD: 903, VTD: 904, VTD: 905, VTD: 907. It has one judge.

(24) District 21C: Forsyth County: VTD: 011, VTD: 012, VTD: 013, VTD: 014, VTD: 015, VTD: 021, VTD: 031, VTD: 032, VTD: 033, VTD: 034, VTD: 061, VTD: 062, VTD: 063, VTD: 064, VTD: 065, VTD: 066, VTD: 067, VTD: 068, VTD: 101, VTD: 111, VTD: 112, VTD: 801, VTD: 802, VTD: 803, VTD: 804, VTD: 805, VTD: 809, VTD: 906, VTD: 908, VTD: 909. It has one judge.

(25) District 21D: Forsyth County: VTD: 081, VTD: 082, VTD: 083, VTD: 201, VTD: 203, VTD: 204, VTD: 205, VTD: 206, VTD: 207, VTD: 301, VTD: 302, VTD: 303, VTD: 304, VTD: 305, VTD: 306, VTD: 401, VTD: 402, VTD: 403, VTD: 404, VTD: 405. It has one judge.

(26) District 26A: Mecklenburg County: VTD 001, VTD 008, VTD 018, VTD 019, VTD 032, VTD 035, VTD 036, VTD 047, VTD 048, VTD 057, VTD 067, VTD 069, VTD 071, VTD 074, VTD 091, VTD 096, VTD 103, VTD 106, VTD 113, VTD 119, VTD 136, VTD 215, VTD 216, VTD 217, VTD 218, VTD 219, VTD 220, VTD 221, VTD 233, VTD 234, VTD 236. It has one judge.

(27) District 26B: Mecklenburg County: VTD 070, VTD 072, VTD 073, VTD 075, VTD 076, VTD 086, VTD 087, VTD 088, VTD 090, VTD 092, VTD 093, VTD 100, VTD 101, VTD 110, VTD 111, VTD 112, VTD 114, VTD 118, VTD 121, VTD 131, VTD 137, VTD 139.1, VTD 140, VTD 144, VTD 226, VTD 227, VTD 232. It has one judge.

(28) District 26C: Mecklenburg County: VTD 127, VTD 133, VTD 134, VTD 142, VTD 143, VTD 150, VTD 151, VTD 202, VTD 206, VTD 207, VTD 208, VTD 209, VTD 223.1, VTD 224, VTD 240, VTD 241, VTD 242. It has one judge.

(29) District 26D: Mecklenburg County: VTD 037, VTD 038, VTD 049, VTD 050, VTD 051, VTD 058, VTD 059, VTD 077, VTD 097, VTD 098, VTD 120, VTD 122, VTD 129, VTD 138, VTD 147, VTD 148, VTD 225, VTD 228, VTD 229, VTD 230, VTD 231, VTD 243. It has one judge.

(30) District 26E: Mecklenburg County: VTD 002, VTD 005, VTD 007, VTD 009, VTD 010, VTD 012, VTD 013, VTD 014, VTD 016, VTD 017, VTD 020, VTD 021, VTD 022, VTD 023, VTD 024, VTD 025, VTD 029, VTD 031, VTD 039, VTD 040, VTD 041, VTD 046, VTD 052, VTD 053, VTD 078.1, VTD 079, VTD 080, VTD 081, VTD 109, VTD 200. It has one judge.

(31) District 26F: Mecklenburg County: VTD 011, VTD 015, VTD 026, VTD 027, VTD 028, VTD 030, VTD 042, VTD 044, VTD 054, VTD 055, VTD 056, VTD 082, VTD 089, VTD 128, VTD 135, VTD 210, VTD 211, VTD 213, VTD 214, VTD 222, VTD 238.1. It has one judge.

(32) District 26G: Mecklenburg County: VTD 003, VTD 004, VTD 043, VTD 060, VTD 061, VTD 104, VTD 105, VTD 107.1, VTD 123, VTD 126, VTD 132, VTD 141, VTD 145, VTD 146, VTD 149, VTD 204.1, VTD 212, VTD 237, VTD 239. It has one judge.

(33) District 26H: Mecklenburg County: VTD 006, VTD 033, VTD 034, VTD 045, VTD 062, VTD 063, VTD 064, VTD 065, VTD 066, VTD 068, VTD 083, VTD 084, VTD 085, VTD 094, VTD 095, VTD 099, VTD 102, VTD 108, VTD 115, VTD 116, VTD 117, VTD 124, VTD 125, VTD 130, VTD 201, VTD 203, VTD 205, VTD 235. It has one judge.

(b1) The qualified voters of District 4 shall elect all judges established for District 4 in subsection (a) of this section, but only persons who reside in Onslow County may be candidates for one of the judgeships and only persons who reside in Duplin, Jones, or Sampson County may be candidates for the remaining judgeship.

(c) In subsection (b) above, the names and boundaries of voting tabulation districts, tracts, block groups, and blocks specified in this section are as shown on the 2010 Census Redistricting TIGER/Line Shapefiles.

(c1) If any voting tabulation district boundary is changed, that change shall not change the boundary of a judicial district, which shall remain the same as it is depicted by the 2010 Census Redistricting TIGER/Line Shapefiles.

(c2) The Legislative Services Officer shall certify a true copy of the block assignment file associated with any mapping software used to generate the language in subsection (b) of this section. The certified true copy of the block assignment file shall be delivered by the Legislative Services Officer to the Principal Clerk of the Senate and the Principal Clerk of the House of Representatives. If any area within North Carolina is not assigned to a specific district by subsection (b) of this section, the certified true copy of the block assignment file delivered to the Principal Clerk of the Senate and the Principal Clerk of the House of Representatives shall control.

(d) The several judges, their terms of office, and their assignments to districts are as follows:

(1) In the first superior court district, J. Herbert Small and Thomas S. Watts serve terms expiring December 31, 1994.

(2) In the second superior court district, William C. Griffin serves a term expiring December 31, 1994.

(3) In the third-A superior court district, David E. Reid serves a term expiring on December 31, 1992.

(4) In the third-B superior court district, Herbert O. Phillips, III, serves a term expiring on December 31, 1994.

(5) In the fourth-A superior court district, Henry L. Stevens, III, serves a term expiring December 31, 1994.

(6) In the fourth-B superior court district, James R. Strickland serves a term expiring December 31, 1992.

(7) In the fifth superior court district, no election shall be held in 1992 for the full term of the seat now occupied by Bradford Tillery, and the holder of that seat shall serve until a successor is elected in 1994 and qualifies. The succeeding term begins January 1, 1995. In the fifth superior court district, Napoleon B. Barefoot serves a term expiring December 31, 1994.

(8) In the sixth-A superior court district, Richard B. Allsbrook serves a term expiring December 31, 1990.

(9) In the sixth-B superior court district, a judge shall be elected in 1988 to serve an eight-year term beginning January 1, 1989.

(10) In the seventh-A superior court district, Charles B. Winberry, serves a term expiring December 31, 1994.

(11) In the seventh-B superior court district, a judge shall be elected in 1988 to serve an eight-year term beginning January 1, 1989.

(12) In the seventh-C superior court district, Franklin R. Brown serves a term expiring December 31, 1990.

(13) In the eighth-A superior court district, James D. Llewellyn serves a term expiring December 31, 1994.

(14) In the eighth-B superior court district, Paul M. Wright serves a term expiring December 31, 1992.

(15) In the ninth superior court district, Robert H. Hobgood and Henry W. Hight, Jr., serve terms expiring December 31, 1994.

(16) In the tenth-A superior court district, a judge shall be elected in 1988 to serve an eight-year term beginning January 1, 1989.

(17) In the tenth-B superior court district, Robert L. Farmer serves a term expiring December 31, 1992. In the tenth-B superior court district, no election shall be held in 1990 for the full term of the seat now occupied by Henry V. Barnette, Jr., and the holder of that seat shall serve until a successor is elected in 1992 and qualifies. The succeeding term begins January 1, 1993.

(18) In the tenth-C superior court district, Edwin S. Preston, serves a term expiring December 31, 1990. In the tenth-D superior court district, Donald Stephens serves a term expiring December 31, 1988.

(19) In the eleventh superior court district, Wiley F. Bowen serves a term expiring December 31, 1990.

(20) In the twelfth-A superior court district, D.B. Herring, Jr., serves a term expiring December 31, 1990.

(21) In the twelfth-B superior court district, a judge shall be elected in 1988 to serve an eight-year term beginning January 1, 1989.

(22) In the twelfth-C superior court district, no election shall be held in 1992 for the full term of the seat now occupied by Coy E. Brewer, Jr., and the holder of that seat shall serve until a successor is elected in 1994 and qualifies. The succeeding term begins January 1, 1995. In the twelfth-C superior court district, E. Lynn Johnson serves a term expiring December 31, 1994.

(23) In the thirteenth superior court district, Giles R. Clark serves a term expiring December 31, 1994.

(24) In the fourteenth-A superior court district, a judge shall be elected in 1988 to serve an eight-year term beginning January 1, 1989.

(25) In the fourteenth-B superior court district, no election shall be held in 1992 for the full term of the seat now occupied by Anthony M. Brannon, and the holder of that seat shall serve until a successor is elected in 1994 and qualifies. The succeeding term begins July 1, 1995.

(26) In the fourteenth-B superior court district, no election shall be held in 1990 for the full term of the seat now occupied by Thomas H. Lee, and the holder of that seat shall serve until a successor is elected in 1994 and qualifies. The succeeding term begins January 1, 1995. In the fourteenth-B superior court district, J. Milton Read, Jr., serves a term expiring December 31, 1994.

(27) In the fifteenth-A superior court district, J.B. Allen, Jr., serves a term expiring December 31, 1994.

(28) In the fifteenth-B superior court district, F. Gordon Battle serves a term expiring December 31, 1994.

(29) In the sixteenth-A superior court district, B. Craig Ellis serves a term expiring December 31, 1994.

(30) In the sixteenth-B superior court district, a judge shall be elected in 1988 to serve an eight-year term beginning January 1, 1989. In the sixteenth-B judicial [superior court] district, a judge shall be appointed by the Governor to serve until the results of the 1990 general election are certified. A person shall be elected in the 1990 general election to serve the remainder of the term expiring December 31, 1996.

(31) In the seventeenth-A superior court district, Melzer A. Morgan, Jr., serves a term expiring December 31, 1990.

(32) In the seventeenth-B superior court district, James M. Long serves a term expiring December 31, 1994.

(33) In the eighteenth-A superior court district, a judge shall be elected in 1988 to serve an eight-year term beginning January 1, 1989.

(34) In the eighteenth-B superior court district, Edward K. Washington's term expired December 31, 1986, but he is holding over because of a court order enjoining an election from being held in 1986. A successor shall be elected in 1988 to serve an eight-year term beginning January 1, 1989.

(35) In the eighteenth-C superior court district, W. Douglas Albright serves a term expiring December 31, 1990.

(36) In the eighteenth-D superior court district, Thomas W. Ross's term expired December 31, 1986, but he is holding over because of a court order enjoining an election from being held in 1986. A successor shall be elected in 1988 to serve an eight-year term beginning January 1, 1989.

(37) In the eighteenth-E superior court district, Joseph John's term expired December 31, 1986, but he is holding over because of a court order enjoining an election from being held in 1986. A successor shall be elected in 1988 to serve an eight-year term beginning January 1, 1989.

(38) In the nineteenth-A superior court district, James C. Davis serves a term expiring December 31, 1992.

(39) In the nineteenth-B1 superior court district, Russell G. Walker, Jr., serves a term expiring December 31, 1990. No election shall be held in 1998 for the full term of the seat now occupied by Russell G. Walker, Jr., and the holder of that seat shall serve until a successor is elected in 2000 and qualifies. The succeeding term shall begin January 1, 2001. The superior court judgeship held on June 12, 1996, in Superior Court District 20A by a resident of Moore County (James M. Webb) is allocated to Superior Court District 19B2. The term of that judge expires December 31, 2000. The judge's successor shall be elected in the 2000 general election.

(40) In the nineteenth-C superior court district, Thomas W. Seay, Jr., serves a term expiring December 31, 1990.

(41) In the twentieth-A superior court district, F. Fetzer Mills serves a term expiring December 31, 1992.

(42) In the twentieth-B superior court district, William H. Helms serves a term expiring December 31, 1990.

(43) In the twenty-first-A superior court district, William Z. Wood serves a term expiring December 31, 1990.

(44) In the twenty-first-B superior court district, Judson D. DeRamus, Jr., serves a term expiring December 31, 1988.

(45) In the twenty-first-C superior court district, William H. Freeman serves a term expiring December 31, 1990.

(46) In the twenty-first-D superior court district, a judge shall be elected in 1988 to serve an eight-year term beginning January 1, 1989.

(47) In the twenty-second superior court district, no election shall be held in 1992 for the full term of the seat now occupied by Preston Cornelius, and the holder of that seat shall serve until a successor is elected in 1994 and qualifies. The succeeding term shall begin January 1, 1995. In the twenty-second superior court district, Robert A. Collier serves a term expiring December 31, 1994.

(48) In the twenty-third superior court district, Julius A. Rousseau, Jr., serves a term expiring December 31, 1990.

(49) In the twenty-fourth superior court district, Charles C. Lamm, Jr., serves a term expiring December 31, 1994.

(50) In the twenty-fifth-A superior court district, Claude S. Sitton serves a term expiring December 31, 1994.

(51) In the twenty-fifth-B superior court district, Forrest A. Ferrell serves a term expiring December 31, 1990.

(52) In the twenty-sixth-A superior court district, no election shall be held in 1994 for the full term of the seat now occupied by W. Terry Sherrill, and the holder of that seat shall serve until a successor is elected in 1996 and qualifies. The succeeding term shall begin January 1, 1997. In the twenty-sixth-A superior court district, a judge shall be elected in 1988 to serve an eight-year term beginning January 1, 1989.

(53) In the twenty-sixth-B superior court district, Frank W. Snepp, Jr., and Kenneth A. Griffin serve terms expiring December 31, 1990.

(54) In the twenty-sixth-C superior court district, no election shall be held in 1992 for the full term of the seat now occupied by Chase Boone Saunders, and the holder of that seat shall serve until a successor is elected in 1994 and qualifies. The succeeding term shall begin January 1, 1995. In the twenty-sixth-C superior court district, Robert M. Burroughs serves a term expiring December 31, 1994.

(55) In the twenty-seventh-A superior court district, no election shall be held in 1988 for the full term of the seat now occupied by Robert E. Gaines, and the holder of that seat shall serve until a successor is elected in 1990 and qualifies. The

succeeding term begins January 1, 1991. In the twenty-seventh-A superior court district, Robert W. Kirby serves a term expiring December 31, 1990.

(56) In the twenty-seventh-B superior court district, John M. Gardner serves a term expiring December 31, 1994.

(57) In the twenty-eighth superior court district, Robert D. Lewis and C. Walter Allen serve terms expiring December 31, 1990.

(58) In the twenty-ninth superior court district, Hollis M. Owens, Jr., serves a term expiring December 31, 1990.

(59) In the thirtieth-A superior court district, James U. Downs serves a term expiring December 31, 1990.

(60) In the thirtieth-B superior court district, Janet M. Hyatt serves a term expiring December 31, 1994.

History.
1969, c. 1171, ss. 1-3; c. 1190, s. 4; 1971, c. 377, s. 5; c. 997; 1973, c. 47, s. 2; c. 646; c. 855, s. 1; 1975, c. 529; c. 956, ss. 1, 2; 1975, 2nd Sess., c. 983, s. 114; 1977, c. 1119, ss. 1, 3, 4; c. 1130, ss. 1, 2; 1977, 2nd Sess., c. 1238, s. 1; c. 1243, s. 4; 1979, c. 838, s. 119; c. 1072, s. 1; 1979, 2nd Sess., c. 1221, s. 1; 1981, c. 964, ss. 1, 2; 1981 (Reg. Sess., 1982), c. 1282, s. 71.2; 1983 (Reg. Sess., 1984), c. 1109, ss. 4, 4.1; 1985, c. 698, s. 11(a); 1987, c. 509, s. 1; c. 549, s. 6.6; c. 738, s. 124; 1987 (Reg. Sess., 1988), c. 1037, s. 1; c. 1056, ss. 14, 15; 1989, c. 795, s. 22(a); 1991, c. 746, s. 1; 1993, c. 321, ss. 200.4(a), 200.5(a), (d); 1995, c. 51, s. 1; c. 509, s. 3; 1995 (Reg. Sess., 1996), c. 589, s. 1(a), (c); 1998-212, s. 16.16A(a); 1998-217, s. 67.3(c); 1999-237, ss. 17.12(b), 17.19(a)-(d), 17.20(a)-(c); 1999-396, s. 1; 2000-67, s. 15.6(a); 2000-140, s. 36; 2001-333, ss. 1, 2; 2001-424, s. 22.4(b); 2001-507, ss. 3, 4; 2003-284, ss. 13.14(a), 13.14(b); 2004-124, s. 14.6(b); 2004-127, s. 2(a); 2005-276, ss. 14.2(a), 14.2(e1); 2006-96, s. 2; 2007-323, s. 14.25(a); 2011-203, ss. 1 -3; 2011-417, s. 1; 2012-182, s. 2(a), (b); 2013-360, s. 18B.22(a); 2017-57, s. 18B.9(a); 2018-5, s. 18B.5(a); 2018-14, s. 1(a); 2018-121, ss. 1(a), 10

§ 7A-41.1. District and set of districts defined; senior resident superior court judges and their authority

(a) In this section and in any other law which refers to this section:

(1) "District" means any superior court district established by G.S. 7A-41 which consists exclusively of one or more entire counties;

(2) "Set of districts" means any set of two or more superior court districts established under G.S. 7A-41, none of which consists exclusively of one or more entire counties, but both or all of which include territory from the same county or counties and together

Chapter 7A

comprise all of the territory of that county or those counties;

(3) "Regular resident superior court judge of the district or set of districts" means a regular superior court judge who is a resident judge of any of the superior court districts established under G.S. 7A-41 which comprise or are included in a district or set of districts as defined herein.

(b) There shall be one and only one senior resident superior court judge for each district or set of districts as defined in subsection (a) of this section, who shall be:

(1) Where there is only one regular resident superior court judge for the district, that judge; and

(2) Where there are two or more regular resident superior court judges for the district or set of districts, the judge who, from among all the regular resident superior court judges of the district or set of districts, has the most continuous service as a regular resident superior court judge; provided if two or more judges are of equal seniority, the oldest of those judges shall be the senior regular resident superior court judge.

(3) Where there is a set of districts, the Chief Justice of the Supreme Court shall designate one of the judges as senior resident superior court judge to serve in that capacity at the pleasure of the Chief Justice, if that set of districts are wholly contained in one county that is specified in law as the sole proper venue for certain actions.

(c) Senior resident superior court judges and regular resident superior court judges possess equal judicial jurisdiction, power, authority and status, but all duties placed by the Constitution or statutes on the resident judge of a superior court district, including the appointment to and removal from office, which are not related to a case, controversy or judicial proceeding and which do not involve the exercise of judicial power, shall be discharged, throughout a district as defined in subsection (a) of this section or throughout all of the districts comprising a set of districts so defined, for each county in that district or set of districts, by the senior resident superior court judge for that district or set of districts. That senior resident superior court judge alone among the superior court judges of that district or set of districts shall receive the salary and benefits of a senior resident superior court judge.

(d) A senior resident superior court judge for a district or set of districts as defined in subsection (a) of this section with two or more regular resident superior court judges, by notice in writing to the Administrative Officer of the Courts, may decline to exercise the authority vested in him by this section, in which event such authority shall be exercised by the regular resident superior court judge who, among the other regular resident superior court judges of the district or set of districts, is next senior in point of service or age, respectively.

(e) In the event a senior resident superior court judge for a district or set of districts with one or more regular resident superior court judges is unable, due to mental or physical incapacity, to exercise the authority vested in him by the statute, and the Chief Justice, in his discretion, has determined that such incapacity exists, the Chief Justice shall appoint an acting senior regular resident superior court judge from the other regular resident judges of the district or set of districts, to exercise, temporarily, the authority of the senior regular resident judge. Such appointee shall serve at the pleasure of the Chief Justice and until his temporary appointment is vacated by appropriate order.

History.
1987 (Reg. Sess., 1988), c. 1037, s. 2; 2010-105, s. 1; 2012-194, s. 63.5

§ 7A-41.2. Nomination and election of regular superior court judges

Candidates for the office of regular superior court judge shall be both nominated and elected by the qualified voters of the superior court district for which the election is sought.

History.
1996, 2nd Ex. Sess., c. 9, s. 1

§ 7A-42. Sessions of superior court in cities other than county seats

(a) Sessions of the superior court shall be held in each city in the State which is not a county seat and which has a population of 35,000 or more, according to the 1960 federal census.

(a1) In addition to the sessions of superior court authorized by subsection (a) of this section, sessions of superior court in the following counties may be held in the additional seats of court listed by order of the Senior Resident Superior Court Judge after consultation with the Chief District Court Judge:

County	Additional Seats of Court
Davidson	Thomasville
Iredell	Mooresville

The courtrooms and related judicial facilities for these sessions of superior court may be provided by the municipality, and in such cases the facilities fee collected for the State by the clerk of superior court shall be remitted to the municipality to assist in meeting the expense of providing those facilities.

(b) For the purpose of segregating the cases to be tried in any city referred to in subsection (a), and to designate the place of trial, the clerk of superior court in any county having one or more such cities shall set up a criminal docket and a civil docket, which dockets shall indicate the cases and proceedings to be tried in each such city in his county. Such dockets shall bear the name of the city in which such sessions of court are to be held, followed by the word "Division." Summons in actions to be tried in any such city shall clearly designate the place of trial.

(c) For the purpose of determining the proper place of trial of any action or proceeding, whether civil or criminal, the county in which any city described in subsection (a) is located shall be divided into divisions, and the territory embraced in the division in which each such city is located shall consist of the township in which such city lies and all contiguous townships within such county, such division of the superior court to be known by the name of such city followed by the word "Division." All other townships of any such county shall constitute a division of the superior court to be known by the name of the county seat followed by the word "Division." All laws, rules, and regulations now or hereafter in force and effect in determining the proper venue as between the superior courts of the several counties of the State shall apply for the purpose of determining the proper place of trial as between such divisions within such county and as between each of such divisions and any other county of the superior court in North Carolina.

(d) The clerk of superior court of any county with an additional seat of superior court may, but shall not be required to, hear matters in any place other than at his office at the county seat.

(e) The grand jury for the several divisions of court of any county in which a city described in subsection (a) is located shall be drawn from the whole county, and may hold hearings and meetings at either the county seat or elsewhere within the county as it may elect, or as it may be directed by the judge holding any session of superior court within such county; provided, however, that in arranging the sessions of the court for the trial of criminal cases for any county in which any such city is located a session of one week or more shall be held at the county seat preceding any session of one week or more to be held in any such city, so as to facilitate the work of the grand jury, and so as to confine its meetings to the county seat as fully as may be practicable. All petit jurors for all sessions of court in the several divisions of such county shall be drawn, as now or hereafter provided by law, from the whole of the county in which any such city is located for all sessions of courts in the several divisions of such county.

(f) Special sessions of court for the trial of either civil or criminal cases in any city described in subsection (a) may be arranged as by law now or hereafter provided for special sessions of the superior court.

(g) All court records of all such divisions of the superior court of any such county shall be kept in the office of the clerk of the superior court at the county seat, but they may be temporarily removed under the direction and supervision of the clerk to any such division or divisions. No judgment or order rendered at any session held in any such city shall become a lien upon or otherwise affect the title to any real estate within such county until it has been docketed in the office of the clerk of the superior court at the county seat as now or may hereafter be provided by law; provided, that nothing herein shall affect the provisions of G.S. 1-233 and the equities therein provided for shall be preserved as to all judgments and orders rendered at any session of the superior court in any such city.

(h) It shall be the duty of the board of county commissioners of the county in which any such city is located to provide a suitable place for holding such sessions of court, and to provide for the payment of the extra expense, if any, of the sheriff and his deputies in attending the sessions of court of any such division, and the expense of keeping, housing and feeding prisoners while awaiting trial.

(i) Notwithstanding the provisions of this section, when exigent circumstances exist, sessions of superior court may be conducted at a location outside a county seat by order of the Senior Resident Superior Court Judge of a county, with the prior approval of the location and the facilities by the Administrative Office of the Courts and after consultation with the Clerk of Superior Court and county officials of the county. An order entered under this subsection shall be filed in the office of the Clerk of Superior Court in the county and posted at the courthouse within the county seat and notice shall be posted in other conspicuous locations. The order shall be limited to such session or sessions as are approved by the Chief Justice of the Supreme Court of North Carolina.

History.
1943, c. 121; 1969, c. 1190, s. 48; 1987 (Reg. Sess., 1988), c. 1037, s. 2.1; 1997-304, s. 4

§ 7A-46. Special sessions

Whenever it appears to the Chief Justice of the Supreme Court that there is need for a special session of superior court in any county, he may order a special session in that county, and order any regular, special, or emergency judge to hold such session. The Chief Justice shall notify the clerk of the superior court of the county, who shall initiate action under Chapter 9 of the General Statutes to provide a jury for the special session, if a jury is required.

Special sessions have all the jurisdiction and powers that regular sessions have.

History.

R.C., c. 31, s. 22; 1868-9, c. 273; 1876-7, c. 44; Code, ss. 914, 915, 916; Rev., ss. 1512, 1513, 1516; C.S., ss. 1450, 1452, 1455; Ex. Sess. 1924, c. 100; 1951, c. 491, ss. 1, 3; 1959, c. 360; 1969, c. 1190, s. 46

§ 7A-47. Powers of regular judges holding courts by assignment or exchange

A regular superior court judge, duly assigned to hold the courts of a county, or holding such courts by exchange, shall have the same powers in the district or set of districts as defined in G.S. 7A-41.1(a) in which that county is located, in open court and in chambers as the resident judge or any judge regularly assigned to hold the courts of the district or set of districts as defined in G.S. 7A-41.1(a) has, and his jurisdiction in chambers shall extend until the session is adjourned or the session expires by operation of law, whichever is later.

History.

1951, c. 740; 1969, c. 1190, s. 42; 1987 (Reg. Sess., 1988), c. 1037, s. 6

§ 7A-47.1. Jurisdiction in vacation or in session

In any case in which the superior court in vacation has jurisdiction, and all the parties unite in the proceedings, they may apply for relief to the superior court in vacation, or during a session of court, at their election. Any regular resident superior court judge of the district or set of districts as defined in G.S. 7A-41.1(a) and any special superior court judge residing in the district or set of districts and the judge regularly presiding over the courts of the district or set of districts have concurrent jurisdiction throughout the district or set of districts in all matters and proceedings in which the superior court has jurisdiction out of session; provided, that in all matters and proceedings not requiring a jury or in which a jury is waived, any regular resident superior court judge of the district or set of districts and any special superior court judge residing in the district or set of districts shall have concurrent jurisdiction throughout the district or set of districts with the judge holding the courts of the district or set of districts and any such regular or special superior court judge, in the exercise of such concurrent jurisdiction, may hear and pass upon such matters and proceedings in vacation, out of session or during a session of court.

History.

1871-2, c. 3; Code, c. 10, s. 230; Rev., s. 1501; C.S., s. 1438; 1939, c. 69; 1945, c. 142; 1951, c. 78, s. 2; 1969, c. 1190, s. 47; 1987 (Reg. Sess., 1988), c. 1037, s. 7

N.C. Gen. Stat. § 7A-47.2

Repealed by Session Laws 1987 (Regular Session, 1988), c. 1037, s. 8.

§ 7A-47.3. Rotation and assignment; sessions

(a) To effect the intent of Article IV, Section 11 of the North Carolina Constitution, each regular resident superior court judge may, upon each rotation, be assigned to hold the courts either of one of the districts or of one of the sets of districts in that judge's judicial division.

(b) All sessions of superior court shall be for an entire county, whether that county comprises or is located in a district or in a set of districts and at each session all matters and proceedings arising anywhere in the county shall be heard.

(c) In making assignment of the judges of the superior court, the Chief Justice of the Supreme Court shall strive to allow each regular resident superior court judge to be assigned to the district or set of districts from which that regular resident superior court judge was elected or appointed no less than one-half of the calendar year.

(d) For purposes of this section, "district or set of districts" shall have the same meaning as in G.S. 7A-41.1(a).

(e) The senior resident superior court judge, in consultation with the parties to the case, shall designate a specific resident judge or a specific judge assigned to hold court in the district to preside over all proceedings in a case subject to G.S. 90-21.11(2).

History.

1987, c. 509, s. 3; 738, s. 124; 1987 (Reg. Sess., 1988), c. 1037, s. 9; 2018-121, s. 5; 2021-47, s. 1(b)

§ 7A-48. Jurisdiction of emergency judges

Emergency superior court judges have the same power and authority in all matters whatsoever, in the courts which they are assigned to hold, that regular judges holding the same courts would have. An emergency judge duly assigned to hold the courts of a county or district or set of districts as defined in G.S. 7A-41.1(a) has the same powers in that county and district or set of districts in open court and in chambers as a resident judge of the district or set of districts or any judge regularly assigned to hold the courts of the district or set of districts would have, but his jurisdiction in chambers extends only until the session is adjourned or the session expires by operation of law, whichever is later.

History.
Ex. Sess. 1921, c. 94, s. 1; C.S., s. 1435(b); 1925, c. 8; 1941, c. 52, s. 2; 1951, c. 88; 1969, c. 1190, s. 39; 1987 (Reg. Sess., 1988), c. 1037, s. 10

§ 7A-49. Orders returnable to another judge; notice

When any special or emergency judge makes any matter returnable before him, and thereafter he is called upon by the Chief Justice to hold court elsewhere, he shall order the matter heard before some other judge, setting forth in the order the time and place where it is to be heard, and he shall send copies of the order to the attorneys representing the parties in such matter.

History.
Ex. Sess. 1921, c. 94, s. 2; C.S., s. 1435(c); 1951, c. 491, s. 1; 1969, c. 1190, s. 40

§ 7A-49.1. Disposition of motions when judge disqualified

Whenever a judge before whom a motion is made, either in open court or in chambers, disqualifies himself from determining it, he may in his discretion refer the motion for disposition to a regular resident superior court judge of, or any judge regularly holding the courts of, the district or set of districts as defined in G.S. 7A-41.1(a) in which the county in which the cause arose is located, or of any adjoining district or set of districts, who shall have full power and authority to hear and determine the motion in the same manner as if he were the presiding judge of a session of superior court for that county.

History.
1939, c. 48; 1961, c. 50; 1969, c. 1190, s. 43; 1987 (Reg. Sess., 1988), c. 1037, s. 11

§ 7A-49.2. Civil business at criminal sessions; criminal business at civil sessions

(a) At criminal sessions of court, motions in civil actions may be heard upon due notice, and trials in civil actions may be heard by consent of parties. Motions for confirmation or rejection of referees' reports may also be heard upon 10 days' notice and judgment may be entered on such reports. The court may also enter consent orders and consent judgments, and try uncontested civil actions.

(b) For sessions of court designated for the trial of civil cases only, no grand juries shall be drawn and no criminal process shall be made returnable to any civil session.

History.
1901, c. 28; Rev., ss. 1507, 1508; 1913, c. 196; Ex. Sess. 1913, c. 23; 1915, cc. 68, 240; 1917, c. 13; C.S., ss. 1444, 1445; 1931, c. 394; 1947, c. 25; 1969, c. 1190, s. 44; 1973, c. 503, s. 1

N.C. Gen. Stat. § 7A-49.3

Repealed by Session Laws 1999-428, s. 2, effective January 1, 2000.

§ 7A-49.4. Superior court criminal case docketing

(a) **Criminal Docketing. --** Criminal cases in superior court shall be calendared by the district attorney at administrative settings according to a criminal case docketing plan developed by the district attorney for each superior court district in consultation with the superior court judges residing in that district and after opportunity for comment by members of the local bar. Each criminal case docketing plan shall, at a minimum, comply with the provisions of this section, but may contain additional provisions not inconsistent with this section.

(b) **Administrative Settings. --** An administrative setting shall be calendared for each felony within 60 days of indictment or service of notice of indictment if required by law, or at the next regularly scheduled session of superior court if later than 60 days from indictment or service if required. At an administrative setting:

(1) The court shall determine the status of the defendant's representation by counsel;

(2) After hearing from the parties, the court shall set deadlines for the delivery of discovery, arraignment if necessary, and filing of motions;

(3) If the district attorney has made a determination regarding a plea arrangement, the district attorney shall inform the defendant as to whether a plea arrangement will be offered and the terms of any proposed plea arrangement, and the court may conduct a plea conference if supported by the interest of justice;

(4) The court may hear pending pretrial motions, set such motions for hearing on a date certain, or defer ruling on motions until the trial of the case; and

(5) The court may schedule more than one administrative setting if requested by the parties or if it is found to be necessary to promote the fair administration of justice in a timely manner.

Whenever practical, administrative settings shall be held by a superior court judge residing within the district, but may otherwise be held by any superior court judge.

If the parties have not otherwise agreed upon a trial date, then upon the conclusion of the final administrative setting, the district attorney shall announce a proposed trial date. The court shall set that date as the tentative trial date unless, after providing the parties an opportunity to be heard, the court determines that the interests of justice require the setting of a different date. In that event, the district attorney shall set another tentative trial date during the final administrative setting. The trial shall occur no sooner than 30 days after the final administrative setting, except by agreement of the State and the defendant.

Nothing in this section precludes the disposition of a criminal case by plea, deferred prosecution, or dismissal prior to an administrative setting.

(c) **Definite Trial Date. --** When a case has not otherwise been scheduled for trial within 120 days of indictment or of service of notice of indictment if required by law, then upon motion by the defendant at any time thereafter, the senior resident superior court judge, or a superior court judge designated by the senior resident superior court judge, may hold a hearing for the purpose of establishing a trial date for the defendant.

(d) **Venue for Administrative Settings. --** Venue for administrative settings may be in any county within the district when necessary to comply with the terms of the criminal case docketing plan. The presence of the defendant is only required for administrative settings held in the county where the case originated.

(e) **Setting and Publishing of Trial Calendar. --** No less than 10 working days before cases are calendared for trial, the district attorney shall publish the trial calendar. The trial calendar shall schedule the cases in the order in which the district attorney anticipates they will be called for trial and should not contain cases that the district attorney does not reasonably expect to be called for trial. In counties in which multiple sessions of court are being held, the district attorney may publish a trial calendar for each session of court.

(f) **Order of Trial. --** The district attorney, after calling the calendar and determining cases for pleas and other disposition, shall announce to the court the order in which the district attorney intends to call for trial the cases remaining on the calendar. Deviations from the announced order require approval by the presiding judge if the defendant whose case is called for trial objects; but the defendant may not object if all the cases scheduled to be heard before the defendant's case have been disposed

of or delayed with the approval of the presiding judge or by consent of the State and the defendant. A case may be continued from the trial calendar only by consent of the State and the defendant or upon order of the presiding judge or resident superior court judge for good cause shown. The district attorney, after consultation with the parties, shall schedule a new trial date for cases not reached during that session of court.

(g) Nothing in this section shall be construed to deprive any victim of the rights granted under Article I, Section 37 of the North Carolina Constitution and Article 46 of Chapter 15A of the General Statutes.

(h) Nothing in this section shall be construed to affect the authority of the court in the call of cases calendared for trial.

History.
1999-428, s. 1

§ 7A-49.5. Statewide electronic filing in courts

(a) The General Assembly finds that the electronic filing of pleadings and other documents required to be filed with the courts may be a more economical, efficient, and satisfactory procedure to handle the volumes of paperwork routinely filed with, handled by, and disseminated by the courts of this State, and therefore authorizes the use of electronic filing in the courts of this State.

(b) The Supreme Court may adopt rules governing this process and associated costs and may supervise its implementation and operation through the Administrative Office of the Courts. The rules adopted under this section shall address the waiver of electronic fees for indigents.

(b1) The Supreme Court shall promulgate rules authorizing electronic filing and electronic signatures in the General Court of Justice. The rules shall require registration to participate in electronic filing and provide security procedures that include a mandatory submission of a form of identification to electronically file pro se.

(c) The Administrative Office of the Courts may contract with a vendor to provide electronic filing in the courts.

(d) Any funds received by the Administrative Office of the Courts from the vendor selected pursuant to subsection (c) of this section, other than applicable statutory court costs, as a result of electronic filing, shall be deposited in the Court Information Technology Fund in accordance with G.S. 7A-343.2.

History.
2006-187, s. 2(c); 2007-323, s. 14.17(c); 2012-142, s. 16.5(f); 2019-243, s. 3(a)

§ 7A-49.6. Proceedings conducted by audio and video transmission.

(a) Except as otherwise provided in this section, judicial officials may conduct proceedings of all types using an audio and video transmission in which the parties, the presiding official, and any other participants can see and hear each other. Judicial officials conducting proceedings by audio and video transmission under this section must safeguard the constitutional rights of those persons involved in the proceeding and preserve the integrity of the judicial process.

(b) Each party to a proceeding involving audio and video transmission must be able to communicate fully and confidentially with his or her attorney if the party is represented by an attorney.

(c) In a civil proceeding involving a jury, the court may allow a witness to testify by audio and video transmission only upon finding in the record that good cause exists for doing so under the circumstances.

(d) A party may object to conducting a civil proceeding by audio and video transmission. If the presiding official finds that the party has demonstrated good cause for the objection, the proceeding must not be held by audio and video transmission. If there is no objection, or if there is an objection and good cause is not shown, the presiding official may conduct the proceeding by audio and video transmission.

(e) Except as otherwise permitted by law, when the right to confront witnesses or be present is implicated in criminal or juvenile delinquency proceedings, the court may not proceed by audio and video transmission unless the court has obtained a knowing, intelligent, and voluntary waiver of the defendant's or juvenile respondent's rights.

(f) Proceedings conducted by audio and video transmission shall be held in a manner that complies with any applicable federal and State laws governing the confidentiality and security of confidential information.

(g) If the proceeding is one that is open to the public, then the presiding official must facilitate access to the proceeding by the public and the media as nearly as practicable to the access that would be available were the proceeding conducted in person.

(h) If the proceeding is required by law to be recorded, then the audio and video transmission must be recorded in accordance with G.S. 7A-95, G.S. 7A-198, and other laws, as applicable.

(i) This section is not intended to limit the court's authority to receive remote testimony pursuant to statutes that otherwise permit it, including G.S. 15A-1225.1, 15A-1225.2, 15A-1225.3, 20-139.1, 8C-1, Rule 616, 50A-111, and 52C-3-315(f).

(j) All proceedings under this section shall be conducted using videoconferencing applications approved by the Administrative Office of the Courts.

(k) As used herein, the term "judicial official" has the same meaning as in G.S. 15A-101(5).

History.
2021-47, s. 9(a)

ARTICLE 9
DISTRICT ATTORNEYS AND PROSECUTORIAL DISTRICTS

§ 7A-60. District attorneys and prosecutorial districts

(a) The State shall be divided into prosecutorial districts, as shown in subsection (a1) of this section. There shall be a district attorney for each prosecutorial district, as provided in subsections (b) and (c) of this section who shall be a resident of the prosecutorial district for which elected. A vacancy in the office of district attorney shall be filled as provided in Article IV, Sec. 19 of the Constitution.

(a1) *(Effective January 1, 2021 through December 31, 2022)* The counties of the State are organized into prosecutorial districts, and each district has the counties and the number of full-time assistant district attorneys set forth in the following table:

Prosecutorial District	Counties	No. of Full-Time Asst. District Attorneys
1	Camden, Chowan, Currituck, Dare, Gates, Pasquotank, Perquimans	12
2	Beaufort, Hyde, Martin, Tyrrell, Washington	8
3	Pitt	12
4	Carteret, Craven, Pamlico	13
5	Duplin, Jones, Onslow, Sampson	20
6	New Hanover, Pender	20
7	Bertie, Halifax, Hertford, Northampton	11

Prosecutorial District	Counties	No. of Full-Time Asst. District Attorneys
8	Edgecombe, Nash, Wilson	19
9	Greene, Lenoir, Wayne	15
11	Franklin, Granville, Person Vance, Warren	15
10	Wake	42
12	Harnett, Lee	12
13	Johnston	11
14	Cumberland	25
15	Bladen, Brunswick, Columbus	15
16	Durham	18
17	Alamance	12
18	Orange, Chatham	10
20	Robeson	13
21	Anson, Richmond, Scotland	9
22	Caswell, Rockingham	9
23	Stokes, Surry	8
24	Guilford	35
25	Cabarrus	10
26	Mecklenburg	58
27	Rowan	9
29	Hoke, Moore	9
28	Montgomery, Stanly	6
30	Union	11
31	Forsyth	27
32	Alexander, Iredell	13
33	Davidson, Davie	12
34	Alleghany, Ashe, Wilkes, Yadkin	9
35	Avery, Madison, Mitchell, Watauga, Yancey	8
36	Burke, Caldwell, Catawba	20
37	Randolph	10
38	Gaston	16
39	Cleveland, Lincoln	13
40	Buncombe	14
41	McDowell, Rutherford	8
42	Henderson, Polk, Transylvania	9
43	Cherokee, Clay, Graham, Haywood, Jackson, Macon, Swain.	13

(a1) *(Effective January 1, 2023)* The counties of the State are organized into prosecutorial districts, and each district has the counties and the number of full-time assistant district attorneys set forth in the following table:

Prosecutorial District	Counties	No. of Full-Time Asst. District Attorneys
1	Camden, Chowan, Currituck, Dare, Gates, Pasquotank, Perquimans	12
2	Beaufort, Hyde, Martin, Tyrrell, Washington	8
3	Pitt	12
4	Carteret, Craven, Pamlico	13
5	Duplin, Jones, Onslow, Sampson	20
6	New Hanover, Pender	20
7	Bertie, Halifax, Hertford, Northampton	11
8	Edgecombe, Nash, Wilson	19
9	Greene, Lenoir, Wayne	15

Prosecutorial District	Counties	No. of Full-Time Asst. District Attorneys
11	Franklin, Granville, Person Vance, Warren	15
10	Wake	42
12	Harnett, Lee	12
13	Johnston	11
14	Cumberland	25
15	Bladen, Brunswick, Columbus	15
16	Durham	18
17	Alamance	12
18	Orange, Chatham	10
20	Robeson	13
21	Anson, Richmond, Scotland	9
22	Caswell, Rockingham	9
23	Stokes, Surry	8
24	Guilford	35
25	Cabarrus	10
26	Mecklenburg	58
27	Rowan	9
29	Hoke, Moore	9
28	Montgomery, Stanly	6
30	Union	11
31	Forsyth	27
32	Alexander, Iredell	13
33	Davidson, Davie	12
34	Alleghany, Ashe, Wilkes, Yadkin	9
35	Avery, Madison, Mitchell, Watauga, Yancey	8
36	Burke, Caldwell	10
37	Randolph	10
38	Gaston	16
39	Cleveland, Lincoln	13
40	Buncombe	14
41	McDowell, Rutherford	8
42	Henderson, Polk, Transylvania	9
43	Cherokee, Clay, Graham, Haywood, Jackson, Macon, Swain.	13
44	Catawba	10

(a2) Repealed by Session Laws 2017-57, s. 18B.9(f), effective June 28, 2017.

(b) Except as provided in subsection (c) of this section, each district attorney for a prosecutorial district as defined in subsection (a1) of this section, other than District 19B, who is in office on December 31, 1988, shall continue in office for that prosecutorial district, for a term expiring December 31, 1990. In the general election of 1990, and every four years thereafter, a district attorney shall be elected for a four-year term for each prosecutorial district other than Districts 16A and 19B, and shall take office on the January 1 following such election. The district attorney for Prosecutorial District 19B, who is elected in the general election of 1988 for a four-year term beginning January 1, 1989, shall serve that term for Prosecutorial District

19B. In the general election of 1992, and every four years thereafter, a district attorney shall be elected for a four-year term for Prosecutorial Districts 16A and 19B and shall take office on the January 1 following such election.

(c) The office and term of the district attorney for Prosecutorial District 12 formerly consisting of Cumberland and Hoke Counties are allocated to Prosecutorial District 12 as defined by subsection (a1) of this section. The office and the term of the district attorney for former Prosecutorial District 16 consisting of Robeson and Scotland Counties are allocated to Prosecutorial District 16B as defined by subsection (a1) of this section. The initial district attorney for Prosecutorial District 16A as defined in subsection (a1) of this section shall be elected in the general election of November 1988, from nominations made in accordance with G.S. 163-114 as if a vacancy had occurred in nomination, and shall serve an initial term expiring December 31, 1992. In all other respects, subsection (b) of this section shall apply to the district attorneys for Prosecutorial Districts 12, 16A, and 16B to the same extent as all other district attorneys.

History.

1967, c. 1049, s. 1; 1975, c. 956, s. 4; 1977, c. 1130, s. 3; 1977, 2nd Sess., c. 1238, s. 2; 1981, c. 964, ss. 2, 3; 1987, c. 509, ss. 4, 5; c. 738, s. 127(a); 1987 (Reg. Sess., 1988), c. 1056, s. 1; c. 1086, s. 111; 1989, c. 770, ss. 1, 56; c. 795, s. 24(a), (e); 1991, c. 742, s. 13; 1991 (Reg. Sess., 1992), c. 900, s. 120(a), (b); 1993, c. 321, ss. 200.4 (*l*), 200.7(a), (b); 1995, c. 507, s. 21.7; 1995 (Reg. Sess., 1996), c. 589, s. 3(a); 1996, 2nd Ex. Sess., c. 18, s. 22(a); 1997-443, s. 18.11(a); 1998-212, s. 16.20(a); 1999-237, s. 17.8(a); 2004-124, s. 14.6(h); 2005-276, s. 14.2 (*l*); 2006-66, ss. 14.3(a), 14.19(a); 2007-323, ss. 14.14(a), (b), 14.25(j); 2008-107, s. 14.6; 2009-451, s. 15.17E(a); 2012-194, s. 1(b); 2013-360, s. 18B.22(k); 2014-100, s. 18B.7(a); 2017-6, s. 3; 2017-57, s. 18B.9(e), (f), (h), (i); 2017-197, s. 5.6(a) -(c); 2018-5, s. 18B.6; 2018-114, s. 24(a), (b); 2018-121, ss. 3(a), 7; 2018-146, ss. 3.1(a), (b), 6.1; 2019-229, s. 1(a) -(c); 2021-91, s. 13(b)

§ 7A-61. Duties of district attorney

The district attorney shall prepare the trial dockets, prosecute in a timely manner in the name of the State all criminal actions and infractions requiring prosecution in the superior and district courts of the district attorney's prosecutorial district and advise the officers of justice in the district attorney's district. The district attorney shall also represent the State in juvenile cases in the superior and district courts in which the juvenile is represented by an attorney. The district attorney shall provide to the Attorney General any case files, records and additional information necessary for the Attorney General to conduct appeals to the Appellate Division for cases from the district attorney's prosecutorial district. The Attorney General shall not delegate to the district attorney, or any other entity, the duty to represent the State in criminal and juvenile appeals. Each district attorney shall devote his full time to the duties of his office and shall not engage in the private practice of law.

History.

1967, c. 1049, s. 1; 1969, c. 1190, s. 5; 1971, c. 377, s. 5.1; 1973, c. 47, s. 2; 1985, c. 764, s. 7; 1985 (Reg. Sess., 1986), c. 852, s. 17; 1987 (Reg. Sess., 1988), c. 1037, s. 12; 1999-428, s. 3; 2017-212, s. 5.2(b)

§ 7A-62. Acting district attorney

When a district attorney becomes for any reason unable to perform his duties, the Governor shall appoint an acting district attorney to serve during the period of disability. An acting district attorney has all the power, authority and duties of the regular district attorney. He shall take the oath of office prescribed for the regular district attorney, and shall receive the same compensation as the regular district attorney.

History.

1967, c. 1049, s. 1; 1973, c. 47, s. 2

§ 7A-63. Assistant district attorneys

Each district attorney shall be entitled to the number of full-time assistant district attorneys set out in this Subchapter to be appointed by the district attorney, to serve at the district attorney's pleasure. A vacancy in the office of assistant district attorney shall be filled in the same manner as the initial appointment. An assistant district attorney shall take the same oath of office as the district attorney, and shall perform such duties as may be assigned by the district attorney. The district attorney shall devote full time to the duties of the office and shall not engage in the private practice of law during his or her term.

History.

1967, c. 1049, s. 1; 1969, c. 1190, s. 6; 1971, c. 377, s. 6; 1973, c. 47, s. 2; 2014-100, s. 18B.7(b); 2017-57, s. 18B.9(g)

§ 7A-64. Temporary assistance for district attorneys

(a) A district attorney may apply to the Director of the Administrative Office of the Courts to:

(1) Temporarily assign an assistant district attorney from another district, after consultation with the district attorney thereof, to assist in the prosecution of cases in the requesting district;

(2) Authorize the temporary appointment, by the requesting district attorney, of a qualified attorney to assist the requesting district attorney; or

(3) Enter into contracts with local governments for the provision of services by the State pursuant to G.S. 153A-212.1 or G.S. 160A-289.1.

(a1) Repealed by Session Laws 2012-7, s. 9, effective June 7, 2012.

(b) The Director of the Administrative Office of the Courts may provide this assistance only upon a showing by the requesting district attorney supported by facts that at least one of the following circumstances apply:

(1) Criminal cases have accumulated on the dockets of the superior or district courts of the district beyond the capacity of the

district attorney and the district attorney's full-time assistants to keep the dockets reasonably current.

(2) The overwhelming public interest warrants the use of additional resources for the speedy disposition of cases involving drug offenses, domestic violence, or other offenses involving a threat to public safety.

(3) There is a conflict of interest.

(4) A county within the jurisdiction of the requesting district attorney is subject to a disaster declaration by the Governor pursuant to G.S. 166A-19.3(3).

(c) The length of service and compensation of any temporary appointee or the terms of any contract entered into with local governments shall be fixed by Director of the Administrative Office of the Courts in each case. Nothing in this section shall be construed to obligate the General Assembly to make any appropriation to implement the provisions of this section or to obligate the Administrative Office of the Courts to provide the administrative costs of establishing or maintaining the positions or services provided for under this section. Further, nothing in this section shall be construed to obligate the Administrative Office of the Courts to maintain positions or services initially provided for under this section.

History.
1967, c. 1049, s. 1; 1973, c. 47, s. 2; 1999-237, s. 17.17(a); 2000-67, s. 15.4(g); 2010-171, s. 2; 2012-7, s. 9; 2017-158, s. 14; 2018-138, s. 2.12(a)

§ 7A-65. Compensation and allowances of district attorneys and assistant district attorneys

(a) The annual salary of:

(1) District attorneys shall be as provided in the Current Operations Appropriations Act.

(2) Full-time assistant district attorneys shall be as provided in the Current Operations Appropriations Act.

When traveling on official business, each district attorney and assistant district attorney is entitled to reimbursement for his or her subsistence expenses to the same extent as State employees generally. When traveling on official business outside his or her county of residence, each district attorney and assistant district attorney is entitled to reimbursement for travel expenses to the same extent as State employees generally. For purposes of this subsection, the term "official business" does not include regular, daily commuting between a person's home and the district attorney's office. Travel distances, for purposes of reimbursement for mileage, shall be determined

according to the travel policy of the Administrative Office of the Courts.

(b) Repealed by Session Laws 1985, c. 689, s. 2.

(c) In lieu of merit and other increment raises paid to regular State employees, a district attorney shall receive as longevity pay an amount equal to four and eight-tenths percent (4.8%) of the annual salary set forth in the Current Operations Appropriations Act payable monthly after five years of service, and nine and six-tenths percent (9.6%) after 10 years of service, fourteen and four-tenths percent (14.4%) after 15 years of service, nineteen and two-tenths percent (19.2%) after 20 years of service, and twenty-four percent (24%) after 25 years of service. Service shall mean service in the elective position of a district attorney and shall not include service as a deputy or acting district attorney. Service shall also mean service as a justice or judge of the General Court of Justice, clerk of superior court, assistant district attorney, public defender, appellate defender, or assistant public or appellate defender.

(d) In lieu of merit and other increment raises paid to regular State employees, an assistant district attorney shall receive as longevity pay an amount equal to four and eight-tenths percent (4.8%) of the annual salary set forth in the Current Operations Appropriations Act payable monthly after five years of service, nine and six-tenths percent (9.6%) after 10 years of service, fourteen and four-tenths percent (14.4%) after 15 years of service, nineteen and two-tenths percent (19.2%) after 20 years of service, and twenty-four percent (24%) after 25 years of service. "Service" means service as an assistant district attorney, district attorney, resource prosecutor, public defender, appellate defender, assistant public or appellate defender, justice or judge of the General Court of Justice, or clerk of superior court. For purposes of this subsection, "resource prosecutor" means a former assistant district attorney who has left the employment of the district attorney's office to serve in a specific, time-limited position with the Conference of District Attorneys.

History.
1967, c. 1049, s. 1; 1973, c. 47, s. 2; 1983, c. 761, ss. 246, 248; 1983 (Reg. Sess., 1984), c. 1034, ss. 92, 165; c. 1109, s. 13.1; 1985, c. 689, s. 2; c. 698, s. 10(b); 1985 (Reg. Sess., 1986), c. 1014, s. 224; 1987, c. 738, s. 33(a); 1995, c. 507, s. 7.4A; 1999-237, s. 28.19(a); 2000-67, s. 26.3A(a); 2003-284, ss. 30.19A(a), 30.19A(b); 2005-276, s. 29.23A; 2007-323, ss. 28.15A, 28.18A(d); 2009-451, s. 15.17B(b)

§ 7A-66. Removal of district attorneys

The following are grounds for suspension of a district attorney or for his removal from office:

(1) Mental or physical incapacity interfering with the performance of his duties which is, or is likely to become, permanent;

(2) Willful misconduct in office;

(3) Willful and persistent failure to perform his duties;

(4) Habitual intemperance;

(5) Conviction of a crime involving moral turpitude;

(6) Conduct prejudicial to the administration of justice which brings the office into disrepute; or

(7) Knowingly authorizing or permitting an assistant district attorney to commit any act constituting grounds for removal, as defined in subdivisions (1) through (6) hereof.

A proceeding to suspend or remove a district attorney is commenced by filing with the clerk of superior court of the county where the district attorney resides a sworn affidavit charging the district attorney with one or more grounds for removal. The clerk shall immediately bring the matter to the attention of the senior regular resident superior court judge for the district or set of districts as defined in G.S. 7A-41.1(a) in which the county is located who shall within 30 days either review and act on the charges or refer them for review and action within 30 days to another superior court judge residing in or regularly holding the courts of that district or set of districts. If the superior court judge upon review finds that the charges if true constitute grounds for suspension, and finds probable cause for believing that the charges are true, he may enter an order suspending the district attorney from performing the duties of his office until a final determination of the charges on the merits. During the suspension the salary of the district attorney continues. If the superior court judge finds that the charges if true do not constitute grounds for suspension or finds that no probable cause exists for believing that the charges are true, he shall dismiss the proceeding.

If a hearing, with or without suspension, is ordered, the district attorney should receive immediate written notice of the proceedings and a true copy of the charges, and the matter shall be set for hearing not less than 10 days nor more than 30 days thereafter. The matter shall be set for hearing before the judge who originally examined the charges or before another regular superior court judge resident in or regularly holding the courts of that district or set of districts. The hearing shall be open to the public. All testimony shall be recorded. At the hearing the superior court judge shall hear evidence and make findings of fact and conclusions of law and if he finds that grounds for removal exist, he shall enter an order permanently removing the district attorney from office, and terminating his salary. If he finds that no grounds exist, he shall terminate the suspension, if any.

The district attorney may appeal from an order of removal to the Court of Appeals on the basis of error of law by the superior court judge. Pending decision of the case on appeal, the district attorney shall not perform any of the duties of his office. If, upon final determination, he is ordered reinstated either by the appellate division or by the superior court upon remand his salary shall be restored from the date of the original order of removal.

History.
1967, c. 1049, s. 1; 1973, c. 47, s. 2; c. 148, s. 1; 1977, c. 21, ss. 1, 2; 1987 (Reg. Sess., 1988), c. 1037, s. 13

§ 7A-66.1. Office of solicitor may be denominated as office of district attorney; "solicitor" and "district attorney" made interchangeable; interchangeable use authorized in proceedings, documents, and quotations

(a) The constitutional office of solicitor may be denominated as the office of "district attorney" for all purposes, and the terms "solicitor" and "district attorney" shall be identical in meaning and interchangeable in use. All terms derived from or related to the term "solicitor" may embody this denomination.

(b) Repealed by Session Laws 1975, c. 956, s. 5.

(c) The interchangeable use authorized in this section includes use in all forms of oral, written, visual, and other communication including:

(1) Oaths of office;

(2) Other oaths or orations required or permitted in court or official proceedings;

(3) Ballots;

(4) Statutes;

(5) Regulations;

(6) Ordinances;

(7) Judgments and other court orders and records;

(8) Opinions in cases;

(9) Contracts;

(10) Bylaws;

(11) Charters;

(12) Official commissions, orders of appointment, proclamations, executive orders, and other official papers or pronouncements of the Governor or any executive, legislative, or judicial official of the State or any of its subdivisions;

(13) Official and unofficial letterheads;

(14) Campaign advertisements;

(15) Official and unofficial public notices; and

(16) In all other contexts not enumerated.

The interchangeability authorized in this section extends to the privilege of substituting terminology in matter quoted in oral, written, and other modes of communication without making indication of such change, except where such change may result in a substantive misunderstanding. Reprints or certifications of the text of the Constitution of North Carolina made by the Secretary of State, however, must retain the original terminology and indicate in brackets beside the original terminology the appropriate alternative words.

History.

1973, c. 47, s. 1; 1975, c. 956, s. 5

N.C. Gen. Stat. § 7A-67

Repealed by Session Laws 1971, c. 377, s. 32.

§ 7A-68. Administrative assistants

(a) Each district attorney shall be entitled to one administrative assistant to be appointed by the district attorney and to serve at his pleasure. The assistant need not be an attorney licensed to practice law in the State of North Carolina.

(b) It shall be the duty of the administrative assistant to assist the district attorney in preparing cases for trial and in expediting the criminal court docket, and to assist in such other duties as may be assigned by the district attorney.

(c) When traveling on official business, each administrative assistant is entitled to reimbursement for his subsistence and travel expenses to the same extent as State employees generally.

History.

1973, c. 807

§ 7A-69. Investigatorial assistants

The district attorney in prosecutorial districts 1, 3B, 4, 5, 7, 8, 11, 12, 13, 14, 15A, 15B, 16A, 18, 19B, 20A, 20B, 21, 22A, 22B, 24, 25, 26, 27A, 27B, 28, 29A, 29B, and 30 is entitled to one investigatorial assistant, and the district attorney in prosecutorial district 10 is entitled to two investigatorial assistants, to be appointed by the district attorney and to serve at his pleasure.

It shall be the duty of the investigatorial assistant to investigate cases preparatory to trial and to perform such other Duties as may be assigned by the district attorney. The investigatorial assistant is entitled to reimbursement for his subsistence and travel expenses to the same extent as State employees generally.

History.

1975, c. 956, s. 6; 1977, c. 969, s. 1; 1981, c. 964, s. 2; 1993, c. 321, s. 200.7(e); 1997-443, s. 18.16; 1998-212, s. 16.21; 1999-237, s. 17.9; 2004-124, s. 14.7(a); 2005-276, s. 14.2(p); 2007-323, s. 14.25(n)

N.C. Gen. Stat. § 7A-69.1

Repealed by Session Laws 1985 (Regular Session, 1986), c. 998, s. 3.

ARTICLE 11
SPECIAL REGULATIONS

§ 7A-95. Reporting of trials

(a) Court reporting personnel shall be utilized if available, for the reporting of trials in the superior court. If court reporters are not available in any county, electronic or other mechanical devices shall be provided by the Administrative Office of the Courts upon the request of the senior regular resident superior court judge.

(b) The Administrative Office of the Courts shall from time to time investigate the state of the art and techniques of recording testimony, and shall provide such electronic or mechanical devices as are found to be most efficient for this purpose.

(c) If an electronic or other mechanical device is utilized, it shall be the duty of the clerk of the superior court or some person designated by the clerk to operate the device while a trial is in progress, and the clerk shall thereafter preserve the record thus produced, which may be transcribed, as required, by any person designated by the Administrative Office of the Courts. If stenotype, shorthand, or stenomask equipment is used, the original tapes, notes, discs or other records are the property of the State, and the clerk shall keep them in his custody.

(d) Reporting of any trial may be waived by consent of the parties.

(e) Appointment of a reporter or reporters for superior court proceedings in each district or set of districts as defined in G.S. 7A-41.1(a) shall be made by the senior regular resident superior court judge of that district or set of districts. The compensation and allowances of reporters in each such district or set of districts shall be fixed by the senior regular resident superior court judge, within limits determined by the Administrative Officer of the Courts, and paid by the State.

(f) Repealed by Session Laws 1971, c. 377, s. 32.

History.

1965, c. 310, s. 1; 1969, c. 1190, s. 7; 1971, c. 377, s. 32; 1987, c. 384, s. 1.; 1987 (Reg. Sess., 1988), c. 1037, s. 14

§ 7A-96. Court adjourned by sheriff when judge not present

If the judge of a superior court shall not be present to hold any session of court at the time fixed therefor, he may order the sheriff to adjourn the court to any day certain during the session, and on failure to hear from the judge it shall be the duty of the sheriff to adjourn the court from day to day, unless he shall be sooner informed that the judge for any reason cannot hold the session.

History.
Code, s. 926; 1887, c. 13; 1901, c. 269; Rev., s. 1510; C.S., s. 1448; 1969, c. 1190, s. 49

§ 7A-97. Court's control of argument

In all trials in the superior courts there shall be allowed two addresses to the jury for the State or plaintiff and two for the defendant, except in capital felonies, when there shall be no limit as to number. The judges of the superior court are authorized to limit the time of argument of counsel to the jury on the trial of actions, civil and criminal as follows: to not less than one hour on each side in misdemeanors and appeals from justices of the peace; to not less than two hours on each side in all other civil actions and in felonies less than capital; in capital felonies, the time of argument of counsel may not be limited otherwise than by consent, except that the court may limit the number of those who may address the jury to three counsel on each side. Where any greater number of addresses or any extension of time are desired, motion shall be made, and it shall be in the discretion of the judge to allow the same or not, as the interests of justice may require. In jury trials the whole case as well of law as of fact may be argued to the jury.

History.
1903, c. 433; Rev., s. 216; C.S., s. 203; 1927, c. 52; 1995, c. 431, s. 7

§ 7A-98. Unsworn declarations under penalty of perjury.

(a) Any matter required or permitted to be supported, evidenced, established, or proved in writing under oath or affirmation may, if filed electronically pursuant to rules promulgated by the Supreme Court under G.S. 7A-49.5, with like force and effect be supported, evidenced, established, or proved by an unsworn declaration in writing, subscribed by the declarant and dated, that the statement is true under penalty of perjury.

(b) Declarations given pursuant to this section shall be deemed sufficient if given in substantially the following form:

"I declare (or certify, verify, or state) under penalty of perjury under the laws of North Carolina that the foregoing is true and correct. Executed on (date). (Signature)."

(c) Except as otherwise provided by law, this section does not apply to, and such unsworn declarations shall not be deemed sufficient for, any of the following:

(1) Oral testimony.

(2) Oaths of office.

(3) Any statement under oath or affirmation required to be taken before a specified official other than a notary public.

(4) Any will or codicil executed pursuant to G.S. 31-11.6.

(5) Any real property deed, contract, or lease requiring an acknowledgment pursuant to G.S. 47-17.

History.
2021-47, s. 17(a)

ARTICLE 12
CLERK OF SUPERIOR COURT

§ 7A-109.2. (Contingent effective date -- see notes) Records of dispositions in criminal cases

Each clerk of superior court shall ensure that all records of dispositions in criminal cases, including those records filed electronically, contain all the essential information about the case, including the identity of the presiding judge and the attorneys representing the State and the defendant.

History.
1998-208, s. 2

EDITOR'S NOTE. --
Session Laws 2006-253, s. 33, provides in part: "Sections 20.1, 20.2, and the requirement that the Administrative Office of the Courts electronically record certain data contained in subsection (c) of G.S. 20-138.4, as amended by Section 19 of this act, become effective after the next rewrite of the superior court clerks system by the Administrative Office of the Courts."

§ 7A-109.2. (Contingent effective date -- see notes) Records of dispositions in criminal cases; impaired driving integrated data system

(a) Each clerk of superior court shall ensure that all records of dispositions in criminal cases, including those records filed electronically, contain all the essential information about the case, including the the name of the presiding judge and the attorneys representing the State and the defendant.

(b) In addition to the information required by subsection (a) of this section for all offenses involving impaired driving as defined by G.S. 20-4.01, all charges of driving while license revoked for an impaired driving license revocation as defined by G.S. 20-28.2, and any other violation of the motor vehicle code involving the operation of a vehicle and the possession, consumption, use, or transportation of alcoholic beverages, the clerk shall include in the electronic records the following information:

(1) The reasons for any pretrial dismissal by the court.

(2) The alcohol concentration reported by the charging officer or chemical analyst, if any.

(3) The reasons for any suppression of evidence.

History.
1998-208, s. 2; 2006-253, s. 20.1

Session Laws 2006-253, s. 33, provides in part: "Sections 20.1, 20.2, and the requirement that the Administrative Office of the Courts electronically record certain data contained in subsection (c) of G.S. 20-138.4, as amended by Section 19 of this act, become effective after the next rewrite of the superior court clerks system by the Administrative Office of the Courts." As of October, 2021, the rewrite of the superior court clerks system has not been completed.

§ 7A-109.3. Delivery of commitment order

(a) Whenever the district court sentences a person to imprisonment and commitment to the custody of the Division of Adult Correction and Juvenile Justice of the Department of Public Safety pursuant to G.S. 15A-1352, the clerk of superior court shall furnish the sheriff with the signed order of commitment within 48 hours of the issuance of the sentence.

(a1) If the district court sentences a person under the age of 18 to imprisonment and commitment, the clerk of superior court shall furnish the detention facility approved by the Juvenile Justice Section of the Division of Adult Correction and Juvenile Justice with the signed order of commitment within 48 hours of the issuance of the sentence.

(b) Whenever the superior court sentences a person to imprisonment and commitment to the custody of the Division of Adult Correction and Juvenile Justice of the Department of Public Safety pursuant to G.S. 15A-1352, the clerk of superior court shall furnish the sheriff with the signed order of commitment within 72 hours of the issuance of the sentence.

(c) If the superior court sentences a person under the age of 18 to imprisonment and commitment, the clerk of superior court shall furnish the detention facility approved by the Juvenile Justice Section of the Division of Adult

Correction and Juvenile Justice with the signed order of commitment within 48 hours of the issuance of the sentence.

History.
1999-237, s. 18.10(c); 2011-145, s. 19.1(h); 2017-186, s. 2(b); 2020-83, s. 8(a)

§ 7A-109.4. Records of offenses involving impaired driving

The clerk of superior court shall maintain all records relating to an offense involving impaired driving as defined in G.S. 20-4.01(24a) for a minimum of 10 years from the date of conviction. Prior to destroying the record, the clerk shall record the name of the defendant, the judge, the prosecutor, and the attorney or whether there was a waiver of attorney, the alcohol concentration or the fact of refusal, the sentence imposed, and whether the case was appealed to superior court and its disposition.

History.
2006-253, s. 24

SUBCHAPTER 04.
DISTRICT COURT DIVISION OF THE GENERAL COURT OF JUSTICE

ARTICLE 13
CREATION AND ORGANIZATION OF THE DISTRICT COURT DIVISION

§ 7A-130. Creation of district court division and district court districts; seats of court

(a) The district court division of the General Court of Justice is hereby created. It consists of various district courts organized in territorial districts. The numbers and boundaries of the districts are as provided by G.S. 7A-133. The district court shall sit in the county seat of each county, and at such additional places in each county as the General Assembly may authorize, except that sessions of court are not required at an additional seat of court unless the chief district judge and the Administrative Officer of the Courts concur in a finding that the facilities are adequate.

(b) Notwithstanding subsection (a) of this section, when exigent circumstances exist within a judicial district, sessions of district court may be conducted at a location outside a county seat by order of the chief district court judge of a county, with the prior approval of the location and facilities by the Administrative Officer of the Courts and after consultation with the clerk of superior court and county officials of the county. An order entered under this subsection shall be filed in the office of the clerk of superior court in the county and posted at the courthouse within the county seat and notice shall be posted in other conspicuous locations.

History.
1965, c. 310, s. 1; 1987, c. 509, s. 14; c. 738, s. 124; 2018-138, s. 2.12(b)

§ 7A-131. Establishment of district courts

District courts are established, within districts, in accordance with the following schedule:

(1) On the first Monday in December, 1966, the first, the twelfth, the fourteenth, the sixteenth, the twenty-fifth, and the thirtieth districts;

(2) On the first Monday in December, 1968, the second, the third, the fourth, the fifth, the sixth, the seventh, the eighth, the ninth, the tenth, the eleventh, the thirteenth, the fifteenth, the eighteenth, the twentieth, the twenty-first, the twenty-fourth, the twenty-sixth, the twenty-seventh, and the twenty-ninth districts;

(3) On the first Monday in December, 1970, the seventeenth, the nineteenth, the twenty-second, the twenty-third, and the twenty-eighth districts.

History.
1965, c. 310, s. 1

§ 7A-132. Judges, district attorneys, full-time assistant district attorneys and magistrates for district court districts

Each district court district shall have one or more judges and one district attorney. Each county within each district shall have at least one magistrate.

For each district the General Assembly shall prescribe the numbers of district judges, and the numbers of full-time assistant district attorneys. For each county within each district the General Assembly shall prescribe a minimum number of magistrates.

History.
1965, c. 310, s. 1; 1967, c. 1049, s. 5; 1973, c. 47, s. 2; 2006-187, s. 7(b)

§ 7A-133. Numbers of judges by districts; numbers of magistrates and additional seats of court, by counties

(a) Each district court district shall have the numbers of judges as set forth in the following table:

District	Judges	County
1	5	Camden
		Chowan
		Currituck
		Dare
		Gates
		Pasquotank
		Perquimans
2	4	Martin
		Beaufort
		Tyrrell
		Hyde
		Washington
3A	6	Pitt
3B	6	Craven
		Pamlico
		Carteret
4	9	Sampson
		Duplin
		Jones
		Onslow
5	9	New Hanover
		Pender
6	4	Northampton
		Bertie
		Hertford
		Halifax
7	7	Nash
		Edgecombe
		Wilson
8	6	Wayne
		Greene
		Lenoir
9	5	Granville
		(part of Vance see subsection (b))
		Franklin
		Person
9B	2	Warren
		(part of Vance see subsection (b))
10A	3	(part of Wake see subsection (b))
10B	3	(part of Wake see subsection (b))
10C	3	(part of Wake see subsection (b))
10D	5	(part of Wake see subsection (b))

District	Judges	County
10E	3	(part of Wake see subsection (b))
10F	3	(part of Wake see subsection (b))
11	11	Harnett Johnston Lee
12	10	Cumberland
13	6	Bladen Brunswick Columbus
14	7	Durham
15A	4	Alamance
15B	5	Orange Chatham
16A	4	Scotland Anson Richmond
16B	6	Robeson
17A	4	Caswell Rockingham
17B	4	Stokes Surry
18	14	Guilford
19A	6	Cabarrus
19B	5	Randolph
19C	5	Rowan
19D	4	Hoke, Moore
20A	3	Montgomery, Stanly
20B	1	(part of Union see subsection (b))
20C	2	(part of Union see subsection (b))
20D	2	Union
21	11	Forsyth
22A	6	Alexander Iredell
22B	6	Davidson Davie
23	4	Alleghany Ashe Wilkes Yadkin
24	4	Avery Madison Mitchell Watauga Yancey
25	10	Burke Caldwell Catawba
26	21	Mecklenburg
27A	7	Gaston
27B	6	Cleveland Lincoln
28	7	Buncombe
29A	4	McDowell

District	Judges	County
29B	4	Rutherford Henderson Polk Transylvania
30	6	Cherokee Clay Graham Haywood Jackson Macon Swain.

(b) For district court districts of less than a whole county, or with part or all of one county with part of another, the composition of the district is as follows:

(1) District Court District 9 consists of Person, Franklin and Granville Counties and the remainder of Vance County not in District Court District 9B.

(2) District Court District 9B consists of Warren County and VTD EH1, VTD MIDD, VTD NH1, VTD NH2, VTD TWNS, VTD WMSB of Vance County.

(3) District Court District 20C consists of the remainder of Union County not in District Court District 20B.

(4) District Court District 20B consists of Precinct 01: Tract 204.01: Block Group 2: Block 2040, Block 2057, Block 2058, Block 2060, Block 2061, Block 2062, Block 2064, Block 2065; Tract 204.02: Block Group 2: Block 2001, Block 2002, Block 2003, Block 2004, Block 2005, Block 2006, Block 2007, Block 2008, Block 2009, Block 2010, Block 2011, Block 2012, Block 2013, Block 2014, Block 2015, Block 2016, Block 2017, Block 2018, Block 2023, Block 2024, Block 2025, Block 2026, Block 2027, Block 2028, Block 2029, Block 2030, Block 2031, Block 2032, Block 2033, Block 2034; Block Group 3: Block 3000, Block 3003, Block 3004, Block 3005, Block 3006, Block 3007, Block 3008, Block 3009, Block 3010, Block 3011, Block 3012, Block 3013, Block 3014, Block 3015, Block 3016, Block 3017, Block 3018, Block 3019, Block 3020, Block 3021, Block 3022, Block 3023, Block 3024, Block 3025, Block 3026, Block 3027, Block 3028, Block 3029, Block 3030, Block 3031, Block 3032, Block 3033, Block 3034, Block 3035, Block 3036, Block 3037, Block 3038, Block 3039, Block 3040, Block 3041, Block 3042, Block 3043, Block 3044, Block 3045, Block 3046, Block 3047; Block Group 4: Block 4035, Block 4054, Block 4055; Precinct 02: Tract 205: Block Group 1: Block 1000, Block 1001, Block 1002, Block 1003, Block 1004, Block 1005, Block 1006, Block 1007, Block 1009, Block 1010, Block 1011, Block 1012, Block

1013, Block 1014, Block 1015, Block 1016, Block 1017, Block 1018, Block 1019, Block 1020, Block 1021, Block 1022, Block 1023, Block 1037, Block 1038; Block Group 2: Block 2081, Block 2082, Block 2092, Block 2099, Block 2100, Block 2101, Block 2102; Tract 206: Block Group 3: Block 3036, Block 3038, Block 3039, Block 3040, Block 3048; Block Group 4: Block 4053; Precinct 03, Precinct 04, Precinct 06: Tract 202.02: Block Group 1: Block 1012, Block 1013, Block 1014, Block 1015, Block 1017, Block 1018, Block 1021, Block 1022, Block 1023; Tract 204.01: Block Group 2: Block 2000, Block 2001, Block 2002, Block 2003, Block 2004, Block 2005, Block 2033, Block 2034, Block 2035, Block 2036, Block 2041, Block 2042, Block 2043, Block 2044, Block 2045, Block 2056, Block 2063, Block 2999; Precinct 08, Precinct 09, Precinct 10, Precinct 13, Precinct 23: Tract 206: Block Group 4: Block 4051; Precinct 25: Tract 206: Block Group 4: Block 4036; Precinct 34, Precinct 36, Precinct 43 of Union County.

(5) District 10A: Wake County: VTD 01-42, VTD 01-47, VTD 02-01, VTD 02-02, VTD 02-03, VTD 02-04, VTD 02-05, VTD 02-06, VTD 07-02, VTD 07-06, VTD 07-07, VTD 08-04, VTD 08-05, VTD 08-07, VTD 09-01, VTD 09-03, VTD 10-01, VTD 13-10, VTD 13-11, VTD 14-01, VTD 14-02, VTD 19-03, VTD 19-04, VTD 19-05, VTD 19-06, VTD 19-07, VTD 19-09, VTD 19-10, VTD 19-11, VTD 19-12.

(6) District 10B: Wake County: VTD 09-02, VTD 10-02, VTD 10-03, VTD 10-04, VTD 13-01, VTD 13-07, VTD 13-08, VTD 13-09, VTD 16-08, VTD 17-02, VTD 17-03, VTD 17-04, VTD 17-06, VTD 17-07, VTD 17-08, VTD 17-09, VTD 17-11, VTD 19-16, VTD 19-17.

(7) District 10C: Wake County: VTD 01-04, VTD 01-09, VTD 01-10, VTD 01-12, VTD 01-13, VTD 01-14, VTD 01-15, VTD 01-17, VTD 01-18, VTD 01-28, VTD 01-30, VTD 01-34, VTD 01-36, VTD 01-37, VTD 01-38, VTD 01-39, VTD 01-43, VTD 01-44, VTD 01-45, VTD 01-46, VTD 01-51, VTD 07-03, VTD 07-04, VTD 07-05, VTD 07-09, VTD 07-11, VTD 07-12, VTD 07-13, VTD 08-02, VTD 08-06, VTD 08-09, VTD 13-02, VTD 13-05, VTD 13-06, VTD 17-01, VTD 17-05, VTD 17-10.

(8) District 10D: Wake County: VTD 01-01, VTD 01-02, VTD 01-03, VTD 01-05, VTD 01-06, VTD 01-07, VTD 01-11, VTD 01-16, VTD 01-29, VTD 01-33, VTD 01-49, VTD 04-01, VTD 04-02, VTD 04-03, VTD 04-04, VTD 04-05, VTD 04-06, VTD 04-07, VTD 04-08, VTD 04-09, VTD 04-10, VTD 04-11, VTD 04-12, VTD 04-14, VTD 04-15, VTD 04-16, VTD 04-17, VTD 04-18, VTD 04-20,

VTD 04-21, VTD 05-05, VTD 06-05, VTD 06-07, VTD 07-01, VTD 07-10, VTD 08-03, VTD 08-08, VTD 08-10, VTD 08-11, VTD 11-01, VTD 11-02, VTD 12-01, VTD 12-02, VTD 12-04, VTD 12-05, VTD 12-06, VTD 12-07, VTD 12-09, VTD 15-01, VTD 15-02, VTD 15-03, VTD 15-04, VTD 16-01, VTD 16-05, VTD 16-09, VTD 18-02, VTD 18-03, VTD 18-05, VTD 20-03, VTD 20-05, VTD 20-09.

(9) District 10E: Wake County: VTD 01-19, VTD 01-20, VTD 01-21, VTD 01-22, VTD 01-23, VTD 01-25, VTD 01-26, VTD 01-27, VTD 01-31, VTD 01-32, VTD 01-35, VTD 01-40, VTD 01-41, VTD 01-48, VTD 01-50, VTD 16-02, VTD 16-03, VTD 16-04, VTD 16-06, VTD 16-07, VTD 18-01, VTD 18-04, VTD 18-06, VTD 18-07, VTD 18-08.

(10) District 10F: Wake County: VTD 03-00, VTD 04-13, VTD 04-19, VTD 05-01, VTD 05-03, VTD 05-04, VTD 05-06, VTD 06-01, VTD 06-04, VTD 06-06, VTD 12-08, VTD 20-01, VTD 20-02, VTD 20-04, VTD 20-06, VTD 20-08, VTD 20-10, VTD 20-11, VTD 20-12.

(11) through (18) Repealed by Session Laws 2020-84, s. 2(a), effective January 1, 2021.

The names and boundaries of voting tabulation districts specified for Wake County, and Vance County in this section are as shown on the 2010 Census Redistricting TIGER/Line Shapefiles. Precinct boundaries for Union County are those shown on the Legislative Services Office's redistricting computer database on January 1, 2005; and for other counties are those reported by the United States Bureau of the Census under Public Law 94-171 for the 1990 Census in the IVTD Version of the TIGER files.

(b1) The qualified voters of District Court District 11 shall elect all eight judges established for the District in subsection (a) of this section, but only persons who reside in Johnston County may be candidates for five of the judgeships, only persons who reside in Harnett County may be candidates for two of the judgeships, and only persons who reside in Lee County may be candidates for the remaining judgeship.

(b2) The qualified voters of District Court District 13 shall elect all six judges established for the District in subsection (a) of this section, but only persons who reside in Bladen County may be candidates for one of those judgeships, only persons who reside in Columbus County may be candidates for two of those judgeships, and only persons who reside in Brunswick County may be candidates for three of those judgeships. These district court judgeships shall be numbered and assigned for residency purposes as follows:

(1) Seat number one, established for residents of Brunswick County by this section, shall be the seat currently held by Judge Barefoot.

(2) Seat number two, established for residents of Brunswick County by this section, shall be the seat currently held by Judge Fairley.

(3) Seat number three, established for residents of Brunswick County by this section, shall be the seat currently held by Judge Warren.

(4) Seat number four, established for residents of Columbus County by this section, shall be the seat currently held by Judge Jolly.

(5) Seat number five, established for residents of Columbus County by this section, shall be the seat currently held by Judge Tyler.

(6) Seat number six, established for residents of Bladen County by this section, shall be the seat currently held by Judge Ussery.

(b3) The qualified voters of District Court District 22A shall elect all five judges established for the District in subsection (a) of this section, but only persons who reside in Alexander County may be candidates for two of the judgeships, and only persons who reside in Iredell County may be candidates for three of the judgeships.

(b4) The qualified voters of District Court District 22B shall elect all six judges established for the District in subsection (a) of this section, but only persons who reside in Davie County may be candidates for two of the judgeships, and only persons who reside in Davidson County may be candidates for four of the judgeships.

(b5) The qualified voters of District 16A shall elect all judges established for District 16A in subsection (a) of this section, but only persons who reside in Anson County may be candidates for one of the judgeships, only persons who reside in Scotland County may be candidates for one of the judgeships, and only persons who reside in Richmond County may be candidates for the remaining judgeships. In order to implement this section the following shall apply in order to transition from at large seats to residency requirements:

(1) In 2020, and every four years thereafter, the district court judgeship requiring a resident of Anson County shall be elected, and a district court judgeship requiring a resident of Richmond County shall be elected.

(2) In 2022, and every four years thereafter, the district court judgeship requiring a resident of Scotland County shall be elected, and a district court judgeship requiring a resident of Richmond County shall be elected.

(b6) *(Effective until January 1, 2023)* The qualified voters of District 20A shall elect all judges established for District 20A in subsection (a) of this section, but only persons who reside in Montgomery County may be candidates for one of the judgeships, and only persons who reside in Montgomery or Stanly County may be candidates for the remaining judgeships.

(b6) *(Effective January 1, 2023, with elections in 2022 to be held accordingly)* The qualified voters of District 20A shall elect all judges established for District 20A in subsection (a) of this section, but only persons who reside in Montgomery County may be candidates for one of the judgeships, and only persons who reside in Stanly County may be candidates for the remaining judgeships.

(b7) Subject to the provisions of this subsection, the qualified voters of District 25 shall elect all judges established for District 25 in subsection (a) of this section, but only persons who reside in Catawba County may be candidates for five of the judgeships, and only persons who reside in Burke or Caldwell County may be candidates for the remaining judgeships. In order to implement this section the following shall apply in order to transition from at large seats to residency requirements:

(1) **Transition of seats; regular elections.** -- For any district court judgeship that is held by a resident of Burke or Caldwell Counties on July 1, 2018, at the next general election after July 1, 2018, that district court judgeship shall be filled only by a person who is a resident of Burke or Caldwell Counties. Until such time as three district court judgeships transition under subdivision (2) of this subsection, for any district court judgeship that is held by a resident of Catawba County on July 1, 2018, that district court judgeship shall, at the next general election after July 1, 2018, be filled only by a person who is a resident of Burke, Caldwell, or Catawba County.

(2) **Transition of seats; vacancies.** -- Upon each of the first three district court judgeship vacancies occurring in District Court District 25 after July 1, 2018, due to death, resignation, removal, or retirement of a person who is a resident of Catawba County holding a judgeship on July 1, 2018, that vacancy shall be filled according to law for the remainder of the unfilled term. At the next general election held for that district court judgeship, only persons who reside in Burke or Caldwell County may be candidates for that district court judgeship. Any primary associated with that general election for that district court judgeship after the completion of the term shall also

be held accordingly, in accordance with this subsection.

(3) **Notification to State Board. --** Upon each of the first three district court judgeship vacancies occurring after July 1, 2018, in District Court District 25 due to the death, resignation, removal, or retirement of a person who is a resident of Catawba County holding a judgeship on July 1, 2018, the Director of the Administrative Office of the Courts shall provide written notice of the vacancy to the State Board of Elections and Ethics Enforcement. During the filing period for that district court judgeship at the next general election held for that district court judgeship, the State Board of Elections and Ethics Enforcement shall ensure that only persons who reside in Burke or Caldwell County may file as candidates for that district court judgeship in accordance [with] this subsection.

(4) **Final transition. --** If a total of three district court judgeships have not transferred under subdivision (2) of this subsection to be eligible to be held by only persons who are residents of Burke or Caldwell Counties by January 1, 2030, a sufficient number of district court judgeships to total three district court judgeships shall be transferred to be held by only persons who are residents of Burke or Caldwell Counties on January 1, 2031, and the 2030 elections shall be held accordingly.

(c) Each county shall have the numbers of magistrates and additional seats of district court, as set forth in the following table:

County	Magistrates Min.	Additional Seats of Court
Camden	3	
Chowan	3	
Currituck	3	
Dare	4	
Gates	2	
Pasquotank	4	
Perquimans	3	
Martin	3	
Beaufort	4	
Tyrrell	3	
Hyde	3.5	
Washington	3	
Pitt	10.5	Farmville Ayden
Craven	8	Havelock
Pamlico	3	
Carteret	6	
Sampson	5	
Duplin	4	
Jones	2	
Onslow	11	

County	Magistrates Min.	Additional Seats of Court
New Hanover	11	
Pender	3.8	
Halifax	7	Roanoke Rapids, Scotland Neck
Northampton	3	
Bertie	3	
Hertford	3	
Nash	9	Rocky Mount
Edgecombe	7	Rocky Mount
Wilson	7	
Wayne	9	Mount Olive
Greene	3	
Lenoir	7	La Grange
Granville	5	
Vance	6	
Warren	3	
Franklin	4	
Person	4	
Caswell	3	
Wake	18.5	Apex, Wendell, Fuquay-Varina, Wake Forest
Harnett	8	Dunn
Johnston	10	Benson, Clayton, Selma
Lee	5	
Cumberland	19	
Bladen	3	
Brunswick	8	
Columbus	5	Tabor City
Durham	13	
Alamance	12	Burlington
Orange	7	Chapel Hill
Chatham	4	Siler City
Scotland	5	
Hoke	3	
Robeson	12	Fairmont, Maxton, Pembroke, Red Springs, Rowland, St. Pauls
Rockingham	7	Reidsville, Eden, Madison
Stokes	3	
Surry	6	Mt. Airy
Guilford	24.4	High Point
Cabarrus	9	Kannapolis
Montgomery	3	
Randolph	9	Liberty

County	Magistrates Min.	Additional Seats of Court
Rowan	9	
Stanly	5	
Union	7	
Anson	3	
Richmond	5	Hamlet
Moore	5	Southern Pines
Forsyth	15	Kernersville
Alexander	3	
Davidson	8	Thomasville
Davie	3	
Iredell	9	Mooresville
Alleghany	2	
Ashe	3	
Wilkes	6	
Yadkin	3	
Avery	3	
Madison	3	
Mitchell	3	
Watauga	4	
Yancey	3	
Burke	5.6	
Caldwell	6	
Catawba	10	Hickory
Mecklenburg	26.50	
Gaston	17	
Cleveland	7	
Lincoln	5	
Buncombe	15	
Henderson	6.5	
McDowell	3	
Polk	3	
Rutherford	6	
Transylvania	3	
Cherokee	3	
Clay	2	
Graham	2	
Haywood	5	Canton
Jackson	3	
Macon	3	
Swain	3.	

History.

1965, c. 310, s. 1; 1967, c. 691, s. 8; 1969, c. 1190, s. 10; c. 1254; 1971, c. 377, s. 7; cc. 727, 840, 841, 842, 843, 865, 866, 898; 1973, cc. 132, 373, 483; c. 838, s. 1; c. 1376; 1975, c. 956, ss. 8, 10; 1977, cc. 121, 122; c. 678, s. 2; c. 947, s. 1; c. 1130, ss. 4, 5; 1977, 2nd Sess., c. 1238, s. 3; c. 1243, ss. 3, 6; 1979, c. 465; c. 838, ss. 117, 118; c. 1072, ss. 2, 3; 1979, 2nd Sess., c. 1221, s. 2; 1981, c. 964, s. 4; 1983, c. 881, s. 5; 1983 (Reg. Sess., 1984), c. 1109, s. 5; 1985, c. 698, ss. 7(a), 12; 1985 (Reg. Sess., 1986), c. 1014, s. 222; 1987, c. 738, ss. 126(a), 130(a); 1987 (Reg. Sess., 1988), c. 1056, s. 4; c. 1075; c. 1100, s. 17.2(a); 1989, c. 795, s. 23(a), (d), (h); 1991, c. 742, ss. 11, 12(a); 1993, c. 321, ss. 200.4(e), 200.6(a), (d); 1993 (Reg. Sess., 1994), c. 769, s. 24.9; 1995, c. 507, s. 21.1(c); 1995 (Reg. Sess., 1996), c. 589, s. 2(a); 1996, 2nd Ex. Sess., c. 18, ss. 22.4, 22.7(a); 1997-443, ss. 18.12(a), 18.13; 1998-212, ss. 16.11, 16.16(a); 1998-217, s. 67.3(a); 1999-237, ss. 17.4, 17.6(a); 2000-67, ss. 15.2, 15.3(a); 2001-400, s. 1; 2001-424, ss. 22.16, 22.17(a); 2003-284, s. 13.8; 2004-124, ss. 14.1(a), 14.6(e); 2005-276, s. 14.2(f), (f1); 2005-345, s. 27(a), (b); 2006-66, ss. 14.4(a), 14.5; 2006-96, s. 1; 2006-187, s. 7(a); 2006-221, s. 14(a); 2006-264, s. 93(a); 2007-323, ss. 14.13(a), (d), 14.25(e), (f); 2007-484, s. 25(a), 36; 2008-107, s. 14.13(a); 2009-341, s. 1; 2012-194, s. 1(c), (d); 2013-360, s. 18B.22(f); 2016-94, s. 19B.3(a); 2017-57, s. 18B.9(c); 2018-14, s. 2(a); 2018-121, s. 2(a); 2019-229, s. 2(a); 2020-84, s. 2(a); 2021-148, s. 1

N.C. Gen. Stat. § 7A-134

Repealed by Session Laws 1973, c. 1339, s. 2.

§ 7A-135. Transfer of pending cases when present inferior courts replaced by district courts

On the date that the district court is established in any county, cases pending in the inferior court or courts of that county shall be transferred to the appropriate division of the General Court of Justice, and all records of these courts shall be transferred to the office of clerk of superior court in that county pursuant to rule of Supreme Court.

History.
1965, c. 310, s. 1

ARTICLE 14
DISTRICT JUDGES

§ 7A-140. Number; election; term; qualification; oath

There shall be at least one district judge for each district. Each district judge shall be elected by the qualified voters of the district court district in which he or she is to serve at the time of the election for members of the General Assembly. The number of judges for each district shall be determined by the General Assembly. Each judge shall be a resident of the district for which elected, and shall serve a term of four years, beginning on the first day in January next after election.

Each district judge shall devote his or her full time to the duties of the office. He or she shall not practice law during the term, nor shall he or she during such term be the partner or associate of any person engaged in the practice of law.

Before entering upon his or her duties, each district judge, in addition to other oaths prescribed by law, shall take the oath of office prescribed for a judge of the General Court of Justice.

History.

1965, c. 310, s. 1; 1969, c. 1190, s. 11; 2005-425, s. 3.1

§ 7A-141. Designation of chief judge; assignment of judge to another district for temporary or specialized duty

When more than one judge is authorized in a district, the Chief Justice of the Supreme Court shall designate one of the judges as chief district judge to serve in such capacity at the pleasure of the Chief Justice. In a single judge district, the judge is the chief district judge.

The Chief Justice may transfer a district judge from one district to another for temporary or specialized duty.

History.

1965, c. 310, s. 1

§ 7A-142. Vacancies in office

A vacancy in the office of district judge shall be filled for the unexpired term by appointment of the Governor. The bar of the judicial district, as defined in G.S. 84-19, shall nominate five persons who are residents of the judicial district who are duly authorized to practice law in the district for consideration by the Governor. The nominees shall be selected by vote of only those bar members who reside in the district. In the event fewer than five persons are nominated, upon providing the nominations to the Governor, the bar shall certify that there were insufficient nominations in the district to comply with this section. Prior to filling the vacancy, the Governor shall give due consideration to the nominations provided by the bar of the judicial district.

History.

1965, c. 310, s. 1; 1975, c. 441; 1981, c. 763, ss. 1, 2; 1985 (Reg. Sess., 1986), c. 1006, s. 1; 1987 (Reg. Sess., 1988), c. 1037, s. 16; c. 1056, s. 7; c. 1086, s. 112(b); 1991, c. 742, s. 16; 1999-237, s. 17.10; 2001-403, s. 2(a); 2002-159, s. 58; 2011-28, s. 2; 2013-387, s. 4

N.C. Gen. Stat. § 7A-143

Repealed by Session Laws 1973, c. 148, s. 6.

§ 7A-144. Compensation

(a) Each judge shall receive the annual salary provided in the Current Operations Appropriations Act, and reimbursement on the same basis as State employees generally, for his or her necessary subsistence expenses and for travel expenses when on official business outside the judge's county of residence. For purposes of this subsection, the term "official business" does not include regular, daily commuting between a judge's home and the court. Travel distances, for purposes of reimbursement for mileage, shall be determined according to the travel policy of the Administrative Office of the Courts.

(b) Notwithstanding merit, longevity and other increment raises paid to regular State employees, a judge of the district court shall receive as longevity pay an annual amount equal to four and eight-tenths percent (4.8%) of the annual salary set forth in the Current Operations Appropriations Act payable monthly after five years of service, nine and six-tenths percent (9.6%) after 10 years of service, fourteen and four-tenths percent (14.4%) after 15 years of service, nineteen and two-tenths percent (19.2%) after 20 years of service, and twenty-four percent (24%) after 25 years of service. "Service" means service as a justice or judge of the General Court of Justice, as a member of the Utilities Commission, as an administrative law judge, or as director or assistant director of the Administrative Office of the Courts. Service shall also mean service as a district attorney or as a clerk of superior court.

History.

1965, c. 310, s. 1; 1967, c. 691, s. 10; 1983, c. 761, s. 245; 1983 (Reg. Sess., 1984), c. 1034, s. 165; c. 1109, ss. 11, 13.1; 1985, c. 698, s. 10(a); 1987 (Reg. Sess., 1988), c. 1100, s. 15(d); 1989, c. 770, s. 5; 2007-323, s. 28.18A(f); 2009-451, s. 15.17B(a); 2017-57, s. 35.4(g)

N.C. Gen. Stat. § 7A-145

Repealed by Session Laws 1971, c. 377, s. 32.

§ 7A-146. Administrative authority and duties of chief district judge

The chief district judge, subject to the general supervision of the Chief Justice of the Supreme Court, has administrative supervision and authority over the operation of the district courts and magistrates in his district. These powers and duties include, but are not limited to, the following:

(1) Arranging schedules and assigning district judges for sessions of district courts.

(2) Arranging or supervising the calendaring of noncriminal matters for trial or hearing.

(3) Supervising the clerk of superior court in the discharge of the clerical functions of the district court.

(4) Assigning matters to magistrates, and consistent with the salaries set by the Administrative Officer of the Courts, prescribing times and places at which magistrates shall be available for the performance of their duties; however, the chief district judge may in writing delegate his authority to prescribe times and places at which

magistrates in a particular county shall be available for the performance of their duties to another district court judge or the clerk of the superior court, or the judge may appoint a chief magistrate to fulfill some or all of the duties under subdivision (12) of this section, and the person to whom such authority is delegated shall make monthly reports to the chief district judge of the times and places actually served by each magistrate.

(5) Making arrangements with proper authorities for the drawing of civil court jury panels and determining which sessions of district court shall be jury sessions.

(6) Arranging for the reporting of civil cases by court reporters or other authorized means.

(7) Arranging sessions, to the extent practicable for the trial of specialized cases, including traffic, domestic relations, and other types of cases, and assigning district judges to preside over these sessions so as to permit maximum practicable specialization by individual judges.

(8) Repealed by Session Laws 1991 (Regular Session, 1992), c. 900, s. 118(b), effective July 15, 1992.

(9) Assigning magistrates when exigent circumstances exist to temporary duty outside the county of their residence but within that district pursuant to the policies and procedures prescribed under G.S. 7A-343(11); and, upon the request of a chief district judge of another district and upon the approval of the Administrative Officer of the Courts, to temporary duty in the district of the requesting chief district judge pursuant to the policies and procedures prescribed under G.S. 7A-343(11).

(10) Designating another district judge of his district as acting chief district judge, to act during the absence or disability of the chief district judge.

(11) Designating certain magistrates to appoint counsel and accept waivers of counsel pursuant to Article 36 of this Chapter. This designation does not give any magistrate the authority to appoint counsel or accept waivers of counsel for potentially capital offenses, as defined by rules adopted by the Office of Indigent Defense Services.

(12) Designating a full-time magistrate in a county to serve as chief magistrate for that county for an indefinite term and at the judge's pleasure. The chief magistrate shall have the derivative administrative authority assigned by the chief district court judge under subdivision (4) of this section. This subdivision applies only to counties in which the chief district court judge determines that designating a chief

magistrate would be in the interest of justice.

History.
1965, c. 310, s. 1; 1971, c. 377, s. 8; 1977, c. 945, s. 1; 1983, c. 586, s. 1; 1983 (Reg. Sess., 1984), c. 1034, s. 85; 1985, c. 425, s. 2; c. 764, s. 8; 1985 (Reg. Sess., 1986), c. 852, s. 17; 1991 (Reg. Sess., 1992), c. 900, s. 118(b); 2009-419, s. 2; 2011-411, s. 2(b); 2013-89, s. 1; 2015-247, s. 3(a); 2018-138, s. 2.12(c)

§ 7A-147. Specialized judgeships

(a) Prior to January 1 of each year in which elections for district court judges are to be held, the Administrative Officer of the Courts may, with the approval of the chief district judge, designate one or more judgeships in districts having three or more judgeships, as specialized judgeships, naming in each case the specialty. Designations shall become effective when filed with the State Board of Elections. Nominees for the position or positions of specialist judge shall be made in the ensuing primary and the position or positions shall be filled at the general election thereafter. The State Board of Elections shall prepare primary and general election ballots to effectuate the purposes of this section.

(b) The designation of a specialized judgeship shall in no way impair the right of the chief district judge to arrange sessions for the trial of specialized cases and to assign any district judge to preside over these sessions. A judge elected to a specialized judgeship has the same powers as a regular district judge.

(c) The policy of the State is to encourage specialization in juvenile cases by district court judges who are qualified by training and temperament to be effective in relating to youth and in the use of appropriate community resources to meet their needs. The Administrative Office of the Courts is therefore authorized to encourage judges who hear juvenile cases to secure appropriate training whether or not they were elected to a specialized judgeship as provided herein. Such training shall be provided within the funds available to the Administrative Office of the Courts for such training, and judges attending such training shall be reimbursed for travel and subsistence expenses at the same rate as is applicable to other State employees.

The Administrative Office of the Courts shall develop a plan whereby a district court judge may be better qualified to hear juvenile cases by reason of training, experience, and demonstrated ability. Any district court judge who completes the training under this plan shall receive a certificate to this effect from the Administrative Office of the Courts. In districts where there is a district court judge who has completed this training as herein provided, the chief district judge shall give due consideration in the assignment of such cases where practical and feasible.

History.
1965, c. 310, s. 1; 1975, c. 823; 1979, c. 622, s. 1; 2017-6, s. 3; 2018-146, ss. 3.1(a), (b), 6.1

§ 7A-148. Annual conference of chief district judges

(a) The chief district judges of the various district court districts shall meet at least once a year upon call of the Chief Justice of the Supreme Court to discuss mutual problems affecting the courts and the improvement of court operations, to prepare and adopt uniform schedules of offenses for the types of offenses specified in G.S. 7A-273(2) and G.S. 7A-273(2a) for which magistrates and clerks of court may accept written appearances, waivers of trial or hearing and pleas of guilty or admissions of responsibility, and establish a schedule of penalties or fines therefor, and to take such further action as may be found practicable and desirable to promote the uniform administration of justice.

(b) The chief district judges shall prescribe a multicopy uniform traffic ticket and complaint for exclusive use in each county of the State not later than December 31, 1970.

History.
1965, c. 310, s. 1; 1967, c. 691, s. 11; 1983, c. 586, s. 2; 1985, c. 425, s. 1; c. 764, s. 9; 1985 (Reg. Sess., 1986), c. 852, s. 17; 1991, c. 151, s. 1; c. 609, s. 2; 1991 (Reg. Sess., 1992), c. 900, s. 118(a); 1999-80, s. 2

§ 7A-149. Jurisdiction; sessions

(a) Notwithstanding any other provision of law, a district court judge of a district court district which is in a set of districts as defined by G.S. 7A-200 has jurisdiction in the entire county or counties in which the district is located to the same extent as if the district encompassed the entire county, and has jurisdiction in the entire set of districts to the same extent as if the district encompassed the entire set of districts.

(b) All sessions of district court shall be for an entire county, whether that county comprises or is located in a district or in a set of districts as defined in G.S. 7A-200, and at each session all matters and proceedings arising anywhere in the county may be heard.

(c) All clerks of court for a county have jurisdiction over the entire county, notwithstanding that the county may be part of a set of districts.

History.
1995, c. 507, s. 21.1(b)

ARTICLE 16
MAGISTRATES

§ 7A-170. Nature of office and oath; age limit for service

(a) A magistrate is an officer of the district court. Before entering upon the duties of his office, a magistrate shall take the oath of office prescribed for a magistrate of the General Court of Justice. A magistrate possesses all the powers of his office at all times during his term.

(b) No magistrate may continue in office beyond the last day of the month in which the magistrate reaches the mandatory retirement age for justices and judges of the General Court of Justice specified in G.S. 7A-4.20.

History.
1965, c. 310, s. 1; 1969, c. 1190, s. 13; 1977, c. 945, s. 2; 2013-277, s. 1

§ 7A-171. Numbers; appointment and terms; vacancies

(a) The General Assembly shall establish a minimum quota of magistrates for each county. In no county shall the minimum quota be less than one. The number of magistrates in a county, above the minimum quota set by the General Assembly, is determined by the Administrative Office of the Courts after consultation with the chief district court judge for the district in which the county is located.

(a1) The initial term of appointment for a magistrate is two years and subsequent terms shall be for a period of four years. The term of office begins on the first day of January of the odd-numbered year after appointment. The service of an individual as a magistrate filling a vacancy as provided in subsection (d) of this section does not constitute an initial term. For purposes of this section, any term of office for a magistrate who has served a two-year term is for four years even if the two-year term of appointment was before the effective date of this section, the term is after a break in service, or the term is for appointment in a different county from the county where the two-year term of office was served.

(b) Not earlier than the Tuesday after the first Monday nor later than the third Monday in December of each even-numbered year, the clerk of the superior court shall submit to the senior regular resident superior court judge of the district or set of districts as defined in G.S. 7A-41.1(a) in which the clerk's county is located the names of two (or more, if requested by the judge) nominees for each magisterial office for the county for which the term of office of the magistrate holding that position shall expire on December 31 of that year. Not later than the fourth Monday in December, the senior regular resident superior court judge shall, from the nominations submitted by the clerk of the superior court, appoint magistrates to fill the positions for each county of the judge's district or set of districts.

(c) If an additional magisterial office for a county is approved to commence on January 1 of an odd-numbered year, the new position shall be filled as provided in subsection (b) of this section. If the additional position takes effect at any other time, it is to be filled as provided in subsection (d) of this section.

(d) Within 30 days after a vacancy in the office of magistrate occurs the clerk of superior court shall submit to the senior regular resident superior court judge the names of two (or more, if so requested by the judge) nominees for the office vacated. Within 15 days after receipt of the nominations the senior regular resident superior court judge shall appoint from the nominations received a magistrate who shall take office immediately and shall serve until December 31 of the even-numbered year, and thereafter the position shall be filled as provided in subsection (b) of this section.

History.
1965, c. 310, s. 1; 1967, c. 691, s. 15; 1971, s. 84, s. 1; 1973, c. 503, s. 2; 1977, c. 945, ss. 3, 4; 1987 (Reg. Sess., 1988), c. 1037, s. 17; 2004-128, s. 19; 2006-187, s. 7(c)

ARTICLE 17
CLERICAL FUNCTIONS IN THE DISTRICT COURT

§ 7A-180. Functions of clerk of superior court in district court matters

The clerk of superior court:

(1) Has and exercises all of the judicial powers and duties in respect of actions and proceedings pending from time to time in the district court of the clerk's county which are now or hereafter conferred or imposed upon the clerk by law in respect of actions and proceedings pending in the superior court of the clerk's county.

(2) Performs all of the clerical, administrative and fiscal functions required in the operation of the district court of the clerk's county in the same manner as the clerk is required to perform functions in the operation of the superior court of the clerk's county.

(3) Maintains, under the supervision of the Administrative Office of the Courts, an office of uniform consolidated records of all judicial proceedings in the superior court division and the district court division of the General Court of Justice in the clerk's county. Those records shall include civil actions, special proceedings, estates, criminal actions, juvenile actions, minutes of the court and all other records required by law to be maintained. The form and procedure for filing, docketing, indexing, and recording shall be as prescribed by the Administrative Officer of the Courts notwithstanding any contrary statutory provision as to the title and form of the record or as a method of indexing.

(4) Has the power to accept written appearances, waivers of trial or hearing and pleas of guilty or admissions of responsibility for the types of offenses specified in G.S. 7A-273(2) and G.S. 7A-273(2a) in accordance with the schedules of offenses promulgated by the Conference of Chief District Judges pursuant to G.S. 7A-148, and in those cases, to enter judgment and collect the fine or penalty and costs.

(5) Has the power to issue warrants of arrest valid throughout the State, and search warrants valid throughout the county of the issuing clerk.

(6) Has the power to conduct an initial appearance in accordance with Chapter 15A, Article 24, Initial Appearance, and to fix conditions of release in accordance with Chapter 15A, Article 26, Bail.

(7) Continues to exercise all powers, duties and authority vested in or imposed upon clerks of superior court by general law, with the exception of jurisdiction in juvenile matters.

(8) Has the power to accept written appearances, waivers of trial and pleas of guilty to violations of G.S. 14-107 when restitution, including service charges and processing fees allowed under G.S. 14-107, is made, the amount of the check is two thousand dollars ($ 2,000) or less, and the warrant does not charge a fourth or subsequent violation of this statute, and, in those cases, to enter judgments as the chief district judge shall direct and, forward the amounts collected as restitution to the appropriate prosecuting witnesses and to collect the costs.

(9) Repealed by Session Laws 1991 (Reg. Sess., 1992), c. 900, s. 118(c).

History.
1965, c. 310, s. 1; 1967, c. 691, s. 16; 1969, c. 1190, s. 14; 1973, c. 503, ss. 3, 4; c. 1286, s. 6; 1975, c. 166, s. 23; c. 626, s. 2; 1981, c. 142; 1983, c. 586, s. 4; 1985, c. 425, s. 3; c. 764, s. 10; 1985 (Reg. Sess., 1986), c. 852, s. 17; 1987, c. 355, s. 3; 1989 (Reg. Sess., 1990), c. 1041, s.

2; 1991, c. 520, s. 1; 1991 (Reg. Sess., 1992), c. 900, s. 118(c); 1993, c. 374, s. 3; 2021-47, s. 7(b)

§ 7A-181. Functions of assistant and deputy clerks of superior court in district court matters

Assistant and deputy clerks of superior court:

(1) Have the same powers and duties with respect to matters in the district court division as they have in the superior court division;

(2) Have the same powers as the clerk of superior court with respect to the issuance of warrants and acceptance of written appearances, waivers of trial and pleas of guilty; and

(3) Have the same power as the clerk of superior court to fix conditions of release in accordance with Chapter 15A, Article 26, Bail, and the same power as the clerk of superior court to conduct an initial appearance in accordance with Chapter 15A, Article 24, Initial Appearance.

History.

1965, c. 310, s. 1; 1967, c. 691, s. 17; 1973, c. 503, s. 5; 1975, c. 166, s. 24; c. 626, s. 3

§ 7A-182. Clerical functions at additional seats of court

(a) In any county in which the General Assembly has authorized the district court to hold sessions at a place or places in addition to the county seat, the clerk of superior court shall furnish assistant and deputy clerks to the extent necessary to process efficiently the judicial business at such additional seat or seats of court. Only such records as are necessary for the expeditious processing of current judicial business shall be kept at the additional seat or seats of court. The office of the clerk of superior court at the county seat shall remain the permanent depository of official records.

(b) If an additional seat of a district court is designated for any municipality located in more than one county of a district, the clerical functions for that seat of court shall be provided by the clerks of superior court of the contiguous counties, in accordance with standing rules issued by the chief district judge, after consultation with the clerks concerned and a committee of the district bar appointed for this purpose. An assistant or deputy clerk assigned to a seat of district court described in this subsection shall have the same powers and authority as if he were acting in his own county.

History.

1965, c. 310, s. 1; 1967, c. 691, s. 18; 1969, c. 1190, s. 15

§ 7A-183. Clerk or assistant clerk as child support hearing officer

A clerk or assistant clerk of superior court who meets the qualifications of G.S. 50-39 and is properly designated pursuant to G.S. Chapter 50, Article 2, to serve as a child support hearing officer, may serve in that capacity and has the authority and responsibility assigned to child support hearing officers by Chapter 50.

History.

1985 (Reg. Sess., 1986), c. 993, s. 3

ARTICLE 18
DISTRICT COURT PRACTICE AND PROCEDURE GENERALLY

§ 7A-190. District courts always open

The district courts shall be deemed always open for the disposition of matters properly cognizable by them. But all trials on the merits shall be conducted at trial sessions regularly scheduled as provided in this Chapter.

History.

1965, c. 310, s. 1

§ 7A-191. Trials; hearings and orders in chambers

All trials on the merits and all hearings on infractions conducted pursuant to Article 66 of Chapter 15A shall be conducted in open court and so far as convenient in a regular courtroom. All other proceedings, hearings, and acts may be done or conducted by a judge in chambers in the absence of the clerk or other court officials and at any place within the district; but no hearing may be held, nor order entered, in any cause outside the district in which it is pending without the consent of all parties affected thereby.

History.

1965, c. 310, s. 1; 1985, c. 764, s. 11; 1985 (Reg. Sess., 1986), c. 852, s. 17

§ 7A-191.1. Recording of proceeding in which defendant pleads guilty or no contest to felony in district court

The trial judge shall require that a true, complete, and accurate record be made of the proceeding in which a defendant pleads guilty or no contest to a Class H or I felony pursuant to G.S. 7A-272.

History.
1995 (Reg. Sess., 1996), c. 725, s. 4

§ 7A-192. By whom power of district court to enter interlocutory orders exercised

Any district judge may hear motions and enter interlocutory orders in causes regularly calendared for trial or for the disposition of motions, at any session to which the district judge has been assigned to preside. The chief district judge and any district judge designated by written order or rule of the chief district judge, may in chambers hear motions and enter interlocutory orders in all causes pending in the district courts of the district, including causes transferred from the superior court to the district court under the provisions of this Chapter. The designation is effective from the time filed in the office of the clerk of superior court of each county of the district until revoked or amended by written order of the chief district judge.

History.
1965, c. 310, s. 1; 1969, c. 1190, s. 16

§ 7A-193. Civil procedure generally

Except as otherwise provided in this Chapter, the civil procedure provided in Chapters 1 and 1A of the General Statutes applies in the district court division of the General Court of Justice. Where there is reference in Chapters 1 and 1A of the General Statutes to the superior court, it shall be deemed to refer also to the district court in respect of causes in the district court division.

History.
1965, c. 310, s. 1; 1969, c. 1190, s. 17

N.C. Gen. Stat. § 7A-194

Repealed by Session Laws 1977, c. 711, s. 33.

N.C. Gen. Stat. § 7A-195

Repealed by Session Laws 1969, c. 911, s. 5.

§ 7A-196. Jury trials

(a) In civil cases in the district court there shall be a right to trial by a jury of 12 in conformity with Rules 38 and 39 of the Rules of Civil Procedure.

(b) In criminal cases there shall be no jury trials in the district court. Upon appeal to superior court trial shall be de novo, with jury trial as provided by law.

(c) In adjudicatory hearings for infractions, there shall be no right to trial by jury in the district court.

History.
1965, c. 310, s. 1; 1967, c. 954, s. 3; 1985, c. 764, s. 12; 1985 (Reg. Sess., 1986), c. 852, s. 17

§ 7A-197. Petit jurors

Unless otherwise provided in this Chapter, the provisions of Chapter 9 of the General Statutes with respect to petit jurors for the trial of civil actions in the superior court are applicable to the trial of civil actions in the district court.

History.
1965, c. 310, s. 1

§ 7A-198. Reporting of civil trials

(a) Court-reporting personnel shall be utilized, if available, for the reporting of civil trials in the district court. If court reporters are not available in any county, electronic or other mechanical devices shall be provided by the Administrative Office of the Courts upon request of the chief district judge.

(b) The Administrative Office of the Courts shall from time to time investigate the state of the art and techniques of recording testimony, and shall provide such electronic or mechanical devices as are found to be most efficient for this purpose.

(c) If an electronic or other mechanical device is utilized, it shall be the duty of the clerk of the superior court or some other person designated by him to operate the device while a trial is in progress, and the clerk shall thereafter preserve the record thus produced, which may be transcribed, as required, by any person designated by the Administrative Office of the Courts. If stenotype, shorthand, or stenomask equipment is used, the original tapes, notes, discs, or other records are the property of the State, and the clerk shall keep them in his custody.

(d) Reporting of any trial may be waived by consent of the parties.

(e) Reporting will not be provided in ex parte or emergency hearings before a judge pursuant to Chapter 50B or 50C of the General Statutes, trials before magistrates, or in hearings to adjudicate and dispose of infractions in the district court.

(f) Appointment of a reporter or reporters for district court proceedings in each district court district shall be made by the chief district judge for that district. The compensation and allowances of reporters in each district shall be fixed by the chief district judge, within limits determined by the Administrative Officer of the Courts, and paid by the State.

(g) A party to a civil trial in district court may request a private agreement from the opposing party or parties to share equally in the cost of a court reporter to be selected from a list provided by the Administrative Office of the Courts. If the opposing party does not consent to share this cost, the requesting party may nevertheless pay to have a court reporter present to record the trial and, in the event that the opposing party appeals the case, that party shall reimburse the party providing the court reporter in full for the costs incurred for the court reporter's services and transcripts.

In the event that the recording device in a civil trial conducted without a court reporter fails for any reason to provide a reasonably accurate record of the trial for purposes of appeal, then the trial judge shall grant a motion for a new trial made by a losing party whose request pursuant to this section to share the cost of a court reporter was not consented to by the opposing party.

History.
1965, c. 310, s. 1; 1969, c. 1190, s. 18; 1985, c. 764, s. 13; 1985 (Reg. Sess., 1986), c. 852, s. 17; 1987, c. 384, s. 2; 1987 (Reg. Sess., 1988), c. 1037, s. 19; 1996, 2nd Ex. Sess., c. 18, s. 22.11; 2015-173, s. 5

§ 7A-199. Special venue rule when district court sits without jury in seat of court lying in more than one county; where judgments recorded

(a) In any nonjury civil action or juvenile matter properly pending in the district court division, regularly assigned for a hearing or trial before a district judge at a seat of the district court in a municipality the corporate limits of which extend into two or more contiguous counties, venue is properly laid for such trial or hearing if by statute or common law it is properly laid in any of the contiguous counties.

(b) In any jury civil action regularly assigned for a hearing or trial before a district judge at a seat of the district court in a municipality the corporate limits of which extend into two or more contiguous counties, venue is properly laid for such jury trial if by statute or common law it is properly laid in any of the contiguous counties; provided, however, any such action shall be instituted in the county of proper venue, and the jurors summoned shall be from the county where such action was instituted. Notwithstanding the fact that the place of trial within such municipality is in a different county from the county where such action was commenced, the sheriff of the county where such action was commenced is authorized to summon the jurors to appear at such place of trial. Such jurors shall be subject to the same challenge as other jurors, except challenges for nonresidence in the county of trial.

(c) A district court judge sitting at a seat of court described in this section may, in criminal cases, conduct preliminary hearings and try misdemeanors arising within the corporate limits of the municipality plus the territory embraced within a distance of one mile in all directions therefrom.

If the corporate limits of the municipality extend into two or more counties, each of which is in a separate district court district, a district court judge assigned to sit at the seat of court has the same authority over criminal cases arising in the municipality and the territory embraced within a distance of one mile in all directions that he would have if the corporate limits of the municipality were solely located in a single district court district. Judges assigned to sit in such a municipality shall be assigned by the chief district court judge serving the district in which a majority of the voters of the municipality reside, but offenses arising in a portion of the municipality in which a minority of the voters reside shall not be disposed of in the municipality unless the chief district court judge for that district consents in writing to the disposition of criminal cases in the municipality. However, for charges brought by municipal law enforcement officers only, if the corporate limits of the municipality extend into four or more counties, each of which is in a separate district court district, offenses arising in a portion of the municipality in which a minority of the voters reside shall be disposed of in the portion of the municipality in which a majority of the voters reside without obtaining the consent of the chief district court judge for the district in which the offense occurred.

(d) The judgment or order rendered in any civil action or juvenile matter heard or tried under the authority of this section shall be recorded in the county where the action was commenced. The judgment or finding of probable cause or other determination in any criminal action heard or tried under the authority of this section shall be recorded in the county where the offense was committed.

History.
1967, c. 691, s. 19; 1989, c. 795, s. 23(c2); 2009-398, s. 1

§ 7A-200. District and set of districts defined; chief district court judges and their authority

(a) In this section:

(1) "District" means any district court district established by G.S. 7A-133 which consists exclusively of one or more entire counties;

(2) "Set of districts" means any set of two or more district court districts established under G.S. 7A-133, none of which consists exclusively of one or more entire counties, but both or all of which include territory from the same county or counties and together comprise all of the territory of that county or those counties; "set of districts" also means a set of three district court districts in one county, one consisting of the entire county and the other two consisting of parts of that county; and

(3) "Chief district court judge" means in the case of a set of districts, the chief district court judge for those districts, designated by the chief justice from among the district court judges for the districts in the set of districts.

(b) Whenever by law a duty is imposed upon the chief district court judge, it means for a set of districts the chief district court judge designated under subsection (a)(3) of this section.

History.
1995, c. 507, s. 21.1(a); 2007-484, s. 25(c)

SUBCHAPTER 05.
JURISDICTION AND POWERS OF THE TRIAL DIVISIONS OF THE GENERAL COURT OF JUSTICE

ARTICLE 22
JURISDICTION OF THE TRIAL DIVISIONS IN CRIMINAL ACTIONS

§ 7A-270. Generally

General jurisdiction for the trial of criminal actions is vested in the superior court and the district court divisions of the General Court of Justice.

History.
1965, c. 310, s. 1

§ 7A-271. Jurisdiction of superior court

(a) The superior court has exclusive, original jurisdiction over all criminal actions not assigned to the district court division by this Article, except that the superior court has jurisdiction to try a misdemeanor:

(1) Which is a lesser included offense of a felony on which an indictment has

been returned, or a felony information as to which an indictment has been properly waived; or

(2) When the charge is initiated by presentment; or

(3) Which may be properly consolidated for trial with a felony under G.S. 15A-926;

(4) To which a plea of guilty or nolo contendere is tendered in lieu of a felony charge; or

(5) When a misdemeanor conviction is appealed to the superior court for trial de novo, to accept a guilty plea to a lesser included or related charge.

(b) Appeals by the State or the defendant from the district court are to the superior court. The jurisdiction of the superior court over misdemeanors appealed from the district court to the superior court for trial de novo is the same as the district court had in the first instance, and when that conviction resulted from a plea arrangement between the defendant and the State pursuant to which misdemeanor charges were dismissed, reduced, or modified, to try those charges in the form and to the extent that they subsisted in the district court immediately prior to entry of the defendant and the State of the plea arrangement.

(c) When a district court is established in a district, any superior court judge presiding over a criminal session of court shall order transferred to the district court any pending misdemeanor which does not fall within the provisions of subsection (a), and which is not pending in the superior court on appeal from a lower court.

(d) The criminal jurisdiction of the superior court includes the jurisdiction to dispose of infractions only in the following circumstances:

(1) If the infraction is a lesser-included violation of a criminal action properly before the court, the court must submit the infraction for the jury's consideration in factually appropriate cases.

(2) If the infraction is a lesser-included violation of a criminal action properly before the court, or if it is a related charge, the court may accept admissions of responsibility for the infraction. A proper pleading for the criminal action is sufficient to support a finding of responsibility for the lesser-included infraction.

(e) The superior court has exclusive jurisdiction over all hearings held pursuant to G.S. 15A-1345(e) where the district court had accepted a defendant's plea of guilty or no contest to a felony under the provisions of G.S. 7A-272(c), except that the district court shall have jurisdiction to hear these matters with the consent of the State and the defendant.

(f) The superior court has exclusive jurisdiction over all hearings to revoke probation pursuant to G.S. 15A-1345(e) where the district court is supervising a drug treatment court or therapeutic court probation judgment under G.S. 7A-272(e), except that the district court has jurisdiction to conduct the revocation proceedings when the chief district court judge and the senior resident superior court judge agree that it is in the interest of justice that the proceedings be conducted by the district court. If the district court exercises jurisdiction under this subsection to revoke probation, appeal of an order revoking probation is to the appellate division.

(g) The superior court has jurisdiction to issue a secure custody order pursuant to G.S. 7B-1903 when a juvenile matter that has been transferred to superior court is remanded to district court pursuant to G.S. 7B-2200.5(d).

History.

1965, c. 310, s. 1; 1967, c. 691, s. 24; 1969, c. 1190, ss. 23, 24; 1971, c. 377, s. 15; 1977, c. 711, s. 6; 1979, 2nd Sess., c. 1328, s. 2; 1985, c. 764, s. 15; 1985 (Reg. Sess., 1986), c. 852, s. 17; 2004-128, s. 2; 2009-452, s. 1; 2009-516, s. 7(a), (b); 2010-96, s. 26(a); 2010-97, s. 13; 2021-123, s. 3(a)

§ 7A-272. Jurisdiction of district court; concurrent jurisdiction in guilty or no contest pleas for certain felony offenses; appellate and appropriate relief procedures applicable

(a) Except as provided in this Article, the district court has exclusive, original jurisdiction for the trial of criminal actions, including municipal ordinance violations, below the grade of felony, and the same are hereby declared to be petty misdemeanors.

(b) The district court has jurisdiction to conduct preliminary examinations and to bind the accused over for trial upon waiver of preliminary examination or upon a finding of probable cause, making appropriate orders as to bail or commitment.

(c) With the consent of the presiding district court judge, the prosecutor, and the defendant, the district court has jurisdiction to accept a defendant's plea of guilty or no contest to a Class H or I felony if:

(1) The defendant is charged with a felony in an information filed pursuant to G.S. 15A-644.1, the felony is pending in district court, and the defendant has not been indicted for the offense; or

(2) The defendant has been indicted for a criminal offense but the defendant's case is transferred from superior court to district court pursuant to G.S. 15A-1029.1.

(d) Provisions in Chapter 15A of the General Statutes apply to a plea authorized under subsection (c) of this section as if the plea had been entered in superior court, so that a district court judge is authorized to act in these matters in the same manner as a superior court judge would be authorized to act if the plea had been entered in superior court, and appeals that are authorized in these matters are to the appellate division.

(e) With the consent of the chief district court judge and the senior resident superior court judge, the district court has jurisdiction to preside over the supervision of a probation judgment entered in superior court in which the defendant is required to participate in a drug treatment court program pursuant to G.S. 15A-1343(b1)(2b) or a therapeutic court as defined in subsection (f) of this section, or is participating in the drug treatment court pursuant to a deferred prosecution agreement under G.S. 15A-1341(a2) or the terms of a conditional discharge under G.S. 15A-1341(a5). The district court may modify or extend the probation judgment, but jurisdiction to revoke probation supervised under this subsection is as provided in G.S. 7A-271(f).

(f) As used in subsection (e) of this section, the term "therapeutic court" refers to a court, other than drug treatment court established pursuant to Article 62 of Chapter 7A of the General Statutes, in which a criminal defendant, either as a condition of probation or pursuant to a deferred prosecution agreement or the terms of a conditional discharge under G.S. 15A-1341, is ordered to participate in specified activities designed to address underlying problems of substance abuse and mental illness that contribute to the person's criminal activity. The ordered activities shall, at a minimum, require the person to participate in treatment and attend regular court sessions of the therapeutic court over an extended period of time. The senior resident superior court judge and the chief district court judge shall agree in writing that the therapeutic court is being established and shall file the written agreement with the Administrative Office of the Courts before jurisdiction established by subsection (e) of this section may be exercised by the district court.

History.

1965, c. 310, s. 1; 1995 (Reg. Sess., 1996), c. 725, ss. 1, 2; 2009-452, s. 2; 2009-516, s. 8(a), (b); 2010-96, s. 26(b); 2010-97, s. 13; 2014-119, s. 2(b)

§ 7A-273. Powers of magistrates in infractions or criminal actions

In criminal actions or infractions, any magistrate has power:

(1) In infraction cases in which the maximum penalty that can be imposed is not more than fifty dollars ($ 50.00), exclusive

of costs, or in Class 3 misdemeanors, other than the types of infractions and misdemeanors specified in subdivision (2) of this section, to accept guilty pleas or admissions of responsibility and enter judgment;

(2) In misdemeanor or infraction cases involving alcohol offenses under Chapter 18B of the General Statutes, traffic offenses, hunting, fishing, State park and recreation area rule offenses under Chapters 113 and 143B of the General Statutes, State forest rule offenses under Articles 74 and 75 of Chapter 106 of the General Statutes, boating offenses under Chapter 75A of the General Statutes, open burning offenses under Article 78 of Chapter 106 of the General Statutes, and littering offenses under G.S. 14-399(c) and G.S. 14-399(c1), to accept written appearances, waivers of trial or hearing and pleas of guilty or admissions of responsibility, in accordance with the schedule of offenses and fines or penalties promulgated by the Conference of Chief District Judges pursuant to G.S. 7A-148, and in such cases, to enter judgment and collect the fines or penalties and costs;

(2a) In misdemeanor cases involving the violation of a county ordinance authorized by law regulating the use of dune or beach buggies or other power-driven vehicles specified by the governing body of the county on the foreshore, beach strand, or the barrier dune system, to accept written appearances, waivers of trial or hearing, and pleas of guilty or admissions of responsibility, in accordance with the schedule of offenses and fines or penalties promulgated by the Conference of Chief District Court Judges pursuant to G.S. 7A-148, and in such cases, to enter judgment and collect the fines or penalties and costs;

(3) To issue arrest warrants valid throughout the State;

(4) To issue search warrants valid throughout the county;

(5) To grant bail before trial for any noncapital offense;

(6) Notwithstanding the provisions of subdivision (1) of this section, to hear and enter judgment as the chief district judge shall direct in all worthless check cases brought under G.S. 14-107, when the amount of the check is two thousand dollars ($ 2,000) or less. Provided, however, that under this section magistrates may not impose a prison sentence longer than 30 days;

(7) To conduct an initial appearance as provided in G.S. 15A-511; and

(8) To accept written appearances, waivers of trial and pleas of guilty in violations

of G.S. 14-107 when the amount of the check is two thousand dollars ($ 2,000) or less, restitution, including service charges and processing fees allowed by G.S. 14-107, is made, and the warrant does not charge a fourth or subsequent violation of this statute, and in these cases to enter judgments as the chief district judge directs.

(9) Repealed by Session Laws 1991 (Regular Session, 1992), c. 900, s. 118(d).

History.

1965, c. 310, s. 1; 1969, c. 876, s. 2; c. 1190, s. 25; 1973, c. 6; c. 503, s. 8; c. 1286, s. 7; 1975, c. 626, s. 4; 1977, c. 873, s. 1; 1979, c. 144, s. 3; 1981, c. 555, s. 3; 1983, c. 586, s. 5; 1985, c. 425, s. 4; c. 764, s. 16; 1985 (Reg. Sess., 1986), c. 852, s. 17; 1987, c. 355, ss. 1, 2; 1989, c. 343; c. 763; 1989 (Reg. Sess., 1990), c. 1041, s. 1; 1991, c. 520, s. 2; 1991 (Reg. Sess., 1992), c. 900, s. 118(d); 1993, c. 374, s. 4; c. 538, s. 35; 1994, Ex. Sess., c. 14, s. 1; c. 24, s. 14(b); 1999-80, s. 1; 2002-159, s. 1; 2014-115, s. 20; 2015-241, s. 14.30(aa1); 2021-78, s. 2(a)

§ 7A-274. Power of mayors, law-enforcement officers, etc., to issue warrants and set bail restricted

The power of mayors, law-enforcement officers, and other persons not officers of the General Court of Justice to issue arrest, search, or peace warrants, or to set bail, is terminated in any district court district upon the establishment of a district court therein.

History.
1965, c. 310, s. 1

ARTICLE 22A
PROHIBITED ORDERS

§ 7A-276.1. Court orders prohibiting publication or broadcast of reports of open court proceedings or reports of public records banned

No court shall make or issue any rule or order banning, prohibiting, or restricting the publication or broadcast of any report concerning any of the following: any evidence, testimony, argument, ruling, verdict, decision, judgment, or other matter occurring in open court in any hearing, trial, or other proceeding, civil or criminal; and no court shall issue any rule or order sealing, prohibiting, restricting the publication or broadcast of the contents of any public record as defined by any statute of this State, which is required to be open to public inspection under any valid statute, regulation, or rule of common law. If any rule or order is made or issued by any court in violation of the provisions of this statute, it shall be null and void and of no effect, and no person shall be punished for contempt for the violation of any such void rule or order.

History.
1977, c. 711, s. 3

ARTICLE 24
JUVENILE SERVICES

§§ 7A-289.1 through 7A-289.6

Repealed by Session Laws 1998-202, s. 1(a).

N.C. Gen. Stat. § 7A-289.7

Repealed by Session Laws 1979, c. 815, s. 1.

ARTICLE 24A
DELINQUENCY PREVENTION AND YOUTH SERVICES

§§ 7A-289.13 through 7A-289.16

Repealed by Session Laws 1998-202, s. 1(a).

ARTICLE 24B
TERMINATION OF PARENTAL RIGHTS

§§ 7A-289.22, 7A-289.23

Repealed by Session Laws 1998-202, s. 5.

N.C. Gen. Stat. § 7A-289.23A

Recodified as § 7B-1102.

§§ 7A-289.24 through 7A-289.35

Repealed by Session Laws 1998-202, s. 5.

ARTICLE 25
JURISDICTION AND PROCEDURE IN CRIMINAL APPEALS FROM DISTRICT COURTS

§ 7A-290. Appeals from district court in criminal cases; notice; appeal bond

Any defendant convicted in district court before the magistrate may appeal to the district court for trial de novo before the district court judge. Any defendant convicted in district court before the judge may appeal to the superior court for trial de novo. Notice of appeal may be given orally in open court, or to the clerk in writing within 10 days of entry of judgment. Upon expiration of the 10-day period in which an appeal may be entered, if an appeal has been entered and not withdrawn, the clerk shall transfer the case to the district or superior court docket. The original bail shall stand pending appeal, unless the judge orders bail denied, increased, or reduced.

History.
1965, c. 310, s. 1; 1967, c. 601, s. 1; 1969, c. 876, s. 3; c. 911, s. 5; c. 1190, s. 26; 1971, c. 377, s. 16

ARTICLE 26
ADDITIONAL POWERS OF DISTRICT COURT JUDGES AND MAGISTRATES

§ 7A-291. Additional powers of district court judges

In addition to the jurisdiction and powers assigned in this Chapter, a district court judge has the following powers:

(1) To administer oaths;

(2) To punish for contempt;

(3) To compel the attendance of witnesses and the production of evidence;

(4) To set bail;

(5) To issue arrest warrants valid throughout the State, and search warrants valid throughout the district of issue; and

(6) To issue all process and orders necessary or proper in the exercise of his powers and authority, and to effectuate his lawful judgments and decrees.

History.
1965, c. 310, s. 1; 1969, c. 1190, s. 27; 1973, c. 1286, s. 11

§ 7A-292. Additional powers of magistrates

(a) In addition to the jurisdiction and powers assigned in this Chapter to the magistrate in civil and criminal actions, each magistrate has the following additional powers:

(1) To administer oaths.

(2) To punish for direct criminal contempt subject to the limitations contained in Chapter 5A of the General Statutes of North Carolina.

(3) When authorized by the chief district judge, to take depositions and examinations before trial.

(4) To issue subpoenas and capiases valid throughout the county.

(5) To take affidavits for the verification of pleadings.

(6) To issue writs of habeas corpus ad testificandum, as provided in G.S. 17-41.

(7) To assign a year's allowance to the surviving spouse and a child's allowance to the children as provided in Chapter 30, Article 4, of the General Statutes.

(8) To take acknowledgments of instruments, as provided in G.S. 47-1.

(9) To perform the marriage ceremony, as provided in G.S. 51-1.

(10) To take acknowledgment of a written contract or separation agreement between husband and wife.

(11) Repealed by Session Laws 1973, c. 503, s. 9.

(12) To assess contribution for damages or for work done on a dam, canal, or ditch, as provided in G.S. 156-15.

(13) Repealed by Session Laws 1973, c. 503, s. 9.

(14) To accept the filing of complaints and to issue summons pursuant to Article 4 of Chapter 42A of the General Statutes in expedited eviction proceedings when the office of the clerk of superior court is closed.

(15) When authorized by the chief district judge, as permitted in G.S. 7A-146(11), to provide for appointment of counsel and acceptance of waivers of counsel pursuant to Article 36 of this Chapter.

(16) To appoint an umpire to determine motor vehicle liability policy diminution in value, as provided in G.S. 20-279.21(d1).

(b) The authority granted to magistrates under G.S. 51-1 and subdivision (a)(9) of this section is a responsibility given collectively to the magistrates in a county and is not a duty imposed upon each individual magistrate. The chief district court judge shall ensure that marriages before a magistrate are available to be performed at least a total of 10 hours per week, over at least three business days per week.

History.
1965, c. 310, s. 1; 1967, c. 691, s. 25; 1971, c. 377, s. 17; 1973, c. 503, s. 9; 1977, c. 375, s. 4; 1979, 2nd Sess., c. 1080, s. 6; 1994, Ex. Sess., c. 4, s. 4; 1999-420, s. 4; 1999-456, s. 9(a), (b); 2009-419, s. 1; 2009-440, s. 2; 2009-566, s. 28; 2009-570, s. 48.2; 2015-75, s. 4; 2015-247, s. 3(b)

§ 7A-293. Special authority of a magistrate assigned to a municipality located in more than one county of a district court district

A magistrate assigned to an incorporated municipality, the boundaries of which lie in more than one county of a district court district, may, in criminal matters, exercise the powers granted by G.S. 7A-273 as if the corporate limits plus the territory embraced within a distance of one mile in all directions therefrom were located wholly within the magistrate's county of residence. Appeals from a magistrate exercising the authority granted by this section shall be taken in the district court in the county in which the offense was committed. A magistrate exercising the special authority granted by this section shall transmit all records, reports, and monies collected to the clerk of the superior court of the county in which the offense was committed. In addition, if a magistrate is assigned to an incorporated municipality, the boundaries of which lie in two or more district court districts, the magistrate may exercise the powers described in this section as if the counties were in the same district court district, if the clerks of superior court and the chief district court judges serving the districts in which the municipality is located agree in writing that the exercise of this special authority would promote the administration of justice in the municipality and in the districts. However, if a magistrate is assigned to an incorporated municipality, the boundaries of which lie in four or more counties, each of which is in a separate district court district, the magistrate may exercise the powers described in this section as if all the counties were in the same district court district, without the necessity of such an agreement between the clerks and judges of the affected counties, and the records, reports, and monies collected in connection with the exercise of that authority shall be transmitted to the clerk of the superior court district for the county in which the offense was committed.

History.
1967, c. 691, s. 26; 1989, c. 795, s. 23(c1); 2009-398, s. 2

SUBCHAPTER 06.
REVENUES AND EXPENSES OF THE JUDICIAL DEPARTMENT

ARTICLE 27
EXPENSES OF THE JUDICIAL DEPARTMENT

§ 7A-300. Expenses paid from State funds

(a) The operating expenses of the Judicial Department shall be paid from State funds, out of appropriations for this purpose made by the General Assembly, or from funds provided by local governments pursuant to G.S. 7A-300.1, 153A-212.1, or 160A-289.1. The Administrative Office of the Courts shall prepare budget estimates to cover these expenses, including therein the following items and such other items as are deemed necessary for the proper functioning of the Judicial Department:

(1) Salaries, departmental expense, printing and other costs of the appellate division;

(2) Salaries and expenses of superior court judges, district attorneys, assistant district attorneys, public defenders, and assistant public defenders, and fees and expenses of counsel assigned to represent indigents under the provisions of Subchapter IX of this Chapter;

(3) Salaries, travel expenses, departmental expense, printing and other costs of the Administrative Office of the Courts;

(4) Salaries and travel expenses of district judges, magistrates, and family court counselors;

(5) Salaries and travel expenses of clerks of superior court, their assistants, deputies, and other employees, and the expenses of their offices, including supplies and materials, postage, telephone and telegraph, bonds and insurance, equipment, and other necessary items;

(6) Fees and travel expenses of jurors, and of witnesses required to be paid by the State;

(7) Compensation and allowances of court reporters;

(8) Briefs for counsel and transcripts and other records for adequate appellate review when an appeal is taken by an indigent person;

(9) Transcripts of preliminary hearings in indigency cases and, in cases in which the defendant pays for a transcript of the preliminary hearing, a copy for the district attorney;

(10) Transcript of the evidence and trial court charge furnished the district attorney when a criminal action is appealed to the appellate division;

(11) All other expenses arising out of the operations of the Judicial Department which by law are made the responsibility of the State; and

(12) Operating expenses of the Judicial Council and the Judicial Standards Commission.

(b) Repealed by Session Laws 1971, c. 377, s. 32.

History.
1965, c. 310, s. 1; 1967, c. 108, s. 9; c. 1049, s. 5; 1969, c. 1013, s. 2; 1971, c. 377, ss. 18, 21; 1973, c. 47, s. 2; c. 503, ss. 10, 11; 2000-67, s. 15.4(c); 2010-31, s. 29.7(a)

§ 7A-300.1. Local supplementation of salaries for certain officers and employees

(a) In order to attract and retain the best qualified officers and employees for positions in the Judicial Branch of government, the Administrative Office of the Courts may contract with the governing body of a city or county for the provision of local funds to supplement the salaries of Judicial Department employees, other than elected officials and magistrates, who serve the superior court district, district court district, or prosecutorial district containing that unit of local government. Any employee who receives salary supplementation under this section shall be notified before receiving it that the supplementation is subject to the availability of local funds, may be discontinued at any time, and is not "compensation" for purposes of the Teachers' and State Employees' Retirement System or the Consolidated Judicial Retirement System.

(b) This section applies only to (i) cities with a population of 300,000 or more according to the most recent estimate of the Office of State Budget and Management and (ii) counties with a population of 300,000 or over according to the most recent estimate of the Office of State Budget and Management.

History.
2010-31, s. 29.7(b)

§ 7A-301. Disbursement of expenses

The salaries and expenses of all personnel in the Judicial Department and other operating expenses shall be paid out of the State treasury upon warrants duly drawn thereon, except that the Administrative Office of the Courts and the Department of Administration, with the approval of the State Auditor, may establish alternative procedures for the prompt payment of juror fees, witness fees, and other small expense items.

History.
1965, c. 310, s. 1

§ 7A-302. Counties and municipalities responsible for physical facilities

In each county in which a district court has been established, courtrooms, office space for juvenile court counselors and support staff as assigned by the Juvenile Justice Section of the Division of Adult Correction and Juvenile Justice of the Department of Public Safety, and related judicial facilities (including furniture), as defined in this Subchapter, shall be provided by the county, except that courtrooms and related judicial facilities may, with the approval of the administrative Officer of the Courts, after consultation with county and municipal authorities, be provided by a municipality in the county. To assist a county or municipality in meeting the expense of providing courtrooms and related judicial facilities, a part of the costs of court, known as the "facilities fee," collected for the State by the clerk of superior court, shall be remitted to the county or municipality providing the facilities.

History.

1965, c. 310, s. 1; 1998-202, s. 15; 2000-137, s. 4(a); 2007-323, s. 14.16; 2008-107, s. 29.8(f); 2011-145, s. 19.1(l); 2017-186, s. 2(c)

§ 7A-303. Equipment and supplies in clerk's office

Upon the establishment of the district court in any county, supplies and all equipment in the office of the clerk of superior court shall become the property of the State.

History.

1965, c. 310, s. 1

ARTICLE 28
UNIFORM COSTS AND FEES IN THE TRIAL DIVISIONS

§ 7A-304. Costs in criminal actions

(a) In every criminal case in the superior or district court, wherein the defendant is convicted, or enters a plea of guilty or nolo contendere, or when costs are assessed against the prosecuting witness, the following costs shall be assessed and collected. No costs may be assessed when a case is dismissed. Only upon entry of a written order, supported by findings of fact and conclusions of law, determining that there is just cause, the court may (i) waive costs assessed under this section or (ii) waive or reduce costs assessed under subdivision (7), (8), (8a), (11), (12), or (13) of this section. No court may waive or remit all or part of any court fines or costs without providing notice and opportunity to be heard by all government entities directly affected. The court shall provide notice to the government entities directly affected of (i) the date and time of the hearing and (ii) the right to be heard and make an objection to the remission or waiver of all or part of the order of court costs at least 15 days prior to hearing. Notice shall be made to the government entities affected by first-class mail to the address provided for receipt of court costs paid pursuant to the order. The

costs referenced in this subsection are listed below:

(1) For each arrest or personal service of criminal process, including citations and subpoenas, the sum of five dollars ($ 5.00), to be remitted to the county wherein the arrest was made or process was served, except that in those cases in which the arrest was made or process served by a law-enforcement officer employed by a municipality, the fee shall be paid to the municipality employing the officer.

(2) For the use of the courtroom and related judicial facilities, the sum of twelve dollars ($ 12.00) in the district court, including cases before a magistrate, and the sum of thirty dollars ($ 30.00) in superior court, to be remitted to the county in which the judgment is rendered. In all cases where the judgment is rendered in facilities provided by a municipality, the facilities fee shall be paid to the municipality. Funds derived from the facilities fees shall be used exclusively by the county or municipality for providing, maintaining, and constructing adequate courtroom and related judicial facilities, including: adequate space and furniture for judges, district attorneys, public defenders and other personnel of the Office of Indigent Defense Services, magistrates, juries, and other court related personnel; office space, furniture and vaults for the clerk; jail and juvenile detention facilities; free parking for jurors; and a law library (including books) if one has heretofore been established or if the governing body hereafter decides to establish one. In the event the funds derived from the facilities fees exceed what is needed for these purposes, the county or municipality may use any or all of the excess to retire outstanding indebtedness incurred in the construction of the facilities, or to reimburse the county or municipality for funds expended in constructing or renovating the facilities (without incurring any indebtedness) within a period of two years before or after the date a district court is established in such county, or to supplement the operations of the General Court of Justice in the county.

(2a) For the upgrade, maintenance, and operation of the judicial and county courthouse telecommunications and data connectivity, the sum of four dollars ($ 4.00), to be credited to the Court Information Technology Fund.

(2b) Repealed by Session Laws 2015-241, s. 18A.11, effective July 1, 2015.

(3) For the retirement and insurance benefits of both State and local government

law-enforcement officers, the sum of six dollars and twenty-five cents ($ 6.25), to be remitted to the State Treasurer. Fifty cents (50 cent(s)) of this sum shall be administered as is provided in Article 12C of Chapter 143 of the General Statutes. Five dollars and seventy-five cents ($ 5.75) of this sum shall be administered as is provided in Article 12E of Chapter 143 of the General Statutes, with one dollar and twenty-five cents ($ 1.25) being administered in accordance with the provisions of G.S. 143-166.50(e).

(3a) For the supplemental pension benefits of sheriffs, the sum of one dollar twenty-five cents ($ 1.25) to be remitted to the Department of Justice and administered under the provisions of Article 12H of Chapter 143 of the General Statutes.

(3b) For the services, staffing, and operations of the Criminal Justice Education and Training Standards Commission, the sum of three dollars ($ 3.00) to be remitted to the Department of Justice.

(3c) For legal representation to indigent defendants and others entitled to counsel under North Carolina law, the sum of two dollars ($ 2.00) to be remitted to the Office of Indigent Defense Services.

(4) For support of the General Court of Justice, the sum of one hundred forty-seven dollars and fifty cents ($ 147.50) in the district court, including cases before a magistrate, and the sum of one hundred fifty-four dollars and fifty cents ($ 154.50) in the superior court, to be remitted to the State Treasurer. For a person convicted of a felony in superior court who has made a first appearance in district court, both the district court and superior court fees shall be assessed. The State Treasurer shall remit the sum of ninety-five cents ($.95) of each fee collected under this subdivision to the North Carolina State Bar for the provision of services described in G.S. 7A-474.19.

(4a) For support of the General Court of Justice, the sum of ten dollars ($ 10.00) for all offenses arising under Chapter 20 of the General Statutes, to be remitted to the State Treasurer.

(4b) For additional support of the General Court of Justice, the sum of fifty dollars ($ 50.00) for all offenses arising under Chapter 20 of the General Statutes and resulting in a conviction of an improper equipment offense, to be remitted to the State Treasurer.

(5) For using pretrial release services, the district or superior court judge shall, upon conviction, impose a fee of fifteen dollars ($ 15.00) to be remitted to the county

providing the pretrial release services. This cost shall be assessed and collected only if the defendant had been accepted and released to the supervision of the agency providing the pretrial release services.

(6) For support of the General Court of Justice, the sum of two hundred dollars ($ 200.00) is payable by a defendant who fails to appear to answer the charge as scheduled, unless within 20 days after the scheduled appearance, the person either appears in court to answer the charge or disposes of the charge pursuant to G.S. 7A-146, and the sum of fifty dollars ($ 50.00) is payable by a defendant who fails to pay a fine, penalty, or costs within 40 days of the date specified in the court's judgment. The fee for failure to appear shall only be collected once in a criminal case. Upon a showing to the court that the defendant failed to appear because of an error or omission of a judicial official, a prosecutor, or a law-enforcement officer, the court shall waive the fee for failure to appear. These fees shall be remitted to the State Treasurer.

(7) For the services of the North Carolina State Crime Laboratory facilities, the district or superior court judge shall, upon conviction, order payment of the sum of six hundred dollars ($ 600.00) to be remitted to the Department of Justice for support of the Laboratory. This cost shall be assessed only in cases in which, as part of the investigation leading to the defendant's conviction, the laboratories have performed DNA analysis of the crime, tests of bodily fluids of the defendant for the presence of alcohol or controlled substances, or analysis of any controlled substance possessed by the defendant or the defendant's agent.

(8) For the services of any crime laboratory facility, the district or superior court judge shall, upon conviction, order payment of the sum of six hundred dollars ($ 600.00) to be remitted to the general fund of the local governmental unit that operates the laboratory or paid for the laboratory services. The funds shall be used for law enforcement purposes. The cost shall be assessed only in cases in which, as part of the investigation leading to the defendant's conviction, the laboratory has performed DNA analysis of the crime, test of bodily fluids of the defendant for the presence of alcohol or controlled substances, or analysis of any controlled substance possessed by the defendant or the defendant's agent. The costs shall be assessed only if the court finds that the work performed at the laboratory is the

equivalent of the same kind of work performed by the North Carolina State Crime Laboratory under subdivision (7) of this subsection.

(8a) For the services of any private hospital performing toxicological testing under contract with a prosecutorial district, the district or superior court judge shall, upon conviction, order payment of the sum of six hundred dollars ($ 600.00) to be remitted to the State Treasurer for the support of the General Court of Justice. The cost shall be assessed only in cases in which, as part of the investigation leading to the defendant's conviction, the laboratory has performed testing of bodily fluids of the defendant for the presence of alcohol or controlled substances. The costs shall be assessed only if the court finds that the work performed by the local hospital is the equivalent of the same kind of work performed by the North Carolina State Crime Laboratory under subdivision (7) of this subsection.

(9) For the support and services of the State DNA Database and DNA Databank, the sum of two dollars ($ 2.00). This amount is annually appropriated to the Department of Justice for this purpose. Notwithstanding the provisions of subsection (e) of this section, this cost does not apply to infractions.

(9a) For the services of the North Carolina State Crime Laboratory facilities, the district or superior court judge shall, upon conviction, order payment of the sum of six hundred dollars ($ 600.00) to be remitted to the Department of Justice to be used for laboratory purposes. This cost shall be assessed only in cases in which, as part of the investigation leading to the defendant's conviction, the laboratories have performed digital forensics, including the seizure, forensic imaging, and acquisition and analysis of digital media.

(9b) For the services of any crime laboratory facility, the district or superior court judge shall, upon conviction, order payment of the sum of six hundred dollars ($ 600.00) to be remitted to the general fund of the local law enforcement unit that operates the laboratory or paid for the laboratory services. The funds shall be used for laboratory services. The cost shall be assessed only in (i) cases in which, as part of the investigation leading to the defendant's conviction, the laboratory has performed digital forensics, including the seizure, forensic imaging, and acquisition and analysis of digital media, and (ii) if the court finds that the work performed at the laboratory is the equivalent of the same kind of work

performed by the North Carolina State Crime Laboratory under subdivision (9a) of this subsection.

(10) For support of the General Court of Justice, the sum of one hundred dollars ($ 100.00) is payable by a defendant convicted under G.S. 20-138.1 or G.S. 20-138.2, for a second or subsequent conviction under G.S. 20-138.2A, or for a second or subsequent conviction under G.S. 20-138.2B, to be remitted to the State Treasurer. This fee shall be in addition to the fee required by subdivision (4a) of this subsection.

(11) For the services of an expert witness employed by the North Carolina State Crime Laboratory who completes a chemical analysis pursuant to G.S. 20-139.1, a forensic analysis pursuant to G.S. 8-58.20, or a digital forensics analysis and provides testimony about that analysis in a defendant's trial, the district or superior court judge shall, upon conviction of the defendant, order payment of the sum of six hundred dollars ($ 600.00) to be remitted to the Department of Justice for support of the State Crime Laboratory. This cost shall be assessed only in cases in which the expert witness provides testimony about the chemical or forensic analysis in the defendant's trial and shall be in addition to any cost assessed under subdivision (7) or (9a) of this subsection.

(12) For the services of an expert witness employed by a crime laboratory who completes a chemical analysis pursuant to G.S. 20-139.1, a forensic analysis pursuant to G.S. 8-58.20, or a digital forensics analysis and provides testimony about that analysis in a defendant's trial, the district or superior court judge shall, upon conviction of the defendant, order payment of the sum of six hundred dollars ($ 600.00) to be remitted to the general fund of the local governmental unit that operates the laboratory or paid for the laboratory services. The funds shall be used for laboratory services. This cost shall be assessed only in cases in which the expert witness provides testimony about the chemical or forensic analysis in the defendant's trial and shall be in addition to any cost assessed under subdivision (8) or (9b) of this subsection.

(13) For the services of an expert witness employed by a private hospital performing toxicological testing under contract with a prosecutorial district who completes a chemical analysis pursuant to G.S. 20-139.1 and provides testimony about that analysis in a defendant's trial, the district or superior court judge shall, upon conviction of the defendant, order payment of the sum of six hundred dollars ($ 600.00) to

be remitted to the State Treasurer for the support of the General Court of Justice. This cost shall be assessed only in cases in which the expert witness provides testimony about the chemical analysis in the defendant's trial and shall be in addition to any cost assessed under subdivision (8a) of this subsection.

(a1) Repealed by Session Laws 1997-475, s. 4.1 .

(a2) The Administrative Office of the Courts shall report on October 1, 2018, and annually thereafter, to the Joint Legislative Oversight Committee on Justice and Public Safety on the implementation of the notice of waiver of costs to the government entities directly affected as required by subsection (a) of this section.

(b) On appeal, costs are cumulative, and costs assessed before a magistrate shall be added to costs assessed in the district court, and costs assessed in the district court shall be added to costs assessed in the superior court, except that the fee for the Law-Enforcement Officers' Benefit and Retirement Fund and the Sheriffs' Supplemental Pension Fund and the fee for pretrial release services shall be assessed only once in each case. No superior court costs shall be assessed against a defendant who gives notice of appeal from the district court but withdraws it prior to the expiration of the 10-day period for entering notice of appeal. When a case is reversed on appeal, the defendant shall not be liable for costs, and the State shall be liable for the cost of printing records and briefs in the Appellate Division.

(c) Witness fees, expenses for blood tests and comparisons incurred by G.S. 8-50.1(a), jail fees and cost of necessary trial transcripts shall be assessed as provided by law in addition to other costs set out in this section. Nothing in this section shall limit the power or discretion of the judge in imposing fines or forfeitures or ordering restitution.

(d) (1) In any criminal case in which the liability for costs, fines, restitution, attorneys' fees, or any other lawful charge has been finally determined, the clerk of superior court shall, unless otherwise ordered by the presiding judge, disburse the funds when paid in accordance with the following priorities:

a. Sums in restitution to the victim entitled thereto;

b. Costs due the county;

c. Costs due the city;

d. Fines to the county school fund;

e. Sums in restitution prorated among the persons other than the victim entitled thereto;

f. Costs due the State;

g. Attorney's fees, including appointment fees assessed pursuant to G.S. 7A-455.1.

(2) Sums in restitution received by the clerk of superior court shall be disbursed when:

a. Complete restitution has been received; or

b. When, in the opinion of the clerk, additional payments in restriction will not be collected; or

c. Upon the request of the person or persons entitled thereto; and

d. In any event, at least once each calendar year.

(e) Unless otherwise provided by law, the costs assessed pursuant to this section for criminal actions disposed of in the district court are also applicable to infractions disposed of in the district court. The costs assessed in superior court for criminal actions appealed from district court to superior court are also applicable to infractions appealed to superior court. If an infraction is disposed of in the superior court pursuant to G.S. 7A-271(d), costs applicable to the original charge are applicable to the infraction.

(f) The court may allow a defendant owing monetary obligations under this section to either make payment in full when costs are assessed or make payment on an installment plan arranged with the court. Defendants making use of an installment plan shall pay a onetime setup fee of twenty dollars ($ 20.00) to cover the additional costs to the court of receiving and disbursing installment payments. Fees collected under this subsection shall be remitted to the State Treasurer for support of the General Court of Justice.

(g) Changes to the costs or fees in this section apply to costs or fees assessed or collected on or after the effective date of the change. However, in misdemeanor or infraction cases disposed of on or after the effective date by written appearance, waiver of trial or hearing, or plea of guilt or admission of responsibility pursuant to G.S. 7A-180(4) or G.S. 7A-273(2), and within the time limit imposed by subdivision (a)(6) of this section, in which the citation or other criminal process was issued before the effective date, the costs or fees shall be the lesser of those specified in this section as amended, or those specified in the notice portion of the defendant's or respondent's copy of the citation or other criminal process, if any costs or fees are specified in that notice.

History.
1965, c. 310, s. 1; 1967, c. 601, s. 2; c. 691, ss. 27-29; c. 1049, s. 5; 1969, c. 1013, s. 3; c. 1190, ss. 28, 29; 1971, c. 377, ss. 19-21; c. 1129; 1973, c. 47, s. 2; 1975, c. 558, ss. 1, 2; 1975, 2nd Sess., c. 980, s. 1; 1979, c. 576, s. 3; 1981, c. 369; c. 691, s. 1; c. 896, s. 2; c. 959, s. 1; 1983, c. 713, ss. 2, 3; 1983 (Reg. Sess., 1984), c. 1034, s. 249; 1985, c. 479, s. 196(a); c. 729, ss. 2-4; c. 764, s. 17; 1986, Ex. Sess., c. 5; 1985 (Reg. Sess., 1986), c. 852,

s. 17; c. 1015, s. 1; 1989, c. 664, ss. 1, 2; c. 786, s. 1; 1989 (Reg. Sess., 1990), c. 1044, s. 1; 1991, c. 742, s. 15(a); 1991 (Reg. Sess., 1992), c. 811, s. 1; 1993, c. 313, s. 2; 1996, 2nd Ex. Sess., c. 18, s. 22.13(a); 1997-475, s. 4.1; 1998-212, ss. 19.4(k), 29A.12(a); 2000-109, s. 4(a); 2000-144, s. 2; 2001-424, s. 22.14(a); 2002-126, ss. 29A.4(a), 29A.8(a), 29A.9(b); 2003-284, s. 30.19B(a); 2004-186, s. 4.4; 2005-250, s. 1; 2005-276, ss. 43.1(a), 29.30(b); 2005-363, s. 1; 2007-323, s. 30.8(a); 2008-107, s. 29.8(a); 2008-118, s. 2.9(a); 2009-451, s. 15.20(a), (b), (c); 2009-516, s. 1; 2009-575, s. 13A; 2010-31, s. 15.5(a); 2010-123, s. 6.1; 2010-147, s. 7.1; 2011-19, s. 5; 2011-145, ss. 15.10(a), 19.1(h), 31.23(a), 31.23B, 31.26(b), (c), 31.26A; 2011-191, s. 4; 2011-192, s. 7(n), (o); 2011-326, s. 2; 2011-391, ss. 63(a), (b), 66; 2012-142, ss. 16.5(b), 16.6(b); 2013-360, ss. 17.6(g), 18B.18(a), 18B.19(a); 2014-100, s. 18B.14(a); 2015-241, ss. 18A.11, 18A.23(b); 2015-247, s. 1(a); 2017-57, ss. 18B.5(a), 18B.6(a), 18B.10(a); 2018-5, s. 18B.1; 2019-150, s. 1; 2019-177, s. 9(a); 2020-68, s. 1; 2020-83, s. 10.1(b)

§ 7A-305. Costs in civil actions

(a) In every civil action in the superior or district court, except for actions brought under Chapter 50B of the General Statutes, shall be assessed:

(1) For the use of the courtroom and related judicial facilities, the sum of twelve dollars ($ 12.00) in cases heard before a magistrate, and the sum of sixteen dollars ($ 16.00) in district and superior court, to be remitted to the county in which the judgment is rendered, except that in all cases in which the judgment is rendered in facilities provided by a municipality, the facilities fee shall be paid to the municipality. Funds derived from the facilities fees shall be used in the same manner, for the same purposes, and subject to the same restrictions, as facilities fees assessed in criminal actions.

(1a) For the upgrade, maintenance, and operation of the judicial and county courthouse telecommunications and data connectivity, the sum of four dollars ($ 4.00), to be credited to the Court Information Technology Fund.

(2) For support of the General Court of Justice, the sum of one hundred eighty dollars ($ 180.00) in the superior court and the sum of one hundred thirty dollars ($ 130.00) in the district court except that if the case is assigned to a magistrate the sum shall be eighty dollars ($ 80.00). If a case is designated as a mandatory complex business case under G.S. 7A-45.4, upon assignment to a Business Court Judge, the party filing the designation shall pay an additional one thousand one hundred dollars ($ 1,100) for support of the General Court of Justice. If a case is designated as

a complex business case under Rule 2.1 and Rule 2.2 of the General Rules of Practice for the Superior and District Courts, upon assignment to a Business Court Judge, the plaintiff shall pay an additional one thousand one hundred dollars ($ 1,100) for support of the General Court of Justice. Sums collected under this subdivision shall be remitted to the State Treasurer. The State Treasurer shall remit the sum of ninety-five cents ($.95) of each fee collected under this subdivision to the North Carolina State Bar for the provision of services described in G.S. 7A-474.19.

(a1) Costs apply to any and all additional and subsequent actions filed by amendment or counterclaim to the original action brought under Chapter 50B of the General Statutes, unless such additional and subsequent amendment or counterclaim to the action is limited to requests for relief authorized by Chapter 50B of the General Statutes.

(a2) In every action for absolute divorce filed in the district court, a cost of seventy-five dollars ($ 75.00) shall be assessed against the person filing the divorce action. Costs collected by the clerk pursuant to this subsection shall be remitted to the State Treasurer, who shall deposit seventy-five dollars ($ 75.00) to the Domestic Violence Center Fund established under G.S. 50B-9. Costs assessed under this subsection shall be in addition to any other costs assessed under this section.

(a3), (a4) Repealed by Session Laws 2008-118, s. 2.9(c), effective July 1, 2008.

(a5) In every civil action in the superior or district court wherein a party files a pleading containing one or more counterclaims, third-party complaints, or cross-claims, except for counterclaim and cross-claim actions brought under Chapter 50B of the General Statutes for which costs are assessed pursuant to subsection (a1) of this section, the following shall be assessed:

(1) For the use of the courtroom and related judicial facilities, the sum of twelve dollars ($ 12.00) in cases heard before a magistrate, and the sum of sixteen dollars ($ 16.00) in district and superior court, to be remitted to the municipality providing the facilities in which the judgment is rendered. If a municipality does not provide the facilities in which the judgment is rendered, the sum is to be remitted to the county in which the judgment is rendered. Funds derived from the facilities' fees shall be used in the same manner, for the same purposes, and subject to the same restrictions as facilities' fees assessed in criminal actions.

(2) For the upgrade, maintenance, and operation of the judicial and county

courthouse phone systems, the sum of four dollars ($ 4.00), to be credited to the Court Information Technology Fund.

(3) For support of the General Court of Justice, the sum of one hundred eighty dollars ($ 180.00) in the superior court, except that if a case is assigned to a special superior court judge as a complex business case under G.S. 7A-45.3, filing fees shall be collected and disbursed in accordance with subsection (a) of this section, and the sum of one hundred thirty dollars ($ 130.00) in the district court, except that if the case is assigned to a magistrate, the sum shall be eighty dollars ($ 80.00). Sums collected under this subdivision shall be remitted to the State Treasurer. The State Treasurer shall remit the sum of ninety-five cents ($.95) of each fee collected under this subdivision to the North Carolina State Bar for the provision of services described in G.S. 7A-474.19.

(b) On appeal, costs are cumulative, and when cases heard before a magistrate are appealed to the district court, the General Court of Justice fee and the facilities fee applicable in the district court shall be added to the fees assessed before the magistrate. When an order of the clerk of the superior court is appealed to either the district court or the superior court, no additional General Court of Justice fee or facilities fee shall be assessed.

(b1) When a defendant files an answer in an action filed as a small claim which requires the entire case to be withdrawn from a magistrate and transferred to the district court, the difference between the General Court of Justice fee and facilities fee applicable to the district court and the General Court of Justice fee and facilities fee applicable to cases heard by a magistrate shall be assessed. The defendant is responsible for paying the fee.

(c) The clerk of superior court, at the time of the filing of the papers initiating the action or the appeal, shall collect as advance court costs, the facilities fee, General Court of Justice fee, and the divorce fee imposed under subsection (a2) of this section, except in suits by an indigent. The clerk shall also collect the fee for discovery procedures under Rule 27(a) and (b) at the time of the filing of the verified petition.

(d) The following expenses, when incurred, are assessable or recoverable, as the case may be. The expenses set forth in this subsection are complete and exclusive and constitute a limit on the trial court's discretion to tax costs pursuant to G.S. 6-20:

(1) Witness fees, as provided by law.

(2) Jail fees, as provided by law.

(3) Counsel fees, as provided by law.

(4) Expense of service of process by certified mail and by publication.

(5) Costs on appeal to the superior court, or to the appellate division, as the case may be, of the original transcript of testimony, if any, insofar as essential to the appeal.

(6) Fees for personal service and civil process and other sheriff's fees, as provided by law. Fees for personal service by a private process server may be recoverable in an amount equal to the actual cost of such service or fifty dollars ($ 50.00), whichever is less, unless the court finds that due to difficulty of service a greater amount is appropriate.

(7) Fees of mediators appointed by the court, mediators agreed upon by the parties, guardians ad litem, referees, receivers, commissioners, surveyors, arbitrators, appraisers, and other similar court appointees, as provided by law. The fee of such appointees shall include reasonable reimbursement for stenographic assistance, when necessary.

(8) Fees of interpreters, when authorized and approved by the court.

(9) Premiums for surety bonds for prosecution, as authorized by G.S. 1-109.

(10) Reasonable and necessary expenses for stenographic and videographic assistance directly related to the taking of depositions and for the cost of deposition transcripts.

(11) Reasonable and necessary fees of expert witnesses solely for actual time spent providing testimony at trial, deposition, or other proceedings.

(12) The fee assessed pursuant to subdivision (2) of subsection (a) of this section upon assignment of a case to a special superior court judge as a complex business case.

Nothing in this subsection or in G.S. 6-20 shall be construed to limit the trial court's authority to award fees and expenses in connection with pretrial discovery matters as provided in Rule 26(b) or Rule 37 of the Rules of Civil Procedure, and no award of costs made pursuant to this section or pursuant to G.S. 6-20 shall reverse or modify any such orders entered in connection with pretrial discovery.

(e) Nothing in this section shall affect the liability of the respective parties for costs as provided by law.

(f) For the support of the General Court of Justice, the sum of twenty dollars ($ 20.00) shall accompany any filing of a notice of hearing on a motion not listed in G.S. 7A-308 that is filed with the clerk. No costs shall be assessed to a notice of hearing on a motion containing as a sole claim for relief the taxing of costs, including attorneys' fees, to a motion filed pursuant to G.S. 1C-1602 or G.S. 1C-1603, or to a motion filed by a child support enforcement agency established pursuant to Part D of Title IV of the Social Security Act. No more than one fee shall be assessed for any motion for which a notice of hearing is filed, regardless of whether the hearing is continued, rescheduled, or otherwise delayed.

History.

1965, c. 310, s. 1; 1967, c. 108, s. 10; c. 691, s. 30; 1971, c. 377, ss. 23, 24; c. 1181, s. 1; 1973, c. 503, ss. 12-14; c. 1267, s. 3; 1975, c. 558, s. 3; 1975, 2nd Sess., c. 980, ss. 2, 3; 1979, 2nd Sess., c. 1234, s. 1; 1981, c. 555, s. 6; c. 691, s. 2; 1983, c. 713, ss. 4-6; 1989, c. 786, s. 2; 1991, c. 742, s. 15(b); 1991 (Reg. Sess., 1992), c. 811, s. 2; 1993, c. 435, s. 6; 1995, c. 275, s. 2; 1998-212, s. 29A.12(b); 1998-219, ss. 2, 3; 2000-109, s. 4(b); 2001-424, s. 22.14(b); 2002-126, ss. 29A.4(b), 29A.6(e); 2004-186, s. 4.3; 2005-276, s. 43.1(b); 2005-405, s. 5; 2005-425, s. 1.2; 2007-212, s. 3; 2007-293, s. 2; 2007-323, ss. 30.8(b), 30.10(a), 30.11(a), (c); 2007-345, ss. 9.1(a), (c); 2008-107, ss. 29.1(a), 29.8(b); 2008-118, s. 2.9(c); 2008-193, s. 2; 2009-451, s. 15.20(d), (e); 2010-31, ss. 15.5(b), 15.8(a); 2010-123, s. 6.1; 2011-145, s. 31.23(b); 2012-142, s. 16.5(c); 2013-225, ss. 2, 3, 4(a); 2013-360, ss. 18B.17(a), 30.2(a), 30.2(a1); 2013-363, s. 7.1; 2014-102, s. 4; 2015-241, s. 18A.23(c); 2017-57, s. 18B.10(b); 2017-197, s. 5.4A(a)

§ 7A-305.1. Discovery, fee on filing verified petition

When discovery procedures under Rule 27 of the Rules of Civil Procedure are utilized, the sum of twenty dollars ($ 20.00) shall be assessed and collected by the clerk at the time of the filing of the verified petition. If a civil action is subsequently initiated, the twenty dollars ($ 20.00) shall be credited against costs in the civil action.

History.
1971, c. 377, s. 22

§ 7A-306. Costs in special proceedings

(a) In every special proceeding in the superior court, the following costs shall be assessed:

(1) For the use of the courtroom and related judicial facilities, the sum of ten dollars ($ 10.00) to be remitted to the county. Funds derived from the facilities fees shall be used in the same manner, for the same purposes, and subject to the same restrictions, as facilities fees assessed in criminal actions.

(1a) For the upgrade, maintenance, and operation of the judicial and county courthouse telecommunications and data connectivity, the sum of four dollars ($ 4.00), to be credited to the Court Information Technology Fund.

(2) For support of the General Court of Justice the sum of one hundred six dollars ($ 106.00). In addition, in proceedings involving land, except boundary disputes, if the fair market value of the land involved is over one hundred dollars ($ 100.00), there shall be an additional sum of thirty cents (30 cent(s)) per one hundred dollars ($ 100.00) of value, or major fraction thereof, not to exceed a maximum additional sum of two hundred dollars ($ 200.00). Fair market value is determined by the sale price if there is a sale, the appraiser's valuation if there is no sale, or the appraised value from the property tax records if there is neither a sale nor an appraiser's valuation. Sums collected under this subdivision shall be remitted to the State Treasurer.

(b) The facilities fee and thirty dollars ($ 30.00) of the General Court of Justice fee are payable at the time the proceeding is initiated.

(c) The following additional expenses, when incurred, are assessable or recoverable, as the case may be:

(1) Witness fees, as provided by law.

(2) Counsel fees, as provided by law.

(3) Costs on appeal, of the original transcript of testimony, if any, insofar as essential to the appeal.

(4) Fees for personal service of civil process, and other sheriff's fees, and for service by publication, as provided by law.

(5) Fees of guardians ad litem, referees, receivers, commissioners, surveyors, arbitrators, appraisers, and other similar court appointees, as provided by law. The fees of such appointees shall include reasonable reimbursement for stenographic assistance, when necessary.

(d) Costs assessed before the clerk shall be added to costs assessable on appeal to the judge or upon transfer to the civil issue docket.

(e) Nothing in this section shall affect the liability of the respective parties for costs, as provided by law.

(f) This section does not apply to a foreclosure under power of sale in a deed of trust or mortgage.

(g) For the support of the General Court of Justice, the sum of twenty dollars ($ 20.00) shall accompany any filing of a notice of hearing on a motion not listed in G.S. 7A-308 that is filed with the clerk. No costs shall be assessed to a notice of hearing on a motion containing as a sole claim for relief the taxing of costs, including attorneys' fees, or to a motion filed pursuant to G.S. 1C-1602 or G.S. 1C-1603. No more than one fee shall be assessed for any motion for which a notice of hearing is filed, regardless of whether the hearing is continued, rescheduled, or otherwise delayed.

History.

1965, c. 310, s. 1; 1967, c. 24, s. 2; 1971, c. 377, s. 25; c. 1181, s. 1; 1973, c. 503, s. 15; 1981, c. 691, s. 3; 1983, c. 713, ss. 7-9; c. 881, s. 4; 1985, c. 511, s. 1; 1989, c. 646, s. 1; 1991 (Reg. Sess., 1992), c. 811, s. 3; 1998-212, s. 29A.12(c); 2000-109, s. 4(c); 2001-424, s. 22.14(c); 2002-135, s. 1; 2005-276, s. 43.1(c); 2007-323, s. 30.8(c); 2008-107, s. 29.8(c); 2009-451, s. 15.20(f), (g); 2011-145, s. 31.23(c); 2012-142, s. 16.5(d); 2013-225, s. 4(b); 2013-360, s. 18B.17(b); 2015-241, s. 18A.23(d); 2017-197, s. 5.4A(b)

§ 7A-307. Costs in administration of estates

(a) In the administration of the estates of decedents, minors, incompetents, of missing persons, in the administration of trusts under wills and under powers of attorney, in trust proceedings under G.S. 36C-2-203, in estate proceedings under G.S. 28A-2-4, in power of attorney proceedings under G.S. 32C-1-116(a), and in collections of personal property by affidavit, the following costs shall be assessed:

(1) For the use of the courtroom and related judicial facilities, the sum of ten dollars ($ 10.00), to be remitted to the county. Funds derived from the facilities fees shall be used in the same manner, for the same purposes, and subject to the same restrictions, as facilities fees assessed in criminal actions.

(1a) For the upgrade, maintenance, and operation of the judicial and county courthouse telecommunications and data connectivity, the sum of four dollars ($ 4.00), to be credited to the Court Information Technology Fund.

(2) For support of the General Court of Justice, the sum of one hundred six dollars ($ 106.00), plus an additional forty cents (40 cent(s)) per one hundred dollars ($ 100.00), or major fraction thereof, of the gross estate, not to exceed six thousand dollars ($ 6,000). Gross estate shall include the fair market value of all personalty when received, and all proceeds from the sale of realty coming into the hands of the fiduciary, but shall not include the value of realty. In collections of personal property by affidavit, the fee based on the gross estate shall be computed from the information in the final affidavit of collection made pursuant to G.S. 28A-25-3 and shall be paid when that affidavit is filed. In all other cases, this fee shall be computed from the information reported in the inventory. If additional gross estate, including income, comes into the hands of the fiduciary after the filing of the inventory, the fee for such additional value shall be computed from the information reported in the account or report disclosing such additional value. For each filing the minimum fee shall be fifteen dollars ($ 15.00). Sums collected under this subdivision shall be remitted to the State Treasurer.

(2a) Notwithstanding subdivision (2) of this subsection, the fee of forty cents (40 cent(s)) per one hundred dollars ($ 100.00), or major fraction, of the gross estate, not to exceed six thousand dollars ($ 6,000), shall not be assessed on personalty received by a trust under a will when the estate of the decedent was administered under Chapters 28 or 28A of the General Statutes. Instead, a fee of twenty dollars ($ 20.00) shall be assessed on the filing of each annual and final account. However, the fee shall be assessed only on newly contributed or acquired assets, all interest or other income that accrues or is earned on or with respect to any existing or newly contributed or acquired assets, and realized gains on the sale of any and all trust assets. Newly contributed or acquired assets do not include assets acquired by the sale, transfer, exchange, or otherwise of the amount of trust property on which fees were previously assessed.

(2b) Notwithstanding subdivisions (1) and (2) of this subsection, the only cost assessed when the estate is administered or settled pursuant to G.S. 28A-25-6 shall be a fee of twenty dollars ($ 20.00) to be assessed upon filing of the application.

(2c) Notwithstanding subdivision (2) of this subsection, the fee of forty cents (40 cent(s)) per one hundred dollars ($ 100.00), or major fraction, of the gross estate shall not be assessed on the gross estate of a trust that is the subject of a proceeding under G.S. 36C-2-203 if there is no requirement in the trust that accountings be filed with the clerk.

(2d) Notwithstanding subdivisions (1) and (2) of this subsection, the only cost assessed in connection with the qualification of a limited personal representative under G.S. 28A-29-1 shall be a fee of twenty dollars ($ 20.00) to be assessed upon the filing of the petition.

(3) For probate of a will without qualification of a personal representative, the clerk shall assess a facilities fee as provided in subdivision (1) of this subsection and shall assess for support of the General Court of Justice, the sum of twenty dollars ($ 20.00).

(4) For the support of the General Court of Justice, the sum of twenty dollars ($ 20.00) shall accompany any filing of a notice of hearing on a motion not listed in G.S. 7A-308 that is filed with the clerk. No costs shall be assessed to a notice of hearing on

a motion containing as a sole claim for relief the taxing of costs, including attorneys' fees, or to a motion filed pursuant to G.S. 1C-1602 or G.S. 1C-1603. No more than one fee shall be assessed for any motion for which a notice of hearing is filed, regardless of whether the hearing is continued, rescheduled, or otherwise delayed.

(5) For the filing of a caveat to a will, the clerk shall assess for support of the General Court of Justice, the sum of two hundred dollars ($ 200.00).

(6) Notwithstanding subdivisions (1) and (2) of this subsection, the only cost assessed in connection with the reopening of an estate administration under G.S. 28A-23-5 shall be forty cents (40 cent(s)) per one hundred dollars ($ 100.00), or major fraction, of any additional gross estate, including income, coming into the hands of the fiduciary after the estate is reopened; provided that the total cost assessed when added to the total cost assessed in all prior administrations of the estate shall not exceed six thousand dollars ($ 6,000).

(7) For the filing of a petition for an elective share proceeding, the clerk shall assess for support of the General Court of Justice, the sum of two hundred dollars ($ 200.00).

(b) In collections of personal property by affidavit, the facilities fee and thirty dollars ($ 30.00) of the General Court of Justice fee shall be paid at the time of filing the qualifying affidavit pursuant to G.S. 28A-25-1. If the sole asset of the estate is a cause of action, these fees shall be paid at the time of the qualification of the fiduciary.

(b1) The clerk shall assess the following miscellaneous fees:

(1) Filing and indexing a will with no probate

-- first page.. $ 1.00

-- each additional page or fraction thereof

.... 25

(2) Issuing letters to fiduciaries, per letter over five letters issued. 1.00

(3) Inventory of safe deposits of a decedent, per box, per day.......................... 15.00

(4) Taking a deposition.................... 10.00

(5) Docketing and indexing a will probated in another county in the State

-- first page.. 6.00

-- each additional page or fraction thereof.

.... 25

(6) Hearing petition for year's allowance to surviving spouse or child, in cases not assigned to a magistrate, and allotting the same.. 20.00

(c) The following additional expenses, when incurred, are also assessable or recoverable, as the case may be:

(1) Witness fees, as provided by law.

(2) Counsel fees, as provided by law.

(3) Costs on appeal, of the original transcript of testimony, if any, insofar as essential to the appeal.

(4) Fees for personal service of civil process, and other sheriff's fees, as provided by law.

(5) Fees of guardians ad litem, referees, receivers, commissioners, surveyors, arbitrators, appraisers, and other similar court appointees, as provided by law.

(d) Costs assessed before the clerk shall be added to costs assessable on appeal to the judge or upon transfer to the civil issue docket.

(e) Nothing in this section shall affect the liability of the respective parties for costs, as provided by law.

History.

1965, c. 310, s. 1; 1967, c. 691, s. 31; 1969, c. 1190, s. 30; 1971, c. 1181, s. 1; 1973, c. 1335, s. 1; 1981, c. 691, s. 4; 1983, c. 713, ss. 10-17; 1985, c. 481, ss. 1-5; 1985 (Reg. Sess., 1986), c. 855; 1987, c. 837; 1989, c. 719; 1991 (Reg. Sess., 1992), c. 811, ss. 4, 5; 1997-310, s. 4; 1998-212, s. 29A.12(d); 2000-109, s. 4(d); 2001-413, s. 1.2; 2001-424, s. 22.14(d); 2002-135, ss. 2, 3; 2005-276, s. 43.1(d); 2007-323, ss. 30.8(d), 30.10(b); 2008-107, s. 29.8(d); 2008-193, s. 2; 2009-444, s. 3; 2009-451, s. 15.20(h), (i); 2009-570, s. 29; 2011-145, s. 31.23(d); 2011-344, s. 2; 2011-391, s. 62; 2012-142, s. 16.5(e); 2013-225, s. 4(c); 2013-360, s. 18B.17(c); 2015-241, s. 18A.23(e); 2017-158, s. 13; 2017-197, s. 5.4A(c); 2018-40, s. 3; 2019-243, s. 11(a); 2020-60, s. 3

§ 7A-308. Miscellaneous fees and commissions

(a) The following miscellaneous fees and commissions shall be collected by the clerk of superior court and remitted to the State for the support of the General Court of Justice:

(1) Foreclosure under power of sale in deed of trust or mortgage .... $ 300.00

If the property is sold under the power of sale, an additional amount will be charged, determined by the following formula: forty-five cents (.45) per one hundred dollars ($ 100.00), or major fraction thereof, of the final sale price. If the amount determined by the formula is less than ten dollars ($ 10.00), a minimum ten dollar ($ 10.00) fee will be collected. If the amount determined by the formula is more than five hundred dollars ($ 500.00), a maximum five hundred-dollar ($ 500.00) fee will be collected.

(1a) In rem foreclosures conducted under G.S. 105-375, if the property is sold under execution .... $ 300.00

(2) Proceeding supplemental to execution 30.00

(3) Confession of judgment 25.00

(4) Taking a deposition 10.00

(5) Execution 25.00

(6) Notice of resumption of former name 10.00

(7) Taking an acknowledgment or administering an oath, or both, with or without seal, each certificate (except that oaths of office shall be administered to public officials without charge) 2.00

(8) Bond, taking justification or approving 10.00

(9) Certificate, under seal 3.00

(10) Exemplification of records 10.00

(11) Recording or docketing (including indexing) any document

-- first page 6.00

-- each additional page or fraction thereof 25

(12) Preparation of copies

-- first page (of each document copied) 2.00

-- each additional page or fraction thereof 25

(13) Preparation and docketing of transcript of judgment 10.00

(14) Substitution of trustee in deed of trust 10.00

(15) Execution of passport application -- the amount allowed by federal law

(16) Repealed by Session Laws 1989, c. 783, s. 2.

(17) Criminal record search except if search is requested by an agency of the State or any of its political subdivisions or by an agency of the United States or by a petitioner in a proceeding under Article 2 of General Statutes Chapter 20 .... 25.00

(18) Filing the affirmations, acknowledgments, agreements and resulting orders entered into under the provisions of G.S. 110-132 and G.S. 110-133 .... 6.00

(19) Repealed by Session Laws 1989, c. 783, s. 3.

(20) Filing a motion to assert a right of access under G.S. 1-72.1. .... 30.00

(21) In civil matters, except in actions commenced or prosecuted by a child support enforcement agency established pursuant to Part D of Title IV of the Social Security Act, all alias and pluries summons issued and all endorsements issued on an original summons 15.00.(b) The fees and commissions set forth in this section are not chargeable when the service is performed as a part of the regular disposition of any action or special proceeding or the administration of an estate. When a transaction involves more than one of the services set forth in this section, only the greater service fee shall be charged. The Director of the Administrative Office of the courts shall issue guidelines pursuant to G.S. 7A-343(3) to be followed in administering this subsection.

(b1) The fees set forth in subdivisions (9) and (12) of subsection (a) of this section are not chargeable when copies or certificates under seal are requested by an attorney who has been appointed or who is under contract with the Office of Indigent Defense Services to represent an indigent person at State expense, if the request is made in connection with the appointed case or the contract and during the duration of the appointment or the contract.

(b2) The fees set forth in subdivision (11) of subsection (a) of this section are not chargeable when service is performed or documents are filed pursuant to the provisions of G.S. 14-112.3 or when an attorney is designating a period of secure leave pursuant to rules adopted by the Supreme Court of North Carolina.

(c) A person who participates in a program for the collection of worthless checks under G.S. 14-107.2 must pay a fee of sixty dollars ($ 60.00). The fee collected under this subsection must be remitted to the State by the clerk of the court in the county in which the program is established and credited to the Collection of Worthless Checks Fund. The Collection of Worthless Checks Fund is created as a special revenue fund. Revenue in the Fund does not revert at the end of the fiscal year, and interest and other investment income earned by the Fund accrues to the Fund. The money in the Fund is subject to appropriation by the General Assembly and may be used solely for the expenses of the programs established under G.S. 14-107.2 for the collection of worthless checks, including personnel, equipment, and other costs of district attorneys' offices that are attributable to the provision of these programs.

History.

1965, c. 310, s. 1; 1967, c. 691, ss. 32, 33; 1969, c. 1190, s. 31; 1971, c. 956, s. 2; 1973, c. 503, s. 16; c. 886; 1975, c. 829; 1981, c. 313, s. 1; 1983, c. 713, s. 18; 1985, c. 475, ss. 2, 3; c. 481, ss. 6-8; c. 511, s. 2; 1989, c. 783, ss. 2 -4; c. 786, ss. 1, 3; 1997-114, s. 1; 1997-443, s. 18.22(a); 1998-23, s. 11; 1998-212, s. 16.3; 1999-237, s. 17.7; 2000-67, s. 15.3A(a); 2000-109, s. 4(e); 2001-516, s. 2; 2002-126, ss. 29A.7(a), 29A.13.1(a); 2002-135, s. 4; 2003-284, s. 36A.2; 2005-251, s. 1; 2007-323, ss. 30.8(e), (f), 30.10(c); 2008-193, s. 2; 2009-317, s. 1; 2009-451, s. 15.20 (*l*); 2011-145, s. 31.23(e), (g); 2011-285, s. 1; 2011-391, s. 66.1; 2013-225, s. 4(d), (e); 2015-182, s. 3.5; 2019-177, s. 1; 2019-243, ss. 4, 12(a)

§ 7A-308.1. Fees on deposits and investments

On all funds received by the clerk by virtue or color of his office and deposited pursuant to G.S. 7A-112.1 or invested pursuant to G.S. 7A-112, one or both of the fees provided for in this section shall be assessed and collected as follows:

(1) On all funds deposited by the clerk in an interest bearing checking account pursuant to G.S. 7A-112.1, a fee of four percent (4%) of each principal amount so deposited shall be assessed and collected, subject to the following conditions:

a. The fee shall be collected from interest earnings only and shall not exceed the amount of the interest earnings on any principal amount so deposited, or seven hundred fifty dollars ($ 750.00), whichever is less;

b. All fees collected pursuant to this subsection shall be paid to the county as court facilities fees and used as prescribed in G.S. 7A-304(a)(2);

c. All interest earnings in excess of the prescribed fee shall be remitted to the beneficial owner or owners of any principal amount when that amount is withdrawn and distributed by the clerk; and

d. If any principal amount is withdrawn from the checking account and invested pursuant to G.S. 7A-112, any interest in excess of the prescribed clerk's fee which is invested with the principal amount shall be included in the fund upon which the fee provided for in subdivision (2) is computed.

(2) On all funds to be invested by the clerk pursuant to G.S. 7A-112, a fee equal to five percent (5%) of each fund shall be assessed and collected, subject to the following conditions:

a. The fee shall be charged and deducted from each fund before the fund is invested, and only the balance shall be invested;

b. Over the life of an account, the fees charged on the initial funds and all funds subsequently placed with the clerk for that account shall not exceed the investment earnings on the account or one thousand dollars ($ 1,000), whichever is less;

c. All fees collected pursuant to this subsection shall be remitted to the State Treasurer for the support of the General Court of Justice; and

d. Any fees charged in excess of the cumulative investment earnings on an account shall be refunded and all investment earnings in excess of the prescribed fee shall be remitted to the beneficial owner or owners when all funds in that account are finally withdrawn and distributed by the clerk.

History.
1989, c. 783, s. 5

§ 7A-309. Magistrate's special fees

The following special fees shall be collected by the magistrate and remitted to the clerk of superior court for the use of the State in support of the General Court of Justice:

(1) Performing marriage ceremony .... $ 50.00

(2) Hearing petition for year's allowance to surviving spouse or child, issuing notices to commissioners, allotting the same, and making return 20.00

(3) Taking a deposition.................... 10.00

(4) Proof of execution or acknowledgment of any instrument 2.00

(5) Performing any other statutory function not incident to a civil or criminal action ....$ 2.00.

History.
1965, c. 310, s. 1; 1973, c. 503, s. 17; 1983, c. 713, s. 19; 2002-126, s. 29A.10(a); 2019-243, s. 11(b)

§ 7A-310. Fees of commissioners and assessors appointed by magistrate

Any person appointed by a magistrate as a commissioner or assessor, and who shall serve, shall be paid the sum of two dollars ($ 2.00), to be taxed as a part of the bill of costs of the proceeding.

History.
1965, c. 310, s. 1

§ 7A-311. Uniform civil process fees

(a) In a civil action or special proceeding, except for actions brought under Chapter 50B of the General Statutes, the following fees and commissions shall be assessed, collected, and remitted to the county:

(1) a. For each item of civil process served, including summons, subpoenas, notices, motions, orders, writs and pleadings, the sum of thirty dollars ($ 30.00). When two or more items of civil process are served simultaneously on one party, only one thirty-dollar ($ 30.00) fee shall be charged.

b. When an item of civil process is served on two or more persons or organizations, a separate service charge shall be made for each person or organization. The process fee shall be remitted to the county. This subsection shall not apply to service of summons to jurors.

c. At least fifty percent (50%) of the fees collected pursuant to this subdivision shall be used by the county to ensure the timely service of process within the county, which may include the hiring of additional law enforcement personnel upon the recommendation of the sheriff.

(2) For the seizure of personal property and its care after seizure, all necessary expenses, in addition to any fees for service of process.

(3) For all sales by the sheriff of property, either real or personal, or for funds collected by the sheriff under any judgment, five percent (5%) on the first five hundred dollars ($ 500.00), and two and one-half percent (2 1/2%) on all sums over five hundred dollars ($ 500.00), plus necessary expenses of sale. Whenever an execution is issued to the sheriff, and subsequently while the execution is in force and outstanding, and after the sheriff has served or attempted to serve such execution, the judgment, or any part thereof, is paid directly or indirectly to the judgment creditor, the fee herein is payable to the sheriff on the amount so paid. The judgment creditor shall be responsible for collecting and paying all execution fees on amounts paid directly to the judgment creditor.

(4) For execution of a judgment of ejectment, all necessary expenses, in addition to any fees for service of process.

(5) For necessary transportation of individuals to or from State institutions or another state, the same mileage and subsistence allowances as are provided for State employees.

(b) All fees that are required to be assessed, collected, and remitted under subsection (a) of this section shall be collected in advance (except in suits in forma pauperis) except those contingent on sales prices or statutory commissions. When the fee is not collected in advance or at the time of assessment, a lien shall exist in favor of the county on all property of the party owing the fee. If the fee remains unpaid it shall be entered as a judgment against the debtor and shall be docketed in the judgment docket in the office of the clerk of superior court.

(c) The process fees and commissions set forth in this section are complete and exclusive and in lieu of any and all other process fees and commissions in civil actions and special proceedings.

History.
1965, c. 310, s. 1; 1967, c. 691, s. 34; 1969, c. 1190, s. 31 1/2; 1973, c. 417, ss. 1, 2; c. 503, s. 18; c. 1139; 1979, c. 801, s. 2; 1989 (Reg. Sess., 1990), c. 1044, s. 2; 1998-212, s. 29A.12(e); 2002-126, ss. 29A.6(f), 29A.6(g); 2004-113, s. 1; 2011-145, s. 31.26(d); 2011-192, s. 7(n); 2015-55, s. 2

§ 7A-312. Uniform fees for jurors; meals

(a) A juror in the General Court of Justice including a petit juror, or a coroner's juror, but excluding a grand juror, shall receive twelve dollars ($ 12.00) for the first day of service and twenty dollars ($ 20.00) per day afterwards, except that if any person serves as a juror for more than five days in any 24-month period, the juror shall receive forty dollars ($ 40.00) per day for each day of service in excess of five days. A grand juror shall receive twenty dollars ($ 20.00) per day. A juror required to remain overnight at the site of the trial shall be furnished adequate accommodations and subsistence. If required by the presiding judge to remain in a body during the trial of a case, meals shall be furnished the jurors during the period of sequestration. Jurors from out of the county summoned to sit on a special venire shall receive mileage at the same rate as State employees. Persons summoned as jurors shall be exempt during their period of service from paying a ferry toll required under G.S. 136-82 to travel to and from their homes and the site of that service.

(b) Notwithstanding subsection (a) of this section, the Administrative Office of the Courts may select a judicial district to operate a pilot program in which a juror may waive payment of the per diem fees provided for in that subsection. A juror waiving the fee may designate that the fee be used for any of the following services, if such services are provided in the district: (i) client treatment and service programs associated with a drug treatment or DWI treatment court program; (ii) courthouse self-help centers; (iii) courthouse child care centers; (iv) legal aid programs operated by a nonprofit corporation operating within the district; and (v) the Crime Victims Compensation Fund. If no such services are provided within the district, then waived fees are transferred to the Crime Victims Compensation Fund.

History.
1965, c. 310, s. 1; 1967, c. 1169; 1969, c. 1190, s. 32; 1971, c. 377, s. 26; 1973, c. 503, s. 19; 1979, c. 985; 1983, c. 881, ss. 2, 3; 1989, c. 646, s. 2; 1995, c. 324, ss. 21.1(a), (c); 2006-66, s. 14.17; 2006-187, s. 9; 2007-393, s. 16; 2012-180, s. 13

§ 7A-313. Uniform jail fees

Persons who are lawfully confined in jail awaiting trial shall be liable to the county or municipality maintaining the jail in the sum of ten dollars ($ 10.00) for each 24 hours' confinement, or fraction thereof, except that a person so confined shall not be liable for this fee if the case or proceeding against him is dismissed, or if acquitted, or if judgment is arrested, or if probable cause is not found, or if the grand jury fails to return a true bill.

Persons who are ordered to pay jail fees pursuant to a probationary sentence shall be liable to the county or municipality maintaining the jail at the same per diem rate paid by the Division of Adult Correction and Juvenile Justice of the Department of Public Safety to local jails for maintaining a prisoner, as set by the General Assembly in its appropriations acts.

History.
1965, c. 310, s. 1; 1969, c. 1190, s. 33; 1973, c. 503, s. 20; 1975, c. 444; 1989, c. 733, s. 1; 2000-109, s. 5; 2000-140, s. 104; 2011-145, ss. 19.1(h), 31.26(e); 2011-192, s. 7(n); 2017-186, s. 2(d)

§ 7A-313.1. Fee for costs of electronic monitoring

A county that provides the personnel, equipment, and other costs of providing electronic monitoring as a condition of an offender's bond or pretrial release may collect a fee from the offender that is the lesser of the amount of the jail fee authorized in G.S. 7A-313 or the actual cost of providing the electronic monitoring. A county may not collect a fee from an offender who is determined to be indigent and entitled to court-appointed counsel.

History.
2011-378, s. 1

§ 7A-314. Uniform fees for witnesses; experts; limit on number

(a) A witness under subpoena, bound over, or recognized, other than a salaried State, county, or municipal law-enforcement officer, or an out-of-state witness in a criminal case, whether to testify before the court, Judicial Standards Commission, jury of view, magistrate, clerk, referee, commissioner, appraiser, or arbitrator shall be entitled to receive five dollars ($ 5.00) per day, or fraction thereof, during his attendance, which, except as to witnesses before the Judicial Standards Commission, must be certified to the clerk of superior court. Compensation of witnesses acting on behalf of the court or prosecutorial offices shall be paid in accordance with the rules established by the Administrative Office of the Courts. Compensation of witnesses provided under G.S. 7A-454 shall be in accordance with rules established by the Office of Indigent Defense Services.

(b) A witness entitled to the fee set forth in subsection (a) of this section, and a law-enforcement officer who qualifies as a witness, shall be entitled to receive reimbursement for travel expenses as follows:

(1) A witness whose residence is outside the county of appearance but within 75 miles of the place of appearance shall be entitled to receive mileage reimbursement at the rate currently authorized for State employees, for each mile necessarily traveled from his place of resident to the place of appearance and return, each day. Reimbursements to witnesses acting on behalf of the court or prosecutorial offices shall be paid in accordance with the rules established by the Administrative Office of the Courts. Reimbursements to witnesses provided under G.S. 7A-454 shall be in accordance with rules established by the Office of Indigent Defense Services.

(2) A witness whose residence is outside the county of appearance and more than 75 miles from the place of appearance shall be entitled to receive mileage reimbursement at the rate currently authorized State employees for one round-trip from his place of residence to the place of appearance. A witness required to appear more than one day shall be entitled to receive reimbursement for actual expenses incurred for lodging and meals not to exceed the maximum currently authorized for State employees, in lieu of daily mileage. Reimbursements to witnesses acting on behalf of the court or prosecutorial offices shall be paid in accordance with the rules established by the Administrative Office of the Courts. Reimbursements to witnesses provided under G.S. 7A-454 shall be in accordance with rules established by the Office of Indigent Defense Services.

(c) A witness who resides in a state other than North Carolina and who appears for the purpose of testifying in a criminal action and proves his attendance may be compensated at the rate allowed to State officers and employees by subdivisions (1) and (2) of G.S. 138-6(a) for one round-trip from his place of residence to the place of appearance, and five dollars ($ 5.00) for each day that he is required to travel and attend as a witness, upon order of the court based upon a finding that the person was a necessary witness. If such a witness is required to appear more than one day, he is also entitled to reimbursement for actual expenses incurred for lodging and meals, not to exceed the maximum currently authorized for State employees. Reimbursements to witnesses acting on behalf of the court or prosecutorial offices shall be paid in accordance with the rules established by the Administrative Office of the Courts. Reimbursements to witnesses provided under G.S. 7A-454 shall be in accordance with rules established by the Office of Indigent Defense Services.

(d) Subject to the specific limitations set forth in G.S. 7A-305(d)(11), an expert witness, other than a salaried State, county, or municipal law-enforcement officer, shall receive such compensation and allowances as the court, or the Judicial Standards Commission, in its discretion, may authorize. A law-enforcement officer who appears as an expert witness shall receive reimbursement for travel expenses only, as provided in subsection (b) of this section. Compensation of experts acting on behalf of the court or prosecutorial offices shall be paid in accordance with the rules established by the Administrative Office of the Courts. Compensation of experts provided under G.S. 7A-454 shall be in accordance with rules established by the Office of Indigent Defense Services.

(e) If more than two witnesses are subpoenaed, bound over, or recognized, to prove a single material fact, the expense of the additional witnesses shall be borne by the party issuing or requesting the subpoena.

(f) Repealed by Session Laws 2012-142, s. 16.3(a), effective July 1, 2012.

History.
1965, c. 310, s. 1; 1969, c. 1190, s. 34; 1971, c. 377, s. 27; 1973, c. 503, ss. 21, 22; 1983, c. 713, s. 20; 1998-212, s. 16.25(a); 2000-144, s. 3; 2006-187, s. 5(a); 2007-323, s. 14.23; 2010-31, s. 15.7; 2011-391, s. 64; 2012-142, s. 16.3(a); 2015-153, s. 2

§ 7A-314.1. Family court fees

(a) The Administrative Office of the Courts may charge a uniform fee of not more than fifty dollars ($ 50.00) per hour to persons receiving the services of a supervised visitation and exchange center through a family court program. The fees collected under this section may be used by the Director of the Administrative Office of the Courts to support the continued operation of supervised visitation and exchange centers which provide services to family court clients regarding domestic violence, substance abuse, mental illness, parental alienation, and other issues.

(b) The Director of the Administrative Office of the Courts may establish a procedure for persons to apply for a reduction in the fee, based upon the person's ability to pay as a result of indigence, status as a victim of domestic violence, or other circumstances.

History.
2004-110, s. 7.1; 2013-304, s. 1

§ 7A-315. Liability of State for witness fees in criminal cases when defendant not liable

In a criminal action, if no prosecuting witness is designated by the court as liable for the costs, and the defendant is acquitted, or convicted and unable to pay, or a nolle prosequi is entered, or judgment is arrested, or probable cause is not found, or the grand jury fails to return a true bill, the State shall be liable for the witness fees allowed per G.S. 7A-314 and any expenses for blood tests and comparisons incurred per G.S. 8-50.1(a).

History.
1965, c. 310, s. 1; 1979, c. 576, s. 4

§ 7A-316. Payment of witness fees in criminal actions

A witness in a criminal action who is entitled to a witness fee and who proves his attendance prior to assessment of the bill of costs shall be paid by the clerk from State funds and the amount disbursed shall be assessed in the bill of costs. When the State is liable for the fee, a witness who proves his attendance not later than the last day of court in the week in which the trial was completed shall be paid by the clerk from State funds. If more than two witnesses shall be subpoenaed, bound over, or recognized, to prove a single material fact, disbursements to such additional witnesses shall be charged against the party issuing or requesting the subpoena.

History.
1965, c. 310, s. 1; 1971, c. 377, s. 28

§ 7A-317. Counties and municipalities required to advance costs and fees

(a) Counties and municipalities required to advance pay all costs and fees due to the court at the time of filing. The clerk of superior court may consent to allow the county or municipality to pay all costs and fees within 45 days of the date of the filing of any action in lieu of paying costs and fees at the time of filing.

(b) The clerk of superior court shall withhold all facilities fees due to be remitted to a county or municipality when the county or municipality does not pay costs and fees due to the court within 90 days of the date of filing any action.

History.
1967, c. 691, s. 35; 2007-323, s. 30.10(d); 2008-193, ss. 1 -3; 2013-225, s. 5

§ 7A-317.1. Disposition of fees in counties with unincorporated seats of court

Notwithstanding any other provision of this Article, if a municipality listed in G.S. 7A-133 as an additional seat of district court is not incorporated, the arrest, facilities, and jail fees which would ordinarily accrue thereto, shall instead accrue to the county in which the unincorporated municipality is located.

History.
1969, c. 1190, s. 34 1/2

§ 7A-318. Determination and disbursement of costs on and after date district court established

(a) On and after the date that the district court is established in a judicial district, costs in every action, proceeding or other matter pending in the General Court of Justice in that district, shall be assessed as provided in this Article, unless costs have been finally assessed according to prior law. In computing costs as provided in this section, the parties shall be given credit for any fees, costs, and commissions paid in the pending action, proceeding or other matter, before the district court was established in the district, except that no refunds are authorized.

(b) In the administration of estates, costs shall be considered finally assessed according to prior law when they have been assessed at the time of the filing of any inventory, account, or other report. Costs at any filing on or after the date the district court is established in a judicial district shall be assessed as provided in this Article.

(c) When the General Court of Justice fee and the facilities fee are assessed as provided in this Article and credit is given for fees, costs, and commissions paid before the district court was established in the district, the actual amount thereafter received by the clerk shall be remitted to the State for the support of the General Court of Justice.

(d) When costs have been finally assessed according to prior law, but come into the hands of the clerk after the district court is established in the district, funds so received shall be disbursed according to prior law.

(e) Cost funds in the hands of the clerk at the time the district court is established shall be disbursed according to prior law.

History.
1965, c. 310, s. 1; 1967, c. 691, s. 35

N.C. Gen. Stat. § 7A-319

Repealed by Session Laws 1971, c. 377, s. 32.

§ 7A-320. Costs are exclusive

The costs set forth in this Article are complete and exclusive, and in lieu of any other costs and fees.

History.
1983, c. 713, s. 1

§ 7A-321. Collection of offender fines and fees assessed by the court; collection assistance fee

(a) The Judicial Department may, in lieu of payment by cash or check, accept payment by credit card, charge card, or debit card for the fines, fees, and costs owed to the courts by offenders.

(b) In attempting to collect the fines, fees, costs, and restitution owed by offenders not sentenced to supervised probation or active time, the Administrative Office of the Courts may do the following:

(1) Assess a collection assistance fee if an amount due remains unpaid for 30 days after the time period allotted by the court. The amount of the collection assistance fee shall not exceed the average cost of collecting the debt or twenty percent (20%) of the amount past due, whichever is less.

(2) Enter into contracts with a collection agency, agencies, or municipal or county government agencies to collect unpaid amounts owed. The Administrative Office of the Courts may provide by such contract for the collection assistance fee to be retained by the agency or agencies that collect the amounts owed.

(3) Intercept tax refund checks under Chapter 105A of the General Statutes, the Setoff Debt Collection Act.

(c) Repealed by Session Laws 2011-323, s. 1, effective July 1, 2011, and applicable to cases adjudicated on or after that date.

(d) The court shall retain a collection assistance fee in the amount of ten percent (10%) of any cost or fee collected by the Department pursuant to this Article or Chapter 20 of the General Statutes and remitted to an agency of the State or any of its political subdivisions, other than a cost or fee listed in this subsection. The court shall remit the collection assistance fee to the State Treasurer for the support of the General Court of Justice.

The collection assistance fee shall not be retained from the following:

(1) Costs and fees designated by law for remission to or use by an agency or program of the Judicial Department or for support of the General Court of Justice.

(2) Costs and fees designated by law for remission to the General Fund.

(3) Costs and fees designated by law for remission to the Statewide Misdemeanant Confinement Fund.

History.
2006-187, s. 1(a); 2007-323, s. 30.9(a); 2009-451, s. 15.20(m); 2009-575, s. 14; 2011-145, s. 31.26(f1); 2011-192, ss. 7(n), 7(p); 2011-323, s. 1

SUBCHAPTER 08.
CONFERENCE OF DISTRICT ATTORNEYS

ARTICLE 32
CONFERENCE OF DISTRICT ATTORNEYS

§ 7A-411. Establishment and purpose

There is created the Conference of District Attorneys of North Carolina, of which every district attorney in North Carolina is a member. The purpose of the Conference is to assist in improving the administration of justice in North Carolina by coordinating the prosecution efforts of the various district attorneys, by assisting them in the administration of their offices, and by exercising the powers and performing the duties provided for in this Article.

History.
1983, c. 761, s. 152

§ 7A-412. Annual meetings; organization; election of officers

(a) **Annual Meetings.** -- The Conference shall meet annually at a time and place selected by the President of the Conference.

(b) **Election of Officers.** -- Officers of the Conference are a President, a President-elect, a Vice-president, and other officers from among its membership that the Conference may designate in its bylaws. Officers are elected for one-year terms at the annual Conference, and take office on July 1 immediately following their election.

(c) **Executive Committee.** -- The Executive Committee of the Conference consists of the President, the President-elect, the Vice-president, and four other members of the Conference. One of these four members shall be the immediate past president if there is one and if he continues to be a member.

(d) **Organization and Functioning; Bylaws.** -- The bylaws may provide for the organization and functioning of the Conference, including the powers and duties of its officers and committees. The bylaws shall state the number of members required to constitute a quorum at any meeting of the Conference or the Executive Committee. The bylaws shall set out the procedure for amending the bylaws.

(e) **Calling Meetings; Duty to Attend.** -- The President or the Executive Committee may call a meeting of the Conference upon 10 days' notice to the members, except upon written waiver of notice signed by at least three-fourths of the members. A member should attend each meeting of the Conference and the Executive Committee of which he is given notice. Members are entitled to reimbursement for travel and subsistence expenses at the rate applicable to State employees.

History.
1983, c. 761, s. 152

§ 7A-413. Powers of Conference

(a) The Conference may:

(1) Cooperate with citizens and other public and private agencies to promote the effective administration of criminal justice.

(2) Assist prosecutors in the effective prosecution and trial of criminal offenses, and develop an advisory trial manual.

(3) Develop advisory manuals to assist prosecutors in the organization and administration of their offices, case management, calendaring, case tracking, filing, and office procedures.

(4) Cooperate with the Administrative Office of the Courts and the School of Government at the University of North Carolina at Chapel Hill concerning education and training programs for prosecutors and staff.

(b) The Conference may not adopt rules pursuant to Chapter 150B of the General Statutes.

History.
1983, c. 761, s. 152; 1987, c. 827, s. 1; 2006-264, s. 29(b)

§ 7A-414. Executive Secretary; clerical support

The Conference may employ an executive secretary and any necessary supporting staff to assist it in carrying out its duties.

History.
1983, c. 761, s. 152

SUBCHAPTER 09.
REPRESENTATION OF INDIGENT PERSONS

ARTICLE 36
ENTITLEMENT OF INDIGENT PERSONS GENERALLY

§ 7A-450. Indigency; definition; entitlement; determination; change of status

(a) An indigent person is a person who is financially unable to secure legal representation and to provide all other necessary expenses of representation in an action or proceeding enumerated in this Subchapter. An interpreter is a necessary expense as defined in Chapter 8B of the General Statutes for a deaf person who is entitled to counsel under this subsection.

(b) Whenever a person, under the standards and procedures set out in this Subchapter, is determined to be an indigent person entitled to counsel, it is the responsibility of the State to provide him with counsel and the other necessary expenses of representation. The professional relationship of counsel so provided to the indigent person he represents is the same as if counsel had been privately retained by the indigent person.

(b1) An indigent person indicted for murder may not be tried where the State is seeking the death penalty without an assistant counsel being appointed in a timely manner. If the indigent person is represented by the public defender's office, the requirement of an assistant counsel may be satisfied by the assignment to the case of an additional attorney from the public defender's staff.

(c) The question of indigency may be determined or redetermined by the court at any stage of the action or proceeding at which an indigent is entitled to representation.

(d) If, at any stage in the action or proceeding, a person previously determined to be indigent becomes financially able to secure legal representation and provide other necessary expenses of representation, he must inform the counsel appointed by the court to represent him of that fact. In such a case, that information is not included in the attorney client privilege, and counsel must promptly inform the court of that information.

History.
1969, c. 1013, s. 1; 1981, c. 409, s. 2; c. 937, s. 3; 1985, c. 698, s. 22(a); 2000-144, s. 5

§ 7A-450.1. Responsibility for payment by certain fiduciaries

It is the intent of the General Assembly that, whenever possible, if an attorney or guardian ad litem is appointed pursuant to G.S. 7A-451 for a person who is less than 18 years old or who is at least 18 years old but remains dependent on and domiciled with a parent or guardian, the parent, guardian, or any trustee in possession of funds or property for the benefit of the person, shall reimburse the State for the attorney or guardian ad litem fees, pursuant to the procedures established in G.S. 7A-450.2 and G.S. 7A-450.3. This section shall not apply in any case in which the person for whom an attorney or guardian ad litem is appointed prevails.

History.
1983, c. 726, s. 1; 1991 (Reg. Sess., 1992), c. 1030, s. 2

§ 7A-450.2. Determination of fiduciaries at indigency determination; summons; service of process

At the same time as a person who is less than 18 years old or who is at least 18 years old but remains dependent on and domiciled with a parent or guardian is determined to be indigent, and has an attorney or guardian ad litem appointed pursuant to G.S. 7A-451, the court shall determine the identity and address of the parent, guardian or any trustee in possession of funds or property for the benefit of the person. The court shall issue a summons to the parent, guardian or trustee to be present at the dispositional hearing or the sentencing hearing or other appropriate hearing and to be a party to these hearings for the purpose of being determined responsible for reimbursing the State for the person's attorney or guardian ad litem fees, or to show cause why he should not be held responsible.

Both the issuance of the summons and the service of process shall be pursuant to G.S. 1A-1, Rule 4.

History.
1983, c. 726, s. 1

§ 7A-450.3. Determination of responsibility at hearing

At the dispositional, sentencing or other hearing of the person who is less than 18 years old or who is at least 18 years old but remains dependent on and domiciled with a parent or guardian, the court shall make a determination whether the parent, guardian or trustee should be held responsible for reimbursing the State for the person's attorney or guardian ad litem fees. This determination shall include the financial situation of the parent, guardian or trustee, the relationship of responsibility the parent, guardian or trustee bears to the person and any showings by the parent, guardian or trustee that the person is emancipated or not dependent. The test of the party's financial ability to pay is the test applied to appointment of an attorney in cases of indigency. Any provision of any deed, trust or other writing, which, if enforced, would defeat the intent or purpose of this section is contrary to the public policy of this State and is void insofar as it may apply to prohibit reimbursement to the State.

If the court determines that the parent, guardian or trustee is responsible for reimbursing the State for the attorney or guardian ad litem fees, the court shall so order. If the party does not comply with the order at the time of disposition, the court shall file a judgment against him for the amount due the State.

History.
1983, c. 726, s. 1; 2005-254, s. 3

§ 7A-450.4. Exemptions

General Statutes 7A-450.1, 7A-450.2 and 7A-450.3 do not authorize the court to require the Department of Health and Human Services or any county Department of Social Services to reimburse the State for fees.

History.
1983, c. 726, s. 1; 1997-443, s. 11A.118(a)

§ 7A-451. Scope of entitlement

(a) An indigent person is entitled to services of counsel in the following actions and proceedings:

(1) Any case in which imprisonment, or a fine of five hundred dollars ($ 500.00), or more, is likely to be adjudged.

(2) A hearing on a petition for a writ of habeas corpus under Chapter 17 of the General Statutes.

(3) A motion for appropriate relief under Chapter 15A of the General Statutes if appointment of counsel is authorized by Chapter 15A of the General Statutes and the defendant has been convicted of a felony, has been fined five hundred dollars ($ 500.00) or more, or has been sentenced to a term of imprisonment.

(4) A hearing for revocation of probation.

(5) A hearing in which extradition to another state is sought.

(6) A proceeding for an inpatient involuntary commitment to a facility under Part 7 of Article 5 of Chapter 122C of the General Statutes, or a proceeding for commitment under Part 8 of Article 5 of Chapter 122C of the General Statutes.

(7) In any case of execution against the person under Chapter 1, Article 28 of the General Statutes, and in any civil arrest and bail proceeding under Chapter 1, Article 34, of the General Statutes.

(8) In the case of a juvenile, a hearing as a result of which commitment to an institution or transfer to the superior court for trial on a felony charge is possible.

(9) A hearing for revocation of parole at which the right to counsel is provided in accordance with the provisions of Chapter 148, Article 4, of the General Statutes.

(10) Repealed by Session Laws 2003, c. 13, s. 2(a), effective April 17, 2003, and applicable to all petitions for sterilization pending and orders authorizing sterilization that have not been executed as of April 17, 2003.

(11) A proceeding for the provision of protective services according to Chapter 108A, Article 6 of the General Statutes.

(12) In the case of a juvenile alleged to be abused, neglected, or dependent under Subchapter I of Chapter 7B of the General Statutes.

(13) A proceeding to find a person incompetent under Subchapter I of Chapter 35A, of the General Statutes.

(14) A proceeding to terminate parental rights where a guardian ad litem is appointed pursuant to G.S. 7B-1101.

(15) An action brought pursuant to Article 11 of Chapter 7B of the General Statutes to terminate an indigent person's parental rights.

(16) A proceeding involving consent for an abortion on an unemancipated minor pursuant to Article 1A, Part 2 of Chapter 90 of the General Statutes. G.S. 7A-450.1, 7A-450.2, and 7A-450.3 shall not apply to this proceeding.

(17) A proceeding involving limitation on freedom of movement or access pursuant to G.S. 130A-475 or G.S. 130A-145.

(18) A proceeding involving placement into satellite monitoring under Part 5 of Article 27A of Chapter 14 of the General Statutes.

(19) A proceeding involving a review of the sex offender registration requirement as provided in G.S. 14-208.12B.

(b) In each of the actions and proceedings enumerated in subsection (a) of this section, entitlement to the services of counsel begins as soon as feasible after the indigent is taken into custody or service is made upon him of the charge, petition, notice or other initiating process. Entitlement continues through any critical stage of the action or proceeding, including, if applicable:

(1) An in-custody interrogation;

(2) A pretrial identification procedure which occurs after formal charges have been preferred and at which the presence of the indigent is required;

(3) A hearing for the reduction of bail, or to fix bail if bail has been earlier denied;

(4) A probable cause hearing;

(5) Trial and sentencing;

(6) Review of any judgment or decree pursuant to G.S. 7A-27, 7A-30(1), 7A-30(2), and Subchapter XIV of Chapter 15A of the General Statutes;

(7) In a capital case in which a defendant is under a sentence of death, subject to rules adopted by the Office of Indigent Defense Services, review of any judgment or decree rendered on direct appeal by the

Supreme Court of North Carolina pursuant to the certiorari jurisdiction of the United States Supreme Court; and

(8) In a noncapital case, subject to rules adopted by the Office of Indigent Defense Services, review of any judgment or decree rendered on direct appeal by a court of the North Carolina Appellate Division pursuant to the certiorari jurisdiction of the United States Supreme Court, when the judgment or decree:

a. Decides an important question of federal law in a way that conflicts with relevant decisions of the United States Supreme Court, a federal Court of Appeals, or the court of last resort of another state;

b. Decides an important question of federal law that has not been, but should be, settled by the United States Supreme Court; or

c. Decides a question of federal law in the indigent's favor and the judgment or decree is challenged by opposing counsel through an attempt to invoke the certiorari jurisdiction of the United States Supreme Court.

(c) In any capital case, an indigent defendant who is under a sentence of death and desires counsel may apply to the Office of Indigent Defense Services for the appointment of counsel to represent the defendant in preparing, filing, and litigating a motion for appropriate relief. The application for the appointment of such postconviction counsel may be made prior to completion of review on direct appeal and shall be made no later than 10 days from the latest of the following:

(1) The mandate has been issued by the Supreme Court of North Carolina on direct appeal pursuant to N.C.R. App. P. 32(b) and the time for filing a petition for writ of certiorari to the United States Supreme Court has expired without a petition being filed;

(2) The United States Supreme Court denied a timely petition for writ of certiorari of the decision on direct appeal by the Supreme Court of North Carolina; or

(3) The United States Supreme Court granted the defendant's or the State's timely petition for writ of certiorari of the decision on direct appeal by the Supreme Court of North Carolina, but subsequently left the defendant's death sentence undisturbed.

(c1) Upon application, supported by the defendant's affidavit, the Office of Indigent Defense Services shall determine whether the defendant was previously adjudicated indigent for purposes of trial or direct appeal. If the defendant was previously adjudicated indigent,

the defendant shall be presumed indigent for purposes of this subsection, and the Office of Indigent Defense Services shall appoint two counsel to represent the defendant. If the defendant was not previously adjudicated indigent, the Office of Indigent Defense Services shall request that the superior court in the district where the defendant was indicted determine whether the defendant is indigent. If the court finds that the defendant is indigent, the Office of Indigent Defense Services shall then appoint two counsel to represent the defendant.

(c2) The defendant does not have a right to be present at the time of appointment of counsel, and the appointment need not be made in open court.

(d) The appointment of counsel as provided in subsection (c) of this section and the procedure for compensation shall comply with rules adopted by the Office of Indigent Defense Services.

(e) No counsel appointed pursuant to subsection (c) of this section shall have previously represented the defendant at trial or on direct appeal in the case for which the appointment is made unless the defendant expressly requests continued representation and understandingly waives future allegations of ineffective assistance of counsel.

(e1) When the Supreme Court of North Carolina files an opinion affirming or reversing the judgment of the trial court in a case in which the defendant was sentenced to death, or files an opinion or decision with regard to such a defendant's postconviction petition for relief from a sentence of death, or when any federal court files or issues an opinion or decision in such circumstances, the Division of Adult Correction and Juvenile Justice of the Department of Public Safety shall, on the day the opinion or decision is filed or issued, permit counsel for the defendant to visit the defendant at the institution at which the defendant is confined. The visit shall be permitted during regular business hours for not less than one hour, unless a visit outside regular business hours is agreed to by both the institution's administrator and counsel for the defendant. This section shall not be construed to abridge the adequate and reasonable opportunity for attorneys to consult with clients sentenced to death generally and shall not be construed to mandate an attorney visit during an emergency at the institution at which a defendant is confined.

(f) A guardian ad litem shall be appointed to represent the best interest of an underage party seeking judicial authorization to marry pursuant to G.S. 51-2A. The appointment and duties of the guardian ad litem shall be governed by G.S. 51-2A. The procedure for compensation of the guardian ad litem shall comply with rules adopted by the Office of Indigent Defense Services.

History.

1969, c. 1013, s. 1; 1973, c. 151, ss. 1, 3; c. 616; c. 726, s. 4; c. 1116, s. 1; c. 1125; c. 1320; c. 1378, s. 2; 1977, c. 711, ss. 7, 8; c. 725, s. 2; 1979, 2nd Sess., c. 1206, s. 3; 1981, c. 966, s. 4; 1983, c. 638, s. 23; c. 864, s. 4; 1985, c. 509, s. 1; c. 589, s. 3; 1987, c. 550, s. 16; 1995, c. 462, s. 3; 1995 (Reg. Sess., 1996), c. 719, s. 7; 1998-202, s. 13(a); 2000-144, s. 6; 2001-62, s. 14; 2002-179, s. 16; 2003-13, s. 2(a); 2005-250, s. 2; 2007-323, s. 14.19(a); 2009-91, s. 1; 2009-387, ss. 3, 5; 2011-145, s. 19.1(h); 2017-176, s. 1(c); 2017-186, s. 2(f); 2020-83, s. 11.5(b)

§ 7A-451.1. Counsel fees for outpatient involuntary commitment proceedings

The State shall pay counsel fees for persons appointed pursuant to G.S. 122C-267(d).

History.

1983, c. 638, s. 24; c. 864, s. 4; 1985, c. 589, s. 4; 1991, c. 761, s. 3

§ 7A-452. Source of counsel; fees; appellate records

(a) Upon the court's determination that a person is indigent and entitled to counsel under this Article, counsel shall be appointed in accordance with rules adopted by the Office of Indigent Defense Services. In noncapital cases, the court shall assign counsel pursuant to rules adopted by the Office of Indigent Defense Services. In capital cases, the Office of Indigent Defense Services or designee of the Office of Indigent Defense Services shall assign counsel; at least one member of each capital defense team, where practicable, shall be a member of the bar in that division. In the courts of those counties which have a public defender, however, the public defender may tentatively assign himself or an assistant public defender to represent an indigent person, subject to subsequent determination of entitlement to counsel by the court and approval by the court in noncapital cases and by the Office of Indigent Defense Services in capital cases.

(b) Fees of assigned counsel and salaries and other operating expenses of the offices of the public defenders shall be borne by the State.

(c) (1) The clerk of superior court is authorized to make a determination of indigency and entitlement to counsel, as authorized by this Article. The word "court," as it is used in this Article and in any rules pursuant to this Article, includes the clerk of superior court.

(2) A judge of superior or district court having authority to determine entitlement to counsel in a particular case may give directions to the clerk with regard to the

determination of entitlement to counsel in that case; may, if he finds it appropriate, change or modify the determination made by the clerk; and may set aside a finding of waiver of counsel made by the clerk.

(d) Unless a public defender or assistant public defender is appointed to serve, standby counsel appointed under G.S. 15A-1243 shall receive reasonable compensation to be paid by the State.

(e) In cases in which an indigent person has entered notice of appeal and appellate counsel has been appointed by the Office of Indigent Defense Services, the clerk of superior court shall make a copy of the complete trial division file in the case, make a copy of documentary exhibits upon request, and furnish those files and any requested documentary exhibits to the appointed attorney.

History.

1969, c. 1013, s. 1; 1971, c. 377, s. 32; 1973, c. 1286, s. 8; 1977, c. 711, s. 9; 1987 (Reg. Sess., 1988), c. 1037, s. 29; 2000-144, s. 7; 2005-148, s. 1

§ 7A-453. Duty of custodian of a possibly indigent person; determination of indigency

(a) In counties designated by the Office of Indigent Defense Services, the authority having custody of a person who is without counsel for more than 48 hours after being taken into custody shall so inform the designee of the Office of Indigent Defense Services. The designee of the Office of Indigent Defense Services shall make a preliminary determination as to the person's entitlement to his services, and proceed accordingly. The court shall make the final determination.

(b) In counties that have not been designated by the Office of Indigent Defense Services, the authority having custody of a person who is without counsel for more than 48 hours after being taken into custody shall so inform the clerk of superior court.

(c) In any county, if a defendant, upon being taken into custody, states that he is indigent and desires counsel, the authority having custody shall immediately inform the designee of the Office of Indigent Defense Services or the clerk of superior court, as the case may be, who shall take action as provided in this Article.

(d) The duties imposed by this section upon authorities having custody of persons who may be indigent are in addition to the duties imposed upon arresting officers under G.S. 15-47.

History.

1969, c. 1013, s. 1; 1973, c. 1286, s. 8; 1987 (Reg. Sess., 1988), c. 1037, s. 30; 2000-144, s. 8

§ 7A-454. Supporting services

Fees for the services of an expert witness or other witnesses, paid in accordance with G.S. 7A-314, including travel expenses, lodging, and other appearance expenses, for an indigent person and other necessary expenses of counsel shall be paid by the State in accordance with rules adopted by the Office of Indigent Defense Services.

History.
1969, c. 1013, s. 1; 2000-144, s. 9; 2011-145, s. 31.23C(b); 2011-391, s. 64

§ 7A-455. Partial indigency; liens; acquittals

(a) If, in the opinion of the court, an indigent person is financially able to pay a portion, but not all, of the value of the legal services rendered for that person by assigned counsel, the public defender, or the appellate defender, and other necessary expenses of representation, the court shall order the partially indigent person to pay such portion to the clerk of superior court for transmission to the State treasury.

(b) In all cases the court shall direct that a judgment be entered in the office of the clerk of superior court for the money value of services rendered by assigned counsel, the public defender, or the appellate defender, plus any sums allowed for other necessary expenses of representing the indigent person, including any fees and expenses that may have been allowed prior to final determination of the action to assigned counsel pursuant to G.S. 7A-458, which shall constitute a lien as prescribed by the general law of the State applicable to judgments. Any reimbursement to the State as provided in subsection (a) of this section or any funds collected by reason of such judgment shall be deposited in the State treasury and credited against the judgment. The value of services shall be determined in accordance with rules adopted by the Office of Indigent Defense Services. The money value of services rendered by the public defender and the appellate defender shall be based upon the factors normally involved in fixing the fees of private attorneys, such as the nature of the case, the time, effort, and responsibility involved, and the fee usually charged in similar cases. A district court judge shall direct entry of judgment for actions or proceedings finally determined in the district court and a superior court judge shall direct entry of judgment for actions or proceedings originating in, heard on appeal in, or appealed from the superior court. Even if the trial, appeal, hearing, or other proceeding is never held, preparation therefor is nevertheless compensable.

(b1) In every case in which the State is entitled to a lien pursuant to this section, the public defender shall at the time of sentencing or other conclusion of the proceedings petition the court to enter judgment for the value of the legal services rendered by the public defender, and the appellate defender shall upon completion of the appeal petition or request the trial court to enter judgment for the value of the legal services rendered by the appellate defender.

(c) No order for partial payment under subsection (a) of this section and no judgment under subsection (b) of this section shall be entered unless the indigent person is convicted. If the indigent person is convicted, the order or judgment shall become effective and the judgment shall be docketed and indexed pursuant to G.S. 1-233 et seq., in the amount then owing, upon the later of (i) the date upon which the conviction becomes final if the indigent person is not ordered, as a condition of probation, to pay the State of North Carolina for the costs of his representation in the case or (ii) the date upon which the indigent person's probation is terminated, is revoked, or expires if the indigent person is so ordered. No order for partial payment under subsection (a) of this section and no judgment under subsection (b) of this section shall be entered for the value of legal services rendered to perfect an appeal to the Appellate Division or in postconviction proceedings, if all of the matters that the person raised in the proceeding are vacated, reversed, or remanded for a new trial or resentencing.

(d) In all cases in which the entry of a judgment is authorized under G.S. 7A-450.1 through G.S. 7A-450.4 or under this section, the attorney, guardian ad litem, public defender, or appellate defender who rendered the services or incurred the expenses for which the judgment is to be entered shall make reasonable efforts to obtain the social security number, if any, of each person against whom judgment is to be entered. This number, a certification that the person has no social security number, or a certification that the social security number cannot be obtained with reasonable efforts shall be included in each fee application submitted by an assigned attorney, guardian ad litem, public defender, or appellate defender, and no order for payment entered upon an application which does not include the required social security number or certification shall be valid to authorize payment to the applicant from the Indigent Persons' Attorney Fee Fund. Each judgment docketed against any person under this section or under G.S. 7A-450.3 shall include the social security number, if any, of the judgment debtor.

History.
1969, c. 1013, s. 1; 1983, c. 135, s. 2; 1983 (Reg. Sess., 1984), c. 1109, s. 12; 1985, c. 474, s. 9; 1989 (Reg. Sess., 1990), c. 946, ss. 5, 6; 1991, c. 761, s. 4; 1991 (Reg.

Sess., 1992), c. 900, s. 116(a); 2000-144, s. 10; 2005-254, s. 1; 2013-41, s. 1

§ 7A-455.1. Appointment fee in criminal cases

(a) In every criminal case in which counsel is appointed at the trial level, the judge shall order the defendant to pay to the clerk of court an appointment fee of seventy-five dollars ($ 75.00). No fee shall be due unless the person is convicted.

(b) The mandatory seventy-five dollar ($ 75.00) fee may not be remitted or revoked by the court and shall be added to any amounts the court determines to be owed for the value of legal services rendered to the defendant and shall be collected in the same manner as attorneys' fees are collected for such representation.

(c) Repealed by Session Laws 2005-250 s. 3, effective August 4, 2005.

(d) Inability, failure, or refusal to pay the appointment fee shall not be grounds for denying appointment of counsel, for withdrawal of counsel, or for contempt.

(e) The appointment fee required by this section shall be assessed only once for each attorney appointment, regardless of the number of cases to which the attorney was assigned. An additional appointment fee shall not be assessed if the charges for which an attorney was appointed were reassigned to a different attorney.

(f) Of each appointment fee collected under this section, the sum of seventy dollars ($ 70.00) shall be credited to the Indigent Persons' Attorney Fee Fund and the sum of five dollars ($ 5.00) shall be credited to the Court Information Technology Fund under G.S. 7A-343.2. These fees shall not revert.

(g) The Office of Indigent Defense Services shall adopt rules and develop forms to govern implementation of this section.

History.
2002-126, s. 29A.9(a); 2003-284, s. 13.11; 2005-250, s. 3; 2009-451, s. 15.17I(a); 2010-31, s. 15.11(a); 2012-142, s. 16.5(h); 2020-83, s. 10.1(a)

§ 7A-456. False statements; penalty

(a) A false material statement made by a person under oath or affirmation in regard to the question of his indigency constitutes a Class I felony.

(b) A judicial official making the determination of indigency shall notify the person of the provisions of subsection (a) of this section.

(c) Repealed by Session Laws 1987 (Reg. Sess., 1988), c. 1100, s. 11.1.

History.
1969, c. 1013, s. 1; 1987 (Reg. Sess., 1988), c. 1086, s. 113(c); c. 1100, s. 11.1; 1993 (Reg. Sess., 1994), c. 767, s. 19

§ 7A-457. Waiver of counsel; pleas of guilty

(a) An indigent person who has been informed of his right to be represented by counsel at any in-court proceeding, may, in writing, waive the right to in-court representation by counsel in accordance with rules adopted by the Office of Indigent Defense Services. Any waiver of counsel shall be effective only if the court finds of record that at the time of waiver the indigent person acted with full awareness of his rights and of the consequences of the waiver. In making such a finding, the court shall consider, among other things, such matters as the person's age, education, familiarity with the English language, mental condition, and the complexity of the crime charged.

(b) If an indigent person waives counsel as provided in subsection (a), and pleads guilty to any offense, the court shall inform him of the nature of the offense and the possible consequences of his plea, and as a condition of accepting the plea of guilty the court shall examine the person and shall ascertain that the plea was freely, understandably and voluntarily made, without undue influence, compulsion or duress, and without promise of leniency.

(c) An indigent person who has been informed of his right to be represented by counsel at any out-of-court proceeding, may, either orally or in writing, waive the right to out-of-court representation by counsel.

History.
1969, c. 1013, s. 1; 1971, c. 1243; 1973, c. 151, s. 3; 2000-144, s. 11

§ 7A-458. Counsel fees

The fee to which an attorney who represents an indigent person is entitled shall be fixed in accordance with rules adopted by the Office of Indigent Defense Services. Fees shall be based on the factors normally considered in fixing attorneys' fees, such as the nature of the case, and the time, effort and responsibility involved. Fees shall not be set or ordered at rates higher than those established by the rules adopted under this section without the approval of the Office of Indigent Defense Services. Even if the trial, appeal, hearing or other proceeding is never held, preparation therefor is nevertheless compensable and, in capital cases and other extraordinary cases pending in superior court, a fee for services rendered and payment for expenses incurred may be allowed pending final determination of the case.

History.
1969, c. 1013, s. 1; 1987 (Reg. Sess., 1988), c. 1086, s. 113(b); 1991 (Reg. Sess., 1992), c. 900, s. 116(b); 2000-144, s. 12; 2005-276, s. 14.13

N.C. Gen. Stat. § 7A-459

Repealed by Session Laws 2000-144, s. 13, as amended by Session Laws 2001-424, s. 22.11(c), effective July 1, 2001.

ARTICLE 37
THE PUBLIC DEFENDER

§§ 7A-465 through 7A-467

Repealed by Session Laws 2000-144, s. 13, as amended by Session Laws 2001-424, s. 22.11(c), effective July 1, 2001.

N.C. Gen. Stat. § 7A-468

Repealed by Session Laws 1987 (Regular Session, 1988), c. 1056, s. 13.

§§ 7A-469 through 7A-471

Repealed by Session Laws 2000-144, s. 13, as amended by Session Laws 2001-424, s. 22.11(c), effective July 1, 2001.

ARTICLE 37A
ACCESS TO CIVIL JUSTICE ACT

§§ 7A-474.1 through 7A-474.5

Repealed by Session Laws 2017-57, s. 18B.10(c), effective June 28, 2017.

History.
G.S. 7A-474.1: 1989, c. 795, s. 25; 2001-424, s. 22.14(e); 2007-323, s. 30.8(g); repealed by 2017-57, s. 18B.10(c), effective June 28, 2017. G.S. 7A-474.2: 1989, c. 795, s. 25; 2001-424, s. 22.14(f); 2007-323, s. 30.8(h); 2007-547, s. 9; 2008-194, s. 3(a); repealed by 2017-57, s. 18B.10(c), effective June 28, 2017. G.S. 7A-474.3: 1989, c. 795, s. 25; 1997-506, s. 29; 2007-547, s. 10; 2008-107, s. 14.9; 2011-145, s. 19.1(h); 2012-83, s. 15; repealed by 2017-57, s. 18B.10(c), effective June 28, 2017. G.S. 7A-474.4: 1989, c. 795, s. 25; 2001-424, s. 22.14(g); 2007-323, s. 30.8(i); 2008-194, s. 3(b); repealed by 2017-57, s. 18B.10(c), effective June 28, 2017. G.S. 7A-474.5: 1989, c. 795, s. 25; 2001-424, s. 22.14(h); 2007-323, s. 30.8(j); repealed by 2017-57, s. 18B.10(c), effective June 28, 2017

ARTICLE 38A
APPELLATE DEFENDER OFFICE

§§ 7A-486 through 7A-486.7

Repealed by Session Laws 2000-144, s. 13, as amended by Session Laws 2001-424, s. 22.11(c), effective July 1, 2001.

ARTICLE 39
GUARDIAN AD LITEM PROGRAM

§§ 7A-489 through 7A-493

Repealed by Session Laws 1998-202, s. 5, effective July 1, 1999.

ARTICLE 39A
CUSTODY AND VISITATION MEDIATION PROGRAM

§ 7A-494. Custody and Visitation Mediation Program established

(a) The Administrative Office of the Courts shall establish a Custody and Visitation Mediation Program to provide statewide and uniform services in accordance with G.S. 50-13.1 in cases involving unresolved issues about the custody or visitation of minor children. The Director of the Administrative Office of the Courts shall appoint such AOC staff support required for planning, organizing, and administering such program on a statewide basis.

The purposes of the Custody and Visitation Mediation Program shall be to provide the services of skilled mediators to further the goals expressed in G.S. 50-13.1(b).

(b) Beginning on July 1, 1989, the Administrative Office of the Courts shall establish in phases a statewide custody mediation program comprised of local district programs to be established in all judicial districts of the State. Each local district program shall consist of: a qualified mediator or mediators to provide mediation services; and such clerical staff as the Administrative Office of the Courts in consultation with the local district program deems necessary. Such personnel, to be employed by the Chief District Court Judge of the district, may serve as full-time or part-time State employees or, in the alternative, such activities may be provided on a contractual basis when determined appropriate by the Administrative Office of the Courts.

The Administrative Office of the Courts may authorize all or part of a program in one judicial district to be operated in conjunction with that of another district or districts. The Director of the Administrative Office of the Courts is authorized to approve contractual agreements for such services as executed by order of the Chief District Court Judge of a district court district; such contracts to be exempt from competitive bidding procedures under Chapter 143 of the General Statutes. The Administrative Office of the Courts shall promulgate rules and regulations necessary and appropriate for the administration of the program. Funds appropriated by the General Assembly for the establishment and maintenance of mediation programs under this Article shall be administered by the Administrative Office of the Courts.

(c) For a person to qualify to provide mediation services under this Article, that person shall show that he or she:

(1) Has at minimum a master's degree in psychology, social work, family counselling, or a comparable human relations discipline; and

(2) Has at least 40 hours of training in mediation techniques by a qualified instructor of mediation as determined by the Administrative Office of the Courts; and

(3) Has had professional training and experience relating to child development, family dynamics, or comparable areas; and

(4) Meets such other criteria as may be specified by the Administrative Office of the Courts.

History.
1989, c. 795, s. 15

§ 7A-495. Implementation and administration

(a) **Local District Program.** -- The Administrative Office of the Courts shall, in cooperation with each Chief District Court Judge and other district personnel, implement and administer the program mandated by this Article.

(b) **Advisory Committee Established.** -- The Director of the Administrative Office of the Courts shall appoint a Custody Mediation Advisory Committee consisting of at least five members to advise the Custody Mediation Program. The members of the Advisory Committee shall receive the same per diem and reimbursement for travel expenses as members of State boards and commissions generally.

History.
1989, c. 795, s. 15

ARTICLE 39B
INDIGENT DEFENSE SERVICES ACT

§ 7A-498. Title

This Article shall be known and may be cited as the "Indigent Defense Services Act of 2000".

History.
2000-144, s. 1

§ 7A-498.1. Purpose

Whenever a person is determined to be indigent and entitled to counsel, it is the responsibility of the State under the federal and state constitutions to provide that person with counsel and the other necessary expenses of representation. The purpose of this Article is to:

(1) Enhance oversight of the delivery of counsel and related services provided at State expense;

(2) Improve the quality of representation and ensure the independence of counsel;

(3) Establish uniform policies and procedures for the delivery of services;

(4) Generate reliable statistical information in order to evaluate the services provided and funds expended; and

(5) Deliver services in the most efficient and cost-effective manner without sacrificing quality representation.

History.
2000-144, s. 1

§ 7A-498.2. Establishment of Office of Indigent Defense Services

(a) The Office of Indigent Defense Services, which is administered by the Director of Indigent Defense Services and includes the Commission on Indigent Defense Services and the Sentencing Services Program established in Article 61 of this Chapter, is created within the Administrative Office of the Courts. As used in this Article, "Office" means the Office of Indigent Defense Services, "Director" means the Director of Indigent Defense Services, and "Commission" means the Commission on Indigent Defense Services.

(b) Except as provided otherwise by this section, the Office of Indigent Defense Services may exercise its prescribed powers independently of the head of the Administrative Office of the Courts. The Office may enter into contracts, own property, and accept funds, grants, and gifts from any public or private source to pay expenses incident to implementing its purposes.

(c) The Director of the Administrative Office of the Courts shall provide general administrative support to the Office of Indigent Defense Services. The term "general administrative support" includes purchasing, payroll, and similar administrative services.

(d) The budget of the Office of Indigent Defense Services shall be a part of the budget of the Administrative Office of the Courts. The Administrative Office of the Courts shall conduct an annual audit of the budget of the Office of Indigent Defense Services.

(e) The Director of the Administrative Office of the Courts may modify the budget of the Office of Indigent Defense Services and may use funds appropriated to the Office without the approval of the Commission or the Office of Indigent Defense Services.

History.
2000-144, s. 1; 2002-126, s. 14.7(b); 2015-241, s. 18A.17(b)

§ 7A-498.3. Responsibilities of Office of Indigent Defense Services

(a) The Office of Indigent Defense Services shall be responsible for establishing, supervising, and maintaining a system for providing legal representation and related services in the following cases:

(1) Cases in which an indigent person is subject to a deprivation of liberty or other constitutionally protected interest and is entitled by law to legal representation;

(2) Cases in which an indigent person is entitled to legal representation under G.S. 7A-451 and G.S. 7A-451.1;

(2a) Cases in which the State is legally obligated to provide legal assistance and access to the courts to inmates in the custody of the Division of Adult Correction and Juvenile Justice of the Department of Public Safety; and

(3) Any other cases in which the Office of Indigent Defense Services is designated by statute as responsible for providing legal representation.

(b) The Office of Indigent Defense Services shall develop policies and procedures for determining indigency in cases subject to this Article, and those policies shall be applied uniformly throughout the State. Except in cases under subdivision (2a) of subsection (a) of this section, the court shall determine in each case whether a person is indigent and entitled to legal representation, and counsel shall be appointed as provided in G.S. 7A-452.

(b1) The Office of Indigent Defense Services shall develop a model appointment plan with minimum qualification standards for appointed private counsel by July 1, 2019, for adoption and promulgation by each judicial district. Judicial districts may request modifications to the model plan and qualification standards. If a judicial district has not adopted an appointment plan with the Indigent Defense Services' minimum qualification standards by January 2, 2021, the model plan and qualification standards developed by Indigent Defense Services will become effective on that date in that judicial district. Indigent Defense Services shall review the model plan and qualification standards every five years and, in the event it modifies the model plan and/or qualification standards, shall notify the judicial districts of the change. Judicial districts will have 18 months from the date Indigent Defense Services gives notice of a change to seek modifications to the revised model plan or to the qualification standards.

(c) In all cases subject to this Article, appointment of counsel, determination of compensation, appointment of experts, and use of funds for experts and other services related to legal representation shall be in accordance with rules and procedures adopted by the Office of Indigent Defense Services.

(d) The Office of Indigent Defense Services shall allocate and disburse funds appropriated for legal representation and related services in cases subject to this Article pursuant to rules and procedures established by the Office.

History.
2000-144, s. 1; 2005-276, s. 14.9(a); 2011-145, s. 19.1(h); 2017-186, s. 2(i); 2018-40, s. 6

§ 7A-498.4. Establishment of Commission on Indigent Defense Services

(a) The Commission on Indigent Defense Services is created within the Office of Indigent Defense Services and shall consist of 13 members. To create an effective working group, assure continuity, and achieve staggered terms, the Commission shall be appointed as provided in this section.

(b) The members of the Commission shall be appointed as follows:

(1) The Chief Justice of the North Carolina Supreme Court shall appoint one member, who shall be an active or former member of the North Carolina judiciary.

(2) The Governor shall appoint one member, who shall be a nonattorney.

(3) The General Assembly shall appoint one member, who shall be an attorney, upon the recommendation of the President Pro Tempore of the Senate.

(4) The General Assembly shall appoint one member, who shall be an attorney, upon

the recommendation of the Speaker of the House of Representatives.

(5) The North Carolina Public Defenders Association shall appoint member, who shall be an attorney.

(6) The North Carolina StateBar shall appoint one member, who shall be an attorney.

(7) The North Carolina Bar Association shall appoint one member, who shall be an attorney.

(8) The North Carolina Academy of Trial Lawyers shall appoint one member, who shall be an attorney.

(9) The North Carolina Association of Black Lawyers shall appoint one member, who shall be an attorney.

(10) The North Carolina Association of Women Lawyers shall appoint one member, who shall be an attorney.

(11) The Commission shall appoint three members, who shall reside in different judicial districts from one another. One appointee shall be a nonattorney, and one appointee may be an active member of the North Carolina judiciary. One appointee shall be Native American. The initial three members satisfying this subdivision shall be appointed as provided in subsection (k) of this section.

(c) The terms of members appointed pursuant to subsection (b) of this section shall be as follows:

(1) The initial appointments by the Chief Justice, the Governor, and the General Assembly shall be for four years.

(2) The initial appointments by the Public Defenders Association and State Bar, and one appointment by the Commission, shall be for three years.

(3) The initial appointments by the Bar Association and Trial Academy, and one appointment by the Commission, shall be for two years.

(4) The initial appointments by the Black Lawyers Association and Women Lawyers Association, and one appointment by the Commission, shall be for one year.

At the expiration of these initial terms, appointments shall be for four years and shall be made by the appointing authorities designated in subsection (b) of this section. No person shall serve more than two consecutive four-year terms plus any initial term of less than four years.

(d) Persons appointed to the Commission shall have significant experience in the defense of criminal or other cases subject to this Article or shall have demonstrated a strong commitment to quality representation in indigent defense matters. No active prosecutors or law enforcement officials, or active employees of such persons, may be appointed to or serve on the Commission. No active judicial officials, or active employees of such persons, may be appointed to or serve on the Commission, except as provided in subsection (b) of this section. No active public defenders, active employees of public defenders, or other active employees of the Office of Indigent Defense Services may be appointed to or serve on the Commission, except that notwithstanding this subsection, G.S. 14-234, or any other provision of law, Commission members may include part-time public defenders employed by the Office of Indigent Defense Services and may include persons, or employees of persons or organizations, who provide legal services subject to this Article as contractors or appointed attorneys.

(e) All members of the Commission are entitled to vote on any matters coming before the Commission unless otherwise provided by rules adopted by the Commission concerning voting on matters in which a member has, or appears to have, a financial or other personal interest.

(f) Each member of the Commission shall serve until a successor in office has been appointed. Vacancies shall be filled by appointment by the appointing authority for the unexpired term. Removal of Commission members shall be in accordance with policies and procedures adopted by the Commission.

(g) A quorum for purposes of conducting Commission business shall be a majority of the members of the Commission.

(h) The Commission shall elect a Commission chair from the members of the Commission for a term of two years.

(i) The Director of Indigent Defense Services shall attend all Commission meetings except those relating to removal or reappointment of the Director or allegations of misconduct by the Director. The Director shall not vote on any matter decided by the Commission.

(j) Commission members shall not receive compensation but are entitled to be paid necessary subsistence and travel expenses in accordance with G.S. 138-5 and G.S. 138-6 as applicable.

(k) The Commission shall hold its first meeting no later than September 15, 2000. All appointments to the Commission specified in subdivisions (1) through (10) of subsection (b) of this section shall be made by the appointing authorities by September 1, 2000. The appointee of the Chief Justice shall convene the first meeting. No later than 30 days after its first meeting, the Commission shall make the appointments specified in subdivision (11) of subsection (b) of this section and shall elect its chair.

History.
2000-144, s. 1; 2001-424, s. 22.11(b)

§ 7A-498.5. Responsibilities of Commission

(a) The Commission shall have as its principal purpose the development and improvement of programs by which the Office of Indigent Defense Services provides legal representation to indigent persons.

(b) The Commission shall appoint the Director of the Office of Indigent Defense Services, who shall be chosen on the basis of training, experience, and other qualifications. The Commission shall consult with the Chief Justice and Director of the Administrative Office of the Courts in selecting a Director, but shall have final authority in making the appointment.

(c) The Commission shall develop standards governing the provision of services under this Article. The standards shall include:

(1) Standards for maintaining and operating regional and district public defender offices and appellate defender offices, including requirements regarding qualifications, training, and size of the legal and supporting staff;

(2) Standards prescribing minimum experience, training, and other qualifications for appointed counsel;

(3) Standards for public defender and appointed counsel caseloads;

(4) Standards for the performance of public defenders and appointed counsel;

(5) Standards for the independent, competent, and efficient representation of clients whose cases present conflicts of interest, in both the trial and appellate courts;

(6) Standards for providing and compensating experts and others who provide services related to legal representation;

(7) Standards for qualifications and performance in capital cases, consistent with any rules adopted by the Supreme Court; and

(8) Standards for determining indigency and for assessing and collecting the costs of legal representation and related services.

(d) The Commission shall determine the methods for delivering legal services to indigent persons eligible for legal representation under this Article and shall establish in each district or combination of districts a system of appointed counsel, contract counsel, part-time public defenders, public defender offices, appellate defender services, and other methods for delivering counsel services, or any combination of these services.

(e) In determining the method of services to be provided in a particular district, the Director shall consult with the district bar as defined in G.S. 84-19 and the judges of the district or districts under consideration. The Commission shall adopt procedures ensuring that affected local bars have the opportunity to be significantly involved in determining the method or methods for delivering services in their districts. The Commission shall solicit written comments from the affected local district bar, senior resident superior court judge, and chief district court judge. Those comments, along with the recommendations of the Commission, shall be forwarded to the members of the General Assembly who represent the affected district and to other interested parties.

(f) Subject to G.S. 7A-498.2(e) the Commission shall establish policies and procedures with respect to the distribution of funds appropriated under this Article, including rates of compensation for appointed counsel, schedules of allowable expenses, appointment and compensation of expert witnesses, and procedures for applying for and receiving compensation. The rate of compensation set for expert witnesses may be no greater than the rate set by the Administrative Office of the Courts under G.S. 7A-314(d).

(g) Repealed by Session Laws 2015-241, s. 18A.17(c), effective July 1, 2015.

(h) The Commission shall adopt such other rules and procedures as it deems necessary for the conduct of business by the Commission and the Office of Indigent Defense Services.

History.
2000-144, s. 1; 2001-392, s. 2; 2011-145, s. 15.20; 2015-241, s. 18A.17(c); 2015-268, s. 6.3

§ 7A-498.6. Director of Indigent Defense Services

(a) The Director of Indigent Defense Services shall be appointed by the Commission for a term of four years. The salary of the Director shall be set by the General Assembly in the Current Operations Appropriations Act, after consultation with the Commission. The Director may be removed during this term in the discretion of the Commission by a vote of two-thirds of all of the Commission members. The Director shall be an attorney licensed and eligible to practice in the courts of this State at the time of appointment and at all times during service as the Director.

(b) The Director shall:

(1) Prepare and submit to the Commission a proposed budget for the Office of Indigent Defense Services, an annual report containing pertinent data on the operations, costs, and needs of the Office, and such other information as the Commission may require;

(2) Assist the Commission in developing rules and standards for the delivery of services under this Article;

(3) Administer and coordinate the operations of the Office and supervise compliance with standards adopted by the Commission;

(4) Subject to policies and procedures established by the Commission, hire such professional, technical, and support personnel as deemed reasonably necessary for the efficient operation of the Office of Indigent Defense Services;

(5) Keep and maintain proper financial records for use in calculating the costs of the operations of the Office of Indigent Defense Services;

(6) Apply for and accept on behalf of the Office of Indigent Defense Services any funds that may become available from government grants, private gifts, donations, or devises from any source;

(6a) Collaborate with the Director of the Administrative Office of the Courts in developing administrative procedures pursuant to G.S. 105A-8(b);

(7) Coordinate the services of the Office of Indigent Defense Services with any federal, county, or private programs established to provide assistance to indigent persons in cases subject to this Article and consult with professional bodies concerning improving the administration of indigent services;

(8) Conduct training programs for attorneys and others involved in the legal representation of persons subject to this Article;

(8a) Administer the Sentencing Services Program established in Article 61 of this Chapter; and

(9) Perform other duties as the Commission may assign.

(c) In lieu of merit and other increment raises paid to regular State employees, the Director of Indigent Defense Services shall receive as longevity pay an amount equal to four and eight-tenths percent (4.8%) of the annual salary set forth in the Current Operations Appropriations Act payable monthly after five years of service, nine and six-tenths percent (9.6%) after 10 years of service, fourteen and four-tenths percent (14.4%) after 15 years of service, nineteen and two-tenths percent (19.2%) after 20 years of service, and twenty-four percent (24%) after 25 years of service. "Service" means service as Director of Indigent Defense Services, a public defender, appellate defender, assistant public or appellate defender, district attorney, assistant district attorney, justice or judge of the General Court of Justice, or clerk of superior court.

History.
2000-144, s. 1; 2002-126, s. 14.7(c); 2008-107, ss. 26.4(b), (c); 2011-284, s. 7; 2019-243, s. 10(c)

§ 7A-498.7. Public Defender Offices

(a) The following counties of the State are organized into the defender districts listed below,

and in each of those defender districts an office of public defender is established:

Defender District	Counties
1	Camden, Chowan, Currituck,Dare, Gates, Pasquotank, Perquimans
3A	Pitt
3B	Craven, Pamlico, Carteret
5	New Hanover
10	Wake
12	Cumberland
14	Durham
15B	Orange, Chatham
16A	Scotland, Hoke
16B	Robeson
18	Guilford
21	Forsyth
26	Mecklenburg
27A	Gaston
28	Buncombe
29A	McDowell, Rutherford
29B	Henderson, Polk,Transylvania

After notice to, and consultation with, the affected district bar, senior resident superior court judge, and chief district court judge, the Commission on Indigent Defense Services may recommend to the General Assembly that a district or regional public defender office be established. A legislative act is required in order to establish a new office or to abolish an existing office.

(b) For each new term, and to fill any vacancy, public defenders shall be appointed from a list of not less than three and not more than four names nominated as follows:

(1) Not less than two and not more than three by written ballot of the attorneys resident in the defender district who are licensed to practice law in North Carolina. The balloting shall be conducted pursuant to rules adopted by the Commission on Indigent Defense Services.

(2) One name submitted by the Administrative Officer of the Courts after consultation with the Director of the Office of Indigent Defense Services.

(b1) The appointment required under subsection (b) of this section shall be made by the senior resident superior court judge of the superior court district or set of districts as defined in G.S. 7A-41.1 that includes the county or counties of the defender district for which the public defender is being appointed.

(c) A public defender shall be an attorney licensed to practice law in North Carolina and shall devote full time to the duties of the office. In lieu of merit and other increment raises paid to regular State employees, a public defender shall receive as longevity pay an amount equal to four and eight-tenths percent (4.8%) of the annual salary set forth in the Current Operations Appropriations Act payable monthly after five years of service, nine and six-tenths percent (9.6%) after 10 years of service, fourteen and four-tenths percent (14.4%) after 15 years of service, nineteen and two-tenths percent (19.2%) after 20 years of service, and twenty-four percent (24%) after 25 years of service. "Service" means service as a public defender, appellate defender, assistant public or appellate defender, district attorney, assistant district attorney, justice or judge of the General Court of Justice, or clerk of superior court.

(c1) When traveling on official business, each public defender and assistant public defender is entitled to reimbursement for his or her subsistence expenses to the same extent as State employees generally. When traveling on official business outside his or her county of residence, each public defender and assistant public defender is entitled to reimbursement for travel expenses to the same extent as State employees generally. For purposes of this subsection, the term "official business" does not include regular, daily commuting between a person's home and the public defender's office. Travel distances, for purposes of reimbursement for mileage, shall be determined according to the travel policy of the Administrative Office of the Courts.

(d) Subject to standards adopted by the Commission, the day-to-day operation and administration of public defender offices shall be the responsibility of the public defender in charge of the office. The public defender shall keep appropriate records and make periodic reports, as requested, to the Director of the Office of Indigent Defense Services on matters related to the operation of the office.

(e) The Office of Indigent Defense Services shall procure office equipment and supplies for the public defender, and provide secretarial and library support from State funds appropriated to the public defender's office for this purpose.

(f) Each public defender is entitled to assistant public defenders, investigators, and other staff, full-time or part-time, as may be authorized by the Commission. Assistants, investigators, and other staff are appointed by the public defender and serve at the pleasure of the public defender. Average and minimum compensation of assistants shall be as provided in the biennial Current Operations Appropriations Act. The actual salaries of assistants shall be set by the public defender in charge of the office, subject to approval by the Commission. The Commission shall fix the compensation of investigators. Assistants and investigators shall perform such duties as may be assigned by the public defender.

(f1) In cases in which a public defender determines that a conflict of interest exists in the office, whenever practical, rather than obtaining private assigned counsel to resolve the conflict, the public defender may request the appointment of an assistant public defender from another office of public defender in the region to resolve the conflict.

(g) In lieu of merit and other increment raises paid to regular State employees, an assistant public defender shall receive as longevity pay an amount equal to four and eight-tenths percent (4.8%) of the annual salary set forth in the Current Operations Appropriations Act payable monthly after five years of service, nine and six-tenths percent (9.6%) after 10 years of service, fourteen and four-tenths percent (14.4%) after 15 years of service, nineteen and two-tenths percent (19.2%) after 20 years of service, and twenty-four percent (24%) after 25 years of service. "Service" means service as a public defender, appellate defender, assistant public or appellate defender, district attorney, assistant district attorney, justice or judge of the General Court of Justice, or clerk of superior court.

(h) The term of office of public defender appointed under this section is four years. A public defender or assistant public defender may be suspended or removed from office, and reinstated, for the same causes and under the same procedures as are applicable to removal of a district attorney.

(i) A public defender may apply to the Director of the Office of Indigent Defense Services to enter into contracts with local governments for the provision by the State of services of temporary assistant public defenders pursuant to G.S. 153A-212.1 or G.S. 160A-289.1.

(j) The Director of the Office of Indigent Defense Services may provide assistance requested pursuant to subsection (i) of this section only upon a showing by the requesting public defender, supported by facts, that the overwhelming public interest warrants the use of additional resources for the speedy disposition of cases involving drug offenses, domestic violence, or other offenses involving a threat to public safety.

(k) The terms of any contract entered into with local governments pursuant to subsection (i) of this section shall be fixed by the Director of the Office of Indigent Defense Services in each case. Nothing in this section shall be construed to obligate the General Assembly to make any appropriation to implement the provisions of this section or to obligate the Office of Indigent Defense Services to provide the administrative costs of establishing or maintaining the positions or services provided for under this section. Further, nothing in this section shall be construed to obligate the Office of Indigent Defense Services to maintain positions or services initially provided for under this section.

History.
2000-144, s. 1; 2001-424, ss. 22.11(a), 22.11(d); 2002-126, s. 14.11(a); 2003-284, ss. 30.19A(c), (d); 2004-124, ss. 14.4(a), (b); 2005-276, s. 14.14(a); 2005-345, s. 50A; 2007-323, ss. 14.4(b), (d), 28.18A(g); 2008-107, s. 14.4; 2009-451, s. 15.17B(c); 2010-96, s. 27; 2011-145, s. 15.16(b); 2013-360, ss. 18A.5(a), 18A.6(a); 2018-5, s. 18A.2(a)

§ 7A-498.8. Appellate Defender

(a) The appellate defender shall be appointed by the Commission on Indigent Defense Services for a term of four years. A vacancy in the office of appellate defender shall be filled by appointment of the Commission on Indigent Defense Services for the unexpired term. The appellate defender may be suspended or removed from office for cause by two-thirds vote of all the members of the Commission on Indigent Defense Services. The Commission shall provide the appellate defender with timely written notice of the alleged causes and an opportunity for hearing before the Commission prior to taking any final action to remove or suspend the appellate defender, and the appellate defender shall be given written notice of the Commission's decision. The appellate defender may obtain judicial review of suspension or removal by the Commission by filing a petition within 30 days of receiving notice of the decision with the Superior Court of Wake County. Review of the Commission's decision shall be heard on the record and not as a de novo review or trial de novo. The Commission shall adopt rules implementing this section.

(b) The appellate defender shall perform such duties as may be directed by the Office of Indigent Defense Services, including:

(1) Representing indigent persons subsequent to conviction in trial courts. The Office of Indigent Defense Services may, following consultation with the appellate defender and consistent with the resources available to the appellate defender to ensure quality criminal defense services by the appellate defender's office, assign appeals, or authorize the appellate defender to assign appeals, to a local public defender's office or to private assigned counsel.

(2) Maintaining a clearinghouse of materials and a repository of briefs prepared by the appellate defender to be made available to private counsel representing indigents in criminal cases.

(3) Providing continuing legal education training to assistant appellate defenders and to private counsel representing

indigents in criminal cases, including capital cases, as resources are available.

(4) Providing consulting services to attorneys representing defendants in capital cases.

(5) Recruiting qualified members of the private bar who are willing to provide representation in State and federal death penalty postconviction proceedings.

(6) In the appellate defender's discretion, serving as counsel of record for indigent defendants in capital cases in State court.

(6a) In the appellate defender's discretion, serving as counsel of record for indigent defendants in the United States Supreme Court pursuant to a petition for writ of certiorari of the decision on direct appeal by a court of the North Carolina Appellate Division.

(7) Undertaking other direct representation and consultation in capital cases pending in federal court only to the extent that such work is fully federally funded.

(c) The appellate defender shall appoint assistants and staff, not to exceed the number authorized by the Office of Indigent Defense Services. The assistants and staff shall serve at the pleasure of the appellate defender.

(d) Funds to operate the office of appellate defender, including office space, office equipment, supplies, postage, telephone, library, staff salaries, training, and travel, shall be provided by the Office of Indigent Defense Services from funds authorized by law. Salaries shall be set by the Office of Indigent Defense Services.

History.
2000-144, s. 1; 2007-323, s. 14.19(b); 2008-187, s. 3

§ 7A-498.9. Annual report on Office of Indigent Defense Services

The Office of Indigent Defense Services shall report to the Chairs of the Joint Legislative Oversight Committee on Justice and Public Safety and to the Chairs of the House of Representatives and Senate Committees on Justice and Public Safety by March 15 of each year on the following:

(1) The volume and cost of cases handled in each district by assigned counsel or public defenders;

(2) Actions taken by the Office to improve the cost-effectiveness and quality of indigent defense services, including the capital case program;

(3) Plans for changes in rules, standards, or regulations in the upcoming year; and

(4) Any recommended changes in law or funding procedures that would assist the Office in improving the management of funds expended for indigent defense

services, including any recommendations concerning the feasibility and desirability of establishing regional public defender offices.

History.
2014-100, s. 18B.1(j); 2015-241, s. 18B.1

SUBCHAPTER 11.
NORTH CAROLINA
JUVENILE CODE

ARTICLE 41
PURPOSE;
DEFINITIONS

§§ 7A-516 through 7A-522

Repealed by Session Laws 1998-202, s. 5 .

ARTICLE 42
JURISDICTION

§§ 7A-523 through 7A-529

Repealed by Session Laws 1998-202, s. 5 .

ARTICLE 43
SCREENING OF
DELINQUENCY AND
UNDISCIPLINED PETITIONS

§§ 7A-530 through 7A-541

Repealed by Session Laws 1998-202, s. 5 .

ARTICLE 44
SCREENING OF ABUSE AND
NEGLECT COMPLAINTS

§§ 7A-542 through 7A-557

Repealed by Session Laws 1998-202, s. 5 .

ARTICLE 45
VENUE; PETITION; SUMMONS

§§ 7A-558 through 7A-570

Repealed by Session Laws 1998-202, s. 5 .

ARTICLE 46
TEMPORARY
CUSTODY; SECURE AND
NONSECURE CUSTODY;
CUSTODY HEARINGS

§§ 7A-571 through 7A-577

Repealed by Session Laws 1998-202, s. 5 .

N.C. Gen. Stat. § 7A-577.1
Recodified as G.S. 7B-507.

§§ 7A-578 through 7A-583

Repealed by Session Laws 1998-202, s. 5 .

ARTICLE 47
BASIC RIGHTS

§§ 7A-584 through 7A-593

Repealed by Session Laws 1998-202, s. 5 .

ARTICLE 48
LAW-ENFORCEMENT
PROCEDURES IN
DELINQUENCY
PROCEEDINGS

§§ 7A-594 through 7A-607

Repealed by Session Laws 1998-202, s. 5 .

ARTICLE 49
TRANSFER TO
SUPERIOR COURT

§§ 7A-608 through 7A-617

Repealed by Session Laws 1998-202, s. 5 .

ARTICLE 50
DISCOVERY

§§ 7A-618 through 7A-626

Repealed by Session Laws 1998-202, s. 5 .

ARTICLE 51
HEARING PROCEDURES

§§ 7A-627 through 7A-645

Repealed by Session Laws 1998-202, s. 5 .

ARTICLE 52
DISPOSITIONS

§§ 7A-646 through 7A-657

Repealed by Session Laws 1998-202, s. 5 .

N.C. Gen. Stat. § 7A-657.1

Recodified as § 7B-907.

§§ 7A-658 through 7A-663

Repealed by Session Laws 1998-202, s. 5 .

ARTICLE 53
MODIFICATION AND ENFORCEMENT OF DISPOSITIONAL ORDERS; APPEALS

§§ 7A-664 through 7A-674

Repealed by Session Laws 1998-202, s. 5 .

ARTICLE 54
JUVENILE RECORDS AND SOCIAL REPORTS

§§ 7A-675 through 7A-683

Repealed by Session Laws 1998-202, s. 5 .

ARTICLE 55
INTERSTATE COMPACT ON JUVENILES

§§ 7A-684 through 7A-716

Repealed by Session Laws 1998-202, s. 5 .

ARTICLE 56
EMANCIPATION

§§ 7A-717 through 7A-731

Repealed by Session Laws 1998-202, s. 5 .

ARTICLE 57
JUDICIAL CONSENT FOR EMERGENCY SURGICAL OR MEDICAL TREATMENT

§§ 7A-732 through 7A-739

Repealed by Session Laws 1998-202, s. 5 .

ARTICLE 58
JUVENILE LAW STUDY COMMISSION

§§ 7A-740 through 7A-744

Repealed by Session Laws 1998-202, s. 5 .

SUBCHAPTER 13.
SENTENCING SERVICES PROGRAM

ARTICLE 61
SENTENCING SERVICES PROGRAM

§ 7A-770. Purpose

This Article shall be known and may be cited as the "Sentencing Services Act." The purpose of this Article is to establish a statewide sentencing services program that will provide the judicial system with information that will assist that system in imposing sentences that make the most effective use of available resources. In furtherance of this purpose, this Article provides for the following:

(1) Establishment of local programs that can provide judges and other court officials with information about local correctional programs that are appropriate for offenders who require a comprehensive sentencing plan that combines punishment, control, and rehabilitation services.

(2) Increased opportunities for certain felons to make restitution to victims of crime through financial reimbursement or community service.

(3) Local involvement in the development of sentencing services to assure that they are specifically designed to meet local needs.

(4) Effective use of available community corrections programs by advising judges and other court officials of the offenders most suited for a particular program.

History.
1983, c. 909, s. 1; 1991, c. 566, ss. 2, 3; 1999-306, s. 1

§ 7A-771. Definitions

As used in this Article:

(1) Recodified as subdivision (3b) by Session Laws 1999-306, s. 1, effective January 1, 2000.

(2) Recodified as subdivision (3a) by Session Laws 1999-306, s. 1, effective January 1, 2000.

(2a) "Director" means the Director of Indigent Defense Services.

(3) Repealed by Session Laws 1999-306, s. 1, effective January 1, 2000.

(3a) "Sentencing plan" means a plan presented in writing to the sentencing judge which provides a detailed assessment and description of the offender's background, including available information about past criminal activity, a matching of the specific offender's needs with available resources, and, if appropriate, the program's recommendations regarding an intermediate sentence.

(3b) "Sentencing services program" means an agency or State-run office within the superior court district which shall (i) prepare sentencing plans; (ii) arrange or contract with public and private agencies for necessary services for offenders; and (iii) assist offenders in initially obtaining services ordered as part of a sentence entered pursuant to a sentencing plan, if the assistance is not available otherwise.

(4) Repealed by Session Laws 1991, c. 566, s. 4.

(4a) "Superior court district" means a superior court district established by G.S. 7A-41 for those districts consisting of one or more entire counties, and otherwise means the applicable set of districts as that term is defined in G.S. 7A-41.1.

(5) Repealed by Session Laws 1999-306, s. 1, effective January 1, 2000.

History.
1983, c. 909, s. 1; 1989, c. 770, s. 58; 1991, c. 566, ss. 2, 4; 1993 (Reg. Sess., 1994), c. 767, s. 14; 1995, c. 324, s. 21.9(c); 1997-57, s. 5; 1999-306, s. 1; 2002-126, s. 14.7(d)

§ 7A-772. Allocation of funds

(a) The Director may award grants in accordance with the policies established by this Article and in accordance with any laws made for that purpose, including appropriations acts and provisions in appropriations acts, and adopt regulations for the implementation, operation, and monitoring of sentencing services programs. Sentencing services programs that are grantees shall use the funds exclusively to develop a sentencing services program that provides sentencing information to judges and other court officials. Grants shall be awarded by the Director to agencies whose comprehensive program plans promise best to meet the goals set forth herein. The Director shall consider the plan required by G.S. 7A-774 in making funding decisions. If a senior resident superior court judge has not formally endorsed the plan, the Director shall consider that fact in making grant decisions, but the Director may, if appropriate, award grants to a program in which the judge has not endorsed the plan as submitted.

(b) The Director may establish local sentencing services programs and appoint those staff as the Director deems necessary. These personnel may serve as full-time or part-time State employees or may be hired on a contractual basis when determined appropriate by the director. Contracts entered under the authority of this subsection shall be exempt from the competitive bidding procedures under Chapter 143 of the General Statutes. The Office of Indigent Defense Services shall adopt rules necessary and appropriate for the administration of the program. Funds appropriated by the General Assembly for the establishment and maintenance of sentencing services programs under this Article shall be administered by the Office of Indigent Defense Services.

History.
1983, c. 909, s. 1; 1991, c. 566, ss. 2, 5; 1995, c. 324, s. 21.9(d); 1999-306, s. 1; 2002-126, s. 14.7(e)

§ 7A-773. Responsibilities of a sentencing services program

A sentencing services program shall be responsible for:

(1) Identifying offenders who:

a. Are charged with or have been offered a plea by the State for a felony offense for which the class of offense and prior record level authorize the court to impose an active punishment, but do not require that it do so;

b. Have a high risk of committing future crimes without appropriate sanctions and interventions; and

c. Would benefit from the preparation of an intensive and comprehensive sentencing plan of the type prepared by sentencing services programs.

(2) Preparing detailed sentencing services plans requested pursuant to G.S. 7A-773.1 for presentation to the sentencing judge.

(3) Contracting or arranging with public or private agencies for services described in the sentencing plan.

(4) Repealed by Session Laws 1999-306, s. 1, effective January 1, 2000.

History.
1983, c. 909, s. 1; 1991, c. 566, s. 2; 1993 (Reg. Sess., 1994), c. 767, s. 15; 1995, c. 324, s. 21.9(e); 1999-306, s. 1

§ 7A-773.1. Who may request plans; disposition of plans; contents of plans

(a) A judge presiding over a case in which the offender meets the criteria set forth in G.S. 7A-773(1) may request, at any time prior to the imposition of sentence, that the sentencing services program provide a sentencing plan. The court may also request, at any time prior to the imposition of sentence, that the program provide a sentencing plan in misdemeanor cases in which the class of offense is Class A1 or Class 1 and the prior conviction level is Level III, if the court determines that the preparation of such a plan is in the interest of justice. In addition, in cases in which the offender meets the criteria set forth in G.S. 7A-773, the defendant or a prosecutor, at any time before the court has accepted a guilty plea or received a guilty verdict, may request that the program provide a plan. However, prior to an adjudication of guilt, a defendant may decline to participate in the preparation of a plan within a reasonable time after the request is made. In that case, no plan shall be prepared or presented to the court by the sentencing services program prior to an adjudication of guilt. A defendant's decision not to participate shall be made in writing and filed with the court. The comprehensive sentencing services program plan prepared pursuant to G.S. 7A-774 shall define what constitutes a reasonable time within the meaning of this subsection.

(b) Any sentencing plan prepared by a sentencing services program shall be presented to the court, the defendant, and the State in an appropriate manner.

(c) Sentencing plans prepared by sentencing services programs may include recommendations for use of any treatment or correctional resources available, unless the sentencing court instructs otherwise. Sentencing plans that identify an offender's needs for education, treatment, control, or other services shall, to the extent feasible, also identify resources to meet those needs. Plans may report that no intermediate punishment is appropriate under the circumstances of the case.

(d) To the extent allowed by law, the sentencing services program shall develop procedures to ensure that the program staff may work with offenders before a plea is entered. To that end, information obtained in the course of preparing a sentencing plan may not be used by the State for any purpose at trial and is subject to the provisions of G.S. 15A-1333.

History.
1999-306, s. 1; 2000-67, s. 15.9(b)

§ 7A-774. Requirements for a comprehensive sentencing services program plan

Agencies applying for grants shall prepare a comprehensive sentencing services program plan for the development, implementation, operation, and improvement of a sentencing services program for the superior court district, as prescribed by the Director. The plan shall be updated annually and shall be submitted to the senior resident superior court judge for the superior court district for the judge's advice and written endorsement. The plan shall then be forwarded to the Director for approval. The plan shall include:

(1) Goals and objectives of the sentencing services program.

(2) Specification of the kinds or categories of offenders for whom the programs will provide sentencing information to the courts.

(3) Proposed procedures for the identification of appropriate offenders to comply with the plan and the criteria in G.S. 7A-773(1).

(4) Procedures for preparing and presenting plans to the court.

(4a) Strategies for ensuring that judges and court officials who are possible referral sources use the program's services in appropriate cases.

(5) Procedures for obtaining services from existing public or private agencies, and a detailed budget for staff, contracted services, and all other costs.

(6) to (8). Repealed by Session Laws 1999-306, s. 1, effective January 1, 2000.

History.
1983, c. 909, s. 1; 1991, c. 566, ss. 2, 7; 1999-306, s. 1

§ 7A-775. Sentencing services board

(a) Each sentencing services program shall establish a sentencing services board to provide direction and assistance to the sentencing services program in the implementation and evaluation of the plan. Sentencing services boards may be organized as nonprofit corporations under Chapter 55A of the General Statutes. The sentencing services board shall consist of not less than 12 members, and shall include, insofar as possible, judges, district attorneys, attorneys, social workers, law-enforcement officers, probation officers, and other interested persons. The sentencing services board shall meet on a regular basis, and its duties include, but are not limited to, the following:

(1) Preparation and submission of the sentencing services program plan to the senior resident superior court judge and the Director annually, as provided in G.S. 7A-772(a);

(1a) Development of an annual budget for the program;

(2) Hiring, firing, and evaluation of program personnel;

(3) Selection of board members;

(4) Arranging for an annual financial audit.

(5) Development of procedures for contracting for services.

(b) If the board serves as an advisory board to a sentencing services program located in a local or State agency, the board's duties do not include budgeting and personnel decisions.

History.
1983, c. 909, s. 1; 1991, c. 566, ss. 2, 6; 1999-306, s. 1; 2006-203, s. 11; 2006-264, s. 1(a)

§ 7A-776. Limitation on use of funds

Funds provided for use under the provisions of this Article shall not be used for the operating costs, construction, or any other costs associated with local jail confinement, or for any purpose other than the operation of a sentencing services program that complies with this Article.

History.
1983, c. 909, s. 1; 1991, c. 566, s. 2; 1999-306, s. 1

§ 7A-777. Evaluation

The Director shall evaluate each sentencing services program on an annual basis to determine the degree to which the program effectively meets the needs of the courts in its judicial district by providing them with sentencing information. In conducting the evaluation, the Director shall consider the goals and objectives established in the program's plan, as well as the extent to which the program is able to ensure that the offenders served by the plan meet the criteria established in G.S. 7A-773(1).

History.
1983, c. 909, s. 1; 1991, c. 566, ss. 2, 7; 1999-306, s. 1

DIVISION 14.
DRUG TREATMENT
COURTS

ARTICLE 62
NORTH CAROLINA DRUG
TREATMENT COURT ACT

§ 7A-790. Short title

This Article shall be known and may be cited as the "North Carolina Drug Treatment Court Act of 1995".

History.
1995, c. 507, s. 21.6(a); 1998-23, s. 9; 1998-212, s. 16.15(a)

§ 7A-791. Purpose

The General Assembly recognizes that a critical need exists in this State for judicial programs that will reduce the incidence of alcohol and other drug abuse or dependence and crimes, including the offense of driving while impaired, delinquent acts, and child abuse and neglect committed as a result of alcohol and other drug abuse or dependence, and child abuse and neglect where alcohol and other drug abuse or dependence are significant factors in the child abuse and neglect. It is the intent of the General Assembly by this Article to create a program to facilitate the creation of local drug treatment court programs and driving while impaired (DWI) treatment court programs.

History.
1995, c. 507, s. 21.6(a); 1998-23, s. 9; 1998-212, s. 16.15(a), (b); 2001-424, s. 22.8(a); 2009-451, s. 15.11

§ 7A-792. Goals.

The goals of the drug treatment court programs funded under this Article include the following:

(1) To reduce alcoholism and other drug dependencies among adult and juvenile offenders and defendants and among respondents in juvenile petitions for abuse, neglect, or both;

(2) To reduce criminal and delinquent recidivism and the incidence of child abuse and neglect;

(3) To reduce the alcohol-related and other drug-related court workload;

(4) To increase the personal, familial, and societal accountability of adult and juvenile offenders and defendants and respondents in juvenile petitions for abuse, neglect, or both; and

(5) To promote effective interaction and use of resources among criminal and juvenile justice personnel, child protective services personnel, and community agencies.

History.
1995, c. 507, s. 21.6(a); 1998-23, s. 9; 1998-212, s. 16.15(a); 2001-424, s. 22.8(b)

§ 7A-793. Establishment of Program.

The North Carolina Drug Treatment Court Program is established in the Administrative Office of the Courts to facilitate the creation and funding of local drug treatment court programs. The Director of the Administrative Office of the Courts shall provide any necessary staff for planning, organizing, and administering the program. Local drug treatment court programs funded pursuant to this Article shall be operated consistently with the guidelines adopted pursuant to G.S. 7A-795. Local drug treatment court programs established and funded pursuant to this Article may consist of adult drug treatment court programs, juvenile drug treatment court programs, family drug treatment court programs, or any combination of these programs.

History.
1995, c. 507, s. 21.6(a); 1998-23, s. 9; 1998-212, s. 16.15(a), (c); 2001-424, s. 22.8(c)

§ 7A-794. Fund administration

The Drug Treatment Court Program Fund is created in the Administrative Office of the Courts and is administered by the Director of the Administrative Office of the Courts in consultation with the State Drug Treatment Court Advisory Committee.

History.
1995, c. 507, s. 21.6(a); 1998-23, s. 9; 1998-212, s. 16.15(a), (d); 2007-393, s. 12

§ 7A-795. State Drug Treatment Court Advisory Committee.

The State Drug Treatment Court Advisory Committee is established to develop and recommend to the Director of the Administrative Office of the Courts guidelines for the drug treatment court program and to monitor local programs wherever they are implemented. The Committee shall be chaired by the Director or the Director's designee and shall consist of not less than seven members appointed by the Director and broadly representative of the courts, law enforcement, corrections, juvenile justice, child protective services, and substance abuse treatment communities. In developing guidelines, the Advisory Committee shall consider the Substance Abuse and the Courts Action Plan and other recommendations of the Substance Abuse and the Courts State Task Force.

History.
1995, c. 507, s. 21.6(a); 1998-23, s. 9; 1998-212, s. 16.15(a), (e); 2001-424, s. 22.8(d)

§ 7A-796. Local drug treatment court management committee.

Each judicial district choosing to establish a drug treatment court shall form a local drug treatment court management committee, which shall be comprised to assure representation appropriate to the type or types of drug treatment court operations to be conducted in the district and shall consist of persons appointed by the senior resident superior court judge with the concurrence of the chief district court judge and the district attorney for that district, chosen from the following list:

(1) A judge of the superior court;

(2) A judge of the district court;

(3) A district attorney or assistant district attorney;

(4) A public defender or assistant public defender in judicial districts served by a public defender;

(5) An attorney representing a county department of social services within the district;

(6) A representative of the guardian ad litem;

(7) A member of the private criminal defense bar;

(8) A member of the private bar who represents respondents in department of social services juvenile matters;

(9) A clerk of superior court;

(10) The trial court administrator in judicial districts served by a trial court administrator;

(11) The director or member of the child welfare services division of a county department of social services within the district;

(12) The chief juvenile court counselor for the district;

(13) A probation officer;

(14) A local law enforcement officer;

(15) A representative of the local school administrative unit;

(16) A representative of the local community college;

(17) A representative of the treatment providers;

(18) A representative of the area mental health program;

(19) Any local drug treatment coordinator; and

(20) Any other persons selected by the local management committee.

The local drug treatment court management committee shall develop local guidelines and procedures, not inconsistent with the State

Chapter 7A

guidelines, that are necessary for the operation and evaluation of the local drug treatment court.

History.
1995, c. 507, s. 21.6(a); 1998-23, s. 9; 1998-212, s. 16.15(a), (f); 2001-424, s. 22.8(e); 2008-187, s. 4

§ 7A-797. Eligible population; drug treatment court procedures

The Director of the Administrative Office of the Courts, in conjunction with the State Drug Treatment Court Advisory Committee, shall develop criteria for eligibility and other procedural and substantive guidelines for drug treatment court operation.

History.
1995, c. 507, s. 21.6(a); 1998-23, s. 9; 1998-212, s. 16.15(a)

N.C. Gen. Stat. § 7A-798

Repealed by Session Laws 2007-393, s. 13, effective October 1, 2007.

§ 7A-799. Treatment not guaranteed

Nothing contained in this Article shall confer a right or an expectation of a right to treatment for a defendant or offender within the criminal or juvenile justice system or a respondent in a juvenile petition for abuse, neglect, or both.

History.
1995, c. 507, s. 21.6(a); 1998-23, s. 9; 1998-212, s. 16.15(a); 2001-424, s. 22.8(f)

§ 7A-800. Payment of costs of treatment program.

Each defendant, offender, or respondent in a juvenile petition for abuse, neglect, or both, who receives treatment under a local drug treatment court program shall contribute to the cost of the alcohol and other drug abuse or dependency treatment received in the drug treatment court program, based upon guidelines developed by the local drug treatment court management committee.

History.
1995, c. 507, s. 21.6(a); 1998-23, s. 9; 1998-212, s. 16.15(a), (h); 2001-424, s. 22.8(g)

§ 7A-801. Monitoring and annual report

The Administrative Office of the Courts shall monitor all State-recognized and funded local drug treatment courts, prepare an annual report on the implementation, operation, and effectiveness of the statewide drug treatment court program, and submit the report to the General Assembly by March 1 of each year. Each local drug treatment court program shall submit evaluation reports to the Administrative Office of the Courts as requested.

History.
1995, c. 507, s. 21.6(a); 1998-23, s. 9; 1998-212, s. 16.15(a), (i); 2007-393, s. 14

§§ 7A-802 through 7A-804

Reserved for future codification purposes.

CHAPTER 7B
JUVENILE CODE

DIVISION 01.
ABUSE, NEGLECT, DEPENDENCY

ARTICLE 1
PURPOSES; DEFINITIONS

§ 7B-100. Purpose

This Subchapter shall be interpreted and construed so as to implement the following purposes and policies:

(1) To provide procedures for the hearing of juvenile cases that assure fairness and equity and that protect the constitutional rights of juveniles and parents;

(2) To develop a disposition in each juvenile case that reflects consideration of the facts, the needs and limitations of the juvenile, and the strengths and weaknesses of the family.

(3) To provide for services for the protection of juveniles by means that respect both the right to family autonomy and the juveniles' needs for safety, continuity, and permanence; and

(4) To provide standards for the removal, when necessary, of juveniles from their homes and for the return of juveniles to their homes consistent with preventing the unnecessary or inappropriate separation of juveniles from their parents.

(5) To provide standards, consistent with the Adoption and Safe Families Act of 1997, P.L. 105-89, for ensuring that the best interests of the juvenile are of paramount consideration by the court and that when it is not in the juvenile's best interest to be returned home, the juvenile will be placed in a safe, permanent home within a reasonable amount of time.

History.
1979, c. 815, s. 1; 1987 (Reg. Sess., 1988), c. 1090, s. 1; 1998-202, s. 6; 1999-456, s. 60; 2003-140, s. 5

§ 7B-101. Definitions

As used in this Subchapter, unless the context clearly requires otherwise, the following words have the listed meanings:

(1) **Abused juveniles. --** Any juvenile less than 18 years of age (i) who is found to be a minor victim of human trafficking under G.S. 14-43.15 or (ii) whose parent, guardian, custodian, or caretaker:

a. Inflicts or allows to be inflicted upon the juvenile a serious physical injury by other than accidental means;

b. Creates or allows to be created a substantial risk of serious physical injury to the juvenile by other than accidental means;

c. Uses or allows to be used upon the juvenile cruel or grossly inappropriate procedures or cruel or grossly inappropriate devices to modify behavior;

d. Commits, permits, or encourages the commission of a violation of the following laws by, with, or upon the juvenile: first-degree forcible rape, as provided in G.S. 14-27.21; second-degree forcible rape as provided in G.S. 14-27.22; statutory rape of a child by an adult as provided in G.S. 14-27.23; first-degree statutory rape as provided in G.S. 14-27.24; first-degree forcible sex offense as provided in G.S. 14-27.26; second-degree forcible sex offense as provided in G.S. 14-27.27; statutory sexual offense with a child by an adult as provided in G.S. 14-27.28; first-degree statutory sexual offense as provided in G.S. 14-27.29; sexual activity by a substitute parent or custodian as provided in G.S. 14-27.31; sexual activity with a student as provided in G.S. 14-27.32; unlawful sale, surrender, or purchase of a minor, as provided in G.S. 14-43.14; crime against nature, as provided in G.S. 14-177; incest, as provided in G.S. 14-178; preparation of obscene photographs, slides, or motion pictures of the juvenile, as provided in G.S. 14-190.5; employing or permitting the juvenile to assist in a violation of the obscenity laws as provided in G.S. 14-190.6; dissemination of obscene material to the juvenile as provided in G.S. 14-190.7 and G.S. 14-190.8; displaying or disseminating material harmful to the juvenile as provided in G.S. 14-190.14 and G.S. 14-190.15; first and second degree sexual exploitation of the juvenile as provided in G.S. 14-190.16 and G.S. 14-190.17; promoting the prostitution of the juvenile as provided in G.S. 14-205.3(b); and taking indecent liberties with the juvenile, as provided in G.S. 14-202.1;

e. Creates or allows to be created serious emotional damage to the juvenile; serious emotional damage is evidenced by a juvenile's severe anxiety, depression, withdrawal, or aggressive behavior toward himself or others;

f. Encourages, directs, or approves of delinquent acts involving moral turpitude committed by the juvenile; or

g. Commits or allows to be committed an offense under G.S. 14-43.11 (human trafficking), G.S. 14-43.12 (involuntary servitude), or G.S. 14-43.13 (sexual servitude) against the child.

(2) Repealed by Session Laws 2015-136, s. 1, effective October 1, 2015, and applicable to actions filed or pending on or after that date.

(3) **Caretaker.** -- Any person other than a parent, guardian, or custodian who has responsibility for the health and welfare of a juvenile in a residential setting. A person responsible for a juvenile's health and welfare means a stepparent; foster parent; an adult member of the juvenile's household; an adult entrusted with the juvenile's care; a potential adoptive parent during a visit or trial placement with a juvenile in the custody of a department; any person such as a house parent or cottage parent who has primary responsibility for supervising a juvenile's health and welfare in a residential child care facility or residential educational facility; or any employee or volunteer of a division, institution, or school operated by the Department of Health and Human Services. Nothing in this subdivision shall be construed to impose a legal duty of support under Chapter 50 or Chapter 110 of the General Statutes. The duty imposed upon a caretaker as defined in this subdivision shall be for the purpose of this Subchapter only.

(4) **Clerk.** -- Any clerk of superior court, acting clerk, or assistant or deputy clerk.

(5) Repealed by Session Laws 2013-129, s. 1, effective October 1, 2013, and applicable to actions filed or pending on or after that date.

(6) **Court.** -- The district court division of the General Court of Justice.

(7) **Court of competent jurisdiction.** -- A court having the power and authority of law to act at the time of acting over the subject matter of the cause.

(7a) **Criminal history.** -- A local, State, or federal criminal history of conviction or pending indictment of a crime, whether a misdemeanor or a felony, involving violence against a person.

(8) **Custodian.** -- The person or agency that has been awarded legal custody of a juvenile by a court.

(8a) **Department.** -- Each county's child welfare agency. Unless the context clearly implies otherwise, when used in this Subchapter, "department" or "department of social services" shall refer to the county agency providing child welfare services, regardless of the name of the agency or whether the county has consolidated human services, pursuant to G.S. 153A-77 and shall include a regional social services department created pursuant to Part 2B of Article 1 of Chapter 108A of the General Statutes.

(9) **Dependent juvenile.** -- A juvenile in need of assistance or placement because (i) the juvenile has no parent, guardian, or custodian responsible for the juvenile's care or supervision or (ii) the juvenile's parent, guardian, or custodian is unable to provide for the juvenile's care or supervision and lacks an appropriate alternative child care arrangement.

(10) **Director.** -- The director of the department of social services in the county in which the juvenile resides or is found, or the director's representative as authorized in G.S. 108A-14.

(11) **District.** -- Any district court district as established by G.S. 7A-133.

(11a) **Family assessment response.** -- A response to selected reports of child neglect and dependency as determined by the Director using a family-centered approach that is protection and prevention oriented and that evaluates the strengths and needs of the juvenile's family, as well as the condition of the juvenile.

(11b) **Investigative assessment response.** -- A response to reports of child abuse and selected reports of child neglect and dependency as determined by the Director using a formal information gathering process to determine whether a juvenile is abused, neglected, or dependent.

(12) **Judge.** -- Any district court judge.

(13) **Judicial district.** -- Any district court district as established by G.S. 7A-133.

(14) **Juvenile.** -- A person who has not reached the person's eighteenth birthday and is not married, emancipated, or a member of the Armed Forces of the United States.

(15) **Neglected juvenile.** -- Any juvenile less than 18 years of age (i) who is found to be a minor victim of human trafficking under G.S. 14-43.15 or (ii) whose parent, guardian, custodian, or caretaker does any of the following:

a. Does not provide proper care, supervision, or discipline.

b. Has abandoned the juvenile.

c. Has not provided or arranged for the provision of necessary medical or remedial care.

d. Creates or allows to be created a living environment that is injurious to the juvenile's welfare.

e. Has participated or attempted to participate in the unlawful transfer of custody of the juvenile under G.S. 14-321.2.

f. Has placed the juvenile for care or adoption in violation of law.

In determining whether a juvenile is a neglected juvenile, it is relevant whether that juvenile lives in a home where another juvenile has died as a result of suspected abuse or neglect or lives in a home where another juvenile has been subjected to abuse or neglect by an adult who regularly lives in the home.

(15a) **Nonrelative kin.** -- An individual having a substantial relationship with the juvenile. In the case of a juvenile member of a State-recognized tribe as set forth in G.S. 143B-407(a), nonrelative kin also includes any member of a State-recognized tribe or a member of a federally recognized tribe, whether or not there is a substantial relationship with the juvenile.

(16) **Petitioner.** -- The individual who initiates court action, whether by the filing of a petition or of a motion for review alleging the matter for adjudication.

(17) **Prosecutor.** -- The district attorney or assistant district attorney assigned by the district attorney to juvenile proceedings.

(18) **Reasonable efforts.** -- The diligent use of preventive or reunification services by a department of social services when a juvenile's remaining at home or returning home is consistent with achieving a safe, permanent home for the juvenile within a reasonable period of time. If a court of competent jurisdiction determines that the juvenile is not to be returned home, then reasonable efforts means the diligent and timely use of permanency planning services by a department of social services to develop and implement a permanent plan for the juvenile.

(18a) **Relative.** -- An individual directly related to the juvenile by blood, marriage, or adoption, including a grandparent, sibling, aunt, or uncle.

(18b) **Responsible individual.** -- A parent, guardian, custodian, caretaker, or individual responsible for subjecting a juvenile to human trafficking under G.S. 14-43.11, 14-43.12, or 14-43.13, who abuses or seriously neglects a juvenile.

(18c) **Return home or reunification.** -- Placement of the juvenile in the home of either parent or placement of the juvenile in the home of a guardian or custodian from whose home the child was removed by court order.

(19) **Safe home.** -- A home in which the juvenile is not at substantial risk of physical or emotional abuse or neglect.

(19a) **Serious neglect.** -- Conduct, behavior, or inaction of the juvenile's parent, guardian, custodian, or caretaker that evidences a disregard of consequences of such magnitude that the conduct, behavior, or inaction constitutes an unequivocal danger to the juvenile's health, welfare, or safety, but does not constitute abuse.

(20) Repealed by Session Laws 2013-129, s. 1, effective October 1, 2013, and applicable to actions filed or pending on or after that date.

(21) **Substantial evidence.** -- Relevant evidence a reasonable mind would accept as adequate to support a conclusion.

(22) **Working day.** -- Any day other than a Saturday, Sunday, or a legal holiday when the courthouse is closed for transactions.

The singular includes the plural, the masculine singular includes the feminine singular and masculine and feminine plural unless otherwise specified.

History.
1979, c. 815, s. 1; 1981, c. 336; c. 359, s. 2; c. 469, ss. 1-3; c. 716, s. 1; 1985, c. 648; c. 757, s. 156(q); 1985 (Reg. Sess., 1986), c. 852, s. 16; 1987, c. 162; c. 695; 1987 (Reg. Sess., 1988), c. 1037, ss. 36, 37; 1989 (Reg. Sess., 1990), c. 815, s. 1; 1991, c. 258, s. 3; c. 273, s. 11; 1991 (Reg. Sess., 1992), c. 1030, s. 3; 1993, c. 324, s. 1; c. 516, ss. 1 -3; 1997-113, s. 1; 1997-390, s. 3; 1997-390, s. 3.2; 1997-443, s. 11A.118(a); 1997-506, s. 30; 1998-202, s. 6; 1998-229, ss. 1, 18; 1999-190, s. 1; 1999-318, s. 1; 1999-456, s. 60; 2005-55, s. 1; 2005-399, s. 1; 2009-38, s. 1; 2010-90, ss. 1, 2; 2011-183, s. 2; 2012-153, s. 2; 2013-129, s. 1; 2013-368, s. 16; 2015-123, s. 1; 2015-136, s. 1; 2015-181, s. 21; 2016-94, s. 12C.1(d); 2016-115, s. 3; 2017-41, s. 4.3; 2018-68, s. 8.1(a), (b); 2018-75, s. 5(a); 2018-145, s. 11(d); 2019-33, s. 1; 2019-245, s. 6(a); 2021-100, s. 1(a); 2021-123, s. 5(a); 2021-132, s. 1(a)

ARTICLE 2
JURISDICTION

§ 7B-200. Jurisdiction

(a) The court has exclusive, original jurisdiction over any case involving a juvenile who is alleged to be abused, neglected, or dependent. This jurisdiction does not extend to cases involving adult defendants alleged to be guilty of abuse or neglect.

The court also has exclusive original jurisdiction of the following proceedings:

(1) Proceedings under the Interstate Compact on the Placement of Children set forth in Article 38 of this Chapter.

(2) Proceedings involving judicial consent for emergency surgical or medical treatment for a juvenile when the juvenile's parent, guardian, custodian, or other person who has assumed the status and obligation of a parent without being awarded legal custody of the juvenile by a court refuses to consent for treatment to be rendered.

(3) Proceedings to determine whether a juvenile should be emancipated.

(4) Proceedings to terminate parental rights.

(4a) Proceedings for reinstatement of parental rights.

(5) Proceedings to review the placement of a juvenile in foster care pursuant to an agreement between the juvenile's parents or guardian and a county department of social services.

(5a) Proceedings to review the placement of a young adult in foster care pursuant to G.S. 108A-48 and G.S. 7B-910.1.

(6) Proceedings in which a person is alleged to have obstructed or interfered with an investigation required by G.S. 7B-302.

(7) Proceedings involving consent for an abortion on an unemancipated minor under Article 1A, Part 2 of Chapter 90 of the General Statutes.

(8) Proceedings by an underage party seeking judicial authorization to marry under Article 1 of Chapter 51 of the General Statutes.

(9) Petitions for judicial review of a director's determination under Article 3A of this Chapter.

(b) The court shall have jurisdiction over the parent, guardian, custodian, or caretaker of a juvenile who has been adjudicated abused, neglected, or dependent, provided the parent, guardian, custodian, or caretaker has (i) been properly served with summons pursuant to G.S. 7B-406, (ii) waived service of process, or (iii) automatically become a party pursuant to G.S. 7B-401.1(c) or (d).

(c) When the court obtains jurisdiction over a juvenile as the result of a petition alleging that the juvenile is abused, neglected, or dependent:

(1) Any other civil action in this State in which the custody of the juvenile is an issue is automatically stayed as to that issue, unless the juvenile proceeding and the civil custody action or claim are consolidated pursuant to subsection (d) of this section or the court in the juvenile proceeding enters an order dissolving the stay. When there is an automatic stay, the court shall ensure that a notice is filed in the stayed action if the county and case file number are made known to the court. The notice shall be on a printed form created by the North Carolina Administrative Office of the Courts, include notice of the stay, and provide the county and case file number for the action under this Article.

(2) If an order entered in the juvenile proceeding and an order entered in another civil custody action conflict, the order in the juvenile proceeding controls as long as the court continues to exercise jurisdiction in the juvenile proceeding.

(d) Notwithstanding G.S. 50-13.5(f), the court in a juvenile proceeding may order that any civil action or claim for custody filed in the district be consolidated with the juvenile proceeding. If a civil action or claim for custody of the juvenile is filed in another district, the court in the juvenile proceeding, for good cause and after consulting with the court in the other district, may: (i) order that the civil action or claim for custody be transferred to the county in which the juvenile proceeding is filed; or (ii) order a change of venue in the juvenile proceeding and transfer the juvenile proceeding to the county in which the civil action or claim is filed. The court in the juvenile proceeding may also proceed in the juvenile proceeding while the civil action or claim remains stayed or dissolve the stay of the civil action or claim and stay the juvenile proceeding pending a resolution of the civil action or claim.

History.
1979, c. 815, s. 1; 1983, c. 837, s. 1; 1985, c. 459, s. 2; 1987, c. 409, s. 2; 1995, c. 328, s. 3; c. 462, s. 2; 1996, 2nd Ex. Sess., c. 18, s. 23.2(c); 1998-202, s. 6; 1999-456, s. 60; 2001-62, s. 13; 2005-320, s. 1; 2005-399, s. 4; 2010-90, s. 3; 2011-295, s. 1; 2013-129, s. 2; 2017-161, s. 1; 2019-33, s. 2

§ 7B-201. Retention and termination of jurisdiction

(a) When the court obtains jurisdiction over a juvenile, jurisdiction shall continue until terminated by order of the court or until the juvenile reaches the age of 18 years or is otherwise emancipated, whichever occurs first.

(b) When the court's jurisdiction terminates, whether automatically or by court order, the court thereafter shall not modify or enforce any order previously entered in the case, including any juvenile court order relating to the custody, placement, or guardianship of the juvenile. The legal status of the juvenile and the custodial rights of the parties shall revert to the status they were before the juvenile petition was filed, unless applicable law or a valid court order in another civil action provides otherwise. Termination of the court's jurisdiction in an abuse, neglect, or dependency proceeding, however, shall not affect any of the following:

(1) A civil custody order entered pursuant to G.S. 7B-911.

(2) An order terminating parental rights.

(3) A pending action to terminate parental rights, unless the court orders otherwise.

(4) Any proceeding in which the juvenile is alleged to be or has been adjudicated undisciplined or delinquent.

(5) The court's jurisdiction in relation to any new abuse, neglect, or dependency petition that is filed.

History.

1979, c. 815, s. 1; 1981, c. 469, s. 4; 1996, 2nd Ex. Sess., c. 18, s. 23.2(d); 1998-202, s. 6; 1999-456, s. 60; 2005-320, s. 2

§ 7B-202. Permanency mediation

(a) The Administrative Office of the Courts shall establish a Permanency Mediation Program to provide statewide and uniform services to resolve issues in cases under this Subchapter in which a juvenile is alleged or has been adjudicated to be abused, neglected, or dependent, or in which a petition or motion to terminate a parent's rights has been filed. Participants in the mediation shall include the parties and their attorneys, including the guardian ad litem and attorney advocate for the child; provided, the court may allow mediation to proceed without the participation of a parent whose identity is unknown, a party who was served and has not made an appearance, or a parent, guardian, or custodian who has not been served despite a diligent attempt to serve the person. Upon a finding of good cause, the court may allow mediation to proceed without the participation of a parent who is unable to participate due to incarceration, illness, or some other cause. Others may participate by agreement of the parties, their attorneys, and the mediator, or by order of the court.

(b) The Administrative Office of the Courts shall establish in phases a statewide Permanency Mediation Program consisting of local district programs to be established in all judicial districts of the State. The Director of the Administrative Office of the Courts is authorized to approve contractual agreements for such services as executed by order of the Chief District Court Judge of a district court district, such contracts to be exempt from competitive bidding procedures under Chapter 143 of the General Statutes. The Administrative Office of the Courts shall promulgate policies and regulations necessary and appropriate for the administration of the program. Any funds appropriated by the General Assembly for the establishment and maintenance of permanency mediation programs under this Article shall be administered by the Administrative Office of the Courts.

(c) Mediation proceedings shall be held in private and shall be confidential. Except as provided otherwise in this section, all verbal or written communications from participants in the mediation to the mediator or between or among the participants in the presence of the mediator are absolutely privileged and inadmissible in court.

(d) Neither the mediator nor any party or other person involved in mediation sessions under this section shall be competent to testify to communications made during or in furtherance of such mediation sessions; provided, there is no confidentiality or privilege as to communications made in furtherance of a crime or fraud. Nothing in this subsection shall be construed as permitting an individual to obtain immunity from prosecution for criminal conduct or as excusing an individual from the reporting requirements of Article 3 of Chapter 7B of the General Statutes or G.S. 108A-102.

(e) Any agreement reached by the parties as a result of the mediation, whether referred to as a "placement agreement," "case plan," or some similar name, shall be reduced to writing, signed by each party, and submitted to the court as soon as practicable. Unless the court finds good reason not to, the court shall incorporate the agreement in a court order, and the agreement shall become enforceable as a court order. If some or all of the issues referred to mediation are not resolved by mediation, the mediator shall report that fact to the court.

History.

2006-187, s. 4(a)

§§ 7B-203 through 7B-299

Reserved for future codification purposes.

ARTICLE 3
SCREENING OF ABUSE AND NEGLECT COMPLAINTS

§ 7B-300. Protective services

The director of the department of social services in each county of the State shall establish protective services for juveniles alleged to be abused, neglected, or dependent.

Protective services shall include the screening of reports, the performance of an assessment using either a family assessment response or an investigative assessment response, casework, or other counseling services to parents, guardians, or other caretakers as provided by the director to help the parents, guardians, or other caretakers and the court to prevent abuse or neglect, to improve the quality of child care, to be more adequate parents, guardians, or caretakers, and to preserve and stabilize family life.

History.

1979, c. 815, s. 1; 1981, c. 359, s. 1; 1991 (Reg. Sess., 1992), c. 923, s. 1; 1997-506, s. 31; 1998-202, s. 6; 1999-456, s. 60; 2005-55, s. 2; 2015-123, s. 2

§ 7B-301. Duty to report abuse, neglect, dependency, or death due to maltreatment

(a) Any person or institution who has cause to suspect that any juvenile is abused, neglected, or dependent, as defined by G.S. 7B-101, or has died as the result of maltreatment, shall report the case of that juvenile to the director of the department of social services in the county where the juvenile resides or is found. The report may be made orally, by telephone, or in writing. The report shall include information as is known to the person making it including the name and address of the juvenile; the name and address of the juvenile's parent, guardian, or caretaker; the age of the juvenile; the names and ages of other juveniles in the home; the present whereabouts of the juvenile if not at the home address; the nature and extent of any injury or condition resulting from abuse, neglect, or dependency; and any other information which the person making the report believes might be helpful in establishing the need for protective services or court intervention. If the report is made orally or by telephone, the person making the report shall give the person's name, address, and telephone number. Refusal of the person making the report to give a name shall not preclude the department's assessment of the alleged abuse, neglect, dependency, or death as a result of maltreatment.

(b) Any person or institution who knowingly or wantonly fails to report the case of a juvenile as required by subsection (a) of this section, or who knowingly or wantonly prevents another person from making a report as required by subsection (a) of this section, is guilty of a Class 1 misdemeanor.

(c) Repealed by Session Laws 2015-123, s. 3, effective January 1, 2016.

History.

1979, c. 815, s. 1; 1991 (Reg. Sess., 1992), c. 923, s. 2; 1993, c. 516, s. 4; 1997-506, s. 32; 1998-202, s. 6; 1999-456, s. 60; 2005-55, s. 3; 2013-52, s. 7; 2015-123, s. 3

§ 7B-302. Assessment by director; military affiliation; access to confidential information; notification of person making the report

(a) When a report of abuse, neglect, or dependency is received, the director of the department of social services shall make a prompt and thorough assessment, using either a family assessment response or an investigative assessment response, in order to ascertain the facts of the case, including collecting information concerning the military affiliation of the parent, guardian, custodian, or caretaker of the juvenile alleged to have been abused or neglected, the extent of the abuse or neglect, and the risk of harm to the juvenile, in order to determine whether protective services should be provided or the complaint filed as a petition. When the report alleges abuse, the director shall immediately, but no later than 24 hours after receipt of the report, initiate the assessment. When the report alleges neglect or dependency, the director shall initiate the assessment within 72 hours following receipt of the report. When the report alleges abandonment of a juvenile or unlawful transfer of custody under G.S. 14-321.2, the director shall immediately initiate an assessment. When the report alleges abandonment, the director shall also take appropriate steps to assume temporary custody of the juvenile, and take appropriate steps to secure an order for nonsecure custody of the juvenile. The assessment and evaluation shall include a visit to the place where the juvenile resides, except when the report alleges abuse or neglect in a child care facility as defined in Article 7 of Chapter 110 of the General Statutes. When a report alleges abuse or neglect in a child care facility as defined in Article 7 of Chapter 110 of the General Statutes, a visit to the place where the juvenile resides is not required. When the report alleges abandonment, the assessment shall include a request from the director to law enforcement officials to investigate through the North Carolina Center for Missing Persons and other national and State resources whether the juvenile is a missing child.

(a1) All information received by the department of social services, including the identity of the reporter, shall be held in strictest confidence by the department, except under the following circumstances:

(1) The department shall disclose confidential information to any federal, State, or local government entity or its agent, or any private child placing or adoption agency licensed by the Department of Health and Human Services, in order to protect a juvenile from abuse or neglect. The disclosure of confidential information pursuant to this subdivision shall include sharing

413

information with the appropriate military authority if the director finds evidence that a juvenile may have been abused or neglected and the parent, guardian, custodian, or caretaker of the juvenile alleged to have been abused or neglected has a military affiliation. Any confidential information disclosed to any federal, State, or local government entity or its agent under this subsection shall remain confidential with the other entity or its agent and shall only be redisclosed for purposes directly connected with carrying out that entity's mandated responsibilities.

(1a) The department shall disclose confidential information regarding the identity of the reporter to any federal, State, or local government entity or its agent with a court order. The department may only disclose confidential information regarding the identity of the reporter to a federal, State, or local government entity or its agent without a court order when the entity demonstrates a need for the reporter's name to carry out the entity's mandated responsibilities.

(2) The juvenile's guardian ad litem or the juvenile, including a juvenile who has reached age 18 or been emancipated is authorized to review the record and request all or part of the record unless prohibited by federal law. The department shall provide electronic or written copies of the requested information within a reasonable period of time.

(3) A district or superior court judge of this State presiding over a civil matter in which the department of social services is not a party may order the department to release confidential information, after providing the department with reasonable notice and an opportunity to be heard and then determining that the information is relevant and necessary to the trial of the matter before the court and unavailable from any other source. This subdivision shall not be construed to relieve any court of its duty to conduct hearings and make findings required under relevant federal law, before ordering the release of any private medical or mental health information or records related to substance abuse or HIV status or treatment. The department of social services may surrender the requested records to the court, for in camera review, if the surrender is necessary to make the required determinations.

(4) A district or superior court judge of this State presiding over a criminal or delinquency matter shall conduct an in camera review prior to releasing to the defendant or juvenile any confidential records maintained by the department of social services, except those records the defendant or juvenile is entitled to pursuant to subdivision (2) of this subsection.

(5) The department may disclose confidential information to a parent, guardian, custodian, or caretaker in accordance with G.S. 7B-700 of this Subchapter.

(a2) If the director, at any time after receiving a report that a juvenile may be abused, neglected, or dependent, determines that the juvenile's legal residence is in another county, the director shall promptly notify the director in the county of the juvenile's residence, and the two directors shall coordinate efforts to ensure that appropriate actions are taken.

(a3) Except where prohibited by federal law, including state plan requirements within federal programs, and notwithstanding other applicable State law, any of the following may request access to confidential information and records maintained pursuant to this Article by the Department or a county department of social services:

(1) An individual member of the North Carolina General Assembly.

(2) A joint legislative oversight committee of the North Carolina General Assembly.

A request made pursuant to this subsection shall be made to the Department or to the director of a county department of social services. The request shall be limited to purposes necessary for oversight of programs related to child protective services. Upon receiving a request pursuant to this subsection, the Department shall coordinate with the county department of social services to obtain all necessary information or records responsive to the request. A county department of social services shall provide the Department with all information and records, or copies of records, as requested. If the request is made to the director of a county department of social services, the Department shall assist the director of the county department of social services in fulfilling the request and providing all necessary information or records in accordance with this subsection. Upon receipt of a request from an individual member of the North Carolina General Assembly, the Department shall make the confidential information and records available for inspection and examination at the county department of social services. Upon the request of a joint legislative oversight committee, the Department shall assist the director of the county department of social services with sharing the confidential information and records with the requesting committee in a closed session in accordance with G.S. 143-318.11(a)(1).

The confidential information or records shared pursuant to this subsection shall be the minimum necessary to satisfy the request. A member of the North Carolina General Assembly or joint legislative oversight committee shall not retain copies of any part of the information and records or take photographs or create electronic images of any information and records reviewed pursuant to a request under this subsection. All information and records shared pursuant to this subsection shall be withheld from public inspection and maintained in a confidential manner. The following information shall remain confidential and shall not be shared or disclosed in response to a request for information and records made pursuant to this subsection:

(1) The identity of a reporter.

(2) Juvenile court records as set forth in Article 29 of Subchapter III of this Chapter and Article 30 of Subchapter III of this Chapter.

(a4) Any violation of subsection (a3) of this section shall be punishable as a Class 1 misdemeanor.

(a5) The disclosure of confidential information pursuant to subsection (a3) of this section may only be requested for information received or created by the agency on or after the effective date of this section.

(b) When a report of a juvenile's death as a result of suspected maltreatment or a report of suspected abuse, neglect, or dependency of a juvenile in a noninstitutional setting is received, the director of the department of social services shall immediately ascertain if other juveniles live in the home, and, if so, initiate an assessment in order to determine whether they require protective services or whether immediate removal of the juveniles from the home is necessary for their protection. When a report of a juvenile's death as a result of maltreatment or a report of suspected abuse, neglect, or dependency of a juvenile in an institutional setting such as a residential child care facility or residential educational facility is received, the director of the department of social services shall immediately ascertain if other juveniles remain in the facility subject to the alleged perpetrator's care or supervision, and, if so, assess the circumstances of those juveniles in order to determine whether they require protective services or whether immediate removal of those juveniles from the facility is necessary for their protection.

(c) If the assessment indicates that abuse, neglect, or dependency has occurred, the director shall decide whether immediate removal of the juvenile or any other juveniles in the home is necessary for their protection. If immediate removal does not seem necessary, the director shall immediately provide or arrange for protective services. If the parent, guardian, custodian, or caretaker refuses to accept the protective services provided or arranged by the director, the director shall sign a petition seeking to invoke the jurisdiction of the court for the protection of the juvenile or juveniles.

(d) If immediate removal seems necessary for the protection of the juvenile or other juveniles in the home, the director shall sign a petition that alleges the applicable facts to invoke the jurisdiction of the court. Where the assessment shows that it is warranted, a protective services worker may assume temporary custody of the juvenile for the juvenile's protection pursuant to Article 5 of this Chapter.

(d1) Whenever a juvenile is removed from the home of a parent, guardian, custodian, stepparent, or adult relative entrusted with the juvenile's care due to physical abuse, the director shall conduct a thorough review of the background of the alleged abuser or abusers. This review shall include a criminal history check and a review of any available mental health records. If the review reveals that the alleged abuser or abusers have a history of violent behavior against people, the director shall petition the court to order the alleged abuser or abusers to submit to a complete mental health evaluation by a licensed psychologist or psychiatrist.

(e) In performing any duties related to the assessment of the report or the provision or arrangement for protective services, the director may consult with any public or private agencies or individuals, including the available State or local law enforcement officers who shall assist in the assessment and evaluation of the seriousness of any report of abuse, neglect, or dependency when requested by the director. The director or the director's representative may make a written demand for any information or reports, whether or not confidential, that may in the director's opinion be relevant to the assessment or provision of protective services. Upon the director's or the director's representative's request and unless protected by the attorney-client privilege, any public or private agency or individual shall provide access to and copies of this confidential information and these records to the extent permitted by federal law and regulations. If a custodian of criminal investigative information or records believes that release of the information will jeopardize the right of the State to prosecute a defendant or the right of a defendant to receive a fair trial or will undermine an ongoing or future investigation, it may seek an order from a court of competent jurisdiction to prevent disclosure of the information. In such an action, the custodian of the records shall have the burden of showing by a preponderance of the evidence that disclosure of the information in question will jeopardize the right of the State to prosecute a defendant or the right of a defendant to receive a fair trial or will undermine an ongoing or future investigation. Actions brought pursuant to this paragraph shall be set down for immediate hearing, and subsequent proceedings in the actions shall be accorded priority by the trial and appellate courts.

(f) Within five working days after receipt of the report of abuse, neglect, or dependency, the director shall give written notice to the person making the report, unless requested by that person not to give notice, as to whether the report was accepted for assessment and whether the report was referred to the appropriate State or local law enforcement agency.

(g) Within five working days after completion of the protective services assessment, the director shall give subsequent written notice to the person making the report, unless requested by that person not to give notice, as to whether there is a finding of abuse, neglect, or dependency, whether the county department of social services is taking action to protect the juvenile, and what action it is taking, including whether or not a petition was filed. The person making the report shall be informed of procedures necessary to request a review by the prosecutor of the director's decision not to file a petition. A request for review by the prosecutor shall be made within five working days of receipt of the second notification. The second notification shall include notice that, if the person making the report is not satisfied with the director's decision, the person may request review of the decision by the prosecutor within five working days of receipt. The person making the report may waive the person's right to this notification, and no notification is required if the person making the report does not identify himself to the director.

(h) The director or the director's representative may not enter a private residence for assessment purposes without at least one of the following:

(1) The reasonable belief that a juvenile is in imminent danger of death or serious physical injury.

(2) The permission of the parent or person responsible for the juvenile's care.

(3) The accompaniment of a law enforcement officer who has legal authority to enter the residence.

(4) An order from a court of competent jurisdiction.

History.
1979, c. 815, s. 1; 1985, c. 205; 1991, c. 593, s. 1; 1991 (Reg. Sess., 1992), c. 923, s. 3; 1993, c. 516, s. 5; 1995, c. 411, s. 1; 1997-390, s. 3.1; 1998-202, s. 6; 1998-229, ss. 2, 19; 1999-190, s. 2; 1999-318, s. 2; 1999-456, s. 60; 2001-291, s. 1; 2003-304, s. 4.1; 2005-55, s. 4; 2006-205,
s. 1; 2009-311, s. 1; 2012-153, s. 6; 2015-123, s. 4; 2016-94, s. 12C.1(e); 2016-115, s. 4; 2017-102, s. 2; 2019-201, s. 3(a); 2021-100, s. 2; 2021-132, s. 1(c)

§ 7B-303. Interference with assessment

(a) If any person obstructs or interferes with an assessment required by G.S. 7B-302, the director may file a petition naming that person as respondent and requesting an order directing the respondent to cease the obstruction or interference. The petition shall contain the name and date of birth and address of the juvenile who is the subject of the assessment; shall include a concise statement of the basis for initiating the assessment, shall specifically describe the conduct alleged to constitute obstruction of or interference with the assessment; and shall be verified.

(b) For purposes of this section, obstruction of or interference with an assessment means refusing to disclose the whereabouts of the juvenile, refusing to allow the director to have personal access to the juvenile, refusing to allow the director to observe or interview the juvenile in private, refusing to allow the director access to confidential information and records upon request pursuant to G.S. 7B-302, refusing to allow the director to arrange for an evaluation of the juvenile by a physician or other expert, or other conduct that makes it impossible for the director to carry out the duty to assess the juvenile's condition.

(c) Upon filing of the petition, the court shall schedule a hearing to be held not less than five days after service of the petition and summons on the respondent. Service of the petition and summons and notice of hearing shall be made as provided by the Rules of Civil Procedure on the respondent; the juvenile's parent, guardian, custodian, or caretaker; and any other person determined by the court to be a necessary party. If at the hearing on the petition the court finds by clear, cogent, and convincing evidence that the respondent, without lawful excuse, has obstructed or interfered with an assessment required by G.S. 7B-302, the court may order the respondent to cease such obstruction or interference. The burden of proof shall be on the petitioner.

(d) If the director has reason to believe that the juvenile is in need of immediate protection or assistance, the director shall so allege in the petition and may seek an ex parte order from the court. If the court, from the verified petition and any inquiry the court makes of the director, finds probable cause to believe both that the juvenile is at risk of immediate harm and that the respondent is obstructing or interfering with the director's ability to assess the juvenile's condition, the court may enter an ex parte order directing the respondent to cease the obstruction or interference. The order shall be limited to provisions necessary to enable the director to conduct an assessment sufficient to determine whether the juvenile is in need of immediate protection or assistance. Within 10 days after the entry of an ex parte order under this subsection, a hearing shall be held to determine whether there is good cause for the continuation of the order or the entry of a different order. An order entered under this subsection shall be served on the respondent along with a copy of the petition, summons, and notice of hearing.

(e) The director may be required at a hearing under this section to reveal the identity of any person who made a report of suspected abuse, neglect, or dependency as required by G.S. 7B-301.

(f) An order entered pursuant to this section is enforceable by civil or criminal contempt as provided in Chapter 5A of the General Statutes.

History.
1987, c. 409, s. 1; 1993, c. 516, s. 6; 1998-202, s. 6; 1999-456, s. 60; 2005-55, s. 5

N.C. Gen. Stat. § 7B-304

Repealed by Session Laws 2003, c. 140, s. 1, effective June 4, 2003.

§ 7B-305. Request for review by prosecutor

The person making the report shall have five working days, from receipt of the decision of the director of the department of social services not to petition the court, to notify the prosecutor that the person is requesting a review. The prosecutor shall notify the person making the report and the director of the time and place for the review, and the director shall immediately transmit to the prosecutor a copy of a summary of the assessment.

History.
1979, c. 815, s. 1; 1998-202, s. 6; 1999-456, s. 60; 2005-55, s. 6

§ 7B-306. Review by prosecutor

The prosecutor shall review the director's determination that a petition should not be filed within 20 days after the person making the report is notified. The review shall include conferences with the person making the report, the protective services worker, the juvenile, if practicable, and other persons known to have pertinent information about the juvenile or the juvenile's family. At the conclusion of the conferences, the prosecutor may affirm the decision made by the director, may request the

appropriate local law enforcement agency to investigate the allegations, or may direct the director to file a petition.

History.
1979, c. 815, s. 1; 1981, c. 469, s. 7; 1993, c. 516, s. 7; 1998-202, s. 6; 1999-456, s. 60

§ 7B-307. Duty of director to report evidence of abuse, neglect; investigation by local law enforcement; notification to appropriate military authority; notification of Department of Health and Human Services

(a) If the director finds evidence that a juvenile may have been abused as defined by G.S. 7B-101, the director shall make an immediate oral and subsequent written report of the findings to the district attorney or the district attorney's designee and the appropriate local law enforcement agency, including notifying the appropriate military authority that there is evidence of abuse or neglect of a juvenile by a parent, guardian, custodian, or caretaker with that military affiliation, within 48 hours after receipt of the report. The local law enforcement agency shall immediately, but no later than 48 hours after receipt of the information, initiate and coordinate a criminal investigation with the protective services assessment being conducted by the county department of social services. Upon completion of the investigation, the district attorney shall determine whether criminal prosecution is appropriate and may request the director or the director's designee to appear before a magistrate.

If the director receives information that a juvenile may have been physically harmed in violation of any criminal statute by any person other than the juvenile's parent, guardian, custodian, or caretaker, the director shall make an immediate oral and subsequent written report of that information to the district attorney or the district attorney's designee and to the appropriate local law enforcement agency within 48 hours after receipt of the information. The local law enforcement agency shall immediately, but no later than 48 hours after receipt of the information, initiate a criminal investigation. Upon completion of the investigation, the district attorney shall determine whether criminal prosecution is appropriate.

If the report received pursuant to G.S. 7B-301 involves abuse or neglect of a juvenile or child maltreatment, as defined in G.S. 110-105.3, in child care, the director shall notify the Department of Health and Human Services within 24 hours or on the next working day of receipt of the report.

The director of the department of social services shall submit a report of alleged abuse, neglect, or dependency cases or child fatalities that are the result of alleged maltreatment to the central registry under the policies adopted by the Social Services Commission.

(b), (c) Repealed by Session Laws 2015-123, s. 5, effective January 1, 2016.

History.

1979, c. 815, s. 1; 1983, c. 199; 1985, c. 757, s. 156(s)-(u); 1991, c. 593, s. 2; 1991 (Reg. Sess., 1992), c. 923, s. 4; 1993, c. 516, s. 8; 1997-443, s. 11A.118(a); 1997-506, s. 33; 1998-202, s. 6; 1999-456, s. 60; 2005-55, s. 7; 2015-123, s. 5; 2019-201, s. 3(b)

§ 7B-308. Authority of medical professionals in abuse cases

(a) Any physician or administrator of a hospital, clinic, or other medical facility to which a suspected abused juvenile is brought for medical diagnosis or treatment shall have the right, when authorized by the chief district court judge of the district or the judge's designee, to retain physical custody of the juvenile in the facility when the physician who examines the juvenile certifies in writing that the juvenile who is suspected of being abused should remain for medical treatment or that, according to the juvenile's medical evaluation, it is unsafe for the juvenile to return to the juvenile's parent, guardian, custodian, or caretaker. This written certification must be signed by the certifying physician and must include the time and date that the judicial authority to retain custody is given. Copies of the written certification must be appended to the juvenile's medical and judicial records and another copy must be given to the juvenile's parent, guardian, custodian, or caretaker. The right to retain custody in the facility shall exist for up to 12 hours from the time and date contained in the written certification.

(b) Immediately upon receipt of judicial authority to retain custody, the physician, the administrator, or that person's designee shall so notify the director of social services for the county in which the facility is located. The director shall treat this notification as a report of suspected abuse and shall immediately begin an assessment of the case.

(1) If the assessment reveals (i) that it is the opinion of the certifying physician that the juvenile is in need of medical treatment to cure or alleviate physical distress or to prevent the juvenile from suffering serious physical injury, and (ii) that it is the opinion of the physician that the juvenile should for these reasons remain in the custody of the facility for 12 hours, but (iii) that the juvenile's parent, guardian, custodian, or caretaker cannot be reached or, upon request, will not consent to the treatment within

the facility, the director shall within the initial 12-hour period file a juvenile petition alleging abuse and setting forth supporting allegations and shall seek a nonsecure custody order. A petition filed and a nonsecure custody order obtained in accordance with this subdivision shall come on for hearing under the regular provisions of this Subchapter unless the director and the certifying physician together voluntarily dismiss the petition.

(2) In all cases except those described in subdivision (1) above, the director shall conduct the assessment and may initiate juvenile proceedings and take all other steps authorized by the regular provisions of this Subchapter. If the director decides not to file a petition, the physician, the administrator, or that person's designee may ask the prosecutor to review this decision according to the provisions of G.S. 7B-305 and G.S. 7B-306.

(c) If, upon hearing, the court determines that the juvenile is found in a county other than the county of legal residence, in accord with G.S. 153A-257, the juvenile may be transferred, in accord with G.S. 7B-903(2), to the custody of the department of social services in the county of residence.

(d) If the court, upon inquiry, determines that the medical treatment rendered was necessary and appropriate, the cost of that treatment may be charged to the parents, guardian, custodian, or caretaker, or, if the parents are unable to pay, to the county of residence in accordance with G.S. 7B-903 and G.S. 7B-904.

(e) Except as otherwise provided, a petition begun under this section shall proceed in like manner with petitions begun under G.S. 7B-302.

(f) The procedures in this section are in addition to, and not in derogation of, the abuse and neglect reporting provisions of G.S. 7B-301 and the temporary custody provisions of G.S. 7B-500. Nothing in this section shall preclude a physician or administrator and a director of social services from following the procedures of G.S. 7B-301 and G.S. 7B-500 whenever these procedures are more appropriate to the juvenile's circumstances.

History.

1979, c. 815, s. 1; 1981, c. 716, s. 2; 1995, c. 255, s. 1; 1998-202, s. 6; 1999-456, s. 60; 2005-55, s. 8

§ 7B-309. Immunity of persons reporting and cooperating in an assessment

Anyone who makes a report pursuant to this Article; cooperates with the county department of social services in a protective services assessment; testifies in any judicial proceeding resulting from a protective services report or assessment; provides information or assistance, including medical evaluations or consultation in connection with a report, investigation, or legal intervention pursuant to a good-faith report of child abuse or neglect; or otherwise participates in the program authorized by this Article; is immune from any civil or criminal liability that might otherwise be incurred or imposed for that action provided that the person was acting in good faith. In any proceeding involving liability, good faith is presumed.

History.
1979, c. 815, s. 1; 1981, s. 469, s. 8; 1993, c. 516, s. 9; 1998-202, s. 6; 1999-456, s. 60; 2005-55, s. 9; 2019-240, s. 18

§ 7B-310. Privileges not grounds for failing to report or for excluding evidence

No privilege shall be grounds for any person or institution failing to report that a juvenile may have been abused, neglected, or dependent, even if the knowledge or suspicion is acquired in an official professional capacity, except when the knowledge or suspicion is gained by an attorney from that attorney's client during representation only in the abuse, neglect, or dependency case. No privilege, except the attorney-client privilege, shall be grounds for excluding evidence of abuse, neglect, or dependency in any judicial proceeding (civil, criminal, or juvenile) in which a juvenile's abuse, neglect, or dependency is in issue nor in any judicial proceeding resulting from a report submitted under this Article, both as this privilege relates to the competency of the witness and to the exclusion of confidential communications.

History.
1979, c. 815, s. 1; 1987, c. 323, s. 1; 1993, c. 514, s. 3; c. 516, s. 10; 1995, c. 509, s. 133; 1998-202, s. 6; 1999-456, s. 60

§ 7B-311. Central registry; responsible individuals list

(a) The Department of Health and Human Services shall maintain a central registry of abuse, neglect, and dependency cases and child fatalities that are the result of alleged maltreatment that are reported under this Article in order to compile data for appropriate study of the extent of abuse and neglect within the State and to identify repeated abuses of the same juvenile or of other juveniles in the same family. This data shall be furnished by county directors of social services to the Department of Health and Human Services and shall be confidential, subject to rules adopted by the Social Services Commission providing for its use for study and research and for other appropriate disclosure. Data shall not be used at any hearing or court proceeding unless based upon a final judgment of a court of law.

(b) The Department shall also maintain a list of responsible individuals. The Department may provide information from this list to child caring institutions, child placing agencies, group home facilities, and other providers of foster care, child care, or adoption services that need to determine the fitness of individuals to care for or adopt children. The name of an individual who has been identified as a responsible individual shall be placed on the responsible individuals list only after one of the following:

(1) The individual is properly notified pursuant to G.S. 7B-320 and fails to file a petition for judicial review in a timely manner.

(2) The court determines that the individual is a responsible individual as a result of a hearing on the individual's petition for judicial review.

(3) The individual is criminally convicted as a result of the same incident involved in an investigative assessment response.

(c) It is unlawful for any public official or public employee to knowingly and willfully release information from either the central registry or the responsible individuals list to a person who is not authorized to receive the information. It is unlawful for any person who is authorized to receive information from the central registry or the responsible individuals list to release that information to an unauthorized person. It is unlawful for any person who is not authorized to receive information from the central registry or the responsible individuals list to access or attempt to access that information. A person who commits an offense described in this subsection is guilty of a Class 3 misdemeanor.

(d) The Social Services Commission shall adopt rules regarding the operation of the central registry and responsible individuals list, including procedures for each of the following:

(1) Filing data.

(2) Notifying an individual that the individual has been determined by the director to be a responsible individual.

(3) Correcting and expunging information.

(4) Determining persons who are authorized to receive information from the responsible individuals list.

(5) Releasing information from the responsible individuals list to authorized requestors.

(6) Gathering statistical information.

(7) Keeping and maintaining information placed in the registry and on the responsible individuals list.

(8) Repealed by Session Laws 2010-90, s. 4, effective July 11, 2010.

History.

1979, c. 815, s. 1; 1993, c. 516, s. 11; 1997-443, s. 11A.118(a); 1998-202, s. 6; 1999-456, s. 60; 2005-399, s. 2; 2010-90, s. 4; 2013-129, s. 3

§§ 7B-312 through 7B-319

Reserved for future codification purposes.

ARTICLE 3A
JUDICIAL REVIEW; RESPONSIBLE INDIVIDUALS LIST

§ 7B-320. Notification to individual determined to be a responsible individual

(a) After the completion of an investigative assessment response that results in a determination of abuse or serious neglect and the identification of a responsible individual, the director shall personally deliver written notice of the determination to the identified individual in an expeditious manner.

(a1) If the director determines that the juvenile is the victim of human trafficking by an individual other than the juvenile's parent, guardian, custodian, or caretaker, the director shall cooperate with the local law enforcement agency and district attorney to determine the safest way, if possible, to provide notification to the identified responsible individual. If the director does not provide notification in accordance with this subsection, the director shall document the reason and basis for not providing the notification.

The director shall not provide notification to the responsible individual or proceed further under this Article if notification is likely to cause any of the following to occur:

(1) Cause mental or physical harm or danger to the juvenile.

(2) Undermine an ongoing or future criminal investigation.

(3) Jeopardize the State's ability to prosecute the identified responsible individual.

(b) If personal written notice is not made within 15 days of the determination and the director has made diligent efforts to locate the identified individual, the director shall send the notice to the individual by registered or certified mail, return receipt requested, and addressed to the individual at the individual's last known address.

(c) The notice shall include all of the following:

(1) A statement informing the individual of the nature of the investigative assessment response and whether the director determined abuse or serious neglect or both.

(1a) A statement that the individual has been identified as a responsible individual.

(2) A statement summarizing the substantial evidence supporting the director's determination without identifying the reporter or collateral contacts.

(3) A statement informing the individual that unless the individual petitions for judicial review, the individual's name will be placed on the responsible individuals list as provided in G.S. 7B-311, and that the Department of Health and Human Services may provide information from this list to child caring institutions, child placing agencies, group home facilities, and other providers of foster care, child care, or adoption services that need to determine the fitness of individuals to care for or adopt children.

(4) A clear description of the actions the individual must take to seek judicial review of the director's determination.

(d) In addition to the notice, the director shall provide the individual with a copy of a petition for judicial review form.

History.

2005-399, s. 3; 2010-90, s. 5; 2013-129, s. 4; 2019-33, s. 3; 2021-132, s. 2(a)

§§ 7B-321, 7B-322

Repealed by Session Laws 2010-90, s. 6, effective July 11, 2010.

History.

§§ 7B-321, 7B-322: 2005-399, s. 3, repealed by 2010-90, s. 6, effective July 11, 2010

§ 7B-323. Petition for judicial review; district court

(a) Within 15 days of the receipt of notice of the director's determination under G.S. 7B-320(a) or (b), an individual may file a petition for judicial review with the district court of the county in which the abuse or serious neglect report arose. The request shall be by a petition for judicial review filed with the appropriate clerk of court's office with a copy delivered in person or by certified mail, return receipt requested, to the director who determined the abuse or serious neglect and identified the individual as a responsible individual. The petition for judicial review shall contain the name, date of birth, and address of the individual seeking judicial review, the name of the juvenile who was the subject of the determination of abuse or serious neglect, and facts that invoke the jurisdiction of the court. Failure to timely file a petition for judicial review constitutes a waiver of the individual's right to a district court hearing and to contest the placement of the individual's name on the responsible individuals list.

(a1) If the director cannot show that the individual has received actual notice, the director shall not place the individual on the responsible individuals list until an ex parte hearing is held at which a district court judge determines that the director made diligent efforts to find the individual. A finding that the individual is evading service is relevant to the determination that the director made diligent efforts.

(b) The clerk of court shall maintain a separate docket for judicial review actions. Upon the filing of a petition for judicial review, the clerk shall calendar the matter for hearing within 45 days from the date the petition is filed at a session of district court hearing juvenile matters or, if there is no such session, at the next session of juvenile court. The clerk shall send notice of the hearing to the petitioner and to the director who determined the abuse or serious neglect and identified the individual as a responsible individual. Upon the request of a party, the court shall close the hearing to all persons, except officers of the court, the parties, their witnesses, and law enforcement investigating the same allegations. At the hearing, the director shall have the burden of proving by a preponderance of the evidence the abuse or serious neglect and the identification of the individual seeking judicial review as a responsible individual. The hearing shall be before a judge without a jury. The rules of evidence applicable in civil cases shall apply. However, the court, in its discretion, may permit the admission of any reliable and relevant evidence, including, but not limited to, child medical evaluation reports and child and family evaluation reports that the director relied on to make the determination that abuse or serious neglect occurred, if the general purposes of the rules of evidence and the interests of justice will best be served by its admission.

(b1) Upon receipt of a notice of hearing for judicial review, the director who identified the individual as a responsible individual shall review all records, reports, and other information gathered during the investigative assessment response. If after a review, the director determines that there is not sufficient evidence to support a determination that the individual abused or seriously neglected the juvenile and is a responsible individual, the director shall prepare a written statement of the director's determination and either deliver the statement personally to the individual seeking judicial review or send the statement by first-class mail. The director shall also give written notice of the director's determination to the clerk to be placed in the court file, and the judicial review hearing shall be cancelled with notice of the cancellation given by the clerk to the petitioner.

(c) At the hearing, the following rights of the parties shall be preserved:

(1) The right to present sworn evidence, law, or rules that bear upon the case.

(2) The right to represent themselves or obtain the services of an attorney at their own expense.

(3) The right to subpoena witnesses, cross-examine witnesses of the other party, and make a closing argument summarizing the party's view of the case and the law.

(d) Within 30 days after completion of the hearing, the court shall enter an order containing findings of fact and conclusions of law. The clerk shall serve a copy of the order on each party or the party's attorney of record. If the court concludes that the director has not established by a preponderance of the evidence abuse or serious neglect or the identification of the responsible individual, the court shall reverse the director's determination and order the director not to place the individual's name on the responsible individuals list. If the court concludes that the director has established by a preponderance of the evidence abuse or serious neglect and the identification of the individual seeking judicial review as a responsible individual, the court shall order the director to place the individual's name on the responsible individuals list, consistent with the court's order.

(e) Notwithstanding any time limitations contained in this section or the provisions of G.S. 7B-324(a)(4), upon the filing of a petition for judicial review by an individual identified by a director as a responsible individual, the district court of the county in which the abuse or neglect report arose may review a director's determination of abuse or serious neglect at any time if the review serves the interests of justice or for extraordinary circumstances. If the district court undertakes such a review, a hearing shall be held pursuant to this section at which the director shall have the burden of establishing by a preponderance of the evidence abuse or serious neglect and the identification of the individual seeking judicial review as a responsible individual. If the court concludes that the director has not established by a preponderance of the evidence abuse or serious neglect or the identification of the responsible individual, the court shall reverse the director's determination and order the director to expunge the individual's name from the responsible individuals list.

(f) A party may appeal the district court's decision under G.S. 7A-27(b)(2).

History.
2005-399, s. 3; 2010-90, s. 7; 2013-129, s. 5; 2015-247, s. 7; 2019-33, s. 4

§ 7B-324. Persons ineligible to petition for judicial review

(a) An individual who has been identified by a director as a responsible individual is not eligible for judicial review if any of the following apply:

(1) The individual is criminally convicted as a result of the same incident. The district attorney shall inform the director of the result of the criminal proceeding.

(2) Repealed by Session Laws 2013-129, s. 6, effective October 1, 2013, and applicable to actions filed or pending on or after that date.

(3) Repealed by Session Laws 2010-90, s. 8, effective July 11, 2010.

(4) After proper notice, the individual fails to file a petition for judicial review with the district court in a timely manner.

(5) Repealed by Session Laws 2010-90, s. 8, effective July 11, 2010.

(a1) If the individual is criminally convicted as a result of the same incident after the petition for judicial review is filed, the court shall dismiss the petition for judicial review with prejudice.

(b) If an individual seeking judicial review is named as a respondent in a juvenile court case or a defendant in a criminal court case resulting from the same incident, the district court judge may stay the judicial review proceeding.

History.
2005-399, s. 3; 2010-90, s. 8; 2013-129, s. 6; 2019-33, s. 5

§§ 7B-325 through 7B-399

Reserved for future codification purposes.

ARTICLE 4
VENUE; PETITIONS

§ 7B-400. Venue

(a) A proceeding in which a juvenile is alleged to be abused, neglected, or dependent may be commenced in the judicial district in which the juvenile resides or is present at the time the petition is filed. If a regional social services department includes counties in more than one judicial district, the department shall file in the judicial district where the child resides or was present when the report required by G.S. 7B-301 was received. Notwithstanding G.S. 153A-257, the absence of a juvenile from the juvenile's home pursuant to a protection plan during an assessment or the provision of case management services by a department of social services shall not change the original venue if it subsequently becomes necessary to file a juvenile petition.

(b) When the director in one county conducts an assessment pursuant to G.S. 7B-302 in another county because a conflict of interest exists, the director in the county conducting the assessment may file a resulting petition in either county.

(c) For good cause, the court may grant motion for change of venue before adjudication. A pre-adjudication change of venue shall not affect the identity of the petitioner.

(d) Any change of venue after adjudication shall be pursuant to G.S. 7B-900.1.

History.
1979, c. 815, s. 1; 1998-202, s. 6; 1999-456, s. 60; 2009-311, s. 2; 2013-129, s. 7; 2017-41, s. 4.4

§ 7B-401. Pleading and process

(a) The pleading in an abuse, neglect, or dependency action is the petition. The process in an abuse, neglect, or dependency action is the summons.

(b) If the court has retained jurisdiction over a juvenile whose custody was granted to a parent and there are no periodic judicial reviews of the placement, the provisions of Article 8 of this subchapter shall apply to any subsequent report of abuse, neglect, or dependency determined by the director of social services to require court action pursuant to G.S. 7B-302.

History.
1979, c. 815, s. 1; 1998-202, s. 6; 1999-456, s. 60; 2013-129, s. 8

§ 7B-401.1. Parties

(a) **Petitioner.** -- Only a county director of social services or the director's authorized representative may file a petition alleging that a juvenile is abused, neglected, or dependent. The petitioner shall remain a party until the court terminates its jurisdiction in the case.

(b) **Parents.** -- The juvenile's parent shall be a party unless one of the following applies:

(1) The parent's rights have been terminated.

(2) The parent has relinquished the juvenile for adoption, unless the court orders that the parent be made a party.

(3) The parent has been convicted under G.S. 14-27.21, 14-27.22, 14-27.23, or 14-27.24 for an offense that resulted in the conception of the juvenile.

(c) **Guardian.** -- A person who is the child's court-appointed guardian of the person or general guardian when the petition is filed shall be a party. A person appointed as the child's guardian pursuant to G.S. 7B-600 shall automatically become a party but only if the court has found that the guardianship is the permanent plan for the juvenile.

(d) **Custodian.** -- A person who is the juvenile's custodian, as defined in G.S. 7B-101(8), when the petition is filed shall be a party. A person to whom custody of the juvenile is awarded in the juvenile proceeding shall automatically become a party but only if the court has found that the custody arrangement is the permanent plan for the juvenile.

(e) **Caretaker.** -- A caretaker shall be a party only if (i) the petition includes allegations relating to the caretaker, (ii) the caretaker has assumed the status and obligation of a parent, or (iii) the court orders that the caretaker be made a party.

(e1) **Foster Parent.** -- A foster parent as defined in G.S. 131D-10.2(9a) providing foster care for the juvenile is not a party to the case and may be allowed to intervene only if the foster parent has authority to file a petition to terminate the parental rights of the juvenile's parents pursuant to G.S. 7B-1103.

(f) **The Juvenile.** -- The juvenile shall be a party.

(g) **Removal of a Party.** -- If a guardian, custodian, or caretaker is a party, the court may discharge that person from the proceeding, making the person no longer a party, if the court finds that the person does not have legal rights that may be affected by the action and that the person's continuation as a party is not necessary to meet the juvenile's needs.

(h) **Intervention.** -- Except as provided in G.S. 7B-1103(b) and subsection (e1) of this section, the court shall not allow intervention by a person who is not the juvenile's parent, guardian, or custodian, but may allow intervention by another county department of social services that has an interest in the proceeding. This section shall not prohibit the court from consolidating a juvenile proceeding with a civil action or claim for custody pursuant to G.S. 7B-200.

(i) **Young Adult in Foster Care.** -- In proceedings held pursuant to G.S. 7B-910.1, the young adult in foster care and the director of the department of social services are parties.

History.

2013-129, s. 9; 2015-136, s. 2; 2015-181, s. 22; 2015-241, s. 12C.9(h); 2015-264, s. 33(a); 2016-94, s. 12C.1(f)

§ 7B-402. Petition

(a) The petition shall contain the name, date of birth, address of the juvenile, the name and last known address of each party as determined by G.S. 7B-401.1, and allegations of facts sufficient to invoke jurisdiction over the juvenile. The petition may contain information on more than one juvenile when the juveniles are from the same home and are before the court for the same reason.

(b) The petition, or an affidavit attached to the petition, shall contain the information required by G.S. 50A-209.

(c) Sufficient copies of the petition shall be prepared so that copies will be available for each party named in the petition, except the juvenile, and for the juvenile's guardian ad litem, the social worker, and any person determined by the court to be a necessary party.

(d) If the petition is filed in a county other than the county of the juvenile's residence, the petitioner shall provide a copy of the petition and any notices of hearing to the director of the department of social services in the county of the juvenile's residence.

History.

1979, c. 815, s. 1; 1981, c. 469, s. 9; 1998-202, s. 6; 1999-456, s. 60; 2004-128, s. 11; 2005-320, s. 3; 2009-311, s. 3; 2010-90, s. 9; 2013-129, s. 10

§ 7B-403. Receipt of reports; filing of petition

(a) All reports concerning a juvenile alleged to be abused, neglected, or dependent shall be referred to the director of the department of social services for screening. Thereafter, if it is determined by the director that a report should be filed as a petition, the petition shall be drawn by the director, verified before an official authorized to administer oaths, and filed by the clerk, recording the date of filing.

(b) A decision of the director of social services not to file a report as a petition shall be reviewed by the prosecutor if review is requested pursuant to G.S. 7B-305.

History.

1979, c. 815, s. 1; 1981, c. 469, ss. 10, 11; 1998-202, s. 6; 1999-456, s. 60

§ 7B-404. Immediate need for petition when clerk's office is closed

(a) When the office of the clerk is closed, a magistrate shall accept for filing the following:

(1) A petition alleging a juvenile to be abused, neglected, or dependent.

(2) A petition alleging the obstruction of or interference with an assessment required by G.S. 7B-302.

(b) The authority of the magistrate under this section is limited to emergency situations when a petition must be filed to obtain a nonsecure custody order or an order under G.S. 7B-303. Any petition accepted for filing under this section shall be delivered to the clerk's office for processing as soon as that office is open for business.

History.

1979, c. 815, s. 1; 1987, c. 409, s. 3; 1998-202, s. 6; 1999-456, s. 60; 2005-55, s. 10; 2017-161, s. 2

§ 7B-405. Commencement of action

An action is commenced by the filing of a petition in the clerk's office when that office is open or by the acceptance of a juvenile petition by a magistrate when the clerk's office is closed, which shall constitute filing.

History.

1979, c. 815, s. 1; 1998-202, s. 6; 1999-456, s. 60; 2017-161, s. 3

§ 7B-406. Issuance of summons

(a) Immediately after a petition has been filed alleging that a juvenile is abused, neglected, or dependent, the clerk shall issue a summons to each party named in the petition, except the juvenile, requiring them to appear for a hearing at the time and place stated in the summons. A copy of the petition shall be attached to each summons. Service of the summons shall be completed as provided in G.S. 7B-407, but the parent of the juvenile shall not be deemed to be under a disability even though the parent is a minor.

(b) A summons shall be on a printed form supplied by the Administrative Office of the Courts and shall include each of the following:

(1) Notice of the nature of the proceeding.

(2) Notice of any right to counsel and information about how a parent may seek the appointment of counsel prior to a hearing if provisional counsel is not identified.

(2a) Repealed by Session Laws 2013-129, s. 11, effective October 1, 2013, and applicable to actions filed or pending on or after that date.

(3) Notice that, if the court determines at the hearing that the allegations of the petition are true, the court will conduct a dispositional hearing to consider the needs of the juvenile and enter an order designed to meet those needs and the objectives of the State.

(4) Notice that the dispositional order or a subsequent order:

   a. May remove the juvenile from the custody of the parent, guardian, or custodian.

   b. May require that the juvenile receive medical, psychiatric, psychological, or other treatment and that the parent participate in the treatment.

   c. May require the parent to undergo psychiatric, psychological, or other treatment or counseling for the purpose of remedying the behaviors or conditions that are alleged in the petition or that contributed to the removal of the juvenile from the custody of that person.

   d. May order the parent to pay for treatment that is ordered for the juvenile or the parent.

   e. May, upon proper notice and hearing and a finding based on the criteria set out in G.S. 7B-1111, terminate the parental rights of the respondent parent.

(c) The summons shall advise the parent that upon service, jurisdiction over that person is obtained and that failure to comply with any order of the court pursuant to G.S. 7B-904 may cause the court to issue a show cause order for contempt.

(d) A summons shall be directed to the person summoned to appear and shall be delivered to any person authorized to serve process.

History.

1979, c. 815, s. 1; 1987 (Reg. Sess., 1988), c. 1090, s. 2; 1995, c. 328, s. 1; 1998-202, s. 6; 1999-456, s. 60; 2000-183, s. 1; 2001-208, s. 1; 2001-487, s. 101; 2004-128, s. 12; 2010-90, s. 10; 2013-129, s. 11

§ 7B-407. Service of summons

The summons shall be served under G.S. 1A-1, Rule 4, upon the parent, guardian, custodian, or caretaker, not less than five days prior to the date of the scheduled hearing. The time for service may be waived in the discretion of the court.

If service by publication under G.S. 1A-1, Rule 4(j1), or service in a foreign country under Rule 4(j3), is required, the cost of the service by publication shall be advanced by the petitioner and may be charged as court costs as the court may direct.

History.

1979, c. 815, s. 1; 1998-202, s. 6; 1999-456, s. 60; 2003-304, s. 1; 2013-129, s. 12; 2017-161, s. 4

§ 7B-408. Copy of petition and notices to guardian ad litem

Immediately after a petition has been filed alleging that a juvenile is abused or neglected, the clerk shall provide a copy of the petition and any notices of hearings to the local guardian ad litem office.

History.

2003-140, s. 6

§§ 7B-409 through 7B-413

Reserved for future codification purposes.

ARTICLE 5
TEMPORARY CUSTODY; NONSECURE CUSTODY; CUSTODY HEARINGS

§ 7B-500. Taking a juvenile into temporary custody; civil and criminal immunity

(a) Temporary custody means the taking of physical custody and providing personal care and supervision until a court order for nonsecure custody can be obtained. A juvenile may be taken into temporary custody without a court order by a law enforcement officer or a department of social services worker if there are reasonable grounds to believe that the juvenile is abused, neglected, or dependent and that the juvenile would be injured or could not be taken into custody if it were first necessary to obtain a court order. If a department of social services worker takes a juvenile into temporary custody under this section, the worker may arrange for the placement, care, supervision, and transportation of the juvenile.

(b) The following individuals shall, without a court order, take into temporary custody an infant under seven days of age that is voluntarily delivered to the individual by the infant's parent who does not express an intent to return for the infant:

    (1) A health care provider, as defined under G.S. 90-21.11, who is on duty or at a hospital or at a local or district health department or at a nonprofit community health center.

    (2) A law enforcement officer who is on duty or at a police station or sheriff's department.

    (3) A social services worker who is on duty or at a local department of social services.

    (4) A certified emergency medical service worker who is on duty or at a fire or emergency medical services station.

(c) An individual who takes an infant into temporary custody under subsection (b) of this section shall perform any act necessary to protect the physical health and well-being of the infant and shall immediately notify the department of social services or a local law enforcement agency. Any individual who takes an infant into temporary custody under subsection (b) of this section may inquire as to the parents' identities and as to any relevant medical history, but the parent is not required to provide the information. The individual shall notify the parent that the parent is not required to provide the information.

(d) Any adult may, without a court order, take into temporary custody an infant under seven days of age that is voluntarily delivered to the individual by the infant's parent who does not express an intent to return for the infant. Any individual who takes an infant into temporary custody under this section shall perform any act necessary to protect the physical health and well-being of the infant and shall immediately notify the department of social services or a local law enforcement agency. An individual who takes an infant into temporary custody under this subsection may inquire as to the parents' identities and as to any relevant medical history, but the parent is not required to provide the information. The individual shall notify the parent that the parent is not required to provide the information.

(e) An individual described in subsection (b) or (d) of this section is immune from any civil or criminal liability that might otherwise be incurred or imposed as a result of any omission or action taken pursuant to the requirements of subsection (c) or (d) of this section as long as that individual was acting in good faith. The immunity established by this subsection does not extend to gross negligence, wanton conduct, or intentional wrongdoing that would otherwise be actionable.

History.

1979, c. 815, s. 1; 1985, c. 408, s. 1; 1985 (Reg. Sess., 1986), c. 863, s. 1; 1994, Ex. Sess., c. 27, s. 2; 1995, c. 391, s. 1; 1997-443, s. 11A.118(a); 1998-202, s. 6; 1999-456, s. 60; 2001-291, s. 2

§ 7B-501. Duties of person taking juvenile into temporary custody

(a) A person who takes a juvenile into custody without a court order under G.S. 7B-500 shall proceed as follows:

    (1) Notify the juvenile's parent, guardian, custodian, or caretaker that the juvenile has been taken into temporary custody and advise the parent, guardian, custodian, or caretaker of the right to be present with the juvenile until a determination is made as to the need for nonsecure custody. Failure to notify the parent that the juvenile is in custody shall not be grounds for release of the juvenile.

    (2) Release the juvenile to the juvenile's parent, guardian, custodian, or caretaker if the person having the juvenile in temporary custody decides that continued custody is unnecessary.

    (3) The person having temporary custody shall communicate with the director of the department of social services who shall consider prehearing diversion. If the decision is made to file a petition, the director shall contact the judge or person delegated authority pursuant to G.S. 7B-502 for a

determination of the need for continued custody.

(b) A juvenile taken into temporary custody under this Article shall not be held for more than 12 hours, or for more than 24 hours if any of the 12 hours falls on a Saturday, Sunday, or legal holiday, unless:

(1) A petition or motion for review has been filed by the director of the department of social services, and

(2) An order for nonsecure custody has been entered by the court.

History.

1979, c. 815, s. 1; 1981, c. 335, ss. 1, 2; 1994, Ex. Sess., c. 17, s. 1; c. 27, s. 3; 1995, c. 391, s. 2; 1998-202, s. 6; 1999-456, s. 60

§ 7B-502. Authority to issue custody orders; delegation

(a) In the case of any juvenile alleged to be within the jurisdiction of the court, the court may order that the juvenile be placed in nonsecure custody pursuant to criteria set out in G.S. 7B-503 when custody of the juvenile is necessary. The order for nonsecure custody may be entered ex parte. Unless the petition is being filed pursuant to G.S. 7B-404, telephonic communication that the department will be seeking nonsecure custody shall be given to counsel, or if unavailable, to a partner or employee at the attorney's office when any of the following occur:

(1) The department has received written notification that a respondent has counsel for the juvenile matter.

(2) The respondent is represented by counsel in a juvenile proceeding within the same county involving another juvenile of the respondent.

Notice is not required to provisional counsel appointed pursuant to G.S. 7B-602.

(b) Any district court judge shall have the authority to issue nonsecure custody orders pursuant to G.S. 7B-503. The chief district court judge may delegate the court's authority to persons other than district court judges by administrative order which shall be filed in the office of the clerk of superior court. The administrative order shall specify which persons shall be contacted for approval of a nonsecure custody order pursuant to G.S. 7B-503.

History.

1979, c. 815, s. 1; 1981, c. 425; 1983, c. 590, s. 1; 1998-202, s. 6; 1999-456, s. 60; 2015-136, s. 3

§ 7B-503. Criteria for nonsecure custody

(a) When a request is made for nonsecure custody, the court shall first consider release of

the juvenile to the juvenile's parent, relative, guardian, custodian, or other responsible adult. An order for nonsecure custody shall be made only when there is a reasonable factual basis to believe the matters alleged in the petition are true, and any of the following apply:

(1) The juvenile has been abandoned.

(2) The juvenile has suffered physical injury, sexual abuse, or serious emotional damage as defined by G.S. 7B-101(1)e.

(3) The juvenile is exposed to a substantial risk of physical injury or sexual abuse because the parent, guardian, custodian, or caretaker has created the conditions likely to cause injury or abuse or has failed to provide, or is unable to provide, adequate supervision or protection.

(4) The juvenile is in need of medical treatment to cure, alleviate, or prevent suffering serious physical harm which may result in death, disfigurement, or substantial impairment of bodily functions, and the juvenile's parent, guardian, custodian, or caretaker is unwilling or unable to provide or consent to the medical treatment.

(5) The parent, guardian, custodian, or caretaker consents to the nonsecure custody order.

(6) The juvenile is a runaway and consents to nonsecure custody.

A juvenile alleged to be abused, neglected, or dependent shall be placed in nonsecure custody only when there is a reasonable factual basis to believe that there are no other reasonable means available to protect the juvenile. In no case shall a juvenile alleged to be abused, neglected, or dependent be placed in secure custody.

(b) Whenever a petition is filed under G.S. 7B-302(d1), the court shall rule on the petition prior to returning the child to a home where the alleged abuser or abusers are or have been present. If the court finds that the alleged abuser or abusers have a history of violent behavior against people, the court shall order the alleged abuser or abusers to submit to a complete mental health evaluation by a licensed psychologist or psychiatrist. The court may order the alleged abuser or abusers to pay the cost of any mental health evaluation required under this section.

History.

1979, c. 815, s. 1; 1981, c. 426, ss. 1-4; c. 526; 1983, c. 590, ss. 2-6; 1987, c. 101; 1987 (Reg. Sess., 1988), c. 1090, s. 3; 1989, c. 550; 1998-202, s. 6; 1999-318, s. 4; 1999-456, s. 60; 2011-295, s. 2; 2019-33, s. 6

§ 7B-504. Order for nonsecure custody

The custody order shall be in writing and shall direct a law enforcement officer or other authorized person to take physical custody of the juvenile and to make due return on the order. A copy of the order shall be given to the juvenile's parent, guardian, custodian, or caretaker by the official executing the order.

An officer receiving an order for custody which is complete and regular on its face may execute it in accordance with its terms. If the court finds on the basis of the petition and request for nonsecure custody or the testimony of the petitioner that a less intrusive remedy is not available, the court may authorize a law enforcement officer to enter private property to take physical custody of the juvenile. If required by exigent circumstances of the case, the court may authorize a law enforcement officer to make a forcible entry at any hour. The officer is not required to inquire into the regularity or continued validity of the order and shall not incur criminal or civil liability for its due service.

History.
1979, c. 815, s. 1; 1989, c. 124; 1998-202, s. 6; 1999-456, s. 60; 2015-43, s. 1

§ 7B-505. Placement while in nonsecure custody

(a) A juvenile meeting the criteria set out in G.S. 7B-503 may be placed in nonsecure custody with the department of social services or a person designated in the order for temporary residential placement in any of the following:

(1) A licensed foster home or a home otherwise authorized by law to provide such care.

(2) A facility operated by the department of social services.

(3) Any other home or facility, including the home of a parent, relative, nonrelative kin, or other person with legal custody of a sibling of the juvenile, approved by the court and designated in the order.

(a1) If juvenile siblings are removed from the home and placed in the nonsecure custody of a county department of social services, the director shall make reasonable efforts to place the juvenile siblings in the same home. The director is not required to make reasonable efforts under this subsection if the director documents that placing the juvenile siblings would be contrary to the safety or well-being of any of the juvenile siblings. If, after making reasonable efforts, the director is unable to place the juvenile siblings in the same home, the director shall make reasonable efforts to provide frequent sibling visitation and ongoing interaction between the juvenile siblings, unless the director documents that frequent visitation or other ongoing interaction between the juvenile siblings would be contrary to the safety or well-being of any of the juvenile siblings.

(b) The court shall order the department of social services to make diligent efforts to notify relatives and other persons with legal custody of a sibling of the juvenile that the juvenile is in nonsecure custody and of any hearings scheduled to occur pursuant to G.S. 7B-506, unless the court finds the notification would be contrary to the best interests of the juvenile. The department of social services shall use due diligence to identify and notify adult relatives and other persons with legal custody of a sibling of the juvenile within 30 days after the initial order removing custody. The department shall file with the court information regarding attempts made to identify and notify adult relatives of the juvenile and persons with legal custody of a sibling of the juvenile. In placing a juvenile in nonsecure custody under this section, the court shall first consider whether a relative of the juvenile is willing and able to provide proper care and supervision of the juvenile in a safe home. If the court finds that the relative is willing and able to provide proper care and supervision in a safe home, then the court shall order placement of the juvenile with the relative unless the court finds that placement with the relative would be contrary to the best interests of the juvenile.

(c) If the court does not place the juvenile with a relative, the court may consider whether an appropriate former foster parent, nonrelative kin, or other persons with legal custody of a sibling of the juvenile are willing and able to provide proper care and supervision of the juvenile in a safe home. The court may order the department to notify the juvenile's State-recognized tribe of the need for nonsecure custody for the purpose of locating relatives or nonrelative kin for placement. The court may order placement of the juvenile with nonrelative kin if the court finds the placement is in the juvenile's best interests.

(d) In placing a juvenile in nonsecure custody under this section, the court shall also consider whether it is in the juvenile's best interest to remain in the juvenile's community of residence. In placing a juvenile in nonsecure custody under this section, the court shall consider the Indian Child Welfare Act, Pub. L. No. 95-608, 25 U.S.C. §§ 1901, et seq., as amended, and the Howard M. Metzenbaum Multiethnic Placement Act of 1994, Pub. L. No. 103-382, 108 Stat. 4056, as amended, as they may apply. Placement of a juvenile with a relative outside of this State must be in accordance with the Interstate Compact on the Placement of Children, Article 38 of this Chapter.

History.
1979, c. 815, s. 1; 1983, c. 639, ss. 1, 2; 1997-390, s. 4; 1997-443, s. 11A.118(a); 1998-202, s. 6; 1998-229, ss. 3, 20; 1999-456, s. 60; 2002-164, s. 4.7; 2013-129, s. 13; 2015-135, s. 2.2; 2015-136, s. 4; 2017-161, s. 5; 2021-100, s. 3; 2021-132, s. 1(d)

§ 7B-505.1. Consent for medical care for a juvenile placed in nonsecure custody of a department of social services

(a) Unless the court orders otherwise, when a juvenile is placed in the nonsecure custody of a county department of social services, the director may arrange for, provide, or consent to any of the following:

(1) Routine medical and dental care or treatment, including, but not limited to, treatment for common pediatric illnesses and injuries that require prompt intervention.

(2) Emergency medical, surgical, psychiatric, psychological, or mental health care or treatment.

(3) Testing and evaluation in exigent circumstances.

(b) When placing a juvenile in nonsecure custody of a county department of social services pursuant to G.S. 7B-502, the court may authorize the director to consent to a Child Medical Evaluation upon written findings that demonstrate the director's compelling interest in having the juvenile evaluated prior to the hearing required by G.S. 7B-506.

(c) The director shall obtain authorization from the juvenile's parent, guardian, or custodian to consent to all care or treatment not covered by subsection (a) or (b) of this section, except that the court may authorize the director to provide consent after a hearing at which the court finds by clear and convincing evidence that the care, treatment, or evaluation requested is in the juvenile's best interest. Care and treatment covered by this subsection includes:

(1) Prescriptions for psychotropic medications.

(2) Participation in clinical trials.

(3) Immunizations when it is known that the parent has a bona fide religious objection to the standard schedule of immunizations.

(4) Child Medical Evaluations not governed by subsection (b) of this section, comprehensive clinical assessments, or other mental health evaluations.

(5) Surgical, medical, or dental procedures or tests that require informed consent.

(6) Psychiatric, psychological, or mental health care or treatment that requires informed consent.

(d) For any care or treatment provided, the director shall make reasonable efforts to promptly notify the parent, guardian, or custodian that care or treatment will be or has been provided and give the parent or guardian frequent status reports on the juvenile's treatment and the care provided. Upon request of the juvenile's parent, guardian, or custodian, the director shall make available to the parent, guardian, or custodian any results or records of the aforementioned evaluations, except when prohibited by G.S. 122C-53(d). The results of a Child Medical Evaluation shall only be disclosed according to the provisions of G.S. 7B-700.

(e) Except as prohibited by federal law, the department may disclose confidential information deemed necessary for the juvenile's assessment and treatment to a health care provider serving the juvenile.

(f) Unless the court has ordered otherwise, except as prohibited by federal law, a health care provider shall disclose confidential information about a juvenile to a director of a county department of social services with custody of the juvenile and a parent, guardian, or custodian.

History.
2015-136, s. 5; 2016-94, s. 12C.1(f1); 2017-161, s. 6

§ 7B-506. Hearing to determine need for continued nonsecure custody

(a) No juvenile shall be held under a nonsecure custody order for more than seven calendar days without a hearing on the merits or a hearing to determine the need for continued custody. A hearing on nonsecure custody conducted under this subsection may be continued for up to 10 business days with the consent of the juvenile's parent, guardian, custodian, or caretaker and, if appointed, the juvenile's guardian ad litem. In addition, the court may require the consent of additional parties or may schedule the hearing on custody despite a party's consent to a continuance. In every case in which an order has been entered by an official exercising authority delegated pursuant to G.S. 7B-502, a hearing to determine the need for continued custody shall be conducted on the day of the next regularly scheduled session of district court in the city or county where the order was entered if such session precedes the expiration of the applicable time period set forth in this subsection: Provided, that if such session does not precede the expiration of the time period, the hearing may be conducted at another regularly scheduled session of district court in the district where the order was entered.

(b) At a hearing to determine the need for continued custody, the court shall receive testimony and shall allow the parties the right to introduce evidence, to be heard in the person's own behalf, and to examine witnesses. The petitioner shall bear the burden at every stage of the proceedings to provide clear and convincing evidence that the juvenile's placement in custody is necessary. The court shall not be bound by the usual rules of evidence at such hearings.

(c) The court shall be bound by criteria set forth in G.S. 7B-503 in determining whether continued custody is warranted.

(c1) In determining whether continued custody is warranted, the court shall consider the opinion of the mental health professional who performed an evaluation under G.S. 7B-503(b) before returning the juvenile to the custody of that individual.

(d) If the court determines that the juvenile meets the criteria in G.S. 7B-503 and should continue in custody, the court shall issue an order to that effect. The order shall be in writing with appropriate findings of fact and signed and entered within 30 days of the completion of the hearing. The findings of fact shall include the evidence relied upon in reaching the decision and purposes which continued custody is to achieve.

(e) If the court orders at the hearing required in subsection (a) of this section that the juvenile remain in custody, a subsequent hearing on continued custody shall be held within seven business days of that hearing, excluding Saturdays, Sundays, and legal holidays when the courthouse is closed for transactions, and pending a hearing on the merits, hearings thereafter shall be held at intervals of no more than 30 calendar days.

(f) Hearings conducted under subsection (e) of this section may be waived only with the consent of the juvenile's parent, guardian, custodian, or caretaker, and, if appointed, the juvenile's guardian ad litem.

The court may require the consent of additional parties or schedule a hearing despite a party's consent to waiver.

(g) In addition to the hearings required under this section, any party may schedule a hearing on the issue of placement.

(g1) The provisions of G.S. 7B-905.1 shall apply to determine visitation.

(h) At each hearing to determine the need for continued custody, the court shall determine the following:

(1) Inquire as to the identity and location of any missing parent and whether paternity is at issue. The court shall include findings as to the efforts undertaken to locate the missing parent and to serve that parent, as well as efforts undertaken to establish paternity when paternity is an issue. The order may provide for specific efforts aimed at determining the identity and location of any missing parent, as well as specific efforts aimed at establishing paternity.

(2) Inquire about efforts made to identify and notify relatives as potential resources for placement or support and as to whether a relative of the juvenile is willing and able to provide proper care and supervision of the juvenile in a safe home. If the court finds that the relative is willing and able to provide proper care and supervision in a safe home, then the court shall order temporary placement of the juvenile with the relative unless the court finds that placement with the relative would be contrary to the best interests of the juvenile. In placing a juvenile in nonsecure custody under this section, the court shall consider the Indian Child Welfare Act, Pub. L. No. 95-608, 25 U.S.C. §§ 1901, et seq., as amended, and the Howard M. Metzenbaum Multiethnic Placement Act of 1994, Pub. L. No. 103-382, 108 Stat. 4056, as amended, as they may apply. Placement of a juvenile with a relative outside of this State must be in accordance with the Interstate Compact on the Placement of Children set forth in Article 38 of this Chapter.

(2a) If the court does not place the juvenile with a relative, the court may consider whether nonrelative kin or other persons with legal custody of a sibling of the juvenile is willing and able to provide proper care and supervision of the juvenile in a safe home. The court may order the department to notify the juvenile's State-recognized tribe of the need for nonsecure custody for the purpose of locating relatives or nonrelative kin for placement. The court may order placement of the juvenile with nonrelative kin or other persons with legal custody of a sibling of the juvenile if the court finds the placement is in the juvenile's best interests.

(3) Inquire as to whether there are other juveniles remaining in the home from which the juvenile was removed and, if there are, inquire as to the specific findings of the assessment conducted under G.S. 7B-302 and any actions taken or services provided by the director for the protection of the other juveniles.

History.
1979, c. 815, s. 1; 1981, c. 469, s. 13; 1987 (Reg. Sess., 1988), c. 1090, s. 4; 1994, Ex. Sess., c. 27, s. 1; 1997-390, ss. 5, 6; 1998-229, s. 4; 1998-202, s. 6; 1998-229, ss. 4.1, 21; 1999-318, s. 5; 1999-456, s. 60; 2001-208, ss. 16, 24; 2001-487, s. 101; 2003-337, s. 9; 2005-55, s. 11; 2007-276, s. 1; 2013-129, s. 14; 2015-136, s. 6; 2017-161, s. 7

§ 7B-507. Juvenile placed in nonsecure custody of a department of social services

(a) An order placing or continuing the placement of a juvenile in the nonsecure custody of a county department of social services:

(1) Shall contain a finding that the juvenile's continuation in or return to the juvenile's own home would be contrary to the juvenile's health and safety.

(2) Shall contain specific findings as to whether a county department of social services has made reasonable efforts to prevent the need for placement of the juvenile. In determining whether efforts to prevent the placement of the juvenile were reasonable, the juvenile's health and safety shall be the paramount concern. The court may find that efforts to prevent the need for the juvenile's placement were precluded by an immediate threat of harm to the juvenile. A finding that reasonable efforts were not made by a county department of social services shall not preclude the entry of an order authorizing the juvenile's placement when the court finds that placement is necessary for the protection of the juvenile.

(3) Repealed by Session Laws 2015-136, s. 7, effective October 1, 2015, and applicable to actions filed or pending on or after that date.

(4) Shall specify that the juvenile's placement and care are the responsibility of the county department of social services and that the department is to provide or arrange for the foster care or other placement of the juvenile, unless after considering the department's recommendations, the court orders a specific placement the court finds to be in the juvenile's best interests.

(5) May order services or other efforts aimed at returning the juvenile to a safe home.

(b) through (d) Repealed by Session Laws 2015-136, s. 7, effective October 1, 2015, and applicable to actions filed or pending on or after that date.

History.
1998-229, ss. 4.1, 21.1; 1999-456, s. 60; 2001-487, s. 2; 2005-398, s. 1; 2011-295, s. 3; 2013-129, s. 15; 2013-378, s. 1; 2015-136, s. 7

§ 7B-508. Telephonic communication authorized

All communications, notices, orders, authorizations, and requests authorized or required by G.S. 7B-501, 7B-503, and 7B-504 may be made by telephone when other means of communication are impractical. All written orders pursuant to telephonic communication shall bear the name and the title of the person communicating by telephone, the signature and the title of the official entering the order, and the hour and the date of the authorization.

History.
1979, c. 815, s. 1; 1981, c. 469, s. 13; 1987 (Reg. Sess., 1988), c. 1090, s. 4; 1994, Ex. Sess., c. 27, s. 1; 1997-390, ss. 5, 6; 1998-202, s. 6; 1998-229, s. 4; 1999-456, s. 60

ARTICLE 6
BASIC RIGHTS

§ 7B-600. Appointment of guardian

(a) In any case when no parent appears in a hearing with the juvenile or when the court finds it would be in the best interests of the juvenile, the court may appoint a guardian of the person for the juvenile. The guardian shall operate under the supervision of the court with or without bond and shall file only such reports as the court shall require. The guardian shall have the care, custody, and control of the juvenile or may arrange a suitable placement for the juvenile and may represent the juvenile in legal actions before any court. The guardian may consent to certain actions on the part of the juvenile in place of the parent including (i) marriage, (ii) enlisting in the Armed Forces of the United States, and (iii) enrollment in school. The guardian may also consent to any necessary remedial, psychological, medical, or surgical treatment for the juvenile. The authority of the guardian shall continue until the guardianship is terminated by court order, until the juvenile is emancipated pursuant to Article 35 of Subchapter IV of this Chapter, or until the juvenile reaches the age of majority.

(b) In any case where the court has determined that the appointment of a relative or other suitable person as guardian of the person for a juvenile is the permanent plan for the juvenile and appoints a guardian under this section, the guardian becomes a party to the proceeding. The court may terminate the guardianship only if (i) the court finds that the relationship between the guardian and the juvenile is no longer in the juvenile's best interest, (ii) the guardian is unfit, (iii) the guardian has neglected a guardian's duties, or (iv) the guardian is unwilling or unable to continue assuming a guardian's duties.

(b1) If a party files a motion under G.S. 7B-906.1 or G.S. 7B-1000, the court may, prior to conducting a review hearing, do one or more of the following:

(1) Order the county department of social services to conduct an investigation and file a written report of the investigation regarding the performance of the guardian of the person of the juvenile and give testimony concerning its investigation.

(2) Utilize the community resources in behavioral sciences and other professions in the investigation and study of the guardian.

(3) Ensure that a guardian ad litem has been appointed for the juvenile in accordance with G.S. 7B-601 and has been notified of the pending motion or petition.

(4) Take any other action necessary in order to make a determination in a particular case.

(c) If the court appoints an individual guardian of the person pursuant to this section, the court shall verify that the person being appointed as guardian of the juvenile understands the legal significance of the appointment and will have adequate resources to care appropriately for the juvenile. The fact that the prospective guardian has provided a stable placement for the juvenile for at least six consecutive months is evidence that the person has adequate resources.

History.
1979, c. 815, s. 1; 1997-390, s. 7; 1998-202, s. 6; 1999-456, s. 60; 2000-124, s. 1; 2003-140, s. 9(a); 2011-183, s. 3; 2011-295, s. 4; 2013-129, s. 16; 2019-33, s. 7(a)

§ 7B-601. Appointment and duties of guardian ad litem

(a) When in a petition a juvenile is alleged to be abused or neglected, the court shall appoint a guardian ad litem to represent the juvenile. When a juvenile is alleged to be dependent, the court may appoint a guardian ad litem to represent the juvenile. The juvenile is a party in all actions under this Subchapter. The guardian ad litem and attorney advocate have standing to represent the juvenile in all actions under this Subchapter where they have been appointed. The appointment shall be made pursuant to the program established by Article 12 of this Chapter unless representation is otherwise provided pursuant to G.S. 7B-1202 or G.S. 7B-1203. The appointment shall terminate when the permanent plan has been achieved for the juvenile and approved by the court. The court may reappoint the guardian ad litem pursuant to a showing of good cause upon motion of any party, including the guardian ad litem, or of the court. In every case where a nonattorney is appointed as a guardian ad litem, an attorney shall be appointed in the case in order to assure protection of the juvenile's legal rights throughout the proceeding. The duties of the guardian ad litem program shall be to make an investigation to determine the facts, the needs of the juvenile, and the available resources within the family and community to meet those needs; to facilitate, when appropriate, the settlement of disputed issues; to offer evidence and examine witnesses at adjudication; to explore options with the court at the dispositional hearing; to conduct follow-up investigations to insure that the orders of the court are being properly executed; to report to the court when the needs of the juvenile are not being met; and to protect and promote the best interests of the juvenile

until formally relieved of the responsibility by the court.

(b) The court may authorize the guardian ad litem to accompany the juvenile to court in any criminal action wherein the juvenile may be called on to testify in a matter relating to abuse.

(c) The guardian ad litem has the authority to obtain any information or reports, whether or not confidential, that may in the guardian ad litem's opinion be relevant to the case. No privilege other than the attorney-client privilege may be invoked to prevent the guardian ad litem and the court from obtaining such information. The confidentiality of the information or reports shall be respected by the guardian ad litem, and no disclosure of any information or reports shall be made to anyone except by order of the court or unless otherwise provided by law.

History.
1979, c. 815, s. 1; 1981, c. 528; 1983, c. 761, s. 159; 1987 (Reg. Sess., 1988), c. 1090, s. 5; 1993, c. 537, s. 1; 1995, c. 324, s. 21.13; 1998-202, s. 6; 1999-432, s. 1; 1999-456, s. 60

§ 7B-602. Parent's right to counsel; guardian ad litem

(a) In cases where the juvenile petition alleges that a juvenile is abused, neglected, or dependent, the parent has the right to counsel and to appointed counsel in cases of indigency unless that person waives the right. When a petition is filed alleging that a juvenile is abused, neglected, or dependent, the clerk shall appoint provisional counsel for each parent named in the petition in accordance with rules adopted by the Office of Indigent Defense Services, shall indicate the appointment on the juvenile summons or attached notice, and shall provide a copy of the petition and summons or notice to the attorney. At the first hearing, the court shall dismiss the provisional counsel if the respondent parent:

(1) Does not appear at the hearing;

(2) Does not qualify for court-appointed counsel;

(3) Has retained counsel; or

(4) Waives the right to counsel.

The court shall confirm the appointment of counsel if subdivisions (1) through (4) of this subsection are not applicable to the respondent parent.

The court may reconsider a parent's eligibility and desire for appointed counsel at any stage of the proceeding.

(a1) A parent qualifying for appointed counsel may be permitted to proceed without the assistance of counsel only after the court examines the parent and makes findings of fact sufficient to show that the waiver is knowing and voluntary. The court's examination shall be reported as provided in G.S. 7B-806.

(b) In addition to the right to appointed counsel set forth above, a guardian ad litem shall be appointed in accordance with the provisions of G.S. 1A-1, Rule 17, to represent a parent who is under the age of 18 years and who is not married or otherwise emancipated. The appointment of a guardian ad litem under this subsection shall not affect the minor parent's entitlement to a guardian ad litem pursuant to G.S. 7B-601 in the event that the minor parent is the subject of a separate juvenile petition.

(c) On motion of any party or on the court's own motion, the court may appoint a guardian ad litem for a parent who is incompetent in accordance with G.S. 1A-1, Rule 17.

(d) The parent's counsel shall not be appointed to serve as the guardian ad litem and the guardian ad litem shall not act as the parent's attorney. Communications between the guardian ad litem appointed under this section and the parent and between the guardian ad litem and the parent's counsel shall be privileged and confidential to the same extent that communications between the parent and the parent's counsel are privileged and confidential.

(e) Repealed by Session Laws 2013-129, s. 17, effective October 1, 2013, and applicable to actions filed or pending on or after that date.

History.
1979, c. 815, s. 1; 1981, c. 469, s. 14; 1998-202, s. 6; 1999-456, s. 60; 2000-144, s. 16; 2001-208, s. 2; 2001-487, s. 101; 2005-398, s. 2; 2011-326, s. 12(a); 2013-129, s. 17; 2021-100, s. 4

§ 7B-603. Payment of court-appointed attorney or guardian ad litem

(a) An attorney or guardian ad litem appointed pursuant to G.S. 7B-601 shall be paid a reasonable fee fixed by the court or by direct engagement for specialized guardian ad litem services through the Administrative Office of the Courts.

(a1) The court may require payment of the fee for an attorney or guardian ad litem appointed pursuant to G.S. 7B-601 from a person other than the juvenile as provided in G.S. 7A-450.1, 7A-450.2, and 7A-450.3. In no event shall the parent or guardian be required to pay the fees for a court-appointed attorney or guardian ad litem in an abuse, neglect, or dependency proceeding unless the juvenile has been adjudicated to be abused, neglected, or dependent or, in a proceeding to terminate parental rights, unless the parent's rights have been terminated. If the party is ordered to reimburse the State for attorney or guardian ad litem fees and fails to comply with the order at the time of disposition,

the court shall file a judgment against the party for the amount due the State.

(b) An attorney or guardian ad litem appointed pursuant to G.S. 7B-602 or pursuant to any other provision of the Juvenile Code for which the Office of Indigent Defense Services is responsible for providing counsel shall be paid a reasonable fee in accordance with rules adopted by the Office of Indigent Defense Services.

(b1) The court may require payment of the fee for an attorney appointed pursuant to G.S. 7B-602 or G.S. 7B-1101.1 from the respondent. In no event shall the respondent be required to pay the fees for a court-appointed attorney in an abuse, neglect, or dependency proceeding unless the juvenile has been adjudicated to be abused, neglected, or dependent or, in a proceeding to terminate parental rights, unless the respondent's rights have been terminated. At the dispositional hearing or other appropriate hearing, the court shall make a determination whether the respondent should be held responsible for reimbursing the State for the respondent's attorneys' fees. This determination shall include the respondent's financial ability to pay.

If the court determines that the respondent is responsible for reimbursing the State for the respondent's attorneys' fees, the court shall so order. If the respondent does not comply with the order at the time of disposition, the court shall file a judgment against the respondent for the amount due the State.

(c) Repealed by Session Laws 2005-254, s. 2, effective October 1, 2005, and applicable to the appointment of counsel on or after that date.

History.
1979, c. 815, s. 1; 1983, c. 726, ss. 2, 3; 1987 (Reg. Sess., 1988), c. 1090, s. 6; 1991, c. 575, s. 1; 1998-202, s. 6; 1999-456, s. 60; 2000-144, s. 17; 2005-254, s. 2 ., 2014-115, s. 21; 2017-158, s. 25

ARTICLE 7
DISCOVERY

§ 7B-700. Sharing of information; discovery

(a) **Sharing of Information.** -- A department of social services is authorized to share with any other party information relevant to the subject matter of an action pending under this Subchapter. However, this subsection does not authorize the disclosure of the identity of the reporter or any uniquely identifying information that would lead to the discovery of the reporter's identity in accordance with G.S. 7B-302 or the identity of any other person where the agency making the information available determines that the disclosure would be likely to endanger the life or safety of the person.

(b) **Local Rules.** -- The chief district court judge may adopt local rules or enter an administrative order addressing the sharing of information among parties and the use of discovery.

(c) **Discovery.** -- Any party may file a motion for discovery. The motion shall contain a specific description of the information sought and a statement that the requesting party has made a reasonable effort to obtain the information pursuant to subsections (a) and (b) of this section or that the information cannot be obtained pursuant to subsections (a) and (b) of this section. The motion shall be served upon all parties pursuant to G.S. 1A-1, Rule 5. The motion shall be heard and ruled upon within 10 business days of the filing of the motion. The court may grant, restrict, defer, or deny the relief requested. Any order shall avoid unnecessary delay of the hearing, establish expedited deadlines for completion, and conform to G.S. 7B-803.

(d) **Protective Order.** -- Any party served with a motion for discovery may request that the discovery be denied, restricted, or deferred and shall submit, for in camera inspection, the document, information, or materials the party seeks to protect. If the court enters any order granting relief, copies of the documents, information, or materials submitted in camera shall be preserved for appellate review in the event of an appeal.

(e) **Redisclosure.** -- Information obtained through discovery or sharing of information under this section may not be redisclosed if the redisclosure is prohibited by State or federal law.

(f) **Guardian Ad Litem.** -- Unless provided otherwise by local rules, information or reports obtained by the guardian ad litem pursuant to G.S. 7B-601 are not subject to disclosure pursuant to this subsection, except that reports and records shall be shared with all parties before submission to the court.

History.
1979, c. 815, s. 1; 1998-202, s. 6; 1999-456, s. 60; 2009-311, s. 4

ARTICLE 8
HEARING PROCEDURES

§ 7B-800. Amendment of petition

The court, in its discretion, may permit a petition to be amended. The court shall direct the manner in which an amended petition shall be served and the time allowed for a party to prepare after the petition has been amended.

History.
1979, c. 815, s. 1; 1998-202, s. 6; 1999-456, s. 60; 2010-90, s. 11

§ 7B-800.1. Pre-adjudication hearing

(a) Prior to the adjudicatory hearing, the court shall consider the following:

(1) Retention or release of provisional counsel.

(2) Identification of the parties to the proceeding.

(3) Whether paternity has been established or efforts made to establish paternity, including the identity and location of any missing parent.

(4) Whether relatives, parents, or other persons with legal custody of a sibling of the juvenile have been identified and notified as potential resources for placement or support.

(5) Whether all summons, service of process, and notice requirements have been met.

(5a) Whether the petition has been properly verified and invokes jurisdiction.

(6) Any pretrial motions, including (i) appointment of a guardian ad litem in accordance with G.S. 7B-602, (ii) discovery motions in accordance with G.S. 7B-700, (iii) amendment of the petition in accordance with G.S. 7B-800, or (iv) any motion for a continuance of the adjudicatory hearing in accordance with G.S. 7B-803.

(7) Any other issue that can be properly addressed as a preliminary matter.

(b) The pre-adjudication hearing may be combined with a hearing on the need for nonsecure custody or any pretrial hearing or conducted in accordance with local rules.

(c) The parties may enter stipulations in accordance with G.S. 7B-807 or enter a consent order in accordance with G.S. 7B-801.

History.
2013-129, s. 18; 2014-16, s. 1; 2015-135, s. 2.3; 2015-136, s. 8

§ 7B-801. Hearing

(a) At any hearing authorized or required under this Subchapter, the court in its discretion shall determine whether the hearing or any part of the hearing shall be closed to the public. In determining whether to close the hearing or any part of the hearing, the court shall consider the circumstances of the case, including, but not limited to, the following factors:

(1) The nature of the allegations against the juvenile's parent, guardian, custodian or caretaker;

(2) The age and maturity of the juvenile;

(3) The benefit to the juvenile of confidentiality;

(4) The benefit to the juvenile of an open hearing; and

(5) The extent to which the confidentiality afforded the juvenile's record pursuant to G.S. 132-1.4(l) and G.S. 7B-2901 will be compromised by an open hearing.

(b) No hearing or part of a hearing shall be closed by the court if the juvenile requests that it remain open.

(b1) Nothing in this Subchapter precludes the court in an abuse, neglect, or dependency proceeding from entering a consent adjudication order, disposition order, review order, or permanency planning order when each of the following apply:

(1) All parties are present or represented by counsel, who is present and authorized to consent.

(2) The juvenile is represented by counsel.

(3) The court makes sufficient findings of fact.

(c) The adjudicatory hearing shall be held in the district at such time and place as the chief district court judge shall designate, but no later than 60 days from the filing of the petition unless the judge pursuant to G.S. 7B-803 orders that it be held at a later time.

History.
1979, c. 815, s. 1; 1998-202, s. 6; 1998-229, ss. 5, 22; 1999-456, s. 60; 2011-295, s. 5

§ 7B-802. Conduct of hearing

The adjudicatory hearing shall be a judicial process designed to adjudicate the existence or nonexistence of any of the conditions alleged in a petition. In the adjudicatory hearing, the court shall protect the rights of the juvenile and the juvenile's parent to assure due process of law.

History.
1979, c. 815, s. 1; 1998-202, s. 6; 1999-456, s. 60

§ 7B-803. Continuances

The court may, for good cause, continue the hearing for as long as is reasonably required to receive additional evidence, reports, or assessments that the court has requested, or other information needed in the best interests of the juvenile and to allow for a reasonable time for the parties to conduct expeditious discovery. Otherwise, continuances shall be granted only in extraordinary circumstances when necessary for the proper administration of justice or in the best interests of the juvenile. Resolution of a pending criminal charge against a respondent

arising out of the same transaction or occurrence as the juvenile petition shall not be the sole extraordinary circumstance for granting a continuance.

History.
1979, c. 815, s. 1; 1987 (Reg. Sess., 1988), c. 1090, s. 9; 1998-202, s. 6; 1999-456, s. 60; 2013-129, s. 19

§ 7B-804. Rules of evidence

Where the juvenile is alleged to be abused, neglected, or dependent, the rules of evidence in civil cases shall apply.

History.
1979, c. 815, s. 1; 1981, ch. 469, s. 17; 1998-202, s. 6; 1999-456, s. 60

§ 7B-805. Quantum of proof in adjudicatory hearing

The allegations in a petition alleging that a juvenile is abused, neglected, or dependent shall be proved by clear and convincing evidence.

History.
1979, c. 815, s. 1; 1998-202, s. 6; 1999-456, s. 60; 2010-90, s. 12; 2013-129, s. 20

§ 7B-806. Record of proceedings

All adjudicatory and dispositional hearings shall be recorded by stenographic notes or by electronic or mechanical means. Records shall be reduced to a written transcript only when timely notice of appeal has been given. The court may order that other hearings be recorded.

History.
1979, c. 815, s. 1; 1998-202, s. 6; 1999-456, s. 60

§ 7B-807. Adjudication

(a) If the court finds from the evidence, including stipulations by a party, that the allegations in the petition have been proven by clear and convincing evidence, the court shall so state. A record of specific stipulated adjudicatory facts shall be made by either reducing the facts to a writing, signed by each party stipulating to them and submitted to the court; or by reading the facts into the record, followed by an oral statement of agreement from each party stipulating to them. If the court finds that the allegations have not been proven, the court shall dismiss the petition with prejudice, and if the juvenile is in nonsecure custody, the juvenile shall be released to the parent, guardian, custodian, or caretaker.

(a1) Repealed by Session Laws 2013-129, s. 21, effective October 1, 2013, and applicable to actions filed or pending on or after that date.

(b) The adjudicatory order shall be in writing and shall contain appropriate findings of fact and conclusions of law. The order shall be reduced to writing, signed, and entered no later than 30 days following the completion of the hearing. If the order is not entered within 30 days following completion of the hearing, the clerk of court for juvenile matters shall schedule a subsequent hearing at the first session of court scheduled for the hearing of juvenile matters following the 30-day period to determine and explain the reason for the delay and to obtain any needed clarification as to the contents of the order. The order shall be entered within 10 days of the subsequent hearing required by this subsection.

History.

1979, c. 815, s. 1; 1998-202, s. 6; 1999-456, s. 60; 2001-208, s. 17; 2001-487, s. 101; 2005-398, s. 3; 2010-90, s. 13; 2011-295, s. 6; 2013-129, s. 21

§ 7B-808. Predisposition report

(a) The court shall proceed to the dispositional hearing upon receipt of sufficient social, medical, psychiatric, psychological, and educational information. No predisposition report shall be submitted to or considered by the court prior to the completion of the adjudicatory hearing. The court may proceed with the dispositional hearing without receiving a predisposition report if the court makes a written finding that a report is not necessary.

(b) The director of the department of social services shall prepare the predisposition report for the court containing the results of any mental health evaluation under G.S. 7B-503, a placement plan, and a treatment plan the director deems appropriate to meet the juvenile's needs.

(c) The chief district court judge may adopt local rules or make an administrative order addressing the sharing of the reports among parties, including an order that prohibits disclosure of the report to the juvenile if the court determines that disclosure would not be in the best interest of the juvenile. Such local rules or administrative order may not:

(1) Prohibit a party entitled by law to receive confidential information from receiving that information.

(2) Allow disclosure of any confidential source protected by statute.

History.

1979, c. 815, s. 1; 1998-202, s. 6; 1999-456, s. 60; 2003-140, s. 2; 2004-203, s. 17

ARTICLE 9
DISPOSITIONS

§ 7B-900. Purpose

The purpose of dispositions in juvenile actions is to design an appropriate plan to meet the needs of the juvenile and to achieve the objectives of the State in exercising jurisdiction. If possible, the initial approach should involve working with the juvenile and the juvenile's family in their own home so that the appropriate community resources may be involved in care, supervision, and treatment according to the needs of the juvenile. Thus, the court should arrange for appropriate community-level services to be provided to the juvenile and the juvenile's family in order to strengthen the home situation.

History.

1979, c. 815, s. 1; 1995 (Reg. Sess., 1996), c. 609, s. 1; 1998-202, s. 6; 1999-456, s. 60

§ 7B-900.1. Post adjudication venue

(a) At any time after adjudication, the court on its own motion or motion of any party may transfer venue to a different county, regardless of whether the action could have been commenced in that county, if the court finds that the forum is inconvenient, that transfer of the action to the other county is in the best interest of the juvenile, and that the rights of the parties are not prejudiced by the change of venue.

(b) Before ordering that a case be transferred to another county, the court shall find that the director of the department of social services in the county in which the action is pending and the director in the county to which transfer is contemplated have communicated about the case and that:

(1) The two directors are in agreement with respect to each county's responsibility for providing financial support for the juvenile and services for the juvenile and the juvenile's family; or

(2) The Director of the Division of Social Services or the Director's designee has made that determination pursuant to G.S. 153A-257(d).

(c) When the court transfers a case to a different county, the court shall join or substitute as a party to the action the director of the department of social services in the county to which the case is being transferred and, if the juvenile is in the custody of the department of social services in the county in which the action is pending, shall transfer custody to the department of social services in the county to which the case is being transferred. The director of the department of social services in the county to which the case is being transferred must be given notice and an opportunity to be heard before the court enters an order pursuant to this subsection. However, the director may waive the right to notice and a hearing.

(d) Before ordering that a case be transferred to a different district, the court shall communicate with the chief district court judge or a judge presiding in juvenile court in the district to which the transfer is contemplated explaining the reasons for the proposed transfer. If the judge in the district to which the transfer is proposed makes a timely objection to the transfer, either verbally or in writing, the court shall order the transfer only after making detailed findings of fact that support a conclusion that the juvenile's best interests require that the case be transferred.

(e) Before ordering that a case be transferred to another county, the court shall consider relevant factors, which may include:

(1) The current residences of the juvenile and the parent, guardian, or custodian and the extent to which those residences have been and are likely to be stable.

(2) The reunification plan or other permanent plan for the juvenile and the likely effect of a change in venue on efforts to achieve permanence for the juvenile expeditiously.

(3) The nature and location of services and service providers necessary to achieve the reunification plan or other permanent plan for the juvenile.

(4) The impact upon the juvenile of the potential disruption of an existing therapeutic relationship.

(5) The nature and location of witnesses and evidence likely to be required in future hearings.

(6) The degree to which the transfer would cause inconvenience to one or more parties.

(7) Any agreement of the parties as to which forum is most convenient.

(8) The familiarity of the departments of social services, the courts, and the local offices of the guardian ad litem with the juvenile and the juvenile's family.

(9) Any other factor the court considers relevant.

(f) The order transferring venue shall be in writing, signed, and entered no later than 30 days from completion of the hearing. The order shall identify the next court action and specify the date within which the next hearing shall be held. If the order is not entered within 30 days following completion of the hearing, the clerk of court for juvenile matters shall schedule a subsequent hearing at the first session of court

scheduled for the hearing of juvenile matters following the 30-day period to determine and explain the reason for the delay and to obtain any needed clarification as to the contents of the order. The order shall be entered within 10 days of the subsequent hearing required by this subsection.

(g) The clerk shall transmit to the court in the county to which the case is being transferred a copy of the complete record of the case within three business days after entry of the order transferring venue.

Upon receiving a case that has been transferred from another county, the clerk shall promptly satisfy the following:

(1) Assign an appropriate file number to the case.

(2) Ensure that any necessary appointments of new attorneys or guardians ad litem are made.

(3) Calendar the next court action as set forth in the order transferring venue and give appropriate notice to all parties.

History.
2009-311, s. 5

§ 7B-901. Initial dispositional hearing

(a) The dispositional hearing shall take place immediately following the adjudicatory hearing and shall be concluded within 30 days of the conclusion of the adjudicatory hearing. The dispositional hearing may be informal and the court may consider written reports or other evidence concerning the needs of the juvenile. The juvenile and the juvenile's parent, guardian, or custodian shall have the right to present evidence, and they may advise the court concerning the disposition they believe to be in the best interests of the juvenile. The court may consider any evidence, including hearsay evidence as defined in G.S. 8C-1, Rule 801, including testimony or evidence from any person who is not a party, that the court finds to be relevant, reliable, and necessary to determine the needs of the juvenile and the most appropriate disposition.

(b) At the dispositional hearing, the court shall inquire as to the identity and location of any missing parent and whether paternity is at issue. The court shall include findings of the efforts undertaken to locate the missing parent and to serve that parent and efforts undertaken to establish paternity when paternity is an issue. The order may provide for specific efforts in determining the identity and location of any missing parent and specific efforts in establishing paternity. The court shall also inquire about efforts made to identify and notify relatives, parents, or other persons with legal custody of a sibling of the juvenile, as potential resources for placement or support.

(c) If the disposition order places a juvenile in the custody of a county department of social services, the court shall direct that reasonable efforts for reunification as defined in G.S. 7B-101 shall not be required if the court makes written findings of fact pertaining to any of the following, unless the court concludes that there is compelling evidence warranting continued reunification efforts:

(1) A court of competent jurisdiction determines or has determined that aggravated circumstances exist because the parent has committed or encouraged the commission of, or allowed the continuation of, any of the following upon the juvenile:

    a. Sexual abuse.

    b. Chronic physical or emotional abuse.

    c. Torture.

    d. Abandonment.

    e. Chronic or toxic exposure to alcohol or controlled substances that causes impairment of or addiction in the juvenile.

    f. Any other act, practice, or conduct that increased the enormity or added to the injurious consequences of the abuse or neglect.

(2) A court of competent jurisdiction has terminated involuntarily the parental rights of the parent to another child of the parent.

(3) A court of competent jurisdiction determines or has determined that (i) the parent has committed murder or voluntary manslaughter of another child of the parent; (ii) has aided, abetted, attempted, conspired, or solicited to commit murder or voluntary manslaughter of the child or another child of the parent; (iii) has committed a felony assault resulting in serious bodily injury to the child or another child of the parent; (iv) has committed sexual abuse against the child or another child of the parent; or (v) has been required to register as a sex offender on any government-administered registry.

(d) When the court determines that reunification efforts are not required, the court shall order concurrent permanent plans as soon as possible, after providing each party with a reasonable opportunity to prepare and present evidence. The court shall schedule a permanency planning hearing within 30 days to address the permanent plans in accordance with G.S. 7B-906.1 and G.S. 7B-906.2.

History.
1979, c. 815, s. 1; 1981, c. 469, s. 18; 1998-202, s. 6; 1999-456, s. 60; 2003-62, s. 1; 2005-398, s. 4; 2007-276, s. 2; 2011-295, s. 7; 2013-129, s. 22; 2015-135, s. 2.4; 2015-136, s. 9; 2015-264, s. 34(a); 2016-94, s. 12C.1(g); 2018-86, s. 2; 2019-33, s. 8; 2021-100, s. 5

N.C. Gen. Stat. § 7B-902

Repealed by Session Laws 2011-295, s. 8, effective October 1, 2011, and applicable to actions filed on or pending on or after that date.

History.
1981, c. 371, s. 1; 1998-202, s. 6; 1999-456, s. 60; repealed by Session Laws 2011-295, s. 8, effective October 1, 2011

§ 7B-903. Dispositional alternatives for abused, neglected, or dependent juvenile

(a) The following alternatives for disposition shall be available to any court exercising jurisdiction, and the court may combine any of the applicable alternatives when the court finds the disposition to be in the best interests of the juvenile:

(1) Dismiss the case or continue the case in order to allow the parent, guardian, custodian, caretaker or others to take appropriate action.

(2) Require that the juvenile be supervised in the juvenile's own home by the department of social services in the juvenile's county or by another individual as may be available to the court, subject to conditions applicable to the parent, guardian, custodian, or caretaker as the court may specify.

(3) Repealed by Session Laws 2015-136, s. 10, effective October 1, 2015, and applicable to actions filed or pending on or after that date.

(4) Place the juvenile in the custody of a parent, relative, private agency offering placement services, or some other suitable person. If the court determines that the juvenile should be placed in the custody of an individual other than a parent, the court shall verify that the person receiving custody of the juvenile understands the legal significance of the placement and will have adequate resources to care appropriately for the juvenile. The fact that the prospective custodian has provided a stable placement for the juvenile for at least six consecutive months is evidence that the person has adequate resources.

(5) Appoint a guardian of the person for the juvenile as provided in G.S. 7B-600.

(6) Place the juvenile in the custody of the department of social services in the county of the juvenile's residence. In the case of a juvenile who has legal residence outside the State, the court may place the juvenile in the physical custody of the department of social services in the county where the juvenile is found so that agency may return the juvenile to the responsible authorities in the juvenile's home state.

(a1) In placing a juvenile in out-of-home care under this section, the court shall first consider whether a relative of the juvenile is willing and able to provide proper care and supervision of the juvenile in a safe home. If the court finds that the relative is willing and able to provide proper care and supervision in a safe home, then the court shall order placement of the juvenile with the relative unless the court finds that the placement is contrary to the best interests of the juvenile. In placing a juvenile in out-of-home care under this section, the court shall also consider whether it is in the juvenile's best interest to remain in the juvenile's community of residence. Placement of a juvenile with a relative outside of this State must be in accordance with the Interstate Compact on the Placement of Children.

(a2) An order under this section placing or continuing the placement of the juvenile in out-of-home care shall contain a finding that the juvenile's continuation in or return to the juvenile's own home would be contrary to the juvenile's health and safety.

(a3) An order under this section placing the juvenile in out-of-home care shall contain specific findings as to whether the department has made reasonable efforts to prevent the need for placement of the juvenile. In determining whether efforts to prevent the placement of the juvenile were reasonable, the juvenile's health and safety shall be the paramount concern.

The court may find that efforts to prevent the need for the juvenile's placement were precluded by an immediate threat of harm to the juvenile. A finding that reasonable efforts were not made by a county department of social services shall not preclude the entry of an order authorizing the juvenile's placement when the court finds that placement is necessary for the protection of the juvenile.

(a4) If the court does not place the juvenile with a relative, the court may consider whether nonrelative kin or other persons with legal custody of a sibling of the juvenile are willing and able to provide proper care and supervision of the juvenile in a safe home. The court may order the department to notify the juvenile's State-recognized tribe of the need for custodial care for the purpose of locating relatives or nonrelative kin for placement. The court may order placement of the juvenile with nonrelative kin if the court finds the placement is in the juvenile's best interests.

(b) When the court has found that a juvenile has suffered physical abuse and that the individual responsible for the abuse has a history of violent behavior against people, the court shall consider the opinion of the mental health professional who performed an evaluation under G.S. 7B-503(b) before returning the juvenile to the custody of that individual.

(c) Repealed by Session Laws 2015-136, s. 10, effective October 1, 2015, and applicable to actions filed or pending on or after that date.

(d) The court may order that the juvenile be examined by a physician, psychiatrist, psychologist, or other qualified expert as may be needed for the court to determine the needs of the juvenile. Upon completion of the examination, the court shall conduct a hearing to determine whether the juvenile is in need of medical, surgical, psychiatric, psychological, or other treatment and who should pay the cost of the treatment. The county manager, or such person who shall be designated by the chairman of the county commissioners, of the juvenile's residence shall be notified of the hearing and allowed to be heard. Subject to G.S. 7B-903.1, if the court finds the juvenile to be in need of medical, surgical, psychiatric, psychological, or other treatment, the court shall permit the parent or other responsible persons to arrange for treatment. If the parent declines or is unable to make necessary arrangements, the court may order the needed treatment, surgery, or care and the court may order the parent to pay the cost of the care pursuant to G.S. 7B-904. If the court finds the parent is unable to pay the cost of treatment, the court shall order the county to arrange for treatment of the juvenile and to pay for the cost of the treatment. The county department of social services shall recommend the facility that will provide the juvenile with treatment.

(e) If the court determines that the juvenile may be mentally ill or developmentally disabled, the court may order the county department of social services to coordinate with the appropriate representative of the area mental health, developmental disabilities, and substance abuse services authority or other managed care organization responsible for managing public funds for mental health and developmental disabilities to develop a treatment plan for the juvenile. The court shall not commit a juvenile directly to a State hospital or developmental center for persons with intellectual and developmental disabilities and orders purporting to commit a juvenile directly to a State hospital or developmental center for persons with intellectual and developmental disabilities shall be void and of no effect. If the court determines that institutionalization is the best service for the juvenile, admission shall be with the voluntary consent of the parent, guardian, or custodian. If the parent, guardian, or custodian refuses to consent to admission to a mental hospital or developmental center for persons with intellectual and developmental disabilities, the signature and consent of the court may be substituted for that purpose. A State hospital or developmental center for persons with intellectual and developmental disabilities that refuses admission to a juvenile referred for admission by a court, or discharges a juvenile previously admitted on court referral prior to completion of treatment, shall submit to the court a written report setting out the reasons for denial of admission or discharge and setting out the juvenile's diagnosis, indications of mental illness or intellectual and developmental disabilities, indications of need for treatment, and a statement as to the location of any facility known to have a treatment program for the juvenile in question.

History.
1979, c. 815, s. 1; 1981, c. 469, s. 19; 1985, c. 589, s. 5; c. 777, s. 1; 1985 (Reg. Sess., 1986), c. 863, s. 2; 1991, c. 636, s. 19(a); 1995 (Reg. Sess., 1996), c. 609, s. 3; 1997-516, s. 1A; 1998-202, s. 6; 1998-229, ss. 6, 23; 1999-318, s. 6; 1999-456, s. 60; 2002-164, s. 4.8; 2003-140, s. 9(b); 2015-136, s. 10; 2019-33, s. 7(b); 2021-132, s. 1(e)

§ 7B-903.1. Juvenile placed in custody of a department of social services

(a) Except as prohibited by federal law, the director of a county department of social services with custody of a juvenile shall be authorized to make decisions about matters not addressed herein that are generally made by a juvenile's custodian, including, but not limited to, educational decisions and consenting to the sharing of the juvenile's information. The court may delegate any part of this authority to the juvenile's parent, foster parent, or another individual.

(b) When a juvenile is in the custody or placement responsibility of a county department of social services, the placement provider may, in accordance with G.S. 131D-10.2A, provide or withhold permission, without prior approval of the court or county department of social services, to allow a juvenile to participate in normal childhood activities. If such authorization is not in the juvenile's best interest, the court shall set out alternative parameters for approving normal childhood activities.

(c) If a juvenile is removed from the home and placed in the custody or placement responsibility of a county department of social services, the director shall not allow unsupervised visitation with or return physical custody of the juvenile to the parent, guardian, custodian, or caretaker without a hearing at which the court finds that the juvenile will receive proper care and supervision in a safe home. Before a county department of social services may recommend unsupervised visits or return of physical custody of the juvenile to the parent, guardian, custodian, or caretaker from whom the juvenile was removed, a county department of social services shall first observe that parent, guardian, custodian, or caretaker with the juvenile for at least two visits that support the

recommendation. Each observation visit shall consist of an observation of not less than one hour with the juvenile, shall be conducted at least seven days apart, and shall occur within 30 days of the hearing at which the department of social services makes the recommendation. A department of social services shall provide documentation of any observation visits that it conducts to the court for its consideration as to whether unsupervised visits or physical custody should be granted to the parent, guardian, custodian, or caretaker from whom the juvenile was removed.

(c1) If juvenile siblings are removed from the home and placed in the nonsecure custody of a county department of social services, the director shall make reasonable efforts to place the juvenile siblings in the same home. The director is not required to make reasonable efforts under this subsection if the director documents that placing the juvenile siblings would be contrary to the safety or well-being of any of the juvenile siblings. If, after making reasonable efforts, the director is unable to place the juvenile siblings in the same home, the director shall make reasonable efforts to provide frequent sibling visitation and ongoing interaction between the juvenile siblings, unless the director documents that frequent visitation or other ongoing interaction between the juvenile siblings would be contrary to the safety or well-being of any of the juvenile siblings.

(d) When a county department of social services having custody or placement responsibility of a juvenile intends to change the juvenile's placement, the department shall give the guardian ad litem for the juvenile notice of its intention unless precluded by emergency circumstances from doing so. Where emergency circumstances exist, the department of social services shall notify the guardian ad litem or the attorney advocate within 72 hours of the placement change, unless local rules require notification within a shorter time period.

(e) When a juvenile is placed in the custody of a county department of social services, the provisions of G.S. 7B-505.1 apply.

History.
2015-135, s. 2.5; 2015-136, s. 11; 2017-41, s. 10; 2021-100, s. 6; 2021-132, s. 1(f)

§ 7B-903.2. Emergency motion for placement and payment

(a) If the requirements of G.S. 122C-142.2(b) through (f) are not satisfied, a party to the juvenile case, the Department of Health and Human Services, the hospital where the juvenile is currently located, the local management entity/managed care organization, or the prepaid health plan may make a limited appearance for the sole purpose of filing a motion in the district court in the county with jurisdiction over the juvenile in the abuse, neglect, and dependency matter regarding the juvenile's continued stay in an emergency department or subsequent admission at the hospital.

(b) The motion shall contain a specific description of the requirements of G.S. 122C-142.2(b) through (f) which were not satisfied.

(c) The motion shall be served on all parties to the juvenile proceeding pursuant to G.S. 1A-1, Rule 5. The motion shall also be served upon the hospital where the juvenile is receiving services, the local management entity/managed care organization or prepaid health plan for the juvenile, and the Department of Health and Human Services. The hospital, the local management entity/managed care organization or prepaid health plan for the juvenile, and the Department of Health and Human Services, upon service of the motion, shall automatically become a party to the juvenile proceeding for the limited purpose of participating in hearings held in relation to and for complying with orders entered by the court pursuant to this section.

(d) Upon request of the movant, the department of social services shall provide the movant with the case file number, the juvenile's name, and the addresses of all parties and attorneys in the juvenile matter, to the extent necessary to effectuate service pursuant to subsection (c) of this section. Nothing in this section shall require the department of social services to provide the name and address of the juvenile who is a party to the action.

(e) The motion shall be heard in the district court with jurisdiction over the juvenile in the abuse, neglect, and dependency matter. The rules of evidence in civil cases shall apply. Any person or party served with notice of the motion pursuant to subsection (b) of this section may request to be heard by the court and present evidence. The hearing shall be conducted in accordance with G.S. 7B-801.

(f) The court shall make written findings of fact and conclusions of law, including whether:

(1) The movant established by clear and convincing evidence that there is no medical necessity for the juvenile to remain in the hospital.

(2) The responsible party has not satisfied the requirements of G.S. 122C-142.2(b) through (f).

(g) When the court finds that there is clear and convincing evidence that there is no medical necessity for the juvenile to remain in the hospital and that the responsible party has not satisfied the requirements of G.S. 122C-142.2(b) through (f), the court may order any of the following:

(1) That the responsible party pay reasonable hospital charges of the juvenile's continued admission at the hospital. The reasonable charges shall be limited to those incurred after the date it was no longer medically necessary for the juvenile to remain in the hospital.

(2) That the responsible party pay for any damage to property caused by the juvenile incurred after the date it was no longer medically necessary for the juvenile to remain in the hospital.

(3) That the responsible party satisfy the requirements of G.S. 122C-142.2(b) through (f).

(4) Any relief the court finds appropriate.

(h) The order shall be reduced to writing, signed, and entered no later than 72 hours following the completion of the hearing. The clerk of court for juvenile matters shall schedule a subsequent hearing for review within 30 days of entry of the order.

(i) If at any time after the motion is filed, the juvenile is discharged from the hospital and placed by the director, the court shall dismiss the motion.

(j) All parties to the hearing shall bear their own costs.

History.
2021-132, s. 5(b)

§ 7B-904. Authority over parents of juvenile adjudicated as abused, neglected, or dependent

(a) If the court orders medical, surgical, psychiatric, psychological, or other treatment pursuant to G.S. 7B-903, the court may order the parent or other responsible parties to pay the cost of the treatment or care ordered.

(b) At the dispositional hearing or a subsequent hearing if the court finds that it is in the best interests of the juvenile for the parent, guardian, custodian, stepparent, adult member of the juvenile's household, or adult entrusted with the juvenile's care to be directly involved in the juvenile's treatment, the court may order the parent, guardian, custodian, stepparent, adult member of the juvenile's household, or adult entrusted with the juvenile's care to participate in medical, psychiatric, psychological, or other treatment of the juvenile. The cost of the treatment shall be paid pursuant to G.S. 7B-903.

(c) At the dispositional hearing or a subsequent hearing the court may determine whether the best interests of the juvenile require that the parent, guardian, custodian, stepparent, adult member of the juvenile's household, or adult entrusted with the juvenile's care undergo psychiatric, psychological, or other treatment or counseling directed toward remediating or remedying behaviors or conditions that led to or contributed to the juvenile's adjudication or to the court's decision to remove custody of the juvenile from the parent, guardian, custodian, stepparent, adult member of the juvenile's household, or adult entrusted with the juvenile's care. If the court finds that the best interests of the juvenile require the parent, guardian, custodian, stepparent, adult member of the juvenile's household, or adult entrusted with the juvenile's care undergo treatment, it may order that individual to comply with a plan of treatment approved by the court or condition legal custody or physical placement of the juvenile with the parent, guardian, custodian, stepparent, adult member of the juvenile's household, or adult entrusted with the juvenile's care upon that individual's compliance with the plan of treatment. The court may order the parent, guardian, custodian, stepparent, adult member of the juvenile's household, or adult entrusted with the juvenile's care to pay the cost of treatment ordered pursuant to this subsection. In cases in which the court has conditioned legal custody or physical placement of the juvenile with the parent, guardian, custodian, stepparent, adult member of the juvenile's household, or adult entrusted with the juvenile's care upon compliance with a plan of treatment, the court may charge the cost of the treatment to the county of the juvenile's residence if the court finds the parent, guardian, custodian, stepparent, adult member of the juvenile's household, or adult entrusted with the juvenile's care is unable to pay the cost of the treatment. In all other cases, if the court finds the parent, guardian, custodian, stepparent, adult member of the juvenile's household, or adult entrusted with the juvenile's care is unable to pay the cost of the treatment ordered pursuant to this subsection, the court may order that individual to receive treatment currently available from the area mental health program that serves the parent's catchment area.

(c1) If the court has ordered an individual to comply with a plan of treatment for substance use disorder, including opioid dependency, that individual shall not be in violation of the terms or conditions of that part of the court's order if he or she is compliant with medication-assisted treatment. For the purposes of this subsection, "medication-assisted treatment" means the use of pharmacological medications administered, dispensed, and prescribed in a Substance Abuse and Mental Health Services Administration (SAMHSA) accredited and certified opioid treatment program (OTP) or by a certified practitioner licensed in this State to practice medicine, in combination with counseling and behavioral therapies, to provide a whole patient approach to the treatment of substance use disorders.

(d) At the dispositional hearing or a subsequent hearing, when legal custody of a juvenile is vested in someone other than the juvenile's parent, if the court finds that the parent is able to do so, the court may order that the parent pay a reasonable sum that will cover, in whole or in part, the support of the juvenile after the order is entered. If the court requires the payment of child support, the amount of the payments shall be determined as provided in G.S. 50-13.4(c). If the court places a juvenile in the custody of a county department of social services and if the court finds that the parent is unable to pay the cost of the support required by the juvenile, the cost shall be paid by the county department of social services in whose custody the juvenile is placed, provided the juvenile is not receiving care in an institution owned or operated by the State or federal government or any subdivision thereof.

(d1) At the dispositional hearing or a subsequent hearing, the court may order the parent, guardian, custodian, or caretaker served with a copy of the summons pursuant to G.S. 7B-407 to do any of the following:

(1) Attend and participate in parental responsibility classes if those classes are available in the judicial district in which the parent, guardian, custodian, or caretaker resides.

(2) Provide, to the extent that person is able to do so, transportation for the juvenile to keep appointments for medical, psychiatric, psychological, or other treatment ordered by the court if the juvenile remains in or is returned to the home.

(3) Take appropriate steps to remedy conditions in the home that led to or contributed to the juvenile's adjudication or to the court's decision to remove custody of the juvenile from the parent, guardian, custodian, or caretaker.

(e) Upon motion of a party or upon the court's own motion, the court may issue an order directing the parent, guardian, custodian, or caretaker served with a copy of the summons pursuant to G.S. 7B-407 to appear and show cause why the parent, guardian, custodian, or caretaker should not be found or held in civil or criminal contempt for willfully failing to comply with an order of the court. Chapter 5A of the General Statutes shall govern contempt proceedings initiated pursuant to this section.

History.
1979, c. 815, s. 1; 1983, c. 837, ss. 2, 3; 1987, c. 598, s. 2; 1989, c. 218; c. 529, s. 7; 1995, c. 328, s. 2; 1995 (Reg. Sess., 1996), c. 609, s. 4; 1997-456, s. 1; 1998-202, s. 6; 1999-318, s. 7; 1999-456, s. 60; 2001-208, s. 3; 2001-487, s. 101; 2021-100, s. 7

§ 7B-905. Dispositional order

(a) The dispositional order shall be in writing, signed, and entered no later than 30 days from the completion of the hearing, and shall contain appropriate findings of fact and conclusions of law. The court shall state with particularity, both orally and in the written order of disposition, the precise terms of the disposition including the kind, duration, and the person who is responsible for carrying out the disposition and the person or agency in whom custody is vested. If the order is not entered within 30 days following completion of the hearing, the clerk of court for juvenile matters shall schedule a subsequent hearing at the first session of court scheduled for the hearing of juvenile matters following the 30-day period to determine and explain the reason for the delay and to obtain any needed clarification as to the contents of the order. The order shall be entered within 10 days of the subsequent hearing required by this subsection.

(b) Repealed by Session Laws 2021-132, s. 1(j), effective October 1, 2021, and applicable to actions filed or pending on or after that date.

(c), (d) Repealed by Session Laws 2015-136, s. 12, effective October 1, 2015, and applicable to actions filed or pending on or after that date.

History.
1979, c. 815, s. 1; 1987 (Reg. Sess., 1988), c. 1090, s. 10; 1991, c. 434, s. 1; 1997-390, s. 8; 1998-202, s. 6; 1998-229, s. 24; 1999-456, s. 60; 2001-208, ss. 4, 18; 2001-487, s. 101; 2005-398, s. 5; 2011-295, s. 9; 2013-129, s. 23; 2015-136, s. 12; 2021-100, s. 8; 2021-132, s. 1(j)

§ 7B-905.1. Visitation

(a) An order that removes custody of a juvenile from a parent, guardian, or custodian or that continues the juvenile's placement outside the home shall provide for visitation that is in the best interests of the juvenile consistent with the juvenile's health and safety, including no visitation. The court may specify in the order conditions under which visitation may be suspended.

(b) If the juvenile is placed or continued in the custody or placement responsibility of a county department of social services, the court may order the director to arrange, facilitate, and supervise a visitation plan expressly approved or ordered by the court. The plan shall indicate the minimum frequency and length of visits and whether the visits shall be supervised. Unless the court orders otherwise, the director shall have discretion to determine who will supervise visits when supervision is required, to determine the location of visits, and to change the day and time of visits in response to scheduling conflicts, illness of the child or party, or extraordinary circumstances. The director shall promptly communicate a limited and temporary change in the visitation schedule to the affected party. Any ongoing change in the visitation

schedule shall be communicated to the party in writing and state the reason for the change.

If the director makes a good faith determination that the visitation plan is not consistent with the juvenile's health and safety, the director may temporarily suspend all or part of the visitation plan. The director shall not be subject to any motion to show cause for this suspension but shall expeditiously file a motion for review and request that a hearing be scheduled within 30 days. However, no motion or notice of hearing is required if a review or permanency planning hearing is already scheduled to be heard within 30 days of the suspension.

(b1) When visitation, whether supervised or unsupervised, is ordered between a juvenile who is placed in or continued in the custody or placement responsibility of a county department of social services and a parent, a parent's positive result from a drug screen alone is insufficient to deny the parent court-ordered visitation with the juvenile. For parents with unsupervised visitation that have a positive result from a drug screen, the department of social services shall expeditiously file a motion for review and request that a hearing be scheduled within 30 days for the court to review the visitation plan to ensure the safety of the child. While the motion is pending, the director may temporarily impose supervision requirements to all or part of the visitation plan. The director shall promptly communicate the limited and temporary change in the visitation plan to the affected party. Nothing in this subsection prevents a visit from being cancelled if, at the time that visitation between the parent and the juvenile occurs, a parent is under the influence of drugs or alcohol and exhibits behavior that may create an unsafe environment for a child, or the parent appears to be actively impaired.

(c) If the juvenile is placed or continued in the custody or guardianship of a relative or other suitable person, any order providing for visitation shall specify the minimum frequency and length of the visits and whether the visits shall be supervised. The court may authorize additional visitation as agreed upon by the respondent and custodian or guardian.

(d) If the court waives permanency planning hearings and retains jurisdiction, all parties shall be informed of the right to file a motion for review of any visitation plan entered pursuant to this section. Upon motion of any party and after proper notice and a hearing, the court may establish, modify, or enforce a visitation plan that is in the juvenile's best interest. Prior to or at the hearing, the court may order the department and guardian ad litem to investigate and make written recommendations as to appropriate visitation and give testimony concerning its recommendations. For resolution of issues related to visitation, the court may order the parents, guardian, or custodian to participate in custody mediation where there is a program established pursuant to G.S. 7A-494. In referring a case to custody mediation, the court shall specify the issue or issues for mediation, including, but not limited to, whether or not visitation shall be supervised and whether overnight visitation may occur. Custody mediation shall not permit the participants to consent to a change in custody. A copy of any agreement reached in custody mediation shall be provided to all parties and counsel and shall be approved by the court. The provisions of G.S. 50-13.1(d) through (f) apply to this section.

History.
2013-129, s. 24; 2019-33, s. 9; 2021-100, s. 9; 2021-132, s. 1(g).

N.C. Gen. Stat. § 7B-906

Repealed by Session Laws 2013-129, s. 25, effective October 1, 2013, and applicable to actions filed or pending on or after that date.

History.
1979, c. 815, s. 1; 1987, c. 810; 1987 (Reg. Sess., 1988), c. 1090, s. 11; 1989, c. 152, s. 1; 1997-390, s. 9; 1998-202, s. 6; 1998-229, ss. 8, 25; 1999-456, s. 60; 2000-124, s. 2; 2001-208, s. 19; 2001-487, s. 101; 2003-62, s. 2; 2003-140, s. 9(c); 2005-398, s. 6; 2007-276, s. 3; 2009-311, s. 6; repealed by 2013-129, s. 25, effective October 1, 2013

§ 7B-906.1. Review and permanency planning hearings

(a) The court shall conduct a review or permanency planning hearing within 90 days from the date of the initial dispositional hearing held pursuant to G.S. 7B-901. Review or permanency planning hearings shall be held at least every six months thereafter. If custody has not been removed from a parent, guardian, caretaker, or custodian, the hearing shall be designated as a review hearing. If custody has been removed from a parent, guardian, or custodian, the hearing shall be designated as permanency planning hearing.

(b) The director of social services shall make a timely request to the clerk to calendar each hearing at a session of court scheduled for the hearing of juvenile matters. The clerk shall give 15 days' notice of the hearing and its purpose to (i) the parents, (ii) the juvenile if 12 years of age or more, (iii) the guardian, (iv) the person providing care for the juvenile, (v) the custodian or agency with custody, (vi) the guardian ad litem, and (vii) any other person or agency the court may specify. The department of social services shall either provide to the clerk the name and address of the person providing care for the

juvenile for notice under this subsection or file written documentation with the clerk that the juvenile's current care provider was sent notice of hearing. Nothing in this subsection shall be construed to make the person providing care for the juvenile a party to the proceeding solely based on receiving notice and the right to be heard.

(c) At each hearing, the court shall consider information from the parents, the juvenile, the guardian, any person providing care for the juvenile, the custodian or agency with custody, the guardian ad litem, and any other person or agency that will aid in the court's review. The court may consider any evidence, including hearsay evidence as defined in G.S. 8C-1, Rule 801, or testimony or evidence from any person that is not a party, that the court finds to be relevant, reliable, and necessary to determine the needs of the juvenile and the most appropriate disposition.

(c) At each hearing, the court shall consider information from the parents, the juvenile, the guardian, any person with whom the juvenile is placed, the custodian or agency with custody, the guardian ad litem, and any other person or agency that will aid in the court's review. The court shall provide any person with whom the child is placed the opportunity to address the court regarding the juvenile's well-being. The court may consider any evidence, including hearsay evidence as defined in G.S. 8C-1, Rule 801, or testimony or evidence from any person that is not a party, that the court finds to be relevant, reliable, and necessary to determine the needs of the juvenile and the most appropriate disposition.

(d) At each hearing, the court shall consider the following criteria and make written findings regarding those that are relevant:

(1) Services which have been offered to prevent the removal or reunite the juvenile with either parent whether or not the juvenile resided with the parent at the time of removal or the guardian or custodian from whom the child was removed.

(1a) Reports on the juvenile's continuation in the home of the parent, guardian, or custodian; and the appropriateness of the juvenile's continuation in that home. If the juvenile is removed from the custody of a parent, guardian, or custodian at a review hearing, the court shall schedule a permanency planning hearing within 30 days of the review, unless the hearing was noticed and heard as a permanency planning hearing.

(2) Reports on visitation that has occurred and whether there is a need to create, modify, or enforce an appropriate visitation plan in accordance with G.S. 7B-905.1.

(3) Whether efforts to reunite the juvenile with either parent clearly would be unsuccessful or inconsistent with the juvenile's health or safety and need for a safe, permanent home within a reasonable period of time. The court shall consider efforts to reunite regardless of whether the juvenile resided with the parent, guardian, or custodian at the time of removal.

(4) Reports on the placements the juvenile has had, the appropriateness of the juvenile's current foster care placement, and the goals of the juvenile's foster care plan, including the role the current foster parent will play in the planning for the juvenile.

(5) If the juvenile is 16 or 17 years of age, a report on an independent living assessment of the juvenile and, if appropriate, an independent living plan developed for the juvenile.

(6) Repealed by Session Laws 2021-132, s. 1(h), effective October 1, 2021, and applicable to actions filed or pending on or after that date.

(7) Any other criteria the court deems necessary.

(d1) At any review hearing, the court may maintain the juvenile's placement under review or order a different placement, appoint an individual guardian of the person pursuant to G.S. 7B-600, or order any disposition authorized by G.S. 7B-903, including the authority to place the child in the custody of either parent or any relative found by the court to be suitable and found by the court to be in the best interests of the juvenile.

(d2) Absent extraordinary circumstances, when the parent, guardian, or custodian has successfully completed the court-ordered services and the juvenile is residing in a safe home, the court may waive further review hearings or terminate its jurisdiction in accordance with this subsection or G.S. 7B-911.

(e) At any permanency planning hearing where the juvenile is not placed with a parent, the court shall additionally consider the following criteria and make written findings regarding those that are relevant:

(1) Whether it is possible for the juvenile to be placed with a parent within the next six months and, if not, why such placement is not in the juvenile's best interests.

(2) Where the juvenile's placement with a parent is unlikely within six months, whether legal guardianship or custody with a relative or some other suitable person should be established and, if so, the rights and responsibilities that should remain with the parents.

(3) Where the juvenile's placement with a parent is unlikely within six months, whether adoption should be pursued and, if so, any barriers to the juvenile's adoption, including when and if termination of parental rights should be considered.

(4) Where the juvenile's placement with a parent is unlikely within six months, whether the juvenile should remain in the current placement, or be placed in another permanent living arrangement and why.

(5) Whether the county department of social services has since the initial permanency plan hearing made reasonable efforts to implement the permanent plan for the juvenile.

(6) Any other criteria the court deems necessary.

(f) In the case of a juvenile who is in the custody or placement responsibility of a county department of social services and has been in placement outside the home for 12 of the most recent 22 months, or a court of competent jurisdiction has determined that the parent (i) has abandoned the child, (ii) has committed murder or voluntary manslaughter of another child of the parent, or (iii) has aided, abetted, attempted, conspired, or solicited to commit murder or voluntary manslaughter of the child or another child of the parent, the director of the department of social services shall initiate a proceeding to terminate the parental rights of the parent unless the court finds any of the following:

(1) The primary permanent plan for the juvenile is guardianship or custody with a relative or some other suitable person.

(2) The court makes specific findings as to why the filing of a petition for termination of parental rights is not in the best interests of the child.

(3) The department of social services has not provided the juvenile's family with services the department deems necessary when reasonable efforts are still required to enable the juvenile's return to a safe home.

(g) At the conclusion of each permanency planning hearing, the court shall make specific findings as to the best permanent plans to achieve a safe, permanent home for the juvenile within a reasonable period of time.

(h) The order shall be reduced to writing, signed, and entered no later than 30 days following the completion of the hearing. If the order is not entered within 30 days following completion of the hearing, the clerk of court for juvenile matters shall schedule a subsequent hearing at the first session of court scheduled for the hearing of juvenile matters following the 30-day period to determine and explain the reason for the delay and to obtain any needed clarification as to the contents of the order. The order shall be entered within 10 days of the subsequent hearing required by this subsection.

(i) The court may maintain the juvenile's placement under review or order a different placement, appoint a guardian of the person for the juvenile pursuant to G.S. 7B-600, or order any disposition authorized by G.S. 7B-903, including the authority to place the child in the custody of either parent or any relative found by the court to be suitable and found by the court to be in the best interests of the juvenile.

(j) If the court determines that the juvenile shall be placed in the custody of an individual other than a parent or appoints an individual guardian of the person pursuant to G.S. 7B-600, the court shall verify that the person receiving custody or being appointed as guardian of the juvenile understands the legal significance of the placement or appointment and will have adequate resources to care appropriately for the juvenile. The fact that the prospective custodian or guardian has provided a stable placement for the juvenile for at least six consecutive months is evidence that the person has adequate resources.

(k) If at any time a juvenile has been removed from a parent and legal custody is awarded to either parent or findings are made in accordance with subsection (n) of this section, the court shall be relieved of the duty to conduct periodic judicial reviews of the placement.

(k1) The court shall not waive or refuse to conduct a review hearing if a party files a motion seeking the review hearing and alleges a significant fact.

(l) If the court continues the juvenile's placement in the custody or placement responsibility of a county department of social services, the provisions of G.S. 7B-903.1 shall apply to any order entered under this section.

(m) If the court finds that a proceeding to terminate the parental rights of the juvenile's parents is necessary in order to perfect the primary permanent plan for the juvenile, the director of the department of social services shall file a petition to terminate parental rights within 60 calendar days from the date of the entry of the order unless the court makes written findings regarding why the petition cannot be filed within 60 days. If the court makes findings to the contrary, the court shall specify the time frame in which any needed petition to terminate parental rights shall be filed.

(n) Notwithstanding other provisions of this Article, the court may waive the holding of hearings required by this section, may require written reports to the court by the agency or person holding custody in lieu of permanency planning hearings, or order that permanency planning hearings be held less often than every six months if the court finds by clear, cogent, and convincing evidence each of the following:

(1) The juvenile has resided in the placement for a period of at least one year or the juvenile has resided in the placement for at least six consecutive months and the court enters a consent order pursuant to G.S. 7B-801(b1).

(2) The placement is stable and continuation of the placement is in the juvenile's best interests.

(3) Neither the juvenile's best interests nor the rights of any party require that permanency planning hearings be held every six months.

(4) All parties are aware that the matter may be brought before the court for review at any time by the filing of a motion for review or on the court's own motion.

(5) The court order has designated the relative or other suitable person as the juvenile's permanent custodian or guardian of the person.

The court may not waive or refuse to conduct a hearing if a party files a motion seeking the hearing. However, if a guardian of the person has been appointed for the juvenile and the court has also made findings in accordance with subsection (n) of this section that guardianship is the permanent plan for the juvenile, the court shall proceed in accordance with G.S. 7B-600(b).

(o) Permanency planning hearings under this section shall be replaced by post termination of parental rights' placement review hearings when required by G.S. 7B-908.

History.
2013-129, s. 26; 2015-136, ss. 13, 17; 2016-94, s. 12C.1(g1); 2017-161, s. 8; 2019-33, s. 10; 2021-100, s. 10; 2021-132, s. 1(h).

§ 7B-906.2. Permanent plans; concurrent planning

(a) At any permanency planning hearing pursuant to G.S. 7B-906.1, the court shall adopt one or more of the following permanent plans the court finds is in the juvenile's best interest:

(1) Reunification as defined by G.S. 7B-101.

(2) Adoption under Article 3 of Chapter 48 of the General Statutes.

(3) Guardianship pursuant to G.S. 7B-600(b).

(4) Custody to a relative or other suitable person.

(5) Another Planned Permanent Living Arrangement (APPLA) pursuant to G.S. 7B-912.

(6) Reinstatement of parental rights pursuant to G.S. 7B-1114.

(a1) Concurrent planning shall continue until a permanent plan is or has been achieved.

(b) At any permanency planning hearing, the court shall adopt concurrent permanent plans and shall identify the primary plan and secondary plan. Reunification shall be a primary or secondary plan unless the court made written findings under G.S. 7B-901(c) or G.S. 7B-906.1(d)(3), the permanent plan is or has been achieved in accordance with subsection (a1) of this section, or the court makes written findings that reunification efforts clearly would be unsuccessful or would be inconsistent with the juvenile's health or safety. The finding that reunification efforts clearly would be unsuccessful or inconsistent with the juvenile's health or safety may be made at any permanency planning hearing. Unless permanence has been achieved, the court shall order the county department of social services to make efforts toward finalizing the primary and secondary permanent plans and may specify efforts that are reasonable to timely achieve permanence for the juvenile.

(c) Unless reunification efforts were previously ceased, at each permanency planning hearing the court shall make a finding about whether the reunification efforts of the county department of social services were reasonable. In every subsequent permanency planning hearing held pursuant to G.S. 7B-906.1, the court shall make written findings about the efforts the county department of social services has made toward the primary permanent plan and any secondary permanent plans in effect prior to the hearing. The court shall make a conclusion about whether efforts to finalize the permanent plan were reasonable to timely achieve permanence for the juvenile.

(d) At any permanency planning hearing under subsections (b) and (c) of this section, the court shall make written findings as to each of the following, which shall demonstrate the degree of success or failure toward reunification:

(1) Whether the parent is making adequate progress within a reasonable period of time under the plan.

(2) Whether the parent is actively participating in or cooperating with the plan, the department, and the guardian ad litem for the juvenile.

(3) Whether the parent remains available to the court, the department, and the guardian ad litem for the juvenile.

(4) Whether the parent is acting in a manner inconsistent with the health or safety of the juvenile.

(e) If the juvenile is 14 years of age or older, the court shall make written findings in accordance with G.S. 7B-912(a), regardless of the juvenile's permanent plan.

History.
2015-136, s. 14; 2016-94, s. 12C.1(h); 2019-33, s. 11; 2021-100, s. 11; 2021-132, s. 1(k)

N.C. Gen. Stat. § 7B-907

Repealed by Session Laws 2013-129, s. 25, effective October 1, 2013, and applicable to actions filed or pending on or after that date.

History.
1998-229, ss. 8.1, 25.1; 1999-456, s. 60; 2001-208, ss. 5, 20; 2001-487, s. 101; 2003-62, s. 3; 2003-140, s. 9(d); 2005-398, s. 7; 2007-276, s. 4; 2009-311, s. 7; repealed by 2013-129, s. 25, effective October 1, 2013

§ 7B-908. Post termination of parental rights' placement court review

(a) The purpose of each placement review is to ensure that every reasonable effort is being made to provide for the permanent plan for the juvenile who has been placed in the custody of a county director or licensed child-placing agency, which is consistent with the juvenile's best interests. At each review hearing the court may consider information from the department of social services, the licensed child-placing agency, the guardian ad litem, the child, the person providing care for the child, and any other person or agency the court determines is likely to aid in the review. The court may consider any evidence, including hearsay evidence as defined in G.S. 8C-1, Rule 801, that the court finds to be relevant, reliable, and necessary to determine the needs of the juvenile and the most appropriate disposition.

(b) The court shall conduct a placement review not later than six months from the date of the termination hearing when both parents' parental rights have been terminated by a petition or motion brought by any person or agency designated in G.S. 7B-1103(a)(2) through (6), or one parent's parental rights have been terminated by court order and the other parent's parental rights have been relinquished under Chapter 48 of the General Statutes, and a county director or licensed child-placing agency has custody of the juvenile. The court shall conduct reviews every six months thereafter until the juvenile is the subject of a decree of adoption:

(1) No more than 30 days and no less than 15 days prior to each review, the clerk shall give notice of the review to the juvenile if the juvenile is at least 12 years of age, the legal custodian or guardian of the juvenile, the person providing care for the juvenile, the guardian ad litem, if any, and any other person or agency the court may specify. The department of social services shall either provide to the clerk the name and address of the person providing care for the child for notice under this subsection or file written documentation with the clerk that the child's current care provider was sent notice of hearing. Only the juvenile, the legal

custodian or guardian of the juvenile, the person providing care for the juvenile, and the guardian ad litem may participate in the review hearings, except as otherwise directed by the court. Nothing in this subdivision shall be construed to make the person a party to the proceeding solely based on receiving notice and the right to be heard. Any individual whose parental rights have been terminated or has executed a relinquishment that is no longer revocable shall not be considered a party to the proceeding unless an appeal of the order terminating parental rights is pending, and a court has stayed the order pending the appeal.

(2) If a guardian ad litem for the juvenile has not been appointed previously by the court in the termination proceeding, the court, at the initial six-month review hearing, may appoint a guardian ad litem to represent the juvenile. The court may continue the case for such time as is necessary for the guardian ad litem to become familiar with the facts of the case.

(c) The court shall consider at least the following in its review and make written findings regarding the following that are relevant:

(1) The adequacy of the permanency plans developed by the county department of social services or a licensed child-placing agency for a permanent placement in the juvenile's best interests and the efforts of the department or agency to implement the plans.

(2) Whether the juvenile has been listed for adoptive placement with NC Kids Adoption and Foster Care Network or any other child-specific recruitment program or whether there is an exemption to listing that the court finds is in the child's best interest.

(3) The efforts previously made by the department or agency to find a permanent placement for the juvenile.

(4) Whether the current placement is in the juvenile's best interest.

(d) The court, after making findings of fact, shall do one of the following it finds to be in the best interests of the child:

(1) Affirm the county department's or child placing agency's plan.

(2) Order a different plan designated in G.S. 7B-906.2(a).

(d1) The court may (i) order concurrent permanent plans if the court finds concurrent permanency planning to be in the best interests of the juvenile and (ii) specify efforts that are necessary to accomplish a permanent plan designated in subdivisions (1) or (2) of subsection (d) of this section that is in the best interests of the juvenile. If a juvenile is not placed with prospective adoptive parents as selected in G.S.

7B-1112.1, the court may order a placement that the court finds to be in the juvenile's best interest after considering the department's recommendations.

(e) If the juvenile is the subject of a decree of adoption prior to the date scheduled for the review, within 10 days of receiving notice that the adoption decree has been entered, the department of social services shall file with the court and serve on any guardian ad litem for the juvenile written notice of the entry. The adoption decree shall not be filed in the court file. The review hearing shall be cancelled with notice of said cancellation given by the clerk to all persons previously notified.

(e1) The order shall be reduced to writing, signed, and entered no later than 30 days following the completion of the hearing. If the order is not entered within 30 days following completion of the hearing, the clerk of court for juvenile matters shall schedule a subsequent hearing at the first session of court scheduled for the hearing of juvenile matters following the 30-day period to determine and explain the reason for the delay and to obtain any needed clarification regarding the contents of the order. The order shall be entered within 10 days of the subsequent hearing required by this subsection.

(f) Repealed by Session Laws 2011-295, s. 10, effective October 1, 2011, and applicable to actions filed or pending on or after that date.

History.

1983, c. 607, s. 1; 1993, c. 537, s. 2; 1998-202, s. 6; 1998-229, ss. 9, 26; 1999-456, s. 60; 2003-62, s. 4; 2005-398, s. 8; 2007-276, s. 5; 2009-311, s. 8; 2011-295, s. 10; 2013-129, s. 27; 2017-161, s. 9; 2019-33, s. 12; 2021-100, s. 12

§ 7B-909. Review of agency's plan for placement

(a) The director of social services or the director of the licensed private child-placing agency shall promptly notify the clerk to calendar the case for review of the department's or agency's plan for the juvenile at a session of court scheduled for the hearing of juvenile matters if the juvenile is in the custody of the department or agency and has not become the subject of a decree of adoption within six months following relinquishment of the juvenile for adoption by a parent, guardian, or guardian ad litem under the provisions of Part 7 of Article 3 of Chapter 48 of the General Statutes.

(b) Repealed by 2007-276, s. 6, effective October 1, 2007.

(b1) If the court finds on motion of a department of social services or licensed child-placing agency that a consent or relinquishment for adoption necessary for the juvenile to be adopted cannot be obtained, and that no further steps are being taken to terminate the parental rights of the parent from whom consent or relinquishment has not been obtained, the court may order, upon finding that it is in the juvenile's best interest, that any relinquishment for adoption signed by a parent who has surrendered the child for adoption shall be voided pursuant to G.S. 48-3-707(a)(4). Before voiding any relinquishment under this subsection, the court shall require the county department of social services or licensed child-placing agency to give at least 15 days' notice to the relinquishing parent whose rights will be restored. The relinquishing parent shall have the right to be heard on (i) whether the relinquishment should be voided and (ii) the parent's plan to provide for the juvenile if the relinquishment is voided. If after due diligence the relinquishing parent cannot be located, the notice of hearing shall be deposited in the United States mail, return receipt requested, and sent to the address of the parent given in the relinquishment. The date of receipt of the notice is deemed the date of delivery or last attempted delivery.

(c) Notification of the court under this section shall be by a petition for review or motion for review, if the court is exercising jurisdiction over the juvenile. The review shall be conducted within 30 days following the filing of the petition for review unless the court shall otherwise direct. The court shall conduct reviews every six months until the juvenile is the subject of a decree of adoption. However, further reviews are not required after the voiding of a relinquishment under subsection (b1) of this section. The initial review and all subsequent reviews, except a review hearing under subsection (b1) of this section, shall be conducted pursuant to G.S. 7B-908. Any individual whose parental rights have been terminated or who has relinquished the juvenile for adoption under the provisions of Part 7 of Article 3 of Chapter 48 of the General Statutes shall not be considered a party to the review unless an appeal of the order terminating parental rights is pending, and a court has stayed the order pending the appeal.

History.
1983, c. 607, s. 2; 1993, c. 537, s. 4; 1995, c. 457, s. 6; 1998-202, s. 6; 1998-229, s. 9; 1999-456, s. 60; 2005-398, s. 9; 2007-276, s. 6; 2013-129, s. 28; 2013-236, s. 1; 2013-410, s. 27

§ 7B-909.1. Relinquishment to a department of social services

Before the relinquishment of a juvenile to a department of social services for the purpose of adoption may be executed by a parent who is a respondent in an action under this Subchapter and (i) whose retained counsel has entered a notice of appearance or (ii) who has an attorney whose

provisional appointment has been confirmed by the court, each of the following shall occur:

(1) Notice shall be given by any reasonable and timely means of communication to the parent's counsel or, if such counsel is unavailable, to the partner or employee at the attorney's office that the department has made arrangements for the parent to execute a relinquishment at a specific date, time, and location.

(2) The parent shall be advised of the right to seek the advice of the parent's counsel prior to executing the relinquishment and to have the parent's counsel present while executing the relinquishment.

History.
2019-33, s. 13

§ 7B-910. Review of voluntary foster care placements

(a) The court shall review the placement of any juvenile in foster care made pursuant to a voluntary agreement between the juvenile's parents or guardian and a county department of social services and shall make findings from evidence presented at a review hearing with regard to:

(1) The voluntariness of the placement;

(2) The appropriateness of the placement;

(3) Whether the placement is in the best interests of the juvenile; and

(4) The services that have been or should be provided to the parents, guardian, foster parents, and juvenile, as the case may be, either (i) to improve the placement or (ii) to eliminate the need for the placement.

(b) The court may approve the continued placement of the juvenile in foster care on a voluntary agreement basis, disapprove the continuation of the voluntary placement, or direct the department of social services to petition the court for legal custody if the placement is to continue.

(c) An initial review hearing shall be held not more than 90 days after the juvenile's placement and shall be calendared by the clerk for hearing within such period upon timely request by the director of social services. An additional review hearing shall be held 90 days thereafter and any review hearings at such times as the court shall deem appropriate and shall direct, either upon its own motion or upon written request of the parents, guardian, foster parents, or director of social services. A juvenile placed under a voluntary agreement between the juvenile's parent or guardian and the county department of social services shall not remain in placement more than six months without the filing of a petition alleging abuse, neglect, or dependency.

(d) The clerk shall give at least 15 days' advance written notice of the initial and subsequent review hearings to the parents or guardian of the juvenile, to the juvenile if 12 or more years of age, to the director of social services, and to any other persons whom the court may specify.

History.
1983, c. 607, s. 2; 1993, c. 537, s. 4; 1995, c. 457, s. 6; 1998-202, s. 6; 1999-456, s. 60; 2001-208, s. 21; 2001-487, s. 101

§ 7B-910.1. Review of voluntary foster care placements with young adults

(a) The court shall review the placement of a young adult in foster care authorized by G.S. 108A-48(c) when the director of social services and a young adult who was in foster care as a juvenile enter into a voluntary placement agreement. The review hearing shall be held not more than 90 days from the date the agreement was executed, and the court shall make findings from evidence presented at this review hearing with regard to all of the following:

(1) Whether the placement is in the best interest of the young adult in foster care.

(2) The services that have been or should be provided to the young adult in foster care to improve the placement.

(3) The services that have been or should be provided to the young adult in foster care to further the young adult's educational or vocational ambitions, if relevant.

(b) Upon written request of the young adult or the director of social services, the court may schedule additional hearings to monitor the placement and progress toward the young adult's educational or vocational ambitions.

(c) No guardian ad litem under G.S. 7B-601 will be appointed to represent the young adult in the initial or any subsequent hearing.

(d) The clerk shall give written notice of the initial and any subsequent review hearings to the young adult in foster care and the director of social services at least 15 days prior to the date of the hearing.

(e) When the young adult elects to terminate the agreement, the agreement may be terminated without a return to court. When the department elects to terminate the agreement over the objection of the young adult, the department shall file a motion to bring the matter back before the court for resolution.

History.
2015-241, s. 12C.9(g); 2017-161, s. 10; 2021-100, s. 13

§ 7B-911. Civil child custody order

(a) Upon placing custody with a parent or other appropriate person, the court shall determine whether or not jurisdiction in the juvenile proceeding should be terminated and custody of the juvenile awarded to a parent or other appropriate person pursuant to G.S. 50-13.1, 50-13.2, 50-13.5, and 50-13.7.

(b) When the court enters a custody order under this section, the court shall either cause the order to be filed in an existing civil action relating to the custody of the juvenile or, if there is no other civil action, instruct the clerk to treat the order as the initiation of a civil action for custody.

If the order is filed in an existing civil action and the person to whom the court is awarding custody is not a party to that action, the court shall order that the person be joined as a party and that the caption of the case be changed accordingly. The order shall resolve any pending claim for custody and shall constitute a modification of any custody order previously entered in the action.

If the court's order initiates a civil action, the court shall designate the parties to the action and determine the most appropriate caption for the case. The civil filing fee is waived unless the court orders one or more of the parties to pay the filing fee for a civil action into the office of the clerk of superior court. The order shall constitute a custody determination, and any motion to enforce or modify the custody order shall be filed in the newly created civil action in accordance with the provisions of Chapter 50 of the General Statutes. The Administrative Office of the Courts may adopt rules and shall develop and make available appropriate forms for establishing a civil file to implement this section.

(c) When entering an order under this section, the court shall satisfy the following:

(1) Make findings and conclusions that support the entry of a custody order in an action under Chapter 50 of the General Statutes or, if the juvenile is already the subject of a custody order entered pursuant to Chapter 50, makes findings and conclusions that support modification of that order pursuant to G.S. 50-13.7.

(2) Make the following findings:

a. There is not a need for continued State intervention on behalf of the juvenile through a juvenile court proceeding.

b. At least six months have passed since the court made a determination that the juvenile's placement with the person to whom the court is awarding custody is the permanent plan for the juvenile, though this finding is not required if the court is awarding custody to a parent or to a person with whom the child was living when the juvenile petition was filed.

449

History.
2005-320, s. 4; 2013-129, s. 29

§ 7B-912. Juveniles 14 years of age and older; Another Planned Permanent Living Arrangement

(a) In addition to the permanency planning requirements under G.S. 7B-906.1, at every permanency planning hearing for a juvenile in the custody of a county department of social services who has attained the age of 14 years, the court shall inquire and make written findings regarding each of the following:

(1) The services provided to assist the juvenile in making a transition to adulthood.

(2) The steps the county department of social services is taking to ensure that the foster family or other licensed placement provider follows the reasonable and prudent parent standard as provided in G.S. 131D-10.2A.

(3) Whether the juvenile has regular opportunities to engage in age-appropriate or developmentally appropriate activities.

(b) At or before the permanency planning hearing immediately following the juvenile's seventeenth birthday and at each permanency planning hearing thereafter, the court shall (i) inquire as to whether the juvenile has a copy of the juvenile's birth certificate, Social Security card, health insurance information, drivers license or other identification card, any educational or medical records the juvenile requests, and information about how the juvenile may participate in the foster care 18-21 program authorized by G.S. 108A-48, and (ii) determine the person or entity that should assist the juvenile in obtaining these documents before the juvenile attains the age of 18 years.

(b1) The department shall include in its report to the court at every hearing after the juvenile's seventeenth birthday all of the following information:

(1) The department's efforts to identify and secure viable placement options for when the juvenile attains the age of 18 years.

(2) A list of appropriate adults who can serve as resources for the juvenile when the juvenile attains the age of 18 years.

(3) Contact information of the person responsible for overseeing voluntary foster care placements with young adults in the county department of social services with custody or placement responsibility of the juvenile and in the county department of social services in the county where the juvenile plans to reside at the age of 18 years.

(4) If appropriate, whether the juvenile has information about how he or she may maintain contact with his or her siblings,

parents, or relatives when the juvenile attains the age of 17 years.

(5) Whether the department has provided the juvenile with a point of contact to secure Medicaid and maintain physical and mental health services for which the juvenile will be eligible when the juvenile attains the age of 18 years.

(6) Whether the department has provided the juvenile with information about educational, vocational, or job plans for when the juvenile attains the age of 18 years.

(c) If the court finds each of the following conditions applies, the court shall approve Another Planned Permanent Living Arrangement (APPLA) as defined by P.L. 113-183, as the juvenile's primary permanent plan:

(1) The juvenile is 16 or 17 years old.

(2) The county department of social services has made diligent efforts to place the juvenile permanently with a parent or relative or in a guardianship or adoptive placement.

(3) Compelling reasons exist that it is not in the best interest of the juvenile to be placed permanently with a parent or relative or in a guardianship or adoptive placement.

(4) APPLA is the best permanency plan for the juvenile.

(d) If the court approves APPLA as the juvenile's permanent plan, the court shall, after questioning the juvenile, make written findings addressing the juvenile's desired permanency outcome.

History.
2015-135, s. 2.6; 2015-136, s. 15; 2021-100, ss. 14, 15

ARTICLE 10
MODIFICATION AND ENFORCEMENT OF DISPOSITIONAL ORDERS; APPEALS

§ 7B-1000. Authority to modify

(a) Upon motion in the cause or petition, and after notice, the court may conduct a modification hearing to determine whether the order of the court is in the best interests of the juvenile. The court may modify the order in light of changes in circumstances or the needs of the juvenile and address the issues raised in the motion that do not require a review or permanency planning hearing pursuant to G.S. 7B-906.1.

(b) In any case where the court finds the juvenile to be abused, neglected, or dependent, the jurisdiction of the court to modify any order or disposition made in the case shall continue during the minority of the juvenile, until terminated by order of the court, or until the juvenile is otherwise emancipated.

(c) When a motion is filed to conduct a modification hearing under this section and the guardian ad litem appointed through G.S. 7B-601 has been previously released, the court shall reappoint a guardian ad litem and an attorney advocate. The clerk shall provide the motion and any notice of hearing to the guardian ad litem and the attorney advocate. The hearing on the motion shall not take place until the guardian ad litem and the attorney advocate have been reappointed.

(d) When a motion is filed to conduct a modification hearing under this section and counsel for respondent parents appointed through G.S. 7B-602 has been released, the court shall appoint provisional counsel in accordance with G.S. 7B-602.

(e) The order shall be reduced to writing, signed, and entered no later than 30 days following the completion of the hearing. If the order is not entered within 30 days following completion of the hearing, the clerk of court for juvenile matters shall schedule a subsequent hearing at the first session of court scheduled for the hearing of juvenile matters following the 30-day period to determine and explain the reason for the delay and to obtain any needed clarification as to the contents of the order. The order shall be entered within 10 days of the subsequent hearing required by this subsection.

History.
1979, c. 815, s. 1; 1998-202, s. 6; 1999-456, s. 60; 2000-124, s. 3; 2013-129, s. 30; 2021-100, s. 16

§ 7B-1001. Right to appeal

(a) In a juvenile matter under this Subchapter, only the following final orders may be appealed directly to the Court of Appeals:

(1) Any order finding absence of jurisdiction.

(2) Any order, including the involuntary dismissal of a petition, which in effect determines the action and prevents a judgment from which appeal might be taken.

(3) Any initial order of disposition and the adjudication order upon which it is based.

(4) Any order, other than a nonsecure custody order, that changes legal custody of a juvenile.

(5) An order under G.S. 7B-906.2(b) eliminating reunification, as defined by G.S. 7B-101(18c), as a permanent plan by either of the following:

a. A parent who is a party and:

1. Has preserved the right to appeal the order in writing within 30 days after entry and service of the order.

2. A termination of parental rights petition or motion has not been filed within 65 days of entry and service of the order.

3. A notice of appeal of the order eliminating reunification is filed within 30 days after the expiration of the 65 days.

b. A party who is a guardian or custodian with whom reunification is not a permanent plan.

(6) Repealed by Session Laws 2017-41, s. 8(a), and Session Laws 2017-102, s. 40(f), effective January 1, 2019, and applicable to appeals filed on or after that date.

(7) Any order that terminates parental rights or denies a petition or motion to terminate parental rights.

(8) An order eliminating reunification as a permanent plan under G.S. 7B-906.2(b), if all of the following conditions are satisfied:

a. The right to appeal the order eliminating reunification has been preserved in writing within 30 days of entry and service of the order.

b. A motion or petition to terminate the parent's rights is filed within 65 days of entry and service of the order eliminating reunification and both of the following occur:

1. The motion or petition to terminate rights is heard and granted.

2. The order terminating parental rights is appealed in a proper and timely manner.

c. A separate notice of appeal of the order eliminating reunification is filed within 30 days after entry and service of a termination of parental rights order.

(a1) Repealed by Session Laws 2021-18, s. 2, effective July 1, 2021, and applicable to appeals filed on or after that date.

(a2) In an appeal filed pursuant to subdivision (a)(8) of this section, the Court of Appeals shall review the order eliminating reunification together with an appeal of the order terminating parental rights. If the order eliminating reunification is vacated or reversed, the order terminating parental rights shall be vacated.

(b) Notice of appeal and notice to preserve the right to appeal shall be given in writing by a proper party as defined in G.S. 7B-1002 and shall be made within 30 days after entry and service of the order in accordance with G.S. 1A-1, Rule 58.

(c) Notice of appeal shall be signed by both the appealing party and counsel for the appealing party, if any. In the case of an appeal by a juvenile, notice of appeal shall be signed by the guardian ad litem attorney advocate.

History.

1979, c. 815, s. 1; 1998-202, s. 6; 1999-456, s. 60; 2001-208, s. 25; 2001-487, s. 101; 2005-398, s. 10; 2011-295, s. 11; 2013-129, s. 31; 2015-136, s. 16; 2017-7, s. 4; 2017-41, s. 8(a); 2017-102, s. 40(f); 2019-33, s. 14(a); 2021-18, s. 2; 2021-100, s. 1(b); 2021-132, s. 1(b)

§ 7B-1002. Proper parties for appeal

Appeal from an order permitted under G.S. 7B-1001 may be taken by:

(1) A juvenile acting through the juvenile's guardian ad litem previously appointed under G.S. 7B-601.

(2) A juvenile for whom no guardian ad litem has been appointed under G.S. 7B-601. If such an appeal is made, the court shall appoint a guardian ad litem pursuant to G.S. 1A-1, Rule 17 for the juvenile for the purposes of that appeal.

(3) A county department of social services.

(4) A parent, a guardian appointed under G.S. 7B-600 or Chapter 35A of the General Statutes, or a custodian as defined in G.S. 7B-101 who is a nonprevailing party.

(5) Any party that sought but failed to obtain termination of parental rights.

History.

1979, c. 815, s. 1; 1998-202, s. 6; 1999-456, s. 60; 2005-398, s. 11

§ 7B-1003. Disposition pending appeal

(a) During an appeal of an order entered under this Subchapter, the trial court may enforce the order unless the trial court or an appellate court orders a stay.

(b) Pending disposition of an appeal, unless directed otherwise by an appellate court or subsection (c) of this section applies, the trial court shall:

(1) Continue to exercise jurisdiction and conduct hearings under this Subchapter with the exception of Article 11 of the General Statutes; and

(2) Enter orders affecting the custody or placement of the juvenile as the court finds to be in the best interests of the juvenile.

(c) Pending disposition of an appeal of an order entered under Article 11 of this Chapter where the petition for termination of parental rights was not filed as a motion in a juvenile matter initiated under Article 4 of this Chapter, the court may enter a temporary order affecting the custody or placement of the juvenile as the court finds to be in the best interests of

the juvenile. Upon the affirmation of the order of adjudication or disposition of the court in a juvenile case by the Court of Appeals, or by the Supreme Court in the event of an appeal, the court shall have authority to modify or alter its original order of adjudication or disposition as the court finds to be in the best interests of the juvenile to reflect any adjustment made by the juvenile or change in circumstances during the period of time the case on appeal was pending, provided that if the modifying order be entered ex parte, the court shall give notice to interested parties to show cause, if there be any, within 10 days thereafter, as to why the modifying order should be vacated or altered.

(d) When the court has found that a juvenile has suffered physical abuse and that the individual responsible for the abuse has a history of violent behavior, the court shall consider the opinion of the mental health professional who performed the evaluation under G.S. 7B-503(b) before returning the juvenile to the custody of that individual pending resolution of an appeal.

(e) The provisions of G.S. 7B-903.1 shall apply to any order entered during an appeal that provides for the placement or continued placement of a juvenile in foster care.

History.

1979, c. 815, s. 1; 1987 (Reg. Sess., 1988), c. 1090, s. 12; 1998-202, s. 6; 1999-318, s. 8; 1999-456, s. 60; 2001-208, s. 27; 2001-487, s. 101; 2003-140, s. 8; 2005-398, s. 12; 2019-33, s. 14(b)

§ 7B-1004. Disposition after appeal

When an order of the court is affirmed by the Court of Appeals or by the Supreme Court, the trial court may modify or alter the original order as the court finds to be in the best interests of the juvenile to reflect any change in circumstances during the period of time the appeal was pending. If the modifying order is entered ex parte, the court shall give notice to interested parties to show cause within 10 days thereafter as to why the modifying order should be vacated or altered.

History.

1979, c. 815, s. 1; 1998-202, s. 6; 1999-456, s. 60; 2005-398, s. 13

ARTICLE 11
TERMINATION OF PARENTAL RIGHTS

§ 7B-1100. Legislative intent; construction of Article

The General Assembly hereby declares as a matter of legislative policy with respect to termination of parental rights:

(1) The general purpose of this Article is to provide judicial procedures for terminating the legal relationship between a juvenile and the juvenile's biological or legal parents when the parents have demonstrated that they will not provide the degree of care which promotes the healthy and orderly physical and emotional well-being of the juvenile.

(2) It is the further purpose of this Article to recognize the necessity for any juvenile to have a permanent plan of care at the earliest possible age, while at the same time recognizing the need to protect all juveniles from the unnecessary severance of a relationship with biological or legal parents.

(3) Action which is in the best interests of the juvenile should be taken in all cases where the interests of the juvenile and those of the juvenile's parents or other persons are in conflict.

(4) This Article shall not be used to circumvent the provisions of Chapter 50A of the General Statutes, the Uniform Child-Custody Jurisdiction and Enforcement Act.

History.
1977, c. 879, s. 8; 1979, c. 110, s. 6; 1998-202, s. 6; 1999-223, s. 5; 1999-456, s. 60

§ 7B-1101. Jurisdiction

The court shall have exclusive original jurisdiction to hear and determine any petition or motion relating to termination of parental rights to any juvenile who resides in, is found in, or is in the legal or actual custody of a county department of social services or licensed child-placing agency in the district at the time of filing of the petition or motion. The court shall have jurisdiction to terminate the parental rights of any parent irrespective of the age of the parent. Provided, that before exercising jurisdiction under this Article, the court shall find that it has jurisdiction to make a child-custody determination under the provisions of G.S. 50A-201, 50A-203, or 50A-204. The court shall have jurisdiction to terminate the parental rights of any parent irrespective of the state of residence of the parent. Provided, that before exercising jurisdiction under this Article regarding the parental rights of a nonresident parent, the court shall find that it has jurisdiction to make a child-custody determination under the provisions of G.S. 50A-201 or G.S. 50A-203, without regard to G.S. 50A-204 and that process was served on the nonresident parent pursuant to G.S. 7B-1106. Provided, further, that the clerk of superior court shall have jurisdiction for

adoptions under Chapter 48 of the General Statutes.

History.
1977, c. 879, s. 8; 1979, c. 110, s. 7; 1979, 2nd Sess., c. 1206, s. 1; 1981, c. 996, s. 1; 1983, c. 89, s. 1; 1995, c. 457, s. 3; 1998-202, s. 6; 1999-223, s. 6; 1999-456, s. 60; 2000-144, s. 18; 2000-183, s. 2; 2003-140, s. 4; 2005-398, s. 14; 2007-152, s. 1

§ 7B-1101.1. Parent's right to counsel; guardian ad litem

(a) The parent has the right to counsel, and to appointed counsel in cases of indigency, unless the parent waives the right. The fees of appointed counsel shall be borne by the Office of Indigent Defense Services. When a petition is filed, unless the parent is already represented by counsel, the clerk shall appoint provisional counsel for each respondent parent named in the petition in accordance with rules adopted by the Office of Indigent Defense Services, shall indicate the appointment on the juvenile summons, and shall provide a copy of the summons and petition to the attorney. At the first hearing after service upon the respondent parent, the court shall dismiss the provisional counsel if the respondent parent:

(1) Does not appear at the hearing;

(2) Does not qualify for court-appointed counsel;

(3) Has retained counsel; or

(4) Waives the right to counsel.

The court shall confirm the appointment of counsel if subdivisions (1) through (4) of this subsection are not applicable to the respondent parent. The court may reconsider a parent's eligibility and desire for appointed counsel at any stage of the proceeding.

(a1) A parent qualifying for appointed counsel may be permitted to proceed without the assistance of counsel only after the court examines the parent and makes findings of fact sufficient to show that the waiver is knowing and voluntary. This examination shall be reported as provided in G.S. 7B-806.

(b) In addition to the right to appointed counsel under subsection (a) of this section, a guardian ad litem shall be appointed in accordance with G.S. 1A-1, Rule 17, to represent any parent who is under the age of 18 years and who is not married or otherwise emancipated.

(c) On motion of any party or on the court's own motion, the court may appoint a guardian ad litem for a parent who is incompetent in accordance with G.S. 1A-1, Rule 17.

(d) The parent's counsel shall not be appointed to serve as the guardian ad litem and the guardian ad litem shall not act as the parent's attorney. Communications between the guardian ad litem appointed under this section and the parent and between the guardian ad litem and the parent's counsel shall be privileged and confidential to the same extent that communications between the parent and the parent's counsel are privileged and confidential.

(e) Repealed by Session Laws 2013-129, s. 32, effective October 1, 2013, and applicable to actions filed or pending on or after that date.

(f) The fees of a guardian ad litem appointed pursuant to this section shall be borne by the Office of Indigent Defense Services when the court finds that the respondent is indigent. In other cases, the fees of the court-appointed guardian ad litem shall be a proper charge against the respondent if the respondent does not secure private legal counsel.

History.
2005-398, s. 15; 2009-311, s. 9; 2011-326, s. 12(b); 2012-194, s. 41; 2013-129, s. 32; 2021-100, s. 17

§ 7B-1102. Pending child abuse, neglect, or dependency proceedings

(a) When the district court is exercising jurisdiction over a juvenile and the juvenile's parent in an abuse, neglect, or dependency proceeding, a person or agency specified in G.S. 7B-1103(a) may file in that proceeding a motion for termination of the parent's rights in relation to the juvenile.

(b) A motion pursuant to subsection (a) of this section and the notice required by G.S. 7B-1106.1 shall be served in accordance with G.S. 1A-1, Rule 5(b), except:

(1) Service must be in accordance with G.S. 1A-1, Rule 4, if one of the following applies:

a. The person or agency to be served was not served originally with summons.

b. The person or agency to be served was served originally by publication that did not include notice substantially in conformity with the notice required by G.S. 7B-406(b)(4)e.

c. Two years has elapsed since the date of the original action.

(2) In any case, the court may order that service of the motion and notice be made pursuant to G.S. 1A-1, Rule 4.

For purposes of this section, the parent of the juvenile shall not be deemed to be under disability even though the parent is a minor.

(b1) If a parent who is served under G.S. 1A-1, Rule 4, with a motion under this section has an attorney of record, a copy of the motion and the notice served upon the parent shall also be sent to the parent's attorney.

(c) When a petition for termination of parental rights is filed in the same district in which there is pending an abuse, neglect, or dependency proceeding involving the same juvenile, the court on its own motion or motion of a party may consolidate the action pursuant to G.S. 1A-1, Rule 42.

History.
1998-229, ss. 9.1, 26.1; 1999-456, s. 60; 2000-183, s. 3; 2011-332, s. 4.1

§ 7B-1103. Who may file a petition or motion

(a) A petition or motion to terminate the parental rights of either or both parents to his, her, or their minor juvenile may only be filed by one or more of the following:

(1) Either parent seeking termination of the right of the other parent.

(2) Any person who has been judicially appointed as the guardian of the person of the juvenile.

(3) Any county department of social services, consolidated county human services agency, or licensed child-placing agency to whom custody of the juvenile has been given by a court of competent jurisdiction.

(4) Any county department of social services, consolidated county human services agency, or licensed child-placing agency to which the juvenile has been surrendered for adoption by one of the parents or by the guardian of the person of the juvenile, pursuant to G.S. 48-3-701.

(5) Any person with whom the juvenile has resided for a continuous period of 18 months or more next preceding the filing of the petition or motion.

(6) Any guardian ad litem appointed to represent the minor juvenile pursuant to G.S. 7B-601 who has not been relieved of this responsibility.

(7) Any person who has filed a petition for adoption pursuant to Chapter 48 of the General Statutes.

(b) Any person or agency that may file a petition under subsection (a) of this section may intervene in a pending abuse, neglect, or dependency proceeding for the purpose of filing a motion to terminate parental rights.

(c) *(See Editor's note)* No person whose actions resulted in a conviction under G.S. 14-27.21, 14-27.22, 14-27.23, or 14-27.24 and the conception of the juvenile may file a petition to terminate the parental rights of another with respect to that juvenile.

History.
1977, c. 879, s. 8; 1983, c. 870, s. 1; 1985, c. 758, s. 1; 1987, c. 371, s. 2; 1995 (Reg. Sess., 1996), c. 690, s. 4;

1998-202, s. 6; 1998-229, s. 9.1; 1999-456, s. 60; 2000-183, s. 4; 2004-128, s. 13; 2015-181, s. 23; 2015-264, s. 33(b); 2021-132, s. 1 (*l*)

EDITOR'S NOTE. --
This section was originally enacted as G.S. 7B-1102. It has been renumbered as this section at the direction of the Revisor of Statutes.

Subsection (c), added by Session Laws 2004-128, s. 13, effective December 1, 2004, and applies to offenses committed on or after that date.

Session Laws 2015-264, s. 33(d) made the amendment to this section by Session Laws 2015-264, s. 33(b), which deleted "G.S." two times preceding "14-27.22" and "14-27.24"; and inserted "14-27.23" in subsection (c), effective December 1, 2015, and applicable to petitions filed on or after that date.

Session Laws 2015-264, s. 91.7 contains a severability clause.

Session Laws 2021-132, s. 1(m), made the substitution of "18 months" for "two years" in subdivision (a)(5) of this section by Session Laws 2021-132, s. 1 (l), effective October 1, 2021, and applicable to actions filed or pending on or after that date.

§ 7B-1104. Petition or motion

The petition, or motion pursuant to G.S. 7B-1102, shall be verified by the petitioner or movant and shall be entitled "In Re (last name of juvenile), a minor juvenile", who shall be a party to the action, and shall set forth such of the following facts as are known; and with respect to the facts which are unknown the petitioner or movant shall so state:

(1) The name of the juvenile as it appears on the juvenile's birth certificate, the date and place of birth, and the county where the juvenile is presently residing.

(2) The name and address of the petitioner or movant and facts sufficient to identify the petitioner or movant as one authorized by G.S. 7B-1103 to file a petition or motion.

(3) *(See Editor's note)* The name and address of the parents of the juvenile. If the name or address of one or both parents is unknown to the petitioner or movant, the petitioner or movant shall set forth with particularity the petitioner's or movant's efforts to ascertain the identity or whereabouts of the parent or parents. The information may be contained in an affidavit attached to the petition or motion and incorporated therein by reference. A person whose actions resulted in a conviction under G.S. 14-27.21, 14-27.22, 14-27.23, or 14-27.24 and the conception of the juvenile need not be named in the petition.

(4) The name and address of any person who has been judicially appointed as guardian of the person of the juvenile.

(5) The name and address of any person or agency to whom custody of the juvenile has been given by a court of this or any other state; and a copy of the custody order shall be attached to the petition or motion.

(6) Facts that are sufficient to warrant a determination that one or more of the grounds for terminating parental rights exist.

(7) That the petition or motion has not been filed to circumvent the provisions of Article 2 of Chapter 50A of the General Statutes, the Uniform Child-Custody Jurisdiction and Enforcement Act.

History.
1977, c. 879, s. 8; 1979, c. 110, s. 8; 1981, c. 469, s. 23; 1987, c. 550, s. 15; 1998-202, s. 6; 1999-223, s. 7; 1999-456, s. 60; 2000-183, s. 5; 2004-128, s. 14; 2009-38, s. 2; 2015-181, s. 24; 2015-264, s. 33(c)

§ 7B-1105. Preliminary hearing; unknown parent

(a) If either the name or identity of any parent whose parental rights the petitioner seeks to terminate is not known to the petitioner, the court shall, within 10 days from the date of filing of the petition, or during the next term of court in the county where the petition is filed if there is no court in the county in that 10-day period, conduct a preliminary hearing to ascertain the name or identity of such parent.

(b) The court may, in its discretion, inquire of any known parent of the juvenile concerning the identity of the unknown parent and may order the petitioner to conduct a diligent search for the parent. Should the court ascertain the name or identity of the parent, it shall enter a finding to that effect; and the parent shall be summoned to appear in accordance with G.S. 7B-1106.

(c) Notice of the preliminary hearing need be given only to the petitioner who shall appear at the hearing, but the court may cause summons to be issued to any person directing the person to appear and testify.

(d) If the court is unable to ascertain the name or identity of the unknown parent, the court shall order publication of notice of the termination proceeding and shall specifically order the place or places of publication and the contents of the notice which the court concludes is most likely to identify the juvenile to such unknown parent. The notice shall be published in a newspaper qualified for legal advertising in accordance with G.S. 1-597 and G.S. 1-598 and published in the counties directed by the court, once a week for three successive weeks. Provided, further, the notice shall:

(1) Designate the court in which the petition is pending;

(2) Be directed to "the father (mother) (father and mother) of a male (female) juvenile born on or about _____(date) in _____ County, _____(city), _____(State), respondent";

(3) Designate the docket number and title of the case (the court may direct the actual name of the title be eliminated and the words "In Re Doe" substituted therefor);

(4) State that a petition seeking to terminate the parental rights of the respondent has been filed;

(5) Direct the respondent to answer the petition within 30 days after a date stated in the notice, exclusive of such date, which date so stated shall be the date of first publication of notice and be substantially in the form as set forth in G.S. 1A-1, Rule 4(j1); and

(6) State that the respondent's parental rights to the juvenile will be terminated upon failure to answer the petition within the time prescribed.

Upon completion of the service, an affidavit of the publisher shall be filed with the court.

(e) The court shall issue the order required by subsections (b) and (d) of this section within 30 days from the date of the preliminary hearing unless the court shall determine that additional time for investigation is required.

(f) Upon the failure of the parent served by publication pursuant to subsection (d) of this section to answer the petition within the time prescribed, the court shall issue an order terminating all parental rights of the unknown parent.

(g) No summons shall be required for a parent whose name or identity is unknown and who is served by publication as provided in this section.

History.

1977, c. 879, s. 8; 1987, c. 282, s. 1; 1998-202, s. 6; 1999-456, s. 60; 2011-295, s. 12; 2018-68, s. 5.1

§ 7B-1106. Issuance of summons

(a) Except as provided in G.S. 7B-1105, upon the filing of the petition, the court shall cause a summons to be issued. The summons shall be directed to the following persons or agency, not otherwise a party petitioner, who shall be named as respondents:

(1) The parents of the juvenile. However, a summons does not need to be directed to or served upon any parent who, under Chapter 48 of the General Statutes, has irrevocably relinquished the juvenile to a county department of social services or licensed child-placing agency or to any

parent who has consented to the adoption of the juvenile by the petitioner.

(2) Any person who has been judicially appointed as guardian of the person of the juvenile.

(3) The custodian of the juvenile appointed by a court of competent jurisdiction.

(4) Any county department of social services or licensed child-placing agency to whom a juvenile has been released by one parent pursuant to Part 7 of Article 3 of Chapter 48 of the General Statutes or any county department of social services to whom placement responsibility for the child has been given by a court of competent jurisdiction.

(5) Repealed by Session Laws 2009-38, s. 3, effective May 27, 2009.

The summons shall notify the respondents to file a written answer within 30 days after service of the summons and petition. Service of the summons shall be completed as provided under the procedures established by G.S. 1A-1, Rule 4. Prior to service by publication under G.S. 1A-1, the court shall make findings of fact that a respondent cannot otherwise be served despite diligent efforts made by petitioner for personal service. The court shall approve the form of the notice before it is published. The parent of the juvenile shall not be deemed to be under a disability even though the parent is a minor.

(a1) If a guardian ad litem has been appointed for the juvenile pursuant to G.S. 7B-601 and has not been relieved of responsibility or if the court appoints a guardian ad litem for the juvenile after the petition is filed, a copy of all pleadings and other papers required to be served shall be served on the juvenile's guardian ad litem or attorney advocate pursuant to procedures established under G.S. 1A-1, Rule 5.

(a2) If an attorney has been appointed for a respondent pursuant to G.S. 7B-602 and has not been relieved of responsibility, a copy of all pleadings and other papers required to be served on the respondent shall be served on the respondent's attorney pursuant to procedures established under G.S. 1A-1, Rule 5.

(b) The summons shall be issued for the purpose of terminating parental rights pursuant to the provisions of subsection (a) of this section and shall include:

(1) The name of the minor juvenile;

(2) Notice that a written answer to the petition must be filed with the clerk who signed the petition within 30 days after service of the summons and a copy of the petition, or the parent's rights may be terminated;

(3) Notice that any counsel appointed previously and still representing the parent in an abuse, neglect, or dependency proceeding shall continue to represent the parent unless otherwise ordered by the court;

(4) Notice that if the parent is indigent and is not already represented by appointed counsel, the parent is entitled to appointed counsel, that provisional counsel has been appointed, and that the appointment of provisional counsel shall be reviewed by the court at the first hearing after service;

(5) Notice that the date, time, and place of any pretrial hearing pursuant to G.S. 7B-1108.1 and the hearing on the petition will be mailed by the petitioner upon filing of the answer or 30 days from the date of service if no answer is filed; and

(6) Notice of the purpose of the hearing and notice that the parents may attend the termination hearing.

(c) If a county department of social services, not otherwise a party petitioner, is served with a petition alleging that the parental rights of the parent should be terminated pursuant to G.S. 7B-1111, the department shall file a written answer and shall be deemed a party to the proceeding.

History.
1977, c. 879, s. 8; 1981, c. 966, s. 2; 1983, c. 581, ss. 1, 2; 1995, c. 457, s. 4; 1998-202, s. 6; 1998-229, ss. 10, 27; 1999-456, s. 60; 2000-183, s. 13; 2001-208, s. 28; 2001-487, s. 101; 2009-38, s. 3; 2009-311, s. 10; 2011-295, s. 13; 2013-129, s. 33; 2017-161, s. 11

§ 7B-1106.1. Notice in pending child abuse, neglect, or dependency cases

(a) Upon the filing of a motion pursuant to G.S. 7B-1102, the movant shall prepare a notice directed to each of the following persons or agency, not otherwise a movant:

(1) The parents of the juvenile. However, notice does not need to be directed to or served upon any parent who, under Chapter 48 of the General Statutes, has irrevocably relinquished the juvenile to a county department of social services or licensed child-placing agency or to any parent who has consented to the adoption of the juvenile by the movant.

(2) Any person who has been judicially appointed as guardian of the person of the juvenile.

(3) The custodian of the juvenile appointed by a court of competent jurisdiction.

(4) Any county department of social services or licensed child-placing agency to whom a juvenile has been released by one parent pursuant to Part 7 of Article 3 of Chapter 48 of the General Statutes or any county department of social services to whom placement responsibility for the juvenile has been given by a court of competent jurisdiction.

(5) The juvenile's guardian ad litem or attorney advocate, if one has been appointed pursuant to G.S. 7B-601 and has not been relieved of responsibility.

(6) Repealed by Session Laws 2009-38, s. 4, effective May 27, 2009.

The notice shall notify the person or agency to whom it is directed to file a written response within 30 days after service of the motion and notice. Service of the motion and notice shall be completed as provided under G.S. 7B-1102(b).

(b) The notice required by subsection (a) of this section shall include all of the following:

(1) The name of the minor juvenile.

(2) Notice that a written response to the motion must be filed with the clerk within 30 days after service of the motion and notice, or the parent's rights may be terminated.

(3) Notice that any counsel appointed previously and still representing the parent in an abuse, neglect, or dependency proceeding will continue to represent the parents unless otherwise ordered by the court.

(4) Notice that if the parent is indigent, the parent is entitled to appointed counsel and if the parent is not already represented by appointed counsel the parent may contact the clerk immediately to request counsel.

(5) Notice that the date, time, and place of any pretrial hearing pursuant to G.S. 7B-1108.1 and the hearing on the motion will be mailed by the moving party upon filing of the response or 30 days from the date of service if no response is filed.

(6) Notice of the purpose of the hearing and notice that the parents may attend the termination hearing.

(c) If a county department of social services, not otherwise a movant, is served with a motion seeking termination of a parent's rights, the director shall file a written response and shall be deemed a party to the proceeding.

History.
2000-183, s. 6; 2009-38, s. 4; 2009-311, s. 11

§ 7B-1107. Failure of parent to answer or respond

Upon the failure of a respondent parent to file written answer to the petition or written response to the motion within 30 days after service of the summons and petition or notice and motion, or within the time period established for a defendant's reply by G.S. 1A-1, Rule 4(j1) if service is by publication, the court may issue an order terminating all parental and custodial rights of that parent with respect to the juvenile; provided the court shall order a hearing on the petition or motion and may examine the petitioner or movant or others on the facts alleged in the petition or motion.

History.
1977, c. 879, s. 8; 1979, c. 525, s. 3; 1987, c. 282, s. 2; 1998-202, s. 6; 1998-229, s. 10; 1999-456, s. 60; 2000-183, s. 7

§ 7B-1108. Answer or response of parent; appointment of guardian ad litem for juvenile

(a) Any respondent may file a written answer to the petition or written response to the motion. Only a district court judge may grant an extension of time in which to answer or respond. The answer or response shall admit or deny the allegations of the petition or motion and shall set forth the name and address of the answering respondent or the respondent's attorney.

(b) If an answer or response denies any material allegation of the petition or motion, the court shall appoint a guardian ad litem for the juvenile to represent the best interests of the juvenile, unless the petition or motion was filed by the guardian ad litem pursuant to G.S. 7B-1103, or a guardian ad litem has already been appointed pursuant to G.S. 7B-601. A licensed attorney shall be appointed to assist those guardians ad litem who are not attorneys licensed to practice in North Carolina. The appointment, duties, and payment of the guardian ad litem shall be the same as in G.S. 7B-601 and G.S. 7B-603, but in no event shall a guardian ad litem who is trained and supervised by the guardian ad litem program be appointed to any case unless the juvenile is or has been the subject of a petition for abuse, neglect, or dependency or with good cause shown the local guardian ad litem program consents to the appointment.

(c) In proceedings under this Article, the appointment of a guardian ad litem shall not be required except, as provided above, in cases in which an answer or response is filed denying material allegations, or as required under G.S. 7B-1101; but the court may, in its discretion, appoint a guardian ad litem for a juvenile, either before or after determining the existence of grounds for termination of parental rights, in order to assist the court in determining the best interests of the juvenile.

(d) If a guardian ad litem has previously been appointed for the juvenile under G.S. 7B-601, and the appointment of a guardian ad litem could also be made under this section, the guardian ad litem appointed under G.S. 7B-601, and any attorney appointed to assist that guardian, shall also represent the juvenile in all proceedings under this Article and shall have the duties and payment of a guardian ad litem appointed under this section, unless the court determines that the best interests of the juvenile require otherwise.

History.
1977, c. 879, s. 8; 1981 (Reg. Sess., 1982), c. 1331, s. 3; 1983, c. 870, s. 2; 1989 (Reg. Sess., 1990), c. 851, s. 1; 1998-202, s. 6; 1999-456, s. 60; 2000-183, s. 8; 2003-140, s. 7; 2009-311, s. 12; 2011-295, s. 14

§ 7B-1108.1. Pretrial hearing

(a) The court shall conduct a pretrial hearing. However, the court may combine the pretrial hearing with the adjudicatory hearing on termination in which case no separate pretrial hearing order is required. At the pretrial hearing, the court shall consider the following:

(1) Retention or release of provisional counsel.

(2) Whether a guardian ad litem should be appointed for the juvenile, if not previously appointed.

(3) Whether all summons, service of process, and notice requirements have been met.

(4) Any pretrial motions.

(5) Any issues raised by any responsive pleading, including any affirmative defenses.

(6) Any other issue which can be properly addressed as a preliminary matter.

(b) Written notice of the pretrial hearing shall be in accordance with G.S. 7B-1106 and G.S. 7B-1106.1.

History.
2009-311, s. 13

§ 7B-1109. Adjudicatory hearing on termination

(a) The hearing on the termination of parental rights shall be conducted by the court sitting without a jury and shall be held in the district at such time and place as the chief district court judge shall designate, but no later than 90 days from the filing of the petition or motion unless the judge pursuant to subsection (d) of this section orders that it be held at a later time. Reporting of the hearing shall be as provided by G.S. 7A-198 for reporting civil trials.

(b) The court shall inquire whether the juvenile's parents are present at the hearing and, if so, whether they are represented by counsel. If the parents are not represented by counsel, the court shall inquire whether the parents desire counsel but are indigent. In the event that the parents desire counsel but are indigent as defined in G.S. 7A-450(a) and are unable to obtain counsel to represent them, counsel shall be appointed to represent them in accordance with rules adopted by the Office of Indigent Defense Services. The court shall grant the parents such an extension of time as is reasonable to permit their appointed counsel to prepare their defense to the termination petition or motion.

(c) The court may, upon finding that reasonable cause exists, order the juvenile to be examined by a psychiatrist, a licensed clinical psychologist, a physician, a public or private agency, or any other expert in order that the juvenile's psychological or physical condition or needs may be ascertained or, in the case of a parent whose ability to care for the juvenile is at issue, the court may order a similar examination of any parent of the juvenile.

(d) The court may for good cause shown continue the hearing for up to 90 days from the date of the initial petition in order to receive additional evidence including any reports or assessments that the court has requested, to allow the parties to conduct expeditious discovery, or to receive any other information needed in the best interests of the juvenile. Continuances that extend beyond 90 days after the initial petition shall be granted only in extraordinary circumstances when necessary for the proper administration of justice, and the court shall issue a written order stating the grounds for granting the continuance.

(e) The court shall take evidence, find the facts, and shall adjudicate the existence or nonexistence of any of the circumstances set forth in G.S. 7B-1111 which authorize the termination of parental rights of the respondent. The adjudicatory order shall be reduced to writing, signed, and entered no later than 30 days following the completion of the termination of parental rights hearing. If the order is not entered within 30 days following completion of the hearing, the clerk of court for juvenile matters shall schedule a subsequent hearing at the first session of court scheduled for the hearing of juvenile matters following the 30-day period to determine and explain the reason for the delay and to obtain any needed clarification as to the contents of the order. The order shall be entered within 10 days of the subsequent hearing required by this subsection.

(f) The burden in such proceedings shall be upon the petitioner or movant and all findings of fact shall be based on clear, cogent, and convincing evidence. The rules of evidence in civil cases shall apply. No husband-wife or physician-patient privilege shall be grounds for excluding any evidence regarding the existence or nonexistence of any circumstance authorizing the termination of parental rights.

History.
1977, c. 879, s. 8; 1979, c. 669, s. 1; 1981, c. 966, s. 3; (Reg. Sess., 1982), c. 1331, s. 3; 1983, c. 870, s. 2; 1989 (Reg. Sess., 1990), c. 851, s. 1; 1998-202, s. 6; 1999-456, s. 60; 2000-144, s. 19; 2000-183, s. 9; 2001-208, ss. 7, 22; 2001-487, s. 101; 2003-304, s. 2; 2005-398, s. 16; 2011-295, s. 15; 2013-129, s. 34

§ 7B-1110. Determination of best interests of the juvenile

(a) After an adjudication that one or more grounds for terminating a parent's rights exist, the court shall determine whether terminating the parent's rights is in the juvenile's best interest. The court may consider any evidence, including hearsay evidence as defined in G.S. 8C-1, Rule 801, that the court finds to be relevant, reliable, and necessary to determine the best interests of the juvenile. In each case, the court shall consider the following criteria and make written findings regarding the following that are relevant:

(1) The age of the juvenile.

(2) The likelihood of adoption of the juvenile.

(3) Whether the termination of parental rights will aid in the accomplishment of the permanent plan for the juvenile.

(4) The bond between the juvenile and the parent.

(5) The quality of the relationship between the juvenile and the proposed adoptive parent, guardian, custodian, or other permanent placement.

(6) Any relevant consideration.

Any order shall be reduced to writing, signed, and entered no later than 30 days following the completion of the termination of parental rights hearing. If the order is not entered within 30 days following completion of the hearing, the clerk of court for juvenile matters shall schedule a subsequent hearing at the first session of court scheduled for the hearing of juvenile matters following the 30-day period to determine and explain the reason for the delay and to obtain any needed clarification as to the contents of the order. The order shall be entered within 10 days of the subsequent hearing required by this subsection.

(b) Should the court conclude that, irrespective of the existence of one or more circumstances authorizing termination of parental rights, the best interests of the juvenile require that rights should not be terminated, the court shall dismiss the petition or deny the motion, but only after setting forth the facts and conclusions upon which the dismissal or denial is based.

(c) Should the court determine that circumstances authorizing termination of parental

459

rights do not exist, the court shall dismiss the petition or deny the motion, making appropriate findings of fact and conclusions.

(d) Counsel for the petitioner or movant shall serve a copy of the termination of parental rights order upon the guardian ad litem for the juvenile, if any, and upon the juvenile if the juvenile is 12 years of age or older.

(e) The court may tax the cost of the proceeding to any party.

History.
1977, c. 879, s. 8; 1981 (Reg. Sess., 1982), c. 1131, s. 1; 1983, c. 581, s. 3; c. 607, s. 3; 1998-202, s. 6; 1999-456, s. 60; 2000-183, s. 10; 2001-208, s. 23; 2001-487, s. 101; 2005-398, s. 17; 2011-295, s. 16

§ 7B-1111. Grounds for terminating parental rights

(a) The court may terminate the parental rights upon a finding of one or more of the following:

(1) The parent has abused or neglected the juvenile. The juvenile shall be deemed to be abused or neglected if the court finds the juvenile to be an abused juvenile within the meaning of G.S. 7B-101 or a neglected juvenile within the meaning of G.S. 7B-101.

(2) The parent has willfully left the juvenile in foster care or placement outside the home for more than 12 months without showing to the satisfaction of the court that reasonable progress under the circumstances has been made in correcting those conditions which led to the removal of the juvenile. No parental rights, however, shall be terminated for the sole reason that the parents are unable to care for the juvenile on account of their poverty.

(3) The juvenile has been placed in the custody of a county department of social services, a licensed child-placing agency, a child-caring institution, or a foster home, and the parent has for a continuous period of six months immediately preceding the filing of the petition or motion willfully failed to pay a reasonable portion of the cost of care for the juvenile although physically and financially able to do so.

(4) One parent has been awarded custody of the juvenile by judicial decree or has custody by agreement of the parents, and the other parent whose parental rights are sought to be terminated has for a period of one year or more next preceding the filing of the petition or motion willfully failed without justification to pay for the care, support, and education of the juvenile, as required by the decree or custody agreement.

(5) The father of a juvenile born out of wedlock has not, prior to the filing of a petition or motion to terminate parental rights, done any of the following:

a. Filed an affidavit of paternity in a central registry maintained by the Department of Health and Human Services. The petitioner or movant shall inquire of the Department of Health and Human Services as to whether such an affidavit has been so filed and the Department's certified reply shall be submitted to and considered by the court.

b. Legitimated the juvenile pursuant to provisions of G.S. 49-10, G.S. 49-12.1, or filed a petition for this specific purpose.

c. Legitimated the juvenile by marriage to the mother of the juvenile.

d. Provided substantial financial support or consistent care with respect to the juvenile and mother.

e. Established paternity through G.S. 49-14, 110-132, 130A-101, 130A-118, or other judicial proceeding.

(6) That the parent is incapable of providing for the proper care and supervision of the juvenile, such that the juvenile is a dependent juvenile within the meaning of G.S. 7B-101, and that there is a reasonable probability that the incapability will continue for the foreseeable future. Incapability under this subdivision may be the result of substance abuse, intellectual disability, mental illness, organic brain syndrome, or any other cause or condition that renders the parent unable or unavailable to parent the juvenile and the parent lacks an appropriate alternative child care arrangement.

(7) The parent has willfully abandoned the juvenile for at least six consecutive months immediately preceding the filing of the petition or motion, or the parent has voluntarily abandoned an infant pursuant to G.S. 7B-500 for at least 60 consecutive days immediately preceding the filing of the petition or motion.

(8) The parent has committed murder or voluntary manslaughter of another child of the parent or other child residing in the home; has aided, abetted, attempted, conspired, or solicited to commit murder or voluntary manslaughter of the child, another child of the parent, or other child residing in the home; has committed a felony assault that results in serious bodily injury to the child, another child of the parent, or other child residing in the home; or has committed murder or voluntary manslaughter of the other parent of the child. The petitioner has the burden of proving any of these offenses in the termination of parental rights hearing by (i) proving the elements of the

offense or (ii) offering proof that a court of competent jurisdiction has convicted the parent of the offense, whether or not the conviction was by way of a jury verdict or any kind of plea. If the parent has committed the murder or voluntary manslaughter of the other parent of the child, the court shall consider whether the murder or voluntary manslaughter was committed in self-defense or in the defense of others, or whether there was substantial evidence of other justification.

(9) The parental rights of the parent with respect to another child of the parent have been terminated involuntarily by a court of competent jurisdiction and the parent lacks the ability or willingness to establish a safe home.

(10) Where the juvenile has been relinquished to a county department of social services or a licensed child-placing agency for the purpose of adoption or placed with a prospective adoptive parent for adoption; the consent or relinquishment to adoption by the parent has become irrevocable except upon a showing of fraud, duress, or other circumstance as set forth in G.S. 48-3-609 or G.S. 48-3-707; termination of parental rights is a condition precedent to adoption in the jurisdiction where the adoption proceeding is to be filed; and the parent does not contest the termination of parental rights.

(11) The parent has been convicted of a sexually related offense under Chapter 14 of the General Statutes that resulted in the conception of the juvenile.

(b) The burden in these proceedings is on the petitioner or movant to prove the facts justifying the termination by clear and convincing evidence.

History.
1977, c. 879, s. 8; 1979, c. 669, s. 2; 1979, 2nd Sess., c. 1088, s. 2; c. 1206, s. 2; 1983, c. 89, s. 2; c. 512; 1985, c. 758, ss. 2, 3; c. 784; 1991 (Reg. Sess., 1992), c. 941, s. 1; 1997-390, ss. 1, 2; 1997-443, s. 11A.118(a); 1998-202, s. 6; 1998-229, ss. 11, 28; 1999-456, s. 60; 2000-183, s. 11; 2001-208, s. 6; 2001-291, s. 3; 2001-487, s. 101; 2003-140, s. 3; 2005-146, s. 1; 2007-151, s. 1; 2007-484, s. 26(a); 2012-40, s. 1; 2013-129, s. 35; 2018-47, s. 2

§ 7B-1112. Effects of termination order

An order terminating the parental rights completely and permanently terminates all rights and obligations of the parent to the juvenile and of the juvenile to the parent arising from the parental relationship, except that the juvenile's right of inheritance from the juvenile's parent shall not terminate until a final order of adoption is issued. The parent is not thereafter entitled to notice of proceedings to adopt the juvenile and may not object thereto or otherwise participate therein:

(1) If the juvenile had been placed in the custody of or released for adoption by one parent to a county department of social services or licensed child-placing agency and is in the custody of the agency at the time of the filing of the petition or motion, including a petition or motion filed pursuant to G.S. 7B-1103(a)(6), that agency shall, upon entry of the order terminating parental rights, acquire all of the rights for placement of the juvenile, except as otherwise provided in G.S. 7B-908(d), as the agency would have acquired had the parent whose rights are terminated released the juvenile to that agency pursuant to the provisions of Part 7 of Article 3 of Chapter 48 of the General Statutes, including the right to consent to the adoption of the juvenile.

(2) Except as provided in subdivision (1) above, upon entering an order terminating the parental rights of one or both parents, the court may place the juvenile in the custody of the petitioner or movant, or some other suitable person, or in the custody of the department of social services or licensed child-placing agency, as may appear to be in the best interests of the juvenile.

History.
1977, c. 879, s. 8; 1983, c. 870, s. 3; 1995, c. 457, s. 5; 1998-202, s. 6; 1998-229, s. 11; 1999-456, s. 60; 2000-183, s. 12; 2011-295, s. 17; 2012-194, s. 2

§ 7B-1112.1. Selection of adoptive parents

The process of selection of specific adoptive parents shall be the responsibility of and within the discretion of the county department of social services or licensed child-placing agency. In selecting the adoptive parents, any current placement provider wanting to adopt the child shall be considered. The guardian ad litem may request information from and consult with the county department or child-placing agency concerning the selection process. If the guardian ad litem requests information about the selection process, the county shall provide the information within five business days. The county department of social services shall notify the guardian ad litem and the foster parents of the selection of prospective adoptive parents within 10 days of the selection and before the filing of the adoption petition. If the guardian ad litem disagrees with the selection of adoptive parents or the foster parents want to adopt the juvenile and were not selected as adoptive parents, the guardian ad litem or foster parents shall file a motion within 10 days of the department's

461

notification and schedule the case for hearing on the next juvenile calendar. The department shall not change the juvenile's placement to the prospective adoptive parents unless the time period for filing a motion has expired and no motion has been filed. The Department shall provide a copy of a motion for judicial review of adoption selection to the foster parents not selected. Nothing in this section shall be construed to make the foster parents a party to the proceeding solely based on receiving notification and the right to be heard by filing a motion. In hearing any motion, the court shall consider the recommendations of the agency and the guardian ad litem and other facts related to the selection of adoptive parents. The court shall then determine whether the proposed adoptive placement is in the juvenile's best interests.

History.
2011-295, s. 18; 2013-129, s. 36

N.C. Gen. Stat. § 7B-1113

Repealed by Session Laws 2005-398, s. 18, effective October 1, 2005.

§ 7B-1114. Reinstatement of parental rights

(a) A juvenile whose parent's rights have been terminated, the guardian ad litem attorney, or a county department of social services with custody of the juvenile may file a motion to reinstate the parent's rights if all of the following conditions are satisfied:

(1) The juvenile is at least 12 years of age or, if the juvenile is younger than 12, the motion alleges extraordinary circumstances requiring consideration of the motion.

(2) The juvenile does not have a legal parent, is not in an adoptive placement, and is not likely to be adopted within a reasonable period of time.

(3) The order terminating parental rights was entered at least three years before the filing of the motion, unless the court has found or the juvenile's attorney advocate and the county department of social services with custody of the juvenile stipulate that the juvenile's permanent plan is no longer adoption.

(b) If a motion could be filed under subsection (a) of this section and the parent whose rights have been terminated contacts the county department of social services with custody of the juvenile or the juvenile's guardian ad litem regarding reinstatement of the parent's rights, the department or the guardian ad litem shall notify the juvenile that the juvenile has a right to file a motion for reinstatement of parental rights.

(c) If a motion to reinstate parental rights is filed and the juvenile does not have a guardian ad litem appointed pursuant to G.S. 7B-601, the court shall appoint a guardian ad litem to represent the best interests of the juvenile. The appointment, duties, and payment of the guardian ad litem and the guardian ad litem attorney shall be the same as in G.S. 7B-601 and G.S. 7B-603.

(d) The party filing a motion to reinstate parental rights shall serve the motion on each of the following who is not the movant:

(1) The juvenile.

(2) The juvenile's guardian ad litem or the guardian ad litem attorney.

(3) The county department of social services with custody of the juvenile.

(4) The former parent whose rights the motion seeks to have reinstated.

A former parent who is served under this subsection is not a party to the proceeding and is not entitled to appointed counsel but may retain counsel at the former parent's own expense.

(e) The movant shall ask the clerk to calendar the case for a preliminary hearing on the motion for reinstatement of parental rights within 60 days of the filing of the motion at a session of court scheduled for the hearing of juvenile matters. The movant shall give at least 15 days' notice of the hearing and state its purpose to the persons listed in subdivisions (d)(1) through (d)(4) of this section. In addition, the movant shall send a notice of the hearing to the juvenile's placement provider. Nothing in this section shall be construed to make the former parent or the juvenile's placement provider a party to the proceeding based solely on being served with the motion or receiving notice and the right to be heard.

(f) At least seven days before the preliminary hearing, the department of social services and the juvenile's guardian ad litem shall provide to the court, the other parties, and the former parent reports that address the factors specified in subsection (g) of this section.

(g) At the preliminary hearing and any subsequent hearing on the motion, the court shall consider information from the county department of social services with custody of the juvenile, the juvenile, the juvenile's guardian ad litem, the juvenile's former parent whose parental rights are the subject of the motion, the juvenile's placement provider, and any other person or agency that may aid the court in its review. The court may consider any evidence, including hearsay evidence as defined in G.S. 8C-1, Rule 801, that the court finds to be relevant, reliable, and necessary to determine the needs of the juvenile and whether reinstatement is in the juvenile's best interest. The court shall consider the following criteria and make written findings regarding the following that are relevant:

(1) What efforts were made to achieve adoption or a permanent guardianship.

(2) Whether the parent whose rights the motion seeks to have reinstated has remedied the conditions that led to the juvenile's removal and termination of the parent's rights.

(3) Whether the juvenile would receive proper care and supervision in a safe home if placed with the parent.

(4) The age and maturity of the child and the ability of the child to express the child's preference.

(5) The parent's willingness to resume contact with the juvenile and to have parental rights reinstated.

(6) The juvenile's willingness to resume contact with the parent and to have parental rights reinstated.

(7) Services that would be needed by the juvenile and the parent if the parent's rights were reinstated.

(8) Any other criteria the court deems necessary.

(h) At the conclusion of the preliminary hearing, the court shall either dismiss the motion or order that the juvenile's permanent plan become reinstatement of parental rights. If the court does not dismiss the motion, the court shall conduct interim hearings at least every six months until the motion is granted or dismissed. Interim hearings may be combined with posttermination of parental rights review hearings required by G.S. 7B-908. At each interim hearing, the court shall assess whether the plan of reinstatement of parental rights continues to be in the juvenile's best interest and whether the department of social services has made reasonable efforts to achieve the permanent plan.

(i) At any hearing under this section, after making proper findings of fact and conclusions of law, the court may do one of the following:

(1) Enter an order for visitation in accordance with G.S. 7B-905.1.

(2) Order that the juvenile be placed in the former parent's home and supervised by the department of social services either directly or, when the former parent lives in a different county, through coordination with the county department of social services in that county, or by other personnel as may be available to the court, subject to conditions applicable to the former parent as the court may specify. Any order authorizing placement with the former parent shall specify that the juvenile's placement and care remain the responsibility of the county department of social services with custody of the juvenile and that the department is to provide or arrange for the placement of the juvenile.

(j) The court shall either dismiss or grant a motion for reinstatement of parental rights within 12 months from the date the motion was filed, unless the court makes written findings why a final determination cannot be made within that time. If the court makes such findings, the court shall specify the time frame in which a final order shall be entered.

(k) An order reinstating parental rights restores all rights, powers, privileges, immunities, duties, and obligations of the parent as to the juvenile, including those relating to custody, control, and support of the juvenile. If a parent's rights are reinstated, the court shall be relieved of the duty to conduct periodic reviews.

(l) An order shall be entered no later than 30 days following the completion of any hearing pursuant to this section. If the order is not entered within 30 days following completion of the hearing, the clerk of court for juvenile matters shall schedule a subsequent hearing at the first session of court scheduled for the hearing of juvenile matters following the 30-day period to determine and explain the reason for the delay and to obtain any needed clarification as to the contents of the order. The order shall be entered within 10 days of the subsequent hearing required by this subsection.

(m) The granting of a motion for reinstatement of parental rights does not vacate or otherwise affect the validity of the original order terminating parental rights.

(n) A parent whose rights are reinstated pursuant to this section is not liable for child support or the costs of any services provided to the juvenile for the period from the date of the order terminating the parent's rights to the date of the order reinstating the parent's rights.

History.
2011-295, s. 18; 2013-129, s. 37

ARTICLE 12
GUARDIAN AD LITEM PROGRAM

§ 7B-1200. Office of Guardian ad Litem Services established

There is established within the Administrative Office of the Courts an Office of Guardian ad Litem Services to provide services in accordance with G.S. 7B-601 to abused, neglected, or dependent juveniles involved in judicial proceedings and to assure that all participants in these proceedings are adequately trained to carry out their responsibilities. Each local program shall consist of volunteer guardians ad litem, at least one program attorney, a program coordinator who is a paid State employee, and any clerical staff as the Administrative Office of the Courts in consultation with the local program deems necessary. The Administrative Office of the Courts shall adopt rules and regulations necessary and appropriate for the administration of the program.

History.

1983, c. 761, s. 160; 1987 (Reg. Sess., 1988), c. 1037, s. 32; c. 1090, s. 7; 1998-202, s. 6

§ 7B-1201. Implementation and administration

(a) **Local Programs. --** The Administrative Office of the Courts shall, in cooperation with each chief district court judge and other personnel in the district, implement and administer the program mandated by this Article. Where a local program has not yet been established in accordance with this Article, the district court district shall operate a guardian ad litem program approved by the Administrative Office of the Courts.

(b) **Advisory Committee Established. --** The Director of the Administrative Office of the Courts shall appoint a Guardian ad Litem Advisory Committee consisting of at least five members to advise the Office of Guardian ad Litem Services in matters related to this program. The members of the Advisory Committee shall receive the same per diem and reimbursement for travel expenses as members of State boards and commissions generally.

History.

1983, c. 761, s. 160; 1987 (Reg. Sess., 1988), c. 1037, s. 33; 1998-202, s. 6

§ 7B-1202. Conflict of interest or impracticality of implementation

If a conflict of interest prohibits a local program from providing representation to an abused, neglected, or dependent juvenile, the court may appoint any member of the district bar to represent the juvenile. If the Administrative Office of the Courts determines that within a particular district court district the implementation of a local program is impractical, or that an alternative plan meets the conditions of G.S. 7B-1203, the Administrative Office of the Courts shall waive the establishment of the program within the district.

History.

1983, c. 761, s. 160; 1987 (Reg. Sess., 1988), c. 1037, s. 34; c. 1090, s. 8; 1998-202, s. 6

§ 7B-1203. Alternative plans

A district court district shall be granted a waiver from the implementation of a local program if the Administrative Office of the Courts determines that the following conditions are met:

(1) An alternative plan has been developed to provide adequate guardian ad litem services for every juvenile consistent with the duties stated in G.S. 7B-601; and

(2) The proposed alternative plan will require no greater proportion of State funds than the district court district's abuse and neglect caseload represents to the State's abuse and neglect caseload. Computation of abuse and neglect caseloads shall include such factors as the juvenile population, number of substantiated abuse and neglect reports, number of abuse and neglect petitions, number of abused and neglected juveniles in care to be reviewed pursuant to G.S. 7B-906.1, nature of the district's district court caseload, and number of petitions to terminate parental rights.

When an alternative plan is approved pursuant to this section, the Administrative Office of the Courts shall retain authority to monitor implementation of the said plan in order to assure compliance with the requirements of this Article and G.S. 7B-601. In any district court district where the Administrative Office of the Courts determines that implementation of an alternative plan is not in compliance with the requirements of this section, the Administrative Office of the Courts may implement and administer a program authorized by this Article.

History.

1983, c. 761, s. 160; 1987 (Reg. Sess., 1988), c. 1037, s. 35; 1998-202, s. 6; 2013-129, s. 38

§ 7B-1204. Civil liability of volunteers

Any volunteer participating in a judicial proceeding pursuant to the program authorized by this Article shall not be civilly liable for acts or omissions committed in connection with the proceeding if the volunteer acted in good faith and was not guilty of gross negligence.

History.

1983, c. 761, s. 160; 1998-202, s. 6

ARTICLE 13
PREVENTION OF ABUSE AND NEGLECT

§ 7B-1300. Purpose

It is the expressed intent of this Article to make the prevention of abuse and neglect, as defined in G.S. 7B-101, a priority of this State and to establish the Children's Trust Fund as a means to that end.

History.
1983, c. 894, s. 1; 1998-202, s. 6

§ 7B-1301. Program on Prevention of Abuse and Neglect

(a) The Department of Health and Human Services, through the Division of Social Services, shall implement the Program on Prevention of Abuse and Neglect. The Division of Social Services shall provide the staff and support services for implementing this program.

(b) In order to carry out the purposes of this Article:

(1) Repealed by Session Laws 2009-451, s. 10.43(b), effective July 1, 2009.

(2) The Division of Social Services shall review applications and contract with public or private nonprofit organizations, agencies, schools, or with qualified individuals to operate community-based educational and service programs designed to prevent the occurrence of abuse and neglect. Every contract entered into by the Division of Social Services shall contain provisions that at least twenty-five percent (25%) of the total funding required for a program be provided by the administering organization in the form of in-kind or other services and that a mechanism for evaluation of services provided under the contract be included in the services to be performed. In addition, every proposal to the Division of Social Services for funding under this Article shall include assurances that the proposal has been forwarded to the local department of social services for comment so that the Division of Social Services may consider coordination and duplication of effort on the local level.

(3) The Division of Social Services shall develop appropriate guidelines and criteria for awarding contracts under this Article. These criteria shall include, but are not limited to: documentation of need within the proposed geographical impact area; diversity of geographical areas of programs funded under this Article; demonstrated effectiveness of the proposed strategy or program for preventing abuse and neglect; reasonableness of implementation plan for achieving stated objectives; utilization of community resources including volunteers; provision for an evaluation component that will provide outcome data;

plan for dissemination of the program for implementation in other communities; and potential for future funding from private sources.

(4) The Division of Social Services shall develop guidelines for regular monitoring of contracts awarded under this Article in order to maximize the investments in prevention programs by the Children's Trust Fund and to establish appropriate accountability measures for administration of contracts.

(5) The Division of Social Services shall develop a State plan for the prevention of abuse and neglect for submission to the Governor, the President of the Senate, and the Speaker of the House of Representatives.

(c) To assist in implementing this Article, the Division of Social Services may accept contributions, grants, or gifts in cash or otherwise from persons, associations, or corporations. All monies received by the Division of Social Services from contributions, grants, or gifts and not through appropriation by the General Assembly shall be deposited in the Children's Trust Fund. Disbursements of the funds shall be on the authorization of the Department of Health and Human Services. In order to maintain an effective expenditure and revenue control, the funds are subject in all respects to State law and regulations, but no appropriation is required to permit expenditure of the funds.

(d) Programs contracted for under this Article are intended to prevent abuse and neglect of juveniles. Abuse and neglect prevention programs are defined to be those programs and services which impact on juveniles and families before any substantiated incident of abuse or neglect has occurred. These programs may include, but are not limited to:

(1) Community-based educational programs on prenatal care, perinatal bonding, child development, basic child care, care of children with special needs, and coping with family stress; and

(2) Community-based programs relating to crisis care, aid to parents, and support groups for parents and their children experiencing stress within the family unit.

(e) No more than twenty percent (20%) of each year's total awards may be utilized for funding State-level programs to coordinate community-based programs.

History.
1983, c. 894, s. 1; 1993 (Reg. Sess., 1994), c. 677, s. 1; 1998-202, s. 6; 2009-451, s. 10.43(b)

§ 7B-1302. Children's Trust Fund

(a) There is established a fund to be known as the "Children's Trust Fund," in the Department of Health and Human Services, Division of Social Services, which shall be funded by a portion of the marriage license fee under G.S. 161-11.1 and a portion of the special license plate fee under G.S. 20-81.12. The money in the Fund shall be used by the Division of Social Services to fund abuse and neglect prevention programs so authorized by this Article.

(b) The Department of Health and Human Services shall report annually on revenues and expenditures of the Children's Trust Fund to the Joint Legislative Commission on Governmental Operations.

History.
1983, c. 894, s. 1; 1998-202, s. 6; 1999-277, s. 5; 2004-124, s. 7.33(b); 2009-451, s. 10.43(c); 2010-31, s. 10.20A(a)

ARTICLE 14
NORTH CAROLINA CHILD FATALITY PREVENTION SYSTEM

§ 7B-1400. Declaration of public policy

The General Assembly finds that it is the public policy of this State to prevent the abuse, neglect, and death of juveniles. The General Assembly further finds that the prevention of the abuse, neglect, and death of juveniles is a community responsibility; that professionals from disparate disciplines have responsibilities for children or juveniles and have expertise that can promote their safety and well-being; and that multidisciplinary reviews of the abuse, neglect, and death of juveniles can lead to a greater understanding of the causes and methods of preventing these deaths. It is, therefore, the intent of the General Assembly, through this Article, to establish a statewide multidisciplinary, multiagency child fatality prevention system consisting of the State Team established in G.S. 7B-1404 and the Local Teams established in G.S. 7B-1406. The purpose of the system is to assess the records of selected cases in which children are being served by child protective services and the records of all deaths of children in North Carolina from birth to age 18 in order to (i) develop a communitywide approach to the problem of child abuse and neglect, (ii) understand the causes of childhood deaths, (iii) identify any gaps or deficiencies that may exist in the delivery of services to children and their families by public agencies that are designed to prevent future child abuse, neglect, or death, and (iv) make and implement recommendations for changes to laws, rules, and policies that will support the safe and healthy development of

our children and prevent future child abuse, neglect, and death.

History.
1991, c. 689, s. 233(a); 1993, c. 321, s. 285(a); 1998-202, s. 6

§ 7B-1401. Definitions

The following definitions apply in this Article:
(1) **Additional Child Fatality.** -- Any death of a child that did not result from suspected abuse or neglect and about which no report of abuse or neglect had been made to the county department of social services within the previous 12 months.
(2) **Local Team.** -- A Community Child Protection Team or a Child Fatality Prevention Team.
(3) **State Team.** -- The North Carolina Child Fatality Prevention Team.
(4) **Task Force.** -- The North Carolina Child Fatality Task Force.
(5) **Team Coordinator.** -- The Child Fatality Prevention Team Coordinator.

History.
1991, c. 689, s. 233(a); 1993, c. 321, s. 285(a); 1998-202, s. 6

§ 7B-1402. Task Force -- creation; membership; vacancies

(a) There is created the North Carolina Child Fatality Task Force within the Department of Health and Human Services for budgetary purposes only.

(b) The Task Force shall be composed of 36 members, 12 of whom shall be ex officio members, four of whom shall be appointed by the Governor, 10 of whom shall be appointed by the Speaker of the House of Representatives, and 10 of whom shall be appointed by the President Pro Tempore of the Senate. The ex officio members other than the Chief Medical Examiner may designate representatives from their particular departments, divisions, or offices to represent them on the Task Force. In making appointments or designating representatives, appointing authorities and ex officio members shall use best efforts to select members or representatives with sufficient knowledge and experience to effectively contribute to the issues examined by the Task Force and, to the extent possible, to reflect the geographical, political, gender, and racial diversity of this State. The members shall be as follows:
(1) The Chief Medical Examiner.
(2) The Attorney General.
(3) The Director of the Division of Social Services.

(4) The Director of the State Bureau of Investigation.

(5) The Director of the Maternal and Child Health Section of the Department of Health and Human Services.

(6) The chair of the Council for Women and Youth Involvement.

(7) The Superintendent of Public Instruction.

(8) The Chairman of the State Board of Education.

(9) The Director of the Division of Mental Health, Developmental Disabilities, and Substance Abuse Services.

(10) The Secretary of the Department of Health and Human Services.

(11) The Director of the Administrative Office of the Courts.

(11a) The Director of the Juvenile Justice Section, Division of Adult Correction and Juvenile Justice, Department of Public Safety.

(12) A director of a county department of social services, appointed by the Governor upon recommendation of the President of the North Carolina Association of County Directors of Social Services.

(13) A representative from a Sudden Infant Death Syndrome or safe infant sleep counseling and education program, appointed by the Governor upon recommendation of the Director of the Maternal and Child Health Section of the Department of Health and Human Services.

(14) A representative from the NC Child, appointed by the Governor upon recommendation of the President of the organization.

(15) A director of a local department of health, appointed by the Governor upon the recommendation of the President of the North Carolina Association of Local Health Directors.

(16) A representative from a private group, other than NC Child, that advocates for children, appointed by the Speaker of the House of Representatives upon recommendation of private child advocacy organizations.

(17) A pediatrician, licensed to practice medicine in North Carolina, appointed by the Speaker of the House of Representatives upon recommendation of the North Carolina Pediatric Society.

(18) A representative from the North Carolina League of Municipalities, appointed by the Speaker of the House of Representatives upon recommendation of the League.

(18a) A representative from the North Carolina Domestic Violence Commission, appointed by the Speaker of the House of Representatives upon recommendation of the Director of the Commission.

(19) One public member, appointed by the Speaker of the House of Representatives.

(20) A county or municipal law enforcement officer, appointed by the President Pro Tempore of the Senate upon recommendation of organizations that represent local law enforcement officers.

(21) A district attorney, appointed by the President Pro Tempore of the Senate upon recommendation of the President of the North Carolina Conference of District Attorneys.

(22) A representative from the North Carolina Association of County Commissioners, appointed by the President Pro Tempore of the Senate upon recommendation of the Association.

(22a) A representative from the North Carolina Coalition Against Domestic Violence, appointed by the President Pro Tempore of the Senate upon recommendation of the Executive Director of the Coalition.

(23) One public member, appointed by the President Pro Tempore of the Senate.

(24) Five members of the Senate, appointed by the President Pro Tempore of the Senate, and five members of the House of Representatives, appointed by the Speaker of the House of Representatives.

(c) All members of the Task Force are voting members. Vacancies in the appointed membership shall be filled by the appointing officer who made the initial appointment. Terms shall be two years. The members shall elect a chair who shall preside for the duration of the chair's term as member. In the event a vacancy occurs in the chair before the expiration of the chair's term, the members shall elect an acting chair to serve for the remainder of the unexpired term.

History.

1991, c. 689, s. 233(a); 1991 (Reg. Sess., 1992), c. 900, s. 169(b); 1993, c. 321, s. 285(a); 1993 (Reg. Sess., 1994), c. 769, s. 27.8(d); 1996, 2nd Ex. Sess., c. 17, s. 3.2; 1997-443, s. 11A.98; 1997-456, s. 27; 1998-202, s. 6; 1998-212, s. 12.44(a), (b); 2004-186, s. 5.1; 2016-94, s. 32.5(h); 2020-78, s. 4F.1(a)

§ 7B-1403. Task Force -- duties

The Task Force shall:

(1) Undertake a statistical study of the incidences and causes of child deaths in this State and establish a profile of child deaths. The study shall include (i) an analysis of all community and private and public agency involvement with the decedents and their families prior to death, and (ii) an analysis of child deaths by age, cause, and geographic distribution;

(2) Develop a system for multidisciplinary review of child deaths. In developing such a system, the Task Force shall study the operation of existing Local Teams. The Task Force shall also consider the feasibility and desirability of local or regional review teams and, should it determine such teams to be feasible and desirable, develop guidelines for the operation of the teams. The Task Force shall also examine the laws, rules, and policies relating to confidentiality of and access to information that affect those agencies with responsibilities for children, including State and local health, mental health, social services, education, and law enforcement agencies, to determine whether those laws, rules, and policies inappropriately impede the exchange of information necessary to protect children from preventable deaths, and, if so, recommend changes to them;

(3) Receive and consider reports from the State Team; and

(4) Perform any other studies, evaluations, or determinations the Task Force considers necessary to carry out its mandate.

History.
1991, c. 689, s. 233(a); 1996, 2nd Ex. Sess., c. 17, s. 3.2; 1998-202, s. 6; 1998-212, s. 12.44(a), (c)

§ 7B-1404. State Team -- creation; membership; vacancies

(a) There is created the North Carolina Child Fatality Prevention Team within the Department of Health and Human Services for budgetary purposes only.

(b) The State Team shall be composed of the following 11 members of whom nine members are ex officio and two are appointed:

(1) The Chief Medical Examiner, who shall chair the State Team;

(2) The Attorney General;

(3) The Director of the Division of Social Services, Department of Health and Human Services;

(4) The Director of the State Bureau of Investigation;

(5) The Director of the Division of Maternal and Child Health of the Department of Health and Human Services;

(6) The Superintendent of Public Instruction;

(7) The Director of the Division of Mental Health, Developmental Disabilities, and Substance Abuse Services, Department of Health and Human Services;

(8) The Director of the Administrative Office of the Courts;

(9) The pediatrician appointed pursuant to G.S. 7B-1402(b) to the Task Force;

(10) A public member, appointed by the Governor; and

(11) The Team Coordinator.

The ex officio members other than the Chief Medical Examiner may designate a representative from their departments, divisions, or offices to represent them on the State Team.

(c) All members of the State Team are voting members. Vacancies in the appointed membership shall be filled by the appointing officer who made the initial appointment.

History.
1991, c. 689, s. 233(a); 1993, c. 321, s. 285(a); 1997-443, s. 11A.99; 1997-456, s. 27; 1998-202, s. 6

§ 7B-1405. State Team -- duties

The State Team shall:

(1) Review current deaths of children when those deaths are attributed to child abuse or neglect or when the decedent was reported as an abused or neglected juvenile pursuant to G.S. 7B-301 at any time before death;

(2) Report to the Task Force during the existence of the Task Force, in the format and at the time required by the Task Force, on the State Team's activities and its recommendations for changes to any law, rule, and policy that would promote the safety and well-being of children;

(3) Upon request of a Local Team, provide technical assistance to the Team;

(4) Periodically assess the operations of the multidisciplinary child fatality prevention system and make recommendations for changes as needed;

(5) Work with the Team Coordinator to develop guidelines for selecting child deaths to receive detailed, multidisciplinary death reviews by Local Teams that review cases of additional child fatalities; and

(6) Receive reports of findings and recommendations from Local Teams that review cases of additional child fatalities and work with the Team Coordinator to implement recommendations.

History.
1991, c. 689, s. 233(a); 1993, c. 321, s. 285(a); 1997-443, s. 11A.99; 1997-456, s. 27; 1998-202, s. 6

§ 7B-1406. Community Child Protection Teams; Child Fatality Prevention Teams; creation and duties

(a) Community Child Protection Teams are established in every county of the State. Each Community Child Protection Team shall:

(1) Review, in accordance with the procedures established by the director of the

county department of social services under G.S. 7B-1409:

    a. Selected active cases in which children are being served by child protective services; and

    b. Cases in which a child died as a result of suspected abuse or neglect, and

        1. A report of abuse or neglect has been made about the child or the child's family to the county department of social services within the previous 12 months, or

        2. The child or the child's family was a recipient of child protective services within the previous 12 months.

  (2) Submit annually to the board of county commissioners recommendations, if any, and advocate for system improvements and needed resources where gaps and deficiencies may exist.

In addition, each Community Child Protection Team may review the records of all additional child fatalities and report findings in connection with these reviews to the Team Coordinator.

(b) Any Community Child Protection Team that determines it will not review additional child fatalities shall notify the Team Coordinator. In accordance with the plan established under G.S. 7B-1408(1), a separate Child Fatality Prevention Team shall be established in that county to conduct these reviews. Each Child Fatality Prevention Team shall:

  (1) Review the records of all cases of additional child fatalities.

  (2) Submit annually to the board of county commissioners recommendations, if any, and advocate for system improvements and needed resources where gaps and deficiencies may exist.

  (3) Report findings in connection with these reviews to the Team Coordinator.

(c) All reports to the Team Coordinator under this section shall include:

  (1) A listing of the system problems identified through the review process and recommendations for preventive actions;

  (2) Any changes that resulted from the recommendations made by the Local Team;

  (3) Information about each death reviewed; and

  (4) Any additional information requested by the Team Coordinator.

History.
1993, c. 321, s. 285(a); 1998-202, s. 6

§ 7B-1407. Local Teams; composition

(a) Each Local Team shall consist of representatives of public and nonpublic agencies in the community that provide services to children and their families and other individuals who represent the community. No single team shall encompass a geographic or governmental area larger than one county.

(b) Each Local Team shall consist of the following persons:

  (1) The director of the county department of social services and a member of the director's staff;

  (2) A local law enforcement officer, appointed by the board of county commissioners;

  (3) An attorney from the district attorney's office, appointed by the district attorney;

  (4) The executive director of the local community action agency, as defined by the Department of Health and Human Services, or the executive director's designee;

  (5) The superintendent of each local school administrative unit located in the county, or the superintendent's designee;

  (6) A member of the county board of social services, appointed by the chair of that board;

  (7) A local mental health professional, appointed by the director of the area authority established under Chapter 122C of the General Statutes;

  (8) The local guardian ad litem coordinator, or the coordinator's designee;

  (9) The director of the local department of public health; and

  (10) A local health care provider, appointed by the local board of health.

(c) In addition, a Local Team that reviews the records of additional child fatalities shall include the following five additional members:

  (1) An emergency medical services provider or firefighter, appointed by the board of county commissioners;

  (2) A district court judge, appointed by the chief district court judge in that district;

  (3) A county medical examiner, appointed by the Chief Medical Examiner;

  (4) A representative of a local child care facility or Head Start program, appointed by the director of the county department of social services; and

  (5) A parent of a child who died before reaching the child's eighteenth birthday, to be appointed by the board of county commissioners.

(d) The Team Coordinator shall serve as an ex officio member of each Local Team that reviews the records of additional child fatalities. The board of county commissioners may appoint a maximum of five additional members to represent county agencies or the community at large to serve on any Local Team. Vacancies on a Local Team shall be filled by the original appointing authority.

(e) Each Local Team shall elect a member to serve as chair at the Team's pleasure.

(f) Each Local Team shall meet at least four times each year.

(g) The director of the local department of social services shall call the first meeting of the Community Child Protection Team. The director of the local department of health, upon consultation with the Team Coordinator, shall call the first meeting of the Child Fatality Prevention Team. Thereafter, the chair of each Local Team shall schedule the time and place of meetings, in consultation with these directors, and shall prepare the agenda. The chair shall schedule Team meetings no less often than once per quarter and often enough to allow adequate review of the cases selected for review. Within three months of election, the chair shall participate in the appropriate training developed under this Article.

History.
1993, c. 321, s. 285(a); 1997-443, s. 11A.100; 1997-456, s. 27; 1997-506, s. 52; 1998-202, s. 6

§ 7B-1408. Child Fatality Prevention Team Coordinator; duties

The Child Fatality Prevention Team Coordinator shall serve as liaison between the State Team and the Local Teams that review records of additional child fatalities and shall provide technical assistance to these Local Teams. The Team Coordinator shall:

(1) Develop a plan to establish Local Teams that review the records of additional child fatalities in each county.

(2) Develop model operating procedures for these Local Teams that address when public meetings should be held, what items should be addressed in public meetings, what information may be released in written reports, and any other information the Team Coordinator considers necessary.

(3) Provide structured training for these Local Teams at the time of their establishment, and continuing technical assistance thereafter.

(4) Provide statistical information on all child deaths occurring in each county to the appropriate Local Team, and assure that all child deaths in a county are assessed through the multidisciplinary system.

(5) Monitor the work of these Local Teams.

(6) Receive reports of findings, and other reports that the Team Coordinator may require, from these Local Teams.

(7) Report the aggregated findings of these Local Teams to each Local Team that reviews the records of additional child fatalities and to the State Team.

(8) Evaluate the impact of local efforts to identify problems and make changes.

History.
1993, c. 321, s. 285(a); 1998-202, s. 6

§ 7B-1409. Community Child Protection Teams; duties of the director of the county department of social services

In addition to any other duties as a member of the Community Child Protection Team, and in connection with the reviews under G.S. 7B-1406(a)(1), the director of the county department of social services shall:

(1) Assure the development of written operating procedures in connection with these reviews, including frequency of meetings, confidentiality policies, training of members, and duties and responsibilities of members;

(2) Assure that the Team defines the categories of cases that are subject to its review;

(3) Determine and initiate the cases for review;

(4) Bring for review any case requested by a Team member;

(5) Provide staff support for these reviews;

(6) Maintain records, including minutes of all official meetings, lists of participants for each meeting of the Team, and signed confidentiality statements required under G.S. 7B-1413, in compliance with applicable rules and law; and

(7) Report quarterly to the county board of social services, or as required by the board, on the activities of the Team.

History.
1993, c. 321, s. 285(a); 1998-202, s. 6

§ 7B-1410. Local Teams; duties of the director of the local department of health

In addition to any other duties as a member of the Local Team and in connection with reviews of additional child fatalities, the director of the local department of health shall:

(1) Distribute copies of the written procedures developed by the Team Coordinator under G.S. 7B-1408 to the administrators of all agencies represented on the Local Team and to all members of the Local Team;

(2) Maintain records, including minutes of all official meetings, lists of participants for each meeting of the Local Team, and signed confidentiality statements required under G.S. 7B-1413, in compliance with applicable rules and law;

(3) Provide staff support for these reviews; and

(4) Report quarterly to the local board of health, or as required by the board, on the activities of the Local Team.

History.
1993, c. 321, s. 285(a); 1998-202, s. 6

§ 7B-1411. Community Child Protection Teams; responsibility for training of team members

The Division of Social Services, Department of Health and Human Services, shall develop and make available, on an ongoing basis, for the members of Local Teams that review active cases in which children are being served by child protective services, training materials that address the role and function of the Local Team, confidentiality requirements, an overview of child protective services law and policy, and Team record keeping.

History.
1993, c. 321, s. 285(a); 1997-443, s. 11A.118(a); 1998-202, s. 6

§ 7B-1412. Task Force -- reports

The Task Force shall report annually to the Governor and General Assembly, within the first week of the convening or reconvening of the General Assembly. The report shall contain at least a summary of the conclusions and recommendations for each of the Task Force's duties, as well as any other recommendations for changes to any law, rule, or policy that it has determined will promote the safety and well-being of children. Any recommendations of changes to law, rule, or policy shall be accompanied by specific legislative or policy proposals and detailed fiscal notes setting forth the costs to the State.

History.
1991, c. 689, s. 233(a); 1991 (Reg. Sess., 1992), c. 900, s. 169(a); 1993 (Reg. Sess., 1994), c. 769, s. 27.8(a); 1996, 2nd Ex. Sess., c. 17, ss. 3.1, 3.2; 1998-202, s. 6; 1998-212, s. 12.44(a), (d)

§ 7B-1413. Access to records

(a) The State Team, the Local Teams, and the Task Force during its existence, shall have access to all medical records, hospital records, and records maintained by this State, any county, or any local agency as necessary to carry out the purposes of this Article, including police investigations data, medical examiner investigative data, health records, mental health records, and social services records. The State Team, the Task Force, and the Local Teams shall not, as

part of the reviews authorized under this Article, contact, question, or interview the child, the parent of the child, or any other family member of the child whose record is being reviewed. Any member of a Local Team may share, only in an official meeting of that Local Team, any information available to that member that the Local Team needs to carry out its duties.

(b) Meetings of the State Team and the Local Teams are not subject to the provisions of Article 33C of Chapter 143 of the General Statutes. However, the Local Teams may hold periodic public meetings to discuss, in a general manner not revealing confidential information about children and families, the findings of their reviews and their recommendations for preventive actions. Minutes of all public meetings, excluding those of executive sessions, shall be kept in compliance with Article 33C of Chapter 143 of the General Statutes. Any minutes or any other information generated during any closed session shall be sealed from public inspection.

(c) All otherwise confidential information and records acquired by the State Team, the Local Teams, and the Task Force during its existence, in the exercise of their duties are confidential; are not subject to discovery or introduction into evidence in any proceedings; and may only be disclosed as necessary to carry out the purposes of the State Team, the Local Teams, and the Task Force. In addition, all otherwise confidential information and records created by a Local Team in the exercise of its duties are confidential; are not subject to discovery or introduction into evidence in any proceedings; and may only be disclosed as necessary to carry out the purposes of the Local Team. No member of the State Team, a Local Team, nor any person who attends a meeting of the State Team or a Local Team, may testify in any proceeding about what transpired at the meeting, about information presented at the meeting, or about opinions formed by the person as a result of the meetings. This subsection shall not, however, prohibit a person from testifying in a civil or criminal action about matters within that person's independent knowledge.

(d) Each member of a Local Team and invited participant shall sign a statement indicating an understanding of and adherence to confidentiality requirements, including the possible civil or criminal consequences of any breach of confidentiality.

(e) Cases receiving child protective services at the time of review by a Local Team shall have an entry in the child's protective services record to indicate that the case was received by that Team. Additional entry into the record shall be at the discretion of the director of the county department of social services.

(f) The Social Services Commission shall adopt rules to implement this section in connection

Chapter 7B

with reviews conducted by Community Child Protection Teams. The Commission for Public Health shall adopt rules to implement this section in connection with Local Teams that review additional child fatalities. In particular, these rules shall allow information generated by an executive session of a Local Team to be accessible for administrative or research purposes only.

History.
1991, c. 689, s. 233(a); 1993, c. 321, s. 285(a); 1998-202, s. 6; 2007-182, s. 1.3

§ 7B-1414. Administration; funding

(a) To the extent of funds available, the chairs of the Task Force and State Team may hire staff or consultants to assist the Task Force and the State Team in completing their duties.

(b) Members, staff, and consultants of the Task Force or State Team shall receive travel and subsistence expenses in accordance with the provisions of G.S. 138-5 or G.S. 138-6, as the case may be, paid from funds appropriated to implement this Article and within the limits of those funds.

(c) With the approval of the Legislative Services Commission, legislative staff and space in the Legislative Building and the Legislative Office Building may be made available to the Task Force.

History.
1991, c. 689, s. 233(a); 1998-202, s. 6

DIVISION 02.
UNDISCIPLINED AND
DELINQUENT JUVENILES

ARTICLE 15
PURPOSES; DEFINITIONS

§ 7B-1500. Purpose

This Subchapter shall be interpreted and construed so as to implement the following purposes and policies:

(1) To protect the public from acts of delinquency.

(2) To deter delinquency and crime, including patterns of repeat offending:

    a. By providing swift, effective dispositions that emphasize the juvenile offender's accountability for the juvenile's actions; and

    b. By providing appropriate rehabilitative services to juveniles and their families.

(3) To provide an effective system of intake services for the screening and evaluation of complaints and, in appropriate cases, where court intervention is not necessary to ensure public safety, to refer juveniles to community-based resources.

(4) To provide uniform procedures that assure fairness and equity; that protect the constitutional rights of juveniles, parents, and victims; and that encourage the court and others involved with juvenile offenders to proceed with all possible speed in making and implementing determinations required by this Subchapter.

History.
1979, c. 815, s. 1; 1987 (Reg. Sess., 1988), c. 1090, s. 1; 1998-202, s. 6

§ 7B-1501. Definitions

In this Subchapter, unless the context clearly requires otherwise, the following words have the listed meanings. The singular includes the plural, unless otherwise specified:

(1) **Chief court counselor. --** The person responsible for administration and supervision of juvenile intake, probation, and post-release supervision in each judicial district, operating under the supervision of the Division of Adult Correction and Juvenile Justice of the Department of Public Safety.

(1a) **Juvenile consultation. --** The provision of services to a vulnerable juvenile and to the parent, guardian, or custodian of a vulnerable juvenile pursuant to G.S. 7B-1706.1. Juvenile consultation cases are subject to confidentiality laws provided in Subchapter III of this Chapter.

(2) **Clerk. --** Any clerk of superior court, acting clerk, or assistant or deputy clerk.

(3) **Community-based program. --** A program providing nonresidential or residential treatment to a juvenile under the jurisdiction of the juvenile court in the community where the juvenile's family lives. A community-based program may include specialized foster care, family counseling, shelter care, and other appropriate treatment.

(4) **Court. --** The district court division of the General Court of Justice.

(5) Repealed by Session Laws 2001-490, s. 2.1, effective June 30, 2001.

(6) **Custodian. --** The person or agency that has been awarded legal custody of a juvenile by a court.

(7) **Delinquent juvenile. --**

    a. Any juvenile who, while less than 16 years of age but at least 10 years of age, commits a crime or infraction under State law or under an ordinance of local government, including violation of the motor vehicle laws, or who commits indirect contempt by a juvenile as defined in G.S. 5A-31.

b. Any juvenile who, while less than 18 years of age but at least 16 years of age, commits a crime or an infraction under State law or under an ordinance of local government, excluding all violations of the motor vehicle laws under Chapter 20 of the General Statutes, or who commits indirect contempt by a juvenile as defined in G.S. 5A-31.

c. Any juvenile who, while less than 10 years of age but at least 8 years of age, commits a Class A, B1, B2, C, D, E, F, or G felony under State law.

d. Any juvenile who, while less than 10 years of age but at least 8 years of age, commits a crime or an infraction under State law or under an ordinance of local government, including violation of the motor vehicle laws, and has been previously adjudicated delinquent.

(8) **Detention.** -- The secure confinement of a juvenile under a court order.

(9) **Detention facility.** -- A facility approved to provide secure confinement and care for juveniles. Detention facilities include both State and locally administered detention homes, centers, and facilities.

(10) **District.** -- Any district court district as established by G.S. 7A-133.

(10a) **Division.** -- The Division of Adult Correction and Juvenile Justice of the Department of Public Safety created under Article 12 of Chapter 143B of the General Statutes.

(11) **Holdover facility.** -- A place in a jail which has been approved by the Department of Health and Human Services as meeting the State standards for detention as required in G.S. 153A-221 providing close supervision where the juvenile cannot converse with, see, or be seen by the adult population.

(12) **House arrest.** -- A requirement that the juvenile remain at the juvenile's residence unless the court or the juvenile court counselor authorizes the juvenile to leave for school, counseling, work, or other similar specific purposes, provided the juvenile is accompanied in transit by a parent, legal guardian, or other person approved by the juvenile court counselor.

(13) **Intake.** -- The process of screening and evaluating a complaint alleging that a juvenile is delinquent or undisciplined to determine whether the complaint should be filed as a petition.

(14) **Interstate Compact on Juveniles.** -- An agreement ratified by 50 states and the District of Columbia providing a formal means of returning a juvenile, who is an absconder, escapee, or runaway, to the juvenile's home state, and codified in Article 28 of this Chapter.

(15) **Judge.** -- Any district court judge.

(16) **Judicial district.** -- Any district court district as established by G.S. 7A-133.

(17) **Juvenile.** -- Except as provided in subdivisions (7) and (27) of this section, any person who has not reached the person's eighteenth birthday and is not married, emancipated, or a member of the Armed Forces of the United States. Wherever the term "juvenile" is used with reference to rights and privileges, that term encompasses the attorney for the juvenile as well.

(18) **Juvenile court.** -- Any district court exercising jurisdiction under this Chapter.

(18a) **Juvenile court counselor.** -- A person responsible for intake services and court supervision services to juveniles under the supervision of the chief court counselor.

(19) Repealed by Session Laws 2000, c. 137, s. 2, effective July 20, 2000.

(20) **Petitioner.** -- The individual who initiates court action by the filing of a petition or a motion for review alleging the matter for adjudication.

(21) **Post-release supervision.** -- The supervision of a juvenile who has been returned to the community after having been committed to the Division for placement in a youth development center.

(22) **Probation.** -- The status of a juvenile who has been adjudicated delinquent, is subject to specified conditions under the supervision of a juvenile court counselor, and may be returned to the court for violation of those conditions during the period of probation.

(23) **Prosecutor.** -- The district attorney or an assistant district attorney.

(24) **Protective supervision.** -- The status of a juvenile who has been adjudicated undisciplined and is under the supervision of a juvenile court counselor.

(24a) **Severe emotional disturbance.** -- A diagnosable mental, behavioral, or emotional disorder of sufficient duration to meet diagnostic criteria specified within the DSM-5 that resulted in functional impairment which substantially interferes with or limits the child's role or functioning in family, school, or community activities in a person who is under the age of 18.

(25) **Teen court program.** -- A community resource for the diversion of cases in which a juvenile has allegedly committed certain offenses for hearing by a jury of the juvenile's peers, which may assign the juvenile to counseling, restitution, curfews, community service, or other rehabilitative measures.

(26) Repealed by Session Laws 2001-95, s. 1, effective May 18, 2001.

(27) **Undisciplined juvenile.** --

a. A juvenile who, while less than 16 years of age but at least 10 years of age, is unlawfully absent from school; or is regularly disobedient to and beyond the disciplinary control of the juvenile's parent, guardian, or custodian; or is regularly found in places where it is unlawful for a juvenile to be; or has run away from home for a period of more than 24 hours; or

b. A juvenile who is 16 or 17 years of age and who is regularly disobedient to and beyond the disciplinary control of the juvenile's parent, guardian, or custodian; or is regularly found in places where it is unlawful for a juvenile to be; or has run away from home for a period of more than 24 hours.

(27a) **Victim.** -- Any individual or entity against whom a crime or infraction is alleged to have been committed by a juvenile based on reasonable grounds that the alleged facts are true. For purposes of Article 17 of this Chapter, the term may also include a parent, guardian, or custodian of a victim under the age of 18 years of age.

(27b) **Vulnerable juvenile.** -- Any juvenile who, while less than 10 years of age but at least 6 years of age, commits a crime or infraction under State law or under an ordinance of local government, including violation of the motor vehicle laws, and is not a delinquent juvenile.

(28) **Wilderness program.** -- A rehabilitative residential treatment program in a rural or outdoor setting.

(29) **Youth development center.** -- A secure residential facility authorized to provide long-term treatment, education, and rehabilitative services for delinquent juveniles committed by the court to the Division.

History.
1979, c. 815, s. 1; 1981, c. 336; c. 359, s. 2; c. 469, ss. 1-3; c. 716, s. 1; 1985, c. 648; c. 757, s. 156(q); 1985 (Reg. Sess., 1986), c. 852, s. 16; 1987, c. 162; c. 695; 1987 (Reg. Sess., 1988), c. 1037, ss. 36, 37; 1989 (Reg. Sess., 1990), c. 815, s. 1; 1991, c. 258, s. 3; c. 273, s. 11; 1991 (Reg. Sess., 1992), c. 1030, s. 3; 1993, c. 324, s. 1; c. 516, ss. 1-3; 1997-113, s. 1; 1997-390, ss. 3, 3.2; 1997-443, s.

11A.118(a); 1997-506, s. 30; 1998-202, s. 6; 1998-229, s. 1; 2000-137, s. 2; 2001-95, ss. 1, 2, 5; 2001-487, s. 3; 2001-490, s. 2.1; 2007-168, s. 2; 2009-545, s. 1; 2009-547, s. 1; 2011-145, s. 19.1(l); 2011-183, s. 4; 2017-57, s. 16D.4(a); 2017-186, s. 2(j); 2018-142, s. 23(b); 2019-186, s. 1(a); 2021-123, ss. 5(b), 8(a)

ARTICLE 16
JURISDICTION

§ 7B-1600. Jurisdiction over undisciplined juveniles

(a) The court has exclusive, original jurisdiction over any case involving a juvenile who is alleged to be undisciplined. For purposes of determining jurisdiction, the age of the juvenile at the time of the alleged offense governs.

(b) When the court obtains jurisdiction over a juvenile under this section, jurisdiction shall continue until terminated by order of the court, the juvenile reaches the age of 18 years, or the juvenile is emancipated.

(c) The court has jurisdiction over the parent, guardian, or custodian of a juvenile who is under the jurisdiction of the court pursuant to this section, if the parent, guardian, or custodian has been served with a summons pursuant to G.S. 7B-1805.

History.
1979, c. 815, s. 1; 1983, c. 837, s. 1; 1985, c. 459, s. 2; 1987, c. 409, s. 2; 1995, c. 328, s. 3; c. 462, s. 2; 1996, 2nd Ex. Sess., c. 18, s. 23.2(c); 1998-202, s. 6

§ 7B-1601. Jurisdiction over delinquent juveniles

(a) The court has exclusive, original jurisdiction over any case involving a juvenile who is alleged to be delinquent. For purposes of determining jurisdiction, the age of the juvenile at the time of the alleged offense governs.

(b) When the court obtains jurisdiction over a juvenile alleged to be delinquent for an offense committed prior to the juvenile reaching the age of 16 years, jurisdiction shall continue until terminated by order of the court or until the juvenile reaches the age of 18 years, except as provided otherwise in this Article.

(b1) When the court obtains jurisdiction over a juvenile alleged to be delinquent for an offense committed while the juvenile was at least 16 years of age but less than 17 years of age, jurisdiction shall continue until terminated by order of the court or until the juvenile reaches the age of 19 years, except as provided otherwise in this Article. If the offense was committed while the juvenile was at least 17 years of age, jurisdiction shall continue until terminated by order of the court or until the juvenile reaches the age of 20 years, except as provided otherwise in this Article.

(c) When delinquency proceedings for a juvenile alleged to be delinquent for an offense committed prior to the juvenile reaching the age of 16 years cannot be concluded before the juvenile reaches the age of 18 years, the court retains jurisdiction for the sole purpose of conducting proceedings pursuant to Article 22 of this Chapter and either transferring the case to superior court for trial as an adult or dismissing the petition.

(c1) When delinquency proceedings for a juvenile alleged to be delinquent for an offense committed while the juvenile was at least 16 years of age but less than 17 years of age cannot be concluded before the juvenile reaches the age of 19 years, the court retains jurisdiction for the sole purpose of conducting proceedings pursuant to Article 22 of this Chapter and either transferring the case to superior court for trial as an adult or dismissing the petition. When delinquency proceedings for a juvenile alleged to be delinquent for an offense committed while the juvenile was at least 17 years of age cannot be concluded before the juvenile reaches the age of 20 years, the court retains jurisdiction for the sole purpose of conducting proceedings pursuant to Article 22 of this Chapter and either transferring the case to superior court for trial as an adult or dismissing the petition.

(d) When the court has not obtained jurisdiction over a juvenile before the juvenile reaches the age of 18, for a felony and any related misdemeanors the juvenile allegedly committed on or after the juvenile's thirteenth birthday and prior to the juvenile's sixteenth birthday, the court has jurisdiction for the sole purpose of conducting proceedings pursuant to Article 22 of this Chapter and either transferring the case to superior court for trial as an adult or dismissing the petition.

(d1) When the court has not obtained jurisdiction over a juvenile before the juvenile reaches the age of 19, for a felony and related misdemeanors the juvenile allegedly committed while the juvenile was at least 16 years of age but less than 17 years of age, the court has jurisdiction for the sole purpose of conducting proceedings pursuant to Article 22 of this Chapter and either transferring the case to superior court for trial as an adult or dismissing the petition. When the court has not obtained jurisdiction over a juvenile before the juvenile reaches the age of 20, for a felony and related misdemeanors the juvenile allegedly committed while the juvenile was at least 17 years of age but less than 18 years of age, the court has jurisdiction for the sole purpose of conducting proceedings pursuant to Article 22 of this Chapter and either transferring the case to superior court for trial as an adult or dismissing the petition.

(e) The court has jurisdiction over delinquent juveniles in the custody of the Division and over proceedings to determine whether a juvenile who is under the post-release supervision of the juvenile court counselor has violated the terms of the juvenile's post-release supervision.

(f) The court has jurisdiction over persons 18 years of age or older who are under the extended jurisdiction of the juvenile court.

(g) The court has jurisdiction over the parent, guardian, or custodian of a juvenile who is under the jurisdiction of the court pursuant to this section if the parent, guardian, or custodian has been served with a summons pursuant to G.S. 7B-1805.

History.

1979, c. 815, s. 1; 1983, c. 837, s. 1; 1985, c. 459, s. 2; 1987, c. 409, s. 2; 1995, c. 328, s. 3; c. 462, s. 2; 1996, 2nd Ex. Sess., c. 18, s. 23.2(c); 1998-202, s. 6; 2000-137, s. 3; 2001-490, s. 2.2; 2011-145, 19.1(*l*); 2017-57, s. 16D.4(b); 2018-142, s. 23(b); 2021-123, s. 1(b)

§ 7B-1602. Extended jurisdiction over a delinquent juvenile under certain circumstances

(a) When a juvenile is committed to the Division for placement in a youth development center for an offense that would be first degree murder pursuant to G.S. 14-17, first-degree forcible rape pursuant to G.S. 14-27.21, first-degree statutory rape pursuant to G.S. 14-27.24, first-degree forcible sexual offense pursuant to G.S. 14-27.26, or first-degree statutory sexual offense pursuant to G.S. 14-27.29 if committed by an adult, jurisdiction shall continue until terminated by order of the court or until the juvenile reaches the age of 21 years, whichever occurs first.

(b) When a juvenile is committed to the Division for placement in a youth development center for an offense committed under the age of 16 that would be a Class B1, B2, C, D, or E felony if committed by an adult, other than an offense set forth in subsection (a) of this section, jurisdiction shall continue until terminated by order of the court or until the juvenile reaches the age of 19 years, whichever occurs first.

(c) When a juvenile is committed to the Division for placement in a youth development center for an offense committed while the juvenile was at least 16 years of age but less than 17 years of age that would be a Class B1, B2, C, D, or E felony if committed by an adult, other than an offense set forth in subsection (a) of this section, jurisdiction shall continue until terminated by order of the court or until the juvenile reaches the age of 20 years, whichever occurs first.

(d) When a juvenile is committed to the Division for placement in a youth development center for an offense committed while at least 17 years of age that would be a Class B1, B2, C, D, or E felony if committed by an adult, other than an offense set forth in subsection (a) of this section, jurisdiction shall continue until terminated by order of the court or until the juvenile reaches the age of 21 years, whichever occurs first.

History.
1979, c. 815, s. 1; 1981, c. 469, s. 4; 1996, 2nd Ex. Sess., c. 18, s. 23.2(d); 1998-202, s. 6; 2000-137, s. 3; 2001-95, s. 5; 2011-145, s. 19.1 (*l*); 2015-181, s. 25; 2021-123, s. 1(c)

§ 7B-1603. Jurisdiction in certain circumstances

The court has exclusive original jurisdiction of all of the following proceedings:
(1) Proceedings under the Interstate Compact on the Placement of Children set forth in Article 38 of this Chapter.
(2) Proceedings involving judicial consent for emergency surgical or medical treatment for a juvenile when the juvenile's parent, guardian, custodian, or person who has assumed the status and obligation of a parent without being awarded legal custody of the juvenile by a court refuses to consent for treatment to be rendered.
(3) Proceedings to determine whether a juvenile should be emancipated.
(4) Proceedings in which a juvenile has been ordered pursuant to G.S. 5A-32(b) to appear and show cause why the juvenile should not be held in contempt.

History.
1979, c. 815, s. 1; 1983, c. 837, s. 1; 1985, c. 459, s. 2; 1987, c. 409, s. 2; 1995, c. 328, s. 3; c. 462, s. 2; 1996, 2nd Ex. Sess., c. 18, s. 23.2(c); 1998-202, s. 6; 2007-168, s. 3

§ 7B-1604. Limitations on juvenile court jurisdiction

(a) Any juvenile, including a juvenile who is under the jurisdiction of the court, who commits a criminal offense on or after the juvenile has reached the age of 18 years is subject to prosecution as an adult. A juvenile who is emancipated shall be prosecuted as an adult for the commission of a criminal offense.
(b) A juvenile shall be prosecuted as an adult for any criminal offense the juvenile commits after a district or superior court conviction if either of the following applies:
(1) The juvenile has previously been transferred to and convicted in superior court.

(2) The juvenile has previously been convicted in either district or superior court for a felony or a misdemeanor. Violations of the motor vehicle laws punishable as a misdemeanor or infraction shall not be considered a conviction for the purposes of this subsection unless the conviction is for an offense involving impaired driving as defined by G.S. 20-4.01(24a).

History.
1979, c. 815, s. 1; 1981, c. 469, s. 4; 1983, c. 837, s. 1; 1985, c. 459, s. 2; 1987, c. 409, s. 2; 1995, c. 328, s. 3; c. 462, s. 2; 1996, 2nd Ex. Sess., c. 18, s. 23.2(c); 1998-202, s. 6; 2017-57, s. 16D.4(c); 2018-142, s. 23(b); 2019-186, s. 2

ARTICLE 17
SCREENING OF DELINQUENCY, UNDISCIPLINED, AND VULNERABLE COMPLAINTS

§ 7B-1700. Intake services

The chief court counselor, under the direction of the Division, shall establish intake services in each judicial district of the State for all delinquency and undisciplined cases and all complaints against vulnerable juveniles.

The purpose of intake services shall be to determine from available evidence whether there are reasonable grounds to believe the facts alleged are true, to determine whether the facts alleged constitute a delinquent or undisciplined offense within the jurisdiction of the court, to determine whether the facts alleged are sufficiently serious to warrant court action, and to obtain assistance from community resources when court referral is not necessary or allowed. The juvenile court counselor shall not engage in field investigations to substantiate complaints or to produce supplementary evidence but may refer complainants to law enforcement agencies for those purposes.

History.
1979, c. 815, s. 1; 1998-202, s. 6; 2000-137, s. 3; 2001-490, s. 2.3; 2011-145, s. 19.1 (*l*); 2021-123, s. 5(c)

§ 7B-1700.1. Duty to report abuse, neglect, dependency

Any time a juvenile court counselor or any person has cause to suspect that a juvenile is abused, neglected, or dependent, or has died as the result of maltreatment, the juvenile court counselor or the person shall make a report to the county department of social services as required by G.S. 7B-301.

History.
2009-311, s. 14

§ 7B-1701. Preliminary inquiry

(a) When a complaint is received against a juvenile at least 10 years of age, the juvenile court counselor shall make a preliminary determination as to whether the juvenile is within the jurisdiction of the court as a delinquent or undisciplined juvenile. If the juvenile court counselor finds that the facts contained in the complaint do not state a case within the jurisdiction of the court, that legal sufficiency has not been established, or that the matters alleged are frivolous, the juvenile court counselor, without further inquiry, shall refuse authorization to file the complaint as a petition.

If a complaint against the juvenile has not been previously received, as determined by the juvenile court counselor, the juvenile court counselor shall make reasonable efforts to meet with the juvenile and the juvenile's parent, guardian, or custodian if the offense is divertible.

When requested by the juvenile court counselor, the prosecutor shall assist in determining the sufficiency of evidence as it affects the quantum of proof and the elements of offenses.

The juvenile court counselor, without further inquiry, shall authorize the complaint to be filed as a petition if the juvenile court counselor finds reasonable grounds to believe that the juvenile has committed one of the following nondivertible offenses:

(1) Murder;

(2) First-degree rape or second degree rape;

(3) First-degree sexual offense or second degree sexual offense;

(4) Arson;

(5) Any violation of Article 5, Chapter 90 of the General Statutes that would constitute a felony if committed by an adult;

(6) First degree burglary;

(7) Crime against nature; or

(8) Any felony which involves the willful infliction of serious bodily injury upon another or which was committed by use of a deadly weapon.

(b) When a complaint is received against a juvenile less than 10 years of age, the juvenile court counselor shall make a preliminary determination as to whether the juvenile is a vulnerable juvenile or is within the jurisdiction of the court as a delinquent juvenile. If the juvenile court counselor determines the juvenile is within the jurisdiction of the court as a delinquent juvenile, the juvenile court counselor shall proceed with the complaint pursuant to subsection (a) of this section. If the juvenile court counselor determines the juvenile is a vulnerable juvenile, the juvenile court counselor shall handle the complaint as a juvenile consultation for a vulnerable juvenile.

History.
1979, c. 815, s. 1; 1983, c. 251, s. 1; 1998-202, s. 6; 2001-490, s. 2.4; 2015-58, s. 2.1; 2021-123, s. 5(c)

§ 7B-1702. Evaluation

Upon a finding of legal sufficiency, except in cases involving nondivertible offenses set out in G.S. 7B-1701(a), the juvenile court counselor shall determine whether a complaint should be filed as a petition, the juvenile diverted pursuant to G.S. 7B-1706, or the case resolved without further action. In making the decision, the counselor shall consider criteria provided by the Department and shall conduct a gang assessment for juveniles who are 12 years of age or older. The intake process shall include the following steps if practicable:

(1) Interviews with the complainant and the victim if someone other than the complainant;

(2) Interviews with the juvenile and the juvenile's parent, guardian, or custodian;

(3) Interviews with persons known to have relevant information about the juvenile or the juvenile's family.

Interviews required by this section shall be conducted in person unless it is necessary to conduct them by telephone.

History.
1979, c. 815, s. 1; 1981, c. 469, s. 5; 1998-202, s. 6; 2000-137, s. 3; 2001-490, s. 2.5; 2011-145, s. 19.1 (*l*); 2017-57, s. 16D.4(ee); 2017-197, s. 5.4; 2018-142, s. 23(b); 2019-186, s. 3; 2021-123, s. 5(c)

§ 7B-1703. Evaluation decision

(a) The juvenile court counselor shall complete evaluation of a complaint within 15 days of receipt of the complaint, with an extension for a maximum of 15 additional days at the discretion of the chief court counselor. The juvenile court counselor shall decide within this time period whether a complaint shall be filed as a juvenile petition, handled as a juvenile consultation for a vulnerable juvenile, or handled in some other manner authorized by this Article.

(b) Except as provided in G.S. 7B-1706, if the juvenile court counselor determines that a complaint should be filed as a petition, the counselor shall file the petition as soon as practicable, but in any event within 15 days after the complaint is received, with an extension for a maximum of 15 additional days at the discretion of the chief court counselor. The juvenile court counselor shall assist the complainant when necessary with the preparation and filing of the petition, shall include on it the date and the words "Approved for Filing", shall sign it, and shall transmit it to the clerk of superior court.

(c) If the juvenile court counselor determines that a petition should not be filed or the complaint handled as a juvenile consultation, the juvenile court counselor shall notify the complainant and the victim, if the complainant is not the victim, immediately in writing with specific reasons for the decision, whether or not legal sufficiency was found, and whether the matter was closed or diverted and retained, and shall include notice of the complainant's and victim's right to have the decision reviewed by the prosecutor. The juvenile court counselor shall sign the complaint after indicating on it:

(1) The date of the determination;

(2) The words "Not Approved for Filing"; and

(3) Whether the matter is "Closed" or "Diverted and Retained".

Except as provided in G.S. 7B-1706, any complaint not approved for filing as a juvenile petition or handled as a juvenile consultation shall be destroyed by the juvenile court counselor after holding the complaint for a temporary period to allow review as provided in G.S. 7B-1705.

(d) If the juvenile court counselor determines that a complaint should be handled as a juvenile consultation, the juvenile court counselor shall obtain referral information.

History.
1979, c. 815, s. 1; 1998-202, s. 6; 2001-490, s. 2.6; 2017-57, s. 16D.4(t); 2018-142, s. 23(b); 2021-123, s. 5(c)

§ 7B-1704. Request for review by prosecutor

The complainant and the victim have five calendar days, from receipt of the juvenile court counselor's decision not to approve the filing of a petition, to request review by the prosecutor. The juvenile court counselor shall notify the prosecutor immediately of such request and shall transmit to the prosecutor a copy of the complaint. The prosecutor shall notify the complainant, the victim, and the juvenile court counselor of the time and place for the review.

History.
1979, c. 815, s. 1; 1998-202, s. 6; 2001-490, s. 2.7; 2017-57, s. 16D.4(u); 2018-142, s. 23(b)

§ 7B-1705. Review of determination that petition should not be filed

No later than 20 days after the complainant and the victim are notified, the prosecutor shall review the juvenile court counselor's determination that a juvenile petition should not be filed. Review shall include conferences with the complainant, the victim, and the juvenile court counselor. At the conclusion of the review, the prosecutor shall: (i) affirm the decision of the juvenile court counselor or direct the filing of a petition and (ii) notify the complainant and the victim of the prosecutor's action.

History.
1979, c. 815, s. 1; 1981, c. 469, s. 6; 1998-202, s. 6; 2001-490, s. 2.8; 2017-57, s. 16D.4(v); 2018-142, s. 23(b)

§ 7B-1706. Diversion plans and referral

(a) Unless the offense is one in which a petition is required by G.S. 7B-1701(a), upon a finding of legal sufficiency the juvenile court counselor may divert the juvenile pursuant to a diversion plan, which may include referring the juvenile to any of the following resources:

(1) An appropriate public or private resource;

(2) Restitution;

(3) Community service;

(4) Victim-offender mediation;

(5) Regimented physical training;

(6) Counseling;

(7) A teen court program, as set forth in subsection (c) of this section.

As part of a diversion plan, the juvenile court counselor may enter into a diversion contract with the juvenile and the juvenile's parent, guardian, or custodian.

(b) Unless the offense is one in which a petition is required by G.S. 7B-1701(a), upon a finding of legal sufficiency the juvenile court counselor may enter into a diversion contract with the juvenile and the parent, guardian, or custodian; provided, a diversion contract requires the consent of the juvenile and the juvenile's parent, guardian, or custodian. A diversion contract shall:

(1) State conditions by which the juvenile agrees to abide and any actions the juvenile agrees to take;

(2) State conditions by which the parent, guardian, or custodian agrees to abide and any actions the parent, guardian, or custodian agrees to take;

(3) Describe the role of the juvenile court counselor in relation to the juvenile and the parent, guardian, or custodian;

(4) Specify the length of the contract, which shall not exceed six months;

(5) Indicate that all parties understand and agree that:

a. The juvenile's violation of the contract may result in the filing of the complaint as a petition; and

b. The juvenile's successful completion of the contract shall preclude the filing of a petition.

After a diversion contract is signed by the parties, the juvenile court counselor shall provide copies of the contract to the juvenile and the juvenile's parent, guardian, or custodian. The juvenile court counselor shall notify any agency or other resource from which the juvenile or the juvenile's parent, guardian, or custodian will be seeking services or treatment pursuant to the terms of the contract. At any time during the term of the contract if the juvenile court counselor determines that the juvenile has failed to comply substantially with the terms of the contract, the juvenile court counselor may file the complaint as a petition. Unless the juvenile court counselor has filed the complaint as a petition, the juvenile court counselor shall close the juvenile's file in regard to the diverted matter within six months after the date of the contract.

(c) If a teen court program has been established in the district, the juvenile court counselor, upon a finding of legal sufficiency, may refer to a teen court program, any case in which a juvenile has allegedly committed an offense that would be an infraction or misdemeanor if committed by an adult. However, the juvenile court counselor shall not refer a case to a teen court program if the juvenile is alleged to have committed any of the following offenses:

(1) Driving while impaired under G.S. 20-138.1, 20-138.2, 20-138.3, 20-138.5, or 20-138.7, or any other motor vehicle violation;

(2) A Class A1 misdemeanor;

(3) An assault in which a weapon is used; or

(4) A controlled substance offense under Article 5 of Chapter 90 of the General Statutes, other than simple possession of a Schedule VI drug or alcohol.

(d) The juvenile court counselor shall maintain diversion plans and contracts entered into pursuant to this section to allow juvenile court counselors to determine when a juvenile has had a complaint diverted previously. Diversion plans and contracts are not public records under Chapter 132 of the General Statutes, shall not be included in the clerk's record pursuant to G.S. 7B-3000, and shall be withheld from public inspection or examination. Diversion plans and contracts shall be destroyed when the juvenile reaches the age of 18 years or when the juvenile is no longer under the jurisdiction of the court, whichever is longer.

(e) No later than 60 days after the juvenile court counselor diverts a juvenile, the juvenile court counselor shall determine whether the juvenile and the juvenile's parent, guardian, or custodian have complied with the terms of the diversion plan or contract. In making this determination, the juvenile court counselor shall contact any referral resources to determine whether the juvenile and the juvenile's parent, guardian, or custodian complied with any recommendations for treatment or services made by the resource. If the juvenile and the juvenile's parent, guardian, or custodian have not complied, the juvenile court counselor shall reconsider the decision to divert and may authorize the filing of the complaint as a petition within 10 days after making the determination. If the juvenile court counselor does not file a petition, the juvenile court counselor may continue to monitor the case for up to six months from the date of the diversion plan or contract. At any point during that time period if the juvenile and the juvenile's parent, guardian, or custodian fail to comply, the juvenile court counselor shall reconsider the decision to divert and may authorize the filing of the complaint as a petition. After six months, the juvenile court counselor shall close the diversion plan or contract file.

History.
1979, c. 815, s. 1; 1998-202, s. 6; 2001-490, s. 2.9; 2019-41, s. 1; 2021-123, s. 5(c)

§ 7B-1706.1. Juvenile consultation services

A juvenile court counselor shall serve a vulnerable juvenile under a juvenile consultation for up to six months providing case management services. An extension of juvenile consultation services may be made for up to three months at the approval of the chief court counselor. As part of case management services, the juvenile court counselor shall provide screenings, assessments, community resources, and programming to the juvenile and the parent, legal guardian, or custodian.

History.
2021-123, s. 5(c)

§ 7B-1707. Direct contempt by juvenile

The preceding sections of this Article do not apply when a juvenile is ordered pursuant to G.S. 5A-32(b) to appear and show cause why the juvenile should not be held in contempt.

History.
2007-168, s. 4

ARTICLE 18
VENUE; PETITION; SUMMONS

§ 7B-1800. Venue

(a) A proceeding in which a juvenile is alleged to be delinquent or undisciplined shall be commenced and adjudicated in the district in which the offense is alleged to have occurred. When a proceeding is commenced in a district other than that of the juvenile's residence, the court shall proceed to adjudication in that district and, if the juvenile is in residential treatment or foster care in that district, the court shall conduct the dispositional hearing in that district as well, unless the judge enters an order, supported by findings of fact, that a transfer would serve the ends of justice or is in the best interests of the juvenile.

(b) Except as provided in subsection (a) of this section, after adjudication, the following procedures shall be available to the court:

(1) The court may transfer the proceeding to the court in the district where the juvenile resides for disposition.

(2) Where the proceeding is not transferred under subdivision (1) of this section, the court shall immediately notify the chief district court judge in the district in which the juvenile resides. If the chief district court judge requests a transfer within five days after receipt of notification, the court shall transfer the proceeding.

(3) Where the proceeding is not transferred under subdivision (1) or (2) of this section, the court, upon motion of the juvenile, shall transfer the proceeding to the court in the district where the juvenile resides for disposition. The court shall advise the juvenile of the juvenile's right to transfer under this section.

History.
1979, c. 815, s. 1; 1998-202, s. 6; 2004-155, s. 1

§ 7B-1801. Pleading and process

The pleading in a juvenile action is the petition. The process in a juvenile action is the summons.

History.
1979, c. 815, s. 1; 1998-202, s. 6

§ 7B-1802. Petition

The petition shall contain the name, date of birth, and address of the juvenile and the name and last known address of the juvenile's parent, guardian, or custodian. The petition shall allege the facts that invoke jurisdiction over the juvenile. The petition shall not contain information on more than one juvenile.

A petition in which delinquency is alleged shall contain a plain and concise statement, without allegations of an evidentiary nature, asserting facts supporting every element of a criminal offense and the juvenile's commission thereof with sufficient precision clearly to apprise the juvenile of the conduct which is the subject of the allegation.

Sufficient copies of the petition shall be prepared so that copies will be available for the juvenile, for each parent if living separate and apart, for the guardian or custodian if any, for the juvenile court counselor, for the prosecutor, and for any person determined by the court to be a necessary party.

History.
1979, c. 815, s. 1; 1981, c. 469, s. 9; 1998-202, s. 6; 2001-490, s. 2.10

§ 7B-1803. Receipt of complaints; filing of petition

(a) All complaints concerning a juvenile alleged to be delinquent or undisciplined shall be referred to the juvenile court counselor for screening and evaluation. Thereafter, if the juvenile court counselor determines that a petition should be filed, the petition shall be drawn by the juvenile court counselor or the clerk, signed by the complainant, and verified before an official authorized to administer oaths. If the circumstances indicate a need for immediate attachment of jurisdiction and if the juvenile court counselor is out of the county or otherwise unavailable to receive a complaint and to draw a petition when it is needed, the clerk shall assist the complainant in communicating the complaint to the juvenile court counselor by telephone and, with the approval of the juvenile court counselor, shall draw a petition and file it when signed and verified. A copy of the complaint and petition shall be transmitted to the juvenile court counselor.

(b) If review is requested pursuant to G.S. 7B-1704, the prosecutor shall review a complaint and any decision of the juvenile court counselor not to authorize that the complaint be filed as a petition. If the prosecutor, after review, authorizes a complaint to be filed as a petition, the prosecutor shall prepare the complaint to be filed by the clerk as a petition, recording the day of filing.

History.
1979, c. 815, s. 1; 1981, c. 469, ss. 10, 11; 1998-202, s. 6; 2001-490, s. 2.11; 2012-172, s. 1

§ 7B-1804. Commencement of action

(a) An action is commenced by the filing of a petition in the clerk's office when that office is open, or by a magistrate's acceptance of a petition for filing pursuant to subsection (b) of this section when the clerk's office is closed.

(b) When the office of the clerk is closed and the juvenile court counselor requests a petition alleging a juvenile to be delinquent or undisciplined, a magistrate may draw and verify the petition and accept it for filing, which acceptance shall constitute filing. The magistrate's authority under this subsection is limited to emergency situations when a petition is required in order to obtain a secure or nonsecure custody order. Any petition accepted for filing under this subsection shall be delivered to the clerk's office for processing as soon as that office is open for business.

History.
1979, c. 815, s. 1; 1987, c. 409, s. 3; 1998-202, s. 6; 2001-490, s. 2.12

§ 7B-1805. Issuance of summons

(a) Immediately after a petition has been filed alleging that a juvenile is undisciplined or delinquent, the clerk shall issue a summons to the juvenile and to the parent, guardian, or custodian requiring them to appear for a hearing at the time and place stated in the summons. A copy of the petition shall be attached to each summons.

(b) A summons shall be on a printed form supplied by the Administrative Office of the Courts and shall include:

(1) Notice of the nature of the proceeding and the purpose of the hearing scheduled on the summons.

(2) Notice of any right to counsel and information about how to seek the appointment of counsel prior to a hearing.

(3) Notice that, if the court determines at the adjudicatory hearing that the allegations of the petition are true, the court will conduct a dispositional hearing and will have jurisdiction to enter orders affecting substantial rights of the juvenile and of the parent, guardian, or custodian, including orders that:

a. Affect the juvenile's custody;

b. Impose conditions on the juvenile;

c. Require that the juvenile receive medical, psychiatric, psychological, or other treatment and that the parent participate in the treatment;

d. Require the parent to undergo psychiatric, psychological, or other treatment or counseling;

e. Order the parent to pay for treatment that is ordered for the juvenile or the parent; and

f. Order the parent to pay support for the juvenile for any period the juvenile does not reside with the parent or to pay attorneys' fees or other fees or expenses as ordered by the court.

(4) Notice that the parent, guardian, or custodian shall be required to attend scheduled hearings and that failure without reasonable cause to attend may result in proceedings for contempt of court.

(5) Notice that the parent, guardian, or custodian shall be responsible for bringing the juvenile before the court at any hearing the juvenile is required to attend and that failure without reasonable cause to bring the juvenile before the court may result in proceedings for contempt of court.

(c) The summons shall advise the parent, guardian, or custodian that upon service, jurisdiction over the parent, guardian, or custodian is obtained and that failure of the parent, guardian, or custodian to appear or bring the juvenile before the court without reasonable cause or to comply with any order of the court pursuant to Article 27 of this Chapter may cause the court to issue a show cause order for contempt. The summons shall contain the following language in bold type:

"TO THE PARENT(S), GUARDIAN(S), OR CUSTODIAN(S): YOUR FAILURE TO APPEAR IN COURT FOR A SCHEDULED HEARING OR TO COMPLY WITH AN ORDER OF THE COURT MAY RESULT IN A FINDING OF CRIMINAL CONTEMPT. A PERSON HELD IN CRIMINAL CONTEMPT MAY BE SUBJECT TO IMPRISONMENT OF UP TO 30 DAYS, A FINE NOT TO EXCEED FIVE HUNDRED DOLLARS ($ 500.00) OR BOTH."

(d) A summons shall be directed to the person summoned to appear and shall be delivered to any person authorized to serve process.

History.
1979, c. 815, s. 1; 1987 (Reg. Sess., 1988), c. 1090, s. 2; 1995, c. 328, s. 1; 1998-202, s. 6

§ 7B-1806. Service of summons

The summons and petition shall be personally served upon the parent, the guardian, or custodian and the juvenile not less than five days prior to the date of the scheduled hearing. The time for service may be waived in the discretion of the court.

If the parent, guardian, or custodian entitled to receive a summons cannot be found by a diligent effort, the court may authorize service of the summons and petition by mail or by publication. The cost of the service by publication shall be advanced by the petitioner and may be charged as court costs as the court may direct.

The court may issue a show cause order for contempt against a parent, guardian, or custodian who is personally served and fails without reasonable cause to appear and to bring the juvenile before the court.

The provisions of G.S. 15A-301(a), (c), (d), and (e) relating to criminal process apply to juvenile process; provided the period of time for return of an unserved summons is 30 days.

History.
1979, c. 815, s. 1; 1998-202, s. 6

§ 7B-1807. Notice to parent and juvenile of scheduled hearings

The clerk shall give to all parties, including both parents of the juvenile, the juvenile's guardian or custodian, and any other person who has assumed the status and obligation of a parent without being awarded legal custody of the juvenile by a court, five days' written notice of the date and time of all scheduled hearings unless the party is notified in open court or the court orders otherwise.

History.
1998-202, s. 6

§ 7B-1808. First appearance for felony cases

(a) A juvenile who is alleged in the petition to have committed an offense that would be a felony if committed by an adult shall be summoned to appear before the court for a first appearance within 10 days of the filing of the petition. If the juvenile is in secure or nonsecure custody, the first appearance shall take place at the initial hearing required by G.S. 7B-1906. Unless the juvenile is in secure or nonsecure custody, the court may continue the first appearance to a time certain for good cause.

(b) At the first appearance, the court shall:

(1) Inform the juvenile of the allegations set forth in the petition;

(2) Determine whether the juvenile has retained counsel or has been assigned counsel;

(3) If applicable, inform the juvenile of the date of the probable cause hearing, which shall be within 15 days of the first appearance; and

(4) Inform the parent, guardian, or custodian that the parent, guardian, or custodian is required to attend all hearings scheduled in the matter and may be held in contempt of court for failure to attend any scheduled hearing.

If the juvenile is not represented by counsel, counsel for the juvenile shall be appointed in accordance with rules adopted by the Office of Indigent Services.

History.
1998-202, s. 6; 2000-144, s. 20; 2001-487, s. 4

ARTICLE 19
TEMPORARY CUSTODY; SECURE AND NONSECURE CUSTODY; CUSTODY HEARINGS

§ 7B-1900. Taking a juvenile into temporary custody

Temporary custody means the taking of physical custody and providing personal care and supervision until a court order for secure or nonsecure custody can be obtained. A juvenile may be taken into temporary custody without a court order under the following circumstances:

(1) By a law enforcement officer if grounds exist for the arrest of an adult in identical circumstances under G.S. 15A-401(b).

(2) By a law enforcement officer or a juvenile court counselor if there are reasonable grounds to believe that the juvenile is an undisciplined juvenile.

(3) By a law enforcement officer, by a juvenile court counselor, by a member of the Black Mountain Center, Alcohol Rehabilitation Center, and Juvenile Evaluation Center Joint Security Force established pursuant to G.S. 122C-421, or by personnel of the Division if there are reasonable grounds to believe the juvenile is an absconder from any residential facility operated by the Division or from an approved detention facility.

History.
1979, c. 815, s. 1; 1985, c. 408, s. 1; 1985 (Reg. Sess., 1986), c. 863, s. 1; 1994, Ex. Sess., c. 27, s. 2; 1995, c. 391, s. 1; 1997-443, s. 11A.118(a); 1998-202, s. 6; 2000-137, s. 3; 2001-490, s. 2.13; 2011-145, s. 19.1 (l)

§ 7B-1901. Duties of person taking juvenile into temporary custody

(a) A person who takes a juvenile into custody without a court order under G.S. 7B-1900(1) or (2) shall proceed as follows:

(1) Notify the juvenile's parent, guardian, or custodian that the juvenile has been taken into temporary custody and advise the parent, guardian, or custodian of the right to be present with the juvenile until a determination is made as to the need for secure or nonsecure custody. Failure to notify the parent, guardian, or custodian that the juvenile is in custody shall not be grounds for release of the juvenile.

(2) Release the juvenile to the juvenile's parent, guardian, or custodian if the person having the juvenile in temporary custody decides that continued custody is unnecessary. In the case of a juvenile unlawfully absent from school, if continued custody is unnecessary, the person having temporary custody may deliver the juvenile to the juvenile's school or, if the local city or county government and the local school board adopt a policy, to a place in the local school administrative unit.

(3) If the juvenile is not released, request that a petition be drawn pursuant to G.S. 7B-1803 or G.S. 7B-1804. Once the petition has been drawn and verified, the person shall communicate with the juvenile court counselor. If the juvenile court counselor approves the filing of the petition, the juvenile court counselor shall contact the judge or the person delegated authority pursuant to G.S. 7B-1902 if other than the juvenile court counselor, for a determination of the need for continued custody.

(b) A juvenile taken into temporary custody under this Article shall not be held for more than 12 hours, or for more than 24 hours if any of the 12 hours falls on a Saturday, Sunday, or legal holiday, unless a petition or motion for review has been filed and an order for secure or nonsecure custody has been entered.

(c) A person who takes a juvenile into custody under G.S. 7B-1900(3), after receiving an order for secure custody, shall transport the juvenile to the nearest approved facility providing secure custody. The person then shall contact the administrator of the facility from which the juvenile absconded, who shall be responsible for returning the juvenile to that facility.

(d) A person who takes an individual who is 21 years of age or older into temporary custody for an offense committed when the individual was a juvenile shall proceed in accordance with this Chapter. If, pursuant to the criteria in G.S. 7B-1903(b), secure custody is ordered for any person 21 years of age or older who falls within the jurisdiction of the court, pursuant to G.S. 7B-1601(d) or G.S. 7B-1601(d1), the order shall designate that the person be temporarily detained in the county jail where the charges arose.

History.
1979, c. 815, s. 1; 1981, c. 335, ss. 1, 2; 1994, Ex. Sess., c. 17, s. 1; c. 27, s. 3; 1995, c. 391, s. 2; 1998-202, s. 6; 2001-490, s. 2.14; 2019-186, s. 4

§ 7B-1902. Authority to issue custody orders; delegation

In the case of any juvenile alleged to be within the jurisdiction of the court, when the court finds it necessary to place the juvenile in custody, the court may order that the juvenile be placed in secure or nonsecure custody pursuant to criteria set out in G.S. 7B-1903.

Any district court judge may issue secure and nonsecure custody orders pursuant to G.S. 7B-1903. The chief district court judge may delegate the court's authority to the chief court counselor or the chief court counselor's counseling staff by administrative order filed in the office of the clerk of superior court. The administrative order shall specify which persons may be contacted for approval of a secure or nonsecure custody order. The chief district court judge shall not delegate the court's authority to detain or house juveniles in holdover facilities pursuant to G.S. 7B-1905 or G.S. 7B-2513.

Any superior court judge may issue a secure custody order pursuant to G.S. 7B-1903 when a juvenile matter that has been transferred to superior court is remanded to district court pursuant to G.S. 7B-2200.5(d).

History.
1979, c. 815, s. 1; 1981, c. 425; 1983, c. 590, s. 1; 1998-202, s. 6; 2021-123, s. 3(b)

§ 7B-1903. Criteria for secure or nonsecure custody

(a) When a request is made for nonsecure custody, the court shall first consider release of the juvenile to the juvenile's parent, guardian, custodian, or other responsible adult. An order for nonsecure custody shall be made only when there is a reasonable factual basis to believe the matters alleged in the petition are true, and that:

(1) The juvenile is a runaway and consents to nonsecure custody; or

(2) The juvenile meets one or more of the criteria for secure custody, but the court finds it in the best interests of the juvenile that the juvenile be placed in a nonsecure placement.

(b) When a request is made for secure custody, the court may order secure custody only where the court finds there is a reasonable factual basis to believe that the juvenile committed the offense as alleged in the petition, and that one of the following circumstances exists:

(1) The juvenile is charged with a felony and has demonstrated that the juvenile is a danger to property or persons.

(2) The juvenile has demonstrated that the juvenile is a danger to persons and is charged with either (i) a misdemeanor at least one element of which is assault on a person or (ii) a misdemeanor in which the juvenile used, threatened to use, or displayed a firearm or other deadly weapon.

(2a) The juvenile has demonstrated that the juvenile is a danger to persons and is charged with a violation of G.S. 20-138.1 or G.S. 20-138.3.

(3) The juvenile has willfully failed to appear on a pending delinquency charge or on charges of violation of probation or post-release supervision, providing the juvenile was properly notified.

(4) A delinquency charge is pending against the juvenile, and there is reasonable cause to believe the juvenile will not appear in court.

(5) The juvenile is an absconder from (i) any residential facility operated by the Division or any detention facility in this State or (ii) any comparable facility in another state.

(6) There is reasonable cause to believe the juvenile should be detained for the juvenile's own protection because the juvenile has recently suffered or attempted self-inflicted physical injury. In such case, the juvenile must have been refused admission by one appropriate hospital, and the period of secure custody is limited to 24 hours to determine the need for inpatient hospitalization. If the juvenile is placed in secure custody, the juvenile shall receive continuous supervision and a physician shall be notified immediately.

(7) The juvenile is alleged to be undisciplined by virtue of the juvenile's being a runaway and is inappropriate for nonsecure custody placement or refuses nonsecure custody, and the court finds that the juvenile needs secure custody for up to 24 hours, excluding Saturdays, Sundays, and State holidays, to evaluate the juvenile's need for medical or psychiatric treatment or to facilitate reunion with the juvenile's parents, guardian, or custodian.

(8) The juvenile is alleged to be undisciplined and has willfully failed to appear in court after proper notice; the juvenile shall be brought to court as soon as possible and in no event should be held more than 24 hours, excluding Saturdays, Sundays, and State holidays.

(c) When a juvenile has been adjudicated delinquent, the court may order secure custody pending the dispositional hearing or pending placement of the juvenile pursuant to G.S. 7B-2506. As long as the juvenile remains in secure custody, further hearings to determine the need for continued secure custody shall be held at intervals of no more than 10 calendar days but may be waived for no more than 30 calendar days only with the consent of the juvenile, through counsel for the juvenile, either orally in open court or in writing. The order for continued secure custody shall be in writing with appropriate findings of fact.

(d) The court may order secure custody for a juvenile who is alleged to have violated the conditions of the juvenile's probation or post-release supervision, but only if the juvenile is alleged to have committed acts that damage property or injure persons.

(e) If the criteria for secure custody as set out in subsection (b), (c), or (d) of this section are met, the court may enter an order directing an officer or other authorized person to assume custody of the juvenile and to take the juvenile to the place designated in the order. If, pursuant to the criteria in subsection (b) of this section, secure custody is ordered for any person 18 years of age or older who falls within the jurisdiction of the court, pursuant to G.S. 7B-1601(d) or G.S. 7B-1601(d1), the order may designate that the person be temporarily detained in the county jail where the charges arose.

(f) If the court finds that there is a need for an evaluation of a juvenile for medical or psychiatric treatment pursuant to subsection (b) of this section and that juvenile is under 10 years of age and does not have a pending delinquency charge, the law enforcement officer or other authorized person assuming custody of the juvenile shall not use physical restraints during the transport of the juvenile to the place designated in the order, unless in the discretion of the officer or other authorized person, the restraints are reasonably necessary for the safety of the officer, authorized person, or the juvenile.

History.
1979, c. 815, s. 1; 1981, c. 426, ss. 1-4; c. 526; 1983, c. 590, ss. 2-6; 1987, c. 101; 1987 (Reg. Sess., 1988), c. 1090, s. 3; 1989, c. 550; 1998-202, s. 6; 2000-137, s. 3; 2001-158, s. 1; 2007-493, s. 31; 2011-145, s. 19.1 (*l*); 2012-172, s. 3; 2015-58, s. 3.1; 2019-186, s. 5

§ 7B-1904. Order for secure or nonsecure custody

The custody order shall be in writing and shall direct a law enforcement officer or other authorized person to assume custody of the juvenile and to make due return on the order. The official executing the order shall give a copy of the order to the juvenile's parent, guardian, or custodian. If the order is for nonsecure custody, the official executing the order shall also give a copy of the petition and order to the person or agency with whom the juvenile is being placed. If the order is for secure custody, copies of the petition and custody order shall accompany the juvenile to the detention facility or holdover facility of the jail. A message of the Department of Public Safety stating that a juvenile petition and secure custody order relating to a specified juvenile are on file in a particular county shall be authority to detain the juvenile in secure custody until a copy of the juvenile petition and secure custody order can be forwarded to the juvenile detention facility. The copies of the juvenile petition and secure custody order shall be transmitted to the detention facility no later than 72 hours after the initial detention of the juvenile.

An officer receiving an order for custody which is complete and regular on its face may execute it in accordance with its terms and need not inquire into its regularity or continued validity, nor does the officer incur criminal or civil liability for its execution.

History.
1979, c. 815, s. 1; 1989, c. 124; 1998-202, s. 6; 2009-311, s. 15; 2014-100, s. 17.1(t).

§ 7B-1905. Place of secure or nonsecure custody

(a) A juvenile meeting the criteria set out in G.S. 7B-1903(a), may be placed in nonsecure custody with a department of social services or a person designated in the order for temporary residential placement in:

(1) A licensed foster home or a home otherwise authorized by law to provide such care;

(2) A facility operated by a department of social services; or

(3) Any other home or facility approved by the court and designated in the order.

In placing a juvenile in nonsecure custody, the court shall first consider whether a relative of the juvenile is willing and able to provide proper care and supervision of the juvenile. If the court finds that the relative is willing and able to provide proper care and supervision, the court shall order placement of the juvenile with the relative unless the court finds that placement with the relative would be contrary to the best interest of the juvenile. Placement of a juvenile outside of this State shall be in accordance with the Interstate Compact on the Placement of Children set forth in Article 38 of this Chapter.

(b) Pursuant to G.S. 7B-1903(b), (c), or (d), a juvenile may be temporarily detained in an approved detention facility. It shall be unlawful for a sheriff or any unit of government to operate a juvenile detention facility unless the facility meets the standards and rules adopted by the Department of Public Safety and has been approved by the Juvenile Justice Section of the Division for operation as a juvenile detention facility.

(c) A juvenile who has allegedly committed an offense that would be a Class A, B1, B2, C, D, or E felony if committed by an adult may be detained in secure custody in a holdover facility up to 72 hours, if the court, based on information provided by the juvenile court counselor, determines that no acceptable alternative placement is available and the protection of the public requires the juvenile be housed in a holdover facility.

(d) If, pursuant to the criteria in G.S. 7B-1903(b), secure custody is ordered for any person 18 years of age or older who falls within the jurisdiction of the court, pursuant to G.S. 7B-1601(d) or G.S. 7B-1601(d1), the person may be temporarily detained in the county jail where the charges arose.

History.
1979, c. 815, s. 1; 1983, c. 639, ss. 1, 2; 1997-390, s. 4; 1997-443, s. 11A.118(a); 1998-202, s. 6; 1998-229, s. 3; 1999-423, s. 14; 2001-490, s. 2.15; 2012-172, s. 4; 2019-186, s. 6

§ 7B-1906. Secure or nonsecure custody hearings

(a) No juvenile shall be held under a secure custody order for more than five calendar days or under a nonsecure custody order for more than seven calendar days without a hearing on the merits or an initial hearing to determine the need for continued custody. A hearing conducted under this subsection may not be continued or waived. In every case in which an order has been entered by an official exercising authority delegated pursuant to G.S. 7B-1902, a hearing to determine the need for continued custody shall be conducted on the day of the next regularly scheduled session of district court in the city or county where the order was entered if the session precedes the expiration of the applicable time period set forth in this subsection. If the session does not precede the expiration of the time period, the hearing may be conducted at another regularly scheduled session of district court in the district where the order was entered.

(b) As long as the juvenile remains in secure or nonsecure custody, further hearings to determine the need for continued secure custody shall be held at intervals of no more than 10 calendar days, except as otherwise provided in this section. A subsequent hearing on continued nonsecure custody shall be held within seven business days, excluding Saturdays, Sundays, and legal holidays when the courthouse is closed for transactions, of the initial hearing required in subsection (a) of this section and hearings thereafter shall be held at intervals of no more than 30 calendar days. In the case of a juvenile alleged to be delinquent, further hearings may be waived only with the consent of the juvenile, through counsel for the juvenile.

(b1) For a juvenile who was 16 years of age or older at the time the juvenile allegedly committed an offense that would be a Class A, B1, B2, C,

485

D, E, F, or G felony if committed by an adult, further hearings to determine the need for secure custody shall be held at intervals of no more than 30 calendar days. Further hearings may be waived only with the consent of the juvenile, through counsel for the juvenile. Upon request of the juvenile, through counsel for the juvenile, and for good cause as determined by the court, further hearings to determine the need for secure custody may be held at intervals of 10 days.

(b2) A hearing to determine the need for continued secure custody shall be held no more than 10 calendar days following the issuance of a secure custody order on remand of the matter from superior court pursuant to G.S. 7B-2200.5(d). A hearing conducted under this subsection may not be continued or waived. Subsequent hearings on the need for continued secure custody shall be held pursuant to subsection (b1) of this section. The district court has authority to modify any secure custody order pursuant to the provisions of this section following the issuance of that order by the superior court.

(c) The court shall determine whether a juvenile who is alleged to be delinquent has retained counsel or has been assigned counsel; if the juvenile is not represented by counsel, counsel for the juvenile shall be appointed in accordance with rules adopted by the Office of Indigent Defense Services.

(d) At a hearing to determine the need for continued custody, the court shall receive testimony and shall allow the juvenile and the juvenile's parent, guardian, or custodian an opportunity to introduce evidence, to be heard in their own behalf, and to examine witnesses. The State shall bear the burden at every stage of the proceedings to provide clear and convincing evidence that restraints on the juvenile's liberty are necessary and that no less intrusive alternative will suffice. The court shall not be bound by the usual rules of evidence at the hearings.

(e) The court shall be bound by criteria set forth in G.S. 7B-1903 in determining whether continued custody is warranted.

(f) The court may impose appropriate restrictions on the liberty of a juvenile who is released from secure custody, including:

    (1) Release on the written promise of the juvenile's parent, guardian, or custodian to produce the juvenile in court for subsequent proceedings;

    (2) Release into the care of a responsible person or organization;

    (3) Release conditioned on restrictions on activities, associations, residence, or travel if reasonably related to securing the juvenile's presence in court; or

    (4) Any other conditions reasonably related to securing the juvenile's presence in court.

(g) If the court determines that the juvenile meets the criteria in G.S. 7B-1903 and should continue in custody, the court shall issue an order to that effect. The order shall be in writing with appropriate findings of fact. The findings of fact shall include the evidence relied upon in reaching the decision and the purposes which continued custody is to achieve.

(h) Repealed by Session Laws 2021-47, s. 10(a), effective June 18, 2021, and applicable to proceedings occurring on or after that date.

History.

1979, c. 815, s. 1; 1981, c. 469, s. 13; 1987 (Reg. Sess., 1988), c. 1090, s. 4; 1994, Ex. Sess., c. 27, s. 1; 1997-390, ss. 5, 6; 1998-202, s. 6; 1998-229, s. 4; 2000-144, s. 21; 2003-337, s. 10; 2019-186, s. 7; 2021-47, s. 10(a); 2021-123, s. 3(c)

§ 7B-1907. Telephonic communication authorized

All communications, notices, orders, authorizations, and requests authorized or required by G.S. 7B-1901, 7B-1903, and 7B-1904 may be made by telephone when other means of communication are impractical. All written orders pursuant to telephonic communication shall bear the name and the title of the person communicating by telephone, the signature and the title of the official entering the order, and the hour and the date of the authorization.

History.

1979, c. 815, s. 1; 1998-202, s. 6

ARTICLE 20
BASIC RIGHTS

§ 7B-2000. Juvenile's right to counsel; presumption of indigence

(a) A juvenile alleged to be within the jurisdiction of the court has the right to be represented by counsel in all proceedings. Counsel for the juvenile shall be appointed in accordance with rules adopted by the Office of Indigent Defense Services, unless counsel is retained for the juvenile, in any proceeding in which the juvenile is alleged to be (i) delinquent or (ii) in contempt of court when alleged or adjudicated to be undisciplined.

(b) All juveniles shall be conclusively presumed to be indigent, and it shall not be necessary for the court to receive from any juvenile an affidavit of indigency.

History.

1979, c. 815, s. 1; 1998-202, s. 6; 2000-144, s. 22

§ 7B-2001. Appointment of guardian

In any case when no parent, guardian, or custodian appears in a hearing with the juvenile or when the court finds it would be in the best interests of the juvenile, the court may appoint a guardian of the person for the juvenile. The guardian shall operate under the supervision of the court with or without bond and shall file only such reports as the court shall require. Unless the court orders otherwise, the guardian:

(1) Shall have the care, custody, and control of the juvenile or may arrange a suitable placement for the juvenile.

(2) May represent the juvenile in legal actions before any court.

(3) May consent to certain actions on the part of the juvenile in place of the parent or custodian, including (i) marriage, (ii) enlisting in the Armed Forces of the United States, and (iii) enrollment in school.

(4) May consent to any necessary remedial, psychological, medical, or surgical treatment for the juvenile.

The authority of the guardian shall continue until the guardianship is terminated by court order, until the juvenile is emancipated pursuant to Subchapter IV of this Chapter, or until the juvenile reaches the age of majority.

History.
1979, c. 815, s. 1; 1997-390, s. 7; 1998-202, s. 6; 2011-183, s. 5

§ 7B-2002. Payment of court-appointed attorney

An attorney appointed pursuant to G.S. 7B-2000 or pursuant to any other provision of this Subchapter shall be paid a reasonable fee in accordance with rules adopted by the Office of Indigent Defense Services. The court may require payment of the attorneys' fees from a person other than the juvenile as provided in G.S. 7A-450.1, 7A-450.2, and 7A-450.3. A person who does not comply with the court's order of payment may be found in civil contempt as provided in G.S. 5A-21.

History.
1979, c. 815, s. 1; 1983, c. 726, ss. 2, 3; 1987 (Reg. Sess., 1988), c. 1090, s. 6; 1991, c. 575, s. 1; 1998-202, s. 6; 2000-144, s. 23

ARTICLE 20A
RIGHTS OF VICTIMS OF DELINQUENT ACTS

§ 7B-2051. Definitions

(a) The following definitions apply in this Article:

(1) **Court proceeding.** -- Any open hearing authorized or required by this Subchapter and any closed hearing or portion of a closed hearing in which the victim, in accordance with G.S. 7B-2402, is permitted to be present. The term shall not include the first appearance described in G.S. 7B-1808 if the juvenile is in secure or nonsecure custody. If it is known by the juvenile court counselor and the district attorney's office that (i) the juvenile and the victim have a personal relationship as defined in G.S. 50B-1(b) and (ii) the hearing may result in the juvenile's release from custody, efforts will be made to contact the victim.

(2) **Family member.** -- A spouse, child, parent, guardian, legal custodian, sibling, or grandparent of the victim. The term does not include the accused.

(3) **Felony property offense.** -- An offense that, if committed by an adult, would constitute a felony violation of one of the following:

a. Subchapter IV of Chapter 14 of the General Statutes.

b. Subchapter V of Chapter 14 of the General Statutes.

(4) **Offense against the person.** -- An offense against or involving the person of the victim that, if committed by an adult, would constitute a violation of one of the following:

a. Subchapter III of Chapter 14 of the General Statutes.

b. Subchapter VII of Chapter 14 of the General Statutes.

c. Article 39 of Chapter 14 of the General Statutes.

d. Chapter 20 of the General Statutes, if an element of the act of delinquency involves impairment of the defendant, or injury or death to the victim.

e. A valid protective order under G.S. 50B-4.1, including, but not limited to, G.S. 14-134.3 and G.S. 14-269.8.

f. Article 35 of Chapter 14 of the General Statutes, if the elements of the act of delinquency involve communicating a threat or stalking.

g. An offense that triggers the enumerated victims' rights, as required by the North Carolina Constitution.

(5) **Victim.** -- A person against whom there is probable cause to believe a juvenile has committed an offense against the person or a felony property offense.

(b) If the victim is a minor or is legally incapacitated, a parent, guardian, or legal custodian may assert the victim's rights under this Article. The accused may not assert the victim's right. If the victim is deceased, then a family member, in the order set forth in the definition contained in this section, may assert the victim's rights under this Article, with the following limitations:

(1) The guardian or legal custodian of a deceased minor has priority over a family member.

(2) The right contained in G.S. 15A-834 may only be exercised by the personal representative of the victim's estate.

(c) An individual entitled to exercise the victim's rights as the appropriate family member in accordance with this section may designate any family member to act on behalf of the victim.

(d) An individual who, in the determination of the district attorney's office, would not act in the best interests of the victim shall not be entitled to assert or exercise the victim's rights. An individual may petition the court to review this determination by the district attorney's office.

History.
2019-216, s. 10

§ 7B-2052. Victim's rights

(a) A victim of a juvenile offense shall be treated with dignity and respect by the juvenile justice system.

(b) A victim has the following rights:

(1) The right, upon request, to reasonable, accurate, and timely notice of court proceedings of the juvenile.

(2) The right, upon request, to be present at court proceedings of the juvenile.

(3) The right to be reasonably heard at court proceedings involving the adjudication, disposition, or release of the juvenile.

(4) The right to receive restitution in a reasonably timely manner, when ordered by the court.

(5) The right to be given information about the offense, how the juvenile justice system works, the rights of victims, and the availability of services for victims.

(6) The right, upon request, to receive information about the adjudication of the juvenile or disposition of the case.

(7) The right, upon request, to receive notification of the escape or release of the juvenile.

(8) The right to reasonably confer with the district attorney's office.

(c) This Article does not create a claim for damages against the State, any county or municipality, or any State or county agencies, instrumentalities, officers, or employees.

History.
2019-216, s. 10

§ 7B-2053. Responsibilities of the district attorney's office

(a) Within 72 hours of the filing of a petition, the district attorney's office shall provide the victim with the following information:

(1) The victim's rights under this Article, including the right to reasonably confer with the district attorney's office.

(2) The responsibilities of the district attorney's office under this Article.

(3) The steps generally taken by the district attorney's office in cases involving juvenile offenses.

(4) Suggestions on what the victim should do if threatened or intimidated by the juvenile or someone acting on the juvenile's behalf.

(5) The name and telephone number of a victim and witness assistant in the district attorney's office whom the victim may contact for further information.

(6) A list of each right enumerated under G.S. 7B-2052(b).

(7) Information about any other rights afforded to victims by law.

(b) On a form provided by the district attorney's office for this purpose, the victim shall indicate whether the victim requests to receive notices of some, all, or none of the court proceedings included under this Article. The form shall also indicate whether the victim wishes to receive information about the adjudication and disposition of the case. If the victim elects to receive notices or information by requesting it on the form provided, the victim shall be responsible for notifying the district attorney's office of any changes in the victim's address and telephone number or other contact information. The victim may alter the request for notification or information at any time by notifying the district attorney's office and completing the form provided by the district attorney's office.

(c) The district attorney's office shall make every effort to ensure that a victim's personal information is not disclosed unless otherwise required by law. The district attorney's office shall inform the victim that personal information such as the victim's telephone number, home address, and bank account number are not relevant in every case, and that the victim may request the district attorney to object to that line of questioning when appropriate.

(d) The district attorney's office shall offer the victim the opportunity to reasonably confer with an attorney in the district attorney's office to obtain the views of the victim about, at a minimum, dismissal, plea or negotiations, disposition, and any dispositional alternatives.

(e) Notwithstanding Articles 30 and 31 of Subchapter III of this Chapter, the district attorney's office shall notify the victim of the date, time, and place of court proceedings as requested by the victim under subsection (b) of this section. All notices required to be given by the district attorney's office shall be reasonable, accurate, and timely and shall be given in a manner that is reasonably calculated to be received by the victim prior to the date of the court proceeding. The district attorney's office shall consider all hearings open, pursuant to G.S. 7B-2402, for the purpose of providing notice to the victim. The district attorney shall inform the victim if the entire hearing has been closed to the victim by the court. The district attorney's office may provide the required notification electronically or by telephone, unless the victim requests otherwise. The notifications required by this section shall be documented by the district attorney's office.

(f) Whenever practical, the district attorney's office shall provide a secure waiting area during court proceedings that does not place the victim in close proximity to the juvenile or the juvenile's family.

(g) Prior to the dispositional hearing, the district attorney's office shall notify the victim that the victim may request in writing to be notified (i) in advance of the juvenile's scheduled release date, if the juvenile is committed to the Division for placement in a youth development center or (ii) in the event that the juvenile escapes, if the juvenile is being held in secure custody or is committed to the Division for placement in a youth development center.

(h) At the dispositional hearing, the prosecutor shall submit to the court a form containing the victim's request for further notices under subsection (g) of this section and any necessary identifying information about the victim, if applicable. The chief court counselor shall include the form with the final disposition and commitment transmitted to the Division, and the form shall be maintained by the Division as a confidential file. The victim shall be responsible for notifying the Division of any changes in the victim's address and telephone number.

(i) Notwithstanding Articles 30 and 31 of Subchapter III of this Chapter, following the completion of the dispositional hearing, the district attorney's office shall provide the victim with information about the adjudication and disposition of the juvenile as requested by the victim pursuant to G.S. 7B-2053(b). The information provided shall be limited to (i) whether or not the juvenile was adjudicated delinquent, and if so, the offense classification, the dispositions available to the court as provided in G.S. 7B-2508, and (ii) no-contact orders as they relate to the victim, and (iii) any order for restitution.

History.
2019-216, s. 10

§ 7B-2054. Responsibilities of judicial officials

(a) In any court proceeding subject to this Article in which the victim may be present, the court shall inquire as to whether a victim is present and wishes to be heard and, if so, shall grant the victim an opportunity to be reasonably heard. The right to be reasonably heard may be exercised, at the victim's discretion, through an oral statement, submission of a written statement, or submission of an audio or video statement.

(b) In the event that an entire hearing has been closed to the victim by the court, the victim shall have the opportunity to be heard by the court regarding the right to be present, if the court has not previously provided this opportunity to the victim.

(c) A judge notified by the clerk of court that a victim has filed a motion alleging a violation of the rights provided in this Article shall review the motion. The judge involved in the proceeding that gave rise to the rights in question may, on the judge's own motion, recuse himself or herself if justice requires it, and report the recusal to the Administrative Office of the Courts. The judge, or a judge appointed by the Administrative Office of the Courts in the event of recusal, shall dispose of the motion or set the motion for hearing as required by G.S. 7B-2058.

(d) The court shall make every effort to provide a secure waiting area during court proceedings that does not place the victim in close proximity to the juvenile or the juvenile's family.

History.
2019-216, s. 10

§ 7B-2055. Responsibilities of the Division of Adult Correction and Juvenile Justice

(a) Notwithstanding Articles 30 and 31 of Subchapter III of this Chapter, if a victim has requested to be notified of the juvenile's release pursuant to G.S. 7B-2053, at least 45 days before releasing to post-release supervision a juvenile who was committed to the Division for placement in a youth development center, the Division shall notify the victim as requested. The notification shall include only the juvenile's initials, offense, date of commitment, projected release date, and any no-contact release conditions related to the victim.

(b) When determining whether a juvenile is ready for release pursuant to G.S. 7B-2514, the Division shall provide the victim an opportunity to be reasonably heard by the Division and shall consider the victim's views regarding release of the juvenile. If the Division determines that the juvenile is ready for release, the victim's views shall be considered during the post-release supervision planning conference process.

(c) Notwithstanding Articles 30 and 31 of Subchapter III of this Chapter, if a victim has requested in writing to be notified of the juvenile's escape pursuant to G.S. 7B-2053, within 24 hours of the time the juvenile escapes from a youth development center or from secure custody, the Division shall notify the victim. If, pursuant to G.S. 7B-3102, disclosure of information about the escaped juvenile will be released to the public, the Division may provide to the victim the same information that will be released to the public, but the Division shall make a reasonable effort to notify the victim prior to releasing the information to the public. The Division shall notify the victim within 24 hours of the juvenile's return to custody, even if the juvenile is returned to custody before the notification of escape is required.

(d) When a form is included with the final disposition and commitment pursuant to G.S. 7B-2053(h), or when the victim has otherwise filed a written request for notification with the Division, the Division shall notify the victim of the procedure for alleging a failure of the Division to notify the victim as required by this section.

History.
2019-216, s. 10

§ 7B-2056. Right to restitution

A victim has the right to receive restitution when ordered by the court pursuant to G.S. 7B-2506(4) and G.S. 7B-2506(22).

History.
2019-216, s. 10

§ 7B-2057. Confidentiality of a juvenile record

No rights under this Article provide grounds for a victim to examine or obtain confidential juvenile records. In providing notice or information to any victim, no agency, department, or official shall permit a victim to examine or obtain copies of any part of the juvenile record. Except as provided in G.S. 7B-2055(c), any agency, department, or official that provides a victim written notice or information under this Article shall not identify the juvenile by name in the notice or information, but shall identify the juvenile by the juvenile's first and last initials only. This Article shall not be construed to require or permit disclosing to any victim any information contained in juvenile records except as specifically provided.

History.
2019-216, s. 10

§ 7B-2058. Enforcement of rights

(a) A victim may assert the rights provided in this Article pursuant to Section 37 of Article I of the North Carolina Constitution. In no event shall any underlying proceeding be subject to undue delay for the enforcement provided in this section. The procedure by which a victim may assert the rights provided under this Article shall be by motion to the court of jurisdiction. For the purposes of this section, the term "victim" includes the following individuals acting on behalf of the victim:

(1) The victim's attorney.

(2) The prosecutor, at the request of the victim.

(3) A parent, guardian, or legal custodian, if the victim is a minor or is legally incapacitated, as provided in G.S. 7B-2051.

(4) A family member, if the victim is deceased, as provided in G.S. 7B-2051.

(b) A victim may allege a violation of the rights provided in this Article by filing a motion with the office of the clerk of superior court. The motion must be filed within the same proceeding giving rise to the rights in question.

(c) If the motion involves an allegation that the district attorney failed to comply with the rights of a victim provided by this Article, the victim must first file a written complaint with the district attorney, to afford the district attorney an opportunity to resolve the issue stated in the written complaint in a timely manner.

(d) A victim has the right to consult with an attorney regarding an alleged violation of the rights provided in this Article, but the victim does not have the right to counsel provided by the State.

(e) The Administrative Office of the Courts shall create a form to serve as the motion to enable a victim to allege a violation of the rights provided in this Article. The form will indicate what specific right has allegedly been violated. The form will also provide the victim the opportunity to describe the substance of the alleged violation in detail. If the motion involves an allegation that the district attorney failed to comply with the rights of a victim provided in this Article, the victim must attach a copy of the written complaint previously filed with the district attorney as required by subsection (c) of the section.

(f) The clerk of superior court of each county shall provide the form necessary to enable a victim to allege a violation of the rights provided in this Article. No fees shall be assessed for the filing of this motion. A copy of the motion required in subsection (b) of this section shall be given to the prosecutor if other than the elected District Attorney, the elected District Attorney, and the judge involved in the criminal proceeding that gave rise to the rights in question.

(g) The judge shall review the motion and dispose of it or set it for hearing in a timely manner. Review may include conferring with the victim, the prosecutor if other than the District Attorney, and the District Attorney, in order to inquire as to compliance with this Article. At the conclusion of the review, the judge shall dispose of the motion or set the motion for hearing.

(h) If the judge fails to review the motion and dispose of it or set it for a hearing in a timely manner, a victim may petition the North Carolina Court of Appeals for a writ of mandamus. The petition shall be filed without unreasonable delay. The court for good cause shown may shorten the time for filing a response.

(i) The failure or inability of any person to provide a right or service under this Article, including a service provided through the Statewide Automated Victim Assistance and Notification System established by the Governor's Crime Commission, may not be used by a juvenile, by any other accused, or by any victim or family member of a victim, as a ground for relief in any criminal, juvenile, or other civil proceeding, except as provided in Section 37 of Article I of the North Carolina Constitution.

History.
2019-216, s. 10

ARTICLE 21
LAW ENFORCEMENT PROCEDURES IN DELINQUENCY PROCEEDINGS

§ 7B-2100. Role of the law enforcement officer

A law enforcement officer who takes a juvenile into temporary custody should select the most appropriate course of action to the situation, the needs of the juvenile, and the protection of the public safety. The officer may:

(1) Release the juvenile, with or without first counseling the juvenile;

(2) Release the juvenile to the juvenile's parent, guardian, or custodian;

(3) Refer the juvenile to community resources;

(4) Seek a petition; or

(5) Seek a petition and request a custody order.

History.
1979, c. 815, s. 1; 1998-202, s. 6

§ 7B-2101. Interrogation procedures

(a) Any juvenile in custody must be advised prior to questioning:

(1) That the juvenile has a right to remain silent;

(2) That any statement the juvenile does make can be and may be used against the juvenile;

(3) That the juvenile has a right to have a parent, guardian, or custodian present during questioning; and

(4) That the juvenile has a right to consult with an attorney and that one will be appointed for the juvenile if the juvenile is not represented and wants representation.

(b) When the juvenile is less than 16 years of age, no in-custody admission or confession resulting from interrogation may be admitted into evidence unless the confession or admission was made in the presence of the juvenile's parent, guardian, custodian, or attorney. If an attorney is not present, the parent, guardian, or custodian as well as the juvenile must be advised of the juvenile's rights as set out in subsection (a) of this section; however, a parent, guardian, or custodian may not waive any right on behalf of the juvenile.

(c) If the juvenile indicates in any manner and at any stage of questioning pursuant to this section that the juvenile does not wish to be questioned further, the officer shall cease questioning.

(d) Before admitting into evidence any statement resulting from custodial interrogation, the court shall find that the juvenile knowingly, willingly, and understandingly waived the juvenile's rights.

History.
1979, c. 815, s. 1; 1998-202, s. 6; 2015-58, s. 1.1

§ 7B-2102. Fingerprinting and photographing juveniles

(a) A law enforcement officer or agency shall fingerprint and photograph a juvenile who was 10 years of age or older at the time the juvenile allegedly committed a nondivertible offense as set forth in G.S. 7B-1701(a), when a complaint has been prepared for filing as a petition and the juvenile is in physical custody of law enforcement or the Division.

(a1) A county juvenile detention facility shall photograph a juvenile who has been committed to that facility. The county detention facility shall release any photograph it makes or receives pursuant to this section to the Division, upon the Division's request. The duty of confidentiality in subsection (d) of this section applies to the Division, except as provided in G.S. 7B-3102.

(b) If a law enforcement officer or agency does not take the fingerprints or a photograph of the juvenile pursuant to subsection (a) of this section or the fingerprints or photograph have been destroyed pursuant to subsection (e) of this section, a law enforcement officer or agency shall fingerprint and photograph a juvenile who has been adjudicated delinquent if the juvenile was 10 years of age or older at the time the juvenile committed an offense that would be a felony if committed by an adult.

(c) A law enforcement officer, facility, or agency who fingerprints or photographs a juvenile pursuant to this section shall do so in a proper format for transfer to the State Bureau of Investigation and the Federal Bureau of Investigation. After the juvenile, who was 10 years of age or older at the time of the offense, is adjudicated delinquent of an offense that would be a felony if committed by an adult, fingerprints obtained pursuant to this section shall be transferred to the State Bureau of Investigation and placed in the Automated Fingerprint Identification System (AFIS) to be used for all investigative and comparison purposes, and may be entered into a local fingerprint database for the same purposes, if the law enforcement agency with jurisdiction is served by a secure crime laboratory facility that maintains a local fingerprint database. Photographs obtained pursuant to this section shall be placed in a format approved by the State Bureau of Investigation and may be used for all investigative or comparison purposes. The State Bureau of Investigation shall release any photograph it receives pursuant to this section to the Division, upon the Division's request. The duty of confidentiality in subsection (d) of this section applies to the Division, except as provided in G.S. 7B-3102.

(d) Fingerprints and photographs taken pursuant to this section are not public records under Chapter 132 of the General Statutes, shall not be included in the clerk's record pursuant to G.S. 7B-3000, shall be withheld from public inspection or examination, and shall not be eligible for expunction pursuant to G.S. 7B-3200. Fingerprints and photographs taken pursuant to this section shall be maintained separately from any juvenile record, other than the electronic file maintained by the State Bureau of Investigation.

(d1) Repealed by Session Laws 2007-458, s. 1, effective October 1, 2007.

(e) If a juvenile is fingerprinted and photographed pursuant to subsection (a) of this section, the custodian of records shall destroy all fingerprints and photographs at the earlier of the following:

(1) The juvenile court counselor or prosecutor does not file a petition against the juvenile within one year of fingerprinting and photographing the juvenile pursuant to subsection (a) of this section;

(2) The court does not find probable cause pursuant to G.S. 7B-2202; or

(3) The juvenile is not adjudicated delinquent of any offense that would be a felony or a misdemeanor if committed by an adult.

The chief court counselor shall notify the local custodian of records, and the local custodian of records shall notify any other record-holding agencies, when a decision is made not to file a petition, the court does not find probable cause, or the court does not adjudicate the juvenile delinquent.

History.
1996, 2nd Ex. Sess., c. 18, s. 23.2(a); 1998-202, s. 6; 2000-137, s. 3; 2001-490, s. 2.16; 2003-297, s. 2; 2007-458, ss. 1, 3(a), (b); 2011-145, s. 19.1 (*l*); 2019-243, s. 19.5; 2021-123, s. 5(d)

§ 7B-2103. Authority to issue nontestimonial identification order where juvenile alleged to be delinquent

Except as provided in G.S. 7B-2102 or G.S. 15A-284.52(c1), nontestimonial identification procedures shall not be conducted on any juvenile without a court order issued pursuant to this Article unless the juvenile has been charged as an adult or transferred to superior court for trial as an adult in which case procedures applicable to adults, as set out in Articles 14 and 23 of Chapter 15A of the General Statutes, shall apply. A nontestimonial identification order authorized by this Article may be issued by any judge of the district court or of the superior court upon request of a prosecutor. As used in this Article, "nontestimonial identification" means identification by fingerprints, palm prints, footprints, measurements, blood specimens, urine specimens, saliva samples, hair samples, or other reasonable physical examination, handwriting exemplars, voice samples, photographs, and lineups or similar identification procedures requiring the presence of a juvenile.

History.
1979, c. 815, s. 1; 1981, c. 454, s. 1; 1998-202, s. 6; 2019-47, s. 1

§ 7B-2104. Time of application for nontestimonial identification order

A request for a nontestimonial identification order may be made prior to taking a juvenile into custody or after custody and prior to the adjudicatory hearing.

History.
1979, c. 815, s. 1; 1981, c. 454, s. 2; 1998-202, s. 6

§ 7B-2105. Grounds for nontestimonial identification order

(a) Except as provided in subsection (b) of this section, a nontestimonial identification order may issue only on affidavit or affidavits sworn to before the court and establishing the following grounds for the order:

(1) That there is probable cause to believe that an offense has been committed that would be a felony if committed by an adult;

(2) That there are reasonable grounds to suspect that the juvenile named or described in the affidavit committed the offense; and

(3) That the results of specific nontestimonial identification procedures will be of material aid in determining whether the juvenile named in the affidavit committed the offense.

(b) A nontestimonial identification order to obtain a blood specimen from a juvenile may issue only on affidavit or affidavits sworn to before the court and establishing the following grounds for the order:

(1) That there is probable cause to believe that an offense has been committed that would be a felony if committed by an adult;

(2) That there is probable cause to believe that the juvenile named or described in the affidavit committed the offense; and

(3) That there is probable cause to believe that obtaining a blood specimen from the juvenile will be of material aid in determining whether the juvenile named in the affidavit committed the offense.

History.
1979, c. 815, s. 1; 1997-80, s. 11; 1998-202, s. 6

§ 7B-2106. Issuance of order

Upon a showing that the grounds specified in G.S. 7B-2105 exist, the judge may issue an order following the same procedure as in the case of adults under G.S. 15A-274, 15A-275, 15A-276, 15A-277, 15A-278, 15A-279, 15A-280, and 15A-282.

History.
1979, c. 815, s. 1; 1998-202, s. 6

§ 7B-2107. Nontestimonial identification order at request of juvenile

A juvenile in custody for or charged with an offense which if committed by an adult would be a felony offense may request that nontestimonial identification procedures be conducted. If it appears that the results of specific nontestimonial identification procedures will be of material aid to the juvenile's defense, the judge to whom the request was directed must order the State to conduct the identification procedures.

History.
1979, c. 815, s. 1; 1997-80, s. 12; 1998-202, s. 6

§ 7B-2108. Destruction of records resulting from nontestimonial identification procedures

The results of any nontestimonial identification procedures shall be retained or disposed of as follows:

(1) If a petition is not filed against a juvenile who has been the subject of nontestimonial identification procedures, all records of the evidence shall be destroyed.

(2) If the juvenile is not adjudicated delinquent or convicted in superior court following transfer, all records resulting from a nontestimonial order shall be destroyed. Further, in the case of a juvenile who is under 13 years of age and who is adjudicated delinquent for an offense that would be less than a felony if committed by an adult, all records shall be destroyed.

(3) If a juvenile 13 years of age or older is adjudicated delinquent for an offense that would be a felony if committed by an adult, all records resulting from a nontestimonial order may be retained in the court file. Special precautions shall be taken to ensure that these records will be maintained in a manner and under sufficient safeguards to limit their use to inspection by law enforcement officers for comparison purposes in the investigation of a crime.

(4) If the juvenile is transferred to and convicted in superior court, all records resulting from nontestimonial identification procedures shall be processed as in the case of an adult.

(5) Any evidence seized pursuant to a nontestimonial order shall be retained by law enforcement officers until further order is entered by the court.

(6) Destruction of nontestimonial identification records pursuant to this section shall be performed by the law enforcement agency having possession of the records. Following destruction, the law enforcement agency shall make written certification to the court of the destruction.

History.
1979, c. 815, s. 1; 1994, Ex. Sess., c. 22, s. 28; 1998-202, s. 6

§ 7B-2109. Penalty for willful violation

Any person who willfully violates provisions of this Article which prohibit conducting nontestimonial identification procedures without an order issued by the court shall be guilty of a Class 1 misdemeanor.

History.
1979, c. 815, s. 1; 1993, c. 539, s. 5; 1994, Ex. Sess., c. 24, s. 14(c); 1998-202, s. 6

ARTICLE 22
PROBABLE CAUSE HEARING AND TRANSFER HEARING

§ 7B-2200. Transfer of jurisdiction of a juvenile under the age of 16 to superior court

Except as otherwise provided in G.S. 7B-2200.5, after notice, hearing, and a finding of probable cause the court may, upon motion of the prosecutor or the juvenile's attorney or upon its own motion, transfer jurisdiction over a juvenile to superior court if the juvenile was at least 13 years of age but less than 16 years of age at the time the juvenile allegedly committed an offense that would be a felony if committed by an adult. If the alleged felony constitutes a Class A felony and the court finds probable cause, the court shall transfer the case to the superior court for trial as in the case of adults.

History.
1979, c. 815, s. 1; 1991 (Reg. Sess., 1992), c. 842, s. 1; 1994, Ex. Sess., c. 22, s. 25; 1998-202, s. 6; 2017-57, s. 16D.4(d); 2018-142, s. 23(b)

§§ 7B-2200.1 through 7B-2200.4

Reserved for future codification purposes.

§ 7B-2200.5. Transfer of jurisdiction of a juvenile at least 16 years of age to superior court

(a) If a juvenile was 16 years of age or older at the time the juvenile allegedly committed an offense that would be a Class A, B1, B2, C, D, E, F, or G felony if committed by an adult, the court shall transfer jurisdiction over the juvenile to superior court for trial as in the case of adults unless the prosecutor declines to prosecute in superior court as provided in subsection (a1) of this section after either of the following:

(1) Notice to the juvenile and a finding by the court that a bill of indictment has been returned against the juvenile charging the commission of an offense that constitutes a Class A, B1, B2, C, D, E, F, or G felony if committed by an adult.

(2) Notice, hearing, and a finding of probable cause that the juvenile committed an offense that constitutes a Class A, B1, B2, C, D, E, F, or G felony if committed by an adult.

(a1) The prosecutor may decline to prosecute in superior court a matter that would otherwise be subject to mandatory transfer pursuant to subsection (a) of this section if the juvenile has allegedly committed an offense that would be a Class D, E, F, or G felony if committed by an adult. If the prosecutor declines to prosecute the matter in superior court, jurisdiction over the juvenile shall remain in juvenile court following a finding of probable cause pursuant to G.S. 7B-2202. Prior to adjudication, the prosecutor may choose to transfer the matter pursuant to subsection (a) of this section if the juvenile has allegedly committed an offense that would be a Class D, E, F, or G felony if committed by an adult.

(b) If the juvenile was 16 years of age or older at the time the juvenile allegedly committed an offense that would be a Class H or I felony if committed by an adult, after notice, hearing, and a finding of probable cause, the court may, upon motion of the prosecutor or the juvenile's attorney or upon its own motion, transfer jurisdiction over a juvenile to superior court pursuant to G.S. 7B-2203.

(c) A probable cause hearing conducted pursuant to subdivision (2) of subsection (a) of this section shall be conducted within 90 days of the date of the juvenile's first appearance. The court may continue the hearing for good cause.

(d) In any case where jurisdiction over a juvenile has been transferred to superior court, upon joint motion of the prosecutor and the juvenile's attorney, the superior court shall remand the case to district court. The prosecutor shall provide the chief court counselor or his or her designee with a copy of the joint motion prior to submitting the motion to the court. The superior court shall expunge the superior court record in accordance with G.S. 15A-145.8 at the time of remand, and, if the juvenile meets the criteria established in G.S. 7B-1903, may issue an order for secure custody upon the request of a prosecutor. The prosecutor shall provide a copy of any secure custody order issued to the chief court counselor or his or her designee, as soon as possible and no more than 24 hours after the order is issued.

History.
2017-57, s. 16D.4(e); 2017-197, s. 5.3; 2018-142, s. 23(b); 2019-186, s. 8(a); 2021-123, ss. 3(d), 4

§ 7B-2201. Fingerprinting and DNA sample from juvenile transferred to superior court

(a) When jurisdiction over a juvenile is transferred to the superior court, the juvenile shall be fingerprinted and the juvenile's fingerprints shall be sent to the State Bureau of Investigation.

(b) When jurisdiction over a juvenile is transferred to the superior court, a DNA sample shall be taken from the juvenile if any of the offenses for which the juvenile is transferred are included in the provisions of G.S. 15A-266.3A.

History.
1981, c. 862, s. 2; 1998-202, s. 6; 2010-94, s. 13

§ 7B-2202. Probable cause hearing

(a) Except as otherwise provided in G.S. 7B-2200.5(a)(1), the court shall conduct a hearing to determine probable cause in all felony cases in which a juvenile was 13 years of age or older when the offense was allegedly committed. Except as otherwise provided in G.S. 7B-2200.5(c), the hearing shall be conducted within 15 days of the date of the juvenile's first appearance. The court may continue the hearing for good cause.

(b) At the probable cause hearing:

(1) A prosecutor shall represent the State;

(2) The juvenile shall be represented by counsel;

(3) The juvenile may testify, call, and examine witnesses, and present evidence; and

(4) Each witness shall testify under oath or affirmation and be subject to cross-examination.

(c) The State shall by nonhearsay evidence, or by evidence that satisfies an exception to the hearsay rule, show that there is probable cause to believe that the offense charged has been committed and that there is probable cause to believe that the juvenile committed it, except:

(1) A report or copy of a report made by a physicist, chemist, firearms identification expert, fingerprint technician, or an expert or technician in some other scientific, professional, or medical field, concerning the results of an examination, comparison, or test performed in connection with the case in issue, when stated in a report by that person, is admissible in evidence;

(2) If there is no serious contest, reliable hearsay is admissible to prove value, ownership of property, possession of property in a person other than the juvenile, lack of consent of the owner, possessor, or custodian of property to the breaking or entering of premises, chain of custody, and authenticity of signatures.

(d) Counsel for the juvenile may waive in writing the right to the hearing and stipulate to a finding of probable cause.

(e) If probable cause is found and transfer to superior court is not required by G.S. 7B-2200 or G.S. 7B-2200.5, upon motion of the prosecutor or the juvenile's attorney or upon its own motion, the court shall either proceed to a transfer hearing or set a date for that hearing. If the juvenile has not received notice of the intention to seek transfer at least five days prior to the probable cause hearing, the court, at the request of the juvenile, shall continue the transfer hearing.

(f) If the court does not find probable cause for a felony offense, the court shall:

(1) Dismiss the proceeding, or

(2) If the court finds probable cause to believe that the juvenile committed a lesser included offense that would constitute a misdemeanor if committed by an adult, either proceed to an adjudicatory hearing or set a date for that hearing. The adjudicatory hearing shall be a separate hearing. The court may continue the adjudicatory hearing for good cause.

History.
1979, c. 815, s. 1; 1981, c. 469, ss. 15, 16; 1994, Ex. Sess., c. 22, s. 26; 1998-202, s. 6; 2015-58, s. 1.2; 2017-57, s. 16D.4(f); 2018-142, s. 23(b); 2019-186, s. 8(b)

§ 7B-2203. Transfer hearing

(a) At the transfer hearing, the prosecutor and the juvenile may be heard and may offer evidence, and the juvenile's attorney may examine any court or probation records, or other records the court may consider in determining whether to transfer the case.

(b) In the transfer hearing, the court shall determine whether the protection of the public and the needs of the juvenile will be served by transfer of the case to superior court and shall consider the following factors:

(1) The age of the juvenile;

(2) The maturity of the juvenile;

(3) The intellectual functioning of the juvenile;

(4) The prior record of the juvenile;

(5) Prior attempts to rehabilitate the juvenile;

(6) Facilities or programs available to the court prior to the expiration of the court's jurisdiction under this Subchapter and the likelihood that the juvenile would benefit from treatment or rehabilitative efforts;

(7) Whether the alleged offense was committed in an aggressive, violent, premeditated, or willful manner; and

(8) The seriousness of the offense and whether the protection of the public requires that the juvenile be prosecuted as an adult.

(c) Any order of transfer shall specify the reasons for transfer. When the case is transferred to superior court, the superior court has jurisdiction over that felony, any offense based on the same act or transaction or on a series of acts or transactions connected together or constituting parts of a single scheme or plan of that felony, and any greater or lesser included offense of that felony.

(d) If the court does not transfer the case to superior court, the court shall either proceed to an adjudicatory hearing or set a date for that hearing. The adjudicatory hearing shall be a separate hearing. The court may continue the adjudicatory hearing for good cause.

History.
1979, c. 815, s. 1; 1983, c. 532, s. 1; 1994, Ex. Sess., c. 22, s. 27; 1998-202, s. 6; 2015-58, s. 1.3

§ 7B-2204. Right to pretrial release; detention

(a) Once the order of transfer has been entered, the juvenile has the right to pretrial release as provided in G.S. 15A-533 and G.S. 15A-534. The release order shall specify the person or persons to whom the juvenile may be released. Pending release, the court shall order that the juvenile be detained in a detention facility while awaiting trial. Personnel of the Juvenile Justice Section of the Division, or personnel approved by the Juvenile Justice Section, shall transport the juvenile from the detention facility to court.

(b) The court may order the juvenile to be held in a holdover facility at any time the presence of the juvenile is required in court for pretrial hearings or trial, if the court finds that it would be inconvenient to return the juvenile to the detention facility. Personnel of the Justice Section of the Division, or personnel approved by the Juvenile Justice Section, shall transport the juvenile from the holdover facility to court and shall transport the juvenile back to the detention center.

(c) If the juvenile reaches the age of 18 years while awaiting the completion of proceedings in superior court, the juvenile shall be transported by personnel of the Juvenile Justice Section of the Division, or personnel approved by the Juvenile Justice Section, to the custody of the sheriff of the county where the charges arose.

(d) Should the juvenile be found guilty, or enter a plea of guilty or no contest to a criminal offense in superior court and receive an active sentence, then immediate transfer to the Division of Adult Correction and Juvenile Justice of the Department of Public Safety shall be ordered. Until such time as the juvenile is transferred to the Division of Adult Correction and Juvenile Justice of the Department of Public Safety, the juvenile may be detained in a holdover facility or detention facility approved by the Juvenile Justice Section.

(e) The juvenile may be kept by the Division of Adult Correction and Juvenile Justice of the Department of Public Safety as a safekeeper until the juvenile is placed in an appropriate correctional program.

History.
1979, c. 815, s. 1; 1987, c. 144; 1991, c. 352, s. 1; 1998-202, s. 6; 2011-145, s. 19.1(h); 2017-186, s. 2(k); 2019-186, s. 9; 2021-123, s. 2

ARTICLE 23
DISCOVERY

§ 7B-2300. Disclosure of evidence by petitioner

(a) **Statement of the Juvenile.** -- Upon motion of a juvenile alleged to be delinquent, the court shall order the petitioner:

(1) To permit the juvenile to inspect and copy any relevant written or recorded statements within the possession, custody, or control of the petitioner made by the juvenile or any other party charged in the same action; and

(2) To divulge, in written or recorded form, the substance of any oral statement made by the juvenile or any other party charged in the same action.

(b) **Names of Witnesses.** -- Upon motion of the juvenile, the court shall order the petitioner to furnish the names of persons to be called as witnesses. A copy of the record of witnesses under the age of 16 shall be provided by the petitioner to the juvenile upon the juvenile's motion if accessible to the petitioner.

(c) **Documents and Tangible Objects.** -- Upon motion of the juvenile, the court shall order the petitioner to permit the juvenile to inspect and copy books, papers, documents, photographs, motion pictures, mechanical or electronic recordings, tangible objects, or portions thereof:

(1) Which are within the possession, custody, or control of the petitioner, the prosecutor, or any law enforcement officer conducting an investigation of the matter alleged; and

(2) Which are material to the preparation of the defense, are intended for use by the petitioner as evidence, or were obtained from or belong to the juvenile.

(d) **Reports of Examinations and Tests.** -- Upon motion of a juvenile, the court shall order the petitioner to permit the juvenile to inspect and copy results of physical or mental examinations or of tests, measurements, or experiments made in connection with the case, within the possession, custody, or control of the petitioner. In addition upon motion of a juvenile, the court shall order the petitioner to permit the juvenile to inspect, examine, and test, subject to appropriate safeguards, any physical evidence or a sample of it or tests or experiments made in connection with the evidence in the case if it is available to the petitioner, the prosecutor, or any law enforcement officer conducting an investigation of the matter alleged, and if the petitioner intends to offer the evidence at trial.

(e) Except as provided in subsections (a) through (d) of this section, this Article does not require the production of reports, memoranda, or other internal documents made by the petitioner, law enforcement officers, or other persons acting on behalf of the petitioner in connection with the investigation or prosecution of the case or of statements made by witnesses or the petitioner to anyone acting on behalf of the petitioner.

(f) Nothing in this section prohibits a petitioner from making voluntary disclosures in the interest of justice.

History.
1979, c. 815, s. 1; 1998-202, s. 6

§ 7B-2301. Disclosure of evidence by juvenile

(a) **Names of Witnesses.** -- Upon motion of the petitioner, the court shall order the juvenile to furnish to the petitioner the names of persons to be called as witnesses.

(b) **Documents and Tangible Objects.** -- If the court grants any relief sought by the juvenile under G.S. 7B-2300, upon motion of the petitioner, the court shall order the juvenile to permit the petitioner to inspect and copy books, papers, documents, photographs, motion pictures, mechanical or electronic recordings, tangible objects, or portions thereof which are within the possession, custody, or control of the juvenile and which the juvenile intends to introduce in evidence.

(c) **Reports of Examinations and Tests.** -- If the court grants any relief sought by the juvenile under G.S. 7B-2300, upon motion of the petitioner, the court shall order the juvenile to permit the petitioner to inspect and copy results of physical or mental examinations or of tests, measurements, or experiments made in connection with the case within the possession and control of the juvenile which the juvenile intends to introduce in evidence or which were prepared by a witness whom the juvenile intends to call if the results relate to the witness's testimony. In addition, upon motion of a petitioner, the court shall order the juvenile to permit the petitioner to inspect, examine, and test, subject to appropriate safeguards, any physical evidence or a sample of it if the juvenile intends

to offer the evidence or tests or experiments made in connection with the evidence in the case.

History.
1979, c. 815, s. 1; 1998-202, s. 6

§ 7B-2302. Regulation of discovery; protective orders

(a) Upon written motion of a party and a finding of good cause, the court may at any time order that discovery or inspection be denied, restricted, or deferred.

(b) The court may permit a party seeking relief under subsection (a) of this section to submit supporting affidavits or statements to the court for in camera inspection. If thereafter the court enters an order granting relief under subsection (a) of this section, the material submitted in camera must be available to the Court of Appeals in the event of an appeal.

History.
1979, c. 815, s. 1; 1998-202, s. 6

§ 7B-2303. Continuing duty to disclose

If a party, subject to compliance with an order issued pursuant to this Article, discovers additional evidence prior to or during the hearing or decides to use additional evidence, and if the evidence is or may be subject to discovery or inspection under this Article, the party shall promptly notify the other party of the existence of the additional evidence or of the name of each additional witness.

History.
1979, c. 815, s. 1; 1998-202, s. 6

ARTICLE 24
HEARING PROCEDURES

§ 7B-2400. Amendment of petition

The court may permit a petition to be amended when the amendment does not change the nature of the offense alleged. If a motion to amend is allowed, the juvenile shall be given a reasonable opportunity to prepare a defense to the amended allegations.

History.
1979, c. 815, s. 1; 1998-202, s. 6

§ 7B-2401. Determination of incapacity to proceed; evidence; temporary commitment; temporary orders

The provisions of G.S. 15A-1001, 15A-1002, and 15A-1003 apply to all cases in which a juvenile is alleged to be delinquent. No juvenile committed under this section may be placed in a situation where the juvenile will come in contact with adults committed for any purpose.

History.
1979, c. 815, s. 1; 1998-202, s. 6

§ 7B-2402. Open hearings

All hearings authorized or required pursuant to this Subchapter shall be open to the public unless the court closes the hearing or part of the hearing for good cause, upon motion of a party or its own motion. If the court closes the hearing or part of the hearing to the public, the court may allow any victim, member of a victim's family, law enforcement officer, witness or any other person directly involved in the hearing to be present at the hearing.

In determining good cause to close a hearing or part of a hearing, the court shall consider the circumstances of the case, including, but not limited to, the following factors:

(1) The nature of the allegations against the juvenile;

(2) The age and maturity of the juvenile;

(3) The benefit to the juvenile of confidentiality;

(4) The benefit to the public of an open hearing; and

(5) The extent to which the confidentiality of the juvenile's file will be compromised by an open hearing.

No hearing or part of a hearing shall be closed by the court if the juvenile requests that it remain open.

History.
1979, c. 815, s. 1; 1998-202, s. 6; 1998-229, s. 5

§ 7B-2402.1. Restraint of juveniles in courtroom

At any hearing authorized or required by this Subchapter, the judge may subject a juvenile to physical restraint in the courtroom only when the judge finds the restraint to be reasonably necessary to maintain order, prevent the juvenile's escape, or provide for the safety of the courtroom. Whenever practical, the judge shall provide the juvenile and the juvenile's attorney an opportunity to be heard to contest the use of restraints before the judge orders the use of restraints. If restraints are ordered, the judge shall make findings of fact in support of the order.

History.
2007-100, s. 1

§ 7B-2403. Adjudicatory hearing

The adjudicatory hearing shall be held within a reasonable time in the district at the time and place the chief district court judge designates.

History.
1979, c. 815, s. 1; 1998-202, s. 6; 1998-229, s. 5

§ 7B-2404. Participation of the prosecutor; voluntary dismissal

(a) A prosecutor shall represent the State in contested delinquency hearings including first appearance, detention, probable cause, transfer, adjudicatory, dispositional, probation revocation, post-release supervision, and extended jurisdiction hearings.

(b) A prosecutor may dismiss any allegations stated in a juvenile petition with or without leave by entering an oral dismissal in open court at any time or by filing a written dismissal with the clerk. The juvenile, the juvenile's parent, guardian, or custodian, and the juvenile's counsel shall be notified of the dismissal by the prosecutor either in open court or by being served with the written dismissal. In addition, the written dismissal shall be served on (i) the chief court counselor or his or her designee and (ii) if the juvenile is being held in a detention center, the director of the detention center. If the prosecutor dismisses the petition with leave because of the failure of the juvenile to appear in court, the prosecutor may refile the petition if the juvenile is apprehended or apprehension is imminent.

History.
1979, c. 815, s. 1; 1981, c. 469, s. 12; 1998-202, s. 6; 2015-58, s. 2.2

§ 7B-2405. Conduct of the adjudicatory hearing

The adjudicatory hearing shall be a judicial process designed to determine whether the juvenile is undisciplined or delinquent. In the adjudicatory hearing, the court shall protect the following rights of the juvenile and the juvenile's parent, guardian, or custodian to assure due process of law:

(1) The right to written notice of the facts alleged in the petition;

(2) The right to counsel;

(3) The right to confront and cross-examine witnesses;

(4) The privilege against self-incrimination;

(5) The right of discovery; and

(6) All rights afforded adult offenders except the right to bail, the right of self-representation, and the right of trial by jury.

History.
1979, c. 815, s. 1; 1998-202, s. 6

§ 7B-2406. Continuances

The court for good cause may continue the hearing for as long as is reasonably required to receive additional evidence, reports, or assessments that the court has requested, or other information needed in the best interests of the juvenile and to allow for a reasonable time for the parties to conduct expeditious discovery. Otherwise, continuances shall be granted only in extraordinary circumstances when necessary for the proper administration of justice or in the best interests of the juvenile.

History.
1979, c. 815, s. 1; 1987 (Reg. Sess., 1988), c. 1090, s. 9; 1998-202, s. 6

§ 7B-2407. When admissions by juvenile may be accepted

(a) The court may accept an admission from a juvenile only after first addressing the juvenile personally and:

(1) Informing the juvenile that the juvenile has a right to remain silent and that any statement the juvenile makes may be used against the juvenile;

(2) Determining that the juvenile understands the nature of the charge;

(3) Informing the juvenile that the juvenile has a right to deny the allegations;

(4) Informing the juvenile that by the juvenile's admissions the juvenile waives the juvenile's right to be confronted by the witnesses against the juvenile;

(5) Determining that the juvenile is satisfied with the juvenile's representation; and

(6) Informing the juvenile of the most restrictive disposition on the charge.

(b) By inquiring of the prosecutor, the juvenile's attorney, and the juvenile personally, the court shall determine whether there were any prior discussions involving admissions, whether the parties have entered into any arrangement with respect to the admissions and the terms thereof, and whether any improper pressure was exerted. The court may accept an admission from a juvenile only after determining that the admission is a product of informed choice.

(c) The court may accept an admission only after determining that there is a factual basis for the admission. This determination may be based upon any of the following information: a statement of the facts by the prosecutor; a written statement of the juvenile; sworn testimony which may include reliable hearsay; or a statement of facts by the juvenile's attorney.

History.
1979, c. 815, s. 1; 1998-202, s. 6

§ 7B-2408. Rules of evidence

If the juvenile denies the allegations of the petition, the court shall proceed in accordance with the rules of evidence applicable to criminal cases. In addition, no statement made by a juvenile to the juvenile court counselor during the preliminary inquiry and evaluation process shall be admissible prior to the dispositional hearing.

History.
1979, c. 815, s. 1; 1981, ch. 469, s. 17; 1998-202, s. 6; 2001-490, s. 2.17

§§ 7B-2408.1 through 7B-2408.4

Reserved for future codification purposes.

§ 7B-2408.5. Motion to suppress evidence in adjudicatory hearings; procedure; appeal

(a) A motion to suppress evidence in court made before the adjudicatory hearing must be in writing and a copy of the motion must be served upon the State. The motion must state the grounds upon which it is made. The motion must be accompanied by an affidavit containing facts supporting the motion. The affidavit may be based upon personal knowledge, or upon information and belief, if the source of the information and the basis for the belief are stated. The State may file an answer denying or admitting any of the allegations. A copy of the answer must be served on the juvenile's counsel or the juvenile's parent, guardian, or custodian, if the juvenile has no counsel.

(b) The judge must summarily grant the motion to suppress evidence if:

(1) The motion complies with the requirements of subsection (a) of this section, it states grounds which require exclusion of the evidence, and the State concedes the truth of allegations of fact which support the motion; or

(2) The State stipulates that the evidence sought to be suppressed will not be offered in evidence in any juvenile proceeding.

(c) The judge may summarily deny the motion to suppress evidence if:

(1) The motion does not allege a legal basis for the motion; or

(2) The affidavit does not as a matter of law support the ground alleged.

(d) If the motion is not determined summarily, the judge must make the determination after a hearing and finding of facts. Testimony at the hearing must be under oath.

(e) A motion to suppress made during the adjudicatory hearing may be made in writing or orally and may be determined in the same manner as when made before the adjudicatory hearing.

(f) The judge must set forth in the record his or her findings of facts and conclusions of law.

(g) An order finally denying a motion to suppress evidence may be reviewed upon an appeal of a final order of the court in a juvenile matter.

(h) The provisions of G.S. 15A-974 shall apply to this section.

History.
2015-58, s. 1.4

§ 7B-2409. Quantum of proof in adjudicatory hearing

The allegations of a petition alleging the juvenile is delinquent shall be proved beyond a reasonable doubt. The allegations in a petition alleging undisciplined behavior shall be proved by clear and convincing evidence.

History.
1979, c. 815, s. 1; 1998-202, s. 6

§ 7B-2410. Record of proceedings

All adjudicatory and dispositional hearings and hearings on probable cause and transfer to superior court shall be recorded by stenographic notes or by electronic or mechanical means. Records shall be reduced to a written transcript only when timely notice of appeal has been given. The court may order that other hearings be recorded.

History.
1979, c. 815, s. 1; 1998-202, s. 6

§ 7B-2411. Adjudication

If the court finds that the allegations in the petition have been proved as provided in G.S. 7B-2409, the court shall so state in a written order of adjudication, which shall include, but not be limited to, the date of the offense, the misdemeanor or felony classification of the offense, and the date of adjudication. If the court finds that the allegations have not been proved, the court shall dismiss the petition with prejudice and the juvenile shall be released from secure or nonsecure custody if the juvenile is in custody.

History.
1979, c. 815, s. 1; 1998-202, s. 6; 2009-545, s. 4

§ 7B-2412. Legal effect of adjudication of delinquency

An adjudication that a juvenile is delinquent or commitment of a juvenile to the Division for placement in a youth development center shall neither be considered conviction of any criminal offense nor cause the juvenile to forfeit any citizenship rights.

History.
1979, c. 815, s. 1; 1998-202, s. 6; 2000-137, s. 3; 2001-95, s. 5; 2011-145, s. 19.1 (*l*)

§ 7B-2413. Predisposition investigation and report

The court shall proceed to the dispositional hearing upon receipt of the predisposition report. A risk and needs assessment, containing information regarding the juvenile's social, medical, psychiatric, psychological, and educational history, as well as any factors indicating the probability of the juvenile committing further delinquent acts, shall be conducted for the juvenile and shall be attached to the predisposition report. In cases where no predisposition report is available and the court makes a written finding that a report is not needed, the court may proceed with the dispositional hearing. No predisposition report or risk and needs assessment of any child alleged to be delinquent or undisciplined shall be made prior to an adjudication that the juvenile is within the juvenile jurisdiction of the court unless the juvenile, the juvenile's parent, guardian, or custodian, or the juvenile's attorney files a written statement with the juvenile court counselor granting permission and giving consent to the predisposition report or risk and needs assessment. No predisposition report shall be submitted to or considered by the court prior to the completion of the adjudicatory hearing. The court shall permit the juvenile to inspect any predisposition report, including any attached risk and needs assessment, to be considered by the court in making the disposition unless the court determines that disclosure would seriously harm the juvenile's treatment or rehabilitation or would violate a promise of confidentiality. Opportunity to offer evidence in rebuttal shall be afforded the juvenile and the juvenile's parent, guardian, or custodian at the dispositional hearing. The court may order counsel not to disclose parts of the report to the juvenile or the juvenile's parent, guardian, or custodian if the court finds that disclosure would seriously harm the treatment or rehabilitation of the juvenile or would violate a promise of confidentiality given to a source of information.

History.
1979, c. 815, s. 1; 1998-202, s. 6; 1999-423, s. 13; 2001-490, s. 2.18

§ 7B-2414. When jeopardy attaches

Jeopardy attaches in an adjudicatory hearing when the court begins to hear evidence.

History.
1979, c. 815, s. 1; 1998-202, s. 6

ARTICLE 25
DISPOSITIONS

§ 7B-2500. Purpose

The purpose of dispositions in juvenile actions is to design an appropriate plan to meet the needs of the juvenile and to achieve the objectives of the State in exercising jurisdiction, including the protection of the public. The court should develop a disposition in each case that:

(1) Promotes public safety;

(2) Emphasizes accountability and responsibility of both the parent, guardian, or custodian and the juvenile for the juvenile's conduct; and

(3) Provides the appropriate consequences, treatment, training, and rehabilitation to assist the juvenile toward becoming a nonoffending, responsible, and productive member of the community.

History.
1979, c. 815, s. 1; 1995 (Reg. Sess., 1996), c. 609, s. 1; 1998-202, s. 6

§ 7B-2501. Dispositional hearing

(a) The dispositional hearing may be informal, and the court may consider written reports or other evidence concerning the needs of the juvenile. The court may consider any evidence, including hearsay evidence as defined in G.S. 8C-1, Rule 801, that the court finds to be relevant, reliable, and necessary to determine the needs of the juvenile and the most appropriate disposition.

(b) The juvenile and the juvenile's parent, guardian, or custodian shall have an opportunity to present evidence, and they may advise the court concerning the disposition they believe to be in the best interests of the juvenile.

(c) In choosing among statutorily permissible dispositions, the court shall select the most appropriate disposition both in terms of kind and duration for the delinquent juvenile. Within the guidelines set forth in G.S. 7B-2508, the court shall select a disposition that is designed to protect the public and to meet the needs and best interests of the juvenile, based upon:

(1) The seriousness of the offense;

(2) The need to hold the juvenile accountable;

(3) The importance of protecting the public safety;

(4) The degree of culpability indicated by the circumstances of the particular case; and

(5) The rehabilitative and treatment needs of the juvenile indicated by a risk and needs assessment.

(d) The court may dismiss the case, or continue the case for no more than six months in order to allow the family an opportunity to meet the needs of the juvenile through more adequate home supervision, through placement in a private or specialized school or agency, through placement with a relative, or through some other plan approved by the court.

History.
1979, c. 815, s. 1; 1981, c. 469, s. 18; 1998-202, s. 6; 2003-62, s. 5

§ 7B-2502. Evaluation and treatment of undisciplined and delinquent juveniles

(a) In any case, the court may order that the juvenile be examined by a physician, psychiatrist, psychologist, or other qualified expert as may be needed for the court to determine the needs of the juvenile.

(a1) In the case of a juvenile adjudicated delinquent for committing an offense that involves the possession, use, sale, or delivery of alcohol or a controlled substance, the court shall require the juvenile to be tested for the use of controlled substances or alcohol within 30 days of the adjudication. In the case of any juvenile adjudicated delinquent, the court may, if it deems it necessary, require the juvenile to be tested for the use of controlled substances or alcohol. The results of these initial tests conducted pursuant to this subsection shall be used for evaluation and treatment purposes only. In placing a juvenile in out-of-home care under this section, the court shall also consider whether it is in the juvenile's best interest to remain in the juvenile's community of residence.

(a2) In the case of a juvenile with a suspected mental illness, developmental disability, or intellectual disability that has been adjudicated delinquent, the court shall order that the Juvenile Justice Section of the Division of Adult Correction and Juvenile Justice of the Department of Public Safety make a referral for a comprehensive clinical assessment or equivalent mental health assessment, unless the court finds a comprehensive clinical assessment or equivalent mental health assessment has been conducted within the last 45 days before the adjudication hearing. An assessment ordered by a court under this subsection shall evaluate the developmental, emotional, behavioral, and mental health needs of the juvenile.

(a3) If an assessment is ordered by the court under subsection (a2) of this section, the court shall review the assessment prior to the date of disposition in the case. If the court finds sufficient evidence that the juvenile has severe emotional disturbance, as defined in G.S. 7B-1501(24a), or a developmental disability, as defined in G.S. 122C-3(12a), or intellectual disability, as defined in G.S. 122C-3(17a), that, in the court's discretion, substantially contributed to the juvenile's delinquent behavior, and the juvenile is eligible for a Juvenile Justice Level 3 disposition and/or is recommended for a Psychiatric Residential Treatment Facility (PRTF) placement, the court shall order a care review team to be convened by the Juvenile Justice Section of the Division of Adult Correction and Juvenile Justice of the Department of Public Safety and assigned to the case.

(a4) If a care review team is assigned to a case by the court under subsection (a3) of this section, the care review team shall develop a recommendation plan for appropriate services and resources that address the identified needs of the juvenile. The care review team shall submit a recommendation to the court within 30 calendar days of the date of the court order convening the care review team. The court shall review the recommendation plan when determining the juvenile's disposition in accordance with G.S. 7B-2501(c). A care review team shall consist of, at a minimum, all of the following:

(1) The juvenile.

(2) The juvenile's parents, guardian, or custodian.

(3) Representatives from the Juvenile Justice Section of the Division of Adult Correction and Juvenile Justice of the Department of Public Safety.

(4) A representative from the local management entity/managed care organization or prepaid health plan (PHP) in which the juvenile is enrolled.

(5) Representatives from any State agency or local department of social services that is currently providing services to the juvenile or the juvenile's family.

(b) If the juvenile does not have health insurance coverage for the recommended treatment, the court shall conduct a hearing to determine who should pay the cost of the assessment, evaluation or treatment pursuant to this section. The county manager, or any other person who is designated by the chair of the board of county commissioners, of the county of the juvenile's residence shall be notified of the hearing, and allowed to be heard. The court shall permit the parent, guardian, custodian, or other responsible persons to arrange for evaluation or treatment. If the parent, guardian, or custodian

declines or is unable to make necessary arrangements, the court may order the needed evaluation or treatment, surgery, or care, and the court may order the parent to pay the cost of the care pursuant to Article 27 of this Chapter. If the court finds the parent or funding from the Juvenile Justice Section of the Division of Adult Correction and Juvenile Justice of the Department of Public Safety is unable to pay the cost of evaluation or treatment, the court shall order the county to arrange for evaluation or treatment of the juvenile and to pay for the cost of the evaluation or treatment.

(c) Repealed by Session Laws 2021-123, s. 8(b), effective December 1, 2021, and applicable to petitions filed on or after that date.

(c1) A juvenile shall not be committed directly to a State hospital or State developmental center, and orders purporting to commit a juvenile directly to a State hospital or State developmental center, except for an examination to determine capacity to proceed, are void and of no effect.

History.
1979, c. 815, s. 1; 1981, c. 469, s. 19; 1985, c. 589, s. 5; c. 777, s. 1; 1985 (Reg. Sess., 1986), c. 863, s. 2; 1991, c. 636, s. 19(a); 1995 (Reg. Sess., 1996), c. 609, s. 3; 1997-516, s. 1A; 1998-202, s. 6; 1998-229, s. 6; 2002-164, s. 4.9; 2019-76, s. 11; 2021-123, s. 8(b)

§ 7B-2503. Dispositional alternatives for undisciplined juveniles

The following alternatives for disposition shall be available to the court exercising jurisdiction over a juvenile who has been adjudicated undisciplined. In placing a juvenile in out-of-home care under this section, the court shall also consider whether it is in the juvenile's best interest to remain in the juvenile's community of residence. The court may combine any of the applicable alternatives when the court finds it to be in the best interests of the juvenile:

(1) In the case of any juvenile who needs more adequate care or supervision or who needs placement, the judge may do any of the following:

a. Require that the juvenile be supervised in the juvenile's own home by a department of social services in the juvenile's county of residence, a juvenile court counselor, or other personnel as may be available to the court, subject to conditions applicable to the parent, guardian, or custodian or the juvenile as the judge may specify.

b. Place the juvenile in the custody of a parent, guardian, custodian, relative, private agency offering placement services, or some other suitable person.

c. If the director of the department of social services has received notice and an opportunity to be heard, place the juvenile in the custody of a department of social services in the county of the juvenile's residence, or in the case of a juvenile who has legal residence outside the State, in the physical custody of a department of social services in the county where the juvenile is found so that agency may return the juvenile to the responsible authorities in the juvenile's home state. An order placing a juvenile in the custody or placement responsibility of a county department of social services shall contain a finding that the juvenile's continuation in the juvenile's own home would be contrary to the juvenile's best interest. This placement shall be reviewed in accordance with G.S. 7B-906.1. A parent who is indigent is entitled to court-appointed counsel for representation in the hearings held pursuant to G.S. 7B-906.1 unless the parent makes a knowing and voluntary waiver of the right to counsel.

(2) Place the juvenile under the protective supervision of a juvenile court counselor for a period of up to three months, with an extension of an additional three months in the discretion of the court.

(3) Excuse the juvenile from compliance with the compulsory school attendance law when the court finds that suitable alternative plans can be arranged by the family through other community resources for one of the following:

a. An education related to the needs or abilities of the juvenile including vocational education or special education;

b. A suitable plan of supervision or placement; or

c. Some other plan that the court finds to be in the best interests of the juvenile.

History.
1979, c. 815, s. 1; 1981, c. 469, s. 19; 1985, c. 589, s. 5; c. 777, s. 1; 1985 (Reg. Sess., 1986), c. 863, s. 2; 1991, c. 636, s. 19(a); 1995 (Reg. Sess., 1996), c. 609, s. 3; 1997-516, s. 1A; 1998-202, s. 6; 1998-229, s. 6; 2001-208, s. 8; 2001-487, s. 101; 2001-490, s. 2.19; 2002-164, s. 4.10; 2009-311, s. 16; 2013-129, s. 39; 2017-161, s. 12; 2019-33, s. 15(a)

§ 7B-2504. Conditions of protective supervision for undisciplined juveniles

The court may place a juvenile on protective supervision pursuant to G.S. 7B-2503 so that the juvenile court counselor may (i) assist the juvenile in securing social, medical, and educational services and (ii) visit and work with the family as a unit to ensure the juvenile is provided proper supervision and care. The court may impose any combination of the following conditions of protective supervision that are related to the needs of the juvenile, including:

(1) That the juvenile shall remain on good behavior and not violate any laws;

(2) That the juvenile attend school regularly;

(3) That the juvenile maintain passing grades in up to four courses during each grading period and meet with the juvenile court counselor and a representative of the school to make a plan for how to maintain those passing grades;

(4) That the juvenile not associate with specified persons or be in specified places;

(5) That the juvenile abide by a prescribed curfew;

(6) That the juvenile report to a juvenile court counselor as often as required by a juvenile court counselor;

(7) That the juvenile be employed regularly if not attending school; and

(8) That the juvenile satisfy any other conditions determined appropriate by the court.

History.
1979, c. 815, s. 1; 1998-202, s. 6; 2001-490, s. 2.20

§ 7B-2505. Violation of protective supervision by undisciplined juvenile

(a) On motion of the juvenile court counselor or the juvenile, or on the court's own motion, the court may review the progress of any juvenile on protective supervision at any time during the period of protective supervision. When the motion is filed during the period of protective supervision and either alleges a violation of protective supervision or seeks an extension of protective supervision as permitted by G.S. 7B-2503(2), the court's review may occur within a reasonable time after the period of protective supervision ends, and the court shall have jurisdiction to enter an order under this section. The conditions or duration of protective supervision may be modified only as provided in this Subchapter and only after notice and a hearing.

(b) If the court, after notice and a hearing, finds by the greater weight of the evidence that the juvenile has violated the conditions of protective supervision set by the court, the court may do one or more of the following:

(1) Continue or modify the conditions of protective supervision.

(2) Order any disposition authorized by G.S. 7B-2503.

(3) Notwithstanding the time limitation in G.S. 7B-2503(2), extend the period

of protective supervision for up to three months.

History.
1998-202, s. 6; 2001-490, s. 2.21; 2012-172, s. 5

§ 7B-2506. Dispositional alternatives for delinquent juveniles

The court exercising jurisdiction over a juvenile who has been adjudicated delinquent may use the following alternatives in accordance with the dispositional structure set forth in G.S. 7B-2508:

(1) In the case of any juvenile under the age of 18 years who needs more adequate care or supervision or who needs placement, the judge may do any of the following:

a. Require that a juvenile be supervised in the juvenile's own home by the department of social services in the juvenile's county, a juvenile court counselor, or other personnel as may be available to the court, subject to conditions applicable to the parent, guardian, or custodian or the juvenile as the judge may specify.

b. Place the juvenile in the custody of a parent, guardian, custodian, relative, private agency offering placement services, or some other suitable person.

c. If the director of the county department of social services has received notice and an opportunity to be heard, place the juvenile in the custody of the department of social services in the county of the juvenile's residence, or in the case of a juvenile who has legal residence outside the State, in the physical custody of a department of social services in the county where the juvenile is found so that agency may return the juvenile to the responsible authorities in the juvenile's home state. An order placing a juvenile in the custody or placement responsibility of a county department of social services shall contain a finding that the juvenile's continuation in the juvenile's own home would be contrary to the juvenile's best interest. This placement shall be reviewed in accordance with G.S. 7B-906.1. A parent who is indigent is entitled to court-appointed counsel for representation in the hearings held pursuant to G.S. 7B-906.1 unless the parent makes a knowing and voluntary waiver of the right to counsel.

(2) Excuse a juvenile under the age of 16 years from compliance with the compulsory school attendance law when the court finds that suitable alternative plans can be arranged by the family through other community resources for one of the following:

a. An education related to the needs or abilities of the juvenile including vocational education or special education;

b. A suitable plan of supervision or placement; or

c. Some other plan that the court finds to be in the best interests of the juvenile.

(3) Order the juvenile to cooperate with a community-based program, an intensive substance abuse treatment program, or a residential or nonresidential treatment program. Participation in the programs shall not exceed 12 months.

(4) Require restitution, full or partial, up to five hundred dollars ($ 500.00), payable within a 12-month period to any person who has suffered loss or damage as a result of the offense committed by the juvenile. The court may determine the amount, terms, and conditions of the restitution. If the juvenile participated with another person or persons, all participants should be jointly and severally responsible for the payment of restitution; however, the court shall not require the juvenile to make restitution if the juvenile satisfies the court that the juvenile does not have, and could not reasonably acquire, the means to make restitution.

(5) Impose a fine related to the seriousness of the juvenile's offense. If the juvenile has the ability to pay the fine, it shall not exceed the maximum fine for the offense if committed by an adult.

(6) Order the juvenile to perform up to 100 hours supervised community service consistent with the juvenile's age, skill, and ability, specifying the nature of the work and the number of hours required. The work shall be related to the seriousness of the juvenile's offense and in no event may the obligation to work exceed 12 months.

(7) Order the juvenile to participate in the victim-offender reconciliation program.

(8) Place the juvenile on probation under the supervision of a juvenile court counselor, as specified in G.S. 7B-2510.

(9) Order that the juvenile shall not be licensed to operate a motor vehicle in the State of North Carolina for as long as the court retains jurisdiction over the juvenile or for any shorter period of time. The clerk of court shall notify the Division of Motor Vehicles of that order.

(10) Impose a curfew upon the juvenile.

(11) Order that the juvenile not associate with specified persons or be in specified places.

(12) Impose confinement on an intermittent basis in an approved detention facility. Confinement shall be limited to not more than five 24-hour periods, the timing and imposition of which is determined by the court in its discretion.

(13) Order the juvenile to cooperate with placement in a wilderness program.

(14) Order the juvenile to cooperate with placement in a residential treatment facility, an intensive nonresidential treatment program, an intensive substance abuse program, or in a group home other than a multipurpose group home operated by a State agency.

(15) Place the juvenile on intensive probation under the supervision of a juvenile court counselor.

(16) Order the juvenile to cooperate with a supervised day program requiring the juvenile to be present at a specified place for all or part of every day or of certain days. In determining whether to order a juvenile to a particular supervised day program, the court shall consider the structure and operations of the program and whether that program will meet the needs of the juvenile. The court also may require the juvenile to comply with any other reasonable conditions specified in the dispositional order that are designed to facilitate supervision.

(17) Order the juvenile to participate in a regimented training program.

(18) Order the juvenile to submit to house arrest.

(19) Suspend imposition of a more severe, statutorily permissible disposition with the provision that the juvenile meet certain conditions agreed to by the juvenile and specified in the dispositional order. The conditions shall not exceed the allowable dispositions for the level under which disposition is being imposed.

(20) Order that the juvenile be confined in an approved juvenile detention facility for a term of up to 14 24-hour periods, which confinement shall not be imposed consecutively with intermittent confinement pursuant to subdivision (12) of this section at the same dispositional hearing. The timing and imposition of this confinement shall be determined by the court in its discretion.

(21) Order the residential placement of a juvenile in a multipurpose group home operated by a State agency.

(22) Require restitution of more than five hundred dollars ($ 500.00), full or partial, payable within a 12-month period to any person who has suffered loss or damage as a result of an offense committed by the juvenile. The court may determine the amount, terms, and conditions of restitution. If the juvenile participated with another person or persons, all participants should be jointly and severally responsible for the payment of the restitution; however, the court shall not require the juvenile to make restitution if the juvenile satisfies the court that the juvenile does not have, and could not reasonably acquire, the means to make restitution.

(23) Order the juvenile to perform up to 200 hours supervised community service consistent with the juvenile's age, skill, and ability, specifying the nature of work and the number of hours required. The work shall be related to the seriousness of the juvenile's offense.

(24) Commit the juvenile to the Division for placement in a youth development center in accordance with G.S. 7B-2513 for a period of not less than six months.

History.
1979, c. 815, s. 1; 1981, c. 469, ss. 19, 20; 1985, c. 589, s. 5; c. 777, s. 1; 1985 (Reg. Sess., 1986), c. 863, s. 2; 1991, c. 353, s. 1; 636, s. 19(a); 1991 (Reg. Sess., 1992), c. 1030, s. 4; 1993, c. 369, s. 1; c. 462, s. 1; 1995 (Reg. Sess., 1996), c. 609, s. 3; 1997-516, s. 1A; 1998-202, s. 6; 1998-229, s. 6; 1999-444, s. 1; 2000-137, s. 3; 2001-95, s. 5; 2001-179, s. 2; 2001-208, s. 9; 2001-487, s. 101; 2001-490, s. 2.22; 2009-311, s. 17; 2011-145, s. 19.1 (*l*); 2013-129, s. 40; 2015-58, s. 3.2; 2017-57, s. 16D.4(g); 2017-161, s. 13; 2018-142, s. 23(b); 2019-33, s. 15(b)

§ 7B-2507. Delinquency history levels

(a) **Generally.** -- The delinquency history level for a delinquent juvenile is determined by calculating the sum of the points assigned to each of the juvenile's prior adjudications or convictions and to the juvenile's probation status, if any, that the court finds to have been proved in accordance with this section. For the purposes of this section, a prior adjudication is an adjudication of an offense that occurs before the adjudication of the offense before the court.

(b) **Points.** -- Points are assigned as follows:

(1) For each prior adjudication of a Class A through E felony offense, 4 points.

(2) For each prior adjudication of a Class F through I felony offense or Class A1 misdemeanor offense, 2 points.

(2a) For each prior conviction of a Class A through E felony offense, 4 points.

(2b) For each prior conviction of a Class F through I felony or Class A1 misdemeanor offense, excluding conviction of the motor vehicle laws, 2 points.

(2c) For each prior misdemeanor conviction of impaired driving (G.S. 20-138.1), impaired driving in a commercial vehicle

(G.S. 20-138.2), and misdemeanor death by vehicle (G.S. 20-141.4(a2)), 2 points.

(3) For each prior adjudication of a Class 1, 2, or 3 misdemeanor offense, 1 point.

(3a) For each prior conviction of a Class 1, 2, or 3 misdemeanor offense, excluding conviction for violation of the motor vehicle laws, 1 point.

(4) If the juvenile was on probation at the time of offense, 2 points.

No points shall be assigned for a prior adjudication that a juvenile is in direct contempt of court or indirect contempt of court.

(c) **Delinquency History Levels.** -- The delinquency history levels are:

(1) Low -- No more than 1 point.

(2) Medium -- At least 2, but not more than 3 points.

(3) High -- At least 4 points.

In determining the delinquency history level, the classification of a prior offense is the classification assigned to that offense at the time the juvenile committed the offense for which disposition is being ordered.

(d) **Multiple Prior Adjudications or Convictions Obtained in One Court Session.** -- For purposes of determining the delinquency history level, if a juvenile is adjudicated delinquent or convicted for more than one offense in a single session of district court or more than one offense in a single superior court during one calendar week, only the adjudication or conviction for the offense with the highest point total is used.

(e) **Classification of Prior Adjudications or Convictions From Other Jurisdictions.** -- Except as otherwise provided in this subsection, an adjudication or conviction occurring in a jurisdiction other than North Carolina is classified as a Class I felony if the jurisdiction in which the offense occurred classifies the offense as a felony, or is classified as a Class 3 misdemeanor if the jurisdiction in which the offense occurred classifies the offense as a misdemeanor. If the juvenile proves by the preponderance of the evidence that an offense classified as a felony in the other jurisdiction is substantially similar to an offense that is a misdemeanor in North Carolina, the adjudication or conviction is treated as that class of misdemeanor for assigning delinquency history level points. If the State proves by the preponderance of the evidence that an offense classified as either a misdemeanor or a felony in the other jurisdiction is substantially similar to an offense in North Carolina that is classified as a Class I felony or higher, the adjudication or conviction is treated as that class of felony for assigning delinquency history level points. If the State proves by the preponderance of the evidence that an offense classified as a misdemeanor in the other jurisdiction is substantially similar to

an offense classified as a Class A1 misdemeanor in North Carolina, the adjudication or conviction is treated as a Class A1 misdemeanor for assigning delinquency history level points.

(f) **Proof of Prior Adjudications or Convictions.** -- A prior adjudication or conviction shall be proved by any of the following methods:

(1) Stipulation of the parties.

(2) An original or copy of the court record of the prior adjudication or conviction.

(3) A copy of records maintained by the Department of Public Safety or by the Division.

(4) Any other method found by the court to be reliable.

The State bears the burden of proving, by a preponderance of the evidence, that a prior adjudication or conviction exists and that the juvenile before the court is the same person as the juvenile named in the prior adjudication or conviction. The original or a copy of the court records or a copy of the records maintained by the Department of Public Safety or of the Division, bearing the same name as that by which the juvenile is charged, is prima facie evidence that the juvenile named is the same person as the juvenile before the court, and that the facts set out in the record are true. For purposes of this subsection, "a copy" includes a paper writing containing a reproduction of a record maintained electronically on a computer or other data processing equipment, and a document produced by a facsimile machine. The prosecutor shall make all feasible efforts to obtain and present to the court the juvenile's full record. Evidence presented by either party at trial may be utilized to prove prior adjudications or convictions. If asked by the juvenile, the prosecutor shall furnish the juvenile's prior adjudications or convictions to the juvenile within a reasonable time sufficient to allow the juvenile to determine if the record available to the prosecutor is accurate.

History.
1998-202, s. 6; 2000-137, s. 3; 2007-168, s. 5; 2011-145, s. 19.1 (*l*); 2014-100, s. 17.1(q); 2015-58, s. 2.3; 2017-57, s. 16D.4(h); 2018-142, s. 23(b)

§ 7B-2508. Dispositional limits for each class of offense and delinquency history level

(a) **Offense Classification.** -- The offense classifications are as follows:

(1) Violent -- Adjudication of a Class A through E felony offense;

(2) Serious -- Adjudication of a Class F through I felony offense or a Class A1 misdemeanor;

(3) Minor -- Adjudication of a Class 1, 2, or 3 misdemeanor or adjudication of indirect contempt by a juvenile.

(b) **Delinquency History Levels.** -- A delinquency history level shall be determined for each delinquent juvenile as provided in G.S. 7B-2507.

(c) **Level 1 -- Community Disposition.** -- A court exercising jurisdiction over a juvenile who has been adjudicated delinquent and for whom the dispositional chart in subsection (f) of this section prescribes a Level 1 disposition may provide for evaluation and treatment under G.S. 7B-2502 and for any of the dispositional alternatives contained in subdivisions (1) through (13) and (16) of G.S. 7B-2506. In determining which dispositional alternative is appropriate, the court shall consider the needs of the juvenile as indicated by the risk and needs assessment contained in the predisposition report, the appropriate community resources available to meet those needs, and the protection of the public.

(d) **Level 2 -- Intermediate Disposition.** -- A court exercising jurisdiction over a juvenile who has been adjudicated delinquent and for whom the dispositional chart in subsection (f) of this section prescribes a Level 2 disposition may provide for evaluation and treatment under G.S. 7B-2502 and for any of the dispositional alternatives contained in subdivisions (1) through (23) of G.S. 7B-2506, but shall provide for at least one of the intermediate dispositions authorized in subdivisions (13) through (23) of G.S. 7B-2506. However, notwithstanding any other provision of this section, a court may impose a Level 3 disposition if the juvenile has previously received a Level 3 disposition in a prior juvenile action. In determining which dispositional alternative is appropriate, the court shall consider the needs of the juvenile as indicated by the risk and needs assessment contained in the predisposition report, the appropriate community resources available to meet those needs, and the protection of the public.

(e) **Level 3 -- Commitment.** -- A court exercising jurisdiction over a juvenile who has been adjudicated delinquent and for whom the dispositional chart in subsection (f) of this section prescribes a Level 3 disposition shall commit the juvenile to the Division for placement in a youth development center in accordance with G.S. 7B-2506(24). However, a court may impose a Level 2 disposition rather than a Level 3 disposition if the court submits written findings on the record that substantiate extraordinary needs on the part of the offending juvenile.

(f) **Dispositions for Each Class of Offense and Delinquency History Level; Disposition Chart Described.** -- The authorized disposition for each class of offense and delinquency history level is as specified in the chart below. Delinquency history levels are indicated horizontally on the top of the chart. Classes of offense are indicated vertically on the left side of the chart. Each cell on the chart indicates which of the dispositional levels described in subsections (c) through (e) of this section are prescribed for that combination of offense classification and delinquency history level:

DELINQUENCY HISTORY

OFFENSE	LOW	MEDIUM	HIGH
VIOLENT	Level 2 or 3	Level 3	Level 3
SERIOUS	Level 1 or 2	Level 2	Level 2 or 3
MINOR	Level 1	Level 1 or 2	Level 2.

(g) Notwithstanding subsection (f) of this section, a juvenile who has been adjudicated for a minor offense may be committed to a Level 3 disposition if the juvenile has been adjudicated of four or more prior offenses. For purposes of determining the number of prior offenses under this subsection, each successive offense is one that was committed after adjudication of the preceding offense.

(g1) Notwithstanding subsection (f) of this section, if a juvenile is adjudicated for an offense that the court finds beyond a reasonable doubt was committed as part of criminal gang activity as defined in G.S. 7B-2508.1, the juvenile shall receive a disposition one level higher than would otherwise be provided for the class of offense and delinquency history level.

(h) If a juvenile is adjudicated of more than one offense during a session of juvenile court, the court shall consolidate the offenses for disposition and impose a single disposition for the consolidated offenses. The disposition shall be specified for the class of offense and delinquency history level of the most serious offense.

History.
1998-202, s. 6; 2000-137, s. 3; 2001-95, s. 5; 2001-179, s. 1; 2007-168, s. 6; 2011-145, s. 19.1 (*l*); 2017-57, s. 16D.4(gg); 2017-197, s. 5.4; 2018-142, s. 23(b); 2019-186, s. 10

§ 7B-2508.1. Criminal gang activity

The following definitions apply in this Article:

(1) **Criminal gang.** -- Any ongoing organization, association, or group of three or more persons, whether formal or informal, that (i) has as one of its primary activities the commission of criminal or delinquent acts and (ii) shares a common name, identification, signs, symbols, tattoos, graffiti, attire, or other distinguishing characteristics, including common activities, customs, or behaviors. The term shall not include three or more persons associated in fact, whether formal or informal, who are not engaged in criminal gang activity.

(2) **Criminal gang activity.** -- The commission of, attempted commission of, or solicitation, coercion, or intimidation of another person to commit (i) any offense under Article 5 of Chapter 90 of the General Statutes or (ii) any offense under Chapter 14 of the General Statutes except Article 9, 22A, 40, 46, or 59 thereof, and further excepting G.S. 14-82, 14-145, 14-183, 14-184, 14-186, 14-190.9, 14-247, 14-248, or 14-313 thereof, and either of the following conditions is met:

a. The offense is committed with the intent to benefit, promote, or further the interests of a criminal gang or for the purposes of increasing a person's own standing or position within a criminal gang.

b. The participants in the offense are identified as criminal gang members acting individually or collectively to further any criminal purpose of a criminal gang.

(3) **Criminal gang member.** -- Any person who meets three or more of the following criteria:

a. The person admits to being a member of a criminal gang.

b. The person is identified as a criminal gang member by a reliable source, including a parent or a guardian.

c. The person has been previously involved in criminal gang activity.

d. The person has adopted symbols, hand signs, or graffiti associated with a criminal gang.

e. The person has adopted the display of colors or the style of dress associated with a criminal gang.

f. The person is in possession of or linked to a criminal gang by physical evidence, including photographs, ledgers, rosters, written or electronic communications, or membership documents.

g. The person has tattoos or markings associated with a criminal gang.

h. The person has adopted language or terminology associated with a criminal gang.

i. The person appears in any form of social media to promote a criminal gang.

History.
2017-57, s. 16D.4(hh); 2017-197, s. 5.4; 2018-142, s. 23(b)

§ 7B-2509. Registration of certain delinquent juveniles

In any case in which a juvenile, who was at least 11 years of age at the time of the offense, is adjudicated delinquent for committing a violation of G.S. 14-27.6 (attempted rape or sexual offense), G.S. 14-27.21 (first-degree forcible rape), G.S. 14-27.22 (second-degree forcible rape), G.S. 14-27.24 (first-degree statutory rape), G.S. 14-27.26 (first-degree forcible sexual offense), G.S. 14-27.27 (second-degree forcible sexual offense), or G.S. 14-27.29 (first-degree statutory sexual offense), the judge, upon a finding that the juvenile is a danger to the community, may order that the juvenile register in accordance with Part 4 of Article 27A of Chapter 14 of the General Statutes.

History.
1997-516, s. 1A; 1998-202, s. 11; 2015-181, s. 26

§ 7B-2510. Conditions of probation; violation of probation

(a) In any case where a juvenile is placed on probation pursuant to G.S. 7B-2506(8), the juvenile court counselor shall have the authority to visit the juvenile where the juvenile resides. The court may impose conditions of probation that are related to the needs of the juvenile and that are reasonably necessary to ensure that the juvenile will lead a law-abiding life, including:

(1) That the juvenile shall remain on good behavior.

(2) That the juvenile shall not violate any laws.

(3) That the juvenile shall not violate any reasonable and lawful rules of a parent, guardian, or custodian.

(4) That the juvenile attend school regularly.

(5) That the juvenile maintain passing grades in up to four courses during each grading period and meet with the juvenile court counselor and a representative of the school to make a plan for how to maintain those passing grades.

(6) That the juvenile not associate with specified persons or be in specified places.

(7) That the juvenile:

a. Refrain from use or possession of any controlled substance included in any schedule of Article 5 of Chapter 90 of the General Statutes, the Controlled Substances Act;

b. Refrain from use or possession of any alcoholic beverage regulated under Chapter 18B of the General Statutes; and

c. Submit to random drug testing.

(8) That the juvenile abide by a prescribed curfew.

(9) That the juvenile submit to a warrantless search at reasonable times.

(10) That the juvenile possess no firearm, explosive device, or other deadly weapon.

(11) That the juvenile report to a juvenile court counselor as often as required by the juvenile court counselor.

(12) That the juvenile make specified financial restitution or pay a fine in accordance with G.S. 7B-2506(4), (5), and (22).

(13) That the juvenile be employed regularly if not attending school.

(14) That the juvenile satisfy any other conditions determined appropriate by the court.

(b) In addition to the regular conditions of probation specified in subsection (a) of this section, the court may, at a dispositional hearing or any subsequent hearing, order the juvenile to comply, if directed to comply by the chief court counselor, with one or more of the following conditions:

(1) Perform up to 20 hours of community service;

(2) Submit to substance abuse monitoring and treatment;

(3) Participate in a life skills or an educational skills program administered by the Division;

(4) Cooperate with electronic monitoring; and

(5) Cooperate with intensive supervision.

However, the court shall not give the chief court counselor discretion to impose the conditions of either subsection (4) or (5) of this section unless the juvenile is subject to Level 2 dispositions pursuant to G.S. 7B-2508 or subsection (d) of this section.

(c) An order of probation shall remain in force for a period not to exceed one year from the date entered. Prior to expiration of an order of probation, the court may extend it for an additional period of one year after notice and a hearing, if the court finds that the extension is necessary to protect the community or to safeguard the welfare of the juvenile. At the discretion of the court, the hearing to determine to extend probation may occur after the expiration of an order of probation at the next regularly scheduled court date or if the juvenile fails to appear in court.

(d) On motion of the juvenile court counselor or the juvenile, or on the court's own motion, the court may review the progress of any juvenile on probation at any time during the period of probation or at the end of probation. The conditions or duration of probation may be modified only as provided in this Subchapter and only after notice and a hearing.

(e) If the court, after notice and a hearing, finds by the greater weight of the evidence that the juvenile has violated the conditions of probation set by the court, the court may continue the original conditions of probation, modify the conditions of probation, or, except as provided in subsection (f) of this section, order a new disposition. In the court's discretion, the court may order a new disposition at the next higher level on the disposition chart or order a term of confinement in a secure juvenile detention facility for up to twice the term authorized by G.S. 7B-2508, in addition to any other Level 2 dispositional option.

(f) A court shall not order a Level 3 disposition for violation of the conditions of probation by a juvenile adjudicated delinquent for an offense classified as minor under G.S. 7B-2508.

History.
1979, c. 815, s. 1; 1981, c. 469, s. 20; 1991, c. 353, s. 1; 1991 (Reg. Sess., 1992), c. 1030, s. 4; 1993, c. 369, s. 1; c. 462, s. 1; 1998-202, s. 6; 2000-137, s. 3; 2001-490, ss. 2.23, 2.24; 2011-145, s. 19.1 (*l*); 2015-58, s. 2.4

§ 7B-2511. Termination of probation

At the end of or at any time during probation, the court may terminate probation by written order upon finding that there is no further need for supervision. The finding and order terminating probation may be entered in chambers in the absence of the juvenile and may be based on a report from the juvenile court counselor or, at the election of the court, the order may be entered with the juvenile present after notice and a hearing.

History.
1979, c. 815, s. 1; 1998-202, s. 6; 2001-490, s. 2.25

§ 7B-2512. Dispositional order

(a) The dispositional order shall be in writing and shall contain appropriate findings of fact and conclusions of law. The court shall state with particularity, both orally and in the written order of disposition, the precise terms of the disposition including the kind, duration, and the person who is responsible for carrying out the disposition and the person or agency in whom custody is vested.

(b) The court shall include information at the time of issuing the dispositional order, either orally in court or in writing, on the expunction of juvenile records as provided for in G.S. 7B-3200 that are applicable to the dispositional order.

History.
1979, c. 815, s. 1; 1987 (Reg. Sess., 1988), c. 1090, s. 10; 1991, c. 434, s. 1; 1997-390, s. 8; 1998-202, s. 6; 1998-229, s. 7; 2015-58, s. 2.5

§ 7B-2513. Commitment of delinquent juvenile to Division

(a) Pursuant to G.S. 7B-2506 and G.S. 7B-2508, the court may commit a delinquent juvenile who is at least 10 years of age to the Division for placement in a youth development center. Commitment shall be for an indefinite term of at least six months.

(a1) For an offense the juvenile committed prior to reaching the age of 16 years, the term shall not exceed:

(1) The twenty-first birthday of the juvenile if the juvenile has been committed to the Division for an offense that would be first-degree murder pursuant to G.S. 14-17, first-degree forcible rape pursuant to G.S. 14-27.21, first-degree statutory rape pursuant to G.S. 14-27.24, first-degree forcible sexual offense pursuant to G.S. 14-27.26, or first-degree statutory sexual offense pursuant to G.S. 14-27.29 if committed by an adult;

(2) The nineteenth birthday of the juvenile if the juvenile has been committed to the Division for an offense that would be a Class B1, B2, C, D, or E felony if committed by an adult, other than an offense set forth in subdivision (1) of this subsection; or

(3) The eighteenth birthday of the juvenile if the juvenile has been committed to the Division for an offense other than an offense that would be a Class A, B1, B2, C, D, or E felony if committed by an adult.

(a2) For an offense the juvenile committed while the juvenile was at least 16 years of age but less than 17 years of age, the term shall not exceed:

(1) The twenty-first birthday of the juvenile if the juvenile has been committed to the Division for an offense that would be first degree murder pursuant to G.S. 14-17, first-degree forcible rape pursuant to G.S. 14-27.21, first-degree statutory rape pursuant to G.S. 14-27.24, first-degree forcible sexual offense pursuant to G.S. 14-27.26, or first-degree statutory sexual offense pursuant to G.S. 14-27.29 if committed by an adult;

(2) The twentieth birthday of the juvenile if the juvenile has been committed to the Division for an offense that would be a Class B1, B2, C, D, or E felony if committed by an adult, other than an offense set forth in subdivision (1) of this subsection; or

(3) The juvenile's nineteenth birthday if the juvenile has been committed to the Division for an offense other than an offense that would be a Class A, B1, B2, C, D, or E felony if committed by an adult.

(a3) For an offense the juvenile committed while the juvenile was at least 17 years of age, the term shall not exceed:

(1) The twenty-first birthday of the juvenile if the juvenile has been committed to the Division for an offense that would be a Class A, B1, B2, C, D, or E felony if committed by an adult; or

(2) The juvenile's twentieth birthday if the juvenile has been committed to the Division for an offense other than an offense that would be a Class A, B1, B2, C, D, or E felony if committed by an adult.

(a4) No juvenile shall be committed to a youth development center beyond the minimum six-month commitment for a period of time in excess of the maximum term of imprisonment for which an adult in prior record level VI for felonies or in prior conviction level III for misdemeanors could be sentenced for the same offense, except when the Division pursuant to G.S. 7B-2515 determines that the juvenile's commitment needs to be continued for an additional period of time to continue care or treatment under the plan of care or treatment developed under subsection (f) of this section. At the time of commitment to a youth development center, the court shall determine the maximum period of time the juvenile may remain committed before a determination must be made by the Division pursuant to G.S. 7B-2515 and shall notify the juvenile of that determination.

(b) The court may commit a juvenile to a definite term of not less than six months and not more than two years if the court finds that the juvenile is 14 years of age or older, has been previously adjudicated delinquent for two or more felony offenses, and has been previously committed to a youth development center.

(c) The chief court counselor shall have the responsibility for transporting the juvenile to the youth development center designated by the Division. The juvenile shall be accompanied to the youth development center by a person of the same sex.

(d) The chief court counselor shall ensure that the records requested by the Division accompany the juvenile upon transportation for admittance to a youth development center or, if not obtainable at the time of admission, are sent to the youth development center within 15 days of the admission. If records requested by the Division for admission do not exist, to the best knowledge of the chief court counselor, the chief court counselor shall so stipulate in writing to the youth development center. If such records do exist, but the chief court counselor is unable to obtain copies of them, a district court may order that the records from public agencies be made available to the youth development center. Records that are confidential by law shall remain confidential and the Division shall be bound by the specific laws governing the confidentiality of these records. All records shall be used in a manner consistent with the best interests of the juvenile.

(e) A commitment order accompanied by information requested by the Division shall be forwarded to the Division. The Division shall place the juvenile in the youth development center that would best provide for the juvenile's needs and shall notify the committing court. The Division may assign a juvenile committed for delinquency to any institution of the Division or licensed by the Division, which program is appropriate to the needs of the juvenile.

The Division, after assessment of the juvenile, may provide commitment services to the juvenile in a program not located in a youth development center or detention facility. If the Division recommends that commitment services for the juvenile are to be provided in a setting that is not located in a youth development center or detention facility, the Division shall file a motion, along with information about the recommended services for the juvenile, with the committing court prior to placing the juvenile in the identified commitment program. The Division shall send notice of the motion to the District Attorney, the juvenile, and the juvenile's attorney. Upon receipt of the motion filed by the Division, the court may enter an order without the appearance of witnesses and without hearing if the court determines that the identified commitment program is appropriate and a hearing is not necessary. The court must hold a hearing if the juvenile or the juvenile's attorney requests a hearing. If the court notifies the Division of its intent to hold a hearing, the date for that hearing shall be set by the court and the Division shall place the juvenile in a youth development center or detention facility until the determination of the court at that hearing.

(f) When the court commits a juvenile to the Division for placement in a youth development center, the Division shall prepare a plan for care or treatment within 30 days after assuming custody of the juvenile.

(g) Commitment of a juvenile to the Division for placement in a youth development center does not terminate the court's continuing jurisdiction over the juvenile and the juvenile's parent, guardian, or custodian. Commitment of a juvenile to the Division for placement in a youth development center transfers only physical custody of the juvenile. Legal custody remains with the parent, guardian, custodian, agency, or institution in whom it was vested.

(h) Pending placement of a juvenile with the Division, the court may house a juvenile who has been adjudicated delinquent for an offense that would be a Class A, B1, B2, C, D, or E felony if committed by an adult in a holdover facility up to 72 hours if the court, based on the information provided by the juvenile court counselor, determines that no acceptable alternative placement is available and the protection of the public requires that the juvenile be housed in a holdover facility.

(i) A juvenile who is committed to the Division for placement in a youth development center shall be tested for the use of controlled substances or alcohol. The results of this initial test shall be incorporated into the plan of care as provided in subsection (f) of this section and used for evaluation and treatment purposes only.

(j) Repealed by Session Laws 2019-216, s. 15, effective August 31, 2019, and applicable to offenses and acts of delinquency committed on or after that date.

History.
1979, c. 815, s. 1; 1983, c. 133, s. 2; 1987, c. 100; c. 372; 1991, c. 434, ss. 2, 3; 1995 (Reg. Sess., 1996), c. 609, s. 2; 1997-443, s. 11A.118(a); 1998-202, s. 6; 1999-423, s. 1; 2000-137, s. 3; 2001-95, s. 5; 2001-490, s. 2.26; 2003-53, s. 1; 2011-145, s. 19.1 (*l*); 2015-181, s. 27; 2017-57, s. 16D.4(i); 2018-142, s. 23(b); 2019-216, s. 15; 2021-123, s. 1(a)

§ 7B-2514. Post-release supervision planning; release

(a) The Division shall be responsible for evaluation of the progress of each juvenile at least once every six months as long as the juvenile remains in the care of the Division. Any determination that the juvenile should remain in the care of the Division for an additional period of time shall be based on the Division's determination that the juvenile requires additional treatment or rehabilitation pursuant to G.S. 7B-2515. If the Division determines that a juvenile is ready for release, the Division shall initiate a post-release supervision planning process. The post-release supervision planning process shall be defined by rules and regulations of the Division, but shall include the following:

(1) Written notification shall be given to the court that ordered commitment.

(2) A post-release supervision planning conference shall be held involving as many as possible of the following: the juvenile, the juvenile's parent, guardian, or custodian, juvenile court counselors who have supervised the juvenile on probation or will supervise the juvenile on post-release supervision, and staff of the facility that found the juvenile ready for release. The planning conference shall include personal contact and evaluation rather than telephonic notification.

(3) The planning conference participants shall consider, based on the individual needs of the juvenile and pursuant to rules adopted by the Division, placement of the juvenile in any program under the auspices of the Division, including the juvenile court services programs that, in the judgment of the Division, would be appropriate transitional placement, pending release under G.S. 7B-2513.

(b) The Division shall develop the plan in writing and base the terms on the needs of the juvenile and the protection of the public. Every plan shall require the juvenile to complete at least 90 days, but not more than one year, of post-release supervision.

(c) The Division shall release a juvenile under a plan of post-release supervision at least 90 days prior to one of the following:

(1) Completion of the juvenile's definite term of commitment.

(2) The juvenile's twenty-first birthday if the juvenile has been committed to the Division for an offense that would be first-degree murder pursuant to G.S. 14-17, first-degree forcible rape pursuant to G.S. 14-27.21, first-degree statutory rape pursuant to G.S. 14-27.24, first-degree forcible sexual offense pursuant to G.S. 14-27.26, or first-degree statutory sexual offense pursuant to G.S. 14-27.29 if committed by an adult.

(3) If the juvenile has been committed to the Division for an offense that would be a Class B1, B2, C, D, or E felony if committed by an adult, other than an offense set forth in G.S. 7B-1602(a):

a. The juvenile's nineteenth birthday, if the juvenile committed the offense prior to reaching the age of 16 years.

b. The juvenile's twentieth birthday, if the juvenile committed the offense while the juvenile was at least 16 years of age but less than 17 years of age.

c. The juvenile's twenty-first birthday, if the juvenile committed the offense while the juvenile was at least 17 years of age.

(4) If the juvenile has been committed to the Division for an offense other than an offense that would be a Class A, B1, B2, C, D, or E felony if committed by an adult:

a. The eighteenth birthday of the juvenile, if the juvenile committed the offense prior to reaching the age of 16 years.

b. The nineteenth birthday of the juvenile, if the juvenile committed the offense while the juvenile was at least 16 years of age but less than 17 years of age.

c. The twentieth birthday of the juvenile, if the juvenile committed the offense while the juvenile was at least 17 years of age.

(d) Notwithstanding Articles 30 and 31 of Subchapter III of this Chapter, and in addition to any notice to the victim required pursuant to G.S. 7B-2055, at least 45 days before releasing to post-release supervision a juvenile who was committed for a Class A or B1 felony, the Division shall notify by first-class mail at the last known address all of the following:

(1) The juvenile.

(2) The juvenile's parent, guardian, or custodian.

(3) The district attorney of the district where the juvenile was adjudicated.

(4) The head of the enforcement agency that took the juvenile into custody.

(5) Repealed by Session Laws 2019-216, s. 11, effective August 31, 2019, and applicable to offenses and acts of delinquency committed on or after that date.

The notification shall include only the juvenile's name, offense, date of commitment, and date proposed for release. A copy of the notice shall be sent to the appropriate clerk of superior court for placement in the juvenile's court file.

(e) The Division may release a juvenile under an indefinite commitment to post-release supervision only after the juvenile has been committed to the Division for placement in a youth development center for a period of at least six months.

(f) A juvenile committed to the Division for placement in a youth development center for a definite term shall receive credit toward that term for the time the juvenile spends on post-release supervision.

(g) A juvenile on post-release supervision shall be supervised by a juvenile court counselor. Post-release supervision shall be terminated by order of the court.

History.
1979, c. 815, s. 1; 1983, c. 133, s. 1; c. 276, s. 1; 1989, c. 235; 1996, 2nd Ex. Sess., c. 18, s. 23.2(e); 1998-202, s. 6; 2000-137, s. 3; 2001-95, s. 5; 2001-490, ss. 2.27, 2.28; 2011-145, s. 19 (*l*); 2015-181, s. 28; 2019-216, s. 11; 2021-123, s. 1(d)

§ 7B-2515. Notification of extended commitment; plan of treatment

(a) In determining whether a juvenile who was committed to the Division for an offense that was committed prior to the juvenile reaching the age of 16 years should be released before the juvenile's 18th birthday, the Division shall consider the protection of the public and the likelihood that continued placement will lead to further rehabilitation. If the Division does not intend to release the juvenile prior to the juvenile's eighteenth birthday, or if the Division determines that the juvenile's commitment should be continued beyond the maximum commitment period as set forth in G.S. 7B-2513(a4), the Division shall notify the juvenile and the juvenile's parent, guardian, or custodian in writing at least 30 days in advance of the juvenile's eighteenth birthday or the end of the maximum commitment period, of the additional specific commitment period proposed by the Division, the basis for extending the commitment period, and the plan for future care or treatment.

(a1) In determining whether a juvenile who was committed to the Division for an offense that was committed while the juvenile was at least 16 years of age but less than 17 years of age should be released before the juvenile's nineteenth birthday, the Division shall consider the protection of the public and the likelihood that continued placement will lead to further rehabilitation. If the Division does not intend to release the juvenile prior to the juvenile's nineteenth birthday, or if the Division determines that the juvenile's commitment should be continued beyond the maximum commitment period as set forth in G.S. 7B-2513(a4), the Division shall notify the juvenile and the juvenile's parent, guardian, or custodian in writing, at least 30 days in advance of the juvenile's nineteenth birthday or the end of the maximum commitment period, of the additional specific commitment period proposed by the Division, the basis for extending the commitment period, and the plan for future care or treatment.

(a2) In determining whether a juvenile who was committed to the Division for an offense that was committed while the juvenile was at least 17 years of age but less than 18 years of age should be released before the juvenile's twentieth birthday, the Division shall consider the protection of the public and the likelihood that continued placement will lead to further rehabilitation. If the Division does not intend to release the juvenile prior to the juvenile's twentieth birthday, or if the Division determines that the juvenile's commitment should be continued beyond the maximum commitment period as set forth in G.S. 7B-2513(a4), the Division shall notify the juvenile and the juvenile's parent, guardian, or custodian in writing, at least 30 days in advance of the juvenile's twentieth birthday or the end of the maximum commitment period, of the additional specific commitment period proposed by the Division, the basis for extending the commitment period, and the plan for future care or treatment.

(b) The Division shall modify the plan of care or treatment developed pursuant to G.S. 7B-2513(f) to specify (i) the specific goals and outcomes that require additional time for care or treatment of the juvenile; (ii) the specific course of treatment or care that will be implemented to achieve the established goals and outcomes; and (iii) the efforts that will be taken to assist the juvenile's family in creating an environment that will increase the likelihood that the efforts to treat and rehabilitate the juvenile will be successful upon release. If appropriate, the Division may place the juvenile in a setting other than a youth development center.

(c) The juvenile and the juvenile's parent, guardian, or custodian may request a review by the court of the Division's decision to extend the juvenile's commitment pursuant to this section,

in which case the court shall conduct a review hearing. The court may modify the Division's decision and the juvenile's maximum commitment period. If the juvenile or the juvenile's parent, guardian, or custodian does not request a review of the Division's decision, the Division's decision shall become the juvenile's new maximum commitment period.

History.
1998-202, s. 6; 1998-217, s. 57(1); 2000-137, s. 3; 2001-95, s. 5; 2011-145, s. 19.1 (*l*); 2017-57, s. 16D.4(j); 2018-142, s. 23(b)

§ 7B-2516. Revocation of post-release supervision

(a) On motion of the juvenile court counselor providing post-release supervision or motion of the juvenile, or on the court's own motion, and after notice, the court may hold a hearing to review the progress of any juvenile on post-release supervision at any time during the period of post-release supervision. With respect to any hearing involving allegations that the juvenile has violated the terms of post-release supervision, the juvenile:

(1) Shall have reasonable notice in writing of the nature and content of the allegations in the motion, including notice that the purpose of the hearing is to determine whether the juvenile has violated the terms of post-release supervision to the extent that post-release supervision should be revoked;

(2) Shall be represented by an attorney at the hearing;

(3) Shall have the right to confront and cross-examine witnesses; and

(4) May admit, deny, or explain the violation alleged and may present proof, including affidavits or other evidence, in support of the juvenile's contentions. A record of the proceeding shall be made and preserved in the juvenile's record.

(b) If the court determines by the greater weight of the evidence that the juvenile has violated the terms of post-release supervision, the court may revoke the post-release supervision or make any other disposition authorized by this Subchapter.

(c) If the court revokes post-release supervision, the juvenile shall be returned to the Division for placement in a youth development center for an indefinite term of at least 90 days, provided, however, that no juvenile shall remain committed to the Division for placement in a youth development center past the maximum term of commitment allowed pursuant to G.S. 7B-2513(a1), 7B-2513(a2), and 7B-2513(a3).

History.

1979, c. 815, s. 1; 1998-202, s. 6; 2000-137, s.3; 2001-95, s. 5; 2001-490, s. 2.29; 2011-145, s. 19.1 (*l*); 2015-181, s. 29; 2021-123, s. 1(e)

§ 7B-2517. Transfer authority of Governor

The Governor may order transfer of any person less than 18 years of age from any jail or penal facility of the State to one of the residential facilities operated by the Division in appropriate circumstances, provided the Governor shall consult with the Division concerning the feasibility of the transfer in terms of available space, staff, and suitability of program.

When an inmate, committed to the Division of Adult Correction and Juvenile Justice of the Department of Public Safety, is transferred by the Governor to a residential program operated by the Division, the Division may release the juvenile based on the needs of the juvenile and the best interests of the State. Transfer shall not divest the probation or parole officer of the officer's responsibility to supervise the inmate on release.

History.

1979, c. 815, s. 1; 1997-443, s. 11A.118(a); 1998-202, s. 6; 2000-137, s. 3; 2011-145, ss. 19.1(h), (*l*); 2017-186, s. 2 (*l*)

ARTICLE 26
MODIFICATION AND ENFORCEMENT OF DISPOSITIONAL ORDERS; APPEALS

§ 7B-2600. Authority to modify or vacate

(a) Upon motion in the cause or petition, and after notice, the court may conduct a review hearing to determine whether the order of the court is in the best interests of the juvenile, and the court may modify or vacate the order in light of changes in circumstances or the needs of the juvenile.

(b) In a case of delinquency, the court may reduce the nature or the duration of the disposition on the basis that it was imposed in an illegal manner or is unduly severe with reference to the seriousness of the offense, the culpability of the juvenile, or the dispositions given to juveniles convicted of similar offenses.

(c) In any case where the court finds the juvenile to be undisciplined, the jurisdiction of the court to modify any order or disposition made in the case shall continue during the minority

of the juvenile or until terminated by order of the court.

(d) In any case where the court finds the juvenile to be delinquent, the jurisdiction of the court to modify any order or disposition made in the case shall continue until one of the following first occurs:

(1) Unless subdivision (4) of this subsection applies, the juvenile reaches the age of 18 for an offense committed prior to the juvenile reaching the age of 16.

(2) Unless subdivision (4) of this subsection applies, the juvenile reaches the age of 19 for an offense committed while the juvenile was at least 16 years of age but less than 17 years of age.

(3) Unless subdivision (4) of this subsection applies, the juvenile reaches the age of 20 for an offense committed while the juvenile was at least 17 years of age.

(4) The juvenile reaches the maximum term of commitment as authorized pursuant to G.S. 7B-2513(a1), 7B-2513(a2), and 7B-2513(a3), if the juvenile was committed to the Division for placement in a youth development center.

(5) Termination by order of the court.

History.

1979, c. 815, s. 1; 1998-202, s. 6; 2000-137, s. 3; 2011-145, s. 19.1 (*l*); 2015-181, s. 30; 2021-123, s. 1(f)

§ 7B-2601. Request for modification for lack of suitable services

If the Division finds that any juvenile committed to the Division's care is not suitable for its program, the Division may make a motion in the cause so that the court may make an alternative disposition that is consistent with G.S. 7B-2508.

History.

1979, c. 815, s. 1; 1998-202, s. 6; 2000-137, s. 3; 2011-145, s. 19.1 (*l*)

§ 7B-2602. Right to appeal

Upon motion of a proper party as defined in G.S. 7B-2604, review of any final order of the court in a juvenile matter under this Article shall be before the Court of Appeals. Notice of appeal shall be given in open court at the time of the hearing or in writing within 10 days after entry of the order. However, if no disposition is made within 60 days after entry of the order, written notice of appeal may be given within 70 days after such entry. A final order shall include:

(1) Any order finding absence of jurisdiction;

(2) Any order which in effect determines the action and prevents a judgment from which appeal might be taken;

(3) Any order of disposition after an adjudication that a juvenile is delinquent or undisciplined; or

(4) Any order modifying custodial rights.

History.

1979, c. 815, s. 1; 1998-202, s. 6

§ 7B-2603. Right to appeal transfer decision

(a) Notwithstanding G.S. 7B-2602, any order transferring jurisdiction of the district court in a juvenile matter to the superior court may be appealed to the superior court for a hearing on the record. Notice of the appeal must be given in open court or in writing within 10 days after entry of the order of transfer in district court. Entry of an order shall be treated in the same manner as entry of a judgment under G.S. 1A-1, Rule 58 of the North Carolina Rules of Civil Procedure. The clerk of superior court shall provide the district attorney with a copy of any written notice of appeal filed by the attorney for the juvenile. Upon expiration of the 10 day period in which an appeal may be entered, if an appeal has been entered and not withdrawn, the clerk shall transfer the case to the superior court docket. The superior court shall, within a reasonable time, review the record of the transfer hearing for abuse of discretion by the juvenile court in the issue of transfer. The superior court shall not review the findings as to probable cause for the underlying offense.

(b) Once an order of transfer has been entered by the district court, the juvenile has the right to be considered for pretrial release as provided in G.S. 15A-533 and G.S. 15A-534. Any detention of the juvenile pending release shall be in accordance with G.S. 7B-2204.

(c) If an appeal of the transfer order is taken, the superior court shall enter an order either (i) remanding the case to the juvenile court for adjudication or (ii) upholding the transfer order. If the superior court remands the case to juvenile court for adjudication and the juvenile has been granted pretrial release provided in G.S 15A-533 and G.S. 15A-534, the obligor shall be released from the juvenile's bond upon the district court's review of whether the juvenile shall be placed in secure or nonsecure custody as provided in G.S. 7B-1903.

(d) The superior court order shall be an interlocutory order, and the issue of transfer may be appealed to the Court of Appeals only after the juvenile has been convicted in superior court.

History.

1979, c. 815, s. 1; 1998-202, s. 6; 1999-309, s. 2; 1999-423, s. 2; 2017-57, s. 16D.4(k); 2018-142, s. 23(b)

§ 7B-2604. Proper parties for appeal

(a) An appeal may be taken by the juvenile, the juvenile's parent, guardian, or custodian, a county, or the State.

(b) The State's appeal is limited to the following orders in delinquency or undisciplined cases:

(1) An order finding a State statute to be unconstitutional; and

(2) Any order which terminates the prosecution of a petition by upholding the defense of double jeopardy, by holding that a cause of action is not stated under a statute, or by granting a motion to suppress.

(c) A county's appeal is limited to orders in which the county has been ordered to pay for medical, surgical, psychiatric, psychological, or other evaluation or treatment of a juvenile pursuant to G.S. 7B-2502, or other medical, psychiatric, psychological, or other evaluation or treatment of a parent pursuant to G.S. 7B-2702.

History.

1979, c. 815, s. 1; 1998-202, s. 6; 2003-171, s. 1

§ 7B-2605. Disposition pending appeal

Pending disposition of an appeal, the release of the juvenile, with or without conditions, should issue in every case unless the court orders otherwise. For compelling reasons which must be stated in writing, the court may enter a temporary order affecting the custody or placement of the juvenile as the court finds to be in the best interests of the juvenile or the State.

History.

1979, c. 815, s. 1; 1987 (Reg. Sess., 1988), c. 1090, s. 12; 1998-202, s. 6

§ 7B-2606. Disposition after appeal

Upon the affirmation of the order of adjudication or disposition of the court by the Court of Appeals or by the Supreme Court in the event of an appeal, the court shall have authority to modify or alter the original order of adjudication or disposition as the court finds to be in the best interests of the juvenile to reflect any adjustment made by the juvenile or change in circumstances during the period of time the appeal was pending. If the modifying order is entered ex parte, the court shall give notice to interested parties to show cause within 10 days thereafter as to why the modifying order should be vacated or altered.

History.

1979, c. 815, s. 1; 1998-202, s. 6

ARTICLE 27
AUTHORITY OVER PARENTS OF JUVENILES ADJUDICATED DELINQUENT OR UNDISCIPLINED

§ 7B-2700. Appearance in court

The parent, guardian, or custodian of a juvenile under the jurisdiction of the juvenile court shall attend the hearings of which the parent, guardian, or custodian receives notice. The court may excuse the appearance of either or both parents or the guardian or custodian at a particular hearing or all hearings. Unless so excused, the willful failure of a parent, guardian, or custodian to attend a hearing of which the parent, guardian, or custodian has notice shall be grounds for contempt.

History.
1998-202, s. 6

§ 7B-2701. Parental responsibility classes

The court may order the parent, guardian, or custodian of a juvenile who has been adjudicated undisciplined or delinquent to attend parental responsibility classes if those classes are available in the judicial district in which the parent, guardian, or custodian resides.

History.
1998-202, s. 6

§ 7B-2702. Medical, surgical, psychiatric, or psychological evaluation or treatment of juvenile or parent

(a) If the court orders medical, surgical, psychiatric, psychological, or other evaluation or treatment pursuant to G.S. 7B-2502, the court may order the parent or other responsible parties to pay the cost of the treatment or care ordered.

(b) At the dispositional hearing or a subsequent hearing, if the court finds that it is in the best interests of the juvenile for the parent to be directly involved in the juvenile's evaluation or treatment, the court may order that person to participate in medical, psychiatric, psychological, or other evaluation or treatment of the juvenile. The cost of the evaluation or treatment shall be paid pursuant to G.S. 7B-2502.

(c) At the dispositional hearing or a subsequent hearing, the court may determine whether the best interests of the juvenile require that the parent undergo psychiatric, psychological, or other evaluation or treatment or counseling directed toward remedying behaviors or conditions that led to or contributed to the juvenile's adjudication or to the court's decision to remove custody of the juvenile from the parent. If the court finds that the best interests of the juvenile require the parent undergo evaluation or treatment, it may order that person to comply with a plan of evaluation or treatment approved by the court or condition legal custody or physical placement of the juvenile with the parent upon that person's compliance with the plan of evaluation or treatment.

(d) In cases in which the court has ordered the parent of the juvenile to comply with or undergo evaluation or treatment, the court may order the parent to pay the cost of evaluation or treatment ordered pursuant to this subsection. In cases in which the court has conditioned legal custody or physical placement of the juvenile with the parent upon the parent's compliance with a plan of evaluation or treatment, the court may charge the cost of the evaluation or treatment to the county of the juvenile's residence if the court finds the parent is unable to pay the cost of the evaluation or treatment. In all other cases, if the court finds the parent is unable to pay the cost of the evaluation or treatment ordered pursuant to this subsection, the court may order the parent to receive evaluation or treatment currently available from the area mental health program that serves the parent's catchment area.

History.
1979, c. 815, s. 1; 1981, c. 469, s. 19; 1983, c. 837, ss. 2, 3; 1985, c. 589, s. 5; c. 777, s. 1; 1985 (Reg. Sess., 1986), c. 863, s. 2; 1987, c. 598, s. 2; 1989, c. 218; c. 529, s. 7; 1991, c. 636, s. 19(a); 1995, c. 328, s. 2; 1995 (Reg. Sess., 1996), c. 609, ss. 3, 4; 1997-456, s. 1; 1997-516, s. 1A; 1998-202, s. 6; 1998-229, s. 6

§ 7B-2703. Compliance with orders of court

(a) The court may order the parent, guardian, or custodian, to the extent that person is able to do so, to provide transportation for a juvenile to keep an appointment with a juvenile court counselor or to comply with other orders of the court.

(b) The court may order a parent, guardian, or custodian to cooperate with and assist the juvenile in complying with the terms and conditions of probation or other orders of the court.

History.
1998-202, s. 6; 2001-490, s. 2.30

§ 7B-2704. Payment of support or other expenses; assignment of insurance coverage

At the dispositional hearing or a subsequent hearing, if the court finds that the parent is able to do so, the court may order the parent to:

(1) Pay a reasonable sum that will cover in whole or in part the support of the juvenile. If the court requires the payment of child support, the amount of the payments shall be determined as provided in G.S. 50-13.4;

(2) Pay a fee for probation supervision or residential facility costs;

(3) Assign private insurance coverage to cover medical costs while the juvenile is in secure detention, youth development center, or other out-of-home placement; and

(4) Pay appointed attorneys' fees.

All money paid by a parent pursuant to this section shall be paid into the office of the clerk of superior court.

If the court places a juvenile in the custody of a county department of social services and if the court finds that the parent is unable to pay the cost of the support required by the juvenile, the cost shall be paid by the county department of social services in whose custody the juvenile is placed, provided the juvenile is not receiving care in an institution owned or operated by the State or federal government or any subdivision thereof.

History.
1979, c. 815, s. 1; 1981, c. 469, s. 19; 1983, c. 837, ss. 2, 3; 1985, c. 589, s. 5; c. 777, s. 1; 1985 (Reg. Sess., 1986), c. 863, s. 2; 1987, c. 598, s. 2; 1989, c. 218; c. 529, s. 7; 1991, c. 636, s. 19(a); 1995, c. 328, s. 2; 1995 (Reg. Sess., 1996), c. 609, ss. 3, 4; 1997-456, s. 1; 1997-516, s. 1A; 1998-202, s. 6; 1998-229, s. 6; 2000-144, s. 24; 2001-95, s. 5

§ 7B-2705. Employment discrimination unlawful

No employer may discharge, demote, or deny a promotion or other benefit of employment to any employee because the employee complies with the provisions of this Article. The Commissioner of Labor shall enforce the provisions of this section according to Article 21 of Chapter 95 of the General Statutes, including the rules and regulations issued pursuant to that Article.

History.
1998-202, s. 6

§ 7B-2706. Contempt for failure to comply

Upon motion of the juvenile court counselor or prosecutor or upon the court's own motion, the court may issue an order directing the parent, guardian, or custodian to appear and show cause why the parent, guardian, or custodian should not be found or held in civil or criminal contempt for willfully failing to comply with an order of the court. Chapter 5A of the General Statutes shall govern contempt proceedings initiated pursuant to this Article.

History.
1998-202, s. 6; 2001-490, s. 2.31

ARTICLE 27A*
AUTHORITY OVER PARENTS, GUARDIANS, OR CUSTODIANS OF VULNERABLE JUVENILES WHO ARE RECEIVING JUVENILE CONSULTATION SERVICES.

§ 7B-2715. Attend all scheduled meetings with juvenile court counselor

The parent, guardian, or custodian of a juvenile being provided services through a juvenile consultation shall attend all scheduled meetings with the juvenile court counselor provided sufficient notice of the meeting was given to the parent, guardian, or custodian.

History.
2021-123, s. 5(e)

§ 7B-2716. Attend parental responsibility classes

The juvenile court counselor may direct the parent, guardian, or custodian of a juvenile who is being provided services through a juvenile consultation to attend parental responsibility classes if those classes are available in the district in which the parent, guardian, or custodian resides.

History.
2021-123, s. 5(e)

§ 7B-2717. Medical, surgical, psychiatric, or psychological evaluation or treatment of vulnerable juveniles who are receiving juvenile consultation services or parents

(a) The juvenile court counselor shall work with the parent, guardian, or custodian of the juvenile receiving juvenile consultation services to obtain for the juvenile any medical, surgical, psychiatric, psychological, or other evaluation or treatment as needed or recommended as part

---

* Session Laws 2021-123, s. 5(e), designated the sections in this Article as G.S. 7B-2710 through 7B-2713. The sections have been renumbered as G.S. 7B-2715 through 7B-2718 at the direction of the Revisor of Statutes.

of the juvenile consultation process. The juvenile court counselor shall work with the parent, guardian, or custodian of the juvenile and other funding resources to find a means for paying for such services, including helping the parent, guardian, or custodian of the juvenile to apply for Health Choice and/or Medicaid.

(b) The juvenile court counselor, with written recommendations of a qualified physician, surgeon, or mental health provider, shall advise the parent, guardian, or custodian of the juvenile receiving juvenile consultation services to be directly involved in the juvenile's evaluation or treatment and participate in medical, psychiatric, psychological, or other evaluation or treatment of the juvenile if it is determined to be in the best interests of the juvenile.

(c) The juvenile court counselor may recommend that the parent, guardian, or custodian of the juvenile receiving juvenile consultation services undergo psychiatric, psychological, or other evaluation or treatment or counseling with written orders or recommendations from a qualified mental or physical health provider directed toward remedying behaviors or conditions that led to or contributed to the juvenile's receipt of a juvenile consultation.

(d) With written orders or recommendations from a qualified mental or physical health provider, the juvenile court counselor may recommend that the parent, guardian, or custodian of the juvenile receiving juvenile consultation services seek funding through the Division of Juvenile Justice and/or the local management entity and managed care organization that serves the catchment area to pay the cost of any evaluation or treatment recommended for the parent, guardian, or custodian of the juvenile.

History.
2021-123, s. 5(e)

§ 7B-2718. Compliance with recommendations of the juvenile court counselor for juveniles receiving juvenile consultation services

(a) In cases in which the juvenile court counselor is providing juvenile consultation services, the juvenile court counselor may transport the parent, guardian, or custodian of a juvenile receiving juvenile consultation services and the juvenile receiving juvenile consultation services, to the extent the juvenile court counselor is able to do so, to keep an appointment or to comply with the recommendations of the juvenile court counselor.

(b) In all cases in which the juvenile court counselor is providing juvenile consultation services, the juvenile court counselor shall work

collaboratively with the parent, guardian, or custodian of the juvenile, the Department of Social Services, the local management entity or managed care organization, the local education authority, and all other community stakeholders involved with the juvenile and family. This will be identified as the Juvenile and Family Team, and all local community agencies involved with the juvenile and family shall be invited to all meetings scheduled with the juvenile and parent, guardian, or custodian of the juvenile.

(c) If a parent, guardian, or custodian of a juvenile refuses to follow the recommendations of the Juvenile and Family Team, and this refusal puts the juvenile at risk of abuse, neglect, or dependency, the juvenile court counselor shall report to the Department of Social Services who may file an abuse, neglect, or dependency petition pursuant to G.S. 7B-403.

History.
2021-123, s. 5(e)

ARTICLE 28
INTERSTATE COMPACT ON JUVENILES

§§ 7B-2800 through 7B-2827

Repealed by Session Laws 2005-194, s. 2 . See editor's note.

History.
G.S. 7B-2800: 1963, c. 910, s. 1; 1965, c. 925, s. 1; 1979, c. 815, s. 1; 1998-202, s. 6 . G.S. 7B-2801: 1963, c. 910, s. 1; 1965, c. 925, s. 1; 1979, c. 815, s. 1; 1998-202, s. 6 . G.S. 7B-2802: 1963, c. 910, s. 1; 1965, c. 925, s. 1; 1979, c. 815, s. 1; 1998-202, s. 6 . G.S. 7B-2803: 1963, c. 910, s. 1; 1965, c. 925, s. 1; 1979, c. 815, s. 1; 1998-202, s. 6 . G.S. 7B-2804: 1963, c. 910, s. 1; c. 1965, c. 925, s. 1; 1979, c. 815, s. 1; 1998-202, s. 6; 2000-144, s. 25 . G.S. 7B-2805: 1963, c. 910, s. 1; 1965, c. 925, s. 1; 1979, c. 815, s. 1; 1998-202, s. 6; 2000-144, s. 26 . G.S. 7B-2806: 1963, c. 910, s. 1; 1965, c. 925, s. 1; 1979, c. 815, s. 1; 1998-202, s. 6 . G.S. 7B-2807: 1963, c. 910, s. 1; 1965, c. 925, s. 1; 1979, c. 815, s. 1; 1998-202, s. 6 . G.S. 7B-2808: 1963, c. 910, s. 1; 1965, c. 925, s. 1; 1979, c. 815, s. 1; 1998-202, s. 6 . G.S. 7B-2809: 1963, c. 910, s. 1; 1965, c. 925, s. 1; 1979, c. 815, s. 1; 1998-202, s. 6 . G.S. 7B-2810: 1963, c. 910, s. 1; 1965, c. 925, s. 1; 1979, c. 815, s. 1; 1998-202, s. 6 . G.S. 7B-2811: 1963, c. 910, s. 1; 1965, c. 925, s. 1; 1979, c. 815, s. 1; 1998-202, s. 6 . G.S. 7B-2812: 1963, c. 910, s. 1; 1965, c. 925, s. 1; 1979, c. 815, s. 1; 1998-202, s. 6 . G.S. 7B-2813: 1963, c. 910, s. 1; 1965, c. 925, s. 1; 1979, c. 815, s. 1; 1998-202, s. 6 . G.S. 7B-2814: 1963, c. 910, s. 1; 1965, c. 925, s. 1; 1979, c. 815, s. 1; 1998-202, s. 6 . G.S. 7B-2815: 1963, c. 910, s. 1; 1965, c. 925, s. 1; 1979, c. 815, s. 1; 1998-202, s. 6 . G.S.

7B-2816: 1963, c. 910, s. 2; 1979, c. 815, s. 1; 1998-202, s. 6 . G.S. 7B-2817: 1963, c. 910, s. 3; 1979, c. 815, s. 1; 1998-202, s. 6 . G.S. 7B-2818: 1963, c. 910, s. 4; 1979, c. 815, s. 1; 1998-202, s. 6 . G.S. 7B-2819: 1963, c. 910, s. 5; 1979, c. 815, s. 1; 1998-202, s. 6 . G.S. 7B-282020: 1963, c. 910, s. 6; 1979, c. 815, s. 1; 1998-202, s. 6 . G.S. 7B-2821: 1965, c. 925, s. 2; 1971, c. 1231, s. 2; 1977, c. 552; 1979, c. 815, s. 1; 1998-202, s. 6 . G.S. 7B-2822: 1979, c. 815, s. 1; 1998-202, s. 6 . G.S. 7B-2823: 1979, c. 815, s. 1; 1998-202, s. 6 . G.S. 7B-2824: 1979, c. 815, s. 1; 1998-202, s. 6 . G.S. 7B-2825: 1979, c. 815, s. 1; 1998-202, s. 6 . G.S. 7B-2826: 1979, c. 815, s. 1; 1998-202, s. 6 . G.S. 7B-2827: 1979, c. 815, s. 1; 1998-202, s. 6

DIVISION 03.
JUVENILE RECORDS

ARTICLE 29
RECORDS AND SOCIAL REPORTS OF CASES OF ABUSE, NEGLECT, AND DEPENDENCY

§ 7B-2900. Definitions

The definitions of G.S. 7B-101 and G.S. 7B-1501 apply to this Subchapter.

History.
1998-202, s. 6

§ 7B-2901. Confidentiality of records

(a) The clerk shall maintain a complete record of all juvenile cases filed in the clerk's office alleging abuse, neglect, or dependency. The records shall be withheld from public inspection and, except as provided in this subsection, may be examined only by order of the court. The record shall include the summons, petition, custody order, court order, written motions, the electronic or mechanical recording of the hearing, and other papers filed in the proceeding. The recording of the hearing shall be reduced to a written transcript only when notice of appeal has been timely given. After the time for appeal has expired with no appeal having been filed, the recording of the hearing may be erased or destroyed upon the written order of the court or in accordance with a retention schedule approved by the Director of the Administrative Office of the Courts and the Department of Natural and Cultural Resources under G.S. 121-5(c).

The following persons may examine the juvenile's record maintained pursuant to this subsection and obtain copies of written parts of the record without an order of the court:

(1) The person named in the petition as the juvenile;

(2) The guardian ad litem;

(3) The county department of social services; and

(4) The juvenile's parent, guardian, or custodian, or the attorney for the juvenile or the juvenile's parent, guardian, or custodian.

(b) The Director of the Department of Social Services shall maintain a record of the cases of juveniles under protective custody by the Department or under placement by the court, which shall include family background information; reports of social, medical, psychiatric, or psychological information concerning a juvenile or the juvenile's family; interviews with the juvenile's family; or other information which the court finds should be protected from public inspection in the best interests of the juvenile. The records maintained pursuant to this subsection may be examined only in the following circumstances:

(1) The juvenile's guardian ad litem or the juvenile, including a juvenile who has reached age 18 or been emancipated, is authorized to review the record and request all or part of the record unless prohibited by federal law. The department shall provide electronic or written copies of the requested information within a reasonable period of time.

(2) A district or superior court judge of this State presiding over a civil matter in which the department is not a party may order the department to release confidential information, after providing the department with reasonable notice and an opportunity to be heard and then determining that the information is relevant and necessary to the trial of the matter before the court and unavailable from any other source. This subsection shall not be construed to relieve any court of its duty to conduct hearings and make findings required under relevant federal law before ordering the release of any private medical or mental health information or records related to substance abuse or HIV status or treatment. The department may surrender the requested records to the court, for in camera review, if surrender is necessary to make the required determinations.

(3) A district or superior court judge of this State presiding over a criminal or delinquency matter shall conduct an in camera review before releasing to the defendant or juvenile any confidential records maintained by the department of social services, except those records the defendant or

519

juvenile is entitled to pursuant to subdivision (1) of this subsection.

(4) The department may disclose confidential information to a parent, guardian, custodian, or caretaker in accordance with G.S. 7B-700.

(c) In the case of a child victim, the court may order the sharing of information among such public agencies as the court deems necessary to reduce the trauma to the victim.

(d) The court's entire record of a proceeding involving consent for an abortion on an unemancipated minor under Article 1A, Part 2 of Chapter 90 of the General Statutes is not a matter of public record, shall be maintained separately from any juvenile record, shall be withheld from public inspection, and may be examined only by order of the court, by the unemancipated minor, or by the unemancipated minor's attorney or guardian ad litem.

History.

1979, c. 815, s. 1; 1987, c. 297; 1994, Ex. Sess., c. 7, s. 1; 1995, c. 462, s. 4; c. 509, s. 5; 1997-459, s. 2; 1998-202, s. 6; 2001-208, s. 10; 2001-487, s. 101; 2009-311, s. 18; 2017-158, s. 23; 2021-100, s. 18

§ 7B-2902. Disclosure in child fatality or near fatality cases

(a) The following definitions apply in this section:

(1) **Child fatality.** -- The death of a child from suspected abuse, neglect, or maltreatment.

(2) **Findings and information.** -- A written summary, as allowed by subsections (c) through (f) of this section, of actions taken or services rendered by a public agency following receipt of information that a child might be in need of protection. The written summary shall include any of the following information the agency is able to provide:

a. The dates, outcomes, and results of any actions taken or services rendered.

b. The results of any review by the State Child Fatality Prevention Team, a local child fatality prevention team, a local community child protection team, the Child Fatality Task Force, or any public agency.

c. Confirmation of the receipt of all reports, accepted or not accepted by the county department of social services, for investigation of suspected child abuse, neglect, or maltreatment, including confirmation that investigations were conducted, the results of the investigations, a description of the conduct of the most recent investigation and the services rendered, and a

statement of basis for the department's decision.

(3) **Near fatality.** -- A case in which a physician determines that a child is in serious or critical condition as the result of sickness or injury caused by suspected abuse, neglect, or maltreatment.

(4) **Public agency.** -- Any agency of State government or its subdivisions as defined in G.S. 132-1(a).

(b) Notwithstanding any other provision of law and subject to the provisions of subsections (c) through (f) of this section, a public agency shall disclose to the public, upon request, the findings and information related to a child fatality or near fatality if:

(1) A person is criminally charged with having caused the child fatality or near fatality; or

(2) The district attorney has certified that a person would be charged with having caused the child fatality or near fatality but for that person's prior death.

(c) Nothing herein shall be deemed to authorize access to the confidential records in the custody of a public agency, or the disclosure to the public of the substance or content of any psychiatric, psychological, or therapeutic evaluations or like materials or information pertaining to the child or the child's family unless directly related to the cause of the child fatality or near fatality, or the disclosure of information that would reveal the identities of persons who provided information related to the suspected abuse, neglect, or maltreatment of the child.

(d) Within five working days from the receipt of a request for findings and information related to a child fatality or near fatality, a public agency shall consult with the appropriate district attorney and provide the findings and information unless the agency has a reasonable belief that release of the information:

(1) Is not authorized by subsections (a) and (b) of this section;

(2) Is likely to cause mental or physical harm or danger to a minor child residing in the deceased or injured child's household;

(3) Is likely to jeopardize the State's ability to prosecute the defendant;

(4) Is likely to jeopardize the defendant's right to a fair trial;

(5) Is likely to undermine an ongoing or future criminal investigation; or

(6) Is not authorized by federal law and regulations.

(e) Any person whose request is denied may apply to the appropriate superior court for an order compelling disclosure of the findings and information of the public agency. The application shall set forth, with reasonable particularity, factors supporting the application. The superior court shall have jurisdiction to issue such orders. Actions brought pursuant to this section shall be set down for immediate hearing, and subsequent proceedings in such actions shall be accorded priority by the appellate courts. After the court has reviewed the specific findings and information, in camera, the court shall issue an order compelling disclosure unless the court finds that one or more of the circumstances in subsection (d) of this section exist.

(f) Access to criminal investigative reports and criminal intelligence information of public law enforcement agencies and confidential information in the possession of the State Child Fatality Prevention Team, the local teams, and the Child Fatality Task Force, shall be governed by G.S. 132-1.4 and G.S. 7B-1413 respectively. Nothing herein shall be deemed to require the disclosure or release of any information in the possession of a district attorney.

(g) Any public agency or its employees acting in good faith in disclosing or declining to disclose information pursuant to this section shall be immune from any criminal or civil liability that might otherwise be incurred or imposed for such action.

(h) Nothing herein shall be deemed to narrow or limit the definition of "public records" as set forth in G.S. 132-1(a).

History.
1997-459, s. 1; 1998-202, s. 6

ARTICLE 30
JUVENILE RECORDS AND SOCIAL REPORTS OF DELINQUENCY AND UNDISCIPLINED CASES

§ 7B-3000. Juvenile court records

(a) The clerk shall maintain a complete record of all juvenile cases filed in the clerk's office to be known as the juvenile record. The record shall include the summons and petition, any secure or nonsecure custody order, any electronic or mechanical recording of hearings, and any written motions, orders, or papers filed in the proceeding.

(b) All juvenile records shall be withheld from public inspection and, except as provided in this subsection, may be examined only by order of the court. Except as provided in subsection (c) of this section, the following persons may examine the juvenile's record and obtain copies of written parts of the record without an order of the court:

    (1) The juvenile or the juvenile's attorney;

    (2) The juvenile's parent, guardian, or custodian, or the authorized representative of the juvenile's parent, guardian, or custodian;

    (3) The prosecutor;

    (4) Court counselors; and

    (5) Probation officers in the Section of Community Corrections of the Division of Adult Correction and Juvenile Justice of the Department of Public Safety, as provided in subsection (e1) of this section and in G.S. 15A-1341(e).

Except as provided in subsection (c) of this section, the prosecutor may, in the prosecutor's discretion, share information obtained from a juvenile's record with magistrates and law enforcement officers sworn in this State, but may not allow a magistrate or law enforcement officer to photocopy any part of the record. A prosecutor shall share information with a victim only as provided in Article 20A of this Chapter and shall not allow a victim to examine or photocopy any part of the record.

(c) The court may direct the clerk to "seal" any portion of a juvenile's record. The clerk shall secure any sealed portion of a juvenile's record in an envelope clearly marked "SEALED: MAY BE EXAMINED ONLY BY ORDER OF THE COURT", or with similar notice, and shall permit examination or copying of sealed portions of a juvenile's record only pursuant to a court order specifically authorizing inspection or copying.

(d) Any portion of a juvenile's record consisting of an electronic or mechanical recording of a hearing shall be transcribed only when notice of appeal has been timely given and shall be copied electronically or mechanically, only by order of the court. After the time for appeal has expired with no appeal having been filed, the court may enter a written order directing the clerk to destroy the recording of the hearing, or the recording may be destroyed in accordance with a retention schedule approved by the Director of the Administrative Office of the Courts and the Department of Natural and Cultural Resources under G.S. 121-5(c).

(e) Notwithstanding any other provision of law, if the defendant in a criminal proceeding involving a Class A1 misdemeanor or a felony was less than 21 years of age at the time of the offense, information obtained pursuant to subsection (b) of this section regarding the juvenile's record of an adjudication of delinquency for an offense that would be a Class A1 misdemeanor or a felony if committed by an adult, where the adjudication occurred after the defendant reached 13 years of age, may be used by law enforcement, the magistrate, the courts, and the prosecutor for pretrial release, plea negotiating decisions, and plea acceptance decisions. Information obtained regarding any juvenile record shall remain confidential and shall not be placed in any public record.

(e1) When a person is subject to probation supervision under Article 82 of Chapter 15A of the General Statutes, for an offense that was committed while the person was less than 25 years of age, that person's juvenile record of an adjudication of delinquency for an offense that would be a felony if committed by an adult may be examined without a court order by the probation officer in the Section of Community Corrections of the Division of Adult Correction and Juvenile Justice assigned to supervise the person for the purpose of assessing risk related to supervision.

Each judicial district manager in the Section of Community Corrections of the Division of Adult Correction and Juvenile Justice shall designate a staff person in each county to obtain from the clerk, at the request of the probation officer assigned to supervise the person, any juvenile records authorized to be examined under this subsection. The judicial district manager shall inform the clerk in each county, in writing, of the designated staff person in the county. The designated staff person shall transfer any juvenile records obtained to the probation officer assigned to supervise the person.

Any copies of juvenile records obtained pursuant to this subsection shall continue to be withheld from public inspection and shall not become part of the public record in any criminal proceeding. Any copies of juvenile records shall be destroyed within 30 days of termination of the person's period of probation supervision. Any other information in the Section of Community Corrections of the Division of Adult Correction and Juvenile Justice records, relating to a person's juvenile record, shall remain confidential and shall be maintained or destroyed pursuant to guidelines established by the Department of Natural and Cultural Resources for the maintenance and destruction of Section of Community Corrections of the Division of Adult Correction and Juvenile Justice records.

(f) The juvenile's record of an adjudication of delinquency for an offense that would be a Class A, B1, B2, C, D, or E felony if committed by an adult may be used in a subsequent criminal proceeding against the juvenile either under G.S. 8C-1, Rule 404(b), or to prove an aggravating factor at sentencing under G.S. 15A-1340.4(a), 15A-1340.16(d), or 15A-2000(e). The record may be so used only by order of the court in the subsequent criminal proceeding, upon motion of the prosecutor, after an in camera hearing to determine whether the record in question is admissible.

(g) Except as provided in subsection (d) of this section, a juvenile's record shall be destroyed only as authorized by G.S. 7B-3200 or by rules adopted by the Administrative Office of the Courts.

History.
1979, c. 815, s. 1; 1987, c. 297; 1994, Ex. Sess., c. 7, s. 1; 1995, c. 462, s. 4; c. 509, s. 5; 1997-459, s. 2; 1998-202, s. 6; 2000-137, s. 3; 2002-159, s. 26; 2009-372, s. 1; 2009-545, s. 2; 2011-145, s. 19.1(h), (k); 2011-277, s. 1; 2012-83, s. 17; 2015-241, s. 14.30(s); 2017-158, s. 24; 2017-186, s. 2(m); 2019-216, s. 12

§ 7B-3001. Other records relating to juveniles

(a) The chief court counselor shall maintain a record of all cases of juveniles under supervision of juvenile court counselors, to be known as the juvenile court counselor's record. The juvenile court counselor's record shall include the juvenile's delinquency record; consultations with law enforcement that did not result in the filing of a complaint; family background information; reports of social, medical, psychiatric, or psychological information concerning a juvenile or the juvenile's family; probation reports; interviews with the juvenile's family; the results of the gang assessment; or other information the court finds should be protected from public inspection in the best interests of the juvenile.

(a1) To assist at the time of investigation of an incident that could result in the filing of a complaint, upon request, a juvenile court counselor shall share with a law enforcement officer sworn in this State information from the juvenile court counselor's record related to a juvenile's delinquency record or prior consultations with law enforcement. A law enforcement officer may not obtain copies of any part of the record, and all information shared pursuant to this subsection shall be withheld from public inspection as provided in subsection (b) of this section.

(b) Unless jurisdiction of the juvenile has been transferred to superior court, all law enforcement records and files concerning a juvenile shall be kept separate from the records and files of adults and shall be withheld from public inspection. The following persons may examine and obtain copies of law enforcement records and files concerning a juvenile without an order of the court:

(1) The juvenile or the juvenile's attorney;

(2) The juvenile's parent, guardian, custodian, or the authorized representative of the juvenile's parent, guardian, or custodian;

(3) The prosecutor;

(4) Juvenile court counselors; and

(5) Law enforcement officers sworn in this State.

Otherwise, the records and files may be examined or copied only by order of the court.

(c) All records and files maintained by the Division pursuant to this Chapter shall be withheld from public inspection. The following persons may examine and obtain copies of the Division records and files concerning a juvenile without an order of the court:

(1) The juvenile and the juvenile's attorney;

(2) The juvenile's parent, guardian, custodian, or the authorized representative of the juvenile's parent, guardian, or custodian;

(3) Professionals in the agency who are directly involved in the juvenile's case; and

(4) Juvenile court counselors.

Otherwise, the records and files may be examined or copied only by order of the court. The court may inspect and order the release of records maintained by the Division.

(d) When the Section of Community Corrections of the Division of Adult Correction and Juvenile Justice of the Department of Public Safety is authorized to access a juvenile record pursuant to G.S. 7B-3000(e1), the Division may, at the request of the Section of Community Corrections of the Division of Adult Correction and Juvenile Justice, notify the Section of Community Corrections of the Division of Adult Correction and Juvenile Justice that there is a juvenile record of an adjudication of delinquency for an offense that would be a felony if committed by an adult for a person subject to probation supervision under Article 82 of Chapter 15A of the General Statutes and may notify the Section of Community Corrections of the Division of Adult Correction and Juvenile Justice of the county or counties where the adjudication of delinquency occurred.

History.
1979, c. 815, s. 1; 1987, c. 297; 1994, Ex. Sess., c. 7, s. 1; 1995, c. 462, s. 4; c. 509, s. 5; 1997-459, s. 2; 1998-202, s. 6; 2000-137, s. 3; 2001-490, s. 2.32; 2009-372, s. 2; 2009-545, s. 3; 2011-145, s. 19.1(h), (k), (l); 2017-57, s. 16D.4(x), (ii); 2017-186, s. 2(n); 2017-197, s. 5.4; 2018-142, s. 23(b)

ARTICLE 31
DISCLOSURE OF JUVENILE INFORMATION

§ 7B-3100. Disclosure of information about juveniles

(a) The Division, after consultation with the Conference of Chief District Court Judges, shall adopt rules designating certain local agencies that are authorized to share information concerning juveniles in accordance with the provisions of this section. Agencies so designated shall share with one another, upon request and to the extent permitted by federal law and regulations, information that is in their possession that is relevant to (i) any assessment of a report of child abuse, neglect, or dependency or the provision or arrangement of protective services in a child abuse, neglect, or dependency case by a local department of social services pursuant to the authority granted under Chapter 7B of the General Statutes, (ii) any case in which a petition is filed alleging that a juvenile is abused, neglected, dependent, undisciplined, or delinquent, or (iii) any case in which a vulnerable juvenile is receiving juvenile consultation services. Agencies shall continue to share information until (i) the protective services case is closed by the local department of social services, (ii) if a petition is filed, until the juvenile is no longer subject to the jurisdiction of juvenile court, or (iii) if a vulnerable juvenile is receiving juvenile consultation services, until the juvenile consultation is closed. Agencies that may be designated as "agencies authorized to share information" include local mental health facilities, local health departments, local departments of social services, local law enforcement agencies, local school administrative units, the district's district attorney's office, the Juvenile Justice Section of the Division of Adult Correction and Juvenile Justice of the Department of Public Safety, and the Office of Guardian ad Litem Services of the Administrative Office of the Courts, and, pursuant to the provisions of G.S. 7B-3000(e1), the Section of Community Corrections of the Division of Adult Correction and Juvenile Justice of the Department of Public Safety. Any information shared among agencies pursuant to this section shall remain confidential, shall be withheld from public inspection, and shall be used only for the protection of the juvenile and others or to improve the educational opportunities of the juvenile, and shall be released in accordance with the provisions of the Family Educational and Privacy Rights Act as set forth in 20 U.S.C. § 1232g. Nothing in this section or any other provision of law shall preclude any other necessary sharing of information among agencies. Nothing herein shall be deemed to require the disclosure or release of any information in the possession of a district attorney.

(b) Disclosure of information concerning any juvenile under investigation, alleged to be within the jurisdiction of the court, or receiving juvenile consultation services that would reveal the identity of that juvenile is prohibited except that publication of pictures of runaways is permitted with the permission of the parents and except as provided in Article 20A of this Chapter and G.S. 7B-3102.

(c) The juvenile's guardian ad litem attorney advocate appointed pursuant to G.S. 7B-601 may share confidential information about the juvenile with the juvenile's attorney appointed or retained pursuant to G.S. 7B-2000.

History.

1979, c. 815, s. 1; 1987, c. 297; 1994, Ex. Sess., c. 7, s. 1; 1995, c. 462, s. 4; c. 509, s. 5; 1997-459, s. 2; 1998-202, s. 6; 2000-137, s. 3; 2006-205, s. 2; 2007-458, s. 4; 2009-372, s. 3; 2011-145, s. 19.1(h), (k), (l); 2017-186, s. 2(o); 2019-33, s. 16; 2019-216, s. 13; 2021-123, s. 5(f)

§ 7B-3101. Notification of schools when juveniles are alleged or found to be delinquent

(a) Notwithstanding G.S. 7B-3000, the juvenile court counselor shall deliver verbal and written notification of any of the following actions to the principal of the school that the juvenile attends:

(1) A petition is filed under G.S. 7B-1802 that alleges delinquency for an offense that would be a felony if committed by an adult.

(2) The court transfers jurisdiction over a juvenile to the superior court under G.S. 7B-2200.5 or G.S. 7B-2200.

(3) The court dismisses under G.S. 7B-2411 the petition that alleges delinquency for an offense that would be a felony if committed by an adult.

(4) The court issues a dispositional order under Article 25 of Chapter 7B of the General Statutes including, but not limited to, an order of probation that requires school attendance, concerning a juvenile alleged or found delinquent for an offense that would be a felony if committed by an adult.

(5) The court modifies or vacates any order or disposition under G.S. 7B-2600 concerning a juvenile alleged or found delinquent for an offense that would be a felony if committed by an adult.

Notification of the school principal in person or by telephone shall be made before the beginning of the next school day. Delivery shall be made as soon as practicable but at least within five days of the action. Delivery shall be made in person or by certified mail. Notification that a petition has been filed shall describe the nature of the offense. Notification of a dispositional order, a modified or vacated order, or a transfer to superior court shall describe the court's action and any applicable disposition requirements. As used in this subsection, the term "offense" does not include any offense under Chapter 20 of the General Statutes.

(b) If the principal of the school the juvenile attends returns any notification as required by G.S. 115C-404, and if the juvenile court counselor learns that the juvenile is transferring to another school, the juvenile court counselor shall deliver the notification to the principal of the school to which the juvenile is transferring. Delivery shall be made as soon as practicable and shall be made in person or by certified mail.

(c) Principals shall handle any notification delivered under this section in accordance with G.S. 115C-404.

(d) For the purpose of this section, "school" means any public or private school in the State that is authorized under Chapter 115C of the General Statutes.

History.

1997-443, s. 8.29(e); 1998-202, s. 6; 2017-57, s. 16D.4 (l); 2018-142, s. 23(b); 2019-177, s. 2

§ 7B-3102. Disclosure of information about juveniles who escape

(a) Notwithstanding G.S. 7B-2102(d) or any other law to the contrary, within 24 hours of the time a juvenile escapes from custody the Division shall release to the public the juvenile's first name, last initial, and photograph; the name and location of the institution from which the juvenile escaped, or if the juvenile's escape was not from an institution, the circumstances and location of the escape; and if deemed appropriate a statement, based on the juvenile's record, of the level of concern of the Division as to the juvenile's threat to self or to others, if the juvenile escapes from a detention facility, secure custody, or a youth development center and the juvenile has been adjudicated delinquent. The determination of the level of threat posed by a juvenile who escapes from custody shall be made by the Deputy Commissioner of Juvenile Justice or the Deputy Commissioner's designee.

(b) When a juvenile escapes from a detention facility or secure custody, the Division may release to the public within 24 hours the juvenile's first name, last initial, and photograph; the name and location of the institution from which the juvenile escaped, or if the juvenile's escape was not from an institution, the circumstances and location of the escape; and a statement, based on the juvenile's record, of the level of concern of the Division as to the juvenile's threat to self or to others if both of the following apply:

(1) The juvenile is alleged to have committed an offense that would be a felony if committed by an adult.

(2) The Division determines, based on the juvenile's record, that the juvenile presents a danger to self or others.

(c) If a juvenile subject to subsection (a) or (b) of this section is returned to custody before the disclosure required or permitted is made, the Division shall not make the disclosure.

(d) The Division shall maintain a photograph of every juvenile in its custody.

(e) Before information is released to the public under this section, the Division shall make a reasonable effort to notify a parent, legal guardian, or custodian of the juvenile, and shall also make a reasonable effort to provide notification to the victim in accordance with G.S. 7B-2055.

History.
2007-458, s. 2; 2008-169, s. 1; 2011-145, s. 19.1 (*l*); 2015-41, s. 1; 2019-216, s. 14

ARTICLE 32
EXPUNCTION OF JUVENILE RECORDS

§ 7B-3200. Expunction of records of juveniles alleged or adjudicated delinquent and undisciplined

(a) Any person who has attained the age of 18 years may file a petition in the court where the person was adjudicated undisciplined for expunction of all records of that adjudication.

(b) Any person who has attained the age of 18 years may file a petition in the court where the person was adjudicated delinquent for expunction of all records of that adjudication provided:

(1) The offense for which the person was adjudicated would have been a crime other than a Class A, B1, B2, C, D, or E felony if committed by an adult.

(1a) The person has been released from juvenile court jurisdiction.

(2) At least 18 months have elapsed since the person was released from juvenile court jurisdiction, and the person has not subsequently been adjudicated delinquent or convicted as an adult of any felony or misdemeanor other than a traffic violation under the laws of the United States or the laws of this State or any other state.

The requirements set forth in subdivision (2) of this subsection shall not apply to a person whose participation in the offense was a result of having been a victim of human trafficking as defined in G.S. 14-43.10 or a victim of a severe form of trafficking in persons as defined in the federal Trafficking Victims Protection Act, 22 U.S.C. § 7102.

Records relating to an adjudication for an offense that would be a Class A, B1, B2, C, D, or E felony if committed by an adult shall not be expunged.

(c) The petition shall contain, but not be limited to, all of the following:

(1) An affidavit by the petitioner that includes all of the following statements:

a. That the petitioner has been of good behavior since the adjudication.

b. If the petition is based on a delinquency adjudication, that the petitioner has been released from juvenile court jurisdiction and has not subsequently been adjudicated delinquent or convicted as an adult of any felony or misdemeanor other than a traffic violation under the laws of the United States, or the laws of this State or any other state.

c. If the petitioner is not subject to the requirements set forth in subdivision (2) of subsection (b) of this section, the affidavit shall state that the petitioner was adjudicated delinquent for an offense the petitioner participated in as a result of having been a victim of human trafficking as defined in G.S. 14-43.10 or a victim of a severe form of trafficking in persons as defined in the federal Trafficking Victims Protection Act, 22 U.S.C. § 7102.

(2) Verified affidavits of two persons, who are not related to the petitioner or to each other by blood or marriage, that they know the character and reputation of the petitioner in the community in which the petitioner lives and that the petitioner's character and reputation are good.

(3) A statement that the petition is a motion in the cause in the case wherein the petitioner was adjudicated delinquent or undisciplined.

The petition shall be served upon the district attorney in the district wherein adjudication occurred. The district attorney shall have 10 days thereafter in which to file any objection thereto and shall be duly notified as to the date of the hearing on the petition.

(d) If the court, after hearing, finds that the petitioner satisfies the conditions set out in subsections (a) or (b) of this section, the court shall order and direct the clerk and all law enforcement agencies to expunge their records of the adjudication including all references to arrests, complaints, referrals, petitions, and orders.

(e) The clerk shall forward a certified copy of the order to the sheriff, chief of police, or other law enforcement agency.

(f) Records of a juvenile adjudicated delinquent or undisciplined being maintained by the chief court counselor, an intake counselor, or a juvenile court counselor shall be retained or disposed of as provided by the Division, except that no records shall be destroyed before the juvenile reaches the age of 18 or 18 months have elapsed since the person was released from juvenile court jurisdiction, whichever occurs last.

(g) Records of a juvenile adjudicated delinquent or undisciplined being maintained by personnel at a residential facility operated by the Division, shall be retained or disposed of as provided by the Division, except that no records shall be destroyed before the juvenile reaches the age of 18 or 18 months have elapsed since the person was released from juvenile court jurisdiction, whichever occurs last.

(h) Any person who was alleged to be delinquent as a juvenile and has attained the age of 16 years, or was alleged to be undisciplined as a juvenile and has attained the age of 18 years, may file a petition in the court in which the person was alleged to be delinquent or undisciplined, for expunction of all juvenile records of the juvenile having been alleged to be delinquent or undisciplined if the court dismissed the juvenile petition without an adjudication that the juvenile was delinquent or undisciplined. The petition shall be served on the chief court counselor in the district where the juvenile petition was filed. The chief court counselor shall have 10 days thereafter in which to file a written objection in the court. If no objection is filed, the court may grant the petition without a hearing. If an objection is filed or the court so directs, a hearing shall be scheduled and the chief court counselor shall be notified as to the date of the hearing. If the court finds at the hearing that the petitioner satisfies the conditions specified herein, the court shall order the clerk and the appropriate law enforcement agencies to expunge their records of the allegations of delinquent or undisciplined acts including all references to arrests, complaints, referrals, juvenile petitions, and orders. The clerk shall forward a certified copy of the order of expunction to the sheriff, chief of police, or other appropriate law enforcement agency, and to the chief court counselor, and these specified officials shall immediately destroy all records relating to the allegations that the juvenile was delinquent or undisciplined.

(i) The clerk of superior court in each county in North Carolina shall, as soon as practicable after each term of court in the clerk's county, file with the Administrative Office of the Courts, the names of those persons granted an expunction under the provisions of this section, and the Administrative Office of the Courts shall maintain a confidential file containing the names of persons granted an expunction. The information contained in such file shall be disclosed only to judges of the General Court of Justice of North Carolina for the purpose of ascertaining whether any person charged with an offense has been previously granted an expunction.

History.
1979, c. 815, s. 1; 1989, c. 186; 1994, Ex. Sess., c. 7, s. 2; 1995, c. 509, s. 6; 1997-443, s. 11A.118(a); 1998-202, s. 6; 2000-137, s. 3; 2001-490, s. 2.33; 2011-145, s. 19.1 (*l*); 2019-158, s. 4(d)

§ 7B-3201. Effect of expunction

(a) Whenever a juvenile's record is expunged, with respect to the matter in which the record was expunged, the juvenile who is the subject of the record and the juvenile's parent may not be held thereafter under any provision of any laws to be guilty of perjury or otherwise giving a false statement by reason of the person's failure to recite or acknowledge such record or response to any inquiry made of the person for any purpose.

(b) Notwithstanding subsection (a) of this section, in any delinquency case if the juvenile is the defendant and chooses to testify or if the juvenile is not the defendant and is called as a witness, the juvenile may be ordered to testify with respect to whether the juvenile was adjudicated delinquent.

History.
1979, c. 815, s. 1; 1983 (Reg. Sess., 1984), c. 1037, s. 7; 1998-202, s. 6

§ 7B-3202. Notice of expunction

Upon expunction of a juvenile's record, the clerk shall send a written notice to the juvenile at the juvenile's last known address informing the juvenile that the record has been expunged and with respect to the matter involved, the juvenile may not be held thereafter under any provision of any laws to be guilty of perjury or otherwise giving a false statement by reason of the juvenile's failure to recite or acknowledge such record or response to any inquiry made of the juvenile for any purpose except that upon testifying in a delinquency proceeding, the juvenile may be required by a court to disclose that the juvenile was adjudicated delinquent.

History.
1979, c. 815, s. 1; 1983 (Reg. Sess., 1984), c. 1037, s. 8; 1998-202, s. 6

ARTICLE 33
COMPUTATION OF
RECIDIVISM RATES

N.C. Gen. Stat. § 7B-3300

Repealed by Session Laws 2005-276, s. 14.19(c), effective July 1, 2005.

DIVISION 04.
PARENTAL AUTHORITY; EMANCIPATION

ARTICLE 34
PARENTAL AUTHORITY OVER JUVENILES

§ 7B-3400. Juvenile under 18 subject to parents' control

Notwithstanding any other provision of law, any juvenile under 18 years of age, except as provided in G.S. 7B-3402 and G.S. 7B-3403, shall be subject to the supervision and control of the juvenile's parents.

History.
1969, c. 1080, s. 1; 1998-202, s. 6

§ 7B-3401. Definitions

The definitions of G.S. 7B-101 and G.S. 7B-1501 apply to this Subchapter.

History.
1998-202, s. 6

§ 7B-3402. Exceptions

This Article shall not apply to any juvenile under the age of 18 who is married or who is serving in the Armed Forces of the United States, or who has been emancipated.

History.
1969, c. 1080, s. 2; 1998-202, s. 6; 2011-183, s. 6

§ 7B-3403. No criminal liability created

This Article shall not be interpreted to place any criminal liability on a parent, guardian, or custodian for any act of the juvenile 16 years of age or older.

History.
1969, c. 1080, s. 3; 1998-202, s. 6

§ 7B-3404. Enforcement

The provisions of this Article may be enforced by the parent, guardian, custodian, or person who has assumed the status and obligation of a parent without being awarded legal custody of the juvenile by a court to the juvenile by filing a civil action in the district court of the county where the juvenile can be found or the county of the plaintiff's residence. Upon the institution of such action by a verified complaint, alleging that the defendant juvenile has left home or has left the place where the juvenile has been residing and refuses to return and comply with the direction and control of the plaintiff, the court may issue an order directing the juvenile personally to appear before the court at a specified time to be heard in answer to the allegations of the plaintiff and to comply with further orders of the court. Such orders shall be served by the sheriff upon the juvenile and upon any other person named as a party defendant in such action. At the time of the issuance of the order directing the juvenile to appear, the court may in the same order, or by separate order, order the sheriff to enter any house, building, structure, or conveyance for the purpose of searching for the juvenile and serving the order and for the purpose of taking custody of the person of the juvenile in order to bring the juvenile before the court. Any order issued at said hearing shall be treated as a mandatory injunction and shall remain in full force and effect until the juvenile reaches the age of 18, or until further orders of the court. Within 30 days after the hearing on the original order, the juvenile, or anyone acting in the juvenile's behalf, may file a verified answer to the complaint. Upon the filing of an answer by or on behalf of the juvenile, any district court judge holding court in the county or district court district as defined in G.S. 7A-133 where the action was instituted shall have jurisdiction to hear the matter, without a jury, and to make findings of fact, conclusions of law, and render judgment thereon. Appeals from the district court to the Court of Appeals shall be allowed as in civil actions generally. The district court issuing the original order or the district court hearing the matter after answer has been filed shall also have authority to order that any person named defendant in the order or judgment shall not harbor, keep, or allow the defendant juvenile to remain on the person's premises or in the person's home. Failure of any defendant to comply with the terms of said order or judgment shall be punishable as for contempt.

History.
1969, c. 1080, s. 4; 1987 (Reg. Sess., 1988), c. 1037, s. 108; 1991 (Reg. Sess., 1992), c. 1031, s. 1; 1998-202, s. 6

ARTICLE 35
EMANCIPATION

§ 7B-3500. Who may petition

Any juvenile who is 16 years of age or older and who has resided in the same county in North Carolina or on federal territory within the boundaries of North Carolina for six months next preceding the filing of the petition may petition the court in that county for a judicial decree of emancipation.

History.

1979, c. 815, s. 1; 1998-202, s. 6

§ 7B-3501. Petition

The petition shall be signed and verified by the petitioner and shall contain the following information:

(1) The full name of the petitioner and the petitioner's birth date, and state and county of birth;

(2) A certified copy of the petitioner's birth certificate;

(3) The name and last known address of the parent, guardian, or custodian;

(4) The petitioner's address and length of residence at that address;

(5) The petitioner's reasons for requesting emancipation; and

(6) The petitioner's plan for meeting the petitioner's needs and living expenses which plan may include a statement of employment and wages earned that is verified by the petitioner's employer.

History.

1979, c. 815, s. 1; 1998-202, s. 6

§ 7B-3502. Summons

A copy of the filed petition along with a summons shall be served upon the petitioner's parent, guardian, or custodian who shall be named as respondents. The summons shall include the time and place of the hearing and shall notify the respondents to file written answer within 30 days after service of the summons and petition. In the event that personal service cannot be obtained, service shall be in accordance with G.S. 1A-1, Rule 4(j).

History.

1979, c. 815, s. 1; 1998-202, s. 6

§ 7B-3503. Hearing

The court, sitting without a jury, shall permit all parties to present evidence and to cross-examine witnesses. The petitioner has the burden of showing by a preponderance of the evidence that emancipation is in the petitioner's best interests. Upon finding that reasonable cause exists, the court may order the juvenile to be examined by a psychiatrist, a licensed clinical psychologist, a physician, or any other expert to evaluate the juvenile's mental or physical condition. The court may continue the hearing and order investigation by a juvenile court counselor or by the county department of social services to substantiate allegations of the petitioner or respondents.

No husband-wife or physician-patient privilege shall be grounds for excluding any evidence in the hearing.

History.

1979, c. 815, s. 1; 1998-202, s. 6; 2001-490, s. 2.34

§ 7B-3504. Considerations for emancipation

In determining the best interests of the petitioner and the need for emancipation, the court shall review the following considerations:

(1) The parental need for the earnings of the petitioner;

(2) The petitioner's ability to function as an adult;

(3) The petitioner's need to contract as an adult or to marry;

(4) The employment status of the petitioner and the stability of the petitioner's living arrangements;

(5) The extent of family discord which may threaten reconciliation of the petitioner with the petitioner's family;

(6) The petitioner's rejection of parental supervision or support; and

(7) The quality of parental supervision or support.

History.

1979, c. 815, s. 1; 1998-202, s. 6

§ 7B-3505. Final decree of emancipation

After reviewing the considerations for emancipation, the court may enter a decree of emancipation if the court determines:

(1) That all parties are properly before the court or were duly served and failed to appear and that time for filing an answer has expired;

(2) That the petitioner has shown a proper and lawful plan for adequately providing for the petitioner's needs and living expenses;

(3) That the petitioner is knowingly seeking emancipation and fully understands the ramifications of the act; and

(4) That emancipation is in the best interests of the petitioner.

The decree shall set out the court's findings.

If the court determines that the criteria in subdivisions (1) through (4) are not met, the court shall order the proceeding dismissed.

History.

1979, c. 815, s. 1; 1998-202, s. 6

§ 7B-3506. Costs of court

The court may tax the costs of the proceeding to any party or may, for good cause, order the costs remitted.

The clerk may collect costs for furnishing to the petitioner a certificate of emancipation which shall recite the name of the petitioner and the fact of the petitioner's emancipation by court decree and shall have the seal of the clerk affixed thereon.

History.

1979, c. 815, s. 1; 1998-202, s. 6

§ 7B-3507. Legal effect of final decree

As of entry of the final decree of emancipation:

(1) The petitioner has the same right to make contracts and conveyances, to sue and to be sued, and to transact business as if the petitioner were an adult.

(2) The parent, guardian, or custodian is relieved of all legal duties and obligations owed to the petitioner and is divested of all rights with respect to the petitioner.

(3) The decree is irrevocable.

Notwithstanding any other provision of this section, a decree of emancipation shall not alter the application of G.S. 14-326.1 or the petitioner's right to inherit property by intestate succession.

History.

1979, c. 815, s. 1; 1998-202, s. 6

§ 7B-3508. Appeals

Any petitioner, parent, guardian, or custodian who is a party to a proceeding under this Article may appeal from any order of disposition to the Court of Appeals provided that notice of appeal is given in open court at the time of the hearing or in writing within 10 days after entry of the order. Entry of an order shall be treated in the same manner as entry of a judgment under G.S. 1A-1, Rule 58 of the North Carolina Rules of Civil Procedure. Pending disposition of an appeal, the court may enter a temporary order affecting the custody or placement of the petitioner as the court finds to be in the best interests of the petitioner or the State.

History.

1979, c. 815, s. 1; 1998-202, s. 6; 1999-309, s. 3

§ 7B-3509. Application of common law

A married juvenile is emancipated by this Article. All other common-law provisions for emancipation are superseded by this Article.

History.

1979, c. 815, s. 1; 1998-202, s. 6

ARTICLE 36
JUDICIAL CONSENT FOR EMERGENCY SURGICAL OR MEDICAL TREATMENT

§ 7B-3600. Judicial authorization of emergency treatment; procedure

A juvenile in need of emergency treatment under Article 1A of Chapter 90 of the General Statutes, whose physician is barred from rendering necessary treatment by reason of parental refusal to consent to treatment, may receive treatment with court authorization under the following procedure:

(1) The physician shall sign a written statement setting out:

a. The treatment to be rendered and the emergency need for treatment;

b. The refusal of the parent, guardian, custodian, or person who has assumed the status and obligation of a parent without being awarded legal custody of the juvenile by a court to consent to the treatment; and

c. The impossibility of contacting a second physician for a concurring opinion on the need for treatment in time to prevent immediate harm to the juvenile.

(2) Upon examining the physician's written statement prescribed in subdivision (1) of this section and finding:

a. That the statement is in accordance with this Article, and

b. That the proposed treatment is necessary to prevent immediate harm to the juvenile.

The court may issue a written authorization for the proposed treatment to be rendered.

(3) In acute emergencies in which time may not permit implementation of the written procedure set out in subdivisions (1) and (2) of this section, the court may authorize treatment in person or by telephone upon receiving the oral statement of a physician satisfying the requirements of subdivision (1) of this section and upon finding that the proposed treatment is necessary to prevent immediate harm to the juvenile.

(4) The court's authorization for treatment overriding parental refusal to consent should not be given without attempting to offer the parent an opportunity to state the reasons for refusal; however, failure of the court to hear the parent's objections shall not invalidate judicial authorization under this Article.

(5) The court's authorization for treatment under subdivisions (1) and (2) of this section shall be issued in duplicate. One copy shall be given to the treating physician and the other copy shall be attached to the physician's written statement and filed as a juvenile proceeding in the office of the clerk of court.

(6) The court's authorization for treatment under subdivision (3) of this section shall be reduced to writing as soon as possible, supported by the physician's written statement as prescribed in subdivision (1) of this section and shall be filed as prescribed in subdivision (5) of this section.

The court's authorization for treatment under this Article shall have the same effect as parental consent for treatment.

Following the court's authorization for treatment and after giving notice to the juvenile's parent, guardian, or custodian the court shall conduct a hearing in order to provide for payment for the treatment rendered. The court may order the parent or other responsible parties to pay the cost of treatment. If the court finds the parent is unable to pay the cost of treatment, the cost shall be a charge upon the county when so ordered.

This Article shall operate as a remedy in addition to the provisions in G.S. 7B-505.1 and G.S. 7B-903.1.

History.
1979, c. 815, s. 1; 1998-202, s. 6; 2017-161, s. 14

DIVISION 05.
PLACEMENT OF JUVENILES

ARTICLE 37
PLACING OR ADOPTION OF JUVENILE DELINQUENTS OR DEPENDENTS

§ 7B-3700. Consent required for bringing child into State for placement or adoption

(a) No person, agency, association, institution, or corporation shall bring or send into the State any child for the purpose of giving custody of the child to some person in the State or procuring adoption by some person in the State without first obtaining the written consent of the Department of Health and Human Services.

(b) The person with whom a child is placed for either of the purposes set out in subsection (a) of this section shall be responsible for the child's proper care and training. The Department of Health and Human Services or its agents shall have the same right of visitation and supervision of the child and the home in which it is placed as in the case of a child placed by the Department or its agents as long as the child shall remain within the State and until the child shall have reached the age of 18 years or shall have been legally adopted.

History.
1931, c. 226, s. 1; 1947, c. 609, s. 1; 1973, c. 476, s. 138; 1997-443, s. 11A.118(a); 1998-202, s. 6

§ 7B-3701. Bond required

The Social Services Commission may, in its discretion, require of a person, agency, association, institution, or corporation which brings or sends a child into the State with the written consent of the Department of Health and Human Services, as provided by G.S. 7B-3700, a continuing bond in a penal sum not in excess of one thousand dollars ($ 1,000) with such conditions as may be prescribed and such sureties as may be approved by the Department of Health and Human Services. Said bond shall be made in favor of and filed with the Department of Health and Human Services with the premium prepaid by the said person, agency, association, institution, or corporation desiring to place such child in the State.

History.
1931, c. 226, s. 2; 1947, c. 609, s. 2; 1969, c. 982; 1973, c. 476, s. 138; 1997-443, s. 11A.118(a); 1998-202, s. 6

§ 7B-3702. Consent required for removing child from State

No child shall be taken or sent out of the State for the purpose of placing the child in a foster home or in a child-caring institution without first obtaining the written consent of the Department of Health and Human Services. The foster home or child-caring institution in which the child is placed shall report to the Department of Health and Human Services at such times as the Department of Health and Human Services may direct as to the location and well-being of such child until the child shall have reached the age of 18 years or shall have been legally adopted.

History.
1931, c. 226, s. 3; 1947, c. 609, s. 3; 1973, c. 476, s. 138; 1997-443, s. 11A.118(a); 1998-202, s. 6

§ 7B-3703. Violation of Article a misdemeanor

Every person acting for himself or for an agency who violates any of the provisions of this Article or who shall intentionally make any false statements to the Social Services Commission or the Secretary or an employee thereof acting for the Department of Health and Human Services in an official capacity in the placing or adoption of juvenile delinquents or dependents shall, upon conviction thereof, be guilty of a Class 2 misdemeanor.

History.
1931, c. 226, s. 7; 1957, c. 100, s. 1; 1973, c. 476, s. 138; 1993, c. 539, s. 823; 1994, Ex. Sess., c. 24, s. 14(c); 1997-443, s. 11A.118(a); 1998-202, s. 6

§ 7B-3704. Definitions

The term "Department" wherever used in this Article shall be construed to mean the Department of Health and Human Services. The term "Secretary" wherever used in this Article shall be construed to mean the Secretary of the Department of Health and Human Services.

History.
1931, c. 226, s. 8; 1957, c. 100, s. 1; 1973, c. 476, s. 138; 1997-443, s. 11A.118(a); 1998-202, s. 6

§ 7B-3705. Application of Article

None of the provisions of this Article shall apply when a child is brought into or sent into, or taken out of, or sent out of the State, by the guardian of the person of such child, or by a parent, stepparent, grandparent, uncle or aunt of such child, or by a brother, sister, half brother, or half sister of such child, if such brother, sister, half brother, or half sister is 18 years of age or older.

History.
1947, c. 609, s. 5; 1971, c. 1231, s. 1; 1998-202, s. 6

ARTICLE 38
INTERSTATE COMPACT ON THE PLACEMENT OF CHILDREN

§ 7B-3800. Adoption of Compact

The Interstate Compact on the Placement of Children is hereby enacted into law and entered into with all other jurisdictions legally joining therein in a form substantially as contained in this Article. It is the intent of the General Assembly that Article 37 of this Chapter shall govern interstate placements of children between North Carolina and any other jurisdictions not a party to this Compact. It is the intent of the General Assembly that Chapter 48 of the General Statutes shall govern the adoption of children within the boundaries of North Carolina.

Article I. Purpose and Policy.

It is the purpose and policy of the party states to cooperate with each other in the interstate placement of children to the end that:

(a) Each child requiring placement shall receive the maximum opportunity to be placed in a suitable environment and with persons or institutions having appropriate qualifications and facilities to provide a necessary and desirable degree and type of care.

(b) The appropriate authorities in a state where a child is to be placed may have full opportunity to ascertain the circumstances of the proposed placement, thereby promoting full compliance with applicable requirements for the protection of the child.

(c) The proper authorities of the state from which the placement is made may obtain the most complete information on the basis of which to evaluate a projected placement before it is made.

(d) Appropriate jurisdictional arrangements for the care of children will be promoted.

Article II. Definitions.

As used in this Compact:

(a) "Child" means a person who, by reason of minority, is legally subject to parental, guardianship or similar control.

(b) "Sending agency" means a party state officer or employee thereof; a subdivision of a party state, or officer or employee thereof; a court of a party state; a person, corporation, association, charitable agency or other entity which sends, brings, or causes to be sent or brought any child to another party state.

(c) "Receiving state" means the state to which a child is sent, brought, or caused to be sent or brought, whether by public authorities or private persons or agencies, and whether for placement with state or local public authorities of [or] for placement with private agencies or persons.

(d) "Placement" means the arrangement for the care of a child in a family free or boarding home or in a child-caring agency or institution but does not include any institution caring for the mentally ill, mentally defective, or epileptic or any institution primarily educational in character, and any hospital or other medical facility.

(e) "Appropriate public authorities" as used in Article III shall, with reference to this State, mean the Department of Health and Human Services and said agency shall receive and act with reference to notices required by Article III.

(f) "Appropriate authority in the receiving state" as used in paragraph (a) of Article V shall, with reference to this State, means the Secretary.

(g) "Executive head" as used in Article VII means the Governor.

Article III. Conditions for Placement.

(a) No sending agency shall send, bring, or cause to be sent or brought into any other party state any child for placement in foster care or as a preliminary to a possible adoption unless the sending agency shall comply with each and every requirement set forth in this Article and with the applicable laws of the receiving state governing the placement of children therein.

(b) Prior to sending, bringing, or causing any child to be sent or brought into a receiving state for placement in foster care or as a preliminary to a possible adoption, the sending agency shall furnish the appropriate public authorities in the receiving state written notice of the intention to send, bring, or place the child in the receiving state. The notice shall contain:

(1) The name, date, and place of birth of the child.

(2) The identity and address or addresses of the parents or legal guardian.

(3) The name and address of the person, agency or institution to or with which the sending agency proposes to send, bring, or place the child.

(4) A full statement of the reasons for such proposed action and evidence of the authority pursuant to which the placement is proposed to be made.

(c) Any public officer or agency in a receiving state which is in receipt of a notice pursuant to paragraph (b) of this Article may request of the sending agency, or any other appropriate officer or agency of or in the sending agency's state, and shall be entitled to receive therefrom, such supporting or additional information as it may deem necessary under the circumstances to carry out the purpose and policy of this Compact.

(d) The child shall not be sent, brought, or caused to be sent or brought into the receiving state until the appropriate public authorities in the receiving state shall notify the sending agency, in writing, to the effect that the proposed placement does not appear to be contrary to the interests of the child.

Article IV. Penalty for Illegal Placement.

The sending, bringing, or causing to be sent or brought into any receiving state of a child in violation of the terms of this Compact shall constitute a violation of the laws respecting the placement of children of both the state in which the sending agency is located or from which it sends or brings the child and of the receiving state. Such violation may be punished or subjected to penalty in either jurisdiction in accordance with its laws. In addition to liability for any such punishment or penalty, any such violation shall constitute full and sufficient grounds for the suspension or revocation of any license, permit, or other legal authorization held by the sending agency which empowers or allows it to place, or care for children.

Article V. Retention of Jurisdiction.

(a) The sending agency shall retain jurisdiction over the child sufficient to determine all matters in relation to the custody, supervision, care, treatment, and disposition of the child which it would have had if the child had remained in the sending agency's state, until the child is adopted, reaches majority, becomes self-supporting or is discharged with the concurrence of the appropriate authority in the receiving state. Such jurisdiction shall also include the power to effect or cause the return of the child or its transfer to another location and custody pursuant to law. The sending agency shall continue to have financial responsibility for support and maintenance of the child during the period of the placement. Nothing contained herein shall defeat a claim of jurisdiction by a receiving state sufficient to deal with an act of delinquency or crime committed therein.

(b) When the sending agency is a public agency, it may enter into an agreement with an authorized public or private agency in the receiving state providing for the performance of one or more services in respect of such case by the latter as agent for the sending agency.

(c) Nothing in this Compact shall be construed to prevent a private charitable agency authorized to place children in the receiving state from performing services or acting as agent in that state for a private charitable agency of the sending state; nor to prevent the agency in the receiving state from discharging financial responsibility for the support and maintenance of a child who has been placed on behalf of the sending agency without relieving the responsibility set forth in paragraph (a) hereof.

Article VI. Institutional Care of Delinquent Children.

A child adjudicated delinquent may be placed in an institution in another party jurisdiction pursuant to this Compact, but no such placement shall be made unless the child is given a court hearing on notice to the parent or guardian with opportunity to be heard, prior to the child's being sent to such other party jurisdiction for institutional care and the court finds that:

(1) Equivalent facilities for the child are not available in the sending agency's jurisdiction; and

(2) Institutional care in the other jurisdiction is in the best interests of the child and will not produce undue hardship.

Article VII. Compact Administrator.

The executive head of each jurisdiction party to this Compact shall designate an officer who shall be general coordinator of activities under this Compact in the officer's jurisdiction and who, acting jointly with like officers of other party jurisdictions, shall have power to promulgate rules and regulations to carry out more effectively the terms and provisions of this Compact.

Article VIII. Limitations.

This Compact shall not apply to: (a) the sending or bringing of a child into a receiving state by the child's parent, stepparent, grandparent, adult brother or sister, adult uncle or aunt, or the child's guardian and leaving the child with any such relative or nonagency guardian in the receiving state. (b) Any placement, sending or bringing of a child into a receiving state pursuant to any other interstate compact to which both the state from which the child is sent or brought and the receiving state are party, or to any other agreement between said states which has the force of law.

Article IX. Enactment and Withdrawal.

This Compact shall be open to joinder by any state, territory or possession of the United States, the District of Columbia, the Commonwealth of Puerto Rico, and, with the consent of Congress, the government of Canada or any province thereof. It shall become effective with respect to any such jurisdiction when such jurisdiction has enacted the same into law. Withdrawal from this Compact shall be by the enactment of a statute repealing the same, but shall not take effect until two years after the effective date of such statute and until written notice of the withdrawal has been given by the withdrawing state to the governor of each other party jurisdiction. Withdrawal of a party state shall not affect the rights, duties, and obligations under this Compact of any sending agency therein with respect to a placement made prior to the effective date of withdrawal.

Article X. Construction and Severability.

The provisions of this Compact shall be liberally construed to effectuate the purposes thereof. The provisions of this Compact shall be severable and if any phrase, clause, sentence, or provision of this Compact is declared to be contrary to the constitution of any party state or of the United States or the applicability thereof to any government, agency, person, or circumstance is held invalid, the validity of the remainder of this Compact and the applicability thereof to any government, agency, person, or circumstance shall not be affected thereby. If this Compact shall be held contrary to the constitution of any state party thereto, the Compact shall remain in full force and effect as to the remaining states and in full force and effect as to the state affected as to all severable matters.

History.
1971, c. 453, s. 1; 1973, c. 476, s. 138; 1983, c. 454, s. 8; 1997-443, s. 11A.118(a); 1998-202, s. 6; 1999-423, s. 3

§ 7B-3801. Financial responsibility under Compact

Financial responsibility for any child placed pursuant to the provisions of the Interstate Compact on the Placement of Children shall be determined in accordance with the provisions of Article V thereof in the first instance. However, in the event of partial or complete default of performance thereunder, the provisions of any other state laws fixing responsibility for the support of children also may be invoked.

History.
1971, c. 453, s. 2; 1998-202, s. 6

§ 7B-3802. Agreements under Compact

The officers and agencies of this State and its subdivisions having authority to place children are hereby empowered to enter into agreements with appropriate officers or agencies of or in other party states pursuant to paragraph (b) of Article V of the Interstate Compact on the Placement of Children. Any such agreement which contains a financial commitment or imposes a financial obligation on this State or subdivision or agency thereof shall not be binding unless it has the approval in writing of the Secretary of the Department of Health and Human Services in the case of the State and of the county director of social services in the case of a county or other subdivision of the State.

History.
1971, c. 453, s. 2; 1973, c. 476, s. 138; 1997-443, s. 11A.118(a); 1998-202, s. 6

§ 7B-3803. Visitation, inspection or supervision

Any requirements for visitation, inspection or supervision of children, homes, institutions or other agencies in another party state which may apply under the laws of this State shall be deemed to be met if performed pursuant to an agreement entered into by appropriate officers or agencies of this State or a subdivision thereof as contemplated by paragraph (b) of Article V of the Interstate Compact on the Placement of Children.

History.
1971, c. 453, s. 2; 1998-202, s. 6

§ 7B-3804. Compact to govern between party states

The provisions of Article 37 of this Chapter shall not apply to placements made pursuant to the Interstate Compact on the Placement of Children.

History.
1971, c. 453, s. 2; 1998-202, s. 6

§ 7B-3805. Placement of delinquents

Any court having jurisdiction to place delinquent children may place such a child in an institution or in another state pursuant to Article VI of the Interstate Compact on the Placement of Children and shall retain jurisdiction as provided in Article V thereof.

History.
1971, c. 453, s. 2; 1998-202, s. 6

§ 7B-3806. Compact Administrator

The Governor is hereby authorized to appoint a Compact Administrator in accordance with the terms of said Article VII.

History.
1971, c. 453, s. 2; 1998-202, s. 6

§ 7B-3807. (Repealed effective October 1, 2021) Adoption of the Interstate Compact on the Placement of Children regulations

History.
2019-172, s. 11; repealed by Session Laws 2021-100, s. 19, effective October 1, 2021

§ 7B-3808. Action for Interstate Compact administrator to forward a request

The Interstate Compact on the Placement of Children office at the Department of Health and Human Services has the authority to request supporting or additional information necessary to carry out the purpose and policy of the compact and to require assurance that the placement meets all applicable North Carolina placement statutes. Any sending agency that intends to place a child into and out of North Carolina shall submit a complete request to the Interstate Compact on the Placement of Children office at the Department of Health and Human Services. To be considered a complete request, the submission must comply with the Interstate Compact on the Placement of Children regulations and include any supporting additional information that the Department of Health and Human Services or the receiving state deems necessary. Unless otherwise provided by the Interstate Compact on the Placement of Children regulations, when the Department of Health and Human Services receives an incomplete request, the Department of Health and Human Services shall provide either the sending agency in North Carolina or the receiving state with written notice of the specific information needed to process the request and shall allow the sending agency 10 business days from the date of the notice to submit the requested information. If after the expiration of the 10 business days the Interstate Compact on the Placement of Children office at the Department of Health and Human Services does not receive the requested information or the sending agency does not withdraw its request, the request shall be deemed expired.

History.
2019-172, s. 12

ARTICLE 39
INTERSTATE COMPACT ON ADOPTION AND MEDICAL ASSISTANCE

§ 7B-3900. Legislative findings and purposes

(a) Finding adoptive families for children, for whom state assistance is desirable pursuant to G.S. 108A-49 and G.S. 108A-50, and assuring the protection of the interests of the children affected during the entire assistance period require special measures when the adoptive parents move to another state or are residents of another state. Additionally, the provision of medical and other necessary services for children receiving State assistance encounters special difficulties when the provision of services takes place in another state.

(b) In recognition of the need for special measures, the General Assembly authorizes the Secretary of the Department of Health and Human Services to enter into interstate agreements with agencies of other states for the protection of children on behalf of whom adoption assistance is being provided by the Department of Health and Human Services and to provide procedures for interstate adoption assistance payments, including payments for medical services.

History.
1999-190, s. 5

§ 7B-3901. Definitions

Unless the context requires otherwise, as used in this Article:

(1) "Adoption assistance state" means the state that is a signatory to an adoption assistance agreement in a particular case.

(2) "Residence state" means the state where the child is living.

(3) "State" means a state of the United States, the District of Columbia, the Commonwealth of Puerto Rico, the Virgin Islands, Guam, the Commonwealth of the Northern Mariana Islands, or any territory or possession subject to the jurisdiction of the United States.

History.
1999-190, s. 5

§ 7B-3902. Compacts authorized

The Secretary of the Department of Health and Human Services may develop, participate in the development of, negotiate, and enter into one or more interstate compacts on behalf of this State with other states to implement this Article. When entered into, and for so long as it remains in force, such a compact shall have the full force and effect of law.

History.
1999-190, s. 5

§ 7B-3903. Content of compacts

(a) A compact under this Article shall contain all of the following provisions:

(1) A provision making it available for joinder by all states.

(2) A provision for withdrawal from the compact upon written notice to the parties, with a period of at least one year between the date of the notice and effective date of the withdrawal.

(3) A requirement that the protections afforded by or under the compact continue in force for the duration of the adoption assistance and apply to all children and their adoptive parents who, on the effective date of the withdrawal, are receiving adoption assistance from a party state other than the state in which they are a resident and have their principal place of abode.

(4) A requirement that each instance of adoption assistance to which the compact applies be covered by an adoption assistance agreement in writing between the adoptive parents and the state child welfare agency of the state which undertakes to provide the adoption assistance and that any such agreement be expressly for the benefit of the adopted child and enforceable by the adoptive parents and the state child welfare agency providing the adoption assistance.

(5) Any other provisions appropriate to implement the proper administration of the compact.

(b) A compact entered into under this Article may contain any of the following provisions:

(1) Provisions establishing procedures and entitlement to medical and other necessary social services for the child in accordance with applicable laws, even though the child and the adoptive parents are in a state other than the one responsible for or providing the services or the funds to defray part or all of the expense thereof.

(2) Any other provisions appropriate or incidental to the proper administration of the compact.

History.
1999-190, s. 5

§ 7B-3904. Medical assistance

(a) A child with special needs who is a resident of this State who is the subject of an adoption assistance agreement with another state shall be accepted as being entitled to receive medical assistance certification from this State upon the filing in the department of social services of the county in which the child resides a certified copy of the adoption assistance agreement obtained from the adoption assistance state.

(b) The Division of Health Benefits shall consider the holder of a medical assistance certification under this section to be entitled to the same medical benefits under the laws of this State as any other holder of a medical assistance certification and shall process and make payment on claims on account of that holder in the same manner and under the same conditions and procedures that apply to other recipients of medical assistance.

(c) The provisions of this section apply only to medical assistance for children under adoption assistance agreements from states that have entered into a compact with this State under which the other state provides medical assistance to children with special needs under adoption assistance agreements made by this State.

History.

1999-190, s. 5; 2019-81, s. 15(a)

§ 7B-3905. Federal participation

The Department of Health and Human Services, in connection with the administration of this Article and any compact entered into pursuant to this Article, shall include the provision of adoption assistance and medical assistance for which the federal government pays some or all of the cost in any state plan made pursuant to the Adoption Assistance and Child Welfare Act of 1980 (P.L. 96-272), Titles IV (E) and XIX of the Social Security Act and any other applicable federal laws. The Department shall apply for and administer all relevant federal aid in accordance with law.

History.

1999-190, s. 5

§ 7B-3906. Compact Administrator

The Secretary of the Department of Health and Human Services may appoint a Compact Administrator who shall be the general coordinator of activities under this Compact in this State and who, acting jointly with like officers of other party states, may promulgate rules to carry out more effectively the terms and provisions of this Compact.

History.

1999-190, s. 5

ARTICLE 40
INTERSTATE COMPACT FOR JUVENILES

§ 7B-4000. Short title

This Article may be cited as "The Interstate Compact for Juveniles".

History.

2005-194, s. 1

§ 7B-4001. Governor to execute Compact; form of Compact

The Governor of North Carolina is authorized and directed to execute a Compact on behalf of the State of North Carolina with any state of the United States legally joining therein in the form substantially as follows:

"Article I. Purpose.

(a) The compacting states to this Interstate Compact recognize that each state is responsible for the proper supervision or return of juveniles, delinquents, and status offenders who are on probation or parole and who have absconded, escaped, or run away from supervision and control and in so doing have endangered their own safety and the safety of others. The compacting states also recognize that each state is responsible for the safe return of juveniles who have run away from home and in doing so have left their state of residence. The compacting states also recognize that Congress, by enacting the Crime Control Act, 4 U.S.C. § 112 (1965), has authorized and encouraged compacts for cooperative efforts and mutual assistance in the prevention of crime.

(b) It is the purpose of this Compact, through means of joint and cooperative action among the compacting states to:

(1) Ensure that the adjudicated juveniles and status offenders subject to this Compact are provided adequate supervision and services in the receiving state as ordered by the adjudicating judge or parole authority in the sending state;

(2) Ensure that the public safety interests of the citizens, including the victims of juvenile offenders, in both the sending and receiving states are adequately protected;

(3) Return juveniles who have run away, absconded, or escaped from supervision or control, or have been accused of an offense to the state requesting their return;

(4) Make contracts for the cooperative institutionalization in public facilities in member states for delinquent youth needing special services;

(5) Provide for the effective tracking and supervision of juveniles;

(6) Equitably allocate the costs, benefits, and obligations of the compacting states;

(7) Establish procedures to manage the movement between states of juvenile offenders released to the community under the jurisdiction of courts, juvenile departments, or any other criminal or juvenile justice agency which has jurisdiction over juvenile offenders;

(8) Ensure immediate notice to jurisdictions where defined offenders are authorized to travel or to relocate across state lines;

(9) Establish procedures to resolve pending charges (detainers) against juvenile offenders prior to transfer or release to the community under the terms of this Compact;

(10) Establish a system of uniform data collection on information pertaining to juveniles subject to this Compact that allows access by authorized juvenile justice and criminal justice officials and regular reporting of Compact activities to heads of state executive, judicial, and legislative branches and juvenile and criminal justice administrators;

(11) Monitor compliance with rules governing interstate movement of juveniles and initiate interventions to address and correct noncompliance;

(12) Coordinate training and education regarding the regulation of interstate movement of juveniles for officials involved in such activity; and

(13) Coordinate the implementation and operation of the Compact with the Interstate Compact for the Placement of Children, the Interstate Compact for Adult Offender Supervision, and other compacts affecting juveniles particularly in those cases where concurrent or overlapping supervision issues arise.

(c) It is the policy of the compacting states that the activities conducted by the Interstate Commission created herein are the formation of public policies and therefore are public business. Furthermore, the compacting states shall cooperate and observe their individual and collective duties and responsibilities for the prompt return and acceptance of juveniles subject to the provisions of this Compact. The provisions of this Compact shall be reasonably and liberally construed to accomplish the purposes and policies of the Compact.

Article II. Definitions.

As used in this Compact, unless the context clearly requires a different construction:

(1) "Bylaws" means those bylaws established by the Interstate Commission for its governance or for directing or controlling its actions or conduct.

(2) "Compact Administrator" means the individual in each compacting state appointed pursuant to the terms of this Compact responsible for the administration and management of the state's supervision and transfer of juveniles subject to the terms of this Compact, the rules adopted by the Interstate Commission, and policies adopted by the State Council under this Compact.

(3) "Compacting State" means any state which has enacted the enabling legislation for this Compact.

(4) "Commissioner" means the voting representative of each compacting state appointed pursuant to Article III of this Compact.

(5) "Court" means any court having jurisdiction over delinquent, neglected, or dependent children.

(6) "Deputy Compact Administrator" means the individual, if any, in each compacting state appointed to act on behalf of a Compact Administrator pursuant to the terms of this Compact responsible for the administration and management of the state's supervision and transfer of juveniles subject to the terms of this compact, the rules adopted by the Interstate Commission, and policies adopted by the State Council under this Compact.

(7) "Interstate Commission" means the Interstate Commission for Juveniles created by Article III of this Compact.

(8) "Juvenile" means any person defined as a juvenile in any member state or by the rules of the Interstate Commission, including:

a. **Accused Delinquent.** -- A person charged with an offense that, if committed by an adult, would be a criminal offense;

b. **Adjudicated Delinquent.** -- A person found to have committed an offense that, if committed by an adult, would be a criminal offense;

c. **Accused Status Offender.** -- A person charged with an offense that would not be a criminal offense if committed by an adult;

d. **Adjudicated Status Offender.** -- A person found to have committed an offense that would not be a criminal offense if committed by an adult; and

e. **Nonoffender.** -- A person in need of supervision who has not been accused or adjudicated a status offender or delinquent.

(9) "Noncompacting State" means any state which has not enacted the enabling legislation for this Compact.

(10) "Probation" or "Parole" means any kind of supervision or conditional release of juveniles authorized under the laws of the compacting states.

(11) "Rule" means a written statement by the Interstate Commission promulgated pursuant to Article VI of this Compact that is of general applicability, implements, interprets, or prescribes a policy or provision of the Compact, or an organizational, procedural, or practice requirement of the Commission, and has the force and effect of statutory law in a compacting state, and includes the amendment, repeal, or suspension of an existing rule.

(12) "State" means a state of the United States, the District of Columbia or its designee, the Commonwealth of Puerto Rico, the

U.S. Virgin Islands, Guam, American Samoa, and the Northern Marianas Islands.

Article III. Interstate Commission for Juveniles.

(a) The compacting states hereby create the "Interstate Commission for Juveniles." The Commission shall be a body corporate and joint agency of the compacting states. The Commission shall have all the responsibilities, powers, and duties set forth herein, and such additional powers as may be conferred upon it by subsequent action of the respective legislatures of the compacting states in accordance with the terms of this Compact.

(b) The Interstate Commission shall consist of commissioners appointed by the appropriate appointing authority in each state pursuant to the rules and requirements of each compacting state and in consultation with the State Council for Interstate Juvenile Supervision created hereunder. The Commissioner shall be the compact administrator, deputy compact administrator, or designee from that state who shall serve on the Interstate Commission in such capacity under or pursuant to the applicable law of the compacting state.

(c) In addition to the commissioners who are the voting representatives of each state, the Interstate Commission shall include individuals who are not commissioners, but who are members of interested organizations. Such noncommissioner members must include a member of the national organizations of governors, legislators, state chief justices, attorneys general, Interstate Compact for Adult Offender Supervision, Interstate Compact for the Placement of Children, juvenile justice and juvenile corrections officials, and crime victims. All noncommissioner members of the Interstate Commission shall be ex officio, nonvoting members. The Interstate Commission may provide in its bylaws for such additional ex officio, nonvoting members, including members of other national organizations, in such numbers as shall be determined by the Commission.

(d) Each compacting state represented at any meeting of the Commission is entitled to one vote. A majority of the compacting states shall constitute a quorum for the transaction of business, unless a larger quorum is required by the bylaws of the Interstate Commission.

(e) The Commission shall meet at least once each calendar year. The chairperson may call additional meetings and, upon the request of a simple majority of the compacting states, shall call additional meetings. Public notice shall be given of all meetings, and meetings shall be open to the public.

(f) The Interstate Commission shall establish an executive committee, which shall include commission officers, members, and others as determined by the bylaws. The executive committee shall have the power to act on behalf of the Interstate Commission during periods when the Interstate Commission is not in session, with the exception of rule making and/or amendment to the Compact. The executive committee shall oversee the day-to-day activities of the administration of the Compact managed by an executive director and Interstate Commission staff, administer enforcement and compliance with the provisions of the Compact, its bylaws and rules, and perform other duties as directed by the Interstate Commission or set forth in the bylaws.

(g) Each member of the Interstate Commission shall have the right and power to cast a vote to which that compacting state is entitled and to participate in the business and affairs of the Interstate Commission. A member shall vote in person and shall not delegate a vote to another compacting state. However, a commissioner, in consultation with the state council, shall appoint another authorized representative, in the absence of the commissioner from that state, to cast a vote on behalf of the compacting state at a specified meeting. The bylaws may provide for members' participation in meetings by telephone or other means of telecommunication or electronic communication.

(h) The Interstate Commission's bylaws shall establish conditions and procedures under which the Interstate Commission shall make its information and official records available to the public for inspection or copying. The Interstate Commission may exempt from disclosure any information or official records to the extent they would adversely affect personal privacy rights or proprietary interests.

(i) Public notice shall be given of all meetings, and all meetings shall be open to the public, except as set forth in the Rules or as otherwise provided in the Compact. The Interstate Commission and any of its committees may close a meeting to the public where it determines by two-thirds vote that an open meeting would be likely to:

(1) Relate solely to the Interstate Commission's internal personnel practices and procedures;

(2) Disclose matters specifically exempted from disclosure by statute;

(3) Disclose trade secrets or commercial or financial information which is privileged or confidential;

(4) Involve accusing any person of a crime or formally censuring any person;

(5) Disclose information of a personal nature where disclosure would constitute a clearly unwarranted invasion of personal privacy;

(6) Disclose investigative records compiled for law enforcement purposes;

(7) Disclose information contained in or related to examination, operating, or condition reports prepared by, or on behalf of or for the use of, the Interstate Commission with respect to a regulated person or entity for the purpose of regulation or supervision of such person or entity;

(8) Disclose information, the premature disclosure of which would significantly endanger the stability of a regulated person or entity; or

(9) Specifically relate to the Interstate Commission's issuance of a subpoena or its participation in a civil action or other legal proceeding.

(j) For every meeting closed pursuant to this provision, the Interstate Commission's legal counsel shall publicly certify that, in the legal counsel's opinion, the meeting may be closed to the public and shall reference each relevant exemptive provision. The Interstate Commission shall keep minutes which shall fully and clearly describe all matters discussed in any meeting and shall provide a full and accurate summary of any actions taken, and the reasons therefor, including a description of each of the views expressed on any item and the record of any roll call vote (reflected in the vote of each member on the question). All documents considered in connection with any action shall be identified in the minutes.

(k) The Interstate Commission shall collect standardized data concerning the interstate movement of juveniles as directed through its rules which shall specify the data to be collected, the means of collection and data exchange, and reporting requirements. Such methods of data collection, exchange, and reporting shall insofar as is reasonably possible conform to up-to-date technology and coordinate its information functions with the appropriate repository of records.

Article IV. Powers and Duties of
the Interstate Commission.

(a) The Interstate Commission shall have the following powers and duties:

(1) To provide for dispute resolution among compacting states.

(2) To promulgate rules to effect the purposes and obligations as enumerated in this Compact, which shall have the force and effect of statutory law and shall be binding in the compacting states to the extent and in the manner provided in this Compact.

(3) To oversee, supervise, and coordinate the interstate movement of juveniles subject to the terms of this Compact and any bylaws adopted and rules promulgated by the Interstate Commission.

(4) To enforce compliance with the Compact provisions, the rules promulgated by the Interstate Commission, and the bylaws, using all necessary and proper means including, but not limited to, the use of judicial process.

(5) To establish and maintain offices which shall be located within one or more of the compacting states.

(6) To purchase and maintain insurance and bonds.

(7) To borrow, accept, hire, or contract for services of personnel.

(8) To establish and appoint committees and hire staff which it deems necessary for the carrying out of its functions including, but not limited to, an executive committee as required by Article III of this Compact, which shall have the power to act on behalf of the Interstate Commission in carrying out its powers and duties hereunder.

(9) To elect or appoint such officers, attorneys, employees, agents, or consultants, and to fix their compensation, define their duties, and determine their qualifications; and to establish the Interstate Commission's personnel policies and programs relating to, inter alia, conflicts of interest, rates of compensation, and qualifications of personnel.

(10) To accept any and all donations and grants of money, equipment, supplies, materials, and services, and to receive, utilize, and dispose of them.

(11) To lease, purchase, accept contributions or donations of, or otherwise to own, hold, improve, or use any property, real, personal, or mixed.

(12) To sell, convey, mortgage, pledge, lease, exchange, abandon, or otherwise dispose of any property, real, personal, or mixed.

(13) To establish a budget and make expenditures and levy dues as provided in Article VIII of this Compact.

(14) To sue and be sued.

(15) To adopt a seal and bylaws governing the management and operation of the Interstate Commission.

(16) To perform such functions as may be necessary or appropriate to achieve the purposes of this Compact.

(17) To report annually to the legislatures, governors, judiciary, and state councils of the compacting states concerning the activities of the Interstate Commission during the preceding year. Such reports shall also include any recommendations that may have been adopted by the Interstate Commission.

(18) To coordinate education, training, and public awareness regarding the interstate movement of juveniles for officials involved in such activity.

(19) To establish uniform standards of the reporting, collecting, and exchanging of data.

(b) The Interstate Commission shall maintain its corporate books and records in accordance with the bylaws.

Article V. Organization and Operation of the Interstate Commission.

(a) **Bylaws.** -- The Interstate Commission shall, by a majority of the members present and voting, within 12 months after the first Interstate Commission meeting, adopt bylaws to govern its conduct as may be necessary or appropriate to carry out the purposes of the Compact, including, but not limited to:

(1) Establishing the fiscal year of the Interstate Commission;

(2) Establishing an executive committee and such other committees as may be necessary;

(3) Providing for the establishment of committees governing any general or specific delegation of any authority or function of the Interstate Commission;

(4) Providing reasonable procedures for calling and conducting meetings of the Interstate Commission and ensuring reasonable notice of each such meeting;

(5) Establishing the titles and responsibilities of the officers of the Interstate Commission;

(6) Providing a mechanism for concluding the operations of the Interstate Commission and the return of any surplus funds that may exist upon the termination of the Compact after the payment and/or reserving of all of its debts and obligations;

(7) Providing "start-up" rules for initial administration of the Compact; and

(8) Establishing standards and procedures for compliance and technical assistance in carrying out the Compact.

(b) **Officers and Staff.** -- The Interstate Commission shall, by a majority of the members, elect annually from among its members a chairperson and a vice-chairperson, each of whom shall have such authority and duties as may be specified in the bylaws. The chairperson or, in the chairperson's absence or disability, the vice-chairperson shall preside at all meetings of the Interstate Commission. The officers so elected shall serve without compensation or remuneration from the Interstate Commission; provided that, subject to the availability of budgeted funds, the officers shall be reimbursed for any ordinary and necessary costs and expenses incurred by them in the performance of their duties and responsibilities as officers of the Interstate Commission.

The Interstate Commission shall, through its executive committee, appoint or retain an executive director for such period, upon such terms and conditions and for such compensation as the Interstate Commission may deem appropriate. The executive director shall serve as secretary to the Interstate Commission, but shall not be a member and shall hire and supervise such other staff as may be authorized by the Interstate Commission.

(c) **Qualified Immunity, Defense, and Indemnification.** -- The Commission's executive director and employees shall be immune from suit and liability, either personally or in their official capacity, for any claim for damage to or loss of property or personal injury or other civil liability caused or arising out of or relating to any actual or alleged act, error, or omission that occurred, or that such person had a reasonable basis for believing occurred within the scope of Commission employment, duties, or responsibilities; provided, that any such person shall not be protected from suit or liability for any damage, loss, injury, or liability caused by the intentional or willful and wanton misconduct of any such person.

The liability of any commissioner, or the employee or agent of a commissioner, acting within the scope of such person's employment or duties for acts, errors, or omissions occurring within such person's state may not exceed the limits of liability set forth under the Constitution and laws of that state for state officials, employees, and agents. Nothing in this subsection shall be construed to protect any such person from suit or liability for any damage, loss, injury, or liability caused by the intentional or willful and wanton misconduct of any such person.

The Interstate Commission shall defend the executive director or the employees or representatives of the Interstate Commission and, subject to the approval of the Attorney General of the state represented by any commissioner of a compacting state, shall defend such commissioner or the commissioner's representatives or employees in any civil action seeking to impose liability arising out of any actual or alleged act, error, or omission that occurred within the scope of Interstate Commission employment, duties, or responsibilities, or that the defendant had a reasonable basis for believing occurred within the scope of Interstate Commission employment, duties, or responsibilities, provided that the actual or alleged act, error, or omission did not result from intentional or willful and wanton misconduct on the part of such person.

The Interstate Commission shall indemnify and hold the commissioner of a compacting state, or the commissioner's representatives or employees, or the Interstate Commission's representatives or employees, harmless in the amount of any settlement or judgment obtained against such persons arising out of any actual or alleged act, error, or omission that occurred within the scope of Interstate Commission employment, duties, or responsibilities, or that such persons had a reasonable basis for believing occurred within the scope of Interstate Commission employment, duties, or responsibilities, provided that the actual or alleged act, error, or omission did not result from intentional or willful and wanton misconduct on the part of such persons.

Article VI. Rule-Making Functions of the Interstate Commission.

(a) The Interstate Commission shall promulgate and publish rules in order to effectively and efficiently achieve the purposes of the Compact.

(b) Rule making shall occur pursuant to the criteria set forth in this Article and the bylaws and rules adopted pursuant thereto. Such rule making shall substantially conform to the principles of the "Model State Administrative Procedures Act," 1981 Act, Uniform Laws Annotated, Vol. 16, p. 1 (2000), or such other administrative procedures acts, as the Interstate Commission deems appropriate consistent with due process requirements under the United States Constitution as now or hereafter interpreted by the United States Supreme Court. All rules and amendments shall become binding as of the date specified, as published with the final version of the rule as approved by the Commission.

(c) When promulgating a rule, the Interstate Commission shall, at a minimum:

(1) Publish the proposed rule's entire text stating the reason for that proposed rule;

(2) Allow and invite any and all persons to submit written data, facts, opinions, and arguments, which information shall be added to the record and be made publicly available;

(3) Provide an opportunity for an informal hearing if petitioned by 10 or more persons;

(4) Promulgate a final rule and its effective date, if appropriate, based on input from state or local officials, or interested parties; and

(5) Allow, not later than 60 days after a rule is promulgated, any interested person to file a petition in the United States District Court for the District of Columbia or in the Federal District Court where the Interstate Commission's principal office is located for judicial review of such rule.

(d) If the court finds that the Interstate Commission's action is not supported by substantial evidence in the rule-making record, the court shall hold the rule unlawful and set it aside. For purposes of this subsection, evidence is substantial if it would be considered substantial evidence under the Model State Administrative Procedures Act.

(e) If a majority of the legislatures of the compacting states rejects a rule, those states may, by enactment of a statute or resolution in the same manner used to adopt the Compact, cause that rule to have no further force and effect in any compacting state.

(f) The existing rules governing the operation of the Interstate Compact on Juveniles superseded by this act shall be null and void when all states, as defined in the Compact, have adopted The Interstate Compact for Juveniles.

(g) Upon determination by the Interstate Commission that a state of emergency exists, it may promulgate an emergency rule which shall become effective immediately upon adoption, provided that the usual rule-making procedures provided hereunder shall be retroactively applied to said rule as soon as reasonably possible but no later than 90 days after the effective date of the emergency rule.

Article VII. Oversight, Enforcement, and Dispute Resolution by the Interstate Commission.

(a) **Oversight.** -- The Interstate Commission shall oversee the administration and operations of the interstate movement of juveniles subject to this Compact in the compacting states and shall monitor such activities being administered in noncompacting states which may significantly affect compacting states.

The courts and executive agencies in each compacting state shall enforce this Compact and shall take all actions necessary and appropriate to effectuate the Compact's purposes and intent. The provisions of this Compact and the rules promulgated hereunder shall be received by all the judges, public officers, commissions, and departments of the state government as evidence of the authorized statute and administrative rules, and all courts shall take judicial notice of the Compact and the rules. In any judicial or administrative proceeding in a compacting state pertaining to the subject matter of this Compact which may affect the powers, responsibilities, or actions of the Interstate Commission, it shall be entitled to receive all service of process in any such proceeding and shall have standing to intervene in the proceeding for all purposes.

(b) **Dispute Resolution.** -- The compacting states shall report to the Interstate Commission on all issues and activities necessary for the administration of the Compact as well as issues and activities pertaining to compliance with the provisions of the Compact and its bylaws and rules.

The Interstate Commission shall attempt, upon the request of a compacting state, to resolve any disputes or other issues which are subject to the Compact and which may arise among compacting states and between compacting and noncompacting states. The Commission shall promulgate a rule providing for both mediation and binding dispute resolution for disputes among the compacting states.

The Interstate Commission, in the reasonable exercise of its discretion, shall enforce the provisions and rules of this Compact using any or all means set forth in Article XI of this Compact.

Article VIII. Finance.

(a) The Interstate Commission shall pay or provide for the payment of the reasonable expenses of its establishment, organization, and ongoing activities.

(b) The Interstate Commission shall levy on and collect an annual assessment from each compacting state to cover the cost of the internal operations and activities of the Interstate Commission and its staff which must be in a total amount sufficient to cover the Interstate Commission's annual budget as approved each year. The aggregate annual assessment amount shall be allocated based upon a formula to be determined by the Interstate Commission, taking into consideration the population of each compacting state and the volume of interstate movement of juveniles in each compacting state and shall promulgate a rule binding upon all compacting states which governs said assessment.

(c) The Interstate Commission shall not incur any obligations of any kind prior to securing the funds adequate to meet the same; nor shall the Interstate Commission pledge the credit of any of the compacting states, except by and with the authority of the compacting state.

(d) The Interstate Commission shall keep accurate accounts of all receipts and disbursements. The receipts and disbursements of the Interstate Commission shall be subject to the audit and accounting procedures established under its bylaws. However, all receipts and disbursements of funds handled by the Interstate Commission shall be audited yearly by a certified or licensed public accountant, and the report of the audit shall be included in and become part of the annual report of the Interstate Commission.

Article IX. The State Council.

Each member state shall create a State Council for Interstate Juvenile Supervision. While each state may determine the membership of its own state council, its membership must include at least one representative from the legislative, judicial, and executive branches of government, victims groups, and the compact administrator, deputy compact administrator, or designee. Each compacting state retains the right to determine the qualifications of the compact administrator or deputy compact administrator. Each state council will advise and may exercise oversight and advocacy concerning that state's participation in Interstate Commission activities and other duties as may be determined by that state, including, but not limited to, development of policy concerning operations

and procedures of the Compact within that state.

Article X. Compacting States, Effective Date, and Amendment.

(a) Any state, the District of Columbia or its designee, the Commonwealth of Puerto Rico, the U.S.Virgin Islands, Guam, American Samoa, and the Northern Marianas Islands, as defined in Article II of this Compact, is eligible to become a compacting state.

(b) The Compact shall become effective and binding upon legislative enactment of the Compact into law by no less than 35 of the states. The initial effective date shall be the later of July 1, 2004, or upon enactment into law by the 35th jurisdiction. Thereafter, it shall become effective and binding as to any other compacting state upon enactment of the Compact into law by that state. The governors of nonmember states or their designees shall be invited to participate in the activities of the Interstate Commission on a nonvoting basis prior to adoption of the Compact by all states and territories of the United States.

(c) The Interstate Commission may propose amendments to the Compact for enactment by the compacting states. No amendment shall become effective and binding upon the Interstate Commission and the compacting states unless and until it is enacted into law by unanimous consent of the compacting states.

Article XI. Withdrawal, Default, Termination, and Judicial Enforcement.

(a) **Withdrawal. --** Once effective, the Compact shall continue in force and remain binding upon each and every compacting state; provided that a compacting state may withdraw from the Compact by specifically repealing the statute which enacted the Compact into law.

The effective date of withdrawal is the effective date of the repeal.

The withdrawing state shall immediately notify the chairperson of the Interstate Commission in writing upon the introduction of legislation repealing this Compact in the withdrawing state. The Interstate Commission shall notify the other compacting states of the withdrawing state's intent to withdraw within 60 days of its receipt thereof.

The withdrawing state is responsible for all assessments, obligations, and liabilities incurred through the effective date of withdrawal, including any obligations, the performance of which extend beyond the effective date of withdrawal.

Reinstatement following withdrawal of any compacting state shall occur upon the withdrawing state reenacting the Compact or upon such later date as determined by the Interstate Commission.

(b) **Technical Assistance, Fines, Suspension, Termination, and Default.** -- If the Interstate Commission determines that any compacting state has at any time defaulted in the performance of any of its obligations or responsibilities under this Compact, or the bylaws or duly promulgated rules, the Interstate Commission may impose any or all of the following penalties:

(1) Remedial training and technical assistance as directed by the Interstate Commission;

(2) Alternative Dispute Resolution;

(3) Fines, fees, and costs in such amounts as are deemed to be reasonable as fixed by the Interstate Commission; and

(4) Suspension or termination of membership in the Compact, which shall be imposed only after all other reasonable means of securing compliance under the bylaws and rules have been exhausted, and the Interstate Commission has therefore determined that the offending state is in default. Immediate notice of suspension shall be given by the Interstate Commission to the Governor, the Chief Justice, or the Chief Judicial Officer of the state, the majority and minority leaders of the defaulting state's legislature, and the state council.

The grounds for default include, but are not limited to, failure of a compacting state to perform such obligations or responsibilities imposed upon it by this Compact, the bylaws, or duly promulgated rules, and any other grounds designated in Commission bylaws and rules. The Interstate Commission shall immediately notify the defaulting state in writing of the penalty imposed by the Interstate Commission and of the default pending a cure of the default. The Commission shall stipulate the conditions and the time period within which the defaulting state must cure its default. If the defaulting state fails to cure the default within the time period specified by the Commission, the defaulting state shall be terminated from the Compact upon an affirmative vote of a majority of the compacting states, and all rights, privileges, and benefits conferred by this Compact shall be terminated from the effective date of termination.

Within 60 days of the effective date of termination of a defaulting state, the Commission shall notify the Governor, the Chief Justice or Chief Judicial Officer, the majority and minority leaders of the defaulting state's legislature, and the state council of the termination.

The defaulting state is responsible for all assessments, obligations, and liabilities incurred through the effective date of termination, including any obligations, the performance of which extends beyond the effective date of termination.

The Interstate Commission shall not bear any costs relating to the defaulting state unless otherwise mutually agreed upon in writing between the Interstate Commission and the defaulting state.

Reinstatement following termination of any compacting state requires both a reenactment of the Compact by the defaulting state and the approval of the Interstate Commission pursuant to the rules.

(c) **Judicial Enforcement.** -- The Interstate Commission may, by majority vote of the members, initiate legal action in the United States District Court for the District of Columbia or, at the discretion of the Interstate Commission, in the federal district where the Interstate Commission has its offices to enforce compliance with the provisions of the Compact and its duly promulgated rules and bylaws, against any compacting state in default. In the event judicial enforcement is necessary, the prevailing party shall be awarded all costs of such litigation, including reasonable attorneys' fees.

(d) **Dissolution of Compact.** -- The Compact dissolves effective upon the date of the withdrawal or default of the compacting state, which reduces membership in the Compact to one compacting state.

Upon the dissolution of this Compact, the Compact becomes null and void and shall be of no further force or effect, and the business and affairs of the Interstate Commission shall be concluded, and any surplus funds shall be distributed in accordance with the bylaws.

Article XII. Severability and Construction.

(a) The provisions of this Compact shall be severable, and if any phrase, clause, sentence, or provision is deemed unenforceable, the remaining provisions of the Compact shall be enforceable.

(b) The provisions of this Compact shall be liberally construed to effectuate its purposes.

Article XIII. Binding Effect of Compact and Other Laws.

(a) **Other Laws.** -- Nothing herein prevents the enforcement of any other law of a compacting state that is not inconsistent with this Compact.

All compacting states' laws, other than state Constitutions and other interstate compacts, conflicting with this Compact are superseded to the extent of the conflict.

(b) **Binding Effect of the Compact.** -- All lawful actions of the Interstate Commission, including all rules and bylaws promulgated by the Interstate Commission, are binding upon the compacting states.

All agreements between the Interstate Commission and the compacting states are binding in accordance with their terms.

Upon the request of a party to a conflict over meaning or interpretation of Interstate Commission actions, and upon a majority vote of the compacting states, the Interstate Commission may issue advisory opinions regarding such meaning or interpretation.

In the event any provision of this Compact exceeds the constitutional limits imposed on the legislature of any compacting state, the obligations, duties, powers, or jurisdiction sought to be conferred by such provision upon the Interstate Commission shall be ineffective, and such obligations, duties, powers, or jurisdiction shall remain in the compacting state and shall be exercised by the agency thereof to which such obligations, duties, powers, or jurisdiction are delegated by law in effect at the time this Compact becomes effective."

History.
2005-194, s. 1

§ 7B-4002. Implementation of the Compact

(a) The North Carolina State Council for Interstate Juvenile Supervision is hereby established. The Secretary of Public Safety, or the Secretary's designee, shall serve as the Compact Administrator for the State of North Carolina and as North Carolina's Commissioner to the Interstate Commission. The Secretary of Public Safety, or the Secretary's designee, is a member of the State Council and serves as chairperson of the State Council. In addition to the chairperson, the State Council shall consist of 10 members as follows:

(1) One member representing the executive branch, to be appointed by the Governor;

(2) One member from a victim's assistance group, to be appointed by the Governor;

(3) One at-large member, to be appointed by the Governor;

(4) One member of the Senate, to be appointed by the President Pro Tempore of the Senate;

(5) One member of the House of Representatives, to be appointed by the Speaker of the House of Representatives;

(6) A district court judge, to be appointed by the Chief Justice of the Supreme Court; and

(7) Four members representing the juvenile court counselors, to be appointed by the Secretary of Public Safety.

(b) The State Council shall meet at least twice a year and may also hold special meetings at the call of the chairperson. All terms are for three years.

(c) The State Council may advise the Compact Administrator on participation in the Interstate Commission activities and administration of the Compact.

(d) The members of the State Council shall serve without compensation but shall be reimbursed for necessary travel and subsistence expenses in accordance with the policies of the Office of State Budget and Management.

(e) The State Council shall act in an advisory capacity to the Secretary of Public Safety concerning this State's participation in Interstate Commission activities and other duties as may be determined by each member state, including recommendations for policy concerning the operations and procedures of the Compact within this State.

(f) The Governor shall by executive order provide for any other matters necessary for implementation of the Compact at the time that it becomes effective, and, except as otherwise provided for in this section, the State Council may promulgate rules or regulations necessary to implement and administer the Compact.

History.
2005-194, s. 1; 2012-194, s. 3

CHAPTER 8
EVIDENCE

ARTICLE 1
STATUTES

§ 8-1. Printed statutes and certified copies evidence

All statutes, or joint resolutions, passed by the General Assembly may be read in evidence from the printed statute book; or a copy of any act of the General Assembly certified by the Secretary of State shall be received in evidence in every court.

History.
1826, c. 7; R.C., c. 44, ss. 4, 5; Code, ss. 1339, 1340; Rev., ss. 1592, 1593; C.S., s. 1747

§ 8-2. Martin's collection of private acts

Any private act published by Francis X. Martin, in his collection of private acts, shall be received in evidence in every court.

History.
1826, c. 7, s. 2; R.C., c. 44, s. 5; Code, s. 1340; Rev., s. 1593; C.S., s. 1748

§ 8-3. Laws of other states or foreign countries

(a) A printed copy of a statute, or other written law, of another state, or of a territory, or of a foreign country, or a printed copy of a proclamation, edict, decree or ordinance, by the executive thereof, contained in a book or publication purporting or proved to have been published by the authority thereof, or proved to be commonly admitted as evidence of the existing law, in the judicial tribunals thereof, shall be evidence of the statute law, proclamation, edict, decree, or ordinance. The unwritten or common law of another state, or of a territory, or of a foreign country, may be proved as a fact by oral evidence. The books of the reports of cases, adjudged in the courts thereof, shall also be admitted as evidence of the unwritten or common law thereof.

(b) Any party may exhibit a copy of the law of another state, territory, or foreign country copied from a printed volume of the laws of such state, territory, or country on file in

    (1) The offices of the Governor or the Secretary of State, and duly certified by the Secretary of State, or

    (2) The State Library and certified as provided in G.S. 125-6, or

    (3) The Supreme Court Library and certified as provided in G.S. 7A-13 (f).

History.
1823, c. 1193, ss. 1, 3, P.R.; R.C., c. 44, s. 3; C.C.P., s. 360; Code, s. 1338; Rev., s. 1594; C.S., s. 1749; 1967, c. 565

§ 8-4. Judicial notice of laws of United States, other states and foreign countries

When any question shall arise as to the law of the United States, or of any other state or territory of the United States, or of the District of Columbia, or of any foreign country, the court shall take notice of such law in the same manner as if the question arose under the law of this State.

History.
1931, c. 30

§ 8-5. Town ordinances certified

In a trial in which the offense charged is the violation of a town ordinance, a copy of the ordinance alleged to have been violated, proven as provided in G.S. 160A-79, shall be prima facie evidence of the existence of such ordinance.

History.
1899, c. 277, s. 2; Rev., s. 1595; C.S., s. 1750; 1971, c. 381, s. 3; 1973, c. 1446, s. 17

ARTICLE 3
PUBLIC RECORDS

§ 8-34. Copies of official writings

(a) Copies of all official bonds, writings, papers, or documents, recorded or filed as records in any court, or public office, or lodged in the office of the Governor, Treasurer, Auditor, Secretary of State, Attorney General, Adjutant General, or the State Department of Natural and Cultural Resources, shall be as competent evidence as the originals, when certified by the keeper of such records or writings under the seal of the keeper's office when there is such seal, or under the keeper's hand when there is no such seal, unless the court shall order the production of the original. Copies of the records of the board of county commissioners shall be evidence when certified by the clerk of the board under the clerk's hand and seal of the county.

(b) The provisions of this section shall apply to records stored on any form of permanent, computer-readable media, such as a CD-ROM, if the medium is not subject to erasure or alteration. Nonerasable, computer-readable storage media may be used for preservation duplicates, as defined in G.S. 132-8.2, or for the preservation of permanently valuable records as provided in G.S. 121-5(d).

History.
1792, c. 368, s. 11, P.R.; R.C., c. 44, s. 8; 1868-9, c. 20, s. 21; 1871-2, c. 91; Code, ss. 715, 1342; Rev., s. 1616; C.S., s. 1779; 1961, c. 739; 1973, c. 476, s. 48; 1999-131, s. 3; 1999-456, s. 47(c); 2011-326, s. 13(a); 2015-241, s. 14.30(s)

§ 8-35. Authenticated copies of public records

All copies of bonds, contracts, notes, mortgages, or other papers relating to or connected with any loan, account, settlement of any account or any part thereof, or other transaction, between the United States or any state thereof or any corporation all of whose stock is beneficially owned by the United States or any state thereof, either directly or indirectly, and any person, natural or artificial; or extracts therefrom when complete on any one subject, or copies from the books or papers on file, or records of any public office of the State or the United States or of any corporation all of whose stock is beneficially owned by the United States or by any state thereof, directly or indirectly, shall be received in evidence and entitled to full faith and credit in any of the courts of this State when certified to by the chief officer or agent in charge of such public office or of such office of such corporation, or by the secretary or an assistant secretary of such corporation, to be true copies, and authenticated under the seal of the office, department, or corporation concerned. Any such certificate shall be prima facie evidence of the genuineness of such certificate and seal, the truth of the statements made in such certificate, and the official character of the person by which it purports to have been executed.

History.
1891, c. 501; Rev., s. 1617; C.S., s. 1780; 1939, c. 149

§ 8-35.1. Division of Motor Vehicles' record admissible as prima facie evidence of convictions of offenses involving impaired driving

Notwithstanding the provisions of G.S. 15A-924(d), a properly certified copy under G.S. 8-35 or G.S. 20-26(b) of the license records of a defendant kept by the Division of Motor Vehicles under G.S. 20-26(a) is admissible as prima facie evidence of any prior conviction of a defendant for an offense involving impaired driving as defined in G.S. 20-4.01(24a).

History.
1975, c. 642, s. 1; c. 716, s. 5; 1983, c. 435, s. 3

§ 8-35.2. Records of clerk of court criminal index admissible in certain cases

Notwithstanding the provisions of G.S. 15A-924(d) or 15A-1340.4(e), certified copies of the records contained in the criminal index or similar records maintained manually or by automatic data processing equipment by the clerk of superior court, are admissible as prima facie evidence of any prior convictions of the person named in the records, if the original documents upon which the records are based have been destroyed pursuant to law. The index must contain at least the following information:

(1) The case file number;
(2) The name, sex, and race of the defendant;
(3) His address;
(4) His driver's license number, if the conviction is for a motor vehicle offense and the number is available;
(5) The date of birth of the defendant, if it is available;
(6) The offense for which he was charged and the date of same;
(7) The disposition of the charge and the date of same;
(8) Whether the defendant was indigent;
(9) Whether he was represented by an attorney, and if so, the name of the attorney;
(10) Whether the defendant waived his right to an attorney, and
(11) The name and address of any victim, if available.

History.
1985, c. 606, s. 1; 1997-456, s. 27

§ 8-36. Authenticated copy of record of administration

When letters testamentary or of administration on the goods and chattels of any person deceased, being an inhabitant in another state or territory, have been granted, or a return or inventory of the estate has been made, a copy of the record of administration or of the letters testamentary, and a copy of an inventory or return of the effects of the deceased, after the same has been granted or made, agreeable to the laws of the state where the same has been done, being properly certified, either according to the act of Congress or by the proper officer of such state or territory, shall be allowed as evidence.

History.
1834, c. 4; R.C., c. 44, s. 7; Code, s. 1343; Rev., s. 1618; C.S., s. 1781

§ 8-37. Certificate of Commissioner of Motor Vehicles as to ownership of automobile

In any civil or criminal action in which the ownership of a motor vehicle is relevant, evidence as to the letters and numbers appearing upon the registration plate attached to such vehicle or of the motor vehicle identification number, together with certified copies of records furnished pursuant to G.S. 20-42 by the Commissioner of Motor Vehicles showing the name of the owner of the vehicle to which such registration plate or vehicle identification number is assigned, or a certified copy of the certificate of title for such motor vehicle on file with the Commissioner of Motor Vehicles, is prima facie evidence of the ownership of such motor vehicle.

History.
1931, c. 88, s. 1; 1943, c. 650; 1979, c. 980

ARTICLE 3A
FINDINGS, RECORDS AND REPORTS OF FEDERAL OFFICERS AND EMPLOYEES

§ 8-37.1. Finding of presumed death

(a) A written finding of presumed death, made by the Secretary of War, the Secretary of the Navy, or other officer or employee of the United States authorized to make such finding, pursuant to the Federal Missing Persons Act (56 Stat. 143, 1092, and P.L. 408, ch. 371, 2d Sess. 78th Cong.; 50 U.S.C. App. Supp. 1001-17), as now or hereafter amended, or a duly certified copy of such finding, shall be received in any court, office or other place in this State as prima facie evidence of the death of the person therein found to be dead, and the date, circumstances and place of his disappearance. This subsection applies only to findings of presumed death made prior to the effective date of Section 5(b) of Public Law 89-554.

(b) A written finding of presumed death, made by the Secretary pursuant to Chapter 10 of Title 37 of the U.S. Code, P.L. 89-554 as now or hereafter amended, or a duly certified copy of such finding, shall be received in any court, office, or other place in this State as prima facie evidence of the death of the person therein found to be dead, and the date, circumstances, and place of his disappearance. This subsection applies only to findings of presumed death made on or after the effective date of Section 5(b) of Public Law 89-554.

History.
1945, c. 731, s. 1; 1995, c. 379, s. 3

§ 8-37.2. Report or record that person missing, interned, captured, etc

An official written report or record, or duly certified copy thereof, that a person is missing, missing in action, interned in a neutral country, or beleaguered, besieged or captured by an enemy, or is dead, or is alive, made by any officer or employee of the United States authorized by the act referred to in § 8-37.1, or by any other law of the United States to make same, shall be received in any court, office or other place in this State as prima facie evidence that such person is missing, missing in action, interned in a neutral country, or beleaguered, besieged or captured by an enemy, or is dead, or is alive, as the case may be.

History.
1945, c. 731, s. 2

§ 8-37.3. Deemed signed and issued pursuant to law; evidence of authority to certify

For the purposes of §§ 8-37.1 and 8-37.2 any finding, report or record, or duly certified copy thereof, purporting to have been signed by such an officer or employee of the United States as is described in said sections, shall prima facie be deemed to have been signed and issued by such an officer or employee pursuant to law, and the person signing same shall prima facie be deemed to have acted within the scope of his authority. If a copy purports to have been certified by a person authorized by law to certify the same, such certified copy shall be prima facie evidence of his authority so to certify.

History.
1945, c. 731, s. 3

ARTICLE 4
OTHER WRITINGS IN EVIDENCE

N.C. Gen. Stat. § 8-38

Repealed by Session Laws 1983 (Regular Session, 1984), c. 1037, s. 13.

§ 8-39. Parol evidence to identify land described

In all actions for the possession of or title to any real estate parol testimony may be introduced to identify the land sued for, and fit it to the description contained in the paper-writing offered as evidence of title or of the right of possession, and if from this evidence the jury is satisfied that the land in question is the identical land intended to be conveyed by the parties to such paper-writing, then such paper-writing shall be deemed and taken to be sufficient in law to pass such title to or interest in such land as it purports to pass: Provided, that such paper-writing is in all other respects sufficient to pass such title or interest.

History.
1891, c. 465, s. 1; Rev., s. 1605; C.S., s. 1783

N.C. Gen. Stat. § 8-40

Repealed by Session Laws 1983 (Regular Session, 1984), c. 1037, s. 12.

N.C. Gen. Stat. § 8-40.1

Repealed by Session Laws 1983 (Regular Session, 1984), c. 1037, s. 10.

§ 8-41. Bills of lading in evidence

In all actions by or against common carriers or in the trial of any criminal action in which it shall be thought necessary to introduce in evidence any bills of lading issued by said common carrier or by a connecting carrier, it shall be competent to introduce in evidence any paper-writing purporting to be the original bill of lading, or a duplicate thereof, upon proof that such paper purporting to be such bill of lading or duplicate was received in due course of mail from consignor or agent of said carrier or connecting carrier, or delivered by said common carrier to the consignee or other person entitled to the possession of the property for which said paper purports to be the bill of lading: Provided, that such purported bill of lading shall not be declared to be the bill of lading unless the said purported bill of lading is first exhibited by the plaintiff or his agent or attorney to the defendant or its attorney, or its agent upon whom process may be served, ten days before the trial where the point of shipment is in the State, and twenty days when the point of shipment is without the State. Upon such proof and introduction of the bill of lading, the due execution thereof shall be prima facie established.

History.
1915, c. 287; C.S., s. 1785; 1945, c. 97

§ 8-42. Book accounts under sixty dollars

When any person shall bring an action upon a contract, or shall plead, or give notice of, a setoff or counterclaim for goods, wares and merchandise by him sold and delivered, or for work done and performed, he shall file his account with his complaint, or with his plea or notice of setoff or counterclaim, and if upon the trial of the issue, or executing a writ of inquiry of damages in such action, he shall declare upon his oath that the matter in dispute is a book account,

and that he hath no means to prove the delivery of any of the articles which he then shall propose to prove by himself but by this book, in that case such book may be given in evidence, if he shall make out by his own oath that it doth contain a true account of all the dealings, or the last settlement of accounts between himself and the opposing party, and that all the articles therein contained, and by him so proved, were bona fide delivered, and that he hath given the opposing party all just credits; and such book and oath shall be received as evidence for the several articles so proved to be delivered within two years next before the commencement of the action, but not for any article of a longer standing, nor for any greater amount than sixty dollars ($ 60.00).

History.
1756, c. 57, ss. 2, 6, 7, P.R.; R.C., c. 15, s. 1; Code, s. 591; Rev., s. 1622; C.S., s. 1786

§ 8-43. Book accounts proved by personal representative

In all actions where executors and administrators are parties, such book account for all articles delivered within two years previous to the death of the deceased may be proved under the like circumstances, rules and conditions; and in such case, the executor or administrator may prove by himself that he found the account so stated on the books of the deceased; that there are no witnesses, to his knowledge, capable of proving the delivery of the articles which he shall propose to prove by said book, and that he believes the same to be just, and doth not know of any other or further credit to be given than what is therein mentioned: Provided, that if two years shall not have elapsed previous to the death of the deceased, the executor or administrator may prove the said book account, if the suit shall be commenced within three years from the delivery of the articles: Provided further, that whenever by the aforesaid proviso the time of proving a book account in manner aforesaid is enlarged as to the one party, to the same extent shall be enlarged the time as to the other party.

History.
1756, c. 57, s. 2, P.R.; 1796, c. 465, P.R.; R.C., c. 15, s. 2; Code, s. 592; Rev., s. 1623; C.S., s. 1787

§ 8-44. Copies of book accounts in evidence

A copy from the book of accounts proved in manner above directed may be given in evidence in any such action or setoff as aforesaid, and shall be as available as if such book had been produced, unless the party opposing such proof shall give notice to the adverse party or his attorney, at the joining of the issue, or 10 days before the trial, that he will require the book to be produced at the trials; and in that case no such copy shall be admitted as evidence.

History.
1756, c. 57, s. 33, P.R.; R.C., c. 15, s. 3; C.C.P., s. 343c; Code, s. 593; Rev., s. 1624; C.S., s. 1788

§ 8-44.1. Hospital medical records

Copies or originals of hospital medical records shall not be held inadmissible in any court action or proceeding on the grounds that they lack certification, identification, or authentication, and shall be received as evidence if otherwise admissible, in any court or quasi-judicial proceeding, if they have been tendered to the presiding judge or designee by the custodian of the records, in accordance with G.S. 1A-1, Rule 45(c), or if they are certified, identified, and authenticated by the live testimony of the custodian of such records.

Hospital medical records are defined for purposes of this section and G.S. 1A-1, Rule 45(c) as records made in connection with the diagnosis, care and treatment of any patient or the charges for such services except that records covered by G.S. 122-8.1, G.S. 90-109.1 and federal statutory or regulatory provisions regarding alcohol and drug abuse, are subject to the requirements of said statutes.

History.
1973, c. 1332, s. 1; 1983, c. 665, s. 2

§ 8-45. Itemized and verified accounts

In any actions instituted in any court of this State upon an account for goods sold and delivered, for rents, for services rendered, or labor performed, or upon any oral contract for money loaned, a verified itemized statement of such account shall be received in evidence, and shall be deemed prima facie evidence of its correctness.

History.
1897, c. 480; Rev., s. 1625; 1917, c. 32; C.S., s. 1789; 1941, c. 104

ARTICLE 4A
PHOTOGRAPHIC COPIES OF BUSINESS AND PUBLIC RECORDS

§ 8-45.1. Photographic reproductions admissible; destruction of originals

(a) If any business, institution, member of a profession or calling, or any department or agency of government, in the regular course of business or activity has kept or recorded any memorandum, writing, entry, print, representation, X ray or combination thereof, of any act, transaction, occurrence or event, and in the regular course of business has caused any or all of the same to be recorded, copied or reproduced by any photographic, photostatic, microfilm, microcard, miniature photographic, or other process which accurately reproduces or forms a durable medium for so reproducing the original, the original may be destroyed in the regular course of business unless held in a custodial or fiduciary capacity or unless its preservation is required by law. Such reproduction, when satisfactorily identified, is as admissible in evidence as the original itself in any judicial or administrative proceeding whether the original is in existence or not and an enlargement or facsimile of such reproduction is likewise admissible in evidence if the original reproduction is in existence and available for inspection under direction of court. The introduction of a reproduced record, enlargement or facsimile, does not preclude admission of the original.

(b) The provisions of subsection (a) of this section shall apply to records stored on any form of permanent, computer-readable media, such as a CD-ROM, if the medium is not subject to erasure or alteration. Nonerasable, computer-readable storage media may be used for preservation duplicates, as defined in G.S. 132-8.2, or for the preservation of permanently valuable records as provided in G.S. 121-5(d).

History.
1951, ch. 262, s. 1; 1977, ch. 569; 1999-131, s. 1; 1999-456, s. 47(a); 2011-326, s. 13(b)

§ 8-45.2. Uniformity of interpretation

This Article shall be so interpreted and construed as to effectuate its general purpose of making uniform the law of those states which enact it.

History.
1951, c. 262, s. 2

§ 8-45.3. Photographic reproduction of records of Department of Revenue and Division of Employment Security

(a) The State Department of Revenue is hereby specifically authorized to have photographed, photocopied, or microphotocopied all records of the Department, including tax returns required by law to be made to the Department, and said photographs, photocopies, or microphotocopies, when certified by the

Department as true and correct photographs, photocopies, or microphotocopies, shall be as admissible in evidence in all actions, proceedings and matters as the originals thereof would have been.

(a1) The Division of Employment Security is hereby specifically authorized to have photographed, photocopied, or microphotocopied all records of the Division, including filings required by law to be made to the Division, and said photographs, photocopies, or microphotocopies, when certified by the Division as true and correct photographs, photocopies, or microphotocopies, shall be as admissible in evidence in all actions, proceedings, and matters as the originals thereof would have been.

(b) The provisions of this section shall apply to records stored on any form of permanent, computer-readable media, such as a CD-ROM, if the medium is not subject to erasure or alteration. Nonerasable, computer-readable storage media may be used for preservation duplicates, as defined in G.S. 132-8.2, or for the preservation of permanently valuable records as provided in G.S. 121-5(d).

History.
1951, c. 262, s. 3; 1999-131, s. 2; 1999-456, s. 47(b); 2001-115, s. 1; 2011-326, s. 13(c); 2011-401, s. 3.2

§ 8-45.4. Title of Article

This Article may be cited as the "Uniform Photographic Copies of Business and Public Records as Evidence Act."

History.
1951, c. 262, s. 4

ARTICLE 4B
EVIDENCE OF FRAUD, DURESS, UNDUE INFLUENCE

§ 8-45.5. Statements, releases, etc., obtained from persons in shock or under the influence of drugs; fraud presumed

Any oral or written statement, waiver, release, receipt, or other representation of any kind by any person made or executed while a patient in any hospital and taken by any person in connection with any type of insurance coverage on or for the benefit of said patient which shall have been taken while such patient was in shock or appreciably under the influence of any drug, including drugs given primarily for sedation, shall be deemed to have been obtained by means of fraud, duress or undue influence on the part of the person or persons taking same, and the same shall be incompetent and inadmissible in evidence to prove or disprove

any fact or circumstance relating to any claim for which any insurance company may be liable under any policy of insurance issued to, or which may indemnify or provide coverage or protection for the person making or executing any such statement or other instrument while a patient in a hospital, nor may any such person making or executing the same be examined or cross-examined in regard thereto.

History.
1967, c. 928

ARTICLE 7
COMPETENCY OF WITNESSES

§ 8-49. Witness not excluded by interest or crime

No person offered as a witness shall be excluded, by reason of incapacity from interest or crime, from giving evidence either in person or by deposition, according to the practice of the court, on the trial of any issue joined, or of any matter or question, or on any inquiry arising in any suit or proceeding, civil or criminal, in any court, or before any judge, justice, jury or other person having, by law, authority to hear, receive and examine evidence; and every person so offered shall be admitted to give evidence, notwithstanding such person may or shall have an interest in the matter in question, or in the event of the trial of the issue, or of the suit or other proceeding in which he is offered as a witness. This section shall not be construed to apply to attesting witnesses to wills.

History.
1866, c. 43, ss. 1, 4; C.C.P., c. 342; 1869-70, c. 177; 1871-2, c. 4; Code, ss. 589, 1350; Rev., ss. 1628, 1629; C.S., s. 1792

§ 8-50. Parties competent as witnesses

(a) On the trial of any issue, or of any matter or question, or on any inquiry arising in any action, suit or other proceeding in court, or before any judge, justice, jury or other person having, by law, authority to hear and examine evidence, the parties themselves and the person in whose behalf any suit or other proceeding may be brought or defended, shall, except as otherwise provided, be competent and compellable to give evidence, either viva voce or by deposition, according to the practice of the court, in behalf of either or any of the parties to said action, suit or other proceeding. Nothing in this section shall be construed to apply to any action or other proceeding in any court instituted in consequence of adultery, or to any action for criminal conversation.

(b), (c) Repealed by Session Laws 1967, c. 954, s. 4.

History.
1866, c. 43, ss. 2, 3; Code, s. 1351; Rev., s. 1630; C.S., s. 1793; 1953, c. 885, s. 1; 1967, c. 954, s. 4

§ 8-50.1. Competency of blood tests; jury charge; taxing of expenses as costs

(a) In the trial of any criminal action or proceeding in any court in which the question of parentage arises, regardless of any presumptions with respect to parentage, the court before whom the matter may be brought, upon motion of the State or the defendant, shall order that the alleged-parent defendant, the known natural parent, and the child submit to any blood tests and comparisons which have been developed and adapted for purposes of establishing or disproving parentage and which are reasonably accessible to the alleged-parent defendant, the known natural parent, and the child. The results of those blood tests and comparisons, including the statistical likelihood of the alleged parent's parentage, if available, shall be admitted in evidence when offered by a duly qualified, licensed practicing physician, duly qualified immunologist, duly qualified geneticist, or other duly qualified person. Upon receipt of a motion and the entry of an order under the provisions of this subsection, the court shall proceed as follows:

(1) Where the issue of parentage is to be decided by a jury, where the results of those blood tests and comparisons are not shown to be inconsistent with the results of any other blood tests and comparisons, and where the results of those blood tests and comparisons indicate that the alleged-parent defendant cannot be the natural parent of the child, the jury shall be instructed that if they believe that the witness presenting the results testified truthfully as to those results, and if they believe that the tests and comparisons were conducted properly, then it will be their duty to decide that the alleged-parent is not the natural parent; whereupon, the court shall enter the special verdict of not guilty; and

(2) By requiring the State or defendant, as the case may be, requesting the blood tests and comparisons pursuant to this subsection to initially be responsible for any of the expenses thereof and upon the entry of a special verdict incorporating a finding of parentage or nonparentage, by taxing the expenses for blood tests and comparisons, in addition to any fees for expert witnesses allowed per G.S. 7A-314 whose testimonies

supported the admissibility thereof, as costs in accordance with G.S. 7A-304; G.S. Chapter 6, Article 7; or G.S. 7A-315, as applicable.

(b) Repealed by Session Laws 1993, c. 333, s. 2.

(b1) In the trial of any civil action in which the question of parentage arises, the court shall, on motion of a party, order the mother, the child, and the alleged father-defendant to submit to one or more blood or genetic marker tests, to be performed by a duly certified physician or other expert. The court shall require the person requesting the blood or genetic marker tests to pay the costs of the tests. The court may, in its discretion, tax as part of costs the expenses for blood or genetic marker tests and comparisons. Verified documentary evidence of the chain of custody of the blood specimens obtained pursuant to this subsection shall be competent evidence to establish the chain of custody. Any party objecting to or contesting the procedures or results of the blood or genetic marker tests shall file with the court written objections setting forth the basis for the objections and shall serve copies thereof upon all other parties not less than 10 days prior to any hearing at which the results may be introduced into evidence. The person contesting the results of the blood or genetic marker tests has the right to subpoena the testing expert pursuant to the Rules of Civil Procedure. If no objections are filed within the time and manner prescribed, the test results are admissible as evidence of paternity without the need for foundation testimony or other proof of authenticity or accuracy. The results of the blood or genetic marker tests shall have the following effect:

(1) If the court finds that the conclusion of all the experts, as disclosed by the evidence based upon the test, is that the probability of the alleged parent's parentage is less than eighty-five percent (85%), the alleged parent is presumed not to be the parent and the evidence shall be admitted. This presumption may be rebutted only by clear, cogent, and convincing evidence;

(2) If the experts disagree in their findings or conclusions, the question of paternity shall be submitted upon all the evidence;

(3) If the tests show that the alleged parent is not excluded and that the probability of the alleged parent's parentage is between eighty-five percent (85%) and ninety-seven percent (97%), this evidence shall be admitted by the court and shall be weighed with other competent evidence;

(4) If the experts conclude that the genetic tests show that the alleged parent is not excluded and that the probability of the alleged parent's parentage is ninety-seven

percent (97%) or higher, the alleged parent is presumed to be the parent and this evidence shall be admitted. This presumption may be rebutted only by clear, cogent, and convincing evidence.

History.
1949, c. 51; 1965, c. 618; 1975, c. 449, ss. 1, 2; 1979, c. 576, s. 1; 1993, c. 333, s. 2; 1993 (Reg. Sess., 1994), c. 733, s. 1

§ 8-50.2. Results of speed-measuring instruments; admissibility

(a) The results of the use of radio microwave, laser, or other speed-measuring instruments shall be admissible as evidence of the speed of an object in any criminal or civil proceeding for the purpose of corroborating the opinion of a person as to the speed of an object based upon the visual observation of the object by such person.

(b) Notwithstanding the provisions of subsection (a) of this section, the results of a radio microwave, laser, or other electronic speed-measuring instrument are not admissible in any proceeding unless it is found that:

(1) The operator of the instrument held, at the time the results of the speed-measuring instrument were obtained, a certificate from the North Carolina Criminal Justice Education and Training Standards Commission (hereinafter referred to as the Commission) authorizing him to operate the speed-measuring instrument from which the results were obtained.

(2) The operator of the instrument operated the speed-measuring instrument in accordance with the procedures established by the Commission for the operation of such instrument.

(3) The instrument employed was approved for use by the Commission and the Secretary of Public Safety pursuant to G.S. 17C-6.

(4) The speed-measuring instrument had been calibrated and tested for accuracy in accordance with the standards established by the Commission for that particular instrument.

(c) All radio microwave, laser, and other electronic speed-measuring instruments shall be tested for accuracy within a 12-month period prior to the alleged violation by a technician possessing at least a General Radiotelephone Operator License from the Federal Communications Commissions or possessing a Certified Electronics Technician certificate issued by a Federal Communications Commission Commercial Operators License Examination Manager or by a laboratory established by the International Association of Chiefs of Police. A written

certificate by the technician or laboratory showing that the test was made within the required period and that the instrument was accurate shall be competent and prima facie evidence of those facts in any proceeding referred to in subsection (a) of this section.

All radio microwave, laser, and other speed enforcement instruments shall be tested in accordance with standards established by the North Carolina Criminal Justice Education and Training Standards Commission. The Commission shall provide for certification of all radio microwave, laser, and other speed enforcement instruments.

(d) In every proceeding where the results of a radio microwave, laser, or other speed-measuring instrument is sought to be admitted, judicial notice shall be taken of the rules approving the use of the models and types of radio microwave, laser, and other speed-measuring instruments and the procedures for operation and calibration or measuring accuracy of such instruments.

History.
1979, 2nd Sess., c. 1184, s. 3; 1983, c. 34; 1987, c. 318; c. 827, s. 60; 1994, Ex. Sess., c. 18, s. 1; 2005-137, s. 1; 2011-145, s. 19.1(g)

N.C. Gen. Stat. § 8-50.3

Expired effective September 30, 2007.

N.C. Gen. Stat. § 8-51

Repealed by Session Laws 1983 (Regular Session, 1984), c. 1037, s. 5.

§ 8-51.1. Dying declarations

Dying declarations admissible in administrative proceedings shall be as provided in G.S. 8C-1, Rule 804.

History.
1973, c. 464, s. 1; 1983 (Reg. Sess., 1984), c. 1037, s. 11

N.C. Gen. Stat. § 8-52

Repealed by Session Laws 1973, c. 41.

§ 8-53. Communications between health care provider and patient

No person, duly authorized to practice under Article 1 of Chapter 90 of the General Statutes, shall be required to disclose any information which he may have acquired in attending a patient in a professional character, and which information was necessary to enable him to prescribe for such patient as a physician, or to do any act for him as a surgeon, and no such information shall be considered public records under G.S. 132-1. Confidential information obtained in medical records shall be furnished only on the authorization of the patient, or if deceased, the executor, administrator, or, in the case of unadministered estates, the next of kin. Any resident or presiding judge in the district, either at the trial or prior thereto, or the Industrial Commission pursuant to law may, subject to G.S. 8-53.6, compel disclosure if in his opinion disclosure is necessary to a proper administration of justice. If the case is in district court the judge shall be a district court judge, and if the case is in superior court the judge shall be a superior court judge.

History.
1885, c. 159; Rev., s. 1621; C.S., s. 1798; 1969, c. 914; 1977, c. 1118; 1983, c. 410, ss. 1, 2; c. 471; 2019-191, s. 41

§ 8-53.1. Physician-patient and nurse privilege; limitations

(a) Notwithstanding the provisions of G.S. 8-53 and G.S. 8-53.13, the physician-patient or nurse privilege shall not be a ground for excluding evidence regarding the abuse or neglect of a child under the age of 16 years or regarding an illness of or injuries to such child or the cause thereof in any judicial proceeding related to a report pursuant to the North Carolina Juvenile Code, Chapter 7B of the General Statutes of North Carolina.

(b) Nothing in this Article shall preclude a health care provider, as defined in G.S. 90-21.11, from disclosing information pursuant to G.S. 90-21.20B.

History.
1965, c. 472, s. 2; 1971, c. 710, s. 2; 1981, c. 469, s. 24; 1998-202, s. 13(b); 2004-186, s. 16.2; 2006-253, s. 18; 2007-115, s. 4

§ 8-53.2. Communications between clergymen and communicants

No priest, rabbi, accredited Christian Science practitioner, or a clergyman or ordained minister of an established church shall be competent to testify in any action, suit or proceeding concerning any information which was communicated to him and entrusted to him in his professional capacity, and necessary to enable him to discharge the functions of his office according to the usual course of his practice or discipline, wherein such person so communicating such information about himself or another is seeking spiritual counsel and advice relative to and growing out of the information so imparted, provided, however, that this section shall not apply where communicant in open court waives the privilege conferred.

History.
1959, c. 646; 1963, c. 200; 1967, c. 794

§ 8-53.3. Communications between psychologist and client or patient

No person, duly authorized as a licensed psychologist or licensed psychological associate, nor any of his or her employees or associates, shall be required to disclose any information which he or she may have acquired in the practice of psychology and which information was necessary to enable him or her to practice psychology. Any resident or presiding judge in the district in which the action is pending may, subject to G.S. 8-53.6, compel disclosure, either at the trial or prior thereto, if in his or her opinion disclosure is necessary to a proper administration of justice. If the case is in district court the judge shall be a district court judge, and if the case is in superior court the judge shall be a superior court judge.

Notwithstanding the provisions of this section, the psychologist-client or patient privilege shall not be grounds for failure to report suspected child abuse or neglect to the appropriate county department of social services, or for failure to report a disabled adult suspected to be in need of protective services to the appropriate county department of social services. Notwithstanding the provisions of this section, the psychologist-client or patient privilege shall not be grounds for excluding evidence regarding the abuse or neglect of a child, or an illness of or injuries to a child, or the cause thereof, or for excluding evidence regarding the abuse, neglect, or exploitation of a disabled adult, or an illness of or injuries to a disabled adult, or the cause thereof, in any judicial proceeding related to a report pursuant to the Child Abuse Reporting Law, Article 3 of Chapter 7B of the General Statutes, or to the Protection of the Abused, Neglected, or Exploited Disabled Adult Act, Article 6 of Chapter 108A of the General Statutes.

History.
1967, c. 910, s. 18; 1983, c. 410, ss. 3, 7; 1987, c. 323, s. 2; 1993, c. 375, s. 2; c. 553, s. 78; 1998-202, s. 13(c)

§ 8-53.4. School counselor privilege

No person certified by the State Department of Public Instruction as a school counselor and duly appointed or designated as such by the governing body of a public school system within this State or by the head of any private school within this State shall be competent to testify in any action, suit, or proceeding concerning any information acquired in rendering counseling services to any student enrolled in such public school system or private school, and which information was necessary to enable him to render counseling services; provided, however, that this section shall not apply where the student in open court waives the privilege conferred. Any resident or presiding judge in the district in which the action is pending may compel disclosure, either at the trial or prior thereto, if in his opinion disclosure is necessary to a proper administration of justice. If the case is in district court the judge shall be the district court judge, and if the case is in superior court the judge shall be a superior court judge.

History.

1971, c. 943; 1983, c. 410, ss. 4, 5

§ 8-53.5. Communications between licensed marital and family therapist and client(s)

No person, duly licensed as a licensed marriage and family therapist, nor any of the person's employees or associates, shall be required to disclose any information which the person may have acquired in rendering professional marriage and family therapy services, and which information was necessary to enable the person to render professional marriage and family therapy services. Any resident or presiding judge in the district in which the action is pending may, subject to G.S. 8-53.6, compel disclosure, either at the trial or prior thereto, if in the court's opinion disclosure is necessary to a proper administration of justice. If the case is in district court the judge shall be a district court judge, and if the case is in superior court the judge shall be a superior court judge.

History.

1979, c. 697, s. 2; 1983, c. 410, ss. 6, 7; 1985, c. 223. s. 1; 2001-487, s. 40(a); 2004-203, s. 18

§ 8-53.6. No disclosure in alimony and divorce actions

In an action pursuant to G.S. 50-5.1, 50-6, 50-7, 50-16.2A, and 50-16.3A if either or both of the parties have sought and obtained marital counseling by a licensed physician, licensed psychologist, licensed psychological associate, licensed clinical social worker, or licensed marriage and family therapist, the person or persons rendering such counseling shall not be competent to testify in the action concerning information acquired while rendering such counseling.

History.

1983, c. 410, s. 8; 2001-152, s. 1

§ 8-53.7. Social worker privilege

No person engaged in delivery of private social work services, duly licensed or certified pursuant to Chapter 90B of the General Statutes shall be required to disclose any information that he or she may have acquired in rendering professional social services, and which information was necessary to enable him or her to render professional social services: provided, that the presiding judge of a superior or district court may compel such disclosure, if in the court's opinion the same is necessary to a proper administration of justice and such disclosure is not prohibited by G.S. 8-53.6 or any other statute or regulation.

History.

1983, c. 495, s. 2; 2001-152, s. 2; 2001-487, s. 40(b)

§ 8-53.8. Counselor privilege

No person, duly licensed pursuant to Chapter 90, Article 24, of the General Statutes, shall be required to disclose any information which he or she may have acquired in rendering clinical mental health counseling services, and which information was necessary to enable him or her to render clinical mental health counseling services: Provided, that the presiding judge of a superior or district court may compel such disclosure, if in the court's opinion the same is necessary to a proper administration of justice and such disclosure is not prohibited by other statute or regulation.

History.

1983, c. 755, s. 2; 1993, c. 514, s. 2; 2019-240, s. 3(a)

§ 8-53.9. Optometrist/patient privilege

No person licensed pursuant to Article 6 of Chapter 90 of the General Statutes shall be required to disclose any information that may have been acquired in rendering professional optometric services and which information was necessary to enable that person to render professional optometric services, except that the presiding judge of a superior or district court may compel this disclosure, if, in the court's opinion, disclosure is necessary to a proper administration of justice and disclosure is not prohibited by other statute or rule.

History.

1997-75, s. 4; 1997-304, s. 3

§ 8-53.10. Peer support group counselors

(a) **Definitions.** -- The following definitions apply in this section:

(1) **Client law enforcement employee.** -- Any law enforcement employee or a member of his or her immediate family who is in need of and receives peer

counseling services offered by the officer's employing law enforcement agency.

(2) **Immediate family.** -- A spouse, child, stepchild, parent, or stepparent.

(3) **Peer counselor.** -- Any law enforcement officer or civilian employee of a law enforcement agency who:

a. Has received training to provide emotional and moral support and counseling to client law enforcement employees and their immediate families; and

b. Was designated by the sheriff, police chief, or other head of a law enforcement agency to counsel a client law enforcement employee.

(4) **Privileged communication.** -- Any communication made by a client law enforcement employee or a member of the client law enforcement employee's immediate family to a peer counselor while receiving counseling.

(b) A peer counselor shall not disclose any privileged communication that was necessary to enable the counselor to render counseling services unless one of the following apply:

(1) The disclosure is authorized by the client or, if the client is deceased, the disclosure is authorized by the client's executor, administrator, or in the case of unadministrated estates, the client's next of kin.

(2) The disclosure is necessary to the proper administration of justice and, subject to G.S. 8-53.6, is compelled by a resident or presiding judge. If the case is in district court the judge shall be a district court judge, and if the case is in superior court the judge shall be a superior court judge.

(c) The privilege established by this section shall not apply:

(1) If the peer counselor was an initial responding officer, a witness, or a party to the incident that prompted the delivery of peer counseling services.

(2) To communications made while the peer counselor was not acting in his or her official capacity as a peer counselor.

(3) To communications related to a violation of criminal law. This subdivision does not require the disclosure of otherwise privileged communications related to an officer's use of force.

(d) Notwithstanding the provisions of this section, the peer counselor privilege shall not be grounds for failure to report suspected child abuse or neglect to the appropriate county department of social services, or for failure to report a disabled adult suspected to be in need of protective services to the appropriate county department of social services. Notwithstanding the provisions of this section, the peer counselor privilege shall not be grounds for excluding evidence regarding the abuse or neglect of a child, or an illness of or injuries to a child, or the cause thereof, or for excluding evidence regarding the abuse, neglect, or exploitation of a disabled adult, or an illness of or injuries to a disabled adult, or the cause thereof, in any judicial proceeding related to a report pursuant to the Child Abuse Reporting Law, Article 3 of Chapter 7B, or to the Protection of the Abused, Neglected, or Exploited Disabled Adult Act, Article 6 of Chapter 108A of the General Statutes.

History.
1999-374, s. 1

§ 8-53.11. Persons, companies, or other entities engaged in gathering or dissemination of news

(a) **Definitions.** -- The following definitions apply in this section:

(1) **Journalist.** -- Any person, company, or entity, or the employees, independent contractors, or agents of that person, company, or entity, engaged in the business of gathering, compiling, writing, editing, photographing, recording, or processing information for dissemination via any news medium.

(2) **Legal proceeding.** -- Any grand jury proceeding or grand jury investigation; any criminal prosecution, civil suit, or related proceeding in any court; and any judicial or quasi-judicial proceeding before any administrative, legislative, or regulatory board, agency, or tribunal.

(3) **News medium.** -- Any entity regularly engaged in the business of publication or distribution of news via print, broadcast, or other electronic means accessible to the general public.

(b) A journalist has a qualified privilege against disclosure in any legal proceeding of any confidential or nonconfidential information, document, or item obtained or prepared while acting as a journalist.

(c) In order to overcome the qualified privilege provided by subsection (b) of this section, any person seeking to compel a journalist to testify or produce information must establish by the greater weight of the evidence that the testimony or production sought:

(1) Is relevant and material to the proper administration of the legal proceeding for which the testimony or production is sought;

(2) Cannot be obtained from alternate sources; and

(3) Is essential to the maintenance of a claim or defense of the person on whose behalf the testimony or production is sought.

Any order to compel any testimony or production as to which the qualified privilege has been asserted shall be issued only after notice to the journalist and a hearing and shall include clear and specific findings as to the showing made by the person seeking the testimony or production.

(d) Notwithstanding subsections (b) and (c) of this section, a journalist has no privilege against disclosure of any information, document, or item obtained as the result of the journalist's eyewitness observations of criminal or tortious conduct, including any physical evidence or visual or audio recording of the observed conduct.

History.
1999-267, s. 1

§ 8-53.12. Communications with agents of rape crisis centers and domestic violence programs privileged

(a) **Definitions.** -- The following definitions apply in this section:

(1) **Agent.** -- An employee or agent of a center who has completed a minimum of 20 hours of training as required by the center, or a volunteer, under the direct supervision of a center supervisor, who has completed a minimum of 20 hours of training as required by the center.

(2) **Center.** -- A domestic violence program or rape crisis center.

(3) **Domestic violence program.** -- A nonprofit organization or program whose primary purpose is to provide services to domestic violence victims.

(4) **Domestic violence victim.** -- Any person alleging domestic violence as defined by G.S. 50B-1, who consults an agent of a domestic violence program for the purpose of obtaining, for himself or herself, advice, counseling, or other services concerning mental, emotional, or physical injuries suffered as a result of the domestic violence. The term shall also include those persons who have a significant relationship with a victim of domestic violence and who have sought, for themselves, advice, counseling, or other services concerning a mental, physical, or emotional condition caused or reasonably believed to be caused by the domestic violence against the victim.

(5) **Rape crisis center.** -- Any publicly or privately funded agency, institution, organization, or facility that offers counseling and other services to victims of sexual assault and their families.

(6) **Services.** -- Includes, but is not limited to, crisis hotlines; safe homes and shelters; assessment and intake; children of violence services; individual counseling; support in medical, administrative, and judicial systems; transportation, relocation,

and crisis intervention. The term does not include investigation of physical or sexual assault of children under the age of 16.

(7) **Sexual assault.** -- Any alleged violation of G.S. 14-27.21, 14-27.22, 14-27.24, 14-27.25, 14-27.26, 14-27.27, 14-27.29, 14-27.30, 14-27.31, 14-27.32, or 14-202.1, whether or not a civil or criminal action arises as a result of the alleged violation.

(8) **Sexual assault victim.** -- Any person alleging sexual assault, who consults an agent of a rape crisis center for the purpose of obtaining, for themselves, advice, counseling, or other services concerning mental, physical, or emotional injuries suffered as a result of sexual assault. The term shall also include those persons who have a significant relationship with a victim of sexual assault and who have sought, for themselves, advice, counseling, or other services concerning a mental, physical, or emotional condition caused or reasonably believed to be caused by sexual assault of a victim.

(9) **Victim.** -- A sexual assault victim or a domestic violence victim.

(b) **Privileged Communications.** -- No agent of a center shall be required to disclose any information which the agent acquired during the provision of services to a victim and which information was necessary to enable the agent to render the services; provided, however, that this subsection shall not apply where the victim waives the privilege conferred. Any agent or center that receives a request for such information shall make every effort to inform the victim of the request and provide the victim a copy of the request if the request was in writing. Any resident or presiding judge in the district in which the action is pending shall compel disclosure, either at the trial or prior thereto, if the court finds, by a preponderance of the evidence, a good faith, specific and reasonable basis for believing that (i) the records or testimony sought contain information that is relevant and material to factual issues to be determined in a civil proceeding, or is relevant, material, and exculpatory upon the issue of guilt, degree of guilt, or sentencing in a criminal proceeding for the offense charged or any lesser included offense, (ii) the evidence is not sought merely for character impeachment purposes, and (iii) the evidence sought is not merely cumulative of other evidence or information available or already obtained by the party seeking the disclosure or the party's counsel. If the case is in district court, the judge shall be a district court judge, and if the case is in superior court, the judge shall be a superior court judge.

The judge in any court proceeding subject to this section shall inquire as to whether the victim is present and wishes to be heard. If the victim is present and wishes to be heard, the court shall grant the victim an opportunity to be reasonably heard. The right to be reasonably heard may be exercised, at the victim's discretion, through an oral statement, submission of a written statement, or submission of an audio or video statement. Before requiring production of records, the court must find that the party seeking disclosure has made a sufficient showing that the records are likely to contain information subject to disclosure under this subsection. If the court finds a sufficient showing has been made, the court shall order that the records be produced for the court under seal, shall examine the records in camera, and may allow disclosure of those portions of the records which the court finds contain information subject to disclosure under this subsection. After all appeals in the action have been exhausted, any records received by the court under seal shall be returned to the center, unless otherwise ordered by the court. The privilege afforded under this subsection terminates upon the death of the victim.

(c) **Duty in Case of Abuse or Neglect. --** Nothing in this section shall be construed to relieve any person of any duty pertaining to abuse or neglect of a child or disabled adult as required by law.

History.
2001-277, s. 1; 2015-181, s. 31; 2019-216, s. 1.5

§ 8-53.13. Nurse privilege

No person licensed pursuant to Article 9A of Chapter 90 of the General Statutes shall be required to disclose any information that may have been acquired in rendering professional nursing services, and which information was necessary to enable that person to render professional nursing services, except that the presiding judge of a superior or district court may compel disclosure if, in the court's opinion, disclosure is necessary to a proper administration of justice and disclosure is not prohibited by other statute or rule. Nothing in this section shall preclude the admission of otherwise admissible written or printed medical records in any judicial proceeding, in accordance with the procedure set forth in G.S. 8-44.1, after a determination by the court that disclosure should be compelled as set forth herein.

History.
2003-342, s. 1; 2004-186, s. 16.1

§ 8-53.14. Communications between behavior analyst and client or patient.

No individual authorized as a licensed behavior analyst, or any of the individual's employees or associates, shall be required to disclose any information that the individual may have acquired in the practice of behavior analysis and which information was necessary to enable the individual to practice behavior analysis. Any resident or presiding judge in the district in which the action is pending may, subject to G.S. 8-53.6, compel disclosure, either at or before trial, if in the judge's opinion, disclosure is necessary to a proper administration of justice. If the case is in district court, the judge shall be a district court judge, and if the case is in superior court, the judge shall be a superior court judge.

Notwithstanding the provisions of this section, the behavior analyst -- client or behavior analyst -- patient privilege shall not be grounds for failure to report suspected child abuse or neglect to the appropriate county department of social services or for failure to report a disabled adult suspected to be in need of protective services to the appropriate county department of social services. Notwithstanding the provisions of this section, the behavior analyst -- client or behavior analyst -- patient privilege shall not be grounds for excluding any evidence of abuse, neglect, illness, or injuries of a child or for excluding any evidence regarding the abuse, neglect, exploitation, illness, or injuries of a disabled adult in any judicial proceeding related to a report pursuant to Article 3 of Chapter 7B of the General Statutes.

History.
2021-22, s. 3

§ 8-54. Defendant in criminal action competent but not compellable to testify

In the trial of all indictments, complaints, or other proceedings against persons charged with the commission of crimes, offenses or misdemeanors, the person so charged is, at his own request, but not otherwise, a competent witness, and his failure to make such request shall not create any presumption against him. But every such person examined as a witness shall be subject to cross-examination as other witnesses. Except as above provided, nothing in this section shall render any person, who in any criminal proceeding is charged with the commission of a criminal offense, competent or compellable to give evidence against himself, nor render any person compellable to answer any question tending to criminate himself.

History.
1856-7, c. 23; 1866, c. 43, s. 3; 1868-9, c. 209, s. 4; 1881, c. 89, s. 3; c. 110, ss. 2, 3; Code ss. 1353, 1354; Rev., ss. 1634, 1635; C.S., s. 1799

§ 8-55. Testimony enforced in certain criminal investigations; immunity

If any justice, judge or magistrate of the General Court of Justice shall have good reason to believe that any person within his jurisdiction has knowledge of the existence and establishment of any faro bank, faro table or other gaming table prohibited by law, or of any place where alcoholic beverages are sold contrary to law, in any town or county within his jurisdiction, such person not being minded to make voluntary information thereof on oath, then it shall be lawful for such justice, magistrate, or judge to issue to the sheriff of the county in which such faro bank, faro table, gaming table, or place where alcoholic beverages are sold contrary to law is supposed to be a subpoena, capias ad testificandum, or other summons in writing, commanding such person to appear immediately before such justice, magistrate, or judge and give evidence on oath as to what he may know touching the existence, establishment and whereabouts of such faro bank, faro table or other gaming table, or place where alcoholic beverages are sold contrary to law, and the name and personal description of the keeper thereof. Such evidence, when obtained, shall be considered and held in law as an information on oath, and the justice, magistrate or judge may thereupon proceed to seize and arrest such keeper and destroy such table, or issue process therefor as provided by law. No person shall be excused, on any prosecution, from testifying touching any unlawful gaming done by himself or others; but no discovery made by the witness upon such examination shall be used against him in any penal or criminal prosecution, and he shall be altogether pardoned of the offenses so done or participated in by him.

History.

R.C., c. 35, s. 50; 1858-9, c. 34, s. 1; Code, ss. 1050, 1215; 1889, c. 355; Rev., ss. 1637, 3721; 1913, c. 141; C.S., s. 1800; 1969, c. 44, s. 22; 1971, c. 381, s. 4; 1981, c. 412, s. 4(4); c. 747, s. 66

§ 8-56. Husband and wife as witnesses in civil action

In any trial or inquiry in any suit, action or proceeding in any court, or before any person having, by law or consent of parties, authority to examine witnesses or hear evidence, the husband or wife of any party thereto, or of any person in whose behalf any such suit, action or proceeding is brought, prosecuted, opposed or defended, shall, except as herein stated, be competent and compellable to give evidence, as any other witness on behalf of any party to such suit, action or proceeding. No husband or wife shall be compellable to disclose any confidential communication made by one to the other during their marriage.

History.

1866, c. 43, ss. 3, 4; C.C.P., s. 341; Code, s. 588; Rev., s. 1636; 1919, c. 18; C.S., s. 1801; 1945, c. 635; 1977, c. 547; 1983 (Reg. Sess., 1984), c. 1037, s. 3

§ 8-57. Husband and wife as witnesses in criminal actions

(a) The spouse of the defendant shall be a competent witness for the defendant in all criminal actions, but the failure of the defendant to call such spouse as a witness shall not be used against him. Such spouse is subject to cross-examination as are other witnesses.

(b) The spouse of the defendant shall be competent but not compellable to testify for the State against the defendant in any criminal action or grand jury proceedings, except that the spouse of the defendant shall be both competent and compellable to so testify:

(1) In a prosecution for bigamy or criminal cohabitation, to prove the fact of marriage and facts tending to show the absence of divorce or annulment;

(2) In a prosecution for assaulting or communicating a threat to the other spouse;

(3) In a prosecution for trespass in or upon the separate lands or residence of the other spouse when living separate and apart from each other by mutual consent or court order;

(4) In a prosecution for abandonment of or failure to provide support for the other spouse or their child;

(5) In a prosecution of one spouse for any other criminal offense against the minor child of either spouse, including any child of either spouse who is born out of wedlock or adopted or a foster child.

(c) No husband or wife shall be compellable in any event to disclose any confidential communication made by one to the other during their marriage.

History.

1856-7, c. 23; 1866, c. 43; 1868-9, c. 209; 1881, c. 110; Code, ss. 588, 1353, 1354; Rev., ss. 1634, 1635, 1636; C.S., s. 1802; 1933, c. 13, s. 1; c. 361; 1951, c. 296; 1957, c. 1036; 1967, c. 116; 1971, c. 800; 1973, c. 1286, s. 11; 1983, c. 170, s. 1; 1985 (Reg. Sess., 1986), c. 843, s. 5; 1987 (Reg. Sess., 1988), c. 1040, s. 1; 1989 (Reg. Sess., 1990), c. 1039, s. 4; 1991, c, 686, s. 3; 2013-198, s. 2

§ 8-57.1. Husband-wife privilege waived in child abuse

Notwithstanding the provisions of G.S. 8-56 and G.S. 8-57, the husband-wife privilege shall not be ground for excluding evidence regarding the abuse or neglect of a child under the age of 16 years or regarding an illness of or injuries to such child or the cause thereof in any judicial proceeding related to a report pursuant to the Child Abuse Reporting Law, Article 3 of Chapter 7B of the General Statutes of North Carolina.

History.
1971, c. 710, s. 3; 1998-202, s. 13(d)

§ 8-57.2. Presumed father or mother as witnesses where paternity at issue

Whenever an issue of paternity of a child born or conceived during a marriage arises in any civil or criminal proceeding, the presumed father or the mother of such child is competent to give evidence as to any relevant matter regarding paternity of the child, including nonaccess to the present or former spouse, regardless of any privilege which may otherwise apply. No parent offering such evidence shall thereafter be prosecuted based upon that evidence for any criminal act involved in the conception of the child whose paternity is in issue and/or for whom support is sought, except for perjury committed in this testimony.

History.
1981, c. 634, s. 1

N.C. Gen. Stat. § 8-58

Repealed by Session Laws 1973, c. 1286, ss. 11, 26.

§ 8-58.1. Injured party as witness when medical charges at issue

(a) Whenever an issue of hospital, medical, dental, pharmaceutical, or funeral charges arises in any civil proceeding, the injured party or his guardian, administrator, or executor is competent to give evidence regarding the amount paid or required to be paid in full satisfaction of such charges, provided that records or copies of such charges showing the amount paid or required to be paid in full satisfaction of such charges accompany such testimony.

(b) The testimony of a person pursuant to subsection (a) of this section establishes a rebuttable presumption of the reasonableness of the amount paid or required to be paid in full satisfaction of the charges. However, in the event that the provider of hospital, medical, dental, pharmaceutical, or funeral services gives sworn testimony that the charge for that provider's service either was satisfied by payment of an amount less than the amount charged, or can be satisfied by payment of an amount less than the amount charged, then with respect to that provider's charge only, the presumption of the reasonableness of the amount charged is rebutted and a rebuttable presumption is established

that the lesser satisfaction amount is the reasonable amount of the charges for the testifying provider's services. For the purposes of this subsection, the word "provider" shall include the agent or employee of a provider of hospital, medical, dental, pharmaceutical, or funeral services, or a person with responsibility to pay a provider of hospital, medical, dental, pharmaceutical, or funeral services on behalf of an injured party.

(c) The fact that a provider charged for services provided to the injured person establishes a permissive presumption that the services provided were reasonably necessary but no presumption is established that the services provided were necessary because of injuries caused by the acts or omissions of an alleged tortfeasor.

History.
1983, c. 776, s. 1; 2011-283, s. 1.2; 2011-317, s. 1.1

ARTICLE 7A
RESTRICTIONS ON EVIDENCE IN RAPE CASES

§§ 8-58.6 through 8-58.11

Repealed by Session Laws 1983 (Regular Session, 1984), c. 1037, s. 2.

ARTICLE 7B
EXPERT TESTIMONY

§§ 8-58.12 through 8-58.14

Repealed by Session Laws 1983 (Regular Session, 1984), c. 1037, s. 9.

ARTICLE 7C
ADMISSIBILITY OF FORENSIC EVIDENCE

§ 8-58.20. Forensic analysis admissible as evidence

(a) In any criminal prosecution, a laboratory report of a written forensic analysis, including an analysis of the defendant's DNA, or a forensic sample alleged to be the defendant's DNA, as that term is defined in G.S. 15A-266.2(2), that states the results of the analysis and that is signed and sworn to by the person performing the analysis may be admissible in evidence without the testimony of the analyst who prepared the report in accordance with the requirements of this section.

(b) A forensic analysis, to be admissible under this section, shall be performed by a laboratory that is accredited by an accrediting body that requires conformance to forensic specific requirements and which is a signatory to the International Laboratory Accreditation Cooperation (ILAC) Mutual Recognition Arrangement For Testing for the submission, identification, analysis, and storage of forensic analyses. The analyses of DNA samples and typing results of DNA samples shall be performed by a laboratory that is accredited by an accrediting body that requires conformance to forensic specific requirements and which is a signatory to the ILAC Mutual Recognition Arrangement For Testing.

(c) The analyst who analyzes the forensic sample and signs the report shall complete an affidavit on a form developed by the State Crime Laboratory. In the affidavit, the analyst shall state (i) that the person is qualified by education, training, and experience to perform the analysis, (ii) the name and location of the laboratory where the analysis was performed, and (iii) that performing the analysis is part of that person's regular duties. The analyst shall also aver in the affidavit that the tests were performed pursuant to the accrediting body's standards for that discipline and that the evidence was handled in accordance with established and accepted procedures while in the custody of the laboratory. The affidavit shall be sufficient to constitute prima facie evidence regarding the person's qualifications. The analyst shall attach the affidavit to the laboratory report and shall provide the affidavit to the investigating officer and the district attorney in the prosecutorial district in which the criminal charges are pending. An affidavit by a forensic analyst sworn to and properly executed before an official authorized to administer oaths is admissible in evidence without further authentication in any criminal proceeding with respect to the forensic analysis administered and the procedures followed.

(d) The district attorney shall serve a copy of the laboratory report and affidavit and indicate whether the report and affidavit will be offered as evidence at any proceeding against the defendant on the attorney of record for the defendant, or on the defendant if that person has no attorney, no later than five business days after receiving the report and affidavit, or 30 business days before any proceeding in which the report may be used against the defendant, whichever occurs first.

(e) Upon receipt of a copy of the laboratory report and affidavit, the attorney of record for the defendant or the defendant if that person has no attorney, shall have 15 business days to file a written objection to the use of the laboratory report and affidavit at any proceeding against the defendant. The written objection shall be filed with the court in which the matter is pending with a copy provided to the district attorney.

(f) If the defendant's attorney of record, or the defendant if that person has no attorney, fails to file a written objection with the court to the use of the laboratory report and affidavit within the time allowed by this section, then the objection shall be deemed waived and the laboratory report and affidavit shall be admitted in evidence in any proceeding without the testimony of the analyst subject to the presiding judge ruling otherwise at the proceeding when offered. If, however, a written objection is filed, this section does not apply and the admissibility of the evidence shall be determined and governed by the appropriate rules of evidence.

(g) **Procedure for Establishing Chain of Custody of Evidence Subject to Forensic Analysis Without Calling Unnecessary Witnesses.** --

(1) For the purpose of establishing the chain of physical custody or control of evidence that has been subjected to forensic analysis performed as provided in subsection (b) of this section, a statement signed by each successive person in the chain of custody that the person delivered it to the other person indicated on or about the date stated is prima facie evidence that the person had custody and made the delivery as stated, without the necessity of a personal appearance in court by the person signing the statement.

(2) The statement shall contain a sufficient description of the material or its container so as to distinguish it as the particular item in question and shall state that the material was delivered in essentially the same condition as received. The statement may be placed on the same document as the report provided for in subsection (a) of this section.

(3) The provisions of this subsection may be utilized by the State only if (i) the State notifies the defendant at least 15 business days before any proceeding at which the statement would be used of its intention to introduce the statement into evidence under this subsection and provides the defendant with a copy of the statement and (ii) the defendant fails to file a written notification with the court, with a copy to the State, at least five business days before the proceeding that the defendant objects to the introduction of the statement into evidence.

(4) In lieu of the notice required in subdivision (3) of this subsection, the State may include the statement with the laboratory report and affidavit, as provided in subsection (d) of this section.

(5) If the defendant's attorney of record, or the defendant if that person has no attorney, fails to file the written objection as provided in this subsection, then the

objection shall be deemed waived and the statement shall be admitted into evidence without the necessity of a personal appearance by the person signing the statement.

(6) Upon filing a timely objection, the admissibility of the statement shall be determined and governed by the appropriate rules of evidence.

Nothing in this subsection precludes the right of any party to call any witness or to introduce any evidence supporting or contradicting the evidence contained in the statement.

(h) This section does not apply to chemical analyses under G.S. 20-139.1.

History.
2004-124, s. 15.2(c); 2007-484, s. 1; 2009-473, s. 7; 2011-19, s. 7; 2011-307, s. 9; 2012-168, s. 6; 2013-171, ss. 2, 3; 2013-194, s. 2; 2013-338, s. 1; 2014-100, s. 17.1(u); 2015-173, s. 1

ARTICLE 8
ATTENDANCE OF WITNESS

§ 8-59. Issue and service of subpoena

In obtaining the testimony of witnesses in causes pending in the trial divisions of the General Court of Justice, subpoenas shall be issued and served in the manner provided in Rule 45 of the Rules of Civil Procedure for civil actions. Provided that in criminal cases any employee of a local law-enforcement agency may effect service of a subpoena for the attendance of witnesses by telephone communication with the person named. However, in the case of a witness served by telephone communication pursuant to this section, neither an order to show cause nor an order for arrest shall be issued until such person has been served personally with the written subpoena.

History.
1777, c. 115, s. 36, P.R.; R.C., c. 31, s. 59; Code, s. 1355; Rev., s. 1639; C.S., s. 1803; 1959, c. 522, s. 2; 1967, c. 954, s. 3; 1971, c. 381, s. 5; 1981, c. 267; 1989, c. 262, s. 2

N.C. Gen. Stat. § 8-60

Repealed by Session Laws 1967, c. 954, s. 4.

§ 8-61. Subpoena for the production of documentary evidence

Subpoenas for the production of records, books, papers, documents, or tangible things may be issued in criminal actions in the same manner as provided for civil actions in Rule 45 of the Rules of Civil Procedure.

History.
1797, c. 476, P.R.; R.C., c. 31, s. 81; Code, s. 1372; Rev., s. 1641; C.S., s. 1805; 1967, c. 954, s. 3; c. 1168

N.C. Gen. Stat. § 8-62

Repealed by Session Laws 1967, c. 954, s. 4.

§ 8-63. Witnesses attend until discharge; effect of nonattendance

Every witness, being summoned to appear in any of the said courts, in manner before directed, shall appear accordingly, and, subject to the provisions of G.S. 6-51, continue to attend from session to session until discharged, when summoned in a civil action or special proceeding, by the court or the party at whose instance such witness shall be summoned, or, when summoned in a criminal prosecution, until discharged by the court, the prosecuting officer, or the party at whose instance he was summoned; and in default thereof shall forfeit and pay, in civil actions or special proceedings, to the party at whose instance the subpoena issued, the sum of forty dollars ($ 40.00), to be recovered by motion in the cause, and shall be further liable to his action for the full damages which may be sustained for the want of such witness's testimony; or if summoned in a criminal prosecution shall forfeit and pay eighty dollars ($ 80.00) for the use of the State, or the party summoning him. If the civil action or special proceeding shall, in the vacation, be compromised and settled between the parties, and the party at whose instance such witness was summoned should omit to discharge him from further attendance, and for want of such discharge he shall attend the next session, in that case the witness, upon oath made of the facts, shall be entitled to a ticket from the clerk in the same manner as other witnesses, and shall recover from the party at whose instance he was summoned the allowance which is given to witnesses for their attendance, with costs.

No execution shall issue against any defaulting witness for the forfeiture aforesaid but after notice made known to him to show cause against the issuing thereof; and if sufficient cause be shown of his incapacity to attend, execution shall not issue, and the witness shall be discharged of the forfeiture without costs; but otherwise the court shall, on motion, award execution for the forfeiture against the defaulting witness.

History.
1777, c. 115, ss. 37, 38, 43, P.R.; 1799, c. 528, P.R.; 1801, c. 591, P.R.; R.C., c. 31, ss. 60, 61, 62; Code, s. 1356; Rev., s. 1643; C.S., s. 1807; 1965, c. 284; 1971, c. 381, s. 12

§ 8-64. Witnesses exempt from civil arrest

Every witness shall be exempt from arrest in civil actions or special proceedings during his attendance at any court, or before a commissioner, arbitrator, referee, or other person authorized to command the attendance of such witness, and during the time such witness is going to and returning from the place of such attendance, allowing one day for every thirty miles such witness has to travel to and from his place of residence.

History.
1777, c. 115, s. 44, P.R.; R.C., c. 31, s. 70; Code, s. 1367; Rev., s. 1644; C.S., s. 1808

ARTICLE 9
ATTENDANCE OF WITNESSES FROM WITHOUT STATE

§§ 8-65 through 8-70

Transferred to G.S. 15A-811 through 15A-816 by Session Laws 1973, c. 1286, s. 9.

ARTICLE 10
DEPOSITIONS

§§ 8-71 through 8-73

Repealed by Session Laws 1967, c. 954, s. 4.

§ 8-74. Depositions for defendant in criminal actions

In all criminal actions, hearings and investigations it shall be lawful for the defendant in any such action to make affidavit before the clerk of the superior court of the county in which said action is pending, that it is important for the defense that he have the testimony of any person, whose name must be given, and that such person is so infirm, or otherwise physically incapacitated, or nonresident of this State, that he cannot procure his attendance at the trial or hearing of said cause. Upon the filing of such affidavit, it shall be the duty of the clerk to appoint some responsible person to take the deposition of such witness, which deposition may be read in the trial of such criminal action under the same rules as now apply by law to depositions in civil actions: provided, that the district attorney or prosecuting attorney of the district, county or town in which such action is pending have 10 days' notice of the taking of such deposition, who may appear in person or by representative to conduct the cross-examination of such witness.

History.
Code, s. 1357; 1891, c. 522; 1893, c. 80; Rev., s. 1652; 1915, c. 251; C.S., s. 1812; 1971, c. 381, s. 6; 1973, c. 47, s. 2

N.C. Gen. Stat. § 8-75

Repealed by Session Laws 1971, c. 381, s. 13.

§ 8-76. Depositions before municipal authorities

Any board of aldermen, board of town or county commissioners or any person interested in any proceeding, investigation, hearing or trial before such board, may take the depositions of all persons whose evidence may be desired for use in said proceeding, investigation, hearing or trial; and to do so, the chairman of such board or such person may apply in person or by attorney to the superior court clerk of that county in which such proceeding, investigation, hearing or trial is pending, for a commission to take the same, and said clerk, upon such application, shall issue such commission, or such deposition may be taken by a notary public of this State or of any other state or foreign country without a commission issuing from the court; and the notice and proceedings upon the taking of said depositions shall be the same as provided for in civil actions; and if the person upon whom the notice of the taking of such deposition is to be served is absent from or cannot after due diligence be found within this State, but can be found within the county in which the deposition is to be taken, then, and in that case, said notice shall be personally served on such person by the commissioner appointed to take such deposition or by the notary taking such deposition, as the case may be; and when any such deposition is returned to the clerk it shall be opened and passed upon by him and delivered to such board, and the reading and using of such deposition shall conform to the rules of the superior court.

History.
1889, c. 151; Rev., s. 1653; C.S., s. 1814; 1943, c. 543

N.C. Gen. Stat. § 8-77

Repealed by Session Laws 1995, c. 379, s. 9.

§ 8-78. Commissioner may subpoena witness and punish for contempt

Commissioners to take depositions appointed by the courts of this State, or by the courts of the states or territories of the United States, arbitrators, referees, and all persons acting under a commission issuing from any court of record in this State, are hereby empowered, they or the clerks of the courts respectively in this State, to which such commission shall be returnable, to issue subpoenas, specifying the time and place for the attendance of witnesses before them, and to administer oaths to said witnesses, to the end that they may give their testimony. And any witness appearing before any of the said persons and refusing to give his testimony on oath touching such matters as he may be lawfully examined unto shall be committed, by warrant of the person before whom he shall so refuse, to the common jail of the county, there to remain until he may be willing to give his evidence; which warrant of commitment shall recite what authority the person has to take the testimony of such witness, and the refusal of the witness to give it.

History.
1777, c. 115, s. 42, P.R.; 1805, c. 685, ss. 1, 2, P.R.; 1848, c. 66; 1850, c. 188; R.C., c. 31, s. 64; Code, s. 1362; Rev., s. 1649; C.S., s. 1816

§ 8-79. Attendance before commissioner enforced

The sheriff of the county where the witness may be shall execute all such subpoenas, and make due return thereof before the commissioner, or other person, before whom the witness is to appear, in the same manner, and under the same penalties, as in case of process of a like kind returnable to court; and when the witness shall be subpoenaed five days before the time of his required attendance, and shall fail to appear according to the subpoena and give evidence, the default shall be noted by the commissioner, arbitrator, or other person aforesaid; and in case the default be made before a commissioner acting under authority from courts without the State, the defaulting witness shall forfeit and pay to the party at whose instance he may be subpoenaed fifty dollars, and on the trial for such penalty the subpoena issued by the commissioner, or other person, as aforesaid, with the indorsement thereon of due service by the officer serving the same, together with the default noted as aforesaid and indorsed on the subpoena, shall be prima facie evidence of the forfeiture, and sufficient to entitle the plaintiff to judgment for the same, unless the witness may show his incapacity to have attended.

History.
1848, c. 66, s. 2; 1850, c. 188, ss. 1, 2; R.C., c. 31, s. 65; Code, s. 1363; Rev., s. 1650; C.S., s. 1817

§ 8-80. Remedies against defaulting witness before commissioner

But in case the default be made before a commissioner, arbitrator, referee or other person,

acting under a commission or authority from any of the courts of this State, then the same shall be certified under his hand, and returned with the subpoena to the court by which he was commissioned or empowered to take the evidence of such witness; and thereupon the court shall adjudge the defaulting witness to pay to the party at whose instance he was summoned the sum of forty dollars ($ 40.00); but execution shall not issue therefor until the same be ordered by the court, after such proceedings had as shall give said witness an opportunity to show cause, if he can, against the issuing thereof.

History.
1850, c. 188, s. 2; R.C., c. 31, s. 66; Code, s. 1364; Rev., s. 1651; C.S., s. 1818

§ 8-81. Objection to deposition before trial

At any time before the trial, or hearing of an action or proceeding, any party may make a motion to the judge or court to reject a deposition for irregularity in the taking of it, either in whole or in part, for scandal, impertinence, the incompetency of the testimony, for insufficient notice, or for any other good cause. The objecting party shall state his exceptions in writing.

History.
1869-70, c. 227, ss. 13, 17; Code, s. 1361; 1895, c. 312; 1903, c. 132; Rev., s. 1648; C.S., s. 1819

§ 8-82. Deposition not quashed after trial begun

No deposition shall be quashed, or rejected, on objection first made after a trial has begun, merely because of an irregularity in taking the same, provided it shall appear that the party objecting had notice that it had been taken, and it was on file long enough before the trial to enable him to present his objection.

History.
1869-70, c. 227, s. 12; Code, s. 1360; Rev., s. 1647; C.S., s. 1820

§ 8-83. When deposition may be read on the trial

Every deposition taken and returned in the manner provided by law may be read on the trial of the action or proceeding, or before any referee, in the following cases, and not otherwise:

(1) If the witness is dead, or has become insane since the deposition was taken.

(2) If the witness is a resident of a foreign country, or of another state, and is not present at the trial.

(3) If the witness is confined in a prison outside the county in which the trial takes place.

(4) If the witness is so old, sick or infirm as to be unable to attend court.

(5) If the witness is the President of the United States, or the head of any department of the federal government, or a judge, district attorney, or clerk of any court of the United States, and the trial shall take place during the term of such court.

(6) If the witness is the Governor of the State, or the head of any department of the State government, or the president of the University, or the head of any other incorporated college in the State, or the superintendent or any physician in the employ of any of the hospitals for the insane for the State.

(7) If the witness is a justice of the Supreme Court, judge of the Court of Appeals, or a judge, presiding officer, clerk or district attorney of any court of record, and the trial shall take place during the term of such court.

(8) If the witness is a member of the Congress of the United States, or a member of the General Assembly, and the trial shall take place during a time that such member is in the service of that body.

(9) Except in actions or proceedings governed by the Rules of Civil Procedure, if the witness has been duly summoned, and at the time of the trial is out of the State, or is more than seventy-five miles by the usual public mode of travel from the place where the court is sitting, without the procurement or consent of the party offering his deposition.

(10) If the action is pending in a magistrate's court the deposition may be read on the trial of the action, provided the witness is more than 75 miles by the usual public mode of travel from the place where the court is sitting.

(11) Except in actions or proceedings governed by the Rules of Civil Procedure, if the witness is a physician duly licensed to practice medicine in the State of North Carolina, and resides or maintains his office outside the county in which the action is pending.

If any provision of this section conflicts with the Rules of Civil Procedure, then those Rules shall control in actions or proceedings governed by them.

History.
1777, c. 115, ss. 39, 40, 41, P.R.; 1803, c. 633, P.R.; 1828, ch. 24, ss. 1, 2; 1836, c. 30; R.C., c. 31, s. 63; 1869-70, c. 227, s. 11; 1881, c. 279, ss. 1, 3; Code, s. 1358; 1905, c. 366; Rev., s. 1645; 1919, c. 324; C.S., s. 1821; 1965, c. 675; 1969, c. 44, s. 23; 1971, c. 381, s. 7; 1973, c. 47, s. 2; 1991, c. 491, s. 1

N.C. Gen. Stat. § 8-84

Repealed by Session Laws 1975, c. 762, s. 4.

ARTICLE 11
PERPETUATION OF TESTIMONY

§ 8-85. Court reporter's certified transcription

Testimony taken and transcribed by a court reporter and certified by the reporter or by the judge who presided at the trial at which the testimony was given, may be offered in evidence in any court as the deposition of the witness whose testimony is so taken and transcribed, in the manner, and under the rules governing the introduction of depositions in civil actions.

History.
1971, c. 377, s. 1

§§ 8-86 through 8-88

Repealed by Session Laws 1967, c. 954, s. 4.

ARTICLE 12
INSPECTION AND PRODUCTION OF WRITINGS

N.C. Gen. Stat. § 8-89

Repealed by Session Laws 1967, c. 954, s. 4.

N.C. Gen. Stat. § 8-89.1

Repealed by Session Laws 1975, c. 762, s. 4.

§§ 8-90, 8-91

Repealed by Session Laws 1967, c. 954, s. 4.

ARTICLE 13
PHOTOGRAPHS

§ 8-97. Photographs as substantive or illustrative evidence

Any party may introduce a photograph, video tape, motion picture, X-ray or other photographic representation as substantive evidence upon laying a proper foundation and meeting other applicable evidentiary requirements. This section does not prohibit a party from introducing a photograph or other pictorial representation solely for the purpose of illustrating the testimony of a witness.

History.
1981, c. 451, s. 1

ARTICLE 14
CHAIN OF CUSTODY

§ 8-103. Courier service and contract carriers

For purposes of maintaining a chain of custody for any item of evidence, depositing the item with the State courier service operated by the Department of Administration or a common or contract carrier shall be considered the same as depositing such item in first class United States mail.

History.
1983, c. 375, s. 1

CHAPTER 8B
INTERPRETERS FOR
DEAF PERSONS

§ 8B-1. Definitions; right to interpreter; determination of competence

As used in this Chapter:

(1) "Appointing authority" means the presiding judge or clerk of superior court in a judicial proceeding, or a hearing officer, examiner, commissioner, chairman, presiding officer or similar official in a legislative or administrative proceeding.

(2) "Deaf person" means a person whose hearing impairment is so significant that the individual is impaired in processing linguistic information through hearing, with or without amplification.

(3) "Qualified interpreter" means an interpreter licensed under Chapter 90D of the General Statutes. If the appointing authority finds that a licensed interpreter is not available, an unlicensed interpreter may be called and used as a qualified interpreter if the interpreter's actual qualifications have otherwise been determined to be adequate for the present need. In no event will an interpreter be considered qualified if the interpreter is unable to communicate effectively with and simultaneously and accurately interpret for the deaf person.

A deaf person who does not utilize sign language may request an aural/oral interpreter. Before this interpreter is appointed, the appointing authority shall satisfy itself that the aural/oral interpreter is competent to interpret the proceedings to the deaf person and to present the testimony, statements, and any other information tendered by the deaf person.

History.
1981, c. 937, s. 1; 1997-443, s. 11A.118(a); 2002-182, s. 2; 2003-56, s. 3

§ 8B-2. Appointment of interpreters in certain judicial, legislative, and administrative proceedings; removal

(a) When a deaf person is a party to or a witness in any civil or criminal proceeding in any superior or district court of the State, including juvenile proceedings, special proceedings, and proceedings before the magistrate, the court shall appoint a qualified interpreter to interpret the proceedings to the deaf person and to interpret the deaf person's testimony, if any.

(b) When a deaf person is a witness before any legislative committee or subcommittee or legislative research or study committee or

subcommittee or commission authorized by the General Assembly, the appointing authority conducting the proceeding shall appoint a qualified interpreter to interpret the proceedings to the deaf person and to interpret the deaf person's testimony.

(c) When a deaf person is a party to or a witness in an administrative proceeding before any department, board, commission, agency or licensing authority of the State, or of any county or city of the State, the appointing authority conducting the proceeding shall appoint a qualified interpreter to interpret the proceedings to the deaf person and to interpret the deaf person's testimony, if any.

(d) If a deaf person is arrested for an alleged violation of criminal law of the State, including a local ordinance, the arresting officer shall immediately procure a qualified interpreter from the appropriate court for any interrogation, warning, notification of rights, arraignment, bail hearing or other preliminary proceeding, but no arrestee otherwise eligible for release on bail under Article 26 of Chapter 15A of the General Statutes shall be held in custody pending the arrival of an interpreter. No answer, statement or admission taken from the deaf person without a qualified interpreter present and functioning is admissible in court for any purpose.

(e) Whenever a juvenile whose parent or parents are deaf is brought before a court for any reason whatsoever, the court shall appoint a qualified interpreter to interpret the proceedings and testimony for the deaf parent or parents, and to interpret any statements or testimony the deaf parent or parents may be called upon to give to the court.

(f) A qualified interpreter shall not be appointed until the appointing authority makes a preliminary determination that the interpreter is able to communicate effectively with and to interpret accurately for the deaf person. If no qualified interpreter can be found who can successfully communicate with this person, he may select his own interpreter without regard to whether the interpreter is "qualified" within the meaning set forth under this statute.

(g) The appointing authority may, on its own motion or on the request of the deaf person, remove an interpreter for inability to communicate or because his services have been waived.

History.
1981, c. 937, s. 1

§ 8B-3. Waiver of appointed interpreter

(a) A deaf person entitled to the services of an interpreter under this Chapter may waive these services. The waiver must be approved in writing by the person's attorney. If the person does not have an attorney, approval must be made in writing by the appointing authority.

(b) A deaf person who has waived an interpreter under this section may provide his own interpreter at his own expense, without regard to whether such interpreter is qualified under this Chapter.

History.
1981, c. 937, s. 1

§ 8B-4. Notice of need for interpreter; proof of deafness

A deaf person entitled to an interpreter under this Chapter shall, if practicable, notify the appropriate appointing authority of his need prior to his appearance. A failure to notify or to request an interpreter is not a waiver of the right to an interpreter. Before appointing an interpreter, an appointing authority may require satisfactory proof of the requesting person's deafness if he has reason to believe the person is not hearing impaired.

History.
1981, c. 937, s. 1

§ 8B-5. Privileged communications

If a communication made by the deaf person through an interpreter is privileged, the privilege extends also to the interpreter.

History.
1981, c. 937, s. 1

§ 8B-6. List of interpreters; coordination of interpreter services

The Department of Health and Human Services shall prepare and maintain an up-to-date list of qualified and available interpreters. A copy of the list shall be provided to each clerk of superior court and to the North Carolina Interpreter and Transliterator Licensing Board created in Chapter 90D of the General Statutes. When requested by an appointing authority to provide an interpreter the Division of Services for the Deaf and the Hard of Hearing shall assist in arranging for an interpreter at the time and place needed through its program of community services for the hearing impaired.

History.
1981, c. 937, s. 1; 1989, c. 533, s. 4; 1997-443, s. 11A.118(a); 2002-182, s. 3; 2003-56, s. 3

§ 8B-7. Oath

Before acting, an interpreter shall take an oath or affirmation that he will make a true interpretation in an understandable manner of the proceedings to the person for whom he is appointed and that he will convey the statements of the person in the English language to the best of his skill and judgment.

History.
1981, c. 937, s. 1

§ 8B-8. Compensation

(a) An interpreter appointed under this Chapter is entitled to a reasonable fee for services, including waiting time, time reserved by the courts for the assignment, and reimbursement for necessary travel and subsistence expenses. The fee shall be fixed by the appointing authority who shall consider any fee schedule for interpreters established by the Department of Health and Human Services. Reimbursement for necessary travel and subsistence expenses shall be at rates provided by law for State employees generally.

(b) The fees and expenses of interpreters who serve before any superior or district court criminal and juvenile proceeding are payable from funds appropriated to the Administrative Office of the Courts.

(c) The fees and expenses of interpreters who serve in civil cases and special proceedings are also payable from funds appropriated to the Administrative Office of the Courts.

(d) Fees and expenses of interpreters who serve before a legislative body described in this Article are payable from funds appropriated for operating expenses of the General Assembly.

(e) Fees and expenses of interpreters who serve before any State administrative agency are payable by that agency.

(f) Fees and expenses of interpreters who serve before city or county administrative proceedings are payable by the respective city or county.

(g) Repealed by Session Laws 1995, c. 277, s. 1, effective July 1, 1995.

History.
1981, c. 937, s. 1; 1989, c. 533, s. 5; 1995, c. 277, s. 1; 1997-443, s. 11A.118(a)

§ 8B-9. Responsibility for payment of funds to implement Chapter

Responsibility for payment of funds to implement this Chapter rests with the particular entity specified in G.S. 8B-8 whose procedure required the service.

History.
1981, c. 937, s. 2

§ 8B-10. North Carolina Training and Licensing Preparation Program fees

The Division of Services for the Deaf and the Hard of Hearing of the Department of Health and Human Services may charge a fee of no more than fifty dollars ($ 50.00) to individuals who participate in interpreter training or workshops offered by the North Carolina Training and Licensing Preparation Program. The Division may charge a fee of no more than one hundred dollars ($ 100.00) for a diagnostic evaluation offered under the Program. This fee is for voluntary diagnostic services only. These fees are to cover the cost of administering the Program and are payable when a participant takes part in a planned activity.

History.
1991, c. 465, s. 1; 1997-443, s. 11A.118(a); 2002-182, s. 4; 2003-56, s. 3

CHAPTER 8C
EVIDENCE CODE

§ 8C-1 RULES OF EVIDENCE

ARTICLE 1
GENERAL PROVISIONS

Rule 101. Scope

These rules govern proceedings in the courts of this State to the extent and with the exceptions stated in Rule 1101.

History.
1983, ch. 701, s. 1

Rule 102. Purpose and construction

(a) *In general.* -- These rules shall be construed to secure fairness in administration, elimination of unjustifiable expense and delay, and promotion of growth and development of the law of evidence to the end that the truth may be ascertained and proceedings justly determined.

(b) *Subordinate divisions.* -- For the purpose of these rules only, the subordinate division of any rule which is labeled with a lower case letter shall be a subdivision.

History.
1983, c. 701, s. 1

Rule 103. Rulings on evidence

(a) *Effect of erroneous ruling.* -- Error may not be predicated upon a ruling which admits or excludes evidence unless a substantial right of the party is affected, and

(1) **Objection.** -- In case the ruling is one admitting evidence, a timely objection or motion to strike appears of record. No particular form is required in order to preserve the right to assert the alleged error upon appeal if the motion or objection clearly presented the alleged error to the trial court;

(2) **Offer of proof.** -- In case the ruling is one excluding evidence, the substance of the evidence was made known to the court by offer or was apparent from the context within which questions were asked.

Once the court makes a definitive ruling on the record admitting or excluding evidence, either at or before trial, a party need not renew an objection or offer of proof to preserve a claim of error for appeal.

(b) *Record of offer and ruling.* -- The court may add any other or further statement which shows the character of the evidence, the form in which it was offered, the objection made, and the ruling thereon. It may direct the making of an offer in question and answer form.

(c) *Hearing of jury.* -- In jury cases, proceedings shall be conducted, to the extent practicable, so as to prevent inadmissible evidence from being suggested to the jury by any means, such as making statements or offers of proof or asking questions in the hearing of the jury.

(d) *Review of errors where justice requires.* -- Notwithstanding the requirements of subdivision (a) of this rule, an appellate court may review errors affecting substantial rights if it determines, in the interest of justice, it is appropriate to do so.

History.
1983, c. 701, s. 1; 2003-101, s. 1; 2006-264, s. 30.5

Rule 104. Preliminary questions

(a) *Questions of admissibility generally.* -- Preliminary questions concerning the qualification of a person to be a witness, the existence of a privilege, or the admissibility of evidence shall be determined by the court, subject to the provisions of subdivision (b). In making its determination it is not bound by the rules of evidence except those with respect to privileges.

(b) *Relevancy conditioned on fact.* -- When the relevancy of evidence depends upon the fulfillment of a condition of fact, the court shall admit it upon, or subject to, the introduction of evidence sufficient to support a finding of the fulfillment of the condition.

(c) *Hearing of jury.* -- Hearings on the admissibility of confessions or other motions to suppress evidence in criminal trials in Superior Court shall in all cases be conducted out of the hearing of the jury. Hearings on other preliminary matters shall be so conducted when the interests of justice require or, when an accused is a witness, if he so requests.

(d) *Testimony by accused.* -- The accused does not, by testifying upon a preliminary matter, subject himself to cross-examination as to other issues in the case.

(e) *Weight and credibility.* -- This rule does not limit the right of a party to introduce before the jury evidence relevant to weight or credibility.

History.
1983, ch. 701, s. 1

Rule 105. Limited admissibility

When evidence which is admissible as to one party or for one purpose but not admissible as to another party or for another purpose is admitted, the court, upon request, shall restrict the evidence to its proper scope and instruct the jury accordingly.

History.
1983, c. 701, s. 1

Rule 106. Remainder of or related writings or recorded statements

When a writing or recorded statement or part thereof is introduced by a party, an adverse party may require him at that time to introduce any other part or any other writing or recorded statement which ought in fairness to be considered contemporaneously with it.

History.
1983, c. 701, s. 1

ARTICLE 2
JUDICIAL NOTICE

Rule 201. Judicial notice of adjudicative facts

(a) *Scope of rule.* -- This rule governs only judicial notice of adjudicative facts.

(b) *Kinds of facts.* -- A judicially noticed fact must be one not subject to reasonable dispute in that it is either (1) generally known within the territorial jurisdiction of the trial court or (2) capable of accurate and ready determination by resort to sources whose accuracy cannot reasonably be questioned.

(c) *When discretionary.* -- A court may take judicial notice, whether requested or not.

(d) *When mandatory.* -- A court shall take judicial notice if requested by a party and supplied with the necessary information.

(e) *Opportunity to be heard.* -- In a trial court, a party is entitled upon timely request to an opportunity to be heard as to the propriety of taking judicial notice and the tenor of the matter noticed. In the absence of prior notification, the request may be made after judicial notice has been taken.

(f) *Time of taking notice.* -- Judicial notice may be taken at any stage of the proceeding.

(g) *Instructing jury.* -- In a civil action or proceeding, the court shall instruct the jury to accept as conclusive any fact judicially noticed. In a criminal case, the court shall instruct the jury that it may, but is not required to, accept as conclusive any fact judicially noticed.

History.
1983, c. 701, s. 1

ARTICLE 3
PRESUMPTIONS IN CIVIL ACTIONS AND PROCEEDINGS

Rule 301. Presumptions in general in civil actions and proceedings

In all civil actions and proceedings when not otherwise provided for by statute, by judicial decision, or by these rules, a presumption imposes on the party against whom it is directed the burden of going forward with evidence to rebut or meet the presumption, but does not shift to such party the burden of proof in the sense of the risk of nonpersuasion, which remains throughout the trial upon the party on whom it was originally cast. The burden of going forward is satisfied by the introduction of evidence sufficient to permit reasonable minds to conclude that the presumed fact does not exist. If the party against whom a presumption operates fails to meet the burden of producing evidence, the presumed fact shall be deemed proved, and the court shall instruct the jury accordingly. When the burden of producing evidence to meet a presumption is satisfied, the court must instruct the jury that it may, but is not required to, infer the existence of the presumed fact from the proved fact.

History.
1983, c. 701, s. 1

Rule 302. Applicability of federal law in civil actions and proceedings

In civil actions and proceedings, the effect of a presumption respecting a fact which is an element of a claim or defense as to which federal law supplies the rule of decision is determined in accordance with federal law.

History.
1983, c. 701, s. 1

ARTICLE 4
RELEVANCY AND ITS LIMITS

Rule 401. Definition of "relevant evidence."

"Relevant evidence" means evidence having any tendency to make the existence of any fact that is of consequence to the determination of the action more probable or less probable than it would be without the evidence.

History.
1983, c. 701, s. 1

Rule 402. Relevant evidence generally admissible; irrelevant evidence inadmissible

All relevant evidence is admissible, except as otherwise provided by the Constitution of the United States, by the Constitution of North Carolina, by Act of Congress, by Act of the General Assembly or by these rules. Evidence which is not relevant is not admissible.

History.
1983, c. 701, s. 1

Rule 403. Exclusion of relevant evidence on grounds of prejudice, confusion, or waste of time

Although relevant, evidence may be excluded if its probative value is substantially outweighed by the danger of unfair prejudice, confusion of the issues, or misleading the jury, or by considerations of undue delay, waste of time, or needless presentation of cumulative evidence.

History.
1983, c. 701, s. 1

Rule 404. Character evidence not admissible to prove conduct; exceptions; other crimes

(a) *Character evidence generally.* -- Evidence of a person's character or a trait of his character is not admissible for the purpose of proving that he acted in conformity therewith on a particular occasion, except:

(1) *Character of accused.* -- Evidence of a pertinent trait of his character offered by an accused, or by the prosecution to rebut the same;

(2) *Character of victim.* -- Evidence of a pertinent trait of character of the victim of the crime offered by an accused, or by the prosecution to rebut the same, or evidence of a character trait of peacefulness of the victim offered by the prosecution in a homicide case to rebut evidence that the victim was the first aggressor;

(3) *Character of witness.* -- Evidence of the character of a witness, as provided in Rules 607, 608, and 609.

(b) *Other crimes, wrongs, or acts.* -- Evidence of other crimes, wrongs, or acts is not admissible to prove the character of a person in order to show that he acted in conformity

therewith. It may, however, be admissible for other purposes, such as proof of motive, opportunity, intent, preparation, plan, knowledge, identity, or absence of mistake, entrapment or accident. Admissible evidence may include evidence of an offense committed by a juvenile if it would have been a Class A, B1, B2, C, D, or E felony if committed by an adult.

History.
1983, c. 701, s. 1; 1994, Ex. Sess., c. 7, s. 3; 1995, c. 509, s. 7

Rule 405. Methods of proving character

(a) *Reputation or opinion.* -- In all cases in which evidence of character or a trait of character of a person is admissible, proof may be made by testimony as to reputation or by testimony in the form of an opinion. On cross-examination, inquiry is allowable into relevant specific instances of conduct. Expert testimony on character or a trait of character is not admissible as circumstantial evidence of behavior.

(b) *Specific instances of conduct.* -- In cases in which character or a trait of character of a person is an essential element of a charge, claim, or defense, proof may also be made of specific instances of his conduct.

History.
1983, c. 701, s. 1

Rule 406. Habit; routine practice

Evidence of the habit of a person or of the routine practice of an organization, whether corroborated or not and regardless of the presence of eyewitnesses, is relevant to prove that the conduct of the person or organization on a particular occasion was in conformity with the habit or routine practice.

History.
1983, c. 701, s. 1

Rule 407. Subsequent remedial measures

When, after an event, measures are taken which, if taken previously, would have made the event less likely to occur, evidence of the subsequent measures is not admissible to prove negligence or culpable conduct in connection with the event. This rule does not require the exclusion of evidence of subsequent measures when offered for another purpose, such as proving ownership, control, or feasibility of precautionary measures, if those issues are controverted, or impeachment.

History.

1983, c. 701, s. 1

Rule 408. Compromise and offers to compromise

Evidence of (1) furnishing or offering or promising to furnish, or (2) accepting or offering or promising to accept, a valuable consideration in compromising or attempting to compromise a claim which was disputed as to either validity or amount, is not admissible to prove liability for or invalidity of the claim or its amount. Evidence of conduct or evidence of statements made in compromise negotiations is likewise not admissible. This rule does not require the exclusion of any evidence otherwise discoverable merely because it is presented in the course of compromise negotiations. This rule also does not require exclusion when the evidence is offered for another purpose, such as proving bias or prejudice of a witness, negativing a contention of undue delay, or proving an effort to obstruct a criminal investigation or prosecution.

History.

1983, c. 701, s. 1

Rule 409. Payment of medical and other expenses

Evidence of furnishing or offering or promising to pay medical, hospital, or other expenses occasioned by an injury is not admissible to prove liability for the injury.

History.

1983, c. 701, s. 1

Rule 410. Inadmissibility of pleas, plea discussions, and related statements

Except as otherwise provided in this rule, evidence of the following is not, in any civil or criminal proceeding, admissible for or against the defendant who made the plea or was a participant in the plea discussions:

(1) A plea of guilty which was later withdrawn;

(2) A plea of no contest;

(3) Any statement made in the course of any proceedings under Article 58 of Chapter 15A of the General Statutes or comparable procedure in district court, or proceedings under Rule 11 of the Federal Rules of Criminal Procedure or comparable procedure in another state, regarding a plea of guilty which was later withdrawn or a plea of no contest;

(4) Any statement made in the course of plea discussions with an attorney for the prosecuting authority which do not result

in a plea of guilty or which result in a plea of guilty later withdrawn.

However, such a statement is admissible in any proceeding wherein another statement made in the course of the same plea or plea discussions has been introduced and the statement ought in fairness be considered contemporaneously with it.

History.

1983, c. 701, s. 1

Rule 411. Liability insurance

Evidence that a person was or was not insured against liability is not admissible upon the issue whether he acted negligently or otherwise wrongfully. This rule does not require the exclusion of evidence of insurance against liability when offered for another purpose, such as proof of agency, ownership, or control, or bias or prejudice of a witness.

History.

1983, c. 701, s. 1

Rule 412. Rape or sex offense cases; relevance of victim's past behavior

(a) As used in this rule, the term "sexual behavior" means sexual activity of the complainant other than the sexual act which is at issue in the indictment on trial.

(b) Notwithstanding any other provision of law, the sexual behavior of the complainant is irrelevant to any issue in the prosecution unless such behavior:

(1) Was between the complainant and the defendant; or

(2) Is evidence of specific instances of sexual behavior offered for the purpose of showing that the act or acts charged were not committed by the defendant; or

(3) Is evidence of a pattern of sexual behavior so distinctive and so closely resembling the defendant's version of the alleged encounter with the complainant as to tend to prove that such complainant consented to the act or acts charged or behaved in such a manner as to lead the defendant reasonably to believe that the complainant consented; or

(4) Is evidence of sexual behavior offered as the basis of expert psychological or psychiatric opinion that the complainant fantasized or invented the act or acts charged.

(c) Sexual behavior otherwise admissible under this rule may not be proved by reputation or opinion.

(d) Notwithstanding any other provision of law, unless and until the court determines that evidence of sexual behavior is relevant under subdivision (b), no reference to this behavior may be made in the presence of the jury and no evidence of this behavior may be introduced at any time during the trial of any of the following:

(1) A charge of rape or a lesser included offense of rape.

(2) A charge of a sex offense or a lesser included offense of a sex offense.

(3) An offense being tried jointly with a charge of rape or a sex offense, or with a lesser included offense of rape or a sex offense.

(4) A charge of sexual servitude under G.S. 14-43.13.

Before any questions pertaining to such evidence are asked of any witness, the proponent of such evidence shall first apply to the court for a determination of the relevance of the sexual behavior to which it relates. The proponent of such evidence may make application either prior to trial pursuant to G.S. 15A-952, or during the trial at the time when the proponent desires to introduce such evidence. When application is made, the court shall conduct an in camera hearing, which shall be transcribed, to consider the proponent's offer of proof and the argument of counsel, including any counsel for the complainant, to determine the extent to which such behavior is relevant. In the hearing, the proponent of the evidence shall establish the basis of admissibility of such evidence. Notwithstanding subdivision (b) of Rule 104, if the relevancy of the evidence which the proponent seeks to offer in the trial depends upon the fulfillment of a condition of fact, the court, at the in camera hearing or at a subsequent in camera hearing scheduled for that purpose, shall accept evidence on the issue of whether that condition of fact is fulfilled and shall determine that issue. If the court finds that the evidence is relevant, it shall enter an order stating that the evidence may be admitted and the nature of the questions which will be permitted.

(e) The record of the in camera hearing and all evidence relating thereto shall be open to inspection only by the parties, the complainant, their attorneys and the court and its agents, and shall be used only as necessary for appellate review. At any probable cause hearing, the judge shall take cognizance of the evidence, if admissible, at the end of the in camera hearing without the questions being repeated or the evidence being resubmitted in open court.

History.
1983, c. 701, s. 1; 2018-75, s. 6(a)

Rule 413. Medical actions; statements to ameliorate or mitigate adverse outcome.

Statements by a health care provider apologizing for an adverse outcome in medical treatment, offers to undertake corrective or remedial treatment or actions, and gratuitous acts to assist affected persons shall not be admissible to prove negligence or culpable conduct by the health care provider in an action brought under Article 1B of Chapter 90 of the General Statutes.

History.
2004-149, s. 3.1

Rule 414. Evidence of medical expenses

Evidence offered to prove past medical expenses shall be limited to evidence of the amounts actually paid to satisfy the bills that have been satisfied, regardless of the source of payment, and evidence of the amounts actually necessary to satisfy the bills that have been incurred but not yet satisfied. This rule does not impose upon any party an affirmative duty to seek a reduction in billed charges to which the party is not contractually entitled.

History.
2011-283, s. 1.1; 2011-317, s. 1.1

ARTICLE 5
PRIVILEGES

Rule 501. General rule

Except as otherwise required by the Constitution of the United States, the privileges of a witness, person, government, state, or political subdivision thereof shall be determined in accordance with the law of this State.

History.
1983, c. 701, s. 1

ARTICLE 6
WITNESSES

Rule 601. General rule of competency; disqualification of witness

(a) *General rule.* -- Every person is competent to be a witness except as otherwise provided in these rules.

(b) *Disqualification of witness in general.* -- A person is disqualified to testify as a witness when the court determines that the person is (1) incapable of expressing himself or herself concerning the matter as to be understood, either directly or through interpretation by one who can understand him or her, or (2) incapable of understanding the duty of a witness to tell the truth.

(c) *Disqualification of interested persons.* -- Upon the trial of an action, or the hearing upon the merits of a special proceeding, a party or a person interested in the event, or a person from, through or under whom such a party or interested person derives his or her interest or title by assignment or otherwise, shall not be examined as a witness in his or her own behalf or interest, or in behalf of the party succeeding to his or her title or interest, against the executor, administrator or survivor of a deceased person, or the guardian of an incompetent person, or a person deriving his or her title or interest from, through or under a deceased or incompetent person by assignment or otherwise, concerning any oral communication between the witness and the deceased or incompetent person. However, this subdivision shall not apply when:

(1) The executor, administrator, survivor, guardian, or person so deriving title or interest is examined in his or her own behalf regarding the subject matter of the oral communication.

(2) The testimony of the deceased or incompetent person is given in evidence concerning the same transaction or communication.

(3) Evidence of the subject matter of the oral communication is offered by the executor, administrator, survivor, guardian or person so deriving title or interest.

Nothing in this subdivision shall preclude testimony as to the identity of the operator of a motor vehicle in any case.

History.
1983, c. 701, s. 1; 2011-29, s. 2

Rule 602. Lack of personal knowledge

A witness may not testify to a matter unless evidence is introduced sufficient to support a finding that he has personal knowledge of the matter. Evidence to prove personal knowledge may, but need not, consist of the testimony of the witness himself. This rule is subject to the provisions of Rule 703, relating to opinion testimony by expert witnesses.

History.
1983, c. 701, s. 1

Rule 603. Oath or affirmation

Before testifying, every witness shall be required to declare that he will testify truthfully, by oath or affirmation administered in a form

calculated to awaken his conscience and impress his mind with his duty to do so.

History.
1983, c. 701, s. 1

Rule 604. Interpreters

An interpreter is subject to the provisions of these rules relating to qualification as an expert and the administration of an oath or affirmation that he will make a true translation.

History.
1983, c. 701, s. 1

Rule 605. Competency of judge as witness

The judge presiding at the trial may not testify in that trial as a witness. No objection need be made in order to preserve the point.

History.
1983, c. 701, s. 1

Rule 606. Competency of juror as witness

(a) *At the trial.* -- A member of the jury may not testify as a witness before that jury in the trial of the case in which he is sitting as a juror. If he is called so to testify, the opposing party shall be afforded an opportunity to object out of the presence of the jury.

(b) *Inquiry into validity of verdict or indictment.* -- Upon an inquiry into the validity of a verdict or indictment, a juror may not testify as to any matter or statement occurring during the course of the jury's deliberations or to the effect of anything upon his or any other juror's mind or emotions as influencing him to assent to or dissent from the verdict or indictment or concerning his mental processes in connection therewith, except that a juror may testify on the question whether extraneous prejudicial information was improperly brought to the jury's attention or whether any outside influence was improperly brought to bear upon any juror. Nor may his affidavit or evidence of any statement by him concerning a matter about which he would be precluded from testifying be received for these purposes.

History.
1983, c. 701, s. 1

Rule 607. Who may impeach

The credibility of a witness may be attacked by any party, including the party calling him.

History.
1983, c. 701, s. 1

Rule 608. Evidence of character and conduct of witness

(a) *Opinion and reputation evidence of character.* -- The credibility of a witness may be attacked or supported by evidence in the form of reputation or opinion as provided in Rule 405(a), but subject to these limitations: (1) the evidence may refer only to character for truthfulness or untruthfulness, and (2) evidence of truthful character is admissible only after the character of the witness for truthfulness has been attacked by opinion or reputation evidence or otherwise.

(b) *Specific instances of conduct.* -- Specific instances of the conduct of a witness, for the purpose of attacking or supporting his credibility, other than conviction of crime as provided in Rule 609, may not be proved by extrinsic evidence. They may, however, in the discretion of the court, if probative of truthfulness or untruthfulness, be inquired into on cross-examination of the witness (1) concerning his character for truthfulness or untruthfulness, or (2) concerning the character for truthfulness or untruthfulness of another witness as to which character the witness being cross-examined has testified.

The giving of testimony, whether by an accused or by any other witness, does not operate as a waiver of his privilege against self-incrimination when examined with respect to matters which relate only to credibility.

History.
1983, c. 701, s. 1

Rule 609. Impeachment by evidence of conviction of crime

(a) *General rule.* -- For the purpose of attacking the credibility of a witness, evidence that the witness has been convicted of a felony, or of a Class A1, Class 1, or Class 2 misdemeanor, shall be admitted if elicited from the witness or established by public record during cross-examination or thereafter.

(b) *Time limit.* -- Evidence of a conviction under this rule is not admissible if a period of more than 10 years has elapsed since the date of the conviction or of the release of the witness from the confinement imposed for that conviction, whichever is the later date, unless the court determines, in the interests of justice, that the probative value of the conviction supported by specific facts and circumstances substantially outweighs its prejudicial effect. However, evidence of a conviction more than 10 years old as calculated herein is not admissible unless the proponent gives to the adverse party sufficient advance written notice of intent to use such evidence to provide the adverse party with a fair opportunity to contest the use of such evidence.

(c) *Effect of pardon.* -- Evidence of a conviction is not admissible under this rule if the conviction has been pardoned.

(d) *Juvenile adjudications.* -- Evidence of juvenile adjudications is generally not admissible under this rule. The court may, however, in a criminal case allow evidence of a juvenile adjudication of a witness other than the accused if conviction of the offense would be admissible to attack the credibility of an adult and the court is satisfied that admission in evidence is necessary for a fair determination of the issue of guilt or innocence.

(e) *Pendency of appeal.* -- The pendency of an appeal therefrom does not render evidence of a conviction inadmissible. Evidence of the pendency of an appeal is admissible.

History.
1983, c. 701, s. 1; 1999-79, s. 1

Rule 610. Religious beliefs or opinions

Evidence of the beliefs or opinions of a witness on matters of religion is not admissible for the purpose of showing that by reason of their nature his credibility is impaired or enhanced; provided, however, such evidence may be admitted for the purpose of showing interest or bias.

History.
1983, c. 701, s. 1

Rule 611. Mode and order of interrogation and presentation

(a) *Control by court.* -- The court shall exercise reasonable control over the mode and order of interrogating witnesses and presenting evidence so as to (1) make the interrogation and presentation effective for the ascertainment of the truth, (2) avoid needless consumption of time, and (3) protect witnesses from harassment or undue embarrassment.

(b) *Scope of cross-examination.* -- A witness may be cross-examined on any matter relevant to any issue in the case, including credibility.

(c) *Leading questions.* -- Leading questions should not be used on the direct examination of a witness except as may be necessary to develop his testimony. Ordinarily leading questions should be permitted on cross-examination. When a party calls a hostile witness, an adverse party, or a witness identified with an adverse party, interrogation may be by leading questions.

History.
1983, c. 701, s. 1

Rule 612. Writing or object used to refresh memory

(a) **While testifying.** -- If, while testifying, a witness uses a writing or object to refresh his memory, an adverse party is entitled to have the writing or object produced at the trial, hearing, or deposition in which the witness is testifying.

(b) **Before testifying.** -- If, before testifying, a witness uses a writing or object to refresh his memory for the purpose of testifying and the court in its discretion determines that the interests of justice so require, an adverse party is entitled to have those portions of any writing or of the object which relate to the testimony produced, if practicable, at the trial, hearing, or deposition in which the witness is testifying.

(c) **Terms and conditions of production and use.** -- A party entitled to have a writing or object produced under this rule is entitled to inspect it, to cross-examine the witness thereon, and to introduce in evidence those portions which relate to the testimony of the witness. If production of the writing or object at the trial, hearing, or deposition is impracticable, the court may order it made available for inspection. If it is claimed that the writing or object contains privileged information or information not directly related to the subject matter of the testimony, the court shall examine the writing or object in camera, excise any such portions, and order delivery of the remainder to the party entitled thereto. Any portion withheld over objections shall be preserved and made available to the appellate court in the event of an appeal. If a writing or object is not produced, made available for inspection, or delivered pursuant to order under this rule, the court shall make any order justice requires, but in criminal cases if the prosecution elects not to comply, the order shall be one striking the testimony or, if justice so requires, declaring a mistrial.

History.
1983, c. 701, s. 1

Rule 613. Prior statements of witnesses

In examining a witness concerning a prior statement made by him, whether written or not, the statement need not be shown nor its contents disclosed to him at that time, but on request the same shall be shown or disclosed to opposing counsel.

History.
1983, c. 701, s. 1

Rule 614. Calling and interrogation of witnesses by court

(a) **Calling by court.** -- The court may, on its own motion or at the suggestion of a party, call witnesses, and all parties are entitled to cross-examine witnesses thus called.

(b) **Interrogation by court.** -- The court may interrogate witnesses, whether called by itself or by a party.

(c) **Objections.** -- No objections are necessary with respect to the calling of a witness by the court or to questions propounded to a witness by the court but it shall be deemed that proper objection has been made and overruled.

History.
1983, c. 701, s. 1

Rule 615. Exclusion of witnesses

At the request of a party the court may order witnesses excluded so that they cannot hear the testimony of other witnesses, and it may make the order of its own motion. This rule does not authorize exclusion of (1) a party who is a natural person, or (2) an officer or employee of a party that is not a natural person designated as its representative by its attorney, or (3) a person whose presence is shown by a party to be essential to the presentation of his cause, or (4) a person whose presence is determined by the court to be in the interest of justice.

History.
1983, c. 701, s. 1

Rule 616. Alternative testimony of witnesses with an intellectual or developmental disability in civil cases and special proceedings.

(a) **Definitions.** -- The following definitions apply to this section:

(1) The definitions set out in G.S. 122C-3.

(2) **Remote testimony.** -- A method by which a witness testifies outside of an open forum and outside of the physical presence of a party or parties.

(b) **Remote Testimony Authorized.** -- An individual with an intellectual or developmental disability who is competent to testify may testify by remote testimony in a civil proceeding or special proceeding if the court determines by clear and convincing evidence that the witness would suffer serious emotional distress from testifying in the presence of a named party or parties or from testifying in an open forum and that the ability of the witness to communicate with the trier of fact would be impaired by testifying in the presence of a named party or parties or from testifying in an open forum.

(c) **Hearing Procedure.** -- Upon motion of a party or the court's own motion, and for good cause shown, the court shall hold an evidentiary hearing to determine whether to allow remote testimony. The hearing shall be recorded unless recordation is waived by all parties. The presence of the witness is not required at the hearing unless so ordered by the presiding judge.

(d) *Order.* -- An order allowing or disallowing the use of remote testimony shall state the findings and conclusions of law that support the court's determination. An order allowing the use of remote testimony also shall do all of the following:

(1) State the method by which the witness is to testify.

(2) List any individual or category of individuals allowed to be in or required to be excluded from the presence of the witness during testimony.

(3) State any special conditions necessary to facilitate the cross-examination of the witness.

(4) State any condition or limitation upon the participation of individuals in the presence of the witness during the testimony.

(5) State any other conditions necessary for taking or presenting testimony.

(e) *Testimony.* -- The method of remote testimony shall allow the trier of fact and all parties to observe the demeanor of the witness as the witness testifies in a similar manner as if the witness were testifying in the open forum. Except as provided in this section, the court shall ensure that the counsel for all parties is physically present where the witness testifies and has a full and fair opportunity for examination and cross-examination of the witness. In a proceeding where a party is representing itself, the court may limit or deny the party from being physically present during testimony if the court finds that the witness would suffer serious emotional distress from testifying in the presence of the party. A party may waive the right to have counsel physically present where the witness testifies.

(f) *Nonexclusive Procedure and Standard.* -- Nothing in this section prohibits the use or application of any other method or procedure authorized or required by law for the introduction into evidence of statements or testimony of an individual with an intellectual or developmental disability.

History.
2009-514, s. 1; 2018-47, s. 3(a)

ARTICLE 7
OPINIONS AND
EXPERT TESTIMONY

Rule 701. Opinion testimony by lay witness

If the witness is not testifying as an expert, his testimony in the form of opinions or inferences is limited to those opinions or inferences which are (a) rationally based on the perception of the witness and (b) helpful to a clear understanding of his testimony or the determination of a fact in issue.

History.
1983, c. 701, s. 1

Rule 702. Testimony by experts

(a) If scientific, technical or other specialized knowledge will assist the trier of fact to understand the evidence or to determine a fact in issue, a witness qualified as an expert by knowledge, skill, experience, training, or education, may testify thereto in the form of an opinion, or otherwise, if all of the following apply:

(1) The testimony is based upon sufficient facts or data.

(2) The testimony is the product of reliable principles and methods.

(3) The witness has applied the principles and methods reliably to the facts of the case.

(a1) Notwithstanding any other provision of law, a witness may give expert testimony solely on the issue of impairment and not on the issue of specific alcohol concentration level relating to the following:

(1) The results of a Horizontal Gaze Nystagmus (HGN) Test when the test is administered in accordance with the person's training by a person who has successfully completed training in HGN.

(2) Whether a person was under the influence of one or more impairing substances, and the category of such impairing substance or substances, if the witness holds a current certification as a Drug Recognition Expert, issued by the State Department of Health and Human Services.

(b) In a medical malpractice action as defined in G.S. 90-21.11, a person shall not give expert testimony on the appropriate standard of health care as defined in G.S. 90-21.12 unless the person is a licensed health care provider in this State or another state and meets the following criteria:

(1) If the party against whom or on whose behalf the testimony is offered is a specialist, the expert witness must:

a. Specialize in the same specialty as the party against whom or on whose behalf the testimony is offered; or

b. Specialize in a similar specialty which includes within its specialty the performance of the procedure that is the subject of the complaint and have prior experience treating similar patients.

(2) During the year immediately preceding the date of the occurrence that is the basis for the action, the expert witness

must have devoted a majority of his or her professional time to either or both of the following:

a. The active clinical practice of the same health profession in which the party against whom or on whose behalf the testimony is offered, and if that party is a specialist, the active clinical practice of the same specialty or a similar specialty which includes within its specialty the performance of the procedure that is the subject of the complaint and have prior experience treating similar patients; or

b. The instruction of students in an accredited health professional school or accredited residency or clinical research program in the same health profession in which the party against whom or on whose behalf the testimony is offered, and if that party is a specialist, an accredited health professional school or accredited residency or clinical research program in the same specialty.

(c) Notwithstanding subsection (b) of this section, if the party against whom or on whose behalf the testimony is offered is a general practitioner, the expert witness, during the year immediately preceding the date of the occurrence that is the basis for the action, must have devoted a majority of his or her professional time to either or both of the following:

(1) Active clinical practice as a general practitioner; or

(2) Instruction of students in an accredited health professional school or accredited residency or clinical research program in the general practice of medicine.

(d) Notwithstanding subsection (b) of this section, a physician who qualifies as an expert under subsection (a) of this Rule and who by reason of active clinical practice or instruction of students has knowledge of the applicable standard of care for nurses, nurse practitioners, certified registered nurse anesthetists, certified registered nurse midwives, physician assistants, or other medical support staff may give expert testimony in a medical malpractice action with respect to the standard of care of which he is knowledgeable of nurses, nurse practitioners, certified registered nurse anesthetists, certified registered nurse midwives, physician assistants licensed under Chapter 90 of the General Statutes, or other medical support staff.

(e) Upon motion by either party, a resident judge of the superior court in the county or judicial district in which the action is pending may allow expert testimony on the appropriate standard of health care by a witness who does not meet the requirements of subsection (b) or (c) of this Rule, but who is otherwise qualified as an expert witness, upon a showing by the movant of extraordinary circumstances and a determination by the court that the motion should be allowed to serve the ends of justice.

(f) In an action alleging medical malpractice, an expert witness shall not testify on a contingency fee basis.

(g) This section does not limit the power of the trial court to disqualify an expert witness on grounds other than the qualifications set forth in this section.

(h) Notwithstanding subsection (b) of this section, in a medical malpractice action as defined in G.S. 90-21.11(2)b. against a hospital, or other health care or medical facility, a person shall not give expert testimony on the appropriate standard of care as to administrative or other nonclinical issues unless the person has substantial knowledge, by virtue of his or her training and experience, about the standard of care among hospitals, or health care or medical facilities, of the same type as the hospital, or health care or medical facility, whose actions or inactions are the subject of the testimony situated in the same or similar communities at the time of the alleged act giving rise to the cause of action.

(i) A witness qualified as an expert in accident reconstruction who has performed a reconstruction of a crash, or has reviewed the report of investigation, with proper foundation may give an opinion as to the speed of a vehicle even if the witness did not observe the vehicle moving.

History.
1983, c. 701, s. 1; 1995, c. 309, s. 1; 2006-253, s. 6; 2007-493, s. 5; 2011-283, s. 1.3; 2011-400, s. 4; 2017-57, s. 17.8(b); 2017-212, s. 5.3

Rule 703. Bases of opinion testimony by experts

The facts or data in the particular case upon which an expert bases an opinion or inference may be those perceived by or made known to him at or before the hearing. If of a type reasonably relied upon by experts in the particular field in forming opinions or inferences upon the subject, the facts or data need not be admissible in evidence.

History.
1983, c. 701, s. 1

Rule 704. Opinion on ultimate issue

Testimony in the form of an opinion or inference is not objectionable because it embraces an ultimate issue to be decided by the trier of fact.

History.
1983, c. 701, s. 1

Rule 705. Disclosure of facts or data underlying expert opinion

The expert may testify in terms of opinion or inference and give his reasons therefor without prior disclosure of the underlying facts or data, unless an adverse party requests otherwise, in which event the expert will be required to disclose such underlying facts or data on direct examination or voir dire before stating the opinion. The expert may in any event be required to disclose the underlying facts or data on cross-examination. There shall be no requirement that expert testimony be in response to a hypothetical question.

History.
1983, c. 701, s. 1

Rule 706. Court appointed experts

(a) *Appointment.* -- The court may on its own motion or on the motion of any party enter an order to show cause why expert witnesses should not be appointed, and may request the parties to submit nominations. The court may appoint any expert witnesses agreed upon by the parties, and may appoint witnesses of its own selection. An expert witness shall not be appointed by the court unless he consents to act. A witness so appointed shall be informed of his duties by the court in writing, a copy of which shall be filed with the clerk, or at a conference in which the parties shall have opportunity to participate. A witness so appointed shall advise the parties of his findings, if any; his deposition may be taken by any party; and he may be called to testify by the court or any party. He shall be subject to cross-examination by each party, including a party calling him as a witness.

(b) *Compensation.* -- Expert witnesses so appointed are entitled to reasonable compensation in whatever sum the court may allow. The compensation thus fixed is payable from funds which may be provided by law in criminal cases and civil actions and proceedings involving just compensation for the taking of property. In other civil actions and proceedings the compensation shall be paid by the parties in such proportion and at such time as the court directs, and thereafter charged in like manner as other costs.

(c) *Disclosure of appointment.* -- In the exercise of its discretion, the court may authorize disclosure to the jury of the fact that the court appointed the expert witness.

(d) *Parties' experts of own selection.* -- Nothing in this rule limits the parties in calling expert witnesses of their own selection.

ARTICLE 8
HEARSAY

Rule 801. Definitions and exception for admissions of a party-opponent

The following definitions apply under this Article:

(a) **Statement.** -- A "statement" is (1) an oral or written assertion or (2) nonverbal conduct of a person, if it is intended by him as an assertion.

(b) **Declarant.** -- A "declarant" is a person who makes a statement.

(c) **Hearsay.** -- "Hearsay" is a statement, other than one made by the declarant while testifying at the trial or hearing, offered in evidence to prove the truth of the matter asserted.

(d) **Exception for Admissions by a Party-Opponent.** -- A statement is admissible as an exception to the hearsay rule if it is offered against a party and it is (A) his own statement, in either his individual or a representative capacity, or (B) a statement of which he has manifested his adoption or belief in its truth, or (C) a statement by a person authorized by him to make a statement concerning the subject, or (D) a statement by his agent or servant concerning a matter within the scope of his agency or employment, made during the existence of the relationship or (E) a statement by a co-conspirator of such party during the course and in furtherance of the conspiracy.

History.
1983, c. 701, s. 1

Rule 802. Hearsay rule

Hearsay is not admissible except as provided by statute or by these rules.

History.
1983, c. 701, s. 1

Rule 803. Hearsay exceptions; availability of declarant immaterial

The following are not excluded by the hearsay rule, even though the declarant is available as a witness:

(1) **Present Sense Impression.** -- A statement describing or explaining an event or condition made while the declarant was

perceiving the event or condition, or immediately thereafter.

(2) **Excited Utterance. --** A statement relating to a startling event or condition made while the declarant was under the stress of excitement caused by the event or condition.

(3) **Then Existing Mental, Emotional, or Physical Condition. --** A statement of the declarant's then existing state of mind, emotion, sensation, or physical condition (such as intent, plan, motive, design, mental feeling, pain, and bodily health), but not including a statement of memory or belief to prove the fact remembered or believed unless it relates to the execution, revocation, identification, or terms of declarant's will.

(4) **Statements for Purposes of Medical Diagnosis or Treatment. --** Statements made for purposes of medical diagnosis or treatment and describing medical history, or past or present symptoms, pain, or sensations, or the inception or general character of the cause or external source thereof insofar as reasonably pertinent to diagnosis or treatment.

(5) **Recorded Recollection. --** A memorandum or record concerning a matter about which a witness once had knowledge but now has insufficient recollection to enable him to testify fully and accurately, shown to have been made or adopted by the witness when the matter was fresh in his memory and to reflect that knowledge correctly. If admitted, the memorandum or record may be read into evidence but may not itself be received as an exhibit unless offered by an adverse party.

(6) **Records of Regularly Conducted Activity. --** A memorandum, report, record, or data compilation, in any form, of acts, events, conditions, opinions, or diagnoses, made at or near the time by, or from information transmitted by, a person with knowledge, if (i) kept in the course of a regularly conducted business activity and (ii) it was the regular practice of that business activity to make the memorandum, report, record, or data compilation, all as shown by the testimony of the custodian or other qualified witness, or by affidavit or by document under seal under Rule 902 of the Rules of Evidence made by the custodian or witness, unless the source of information or the method or circumstances of preparation indicate lack of trustworthiness. Authentication of evidence by affidavit shall be confined to the records of nonparties, and the proponent of that evidence shall give advance notice to all other parties of intent to offer the evidence with authentication

by affidavit. The term "business" as used in this paragraph includes business, institution, association, profession, occupation, and calling of every kind, whether or not conducted for profit.

(7) **Absence of Entry in Records Kept in Accordance with the Provisions of Paragraph (6). --** Evidence that a matter is not included in the memoranda, reports, records, or data compilations, in any form, kept in accordance with the provisions of paragraph (6), to prove the nonoccurrence or nonexistence of the matter, if the matter was of a kind of which a memorandum, report, record, or data compilation was regularly made and preserved, unless the sources of information or other circumstances indicate lack of trustworthiness.

(8) **Public Records and Reports. --** Records, reports, statements, or data compilations, in any form, of public offices or agencies, setting forth (A) the activities of the office or agency, or (B) matters observed pursuant to duty imposed by law as to which matters there was a duty to report, excluding, however, in criminal cases matters observed by police officers and other law-enforcement personnel, or (C) in civil actions and proceedings and against the State in criminal cases, factual findings resulting from an investigation made pursuant to authority granted by law, unless the sources of information or other circumstances indicate lack of trustworthiness.

(9) **Records of Vital Statistics. --** Records or data compilations, in any form, of births, fetal deaths, deaths, or marriages, if the report thereof was made to a public office pursuant to requirements of law.

(10) **Absence of Public Record or Entry. --** To prove the absence of a record, report, statement, or data compilation, in any form, or the nonoccurrence or nonexistence of a matter of which a record, report, statement, or data compilation, in any form, was regularly made and preserved by a public office or agency, evidence in the form of a certification in accordance with Rule 902, or testimony, that diligent search failed to disclose the record, report, statement, or data compilation, or entry.

(11) **Records of Religious Organizations. --** Statements of births, marriages, divorces, deaths, legitimacy, ancestry, relationship by blood or marriage, or other similar facts of personal or family history, contained in a regularly kept record of a religious organization.

(12) **Marriage, Baptismal, and Similar Certificates. --** Statements of fact contained in a certificate that the maker performed a marriage or other ceremony or

Chapter 8C

administered a sacrament, made by a clergyman, public official, or other person authorized by the rules or practices of a religious organization or by law to perform the act certified, and purporting to have been issued at the time of the act or within a reasonable time thereafter.

(13) **Family Records.** -- Statements of fact concerning personal or family history contained in family Bibles, genealogies, charts, engravings on rings, inscriptions on family portraits, engravings on urns, crypts, or tombstones, or the like.

(14) **Records of Documents Affecting an Interest in Property.** -- The record of a document purporting to establish or affect an interest in property, as proof of the content of the original recorded document and its execution and delivery by each person by whom it purports to have been executed, if the record is a record of a public office and an applicable statute authorizes the recording of documents of that kind in that office.

(15) **Statements in Documents Affecting an Interest in Property.** -- A statement contained in a document purporting to establish or affect an interest in property if the matter stated was relevant to the purpose of the document, unless dealings with the property since the document was made have been inconsistent with the truth of the statement or the purport of the document.

(16) **Statements in Ancient Documents.** -- Statements in a document in existence 20 years or more the authenticity of which is established.

(17) **Market Reports, Commercial Publications.** -- Market quotations, tabulations, lists, directories, or other published compilations, generally used and relied upon by the public or by persons in particular occupations.

(18) **Learned Treatises.** -- To the extent called to the attention of an expert witness upon cross-examination or relied upon by him in direct examination, statements contained in published treatises, periodicals, or pamphlets on a subject of history, medicine, or other science or art, established as a reliable authority by the testimony or admission of the witness or by other expert testimony or by judicial notice. If admitted, the statements may be read into evidence but may not be received as exhibits.

(19) **Reputation Concerning Personal or Family History.** -- Reputation among members of his family by blood, adoption, or marriage, or among his associates, or in the community, concerning a person's birth, adoption, marriage, divorce, death, legitimacy, relationship by blood, adoption, or marriage, ancestry, or other similar fact of his personal or family history.

(20) **Reputation Concerning Boundaries or General History.** -- Reputation in a community, arising before the controversy, as to boundaries of or customs affecting lands in the community, and reputation as to events of general history important to the community or state or nation in which located.

(21) **Reputation as to Character.** -- Reputation of a person's character among his associates or in the community.

(22) (Reserved).

(23) **Judgment as to Personal, Family or General History, or Boundaries.** -- Judgments as proof of matters of personal, family or general history, or boundaries, essential to the judgment, if the same would be provable by evidence of reputation.

(24) **Other Exceptions.** -- A statement not specifically covered by any of the foregoing exceptions but having equivalent circumstantial guarantees of trustworthiness, if the court determines that (A) the statement is offered as evidence of a material fact; (B) the statement is more probative on the point for which it is offered than any other evidence which the proponent can procure through reasonable efforts; and (C) the general purposes of these rules and the interests of justice will best be served by admission of the statement into evidence. However, a statement may not be admitted under this exception unless the proponent of it gives written notice stating his intention to offer the statement and the particulars of it, including the name and address of the declarant, to the adverse party sufficiently in advance of offering the statement to provide the adverse party with a fair opportunity to prepare to meet the statement.

History.
1983, c. 701, s. 1; 2015-247, s. 11(a)

Rule 804. Hearsay exceptions; declarant unavailable

(a) *Definition of unavailability.* -- "Unavailability as a witness" includes situations in which the declarant:

(1) Is exempted by ruling of the court on the ground of privilege from testifying concerning the subject matter of his statement; or

(2) Persists in refusing to testify concerning the subject matter of his statement despite an order of the court to do so; or

(3) Testifies to a lack of memory of the subject matter of his statement; or

(4) Is unable to be present or to testify at the hearing because of death or then existing physical or mental illness or infirmity; or

(5) Is absent from the hearing and the proponent of his statement has been unable to procure his attendance (or in the case of a hearsay exception under subdivision (b) (2), (3), or (4), his attendance or testimony) by process or other reasonable means.

A declarant is not unavailable as a witness if his exemption, refusal, claim of lack of memory, inability, or absence is due to the procurement or wrongdoing of the proponent of his statement for the purpose of preventing the witness from attending or testifying.

(b) *Hearsay exceptions.* -- The following are not excluded by the hearsay rule if the declarant is unavailable as a witness:

(1) **Former Testimony.** -- Testimony given as a witness at another hearing of the same or a different proceeding, or in a deposition taken in compliance with law in the course of the same or another proceeding, if the party against whom the testimony is now offered, or, in a civil action or proceeding, a predecessor in interest, had an opportunity and similar motive to develop the testimony by direct, cross, or redirect examination.

(2) **Statement Under Belief of Impending Death.** -- A statement made by a declarant while believing that his death was imminent, concerning the cause or circumstances of what he believed to be his impending death.

(3) **Statement Against Interest.** -- A statement which was at the time of its making so far contrary to the declarant's pecuniary or proprietary interest, or so far tended to subject him to civil or criminal liability, or to render invalid a claim by him against another, that a reasonable man in his position would not have made the statement unless he believed it to be true. A statement tending to expose the declarant to criminal liability is not admissible in a criminal case unless corroborating circumstances clearly indicate the trustworthiness of the statement.

(4) **Statement of Personal or Family History.** -- (A) A statement concerning the declarant's own birth, adoption, marriage, divorce, legitimacy, relationship by blood, adoption, or marriage, ancestry, or other similar fact of personal or family history, even though declarant had no means of acquiring personal knowledge of the matter stated; or (B) a statement concerning the foregoing matters, and death also, of another person, if the declarant was related

to the other by blood, adoption, or marriage or was so intimately associated with the other's family as to be likely to have accurate information concerning the matter declared.

(5) **Other Exceptions.** -- A statement not specifically covered by any of the foregoing exceptions but having equivalent circumstantial guarantees of trustworthiness, if the court determines that (A) the statement is offered as evidence of a material fact; (B) the statement is more probative on the point for which it is offered than any other evidence which the proponent can procure through reasonable efforts; and (C) the general purposes of these rules and the interests of justice will best be served by admission of the statement into evidence. However, a statement may not be admitted under this exception unless the proponent of it gives written notice stating his intention to offer the statement and the particulars of it, including the name and address of the declarant, to the adverse party sufficiently in advance of offering the statement to provide the adverse party with a fair opportunity to prepare to meet the statement.

History.
1983, c. 701, s. 1

Rule 805. Hearsay within hearsay

Hearsay included within hearsay is not excluded under the hearsay rule if each part of the combined statements conforms with an exception to the hearsay rule provided in these rules.

History.
1983, c. 701, s. 1

Rule 806. Attacking and supporting credibility of declarant

When a hearsay statement has been admitted in evidence, the credibility of the declarant may be attacked, and if attacked may be supported, by any evidence which would be admissible for those purposes if declarant had testified as a witness. Evidence of a statement or conduct by the declarant at any time, inconsistent with his hearsay statement, is not subject to any requirement that he may have been afforded an opportunity to deny or explain. If the party against whom a hearsay statement has been admitted calls the declarant as a witness, the party is entitled to examine him on the statement as if under cross-examination.

History.
1983, c. 701, s. 1

ARTICLE 9
AUTHENTICATION AND IDENTIFICATION

Rule 901. Requirement of authentication or identification

(a) *General provision.* -- The requirement of authentication or identification as a condition precedent to admissibility is satisfied by evidence sufficient to support a finding that the matter in question is what its proponent claims.

(b) *Illustrations.* -- By way of illustration only, and not by way of limitation, the following are examples of authentication or identification conforming with the requirements of this rule:

(1) **Testimony of Witness with Knowledge.** -- Testimony that a matter is what it is claimed to be.

(2) **Nonexpert Opinion on Handwriting.** -- Nonexpert opinion as to the genuineness of handwriting, based upon familiarity not acquired for purposes of the litigation.

(3) **Comparison by Trier or Expert Witness.** -- Comparison by the trier of fact or by expert witnesses with specimens which have been authenticated.

(4) **Distinctive Characteristics and the Like.** -- Appearance, contents, substance, internal patterns, or other distinctive characteristics, taken in conjunction with circumstances.

(5) **Voice Identification.** -- Identification of a voice, whether heard firsthand or through mechanical or electronic transmission or recording, by opinion based upon hearing the voice at any time under circumstances connecting it with the alleged speaker.

(6) **Telephone Conversations.** -- Telephone conversations, by evidence that a call was made to the number assigned at the time by the telephone company to a particular person or business, if (A) in the case of a person, circumstances, including self-identification, show the person answering to be the one called, or (B) in the case of a business, the call was made to a place of business and the conversation related to business reasonably transacted over the telephone.

(7) **Public Records or Reports.** -- Evidence that a writing authorized by law to be recorded or filed and in fact recorded or filed in a public office, or a purported public record, report, statement, or data compilation, in any form, is from the public office where items of this nature are kept.

(8) **Ancient Documents or Data Compilations.** -- Evidence that a document or data compilation, in any form, (A) is in such condition as to create no suspicion concerning its authenticity, (B) was in a place where it, if authentic, would likely be, and (C) has been in existence 20 years or more at the time it is offered.

(9) **Process or System.** -- Evidence describing a process or system used to produce a result and showing that the process or system produces an accurate result.

(10) **Methods Provided by Statute.** -- Any method of authentication or identification provided by statute.

History.
1983, c. 701, s. 1

Rule 902. Self-authentication

Extrinsic evidence of authenticity as a condition precedent to admissibility is not required with respect to the following:

(1) **Domestic Public Documents Under Seal.** -- A document bearing a seal purporting to be that of the United States, or of any state, district, commonwealth, territory or insular possession thereof, or the Trust Territory of the Pacific Islands, or of a political subdivision, department, officer, or agency thereof, and a signature purporting to be an attestation or execution.

(2) **Domestic Public Documents Not Under Seal.** -- A document purporting to bear the signature in his official capacity of an officer or employee of any entity included in paragraph (1) hereof, having no seal, if a public officer having a seal and having official duties in the district or political subdivision of the officer or employee certifies under seal that the signer has the official capacity and that the signature is genuine.

(3) **Foreign Public Documents.** -- A document purporting to be executed or attested in his official capacity by a person authorized by the laws of a foreign country to make the execution or attestation, and accompanied by a final certification as to the genuineness of the signature and official position (A) of the executing or attesting person, or (B) of any foreign official whose certificate of genuineness of signature and official position relates to the execution or attestation or is in a chain of certificates of genuineness of signature and official position relating to the execution or attestation. A final certification may be made by a secretary of embassy or legation, consul general, consul, vice consul, or consular agent of the United States, or a diplomatic or

consular official of the foreign country assigned or accredited to the United States. If reasonable opportunity has been given to all parties to investigate the authenticity and accuracy of official documents, the court may, for good cause shown, order that they be treated as presumptively authentic without final certification or permit them to be evidenced by an attested summary with or without final certification.

(4) **Certified Copies of Public Records.** -- A copy of an official record or report or entry therein, or of a document authorized by law to be recorded or filed and actually recorded or filed in a public office, including data compilations in any form, certified as correct by the custodian or other person authorized to make the certification, by certificate complying with paragraph (1), (2), or (3) or complying with any law of the United States or of this State.

(5) **Official Publications.** -- Books, pamphlets, or other publications purporting to be issued by public authority.

(6) **Newspapers and Periodicals.** -- Printed materials purporting to be newspapers or periodicals.

(7) **Trade Inscriptions and the Like.** -- Inscriptions, signs, tags, or labels purporting to have been affixed in the course of business and indicating ownership, control, or origin.

(8) **Acknowledged Documents.** -- Documents accompanied by a certificate of acknowledgment executed in the manner provided by law by a notary public or other officer authorized by law to take acknowledgments.

(9) **Commercial Paper and Related Documents.** -- Commercial paper, signatures thereon, and documents relating thereto to the extent provided by general commercial law.

(10) **Presumptions Created by Law.** -- Any signature, document, or other matter declared by any law of the United States or of this State to be presumptively or prima facie genuine or authentic.

History.
1983, c. 701, s. 1

Rule 903. Subscribing witness' testimony unnecessary

The testimony of a subscribing witness is not necessary to authenticate a writing unless required by the laws of the jurisdiction whose laws govern the validity of the writing.

History.
1983, c. 701, s. 1

ARTICLE 10
CONTENTS OF WRITINGS, RECORDINGS AND PHOTOGRAPHS

Rule 1001. Definitions

For the purposes of this Article the following definitions are applicable:

(1) **Writings and Recordings.** -- "Writings" and "recordings" consist of letters, words, sounds, or numbers, or their equivalent, set down by handwriting, typewriting, printing, photostating, photographing, magnetic impulse, mechanical or electronic recording, or other form of data compilation.

(2) **Photographs.** -- "Photographs" include still photographs, x-ray films, video tapes, and motion pictures.

(3) **Original.** -- An "original" of a writing or recording is the writing or recording itself or any counterpart intended to have the same effect by a person executing or issuing it. An "original" of a photograph includes the negative or any print therefrom. If data are stored in a computer or similar device, any printout or other output readable by sight, shown to reflect the data accurately, is an "original."

(4) **Duplicate.** -- A "duplicate" is a counterpart produced by the same impression as the original, or from the same matrix, or by means of photography, including enlargements and miniatures, or by mechanical or electronic re-recording, or by chemical reproduction, or by other equivalent techniques which accurately reproduce the original.

History.
1983, c. 701, s. 1

Rule 1002. Requirement of original

To prove the content of a writing, recording, or photograph, the original writing, recording, or photograph is required, except as otherwise provided in these rules or by statute.

History.
1983, c. 701, s. 1

Rule 1003. Admissibility of duplicates

A duplicate is admissible to the same extent as an original unless (1) a genuine question is raised as to the authenticity of the original or (2) in the circumstances it would be unfair to admit the duplicate in lieu of the original.

History.
1983, c. 701, s. 1

Rule 1004. Admissibility of other evidence of contents

The original is not required, and other evidence of the contents of a writing, recording, or photograph is admissible if:

(1) **Originals Lost or Destroyed. --** All originals are lost or have been destroyed, unless the proponent lost or destroyed them in bad faith; or

(2) **Original Not Obtainable. --** No original can be obtained by any available judicial process or procedure; or

(3) **Original in Possession of Opponent. --** At a time when an original was under the control of a party against whom offered, he was put on notice, by the pleadings or otherwise, that the contents would be a subject of proof at the hearing, and he does not produce the original at the hearing; or

(4) **Collateral Matters. --** The writing, recording, or photograph is not closely related to a controlling issue.

History.
1983, c. 701, s. 1

Rule 1005. Public records

The contents of an official record, or of a document authorized to be recorded or filed and actually recorded or filed, including data compilations in any form, if otherwise admissible, may be proved by copy, certified as correct in accordance with Rule 902 or testified to be correct by a witness who has compared it with the original. If a copy which complies with the foregoing cannot be obtained by the exercise of reasonable diligence, then other evidence of the contents may be given.

History.
1983, c. 701, s. 1

Rule 1006. Summaries

The contents of voluminous writings, recordings, or photographs which cannot conveniently be examined in court may be presented in the form of a chart, summary, or calculation. The originals, or duplicates, shall be made available for examination or copying, or both, by other parties at a reasonable time and place. The court may order that they be produced in court.

History.
1983, c. 701, s. 1

Rule 1007. Testimony or written admission of party

Contents of writings, recordings, or photographs may be proved by the testimony or deposition of the party against whom offered or by his written admission, without accounting for the nonproduction of the original.

History.
1983, c. 701, s. 1

Rule 1008. Functions of court and jury

When the admissibility of other evidence of contents of writings, recordings, or photographs under these rules depends upon the fulfillment of a condition of fact, the question whether the condition has been fulfilled is ordinarily for the court to determine in accordance with the provisions of Rule 104. However, when an issue is raised (a) whether the asserted writing ever existed, or (b) whether another writing, recording, or photograph produced at the trial is the original, or (c) whether other evidence of contents correctly reflects the contents, the issue is for the trier of fact to determine as in the case of other issues of fact.

History.
1983, c. 701, s. 1

ARTICLE 11
MISCELLANEOUS RULES

Rule 1101. Applicability of rules

(a) *Proceedings generally.* -- Except as otherwise provided in subdivision (b) or by statute, these rules apply to all actions and proceedings in the courts of this State.

(b) *Rules inapplicable.* -- The rules other than those with respect to privileges do not apply in the following situations:

(1) **Preliminary Questions of Fact. --** The determination of questions of fact preliminary to admissibility of evidence when the issue is to be determined by the court under Rule 104(a).

(2) **Grand Jury. --** Proceedings before grand juries.

(3) **Miscellaneous Proceedings. --** Proceedings for extradition or rendition; first appearance before district court judge or probable cause hearing in criminal cases; sentencing, or granting or revoking probation; issuance of warrants for arrest, criminal summonses, and search warrants; proceedings with respect to release on bail or otherwise.

Chapter 8C

(4) **Contempt Proceedings. --** Contempt proceedings in which the court is authorized by law to act summarily.

History.

1983, c. 701, s. 1; 1983 (Reg. Sess., 1984), c. 1037, s. 14; 1985, c. 509, s. 2

Rule 1102. Short title

These rules shall be known and may be cited as the "North Carolina Rules of Evidence."

History.

1983, c. 701, s. 1

CHAPTER 9
JURORS

ARTICLE 1
JURY COMMISSIONS, PREPARATION OF JURY LISTS, AND DRAWING OF PANELS

§ 9-1. Jury commission in each county; membership; selection; oath; terms; expenses of jury system

Not later than July 1, 1967, there shall be appointed in each county a jury commission of three members. One member of the commission shall be appointed by the senior regular resident superior court judge, one member by the clerk of superior court, and one member by the board of county commissioners. The appointees shall be qualified voters of the county, and shall serve for terms of two years. Appointees may be reappointed to successive terms. A vacancy in the commission shall be filled in the same manner as the original appointment, for the unexpired term. Each commissioner shall take an oath or affirmation that, without favor or prejudice, he will honestly perform the duties of a member of the jury commission during his term of service. The compensation of commissioners shall be fixed by the board of county commissioners, and shall be paid from the general fund of the county. All expenses necessary to carry out the provisions of this Chapter and to administer the jury system, including all data processing, document processing, supplies, postage, and other similar expenses, except as otherwise provided in this Chapter, shall be paid from the general fund of the county, except that the clerk of superior court shall furnish clerical or other personnel assistance, as the commission may reasonably require.

History.
1967, c. 218, s. 1; 1981, c. 720, s. 3; 1991, c. 729, s. 1

§ 9-2. Preparation of master jury list; sources of names

(a) It shall be the duty of the jury commission during every odd-numbered year to prepare a master list of prospective jurors qualified under this Chapter to serve in the biennium beginning on January 1 of the next year. Instead of providing a master list for an entire biennium, the commission may prepare a master list each year if the senior regular resident superior court judge requests in writing that it do so.

(b) In preparing the master list, the jury commission shall use the list of registered voters and persons with drivers license records supplied to the county by the Commissioner of Motor Vehicles pursuant to G.S. 20-43.4. The commission may use fewer than all the names from the list if it uses a random method of selection. The commission may use other sources of names deemed by it to be reliable.

(c), (d) Repealed by Session Laws 2003-226, s. 7(d), effective January 1, 2004.

(e) The jury commission shall merge the entire list of names of each source used and randomly select the desired number of names to form the master list.

(f) The master list shall contain not less than one and one-quarter times and not more than three times as many names as were drawn for jury duty in all courts in the county during the previous biennium, or, if an annual list is being prepared as requested under subsection (a) of this section the master list shall contain not less than one and one-quarter times and not more than three times as many names as were drawn for jury duty in all courts in the county during the previous year but in no event shall the list include fewer than 500 names, except that in counties in which a different panel of jurors is selected for each day of the week, there is no limit to the number of names that may be placed on the master list.

(g) Repealed by Session Laws 2003-226, s. 7(d), effective January 1, 2004.

(h) As used in this section "random" or "randomly" refers to a method of selection that results in each name on a list having an equal opportunity to be selected.

(i) To facilitate random selection of jurors, all the names on the master list may be sorted into random order before the first panel is drawn. Thereafter, names may be selected sequentially from the randomized list without further randomization, except as required by G.S. 15A-1214.

(j) The procedure for performing the preparation of the master list shall be in writing, adopted by the jury commission, and kept available for public inspection in the office of the clerk of court. The procedure must effectively preserve the authorized grounds for disqualification, the right of public access to the master list of prospective jurors as provided by G.S. 9-4, and the time sequence for drawing and summoning a jury panel.

(k) In counties utilizing electronic data processing equipment, the functions of preparing and maintaining custody of the master list of prospective jurors, the procedure for drawing and summoning panels of jurors, and the procedure for maintaining records of names of jurors who have served, been excused or disqualified, or whose service has been deferred may be performed by this equipment, except that decisions as to mental or physical competence of prospective jurors shall continue to be made by jury commissioners.

History.

1806, c. 694, P.R.; Code, ss. 1722, 1723; 1889, c. 559; 1897, cc. 117, 539; 1899, c. 729; Rev., s. 1957; C.S., s. 2312; 1947, c. 1007, s. 1; 1967, c. 218, s. 1; 1969, c. 205, s. 1; c. 1190, s. 491/2; 1973, c. 83, ss. 1, 2; 1981, c. 430, s. 1; c. 720, s. 1; 1981 (Reg. Sess., 1982), c. 1226, s. 1; 1983, c. 197, s. 2; 2003-226, s. 7(d); 2007-512, s. 1; 2012-180, s. 1

N.C. Gen. Stat. § 9-2.1

Repealed by Session Laws 2012-180, s. 2, effective July 12, 2012.

History.

1977, c. 220, s. 1; 1981, c. 430, s. 3; 1985, c. 368; repealed by 2012-180, s. 2, effective July 12, 2012

§ 9-3. Qualifications of prospective jurors

All persons are qualified to serve as jurors and to be included on the master jury list who are citizens of the State and residents of the county, who have not served as jurors during the preceding two years or who have not served a full term of service as grand jurors during the preceding six years, who are 18 years of age or over, who are physically and mentally competent, who can understand the English language, who have not been convicted of a felony or pleaded guilty or nolo contendere to an indictment charging a felony (or if convicted of a felony or having pleaded guilty or nolo contendere to an indictment charging a felony have had their citizenship restored pursuant to law), and who have not been adjudged non compos mentis. Persons not qualified under this section are subject to challenge for cause.

History.

1806, c. 694, P.R.; Code, ss. 1722, 1723; 1889, c. 559; 1897, cc. 117, 539; 1899, c. 729; Rev., s. 1957; C.S., s. 2312; 1947, c. 1007, s. 1; 1967, c. 218, s. 1; 1971, c. 1231, s. 1; 1973, c. 230, ss. 1, 2; 1977, c. 711, s. 10; 2011-42, s. 1; 2012-180, s. 3; 2013-148, s. 1

§ 9-4. Preparation and custody of alphabetized list; access to list.

(a) As the master jury list is prepared, the name of each qualified person selected for the list shall be recorded and alphabetically arranged. The alphabetized list shall be maintained in the office of the clerk of court, together with a statement of the sources used and procedures followed in preparing the list. The alphabetized list shall be kept under lock and key, but shall be available for public inspection during regular office hours. The clerk of court may elect to store an electronic copy of the alphabetized list for the county.

(b) Public access to juror information shall be limited to the alphabetized list of the names. The addresses and dates of birth of prospective jurors are confidential and not subject to disclosure without an order of the court.

History.

1967, c. 218, s. 1; 1969, c. 205, s. 2; 2009-518, s. 1; 2012-18, s. 1.1; 2012-180, s. 4; 2013-166, s. 2

§ 9-5. Procedure for drawing panel of jurors

At least 30 days prior to any session or sessions of superior or district court requiring a jury, the clerk of superior court or assistant or deputy clerk shall prepare or have electronically prepared a randomized list of names from the master jury list equal to the number of jurors required for the session or sessions scheduled. The clerk of superior court may decrease the number of randomized names to account for the addition of names of previously selected jurors whose service has been deferred to this session. For each week of a superior court session, the senior resident superior court judge for the district or set of districts as defined in G.S. 7A-41.1(a) in which the county is located shall specify the number of jurors to be drawn. For each week of a district court jury session, the chief district judge of the district court district in which the county is located shall specify the number of jurors to be drawn. Pooling of jurors between or among concurrent sessions of various courts is authorized in the discretion of the senior regular resident superior court judge. When pooling is utilized, the senior regular resident superior court judge, after consultation with the chief district judge when a district court jury is required, shall specify the total number of jurors to be drawn for such concurrent sessions. When grand jurors are needed, at least nine additional names shall be drawn.

The clerk of superior court shall either (i) prepare and issue the summonses or (ii) deliver the printed summonses or the list of names and addresses of jurors to the sheriff, who shall issue the summonses in accordance with the provisions of G.S. 9-10(a). The persons so summoned may serve as jurors in either the superior or the district court, or both, for the week for which summoned. Jurors who serve each week shall be discharged at the close of the weekly session or sessions, unless actually engaged in the trial of a case, and then they shall not be discharged until their service in that case is completed.

History.

1806, c. 694, P.R.; 1868-9, c. 9, ss. 5, 6; c. 175; Code, ss. 1726, 1727, 1731; 1889, c. 559; 1897, c. 117; 1901, c. 28, s. 3; c. 636; 1903, c. 11; 1905, c. 38; c. 76, s. 4; c. 285; Rev., ss. 1958, 1959; C.S., ss. 2313, 2314; 1967, c. 218, s. 1; 1969, c. 205, s. 3; 1987 (Reg. Sess., 1988), c. 1037, s. 38; 2012-180, s. 5

§ 9-6. Jury service a public duty; excuses to be allowed in exceptional cases; procedure

(a) The General Assembly hereby declares the public policy of this State to be that jury service is the solemn obligation of all qualified citizens, and that excuses from the discharge of this responsibility should be granted only for reasons of compelling personal hardship or because requiring service would be contrary to the public welfare, health, or safety.

(b) Pursuant to the foregoing policy, each chief district court judge shall promulgate procedures whereby he or any district court judge of his district court district designated by him, prior to the date that a jury session (or sessions) of superior or district court convenes, shall receive, hear, and pass on applications for excuses from jury duty. The procedures shall provide for the time and place, publicly announced, at which applications for excuses will be heard, and prospective jurors who have been summoned for service shall be so informed. In counties located in a district or set of districts as defined in G.S. 7A-41.1(a) which have a trial court administrator, the chief district judge may assign the duty of passing on applications for excuses from jury service to the administrator. In all cases concerning excuses, the clerk of court or the trial court administrator shall notify prospective jurors of the disposition of their excuses.

(b1) A prospective juror who is summoned for jury service in a session of court scheduled during a period of time when the prospective juror is taking classes or exams as a full-time student enrolled at an out-of-state postsecondary public or private educational institution, including any out-of-state trade or professional institution, college, or university, shall be excused from jury service upon request made pursuant to G.S. 9-6.1(a) and supported by documentation showing enrollment at the out-of-state educational institution.

(c) A prospective juror excused by a judge in the exercise of the discretion conferred by subsection (b) of this section or excused pursuant to subsection (b1) of this section may be required by the judge to serve as a juror in a subsequent session of court. If required to serve subsequently, the juror shall be considered on such occasion the same as if he were a member of the panel regularly summoned for jury service at that time.

(d) A judge hearing applications for excuses from jury duty shall excuse any person disqualified under § 9-3.

(e) The judge shall inform the clerk of superior court of persons excused under this section, and the clerk shall keep a record of excuses separate from the master jury list.

(f) The discretionary authority of a presiding judge to excuse a juror at the beginning of or during a session of court is not affected by this section.

History.

1967, c. 218, s. 1; 1969, c. 205, ss. 4, 5; 1971, c. 377, s. 30; 1979, 2nd Sess., c. 1207, s. 1; 1981, c. 430, s. 2; 1985, c. 609, s. 2; 1987 (Reg. Sess., 1988), c. 1037, s. 47; 2012-180, s. 6; 2015-210, s. 2

§ 9-6.1. Requests to be excused

(a) Any person summoned as a juror who is a full-time student and who wishes to be excused pursuant to G.S. 9-6.1(b1) [G.S. 9-6(b1)] or who is 72 years or older and who wishes to be excused, deferred, or exempted, may make the request without appearing in person by filing a signed statement of the ground of the request with the chief district court judge of that district, or the district court judge or trial court administrator designated by the chief district court judge pursuant to G.S. 9-6(b), at any time five business days before the date upon which the person is summoned to appear.

(b) Any person summoned as a juror who has a disability that could interfere with the person's ability to serve as a juror and who wishes to be excused, deferred, or exempted may make the request without appearing in person by filing a signed statement of the ground of the request, including a brief explanation of the disability that interferes with the person's ability to serve as a juror, with the chief district court judge of that district, or the district court judge or trial court administrator designated by the chief district court judge pursuant to G.S. 9-6(b), at any time five business days before the date upon which the person is summoned to appear. Upon request of the court, medical documentation of any disability may be submitted. Any privileged medical information or protected health information described in this section shall be confidential and shall be exempt from the provisions of Chapter 132 of the General Statutes or any other provision requiring information and records held by State agencies to be made public or accessible to the public.

(c) A person may request either a temporary or permanent exemption under this section, and the judge or trial court administrator may accept or reject either in the exercise of discretion conferred by G.S. 9-6(b), including the substitution of a temporary exemption for a requested permanent exemption. In the case of supplemental jurors summoned under G.S. 9-11, notice may be given when summoned. In case the chief district court judge, or the judge or trial court administrator designated by the chief district court judge pursuant to G.S. 9-6(b), rejects the request for exemption, the prospective juror shall be immediately notified by the trial court administrator or the clerk of court by telephone, letter, or personally.

History.
1979, 2nd Sess., c. 1207, s. 2; 1981, c. 9, ss. 1, 2; c. 430, ss. 4, 5; 2005-149, s. 1; 2011-42, s. 2; 2012-180, s. 7; 2015-210, s. 3

§ 9-7. Notation on master jury list of names of jurors who have served; retention

(a) The names of persons summoned for jury service and the date or dates on which each person served shall be noted on the master jury list. This information shall be retained for two years, and persons shall be exempt from jury service for a period of two years from the date on which they were discharged from their prior service, except as provided in subsection (b) of this section.

(b) The names of persons summoned for jury service who served a full term on the grand jury pursuant to G.S. 15A-622, the date or dates on which each person served, and a notation that the person served the full term of service as a grand juror shall be noted on the master list. This information shall be retained for six years, and persons shall be exempt from jury service for a period of six years from the date on which they were discharged from their prior service.

History.
1967, c. 218, s. 1; 2012-180, s. 8; 2013-148, s. 2

§ 9-7.1. Trial court administrator may assist clerk with performance of duties

Upon the request of the clerk of superior court and with the agreement of the clerk of superior court and the senior resident superior court judge, the duties and responsibilities of the clerk of superior court under this Article may be assigned to the trial court administrator pursuant to G.S. 7A-356.

History.
2012-180, s. 10

§§ 9-8, 9-9

Repealed by Session Laws 1967, c. 218, s. 1.

ARTICLE 2
PETIT JURORS

§ 9-10. Summons to jurors

(a) The clerk of court shall serve the summons by first-class mail, or shall deliver either printed summonses or the list of the panel of prospective jurors to the sheriff of the county, who shall summon the persons named therein. The summons shall be served personally, or by leaving a copy thereof at the place of residence of the juror, or by telephone or first-class mail, at least 15 days before the session of court for which the juror is summoned. Service by telephone, or by first-class mail if mailed to the correct current address of the juror on or before the fifteenth day before the day the court convenes, shall be valid and binding on the person served, and he shall be bound to appear in the same manner as if personally served. The summons shall contain information as to the time, place, and authority before whom applications for excuses from jury service may be heard.

(b) All summons served personally or by mail under this section or under G.S. 9-11 shall inform the prospective juror that persons 72 years of age or older are entitled to establish in writing exemption from jury service for good cause, shall contain a statement for claiming such exemption and stating the cause and a place for the prospective juror's signature, and shall state the mailing address of the clerk of superior court and the date by which such request for exemption must be received.

History.
1779, c. 157, ss. 4, 6, P.R.; R.C., c. 31, s. 29; 1868-9, c. 9, s. 12; Code, s. 1733; Rev., s. 1976; C.S., s. 2320; 1967, c. 218, s. 1; 1979, 2nd Sess., c. 1207, s. 3; 1985, c. 609, s. 3; 2006-226, s. 8; 2006-264, ss. 30(a), 30(c); 2012-180, s. 9

§ 9-11. Supplemental jurors; special venire

(a) If necessary, the court may, without using the jury list, order the sheriff to summon from day to day additional jurors to supplement the original venire. Jurors so summoned shall have the same qualifications and be subject to the same challenges as jurors selected for the regular jury list. If the presiding judge finds that service of summons by the sheriff is not suitable because of his direct or indirect interest in the action to be tried, the judge may appoint some suitable person in place of the sheriff to summon supplemental jurors. The clerk of superior court shall keep a record of the names of those additional jurors who are so summoned and who report for jury service.

(b) The presiding judge may, in his discretion, at any time before or during a session direct that supplemental jurors or a special venire be selected from the jury list in the same manner as is provided for the selection of regular jurors. Jurors summoned under this subsection may be discharged by the court at any time during the session and are subject to the same challenges as regular jurors, and to no other challenges.

History.

1779, c. 156, s. 69, P.R.; 1830, c. 27; R.C., c. 31, s. 29; c. 35, ss. 30, 31; Code, ss. 1733, 1738, 1739, 1740; 1887, c. 53; 1889, c. 441; 1897, c. 364; Rev., ss. 1967, 1968, 1973, 1974, 1975, 3265, 3602; 1911, c. 15; 1913, c. 31, ss. 1, 2; 1915, c. 210; C.S., ss. 2321, 2322, 2338, 2339, 2340, 4635; 1967, c. 218, s. 1; 1969, c. 205, s. 6; 2012-180, s. 11

§ 9-12. Supplemental jurors from other counties

(a) On motion of any party or the State, or on his own motion, any judge of the superior court, if he is of the opinion that it is necessary in order to provide a fair trial in any case, and regardless of whether he will preside over the trial of that case, may order as many jurors as he deems necessary to be summoned from any county or counties in the district or set of districts as defined in G.S. 7A-41.1(a) in which the county of trial is located or in any adjoining district or set of districts. These jurors shall be selected and shall serve in the manner provided for selection and service of supplemental jurors selected from the jury list. These jurors shall be subject to the same challenges as other jurors, except challenges for nonresidence in the county of trial.

(b) Transportation may be furnished in lieu of mileage.

(c) Repealed by Session Laws 1971, c. 377, s. 32.

History.

1913, c. 4, ss. 1, 2; C.S., s. 473; 1931, c. 308; 1933, c. 248; 1961, c. 110; 1967, c. 218, s. 1; 1971, c. 377, s. 32; 1987 (Reg. Sess., 1988), c. 1037, s. 48

§ 9-13. Penalty for disobeying summons

Every person summoned to appear as a juror who has not been excused, and who fails to appear and attend until duly discharged, shall be subject to a fine of not more than fifty dollars ($ 50.00), to be imposed by the court, unless he renders an excuse deemed sufficient. The forfeiture so imposed if not paid forthwith shall be entered as a judgment against the defaulting juror, and the clerk of superior court shall issue an execution against his estate.

History.

1779, c. 157, s. 4, P.R.; 1783, c. 189, P.R.; 1806, c. 694, P.R.; R.C., c. 31, s. 30; Code, ss. 405, 1734; Rev., s. 1977; C.S., s. 2323; 1967, c. 218, s. 1

§ 9-14. Jury sworn; judge decides competency

The clerk shall, at the beginning of court, swear all jurors who have not been selected as grand jurors. Each juror shall take (i) the oath required by Section 7 of Article VI of the Constitution of North Carolina, by swearing or affirming to support and maintain the Constitution of the United States and the Constitution and laws of North Carolina not inconsistent therewith and (ii) the oath required under G.S. 11-11, by swearing or affirming to truthfully and without prejudice or partiality try all issues in criminal or civil actions that come before the juror and give true verdicts according to the evidence. Nothing herein shall be construed to disallow the usual challenges in law to the whole jury so sworn or to any juror; and if by reason of such challenge any juror is withdrawn from a jury being selected to try a case, his place on that jury shall be taken by another qualified juror. The presiding judge shall decide all questions as to the competency of jurors.

History.

1790, c. 321, P.R.; 1822, c. 1133, s. 1, P.R.; R.C., c. 31, s. 34; Code, s. 405; Rev., s. 1966; C.S., s. 2324; 1967, c. 218, s. 1; 2013-164, s. 1

§ 9-15. Questioning jurors without challenge; challenges for cause

(a) The court, and any party to an action, or his counsel of record shall be allowed, in selecting the jury, to make direct oral inquiry of any prospective juror as to the fitness and competency of any person to serve as a juror, without having such inquiry treated as a challenge of such person, and it shall not be considered by the court that any person is challenged as a juror until the party shall formally state that such person is so challenged.

(b) It shall not be a valid cause for challenge that any juror, regular or supplemental, is not a freeholder or has not paid the taxes assessed against him.

(c) In civil cases if any juror has a suit pending and at issue in the court in which he is serving, he may be challenged for cause, and he shall be withdrawn from the trial panel, and may be withdrawn from the venire in the discretion of the presiding judge. In criminal cases challenges are governed by Article 72, Selecting and Impaneling the Jury, of Chapter 15A of the General Statutes.

History.

1806, c. 694, P.R.; 1868-9, c. 9, s. 7; Code, s. 1728; Rev., s. 1960; 1913, c. 31, ss. 5, 6, 7; C.S., ss. 2316, 2325, 2326; 1933, c. 130; 1967, c. 218, s. 1; 1973, c. 95; 1977, c. 711, s. 11

§ 9-16. Exemption from civil arrest

No sheriff or other officer shall arrest under civil process any juror during his attendance at or going to and returning from any session of the superior or district court. Any such arrest shall be invalid, and the defendant on motion shall be discharged.

History.

1779, c. 157, s. 10, P.R.; R.C., c. 31, s. 31; Code, s. 1735; Rev., s. 1979, C.S., s. 2328; 1967, c. 218, s. 1

§ 9-17. Jurors impaneled to try case furnished with accommodations; separation of jurors

A jury, impaneled to try any cause, shall be put in charge of an officer of the court and shall be furnished with such accommodations as the court may order, and the accommodations shall be paid for by the parties or by the State, as ordered by the presiding judge. When sequestration of the jury is ordered in a criminal case, however, the State shall pay for all accommodations of jurors.

The presiding judge, in his discretion, may direct any jury to be sequestered while it has a case or issue under consideration.

History.

1876-7, c. 173; Code, s. 1736; 1889, c. 44; Rev., s. 1978, C.S., s. 2327; 1947, c. 1007, s. 2; 1967, c. 218, s. 1; 1977, c. 711, s. 12

§ 9-18. Alternate jurors

(a) Civil Cases. Whenever the presiding judge deems it appropriate, one or more alternate jurors may be selected in the same manner as the regular trial panel of jurors in the case. Each party shall be entitled to two peremptory challenges as to each such alternate juror, in addition to any unexpended challenges the party may have after the selection of the regular trial panel. Alternate jurors shall be sworn and seated near the jury with equal opportunity to see and hear the proceedings and shall attend the trial at all times with the jury and shall obey all orders and admonitions of the court to the jury. When the jurors are ordered kept together in any case, the alternate jurors shall be kept with them. An alternate juror shall receive the same compensation as other jurors and, except as hereinafter provided, shall be discharged upon the final submission of the case to the jury.

If before that time any juror dies, becomes incapacitated or disqualified, or is discharged for any reason, an alternate juror shall become a part of the jury and serve in all respects as those selected on the regular trial panel. If more than one alternate juror has been selected, they shall be available to become a part of the jury in the order in which they were selected.

(b) Criminal Cases. Procedures relating to alternate jurors in criminal cases are governed by Article 72, Selecting and Impaneling the Jury, of Chapter 15A of the General Statutes.

History.

1931, c. 103; 1939, c. 35; 1951, cc. 82, 1043; 1967, c. 218, s. 1; 1977, c. 406, ss. 3-5; c. 711, s. 13; 1979, c. 711, s. 2

ARTICLE 3
PEREMPTORY CHALLENGES

§ 9-19. Peremptory challenges in civil cases

The clerk, before a jury is impaneled to try the issues in any civil suit, shall read over the names of the prospective jurors in the presence and hearing of the parties or their counsel; and the parties, or their counsel for them, may challenge peremptorily eight jurors without showing any cause therefor, and the challenges shall be allowed by the court.

History.

1796, c. 452, s. 2, P.R.; 1812, c. 833, P.R.; R.C., c. 31, s. 35; Code, s. 406; Rev., s. 1964; C.S., s. 2331; 1935, c. 475, s. 1; 1965, c. 1182; 1967, c. 218, s. 1

§ 9-20. Civil cases having several plaintiffs or several defendants; challenges apportioned; discretion of judge

(a) When there are two or more defendants in a civil action, the presiding judge, if it appears that there are antagonistic interests between the defendants, may in the judge's discretion apportion among the defendants the challenges now allowed by law, or the judge may increase the number of challenges to not exceeding six for each defendant or class of defendants representing the same interest.

(b) When there are two or more plaintiffs in a civil action, the presiding judge, if it appears that there are antagonistic interests between the plaintiffs, may, in the judge's discretion, apportion among the plaintiffs the challenges now allowed by law, or the judge may increase the number of challenges to not exceeding six for each plaintiff or class of plaintiffs representing the same interest.

(c) Whenever a judge exercises the discretion authorized by subsection (a) or (b) of this section to increase the number of challenges for either the plaintiffs or the defendants, the judge may, in the judge's discretion, increase the number of challenges for the opposing side, not to exceed the total number given to the other side.

History.
1905, c. 357; Rev., s. 1965; C.S., s. 2332; 1967, c. 218, s. 1; 2007-210, s. 1

§ 9-21. Peremptory challenges in criminal cases governed by Chapter 15A

Peremptory challenges in criminal cases are governed by Article 72, Selecting and Impaneling the Jury, of Chapter 15A of the General Statutes.

History.
22 Hen. VIII, c. 14, s. 6; 33 Edw. I, c. 4; 1777, c. 115, s. 85, P.R.; 1801, c. 592, s. 1, P.R.; 1812, c. 833, P.R.; 1826, c. 9; 1827, c. 10; R.S., c. 35, ss. 19, 21; R.C., c. 35, ss. 32, 33; 1871-2, c. 39; Code, ss. 1199, 1200; 1887, c. 53; Rev., ss. 3263, 3264; 1907, c. 415; 1913, c. 31, ss. 3, 4; C.S., ss. 4633, 4634; 1935, c. 475, ss. 2, 3; 1967, c. 218, s. 1; 1969, c. 205, s. 7; 1971, c. 75; 1977, c. 711, s. 14

ARTICLE 4
GRAND JURORS

§§ 9-22 through 9-26

Repealed by Session Laws 1973, c. 1286, s. 26.

§§ 9-27 through 9-31

Repealed by Session Laws 1967, c. 218, s. 1.

ARTICLE 5
DISCHARGE OF JURORS PROHIBITED

§ 9-32. Discharge of juror unlawful

(a) No employer may discharge or demote any employee because the employee has been called for jury duty, or is serving as a grand juror or petit juror.

(b) Any employer who violates any provision of this section shall be liable in a civil action for reasonable damages suffered by an employee as a result of the violation, and an employee discharged or demoted in violation of this section shall be entitled to be reinstated to his former position. The burden of proof shall be upon the employee.

(c) The statute of limitations for actions under this section shall be one year pursuant to G.S. 1-54.

History.
1987, c. 702, s. 1

CHAPTER 12
STATUTORY
CONSTRUCTION

N.C. Gen. Stat. § 12-1

Repealed by Session Laws 1957, c. 783, s. 3.

§ 12-2. Repeal of statute not to affect actions

The repeal of a statute shall not affect any action brought before the repeal, for any forfeitures incurred, or for the recovery of any rights accruing under such statute.

History.
1830, c. 44; R.C., c. 108, s. 1; 1879, c. 163; 1881, c. 48; Code, s. 3764; Rev., s. 2830; C.S., s. 3948

§ 12-3. Rules for construction of statutes

In the construction of all statutes the following rules shall be observed, unless such construction would be inconsistent with the manifest intent of the General Assembly, or repugnant to the context of the same statute, that is to say:

(1)   **Singular and Plural Number, Masculine Gender, etc.** -- Every word importing the singular number only shall extend and be applied to several persons or things, as well as to one person or thing; and every word importing the plural number only shall extend and be applied to one person or thing, as well as to several persons or things; and every word importing the masculine gender only shall extend and be applied to females as well as to males, unless the context clearly shows to the contrary.

(2) **Authority, to Three or More Exercised by Majority.** -- All words purporting to give a joint authority to three or more public officers or other persons shall be construed as giving such authority to a majority of such officers or other persons, unless it shall be otherwise expressly declared in the law giving the authority.

(3) **"Month" and "Year".** -- The word "month" shall be construed to mean a calendar month, unless otherwise expressed; and the word "year," a calendar year, unless otherwise expressed; and the word "year" alone shall be equivalent to the expression "year of our Lord." When a statute refers to a period of one or more months and the last month does not have a date corresponding to the initial date, the period shall expire on the last day of the last month.

(4) **Leap Year, How Counted.** -- In every leap year the increasing day and the day before, in all legal proceedings, shall be counted as one day.

(5) **"Oath" and "Sworn".** -- The word "oath" shall be construed to include "affirmation," in all cases where by law an affirmation may be substituted for an oath, and in like cases the word "sworn" shall be construed to include the word "affirmed."

(6) **"Person" and "Property".** -- The word "person" shall extend and be applied to bodies politic and corporate, as well as to individuals, unless the context clearly shows to the contrary. The words "real property" shall be coextensive with lands, tenements and hereditaments. The words "personal property" shall include moneys, goods, chattels, choses in action and evidences of debt, including all things capable of ownership, not descendable to heirs at law. The word "property" shall include all property, both real and personal.

(7) **"Preceding" and "Following".** -- The words "preceding" and "following," when used by way of reference to any section of a statute, shall be construed to mean the section next preceding or next following that in which such reference is made; unless when some other section is expressly designated in such reference.

(8) **"Seal".** -- In all cases in which the seal of any court or public office shall be required by law to be affixed to any paper issuing from such court or office, the word "seal" shall be construed to include an impression of such official seal, made upon the paper alone, as well as an impression made by means of a wafer or of wax affixed thereto.

(9) **"Will".** -- The term "will" shall be construed to include codicils as well as wills.

(10) **"Written" and "in Writing".** -- The words "written" and "in writing" may be construed to include printing, engraving, lithographing, and any other mode of representing words and letters: Provided, that in all cases where a written signature is required by law, the same shall be in a proper handwriting, or in a proper mark.

(11) **"State" and "United States".** -- The word "state," when applied to the different parts of the United States, shall be construed to extend to and include the District of Columbia and the several territories, so called; and the words "United States" shall be construed to include the said district and territories and all dependencies.

(12) **"Imprisonment for One Month," How Construed.** -- The words "imprisonment for one month," wherever used in any

of the statutes, shall be construed to mean "imprisonment for thirty days."

(13) **"Governor," "Senator," "Solicitor," "Elector," "Executor," "Administrator," "Collector," "Juror," and "Auditor".** -- The words "Governor," "Senator," "district attorney," "elector," "executor," "administrator," "collector," "juror," "auditor," and any other words of like character shall when applied to the holder of such office, or occupant of such position, be words of common gender, and they shall be a sufficient designation of the person holding such office or position, whether the holder be a man or woman.

(14) **"Devisee" and "Devise".** -- The word "devisee," wherever used in any of the statutes, shall be construed to mean "devisee" as defined in G.S. 28A-1-1. The word "devise," wherever used in any of the statutes as a noun, shall be construed to mean a testamentary disposition of real or personal property and, wherever used in any of the statutes as a verb, shall be construed to mean to dispose of real or personal property by will.

(15) **Requirement to consult with a committee or commission of the General Assembly.** -- All words purporting to require an individual or other entity to consult with a committee or commission of the General Assembly before taking an action shall be construed to require the entity to do all of the following:

　　a. Submit a report of the action under consideration to the chairs and staff of the committee or commission. The report shall include all information required by statute and the rules of that committee or commission. The staff of the committee or commission shall make the report available electronically to the members of the committee or commission and to the public.

　　b. Appear at a meeting of the committee or commission at which the matter is heard. Unless another period of time is specified by statute, the requirement to appear is satisfied if the committee or commission does not have a meeting at which the matter is heard within 90 days of receiving the required submission.

(16) **"Husband and Wife" and similar terms.** -- The words "husband and wife," "wife and husband," "man and wife," "woman and husband," "husband or wife," "wife or husband," "man or wife," "woman or husband," or other terms suggesting two individuals who are then lawfully married to each other shall be construed to include any two individuals who are then lawfully married to each other.

(17) **"Widow" and "Widower."** -- The words "widow" and "widower" mean the surviving spouse of a deceased individual.

History.
21 Hen. III; R.S., c. 31, s. 113; R.C., c. 31, s. 108; c. 108; Code, s. 3765; Rev., s. 2831; C.S., s. 3949; 1921, c. 30; 1973, c. 47, s. 2; 1977, c. 446, s. 4; 2011-284, s. 1; 2012-142, s. 6.11; 2017-102, s. 35

§ 12-3.1. Fees and charges by agencies

(a) **Authority.** -- Only the General Assembly has the power to authorize an agency to establish or increase a fee or charge for the rendering of any service or fulfilling of any duty to the public. In the construction of a statute, unless that construction would be inconsistent with the manifest intent of the General Assembly or repugnant to the context of the statute, the legislative grant of authority to an agency to adopt rules shall not be construed as a grant of authority to the agency to establish by rule a fee or a charge for the rendering of any service or fulfilling of any duty to the public, unless the statute expressly provides for the grant of authority to establish a fee or charge for that specific service. Notwithstanding any other law, a rule adopted by an agency to establish or increase a fee or charge shall not go into effect until the agency has consulted with the Joint Legislative Commission on Governmental Operations on the amount and purpose of the fee or charge to be established or increased. Where a rule provides for a periodic automatic adjustment to a fee, the agency that adopts the rule is not required to consult with the Commission every time the fee automatically adjusts. The agency shall submit a request for consultation to all members of the Commission, the Commission Assistant, and the Fiscal Research Division of the General Assembly on the same date the notice of text of the rule is published. The request for consultation shall consist of a written report stating (i) the amount of the current fee or charge, if applicable, (ii) the amount of the proposed new or increased fee or charge, (iii) the statutory authority for the fee or charge, and (iv) a detailed explanation of the need for the establishment or increase of the fee or charge.

(a1) If the Commission does not hold a meeting to hear the consultation required by subsection (a) of this section within 90 days after the notice of text of the rule has been published and the consultation request required by subsection (a) of this section has been submitted, the consultation requirement is satisfied.

(b) **Definitions.** -- The following definitions apply in this section:

　　(1) **Agency.** -- Every agency, institution, board, commission, bureau, department, division, council, member of the Council of

State, or officer of the legislative, executive or judicial branches of State government. The term does not include counties, cities, towns, villages, other municipal corporations or political subdivisions of the State or any agencies of these subdivisions, the University of North Carolina, community colleges, hospitals, county or city boards of education, other local public districts, units, or bodies of any kind, or private corporations created by act of the General Assembly.

(2) **Rule.** -- Every rule, regulation, ordinance, standard, and amendment thereto adopted by any agency, including rules and regulations regarding substantive matters, standards for products, procedural rules for complying with statutory or regulatory authority or requirements and executive orders of the Governor.

(c) **Exceptions.** -- This section does not apply to any of the following:

(1) Rules establishing fees or charges to State, federal or local governmental units.

(2) A reasonable fee or charge for copying, transcripts of public hearings, State publications, or mailing a document or other item.

(3) Reasonable registration fees covering the cost of a conference or workshop.

(4) Reasonable user fees covering the cost of providing data processing services.

(d) In lieu of the requirements of subsections (a) and (a1) of this section, the North Carolina State Ports Authority shall report the establishment or increase of any fee to the Joint Legislative Commission on Governmental Operations as provided in G.S. 136-262(a)(11).

History.
1979, c. 559, s. 1; 1981, c. 695, ss. 1, 2; 1987, c. 564, s. 35; 1991, c. 418, s. 6; 2001-427, s. 8(a); 2002-99, s. 7(c); 2005-276, s. 6.8(b); 2011-145, s. 14.6(k); 2015-241, s. 6.18

§ 12-4. Construction of amended statute

Where a part of a statute is amended it is not to be considered as having been repealed and reenacted in the amended form; but the portions which are not altered are to be considered as having been the law since their enactment, and the new provisions as having been enacted at the time of the amendment.

Whenever the General Assembly (i) enacts a bill which purports to amend an existing general statute by deleting, adding, or substituting specific words or figures, and (ii) such bill also purports to set out the wording of the amended statute, or a portion thereof, as it will read after the amendment is accomplished, and (iii) there is a variance between the latter and the former, then, in such case, the latter shall control and be presumed to express the amendatory intent of the General Assembly.

History.
1868-9, c. 270, s. 22; 1870-1, c. 111; Code, s. 3766; Rev., s. 2832; C.S., s. 3950; 1971, c. 115

CHAPTER 13
CITIZENSHIP
RESTORED

§ 13-1. Restoration of citizenship

Any person convicted of a crime, whereby the rights of citizenship are forfeited, shall have such rights automatically restored upon the occurrence of any one of the following conditions:

(1) The unconditional discharge of an inmate, of a probationer, or of a parolee by the agency of the State having jurisdiction of that person or of a defendant under a suspended sentence by the court.

(2) The unconditional pardon of the offender.

(3) The satisfaction by the offender of all conditions of a conditional pardon.

(4) With regard to any person convicted of a crime against the United States, the unconditional discharge of such person by the agency of the United States having jurisdiction of such person, the unconditional pardon of such person or the satisfaction by such person of a conditional pardon.

(5) With regard to any person convicted of a crime in another state, the unconditional discharge of such person by the agency of that state having jurisdiction of such person, the unconditional pardon of such person or the satisfaction by such person of a conditional pardon.

History.
1971, c. 902; 1973, c. 251; c. 1262, s. 10; 1977, c. 813, s. 1; 1991, c. 274, s. 1; 2011-145, s. 19.1(h); 2012-83, s. 18; 2013-410, s. 2

§ 13-2. Issuance and filing of certificate or order of restoration

(a) The agency, department, or court having jurisdiction over the inmate, probationer, parolee or defendant at the time his rights of citizenship are restored under the provisions of G.S. 13-1(1) shall immediately issue a certificate or order in duplicate evidencing the offender's unconditional discharge and specifying the restoration of his rights of citizenship.

The original of such certificate or order shall be promptly transmitted to the clerk of the General Court of Justice in the county where the official record of the case from which the conviction arose is filed. The clerk shall then file the certificate or order without charge with the official record of the case.

(b) In the case of a person convicted of a crime against another state or the United States, whose rights to citizenship have been restored according to G.S. 13-1, the following provisions shall apply:

(1) It shall be the duty of the clerk of the court in the county where such person resides, upon a showing by such person or his representative that the conditions of G.S. 13-1 have been met, to issue the certificate evidencing the offender's unconditional discharge and specifying the restoration of his rights of citizenship. For purposes of this subsection, the fulfillment of the conditions of G.S. 13-1 shall be considered met upon the presentation to the clerk of any paper writing from the agency of any other state or of the United States which had jurisdiction over such person, which shows that the conditions of G.S. 13-1 have been met.

(2) The certificate described in subdivision (b)(1) shall be filed by the clerk of the General Court of Justice in the county in which such person resides.

The provisions of this subsection apply equally to conditional and unconditional pardons by the governor of any other state or by the President of the United States, as well as unconditional discharges by the agency of another state or of the United States having jurisdiction over said person.

History.
1971, c. 902; 1973, c. 251; 1977, c. 813, s. 2; 1991, c. 274, s. 2

§ 13-3. Issuance, service and filing of warrant of unconditional pardon

In the event the rights of citizenship are restored by an unconditional pardon as specified in G.S. 13-1(2), the Governor, under the provisions of G.S. 147-23, shall issue his warrant therefor specifying the restoration of rights of citizenship to the offender; and the officer to whom the Governor issues his warrant to effect the release of the offender shall deliver a copy of the warrant to the offender under the provisions of G.S. 147-25. The original warrant bearing the officer's return as specified in G.S. 147-25 shall be filed by the clerk of the General Court of Justice without charge in the county where the official record of the case from which the conviction arose is filed.

History.
1971, c. 902; 1973, c. 251

§ 13-4. Endorsement of warrant, service and filing of conditional pardon

When the offender has satisfied all of the conditions of a conditional pardon, and his rights of citizenship have been restored under the provisions of G.S. 13-1(3), the Governor shall issue an endorsement to the original warrant which specified the conditions of the pardon. Such endorsement shall acknowledge that the offender has satisfied all of the conditions of the pardon.

The Governor shall then deliver the endorsement to the officer specified in G.S. 147-25 for service and delivery to the clerk. Service and delivery to the clerk and filing by the clerk shall be done in accordance with the provisions of G.S. 13-3 so that the endorsement reflecting satisfaction of all conditions of the pardon will be served and recorded as if it were a warrant of unconditional pardon.

History.
1973, c. 251

CHAPTER 14
CRIMINAL LAW

SUBCHAPTER 01.
GENERAL PROVISIONS

ARTICLE 1
FELONIES AND MISDEMEANORS

§ 14-1. Felonies and misdemeanors defined

A felony is a crime which:
(1) Was a felony at common law;
(2) Is or may be punishable by death;
(3) Is or may be punishable by imprisonment in the State's prison; or
(4) Is denominated as a felony by statute.
Any other crime is a misdemeanor.

History.
1891, c. 205, s. 1; Rev., s. 3291; C.S., s. 4171; 1967, c. 1251, s. 1

N.C. Gen. Stat. § 14-1.1

Repealed by Session Laws 1993, c. 538, s. 2.

N.C. Gen. Stat. § 14-2

Repealed by Session Laws 1993, c. 538, s. 2.1.

N.C. Gen. Stat. § 14-2.1

Repealed by Session Laws 1993, c. 538, s. 3.

N.C. Gen. Stat. § 14-2.2

Repealed by Session Laws 2003-0378, s. 1, effective August 1, 2003.

§ 14-2.3. Forfeiture of gain acquired through criminal activity

(a) Except as is otherwise provided in Article 3 of Chapter 31A, in the case of any violation of Article 13A of Chapter 14, or a general statute constituting a felony other than a nonwillful homicide, any money or other property or interest in property acquired thereby shall be forfeited to the State of North Carolina, including any profits, gain, remuneration, or compensation directly or indirectly collected by or accruing to any offender.

(b) An action to recover such property shall be brought by either a District Attorney or the Attorney General pursuant to G.S. 1-532. The action must be brought within three years from the date of the conviction for the offense.

(c) Nothing in this section shall be construed to require forfeiture of any money or property recovered by law-enforcement officers pursuant to the investigation of an offense when the money or property is readily identifiable by the owner or guardian of the property or is traceable to him.

History.
1981, c. 840, s. 1; 2008-214, s. 1

§ 14-2.4. Punishment for conspiracy to commit a felony

(a) Unless a different classification is expressly stated, a person who is convicted of a conspiracy to commit a felony is guilty of a felony that is one class lower than the felony he or she conspired to commit, except that a conspiracy to commit a Class A or Class B1 felony is a Class B2 felony, a conspiracy to commit a Class B2 felony is a Class C felony, and a conspiracy to commit a Class I felony is a Class 1 misdemeanor.

(b) Unless a different classification is expressly stated, a person who is convicted of a conspiracy to commit a misdemeanor is guilty of a misdemeanor that is one class lower than the misdemeanor he or she conspired to commit, except that a conspiracy to commit a Class 3 misdemeanor is a Class 3 misdemeanor.

History.
1983, c. 451, s. 1; 1993, c. 538, s. 5; 1994, Ex. Sess., c. 22, s. 12; c. 24, s. 14(b)

§ 14-2.5. Punishment for attempt to commit a felony or misdemeanor

Unless a different classification is expressly stated, an attempt to commit a misdemeanor or a felony is punishable under the next lower classification as the offense which the offender attempted to commit. An attempt to commit a Class A or Class B1 felony is a Class B2 felony, an attempt to commit a Class B2 felony is a Class C felony, an attempt to commit a Class I felony is a Class 1 misdemeanor, and an attempt to commit a Class 3 misdemeanor is a Class 3 misdemeanor.

History.
1993, c. 538, s. 6; 1994, Ex. Sess., c. 22, s. 11; c. 24, s. 14(b)

§ 14-2.6. Punishment for solicitation to commit a felony or misdemeanor

(a) Unless a different classification is expressly stated, a person who solicits another person to commit a felony is guilty of a felony that is two classes lower than the felony the person solicited the other person to commit, except that a solicitation to commit a Class A or Class B1 felony is a Class C felony, a solicitation to commit a Class B2 felony is a Class D felony, a solicitation to commit a Class H felony is a Class 1 misdemeanor, and a solicitation to commit a Class I felony is a Class 2 misdemeanor.

(b) Unless a different classification is expressly stated, a person who solicits another person to commit a misdemeanor is guilty of a Class 3 misdemeanor.

History.
1993, c. 538, s. 6.1; 1994, Ex. Sess., c. 22, s. 13; c. 24, s. 14(b)

§ 14-3. Punishment of misdemeanors, infamous offenses, offenses committed in secrecy and malice, or with deceit and intent to defraud, or with ethnic animosity

(a) Except as provided in subsections (b) and (c), every person who shall be convicted of any misdemeanor for which no specific classification and no specific punishment is prescribed by statute shall be punishable as a Class 1 misdemeanor. Any misdemeanor that has a specific punishment, but is not assigned a classification by the General Assembly pursuant to law is classified as follows, based on the maximum punishment allowed by law for the offense as it existed on the effective date of Article 81B of Chapter 15A of the General Statutes:

    (1) If that maximum punishment is more than six months imprisonment, it is a Class 1 misdemeanor;

    (2) If that maximum punishment is more than 30 days but not more than six months imprisonment, it is a Class 2 misdemeanor; and

    (3) If that maximum punishment is 30 days or less imprisonment or only a fine, it is a Class 3 misdemeanor.

Misdemeanors that have punishments for one or more counties or cities pursuant to a local act of the General Assembly that are different from the generally applicable punishment are classified pursuant to this subsection if not otherwise specifically classified.

(b) If a misdemeanor offense as to which no specific punishment is prescribed be infamous, done in secrecy and malice, or with deceit and intent to defraud, the offender shall, except where the offense is a conspiracy to commit a misdemeanor, be guilty of a Class H felony.

(c) If any Class 2 or Class 3 misdemeanor is committed because of the victim's race, color, religion, nationality, or country of origin, the offender shall be guilty of a Class 1 misdemeanor. If any Class A1 or Class 1 misdemeanor offense is committed because of the victim's race, color, religion, nationality, or country of origin, the offender shall be guilty of a Class H felony.

History.
R.C., c. 34, s. 120; Code, s. 1097; Rev., s. 3293; C.S., s. 4173; 1927, c. 1; 1967, c. 1251, s. 3; 1979, c. 760, s. 5; 1979, 2nd Sess., c. 1316, ss. 2, 47, 48; 1981, c. 63, s. 1; c. 179, s. 14; 1991, c. 702, s. 2; 1993, c. 538, s. 7; 1994, Ex. Sess., c. 14, s. 2; c. 24, s. 14(b); 1995 (Reg. Sess., 1996), c. 742, s. 6; 2008-197, s. 4.1

§ 14-3.1. Infraction defined; sanctions

(a) An infraction is a noncriminal violation of law not punishable by imprisonment. Unless otherwise provided by law, the sanction for a person found responsible for an infraction is a penalty of not more than one hundred dollars ($ 100.00). The proceeds of penalties for infractions are payable to the county in which the infraction occurred for the use of the public schools.

(b) The procedure for disposition of infractions is as provided in Article 66 of Chapter 15A of the General Statutes.

History.
1985, c. 764, s. 1; 1985 (Reg. Sess., 1986), c. 852, s. 17

§ 14-4. Violation of local ordinances misdemeanor

(a) Except as provided in subsection (b) or (c) of this section, if any person shall violate an ordinance of a county, city, town, or metropolitan sewerage district created under Article 5 of Chapter 162A, he shall be guilty of a Class 3 misdemeanor and shall be fined not more than five hundred dollars ($ 500.00). No fine shall exceed fifty dollars ($ 50.00) unless the ordinance expressly states that the maximum fine is greater than fifty dollars ($ 50.00).

(b) If any person shall violate an ordinance of a county, city, or town regulating the operation or parking of vehicles, he shall be responsible for an infraction and shall be required to pay a penalty of not more than fifty dollars ($ 50.00).

(c) A person may not be found responsible or guilty of a local ordinance violation punishable pursuant to subsection (a) of this section if, when tried for that violation, the person produces proof of compliance with the local ordinance through any of the following:

    (1) No new alleged violations of the local ordinance within 30 days from the date of the initial alleged violation.

(2) The person provides proof of a good-faith effort to seek assistance to address any underlying factors related to unemployment, homelessness, mental health, or substance abuse that might relate to the person's ability to comply with the local ordinance.

History.
1871-2, c. 195, s. 2; Code, s. 3820; Rev., s. 3702; C.S., s. 4174; 1969, c. 36, s. 2; 1985, c. 764, s. 2; 1985 (Reg. Sess., 1986), c. 852, s. 17; 1991, c. 415, s. 1; c. 446, s. 1; 1993, c. 538, s. 8; c. 539, s. 9; 1994, Ex. Sess., c. 24, ss. 14(b), 14(c); 1995, c. 509, s. 133.1; 2021-138, s. 13(c)

§ 14-4.1. Legislative review of regulatory crimes

(a) Any rule adopted or amended pursuant to Article 2A of Chapter 150B of the General Statutes that creates a new criminal offense or otherwise subjects a person to criminal penalties is subject to G.S. 150B-21.3(b1) regardless of whether the rule received written objections from 10 or more persons pursuant to G.S. 150B-21.3(b2).

(b) This section applies to rules adopted on or after January 1, 2020.

History.
2019-198, s. 1

ARTICLE 2
PRINCIPALS AND ACCESSORIES

§§ 14-5, 14-5.1

Repealed by Session Laws 1981, c. 686, s. 2.

§ 14-5.2. Accessory before fact punishable as principal felon

All distinctions between accessories before the fact and principals to the commission of a felony are abolished. Every person who heretofore would have been guilty as an accessory before the fact to any felony shall be guilty and punishable as a principal to that felony. However, if a person who heretofore would have been guilty and punishable as an accessory before the fact is convicted of a capital felony, and the jury finds that his conviction was based solely on the uncorroborated testimony of one or more principals, coconspirators, or accessories to the crime, he shall be guilty of a Class B2 felony.

History.
1981, c. 686, s. 1; 1994, Ex. Sess., c. 22, s. 6

N.C. Gen. Stat. § 14-6

Repealed by Session Laws 1981, c. 686, s. 2.

§ 14-7. Accessories after the fact; trial and punishment

If any person shall become an accessory after the fact to any felony, whether the same be a felony at common law or by virtue of any statute made, or to be made, such person shall be guilty of a crime, and may be indicted and convicted together with the principal felon, or after the conviction of the principal felon, or may be indicted and convicted for such crime whether the principal felon shall or shall not have been previously convicted, or shall or shall not be amenable to justice. Unless a different classification is expressly stated, that person shall be punished for an offense that is two classes lower than the felony the principal felon committed, except that an accessory after the fact to a Class A or Class B1 felony is a Class C felony, an accessory after the fact to a Class B2 felony is a Class D felony, an accessory after the fact to a Class H felony is a Class 1 misdemeanor, and an accessory after the fact to a Class I felony is a Class 2 misdemeanor. The offense of such person may be inquired of, tried, determined and punished by any court which shall have jurisdiction of the principal felon, in the same manner as if the act, by reason whereof such person shall have become an accessory, had been committed at the same place as the principal felony, although such act may have been committed without the limits of the State; and in case the principal felony shall have been committed within the body of any county, and the act by reason whereof any person shall have become accessory shall have been committed within the body of any other county, the offense of such person guilty of a felony as aforesaid may be inquired of, tried, determined, and punished in either of said counties: Provided, that no person who shall be once duly tried for such felony shall be again indicted or tried for the same offense.

History.
1797, c. 485, s. 1, P.R.; 1852, c. 58; R.C., c. 34, s. 54; Code, s. 978; Rev., s. 3289; C.S., s. 4177; 1979, c. 760, s. 5; 1979, 2nd Sess., c. 1316, s. 47; 1981, c. 63, s. 1; c. 179, s. 14; 1997-443, s. 19.25(p)

ARTICLE 2A
HABITUAL FELONS

§ 14-7.1. Persons defined as habitual felons

(a) Any person who has been convicted of or pled guilty to three felony offenses in any federal court or state court in the United States or combination thereof is declared to be an habitual felon and may be charged as a status offender pursuant to this Article.

(b) For the purpose of this Article, a felony offense is defined to include all of the following:

(1) An offense that is a felony under the laws of this State.

(2) An offense that is a felony under the laws of another state or sovereign that is substantially similar to an offense that is a felony in North Carolina, and to which a plea of guilty was entered, or a conviction was returned regardless of the sentence actually imposed.

(3) An offense that is a crime under the laws of another state or sovereign that does not classify any crimes as felonies if all of the following apply:

a. The offense is substantially similar to an offense that is a felony in North Carolina.

b. The offense may be punishable by imprisonment for more than a year in state prison.

c. A plea of guilty was entered or a conviction was returned regardless of the sentence actually imposed.

(4) An offense that is a felony under federal law. Provided, however, that federal offenses relating to the manufacture, possession, sale and kindred offenses involving intoxicating liquors shall not be considered felonies for the purposes of this Article.

(c) For the purposes of this Article, felonies committed before a person attains the age of 18 years shall not constitute more than one felony. The commission of a second felony shall not fall within the purview of this Article unless it is committed after the conviction of or plea of guilty to the first felony. The commission of a third felony shall not fall within the purview of this Article unless it is committed after the conviction of or plea of guilty to the second felony. Pleas of guilty to or convictions of felony offenses prior to July 6, 1967, shall not be felony offenses within the meaning of this Article. Any felony offense to which a pardon has been extended shall not for the purpose of this Article constitute a felony. The burden of proving such pardon shall rest with the defendant and the State shall not be required to disprove a pardon.

History.
1967, c. 1241, s. 1; 1971, c. 1231, s. 1; 1979, c. 760, s. 4; 1981, c. 179, s. 10; 2011-192, s. 3(b); 2017-176, s. 2(a)

§ 14-7.2. Punishment

When any person is charged by indictment with the commission of a felony under the laws of the State of North Carolina and is also charged with being an habitual felon as defined in G.S. 14-7.1, he must, upon conviction, be sentenced and punished as an habitual felon, as in this Chapter provided, except in those cases where the death penalty or a life sentence is imposed.

History.
1967, c. 1241, s. 2; 1981, c. 179, s. 11

§ 14-7.3. Charge of habitual felon

The district attorney, in his or her discretion, may charge a person as an habitual felon pursuant to this Article. An indictment which charges a person who is an habitual felon within the meaning of G.S. 14-7.1 with the commission of any felony under the laws of the State of North Carolina must, in order to sustain a conviction of habitual felon, also charge that said person is an habitual felon. The indictment charging the defendant as an habitual felon shall be separate from the indictment charging him with the principal felony. An indictment which charges a person with being an habitual felon must set forth the date that prior felony offenses were committed, the name of the state or other sovereign against whom said felony offenses were committed, the dates that pleas of guilty were entered to or convictions returned in said felony offenses, and the identity of the court wherein said pleas or convictions took place. No defendant charged with being an habitual felon in a bill of indictment shall be required to go to trial on said charge within 20 days of the finding of a true bill by the grand jury; provided, the defendant may waive this 20-day period.

History.
1967, c. 1241, s. 3; 2011-192, s. 3(c)

§ 14-7.4. Evidence of prior convictions of felony offenses

In all cases where a person is charged under the provisions of this Article with being an habitual felon, the record or records of prior convictions of felony offenses shall be admissible in evidence, but only for the purpose of proving that said person has been convicted of former felony offenses. A prior conviction may be proved by stipulation of the parties or by the original or a certified copy of the court record of the prior conviction. The original or certified copy of the court record, bearing the same name as that by which the defendant is charged, shall be prima facie evidence that the defendant named therein is the same as the defendant before the court, and shall be prima facie evidence of the facts set out therein.

History.
1967, c. 1241, s. 4; 1981, c. 179, s. 12

§ 14-7.5. Verdict and judgment

When an indictment charges an habitual felon with a felony as above provided and an indictment also charges that said person is an habitual felon as provided herein, the defendant shall be tried for the principal felony as provided by law. The indictment that the person is an habitual felon shall not be revealed to the jury unless the jury shall find that the defendant is guilty of the principal felony or other felony with which he is charged. If the jury finds the defendant guilty of a felony, the bill of indictment charging the defendant as an habitual felon may be presented to the same jury. Except that the same jury may be used, the proceedings shall be as if the issue of habitual felon were a principal charge. If the jury finds that the defendant is an habitual felon, the trial judge shall enter judgment according to the provisions of this Article. If the jury finds that the defendant is not an habitual felon, the trial judge shall pronounce judgment on the principal felony or felonies as provided by law.

History.
1967, c. 1241, s. 5

§ 14-7.6. Sentencing of habitual felons

When an habitual felon as defined in this Article commits any felony under the laws of the State of North Carolina, the felon must, upon conviction or plea of guilty under indictment as provided in this Article (except where the felon has been sentenced as a Class A, B1, or B2 felon) be sentenced at a felony class level that is four classes higher than the principal felony for which the person was convicted; but under no circumstances shall an habitual felon be sentenced at a level higher than a Class C felony. In determining the prior record level, convictions used to establish a person's status as an habitual felon shall not be used. Sentences imposed under this Article shall run consecutively with and shall commence at the expiration of any sentence being served by the person sentenced under this section.

History.
1967, c. 1241, s. 6; 1981, c. 179, s. 13; 1993, c. 538, s. 9; 1994, Ex. Sess., c. 22, ss. 15, 16; c. 24, s. 14(b); 1993 (Reg. Sess., 1994), c. 767, s. 16; 2011-192, s. 3(d)

ARTICLE 2B
VIOLENT HABITUAL FELONS

§ 14-7.7. Persons defined as violent habitual felons

(a) Any person who has been convicted of two violent felonies in any federal court, in a court of this or any other state of the United States, or in a combination of these courts is declared to be a violent habitual felon. For purposes of this Article, "convicted" means the person has been adjudged guilty of or has entered a plea of guilty or no contest to the violent felony charge, and judgment has been entered thereon when such action occurred on or after July 6, 1967. This Article does not apply to a second violent felony unless it is committed after the conviction or plea of guilty or no contest to the first violent felony. Any felony to which a pardon has been extended shall not, for the purposes of this Article, constitute a felony. The burden of proving a pardon shall rest with the defendant, and this State shall not be required to disprove a pardon. Conviction as an habitual felon shall not, for purposes of this Article, constitute a violent felony.

(b) For purposes of this Article, "violent felony" includes the following offenses:

(1) All Class A through E felonies.

(2) Any repealed or superseded offense substantially equivalent to the offenses listed in subdivision (1).

(3) Any offense committed in another jurisdiction substantially similar to the offenses set forth in subdivision (1) or (2).

History.
1994, Ex. Sess., c. 22, ss. 31, 32; 2000-155, s. 14

§ 14-7.8. Punishment

When a person is charged by indictment with the commission of a violent felony and is also charged with being a violent habitual felon as defined in G.S. 14-7.7, the person must, upon conviction, be sentenced in accordance with this Article, except in those cases where the death penalty is imposed.

History.
1994, Ex. Sess., c. 22, s. 31

§ 14-7.9. Charge of violent habitual felon.

An indictment that charges a person who is a violent habitual felon within the meaning of G.S. 14-7.7 with the commission of any violent felony must, in order to sustain a conviction of violent habitual felon, also charge that the person is a violent habitual felon. The indictment charging the defendant as a violent habitual felon shall be separate from the indictment charging the defendant with the principal violent felony. An indictment that charges a person with being a violent habitual felon must set forth the date that prior violent felonies were committed, the name of the state or other

603

sovereign against whom the violent felonies were committed, the dates of convictions of the violent felonies, and the identity of the court in which the convictions took place. A defendant charged with being a violent habitual felon in a bill of indictment shall not be required to go to trial on that charge within 20 days after the finding of a true bill by the grand jury unless the defendant waives this 20-day period.

History.
1994, Ex. Sess., c. 22, s. 31

§ 14-7.10. Evidence of prior convictions of violent felonies

In all cases where a person is charged under this Article with being a violent habitual felon, the records of prior convictions of violent felonies shall be admissible in evidence, but only for the purpose of proving that the person has been convicted of former violent felonies. A prior conviction may be proved by stipulation of the parties or by the original or a certified copy of the court record of the prior conviction. The original or certified copy of the court record, bearing the same name as that by which the defendant is charged, shall be prima facie evidence that the defendant named therein is the same as the defendant before the court, and shall be prima facie evidence of the facts set out therein.

History.
1994, Ex. Sess., c. 22, s. 31

§ 14-7.11. Verdict and judgment

When an indictment charges a violent habitual felon with a violent felony as provided in this Article and an indictment also charges that the person is a violent habitual felon as provided in this Article, the defendant shall be tried for the principal violent felony as provided by law. The indictment that the person is a violent habitual felon shall not be revealed to the jury unless the jury finds that the defendant is guilty of the principal violent felony or another violent felony with which the defendant is charged. If the jury finds the defendant guilty of a violent felony, the bill of indictment charging the defendant as a violent habitual felon may be presented to the same jury. Except that the same jury may be used, the proceedings shall be as if the issue of violent habitual felon were a principal charge. If the jury finds that the defendant is a violent habitual felon, the trial judge shall enter judgment according to the provisions of this Article. If the jury finds that the defendant is not a violent habitual felon, the trial judge shall pronounce judgment on the principal violent felony or felonies as provided by law.

History.
1994, Ex. Sess., c. 22, s. 31

§ 14-7.12. Sentencing of violent habitual felons

A person who is convicted of a violent felony and of being a violent habitual felon must, upon conviction (except where the death penalty is imposed), be sentenced to life imprisonment without parole. Life imprisonment without parole means that the person will spend the remainder of the person's natural life in prison. The sentencing judge may not suspend the sentence and may not place the person sentenced on probation. Sentences for violent habitual felons imposed under this Article shall run consecutively with and shall commence at the expiration of any other sentence being served by the person.

History.
1994, Ex. Sess., c. 22, s. 31

§§ 14-7.13 through 14-7.19

Reserved for future codification purposes.

ARTICLE 2C
CONTINUING CRIMINAL ENTERPRISE

§ 14-7.20. Continuing criminal enterprise

(a) Except as otherwise provided in subsection (a1) of this section, any person who engages in a continuing criminal enterprise shall be punished as a Class H felon and in addition shall be subject to the forfeiture prescribed in subsection (b) of this section.

(a1) Any person who engages in a continuing criminal enterprise where the felony violation required by subdivision (c)(1) of this section is a violation of G.S. 14-10.1 shall be punished as a Class D felon and, in addition, shall be subject to the forfeiture prescribed in subsection (b) of this section.

(b) Any person who is convicted under subsection (a) or (a1) of this section of engaging in a continuing criminal enterprise shall forfeit to the State of North Carolina:

    (1) The profits obtained by the person in the enterprise, and

    (2) Any of the person's interest in, claim against, or property or contractual rights of any kind affording a source of influence over, such enterprise.

(c) For purposes of this section, a person is engaged in a continuing criminal enterprise if:

(1) The person violates any provision of this Chapter, the punishment of which is a felony; and

(2) The violation is a part of a continuing series of violations of this Chapter:

    a. Which are undertaken by the person in concert with five or more other persons with respect to whom the person occupies a position of organizer, a supervisory position, or any other position of management; and

    b. From which the person obtains substantial income or resources.

History.
1995, c. 378, s. 1; 2012-38, s. 2

§§ 14-7.21 through 14-7.24

Reserved for future codification purposes.

ARTICLE 2D
HABITUAL BREAKING AND ENTERING STATUS OFFENSE

§ 14-7.25. Definitions

The following definitions apply in this Article:

(1) "Breaking and entering." -- The term means any of the following felony offenses:

    a. First degree burglary (G.S. 14-51).

    b. Second degree burglary (G.S. 14-51).

    c. Breaking out of dwelling house burglary (G.S. 14-53).

    d. Breaking or entering buildings generally (G.S. 14-54(a)).

    d1. Breaking or entering with intent to terrorize or injure an occupant of the building (G.S. 14-54(a1)).

    e. Breaking or entering a building that is a place of religious worship (G.S. 14-54.1).

    f. Any repealed or superseded offense substantially equivalent to any of the offenses in sub-subdivision a., b., c., d., or e. of this subdivision.

    g. Any offense committed in another jurisdiction substantially similar to any of the offenses in sub-subdivision a., b., c., d., or e. of this subdivision.

(2) "Convicted." -- The person has been adjudged guilty of or has entered a plea of guilty or no contest to the offense of breaking and entering.

(3) "Status offender." -- A person who is a habitual breaking and entering status offender as described in G.S. 14-7.26.

History.
2011-192, s. 3(a); 2017-176, s. 3(a)

§ 14-7.26. Habitual breaking and entering status offender

Any person who has been convicted of or pled guilty to one or more prior felony offenses of breaking and entering in any federal court or state court in the United States, or combination thereof, is guilty of the status offense of habitual breaking and entering and may be charged with that status offense pursuant to this Article.

This Article does not apply to a second felony offense of breaking and entering unless it is committed after the conviction of the first felony offense of breaking and entering. For purposes of this Article, felony offenses of breaking and entering committed before the person is 18 years of age shall not constitute more than one felony of breaking and entering. Any felony to which a pardon has been extended shall not, for the purposes of this Article, constitute a felony offense of breaking and entering.

History.
2011-192, s. 3(a)

§ 14-7.27. Punishment

When any person is charged with a felony offense of breaking and entering and is also charged with being a status offender as defined in G.S. 14-7.26, the person must, upon conviction, be sentenced and punished as a status offender as provided by this Article.

History.
2011-192, s. 3(a)

§ 14-7.28. Charge of habitual breaking and entering status offender

(a) The district attorney, in his or her discretion, may charge a person with the status offense of habitual breaking and entering pursuant to this Article. To sustain a conviction of a person as a status offender, the person must be charged separately for the felony offense of breaking and entering and for the habitual breaking and entering status offense. The indictment charging the defendant as a status offender shall be separate from the indictment charging the person with the principal felony offense of breaking and entering.

(b) An indictment that charges a person with being a status offender must set forth the date that the prior felony offense of breaking and entering was committed, the name of the state or other sovereign against whom the felony offense of breaking and entering was committed, the dates that the plea of guilty was entered into or conviction returned in the felony offense of breaking and entering, and the identity of the court in which the plea or conviction took place. No defendant charged with being a status offender in a bill of indictment shall be required to go to trial on the charge within 20 days of the finding of a true bill by the grand jury; provided, the defendant may waive this 20-day period.

History.
2011-192, s. 3(a)

§ 14-7.29. Evidence of prior convictions of breaking and entering

In all cases in which a person is charged under the provisions of this Article with being a status offender, the record of prior conviction of the felony offense of breaking and entering shall be admissible in evidence, but only for the purpose of proving that the person has been convicted of a former felony offense of breaking and entering. A prior conviction may be proved by stipulation of the parties or by the original or a certified copy of the court record of the prior conviction. The original or certified copy of the court record, bearing the same name as that by which the defendant is charged, shall be prima facie evidence that the defendant named therein is the same as the defendant before the court and shall be prima facie evidence of the facts set out therein.

History.
2011-192, s. 3(a)

§ 14-7.30. Verdict and judgment

(a) When an indictment charges a person with a felony offense of breaking and entering as provided by this Article and an indictment also charges that the person is a status offender, the defendant shall be tried for the principal offense of breaking and entering as provided by law. The indictment that the person is a status offender shall not be revealed to the jury unless the jury shall find that the defendant is guilty of the principal felony offense of breaking and entering with which the defendant is charged.

(b) If the jury finds the defendant guilty of the felony offense of breaking and entering, the bill of indictment charging the defendant as a status offender may be presented to the same jury. Except that the same jury may be used, the proceedings shall be as if the issue of status offender were a principal charge.

(c) If the jury finds that the defendant is a status offender, the trial judge shall enter

judgment according to the provisions of this Article. If the jury finds that the defendant is not a status offender, the trial judge shall pronounce judgment on the principal felony offense of breaking and entering as provided by law.

History.
2011-192, s. 3(a)

§ 14-7.31. Sentencing of status offenders

(a) When a status offender as defined in this Article commits a felony offense of breaking and entering under the laws of the State of North Carolina, the status offender must, upon conviction or plea of guilty under indictment as provided in this Article, be sentenced as a Class E felon.

(b) In determining the prior record level, any conviction used to establish a person's status as a status offender shall not be used. Sentences imposed under this Article shall run consecutively with and shall commence at the expiration of any sentence being served by the person sentenced under this section.

(c) A conviction as a status offender under this Article shall not constitute commission of a felony for the purpose of either Article 2A or Article 2B of Chapter 14 of the General Statutes.

History.
2011-192, s. 3(a)

§§ 14-7.32 through 14-7.34

Reserved for future codification purposes.

ARTICLE 2E
ARMED HABITUAL FELON

§ 14-7.35. Definitions

The following definitions apply in this Article:

(1) "Convicted." -- The person has been adjudged guilty of or has entered a plea of guilty or no contest to the firearm-related felony.

(2) "Firearm-related felony." -- Any felony committed by a person in which the person used or displayed a firearm while committing the felony.

(3) "Status offender." -- A person who is an armed habitual felon as described in G.S. 14-7.36.

History.
2013-369, s. 26

§ 14-7.36. Armed habitual felon

Any person who has been convicted of or pled guilty to one or more prior firearm-related felony offenses in any federal court or state court in the United States, or combination thereof, is guilty of the status offense of armed habitual felon and may be charged with that status offense pursuant to this Article.

This Article does not apply to a second firearm-related felony unless it is committed after the conviction of a firearm-related felony in which evidence of the person's use, display, or threatened use or display of a firearm was needed to prove an element of the felony or was needed to establish the requirement for an enhanced or aggravated sentence. For purposes of this Article, firearm-related felonies committed before the person is 18 years of age shall not constitute more than one firearm-related felony. Any firearm-related felony to which a pardon has been extended shall not, for the purposes of this Article, constitute a firearm-related felony.

History.
2013-369, s. 26

§ 14-7.37. Punishment

When any person is charged with a firearm-related felony and is also charged with being a status offender, the person must, upon conviction, be sentenced and punished as a status offender as provided by this Article.

History.
2013-369, s. 26

§ 14-7.38. Charge of status offense as an armed habitual felon

(a) The district attorney, in the district attorney's discretion, may charge a person as a status offender pursuant to this Article. To sustain a conviction of a person as a status offender, the person must be charged separately for the principal firearm-related felony and for the status offense of armed habitual felon. The indictment charging the defendant as a status offender shall be separate from the indictment charging the person with the principal firearm-related felony.

(b) An indictment that charges a person with being a status offender must set forth all of the following information regarding the prior firearm-related felony:

(1) The date the offense was committed.

(2) The name of the state or other sovereign against whom the offense was committed.

(3) The dates that the plea of guilty was entered into or conviction returned in the offense.

(4) The identity of the court in which the plea or conviction took place.

(c) No defendant charged with being a status offender in a bill of indictment shall be required to go to trial on the charge within 20 days of the finding of a true bill by the grand jury; provided, the defendant may waive this 20-day period.

History.
2013-369, s. 26

§ 14-7.39. Evidence of prior convictions of firearm-related felonies

In all cases in which a person is charged under the provisions of this Article with being a status offender, the record of prior conviction of the firearm-related felony shall be admissible in evidence, but only for the purpose of proving that the person has been convicted of a former firearm-related felony. A prior conviction may be proved by stipulation of the parties or by the original or a certified copy of the court record of the prior conviction. The original or certified copy of the court record, bearing the same name as that by which the defendant is charged, shall be prima facie evidence that the defendant named therein is the same as the defendant before the court and shall be prima facie evidence of the facts set out therein.

History.
2013-369, s. 26

§ 14-7.40. Verdict and judgment

(a) When an indictment charges a person with a firearm-related felony as provided by this Article and an indictment also charges that the person is a status offender, the defendant shall be tried for the principal firearm-related felony as provided by law. The indictment that the person is a status offender shall not be revealed to the jury unless the jury shall find that the defendant is guilty of the principal firearm-related felony with which the defendant is charged.

(b) If the jury finds the defendant guilty of the principal firearm-related felony, and it is found as provided in this section that (i) the person committed the felony by using, displaying, or threatening the use or display of a firearm or deadly weapon and (ii) the person actually possessed the firearm or deadly weapon about his or her person, the bill of indictment charging the defendant as a status offender may be presented to the same jury. Except that the same jury may be used, the proceedings shall be as if the issue of status offender were a principal charge.

(c) If the jury finds that the defendant is a status offender, the trial judge shall enter judgment according to the provisions of this Article. If the jury finds that the defendant is not a status offender, the trial judge shall pronounce judgment on the principal firearm-related felony offense as provided by law.

History.
2013-369, s. 26

§ 14-7.41. Sentencing of armed habitual felon

(a) A person who is convicted of a firearm-related felony and is also convicted of the status offense must, upon conviction or plea of guilty under indictment as provided in this Article, be sentenced as a Class C felon (except where the felon has been sentenced as a Class A, B1, or B2 felon). However, in no case shall the person receive a minimum term of imprisonment of less than 120 months. The court may not suspend the sentence and may not place the person sentenced on probation.

(b) In determining the prior record level, any conviction used to establish a person's status as an armed habitual felon shall not be used. Sentences imposed under this Article shall run consecutively with and shall commence at the expiration of any sentence being served by the person sentenced under this section.

(c) A conviction as a status offender under this Article shall not constitute commission of a felony for the purpose of either Article 2A or Article 2B of Chapter 14 of the General Statutes.

(d) A sentence imposed under this Article may not be enhanced pursuant to G.S. 15A-1340.16A.

History.
2013-369, s. 26

ARTICLE 2F
CRIMES BY UNMANNED AIRCRAFT SYSTEMS

§ 14-7.45. Crimes committed by use of unmanned aircraft systems

All crimes committed by use of an unmanned aircraft system, as defined in G.S. 15A-300.1, while in flight over this State shall be governed by the laws of this State, and the question of whether the conduct by an unmanned aircraft system while in flight over this State constitutes a crime by the owner of the unmanned

aircraft system shall be determined by the laws of this State.

History.
2014-100, 34.30(b)

SUBCHAPTER 02.
OFFENSES AGAINST THE STATE

ARTICLE 3
REBELLION

§ 14-8. Rebellion against the State

If any person shall incite, set on foot, assist or engage in a rebellion or insurrection against the authority of the State of North Carolina or the laws thereof, or shall give aid or comfort thereto, every person so offending in any of the ways aforesaid shall be guilty of a felony, and shall be punished as a Class F felon.

History.
Const., art. 4, s. 5; 1861, c. 18; 1866, c. 64; 1868, c. 60, s. 2; Code, s. 1106; Rev., s. 3437; C.S., s. 4178; 1979, c. 760, s. 5; 1979, 2nd Sess., c. 1316, s. 47; 1981, c. 63, s. 1; c. 179, s. 14; 1993, c. 539, s. 1122; 1994, Ex. Sess., c. 24, s. 14(c)

N.C. Gen. Stat. § 14-9

Repealed by Session Laws 1994, Extra Session, c. 14, s. 71(1).

§ 14-10. Secret political and military organizations forbidden

If any person, for the purpose of compassing or furthering any political object, or aiding the success of any political party or organization, or resisting the laws, shall join or in any way connect or unite himself with any oath-bound secret political or military organization, society or association of whatsoever name or character; or shall form or organize or combine and agree with any other person or persons to form or organize any such organization; or as a member of any secret political or military party or organization shall use, or agree to use, any certain signs or grips or passwords, or any disguise of the person or voice, or any disguise whatsoever for the advancement of its object, and shall take or administer any extrajudicial oath or other secret, solemn pledge, or any like secret means; or if any two or more persons, for the purpose of compassing or furthering any political object, or aiding the success of any political party or organization, or circumventing the laws, shall secretly assemble, combine or agree together, and the more effectually to accomplish such purposes, or any of them, shall use any certain signs, or grips, or passwords, or any disguise of the person or voice, or other disguise whatsoever, or shall take or administer any extrajudicial oath or other secret, solemn pledge; or if any persons shall band together and assemble to muster, drill or practice any military evolutions except by virtue of the authority of an officer recognized by law, or of an instructor in institutions or schools in which such evolutions form a part of the course of instruction; or if any person shall knowingly permit any of the acts and things herein forbidden to be had, done or performed on his premises, or on any premises under his control; or if any person being a member of any such secret political or military organization shall not at once abandon the same and separate himself entirely therefrom, every person so offending shall be guilty of a Class 1 misdemeanor.

History.
1868-9, c. 267; 1870-1, c. 133; 1871-2, c. 143; Code, s. 1095; Rev., s. 3439; C.S., s. 4180; 1993, c. 539, s. 10; 1994, Ex. Sess., c. 24, s. 14(c).

ARTICLE 3A
TERRORISM

§ 14-10.1. Terrorism

(a) As used in this section, the term "act of violence" means a violation of G.S. 14-17; a felony punishable pursuant to G.S. 14-18; any felony offense in this Chapter that includes an assault, or use of violence or force against a person; any felony offense that includes either the threat or use of any explosive or incendiary device; or any offense that includes the threat or use of a nuclear, biological, or chemical weapon of mass destruction.

(b) A person is guilty of the separate offense of terrorism if the person commits an act of violence with the intent to do either of the following:

(1) Intimidate the civilian population at large, or an identifiable group of the civilian population.

(2) Influence, through intimidation, the conduct or activities of the government of the United States, a state, or any unit of local government.

(c) A violation of this section is a felony that is one class higher than the offense which is the underlying act of violence, except that a violation is a Class B1 felony if the underlying act of violence is a Class A or Class B1 felony offense. A violation of this section is a separate

offense from the underlying offense and shall not merge with other offenses.

(d) All real and personal property of every kind used or intended for use in the course of, derived from, or realized through an offense punishable pursuant to this Article shall be subject to lawful seizure and forfeiture to the State as set forth in G.S. 14-2.3 and G.S. 14-7.20. However, the forfeiture of any real or personal property shall be subordinate to any security interest in the property taken by a lender in good faith as collateral for the extension of credit and recorded as provided by law, and no real or personal property shall be forfeited under this section against an owner who made a bona fide purchase of the property, or a person with rightful possession of the property, without knowledge of a violation of this Article.

(e) Any person whose property or person is injured by reason of a violation of this section may sue for and recover treble damages, costs, and attorneys' fees pursuant to G.S. 1-539.2D.

History.
2012-38, s. 1; 2015-215, s. 2

ARTICLE 4
SUBVERSIVE ACTIVITIES

§ 14-11. Activities aimed at overthrow of government; use of public buildings

It shall be unlawful for any person, by word of mouth or writing, willfully and deliberately to advocate, advise or teach a doctrine that the government of the United States, the State of North Carolina or any political subdivision thereof shall be overthrown or overturned by force or violence or by any other unlawful means. It shall be unlawful for any public building in the State, owned by the State of North Carolina, any political subdivision thereof, or by any department or agency of the State or any institution supported in whole or in part by State funds, to be used by any person for the purpose of advocating, advising or teaching a doctrine that the government of the United States, the State of North Carolina or any political subdivision thereof should be overthrown by force, violence or any other unlawful means.

History.
1941, c. 37, s. 1

§ 14-12. Punishment for violations

Any person or persons violating any of the provisions of this Article shall, for the first offense, be guilty of a Class 1 misdemeanor and be punished accordingly, and for the second offense shall be punished as a Class H felon.

History.
1941, c. 37, s. 2; 1979, c. 760, s. 5; 1979, 2nd Sess., c. 1316, s. 47; 1981, c. 63, s. 1; c. 179, s. 14; 1993, c. 539, s. 11; 1994, Ex. Sess., c. 24, s. 14(c)

§ 14-12.1. Certain subversive activities made unlawful

It shall be unlawful for any person to:
(1) By word of mouth or writing advocate, advise or teach the duty, necessity or propriety of overthrowing or overturning the government of the United States or a political subdivision of the United States by force or violence; or,
(2) Print, publish, edit, issue or knowingly circulate, sell, distribute or publicly display any book, paper, document, or written or printed matter in any form, containing or advocating, advising or teaching the doctrine that the government of the United States or a political subdivision of the United States should be overthrown by force, violence or any unlawful means; or,
(3) Organize or help to organize or become a member of or voluntarily assemble with any society, group or assembly of persons formed to teach or advocate the doctrine that the government of the United States or a political subdivision of the United States should be overthrown by force, violence or any unlawful means.
Any person violating the provisions of this section shall be punished as a Class H felon.
Whenever two or more persons assemble for the purpose of advocating or teaching the doctrine that the government of the United States or a political subdivision of the United States should be overthrown by force, violence or any unlawful means, such an assembly is unlawful, and every person voluntarily participating therein by his presence, aid or instigation, shall be punished as a Class H felon.
Every editor or proprietor of a book, newspaper or serial and every manager of a partnership or incorporated association by which a book, newspaper or serial is issued, is chargeable with the publication of any matter contained in such book, newspaper or serial. But in every prosecution therefor, the defendant may show in his defense that the matter complained of was published without his knowledge or fault and against his wishes, by another who had no authority from him to make the publication and whose act was disavowed by him as soon as known.

No person shall be employed by any department, bureau, institution or agency of the State of North Carolina who has participated in any of the activities described in this section, and any person now employed by any department, bureau, institution or agency and who has been or is engaged in any of the activities described in this section shall be forthwith discharged. Evidence satisfactory to the head of such department, bureau, institution or agency of the State shall be sufficient for refusal to employ any person or cause for discharge of any employee for the reasons set forth in this paragraph.

History.
1947, c. 1028; 1953, c. 675, s. 2; 1979, c. 760, s. 5; 1979, 2nd Sess., c. 1316, s. 47; 1981, c. 63, s. 1; c. 179, s. 14

ARTICLE 4A
PROHIBITED SECRET SOCIETIES AND ACTIVITIES

§ 14-12.2. Definitions

The terms used in this Article are defined as follows:
(1) The term "secret society" shall mean any two or more persons organized, associated together, combined or united for any common purpose whatsoever, who shall use among themselves any certain grips, signs or password, or who shall use for the advancement of any of their purposes or as a part of their ritual any disguise of the person, face or voice or any disguise whatsoever, or who shall take any extrajudicial oath or secret solemn pledge or administer such oath or pledge to those associated with them, or who shall transact business and advance their purposes at secret meeting or meetings which are tiled and guarded against intrusion by persons not associated with them.
(2) The term "secret political society" shall mean any secret society, as hereinbefore defined, which shall at any time have for a purpose the hindering or aiding the success of any candidate for public office, or the hindering or aiding the success of any political party or organization, or violating any lawfully declared policy of the government of the State or any of the laws and constitutional provisions of the State.
(3) The term "secret military society" shall mean any secret society, as hereinbefore defined, which shall at any time meet, assemble or engage in a venture when members thereof are illegally armed, or which shall at any time have for a purpose the engaging in any venture by members

thereof which shall require illegal armed force or in which illegal armed force is to be used, or which shall at any time muster, drill or practice any military evolutions while illegally armed.

History.
1953, c. 1193, s. 1

§ 14-12.3. Certain secret societies prohibited

It shall be unlawful for any person to join, unite himself with, become a member of, apply for membership in, form, organize, solicit members for, combine and agree with any person or persons to form or organize, or to encourage, aid or assist in any way any secret political society or any secret military society or any secret society having for a purpose the violating or circumventing the laws of the State.

History.
1953, c. 1193, s. 2

§ 14-12.4. Use of signs, grips, passwords or disguises or taking or administering oath for illegal purposes

It shall be unlawful for any person to use, agree to use, or to encourage, aid or assist in the using of any signs, grips, passwords, disguise of the face, person or voice, or any disguise whatsoever in the furtherance of any illegal secret political purpose, any illegal secret military purpose, or any purpose of violating or circumventing the laws of the State; and it shall be unlawful for any person to take or administer, or agree to take or administer, any extrajudicial oath or secret solemn pledge to further any illegal secret political purpose, any illegal secret military purpose, or any purpose of violating or circumventing the laws of the State.

History.
1953, c. 1193, s. 3

§ 14-12.5. Permitting, etc., meetings or demonstrations of prohibited secret societies

It shall be unlawful for any person to permit or agree to permit any members of a secret political society or a secret military society or a secret society having for a purpose the violating or circumventing the laws of the State to meet or to hold any demonstration in or upon any property owned or controlled by him.

History.
1953, c. 1193, s. 4

§ 14-12.6. Meeting places and meetings of secret societies regulated

Every secret society which has been or is now being formed and organized within the State, and which has members within the State shall forthwith provide or cause to be provided for each unit, lodge, council, group of members, grand lodge or general supervising unit a regular meeting place in some building or structure, and shall forthwith place and thereafter regularly keep a plainly visible sign or placard on the immediate exterior of such building or structure or on the immediate exterior of the meeting room or hall within such building or structure, if the entire building or structure is not controlled by such secret society, bearing upon said sign or placard the name of the secret society, the name of the particular unit, lodge, council, group of members, grand lodge or general supervising unit thereof and the name of the secretary, officer, organizer or member thereof who knows the purposes of the secret society and who knows or has a list of the names and addresses of the members thereof, and as such secretary, officer, organizer or member dies, removes, resigns or is replaced, his or her successor's name shall be placed upon such sign or placard; any person or persons who shall hereafter undertake to form and organize any secret society or solicit membership for a secret society within the State shall fully comply with the foregoing provisions of this section before forming and organizing such secret society and before soliciting memberships therein; all units, lodges, councils, groups of members, grand lodge and general supervising units of all secret societies within the State shall hold all of their secret meetings at the regular meeting place of their respective units, lodges, councils, group of members, grand lodge or general supervising units or at the regular meeting place of some other unit, lodge, council, group of members, grand lodge or general supervising unit of the same secret society, and at no other place unless notice is given of the time and place of the meeting and the name of the secret society holding the meeting in some newspaper having circulation in the locality where the meeting is to be held at least two days before the meeting.

History.
1953, c. 1193, s. 5

§ 14-12.7. Wearing of masks, hoods, etc., on public ways

No person or persons at least 16 years of age shall, while wearing any mask, hood or device whereby the person, face or voice is disguised so as to conceal the identity of the wearer, enter, be or appear upon any lane, walkway, alley, street, road, highway or other public way in this State.

History.
1953, c. 1193, s. 6; 1983, c. 175, ss. 1, 10; c. 720, s. 4

§ 14-12.8. Wearing of masks, hoods, etc., on public property

No person or persons shall in this State, while wearing any mask, hood or device whereby the person, face or voice is disguised so as to conceal the identity of the wearer, enter, or appear upon or within the public property of any municipality or county of the State, or of the State of North Carolina.

History.
1953, c. 1193, s. 7

§ 14-12.9. Entry, etc., upon premises of another while wearing mask, hood or other disguise

No person or persons at least 16 years of age shall, while wearing a mask, hood or device whereby the person, face or voice is disguised so as to conceal the identity of the wearer, demand entrance or admission, enter or come upon or into, or be upon or in the premises, enclosure or house of any other person in any municipality or county of this State.

History.
1953, c. 1193, s. 8; 1983, c. 175, ss. 2, 10; c. 720, s. 4

§ 14-12.10. Holding meetings or demonstrations while wearing masks, hoods, etc

No person or persons at least 16 years of age shall while wearing a mask, hood or device whereby the person, face or voice is disguised so as to conceal the identity of the wearer, hold any manner of meeting, or make any demonstration upon the private property of another unless such person or persons shall first obtain from the owner or occupier of the property his or her written permission to do so, which said written permission shall be recorded in the office of the register of deeds of the county in which said property is located before the beginning of such meeting or demonstration.

History.
1953, c. 1193, s. 9; 1983, c. 175, ss. 3, 10; c. 720, s. 4

§ 14-12.11. Exemptions from provisions of Article

(a) Any of the following are exempted from the provisions of G.S. 14-12.7, 14-12.8, 14-12.9, 14-12.10 and 14-12.14:

(1) Any person or persons wearing traditional holiday costumes in season.

(2) Any person or persons engaged in trades and employment where a mask is worn for the purpose of ensuring the physical safety of the wearer, or because of the nature of the occupation, trade or profession.

(3) Any person or persons using masks in theatrical productions including use in Mardi Gras celebrations and masquerade balls.

(4) Persons wearing gas masks prescribed in civil defense drills and exercises or emergencies.

(5) Any person or persons, as members or members elect of a society, order or organization, engaged in any parade, ritual, initiation, ceremony, celebration or requirement of such society, order or organization, and wearing or using any manner of costume, paraphernalia, disguise, facial makeup, hood, implement or device, whether the identity of such person or persons is concealed or not, on any public or private street, road, way or property, or in any public or private building, provided permission shall have been first obtained therefor by a representative of such society, order or organization from the governing body of the municipality in which the same takes place, or, if not in a municipality, from the board of county commissioners of the county in which the same takes place.

(6) Any person wearing a mask for the purpose of ensuring the physical health or safety of the wearer or others.

(a1) This Article shall not apply to any preliminary meetings held in good faith for the purpose of organizing, promoting or forming a labor union or a local organization or subdivision of any labor union nor shall the provisions of this Article apply to any meetings held by a labor union or organization already organized, operating and functioning and holding meetings for the purpose of transacting and carrying out functions, pursuits and affairs expressly pertaining to such labor union.

(b) Notwithstanding G.S. 14-12.7 and G.S. 14-12.8, a person may wear a mask for the purpose of protecting the person's head, face, or head and face, when operating a motorcycle, as defined in G.S. 20-4.01. A person wearing a mask when operating a motorcycle shall remove the mask during a traffic stop, including at a checkpoint or roadblock under G.S. 20-16.3A, or when approached by a law enforcement officer.

(c) Notwithstanding subdivision (a)(6) of this section, a person wearing a mask for the purpose of ensuring the physical health or safety of the wearer or others shall remove the mask, upon request by a law enforcement officer, in any of the following circumstances:

(1) During a traffic stop, including a checkpoint or roadblock pursuant to G.S. 20-16.3A.

(2) When a law enforcement officer has reasonable suspicion or probable cause during a criminal investigation.

History.
1953, c. 1193, s. 10; 2019-115, s. 1; 2020-3, s. 4.3(a); 2020-93, ss. 2, 3

§ 14-12.12. Placing burning or flaming cross on property of another or on public street or highway or on any public place

(a) It shall be unlawful for any person or persons to place or cause to be placed on the property of another in this State a burning or flaming cross or any manner of exhibit in which a burning or flaming cross, real or simulated, is a whole or a part, without first obtaining written permission of the owner or occupier of the premises so to do.

(b) It shall be unlawful for any person or persons to place or cause to be placed on the property of another in this State or on a public street or highway, or on any public place a burning or flaming cross or any manner of exhibit in which a burning or flaming cross real or simulated, is a whole or a part, with the intention of intimidating any person or persons or of preventing them from doing any act which is lawful, or causing them to do any act which is unlawful.

History.
1953, c. 1193, s. 11; 1967, c. 522, ss. 1, 2; 2008-197, s. 1

§ 14-12.13. Placing exhibit with intention of intimidating, etc., another

It shall be unlawful for any person or persons to place or cause to be placed anywhere in this State any exhibit of any kind whatsoever, while masked or unmasked, with the intention of intimidating any person or persons, or of preventing them from doing any act which is lawful, or of causing them to do any act which is unlawful. For the purposes of this section, the term "exhibit" includes items such as a noose.

History.
1953, c. 1193, s. 12; 2008-197, s. 2

§ 14-12.14. Placing exhibit while wearing mask, hood, or other disguise

It shall be unlawful for any person or persons, while wearing a mask, hood or device whereby the person, face or voice is disguised so as to conceal the identity of the wearer, to place or cause to be placed at or in any place in the State any exhibit of any kind whatsoever, with the intention of intimidating any person or persons, or of preventing them from doing any act which is lawful, or of causing them to do any act which is unlawful. For the purposes of this section, the term "exhibit" includes items such as a noose.

History.
1953, c. 1193, s. 13; 1967, c. 522, s. 3; 2008-197, s. 3

§ 14-12.15. Punishment for violation of Article

All persons violating any of the provisions of this Article, except for G.S. 14-12.12(b), 14-12.13, and 14-12.14, shall be guilty of a Class 1 misdemeanor. All persons violating the provisions of G.S. 14-12.12(b), 14-12.13, and 14-12.14 shall be punished as a Class H felon.

History.
1953, c. 1193, s. 14; 1967, c. 602; 1979, c. 760, s. 5; 1979, 2nd Sess., c. 1316, s. 47; 1981, c. 63, s. 1; c. 179, s. 14; 1993, c. 539, s. 12; 1994, Ex. Sess., c. 24, s. 14(c); 2008-197, s. 4

ARTICLE 5
COUNTERFEITING AND ISSUING MONETARY SUBSTITUTES

§ 14-13. Counterfeiting coin and uttering coin that is counterfeit

If any person shall falsely make, forge or counterfeit, or cause or procure to be falsely made, forged or counterfeited, or willingly aid or assist in falsely making, forging or counterfeiting the resemblance or similitude or likeness of any coin of gold or silver which is in common use and received in the discharge of contracts by the citizens of the State; or shall pass, utter, publish or sell, or attempt to pass, utter, publish or sell, or bring into the State from any other place with intent to pass, utter, publish or sell as true, any such false, forged or counterfeited coin, knowing the same to be false, forged or counterfeited, with intent to defraud any person whatsoever, every person so offending shall be punished as a Class I felon.

History.
1811, c. 814, s. 3, P.R.; R.C., c. 34, s. 64; Code, s. 1035; Rev., s. 3422; C.S., s. 4181; 1979, c. 760, s. 5; 1979, 2nd Sess., c. 1316, s. 47; 1981, c. 63, s. 1; c. 179, s. 14;

Chapter 14

1993, c. 539, s. 1123; 1994, Ex. Sess., c. 24, s. 14(c); 1995, c. 379, s. 1(a)

§ 14-14. Possessing tools for counterfeiting

If any person shall have in his possession any instrument for the purpose of making any counterfeit similitude or likeness of any coin made of gold or silver which is in common use and received in discharge of contracts by the citizens of the State, and shall be duly convicted thereof, the person so offending shall be punished as a Class I felon.

History.

1811, c. 814, s. 4, P.R.; R.C., c. 34, s. 65; Code, s. 1036; Rev., s. 3423; C.S., s. 4182; 1979, c. 760, s. 5; 1979, 2nd Sess., c. 1316, s. 47; 1981, c. 63, s. 1; c. 179, s. 14; 1993, c. 539, s. 1124; 1994, Ex. Sess., c. 24, s. 14(c); 1995, c. 379, s. 1(b)

§ 14-15. Issuing substitutes for money without authority

If any person or corporation, unless the same be expressly allowed by law, shall issue any bill, due bill, order, ticket, certificate of deposit, promissory note or obligation, or any other kind of security, whatever may be its form or name, with the intent that the same shall circulate or pass as the representative of, or as a substitute for, money, he shall be guilty of a Class 3 misdemeanor and only punishable by a fine not to exceed the sum of fifty dollars ($ 50.00); and if the offender be a corporation, it shall in addition forfeit its charter. Every person or corporation offending against this section, or aiding or assisting therein, shall be guilty of a Class 3 misdemeanor and only punishable by a fine not to exceed fifty dollars ($ 50.00).

History.

R.C., c. 36, s. 5; Code, s. 2493; 1895, c. 127; Rev., s. 3711; C.S., s. 4183; 1993, c. 539, s. 13; 1994, Ex. Sess., c. 24, s. 14(c)

§ 14-16. Receiving or passing unauthorized substitutes for money

If any person or corporation shall pass or receive, as the representative of, or as the substitute for, money, any bill, check, certificate, promissory note, or other security of the kind mentioned in G.S. 14-15, whether the same be issued within or without the State, such person or corporation, and the officers and agents of such corporation aiding therein, who shall offend against this section shall be guilty of a Class 3 misdemeanor and only punishable by a fine not to exceed five dollars ($ 5.00).

History.

R.C., c. 36, s. 6; Code, s. 2494; 1895, c. 127; Rev., s. 3712; C.S., s. 4184; 1993, c. 539, s. 14; 1994, Ex. Sess., c. 24, s. 14(c)

§§ 14-16.1 through 14-16.5

Reserved for future codification purposes.

ARTICLE 5A
ENDANGERING EXECUTIVE, LEGISLATIVE, AND COURT OFFICERS

§ 14-16.6. Assault on executive, legislative, or court officer

(a) Any person who assaults any legislative officer, executive officer, or court officer, or assaults another person as retaliation against any legislative officer, executive officer, or court officer because of the exercise of that officer's duties, or any person who makes a violent attack upon the residence, office, temporary accommodation or means of transport of any one of those officers or persons in a manner likely to endanger the officer or person, shall be guilty of a felony and shall be punished as a Class I felon.

(b) Any person who commits an offense under subsection (a) and uses a deadly weapon in the commission of that offense shall be punished as a Class F felon.

(c) Any person who commits an offense under subsection (a) and inflicts serious bodily injury to any legislative officer, executive officer, or court officer, shall be punished as a Class F felon.

History.

1981, c. 822, s. 1; 1993, c. 539, s. 1125; 1994, Ex. Sess., c. 24, s. 14(c); 1999-398, s. 1; 2014-119, s. 6(a)

§ 14-16.7. Threats against executive, legislative, or court officers

(a) Any person who knowingly and willfully makes any threat to inflict serious bodily injury upon or to kill any legislative officer, executive officer, or court officer, or who knowingly and willfully makes any threat to inflict serious bodily injury upon or kill any other person as retaliation against any legislative officer, executive officer, or court officer because of the exercise of that officer's duties, shall be guilty of a felony and shall be punished as a Class I felon.

(b) Any person who knowingly and willfully deposits for conveyance in the mail any letter, writing, or other document containing a threat to commit an offense described in subsection (a) of this section shall be guilty of a felony and shall be punished as a Class I felon.

History.

1981, c. 822, s. 1; 1993, c. 539, s. 1126; 1994, Ex. Sess., c. 24, s. 14(c); 1999-398, s. 1; 2014-119, s. 6(b)

§ 14-16.8. No requirement of receipt of the threat

In prosecutions under G.S. 14-16.7 of this Article it shall not be necessary to prove that any legislative officer, executive officer, or court officer actually received the threatening communication or actually believed the threat.

History.

1981, c. 822, s. 1; 1999-398, s. 1

§ 14-16.9. Officers-elect to be covered

Any person who has been elected to any office covered by this Article but has not yet taken the oath of office shall be considered to hold the office for the purpose of this Article and G.S. 143B-919.

History.

1981, c. 822, s. 1; 2011-145, s. 19.1(dd1); 2011-391, s. 43 (*l*); 2014-100, s. 17.1(v)

§ 14-16.10. Definitions

The following definitions apply in this Article:

(1) **Court officer.** -- Magistrate, clerk of superior court, acting clerk, assistant or deputy clerk, judge, or justice of the General Court of Justice; district attorney, assistant district attorney, or any other attorney designated by the district attorney to act for the State or on behalf of the district attorney; public defender or assistant defender; court reporter; juvenile court counselor as defined in G.S. 7B-1501(18a); any attorney or other individual employed by or acting on behalf of the department of social services in proceedings pursuant to Subchapter I of Chapter 7B of the General Statutes; any attorney or other individual appointed pursuant to G.S. 7B-601 or G.S. 7B-1108 or employed by the Guardian ad Litem Services Division of the Administrative Office of the Courts.

(2) **Executive officer.** -- A person named in G.S. 147-3(c).

(3) **Legislative officer.** -- A person named in G.S. 147-2(1), (2), or (3).

History.

1999-398, s. 1; 2001-490, s. 2.35; 2003-140, s. 10

SUBCHAPTER 03. OFFENSES AGAINST THE PERSON

ARTICLE 6 HOMICIDE

§ 14-17. Murder in the first and second degree defined; punishment

(a) A murder which shall be perpetrated by means of a nuclear, biological, or chemical weapon of mass destruction as defined in G.S. 14-288.21, poison, lying in wait, imprisonment, starving, torture, or by any other kind of willful, deliberate, and premeditated killing, or which shall be committed in the perpetration or attempted perpetration of any arson, rape or a sex offense, robbery, kidnapping, burglary, or other felony committed or attempted with the use of a deadly weapon shall be deemed to be murder in the first degree, a Class A felony, and any person who commits such murder shall be punished with death or imprisonment in the State's prison for life without parole as the court shall determine pursuant to G.S. 15A-2000, except that any such person who was under 18 years of age at the time of the murder shall be punished in accordance with Part 2A of Article 81B of Chapter 15A of the General Statutes.

(a1) If a murder was perpetrated with malice as described in subdivision (1) of subsection (b) of this section, and committed against a spouse, former spouse, a person with whom the defendant lives or has lived as if married, a person with whom the defendant is or has been in a dating relationship as defined in G.S. 50B-1(b)(6), or a person with whom the defendant shares a child in common, there shall be a rebuttable presumption that the murder is a "willful, deliberate, and premeditated killing" under subsection (a) of this section and shall be deemed to be murder in the first degree, a Class A felony, if the perpetrator has previously been convicted of one of the following offenses involving the same victim:

(1) An act of domestic violence as defined in G.S. 50B-1(a).

(2) A violation of a domestic violence protective order under G.S. 50B-4.1(a), (f), (g), or (g1) or G.S. 14-269.8 when the same victim is the subject of the domestic violence protective order.

(3) Communicating a threat under G.S. 14-277.1.

(4) Stalking as defined in G.S. 14-277.3A.

(5) Cyberstalking as defined in G.S. 14-196.3.

(6) Domestic criminal trespass as defined in G.S. 14-134.3.

(b) A murder other than described in subsection (a) or (a1) of this section or in G.S. 14-23.2 shall be deemed second degree murder. Any person who commits second degree murder shall be punished as a Class B1 felon, except that a person who commits second degree murder shall be punished as a Class B2 felon in either of the following circumstances:

(1) The malice necessary to prove second degree murder is based on an inherently dangerous act or omission, done in such a reckless and wanton manner as to manifest a mind utterly without regard for human life and social duty and deliberately bent on mischief.

(2) The murder is one that was proximately caused by the unlawful distribution of any opium, opiate, or opioid; any synthetic or natural salt, compound, derivative, or preparation of opium, or opiate, or opioid; cocaine or other substance described in G.S. 90-90(1)d.; methamphetamine; or a depressant described in G.S. 90-92(a)(1), and the ingestion of such substance caused the death of the user.

(c) For the purposes of this section, it shall constitute murder where a child is born alive but dies as a result of injuries inflicted prior to the child being born alive. The degree of murder shall be determined as described in subsections (a) and (b) of this section.

History.
1893, cc. 85, 281; Rev., s. 3631; C.S., s. 4200; 1949, c. 299, s. 1; 1973, c. 1201, s. 1; 1977, c. 406, s. 1; 1979, c. 682, s. 6; 1979, c. 760, s. 5; 1979, 2nd Sess., c. 1251, ss. 1, 2; c. 1316, s. 47; 1981, c. 63, s. 1; c. 179, s. 14; c. 662, s. 1; 1987, c. 693; 1989, c. 694; 1993, c. 539, s. 112; 1994, Ex. Sess., c. 21, s. 1; c. 22, s. 4; c. 24, s. 14(c); 2001-470, s. 2; 2004-178, s. 1; 2007-81, s. 1; 2012-165, s. 1; 2013-47, s. 2; 2013-410, s. 3(a); 2017-94, s. 1; 2017-115, s. 9

§ 14-17.1. Crime of suicide abolished

The common-law crime of suicide is hereby abolished as an offense.

History.
1973, c. 1205

§ 14-18. Punishment for manslaughter

Voluntary manslaughter shall be punishable as a Class D felony, and involuntary manslaughter shall be punishable as a Class F felony.

History.
4 Hen. VII, s. 13; 1816, c. 918, P.R.; R.C., c. 34, s. 24; 1879, c. 255; Code, s. 1055; Rev., s. 3632; C.S., s. 4201; 1933, c. 249; 1979, c. 760, s. 5; 1979, 2nd Sess., c. 1316, s. 47; 1981, c. 63, s. 1; c. 179, s. 14; 1993, c. 539, s. 112; 1994, Ex. Sess., c. 24, s. 14(c); 1997-443, s. 19.25(q)

N.C. Gen. Stat. § 14-18.1

Repealed by Session Laws 1994, Extra Session, c. 14, s. 73.

N.C. Gen. Stat. § 14-18.2

Repealed by Session Laws 2011-60, s. 3, effective December 1, 2011, and applicable to offenses committed on or after that date.

History.
1998-212, s. 17.16(b); repealed by 2011-60, s. 3, effective December 1, 2011

§ 14-18.4. Death by distribution of certain controlled substances; aggravated death by distribution of certain controlled substances; penalties

(a) **Legislative Intent.** -- The General Assembly recognizes that deaths due to the opioid epidemic are devastating families and communities across North Carolina. The General Assembly finds that the opioid crisis is overwhelming medical providers engaged in the lawful distribution of controlled substances and is straining prevention and treatment efforts. Therefore, the General Assembly enacts this law to encourage effective intervention by the criminal justice system to hold illegal drug dealers accountable for criminal conduct that results in death.

(b) **Death by Distribution of Certain Controlled Substances.** -- A person is guilty of death by distribution of certain controlled substances if all of the following requirements are met:

(1) The person unlawfully sells at least one certain controlled substance.

(2) The ingestion of the certain controlled substance or substances causes the death of the user.

(3) The commission of the offense in subdivision (1) of this subsection was the proximate cause of the victim's death.

(4) The person did not act with malice.

(c) **Aggravated Death by Distribution of Certain Controlled Substances.** -- A person is guilty of aggravated death by distribution of certain controlled substances if all of the following requirements are met:

(1) The person unlawfully sells at least one certain controlled substance.

(2) The ingestion of the certain controlled substance or substances causes the death of the user.

(3) The commission of the offense in subdivision (1) of this subsection was the proximate cause of the victim's death.

(4) The person did not act with malice.

(5) The person has a previous conviction under this section, G.S. 90-95(a)(1), 90-95.1, 90-95.4, 90-95.6, or trafficking in violation of G.S. 90-95(h), or a prior conviction in any federal or state court in the United States that is substantially similar to an offense listed, within seven years of the date of the offense. In calculating the seven-year period under this subdivision, any period of time during which the person was incarcerated in a local, state, or federal detention center, jail, or prison shall be excluded.

(d) **Certain Controlled Substance.** -- For the purposes of this section, the term "certain controlled substance" includes any opium, opiate, or opioid; any synthetic or natural salt, compound, derivative, or preparation of opium, opiate, or opioid; cocaine or any other substance described in G.S. 90-90(1)(d); methamphetamine; a depressant described in G.S. 90-92(a) (1); or a mixture of one or more of these substances.

(e) **Lesser Included Offense.** -- Death by distribution of certain controlled substances constitutes a lesser included offense of aggravated death by distribution of certain controlled substances in violation of this section.

(f) **Samaritan Protection.** -- Nothing in this section shall be construed to restrict or interfere with the rights and immunities provided under G.S. 90-96.2.

(g) **Lawful Distribution.** -- This section shall not apply to any of the following:

(1) Issuing a valid prescription for a controlled substance for a legitimate medical purpose by an individual practitioner acting in the usual course of professional practice.

(2) Dispensing, delivering, or administering a controlled substance pursuant to a prescription, by a pharmacy permitted under G.S. 90-85.21, a pharmacist, or an individual practitioner.

(h) **Penalties.** -- Unless the conduct is covered under some other provision of law providing greater punishment, the following classifications apply to the offenses set forth in this section:

(1) Death by distribution of certain controlled substances is a Class C felony.

(2) Aggravated death by distribution of certain controlled substances is a Class B2 felony.

History.
2019-83, s. 1

N.C. Gen. Stat. § 14-19

Repealed by Session Laws 1979, c. 760, s. 5.

N.C. Gen. Stat. § 14-20

Repealed by Session Laws 1993 (Reg. Sess., 1994), c. 767, s. 29(1).

§§ 14-21 through 14-23

Repealed by Session Laws 1979, c. 682, s. 7.

ARTICLE 6A
UNBORN VICTIMS

§ 14-23.1. Definition

As used in this Article only, "unborn child" means a member of the species homo sapiens, at any stage of development, who is carried in the womb.

History.
2011-60, s. 2

§ 14-23.2. Murder of an unborn child; penalty

(a) A person who unlawfully causes the death of an unborn child is guilty of the separate offense of murder of an unborn child if the person does any one of the following:

(1) Willfully and maliciously commits an act with the intent to cause the death of the unborn child.

(2) Causes the death of the unborn child in perpetration or attempted perpetration of any of the criminal offenses set forth under G.S. 14-17.

(3) Commits an act causing the death of the unborn child that is inherently dangerous to human life and is done so recklessly and wantonly that it reflects disregard of life.

(b) **Penalty.** -- An offense under:

(1) Subdivision (a)(1) or (a)(2) of this section shall be a Class A felony, and any person who commits such offense shall be punished with imprisonment in the State's prison for life without parole.

(2) Subdivision (a)(3) of this section shall be subject to the same sentence as if the person had been convicted of second degree murder pursuant to G.S. 14-17.

History.
2011-60, s. 2

§ 14-23.3. Voluntary manslaughter of an unborn child; penalty

(a) A person is guilty of the separate offense of voluntary manslaughter of an unborn child if the person unlawfully causes the death of an unborn child by an act that would be voluntary manslaughter if it resulted in the death of the mother.

(b) **Penalty.** -- Any person who commits an offense under this section shall be guilty of a Class D felony.

History.
2011-60, s. 2

§ 14-23.4. Involuntary manslaughter of an unborn child; penalty

(a) A person is guilty of the separate offense of involuntary manslaughter of an unborn child if the person unlawfully causes the death of an unborn child by an act that would be involuntary manslaughter if it resulted in the death of the mother.

(b) **Penalty.** -- Any person who commits an offense under this section shall be guilty of a Class F felony.

History.
2011-60, s. 2

§ 14-23.5. Assault inflicting serious bodily injury on an unborn child; penalty

(a) A person is guilty of the separate offense of assault inflicting serious bodily injury on an unborn child if the person commits a battery on the mother of the unborn child and the child is subsequently born alive and suffered serious bodily harm as a result of the battery.

(b) For purposes of this section, "serious bodily harm" is defined as bodily injury that creates a substantial risk of death, or that causes serious permanent disfigurement, coma, a permanent or protracted condition that causes extreme pain, or permanent or protracted loss or impairment of the function of any bodily member or organ, or that results in prolonged hospitalization, or causes the birth of the unborn child prior to 37-weeks gestation, if the child weighs 2,500 grams or less at the time of birth.

(c) **Penalty.** -- Any person who commits an offense under this section shall be guilty of a Class F felony.

History.
2011-60, s. 2

§ 14-23.6. Battery on an unborn child

(a) A person is guilty of the separate offense of battery on an unborn child if the person commits a battery on a pregnant woman. This offense is a lesser-included offense of G.S. 14-23.5.

(b) **Penalty.** -- Any person who commits an offense under this section is guilty of a Class A1 misdemeanor.

History.
2011-60, s. 2

§ 14-23.7. Exceptions

Nothing in this Article shall be construed to permit the prosecution under this Article of any of the following:

(1) Acts which cause the death of an unborn child if those acts were lawful, pursuant to the provisions of G.S. 14-45.1.

(2) Acts which are committed pursuant to usual and customary standards of medical practice during diagnostic testing or therapeutic treatment.

(3) Acts committed by a pregnant woman with respect to her own unborn child, including, but not limited to, acts which result in miscarriage or stillbirth by the woman. The following definitions shall apply in this section:

a. **Miscarriage.** -- The interruption of the normal development of an unborn child, other than by a live birth, and which is not an induced abortion permitted under G.S. 14-45.1, resulting in the complete expulsion or extraction from a pregnant woman of the unborn child.

b. **Stillbirth.** -- The death of an unborn child prior to the complete expulsion or extraction from a woman, irrespective of the duration of pregnancy and which is not an induced abortion permitted under G.S. 14-45.1.

History.
2011-60, s. 2

§ 14-23.8. Knowledge not required

Except for an offense under G.S. 14-23.2(a)(1), an offense under this Article does not require proof of either of the following:

(1) The person engaging in the conduct had knowledge or should have had knowledge that the victim of the underlying offense was pregnant.

(2) The defendant intended to cause the death of, or bodily injury to, the unborn child.

History.
2011-60, s. 2

ARTICLE 7
RAPE AND KINDRED OFFENSES

§§ 14-24, 14-25

Repealed by Session Laws, 1975, c. 402.

§§ 14-26, 14-27

Repealed by Session Laws 1979, c. 682, s. 7.

ARTICLE 7A
RAPE AND OTHER SEX OFFENSES

N.C. Gen. Stat. § 14-27.1

Recodified as G.S. 14-27.20 by Session Laws 2015-181, s. 2, effective December 1, 2015, and applicable to offenses committed on or after that date.

N.C. Gen. Stat. § 14-27.2

Recodified as G.S. 14-27.21 by Session Laws 2015-181, s. 3(a), effective December 1, 2015, and applicable to offenses committed on or after that date.

N.C. Gen. Stat. § 14-27.2A

Recodified as G.S. 14-27.23 by Session Laws 2015-181, s. 5(a), effective December 1, 2015, and applicable to offenses committed on or after that date.

N.C. Gen. Stat. § 14-27.3

Recodified as G.S. 14-27.22 by Session Laws 2015-181, s. 4(a), effective December 1, 2015, and applicable to offenses committed on or after that date.

N.C. Gen. Stat. § 14-27.4

Recodified as G.S. 14-27.26 by Session Laws 2015-181, s. 8(a), effective December 1, 2015, and applicable to offenses committed on or after that date.

N.C. Gen. Stat. § 14-27.4A

Recodified as G.S. 14-27.28 by Session Laws 2015-181, s. 10(a), effective December 1, 2015, and applicable to offenses committed on or after that date.

N.C. Gen. Stat. § 14-27.5

Recodified as G.S. 14-27.27 by Session Laws 2015-181, s. 9(a), effective December 1, 2015, and applicable to offenses committed on or after that date.

N.C. Gen. Stat. § 14-27.5A

Recodified as G.S. 14-27.33 by Session Laws 2015-181, s. 15, effective December 1, 2015, and applicable to offenses committed on or after that date.

N.C. Gen. Stat. § 14-27.6

Repealed by Session Laws 1994, Extra Session, c. 14, s. 71(3).

N.C. Gen. Stat. § 14-27.7

Recodified as G.S. 14-27.31 and 14-27.32 by Session Laws 2015-181, ss. 13(a) and 14(a), effective December 1, 2015, and applicable to offenses committed on or after that date.

N.C. Gen. Stat. § 14-27.7A

Recodified as G.S. 14-27.25 by Session Laws 2015-181, s. 7(a), effective December 1, 2015, and applicable to offenses committed on or after that date.

N.C. Gen. Stat. § 14-27.8

Recodified as G.S. 14-27.34 by Session Laws 2015-181, s. 15, effective December 1, 2015, and applicable to offenses committed on or after that date.

N.C. Gen. Stat. § 14-27.9

Recodified as G.S. 14-27.35 by Session Laws 2015-181, s. 15, effective December 1, 2015, and applicable to offenses committed on or after that date.

N.C. Gen. Stat. § 14-27.10

Recodified as G.S. 14-27.36 by Session Laws 2015-181, s. 15, effective December 1, 2015, and applicable to offenses committed on or after that date.

ARTICLE 7B
RAPE AND OTHER SEX OFFENSES

Chapter 14

§ 14-27.20. Definitions

The following definitions apply in this Article:

(1) Repealed by Session Laws 2018-47, s. 4(a), effective December 1, 2018.

(1a) **Against the will of the other person.** -- Either of the following:

a. Without consent of the other person.

b. After consent is revoked by the other person, in a manner that would cause a reasonable person to believe consent is revoked.

(2) **Mentally incapacitated.** -- A victim who due to any act is rendered substantially incapable of either appraising the nature of his or her conduct, or resisting the act of vaginal intercourse or a sexual act.

(2a) **Person who has a mental disability.** -- A victim who has an intellectual disability or a mental disorder that temporarily or permanently renders the victim substantially incapable of appraising the nature of his or her conduct, or of resisting the act of vaginal intercourse or a sexual act, or of communicating unwillingness to submit to the act of vaginal intercourse or a sexual act.

(3) **Physically helpless.** -- Any of the following:

a. A victim who is unconscious.

b. A victim who is physically unable to resist an act of vaginal intercourse or a sexual act or communicate unwillingness to submit to an act of vaginal intercourse or a sexual act.

(4) **Sexual act.** -- Cunnilingus, fellatio, analingus, or anal intercourse, but does not include vaginal intercourse. Sexual act also means the penetration, however slight, by any object into the genital or anal opening of another person's body. It is an affirmative defense that the penetration was for accepted medical purposes.

(5) **Sexual contact.** -- Any of the following:

a. Touching the sexual organ, anus, breast, groin, or buttocks of any person.

b. A person touching another person with their own sexual organ, anus, breast, groin, or buttocks.

c. A person ejaculating, emitting, or placing semen, urine, or feces upon any part of another person.

(6) **Touching.** -- As used in subdivision (5) of this section, means physical contact with another person, whether accomplished directly, through the clothing of the person committing the offense, or through the clothing of the victim.

History.

1979, c. 682, s. 1; 2002-159, s. 2(a); 2003-252, s. 1; 2006-247, s. 12(a); 2015-181, s. 2; 2018-47, s. 4(a); 2019-245, ss. 5(a), 6(c)

§ 14-27.21. First-degree forcible rape

(a) A person is guilty of first-degree forcible rape if the person engages in vaginal intercourse with another person by force and against the will of the other person, and does any of the following:

(1) Uses, threatens to use, or displays a dangerous or deadly weapon or an article which the other person reasonably believes to be a dangerous or deadly weapon.

(2) Inflicts serious personal injury upon the victim or another person.

(3) The person commits the offense aided and abetted by one or more other persons.

(b) Any person who commits an offense defined in this section is guilty of a Class B1 felony.

(c) Upon conviction, a person convicted under this section has no rights to custody of or rights of inheritance from any child born as a result of the commission of the rape, nor shall the person have any rights related to the child under Chapter 48 or Subchapter 1 of Chapter 7B of the General Statutes.

History.

1979, c. 682, s. 1; 1979, 2nd Sess., c. 1316, s. 4; 1981, c. 63; c. 106, ss. 1, 2; c. 179, s. 14; 1983, c. 175, ss. 4, 10; c. 720, s. 4; 1994, Ex. Sess., c. 22, s. 2; 2004-128, s. 7; 2015-181, s. 3(a), (b); 2017-30, s. 1

§ 14-27.22. Second-degree forcible rape

(a) A person is guilty of second-degree forcible rape if the person engages in vaginal intercourse with another person:

(1) By force and against the will of the other person; or

(2) Who has a mental disability or who is mentally incapacitated or physically helpless, and the person performing the act knows or should reasonably know the other person has a mental disability or is mentally incapacitated or physically helpless.

(b) Any person who commits the offense defined in this section is guilty of a Class C felony.

(c) Upon conviction, a person convicted under this section has no rights to custody of or rights of inheritance from any child conceived during the commission of the rape, nor does the person have any rights related to the child under Chapter 48 of the General Statutes or Subchapter I of Chapter 7B of the General Statutes.

History.

1979, c. 682, s. 1; 1979, 2nd Sess., c. 1316, s. 5; 1981, cc. 63, 179; 1993, c. 539, s. 1130; 1994, Ex. Sess., c. 24,

Chapter 14

s. 14(c); 2002-159, s. 2(b); 2004-128, s. 8; 2015-181, s. 4(a), (b); 2018-47, s. 4(b)

§ 14-27.23. Statutory rape of a child by an adult

(a) A person is guilty of statutory rape of a child by an adult if the person is at least 18 years of age and engages in vaginal intercourse with a victim who is a child under the age of 13 years.

(b) A person convicted of violating this section is guilty of a Class B1 felony and shall be sentenced pursuant to Article 81B of Chapter 15A of the General Statutes, except that in no case shall the person receive an active punishment of less than 300 months, and except as provided in subsection (c) of this section. Following the termination of active punishment, the person shall be enrolled in satellite-based monitoring for life pursuant to Part 5 of Article 27A of Chapter 14 of the General Statutes.

(c) Notwithstanding the provisions of Article 81B of Chapter 15A of the General Statutes, the court may sentence the defendant to active punishment for a term of months greater than that authorized pursuant to G.S. 15A-1340.17, up to and including life imprisonment without parole, if the court finds that the nature of the offense and the harm inflicted are of such brutality, duration, severity, degree, or scope beyond that normally committed in such crimes, or considered in basic aggravation of these crimes, so as to require a sentence to active punishment in excess of that authorized pursuant to G.S. 15A-1340.17. If the court sentences the defendant pursuant to this subsection, it shall make findings of fact supporting its decision, to include matters it considered as egregious aggravation. Egregious aggravation can include further consideration of existing aggravating factors where the conduct of the defendant falls outside the heartland of cases even the aggravating factors were designed to cover. Egregious aggravation may also be considered based on the extraordinarily young age of the victim, or the depraved torture or mutilation of the victim, or extraordinary physical pain inflicted on the victim.

(d) Upon conviction, a person convicted under this section has no rights to custody of or rights of inheritance from any child born as a result of the commission of the rape, nor shall the person have any rights related to the child under Chapter 48 or Subchapter 1 of Chapter 7B of the General Statutes.

(e) The offense under G.S. 14-27.24 is a lesser included offense of the offense in this section.

History.
2008-117, s. 1; 2015-181, s. 5(a), 5(b)

§ 14-27.24. First-degree statutory rape

(a) A person is guilty of first-degree statutory rape if the person engages in vaginal intercourse with a victim who is a child under the age of 13 years and the defendant is at least 12 years old and is at least four years older than the victim.

(b) Any person who commits an offense defined in this section is guilty of a Class B1 felony.

(c) Upon conviction, a person convicted under this section has no rights to custody of or rights of inheritance from any child born as a result of the commission of the rape, nor shall the person have any rights related to the child under Chapter 48 or Subchapter 1 of Chapter 7B of the General Statutes.

History.
1979, c. 682, s. 1; 1979, 2nd Sess., c. 1316, s. 4; 1981, c. 63; c. 106, ss. 1, 2; c. 179, s. 14; 1983, c. 175, ss. 4, 10; c. 720, s. 4; 1994, Ex. Sess., c. 22, s. 2; 2004-128, s. 7; 2015-181, s. 6

§ 14-27.25. Statutory rape of person who is 15 years of age or younger

(a) A defendant is guilty of a Class B1 felony if the defendant engages in vaginal intercourse with another person who is 15 years of age or younger and the defendant is at least 12 years old and at least six years older than the person, except when the defendant is lawfully married to the person.

(b) Unless the conduct is covered under some other provision of law providing greater punishment, a defendant is guilty of a Class C felony if the defendant engages in vaginal intercourse with another person who is 15 years of age or younger and the defendant is at least 12 years old and more than four but less than six years older than the person, except when the defendant is lawfully married to the person.

History.
1995, c. 281, s. 1; 2015-62, s. 1(a); 2015-181, s. 7(a), (b)

§ 14-27.26. First-degree forcible sexual offense

(a) A person is guilty of a first degree forcible sexual offense if the person engages in a sexual act with another person by force and against the will of the other person, and does any of the following:

(1) Uses, threatens to use, or displays a dangerous or deadly weapon or an article which the other person reasonably believes to be a dangerous or deadly weapon.

(2) Inflicts serious personal injury upon the victim or another person.

(3) The person commits the offense aided and abetted by one or more other persons.

(b) Any person who commits an offense defined in this section is guilty of a Class B1 felony.

History.
1979, c. 682, s. 1; 1979, 2nd Sess., c. 1316, s. 6; 1981, c. 63; c. 106, ss. 3, 4; c. 179, s. 14; 1983, c. 175, ss. 5, 10; c. 720, s. 4; 1994, Ex. Sess., c. 22, s. 3; 2015-181, s. 8(a), (b); 2017-30, s. 2

§ 14-27.27. Second-degree forcible sexual offense

(a) A person is guilty of second degree forcible sexual offense if the person engages in a sexual act with another person:

(1) By force and against the will of the other person; or

(2) Who has a mental disability or who is mentally incapacitated or physically helpless, and the person performing the act knows or should reasonably know that the other person has a mental disability or is mentally incapacitated or physically helpless.

(b) Any person who commits the offense defined in this section is guilty of a Class C felony.

History.
1979, c. 682, s. 1; 1979, 2nd Sess., c. 1316, s. 7; 1981, c. 63; c. 179, s. 14; 1993, c. 539, s. 1131; 1994, Ex. Sess., c. 24, s. 14(c); 2002-159, s. 2(c); 2015-181, s. 9(a), (b); 2018-47, s. 4(c)

§ 14-27.28. Statutory sexual offense with a child by an adult

(a) A person is guilty of statutory sexual offense with a child by an adult if the person is at least 18 years of age and engages in a sexual act with a victim who is a child under the age of 13 years.

(b) A person convicted of violating this section is guilty of a Class B1 felony and shall be sentenced pursuant to Article 81B of Chapter 15A of the General Statutes, except that in no case shall the person receive an active punishment of less than 300 months, and except as provided in subsection (c) of this section. Following the termination of active punishment, the person shall be enrolled in satellite-based monitoring for life pursuant to Part 5 of Article 27A of Chapter 14 of the General Statutes.

(c) Notwithstanding the provisions of Article 81B of Chapter 15A of the General Statutes, the court may sentence the defendant to active punishment for a term of months greater than that authorized pursuant to G.S. 15A-1340.17, up to and including life imprisonment without parole, if the court finds that the nature of the offense

and the harm inflicted are of such brutality, duration, severity, degree, or scope beyond that normally committed in such crimes, or considered in basic aggravation of these crimes, so as to require a sentence to active punishment in excess of that authorized pursuant to G.S. 15A-1340.17. If the court sentences the defendant pursuant to this subsection, it shall make findings of fact supporting its decision, to include matters it considered as egregious aggravation. Egregious aggravation can include further consideration of existing aggravating factors where the conduct of the defendant falls outside the heartland of cases even the aggravating factors were designed to cover. Egregious aggravation may also be considered based on the extraordinarily young age of the victim, or the depraved torture or mutilation of the victim, or extraordinary physical pain inflicted on the victim.

(d) The offense under G.S. 14-27.29 is a lesser included offense of the offense in this section.

History.
2008-117, s. 2; 2015-181, s. 10(a), (b)

§ 14-27.29. First-degree statutory sexual offense

(a) A person is guilty of first-degree statutory sexual offense if the person engages in a sexual act with a victim who is a child under the age of 13 years and the defendant is at least 12 years old and is at least four years older than the victim.

(b) Any person who commits an offense defined in this section is guilty of a Class B1 felony.

History.
1979, c. 682, s. 1; 1979, 2nd Sess., c. 1316, s. 6; 1981, c. 63; c. 106, ss. 3, 4; c. 179, s. 14; 1983, c. 175, ss. 5, 10; c. 720, s. 4; 1994, Ex. Sess., c. 22, s. 3; 2015-181, s. 11

§ 14-27.30. Statutory sexual offense with a person who is 15 years of age or younger

(a) A defendant is guilty of a Class B1 felony if the defendant engages in a sexual act with another person who is 15 years of age or younger and the defendant is at least 12 years old and at least six years older than the person, except when the defendant is lawfully married to the person.

(b) Unless the conduct is covered under some other provision of law providing greater punishment, a defendant is guilty of a Class C felony if the defendant engages in a sexual act with another person who is 15 years of age or younger and the defendant is at least 12 years old and more than four but less than six years older than the person, except when the defendant is lawfully married to the person.

§ 14-27.31. Sexual activity by a substitute parent or custodian

(a) If a defendant who has assumed the position of a parent in the home of a minor victim engages in vaginal intercourse or a sexual act with a victim who is a minor residing in the home, the defendant is guilty of a Class E felony.

(b) If a person having custody of a victim of any age or a person who is an agent or employee of any person, or institution, whether such institution is private, charitable, or governmental, having custody of a victim of any age engages in vaginal intercourse or a sexual act with such victim, the defendant is guilty of a Class E felony.

(c) Consent is not a defense to a charge under this section.

History.
1979, c. 682, s. 1; 1979, 2nd Sess., c. 1316, s. 9; 1981, c. 63; c. 179, s. 14; 1993, c. 539, s. 1132; 1994, Ex. Sess., c. 24, s. 14(c); 1999-300, s. 2; 2003-98, s. 1; 2015-181, s. 13(a), (b)

§ 14-27.32. Sexual activity with a student

(a) If a defendant, who is a teacher, school administrator, student teacher, school safety officer, or coach, at any age, or who is other school personnel, and who is at least four years older than the victim engages in vaginal intercourse or a sexual act with a victim who is a student, at any time during or after the time the defendant and victim were present together in the same school, but before the victim ceases to be a student, the defendant is guilty of a Class G felony, except when the defendant is lawfully married to the student. The term "same school" means a school at which the student is enrolled and the defendant is employed, assigned, or volunteers.

(b) A defendant who is school personnel, other than a teacher, school administrator, student teacher, school safety officer, or coach, and is less than four years older than the victim and engages in vaginal intercourse or a sexual act with a victim who is a student, is guilty of a Class I felony.

(c) This section shall apply unless the conduct is covered under some other provision of law providing for greater punishment.

(d) Consent is not a defense to a charge under this section.

(e) For purposes of this section, the terms "school", "school personnel", and "student" shall have the same meaning as in G.S. 14-202.4(d). For purposes of this section, the term "school safety officer" shall include a school resource officer or any other person who is regularly present in a school for the purpose of promoting and maintaining safe and orderly schools.

History.
1979, c. 682, s. 1; 1979, 2nd Sess., c. 1316, s. 9; 1981, c. 63; c. 179, s. 14; 1993, c. 539, s. 1132; 1994, Ex. Sess., c. 24, s. 14(c); 1999-300, s. 2; 2003-98, s. 1; 2015-44, s. 2; 2015-181, s. 14(a), (b)

§ 14-27.33. Sexual battery

(a) A person is guilty of sexual battery if the person, for the purpose of sexual arousal, sexual gratification, or sexual abuse, engages in sexual contact with another person:

(1) By force and against the will of the other person; or

(2) Who has a mental disability or who is mentally incapacitated or physically helpless, and the person performing the act knows or should reasonably know that the other person has a mental disability or is mentally incapacitated or physically helpless.

(b) Any person who commits the offense defined in this section is guilty of a Class A1 misdemeanor.

History.
2003-252, s. 2; 2015-181, s. 15; 2018-47, s. 4(d)

§ 14-27.33A. Sexual contact or penetration under pretext of medical treatment

(a) **Definitions.** -- The following definitions apply in this section:

(1) **Incapacitated.** -- A patient's incapability of appraising the nature of a medical treatment, either because the patient is unconscious or under the influence of an impairing substance, including, but not limited to, alcohol, anesthetics, controlled substances listed under Chapter 90 of the General Statutes, or any other drug or psychoactive substance capable of impairing a person's physical or mental faculties.

(2) **Medical treatment.** -- Includes an examination or a procedure.

(3) **Patient.** -- A person who has undergone or is seeking to undergo medical treatment.

(4) **Sexual contact.** -- The intentional touching of a person's intimate parts or the intentional touching of the clothing covering the immediate area of the person's intimate parts, if that intentional touching can reasonably be construed as being for the purpose of sexual arousal or gratification, done for a sexual purpose, or done in a sexual manner.

(5) **Sexual penetration.** -- Sexual intercourse, cunnilingus, fellatio, anal

Chapter 14

intercourse, or any other intrusion, however slight, of any part of a person's body or of any object into the genital or anal openings of another person's body, regardless of whether semen is emitted, if that intrusion can reasonably be construed as being for the purpose of sexual arousal or gratification, done for a sexual purpose, or done in a sexual manner.

(b) **Offense; Penalty. --** Unless the conduct is covered under some other provision of law providing greater punishment, a person who undertakes medical treatment of a patient is guilty of a Class C felony if the person does any of the following in the course of that medical treatment:

(1) Represents to the patient that sexual contact between the person and the patient is necessary or will be beneficial to the patient's health and induces the patient to engage in sexual contact with the person by means of the representation.

(2) Represents to the patient that sexual penetration between the person and the patient is necessary or will be beneficial to the patient's health and induces the patient to engage in sexual penetration with the person by means of the representation.

(3) Engages in sexual contact with the patient while the patient is incapacitated.

(4) Engages in sexual penetration with the patient while the patient is incapacitated.

(c) This section does not prohibit a person from being charged with, convicted of, or punished for any other violation of law that is committed by that person while violating this section.

(d) The court may order a term of imprisonment imposed for a violation of this section to be served consecutively to a term of imprisonment imposed for any other crime, including any other violation of law arising out of the same transaction as the violation of this section.

History.
2019-191, s. 43(a)

§ 14-27.34. No defense that victim is spouse of person committing act

A person may be prosecuted under this Article whether or not the victim is the person's legal spouse at the time of the commission of the alleged rape or sexual offense.

History.
1979, c. 682, s. 1; 1987, c. 742; 1993, c. 274, s. 1; 2015-181, s. 15

§ 14-27.35. No presumption as to incapacity

In prosecutions under this Article, there shall be no presumption that any person under the age of 14 years is physically incapable of committing a sex offense of any degree or physically incapable of committing rape, or that a male child under the age of 14 years is incapable of engaging in sexual intercourse.

History.
1979, c. 682, s. 1; 2015-181, s. 15

§ 14-27.36. Evidence required in prosecutions under this Article

It shall not be necessary upon the trial of any indictment for an offense under this Article where the sex act alleged is vaginal intercourse or anal intercourse to prove the actual emission of semen in order to constitute the offense; but the offense shall be completed upon proof of penetration only. Penetration, however slight, is vaginal intercourse or anal intercourse.

History.
1979, c. 682, s. 1; 2015-181, s. 15

ARTICLE 8
ASSAULTS

§ 14-28. Malicious castration

If any person, of malice aforethought, shall unlawfully castrate any other person, or cut off, maim or disfigure any of the privy members of any person, with intent to murder, maim, disfigure, disable or render impotent such person, the person so offending shall be punished as a Class C felon.

History.
1831, c. 40, s. 1; R.C., c. 34, s. 4; 1868-9, c. 167, s. 6; Code, s. 999; Rev., s. 3627; C.S., s. 4210; 1979, c. 760, s. 5; 1979, 2nd Sess., c. 1316, s. 47; 1981, c. 63, s. 1; c. 179, s. 14; 1993, c. 539, s. 1133; 1994, Ex. Sess., c. 24, s. 14(c)

§ 14-28.1. Female genital mutilation of a child

(a) **Legislative Intent. --** The General Assembly finds that female genital mutilation is a crime that causes a long-lasting impact on the victim's quality of life and has been recognized internationally as a violation of the human rights of girls and women. The practice is mostly carried out on girls under the age of 15 years old. The General Assembly also recognizes that the practice includes any procedure that intentionally alters or injures the female genital organs for nonmedical reasons. These procedures can cause severe pain, excessive bleeding, urinary problems, and death. Therefore, the General Assembly enacts this law to protect these vulnerable victims.

(b) **Mutilation.** -- A person who knowingly and unlawfully circumcises, excises, or infibulates the whole or any part of the labia majora, labia minora, or clitoris of a child less than 18 years of age is guilty of a Class C felony.

(c) **Consent to Mutilation.** -- A parent, or a person providing care to or supervision of a child less than 18 years of age, who consents to or permits the unlawful circumcision, excision, or infibulation, in whole or in any part, of the labia majora, labia minora, or clitoris of the child, is guilty of a Class C felony.

(d) **Removal for Mutilation.** -- A parent, or a person providing care to or supervision of a child less than 18 years of age, who knowingly removes or permits the removal of the child from the State for the purpose of having the child's labia majora, labia minora, or clitoris circumcised, excised, or infibulated, is guilty of a Class C felony.

(e) **Exceptions.** -- A surgical operation is not a violation of this section if the operation meets either of the following requirements:

(1) The operation is necessary to the health of the person on whom it is performed and is performed by a person licensed in the State as a medical practitioner.

(2) The operation is performed on a person in labor who has just given birth and is performed for medical purposes connected with that labor or birth by a person licensed in this State as a medical practitioner or certified nurse midwife, or a person in training to become licensed as a medical practitioner or certified nurse midwife.

(f) **No Defense.** -- It is not a defense to prosecution under this section that the person on whom the circumcision, excision, or infibulation is performed, or any other person, believes that the circumcision, excision, or infibulation is required as a matter of custom or ritual, or that the person on whom the circumcision, excision, or infibulation is performed consented to the circumcision, excision, or infibulation.

History.
2019-183, s. 1

§ 14-29. Castration or other maiming without malice aforethought

If any person shall, on purpose and unlawfully, but without malice aforethought, cut, or slit the nose, bite or cut off the nose, or a lip or an ear, or disable any limb or member of any other person, or castrate any other person, or cut off, maim or disfigure any of the privy members of any other person, with intent to kill, maim, disfigure, disable or render impotent such person, the person so offending shall be punished as a Class E felon.

History.
1754, c. 56, P.R.; 1791, c. 339, ss. 2, 3, P.R.; 1831, c. 40, s. 2; R.C., c. 34, s. 47; Code, s. 1000; Rev., s. 3626; C.S., s. 4211; 1979, c. 760, s. 5; 1979, 2nd Sess., c. 1316, s. 47; 1981, c. 63, s. 1; c. 179, s. 14; 1993, c. 539, s. 1134; 1994, Ex. Sess., c. 24, s. 14(c)

§ 14-30. Malicious maiming

If any person shall, of malice aforethought, unlawfully cut out or disable the tongue or put out an eye of any other person, with intent to murder, maim or disfigure, the person so offending, his counselors, abettors and aiders, knowing of and privy to the offense, shall be punished as a Class C felon.

History.
22 and 23 Car. II, c. 1 (Coventry Act); 1754, c. 56, P.R.; 1791, c. 339, s. 1, P.R.; 1831, c. 12; R.C., c. 34, s. 14; Code, s. 1080; Rev., s. 3636; C.S., s. 4212; 1979, c. 760, s. 5; 1979, 2nd Sess., c. 1316, s. 47; 1981, c. 63, s. 1; c. 179, s. 14; 1993, c. 539, s. 1135; 1994, Ex. Sess., c. 24, s. 14(c)

§ 14-30.1. Malicious throwing of corrosive acid or alkali

If any person shall, of malice aforethought, knowingly and willfully throw or cause to be thrown upon another person any corrosive acid or alkali with intent to murder, maim or disfigure and inflicts serious injury not resulting in death, he shall be punished as a Class E felon.

History.
1963, c. 354; 1979, c. 760, s. 5; 1979, 2nd Sess., c. 1316, s. 47; 1981, c. 63, s. 1; c. 179, s. 14; 1993, c. 539, s. 1136; 1994, Ex. Sess., c. 24, s. 14(c)

§ 14-31. Maliciously assaulting in a secret manner

If any person shall in a secret manner maliciously commit an assault and battery with any deadly weapon upon another by waylaying or otherwise, with intent to kill such other person, notwithstanding the person so assaulted may have been conscious of the presence of his adversary, he shall be punished as a Class E felon.

History.
1887, c. 32; Rev., s. 3621; 1919, c. 25; C.S., s. 4213; 1969, c. 602, s. 1; 1979, c. 760, s. 5; 1979, 2nd Sess.,

Chapter 14

c. 1316, s. 47; 1981, c. 63, s. 1; c. 179, s. 14; 1993, c. 539, s. 1137; 1994, Ex. Sess., c. 24, s. 14(c)

§ 14-32. Felonious assault with deadly weapon with intent to kill or inflicting serious injury; punishments

(a) Any person who assaults another person with a deadly weapon with intent to kill and inflicts serious injury shall be punished as a Class C felon.

(b) Any person who assaults another person with a deadly weapon and inflicts serious injury shall be punished as a Class E felon.

(c) Any person who assaults another person with a deadly weapon with intent to kill shall be punished as a Class E felon.

History.
1919, c. 101; C.S., s. 4214; 1931, c. 145, s. 30; 1969, c. 602, s. 2; 1971, c. 765, s. 1; c. 1093, s. 12; 1973, c. 229, ss. 1-3; 1979, c. 760, s. 5; 1979, 2nd Sess., c. 1316, s. 47; 1981, c. 63, s. 1; c. 179, s. 14; 1993, c. 539, s. 1138; 1994, Ex. Sess., c. 24, s. 14(c)

§ 14-32.1. Assaults on individuals with a disability; punishments

(a) For purposes of this section, an "individual with a disability" is an individual who has one or more of the following that would substantially impair the ability to defend oneself:

(1) A physical or mental disability, such as a decreased use of arms or legs, blindness, deafness, intellectual disability, or mental illness.

(2) An infirmity.

(b) through (d) Repealed by Session Laws 1993 (Reg. Sess., 1994), c. 767, s. 31, effective October 1, 1994.

(e) Unless the conduct is covered under some other provision of law providing greater punishment, any person who commits any aggravated assault or assault and battery on an individual with a disability is guilty of a Class F felony. A person commits an aggravated assault or assault and battery upon an individual with a disability if, in the course of the assault or assault and battery, that person does any of the following:

(1) Uses a deadly weapon or other means of force likely to inflict serious injury or serious damage to an individual with a disability.

(2) Inflicts serious injury or serious damage to an individual with a disability.

(3) Intends to kill an individual with a disability.

(f) Any person who commits a simple assault or battery upon an individual with a disability is guilty of a Class A1 misdemeanor.

History.
1981, c. 780, s. 1; 1993, c. 539, ss. 15, 1139; 1994, Ex. Sess., c. 24, s. 14(c); 1993 (Reg. Sess., 1994), c. 767, s. 31; 2006-179, s. 1; 2018-47, s. 4(m)

§ 14-32.2. Patient abuse and neglect; punishments; definitions

(a) It is unlawful for any person to physically abuse a patient of a health care facility or a resident of a residential care facility, when the abuse results in death or bodily injury.

(b) Unless the conduct is prohibited by some other provision of law providing for greater punishment, a violation of subsection (a) of this section is the following:

(1) A Class C felony where intentional conduct proximately causes the death of the patient or resident.

(2) A Class E felony where culpably negligent conduct proximately causes the death of the patient or resident.

(3) A Class F felony where such conduct is willful or culpably negligent and proximately causes serious bodily injury to the patient or resident.

(4) A Class H felony where such conduct evinces a pattern of conduct and the conduct is willful or culpably negligent and proximately causes bodily injury to a patient or resident.

(c) through (e1) Repealed by Session Laws 2019-76, s. 12(a), effective January 1, 2020, and applicable to offenses committed on or after that date.

(f) Any defense which may arise under G.S. 90-321(h) or G.S. 90-322(d) pursuant to compliance with Article 23 of Chapter 90 of the General Statutes is fully applicable to any prosecution initiated under this section.

(g) Criminal process for a violation of this section may be issued only upon the request of a district attorney.

(h) The provisions of this section do not supersede any other applicable statutory or common law offenses.

(i) The following definitions apply in this section:

(1) **Abuse.** -- The willful or culpably negligent infliction of physical injury or the willful or culpably negligent violation of any law designed for the health or welfare of a patient or resident.

(2) **Culpably negligent.** -- Conduct of a willful, gross, and flagrant character, evincing reckless disregard of human life.

(3) **Health care facility.** -- Includes hospitals, skilled nursing facilities, intermediate care facilities, intermediate care facilities for individuals with intellectual disabilities, psychiatric facilities, rehabilitation facilities, kidney disease treatment

centers, home health agencies, ambulatory surgical facilities, and any other health care related facility whether publicly or privately owned.

(4) **Person.** -- Includes any individual, association, corporation, partnership, or other entity.

(5) **Residential care facility.** -- Includes adult care homes and any other residential care related facility whether publicly or privately owned.

History.
1987, c. 527, s. 1; 1993, c. 539, s. 1140; 1994, Ex. Sess., c. 24, s. 14(c); 1995, c. 535, s. 1; 1995 (Reg. Sess., 1996), c. 742, ss. 7, 8; 1999-334, s. 3.15; 1999-456, s. 61(b); 2007-188, s. 1; 2019-76, s. 12(a)

§ 14-32.3. Domestic abuse, neglect, and exploitation of disabled or elder adults

(a) **Abuse.** -- A person is guilty of abuse if that person is a caretaker of a disabled or elder adult who is residing in a domestic setting and, with malice aforethought, knowingly and willfully: (i) assaults, (ii) fails to provide medical or hygienic care, or (iii) confines or restrains the disabled or elder adult in a place or under a condition that is cruel or unsafe, and as a result of the act or failure to act the disabled or elder adult suffers mental or physical injury.

If the disabled or elder adult suffers serious injury from the abuse, the caretaker is guilty of a Class F felony. If the disabled or elder adult suffers injury from the abuse, the caretaker is guilty of a Class H felony.

A person is not guilty of an offense under this subsection if the act or failure to act is in accordance with G.S. 90-321 or G.S. 90-322.

(b) **Neglect.** -- A person is guilty of neglect if that person is a caretaker of a disabled or elder adult who is residing in a domestic setting and, wantonly, recklessly, or with gross carelessness: (i) fails to provide medical or hygienic care, or (ii) confines or restrains the disabled or elder adult in a place or under a condition that is unsafe, and as a result of the act or failure to act the disabled or elder adult suffers mental or physical injury.

If the disabled or elder adult suffers serious injury from the neglect, the caretaker is guilty of a Class G felony. If the disabled or elder adult suffers injury from the neglect, the caretaker is guilty of a Class I felony.

A person is not guilty of an offense under this subsection if the act or failure to act is in accordance with G.S. 90-321 or G.S. 90-322.

(c) Repealed by Session Laws 2005-272, s. 1, effective December 1, 2005, and applicable to offenses committed on or after that date.

(d) **Definitions.** -- The following definitions apply in this section:

(1) **Caretaker.** -- A person who has the responsibility for the care of a disabled or elder adult as a result of family relationship or who has assumed the responsibility for the care of a disabled or elder adult voluntarily or by contract.

(2) **Disabled adult.** -- A person 18 years of age or older or a lawfully emancipated minor who is present in the State of North Carolina and who is physically or mentally incapacitated as defined in G.S. 108A-101(d).

(3) **Domestic setting.** -- Residence in any residential setting except for a health care facility or residential care facility as these terms are defined in G.S. 14-32.2.

(4) **Elder adult.** -- A person 60 years of age or older who is not able to provide for the social, medical, psychiatric, psychological, financial, or legal services necessary to safeguard the person's rights and resources and to maintain the person's physical and mental well-being.

History.
1995, c. 246, s. 1; 1995 (Reg. Sess., 1996), c. 742, s. 9; 2005-272, s. 1

§ 14-32.4. Assault inflicting serious bodily injury; strangulation; penalties.

(a) Unless the conduct is covered under some other provision of law providing greater punishment, any person who assaults another person and inflicts serious bodily injury is guilty of a Class F felony. "Serious bodily injury" is defined as bodily injury that creates a substantial risk of death, or that causes serious permanent disfigurement, coma, a permanent or protracted condition that causes extreme pain, or permanent or protracted loss or impairment of the function of any bodily member or organ, or that results in prolonged hospitalization.

(b) Unless the conduct is covered under some other provision of law providing greater punishment, any person who assaults another person and inflicts physical injury by strangulation is guilty of a Class H felony.

History.
1996, 2nd Ex. Sess., c. 18, s. 20.13(a); 2004-186, s. 9.1

§ 14-33. Misdemeanor assaults, batteries, and affrays, simple and aggravated; punishments

(a) Any person who commits a simple assault or a simple assault and battery or participates in a simple affray is guilty of a Class 2 misdemeanor.

(b) Unless his conduct is covered under some other provision of law providing greater punishment, any person who commits any assault, assault and battery, or affray is guilty of a Class 1 misdemeanor if, in the course of the assault, assault and battery, or affray, he:

(1) through (3) Repealed by Session Laws 1995, c. 507, s. 19.5(b);

(4) through (7) Repealed by Session Laws 1991, c. 525, s. 1;

(8) Repealed by Session Laws 1995, c. 507, s. 19.5(b);

(9) Commits an assault and battery against a sports official when the sports official is discharging or attempting to discharge official duties at a sports event, or immediately after the sports event at which the sports official discharged official duties. A "sports official" is a person at a sports event who enforces the rules of the event, such as an umpire or referee, or a person who supervises the participants, such as a coach. A "sports event" includes any interscholastic or intramural athletic activity in a primary, middle, junior high, or high school, college, or university, any organized athletic activity sponsored by a community, business, or nonprofit organization, any athletic activity that is a professional or semiprofessional event, and any other organized athletic activity in the State.

(c) Unless the conduct is covered under some other provision of law providing greater punishment, any person who commits any assault, assault and battery, or affray is guilty of a Class A1 misdemeanor if, in the course of the assault, assault and battery, or affray, he or she:

(1) Inflicts serious injury upon another person or uses a deadly weapon;

(2) Assaults a female, he being a male person at least 18 years of age;

(3) Assaults a child under the age of 12 years;

(4) Assaults an officer or employee of the State or any political subdivision of the State, when the officer or employee is discharging or attempting to discharge his official duties;

(5) Repealed by Session Laws 1999-105, s. 1, effective December 1, 1999; or

(6) Assaults a school employee or school volunteer when the employee or volunteer is discharging or attempting to discharge his or her duties as an employee or volunteer, or assaults a school employee or school volunteer as a result of the discharge or attempt to discharge that individual's duties as a school employee or school volunteer. For purposes of this subdivision, the following definitions shall apply:

a. "Duties" means:

1. All activities on school property;

2. All activities, wherever occurring, during a school authorized event or the accompanying of students to or from that event; and

3. All activities relating to the operation of school transportation.

b. "Employee" or "volunteer" means:

1. An employee of a local board of education; or a charter school authorized under G.S. 115C-218.5, or a nonpublic school which has filed intent to operate under Part 1 or Part 2 of Article 39 of Chapter 115C of the General Statutes;

2. An independent contractor or an employee of an independent contractor of a local board of education, charter school authorized under G.S. 115C-218.5, or a nonpublic school which has filed intent to operate under Part 1 or Part 2 of Article 39 of Chapter 115C of the General Statutes, if the independent contractor carries out duties customarily performed by employees of the school; and

3. An adult who volunteers his or her services or presence at any school activity and is under the supervision of an individual listed in sub-sub-subdivision 1. or 2. of this sub-subdivision.

(7) Assaults a public transit operator, including a public employee or a private contractor employed as a public transit operator, when the operator is discharging or attempting to discharge his or her duties.

(8) Assaults a company police officer certified pursuant to the provisions of Chapter 74E of the General Statutes or a campus police officer certified pursuant to the provisions of Chapter 74G, Article 1 of Chapter 17C, or Chapter 116 of the General Statutes in the performance of that person's duties.

(9) Assaults a transportation network company (TNC) driver providing a transportation network company (TNC) service. For the purposes of this subdivision, the definitions for "TNC driver" and "TNC service" as defined in G.S. 20-280.1 shall apply.

(c1) No school personnel as defined in G.S. 14-33(c)(6) who takes reasonable actions in good faith to end a fight or altercation between students shall incur any civil or criminal liability as the result of those actions.

(d) Any person who, in the course of an assault, assault and battery, or affray, inflicts serious injury upon another person, or uses a deadly weapon, in violation of subdivision (c)(1) of this section, on a person with whom the person has a personal relationship, and in the presence of a minor, is guilty of a Class A1 misdemeanor. A person convicted under this subsection, who is sentenced to a community punishment, shall be placed on supervised probation in addition to any other punishment imposed by the court.

A person committing a second or subsequent violation of this subsection shall be sentenced to an active punishment of no less than 30 days in addition to any other punishment imposed by the court.

The following definitions apply to this subsection:

(1) "Personal relationship" is as defined in G.S. 50B-1(b).

(2) "In the presence of a minor" means that the minor was in a position to see or hear the assault.

(3) "Minor" is any person under the age of 18 years who is residing with or is under the care and supervision of, and who has a personal relationship with, the person assaulted or the person committing the assault.

History.
1870-1, c. 43, s. 2; 1873-4, c. 176, s. 6; 1879, c. 92, ss. 2, 6; Code, s. 987; Rev., s. 3620, 1911, c. 193; C.S., s. 4215; 1933, c. 189; 1949, c. 298; 1969, c. 618, s. 1; 1971, c. 765, s. 2; 1973, c. 229, s. 4; c. 1413; 1979, cc. 524, 656; 1981, c. 180; 1983, c. 175, ss. 6, 10; c. 720, s. 4; 1985, c. 321; 1991, c. 525, s. 1; 1993, c. 286, s. 1; c. 539, s. 16; 1994, Ex. Sess., c. 14, s. 3; c. 24, s. 14(c); 1993 (Reg. Sess., 1994), c. 687, s. 1; 1995, c. 352, s. 1; 1995, c. 507, s. 19.5(b); 1999-105, s. 1; 2003-409, s. 1; 2004-26, s. 1; 2004-199, s. 7; 2005-231, s. 6.2; 2012-149, s. 1; 2014-101, s. 7; 2015-62, s. 4(b); 2019-194, s. 3.5(a)

§ 14-33.1. Evidence of former threats upon plea of self-defense

In any case of assault, assault and battery, or affray in which the plea of the defendant is self-defense, evidence of former threats against the defendant by the person alleged to have been assaulted by him, if such threats shall have been communicated to the defendant before the altercation, shall be competent as bearing upon the reasonableness of the claim of apprehension by the defendant of bodily harm, and also as bearing upon the amount of force which reasonably appeared necessary to the defendant, under the circumstances, to repel his assailant.

History.
1969, c. 618, s. 2

§ 14-33.2. Habitual misdemeanor assault

A person commits the offense of habitual misdemeanor assault if that person violates any of the provisions of G.S. 14-33 and causes physical injury, or G.S. 14-34, and has two or more prior

convictions for either misdemeanor or felony assault, with the earlier of the two prior convictions occurring no more than 15 years prior to the date of the current violation. A conviction under this section shall not be used as a prior conviction for any other habitual offense statute. A person convicted of violating this section is guilty of a Class H felony.

History.
1995, c. 507, s. 19.5(c); 2004-186, s. 10.1

§ 14-34. Assaulting by pointing gun

If any person shall point any gun or pistol at any person, either in fun or otherwise, whether such gun or pistol be loaded or not loaded, he shall be guilty of a Class A1 misdemeanor.

History.
1889, c. 527; Rev., s. 3622; C.S., s. 4216; 1969, c. 618, s. 21/2; 1993, c. 539, s. 17; 1994, Ex. Sess., c. 24, s. 14(c); 1995, c. 507, s. 19.5(d)

§ 14-34.1. Discharging certain barreled weapons or a firearm into occupied property

(a) Any person who willfully or wantonly discharges or attempts to discharge any firearm or barreled weapon capable of discharging shot, bullets, pellets, or other missiles at a muzzle velocity of at least 600 feet per second into any building, structure, vehicle, aircraft, watercraft, or other conveyance, device, equipment, erection, or enclosure while it is occupied is guilty of a Class E felony.

(b) A person who willfully or wantonly discharges a weapon described in subsection (a) of this section into an occupied dwelling or into any occupied vehicle, aircraft, watercraft, or other conveyance that is in operation is guilty of a Class D felony.

(c) If a person violates this section and the violation results in serious bodily injury to any person, the person is guilty of a Class C felony.

History.
1969, c. 341; c. 869, s. 7; 1979, c. 760, s. 5; 1979, 2nd Sess., c. 1316, s. 47; 1981, c. 63, s. 1; c. 179, s. 14; c. 755; 1993, c. 539, s. 1141; 1994, Ex. Sess., c. 24, s. 14(c); 2005-461, s. 1

§ 14-34.2. Assault with a firearm or other deadly weapon upon governmental officers or employees, company police officers, or campus police officers

Unless a person's conduct is covered under some other provision of law providing greater punishment, any person who commits an assault with a firearm or any other deadly weapon upon an officer or employee of the State or of any political subdivision of the State, a company police officer certified pursuant to the provisions of Chapter 74E of the General Statutes, or a campus police officer certified pursuant to the provisions of Chapter 74G, Article 1 of Chapter 17C or Chapter 116 of the General Statutes, in the performance of his duties shall be guilty of a Class F felony.

History.
1969, c. 1134; 1977, c. 829; 1979, c. 760, s. 5; 1979, 2nd Sess., c. 1316, s. 47; 1981, c. 63, s. 1; c. 179, s. 14; 1981, c. 535, s. 1; 1991, c. 525, s. 2; 1993, c. 539, s. 1142; 1994, Ex. Sess., c. 24, s. 14(c); 1993 (Reg. Sess., 1994), c. 687, s. 2; 1995, c. 507, s. 19.5(i); 2005-231, s. 6.1

§ 14-34.3. Manufacture, sale, purchase, or possession of teflon-coated types of bullets prohibited

(a) It is unlawful for any person to import, manufacture, possess, store, transport, sell, offer to sell, purchase, offer to purchase, deliver or give to another, or acquire any teflon-coated bullet.

(b) This section does not apply to:

(1) Officers and enlisted personnel of the Armed Forces of the United States when in discharge of their official duties as such and acting under orders requiring them to carry arms or weapons, civil officers of the United States while in the discharge of their official duties, officers and soldiers of the militia when called into actual service, officers of the State, or of any county, city or town, charged with the execution of the laws of the State, when acting in the discharge of their official duties;

(2) Importers, manufacturers, and dealers validly licensed under the laws of the United States or the State of North Carolina who possess for the purpose of sale to authorized law-enforcement agencies only;

(3) Inventors, designers, ordinance consultants and researchers, chemists, physicists, and other persons employed by or under contract with a manufacturing company engaged in making or doing research designed to enlarge knowledge or to facilitate the creation, development, or manufacture of more effective police-type body armor.

(c) Any person who violates any provision of this section is guilty of a Class 1 misdemeanor.

History.
1981 (Reg. Sess., 1982), c. 1272, s. 1; 1993, c. 539, s. 18; 1994, Ex. Sess., c. 24, s. 14(c); 1999-456, s. 33(a); 2011-183, s. 8

§ 14-34.4. Adulterated or misbranded food, drugs, or cosmetics; intent to cause serious injury or death; intent to extort

(a) Any person who with the intent to cause serious injury or death manufactures, sells, delivers, offers, or holds for sale, any food, drug, or cosmetic that is adulterated or misbranded, or adulterates or misbrands any food, drug, or cosmetic, in violation of G.S. 106-122, is guilty of a Class C felony.

(b) Any person who with the intent to wrongfully obtain, directly or indirectly, anything of value or any acquittance, advantage, or immunity communicates to another that he has violated, or intends to violate, subsection (a) of this section, is guilty of a Class C felony.

History.
1987, c. 313, s. 1

§ 14-34.5. Assault with a firearm on a law enforcement, probation, or parole officer, or on a member of the North Carolina National Guard, or on a person employed at a State or local detention facility

(a) Any person who commits an assault with a firearm upon a law enforcement officer, probation officer, or parole officer while the officer is in the performance of his or her duties is guilty of a Class D felony.

(a1) Any person who commits an assault with a firearm upon a member of the North Carolina National Guard while the member is in the performance of his or her duties is guilty of a Class E felony.

(b) Anyone who commits an assault with a firearm upon a person who is employed at a detention facility operated under the jurisdiction of the State or a local government while the employee is in the performance of the employee's duties is guilty of a Class D felony.

History.
1995, c. 507, s. 19.5(j); 1995 (Reg. Sess., 1996), c. 742, s. 10; 1997-443, s. 19.25(gg); 2015-74, s. 2; 2019-116, s. 1; 2019-228, s. 1(a)

§ 14-34.6. Assault or affray on a firefighter, an emergency medical technician, medical responder, and hospital personnel

(a) A person is guilty of a Class I felony if the person commits an assault or affray causing physical injury on any of the following persons who are discharging or attempting to discharge their official duties:

(1) An emergency medical technician or other emergency health care provider.

(2) A medical responder.

(3) Hospital personnel and licensed healthcare providers who are providing or attempting to provide health care services to a patient.

(4) Repealed by Session Laws 2011-356, s. 2, effective December 1, 2011, and applicable to offenses committed on or after that date.

(5) A firefighter.

(6) Hospital security personnel.

(b) Unless a person's conduct is covered under some other provision of law providing greater punishment, a person is guilty of a Class G felony if the person violates subsection (a) of this section and (i) inflicts serious bodily injury or (ii) uses a deadly weapon other than a firearm.

(c) Unless a person's conduct is covered under some other provision of law providing greater punishment, a person is guilty of a Class E felony if the person violates subsection (a) of this section and uses a firearm.

History.
1995, c. 507, s. 19.6(a); 1996, 2nd Ex. Sess., c. 18, s. 20.14B(b); 1997-9, s. 2; 1997-443, s. 11A.129A; 1998-217, s. 1; 2011-356, s. 2; 2015-97, s. 1; 2017-57, s. 16B.3(a); 2019-228, s. 1(b)

§ 14-34.7. Certain assaults on a law enforcement, probation, or parole officer, or on a member of the North Carolina National Guard, or on a person employed at a State or local detention facility; penalty

(a) Unless covered under some other provision of law providing greater punishment, a person is guilty of a Class F felony if the person assaults a law enforcement officer, probation officer, or parole officer while the officer is discharging or attempting to discharge his or her official duties and inflicts serious bodily injury on the officer.

(a1) Unless covered under some other provision of law providing greater punishment, a person is guilty of a Class F felony if the person assaults a member of the North Carolina National Guard while he or she is discharging or attempting to discharge his or her official duties and inflicts serious bodily injury on the member.

(b) Unless covered under some other provision of law providing greater punishment, a person is guilty of a Class F felony if the person assaults a person who is employed at a detention facility operated under the jurisdiction of the State or a local government while the employee is in the performance of the employee's duties and inflicts serious bodily injury on the employee.

(c) Unless covered under some other provision of law providing greater punishment, a person is guilty of a Class I felony if the person does any of the following:

(1) Assaults a law enforcement officer, probation officer, or parole officer while the officer is discharging or attempting to discharge his or her official duties and inflicts physical injury on the officer.

(2) Assaults a person who is employed at a detention facility operated under the jurisdiction of the State or a local government while the employee is in the performance of the employee's duties and inflicts physical injury on the employee.

(3) Assaults a member of the North Carolina National Guard while he or she is discharging or attempting to discharge his or her official duties and inflicts physical injury on the member.

For the purposes of this subsection, "physical injury" includes cuts, scrapes, bruises, or other physical injury which does not constitute serious injury.

History.
1996, 2nd Ex. Sess., c. 18, s. 20.14B(a); 1997-443, s. 19.25(hh); 2001-487, s. 41; 2011-356, s. 1; 2015-74, s. 1

§ 14-34.8. Criminal use of laser device

(a) For purposes of this section, the term "laser" means light amplification by stimulated emission of radiation.

(b) It is unlawful intentionally to point a laser device at a law enforcement officer, or at the head or face of another person, while the device is emitting a laser beam.

(c) A violation of this section is an infraction.

(d) This section does not apply to a law enforcement officer who uses a laser device in discharging or attempting to discharge the officer's official duties. This section does not apply to a health care professional who uses a laser device in providing services within the scope of practice of that professional nor to any other person who is licensed or authorized by law to use a laser device or uses it in the performance of the person's official duties.

(e) This section does not apply to laser tag, paintball guns, and other similar games and devices using light emitting diode (LED) technology.

History.
1999-401, s. 1

§ 14-34.9. Discharging a firearm from within an enclosure

Unless covered under some other provision of law providing greater punishment, any person who willfully or wantonly discharges or attempts to discharge a firearm, as a part of criminal gang activity, from within any building, structure, motor vehicle, or other conveyance, erection, or enclosure toward a person or persons not within that enclosure shall be punished as a Class E felon.

History.
2008-214, s. 2; 2017-194, s. 6

§ 14-34.10. Discharge firearm within enclosure to incite fear

Unless covered under some other provision of law providing greater punishment, any person who willfully or wantonly discharges or attempts to discharge a firearm within any occupied building, structure, motor vehicle, or other conveyance, erection, or enclosure with the intent to incite fear in another shall be punished as a Class F felon.

History.
2013-144, s. 1

ARTICLE 9
HAZING

§ 14-35. Hazing; definition and punishment

It is unlawful for any student in attendance at any university, college, or school in this State to engage in hazing, or to aid or abet any other student in the commission of this offense. For the purposes of this section hazing is defined as follows: "to subject another student to physical injury as part of an initiation, or as a prerequisite to membership, into any organized school group, including any society, athletic team, fraternity or sorority, or other similar group." Any violation of this section shall constitute a Class 2 misdemeanor.

History.
1913, c. 169, ss. 1, 2, 3, 4; C.S., s. 4217; 1969, c. 1224, s. 1; 1993, c. 539, s. 19; 1994, Ex. Sess., c. 24, s. 14(c); 2003-299, s. 1

N.C. Gen. Stat. § 14-36

Repealed by Session Laws 2003-299, § 2, effective December 1, 2003, and applicable to offenses committed on or after that date.

N.C. Gen. Stat. § 14-37

Repealed by Session Laws 1979, c. 7, s. 1.

§ 14-38. Witnesses in hazing trials; no indictment to be founded on self-criminating testimony

In all trials for the offense of hazing any student or other person subpoenaed as a witness in behalf of the State shall be required to testify if called upon to do so: Provided, however, that no student or other person so testifying shall be amenable or subject to indictment on account of, or by reason of, such testimony.

History.
1913, c. 169, s. 8; C.S., s. 4220

ARTICLE 10
KIDNAPPING AND ABDUCTION

§ 14-39. Kidnapping

(a) Any person who shall unlawfully confine, restrain, or remove from one place to another, any other person 16 years of age or over without the consent of such person, or any other person under the age of 16 years without the consent of a parent or legal custodian of such person, shall be guilty of kidnapping if such confinement, restraint or removal is for the purpose of:

(1) Holding such other person for a ransom or as a hostage or using such other person as a shield; or

(2) Facilitating the commission of any felony or facilitating flight of any person following the commission of a felony; or

(3) Doing serious bodily harm to or terrorizing the person so confined, restrained or removed or any other person; or

(4) Holding such other person in involuntary servitude in violation of G.S. 14-43.12.

(5) Trafficking another person with the intent that the other person be held in involuntary servitude or sexual servitude in violation of G.S. 14-43.11.

(6) Subjecting or maintaining such other person for sexual servitude in violation of G.S. 14-43.13.

(b) There shall be two degrees of kidnapping as defined by subsection (a). If the person kidnapped either was not released by the defendant in a safe place or had been seriously injured or sexually assaulted, the offense is kidnapping in the first degree and is punishable as a Class C felony. If the person kidnapped was released in a safe place by the defendant and had not been seriously injured or sexually assaulted, the offense is kidnapping in the second degree and is punishable as a Class E felony.

(c) Any firm or corporation convicted of kidnapping shall be punished by a fine of not less than five thousand dollars ($ 5,000) nor more than one hundred thousand dollars ($ 100,000), and its charter and right to do business in the State of North Carolina shall be forfeited.

History.

1933, c. 542; 1975, c. 843, s. 1; 1979, c. 760, s. 5; 1979, 2nd Sess., c. 1316, s. 47; 1981, c. 63, s. 1; c. 179, s. 14; 1983, c. 746, s. 2; 1993, c. 539, s. 1143; 1994, Ex. Sess., c. 24, s. 14(c); 1995, c. 509, s. 8; 2006-247, s. 20(c)

§ 14-40. Enticing minors out of the State for the purpose of employment

If any person shall employ and carry beyond the limits of this State any minor, or shall induce any minor to go beyond the limits of this State, for the purpose of employment without the consent in writing, duly authenticated, of the parent, guardian or other person having authority over such minor, he shall be guilty of a Class 2 misdemeanor. The fact of the employment and going out of the State of the minor, or of the going out of the State by the minor, at the solicitation of the person for the purpose of employment, shall be prima facie evidence of knowledge that the person employed or solicited to go beyond the limits of the State is a minor.

History.

1891, c. 45; Rev., s. 3630; C.S., s. 4222; 1969, c. 1224, s. 4; 1993, c. 539, s. 21; 1994, Ex. Sess., c. 24, s. 14(c)

§ 14-41. Abduction of children

(a) Any person who, without legal justification or defense, abducts or induces any minor child who is at least four years younger than the person to leave any person, agency, or institution lawfully entitled to the child's custody, placement, or care shall be guilty of a Class F felony.

(b) The provisions of this section shall not apply to any public officer or employee in the performance of his or her duty.

History.

1879, c. 81; Code, s. 973; Rev., s. 3358; C.S., s. 4223; 1979, c. 760, s. 5; 1979, 2nd Sess., c. 1316, s. 47; 1981, c. 63, s. 1; c. 179, s. 14; 1993, c. 539, s. 1144; 1994, Ex. Sess., c. 24, s. 14(c); 1995 (Reg. Sess., 1996), c. 745, s. 1

N.C. Gen. Stat. § 14-42

Repealed by Session Laws 1993, c. 539, s. 1358.2.

N.C. Gen. Stat. § 14-43

Repealed by Session Laws 1993 (Reg. Sess., 1994), c. 767, s. 29(2).

§ 14-43.1. Unlawful arrest by officers from other states

A law-enforcement officer of a state other than North Carolina who, knowing that he is in the State of North Carolina and purporting to act by authority of his office, arrests a person in the State of North Carolina, other than as is permitted by G.S. 15A-403, is guilty of a Class 2 misdemeanor.

History.

1973, c. 1286, s. 10; 1993, c. 539, s. 22; 1994, Ex. Sess., c. 24, s. 14(c)

N.C. Gen. Stat. § 14-43.2

Repealed by Session Laws 2006-247, s. 20(a), effective December 1, 2006, and applicable to offenses committed on or after that date.

§ 14-43.3. Felonious restraint

A person commits the offense of felonious restraint if he unlawfully restrains another person without that person's consent, or the consent of the person's parent or legal custodian if the person is less than 16 years old, and moves the person from the place of the initial restraint by transporting him in a motor vehicle or other conveyance. Violation of this section is a Class F felony. Felonious restraint is considered a lesser included offense of kidnapping.

History.

1985, c. 545, s. 1; 1993, c. 539, s. 1147; 1994, Ex. Sess., c. 24, s. 14(c)

§§ 14-43.4 through 14-43.9

Reserved for future codification purposes.

ARTICLE 10A
HUMAN TRAFFICKING

§ 14-43.10. Definitions

(a) **Definitions.** -- The following definitions apply in this Article:

(1) **Coercion.** -- The term includes all of the following:

a. Causing or threatening to cause bodily harm to any person, physically restraining or confining any person, or threatening to physically restrain or confine any person.

b. Exposing or threatening to expose any fact or information that if revealed would tend to subject a person to criminal or immigration proceedings, hatred, contempt, or ridicule.

c. Destroying, concealing, removing, confiscating, or possessing any actual or purported passport or other immigration document, or any other actual or purported government identification document, of any person.

d. Providing a controlled substance, as defined by G.S. 90-87, to a person.

(2) **Deception.** -- The term includes all of the following:

a. Creating or confirming another's impression of an existing fact or past event that is false and which the accused knows or believes to be false.

b. Maintaining the status or condition of a person arising from a pledge by that person of his or her personal services as security for a debt, if the value of those services as reasonably assessed is not applied toward the liquidation of the debt or the length and nature of those services are not respectively limited and defined, or preventing a person from acquiring information pertinent to the disposition of such debt.

c. Promising benefits or the performance of services that the accused does not intend to deliver or perform or knows will not be delivered or performed.

(3) **Involuntary servitude.** -- The term includes the following:

a. The performance of labor, whether or not for compensation, or whether or not for the satisfaction of a debt; and

b. By deception, coercion, or intimidation using violence or the threat of violence or by any other means of coercion or intimidation.

(4) **Minor.** -- A person who is less than 18 years of age.

(5) **Sexual servitude.** -- The term includes the following:

a. Any sexual activity as defined in G.S. 14-190.13 for which anything of value is directly or indirectly given, promised to, or received by any person, which conduct is induced or obtained by coercion or deception or which conduct is induced or obtained from a person under the age of 18 years; or

b. Any sexual activity as defined in G.S. 14-190.13 that is performed or provided by any person, which conduct is induced or obtained by coercion or deception or which conduct is induced or obtained from a person under the age of 18 years.

(6) **Victim.** -- Unless the context requires otherwise, a person subjected to the practices set forth in G.S. 14-43.11, 14-43.12, or 14-43.13.

(b) Reserved.

History.
2006-247, s. 20(b); 2018-75, s. 1; 2018-145, s. 11(e)

§ 14-43.11. Human trafficking

(a) A person commits the offense of human trafficking when that person (i) knowingly or in reckless disregard of the consequences of the action recruits, entices, harbors, transports, provides, or obtains by any means another person with the intent that the other person be held in involuntary servitude or sexual servitude or (ii) willfully or in reckless disregard of the consequences of the action causes a minor to be held in involuntary servitude or sexual servitude.

(b) A person who violates this section is guilty of a Class C felony if the victim of the offense is an adult. A person who violates this section is guilty of a Class B2 felony if the victim of the offense is a minor.

(c) Each violation of this section constitutes a separate offense and shall not merge with any other offense. Evidence of failure to deliver benefits or perform services standing alone shall not be sufficient to authorize a conviction under this section.

(c1) Mistake of age is not a defense to prosecution under this section. Consent of a minor is not a defense to prosecution under this section.

(d) A person who is not a legal resident of North Carolina, and would consequently be ineligible for State public benefits or services, shall be eligible for the public benefits and services of any State agency if the person is otherwise eligible for the public benefit and is a victim of an offense charged under this section. Eligibility for public benefits and services shall terminate at such time as the victim's eligibility to remain in the United States is terminated under federal law.

History.
2006-247, s. 20(b); 2007-547, s. 1; 2013-368, s. 1; 2017-151, s. 1

§ 14-43.12. Involuntary servitude

(a) A person commits the offense of involuntary servitude when that person knowingly and willfully or in reckless disregard of the consequences of the action holds another in involuntary servitude.

(b) A person who violates this section is guilty of a Class F felony if the victim of the offense is an adult. A person who violates this section is guilty of a Class C felony if the victim of the offense is a minor.

(c) Each violation of this section constitutes a separate offense and shall not merge with any other offense. Evidence of failure to deliver benefits or perform services standing alone shall not be sufficient to authorize a conviction under this section.

(c1) Mistake of age is not a defense to prosecution under this section. Consent of a minor is not a defense to prosecution under this section.

(d) Nothing in this section shall be construed to affect the laws governing the relationship between an unemancipated minor and his or her parents or legal guardian.

(e) If any person reports a violation of this section, which violation arises out of any contract for labor, to any party to the contract, the party shall immediately report the violation to the sheriff of the county in which the violation is alleged to have occurred for appropriate action. A person violating this subsection shall be guilty of a Class 1 misdemeanor.

History.
1983, ch. 746, s. 1; 1993, c. 539, ss. 23, 1146; 1994, Ex. Sess., c. 24, s. 14(c); 2006-247, s. 20(b); 2013-368, s. 2

§ 14-43.13. Sexual servitude

(a) A person commits the offense of sexual servitude when that person knowingly or in reckless disregard of the consequences of the action subjects, maintains, or obtains another for the purposes of sexual servitude.

(b) A person who violates this section is guilty of a Class D felony if the victim of the offense is an adult. A person who violates this section is guilty of a Class C felony if the victim of the offense is a minor.

(b1) Mistake of age is not a defense to prosecution under this section. Consent of a minor is not a defense to prosecution under this section.

(c) Each violation of this section constitutes a separate offense and shall not merge with any other offense. Evidence of failure to deliver benefits or perform services standing alone shall not be sufficient to authorize a conviction under this section.

History.
2006-247, s. 20(b); 2013-368, s. 3; 2019-158, s. 1(a)

§ 14-43.14. Unlawful sale, surrender, or purchase of a minor

(a) A person commits the offense of unlawful sale, surrender, or purchase of a minor when that person, acting with willful or reckless disregard for the life or safety of a minor, participates in any of the following: the acceptance, solicitation, offer, payment, or transfer of any compensation, in money, property, or other thing of value, at any time, by any person

in connection with the unlawful acquisition or transfer of the physical custody of a minor, except as ordered by the court. This section does not apply to actions that are ordered by a court, authorized by statute, or otherwise lawful.

(b) A person who violates this section is guilty of a Class F felony and shall pay a minimum fine of five thousand dollars ($ 5,000). For each subsequent violation, a person is guilty of a Class F felony and shall pay a minimum fine of ten thousand dollars ($ 10,000).

(c) A minor whose parent, guardian, or custodian has sold or attempted to sell a minor in violation of this Article is an abused juvenile as defined by G.S. 7B-101(1). The court may place the minor in the custody of the Department of Social Services or with such other person as is in the best interest of the minor.

(d) A violation of this section is a lesser included offense of G.S. 14-43.11.

(e) When a person is convicted of a violation of this section, the sentencing court shall consider whether the person is a danger to the community and whether requiring the person to register as a sex offender pursuant to Article 27A of this Chapter would further the purposes of that Article as stated in G.S. 14-208.5. If the sentencing court rules that the person is a danger to the community and that the person shall register, then an order shall be entered requiring the person to register.

History.
2012-153, s. 1

§ 14-43.15. Minor victims

Any minor victim of a violation of G.S. 14-43.11, 14-43.12, or 14-43.13 shall be alleged to be abused and neglected and the provisions of Subchapter I of Chapter 7B of the General Statutes shall apply.

History.
2018-68, s. 8.1(c); 2019-177, s. 3

§ 14-43.16. Affirmative defense

(a) **Affirmative Defense.** -- It is an affirmative defense to a prosecution under this Article that the person charged with the offense was a victim at the time of the offense and was coerced or deceived into committing the offense as a direct result of the person's status as a victim.

(b) **Construction.** -- Nothing in this section shall be construed to limit or abrogate any other affirmative defense to a prosecution under this Article available to a person by statute or common law.

History.
2018-75, s. 2(a); 2018-145, s. 11(a)

§ 14-43.17. Victim confidentiality; penalty for unlawful disclosure

(a) **Confidentiality Requirement.** -- Except as otherwise provided in subsections (b) and (d) of this section, the name, address, or other information that reasonably could be expected to lead directly to the identity of any of the following, is confidential and shall not be considered a public record as that term is defined in G.S. 132-1:

(1) A victim.

(2) An alleged victim.

(3) An immediate family member of a victim or alleged victim. For purposes of this subdivision, the term "immediate family member" means a spouse, child, sibling, parent, grandparent, grandchild, or the spouse of an immediate family member. This term includes stepparents, stepchildren, stepsiblings, and adoptive relationships.

(b) **Exceptions.** -- Information subject to the confidentiality requirement set forth in subsection (a) of this section may be disclosed only for the following purposes:

(1) For use in a law enforcement investigation or criminal prosecution.

(2) To ensure the provision of medical care, housing, or family services or benefits to any of the persons listed in subdivisions (1) through (3) of subsection (a) of this section.

(3) Upon written request by any of the persons listed in subdivisions (1) through (3) of subsection (a) of this section.

(4) As required by federal law or court order.

(c) **Penalty.** -- A person who knowingly violates subsection (a) of this section is guilty of a Class 3 misdemeanor.

(d) **Court Records.** -- This section does not apply to records that have been made part of a court file in the custody of the General Court of Justice.

History.
2018-75, s. 3(a); 2018-145, ss. 11(b), 23

§ 14-43.18. Civil cause of action; damages and attorneys' fees; limitation

(a) **Cause of Action.** -- An individual who is a victim may bring a civil action against a person who violates this Article or a person who knowingly benefits financially or by receiving anything of value from participation in a venture which that person knew or should have known violates this Article.

(b) **Relief and Damages.** -- The victim may seek and the court may award any or all of the following types of relief:

(1) An injunction to enjoin continued violation of this Article.

(2) Compensatory damages, which includes the following:

a. The greater of (i) the gross income or value to the defendant of the victim's labor; or (ii) value of the victim's labor as guaranteed under the Minimum Wage Law and overtime provisions of the Fair Labor Standards Act (FLSA).

b. Any costs reasonably incurred by the victim for medical care, psychological treatment, temporary housing, transportation, and any other services designed to assist a victim in recovering from any injuries or loss resulting from a violation of this Article.

(3) General damages for noneconomic losses.

(c) **Attorneys' Fees.** -- The court may award to the plaintiff and assess against the defendant the reasonable costs and expenses, including attorneys' fees, of the plaintiff in bringing an action pursuant to this section. If the court determines that the plaintiff's action is frivolous, it may award to the defendant and assess against the plaintiff the reasonable costs and expenses, including attorneys' fees, of the defendant in defending the action brought pursuant to this section.

(d) **Stay Pending Criminal Action.** -- Any civil action filed under this section shall be stayed during the pendency of any criminal action arising out of the same occurrence in which the plaintiff is the victim. The term "criminal action" includes investigation and prosecution and is pending until final adjudication in the trial court.

(e) **Statute of Limitations.** -- No action may be maintained under subsection (a) of this section unless it is commenced no later than either of the following:

(1) Ten years after the cause of action arose.

(2) Ten years after the victim reaches 18 years of age if the victim was a minor at the time of the alleged offense.

(f) **Jury Trial.** -- Parties to a civil action brought pursuant to this section shall have the right to a jury trial as provided under G.S. 1A-1, Rules of Civil Procedure.

History.
2019-158, s. 3(a)

§§ 14-43.18 through 14-43.19

Reserved for future codification purposes.

§ 14-43.20. Mandatory restitution; victim services; forfeiture

(a) Repealed by Session Laws 2018-75, s. 4(a), effective December 1, 2018.

(b) **Restitution.** -- Restitution for a victim is mandatory under this Article. At a minimum, the court shall order restitution in an amount equal to the value of the victim's labor as guaranteed under the Minimum Wage Law and overtime provisions of the Fair Labor Standards Act (FLSA). In addition, the judge may order any other amount of loss identified, including the gross income or value to the defendant of the victim's labor or services and any costs reasonably certain to be incurred by or on behalf of the victim for medical care, psychological treatment, temporary housing, transportation, funeral services, and any other services designed to assist a victim recover from any injuries or loss resulting from an offense committed under G.S. 14-43.11, 14-43.12, or 14-43.13.

(c) **Trafficking Victim Services.** -- Subject to the availability of funds, the Department of Health and Human Services may provide or fund emergency services and assistance to individuals who are victims of one or more offenses under G.S. 14-43.11, 14-43.12, or 14-43.13.

(d) **Certification.** -- The Attorney General, a district attorney, or any law enforcement official shall certify in writing to the United States Department of Justice or other federal agency, such as the United States Department of Homeland Security, that an investigation or prosecution under this Article for a violation of G.S. 14-43.11, 14-43.12, or 14-43.13 has begun and the individual who is a likely victim of one of those crimes is willing to cooperate or is cooperating with the investigation to enable the individual, if eligible under federal law, to qualify for an appropriate special immigrant visa and to access available federal benefits. Cooperation with law enforcement shall not be required of victims who are under 18 years of age. This certification shall be made available to the victim and the victim's designated legal representative.

(e) **Forfeiture.** -- A person who commits a violation of G.S. 14-43.11, 14-43.12, or 14-43.13 is subject to the property forfeiture provisions set forth in G.S. 14-2.3.

(f) **Escheat.** -- If a judge finds that the victim to whom restitution is due under this Article is unavailable to claim the restitution award, then the judge shall order the restitution be made payable to the clerk of superior court in the county in which the conviction for the offense requiring restitution occurred. If the victim fails to claim the restitution award within two years of the date of the restitution order issued by the judge, the clerk shall remit the restitution proceeds to the Crime Victims Compensation Fund established pursuant to G.S. 15B-23. Notwithstanding any provision of G.S. 15B-23 to the contrary, funds remitted to the Crime Victims Compensation Fund shall be used only to provide aid to victims who are (i) worthy and needy as determined by the Crime Victims Compensation Commission and (ii) enrolled in public institutions of higher education of this State.

History.
2013-368, s. 17; 2018-75, s. 4(a); 2018-145, s. 11(c)

ARTICLE 11
ABORTION AND KINDRED OFFENSES

§ 14-44. Using drugs or instruments to destroy unborn child

If any person shall willfully administer to any woman, either pregnant or quick with child, or prescribe for any such woman, or advise or procure any such woman to take any medicine, drug or other substance whatever, or shall use or employ any instrument or other means with intent thereby to destroy such child, he shall be punished as a Class H felon.

History.
1881, c. 351, s. 1; Code, s. 975; Rev., s. 3618; C.S., s. 4226; 1967, c. 367, s. 1; 1979, c. 760, s. 5; 1979, 2nd Sess., c. 1316, s. 47; 1981, c. 63, s. 1; c. 179, s. 14

§ 14-45. Using drugs or instruments to produce miscarriage or injure pregnant woman

If any person shall administer to any pregnant woman, or prescribe for any such woman, or advise and procure such woman to take any medicine, drug or anything whatsoever, with intent thereby to procure the miscarriage of such woman, or to injure or destroy such woman, or shall use any instrument or application for any of the above purposes, he shall be punished as a Class I felon.

History.
1881, c. 351, s. 2; Code, s. 976; Rev., s. 3619; C.S., s. 4227; 1979, c. 760, s. 5; 1979, 2nd Sess., c. 1316, s. 47; 1981, c. 63, s. 1; c. 179, s. 14

§ 14-45.1. When abortion not unlawful

(a) Notwithstanding any of the provisions of G.S. 14-44 and 14-45, it shall not be unlawful, during the first 20 weeks of a woman's pregnancy, to advise, procure, or cause a miscarriage or abortion when the procedure is performed by a qualified physician licensed to practice medicine in North Carolina in a hospital or clinic certified by the Department of Health and

Human Services to be a suitable facility for the performance of abortions.

(a1) The Department of Health and Human Services shall annually inspect any clinic, including ambulatory surgical facilities, where abortions are performed. The Department of Health and Human Services shall publish on the Department's Web site and on the State Web site established under G.S. 90-21.84 the results and findings of all inspections conducted on or after January 1, 2013, of clinics, including ambulatory surgical facilities, where abortions are performed, including any statement of deficiencies and any notice of administrative action resulting from the inspection. No person who is less than 18 years of age shall be employed at any clinic, including ambulatory surgical facilities, where abortions are performed. The requirements of this subsection shall not apply to a hospital required to be licensed under Chapter 131E of the General Statutes.

(b) Notwithstanding any of the provisions of G.S. 14-44 and 14-45, it shall not be unlawful, after the twentieth week of a woman's pregnancy, to advise, procure or cause a miscarriage or abortion when the procedure is performed by a qualified physician licensed to practice medicine in North Carolina in a hospital licensed by the Department of Health and Human Services, if there is a medical emergency as defined by G.S. 90-21.81(5).

(b1) A qualified physician who advises, procures, or causes a miscarriage or abortion after the sixteenth week of a woman's pregnancy shall record all of the following: the method used by the qualified physician to determine the probable gestational age of the unborn child at the time the procedure is to be performed; the results of the methodology, including the measurements of the unborn child; and an ultrasound image of the unborn child that depicts the measurements. The qualified physician shall provide this information, including the ultrasound image, to the Department of Health and Human Services pursuant to G.S. 14-45.1(c).

A qualified physician who procures or causes a miscarriage or abortion after the twentieth week of a woman's pregnancy shall record the findings and analysis on which the qualified physician based the determination that there existed a medical emergency as defined by G.S. 90-21.81(5) and shall provide that information to the Department of Health and Human Services pursuant to G.S. 14-45.1(c). Materials generated by the physician or provided by the physician to the Department of Health and Human Services pursuant to this section shall not be public records under G.S. 132-1.

The information provided under this subsection shall be for statistical purposes only, and the confidentiality of the patient and the physician shall be protected. It is the duty of the qualified physician to submit information to the Department of Health and Human Services that omits identifying information of the patient and complies with Health Insurance Portability and Accountability Act of 1996 (HIPAA).

(c) The Department of Health and Human Services shall prescribe and collect on an annual basis, from hospitals or clinics, including ambulatory surgical facilities, where abortions are performed, statistical summary reports concerning the medical and demographic characteristics of the abortions provided for in this section, including the information described in subsection (b1) of this section as it shall deem to be in the public interest. Hospitals or clinics where abortions are performed shall be responsible for providing these statistical summary reports to the Department of Health and Human Services. The reports shall be for statistical purposes only and the confidentiality of the patient relationship shall be protected. Materials generated by the physician or provided by the physician to the Department of Health and Human Services pursuant to this section shall not be public records under G.S. 132-1.

(d) The requirements of G.S. 130A-114 are not applicable to abortions performed pursuant to this section.

(e) No physician, nurse, or any other health care provider who shall state an objection to abortion on moral, ethical, or religious grounds shall be required to perform or participate in medical procedures which result in an abortion. The refusal of a physician, nurse, or health care provider to perform or participate in these medical procedures shall not be a basis for damages for the refusal, or for any disciplinary or any other recriminatory action against the physician, nurse, or health care provider. For purposes of this section, the phrase "health care provider" shall have the same meaning as defined under G.S. 90-410(1).

(f) Nothing in this section shall require a hospital, other health care institution, or other health care provider to perform an abortion or to provide abortion services.

(g) For purposes of this section, "qualified physician" means (i) a physician who possesses, or is eligible to possess, board certification in obstetrics or gynecology, (ii) a physician who possesses sufficient training based on established medical standards in safe abortion care, abortion complications, and miscarriage management, or (iii) a physician who performs an abortion in a medical emergency as defined by G.S. 90-21.81(5).

History.
1967, c. 367, s. 2; 1971, c. 383, ss. 1, 1 1/2; 1973, c. 139; c. 476, s. 128; c. 711; 1997-443, s. 11A.118(a); 2013-366, s. 1(a), (b); 2015-62, s. 7(a)

§ 14-46. Concealing birth of child

If any person shall, by secretly burying or otherwise disposing of the dead body of a new-born child, endeavor to conceal the birth of such child, such person shall be punished as a Class I felon. Any person aiding, counseling or abetting any other person in concealing the birth of a child in violation of this statute shall be guilty of a Class 1 misdemeanor.

History.
21 Jac. I, c. 27; 43 Geo. III, c. 58, s. 3; 9 Geo. IV, c. 31, s. 14; 1818, c. 985, P.R.; R.C., c. 34, s. 28; 1883, c. 390; Code, s. 1004; Rev., s. 3623; C.S., s. 4228; 1977, c. 577; 1979, c. 760, s. 5; 1979, 2nd Sess., c. 1316, s. 47; 1981, c. 63, s. 1; c. 179, s. 14; 1993, c. 539, ss. 24, 1148; 1994, Ex. Sess., c. 24, s. 14(c)

§ 14-46.1. Prohibit sale of the remains of an unborn child resulting from an abortion or miscarriage

(a) No person shall sell the remains of an unborn child resulting from an abortion or a miscarriage or any aborted or miscarried material.

(b) For purposes of this section, the term "sell" shall mean the transfer from one person to another in exchange for any consideration whatsoever. The term shall not include payment for incineration, burial, cremation, or any services performed pursuant to G.S. 130A-131.10(f).

(c) A person convicted of a violation of this section is guilty of a Class I felony.

History.
2015-265, s. 2

ARTICLE 12
LIBEL AND SLANDER

§ 14-47. Communicating libelous matter to newspapers

If any person shall state, deliver or transmit by any means whatever, to the manager, editor, publisher or reporter of any newspaper or periodical for publication therein any false and libelous statement concerning any person or corporation, and thereby secure the publication of the same, he shall be guilty of a Class 2 misdemeanor.

History.
1901, c. 557, ss. 2, 3; Rev., s. 3635; C.S., s. 4229; 1969, c. 1224, s. 1; 1993, c. 539, s. 25; 1994, Ex. Sess., c. 24, s. 14(c)

N.C. Gen. Stat. § 14-48

Repealed by Session Laws 1975, c. 402.

ARTICLE 13
MALICIOUS INJURY OR DAMAGE BY USE OF EXPLOSIVE OR INCENDIARY DEVICE OR MATERIAL

§ 14-49. Malicious use of explosive or incendiary; punishment

(a) Any person who willfully and maliciously injures another by the use of any explosive or incendiary device or material is guilty of a Class D felony.

(b) Any person who willfully and maliciously damages any real or personal property of any kind or nature belonging to another by the use of any explosive or incendiary device or material is guilty of a Class G felony.

(b1) Any person who willfully and maliciously damages, aids, counsels, or procures the damaging of any church, chapel, synagogue, mosque, masjid, or other building of worship by the use of any explosive or incendiary device or material is guilty of a Class E felony.

(b2) Any person who willfully and maliciously damages, aids, counsels, or procures the damaging of the State Capitol, the Legislative Building, the Justice Building, or any building owned or occupied by the State or any of its agencies, institutions, or subdivisions or by any county, incorporated city or town, or other governmental entity by the use of any explosive or incendiary device or material is guilty of a Class E felony.

(c) Repealed by Session Laws 1993, c. 539, s. 1149, effective October 1, 1994.

History.
1923, c. 80, s. 1; C.S., s. 4231(a); 1951, c. 1126, s. 1; 1969, c. 869, s. 6; 1979, c. 760, s. 5; 1979, 2nd Sess., c. 1316, s. 47; 1981, c. 63, s. 1; c. 179, s. 14; 1993, c. 539, s. 1149; 1994, Ex. Sess., c. 24, s. 14(c); 1995 (Reg. Sess., 1996), c. 751, s. 1; 2003-392, s. 3(c)

§ 14-49.1. Malicious damage of occupied property by use of explosive or incendiary; punishment

Any person who willfully and maliciously damages any real or personal property of any kind or nature, being at the time occupied by another, by the use of any explosive or incendiary device or material is guilty of a felony punishable as a Class D felony.

History.
1967, c. 342; 1969, c. 869, s. 6; 1979, c. 760, s. 5; 1979, 2nd Sess., c. 1316, s. 47; 1981, c. 63, s. 1; c. 179, s. 14; 1993, c. 539, s. 1150; 1994, Ex. Sess., c. 24, s. 14(c)

N.C. Gen. Stat. § 14-50

Repealed by Session Laws 1994, Extra Session, c. 14, s. 71(4).

§ 14-50.1. Explosive or incendiary device or material defined

As used in this Article, "explosive or incendiary device or material" means nitroglycerine, dynamite, gunpowder, other high explosive, incendiary bomb or grenade, other destructive incendiary device, or any other destructive incendiary or explosive device, compound, or formulation; any instrument or substance capable of being used for destructive explosive or incendiary purposes against persons or property, when the circumstances indicate some probability that such instrument or substance will be so used; or any explosive or incendiary part or ingredient in any instrument or substance included above, when the circumstances indicate some probability that such part or ingredient will be so used.

History.
1969, c. 869, s. 6

§§ 14-50.2 through 14-50.14

Reserved for future codification purposes.

ARTICLE 13A
NORTH CAROLINA CRIMINAL GANG SUPPRESSION ACT

§ 14-50.15. Short title

This Article shall be known and may be cited as the "North Carolina Criminal Gang Suppression Act."

History.
2008-214, s. 3; 2017-194, s. 3

ARTICLE 13A
NORTH CAROLINA STREET GANG SUPPRESSION ACT

§ 14-50.16. Pattern of criminal street gang activity

(a) It is unlawful for any person employed by or associated with a criminal street gang to do either of the following:

(1) To conduct or participate in a pattern of criminal street gang activity.

(2) To acquire or maintain any interest in or control of any real or personal property through a pattern of criminal street gang activity.

A violation of this section is a Class H felony, except that a person who violates subdivision (a)(1) of this section, and is an organizer, supervisor, or acts in any other position of management with regard to the criminal street gang, shall be guilty of a Class F felony.

(b) As used in this Article, "criminal street gang" or "street gang" means any ongoing organization, association, or group of three or more persons, whether formal or informal, that:

(1) Has as one of its primary activities the commission of one or more felony offenses, or delinquent acts that would be felonies if committed by an adult;

(2) Has three or more members individually or collectively engaged in, or who have engaged in, criminal street gang activity; and

(3) May have a common name, common identifying sign or symbol.

(c) As used in this Article, "criminal street gang activity" means to commit, to attempt to commit, or to solicit, coerce, or intimidate another person to commit an act or acts, with the specific intent that such act or acts were intended or committed for the purpose, or in furtherance, of the person's involvement in a criminal street gang or street gang. An act or acts are included if accompanied by the necessary mens rea or criminal intent and would be chargeable by indictment under the following laws of this State:

(1) Any offense under Article 5 of Chapter 90 of the General Statutes (Controlled Substances Act).

(2) Any offense under Chapter 14 of the General Statutes except Articles 9, 22A, 40, 46, 47, 59 thereof; and further excepting G.S. 14-78.1, 14-82, 14-86, 14-145, 14-179, 14-183, 14-184, 14-186, 14-190.9, 14-195, 14-197, 14-201, 14-247, 14-248, 14-313 thereof.

(d) As used in this Article, "pattern of criminal street gang activity" means engaging in, and having a conviction for, at least two prior incidents of criminal street gang activity, that have the same or similar purposes, results, accomplices, victims, or methods of commission or otherwise are interrelated by common characteristics and are not isolated and unrelated incidents, provided that at least one of these offenses occurred after December 1, 2008, and the last of the offenses occurred within three years, excluding any periods of imprisonment, of prior criminal street gang activity. Any offenses committed by a defendant prior to indictment for an offense based upon a pattern of street gang activity shall not be used as the basis for any subsequent indictments for offenses involving a pattern of street gang activity.

History.
2008-214, s. 3.

§ 14-50.16A. Criminal gang activity

Definitions. -- The following definitions apply in this Article:

(1) **Criminal gang.** -- Any ongoing organization, association, or group of three or more persons, whether formal or informal, that (i) has as one of its primary activities the commission of criminal or delinquent acts and (ii) shares a common name, identification, signs, symbols, tattoos, graffiti, attire, or other distinguishing characteristics, including common activities, customs, or behaviors. The term shall not include three or more persons associated in fact, whether formal or informal, who are not engaged in criminal gang activity.

(2) **Criminal gang activity.** -- The commission of, attempted commission of, or solicitation, coercion, or intimidation of another person to commit (i) any offense under Article 5 of Chapter 90 of the General Statutes or (ii) any offense under Chapter 14 of the General Statutes except Article 9, 22A, 40, 46, or 59 thereof, and further excepting G.S. 14-82, 14-145, 14-183, 14-184, 14-186, 14-190.9, 14-247, 14-248, or 14-313 thereof, and either of the following conditions is met:

a. The offense is committed with the intent to benefit, promote, or further the interests of a criminal gang or for the purposes of increasing a person's own standing or position within a criminal gang.

b. The participants in the offense are identified as criminal gang members acting individually or collectively to further any criminal purpose of a criminal gang.

(3) **Criminal gang leader or organizer.** -- Any criminal gang member who acts in any position of management with regard to the criminal gang and who meets two or more of the following criteria:

a. Exercises decision-making authority over matters regarding a criminal gang.

b. Participates in the direction, planning, organizing, or commission of criminal gang activity.

c. Recruits other gang members.

d. Receives a larger portion of the proceeds of criminal gang activity.

e. Exercises control and authority over other criminal gang members.

(4) **Criminal gang member.** -- Any person who meets three or more of the following criteria:

a. The person admits to being a member of a criminal gang.

b. The person is identified as a criminal gang member by a reliable source, including a parent or a guardian.

c. The person has been previously involved in criminal gang activity.

d. The person has adopted symbols, hand signs, or graffiti associated with a criminal gang.

e. The person has adopted the display of colors or the style of dress associated with a criminal gang.

f. The person is in possession of or linked to a criminal gang by physical evidence, including photographs, ledgers, rosters, written or electronic communications, or membership documents.

g. The person has tattoos or markings associated with a criminal gang.

h. The person has adopted language or terminology associated with a criminal gang.

i. The person appears in any form of social media to promote a criminal gang.

History.
2017-194, s. 4

§ 14-50.17. Soliciting; encouraging participation

(a) It is unlawful for any person to cause, encourage, solicit, or coerce a person 16 years of age or older to participate in criminal gang activity.

(b) A violation of this section is a Class H felony.

History.
2008-214, s. 3; 2017-194, s. 7

§ 14-50.18. Soliciting; encouraging participation; minor

(a) It is unlawful for any person to cause, encourage, solicit, or coerce a person under 16 years of age to participate in criminal gang activity.

(b) A violation of this section is a Class F felony.

(c) Nothing in this section shall preclude a person who commits a violation of this section from criminal culpability for the underlying offense committed by the minor under any other provision of law.

History.
2008-214, s. 3; 2017-194, s. 8

§ 14-50.19. Intimidation to deter from gang withdrawal

(a) It is unlawful for any person to communicate a threat of injury to a person, or to damage the property of another, with the intent to deter a person from assisting another to withdraw from membership in a criminal gang.

(a1) It is unlawful for any person to injure a person with the intent to deter a person from assisting another to withdraw from membership in a criminal gang.

(b) A violation of subsection (a) of this section is a Class G felony. A violation of subsection (a1) of this section is a Class F felony.

History.
2008-214, s. 3; 2017-194, s. 9

§ 14-50.20. Punishment or retaliation for gang withdrawal

(a) It is unlawful for any person to communicate a threat of injury to a person, or to damage the property of another, as punishment or retaliation against a person for having withdrawn from a criminal gang.

(a1) It is unlawful for any person to injure a person as punishment or retaliation against a person for having withdrawn from a criminal gang.

(b) A violation of subsection (a) of this section is a Class G felony. A violation of subsection (a1) of this section is a Class F felony.

History.
2008-214, s. 3; 2017-194, s. 10

§ 14-50.21. Separate offense

Any offense committed in violation of G.S. 14-50.17 through G.S. 14-50.20 shall be considered a separate offense.

History.
2008-214, s. 3; 2019-177, s. 4(a)

§ 14-50.22. Enhanced offense for misdemeanor criminal gang activity

A person age 15 or older who is convicted of a misdemeanor offense that is committed for the benefit of, at the direction of, or in association with, any criminal gang is guilty of an offense that is one class higher than the offense committed. A Class A1 misdemeanor shall be enhanced to a Class I felony under this section.

History.
2008-214, s. 3; 2017-194, s. 11

§ 14-50.23. Contraband, seizure, and forfeiture

(a) All property of every kind used or intended for use in the course of, derived from, or realized through criminal gang activity is subject to the seizure and forfeiture provisions of G.S. 14-2.3.

(b) In any action under this section, the court may enter a restraining order in connection with any interest that is subject to forfeiture.

(c) **Innocent Activities. --** The provisions of this section shall not apply to property used for criminal gang activity where the owner or person who has legal possession of the property does not have actual knowledge that the property is being used for criminal gang activity.

History.
2008-214, s. 3; 2017-194, s. 12

N.C. Gen. Stat. § 14-50.24

Repealed by Session Laws 2012-28, s. 2, effective October 1, 2012.

History.
2008-214, s. 3; repealed by 2012-28, s. 2, effective October 1, 2012

§ 14-50.25. Reports of disposition; criminal gang activity

When a defendant is found guilty of a criminal offense, other than an offense under G.S. 14-50.17 through G.S. 14-50.20, the presiding judge shall determine whether the offense involved criminal gang activity. If the judge so determines, then the judge shall indicate on the form reflecting the judgment that the offense involved criminal gang activity. The clerk of court shall ensure that the official record of the defendant's conviction includes a notation of the court's determination.

History.
2008-214, s. 3; 2017-194, s. 13; 2019-177, s. 4(b)

§ 14-50.26. Matters proved in criminal trial court

A conviction of an offense defined as criminal gang activity shall preclude the defendant from contesting any factual matters determined in the criminal proceeding in any subsequent civil action or proceeding based on the same conduct.

History.
2008-214, s. 3

§ 14-50.27. Local ordinances not preempted by State law

Nothing in this Article shall prevent a local governing body from adopting and enforcing ordinances relating to gangs and gang violence that are consistent with this Article. Where local laws duplicate or supplement the provisions of this Article, this Article shall be construed as providing alternative remedies and not as preempting the field.

History.
2008-214, s. 3

§ 14-50.27A. Dissemination of criminal intelligence information

A law enforcement agency may disseminate an assessment of criminal intelligence information to the principal of a school when necessary to avoid imminent danger to the life of a student or employee of the school or to the public school property pursuant to 28 C.F.R. § 23.20. The notification may be made in person or by telephone. As used in this subsection, the term "school" means any public or private school in the State under Chapter 115C of the General Statutes.

History.
2009-93, s. 1

§ 14-50.28. Applicability to juveniles under the age of 16

Except as provided in G.S. 14-50.22, 14-50.29, and 14-50.30, the provisions of this Article shall not apply to juveniles under the age of 16.

History.
2008-214, s. 3

§ 14-50.29. Conditional discharge for first offenders under the age of 18

(a) Whenever any person who has not previously been convicted of any felony or misdemeanor other than a traffic violation under the laws of the United States or the laws of this State or any other state, pleads guilty to or is guilty of (i) a Class H felony under this Article or (ii) an enhanced offense under G.S. 14-50.22, and the offense was committed before the person attained the age of 18 years, the court may, without entering a judgment of guilt and with the consent of the defendant, defer further proceedings and place the defendant on probation

upon such reasonable terms and conditions as the court may require.

(b) If the court, in its discretion, defers proceedings pursuant to this section, it shall place the defendant on supervised probation for not less than one year, in addition to any other conditions. Prior to taking any action to discharge and dismiss under this section, the court shall make a finding that the defendant has no previous criminal convictions. Upon fulfillment of the terms and conditions of the probation provided for in this section, the court shall discharge the defendant and dismiss the proceedings against the defendant.

(c) Discharge and dismissal under this section shall be without court adjudication of guilt and shall not be deemed a conviction for purposes of this section or for purposes of disqualifications or disabilities imposed by law upon conviction of a crime. Discharge and dismissal under this section may occur only once with respect to any person. Disposition of a case to determine discharge and dismissal under this section at the district court division of the General Court of Justice shall be final for the purpose of appeal. Upon violation of a term or condition of the probation provided for in this section, the court may enter an adjudication of guilt and proceed as otherwise provided.

(d) Upon discharge and dismissal pursuant to this section, the person may apply for an order to expunge the complete record of the proceedings resulting in the dismissal and discharge, pursuant to the procedures and requirements set forth in G.S. 15A-145.1.

(e) The clerk shall notify State and local agencies of the court's order as provided in G.S. 15A-150.

History.
2008-214, s. 3; 2009-510, s. 2; 2009-577, s. 4

§ 14-50.30. Expunction of records

Any person who has not previously been convicted of any felony or misdemeanor other than a traffic violation under the laws of the United States or the laws of this State or any other state, may, if the offense was committed before the person attained the age of 18 years, be eligible to apply for expunction of certain offenses under this Article pursuant to G.S. 15A-145.1.

History.
2008-214, s. 3; 2009-510, s. 3; 2009-577, s. 5; 2010-174, s. 1

§§ 14-50.31 through 14-50.40

Reserved for future codification purposes.

ARTICLE 13B
NORTH CAROLINA CRIMINAL GANG NUISANCE ABATEMENT ACT

§ 14-50.41. Short title

This Article shall be known and may be cited as the "North Carolina Criminal Gang Nuisance Abatement Act."

History.
2012-28, s. 1; 2018-142, s. 1

§ 14-50.42. Real property used by criminal gangs declared a public nuisance: abatement

(a) **Public Nuisance.** -- Any real property that is erected, established, maintained, owned, leased, or used by any criminal gang for the purpose of conducting criminal gang activity, as defined in G.S. 14-50.16A(2), shall constitute a public nuisance and may be abated as provided by and subject to the provisions of Article 1 of Chapter 19 of the General Statutes.

Proof that criminal gang activity by a criminal gang member is regularly committed at any real property or proof that the real property is regularly used for engaging in criminal gang activity by a criminal gang member is prima facie evidence that the owner or person who has legal possession of the real property knowingly permitted the act unless the owner or person who has legal possession of the real property is making or has made a good-faith attempt to terminate the criminal gang activity or remove criminal gang members from the property through legal means, including trespass or summary ejectment. For purposes of this section, the term "regularly" means at least five times in a period of not more than 12 months.

(b) **Innocent Activities.** -- The provisions of this section shall not apply to real property used for criminal gang activity where any of the following conditions are met:

(1) The owner or person who has legal possession of the real property does not have actual knowledge that the real property is being used for criminal gang activity.

(2) The owner or person who has legal possession of the real property is being coerced into allowing the property to be used for criminal gang activity.

(3) The owner or person who has legal possession of the real property is making or has made a good-faith attempt to terminate the criminal gang activity or remove

criminal gang members from the property through legal means, including trespass or summary ejectment.

For purposes of this subsection, evidence that the defendant knew, or by the exercise of due diligence should have known, of the criminal gang activity constitutes proof of actual knowledge.

History.
2008-214, s. 3; 2012-28, ss. 1, 2; 2017-194, s. 15

§ 14-50.43. Criminal gangs declared a public nuisance

(a) A criminal gang, as defined in G.S. 14-50.16A(a), that regularly engages in criminal gang activity, as defined in G.S. 14-50.16A(2), constitutes a public nuisance. For the purposes of this section, the term "regularly" means at least five times in a period of not more than 12 months.

(b) Any person who regularly associates with others to engage in criminal gang activity, as defined in G.S. 14-50.16A(2), may be made a defendant in a suit, brought pursuant to Chapter 19 of the General Statutes, to abate any public nuisance resulting from criminal gang activity.

(c) If the court finds that a public nuisance exists under this section, the court may enter an order enjoining the defendant in the suit from engaging in criminal gang activities and impose other reasonable requirements to prevent the defendant or a gang from engaging in future criminal gang activities.

(d) An order entered under this section shall expire three years after entry unless extended by the court for good cause established by the plaintiff after a hearing. The order may be modified, rescinded, or vacated at any time prior to its expiration date upon the motion of any party if it appears to the court that one or more of the defendants is no longer engaging in criminal gang activities.

History.
2012-28, s. 1; 2015-91, s. 4; 2017-194, s. 16

SUBCHAPTER 04.
OFFENSES AGAINST THE HABITATION AND OTHER BUILDINGS

ARTICLE 14
BURGLARY AND OTHER HOUSEBREAKINGS

§ 14-51. First and second degree burglary

There shall be two degrees in the crime of burglary as defined at the common law. If the crime be committed in a dwelling house, or in a room used as a sleeping apartment in any building, and any person is in the actual occupation of any part of said dwelling house or sleeping apartment at the time of the commission of such crime, it shall be burglary in the first degree. If such crime be committed in a dwelling house or sleeping apartment not actually occupied by anyone at the time of the commission of the crime, or if it be committed in any house within the curtilage of a dwelling house or in any building not a dwelling house, but in which is a room used as a sleeping apartment and not actually occupied as such at the time of the commission of the crime, it shall be burglary in the second degree. For the purposes of defining the crime of burglary, larceny shall be deemed a felony without regard to the value of the property in question.

History.
1889, c. 434, s. 1; Rev., s. 3331; C.S., s. 4232; 1969, c. 543, s. 1

N.C. Gen. Stat. § 14-51.1

Repealed by Session Laws 2011-268, s. 2, effective December 1, 2011.

History.
1993 (Reg. Sess., 1994), c. 673, s. 1; repealed by 2011-268, s. 26, effective December 1, 2011

§ 14-51.2. Home, workplace, and motor vehicle protection; presumption of fear of death or serious bodily harm

(a) The following definitions apply in this section:

(1) **Home.** -- A building or conveyance of any kind, to include its curtilage, whether the building or conveyance is temporary or permanent, mobile or immobile, which has a roof over it, including a tent, and is designed as a temporary or permanent residence.

(2) **Law enforcement officer.** -- Any person employed or appointed as a full-time, part-time, or auxiliary law enforcement officer, correctional officer, probation officer, post-release supervision officer, or parole officer.

(3) **Motor vehicle.** -- As defined in G.S. 20-4.01(23).

(4) **Workplace.** -- A building or conveyance of any kind, whether the building or conveyance is temporary or permanent, mobile or immobile, which has a roof over it, including a tent, which is being used for commercial purposes.

(b) The lawful occupant of a home, motor vehicle, or workplace is presumed to have held a reasonable fear of imminent death or serious bodily harm to himself or herself or another when using defensive force that is intended or likely to cause death or serious bodily harm to another if both of the following apply:

(1) The person against whom the defensive force was used was in the process of unlawfully and forcefully entering, or had unlawfully and forcibly entered, a home, motor vehicle, or workplace, or if that person had removed or was attempting to remove another against that person's will from the home, motor vehicle, or workplace.

(2) The person who uses defensive force knew or had reason to believe that an unlawful and forcible entry or unlawful and forcible act was occurring or had occurred.

(c) The presumption set forth in subsection (b) of this section shall be rebuttable and does not apply in any of the following circumstances:

(1) The person against whom the defensive force is used has the right to be in or is a lawful resident of the home, motor vehicle, or workplace, such as an owner or lessee, and there is not an injunction for protection from domestic violence or a written pretrial supervision order of no contact against that person.

(2) The person sought to be removed from the home, motor vehicle, or workplace is a child or grandchild or is otherwise in the lawful custody or under the lawful guardianship of the person against whom the defensive force is used.

(3) The person who uses defensive force is engaged in, attempting to escape from, or using the home, motor vehicle, or workplace to further any criminal offense that involves the use or threat of physical force or violence against any individual.

(4) The person against whom the defensive force is used is a law enforcement officer or bail bondsman who enters or attempts to enter a home, motor vehicle, or workplace in the lawful performance of his or her official duties, and the officer or bail bondsman identified himself or herself in accordance with any applicable law or the person using force knew or reasonably should have known that the person entering or attempting to enter was a law enforcement officer or bail bondsman in the lawful performance of his or her official duties.

(5) The person against whom the defensive force is used (i) has discontinued all efforts to unlawfully and forcefully enter the home, motor vehicle, or workplace and

Chapter 14

(ii) has exited the home, motor vehicle, or workplace.

(d) A person who unlawfully and by force enters or attempts to enter a person's home, motor vehicle, or workplace is presumed to be doing so with the intent to commit an unlawful act involving force or violence.

(e) A person who uses force as permitted by this section is justified in using such force and is immune from civil or criminal liability for the use of such force, unless the person against whom force was used is a law enforcement officer or bail bondsman who was lawfully acting in the performance of his or her official duties and the officer or bail bondsman identified himself or herself in accordance with any applicable law or the person using force knew or reasonably should have known that the person was a law enforcement officer or bail bondsman in the lawful performance of his or her official duties.

(f) A lawful occupant within his or her home, motor vehicle, or workplace does not have a duty to retreat from an intruder in the circumstances described in this section.

(g) This section is not intended to repeal or limit any other defense that may exist under the common law.

History.
2011-268, s. 1

§ 14-51.3. Use of force in defense of person; relief from criminal or civil liability

(a) A person is justified in using force, except deadly force, against another when and to the extent that the person reasonably believes that the conduct is necessary to defend himself or herself or another against the other's imminent use of unlawful force. However, a person is justified in the use of deadly force and does not have a duty to retreat in any place he or she has the lawful right to be if either of the following applies:

(1) He or she reasonably believes that such force is necessary to prevent imminent death or great bodily harm to himself or herself or another.

(2) Under the circumstances permitted pursuant to G.S. 14-51.2.

(b) A person who uses force as permitted by this section is justified in using such force and is immune from civil or criminal liability for the use of such force, unless the person against whom force was used is a law enforcement officer or bail bondsman who was lawfully acting in the performance of his or her official duties and the officer or bail bondsman identified himself or herself in accordance with any applicable law or the person using force knew or reasonably should have known that the person was a law enforcement officer or bail bondsman in the lawful performance of his or her official duties.

History.
2011-268, s. 1

§ 14-51.4. Justification for defensive force not available

The justification described in G.S. 14-51.2 and G.S. 14-51.3 is not available to a person who used defensive force and who:

(1) Was attempting to commit, committing, or escaping after the commission of a felony.

(2) Initially provokes the use of force against himself or herself. However, the person who initially provokes the use of force against himself or herself will be justified in using defensive force if either of the following occur:

a. The force used by the person who was provoked is so serious that the person using defensive force reasonably believes that he or she was in imminent danger of death or serious bodily harm, the person using defensive force had no reasonable means to retreat, and the use of force which is likely to cause death or serious bodily harm to the person who was provoked was the only way to escape the danger.

b. The person who used defensive force withdraws, in good faith, from physical contact with the person who was provoked, and indicates clearly that he or she desires to withdraw and terminate the use of force, but the person who was provoked continues or resumes the use of force.

History.
2011-268, s. 1

§ 14-52. Punishment for burglary

Burglary in the first degree shall be punishable as a Class D felony, and burglary in the second degree shall be punishable as a Class G felony.

History.
1870-1, c. 222; Code, s. 994; 1889, c. 434, s. 2; Rev., s. 3330; C.S., s. 4233; 1941, c. 215, s. 1; 1949, c. 299, s. 2; 1973, c. 1201, s. 3; 1977, c. 871, s. 2; 1979, c. 672; 1979, c. 760, s. 5; 1979, 2nd Sess., c. 1316, s. 47; 1981, c. 63, s. 1; c. 179, s. 14; 1993, c. 539, s. 1151; 1994, Ex. Sess., c. 24, s. 14(c)

§ 14-53. Breaking out of dwelling house burglary

If any person shall enter the dwelling house of another with intent to commit any felony or larceny therein, or being in such dwelling house, shall commit any felony or larceny therein, and shall, in either case, break out of such dwelling house in the nighttime, such person shall be punished as a Class D felon.

History.
12 Anne, c. 7, s. 3; R.C., c. 34, s. 8; Code, s. 995; Rev., s. 3332; C.S., s. 4234; 1969, c. 543, s. 2; 1979, c. 760, s. 5; 1979, 2nd Sess., c. 1316, s. 47; 1981, c. 63, s. 1; c. 179, s. 14

§ 14-54. Breaking or entering buildings generally

(a) Any person who breaks or enters any building with intent to commit any felony or larceny therein shall be punished as a Class H felon.

(a1) Any person who breaks or enters any building with intent to terrorize or injure an occupant of the building is guilty of a Class H felony.

(b) Any person who wrongfully breaks or enters any building is guilty of a Class 1 misdemeanor.

(c) As used in this section, "building" shall be construed to include any dwelling, dwelling house, uninhabited house, building under construction, building within the curtilage of a dwelling house, and any other structure designed to house or secure within it any activity or property.

History.
1874-5, c. 166; 1879, c. 323; Code, s. 996; Rev., s. 3333; C.S., s. 4235; 1955, c. 1015; 1969, c. 543, s. 3; 1979, c. 760, s. 5; 1979, 2nd Sess., c. 1316, s. 47; 1981, c. 63, s. 1; c. 179, s. 14; 1993, c. 539, s. 26; 1994, Ex. Sess., c. 24, s. 14(c); 2013-95, s. 1

§ 14-54.1. Breaking or entering a building that is a place of religious worship

(a) Any person who wrongfully breaks or enters any building that is a place of religious worship with intent to commit any felony or larceny therein is guilty of a Class G felony.

(b) As used in this section, a "building that is a place of religious worship" shall be construed to include any church, chapel, meetinghouse, synagogue, temple, longhouse, or mosque, or other building that is regularly used, and clearly identifiable, as a place for religious worship.

History.
2005-235, s. 1

§ 14-54.2. Breaking or entering a pharmacy

(a) **Definition.** -- The following definitions apply to this section:

(1) **Pharmacy.** -- A business that has a pharmacy permit under G.S. 90-85.21.

(2) **Controlled substance.** -- As defined in G.S. 90-87(5).

(b) **Offense.** -- A person who breaks or enters a pharmacy with the intent to commit a larceny of a controlled substance is guilty of a Class E felony.

(c) **Additional Offense.** -- Unless the conduct is covered under some other provision of law providing greater punishment, a person who receives or possesses any controlled substance stolen in violation of subsection (b) of this section, knowing or having reasonable grounds to believe the controlled substance was stolen, is guilty of a Class F felony.

(d) **Forfeiture.** -- Any interest a person has acquired or maintained in property obtained in violation of this section shall be subject to forfeiture pursuant to the procedures for forfeiture as set forth in G.S. 90-112.

History.
2019-40, s. 1

§ 14-55. Preparation to commit burglary or other housebreakings

If any person shall be found armed with any dangerous or offensive weapon, with the intent to break or enter a dwelling, or other building whatsoever, and to commit any felony or larceny therein; or shall be found having in his possession, without lawful excuse, any picklock, key, bit, or other implement of housebreaking; or shall be found in any such building, with intent to commit any felony or larceny therein, such person shall be punished as a Class I felon.

History.
Code, s. 997; Rev., s. 3334; 1907, c. 822; C.S., s. 4236; 1969, c. 543, s. 4; 1979, c. 760, s. 5; 1979, 2nd Sess., c. 1316, s. 47; 1981, c. 63, s. 1; c. 179, s. 14; 1993, c. 539, s. 1152; 1994, Ex. Sess., c. 24, s. 14(c)

§ 14-56. Breaking or entering into or breaking out of railroad cars, motor vehicles, trailers, aircraft, boats, or other watercraft*

(a) If any person, with intent to commit any felony or larceny therein, breaks or enters any railroad car, motor vehicle, trailer, aircraft, boat, or other watercraft of any kind, containing any goods, wares, freight, or other thing of value, or, after having committed any felony or larceny therein, breaks out of any railroad car, motor vehicle, trailer, aircraft, boat, or other watercraft of any kind containing any goods, wares, freight, or other thing of value, that person is guilty of a Class I felony. It is prima facie evidence that a person entered in violation of this section if he is found unlawfully in such a railroad car, motor vehicle, trailer, aircraft, boat, or other watercraft.

(b) It shall not be a violation of this section for any person to break or enter any railroad car, motor vehicle, trailer, aircraft, boat, or other watercraft of any kind to provide assistance to a person inside the railroad car, motor vehicle, trailer, aircraft, boat, or watercraft of any kind if one or more of the following circumstances exist:

(1) The person acts in good faith to access the person inside the railroad car, motor vehicle, trailer, aircraft, boat, or watercraft of any kind in order to provide first aid or emergency health care treatment or because the person inside is, or is in imminent danger of becoming unconscious, ill, or injured.

(2) It is reasonably apparent that the circumstances require prompt decisions and actions in medical, other health care, or other assistance for the person inside the railroad car, motor vehicle, trailer, aircraft, boat, or watercraft of any kind.

(3) The necessity of immediate health care treatment or removal of the person from the railroad car, motor vehicle, trailer, aircraft, boat, or other watercraft of any kind is so reasonably apparent that any delay in the rendering of treatment or removal would seriously worsen the physical condition or endanger the life of the person.

History.
1907, c. 468; C.S., s. 4237; 1969, c. 543, s. 5; 1979, c. 437; c. 760, s. 5; 1979, 2nd Sess., c. 1316, s. 10; 1981, c. 63, s. 1; c. 179, s. 14; 2015-286, s. 3.3(a)

*See Session Law 2021-167, included in frontmatter of this book, for 2021 amendment details.

§ 14-56.1. Breaking into or forcibly opening coin- or currency-operated machines

Any person who forcibly breaks into, or by the unauthorized use of a key or other instrument opens, any coin- or currency-operated machine with intent to steal any property or moneys therein shall be guilty of a Class 1 misdemeanor, but if such person has previously been convicted of violating this section, such person shall be punished as a Class I felon. The term "coin- or currency-operated machine" shall mean any coin- or currency-operated vending machine, pay telephone, telephone coin or currency receptacle, or other coin- or currency-activated machine or device.

There shall be posted on the machines referred to in G.S. 14-56.1 a decal stating that it is a crime to break into vending machines, and that a second offense is a felony. The absence of such a decal is not a defense to a prosecution for the crime described in this section.

History.
1963, c. 814, s. 1; 1977, c. 723, ss. 1, 3; 1979, c. 760, s. 5; c. 767, s. 1; 1979, 2nd Sess., c. 1316, s. 47; 1981, c. 63, s. 1; c. 179, s. 14; 1993, c. 539, ss. 27, 1153; 1994, Ex. Sess., c. 24, s. 14(c)

§ 14-56.2. Damaging or destroying coin- or currency-operated machines

Any person who shall willfully and maliciously damage or destroy any coin- or currency-operated machine shall be guilty of a Class 1 misdemeanor. The term "coin- or currency-operated machine" shall be defined as set out in G.S. 14-56.1.

History.
1963, c. 814, s. 2; 1977, c. 723, s. 2; 1993, c. 539, s. 28; 1994, Ex. Sess., c. 24, s. 14(c)

§ 14-56.3. Breaking into paper currency machines

Any person, who with intent to steal any moneys therein forcibly breaks into any vending or dispensing machine or device which is operated or activated by the use, deposit or insertion of United States paper currency, shall be guilty of a Class 1 misdemeanor, but if such person has previously been convicted of violating this section, such person shall be punished as a Class I felon.

There shall be posted on the machines referred to in this section a decal stating that it is a crime to break into paper currency machines. The absence of such a decal is not a defense to a prosecution for the crime described in this section.

History.
1977, c. 853, ss. 1, 2; 1979, c. 760, s. 5; c. 767, s. 2; 1979, 2nd Sess., c. 1316, s. 47; 1981, c. 63, s. 1; c. 179, s. 14; 1993, c. 539, ss. 29, 115; 1994, Ex. Sess., c. 24, s. 14(c)

§ 14-56.4. Preparation to commit breaking or entering into motor vehicles

(a) For purposes of this section:
(1) "Manipulative key" means a key, device or instrument, other than a key that is designed to operate a specific lock, that can be variably positioned and manipulated in a vehicle keyway to operate a lock or cylinder or multiple locks or cylinders, including a wiggle key, jiggle key, or rocket key.

(2) "Master key" means a key that operates all the keyed locks or cylinders in a similar type or group of locks.

(b) It is unlawful for any person to possess any motor vehicle master key, manipulative

Chapter 14

key, or other motor vehicle lock-picking device or hot wiring device, with the intent to commit any felony, larceny, or unauthorized use of a motor propelled conveyance.

(c) It is unlawful for a person to willfully buy, sell, or transfer a motor vehicle master key, manipulative key or device, key-cutting device, lock pick or lock-picking device, or hot wiring device, designed to open or capable of opening the door or trunk of any motor vehicle or of starting the engine of a motor vehicle for use in any manner prohibited by this section.

(d) Violation of this section is a Class 1 misdemeanor. A second or subsequent violation of this section is a Class I felony.

(e) This section shall not apply to any person who is a dealer of new or used motor vehicles, a car rental agent, a locksmith, an employee of a towing service, an employee of an automotive repair business, a person who is lawfully repossessing a vehicle, or a state, county, or municipal law enforcement officer, when that person is acting within the scope of the person's official duties or employment. This section shall not apply to a business which has a key-cutting device located and used on the premises for the purpose of making replacement keys for the owner or person who is in lawful custody of a vehicle.

History.
2005-352, s. 1

§ 14-57. Burglary with explosives

Any person who, with intent to commit any felony or larceny therein, breaks and enters, either by day or by night, any building, whether inhabited or not, and opens or attempts to open any vault, safe, or other secure place by use of nitroglycerine, dynamite, gunpowder, or any other explosive, or acetylene torch, shall be deemed guilty of burglary with explosives. Any person convicted under this section shall be punished as a Class D felon.

History.
1921, c. 5; C.S., s. 4237(a); 1969, c. 543, s. 6; 1979, c. 760, s. 5; 1979, 2nd Sess., c. 1316, s. 47; 1981, c. 63, s. 1; c. 179, s. 14; 1993, c. 539, s. 1155; 1994, Ex. Sess., c. 24, s. 14(c)

ARTICLE 15
ARSON AND OTHER BURNINGS

§ 14-58. Punishment for arson

There shall be two degrees of arson as defined at the common law. If the dwelling burned was occupied at the time of the burning, the offense

is arson in the first degree and is punishable as a Class D felony. If the dwelling burned was unoccupied at the time of the burning, the offense is arson in the second degree and is punishable as a Class G felony.

History.
R.C., c. 34, s. 2; 1870-1, c. 222; Code, s. 985; Rev., s. 3335; C.S., s. 4238; 1941, c. 215, s. 2; 1949, c. 299, s. 3; 1973, c. 1201, s. 4; 1979, c. 760, s. 5; 1979, 2nd Sess., c. 1316, s. 47; 1981, c. 63, s. 1; c. 179, s. 14; 1993, c. 539, s. 1156; 1994, Ex. Sess., c. 24, s. 14(c)

§ 14-58.1. Definition of "house" and "building."

As used in this Article, the terms "house" and "building" shall be defined to include mobile and manufactured-type housing and recreational trailers.

History.
1973, c. 1374

§ 14-58.2. Burning of mobile home, manufactured-type house or recreational trailer home

If any person shall willfully and maliciously burn any mobile home or manufactured-type house or recreational trailer home which is the dwelling house of another and which is occupied at the time of the burning, the same shall constitute the crime of arson in the first degree.

History.
1973, c. 1374; 1979, c. 760, s. 5; 1979, 2nd Sess., c. 1316, s. 47; 1981, c. 63, s. 1; c. 179, s. 14

§ 14-59. Burning of certain public buildings

If any person shall wantonly and willfully set fire to or burn or cause to be burned or aid, counsel or procure the burning of, the State Capitol, the Legislative Building, the Justice Building or any building owned or occupied by the State or any of its agencies, institutions or subdivisions or by any county, incorporated city or town or other governmental or quasi-governmental entity, he shall be punished as a Class F felon.

History.
1830, c. 41, s. 1; R.C., c. 34, s. 7; 1868-9, c. 167, s. 5; Code, s. 985, subsec. 3; Rev., s. 3344; C.S., s. 4239; 1965, c. 14; 1971, c. 816, s. 1; 1979, c. 760, s. 5; 1979, 2nd Sess., c. 1316, s. 47; 1981, c. 63, s. 1; c. 179, s. 14; 1993, c. 539, s. 115; 1994, Ex. Sess., c. 24, s. 14(c)

§ 14-60. Burning of schoolhouses or buildings of educational institutions

If any person shall wantonly and willfully set fire to or burn or cause to be burned or aid, counsel or procure the burning of, any schoolhouse or building owned, leased or used by any public or private school, college or educational institution, he shall be punished as a Class F felon.

History.

1901, c. 4, s. 28; Rev., s. 3345; 1919, c. 70; C.S., s. 4240; 1965, c. 870; 1971, c. 816, s. 2; 1979, c. 760, s. 5; 1979, 2nd Sess., c. 1316, s. 47; 1981, c. 63, s. 1; c. 179, s. 14; 1993, c. 539, s. 1158; 1994, Ex. Sess., c. 24, s. 14(c)

§ 14-61. Burning of certain bridges and buildings

If any person shall wantonly and willfully set fire to or burn or cause to be burned, or aid, counsel or procure the burning of, any public bridge, or private toll bridge, or the bridge of any incorporated company, or any fire-engine house or rescue-squad building, or any house belonging to an incorporated company or unincorporated association and used in the business of such company or association, he shall be punished as a Class F felon.

History.

1825, c. 1278, P.R.; R.C., c. 34, s. 30; Code, s. 985, subsec. 4; Rev., s. 3337; C.S., s. 4241; 1971, c. 816, s. 3; 1979, c. 760, s. 5; 1979, 2nd Sess., c. 1316, s. 47; 1981, c. 63, s. 1; c. 179, s. 14; 1993, c. 539, s. 1159; 1994, Ex. Sess., c. 24, s. 14(c)

§ 14-62. Burning of certain buildings

If any person shall wantonly and willfully set fire to or burn or cause to be burned, or aid, counsel or procure the burning of, any uninhabited house, or any stable, coach house, outhouse, warehouse, office, shop, mill, barn or granary, or any building, structure or erection used or intended to be used in carrying on any trade or manufacture, or any branch thereof, whether the same or any of them respectively shall then be in the possession of the offender, or in the possession of any other person, he shall be punished as a Class F felon.

History.

1874-5, c. 228; Code, s. 985, subsec. 6; 1885, c. 66; 1903, c. 665, s. 2; Rev., s. 3338; C.S., s. 4242; 1927, c. 11, s. 1; 1953, c. 815; 1959, c. 1298, s. 1; 1971, c. 816, s. 4; 1979, c. 760, s. 5; 1979, 2nd Sess., c. 1316, s. 47; 1981, c. 63, s. 1; c. 179, s. 14; 1993, c. 539, s. 1160; 1994, Ex. Sess., c. 24, s. 14(c); 1995 (Reg. Sess., 1996), c. 751, s. 2

§ 14-62.1. Burning of building or structure in process of construction

If any person shall wantonly and willfully set fire to or burn or cause to be burned, or aid, counsel or procure the burning of, any building or structure in the process of construction for use or intended to be used as a dwelling house or in carrying on any trade or manufacture, or otherwise, whether the same or any of them respectively shall then be in the possession of the offender, or in the possession of any other person, he shall be punished as a Class H felon.

History.

1957, c. 792; 1971, c. 816, s. 5; 1979, c. 760, s. 5; 1979, 2nd Sess., c. 1316, s. 47; 1981, c. 63, s. 1; c. 179, s. 14; 1993, c. 539, s. 1161; 1994, Ex. Sess., c. 24, s. 14(c)

§ 14-62.2. Burning of churches and certain other religious buildings

If any person shall wantonly and willfully set fire to or burn or cause to be burned, or aid, counsel or procure the burning of any church, chapel, or meetinghouse, the person shall be punished as a Class E felon.

History.

1995 (Reg. Sess., 1996), c. 751, s. 3

§ 14-63. Burning of boats and barges

If any person shall wantonly and willfully set fire to or burn or cause to be burned or aid, counsel or procure the burning of, any boat, barge, ferry or float, without the consent of the owner thereof, he shall be punished as a Class H felon. In the event the consent of the owner is given for an unlawful or fraudulent purpose, however, the penalty provisions of this section shall remain in full force and effect.

History.

1909, c. 854; C.S., s. 4243; 1971, c. 816, s. 6; 1979, c. 760, s. 5; 1979, 2nd Sess., c. 1316, s. 47; 1981, c. 63, s. 1; c. 179, s. 14

§ 14-64. Burning of ginhouses and tobacco houses

If any person shall wantonly and willfully set fire to or burn or cause to be burned, or aid, counsel or procure the burning of, any ginhouse or tobacco house, or any part thereof, he shall be punished as a Class H felon.

History.

1863, c. 17; 1868-9, c. 167, s. 5; Code, s. 985, subsec. 2; 1903, c. 665, s. 1; Rev., s. 3341; C.S., s. 4244; 1971, c. 816, s. 7; 1979, c. 760, s. 5; 1979, 2nd Sess., c. 1316, s. 47; 1981, c. 63, s. 1; c. 179, s. 14

Chapter 14

§ 14-65. Fraudulently setting fire to dwelling houses

If any person, being the occupant of any building used as a dwelling house, whether such person be the owner thereof or not, or, being the owner of any building designed or intended as a dwelling house, shall wantonly and willfully or for a fraudulent purpose set fire to or burn or cause to be burned, or aid, counsel or procure the burning of such building, he shall be punished as a Class H felon.

History.
Code, s. 985; 1903, c. 665, s. 3; Rev., s. 3340; 1909, c. 862; C.S., s. 4245; 1927, c. 11, s. 2; 1971, c. 816, s. 8; 1979, c. 760, s. 5; 1979, 2nd Sess., c. 1316, s. 47; 1981, c. 63, s. 1; c. 179, s. 14

§ 14-66. Burning of personal property

If any person shall wantonly and willfully set fire to or burn, or cause to be burned, or aid, counsel or procure the burning of, any goods, wares, merchandise or other chattels or personal property of any kind, whether or not the same shall at the time be insured by any person or corporation against loss or damage by fire, with intent to injure or prejudice the insurer, the creditor or the person owning the property, or any other person, whether the property is that of such person or another, he shall be punished as a Class H felon.

History.
1921, c. 119; C.S., s. 4245(a); 1971, c. 816, s. 9; 1979, c. 760, s. 5; 1979, 2nd Sess., c. 1316, s. 47; 1981, c. 63, s. 1; c. 179, s. 14

N.C. Gen. Stat. § 14-67

Repealed by Session Laws 1993, c. 539, s. 1358.2.

§ 14-67.1. Burning other buildings

If any person shall wantonly and willfully set fire to or burn or cause to be burned or aid, counsel or procure the burning of any building or other structure of any type not otherwise covered by the provisions of this Article, he shall be punished as a Class H felon.

History.
1971, c. 816, s. 11; 1979, c. 760, s. 5; 1979, 2nd Sess., c. 1316, s. 47; 1981, c. 63, s. 1; c. 179, s. 14; 1993, c. 539, s. 1192.1; 1994, Ex. Sess., c. 24, s. 14(c)

§ 14-67.2. Burning caused during commission of another felony

(a) If any person, during the commission of a felony, knowingly damages any dwelling, structure, building, or conveyance referenced in this Article by means of fire or explosive that results in damages valued at ten thousand dollars ($ 10,000) or more, the person shall be punished as a Class D felon unless the person's conduct is covered under some other provision of law providing greater punishment.

(b) If any person, during the commission of a felony, knowingly causes, aids, abets, advises, encourages, hires, counsels, or procures another person to damage any dwelling, structure, building, or conveyance referenced in this Article by means of fire or explosive that results in damages valued at ten thousand dollars ($ 10,000) or more, the person shall be punished as a Class D felon unless the person's conduct is covered under some other provision of law providing greater punishment.

History.
2018-31, s. 1

§ 14-68. Failure of owner of property to comply with orders of public authorities

If the owner or occupant of any building or premises shall fail to comply with the duly authorized orders of the chief of the fire department, or of the Commissioner of Insurance, or of any municipal or county inspector of buildings or of particular features, facilities, or installations of buildings, he shall be guilty of a Class 3 misdemeanor, and punished only by a fine of not less than ten ($ 10.00) nor more than fifty dollars ($ 50.00) for each day's neglect, failure, or refusal to obey such orders.

History.
1899, c. 58, s. 4; Rev., s. 3343; C.S., s. 4247; 1969, c. 1063, s. 1; 1993, c. 539, s. 30; 1994, Ex. Sess., c. 24, s. 14(c)

§ 14-69. Failure of officers to investigate incendiary fires

If any town or city officer shall fail, neglect or refuse to comply with any of the requirements of the law in regard to the investigation of incendiary fires, he shall be guilty of a Class 3 misdemeanor and shall only be punished by a fine not less than twenty-five ($ 25.00) nor more than two hundred dollars ($ 200.00).

History.
1899, c. 58, s. 5; Rev., s. 3342; C.S., s. 4248; 1993, c. 539, s. 3; 1994, Ex. Sess., c. 24, s. 14(c); 1994, Ex. Sess., c. 24, s. 14(c)

§ 14-69.1. Making a false report concerning destructive device

(a) Except as provided in subsection (c) of this section, any person who, by any means of communication to any person or group of persons, makes a report, knowing or having reason to know the report is false, that there is located in or in sufficient proximity to cause damage to any building, house or other structure whatsoever or any vehicle, aircraft, vessel or boat any device designed to destroy or damage the building, house or structure or vehicle, aircraft, vessel or boat by explosion, blasting or burning, is guilty of a Class H felony.

(b) Repealed by S.L. 1997-443, s. 19.25(cc).

(c) Any person who, by any means of communication to any person or groups of persons, makes a report, knowing or having reason to know the report is false, that there is located in or in sufficient proximity to cause damage to any public building any device designed to destroy or damage the public building by explosion, blasting, or burning, is guilty of a Class H felony. Any person who receives a second conviction for a violation of this subsection within five years of the first conviction for violation of this subsection is guilty of a Class G felony. For purposes of this subsection, "public building" means educational property as defined in G.S. 14-269.2(a)(1), a hospital as defined in G.S. 131E-76(3), a building housing only State, federal, or local government offices, or the offices of State, federal, or local government located in a building that is not exclusively occupied by the State, federal, or local government.

(d) The court may order a person convicted under this section to pay restitution, including costs and consequential damages resulting from the disruption of the normal activity that would have otherwise occurred on the premises but for the false report, pursuant to Article 81C of Chapter 15A of the General Statutes.

(e) For purposes of this section, the term "report" shall include making accessible to another person by computer.

History.
1959, c. 555, s. 1; 1991, c. 648, s. 1; 1993, c. 539, ss. 32, 116; 1994, Ex. Sess., c. 24, s. 14(c); 1997-443, s. 19.25(cc); 1999-257, s. 1; 2005-311, s. 1

§ 14-69.2. Perpetrating hoax by use of false bomb or other device

(a) Except as provided in subsection (c) of this section, any person who, with intent to perpetrate a hoax, conceals, places, or displays any device, machine, instrument or artifact, so as to cause any person reasonably to believe the same to be a bomb or other device capable of causing injury to persons or property is guilty of a Class H felony.

(b) Repealed by S.L. 1997-443, s. 19.25(dd).

(c) Any person who, with intent to perpetrate a hoax, conceals, places, or displays in or at a public building any device, machine, instrument, or artifact, so as to cause any person reasonably to believe the same to be a bomb or other device capable of causing injury to persons or property is guilty of a Class H felony. Any person who receives a second conviction for a violation of this subsection within five years of the first conviction for violation of this subsection is guilty of a Class G felony. For purposes of this subsection "public building" means educational property as defined in G.S. 14-269.2(a)(1), a hospital as defined in G.S. 131E-76(3), a building housing only State, federal, or local government offices, or the offices of State, federal, or local government located in a building that is not exclusively occupied by the State, federal, or local government.

(d) The court may order a person convicted under this section to pay restitution, including costs and consequential damages resulting from the disruption of the normal activity that would have otherwise occurred on the premises but for the hoax, pursuant to Article 81C of Chapter 15A of the General Statutes.

History.
1959, c. 555, s. 1; 1991, c. 648, s. 2; 1993, c. 539, s. 33; 1994, Ex. Sess., c. 24, s. 14(c); 1997-443, s. 19.25(dd); 1999-257, s. 2

§ 14-69.3. Arson or other unlawful burning that results in serious bodily injury to a firefighter, law enforcement officer, fire investigator, or emergency medical technician

(a) The following definitions apply in this section:

(1) **Emergency medical technician.** -- The term includes an emergency medical technician, an emergency medical technician-intermediate, and an emergency medical technician-paramedic, as those terms are defined in G.S. 131E-155.

(2) **Fire investigator.** -- The term includes any person who, individually or as part of an investigative team, has the responsibility and authority to determine the origin, cause, or development of a fire or explosion.

(b) A person is guilty of a Class E felony if the person commits a felony under Article 15 of Chapter 14 of the General Statutes and a firefighter, law enforcement officer, fire investigator, or emergency medical technician suffers serious bodily injury while discharging or attempting to discharge official duties on the property, or proximate to the property, that is the subject of the firefighter's, law enforcement officer's, fire investigator's, or emergency medical technician's discharge or attempt to discharge his or her respective duties.

History.
2003-392, s. 3(a); 2018-31, s. 2

SUBCHAPTER 05. OFFENSES AGAINST PROPERTY

ARTICLE 16 LARCENY

§ 14-70. Distinctions between grand and petit larceny abolished; punishment; accessories to larceny

All distinctions between petit and grand larceny are abolished. Unless otherwise provided by statute, larceny is a Class H felony and is subject to the same rules of criminal procedure and principles of law as to accessories before and after the fact as other felonies.

History.
R.C., c. 34, s. 26; Code, s. 1075; Rev., s. 3500; C.S., s. 4249; 1969, c. 522, s. 1; 1993, c. 539, s. 1163; 1994, Ex. Sess., c. 24, s. 14(c)

§ 14-71. Receiving stolen goods; receiving or possessing goods represented as stolen

(a) If any person shall receive any chattel, property, money, valuable security or other thing whatsoever, the stealing or taking whereof amounts to larceny or a felony, either at common law or by virtue of any statute made or hereafter to be made, such person knowing or having reasonable grounds to believe the same to have been feloniously stolen or taken, he shall be guilty of a Class H felony, and may be indicted and convicted, whether the felon stealing and taking such chattels, property, money, valuable security or other thing, shall or shall not have been previously convicted, or shall or shall not be amenable to justice; and any such receiver may be dealt with, indicted, tried and punished in any county in which he shall have, or shall have had, any such property in his possession or in any county in which the thief may be tried, in the same manner as such receiver may be dealt with, indicted, tried and punished in the county where he actually received such chattel, money, security, or other thing; and such receiver shall be punished as one convicted of larceny.

(b) If a person knowingly receives or possesses property in the custody of a law enforcement agency that was explicitly represented to the person by an agent of the law enforcement agency or a person authorized to act on behalf of a law enforcement agency as stolen, the person is guilty of a Class H felony and may be indicted, tried, and punished in any county in which the person received or possessed the property.

History.
1797, c. 485, s. 2; R.C., c. 34, s. 56; Code, s. 1074; Rev., s. 3507; C.S., s. 4250; 1949, c. 145, s. 1; 1975, c. 163, s. 1; 1993, c. 539, s. 1164; 1994, Ex. Sess., c. 24, s. 14(c); 2007-373, s. 1; 2008-187, s. 34(a)

§ 14-71.1. Possessing stolen goods

If any person shall possess any chattel, property, money, valuable security or other thing whatsoever, the stealing or taking whereof amounts to larceny or a felony, either at common law or by virtue of any statute made or hereafter to be made, such person knowing or having reasonable grounds to believe the same to have been feloniously stolen or taken, he shall be guilty of a Class H felony, and may be indicted and convicted, whether the felon stealing and taking such chattels, property, money, valuable security or other thing shall or shall not have been previously convicted, or shall or shall not be amenable to justice; and any such possessor may be dealt with, indicted, tried and punished in any county in which he shall have, or shall have had, any such property in his possession or in any county in which the thief may be tried, in the same manner as such possessor may be dealt with, indicted, tried and punished in the county where he actually possessed such chattel, money, security, or other thing; and such possessor shall be punished as one convicted of larceny.

History.
1977, c. 978, s. 1; 1993, c. 539, s. 1165; 1994, Ex. Sess., c. 24, s. 14(c)

§ 14-71.2. Receiving or transferring stolen vehicles

Any person who, with intent to procure or pass title to a vehicle which he knows or has reason to believe has been stolen or unlawfully taken, receives or transfers possession of the same from or to another, or who has in his possession any vehicle which he knows or has reason to believe has been stolen or unlawfully taken, and who is not an officer of the law engaged at the time in the performance of his duty as such officer shall be punished as a Class H felon.

Chapter 14

History.

1937, c. 407, s. 70; 1979, c. 760, s. 5; 1979, 2nd Sess., c. 1316, s. 47; 1981, c. 63, s. 1; c. 179, s. 14; 1993, c. 539, s. 1252; 1994, Ex. Sess., c. 24, s. 14(c); 2019-186, s. 1(c)

§ 14-72. Larceny of property; receiving stolen goods or possessing stolen goods

(a) Larceny of goods of the value of more than one thousand dollars ($ 1,000) is a Class H felony. The receiving or possessing of stolen goods of the value of more than one thousand dollars ($ 1,000) while knowing or having reasonable grounds to believe that the goods are stolen is a Class H felony. Larceny as provided in subsection (b) of this section is a Class H felony. Receiving or possession of stolen goods as provided in subsection (c) of this section is a Class H felony. Except as provided in subsections (b) and (c) of this section, larceny of property, or the receiving or possession of stolen goods knowing or having reasonable grounds to believe them to be stolen, where the value of the property or goods is not more than one thousand dollars ($ 1,000), is a Class 1 misdemeanor. In all cases of doubt, the jury shall, in the verdict, fix the value of the property stolen.

(b) The crime of larceny is a felony, without regard to the value of the property in question, if the larceny is any of the following:

(1) From the person.

(2) Committed pursuant to a violation of G.S. 14-51, 14-53, 14-54, 14-54.1, or 14-57.

(3) Of any explosive or incendiary device or substance. As used in this section, the phrase "explosive or incendiary device or substance" shall include any explosive or incendiary grenade or bomb; any dynamite, blasting powder, nitroglycerin, TNT, or other high explosive; or any device, ingredient for such device, or type or quantity of substance primarily useful for large-scale destruction of property by explosive or incendiary action or lethal injury to persons by explosive or incendiary action. This definition shall not include fireworks; or any form, type, or quantity of gasoline, butane gas, natural gas, or any other substance having explosive or incendiary properties but serving a legitimate nondestructive or nonlethal use in the form, type, or quantity stolen.

(4) Of any firearm. As used in this section, the term "firearm" shall include any instrument used in the propulsion of a shot, shell or bullet by the action of gunpowder or any other explosive substance within it. A "firearm," which at the time of theft is not capable of being fired, shall be included within this definition if it can be made to work. This definition shall not include air rifles or air pistols.

(5) Of any record or paper in the custody of the North Carolina State Archives as defined by G.S. 121-2(7) and G.S. 121-2(8).

(6) Committed after the defendant has been convicted in this State or in another jurisdiction for any offense of larceny under this section, or any offense deemed or punishable as larceny under this section, or of any substantially similar offense in any other jurisdiction, regardless of whether the prior convictions were misdemeanors, felonies, or a combination thereof, at least four times. A conviction shall not be included in the four prior convictions required under this subdivision unless the defendant was represented by counsel or waived counsel at first appearance or otherwise prior to trial or plea. If a person is convicted of more than one offense of misdemeanor larceny in a single session of district court, or in a single week of superior court or of a court in another jurisdiction, only one of the convictions may be used as a prior conviction under this subdivision; except that convictions based upon offenses which occurred in separate counties shall each count as a separate prior conviction under this subdivision.

(c) The crime of possessing stolen goods knowing or having reasonable grounds to believe them to be stolen in the circumstances described in subsection (b) is a felony or the crime of receiving stolen goods knowing or having reasonable grounds to believe them to be stolen in the circumstances described in subsection (b) is a felony, without regard to the value of the property in question.

(d) Where the larceny or receiving or possession of stolen goods as described in subsection (a) of this section involves the merchandise of any store, a merchant, a merchant's agent, a merchant's employee, or a peace officer who detains or causes the arrest of any person shall not be held civilly liable for detention, malicious prosecution, false imprisonment, or false arrest of the person detained or arrested, when such detention is upon the premises of the store or in a reasonable proximity thereto, is in a reasonable manner for a reasonable length of time, and, if in detaining or in causing the arrest of such person, the merchant, the merchant's agent, the merchant's employee, or the peace officer had, at the time of the detention or arrest, probable cause to believe that the person committed an offense under subsection (a) of this section. If the person being detained by the merchant, the merchant's agent, or the merchant's employee, is a minor under the age of 18 years, the merchant, the merchant's agent, or the merchant's employee, shall call or notify, or make a reasonable effort to call or notify the parent or guardian of the minor, during the period of detention. A merchant, a merchant's agent, or a merchant's employee, who makes a reasonable effort to call or notify the parent or guardian of the minor shall not be held civilly liable for failing to notify the parent or guardian of the minor.

History.

1895, c. 285; Rev., s. 3506; 1913, c. 118, s. 1; C.S., s. 4251; 1941, c. 178, s. 1; 1949, c. 145, s. 2; 1959, c. 1285; 1961, c. 39, s. 1; 1965, c. 621, s. 5; 1969, c. 522, s. 2; 1973, c. 238, ss. 1, 2; 1975, c. 163, s. 2; c. 696, s. 4; 1977, c. 978, ss. 2, 3; 1979, c. 408, s. 1; c. 760, s. 5; 1979, 2nd Sess., c. 1316, ss. 11, 47; 1981, c. 63, s. 1; c. 179, s. 14; 1991, c. 523, s. 2; 1993, c. 539, s. 34; 1994, Ex. Sess., c. 24, s. 14(c); 1995, c. 185, s. 2; 2006-259, s. 4(a); 2012-154, s. 1

§ 14-72.1. Concealment of merchandise in mercantile establishments

(a) Whoever, without authority, willfully conceals the goods or merchandise of any store, not theretofore purchased by such person, while still upon the premises of such store, shall be guilty of a misdemeanor and, upon conviction, shall be punished as provided in subsection (e). Such goods or merchandise found concealed upon or about the person and which have not theretofore been purchased by such person shall be prima facie evidence of a willful concealment.

(b) Repealed by Session Laws 1985 (Regular Session, 1986), c. 841, s. 2.

(c) A merchant, or the merchant's agent or employee, or a peace officer who detains or causes the arrest of any person shall not be held civilly liable for detention, malicious prosecution, false imprisonment, or false arrest of the person detained or arrested, where such detention is upon the premises of the store or in a reasonable proximity thereto, is in a reasonable manner for a reasonable length of time, and, if in detaining or in causing the arrest of such person, the merchant, or the merchant's agent or employee, or the peace officer had at the time of the detention or arrest probable cause to believe that the person committed the offense created by this section. If the person being detained by the merchant, or the merchant's agent or employee, is a minor under the age of 18 years, the merchant or the merchant's agent or employee, shall call or notify, or make a reasonable effort to call or notify the parent or guardian of the minor, during the period of detention. A merchant, or the merchant's agent or employee, who makes a reasonable effort to call or notify the parent or guardian of the minor shall not be held civilly liable for failing to notify the parent or guardian of the minor.

(d) Whoever, without authority, willfully transfers any price tag from goods or merchandise to other goods or merchandise having a higher selling price or marks said goods at a lower price or substitutes or superimposes thereon a false price tag and then presents said goods or merchandise for purchase shall be guilty of a misdemeanor and, upon conviction, shall be punished as provided in subsection (e).

Nothing herein shall be construed to provide that the mere possession of goods or the production by shoppers of improperly priced merchandise for checkout shall constitute prima facie evidence of guilt.

(d1) Notwithstanding subsection (e) of this section, any person who violates subsection (a) of this section by using a lead-lined or aluminum-lined bag, a lead-lined or aluminum-lined article of clothing, or a similar device to prevent the activation of any antishoplifting or inventory control device is guilty of a Class H felony.

(e) **Punishment.** -- For a first conviction under subsection (a) or (d), or for a subsequent conviction for which the punishment is not specified by this subsection, the defendant shall be guilty of a Class 3 misdemeanor. The term of imprisonment may be suspended only on condition that the defendant perform community service for a term of at least 24 hours. For a second offense committed within three years after the date the defendant was convicted of an offense under this section, the defendant shall be guilty of a Class 2 misdemeanor. The term of imprisonment may be suspended only on condition that the defendant be imprisoned for a term of at least 72 hours as a condition of special probation, perform community service for a term of at least 72 hours, or both. For a third or subsequent offense committed within five years after the date the defendant was convicted of two other offenses under this section, the defendant shall be guilty of a Class 1 misdemeanor. The term of imprisonment may be suspended only if a condition of special probation is imposed to require the defendant to serve a term of imprisonment of at least 11 days. However, if the sentencing judge finds that the defendant is unable, by reason of mental or physical infirmity, to perform the service required under this section, and the reasons for such findings are set forth in the judgment, the judge may pronounce such other sentence as the judge finds appropriate.

(f) Repealed by Session Laws 2009-372, s. 12, effective December 1, 2009, and applicable to offenses committed on or after that date.

(g) **Limitations.** -- For active terms of imprisonment imposed under this section:

(1) The judge may not give credit to the defendant for the first 24 hours of time spent in incarceration pending trial;

(2) The defendant must serve the mandatory minimum period of imprisonment and

good or gain time credit may not be used to reduce that mandatory minimum period; and

(3) The defendant may not be released or paroled unless he is otherwise eligible and has served the mandatory minimum period of imprisonment.

History.
1957, c. 301; 1971, c. 238; 1973, c. 457, ss. 1, 2; 1985 (Reg. Sess., 1986), c. 841, ss. 1-3; 1987, c. 660; 1993, c. 539, s. 35; 1994, Ex. Sess., c. 24, s. 14(c); c. 28, s. 1; 1995, c. 185, s. 3; c. 509, s. 9; 1997-80, s. 1; 1997-443, s. 19.25(ff); 2009-372, s. 12

§ 14-72.2. Unauthorized use of a motor-propelled conveyance

(a) A person is guilty of an offense under this section if, without the express or implied consent of the owner or person in lawful possession, he takes or operates an aircraft, motorboat, motor vehicle, or other motor-propelled conveyance of another.

(b) Unauthorized use of an aircraft is a Class H felony. All other unauthorized use of a motor-propelled conveyance is a Class 1 misdemeanor.

(c) Unauthorized use of a motor-propelled conveyance shall be a lesser-included offense of unauthorized use of an aircraft.

(d) As used in this section, "owner" means any person with a property interest in the motor-propelled conveyance.

History.
1973, c. 1330, s. 38; 1977, c. 919; 1979, c. 760, s. 5; 1979, 2nd Sess., c. 1316, s. 47; 1981, c. 63, s. 1; c. 179, s. 14; 1993, c. 539, ss. 36, 1166; 1994, Ex. Sess., c. 24, s. 14(c)

§ 14-72.3. Removal of shopping cart from shopping premises

(a) As used in this section:
(1) "Shopping cart" means the type of push cart commonly provided by grocery stores, drugstores, and other retail stores for customers to transport commodities within the store and from the store to their motor vehicles outside the store.
(2) "Premises" includes the motor vehicle parking area set aside for customers of the store.

(b) It is unlawful for any person to remove a shopping cart from the premises of a store without the consent, given at the time of the removal, of the store owner, manager, agent or employee.

(c) Violation of this section is a Class 3 misdemeanor.

History.
1983, c. 705, s. 1; 1994, Ex. Sess., c. 14, s. 3.1

§ 14-72.4. Unauthorized taking or sale of labeled dairy milk cases or milk crates bearing the name or label of owner

(a) A person is guilty of the unauthorized taking or sale of a dairy milk case or milk crate on or after January 1, 1990, if he:
(1) Takes, buys, sells or disposes of any dairy milk case or milk crate, bearing the name or label of the owner, without the express or implied consent of the owner or his designated agent; or
(2) Refuses upon demand of the owner or his designated agent to return to the owner or his designated agent any dairy milk case or milk crate, bearing the name or label of the owner; or
(3) Defaces, obliterates, erases, covers up, or otherwise removes or conceals any name, label, registered trademark, insignia, or other business identification of an owner of a dairy milk case or milk crate, for the purpose of destroying or removing from the milk case or milk crate evidence of its ownership.

(b) For purposes of this section dairy milk cases or milk crates shall be deemed to bear a name or label of an owner when there is imprinted or attached on the case or crate a name, insignia, mark, business identification or label showing ownership or sufficient information to ascertain ownership. For purposes of this section, the term "dairy case" shall be defined as a wire or plastic container which holds 16 quarts or more of beverage and is used by distributors or retailers, or their agents, as a means to transport, store, or carry dairy products.

(c) A violation of this section is a Class 2 misdemeanor.

(d) Nothing in this section shall preclude the prosecution of any misdemeanor or felony offense that is applicable under any other statute or common law.

History.
1989, c. 303, s. 1; 1994, Ex. Sess., c. 14, s. 3.2

§ 14-72.5. Larceny of motor fuel

(a) If any person shall take and carry away motor fuel valued at less than one thousand dollars ($ 1,000) from an establishment where motor fuel is offered for retail sale with the intent to steal the motor fuel, that person shall be guilty of a Class 1 misdemeanor.

(b) The term "motor fuel" as used in this section shall have the same meaning as found in G.S. 105-449.60(20).

(c) **Conviction Report Sent to Division of Motor Vehicles.** -- The court shall report final convictions of violations of this section to the Division of Motor Vehicles. The Division of Motor Vehicles shall revoke a person's drivers license for a second or subsequent conviction under this section in accordance with G.S. 20-17(a)(16).

History.
2001-352, s. 1

§ 14-72.6. Felonious larceny, possession, or receiving of stolen goods from a permitted construction site

(a) A person is guilty of a Class I felony if he commits any of the following offenses, where the goods are valued in excess of three hundred dollars ($ 300.00) but less than one thousand dollars ($ 1,000):

(1) Larceny of goods from a permitted construction site.

(2) Possessing or receiving of stolen goods, with actual knowledge or having reasonable grounds to believe that the goods were stolen from a permitted construction site.

(b) As used in this section, a "permitted construction site" is a site where a permit, license, or other authorization has been issued by the State or a local governmental entity for the placement of new construction or improvements to real property.

History.
2005-208, s. 1

§ 14-72.7. Chop shop activity

(a) A person is guilty of a Class G felony if that person engages in any of the following activities, without regard to the value of the property in question:

(1) Altering, destroying, disassembling, dismantling, reassembling, or storing any motor vehicle or motor vehicle part the person knows or has reasonable grounds to believe has been illegally obtained by theft, fraud, or other illegal means.

(2) Permitting a place to be used for any activity prohibited by this section, where the person either owns or has legal possession of the place, and knows or has reasonable grounds to believe that the place is being used for any activity prohibited by this section.

(3) Purchasing, disposing of, selling, transferring, receiving, or possessing a motor vehicle or motor vehicle part either knowing or having reasonable grounds to believe that the vehicle identification number of the motor vehicle, or vehicle part

identification number of the vehicle part, has been altered, counterfeited, defaced, destroyed, disguised, falsified, forged, obliterated, or removed.

(4) Purchasing, disposing of, selling, transferring, receiving, or possessing a motor vehicle or motor vehicle part to or from a person engaged in any activity prohibited by this section, knowing or having reasonable grounds to believe that the person is engaging in that activity.

(b) **Innocent Activities.** -- The provisions of this section shall not apply to either of the following:

(1) Purchasing, disposing of, selling, transferring, receiving, possessing, crushing, or compacting a motor vehicle or motor vehicle part in good faith and without knowledge of previous illegal activity in regard to that vehicle or part, as long as the person engaging in the activity does not remove a vehicle identification number or vehicle part identification number before or during the activity.

(2) Purchasing, disposing of, selling, transferring, receiving, possessing, crushing, or compacting a motor vehicle or motor vehicle part after law enforcement proceedings are completed or as a part of law enforcement proceedings, as long as the activity is not in conflict with law enforcement proceedings.

(c) **Civil Penalty.** -- Any court with jurisdiction of a criminal prosecution under this section may also assess a civil penalty. The clear proceeds of the civil penalties shall be remitted to the Civil Penalty and Forfeiture Fund in accordance with G.S. 115C-457.2. The civil penalty shall not exceed three times the assets obtained by the defendant as a result of violations of this section.

(d) **Private Actions.** -- Any person aggrieved by a violation of this section may, in a civil action in any court of competent jurisdiction, obtain appropriate relief, including preliminary and other equitable or declaratory relief, compensatory and punitive damages, reasonable investigation expenses, costs of suit, and any attorneys' fees as may be provided by law.

(e) **Seizure and Forfeiture.** -- Any instrumentality possessed or used to engage in the activities prohibited by this section are subject to the seizure and forfeiture provisions of G.S. 14-86.1. The real property of a place used to engage in the activities prohibited by this section is subject to the abatement and forfeiture provisions of Chapter 19 of the General Statutes.

(f) **Definitions.** -- For the purposes of this section, the following definitions apply:

(1) **Instrumentality.** -- Motor vehicle, motor vehicle part, other conveyance, tool, implement, or equipment possessed or used

in the activities prohibited under this section.

(2) **Vehicle identification number.** -- A number, a letter, a character, a datum, a derivative, or a combination thereof, used by the manufacturer or the Division of Motor Vehicles for the purpose of uniquely identifying a motor vehicle.

(3) **Vehicle part identification number.** -- A number, a letter, a character, a datum, a derivative, or a combination thereof, used by the manufacturer for the purpose of uniquely identifying a motor vehicle part.

History.
2007-178, s. 1; 2013-323, s. 1

§ 14-72.8. Felony larceny of motor vehicle parts

(a) **Offense; Punishment.** -- Unless the conduct is covered under some other provision of law providing greater punishment, larceny of a motor vehicle part is a Class I felony if (i) the cost of repairing the motor vehicle is one thousand dollars ($ 1,000) or more or (ii) the motor vehicle part is a catalytic converter.

(b) **Presumption.** -- A person in possession of a catalytic converter that has been removed from a motor vehicle is presumed to have obtained the catalytic converter under circumstances constituting a violation of subsection (a) of this section unless the person is any of the following:

(1) An employee or agent of a company, or an individual, acting in their official duties for a motor vehicle dealer, motor vehicle repair shop, secondary metals recycler, or salvage yard that is licensed, permitted, or registered pursuant to State law.

(2) An individual who possesses vehicle registration documentation indicating that the catalytic converter in the individual's possession is the result of a replacement of a catalytic converter from a vehicle registered in that individual's name.

(c) **Determining Cost.** -- For purposes of this section, the cost of repairing a motor vehicle means the cost of any replacement part and any additional costs necessary to install the replacement part in the motor vehicle.

History.
2009-379, s. 1; 2021-154, s. 1

§§ 14-72.9, 14-72.10

Reserved for future codification purposes*
*See Session Law 2021-167, included in frontmatter of this book, for 2021 amendment details.

§ 14-72.11. Larceny from a merchant

A person is guilty of a Class H felony if the person commits larceny against a merchant under any of the following circumstances:

(1) By taking property that has a value of more than two hundred dollars ($ 200.00), using an exit door erected and maintained to comply with the requirements of 29 C.F.R. § 1910.36 and 29 C.F.R. § 1910.37, to exit the premises of a store.

(2) By removing, destroying, or deactivating a component of an antishoplifting or inventory control device to prevent the activation of any antishoplifting or inventory control device.

(3) By affixing a product code created for the purpose of fraudulently obtaining goods or merchandise from a merchant at less than its actual sale price.

(4) When the property is infant formula valued in excess of one hundred dollars ($ 100.00). As used in this subsection, the term "infant formula," has the same meaning as found in 21 U.S.C. § 321(z).

(5) By exchanging property for cash, a gift card, a merchandise card, or some other item of value, knowing or having reasonable grounds to believe the property is stolen.

History.
2007-373, s. 2; 2008-187, s. 34(b); 2017-162, s. 1

§ 14-73. Jurisdiction of the superior courts in cases of larceny and receiving stolen goods

The superior courts shall have exclusive jurisdiction of the trial of all cases of the larceny of property, or the receiving of stolen goods knowing them to be stolen, of the value of more than one thousand dollars ($ 1,000).

History.
1913, c. 118, s. 2; C.S., s. 4252; 1941, c. 178, s. 2; 1949, c. 145, s. 3; 1961, c. 39, s. 2; 1979, c. 408, s. 2; 1991, c. 523, s. 3

§ 14-73.1. Petty misdemeanors

The offenses of larceny and the receiving of stolen goods knowing the same to have been stolen, which are made misdemeanors by Article 16, Subchapter V, Chapter 14 of the General Statutes, as amended, are hereby declared to be petty misdemeanors.

History.
1949, c. 145, s. 4; 1973, c. 108, s. 1

§ 14-74. Larceny by servants and other employees

If any servant or other employee, to whom any money, goods or other chattels, or any of the articles, securities or choses in action mentioned in G.S. 14-75, by his master shall be delivered safely to be kept to the use of his master, shall withdraw himself from his master and go away with such money, goods or other chattels, or any of the articles, securities or choses in action mentioned as aforesaid, or any part thereof, with intent to steal the same and defraud his master thereof, contrary to the trust and confidence in him reposed by his said master; or if any servant, being in the service of his master, without the assent of his master, shall embezzle such money, goods or other chattels, or any of the articles, securities or choses in action mentioned as aforesaid, or any part thereof, or otherwise convert the same to his own use, with like purpose to steal them, or to defraud his master thereof, the servant so offending shall be guilty of a felony: Provided, that nothing contained in this section shall extend to apprentices or servants within the age of 16 years. If the value of the money, goods, or other chattels, or any of the articles, securities, or choses in action mentioned in G.S. 14-75, is one hundred thousand dollars ($ 100,000) or more, the person is guilty of a Class C felony. If the value of the money, goods, or other chattels, or any of the articles, securities, or choses in action mentioned in G.S. 14-75, is less than one hundred thousand dollars ($ 100,000), the person is guilty of a Class H felony.

History.
21 Hen. VIII, c. 7, ss. 1, 2; R.C., c. 34, s. 18; Code, s. 1065; Rev., s. 3499; C.S., s. 4253; 1979, c. 760, s. 5; 1979, 2nd Sess., c. 1316, s. 47; 1981, c. 63, s. 1; c. 179, s. 14; 1997-443, s. 19.25(c); 1998-217, s. 4(a)

§ 14-75. Larceny of chose in action

If any person shall feloniously steal, take and carry away, or take by robbery, any bank note, check or other order for the payment of money issued by or drawn on any bank or other society or corporation within this State or within any of the United States, or any treasury warrant, debenture, certificate of stock or other public security, or certificate of stock in any corporation, or any order, bill of exchange, bond, promissory note or other obligation, either for the payment of money or for the delivery of specific articles, being the property of any other person, or of any corporation (notwithstanding any of the said particulars may be termed in law a chose in action), that person is guilty of a Class H felony.

History.
1811, c. 814, s. 1; R.C., c. 34, s. 20; Code, s. 1064; Rev., s. 3498; C.S., s. 4254; 1945, c. 635; 1993, c. 539, s. 1167; 1994, Ex. Sess., c. 24, s. 14(c)

§ 14-75.1. Larceny of secret technical processes

Any person who steals property consisting of a sample, culture, microorganism, specimen, record, recording, document, drawing, or any other article, material, device, or substance which constitutes, represents, evidences, reflects, or records a secret scientific or technical process, invention, formula, or any phase or part thereof shall be punished as a Class H felon. A process, invention, or formula is "secret" when it is not, and is not intended to be, available to anyone other than the owner thereof or selected persons having access thereto for limited purposes with his consent, and when it accords or may accord the owner an advantage over competitors or other persons who do not have knowledge or the benefit thereof.

History.
1967, c. 1175; 1979, c. 760, s. 5; 1979, 2nd Sess., c. 1316, s. 47; 1981, c. 63, s. 1; c. 179, s. 14

§ 14-76. Larceny, mutilation, or destruction of public records and papers

If any person shall steal, or for any fraudulent purpose shall take from its place of deposit for the time being, or from any person having the lawful custody thereof, or shall unlawfully and maliciously obliterate, injure or destroy any record, writ, return, panel, process, interrogatory, deposition, affidavit, rule, order or warrant of attorney or any original document whatsoever, of or belonging to any court of record, or relating to any matter, civil or criminal, begun, pending or terminated in any such court, or any bill, answer, interrogatory, deposition, affidavit, order or decree or any original document whatsoever, of or belonging to any court or relating to any cause or matter begun, pending or terminated in any such court, every such offender shall be guilty of a Class 1 misdemeanor; and in any indictment for such offense it shall not be necessary to allege that the article, in respect to which the offense is committed, is the property of any person or that the same is of any value. If any person shall steal or for any fraudulent purpose shall take from the register's office, or from any person having the lawful custody thereof, or shall unlawfully and willfully obliterate, injure or destroy any book wherein deeds or other instruments of writing are registered, or any other book of registration or record required to be kept by the register of deeds or shall unlawfully destroy, obliterate, deface or remove any records of proceedings of the board of county commissioners, or unlawfully and fraudulently abstract any record, receipt, order or voucher or other paper writing required to be kept by the clerk of the board of commissioners of any county, he shall be guilty of a Class 1 misdemeanor.

History.
8 Hen. VI, c. 12, s. 3; R.C., c. 34, s. 31; 1881, c. 17; Code, s. 1071; Rev., s. 3508; C.S., s. 4255; 1993, c. 539, s. 37; 1994, Ex. Sess., c. 24, s. 14(c).

§ 14-76.1. Mutilation or defacement of records and papers in the North Carolina State Archives

If any person shall willfully or maliciously obliterate, injure, deface, or alter any record or paper in the custody of the North Carolina State Archives as defined by G.S. 121-2(7) and 121-2(8), he shall be guilty of a Class 1 misdemeanor. The provisions of this section do not apply to employees of the Department of Natural and Cultural Resources who may destroy any accessioned records or papers that are approved for destruction by the North Carolina Historical Commission pursuant to the authority contained in G.S. 121-4(12).

History.
1975, c. 696, s. 3; 1993, c. 539, s. 38; 1994, Ex. Sess., c. 24, s. 14(c); 2015-241, s. 14.30(s).

§ 14-77. Larceny, concealment or destruction of wills

If any person, either during the life of the testator or after his death, shall steal or, for any fraudulent purpose, shall destroy or conceal any will, codicil or other testamentary instrument, he shall be guilty of a Class 1 misdemeanor.

History.
R.C., c. 34, s. 32; Code, s. 1072; Rev., s. 3510; C.S., s. 4256; 1993, c. 539, s. 39; 1994, Ex. Sess., c. 24, s. 14(c)

§ 14-78. Larceny of ungathered crops

If any person shall steal or feloniously take and carry away any maize, corn, wheat, rice or other grain, or any cotton, tobacco, potatoes, peanuts, pulse, fruit, vegetable or other product cultivated for food or market, growing, standing or remaining ungathered in any field or ground, that person is guilty of a Class H felony.

History.
1811, c. 816, P.R.; R.C., c. 34, s. 21; 1868-9, c. 251; Code, s. 1069; Rev., s. 3503; C.S., s. 4257; 1975, c. 697; 1993, c. 539, s. 1168; 1994, Ex. Sess., c. 24, s. 14(c)

N.C. Gen. Stat. § 14-78.1

Repealed by Session Laws 1994, Extra Session, c. 14, s. 72(1).

§ 14-79. Larceny of ginseng

If any person shall take and carry away, or shall aid in taking or carrying away, any ginseng growing upon the lands of another person, with intent to steal the same, he shall be punished as a Class H felon.

History.
1905, c. 211; Rev., s. 3502; C.S., s. 4258; 1979, c. 760, s. 5; 1979, 2nd Sess., c. 1316, s. 47; 1981, c. 63, s. 1; c. 179, s. 14; 1993, c. 539, s. 1169; 1994, Ex. Sess., c. 24, s. 14(c); 1999-107, s. 1

§ 14-79.1. Larceny of pine needles or pine straw

If any person shall take and carry away, or shall aid in taking or carrying away, any pine needles or pine straw being produced on the land of another person upon which land notices, signs, or posters prohibiting the raking or removal of pine needles or pine straw have been placed in accordance with the provisions of G.S. 14-159.7, or upon which posted notices have been placed in accordance with the provisions of G.S. 14-159.7, with the intent to steal the pine needles or pine straw, that person shall be guilty of a Class H felony.

History.
1997-443, s. 19.25(aa)

§ 14-79.2. Waste kitchen grease; unlawful acts and penalties

(a) It shall be unlawful for any person to do any of the following:

(1) Take and carry away, or aid in taking or carrying away, any waste kitchen grease container or the waste kitchen grease contained therein, which container bears a notice that unauthorized removal is prohibited without written consent of the owner of the container.

(2) Intentionally contaminate or purposely damage any waste kitchen grease container or grease therein.

(3) Place a label on a waste kitchen grease container knowing that it is owned by another person in order to claim ownership of the container.

(b) Any person who violates subsection (a) of this section shall be penalized as follows:

(1) If the value of the waste kitchen grease container, or the container and the waste kitchen grease contained therein, is one thousand dollars ($ 1,000) or less, it shall be a Class 1 misdemeanor.

(2) If the value of the waste kitchen grease container, or the container and the waste kitchen grease contained therein, is

more than one thousand dollars ($ 1,000), it shall be a Class H felony.

(c) A container in which waste kitchen grease is deposited that bears a name on the container shall be presumed to be owned by that person named on the container.

(d) As used in this section, "waste kitchen grease" has the same meaning as in G.S. 106-168.1.

History.
2012-127, s. 6

N.C. Gen. Stat. § 14-80

Repealed by Session Laws 1994, Extra Session, c. 14, s. 72(2).

§ 14-81. Larceny of horses, mules, swine, cattle, or dogs

(a) Larceny of horses, mules, swine, or cattle is a Class H felony.

(a1) Larceny of a dog is a Class I felony.

(b) In sentencing a person convicted of violating this section, the judge shall, as a minimum punishment, place a person on probation subject to the following conditions:

(1) A person must make restitution for the damage or loss caused by the larceny of the livestock or dogs, and

(2) A person must pay a fine of not less than the amount of the damages or loss caused by the larceny of the livestock or dogs.

(c) No provision in this section shall limit the authority of the judge to sentence the person convicted of violating this section to an active sentence.

History.
1866-7, c. 62; 1868, c. 37, s. 1; 1879, c. 234, s. 2; Code, s. 1066; Rev., s. 3505; 1917, c. 162, s. 2; C.S., s. 4260; 1965, c. 621, s. 6; 1981, c. 664, s. 2; 1989, c. 773, s. 2; 1993, c. 539, s. 1171; 1994, Ex. Sess., c. 24, s. 14(c)

§ 14-82. Taking horses, mules, or dogs for temporary purposes

If any person shall unlawfully take and carry away any horse, gelding, mare, mule, or dog, the property of another person, secretly and against the will of the owner of such property, with intent to deprive the owner of the special or temporary use of the same, or with the intent to use such property for a special or temporary purpose, the person so offending shall be guilty of a Class 2 misdemeanor.

History.
1879, c. 234, s. 1; Code, s. 1067; Rev., s. 3509; 1913, c. 11; C.S., s. 4261; 1969, c. 1224, s. 3; 1989, c. 773, s. 3; 1994, Ex. Sess., c. 14, s. 3.3

N.C. Gen. Stat. § 14-83

Repealed by Session Laws 1943, c. 543.

§ 14-83.1. Fixtures subject to larceny

All common law distinctions providing that personal property that has become affixed to real property is not subject to a charge of larceny are abolished. Any person who shall remove or take and carry away, or shall aid another in removing, taking or carrying away, any property that is affixed to real property, with the intent to steal the property, shall be guilty of larceny and shall be punished as provided by statute.

History.
2008-128, s. 2

§ 14-84. Animals subject to larceny

All common-law distinctions among animals with respect to their being subject to larceny are abolished. Any animal that is in a person's possession is the subject of larceny.

History.
1919, c. 116, s. 9; C.S., s. 4263; 1955, c. 804; 1983, c. 35, s. 1

§ 14-85. Pursuing or injuring livestock with intent to steal

If any person shall pursue, kill or wound any horse, mule, ass, jennet, cattle, hog, sheep or goat, the property of another, with the intent unlawfully and feloniously to convert the same to his own use, he shall be guilty of a Class H felony, and shall be punishable, in all respects, as if convicted of larceny, though such animal may not have come into the actual possession of the person so offending.

History.
1866, c. 57; Code, s. 1068; Rev., s. 3504; C.S., s. 4264; 1993, c. 539, s. 1172; 1994, Ex. Sess., c. 24, s. 14(c)

N.C. Gen. Stat. § 14-86

Repealed by Session Laws 1994, Extra Session, c. 14, s. 72(3), effective October 1, 1994.

§ 14-86.1. Seizure and forfeiture of conveyances used in committing larceny and similar crimes

(a) All conveyances, including vehicles, watercraft or aircraft, used to unlawfully conceal, convey or transport property in violation of G.S. 14-71, 14-71.1, or 14-71.2 or used by any person in the commission of armed or common-law robbery, or used in violation of G.S. 14-72.7, or used by any person in the commission of any larceny when the value of the property taken is more than two thousand dollars ($ 2,000) shall be subject to forfeiture as provided herein, except that:

(1) No conveyance used by any person as a common carrier in the transaction of the business of the common carrier shall be forfeited under the provisions of this section unless it shall appear that the owner or other person in custody or control of such conveyance was a consenting party or privy to a violation that may subject the conveyance to forfeiture under this section;

(2) No conveyance shall be forfeited under the provisions of this section by reason of any act or omission committed or omitted while such conveyance was unlawfully in the possession of a person other than the owner in violation of the criminal laws of the United States, or any state;

(3) No conveyance shall be forfeited pursuant to this section unless the violation involved is a felony;

(4) A forfeiture of a conveyance encumbered by a bona fide security interest is subject to the interest of the secured party who neither had knowledge of nor consented to the act or omission;

(5) No conveyance shall be forfeited under the provisions of this section unless the owner knew or had reason to believe the vehicle was being used in the commission of any violation that may subject the conveyance to forfeiture under this section;

(6) The trial judge in the criminal proceeding which may subject the conveyance to forfeiture may order the seized conveyance returned to the owner if he finds forfeiture inappropriate. If the conveyance is not returned to the owner the procedures provided in subsection (e) shall apply.

As used in this section concerning a violation of G.S. 14-72.7, the term "conveyance" includes any "instrumentality" as defined in that section.

(b) Any conveyance subject to forfeiture under this section may be seized by any law-enforcement officer upon process issued by any district or superior court having original jurisdiction over the offense except that seizure without such process may be made when:

(1) The seizure is incident to an arrest or subject to a search under a search warrant; or

(2) The property subject to seizure has been the subject of a prior judgment in favor of the State in a criminal injunction or forfeiture proceeding under this section.

(c) The conveyance shall be deemed to be in custody of the law-enforcement agency seizing it. The law-enforcement agency may remove the property to a place designated by it or request that the North Carolina Department of Justice or Department of Public Safety take custody of the property and remove it to an appropriate location for disposition in accordance with law; provided, the conveyance shall be returned to the owner upon execution by him of a good and valid bond, with sufficient sureties, in a sum double the value of the property, which said bond shall be approved by an officer of the agency seizing the conveyance and shall be conditioned upon the return of said property to the custody of said officer on the day of trial to abide the judgment of the court.

(d) Whenever a conveyance is forfeited under this section, the law-enforcement agency having custody of it may:

(1) Retain the conveyance for official use; or

(2) Transfer the conveyance which was forfeited under the provisions of this section to the North Carolina Department of Justice or to the North Carolina Department of Public Safety when, in the discretion of the presiding judge and upon application of the North Carolina Department of Justice or the North Carolina Department of Public Safety, said conveyance may be of official use to the North Carolina Department of Justice or the North Carolina Department of Public Safety; or

(3) Upon determination by the director of any law-enforcement agency that a conveyance transferred pursuant to the provisions of this section is of no further use to said agency, such conveyance may be sold as surplus property in the same manner as other conveyances owned by the law-enforcement agency. The proceeds from such sale, after deducting the cost thereof, shall be paid to the school fund of the county in which said conveyance was seized. Any conveyance transferred to any law-enforcement agency under the provisions of this section which has been modified or especially equipped from its original manufactured condition so as to increase its speed shall be used in the performance of official duties only. Such conveyance shall not be resold, transferred or disposed of other than as junk unless the special equipment or modification has been removed and destroyed, and the vehicle restored to its original manufactured condition.

(e) All conveyances subject to forfeiture under the provisions of this section shall be forfeited pursuant to the procedures for forfeiture of conveyances used to conceal, convey, or transport intoxicating beverages found in G.S. 18B-504. Provided, nothing in this section or G.S. 18B-504 shall be construed to require a conveyance to be sold when it can be used in the performance of official duties of the law-enforcement agency.

History.
1979, c. 592; 1983, c. 74; c. 768, s. 2; 1991, c. 523, s. 4; 2007-178, s. 2; 2011-145, s. 19.1(g); 2021-134, s. 1.2(b)

§ 14-86.2. Larceny, destruction, defacement, or vandalism of portable toilets or pumper trucks

Unless the conduct is covered under some other provision of law providing greater punishment, if any person steals, takes from its temporary location or from any person having the lawful custody thereof, or willfully destroys, defaces, or vandalizes a chemical or portable toilet as defined in G.S. 130A-290 or a pumper truck that is operated by a septage management firm that is permitted by the Department of Environmental Quality under G.S. 130A-291.1, the person is guilty of a Class 1 misdemeanor.

History.
2009-37, s. 1; 2015-241, s. 14.30(u)

§§ 14-86.3, 14-86.4

Reserved for future codification purposes.

ARTICLE 16A
ORGANIZED RETAIL THEFT

§ 14-86.5. Definitions

The following definitions apply in this Article:
(1) "Retail property." -- Any new article, product, commodity, item, or component intended to be sold in retail commerce.
(2) "Retail property fence." -- A person or business that buys retail property knowing or believing that retail property is stolen.
(3) "Theft." -- To take possession of, carry away, transfer, or cause to be carried away the retail property of another with the intent to steal the retail property.
(4) "Value." -- The retail value of an item as advertised by the affected retail establishment, to include all applicable taxes.

History.
2007-373, s. 3

§ 14-86.6. Organized retail theft

(a) A person is guilty of a Class H felony if the person does either of the following:
(1) Conspires with another person to commit theft of retail property from

retail establishments, with a value exceeding one thousand five hundred dollars ($ 1,500) aggregated over a 90-day period, with the intent to sell that retail property for monetary or other gain, and who takes or causes that retail property to be placed in the control of a retail property fence or other person in exchange for consideration.
(2) Receives or possesses any retail property that has been taken or stolen in violation of subdivision (1) of this subsection while knowing or having reasonable grounds to believe the property is stolen.
(a1) A person is guilty of a Class G felony if the person does either of the following:
(1) Conspires with another person to commit theft of retail property from one or more retail establishments, with a value exceeding twenty thousand dollars ($ 20,000) aggregated over a 90-day period, with the intent to sell that retail property for monetary or other gain, and who takes or causes that retail property to be placed in the control of a retail property fence or other person in exchange for consideration.
(2) Conspires with two or more other persons as an organizer, supervisor, financier, leader, or manager to engage for profit in a scheme or course of conduct to effectuate the transfer or sale of property stolen from a merchant in violation of this section.
(b) Any interest a person has acquired or maintained in violation of this section shall be subject to forfeiture pursuant to the procedures for forfeiture set out in G.S. 18B-504.
(c) Thefts of retail property occurring in more than one county may be aggregated into an alleged violation of this section. Each county where a part of the charged offense occurs has concurrent venue as described in G.S. 15A-132.

History.
2007-373, s. 3; 2008-187, s. 34(c); 2017-162, s. 2

ARTICLE 17
ROBBERY

§ 14-87. Robbery with firearms or other dangerous weapons

(a) Any person or persons who, having in possession or with the use or threatened use of any firearms or other dangerous weapon, implement or means, whereby the life of a person is endangered or threatened, unlawfully takes or attempts to take personal property from another or from any place of business, residence or banking institution or any other place where there is a person or persons in attendance, at any time, either day or night, or who aids or abets any such person or persons in the commission of such crime, shall be guilty of a Class D felony.

(a1) Attempted robbery with a dangerous weapon shall constitute a lesser included offense of robbery with a dangerous weapon, and evidence sufficient to prove robbery with a dangerous weapon shall be sufficient to support a conviction of attempted robbery with a dangerous weapon.

(b), (c) Repealed by Session Laws 1979, c. 760, s. 5.

(d) Repealed by Session Laws 1993, c. 539, s. 1173.

History.

1929, c. 187, s. 1; 1975, cc. 543, 846; 1977, c. 871, ss. 1, 6; 1979, c. 760, s. 5; 1979, 2nd Sess., c. 1316, ss. 12, 47; 1981, c. 63, s. 1; c. 179, s. 14; 1993, c. 539, s. 1173; 1994, Ex. Sess., c. 24, s. 14(c); 2017-31, s. 1

§ 14-87.1. Punishment for common-law robbery

Robbery as defined at common law, other than robbery with a firearm or other dangerous weapon as defined by G.S. 14-87, shall be punishable as a Class G felony.

History.

1979, c. 760, s. 5; 1993, c. 539, s. 1174; 1994, Ex. Sess., c. 24, s. 14(c)

§ 14-88. Train robbery

If any person shall enter upon any locomotive engine or car on any railroad in this State, and by threats, the exhibition of deadly weapons or the discharge of any pistol or gun, in or near any such engine or car, shall induce or compel any person on such engine or car to submit and deliver up, or allow to be taken therefrom, or from him, anything of value, he shall be guilty of train robbery, and on conviction thereof shall be punished as a Class D felon.

History.

1895, c. 204, s. 2; Rev., s. 3765; C.S., s. 4266; 1979, c. 760, s. 5; 1979, 2nd Sess., c. 1316, s. 47; 1981, c. 63, s. 1; c. 179, s. 14; 1993, c. 539, s. 1175; 1994, Ex. Sess., c. 24, s. 14(c)

N.C. Gen. Stat. § 14-89

Repealed by Session Laws 1994, Extra Session, c. 14, s. 71(5), effective October 1, 1994.

§ 14-89.1. Safecracking

(a) A person is guilty of safecracking if he unlawfully opens, enters, or attempts to open or enter a safe or vault:

(1) By the use of explosives, drills, or tools; or

(2) Through the use of a stolen combination, key, electronic device, or other fraudulently acquired implement or means; or

(3) Through the use of a master key, duplicate key or device made or obtained in an unauthorized manner, stethoscope or other listening device, electronic device used for unauthorized entry in a safe or vault, or other surreptitious means; or

(4) By the use of any other safecracking implement or means.

(b) A person is also guilty of safecracking if he unlawfully removes from its premises a safe or vault for the purpose of stealing, tampering with, or ascertaining its contents.

(c) Safecracking shall be punishable as a Class I felony.

History.

1961, c. 653; 1973, c. 235, s. 1; 1977, c. 1106; 1979, c. 760, s. 5; 1979, 2nd Sess., c. 1316, s. 47; 1981, c. 63, s. 1; c. 179, s. 14; 1993, c. 539, s. 1176; 1994, Ex. Sess., c. 24, s. 14(c)

ARTICLE 18
EMBEZZLEMENT

§ 14-90. Embezzlement of property received by virtue of office or employment

(a) This section shall apply to any person:

(1) Exercising a public trust.

(2) Holding a public office.

(3) Who is a guardian, administrator, executor, trustee, or any receiver, or any other fiduciary, including, but not limited to, a settlement agent, as defined in G.S. 45A-3.

(4) Who is an officer or agent of a corporation, or any agent, consignee, clerk, bailee or servant, except persons under the age of 16 years, of any person.

(b) Any person who shall:

(1) Embezzle or fraudulently or knowingly and willfully misapply or convert to his own use, or

(2) Take, make away with or secrete, with intent to embezzle or fraudulently or knowingly and willfully misapply or convert to his own use,

any money, goods or other chattels, bank note, check or order for the payment of money issued by or drawn on any bank or other corporation, or any treasury warrant, treasury note, bond or obligation for the payment of money issued by the United States or by any state, or any other valuable security whatsoever that (i) belongs to any other person or corporation, unincorporated association or organization or (ii) are closing funds as defined in G.S. 45A-3, which shall have come into his possession or under his care, shall be guilty of a felony.

(c) If the value of the property described in subsection (b) of this section is one hundred thousand dollars ($ 100,000) or more, the person is guilty of a Class C felony. If the value of the property is less than one hundred thousand dollars ($ 100,000), the person is guilty of a Class H felony.

History.
21 Hen. VII, c. 7; 1871-2, c. 145, s. 2; Code, s. 1014; 1889, c. 226; 1891, c. 188; 1897, c. 31; Rev., s. 3406; 1919, c. 97, s. 25; C.S., s. 4268; 1931, c. 158; 1939, c. 1; 1941, c. 31; 1967, c. 819; 1979, c. 760, s. 5; 1979, 2nd Sess., c. 1316, s. 47; 1981, c. 63, s. 1; c. 179, s. 14; 1997-443, s. 19.25(d); 2009-348, s. 1; 2009-570, s. 31

§ 14-91. Embezzlement of State property by public officers and employees

If any officer, agent, or employee of the State, or other person having or holding in trust for the same any bonds issued by the State, or any security, or other property and effects of the same, shall embezzle or knowingly and willfully misapply or convert the same to his own use, or otherwise willfully or corruptly abuse such trust, such offender and all persons knowingly and willfully aiding and abetting or otherwise assisting therein shall be guilty of a felony. If the value of the property is one hundred thousand dollars ($ 100,000) or more, a violation of this section is a Class C felony. If the value of the property is less than one hundred thousand dollars ($ 100,000), a violation of this section is a Class F felony.

History.
1874-5, c. 52; Code, s. 1015; Rev., s. 3407; C.S., s. 4269; 1979, c. 716; c. 760, s. 5; 1979, 2nd Sess., c. 1316, s. 47; 1981, c. 63, s. 1; c. 179, s. 14; 1997-443, s. 19.25(e)

§ 14-92. Embezzlement of funds by public officers and trustees

If an officer, agent, or employee of an entity listed below, or a person having or holding money or property in trust for one of the listed entities, shall embezzle or otherwise willfully and corruptly use or misapply the same for any purpose other than that for which such moneys or property is held, such person shall be guilty of a felony. If the value of the money or property is one hundred thousand dollars ($ 100,000) or more, the person is guilty of a Class C felony. If the value of the money or property is less than one hundred thousand dollars ($ 100,000), the person is guilty of a Class F felony. If any clerk

of the superior court or any sheriff, treasurer, register of deeds or other public officer of any county, unit or agency of local government, or local board of education shall embezzle or wrongfully convert to his own use, or corruptly use, or shall misapply for any purpose other than that for which the same are held, or shall fail to pay over and deliver to the proper persons entitled to receive the same when lawfully required so to do, any moneys, funds, securities or other property which such officer shall have received by virtue or color of his office in trust for any person or corporation, such officer shall be guilty of a felony. If the value of the money, funds, securities, or other property is one hundred thousand dollars ($ 100,000) or more, the person is guilty of a Class C felony. If the value of the money, funds, securities, or other property is less than one hundred thousand dollars ($ 100,000), the person is guilty of a Class F felony. The provisions of this section shall apply to all persons who shall go out of office and fail or neglect to account to or deliver over to their successors in office or other persons lawfully entitled to receive the same all such moneys, funds and securities or property aforesaid. The following entities are protected by this section: a county, a city or other unit or agency of local government, a local board of education, and a penal, charitable, religious, or educational institution.

History.
1876-7, c. 47; Code, s. 1016; 1891, c. 241; Rev., s. 3408; C.S., s. 4270; 1979, c. 760, s. 5; 1979, 2nd Sess., c. 1316, s. 47; 1981, c. 63, s. 1; c. 179, s. 14; 1985, c. 509, s. 3; 1993, c. 539, s. 1177; 1994, Ex. Sess., c. 24, s. 14(c); 1997-443, s. 19.25(f)

§ 14-93. Embezzlement by treasurers of charitable and religious organizations

If any treasurer or other financial officer of any benevolent or religious institution, society or congregation shall lend any of the moneys coming into his hands to any other person or association without the consent of the institution, association or congregation to whom such moneys belong; or, if he shall fail to account for such moneys when called on, he shall be guilty of a felony. If the violation of this section involves money with a value of one hundred thousand dollars ($ 100,000) or more, the person is guilty of a Class C felony. If the violation of this section involves money with a value of less than one hundred thousand dollars ($ 100,000) or less, a violation of this section is a Class H felony.

History.
1879, c. 105; Code, s. 1017; Rev., s. 3409; C.S., s. 4271; 1993, c. 539, s. 1178; 1994, Ex. Sess., c. 24, s. 14(c); 1997-443, s. 19.25(g)

§ 14-94. Embezzlement by officers of railroad companies

If any president, secretary, treasurer, director, engineer, agent or other officer of any railroad company shall embezzle any moneys, bonds or other valuable funds or securities, with which such president, secretary, treasurer, director, engineer, agent or other officer shall be charged by virtue of his office or agency, or shall in any way, directly or indirectly, apply or appropriate the same for the use or benefit of himself or any other person, state or corporation, other than the company of which he is president, secretary, treasurer, director, engineer, agent or other officer, for every such offense the person so offending shall be guilty of a felony, and on conviction in the superior or criminal court of any county through which the railroad of such company shall pass, shall be punished as a felon. If the value of the money, bonds, or other valuable funds or securities is one hundred thousand dollars ($ 100,000) or more, a violation of this section is a Class C felony. If the value of the money, bonds, or other valuable funds or securities is less than one hundred thousand dollars ($ 100,000), a violation of this section is a Class H felony.

History.
1870-1, c. 103, s. 1; Code, s. 1018; Rev., s. 3403; C.S., s. 4272; 1979, c. 760, s. 5; 1979, 2nd Sess., c. 1316, s. 47; 1981, c. 63, s. 1; c. 179, s. 14; 1997-443, s. 19.25(h).

N.C. Gen. Stat. § 14-95

Repealed by Session Laws 1994, Extra Session, c. 14, s. 71(6).

§§ 14-96, 14-96.1

Repealed by Session Laws 1989 (Regular Session, 1990), c. 1054, s. 6.

§ 14-97. Appropriation of partnership funds by partner to personal use

Any person engaged in a partnership business in the State of North Carolina who shall, without the knowledge and consent of his co-partner or copartners, take funds belonging to the partnership business and appropriate the same to his own personal use with the fraudulent intent of depriving his copartners of the use thereof, shall be guilty of a felony. Appropriation of partnership funds with a value of one hundred thousand dollars ($ 100,000) or more by a partner is a Class C felony. Appropriation of partnership funds with the value of less than one hundred thousand dollars ($ 100,000) by a partner is a Class H felony.

History.
1921, c. 127; C.S., s. 4274(a); 1993, c. 539, s. 1179; 1994, Ex. Sess., c. 24, s. 14(c); 1997-443, s. 19.25(i)

§ 14-98. Embezzlement by surviving partner

If any surviving partner shall willfully and intentionally convert any of the property, money or effects belonging to the partnership to his own use, and refuse to account for the same on settlement, he shall be guilty of a felony. If the property, money, or effects has a value of one hundred thousand dollars ($ 100,000) or more, a violation of this section is a Class C felony. If the property, money, or effects has a value of less than one hundred thousand dollars ($ 100,000), a violation of this section is a Class H felony.

History.
1901, c. 640, s. 9; Rev., s. 3405; C.S., s. 4275; 1979, c. 760, s. 5; 1979, 2nd Sess., c. 1316, s. 47; 1981, c. 63, s. 1; c. 179, s. 14; 1997-443, s. 19.25(j)

§ 14-99. Embezzlement of taxes by officers

If any officer appropriates to his own use the State, county, school, city or town taxes, he shall be guilty of embezzlement, and shall be punished as a felon. If the value of the taxes is one hundred thousand dollars ($ 100,000) or more, a violation of this section is a Class C felony. If the value of the taxes is less than one hundred thousand dollars ($ 100,000), a violation of this section is a Class F felony.

History.
1883, c. 136, s. 49; Code, s. 3705; Rev., s. 3410; C.S., s. 4276; 1979, c. 760, s. 5; 1979, 2nd Sess., c. 1316, s. 47; 1981, c. 63, s. 1; c. 179, s. 14; 1993, c. 539, s. 1180; 1994, Ex. Sess., c. 24, s. 14(c); 1997-443, s. 19.25(k)

ARTICLE 19
FALSE PRETENSES AND CHEATS

§ 14-100. Obtaining property by false pretenses

(a) If any person shall knowingly and designedly by means of any kind of false pretense whatsoever, whether the false pretense is of a past or subsisting fact or of a future fulfillment or event, obtain or attempt to obtain from any person within this State any money, goods, property, services, chose in action, or other thing of value with intent to cheat or defraud any person of such money, goods, property, services, chose in action or other thing of value, such person shall be guilty of a felony: Provided, that if, on the trial of anyone indicted for such crime, it shall be proved that he obtained the property in such manner as to amount to larceny or embezzlement, the jury shall have submitted to them such other felony proved; and no person tried for such felony shall be liable to be afterwards prosecuted for larceny or embezzlement upon the same facts: Provided, further, that it shall be sufficient in any indictment for obtaining or attempting to obtain any such money, goods, property, services, chose in action, or other thing of value by false pretenses to allege that the party accused did the act with intent to defraud, without alleging an intent to defraud any particular person, and without alleging any ownership of the money, goods, property, services, chose in action or other thing of value; and upon the trial of any such indictment, it shall not be necessary to prove either an intent to defraud any particular person or that the person to whom the false pretense was made was the person defrauded, but it shall be sufficient to allege and prove that the party accused made the false pretense charged with an intent to defraud. If the value of the money, goods, property, services, chose in action, or other thing of value is one hundred thousand dollars ($ 100,000) or more, a violation of this section is a Class C felony. If the value of the money, goods, property, services, chose in action, or other thing of value is less than one hundred thousand dollars ($ 100,000), a violation of this section is a Class H felony.

(b) Evidence of nonfulfillment of a contract obligation standing alone shall not establish the essential element of intent to defraud.

(b1) In any prosecution for violation of this section, the State is not required to establish that all of the acts constituting the crime occurred in this State or within a single city, county, or local jurisdiction of this State, and it is no defense that not all of the acts constituting the crime occurred in this State or within a single city, county, or local jurisdiction of this State.

(c) For purposes of this section, "person" means person, association, consortium, corporation, body politic, partnership, or other group, entity, or organization.

History.
33 Hen. VIII, c. 1, ss. 1, 2; 30 Geo. II, c. 24, s. 1; 1811, c. 814, s. 2, P.R.; R.C., c. 34, s. 67; Code, s. 1025; Rev., s. 3432; C.S., s. 4277; 1975, c. 783; 1979, c. 760, s. 5; 1979, 2nd Sess., c. 1316, s. 47; 1981, c. 63, s. 1; c. 179, s. 14; 1997-443, s. 19.25(l); 2019-193, s. 2(a)

§ 14-100.1. Possession or manufacture of certain fraudulent forms of identification

(a) Except as otherwise made unlawful by G.S. 20-30, it shall be unlawful for any person to knowingly possess or manufacture a false or fraudulent form of identification as defined in this section for the purpose of deception, fraud, or other criminal conduct.

(b) Except as otherwise made unlawful by G.S. 20- 30, it shall be unlawful for any person to knowingly obtain a form of identification by the use of false, fictitious, or fraudulent information.

(c) Possession of a form of identification obtained in violation of subsection (b) of this section shall constitute a violation of subsection (a) of this section.

(d) For purposes of this section, a "form of identification" means any of the following or any replica thereof:

(1) An identification card containing a picture, issued by any department, agency, or subdivision of the State of North Carolina, the federal government, or any other state.

(2) A military identification card containing a picture.

(3) A passport.

(4) An alien registration card containing a picture.

(e) A violation of this section shall be punished as a Class 1 misdemeanor.

History.
2001-461, s. 1; 2001-487, s. 42(a)

§ 14-101. Obtaining signatures by false pretenses

If any person, with intent to defraud or cheat another, shall designedly, by color of any false token or writing, or by any other false pretense, obtain the signature of any person to any written instrument, the false making of which would be punishable as forgery, he shall be punished as a Class H felon.

History.
1871-2, c. 92; Code, s. 1026; Rev., s. 3433; C.S., s. 4278; 1945, c. 635; 1979, c. 760, s. 5; 1979, 2nd Sess., c. 1316, s. 47; 1981, c. 63, s. 1; c. 179, s. 14; 1993, c. 539, s. 1181

§ 14-102. Obtaining property by false representation of pedigree of animals

If any person shall, with intent to defraud or cheat, knowingly represent any animal for breeding purposes as being of greater degree of any particular strain of blood than such animal actually possesses, and by such representation obtain from any other person money or other thing of value, he shall be guilty of a Class 2 misdemeanor.

History.
1891, c. 94, s. 2; Rev., s. 3307; C.S., s. 4279; 1993, c. 539, s. 40; 1994, Ex. Sess., c. 24, s. 14(c)

§ 14-103. Obtaining certificate of registration of animals by false representation

If any person shall, by any false representation or pretense, with intent to defraud or cheat, obtain from any club, association, society or company for the improvement of the breed of cattle, horses, sheep, swine, fowls or other domestic animals or birds, a certificate of registration of any animal in the herd register of any such association, society or company, or a transfer of any such registration, upon conviction thereof, the person is guilty of a Class 3 misdemeanor.

History.
1891, c. 94, s. 1; Rev. s. 3308; C.S., s. 4280; 1993, c. 539, s. 41; 1994, Ex. Sess., c. 24, s. 14(c)

§ 14-104. Obtaining advances under promise to work and pay for same

If any person, with intent to cheat or defraud another, shall obtain any advances in money, provisions, goods, wares or merchandise of any description from any other person or corporation upon and by color of any promise or agreement that the person making the same will begin any work or labor of any description for such person or corporation from whom the advances are obtained, and the person making the promise or agreement shall willfully fail, without a lawful excuse, to commence or complete such work according to contract, he shall be guilty of a Class 2 misdemeanor.

History.
1889, c. 444; 1891, c. 106; 1905, c. 411; Rev., s. 3431; C.S., s. 4281; 1993, c. 539, s. 42; 1994, Ex. Sess., c. 24, s. 14(c)

§ 14-105. Obtaining advances under written promise to pay therefor out of designated property

If any person shall obtain any advances in money, provisions, goods, wares or merchandise of any description from any other person or corporation, upon any written representation that the person making the same is the owner of any article of produce, or of any other specific chattel or personal property, which property, or the proceeds of which the owner in such representation thereby agrees to apply to the discharge of the debt so created, and the owner shall fail to apply such produce or other property, or the proceeds thereof, in accordance with such agreement, or shall dispose of the same in any other manner than is so agreed upon by the parties to the transaction, the person so offending shall be guilty of a misdemeanor, whether he shall or shall not have been the owner of any

such property at the time such representation was made. Any person violating any provision of this section shall be guilty of a Class 2 misdemeanor.

History.
1879, cc. 185, 186; Code, s. 1027; 1905, c. 104; Rev., s. 3434; C.S., s. 4282; 1969, c. 1224, s. 9; 1993, c. 539, s. 43; 1994, Ex. Sess., c. 24, s. 14(c)

§ 14-106. Obtaining property in return for worthless check, draft or order

Every person who, with intent to cheat and defraud another, shall obtain money, credit, goods, wares or any other thing of value by means of a check, draft or order of any kind upon any bank, person, firm or corporation, not indebted to the drawer, or where he has not provided for the payment or acceptance of the same, and the same be not paid upon presentation, shall be guilty of a Class 3 misdemeanor. The giving of the aforesaid worthless check, draft, or order shall be prima facie evidence of an intent to cheat and defraud.

History.
1907, c. 975; 1909, c. 647; C.S., s. 4283; 1993, c. 539, s. 44; 1994, Ex. Sess., c. 24, s. 14(c); 2013-360, s. 18B.14(a)

§ 14-107. Worthless checks; multiple presentment of checks

(a) It is unlawful for any person, firm or corporation, to draw, make, utter or issue and deliver to another, any check or draft on any bank or depository, for the payment of money or its equivalent, knowing at the time of the making, drawing, uttering, issuing and delivering the check or draft, that the maker or drawer of it:

    (1) Has not sufficient funds on deposit in or credit with the bank or depository with which to pay the check or draft upon presentation, or

    (2) Has previously presented the check or draft for the payment of money or its equivalent.

(b) It is unlawful for any person, firm or corporation to solicit or to aid and abet any other person, firm or corporation to draw, make, utter or issue and deliver to any person, firm or corporation, any check or draft on any bank or depository for the payment of money or its equivalent, being informed, knowing or having reasonable grounds for believing at the time of the soliciting or the aiding and abetting that the maker or the drawer of the check or draft:

    (1) Has not sufficient funds on deposit in, or credit with, the bank or depository with which to pay the check or draft upon presentation, or

(2) Has previously presented the check or draft for the payment of money or its equivalent.

(c) The word "credit" as used in this section means an arrangement or understanding with the bank or depository for the payment of a check or draft.

(d) A violation of this section is a Class I felony if the amount of the check or draft is more than two thousand dollars ($ 2,000). If the amount of the check or draft is two thousand dollars ($ 2,000) or less, a violation of this section is a misdemeanor punishable as follows:

(1) Except as provided in subdivision (3) or (4) of this subsection, the person is guilty of a Class 3 misdemeanor. Provided, however, if the person has been convicted three times of violating this section, the person shall on the fourth and all subsequent convictions (i) be punished as for a Class 1 misdemeanor and (ii) be ordered, as a condition of probation, to refrain from maintaining a checking account or making or uttering a check for three years.

(2) Repealed by Session Laws 1999-408, s. 1, effective December 1, 1999.

(3) If the check or draft is drawn upon a nonexistent account, the person is guilty of a Class 1 misdemeanor.

(4) If the check or draft is drawn upon an account that has been closed by the drawer, or that the drawer knows to have been closed by the bank or depository, prior to time the check is drawn, the person is guilty of a Class 1 misdemeanor.

(e) In deciding to impose any sentence other than an active prison sentence, the sentencing judge shall consider and may require, in accordance with the provisions of G.S. 15A-1343, restitution to the victim for (i) the amount of the check or draft, (ii) any service charges imposed on the payee by a bank or depository for processing the dishonored check, and (iii) any processing fees imposed by the payee pursuant to G.S. 25-3-506, and each prosecuting witness (whether or not under subpoena) shall be entitled to a witness fee as provided by G.S. 7A-314 which shall be taxed as part of the cost and assessed to the defendant.

History.
1925, c. 14; 1927, c. 62; 1929, c. 273, ss. 1, 2; 1931, cc. 63, 138; 1933, cc. 43, 64, 93, 170, 265, 362, 458; 1939, c. 346; 1949, cc. 183, 332; 1951, c. 356; 1961, c. 89; 1963, cc. 73, 547, 870; 1967, c. 49, s. 1; c. 661, s. 1; 1969, c. 157; c. 876, s. 1; cc. 909, 1014; c. 1224, s. 10; 1971, c. 243, s. 1; 1977, c. 885; 1979, c. 837; 1983, c. 741; 1991, c. 523, s. 1; 1993, c. 374, s. 2; c. 539, ss. 45, 1182; 1994, Ex. Sess., c. 24, s. 14(c); 1995 (Reg. Sess., 1996), c. 742, s. 11; 1999-408, s. 1; 2013-244, s. 4; 2013-360, s. 18B.14(b)

§ 14-107.1. Prima facie evidence in worthless check cases

(a) Unless the context otherwise requires, the following definitions apply in this section:

(1) **Check Passer.** -- A natural person who draws, makes, utters, or issues and delivers, or causes to be delivered to another any check or draft on any bank or depository for the payment of money or its equivalent.

(2) **Acceptor.** -- A person, firm, corporation or any authorized employee thereof accepting a check or draft from a check passer.

(3) **Check Taker.** -- A natural person who is an acceptor, or an employee or agent of an acceptor, of a check or draft in a face-to-face transaction.

(b) In prosecutions under G.S. 14-107 the prima facie evidence provisions of subsections (d) and (e) apply if all the conditions of subdivisions (1) through (7) below are met. The prima facie evidence provisions of subsection (e) apply if only conditions (5) through (7) are met. The conditions are:

(1) The check or draft is delivered to a check taker.

(2) The name and mailing address of the check passer are written or printed on the check or draft, and the check taker or acceptor shall not be required to write or print the race or gender of the check passer on the check or draft.

(3) The check taker identifies the check passer at the time of accepting the check by means of a North Carolina driver's license, a special identification card issued pursuant to G.S. 20-37.7, or other reliable serially numbered identification card containing a photograph and mailing address of the person in question.

(4) The license or identification card number of the check passer appears on the check or draft.

(5) After dishonor of the check or draft by the bank or depository, the acceptor sends the check passer a letter by certified mail, to the address recorded on the check, identifying the check or draft, setting forth the circumstances of dishonor, and requesting rectification of any bank error or other error in connection with the transaction within 10 days.

An acceptor may advise the check passer in a letter that legal action may be taken against him if payment is not made within the prescribed time period. Such letter, however, shall be in a form which does not violate applicable provisions of Article 2 of Chapter 75.

(6) The acceptor files the affidavit described in subdivision (7) with a judicial

official, as defined in G.S. 15A-101(5), before issuance of the first process or pleading in the prosecution under G.S. 14-107. The affidavit must be kept in the case file (attached to the criminal pleading in the case).

(7) The affidavit of the acceptor, sworn to before a person authorized to administer oaths, must:

a. State the facts surrounding acceptance of the check or draft. If the conditions set forth in subdivisions (1) through (5) have been met, the specific facts demonstrating observance of those conditions must be stated.

b. Indicate that at least 15 days have elapsed since the mailing of the letter required under subdivision (5) and that the check passer has failed to rectify any error that may have occurred with respect to the dishonored check or draft.

c. Have attached a copy of the letter sent to the check passer pursuant to subdivision (5).

d. Have attached the receipt, or a copy of it, from the United States Postal Service certifying the mailing of the letter described in subdivision (5).

e. Have attached the check or draft or a copy thereof, including any stamp, marking or attachment indicating the reason for dishonor.

(c) In prosecutions under G.S. 14-107, where the check or draft is delivered to the acceptor by mail, or delivered other than in person, the prima facie evidence rule in subsections (d) and (e) shall apply if all the conditions below are met. The prima facie evidence rule in subsection (e) shall apply if conditions (5) through (7) below are met. The conditions are:

(1) The check or draft is delivered to the acceptor by United States mail, or by some person or instrumentality other than a check passer.

(2) The name and mailing address of the check passer are recorded on the check or draft.

(3) The acceptor has previously identified the check passer, at the time of opening the account, establishing the course of dealing, or initiating the lease or contract, by means of a North Carolina driver's license, a special identification card issued pursuant to G.S. 20-37.7, or other reliable serially numbered identification card containing a photograph and mailing address of the person in question, and obtained the signature of the person or persons who will be making payments on the account, course of dealing, lease or contract, and such signature is retained in the account file.

(4) The acceptor compares the name, address, and signature on the check with the name, address, and signature on file in the account, course of dealing, lease, or contract, and notes that the information contained on the check corresponds with the information contained in the file, and the signature on the check appears genuine when compared to the signature in the file.

(5) After dishonor of the check or draft by the bank or depository, the acceptor sends the check passer a letter by certified mail to the address recorded on the check or draft identifying the check or draft, setting forth the circumstances of dishonor and requesting rectification of any bank error or other error in connection with the transaction within 10 days.

An acceptor may advise the check passer in a letter that legal action may be taken against him if payment is not made within the prescribed time period. Such letter, however, shall be in a form which does not violate applicable provisions of Article 2 of Chapter 75.

(6) The acceptor files the affidavits described in subdivision (7) of this subsection with a judicial official, as defined in G.S. 15A-101(5), before issuance of the first process or pleading in the prosecution under G.S. 14-107. The affidavit must be kept in the case file (attached to the criminal pleading in the case).

(7) The affidavit of the acceptor, sworn to before a person authorized to administer oaths, must:

a. State the facts surrounding acceptance of the check or draft. If the conditions set forth in subdivisions (1) through (5) have been met, the specific facts demonstrating observance of those conditions must be stated.

b. Indicate that at least 15 days have elapsed since the mailing of the letter required under subdivision (5) and that the check passer has failed to rectify any error that may have occurred with respect to the dishonored check or draft.

c. Have attached a copy of the letter sent to the check passer pursuant to subdivision (5).

d. Have attached the receipt, or a copy of it, from the United States Postal Service certifying the mailing of the letter described in subdivision (5).

e. Have attached the check or draft or a copy thereof, including any stamp, marking or attachment indicating the reason for dishonor.

(d) If the conditions of subsection (b) or (c) have been met, proof of meeting them is prima facie evidence that the person charged was in fact the identified check passer.

(e) If the bank or depository dishonoring a check or draft has returned it in the regular course of business stamped or marked or with an attachment indicating the reason for dishonor, the check or draft and any attachment may be introduced in evidence and constitute prima facie evidence of the facts of dishonor if the conditions of subdivisions (5) through (7) of subsection (b) or subdivisions (5) through (7) of subsection (c) have been met. The reason for dishonor may be indicated with terms that include, but are not limited to, the following: "insufficient funds," "no account," "account closed," "NSF," "uncollected," "unable to locate," "stale dated," "postdated," "endorsement irregular," "signature irregular," "nonnegotiable," "altered," "unable to process," "refer to maker," "duplicate presentment," "forgery," "noncompliant," or "UCD noncompliant." The fact that the check or draft was returned dishonored may be received as evidence that the check passer had no credit with the bank or depository for payment of the check or draft.

(f) An affidavit by an employee of a bank or depository who has personal knowledge of the facts stated in the affidavit sworn to and properly executed before an official authorized to administer oaths is admissible in evidence without further authentication in a hearing or trial pursuant to a prosecution under G.S. 14-107 in the District Court Division of the General Court of Justice with respect to the facts of dishonor of the check or draft, including the existence of an account, the date the check or draft was processed, whether there were sufficient funds in an account to pay the check or draft, and other related matters. If the defendant requests that the bank or depository employee personally testify in the hearing or trial, the defendant may subpoena the employee. The defendant shall be provided a copy of the affidavit prior to trial and shall have the opportunity to subpoena the affiant for trial.

History.
1979, c. 615, s. 1; 1985, c. 650, s. 1; 1989, c. 421; 1997-149, s. 1; 2013-244, s. 5

§ 14-107.2. Program for collection in worthless check cases

(a) As used in this section, the terms "check passer" and "check taker" have the same meaning as defined in G.S. 14-107.1.

(a1) The Administrative Office of the Courts may authorize the establishment of a program for the collection of worthless checks in any prosecutorial district where economically feasible. The Administrative Office of the Courts

may consider the following factors when making a feasibility determination:

(1) The population of the district.

(2) The number of worthless check prosecutions in the district.

(3) The availability of personnel and equipment in the district.

(b) Upon authorization by the Administrative Office of the Courts, a district attorney may establish a program for the collection of worthless checks in cases that may be prosecuted under G.S. 14-107. The district attorney may establish a program for the collection of worthless checks in cases that would be punishable as misdemeanors, in cases that would be punishable as felonies, or both. The district attorney shall establish criteria for the types of worthless check cases that will be eligible under the program.

(b1) A community mediation center may establish and charge fees for its services in the collection of worthless checks as part of a program established under this section and may assist the Administrative Office of the Courts and district attorneys in the establishment of worthless check programs in any districts in which worthless check programs have not been established.

(c) If a check passer participates in the program by paying the fee under G.S.7A-308(c) and providing restitution to the check taker for (i) the amount of the check or draft, (ii) any service charges imposed on the check taker by a bank or depository for processing the dishonored check, and (iii) any processing fees imposed by the check taker pursuant to G.S. 25-3-506, then the district attorney shall not prosecute the worthless check case under G.S. 14-107.

(d) The Administrative Office of the Courts shall establish procedures for remitting the fee and providing restitution to the check taker.

(e) Repealed by Session Laws 2003-377, s. 3, effective August 1, 2003.

History.
1997-443, s. 18.22(b); 1998-23, s. 11(a); 1998-212, s. 16.3(a); 1999-237, s. 17.7; 2000-67, s. 15.3A(a); 2001-61, s. 1; 2003-377, ss. 1, 2, 3; 2011-145, s. 31.24(a)

§ 14-108. Obtaining property or services from slot machines, etc., by false coins or tokens

Any person who shall operate, or cause to be operated, or who shall attempt to operate, or attempt to cause to be operated any automatic vending machine, slot machine, coin-box telephone or other receptacle designed to receive lawful coin of the United States of America in connection with the sale, use or enjoyment of property or service, by means of a slug or any false, counterfeited, mutilated, sweated or foreign coin, or by any means, method, trick or device whatsoever not lawfully authorized by the owner, lessee or licensee, of such machine, coin-box telephone or receptacle, or who shall take, obtain or receive from or in connection with any automatic vending machine, slot machine, coin-box telephone or other receptacle designed to receive lawful coin of the United States of America in connection with the sale, use or enjoyment of property or service, any goods, wares, merchandise, gas, electric current, article of value, or the use or enjoyment of any telephone or telegraph facilities or service, or of any musical instrument, phonograph or other property, without depositing in and surrendering to such machine, coin-box telephone or receptacle lawful coin of the United States of America to the amount required therefor by the owner, lessee or licensee of such machine, coin-box telephone or receptacle, shall be guilty of a Class 2 misdemeanor.

History.
1927, c. 68, s. 1; 1969, c. 1224, s. 3; 1993, c. 539, s. 46; c. 553, s. 8; 1994, Ex. Sess., c. 24, s. 14(c)

§ 14-109. Manufacture, sale, or gift of devices for cheating slot machines, etc

Any person who, with intent to cheat or defraud the owner, lessee, licensee or other person entitled to the contents of any automatic vending machine, slot machine, coin-box telephone or other receptacle, depository or contrivance designed to receive lawful coin of the United States of America in connection with the sale, use or enjoyment of property or service, or who, knowing that the same is intended for unlawful use, shall manufacture for sale, or sell or give away any slug, device or substance whatsoever intended or calculated to be placed or deposited in any such automatic vending machine, slot machine, coin-box telephone or other such receptacle, depository or contrivance, shall be guilty of a Class 2 misdemeanor.

History.
1927, c. 68, s. 2; 1969, c. 1224, s. 3; 1993, c. 539, s. 47; 1994, Ex. Sess., c. 24, s. 14(c)

§ 14-110. Defrauding innkeeper or campground owner

No person shall, with intent to defraud, obtain food, lodging, or other accommodations at a hotel, inn, boardinghouse, eating house, or campground. Whoever violates this section shall be guilty of a Class 2 misdemeanor. Obtaining such lodging, food, or other accommodation by false pretense, or by false or fictitious show of pretense of baggage or other property, or absconding without paying or offering to pay therefor, or surreptitiously removing or

attempting to remove such baggage, shall be prima facie evidence of such fraudulent intent, but this section shall not apply where there has been an agreement in writing for delay in such payment.

History.
1907, c. 816; C.S., s. 4284; 1969, c. 947; c. 1224, s. 3; 1985, c. 391; 1993, c. 539, s. 48; 1994, Ex. Sess., c. 24, s. 14(c)

N.C. Gen. Stat. § 14-111

Repealed by Session Laws 1994, Extra Session, c. 14, s. 72(4).

§ 14-111.1. Obtaining ambulance services without intending to pay therefor -- Buncombe, Haywood and Madison Counties

Any person who with the intent to defraud shall obtain ambulance services for himself or other persons without intending at the time of obtaining such services to pay a reasonable charge therefor, shall be guilty of a Class 2 misdemeanor. If a person or persons obtaining such services willfully fails to pay for the services within a period of 90 days after request for payment, such failure shall raise a presumption that the services were obtained with the intention to defraud, and with the intention not to pay therefor.

This section shall apply only to the Counties of Buncombe, Haywood and Madison.

History.
1965, c. 976, s. 1; 1969, c. 1224, s. 4; 1993, c. 539, s. 49; 1994, Ex. Sess., c. 24, s. 14(c)

§ 14-111.2. Obtaining ambulance services without intending to pay therefor -- certain named counties

Any person who with intent to defraud shall obtain ambulance services without intending at the time of obtaining such services to pay, if financially able, any reasonable charges therefor shall be guilty of a Class 2 misdemeanor. A determination by the court that the recipient of such services has willfully failed to pay for the services rendered for a period of 90 days after request for payment, and that the recipient is financially able to do so, shall raise a presumption that the recipient at the time of obtaining the services intended to defraud the provider of the services and did not intend to pay for the services.

The section shall apply to Alamance, Anson, Ashe, Beaufort, Cabarrus, Caldwell, Camden, Carteret, Caswell, Catawba, Chatham, Cherokee, Clay, Cleveland, Cumberland, Davie,

Duplin, Durham, Forsyth, Gaston, Graham, Guilford, Halifax, Haywood, Henderson, Hoke, Hyde, Iredell, Macon, Mecklenburg, Montgomery, New Hanover, Onslow, Orange, Pasquotank, Pender, Person, Polk, Randolph, Robeson, Rockingham, Scotland, Stanly, Surry, Transylvania, Union, Vance, Washington, Wilkes and Yadkin Counties only.

History.

1967, c. 964; 1969, cc. 292, 753; c. 1224, s. 4; 1971, cc. 125, 203, 300, 496; 1973, c. 880, s. 2; 1977, cc. 63, 144; 1983, c. 42, s. 1; 1985, c. 335, s. 1; 1987 (Reg. Sess., 1988), c. 910, s. 1; 1993, c. 539, s. 50; 1994, Ex. Sess., c. 24, s. 14(c); 1995, c. 9, s. 2; 1999-64, s. 1; 2000-15, s. 1; 2001-106, s. 1

§ 14-111.3. Making unneeded ambulance request in certain counties

It shall be unlawful for any person or persons to willfully obtain or attempt to obtain ambulance service that is not needed, or to make a false request or report that an ambulance is needed. Every person convicted of violating this section shall be guilty of a Class 3 misdemeanor.

This section shall apply only to the Counties of Alamance, Ashe, Buncombe, Cabarrus, Camden, Carteret, Cherokee, Clay, Cleveland, Davie, Duplin, Durham, Graham, Greene, Halifax, Haywood, Hoke, Macon, Madison, New Hanover, Onslow, Pender, Polk, Robeson, Rockingham, Washington, Wilkes and Yadkin.

History.

1965, c. 976, s. 2; 1971, c. 496; 1977, c. 96; 1983, c. 42, s. 2; 1985, c. 335, s. 2; 1987 (Reg. Sess., 1988), c. 910, s. 2; 1989, c. 514; 1989 (Reg. Sess., 1990), c. 834; 1993, c. 539, s. 51; 1994, Ex. Sess., c. 24, s. 14(c); 1995, c. 9, s. 3; 1999-64, s. 2; 2000-15, s. 2; 2001-106, s. 2

§ 14-111.4. Misuse of 911 system

It is unlawful for an individual who is not seeking public safety assistance, is not providing 911 service, or is not responding to a 911 call to access or attempt to access the 911 system for a purpose other than an emergency communication. A person who knowingly violates this section commits a Class 1 misdemeanor.

History.

2007-383, s. 1(b); 2013-286, s. 1

§ 14-112. Obtaining merchandise on approval

If any person, with intent to cheat and defraud, shall solicit and obtain from any merchant any article of merchandise on approval, and shall thereafter, upon demand, refuse or fail to return the same to such merchant in an

unused and undamaged condition, or to pay for the same, such person so offending shall be guilty of a Class 2 misdemeanor. Evidence that a person has solicited a merchant to deliver to him any article of merchandise for examination or approval and has obtained the same upon such solicitation, and thereafter, upon demand, has refused or failed to return the same to such merchant in an unused and undamaged condition, or to pay for the same, shall constitute prima facie evidence of the intent of such person to cheat and defraud, within the meaning of this section: Provided, this section shall not apply to merchandise sold upon a written contract which is signed by the purchaser.

History.

1911, c. 185; C.S., s. 4285; 1941, c. 242; 1969, c. 1224, s. 2; 1993, c. 539, s. 52; 1994, Ex. Sess., c. 24, s. 14(c)

N.C. Gen. Stat. § 14-112.1

Repealed by Session Laws 1967, c. 1088, s. 2.

§ 14-112.2. Exploitation of an older adult or disabled adult

(a) The following definitions apply in this section:

(1) **Disabled adult.** -- A person 18 years of age or older or a lawfully emancipated minor who is present in the State of North Carolina and who is physically or mentally incapacitated as defined in G.S. 108A-101(d).

(2) **Older adult.** -- A person 65 years of age or older.

(b) It is unlawful for a person: (i) who stands in a position of trust and confidence with an older adult or disabled adult, or (ii) who has a business relationship with an older adult or disabled adult to knowingly, by deception or intimidation, obtain or use, or endeavor to obtain or use, an older adult's or disabled adult's funds, assets, or property with the intent to temporarily or permanently deprive the older adult or disabled adult of the use, benefit, or possession of the funds, assets, or property, or to benefit someone other than the older adult or disabled adult.

(c) It is unlawful for a person to knowingly, by deception or intimidation, obtain or use, endeavor to obtain or use, or conspire with another to obtain or use an older adult's or disabled adult's funds, assets, or property with the intent to temporarily or permanently deprive the older adult or disabled adult of the use, benefit, or possession of the funds, assets, or property, or benefit someone other than the older adult or disabled adult. This subsection shall not apply to a person acting within the scope of that person's lawful authority as the agent for the older adult or disabled adult.

(d) A violation of subsection (b) of this section is punishable as follows:

(1) If the funds, assets, or property involved in the exploitation of the older adult or disabled adult is valued at one hundred thousand dollars ($ 100,000) or more, then the offense is a Class F felony.

(2) If the funds, assets, or property involved in the exploitation of the older adult or disabled adult is valued at twenty thousand dollars ($ 20,000) or more but less than one hundred thousand dollars ($ 100,000), then the offense is a Class G felony.

(3) If the funds, assets, or property involved in the exploitation of the older adult or disabled adult is valued at less than twenty thousand dollars ($ 20,000), then the offense is a Class H felony.

(e) A violation of subsection (c) of this section is punishable as follows:

(1) If the funds, assets, or property involved in the exploitation of the older adult or disabled adult is valued at one hundred thousand dollars ($ 100,000) or more, then the offense is a Class G felony.

(2) If the funds, assets, or property involved in the exploitation of the older adult or disabled adult is valued at twenty thousand dollars ($ 20,000) or more but less than one hundred thousand dollars ($ 100,000), then the offense is a Class H felony.

(3) If the funds, assets, or property involved in the exploitation of the older adult or disabled adult is valued at less than twenty thousand dollars ($ 20,000), then the offense is a Class I felony.

(f) If a person is charged with a violation of this section that involves funds, assets, or property valued at more than five thousand dollars ($ 5,000), the district attorney may file a petition in the pending criminal proceeding before the court with jurisdiction over the pending charges to freeze the funds, assets, or property of the defendant in an amount up to one hundred fifty percent (150%) of the alleged value of funds, assets, or property in the defendant's pending criminal proceeding for purposes of restitution to the victim. The standard of proof required to freeze the defendant's funds, assets, or property shall be by clear and convincing evidence. The procedure for petitioning the court under this subsection shall be governed by G.S. 14-112.3.

History.
2005-272, s. 2; 2006-264, s. 99; 2013-203, s. 1; 2013-337, s. 1

§ 14-112.3. Asset freeze or seizure; proceeding

(a) For purposes of this section, the term "assets" includes funds and property as well as other assets that may be involved in a violation of G.S. 14-112.2.

(b) Whenever it appears by clear and convincing evidence that any defendant is about to or intends to divest himself or herself of assets in a manner that would render the defendant insolvent for purposes of restitution, the district attorney may make an application to the court to freeze or seize the assets of the defendant. Upon a showing by clear and convincing evidence in the hearing, the court shall issue an order to freeze or seize the assets of the defendant in the amount calculated pursuant to G.S. 14-112.2(f). The procedure for petitioning the court under this section shall be governed by G.S. 1A-1, Rule 65, except as otherwise provided in this section.

(b1) An order to freeze or seize assets shall direct the appropriate State or local law enforcement agency with territorial jurisdiction over the assets to serve and execute the order as follows:

(1) Personal property or financial assets in the defendant's possession that are not held by a financial institution shall be seized and held until final disposition as directed by the order.

(2) If the asset is an account, intangible, or other financial asset held by a financial institution, the State or local law enforcement agency shall serve the order on the entity or institution in possession of the asset with return of service to the clerk of superior court.

(3) If the asset is real property, then a lis pendens shall be filed as directed by the court with the clerk in the county or counties where the property is located in accordance with Article 11 of Chapter 1 of the General Statutes. If property is located in multiple counties, a lis pendens shall be filed in each county.

(4) For all orders served and executed in accordance with subsection (b1) of this section, a return of service shall be filed with the clerk of superior court by the State or local law enforcement agency with an inventory of items seized. If assets identified are financial assets as listed in subdivision (2) of this subsection, then the law enforcement agency shall list the financial institution wherein such funds are held and the amount of said funds. Said inventory should also identify any and all available real property and identify the counties wherein lis pendens were filed in accordance with subdivision (3) of this subsection.

(b2) A record of any personal property seized by a law enforcement agency pursuant to this section shall be kept and maintained as provided in Article 2 of Chapter 15 of the General Statutes, except that the property shall not be disposed of other than pursuant to an order of the court entered pursuant to this section. Property frozen or seized pursuant to this section shall be deemed to be in the custody of the law enforcement agency seizing it and shall be removed and stored in the discretion of that law enforcement agency, which may do any of the following:

(1) Place the property under seal.

(2) Remove the property to a place designated by the law enforcement agency.

(3) Request that the North Carolina Department of Justice take custody of the property and remove it to an appropriate location pending an order of the court for disposition.

(c) At any time after service of the order to freeze or seize assets, the defendant or any person claiming an interest in the assets may file a motion to release the assets.

(d) In any proceeding to release assets, the burden of proof shall be by clear and convincing evidence and shall be on the State to show that the defendant is about to, intends to, or did divest himself or herself of assets in a manner that would render the defendant insolvent for purposes of restitution. If the court finds that the defendant is about to, intends to, or did divest himself or herself of assets in a manner that would render the defendant insolvent for purposes of restitution, the court shall deny the motion.

(e) If the prosecution of the charge under G.S. 14-112.2 is terminated by voluntary dismissal without leave by the State or the court, or if a judgment of acquittal is entered, the court shall vacate the order to freeze or seize the assets. If assets are released pursuant to this subsection, accrued costs incident to the seizure, freeze, or storage of the assets shall not be charged against the defendant and shall be borne by the agency incurring those costs.

(e1) Upon conviction of the defendant, or entry of a plea of no contest, any frozen or seized assets shall be used to satisfy the defendant's restitution obligation as ordered by the court, accounting for costs incident to seizure, including costs of sale. However, if the defendant can satisfy the restitution order within a period of time designated by the court, the court may accept an alternate form of restitution satisfaction. Any excess assets shall be returned to the defendant.

In order to satisfy an order of restitution, frozen or seized assets shall be handled as follows:

(1) Assets shall be sold, transferred, paid out, or otherwise applied to the defendant's restitution obligation as follows:

a. If the asset is personal property or liquid assets already seized, the property shall be disposed of in accordance with the court order.

b. If the asset is held by a financial institution, the court shall enter an order directing the payment of those funds to the clerk in the amount specified in the restitution order or, if the amount is less than the full restitution award, the full amount of liquid assets shall be paid. The law enforcement agency shall deliver those funds to the clerk.

c. If the asset is real property, the court shall enter an order directing the sale of the property. The sale shall be conducted pursuant to Article 29A of Chapter 1 of the General Statutes. A private sale may be conducted pursuant to G.S. 1-339.33 through G.S. 1-339.40, if, upon receipt of the petition and satisfactory proof, it appears to the person directed to oversee the sale that a private sale is in the best interest of the victim.

(2) The proceeds of any sale, transfer, or conversion shall be disbursed as follows:

a. The law enforcement agency shall pay all proceeds to the clerk of superior court and shall provide an accounting of personal property sold or liquid assets seized.

b. All proceeds received by the clerk shall be distributed according to the following priority:

1. Payment to the victim in the full amount of the restitution order.

2. The costs and expenses of the sale.

3. All other necessary expenses incident to compliance with this section.

4. Any remaining balance to the defendant within 30 days of the clerk's receipt of the proceeds of the sale, unless the defendant directs the clerk to apply any excess to the defendant's other monetary obligations contained in the judgment of conviction.

(e2) In the event proceeds from the sale, transfer, or conversion of the seized or frozen assets under subsection (e1) of this section are not sufficient to cover the expenses allowed under sub-sub-subdivisions 2. and 3. of subsubdivision b. of subdivision (2) of subsection (e1) of this section, after notice and a hearing at which the defendant is present, the court may enter a supplemental order of restitution for the unpaid portion of those expenses for the benefit of the agency that incurred the expenses, to be paid as part of the criminal judgment and as provided under G.S. 7A-304(d)(1)e.

(f) Any person holding any interest in the frozen or seized assets may commence a separate civil proceeding in the manner provided by law.

(g) Any filing fees, service fees, or other expenses incurred by any State or county agency for the administration or use of this section shall be recoverable only as provided in sub-sub-subdivision 2. of sub-subdivision b. of subdivision (2) of subsection (e1) of this section.

History.
2013-203, s. 2; 2015-182, s. 1

§ 14-113. Obtaining money by false representation of physical disability

It shall be unlawful for any person to falsely represent himself or herself in any manner whatsoever as blind, deaf, unable to speak, or otherwise physically disabled for the purpose of obtaining money or other thing of value or of making sales of any character of personal property. Any person so falsely representing himself or herself and securing aid or assistance on account of such representation, shall be deemed guilty of a Class 2 misdemeanor.

History.
1919, c. 104; C.S., s. 4286; 1969, c. 1224, s. 1; 1993, c. 539, s. 53; 1994, Ex. Sess., c. 24, s. 14(c); 2011-29, s. 3

ARTICLE 19A
OBTAINING PROPERTY OR SERVICES BY FALSE OR FRAUDULENT USE OF CREDIT DEVICE OR OTHER MEANS

§ 14-113.1. Use of false or counterfeit credit device; unauthorized use of another's credit device; use after notice of revocation

It shall be unlawful for any person knowingly to obtain or attempt to obtain credit, or to purchase or attempt to purchase any goods, property or service, by the use of any false, fictitious, or counterfeit telephone number, credit number or other credit device, or by the use of any telephone number, credit number or other credit device of another without the authority of the person to whom such number or device was issued, or by the use of any telephone number, credit number or other credit device in any case where such number or device has been revoked and notice of revocation has been given to the person to whom issued or he has knowledge or

reason to believe that such revocation has occurred.

History.
1961, c. 223, s. 1; 1965, c. 1147; 1967, c. 1244, s. 1; 1971, c. 1213, s. 1

§ 14-113.2. Notice defined; prima facie evidence of receipt of notice

The word "notice" as used in G.S. 14-113.1 shall be construed to include either notice given in person or notice given in writing to the person to whom the number or device was issued. The sending of a notice in writing by registered or certified mail in the United States mail, duly stamped and addressed to such person at his last address known to the issuer, shall be prima facie evidence that such notice was duly received after five days from the date of the deposit in the mail.

History.
1961, c. 223, s. 3; 1965, c. 1147; 1967, c. 1244, s. 1

§ 14-113.3. Use of credit device as prima facie evidence of knowledge

The presentation or use of a revoked, false, fictitious or counterfeit telephone number, credit number, or other credit device for the purpose of obtaining credit or the privilege of making a deferred payment for the article or service purchased shall be prima facie evidence of knowledge that the said credit device is revoked, false, fictitious or counterfeit; and the unauthorized use of any telephone number, credit number or other credit device of another shall be prima facie evidence of knowledge that such use was without the authority of the person to whom such number or device was issued.

History.
1961, c. 223, s. 4; 1965, c. 1147; 1967, c. 1244, s. 1

§ 14-113.4. Avoiding or attempting to avoid payment for telecommunication services

It shall be unlawful for any person to avoid or attempt to avoid, or to cause another to avoid, the lawful charges, in whole or in part, for any telephone or telegraph service or for the transmission of a message, signal or other communication by telephone or telegraph, or over telephone or telegraph facilities by the use of any fraudulent scheme, device, means or method.

History.
1961, c. 223, s. 2; 1965, c. 1147

§ 14-113.5. Making, distributing, possessing, transferring, or programming device for theft of telecommunication service; publication of information regarding schemes, devices, means, or methods for such theft; concealment of existence, origin or destination of any telecommunication

(a) It shall be unlawful for any person knowingly to:

(1) Make, distribute, possess, use, or assemble an unlawful telecommunications device or modify, alter, program, or reprogram a telecommunication device designed, adapted, or which is used:

a. For commission of a theft of telecommunication service or to acquire or facilitate the acquisition of telecommunications service without the consent of the telecommunication service provider in violation of this Article, or

b. To conceal, or assist another to conceal, from any supplier of a telecommunication service provider or from any lawful authority the existence or place of origin or of destination of any telecommunication, or

(2) Sell, possess, distribute, give, transport, or otherwise transfer to another or offer or advertise for sale any:

a. Unlawful telecommunication device, or plans or instructions for making or assembling the same under circumstances evincing an intent to use or employ the unlawful telecommunication device, or to allow the same to be used or employed, for a purpose described in (1)a or (1)b above, or knowing or having reason to believe that the same is intended to be so used, or that the aforesaid plans or instructions are intended to be used for making or assembling the unlawful telecommunication device; or

b. Material, including hardware, cables, tools, data, computer software or other information or equipment, knowing that the purchaser or a third person intends to use the material in the manufacture of an unlawful telecommunication device; or

(3) Publish plans or instructions for making or assembling or using any unlawful telecommunication device, or

(4) Publish the number or code of an existing, cancelled, revoked or nonexistent telephone number, credit number or other credit device, or method of numbering or coding which is employed in the issuance of telephone numbers, credit numbers or other credit devices with knowledge or reason to believe that it may be used to avoid the payment of any lawful telephone or telegraph toll charge under circumstances evincing an intent to have the telephone number, credit number, credit device or method of numbering or coding so used.

(5) Repealed by Session Laws 1995, c. 425, s. 1.

(b) Any unlawful telecommunication device, plans, instructions, or publications described in this section may be seized under warrant or incident to a lawful arrest for a violation of this section. Upon the conviction of a person for a violation of this section, the court may order the sheriff of the county in which the person was convicted to destroy as contraband or to otherwise lawfully dispose of the unlawful telecommunication device, plans, instructions, or publication.

(c) The following definitions apply in this section and in G.S. 14-113.6:

(1) **Manufacture of an unlawful telecommunication device.** -- The production or assembly of an unlawful telecommunication device or the modification, alteration, programming or reprogramming of a telecommunication device to be capable of acquiring or facilitating the acquisition of telecommunication service without the consent of the telecommunication service provider.

(2) **Publish.** -- The communication or dissemination of information to any one or more persons, either orally, in person or by telephone, radio or television, or in a writing of any kind, including without limitation a letter or memorandum, circular or handbill, newspaper or magazine article, or book.

(3) **Telecommunication device.** -- Any type of instrument, device, machine or equipment that is capable of transmitting or receiving telephonic, electronic or radio communications, or any part of such instrument, device, machine or equipment, or any computer circuit, computer chip, electronic mechanism or other component that is capable of facilitating the transmission or reception of telephonic, electronic or radio communications.

(4) **Telecommunication service.** -- Any service provided for a charge or compensation to facilitate the origination, transmission, emission or reception of signs, signals, data, writings, images, sounds or intelligence of any nature of telephone, including cellular or other wireless telephones, wire, radio, electromagnetic, photoelectronic or photo-optical system.

(5) **Telecommunication service provider.** -- A person or entity providing telecommunication service, including, a

Chapter 14

cellular, paging or other wireless communications company or other person or entity which, for a fee, supplies the facility, cell site, mobile telephone switching office or other equipment or telecommunication service.

(6) **Unlawful telecommunication device.** -- Any telecommunication device that is capable, or has been altered, modified, programmed or reprogrammed alone or in conjunction with another access device or other equipment so as to be capable, of acquiring or facilitating the acquisition of any electronic serial number, mobile identification number, personal identification number or any telecommunication service without the consent of the telecommunication service provider. The term includes, telecommunications devices altered to obtain service without the consent of the telecommunication service provider, tumbler phones, counterfeit or clone microchips, scanning receivers of wireless telecommunication service of a telecommunication service provider and other instruments capable of disguising their identity or location or of gaining access to a communications system operated by a telecommunication service provider. This section shall not apply to any device operated by a law enforcement agency in the normal course of its activities.

History.

1965, c. 1147; 1971, c. 1213, s. 2; 1995, c. 425, s. 1

§ 14-113.6. Penalties for violation; civil action

(a) Any person violating any of the provisions of this Article shall be guilty of a Class 2 misdemeanor. However, if the offense is a violation of G.S. 14-113.5 and involves five or more unlawful telecommunication devices the person shall be guilty of a Class G felony.

(b) The court may, in addition to any other sentence authorized by law, order a person convicted of violating G.S. 14-113.5 to make restitution for the offense.

(c) Any person or entity aggrieved by a violation of G.S. 14-113.5 may, in a civil action in any court of competent jurisdiction, obtain appropriate relief, including preliminary and other equitable or declaratory relief, compensatory and punitive damages, reasonable investigation expenses, costs of suit and any attorney fees as may be provided by law.

History.

1961, c. 223, s. 5; 1965, c. 1147; 1969, c. 1224, s. 6; 1993, c. 539, s. 54; 1994, Ex. Sess., c. 24, s. 14(c); 1995, c. 425, s. 2

§ 14-113.6A. Venue of offenses

(a) Any of the offenses described in Article 19A which involve the placement of telephone calls may be deemed to have been committed at either the place at which the telephone call or calls were made or at the place where the telephone call or calls were received.

(b) An offense under former G.S. 14-113.5(3) or 14-113.5(4) (see now G.S. 14-113.5(a)(3) or 14-113.5(a)(4)) may be deemed to have been committed at either the place at which the publication was initiated or at which the publication was received or at which the information so published was utilized to avoid or attempt to avoid the payment of any lawful telephone or telegraph toll charge.

History.

1971, c. 1213, s. 3

§ 14-113.7. Article not construed as repealing § 14-100

This Article shall not be construed as repealing G.S. 14-100.

History.

1961, c. 223, s. 6; 1065, c. 1147

§ 14-113.7A. Application of Article to credit cards

This Article shall not be construed as being applicable to any credit card as the term is defined in G.S. 14-113.8.

History.

1967, c. 1244, s. 1

ARTICLE 19B
FINANCIAL TRANSACTION CARD CRIME ACT

§ 14-113.8. Definitions

The following words and phrases as used in this Chapter, unless a different meaning is plainly required by the context, shall have the following meanings:

(1) **Acquirer.** -- "Acquirer" means a business organization, financial institution, or an agent of a business organization or financial institution that authorizes a merchant to accept payment by financial transaction card for money, goods, services or anything else of value.

(1a) **Automated Banking Device.** -- "Automated banking device" means any machine which when properly activated by a financial transaction card and/or personal identification code may be used for any of the purposes for which a financial transaction card may be used.

(2) **Cardholder.** -- "Cardholder" means the person or organization named on the face of a financial transaction card to whom or for whose benefit the financial transaction card is issued by an issuer.

(3) **Expired Financial Transaction Card.** -- "Expired financial transaction card" means a financial transaction card which is no longer valid because the term shown on it has elapsed.

(4) **Financial Transaction Card.** -- "Financial transaction card" or "FTC" means any instrument or device whether known as a credit card, credit plate, bank services card, banking card, check guarantee card, debit card, or by any other name, issued with or without fee by an issuer for the use of the cardholder:

a. In obtaining money, goods, services, or anything else of value on credit; or

b. In certifying or guaranteeing to a person or business the availability to the cardholder of funds on deposit that are equal to or greater than the amount necessary to honor a draft or check payable to the order of such person or business; or

c. In providing the cardholder access to a demand deposit account or time deposit account for the purpose of:

1. Making deposits of money or checks therein; or

2. Withdrawing funds in the form of money, money orders, or traveler's checks therefrom; or

3. Transferring funds from any demand deposit account or time deposit account to any other demand deposit account or time deposit account; or

4. Transferring funds from any demand deposit account or time deposit account to any credit card accounts, overdraft privilege accounts, loan accounts, or any other credit accounts in full or partial satisfaction of any outstanding balance owed existing therein; or

5. For the purchase of goods, services or anything else of value; or

6. Obtaining information pertaining to any demand deposit account or time deposit account;

d. But shall not include a telephone number, credit number, or other credit device which is covered by the provisions of Article 19A of this Chapter.

(5) **Issuer.** -- "Issuer" means the business organization or financial institution or its duly authorized agent which issues a financial transaction card.

(6) **Personal Identification Code.** -- "Personal identification code" means a numeric and/or alphabetical code assigned to the cardholder of a financial transaction card by the issuer to permit authorized electronic use of that FTC.

(7) **Presenting.** -- "Presenting" means, as used herein, those actions taken by a cardholder or any person to introduce a financial transaction card into an automated banking device, including utilization of a personal identification code, or merely displaying or showing a financial transaction card to the issuer, or to any person or organization providing money, goods, services, or anything else of value, or any other entity with intent to defraud.

(8) **Receives.** -- "Receives" or "receiving" means acquiring possession or control or accepting a financial transaction card as security for a loan.

(9) **Revoked Financial Transaction Card.** -- "Revoked financial transaction card" means a financial transaction card which is no longer valid because permission to use it has been suspended or terminated by the issuer.

(10) **Scanning Device.** -- "Scanning device" means a scanner, reader, or any other device that is used to access, read, scan, obtain, memorize, or store, temporarily or permanently, information encoded on a financial transaction card. This term does not include a skimming device.

(11) **Skimming Device.** -- A self-contained device that (i) is designed to read and store in the device's internal memory information encoded on the computer chip, magnetic strip or stripe, or other storage mechanism of a financial transaction card or from another device that directly reads the information from a financial transaction card and (ii) is incapable of processing the financial transaction card information for the purpose of obtaining, purchasing, or receiving goods, services, money, or anything else of value from a merchant.

History.
1967, c. 1244, s. 2; 1971, c. 1213, s. 4; 1979, c. 741, s. 1; 1989, c. 161, s. 1; 2002-175, s. 2; 2021-68, s. 1

§ 14-113.9. Financial transaction card theft

(a) A person is guilty of financial transaction card theft when the person does any of the following:

(1) Takes, obtains, or withholds a financial transaction card from the person, possession, custody, or control of another without the cardholder's consent and with the intent to use it; or who, with knowledge that it has been so taken, obtained, or withheld, receives the financial transaction card with intent to use it or to sell it, or to transfer it to a person other than the issuer or the cardholder.

(2) Receives a financial transaction card that he or she knows to have been lost, mislaid, or delivered under a mistake as to the identity or address of the cardholder, and retains possession with intent to use it or to sell it or to transfer it to a person other than the issuer or the cardholder.

(3) Not being the issuer, sells a financial transaction card or buys a financial transaction card from a person other than the issuer.

(4) Not being the issuer, during any 12-month period, receives financial transaction cards issued in the names of two or more persons which he or she has reason to know were taken or retained under circumstances that constitute a violation of G.S. 14-113.13(a)(3) and subdivision (3) of subsection (a) of this section.

(5) With the intent to defraud any person, either (i) uses a scanning device to access, read, obtain, memorize, or store, temporarily or permanently, information encoded on another person's financial transaction card, or (ii) receives the encoded information from another person's financial transaction card.

(6) Knowingly possesses, sells, or delivers a skimming device. The prohibition set forth in this subdivision does not apply to an employee, officer, or agent of any of the following while acting within the scope of the person's official duties:

a. A law enforcement agency.

b. A State or federal court.

c. An agency or department of the State, local, or federal government.

d. A financial or retail security investigator employed by a merchant.

(b) Financial transaction card theft is punishable as provided by G.S. 14-113.17(b).

History.
1967, c. 1244, s. 2; 1979, c. 741, s. 1; c. 760, s. 5; 1979, 2nd Sess., c. 1316, s. 47; 1981, c. 63, s. 1; c. 179, s. 14; 2002-175, s. 3; 2021-68, s. 2; 2021-88, s. 2

§ 14-113.10. Prima facie evidence of theft

When a person has in his possession or under his control financial transaction cards issued in the names of two or more other persons other than members of his immediate family, such possession shall be prima facie evidence that such financial transaction cards have been obtained in violation of G.S. 14-113.9(a).

History.
1967, c. 1244, s. 2; 1979, c. 741, s. 1

§ 14-113.11. Forgery of financial transaction card

(a) A person is guilty of financial transaction card forgery when:

(1) With intent to defraud a purported issuer, a person or organization providing money, goods, services or anything else of value, or any other person, he falsely makes or falsely embosses a purported financial transaction card or utters such a financial transaction card; or

(2) With intent to defraud a purported issuer, a person or organization providing money, goods, services or anything else of value, or any other person, he falsely encodes, duplicates or alters existing encoded information on a financial transaction card or utters such a financial transaction card; or

(3) He, not being the cardholder or a person authorized by him, with intent to defraud the issuer, or a person or organization providing money, goods, services or anything else of value, or any other person, signs a financial transaction card.

(b) A person falsely makes a financial transaction card when he makes or draws, in whole or in part, a device or instrument which purports to be the financial transaction card of a named issuer but which is not such a financial transaction card because the issuer did not authorize the making or drawing, or alters a financial transaction card which was validly issued.

(c) A person falsely embosses a financial transaction card when, without authorization of the named issuer, he completes a financial transaction card by adding any of the matter, other than the signature of the cardholder, which an issuer requires to appear on the financial transaction card before it can be used by a cardholder.

(d) A person falsely encodes a financial transaction card when, without authorization of the purported issuer, he records magnetically, electronically, electro-magnetically or by any other means whatsoever, information on a financial transaction card which will permit acceptance of that card by any automated banking device. Conviction of financial transaction card forgery shall be punishable as provided in G.S. 14-113.17(b).

History.

1967, c. 1244, s. 2; 1979, c. 741, s. 1

§ 14-113.12. Prima facie evidence of forgery

(a) When a person, other than the purported issuer, possesses two or more financial transaction cards which are falsely made or falsely embossed, such possession shall be prima facie evidence that said cards were obtained in violation of G.S. 14-113.11(a)(1) or 14-113.11(a)(2).

(b) When a person, other than the cardholder or a person authorized by him possesses two or more financial transaction cards which are signed, such possession shall be prima facie evidence that said cards were obtained in violation of G.S. 14-113.11(a)(3).

History.

1967, c. 1244, s. 2; 1979, c. 741, s. 1

§ 14-113.13. Financial transaction card fraud

(a) A person is guilty of financial transaction card fraud when, with intent to defraud the issuer, a person or organization providing money, goods, services or anything else of value, or any other person, he

(1) Uses for the purpose of obtaining money, goods, services or anything else of value a financial transaction card obtained or retained, or which was received with knowledge that it was obtained or retained, in violation of G.S. 14-113.9 or 14-113.11 or a financial transaction card which he knows is forged, altered, expired, revoked or was obtained as a result of a fraudulent application in violation of G.S. 14-113.13(c); or

(2) Obtains money, goods, services, or anything else of value by:

    a. Representing without the consent of the cardholder that he is the holder of a specified card; or

    b. Presenting the financial transaction card without the authorization or permission of the cardholder; or

    c. Representing that he is the holder of a card and such card has not in fact been issued; or

    d. Using a financial transaction card to knowingly and willfully exceed:

        1. The actual balance of a demand deposit account or time deposit account; or

        2. An authorized credit line in an amount which exceeds such authorized credit line in the amount of five hundred dollars ($ 500.00), or fifty percent (50%) of such authorized credit line, whichever is greater; or

(3) Obtains control over a financial transaction card as security for debt; or

(4) Deposits into his account or any account, by means of an automated banking device, a false, fictitious, forged, altered or counterfeit check, draft, money order, or any other such document not his lawful or legal property; or

(5) Receives money, goods, services or anything else of value as a result of a false, fictitious, forged, altered, or counterfeit check, draft, money order or any other such document having been deposited into an account via an automated banking device, knowing at the time of receipt of the money, goods, services, or item of value that the document so deposited was false, fictitious, forged, altered or counterfeit or that the above deposited item was not his lawful or legal property.

(b) A person who is authorized by an issuer to furnish money, goods, services or anything else of value upon presentation of a financial transaction card by the cardholder, or any agent or employee of such person is guilty of a financial transaction card fraud when, with intent to defraud the issuer or the cardholder, he

(1) Furnishes money, goods, services or anything else of value upon presentation of a financial transaction card obtained or retained in violation of G.S. 14-113.9, or a financial transaction card which he knows is forged, expired or revoked; or

(2) Fails to furnish money, goods, services or anything else of value which he represents in writing to the issuer that he has furnished.

Conviction of financial transaction card fraud as provided in subsection (a) or (b) of this section is punishable as provided in G.S. 14-113.17(a) if the value of all money, goods, services and other things of value furnished in violation of this section, or if the difference between the value actually furnished and the value represented to the issuer to have been furnished in violation of this section, does not exceed five hundred dollars ($ 500.00) in any six-month period. Conviction of financial transaction card fraud as provided in subsection (a) or (b) of this section is punishable as provided in G.S. 14-113.17(b) if such value exceeds five hundred dollars ($ 500.00) in any six-month period.

(c) A person is guilty of financial transaction card fraud when, upon application for a financial transaction card to an issuer, he knowingly makes or causes to be made a false statement or report relative to his name, occupation, financial condition, assets, or liabilities; or willfully and substantially overvalues any assets, or willfully omits or substantially undervalues any indebtedness for the purpose of influencing the issuer to issue a financial transaction card.

Conviction of financial transaction card fraud as provided in this subsection is punishable as provided in G.S. 14-113.17(a).

(c1) A person authorized by an acquirer to furnish money, goods, services or anything else of value upon presentation of a financial transaction card or a financial transaction card account number by a cardholder, or any agent or employee of such person, who, with intent to defraud the issuer, acquirer, or cardholder, remits to an issuer or acquirer, for payment, a financial transaction card record of a sale, which sale was not made by such person, his agent or employee, is guilty of financial transaction card fraud.

Conviction of financial transaction card fraud as provided in this subsection is punishable as provided in G.S. 14-113.17(a).

(d) A cardholder is guilty of financial transaction card fraud when he willfully, knowingly, and with an intent to defraud the issuer, a person or organization providing money, goods, services, or anything else of value, or any other person, submits, verbally or in writing, to the issuer or any other person, any false notice or report of the theft, loss, disappearance, or non-receipt of his financial transaction card.

Conviction of financial transaction card fraud as provided in this subsection is punishable as provided in G.S. 14-113.17(a).

(e) In any prosecution for violation of G.S. 14-113.13, the State is not required to establish and it is no defense that some of the acts constituting the crime did not occur in this State or within one city, county, or local jurisdiction.

(f) For purposes of this section, revocation shall be construed to include either notice given in person or notice given in writing to the person to whom the financial transaction card and/or personal identification code was issued. Notice of revocation shall be immediate when notice is given in person. The sending of a notice in writing by registered or certified mail in the United States mail, duly stamped and addressed to such person at his last address known to the issuer, shall be prima facie evidence that such notice was duly received after seven days from the date of the deposit in the mail. If the address is located outside the United States, Puerto Rico, the Virgin Islands, the Canal Zone and Canada, notice shall be presumed to have been received 10 days after mailing by registered or certified mail.

History.
1967, c. 1244, s. 2; 1979, c. 741, s. 1; 1989, c. 161, s. 2

§ 14-113.14. Criminal possession of financial transaction card forgery devices

(a) A person is guilty of criminal possession of financial transaction card forgery devices when:

(1) He is a person other than the cardholder and possesses two or more incomplete financial transaction cards, with intent to complete them without the consent of the issuer; or

(2) He possesses, with knowledge of its character, machinery, plates, or any other contrivance designed to reproduce instruments purporting to be financial transaction cards of an issuer who has not consented to the preparation of such financial transaction cards.

(b) A financial transaction card is incomplete if part of the matter other than the signature of the cardholder, which an issuer requires to appear on the financial transaction card before it can be used by a cardholder, has not yet been stamped, embossed, imprinted, encoded or written upon it.

Conviction of criminal possession of financial transaction card forgery devices is punishable as provided in G.S. 14-113.17(b).

History.
1967, c. 1244, s. 2; 1979, c. 741, s. 1

§ 14-113.15. Criminal receipt of goods and services fraudulently obtained

A person is guilty of criminally receiving goods and services fraudulently obtained when he receives money, goods, services or anything else of value obtained in violation of G.S. 14-113.13(a) with the knowledge or belief that the same were obtained in violation of G.S. 14-113.13(a). Conviction of criminal receipt of goods and services fraudulently obtained is punishable as provided in G.S. 14-113.17(a) if the value of all the money, goods, services and anything else of value, obtained in violation of this section, does not exceed five hundred dollars ($ 500.00) in any six-month period; conviction of criminal receipt of goods and services fraudulently obtained is punishable as provided in G.S. 14-113.17(b) if such value exceeds five hundred dollars ($ 500.00) in any six-month period.

History.
1967, c. 1244, s. 2; 1979, c. 741, s. 1

§ 14-113.15A. Criminal factoring of financial transaction card records

Any person who, without the acquirer's express authorization, employs or solicits an authorized merchant, or any agent or employee of such merchant, to remit to an issuer or acquirer, for payment, a financial transaction card record of a sale, which sale was not made by such merchant, his agent or employee, is guilty of a felony punishable as provided in G.S. 14-113.17(b).

History.
1989, c. 161, s. 3

§ 14-113.16. Presumption of criminal receipt of goods and services fraudulently obtained

A person who obtains at a discount price a ticket issued by an airline, railroad, steamship or other transportation company from other than an authorized agent of such company which was acquired in violation of G.S. 14-113.13(a) without reasonable inquiry to ascertain that the person from whom it was obtained had a legal right to possess it shall be presumed to know that such ticket was acquired under circumstances constituting a violation of G.S. 14-113.13(a).

History.
1967, c. 1244, s. 2; 1979, c. 741, s. 1

§ 14-113.17. Punishment and penalties

(a) A person who is subject to the punishment and penalties of this Article shall be guilty of a Class 2 misdemeanor.

(b) A crime punishable under this Article is punishable as a Class I felony.

History.
1967, c. 1244, s. 2; 1979, c. 741, s. 1; c. 760, s. 5; 1979, 2nd Sess., c. 1316, s. 47; 1981, c. 63, s. 1; c. 179, s. 14; 1993, c. 539, ss. 55, 1183; 1994, Ex. Sess., c. 24, s. 14(c)

§§ 14-113.18, 14-113.19

Reserved for future codification purposes.

ARTICLE 19C
IDENTITY THEFT

§ 14-113.20. Identity theft

(a) A person who knowingly obtains, possesses, or uses identifying information of another person, living or dead, with the intent to fraudulently represent that the person is the other person for the purposes of making financial or credit transactions in the other person's name, to obtain anything of value, benefit, or advantage, or for the purpose of avoiding legal consequences is guilty of a felony punishable as provided in G.S. 14-113.22(a).

(b) The term "identifying information" as used in this Article includes the following:

(1) Social security or employer taxpayer identification numbers.

(2) Drivers license, State identification card, or passport numbers.

(3) Checking account numbers.

(4) Savings account numbers.

(5) Credit card numbers.

(6) Debit card numbers.

(7) Personal Identification (PIN) Code as defined in G.S. 14-113.8(6).

(8) Electronic identification numbers, electronic mail names or addresses, Internet account numbers, or Internet identification names.

(9) Digital signatures.

(10) Any other numbers or information that can be used to access a person's financial resources.

(11) Biometric data.

(12) Fingerprints.

(13) Passwords.

(14) Parent's legal surname prior to marriage.

(c) It shall not be a violation under this Article for a person to do any of the following:

(1) Lawfully obtain credit information in the course of a bona fide consumer or commercial transaction.

(2) Lawfully exercise, in good faith, a security interest or a right of offset by a creditor or financial institution.

(3) Lawfully comply, in good faith, with any warrant, court order, levy, garnishment, attachment, or other judicial or administrative order, decree, or directive, when any party is required to do so.

History.
1999-449, s. 1; 2000-140, s. 37; 2002-175, s. 4; 2005-414, s. 6

§ 14-113.20A. Trafficking in stolen identities

(a) It is unlawful for a person to sell, transfer, or purchase the identifying information of another person with the intent to commit identity theft, or to assist another person in committing identity theft, as set forth in G.S. 14-113.20.

(b) A violation of this section is a felony punishable as provided in G.S. 14-113.22(a1).

History.
2002-175, s. 5; 2005-414, s. 7(2)

§ 14-113.21. Venue of offenses

In any criminal proceeding brought under G.S. 14-113.20, the crime is considered to be committed in the county where the victim resides, where the perpetrator resides, where any part of the identity theft took place, or in any other county instrumental to the completion of the offense, regardless of whether the defendant was ever actually present in that county.

History.
1999-449, s. 1; 2005-414, ss. 2, 7

§ 14-113.21A. Investigation of offenses

(a) A person who has learned or reasonably suspects that the person has been the victim of identity theft may contact the local law enforcement agency that has jurisdiction over the person's actual residence. Notwithstanding the fact that jurisdiction may lie elsewhere for investigation and prosecution of a crime of identity theft, the local law enforcement agency may take the complaint, issue an incident report, and provide the complainant with a copy of the report and may refer the report to a law enforcement agency in that different jurisdiction.

(b) Nothing in this section interferes with the discretion of a local law enforcement agency to allocate resources for investigations of crimes. A complaint filed or report issued under this section is not required to be counted as an open case for purposes of compiling open case statistics.

History.
2005-414, s. 3

§ 14-113.22. Punishment and liability

(a) A violation of G.S.14-113.20(a) is punishable as a Class G felony, except it is punishable as a Class F felony if: (i) the victim suffers arrest, detention, or conviction as a proximate result of the offense, or (ii) the person is in possession of the identifying information pertaining to three or more separate persons.

(a1) A violation of G.S. 14-113.20A is punishable as a Class E felony.

(a2) The court may order a person convicted under G.S. 14-113.20 or G.S. 14-113.20A to pay restitution pursuant to Article 81C of Chapter 15A of the General Statutes for financial loss caused by the violation to any person. Financial loss included under this subsection may include, in addition to actual losses, lost wages, attorneys' fees, and other costs incurred by the victim in correcting his or her credit history or credit rating, or in connection with any criminal, civil, or administrative proceeding brought against the victim resulting from the misappropriation of the victim's identifying information.

(b) Notwithstanding subsection (a), (a1), or (a2) of this section, any person who commits an act made unlawful by G.S. 14-113.20 or G.S. 14-113.20A may also be liable for damages under G.S. 1-539.2C.

(c) In any case in which a person obtains identifying information of another person in violation of this Article, uses that information to commit a crime in addition to a violation of this Article, and is convicted of that additional crime, the court records shall reflect that the person whose identity was falsely used to commit the crime did not commit the crime.

History.
1999-449, s. 1; 2002-175, ss. 6, 7; 2003-206, s. 3

§ 14-113.23. Authority of the Attorney General

The Attorney General may investigate any complaint regarding identity theft under this Article. In conducting these investigations, the Attorney General has all the investigative powers available to the Attorney General under Article 1 of Chapter 75 of the General Statutes. The Attorney General shall refer all cases of identity theft under G.S. 14-113.20 to the district attorney in the county where the crime was deemed committed in accordance with G.S. 14-113.21.

History.
1999-449, s. 1; 2005-414, s. 7(2)

§ 14-113.24. Credit, charge, or debit card numbers on receipts

(a) For purposes of this section, the word "person" means the person that owns or leases the cash register or other machine or device that electronically prints receipts of credit, charge, or debit card transactions.

(b) Except as provided in this section, no person that accepts credit, charge, or debit cards for the transaction of business shall print more than five digits of the credit, charge, or debit card account number or the expiration date upon any receipt with the intent to provide the receipt to the cardholder at the point of sale. This section applies to a person who employs a cash register or other machine or device that electronically prints receipts for credit, charge, or debit card transactions. This section does not apply to a person whose sole means of recording a credit, charge, or debit card number for the transaction of business is by handwriting or by an imprint or copy of the credit, charge, or debit card.

(c) A person who violates this section commits an infraction as defined in G.S. 14-3.1 and is subject to a penalty of up to five hundred dollars ($ 500.00) per violation, not to exceed five hundred dollars ($ 500.00) in any calendar month or two thousand dollars ($ 2,000) in any calendar year. A person who receives a citation for violation of this section is not subject to the penalty provided in this subsection if the person establishes in court that the person came into compliance with this section within 30 days of the issuance of the citation and the person has remained in compliance with this section.

History.
2003-206, s. 1; 2003-206, s. 2

§ 14-113.25. Sale of certain cash registers and other receipt printing machines

(a) No person shall sell or offer to sell a cash register or other machine or device that electronically prints receipts of credit, charge, or debit card transactions that cannot be programmed or operated to produce a receipt with five or fewer digits of the credit, charge, or debit card account number and no expiration date printed on the receipt. This subsection applies to cash registers or other machines or devices sold or offered for sale for use in the ordinary course of business in this State.

(b) A person who violates this section commits an infraction as defined in G.S. 14-3.1 and is subject to a penalty of up to five hundred dollars ($ 500.00) per violation. For purposes of assessing penalties pursuant to this subsection, the sale or offer for sale of each individual cash register or other machine or device that electronically prints receipts of credit, charge, or debit card transactions in violation of this section is treated as a separate violation.

History.
2003-206, s. 1

§§ 14-113.26 through 14-113.29

Reserved for future codification purposes.

ARTICLE 19D
TELEPHONE RECORDS PRIVACY PROTECTION ACT

§ 14-113.30. Definitions

The following definitions apply in this Article:

(1) **Caller identification record.** -- A record collected and retained by or on behalf of a customer utilizing caller identification or similar technology that is delivered electronically to the recipient of a telephone call simultaneously with the reception of the telephone call and that indicates the telephone number from which the telephone call was initiated or similar information regarding the telephone call.

(2) **Customer.** -- A person or the legal guardian of a person or a representative of a business to whom a telephone service provider provides telephone service to a number subscribed or listed in the name of the person or business.

(3) **Person.** -- An individual, business association, partnership, limited partnership, corporation, limited liability company, or other legal entity.

(4) **Telephone record.** -- A record in written, electronic, or oral form, except a caller identification record, Directory Assistance information, and subscriber list information, that is created by a telephone service provider and that contains any of the following information with respect to a customer:

    a. Telephone numbers that have been dialed by the customer.

    b. Telephone numbers that pertain to calls made to the customer.

    c. The time when calls were made by the customer or to the customer.

    d. The duration of calls made by the customer or to the customer.

    e. The charges applied to calls, if any.

(5) **Telephone service.** -- The conveyance of two-way communication in analog, digital, or other form by any medium, including wire, cable, fiber optics, cellular, broadband personal communications services, or other wireless technologies, satellite, microwave, or at any frequency over any part of the electromagnetic spectrum. The term also includes the conveyance of voice communication over the Internet and telephone relay service.

(6) **Telephone service provider.** -- A person who provides telephone service to a customer without regard to the form of technology used, including traditional wire-line or cable communications service; cellular, broadband PCS, or other wireless communications service; microwave, satellite, or other terrestrial communications service; or voice over Internet communications service.

History.
2007-374, s. 1

§ 14-113.31. Prohibition of falsely obtaining, selling, or soliciting telephone records

(a) No person shall obtain, or attempt to obtain, by any means, whether electronically, in writing, or in oral form, with or without consideration, a telephone record that pertains to a customer who is a resident of this State without the customer's consent by doing any of the following:

(1) Making a false statement or representation to an agent, representative, or employee of a telephone service provider.

(2) Making a false statement or representation to a customer of a telephone service provider.

(3) Knowingly providing to a telephone service provider a document that is fraudulent, that has been lost or stolen, or that has been obtained by fraud, or that contains a false, fictitious, or fraudulent statement or representation.

(4) Accessing customer accounts of a telephone service provider via the Internet without prior authorization from the customer to whom the telephone records relate.

(b) No person shall knowingly purchase, receive, or solicit another to purchase or receive a telephone record that pertains to a customer without the prior authorization of that customer, or if the purchaser or receiver knows or has reason to know that the record has been obtained fraudulently.

(c) No person shall sell or offer to sell a telephone record that was obtained without the customer's prior consent, or if the person knows or has reason to know that the telephone record was obtained fraudulently.

History.
2007-374, s. 1

§ 14-113.32. Exceptions

(a) The provisions of G.S. 14-113.31 shall not apply to any of the following:

(1) Any lawfully authorized investigative, protective, or intelligence activity of a law enforcement agency in connection with the official duties of the law enforcement agency.

(2) A disclosure by a telephone service provider if the telephone service provider reasonably believes the disclosure is necessary to: (i) provide telephone service to a customer, including sharing telephone records with one of the provider's affiliates or (ii) protect an individual or service provider from fraudulent, abusive, or unlawful use of telephone service or a telephone record.

(3) A disclosure by a telephone service provider to the National Center for Missing and Exploited Children.

(4) A disclosure by a telephone service provider that is authorized by State or federal law or regulation.

(5) A disclosure by a telephone service provider to a governmental entity if the provider reasonably believes there is an emergency involving immediate danger of death or serious physical injury.

(6) Testing of a telephone service provider's security procedures or systems for maintaining the confidentiality of customers' telephone records.

(b) Nothing in this Article shall be construed to expand the obligation or duty of a telephone service provider to maintain the confidentiality of telephone records beyond the requirements of this Article or federal law or regulation. Any telephone service provider or agent, employee, or representative of a telephone service provider who reasonably and in good faith discloses telephone records shall not be criminally or civilly liable if the disclosure is later determined to be in violation of this Article.

History.
2007-374, s. 1

§ 14-113.33. Punishment; liability

(a) Unless the conduct is covered under some other provision of law providing greater punishment, any person who violates this Article is guilty of a Class H felony. In any criminal proceeding brought under this Article, the crime is considered to be committed in the county where the customer resides, where the defendant resides, where any part of the offense took place, or in any other county instrumental to the completion of the offense, regardless of whether the defendant was ever actually present in that county.

(b) A violation of G.S. 14-331.31 is a violation of G.S. 75-1.1, except that a customer whose telephone records were obtained, sold, or solicited in violation of this Article shall be entitled to damages pursuant to G.S. 75-16, or one thousand dollars ($ 1,000), whichever is greater.

History.
2007-374, s. 1

ARTICLE 20
FRAUDS

§ 14-114. Fraudulent disposal of personal property on which there is a security interest

(a) If any person, after executing a security agreement on personal property for a lawful purpose, shall make any disposition of any property embraced in such security agreement, with intent to defeat the rights of the secured party, every person so offending and every person with a knowledge of the security interest buying any property embraced in which security agreement, and every person assisting, aiding or abetting the unlawful disposition of such property, with intent to defeat the rights of any secured party in such security agreement, shall be guilty of a Class 2 misdemeanor.

A person's refusal to turn over secured property to a secured party who is attempting to repossess the property without a judgment or order for possession shall not, by itself, be a violation of this section.

(b) Intent to commit the crime as set forth in subsection (a) may be presumed from proof of possession of the property embraced in such security agreement by the grantor thereof after execution of the security agreement, and while it is in force, the further proof of the fact that the sheriff or other officer charged with the execution of process cannot after due diligence find such property under process directed to him for its seizure, for the satisfaction of such security agreement. However, this presumption may be rebutted by evidence that the property has, through no fault of the defendant, been stolen, lost, damaged beyond repair, or otherwise disposed of by the defendant without intent to defeat the rights of the secured party.

History.
1873-4, c. 31; 1874-5, c. 215; 1883, c. 61; Code, s. 1089; 1887, c. 14; Rev., s. 3435; C.S., s. 4287; 1969, c. 984, s. 2; c. 1224, s. 4; 1987 (Reg. Sess., 1988), c. 1065, s. 1; 1993, c. 539, s. 56; 1994, Ex. Sess., c. 24, s. 14(c)

§ 14-115. Secreting property to hinder enforcement of lien or security interest

Any person who, with intent to prevent or hinder the enforcement of a lien or security interest after a judgment or order has been issued for possession for that personal property subject to said lien or security interest, either refuses to surrender such personal property in his possession to a law enforcement officer, or removes, or exchanges, or secretes such personal property, shall be guilty of a Class 2 misdemeanor.

History.
1887, c. 14; Rev., s. 3436; C.S., s. 4288; 1969, c. 984, s. 3; c. 1224, s. 1; 1987 (Reg. Sess., 1988), c. 1065, s. 2; 1989, c. 401; 1993, c. 539, s. 57; 1994, Ex. Sess., c. 24, s. 14(c)

N.C. Gen. Stat. § 14-116

Repealed by Session Laws 1993 (Reg. Sess., 1994), c. 767, s. 30(1).

§ 14-117. Fraudulent and deceptive advertising

It shall be unlawful for any person, firm, corporation or association, with intent to sell or in anywise to dispose of merchandise, securities, service or any other thing offered by such person, firm, corporation or association, directly or indirectly, to the public for sale or distribution, or with intent to increase the consumption thereof, or to induce the public in any manner to enter into any obligation relating thereto, or to acquire title thereto, or an interest therein, to make public, disseminate, circulate or place before the public or cause directly or indirectly to be made, published, disseminated, circulated or placed before the public in this State, in a newspaper or other publication, or in the form of a book, notice, handbill, poster, bill, circular, pamphlet or letter, or in any other way, an advertisement of any sort regarding merchandise, securities, service or any other thing so offered to the public, which advertisement contains any assertion, representation or statement of fact which is untrue, deceptive or misleading: Provided, that such advertising shall be done willfully and with intent to mislead. Any person who shall violate the provisions of this section shall be guilty of a Class 2 misdemeanor.

History.
1915, c. 218; C.S., s. 4290; 1993, c. 539, s. 59; 1994, Ex. Sess., c. 24, s. 14(c)

N.C. Gen. Stat. § 14-117.1

Repealed by Session Laws 1994, Extra Session, c. 14, s. 72(5).

§ 14-117.2. Gasoline price advertisements

(a) Advertisements by any person or firm of the price of any grade of motor fuel must clearly so indicate if such price is dependent upon purchaser himself drawing or pumping the fuel.

(b) Any person or firm violating the provisions of this section shall be guilty of a Class 3 misdemeanor.

History.
1971, c. 324, ss. 1, 2; 1993, c. 539, s. 60; 1994, Ex. Sess., c. 24, s. 14(c)

§ 14-118. Blackmailing

If any person shall knowingly send or deliver any letter or writing demanding of any other person, with menaces and without any reasonable or probable cause, any chattel, money or valuable security; or if any person shall accuse, or threaten to accuse, or shall knowingly send or deliver any letter or writing accusing or threatening to accuse any other person of any crime punishable by law with death or by imprisonment in the State's prison, with the intent to extort or gain from such person any chattel, money or valuable security, every such offender shall be guilty of a Class 1 misdemeanor.

History.
R.C., c. 34, s. 110; Code, s. 989; Rev., s. 3428; C.S., s. 4291; 1993, c. 539, s. 61; 1994, Ex. Sess., c. 24, s. 14(c)

§ 14-118.1. Simulation of court process in connection with collection of claim, demand or account

It shall be unlawful for any person, firm, corporation, association, agent or employee in any manner to coerce, intimidate, or attempt to coerce or intimidate any person in connection with any claim, demand or account, by the issuance, utterance or delivery of any matter, printed, typed or written, which (i) simulates or resembles a summons, warrant, writ or other court process or pleading; or (ii) by its form, wording, use of the name of North Carolina or any officer, agency or subdivision thereof, use of seals or insignia, or general appearance has a tendency to create in the mind of the ordinary person the false impression that it has judicial or other official authorization, sanction or approval. Any violation of the provisions of this section shall be a Class I felony.

History.
1961, c. 1188; 1979, c. 263; 1993, c. 539, s. 62; 1994, Ex. Sess., c. 24, s. 14(c); 2012-150, s. 3

§ 14-118.2. Assisting, etc., in obtaining academic credit by fraudulent means

(a) It shall be unlawful for any person, firm, corporation or association to assist any student, or advertise, offer or attempt to assist any student, in obtaining or in attempting to obtain, by fraudulent means, any academic credit, grade or test score, or any diploma, certificate or other instrument purporting to confer any literary, scientific, professional, technical or other degree in any course of study in any university, college, academy or other educational institution. The activity prohibited by this subsection includes, but is not limited to, preparing or advertising, offering, or attempting to prepare a term paper, thesis, or dissertation for another; impersonating or advertising, offering or attempting to impersonate another in taking or attempting to take an examination; and the giving or changing of a grade or test score or offering to give or change a grade or test score in exchange for an article of value or money.

(b) Any person, firm, corporation or association violating any of the provisions of this section shall be guilty of a Class 2 misdemeanor. This section includes the acts of a teacher or other school official; however, the provisions of this section shall not apply to the acts of one student in assisting another student as herein defined if the former is duly registered in an educational institution in North Carolina and is subject to the disciplinary authority thereof.

History.
1963, c. 781; 1969, c. 1224, s. 7; 1989, c. 144; 1993, c. 539, s. 63; 1994, Ex. Sess., c. 24, s. 14(c)

§ 14-118.3. Acquisition and use of information obtained from patients in hospitals for fraudulent purposes

It shall be unlawful for any person, firm or corporation, or any officer, agent or other representative of any person, firm or corporation to obtain or seek to obtain from any person while a patient in any hospital information concerning any illness, injury or disease of such patient, other than information concerning the illness, injury or disease for which such patient is then hospitalized and being treated, for a fraudulent purpose, or to use any information so obtained in regard to such other illness, injury or disease for a fraudulent purpose.

Any person, firm or corporation violating the provisions of this section shall be guilty of a Class 2 misdemeanor.

History.
1967, c. 974; 1969, c. 1224, s. 5; 1993, c. 539, s. 64; 1994, Ex. Sess., c. 24, s. 14(c)

§ 14-118.4. Extortion

Any person who threatens or communicates a threat or threats to another with the intention thereby wrongfully to obtain anything of value or any acquittance, advantage, or immunity is guilty of extortion and such person shall be punished as a Class F felon.

History.
1973, c. 1032; 1979, c. 760, s. 5; 1979, 2nd Sess., c. 1316, s. 47; 1981, c. 63, s. 1; c. 179, s. 14; 1993, c. 539, s. 1184; 1994, Ex. Sess., c. 24, s. 14(c)

§ 14-118.5. Theft of cable television service

(a) Any person, firm or corporation who, after October 1, 1984, knowingly and willfully attaches or maintains an electronic, mechanical or other connection to any cable, wire, decoder, converter, device or equipment of a cable television system or removes, tampers with, modifies or alters any cable, wire, decoder, converter, device or equipment of a cable television system for the purpose of intercepting or receiving any programming or service transmitted by such cable television system which person, firm or corporation is not authorized by the cable television system to receive, is guilty of a Class 3 misdemeanor which may include a fine not exceeding five hundred dollars ($ 500.00). Each unauthorized connection, attachment, removal, modification or alteration shall constitute a separate violation.

(b) Any person, firm or corporation who knowingly and willfully, without the authorization of a cable television system, distributes, sells, attempts to sell or possesses for sale in North Carolina any converter, decoder, device, or kit, that is designed to decode or descramble any encoded or scrambled signal transmitted by such cable television system, is guilty of a Class 3 misdemeanor which may include a fine not exceeding five hundred dollars ($ 500.00). The term "encoded or scrambled signal" shall include any signal or transmission that is not intended to produce an intelligible program or service without the aid of a decoder, descrambler, filter, trap or other electronic or mechanical device.

(c) Any cable television system may institute a civil action to enjoin and restrain any violation of this section, and in addition, such cable television system shall be entitled to civil damages in the following amounts:

(1) For each violation of subsection (a), three hundred dollars ($ 300.00) or three times the amount of actual damages, if any, sustained by the plaintiff, whichever amount is greater.

(2) For each violation of subsection (b), one thousand dollars ($ 1,000) or three times the amount of actual damages, if any, sustained by the plaintiff, whichever amount is greater.

(d) It is not a necessary prerequisite to a civil action instituted pursuant to this section that the plaintiff has suffered or will suffer actual damages.

(e) Proof that any equipment, cable, wire, decoder, converter or device of a cable television system was modified, removed, altered, tampered with or connected without the consent of such cable system in violation of this section shall be prima facie evidence that such action was taken knowingly and willfully by the person or persons in whose name the cable system's equipment, cable, wire, decoder, converter or device is installed or the person or persons regularly receiving the benefits of cable services resulting from such unauthorized modification, removal, alteration, tampering or connection.

(f) The receipt, decoding or converting of a signal from the air by the use of a satellite dish or antenna shall not constitute a violation of this section.

(g) Cable television systems may refuse to provide service to anyone who violates subsection (a) of this section whether or not the alleged violator has been prosecuted thereunder.

History.
1977, 2nd Sess., c. 1185, s. 1; 1983 (Reg. Sess., 1984), c. 1088, s. 1; 1993, c. 539, s. 65; 1994, Ex. Sess., c. 24, s. 14(c)

§ 14-118.6. Filing false lien or encumbrance

(a) It shall be unlawful for any person to present for filing or recording in a public record or a private record generally available to the public a false lien or encumbrance against the real or personal property of an owner or beneficial interest holder, knowing or having reason to know that the lien or encumbrance is false or contains a materially false, fictitious, or fraudulent statement or representation. Any person who violates this subsection shall be guilty of a Class I felony.

(b) When presented to the register of deeds for recording, if a register of deeds has a reasonable suspicion that an instrument purporting to be a lien or encumbrance is materially false, fictitious, or fraudulent, the register of deeds may refuse to record the purported lien or encumbrance. Neither the register of deeds nor any other entity shall be liable for recording or the refusal to record a purported lien or encumbrance as described in this section. If the recording of the purported lien or encumbrance is denied, the register of deeds shall allow the recording of a Notice of Denied Lien or Encumbrance Filing on a form adopted by the Secretary of State, for which no filing fee shall be collected. The Notice of Denied Lien or Encumbrance Filing shall not itself constitute a lien or encumbrance. When recording is denied, any interested person may initiate a special proceeding in the county where the recording was denied within ten (10) business days of the filing of the Notice of Denied Lien or Encumbrance Filing asking the superior court of the respective county to find that the proposed recording has a statutory or contractual basis and to order that the document be recorded. If, after hearing, upon a minimum of five (5) days' notice as provided in Rule 5 of the Rules of Civil Procedure and opportunity to be heard to all interested persons and all persons claiming an ownership interest in the property, the court finds that there is a statutory or contractual basis for the proposed recording, the court shall order the document recorded, and the party submitting the instrument shall pay the filing fee in accordance with G.S. 161-10. A lien or encumbrance recorded upon order of the court under this subsection shall have a priority interest as of the time of the filing of the Notice of Denied Lien or Encumbrance Filing. If the court finds that there is no statutory or contractual basis for the proposed recording, the court shall enter an order finding that the proposed recording is null and void and that it shall not be filed, indexed, or recorded and a certified copy of that order shall be recorded by the register of deeds that originally denied the recording, for which the party who submitted the instrument shall pay the filing fee in accordance with G.S. 161-10. The review by the judge under this subsection shall not be deemed a finding as to any underlying claim of the parties involved. If a special proceeding is not initiated under this subsection within ten (10) business days of the filing of the Notice of Denied Lien or Encumbrance Filing, the purported lien or encumbrance is deemed null and void as a matter of law.

(b1) When a purported lien or encumbrance is presented to a clerk of superior court for filing and the clerk of court has a reasonable suspicion that the purported lien or encumbrance is materially false, fictitious, or fraudulent, the clerk of court may refuse to file the purported lien or encumbrance. Neither the clerk of court nor the clerk's staff shall be liable for filing or the refusal to file a purported lien or encumbrance under this subsection. The clerk of superior court shall not file, index, or docket the document against the property until that document is approved by any judge of the judicial district having subject matter jurisdiction for filing by the clerk of superior court. If the judge determines that the filing is not false, the clerk shall index the claim of lien. A lien or encumbrance filed upon order of the court under this subsection shall have a priority interest as of the date and time of indexing by the clerk of superior court. If the court finds that there is no statutory or contractual basis for the proposed filing, the court shall enter an order that the proposed filing is null and void as a matter of law, and that it shall not be filed or indexed. The clerk of superior court shall serve the order and return the original denied filing to the person or entity that presented it. The person or entity shall have 30 days from the entry of the order to appeal the order. If the order is not appealed within the applicable time period, the clerk may destroy the filing.

(c) Upon being presented with an order duly issued by a court of competent jurisdiction of this State declaring that a lien or encumbrance already recorded or filed is false, and therefore null and void as a matter of law, the register of deeds or clerk of court that received the recording or filing, in addition to recording or filing the court's order finding the lien or encumbrance to be false, shall conspicuously mark on the first page of the original record previously filed the following statement: "THE CLAIM ASSERTED IN THIS DOCUMENT IS FALSE AND IS NOT PROVIDED FOR BY THE GENERAL LAWS OF THIS STATE."

(d) In addition to any criminal penalties provided for in this section, the presentation of an instrument for recording or filing with a register of deeds or clerk of superior court that purports to be a lien or encumbrance that is determined to be materially false, fictitious, or fraudulent shall constitute a violation of G.S. 75-1.1.

(e) Subsections (b), (b1), and (c) of this section shall not apply to filings under Article 9 of Chapter 25 of the General Statutes or under Chapter 44A of the General Statutes.

History.
2012-150, s. 4; 2013-170, s. 1; 2013-410, s. 27.8; 2015-87, s. 1; 2017-102, s. 3; 2019-117, s. 3; 2019-243, s. 29(a)

§ 14-118.7. Possession, transfer, or use of automated sales suppression device

(a) **Definitions.** -- The following definitions apply in this section:

(1) **Automated sales suppression device or zapper.** -- A software program that falsifies the electronic records of electronic cash registers and other point-of-sale systems, including transaction data and transaction reports. The term includes the software program, any device that carries the software program, or an Internet link to the software program.

(2) **Electronic cash register.** -- A device that keeps a register or supporting documents through the use of an electronic device or computer system designed to record transaction data for the purpose of computing, compiling, or processing retail sales transaction data in whatever manner.

(3) **Phantom-ware.** -- A hidden programming option embedded in the operating system of an electronic cash register or hardwired into the electronic cash register that can be used to create a second set of records or may eliminate or manipulate transaction records, which may or may not be preserved in digital formats, to represent the true or manipulated record of transactions in the electronic cash register.

(4) **Transaction data.** -- The term includes items purchased by a customer, the price for each item, a taxability determination for each item, a segregated tax amount for each of the taxed items, the amount of cash or credit tendered, the net amount returned to the customer in change, the date and time of the purchase, the name, address, and identification number of the vendor, and the receipt or invoice number of the transaction.

(5) **Transaction report.** -- A report that documents, but is not limited to documenting, the sales, taxes, or fees collected, media totals, and discount voids at an electronic cash register and that is printed on cash register tape at the end of a day or shift, or a report that documents every action at an electronic cash register and that is stored electronically.

(b) **Offense.** -- No person shall knowingly sell, purchase, install, transfer, possess, use, or

Chapter 14

access any automated sales suppression device, zapper, or phantom-ware.

(c) **Penalty.** -- Any person convicted of a violation of this section is guilty of a Class H felony with a fine of up to ten thousand dollars ($ 10,000).

(d) **Liability.** -- Any person who violates this section is liable for all taxes, fees, penalties, and interest due the State as the result of the use of an automated sales suppression device, zapper, or phantom-ware and shall forfeit to the State as an additional penalty all profits associated with the sale or use of an automated sales suppression device, zapper, or phantom-ware.

(e) **Contraband.** -- An automated sales suppression device, zapper, or phantom-ware, or any device containing such device or software, is contraband.

History.
2013-301, s. 1

§§ 14-118.8, 14-118.9

Reserved for future codification purposes.

ARTICLE 20A
RESIDENTIAL MORTGAGE FRAUD ACT

§ 14-118.10. Title

This Article shall be known and cited as the "Residential Mortgage Fraud Act."

History.
2007-163, s. 1

§ 14-118.11. Definitions

Unless otherwise provided in this Article, the following definitions apply in this Article:

(1) **Mortgage lending process.** -- The process through which a person seeks or obtains a mortgage loan including solicitation, application, origination, negotiation of terms, underwriting, signing, closing, and funding of a mortgage loan and services provided incident to a mortgage loan, including the appraisal of the residential real property. Documents involved in the mortgage lending process include (i) uniform residential loan applications or other loan applications, (ii) appraisal reports, (iii) settlement statements, (iv) supporting personal documentation for loan applications, including W-2 or other earnings or income statements, verifications of rent, income, and employment, bank statements, tax

returns, and payroll stubs, and (v) any required mortgage-related disclosures.

(2) **Mortgage loan.** -- A loan primarily secured by either (i) a mortgage or a deed of trust on residential real property or (ii) a security interest in a manufactured home (as defined by G.S. 143-145(7)) located or to be located on residential real property.

(3) **Pattern of residential mortgage fraud.** -- Residential mortgage fraud that involves five or more mortgage loans, which have the same or similar intents, results, accomplices, victims, or methods of commission or otherwise are interrelated by distinguishing characteristics.

(4) **Person.** -- An individual, partnership, limited liability company, limited partnership, corporation, association, or other entity, however organized.

(5) **Residential real property.** -- Real property located in the State of North Carolina upon which there is located or is to be located a structure or structures designed principally for residential purposes, including, but not limited to, individual units of townhouses, condominiums, and cooperatives.

History.
2007-163, s. 1

§ 14-118.12. Residential mortgage fraud

(a) A person is guilty of residential mortgage fraud when, for financial gain and with the intent to defraud, that person does any of the following:

(1) Knowingly makes or attempts to make any material misstatement, misrepresentation, or omission within the mortgage lending process with the intention that a mortgage lender, mortgage broker, borrower, or any other person or entity that is involved in the mortgage lending process relies on it.

(2) Knowingly uses or facilitates or attempts to use or facilitate the use of any misstatement, misrepresentation, or omission within the mortgage lending process with the intention that a mortgage lender, borrower, or any other person or entity that is involved in the mortgage lending process relies on it.

(3) Receives or attempts to receive proceeds or any other funds in connection with a residential mortgage closing that the person knew, or should have known, resulted from a violation of subdivision (1) or (2) of this subsection.

(4) Conspires or solicits another to violate any of the provisions of subdivision (1), (2), or (3) of this subsection.

(5) Knowingly files in a public record or a private record generally available to the public a document falsely claiming that a mortgage loan has been satisfied, discharged, released, revoked, or terminated or is invalid.

(b) It shall be sufficient in any prosecution under this Article for residential mortgage fraud to show that the party accused did the act with the intent to deceive or defraud. It shall be unnecessary to show that any particular person or entity was harmed financially in the transaction or that the person or entity to whom the deliberate misstatement, misrepresentation, or omission was made relied upon the misstatement, misrepresentation, or omission.

History.
2007-163, s. 1; 2012-150, s. 5

§ 14-118.13. Venue

In any criminal proceeding brought under this Article, the crime shall be construed to have been committed:

(1) In the county in which the residential real property for which a mortgage loan is being sought is located;

(2) In any county in which any act was performed in furtherance of the violation;

(3) In any county in which any person alleged to have violated this Article had control or possession of any proceeds of the violation;

(4) If a closing occurred, in any county in which the closing occurred; or

(5) In any county in which a document containing a deliberate misstatement, misrepresentation, or omission is filed with the official registrar of deeds or with the Division of Motor Vehicles.

History.
2007-163, s. 1

§ 14-118.14. Authority to investigate and prosecute

Upon its own investigation or upon referral by the Office of the Commissioner of Banks, the North Carolina Real Estate Commission, the Attorney General, the North Carolina Appraisal Board, or other parties, of available evidence concerning violations of this Article, the proper district attorney may institute the appropriate criminal proceedings under this Article.

History.
2007-163, s. 1

§ 14-118.15. Penalty for violation of Article

(a) Unless the conduct is prohibited by some other provision of law providing for greater punishment, a violation of this Article involving a single mortgage loan is a Class H felony.

(b) Unless the conduct is prohibited by some other provision of law providing for greater punishment, a violation of this Article involving a pattern of residential mortgage fraud is a Class E felony.

History.
2007-163, s. 1

§ 14-118.16. Forfeiture

(a) All real and personal property of every kind used or intended for use in the course of, derived from, or realized through a violation of this Article shall be subject to forfeiture to the State as set forth in G.S. 14-2.3 and G.S. 14-7.20. However, the forfeiture of any real or personal property shall be subordinate to any security interest in the property taken by a lender in good faith as collateral for the extension of credit and recorded as provided by law, and no real or personal property shall be forfeited under this section against an owner who made a bona fide purchase of the property without knowledge of a violation of this Article.

(b) In addition to the provisions of subsection (a) of this section, courts may order restitution to any person that has suffered a financial loss due to violation of this Article.

History.
2007-163, s. 1

§ 14-118.17. Liability for reporting suspected mortgage fraud

In the absence of fraud, bad faith, or malice, a person shall not be subject to an action for civil liability for filing reports or furnishing other information regarding suspected residential mortgage fraud to a regulatory or law enforcement agency.

History.
2007-163, s. 1

ARTICLE 21
FORGERY

§ 14-119. Forgery of notes, checks, and other securities; counterfeiting of instruments

(a) It is unlawful for any person to forge or counterfeit any instrument, or possess any counterfeit instrument, with the intent to injure or defraud any person, financial institution, or governmental unit. Any person in violation of this subsection is guilty of a Class I felony.

(b) Any person who transports or possesses five or more counterfeit instruments with the intent to injure or defraud any person, financial institution, or governmental unit is guilty of a Class G felony.

(c) As used in this Article, the term:

(1) "Counterfeit" means to manufacture, copy, reproduce, or forge an instrument that purports to be genuine, but is not, because it has been falsely copied, reproduced, forged, manufactured, embossed, encoded, duplicated, or altered.

(2) "Financial institution" means any mutual fund, money market fund, credit union, savings and loan association, bank, or similar institution, either foreign or domestic.

(3) "Governmental unit" means the United States, any United States territory, any state of the United States, any political subdivision, agency, or instrumentality of any state, or any foreign jurisdiction.

(4) "Instrument" means (i) any currency, bill, note, warrant, check, order, or similar instrument of or on any financial institution or governmental unit, or any cashier or officer of the institution or unit; or (ii) any security issued by, or on behalf of, any corporation, financial institution, or governmental unit.

History.
1819, c. 994, s. 1, P.R.; R.C., c. 34, s. 60; Code, s. 1030; Rev., s. 3419; C.S., s. 4293; 1979, c. 760, s. 5; 1979, 2nd Sess., c. 1316, s. 47; 1981, c. 63, s. 1; c. 179, s. 14; 1983, c. 397, s. 1; 2002-175, s. 1

§ 14-120. Uttering forged paper or instrument containing a forged endorsement

If any person, directly or indirectly, whether for the sake of gain or with intent to defraud or injure any other person, shall utter or publish any such false, forged or counterfeited instrument as is mentioned in G.S. 14-119, or shall pass or deliver, or attempt to pass or deliver, any of them to another person (knowing the same to be falsely forged or counterfeited) the person so offending shall be punished as a Class I felon. If any person, directly or indirectly, whether for the sake of gain or with intent to defraud or injure any other person, shall falsely make, forge or counterfeit any endorsement on any instrument described in the preceding section, whether such instrument be genuine or false,

or shall knowingly utter or publish any such instrument containing a false, forged or counterfeited endorsement or, knowing the same to be falsely endorsed, shall pass or deliver or attempt to pass or deliver any such instrument containing a forged endorsement to another person, the person so offending shall be guilty of a Class I felony.

History.
1819, c. 994, s. 2, P.R.; R.C., c. 34, s. 61; Code, s. 1031; Rev., s. 3427; 1909, c. 666; C.S., s. 4294; 1961, c. 94; 1979, c. 760, s. 5; 1979, 2nd Sess., c. 1316, s. 47; 1981, c. 63, s. 1; c. 179, s. 14; 1983, c. 397, s. 2; 1993, c. 539, s. 1185; 1994, Ex. Sess., c. 24, s. 14(c)

§ 14-121. Selling of certain forged securities

If any person shall sell, by delivery, endorsement or otherwise, to any other person, any judgment for the recovery of money purporting to have been rendered by a magistrate, or any bond, promissory note, bill of exchange, order, draft or liquidated account purporting to be signed by the debtor (knowing the same to be forged), the person so offending shall be punished as a Class H felon.

History.
R.C., c. 34, s. 63; Code, s. 1033; Rev., s. 3425; C.S., s. 4295; 1973, c. 108, s. 2; 1979, c. 760, s. 5; 1979, 2nd Sess., c. 1316, s. 47; 1981, c. 63, s. 1; c. 179, s. 14; 1993, c. 539, s. 1186; 1994, Ex. Sess., c. 24, s. 14(c)

§ 14-122. Forgery of deeds, wills and certain other instruments

If any person, of his own head and imagination, or by false conspiracy or fraud with others, shall wittingly and falsely forge and make, or shall cause or wittingly assent to the forging or making of, or shall show forth in evidence, knowing the same to be forged, any deed, lease or will, or any bond, writing obligatory, bill of exchange, promissory note, endorsement or assignment thereof; or any acquittance or receipt for money or goods; or any receipt or release for any bond, note, bill or any other security for the payment of money; or any order for the payment of money or delivery of goods, with intent, in any of said instances, to defraud any person or corporation, and thereof shall be duly convicted, the person so offending shall be punished as a Class H felon.

History.
5 Eliz., c. 14, ss. 2, 3; 21 James I, c. 26; 1801, c. 572, P.R.; R.C., c. 34, s. 59; Code, s. 1029; Rev., s. 3424; C.S., s. 4296; 1979, c. 760, s. 5; 1979, 2nd Sess., c. 1316, s. 47; 1981, c. 63, s. 1; c. 179, s. 14; 1993, c. 539, s. 1187; 1994, Ex. Sess., c. 24, s. 14(c)

§ 14-122.1. Falsifying documents issued by a secondary school, postsecondary educational institution, or governmental agency

(a) It shall be unlawful for any person knowingly and willfully:

(1) To make falsely or alter falsely, or to procure to be made falsely or altered falsely, or to aid or assist in making falsely or altering falsely, a diploma, certificate, license, or transcript signifying merit or achievement in an educational program issued by a secondary school, a postsecondary educational institution, or a governmental agency;

(2) To sell, give, buy, or obtain, or to procure to be sold, given, bought, or obtained, or to aid or assist in selling, giving, buying, or obtaining, a diploma, certificate, license, or transcript, which he knows is false, signifying merit or achievement in an educational program issued by a secondary school, a postsecondary educational institution, or a governmental agency;

(3) To use, offer, or present as genuine a falsely made or falsely altered diploma, certificate, license, or transcript signifying merit or achievement in an educational program issued by a secondary school, a postsecondary educational institution, or a governmental agency, which he knows is false; or

(4) To make a false written representation of fact that he has received a degree or other certification signifying merit, achievement, or completion of an educational program involving study, experience, or testing from a secondary school, a postsecondary educational institution or governmental agency in an application for:

(a) Employment;

(b) Admission to an educational program;

(c) Award; or

(d) For the purpose of inducing another to issue a diploma, certificate, license, or transcript signifying merit or achievement in an educational program of a secondary school, postsecondary educational institution, or a governmental agency.

(b) As used in this section, "postsecondary educational institution" means a technical college, community college, junior college, college, or university. As used in this section, "governmental agency" means any agency of a State or local government or of the federal government. As used in this section, "secondary school" means grades 9 through 12.

(c) Any person who violates a provision of this section shall be guilty of a Class 1 misdemeanor.

History.
1981, c. 146, s. 1; 1987, c. 388, s. 1; 1993, c. 539, s. 66; 1994, Ex. Sess., c. 24, s. 14(c)

§ 14-123. Forging names to petitions and uttering forged petitions

If any person shall willfully sign, or cause to be signed, or willfully assent to the signing of the name of any person without his consent, or of any deceased or fictitious person, to any petition or recommendation with the intent of procuring any commutation of sentence, pardon or reprieve of any person convicted of any crime or offense, or for the purpose of procuring such pardon, reprieve or commutation to be refused or delayed by any public officer, or with the intent of procuring from any person whatsoever, either for himself or another, any appointment to office, or to any position of honor or trust, or with the intent to influence the official action of any public officer in the management, conduct or decision of any matter affecting the public, he shall be punished as a Class I felon; and if any person shall willfully use any such paper for any of the purposes or intents above recited, knowing that any part of the signatures to such petition or recommendation has been signed thereto without the consent of the alleged signers, or that names of any dead or fictitious persons are signed thereto, he shall be guilty of a felony, and shall be punished in like manner.

History.
1883, c. 275; Code, s. 1034; Rev., s. 3426; C.S., s. 4297; 1979, c. 760, s. 5; 1979, 2nd Sess., c. 1316, s. 47; 1981, c. 63, s. 1; c. 179, s. 14

§ 14-124. Forging certificate of corporate stock and uttering forged certificates

If any officer or agent of a corporation shall, falsely and with a fraudulent purpose, make, with the intent that the same shall be issued and delivered to any other person by name or as holder or bearer thereof, any certificate or other writing, whereby it is certified or declared that such person, holder or bearer is entitled to or has an interest in the stock of such corporation, when in fact such person, holder or bearer is not so entitled, or is not entitled to the amount of stock in such certificate or writing specified; or if any officer or agent of such corporation, or other person, knowing such certificate or other writing to be false or untrue, shall transfer, assign or deliver the same to another person, for the sake of gain, or with the intent to defraud the corporation, or any member thereof, or such person to whom the same shall be transferred, assigned or delivered, the person so offending shall be punished as a Class I felon.

History.

R.C., c. 34, s. 62; Code, s. 1032; Rev., s. 3421; C.S., s. 4298; 1979, c. 760, s. 5; 1979, 2nd Sess., c. 1316, s. 47; 1981, c. 63, s. 1; c. 179, s. 14

§ 14-125. Forgery of bank notes and other instruments by connecting genuine parts

If any person shall fraudulently connect together different parts of two or more bank notes, or other genuine instruments, in such a manner as to produce another note or instrument, with intent to pass all of them as genuine, the same shall be deemed a forgery, and the instrument so produced a forged note, or forged instrument, in like manner as if each of them had been falsely made or forged.

History.

R.C., c. 34, s. 66; Code, s. 1037; Rev., s. 3420; C.S., s. 4299

SUBCHAPTER 06.
CRIMINAL TRESPASS

ARTICLE 22
DAMAGES AND OTHER OFFENSES TO LAND AND FIXTURES

N.C. Gen. Stat. § 14-126

Repealed by Session Laws 1987, c. 700, s. 2.

§ 14-127. Willful and wanton injury to real property

If any person shall willfully and wantonly damage, injure or destroy any real property whatsoever, either of a public or private nature, he shall be guilty of a Class 1 misdemeanor.

History.

R.C., c. 34, s. 111; 1873-4, c. 176, s. 5; Code, s. 1081; Rev., s. 3677; C.S., s. 4301; 1967, c. 1083; 1993, c. 539, s. 67; 1994, Ex. Sess., c. 24, s. 14(c)

§ 14-127.1. Graffiti vandalism

(a) As used in this section, "graffiti vandalism" means to unlawfully write or scribble on, mark, paint, deface, or besmear the walls of (i) any real property, whether public or private, including cemetery tombstones and monuments, (ii) any public building or facility as defined in G.S. 14-132, or (iii) any statue or monument situated in any public place, by any type of pen, paint, or marker regardless of whether the pen

or marker contains permanent ink, paint, or spray paint.

(b) Except as otherwise provided in this section, any person who engages in graffiti vandalism is guilty of a Class 1 misdemeanor. A person convicted of a Class 1 misdemeanor under this subsection shall be fined a minimum of five hundred dollars ($ 500.00) and, if community or intermediate punishment is imposed, shall be required to perform 24 hours of community service.

(c) Any person who violates subsection (a) of this section shall be guilty of a Class H felony if all of the following apply:

(1) The person has two or more prior convictions for violation of this section.

(2) The current violation was committed after the second conviction for violation of this section.

(3) The violation resulting in the second conviction was committed after the first conviction for violation of this section.

History.

2015-72, s. 1

§ 14-128. Injury to trees, crops, lands, etc., of another

Any person, not being on his own lands, who shall without the consent of the owner thereof, willfully commit any damage, injury, or spoliation to or upon any tree, wood, underwood, timber, garden, crops, vegetables, plants, lands, springs, or any other matter or thing growing or being thereon, or who cuts, breaks, injures, or removes any tree, plant, or flower, shall be guilty of a Class 1 misdemeanor: Provided, however, that this section shall not apply to the officers, agents, and employees of the Department of Transportation while in the discharge of their duties within the right-of-way or easement of the Department of Transportation.

History.

Ex. Sess. 1924, c. 54; 1957, c. 65, s. 11; c. 754; 1965, c. 300, s. 1; 1969, c. 22, s. 1; 1973, c. 507, s. 5; 1977, c. 464, s. 34; 1993, c. 539, s. 68; 1994, Ex. Sess., c. 24, s. 14(c)

N.C. Gen. Stat. § 14-128.1

Repealed by Session Laws 1979, c. 964, s. 2.

§ 14-129. Taking, etc., of certain wild plants from land of another

No person, firm or corporation shall dig up, pull up or take from the land of another or from any public domain, the whole or any part of any trailing arbutus, Aaron's Rod (Thermopsis caroliniana), Bird-foot Violet (Viola pedata), Bloodroot (Sanguinaria canadensis), Blue Dogbane (Amsonia tabernaemontana), Cardinalflower (Lobelia cardinalis), Columbine (Aquilegia canadensis), Dutchman's Breeches (Dicentra cucullaria), Maidenhair Fern (Adiantum pedatum), Walking Fern (Camptosorus rhizophyllus), Gentians (Gentiana), Ground Cedar, Running Cedar, Hepatica (Hepatica americana and acutiloba), Jack-in-the-Pulpit (Arisaema triphyllum), Lily (Lilium), Lupine (Lupinus), Monkshood (Aconitum uncinatum and reclinatum), May Apple (Podophyllum peltatum), Orchids (all species), Pitcher Plant (Sarracenia), Shooting Star (Dodecatheon meadia), Oconee Bells (Shortia galacifolia), Solomon's Seal (Polygonatum), Trailing Christmas (Greens-Lycopodium), Trillium (Trillium), Virginia Bluebells (Mertensia virginica), and Fringe Tree (Chionanthus virginicus), American holly, white pine, red cedar, hemlock or other coniferous trees, or any flowering dogwood, any mountain laurel, any rhododendron, or any ground pine, or any Christmas greens, or any Judas tree, or any leucothea, or any azalea, without having in his possession a permit to dig up, pull up or take such plants, signed by the owner of such land, or by his duly authorized agent. Any person convicted of violating the provisions of this section shall be guilty of a Class 3 misdemeanor only punished by a fine of not less than seventy-five dollars ($ 75.00) nor more than one hundred seventy-five dollars ($ 175.00) for each offense, with each plant taken in violation of this section constituting a separate offense. The Clerk of Court for the jurisdiction in which a conviction occurs under this section involving any species listed in this section that also appears on the North Carolina Protected Plants list created under the authority granted by Article 19B of Chapter 106 of the General Statutes shall report the conviction to the Plant Conservation Board so the Board may consider a civil penalty under the authority of that Article.

History.

1941, c. 253; 1951, c. 367, s. 1; 1955, cc. 251, 962; 1961, c. 1021; 1967, c. 355; 1971, c. 951; 1993, c. 539, s. 69; c. 553, s. 9; 1994, Ex. Sess., c. 24, s. 14(c); 2001-93, s. 1; 2001-487, s. 43(a); 2014-120, s. 52(b)

N.C. Gen. Stat. § 14-129.1

Repealed by Session Laws 1979, c. 964, s. 2.

§ 14-129.2. Unlawful to take sea oats

(a) It is unlawful to dig up, pull up, or take from the land of another or from any public domain the whole or any part of any Sea Oats (Uniola paniculata) without the consent of the owner of that land.

(b) Any person convicted of violating the provisions of this section shall be guilty of a Class 3 misdemeanor and shall be punished by a fine of not less than twenty-five dollars ($ 25.00) nor more than two hundred dollars ($ 200.00) for each offense.

History.

2001-93, s. 2

§ 14-129.3. Felony taking of Venus flytrap

(a) Any person, firm, or corporation who digs up, pulls up, takes, or carries away, or aids in taking or carrying away, any Venus flytrap (Dionaea muscipula) plant or the seed of any Venus flytrap plant growing upon the lands of another person, or from the public domain, with the intent to steal the Venus flytrap plant or seed is guilty of a Class H felony.

(b) This section shall not apply to any person, firm, or corporation that has a permit to dig up, pull up, take, or carry away the plant or seed, signed by the owner of the land, or the owner's duly authorized agent. At the time of the digging, pulling, taking, or carrying away, the permit shall be in the possession of the person, firm, or corporation on the land.

History.

2014-120, s. 52(a)

§ 14-130. Trespass on public lands

If any person shall erect a building on any state-owned lands, or cultivate or remove timber from any such lands, without the permission of the State, he shall be guilty of a Class 1 misdemeanor. Moreover, the State can recover from any person cutting timber on its land three times the value of the timber which is cut.

History.

1823, c. 1190, P.R.; 1842, c. 36, s. 4; R.C., c. 34, s. 42; Code, s. 1121; Rev., s. 3746; 1909, c. 891; C.S., s. 4302; 1979, c. 15; 1993, c. 539, s. 70; 1994, Ex. Sess., c. 24, s. 14(c)

§ 14-131. Trespass on land under option by the federal government

On lands under option which have formally or informally been offered to and accepted by either the North Carolina Department of Natural and Cultural Resources or the Department of Environmental Quality by the acquiring federal agency and tentatively accepted by a Department for administration as State forests, State parks, State game refuges or for other public purposes, it shall be unlawful to cut, dig, break, injure or remove any timber, lumber, firewood, trees, shrubs or other plants; or any fence, house, barn or other structure; or to pursue, trap, hunt or kill any bird or other wild animals or take fish from streams or lakes within the boundaries of such areas without the written consent of the local official of the United States having charge of the acquisition of such lands.

Any person, firm or corporation convicted of the violation of this section shall be guilty of a Class 3 misdemeanor.

The Department of Environmental Quality through its legally appointed forestry, fish and game wardens is hereby authorized and empowered to assist the county law-enforcement officers in the enforcement of this section.

History.
1935, c. 317; 1973, c. 1262, s. 86; 1977, c. 771, s. 4; 1989, c. 727, s. 218(2); 1993, c. 539, s. 71; 1994, Ex. Sess., c. 24, s. 14(c); 1997-443, s. 11A.119(a); 2015-241, s. 14.30(bb)

§ 14-132. Disorderly conduct in and injuries to public buildings and facilities

(a) It is a misdemeanor if any person shall:

(1) Make any rude or riotous noise, or be guilty of any disorderly conduct, in or near any public building or facility; or

(2) Unlawfully write or scribble on, mark, deface, besmear, or injure the walls of any public building or facility, or any statue or monument situated in any public place; or

(3) Commit any nuisance in or near any public building or facility.

(b) Any person in charge of any public building or facility owned or controlled by the State, any subdivision of the State, or any other public agency shall have authority to arrest summarily and without warrant for a violation of this section.

(c) The term "public building or facility" as used in this section includes any building or facility which is:

(1) One to which the public or a portion of the public has access and is owned or controlled by the State, any subdivision of the State, any other public agency, or any private institution or agency of a charitable, educational, or eleemosynary nature; or

(2) Dedicated to the use of the general public for a purpose which is primarily concerned with public recreation, cultural activities, and other events of a public nature or character.

(3) Designated by the Director of the State Bureau of Investigation in accordance with G.S. 143B-987.

The term "building or facility" as used in this section also includes the surrounding grounds and premises of any building or facility used in connection with the operation or functioning of such building or facility.

(d) Unless the conduct is covered under some other provision of law providing greater punishment, any person who violates any provision of this section is guilty of a Class 2 misdemeanor.

History.
1829, c. 29, ss. 1, 2; 1842, c. 47; R.C., c. 103, ss. 7, 8; Code, s. 2308; Rev., s. 3742; 1915, c. 269; C.S., s. 4303; 1969, c. 869, s. 71/2; c. 1224, s. 2; 1981, c. 499, s. 2; 1993, c. 539, s. 72; 1994, Ex. Sess., c. 24, s. 14(c); 2014-100, s. 17.1(w); 2015-72, s. 2

N.C. Gen. Stat. § 14-132.1

Repealed by Session Laws 1987, c. 700, s. 2.

§ 14-132.2. Willfully trespassing upon, damaging, or impeding the progress of a public school bus

(a) Any person who shall unlawfully and willfully demolish, destroy, deface, injure, burn or damage any public school bus or public school activity bus shall be guilty of a Class 1 misdemeanor.

(b) Any person who shall enter a public school bus or public school activity bus after being forbidden to do so by the authorized school bus driver in charge thereof, or the school principal to whom the public school bus or public school activity bus is assigned, shall be guilty of a Class 1 misdemeanor.

(c) Any occupant of a public school bus or public school activity bus who shall refuse to leave said bus upon demand of the authorized driver in charge thereof, or upon demand of the principal of the school to which said bus is assigned, shall be guilty of a Class 1 misdemeanor.

(c1) Any person who shall unlawfully and willfully stop, impede, delay, or detain any public school bus or public school activity bus being operated for public school purposes shall be guilty of a Class 1 misdemeanor.

(d) Subsections (b) and (c) of this section shall not apply to a child less than 12 years of age, or authorized professional school personnel.

History.
1975, c. 191, s. 1; 1993, c. 539, s. 73; 1994, Ex. Sess., c. 24, s. 14(c); 2001-26, s. 1

N.C. Gen. Stat. § 14-133

Repealed by Session Laws 1993 (Reg. Sess., 1994), c. 767, s. 30(2).

N.C. Gen. Stat. § 14-134

Repealed by Session Laws 1987, c. 700, s. 2.

N.C. Gen. Stat. § 14-134.1

Repealed by Session Laws 1977, c. 887, s. 2.

§ 14-134.2. Operating motor vehicle upon utility easements after being forbidden to do so

If any person, without permission, shall ride, drive or operate a minibike, motorbike, motorcycle, jeep, dune buggy, automobile, truck or any other motor vehicle, other than a motorized all-terrain vehicle as defined in G.S. 14-159.3, upon a utility easement upon which the owner or holder of the easement or agent of the owner or holder of the easement has posted on the easement a "no trespassing" sign or has otherwise given oral or written notice to the person not to so ride, drive or operate such a vehicle upon the said easement, he shall be guilty of a Class 3 misdemeanor, provided, however, neither the owner of the property nor the holder of the easement or their agents, employees, guests, invitees or permittees shall be guilty of a violation under this section.

History.
1975, c. 636, s. 1; 1993, c. 539, s. 75; 1994, Ex. Sess., c. 24, s. 14(c); 1997-487, s. 2; 2015-26, s. 2.1

§ 14-134.3. Domestic criminal trespass

(a) Any person who enters after being forbidden to do so or remains after being ordered to leave by the lawful occupant, upon the premises occupied by a present or former spouse or by a person with whom the person charged has lived as if married, shall be guilty of a misdemeanor if the complainant and the person charged are living apart; provided, however, that no person shall be guilty if said person enters upon the premises pursuant to a judicial order or written separation agreement which gives the person the right to enter upon said premises for the purpose of visiting with minor children. Evidence that the parties are living apart shall include but is not necessarily limited to:

(1) A judicial order of separation;
(2) A court order directing the person charged to stay away from the premises occupied by the complainant;
(3) An agreement, whether verbal or written, between the complainant and the person charged that they shall live separate and apart, and such parties are in fact living separate and apart; or
(4) Separate places of residence for the complainant and the person charged.

Except as provided in subsection (b) of this section, upon conviction, said person is guilty of a Class 1 misdemeanor.

(b) A person convicted of a violation of this section is guilty of a Class G felony if the person is trespassing upon property operated as a safe house or haven for victims of domestic violence and the person is armed with a deadly weapon at the time of the offense.

History.
1979, c. 561, s. 2; 1993, c. 539, s. 76; 1994, Ex. Sess., c. 24, s. 14(c); 1998-212, s. 17.19(a)

§ 14-135. Larceny of timber

(a) **Offense.** -- Except as otherwise provided in subsection (b) of this section, a person commits the offense of larceny of timber if the person does any of the following:

(1) Knowingly and willfully cuts down, injures, or removes any timber owned by another person, without the consent of the owner of the land or the owner of the timber, or without a lawful easement running with the land.
(2) Buys timber directly from the owner of the timber and fails to make payment in full to the owner by (i) the date specified in the written timber sales agreement or (ii) if there is no such agreement, 60 days from the date that the buyer removes the timber from the property.

(b) **Exceptions.** -- The following are exceptions to the offense set forth in subsection (a) of this section:

(1) A person is not guilty of an offense under subdivision (1) of subsection (a) of this section if the person is an employee or agent of an electric power supplier, as defined in G.S. 62-133.8, and either of the following conditions is met:
   a. The person believed in good faith that consent of the owner had been obtained prior to cutting down, injuring, or removing the timber.
   b. The person believed in good faith that the cutting down, injuring, or removing of the timber was permitted by a utility easement or was necessary to remove a tree hazard. For purposes of this sub-subdivision, the term "tree hazard" includes a dead or dying tree, dead parts of a living tree, or an unstable living tree that is within striking distance of an electric transmission line, electric distribution line, or electric equipment and constitutes a hazard to the line or equipment in the event of a tree failure.
(2) A person is not guilty of an offense under subdivision (2) of subsection (a) of this section if either of the following conditions is met:

a. The person remitted payment in full within the time period set in subdivision (2) of subsection (a) of this section to a person he or she believed in good faith to be the rightful owner of the timber.

b. The person remitted payment in full to the owner of the timber within the 10-day period set forth in subsection (c) of this section.

(c) **Prima Facie Evidence.** -- An owner of timber who does not receive payment in full within the time period set in subdivision (2) of subsection (a) of this section may notify the timber buyer in writing of the owner's demand for payment at the timber buyer's last known address by certified mail or by personal delivery. The timber buyer's failure to make payment in full within 10 days after the mailing or personal delivery authorized under this subsection shall constitute prima facie evidence of the timber buyer's intent to commit an offense under subdivision (2) of subsection (a) of this section.

(d) **Penalty; Restitution.** -- A person who commits an offense under subsection (a) of this section is guilty of a Class G felony. Additionally, a defendant convicted of an offense under subsection (a) of this section shall be ordered to make restitution to the timber owner in an amount equal to either of the following:

(1) Three times the value of the timber cut down, injured, or removed in violation of subdivision (1) of subsection (a) of this section.

(2) Three times the value of the timber bought but not paid for in violation of subdivision (2) of subsection (a) of this section.

Restitution shall also include the cost incurred by the owner to determine the value of the timber. For purposes of subdivisions (1) and (2) of this subsection, "value of the timber" shall be based on the stumpage rate of the timber.

(e) **Civil Remedies.** -- Nothing in this section shall affect any civil remedies available for a violation of subsection (a) of this section.

History.
1889, c. 168; Rev., s. 3687; C.S., s. 4306; 1957, c. 1437, s. 1; 1993, c. 539, s. 77; 1994, Ex. Sess., c. 24, s. 14(c); 2009-508, s. 1; 2021-78, s. 5(a)

§ 14-135.1. Wood load tickets required for certain wood product sales; exceptions; penalties

(a) **Definition.** -- For purposes of this section, the term "wood product" means trees, timber, wood, or any combination thereof.

(b) **Requirement.** -- Except as provided in this section, whenever a timber buyer or timber operator purchases wood product by the load directly from a timber grower or seller and the load is sold by weight, cord, or measure of board feet, the timber buyer or operator shall furnish the timber grower or seller, within 30 days of the completion of the wood product harvest, a separate, true, and accurate wood load ticket for each load of wood product removed from the timber grower's or seller's property. At a minimum, each wood load ticket shall include all of the following information provided by the timber grower or seller who sold the wood product:

(1) The name of the timber grower or seller.

(2) The county from which the wood product was severed.

(3) The amount of wood product severed.

(4) The date the wood product was delivered to the timber buyer or timber operator.

(c) **Applicability.** -- The provisions of this section do not apply to the following:

(1) The sale of wood for firewood only.

(2) A landowner harvesting and processing their own timber.

(3) Bulk or lump sum sales for an agreed total price for all timber purchased and sold in one transaction.

(d) **Punishment.** -- Any person who violates this section is guilty of a Class 2 misdemeanor.

History.
2021-78, s. 6(a)

§ 14-136. Setting fire to grass and brushlands and woodlands

If any person shall intentionally set fire to any grassland, brushland or woodland, except it be his own property, or in that case without first giving notice to all persons owning or in charge of lands adjoining the land intended to be fired, and without also taking care to watch such fire while burning and to extinguish it before it shall reach any lands near to or adjoining the lands so fired, he shall for every such offense be guilty of a Class 2 misdemeanor for the first offense, and for a second or any subsequent similar offense shall be guilty of a Class 1 misdemeanor. If intent to damage the property of another shall be shown, said person shall be punished as a Class I felon. This section shall not prevent an action for the damages sustained by the owner of any property from such fires. For the purposes of this section, the term "woodland" is to be taken to include all forest areas, both timber and cutover land, and all second-growth stands on areas that have at one time been cultivated. Any person who shall furnish to the State, evidence sufficient for the conviction of a violation of this section shall receive the sum of five hundred dollars ($ 500.00) to be paid from the State Fire Suppression Fund.

History.

1777, c. 123, ss. 1, 2, P.R.; R.C., c. 16, ss. 1, 2; Code, ss. 52, 53; Rev., s. 3346; 1915, c. 243, ss. 8, 11; 1919, c. 318; C.S., s. 4309; 1925, c. 61, s. 1; 1943, c. 661; 1979, c. 760, s. 5; 1979, 2nd Sess., c. 1316, s. 47; 1981, c. 63, s. 1; c. 179, s. 14; 1993, c. 539, ss. 78, 1188; c. 892; 1994, Ex. Sess., c. 24, s. 14(c)

§ 14-137. Willfully or negligently setting fire to woods and fields

If any person, firm or corporation shall willfully or negligently set on fire, or cause to be set on fire, any woods, lands or fields, whatsoever, every such offender shall be guilty of a Class 2 misdemeanor. This section shall apply only in those counties under the protection of the Department of Agriculture and Consumer Services in its work of forest fire control. It shall not apply in the case of a landowner firing, or causing to be fired, his own open, nonwooded lands, or fields in connection with farming or building operations at the time and in the manner now provided by law: Provided, he shall have confined the fire at his own expense to said open lands or fields.

History.

1907, c. 320, ss. 4, 5; C.S., s. 4310; 1925, c. 61, s. 2; 1941, c. 258; 1973, c. 1262, s. 86; 1977, c. 771, s. 4; 1989, c. 727, s. 218(3); 1993, c. 539, s. 79; 1994, Ex. Sess., c. 24, s. 14(c); 1997-443, s. 11A.119(a); 2015-241, s. 14.30(u); 2015-263, s. 36(a)

N.C. Gen. Stat. § 14-138

Repealed by Session Laws 1994, Extra Session, c. 14, s. 72(6).

§ 14-138.1. Setting fire to grassland, brushland, or woodland

Any person, firm, corporation, or other legal entity who shall in any manner whatsoever start any fire upon any grassland, brushland, or woodland without fully extinguishing the same, shall be guilty of a Class 3 misdemeanor which may include a fine of not less than ten dollars ($ 10.00) or more than fifty dollars ($ 50.00). For the purpose of this section, the term "woodland" includes timber and cutover land and all second growth stands on areas that were once cultivated.

History.

1995, c. 210, s. 1

N.C. Gen. Stat. § 14-139

Repealed by Session Laws 1981, c. 1100, s. 1.

N.C. Gen. Stat. § 14-140

Repealed by Session Laws 1993 (Reg. Sess., 1994), c. 767, s. 30(3).

§ 14-140.1. Certain fire to be guarded by watchman

Any person, firm, corporation, or other legal entity who shall burn any brush, grass, or other material whereby any property may be endangered or destroyed, without keeping and maintaining a careful watchman in charge of the burning, shall be guilty of an infraction which may include a fine of not more than fifty dollars ($ 50.00). Fire escaping from the brush, grass, or other material while burning shall be prima facie evidence of violation of this provision.

History.

1995, c. 210, s. 2; 2015-263, s. 27

§ 14-141. Burning or otherwise destroying crops in the field

Any person who shall willfully burn or destroy any other person's lawfully grown crop, pasture, or provender shall be punished as follows:

(1) If the damage is two thousand dollars ($ 2,000) or less, the person is guilty of a Class 1 misdemeanor.

(2) If the damage is more than two thousand dollars ($ 2,000), the person is guilty of a Class I felony.

History.

1874-5, c. 133; Code, s. 985, subsec. 2; 1885, c. 42; Rev., s. 3339; C.S., s. 4313; 1979, c. 760, s. 5; 1979, 2nd Sess., c. 1316, s. 47; 1981, c. 63, s. 1; c. 179, s. 14; 1991, c. 534, s. 1; 1993, c. 539, s. 81; 1994, Ex. Sess., c. 24, s. 14(c)

§ 14-142. Injuries to dams and water channels of mills and factories

If any person shall cut away, destroy or otherwise injure any dam, or part thereof, or shall obstruct or damage any race, canal or other water channel erected, opened, used or constructed for the purpose of furnishing water for the operation of any mill, factory or machine works, or for the escape of water therefrom, he shall be guilty of a Class 2 misdemeanor.

History.

1866, c. 48; Code, s. 1087; Rev., s. 3678; C.S., s. 4315; 1969, c. 1224, s. 13; 1993, c. 539, s. 82; 1994, Ex. Sess., c. 24, s. 14(c)

N.C. Gen. Stat. § 14-143

Repealed by Session Laws 1987, c. 700, s. 2.

§ 14-144. Injuring houses, churches, fences and walls

If any person shall, by any other means than burning or attempting to burn, unlawfully and willfully demolish, destroy, deface, injure or damage any of the houses or other buildings mentioned in Article 15 (Arson and Other Burnings) of this Chapter; or shall by any other means than burning or attempting to burn unlawfully and willfully demolish, pull down, destroy, deface, damage or injure any church, uninhabited house, outhouse or other house or building not mentioned in such article; or shall unlawfully and willfully burn, destroy, pull down, injure or remove any fence, wall or other enclosure, or any part thereof, surrounding or about any yard, garden, cultivated field or pasture, or about any church or graveyard, or about any factory or other house in which machinery is used, every person so offending shall be punished as follows:

(1) If the damage is five thousand dollars ($ 5,000) or less, the person is guilty of a Class 2 misdemeanor.

(2) If the damage is more than five thousand dollars ($ 5,000), the person is guilty of a Class I felony.

History.
R.C., c. 34, s. 103; Code, s. 1062; Rev., s. 3673; C.S., s. 4317; 1957, c. 250, s. 2; 1969, c. 1224, s. 1; 1993, c. 539, s. 83; 1994, Ex. Sess., c. 24, s. 14(c); 2008-15, s. 1; 2009-570, s. 3

§ 14-145. Unlawful posting of advertisements

Any person who in any manner paints, prints, places, or affixes, or causes to be painted, printed, placed, or affixed, any business or commercial advertisement on or to any stone, tree, fence, stump, pole, automobile, building, or other object, which is the property of another without first obtaining the written consent of such owner thereof, or who in any manner paints, prints, places, puts, or affixes, or causes to be painted, printed, placed, or affixed, such an advertisement on or to any stone, tree, fence, stump, pole, mile-board, milestone, danger-sign, danger-signal, guide-sign, guide-post, automobile, building or other object within the limits of a public highway, shall be guilty of a Class 3 misdemeanor.

History.
Ex. Sess. 1924, c. 109; 1993, c. 539, s. 84; 1994, Ex. Sess., c. 24, s. 14(c)

§ 14-146. Injuring bridges

If any person shall unlawfully and willfully demolish, destroy, break, tear down, injure or damage any bridge across any of the creeks or rivers or other streams in the State, he shall be guilty of a Class 1 misdemeanor.

History.
1883, c. 271; Code, s. 993; Rev., s. 3771; C.S., s. 4318; 1993, c. 539, s. 85; 1994, Ex. Sess., c. 24, s. 14(c)

§ 14-147. Removing, altering or defacing landmarks

If any person, firm or corporation shall knowingly remove, alter or deface any landmark in anywise whatsoever, or shall knowingly cause such removal, alteration or defacement to be done, such person, firm or corporation shall be guilty of a Class 2 misdemeanor. This section shall not apply to landmarks, such as creeks and other small streams, which the interest of agriculture may require to be altered or turned from their channels, nor to such persons, firms or corporations as own the fee simple in the lands on both sides of the lines designated by the landmarks removed, altered or defaced. Nor shall this section apply to those adjoining landowners who may by agreement remove, alter or deface landmarks in which they alone are interested.

History.
1858-9, c. 17; Code, s. 1063; Rev., s. 3674; 1915, c. 248; C.S., s. 4319; 1993, c. 539, s. 86; 1994, Ex. Sess., c. 24, s. 14(c)

§ 14-148. Defacing or desecrating grave sites

(a) It is unlawful to willfully:

(1) Throw, place or put any refuse, garbage or trash in or on any cemetery.

(2) Take away, disturb, vandalize, destroy or change the location of any stone, brick, iron or other material or fence enclosing a cemetery without authorization of law or consent of the surviving spouse or next of kin of the deceased.

(3) Take away, disturb, vandalize, destroy, or tamper with any shrubbery, flowers, plants or other articles planted or placed within any cemetery to designate where human remains are interred or to preserve and perpetuate the memory and name of any person, without authorization of law or the consent of the surviving spouse or next of kin.

(b) The provisions of this section shall not apply to:

(1) Ordinary maintenance and care of a cemetery by the owner, caretaker, or other person acting to facilitate cemetery operations by keeping the cemetery free from accumulated debris or other signs of neglect.

Chapter 14

(2) Conduct that is punishable under G.S. 14-149.

(3) A professional archaeologist as defined in G.S. 70-28(4) acting pursuant to the provisions of Article 3 of Chapter 70 of the General Statutes.

(c) Violation of this section is a Class I felony if the damage caused by the violation is one thousand dollars ($ 1,000) or more. Any other violation of this section is a Class 1 misdemeanor. In passing sentence, the court shall consider the appropriateness of restitution or reparation as a condition of probation under G.S. 15A-1343(b) (9) as an alternative to actual imposition of a fine, jail term, or both.

History.
1840, c. 6; R.C., c. 34, s. 102; Code, s. 1088; Rev., s. 3680; C.S., s. 4320; 1969, c. 987; 1981, c. 752, s. 1; c. 853, s. 4; 1993, c. 539, s. 87; 1994, Ex. Sess., c. 24, s. 14(c); 2007-122, s. 1

§ 14-149. Desecrating, plowing over or covering up graves; desecrating human remains

(a) It is a Class I felony, without authorization of law or the consent of the surviving spouse or next of kin of the deceased, to knowingly and willfully:

(1) Open, disturb, destroy, remove, vandalize or desecrate any casket or other repository of any human remains, by any means including plowing under, tearing up, covering over or otherwise obliterating or removing any grave or any portion thereof.

(2) Take away, disturb, vandalize, destroy, tamper with, or deface any tombstone, headstone, monument, grave marker, grave ornamentation, or grave artifacts erected or placed within any cemetery to designate the place where human remains are interred or to preserve and perpetuate the memory and the name of any person. This subdivision shall not apply to the ordinary maintenance and care of a cemetery.

(3) Repealed by Session Laws 2007-122, s. 2, effective December 1, 2007, and applicable to offenses committed on or after that date.

(a1) It is a Class H felony, without authorization of law or the consent of the surviving spouse or next of kin of the deceased, to knowingly and willfully disturb, destroy, remove, vandalize, or desecrate any human remains that have been interred in a cemetery.

(b) The provisions of this section shall not apply to a professional archaeologist as defined in G.S. 70-28(4) acting pursuant to the provisions of Article 3 of Chapter 70 of the General Statutes.

History.
1889, c. 130; Rev., s. 3681; 1919, c. 218; C.S., s. 4321; 1981, c. 752, s. 2; c. 853, s. 5; 2007-122, s. 2

§§ 14-150, 14-150.1

Repealed by Session Laws 1981, c. 752, s. 3.

§ 14-151. Interfering with gas, electric, and steam appliances or meters; penalties

(a) It is unlawful for any person to willfully, with intent to injure or defraud, commit any of the following acts:

(1) Connect a tube, pipe, wire, or other instrument or contrivance with a pipe or wire used for conducting or supplying illuminating gas, fuel, natural gas, or electricity in such a manner as to supply the gas or electricity to any burner, orifice, lamp, or motor where the gas or electricity is or can be burned or used without passing through the meter or other instrument provided for registering the quantity consumed.

(2) Obstruct, alter, bypass, tamper with, injure, or prevent the action of a meter or other instrument used to measure or register the quantity of illuminating fuel, natural gas, water, or electricity passing through the meter by a person other than an employee of the company owning or supplying any gas, water, or electric meter, who willfully detaches or disconnects the meter, or makes or reports any test of, or examines for the purpose of testing any meter so detached or disconnected.

(3) In any manner whatever change, extend, or alter any service or other pipe, wire, or attachment of any kind, connecting with or through which natural or artificial gas or electricity is furnished from the gas mains or pipes of any person, without first procuring from the person written permission to make the change, extension, or alterations.

(4) Make any connection or reconnection with the gas mains, water pipes, service pipes, or wires of any person, furnishing to consumers natural or artificial gas, water, or electricity, or turn on or off or in any manner interfere with any valve or stopcock or other appliance belonging to that person, and connected with the person's service or other pipes or wires, or enlarge the orifices of mixers, or use natural gas for heating purposes except through mixers, or electricity for any purpose without first procuring from the person a written permit to turn on or off the stopcock or valve, or to make the connection or reconnections, or to enlarge the orifice of mixers, or to use for

heating purposes without mixers, or to interfere with the valves, stopcocks, wires, or other appliances of them, as the case may be.

(5) Retain possession of or refuse to deliver any mixer, meter, lamp, or other appliance which may be leased or rented by any person, for the purpose of furnishing gas, water, electricity, or power through the appliance, or sell, lend, or in any other manner dispose of the appliance to any person other than the person entitled to the possession of the appliance.

(6) Set on fire any gas escaping from wells, broken or leaking mains, pipes, valves, or other appliances used by any person in conveying gas to consumers, or interfere in any manner with the wells, pipes, mains, gateboxes, valves, stopcocks, wires, cables, conduits, or any other appliances, machinery, or property of any person engaged in furnishing gas to consumers unless employed by or acting under the authority and direction of that person.

(7) Open or cause to be opened, or reconnect or cause to be reconnected any valve lawfully closed or disconnected by a district steam corporation.

(8) Turn on steam or cause it to be turned on or to reenter any premises when the steam has been lawfully stopped from entering the premises.

(9) Reconnect electricity, gas, or water connections or otherwise turn back on one or more of those utilities when they have been lawfully disconnected or turned off by the provider of the utility.

(10) Alter, bypass, interfere with, or cut off any load management device, equipment, or system which has been installed by the electricity supplier for the purpose of limiting the use of electricity at peak-load periods. However, if there has been a written request to remove the load management device, equipment, or system to the electric supplier and the electric supplier has not removed the device within two working days, there is no violation of this section.

(b) Any meter or service entrance facility found to have been altered, tampered with, or bypassed in a manner that would cause the meter to inaccurately measure and register the electricity, gas, or water consumed or which would cause the electricity, gas, or water to be diverted from the recording apparatus of the meter is prima facie evidence of intent to violate and of the violation of this section by the person in whose name the meter is installed or the person or persons so using or receiving the benefits of the unmetered, unregistered, or diverted electricity, gas, or water.

(c) For the purposes of this section, the term "gas" means all types and forms of gas, including, but not limited to, natural gas.

(d) Criminal violations of this section are punishable as follows:

(1) A violation of this section is a Class 1 misdemeanor.

(2) A second or subsequent violation of this section is a Class H felony.

(3) A violation of this section that results in significant property damage or public endangerment is a Class F felony.

(4) Unless the conduct is covered under some other provision of law providing greater punishment, a violation that results in the death of another is a Class D felony.

(e) Whoever is found in a civil action to have violated any provision of this section is liable to the electric, gas, or water supplier in triple the amount of losses and damages sustained or five thousand dollars ($ 5,000), whichever is greater.

(f) Nothing in this section applies to licensed contractors while performing usual and ordinary services in accordance with recognized customs and standards.

History.

1901, c. 735; Rev., s. 3666; C.S., s. 4323; 1993, c. 539, s. 88; 1994, Ex. Sess., c. 24, s. 14(c); 2013-88, s. 1; 2018-142, s. 2(a)

N.C. Gen. Stat. § 14-151.1

Repealed by Session Laws 2013-88, s. 2, effective December 1, 2013, and applicable to offenses committed on or after that date.

History.

1977, c. 735, s. 1; 1983, c. 508, ss. 1, 2; 1989, c. 119; 1993, c. 539, s. 89; 1994, Ex. Sess., c. 24, s. 14(c); repealed by 2013-88, s. 2, effective December 1, 2013

§ 14-152. Injuring fixtures and other property of gas companies; civil liability

If any person shall willfully, wantonly or maliciously remove, obstruct, injure or destroy any part of the plant, machinery, fixtures, structures or buildings, or anything appertaining to the works of any gas company, or shall use, tamper or interfere with the same, he shall be deemed guilty of a Class 3 misdemeanor. Such person shall also forfeit and pay to the company so injured, to be sued for and recovered in a civil action, double the amount of the damages sustained by any such injury.

History.

1889 (Pr.), c. 35, s. 3; Rev., s. 3671; C.S., s. 4324; 1993, c. 539, s. 90; 1994, Ex. Sess., c. 24, s. 14(c)

§ 14-153. Tampering with engines and boilers

If any person shall willfully turn out water from any boiler or turn the bolts of any engine or boiler, or meddle or tamper with such boiler or engine, or any other machinery in connection with any boiler or engine, causing loss, damage, danger or delay to the owner in the prosecution of his work, he shall be guilty of a Class 2 misdemeanor.

History.
1901, c. 733; Rev., s. 3667; C.S., s. 4325; 1993, c. 539, s. 91; 1994, Ex. Sess., c. 24, s. 14(c)

§ 14-154. Injuring wires and other fixtures of telephone, telegraph, and electric-power companies

If any person shall willfully injure, destroy or pull down any telegraph, telephone, cable telecommunications, or electric-power-transmission pedestal or pole, or any telegraph, telephone, cable telecommunications, or electric power line, wire or fiber insulator, power supply, transformer, transmission or other apparatus, equipment or fixture used in the transmission of telegraph, telephone, cable telecommunications, or electrical power service or any equipment related to wireless communications regulated by the Federal Communications Commission, that person shall be guilty of a Class I Felony.

History.
1881, c. 4; 1883, c. 103; Code, s. 1118; Rev., s. 3847; 1907, c. 827, s. 1; C.S., s. 4326; 1993, c. 539, s. 92; 1994, Ex. Sess., c. 24, s. 14(c); 2007-301, s. 2

§ 14-155. Unauthorized connections with telephone or telegraph

It shall be unlawful for any person to tap or make any connection with any wire or apparatus of any telephone or telegraph company operating in this State, except such connection as may be authorized by the person or corporation operating such wire or apparatus. Any person violating this section shall be guilty of a Class 3 misdemeanor. Each day's continuance of such unlawful connection shall be a separate offense. No connection approved by the Federal Communications Commission or the North Carolina Utilities Commission shall be a violation of this section.

History.
1911, c. 113; C.S., s. 4327; 1973, c. 648; 1977, 2nd Sess., c. 1185, s. 2; 1993, c. 539, s. 93; 1994, Ex. Sess., c. 24, s. 14(c)

§ 14-156. Injuring fixtures and other property of electric-power companies

It shall be unlawful for any person willfully and wantonly, and without the consent of the owner, to take down, remove, injure, obstruct, displace or destroy any line erected or constructed for the transmission of electrical current, or any poles, towers, wires, conduits, cables, insulators or any support upon which wires or cables may be suspended, or any part of any such line or appurtenances or apparatus connected therewith, or to sever any wire or cable thereof, or in any manner to interrupt the transmission of electrical current over and along any such line, or to take down, remove, injure or destroy any house, shop, building or other structure or machinery connected with or necessary to the use of any line erected or constructed for the transmission of electrical current, or to wantonly or willfully cause injury to any of the property mentioned in this section by means of fire. Any person violating any of the provisions of this section shall be guilty of a Class 2 misdemeanor.

History.
1907, c. 919; C.S., s. 4328; 1993, c. 539, s. 94; 1994, Ex. Sess., c. 24, s. 14(c)

§ 14-157. Felling trees on telephone and electric-power wires

If any person shall negligently and carelessly cut or fell any tree, or any limb or branch therefrom, in such a manner as to cause the same to fall upon and across any telephone, electric light or electric-power-transmission wire, from which any injury to such wire shall be occasioned, he shall be guilty of a Class 3 misdemeanor, and shall also be liable to penalty of fifty dollars ($ 50.00) for each and every offense.

History.
1903, c. 616; Rev., s. 3849; 1907, c. 827, s. 2; C.S., s. 4329; 1969, c. 1224, s. 9; 1993, c. 539, s. 95; 1994, Ex. Sess., c. 24, s. 14(c)

§ 14-158. Interfering with telephone lines

If any person shall unnecessarily disconnect the wire or in any other way render any telephone line, or any part of such line, unfit for use in transmitting messages, or shall unnecessarily cut, tear down, destroy or in any way render unfit for the transmission of messages any part of the wire of a telephone line, he shall be guilty of a Class 2 misdemeanor.

History.
1901, c. 318; Rev., s. 3845; C.S., s. 4330; 1969, c. 1224, s. 3; 1993, c. 539, s. 96; 1994, Ex. Sess., c. 24, s. 14(c)

Chapter 14

§ 14-159. Injuring buildings or fences; taking possession of house without consent

If any person shall deface, injure or damage any house, uninhabited house or other building belonging to another; or deface, damage, pull down, injure, remove or destroy any fence or wall enclosing, in whole or in part, the premises belonging to another; or shall move into, take possession of and/or occupy any house, uninhabited house or other building situated on the premises belonging to another, without having first obtained authority so to do and consent of the owner or agent thereof, he shall be guilty of a Class 3 misdemeanor.

History.
1929, c. 192, s. 1; 1993, c. 539, s. 97; 1994, Ex. Sess., c. 24, s. 14(c)

§ 14-159.1. Contaminating a public water system

(a) A person commits the offense of contaminating a public water system, as defined in G.S. 130A-313(10), if he willfully or wantonly:

(1) Contaminates, adulterates or otherwise impurifies or attempts to contaminate, adulterate or otherwise impurify the water in a public water system, including the water source, with any toxic chemical, biological agent or radiological substance that is harmful to human health, except those added in approved concentrations for water treatment operations; or

(2) Damages or tampers with the property or equipment of a public water system with the intent to impair the services of the public water system.

(b) Any person who commits the offense defined in this section is guilty of a Class C felony.

History.
1983, c. 507, s. 1; 1985, c. 509, s. 4; c. 689, s. 5; 1993, c. 539, s. 1189; 1994, Ex. Sess., c. 24, s. 14(c)

§ 14-159.2. Interference with animal research

(a) It is unlawful for a person willfully to commit any of the following acts:

(1) The unauthorized entry into any research facility where animals are kept within the facility for research in the advancement of medical, veterinary, dental, or biological sciences, with the intent to (i) disrupt the normal operation of the research facility, or (ii) damage the research facility or any personal property located thereon, or (iii) release from any enclosure or restraining device any animal kept within the research facility, or (iv) interfere with the care of any animal kept within the research facility;

(2) The damaging of any such research facility or any personal property located thereon;

(3) The unauthorized release from any enclosure or restraining device of any animal kept within any research facility; or

(4) The interference with the care of any animal kept within any research facility.

(b) Any person who commits an offense under subsection (a) of this section shall be guilty of a Class 1 misdemeanor.

(c) Any person who commits an offense under subsection (a) of this section that involves the release from any enclosure or restraining device of any animal having an infectious disease shall be guilty of a Class I felony.

(d) As a condition of probation, the court may order a person convicted under this section to make restitution to the owner of the animal for damages, including the cost of restoring the animal to confinement and of restoring the animal to its health condition prior to any release, and for damages to personal property, including materials, equipment, data, and records, and real property caused by the interference. If the interference causes the failure of an experiment, the restitution may include all costs of repeating the experiment, including replacement of the animals, labor, and materials.

(e) Nothing in this section shall be construed to affect any rights or causes of action of a person damaged through interference with animal research.

History.
1991, c. 203, s. 1; 1993, c. 539, ss. 98, 1190; 1994, Ex. Sess., c. 24, s. 14(c)

§ 14-159.3. Trespass to land on motorized all-terrain vehicle

(a) No person shall operate any motorized all-terrain vehicle:

(1) On any private property not owned by the operator, without the written consent of the owner; or

(2) Within the banks of any stream or waterway, but excluding a sound or the Atlantic Ocean, the adjacent lands of which are not owned by the operator, without the consent of the owner or outside the restrictions imposed by the owner.

(a1) A landowner who gives a person written consent to operate an all-terrain vehicle on the landowner's property owes the person the same duty of care that the landowner owes a trespasser.

(b) A "motorized all-terrain vehicle", as used in this section, is a two or more wheeled vehicle designed for recreational off-road use.

(c) A violation of this section shall be a Class 2 misdemeanor.

History.
1997-456, s. 56.8; 1997-487, s. 1; 2014-103, s. 11(a); 2015-26, s. 2.1; 2017-102, s. 4

§ 14-159.4. Cutting, mutilating, defacing, or otherwise injuring property to obtain nonferrous metals

(a) **Definition of Nonferrous Metals.** -- For purposes of this section, the term "nonferrous metals" means metals not containing significant quantities of iron or steel, including, but not limited to, copper wire, copper clad steel wire, copper pipe, copper bars, copper sheeting, aluminum other than aluminum cans, a product that is a mixture of aluminum and copper, catalytic converters, lead-acid batteries, and stainless steel beer kegs or containers.

(b) **Prohibited Act.** -- It is unlawful for a person to willfully and wantonly cut, mutilate, deface, or otherwise injure any personal or real property of another, including any fixtures or improvements, for the purpose of obtaining nonferrous metals in any amount.

(c) **Punishment.** -- Violations of this section are punishable as follows:

(1) **Default.** -- If the direct injury is to property, and the amount of loss in value to the property, the amount of repairs necessary to return the property to its condition before the act, or the property loss (including fixtures or improvements) is less than one thousand dollars ($ 1,000), a violation shall be punishable as a Class 1 misdemeanor. If the applicable amount is one thousand dollars ($ 1,000) or more, but less than ten thousand dollars ($ 10,000), a violation shall be punishable as a Class H felony. If the applicable amount is ten thousand dollars ($ 10,000) or more, a violation shall be deemed an aggravated offense and shall be punishable as a Class F felony.

(2) **When person suffers serious injury.** -- Unless the conduct is covered under some other provision of law providing greater punishment, a violation of this section that results in a serious injury to another person is punishable as a Class A1 misdemeanor.

(3) **When person suffers a serious bodily injury.** -- Unless the conduct is covered under some other provision of law providing greater punishment, a violation of this section that results in serious bodily injury to another person is punishable as a Class F felony. For purposes of this subdivision, "serious bodily injury" is as defined in G.S. 14-32.4.

(4) **When person is killed.** -- Unless the conduct is covered under some other provision of law providing greater punishment, a violation of this section that results in the death of another person is punishable as a Class D felony.

(5) **When critical infrastructure affected.** -- Unless the conduct is covered under some other provision of law providing greater punishment, a violation of this section that results in the disruption of communication or electrical service to critical infrastructure or to more than 10 customers of the communication or electrical service is guilty of a Class 1 misdemeanor.

(d) **Liability.** -- This section does not create or impose a duty of care upon the owner of personal or real property that would not otherwise exist under common law. A public or private owner of personal or real property shall not be civilly liable:

(1) To a person who is injured while committing or attempting to commit a violation of this section.

(2) To a person who is injured while a third party is committing or attempting to commit a violation of this section.

(3) For a person's injuries caused by a dangerous condition created as a result of a violation of this section, when the owner does not know and could not have reasonably known of the dangerous condition.

History.
2012-46, s. 31

N.C. Gen. Stat. § 14-159.5

Reserved for future codification purposes.

ARTICLE 22A

TRESPASSING UPON "POSTED" PROPERTY TO HUNT, FISH, TRAP, OR REMOVE PINE NEEDLES/ STRAW

§ 14-159.6. Trespass for purposes of hunting, etc., without written consent a misdemeanor; defense

(a) Any person who willfully goes on the land, waters, ponds, or a legally established waterfowl blind of another that has been posted in accordance with the provisions of G.S. 14-159.7, to hunt, fish or trap without written permission of the landowner, lessee, or his agent shall be guilty of a Class 2 misdemeanor. Written permission shall be carried on one's person, signed by the landowner, lessee, or agent, and dated within the last 12 months. The written permission shall be displayed upon request of any law enforcement officer of the Wildlife Resources Commission, sheriff or deputy sheriff, or other law enforcement officer with general subject matter jurisdiction. A person shall have written permission for purposes of this section if a landowner, lessee, or agent has granted permission to a club to hunt, fish, or trap on the land and the person is carrying both a current membership card demonstrating the person's membership in the club and a copy of written permission granted to the club that complies with the requirements of this section.

(b) Any person who willfully goes on the land of another that has been posted in accordance with the provisions of G.S. 14-159.7(1), to rake or remove pine needles or pine straw without the written consent of the owner or his agent shall be guilty of a Class 1 misdemeanor.

(c) It is an affirmative defense to a prosecution under subsection (a) or (b) of this section that the person had in fact obtained prior permission of the owner, lessee, or agent as required by those subsections but did not have on his or her person valid written permission at the time of citation or arrest.

History.
1949, c. 887, s. 1; 1953, c. 1226; 1965, c. 1134; 1975, c. 280, s. 1; 1979, c. 830, s. 11; 1991, c. 435, s. 4; 1993, c. 539, s. 99; 1994, Ex. Sess., c. 24, s. 14(c); 1997-443, s. 19.25(z); 2011-231, s. 1

§ 14-159.7. Regulations as to posting of property

For purposes of posting property under G.S. 14-159.7, the owner or lessee of the property may use either of the following methods:

(1) The owner or lessee of the property may place notices, signs, or posters on the property. The notices, signs or posters shall measure not less than 120 square inches and shall be conspicuously posted on private lands not more than 200 yards apart close to and along the boundaries. At least one such notice, sign, or poster shall be posted on each side of such land, and one at each corner thereof, provided that said corner can be reasonably ascertained. For the purpose of prohibiting fishing, or the taking of fish by any means, in any stream, lake, or pond, it shall only be necessary that the signs, notices, or posters be posted along the stream or shoreline of a pond or lake at intervals of not more than 200 yards apart.

(2) The owner or lessee of the property may place identifying purple paint marks on trees or posts around the area to be posted. Each paint mark shall be a vertical line of at least eight inches in length, and the bottom of the mark shall be no less than three feet nor more than five feet from the base of the tree or post. The paint marks shall be placed no more than 100 yards apart and shall be readily visible to any person approaching the property. For the purpose of prohibiting fishing, or the taking of fish by any means, in any stream, lake, or pond, it shall only be necessary that the paint marks be placed along the stream or shoreline of a pond or lake at intervals of not more than 100 yards apart.

History.
1949, c. 887, s. 2; 1953, c. 1226; 1965, c. 923; 1975, c. 280, ss. 2, 3; 1979, c. 830, s. 11; 2011-231, s. 2

§ 14-159.8. Mutilation, etc., of "posted" signs; posting signs without consent of owner or agent

Any person who shall mutilate, destroy or take down any "posted," "no hunting" or similar notice, sign or poster on the lands, waters, or legally established waterfowl blind of another, or who shall post such sign or poster on the lands, waters or legally established waterfowl blind of another, without the consent of the owner or his agent, shall be deemed guilty of a Class 3 misdemeanor and only punished by a fine of not more than one hundred dollars ($ 100.00).

History.
1949, c. 887, s. 3; 1953, c. 1226; 1969, c. 51; 1979, c. 830, s. 11; 1993, c. 539, s. 100; 1994, Ex. Sess., c. 24, s. 14(c)

§ 14-159.9. Entrance on navigable waters, etc., for purpose of fishing, hunting or trapping not prohibited

Nothing in this Article shall be construed to prohibit the entrance of any person upon navigable waters and the bays and sounds adjoining such waters for the purpose of fishing, hunting or trapping.

History.
1949, c. 887, s. 4; 1953, c. 1226; 1979, c. 830, s. 11

§ 14-159.10. Enforcement of Article

This Article may be enforced by sheriffs or deputy sheriffs, law enforcement officers of the Wildlife Resources Commission, and other peace officers with general subject matter jurisdiction.

History.
1979, c. 830, s. 11; 2011-231, s. 3

Chapter 14

ARTICLE 22B
FIRST AND SECOND DEGREE TRESPASS

§ 14-159.11. Definition

As used in this Article, "building" means any structure or part of a structure, other than a conveyance, enclosed so as to permit reasonable entry only through a door and roofed to protect it from the elements.

History.
1987, c. 700, s. 1

§ 14-159.12. First degree trespass

(a) **Offense.** -- A person commits the offense of first degree trespass if, without authorization, he enters or remains:

(1) On premises of another so enclosed or secured as to demonstrate clearly an intent to keep out intruders;

(2) In a building of another; or

(3) On the lands of the Eastern Band of Cherokee Indians after the person has been excluded by a resolution passed by the Eastern Band of Cherokee Indian Tribal Council.

(b) Except as otherwise provided in subsection (c), (d), or (f) of this section, first degree trespass is a Class 2 misdemeanor.

(c) Except as otherwise provided in subsection (d) of this section, a violation of subsection (a) of this section is a Class A1 misdemeanor if all of the following circumstances exist:

(1) The offense is committed on the premises of any of the following:

a. A facility that is owned or operated by an electric power supplier as defined in G.S. 62-133.8(a)(3) and that is either an electric generation facility, a transmission substation, a transmission switching station, a transmission switching structure, or a control center used to manage transmission operations or electrical power generating at multiple plant locations.

b. Any facility used or available for use in the collection, treatment, testing, storing, pumping, or distribution of water for a public water system.

c. Any facility, including any liquefied natural gas storage facility or propane air facility, that is owned or operated by a natural gas local distribution company, natural gas pipeline carrier operating under a certificate of public convenience and necessity from the Utilities Commission, municipal corporation operating a municipally owned gas distribution system, or regional natural gas district organized and operated pursuant to Article 28 of Chapter 160A of the General Statutes used for transmission, distribution, measurement, testing, regulating, compression, control, or storage of natural gas.

d. Any facility used or operated for agricultural activities, as that term is defined in G.S. 106-581.1.

(2) The person actually entered a building, or it was necessary for the person to climb over, go under, or otherwise surmount a fence or other barrier to reach the facility.

(d) If, in addition to the circumstances set out in subsection (c) of this section, the violation also includes any of the following elements, then the offense is a Class H felony:

(1) The offense is committed with the intent to disrupt the normal operation of any of the facilities described in subdivision (1) of subsection (c) of this section.

(2) The offense involves an act that places either the offender or others on the premises at risk of serious bodily injury.

(e) As used in subsections (c) and (d) of this section, the term "facility" shall mean a building or other infrastructure.

(f) A violation of subsection (a) of this section is a Class I felony and shall include a fine of not less than one thousand dollars ($ 1,000) for each violation, if any of the following circumstances exist:

(1) The offense occurs on real property where the person has reentered after having previously been removed pursuant to the execution of a valid order or writ for possession.

(2) The offense occurs under color of title where the person has knowingly created or provided materially false evidence of an ownership or possessory interest.

(3) The offense is the person's second or subsequent violation of subdivision (a)(3) of this section.

History.
1987, c. 700, s. 1; 1993, c. 539, s. 101; 1994, Ex. Sess., c. 24, s. 14(c); 2012-168, s. 1; 2014-103, s. 10(a); 2016-26, s. 1; 2018-66, s. 1

§ 14-159.13. Second degree trespass

(a) **Offense.** -- A person commits the offense of second degree trespass if, without authorization, he enters or remains on premises of another:

(1) After he has been notified not to enter or remain there by the owner, by a person in charge of the premises, by a lawful

Chapter 14

occupant, or by another authorized person; or

(2) That are posted, in a manner reasonably likely to come to the attention of intruders, with notice not to enter the premises.

(b) **Classification.** -- Second degree trespass is a Class 3 misdemeanor.

History.
1987, c. 700, s. 1; 1993, c. 539, s. 102; 1994, Ex. Sess., c. 24, s. 14(c)

§ 14-159.14. Lesser included offenses

The offenses created by this act shall constitute lesser included offenses of breaking or entering as provided in G.S. 14-54 and G.S. 14-56.

History.
1987, c. 700, s. 1

§§ 14-159.15 through 14-159.19

Reserved for future codification purposes.

ARTICLE 22C
CAVE PROTECTION ACT

§ 14-159.20. Definitions

The terms listed below have the following definitions as used in this Article, unless the context clearly requires a different meaning:

(1) "Cave" means any naturally occurring subterranean cavity. The word "cave" includes or is synonymous with cavern, pit, well, sinkhole, and grotto;

(2) "Commercial cave" means any cave with improved trails and lighting utilized by the owner for the purpose of exhibition to the general public as a profit or nonprofit enterprise, wherein a fee is collected for entry;

(3) "Gate" means any structure or device located to limit or prohibit access or entry to any cave;

(4) "Person" means any individual, partnership, firm, association, trust or corporation;

(5) "Speleothem" means a natural mineral formation or deposit occurring in a cave. This includes or is synonymous with stalagmites, stalactites, helectites, anthodites, gypsum flowers, needles, angel's hair, soda straws, draperies, bacon, cave pearls, popcorn (coral), rimstone dams, columns, palettes, and flowstone. Speleothems are commonly composed of calcite, epsomite,

gypsum, aragonite, celestite and other similar minerals; and

(6) "Owner" means a person who has title to land where a cave is located, including a person who owns title to a leasehold estate in such land.

History.
1987, c. 449, s. 1

§ 14-159.21. Vandalism; penalties

It is unlawful for any person, without express, prior, written permission of the owner, to willfully or knowingly:

(1) Break, break off, crack, carve upon, write, burn or otherwise mark upon, remove, or in any manner destroy, disturb, deface, mar or harm the surfaces of any cave or any natural material therein, including speleothems;

(2) Disturb or alter in any manner the natural condition of any cave;

(3) Break, force, tamper with or otherwise disturb a lock, gate, door or other obstruction designed to control or prevent access to any cave, even though entrance thereto may not be gained.

Any person violating a provision of this section shall be guilty of a Class 3 misdemeanor.

History.
1987, c. 449, s. 1; 1993, c. 539, s. 103; 1994, Ex. Sess., c. 24, s. 14(c)

§ 14-159.22. Sale of speleothems unlawful; penalties

It is unlawful to sell or offer for sale any speleothems in this State, or to export them for sale outside the State. A person who violates any of the provisions of this section shall be guilty of a Class 3 misdemeanor.

History.
1987, c. 449, s. 1; 1993, c. 539, s. 104; 1994, Ex. Sess., c. 24, s. 14(c)

§ 14-159.23. Limitation of liability of owners and agents

The owner of a cave, and his agents and employees, shall not be liable for any injury to, or for the death of any person, or for any loss or damage to property, by reason of any act or omission unless it is established that the injury, death, loss, or damage occurred as a result of gross negligence, wanton conduct, or intentional wrongdoing. The limitation of liability provided by this section applies only with respect to injury, death, loss, or damage occurring within a cave, or in connection with entry into or exit from a cave, and applies only with respect to persons to whom no charge has been made for admission to the cave.

History.
1987, c. 449, s. 1

ARTICLE 23
TRESPASSES TO PERSONAL PROPERTY

§ 14-160. Willful and wanton injury to personal property; punishments

(a) If any person shall wantonly and willfully injure the personal property of another he shall be guilty of a Class 2 misdemeanor.

(b) Notwithstanding the provisions of subsection (a), if any person shall wantonly and willfully injure the personal property of another, causing damage in an amount in excess of two hundred dollars ($ 200.00), he shall be guilty of a Class 1 misdemeanor.

(c) This section applies to injuries to personal property without regard to whether the property is destroyed or not.

History.
1876-7, c. 18; Code, s. 1082; 1885, c. 53; Rev., s. 3676; C.S., s. 4331; 1969, c. 1224, s. 14; 1993, c. 539, s. 105

§ 14-160.1. Alteration, destruction or removal of permanent identification marks from personal property

(a) It shall be unlawful for any person to alter, deface, destroy or remove the permanent serial number, manufacturer's identification plate or other permanent, distinguishing number or identification mark from any item of personal property with the intent thereby to conceal or misrepresent the identity of said item.

(b) It shall be unlawful for any person knowingly to sell, buy or be in possession of any item of personal property, not his own, on which the permanent serial number, manufacturer's identification plate or other permanent, distinguishing number or identification mark has been altered, defaced, destroyed or removed for the purpose of concealing or misrepresenting the identity of said item.

(c) Unless the conduct is covered under some other provision of law providing greater punishment, a violation of any of the provisions of this section shall be (i) a Class 1 misdemeanor if the personal property was valued at not more than one thousand dollars ($ 1,000) at the time of the offense or (ii) a Class H felony if the personal property was valued at more than one thousand dollars ($ 1,000) at the time of the offense.

(d) This section shall not in any way affect the provisions of G.S. 20-108, 20-109(a) or 20-109(b).

History.
1977, c. 767, s. 1; 1993, c. 539, s. 106; 1994, Ex. Sess., c. 24, s. 14(c); 2009-204, s. 1; 2021-36, s. 1

§ 14-160.2. Alteration, destruction, or removal of serial number from firearm; possession of firearm with serial number removed

(a) It shall be unlawful for any person to alter, deface, destroy, or remove the permanent serial number, manufacturer's identification plate, or other permanent distinguishing number or identification mark from any firearm with the intent thereby to conceal or misrepresent the identity of the firearm.

(b) It shall be unlawful for any person knowingly to sell, buy, or be in possession of any firearm on which the permanent serial number, manufacturer's identification plate, or other permanent distinguishing number or identification mark has been altered, defaced, destroyed, or removed for the purpose of concealing or misrepresenting the identity of the firearm.

(c) A violation of any of the provisions of this section shall be a Class H felony.

History.
2009-204, s. 2

§ 14-160.3. Injuring, destroying, removing, vandalizing, or tampering with firefighting or emergency medical services machinery or equipment

A person is guilty of a Class 1 misdemeanor if the person intentionally injures, destroys, removes, vandalizes, or tampers with or otherwise intentionally interferes with the operation of any of the following:

(1) Any machinery, apparatus, or equipment used by a fire department or the North Carolina Forest Services for fighting fires, protecting property, or protecting human life.

(2) Any ambulance as defined in G.S. 131E-155 or rescue squad emergency medical services vehicle or any equipment or apparatus used for emergency medical services as defined in G.S. 131E-155.

History.
2017-89, s. 1

N.C. Gen. Stat. § 14-161

Repealed by Session Laws 1994, Extra Session, c. 14, s. 72(7).

§ 14-162. Removing boats

If any person shall loose, unmoor, or turn adrift from any landing or other place wherever the same shall be, any boat, canoe, or other marine vessel, or if any person shall direct the same to be done without the consent of the owner, or the person having the lawful custody or possession of such vessel, he shall be guilty of a Class 2 misdemeanor. The owner may also have his action for such injury. The penalties aforesaid shall not extend to any person who shall press any such property by public authority.

History.

R.C., c. 14, ss. 1, 3; Code, s. 2288; 1889, c. 378; Rev., s. 3544; C.S., s. 4333; 1977, c. 729; 1993, c. 539, s. 107; 1994, Ex. Sess., c. 24, s. 14(c)

§ 14-163. Poisoning livestock

If any person shall willfully and unlawfully poison any horse, mule, hog, sheep or other livestock, the property of another, such person shall be punished as a Class I felon.

History.

1898-9, c. 253; Code, s. 1003; Rev., s. 3313; C.S., s. 4334; 1969, c. 1224, s. 3; 1973, c. 1388; 1979, c. 760, s. 5; 1979, 2nd Sess., c. 1316, s. 47; 1981, c. 63, s. 1; c. 179, s. 14

§ 14-163.1. Assaulting a law enforcement agency animal, an assistance animal, or a search and rescue animal

(a) The following definitions apply in this section:

(1) **Assistance animal.** -- An animal that is trained and may be used to assist a "person with a disability" as defined in G.S. 168A-3. The term "assistance animal" is not limited to a dog and includes any animal trained to assist a person with a disability as provided in Article 1 of Chapter 168 of the General Statutes.

(2) **Law enforcement agency animal.** -- An animal that is trained and may be used to assist a law enforcement officer in the performance of the officer's official duties.

(3) **Harm.** -- Any injury, illness, or other physiological impairment; or any behavioral impairment that impedes or interferes with duties performed by a law enforcement agency animal or an assistance animal.

(3a) **Search and rescue animal.** -- An animal that is trained and may be used to assist in a search and rescue operation.

(4) **Serious harm.** -- Harm that does any of the following:

a. Creates a substantial risk of death.

b. Causes maiming or causes substantial loss or impairment of bodily function.

c. Causes acute pain of a duration that results in substantial suffering.

d. Requires retraining of the law enforcement agency animal or assistance animal.

e. Requires retirement of the law enforcement agency animal or assistance animal from performing duties.

(a1) Any person who knows or has reason to know that an animal is a law enforcement agency animal, an assistance animal, or a search and rescue animal and who willfully kills the animal is guilty of a Class H felony.

(b) Any person who knows or has reason to know that an animal is a law enforcement agency animal, an assistance animal, or a search and rescue animal and who willfully causes or attempts to cause serious harm to the animal is guilty of a Class I felony.

(c) Unless the conduct is covered under some other provision of law providing greater punishment, any person who knows or has reason to know that an animal is a law enforcement agency animal, an assistance animal, or a search and rescue animal and who willfully causes or attempts to cause harm to the animal is guilty of a Class 1 misdemeanor.

(d) Unless the conduct is covered under some other provision of law providing greater punishment, any person who knows or has reason to know that an animal is a law enforcement agency animal, an assistance animal, or a search and rescue animal and who willfully taunts, teases, harasses, delays, obstructs, or attempts to delay or obstruct the animal in the performance of its duty as a law enforcement agency animal, an assistance animal, or a search and rescue animal is guilty of a Class 2 misdemeanor.

(d1) A defendant convicted of a violation of this section shall be ordered to make restitution to the person with a disability, or to a person, group, or law enforcement agency who owns or is responsible for the care of the law enforcement agency animal or search and rescue animal for any of the following as appropriate:

(1) Veterinary, medical care, and boarding expenses for the law enforcement agency animal, the assistance animal, or the search and rescue animal.

(2) Medical expenses for the person with the disability relating to the harm inflicted upon the assistance animal.

(3) Replacement and training or retraining expenses for the law enforcement agency animal, the assistance animal, or the search and rescue animal.

(4) Expenses incurred to provide temporary mobility services to the person with a disability.

(5) Wages or income lost while the person with a disability is with the assistance animal receiving training or retraining.

(6) The salary of the law enforcement agency animal handler as a result of the lost services to the agency during the time the handler is with the law enforcement agency animal receiving training or retraining.

(6a) The salary of the search and rescue animal handler as a result of the search and rescue services lost during the time the handler is with the search and rescue animal receiving training or retraining.

(7) Any other expense reasonably incurred as a result of the offense.

(e) This section shall not apply to a licensed veterinarian whose conduct is in accordance with Article 11 of Chapter 90 of the General Statutes.

(f) Self-defense is an affirmative defense to a violation of this section.

(g) Nothing in this section shall affect any civil remedies available for violation of this section.

History.
1983, c. 646, s. 1; 1993, c. 539, s. 108; 1994, Ex. Sess., c. 24, s. 14(c); 1995, c. 258, s. 1; 2001-411, s. 1; 2005-184, s. 1; 2007-80, s. 1; 2009-460, s. 1

N.C. Gen. Stat. § 14-164

Repealed by Session Laws 1994, Extra Session, c. 14, s. 72(8).

ARTICLE 24
VEHICLES AND DRAFT ANIMALS -- PROTECTION OF BAILOR AGAINST ACTS OF BAILEE

§ 14-165. Malicious or willful injury to hired personal property

Any person who shall rent or hire from any person, firm or corporation, any horse, mule or like animal, or any buggy, wagon, truck, automobile, or other like vehicle, aircraft, motor, trailer, appliance, equipment, tool, or other thing of value, who shall maliciously or willfully injure or damage the same by in any way using or driving the same in violation of any statute of the State of North Carolina, or who shall permit any other person so to do, shall be guilty of a Class 2 misdemeanor.

History.
1927, c. 61, s. 1; 1965, c. 1073, s. 1; 1993, c. 539, s. 109; 1994, Ex. Sess., c. 24, s. 14(c)

§ 14-166. Subletting of hired property

Any person who shall rent or hire, any horse, mule, or other like animal, or any buggy, wagon, truck, automobile, or other like vehicle, aircraft, motor, trailer, appliance, equipment, tool, or other thing of value, who shall, without the permission of the person, firm or corporation from whom such property is rented or hired, sublet or rent the same to any other person, firm or corporation, shall be guilty of a Class 2 misdemeanor.

History.
1927, c. 61, s. 2; 1965, c. 1073, s. 2; 1969, c. 1224, s. 15; 1993, c. 539, s. 110; 1994, Ex. Sess., c. 24, s. 14(c)

§ 14-167. Failure to return hired property

Any person who shall rent or hire, any horse, mule or other like animal, or any buggy, wagon, truck, automobile, or other vehicle, aircraft, motor, trailer, appliance, equipment, tool, or other thing of value, and who shall willfully fail to return the same to the possession of the person, firm or corporation from whom such property has been rented or hired at the expiration of the time for which such property has been rented or hired, shall be guilty of a Class 3 misdemeanor.

If the value at the time of the rental or hiring of the truck, automobile, or other motor vehicle that is not returned is in excess of four thousand dollars ($ 4,000), the person who rented or hired it and failed to return it shall be guilty of a Class H felony.

History.
1927, c. 61, s. 3; 1965, c. 1073, s. 3; 1969, c. 1224, s. 15; 1993, c. 539, s. 111; 1994, Ex. Sess., c. 24, s. 14(c); 2005-182, s. 1; 2013-360, s. 18B.14(c)

§ 14-168. Hiring with intent to defraud

Any person who shall, with intent to cheat and defraud the owner thereof of the rental price therefor, hire or rent any horse or mule or any other like animal, or any buggy, wagon, truck, automobile or other like vehicle, aircraft, motor, trailer, appliance, equipment, tool, or other thing of value, or who shall obtain the possession of the same by false and fraudulent statements made with intent to deceive, which are calculated to deceive, and which do deceive, shall be guilty of a Class 2 misdemeanor.

History.
1927, c. 61, s. 4; 1965, c. 1073, s. 4; 1969, c. 1224, s. 15; 1993, c. 539, s. 112; 1994, Ex. Sess., c. 24, s. 14(c)

§ 14-168.1. Conversion by bailee, lessee, tenant or attorney-in-fact

Every person entrusted with any property as bailee, lessee, tenant or lodger, or with any power of attorney for the sale or transfer thereof, who fraudulently converts the same, or the proceeds thereof, to his own use, or secretes it with a fraudulent intent to convert it to his own use, shall be guilty of a Class 3 misdemeanor.

If, however, the value of the property converted or secreted, or the proceeds thereof, is in excess of four hundred dollars ($ 400.00), every person so converting or secreting it is guilty of a Class H felony. In all cases of doubt the jury shall, in the verdict, fix the value of the property converted or secreted.

History.
1965, c. 1073, s. 5; 1979, c. 468; 1979, 2nd Sess., c. 1316, s. 13; 1981, c. 63, s. 1; c. 179, s. 14; 1993, c. 539, s. 113; 1994, Ex. Sess., c. 24, s. 14(c); 2013-360, s. 18B.14(d)

§ 14-168.2. Definitions

For the purposes of this Article, the terms "rent," "hire" and "lease" are used to designate the letting for hire of any horse, mule or other like animal, or any buggy, wagon, truck, automobile, aircraft, motor, trailer, appliance, equipment, tool, or other thing of value by lease, bailment, or rental agreement.

History.
1965, c. 1073, s. 5

§ 14-168.3. Prima facie evidence of intent to convert property

It shall be prima facie evidence of intent to commit a crime as set forth in G.S. 14-167, 14-168, and 14-168.1 with respect to any property other than a truck, automobile, or other motor vehicle when one who has, by written instrument, leased or rented the personal property of another:

(1) Failed or refused to return such property to its owner after the lease, bailment, or rental agreement has expired,
    a. Within 10 days, and
    b. Within 48 hours after written demand for return thereof is personally served or given by registered mail delivered to the last known address provided in such lease or rental agreement, or
(2) When the leasing or rental of such personal property is obtained by presentation of identification to the lessor or rentor thereof which is false, fictitious, or

knowingly not current as to name, address, place of employment, or other identification.

History.
1965, c. 1118; 2005-182, s. 2

§ 14-168.4. Failing to return rented property on which there is purchase option

(a) It shall be a Class 3 misdemeanor for any person to fail to return rented property with intent to defeat the rights of the owner, which is rented pursuant to a written rental agreement in which there is an option to purchase the property, after the date of termination provided in the agreement has occurred or, if the termination date is the occurrence of a specified event, then that such event has in fact occurred.

(b) Intent to commit the crime set forth in subsection (a) may be presumed from the following evidence:
(1) Evidence that the defendant has disposed of the property, or has encumbered the property by allowing a security interest to be placed on the property or by delivering the property to a pawnbroker; or
(2) Evidence that the defendant has refused to deliver the property to the sheriff or other officer charged with the execution of process directed to him for its seizure, after a judgment for possession of the property or a claim and delivery order for the property has been issued; or
(3) Evidence that the defendant has moved the rented property out of state and has failed to notify the owner of the new location of the property.
However, this presumption may be rebutted by evidence from the defendant that he has no intent to defeat the rights of the owner of the property.

(c) Violations of this Article for failure to return rented property which is rented pursuant to a written rental agreement in which there is an option to purchase shall be prosecuted only under this section.

History.
1987 (Reg. Sess., 1988), c. 1065, s. 3; 1993, c. 539, s. 114; 1994, Ex. Sess., c. 24, s. 14(c); 2013-360, s. 18B.14(e)

§ 14-168.5. Prima facie evidence of intent to convert a truck, automobile, or other motor vehicle; demand for return or payment

(a) **Prima Facie Evidence.** -- It shall be prima facie evidence of intent to commit a crime as set forth in G.S. 14-167, 14-168, and 14-168.1 when one who has, by written instrument, leased or rented a truck, automobile, or other motor vehicle owned by another:

(1) Failed or refused to return the vehicle to the lessor or rentor at the place specified after the lease, bailment, or rental agreement has expired, within 72 hours after written demand for the vehicle is made in accordance with subsection (b) of this section; or

(2) When the leasing or rental of the vehicle is obtained by presentation of identification to the lessor or rentor of the vehicle which is false, fictitious, or knowingly not current as to name, address, place of employment, or other identification.

(b) **Method of Demand; When Effective.**
--

(1) Demand for return of a leased or rented truck, automobile, or other motor vehicle may be made in one of three ways:

a. By personal service in accordance with Rule 4(j) of the North Carolina Rules of Civil Procedure.

b. By certified mail, return receipt requested, addressed to the last known address provided in the lease, bailment, or rental agreement.

c. By depositing the demand with a designated delivery service authorized pursuant to 26 U.S.C. § 7502(f)(2) addressed to the last known address provided in the lease, bailment, or rental agreement.

(2) Demand is effective upon hand delivery to the last known address, three days after deposit by mail (even if the demand is returned as undeliverable), or upon delivery by a designated delivery service to the last known address.

History.
2005-182, s. 3

§ 14-169. Violation made misdemeanor

Except as otherwise provided, any person violating the provisions of this Article shall be guilty of a Class 1 misdemeanor.

History.
1927, c. 61, s. 5; 1929, c. 38, s. 1; 1969, c. 1224, s. 15; 1993, c. 539, s. 115; 1994, Ex. Sess., c. 24, s. 14(c)

ARTICLE 25
REGULATING THE LEASING OF STORAGE BATTERIES

§§ 14-170 through 14-176

Repealed by Session Laws 1993 (Reg. Sess., 1994), c. 767, s. 30(4)-(10).

SUBCHAPTER 07.
OFFENSES AGAINST PUBLIC MORALITY AND DECENCY

ARTICLE 26
OFFENSES AGAINST PUBLIC MORALITY AND DECENCY

§ 14-177. Crime against nature

If any person shall commit the crime against nature, with mankind or beast, he shall be punished as a Class I felon.

History.
25 Hen. VIII, c. 6; 5 Eliz., c. 17; R.C., c. 34, s. 6; 1868-9, c. 167, s. 6; Code, s. 1010; Rev., s. 3349; C.S., s. 4336; 1965, c. 621, s. 4; 1979, c. 760, s. 5; 1979, 2nd Sess., c. 1316, s. 47; 1981, c. 63, s. 1; c. 179, s. 14; 1993, c. 539, s. 1191; 1994, Ex. Sess., c. 24, s. 14(c)

§ 14-178. Incest

(a) **Offense.** -- A person commits the offense of incest if the person engages in carnal intercourse with the person's (i) grandparent or grandchild, (ii) parent or child or stepchild or legally adopted child, (iii) brother or sister of the half or whole blood, or (iv) uncle, aunt, nephew, or niece.

(b) **Punishment and Sentencing.** --

(1) A person is guilty of a Class B1 felony if either of the following occurs:

a. The person commits incest against a child under the age of 13 and the person is at least 12 years old and is at least four years older than the child when the incest occurred.

b. The person commits incest against a child who is 13, 14, or 15 years old and the person is at least six years older than the child when the incest occurred.

(2) A person is guilty of a Class C felony if the person commits incest against a child who is 13, 14, or 15 and the person is more than four but less than six years older than the child when the incest occurred.

(3) In all other cases of incest, the parties are guilty of a Class F felony.

(c) **No Liability for Children Under 16.** -- No child under the age of 16 is liable under this section if the other person is at least four years older when the incest occurred.

History.
1879, c. 16, s. 1; Code, s. 1060; Rev., s. 3351; 1911, c. 16; C.S., s. 4337; 1965, c. 132; 1979, c. 760, s. 5; 1979, 2nd Sess., c. 1316, s. 47; 1981, c. 63, s. 1; c. 179, s. 14; 1993, c. 539, s. 1192; 1994, Ex. Sess., c. 24, s. 14(c); 2002-119, s. 1

N.C. Gen. Stat. § 14-179

Repealed by Session Laws 2002-119, s. 2, effective December 1, 2002.

N.C. Gen. Stat. § 14-180

Repealed by Session Laws 1975, c. 402.

§§ 14-181, 14-182

Repealed by Session Laws 1973, c. 108, s. 4.

§ 14-183. Bigamy

If any person, being married, shall marry any other person during the life of the former husband or wife, every such offender, and every person counseling, aiding or abetting such offender, shall be punished as a Class I felon. Any such offense may be dealt with, tried, determined and punished in the county where the offender shall be apprehended, or be in custody, as if the offense had been actually committed in that county. If any person, being married, shall contract a marriage with any other person outside of this State, which marriage would be punishable as bigamous if contracted within this State, and shall thereafter cohabit with such person in this State, he shall be guilty of a felony and shall be punished as in cases of bigamy. Nothing contained in this section shall extend to any person marrying a second time, whose husband or wife shall have been continually absent from such person for the space of seven years then last past, and shall not have been known by such person to have been living within that time; nor to any person who at the time of such second marriage shall have been lawfully divorced from the bond of the first marriage; nor to any person whose former marriage shall have been declared void by the sentence of any court of competent jurisdiction.

History.
See 9 Geo. IV, c. 31, s. 22; 1790, c. 323, P.R.; 1809, c. 783, P.R.; 1829, c. 9; R.C., c. 34, s. 15; Code, s. 988; Rev., s. 3361; 1913, c. 26; C.S., s. 4342; 1979, c. 760, s. 5; 1979, 2nd Sess., c. 1316, s. 47; 1981, c. 63, s. 1;

c. 179, s. 14; 1993, c. 539, s. 1193; 1994, Ex. Sess., c. 24, s. 14(c)

§ 14-184. Fornication and adultery

If any man and woman, not being married to each other, shall lewdly and lasciviously associate, bed and cohabit together, they shall be guilty of a Class 2 misdemeanor: Provided, that the admissions or confessions of one shall not be received in evidence against the other.

History.
1805, c. 684, P.R.; R.C., c. 34, s. 45; Code, s. 1041; Rev., s. 3350; C.S., s. 4343; 1969, c. 1224, s. 9; 1993, c. 539, s. 119; 1994, Ex. Sess., c. 24, s. 14(c)

N.C. Gen. Stat. § 14-185

Repealed by Session Laws 1975, c. 402.

§ 14-186. Opposite sexes occupying same bedroom at hotel for immoral purposes; falsely registering as husband and wife

Any man and woman found occupying the same bedroom in any hotel, public inn or boardinghouse for any immoral purpose, or any man and woman falsely registering as, or otherwise representing themselves to be, husband and wife in any hotel, public inn or boardinghouse, shall be deemed guilty of a Class 2 misdemeanor.

History.
1917, c. 158, s. 2; C.S., s. 4345; 1969, c. 1224, s. 3; 1993, c. 539, s. 120; 1994, Ex. Sess., c. 24, s. 14(c)

N.C. Gen. Stat. § 14-187

Repealed by Session Laws 1975, c. 402.

§ 14-188. Certain evidence relative to keeping disorderly houses admissible; keepers of such houses defined; punishment

(a) On a prosecution in any court for keeping a disorderly house or bawdy house, or permitting a house to be used as a bawdy house, or used in such a way as to make it disorderly, or a common nuisance, evidence of the general reputation or character of the house shall be admissible and competent; and evidence of the lewd, dissolute and boisterous conversation of the inmates and frequenters, while in and around such house, shall be prima facie evidence of the bad character of the inmates and frequenters, and of the disorderly character of the house. The manager or person having the care, superintendency or government of a disorderly house or bawdy house is the "keeper" thereof, and one who employs another to manage and conduct a disorderly house or bawdy house is also "keeper" thereof.

(b) On a prosecution in any court for keeping a disorderly house or a bawdy house, or permitting a house to be used as a bawdy house or used in such a way to make it disorderly or a common nuisance, the offense shall constitute a Class 2 misdemeanor.

History.
1907, c. 779; C.S., s. 4347; 1969, c. 1224, s. 22; 1993, c. 539, s. 121; 1994, Ex. Sess., c. 24, s. 14(c)

§§ 14-189, 14-189.1

Repealed by Session Laws 1971, c. 405, s. 4.

§§ 14-189.2, 14-190

Repealed by Session Laws 1971, c. 591, s. 4.

§ 14-190.1. Obscene literature and exhibitions

(a) It shall be unlawful for any person, firm or corporation to intentionally disseminate obscenity. A person, firm or corporation disseminates obscenity within the meaning of this Article if he or it:

(1) Sells, delivers or provides or offers or agrees to sell, deliver or provide any obscene writing, picture, record or other representation or embodiment of the obscene; or

(2) Presents or directs an obscene play, dance or other performance or participates directly in that portion thereof which makes it obscene; or

(3) Publishes, exhibits or otherwise makes available anything obscene; or

(4) Exhibits, presents, rents, sells, delivers or provides; or offers or agrees to exhibit, present, rent or to provide: any obscene still or motion picture, film, filmstrip, or projection slide, or sound recording, sound tape, or sound track, or any matter or material of whatever form which is a representation, embodiment, performance, or publication of the obscene.

(b) For purposes of this Article any material is obscene if:

(1) The material depicts or describes in a patently offensive way sexual conduct specifically defined by subsection (c) of this section; and

(2) The average person applying contemporary community standards relating to the depiction or description of sexual matters would find that the material taken as a whole appeals to the prurient interest in sex; and

(3) The material lacks serious literary, artistic, political, or scientific value; and

(4) The material as used is not protected or privileged under the Constitution of the United States or the Constitution of North Carolina.

(c) As used in this Article, "sexual conduct" means:

(1) Vaginal, anal, or oral intercourse, whether actual or simulated, normal or perverted; or

(2) Masturbation, excretory functions, or lewd exhibition of uncovered genitals; or

(3) An act or condition that depicts torture, physical restraint by being fettered or bound, or flagellation of or by a nude person or a person clad in undergarments or in revealing or bizarre costume.

(d) Obscenity shall be judged with reference to ordinary adults except that it shall be judged with reference to children or other especially susceptible audiences if it appears from the character of the material or the circumstances of its dissemination to be especially designed for or directed to such children or audiences.

(e) It shall be unlawful for any person, firm or corporation to knowingly and intentionally create, buy, procure or possess obscene material with the purpose and intent of disseminating it unlawfully.

(f) It shall be unlawful for a person, firm or corporation to advertise or otherwise promote the sale of material represented or held out by said person, firm or corporation as obscene.

(g) Violation of this section is a Class I felony.

(h) Obscene material disseminated, procured, or promoted in violation of this section is contraband.

(i) Nothing in this section shall be deemed to preempt local government regulation of the location or operation of sexually oriented businesses to the extent consistent with the constitutional protection afforded free speech.

History.
1971, c. 405, s. 1; 1973, c. 1434, s. 1; 1985, c. 703, s. 1; 1993, c. 539, s. 1194; 1994, Ex. Sess., c. 24, s. 14(c); 1998-46, s. 2

N.C. Gen. Stat. § 14-190.2

Repealed by Session Laws 1985, c. 703, s. 2.

N.C. Gen. Stat. § 14-190.3

Repealed by Session Laws 1985, c. 703, s. 3.

§ 14-190.4. Coercing acceptance of obscene articles or publications

No person, firm or corporation shall, as a condition to any sale, allocation, consignment or delivery for resale of any paper, magazine, book, periodical or publication require that the purchaser or consignee receive for resale any other article, book, or publication which is obscene within the meaning of G.S. 14-190.1; nor shall any person, firm or corporation deny or threaten to deny any franchise or impose or threaten to impose any penalty, financial or otherwise, by reason of the failure or refusal of any person to accept such articles, books, or publications, or by reason of the return thereof. Violation of this section is a Class 1 misdemeanor.

History.
1971, c. 405, s. 1; 1985, c. 703, s. 4; 1993, c. 539, s. 122; 1994, Ex. Sess., c. 24, s. 14(c)

§ 14-190.5. Preparation of obscene photographs, slides and motion pictures

Every person who knowingly:

(1) Photographs himself or any other person, for purposes of preparing an obscene film, photograph, negative, slide or motion picture for the purpose of dissemination; or

(2) Models, poses, acts, or otherwise assists in the preparation of any obscene film, photograph, negative, slide or motion picture for the purpose of dissemination,

shall be guilty of a Class 1 misdemeanor.

History.
1971, c. 405, s. 1; 1985, c. 703, s. 5; 1993, c. 539, s. 123; 1994, Ex. Sess., c. 24, s. 14(c)

§ 14-190.5A. Disclosure of private images; civil action

(a) **Definitions.** -- The following definitions apply in this section:

(1) **Disclose.** -- Transfer, publish, distribute, or reproduce.

(2) **Image.** -- A photograph, film, videotape, recording, live transmission, digital or computer-generated visual depiction, or any other reproduction that is made by electronic, mechanical, or other means.

(3) **Intimate parts.** -- Any of the following naked human parts: (i) male or female genitals, (ii) male or female pubic area, (iii) male or female anus, or (iv) the nipple of a female over the age of 12.

(4), (5) Repealed by Session Laws 2017-93, s. 1, effective December 1, 2017, and applicable to offenses committed on or after that date.

(6) **Sexual conduct.** -- Includes any of the following:

a. Vaginal, anal, or oral intercourse, whether actual or simulated, normal or perverted.

b. Masturbation, excretory functions, or lewd exhibition of uncovered genitals.

c. An act or condition that depicts torture, physical restraint by being fettered or bound, or flagellation of or by a nude person or a person clad in undergarments or in revealing or bizarre costume.

(b) **Offense.** -- A person is guilty of disclosure of private images if all of the following apply:

(1) The person knowingly discloses an image of another person with the intent to do either of the following:

a. Coerce, harass, intimidate, demean, humiliate, or cause financial loss to the depicted person.

b. Cause others to coerce, harass, intimidate, demean, humiliate, or cause financial loss to the depicted person.

(2) The depicted person is identifiable from the disclosed image itself or information offered in connection with the image.

(3) The depicted person's intimate parts are exposed or the depicted person is engaged in sexual conduct in the disclosed image.

(4) The person discloses the image without the affirmative consent of the depicted person.

(5) The person obtained the image without consent of the depicted person or under circumstances such that the person knew or should have known that the depicted person expected the images to remain private.

(c) **Penalty.** -- A violation of this section shall be punishable as follows:

(1) For an offense by a person who is 18 years of age or older at the time of the offense, the violation is a Class H felony.

(2) For a first offense by a person who is under 18 years of age at the time of the offense, the violation is a Class 1 misdemeanor.

(3) For a second or subsequent offense by a person who is under the age of 18 at the time of the offense, the violation is a Class H felony.

(d) **Exceptions.** -- This section does not apply to any of the following:

(1) Images involving voluntary exposure in public or commercial settings.

(2) Disclosures made in the public interest, including, but not limited to, the reporting of unlawful conduct or the lawful and common practices of law enforcement, criminal reporting, legal proceedings, medical treatment, or scientific or educational activities.

(3) Providers of an interactive computer service, as defined in 47 U.S.C. § 230(f), for images provided by another person.

(e) Destruction of Image. -- In addition to any penalty or other damages, the court may award the destruction of any image made in violation of this section.

(f) Other Sanctions or Remedies Not Precluded. -- A violation of this section is an offense additional to other civil and criminal provisions and is not intended to repeal or preclude any other sanctions or remedies.

(g) Civil Action. -- In addition to any other remedies at law or in equity, including an order by the court to destroy any image disclosed in violation of this section, any person whose image is disclosed, or used, as described in subsection (b) of this section, has a civil cause of action against any person who discloses or uses the image and is entitled to recover from the other person any of the following:

(1) Actual damages, but not less than liquidated damages, to be computed at the rate of one thousand dollars ($ 1,000) per day for each day of the violation or in the amount of ten thousand dollars ($ 10,000), whichever is higher.

(2) Punitive damages.

(3) A reasonable attorneys' fee and other litigation costs reasonably incurred.

The civil cause of action may be brought no more than one year after the initial discovery of the disclosure, but in no event may the action be commenced more than seven years from the most recent disclosure of the private image.

History.
2015-250, s. 1; 2017-93, s. 1

§ 14-190.6. Employing or permitting minor to assist in offense under Article

Every person 18 years of age or older who intentionally, in any manner, hires, employs, uses or permits any minor under the age of 16 years to do or assist in doing any act or thing constituting an offense under this Article and involving any material, act or thing he knows or reasonably should know to be obscene within the meaning of G.S. 14-190.1, shall be guilty of a Class I felony.

History.
1971, c. 405, s. 1; 1983, c. 916, s. 2; 1985, c. 703, s. 6

§ 14-190.7. Dissemination to minors under the age of 16 years

Every person 18 years of age or older who knowingly disseminates to any minor under the age of 16 years any material which he knows or reasonably should know to be obscene within the meaning of G.S. 14-190.1 shall be guilty of a Class I felony.

History.
1971, c. 405, s. 1; 1977, c. 440, s. 2; 1985, c. 703, s. 7

§ 14-190.8. Dissemination to minors under the age of 13 years

Every person 18 years of age or older who knowingly disseminates to any minor under the age of 13 years any material which he knows or reasonably should know to be obscene within the meaning of G.S. 14-190.1 shall be punished as a Class I felon.

History.
1971, c. 405, s. 1; 1977, c. 440, s. 3; 1979, c. 760, s. 5; 1979, 2nd Sess., c. 1316, s. 47; 1981, c. 63, s. 1; c. 179, s. 14; 1983, c. 175, ss. 7, 10; c. 720, ss. 4, 10; 1985, c. 703, s. 8; 1993, c. 539, s. 1195; 1994, Ex. Sess., c. 24, s. 14(c)

§ 14-190.9. Indecent exposure

(a) Unless the conduct is punishable under subsection (a1) of this section, any person who shall willfully expose the private parts of his or her person in any public place and in the presence of any other person or persons, except for those places designated for a public purpose where the same sex exposure is incidental to a permitted activity, or aids or abets in any such act, or who procures another to perform such act; or any person, who as owner, manager, lessee, director, promoter or agent, or in any other capacity knowingly hires, leases or permits the land, building, or premises of which he is owner, lessee or tenant, or over which he has control, to be used for purposes of any such act, shall be guilty of a Class 2 misdemeanor.

(a1) Unless the conduct is prohibited by another law providing greater punishment, any person at least 18 years of age who shall willfully expose the private parts of his or her person in any public place in the presence of any other person less than 16 years of age for the purpose of arousing or gratifying sexual desire shall be guilty of a Class H felony. An offense committed under this subsection shall not be considered to be a lesser included offense under G.S. 14-202.1.

(a2) Unless the conduct is prohibited by another law providing greater punishment, any person who shall willfully expose the private parts of his or her person in the presence of anyone other than a consenting adult on the private premises of another or so near thereto as to be seen from such private premises for the purpose of arousing or gratifying sexual desire is guilty of a Class 2 misdemeanor.

(a4) Unless the conduct is punishable by another law providing greater punishment, any person at least 18 years of age who shall willfully expose the private parts of his or her person in a private residence of which they are not a resident and in the presence of any other person less than 16 years of age who is a resident of that private residence shall be guilty of a Class 2 misdemeanor.

(a5) Unless the conduct is prohibited by another law providing greater punishment, any person located in a private place who shall willfully expose the private parts of his or her person with the knowing intent to be seen by a person in a public place shall be guilty of a Class 2 misdemeanor.

(b) Notwithstanding any other provision of law, a woman may breast feed in any public or private location where she is otherwise authorized to be, irrespective of whether the nipple of the mother's breast is uncovered during or incidental to the breast feeding.

(c) Notwithstanding any other provision of law, a local government may regulate the location and operation of sexually oriented businesses. Such local regulation may restrict or prohibit nude, seminude, or topless dancing to the extent consistent with the constitutional protection afforded free speech.

History.
1971, c. 591, s. 1; 1993, c. 301, s. 1; c. 539, s. 124; 1994, Ex. Sess., c. 24, s. 14(c); 1998-46, s. 3; 2005-226, s. 1; 2015-250, ss. 2, 2.1, 2.3

§§ 14-190.10 through 14-190.12

Repealed by Session Laws 1985, c. 703, s. 9.

§ 14-190.13. Definitions for certain offenses concerning minors

The following definitions apply to G.S. 14-190.14, displaying material harmful to minors; G.S. 14-190.15, disseminating or exhibiting to minors harmful material or performances; G.S. 14-190.16, first degree sexual exploitation of a minor; G.S. 14-190.17, second degree sexual exploitation of a minor; G.S. 14-190.17A, third degree sexual exploitation of a minor.

(1) **Harmful to Minors.** -- That quality of any material or performance that depicts sexually explicit nudity or sexual activity and that, taken as a whole, has the following characteristics:

a. The average adult person applying contemporary community standards would find that the material or performance has a predominant tendency to appeal to a prurient interest of minors in sex; and

b. The average adult person applying contemporary community standards would find that the depiction of sexually explicit nudity or sexual activity in the material or performance is patently offensive to prevailing standards in the adult community concerning what is suitable for minors; and

c. The material or performance lacks serious literary, artistic, political, or scientific value for minors.

(2) **Material.** -- Pictures, drawings, video recordings, films or other visual depictions or representations but not material consisting entirely of written words.

(3) **Minor.** -- An individual who is less than 18 years old and is not married or judicially emancipated.

(4) **Prostitution.** -- Engaging or offering to engage in sexual activity with or for another in exchange for anything of value.

(5) **Sexual Activity.** -- Any of the following acts:

a. Masturbation, whether done alone or with another human or an animal.

b. Vaginal, anal, or oral intercourse, whether done with another human or with an animal.

c. Touching, in an act of apparent sexual stimulation or sexual abuse, of the clothed or unclothed genitals, pubic area, or buttocks of another person or the clothed or unclothed breasts of a human female.

d. An act or condition that depicts torture, physical restraint by being fettered or bound, or flagellation of or by a person clad in undergarments or in revealing or bizarre costume.

e. Excretory functions; provided, however, that this sub-subdivision shall not apply to G.S. 14-190.17A.

f. The insertion of any part of a person's body, other than the male sexual organ, or of any object into another person's anus or vagina, except when done as part of a recognized medical procedure.

g. The lascivious exhibition of the genitals or pubic area of any person.

(6) **Sexually Explicit Nudity.** -- The showing of:

a. Uncovered, or less than opaquely covered, human genitals, pubic area, or buttocks, or the nipple or any portion of the areola of the human female breast, except as provided in G.S. 14-190.9(b); or

b. Covered human male genitals in a discernibly turgid state.

History.
1985, c. 703, s. 9; 1989 (Reg. Sess., 1990), c. 1022, s. 2; 1993, c. 301, s. 2; 2008-218, s. 1; 2013-368, s. 18

§ 14-190.14. Displaying material harmful to minors

719

(a) **Offense.** -- A person commits the offense of displaying material that is harmful to minors if, having custody, control, or supervision of a commercial establishment and knowing the character or content of the material, he displays material that is harmful to minors at that establishment so that it is open to view by minors as part of the invited general public. Material is not considered displayed under this section if the material is placed behind "blinder racks" that cover the lower two thirds of the material, is wrapped, is placed behind the counter, or is otherwise covered or located so that the portion that is harmful to minors is not open to the view of minors.

(b) **Punishment.** -- Violation of this section is a Class 2 misdemeanor. Each day's violation of this section is a separate offense.

History.
1985, c. 703, s. 9; 1993, c. 539, s. 125; 1994, Ex. Sess., c. 24, s. 14(c).

§ 14-190.15. Disseminating harmful material to minors; exhibiting harmful performances to minors

(a) **Disseminating Harmful Material.** -- A person commits the offense of disseminating harmful material to minors if, with or without consideration and knowing the character or content of the material, he:

(1) Sells, furnishes, presents, or distributes to a minor material that is harmful to minors; or

(2) Allows a minor to review or peruse material that is harmful to minors.

(b) **Exhibiting Harmful Performance.** -- A person commits the offense of exhibiting a harmful performance to a minor if, with or without consideration and knowing the character or content of the performance, he allows a minor to view a live performance that is harmful to minors.

(c) **Defenses.** -- Except as provided in subdivision (3), a mistake of age is not a defense to a prosecution under this section. It is an affirmative defense to a prosecution under this section that:

(1) The defendant was a parent or legal guardian of the minor.

(2) The defendant was a school, church, museum, public library, governmental agency, medical clinic, or hospital carrying out its legitimate function; or an employee or agent of such an organization acting in that capacity and carrying out a legitimate duty of his employment.

(3) Before disseminating or exhibiting the harmful material or performance, the defendant requested and received a driver's license, student identification card, or other official governmental or educational identification card or paper indicating that the minor to whom the material or performance was disseminated or exhibited was at least 18 years old, and the defendant reasonably believed the minor was at least 18 years old.

(4) The dissemination was made with the prior consent of a parent or guardian of the recipient.

(d) **Punishment.** -- Violation of this section is a Class 1 misdemeanor.

History.
1985, c. 703, s. 9; 1993, c. 539, s. 126; 1994, Ex. Sess., c. 24, s. 14(c)

§ 14-190.16. First degree sexual exploitation of a minor

(a) **Offense.** -- A person commits the offense of first degree sexual exploitation of a minor if, knowing the character or content of the material or performance, he:

(1) Uses, employs, induces, coerces, encourages, or facilitates a minor to engage in or assist others to engage in sexual activity for a live performance or for the purpose of producing material that contains a visual representation depicting this activity; or

(2) Permits a minor under his custody or control to engage in sexual activity for a live performance or for the purpose of producing material that contains a visual representation depicting this activity; or

(3) Transports or finances the transportation of a minor through or across this State with the intent that the minor engage in sexual activity for a live performance or for the purpose of producing material that contains a visual representation depicting this activity; or

(4) Records, photographs, films, develops, or duplicates for sale or pecuniary gain material that contains a visual representation depicting a minor engaged in sexual activity.

(b) **Inference.** -- In a prosecution under this section, the trier of fact may infer that a participant in sexual activity whom material through its title, text, visual representations, or otherwise represents or depicts as a minor is a minor.

(c) **Mistake of Age.** -- Mistake of age is not a defense to a prosecution under this section.

(d) **Punishment and Sentencing.** -- Violation of this section is a Class C felony.

History.
1985, c. 703, s. 9; 1993, c. 539, s. 1196; 1994, Ex. Sess., c. 24, s. 14(c); 1995, c. 507, s. 19.5(o); 2008-117, s. 3; 2008-218, s. 2

§ 14-190.17. Second degree sexual exploitation of a minor

(a) **Offense.** -- A person commits the offense of second degree sexual exploitation of a minor if, knowing the character or content of the material, he:

(1) Records, photographs, films, develops, or duplicates material that contains a visual representation of a minor engaged in sexual activity; or

(2) Distributes, transports, exhibits, receives, sells, purchases, exchanges, or solicits material that contains a visual representation of a minor engaged in sexual activity.

(b) **Inference.** -- In a prosecution under this section, the trier of fact may infer that a participant in sexual activity whom material through its title, text, visual representations or otherwise represents or depicts as a minor is a minor.

(c) **Mistake of Age.** -- Mistake of age is not a defense to a prosecution under this section.

(d) **Punishment and Sentencing.** -- Violation of this section is a Class E felony.

History.
1985, c. 703, s. 9; 1993, c. 539, s. 1197; 1994, Ex. Sess., c. 24, s. 14(c); 2008-117, s. 4; 2008-218, s. 3

§ 14-190.17A. Third degree sexual exploitation of a minor

(a) **Offense.** -- A person commits the offense of third degree sexual exploitation of a minor if, knowing the character or content of the material, he possesses material that contains a visual representation of a minor engaging in sexual activity.

(b) **Inference.** -- In a prosecution under this section, the trier of fact may infer that a participant in sexual activity whom material through its title, text, visual representations or otherwise represents or depicts as a minor is a minor.

(c) **Mistake of Age.** -- Mistake of age is not a defense to a prosecution under this section.

(d) **Punishment and Sentencing.** -- Violation of this section is a Class H felony.

History.
1989 (Reg. Sess., 1990), c. 1022, s. 1; 1993, c. 539, s. 1198; 1994, Ex. Sess., c. 24, s. 14(c); 2008-117, s. 5; 2008-218, s. 4

§§ 14-190.18, 14-190.19

Repealed by Session Laws 2013-368, s. 4, effective October 1, 2013, and applicable to offenses committed on or after that date.

History.
§ 14-190.18: 1985, c. 703, s. 9; 1993, c. 539, s. 1199; 1994, Ex. Sess., c. 24, s. 14(c); 1995, c. 507, s. 19.5(p); 2008-117, s. 6; repealed by 2013-368, s. 4, effective

October 1, 2013. § 14-190.19: 1985, c. 703, s. 9; 1993, c. 539, s. 1200; 1994, Ex. Sess., c. 24, s. 14(c); repealed by 2013-368, s. 4, effective October 1, 2013

§ 14-190.20. Warrants for obscenity offenses

A search warrant or criminal process for a violation of G.S. 14-190.1 through 14-190.5 may be issued only upon the request of a prosecutor.

History.
1985, c. 703, s. 9.1

N.C. Gen. Stat. § 14-191

Repealed by Session Laws 1971, c. 591, s. 4.

§§ 14-192, 14-193

Repealed by Session Laws 1971, c. 405, s. 4.

N.C. Gen. Stat. § 14-194

Repealed by Session Laws 1971, c. 591, s. 4.

N.C. Gen. Stat. § 14-195

Repealed by Session Laws 1993 (Reg. Sess., 1994), c. 767, s. 30(11).

§ 14-196. Using profane, indecent or threatening language to any person over telephone; annoying or harassing by repeated telephoning or making false statements over telephone

(a) It shall be unlawful for any person:

(1) To use in telephonic communications any words or language of a profane, vulgar, lewd, lascivious or indecent character, nature or connotation;

(2) To use in telephonic communications any words or language threatening to inflict bodily harm to any person or to that person's child, sibling, spouse, or dependent or physical injury to the property of any person, or for the purpose of extorting money or other things of value from any person;

(3) To telephone another repeatedly, whether or not conversation ensues, for the purpose of abusing, annoying, threatening, terrifying, harassing or embarrassing any person at the called number;

(4) To make a telephone call and fail to hang up or disengage the connection with the intent to disrupt the service of another;

(5) To telephone another and to knowingly make any false statement concerning death, injury, illness, disfigurement, indecent conduct or criminal conduct of

the person telephoned or of any member of his family or household with the intent to abuse, annoy, threaten, terrify, harass, or embarrass;

(6) To knowingly permit any telephone under his control to be used for any purpose prohibited by this section.

(b) Any of the above offenses may be deemed to have been committed at either the place at which the telephone call or calls were made or at the place where the telephone call or calls were received. For purposes of this section, the term "telephonic communications" shall include communications made or received by way of a telephone answering machine or recorder, telefacsimile machine, or computer modem.

(c) Anyone violating the provisions of this section shall be guilty of a Class 2 misdemeanor.

History.
1913, c. 35; 1915, c. 41; C.S., s. 4351; 1967, c. 833, s. 1; 1989, c. 305; 1993, c. 539, s. 128; 1994, Ex. Sess., c. 24, s. 14(c); 1999-262, s. 1; 2000-125, s. 2

§§ 14-196.1, 14-196.2

Repealed by Session Laws 1967, c. 833, s. 3.

§ 14-196.3. Cyberstalking

(a) The following definitions apply in this section:

(1) **Electronic communication.** -- Any transfer of signs, signals, writing, images, sounds, data, or intelligence of any nature, transmitted in whole or in part by a wire, radio, computer, electromagnetic, photoelectric, or photo-optical system.

(2) **Electronic mail.** -- The transmission of information or communication by the use of the Internet, a computer, a facsimile machine, a pager, a cellular telephone, a video recorder, or other electronic means sent to a person identified by a unique address or address number and received by that person.

(3) **Electronic tracking device.** -- An electronic or mechanical device that permits a person to remotely determine or track the position and movement of another person.

(4) **Fleet vehicle.** -- Any of the following: (i) one or more motor vehicles owned by a single entity and operated by employees or agents of the entity for business or government purposes, (ii) motor vehicles held for lease or rental to the general public, or (iii) motor vehicles held for sale, or used as demonstrators, test vehicles, or loaner vehicles, by motor vehicle dealers.

(b) It is unlawful for a person to:

(1) Use in electronic mail or electronic communication any words or language

threatening to inflict bodily harm to any person or to that person's child, sibling, spouse, or dependent, or physical injury to the property of any person, or for the purpose of extorting money or other things of value from any person.

(2) Electronically mail or electronically communicate to another repeatedly, whether or not conversation ensues, for the purpose of abusing, annoying, threatening, terrifying, harassing, or embarrassing any person.

(3) Electronically mail or electronically communicate to another and to knowingly make any false statement concerning death, injury, illness, disfigurement, indecent conduct, or criminal conduct of the person electronically mailed or of any member of the person's family or household with the intent to abuse, annoy, threaten, terrify, harass, or embarrass.

(4) Knowingly permit an electronic communication device under the person's control to be used for any purpose prohibited by this section.

(5) Knowingly install, place, or use an electronic tracking device without consent, or cause an electronic tracking device to be installed, placed, or used without consent, to track the location of any person. The provisions of this subdivision do not apply to the installation, placement, or use of an electronic tracking device by any of the following:

a. A law enforcement officer, judicial officer, probation or parole officer, or employee of the Division of Corrections, Department of Public Safety, when any such person is engaged in the lawful performance of official duties and in accordance with State or federal law.

b. The owner or lessee of any vehicle on which the owner or lessee installs, places, or uses an electronic tracking device, unless the owner or lessee is subject to (i) a domestic violence protective order under Chapter 50B of the General Statutes or (ii) any court order that orders the owner or lessee not to assault, threaten, harass, follow, or contact a driver or occupant of the vehicle.

c. A legal guardian for a disabled adult, as defined in G.S. 108A-101(d), or a legally authorized individual or organization designated to provide protective services to a disabled adult pursuant to G.S. 108A-105(c), when the electronic tracking device is installed, placed, or used to track the location of the disabled adult for which the person

Chapter 14

is a legal guardian or the individual or organization is designated to provide protective services.

d. The owner of fleet vehicles, when tracking such vehicles.

e. A creditor or other secured party under a retail installment agreement involving the sale of a motor vehicle or the lessor under a retail lease of a motor vehicle, and any assignee or successor in interest to that creditor, secured party, or lessor, when tracking a motor vehicle identified as security under the retail installment sales agreement or leased pursuant to a retail lease agreement, including the installation, placement, or use of an electronic tracking device to locate and remotely disable the motor vehicle, with the express written consent of the purchaser, borrower, or lessee of the motor vehicle.

f. The installation, placement, or use of an electronic tracking device authorized by an order of a State or federal court.

g. A motor vehicle manufacturer, its subsidiary, or its affiliate that installs or uses an electronic tracking device in conjunction with providing a vehicle subscription telematics service, provided that the customer subscribes or consents to that service.

h. A parent or legal guardian of a minor when the electronic tracking device is installed, placed, or used to track the location of that minor unless the parent or legal guardian is subject to a domestic violence protective order under Chapter 50B of the General Statutes or any court order that orders the parent or legal guardian not to assault, threaten, harass, follow, or contact that minor or that minor's parent, legal guardian, custodian, or caretaker as defined in G.S. 7B-101.

i. An employer, when providing a communication device to an employee or contractor for use in connection with his or her work for the employer.

j. A business, if the tracking is incident to the provision of a product or service requested by the person, except as limited in sub-subdivision k. of this subdivision.

k. A private detective or private investigator licensed under Chapter 74C of the General Statutes, provided that (i) the tracking is pursuant to authority under G.S. 74C-3(a)(8), (ii) the tracking is not otherwise contrary to law, and (iii) the person being tracked is not under the protection of a domestic

violence protective order under Chapter 50B of the General Statutes or any other court order that protects against assault, threat, harassment, following, or contact.

(c) Any offense under this section committed by the use of electronic mail or electronic communication may be deemed to have been committed where the electronic mail or electronic communication was originally sent, originally received in this State, or first viewed by any person in this State.

(d) Any person violating the provisions of this section shall be guilty of a Class 2 misdemeanor.

(e) This section does not apply to any peaceable, nonviolent, or nonthreatening activity intended to express political views or to provide lawful information to others. This section shall not be construed to impair any constitutionally protected activity, including speech, protest, or assembly.

History.

2000-125, s. 1; 2000-140, s. 91; 2015-282, s. 1

N.C. Gen. Stat. § 14-197

Repealed by Session Laws 2015-286, s. 1.1(1), effective October 22, 2015.

History.

1913, c. 40; C.S., s. 4352; Pub. Loc. Ex. Sess., 1924, c. 65; 1933, c. 309; 1937, c. 9; 1939, c. 73; 1945, c. 398; 1947, cc. 144, 959; 1949, c. 845; 1957, c. 348; 1959, c. 733; 1963, cc. 39, 123; 1969, c. 300; 1971, c. 718; 1973, cc. 120, 233; 1993, c. 539, s. 129; 1994, Ex. Sess., c. 24, s. 14(c); Repealed by 2015-286, s. 1.1(1), effective October 22, 2015

N.C. Gen. Stat. § 14-198

Repealed by Session Laws 1975, c. 402.

§ 14-199. Obstructing way to places of public worship

If any person shall maliciously stop up or obstruct the way leading to any place of public worship, or to any spring or well commonly used by the congregation, he shall be guilty of a Class 2 misdemeanor.

History.

1785, c. 241, P.R.; R.C., c. 97, s. 5; Code, s. 3669; Rev., s. 3776; C.S., s. 4354; 1945, c. 635; 1969, c. 1224, s. 1; 1993, c. 539, s. 130; 1994, Ex. Sess., c. 24, s. 14(c)

§§ 14-200, 14-201

Repealed by Session Laws 1994, Extra Session, c. 14, ss. 72(9), 72(10).

§ 14-202. Secretly peeping into room occupied by another person

(a) Any person who shall peep secretly into any room occupied by another person shall be guilty of a Class 1 misdemeanor.

(a1) Unless covered by another provision of law providing greater punishment, any person who secretly or surreptitiously peeps underneath or through the clothing being worn by another person, through the use of a mirror or other device, for the purpose of viewing the body of, or the undergarments worn by, that other person without their consent shall be guilty of a Class 1 misdemeanor.

(b) For purposes of this section:

(1) The term "photographic image" means any photograph or photographic reproduction, still or moving, or any videotape, motion picture, or live television transmission, or any digital image of any individual.

(2) The term "room" shall include, but is not limited to, a bedroom, a rest room, a bathroom, a shower, and a dressing room.

(c) Unless covered by another provision of law providing greater punishment, any person who, while in possession of any device which may be used to create a photographic image, shall secretly peep into any room shall be guilty of a Class A1 misdemeanor.

(d) Unless covered by another provision of law providing greater punishment, any person who, while secretly peeping into any room, uses any device to create a photographic image of another person in that room for the purpose of arousing or gratifying the sexual desire of any person shall be guilty of a Class I felony.

(e) Any person who secretly or surreptitiously uses any device to create a photographic image of another person underneath or through the clothing being worn by that other person for the purpose of viewing the body of, or the undergarments worn by, that other person without their consent shall be guilty of a Class I felony.

(f) Any person who, for the purpose of arousing or gratifying the sexual desire of any person, secretly or surreptitiously uses or installs in a room any device that can be used to create a photographic image with the intent to capture the image of another without their consent shall be guilty of a Class I felony.

(g) Any person who knowingly possesses a photographic image that the person knows, or has reason to believe, was obtained in violation of this section shall be guilty of a Class I felony.

(h) Any person who disseminates or allows to be disseminated images that the person knows, or should have known, were obtained as a result of the violation of this section shall be guilty of a Class H felony if the dissemination is without the consent of the person in the photographic image.

(i) A second or subsequent felony conviction under this section shall be punished as though convicted of an offense one class higher. A second or subsequent conviction for a Class 1 misdemeanor shall be punished as a Class A1 misdemeanor. A second or subsequent conviction for a Class A1 misdemeanor shall be punished as a Class I felony.

(j) If the defendant is placed on probation as a result of violation of this section:

(1) For a first conviction under this section, the judge may impose a requirement that the defendant obtain a psychological evaluation and comply with any treatment recommended as a result of that evaluation.

(2) For a second or subsequent conviction under this section, the judge shall impose a requirement that the defendant obtain a psychological evaluation and comply with any treatment recommended as a result of that evaluation.

(k) Any person whose image is captured or disseminated in violation of this section has a civil cause of action against any person who captured or disseminated the image or procured any other person to capture or disseminate the image and is entitled to recover from those persons actual damages, punitive damages, reasonable attorneys' fees and other litigation costs reasonably incurred.

(l) When a person violates subsection (d), (e), (f), (g), or (h) of this section, or is convicted of a second or subsequent violation of subsection (a), (a1), or (c) of this section, the sentencing court shall consider whether the person is a danger to the community and whether requiring the person to register as a sex offender pursuant to Article 27A of this Chapter would further the purposes of that Article as stated in G.S. 14-208.5. If the sentencing court rules that the person is a danger to the community and that the person shall register, then an order shall be entered requiring the person to register.

(m) The provisions of subsections (a), (a1), (c), (e), (g), (h), and (k) of this section do not apply to:

(1) Law enforcement officers while discharging or attempting to discharge their official duties; or

(2) Personnel of the Division of Adult Correction and Juvenile Justice of the Department of Public Safety or of a local confinement facility for security purposes or during investigation of alleged misconduct by a person in the custody of the Division or the local confinement facility.

(n) This section does not affect the legal activities of those who are licensed pursuant to Chapter 74C, Private Protective Services, or Chapter 74D, Alarm Systems, of the General Statutes, who are legally engaged in the discharge of their official duties within their respective professions, and who are not engaging in activities for an improper purpose as described in this section.

History.
1923, c. 78; C.S., s. 4356(a); 1957, c. 338; 1993, c. 539, s. 131; 1994, Ex. Sess., c. 24, s. 14(c); 2003-303, s. 1; 2004-109, s. 7; 2011-145, s. 19.1(h); 2012-83, s. 1; 2017-186, s. 2(p).

§ 14-202.1. Taking indecent liberties with children

(a) A person is guilty of taking indecent liberties with children if, being 16 years of age or more and at least five years older than the child in question, he either:

(1) Willfully takes or attempts to take any immoral, improper, or indecent liberties with any child of either sex under the age of 16 years for the purpose of arousing or gratifying sexual desire; or

(2) Willfully commits or attempts to commit any lewd or lascivious act upon or with the body or any part or member of the body of any child of either sex under the age of 16 years.

(b) Taking indecent liberties with children is punishable as a Class F felony.

History.
1955, c. 764; 1975, c. 779; 1979, c. 760, s. 5; 1979, 2nd Sess., c. 1316, s. 47; 1981, c. 63, s. 1; 179, s. 14; 1993, c. 539, s. 1201; 1994, Ex. Sess., c. 24, s. 14(c)

§ 14-202.2. Indecent liberties between children

(a) A person who is under the age of 16 years is guilty of taking indecent liberties with children if the person either:

(1) Willfully takes or attempts to take any immoral, improper, or indecent liberties with any child of either sex who is at least three years younger than the defendant for the purpose of arousing or gratifying sexual desire; or

(2) Willfully commits or attempts to commit any lewd or lascivious act upon or with the body or any part or member of the body of any child of either sex who is at least three years younger than the defendant for the purpose of arousing or gratifying sexual desire.

(b) A violation of this section is punishable as a Class 1 misdemeanor.

History.
1995, c. 494, s. 1; 1995 (Reg. Sess., 1996), c. 742, s. 12

§ 14-202.3. Solicitation of child by computer or certain other electronic devices to commit an unlawful sex act

(a) **Offense.** -- A person is guilty of solicitation of a child by a computer if the person is 16 years of age or older and the person knowingly, with the intent to commit an unlawful sex act, entices, advises, coerces, orders, or commands, by means of a computer or any other device capable of electronic data storage or transmission, a child who is less than 16 years of age and at least five years younger than the defendant, or a person the defendant believes to be a child who is less than 16 years of age and who the defendant believes to be at least five years younger than the defendant, to meet with the defendant or any other person for the purpose of committing an unlawful sex act. Consent is not a defense to a charge under this section.

(b) **Jurisdiction.** -- The offense is committed in the State for purposes of determining jurisdiction, if the transmission that constitutes the offense either originates in the State or is received in the State.

(c) **Punishment.** -- A violation of this section is punishable as follows:

(1) A violation is a Class H felony except as provided by subdivision (2) of this subsection.

(2) If either the defendant, or any other person for whom the defendant was arranging the meeting in violation of this section, actually appears at the meeting location, then the violation is a Class G felony.

History.
1995 (Reg. Sess., 1996), c. 632, s. 1; 2005-121, s. 1; 2008-218, s. 5; 2009-336, s. 1

§ 14-202.4. Taking indecent liberties with a student

(a) If a defendant, who is a teacher, school administrator, student teacher, school safety officer, or coach, at any age, or who is other school personnel and is at least four years older than the victim, takes indecent liberties with a victim who is a student, at any time during or after the time the defendant and victim were present together in the same school but before the victim ceases to be a student, the defendant is guilty of a Class I felony, unless the conduct is covered under some other provision of law providing for greater punishment. A person is not guilty of taking indecent liberties with a student if the person is lawfully married to the student.

(b) If a defendant, who is school personnel, other than a teacher, school administrator, student teacher, school safety officer, or coach, and who is less than four years older than the victim, takes indecent liberties with a student as provided in subsection (a) of this section, the defendant is guilty of a Class I felony.

(c) Consent is not a defense to a charge under this section.

(d) For purposes of this section, the following definitions apply:

(1) "Indecent liberties" means:

a. Willfully taking or attempting to take any immoral, improper, or indecent liberties with a student for the purpose of arousing or gratifying sexual desire; or

b. Willfully committing or attempting to commit any lewd or lascivious act upon or with the body or any part or member of the body of a student.

For purposes of this section, the term indecent liberties does not include vaginal intercourse or a sexual act as defined by G.S. 14-27.20.

(1a) "Same school" means a school at which (i) the student is enrolled or is present for a school-sponsored or school-related activity and (ii) the school personnel is employed, volunteers, or is present for a school-sponsored or school-related activity.

(2) "School" means any public school, charter school, or nonpublic school under Parts 1 and 2 of Article 39 of Chapter 115C of the General Statutes.

(3) "School personnel" means any person included in the definition contained in G.S. 115C-332(a)(2), including those employed by a nonpublic, charter, or regional school, and any person who volunteers at a school or a school-sponsored activity.

(3a) "School safety officer" means any other person who is regularly present in a school for the purpose of promoting and maintaining safe and orderly schools and includes a school resource officer.

(4) "Student" means a person enrolled in kindergarten, or in grade one through grade 12 in any school.

History.
1999-300, s. 1; 2003-98, s. 2; 2004-203, s. 19(a); 2015-44, s. 3; 2015-181, s. 16

§ 14-202.5. Ban online conduct by high-risk sex offenders that endangers children

(a) **Offense.** -- It is unlawful for a high-risk sex offender to do any of the following online:

(1) To communicate with a person that the offender believes is under 16 years of age.

(2) To contact a person that the offender believes is under 16 years of age.

(3) To pose falsely as a person under 16 years of age with the intent to commit

an unlawful sex act with a person the offender believes is under 16 years of age.

(4) To use a Web site to gather information about a person that the offender believes is under 16 years of age.

(5) To use a commercial social networking Web site in violation of a policy, posted in a manner reasonably likely to come to the attention of users, prohibiting convicted sex offenders from using the site.

(b) **Definition of Commercial Social Networking Web Site.** -- For the purposes of this section, a "commercial social networking Web site" includes any Web site, application, portal, or other means of accessing the Internet that meets all of the following requirements:

(1) Is operated by a person who derives revenue from membership fees, advertising, or other sources related to the operation of the Web site.

(2) Repealed by Session Laws 2019-245, s. 3(a), effective December 1, 2019, and applicable to offenses committed on or after that date.

(3) Allows users to create personal Web pages or profiles that contain the user's name or nickname, photographs of the user, and other personal information.

(4) Provides users or visitors a mechanism to communicate with others, such as a message board, chat room, or instant messenger.

(c) **Exclusions from Commercial Social Networking Web Site Definition.** -- A commercial social networking Web site does not include a Web site that meets either of the following requirements:

(1) Repealed by Session Laws 2019-245, s. 3(a), effective December 1, 2019, and applicable to offenses committed on or after that date.

(2) Has as its primary purpose the facilitation of commercial transactions, the dissemination of news, the discussion of political or social issues, or professional networking.

(3) Is a Web site owned or operated by a local, State, or federal governmental entity.

(c1) **Definition of High-Risk Sex Offender.** -- For purposes of this section, the term "high-risk sex offender" means any person registered in accordance with Article 27A of Chapter 14 of the General Statutes that meets any of the following requirements:

(1) Was convicted of an aggravated offense, as that term is defined in G.S. 14-208.6, against a person under 18 years of age.

(2) Is a recidivist, as that term is defined in G.S. 14-208.6, and one offense is against a person under 18 years of age.

(3) Was convicted of an offense against a minor, as that term is defined in G.S. 14-208.6.

(4) Was convicted of a sexually violent offense, as that term is defined in G.S. 14-208.6, against a person under 18 years of age.

(5) Was found by a court to be a sexually violent predator, as that term is defined in G.S. 14-208.6, based on a conviction of a sexually violent offense committed against a minor.

(d) **Jurisdiction.** -- The offense is committed in the State for purposes of determining jurisdiction, if the transmission that constitutes the offense either originates in the State or is received in the State.

(e) **Punishment.** -- A violation of this section is a Class H felony.

(f) **Severability.** -- If any provision of this section or its application is held invalid, the invalidity does not affect other provisions or applications of this section that can be given effect without the invalid provisions or applications, and, to this end, the provisions of this section are severable.

History.
2008-218, s. 6; 2009-570, s. 4; 2019-245, s. 3(a)

§ 14-202.5A. Liability of commercial social networking sites

(a) A commercial social networking site, as defined in G.S. 14-202.5, that complies with G.S. 14-208.15A or makes other reasonable efforts to prevent a high-risk sex offender, as defined in G.S. 14-202.5, from using its Web site to endanger children shall not be held civilly liable for damages arising out of the sex offender's communications on the social networking site's system or network.

(b) Repealed by Session Laws 2019-245, s. 3(b), effective December 1, 2019, and applicable to offenses committed on or after that date.

History.
2008-218, s. 7; 2009-272, s. 1; 2019-245, s. 3(b)

§ 14-202.6. Ban on name changes by sex offenders

It is unlawful for a sex offender who is registered in accordance with Article 27A of Chapter 14 of the General Statutes to obtain a change of name under Chapter 101 of the General Statutes.

History.
2008-218, s. 8

§§ 14-202.7 through 14-202.9

Reserved for future codification purposes.

ARTICLE 26A
ADULT ESTABLISHMENTS

§ 14-202.10. Definitions

As used in this Article:

(1) "Adult bookstore" means a bookstore:

a. Which receives a majority of its gross income during any calendar month from the sale or rental of publications (including books, magazines, other periodicals, videotapes, compact discs, other photographic, electronic, magnetic, digital, or other imaging medium) which are distinguished or characterized by their emphasis on matter depicting, describing, or relating to specified sexual activities or specified anatomical areas, as defined in this section; or

b. Having as a preponderance (either in terms of the weight and importance of the material or in terms of greater volume of materials) of its publications (including books, magazines, other periodicals, videotapes, compact discs, other photographic, electronic, magnetic, digital, or other imaging medium) which are distinguished or characterized by their emphasis on matter depicting, describing, or relating to specified sexual activities or specified anatomical areas, as defined in this section.

(2) "Adult establishment" means an adult bookstore, adult motion picture theatre, adult mini motion picture theatre, or adult live entertainment business as defined in this section.

(3) "Adult live entertainment" means any performance of or involving the actual presence of real people which exhibits specified sexual activities or specified anatomical areas, as defined in this section.

(4) "Adult live entertainment business" means any establishment or business wherein adult live entertainment is shown for observation by patrons.

(5) "Adult motion picture theatre" means an enclosed building or premises used for presenting motion pictures, a preponderance of which are distinguished or characterized by an emphasis on matter depicting, describing, or relating to specified sexual activities or specified anatomical areas, as defined in this section, for observation by

patrons therein. "Adult motion picture theatre" does not include any adult mini motion picture theatre as defined in this section.

(6) "Adult mini motion picture theatre" means an enclosed building with viewing booths designed to hold patrons which is used for presenting motion pictures, a preponderance of which are distinguished or characterized by an emphasis on matter depicting, describing or relating to specified sexual activities or specified anatomical areas as defined in this section, for observation by patrons therein.

(7), (8) Repealed by Session Laws 2017-151, s. 2(b), effective October 1, 2017.

(9) "Sexually oriented devices" means without limitation any artificial or simulated specified anatomical area or other device or paraphernalia that is designed principally for specified sexual activities but shall not mean any contraceptive device.

(10) "Specified anatomical areas" means:
a. Less than completely and opaquely covered: (i) human genitals, pubic region, (ii) buttock, or (iii) female breast below a point immediately above the top of the areola; or
b. Human male genitals in a discernibly turgid state, even if completely and opaquely covered.

(11) "Specified sexual activities" means:
a. Human genitals in a state of sexual stimulation or arousal;
b. Acts of human masturbation, sexual intercourse or sodomy; or
c. Fondling or other erotic touchings of human genitals, pubic regions, buttocks or female breasts.

History.
1977, c. 987, s. 1; 1985, c. 731, s. 1; 1998-46, s. 4; 2017-151, s. 2(a), (b).

§ 14-202.11. Restrictions as to adult establishments

(a) No person shall permit any building, premises, structure, or other facility that contains any adult establishment to contain any other kind of adult establishment. No person shall permit any building, premises, structure, or other facility in which sexually oriented devices are sold, distributed, exhibited, or contained to contain any adult establishment.

(a1) No person shall permit the practice of massage and bodywork therapy, as defined in Article 36 of Chapter 90 of the General Statutes, in an adult establishment.

(b) No person shall permit any viewing booth in an adult mini motion picture theatre to be occupied by more than one person at any time.

(c) Nothing in this section shall be deemed to preempt local government regulation of the location or operation of adult establishments or other sexually oriented businesses to the extent consistent with the constitutional protection afforded free speech.

History.
1977, c. 987, s. 1; 1985, c. 731, s. 2; 1998-46, s. 5; 2017-151, s. 2(c).

§ 14-202.12. Violations; penalties

Any person who violates G.S. 14-202.11 shall be guilty of a Class 3 misdemeanor. Any person who has been previously convicted of a violation of G.S. 14-202.11, upon conviction for a second or subsequent violation of G.S. 14-202.11, shall be guilty of a Class 2 misdemeanor.

As used herein, "person" shall include:
(1) The agent in charge of the building, premises, structure or facility; or
(2) The owner of the building, premises, structure or facility when such owner knew or reasonably should have known the nature of the business located therein, and such owner refused to cooperate with the public officials in reasonable measures designed to terminate the proscribed use; provided, however, that if there is an agent in charge, and if the owner did not have actual knowledge, the owner shall not be prosecuted; or
(3) The owner of the business; or
(4) The manager of the business.

History.
1977, c. 987, s. 1; 1985, c. 731, s. 3; 1993, c. 539, s. 132; 1994, Ex. Sess., c. 24, s. 14(c).

§ 14-202.13. Human trafficking public awareness sign

An adult establishment, as defined in G.S. 14-202.10, shall prominently display on the premises in a place that is clearly conspicuous and visible to employees and the public a public awareness sign created and provided by the North Carolina Human Trafficking Commission that contains the National Human Trafficking Resource hotline information.

History.
2017-57, s. 17.4(a); 2017-197, s. 5.8.

ARTICLE 27
PROSTITUTION

§ 14-203. Definition of terms

The following definitions apply in this Article:

(1) **Advance prostitution.** -- The term includes all of the following:

a. Soliciting for a prostitute by performing any of the following acts when acting as other than a prostitute or a patron of a prostitute:

1. Soliciting another for the purpose of prostitution.

2. Arranging or offering to arrange a meeting of persons for the purpose of prostitution.

3. Directing another to a place knowing the direction is for the purpose of prostitution.

4. Using the Internet, including any social media Web site, to solicit another for the purpose of prostitution.

b. Keeping a place of prostitution by controlling or exercising control over the use of any place that could offer seclusion or shelter for the practice of prostitution and performing any of the following acts when acting as other than a prostitute or a patron of a prostitute:

1. Knowingly granting or permitting the use of the place for the purpose of prostitution.

2. Granting or permitting the use of the place under circumstances from which the person should reasonably know that the place is used or is to be used for purposes of prostitution.

3. Permitting the continued use of the place after becoming aware of facts or circumstances from which the person should know that the place is being used for the purpose of prostitution.

(2) **Minor.** -- Any person who is less than 18 years of age.

(3) **Profit from prostitution.** -- When acting as other than a prostitute, to receive anything of value for personally rendered prostitution services or to receive anything of value from a prostitute, if the thing received is not for lawful consideration and the person knows it was earned in whole or in part from the practice of prostitution.

(4) **Prostitute.** -- A person who engages in prostitution.

(5) **Prostitution.** -- The performance of, offer of, or agreement to perform vaginal intercourse, any sexual act as defined in G.S. 14-27.20, or any sexual contact as defined in G.S. 14-27.20, for the purpose of sexual arousal or gratification for any money or other consideration.

History.
1919, c. 215, s. 2; C.S., s. 4357; 2013-368, s. 5; 2015-181, s. 17

§ 14-204. Prostitution

(a) **Offense.** -- Any person who willfully engages in prostitution is guilty of a Class 1 misdemeanor.

(b) **First Offender; Conditional Discharge.** --

(1) Whenever any person who has not previously been convicted of or placed on probation for a violation of this section pleads guilty to or is found guilty of a violation of this section, the court, without entering a judgment and with the consent of such person, shall place the person on probation pursuant to this subsection.

(2) When a person is placed on probation, the court shall enter an order specifying a period of probation of 12 months and shall defer further proceedings in the case until the conclusion of the period of probation or until the filing of a petition alleging violation of a term or condition of probation.

(3) The conditions of probation shall be that the person (i) not violate any criminal statute of any jurisdiction, (ii) refrain from possessing a firearm or other dangerous weapon, (iii) submit to periodic drug testing at a time and in a manner as ordered by the court, but no less than three times during the period of the probation, with the cost of the testing to be paid by the probationer, (iv) obtain a vocational assessment administered by a program approved by the court, and (v) attend no fewer than 10 counseling sessions administered by a program approved by the court.

(4) The court may, in addition to other conditions, require that the person do any of the following:

a. Make a report to and appear in person before or participate with the court or such courts, person, or social service agency as directed by the court in the order of probation.

b. Pay a fine and costs.

c. Attend or reside in a facility established for the instruction or residence of defendants on probation.

d. Support the person's dependents.

e. Refrain from having in the person's body the presence of any illicit drug prohibited by the North Carolina Controlled Substances Act, unless prescribed by a physician, and submit samples of the person's blood or urine or both for tests to determine the presence of any illicit drug.

(5) Upon violation of a term or condition of probation, the court may enter a judgment on its original finding of guilt and proceed as otherwise provided.

(6) Upon fulfillment of the terms and conditions of probation, the court shall discharge the person and dismiss the proceedings against the person. Upon the discharge of the person and dismissal of the proceedings against the person under this subsection, the person is eligible to apply for expunction of records pursuant to G.S. 15A-145.6.

(7) Discharge and dismissal under this subsection shall not be deemed a conviction for purposes of structured sentencing or for purposes of disqualifications or disabilities imposed by law upon conviction of a crime.

(8) There may be only one discharge and dismissal under this section.

(c) **Immunity From Prosecution for Minors.** -- Notwithstanding any other provision of this section, if it is determined, after a reasonable detention for investigative purposes, that a person suspected of or charged with a violation of this section is a minor, that person shall be immune from prosecution under this section and instead shall be taken into temporary protective custody as an undisciplined juvenile pursuant to Article 19 of Chapter 7B of the General Statutes. Pursuant to the provisions of G.S. 7B-301, a law enforcement officer who takes a minor into custody under this section shall immediately report an allegation of a violation of G.S. 14-43.11 and G.S. 14-43.13 to the director of the department of social services in the county where the minor resides or is found, as appropriate, which shall commence an initial investigation into child abuse or child neglect within 24 hours pursuant to G.S. 7B-301 and G.S. 7B-302.

History.
1919, c. 215, s. 1; C.S., s. 4358; 2013-368, s. 5

§§ 14-204.1, 14-205

Repealed by Session Laws 2013-368, s. 4, effective October 1, 2013, and applicable to offenses committed on or after that date.

History.
14-204.1: 1979, c. 873, s. 2; 1993, c. 539, s. 133; 1994, Ex. Sess., c. 24, s. 14(c); repealed by 2013-368, s. 4, effective October 1, 2013. 14-205: 1919, c. 215, s. 6; C.S., s. 4359; repealed by 2013-368, s. 4, effective October 1, 2013

§ 14-205.1. Solicitation of prostitution

(a) Except as otherwise provided in this section, any person who solicits another for the

purpose of prostitution is guilty of a Class 1 misdemeanor for a first offense and a Class H felony for a second or subsequent offense. Any person 18 years of age or older who willfully solicits a minor for the purpose of prostitution is guilty of a Class G felony. Any person who willfully solicits a person who has a severe or profound mental disability for the purpose of prostitution is guilty of a Class E felony. Punishment under this section may include participation in a program devised for the education and prevention of sexual exploitation (i.e. "John School"), where available. A person who violates this subsection is not eligible for a disposition of prayer for judgment continued under any circumstances.

(b) **Immunity From Prosecution for Minors.** -- Notwithstanding any other provision of this section, if it is determined, after a reasonable detention for investigative purposes, that a person suspected of or charged with a violation of this section is a minor who is soliciting as a prostitute, that person shall be immune from prosecution under this section and instead shall be taken into temporary protective custody as an undisciplined juvenile pursuant to Article 19 of Chapter 7B of the General Statutes. Pursuant to G.S. 7B-301, a law enforcement officer who takes a minor into custody under this section shall immediately report an allegation of a violation of G.S. 14-43.11 and G.S. 14-43.13 to the director of the department of social services in the county where the minor resides or is found, as appropriate, which shall commence an initial investigation into child abuse or child neglect within 24 hours pursuant to G.S. 7B-301 and G.S. 7B-302.

History.
2013-368, s. 5; 2015-183, s. 1; 2018-47, s. 4(e)

§ 14-205.2. Patronizing a prostitute

(a) Any person who willfully performs any of the following acts with a person not his or her spouse commits the offense of patronizing a prostitute:

(1) Engages in vaginal intercourse, any sexual act as defined in G.S. 14-27.20, or any sexual contact as defined in G.S. 14-27.20, for the purpose of sexual arousal or gratification with a prostitute.

(2) Enters or remains in a place of prostitution with intent to engage in vaginal intercourse, any sexual act as defined in G.S. 14-27.20, or any sexual contact as defined in G.S. 14-27.20, for the purpose of sexual arousal or gratification.

(b) Except as provided in subsections (c) and (d) of this section, a first violation of this section is a Class A1 misdemeanor. Unless a higher penalty applies, a second or subsequent violation of this section is a Class G felony.

(c) A violation of this section is a Class F felony if the defendant is 18 years of age or older and the prostitute is a minor.

(d) A violation of this section is a Class D felony if the prostitute has a severe or profound mental disability.

History.
2013-368, s. 5; 2015-181, s. 18; 2018-47, s. 4(f)

§ 14-205.3. Promoting prostitution

(a) Any person who willfully performs any of the following acts commits promoting prostitution:

(1) Advances prostitution as defined in G.S. 14-203.

(2) Profits from prostitution by doing any of the following:

a. Compelling a person to become a prostitute.

b. Receiving a portion of the earnings from a prostitute for arranging or offering to arrange a situation in which the person may practice prostitution.

c. Any means other than those described in sub-subdivisions a. and b. of this subdivision, including from a person who patronizes a prostitute. This sub-subdivision does not apply to a person engaged in prostitution who is a minor. A person cannot be convicted of promoting prostitution under this sub-subdivision if the practice of prostitution underlying the offense consists exclusively of the accused's own acts of prostitution under G.S. 14-204.

(b) Any person who willfully performs any of the following acts commits the offense of promoting prostitution of a minor or person who has a mental disability:

(1) Advances prostitution as defined in G.S. 14-203, where a minor or person who has a severe or profound mental disability engaged in prostitution, or any person engaged in prostitution in the place of prostitution is a minor or has a severe or profound mental disability at the time of the offense.

(2) Profits from prostitution by any means where the prostitute is a minor or has a severe or profound mental disability at the time of the offense.

(3) Confines a minor or a person who has a severe or profound mental disability against the person's will by the infliction or threat of imminent infliction of great bodily harm, permanent disability, or disfigurement or by administering to the minor or person who has a severe or profound mental disability, without the person's consent or by threat or deception and for other than medical purposes, any alcoholic intoxicant or a drug as defined in Article 5 of Chapter 90 of the General Statutes (North Carolina Controlled Substances Act) and does any of the following:

a. Compels the minor or person who has a severe or profound mental disability to engage in prostitution.

b. Arranges a situation in which the minor or person who has a severe or profound mental disability may practice prostitution.

c. Profits from prostitution by the minor or person who has a severe or profound mental disability.

For purposes of this subsection, administering drugs or an alcoholic intoxicant to a minor or a person who has a severe or profound mental disability, as described in subdivision (3) of this subsection, shall be deemed to be without consent if the administering is done without the consent of the parents or legal guardian or if the administering is performed or permitted by the parents or legal guardian for other than medical purposes. Mistake of age is not a defense to a prosecution under this subsection.

(c) Unless a higher penalty applies, a violation of subsection (a) of this section is a Class F felony. A violation of subsection (a) of this section by a person with a prior conviction for a violation of this section or a violation of G.S. 14-204 (prostitution), G.S. 14-204.1 (solicitation of prostitution), or G.S. 14-204.2 (patronizing a prostitute) is a Class E felony.

(d) Unless a higher penalty applies, a violation of subdivision (1) or (2) of subsection (b) of this section is a Class D felony. A violation of subdivision (3) of subsection (b) of this section is a Class C felony. Any violation of subsection (b) of this section by a person with a prior conviction for a violation of this section or a violation of G.S. 14-204 (prostitution), G.S. 14-204.1 (solicitation of prostitution), G.S. 14-204.2 (patronizing a prostitute) is a Class C felony.

History.
2013-368, s. 5; 2018-47, s. 4(g)

§ 14-205.4. Certain probation conditions

(a) The court may order any convicted defendant to be examined for sexually transmitted infections. If a person convicted of a crime under this Article receives a sentence which includes probation and that person is infected with a sexually transmitted infection, the period of probation may commence only upon such terms and conditions as shall ensure medical treatment and prevent the spread of the infection.

(b) No female convicted under this Article shall be placed on probation in the care or charge of any person except a female probation officer.

History.
2013-368, s. 5

§ 14-206. Reputation and prior conviction admissible as evidence

In the trial of any person charged with a violation of any of the provisions of this Article, testimony of a prior conviction, or testimony concerning the reputation of any place, structure, or building, and of the person or persons who reside in or frequent the same, and of the defendant, shall be admissible in evidence in support of the charge.

History.
1919, c. 215, s. 3; C.S., s. 4360

§§ 14-207, 14-208

Repealed by Session Laws 2013-368, s. 4, effective October 1, 2013, and applicable to offenses committed on or after that date.

History.
14-207: 1919, c. 215, s. 4; C.S., s. 4361; repealed by 2013-368, s. 4, effective October 1, 2013. 14-208: 1919, c. 215, s. 5; C.S., s. 4362; 1921, c. 101; 1981, c. 969, ss. 1, 2; 1993, c. 539, s.134; 1994, Ex. Sess., c. 24, s. 14(c); repealed by 2013-368, s. 4, effective October 1, 2013

§ 14-208.1. Promoting travel for unlawful sexual conduct

(a) **Definition.** -- For purposes of this section, the term "travel services" means transportation by air, sea, or ground; hotel or other lodging accommodations; package tours, or the provision of vouchers or coupons to be redeemed for future travel; or accommodations for a fee, commission, or other valuable consideration.

(b) **Offense.** -- A person commits the offense of promoting travel for unlawful sexual conduct if the person sells or offers to sell travel services that the person knows to include travel for the purpose of committing any of the following offenses in this State or for the purpose of engaging in conduct that would constitute any one of the following offenses if occurring within this State:

(1) An offense under Article 7B of Chapter 14 of the General Statutes.

(2) Any of the following offenses involving the sexual exploitation of a minor:

a. G.S. 14-190.16.
b. G.S. 14-190.17.
c. G.S. 14-190.17A.

(3) Any of the following offenses involving indecent liberties with a minor:

a. G.S. 14-202.1.
b. G.S. 14-202.4.

(4) Any of the following prostitution offenses:

a. G.S. 14-204.
b. G.S. 14-205.1.
c. G.S. 14-205.2.
d. G.S. 14-205.3.

(c) **Punishment.** -- A violation of this section is a Class G felony.

History.
2019-158, s. 2(a)

§§ 14-208.2 through 14-208.4

Reserved for future codification purposes.

ARTICLE 27A
SEX OFFENDER AND PUBLIC PROTECTION REGISTRATION PROGRAMS

PART 1
REGISTRATION PROGRAMS, PURPOSE AND DEFINITIONS GENERALLY

§ 14-208.5. Purpose

The General Assembly recognizes that sex offenders often pose a high risk of engaging in sex offenses even after being released from incarceration or commitment and that protection of the public from sex offenders is of paramount governmental interest.

The General Assembly also recognizes that persons who commit certain other types of offenses against minors, such as kidnapping, pose significant and unacceptable threats to the public safety and welfare of the children in this State and that the protection of those children is of great governmental interest. Further, the General Assembly recognizes that law enforcement officers' efforts to protect communities, conduct investigations, and quickly apprehend offenders who commit sex offenses or certain offenses against minors are impaired by the lack of information available to law enforcement agencies about convicted offenders who live within the agency's jurisdiction.

Release of information about these offenders will further the governmental interests of public safety so long as the information released is rationally related to the furtherance of those goals.

Therefore, it is the purpose of this Article to assist law enforcement agencies' efforts to protect communities by requiring persons who are convicted of sex offenses or of certain other offenses committed against minors to register with law enforcement agencies, to require the exchange of relevant information about those offenders among law enforcement agencies, and to authorize the access to necessary and relevant information about those offenders to others as provided in this Article.

History.
1995, c. 545, s. 1; 1997-516, s. 1

§14-208.6. Definitions

The following definitions apply in this Article:

(1a) **Aggravated offense.** -- Any criminal offense that includes either of the following: (i) engaging in a sexual act involving vaginal, anal, or oral penetration with a victim of any age through the use of force or the threat of serious violence; or (ii) engaging in a sexual act involving vaginal, anal, or oral penetration with a victim who is less than 12 years old.

(1b) **County registry.** -- The information compiled by the sheriff of a county in compliance with this Article.

(1c) **Department.** -- The Department of Public Safety.

(1d) **Electronic mail.** -- The transmission of information or communication by the use of the Internet, a computer, a facsimile machine, a pager, a cellular telephone, a video recorder, or other electronic means sent to a person identified by a unique address or address number and received by that person.

(1e) **Employed.** -- Includes employment that is full-time or part-time for a period of time exceeding 14 days or for an aggregate period of time exceeding 30 days during any calendar year, whether financially compensated, volunteered, or for the purpose of government or educational benefit.

(1f) **Entity.** -- A business or organization that provides Internet service, electronic communications service, remote computing service, online service, electronic mail service, or electronic instant message or chat services whether the business or organization is inside or outside the State.

(1g) **Instant message.** -- A form of real-time text communication between two or more people. The communication is conveyed via computers connected over a network such as the Internet.

(1h) **Institution of higher education.** -- Any postsecondary public or private educational institution, including any trade or professional institution, college, or university.

(1i) **Internet.** -- The global information system that is logically linked together by a globally unique address space based on the Internet Protocol or its subsequent extensions; that is able to support communications using the Transmission Control Protocol/Internet Protocol suite, its subsequent extensions, or other Internet Protocol compatible protocols; and that provides, uses, or makes accessible, either publicly or privately, high-level services layered on the communications and related infrastructure described in this subdivision.

(1j) **Mental abnormality.** -- A congenital or acquired condition of a person that affects the emotional or volitional capacity of the person in a manner that predisposes that person to the commission of criminal sexual acts to a degree that makes the person a menace to the health and safety of others.

(1k) **Nonresident student.** -- A person who is not a resident of North Carolina but who is enrolled in any type of school in the State on a part-time or full-time basis.

(1*l*) Nonresident worker. -- A person who is not a resident of North Carolina but who has employment or carries on a vocation in the State, on a part-time or full-time basis, with or without compensation or government or educational benefit, for more than 14 days, or for an aggregate period exceeding 30 days in a calendar year.

(1m) **Offense against a minor.** -- Any of the following offenses if the offense is committed against a minor, and the person committing the offense is not the minor's parent: G.S. 14-39 (kidnapping), G.S. 14-41 (abduction of children), and G.S. 14-43.3 (felonious restraint). The term also includes the following if the person convicted of the following is not the minor's parent: a solicitation or conspiracy to commit any of these offenses; aiding and abetting any of these offenses.

(1n) **Online identifier.** -- Electronic mail address, instant message screen name, user ID, chat or other Internet communication name, but it does not mean social security number, date of birth, or pin number.

(2) **Penal institution.** -- Any of the following:

a. A detention facility operated under the jurisdiction of the Section of Prisons of the Division of Adult

Correction and Juvenile Justice of the Department of Public Safety.

b. A detention facility operated under the jurisdiction of another state or the federal government.

c. A detention facility operated by a local government in this State or another state.

(2a) **Personality disorder.** -- An enduring pattern of inner experience and behavior that deviates markedly from the expectations of the individual's culture, is pervasive and inflexible, has an onset in adolescence or early adulthood, is stable over time, and leads to distress or impairment.

(2b) **Recidivist.** -- A person who has a prior conviction for an offense that is described in G.S. 14-208.6(4).

(3) **Release.** -- Discharged or paroled.

(3e) **Reoffender.** -- A person who has two or more convictions for a felony that is described in G.S. 14-208.6(4). For purposes of this definition, if an offender is convicted of more than one offense in a single session of court, only one conviction is counted.

(4) **Reportable conviction.** -- Any of the following:

a. A final conviction for an offense against a minor, a sexually violent offense, or an attempt to commit any of those offenses unless the conviction is for aiding and abetting. A final conviction for aiding and abetting is a reportable conviction only if the court sentencing the individual finds that the registration of that individual under this Article furthers the purposes of this Article as stated in G.S. 14-208.5.

b. A final conviction in another state of an offense, which if committed in this State, is substantially similar to an offense against a minor or a sexually violent offense as defined by this section, or a final conviction in another state of an offense that requires registration under the sex offender registration statutes of that state.

c. A final conviction in a federal jurisdiction (including a court martial) of an offense, which is substantially similar to an offense against a minor or a sexually violent offense as defined by this section.

d. A final conviction for a violation of G.S. 14-202(d), (e), (f), (g), or (h), or a second or subsequent conviction for a violation of G.S. 14-202(a), (a1), or (c), only if the court sentencing the individual issues an order pursuant to G.S. 14-202(l) requiring the individual to register.

e. A final conviction for a violation of G.S. 14-43.14, only if the court sentencing the individual issues an order pursuant to G.S. 14-43.14(e) requiring the individual to register.

(5) **Sexually violent offense.** -- A violation of former G.S. 14-27.6 (attempted rape or sexual offense), G.S. 14-27.21 (first-degree forcible rape), G.S. 14-27.22 (second-degree forcible rape), G.S. 14-27.23 (statutory rape of a child by an adult), G.S. 14-27.24 (first-degree statutory rape), G.S. 14-27.25(a) (statutory rape of a person who is 15 years of age or younger and where the defendant is at least six years older), G.S. 14-27.26 (first-degree forcible sexual offense), G.S. 14-27.27 (second-degree forcible sexual offense), G.S. 14-27.28 (statutory sexual offense with a child by an adult), G.S. 14-27.29 (first-degree statutory sexual offense), G.S. 14-27.30(a) (statutory sexual offense with a person who is 15 years of age or younger and where the defendant is at least six years older), G.S. 14-27.31 (sexual activity by a substitute parent or custodian), G.S. 14-27.32 (sexual activity with a student), G.S. 14-27.33 (sexual battery), G.S. 14-43.11 (human trafficking) if (i) the offense is committed against a minor who is less than 18 years of age or (ii) the offense is committed against any person with the intent that they be held in sexual servitude, G.S. 14-43.13 (subjecting or maintaining a person for sexual servitude), G.S. 14-178 (incest between near relatives), G.S. 14-190.6 (employing or permitting minor to assist in offenses against public morality and decency), G.S. 14-190.9(a1) (felonious indecent exposure), G.S. 14-190.16 (first degree sexual exploitation of a minor), G.S. 14-190.17 (second degree sexual exploitation of a minor), G.S. 14-190.17A (third degree sexual exploitation of a minor), G.S. 14-202.1 (taking indecent liberties with children), G.S. 14-202.3 (Solicitation of child by computer or certain other electronic devices to commit an unlawful sex act), G.S. 14-202.4(a) (taking indecent liberties with a student), G.S. 14-205.2(c) or (d) (patronizing a prostitute who is a minor or has a mental disability), G.S. 14-205.3(b) (promoting prostitution of a minor or a person who has a mental disability), G.S. 14-318.4(a1) (parent or caretaker commit or permit act of prostitution with or by a juvenile), or G.S. 14-318.4(a2) (commission or allowing of sexual act upon a juvenile by parent or guardian). The term also includes the following: a solicitation or conspiracy to commit any of these offenses; aiding and abetting any of these offenses.

(6) **Sexually violent predator.** -- A person who has been convicted of a sexually violent offense and who suffers from a mental abnormality or personality disorder that makes the person likely to engage in sexually violent offenses directed at strangers or at a person with whom a relationship has been established or promoted for the primary purpose of victimization.

(7) **Sheriff.** -- The sheriff of a county in this State.

(8) **Statewide registry.** -- The central registry compiled by the Department in accordance with G.S. 14-208.14.

(9) **Student.** -- A person who is enrolled on a full-time or part-time basis, in any postsecondary public or private educational institution, including any trade or professional institution, or other institution of higher education.

History.
1995, c. 545, s. 1; 1997-15, ss. 1, 2; 1997-516, s. 1; 1999-363, s. 1; 2001-373, s. 1; 2002-147, s. 16; 2003-303, s. 2; 2004-109, s. 8; 2005-121, s. 2; 2005-130, s. 1; 2005-226, s. 2; 2006-247, ss. 1(b), 19(a), 20(d); 2008-117, s. 6.1; 2008-220, s. 1; 2009-498, s. 1; 2010-174, s. 16(a); 2011-145, s. 19.1(h), (j); 2012-153, s. 3; 2012-194, s. 4(a); 2013-33, s. 1; 2013-368, s. 19; 2014-100, s. 17.1(x); 2015-62, s. 1(b); 2015-181, s. 32; 2017-102, s. 5; 2017-186, s. 2(q); 2018-47, s. 4(h); 2021-138, s. 18(b)

§ 14-208.6A. Lifetime registration requirements for criminal offenders

It is the objective of the General Assembly to establish a 30-year registration requirement for persons convicted of certain offenses against minors or sexually violent offenses with an opportunity for those persons to petition in superior court to shorten their registration time period after 10 years of registration. It is the further objective of the General Assembly to establish a more stringent set of registration requirements for recidivists, persons who commit aggravated offenses, and for a subclass of highly dangerous sex offenders who are determined by a sentencing court with the assistance of a board of experts to be sexually violent predators.

To accomplish this objective, there are established two registration programs: the Sex Offender and Public Protection Registration Program and the Sexually Violent Predator Registration Program. Any person convicted of an offense against a minor or of a sexually violent offense as defined by this Article shall register in person as an offender in accordance with Part 2 of this Article. Any person who is a recidivist, who commits an aggravated offense, or who is determined to be a sexually violent predator shall register in person as such in accordance with Part 3 of this Article.

The information obtained under these programs shall be immediately shared with the appropriate local, State, federal, and out-of-state law enforcement officials and penal institutions. In addition, the information designated under G.S. 14-208.10(a) as public record shall be readily available to and accessible by the public. However, the identity of the victim is not public record and shall not be released as a public record.

History.
1997-516, s. 1; 2001-373, s. 2; 2006-247, s. 2(a); 2008-117, s. 7

§ 14-208.6B. Registration requirements for juveniles transferred to and convicted in superior court

A juvenile transferred to superior court pursuant to G.S. 7B-2200 or G.S. 7B-2200.5 who is convicted of a sexually violent offense or an offense against a minor as defined in G.S. 14-208.6 shall register in person in accordance with this Article just as an adult convicted of the same offense must register.

History.
1997-516, s. 1; 1998-202, s. 13(e); 2006-247, s. 3(a); 2017-57, s. 16D.4(o); 2018-142, s. 23(b)

§ 14-208.6C. Discontinuation of registration requirement

The period of registration required by any of the provisions of this Article shall be discontinued only if the conviction requiring registration is reversed, vacated, or set aside, or if the registrant has been granted an unconditional pardon of innocence for the offense requiring registration.

History.
2001-373, s. 3

PART 2
SEX OFFENDER AND PUBLIC PROTECTION REGISTRATION PROGRAM

§ 14-208.7. Registration

(a) A person who is a State resident and who has a reportable conviction shall be required to maintain registration with the sheriff of the county where the person resides. If the person moves to North Carolina from outside this State, the person shall register within three business days of establishing residence in this State, or whenever the person has been present in the State for 15 days, whichever comes first. If the person is a current resident of North Carolina, the person shall register:

(1) Within three business days of release from a penal institution or arrival in a county to live outside a penal institution; or

(2) Immediately upon conviction for a reportable offense where an active term of imprisonment was not imposed.

Registration shall be maintained for a period of at least 30 years following the date of initial county registration unless the person, after 10 years of registration, successfully petitions the superior court to shorten his or her registration time period under G.S. 14-208.12A.

(a1) A person who is a nonresident student or a nonresident worker and who has a reportable conviction, or is required to register in the person's state of residency, is required to maintain registration with the sheriff of the county where the person works or attends school. In addition to the information required under subsection (b) of this section, the person shall also provide information regarding the person's school or place of employment as appropriate and the person's address in his or her state of residence.

(b) The Department of Public Safety shall provide each sheriff with forms for registering persons as required by this Article. The registration form shall require all of the following:

(1) The person's full name, each alias, date of birth, sex, race, height, weight, eye color, hair color, drivers license number, and home address.

(1a) A statement indicating what the person's name was at the time of the conviction for the offense that requires registration; what alias, if any, the person was using at the time of the conviction of that offense; and the name of the person as it appears on the judgment imposing the sentence on the person for the conviction of the offense.

(2) The type of offense for which the person was convicted, the date of conviction, and the sentence imposed.

(3) A current photograph taken by the sheriff, without charge, at the time of registration.

(4) The person's fingerprints taken by the sheriff, without charge, at the time of registration.

(5) A statement indicating whether the person is a student or expects to enroll as a student within a year of registering. If the person is a student or expects to enroll as a student within a year of registration, then the registration form shall also require the name and address of the educational institution at which the person is a student or expects to enroll as a student.

(6) A statement indicating whether the person is employed or expects to be employed at an institution of higher education within a year of registering. If the person is employed or expects to be employed at an institution of higher education within a year of registration, then the registration form shall also require the name and address of the educational institution at which the person is or expects to be employed.

(7) Any online identifier that the person uses or intends to use.

(c) When a person registers, the sheriff with whom the person registered shall immediately send the registration information to the Department of Public Safety in a manner determined by the Department of Public Safety. The sheriff shall retain the original registration form and other information collected and shall compile the information that is a public record under this Part into a county registry.

(d) Any person required to register under this section shall report in person at the appropriate sheriff's office to comply with the registration requirements set out in this section. The sheriff shall provide the registrant with written proof of registration at the time of registration.

History.
1995, c. 545, s. 1; 1997-516, s. 1; 2001-373, s. 4; 2002-147, s. 17; 2006-247, s. 5(a); 2008-117, s. 8; 2008-220, s. 2; 2011-61, s. 1; 2014-100, s. 17.1(r)

§ 14-208.8. Prerelease notification

(a) At least 10 days, but not earlier than 30 days, before a person who will be subject to registration under this Article is due to be released from a penal institution, an official of the penal institution shall do all of the following:

(1) Inform the person of the person's duty to register under this Article and require the person to sign a written statement that the person was so informed or, if the person refuses to sign the statement, certify that the person was so informed.

(2) Obtain the registration information required under G.S. 14-208.7(b)(1), (2), (5), (6), and (7), as well as the address where the person expects to reside upon the person's release.

(3) Send the Department of Public Safety and the sheriff of the county in which the person expects to reside the information collected in accordance with subdivision (2) of this subsection.

(b) If a person who is subject to registration under this Article does not receive an active term of imprisonment, the court pronouncing sentence shall conduct, at the time of sentencing, the notification procedures specified in subsection (a) of this section.

History.
1995, c. 545, s. 1; 1997-516, s. 1; 2002-147, s. 18; 2008-220, s. 3; 2014-100, s. 17.1(r)

§ 14-208.8A. Notification requirement for out-of-county employment if temporary residence established

(a) **Notice Required.** -- A person required to register under G.S. 14-208.7 shall notify the sheriff of the county with whom the person is registered of the person's place of employment and temporary residence, which includes a hotel, motel, or other transient lodging place, if the person meets both of the following conditions:

(1) Is employed or carries on a vocation in a county in the State other than the county in which the person is registered for more than 10 business days within a 30-day period, or for an aggregate period exceeding 30 days in a calendar year, on a part-time or full-time basis, with or without compensation or government or educational benefit.

(2) Maintains a temporary residence in that county for more than 10 business days within a 30-day period, or for an aggregate period exceeding 30 days in a calendar year.

(b) **Time Period.** -- The notice required by subsection (a) of this section shall be provided within 72 hours after the person knows or should know that he or she will be working and maintaining a temporary residence in a county other than the county in which the person resides for more than 10 business days within a 30-day period, or within 10 days after the person knows or should know that he or she will be working and maintaining a temporary residence in a county other than the county in which the person resides for an aggregate period exceeding 30 days in a calendar year.

(c) **Notice to Department of Public Safety.** -- Upon receiving the notice required under subsection (a) of this section, the sheriff shall immediately forward the information to the Department of Public Safety. The Department of Public Safety shall notify the sheriff of the county where the person is working and maintaining a temporary residence of the person's place of employment and temporary address in that county.

History.
2006-247, s. 4(a); 2007-484, s. 2; 2014-100, s. 17.1(r)

§ 14-208.9. Change of address; change of academic status or educational employment status; change of online identifier; change of name

(a) If a person required to register changes address, the person shall report in person and provide written notice of the new address not later than the third business day after the change to the sheriff of the county with whom the person had last registered. If the person moves to another county, the person shall also report in person to the sheriff of the new county and provide written notice of the person's address not later than the tenth day after the change of address. Upon receipt of the notice, the sheriff shall immediately forward this information to the Department of Public Safety. When the Department of Public Safety receives notice from a sheriff that a person required to register is moving to another county in the State, the Department of Public Safety shall inform the sheriff of the new county of the person's new residence.

(b) If a person required to register intends to move to another state, the person shall report in person to the sheriff of the county of current residence at least three business days before the date the person intends to leave this State to establish residence in another state or jurisdiction. The person shall provide to the sheriff a written notification that includes all of the following information: the address, municipality, county, and state of intended residence.

(1) If it appears to the sheriff that the record photograph of the sex offender no longer provides a true and accurate likeness of the sex offender, then the sheriff shall take a photograph of the offender to update the registration.

(2) The sheriff shall inform the person that the person must comply with the registration requirements in the new state of residence. The sheriff shall also immediately forward the information included in the notification to the Department of Public Safety, and the Department of Public Safety shall inform the appropriate state official in the state to which the registrant moves of the person's notification and new address.

(b1) A person who indicates his or her intent to reside in another state or jurisdiction and later decides to remain in this State shall, within three business days after the date upon which the person indicated he or she would leave this State, report in person to the sheriff's office to which the person reported the intended change of residence, of his or her intent to remain in this State. If the sheriff is notified by the sexual offender that he or she intends to remain in this State, the sheriff shall promptly report this information to the Department of Public Safety.

(c) If a person required to register changes his or her academic status either by enrolling as a student or by terminating enrollment as a student, then the person shall, within three business days, report in person to the sheriff of the county with whom the person registered and provide written notice of the person's new status. The written notice shall include the name and address of the institution of higher education at which the student is or was enrolled. The sheriff shall immediately forward this information to the Department of Public Safety.

(d) If a person required to register changes his or her employment status either by obtaining employment at an institution of higher education or by terminating employment at an institution of higher education, then the person shall, within three business days, report in person to the sheriff of the county with whom the person registered and provide written notice of the person's new status not later than the tenth day after the change to the sheriff of the county with whom the person registered. The written notice shall include the name and address of the institution of higher education at which the person is or was employed. The sheriff shall immediately forward this information to the Department of Public Safety.

(e) If a person required to register changes an online identifier, or obtains a new online identifier, then the person shall, within 10 days, report in person to the sheriff of the county with whom the person registered to provide the new or changed online identifier information to the sheriff. The sheriff shall immediately forward this information to the Department of Public Safety.

(f) If a person required to register changes his or her name pursuant to Chapter 101 of the General Statutes or by any other method, then the person shall, within three business days, report in person to the sheriff of the county with whom the person registered to provide the name change to the sheriff. The sheriff shall immediately forward this information to the Department of Public Safety.

History.
1995, c. 545, s. 1; 1997-516, s. 1; 2001-373, s. 5; 2002-147, s. 19; 2006-247, s. 6(a); 2007-213, s. 9A; 2007-484, s. 42(b); 2008-117, s. 9; 2008-220, ss. 4, 5; 2011-61, ss. 2, 3; 2014-100, s. 17.1(r)

§ 14-208.9A. Verification of registration information

(a) The information in the county registry shall be verified semiannually for each registrant as follows:

(1) Every year on the anniversary of a person's initial registration date, and again six months after that date, the Department of Public Safety shall mail a nonforwardable verification form to the last reported address of the person.

(2) The person shall return the verification form in person to the sheriff within three business days after the receipt of the form.

(3) The verification form shall be signed by the person and shall indicate the following:

a. Whether the person still resides at the address last reported to the sheriff. If the person has a different address, then the person shall indicate that fact and the new address.

b. Whether the person still uses or intends to use any online identifiers last reported to the sheriff. If the person has any new or different online identifiers, then the person shall provide those online identifiers to the sheriff.

c. Whether the person still uses or intends to use the name under which the person registered and last reported to the sheriff. If the person has any new or different name, then the person shall provide that name to the sheriff.

(3a) If it appears to the sheriff that the record photograph of the sex offender no longer provides a true and accurate likeness of the sex offender, then the sheriff shall take a photograph of the offender to include with the verification form.

(4) If the person fails to return the verification form in person to the sheriff within three business days after receipt of the form, the person is subject to the penalties provided in G.S. 14-208.11. If the person fails to report in person and provide the written verification as provided by this section, the sheriff shall make a reasonable attempt to verify that the person is residing at the registered address. If the person cannot be found at the registered address and has failed to report a change of address, the person is subject to the penalties provided in G.S. 14-208.11, unless the person reports in person to the sheriff and proves that the person has not changed his or her residential address.

(b) **Additional Verification May Be Required.** -- During the period that an offender is required to be registered under this Article, the sheriff is authorized to attempt to verify that the offender continues to reside at the address last registered by the offender.

(c) **Additional Photograph May Be Required.** -- If it appears to the sheriff that the current photograph of the sex offender no longer provides a true and accurate likeness of the sex offender, upon in-person notice from the sheriff, the sex offender shall allow the sheriff to take another photograph of the sex offender at the time of the sheriff's request. If requested by the sheriff, the sex offender shall appear in person at the sheriff's office during normal business hours within three business days of being requested to do so and shall allow the sheriff to take another photograph of the sex offender. A person who willfully fails to comply with this subsection is guilty of a Class 1 misdemeanor.

History.
1997-516, s. 1; 2006-247, s. 7(a); 2008-117, s. 10; 2008-220, s. 6; 2011-61, s. 4; 2014-100, s. 17.1(r)

§ 14-208.10. Registration information is public record; access to registration information

(a) The following information regarding a person required to register under this Article is public record and shall be available for public inspection: name, sex, address, physical description, picture, conviction date, offense for which registration was required, the sentence imposed as a result of the conviction, and registration status. The information obtained under G.S. 14-208.22 regarding a person's medical records or documentation of treatment for the person's mental abnormality or personality disorder shall not be a part of the public record.

The sheriff shall release any other relevant information that is necessary to protect the public concerning a specific person, but shall not release the identity of the victim of the offense that required registration under this Article.

(b) Any person may obtain a copy of an individual's registration form, a part of the county registry, or all of the county registry, by submitting a written request for the information to the sheriff. However, the identity of the victim of an offense that requires registration under this Article shall not be released. The sheriff may charge a reasonable fee for duplicating costs and for mailing costs when appropriate.

History.
1995, c. 545, s. 1; 1997-516, s. 1

§ 14-208.11. Failure to register; falsification of verification notice; failure to return verification form; order for arrest

(a) A person required by this Article to register who willfully does any of the following is guilty of a Class F felony:

(1) Fails to register as required by this Article, including failure to register with the sheriff in the county designated by the person, pursuant to G.S. 14-208.8, as their expected county of residence.

(2) Fails to notify the last registering sheriff of a change of address as required by this Article.

(3) Fails to return a verification notice as required under G.S. 14-208.9A.

(4) Forges or submits under false pretenses the information or verification notices required under this Article.

(5) Fails to inform the registering sheriff of enrollment or termination of enrollment as a student.

(6) Fails to inform the registering sheriff of employment at an institution of higher education or termination of employment at an institution of higher education.

(7) Fails to report in person to the sheriff's office as required by G.S. 14-208.7, 14-208.9, and 14-208.9A.

(8) Reports his or her intent to reside in another state or jurisdiction but remains in this State without reporting to the sheriff in the manner required by G.S. 14-208.9.

(9) Fails to notify the registering sheriff of out-of-county employment if temporary residence is established as required under G.S. 14-208.8A.

(10) Fails to inform the registering sheriff of any new or changes to existing online identifiers that the person uses or intends to use.

(a1) If a person commits a violation of subsection (a) of this section, the probation officer, parole officer, or any other law enforcement officer who is aware of the violation shall immediately arrest the person in accordance with G.S. 15A-401, or seek an order for the person's arrest in accordance with G.S. 15A-305.

(a2) A person arrested pursuant to subsection (a1) of this section shall be subject to the jurisdiction of the prosecutorial and judicial district that includes the sheriff's office in the county where the person failed to register, pursuant to this Article. If the arrest is made outside of the applicable prosecutorial district, the person shall be transferred to the custody of the sheriff of the county where the person failed to register and all further criminal and judicial proceedings shall be held in that county.

(b) Before a person convicted of a violation of this Article is due to be released from a penal institution, an official of the penal institution shall conduct the prerelease notification procedures specified under G.S. 14-208.8(a)(2) and (3). If upon a conviction for a violation of this Article, no active term of imprisonment is imposed, the court pronouncing sentence shall, at the time of sentencing, conduct the notification procedures specified under G.S. 14-208.8(a)(2) and (3).

(c) A person who is unable to meet the registration or verification requirements of this Article shall be deemed to have complied with its requirements if:

(1) The person is incarcerated in, or is in the custody of, a local, State, private, or federal correctional facility,

(2) The person notifies the official in charge of the facility of their status as a

Chapter 14

person with a legal obligation or requirement under this Article and

(3) The person meets the registration or verification requirements of this Article no later than 10 days after release from confinement or custody.

History.
1995, c. 545, s. 1; 1997-516, s. 1; 2002-147, s. 20; 2006-247, ss. 8(a), 8(b); 2008-220, s. 7; 2013-205, s. 1

§ 14-208.11A. Duty to report noncompliance of a sex offender; penalty for failure to report in certain circumstances

(a) It shall be unlawful and a Class H felony for any person who has reason to believe that an offender is in violation of the requirements of this Article, and who has the intent to assist the offender in eluding arrest, to do any of the following:

(1) Withhold information from, or fail to notify, a law enforcement agency about the offender's noncompliance with the requirements of this Article, and, if known, the whereabouts of the offender.

(2) Harbor, attempt to harbor, or assist another person in harboring or attempting to harbor, the offender.

(3) Conceal, or attempt to conceal, or assist another person in concealing or attempting to conceal, the offender.

(4) Provide information to a law enforcement agency regarding the offender that the person knows to be false information.

(b) This section does not apply if the offender is incarcerated in or is in the custody of a local, State, private, or federal correctional facility.

History.
2006-247, s. 9.1(a)

N.C. Gen. Stat. § 14-208.12

Repealed by S.L. 1997-516, s. 1, effective April 1, 1998.

§ 14-208.12A. Request for termination of registration requirement

(a) Ten years from the date of initial county registration, a person required to register under this Part may petition the superior court to terminate the 30-year registration requirement if the person has not been convicted of a subsequent offense requiring registration under this Article.

If the reportable conviction is for an offense that occurred in North Carolina, the petition shall be filed in the district where the person was convicted of the offense.

If the reportable conviction is for an offense that occurred in another state, the petition shall be filed in the district where the person resides. A person who petitions to terminate the registration requirement for a reportable conviction that is an out-of-state offense shall also do the following: (i) provide written notice to the sheriff of the county where the person was convicted that the person is petitioning the court to terminate the registration requirement and (ii) include with the petition at the time of its filing, an affidavit, signed by the petitioner, that verifies that the petitioner has notified the sheriff of the county where the person was convicted of the petition and that provides the mailing address and contact information for that sheriff.

Regardless of where the offense occurred, if the defendant was convicted of a reportable offense in any federal court, the conviction will be treated as an out-of-state offense for the purposes of this section.

(a1) The court may grant the relief if:

(1) The petitioner demonstrates to the court that he or she has not been arrested for any crime that would require registration under this Article since completing the sentence,

(2) The requested relief complies with the provisions of the federal Jacob Wetterling Act, as amended, and any other federal standards applicable to the termination of a registration requirement or required to be met as a condition for the receipt of federal funds by the State, and

(3) The court is otherwise satisfied that the petitioner is not a current or potential threat to public safety.

(a2) The district attorney in the district in which the petition is filed shall be given notice of the petition at least three weeks before the hearing on the matter. The petitioner may present evidence in support of the petition and the district attorney may present evidence in opposition to the requested relief or may otherwise demonstrate the reasons why the petition should be denied.

(a3) If the court denies the petition, the person may again petition the court for relief in accordance with this section one year from the date of the denial of the original petition to terminate the registration requirement. If the court grants the petition to terminate the registration requirement, the clerk of court shall forward a certified copy of the order to the Department of Public Safety to have the person's name removed from the registry.

(b) If there is a subsequent offense, the county registration records shall be retained until the registration requirement for the subsequent offense is terminated by the court under subsection (a1) of this section.

(c) The victim of the underlying offense may appear and be heard by the court in a proceeding regarding a request for termination of the sex offender registration requirement. If the victim has elected to receive notices of such proceedings, the district attorney's office shall notify the victim of the date, time, and place of the hearing. The district attorney's office may provide the required notification electronically or by telephone, unless the victim requests otherwise. The victim shall be responsible for notifying the district attorney's office of any changes in the victim's address and telephone number or other contact information. The judge in any court proceeding subject to this section shall inquire as to whether the victim is present and wishes to be heard. If the victim is present and wishes to be heard, the court shall grant the victim an opportunity to be reasonably heard. The right to be reasonably heard may be exercised, at the victim's discretion, through an oral statement, submission of a written statement, or submission of an audio or video statement.

History.

1997-516, s. 1; 2006-247, s. 10(a); 2008-117, s. 11; 2011-61, s. 5; 2014-100, s. 17.1(r); 2017-158, s. 22; 2019-245, s. 7(a).

§ 14-208.12B. Registration requirement review

(a) When a person is notified by a sheriff that the person may be required to register based on an out-of-state conviction as provided in G.S. 14-208.6(4)(b), or a federal conviction as provided in G.S. 14-208.6(4)(c), that is substantially similar to a North Carolina sexually violent offense, or an offense against a minor, the sheriff shall notify the person of the right to petition the court for a judicial determination of the requirement to register. Notification shall be served on the person and the district attorney, as provided in G.S. 1A-1, Rule 4(j), or delivery by any other means that the person consented to in writing. The person may petition the court to contest the requirement to register by filing a petition to obtain a judicial determination as to whether the person is required to register under this Article. The judicial review shall be by a superior court judge presiding in the district where the petition is filed. The review under this section is limited to determine whether or not the person's out-of-state or federal conviction is substantially similar to a reportable conviction, as defined in G.S. 14-208.6(4)(a).

(b) The petition shall be filed in the county in which the person resides using a form created by the Administrative Office of the Courts. The petition must be filed with the clerk of court within 30 days of the person's receipt of the notification of the requirement to register from

the sheriff. The person filing the petition must serve a copy of the petition on the office of the district attorney and the sheriff in the county where the person resides within three days of filing the petition with the clerk of court. The petition shall be calendared at the next regularly scheduled term of superior court. At the first setting, the petitioner must be advised of the right to have counsel present at the hearing and to the appointment of counsel if the petitioner cannot afford to retain counsel. Appointment of counsel shall be in accordance with rules adopted by the Office of Indigent Defense Services.

(c) At the hearing, the district attorney has the burden to prove by a preponderance of the evidence, that the person's out-of-state or federal conviction is for an offense, which if committed in North Carolina, was substantially similar to a sexually violent offense, or an offense against a minor. The person may present evidence in support of the lack of substantial similarity between the out-of-state or federal conviction, but may not contest the validity of the conviction. The court may review copies of the relevant out-of-state or federal criminal law and compare the elements of the out-of-state or federal offense to those purportedly similar to a North Carolina offense.

(d) After reviewing the petition, receiving any and all evidence presented by the parties at the hearing, considering any arguments of the parties, the presiding superior court judge shall determine whether the out-of-state or federal conviction is substantially similar to a reportable conviction. If the presiding superior court judge determines the out-of-state or federal conviction is substantially similar to a reportable conviction, the judge shall order the person to register as a sex offender pursuant to this Article. If the presiding superior court judge determines the out-of-state or federal conviction is not substantially similar to a reportable conviction, the judge shall indicate in an order that the person is not required to register as a sex offender pursuant to this Article, based on the out-of-state or federal conviction presented in the hearing. The judge shall prepare a written order and shall direct such order be filed with the clerk of court and copied to the district attorney and the sheriff.

(e) A person who properly files a petition in accordance with this provision shall not be required to register with the sheriff until such petition is decided by the court. No person who properly files a petition in accordance with this provision may be charged with failing to register or any other violation applicable to registrants under this Article, while such petition is pending judicial review as provided in this section.

(f) Any person who is notified by the sheriff of the person's requirement to register as a result of an out-of-state or federal conviction and fails to file a petition under this provision within 30 days of receipt of the notification shall be deemed to have waived judicial review of the person's requirement to register.

(g) A person notified of a requirement to register as a result of a conviction for an offense under G.S. 14-208.6(4)(b) or G.S. 14-208.6(4)(c), who willfully (i) does not file a petition under this section and (ii) does not register in accordance with this Article, shall be in violation of G.S. 14-208.11(a)(1) and shall be guilty of a Class F Felony as provided in that section.

(h) This section shall not be used in lieu of the process to terminate the period of registration pursuant to G.S. 14-208.12A.

(i) No sheriff, or employee of a sheriffs' office, district attorney's office, or the North Carolina State Bureau of Investigation shall incur any civil or criminal liability under North Carolina law as the result of the performance of official duties under this Article.

History.
2020-83, s. 11.5(a)

§ 14-208.13. File with Criminal Information Network

(a) The Department of Public Safety shall include the registration information in the Criminal Information Network as set forth in G.S. 143B-905.

(b) The Department of Public Safety shall maintain the registration information permanently even after the registrant's reporting requirement expires.

History.
1995, c. 545, s. 1; 1997-516, s. 1; 2014-100, s. 17.1(y)

§ 14-208.14. Statewide registry; Department of Public Safety designated custodian of statewide registry

(a) The Department of Public Safety shall compile and keep current a central statewide sex offender registry. The Department is the State agency designated as the custodian of the statewide registry. As custodian the Department has the following responsibilities:

(1) To receive from the sheriff or any other law enforcement agency or penal institution all sex offender registrations, changes of address, changes of academic or educational employment status, and prerelease notifications required under this Article or under federal law. The Department shall also receive notices of any violation of this Article, including a failure to register or a failure to report a change of address.

(2) To provide all need-to-know law enforcement agencies (local, State, campus, federal, and those located in other states) immediately upon receipt by the Department of any of the following: registration information, a prerelease notification, a change of address, a change of academic or educational employment status, or notice of a violation of this Article.

(2a) To notify the appropriate law enforcement unit at an institution of higher education as soon as possible upon receipt by the Department of relevant information based on registration information or notice of a change of academic or educational employment status. If an institution of higher education does not have a law enforcement unit, then the Department shall provide the information to the local law enforcement agency that has jurisdiction for the campus.

(3) To coordinate efforts among law enforcement agencies and penal institutions to ensure that the registration information, changes of address, change of name, prerelease notifications, and notices of failure to register or to report a change of address are conveyed in an appropriate and timely manner.

(4) To provide public access to the statewide registry in accordance with this Article.

(4a) To maintain the system for public access so that a registrant's full name, any aliases, and any legal name changes are cross-referenced and a member of the public may conduct a search of the system for a registrant under any of those names.

(5) To maintain a system allowing an entity to access a list of online identifiers of persons in the central sex offender registry.

(b) The statewide registry shall include the following:

(1) Registration information obtained by a sheriff or penal institution under this Article or from any other local or State law enforcement agency.

(2) Registration information received from a state or local law enforcement agency or penal institution in another state.

(3) Registration information received from a federal law enforcement agency or penal institution.

History.
1997-516, s. 1; 2002-147, s. 21; 2008-220, s. 8; 2011-61, ss. 6, 7; 2014-100, s. 17.1(z)

§ 14-208.15. Certain statewide registry information is public record: access to statewide registry

(a) The information in the statewide registry that is public record is the same as in G.S. 14-208.10. The Department of Public Safety shall release any other relevant information that is necessary to protect the public concerning a specific person, but shall not release the identity of the victim of the offense that required registration under this Article.

(b) The Department of Public Safety shall provide free public access to automated data from the statewide registry, including photographs provided by the registering sheriffs, via the Internet. The public will be able to access the statewide registry to view an individual registration record, a part of the statewide registry, or all of the statewide registry. The Department of Public Safety may also provide copies of registry information to the public upon written request and may charge a reasonable fee for duplicating costs and mailings costs.

(c) Upon request of an institution of higher education, the Sheriff of the county in which the educational institution is located shall provide a report containing the registry information for any registrant who has stated that the registrant is a student or employee, or expects to become a student or employee, of that institution of higher education. The Department of Public Safety shall provide each sheriff with the ability to generate the report from the statewide registry. The report shall be provided electronically without charge. The institution of higher education may receive a written report upon payment of reasonable duplicating costs and mailing costs.

History.
1997-516, s. 1; 2014-100, s. 17.1(r); 2015-44, s. 4

§ 14-208.15A. Release of online identifiers to entity; fee

(a) The Department of Public Safety may release registry information regarding a registered offender's online identifier to an entity for the purpose of allowing the entity to prescreen users or to compare the online identifier information with information held by the entity as provided by this section.

(b) An entity desiring to prescreen its users or compare its database of registered users to the list of online identifiers of persons in the statewide registry may apply to the Department of Public Safety to access the information. An entity that complies with the criteria developed by the Department of Public Safety regarding the release and use of the online identifier information and pays the fee may screen new users or compare its database of registered users to the list of online identifiers of persons in the statewide registry as frequently as the Department of Public Safety may allow for the purpose of identifying a registered user associated with an online identifier contained in the statewide registry.

(c) The Department of Public Safety may charge an entity that submits a request for the online identifiers of persons in the statewide registry an annual fee of one hundred dollars ($ 100.00). Fees collected under this section shall be credited to the Department of Public Safety and applied to the cost of providing this service.

(d) The Department of Public Safety shall develop standards regarding the release and use of online identifier information. The standards shall include a requirement that the information obtained from the statewide registry shall not be disclosed for any purpose other than for prescreening its users or comparing the database of registered users of the entity against the list of online identifiers of persons in the statewide registry.

(e) An entity that receives:

(1) A complaint from a user of the entity's services that a person uses its service to solicit a minor by computer to commit an unlawful sex act as defined in G.S. 14-202.3, or

(2) A report that a user may be violating G.S. 14-190.17 or G.S. 14-190.17A by posting or transmitting material that contains a visual representation of a minor engaged in sexual activity,

shall report that information and the online identifier information of the person allegedly committing the offense, including whether that online identifier is included in the statewide registry, to the Cyber Tip Line at the National Center for Missing and Exploited Children, which shall forward that report to an appropriate law enforcement official in this State. The offense is committed in the State for purposes of determining jurisdiction, if the transmission that constitutes the offense either originates in the State or is received in the State.

(f) An entity that complies with this section in good faith is immune from civil or criminal liability resulting from either of the following:

(1) The entity's refusal to provide system service to a person on the basis that the entity reasonably believed that the person was subject to registration under State sex offender registry laws.

(2) A person's criminal or tortious acts against a minor with whom the person had communicated on the entity's system.

History.
2008-220, s. 9; 2009-272, s. 2; 2014-100, s. 17.1(o), (r)

§ 14-208.16. Residential restrictions

(a) A registrant under this Article shall not knowingly reside at one of the following:

(1) Any location which is within 1,000 feet of any property line of a property on which any public or nonpublic school or child care center is located.

(2) Within any structure, any portion of which is within 1,000 feet of any property line of a property on which any public or nonpublic school or child care center is located.

This subsection applies to any registrant who did not establish his or her residence, in accordance with subsection (d) of this section, prior to August 16, 2006.

(b) As used in this section, "school" does not include home schools as defined in G.S. 115C-563 or institutions of higher education; however, for the purposes of this section, the term "school" shall include any construction project designated for use as a public school if the governing body has notified the sheriff or sheriffs with jurisdiction within 1,000 feet of the construction project of the construction of the public school. The term "child care center" is defined by G.S. 110-86(3); however, for purposes of this section, the term "child care center" does include the permanent locations of organized clubs of Boys and Girls Clubs of America. The term "registrant" means a person who is registered, or is required to register, under this Article.

(c) This section does not apply to child care centers that are located on or within 1,000 feet of the property of an institution of higher education where the registrant is a student or is employed.

(d) Changes in the ownership of or use of property within 1,000 feet of a registrant's registered address that occur after a registrant establishes residency at the registered address shall not form the basis for finding that an offender is in violation of this section. For purposes of this subsection, a residence is established when the registrant does any of the following:

(1) Purchases the residence or enters into a specifically enforceable contract to purchase the residence.

(2) Enters into a written lease contract for the residence and for as long as the person is lawfully entitled to remain on the premises.

(3) Resides with an immediate family member who established residence in accordance with this subsection. For purposes of this subsection, "immediate family member" means a child or sibling who is 18 years of age or older, or a parent, grandparent, legal guardian, or spouse of the registrant.

(e) Nothing in this section shall be construed as creating a private cause of action against a real estate agent or landlord for any act or omission arising out of the residential restriction in this section.

(f) A violation of this section is a Class G felony.

History.
2006-247, s. 11(a); 2007-213, s. 10; 2013-28, s. 1; 2014-21, s. 1; 2019-245, s. 8(a); 2021-115, s. 3

§ 14-208.17. Sexual predator prohibited from working or volunteering for child-involved activities; limitation on residential use

(a) It shall be unlawful for any person required to register under this Article to work for any person or as a sole proprietor, with or without compensation, at any place where a minor is present and the person's responsibilities or activities would include instruction, supervision, or care of a minor or minors.

(b) It shall be unlawful for any person to conduct any activity at his or her residence where the person:

(1) Accepts a minor or minors into his or her care or custody from another, and

(2) Knows that a person who resides at that same location is required to register under this Article.

(c) A violation of this section is a Class F felony.

History.
2006-247, s. 11(b)

§ 14-208.18. Sex offender unlawfully on premises

(a) It shall be unlawful for any person required to register under this Article, if the offense requiring registration is described in subsection (c) of this section, to knowingly be at any of the following locations:

(1) On the premises of any place intended primarily for the use, care, or supervision of minors, including, but not limited to, schools, children's museums, child care centers, nurseries, and playgrounds.

(2) Within 300 feet of any location intended primarily for the use, care, or supervision of minors when the place is located on premises that are not intended primarily for the use, care, or supervision of minors, including, but not limited to, places described in subdivision (1) of this subsection that are located in malls, shopping centers, or other property open to the general public.

(3) At any place where minors frequently congregate, including, but not limited to, libraries, arcades, amusement parks, recreation parks, and swimming pools, when minors are present.

(4) On the State Fairgrounds during the period of time each year that the State Fair is conducted, on the Western North Carolina Agricultural Center grounds during the period of time each year that the North Carolina Mountain State Fair is conducted, and on any other fairgrounds during the period of time that an agricultural fair is being conducted.

(b) Notwithstanding any provision of this section, a person subject to subsection (a) of this section who is the parent or guardian of a minor may take the minor to any location that can provide emergency medical care treatment if the minor is in need of emergency medical care.

(c) The subdivisions of subsection (a) of this section are applicable as follows:

(1) Subdivisions (1), (3), and (4) of subsection (a) of this section apply to persons required to register under this Article who have committed any of the following offenses:

a. Any offense in Article 7B of this Chapter or any federal offense or offense committed in another state, which if committed in this State, is substantially similar to an offense in Article 7B of this Chapter.

b. Any offense where the victim of the offense was under the age of 18 years at the time of the offense.

c. Any offense in violation of G.S. 14-190.16, 14-190.17, or 14-190.17A or any federal offense or offense committed in another state, which if committed in this State is substantially similar to an offense in violation of G.S. 14-190.16, 14-190.17, or 14-190.17A.

(2) Subdivision (2) of subsection (a) of this section applies to persons required to register under this Article if any of the following apply:

a. The person has committed any offense in Article 7B of this Chapter or any federal offense or offense committed in another state, which if committed in this State is substantially similar to an offense in Article 7B of this Chapter, and a finding has been made in any criminal or civil proceeding that the person presents, or may present, a danger to minors under the age of 18.

b. The person has committed any offense where the victim of the offense was under the age of 18 years at the time of the offense.

c. The person has committed an offense in violation of G.S. 14-190.16, 14-190.17, or 14-190.17A or any federal offense or offense committed in another state, which if committed in this State is substantially similar to an offense in

violation of G.S. 14-190.16, 14-190.17, or 14-190.17A.

(d) A person subject to subsection (a) of this section who is a parent or guardian of a student enrolled in a school may be present on school property if all of the following conditions are met:

(1) The parent or guardian is on school property for the purpose for one of the following:

a. To attend a conference at the school with school personnel to discuss the academic or social progress of the parents' or guardians' child; or

b. The presence of the parent or guardian has been requested by the principal or his or her designee for any other reason relating to the welfare or transportation of the child.

(2) The parent or guardian complies with all of the following:

a. Notice: The parent or guardian shall notify the principal of the school of the parents' or guardians' registration under this Article and of his or her presence at the school unless the parent or guardian has permission to be present from the superintendent or the local board of education, or the principal has granted ongoing permission for regular visits of a routine nature. If permission is granted by the superintendent or the local board of education, the superintendent or chairman of the local board of education shall inform the principal of the school where the parents' or guardians' will be present. Notification includes the nature of the parents' or guardians' visit and the hours when the parent or guardian will be present at the school. The parent or guardian is responsible for notifying the principal's office upon arrival and upon departure. Any permission granted under this sub-subdivision shall be in writing.

b. Supervision: At all times that a parent or guardian is on school property, the parent or guardian shall remain under the direct supervision of school personnel. A parent or guardian shall not be on school property even if the parent or guardian has ongoing permission for regular visits of a routine nature if no school personnel are reasonably available to supervise the parent or guardian on that occasion.

(e) A person subject to subsection (a) of this section who is eligible to vote may be present at a location described in subsection (a) used as a voting place as defined by G.S. 163-165 only for the purposes of voting and shall not be outside the voting enclosure other than for the purpose of entering and exiting the voting place. If the voting place is a school, then the person subject to subsection (a) shall notify the principal of the school that he or she is registered under this Article.

(f) A person subject to subsection (a) of this section who is eligible under G.S. 115C-378 to attend public school may be present on school property if permitted by the local board of education pursuant to G.S. 115C-390.11(a)(2).

(g) A juvenile subject to subsection (a) of this section may be present at a location described in that subsection if the juvenile is at the location to receive medical treatment or mental health services and remains under the direct supervision of an employee of the treating institution at all times.

(g1) Notwithstanding any provision of this section, a person subject to subsection (a) of this section who is required to wear an electronic monitoring device shall wear an electronic monitoring device that provides exclusion zones around the premises of all elementary and secondary schools in North Carolina.

(h) A violation of this section is a Class H felony.

History.
2008-117, s. 12; 2009-570, s. 5; 2011-245, s. 2(b); 2011-282, s. 14; 2015-62, s. 5(a); 2015-181, s. 47; 2016-102, s. 1; 2017-6, s. 3; 2017-102, s. 33.1; 2018-146, ss. 3.1(a), (b), 6.1; 2021-115, s. 1.

§ 14-208.19. Community and public notification

The licensee for each licensed day care center and the principal of each elementary school, middle school, and high school shall register with the North Carolina Sex Offender and Public Protection Registry to receive e-mail notification when a registered sex offender moves within a one-mile radius of the licensed day care center or school.

History.
2008-117, s. 13

§ 14-208.19A. Commercial drivers license restrictions

(a) The Division of Motor Vehicles, in compliance with G.S. 20-37.14A, shall not issue or renew a commercial drivers license with a P or S endorsement to any person required to register under this Article.

(b) The Division of Motor Vehicles, in compliance with G.S. 20-37.13(f) shall not issue a commercial driver learner's permit with a P or S endorsement to any person required to register under this Article.

(c) A person who is convicted of a violation that requires registration under Article 27A of Chapter 14 of the General Statutes is disqualified under G.S. 20-17.4 from driving a commercial motor vehicle that requires a commercial drivers license with a P or S endorsement for the period of time during which the person is required to maintain registration under Article 27A of Chapter 14 of the General Statutes.

(d) A person who drives a commercial passenger vehicle or a school bus and who does not have a commercial drivers license with a P or S endorsement because the person was convicted of a violation that requires registration under Article 27A of Chapter 14 of the General Statutes shall be punished as provided by G.S. 20-27.1.

History.
2009-491, s. 1

PART 3
SEXUALLY VIOLENT PREDATOR REGISTRATION PROGRAM

§ 14-208.20. Sexually violent predator determination; notice of intent; presentence investigation

(a) When a person is charged by indictment or information with the commission of a sexually violent offense, the district attorney shall decide whether to seek classification of the offender as a sexually violent predator if the person is convicted. If the district attorney intends to seek the classification of a sexually violent predator, the district attorney shall within the time provided for the filing of pretrial motions under G.S. 15A-952 file a notice of the district attorney's intent. The court may for good cause shown allow late filing of the notice, grant additional time to the parties to prepare for trial, or make other appropriate orders.

(b) Prior to sentencing a person as a sexually violent predator, the court shall order a presentence investigation in accordance with G.S. 15A-1332(c). However, the study of the defendant and whether the defendant is a sexually violent predator shall be conducted by a board of experts selected by the Division of Adult Correction and Juvenile Justice of the Department of Public Safety. The board of experts shall be composed of at least four people. Two of the board members shall be experts in the field of the behavior and treatment of sexual offenders, one of whom shall be selected from a panel of experts in those fields provided by the North Carolina Medical Society and not employed with the Division of Adult Correction and Juvenile Justice of the Department of Public Safety or employed on a full-time basis with any other State agency. One of the board members shall be a victims' rights advocate, and one of the board members shall be a representative of law enforcement agencies.

(c) When the defendant is returned from the presentence commitment, the court shall hold a sentencing hearing in accordance with G.S. 15A-1334. At the sentencing hearing, the court shall, after taking the presentencing report under advisement, make written findings as to whether the defendant is classified as a sexually violent predator and the basis for the court's findings.

History.
1997-516, s. 1; 2001-373, s. 6; 2011-145, s. 19.1(h); 2017-186, s. 2(r)

§ 14-208.21. Lifetime registration procedure; application of Part 2 of this Article

Unless provided otherwise by this Part, the provisions of Part 2 of this Article apply to a person classified as a sexually violent predator, a person who is a recidivist, or a person who is convicted of an aggravated offense. The procedure for registering as a sexually violent predator, a recidivist, or a person convicted of an aggravated offense is the same as under Part 2 of this Article.

History.
1997-516, s. 1; 2001-373, s. 7

§ 14-208.22. Additional registration information required

(a) In addition to the information required by G.S. 14-208.7, the following information shall also be obtained in the same manner as set out in Part 2 of this Article from a person who is a recidivist, who is convicted of an aggravated offense, or who is classified as a sexually violent predator:

(1) Identifying factors.
(2) Offense history.
(3) Documentation of any treatment received by the person for the person's mental abnormality or personality disorder.

(b) The Department of Public Safety shall provide each sheriff with forms for registering persons as required by this Article.

(c) The Division of Adult Correction and Juvenile Justice of the Department of Public Safety shall also obtain the additional information set out in subsection (a) of this section and shall include this information in the prerelease notice forwarded to the sheriff or other appropriate law enforcement agency.

History.
1997-516, s. 1; 2001-373, s. 8; 2011-145, s. 19.1(h); 2014-100, s. 17.1(r); 2017-186, s. 2(s)

§ 14-208.23. Length of registration

A person who is a recidivist, who is convicted of an aggravated offense, or who is classified as a sexually violent predator shall maintain registration for the person's life. Except as provided under G.S. 14-208.6C, the requirement of registration shall not be terminated.

History.
1997-516, s. 1; 2001-373, s. 9

§ 14-208.24. Verification of registration information

(a) The information in the county registry shall be verified by the sheriff for each registrant who is a recidivist, who is convicted of an aggravated offense, or who is classified as a sexually violent predator every 90 days after the person's initial registration date.

(b) The procedure for verifying the information in the criminal offender registry is the same as under G.S. 14-208.9A, except that verification shall be every 90 days as provided by subsection (a) of this section.

History.
1997-516, s. 1; 2001-373, s. 10

N.C. Gen. Stat. § 14-208.25

Repealed by Session Laws 2001-373, s. 11, effective October 1, 2001.

PART 4
REGISTRATION OF CERTAIN JUVENILES ADJUDICATED FOR COMMITTING CERTAIN OFFENSES

§ 14-208.26. Registration of certain juveniles adjudicated for committing certain offenses

(a) When a juvenile is adjudicated delinquent for a violation of former G.S. 14-27.6 (attempted rape or sexual offense), G.S. 14-27.21 (first-degree forcible rape), G.S. 14-27.22 (second-degree forcible rape), G.S. 14-27.24 (first-degree statutory rape), G.S. 14-27.26 (first-degree forcible sexual offense), G.S. 14-27.27 (second-degree forcible sexual offense), or G.S. 14-27.29 (first-degree statutory sexual offense), and the juvenile was at least eleven years of age at the time of the commission of the offense, the court shall consider whether the juvenile is a danger to the community. If the court finds that the juvenile is a danger to the community, then the court shall consider whether the juvenile should be required to register with the county sheriff in accordance with this Part. The determination as to whether the juvenile is a danger to the community and whether the juvenile shall be ordered to register shall be made by the presiding judge at the dispositional hearing. If the judge rules that the juvenile is a danger to the community and that the juvenile shall register, then an order shall be entered requiring the juvenile to register. The court's findings regarding whether the juvenile is a danger to the community and whether the juvenile shall register shall be entered into the court record. No juvenile may be required to register under this Part unless the court first finds that the juvenile is a danger to the community.

A juvenile ordered to register under this Part shall register and maintain that registration as provided by this Part.

(a1) For purposes of this section, a violation of any of the offenses listed in subsection (a) of this section includes all of the following: (i) the commission of any of those offenses, (ii) the attempt, conspiracy, or solicitation of another to commit any of those offenses, (iii) aiding and abetting any of those offenses.

(b) If the court finds that the juvenile is a danger to the community and must register, the presiding judge shall conduct the notification procedures specified in G.S. 14-208.8. The chief court counselor of that district shall file the registration information for the juvenile with the appropriate sheriff.

History.
1997-516, s. 1; 1999-363, s. 2; 2012-194, s. 4(b); 2015-181, s. 33

§ 14-208.27. Change of address

If a juvenile who is adjudicated delinquent and required to register changes address, the juvenile court counselor for the juvenile shall provide written notice of the new address not later than the third business day after the change to the sheriff of the county with whom the juvenile had last registered. Upon receipt of the notice, the sheriff shall immediately forward this information to the Department of Public Safety. If the juvenile moves to another county in this State, the Department of Public Safety shall inform the sheriff of the new county of the juvenile's new residence.

History.
1997-516, s. 1; 2001-490, s. 2.36; 2008-117, s. 14; 2014-100, s. 17.1(r)

§ 14-208.28. Verification of registration information

The information provided to the sheriff shall be verified semiannually for each juvenile registrant as follows:

(1) Every year on the anniversary of a juvenile's initial registration date and six months after that date, the sheriff shall mail a verification form to the juvenile court counselor assigned to the juvenile.

(2) The juvenile court counselor for the juvenile shall return the verification form to the sheriff within three business days after the receipt of the form.

(3) The verification form shall be signed by the juvenile court counselor and the juvenile and shall indicate whether the juvenile still resides at the address last reported to the sheriff. If the juvenile has a different address, then that fact and the new address shall be indicated on the form.

History.
1997-516, s. 1; 2001-490, s. 2.37; 2006-247, s. 13; 2008-117, s. 15

§ 14-208.29. Registration information is not public record; access to registration information available only to law enforcement agenciesand local boards of education

(a) Notwithstanding any other provision of law, the information regarding a juvenile required to register under this Part is not public record and is not available for public inspection.

(b) The registration information of a juvenile adjudicated delinquent and required to register under this Part shall be maintained separately by the sheriff and released only to law enforcement agencies and local boards of education. Registry information for any juvenile enrolled in the local school administrative unit shall be forwarded to the local board of education. Under no circumstances shall the registration of a juvenile adjudicated delinquent be included in the county or statewide registries, or be made available to the public via internet.

History.
1997-516, s. 1; 2008-117, s. 12.2

§ 14-208.30. Termination of registration requirement

The requirement that a juvenile adjudicated delinquent register under this Part automatically terminates on the juvenile's eighteenth birthday or when the jurisdiction of the juvenile court with regard to the juvenile ends, whichever occurs first.

History.
1997-516, s. 1

§ 14-208.31. File with Criminal Information Network

(a) The Department of Public Safety shall include the registration information in the Criminal Information Network as set forth in G.S. 143B-905.

(b) The Department of Public Safety shall maintain the registration information permanently even after the registrant's reporting requirement expires; however, the records shall remain confidential in accordance with Article 32 of Chapter 7B of the General Statutes.

History.
1997-516, s. 1; 1998-202, s. 14; 2014-100, s. 17.1(aa)

§ 14-208.32. Application of Part

This Part does not apply to a juvenile who is tried and convicted as an adult for committing or attempting to commit a sexually violent offense or an offense against a minor. A juvenile who is convicted of one of those offenses as an adult is subject to the registration requirements of Part 2 and Part 3 of this Article.

History.
1997-516, s. 1

§§ 14-208.33 through 14-208.39

Reserved for future codification purposes.

PART 5
SEX OFFENDER MONITORING

§ 14-208.39. Legislative finding of efficacy

The General Assembly finds that empirical and statistical reports such as the 2015 California Study, "Does GPS Improve Recidivism among High Risk Sex Offenders? Outcomes for California's GPS Pilot for High Risk Sex Offender Parolees," show that sex offenders monitored with the global positioning system (GPS) are less likely than other sex offenders to receive a violation for committing a new crime, and that offenders monitored by GPS demonstrated significantly better outcomes for both increasing compliance and reducing recidivism. It is the intent of the General Assembly to protect the public from victimization. Therefore, the General Assembly recognizes that the GPS monitoring program is an effective tool to deter criminal behavior among sex offenders.

History.
2021-138, s. 18(a)

§ 14-208.40. Establishment of program; creation of guidelines; duties

(a) The Division of Adult Correction and Juvenile Justice of the Department of Public Safety shall establish a sex offender monitoring program that uses a continuous satellite-based monitoring system and shall create guidelines to govern the program. The program shall be designed to monitor three categories of offenders as follows:

(1) Any offender who is convicted of a reportable conviction as defined by G.S. 14-208.6(4) and who is required to register under Part 3 of Article 27A of Chapter 14 of the General Statutes because the defendant is classified as a sexually violent predator, is a reoffender, or was convicted of an aggravated offense as those terms are defined in G.S. 14-208.6 and based on the Division of Adult Correction and Juvenile Justice's risk assessment program requires the highest possible level of supervision and monitoring.

(2) Any offender who satisfies all of the following criteria: (i) is convicted of a reportable conviction as defined by G.S. 14-208.6(4), (ii) is required to register under Part 2 of Article 27A of Chapter 14 of the General Statutes, (iii) has committed an offense involving the physical, mental, or sexual abuse of a minor, and (iv) based on the Division of Adult Correction and Juvenile Justice's risk assessment program requires the highest possible level of supervision and monitoring.

(3) Any offender who is convicted of G.S. 14-27.23 or G.S. 14-27.28 and based on the Division of Adult Correction and Juvenile Justice's risk assessment program requires the highest possible level of supervision and monitoring.

(b) In developing the guidelines for the program, the Division of Adult Correction and Juvenile Justice shall require that any offender who is enrolled in the satellite-based program submit to an active continuous satellite-based monitoring program, unless an active program will not work as provided by this section. If the Division of Adult Correction and Juvenile Justice determines that an active program will not work as provided by this section, then the Division of Adult Correction and Juvenile Justice shall require that the defendant submit to a passive continuous satellite-based program that works within the technological or geographical limitations.

(c) The satellite-based monitoring program shall use a system that provides all of the following:

(1) Time-correlated and continuous tracking of the geographic location of the subject using a global positioning system based on satellite and other location tracking technology.

(2) Reporting of subject's violations of prescriptive and proscriptive schedule or location requirements. Frequency of reporting may range from once a day (passive) to near real-time (active).

(d) The Division of Adult Correction and Juvenile Justice may contract with a single vendor for the hardware services needed to monitor subject offenders and correlate their movements to reported crime incidents. The contract may provide for services necessary to implement or facilitate any of the provisions of this Part.

History.
2006-247, s. 15(a); 2007-213, s. 1; 2007-484, s. 42(b); 2008-117, s. 16; 2011-145, s. 19.1(h); 2015-181, s. 40; 2017-186, s. 2(t); 2021-138, s. 18(c)

§ 14-208.40A. Determination of satellite-based monitoring requirement by court

(a) When an offender is convicted of a reportable conviction as defined by G.S. 14-208.6(4), during the sentencing phase, the district attorney shall present to the court any evidence that (i) the offender has been classified as a sexually violent predator pursuant to G.S. 14-208.20, (ii) the offender is a reoffender, (iii) the conviction offense was an aggravated offense, (iv) the conviction offense was a violation of G.S. 14-27.23 or G.S. 14-27.28, or (v) the offense involved the physical, mental, or sexual abuse of a minor. The district attorney shall have no discretion to withhold any evidence required to be submitted to the court pursuant to this subsection.

The offender shall be allowed to present to the court any evidence that the district attorney's evidence is not correct.

(b) After receipt of the evidence from the parties, the court shall determine whether the offender's conviction places the offender in one of the categories described in G.S. 14-208.40(a), and if so, shall make a finding of fact of that determination, specifying whether (i) the offender has been classified as a sexually violent predator pursuant to G.S. 14-208.20, (ii) the offender is a reoffender, (iii) the conviction offense was an aggravated offense, (iv) the conviction offense was a violation of G.S. 14-27.23 or G.S. 14-27.28, or (v) the offense involved the physical, mental, or sexual abuse of a minor.

(c) If the court finds that the offender has been classified as a sexually violent predator, is a reoffender, has committed an aggravated offense, or was convicted of G.S. 14-27.23 or G.S. 14-27.28, the court shall order that the Division of Adult Correction and Juvenile Justice do a risk assessment of the offender. The Division of Adult Correction and Juvenile Justice shall have up to 60 days to complete the risk assessment of the offender and report the results to the court.

(c1) Upon receipt of a risk assessment from the Division of Adult Correction and Juvenile Justice pursuant to subsection (c) of this section, the court shall determine whether, based on the Division of Adult Correction and Juvenile Justice's risk assessment, the offender requires the highest possible level of supervision and monitoring. If the court determines that the offender does require the highest possible level of supervision and monitoring, the court shall order the offender to enroll in a satellite-based monitoring program for a period of 10 years.

(d) If the court finds that the offender committed an offense that involved the physical, mental, or sexual abuse of a minor, that the offense is not an aggravated offense or a violation of G.S. 14-27.23 or G.S. 14-27.28 and the offender is not a reoffender, the court shall order that the Division of Adult Correction do a risk assessment of the offender. The Division of Adult Correction and Juvenile Justice shall have up to 60 days to complete the risk assessment of the offender and report the results to the court.

(e) Upon receipt of a risk assessment from the Division of Adult Correction and Juvenile Justice pursuant to subsection (d) of this section, the court shall determine whether, based on the Division of Adult Correction and Juvenile Justice's risk assessment, the offender requires the highest possible level of supervision and monitoring. If the court determines that the offender does require the highest possible level of supervision and monitoring, the court shall order the offender to enroll in a satellite-based monitoring program for a period of time to be specified by the court, not to exceed 10 years.

History.
2007-213, s. 2; 2008-117, s. 16.1; 2011-145, s. 19.1(h); 2015-181, s. 41; 2017-186, s. 2(u); 2021-138, s. 18(d)

§ 14-208.40B. Determination of satellite-based monitoring requirement in certain circumstances

(a) When an offender is convicted of a reportable conviction as defined by G.S. 14-208.6(4), and there has been no determination by a court on whether the offender shall be required to enroll in satellite-based monitoring, the Division of Adult Correction and Juvenile Justice shall make an initial determination on whether the offender falls into one of the categories described in G.S. 14-208.40(a).

(b) If the Division of Adult Correction and Juvenile Justice determines that the offender falls into one of the categories described in G.S. 14-208.40(a), the district attorney, representing the Division of Adult Correction and Juvenile Justice, shall schedule a hearing in superior court for the county in which the offender resides. The Division of Adult Correction and Juvenile Justice shall notify the offender of the Division of Adult Correction and Juvenile Justice's determination and the date of the scheduled hearing by certified mail sent to the address provided by the offender pursuant to G.S. 14-208.7. The hearing shall be scheduled no sooner than 15 days from the date the notification is mailed. Receipt of notification shall be presumed to be the date indicated by the certified mail receipt. Upon the court's determination that the offender is indigent and entitled to counsel, the court shall assign counsel to represent the offender at the hearing pursuant to rules adopted by the Office of Indigent Defense Services.

(c) At the hearing, the court shall determine if the offender falls into one of the categories described in G.S. 14-208.40(a). The court shall hold the hearing and make findings of fact pursuant to G.S. 14-208.40A.

If the court finds that (i) the offender has been classified as a sexually violent predator pursuant to G.S. 14-208.20, (ii) the offender is a reoffender, (iii) the conviction offense was an aggravated offense, or (iv) the conviction offense was a violation of G.S. 14-27.23 or G.S. 14-27.28, the court shall order that the Division of Adult Correction and Juvenile Justice do a risk assessment of the offender. The Division of Adult Correction and Juvenile Justice shall have up to 60 days to complete the risk assessment of the offender and report the results to the court.

(c1) Upon receipt of a risk assessment from the Division of Adult Correction and Juvenile Justice pursuant to subsection (c) of this section, the court shall determine whether, based on the Division of Adult Correction and Juvenile Justice's risk assessment, the offender requires the highest possible level of supervision and monitoring. If the court determines that the offender does require the highest possible level of supervision and monitoring, the court shall order the offender to enroll in a satellite-based monitoring program for a period of 10 years.

If the court finds that the offender committed an offense that involved the physical, mental, or sexual abuse of a minor, that the offense is not an aggravated offense or a violation of G.S. 14-27.23 or G.S. 14-27.28, and the offender is not a reoffender, the court shall order that the Division of Adult Correction and Juvenile Justice do a risk assessment of the offender. The Division of Adult Correction and Juvenile Justice shall have up to 60 days to complete the risk

assessment of the offender and report the results to the court. The Division of Adult Correction and Juvenile Justice may use a risk assessment of the offender done within six months of the date of the hearing.

Upon receipt of a risk assessment from the Division of Adult Correction and Juvenile Justice, the court shall determine whether, based on the Division of Adult Correction and Juvenile Justice's risk assessment, the offender requires the highest possible level of supervision and monitoring. If the court determines that the offender does require the highest possible level of supervision and monitoring, the court shall order the offender to enroll in a satellite-based monitoring program for a period of time to be specified by the court, not to exceed 10 years.

History.
2007-213, s. 3; 2007-484, s. 42(b); 2008-117, s. 16.2; 2009-387, s. 4; 2011-145, s. 19.1(h); 2015-181, ss. 42, 47; 2017-186, s. 2(v); 2021-138, s. 18(e)

§ 14-208.40C. Requirements of enrollment

(a) Any offender required to enroll in satellite-based monitoring pursuant to G.S. 14-208.40A or G.S. 14-208.40B who receives an active sentence shall be enrolled and receive the appropriate equipment immediately upon the offender's release from the Section of Prisons of the Division of Adult Correction and Juvenile Justice.

(b) Any offender required to enroll in satellite-based monitoring pursuant to G.S. 14-208.40A or G.S. 14-208.40B who receives an intermediate punishment shall, immediately upon sentencing, report to the Section of Community Corrections of the Division of Adult Correction and Juvenile Justice for enrollment in the satellite-based monitoring program, and, if necessary, shall return at any time designated by that Division to receive the appropriate equipment. If the intermediate sentence includes a required period of imprisonment, the offender shall not be required to be enrolled in the satellite-based monitoring program during the period of imprisonment.

(c) Any offender required to enroll in satellite-based monitoring pursuant to G.S. 14-208.40A or G.S. 14-208.40B who receives a community punishment shall, immediately upon sentencing, report to the Section of Community Corrections of the Division of Adult Correction and Juvenile Justice for enrollment in the satellite-based monitoring program, and, if necessary, shall return at any time designated by that Section to receive the appropriate equipment.

History.
2007-213, s. 4; 2007-484, s. 42(b); 2011-145, s. 19.1(j), (k); 2017-186, s. 2(w)

§ 14-208.41. Enrollment in satellite-based monitoring programs mandatory; length of enrollment; tolling

(a) Any person described by G.S. 14-208.40(a)(1) shall enroll in a satellite-based monitoring program with the Section of Community Corrections of the Division of Adult Correction and Juvenile Justice office in the county where the person resides. The person shall remain enrolled in the satellite-based monitoring program for the registration period imposed for a period required by G.S. 14-208.40A or G.S. 14-208.40B unless the requirement to enroll in the satellite-based monitoring program is terminated or modified pursuant to G.S. 14-208.43.

(b) Any person described by G.S. 14-208.40(a)(2) who is ordered by the court pursuant to G.S. 14-208.40A or G.S. 14-208.40B to enroll in a satellite-based monitoring program shall do so with the Section of Community Corrections of the Division of Adult Correction and Juvenile Justice office in the county where the person resides. The person shall remain enrolled in the satellite-based monitoring program for the period of time ordered by the court.

(c) Any person described by G.S. 14-208.40(a)(3), upon completion of active punishment, shall enroll in a satellite-based monitoring program with the Section of Community Corrections of the Division of Adult Correction and Juvenile Justice office in the county where the person resides. The person shall enroll in the satellite-based monitoring program for the entire period of post-release supervision and shall remain enrolled in the satellite-based monitoring program for the period required by G.S. 14-208.40A or G.S. 14-208.40B unless the requirement to enroll in the satellite-based monitoring program is terminated or modified pursuant to G.S. 14-208.43. Any term of imprisonment based on revocation of probation or post-release supervision for the conviction which resulted in satellite-based monitoring tolls the period of enrollment.

History.
2006-247, s. 15(a); 2007-213, s. 13; 2007-484, s. 42(b); 2008-117, s. 17; 2008-187, s. 5; 2011-145, s. 19.1(k); 2017-186, s. 2(x); 2021-138, s. 18(f)

§ 14-208.42. Offenders required to submit to satellite-based monitoring required to cooperate with Division of Adult Correction and Juvenile Justice upon completion of sentence

Notwithstanding any other provision of law, when an offender is required to enroll in satellite-based monitoring pursuant to G.S. 14-208.40A or G.S. 14-208.40B, upon completion of the offender's sentence and any term of parole, post-release supervision, intermediate punishment, or supervised probation that follows the sentence, the offender shall continue to be enrolled in the satellite-based monitoring program for the period required by G.S. 14-208.40A or G.S. 14-208.40B unless the requirement that the person enroll in a satellite-based monitoring program is terminated or modified pursuant to G.S. 14-208.43.

The Division of Adult Correction and Juvenile Justice shall have the authority to have contact with the offender at the offender's residence or to require the offender to appear at a specific location as needed for the purpose of enrollment, to receive monitoring equipment, to have equipment examined or maintained, and for any other purpose necessary to complete the requirements of the satellite-based monitoring program. The offender shall cooperate with the Division of Adult Correction and Juvenile Justice and the requirements of the satellite-based monitoring program until the offender's requirement to enroll is terminated and the offender has returned all monitoring equipment to the Division of Adult Correction and Juvenile Justice.

History.
2006-247, s. 15(a); 2007-213, s. 5; 2007-484, s. 42(b); 2011-145, s. 19.1(h); 2017-186, s. 2(y); 2021-138, s. 18(g)

§ 14-208.43. Petition for termination or modification of the satellite-based monitoring requirement

(a) An offender described by G.S. 14-208.40(a)(1) or G.S. 14-208.40(a)(3) who is required to submit to satellite-based monitoring may file a petition for termination or modification of the monitoring requirement with the superior court in the county where the conviction occurred five years after the date of initial enrollment.

(b) The district attorney in the district in which the petition is filed shall be given notice of the petition at least three weeks before the hearing on the matter. The petitioner may present evidence in support of the petition, and the district attorney may present evidence in opposition to the requested relief or may otherwise demonstrate the reasons why the petition should be denied.

(c) The victim of the underlying offense may appear and be heard by the court in a proceeding regarding a petition for termination or modification of satellite-based monitoring requirement. If the victim has elected to receive notices of such proceedings, the district attorney's office shall notify the victim of the date, time, and place of the hearing. The district attorney's office may provide the required notification electronically or by telephone, unless the victim requests otherwise. The victim shall be responsible for notifying the district attorney's office of any changes in the victim's address and telephone number or other contact information. The judge in any court proceeding subject to this section shall inquire as to whether the victim is present and wishes to be heard. If the victim is present and wishes to be heard, the court shall grant the victim an opportunity to be reasonably heard. The right to be reasonably heard may be exercised, at the victim's discretion, through an oral statement, submission of a written statement, or submission of an audio or video statement.

(d) The petition may be granted only if the court makes all of the following findings:

(1) The petitioner has been enrolled in the satellite-based monitoring program for at least five years.

(2) The petitioner no longer requires the highest possible level of supervision and monitoring for 10 years.

(e) The court may order any of the following:

(1) The petitioner to remain enrolled in the satellite-based monitoring program for a period of time to be specified by the court, not to exceed a total of 10 years.

(2) The petitioner's requirement to enroll in the satellite-based monitoring program be terminated.

(f) If the court denies the petition, the person may again petition the court for relief in accordance with this section two years from the date of the denial of the original petition to terminate the satellite-based monitoring requirement. If the court grants the petition, the clerk of court shall forward a certified copy of the order to the Post Release Supervision and Parole Commission. The court has no authority to consider or terminate a monitoring requirement for an offender described in G.S. 14-208.40(a)(2).

History.

2006-247, s. 15(a); 2007-213, s. 11; 2007-484, s. 42(b); 2008-117, s. 18; 2011-145, s. 19.1(h); 2017-186, s. 2(z); 2021-138, s. 18(h).

§ 14-208.44. Failure to enroll; tampering with device

(a) Any person required to enroll in a satellite-based monitoring program who fails to enroll shall be guilty of a Class F felony.

(b) Any person who intentionally tampers with, removes, vandalizes, or otherwise interferes with the proper functioning of a device issued pursuant to a satellite-based monitoring program to a person duly enrolled in the program shall be guilty of a Class E felony.

(c) Any person required to enroll in a satellite-based monitoring program who fails to provide necessary information to the Division of Adult Correction and Juvenile Justice or fails to cooperate with the Division of Adult Correction and Juvenile Justice's guidelines and regulations for the program shall be guilty of a Class 1 misdemeanor.

(d) For purposes of this section, "enroll" shall include appearing, as directed by the Division of Adult Correction and Juvenile Justice to receive the necessary equipment.

History.

2006-247, s. 15(a); 2007-213, s. 6; 2011-145, s. 19.1(h); 2017-186, s. 2(aa).

§ 14-208.45. Fees

(a) Except as provided in subsections (b) and (b1) of this section, each person required to enroll pursuant to this Part shall pay a one-time fee of ninety dollars ($ 90.00). The fee shall be payable to the clerk of superior court, and the fees shall be remitted quarterly to the Division of Adult Correction and Juvenile Justice of the Department of Public Safety. This fee is intended to offset only the costs associated with the time-correlated tracking of the geographic location of subjects using the location tracking crime correlation system.

(b) When a court determines a person is required to enroll pursuant to G.S. 14-208.40A or G.S. 14-208.40B, the court may exempt a person from paying the fee required by subsection (a) of this section only for good cause and upon motion of the person required to enroll in satellite-based monitoring. The court may require that the fee be paid in advance or in a lump sum or sums, and a probation officer may require payment by those methods.

(c) When a person is required to enroll based on a determination by the Division of Adult Correction and Juvenile Justice pursuant to G.S. 14-208.40B, the Division of Adult Correction and Juvenile Justice shall have the authority to exempt the person from paying the fee only for good cause and upon request of the person required to enroll in satellite-based monitoring. The Division of Adult Correction and Juvenile Justice may require that the fee be paid in advance or in a lump sum or sums, and a probation officer may require payment by those methods.

History.

2006-247, s. 15(a); 2007-213, s. 12; 2007-484, ss. 42(a), (b); 2011-145, s. 19.1(h); 2017-186, s. 2(bb).

§ 14-208.46. Petition for postenrollment determination for lifetime satellite-based monitoring enrollees

(a) An offender who is enrolled in a satellite-based monitoring for life may file a petition for termination or modification of the monitoring requirement with the superior court in the county where the conviction occurred five years after the date of initial enrollment.

(b) The district attorney in the district in which the petition is filed shall be given notice of the petition at least three weeks before the hearing on the matter. The petitioner may present evidence in support of the petition, and the district attorney may present evidence in opposition to the requested relief or may otherwise demonstrate the reasons why the petition should be denied.

(c) The victim of the underlying offense may appear and be heard by the court in a proceeding regarding a petition for termination or modification of satellite-based monitoring requirement. If the victim has elected to receive notices of such proceedings, the district attorney's office shall notify the victim of the date, time, and place of the hearing. The district attorney's office may provide the required notification electronically or by telephone, unless the victim requests otherwise. The victim shall be responsible for notifying the district attorney's office of any changes in the victim's address and telephone number or other contact information. The judge in any court proceeding subject to this section shall inquire as to whether the victim is present and wishes to be heard. If the victim is present and wishes to be heard, the court shall grant the victim an opportunity to be reasonably heard. The right to be reasonably heard may be exercised, at the victim's discretion, through an oral statement, submission of a written statement, or submission of an audio or video statement.

(d) If the petitioner has not been enrolled in the satellite-based monitoring program for at least 10 years, the court shall order the petitioner to remain enrolled in the satellite-based monitoring program for a total of 10 years.

(e) If the petitioner has been enrolled in the satellite-based monitoring program for more than 10 years, the court shall order the petitioner's requirement to enroll in the satellite-based monitoring program be terminated.

(f) The court has no authority to terminate the satellite-based monitoring requirement for an offender ordered to satellite-based monitoring for life prior to 10 years of enrollment.

History.
2021-138, s. 18(i)

SUBCHAPTER 08.
OFFENSES AGAINST PUBLIC JUSTICE

ARTICLE 28
PERJURY

§ 14-209. Punishment for perjury.

If any person knowingly and intentionally makes a false statement under oath or affirmation in any suit, controversy, matter or cause, or in any unsworn declaration deemed sufficient pursuant to G.S. 7A-98 depending in any of the courts of the State; in any deposition or affidavit taken pursuant to law; in any oath or affirmation duly administered of or concerning any matter or thing where such person is lawfully required to be sworn or affirmed, that person is guilty of perjury, and punished as a Class F felon.

History.
1791, c. 338, s. 1, P.R.; R.C., c. 34, s. 49; Code, s. 1092; Rev., s. 3615; C.S., s. 4364; 1979, c. 760, s. 5; 1979, 2nd Sess., c. 1316, s. 47; 1981, c. 63, s. 1; c. 179, s. 14; 1993, c. 539, s. 1202; 1994, Ex. Sess., c. 24, s. 14(c); 2019-243, s. 3(c); 2021-47, s. 17(b)

§ 14-210. Subornation of perjury

If any person shall, by any means, procure another person to commit such willful and corrupt perjury as is mentioned in G.S. 14-209, the person so offending shall be punished as a Class I felon.

History.
1791, c. 338, s. 2, P.R.; R.C., c. 34, s. 50; Code, s. 1093; Rev., s. 3616; C.S., s. 4365; 1993, c. 539, s. 1203; 1994, Ex. Sess., c. 24, s. 14(c)

§ 14-211. Perjury before legislative committees

If any person shall willfully and corruptly swear falsely to any fact material to the investigation of any matter before any committee or commission of either house of the General Assembly, he shall be subject to all the pains and penalties of willful and corrupt perjury, and, on conviction in the Superior Court of Wake County, shall be punished as a Class I felon.

History.
1869-70, c. 5, s. 4; Code, s. 2857; Rev., s. 3611; C.S., s. 4366; 1977, c. 344, s. 4; 1979, c. 760, s. 5; 1979, 2nd Sess., c. 1316, s. 47; 1981, c. 63, s. 1; c. 179, s. 14; 1993, c. 539, s. 1204; 1994, Ex. Sess., c. 24, s. 14(c)

N.C. Gen. Stat. § 14-212

Repealed by Session Laws 1994, Extra Session, c. 14, s. 71(7).

§§ 14-213 through 14-216

Repealed by Session Laws 1989 (Regular Session, 1990), c. 1054, s. 6.

ARTICLE 29
BRIBERY

§ 14-217. Bribery of officials

(a) If any person holding office, or who has filed a notice of candidacy for or been nominated for such office, under the laws of this State who, except in payment of his legal salary, fees or perquisites, shall receive, or consent to receive, directly or indirectly, anything of value or personal advantage, or the promise thereof, for performing or omitting to perform any official act, which lay within the scope of his official authority and was connected with the discharge of his official and legal duties, or with the express or implied understanding that his official action, or omission to act, is to be in any degree influenced thereby, he shall be punished as a Class F felon.

(b) Indictments issued under these provisions shall specify:

   (1) The thing of value or personal advantage sought to be obtained; and

   (2) The specific act or omission sought to be obtained; and

   (3) That the act or omission sought to be obtained lay within the scope of the defendant's official authority and was connected with the discharge of his official and legal duties.

(c) Repealed by Session Laws 1993 (Reg. Sess., 1994), c. 539, s. 1207.

(d) For purposes of this section, a thing of value or personal advantage shall include a campaign contribution made or received under Article 22A of Chapter 163 of the General Statutes.

History.
1868-9, c. 176, s. 2; Code, s. 991; Rev., s. 3568; C.S., s. 4372; 1979, c. 760, s. 5; 1979, 2nd Sess., c. 1316, s. 47; 1981, c. 63, s. 1; c. 179, s. 14; 1983 (Reg. Sess., 1984), c. 1050, s. 1; 1993, c. 539, ss. 1206, 1207; 1994, Ex. Sess., c. 24, s. 14(c); 2010-169, s. 3(a); 2017-6, s. 3; 2018-146, ss. 3.1(a), (b), 6.1

§ 14-218. Offering bribes

If any person shall offer a bribe, whether it be accepted or not, he shall be punished as a Class F felon.

History.
1870-1, c. 232; Code, s. 992; Rev., s. 3569; C.S., s. 4373; 1979, c. 760, s. 5; 1979, 2nd Sess., c. 1316, s. 47; 1981, c. 63, s. 1; c. 179, s. 14; 1993, c. 539, s. 1208; 1994, Ex. Sess., c. 24, s. 14(c)

N.C. Gen. Stat. § 14-219

Repealed by Session Laws 1983, c. 780, s. 1.

§ 14-220. Bribery of jurors

If any juror, either directly or indirectly, shall take anything from the plaintiff or defendant in a civil suit, or from any defendant in a State prosecution, or from any other person, to give his verdict, every such juror, and the person who shall give such juror any fee or reward to influence his verdict, or induce or procure him to make any gain or profit by his verdict, shall be punished as a Class F felon.

History.
5 Edw. III, c. 10; 34 Edw. III, c. 8; 38 Edw. III, c. 12; R.C., c. 34, s. 34; Code, s. 990; Rev., s. 3697; C.S., s. 4375; 1979, c. 760, s. 5; 1979, 2nd Sess., c. 1316, s. 47; 1981, c. 63, s. 1; c. 179, s. 14; 1993, c. 539, s. 1209; 1994, Ex. Sess., c. 24, s. 14(c)

ARTICLE 30
OBSTRUCTING JUSTICE

§ 14-221. Breaking or entering jails with intent to injure prisoners

If any person shall conspire to break or enter any jail or other place of confinement of prisoners charged with crime or under sentence, for the purpose of killing or otherwise injuring any prisoner confined therein; or if any person shall engage in breaking or entering any such jail or other place of confinement of such prisoners with intent to kill or injure any prisoner, he shall be punished as a Class F felon.

History.
1893, c. 461, s. 1; Rev., s. 3698; C.S., s. 4376; 1979, c. 760, s. 5; 1979, 2nd Sess., c. 1316, s. 47; 1981, c. 63, s. 1; c. 179, s. 14; 1993, c. 539, s. 1210; 1994, Ex. Sess., c. 24, s. 14(c)

§ 14-221.1. Altering, destroying, or stealing evidence of criminal conduct

Any person who breaks or enters any building, structure, compartment, vehicle, file, cabinet, drawer, or any other enclosure wherein evidence relevant to any criminal offense or court proceeding is kept or stored with the purpose of altering, destroying or stealing such evidence; or any person who alters, destroys, or steals any evidence relevant to any criminal offense or court proceeding shall be punished as a Class I felon.

As used in this section, the word evidence shall mean any article or document in the possession of a law-enforcement officer or officer of the General Court of Justice being retained for the purpose of being introduced in evidence or having been introduced in evidence or being preserved as evidence.

History.

1975, c. 806, ss. 1, 2; 1979, c. 760, s. 5; 1979, 2nd Sess., c. 1316, s. 47; 1981, c. 63, s. 1; c. 179, s. 14

§ 14-221.2. Altering court documents or entering unauthorized judgments

Any person who without lawful authority intentionally enters a judgment upon or materially alters or changes any criminal or civil process, criminal or civil pleading, or other official case record is guilty of a Class H felony.

History.

1979, c. 526; 1979, 2nd Sess., c. 1316, s. 14; 1981, c. 63, s. 1; c. 179, s. 14

N.C. Gen. Stat. § 14-222

Repealed by Session Laws 1993 (Reg. Sess., 1994), c. 767, s. 30(12).

§ 14-223. Resisting officers

(a) If any person shall willfully and unlawfully resist, delay or obstruct a public officer in discharging or attempting to discharge an official duty, the person is guilty of a Class 2 misdemeanor.

(b) If any person shall willfully and unlawfully resist, delay, or obstruct a public officer in discharging or attempting to discharge an official duty, and the resistance, delay, or obstruction is the proximate cause of a public officer's serious injury, the person is guilty of a Class I felony.

(c) If any person shall willfully and unlawfully resist, delay, or obstruct a public officer in discharging or attempting to discharge an official duty, and the resistance, delay, or obstruction is the proximate cause of a public officer's serious bodily injury, the person is guilty of a Class F felony.

(d) "Serious bodily injury" is defined as bodily injury that creates a substantial risk of death, or that causes serious permanent disfigurement, coma, a permanent or protracted condition that causes extreme pain, or permanent or protracted loss or impairment of the function of any bodily member or organ, or that results in prolonged hospitalization.

History.

1889, c. 51, s. 1; Rev., s. 3700; C.S., s. 4378; 1969, c. 1224, s. 1; 1993, c. 539, s. 136; 1994, Ex. Sess., c. 24, s. 14(c); 2021-138, s. 19(a)

N.C. Gen. Stat. § 14-224

Repealed by Session Laws 1973, c. 1286, s. 26.

§ 14-225. False reports to law enforcement agencies or officers

(a) Except as provided in subsection (b) of this section, any person who shall willfully make or cause to be made to a law enforcement agency or officer any false, deliberately misleading or unfounded report, for the purpose of interfering with the operation of a law enforcement agency, or to hinder or obstruct any law enforcement officer in the performance of his duty, shall be guilty of a Class 2 misdemeanor.

(b) A violation of subsection (a) of this section is punishable as a Class H felony if the false, deliberately misleading, or unfounded report relates to a law enforcement investigation involving the disappearance of a child as that term is defined in G.S. 14-318.5 or child victim of a Class A, B1, B2, or C felony offense. For purposes of this subsection, a child is any person who is less than 16 years of age.

History.

1941, c. 363; 1969, c. 1224, s. 3; 1993, c. 539, s. 137; 1994, Ex. Sess., c. 23, ss. 1 -3; c. 24, s. 14(c); 2013-52, s. 6

§ 14-225.1. Picketing or parading

Any person who, with intent to interfere with, obstruct, or impede the administration of justice, or with intent to influence any justice or judge of the General Court of Justice, juror, witness, district attorney, assistant district attorney, or court officer, in the discharge of his duty, pickets, parades, or uses any sound truck or similar device within 300 feet of an exit from any building housing any court of the General Court of Justice, or within 300 feet of any building or residence occupied or used by such justice, judge, juror, witness, district attorney, assistant district attorney, or court officer, shall upon plea or conviction be guilty of a Class 1 misdemeanor.

History.

1977, c. 266, s. 1; 1993, c. 539, s. 138; 1994, Ex. Sess., c. 24, s. 14(c)

§ 14-225.2. Harassment of and communication with jurors

(a) A person is guilty of harassment of a juror if he:

(1) With intent to influence the official action of another as a juror, harasses, intimidates, or communicates with the juror or his spouse; or

(2) As a result of the prior official action of another as a juror in a grand jury proceeding or trial, threatens in any manner or in any place, or intimidates the former juror or his spouse.

(b) In this section "juror" means a grand juror or a petit juror and includes a person who has been drawn or summoned to attend as a prospective juror.

(c) A person who commits the offense defined in subdivision (a)(1) of this section is guilty of a Class H felony. A person who commits the offense defined in subdivision (a)(2) of this section is guilty of a Class I felony.

History.
1977, c. 711, s. 16; 1979, 2nd Sess., c. 1316, s. 15; 1981, c. 63, s. 1; c. 179, s. 14; 1985, c. 691; 1993, c. 539, s. 1211; 1994, Ex. Sess., c. 24, s. 14(c)

§ 14-226. Intimidating or interfering with witnesses

(a) If any person shall by threats, menaces or in any other manner intimidate or attempt to intimidate any person who is summoned or acting as a witness in any of the courts of this State, or prevent or deter, or attempt to prevent or deter any person summoned or acting as such witness from attendance upon such court, the person shall be guilty of a Class G felony.

(b) A defendant in a criminal proceeding who threatens a witness in the defendant's case with the assertion or denial of parental rights shall be in violation of this section.

History.
1891, c. 87; Rev., s. 3696; C.S., s. 4380; 1977, c. 711, s. 16; 1993, c. 539, s. 1212; 1994, Ex. Sess., c. 24, s. 14(c); 2004-128, s. 15; 2006-264, s. 2; 2011-190, s. 1

§ 14-226.1. Violating orders of court

Any person who shall willfully disobey or violate any injunction, restraining order, or any order lawfully issued by any court for the purpose of maintaining or restoring public safety and public order, or to afford protection for lives or property during times of a public crisis, disaster, riot, catastrophe, or when such condition is imminent, or for the purpose of preventing and abating disorderly conduct as defined in G.S. 14-288.4 shall be guilty of a Class 3 misdemeanor which may include a fine not to exceed two hundred fifty dollars ($ 250.00). This section shall not in any manner affect the court's power to punish for contempt.

History.
1969, c. 1128; 1993, c. 539, s. 139; 1994, Ex. Sess., c. 24, s. 14(c)

§ 14-226.2. Harassment of participant in neighborhood crime watch program

Any person who willfully threatens or intimidates an identifiable member or a resident in the same household as the member of a neighborhood crime watch program for the purpose of intimidating or retaliating against that person for the person's participation in a neighborhood crime watch program is guilty of a Class 1 misdemeanor including a fine of at least three hundred dollars ($ 300.00). It is a violation of this section for a person to threaten or intimidate an identifiable member or a resident in the same household as the member of a neighborhood crime watch program while that member is traveling to or from a neighborhood crime watch meeting, actively participating in a neighborhood crime watch program activity, or actively participating in an ongoing criminal investigation.

History.
2006-181, s. 3

§ 14-226.3. Interference with electronic monitoring devices

(a) For purposes of this section, the term "electronic monitoring device" includes any electronic device that is used to track the location of a person.

(b) It is unlawful for any person to knowingly and without authority remove, destroy, or circumvent the operation of an electronic monitoring device that is being used for the purpose of monitoring a person who is:

(1) Complying with a house arrest program;

(2) Wearing an electronic monitoring device as a condition of bond or pretrial release;

(3) Wearing an electronic monitoring device as a condition of probation;

(4) Wearing an electronic monitoring device as a condition of parole; or

(5) Wearing an electronic monitoring device as a condition of post-release supervision.

(c) It is unlawful for any person to knowingly and without authority request or solicit any other person to remove, destroy, or circumvent the operation of an electronic monitoring device that is being used for the purposes described in subsection (b) of this section.

(d) This section does not apply to persons who are being monitored by an electronic monitoring device pursuant to the provisions of Article 27A of Chapter 14 of the General Statutes, or Chapter 7B of the General Statutes.

(e) Violation of this section by a person who is required to comply with electronic monitoring as a result of a conviction for a criminal offense is a felony one class lower than the most serious underlying felony or a misdemeanor one class lower than the most serious underlying misdemeanor, except that, if the most serious underlying felony is a Class I felony, then violation of this section is a Class A1 misdemeanor. Violation of this section by a person who is required to comply with electronic monitoring as a condition of bond or pretrial release is a Class 1 misdemeanor. Violation of this section by any other person is a Class 2 misdemeanor.

History.
2009-415, s. 1

§ 14-227. Failing to attend as witness before legislative committees

If any person shall willfully fail or refuse to attend or produce papers, on summons of any committee of investigation of either house of the General Assembly, either select or committee of the whole, he shall be guilty of a Class 3 misdemeanor and fined not less than five hundred dollars ($ 500.00) nor more than one thousand dollars ($ 1,000).

History.
1869-70, c. 5, s. 2; Code, s. 2854; Rev., s. 3692; C.S., s. 4381; 1993, c. 539, s. 140; 1994, Ex. Sess., c. 24, s. 14(c)

ARTICLE 30A
SECRET LISTENING

§ 14-227.1. Secret listening to conference between prisoner and his attorney

(a) It shall be unlawful for any person willfully to overhear, or procure any other person to overhear, or attempt to overhear any spoken words between a person who is in the physical custody of a law-enforcement agency or other public agency and such person's attorney, by using any electronic amplifying, transmitting, or recording device, or by any similar or other mechanical or electrical device or arrangement, without the consent or knowledge of all persons engaging in the conversation.

(b) No evidence procured in violation of this section shall be admissible over objection against any person participating in such conference in any court in this State.

History.
1967, c. 187, s. 1

§ 14-227.2. Secret listening to deliberations of grand or petit jury

It shall be unlawful for any person willfully to overhear, or procure any other person to overhear, or attempt to overhear the investigations and deliberations of, or the taking of votes by, a grand jury or a petit jury in a criminal case, by using any electronic amplifying, transmitting,

or recording device, or by any similar or other mechanical or electrical device or arrangement, without the consent or knowledge of said grand jury or petit jury.

History.
1967, c. 187, s. 1

§ 14-227.3. Violation made misdemeanor

All persons violating the provisions of G.S. 14-227.1 or 14-227.2 shall be guilty of a Class 2 misdemeanor.

History.
1967, c. 187, s. 2; 1969, c. 1224, s. 6; 1993, c. 539, s. 141; 1994, Ex. Sess., c. 24, s. 14(c)

ARTICLE 31
MISCONDUCT IN PUBLIC OFFICE

§ 14-228. Buying and selling offices

If any person shall bargain away or sell an office or deputation of an office, or any part or parcel thereof, or shall take money, reward or other profit, directly or indirectly, or shall take any promise, covenant, bond or assurance for money, reward or other profit, for an office or the deputation of an office, or any part thereof, which office, or any part thereof, shall touch or concern the administration or execution of justice, or the receipt, collection, control or disbursement of the public revenue, or shall concern or touch any clerkship in any court of record wherein justice is administered; or if any person shall give or pay money, reward or other profit, or shall make any promise, agreement, bond or assurance for any of such offices, or for the deputation of any of them, or for any part of them, the person so offending in any of the cases aforesaid shall be guilty of a Class I felony.

History.
5, 6 Edw. VI, c. 16, ss. 1, 5; R.C., c. 34, s. 33; Code, s. 998; Rev., s. 3571; C.S., s. 4382; 1993, c. 539, s. 1213; 1994, Ex. Sess., c. 24, s. 14(c)

§ 14-229. Acting as officer before qualifying as such

If any officer shall enter on the duties of his office before he executes and delivers to the authority entitled to receive the same the bonds required by law, and qualifies by taking and subscribing and filing in the proper office the oath of office prescribed, he shall be guilty of a

Class 1 misdemeanor and shall be ejected from his office.

History.
Code, s. 79; Rev., s. 3565; C.S., s. 4383; 1999-408, s. 2

§ 14-230. Willfully failing to discharge duties

(a) If any clerk of any court of record, sheriff, magistrate, school board member, county commissioner, county surveyor, coroner, treasurer, or official of any of the State institutions, or of any county, city or town, shall willfully omit, neglect or refuse to discharge any of the duties of his office, for default whereof it is not elsewhere provided that he shall be indicted, he shall be guilty of a Class 1 misdemeanor. If it shall be proved that such officer, after his qualification, willfully and corruptly omitted, neglected or refused to discharge any of the duties of his office, or willfully and corruptly violated his oath of office according to the true intent and meaning thereof, such officer shall be guilty of misbehavior in office, and shall be punished by removal therefrom under the sentence of the court as a part of the punishment for the offense.

(b) No magistrate recusing in accordance with G.S. 51-5.5 may be charged under this section for recusal to perform marriages in accordance with Chapter 51 of the General Statutes.

History.
1901, c. 270, s. 2; Rev., s. 3592; C.S., s. 4384; 1943, c. 347; 1973, c. 108, s. 5; 1993, c. 539, s. 142; 1994, Ex. Sess., c. 24, s. 14(c); 2009-107, s. 1; 2015-75, s. 2

§ 14-231. Failing to make reports and discharge other duties

If any State or county officer shall fail, neglect or refuse to make, file or publish any report, statement or other paper, or to deliver to his successor all books and other property belonging to his office, or to pay over or deliver to the proper person all moneys which come into his hands by virtue or color of his office, or to discharge any duty devolving upon him by virtue of his office and required of him by law, he shall be guilty of a Class 1 misdemeanor.

History.
Rev., s. 3576; C.S., s. 4385; 1993, c. 539, s. 143; 1994, Ex. Sess., c. 24, s. 14(c)

§ 14-232. Swearing falsely to official reports

If any clerk, sheriff, register of deeds, county commissioner, county treasurer, magistrate or other county officer shall willfully swear falsely to any report or statement required by law to be made or filed, concerning or touching the county, State or school revenue, he shall be guilty of a Class 1 misdemeanor.

History.
1874-5, c. 151, s. 4; 1876-7, c. 276, s. 4; Code, s. 731; Rev., s. 3605; C.S., s. 4386; 1973, c. 108, s. 6; 1993, c. 539, s. 144; 1994, Ex. Sess., c. 24, s. 14(c)

§ 14-233. Making of false report by bank examiners; accepting bribes

If any bank examiner shall knowingly and willfully make any false or fraudulent report of the condition of any bank, which shall have been examined by him, with the intent to aid or abet the officers, owners, or agents of such bank in continuing to operate an insolvent bank, or if any such examiner shall keep or accept any bribe or gratuity given for the purpose of inducing him not to file any report of examination of any bank made by him, or shall neglect to make an examination of any bank by reason of having received or accepted any bribe or gratuity, he shall be punished as a Class I felon.

History.
1903, c. 275, s. 24; Rev., s. 3324; 1921, c. 4, s. 79; C.S., s. 4387; 1979, c. 760, s. 5; 1979, 2nd Sess., c. 1316, s. 47; 1981, c. 63, s. 1; c. 179, s. 14; 1993, c. 539, s. 1214; 1994, Ex. Sess., c. 24, s. 14(c)

§ 14-234. Public officers or employees benefiting from public contracts; exceptions

(a) (1) No public officer or employee who is involved in making or administering a contract on behalf of a public agency may derive a direct benefit from the contract except as provided in this section, or as otherwise allowed by law.

(2) A public officer or employee who will derive a direct benefit from a contract with the public agency he or she serves, but who is not involved in making or administering the contract, shall not attempt to influence any other person who is involved in making or administering the contract.

(3) No public officer or employee may solicit or receive any gift, favor, reward, service, or promise of reward, including a promise of future employment, in exchange for recommending, influencing, or attempting to influence the award of a contract by the public agency he or she serves.

(a1) For purposes of this section:

(1) As used in this section, the term "public officer" means an individual who is elected or appointed to serve or represent a public agency, other than an employee or independent contractor of a public agency.

(2) A public officer or employee is involved in administering a contract if he or she oversees the performance of the contract or has authority to make decisions regarding the contract or to interpret the contract.

(3) A public officer or employee is involved in making a contract if he or she participates in the development of specifications or terms or in the preparation or award of the contract. A public officer is also involved in making a contract if the board, commission, or other body of which he or she is a member takes action on the contract, whether or not the public officer actually participates in that action, unless the contract is approved under an exception to this section under which the public officer is allowed to benefit and is prohibited from voting.

(4) A public officer or employee derives a direct benefit from a contract if the person or his or her spouse: (i) has more than a ten percent (10%) ownership or other interest in an entity that is a party to the contract; (ii) derives any income or commission directly from the contract; or (iii) acquires property under the contract.

(5) A public officer or employee is not involved in making or administering a contract solely because of the performance of ministerial duties related to the contract.

(b) Subdivision (a)(1) of this section does not apply to any of the following:

(1) Any contract between a public agency and a bank, banking institution, savings and loan association, or with a public utility regulated under the provisions of Chapter 62 of the General Statutes.

(2) An interest in property conveyed by an officer or employee of a public agency under a judgment, including a consent judgment, entered by a superior court judge in a condemnation proceeding initiated by the public agency.

(3) Any employment relationship between a public agency and the spouse of a public officer of the agency.

(3a) Any employment relationship between a local board of education and the spouse of the superintendent of that local school administrative unit, if that employment relationship has been approved by that board in an open session meeting pursuant to the board's policy adopted as provided in G.S. 115C-47(17a).

(4) Remuneration from a public agency for services, facilities, or supplies furnished directly to needy individuals by a public officer or employee of the agency under any program of direct public assistance being rendered under the laws of this State or the United States to needy persons administered in whole or in part by the agency if: (i) the programs of public assistance to needy persons are open to general participation on a nondiscriminatory basis to the practitioners of any given profession, professions or occupation; (ii) neither the agency nor any of its employees or agents, have control over who, among licensed or qualified providers, shall be selected by the beneficiaries of the assistance; (iii) the remuneration for the services, facilities or supplies are in the same amount as would be paid to any other provider; and (iv) although the public officer or employee may participate in making determinations of eligibility of needy persons to receive the assistance, he or she takes no part in approving his or her own bill or claim for remuneration.

(b1) No public officer who will derive a direct benefit from a contract entered into under subsection (b) of this section may deliberate or vote on the contract or attempt to influence any other person who is involved in making or administering the contract.

(c) through (d) Repealed by Session Laws 2001-409, s. 1, effective July 1, 2002.

(d1) Subdivision (a)(1) of this section does not apply to (i) any elected official or person appointed to fill an elective office of a village, town, or city having a population of no more than 20,000 according to the most recent official federal census, (ii) any elected official or person appointed to fill an elective office of a county within which there is located no village, town, or city with a population of more than 20,000 according to the most recent official federal census, (iii) any elected official or person appointed to fill an elective office on a city board of education in a city having a population of no more than 20,000 according to the most recent official federal census, (iv) any elected official or person appointed to fill an elective office as a member of a county board of education in a county within which there is located no village, town or city with a population of more than 20,000 according to the most recent official federal census, (v) any physician, pharmacist, dentist, optometrist, veterinarian, or nurse appointed to a county social services board, local health board, or area mental health, developmental disabilities, and substance abuse board serving one or more counties within which there is located no village, town, or city with a population of more than 20,000 according to the most recent official federal census, and (vi) any member of the board of directors of a public hospital if all of the following apply:

(1) The undertaking or contract or series of undertakings or contracts between the village, town, city, county, county social services board, county or city board of

education, local health board or area mental health, developmental disabilities, and substance abuse board, or public hospital and one of its officials is approved by specific resolution of the governing body adopted in an open and public meeting, and recorded in its minutes and the amount does not exceed twenty thousand dollars ($ 20,000) for medically related services and sixty thousand dollars ($ 60,000) for other goods or services within a 12-month period.

(2) The official entering into the contract with the unit or agency does not participate in any way or vote.

(3) The total annual amount of contracts with each official, shall be specifically noted in the audited annual financial statement of the village, town, city, or county.

(4) The governing board of any village, town, city, county, county social services board, county or city board of education, local health board, area mental health, developmental disabilities, and substance abuse board, or public hospital which contracts with any of the officials of their governmental unit shall post in a conspicuous place in its village, town, or city hall, or courthouse, as the case may be, a list of all such officials with whom such contracts have been made, briefly describing the subject matter of the undertakings or contracts and showing their total amounts; this list shall cover the preceding 12 months and shall be brought up-to-date at least quarterly.

(d2) Subsection (d1) of this section does not apply to contracts that are subject to Article 8 of Chapter 143 of the General Statutes, Public Building Contracts.

(d3) Subsection (a) of this section does not apply to an application for or the receipt of a grant under the Agriculture Cost Share Program for Nonpoint Source Pollution Control created pursuant to Article 72 of Chapter 106 of the General Statutes, the Community Conservation Assistance Program created pursuant to Article 73 of Chapter 106 of the General Statutes, or the Agricultural Water Resources Assistance Program created pursuant to Article 5 of Chapter 139 of the General Statutes by a member of the Soil and Water Conservation Commission if the requirements of G.S. 139-4(e) are met, and does not apply to a district supervisor of a soil and water conservation district if the requirements of G.S. 139-8(b) are met.

(d4) Subsection (a) of this section does not apply to an application for, or the receipt of a grant or other financial assistance from, the Tobacco Trust Fund created under Article 75 of Chapter 143 of the General Statutes by a member of the Tobacco Trust Fund Commission or an entity in which a member of the Commission has an interest provided that the requirements of G.S. 143-717(h) are met.

(d5) This section does not apply to a public hospital subject to G.S. 131E-14.2 or a public hospital authority subject to G.S. 131E-21.

(d6) Repealed by Session Laws 2016-126, 4th Ex. Sess., s. 13, effective January 1, 2017.

(e) Anyone violating this section shall be guilty of a Class 1 misdemeanor.

(f) A contract entered into in violation of this section is void. A contract that is void under this section may continue in effect until an alternative can be arranged when: (i) immediate termination would result in harm to the public health or welfare, and (ii) the continuation is approved as provided in this subsection. A public agency that is a party to the contract may request approval to continue contracts under this subsection as follows:

(1) Local governments, as defined in G.S. 159-7(15), public authorities, as defined in G.S. 159-7(10), local school administrative units, and community colleges may request approval from the chair of the Local Government Commission.

(2) All other public agencies may request approval from the State Director of the Budget.

Approval of continuation of contracts under this subsection shall be given for the minimum period necessary to protect the public health or welfare.

History.

1825, c. 1269, P.R.; 1826, c. 29; R.C., c. 34, s. 38; Code, s. 1011; Rev., s. 3572; C.S., s. 4388; 1929, c. 19, s. 1; 1969, c. 1027; 1975, c. 409; 1977, cc. 240, 761; 1979, c. 720; 1981, c. 103, ss. 1, 2, 5; 1983, c. 544, ss. 1, 2; 1985, c. 190; 1987, c. 570; 1989, c. 231; 1991 (Reg. Sess., 1992), c. 1030, s. 5; 1993, c. 539, s. 145; 1994, Ex. Sess., c. 24, s. 14(c); 1995, c. 519, s. 4; 2000-147, s. 6; 2001-409, s. 1; 2001-487, ss. 44(a), 44(b), 45; 2002-159, s. 28; 2006-78, s. 2; 2009-2, s. 2; 2009-226, s. 1; 2010-169, s. 2(a); 2011-145, ss. 13.22A(dd), 13.23(b); 2016-126, 4th Ex. Sess., s. 13; 2018-26, s. 1; 2021-117, s. 1(a)

§ 14-234.1. Misuse of confidential information

(a) It is unlawful for any officer or employee of the State or an officer or an employee of any of its political subdivisions, in contemplation of official action by himself or by a governmental unit with which he is associated, or in reliance on information which was made known to him in his official capacity and which has not been made public, to commit any of the following acts:

(1) Acquire a pecuniary interest in any property, transaction, or enterprise or gain any pecuniary benefit which may be affected by such information or official action; or

(2) Intentionally aid another to do any of the above acts.

(b) Violation of this section is a Class 1 misdemeanor.

History.
1987, c. 616, s. 1; 1993, c. 539, s. 146; 1994, Ex. Sess., c. 24, s. 14(c)

N.C. Gen. Stat. § 14-235

Repealed by Session Laws 1994, Extra Session, c. 14, s. 72(11).

§§ 14-236, 14-237

Repealed by Session Laws 2001-409, ss. 2, 3, effective July 1, 2002.

§ 14-238. Soliciting during school hours without permission of school head

No person, agent, representative or salesman shall solicit or attempt to sell or explain any article of property or proposition to any teacher or pupil of any public school on the school grounds or during the school day without having first secured the written permission and consent of the superintendent, principal or person actually in charge of the school and responsible for it.

Any person violating the provisions of this section shall be guilty of a Class 2 misdemeanor.

History.
1933, c. 220; 1969, c. 1224, s. 8; 1993, c. 539, s. 149; 1994, Ex. Sess., c. 24, s. 14(c)

§ 14-239. Allowing prisoners to escape; punishment

If any sheriff, deputy sheriff, jailer, or other custodial personnel shall willfully or wantonly allow the escape of any person committed to that person's custody who is (i) a person charged with a crime, (ii) a person sentenced by the court upon conviction of any offense, or (iii) committed to the Juvenile Justice Section of the Division of Adult Correction and Juvenile Justice of the Department of Public Safety, that person shall be guilty of a Class 1 misdemeanor. No prosecution shall be brought against any such officer pursuant to this section by reason of a prisoner being allowed to participate pursuant to court order in any work release, work study, community service, or other lawful program, or by reason of any such prisoner failing to return from participation in any such program.

History.
1791, c. 343, s. 1, P.R.; R.C., c. 34, s. 35; Code, s. 1022; 1905, c. 350; Rev., s. 3577; C.S., s. 4393; 1973, c. 108, s. 7; 1983, c. 694; 1993, c. 539, s. 150; 1994, Ex. Sess.,

c. 24, s. 14(c); 2003-297, s. 1; 2011-145, s. 19.1(l); 2017-186, s. 2(cc)

§ 14-240. District attorney to prosecute officer for escape

It shall be the duty of district attorneys, when they shall be informed or have knowledge of any felon, or person otherwise charged with any crime or offense against the State, having within their respective districts escaped out of the custody of any sheriff, deputy sheriff, coroner, or jailer, to take the necessary measures to prosecute such sheriff or other officer so offending.

History.
1791, c. 343, s. 2, P.R.; R.C., c. 34, s. 36; Code, s. 1023; Rev., s. 2822; C.S., s. 4394; 1973, c. 47, s. 2; c. 108, s. 8

§ 14-241. Disposing of public documents or refusing to deliver them over to successor

It shall be the duty of the clerk of the superior court of each county, and every other person to whom the acts of the General Assembly, appellate division reports or other public documents are transmitted or deposited for the use of the county or the State, to keep the same safely in their respective offices; and if any such person having the custody of such books and documents, for the uses aforesaid, shall negligently and willfully dispose of the same, by sale or otherwise, or refuse to deliver over the same to his successor in office, he shall be guilty of a Class 1 misdemeanor. If the clerk of superior court or other custodian determines that the acts of the General Assembly or the appellate division reports no longer are necessary to the effective operation of his or her office, the clerk or other custodian may transfer these materials to the proper recipient for disposition as surplus State property or as otherwise directed by the State Surplus Property Agency of the Department of Administration.

History.
1881, c. 151; Code, s. 1073; Rev., s. 3598; C.S., s. 4395; 1969, c. 44, s. 26; 1993, c. 539, s. 151; 1994, Ex. Sess., c. 24, s. 14(c); 2015-40, s. 2

§ 14-242. Failing to return process or making false return

If any sheriff, deputy, or other officer, whether State or municipal, or any person who presumes to act as any such officer, not being by law authorized so to do, willfully refuses to return any precept, notice or process, to him tendered or delivered, which it is his duty to execute, or willfully makes a false return thereon, the person who willfully refused to make the return or willfully made the false return shall be guilty of a Class 1 misdemeanor.

History.

1818, c. 980, s. 3, P.R.; 1827, c. 20, s. 4; R.C., c. 34, s. 118; Code, s. 1112; Rev., s. 3604; C.S., s. 4396; 1989, c. 462; 1993, c. 539, s. 152; 1994, Ex. Sess., c. 24, s. 14(c)

§ 14-243. Failing to surrender tax list for inspection and correction

If any tax collector shall refuse or fail to surrender his tax list for inspection or correction upon demand by the authorities imposing the tax, or their successors in office, he shall be guilty of a Class 1 misdemeanor.

History.

1870-1, c. 177, s. 2; Code, s. 3823; Rev., s. 3788; C.S., s. 4397; 1983, c. 670, s. 23; 1993, c. 539, s. 153; 1994, Ex. Sess., c. 24, s. 14(c)

§ 14-244. Failing to file report of fines or penalties

If any officer who is by law required to file any report or statement of fines or penalties with the county board of education shall fail so to do at or before the time fixed by law for the filing of such report, he shall be guilty of a Class 1 misdemeanor.

History.

1901, c. 4, s. 62; Rev., s. 3579; C.S., s. 4398; 1993, c. 539, s. 154; 1994, Ex. Sess., c. 24, s. 14(c)

N.C. Gen. Stat. § 14-245

Repealed by Session Laws 1973, c. 108, s. 9.

§ 14-246. Failure of ex-magistrate to turn over books, papers and money

If any magistrate, on expiration of his term of office, or if any personal representative of a deceased magistrate shall, after demand upon him by the clerk of the superior court, willfully fail and refuse to deliver to the clerk of the superior court all dockets, all law and other books, all money, and all official papers which came into his hands by virtue or color of his office, he shall be guilty of a Class 1 misdemeanor.

History.

Code, ss. 828, 829; 1885, c. 402; Rev., s. 3578; C.S., s. 4399; 1973, c. 108, s. 10; 1993, c. 539, s. 155; 1994, Ex. Sess., c. 24, s. 14(c)

§ 14-247. Private use of publicly owned vehicle

(a) It shall be unlawful for any officer, agent or employee of the State of North Carolina, or of any county or of any institution or agency of the State, to use for any private purpose whatsoever any motor vehicle of any type or description whatsoever belonging to the State, or to any county, or to any institution or agency of the State. It is not a private purpose to drive a permanently assigned state-owned motor vehicle between one's official work station and one's home as provided in G.S. 143-341(8)i7a.

It shall be unlawful for any person to violate a rule or regulation adopted by the Department of Administration and approved by the Governor concerning the control of all state-owned passenger motor vehicles as provided in G.S. 143-341(8)i with the intent to defraud the State of North Carolina.

(b) Notwithstanding the provisions of subsection (a) of this section, county employees may carpool with each other in county vehicles as lawfully permitted by the county.

History.

1925, c. 239, s. 1; 1981, c. 859, ss. 52, 53; 1983, c. 717, s. 75

§ 14-248. Obtaining repairs and supplies for private vehicle at expense of State

It shall be unlawful for any officer, agent or employee to have any privately owned motor vehicle repaired at any garage belonging to the State or to any county, or any institution or agency of the State, or to use any tires, oils, gasoline or other accessories purchased by the State, or any county, or any institution or agency of the State, in or on any such private car.

History.

1925, c. 239, s. 2

N.C. Gen. Stat. § 14-249

Repealed by Session Laws 1981, c. 268, s. 1.

N.C. Gen. Stat. § 14-250

Repealed by Session Laws 2001-424, s. 6.14(d), effective September 26, 2001.

§ 14-251. Violation made misdemeanor

Any person, firm or corporation violating any of the provisions of G.S. 14-247 to 14-250 shall be guilty of a Class 2 misdemeanor. Nothing in G.S. 14-247 through 14-251 shall apply to the purchase, use or upkeep or expense account of the car for the executive mansion and the Governor.

History.
1925, c. 239, s. 5; 1969, c. 1224, s. 16; 1993, c. 539, s. 156; 1994, Ex. Sess., c. 24, s. 14(c)

§ 14-252. Five preceding sections applicable to cities and towns

General Statutes 14-247 through 14-251 in every respect shall also apply to cities and incorporated towns.

History.
1931, c. 31

ARTICLE 32
MISCONDUCT IN PRIVATE OFFICE

§ 14-253. Failure of certain railroad officers to account with successors

If the president and directors of any railroad company, and any person acting under them, shall, upon demand, fail or refuse to account with the president and directors elected or appointed to succeed them, and to transfer to them forthwith all the money, books, papers, choses in action, property and effects of every kind and description belonging to such company, they shall be guilty of a Class I felony. The Governor is hereby authorized, at the request of the president, directors and other officers of any railroad company, to make requisition upon the governor of any other state for the apprehension of any such president failing to comply with this section.

History.
1870-1, c. 72, ss. 1-3; Code, ss. 2001, 2002; Rev., s. 3760; C.S., s. 4400; 1993 c. 539, ss. 157, 1215; 1993 (Reg. Sess., 1994), c. 767, s. 20

§ 14-254. Malfeasance of corporation officers and agents

(a) If any president, director, cashier, teller, clerk or agent of any corporation shall embezzle, abstract or willfully misapply any of the moneys, funds or credits of the corporation, or shall, without authority from the directors, issue or put forth any certificate of deposit, draw any order or bill of exchange, make any acceptance, assign any note, bond, draft, bill of exchange, mortgage, judgment or decree, or make any false entry in any book, report or statement of the corporation with the intent in either case to injure or defraud or to deceive any person, or if any person shall aid and abet in the doing of

any of these things, he shall be punished as a Class H felon.

(b) For purposes of this section, "person" means a natural person, association, consortium, corporation, body politic, partnership, or other group, entity, or organization.

History.
1903, c. 275, s. 15; Rev., s. 3325; C.S., s. 4401; 1977, c. 809, ss. 1, 2; 1979, c. 760, s. 5; 1979, 2nd Sess., c. 1316, s. 47; 1981, c. 63, s. 1; c. 179, s. 14; 1993, c. 539, s. 1216; 1994, Ex. Sess., c. 24, s. 14(c)

ARTICLE 33
PRISON BREACH AND PRISONERS

§ 14-254.5. Definitions

The following definitions apply in this Article:

(1) **Employee.** -- Any person who is hired or contracted to work for the State or a local government.

(2) **Prisoner.** -- Any person in the custody of (i) the Division of Adult Correction and Juvenile Justice of the Department of Public Safety, (ii) any law enforcement officer, or (iii) any local confinement facility as defined in G.S. 153A-217 or G.S. 153A-230.1, including persons pending trial, appellate review, or presentence diagnostic evaluation.

History.
2018-67, s. 1

§ 14-255. Escape of working prisoners from custody

If any prisoner removed from the local confinement facility or satellite jail/work release unit of a county pursuant to G.S. 162-58 shall escape from the person having him in custody or the person supervising him, he shall be guilty of a Class 1 misdemeanor.

History.
1876-7, c. 196, s. 4; Code, s. 3455; Rev., s. 3658; C.S., s. 4403; 1991 (Reg. Sess., 1992), c. 841, s. 2.; 1993, c. 539, s. 158; 1994, Ex. Sess., c. 24, s. 14(c); 1997-443, s. 19.25(r)

§ 14-256. Prison breach and escape from county or municipal confinement facilities or officers

If any person shall break any prison, jail or lockup maintained by any county or municipality in North Carolina, being lawfully confined therein, or shall escape from the lawful custody of any superintendent, guard or officer of such prison, jail or lockup, he shall be guilty of a Class 1 misdemeanor, except that the person is guilty of a Class H felony if:

(1) He has been charged with or convicted of a felony and has been committed to the facility pending trial or transfer to the State prison system; or

(2) He is serving a sentence imposed upon conviction of a felony.

History.
1 Edw. II, st. 2d; R.C., c. 34, s. 19; Code, s. 1021; Rev., s. 3657; 1909, c. 872; C.S., s. 4404; 1955, c. 279, s. 1; 1983, c. 455, s. 1; 1993, c. 539, ss. 159, 1217; 1994, Ex. Sess., c. 24, s. 14(c); 1997-443, s. 19.25(s); 2013-389, s. 3

§ 14-256.1. Escape from private correctional facility

It is unlawful for any person convicted in a jurisdiction other than North Carolina but housed in a private correctional facility located in North Carolina to escape from that facility. Violation of this section is a Class H felony.

History.
1998-212, s. 17.23(a)

N.C. Gen. Stat. § 14-257

Repealed by Session Laws 1994, Extra Session, c. 14, s. 72(12).

§ 14-258. Providing forbidden articles or tools for escape; possessing tools for escape

(a) **Providing Forbidden Articles or Tools for Escape.** -- Any person who sells, trades, conveys, or provides any of the following to a prisoner is guilty of a Class H felony:

(1) An article forbidden by prison rules.

(2) A letter, oral message, weapon, tool, good, clothing, device, or instrument, to effect an escape, or aide in an assault or insurrection.

(b) **Increased Penalty.** -- Any violation of subdivision (2) of subsection (a) of this section that does effect an escape, assault, or insurrection is a Class F felony.

(c) **Possessing Tools for Escape.** -- Any prisoner who possesses a letter, weapon, tool, good, article of clothing, device, or instrument to do any of the following is guilty of a Class H felony:

(1) To effect an escape.

(2) Aide in an assault or insurrection.

(d) **Application.** -- The provisions of this section apply to violations committed inside or outside of the prison, jail, detention center, or other confinement facility.

History.
1873-4, c. 158; s. 12; Code, s. 3441; Rev., s. 3662; 1911, c. 11; C.S., s. 4406; 1979, c. 760, s. 5; 1979, 2nd Sess., c. 1316, s. 47; 1981, c. 63, s. 1; c. 179, s. 14; 1993, c. 539, s. 1218; 1994, Ex. Sess., c. 24, s. 14(c); 2018-67, s. 3

§ 14-258.1. Furnishing poison, controlled substances, deadly weapons, cartridges, ammunition or alcoholic beverages to inmates of charitable, mental or penal institutions or local confinement facilities; furnishing tobacco products including vapor products; or furnishing mobile phones to inmates or delinquent juveniles

(a) If any person shall give or sell to any inmate of any charitable, mental or penal institution, or local confinement facility, or if any person shall combine, confederate, conspire, aid, abet, solicit, urge, investigate, counsel, advise, encourage, attempt to procure, or procure another or others to give or sell to any inmate of any charitable, mental or penal institution, or local confinement facility, any deadly weapon, or any cartridge or ammunition for firearms of any kind, or any controlled substances included in Schedules I through VI contained in Article 5 of Chapter 90 of the General Statutes except under the general supervision of a practitioner, poison or poisonous substance, except upon the prescription of a physician, he shall be punished as a Class H felon; and if he be an officer or employee of any institution of the State, or of any local confinement facility, he shall be dismissed from his position or office.

(b) Any person who shall knowingly give or sell any alcoholic beverages to any inmate of any State mental or penal institution, or to any inmate of any local confinement facility, except for medical purposes as prescribed by a duly licensed physician and except for an ordained minister or rabbi who gives sacramental wine to an inmate as part of a religious service; or any person who shall combine, confederate, conspire, procure, or procure another or others to give or sell any alcoholic beverages to any inmate of any such State institution or local confinement facility, except for medical purposes as prescribed by a duly licensed physician and except for an ordained minister or rabbi who gives sacramental wine to an inmate as part of a religious service; or any person who shall bring into the buildings, grounds or other facilities of such institution any alcoholic beverages, except for medical purposes as prescribed by a duly licensed physician or sacramental wine brought by an ordained minister or rabbi for use as part of a religious service, shall be guilty of a Class 1 misdemeanor. If such person is an officer or employee of any institution of the State, such person shall be dismissed from office.

(c) Any person who knowingly gives or sells any tobacco products, including vapor products, as defined in G.S. 148-23.1, to an inmate in the custody of the Division of Adult Correction and Juvenile Justice of the Department of Public Safety and on the premises of a correctional facility or to an inmate in the custody of a local confinement facility, or any person who knowingly gives or sells any tobacco products, including vapor products, to a person who is not an inmate for delivery to an inmate in the custody of the Division of Adult Correction and Juvenile Justice of the Department of Public Safety and on the premises of a correctional facility or to an inmate in the custody of a local confinement facility, other than for authorized religious purposes, is guilty of a Class 1 misdemeanor.

(d) Any person who knowingly gives or sells a mobile telephone or other wireless communications device, or a component of one of those devices, to an inmate in the custody of the Division of Adult Correction and Juvenile Justice of the Department of Public Safety, to a delinquent juvenile in the custody of the Juvenile Justice Section of the Division of Adult Correction and Juvenile Justice of the Department of Public Safety, or to an inmate in the custody of a local confinement facility, or any person who knowingly gives or sells any such device or component to a person who is not an inmate or delinquent juvenile for delivery to an inmate or delinquent juvenile, is guilty of a Class H felony.

For purposes of this subsection, a delinquent juvenile in the custody of the Juvenile Justice Section of the Division of Adult Correction and Juvenile Justice of the Department of Public Safety shall mean a juvenile confined in a youth development center or a detention facility as defined in G.S. 7B-1501, and shall include transportation of a juvenile to or from confinement.

(e) Any inmate of a local confinement facility who possesses any tobacco product, as defined in G.S. 148-23.1, other than for authorized religious purposes, is guilty of a Class 1 misdemeanor.

(f) Notwithstanding subsection (c) of this section, local confinement facilities may give or sell vapor products or FDA-approved tobacco cessation products, such as over-the-counter nicotine replacement therapies, including nicotine gum, patches, and lozenges, to inmates while in the custody of the local confinement facility.

(g) Any inmate in the custody of the Division of Adult Correction of the Department of Public Safety or an inmate of a local confinement facility who possesses a mobile telephone or other wireless communication device or a component of one of those devices is guilty of a Class H felony.

(h) The prohibitions in subsections (d) and (g) of this section shall not apply to any mobile telephone or other wireless communications device provided to or possessed by an inmate of a local confinement facility if the mobile telephone or other wireless communications device has been approved by the sheriff or other person in charge of a local confinement facility for use by inmates and is provided to the inmate in a manner consistent with the approved use of that device.

History.
1961, c. 394, s. 2; 1969, c. 970, s. 6; 1971, c. 929; 1973, c. 1093; 1975, c. 804, ss. 1, 2; 1979, c. 760, s. 5; 1979, 2nd Sess., c. 1316, s. 47; 1981, c. 63, s. 1; c. 179, s. 14; c. 412, s. 4; c. 747, s. 66; 1989, c. 106; 1993, c. 539, s. 160; 1994, Ex. Sess., c. 24, s. 14(c); 2009-560, s. 3; 2011-145, s. 19.1(h); 2014-3, s. 15.2(b); 2014-115, s. 23(a); 2014-119, s. 5(a); 2015-47, s. 1; 2017-186, s. 2(dd); 2020-74, s. 26(a)

§ 14-258.2. Possession of dangerous weapon in prison

(a) Any person while in the custody of the Section of Prisons of the Division of Adult Correction and Juvenile Justice, or any person under the custody of any local confinement facility as defined in G.S. 153A-217, who shall have in his possession without permission or authorization a weapon capable of inflicting serious bodily injuries or death, or who shall fabricate or create such a weapon from any source, shall be guilty of a Class H felony; and any person who commits any assault with such weapon and thereby inflicts bodily injury or by the use of said weapon effects an escape or rescue from imprisonment shall be punished as a Class F felon.

(b) A person is guilty of a Class H felony if he assists a prisoner in the custody of the Section of Prisons of the Division of Adult Correction and Juvenile Justice or of any local confinement facility as defined in G.S. 153A-217 in escaping or attempting to escape and:

    (1) In the perpetration of the escape or attempted escape he commits an assault with a deadly weapon and inflicts bodily injury; or

    (2) By the use of a deadly weapon he effects the escape of the prisoner.

History.
1975, c. 316, s. 1; 1979, c. 760, s. 5; 1979, 2nd Sess., c. 1316, s. 47; 1981, c. 63, s. 1; c. 179, s. 14; 1983, c. 455, s. 2; 1993, c. 539, s. 1219; 1994, Ex. Sess., c. 24, s. 14(c); 2011-145, s. 19.1(j); 2017-186, ss. 2(ee), 3(a)

§ 14-258.3. Taking of hostage, etc., by prisoner

Any prisoner in the custody of the Division of Adult Correction and Juvenile Justice of the Department of Public Safety, including persons in the custody of the Division of Adult Correction and Juvenile Justice of the Department of Public Safety pending trial or appellate review or for presentence diagnostic evaluation, or any prisoner in the custody of any local confinement facility (as defined in G.S. 153A-217), or any person in the custody of any local confinement facility (as defined in G.S. 153A-217) pending trial or appellate review or for any lawful purpose, who by threats, coercion, intimidation or physical force takes, holds, or carries away any person, as hostage or otherwise, shall be punished as a Class F felon. The provisions of this section apply to: (i) violations committed by any prisoner in the custody of the Division of Adult Correction and Juvenile Justice of the Department of Public Safety, whether inside or outside of the facilities of the Division of Adult Correction and Juvenile Justice of the Department of Public Safety; (ii) violations committed by any prisoner or by any other person lawfully under the custody of any local confinement facility (as defined in G.S. 153A-217), whether inside or outside the local confinement facilities (as defined in G.S. 153A-217).

History.
1975, c. 315; 1979, c. 760, s. 5; 1979, 2nd Sess., c. 1316, s. 47; 1981, c. 63, s. 1; c. 179, s. 14; 1993, c. 539, s. 1220; 1994, Ex. Sess., c. 24, s. 14(c); 2011-145, s. 19.1(h); 2012-83, s. 19; 2017-186, s. 2(ff).

§ 14-258.4. Malicious conduct by prisoner

(a) Any prisoner who knowingly and willfully throws, emits, or causes to be used as a projectile, any bodily fluids, excrement, or unknown substance at an employee, while the employee is in the performance of the employee's duties, is guilty of a Class F felony.

(b) Any prisoner who knowingly and willfully exposes genitalia to an employee while the employee is in the performance of the employee's duties is guilty of a Class I felony.

(c) The provisions of this section apply to violations committed inside or outside of the prison, jail, detention center, or other confinement facility.

(d) Sentences imposed under this Article shall run consecutively to and shall commence at the expiration of any sentence being served by the person sentenced under this section.

History.
2001-360, s. 1; 2011-145, ss. 19.1(h), (l); 2017-186, s. 2(gg); 2018-67, s. 2.

§ 14-258.7. Annual reports of violations

(a) The Department of Public Safety and Juvenile Justice shall report the following to the chairs of the Joint Legislative Oversight Committee on Justice and Public Safety by March 15 of each year:

(1) The number of incidents of any violation of this Article, G.S. 14-34.5(b), 14-34.7(b), or 14-34.7(c)(2) involving an employee or contractor of a detention facility operated by the State.

(2) The nature of the resolution of every incident of any violation of this Article, G.S. 14-34.5(b), 14-34.7(b), or 14-34.7(c)(2) involving an employee or contractor of a detention facility operated by the State.

(b) The Conference of District Attorneys shall report the following to the chairs of the Joint Legislative Oversight Committee on Justice and Public Safety by March 15 of each year:

(1) The number of criminal charges pursuant to this Article, G.S. 14-34.5(b), 14-34.7(b), or 14-34.7(c)(2) that resulted in trial.

(2) The number of criminal charges pursuant to this Article, G.S. 14-34.5(b), 14-34.7(b), or 14-34.7(c)(2) that were resolved by a plea to a lesser-included offense.

(3) The number of criminal charges pursuant to this Article, G.S. 14-34.5(b), 14-34.7(b), or 14-34.7(c)(2) that were resolved by a voluntary dismissal or other discretionary action that effectively dismissed or reduced the original charge.

(c) The Administrative Office of the Courts shall report the following to the chairs of the Joint Legislative Oversight Committee on Justice and Public Safety by March 15 of each year:

(1) The number of violations of this Article, G.S. 14-34.5(b), 14-34.7(b), and 14-34.7(c)(2) charged.

(2) The number of violations of this Article, G.S. 14-34.5(b), 14-34.7(b), and 14-34.7(c)(2) that ended in a conviction.

(3) The number of violations of this Article, G.S. 14-34.5(b), 14-34.7(b), and 14-34.7(c)(2) that were dismissed.

History.
2018-67, s. 1.2

§ 14-259. Harboring or aiding certain persons

It shall be unlawful for any person knowing or having reasonable cause to believe, that any person has escaped from any prison, jail, reformatory, or from the criminal insane department of any State hospital, or from the custody of any peace officer who had such person in charge, or that such person is a convict or prisoner whose parole has been revoked, or that such person is a fugitive from justice or is otherwise the subject of an outstanding warrant for arrest or order of arrest, to conceal, hide, harbor, feed, clothe or otherwise aid and comfort in any manner to any such person. Fugitive from justice shall, for the purpose of this provision, mean any person who has fled from any other jurisdiction to avoid prosecution for a crime.

Every person who shall conceal, hide, harbor, feed, clothe, or offer aid and comfort to any other person in violation of this section shall be guilty of a felony, if such other person has been convicted of, or was in custody upon the charge of a felony, and shall be punished as a Class I felon; and shall be guilty of a Class 1 misdemeanor, if such other person had been convicted of, or was in custody upon a charge of a misdemeanor, and shall be punished in the discretion of the court.

The provisions of this section shall not apply to members of the immediate family of such person. For the purposes of this section "immediate family" shall be defined to be the mother, father, brother, sister, wife, husband and child of said person.

History.
1939, c. 72; 1979, c. 760, s. 5; 1979, 2nd Sess., c. 1316, s. 47; 1981, c. 63, s. 1; c. 179, s. 14; 1983, c. 564, ss. 1-3; 1993, c. 539, s. 161; 1994, Ex. Sess., c. 24, s. 14(c)

N.C. Gen. Stat. § 14-260

Recodified as § 162-55 by Session Laws 1983, c. 631, s.1.

N.C. Gen. Stat. § 14-261

Recodified as § 162-56 by Session Laws 1983, c. 631, s.2.

N.C. Gen. Stat. § 14-262

Repealed by Session Laws 1975, c. 402.

N.C. Gen. Stat. § 14-263

Repealed by Session Laws 1979, c. 760, s. 4.

N.C. Gen. Stat. § 14-264

Recodified as § 162-57 by Session Laws 1983, c. 631, s.3.

N.C. Gen. Stat. § 14-265

Repealed by Session Laws 1977, c. 711, s. 33.

ARTICLE 34
CUSTODIAL INSTITUTIONS

§ 14-266. Persuading inmates to escape

It shall be unlawful for any parent, guardian, brother, sister, uncle, aunt, or any person whatsoever to persuade or induce to leave, carry away, or accompany from any State institution, except with the permission of the superintendent or other person next in authority, any boy or girl, man or woman, who has been legally committed or admitted under suspended sentence to said institution by juvenile, recorder's, superior or any other court of competent jurisdiction.

History.
1935, c. 307, s. 1; 1937, c. 189, s. 1

§ 14-267. Harboring fugitives

It shall be unlawful for any person to harbor, conceal, or give succor to, any known fugitive from any institution whose inmates are committed by court or are admitted under suspended sentence.

History.
1935, c. 307, s. 2; 1937, c. 189, s. 2

§ 14-268. Violation made misdemeanor

Any person violating the provisions of this Article shall be guilty of a Class 1 misdemeanor.

History.
1935, c. 307, s. 3; 1993, c. 539, s. 162; 1994, Ex. Sess., c. 24, s. 14(c)

SUBCHAPTER 09.
OFFENSES AGAINST THE PUBLIC PEACE

ARTICLE 35
OFFENSES AGAINST THE PUBLIC PEACE

§ 14-269. Carrying concealed weapons

(a) It shall be unlawful for any person willfully and intentionally to carry concealed about his or her person any bowie knife, dirk, dagger, slung shot, loaded cane, metallic knuckles, razor, shuriken, stun gun, or other deadly weapon of like kind, except when the person is on the person's own premises.

(a1) It shall be unlawful for any person willfully and intentionally to carry concealed about his or her person any pistol or gun except in the following circumstances:

(1) The person is on the person's own premises.

(2) The deadly weapon is a handgun, the person has a concealed handgun permit issued in accordance with Article 54B of this Chapter or considered valid under G.S. 14-415.24, and the person is carrying the concealed handgun in accordance with the scope of the concealed handgun permit as set out in G.S. 14-415.11(c).

(3) The deadly weapon is a handgun and the person is a military permittee as defined under G.S. 14-415.10(2a) who provides to the law enforcement officer proof of deployment as required under G.S. 14-415.11(a).

(a2) This prohibition does not apply to a person who has a concealed handgun permit issued in accordance with Article 54B of this Chapter, has a concealed handgun permit considered valid under G.S. 14-415.24, or is exempt from obtaining a permit pursuant to G.S. 14-415.25, provided the weapon is a handgun, is in a closed compartment or container within the person's locked vehicle, and the vehicle is in a parking area that is owned or leased by State government. A person may unlock the vehicle to enter or exit the vehicle, provided the handgun remains in the closed compartment at all times and the vehicle is locked immediately following the entrance or exit.

(b) This prohibition shall not apply to the following persons:

(1) Officers and enlisted personnel of the Armed Forces of the United States when in discharge of their official duties as such and acting under orders requiring them to carry arms and weapons;

(2) Civil and law enforcement officers of the United States;

(3) Officers and soldiers of the militia and the National Guard when called into actual service;

(3a) A member of the North Carolina National Guard who has been designated in writing by the Adjutant General, State of North Carolina, who has a concealed handgun permit issued in accordance with Article 54B of this Chapter or considered valid under G.S. 14-415.24, and is acting in the discharge of his or her official duties, provided that the member does not carry a concealed weapon while consuming alcohol or an unlawful controlled substance or while alcohol or an unlawful controlled substance remains in the member's body.

(4) Officers of the State, or of any county, city, town, or company police agency charged with the execution of the laws of the State, when acting in the discharge of their official duties;

(4a) Any person who is a district attorney, an assistant district attorney, or an investigator employed by the office of a district attorney and who has a concealed handgun permit issued in accordance with Article 54B of this Chapter or considered valid under G.S. 14-415.24; provided that the person shall not carry a concealed weapon at any time while in a courtroom or while consuming alcohol or an unlawful controlled substance or while alcohol or an unlawful controlled substance remains in the person's body. The district attorney, assistant district attorney, or investigator shall secure the weapon in a locked compartment when the weapon is not on the person of the district attorney, assistant district attorney, or investigator. Notwithstanding the provisions of this subsection, a district attorney may carry a concealed weapon while in a courtroom;

(4b) Any person who is a qualified retired law enforcement officer as defined in G.S. 14-415.10 and meets any one of the following conditions:

a. Is the holder of a concealed handgun permit in accordance with Article 54B of this Chapter.

b. Is exempt from obtaining a permit pursuant to G.S. 14-415.25.

c. Is certified by the North Carolina Criminal Justice Education and Training Standards Commission pursuant to G.S. 14-415.26;

(4c) Detention personnel or correctional officers employed by the State or a unit of local government who park a vehicle in a space that is authorized for their use in the course of their duties may transport a firearm to the parking space and store that firearm in the vehicle parked in the parking space, provided that: (i) the firearm is in a closed compartment or container within the locked vehicle, or (ii) the firearm is in a locked container securely affixed to the vehicle;

(4d) Any person who is a North Carolina district court judge, North Carolina superior court judge, or a North Carolina magistrate and who has a concealed handgun permit issued in accordance with Article 54B of this Chapter or considered valid under G.S. 14-415.24; provided that the person shall not carry a concealed weapon at any time while consuming alcohol or an unlawful controlled substance or while alcohol or an unlawful controlled substance remains in the person's body. The judge or magistrate shall secure the weapon in a locked compartment when the weapon is not on the person of the judge or magistrate;

(4e) Any person who is serving as a clerk of court or as a register of deeds and who has a concealed handgun permit issued in accordance with Article 54B of this Chapter or considered valid under G.S. 14-415.24; provided that the person shall not carry a concealed weapon at any time while consuming alcohol or an unlawful controlled substance or while alcohol or an unlawful controlled substance remains in the person's body. The clerk of court or register of deeds shall secure the weapon in a locked compartment when the weapon is not on the person of the clerk of court or register of deeds. This subdivision does not apply to assistants, deputies, or other employees of the clerk of court or register of deeds;

(5) Sworn law-enforcement officers, when off-duty, provided that an officer does not carry a concealed weapon while consuming alcohol or an unlawful controlled substance or while alcohol or an unlawful controlled substance remains in the officer's body;

(6) State probation or parole certified officers, when off-duty, provided that an officer does not carry a concealed weapon while consuming alcohol or an unlawful controlled substance or while alcohol or an unlawful controlled substance remains in the officer's body.

(7) A person employed by the Department of Public Safety who has been designated in writing by the Secretary of the Department, who has a concealed handgun permit issued in accordance with Article 54B of this Chapter or considered valid under G.S. 14-415.24, and has in the person's possession written proof of the designation by the Secretary of the Department, provided that the person shall not carry a concealed weapon at any time while consuming alcohol or an unlawful controlled substance or while alcohol or an unlawful controlled substance remains in the person's body.

(8) Any person who is an administrative law judge described in Article 60 of Chapter 7A of the General Statutes and who has a concealed handgun permit issued in accordance with Article 54B of this Chapter or considered valid under G.S. 14-415.24, provided that the person shall not carry a concealed weapon at any time while consuming alcohol or an unlawful controlled substance or while alcohol or an unlawful controlled substance remains in the person's body.

(9) State correctional officers, when off-duty, provided that an officer does not carry a concealed weapon while consuming alcohol or an unlawful controlled substance or while alcohol or an unlawful controlled substance remains in the officer's body. If the concealed weapon is a handgun, the correctional officer must meet the firearms training standards of the Division of Adult Correction and Juvenile Justice of the Department of Public Safety.

(b1) It is a defense to a prosecution under this section that:

(1) The weapon was not a firearm;

(2) The defendant was engaged in, or on the way to or from, an activity in which the defendant legitimately used the weapon;

(3) The defendant possessed the weapon for that legitimate use; and

(4) The defendant did not use or attempt to use the weapon for an illegal purpose.

The burden of proving this defense is on the defendant.

(b2) It is a defense to a prosecution under this section that:

(1) The deadly weapon is a handgun;

(2) The defendant is a military permittee as defined under G.S. 14-415.10(2a); and

(3) The defendant provides to the court proof of deployment as defined under G.S. 14-415.10(3a).

(c) Any person violating the provisions of subsection (a) of this section shall be guilty of a Class 2 misdemeanor. Any person violating the provisions of subsection (a1) of this section shall be guilty of a Class 2 misdemeanor for the first offense and a Class H felony for a second or subsequent offense. A violation of subsection (a1) of this section punishable under G.S. 14-415.21(a) is not punishable under this section.

(d) This section does not apply to an ordinary pocket knife carried in a closed position. As used in this section, "ordinary pocket knife" means a small knife, designed for carrying in a pocket or purse, that has its cutting edge and point entirely enclosed by its handle, and that may not be opened by a throwing, explosive, or spring action.

History.

Code, s. 1005; Rev., s. 3708; 1917, c. 76; 1919, c. 197, s. 8; C.S., s. 4410; 1923, c. 57; Ex. Sess. 1924, c. 30; 1929, cc. 51, 224; 1947, c. 459; 1949, c. 1217; 1959, c. 1073, s. 1; 1965, c. 954, s. 1; 1969, c. 1224, s. 7; 1977, c. 616; 1981, c. 412, s. 4; c. 747, s. 66; 1983, c. 86; 1985, c. 432, ss. 1-3; 1993, c. 539, s. 163; 1994, Ex. Sess., c. 24, s. 14(c); 1995, c. 398, s. 2; 1997-238, s. 1; 2003-199, s. 2; 2005-232, ss. 4, 5; 2005-337, s. 1; 2006-259, s. 5(a); 2009-281, s. 1; 2011-183, s. 127(a); 2011-243, s. 1; 2011-268, s. 3; 2013-369, ss. 1, 21, 25; 2014-119, s. 12(a); 2015-5, s. 1; 2015-195, s. 1(a); 2015-215, s. 2.5; 2015-264, s. 3; 2017-186, s. 2(hh)

§ 14-269.1. Confiscation and disposition of deadly weapons

Upon conviction of any person for violation of G.S. 14-269, G.S. 14-269.7, or any other offense involving the use of a deadly weapon of a type referred to in G.S. 14-269, the deadly weapon with reference to which the defendant shall have been convicted shall be ordered confiscated and disposed of by the presiding judge at the trial in one of the following ways in the discretion of the presiding judge.

(1) By ordering the weapon returned to its rightful owner, but only when such owner is a person other than the defendant and has filed a petition for the recovery of such weapon with the presiding judge at the time of the defendant's conviction, and upon a finding by the presiding judge that petitioner is entitled to possession of same and that he was unlawfully deprived of the same without his consent.

(2), (3) Repealed by Session Laws 1994, Ex. Sess., c. 16, s. 2.

(4) By ordering such weapon turned over to the sheriff of the county in which the trial is held or his duly authorized agent to be destroyed if the firearm does not have a legible, unique identification number or is unsafe for use because of wear, damage, age, or modification. The sheriff shall maintain a record of the destruction thereof.

(4a) Repealed by Session Laws 2005-287, s. 3, effective August 22, 2005.

(4b) By ordering the weapon turned over to a law enforcement agency in the county of trial for (i) the official use of the agency or (ii) sale, trade, or exchange by the agency to a federally licensed firearm dealer in accordance with all applicable State and federal firearm laws. The court may order a disposition of the firearm pursuant to this subdivision only upon the written request of the head or chief of the law enforcement agency or a designee of the head or chief of the law enforcement agency and only if the firearm has a legible, unique identification number. If the law enforcement agency sells the firearm, then the proceeds of the sale shall be remitted to the appropriate county finance officer as provided by G.S. 115C-452 to be used to maintain free public schools. The receiving law enforcement agency shall maintain a record and inventory of all firearms received pursuant to this subdivision.

(5) By ordering such weapon turned over to the North Carolina State Crime Laboratory's weapons reference library for official use by that agency. The Laboratory shall maintain a record and inventory of all such weapons received.

(6) By ordering such weapons turned over to the North Carolina Justice Academy for official use by that agency. The North Carolina Justice Academy shall maintain a record and inventory of all such weapons received.

History.

1965, c. 954, s. 2; 1967, c. 24, s. 3; 1983, c. 517; 1989, c. 216; 1993, c. 259, s. 2; 1994, Ex. Sess., c. 16, s. 2; c. 22, s. 23; 1997-356, s. 1; 2003-378, s. 5; 2005-287, s. 3; 2011-19, s. 5; 2013-158, s. 3; 2013-360, s. 17.6(h); 2016-87, s. 2

§ 14-269.2. Weapons on campus or other educational property

(a) The following definitions apply to this section:

(1) **Educational property.** -- Any school building or bus, school campus, grounds, recreational area, athletic field, or other property owned, used, or operated by any board of education or school board of trustees, or directors for the administration of any school.

(1a) **Employee.** -- A person employed by a local board of education or school whether the person is an adult or a minor.

(1b) **School.** -- A public or private school, community college, college, or university.

(2) **Student.** -- A person enrolled in a school or a person who has been suspended or expelled within the last five years from a school, whether the person is an adult or a minor.

(3) **Switchblade knife.** -- A knife containing a blade that opens automatically by the release of a spring or a similar contrivance.

(3a) **Volunteer school safety resource officer.** -- A person who volunteers as a school safety resource officer as provided by G.S. 162-26 or G.S. 160A-288.4.

(4) **Weapon.** -- Any device enumerated in subsection (b), (b1), or (d) of this section.

(b) It shall be a Class I felony for any person knowingly to possess or carry, whether openly or concealed, any gun, rifle, pistol, or other firearm of any kind on educational property or to a curricular or extracurricular activity sponsored by a school. Unless the conduct is covered under some other provision of law providing greater punishment, any person who willfully discharges a firearm of any kind on educational property is guilty of a Class F felony. However, this subsection does not apply to a BB gun, stun gun, air rifle, or air pistol.

(b1) It shall be a Class G felony for any person to possess or carry, whether openly or concealed, any dynamite cartridge, bomb, grenade, mine, or powerful explosive as defined in G.S. 14-284.1, on educational property or to a curricular or extracurricular activity sponsored by a school. This subsection shall not apply to fireworks.

(c) It shall be a Class I felony for any person to cause, encourage, or aid a minor who is less than 18 years old to possess or carry, whether openly or concealed, any gun, rifle, pistol, or other firearm of any kind on educational property. However, this subsection does not apply to a BB gun, stun gun, air rifle, or air pistol.

(c1) It shall be a Class G felony for any person to cause, encourage, or aid a minor who is less than 18 years old to possess or carry, whether openly or concealed, any dynamite cartridge, bomb, grenade, mine, or powerful explosive as defined in G.S. 14-284.1 on educational property. This subsection shall not apply to fireworks.

(d) It shall be a Class 1 misdemeanor for any person to possess or carry, whether openly or concealed, any BB gun, stun gun, air rifle, air pistol, bowie knife, dirk, dagger, slungshot, leaded cane, switchblade knife, blackjack, metallic knuckles, razors and razor blades (except solely for personal shaving), firework, or any sharp-pointed or edged instrument except instructional supplies, unaltered nail files and clips and tools used solely for preparation of food, instruction, and maintenance, on educational property.

(e) It shall be a Class 1 misdemeanor for any person to cause, encourage, or aid a minor who is less than 18 years old to possess or carry, whether openly or concealed, any BB gun, stun gun, air rifle, air pistol, bowie knife, dirk, dagger, slungshot, leaded cane, switchblade knife, blackjack, metallic knuckles, razors and razor blades (except solely for personal shaving), firework, or any sharp-pointed or edged instrument except instructional supplies, unaltered nail files and clips and tools used solely for preparation of food, instruction, and maintenance, on educational property.

(f) Notwithstanding subsection (b) of this section it shall be a Class 1 misdemeanor rather than a Class I felony for any person to possess or carry, whether openly or concealed, any gun, rifle, pistol, or other firearm of any kind, on educational property or to a curricular or extracurricular activity sponsored by a school if:

(1) The person is not a student attending school on the educational property or an employee employed by the school working on the educational property; and

(1a) The person is not a student attending a curricular or extracurricular activity sponsored by the school at which the student is enrolled or an employee attending a curricular or extracurricular activity sponsored by the school at which the employee is employed; and

(2) Repealed by Session Laws 1999-211, s. 1, effective December 1, 1999, and applicable to offenses committed on or after that date.

(3) The firearm is not loaded, is in a motor vehicle, and is in a locked container or a locked firearm rack.

(4) Repealed by Session Laws 1999-211, s. 1, effective December 1, 1999, and

applicable to offenses committed on or after that date.

(g) This section shall not apply to any of the following:

(1) A weapon used solely for educational or school-sanctioned ceremonial purposes, or used in a school-approved program conducted under the supervision of an adult whose supervision has been approved by the school authority.

(1a) A person exempted by the provisions of G.S. 14-269(b).

(2) Firefighters, emergency service personnel, North Carolina Forest Service personnel, detention officers employed by and authorized by the sheriff to carry firearms, and any private police employed by a school, when acting in the discharge of their official duties.

(3) Home schools as defined in G.S. 115C-563(a).

(4) Weapons used for hunting purposes on the Howell Woods Nature Center property in Johnston County owned by Johnston Community College when used with the written permission of Johnston Community College or for hunting purposes on other educational property when used with the written permission of the governing body of the school that controls the educational property.

(5) A person registered under Chapter 74C of the General Statutes as an armed armored car service guard or an armed courier service guard when acting in the discharge of the guard's duties and with the permission of the college or university.

(6) A person registered under Chapter 74C of the General Statutes as an armed security guard while on the premises of a hospital or health care facility located on educational property when acting in the discharge of the guard's duties with the permission of the college or university.

(7) A volunteer school safety resource officer providing security at a school pursuant to an agreement as provided in G.S. 115C-47(61) and either G.S. 162-26 or G.S. 160A-288.4, provided that the volunteer school safety resource officer is acting in the discharge of the person's official duties and is on the educational property of the school that the officer was assigned to by the head of the appropriate local law enforcement agency.

(h) No person shall be guilty of a criminal violation of this section with regard to the possession or carrying of a weapon so long as both of the following apply:

(1) The person comes into possession of a weapon by taking or receiving the weapon

from another person or by finding the weapon.

(2) The person delivers the weapon, directly or indirectly, as soon as practical to law enforcement authorities.

(i) The provisions of this section shall not apply to an employee of an institution of higher education as defined in G.S. 116-143.1 or a nonpublic post-secondary educational institution who resides on the campus of the institution at which the person is employed when all of the following criteria are met:

(1) The employee's residence is a detached, single-family dwelling in which only the employee and the employee's immediate family reside.

(2) The institution is either:

    a. An institution of higher education as defined by G.S. 116-143.1.

    b. A nonpublic post-secondary educational institution that has not specifically prohibited the possession of a handgun pursuant to this subsection.

(3) The weapon is a handgun.

(4) The handgun is possessed in one of the following manners as appropriate:

    a. If the employee has a concealed handgun permit that is valid under Article 54B of this Chapter, or who is exempt from obtaining a permit pursuant to that Article, the handgun may be on the premises of the employee's residence or in a closed compartment or container within the employee's locked vehicle that is located in a parking area of the educational property of the institution at which the person is employed and resides. Except for direct transfer between the residence and the vehicle, the handgun must remain at all times either on the premises of the employee's residence or in the closed compartment of the employee's locked vehicle. The employee may unlock the vehicle to enter or exit, but must lock the vehicle immediately following the entrance or exit if the handgun is in the vehicle.

    b. If the employee is not authorized to carry a concealed handgun pursuant to Article 54B of this Chapter, the handgun may be on the premises of the employee's residence, and may only be in the employee's vehicle when the vehicle is occupied by the employee and the employee is immediately leaving the campus or is driving directly to their residence from off campus. The employee may possess the handgun on the employee's person outside the premises of the employee's residence when making a direct transfer of the

handgun from the residence to the employee's vehicle when the employee is immediately leaving the campus or from the employee's vehicle to the residence when the employee is arriving at the residence from off campus.

(j) The provisions of this section shall not apply to an employee of a public or nonpublic school who resides on the campus of the school at which the person is employed when all of the following criteria are met:

(1) The employee's residence is a detached, single-family dwelling in which only the employee and the employee's immediate family reside.

(2) The school is either:

    a. A public school which provides residential housing for enrolled students.

    b. A nonpublic school which provides residential housing for enrolled students and has not specifically prohibited the possession of a handgun pursuant to this subsection.

(3) The weapon is a handgun.

(4) The handgun is possessed in one of the following manners as appropriate:

    a. If the employee has a concealed handgun permit that is valid under Article 54B of this Chapter, or who is exempt from obtaining a permit pursuant to that Article, the handgun may be on the premises of the employee's residence or in a closed compartment or container within the employee's locked vehicle that is located in a parking area of the educational property of the school at which the person is employed and resides. Except for direct transfer between the residence and the vehicle, the handgun must remain at all times either on the premises of the employee's residence or in the closed compartment of the employee's locked vehicle. The employee may unlock the vehicle to enter or exit, but must lock the vehicle immediately following the entrance or exit if the handgun is in the vehicle.

    b. If the employee is not authorized to carry a concealed handgun pursuant to Article 54B of this Chapter, the handgun may be on the premises of the employee's residence, and may only be in the employee's vehicle when the vehicle is occupied by the employee and the employee is immediately leaving the campus or is driving directly to their residence from off campus. The employee may possess the handgun on the employee's person outside the premises of the employee's residence when making a direct transfer of the

Chapter 14

handgun from the residence to the employee's vehicle when the employee is immediately leaving the campus or from the employee's vehicle to the residence when the employee is arriving at the residence from off campus.

(k) The provisions of this section shall not apply to a person who has a concealed handgun permit that is valid under Article 54B of this Chapter, or who is exempt from obtaining a permit pursuant to that Article, if any of the following conditions are met:

(1) The person has a handgun in a closed compartment or container within the person's locked vehicle or in a locked container securely affixed to the person's vehicle and only unlocks the vehicle to enter or exit the vehicle while the firearm remains in the closed compartment at all times and immediately locks the vehicle following the entrance or exit.

(2) The person has a handgun concealed on the person and the person remains in the locked vehicle and only unlocks the vehicle to allow the entrance or exit of another person.

(3) The person is within a locked vehicle and removes the handgun from concealment only for the amount of time reasonably necessary to do either of the following:

a. Move the handgun from concealment on the person to a closed compartment or container within the vehicle.

b. Move the handgun from within a closed compartment or container within the vehicle to concealment on the person.

(*l*) It is an affirmative defense to a prosecution under subsection (b) or (f) of this section that the person was authorized to have a concealed handgun in a locked vehicle pursuant to subsection (k) of this section and removed the handgun from the vehicle only in response to a threatening situation in which deadly force was justified pursuant to G.S. 14-51.3.

History.
1971, c. 241, ss. 1, 2; c. 1224; 1991, c. 622, s. 1; 1993, c. 539, s. 164; c. 558, s. 1; 1994, Ex. Sess., c. 14, s. 4(a), (b); 1995, c. 49, s. 1; 1997-238, s. 2; 1999-211, s. 1; 1999-257, s. 3, 3.1; 2003-217, s. 1; 2004-198, ss. 1, 2, 3; 2006-264, s. 31; 2007-427, s. 6; 2007-511, s. 12; 2011-268, s. 4; 2013-360, s. 8.45(a), (b); 2013-369, s. 2; 2014-119, s. 9(a); 2015-195, ss. 2, 3

§ 14-269.3. Carrying weapons into assemblies and establishments where alcoholic beverages are sold and consumed

(a) It shall be unlawful for any person to carry any gun, rifle, or pistol into any assembly where a fee has been charged for admission thereto, or into any establishment in which alcoholic beverages are sold and consumed. Any person violating the provisions of this section shall be guilty of a Class 1 misdemeanor.

(b) This section shall not apply to any of the following:

(1) A person exempted from the provisions of G.S. 14-269.

(2) The owner or lessee of the premises or business establishment.

(3) A person participating in the event, if the person is carrying a gun, rifle, or pistol with the permission of the owner, lessee, or person or organization sponsoring the event.

(4) A person registered or hired as a security guard by the owner, lessee, or person or organization sponsoring the event.

(5) A person carrying a handgun if the person has a valid concealed handgun permit issued in accordance with Article 54B of this Chapter, has a concealed handgun permit considered valid under G.S. 14-415.24, or is exempt from obtaining a permit pursuant to G.S. 14-415.25. This subdivision shall not be construed to permit a person to carry a handgun on any premises where the person in legal possession or control of the premises has posted a conspicuous notice prohibiting the carrying of a concealed handgun on the premises in accordance with G.S. 14-415.11(c).

History.
1977, c. 1016, s. 1; 1981, c. 412, s. 4; c. 747, s. 66; 1993, c. 539, s. 165; 1994, Ex. Sess., c. 24, s. 14(c); 2013-369, s. 3

§ 14-269.4. Weapons on certain State property and in courthouses

It shall be unlawful for any person to possess, or carry, whether openly or concealed, any deadly weapon, not used solely for instructional or officially sanctioned ceremonial purposes in the State Capitol Building, the Executive Mansion, the Western Residence of the Governor, or on the grounds of any of these buildings, and in any building housing any court of the General Court of Justice. If a court is housed in a building containing nonpublic uses in addition to the court, then this prohibition shall apply only to that portion of the building used for court purposes while the building is being used for court purposes.

This section shall not apply to any of the following:

(1) Repealed by S.L. 1997-238, s. 3, effective June 27, 1997.

(1a) A person exempted by the provisions of G.S. 14-269(b).

(2) through (4) Repealed by S.L. 1997-238, s. 3, effective June 27, 1997,

(4a) Any person in a building housing a court of the General Court of Justice in possession of a weapon for evidentiary purposes, to deliver it to a law-enforcement agency, or for purposes of registration.

(4b) Any district court judge or superior court judge who carries or possesses a concealed handgun in a building housing a court of the General Court of Justice if the judge is in the building to discharge his or her official duties and the judge has a concealed handgun permit issued in accordance with Article 54B of this Chapter or considered valid under G.S. 14-415.24.

(4c) Firearms in a courthouse, carried by detention officers employed by and authorized by the sheriff to carry firearms.

(4d) Any magistrate who carries or possesses a concealed handgun in any portion of a building housing a court of the General Court of Justice other than a courtroom itself unless the magistrate is presiding in that courtroom, if the magistrate (i) is in the building to discharge the magistrate's official duties, (ii) has a concealed handgun permit issued in accordance with Article 54B of this Chapter or considered valid under G.S. 14-415.24, (iii) has successfully completed a one-time weapons retention training substantially similar to that provided to certified law enforcement officers in North Carolina, and (iv) secures the weapon in a locked compartment when the weapon is not on the magistrate's person.

(5) State-owned rest areas, rest stops along the highways, and State-owned hunting and fishing reservations.

(6) A person with a permit issued in accordance with Article 54B of this Chapter, with a permit considered valid under G.S. 14-415.24, or who is exempt from obtaining a permit pursuant to G.S. 14-415.25, who has a firearm in a closed compartment or container within the person's locked vehicle or in a locked container securely affixed to the person's vehicle. A person may unlock the vehicle to enter or exit the vehicle provided the firearm remains in the closed compartment at all times and the vehicle is locked immediately following the entrance or exit.

(7) Any person who carries or possesses an ordinary pocket knife, as defined in G.S. 14-269(d), carried in a closed position into the State Capitol Building or on the grounds of the State Capitol Building.

Any person violating the provisions of this section shall be guilty of a Class 1 misdemeanor.

History.
1981, c. 646; 1987, c. 820, s. 1; 1993, c. 539, s. 166; 1994, Ex. Sess., c. 24, s. 14(c); 1997-238, s. 3; 2007-412, s. 1; 2007-474, s. 1; 2009-513, s. 1; 2011-268, s. 5; 2013-369, s. 14; 2015-195, s. 1(b)

N.C. Gen. Stat. § 14-269.5

Reserved for future codification purposes.

§ 14-269.6. Possession and sale of spring-loaded projectile knives prohibited

(a) On and after October 1, 1986, it shall be unlawful for any person including law-enforcement officers of the State, or of any county, city, or town to possess, offer for sale, hold for sale, sell, give, loan, deliver, transport, manufacture or go armed with any spring-loaded projectile knife, a ballistic knife, or any weapon of similar character. Except that it shall be lawful for a law-enforcement agency to possess such weapons solely for evidentiary, education or training purposes.

(b) Any person violating the provisions of this section shall be guilty of a Class 1 misdemeanor.

History.
1985 (Reg. Sess., 1986), c. 810, s. 1; 1993, c. 539, s. 167; 1994, Ex. Sess., c. 24, s. 14(c)

§ 14-269.7. Prohibitions on handguns for minors

(a) Any minor who willfully and intentionally possesses or carries a handgun is guilty of a Class 1 misdemeanor.

(b) This section does not apply:

(1) To officers and enlisted personnel of the Armed Forces of the United States when in discharge of their official duties or acting under orders requiring them to carry handguns.

(2) To a minor who possesses a handgun for educational or recreational purposes while the minor is supervised by an adult who is present.

(3) To an emancipated minor who possesses such handgun inside his or her residence.

(4) To a minor who possesses a handgun while hunting or trapping outside the limits of an incorporated municipality if he has on his person written permission from a parent, guardian, or other person standing in loco parentis.

(c) The following definitions apply in this section:

(1) **Handgun.** -- A firearm that has a short stock and is designed to be fired by the use of a single hand, or any combination

of parts from which such a firearm can be assembled.

(2) **Minor.** -- Any person under 18 years of age.

History.
1993, c. 259, s. 1; 1994, Ex. Sess., c. 14, s. 5; 1993 (Reg. Sess., 1994), c. 597, s. 1; 2011-183, s. 9; 2011-268, s. 6

§ 14-269.8. Purchase or possession of firearms by person subject to domestic violence order prohibited

(a) In accordance with G.S. 50B 3.1, it is unlawful for any person to possess, purchase, or receive or attempt to possess, purchase, or receive a firearm, as defined in G.S. 14-409.39(2), machine gun, ammunition, or permits to purchase or carry concealed firearms if ordered by the court for so long as that protective order or any successive protective order entered against that person pursuant to Chapter 50B of the General Statutes is in effect.

(b) Any person violating the provisions of this section shall be guilty of a Class H felony.

History.
1995, c. 527, s. 2; 2003-410, s. 2; 2011-268, s. 7

§§ 14-270, 14-271

Repealed by Session Laws 1994, Extra Session, c. 14, ss. 72, 73.

§§ 14-272 through 14-275

Repealed by Session Laws 1983, c. 39, ss. 1-4.

§ 14-275.1. Disorderly conduct at bus or railroad station or airport

Any person shall be guilty of a Class 3 misdemeanor, if such person while at, or upon the premises of,

(1) Any bus station, depot or terminal, or

(2) Any railroad passenger station, depot or terminal, or

(3) Any airport or air terminal used by any common carrier, or

(4) Any airport or air terminal owned or leased, in whole or in part, by any county, municipality or other political subdivision of the State, or privately owned airport shall

(1) Engage in disorderly conduct, or

(2) Use vulgar, obscene or profane language, or

(3) On any one occasion, without having necessary business there, loiter and loaf upon the premises after being requested to leave by any peace officer

or by any person lawfully in charge of such premises.

History.
1947, c. 310; 1993, c. 539, s. 168; 1994, Ex. Sess., c. 24, s. 14(c)

N.C. Gen. Stat. § 14-276

Repealed by Session Laws 1971, c. 357.

§ 14-276.1. Impersonation of firemen or emergency medical services personnel

It is a Class 3 misdemeanor, for any person, with intent to deceive, to impersonate a fireman or any emergency medical services personnel, whether paid or voluntary, by a false statement, display of insignia, emblem, or other identification on his person or property, or any other act, which indicates a false status of affiliation, membership, or level of training or proficiency, if:

(1) The impersonation is made with intent to impede the performance of the duties of a fireman or any emergency medical services personnel, or

(2) Any person reasonably relies on the impersonation and as a result suffers injury to person or property.

For purposes of this section, emergency medical services personnel means an emergency medical responder, emergency medical technician, advanced emergency medical technician, paramedic, or other member of a rescue squad or other emergency medical organization.

History.
1981, c. 432, s. 1; 1993, c. 539, s. 169; 1994, Ex. Sess., c. 24, s. 14(c); 1997-443, s. 11A.129B; 2015-290, s. 4

§ 14-277. Impersonation of a law-enforcement or other public officer

(a) No person shall falsely represent to another that he is a sworn law-enforcement officer. As used in this section, a person represents that he is a sworn law-enforcement officer if he:

(1) Verbally informs another that he is a sworn law-enforcement officer, whether or not the representation refers to a particular agency;

(2) Displays any badge or identification signifying to a reasonable individual that the person is a sworn law-enforcement officer, whether or not the badge or other identification refers to a particular law-enforcement agency;

(3) Unlawfully operates a vehicle on a public street, highway or public vehicular area with an operating red light as defined in G.S. 20-130.1(a); or

(4) Unlawfully operates a vehicle on a public street, highway, or public vehicular area with an operating blue light as defined in G.S. 20-130.1(c).

(b) No person shall, while falsely representing to another that he is a sworn law-enforcement officer, carry out any act in accordance with the authority granted to a law-enforcement officer. For purposes of this section, an act in accordance with the authority granted to a law-enforcement officer includes:

(1) Ordering any person to remain at or leave from a particular place or area;

(2) Detaining or arresting any person;

(3) Searching any vehicle, building, or premises, whether public or private, with or without a search warrant or administrative inspection warrant;

(4) Unlawfully operating a vehicle on a public street or highway or public vehicular area equipped with an operating red light or siren in such a manner as to cause a reasonable person to yield the right-of-way or to stop his vehicle in obedience to such red light or siren;

(5) Unlawfully operating a vehicle on a public street or highway or public vehicular area equipped with an operating blue light in such a manner as to cause a reasonable person to yield the right-of-way or to stop his vehicle in obedience to such blue light.

(c) Nothing in this section shall prohibit any person from detaining another as provided by G.S. 15A-404 or assisting a law-enforcement officer as provided by G.S. 15A-405.

(d) Repealed by Session Laws 1995 (Reg. Sess., 1996), c. 712, s. 1.

(d1) Violations under this section are punishable as follows:

(1) A violation of subdivision (a)(1), (2), or (3) is a Class 1 misdemeanor.

(2) A violation of subdivision (b)(1), (2), (3), or (4) is a Class 1 misdemeanor. Notwithstanding the disposition in G.S. 15A-1340.23, the court may impose an intermediate punishment on a person sentenced under this subdivision.

(3) A violation of subdivision (a)(4) is a Class I felony.

(4) A violation of subdivision (b)(5) is a Class H felony.

(e) It shall be unlawful for any person other than duly authorized employees of a county, a municipality or the State of North Carolina, including but not limited to, the Department of Social Services, Health, Area Mental Health, Developmental Disabilities, and Substance Abuse Authority or Building Inspector to represent to any person that they are duly authorized employees of a county, a municipality or the State of North Carolina or one of the above-enumerated departments and acting upon such

representation to perform any act, make any investigation, seek access to otherwise confidential information, perform any duty of said office, gain access to any place not otherwise open to the public, or seek to be afforded any privilege which would otherwise not be afforded to such person except for such false representation or make any attempt to do any of said enumerated acts. Any person, corporation, or business association violating the provisions of this section shall be guilty of a Class 1 misdemeanor.

History.
1927, c. 229; 1985, c. 477; 1985, c. 761, s. 1; 1985 (Reg. Sess., 1986), c. 863, s. 3; 1991 (Reg. Sess., 1992), c. 1030, s. 7; 1993, c. 539, ss. 170, 171; 1994, Ex. Sess., c. 24, s. 14(c); 1995 (Reg. Sess., 1996), c. 712, s. 1; 1997-456, s. 2

§ 14-277.1. Communicating threats

(a) A person is guilty of a Class 1 misdemeanor if without lawful authority:

(1) He willfully threatens to physically injure the person or that person's child, sibling, spouse, or dependent or willfully threatens to damage the property of another;

(2) The threat is communicated to the other person, orally, in writing, or by any other means;

(3) The threat is made in a manner and under circumstances which would cause a reasonable person to believe that the threat is likely to be carried out; and

(4) The person threatened believes that the threat will be carried out.

(b) A violation of this section is a Class 1 misdemeanor.

History.
1973, c. 1286, s. 11; 1993, c. 539, s. 172; 1994, Ex. Sess., c. 24, s. 14(c); 1999-262, s. 2

§ 14-277.2. Weapons at parades, etc., prohibited

(a) It shall be unlawful for any person participating in, affiliated with, or present as a spectator at any parade, funeral procession, picket line, or demonstration upon any private health care facility or upon any public place owned or under the control of the State or any of its political subdivisions to willfully or intentionally possess or have immediate access to any dangerous weapon. Violation of this subsection shall be a Class 1 misdemeanor. It shall be presumed that any rifle or gun carried on a rack in a pickup truck at a holiday parade or in a funeral procession does not violate the terms of this act.

(b) For the purposes of this section the term "dangerous weapon" shall include those weapons specified in G.S. 14-269, 14-269.2, 14-284.1, or 14-288.8 or any other object capable of inflicting serious bodily injury or death when used as a weapon.

(c) The provisions of this section shall not apply to a person exempted by the provisions of G.S. 14-269(b) or to persons authorized by State or federal law to carry dangerous weapons in the performance of their duties or to any person who obtains a permit to carry a dangerous weapon at a parade, funeral procession, picket line, or demonstration from the sheriff or police chief, whichever is appropriate, of the locality where such parade, funeral procession, picket line, or demonstration is to take place.

(d) The provisions of this section shall not apply to concealed carry of a handgun at a parade or funeral procession by a person with a valid permit issued in accordance with Article 54B of this Chapter, with a permit considered valid under G.S. 14-415.24, or who is exempt from obtaining a permit pursuant to G.S. 14-415.25. This subsection shall not be construed to permit a person to carry a concealed handgun on any premises where the person in legal possession or control of the premises has posted a conspicuous notice prohibiting the carrying of a concealed handgun on the premises in accordance with G.S. 14-415.11(c).

History.
1981, c. 684, s. 1; 1983, c. 633; 1993, c. 412, s. 2; c. 539, s. 174; 1994, Ex. Sess., c. 24, s. 14(c); 1997-238, s. 4; 2013-369, s. 15

N.C. Gen. Stat. § 14-277.3

Repealed by Session Laws 2008-167, s. 1, effective December 1, 2008.

§ 14-277.3A. Stalking

(a) **Legislative Intent.** -- The General Assembly finds that stalking is a serious problem in this State and nationwide. Stalking involves severe intrusions on the victim's personal privacy and autonomy. It is a crime that causes a long-lasting impact on the victim's quality of life and creates risks to the security and safety of the victim and others, even in the absence of express threats of physical harm. Stalking conduct often becomes increasingly violent over time.

The General Assembly recognizes the dangerous nature of stalking as well as the strong connections between stalking and domestic violence and between stalking and sexual assault. Therefore, the General Assembly enacts this law to encourage effective intervention by the criminal justice system before stalking escalates into behavior that has serious or lethal consequences. The General Assembly intends to enact a stalking statute that permits the criminal justice system to hold stalkers accountable for a wide range of acts, communications, and conduct. The General Assembly recognizes that stalking includes, but is not limited to, a pattern of following, observing, or monitoring the victim, or committing violent or intimidating acts against the victim, regardless of the means.

(b) **Definitions.** -- The following definitions apply in this section:

(1) **Course of conduct.** -- Two or more acts, including, but not limited to, acts in which the stalker directly, indirectly, or through third parties, by any action, method, device, or means, is in the presence of, or follows, monitors, observes, surveils, threatens, or communicates to or about a person, or interferes with a person's property.

(2) **Harasses or harassment.** -- Knowing conduct, including written or printed communication or transmission, telephone, cellular, or other wireless telephonic communication, facsimile transmission, pager messages or transmissions, answering machine or voice mail messages or transmissions, and electronic mail messages or other computerized or electronic transmissions directed at a specific person that torments, terrorizes, or terrifies that person and that serves no legitimate purpose.

(3) **Reasonable person.** -- A reasonable person in the victim's circumstances.

(4) **Substantial emotional distress.** -- Significant mental suffering or distress that may, but does not necessarily, require medical or other professional treatment or counseling.

(c) **Offense.** -- A defendant is guilty of stalking if the defendant willfully on more than one occasion harasses another person without legal purpose or willfully engages in a course of conduct directed at a specific person without legal purpose and the defendant knows or should know that the harassment or the course of conduct would cause a reasonable person to do any of the following:

(1) Fear for the person's safety or the safety of the person's immediate family or close personal associates.

(2) Suffer substantial emotional distress by placing that person in fear of death, bodily injury, or continued harassment.

(d) **Classification.** -- A violation of this section is a Class A1 misdemeanor. A defendant convicted of a Class A1 misdemeanor under this section, who is sentenced to a community punishment, shall be placed on supervised probation in addition to any other punishment imposed by the court. A defendant who commits the offense of stalking after having been previously convicted of a stalking offense is guilty of

Chapter 14

a Class F felony. A defendant who commits the offense of stalking when there is a court order in effect prohibiting the conduct described under this section by the defendant against the victim is guilty of a Class H felony.

(e) **Jurisdiction.** -- Pursuant to G.S. 15A-134, if any part of the offense occurred within North Carolina, including the defendant's course of conduct or the effect on the victim, then the defendant may be prosecuted in this State.

History.
2008-167, s. 2

§ 14-277.4. Obstruction of health care facilities

(a) No person shall obstruct or block another person's access to or egress from a health care facility or from the common areas of the real property upon which the facility is located in a manner that deprives or delays the person from obtaining or providing health care services in the facility.

(b) No person shall injure or threaten to injure a person who is or has been:
(1) Obtaining health care services;
(2) Lawfully aiding another to obtain health care services; or
(3) Providing health care services.

(c) A violation of subsection (a) or (b) of this section is a Class 2 misdemeanor. A second conviction for a violation of either subsection (a) or (b) of this section within three years of the first shall be punishable as a Class 1 misdemeanor. A third or subsequent conviction for a violation of either subsection (a) or (b) of this section within three years of the second or most recent conviction shall be punishable as a Class I felony.

(d) Any person aggrieved under this section may seek injunctive relief in a court of competent jurisdiction to prevent threatened or further violations of this section. Any violation of an injunction obtained pursuant to this section constitutes criminal contempt and shall be punishable by a term of imprisonment of not less than 30 days and no more than 12 months.

(e) This section shall not prohibit any person from engaging in lawful speech or picketing which does not impede or deny another person's access to health care services or to a health care facility or interfere with the delivery of health care services within a health care facility.

(f) "Health care facility" as used in this section means any hospital, clinic, or other facility that is licensed to administer medical treatment or the primary function of which is to provide medical treatment in this State.

(g) "Health care services" as used in this section means services provided in a health care facility.

(h) Persons subject to the prohibitions in subsection (a) of this section do not include owners, officers, agents, or employees of the health care facility or law enforcement officers acting to protect real or personal property.

History.
1993, c. 412, s. 1; 1994, Ex. Sess., c. 14, s. 6; 1993 (Reg. Sess., 1994), c. 767, s. 21

§ 14-277.4A. Targeted picketing of a residence

(a) **Definitions.** -- As used in this section:
(1) "Residence" means any single-family or multifamily dwelling unit that is not being used as a targeted occupant's sole place of business or as a place of public meeting.
(2) "Targeted picketing" means picketing, with or without signs, that is specifically directed toward a residence, or one or more occupants of the residence, and that takes place on that portion of a sidewalk or street in front of the residence, in front of an adjoining residence, or on either side of the residence.

(b) It shall be unlawful for a person to engage in targeted picketing when the person knows or should know that the manner in which they are picketing would cause in a reasonable person any of the following:
(1) Fear for the person's safety or the safety of the person's immediate family or close personal associates.
(2) Substantial emotional distress. For the purposes of this subdivision, "substantial emotional distress" is defined as in G.S. 14-277.3A(b)(4).

(c) Any person who commits the offense defined in this section is guilty of a Class 2 misdemeanor.

(d) Any person aggrieved under this section may seek injunctive relief in a court of competent jurisdiction to prevent threatened or further violations of this section. Any violation of an injunction obtained pursuant to this section constitutes criminal contempt and shall be punishable by a term of imprisonment of not less than 30 days and no more than 12 months.

(e) Nothing in this section shall be construed to prohibit general picketing that proceeds through residential neighborhoods or that proceeds past residences.

History.
2009-300, s. 1

§ 14-277.5. Making a false report concerning mass violence on educational property

Chapter 14

(a) The following definitions apply in this section:

(1) **Educational property.** -- As defined in G.S. 14-269.2.

(2) **Mass violence.** -- Physical injury that a reasonable person would conclude could lead to permanent injury (including mental or emotional injury) or death to two or more people.

(3) **School.** -- As defined in G.S. 14-269.2.

(b) A person who, by any means of communication to any person or groups of persons, makes a report, knowing or having reason to know the report is false, that an act of mass violence is going to occur on educational property or at a curricular or extracurricular activity sponsored by a school, is guilty of a Class H felony.

(c) The court may order a person convicted under this section to pay restitution, including costs and consequential damages resulting from the disruption of the normal activity that would have otherwise occurred on the premises but for the false report, pursuant to Article 81C of Chapter 15A of the General Statutes.

History.
2007-196, s. 1

§ 14-277.6. Communicating a threat of mass violence on educational property

(a) A person who, by any means of communication to any person or groups of persons, threatens to commit an act of mass violence on educational property or at a curricular or extracurricular activity sponsored by a school is guilty of a Class H felony.

(b) The definitions in G.S. 14-277.5 apply to this section.

History.
2018-72, s. 1

§ 14-277.7. Communicating a threat of mass violence at a place of religious worship

(a) A person who, by any means of communication to any person or groups of persons, threatens to commit an act of mass violence at a place of religious worship is guilty of a Class H felony.

(b) The following definitions apply to this section:

(1) **Mass violence.** -- As defined in G.S. 14-277.5(a)(2).

(2) **Place of religious worship.** -- Any church, chapel, meetinghouse, synagogue, temple, longhouse, or mosque, or other building that is regularly used, and clearly identifiable, as a place for religious worship.

History.
2018-72, s. 2

§ 14-277.8. Conditional discharge for first offenders under the age of 20 years

(a) Whenever any person who has not previously been convicted of any felony or misdemeanor other than a traffic violation under the laws of the United States or the laws of this State or any other state pleads guilty to or is guilty of a violation of G.S. 14-277.5, 14-277.6, or 14-277.7, and the offense was committed before the person attained the age of 20 years, the court shall, without entering a judgment of guilt and with the consent of the defendant and the District Attorney, defer further proceedings and place the defendant on probation upon such reasonable terms and conditions as the court may require.

(b) If the court, in its discretion, defers proceedings pursuant to this section, it shall place the defendant on supervised probation for not less than one year. In addition to any other conditions of probation, the court shall require the defendant to complete a minimum of 30 hours of community service, to obtain a mental health evaluation, and to comply with any treatment recommended as a result of the mental health evaluation. Prior to taking any action to discharge and dismiss under this section, the court shall make a finding that the defendant has no previous criminal convictions. Upon fulfillment of the terms and conditions of the probation provided for in this section, the court shall discharge the defendant and dismiss the proceedings against the defendant.

(c) Discharge and dismissal under this section shall be without court adjudication of guilt and shall not be deemed a conviction for purposes of this section or for purposes of disqualifications or disabilities imposed by law upon conviction of a crime. Discharge and dismissal under this section may occur only once with respect to any person. Disposition of a case to determine discharge and dismissal under this section at the district court division of the General Court of Justice shall be final for the purpose of appeal. Upon violation of a term or condition of the probation provided for in this section, the court may enter an adjudication of guilt and proceed as otherwise provided.

(d) Upon discharge and dismissal pursuant to this section, the person may apply for an order to expunge the complete record of the proceedings resulting in the dismissal and discharge, pursuant to the procedures and requirements set forth in G.S. 15A-145.7.

(e) The clerk shall notify State and local agencies of the court's order as provided in G.S. 15A-150.

History.
2018-72, s. 3

SUBCHAPTER 10.
OFFENSES AGAINST THE PUBLIC SAFETY

ARTICLE 36
OFFENSES AGAINST THE PUBLIC SAFETY

§ 14-278. Willful injury to property of railroads

It shall be unlawful for any person to willfully, with intent to cause injury to any person passing over the railroad or damage to the equipment traveling on such road, put or place any matter or thing upon, over or near any railroad track, or destroy, injure, tamper with, or remove the roadbed, or any part thereof, or any rail, sill or other part of the fixtures appurtenant to or constituting or supporting any portion of the track of such railroad, and the person so offending shall be punished as a Class I felon.

History.
1838, c. 38; R.C., c. 34, ss. 99, 100; 1879, c. 255, s. 2; Code, s. 1098; Rev., s. 3754; 1911, c. 200; C.S., s. 4417; 1967, c. 1082, s. 1; 1979, c. 760, s. 5; 1979, 2nd Sess., c. 1316, s. 47; 1981, c. 63, s. 1; c. 179, s. 14; 1985, c. 577, s. 1; 1993, c. 539, s. 1221; 1994, Ex. Sess., c. 24, s. 14(c)

§ 14-279. Unlawful injury to property of railroads

Any person who, without intent to cause injury to any person or damage to equipment, commits any of the acts referred to in G.S. 14-278 shall be guilty of a Class 2 misdemeanor.

History.
R.C., c. 34, s. 101; Code, s. 1099; Rev., s. 3755; C.S., s. 4418; 1967, c. 1082, s. 2; 1985, c. 577, s. 2; 1993, c. 539, s. 175; 1994, Ex. Sess., c. 24, s. 14(c)

§ 14-279.1. Unlawful impairment of operation of railroads

Any person who, without authorization of the affected railroad company, shall willfully do or cause to be done any act to railroad engines, equipment, or rolling stock so as to impede or prevent movement of railroad trains or so as to impair the operation of railroad equipment shall be guilty of a Class 2 misdemeanor.

History.
1979, c. 387, s. 1; 1993, c. 539, s. 176; 1994, Ex. Sess., c. 24, s. 14(c)

§ 14-280. Shooting or throwing at trains or passengers

If any person shall willfully cast, throw or shoot any stone, rock, bullet, shot, pellet or other missile at, against, or into any railroad car, locomotive or train, or any person thereon, while such car or locomotive shall be in progress from one station to another, or while such car, locomotive or train shall be stopped for any purpose, the person so offending shall be guilty of a Class I felony.

History.
1876-7, c. 4; Code, s. 1100; 1887, c. 19; Rev., s. 3763; 1911, c. 179; C.S., s. 4419; 1985, c. 577, s. 3; 1993, c. 539, s. 1222; 1994, Ex. Sess., c. 24, s. 14(c)

§ 14-280.1. Trespassing on railroad right-of-way

(a) **Offense.** -- A person commits the offense of trespassing on railroad right-of-way if the person enters and remains on the railroad right-of-way without the consent of the railroad company or the person operating the railroad or without authority granted pursuant to State or federal law.

(b) **Crossings.** -- Nothing in this section shall apply to a person crossing the railroad right-of-way at a public or private crossing.

(c) **Legally Abandoned Rights-of-Way.** -- This section shall not apply to any right-of-way that has been legally abandoned pursuant to an order of a federal or State agency having jurisdiction over the right-of-way and is not being used for railroad services.

(d) **Classification.** -- Trespassing on railroad right-of-way is a Class 3 misdemeanor.

History.
2000-146, s. 10

§ 14-280.2. Use of a laser device towards an aircraft

(a) Any person who, willfully points a laser device at an aircraft, while the device is emitting a laser beam, and while the aircraft is taking off, landing, in flight, or otherwise in motion, is guilty of a Class H felony.

(b) The following definitions apply to this section:

(1) "Aircraft" is as defined in G.S. 63-1.

(2) "Laser" is as defined in G.S. 14-34.8.

(c) This section shall not apply where the laser use had been approved by a State or federal agency.

History.
2005-329, s. 1

§ 14-280.3. Interference with manned aircraft by unmanned aircraft systems

(a) Any person who willfully damages, disrupts the operation of, or otherwise interferes with a manned aircraft through use of an unmanned aircraft system, while the manned aircraft is taking off, landing, in flight, or otherwise in motion, is guilty of a Class H felony.

(b) The following definitions apply to this section:

(1) **Manned aircraft.** -- As defined in G.S. 15A-300.1.

(2) **Unmanned aircraft system.** -- As defined in G.S. 15A-300.1.

History.
2014-100, s. 34.30(c)

§ 14-281. Operating trains and streetcars while intoxicated

Any train dispatcher, telegraph operator, engineer, fireman, flagman, brakeman, switchman, conductor, motorman, or other employee of any steam, street, suburban or interurban railway company, who shall be intoxicated while engaged in running or operating, or assisting in running or operating, any railway train, shifting-engine, or street or other electric car, shall be guilty of a Class 2 misdemeanor.

History.
1871-2, c. 138, s. 38; Code, s. 1972; 1891, c. 114; Rev., s. 3758; 1907, c. 330; C.S., s. 4420; 1969, c. 1224, s. 3; 1993, c. 539, s. 177; 1994, Ex. Sess., c. 24, s. 14(c)

§ 14-281.1. Throwing, dropping, etc., objects at sporting events

It shall be unlawful for any person to throw, drop, pour, release, discharge, expose or place in an area where an athletic contest or sporting event is taking place any substance or object that shall be likely to cause injury to persons participating in or attending such contests or events or to cause damage to animals, vehicles, equipment, devices, or other things used in connection with such contests or events. Any person violating the provisions of this section shall be guilty of a Class 3 misdemeanor.

History.
1977, c. 772, s. 1; 1993, c. 539, s. 178; 1994, Ex. Sess., c. 24, s. 14(c)

§ 14-282. Displaying false lights on seashore

If any person shall make or display, or cause to be made or displayed, any false light or beacon on or near the seacoast, for the purpose of deceiving and misleading masters of vessels, and thereby putting them in danger of shipwreck, he shall be guilty of a Class I felony.

History.
1831, c. 42; R.C., c. 34, s. 58; Code, s. 1024; Rev., s. 3430; C.S., s. 4421; 1979, 2nd Sess., c. 1316, s. 16; 1981, c. 63, s. 1; c. 179, s. 14; 1993, c. 539, s. 1223; 1994, Ex. Sess., c. 24, s. 14(c)

§ 14-283. Exploding dynamite cartridges and bombs

If any person shall fire off or explode, or cause to be fired off or exploded, except for mechanical purposes in a legitimate business, any dynamite cartridge, bomb or other explosive of a like nature, he shall be guilty of a Class 1 misdemeanor.

History.
1887, c. 364, s. 53; Rev., s. 3794; C.S., s. 4423; 1993, c. 539, s. 179; 1994, Ex. Sess., c. 24, s. 14(c)

§ 14-284. Keeping for sale or selling explosives without a license

If any dealer or other person shall sell or keep for sale any dynamite cartridges, bombs or other combustibles of a like kind, without first having obtained from the board of commissioners of the county where such person or dealer resides a license for that purpose, he shall be guilty of a Class 1 misdemeanor.

History.
1887, c. 364, ss. 1, 4; Rev., s. 3817; C.S., s. 4425; 1993, c. 539, s. 180; 1994, Ex. Sess., c. 24, s. 14(c)

§ 14-284.1. Regulation of sale of explosives; reports; storage

(a) No person shall sell or deliver any dynamite or other powerful explosives as hereinafter defined without being satisfied as to the identity of the purchaser or the one to receive such explosives and then only upon the written application signed by the person or agent of the person purchasing or receiving such explosive, which application must contain a statement of the purpose for which such explosive is to be used.

(b) All persons delivering or selling such explosives shall keep a complete record of all sales or deliveries made, including the amounts sold and delivered, the names of the purchasers or the one to whom the deliveries were made, the dates of all such sales or such deliveries and the use to be made of such explosive, and shall preserve such record and make the same available to any law-enforcement officer during business hours for a period of 12 months thereafter.

(c) All persons having dynamite or other powerful explosives in their possession or under their control shall at all times keep such explosives in a safe and secure manner, and when such explosives are not in the course of being used they shall be stored and protected against theft or other unauthorized possession.

(d) As used in this section, the term "powerful explosives" includes, but shall not be limited to, nitroglycerin, trinitrotoluene, and blasting caps, detonators and fuses for the explosion thereof.

(e) Any person violating the provisions of this section shall be guilty of a Class 2 misdemeanor.

(f) The provisions of this section are intended to apply only to sales to those who purchase for use. Nothing herein contained is intended to apply to a sale made by a manufacturer, jobber, or wholesaler to a retail merchant for resale by said merchant.

(g) Nothing herein contained shall be construed as repealing any law now prohibiting the sale of firecrackers or other explosives; nor shall this section be construed as authorizing the sale of explosives now prohibited by law.

History.
1953, c. 877; 1969, c. 1224, s. 6; 1993, c. 539, s. 181; 1994, Ex. Sess., c. 24, s. 14(c).

§ 14-284.2. Dumping of toxic substances

(a) It shall be unlawful to deposit, place, dump, discharge, spill, release, burn, incinerate, or otherwise dispose of any toxic substances as defined in this section or radioactive material as defined in G.S. 104E-5 into the atmosphere, in the waters, or on land, except where such disposal is conducted pursuant to federal or State law, regulation, or permit. Any person who willfully violates the provisions of this section shall be guilty of a Class F felony. The fine authorized by G.S. 14-1.1(a)(8) for a conviction under this section may include a fine of up to one hundred thousand dollars ($ 100,000) per day of violation.

(b) Within the meaning of this section, toxic substances are defined as the following heavy metals and halogenated hydrocarbons:

(1) Heavy metals: mercury, plutonium, selenium, thallium and uranium;

(2) Halogenated hydrocarbons: polychlorinated biphenyls, kepone.

(c) Within the meaning of this section, the phrase "law, regulation or permit" includes controls over equipment or machinery that emits substances into the atmosphere, in waters, or on land (such as federal or State controls over motor vehicle emissions) and controls over sources of substances that are publicly consumed (such

as drinking water standards), as well as controls over substances directly released into the atmosphere, in waters, or on land (such as pesticide controls and water pollution controls).

(d) Within the meaning of this section the term "person" includes any individual, firm, partnership, limited partnership, corporation or association.

History.
1979, c. 981, s. 2; 1979, 2nd Sess., c. 1316, s. 17; 1981, c. 63, s. 1; c. 179, s. 14; 1993, c. 539, s. 1224; 1994, Ex. Sess., c. 24, s. 14(c)

N.C. Gen. Stat. § 14-285

Repealed by Session Laws 1994, Extra Session, c. 14, s. 72.

§ 14-286. Giving false fire alarms; molesting fire-alarm, fire-detection or fire-extinguishing system

(a) **Offense.** -- It shall be unlawful for any person or persons to wantonly and willfully give or cause to be given, or to advise, counsel, or aid and abet anyone in giving, a false alarm of fire, or to break the glass key protector, or to pull the slide, arm, or lever of any station or signal box of any fire-alarm system, except in case of fire, or willfully misuse or damage a portable fire extinguisher, or in any way to willfully interfere with, damage, deface, molest, or injure any part or portion of any fire-alarm, fire-detection, smoke-detection or fire-extinguishing system.

(b) **Penalty.** -- Any person who willfully interferes with, damages, defaces, molests, or injures any part or portion of a fire-alarm, fire-detection, smoke-detection, or fire-extinguishing system in a prison or local confinement facility is guilty of a Class H felony. Any person who commits any other violation of this section is guilty of a Class 2 misdemeanor. For purposes of this subsection, the term "local confinement facility" means a county or city jail, a local lockup, or a detention facility for adults operated by a local government.

History.
1921, c. 46; C.S., s. 4426(a); 1961, c. 594; 1969, c. 1224, s. 5; 1975, c. 346; 1993, c. 539, s. 182; 1994, Ex. Sess., c. 24, s. 14(c); 2019-134, s. 1

§ 14-286.1. Making false ambulance request

It shall be unlawful for any person to willfully summon an ambulance or willfully report that an ambulance is needed when such person does not have good cause to believe that the services of an ambulance are needed. Every person convicted of willfully violating this section shall be guilty of a Class 3 misdemeanor.

History.

1967, c. 343, s. 6; 1993, c. 539, s. 183; 1994, Ex. Sess., c. 24, s. 14(c)

§ 14-286.2. Interfering with emergency communication

(a) **Offense.** -- A person who intentionally interferes with an emergency communication, knowing that the communication is an emergency communication, and who is not making an emergency communication himself, is guilty of a Class A1 misdemeanor. In addition, a person who interferes with a communications instrument or other emergency equipment with the intent to prevent an emergency communication is guilty of a Class A1 misdemeanor.

(b) Repealed by Session Laws 2001-148, s. 1, effective December 1, 2001.

(b1) **Definitions.** -- The following definitions apply in this section:

(1) **Emergency communication.** -- The term includes communications to law enforcement agencies or other emergency personnel, or other individuals, relating or intending to relate that an individual is or is reasonably believed to be, or reasonably believes himself or another person to be, in imminent danger of bodily injury, or that an individual reasonably believes that his property or the property of another is in imminent danger of substantial damage, injury, or theft.

(2) **Intentional interference.** -- The term includes forcefully removing a communications instrument or other emergency equipment from the possession of another, hiding a communications instrument or other emergency equipment from another, or otherwise making a communications instrument or other emergency equipment unavailable to another, disconnecting a communications instrument or other emergency equipment, removing a communications instrument from its connection to communications lines or wavelengths, damaging or otherwise interfering with communications equipment or connections between a communications instrument and communications lines or wavelengths, disabling a theft-prevention alarm system, providing false information to cancel an earlier call or otherwise falsely indicating that emergency assistance is no longer needed when it is, and any other type of interference that makes it difficult or impossible to make an emergency communication or that conveys a false impression that emergency assistance is unnecessary when it is needed.

History.

1987, c. 690, s. 1; 1993, c. 539, s. 184; 1994, Ex. Sess., c. 24, s. 14(c); 2001-148, s. 1

§ 14-287. Leaving unused well open and exposed

It shall be unlawful for any person, firm or corporation, after discontinuing the use of any well, to leave said well open and exposed; said well, after the use of same has been discontinued, shall be carefully and securely filled: Provided, that this shall not apply to wells on farms that are protected by curbing or board walls. Any person violating any of the provisions of this section shall be guilty of a Class 2 misdemeanor.

History.

1923, c. 125; C.S., s. 4426(c); 1969, c. 1224, s. 5; 1993, c. 539, s. 185; 1994, Ex. Sess., c. 24, s. 14(c)

§ 14-288. Unlawful to pollute any bottles used for beverages

It shall be unlawful for any person, firm or corporation having custody for the purpose of sale, distribution or manufacture of any beverage bottle, to place, cause or permit to be placed therein turpentine, varnish, wood alcohol, bleaching water, bluing, kerosene, oils, or any unclean or foul substance, or other offensive material, or to send, ship, return and deliver or cause or permit to be sent, shipped, returned or delivered to any producer of beverages, any bottle used as a container for beverages, and containing any turpentine, varnish, wood alcohol, bleaching water, bluing, kerosene, oils, or any unclean or foul substance, or other offensive material. Any person, firm or corporation violating the provisions of this section shall be guilty of a Class 3 misdemeanor, and upon conviction shall be fined on the first offense, one dollar ($ 1.00) for each bottle so defiled, and for any subsequent offense not more than ten dollars ($ 10.00) for each bottle so defiled.

History.

1929, c. 324, s. 1; 1993, c. 539, s. 186; 1994, Ex. Sess., c. 24, s. 14(c)

ARTICLE 36A
RIOTS, CIVIL DISORDERS, AND EMERGENCIES

§ 14-288.1. Definitions

Unless the context clearly requires otherwise, the following definitions apply in this Article:

(1) **Chairman of the board of county commissioners.** -- The chairman of the board of county commissioners or, in case of the chairman's absence or disability, the person authorized to act in the chairman's

stead. Unless the governing body of the county has specified who is to act in lieu of the chairman with respect to a particular power or duty set out in this Article, the term "chairman of the board of county commissioners" shall apply to the person generally authorized to act in lieu of the chairman.

(2) **Dangerous weapon or substance.** -- Any deadly weapon, ammunition, explosive, incendiary device, radioactive material or device, as defined in G.S. 14-288.8(c) (5), or any instrument or substance designed for a use that carries a threat of serious bodily injury or destruction of property; or any instrument or substance that is capable of being used to inflict serious bodily injury, when the circumstances indicate a probability that such instrument or substance will be so used; or any part or ingredient in any instrument or substance included above, when the circumstances indicate a probability that such part or ingredient will be so used.

(3) **Declared state of emergency.** -- A state of emergency as that term is defined in G.S. 166A-19.3 or a state of emergency found and declared by any chief executive official or acting chief executive official of any county or municipality acting under the authority of any other applicable statute or provision of the common law to preserve the public peace in a state of emergency, or by any executive official or military commanding officer of the United States or the State of North Carolina who becomes primarily responsible under applicable law for the preservation of the public peace within any part of North Carolina.

(4) **Disorderly conduct.** -- As defined in G.S. 14-288.4(a).

(4a) **Emergency.** -- As defined in G.S. 166A-19.3.

(5) **Law enforcement officer.** -- Any officer of the State of North Carolina or any of its political subdivisions authorized to make arrests; any other person authorized under the laws of North Carolina to make arrests and either acting within that person's territorial jurisdiction or in an area in which that person has been lawfully called to duty by the Governor or any mayor or chairman of the board of county commissioners; any member of the Armed Forces of the United States, the North Carolina National Guard, or the North Carolina State Defense Militia called to duty in a state of emergency in North Carolina and made responsible for enforcing the laws of North Carolina or preserving the public peace; or any officer of the United States authorized to make arrests without

warrant and assigned to duties that include preserving the public peace in North Carolina.

(6) **Mayor.** -- The mayor or other chief executive official of a municipality or, in case of that person's absence or disability, the person authorized to act in that person's stead. Unless the governing body of the municipality has specified who is to act in lieu of the mayor with respect to a particular power or duty set out in this Article, the word "mayor" shall apply to the person generally authorized to act in lieu of the mayor.

(7) **Municipality.** -- Any active incorporated city or town, but not including any sanitary district or other municipal corporation that is not a city or town. An "active" municipality is one which has conducted the most recent election required by its charter or the general law, whichever is applicable, and which has the authority to enact general police-power ordinances.

(8) **Public disturbance.** -- Any annoying, disturbing, or alarming act or condition exceeding the bounds of social toleration normal for the time and place in question which occurs in a public place or which occurs in, affects persons in, or is likely to affect persons in a place to which the public or a substantial group has access. The places covered by this definition shall include, but not be limited to, highways, transport facilities, schools, prisons, apartment houses, places of business or amusement, or any neighborhood.

(9) **Riot.** -- As defined in G.S. 14-288.2(a).

(10) Repealed by Session Laws 2012-12, s. 2(a), effective October 1, 2012.

History.
1969, c. 869, s. 1; 1975, c. 718, s. 5; 2009-281, s. 1; 2011-183, s. 10; 2012-12, s. 2(a)

§ 14-288.2. Riot; inciting to riot; punishments

(a) A riot is a public disturbance involving an assemblage of three or more persons which by disorderly and violent conduct, or the imminent threat of disorderly and violent conduct, results in injury or damage to persons or property or creates a clear and present danger of injury or damage to persons or property.

(b) Any person who willfully engages in a riot is guilty of a Class 1 misdemeanor.

(c) Any person who willfully engages in a riot is guilty of a Class H felony, if:

(1) In the course and as a result of the riot there is property damage in excess of fifteen hundred dollars ($ 1,500) or serious bodily injury; or

(2) Such participant in the riot has in his possession any dangerous weapon or substance.

(d) Any person who willfully incites or urges another to engage in a riot, so that as a result of such inciting or urging a riot occurs or a clear and present danger of a riot is created, is guilty of a Class 1 misdemeanor.

(e) Any person who willfully incites or urges another to engage in a riot, and such inciting or urging is a contributing cause of a riot in which there is property damage in excess of fifteen hundred dollars ($ 1,500) or serious bodily injury, shall be punished as a Class F felon.

History.
1969, c. 869, s. 1; 1979, c. 760, s. 5; 1979, 2nd Sess., c. 1316, s. 47; 1981, c. 63, s. 1; c. 179, s. 14; 1993, c. 539, ss. 187, 188, 1225, 1226; 1994, Ex. Sess., c. 24, s. 14(c).

§ 14-288.3. Provisions of Article intended to supplement common law and other statutes

The provisions of this Article are intended to supersede and extend the coverage of the common-law crimes of riot and inciting to riot. To the extent that such common-law offenses may embrace situations not covered under the provisions of this Article, however, criminal prosecutions may be brought for such crimes under the common law. All other provisions of the Article are intended to be supplementary and additional to the common law and other statutes of this State and, except as specifically indicated, shall not be construed to abrogate, abolish, or supplant other provisions of law. In particular, this Article shall not be deemed to abrogate, abolish, or supplant such common-law offenses as unlawful assembly, rout, conspiracy to commit riot or other criminal offenses, false imprisonment, and going about armed to the terror of the populace and other comparable public-nuisance offenses.

History.
1969, c. 869, s. 1

§ 14-288.4. Disorderly conduct

(a) Disorderly conduct is a public disturbance intentionally caused by any person who does any of the following:

(1) Engages in fighting or other violent conduct or in conduct creating the threat of imminent fighting or other violence.

(2) Makes or uses any utterance, gesture, display or abusive language which is intended and plainly likely to provoke violent retaliation and thereby cause a breach of the peace.

(3) Takes possession of, exercises control over, or seizes any building or facility of any public or private educational institution without the specific authority of the chief administrative officer of the institution, or his authorized representative.

(4) Refuses to vacate any building or facility of any public or private educational institution in obedience to any of the following:

a. An order of the chief administrative officer of the institution, or the officer's representative, who shall include for colleges and universities the vice chancellor for student affairs or the vice-chancellor's equivalent for the institution, the dean of students or the dean's equivalent for the institution, the director of the law enforcement or security department for the institution, and the chief of the law enforcement or security department for the institution.

b. An order given by any fireman or public health officer acting within the scope of the fireman's or officer's authority.

c. If an emergency is occurring or is imminent within the institution, an order given by any law-enforcement officer acting within the scope of the officer's authority.

(5) Shall, after being forbidden to do so by the chief administrative officer, or the officer's authorized representative, of any public or private educational institution:

a. Engage in any sitting, kneeling, lying down, or inclining so as to obstruct the ingress or egress of any person entitled to the use of any building or facility of the institution in its normal and intended use; or

b. Congregate, assemble, form groups or formations (whether organized or not), block, or in any manner otherwise interfere with the operation or functioning of any building or facility of the institution so as to interfere with the customary or normal use of the building or facility.

(6) Disrupts, disturbs or interferes with the teaching of students at any public or private educational institution or engages in conduct which disturbs the peace, order or discipline at any public or private educational institution or on the grounds adjacent thereto.

(6a) Engages in conduct which disturbs the peace, order, or discipline on any public school bus or public school activity bus.

(7) Except as provided in subdivision (8) of this subsection, disrupts, disturbs, or

interferes with a religious service or assembly or engages in conduct which disturbs the peace or order at any religious service or assembly.

(8) Engages in conduct with the intent to impede, disrupt, disturb, or interfere with the orderly administration of any funeral, memorial service, or family processional to the funeral or memorial service, including a military funeral, service, or family processional, or with the normal activities and functions occurring in the facilities or buildings where a funeral or memorial service, including a military funeral or memorial service, is taking place. Any of the following conduct that occurs within two hours preceding, during, or within two hours after a funeral or memorial service shall constitute disorderly conduct under this subdivision:

a. Displaying, within 500 feet of the ceremonial site, location being used for the funeral or memorial, or the family's processional route to the funeral or memorial service, any visual image that conveys fighting words or actual or imminent threats of harm directed to any person or property associated with the funeral, memorial service, or processional route.

b. Uttering, within 500 feet of the ceremonial site, location being used for the funeral or memorial service, or the family's processional route to the funeral or memorial service, loud, threatening, or abusive language or singing, chanting, whistling, or yelling with or without noise amplification in a manner that would tend to impede, disrupt, disturb, or interfere with a funeral, memorial service, or processional route.

c. Attempting to block or blocking pedestrian or vehicular access to the ceremonial site or location being used for a funeral or memorial.

As used in this section the term "building or facility" includes the surrounding grounds and premises of any building or facility used in connection with the operation or functioning of such building or facility.

(b) Except as provided in subsection (c) of this section, any person who willfully engages in disorderly conduct is guilty of a Class 2 misdemeanor.

(c) A person who commits a violation of subdivision (8) of subsection (a) of this section is guilty of:

(1) A Class 1 misdemeanor for a first offense.

(2) A Class I felony for a second offense.

(3) A Class H felony for a third or subsequent offense.

History.

1969, c. 869, s. 1; 1971, c. 668, s. 1; 1973, c. 1347; 1975, c. 19, s. 4; 1983, c. 39, s. 5; 1987, c. 671, s. 1; 1993, c. 539, s. 189; 1994, Ex. Sess., c. 24, s. 14(c); 2001-26, s. 2; 2006-169, s. 1; 2012-12, s. 2(b); 2013-6, s. 1

§ 14-288.5. Failure to disperse when commanded a misdemeanor; prima facie evidence

(a) Any law-enforcement officer or public official responsible for keeping the peace may issue a command to disperse in accordance with this section if he reasonably believes that a riot, or disorderly conduct by an assemblage of three or more persons, is occurring. The command to disperse shall be given in a manner reasonably calculated to be communicated to the assemblage.

(b) Any person who fails to comply with a lawful command to disperse is guilty of a Class 2 misdemeanor.

(c) If any person remains at the scene of any riot, or disorderly conduct by an assemblage of three or more persons, following a command to disperse and after a reasonable time for dispersal has elapsed, it is prima facie evidence that the person so remaining is willfully engaging in the riot or disorderly conduct, as the case may be.

History.

1969, c. 869, s. 1; 1993, c. 539, s. 190; 1994, Ex. Sess., c. 24, s. 14(c)

§ 14-288.6. Looting; trespass during emergency

(a) Any person who enters upon the premises of another without legal justification when the usual security of property is not effective due to the occurrence or aftermath of riot, insurrection, invasion, storm, fire, explosion, flood, collapse, or other disaster or calamity is guilty of a Class 1 misdemeanor of trespass during an emergency.

(b) Any person who commits the crime of trespass during emergency and, without legal justification, obtains or exerts control over, damages, ransacks, or destroys the property of another is guilty of the felony of looting and shall be punished as a Class H felon.

History.

1969, c. 869, s. 1; 1979, c. 760, s. 5; 1979, 2nd Sess., c. 1316, s. 47; 1981, c. 63, s. 1; c. 179, s. 14; 1993, c. 539, ss. 191, 1227; 1994, Ex. Sess., c. 24, s. 14(c)

Chapter 14

N.C. Gen. Stat. § 14-288.7

Repealed by Session Laws 2012-12, s. 2(c), effective October 1, 2012.

History.

1969, c. 869, s. 1; 1993, c. 539, s. 192; 1994, Ex. Sess., c. 24, s. 14(c); repealed by 2012-12, s. 2(c), effective October 1, 2012

§ 14-288.8. Manufacture, assembly, possession, storage, transportation, sale, purchase, delivery, or acquisition of weapon of mass death and destruction; exceptions

(a) Except as otherwise provided in this section, it is unlawful for any person to manufacture, assemble, possess, store, transport, sell, offer to sell, purchase, offer to purchase, deliver or give to another, or acquire any weapon of mass death and destruction.

(b) This section does not apply to any of the following:

(1) Persons exempted from the provisions of G.S. 14-269 with respect to any activities lawfully engaged in while carrying out their duties.

(2) Importers, manufacturers, dealers, and collectors of firearms, ammunition, or destructive devices validly licensed under the laws of the United States or the State of North Carolina, while lawfully engaged in activities authorized under their licenses.

(3) Persons under contract with the United States, the State of North Carolina, or any agency of either government, with respect to any activities lawfully engaged in under their contracts.

(4) Inventors, designers, ordnance consultants and researchers, chemists, physicists, and other persons lawfully engaged in pursuits designed to enlarge knowledge or to facilitate the creation, development, or manufacture of weapons of mass death and destruction intended for use in a manner consistent with the laws of the United States and the State of North Carolina.

(5) Persons who lawfully possess or own a weapon as defined in subsection (c) of this section in compliance with 26 U.S.C. Chapter 53, §§ 5801-5871. Nothing in this subdivision shall limit the discretion of the sheriff in executing the paperwork required by the United States Bureau of Alcohol, Tobacco and Firearms for such person to obtain the weapon.

(c) The term "weapon of mass death and destruction" includes:

(1) Any explosive or incendiary:

a. Bomb; or

b. Grenade; or

c. Rocket having a propellant charge of more than four ounces; or

d. Missile having an explosive or incendiary charge of more than one-quarter ounce; or

e. Mine; or

f. Device similar to any of the devices described above; or

(2) Any type of weapon (other than a shotgun or a shotgun shell of a type particularly suitable for sporting purposes) which will, or which may be readily converted to, expel a projectile by the action of an explosive or other propellant, and which has any barrel with a bore of more than one-half inch in diameter; or

(3) Any firearm capable of fully automatic fire, any shotgun with a barrel or barrels of less than 18 inches in length or an overall length of less than 26 inches, any rifle with a barrel or barrels of less than 16 inches in length or an overall length of less than 26 inches, any muffler or silencer for any firearm, whether or not such firearm is included within this definition. For the purposes of this section, rifle is defined as a weapon designed or redesigned, made or remade, and intended to be fired from the shoulder; or

(4) Any combination of parts either designed or intended for use in converting any device into any weapon described above and from which a weapon of mass death and destruction may readily be assembled.

The term "weapon of mass death and destruction" does not include any device which is neither designed nor redesigned for use as a weapon; any device, although originally designed for use as a weapon, which is redesigned for use as a signaling, pyrotechnic, line-throwing, safety, or similar device; surplus ordnance sold, loaned, or given by the Secretary of the Army pursuant to the provisions of section 4684(2), 4685, or 4686 of Title 10 of the United States Code; or any other device which the Secretary of the Treasury finds is not likely to be used as a weapon, is an antique, or is a rifle which the owner intends to use solely for sporting purposes, in accordance with Chapter 44 of Title 18 of the United States Code.

(d) Any person who violates any provision of this section is guilty of a Class F felony.

History.

1969, c. 869, s. 1; 1975, c. 718, ss. 6, 7; 1977, c. 810; 1983, c. 413, ss. 1, 2; 1993, c. 539, s. 1228; 1994, Ex. Sess., c. 24, s. 14(c); 2001-470, s. 3; 2011-268, s. 8

§ 14-288.9. Assault on emergency personnel; punishments

(a) An assault upon emergency personnel is an assault upon any person coming within the definition of "emergency personnel" which is committed in an area:

    (1) In which a declared state of emergency exists; or

    (2) Within the immediate vicinity of which a riot is occurring or is imminent.

(b) The term "emergency personnel" includes law-enforcement officers, firemen, ambulance attendants, utility workers, doctors, nurses, and other persons lawfully engaged in providing essential services during the emergency.

(c) Any person who commits an assault causing physical injury upon emergency personnel is guilty of a Class I felony. Any person who commits an assault upon emergency personnel with or through the use of any dangerous weapon or substance shall be punished as a Class F felon.

History.
1969, c. 869, s. 1; 1979, c. 760, s. 5; 1979, 2nd Sess., c. 1316, s. 47; 1981, c. 63, s. 1; c. 179, s. 14; 1993, c. 539, ss. 193, 1229; 1994, Ex. Sess., c. 24, s. 14(c); 2011-356, s. 3

§ 14-288.10. Frisk of persons during violent disorders; frisk of curfew violators

(a) Any law-enforcement officer may frisk any person in order to discover any dangerous weapon or substance when he has reasonable grounds to believe that the person is or may become unlawfully involved in an existing riot and when the person is close enough to such riot that he could become immediately involved in the riot. The officer may also at that time inspect for the same purpose the contents of any personal belongings that the person has in his possession.

(b) Any law-enforcement officer may frisk any person he finds violating the provisions of a curfew proclaimed under the authority of G.S. 14-288.12, 14-288.13, 14-288.14, or 14-288.15 or any other applicable statutes or provisions of the common law in order to discover whether the person possesses any dangerous weapon or substance. The officer may also at that time inspect for the same purpose the contents of any personal belongings that the person has in his possession.

History.
1969, c. 869, s. 1

§ 14-288.11. Warrants to inspect vehicles in riot areas or approaching municipalities during emergencies

(a) Notwithstanding the provisions of Article 4 of Chapter 15, any law-enforcement officer may, under the conditions specified in this section, obtain a warrant authorizing inspection of vehicles under the conditions and for the purpose specified in subsection (b).

(b) The inspection shall be for the purpose of discovering any dangerous weapon or substance likely to be used by one who is or may become unlawfully involved in a riot. The warrant may be sought to inspect:

    (1) All vehicles entering or approaching a municipality in which an emergency exists; or

    (2) All vehicles which might reasonably be regarded as being within or approaching the immediate vicinity of an existing riot.

(c) The warrant may be issued by any judge or justice of the General Court of Justice.

(d) The issuing official shall issue the warrant only when he has determined that the one seeking the warrant has been specifically authorized to do so by the head of the law-enforcement agency of which the affiant is a member, and:

    (1) If the warrant is being sought for the inspection of vehicles entering or approaching a municipality, that an emergency exists within the municipality; or

    (2) If the warrant being sought is for the inspection of vehicles within or approaching the immediate vicinity of a riot, that a riot is occurring within that area.

    Facts indicating the basis of these determinations must be stated in an affidavit and signed by the affiant under oath or affirmation.

(e) The warrant must be signed by the issuing official and must bear the hour and date of its issuance.

(f) The warrant must indicate whether it is for the inspection of vehicles entering or approaching a municipality or whether it is for the inspection of vehicles within or approaching the immediate vicinity of a riot. In either case, it must also specify with reasonable precision the area within which it may be exercised.

(g) The warrant shall become invalid 24 hours following its issuance and must bear a notation to that effect.

(h) Warrants authorized under this section shall not be regarded as search warrants for the purposes of application of Article 4 of Chapter 15.

(i) Nothing in this section is intended to prevent warrantless frisks, searches, and inspections to the extent that they may be constitutional and consistent with common law and governing statutes.

History.
1969, c. 869, s. 1; 2012-12, s. 2(d)

§§ 14-288.12 through 14-288.17

Repealed by Session Laws 2012-12, s. 2(e), effective October 1, 2012.

History.

§ 14-288.12: 1969, c. 869, s. 1; 1981, c. 412, s. 4(4); c. 747, s. 66; 1989, c. 770, s. 2; 1993, c. 539, s. 194; 1994, Ex. Sess., c. 24, s. 14(c); 2009-146, s. 1; repealed by 2012-12, s. 2(e), effective October 1, 2012. § 14-288.13: 1969, c. 869, s. 1; 1993, c. 539, s. 195; 1994, Ex. Sess., c. 24, s. 14(c); repealed by 2012-12, s. 2(e), effective October 1, 2012. § 14-288.14: 1969, c. 869, s. 1; 1993, c. 539, s. 196; 1994, Ex. Sess., c. 14, s. 7; c. 24, s. 14(c); repealed by 2012-12, s. 2(e), effective October 1, 2012. § 14-288.15: 1969, c. 869, s. 1; 1993, c. 539, s. 197; 1994, Ex. Sess., c. 24, s. 14(c); repealed by 2012-12, s. 2(e), effective October 1, 2012. § 14-288.16: 1969, c. 869, s. 1; repealed by 2012-12, s. 2(e), effective October 1, 2012. § 14-288.17: 1969, c. 869, s. 1; repealed by 2012-12, s. 2(e), effective October 1, 2012

§ 14-288.18. Injunction to cope with emergencies at public and private educational institutions

(a) The chief administrative officer, or his authorized representative, of any public or private educational institution may apply to any superior court judge for injunctive relief if an emergency exists within his institution. For the purposes of this section, the superintendent of any city or county administrative school unit shall be deemed the chief administrative officer of any public elementary or secondary school within his unit.

(b) Upon a finding by a superior court judge, to whom application has been made under the provisions of this section, that an emergency exists within a public or private educational institution by reason of riot, disorderly conduct by three or more persons, or the imminent threat of riot, the judge may issue an injunction containing provisions appropriate to cope with the emergency then occurring or threatening. The injunction may be addressed to named persons or named or described groups of persons as to whom there is satisfactory cause for believing that they are contributing to the emergency, and ordering such persons or groups of persons to take or refrain or desist from taking such various actions as the judge finds it appropriate to include in his order.

History.

1969, c. 869, s. 1; 2012-12, s. 2(f)

N.C. Gen. Stat. § 14-288.19

Repealed by Session Laws 2012-12, s. 2(e), effective October 1, 2012.

History.

1969, c. 1129; 1993, c. 539, s. 198; 1994, Ex. Sess., c. 24, s. 14(c); 2009-281, s. 1; repealed by 2012-12, s. 2(e), effective October 1, 2012

§ 14-288.20. Certain weapons at civil disorders

(a) The definitions in G.S. 14-288.1 do not apply to this section. As used in this section:

(1) The term "civil disorder" means any public disturbance involving acts or violence by assemblages of three or more persons, which causes an immediate danger of damage or injury to the property or person of any other individual or results in damage or injury to the property or person of any other individual.

(2) The term "firearm" means any weapon which is designed to or may readily be converted to expel any projectile by the action of an explosive; or the frame or receiver of such a weapon.

(3) The term "explosive or incendiary device" means (i) dynamite and all other forms of high explosives, (ii) any explosive bomb, grenade, missile, or similar device, and (iii) any incendiary bomb or grenade, fire bomb, or similar device, including any device which (i) consists of or includes a breakable container including a flammable liquid or compound, and a wick composed of any material which, when ignited, is capable of igniting that flammable liquid or compound, and (ii) can be carried or thrown by one individual acting alone.

(4) The term "law-enforcement officer" means any officer of the United States, any state, any political subdivision of a state, or the District of Columbia charged with the execution of the laws thereof; civil officers of the United States; officers and soldiers of the organized militia and state guard of any state or territory of the United States, the Commonwealth of Puerto Rico, or the District of Columbia; and members of the Armed Forces of the United States.

(b) A person is guilty of a Class H felony, if he:

(1) Teaches or demonstrates to any other person the use, application, or making of any firearm, explosive or incendiary device, or technique capable of causing injury or death to persons, knowing or having reason to know or intending that the same will be unlawfully employed for use in, or in furtherance of, a civil disorder; or

(2) Assembles with one or more persons for the purpose of training with, practicing with, or being instructed in the use of any firearm, explosive or incendiary device, or technique capable of causing injury or death to persons, intending to employ unlawfully the training, practicing, instruction, or technique for use in, or in furtherance of, a civil disorder.

(c) Nothing contained in this section shall make unlawful any act of any law-enforcement officer which is performed in the lawful performance of his official duties.

History.
1981, c. 880, ss. 1, 2; 1993, c. 539, s. 1230; 1994, Ex. Sess., c. 24, s. 14(c); 2011-183, s. 11

§ 14-288.20A. Violation of emergency prohibitions and restrictions

Any person who does any of the following is guilty of a Class 2 misdemeanor:

(1) Violates any provision of an ordinance or a declaration enacted or declared pursuant to G.S. 166A-19.31.

(2) Violates any provision of a declaration or executive order issued pursuant to G.S. 166A-19.30.

(3) Willfully refuses to leave the building as directed in a Governor's order issued pursuant to G.S. 166A-19.78.

History.
2012-12, s. 1(d)

ARTICLE 36B
NUCLEAR, BIOLOGICAL, OR CHEMICAL WEAPONS OF MASS DESTRUCTION

§ 14-288.21. Unlawful manufacture, assembly, possession, storage, transportation, sale, purchase, delivery, or acquisition of a nuclear, biological, or chemical weapon of mass destruction; exceptions; punishment

(a) Except as otherwise provided in this section, it is unlawful for any person to knowingly manufacture, assemble, possess, store, transport, sell, offer to sell, purchase, offer to purchase, deliver or give to another, or acquire a nuclear, biological, or chemical weapon of mass destruction.

(b) This section does not apply to:

(1) Persons listed in G.S. 14-269(b) with respect to any activities lawfully engaged in while carrying out their duties.

(2) Persons under contract with, or working under the direction of, the United States, the State of North Carolina, or any agency of either government, with respect to any activities lawfully engaged in under their contracts or pursuant to lawful direction.

(3) Persons lawfully engaged in the development, production, manufacture, assembly, possession, transport, sale, purchase, delivery or acquisition of any biological agent, disease organism, toxic or poisonous

chemical, radioactive substance or their immediate precursors, for preventive, protective, or other peaceful purposes.

(4) Persons lawfully engaged in accepted agricultural, horticultural, or forestry practices; aquatic weed control; or structural pest and rodent control, in a manner approved by the federal, State, county, or local agency charged with authority over such activities.

(c) The term "nuclear, biological, or chemical weapon of mass destruction", as used in this Article, means any of the following:

(1) Any weapon, device, or method that is designed or has the capability to cause death or serious injury through the release, dissemination, or impact of:

a. Radiation or radioactivity;

b. A disease organism; or

c. Toxic or poisonous chemicals or their immediate precursors.

(2) Any substance that is designed or has the capability to cause death or serious injury and:

a. Contains radiation or radioactivity;

b. Is or contains toxic or poisonous chemicals or their immediate precursors; or

c. Is or contains one or more of the following:

1. Any select agent that is a microorganism, virus, bacterium, fungus, rickettsia, or toxin listed in Appendix A of Part 72 of Title 42 of the Code of Federal Regulations.

2. Any genetically modified microorganisms or genetic elements from an organism on Appendix A of Part 72 of Title 42 of the Code of Federal Regulations, shown to produce or encode for a factor associated with a disease.

3. Any genetically modified microorganisms or genetic elements that contain nucleic acid sequences coding for any of the toxins listed on Appendix A of Part 72 of Title 42 of the Code of Federal Regulations, or their toxic submits.

The term "nuclear, biological, or chemical weapon of mass destruction" also includes any combination of parts or substances either designed or intended for use in converting any device or substance into any nuclear, biological, or chemical weapon of mass destruction or from which a nuclear, biological, or chemical weapon of mass destruction may be readily assembled or created.

(d) Any person who violates any provision of this section is guilty of a Class B1 felony.

History.
2001-470, s. 1

§ 14-288.22. Unlawful use of a nuclear, biological, or chemical weapon of mass destruction; punishment

(a) Any person who unlawfully and willfully injures another by the use of a nuclear, biological, or chemical weapon of mass destruction is guilty of a Class A felony and shall be sentenced to life imprisonment without parole.

(b) Any person who attempts, solicits another, or conspires to injure another by the use of a nuclear, biological, or chemical weapon of mass destruction is guilty of a Class B1 felony.

(c) Any person who for the purpose of violating any provision of this Article, deposits for delivery or attempts to have delivered, a nuclear, biological, or chemical weapon of mass destruction by the United States Postal Service or other public or private business engaged in the delivery of mail, packages, or parcels is guilty of a Class B1 felony.

History.
2001-470, s. 1

§ 14-288.23. Making a false report concerning a nuclear, biological, or chemical weapon of mass destruction; punishment; restitution

(a) Any person who, by any means of communication to any person or group of persons, makes a report, knowing or having reason to know the report is false, that causes any person to reasonably believe that there is located at any place or structure whatsoever any nuclear, biological, or chemical weapon of mass destruction is guilty of a Class D felony.

(b) The court may order a person convicted under this section to pay restitution, including costs and consequential damages resulting from disruption of the normal activity that would have otherwise occurred but for the false report, pursuant to Article 81C of Chapter 15A of the General Statutes.

(c) For purposes of this section, the term "report" shall include making accessible to another person by computer.

History.
2001-470, s. 1

§ 14-288.24. Perpetrating hoax by use of false nuclear, biological, or chemical

weapon of mass destruction; punishment; restitution

(a) Any person who, with intent to perpetrate a hoax, conceals, places, or displays any device, object, machine, instrument, or artifact, so as to cause any person reasonably to believe the same to be a nuclear, biological, or chemical weapon of mass destruction is guilty of a Class D felony.

(b) The court may order a person convicted under this section to pay restitution, including costs and consequential damages resulting from disruption of the normal activity that would have otherwise occurred but for the hoax, pursuant to Article 81C of Chapter 15A of the General Statutes.

History.
2001-470, s. 1

SUBCHAPTER 11.
GENERAL POLICE REGULATIONS

ARTICLE 37
LOTTERIES, GAMING, BINGO AND RAFFLES

PART 1
LOTTERIES AND GAMING

§ 14-289. Advertising lotteries

Except as provided in Chapter 18C of the General Statutes or in connection with a lawful raffle as provided in Part 2 of this Article, if anyone by writing or printing or by circular or letter or in any other way, advertises or publishes an account of a lottery, whether within or without this State, stating how, when or where the same is to be or has been drawn, or what are the prizes therein or any of them, or the price of a ticket or any share or interest therein, or where or how it may be obtained, he shall be guilty of a Class 2 misdemeanor. News medium as defined in G.S. 8-53.11 shall be exempt from this section provided the publishing is in connection with a lawful activity of the news medium.

History.
1887, c. 211; Rev., s. 3725; C.S., s. 4427; 1979, c. 893, s. 3; 1983, c. 896, s. 1; 1993, c. 539, s. 199; 1994, Ex. Sess., c. 24, s. 14(c); 2005-276, s. 31.1(v2); 2005-344, s. 3(a)

§ 14-290. Dealing in lotteries

Except as provided in Chapter 18C of the General Statutes or in connection with a lawful raffle as provided in Part 2 of this Article, if any person shall open, set on foot, carry on, promote, make or draw, publicly or privately, a lottery, by whatever name, style or title the same may be denominated or known; or if any person shall, by such way and means, expose or set to sale any house, real estate, goods, chattels, cash, written evidence of debt, certificates of claims or any other thing of value whatsoever, every person so offending shall be guilty of a Class 2 misdemeanor which may include a fine not to exceed two thousand dollars ($ 2,000). Any person who engages in disposing of any species of property whatsoever, including money and evidences of debt, or in any manner distributes gifts or prizes upon tickets, bottle crowns, bottle caps, seals on containers, other devices or certificates sold for that purpose, shall be held liable to prosecution under this section. Any person who shall have in his possession any tickets, certificates or orders used in the operation of any lottery shall be held liable under this section, and the mere possession of such tickets shall be prima facie evidence of the violation of this section. This section shall not apply to the possession of a lottery ticket or share for a lottery game being lawfully conducted in another state.

History.

1834, c. 19, s. 1; R.C., c. 34, s. 69; 1874-5, c. 96; Code, s. 1047; Rev., s. 3726; C.S., s. 4428; 1933, c. 434; 1937, c. 157; 1979, c. 893, s. 4; 1983, c. 896, s. 1; 1993, c. 539, s. 200; 1994, Ex. Sess., c. 24, s. 14(c); 2005-344, s. 3(b)

§ 14-291. Selling lottery tickets and acting as agent for lotteries

Except as provided in Chapter 18C of the General Statutes or in connection with a lawful raffle as provided in Part 2 of this Article, if any person shall sell, barter or otherwise dispose of any lottery ticket or order for any number of shares in any lottery, or shall in anywise be concerned in such lottery, by acting as agent in the State for or on behalf of any such lottery, to be drawn or paid either out of or within the State, such person shall be guilty of a Class 2 misdemeanor.

History.

1834, c. 19, s. 2; R.C., c. 34, s. 70; Code, s. 1048; Rev., s. 3727; C.S., s. 4429; 1979, c. 893, s. 5; 1983, c. 896, s. 1; 1993, c. 539, s. 201; 1994, Ex. Sess., c. 24, s. 14(c); 2005-344, s. 3(c)

§ 14-291.1. Selling "numbers" tickets; possession prima facie evidence of violation

Except as provided in Chapter 18C of the General Statutes, in connection with a lawful lottery conducted in another state, or in connection with a lawful raffle as provided in Part 2 of this Article, if any person shall sell, barter or cause to be sold or bartered, any ticket, token, certificate or order for any number or shares in any lottery, commonly known as the numbers or butter and egg lottery, or lotteries of similar character, to be drawn or paid within or without the State, such person shall be guilty of a Class 2 misdemeanor. Any person who shall have in his possession any tickets, tokens, certificates or orders used in the operation of any such lottery shall be guilty under this section, and the possession of such tickets shall be prima facie evidence of the violation of this section.

History.

1943, c. 550; 1979, c. 893, s. 6; 1983, c. 896, s. 1; 1993, c. 539, s. 202; 1994, Ex. Sess., c. 24, s. 14(c); 2005-344, s. 3(d)

§ 14-291.2. Pyramid and chain schemes prohibited

(a) No person shall establish, operate, participate in, or otherwise promote any pyramid distribution plan, program, device or scheme whereby a participant pays a valuable consideration for the opportunity or chance to receive a fee or compensation upon the introduction of other participants into the program, whether or not such opportunity or chance is received in conjunction with the purchase of merchandise. A person who establishes or operates a pyramid distribution plan is guilty of a Class H felony. A person who participates in or otherwise promotes a pyramid distribution plan is deemed to participate in a lottery and is guilty of a Class 2 misdemeanor.

(b) "Pyramid distribution plan" means any program utilizing a pyramid or chain process by which a participant gives a valuable consideration for the opportunity to receive compensation or things of value in return for inducing other persons to become participants in the program; and

"Compensation" does not mean payment based on sales of goods or services to persons who are not participants in the scheme, and who are not purchasing in order to participate in the scheme.

(c) Any judge of the superior court shall have jurisdiction, upon petition by the Attorney General of North Carolina or district attorney of the superior court, to enjoin, as an unfair or deceptive trade practice, the continuation of the scheme described in subsection (a); in such proceeding the court may assess civil penalties and attorneys' fees to the Attorney General or the District Attorney pursuant to G.S. 75-15.2 and

75-16.1; and the court may appoint a receiver to secure and distribute assets obtained by any defendant through participation in any such scheme. The clear proceeds of civil penalties provided for in this subsection shall be remitted to the Civil Penalty and Forfeiture Fund in accordance with G.S. 115C-457.2.

(d) Any contract hereafter created for which a part of the consideration consisted of the opportunity or chance to participate in a program described in subsection (a) is hereby declared to be contrary to public policy and therefore void and unenforceable.

History.
1971, c. 875, s. 1; 1973, c. 47, s. 2; 1983, c. 721, s. 2; 1993, c. 539, s. 203; 1994, Ex. Sess., c. 24, s. 14(c); 1997-443, s. 19.25(x); 1998-215, s. 96

§ 14-292. Gambling

Except as provided in Chapter 18C of the General Statutes or in Part 2 or Part 4 of this Article, any person or organization that operates any game of chance or any person who plays at or bets on any game of chance at which any money, property or other thing of value is bet, whether the same be in stake or not, shall be guilty of a Class 2 misdemeanor. This section shall not apply to a person who plays at or bets on any lottery game being lawfully conducted in any state.

History.
1891, c. 29; Rev., s. 3715; C.S., s. 4430; 1979, c. 893, s. 1; 1983, c. 896, s. 1; 1993, c. 539, s. 204; 1994, Ex. Sess., c. 24, s. 14(c); 2005-344, s. 3(e); 2019-13, s. 1

N.C. Gen. Stat. § 14-292.1

Repealed by Session Laws 1983, c. 896, s. 2.

§ 14-292.2. Class III gaming on Indian lands

(a) Except as otherwise provided in this section, and notwithstanding any laws which make Class III gaming, as defined by the federal Indian Gaming Regulatory Act, 25 U.S.C. § 2701, et seq., unlawful in this State, the Class III gaming activities listed in subsection (b) of this section may legally be conducted on Indian lands that are held in trust by the United States government for and on behalf of federally recognized Indian tribes, if all the following apply:

(1) The Class III games are conducted in accordance with a valid Class III Tribal-State Gaming Compact or an amendment to a Compact, applicable to the tribe, that has been negotiated and entered into by the Governor under the authority provided in G.S. 147-12(a)(14) and G.S. 71A-8.

(2) The Tribal-State Gaming Compact has been approved by the U.S. Department of the Interior.

(3) The Tribal-State Gaming Compact requires that all monies paid by the tribe under the Compact be paid to the Indian Gaming Education Revenue Fund established by law.

(b) The following Class III games may lawfully be conducted pursuant to subsection (a) of this section:

(1) Gaming machines.
(2) Live table games.
(3) Raffles, as defined in G.S. 14-309.15(b).
(4) Video games, as defined in G.S. 14-306 and G.S. 14-306.1A.
(5) Sports and horse race wagering.

(c) Nothing in this section shall modify or affect laws applicable to persons or entities other than federally recognized Indian tribes operating games in accordance with subsection (a) of this section.

(d) Notwithstanding any other provision of law, there shall be no more than three Class III gaming facilities authorized by a Compact entered under subsection (a) of this section on the lands of any single Indian tribe, and a Compact that authorizes or allows for the operation of more than three such facilities shall be invalid.

(e) As used in this section, the following terms mean:

(1) **Gaming machine.** -- A machine that meets the definition of any of the following:
a. As set forth in G.S. 14-306.
b. "Gaming machine" as set forth in 25 C.F.R. § 542.2.
c. "Gambling device" as set forth in 15 U.S.C. § 1171.

(2) **Live table games.** -- Games that utilize real nonelectronic cards, dice, chips, or equipment in the play and operation of the game.

(3) **Sports wagering.** -- The placing of wagers on the outcome of professional and collegiate sports contests. For purposes of this subdivision, the wager shall be deemed to occur where it is initiated and received, all of which must occur on Indian lands within the State lawfully permitted to conduct Class III gaming activities pursuant to G.S. 14-292.2(a).

(4) **Horse race wagering.** -- Fixed odds or pari-mutuel wagering on thoroughbred, harness or other racing of horses, including simulcasting and off-track betting. For purposes of this subdivision, the wager shall be deemed to occur where it is initiated and received, all of which must occur on Indian lands within the State lawfully permitted to conduct Class III gaming activities pursuant to G.S. 14-292.2(a).

History.
2012-6, s. 2; 2019-163, s. 1

§ 14-293. Allowing gambling in houses of public entertainment; penalty

Except as provided in Chapter 18C of the General Statutes, if any keeper of an ordinary or other house of entertainment, or of a house wherein alcoholic beverages are retailed, shall knowingly suffer any game, at which money or property, or anything of value, is bet, whether the same be in stake or not, to be played in any such house, or in any part of the premises occupied therewith; or shall furnish persons so playing or betting either on said premises or elsewhere with drink or other thing for their comfort or subsistence during the time of play, he shall be guilty of a Class 2 misdemeanor. Any person who shall be convicted under this section shall, upon such conviction, forfeit his license to do any of the businesses mentioned in this section, and shall be forever debarred from doing any of such businesses in this State. The court shall embody in its judgment that such person has forfeited his license, and no board of county commissioners, board of town commissioners or board of aldermen shall thereafter have power or authority to grant to such convicted person or his agent a license to do any of the businesses mentioned herein.

History.
1799, c. 526, P.R.; 1801, c. 581, P.R.; 1831, c. 26; R.C., c. 34, s. 76; Code, s. 1043; 1901, c. 753; Rev., s. 3716; C.S., 4431; 1967, c. 101, s. 1; 1981, c. 412, s. 4(4); c. 747, s. 66; 1993, c. 539, s. 205; 1994, Ex. Sess., c. 24, s. 14(c); 2005-344, s. 3(f)

§ 14-294. Gambling with faro banks and tables

If any person shall open, establish, use or keep a faro bank, or a faro table, with the intent that games of chance may be played thereat, or shall play or bet thereat any money, property or other thing of value, whether the same be in stake or not, he shall be guilty of a Class 2 misdemeanor.

History.
1848, c. 34; R.C., c. 71; 1856-7, c. 25; Code, s. 1044; Rev., s. 3717; C.S., s. 4432; 1993, c. 539, s. 206; 1994, Ex. Sess., c. 24, s. 14(c)

§ 14-295. Keeping gaming tables, illegal punchboards or slot machines, or betting thereat

If any person shall establish, use or keep any gaming table (other than a faro bank), by whatever name such table may be called, an

illegal punchboard or an illegal slot machine, at which games of chance shall be played, he shall be guilty of a Class 2 misdemeanor; and every person who shall play thereat or thereat bet any money, property or other thing of value, whether the same be in stake or not, shall be guilty of a Class 2 misdemeanor.

History.
1791, c. 336, P.R.; 1798, c. 502, s. 2, P.R.; R.C., c. 34, s. 72; Code, s. 1045; Rev., s. 3718; C.S., s. 4433; 1931, c. 14, s. 2; 1993, c. 539, s. 207; 1994, Ex. Sess., c. 24, s. 14(c)

§ 14-296. Illegal slot machines and punchboards defined

An illegal slot machine or punchboard within the contemplation of G.S. 14-295 through 14-298 is defined as a device where the user may become entitled to receive any money, credit, allowance, or any thing of value, as defined in G.S. 14-306.

History.
1931, c. 14, s. 1; 1989, c. 406, s. 2

§ 14-297. Allowing gaming tables, illegal punchboards or slot machines on premises

If any person shall knowingly suffer to be opened, kept or used in his house or on any part of the premises occupied therewith, any of the gaming tables prohibited by G.S. 14-289 through 14-300 or any illegal punchboard or illegal slot machine, he shall forfeit and pay to any one who will sue therefor two hundred dollars ($ 200.00), and shall also be guilty of a Class 2 misdemeanor.

History.
1798, c. 502, s. 3, P.R.; 1800, c. 5, s. 2, P.R.; R.C., c. 34, s. 73; Code, s. 1046; Rev., s. 3719; C.S., s. 4434; 1931, c. 14, s. 3; 1993, c. 539, s. 208; 1994, Ex. Sess., c. 24, s. 14(c)

§ 14-298. Seizure of illegal gaming items

Upon a determination that probable cause exists to believe that any gaming table prohibited to be used by G.S. 14-289 through G.S. 14-300, any illegal punchboard or illegal slot machine, any video game machine prohibited to be used by G.S. 14-306 or G.S. 14-306.1A, any game terminal described in G.S. 14-306.3(b), or any electronic machine or device using an entertaining display in violation of G.S. 14-306.4 is in the illegal possession or use of any person within the limits of their jurisdiction, all sheriffs and law enforcement officers are authorized to seize the items in accordance with applicable State law. Any law

Chapter 14

enforcement agency in possession of that item shall retain the item pending a disposition order from a district or superior court judge. Upon application by the law enforcement agency, district attorney, or owner, and after notice and opportunity to be heard by all parties, if the court determines that the item is unlawful to possess, it shall enter an order releasing the item to the law enforcement agency for destruction or for training purposes. If the court determines that the item is not unlawful to possess and will not be used in violation of the law, the item shall be ordered released to its owner upon satisfactory proof of ownership. The foregoing procedures for release shall not apply, however, with respect to an item seized for use as evidence in any criminal action or proceeding until after entry of final judgment.

History.

1791, c. 336, P.R.; 1798, c. 502, s. 2, P.R.; R.C., c. 34, s. 74; Code, s. 1049; Rev., s. 3720; C.S., s. 4435; 1931, c. 14, s. 4; 1973, c. 108, s. 11; 2000-151, s. 5; 2004-199, ss. 47(a), 47(b); 2004-203, s. 20(a); 2007-484, s. 3(a); 2008-122, s. 2; 2010-103, s. 2

§ 14-299. Property exhibited by gamblers to be seized; disposition of same

Except as provided in Chapter 18C of the General Statutes or in G.S. 14-292, all moneys or other property or thing of value exhibited for the purpose of alluring persons to bet on any game, or used in the conduct of any such game, including any motor vehicle used in the conduct of a lottery within the purview of G.S. 14-291.1, shall be liable to be seized by any court of competent jurisdiction or by any person acting under its warrant. Moneys so seized shall be turned over to and paid to the treasurer of the county wherein they are seized, and placed in the general fund of the county. Any property seized which is used for and is suitable only for gambling shall be destroyed, and all other property so seized shall be sold in the manner provided for the sale of personal property by execution, and the proceeds derived from said sale shall (after deducting the expenses of keeping the property and the costs of the sale and after paying, according to their priorities all known prior, bona fide liens which were created without the lienor having knowledge or notice that the motor vehicle or other property was being used or to be used in connection with the conduct of such game or lottery) be turned over and paid to the treasurer of the county wherein the property was seized, to be placed by said treasurer in the general fund of the county.

History.

1798, c. 502, s. 3, P.R.; R.C., c. 34, s. 77; Code, s. 1051; Rev., s. 3722; C.S., s. 4436; 1943, c. 84; 1957, c. 501; 1973, c. 108, s. 12; 2005-344, s. 3(g)

§ 14-300. Opposing destruction of gaming tables and seizure of property

If any person shall oppose the destruction of any prohibited gaming table, or the seizure of any moneys, property or other thing staked on forbidden games, or shall take and carry away the same or any part thereof after seizure, he shall forfeit and pay to the person so opposed one thousand dollars ($ 1,000), for the use of the State and the person so opposed, and shall, moreover, be guilty of a Class 2 misdemeanor.

History.

1798, c. 502, s. 4, P.R.; R.C., c. 34, s. 78; Code, s. 1052; Rev., s. 3723; C.S., s. 4437; 1993, c. 539, s. 209; 1994, Ex. Sess., c. 24, s. 14(c)

§ 14-301. Operation or possession of slot machine; separate offenses

It shall be unlawful for any person, firm or corporation to operate, keep in his possession or in the possession of any other person, firm or corporation, for the purpose of being operated, any slot machine or device where the user may become entitled to receive any money, credit, allowance, or any thing of value, as defined in G.S. 14-306. Each time said machine is operated as aforesaid shall constitute a separate offense.

History.

1923, c. 138, ss. 1, 2; C.S., s. 4437(a); 1989, c. 406, s. 3

§ 14-302. Punchboards, vending machines, and other gambling devices; separate offenses

It shall be unlawful for any person, firm or corporation to operate or keep in his possession, or the possession of any other person, firm or corporation, for the purpose of being operated, any punchboard, slot machine or device where the user may become entitled to receive any money, credit, allowance, or any thing of value, as defined in G.S. 14-306. Each time said punchboard, slot machine or device where the user may become entitled to receive any money, credit, allowance, or any thing of value, as defined in G.S. 14-306 is operated, played, or patronized by the paying of money or other thing of value therefor, shall constitute a separate violation of this section as to operation thereunder.

History.

1923, c. 138, ss. 3, 4; C.S., s. 4437(b); 1989, c. 406, s. 4

§ 14-303. Violation of two preceding sections a misdemeanor

A violation of any of the provisions of G.S. 14-301 or 14-302 shall be a Class 2 misdemeanor.

History.
1923, c. 138, s. 5; C.S., s. 4437(c); 1993, c. 366, s. 2, c. 539, s. 210; 1994, Ex. Sess., c. 14, s. 8(a), (b)

§ 14-304. Manufacture, sale, etc., of slot machines and devices

It shall be unlawful to manufacture, own, store, keep, possess, sell, rent, lease, let on shares, lend or give away, transport, or expose for sale or lease, or to offer to sell, rent, lease, let on shares, lend or give away, or to permit the operation of, or for any person to permit to be placed, maintained, used or kept in any room, space or building owned, leased or occupied by him or under his management or control, any slot machine or device where the user may become entitled to receive any money, credit, allowance, or any thing of value, as defined in G.S. 14-306.

History.
1937, c. 196, s. 1; 1989, c. 406, s. 5

§ 14-305. Agreements with reference to slot machines or devices made unlawful

It shall be unlawful to make or permit to be made with any person any agreement with reference to any slot machines or device where the user may become entitled to receive any money, credit, allowance, or any thing of value, as defined in G.S. 14-306 pursuant to which the user thereof may become entitled to receive any money, credit, allowance, or anything of value or additional chance or right to use such machines or devices, or to receive any check, slug, token or memorandum entitling the holder to receive any money, credit, allowance or thing of value.

History.
1937, c. 196, s. 2; 1989, c. 406, s. 6

§ 14-306. Slot machine or device defined

(a) Any machine, apparatus or device is a slot machine or device within the provisions of G.S. 14-296 through 14-309, if it is one that is adapted, or may be readily converted into one that is adapted, for use in such a way that, as a result of the payment of any piece of money or coin or token or any credit card, debit card, prepaid card, or any other method that requires payment to activate play, whether directly into the slot machine or device or resulting in remote activation, such machine or device is caused to operate or may be operated in such manner that the user may receive or become entitled to receive any piece of money, credit, allowance or thing of value, or any check, slug, token or memorandum, whether of value or otherwise, or which may be exchanged for any money, credit, allowance or any thing of value, or which may be given in trade, or the user may secure additional chances or rights to use such machine, apparatus or device; or any other machine or device designed and manufactured primarily for use in connection with gambling and which machine or device is classified by the United States as requiring a federal gaming device tax stamp under applicable provisions of the Internal Revenue Code. This definition is intended to embrace all slot machines and similar devices except slot machines in which is kept any article to be purchased by depositing any coin or thing of value, and for which may be had any article of merchandise which makes the same return or returns of equal value each and every time it is operated, or any machine wherein may be seen any pictures or heard any music by depositing therein any coin or thing of value, or any slot weighing machine or any machine for making stencils by the use of contrivances operated by depositing in the machine any coin or thing of value, or any lock operated by slot wherein money or thing of value is to be deposited, where such slot machines make the same return or returns of equal value each and every time the same is operated and does not at any time it is operated offer the user or operator any additional money, credit, allowance, or thing of value, or check, slug, token or memorandum, whether of value or otherwise, which may be exchanged for money, credit, allowance or thing of value or which may be given in trade or by which the user may secure additional chances or rights to use such machine, apparatus, or device, or in the playing of which the operator does not have a chance to make varying scores or tallies.

(b) The definition contained in subsection (a) of this section and G.S. 14-296, 14-301, 14-302, and 14-305 does not include coin-operated machines, video games, pinball machines, and other computer, electronic or mechanical devices that are operated and played for amusement, that involve the use of skill or dexterity to solve problems or tasks or to make varying scores or tallies and that:

(1) Do not emit, issue, display, print out, or otherwise record any receipt, paper, coupon, token, or other form of record which is capable of being redeemed, exchanged, or repurchased for cash, cash equivalent, or prizes, or award free replays; or

(2) In actual operation, limit to eight the number of accumulated credits or replays that may be played at one time and which may award free replays or paper coupons that may be exchanged for prizes or merchandise with a value not exceeding ten dollars ($ 10.00), but may not be exchanged or converted to money.

(c) Any video machine, the operation of which is made lawful by subsection (b)(2) of this section, shall have affixed to it in view of the player a sticker informing that person that it is a criminal offense with the potential of imprisonment to pay more than that which is allowed by law. In addition, if the machine has an attract chip which allows programming, the static display shall contain the same message.

(d) The exception in subsection (b)(2) of this section does not apply to any machine that pays off in cash. The exemption in subsection (b)(2) of this section does not apply where the prizes, merchandise, credits, or replays are (i) repurchased for cash or rewarded by cash, (ii) exchanged for merchandise of a value of more than ten dollars ($ 10.00), or (iii) where there is a cash payout of any kind, by the person operating or managing the machine or the premises, or any agent or employee of that person. It is also a criminal offense, punishable under G.S. 14-309, for the person making the unlawful payout to the player of the machine to violate this section, in addition to any other person whose conduct may be unlawful.

History.
1937, c. 196, s. 3; 1967, c. 1219; 1977, c. 837; 1985, c. 644; 1989, c. 406, s. 1; 1993, c. 366, s. 1; 2000-151, s. 4; 2010-103, s. 3

N.C. Gen. Stat. § 14-306.1

Repealed by Session 2006-6, s. 3, effective July 1, 2007, and applicable to offenses committed on or after that date.

§ 14-306.1A. Types of machines and devices prohibited by law; penalties

(a) **Ban on Machines.** -- It shall be unlawful for any person to operate, allow to be operated, place into operation, or keep in that person's possession for the purpose of operation any video gaming machine as defined in subsection (b) of this section, except for the exemption for a federally recognized Indian tribe under subsection (e) of this section for whom it shall be lawful to operate and possess machines as listed in subsection (b) of this section if conducted in accordance with an approved Class III Tribal-State Compact applicable to that tribe, as provided in G.S. 147-12(14) and G.S. 71A-8.

(b) **Definitions.** -- As used in this section, a video gaming machine means a slot machine as defined in G.S. 14-306(a) and other forms of electrical, mechanical, or computer games such as, by way of illustration and not exclusion:
    (1) A video poker game or any other kind of video playing card game.
    (2) A video bingo game.
    (3) A video craps game.
    (4) A video keno game.
    (5) A video lotto game.

    (6) Eight liner.
    (7) Pot-of-gold.
    (8) A video game based on or involving the random or chance matching of different pictures, words, numbers, or symbols not dependent on the skill or dexterity of the player.
    (9) Any other video game not dependent on skill or dexterity that is played while revealing a prize as the result of an entry into a sweepstakes.

For the purpose of this section, a video gaming machine is a video machine which requires deposit of any coin or token, or use of any credit card, debit card, prepaid card, or any other method that requires payment, whether directly into the video gaming machine or resulting in remote activation, to activate play of any of the games listed in this subsection.

For the purpose of this section, a video gaming machine includes those that are within the scope of the exclusion provided in G.S. 14-306(b)(2) unless conducted in accordance with an approved Class III Tribal-State Compact applicable to that tribe as provided in G.S. 147-12(14) and G.S. 71A-8. For the purpose of this section, a video gaming machine does not include those that are within the scope of the exclusion provided in G.S. 14-306(b)(1).

(c) **Exemption for Certain Machines.** -- This section shall not apply to:
    (1) Assemblers, repairers, manufacturers, sellers, lessors, or transporters of video gaming machines who assemble, repair, manufacture, sell, lease, or transport them for use out-of-state, or
    (2) Assemblers, repairers, manufacturers, sellers, lessors, or transporters of video gaming machines who assemble, repair, manufacture, sell, or lease video gaming machines for use only by a federally recognized Indian tribe if such machines may be lawfully used on Indian land under the Indian Gaming Regulatory Act.

To qualify for an exemption under this subsection, the machines must be disabled and not operable, unless the machines are located on Indian land where they may be lawfully operated under a Tribal-State Compact.

(d) **Ban on Warehousing.** -- It is unlawful to warehouse any video gaming machine except in conjunction with the activities permitted under subsection (c) of this section.

(e) Repealed by Session Laws 2012-6, s. 3, effective June 6, 2012.

(f) Machines described in G.S. 14-306(b)(1) are excluded from this section.

History.
2006-6, s. 4; 2006-259, s. 6; 2010-103, s. 4; 2012-6, s. 3

§ 14-306.2. Violation of G.S. 14-306.1A a violation of the ABC laws

Violation of G.S. 14-306.1A is a violation of the gambling statutes for the purposes of G.S. 18B-1005(a)(3).

History.
2000-151, s. 2.; 2006-6, s. 5

§ 14-306.3. Certain game promotions unlawful

(a) It is unlawful to promote, operate, or conduct a server-based electronic game promotion.

(b) It is unlawful for any person to possess any game terminal with a display that simulates a game ordinarily played on a slot machine regulated under G.S. 14-306 or a video gaming machine regulated under G.S. 14-306.1A for the purpose of promoting, operating, or conducting a server-based electronic game promotion.

(c) As used in this section, "server-based electronic game promotion" means a system that meets all of the following criteria:

(1) A database contains a pool of entries with each entry associated with a prize value.

(2) Participants purchase, or otherwise obtain by any means, a prepaid card.

(3) With each prepaid card purchased or obtained, the participant also obtains one or more entries.

(4) Entries may be revealed in any of the following ways:

a. At a point-of-sale terminal at the time of purchase or later.

b. At a game terminal with a display that simulates a game ordinarily played on a slot machine regulated under G.S. 14-306 or a video gaming machine regulated under G.S. 14-306.1A.

(d) Upon conviction or plea of guilty, all of the following held by the person shall be automatically revoked:

(1) A permit issued under Chapter 18B of the General Statutes.

(2) A contract to sell tickets or shares under Article 5 of Chapter 18C of the General Statutes.

(e) Nothing in this section shall apply to the form of Class III gaming legally conducted on Indian lands which are held in trust by the United States government for and on behalf of federally recognized Indian tribes if conducted in accordance with an approved Class III Tribal-State Gaming Compact applicable to that tribe as provided in G.S. 147-12(14) and G.S. 71A-8.

History.
2008-122, s. 1

§ 14-306.4. Electronic machines and devices for sweepstakes prohibited

(a) **Definitions.** -- For the purposes of this section, the following definitions apply:

(1) "Electronic machine or device" means a mechanically, electrically or electronically operated machine or device, that is owned, leased or otherwise possessed by a sweepstakes sponsor or promoter, or any of the sweepstakes sponsor's or promoter's partners, affiliates, subsidiaries or contractors, that is intended to be used by a sweepstakes entrant, that uses energy, and that is capable of displaying information on a screen or other mechanism. This section is applicable to an electronic machine or device whether or not:

a. It is server-based.

b. It uses a simulated game terminal as a representation of the prizes associated with the results of the sweepstakes entries.

c. It utilizes software such that the simulated game influences or determines the winning or value of the prize.

d. It selects prizes from a predetermined finite pool of entries.

e. It utilizes a mechanism that reveals the content of a predetermined sweepstakes entry.

f. It predetermines the prize results and stores those results for delivery at the time the sweepstakes entry results are revealed.

g. It utilizes software to create a game result.

h. It requires deposit of any money, coin, or token, or the use of any credit card, debit card, prepaid card, or any other method of payment to activate the electronic machine or device.

i. It requires direct payment into the electronic machine or device, or remote activation of the electronic machine or device.

j. It requires purchase of a related product.

k. The related product, if any, has legitimate value.

l. It reveals the prize incrementally, even though it may not influence if a prize is awarded or the value of any prize awarded.

m. It determines and associates the prize with an entry or entries at the time the sweepstakes is entered.

n. It is a slot machine or other form of electrical, mechanical, or computer game.

(2) "Enter" or "entry" means the act or process by which a person becomes eligible to receive any prize offered in a sweepstakes.

(3) "Entertaining display" means visual information, capable of being seen by a sweepstakes entrant, that takes the form of actual game play, or simulated game play, such as, by way of illustration and not exclusion:

    a. A video poker game or any other kind of video playing card game.

    b. A video bingo game.

    c. A video craps game.

    d. A video keno game.

    e. A video lotto game.

    f. Eight liner.

    g. Pot-of-gold.

    h. A video game based on or involving the random or chance matching of different pictures, words, numbers, or symbols not dependent on the skill or dexterity of the player.

    i. Any other video game not dependent on skill or dexterity that is played while revealing a prize as the result of an entry into a sweepstakes.

(4) "Prize" means any gift, award, gratuity, good, service, credit, or anything else of value, which may be transferred to a person, whether possession of the prize is actually transferred, or placed on an account or other record as evidence of the intent to transfer the prize.

(5) "Sweepstakes" means any game, advertising scheme or plan, or other promotion, which, with or without payment of any consideration, a person may enter to win or become eligible to receive any prize, the determination of which is based upon chance.

(b) Notwithstanding any other provision of this Part, it shall be unlawful for any person to operate, or place into operation, an electronic machine or device to do either of the following:

(1) Conduct a sweepstakes through the use of an entertaining display, including the entry process or the reveal of a prize.

(2) Promote a sweepstakes that is conducted through the use of an entertaining display, including the entry process or the reveal of a prize.

(c) It is the intent of this section to prohibit any mechanism that seeks to avoid application of this section through the use of any subterfuge or pretense whatsoever.

(d) Nothing in this section shall be construed to make illegal any activity which is lawfully conducted on Indian lands pursuant to, and in accordance with, an approved Tribal-State Gaming Compact applicable to that Tribe as provided in G.S. 147-12(14) and G.S. 71A-8.

(e) Each violation of this section shall be considered a separate offense.

(f) Any person who violates this section is guilty of a Class 1 misdemeanor for the first offense and is guilty of a Class H felony for a second offense and a Class G felony for a third or subsequent offense.

History.
2010-103, s. 1

§ 14-307. Issuance of license prohibited

There shall be no State, county, or municipal tax levied for the privilege of operating the machines or devices the operation of which is prohibited by G.S. 14-304 through 14-309.

History.
1937, c. 196, s. 4

§ 14-308. Declared a public nuisance

An article or apparatus maintained or kept in violation of G.S. 14-304 through 14-309 is a public nuisance.

History.
1937, c. 196, s. 5

§ 14-309. Violation made criminal

(a) Any person who violates any provision of G.S. 14-304 through 14-309 is guilty of a Class 1 misdemeanor for the first offense, and is guilty of a Class H felony for a second offense and a Class G felony for a third or subsequent offense.

(b) Notwithstanding the provisions of subsection (a) of this section, any person violating the provisions of G.S. 14-306.1A involving the operation of five or more machines prohibited by that section is guilty of a Class G felony.

(c) Notwithstanding the provisions of subsection (a) of this section, any person violating the provisions of G.S. 14-306.3(b) involving the possession of five or more machines prohibited by that subsection is guilty of a Class G felony.

History.
1937, c. 196, s. 6; 1993, c. 366, s. 3, c. 539, s. 211; 1994, Ex. Sess., c. 14, s. 9(a), (b); 2000-151, s. 3; 2006-6, s. 11; 2008-122, s. 3

§ 14-309.1. Defense to possession; antique slot machines

(a) In any prosecution for possession of a slot machine or device as defined in G.S. 14-306, it is a defense that the slot machine was not intended to be used in the operation or promotion of unlawful gambling activity or enterprise and that the slot machine is an antique. For purposes of this section a slot machine manufactured 25 years ago or earlier is conclusively presumed to be an antique.

(b) When a defendant raises the defense provided in subsection (a), any slot machine seized from the defendant shall not be destroyed or otherwise altered until a final court determination is rendered. If the court determines that the defense has been proved the slot machine shall be returned immediately to the defendant.

History.
1979, 2nd Sess., c. 1090

N.C. Gen. Stat. § 14-309.2

Repealed by Session Laws 2005-276, s. 31.1(v2), effective July 1, 2005.

§§ 14-309.3, 14-309.4

Reserved for future codification purposes.

PART 2
BINGO AND RAFFLES

§ 14-309.5. Bingo

(a) The purpose of the conduct of bingo is to insure a maximum availability of the net proceeds exclusively for application to the charitable, nonprofit causes and undertakings specified herein; that the only justification for this Part is to support such charitable, nonprofit causes; and such purpose should be carried out to prevent the operation of bingo by professionals for profit, prevent commercialized gambling, prevent the disguise of bingo and other game forms or promotional schemes, prevent participation by criminal and other undesirable elements, and prevent the diversion of funds for the purpose herein authorized.

(b) It is lawful for an exempt organization to conduct bingo games in accordance with the provisions of this Part. Any licensed exempt organization who conducts a bingo game in violation of any provision of this Part shall be guilty of a Class 2 misdemeanor. Upon conviction such person shall not conduct a bingo game for a period of one year. It is lawful to participate in a bingo game conducted pursuant to this Part. It shall be a Class I felony for any person: (i) to operate a bingo game without a license; (ii) to operate a bingo game while license is revoked or suspended; (iii) to willfully misuse or misapply any moneys received in connection with any bingo game; or (iv) to contract with or provide consulting services to any licensee. It shall not constitute a violation of any State law to advertise a bingo game conducted in accordance with this Part.

History.
1983, c. 896, s. 3; 1983 (Reg. Sess., 1984), c. 1107, ss. 1-4; 1989 (Reg. Sess., 1990), c. 826, s. 1; 1993, c. 539, ss. 212, 1231; 1994, Ex. Sess., c. 24, s. 14(c)

§ 14-309.6. Definitions

For purposes of this Part, the term:

(1) "Exempt organization" means an organization that has been in continuous existence in the county of operation of the bingo game for at least one year and that is exempt from taxation under section 501(c)(3), 501(c)(4), 501(c)(8), 501(c)(10), 501(c)(19), or 501(d) of the Internal Revenue Code and is exempt under similar provisions of the General Statutes as a bona fide nonprofit charitable, civic, religious, fraternal, patriotic or veterans' organization or as a nonprofit volunteer fire department, or as a nonprofit volunteer rescue squad or a bona fide homeowners' or property owners' association. (If the organization has local branches or chapters, the term "exempt organization" means the local branch or chapter operating the bingo game);

(2) "Bingo game" means a specific game of chance played with individual cards having numbered squares ranging from one to 75, in which prizes are awarded on the basis of designated numbers on such cards conforming to a predetermined pattern of numbers (but shall not include "instant bingo" which is a game of chance played by the selection of one or more prepackaged cards, with winners determined by the appearance of a preselected designation on the card);

(3) Repealed by Session Laws 1983 (Regular Session 1984), c. 1107, s. 5.

(4) "Local law-enforcement agency" means for any bingo game conducted outside the corporate limits of a municipality or inside the corporate limits of a municipality having no municipal police force:

　　a. The county police force; or

　　b. The county sheriff's office in a county with no county police force;

(5) "Local law-enforcement agency" means the municipal police for any bingo game conducted within the corporate limits of a municipality having a police force;

(6) "Beach bingo games" means bingo games which have prizes of ten dollars ($ 10.00) or less or merchandise that is not redeemable for cash and that has a value of ten dollars ($ 10.00) or less; and

(7) "Licensed exempt organization" means an exempt organization which possesses a currently valid license.

(8) "Nonprofit organization" means an organization or association recognized by

the Department of Revenue as tax exempt pursuant to G.S. 105-130.11(a), or any bona fide branch, chapter, or affiliate of that organization.

History.
1983, c. 896, s. 3; 1983 (Reg. Sess., 1984), c. 1107, ss. 2, 5; 2018-100, s. 5(a).

§ 14-309.7. Licensing procedure

(a) An exempt organization shall not operate a bingo game at a location without a license. Application for a bingo license shall be made to the Alcohol Law Enforcement Division of the Department of Public Safety on a form prescribed by the Division. The Division shall charge an annual application fee of two hundred dollars ($ 200.00) to defray the cost of issuing bingo licenses and handling bingo audit reports. The fees collected shall be deposited in the General Fund of the State. The license shall expire one year after issuance and may be renewed annually if the applicant pays the application fee and files an audit with the Division pursuant to G.S. 14-309.11. A copy of the application and license shall be furnished to the local law-enforcement agency in the county or municipality in which the licensee intends to operate before bingo is conducted by the licensee.

(b) Each application and renewal application shall contain the following information:

(1) The name and address of the applicant and if the applicant is a corporation, association, or other similar legal entity, the name and home address of each of the officers of the organization as well as the name and address of the directors, or other persons similarly situated, of the organization.

(2) The name and home address of each member of the special committee described in G.S. 14-309.10.

(3) A copy of the application for recognition of exemptions and a determination letter from the Internal Revenue Service and the Department of Revenue that indicates the applicant is an exempt organization and stating the section under which that exemption is granted. If the applicant is a State or local branch, lodge, post, or chapter of a national organization, a copy of the determination letter of the national organization satisfies this requirement.

(4) The location at which the applicant will conduct the bingo games. If the premises are leased, a copy of the lease or rental agreement.

(c) In order for an exempt organization to have a member familiar with the operation of bingo present on the premises at all times when bingo is being played and for this member to be responsible for the receiving, reporting, and depositing of all revenues received, the exempt organization may pay one member for conducting a bingo game. The pay shall be on an hourly basis only for the time bingo is actually being played and shall not exceed one and one-half times the existing minimum wage in North Carolina. The member paid under this subsection shall be a member in good standing of the exempt organization for at least one year and shall not be the lessor or an employee or agent of the lessor. No other person shall be compensated for conducting a bingo game from funds derived from any activities occurring in, or simultaneously with, the playing of bingo, including funds derived from concessions. An exempt organization shall not contract with any person for the purpose of conducting a bingo game.

(c1) Except as provided in subsection (e) of this section, an exempt organization may hold a bingo game only in or on property owned, either legally or equitably, or leased, but not subleased, by the organization from the owner or bona fide property management agent. The buildings shall be permanent with approved plumbing for bathrooms and shall not be movable or temporary such as a tent or lean-to. The total monthly payment for leased premises shall not exceed one and one-quarter percent (1 1/4%) of the total assessed ad valorem tax value of the portion of the building actually used for the bingo games and the land on which the building is located; the land shall not exceed two acres. The lease shall be for all activities conducted on the leased premises, including the playing of bingo for a period of not less than one year, and the leased premises shall be actually occupied and used by that organization on a regular basis for purposes other than bingo for at least six months before the first game. All equipment used by the exempt organization in conducting the bingo game shall be owned by the organization. Unless the exempt organization leases the property in accordance with this subsection, an exempt organization may conduct a bingo game only in or on property that is exempt from property taxes levied under Subchapter II of Chapter 105 of the General Statutes, or that is classified and not subject to any property taxes levied under Subchapter II of Chapter 105 of the General Statutes. It is unlawful for any person to operate beach bingo games at a location that is being used by any licensed exempt organization for the purpose of conducting bingo games.

(d) Conduct of a bingo game or raffle in accordance with this Part does not operate to defeat an exemption or classification under Subchapter II of Chapter 105 of the General Statutes.

(e) An exempt organization that wants to conduct only an annual or semiannual bingo game may apply to the Alcohol Law Enforcement Division of the Department of Public Safety for a limited occasion permit. The Division may require any information necessary to determine that the bingo game is conducted in accordance with this Part. The Division shall not require more information for a limited occasion permit than it requires for a license under this section. The application shall be made to the Division on prescribed forms at least 30 days prior to the scheduled date of the bingo game. In lieu of the reporting requirements of G.S. 14-309.11(b), the exempt organization shall file with the Division and local law-enforcement a report on prescribed forms no later than 30 days following the bingo game for which the permit was obtained. The forms may require any information necessary to determine that the bingo game was conducted in accordance with this Part. The forms shall not require more information than specified in G.S. 14-309.11(b). Any licensed exempt organization may donate or loan its equipment or use of its premises to an exempt organization that has secured a limited occasion permit as long as the arrangement is disclosed in the limited occasion permit application and is approved by the Division. Except as provided in this subsection, all provisions of this Part apply to an exempt organization operating a bingo game under this subsection.

History.
1983, c. 896, s. 3; c. 923, s. 217; 1983 (Reg. Sess., 1984), c. 1107, ss. 2, 4, 6; 1987, c. 866, ss. 1, 2; 1987 (Reg. Sess., 1988), c. 1001, s. 1; 1997-443, s. 11A.118(a); 2002-159, ss. 3(a), 3(b); 2009-451, s. 17.6; 2011-145, s. 19.1(g); 2016-27, s. 3; 2017-102, s. 5.1(a); 2020-72, s. 1(a)

§ 14-309.8. Limit on sessions

The number of sessions of bingo conducted or sponsored by an exempt organization shall be limited to two sessions per week and such sessions must not exceed a period of five hours each per session. No two sessions of bingo shall be held within a 48-hour period of time. No more than two sessions of bingo shall be operated or conducted in any one building, hall or structure during any one calendar week and if two sessions are held, they must be held by the same exempt organization. This section shall not apply to bingo games conducted at a fair or other exhibition conducted pursuant to Article 45 of Chapter 106 of the General Statutes.

History.
1983, c. 896, s. 3; c. 923, s. 217; 1983 (Reg. Sess., 1984), c. 1107, ss. 6, 7

§ 14-309.9. Bingo prizes

(a) The maximum prize in cash or merchandise that may be offered or paid for any one game of bingo is five hundred dollars ($ 500.00). The maximum aggregate amount of prizes, in cash and/or merchandise, that may be offered or paid at any one session of bingo is one thousand five hundred dollars ($ 1,500). Provided, however, that if an exempt organization holds only one session of bingo during a calendar week, the maximum aggregate amount of prizes, in cash and/or merchandise, that may be offered or paid at any one session is two thousand five hundred dollars ($ 2,500).

(b) Repealed by Session Laws 1983 (Regular Session 1984), c. 1107, s. 8.

(c) This section shall not apply to bingo games conducted at a fair or other exhibition conducted pursuant to Article 45 of Chapter 106 of the General Statutes.

History.
1983, c. 896, s. 3; 1983 (Reg. Sess., 1984), c. 1107, ss. 6, 8

§ 14-309.10. Operation of bingo

The operation of bingo games shall be the direct responsibility of, and controlled by, a special committee selected by the governing body of the exempt organization in the manner provided by the rules of the exempt organization.

History.
1983, c. 896, s. 3; 1983 (Reg. Sess., 1984), c. 1107, s. 9

§ 14-309.11. Accounting and use of proceeds

(a) All funds received in connection with a bingo game shall be placed in a separate bank account. No funds may be disbursed from this account except the exempt organization may expend proceeds for prizes, advertising, utilities, and the purchase of supplies and equipment used [in conducting the raffle and] in playing bingo, taxes and license fees related to bingo and the payment of compensation as authorized by G.S. 14-309.7(c) and for the purposes set forth below for the remaining proceeds. Such payments shall be made by consecutively numbered checks. Any proceeds available in the account after payment of the above expenses shall inure to the exempt organization to be used for religious, charitable, civic, scientific, testing, public safety, literary, or educational purposes or for purchasing, constructing, maintaining, operating or using equipment or land or a building or improvements thereto owned by and for the exempt organization and used for civic purposes or made available by the exempt organization for use by the general public from time to time, or to foster amateur sports competition, or for the prevention of cruelty to children or animals, provided that no proceeds shall be used or expended for social functions for the members of the exempt organization.

(b) An audit of the account required by subsection (a) of this section shall be prepared annually for the period of January 1 through December 31 or otherwise as directed by the Alcohol Law Enforcement Division of the Department of Public Safety and shall be filed with the Division and the local law-enforcement agency at a time directed by the Division. The audit shall be prepared on a form approved by the Division and shall include the following information:

(1) The number of bingo games conducted or sponsored by the exempt organization;

(2) The location and date at which each bingo game was conducted and the prize awarded;

(3) The gross receipts of each bingo game;

(4) The cost or amount of any prize given at each bingo game;

(5) The amount paid in prizes at each session;

(6) The net return to the exempt organization; and

(7) The disbursements from the separate account and the purpose of those disbursements, including the date of each transaction and the name and address of each payee.

(c) Any person who shall willfully furnish, supply, or otherwise give false information in any audit or statement filed pursuant to this section shall be guilty of a Class 2 misdemeanor.

(d) All books, papers, records and documents relevant to determining whether an organization has acted or is acting in compliance with this section shall be open to inspection by the law-enforcement agency or its designee, or the district attorney or his designee, or the Alcohol Law Enforcement Division of the Department of Public Safety at reasonable times and during reasonable hours.

History.
1983, c. 896, s. 3; 1983 (Reg. Sess., 1984), c. 1107, ss. 2, 3, 9; 1987, c. 866, s. 3; 1987 (Reg. Sess., 1988), c. 1001, s. 1; 1993, c. 539, s. 213; 1994, Ex. Sess., c. 24, s. 14(c); 1997-443, s. 11A.118(a); 2002-159, ss. 4(a), (b); 2011-145, s. 19.1(g); 2016-27, s. 3; 2020-72, s. 1(b)

§ 14-309.12. Violation is gambling

A bingo game conducted otherwise than in accordance with the provisions of this Part is "gambling" within the meaning of G.S. 19-1 et seq., and proceedings against such bingo game may be instituted as provided for in Chapter 19 of the General Statutes.

History.
1983, c. 896, s. 3; 1983 (Reg. Sess., 1984), c. 1107, s. 2

§ 14-309.13. Public sessions

Any exempt organization operating a bingo game which is open to persons other than members of the exempt organization, their spouses, and their children shall make such bingo game open to the general public.

History.
1983, c. 896, s. 3; 1983 (Reg. Sess., 1984), c. 1107, s. 4

§ 14-309.14. Beach bingo

Nothing in this Article shall apply to "beach bingo" games except for the following subdivisions:

(1) No beach bingo game may offer a prize having a value greater than ten dollars ($ 10.00). Any person offering a greater than ten-dollar ($ 10.00) but less than fifty-dollar ($ 50.00) prize is guilty of a Class 2 misdemeanor. Any person offering a prize of fifty dollars ($ 50.00) or greater is guilty of a Class I felony.

(2) No beach bingo game may be held in conjunction with any other lawful bingo game, with any "promotional bingo game", or with any offering of an opportunity to obtain anything of value, whether for valuable consideration or not. No beach bingo game may offer free bingo games as a promotion, for prizes or otherwise. Any person who violates this subsection is guilty of a Class I felony.

(3) Repealed by Session Laws 2019-182, s. 14(b), effective September 1, 2019, and applicable to offenses committed on or after that date.

(4) Upon conviction under any provision of this section, such person shall not conduct a bingo game for a period of at least one year.

(5) A person shall not operate a beach bingo game at any location without first obtaining a license as provided by this subdivision. Any person operating a beach bingo game without a license is guilty of a Class 2 misdemeanor. The procedure for obtaining an application for a beach bingo license shall be as follows:

a. The application for a beach bingo license shall be made to the Alcohol Law Enforcement Division of the Department of Public Safety on a form prescribed by the Division. The Division shall charge an initial application fee of three hundred dollars ($ 300.00) and an annual renewal fee of three hundred dollars ($ 300.00) to defray the cost of issuing beach bingo licenses and handling enforcement. The fees collected shall be deposited in the General Fund of the State. This license shall expire one year after the granting of the license but may be renewed yearly upon payment of the renewal fee.

b. Each application and renewal application shall contain all of the following information:

1. The name and address of the applicant and if the applicant is a corporation, association, or other similar legal entity, the name and home address of each of the officers of the organization as well as the name and address of the directors, or other persons similarly situated, of the organization.

2. The location at which the applicant will conduct the bingo games. If the premises are leased, a copy of the lease or rental agreement.

c. Any false information provided in an application for a beach bingo license is cause for suspension of that license and is also a Class 2 misdemeanor.

d. All books, papers, records, and documents relevant to determining whether an individual has acted or is acting in compliance with this section shall be open to inspection by the Alcohol Law Enforcement Division of the Department of Public Safety at reasonable times and during reasonable hours.

History.
1983, c. 896, s. 3; 1983 (Reg. Sess., 1984), c. 1107, s. 10; 1987, c. 701; 1989 (Reg. Sess., 1990), c. 826, s. 2; 1993, c. 539, ss. 214, 1232; 1994, Ex. Sess., c. 24, s. 14(c); 2016-27, s. 1; 2017-102, s. 5.1(b); 2019-182, s. 14(b); 2020-72, s. 1(c)

§ 14-309.15. Raffles

(a) It is lawful for any nonprofit organization, candidate, political committee, or any government entity within the State, to conduct raffles in accordance with this section. Each regional or county chapter of a nonprofit organization is eligible to conduct raffles in accordance with this section independently of its parent organization. Any person who conducts a raffle in violation of any provision of this section is guilty of a Class 2 misdemeanor. Upon conviction that person shall not conduct a raffle for a period of one year. It is lawful to participate in a raffle conducted pursuant to this section. It is not a violation of State law to advertise a raffle conducted in accordance with this section. A raffle conducted pursuant to this section is not "gambling." For the purpose of this section, "candidate" and "political committee" have

the meaning provided by Article 22A of Chapter 163 of the General Statutes, who have filed organization reports under that Article, and who are in good standing with the appropriate board of elections. Receipts and expenditures of a raffle by a candidate or political committee shall be reported in accordance with Article 22A of Chapter 163 of the General Statutes, and ticket purchases are contributions within the meaning of that Article.

(b) For purposes of this section "raffle" means a game in which the prize is won by random drawing of the name or number of one or more persons purchasing chances.

(c) A nonprofit organization may hold no more than four raffles per year.

(d) Except as provided in subsection (g) of this section, the maximum cash prize that may be offered or paid for any one raffle is one hundred twenty-five thousand dollars ($ 125,000) and if merchandise is used as a prize, and it is not redeemable for cash, the maximum fair market value of that prize may be one hundred twenty-five thousand dollars ($ 125,000). The total cash prizes offered or paid by any nonprofit organization shall not exceed two hundred fifty thousand dollars ($ 250,000) in any calendar year. The total fair market value of all prizes offered by any nonprofit organization, either in cash or in merchandise that is not redeemable for cash, shall not exceed two hundred fifty thousand dollars ($ 250,000) in any calendar year.

(e) Raffles shall not be conducted in conjunction with bingo.

(f) As used in this subsection, "net proceeds of a raffle" means the receipts less the cost of prizes awarded. No less than ninety percent (90%) of the net proceeds of a raffle shall be used by the nonprofit organization for charitable, religious, educational, civic, or other nonprofit purposes. None of the net proceeds of the raffle shall be used to pay any person to conduct the raffle, or to rent a building where the tickets are received or sold or the drawing is conducted.

(g) Real property may be offered as a prize in a raffle. The maximum appraised value of real property that may be offered for any one raffle is five hundred thousand dollars ($ 500,000). The total appraised value of all real estate prizes offered by any nonprofit organization shall not exceed five hundred thousand dollars ($ 500,000) in any calendar year.

(h) Notwithstanding any other subsection of this section, it is lawful for a federally insured depository institution to conduct a savings promotion raffle under G.S. 53C-6-20, 54-109.64, 54B-140, or 54C-180.

History.
1983 (Reg. Sess., 1984), c. 1107, s. 11; 1993, c. 219, s. 1; c. 539, s. 215; 1994, Ex. Sess., c. 24, s. 14(c); 1997-10, s. 1; 2005-276, s. 17.31; 2005-345, s. 31; 2006-264, s. 3(a);

2009-49, s. 1; 2011-146, s. 1; 2013-381, s. 59.1; 2018-100, s. 5(b); 2019-173, s. 2(a)

§§ 14-309.16 through 14-309.19

Reserved for future codification purposes.

PART 3
GREYHOUND RACING

§ 14-309.20. Greyhound racing prohibited

(a) No person shall hold, conduct, or operate any greyhound races for public exhibition in this State for monetary remuneration.

(b) No person shall transmit or receive interstate or intrastate simulcasting of greyhound races for commercial purposes in this State.

(c) Any person who violates this section shall be guilty of a Class 1 misdemeanor.

History.
1998-212, s. 17.16(d)

PART 4
GAME NIGHTS

§ 14-309.25. Definitions

The following definitions apply in this Part:

(1) **Exempt organization. --** An organization that has been in continuous existence for at least five years and that is exempt from taxation under section 501(c)(3), 501(c)(4), 501(c)(5), or 501(c)(6) of the United States Internal Revenue Code.

(2) **Game night. --** A specific event at which games of chance are played and prizes are awarded by raffle and that is sponsored by or on behalf of an exempt organization for the primary purpose of raising funds for the exempt organization or is sponsored by an employer or trade association pursuant to G.S. 14-309.34.

(3) **Local law enforcement agency. --** Any county or municipal law enforcement agency that has territorial and subject matter jurisdiction over the location at which the game night is being held.

(4) **Qualified facility. --** As defined in G.S. 18B-1000.

History.
2019-13, s. 2

§ 14-309.26. Game nights

(a) It is lawful for an exempt organization to conduct a game night at a qualified facility in accordance with the provisions of this Part.

Each regional or county chapter of an exempt organization shall be eligible to conduct game nights in accordance with this Part independently of its parent organization, provided that the regional or county chapter has been in continuous existence for at least five years. It is lawful for persons to participate in a game night conducted pursuant to this Part. It shall not constitute a violation of any State law to advertise a game night conducted in accordance with this Part.

(a1) Notwithstanding subsection (a) of this section, an exempt organization that is exempt from taxation under section 501(c)(3) of the Internal Revenue Code and operates a specialized community residential center for individuals with developmental disabilities licensed pursuant to G.S. 122C-23 may conduct a game night in accordance with this Part in a location that is not a qualified facility if the exempt organization has been issued a special one-time permit under G.S. 18B-1002(a)(5) to be used for the game night.

(b) If any exempt organization conducts a game night in violation of any provision of this Part, the person indicated in G.S. 14-309.27(b)(2) is guilty of a Class 2 misdemeanor. In addition to any fine that may be imposed, an exempt organization convicted of a violation under this Part shall not conduct a game night for a period of one year from the date of the conviction.

History.
2019-13, s. 2; 2021-150, s. 32.1

§ 14-309.27. Permit procedure

(a) An exempt organization shall not operate a game night without first obtaining a permit as provided by this Part. The application for a game night permit shall be on a form prescribed by the Alcohol Law Enforcement Division of the Department of Public Safety and shall be submitted to the Alcohol Law Enforcement Headquarters at least 30 days in advance of the date for the game night event.

(b) Each application for a permit under this Part shall contain the following information:

(1) The name and address of the exempt organization that is applying for the permit.

(2) The name, address, and signature of the person applying on behalf of the exempt organization and who will be responsible for the event.

(3) Verification of the tax-exempt status of the exempt organization, except, if the applicant is a local chapter, division, lodge, or branch of the exempt organization, then verification of the tax-exempt status of the parent organization.

(4) Verification of the exempt organization's status as a licensed or exempt charitable or sponsor organization pursuant to Chapter 131F of the General Statutes.

(5) The time, duration, date, and place of the event.

(6) The games proposed to be operated.

(7) The name and address of the person, firm, or corporation who will operate the games and the relationship, if any, of such person, firm, or corporation to the exempt organization or qualified facility.

(7a) The location of the facility at which the event will be held.

(8) The area of the facility in which the event will be held.

(c) A separate application shall be required for each game night event. A fee of one hundred dollars ($ 100.00) shall be charged for each permit. The permit fees assessed under this Part are payable to the Alcohol Law Enforcement Division of the Department of Public Safety and shall be collected and used by the Alcohol Law Enforcement Division to defray the costs of issuing game night permits. The permit shall be displayed at the event. A qualified facility shall not be subject to civil or criminal liability for violating this Part if the exempt organization provides the facility with a permit for the game night event.

History.
2019-13, s. 2; 2021-150, s. 32.1

§ 14-309.28. Limits on game night events

The following limitations apply to game night events:

(1) The number of game night events conducted or sponsored by an exempt organization shall be limited to four events per year.

(2) The event shall not exceed a period of five hours each per event. No more than one game night event shall be held in any quarter of a calendar year that begins January 1.

(3) No more than two game night events shall be operated or conducted in any one building, hall, or structure during any one calendar week, and if two events are held, they must be held by different exempt organizations on different nights of the week.

(4) There shall be no operation of a game night event between the hours of 2:00 A.M. and 12:00 noon Monday through Saturday or between the hours of 2:00 A.M. and 2:00 P.M. Sunday.

(5) A facility authorized to host a game night under this Part shall not host more than two game nights in any calendar month.

History.
2019-13, s. 2; 2021-150, s. 32.1

§ 14-309.29. Game night; prizes and costs

(a) **Prizes.** -- No games at a game night event may be played for cash or a cash prize. Prizes shall be awarded only through a raffle. Participants may exchange chips, markers, or tokens from the game night event for raffle tickets. For purposes of this subsection, the term "cash prize" includes gift cards that are issued by a financial institution or its operating subsidiary and that are usable at multiple unaffiliated sellers of goods or services.

(b) **Costs.** -- The cost of the prizes and expenses to operate the game night event, excluding the cost of food, beverages, and entertainment, shall not exceed the proceeds derived from the event. If the exempt organization hires a game night vendor for the event, payment shall be by fixed fee.

History.
2019-13, s. 2

§ 14-309.30. Operation of game night events

The following games are the only games that may be played at a game night event:

(1) Roulette.
(2) Blackjack.
(3) Poker.
(4) Craps.
(5) Simulated horse race.
(6) Merchandise wheel of fortune.

History.
2019-13, s. 2

§ 14-309.31. Use of proceeds

The exempt organization may use its own funds or funds received in connection with the game night for prizes, advertising, utilities, space rental, and the purchase or rental of supplies and equipment, including game night tables and related equipment, used in conducting the games. Net proceeds from the game night shall inure to the benefit of the exempt organization and shall be used to further the organization's tax-exempt purposes.

History.
2019-13, s. 2

§ 14-309.32. Violation is gambling

A game night conducted other than in accordance with the provisions of this Part is "gambling" within the meaning of G.S. 14-292 and

G.S. 19-1, et seq., and proceedings against such game night may be instituted as provided for in Chapter 19 of the General Statutes.

History.
2019-13, s. 2

§ 14-309.33. Applicability

This Part is only applicable in areas of the State located east of I-26 as that interstate highway was located on November 28, 2011.

History.
2019-13, s. 2

§ 14-309.34. Applicability to employer paid events

(a) It shall be lawful (i) for an employer, with 25 or more employees, to hold a game night event for employees and guests or a trade association, with 25 or more members, to hold a game night event for its members and guests, and (ii) for persons to participate in a game night conducted pursuant to this section, provided all of the following conditions are met:

(1) There is no cost or charge to the attendees.

(2) The employer or trade association obtains a permit and pays the required fee, as provided in G.S. 14-309.27.

(3) The game night event is held at a qualified facility.

(b) Game night events conducted pursuant to this section shall be subject to the limitations of G.S. 14-309.28, 14-309.29(a), and 14-309.30.

(c) For purposes of this section, any reference to "exempt organization" in G.S. 14-309.27 shall include the employer or trade association submitting an application as required by this section, except that the verification required by subdivisions (3) and (4) of subsection (b) of G.S. 14-309.27 shall not be required from an applicant for a permit if the applicant is required to obtain the permit pursuant to subsection (a) of this section.

(d) If any employer or trade association conducts a game night in violation of any provision of this section, the person indicated in G.S. 14-309.27(b)(2) is guilty of a Class 2 misdemeanor. In addition to any fine that may be imposed, the employer or trade association convicted of a violation of this section shall not conduct a game night for a period of one year from the date of the conviction.

History.
2019-13, s. 2

§ 14-309.35. Registration, possession, and transportation of gaming equipment

(a) Notwithstanding the provisions of G.S. 14-295 or G.S. 14-297, it shall be lawful to possess or transport gaming tables and other gaming equipment, if the possession or transportation is solely for use in game night events conducted pursuant to this Part. Gaming tables and other gaming equipment possessed or transported pursuant to this Part shall not be subject to seizure pursuant to G.S. 14-298 if they have been registered pursuant to the provisions of this Article and are used solely in game night events conducted pursuant to this Part.

(b) A gaming table or other gaming equipment possessed or transported for use in a game night event must be registered with the Alcohol Law Enforcement Division of the Department of Public Safety and must have a sticker affixed with a unique number. A fee of twenty-five dollars ($ 25.00) shall be charged for each sticker and each sticker shall be renewed annually. The sticker fees assessed under this section are payable to the Alcohol Law Enforcement Division of the Department of Public Safety and shall be collected and used by the Alcohol Law Enforcement Division to defray the costs of registering the gaming tables and gaming equipment. The Alcohol Law Enforcement Division may inspect, without prior notice, any gaming table or other gaming equipment used in a game night event at any time immediately prior to or during the game night event. Use of a gaming table or gaming equipment in a game night event that does not comply with the requirements of this subsection shall be a Class 1 misdemeanor.

History.
2019-13, s. 2; 2021-150, s. 32.1

§ 14-309.36. Permit procedure for game night vendors

(a) No person, firm, or corporation may receive compensation for providing gaming tables or gaming equipment for use in a game night without first obtaining a permit as provided by this section. The application for a game night vendor permit shall be on a form prescribed by the Alcohol Law Enforcement Division of the Department of Public Safety and shall be submitted to the Alcohol Law Enforcement Headquarters.

(b) A fee of two thousand five hundred dollars ($ 2,500) shall be charged annually for each permit. The permit fees assessed under this section are payable to the Alcohol Law Enforcement Division of the Department of Public Safety and shall be collected and used by the Alcohol Law Enforcement Division to defray the costs of issuing game night vendor permits and ensuring compliance with this section. The game night vendor permit shall be displayed at any event the game night vendor conducts.

(c) The Alcohol Law Enforcement Division shall deny a permit to a person, firm, or corporation that meets any of the following disqualifying conditions:

(1) Has a conviction for any violation of State or federal gambling laws within the five years prior to the date of application.

(2) Has pending charges for any violation of State or federal gambling laws.

(3) Is subject to an active criminal or civil court order prohibiting involvement in gambling activities.

(4) Has a conviction for any felony.

(d) A person, firm, or corporation with a game night vendor permit may not employ a person that meets any of the following disqualifying conditions:

(1) Has a conviction for any violation of State or federal gambling laws within the five years prior to the date of employment.

(2) Has pending charges for any violation of State or federal gambling laws.

(3) Is subject to an active criminal or civil court order prohibiting involvement in gambling activities.

(4) Has a conviction for any felony.

(e) All gaming tables and gaming equipment owned or possessed by a game night vendor must be registered pursuant to G.S. 14-309.35. The Alcohol Law Enforcement Division of the Department of Public Safety shall inspect the gaming tables and equipment of each game night vendor at least one time per calendar year and may conduct any additional inspections reasonably necessary to ensure compliance with G.S. 14-309.35 and this section. Inspections of gaming tables and equipment shall occur (i) on the premises of a game night event that the game night vendor has been employed to conduct, (ii) immediately prior to or during the game night event, (iii) at locations, times, and dates chosen by the Alcohol Law Enforcement Division, and (iv) without prior notice to the game night vendor or any party that has obtained a permit pursuant to G.S. 14-309.27.

History.
2019-13, s. 2; 2021-150, s. 32.1

§ 14-309.37. Slot machines, video gaming machines, electronic sweepstakes machines not authorized

Nothing in this Part shall be construed to authorize the possession, transportation, or use of any slot machine, video gaming machine, or electronic machine or device prohibited pursuant to G.S. 14-304 through 14-309.

History.
2019-13, s. 2

ARTICLE 38
MARATHON DANCES AND SIMILAR ENDURANCE CONTESTS

§§ 14-310 through 14-312

Repealed by Session Laws 1993 (Reg. Sess., 1994), c. 767, s. 30(13)-(15), effective October 1, 1994.

ARTICLE 39
PROTECTION OF MINORS

§ 14-313. Youth access to tobacco products, tobacco-derived products, vapor products, and cigarette wrapping papers

(a) **Definitions.** -- The following definitions apply in this section:

(1) **Distribute.** -- To sell, furnish, give, or provide tobacco products, including tobacco product samples or cigarette wrapping papers, to the ultimate consumer.

(2) **Proof of age.** -- A drivers license or other photographic identification that includes the bearer's date of birth that purports to establish that the person is 18 years of age or older.

(3) **Sample.** -- A tobacco product distributed to members of the general public at no cost for the purpose of promoting the product.

(3a) **Tobacco-derived product.** -- Any noncombustible product derived from tobacco that contains nicotine and is intended for human consumption, whether chewed, absorbed, dissolved, ingested, or by other means. This term does not include a vapor product or any product regulated by the United States Food and Drug Administration under Chapter V of the federal Food, Drug, and Cosmetic Act.

(4) **Tobacco product.** -- Any product that contains tobacco and is intended for human consumption. For purposes of this section, the term includes a tobacco-derived product, vapor product, or components of a vapor product.

(5) **Vapor product.** -- Any noncombustible product that employs a mechanical heating element, battery, or electronic circuit regardless of shape or size and that can be used to heat a liquid nicotine solution contained in a vapor cartridge. The term includes an electronic cigarette,

electronic cigar, electronic cigarillo, and electronic pipe. The term does not include any product regulated by the United States Food and Drug Administration under Chapter V of the federal Food, Drug, and Cosmetic Act.

(b) **Sale or distribution to persons under the age of 18 years.** -- If any person shall distribute, or aid, assist, or abet any other person in distributing tobacco products or cigarette wrapping papers to any person under the age of 18 years, or if any person shall purchase tobacco products or cigarette wrapping papers on behalf of a person under the age of 18 years, the person shall be guilty of a Class 2 misdemeanor; provided, however, that it shall not be unlawful to distribute tobacco products or cigarette wrapping papers to an employee when required in the performance of the employee's duties. Retail distributors of tobacco products shall prominently display near the point of sale a sign in letters at least five-eighths of an inch high which states the following:

N.C. LAW STRICTLY PROHIBITS

THE PURCHASE OF TOBACCO PRODUCTS, TOBACCO-DERIVED PRODUCTS, VAPOR PRODUCTS, AND CIGARETTE WRAPPING PAPERS

BY PERSONS UNDER THE AGE OF 18.

PROOF OF AGE REQUIRED.

Failure to post the required sign shall be an infraction punishable by a fine of twenty-five dollars ($ 25.00) for the first offense and seventy-five dollars ($ 75.00) for each succeeding offense.

A person engaged in the sale of tobacco products or cigarette wrapping papers shall demand proof of age from a prospective purchaser if the person has reasonable grounds to believe that the prospective purchaser is under 18 years of age. Failure to demand proof of age as required by this subsection is a Class 2 misdemeanor if in fact the prospective purchaser is under 18 years of age. Retail distributors of tobacco products or cigarette wrapping papers shall train their sales employees in the requirements of this law. Proof of any of the following shall be a defense to any action brought under this subsection:

(1) The defendant demanded, was shown, and reasonably relied upon proof of age in the case of a retailer, or any other documentary or written evidence of age in the case of a nonretailer.

(2) The defendant relied on the electronic system established and operated by the Division of Motor Vehicles pursuant to G.S. 20-37.02.

(3) The defendant relied on a biometric identification system that demonstrated (i) the purchaser's age to be at least the required age for the purchase and (ii) the purchaser had previously registered with the seller or seller's agent a drivers license, a special identification card issued under G.S. 20-37.7, a military identification card, or a passport showing the purchaser's date of birth and bearing a physical description of the person named on the card.

(b1) **Distribution of tobacco products.** -- Tobacco products shall not be distributed in vending machines; provided, however, vending machines distributing tobacco products are permitted (i) in any establishment which is open only to persons 18 years of age and older; or (ii) in any establishment if the vending machine is under the continuous control of the owner or licensee of the premises or an employee thereof and can be operated only upon activation by the owner, licensee, or employee prior to each purchase and the vending machine is not accessible to the public when the establishment is closed. The owner, licensee, or employee shall demand proof of age from a prospective purchaser if the person has reasonable grounds to believe that the prospective purchaser is under 18 years of age. Failure to demand proof of age as required by this subsection is a Class 2 misdemeanor if in fact the prospective purchaser is under 18 years of age. Proof that the defendant demanded, was shown, and reasonably relied upon proof of age shall be a defense to any action brought under this subsection. Vending machines distributing tobacco products in establishments not meeting the above conditions shall be removed prior to December 1, 1997. Vending machines distributing tobacco-derived products, vapor products, or components of vapor products in establishments not meeting the above conditions shall be removed prior to August 1, 2013. Any person distributing tobacco products through vending machines in violation of this subsection shall be guilty of a Class 2 misdemeanor.

(b2) **Internet distribution of tobacco products.** -- A person engaged in the distribution of tobacco products through the Internet or other remote sales methods shall perform an age verification through an independent, third-party age verification service that compares information available from public records to the personal information entered by the individual during the ordering process to establish that the individual ordering the tobacco products is 18 years of age or older.

(c) **Purchase by persons under the age of 18 years.** -- If any person under the age of 18 years purchases or accepts receipt, or attempts to purchase or accept receipt, of tobacco products or cigarette wrapping papers, or presents or offers to any person any purported proof of age which is false, fraudulent, or not actually his or her own, for the purpose of purchasing or receiving any tobacco product or cigarette wrapping papers, the person shall be guilty of a Class 2 misdemeanor; provided, however, that it shall not be unlawful for an employee to purchase or accept receipt of tobacco products or cigarette wrapping papers when required in the performance of the employee's duties.

(d) **Sending or assisting a person [less than] 18 years to purchase or receive tobacco products or cigarette wrapping papers.** -- If any person shall send a person less than 18 years of age to purchase, acquire, receive, or attempt to purchase, acquire, or receive tobacco products or cigarette wrapping papers, or if any person shall aid or abet a person who is less than 18 years of age in purchasing, acquiring, or receiving or attempting to purchase, acquire, or receive tobacco products or cigarette wrapping papers, the person shall be guilty of a Class 2 misdemeanor; provided, however, persons under the age of 18 may be enlisted by police or local sheriffs' departments to test compliance if the testing is under the direct supervision of that law enforcement department and written parental consent is provided; provided further, that the Department of Health and Human Services shall have the authority, pursuant to a written plan prepared by the Secretary of Health and Human Services, to use persons under 18 years of age in annual, random, unannounced inspections, provided that prior written parental consent is given for the involvement of these persons and that the inspections are conducted for the sole purpose of preparing a scientifically and methodologically valid statistical study of the extent of success the State has achieved in reducing the availability of tobacco products to persons under the age of 18, and preparing any report to the extent required by section 1926 of the federal Public Health Service Act (42 USC § 300x-26).

(e) **Statewide uniformity.** -- It is the intent of the General Assembly to prescribe this uniform system for the regulation of tobacco products and cigarette wrapping papers to ensure the eligibility for and receipt of any federal funds or grants that the State now receives or may receive relating to the provisions of this section. To ensure uniformity, no political subdivisions, boards, or agencies of the State nor any county, city, municipality, municipal corporation, town, township, village, nor any department or agency thereof, may enact ordinances, rules or regulations concerning the sale, distribution, display or promotion of (i) tobacco products or cigarette wrapping papers on or after September 1, 1995, or (ii) tobacco-derived products or vapor products on or after August 1, 2013. This subsection does not apply to the regulation of vending machines, nor

does it prohibit the Secretary of Revenue from adopting rules with respect to the administration of the tobacco products taxes levied under Article 2A of Chapter 105 of the General Statutes.

(f) **Deferred Prosecution or Conditional Discharge.** -- Notwithstanding G.S. 15A-1341(a1) or G.S. 15A-1341(a4), any person charged with a misdemeanor under this section shall be qualified for deferred prosecution or a conditional discharge pursuant to Article 82 of Chapter 15A of the General Statutes provided the defendant has not previously been placed on probation for a violation of this section and so states under oath.

History.
1891, c. 276; Rev., s. 3804; C.S., s. 4438; 1969, c. 1224, s. 3; 1991, c. 628, s. 1; 1993, c. 539, s. 216; 1994, Ex. Sess., c. 24, s. 14(c); 1995, c. 241, s. 1; 1997-434, ss. 1 -6; 1997-443, s. 11A.118(a); 2001-461, s. 5; 2002-159, s. 5; 2005-350, s. 6(b); 2013-165, s. 1; 2014-119, s. 2(c); 2015-264, s. 4

N.C. Gen. Stat. § 14-314

Repealed by Session Laws 1971, c. 31.

§ 14-315. Selling or giving weapons to minors

(a) **Sale of Weapons Other Than Handguns.** -- If a person sells, offers for sale, gives, or in any way transfers to a minor any pistol cartridge, brass knucks, bowie knife, dirk, shurikin, leaded cane, or slungshot, the person is guilty of a Class 1 misdemeanor and, in addition, shall forfeit the proceeds of any sale made in violation of this section.

(a1) **Sale of Handguns.** -- If a person sells, offers for sale, gives, or in any way transfers to a minor any handgun as defined in G.S. 14-269.7, the person is guilty of a Class H felony and, in addition, shall forfeit the proceeds of any sale made in violation of this section. This section does not apply in any of the following circumstances:

    (1) The handgun is lent to a minor for temporary use if the minor's possession of the handgun is lawful under G.S. 14-269.7 and G.S. 14-316 and is not otherwise unlawful.

    (2) The handgun is transferred to an adult custodian pursuant to Chapter 33A of the General Statutes, and the minor does not take possession of the handgun except that the adult custodian may allow the minor temporary possession of the handgun in circumstances in which the minor's possession of the handgun is lawful under G.S. 14-269.7 and G.S. 14-316 and is not otherwise unlawful.

(3) The handgun is a devise and is distributed to a parent or guardian under G.S. 28A-22-7, and the minor does not take possession of the handgun except that the parent or guardian may allow the minor temporary possession of the handgun in circumstances in which the minor's possession of the handgun is lawful under G.S. 14-269.7 and G.S. 14-316 and is not otherwise unlawful.

(b) Repealed by Session Laws 1993 (Reg. Sess., 1994), c. 597, s. 2.

(b1) **Defense.** -- It shall be a defense to a violation of this section if all of the following conditions are met:

(1) The person shows that the minor produced an apparently valid permit to receive the weapon, if such a permit would be required under G.S. 14-402 for transfer of the weapon to an adult.

(2) The person reasonably believed that the minor was not a minor.

(3) The person either:

a. Shows that the minor produced a drivers license, a special identification card issued under G.S. 20-37.7, a military identification card, or a passport, showing the minor's age to be at least the required age for purchase and bearing a physical description of the person named on the card reasonably describing the minor; or

b. Produces evidence of other facts that reasonably indicated at the time of sale that the minor was at least the required age.

History.
1893, c. 514; Rev., s. 3832; C.S., s. 4440; 1985, c. 199; 1993, c. 259, s. 3; 1993, c. 539, s. 217; 1994, Ex. Sess., c. 24, s. 14(c); 1993 (Reg. Sess., 1994), c. 597, s. 2; 1996, 2nd Ex. Sess., c. 18, s. 20.13(b); 2011-284, s. 9; 2013-369, s. 18

§ 14-315.1. Storage of firearms to protect minors

(a) Any person who resides in the same premises as a minor, owns or possesses a firearm, and stores or leaves the firearm (i) in a condition that the firearm can be discharged and (ii) in a manner that the person knew or should have known that an unsupervised minor would be able to gain access to the firearm, is guilty of a Class 1 misdemeanor if a minor gains access to the firearm without the lawful permission of the minor's parents or a person having charge of the minor and the minor:

(1) Possesses it in violation of G.S. 14-269.2(b);

(2) Exhibits it in a public place in a careless, angry, or threatening manner;

(3) Causes personal injury or death with it not in self defense; or

(4) Uses it in the commission of a crime.

(b) Nothing in this section shall prohibit a person from carrying a firearm on his or her body, or placed in such close proximity that it can be used as easily and quickly as if carried on the body.

(c) This section shall not apply if the minor obtained the firearm as a result of an unlawful entry by any person.

(d) "Minor" as used in this section means a person under 18 years of age who is not emancipated.

History.
1993, c. 558, s. 2; 1994, Ex. Sess., c. 14, s. 11

§ 14-315.2. Warning upon sale or transfer of firearm to protect minor

(a) Upon the retail commercial sale or transfer of any firearm, the seller or transferor shall deliver a written copy of G.S. 14-315.1 to the purchaser or transferee.

(b) Any retail or wholesale store, shop, or sales outlet that sells firearms shall conspicuously post at each purchase counter the following warning in block letters not less than one inch in height the phrase: "IT IS UNLAWFUL TO STORE OR LEAVE A FIREARM THAT CAN BE DISCHARGED IN A MANNER THAT A REASONABLE PERSON SHOULD KNOW IS ACCESSIBLE TO A MINOR."

(c) A violation of subsection (a) or (b) of this section is a Class 1 misdemeanor.

History.
1993, c. 558, s. 2; 1994, Ex. Sess., c. 14, s. 12

§ 14-316. Permitting young children to use dangerous firearms

(a) It shall be unlawful for any person to knowingly permit a child under the age of 12 years to have access to, or possession, custody or use in any manner whatever, of any gun, pistol or other dangerous firearm, whether such weapon be loaded or unloaded, unless the person has the permission of the child's parent or guardian, and the child is under the supervision of an adult. Any person violating the provisions of this section shall be guilty of a Class 2 misdemeanor.

(b) Air rifles, air pistols, and BB guns shall not be deemed "dangerous firearms" within the meaning of subsection (a) of this section except in the following counties: Caldwell, Durham, Forsyth, Gaston, Haywood, Mecklenburg, Stokes, Union, Vance.

History.
1913, c. 32; C.S., s. 4441; 1965, c. 813; 1971, c. 309; 1993, c. 539, s. 218; 1994, Ex. Sess., c. 24, s. 14(c); 2013-369, s. 4; 2014-119, s. 10(a)

§ 14-316.1. Contributing to delinquency and neglect by parents and others

Any person who is at least 18 years old who knowingly or willfully causes, encourages, or aids any juvenile within the jurisdiction of the court to be in a place or condition, or to commit an act whereby the juvenile could be adjudicated delinquent, undisciplined, abused, or neglected as defined by G.S. 7B-101 and G.S. 7B-1501 shall be guilty of a Class 1 misdemeanor.

It is not necessary for the district court exercising juvenile jurisdiction to make an adjudication that any juvenile is delinquent, undisciplined, abused, or neglected in order to prosecute a parent or any person, including an employee of the Juvenile Justice Section of the Division of Adult Correction and Juvenile Justice of the Department of Public Safety under this section. An adjudication that a juvenile is delinquent, undisciplined, abused, or neglected shall not preclude a subsequent prosecution of a parent or any other person including an employee of the Juvenile Justice Section of the Division of Adult Correction and Juvenile Justice of the Department of Public Safety, who contributes to the delinquent, undisciplined, abused, or neglected condition of any juvenile.

History.
1919, c. 97, s. 19; C.S., s. 5057; 1959, c. 1284; 1969, c. 911, s. 4; 1971, c. 1180, s. 5; 1979, c. 692; 1983, c. 175, ss. 8, 10; c. 720, s. 4; 1993, c. 539, s. 219; 1994, Ex. Sess., c. 24, s. 14(c); 1997-443, s. 11A.118(a); 1998-202, s. 4(b); 2000-137, s. 4(c); 2011-145, s. 19.1(l); 2017-57, s. 16D.4(p); 2017-186, s. 2(ii); 2018-142, s. 23(b)

§ 14-317. Permitting minors to enter barrooms or billiard rooms

If the manager or owner of any barroom, wherein beer, wine, or any alcoholic beverages are sold or consumed, or billiard room shall knowingly allow any minor under 18 years of age to enter or remain in such barroom or billiard room, where before such minor under 18 years of age enters or remains in such barroom or billiard room, the manager or owner thereof has been notified in writing by the parents or guardian of such minor under 18 years of age not to allow him to enter or remain in such barroom or billiard room, he shall be guilty of a Class 3 misdemeanor.

History.
1897, c. 278; Rev., s. 3729; C.S., s. 4442; 1967, c. 1089; 1993, c. 539, s. 220; 1994, Ex. Sess., c. 24, s. 14(c)

§ 14-318. Exposing children to fire

If any person shall leave any child under the age of eight years locked or otherwise confined in any dwelling, building or enclosure, and go away from such dwelling, building or enclosure without leaving some person of the age of discretion in charge of the same, so as to expose the child to danger by fire, the person so offending shall be guilty of a Class 1 misdemeanor.

History.
1893, c. 12; Rev., s. 3795; C.S., s. 4443; 1983, c. 175, s. 9, 10; c. 720, s. 4; 1993, c. 539, s. 221; 1994, Ex. Sess., c. 24, s. 14(c)

§ 14-318.1. Discarding or abandoning iceboxes, etc.; precautions required

It shall be unlawful for any person, firm or corporation to discard, abandon, leave or allow to remain in any place any icebox, refrigerator or other container, device or equipment of any kind with an interior storage area of more than one and one-half cubic feet of clear space which is airtight, without first removing the door or doors or hinges from such icebox, refrigerator, container, device or equipment. This section shall not apply to any icebox, refrigerator, container, device or equipment which is being used for the purpose for which it was originally designed, or is being used for display purposes by any retail or wholesale merchant, or is crated, strapped or locked to such an extent that it is impossible for a child to obtain access to any airtight compartment thereof. Any person violating the provisions of this section shall be guilty of a Class 1 misdemeanor.

History.
1955, c. 305; 1993, c. 539, s. 222; 1994, Ex. Sess., c. 24, s. 14(c)

§ 14-318.2. Child abuse a misdemeanor

(a) Any parent of a child less than 16 years of age, or any other person providing care to or supervision of such child, who inflicts physical injury, or who allows physical injury to be inflicted, or who creates or allows to be created a substantial risk of physical injury, upon or to such child by other than accidental means is guilty of the Class A1 misdemeanor of child abuse.

(b) The Class A1 misdemeanor of child abuse is an offense additional to other civil and criminal provisions and is not intended to repeal or preclude any other sanctions or remedies.

(c) A parent who abandons an infant less than seven days of age pursuant to G.S. 14-322.3 shall not be prosecuted under this section for any acts or omissions related to the care of that infant.

History.

1965, c. 472, s. 1; 1971, c. 710, s. 6; 1993, c. 539, s. 223; 1994, Ex. Sess., c. 14, s. 13; c. 24, s. 14(c); 2001-291, s. 4; 2008-191, s. 1; 2009-570, s. 6

N.C. Gen. Stat. § 14-318.3

Repealed by Session Laws 1971, c. 710, s. 7.

§ 14-318.4. Child abuse a felony

(a) A parent or any other person providing care to or supervision of a child less than 16 years of age who intentionally inflicts any serious physical injury upon or to the child or who intentionally commits an assault upon the child which results in any serious physical injury to the child is guilty of a Class D felony, except as otherwise provided in subsection (a3) of this section.

(a1) Any parent of a child less than 16 years of age, or any other person providing care to or supervision of the child, who commits, permits, or encourages any act of prostitution with or by the child is guilty of child abuse and shall be punished as a Class D felon.

(a2) Any parent or legal guardian of a child less than 16 years of age who commits or allows the commission of any sexual act upon the child is guilty of a Class D felony.

(a3) A parent or any other person providing care to or supervision of a child less than 16 years of age who intentionally inflicts any serious bodily injury to the child or who intentionally commits an assault upon the child which results in any serious bodily injury to the child, or which results in permanent or protracted loss or impairment of any mental or emotional function of the child, is guilty of a Class B2 felony.

(a4) A parent or any other person providing care to or supervision of a child less than 16 years of age whose willful act or grossly negligent omission in the care of the child shows a reckless disregard for human life is guilty of a Class E felony if the act or omission results in serious bodily injury to the child.

(a5) A parent or any other person providing care to or supervision of a child less than 16 years of age whose willful act or grossly negligent omission in the care of the child shows a reckless disregard for human life is guilty of a Class G felony if the act or omission results in serious physical injury to the child.

(a6) For purposes of this section, a "grossly negligent omission" in providing care to or supervision of a child includes the failure to report a child as missing to law enforcement as provided in G.S. 14-318.5(b).

(b) The felony of child abuse is an offense additional to other civil and criminal provisions and is not intended to repeal or preclude any other sanctions or remedies.

(c) Abandonment of an infant less than seven days of age pursuant to G.S. 14-322.3 may be treated as a mitigating factor in sentencing for a conviction under this section involving that infant.

(d) The following definitions apply in this section:

(1) **Serious bodily injury.** -- Bodily injury that creates a substantial risk of death or that causes serious permanent disfigurement, coma, a permanent or protracted condition that causes extreme pain, or permanent or protracted loss or impairment of the function of any bodily member or organ, or that results in prolonged hospitalization.

(2) **Serious physical injury.** -- Physical injury that causes great pain and suffering. The term includes serious mental injury.

History.

1979, c. 897, s. 1; 1979, 2nd Sess., c. 1316, s. 18; 1981, c. 63, s. 1; c. 179, s. 14; 1983, c. 653, s. 1; c. 916, § 1; 1985, c. 509, s. 5; c. 668; 1993, c. 539, s. 1233; 1994, Ex. Sess., c. 24, s. 14(c); 1999-451, s. 1; 2001-291, s. 5; 2008-191, s. 2; 2013-35, s. 1; 2013-52, s. 3

§ 14-318.5. Failure to report the disappearance of a child to law enforcement; immunity of person reporting in good faith

(a) The following definitions apply in this section:

(1) **Child.** -- Any person who is less than 16 years of age.

(2) **Disappearance of a child.** -- When the parent or other person providing supervision of a child does not know the location of the child and has not had contact with the child for a 24-hour period.

(b) A parent or any other person providing care to or supervision of a child who knowingly or wantonly fails to report the disappearance of a child to law enforcement is in violation of this subsection. Unless the conduct is covered under some other provision of law providing greater punishment, a violation of this subsection is punishable as a Class I felony.

(c) Any person who reasonably suspects the disappearance of a child and who reasonably suspects that the child may be in danger shall report those suspicions to law enforcement within a reasonable time. Unless the conduct is covered under some other provision of law providing greater punishment, a violation of this subsection is punishable as a Class 1 misdemeanor.

(d) This section does not apply if G.S. 110-102.1 is applicable.

(e) Notwithstanding subsection (b) or (c) of this section, if a child is absent from school, a teacher is not required to report the child's absence to law enforcement officers under this section, provided the teacher reports the child's absence from school pursuant to Article 26 of Chapter 115C of the General Statutes.

(f) The felony of failure to report the disappearance of a child as required by subsection (b) of this section is an offense additional to other civil and criminal provisions and is not intended to repeal or preclude any other sanctions or remedies.

(g) Any person who reports the disappearance of a child as required by this section is immune from any civil or criminal liability that might otherwise be incurred or imposed for that action, provided that the person was acting in good faith. In any proceeding involving liability, good faith is presumed.

History.
2013-52, s. 2

§ 14-318.6. Failure to report crimes against juveniles; penalty

(a) **Definitions.** -- As used in this section, the following definitions apply:

(1) **Juvenile.** -- As defined in G.S. 7B-101. For the purposes of this section, the age of the juvenile at the time of the abuse or offense governs.

(2) **Serious bodily injury.** -- As defined in G.S. 14-318.4(d).

(3) **Serious physical injury.** -- As defined in G.S. 14-318.4(d).

(4) **Sexually violent offense.** -- An offense committed against a juvenile that is a sexually violent offense as defined in G.S. 14-208.6(5). This term also includes the following: an attempt, solicitation, or conspiracy to commit any of these offenses; aiding and abetting any of these offenses.

(5) **Violent offense.** -- Any offense that inflicts upon the juvenile serious bodily injury or serious physical injury by other than accidental means. This term also includes the following: an attempt, solicitation, or conspiracy to commit any of these offenses; aiding and abetting any of these offenses.

(b) **Requirement.** -- Any person 18 years of age or older who knows or should have reasonably known that a juvenile has been or is the victim of a violent offense, sexual offense, or misdemeanor child abuse under G.S. 14-318.2 shall immediately report the case of that juvenile to the appropriate local law enforcement agency in the county where the juvenile resides or is found. The report may be made orally or by telephone. The report shall include information as is known to the person making it, including the name, address, and age of the juvenile; the name and address of the juvenile's parent,

guardian, custodian, or caretaker; the name, address, and age of the person who committed the offense against the juvenile; the location where the offense was committed; the names and ages of other juveniles present or in danger; the present whereabouts of the juvenile, if not at the home address; the nature and extent of any injury or condition resulting from the offense or abuse; and any other information which the person making the report believes might be helpful in establishing the need for law enforcement involvement. The person making the report shall give his or her name, address, and telephone number.

(c) **Penalty.** -- Any person 18 years of age or older, who knows or should have reasonably known that a juvenile was the victim of a violent offense, sexual offense, or misdemeanor child abuse under G.S. 14-318.2, and knowingly or willfully fails to report as required by subsection (b) of this section, or who knowingly or willfully prevents another person from reporting as required by subsection (b) of this section, is guilty of a Class 1 misdemeanor.

(d) **Construction.** -- Nothing in this section shall be construed as relieving a person subject to the requirement set forth in subsection (b) of this section from any other duty to report required by law.

(e) **Protection.** -- The identity of a person making a report pursuant to this section must be protected and only revealed as provided in G.S. 132-1.4(c)(4).

(f) **Good-Faith Immunity.** -- A person who makes a report in good faith under this Article, cooperates with law enforcement in an investigation, or testifies in any judicial proceeding resulting from a law enforcement report or investigation is immune from any civil or criminal liability that might otherwise be incurred or imposed for that action, provided that person was acting in good faith.

(g) **Law Enforcement Duty to Report Evidence to the Department of Social Services.** -- If any law enforcement officer, as the result of a report, finds evidence that a juvenile may be abused, neglected, or dependent as defined in G.S. 7B-101, the law enforcement officer shall make an oral report as soon as practicable and make a subsequent written report of the findings to the director of the department of social services within 48 hours after discovery of the evidence. When a report of abuse, neglect, or dependency is received, the director of the department of social services shall make a prompt and thorough assessment, in accordance with G.S. 7B-302, to determine whether protective services should be provided or the complaint filed as a petition.

(h) Nothing in this section shall be construed as to require a person with a privilege under G.S. 8-53.3, 8-53.7, 8-53.8, or 8-53.12 or with

Chapter 14

attorney-client privilege to report pursuant to this section if that privilege would prevent them from doing so.

History.
2019-245, s. 1(a)

N.C. Gen. Stat. § 14-319

Repealed by Session Laws 1975, c. 402.

N.C. Gen. Stat. § 14-320

Repealed by Session Laws 1987, c. 716, s. 2.

§ 14-320.1. Transporting child outside the State with intent to violate custody order

When any federal court or state court in the United States shall have awarded custody of a child under the age of 16 years, it shall be a felony for any person with the intent to violate the court order to take or transport, or cause to be taken or transported, any such child from any point within this State to any point outside the limits of this State or to keep any such child outside the limits of this State. Such crime shall be punishable as a Class I felony. Provided that keeping a child outside the limits of the State in violation of a court order for a period in excess of 72 hours shall be prima facie evidence that the person charged intended to violate the order at the time of taking.

History.
1969, c. 81; 1979, c. 760, s. 5; 1979, 2nd Sess., c. 1316, s. 47; 1981, c. 63, s. 1; c. 179, s. 14; 1983, c. 563, s. 1; 1993, c. 539, s. 1234; 1994, Ex. Sess., c. 24, s. 14(c)

§ 14-321. Failing to pay minors for doing certain work

Whenever any person, having a contract with any corporation, company or person for the manufacture or change of any raw material by the piece or pound, shall employ any minor to assist in the work upon the faith of and by color of such contract, with intent to cheat and defraud such minor, and, having secured the contract price, shall willfully fail to pay the minor when he shall have performed his part of the contract work, whether done by the day or by the job, the person so offending shall be guilty of a Class 3 misdemeanor.

History.
1893, c. 309; Rev., s. 3428a; C.S., s. 4446; 1993, c. 539, s. 224; 1994, Ex. Sess., c. 24, s. 14(c)

§ 14-321.1. Prohibit baby sitting service by sex offender or in the home of a sex offender

(a) For purposes of this section the term "baby sitting service" means providing, for profit, supervision or care for a child under the age of 13 years who is unrelated to the provider by blood, marriage, or adoption, for more than two hours per day while the child's parents or guardian are not on the premises.

(b) Notwithstanding any other provision of law, no person who is an adult may provide or offer to provide a baby sitting service in any of the following circumstances:

(1) The baby sitting service is offered in a home and a resident of the home is a sex offender who is registered in accordance with Article 27A of Chapter 14 of the General Statutes.

(2) A provider of care for the baby sitting service is a sex offender who is registered in accordance with Article 27A of Chapter 14 of the General Statutes.

(c) A violation of this section that is a first offense is a Class 1 misdemeanor. A violation of this section that is a second or subsequent offense is a Class H felony.

History.
2005-416, s. 4

§ 14-321.2. Prohibit unlawful transfer of custody of minor child

(a) It shall be unlawful for:

(1) A parent to effect or attempt to effect an unlawful transfer of custody of that parent's minor child.

(2) A person to accept or attempt to accept custody pursuant to an unlawful transfer of custody of a minor child; except that it shall not be unlawful for a person to receive custody of a child from a parent who intends to effect an unlawful transfer of custody of that parent's minor child if the person promptly notifies law enforcement or child protective services in the county where the child resides or is found and promptly makes the child available to law enforcement or child protective services.

(3) A person to advertise, recruit, or solicit, or to aid, abet, conspire, or seek the assistance of another to advertise, recruit, or solicit the unlawful transfer of custody of a minor child.

(b) **Definitions.** -- As used in this section, the following definitions apply:

(1) "Minor child" means a child under the age of 18 and includes an adopted minor child, as defined in G.S. 48-1-101(14a).

(2) "Parent" means a biological parent, adoptive parent, legal guardian, or legal custodian.

(3) "Relative" means the child's other parent, stepparent, grandparent, adult

sibling, aunt, uncle, first cousin, great-aunt, great-uncle, great-grandparent, or a parent's first cousin.

(4) "Unlawful transfer of custody" means the transfer of physical custody of a minor child, in willful violation of applicable adoption law or by grossly negligent omission in the care of the child, by the child's parent, without a court order or other authorization under law, to a person other than a relative or another individual having a substantial relationship with the child. Compensation in the form of money, property, or other item of value is not required in order for an unlawful transfer of custody to occur. Unlawful transfer of custody does not include any of the following:

a. Placement of a minor child with a prospective adoptive parent in accordance with Part 2 of Article 3 of Chapter 48 of the General Statutes.

b. A consent to adoption of a minor child in accordance with Part 6 of Article 3 of Chapter 48 of the General Statutes.

c. Relinquishment of a minor child in accordance with Part 7 of Article 3 of Chapter 48 of the General Statutes.

d. Placement of a minor child in accordance with the Interstate Compact on the Placement of Children under Article 38 of Chapter 7B of the General Statutes or the Convention of 29 May 1993 on Protection of Children and Co-operation in respect of Intercountry Adoption.

e. Temporary transfer of physical custody of a minor child to an individual with a prior substantial relationship with the child for a specified period of time due to (i) the child's medical, mental health, educational, or recreational needs or (ii) the parent's inability to provide proper care or supervision for the minor child, which may be due to the parent's incarceration, military service, employment, medical treatment, incapacity, or other voluntary or involuntary absence.

f. Transfer of physical custody of a minor child to a relative.

g. Temporary transfer of physical custody of a minor child to a behavioral health facility or other health care provider, an educational institution, or a recreational facility by a parent for a specified period of time due to the child's medical, mental health, educational, or recreational needs.

h. A voluntary foster care placement of the minor child made pursuant to an agreement between the minor child's parent and a county department of social services as described in G.S. 7B-910.

i. Placement of a minor child with a prospective adoptive parent in substantial compliance with the applicable adoption laws of this State or of another state.

(c) Any person who commits an offense under subsection (a) of this section is guilty of a Class A1 misdemeanor.

(d) Any person who commits an offense under subsection (a) of this section that results in serious physical injury to the child is guilty of a Class G felony.

History.
2016-115, s. 1

ARTICLE 40
PROTECTION OF THE FAMILY

§ 14-322. Abandonment and failure to support spouse and children

(a) For purposes of this Article:

(1) "Supporting spouse" means a spouse, whether husband or wife, upon whom the other spouse is actually substantially dependent or from whom such other spouse is substantially in need of maintenance and support.

(2) "Dependent spouse" means a spouse, whether husband or wife, who is actually substantially dependent upon the other spouse for his or her maintenance and support or is substantially in need of maintenance and support from the other spouse.

(b) Any supporting spouse who shall willfully abandon a dependent spouse without providing that spouse with adequate support shall be guilty of a Class 1 or 2 misdemeanor and upon conviction shall be punished according to subsection (f).

(c) Any supporting spouse who, while living with a dependent spouse, shall willfully neglect to provide adequate support for that dependent spouse shall be guilty of a misdemeanor and upon conviction shall be punished according to subsection (f).

(d) Any parent who shall willfully neglect or refuse to provide adequate support for that parent's child, whether natural or adopted, and whether or not the parent abandons the child, shall be guilty of a misdemeanor and upon conviction shall be punished according to subsection (f). Willful neglect or refusal to provide adequate support of a child shall constitute a continuing offense and shall not be barred by any statute of limitations until the youngest living child of the parent shall reach the age of 18 years.

(e) Upon conviction for an offense under this section, the court may make such order as will best provide for the support, as far as may be necessary, of the abandoned spouse or child, or both, from the property or labor of the defendant. If the court requires the payment of child support, the amount of the payments shall be determined as provided in G.S. 50-13.4(c). For child support orders initially entered on or after January 1, 1994, the immediate income withholding provisions of G.S. 110-136.5(c1) shall apply.

(f) A first offense under this section is a Class 2 misdemeanor. A second or subsequent offense is a Class 1 misdemeanor.

History.
1868-9, c. 209, s. 1; 1873-4, c. 176, s. 10; 1879, c. 92; Code, s. 970; Rev., s. 3355; C.S., s. 4447; 1925, c. 290; 1949, c. 810; 1957, c. 369; 1969, c. 1045, s. 1; 1981, c. 683, s. 1; 1989, c. 529, s. 4; 1993, c. 517, s. 3; c. 539, ss. 225, 226; 1994, Ex. Sess., c. 24, s. 14(c)

§ 14-322.1. Abandonment of child or children for six months

Any man or woman who, without just cause or provocation, willfully abandons his or her child or children for six months and who willfully fails or refuses to provide adequate means of support for his or her child or children during the six months' period, and who attempts to conceal his or her whereabouts from his or her child or children with the intent of escaping his lawful obligation for the support of said child or children, shall be punished as a Class I felon.

History.
1963, c. 1227; 1979, c. 760, s. 5; 1979, 2nd Sess., c. 1316, s. 47; 1981, c. 63, s. 1; c. 179, s. 14; 1983, c. 653, s. 2

N.C. Gen. Stat. § 14-322.2

Repealed by Session Laws 1979, c. 838, s. 28.

§ 14-322.3. Abandonment of an infant under seven days of age

When a parent abandons an infant less than seven days of age by voluntarily delivering the infant as provided in G.S. 7B-500(b) or G.S. 7B-500(d) and does not express an intent to return for the infant, that parent shall not be prosecuted under G.S. 14-322, 14-322.1, or 14-43.14.

History.
2001-291, s. 7; 2012-153, s. 4

§§ 14-323 through 14-325

Repealed by Session Laws 1981, c. 683, s. 3.

§ 14-325.1. When offense of failure to support child deemed committed in State

The offense of willful neglect or refusal of a parent to support and maintain a child, and the offense of willful neglect or refusal to support and maintain one's child born out of wedlock, shall be deemed to have been committed in this State whenever the child is living in this State at the time of the willful neglect or refusal to support and maintain the child.

History.
1953, c. 677; 1981, c. 683, s. 2; 2013-198, s. 3

N.C. Gen. Stat. § 14-326

Repealed by Session Laws 1981, c. 683, s. 3.

§ 14-326.1. Parents; failure to support

If any person being of full age, and having sufficient income after reasonably providing for his or her own immediate family shall, without reasonable cause, neglect to maintain and support his or her parent or parents, if such parent or parents be sick or not able to work and have not sufficient means or ability to maintain or support themselves, such person shall be deemed guilty of a Class 2 misdemeanor; upon conviction of a second or subsequent offense such person shall be guilty of a Class 1 misdemeanor.

If there be more than one person bound under the provisions of the next preceding paragraph to support the same parent or parents, they shall share equitably in the discharge of such duty.

History.
1955, c. 1099; 1969, c. 1045, s. 3; 1993, c. 539, s. 227; 1994, Ex. Sess., c. 24, s. 14(c)

ARTICLE 41
ALCOHOLIC BEVERAGES

§§ 14-327, 14-328

Repealed by Session Laws 1971, c. 872, s. 3.

§ 14-329. Manufacturing, trafficking in, transporting, or possessing poisonous alcoholic beverages

(a) Any person who, either individually or as an agent for any person, firm or corporation, shall manufacture for use as a beverage, any spirituous liquor which is found to contain any foreign properties or ingredients poisonous to the human system, shall be punished as a Class H felon.

(b) Any person who, either individually or as agent for any person, firm or corporation, shall, knowing or having reasonable grounds to know of the poisonous qualities thereof, transport for other than personal use, sell or possess for purpose of sale, for use as a beverage, any spirituous liquor which is found to contain any foreign properties or ingredients poisonous to the human system, shall be punished as a Class F felon.

(c) Any person who, either individually or as agent for any person, firm or corporation, shall transport for other than personal use, sell or possess for purpose of sale, any spirituous liquor to be used as a beverage which is found to contain any foreign properties or ingredients poisonous to the human system, shall be guilty of a Class 2 misdemeanor. In prosecutions under this subsection and under subsection (b) above, proof of transportation of more than one gallon of spirituous liquor will be prima facie evidence of transportation for other than personal use, and proof of possession of more than one gallon of spirituous liquor will be prima facie evidence of possession for purpose of sale.

(d) Any person who, either individually or as agent for any person, firm or corporation, shall transport or possess, for use as a beverage, any illicit spirituous liquor which is found to contain any foreign properties or ingredients poisonous to the human system, shall be guilty of a Class 1 misdemeanor: Provided, anyone charged under this subsection may show as a complete defense that the spirituous liquor in question was legally obtained and possessed and that he had no knowledge of the poisonous nature of the beverage.

History.
1873-4, c. 180, ss. 1, 2; Code, s. 983; Rev., s. 3522; C.S., s. 4453; 1961, c. 897; 1979, c. 760, s. 5; 1979, 2nd Sess., c. 1316, s. 47; 1981, c. 63, s. 1; c. 179, s. 14; 1993, c. 539, ss. 228, 229, 1235; 1994, Ex. Sess., c. 24, s. 14(c)

§§ 14-330 through 14-332

Repealed by Session Laws 1971, c. 872, s.3.

ARTICLE 42
PUBLIC
DRUNKENNESS

N.C. Gen. Stat. § 14-333

Repealed by Session Laws 1971, c. 872, s. 3.

§§ 14-334 through 14-335.1

Repealed by Session Laws 1977, 2nd Session, c. 1134, s. 6.

ARTICLE 43
VAGRANTS AND TRAMPS

N.C. Gen. Stat. § 14-336

Repealed by Session Laws 1983, c. 17, s. 1.

N.C. Gen. Stat. § 14-337

Repealed by Session Laws 1973, c. 108, s. 13.

§§ 14-338, 14-339

Repealed by Session Laws 1983, c. 17, ss. 2, 3.

N.C. Gen. Stat. § 14-340

Repealed by Session Laws 1971, c. 700.

N.C. Gen. Stat. § 14-341

Repealed by Session Laws 1971, c. 699.

ARTICLE 44
REGULATION OF SALES

§ 14-342. Selling or offering to sell meat of diseased animals

If any person shall knowingly and willfully slaughter any diseased animal and sell or offer for sale any of the meat of such diseased animal for human consumption, or if any person knows that the meat offered for sale or sold for human consumption by him is that of a diseased animal, he shall be guilty of a Class 1 misdemeanor.

History.
1905, c. 303; Rev., s. 3442; C.S., s. 4465; 1993, c. 539, s. 230; 1994, Ex. Sess., c. 24, s. 14(c)

§ 14-343. Unauthorized dealing in railroad tickets

If any person shall sell or deal in tickets issued by any railroad company, unless he is a duly authorized agent of the railroad company, or shall refuse upon demand to exhibit his authority to sell or deal in such tickets, he shall be guilty of a Class 2 misdemeanor.

History.
1895, c. 83, s. 1; Rev., s. 3764; C.S., s. 4466; 1969, c. 1224, s. 1; 1993, c. 539, s. 231; 1994, Ex. Sess., c. 24, s. 14(c)

§ 14-344. Sale of admission tickets in excess of printed price

Any person, firm, or corporation shall be allowed to add a reasonable service fee to the face value of the tickets sold, and the person, firm, or corporation which sells or resells such tickets shall not be permitted to recoup funds greater than the combined face value of the ticket, tax, and the authorized service fee. This service fee may not exceed three dollars ($ 3.00) for each ticket except that a promoter or operator of the property where the event is to be held and a ticket sales agency may agree in writing on a reasonable service fee greater than three dollars ($ 3.00) for the first sale of tickets by the ticket sales agent. This service fee may be a pre-established amount per ticket or a percentage of each ticket. The existence of the service fee shall be made known to the public by printing or writing the amount of the fee on the tickets which are printed for the event. Any person, firm or corporation which sells or offers to sell a ticket for a price greater than the price permitted by this section or as permitted by G.S. 14-344.1 shall be guilty of a Class 2 misdemeanor.

History.
1941, c. 180; 1969, c. 1224, s. 8; 1977, c. 9; 1979, c. 909; 1981, c. 36; 1985, c. 434; 1991, c. 165, s. 1; 1993, c. 539, s. 232; 1994, Ex. Sess., c. 24, s. 14(c); 2008-158, ss. 3, 4; 2009-255, s. 1

§ 14-344.1. (Contingent repeal, see note) Internet sale of admission tickets in excess of printed price

(a) Internet Resale. -- A person may resell an admission ticket under this section on the Internet at a price greater than the price on the face of the ticket only if all of the following conditions are met:

(1) The venue where the event will occur has not prohibited the Internet ticket resale as provided under subsection (b) of this section.

(2) The person reselling the ticket offers the ticket for resale on a Web site with a ticket guarantee that meets the requirements of subsection (c) of this section. A prospective purchaser must be directed to the guarantee before completion of the resale transaction.

(3) The person has obtained a certificate of registration under G.S. 105-164.29 and collects and remits to the State the sales and use tax in accordance with Article 5 of Chapter 105 of the General Statutes.

(b) Resale Prohibited. -- The venue where an event will occur may prohibit the resale of admission tickets for the event at a price greater than the price on the face of the ticket. To prohibit the resale of tickets under this section, the venue must file a notice of prohibition of the resale of admission tickets for a specified event with the Secretary of State and must post the notice of prohibition conspicuously on its Web site. The primary ticket seller for the event must also post the notice conspicuously on its Web site. A prohibition under this subsection may not become valid until 30 days after the notice is posted on the venue's Web site. The prohibition expires on December 31 of each year unless the prohibition is renewed. To renew a prohibition, a venue must renew its notice of prohibition filed with the Secretary of State and must post the notice as required under this subsection. A venue who files a notice of prohibition must pay a fee in the amount set in G.S. 55-1-22 for filing articles of incorporation. A venue that renews a notice of prohibition must pay a fee in the amount set in G.S. 55-1-22 for filing a paper annual report.

(c) Ticket Guarantee. -- A person who resells or offers to resell admission tickets under this section must guarantee to the purchaser a full refund of the amount paid for the ticket under each of the following conditions:

(1) The ticketed event is cancelled. Reasonable handling and delivery fees may be withheld from the refund price of a cancelled ticketed event if the ticket guarantee on the Web site specifically informs the purchaser that handling and delivery fees will be withheld from the refunded amount.

(2) The purchaser is denied admission to the ticketed event. This subdivision does not apply if admission to the ticketed event is denied to the purchaser because of an action or omission of the purchaser.

(3) The ticket is not delivered to the purchaser in the manner described on the Web site or pursuant to the delivery guarantee made by the reseller, and the failure results in the purchaser's inability to attend the ticketed event.

(d) Student Tickets. -- This section does not apply to student tickets issued by institutions of higher education in North Carolina for sporting events.

(e) Repealed by Session Laws 2010-31, s. 31.7(c), effective June 30, 2010.

History.
2008-158, s. 1; 2009-255, s. 1; 2010-31, ss. 31.7(b), (c); 2014-3, s. 14.27(a)

§ 14-344.2. Prohibition on ticket purchasing software

(a) **Definition.** -- The term "ticket seller" means a person who has executed a written agreement with the management of any venue in North Carolina for a sporting event, theater, musical performance, or public entertainment of any kind to sell tickets to the event over the Internet.

(b) **Unfair Trade Practice.** -- A person who knowingly sells, gives, transfers, uses, distributes, or possesses software that is primarily designed or produced for the purpose of interfering with the operation of a ticket seller who sells, over the Internet, tickets of admission to a sporting event, theater, musical performance, or public entertainment of any kind by circumventing any security measures on the ticket seller's Web site, circumventing any access control systems of the ticket seller's Web site, circumventing any access control solutions of the ticket seller's Web site, or circumventing any controls or measures that are instituted by the ticket seller on its Web site to ensure an equitable ticket buying process shall be in violation of G.S. 75-1.1. The ticket seller and venue hosting the ticketed event have standing to bring a private right of action under G.S. 75-1.1 for violation of this section.

(c) **Original Ticket Seller.** -- A person or firm is not liable under this section with respect to tickets for which the person or firm is the original ticket seller.

History.
2008-158, s. 2; 2009-255, s. 1

N.C. Gen. Stat. § 14-345

Repealed by Session Laws 1994, Extra Session, c. 14, s. 72(16), effective October 1, 1994.

§ 14-346. Sale of convict-made goods prohibited

(a) It shall be unlawful to sell or to offer for sale anywhere within the State of North Carolina any articles or commodities manufactured or produced, wholly or in part, in this State or elsewhere by convicts or prisoners, except

(1) Articles or commodities manufactured or produced by convicts on probation or parole or prisoners released part time for regular employment in the free community, and

(2) Products of agricultural or forestry enterprises or quarrying or mining operations in which inmates of any penal or correctional institution of this State are employed, and

(3) Articles and commodities manufactured or produced in any penal or correctional institution of this State for sale to

departments, institutions, and agencies supported in whole or in part by the State, or to any political subdivision of this State, for the use of these departments, institutions, agencies, and political subdivisions of the State and not for resale, and

(4) Articles of handicraft made by the inmates of any penal or correctional institution of this State during their leisure hours and with their own materials.

(b) Any person, firm or corporation selling, undertaking to sell, or offering for sale any prison-made or convict-made goods, wares or merchandise, anywhere within the State, in violation of the provisions of this section, shall be guilty of a Class 2 misdemeanor. Each sale or offer to sell, in violation of the provisions of this section, shall constitute a separate offense.

History.
1933, c. 146, ss. 1-4; 1959, c. 170, s. 1; 1969, c. 1224, s. 4; 1993, c. 539, s. 233; 1994, Ex. Sess., c. 24, s. 14(c)

§§ 14-346.1, 14-346.2

Repealed by Session Laws 1994, Extra Session, c. 14, s. 72(17), (18).

ARTICLE 45
REGULATION OF EMPLOYER AND EMPLOYEE

N.C. Gen. Stat. § 14-347

Repealed by Session Laws 1971, c. 350.

N.C. Gen. Stat. § 14-348

Repealed by Session Laws 1971, c. 701.

N.C. Gen. Stat. § 14-349

Repealed by Session Laws 1971, c. 351.

N.C. Gen. Stat. § 14-350

Repealed by Session Laws 1971, c. 352.

N.C. Gen. Stat. § 14-351

Repealed by Session Laws 1971, c. 353.

N.C. Gen. Stat. § 14-352

Repealed by Session Laws 1971, c. 354.

§ 14-353. Influencing agents and servants in violating duties owed employers

Any person who gives, offers or promises to an agent, employee or servant any gift or gratuity whatever with intent to influence his action in relation to his principal's, employer's or master's business; any agent, employee or servant who requests or accepts a gift or gratuity or a promise to make a gift or to do an act beneficial to himself, under an agreement or with an understanding that he shall act in any particular manner in relation to his principal's, employer's or master's business; any agent, employee or servant who, being authorized to procure materials, supplies or other articles either by purchase or contract for his principal, employer or master, or to employ service or labor for his principal, employer or master, receives, directly or indirectly, for himself or for another, a commission, discount or bonus from the person who makes such sale or contract, or furnishes such materials, supplies or other articles, or from a person who renders such service or labor; and any person who gives or offers such an agent, employee or servant such commission, discount or bonus, shall be guilty of a Class 2 misdemeanor.

History.

1913, c. 190, s. 1; C.S., s. 4475; 1969, c. 1224, s. 6; 1993, c. 539, s. 234; 1994, Ex. Sess., c. 24, s. 14(c)

§ 14-354. Witness required to give self-incriminating evidence; no suit or prosecution to be founded thereon

No person shall be excused from attending, testifying or producing books, papers, contracts, agreements and other documents before any court, or in obedience to the subpoena of any court, having jurisdiction of the crime denounced in G.S. 14-353, on the ground or for the reason that the testimony or evidence, documentary or otherwise, required of him may tend to incriminate him or to subject him to a penalty or to a forfeiture; but no person shall be liable to any suit or prosecution, civil or criminal, for or on account of any transaction, matter or thing concerning which he may testify or produce evidence, documentary or otherwise, before such court or in obedience to its subpoena or in any such case or proceeding: Provided, that no person so testifying or producing any such books, papers, contracts, agreements or other documents shall be exempted from prosecution and punishment for perjury committed in so testifying.

History.

1913, c. 190, s. 2; C.S., s. 4476

§ 14-355. Blacklisting employees

If any person, agent, company or corporation, after having discharged any employee from his or its service, shall prevent or attempt to prevent, by word or writing of any kind, such discharged employee from obtaining employment with any other person, company or corporation, such person, agent or corporation shall be guilty of a Class 3 misdemeanor and shall be punished by a fine not exceeding five hundred dollars ($ 500.00); and such person, agent, company or corporation shall be liable in penal damages to such discharged person, to be recovered by civil action. This section shall not be construed as prohibiting any person or agent of any company or corporation from furnishing in writing, upon request, any other person, company or corporation to whom such discharged person or employee has applied for employment, a truthful statement of the reason for such discharge.

History.

1909, c. 858, s. 1; C.S., s. 4477; 1993, c. 539, s. 235; 1994, Ex. Sess., c. 24, s. 14(c)

N.C. Gen. Stat. § 14-356

Repealed by Session Laws 1993 (Reg. Sess., 1994), c. 767, s. 30(16).

N.C. Gen. Stat. § 14-357

Repealed by Session Laws 1994, Extra Session, c. 14, s. 72(19).

§ 14-357.1. Requiring payment for medical examination, etc., as condition of employment

(a) It shall be unlawful for any employer, as defined in subsection (b) of this section, to require any applicant for employment, as defined in subsection (c), to pay the cost of a medical examination or the cost of furnishing any records required by the employer as a condition of the initial act of hiring.

(b) The term "employer" as used in this section shall mean and include an individual, a partnership, an association, a corporation, a legal representative, trustee, receiver, trustee in bankruptcy, and any common carrier by rail, motor, water, air, or express company, doing business in or operating within the State.

Provided that this section shall not apply to any employer as defined in this subsection who employs less than 25 employees.

(c) The term "applicant for employment" shall mean and include any person who seeks to be permitted, required or directed by any employer, as defined in subsection (b) hereof, in consideration of direct or indirect gain or profit, to engage in employment.

(d) Any employer who violates the provisions of this section shall be liable to a fine of not more than one hundred dollars ($ 100.00) for each and every violation. It shall be the duty of the Commissioner of Labor to enforce this section.

History.

1951, c. 1094

ARTICLE 46
REGULATION OF LANDLORD AND TENANT

§ 14-358. Local: Violation of certain contracts between landlord and tenant

If any tenant or cropper shall procure advances from his landlord to enable him to make a crop on the land rented by him, and then willfully abandon the same without good cause and before paying for such advances with intent to defraud the landlord; or if any landlord shall contract with a tenant or cropper to furnish him advances to enable him to make a crop, and shall willfully fail or refuse, without good cause, to furnish such advances according to his agreement with intent to defraud the tenant, he shall be guilty of a Class 3 misdemeanor. Any person employing a tenant or cropper who has violated the provisions of this section, with knowledge of such violation, shall be liable to the landlord furnishing such advances for the amount thereof, and shall also be guilty of a Class 3 misdemeanor. This section shall apply to the following counties only: Alamance, Alexander, Beaufort, Bertie, Bladen, Cabarrus, Camden, Caswell, Chowan, Cleveland, Columbus, Craven, Cumberland, Currituck, Duplin, Edgecombe, Gaston, Gates, Greene, Halifax, Harnett, Hertford, Johnston, Jones, Lee, Lenoir, Lincoln, Martin, Mecklenburg, Montgomery, Nash, Northampton, Onslow, Pamlico, Pender, Perquimans, Person, Pitt, Randolph, Robeson, Rockingham, Rowan, Rutherford, Sampson, Stokes, Surry, Tyrrell, Vance, Wake, Warren, Washington, Wayne, Wilson and Yadkin.

History.

1905, cc. 297, 383, 445, 820; Rev., s. 3366; 1907, c. 8; c. 84, s. 1; c. 595, s. 1; cc. 639, 719, 869; Pub. Loc. 1915, c. 18; C.S., s. 4480; Ex. Sess. 1920, c. 26; 1925, c. 285, s. 2; Pub. Loc. 1925, c. 211; Pub. Loc. 1927, c. 614; 1931, c. 136, s. 1; 1945, c. 635; 1953, c. 474; 1983, c. 623; 1993, c. 539, s. 237; 1994, Ex. Sess., c. 24, s. 14(c)

§ 14-359. Local: Tenant neglecting crop; landlord failing to make advances; harboring or employing delinquent tenant

If any tenant or cropper shall procure advances from his landlord to enable him to make a crop on the land rented by him, and then willfully refuse to cultivate such crops or negligently or willfully abandon the same without good cause and before paying for such advances with intent to defraud the landlord; or if any landlord who induces another to become tenant or cropper by agreeing to furnish him advances to enable him to make a crop, shall willfully fail or refuse without good cause to furnish such advances according to his agreement with intent to defraud the tenant, or if any person shall entice, persuade or procure any tenant, lessee or cropper, who has made a contract agreeing to cultivate the land of another, to abandon or to refuse or fail to cultivate such land with intent to defraud the landlord, or after notice shall harbor or detain on his own premises, or on the premises of another, any such tenant, lessee or cropper, he shall be guilty of a Class 3 misdemeanor. Any person who employs a tenant or cropper who has violated the provisions of this section, with knowledge of such violation, shall be liable to the landlord furnishing such advances, for the amount thereof. This section shall apply only to the following counties: Alamance, Anson, Cabarrus, Caswell, Davidson, Franklin, Granville, Halifax, Harnett, Hertford, Hoke, Hyde, Lee, Lincoln, Moore, Person, Randolph, Richmond, Rockingham, Rowan, Rutherford, Sampson, Stanly, Stokes, Union, Vance, Wake and Washington.

History.

1905, c. 299, ss. 1-7; Rev., s. 3367; 1907, c. 84, s. 2; c. 238, s. 1; c. 543; c. 595, s. 2; c. 810; C.S., s. 4481; Ex. Sess. 1920, cc. 20, 26; 1923, c. 32; 1925, c. 285, s. 3; Pub. Loc. 1927, c. 614; 1929, c. 5, s. 1; 1931, c. 44; c. 136, s. 2; 1939, c. 95; 1945, c. 635; 1949, c. 83; 1951, c. 615; 1993, c. 539, s. 238; 1994, Ex. Sess., c. 24, s. 14(c)

ARTICLE 47
CRUELTY TO ANIMALS

§ 14-360. Cruelty to animals; construction of section

(a) If any person shall intentionally overdrive, overload, wound, injure, torment, kill, or deprive of necessary sustenance, or cause or procure to be overdriven, overloaded, wounded, injured, tormented, killed, or deprived of necessary sustenance, any animal, every such

823

offender shall for every such offense be guilty of a Class 1 misdemeanor.

(a1) If any person shall maliciously kill, or cause or procure to be killed, any animal by intentional deprivation of necessary sustenance, that person shall be guilty of a Class H felony.

(b) If any person shall maliciously torture, mutilate, maim, cruelly beat, disfigure, poison, or kill, or cause or procure to be tortured, mutilated, maimed, cruelly beaten, disfigured, poisoned, or killed, any animal, every such offender shall for every such offense be guilty of a Class H felony. However, nothing in this section shall be construed to increase the penalty for cockfighting provided for in G.S. 14-362.

(c) As used in this section, the words "torture", "torment", and "cruelly" include or refer to any act, omission, or neglect causing or permitting unjustifiable pain, suffering, or death. As used in this section, the word "intentionally" refers to an act committed knowingly and without justifiable excuse, while the word "maliciously" means an act committed intentionally and with malice or bad motive. As used in this section, the term "animal" includes every living vertebrate in the classes Amphibia, Reptilia, Aves, and Mammalia except human beings. However, this section shall not apply to the following activities:

(1) The lawful taking of animals under the jurisdiction and regulation of the Wildlife Resources Commission, except that this section shall apply to those birds other than pigeons exempted by the Wildlife Resources Commission from its definition of "wild birds" pursuant to G.S. 113-129(15a).

(2) Lawful activities conducted for purposes of biomedical research or training or for purposes of production of livestock, poultry, or aquatic species.

(2a) Lawful activities conducted for the primary purpose of providing food for human or animal consumption.

(3) Activities conducted for lawful veterinary purposes.

(4) The lawful destruction of any animal for the purposes of protecting the public, other animals, property, or the public health.

(5) The physical alteration of livestock or poultry for the purpose of conforming with breed or show standards.

History.
1881, c. 34, s. 1; c. 368, ss. 1, 15; Code, ss. 2482, 2490; 1891, c. 65; Rev., s. 3299; 1907, c. 42; C.S., s. 4483; 1969, c. 1224, s. 2; 1979, c. 641; 1985 (Reg. Sess., 1986), c. 967, s. 1; 1989, c. 670, s. 1; 1993, c. 539, s. 239; 1994, Ex. Sess., c. 24, s. 14(c); 1998-212, s. 17.16(c); 1999-209, s. 8; 2007-211, ss. 1, 2; 2010-16, ss. 1, 2; 2015-286, s. 4.32(a)

§ 14-360.1. Immunity for veterinarian reporting animal cruelty

Any veterinarian licensed in this State who has reasonable cause to believe that an animal has been the subject of animal cruelty in violation of G.S. 14-360 and who makes a report of animal cruelty, or who participates in any investigation or testifies in any judicial proceeding that arises from a report of animal cruelty, shall be immune from civil liability, criminal liability, and liability from professional disciplinary action and shall not be in breach of any veterinarian-patient confidentiality, unless the veterinarian acted in bad faith or with a malicious purpose. It shall be a rebuttable presumption that the veterinarian acted in good faith. A failure by a veterinarian to make a report of animal cruelty shall not constitute grounds for disciplinary action under G.S. 90-187.8.

History.
2007-232, s. 1

§ 14-361. Instigating or promoting cruelty to animals

If any person shall willfully set on foot, or instigate, or move to, carry on, or promote, or engage in, or do any act towards the furtherance of any act of cruelty to any animal, he shall be guilty of a Class 1 misdemeanor.

History.
1881, c. 368, s. 6; Code, s. 2487; 1891, c. 65; Rev., s. 3300; C.S., s. 4484; 1953, c. 857, s. 1; 1969, c. 1224, s. 3; 1985 (Reg. Sess., 1986), c. 967, s. 1; 1989, c. 670, s. 2; 1993, c. 539, s. 240; 1994, Ex. Sess., c. 24, s. 14(c)

§ 14-361.1. Abandonment of animals

Any person being the owner or possessor, or having charge or custody of an animal, who willfully and without justifiable excuse abandons the animal is guilty of a Class 2 misdemeanor.

History.
1979, c. 687; 1985 (Reg. Sess., 1986), c. 967, s. 2; 1989, c. 670, s. 3; 1993, c. 539, s. 241; 1994, Ex. Sess., c. 24, s. 14(c)

§ 14-362. Cockfighting

A person who instigates, promotes, conducts, is employed at, allows property under his ownership or control to be used for, participates as a spectator at, or profits from an exhibition featuring the fighting of a cock is guilty of a Class I felony. A lease of property that is used or is intended to be used for an exhibition featuring the fighting of a cock is void, and a lessor who knows this use is made or is intended to be made of his property is under a duty to evict the lessee immediately.

History.
1881, c. 368, s. 2; Code, s. 2483; 1891, c. 65; Rev., s. 3301; C.S., s. 4485; 1953, c. 857, s. 2; 1969, c. 1224, s. 3; 1985 (Reg. Sess., 1986), c. 967, s. 3; 1993, c. 539, s. 242; 1994, Ex. Sess., c. 24, s. 14(c); 2005-437, s. 1

§ 14-362.1. Animal fights and baiting, other than cock fights, dog fights and dog baiting

(a) A person who instigates, promotes, conducts, is employed at, provides an animal for, allows property under his ownership or control to be used for, or profits from an exhibition featuring the fighting or baiting of an animal, other than a cock or a dog, is guilty of a Class 2 misdemeanor. A lease of property that is used or is intended to be used for an exhibition featuring the fighting or baiting of an animal, other than a cock or a dog, is void, and a lessor who knows this use is made or is intended to be made of his property is under a duty to evict the lessee immediately.

(b) A person who owns, possesses, or trains an animal, other than a cock or a dog, with the intent that the animal be used in an exhibition featuring the fighting or baiting of that animal or any other animal is guilty of a Class 2 misdemeanor.

(c) A person who participates as a spectator at an exhibition featuring the fighting or baiting of an animal, other than a cock or a dog, is guilty of a Class 2 misdemeanor.

(d) A person who commits an offense under subsection (a) within three years after being convicted of an offense under this section is guilty of a Class I felony.

(e) This section does not prohibit the lawful taking or training of animals under the jurisdiction and regulation of the Wildlife Resources Commission.

History.
1985 (Reg. Sess., 1986), c. 967, s. 5; 1993, c. 539, ss. 243, 1236; 1994, Ex. Sess., c. 24, s. 14(c); 1997-78, s. 2

§ 14-362.2. Dog fighting and baiting

(a) A person who instigates, promotes, conducts, is employed at, provides a dog for, allows property under the person's ownership or control to be used for, gambles on, or profits from an exhibition featuring the baiting of a dog or the fighting of a dog with another dog or with another animal is guilty of a Class H felony. A lease of property that is used or is intended to be used for an exhibition featuring the baiting of a dog or the fighting of a dog with another dog or with another animal is void, and a lessor

who knows this use is made or is intended to be made of the lessor's property is under a duty to evict the lessee immediately.

(b) A person who owns, possesses, or trains a dog with the intent that the dog be used in an exhibition featuring the baiting of that dog or the fighting of that dog with another dog or with another animal is guilty of a Class H felony.

(c) A person who participates as a spectator at an exhibition featuring the baiting of a dog or the fighting of a dog with another dog or with another animal is guilty of a Class H felony.

(d) This section does not prohibit the use of dogs in the lawful taking of animals under the jurisdiction and regulation of the Wildlife Resources Commission.

(e) This section does not prohibit the use of dogs in earthdog trials that are sanctioned or sponsored by entities approved by the Commissioner of Agriculture that meet standards that protect the health and safety of the dogs. Quarry at an earthdog trial shall at all times be kept separate from the dogs by a sturdy barrier, such as a cage, and have access to food and water.

(f) This section does not apply to the use of herding dogs engaged in the working of domesticated livestock for agricultural, entertainment, or sporting purposes.

History.
1997-78, s. 1; 2006-113, s. 3.1; 2006-259, s. 37; 2007-180, s. 1; 2007-181, s. 1

§ 14-362.3. Restraining dogs in a cruel manner

A person who maliciously restrains a dog using a chain or wire grossly in excess of the size necessary to restrain the dog safely is guilty of a Class 1 misdemeanor. For purposes of this section, "maliciously" means the person imposed the restraint intentionally and with malice or bad motive.

History.
2001-411, s. 2

§ 14-363. Conveying animals in a cruel manner

If any person shall carry or cause to be carried in or upon any vehicle or other conveyance, any animal in a cruel or inhuman manner, he shall be guilty of a Class 1 misdemeanor. Whenever an offender shall be taken into custody therefor by any officer, the officer may take charge of such vehicle or other conveyance and its contents, and deposit the same in some safe place of custody. The necessary expenses which may be incurred for taking charge of and keeping and sustaining the vehicle or other conveyance shall be a lien thereon, to be paid before the same can be lawfully reclaimed; or the said expenses, or any part thereof remaining unpaid, may be recovered by the person incurring the same of the owner of such animal in an action therefor.

History.
1881, c. 368, s. 5; Code, s. 2486; 1891, c. 65; Rev., s. 3302; C.S., s. 4486; 1953, c. 857, s. 3; 1969, c. 1224, s. 4; 1985 (Reg. Sess., 1986), c. 967, s. 1; 1989, c. 670, s. 4; 1993, c. 539, s. 244; 1994, Ex. Sess., c. 24, s. 14(c)

§ 14-363.1. Living baby chicks or other fowl, or rabbits under eight weeks of age; disposing of as pets or novelties forbidden

If any person, firm or corporation shall sell, or offer for sale, barter or give away as premiums living baby chicks, ducklings, or other fowl or rabbits under eight weeks of age as pets or novelties, such person, firm or corporation shall be guilty of a Class 3 misdemeanor. Provided, that nothing contained in this section shall be construed to prohibit the sale of nondomesticated species of chicks, ducklings, or other fowl, or of other fowl from proper brooder facilities by hatcheries or stores engaged in the business of selling them for purposes other than for pets or novelties.

History.
1973, c. 466, s. 1; 1985 (Reg. Sess., 1986), c. 967, s. 4; 1993, c. 539, s. 245; 1994, Ex. Sess., c. 24, s. 14(c)

§ 14-363.2. Confiscation of cruelly treated animals

Conviction of any offense contained in this Article may result in confiscation of cruelly treated animals belonging to the accused and it shall be proper for the court in its discretion to order a final determination of the custody of the confiscated animals.

History.
1979, c. 640

§ 14-363.3. Confinement of animals in motor vehicles

(a) In order to protect the health and safety of an animal, any animal control officer, animal cruelty investigator appointed under G.S. 19A-45, law enforcement officer, firefighter, or rescue squad worker, who has probable cause to believe that an animal is confined in a motor vehicle under conditions that are likely to cause suffering, injury, or death to the animal due to heat, cold, lack of adequate ventilation, or under other endangering conditions, may enter the motor vehicle by any reasonable means under the circumstances after making a reasonable effort to locate the owner or other person responsible for the animal.

(b) Nothing in this section shall be construed to apply to the transportation of horses, cattle, sheep, swine, poultry, or other livestock.

History.
2013-377, s. 6

ARTICLE 48
ANIMAL DISEASES

N.C. Gen. Stat. § 14-364

Repealed by Session Laws 1945, c. 635.

ARTICLE 49
PROTECTION OF LIVESTOCK RUNNING AT LARGE

N.C. Gen. Stat. § 14-365

Repealed by Session Laws 1971, c. 110.

§ 14-366. Molesting or injuring livestock

If any person shall unlawfully and on purpose drive any livestock, lawfully running at large in the range, from said range, or shall kill, maim or injure any livestock, lawfully running at large in the range or in the field or pasture of the owner, whether done with actual intent to injure the owner, or to drive the stock from the range, or with any other unlawful intent, every such person, his counselors, aiders, and abettors, shall be guilty of a Class 2 misdemeanor: provided, that nothing herein contained shall prohibit any person from driving out of the range any stock unlawfully brought from other states or places. In any indictment under this section it shall not be necessary to name in the bill or prove on the trial the owner of the stock molested, maimed, killed or injured. Any person violating any provision of this section shall be guilty of a Class 2 misdemeanor.

History.
1850, c. 94, ss. 1, 2; R.C., c. 34, s. 104; Code, s. 1002; 1885, c. 383; 1887, c. 368; 1895, c. 190; Rev., s. 3314; C.S., s. 4494; 1969, c. 1224, s. 9; 1993, c. 539, s. 246; 1994, Ex. Sess., c. 24, s. 14(c)

§ 14-367. Altering the brands of and misbranding another's livestock

If any person shall knowingly alter or deface the mark or brand of any other person's horse, mule, ass, neat cattle, sheep, goat, or hog, or shall knowingly mismark or brand any such beast that may be unbranded or unmarked, not properly his own, with intent to defraud any other person, the person so offending shall be guilty of a Class H felony.

History.

1797, c. 485, s. 2, P.R.; R.C., c. 34, s. 57; Code, s. 1001; Rev., s. 3317; C.S., s. 4495; 1993, c. 539, s. 1237; 1994, Ex. Sess., c. 24, s. 14(c)

§ 14-368. Placing poisonous shrubs and vegetables in public places

If any person shall throw into or leave exposed in any public square, street, lane, alley or open lot in any city, town or village, or in any public road, any mock orange or other poisonous shrub, plant, tree or vegetable, he shall be liable in damages to any person injured thereby and shall also be guilty of a Class 2 misdemeanor.

History.

1887, c. 338; Rev., s. 3318; C.S., s. 4496; 1969, c. 1224, s. 3; 1993, c. 539, s. 247; 1994, Ex. Sess., c. 24, s. 14(c)

N.C. Gen. Stat. § 14-369

Repealed by Session Laws 1994, Extra Session, c. 14, s. 72(20).

ARTICLE 50
PROTECTION OF LETTERS, TELEGRAMS, AND TELEPHONE MESSAGES

§ 14-370. Wrongfully obtaining or divulging knowledge of telephonic messages

If any person wrongfully obtains, or attempts to obtain, any knowledge of a telephonic message by connivance with a clerk, operator, messenger or other employee of a telephone company, or, being such clerk, operator, messenger or employee, willfully divulges to any but the person for whom it was intended, the contents of a telephonic message or dispatch intrusted to him for transmission or delivery, or the nature thereof, he shall be guilty of a Class 2 misdemeanor.

History.

1903, c. 599; Rev., s. 3848; C.S., s. 4497; 1993, c. 539, s. 248; 1994, Ex. Sess., c. 24, s. 14(c)

§ 14-371. Violating privacy of telegraphic messages; failure to transmit and deliver same promptly

If any person wrongfully obtains, or attempts to obtain, any knowledge of a telegraphic message by connivance with a clerk, operator, messenger, or other employee of a telegraph company, or, being such clerk, operator, messenger, or other employee, willfully divulges to any but the person for whom it was intended, the contents of a telegraphic message or dispatch intrusted to him for transmission or delivery, or the nature thereof, or willfully refuse or neglect duly to transmit or deliver the same, he shall be guilty of a Class 2 misdemeanor.

History.

1889, c. 41, s. 1; Rev., s. 3846; C.S., s. 4498; 1993, c. 539, s. 249; 1994, Ex. Sess., c. 24, s. 14(c)

§ 14-372. Unauthorized opening, reading or publishing of sealed letters and telegrams

If any person shall willfully, and without authority, open or read, or cause to be opened or read, a sealed letter or telegram, or shall publish the whole or any portion of such letter or telegram, knowing it to have been opened or read without authority, he shall be guilty of a Class 2 misdemeanor.

History.

1889, c. 41, s. 2; Rev., s. 3728; C.S., s. 4499; 1993, c. 539, s. 250; 1994, Ex. Sess., c. 24, s. 14(c)

ARTICLE 51
PROTECTION OF ATHLETIC CONTESTS

§ 14-373. Bribery of players, managers, coaches, referees, umpires or officials

If any person shall bribe or offer to bribe or shall aid, advise, or abet in any way another in such bribe or offer to bribe, any player or participant in any athletic contest with intent to influence his play, action, or conduct and for the purpose of inducing the player or participant to lose or try to lose or cause to be lost any athletic contest or to limit or try to limit the margin of victory or defeat in such contest; or if any person shall bribe or offer to bribe or shall aid, advise, or abet in any way another in such bribe or offer to bribe, any referee, umpire, manager, coach, or any other official or an athletic club or team, league, association, institution or conference, by whatever name called connected with said athletic contest with intent to influence his decision or bias his opinion or judgment for the purpose of losing or trying to lose or causing to be lost said athletic contest or of limiting or trying to limit the margin of victory or defeat in such contest, such person shall be punished as a Class I felon.

History.
1921, c. 23, s. 1; C.S., s. 4499(a); 1951, c. 364, s. 1; 1961, c. 1054, s. 1; 1979, c. 760, s. 5; 1979, 2nd Sess., c. 1316, s. 47; 1981, c. 63, s. 1; c. 179, s. 14; 1993, c. 539, s. 1238; 1994, Ex. Sess., c. 24, s. 14(c)

§ 14-374. Acceptance of bribes by players, managers, coaches, referees, umpires or officials

If any player or participant in any athletic contest shall accept, or agree to accept, a bribe given for the purpose of inducing the player or participant to lose or try to lose or cause to be lost or limit or try to limit the margin of victory or defeat in such contest; or if any referee, umpire, manager, coach, or any other official of an athletic club, team, league, association, institution, or conference connected with an athletic contest shall accept or agree to accept a bribe given with the intent to influence his decision or bias his opinion or judgment and for the purpose of losing or trying to lose or causing to be lost said athletic contest or of limiting or trying to limit the margin of victory or defeat in such contest, such person shall be punished as a Class I felon.

History.
1921, c. 23, s. 2; C.S., s. 4499(b); 1951, c. 364, s. 2; 1961, c. 1054, s. 2; 1979, c. 760, s. 5; 1979, 2nd Sess., c. 1316, s. 47; 1981, c. 63, s. 1; c. 179, s. 14; 1993, c. 539, s. 1239; 1994, Ex. Sess., c. 24, s. 14(c)

§ 14-375. Completion of offenses set out in §§ 14-373 and 14-374

To complete the offenses mentioned in G.S. 14-373 and 14-374, it shall not be necessary that the player, manager, coach, referee, umpire, or official shall, at the time, have been actually employed, selected, or appointed to perform his respective duties; it shall be sufficient if the bribe be offered, accepted, or agreed to with the view of probable employment, selection, or appointment of the person to whom the bribe is offered or by whom it is accepted. It shall not be necessary that such player, referee, umpire, manager, coach, or other official actually play or participate in any athletic contest, concerning which said bribe is offered or accepted; it shall be sufficient if the bribe be given, offered, or accepted in view of his or their possibly participating therein.

History.
1921, c. 23, s. 3; C.S., s. 4499(c); 1951, c. 364, s. 3; 1961, c. 1054, s. 3

§ 14-376. Bribe defined

By a "bribe," as used in this article, is meant any gift, emolument, money or thing of value, testimonial, privilege, appointment or personal advantage, or in the promise of either, bestowed or promised for the purpose of influencing, directly or indirectly, any player, referee, manager, coach, umpire, club or league official, to see which game an admission fee may be charged, or in which athletic contest any player, manager, coach, umpire, referee, or other official is paid any compensation for his services. Said bribe as defined in this article need not be direct; it may be such as is hidden under the semblance of a sale, bet, wager, payment of a debt, or in any other manner defined to cover the true intention of the parties.

History.
1921, c. 23, s. 4; C.S., s. 4499(d); 1951, c. 364, s. 4; 1961, c. 1054, s. 4

§ 14-377. Intentional losing of athletic contest or limiting margin of victory or defeat

If any player or participant shall commit any willful act of omission or commission, in playing of an athletic contest, with intent to lose or try to lose or to cause to be lost or to limit or try to limit the margin of victory or defeat in such contest for the purpose of material gain to himself, or if any referees, umpire, manager, coach, or other official of an athletic club, team, league, association, institution or conference connected with an athletic contest shall commit any willful act of omission or commission connected with his official duties with intent to try to lose or to cause to be lost or to limit or try to limit the margin of victory or defeat in such contest for the purpose of material gain to himself, such person shall be punished as a Class I felon.

History.
1921, c. 23, s. 5; C.S., s. 4499(e); 1951, c. 364, s. 5; 1961, c. 1054, s. 5; 1979, c. 760, s. 5; 1979, 2nd Sess., c. 1316, s. 47; 1981, c. 63, s. 1; c. 179, s. 14; 1993, c. 539, s. 1240; 1994, Ex. Sess., c. 24, s. 14(c)

§ 14-378. Venue

In all prosecutions under this Article, the venue may be laid in any county where the bribe herein referred to was given, offered, or accepted, or in which the athletic contest was carried on in relation to which the bribe was offered, given, or accepted, or the acts referred to in G.S. 14-377 were committed.

History.

1921, c. 23, s. 6; C.S., s. 4606(c); 1951, c. 364, s. 6

§ 14-379. Bonus or extra compensation not forbidden

Nothing in this Article shall be construed to prohibit the giving or offering of any bonus or extra compensation to any manager, coach, or professional player, or to any league, association, or conference for the purpose of encouraging such manager, coach, or player to a higher degree of skill, ability, or diligence in the performance of his duties.

History.

1921, c. 23, s. 7; C.S., s. 4499(f); 1951, c. 364, s. 7; 1961, c. 1054, s. 6

N.C. Gen. Stat. § 14-380

Repealed by Session Laws 1951, c. 364, s. 8.

ARTICLE 51A
PROTECTION OF HORSE SHOWS

§ 14-380.1. Bribery of horse show judges or officials

Any person who bribes, or offers to bribe, any judge or other official in any horse show, with intent to influence his decision or judgment concerning said horse show, shall be guilty of a Class 2 misdemeanor.

History.

1963, c. 1100, s. 1; 1969, c. 1224, s. 1; 1993, c. 539, s. 251; 1994, Ex. Sess., c. 24, s. 14(c)

§ 14-380.2. Bribery attempts to be reported

Any judge or other official of any horse show shall report to the resident superior court district attorney any attempt to bribe him with respect to his decisions in any horse show, and a failure to so report shall constitute a Class 2 misdemeanor.

History.

1963, c. 1100, s. 2; 1969, c. 1224, s. 1; 1973, c. 47, s. 2; 1993, c. 539, s. 252; 1994, Ex. Sess., c. 24, s. 14(c)

§ 14-380.3. Bribe defined

The word "bribe," as used in this Article, shall have the same meaning as set forth in G.S. 14-376, in relation to athletic contests.

History.

1963, c. 1100, s. 3

§ 14-380.4. Printing Article in horse show schedules

The provisions of this Article shall be printed on all schedules for any horse show held prior to January 1, 1965.

History.

1963, c. 1100, s. 4

ARTICLE 52
MISCELLANEOUS POLICE REGULATIONS

§ 14-381. Desecration of State and United States flag

It shall be unlawful for any person willfully and knowingly to cast contempt upon any flag of the United States or upon any flag of North Carolina by public acts of physical contact including, but not limited to, mutilation, defiling, defacing or trampling. Any person violating this section shall be deemed guilty of a Class 2 misdemeanor.

The flag of the United States, as used in this section, shall be the same as defined in 4 U.S.C.A. 1 and 4 U.S.C.A. 2. The flag of North Carolina, as used in this section, shall be the same as defined in G.S. 144-1.

History.

1917, c. 271; C.S., s. 4500; 1971, c. 295; 1993, c. 539, s. 253; 1994, Ex. Sess., c. 24, s. 14(c)

§ 14-382. Pollution of water on lands used for dairy purposes

It shall be unlawful for any person, firm, or corporation owning lands adjoining the lands of any person, firm, or corporation which are or may be used for dairy purposes or for grazing milk cows, to dispose of or permit disposal of any animal, mineral, chemical, or vegetable refuse, sewage or other deleterious matter in such way as to pollute the water on the lands so used or which may be used for dairy purposes or for grazing milk cows, or to render unfit or unsafe for use the milk produced from cows feeding upon the grasses and herbage growing on such lands. This section shall not apply to incorporated towns maintaining a sewer system. Anyone violating the provisions of this section shall be guilty of a Class 3 misdemeanor, and each day that such pollution is committed or exists shall constitute a separate offense.

History.
1919, c. 222; C.S., s. 4501; 1993, c. 539, s. 254; 1994, Ex. Sess., c. 24, s. 14(c)

§ 14-383. Cutting timber on town watershed without disposing of boughs and debris; misdemeanor

Any person, firm or corporation owning lands or the standing timber on lands within 400 feet of any watershed held or owned by any city or town, for the purpose of furnishing a city or town water supply, upon cutting or removing the timber or permitting the same cut or removed from lands so within 400 feet of said watershed, or any part thereof, shall, within three months after cutting, or earlier upon written notice by said city or town, remove or cause to be burned under proper supervision all treetops, boughs, laps and other portions of timber not desired to be taken for commercial or other purposes, within 400 feet of the boundary line of such part of such watershed as is held or owned by such town or city, so as to leave such space of 400 feet immediately adjoining the boundary line of such watershed, so held or owned, free and clear of all such treetops, laps, boughs and other inflammable material caused by or left from cutting such standing timber, so as to prevent the spread of fire from such cutover area and the consequent damage to such watershed. Any such person, firm or corporation violating the provisions of this section shall be guilty of a Class 2 misdemeanor.

History.
1913, c. 56; C.S., s. 4502; 1969, c. 1224, s. 1; 1993, c. 539, s. 255; 1994, Ex. Sess., c. 24, s. 14(c)

§ 14-384. Injuring notices and advertisements

If any person shall wantonly or maliciously mutilate, deface, pull or tear down, destroy or otherwise damage any notice, sign or advertisement, unless immoral or obscene, whether put up by an officer of the law in performance of the duties of his office or by some other person for a lawful purpose, before the object for which such notice, sign or advertisement was posted shall have been accomplished, he shall be guilty of a Class 3 misdemeanor. Nothing herein contained shall apply to any person mutilating, defacing, pulling or tearing down, destroying or otherwise damaging notices, signs or advertisements put upon his own land or lands of which he may have charge or control, unless consent of such person to put up such notice, sign or advertisement shall have first been obtained, except those put up by an officer of the law in the performance of the duties of his office.

History.
1885, c. 302; Rev., s. 3709; C.S., s. 4503; 1993, c. 539, s. 256; 1994, Ex. Sess., c. 24, s. 14(c)

§ 14-385. Defacing or destroying public notices and advertisements

If any person shall willfully and unlawfully deface, tear down, remove or destroy any legal notice or advertisement authorized by law to be posted by any officer or other person, the same being actually posted at the time of such defacement, tearing down, removal or destruction, during the time for which such legal notice or advertisement shall be authorized by law to be posted, he shall be guilty of a Class 3 misdemeanor.

History.
1876-7, c. 215; Code, s. 981; Rev., s. 3710; C.S., s. 4504; 1993, c. 539, s. 257; 1994, Ex. Sess., c. 24, s. 14(c)

N.C. Gen. Stat. § 14-386

Repealed by Session Laws 1994, Extra Session, c. 14, s. 72(21).

N.C. Gen. Stat. § 14-387

Repealed by Session Laws 1945, c. 635.

N.C. Gen. Stat. § 14-388

Repealed by Session Laws 1943, c. 543.

N.C. Gen. Stat. § 14-389

Repealed by Session Laws 1993 (Reg. Sess., 1994), c. 767, s. 30(17).

§§ 14-390, 14-390.1

Repealed by Session Laws 1969, c. 970, s. 11.

§ 14-391. Usurious loans on household and kitchen furniture or assignment of wages

Any person, firm or corporation who shall lend money in any manner whatsoever by note, chattel mortgage, conditional sale, or purported conditional sale or otherwise, upon any article of household or kitchen furniture, or any assignment of wages, earned or to be earned, and shall willfully:

(1) Take, receive, reserve or charge a greater rate of interest than permitted by law, either before or after the interest may accrue; or

(2) Refuse to give receipts for payments on interest or principal of such loan; or

(3) Fail or refuse to surrender the note and security when the same is paid off or a

new note and mortgage is given in renewal, unless such new mortgage shall state the amount still due by the old note or mortgage and that the new one is given as additional security;

shall be guilty of a Class 1 misdemeanor and in addition thereto shall be subject to the provisions of G.S. 24-2.

History.
1907, c. 110; C.S., s. 4509; 1927, c. 72; 1959, c. 195; 1977, c. 807; 1993, c. 539, s. 259; 1994, Ex. Sess., c. 24, s. 14(c)

§§ 14-392, 14-393

Repealed by Session Laws 1989, c. 508, s. 4.

§ 14-394. Anonymous or threatening letters, mailing or transmitting

It shall be unlawful for any person, firm, or corporation, or any association of persons in this State, under whatever name styled, to write and transmit any letter, note, or writing, whether written, printed, or drawn, without signing his, her, their, or its true name thereto, threatening any person or persons, firm or corporation, or officers thereof with any personal injury or violence or destruction of property of such individuals, firms, or corporations, or using therein any language or threats of any kind or nature calculated to intimidate or place in fear any such persons, firms or corporations, or officers thereof, as to their personal safety or the safety of their property, or using vulgar or obscene language, or using such language which if published would bring such persons into public contempt and disgrace, and any person, firm, or corporation violating the provisions of this section shall be guilty of a Class 1 misdemeanor.

History.
1921, c. 112; C.S., s. 4511(a); 1993, c. 539, s. 260; 1994, Ex. Sess., c. 24, s. 14(c)

§ 14-395. Commercialization of American Legion emblem; wearing by nonmembers

It shall be unlawful for anyone not a member of the American Legion, an organization consisting of ex-members of the United States Army, Navy and Marine Corps, who served as members of such organizations in the recent world war, to wear upon his or her person the recognized emblem of the American Legion, or to use the said emblem for advertising purposes, or to commercialize the same in any way whatsoever; or to use the said emblem in display upon his or her property or place of business, or at any place whatsoever. Anyone violating the provisions of this section shall be guilty of a Class 3 misdemeanor.

History.
1923, c. 89; C.S., s. 4511(b); 1993, c. 539, s. 261; 1994, Ex. Sess., c. 24, s. 14(c); 2011-183, s. 127(b)

§ 14-395.1. Sexual harassment

(a) **Offense.** -- Any lessor of residential real property or the agent of any lessor of residential real property who shall harass on the basis of sex any lessee or prospective lessee of the property shall be guilty of a Class 2 misdemeanor.

(b) **Definitions.** -- For purposes of this section:

(1) "Harass on the basis of sex" means unsolicited overt requests or demands for sexual acts when (i) submission to such conduct is made a term of the execution or continuation of the lease agreement, or (ii) submission to or rejection of such conduct by an individual is used to determine whether rights under the lease are accorded;

(2) "Lessee" means a person who enters into a residential rental agreement with the lessor and all other persons residing in the lessee's rental unit; and

(3) "Prospective lessee" means a person seeking to enter into a residential rental agreement with a lessor.

History.
1989, c. 712, s. 1; 1993, c. 539, s. 262; 1994, Ex. Sess., c. 24, s. 14(c)

§§ 14-396, 14-397

Repealed by Session Laws 1993 (Reg. Sess., 1994), c. 767, s. 30(18), (19).

§ 14-398. Theft or destruction of property of public libraries, museums, etc

Any person who shall steal or unlawfully take or detain, or willfully or maliciously or wantonly write upon, cut, tear, deface, disfigure, soil, obliterate, break or destroy, or who shall sell or buy or receive, knowing the same to have been stolen, any book, document, newspaper, periodical, map, chart, picture, portrait, engraving, statue, coin, medal, apparatus, specimen, or other work of literature or object of art or curiosity deposited in a public library, gallery, museum, collection, fair or exhibition, or in any department or office of State or local government, or in a library, gallery, museum, collection, or exhibition, belonging to any incorporated college or university, or any incorporated institution devoted to educational, scientific, literary, artistic, historical or charitable purposes, shall, if the value of the property stolen, detained, sold, bought or received knowing same to have been stolen, or if the damage done by writing upon, cutting, tearing, defacing, disfiguring, soiling, obliterating, breaking or destroying any such property, shall not exceed fifty dollars ($ 50.00), be guilty of a Class 1 misdemeanor. If the value of the property stolen, detained, sold or received knowing same to have been stolen, or the amount of damage done in any of the ways or manners hereinabove set out, shall exceed the sum of fifty dollars ($ 50.00), the person committing same shall be punished as a Class H felon.

History.

1935, c. 300; 1943, c. 543; 1979, c. 760, s. 5; 1979, 2nd Sess., c. 1316, s. 47; 1981, c. 63, s. 1; c. 179, s. 14; 1993, c. 539, s. 265; 1994, Ex. Sess., c. 24, s. 14(c)

§ 14-399. Littering

(a) No person, including any firm, organization, private corporation, or governing body, agents or employees of any municipal corporation shall intentionally or recklessly throw, scatter, spill or place or intentionally or recklessly cause to be blown, scattered, spilled, thrown or placed or otherwise dispose of any litter upon any public property or private property not owned by the person within this State or in the waters of this State including any public highway, public park, lake, river, ocean, beach, campground, forestland, recreational area, trailer park, highway, road, street or alley except:

(1) When the property is designated by the State or political subdivision thereof for the disposal of garbage and refuse, and the person is authorized to use the property for this purpose; or

(2) Into a litter receptacle in a manner that the litter will be prevented from being carried away or deposited by the elements upon any part of the private or public property or waters.

(a1) No person, including any firm, organization, private corporation, or governing body, agents, or employees of any municipal corporation shall scatter, spill, or place or cause to be blown, scattered, spilled, or placed or otherwise dispose of any litter upon any public property or private property not owned by the person within this State or in the waters of this State including any public highway, public park, lake, river, ocean, beach, campground, forestland, recreational area, trailer park, highway, road, street, or alley except:

(1) When the property is designated by the State or political subdivision thereof for the disposal of garbage and refuse, and the person is authorized to use the property for this purpose; or

(2) Into a litter receptacle in a manner that the litter will be prevented from being carried away or deposited by the elements upon any part of the private or public property or waters.

(a2) Subsection (a1) of this section does not apply to the accidental blowing, scattering, or spilling of an insignificant amount of municipal solid waste, as defined in G.S. 130A-290(18a), during the automated loading of a vehicle designed and constructed to transport municipal solid waste if the vehicle is operated in a reasonable manner and according to manufacturer specifications.

(b) When litter is blown, scattered, spilled, thrown or placed from a vehicle or watercraft, the operator thereof shall be presumed to have committed the offense. This presumption, however, does not apply to a vehicle transporting nontoxic and biodegradable agricultural or garden products or supplies, including mulch, tree bark, wood chips, and raw logs.

(c) Any person who violates subsection (a) of this section in an amount not exceeding 15 pounds and not for commercial purposes is guilty of a Class 3 misdemeanor punishable by a fine of not less than two hundred fifty dollars ($ 250.00) nor more than one thousand dollars ($ 1,000) for the first offense. In addition, the court may require the violator to perform community service of not less than eight hours nor more than 24 hours. The community service required shall be to pick up litter if feasible, and if not feasible, to perform other labor commensurate with the offense committed. Any second or subsequent violation of subsection (a) of this section in an amount not exceeding 15 pounds and not for commercial purposes within three years after the date of a prior violation is a Class 3 misdemeanor punishable by a fine of not less than five hundred dollars ($ 500.00) nor more than two thousand dollars ($ 2,000). In addition, the court may require the violator to perform community service of not less than 16 hours nor more than 50 hours. The community service required shall be to pick up litter if feasible, and if not feasible, to perform other labor commensurate with the offense committed.

(c1) Any person who violates subsection (a1) of this section in an amount not exceeding 15 pounds is guilty of an infraction punishable by a fine of not more than one hundred dollars ($ 100.00). In addition, the court may require the violator to perform community service of not less than four hours nor more than 12 hours. The community service required shall be to pick up litter if feasible, and if not feasible, to perform other labor commensurate with the offense committed. Any second or subsequent violation of subsection (a1) of this section in an amount not exceeding 15 pounds within three years after the date of a prior violation is an infraction punishable by a fine of not more than two hundred dollars ($ 200.00). In addition, the court may require the violator to perform community service of not less than eight hours nor more than 24 hours. The community service required shall be to pick up litter if feasible, and if not feasible, to perform other labor commensurate with the offense committed. For purposes of this subsection, the term "litter" shall not include nontoxic and biodegradable agricultural or garden products or supplies, including mulch, tree bark, and wood chips.

(d) Any person who violates subsection (a) of this section in an amount exceeding 15 pounds but not exceeding 500 pounds and not for commercial purposes is guilty of a Class 3 misdemeanor punishable by a fine of not less than five hundred dollars ($ 500.00) nor more than two thousand dollars ($ 2,000). In addition, the court shall require the violator to perform community service of not less than 24 hours nor more than 100 hours. The community service required shall be to pick up litter if feasible, and if not feasible, to perform other community service commensurate with the offense committed.

(d1) Any person who violates subsection (a1) of this section in an amount exceeding 15 pounds but not exceeding 500 pounds is guilty of an infraction punishable by a fine of not more than two hundred dollars ($ 200.00). In addition, the court may require the violator to perform community service of not less than eight hours nor more than 24 hours. The community service required shall be to pick up litter if feasible, and if not feasible, to perform other labor commensurate with the offense committed.

(e) Any person who violates subsection (a) of this section in an amount exceeding 500 pounds or in any quantity for commercial purposes, or who discards litter that is a hazardous waste as defined in G.S. 130A-290 is guilty of a Class I felony.

(e1) Any person who violates subsection (a1) of this section in an amount exceeding 500 pounds is guilty of an infraction punishable by a fine of not more than three hundred dollars ($ 300.00). In addition, the court may require the violator to perform community service of not less than 16 hours nor more than 50 hours. The community service required shall be to pick up litter if feasible, and if not feasible, to perform other labor commensurate with the offense committed.

(e2) If any person violates subsection (a) or (a1) of this section in an amount exceeding 15 pounds or in any quantity for commercial purposes, or discards litter that is a hazardous waste as defined in G.S. 130A-290, the court shall order the violator to:

(1) Remove, or render harmless, the litter that he discarded in violation of this section;

(2) Repair or restore property damaged by, or pay damages for any damage arising

out of, his discarding litter in violation of this section; or

(3) Perform community public service relating to the removal of litter discarded in violation of this section or to the restoration of an area polluted by litter discarded in violation of this section.

(f) A court may enjoin a violation of this section.

(f1) If a violation of subsection (a) of this section involves the operation of a motor vehicle, upon a finding of guilt, the court shall forward a record of the finding to the Department of Transportation, Division of Motor Vehicles, which shall record a penalty of one point on the violator's drivers license pursuant to the point system established by G.S. 20-16. There shall be no insurance premium surcharge or assessment of points under the classification plan adopted under G.S. 58-36-65 for a finding of guilt under this section.

(g) A motor vehicle, vessel, aircraft, container, crane, winch, or machine involved in the disposal of more than 500 pounds of litter in violation of subsection (a) of this section is declared contraband and is subject to seizure and summary forfeiture to the State.

(h) If a person sustains damages arising out of a violation of subsection (a) of this section that is punishable as a felony, a court, in a civil action for the damages, shall order the person to pay the injured party threefold the actual damages or two hundred dollars ($ 200.00), whichever amount is greater. In addition, the court shall order the person to pay the injured party's court costs and attorney's fees.

(i) For the purpose of the section, unless the context requires otherwise:

(1) "Aircraft" means a motor vehicle or other vehicle that is used or designed to fly, but does not include a parachute or any other device used primarily as safety equipment.

(2) Repealed by Session Laws 1999-454, s. 1.

(2a) "Commercial purposes" means litter discarded by a business, corporation, association, partnership, sole proprietorship, or any other entity conducting business for economic gain, or by an employee or agent of the entity.

(3) "Law enforcement officer" means any law enforcement officer sworn and certified pursuant to Article 1 of Chapter 17C or 17E of the General Statutes, except company police officers as defined in G.S. 74E-6(b) (3). In addition, and solely for the purposes of this section, "law enforcement officer" means any employee of a county or municipality designated by the county or municipality as a litter enforcement officer.

(4) "Litter" means any garbage, rubbish, trash, refuse, can, bottle, box, container,

wrapper, paper, paper product, tire, appliance, mechanical equipment or part, building or construction material, tool, machinery, wood, motor vehicle or motor vehicle part, vessel, aircraft, farm machinery or equipment, sludge from a waste treatment facility, water supply treatment plant, or air pollution control facility, dead animal, or discarded material in any form resulting from domestic, industrial, commercial, mining, agricultural, or governmental operations. While being used for or distributed in accordance with their intended uses, "litter" does not include political pamphlets, handbills, religious tracts, newspapers, and other similar printed materials the unsolicited distribution of which is protected by the Constitution of the United States or the Constitution of North Carolina.

(5) "Vehicle" has the same meaning as in G.S. 20-4.01(49).

(6) "Watercraft" means any boat or vessel used for transportation across the water.

(j) It shall be the duty of all law enforcement officers to enforce the provisions of this section.

(k) This section does not limit the authority of any State or local agency to enforce other laws, rules or ordinances relating to litter or solid waste management.

History.

1935, c. 457; 1937, c. 446; 1943, c. 543; 1951, c. 975, s. 1; 1953, cc. 387, 1011; 1955, c. 437; 1957, cc. 73, 175; 1959, c. 1173; 1971, c. 165; 1973, c. 877; 1977, c. 887, s. 1; 1979, c. 1065, s. 1; 1983, c. 890; 1987, cc. 208, 757; 1989, c. 784, ss. 7.1, 8; 1991, c. 609, s. 1; c. 720, s. 49; c. 725, s. 1; 1993, c. 539, ss. 266, 267, 1241; 1994, Ex. Sess., c. 24, s. 14(c); 1997-518, s. 1; 1998-217, s. 2; 1999-294, s. 4; 1999-454, s. 1; 2001-512, s. 1

N.C. Gen. Stat. § 14-399.1

Repealed by Session Laws 1989, c. 784, s. 7.

§ 14-399.2. Certain plastic yoke and ring type holding devices prohibited

(a) As used in this section:

(1) "Degradable" means that within one year after being discarded, the yoke or ring type holding device is capable of becoming embrittled or decomposing by photodegradation, biodegradation, or chemo-degradation under average seasonal conditions into components other than heavy metals or other toxic substances.

(2) "Recyclable" means that the yoke or ring type holding device is capable of being collected and processed for reuse as a product or raw material.

(b) No person may sell or distribute for sale in this State any container connected to another by a yoke or ring type holding device constructed of plastic that is neither degradable nor recyclable. No person may sell or distribute for sale in this State any container connected to another by a yoke or ring type holding device constructed of plastic that is recyclable but that is not degradable unless such device does not have an orifice larger than one and three-fourths inches. The manufacturer of a degradable yoke or ring type holding device shall emboss or mark the device with a nationally recognized symbol indicating that the device is degradable. The manufacturer of a recyclable yoke or ring type holding device shall emboss or mark the device with a symbol of the type specified in G.S. 130A-309.10(e) indicating the plastic resin used to produce the device and that the device is recyclable. The manufacturer shall register the symbol with the Secretary of State with a sample of the device.

(c) Any person who sells or distributes for sale a yoke or ring type holding device in violation of this section shall be guilty of a Class 3 misdemeanor punishable by a fine of not less than fifty dollars ($ 50.00) nor more than two hundred dollars ($ 200.00). In lieu of a fine or any portion thereof or in addition to a fine, any violation of this section may also be punished by a term of community service.

(d) Other than a manufacturer required to use and register a symbol under subsection (b), a person may not be prosecuted under this section if, at the time of sale or distribution for sale, the yoke or holding device bears a symbol meeting the requirements of this section which has been registered with the Secretary of State.

History.

1989, c. 371, s. 1; 1991, c. 236, s. 1; c. 621, s. 14; 1993, c. 539, s. 268; 1994, Ex. Sess., c. 24, s. 14(c)

§ 14-400. Tattooing; body piercing prohibited

(a) It shall be unlawful for any person or persons to tattoo the arm, limb, or any part of the body of any other person under 18 years of age. Anyone violating the provisions of this section shall be guilty of a Class 2 misdemeanor.

(b) It shall be unlawful for any person to pierce any part of the body other than ears of another person under the age of 18 for the purpose of allowing the insertion of earrings, jewelry, or similar objects into the body, unless the prior consent of a custodial parent or guardian is obtained. Anyone violating the provisions of this section is guilty of a Class 2 misdemeanor.

History.

1937, c. 112, ss. 1, 2; 1969, c. 1224, s. 8; 1971, c. 1231, s. 1; 1993, c. 539, s. 269; 1994, Ex. Sess., c. 24, s. 14(c); 1998-230, s. 9

§ 14-401. Putting poisonous foodstuffs, antifreeze, etc., in certain public places, prohibited

It shall be unlawful for any person, firm or corporation to put or place (i) any strychnine, other poisonous compounds or ground glass on any beef or other foodstuffs of any kind, or (ii) any antifreeze that contains ethylene glycol and is not in a closed container, in any public square, street, lane, alley or on any lot in any village, town or city or on any public road, open field, woods or yard in the country. Any person, firm or corporation who violates the provisions of this section shall be liable in damages to the person injured thereby and also shall be guilty of a Class 1 misdemeanor. This section shall not apply to the poisoning of insects or worms for the purpose of protecting crops or gardens by spraying plants, crops, or trees, to poisons used in rat extermination, or to the accidental release of antifreeze containing ethylene glycol.

History.
1941, c. 181; 1953, c. 1239; 1993, c. 143, s. 1; c. 539, s. 270; 1994, Ex. Sess., c. 24, s. 14(c)

§ 14-401.1. Misdemeanor to tamper with examination questions

Any person who, without authority of the entity who prepares or administers the examination, purloins, steals, buys, receives, or sells, gives or offers to buy, give, or sell any examination questions or copies thereof of any examination provided and prepared by law shall be guilty of a Class 2 misdemeanor.

History.
1917, c. 146, s. 10; C.S., s. 5658; 1969, c. 1224, s. 3; 1991, c. 360, s. 2; 1993, c. 539, s. 271; 1994, Ex. Sess., c. 24, s. 14(c)

§ 14-401.2. Misdemeanor for detective to collect claims, accounts, etc

It shall be unlawful for any person, firm, or corporation, who or which is engaged in business as a detective, detective agency, or what is ordinarily known as "secret service work," or conducts such business, to engage in the business of collecting claims, accounts, bills, notes, or other money obligations for others, or to engage in the business known as a collection agency. Violation of the provisions hereof shall be a Class 2 misdemeanor.

History.
1943, c. 383; 1969, c. 1224, s. 5; 1993, c. 539, s. 272; 1994, Ex. Sess., c. 24, s. 14(c)

§ 14-401.3. Inscription on gravestone or monument charging commission of crime

It shall be illegal for any person to erect or cause to be erected any gravestone or monument bearing any inscription charging any person with the commission of a crime, and it shall be illegal for any person owning, controlling or operating any cemetery to permit such gravestone to be erected and maintained therein. If such gravestone has been erected in any graveyard, cemetery or burial plot, it shall be the duty of the person having charge thereof to remove and obliterate such inscription. Any person violating the provisions of this section shall be guilty of a Class 2 misdemeanor.

History.
1949, c. 1075; 1969, c. 1224, s. 8; 1993, c. 539, s. 273; 1994, Ex. Sess., c. 24, s. 14(c)

§ 14-401.4. Identifying marks on machines and apparatus; application to Division of Motor Vehicles for numbers

(a) No person, firm or corporation shall willfully remove, deface, destroy, alter or cover over the manufacturer's serial or engine number or any other manufacturer's number or other distinguishing number or identification mark upon any machine or other apparatus, including but not limited to farm equipment, machinery and apparatus, but excluding electric storage batteries, nor shall any person, firm or corporation place or stamp any serial, engine, or other number or mark upon such machinery, apparatus or equipment except as provided for in this section, nor shall any person, firm or corporation purchase or take into possession or sell, trade, transfer, devise, give away or in any manner dispose of such machinery, apparatus, or equipment except by intestate succession or as junk or scrap after the manufacturer's serial or engine number or mark has been willfully removed, defaced, destroyed, altered or covered up unless a new number or mark has been added as provided in this section: Provided, however, that this section shall not prohibit or prevent the owner or holder of a mortgage, conditional sales contract, title retaining contract, or a trustee under a deed of trust from taking possession for the purpose of foreclosure under a power of sale or by court order, of such machinery, apparatus, or equipment, or from selling the same by foreclosure sale under a power contained in a mortgage, conditional sales contract, title retaining contract, deed of trust, or court order; or from taking possession thereof in satisfaction of the indebtedness secured by the mortgage, deed of trust, conditional sales contract, or title retaining contract pursuant to an agreement with the owner.

(b) Each seller of farm machinery, farm equipment or farm apparatus covered by this section shall give the purchaser a bill of sale for such machinery, equipment or apparatus and shall include in the bill of sale the manufacturer's serial number or distinguishing number or identification mark, which the seller warrants to be true and correct according to his invoice or bill of sale as received from his manufacturer, supplier, or distributor or dealer.

(c) Each user of farm machinery, farm equipment or farm apparatus whose manufacturer's serial number, distinguishing number or identification mark has been obliterated or is now unrecognizable, may obtain a valid identification number for any such machinery, equipment or apparatus upon application for such number to the Division of Motor Vehicles accompanied by satisfactory proof of ownership and a subsequent certification to the Division by a member of the North Carolina Highway Patrol that said applicant has placed the number on the proper machinery, equipment or apparatus. The Division of Motor Vehicles is hereby authorized and empowered to issue appropriate identification marks or distinguishing numbers for machinery, equipment or apparatus upon application as provided in this section and the Division is further authorized and empowered to designate the place or places on the machinery, equipment or apparatus at which the identification marks or distinguishing numbers shall be placed. The Division is also authorized to designate the method to be used in placing the identification marks or distinguishing numbers on the machinery, equipment or apparatus: Provided, however, that the owner or holder of the mortgage conditional sales contract, title retaining contract, or trustee under a deed of trust in possession of such encumbered machinery, equipment, or apparatus from which the manufacturer's serial or engine number or other manufacturer's number or distinguishing mark has been obliterated or has become unrecognizable or the purchaser at the foreclosure sale thereof, may at any time obtain a valid identification number for any such machinery, equipment or apparatus upon application therefor to the Division of Motor Vehicles.

(d) Except as otherwise provided in this subsection, any person, firm, or corporation who shall violate any part of this section shall be guilty of a Class 1 misdemeanor. If the machine or other apparatus was valued at more than one thousand dollars ($ 1,000) at the time of the offense, then the person, firm, or corporation shall be guilty of a Class H felony.

History.
1949, c. 928; 1951, c. 1110 s. 1; 1953, c. 257; 1975, c. 716, s. 5; 1993, c. 539, s. 274; 1994, Ex. Sess., c. 24, s. 14(c); 2021-36, s. 2

N.C. Gen. Stat. § 14-401.5

Repealed by Session Laws 2004-203, s. 21, effective August 17, 2004.

§ 14-401.6. Unlawful to possess, etc., tear gas except for certain purposes

(a) It is unlawful for any person, firm, corporation or association to possess, use, store, sell, or transport within the State of North Carolina, any form of that type of gas generally known as "tear gas," or any container or device for holding or releasing that gas; except this section does not apply to the possession, use, storage, sale or transportation of that gas or any container or device for holding or releasing that gas:

(1) By officers and enlisted personnel of the Armed Forces of the United States or this State while in the discharge of their official duties and acting under orders requiring them to carry arms or weapons;

(2) By or for any governmental agency for official use of the agency;

(3) By or for county, municipal or State law-enforcement officers in the discharge of their official duties;

(4) By or for security guards registered under Chapter 74C of the General Statutes, company police officers commissioned under Chapter 74E of the General Statutes, or campus police officers commissioned under Chapter 74G of the General Statutes provided they are on duty and have received training according to standards prescribed by the State Bureau of Investigation;

(5) For bona fide scientific, educational, or industrial purposes;

(6) In safes, vaults, and depositories, as a means or protection against robbery;

(7) For use in the home for protection and elsewhere by individuals, who have not been convicted of a felony, for self-defense purposes only, as long as the capacity of any:

a. Tear gas device or container does not exceed 150 cubic centimeters,

b. Tear gas cartridge or shell does not exceed 50 cubic centimeters, and

c. Tear gas device or container does not have the capability of discharging any cartridge, shell, or container larger than 50 cubic centimeters.

(b) Violation of this section is a Class 2 misdemeanor.

(c) Tear gas for the purpose of this section shall mean any solid, liquid or gaseous substance or combinations thereof which will, upon dispersion in the atmosphere, cause tears in the eyes, burning of the skin, coughing, difficulty in breathing or any one or more of these reactions and which will not cause permanent damage to the human body, and the substance and container or device is designed, manufactured, and intended to be used as tear gas.

History.
1951, c. 592; 1969, c. 1224, s. 8; 1977, c. 126; 1979, c. 661; 1983, c. 794, s. 9; 1991 (Reg. Sess., 1992), c. 1043, s. 2; 1993, c. 151, s. 1; c. 539, s. 276; 1994, Ex. Sess., c. 24, s. 14(c); 2005-231, s. 10; 2011-183, s. 12

§ 14-401.7. Persons, firms, banks and corporations dealing in securities on commission taxed as a private banker

No person, bank, or corporation, without a license authorized by law, shall act as a stockbroker or private banker. Any person, bank, or corporation that deals in foreign or domestic exchange certificates of debt, shares in any corporation or charter companies, bank or other notes, for the purpose of selling the same or any other thing for commission or other compensation, or who negotiates loans upon real estate securities, shall be deemed a security broker. Any person, bank, or corporation engaged in the business of negotiating loans on any class of security or in discounting, buying or selling negotiable or other papers or credits, whether in an office for the purpose or elsewhere shall be deemed to be a private banker. Any person, firm, or corporation violating this section shall be guilty of a Class 3 misdemeanor and pay a fine of not less than one hundred dollars ($ 100.00) nor more than five hundred dollars ($ 500.00) for each offense.

History.
1939, c. 310, s. 1004; 1953, c. 970, s. 9; 1993, c. 539, s. 277; 1994, Ex. Sess., c. 24, s. 14(c)

N.C. Gen. Stat. § 14-401.8

Repealed by Session Laws 2015-286, s. 1.1(2), effective October 22, 2015.

History.
1955, c. 958; 1993, c. 539, s. 278; 1994, Ex. Sess., c. 24, s. 14(c); repealed by Session Laws 2015-286, s. 1.1(2), effective October 22, 2015

§ 14-401.9. Parking vehicle in private parking space without permission

It shall be unlawful for any person other than the owner or lessee of a privately owned or leased parking space to park a motor or other vehicle in such private parking space without the express permission of the owner or lessee of such space; provided, that such private parking lot be clearly designated as such by a sign no smaller than 24 inches by 24 inches prominently displayed at the entrance thereto, and provided further, that the parking spaces within

the lot be clearly marked by signs setting forth the name of each individual lessee or owner.

Any person violating any of the provisions of this section shall be guilty of a Class 3 misdemeanor and upon conviction shall be fined not more than ten dollars ($ 10.00) in the discretion of the court.

History.
1955, c. 1019; 1977, c. 398, s. 2; 1993, c. 539, s. 279; 1994, Ex. Sess., c. 24, s. 14(c)

§ 14-401.10. Soliciting advertisements for official publications of law-enforcement officers' associations

Every person, firm or corporation who solicits any advertisement to be published in any law-enforcement officers' association's official magazine, yearbook, or other official publication, shall disclose to the person so solicited, whether so requested or not, the name of the law-enforcement association for which such advertisement is solicited, together with written authority from the president or secretary of such association to solicit such advertising on its behalf.

Any person, firm or corporation violating the provisions of this section shall be guilty of a Class 2 misdemeanor.

History.
1961, c. 518; 1969, c. 1224, s. 8; 1993, c. 539, s. 280; 1994, Ex. Sess., c. 24, s. 14(c)

§ 14-401.11. Distribution of certain food or beverage prohibited

(a) It shall be unlawful for any person to knowingly distribute, sell, give away or otherwise cause to be placed in a position of human accessibility or ingestion, any food, beverage, or other eatable or drinkable substance which that person knows to contain any of the following:

(1) Any noxious or deleterious substance, material or article which might be injurious to a person's health or might cause a person any physical discomfort.

(2) Any controlled substance included in any schedule of the Controlled Substances Act.

(3) Any poisonous chemical or compound or any foreign substance such as, but not limited to, razor blades, pins, and ground glass, which might cause death, serious physical injury or serious physical pain and discomfort.

(b) Penalties.

(1) Any person violating the provisions of G.S. 14-401.11(a)(1):

a. Where the actual or possible effect on a person eating or drinking the

Chapter 14

food, beverage, or other substance was or would be limited to mild physical discomfort without any lasting effect, shall be guilty of a Class I felony.

b. Where the actual or possible effect on a person eating or drinking the food, beverage, or other substance was or would be greater than mild physical discomfort without any lasting effect, shall be punished as a Class H felon.

(2) Any person violating the provisions of G.S. 14-401.11(a)(2) shall be punished as a Class F felon.

(3) Any person violating the provisions of G.S. 14-401.11(a)(3) shall be punished as a Class C felon.

History.
1971, c. 564; 1973, c. 540, s. 1; 1979, c. 760, s. 5; 1979, 2nd Sess., c. 1316, s. 47; 1981, c. 63, s. 1; c. 179, s. 14; 1993, c. 539, s. 1242; 1994, Ex. Sess., c. 24, s. 14(c); 2019-245, s. 6(b)

§ 14-401.12. Soliciting charitable contributions by telephone

(a) Any professional solicitor who solicits by telephone contributions for charitable purposes or in any way compensates another person to solicit by telephone contributions for charitable purposes shall be guilty of a Class 1 misdemeanor. Any person compensated by a professional solicitor to solicit by telephone contributions for charitable purposes shall be guilty of a Class 1 misdemeanor.

(b) **Definitions.** -- Unless a different meaning is required by the context, the following terms as used in this section have the meanings hereinafter respectively ascribed to them:

(1) "Charitable purpose" shall mean any charitable, benevolent, religious, philanthropic, environmental, public or social advocacy or eleemosynary purpose for religion, health, education, social welfare, art and humanities, civic and public interest.

(2) "Contribution" shall mean any promise, gift, devise or other grant for consideration or otherwise, of any money or property of any kind or value, including the promise to pay, which contribution is wholly or partly induced by a solicitation. The term "contribution" shall not include payments by members of an organization for membership fees, dues, fines or assessments, or for services rendered to individual members, if membership in such organization confers a bona fide right, privilege, professional standing, honor or other direct benefit, other than the right to vote, elect officers, or hold offices; nor any money, credit, financial assistance or property received from any governmental authority; nor any donation of blood or any anatomical gift made pursuant to the Revised Uniform Anatomical Gift Act. Reference to dollar amounts of "contributions" or "solicitations" in this section means, in the case of payments or promises to pay for merchandise or rights of any description, the value of the total amount paid or promised to be paid for such merchandise or rights, and not merely that portion of the purchase price to be applied to a charitable purpose.

(3) "Professional fund-raising counsel" shall mean any person who for a flat fixed fee under a written agreement plans, conducts, manages, carries on, or acts as a consultant, whether directly or indirectly, in connection with soliciting contributions for, or on behalf of any charitable organization but who actually solicits no contributions as a part of such services.

(4) "Professional solicitor" shall mean any person who, for a financial or other consideration, solicits contributions for or on behalf of a charitable organization, whether such solicitation is performed personally or through its agents, servants or employees specially employed by or for a charitable organization, who are engaged in the solicitation of contributions under the direction of such person; or a person who plans, conducts, manages, carries on, advises or acts as a consultant, whether directly or indirectly, to a charitable organization in connection with the solicitation of contributions but does not qualify as "professional fund-raising counsel" as defined in this section. A bona fide salaried officer or employee of a charitable organization maintaining a permanent establishment within the State or the bona fide salaried officer or employee of a parent organization certified as tax exempt shall not be deemed to be a professional solicitor.

(5) The words "solicit" and "solicitation" shall mean the request or appeal, directly or indirectly, for any contribution on the plea or representation that such contribution will be used for a charitable purpose. Solicitation as defined herein shall be deemed to occur when the request is made, at the place the request is received, whether or not the person making the same actually receives any contribution.

(c) A solicitation by telephone is presumed to be for a charitable purpose if the person making the solicitation states or implies that some other named person or organization, other than the professional solicitor or his employees, is a sponsor or endorser of the solicitation who will share in the proceeds that result from the telephone solicitation.

History.
1981, c. 805, s. 1; 1993, c. 539, s. 281; 1994, Ex. Sess., c. 24, s. 14(c); 2007-538, s. 8; 2011-284, s. 10

§ 14-401.13. Failure to give right to cancel in off-premises sales

(a) It shall be a Class 3 misdemeanor for any sellers, as defined hereinafter, in connection with an off-premises sale, as defined hereinafter, willfully to:

(1) Fail to furnish the buyer with a fully completed receipt or copy of any contract pertaining to such sale at the time of its execution, which is in the same language, e.g., Spanish, as that principally used in the oral sales presentation and which shows the date of the transaction and contains the name and address of the seller, and in immediate proximity to the space reserved in the contract for the signature of the buyer or on the front page of the receipt if a contract is not used and in boldface type of a minimum size of 10 points, a statement in substantially the following form: "You, the buyer, may cancel this transaction at any time prior to midnight of the third business day after the date of this transaction. See the attached notice of cancellation form for an explanation of this right."

(2) Fail to furnish each buyer, at the time he signs the off-premises sales contract or otherwise agrees to buy consumer goods or services from the seller, a completed form in duplicate, captioned "NOTICE OF CANCELLATION", which shall be attached to the contract or receipt and easily detachable, and which shall contain in boldface type in a minimum size of 10 points, the following information and statements in the same language, e.g., Spanish, as that used in the contract:

"NOTICE OF CANCELLATION
(enter date of transaction)

_____
(date)
You may cancel this transaction, without any penalty or obligation, within three business days from the above date.

If you cancel, any property traded in, any payments made by you under the contract or sale, and any negotiable instrument executed by you will be returned within 10 business days following receipt by the seller of your cancellation notice and any security interest arising out of the transaction will be canceled.

If you cancel, you must make available to the seller at your residence, in substantially as good condition as when received, any goods delivered to you under this contract or sale; or you may, if you wish, comply with the instructions of the seller regarding the return shipment of the goods at the seller's expense and risk. In the event you purchased antiques at an antique show and cancel, and your residence is out-of-state, you must deliver the purchased goods to the seller.

If you do make the goods available to the seller and the seller does not pick them up within 20 days of the date of your notice of cancellation, you may retain or dispose of the goods without any further obligation. If you fail to make the goods available to the seller, or if you agree to return the goods to the seller and fail to do so, then you remain liable for performance of all obligations under the contract.

To cancel this transaction, mail or deliver a signed and dated copy of this cancellation notice, or any other written notice, or send a telegram, to

_____
(name of seller)
at _____
(address of seller's place of business)
not later than midnight of _____
(date)
I hereby cancel this transaction.

_____
(date)

_____"
(buyer's signature)

(3) Fail, before furnishing copies of the "Notice of Cancellation" to the buyer, to complete both copies by entering the name of the seller, the address of the seller's place of business, the date of the transaction, and the date, not earlier than the third business day following the date of the transaction, by which the buyer may give notice of cancellation.

(4) Fail to inform each buyer orally, at the time he signs the contract or purchases the goods or services, of his right to cancel.

(5) Misrepresent in any manner the buyer's right to cancel.

(b) Regardless of the seller's compliance or noncompliance with the requirements of the preceding subsection, it shall be a Class 3 misdemeanor for any seller, as defined hereinafter, to willfully fail or refuse to honor any valid notice of cancellation by a buyer and within 10 business days after the receipt of such notice, to (i) refund all payments made under the contract or sale; (ii) return any goods or property traded in, in substantially as good condition as when received by the seller; (iii) cancel and return any

Chapter 14

negotiable instrument executed by the buyer in connection with the contract or sale and take any action necessary or appropriate to terminate promptly any security interest created in the transaction. If the seller failed to provide a form Notice of Cancellation to the buyer, then oral notice of cancellation by the buyer is sufficient for purposes of this subsection.

(c) For the purposes of this section, the following definitions shall apply:

(1) **Off-Premises Sale.** -- A sale, lease, or rental of consumer goods or services with a purchase price of twenty-five dollars ($ 25.00) or more, whether under single or multiple contracts, in which the seller or his representative personally solicits the sale, including those in response to or following an invitation by the buyer, and the buyer's agreement or offer to purchase is made at a place other than the place of business of the seller. The term "off-premises sale" does not include a transaction:

a. Made pursuant to prior negotiations in the course of a visit by the buyer to a retail business establishment having a fixed permanent location where the goods are exhibited or the services are offered for sale on a continuing basis; or

b. In which the consumer is accorded the right of rescission by the provisions of the Consumer Credit Protection Act (15 U.S.C. 1635) or regulations issued pursuant thereto; or

c. In which the buyer has initiated the contact and the goods or services are needed to meet a bona fide immediate personal emergency of the buyer, and the buyer furnishes the seller with a separate dated and signed personal statement in the buyer's handwriting describing the situation requiring immediate remedy and expressly acknowledging and waiving the right to cancel the sale within three business days; or

d. Conducted and consummated entirely by mail or telephone; and without any other contact between the buyer and the seller or its representative prior to delivery of the goods or performance of the services; or

e. In which the buyer has initiated the contact and specifically requested the seller to visit his home for the purpose of repairing or performing maintenance upon the buyer's property. If in the course of such a visit, the seller sells the buyer the right to receive additional services or goods other than replacement parts necessarily used in performing the maintenance or in making the repairs, the sale of those additional goods or services would not fall within this exclusion; or

f. Pertaining to the sale or rental of real property, to the sale of insurance or to the sale of securities or commodities by a broker-dealer registered with the Securities and Exchange Commission; or

g. Executed at an auction; or

h. Sales of motor vehicles defined in G.S. 20-286(10) by motor vehicle sales representatives licensed pursuant to G.S. 20-287 et seq.

(2) **Consumer Goods or Services.** -- Goods or services purchased, leased, or rented primarily for personal, family, or household purposes, including courses of instruction or training regardless of the purpose for which they are taken.

(3) **Seller.** -- Any person, partnership, corporation, or association engaged in the off-premises sale of consumer goods or services. However, a nonprofit corporation or association, or member or employee thereof acting on behalf of such an association or corporation, shall not be a seller within the meaning of this section.

(4) **Place of Business.** -- The main or permanent branch office or local address of a seller.

(5) **Purchase Price.** -- The total price paid or to be paid for the consumer goods or services, including all interest and service charges.

(6) **Business Day.** -- Any calendar day except Sunday, or the following business holidays: New Year's Day, Washington's Birthday, Memorial Day, Independence Day, Labor Day, Columbus Day, Veterans' Day, Thanksgiving Day, Christmas Day, and Good Friday.

History.
1985, c. 652, s. 1; 1987, c. 551, ss. 1, 2; 1993, c. 141, s. 1; c. 539, s. 282; 1994, Ex. Sess., c. 24, s. 14(c)

§ 14-401.14. Ethnic intimidation; teaching any technique to be used for ethnic intimidation

(a) If a person shall, because of race, color, religion, nationality, or country of origin, assault another person, or damage or deface the property of another person, or threaten to do any such act, he shall be guilty of a Class 1 misdemeanor.

(b) A person who assembles with one or more persons to teach any technique or means to be used to commit any act in violation of subsection (a) of this section is guilty of a Class 1 misdemeanor.

History.

1991, c. 493, s. 1; 1993, c. 332, s. 1; c. 539, s. 283; 1994, Ex. Sess., c. 14, s. 14(b); c. 24, s. 14(a), (c); 1995, c. 509, s. 10

§ 14-401.15. Telephone sales recovery services

(a) Except as provided in subsection (c) of this section, it shall be unlawful for any person or firm to solicit or require payment of money or other consideration in exchange for recovering or attempting to recover:

    (1) Money or other valuable consideration previously tendered to a telephonic seller, as defined in G.S. 66-260; or

    (2) Prizes, awards, or other things of value that the telephonic seller represented would be delivered.

(b) A violation of this section shall be punishable as a Class 1 misdemeanor. Any violation involving actual collection of money or other consideration from a customer shall be punishable as a Class H felony.

(c) This section does not apply to attorneys licensed to practice law in this State, to persons licensed by the North Carolina Private Protective Services Board, or to any collection agent properly holding a permit issued by the Department of Insurance to do business in this State.

History.

1997-482, s. 2

§ 14-401.16. Contaminate food or drink to render one mentally incapacitated or physically helpless

(a) It is unlawful knowingly to contaminate any food, drink, or other edible or potable substance with a controlled substance as defined in G.S. 90-87(5) that would render a person mentally incapacitated or physically helpless with the intent of causing another person to be mentally incapacitated or physically helpless.

(b) It is unlawful knowingly to manufacture, sell, deliver, or possess with the intent to manufacture, sell, deliver, or possess a controlled substance as defined in G.S. 90-87(5) for the purpose of violating this section.

(c) A violation of this section is a Class H felony. However, if a person violates this section with the intent of committing an offense under G.S. 14-27.22 or G.S. 14-27.27, the violation is a Class G felony.

(d) This act does not apply if the controlled substance added to the food, drink, or other edible or potable substance is done at the direction of a licensed physician as part of a medical procedure or treatment with the patient's consent.

History.

1997-501, s. 2; 2015-181, s. 39

§ 14-401.17. Unlawful removal or destruction of electronic dog collars

(a) It is unlawful to intentionally remove or destroy an electronic collar or other electronic device placed on a dog by its owner to maintain control of the dog.

(b) A first conviction for a violation of this section is a Class 3 misdemeanor. A second or subsequent conviction for a violation of this section is a Class 2 misdemeanor.

(c) This act is enforceable by officers of the Wildlife Resources Commission, by sheriffs and deputy sheriffs, and peace officers with general subject matter jurisdiction.

(d) Repealed by Session Laws 2005-94, s. 1, effective December 1, 2005, and applicable to offenses committed on or after that date.

History.

1993 (Reg. Sess., 1994), c. 699, s. 1-4; 1995 (Reg. Sess., 1996) c. 682; 1997-150; 1998-6, s. 1; 1999-51, s. 1; 2000-12, s. 1; 2004-60, s. 3; 2005-94, s. 1; 2005-305, s. 4

§ 14-401.18. Sale of certain packages of cigarettes prohibited

(a) **Definitions.** -- The following definitions apply in this section:

    (1) **Cigarette.** -- Defined in G.S. 105-113.4.

    (2) **Package.** -- Defined in G.S. 105-113.4.

(b) **Offenses.** -- A person who sells or holds for sale (other than for export to a foreign country) a package of cigarettes that meets one or more of the following descriptions commits a Class A1 misdemeanor and engages in an unfair trade practice prohibited by G.S. 75-1.1:

    (1) The package differs in any respect with the requirements of the Federal Cigarette Labeling and Advertising Act, 15 U.S.C. § 1331, for the placement of labels, warnings, or any other information upon a package of cigarettes that is to be sold within the United States.

    (2) The package is labeled "For Export Only," "U.S. Tax Exempt," "For Use Outside U.S.," or has similar wording indicating that the manufacturer did not intend that the product be sold in the United States.

    (3) The package was altered by adding or deleting the wording, labels, or warnings described in subdivision (1) or (2) of this subsection.

Chapter 14

(4) The package was imported into the United States after January 1, 2000, in violation of 26 U.S.C. § 5754.

(5) The package violates federal trademark or copyright laws, federal laws governing the submission of ingredient information to federal authorities pursuant to 15 U.S.C. § 1335a, federal laws governing the import of certain cigarettes pursuant to 19 U.S.C. § 1681 and 19 U.S.C. § 1681b, or any other provision of federal law or regulation.

(c) **Contraband.** -- A package of cigarettes described in subsection (b) of this section is contraband and may be seized by a law enforcement officer. The procedure for seizure and disposition of this contraband is the same as the procedure under G.S. 105-113.31 and G.S. 105-113.32 for non-tax-paid cigarettes.

History.
1999-333, s. 5; 2002-145, s. 4

§ 14-401.18A. Sale of certain e-liquid containers prohibited

(a) The following definitions apply in this section:

(1) **Child-resistant packaging.** -- Packaging that is designed or constructed to be significantly difficult for children under five years of age to open or obtain a toxic or harmful amount of the substance contained therein within a reasonable time and not difficult for adults to use properly, but does not mean packaging which all such children cannot open or obtain a toxic or harmful amount within a reasonable time.

(2) **E-liquid.** -- A liquid product, whether or not it contains nicotine, that is intended to be vaporized and inhaled using a vapor product.

(3) **E-liquid container.** -- A bottle or other container of e-liquid. The term does not include a container holding liquid that is intended for use in a vapor product if the container is pre-filled and sealed by the manufacturer and is not intended to be opened by the consumer.

(4) **Vapor product.** -- Any noncombustible product that employs a mechanical heating element, battery, or electronic circuit regardless of shape or size and that can be used to heat a liquid solution contained in a vapor cartridge. The term includes an electronic cigarette, electronic cigar, electronic cigarillo, and electronic pipe.

(b) It shall be unlawful for any person, firm, or corporation to sell, offer for sale, or introduce into commerce in this State an e-liquid container unless the container constitutes child-resistant packaging. Any person who violates this section is guilty of a Class A1 misdemeanor.

(c) It shall be unlawful for any person, firm, or corporation to sell, offer for sale, or introduce into commerce in this State an e-liquid container for an e-liquid product containing nicotine unless the packaging for the e-liquid product states that the product contains nicotine. Any person who violates this section is guilty of a Class A1 misdemeanor.

(d) Any person, firm, or corporation that violates the provisions of this section shall be liable in damages to any person injured as a result of the violation.

History.
2015-141, s. 1

§ 14-401.19. Filing false security agreements

It shall be unlawful for any person, firm, corporation, or any other association of persons in this State, under whatever name styled, to present a record for filing under the provisions of Article 9 of Chapter 25 of the General Statutes with knowledge that the record is not related to a valid security agreement or with the intention that the record be filed for an improper purpose, such as to hinder, harass, or otherwise wrongfully interfere with any person. A violation of this section shall be a Class I felony.

History.
2001-231, s. 5; 2012-150, s. 6

§ 14-401.20. Defrauding drug and alcohol screening tests; penalty

(a) It is unlawful for a person to do any of the following:

(1) Sell, give away, distribute, or market urine in this State or transport urine into this State with the intent that it be used to defraud a drug or alcohol screening test.

(2) Attempt to foil or defeat a drug or alcohol screening test by the substitution or spiking of a sample or the advertisement of a sample substitution or other spiking device or measure.

(b) It is unlawful for a person to do any of the following:

(1) Adulterate a urine or other bodily fluid sample with the intent to defraud a drug or alcohol screening test.

(2) Possess adulterants that are intended to be used to adulterate a urine or other bodily fluid sample for the purpose of defrauding a drug or alcohol screening test.

(3) Sell adulterants with the intent that they be used to adulterate a urine or other

bodily fluid sample for the purpose of defrauding a drug or alcohol screening test.

(c) A violation of this section is punishable as follows:

(1) For a first offense under this section, the person is guilty of a Class 1 misdemeanor.

(2) For a second or subsequent offense under this section, the person is guilty of a Class I felony.

History.
2002-183, s. 1

§ 14-401.21. Practicing "rebirthing technique"; penalty

(a) It is unlawful for a person to practice a technique, whether known as a "rebirthing technique" or referred to by any other name, to reenact the birthing process in a manner that includes restraint and creates a situation in which a patient may suffer physical injury or death.

(b) A violation of this section is punishable as follows:

(1) For a first offense under this section, the person is guilty of a Class A1 misdemeanor.

(2) For a second or subsequent offense under this section, the person is guilty of a Class I felony.

(c) No State funds shall be used to pay for the rebirthing technique made unlawful by this section and performed in another state notwithstanding that the technique, whether known as a rebirthing technique or referred to by any other name, is lawful in that other state.

History.
2003-205, s. 1; 2004-124, s. 10.2F

§ 14-401.22. Concealment of death; disturbing human remains; dismembering human remains

(a) Except as provided in subsection (a1) of this section, any person who, with the intent to conceal the death of a person, fails to notify a law enforcement authority of the death or secretly buries or otherwise secretly disposes of a dead human body is guilty of a Class I felony.

(a1) Any person who, with the intent to conceal the death of a child, fails to notify a law enforcement authority of the death or secretly buries or otherwise secretly disposes of a dead child's body is guilty of a Class H felony. For purposes of this subsection, a child is any person who is less than 16 years of age.

(b) Any person who aids, counsels, or abets any other person in concealing the death of a person is guilty of a Class A1 misdemeanor.

(c) Any person who willfully (i) disturbs, vandalizes, or desecrates human remains, by any means, including any physical alteration or manipulation of the human remains, or (ii) commits or attempts to commit upon any human remains any act of sexual penetration is guilty of a Class I felony. This subsection does not apply to:

(1) Acts by a first responder or others providing medical care.

(2) Acts committed as part of scientific or medical research, treatment, or diagnosis.

(3) Acts performed by a licensed funeral director or embalmer consistent with standard practice.

(4) Acts committed for the purpose of extracting body parts in accordance with usual and customary standards of medical practice.

(5) Acts by a professional archaeologist as defined in G.S. 70-28(4) acting pursuant to the provisions of Article 3 of Chapter 70 of the General Statutes.

(6) Acts committed for any other lawful purpose.

(d) Any person who attempts to conceal evidence of the death of another by knowingly and willfully dismembering or destroying human remains, by any means, including removing body parts or otherwise obliterating any portion thereof, shall be guilty of a Class H felony.

(e) Any person who violates subsection (a), (a1), or (d) of this section, knowing or having reason to know the body or human remains are of a person that did not die of natural causes, shall be guilty of a Class D felony.

(f) As used in this section, "human remains" means any dead human body in any condition of decay or any significant part of a dead human body, including any limb, organ, or bone.

History.
2005-288, s. 1; 2011-193, s. 1; 2013-52, s. 5

§ 14-401.23. Unlawful manufacture, sale, delivery, or possession of Salvia divinorum

(a) It shall be unlawful for any person to knowingly or intentionally manufacture, sell or deliver, or possess with intent to manufacture, sell or deliver Salvia divinorum or Salvinorin A.

(b) It shall be unlawful for any person to knowingly or intentionally possess Salvia divinorum or Salvinorin A.

(c) A violation of this section is punishable as follows:

(1) For a first or second offense under this section, the person is responsible for an infraction and shall be required to pay a fine of not less than twenty-five dollars ($ 25.00).

(2) For a third or subsequent offense under this section, the person is guilty of a Class 3 misdemeanor.

(d) For purposes of this section:

(1) "Deliver" means the actual constructive or attempted transfer of Salvia divinorum or Salvinorin A from one person to another.

(2) "Manufacture" means the production, preparation, propagation, compounding, conversion or processing of Salvia divinorum or Salvinorin A by any means, whether directly or indirectly, artificially or naturally, or by extraction from substances of a natural origin, or independently by means of chemical synthesis, or by a combination of extraction and chemical synthesis. Manufacture includes any packaging or repackaging of the substance, or labeling or relabeling of its container, except that this term does not include the preparation or compounding of the substance by an individual for the individual's own use.

(3) "Production" includes the manufacture, planting, cultivation, growing, or harvesting of a plant.

(e) The provisions of this section shall not apply to:

(1) Employees or contractors of any accredited college or school of medicine or pharmacy at a public or private university in this State while performing medical or pharmacological research for such institution.

(2) The possession, planting, cultivation, growing, or harvesting of a plant strictly for aesthetic, landscaping, or decorative purposes.

History.
2009-538, s. 1

§ 14-401.24. Unlawful possession and use of unmanned aircraft systems

(a) It shall be a Class E felony for any person to possess or use an unmanned aircraft or unmanned aircraft system that has a weapon attached.

(b) It shall be a Class 1 misdemeanor for any person to fish or to hunt using an unmanned aircraft system.

(c) The following definitions apply to this section:

(1) **To fish.** -- As defined in G.S. 113-130.

(2) **To hunt.** -- As defined in G.S. 113-130.

(3) **Unmanned aircraft.** -- As defined in G.S. 15A-300.1.

(4) **Unmanned aircraft system.** -- As defined in G.S. 15A-300.1.

(5) **Weapon.** -- Those weapons specified in G.S. 14-269, 14-269.2, 14-284.1, or 14-288.8 and any other object capable of inflicting serious bodily injury or death when used as a weapon.

(d) This section shall not prohibit possession or usage of an unmanned aircraft or unmanned aircraft system that is authorized by federal law or regulation.

History.
2014-100, s. 34.30(d)

§ 14-401.25. Unlawful distribution of images

It shall be a Class A1 misdemeanor to publish or disseminate, for any purpose, recorded images taken by a person or non-law enforcement entity through the use of infrared or other similar thermal imaging technology attached to an unmanned aircraft system, as defined in G.S. 15A-300.1, and revealing individuals, materials, or activities inside of a structure without the consent of the property owner.

History.
2014-100, s. 34.30(e)

§ 14-401.26. TNC driver failure to display license plate information

It shall be unlawful for a transportation network company (TNC) driver, as defined in G.S. 20-280.1, to fail to display the license plate number of the TNC driver's vehicle as required by G.S. 20-280.5(d). A violation of this section shall be an infraction and shall be punishable by a fine of two hundred fifty dollars ($ 250.00).

History.
2019-194, s. 3(a)

§ 14-401.27. Impersonation of a transportation network company driver

It shall be unlawful for any person to impersonate a transportation network company (TNC) driver, as defined in G.S. 20-280.1, by a false statement, false display of distinctive signage or emblems known as a trade dress, trademark, branding, or logo of the TNC, or any other act which falsely represents that the person has a current connection with a transportation network company or falsely represents that the person is responding to a passenger ride request for a transportation network company. A violation of this section is a Class H felony if the person impersonates a TNC driver during the commission of a separate felony offense. Any other violation of this section is a Class 2 misdemeanor.

History.
2019-194, s. 3.3(a)

ARTICLE 52A
SALE OF WEAPONS IN CERTAIN COUNTIES

§ 14-402. Sale of certain weapons without permit forbidden

(a) It is unlawful for any person, firm, or corporation in this State to sell, give away, or transfer, or to purchase or receive, at any place within this State from any other place within or without the State any pistol unless: (i) a license or permit is first obtained under this Article by the purchaser or receiver from the sheriff of the county in which the purchaser or receiver resides; or (ii) a valid North Carolina concealed handgun permit is held under Article 54B of this Chapter by the purchaser or receiver who must be a resident of the State at the time of the purchase.

It is unlawful for any person or persons to receive from any postmaster, postal clerk, employee in the parcel post department, rural mail carrier, express agent or employee, railroad agent or employee within the State of North Carolina any pistol without having in his or their possession and without exhibiting at the time of the delivery of the same and to the person delivering the same the permit from the sheriff as provided in G.S. 14-403. Any person violating the provisions of this section is guilty of a Class 2 misdemeanor.

(b) This section does not apply to an antique firearm or an historic edged weapon.

(c) The following definitions apply in this Article:

(1) **Antique firearm. --** Defined in G.S. 14-409.11.

(2), (3) Repealed by Session Laws 2011-56, s. 1, effective April 28, 2011.

(4) **Historic edged weapon. --** Defined in G.S. 14-409.12.

(5) through (7) Repealed by Session Laws 2011-56, s. 1, effective April 28, 2011.

History.
1919, c. 197, s. 1; C.S., s. 5106; 1923, c. 106; 1947, c. 781; 1959, c. 1073, s. 2; 1971, c. 133, s. 2; 1979, c. 895, ss. 1, 2; 1993, c. 287, s. 1; c. 539, s. 284; 1994, Ex. Sess., c. 24, s. 14(c); 2004-183, s. 1; 2004-203, s. 1; 2009-6, s. 2; 2011-56, s. 1

§ 14-403. Permit issued by sheriff; form of permit; expiration of permit

The sheriffs of any and all counties of this State shall issue to any person, firm, or corporation in any county a permit to purchase or receive any weapon mentioned in this Article from any person, firm, or corporation offering to sell or dispose of the weapon. The permit shall expire five years from the date of issuance. The permit shall be a standard form created by the State Bureau of Investigation in consultation with the North Carolina Sheriffs' Association, shall be of a uniform size and material, and shall be designed with security features intended to minimize the ability to counterfeit or replicate the permit and shall be set forth as follows:

North Carolina,

County.

I, _____, Sheriff of said County, do hereby certify that I have conducted a criminal background check of the applicant, _____ whose place of residence is _____ in _____ ____ (or) in _____ Township, County, North Carolina, and have received no information to indicate that it would be a violation of State or federal law for the applicant to purchase, transfer, receive, or possess a handgun. The applicant has further satisfied me as to his, her (or) their good moral character. Therefore, a permit is issued to _____ to purchase one pistol from any person, firm or corporation authorized to dispose of the same.

This permit expires five years from its date of issuance.

This _____ day of _____, _____.

_____

Sheriff.

The standard permit created by this section shall be used statewide by the sheriffs of any and all counties and, when issued by a sheriff, shall also contain an embossed seal unique to the office of the issuing sheriff.

History.
1919, c. 197, s. 2; C.S., s. 5107; 1959, c. 1073, s. 2; 1981 (Reg. Sess., 1982), c. 1395, s. 3; 1995, c. 487, s. 1; 1999-456, s. 59; 2013-369, s. 17.1; 2015-195, s. 10(a)

§ 14-404. Issuance or refusal of permit; appeal from refusal; grounds for refusal; sheriff's fee

(a) Upon application, and such application must be provided by the sheriff electronically, the sheriff shall issue the permit to a resident of that county, unless the purpose of the permit is for collecting, in which case a sheriff can issue a permit to a nonresident, when the sheriff has done all of the following:

(1) Verified, before the issuance of a permit, by a criminal history background investigation that it is not a violation of State or federal law for the applicant to purchase, transfer, receive, or possess a handgun.

The sheriff shall determine the criminal and background history of any applicant by accessing computerized criminal history records as maintained by the State Bureau of Investigation and the Federal Bureau of Investigation, by conducting a national criminal history records check, by conducting a check through the National Instant Criminal Background Check System (NICS), and by conducting a criminal history check through the Administrative Office of the Courts.

(2) Fully satisfied himself or herself by affidavits, oral evidence, or otherwise, as to the good moral character of the applicant. For purposes of determining an applicant's good moral character to receive a permit, the sheriff shall only consider an applicant's conduct and criminal history for the five-year period immediately preceding the date of the application.

(3) Fully satisfied himself or herself that the applicant desires the possession of the weapon mentioned for (i) the protection of the home, business, person, family or property, (ii) target shooting, (iii) collecting, or (iv) hunting.

(b) If the sheriff is not fully satisfied, the sheriff may, for good cause shown, decline to issue the permit and shall provide to the applicant within seven days of the refusal a written statement of the reason(s) for the refusal. The statement shall cite the specific facts upon which the sheriff concluded that the applicant was not qualified for the issuance of a permit and list, by statute number, the applicable law upon which the denial is based. An appeal from the refusal shall lie by way of petition to the superior court in the district in which the application was filed. The determination by the court, on appeal, shall be upon the facts, the law, and the reasonableness of the sheriff's refusal, and shall be final.

(b1) The sheriff shall keep a list of all permit denials, with the specific reasons for the denials noted. The list shall not include any information that would identify the applicant whose application was denied. The list, as described in this subsection, shall be a public record, and the sheriff shall make the list available upon request to any member of the public. The list shall be organized by the quarters of the year, showing the number of denials and the reasons in each three-month period, and the list shall only be released for past, completed quarters.

(c) A permit may not be issued to the following persons:

(1) One who is under an indictment or information for or has been convicted in any state, or in any court of the United States, of a felony (other than an offense pertaining to antitrust violations, unfair trade practices, or restraints of trade). However, a person who has been convicted of a felony in a court of any state or in a court of the United States and (i) who is later pardoned, or (ii) whose firearms rights have been restored pursuant to G.S. 14-415.4, may obtain a permit, if the purchase or receipt of a pistol permitted in this Article does not violate a condition of the pardon or restoration of firearms rights.

(2) One who is a fugitive from justice.

(3) One who is an unlawful user of or addicted to marijuana or any depressant, stimulant, or narcotic drug (as defined in 21 U.S.C. § 802).

(4) One who has been adjudicated mentally incompetent or has been committed to any mental institution.

(5) One who is an alien illegally or unlawfully in the United States.

(6) One who has been discharged from the Armed Forces of the United States under dishonorable conditions.

(7) One who, having been a citizen of the United States, has renounced his or her citizenship.

(8) One who is subject to a court order that:

a. Was issued after a hearing of which the person received actual notice, and at which the person had an opportunity to participate;

b. Restrains the person from harassing, stalking, or threatening an intimate partner of the person or child of the intimate partner of the person, or engaging in other conduct that would place an intimate partner in reasonable fear of bodily injury to the partner or child; and

c. Includes a finding that the person represents a credible threat to the physical safety of the intimate partner or child; or by its terms explicitly prohibits the use, attempted use, or threatened use of physical force against the intimate partner or child that would reasonably be expected to cause bodily injury.

(c1) Repealed by Session Laws 2015-195, s. 11(c), effective August 5, 2015.

(d) Nothing in this Article shall apply to officers authorized by law to carry firearms if the officers identify themselves to the vendor or donor as being officers authorized by law to carry firearms and provide any of the following:

(1) A letter signed by the officer's supervisor or superior officer stating that the officer is authorized by law to carry a firearm.

(2) A current photographic identification card issued by the officer's employer.

(3) A current photographic identification card issued by a State agency that identifies the individual as a law enforcement officer or a probation and parole officer certified by the State of North Carolina.

(4) A current identification card issued by the officer's employer and another form of current photographic identification.

(e) The sheriff shall charge for the sheriff's services upon receipt of an application a fee of five dollars ($ 5.00) for each permit requested. There shall be no limit as to the number or frequency of permit applications and no other costs or fees other than provided in this subsection shall be charged for the permit, including, but not limited to, any costs for investigation, processing, or medical background checks by the sheriff or others providing records to the sheriff.

(e1) The application for a permit shall be on a form created by the State Bureau of Investigation in consultation with the North Carolina Sheriffs' Association. This application shall be used by all sheriffs and must be provided by the sheriff both electronically and in paper form. Only the following shall be required to be submitted by an applicant for a permit:

(1) The permit application developed pursuant to this subsection.

(2) Five dollars for each permit requested pursuant to subsection (e) of this section.

(3) A government issued identification confirming the identity of the applicant.

(4) Proof of residency.

(5) A signed release, in a form to be prescribed by the Administrative Office of the Court, that authorizes and requires disclosure to the sheriff of any court orders concerning the mental health or capacity of the applicant to be used for the sole purpose of determining whether the applicant is disqualified to receive a permit pursuant to this section.

No additional document or evidence shall be required from any applicant.

(f) Each applicant for a license or permit shall be informed by the sheriff within 14 days of the date of the application whether the license or permit will be granted or denied and, if granted, the license or permit shall be immediately issued to the applicant.

(g) An applicant shall not be ineligible to receive a permit under subdivision (c)(4) of this section because of involuntary commitment to mental health services if the individual's rights have been restored under G.S. 14-409.42.

(h) The sheriff shall revoke any permit upon the occurrence of any event or condition subsequent to the issuance of the permit, or the applicant's subsequent inability to meet a requirement under this Article, which would have resulted in a denial of the application submitted to obtain the permit if the event, condition, or the applicant's current inability to meet a statutory requirement had existed at the time of the application and prior to the issuance of the permit. The following procedures apply to a revocation:

(1) The sheriff shall provide written notice to the permittee, pursuant to the provisions of G.S. 1A-1, Rule 4(j), that the permit is revoked upon the service of the notice. The notice shall provide the permittee with information on the process to appeal the revocation.

(2) Upon receipt of the written notice of revocation, the permittee shall surrender the permit to the sheriff. Any law enforcement officer serving the notice is authorized to take immediate possession of the permit from the permittee. If the notice is served by means other than by a law enforcement officer, the permittee shall surrender the permit to the sheriff no later than 48 hours after service of the notice.

(3) The sheriff shall insure that the list of permits which have been revoked is immediately updated so that any potential transferor calling to check the validity of the permit will be informed of the revocation.

(4) A permittee may appeal the revocation of a permit pursuant to this subsection by petitioning a district court judge of the district in which the permittee resides.

(5) Any person who willfully fails to surrender a permit upon notice of revocation shall be guilty of a Class 2 misdemeanor.

(i) A person or entity shall promptly disclose to the sheriff, upon presentation by the applicant or sheriff of an original or photocopied release form described in subdivision (5) of subsection (e1) of this section, any court orders concerning the mental health or capacity of the applicant who signed the release form.

History.

1919, c. 197, s. 3; C.S., s. 5108; 1959, c. 1073, s. 2; 1969, c. 73; 1981 (Reg. Sess., 1982), c. 1395, s. 1; 1987, c. 518, s. 1; 1995, c. 487, s. 2; 2006-39, s. 1; 2006-264, s. 4; 2008-210, s. 3(a); 2009-570, s. 7; 2010-108, s. 4; 2011-2, s. 1; 2011-56, s. 2; 2011-183, s. 13; 2011-268, s. 10; 2013-369, s. 17.2(a); 2013-389, s. 2; 2014-115, s. 23.5(a); 2015-195, ss. 10(d), 11(c), (f), (j); 2016-77, s. 9(a)

§ 14-405. Record of permits kept by sheriff; confidentiality of permit information

(a) The sheriff shall keep a record of all permits issued under this article, including the name, date, place of residence, age, former place of residence, etc., of each such person, firm, or corporation to whom or which a permit is issued. The record shall include the date that a permit was revoked, the date that the permittee received notice of the revocation, whether the permit was surrendered, and the reason for the revocation.

(b) The records maintained by the sheriff pursuant to this section are confidential and are not a public record under G.S. 132-1; provided, however, that the sheriff shall make the records available upon request to any federal, State, and local law enforcement agencies and shall also make the records available to the court if the records are required to be released pursuant to a court order. Any application to a court for release of the list of permit holders and permit application information shall be by a petition to the chief judge of the district court for the district in which the person seeking the information resides.

History.
1919, c. 197, s. 4; C.S., s. 5109; 1959, c. 1073, s. 2; 2013-369, s. 17.4

§ 14-406. Dealer to keep record of sales; confidentiality of records

(a) Every dealer in pistols and other weapons mentioned in this Article shall keep an accurate record of all sales thereof, including the name, place of residence, date of sale, etc., of each person, firm, or corporation to whom or which such sales are made. The records maintained by a dealer pursuant to this section are confidential and are not a public record under G.S. 132-1; provided, however, that the dealer shall make the records available upon request to all State and local law enforcement agencies.

(b) Repealed by Session Laws 2011-56, s. 3, effective April 28, 2011.

History.
1919, c. 197, s. 5; C.S., s. 5110; 1987, c. 115, s. 1; 2009-6, s. 3; 2011-56, s. 3; 2013-369, s. 13

N.C. Gen. Stat. § 14-406.1

Repealed by Session Laws 2011-56, s. 4, effective April 28, 2011.

History.
2009-6, s. 1; Repealed by 2011-56, s. 4, effective April 28, 2011

N.C. Gen. Stat. § 14-407

Repealed by Session Laws 1997-6, s. 1, effective March 21, 1997.

§ 14-407.1. Sale of blank cartridge pistols

The provisions of G.S. 14-402, 14-405, and 14-406 shall apply to the sale of pistols suitable for firing blank cartridges. The sheriffs of all the counties of this State are authorized and may in their discretion issue to any person, firm or corporation, in any such county, a license or permit to purchase or receive any pistol suitable for firing blank cartridges from any person, firm or corporation offering to sell or dispose of the same, which said permit shall be in substantially the following form:

North Carolina

_____ County

I, _____, sheriff of said county, do hereby certify that _____, whose place of residence is _____ Street in _____ (or) in _____ Township in County, North Carolina, having this day satisfied me that the possession of a pistol suitable for firing blank cartridges will be used only for lawful purposes, a permit is therefore given said _____ to purchase said pistol from any person, firm or corporation authorized to dispose of the same, this _____ day of _____, _____.

_____
Sheriff

The sheriff shall charge for the sheriff's services, upon issuing such permit, a fee of fifty cents (50 cent(s)).

History.
1959, c. 1068; 1999-456, s. 59; 2006-264, s. 5

§ 14-408. Violation of § 14-406 a misdemeanor

Any person, firm, or corporation violating any of the provisions of G.S. 14-406 shall be guilty of a Class 2 misdemeanor.

History.
1919, c. 197, s. 7; C.S., s. 5112; 1969, c. 1224, s. 6; 1993, c. 539, s. 285; 1994, Ex. Sess., c. 24, s. 14(c); 1998-217, s. 3(a)

§ 14-408.1. Solicit unlawful purchase of firearm; unlawful to provide materially false information regarding legality of firearm or ammunition transfer

(a) The following definitions apply in this section:

(1) **Ammunition.** -- Any cartridge, shell, or projectile designed for use in a firearm.

(2) **Firearm.** -- A handgun, shotgun, or rifle which expels a projectile by action of an explosion.

(3) **Handgun.** -- A pistol, revolver, or other gun that has a short stock and is

designed to be held and fired by the use of a single hand.

(4) **Licensed dealer.** -- A person who is licensed pursuant to 18 U.S.C. § 923 to engage in the business of dealing in firearms.

(5) **Materially false information.** -- Information that portrays an illegal transaction as legal or a legal transaction as illegal.

(6) **Private seller.** -- A person who sells or offers for sale any firearm, as defined in G.S. 14-409.39, or ammunition.

(b) Any person who knowingly solicits, persuades, encourages, or entices a licensed dealer or private seller of firearms or ammunition to transfer a firearm or ammunition under circumstances that the person knows would violate the laws of this State or the United States is guilty of a Class F felony.

(c) Any person who provides to a licensed dealer or private seller of firearms or ammunition information that the person knows to be materially false information with the intent to deceive the dealer or seller about the legality of a transfer of a firearm or ammunition is guilty of a Class F felony.

(d) Any person who willfully procures another to engage in conduct prohibited by this section shall be held accountable as a principal.

(e) This section does not apply to a law enforcement officer acting in his or her official capacity or to a person acting at the direction of the law enforcement officer.

History.
2011-268, s. 11

§ 14-409. Machine guns and other like weapons

(a) As used in this section, "machine gun" or "submachine gun" means any weapon which shoots, is designed to shoot, or can be readily restored to shoot, automatically more than one shot, without manual reloading, by a single function of the trigger. The term shall also include the frame or receiver of any such weapon, any combination of parts designed and intended for use in converting a weapon into a machine gun, and any combination of parts from which a machine gun can be assembled if such parts are in the possession or under the control of a person.

(b) It shall be unlawful for any person, firm or corporation to manufacture, sell, give away, dispose of, use or possess machine guns, submachine guns, or other like weapons as defined by subsection (a) of this section: Provided, however, that this subsection shall not apply to the following:

Banks, merchants, and recognized business establishments for use in their respective places of business, who shall first apply to and receive from the sheriff of the county in which said business is located, a permit to possess the said weapons for the purpose of defending the said business; officers and soldiers of the United States Army, when in discharge of their official duties, officers and soldiers of the militia when called into actual service, officers of the State, or of any county, city or town, charged with the execution of the laws of the State, when acting in the discharge of their official duties; the manufacture, use or possession of such weapons for scientific or experimental purposes when such manufacture, use or possession is lawful under federal laws and the weapon is registered with a federal agency, and when a permit to manufacture, use or possess the weapon is issued by the sheriff of the county in which the weapon is located; a person who lawfully possesses or owns a weapon as defined by subsection (a) of this section in compliance with 26 U.S.C. Chapter 53, §§ 5801-5871. Nothing in this subdivision shall limit the discretion of the sheriff in executing the paperwork required by the United States Bureau of Alcohol, Tobacco and Firearms for such person to obtain the weapon. Provided, further, that any bona fide resident of this State who now owns a machine gun used in former wars, as a relic or souvenir, may retain and keep same as his or her property without violating the provisions of this section upon his reporting said ownership to the sheriff of the county in which said person lives.

(c) Any person violating any of the provisions of this section shall be guilty of a Class I felony.

History.
1933, c. 261, s. 1; 1959, c. 1073, s. 2; 1965, c. 1200; 1989, c. 680, s. 1; 1993, c. 539, s. 1243; 1994, Ex. Sess., c. 24, s. 14(c); 1999-456, s. 33(b); 2011-268, s. 9

ARTICLE 53
SALE OF WEAPONS IN CERTAIN OTHER COUNTIES

§§ 14-409.1 through 14-409.9

Repealed by Session Laws 1995, c. 487, s. 4.

ARTICLE 53A
OTHER FIREARMS

§ 14-409.10. Purchase of rifles and shotguns out of State

Unless otherwise prohibited by law, a citizen of this State may purchase a firearm in another state if the citizen undergoes a background check that satisfies the law of the state

Chapter 14

of purchase and that includes an inquiry of the National Instant Background Check System.

History.
1969, c. 101, s. 1; 2011-268, s. 12

§ 14-409.11. "Antique firearm" defined

(a) The term "antique firearm" means any of the following:

    (1) Any firearm (including any firearm with a matchlock, flintlock, percussion cap, or similar type of ignition system) manufactured on or before 1898.

    (2) Any replica of any firearm described in subdivision (1) of this subsection if the replica is not designed or redesigned for using rimfire or conventional centerfire fixed ammunition.

    (3) Any muzzle loading rifle, muzzle loading shotgun, or muzzle loading pistol, which is designed to use black powder substitute, and which cannot use fixed ammunition.

(b) For purposes of this section, the term "antique firearm" shall not include any weapon which:

    (1) Incorporates a firearm frame or receiver.

    (2) Is converted into a muzzle loading weapon.

    (3) Is a muzzle loading weapon that can be readily converted to fire fixed ammunition by replacing the barrel, bolt, breechblock, or any combination thereof.

History.
1969, c. 101, s. 2; 2006-259, s. 7(a)

§ 14-409.12. "Historic edged weapons" defined

The term "historic edged weapon" means any bayonet, trench knife, sword or dagger manufactured during or prior to World War II but in no event later than January 1, 1946.

History.
1971, c. 133, s. 1

§§ 14-409.13 through 14-409.38

Reserved for future codification purposes.

ARTICLE 53B
FIREARM REGULATION

§ 14-409.39. Definitions

The following definitions apply in this Article:

    (1) **Dealer.** -- Any person licensed as a dealer pursuant to 18 U.S.C. § 921, et seq., or G.S. 105-80.

    (2) **Firearm.** -- A handgun, shotgun, or rifle which expels a projectile by action of an explosion.

    (3) **Handgun.** -- A pistol, revolver, or other gun that has a short stock and is designed to be held and fired by the use of a single hand.

History.
1995 (Reg. Sess., 1996), c. 727, s. 1

§ 14-409.40. Statewide uniformity of local regulation

(a) It is declared by the General Assembly that the regulation of firearms is properly an issue of general, statewide concern, and that the entire field of regulation of firearms is preempted from regulation by local governments except as provided by this section.

(a1) The General Assembly further declares that the lawful design, marketing, manufacture, distribution, sale, or transfer of firearms or ammunition to the public is not an unreasonably dangerous activity and does not constitute a nuisance per se and furthermore, that it is the unlawful use of firearms and ammunition, rather than their lawful design, marketing, manufacture, distribution, sale, or transfer that is the proximate cause of injuries arising from their unlawful use. This subsection applies only to causes of action brought under subsection (g) of this section.

(b) Unless otherwise permitted by statute, no county or municipality, by ordinance, resolution, or other enactment, shall regulate in any manner the possession, ownership, storage, transfer, sale, purchase, licensing, taxation, manufacture, transportation, or registration of firearms, firearms ammunition, components of firearms, dealers in firearms, or dealers in handgun components or parts.

(c) Notwithstanding subsection (b) of this section, a county or municipality, by zoning or other ordinance, may regulate or prohibit the sale of firearms at a location only if there is a lawful, general, similar regulation or prohibition of commercial activities at that location. Nothing in this subsection shall restrict the right of a county or municipality to adopt a general zoning plan that prohibits any commercial activity within a fixed distance of a school or other educational institution except with a special use permit issued for a commercial activity found not to pose a danger to the health, safety, or general welfare of persons attending the school or educational institution within the fixed distance.

(d) No county or municipality, by zoning or other ordinance, shall regulate in any manner firearms shows with regulations more stringent than those applying to shows of other types of items.

(e) A county or municipality may regulate the transport, carrying, or possession of firearms by employees of the local unit of government in the course of their employment with that local unit of government.

(f) Nothing contained in this section prohibits municipalities or counties from application of their authority under G.S. 153A-129, 160A-189, 14-269, 14-269.2, 14-269.3, 14-269.4, 14-277.2, 14-415.11, 14-415.23, including prohibiting the possession of firearms in public-owned buildings, on the grounds or parking areas of those buildings, or in public parks or recreation areas, except nothing in this subsection shall prohibit a person from storing a firearm within a motor vehicle while the vehicle is on these grounds or areas. Nothing contained in this section prohibits municipalities or counties from exercising powers provided by law in states of emergency declared under Article 1A of Chapter 166A of the General Statutes.

(g) The authority to bring suit and the right to recover against any firearms or ammunition marketer, manufacturer, distributor, dealer, seller, or trade association by or on behalf of any governmental unit, created by or pursuant to an act of the General Assembly or the Constitution, or any department, agency, or authority thereof, for damages, abatement, injunctive relief, or any other remedy resulting from or relating to the lawful design, marketing, manufacture, distribution, sale, or transfer of firearms or ammunition to the public is reserved exclusively to the State. Any action brought by the State pursuant to this section shall be brought by the Attorney General on behalf of the State. This section shall not prohibit a political subdivision or local governmental unit from bringing an action against a firearms or ammunition marketer, manufacturer, distributor, dealer, seller, or trade association for breach of contract or warranty for defect of materials or workmanship as to firearms or ammunition purchased by the political subdivision or local governmental unit.

(h) A person adversely affected by any ordinance, rule, or regulation promulgated or caused to be enforced by any county or municipality in violation of this section may bring an action for declaratory and injunctive relief and for actual damages arising from the violation. The court shall award the prevailing party in an action brought under this subsection reasonable attorneys' fees and court costs as authorized by law.

History.
1995 (Reg. Sess., 1996), c. 727, s. 1; 2002-77, s. 1; 2012-12, s. 2(z); 2015-195, s. 12

§ 14-409.41. Chief law enforcement officer certification; certain firearms

(a) **Definitions.** -- The following definitions apply in this section:

(1) **Certification.** -- The participation and assent of the chief law enforcement officer necessary under federal law for the approval of the application to transfer or make a firearm.

(2) **Chief law enforcement officer.** -- Any official that the United States Bureau of Alcohol, Tobacco, Firearms, and Explosives, or any successor agency, has identified by regulation or otherwise as eligible to provide any required certification for the transfer or making of a firearm.

(3) **Firearm.** -- Any firearm that meets the definition of firearm in 26 U.S.C. § 5845.

(b) When a chief law enforcement officer's certification is required by federal law or regulation for the transfer or making of a firearm, the chief law enforcement officer shall, within 15 days of receipt of a request for certification, provide the certification if the applicant is not prohibited by State or federal law from receiving or possessing the firearm and is not the subject of a proceeding that could result in the applicant being prohibited by State or federal law from receiving or possessing the firearm. If the chief law enforcement officer is unable to make a certification as required by this section, the chief law enforcement officer shall provide the applicant with a written notification of the denial and the reason for the denial.

Nothing in this section shall require a chief law enforcement officer to make a certification the chief law enforcement officer knows to be untrue, but the chief law enforcement officer may not refuse to provide certification based on a generalized objection to private persons or entities making, possessing, or receiving firearms or any certain type of firearm the possession of which is not prohibited by law.

(c) An applicant whose request for certification is denied may appeal the decision of the chief law enforcement officer to the district court of the district in which the request for certification was made. The court shall make a de novo review of the chief law enforcement officer's decision to deny the certification. If the court finds that the applicant is not prohibited by State or federal law from receiving or possessing the firearm, is not the subject of a proceeding that could result in the applicant being prohibited by State or federal law from receiving or possessing the firearm, and that no substantial evidence supports the chief law enforcement officer's determination that the chief law enforcement officer cannot truthfully make the certification, the court shall order the chief law enforcement officer to issue the certification and award court costs and reasonable attorneys' fees to the applicant.

(d) Chief law enforcement officers and their employees who act in good faith are immune from liability arising from any act or omission in making a certification as required by this section.

History.
2015-195, s. 13

§ 14-409.42. Restoration process to remove mental commitment bar

(a) Any individual over the age of 18 may petition for the removal of the disabilities pursuant to 18 U.S.C. § 922(d)(4) and (g)(4), G.S. 14-415.3, and G.S. 14-415.12 arising out of a determination or finding required to be transmitted to the National Instant Criminal Background Check System by subdivisions (1) through (6) of subsection (a) of G.S. 14-409.43. The individual may file the petition with a district court judge upon the expiration of any current inpatient or outpatient commitment.

(b) The petition must be filed in the district court of the county where the respondent was the subject of the most recent judicial determination or finding or in the district court of the county of the petitioner's residence. The clerk of court upon receipt of the petition shall schedule a hearing using the regularly scheduled commitment court time and provide notice of the hearing to the petitioner and the attorney who represented the State in the underlying case, or that attorney's successor. Copies of the petition must be served on the director of the relevant inpatient or outpatient treatment facility and the district attorney in the petitioner's current county of residence.

(c) The burden is on the petitioner to establish by a preponderance of the evidence that the petitioner will not be likely to act in a manner dangerous to public safety and that the granting of the relief would not be contrary to the public interest. The district attorney shall present any and all relevant information to the contrary. For these purposes, the district attorney may access and use any and all mental health records, juvenile records, and criminal history of the petitioner wherever maintained. The applicant must sign a release for the district attorney to receive any mental health records of the applicant. This hearing shall be closed to the public, unless the court finds that the public interest would be better served by conducting the hearing in public. If the court determines the hearing should be open to the public, upon motion by the petitioner, the court may allow for the in camera inspection of any mental health records. The court may allow the use of the record but shall restrict it from

public disclosure, unless it finds that the public interest would be better served by making the record public. The district court shall enter an order that the petitioner is or is not likely to act in a manner dangerous to public safety and that the granting of the relief would or would not be contrary to the public interest. The court shall include in its order the specific findings of fact on which it bases its decision. In making its determination, the court shall consider the circumstances regarding the firearm disabilities from which relief is sought, the petitioner's mental health and criminal history records, the petitioner's reputation, developed at a minimum through character witness statements, testimony, or other character evidence, and any changes in the petitioner's condition or circumstances since the original determination or finding relevant to the relief sought. The decision of the district court may be appealed to the superior court for a hearing de novo. After a denial by the superior court, the applicant must wait a minimum of one year before reapplying. Attorneys designated by the Attorney General shall be available to represent the State, or assist in the representation of the State, in a restoration proceeding when requested to do so by a district attorney and approved by the Attorney General. An attorney so designated shall have all the powers of the district attorney under this section.

(d) Upon a judicial determination to grant a petition under this section, the clerk of superior court in the county where the petition was granted shall forward the order to the National Instant Criminal Background Check System (NICS) for updating of the respondent's record.

History.
2008-210, s. 2; 2013-369, s. 9; 2015-195, s. 11(b), (m).

§ 14-409.43. Reporting of certain disqualifiers to the National Instant Criminal Background Check System (NICS)

(a) Excluding Saturdays, Sundays, and holidays, not later than 48 hours after receiving notice of any of the following judicial determinations or findings, the clerk of superior court in the county where the determination or finding was made shall work through the Administrative Office of the Courts to cause a record of the determination or finding to be transmitted to the National Instant Criminal Background Check System (NICS):

(1) A determination that an individual shall be involuntarily committed to a facility for inpatient mental health treatment upon a finding that the individual is mentally ill and a danger to self or others.

(2) A determination that an individual shall be involuntarily committed to a facility for outpatient mental health treatment upon a finding that the individual is mentally ill and, based on the individual's treatment history, in need of treatment in order to prevent further disability or deterioration that would predictably result in a danger to self or others.

(3) A determination that an individual shall be involuntarily committed to a facility for substance abuse treatment upon a finding that the individual is a substance abuser and a danger to self or others.

(4) A finding that an individual is not guilty by reason of insanity.

(5) A finding that an individual is mentally incompetent to proceed to criminal trial.

(6) A finding that an individual lacks the capacity to manage the individual's own affairs due to marked subnormal intelligence or mental illness, incompetency, condition, or disease.

(7) A determination to grant a petition to an individual for the removal of disabilities pursuant to G.S. 14-409.42 or any applicable federal law.

The 48-hour period for transmitting a record of a judicial determination or finding to the NICS under subsection (a) of this section begins upon receipt by the clerk of a copy of the judicial determination or finding. The Administrative Office of the Courts shall adopt rules to require clerks of court to transmit information to the NICS in a uniform manner.

(b) Excluding Saturdays, Sundays, and holidays, not later than 48 hours after receiving notice of the issuance of a felony warrant, indictment, criminal summons, or order for arrest, the Administrative Office of the Courts shall transmit any unserved felony warrants, indictments, criminal summons, or order for arrests to the NCIC (or National Instant Criminal Background Check System (NICS)).

(c) Excluding Saturdays, Sundays, and holidays, not later than 48 hours after service by the sheriff of an order issued by a judge pursuant to Chapter 50B of the General Statutes and pursuant to G.S. 50B-3(d) the sheriff shall cause a record of the order to be transmitted to the National Instant Criminal Information System.

History.
2015-195, s. 11(d)

N.C. Gen. Stat. § 14-409.44

Reserved for future codification purposes.

ARTICLE 53C
SPORT SHOOTING RANGE PROTECTION ACT OF 1997

§ 14-409.45. Definitions

The following definitions apply in this Article:

(1) **Person.** -- An individual, proprietorship, partnership, corporation, club, or other legal entity.

(2) **Sport shooting range or range.** -- An area designed and operated for the use of rifles, shotguns, pistols, silhouettes, skeet, trap, black powder, or any other similar sport shooting.

(3) **Substantial change in use.** -- The current primary use of the range no longer represents the activity previously engaged in at the range.

History.
1997-465, s. 1

§ 14-409.46. Sport shooting range protection

(a) Notwithstanding any other provision of law, a person who owns, operates, or uses a sport shooting range in this State shall not be subject to civil liability or criminal prosecution in any matter relating to noise or noise pollution resulting from the operation or use of the range if the range is in compliance with any noise control laws or ordinances that applied to the range and its operation at the time the range began operation.

(b) A person who owns, operates, or uses a sport shooting range is not subject to an action for nuisance on the basis of noise or noise pollution, and a State court shall not enjoin the use or operation of a range on the basis of noise or noise pollution, if the range is in compliance with any noise control laws or ordinances that applied to the range and its operation at the time the range began operation.

(c) Rules adopted by any State department or agency for limiting levels of noise in terms of decibel level that may occur in the outdoor atmosphere shall not apply to a sport shooting range that was in operation prior to the adoption of the rule.

(d) A person who acquires title to real property adversely affected by the use of property with a permanently located and improved sport shooting range constructed and initially operated prior to the time the person acquires title shall not maintain a nuisance action on the basis of noise or noise pollution against the person who owns the range to restrain, enjoin, or impede the use of the range. If there is a substantial change in use of the range after the person acquires title, the person may maintain a nuisance action if the action is brought within one year of the date of a substantial change in use. This section does not prohibit actions for negligence or recklessness in the operation of the range or by a person using the range.

(e) A sport shooting range that is operated and is not in violation of existing law at the time of the enactment of an ordinance shall be permitted to continue in operation even if the operation of the sport shooting range at a later date does not conform to the new ordinance or an amendment to an existing ordinance, provided there has been no substantial change in use.

History.
1997-465, s. 1; 2015-195, s. 5(a)

§ 14-409.47. Application of Article

Except as otherwise provided in this Article, this Article does not prohibit a local government from regulating the location and construction of a sport shooting range after September 1, 1997.

History.
1997-465, s. 1; 2015-195, s. 5(b)

ARTICLE 54
SALE, ETC., OF PYROTECHNICS

§ 14-410. Manufacture, sale and use of pyrotechnics prohibited; exceptions; license required; sale to persons under the age of 16 prohibited

(a) Except as otherwise provided in this section, it shall be unlawful for any individual, firm, partnership or corporation to manufacture, purchase, sell, deal in, transport, possess, receive, advertise, use, handle, exhibit, or discharge any pyrotechnics of any description whatsoever within the State of North Carolina.

(a1) It shall be permissible for pyrotechnics to be exhibited, used, handled, manufactured, or discharged within the State, provided all of the following apply:

(1) The exhibition, use, or discharge is at a concert or public exhibition.

(2) All individuals who exhibit, use, handle, or discharge pyrotechnics in connection with a concert or public exhibition have completed the training and licensing required under Article 82A of Chapter 58 of the General Statutes. The display operator or proximate audience display operator, as required under Article 82A of Chapter 58 of the General Statutes, must be present at the concert or public exhibition and must personally direct all aspects of exhibiting, using, handling, or discharging the pyrotechnics. Notwithstanding this subdivision, the display operator for the University of North Carolina School of the Arts may appoint an on-site representative to supervise any performances that include a proximate audience display subsequent to the opening performance, provided that the representative (i) is a minimum of 21 years of age and (ii) is properly trained in the safe discharge of proximate audience displays.

(3) The display operator has secured written authority under G.S. 14-413 from the board of county commissioners of the county, or the city if authorized under G.S. 14-413(a1), in which the pyrotechnics are to be exhibited, used or discharged. Written authority from the board of commissioners or city is not required under this subdivision for a concert or public exhibition provided the display operator has secured written authority from (i) The University of North Carolina or the University of North Carolina at Chapel Hill under G.S. 14-413, and pyrotechnics are exhibited on lands or buildings in Orange County owned by The University of North Carolina or the University of North Carolina at Chapel Hill, (ii) the University of North Carolina School of the Arts and pyrotechnics are exhibited on lands or in buildings owned by the State and used by the University of North Carolina School of the Arts, or (iii) The University of North Carolina or North Carolina State University under G.S. 14-413, and pyrotechnics are exhibited on lands or buildings in Wake County owned by The University of North Carolina or North Carolina State University.

(a2) Notwithstanding any provision of this section, it shall not be unlawful for a common carrier to receive, transport, and deliver pyrotechnics in the regular course of its business.

(a3) The requirements of this section apply to G.S. 14-413(b) and G.S. 14-413(c).

(a4) It shall be permissible for pyrotechnics to be exhibited, used, handled, manufactured, or discharged within the State as a special effect by a production company, as defined in G.S. 105-164.3(185), for a motion picture production, if the motion picture set is closed to the public or is separated from the public by a minimum distance of 500 feet.

(a5) It shall be permissible for pyrotechnics to be exhibited, used, handled, manufactured, or discharged within the State for pyrotechnic or proximate audience display instruction consisting of classroom and practical skills training approved by the Office of State Fire Marshal.

(b) Notwithstanding the provisions of G.S. 14-414, it shall be unlawful for any individual, firm, partnership, or corporation to sell pyrotechnics as defined in G.S. 14-414(2), (3), (4)c., (5), or (6) to persons under the age of 16.

(c) The following definitions apply in this Article:

(1) **Concert or public exhibition.** -- A fair, carnival, show of any description, or public celebration.

(2) **Display operator.** -- An individual issued a display operator license under G.S. 58-82A-3.

(3) **State Fire Marshal.** -- Defined in G.S. 58-80-1.

History.
1947, c. 210, s. 1; 1993 (Reg. Sess., 1994), c. 660, s. 3; 1995, c. 475, s. 1; 2003-298, s. 2; 2007-38, s. 1; 2009-507, s. 1; 2010-22, s. 8; 2013-275, s. 1; 2015-124, s. 1

§ 14-411. Sale deemed made at site of delivery

In case of sale or purchase of pyrotechnics, where the delivery thereof was made by a common or other carrier, the sale shall be deemed to be made in the county wherein the delivery was made by such carrier to the consignee.

History.
1947, c. 210, s. 2

§ 14-412. Possession prima facie evidence of violation

Possession of pyrotechnics by any person, for any purpose other than those permitted under this article, shall be prima facie evidence that such pyrotechnics are kept for the purpose of being manufactured, sold, bartered, exchanged, given away, received, furnished, otherwise disposed of, or used in violation of the provisions of this article.

History.
1947, c. 210, s. 3

§ 14-413. Permits for use at public exhibitions

(a) For the purpose of enforcing the provisions of this Article, the board of county commissioners of any county, or the governing board of a city authorized pursuant to subsection (a1) of this section, may issue permits for use in connection with the conduct of concerts or public exhibitions, such as fairs, carnivals, shows of all descriptions and public celebrations, but only after satisfactory evidence is produced to the effect that said pyrotechnics will be used for the aforementioned purposes and none other. Provided that no such permit shall be required for a public exhibition under any of the following circumstances:

(1) The exhibition is authorized by The University of North Carolina or the University of North Carolina at Chapel Hill and conducted on lands or in buildings in Orange County owned by The University of North Carolina or the University of North Carolina at Chapel Hill.

(2) The exhibition is authorized by the University of North Carolina School of the Arts and conducted on lands or in buildings owned by the State and used by the University of North Carolina School of the Arts.

(3) The exhibition is authorized by The University of North Carolina or North Carolina State University and conducted on lands or in buildings in Wake County owned by The University of North Carolina or North Carolina State University.

(a1) For the purpose of enforcing the provisions of this Article, a board of county commissioners may authorize the governing body of any city in the county to issue permits pursuant to the provisions of this Article for pyrotechnics to be exhibited, used, or discharged within the corporate limits of the city for use in connection with the conduct of concerts or public exhibitions. The board of county commissioners shall adopt a resolution granting the authority to the city, and it shall remain in effect until withdrawn by the board of county commissioners adopting a subsequent resolution withdrawing the authority. If a city lies in more than one county, the board of county commissioners of each county in which the city lies must adopt an authorizing resolution. If any county in which the city lies withdraws the authority of the city to issue permits for the use of pyrotechnics, the authority of the city to issue permits for the use of pyrotechnics will end, and all counties within which the city lies must resume their authority to issue the permits.

(b) For any indoor use of pyrotechnics at a concert or public exhibition, the board of commissioners or the governing body of an authorized city may not issue any permit unless the local fire marshal or the State Fire Marshal (or in the case of The University of North Carolina, the University of North Carolina at Chapel Hill, or North Carolina State University it may not authorize such concert or public exhibition unless the State Fire Marshal) has certified that:

(1) Adequate fire suppression will be used at the site.

(2) The structure is safe for the use of such pyrotechnics with the type of fire suppression to be used.

(3) Adequate egress from the building is available based on the size of the expected crowd.

(c) The requirements of subsection (b) of this section also apply to any city authorized to grant pyrotechnic permits by local act and to the officer delegated the power to grant such permits by local act.

(d) A board of county commissioners or the governing board of a city shall not issue a permit under this section unless the display operator provides proof of insurance in the amount of at least five hundred thousand dollars ($ 500,000) or the minimum amount required under the North Carolina State Building Code pursuant to G.S. 143-138(e), whichever is greater. A board of county commissioners or the governing board of a city may require proof of insurance that exceeds these minimum requirements.

History.
1947, c. 210, s. 4; 1993 (Reg. Sess., 1994), c. 660, s. 3.1; 1995, c. 509, s. 11; 2003-298, s. 1; 2007-38, s. 2; 2009-507, s. 2; 2013-275, s. 2; 2015-124, s. 2

§ 14-414. Pyrotechnics defined; exceptions

For the proper construction of the provisions of this Article, "pyrotechnics," as is herein used, shall be deemed to be and include any and all kinds of fireworks and explosives, which are used for exhibitions or amusement purposes: provided, however, that nothing herein contained shall prevent the manufacture, purchase, sale, transportation, and use of explosives or signaling flares used in the course of ordinary business or industry, or shells or cartridges used as ammunition in firearms. This Article shall not apply to the sale, use, or possession of the following:

(1) Explosive caps designed to be fired in toy pistols, provided that the explosive mixture of the explosive caps shall not exceed twenty-five hundredths (.25) of a gram for each cap.

(2) Snake and glow worms composed of pressed pellets of a pyrotechnic mixture that produce a large, snake-like ash when burning.

(3) Smoke devices consisting of a tube or sphere containing a pyrotechnic mixture that produces white or colored smoke.

(4) Trick noisemakers which produce a small report designed to surprise the user and which include:

  a. A party popper, which is a small plastic or paper item containing not in excess of 16 milligrams of explosive mixture. A string protruding from the device is pulled to ignite the device, expelling paper streamers and producing a small report.

  b. A string popper, which is a small tube containing not in excess of 16 milligrams of explosive mixture with string protruding from both ends. The strings are pulled to ignite the friction-sensitive mixture, producing a small report.

  c. A snapper or drop pop, which is a small, paper-wrapped item containing no more than 16 milligrams of explosive mixture coated on small bits of sand. When dropped, the device produces a small report.

(5) Wire sparklers consisting of wire or stick coated with nonexplosive pyrotechnic mixture that produces a shower of sparks upon ignition. These items must not exceed 100 grams of mixture per item.

(6) Other sparkling devices which emit showers of sparks and sometimes a whistling or crackling effect when burning, do not detonate or explode, do not spin, are hand-held or ground-based, cannot propel themselves through the air, and contain not more than 75 grams of chemical compound per tube, or not more than a total of 200 grams if multiple tubes are used.

History.
1947, c. 210, s. 5; 1955, c. 674, s. 1; 1993, c. 437, s. 1

§ 14-415. Violation made misdemeanor

Any person violating any of the provisions of this Article, except as otherwise specified in said Article, shall be guilty of a Class 2 misdemeanor, except that it is a Class 1 misdemeanor if the exhibition is indoors.

History.
1947, c. 210, s. 6; 1969, c. 1224, s. 3; 1993, c. 539, s. 288; 1994, Ex. Sess., c. 24, s. 14(c); 2003-298, s. 3

ARTICLE 54A
THE FELONY FIREARMS ACT

§ 14-415.1. Possession of firearms, etc., by felon prohibited

(a) It shall be unlawful for any person who has been convicted of a felony to purchase, own, possess, or have in his custody, care, or control any firearm or any weapon of mass death and destruction as defined in G.S. 14-288.8(c). For the purposes of this section, a firearm is (i) any weapon, including a starter gun, which will or is designed to or may readily be converted to expel a projectile by the action of an explosive, or its frame or receiver, or (ii) any firearm muffler or firearm silencer. This section does not apply to an antique firearm, as defined in G.S. 14-409.11.

Every person violating the provisions of this section shall be punished as a Class G felon.

(b) Prior convictions which cause disentitlement under this section shall only include:

(1) Felony convictions in North Carolina that occur before, on, or after December 1, 1995; and

(2) Repealed by Session Laws 1995, c. 487, s. 3, effective December 1, 1995.

(3) Violations of criminal laws of other states or of the United States that occur before, on, or after December 1, 1995, and that are substantially similar to the crimes covered in subdivision (1) which are punishable where committed by imprisonment for a term exceeding one year.

When a person is charged under this section, records of prior convictions of any offense, whether in the courts of this State, or in the courts of any other state or of the United States, shall be admissible in evidence for the purpose of proving a violation of this section. The term "conviction" is defined as a final judgment in any case in which felony punishment, or imprisonment for a term exceeding one year, as the case may be, is authorized, without regard to the plea entered or to the sentence imposed. A judgment of a conviction of the defendant or a plea of guilty by the defendant to such an offense certified to a superior court of this State from the custodian of records of any state or federal court shall be prima facie evidence of the facts so certified.

(c) The indictment charging the defendant under the terms of this section shall be separate from any indictment charging him with other offenses related to or giving rise to a charge under this section. An indictment which charges the person with violation of this section must set forth the date that the prior offense was committed, the type of offense and the penalty therefor, and the date that the defendant was convicted or plead guilty to such offense, the identity of the court in which the conviction or plea of guilty took place and the verdict and judgment rendered therein.

(d) This section does not apply to a person who, pursuant to the law of the jurisdiction in which the conviction occurred, has been pardoned or has had his or her firearms rights restored if such restoration of rights could also be granted under North Carolina law.

(e) This section does not apply and there is no disentitlement under this section if the felony conviction is a violation under the laws of North Carolina, another state, or the United States that pertains to antitrust violations, unfair trade practices, or restraints of trade.

History.

1971, c. 954, s. 1; 1973, c. 1196; 1975, c. 870, ss. 1, 2; 1977, c. 1105, ss. 1, 2; 1979, c. 760, s. 5; 1979, 2nd Sess., c. 1316, s. 47; 1981, c. 63, s. 1; c. 179, s. 14; 1989, c. 770, s. 3; 1993, c. 539, s. 1245; 1994, Ex. Sess., c. 24, s. 14(c); 1995, c. 487, s. 3; c. 507, s. 19.5(k); 2004-186, s. 14.1; 2006-259, s. 7(b); 2010-108, s. 3; 2011-2, s. 1; 2011-268, s. 13

N.C. Gen. Stat. § 14-415.2

Repealed by Session Laws 1975, c. 870, s. 3.

§ 14-415.3. Possession of a firearm or weapon of mass destruction by persons acquitted of certain crimes by reason of insanity or personsdetermined to be incapable to proceed prohibited

(a) It is unlawful for the following persons to purchase, own, possess, or have in the person's custody, care, or control, any firearm or any weapon of mass death and destruction as defined by G.S. 14-288.8(c):

(1) A person who has been acquitted by reason of insanity of any crime set out in G.S. 14-415.1(b) or any violation of G.S. 14-33(b)(1), 14-33(b)(8), or 14-34.

(2) A person who has been determined to lack capacity to proceed as provided in G.S. 15A-1002 for any crime set out in G.S. 14-415.1(b) or any violation of G.S. 14-33(b)(1), 14-33(b)(8), or 14-34.

(b) A violation of this section is a Class H felony. Any firearm or weapon of mass death and destruction lawfully seized for a violation of this section shall be forfeited to the State and disposed of as provided in G.S. 15-11.1.

(c) The provisions of this section shall not apply to a person whose rights have been restored pursuant to G.S. 14-409.42.

History.

1994, Ex. Sess., c. 13, s. 1; 2013-369, s. 10; 2015-195, s. 11(k)

§ 14-415.4. Restoration of firearms rights

(a) **Definitions.** -- The following definitions apply in this section:

(1) **Firearms rights.** -- The legal right in this State of a person to purchase, own, possess, or have in the person's custody, care, or control any firearm or any weapon of mass death and destruction as those terms are defined in G.S. 14-415.1 and G.S. 14-288.8(c).

(2) **Nonviolent felony.** -- The term nonviolent felony does not include any felony that is a Class A, Class B1, or Class B2 felony. Also, the term nonviolent felony does

not include any Class C through Class I felony that is one of the following:

    a. An offense that includes assault as an essential element of the offense.

    b. An offense that includes the possession or use of a firearm or other deadly weapon as an essential or non-essential element of the offense, or the offender was in possession of a firearm or other deadly weapon at the time of the commission of the offense.

    c. An offense for which the offender was armed with or used a firearm or other deadly weapon.

    d. An offense for which the offender must register under Article 27A of Chapter 14 of the General Statutes.

(b) **Purpose.** -- It is the purpose of this section to establish a procedure that allows a North Carolina resident who was convicted of a single nonviolent felony and whose citizenship rights have been restored pursuant to Chapter 13 of the General Statutes to petition the court to remove the petitioner's disentitlement under G.S. 14-415.1 and to restore the person's firearms rights in this State. If the single nonviolent felony conviction was an out-of-state conviction or a federal conviction, then the North Carolina resident shall show proof of the restoration of his or her civil rights and the right to possess a firearm in the jurisdiction where the conviction occurred. Restoration of a person's firearms rights under this section means that the person may purchase, own, possess, or have in the person's custody, care, or control any firearm or any weapon of mass death and destruction as those terms are defined in G.S. 14-415.1 and G.S. 14-288.8(c) without being in violation of G.S. 14-415.1, if otherwise qualified.

(c) **Petition for Restoration of Firearms Rights.** -- A person who was convicted of a non-violent felony in North Carolina but whose civil rights have been restored pursuant to Chapter 13 of the General Statutes for a period of at least 20 years may petition the district court in the district where the person resides to restore the person's firearms rights pursuant to this section. A person who was convicted of a non-violent felony in a jurisdiction other than North Carolina may petition the district court in the district where the person resides to restore the person's firearms rights pursuant to this section only if (i) a period of at least 20 years has passed since the unconditional discharge or unconditional pardon of the person by the agency having jurisdiction where the conviction occurred, and (ii) the person's civil rights, including the right to possess a firearm, have been restored, pursuant to the law of the jurisdiction where the conviction occurred. The court may restore a petitioner's firearms rights after

a hearing in court if the court determines that the petitioner meets the criteria set out in this section and is not otherwise disqualified to have that right restored.

(d) **Criteria.** -- The court may grant a petition to restore a person's firearms rights under this section if the petitioner satisfies all of the following criteria and is not otherwise disqualified to have that right restored:

(1) The petitioner is a resident of North Carolina and has been a resident of the State for one year or longer immediately preceding the filing of the petition.

(2) The petitioner has only one felony conviction and that conviction is for a non-violent felony. For purposes of this subdivision, multiple felony convictions arising out of the same event and consolidated for sentencing shall count as one felony only.

(3) The petitioner's rights of citizenship have been restored pursuant to Chapter 13 of the General Statutes or, if the conviction was in a jurisdiction other than North Carolina, have been restored, pursuant to the laws of the jurisdiction where the conviction occurred, and the petitioner satisfied the applicable 20-year requirement set forth in subsection (c) of this section, before the date of the filing of the petition.

(4) The petitioner has not been convicted under the laws of the United States, the laws of this State, or the laws of any other state of any misdemeanor as described in subdivision (6) of subsection (e) of this section since the conviction of the nonviolent felony.

(5) The petitioner submits his or her fingerprints to the sheriff of the county in which the petitioner resides for a criminal background check pursuant to G.S. 143B-959.

(6) The petitioner is not disqualified under subsection (e) of this section.

(e) **Disqualifiers Requiring Denial of Petition.** -- The court shall deny the petition to restore the firearms rights of any petitioner if the court finds any of the following:

(1) The petitioner is ineligible to purchase, own, possess, or have in the person's custody, care, or control a firearm under the provisions of any law in North Carolina other than G.S. 14-415.1.

(2) The petitioner is under indictment for a felony or a finding of probable cause exists against the petitioner for a felony.

(3) The petitioner is a fugitive from justice.

(4) The petitioner is an unlawful user of, or addicted to, marijuana, alcohol, or any depressant, stimulant, or narcotic drug, or any other controlled substance as defined in 21 U.S.C. § 802.

(5) The petitioner is or has been dishonorably discharged from the Armed Forces of the United States.

(6) The petitioner is or has been adjudicated guilty of or received a prayer for judgment continued or suspended sentence for one or more crimes of violence constituting a misdemeanor, including a misdemeanor under Article 8 of Chapter 14 of the General Statutes, or a misdemeanor under G.S. 14-225.2, 14-226.1, 14-258.1, 14-269.2, 14-269.3, 14-269.4, 14-269.6, 14-276.1, 14-277, 14-277.1, 14-277.2, 14-277.3, 14-281.1, 14-283, 14-288.2, 14-288.4(a)(1) or (2), 14-288.6, 14-288.9, former 14-288.12, former 14-288.13, former 14-288.14, 14-288.20A, 14-318.2, 14-415.21(b), or 14-415.26(d), or a substantially similar out-of-state or federal offense.

(7) The petitioner has had entry of a prayer for judgment continued for a felony, in addition to the nonviolent felony conviction.

(8) The petitioner is free on bond or personal recognizance pending trial, appeal, or sentencing for a crime which would prohibit the person from having his or her firearms rights restored under this section.

(9) An emergency order, ex parte order, or protective order has been issued pursuant to Chapter 50B of the General Statutes or a similar out-of-state or federal order has been issued against the petitioner and the court order issued is still in effect.

(10) A civil no-contact order has been issued pursuant to Chapter 50C of the General Statutes or a similar out-of-state or federal order has been issued against the petitioner and the court order issued is still in effect.

(f) **Notice of Hearing and Hearing Procedure. --** The clerk of court shall provide notice of the hearing to the district attorney in the district in which the petition is filed at least four weeks before the hearing on the matter. The petitioner may present evidence in support of the petition, and the district attorney may present evidence in opposition to the requested restoration of firearms rights or may otherwise demonstrate the reasons why the petition should be denied. The burden is on the petitioner to establish by a preponderance of the evidence that the petitioner is qualified to receive the restoration under subsection (d) of this section and that the petitioner is not disqualified under subsection (e) of this section.

(g) **Right to Petition Again Upon Denial of Petition. --** If the court denies the petition, the person may again petition the court for restoration of his or her firearms rights in accordance with this section one year from the date of the denial of the original petition. However, if the sole basis for the denial of the petition are the grounds set out under G.S. 14-415.4(e)(9) or (10), then the person does not have to wait for one year from the date of denial of the original petition but may petition again upon the expiration of the order.

(h) **Certified Copies of Order Granting Petition to Sheriff, Department of Justice, and National Instant Background Check System Index. --** If the court grants the petition to restore the petitioner's firearms rights, the clerk of court shall forward within 10 days of the entry of the order a certified copy of the order to the sheriff of the county in which the petitioner resides, the North Carolina Department of Justice, and the denied person's file of the national instant criminal background check system index.

(i) **Restoration is Not an Expunction or Pardon. --** A restoration of firearms rights under this section does not result in the expunction of any criminal history record information nor does it constitute a pardon.

(j) **Automatic Revocation Upon Conviction of a Subsequent Felony. --** If a person's firearms rights are restored under this section and the person is convicted of a second or subsequent felony, then the person's firearms rights are automatically revoked and shall not be restored under this section.

(k) **Fee. --** A person who files a petition for restoration of firearms rights under this section shall pay the clerk of court a fee of two hundred dollars ($ 200.00) at the time the petition is filed. Fees collected under this subsection shall be deposited in the General Fund. This subsection does not apply to petitions filed by an indigent.

(l) **Criminal Offense to Submit False Information. --** A person who knowingly and willfully submits false information under this section is guilty of a Class 1 misdemeanor. In addition, a person who is convicted of an offense under this subsection is permanently prohibited from petitioning to restore his or her firearms rights under this section.

History.
2010-108, s. 1; 2011-2, s. 1; 2011-183, s. 14; 2012-12, s. 2(aa); 2014-100, s. 17.1(bb); 2015-195, s. 6; 2021-116, s. 1.2(a)

§§ 14-415.5 through 14-415.9

Reserved for future codification purposes.

ARTICLE 54B
CONCEALED
HANDGUN PERMIT

§ 14-415.10. Definitions

The following definitions apply to this Article:

(1) **Carry a concealed handgun. --** The term includes possession of a concealed handgun.

(1a) **Deployed or deployment. --** Any military duty that removes a military permittee from the permittee's county of residence during which time the permittee's permit expires or will expire.

(2) **Handgun. --** A firearm that has a short stock and is designed to be held and fired by the use of a single hand.

(2a) **Military permittee. --** A person who holds a permit who is also a member of the Armed Forces of the United States, the reserve components of the Armed Forces of the United States, the North Carolina Army National Guard, or the North Carolina Air National Guard.

(3) **Permit. --** A concealed handgun permit issued in accordance with the provisions of this Article.

(3a) **Proof of deployment. --** A copy of the military permittee's deployment orders or other written notification from the permittee's command indicating the start and end date of deployment and that orders the permittee to travel outside the permittee's county of residence.

(4) **Qualified former sworn law enforcement officer. --** An individual who retired from service as a law enforcement officer with a local, State, campus police, or company police agency in North Carolina, other than for reasons of mental disability, who has been retired as a sworn law enforcement officer two years or less from the date of the permit application, and who satisfies all of the following:

a. Immediately before retirement, the individual was a qualified law enforcement officer with a local, State, or company police agency in North Carolina.

b. The individual has a nonforfeitable right to benefits under the retirement plan of the local, State, or company police agency as a law enforcement officer; or has 20 or more aggregate years of law enforcement service and has retired from a company police agency that does not have a retirement plan; or has 20 or more aggregate years of part-time or auxiliary law enforcement service.

c. The individual is not prohibited by State or federal law from receiving a firearm.

(4a) **Qualified retired correctional officer. --** An individual who retired from service as a State correctional officer, other than for reasons of mental disability, who has been retired as a correctional officer two years or less from the date of the permit application and who meets all of the following criteria:

a. Immediately before retirement, the individual met firearms training standards of the Division of Adult Correction and Juvenile Justice of the Department of Public Safety and was authorized by the Division of Adult Correction and Juvenile Justice of the Department of Public Safety to carry a handgun in the course of assigned duties.

b. The individual retired in good standing and was never a subject of a disciplinary action by the Division of Adult Correction and Juvenile Justice of the Department of Public Safety that would have prevented the individual from carrying a handgun.

c. The individual has a vested right to benefits under the Teachers' and State Employees' Retirement System of North Carolina established under Article 1 of Chapter 135 of the General Statutes.

d. The individual is not prohibited by State or federal law from receiving a firearm.

(4b) **Qualified retired law enforcement officer. --** An individual who meets the definition of "qualified retired law enforcement officer" contained in section 926C of Title 18 of the United States Code.

(4c) **Qualified retired probation or parole certified officer. --** An individual who retired from service as a State probation or parole certified officer, other than for reasons of mental disability, who has been retired as a probation or parole certified officer two years or less from the date of the permit application and who meets all of the following criteria:

a. Immediately before retirement, the individual met firearms training standards of the Division of Adult Correction and Juvenile Justice of the Department of Public Safety and was authorized by the Division of Adult Correction and Juvenile Justice of the Department of Public Safety to carry a handgun in the course of duty.

b. The individual retired in good standing and was never a subject of a disciplinary action by the Division of Adult Correction and Juvenile Justice of the Department of Public Safety that would have prevented the individual from carrying a handgun.

c. The individual has a vested right to benefits under the Teachers' and State Employees' Retirement System of North Carolina established under Article 1 of Chapter 135 of the General Statutes.

d. The individual is not prohibited by State or federal law from receiving a firearm.

(5) **Qualified sworn law enforcement officer.** -- A law enforcement officer employed by a local, State, campus police, or company police agency in North Carolina who satisfies all of the following:

a. The individual is authorized by the agency to carry a handgun in the course of duty.

b. The individual is not the subject of a disciplinary action by the agency that prevents the carrying of a handgun.

c. The individual meets the requirements established by the agency regarding handguns.

History.
1995, c. 398, s. 1; 1997-274, s. 2; 1997-441, ss. 2, 3; 2005-231, ss. 4, 5; 2005-232, s. 1; 2007-427, s. 1; 2009-307, s. 2; 2010-104, s. 1; 2011-145, s. 19.1(h); 2011-183, s. 15; 2013-369, s. 24; 2014-119, s. 7(a); 2017-186, s. 2(jj), 3(a)

§ 14-415.11. Permit to carry concealed handgun; scope of permit

(a) Any person who has a concealed handgun permit may carry a concealed handgun unless otherwise specifically prohibited by law. The person shall carry the permit together with valid identification whenever the person is carrying a concealed handgun, shall disclose to any law enforcement officer that the person holds a valid permit and is carrying a concealed handgun when approached or addressed by the officer, and shall display both the permit and the proper identification upon the request of a law enforcement officer. In addition to these requirements, a military permittee whose permit has expired during deployment may carry a concealed handgun during the 90 days following the end of deployment and before the permit is renewed provided the permittee also displays proof of deployment to any law enforcement officer.

(b) The sheriff shall issue a permit to carry a concealed handgun to a person who qualifies for a permit under G.S. 14-415.12. The permit shall be valid throughout the State for a period of five years from the date of issuance.

(c) Except as provided in G.S. 14-415.27, a permit does not authorize a person to carry a concealed handgun in any of the following:

(1) Areas prohibited by G.S. 14-269.2, 14-269.3, and 14-277.2.

(2) Areas prohibited by G.S. 14-269.4, except as allowed under G.S. 14-269.4(6).

(3) In an area prohibited by rule adopted under G.S. 120-32.1.

(4) In any area prohibited by 18 U.S.C. § 922 or any other federal law.

(5) In a law enforcement or correctional facility.

(6) In a building housing only State or federal offices.

(7) In an office of the State or federal government that is not located in a building exclusively occupied by the State or federal government.

(8) On any private premises where notice that carrying a concealed handgun is prohibited by the posting of a conspicuous notice or statement by the person in legal possession or control of the premises.

(c1) Any person who has a concealed handgun permit may carry a concealed handgun on the grounds or waters of a park within the State Parks System as defined in G.S. 143B-135.44.

(c2) It shall be unlawful for a person, with or without a permit, to carry a concealed handgun while consuming alcohol or at any time while the person has remaining in the person's body any alcohol or in the person's blood a controlled substance previously consumed, but a person does not violate this condition if a controlled substance in the person's blood was lawfully obtained and taken in therapeutically appropriate amounts or if the person is on the person's own property.

(c3) As provided in G.S. 14-269.4(5), it shall be lawful for a person to carry any firearm openly, or to carry a concealed handgun with a concealed carry permit, at any State-owned rest area, at any State-owned rest stop along the highways, and at any State-owned hunting and fishing reservation.

(d) A person who is issued a permit shall notify the sheriff who issued the permit of any change in the person's permanent address within 30 days after the change of address. If a permit is lost or destroyed, the person to whom the permit was issued shall notify the sheriff who issued the permit of the loss or destruction of the permit. A person may obtain a duplicate permit by submitting to the sheriff a notarized statement that the permit was lost or destroyed and paying the required duplicate permit fee.

History.
1995, c. 398, s. 1; c. 507, s. 22.1(c); c. 509, s. 135.3(e); 1997, c. 238, s. 6; 2000-140, s. 103; 2000-191, s. 5; 2005-232, s. 3; 2011-268, s. 14; 2015-241, s. 14.30(cc)

§ 14-415.12. Criteria to qualify for the issuance of a permit

(a) The sheriff shall issue a permit to an applicant if the applicant qualifies under the following criteria:

(1) The applicant is a citizen of the United States or has been lawfully admitted for permanent residence as defined in 8 U.S.C. § 1101(a)(20), and has been a resident of the State 30 days or longer immediately preceding the filing of the application.

(2) The applicant is 21 years of age or older.

(3) The applicant does not suffer from a physical or mental infirmity that prevents the safe handling of a handgun.

(4) The applicant has successfully completed an approved firearms safety and training course which involves the actual firing of handguns and instruction in the laws of this State governing the carrying of a concealed handgun and the use of deadly force. The North Carolina Criminal Justice Education and Training Standards Commission shall prepare and publish general guidelines for courses and qualifications of instructors which would satisfy the requirements of this subdivision. An approved course shall be any course which satisfies the requirements of this subdivision and is certified or sponsored by:

    a. The North Carolina Criminal Justice Education and Training Standards Commission,

    b. The National Rifle Association, or

    c. A law enforcement agency, college, private or public institution or organization, or firearms training school, taught by instructors certified by the North Carolina Criminal Justice Education and Training Standards Commission or the National Rifle Association.

Every instructor of an approved course shall file a copy of the firearms course description, outline, and proof of certification annually, or upon modification of the course if more frequently, with the North Carolina Criminal Justice Education and Training Standards Commission.

(5) The applicant is not disqualified under subsection (b) of this section.

(b) The sheriff shall deny a permit to an applicant who:

(1) Is ineligible to own, possess, or receive a firearm under the provisions of State or federal law.

(2) Is under indictment or against whom a finding of probable cause exists for a felony.

(3) Has been adjudicated guilty in any court of a felony, unless: (i) the felony is an offense that pertains to antitrust violations, unfair trade practices, or restraints of trade, or (ii) the person's firearms rights have been restored pursuant to G.S. 14-415.4.

(4) Is a fugitive from justice.

(5) Is an unlawful user of, or addicted to marijuana, alcohol, or any depressant, stimulant, or narcotic drug, or any other controlled substance as defined in 21 U.S.C. § 802.

(6) Is currently, or has been previously adjudicated by a court or administratively determined by a governmental agency whose decisions are subject to judicial review to be, lacking mental capacity or mentally ill. Receipt of previous consultative services or outpatient treatment alone shall not disqualify an applicant under this subdivision.

(7) Is or has been discharged from the Armed Forces of the United States under conditions other than honorable.

(8) Except as provided in subdivision (8a), (8b), or (8c) of this section, is or has been adjudicated guilty of or received a prayer for judgment continued or suspended sentence for one or more crimes of violence constituting a misdemeanor, including but not limited to, a violation of a misdemeanor under Article 8 of Chapter 14 of the General Statutes except for a violation of G.S. 14-33(a), or a violation of a misdemeanor under G.S. 14-226.1, 4-258.1, 14-269.2, 14-269.3, 14-269.4, 14-269.6, 14-277, 14-277.1, 14-277.2, 14-283 except for a violation involving fireworks exempted under G.S. 14-414, 14-288.2, 14-288.4(a)(1), 14-288.6, 14-288.9, former 14-288.12, former 14-288.13, former 14-288.14, 14-415.21(b), or 14-415.26(d) within three years prior to the date on which the application is submitted.

(8a) Is or has been adjudicated guilty of or received a prayer for judgment continued or suspended sentence for one or more crimes of violence constituting a misdemeanor under G.S. 14-33(c)(1), 14-33(c)(2), 14-33(c)(3), 14-33(d), 14-277.3A, 14-318.2, 14-134.3, 50B-4.1, or former G.S. 14-277.3.

(8b) Is prohibited from possessing a firearm pursuant to 18 U.S.C. § 922(g) as a result of a conviction of a misdemeanor crime of domestic violence.

(8c) Has been adjudicated guilty of or received a prayer for judgment continued or suspended sentence for one or more crimes involving an assault or a threat to assault a law enforcement officer, probation or parole officer, person employed at a State or local detention facility, firefighter, emergency medical technician, medical responder, or emergency department personnel.

(9) Has had entry of a prayer for judgment continued for a criminal offense

which would disqualify the person from obtaining a concealed handgun permit.

(10) Is free on bond or personal recognizance pending trial, appeal, or sentencing for a crime which would disqualify him from obtaining a concealed handgun permit.

(11) Has been convicted of an impaired driving offense under G.S. 20-138.1, 20-138.2, or 20-138.3 within three years prior to the date on which the application is submitted.

(c) An applicant shall not be ineligible to receive a concealed carry permit under subdivision (6) of subsection (b) of this section because of an adjudication of mental incapacity or illness or an involuntary commitment to mental health services if the individual's rights have been restored under G.S. 14-409.42.

History.
1995, c. 398, s. 1; c. 509, s. 135.3(d); 1997-441, s. 4; 2007-427, s. 5; 2008-210, s. 3(b); 2009-58, s. 1; 2010-108, s. 5; 2011-2, s. 1; 2011-183, s. 16; 2012-12, s. 2(bb); 2013-369, s. 11; 2015-195, ss. 7, 11(l), 17

§ 14-415.12A. Firearms safety and training course exemption for qualified sworn law enforcement officers and certain other persons

(a) A person who is a qualified sworn law enforcement officer, a qualified former sworn law enforcement officer, a qualified retired correctional officer, or a qualified retired probation or parole certified officer is deemed to have satisfied the requirement under G.S. 14-415.12(a)(4) that an applicant successfully complete an approved firearms safety and training course.

(a1) An individual who is a qualified retired law enforcement officer and has met the standards, as approved by the North Carolina Criminal Justice Education and Training Standards Commission, for handgun qualification for active law enforcement officers within the last 12 months is deemed to have satisfied the requirement under G.S. 14-415.12(a)(4) that an applicant successfully complete an approved firearms safety and training course.

(b) A person who is licensed or registered by the North Carolina Private Protective Services Board under Article 1 of Chapter 74C of the General Statutes as an armed security guard, who also has a firearm registration permit issued by the Board in compliance with G.S. 74C-13, is deemed to have satisfied the requirement under G.S. 14-415.12(a)(4) that an applicant successfully complete an approved firearms safety and training course.

History.
1997-274, s. 1; 2005-211, s. 2; 2010-104, s. 2; 2014-119, s. 7(b); 2015-105, s. 1; 2015-264, s. 36(a)

§ 14-415.13. Application for a permit; fingerprints

(a) A person shall apply to the sheriff of the county in which the person resides to obtain a concealed handgun permit. The applicant shall submit to the sheriff all of the following:

(1) An application, completed under oath, on a form provided by the sheriff, and such application form must be provided by the sheriff electronically. The sheriff shall not request employment information, character affidavits, additional background checks, photographs, or other information unless specifically permitted by this Article.

(2) A nonrefundable permit fee.

(3) A full set of fingerprints of the applicant administered by the sheriff.

(4) An original certificate of completion of an approved course, adopted and distributed by the North Carolina Criminal Justice Education and Training Standards Commission, signed by the certified instructor of the course attesting to the successful completion of the course by the applicant which shall verify that the applicant is competent with a handgun and knowledgeable about the laws governing the carrying of a concealed handgun and the use of deadly force.

(5) A release, in a form to be prescribed by the Administrative Office of the Courts, that authorizes and requires disclosure to the sheriff of any records concerning the mental health or capacity of the applicant to be used for the sole purpose of determining whether the applicant is disqualified for a permit under the provisions of G.S. 14-415.12. This provision does not prohibit submitting information related to involuntary commitment to the National Instant Criminal Background Check System (NICS).

(b) The sheriff shall submit the fingerprints to the State Bureau of Investigation for a records check of State and national databases. The State Bureau of Investigation shall submit the fingerprints to the Federal Bureau of Investigation as necessary. The sheriff shall determine the criminal and background history of an applicant also by conducting a check through the National Instant Criminal Background Check System (NICS). The cost of processing the set of fingerprints shall be charged to an applicant as provided by G.S. 14-415.19.

History.
1995, c. 398, s. 1; c. 507, ss. 22.2(a), 22.1(b); 2006-39, s. 2; 2011-268, s. 15; 2015-195, s. 11(g)

§ 14-415.14. Application form to be provided by sheriff; information to be included in application form

(a) The sheriff shall make permit applications readily available at the office of the sheriff or at other public offices in the sheriff's jurisdiction. The permit application shall be in triplicate, in a form to be prescribed by the State Bureau of Investigation, and shall include the following information with regard to the applicant: name, address, physical description, signature, date of birth, social security number, military status, law enforcement status, and the drivers license number or State identification card number of the applicant if used for identification in applying for the permit.

(b) The permit application shall also contain a warning substantially as follows:

"CAUTION: Federal law and State law on the possession of handguns and firearms may differ. If you are prohibited by federal law from possessing a handgun or a firearm, you may be prosecuted in federal court. A State permit is not a defense to a federal prosecution."

(c) Any person or entity who is presented by the applicant or by the sheriff with an original or photocopied release form as described in G.S. 14-415.13(a)(5) shall promptly disclose to the sheriff any records concerning the mental health or capacity of the applicant who signed the form and authorized the release of the records.

History.
1995, c. 398, s. 1; 1997-274, s. 3; 2000-140, s. 103; 2000-191, s. 3; 2011-268, s. 16; 2014-115, s. 24(a)

§ 14-415.15. Issuance or denial of permit

(a) Except as permitted under subsection (b) of this section, within 45 days after receipt of the items listed in G.S. 14-415.13 from an applicant, and receipt of the required records concerning the mental health or capacity of the applicant, the sheriff shall either issue or deny the permit. The sheriff may conduct any investigation necessary to determine the qualification or competency of the person applying for the permit, including record checks. The sheriff shall make the request for any records concerning the mental health or capacity of the applicant within 10 days of receipt of the items listed in G.S. 14-415.13. No person, company, mental health provider, or governmental entity may charge additional fees to the applicant for background checks conducted under this subsection. A permit shall not be denied unless the applicant is determined to be ineligible pursuant to G.S. 14-415.12.

(b) Upon presentment to the sheriff of the items required under G.S. 14-415.13 (a)(1), (2), and (3), the sheriff may issue a temporary permit for a period not to exceed 45 days to a person who the sheriff reasonably believes is in an emergency situation that may constitute a risk of safety to the person, the person's family or property. The applicant may submit proof of a protective order issued under G.S. 50B-3 for the protection of the applicant as evidence of an emergency situation. The temporary permit may not be renewed and may be revoked by the sheriff without a hearing.

(c) A person's application for a permit shall be denied only if the applicant fails to qualify under the criteria listed in this Article. If the sheriff denies the application for a permit, the sheriff shall, within 45 days, notify the applicant in writing, stating the grounds for denial. An applicant may appeal the denial, revocation, or nonrenewal of a permit by petitioning a district court judge of the district in which the application was filed. The determination by the court, on appeal, shall be upon the facts, the law, and the reasonableness of the sheriff's refusal. The determination by the court shall be final.

History.
1995, c. 398, s. 1; 2005-343, s. 1; 2011-268, s. 17; 2015-195, s. 14

§ 14-415.16. Renewal of permit

(a) At least 45 days prior to the expiration date of a permit, the sheriff of the county where the permit was issued shall send a written notice to the permittee explaining that the permit is about to expire and including information about the requirements for renewal of the permit. The notice shall be sent by first class mail to the last known address of the permittee. Failure to receive a renewal notice shall not relieve a permittee of requirements imposed in this section for renewal of the permit.

(b) The holder of a permit shall apply to renew the permit within the 90-day period prior to its expiration date by filing with the sheriff of the county in which the person resides a renewal form provided by the sheriff's office, an affidavit stating that the permittee remains qualified under the criteria provided in this Article, a newly administered full set of the permittee's fingerprints, and a renewal fee.

(c) Upon receipt of the completed renewal application and the appropriate payment of fees, the sheriff shall determine if the permittee remains qualified to hold a permit in accordance with the provisions of G.S. 14-415.12. The permittee's criminal history shall be updated, including with another inquiry of the National Instant Criminal Background Check System (NICS), and the sheriff may waive the requirement of taking another firearms safety and training course. If the permittee applies for a renewal of the permit within the 90-day period prior to its expiration date and if the permittee remains qualified to have a permit under G.S.

14-415.12, the sheriff shall renew the permit. The permit of a permittee who complies with this section shall remain valid beyond the expiration date of the permit until the permittee either receives a renewal permit or is denied a renewal permit by the sheriff.

(d) No fingerprints shall be required for a renewal permit if the applicant's fingerprints were submitted to the State Bureau of Investigation after June 30, 2001, on the Automated Fingerprint Information System (AFIS) as prescribed by the State Bureau of Investigation.

(e) If the permittee does not apply to renew the permit prior to its expiration date, but does apply to renew the permit within 60 days after the permit expires, the sheriff may waive the requirement of taking another firearms safety and training course. This subsection does not extend the expiration date of the permit.

History.
1995, c. 398, s. 1; c. 507, s. 22.2(b); 2000-140, s. 103; 2000-191, s. 1; 2009-307, s. 1; 2011-268, s. 18

§ 14-415.16A. Permit extensions and renewals for deployed military permittees

(a) A deployed military permittee whose permit will expire during the permittee's deployment, or the permittee's agent, may apply to the sheriff for an extension of the military permittee's permit by providing the sheriff with a copy of the permittee's proof of deployment. Upon receipt of the proof, the sheriff shall extend the permit for a period to end 90 days after the permittee's deployment is scheduled to end. A permit that has been extended under this section shall be valid throughout the State during the period of its extension.

(b) A military permittee's permit that is not extended under subsection (a) of this section and that expires during deployment shall remain valid during the deployment and for 90 days after the end of the deployment as if the permit had not expired. The military permittee may carry a concealed handgun during this period provided the permittee meets all the requirements of G.S. 14-415.11(a).

(c) A military permittee under subsection (a) or subsection (b) of this section shall have 90 days after the end of the permittee's deployment to renew the permit. In addition to the requirements of G.S. 14-415.16, the permittee shall provide to the sheriff proof of deployment. The sheriff shall renew the permit upon receipt of this documentation provided the permittee otherwise remains qualified to hold a concealed handgun permit.

History.
2005-232, s. 2

§ 14-415.17. Permit; sheriff to retain a list of permittees; confidentiality of list and permit application information; availability to law enforcement agencies

(a) The permit shall be in a certificate form, as prescribed by the State Bureau of Investigation, that is approximately the size of a North Carolina drivers license. It shall bear the signature, name, address, date of birth, and the drivers license identification number used in applying for the permit.

(b) The sheriff shall maintain a listing, including the identifying information, of those persons who are issued a permit. Within five days of the date a permit is issued, the sheriff shall send a copy of the permit to the State Bureau of Investigation.

(c) Except as provided otherwise by this subsection, the list of permit holders and the information collected by the sheriff to process an application for a permit are confidential and are not a public record under G.S. 132-1. The sheriff shall make the list of permit holders and the permit information available upon request to all State and local law enforcement agencies. The State Bureau of Investigation shall make the list of permit holders and the information collected by the sheriff to process an application for a permit available to law enforcement officers and clerks of court on a statewide system.

History.
1995, c. 398, s. 1; 2011-268, s. 19; 2013-369, s. 12; 2014-115, s. 24(b)

§ 14-415.18. Revocation or suspension of permit

(a) The sheriff of the county where the permit was issued or the sheriff of the county where the person resides may revoke a permit subsequent to a hearing for any of the following reasons:

(1) Fraud or intentional and material misrepresentation in the obtaining of a permit.

(2) Misuse of a permit, including lending or giving a permit or a duplicate permit to another person, materially altering a permit, or using a permit with the intent to unlawfully cause harm to a person or property. It shall not be considered misuse of a permit to provide a duplicate of the permit to a vender for record-keeping purposes.

(3) The doing of an act or existence of a condition which would have been grounds for the denial of the permit by the sheriff.

(4) The violation of any of the terms of this Article.

(5) Repealed by Session Laws 2013-369, s. 20, effective October 1, 2013.

A permittee may appeal the revocation, or nonrenewal of a permit by petitioning a district court judge of the district in which the applicant resides. The determination by the court, on appeal, shall be upon the facts, the law, and the reasonableness of the sheriff's refusal.

(a1) The sheriff of the county where the permit was issued or the sheriff of the county where the person resides shall revoke a permit of any permittee who is adjudicated guilty of or receives a prayer for judgment continued for a crime which would have disqualified the permittee from initially receiving a permit. Upon determining that a permit should be revoked pursuant to this subsection, the sheriff shall provide written notice to the permittee, pursuant to the provisions of G.S. 1A-1, Rule 4(j), that the permit is revoked upon the service of the notice. The notice shall provide the permittee with information on the process to appeal the revocation.

Upon receipt of the written notice of revocation, the permittee shall surrender the permit to the sheriff. Any law enforcement officer serving the notice is authorized to take immediate possession of the permit from the permittee. If the notice is served by means other than by a law enforcement officer, the permittee shall surrender the permit to the sheriff no later than 48 hours after service of the notice.

A permittee may appeal the revocation of a permit pursuant to this subsection by petitioning a district court judge of the district in which the permittee resides. The determination by the court, on appeal, shall be limited to whether the permittee was adjudicated guilty of or received a prayer for judgment continued for a crime which would have disqualified the permittee from initially receiving a permit. Revocation of the permit is not stayed pending appeal.

(b) The court may suspend a permit as part of and for the duration of any orders permitted under Chapter 50B of the General Statutes.

History.
1995, c. 398, s. 1; 2011-268, s. 20; 2013-369, s. 20

§ 14-415.19. Fees

(a) The permit fees assessed under this Article are payable to the sheriff. The sheriff shall transmit the proceeds of these fees to the county finance officer to be remitted or credited by the county finance officer in accordance with the provisions of this section. Except as otherwise provided by this section, the permit fees are as follows:

Application fee......................$ 80.00
Renewal fee........................$ 75.00
Duplicate permit fee...............$ 15.00

The county finance officer shall remit forty-five dollars ($ 45.00) of each new application fee and forty dollars ($ 40.00) of each renewal fee assessed under this subsection to the North Carolina Department of Public Safety for the costs of State and federal criminal record checks performed in connection with processing applications and for the implementation of the provisions of this Article. The remaining thirty-five dollars ($ 35.00) of each application or renewal fee shall be used by the sheriff to pay the costs of administering this Article and for other law enforcement purposes. The county shall expend the restricted funds for these purposes only.

(a1) The permit fees for a retired sworn law enforcement officer who provides the information required by subdivisions (1) and (2) of this subsection to the sheriff, in addition to any other information required under this Article, are as follows:

Application fee........................$ 45.00
Renewal fee..........................$ 40.00

(1) A copy of the officer's letter of retirement from either the North Carolina Teachers' and State Employees' Retirement System or the North Carolina Local Governmental Employees' Retirement System.

(2) Written documentation from the head of the agency where the person was previously employed indicating that the person was neither involuntarily terminated nor under administrative or criminal investigation within six months of retirement.

The county finance officer shall remit the proceeds of the fees assessed under this subsection to the North Carolina Department of Public Safety to cover the cost of performing the State and federal criminal record checks performed in connection with processing applications and for the implementation of the provisions of this Article.

(b) An additional fee, not to exceed ten dollars ($ 10.00), shall be collected by the sheriff from an applicant for a permit to pay for the costs of processing the applicant's fingerprints, if fingerprints were required to be taken. This fee shall be retained by the sheriff.

History.
1995, c. 398, s. 1; c. 507, s. 22.1(a); 1997-470, s. 1; 2000-140, s. 103; 2000-191, s. 2; 2003-379, s. 1; 2014-100, s. 17.1(o)

§ 14-415.20. No liability of sheriff

A sheriff who issues or refuses to issue a permit to carry a concealed handgun under this Article shall not incur any civil or criminal liability as the result of the performance of the sheriff's duties under this Article.

History.

1995, c. 398, s. 1

§ 14-415.21. Violations of this Article punishable as an infraction

(a) A person who has been issued a valid permit who is found to be carrying a concealed handgun without the permit in the person's possession or who fails to disclose to any law enforcement officer that the person holds a valid permit and is carrying a concealed handgun, as required by G.S. 14-415.11, shall be guilty of an infraction and shall be punished in accordance with G.S. 14-3.1. Any person who has been issued a valid permit who is found to be carrying a concealed handgun in violation of G.S. 14-415.11(c)(8) shall be guilty of an infraction and may be required to pay a fine of up to five hundred dollars ($ 500.00). In lieu of paying a fine the person may surrender the permit.

(a1) A person who has been issued a valid permit who is found to be carrying a concealed handgun in violation of subsection (c2) of G.S. 14-415.11 shall be guilty of a Class 1 misdemeanor.

(b) A person who violates the provisions of this Article other than as set forth in subsection (a) or (a1) of this section is guilty of a Class 2 misdemeanor.

History.

1995, c. 398, s. 1; 2011-268, s. 21(a); 2013-369, s. 16; 2015-195, s. 9

§ 14-415.22. Construction of Article

This Article shall not be construed to require a person who may carry a concealed handgun under the provisions of G.S. 14-269(b) to obtain a concealed handgun permit. The provisions of this Article shall not apply to a person who may lawfully carry a concealed weapon or handgun pursuant to G.S. 14-269(b). A person who may lawfully carry a concealed weapon or handgun pursuant to G.S. 14-269(b) shall not be prohibited from carrying the concealed weapon or handgun on property on which a notice is posted prohibiting the carrying of a concealed handgun, unless otherwise prohibited by statute.

History.

1995, c. 398, s. 1; 1997-238, s. 5

§ 14-415.23. Statewide uniformity

(a) It is the intent of the General Assembly to prescribe a uniform system for the regulation of legally carrying a concealed handgun. To insure uniformity, no political subdivisions, boards, or agencies of the State nor any county,

city, municipality, municipal corporation, town, township, village, nor any department or agency thereof, may enact ordinances, rules, or regulations concerning legally carrying a concealed handgun. A unit of local government may adopt an ordinance to permit the posting of a prohibition against carrying a concealed handgun, in accordance with G.S. 14-415.11(c), on local government buildings and their appurtenant premises.

(b) A unit of local government may adopt an ordinance to prohibit, by posting, the carrying of a concealed handgun on municipal and county recreational facilities that are specifically identified by the unit of local government. If a unit of local government adopts such an ordinance with regard to recreational facilities, then the concealed handgun permittee may, nevertheless, secure the handgun in a locked vehicle within the trunk, glove box, or other enclosed compartment or area within or on the motor vehicle.

(c) For purposes of this section, the term "recreational facilities" includes only the following:

(1) An athletic field, including any appurtenant facilities such as restrooms, during an organized athletic event if the field had been scheduled for use with the municipality or county office responsible for operation of the park or recreational area.

(2) A swimming pool, including any appurtenant facilities used for dressing, storage of personal items, or other uses relating to the swimming pool.

(3) A facility used for athletic events, including, but not limited to, a gymnasium.

(d) For the purposes of this section, the term "recreational facilities" does not include any greenway, designated biking or walking path, an area that is customarily used as a walkway or bike path although not specifically designated for such use, open areas or fields where athletic events may occur unless the area qualifies as an "athletic field" pursuant to subdivision (1) of subsection (c) of this section, and any other area that is not specifically described in subsection (c) of this section.

(e) A person adversely affected by any ordinance, rule, or regulation promulgated or caused to be enforced by any unit of local government in violation of this section may bring an action for declaratory and injunctive relief and for actual damages arising from the violation. The court shall award the prevailing party in an action brought under this subsection reasonable attorneys' fees and court costs as authorized by law.

History.

1995, c. 398, s. 1; 2011-268, s. 21(b); 2013-369, s. 6; 2015-195, s. 15

§ 14-415.24. Reciprocity; out-of-state handgun permits

(a) A valid concealed handgun permit or license issued by another state is valid in North Carolina.

(b) Repealed by Session Laws 2011-268, s. 22(a), effective December 1, 2011.

(c) Every 12 months after the effective date of this subsection, the Department of Justice shall make written inquiry of the concealed handgun permitting authorities in each other state as to: (i) whether a North Carolina resident may carry a concealed handgun in their state based upon having a valid North Carolina concealed handgun permit and (ii) whether a North Carolina resident may apply for a concealed handgun permit in that state based upon having a valid North Carolina concealed handgun permit. The Department of Justice shall attempt to secure from each state permission for North Carolina residents who hold a valid North Carolina concealed handgun permit to carry a concealed handgun in that state, either on the basis of the North Carolina permit or on the basis that the North Carolina permit is sufficient to permit the issuance of a similar license or permit by the other state.

History.

2003-199, s. 1; 2011-268, s. 22(a)

§ 14-415.25. Exemption from permit requirement

Law enforcement officers and qualified retired law enforcement officers authorized by federal law to carry a concealed handgun pursuant to section 926B or 926C of Title 18 of the United States Code, who are in compliance with the requirements of those sections, are exempt from obtaining the permit described in G.S. 14-415.11.

History.

2007-427, s. 3

§ 14-415.26. Certification of qualified retired law enforcement officers

(a) In lieu of obtaining a permit under this Article, a qualified retired law enforcement officer may apply to the North Carolina Criminal Justice Education and Training Standards Commission for certification. The application shall include all of the following:

(1) Verification of completion of the firearms qualification criteria established by the Commission.

(2) Photographic identification indicating retirement status issued by the agency from which the applicant retired from service.

(3) Any other application information required by the Commission.

(b) The Commission shall include with the certification a notice of the limitations applicable under federal or State law to the concealed carry of firearms in this State. The failure to receive a notification under this subsection shall not be a defense to any offense or violation of applicable State or federal laws.

(b1) The Commission shall coordinate with local and State law enforcement officers and with the community college system to provide multiple firearms qualification sites throughout the State where a qualified retired law enforcement officer may satisfy the firearms qualification criteria required for certification under this section.

(c) The Commission shall not incur any civil or criminal liability as the result of the performance of its duties under this section.

(d) It shall be unlawful for an applicant, or any person assisting an applicant, to make a willful and intentional misrepresentation on any form or application submitted to the Commission. A violation of this subsection shall be a Class 2 misdemeanor, and shall result in the immediate revocation of any certification issued by the Commission. A person convicted under this subsection shall be ineligible for certification under this section, or from obtaining a concealed carry permit under State law.

(e) This section shall not exempt any individual engaged in the private protective services profession in this State from fulfilling the registration and training requirements in Chapter 74C of the General Statutes.

History.

2007-427, s. 4; 2009-546, s. 1

§ 14-415.27. Expanded permit scope for certain persons

Notwithstanding G.S. 14-415.11(c), any of the following persons who has a concealed handgun permit issued pursuant to this Article or that is considered valid under G.S. 14-415.24 is not subject to the area prohibitions set out in G.S. 14-415.11(c) and may carry a concealed handgun in the areas listed in G.S. 14-415.11(c) unless otherwise prohibited by federal law:

(1) A district attorney.

(2) An assistant district attorney.

(3) An investigator employed by the office of a district attorney.

(4) A North Carolina district or superior court judge.

(5) A magistrate.

(6) A person who is elected and serving as a clerk of court.

(7) A person who is elected and serving as a register of deeds.

(8) A person employed by the Department of Public Safety who has been designated in writing by the Secretary of the Department and who has in the person's possession written proof of the designation.

(9) A North Carolina administrative law judge.

History.
2011-268, s. 22(b); 2011-326, s. 21; 2013-369, s. 22; 2015-195, s. 1(c)

ARTICLE 55
REGULATION OF CERTAIN REPTILES

§ 14-416. Mishandling of certain reptiles declared public nuisance and criminal offense

The intentional or negligent exposure of other human beings to unsafe contact with venomous reptiles, large constricting snakes, or crocodilians is essentially dangerous and injurious and detrimental to public health, safety and welfare, and is therefore declared to be a public nuisance and a criminal offense, to be abated and punished as provided in this Article.

History.
1949, c. 1084, s. 1; 2009-344, s. 1

§ 14-417. Regulation of ownership or use of venomous reptiles

(a) It shall be unlawful for any person to own, possess, use, transport, or traffic in any venomous reptile that is not housed in a sturdy and secure enclosure. Enclosures shall be designed to be escape-proof, bite-proof, and have an operable lock.

(b) Each enclosure shall be clearly and visibly labeled "Venomous Reptile Inside" with scientific name, common name, appropriate antivenin, and owner's identifying information noted on the container. A written bite protocol that includes emergency contact information, local animal control office, the name and location of suitable antivenin, first aid procedures, and treatment guidelines, as well as an escape recovery plan must be within sight of permanent housing, and a copy must accompany the transport of any venomous reptile.

(c) In the event of an escape of a venomous reptile, the owner or possessor of the venomous reptile shall immediately notify local law enforcement.

History.
1949, c. 1084, s. 2; 2009-344, s. 1; 2013-413, s. 38(a); 2014-115, s. 17; 2019-204, s. 10(a)

§ 14-417.1. Regulation of ownership or use of large constricting snakes

(a) As used in this Article, large constricting snakes shall mean: Reticulated Python, Python reticulatus; Burmese Python, Python molurus; African Rock Python, Python sebae; Amethystine Python, Morelia amethistina; and Green Anaconda, Eunectes murinus; or any of their subspecies or hybrids.

(b) It shall be unlawful for any person to own, possess, use, transport, or traffic in any of the large constricting snakes that are not housed in a sturdy and secure enclosure. Enclosures shall be designed to be escape-proof and shall have an operable lock.

(c) Each enclosure shall be labeled clearly and visibly with the scientific name, common name, number of specimens, and owner's identifying information. A written safety protocol and escape recovery plan shall be within sight of permanent housing, and a copy shall accompany the transport of any of the large constricting snakes. The safety protocol shall include emergency contact information, identification of the local animal control office, and first aid procedures.

(d) In the event of an escape of a large constricting snake, the owner or possessor shall immediately notify local law enforcement.

History.
2009-344, s. 1; 2019-204, s. 10(b)

§ 14-417.2. Regulation of ownership or use of crocodilians

(a) All crocodilians, excluding the American alligator, shall be regulated under this Article. It shall be unlawful for any person to own, possess, use, transport, or traffic in any crocodilian that is not housed in a sturdy and secure enclosure. Permanent enclosures shall be designed to be escape-proof and have a fence of sufficient strength to prevent contact between an observer and the crocodilian and shall have an operable lock. Transport containers shall be designed to be escape-proof and shall be locked.

(b) A written safety protocol and escape recovery plan shall be within sight of permanent housing, and a copy must accompany the transport of any crocodilian.

(c) In the event of the escape of a crocodilian, the owner or possessor shall immediately notify local law enforcement.

History.
2009-344, s. 1; 2019-204, s. 10(c)

Chapter 14

§ 14-418. Prohibited handling of reptiles or suggesting or inducing others to handle

(a) It shall be unlawful for any person to handle any reptile regulated under this Article in a manner that intentionally or negligently exposes another person to unsafe contact with the reptile.

(b) It shall be unlawful for any person to intentionally or negligently suggest, entice, invite, challenge, intimidate, exhort or otherwise induce or aid any person to handle or expose himself in an unsafe manner to any reptile regulated under this Article.

(c) Safe and responsible handling of reptiles for purposes of animal husbandry, exhibition, training, transport, and education is permitted under this section.

History.
1949, c. 1084, s. 3; 2009-344, s. 1

§ 14-419. Investigation of suspected violations; seizure and examination of reptiles; disposition of reptiles

(a) In any case in which a law-enforcement officer or animal control officer has probable cause to believe that any of the provisions of this Article have been or are about to be violated, the officer is authorized and empowered to immediately investigate the violation or impending violation and to consult with representatives of the North Carolina Museum of Natural Sciences or the North CarolinaZoological Park or a designated representative of the North Carolina Department of Natural and Cultural Resources to identify the species, assist with determining interim disposition, and recommend appropriate and safe methods to handle and seize the reptile or reptiles involved. In the case of escape, or if an officer, with probable cause to believe that reptile is being owned, possessed, used, transported, or trafficked in violation of this Article, determines that there is an immediate risk to officer safety or public safety, the officer shall not be required to consult with representatives as provided by this subsection and may kill the reptile.

(b) If, based on available information, the officer, the Museum, the Zoological Park or a designated representative of the Department of Natural and Cultural Resources finds that a seized reptile is a venomous reptile, large constricting snake, or crocodilian regulated under this Article, the Museum or the Zoological Park or a designated representative of the Department of Natural and Cultural Resources shall assist the officer with determining an interim disposition of the reptile in a manner consistent with the safety of the public, until a final disposition is determined by a court of competent jurisdiction.

In the case of a venomous reptile for which antivenin approved by the United States Food and Drug Administration is not readily available, the reptile may be euthanized unless the species is protected under the federal Endangered Species Act of 1973. Where euthanasia is determined to be the appropriate interim disposition, or where a reptile seized pursuant to this Article dies of natural or unintended causes, the parties involved shall not be liable to the reptile's owner.

(b1) Upon conviction of any offense contained in this Article, the court shall order a final disposition of the confiscated venomous reptiles, large constricting snakes, or crocodilians, which may include the transfer of title to the State of North Carolina and shall include reimbursement by the owner for the expenses incurred in the seizure, delivery, and storage thereof.

(c) If the reptile is not a venomous reptile, large constricting snake, or crocodilian regulated under this Article, and either no criminal citations, warrants, or indictments are initiated against the owner in connection with the reptile within 10 days of initial seizure, or a court of law determines that the reptile is not being owned, possessed, used, transported, or trafficked in violation of this Article, then it shall be the duty of the law enforcement officer to return the reptile or reptiles to the person from whom they were seized within 15 days of the seizure.

History.
1949, c. 1084, s. 4; 1981, c. 203, s. 1; 1993, c. 561, s. 116(g); 2009-344, s. 1; 2013-413, s. 38(b); 2014-115, s. 17; 2014-120, s. 39; 2017-10, s. 3.17(a); 2019-204, s. 10(d)

§ 14-420. Arrest of persons violating provisions of Article

If an examination made by the North Carolina State Museum of Natural Sciences or the North CarolinaZoological Park or their designated representatives conducted pursuant to this Article shows that the reptile is a venomous reptile, large constricting snake, or crocodilian subject to this Article, it shall be the duty of the officer making the seizure with probable cause to believe that the reptile is being owned, possessed, used, transported, or trafficked in violation of this Article, to arrest all persons violating any of the provisions of this Article.

History.
1949, c. 1084, s. 5; 1981, c. 203, s. 2; 1993, c. 561, s. 116(h); 2009-344, s. 1.

§ 14-421. Exemptions from provisions of Article

This Article shall not apply to the possession, exhibition, or handling of reptiles by employees or agents of duly constituted veterinarians, zoos, serpentariums, museums, laboratories, educational or scientific institutions, public and private, in the course of their educational or scientific work, or Wildlife Damage Control Agents in the course of the work for which they are approved by the Wildlife Resources Commission.

History.
1949, c. 1084, s. 6; 2009-344, s. 1

§ 14-422. Criminal penalties and civil remedies for violation

(a) Any person violating any of the provisions of this Article shall be guilty of a Class 2 misdemeanor.

(b) If any person, other than the owner of a venomous reptile, large constricting snake, or crocodilian, the owner's agent, employee, or a member of the owner's immediate family, suffers a life threatening injury or is killed as the result of a violation of this Article, the owner of the reptile shall be guilty of a Class A1 misdemeanor. This subsection shall not apply to violations that result from incidents that could not have been prevented or avoided by the owner's exercise of due care or foresight, such as natural disasters or other acts of God, or in the case of thefts of the reptile from the owner.

(c) Any person intentionally releasing into the wild a nonnative venomous reptile, a large constricting snake, or a crocodilian shall be guilty of a Class A1 misdemeanor.

(d) Violations of this Article as set forth in subsections (b) or (c) of this section shall constitute wanton conduct within the meaning of G.S. 1D-5(7) and subject the violator to punitive damages in any civil action that may be filed as a result of the violator's actions.

History.
1949, c. 1084, s. 7; 1969, c. 1224, s. 3; 1993, c. 539, s. 289; 1994, Ex. Sess., c. 24, s. 14(c); 2009-344, s. 1

ARTICLE 56
DEBT ADJUSTING

§ 14-423. Definitions

As used in this Article, the following definitions apply:

(1) "Debt adjuster" means a person who engages in, attempts to engage in, or offers to engage in the practice or business of debt adjusting.

(2) "Debt adjusting" means entering into or making a contract, express or implied, with a particular debtor whereby the debtor agrees to pay a certain amount of money periodically to the person engaged in the debt adjusting business and that person, for consideration, agrees to distribute, or distributes the same among certain specified creditors in accordance with a plan agreed upon. Debt adjusting includes the business or practice of any person who holds himself out as acting or offering or attempting to act for consideration as an intermediary between a debtor and his creditors for the purpose of settling, compounding, or in any way altering the terms of payment of any debt of a debtor, and to that end receives money or other property from the debtor, or on behalf of the debtor, for the payment to, or distribution among, the creditors of the debtor. Debt adjusting also includes the business or practice of debt settlement or foreclosure assistance whereby any person holds himself or herself out as acting for consideration as an intermediary between a debtor and the debtor's creditors for the purpose of reducing, settling, or altering the terms of the payment of any debt of the debtor, whether or not the person distributes the debtor's funds or property among the creditors, and receives a fee or other consideration for reducing, settling, or altering the terms of the payment of the debt in advance of the debt settlement having been completed or in advance of all the services agreed to having been rendered in full.

(3) "Debtor" means an individual who resides in North Carolina, and includes two or more individuals who are jointly and severally, or jointly or severally, indebted to a creditor or creditors.

(3a) "Nominal consideration" means a fee or a contribution to cover the cost of administering a debt management plan not to exceed forty dollars ($ 40.00) for origination or setup of the debt management plan and ten percent (10%) of the monthly payment disbursed under the debt management plan, not to exceed forty dollars ($ 40.00) per month.

(4) "Person" means an individual, firm, partnership, limited partnership, corporation, or association.

History.
1963, c. 394, s. 1; 2005-408, s. 2; 2007-79, s. 1

§ 14-424. Engaging, etc., in business of debt adjusting a misdemeanor

If any person shall engage in, or offer to or attempt to, engage in the business or practice of debt adjusting, or if any person shall hereafter act, offer to act, or attempt to act as a debt adjuster, he shall be guilty of a Class 2 misdemeanor.

History.

1963, c. 394, s. 2; 1969, c. 1224, s. 6; 1993, c. 539, s. 290; 1994, Ex. Sess., c. 24, s. 14(c)

§ 14-425. Enjoining practice of debt adjusting; appointment of receiver for money and property employed

The superior court shall have jurisdiction, in an action brought in the name of the State by the Attorney General or the district attorney of the prosecutorial district as defined in G.S. 7A-60, to enjoin, as an unfair or deceptive trade practice, the continuation of any debt adjusting business or the offering of any debt adjusting services. The Attorney General or the district attorney who brings an action under this section may appoint a receiver for the property and money employed in the transaction of business by such person as a debt adjuster, to ensure, so far as may be possible, the return to debtors of so much of their money and property as has been received by the debt adjuster, and has not been paid to the creditors of the debtors. The court may also assess civil penalties under G.S. 75-15.2 and award attorneys' fees to the State under G.S. 75-16.1.

History.

1963, c. 394, s. 3; 1973, c. 47, s. 2; 1987 (Reg. Sess., 1998), c. 1037, s. 49; 2005-408, s. 3; 2007-79, s. 1

§ 14-426. Certain persons and transactions not deemed debt adjusters or debt adjustment

The following individuals or transactions shall not be deemed debt adjusters or as being engaged in the business or practice of debt adjusting:

(1) Any person or individual who is a regular full-time employee of a debtor, and who acts as an adjuster of his employer's debts.

(2) Any person or individual acting pursuant to any order or judgment of a court, or pursuant to authority conferred by any law of this State or of the United States.

(3) Any person who is a creditor of the debtor, or an agent of one or more creditors of the debtor, and whose services in adjusting the debtor's debts are rendered without cost to the debtor.

(4) Any person who at the request of a debtor, arranges for or makes a loan to the debtor, and who, at the authorization of the debtor, acts as an adjuster of the debtor's debts in the disbursement of the proceeds of the loan, without compensation for the services rendered in adjusting such debts.

(5) An intermittent or casual adjustment of a debtor's debts, for compensation, by an individual or person who is not a debt adjuster or who is not engaged in the business or practice of debt adjusting, and who does not hold himself out as being regularly engaged in debt adjusting.

(6) An attorney-at-law licensed to practice in this State who is not employed by a debt adjuster.

(7) An organization that provides credit counseling, education, and debt management services to debtors if the organization also does all of the following:

a. Provides individualized credit counseling and budgeting assistance to the debtor without charge prior to the debtor's enrollment in a debt management plan provided by the organization.

b. Determines that the debtor has the financial ability to make payments to complete the debt management plan and that the plan is suitable for the debtor.

c. Disburses the debtor's funds to creditors pursuant to a debt management plan that the debtor has paid for with no more than nominal consideration and has agreed to in writing.

d. Provides to the debtor, periodically and on no less than a quarterly basis, an individualized accounting for the most recent period of all of the debtor's payments and disbursements under the debt management plan and all charges paid by the debtor.

e. Does not directly or indirectly require the debtor to purchase other services or materials as a condition to participating in the debt management plan.

f. Does not receive a payment, commission, or other benefit for referring the debtor to a provider of services.

g. Is accredited by an accrediting organization that the Commissioner of Banks approves as being independent and nationally recognized for providing accreditation to organizations that provide credit counseling and debt management services.

History.

1963, c. 394, s. 4; 2005-408, s. 1; 2007-79, s. 1

ARTICLE 57
USE, SALE, ETC., OF GLUES RELEASING TOXIC VAPORS

§§ 14-427 through 14-431

Repealed by Session Laws 1969, c. 970, s. 11.

ARTICLE 58
RECORDS, TAPES
AND OTHER RECORDED
DEVICES

§ 14-432. Definitions

The following definitions apply in this Article:

(1) "Article" means the tangible medium upon which sounds or images are recorded or otherwise stored, including any original phonograph record, disc, tape, audio or video cassette, wire, film, or other medium now known or later developed on which sounds or images, or both, can be recorded or otherwise stored, or any copy or reproduction which duplicates, in whole or in part, the original.

(2) "Fixed" means that the work has been recorded in a tangible medium of expression, by or under the authority of the author, and its embodiment is sufficiently permanent or stable to permit it to be perceived, reproduced, or otherwise communicated for a period of more than transitory duration. A work consisting of sounds or images, or both, that are being transmitted is "fixed" for the purposes of this section if a fixation of the work is being made simultaneously with its transmission.

(3) "Owner" means the person who owns the sounds fixed in any master phonograph record, master disc, master tape, master film, or other device used for reproducing recorded sounds on phonograph records, discs, tapes, films, or other articles on which sound is or can be recorded and from which the transferred sounds are directly or indirectly derived, or the person who owns the rights to record or authorize the recording of a live performance.

History.

1973, c. 1279, s. 1; 1989, c. 589, s. 1; 2003-159, s. 1

§ 14-433. Recording of live performances or recorded sounds and distribution, etc., of such recordings unlawful in certain circumstances

(a) It shall be unlawful for any person to:

(1) Knowingly transfer or cause to be transferred, directly or indirectly by any means, any sounds recorded on a phonograph record, disc, wire, tape, film or other article on which sounds are recorded, with the intent to sell or cause to be sold, or to use or cause to be used for profit through public performance, such article on which sounds are so transferred, without consent of the, owner.

(2) Manufacture, distribute, wholesale or transport any article for profit, or possess for these purposes with the knowledge that the sounds recorded on the article were transferred in violation of subdivision (a)(1) of this section.

(3) Recodified as G.S. 14-433(a1)(1) by Session Laws 2003-159, s. 2.

(4) Recodified as G.S. 14-433(a1)(2) by Session Laws 2003-159, s. 2.

(a1) It shall be unlawful for any person to:

(1) Knowingly transfer or cause to be transferred, directly or indirectly by any means, any sounds at a live performance, with the intent to sell or cause to be sold, or to use or cause to be used for profit through public performance, the article on which sounds are so transferred, without consent of the owner.

(2) Manufacture, distribute, transport or wholesale any article for profit, or possess for those purposes with the knowledge that the sounds recorded on the article were transferred in violation of subdivision (a1)(1) of this section.

(b) Subdivisions (a)(1) and (a)(2) of this section shall apply only to sound recordings that were initially fixed prior to February 15, 1972. Federal copyright law, 17 U.S.C. § 101 et seq., preempts State prosecution of the acts described in subdivisions (a)(1) and (a)(2) with respect to sound recordings initially fixed on or after February 15, 1972.

(c) This section shall not apply to any person engaged in webcasting or radio or television broadcasting who transfers, or causes to be transferred, any such sounds other than from the sound track of a motion picture intended for, or in connection with webcast, broadcast or telecast transmission or related uses, or for archival purposes. An Internet service provider who is solely providing a conduit for access to the Internet, shall not be deemed to be using, or causing to be used, recordings that may be transferred over the Internet by third parties in violation of this Article.

History.

1973, c. 1279, s. 1; 1989, c. 589, s. 1; 2003-159, s. 2

§ 14-434. Retailing, etc., of certain recorded devices unlawful

It shall be unlawful for any person to knowingly retail, advertise or offer for sale or resale, sell or resell or cause the sale or resale, rent or cause to rent, or possess for any of these purposes any article that has been produced, manufactured, distributed, or acquired at wholesale in violation of any provision of this Chapter.

History.
1973, c. 1279, s. 1, 1989, c. 589, s. 1

§ 14-435. Recorded devices to show true name and address of manufacturer

(a) A person is guilty of failure to disclose the origin of an article when, for commercial advantage or private financial gain, the person knowingly advertises or offers for sale or resale, or sells or resells, or causes the rental, sale, or resale, or rents, or manufactures, or possesses for these purposes, any article, the packaging, cover, box, jacket, or label of which does not clearly and conspicuously disclose the actual true name and address of the manufacturer of the article and the name of the actual author, artist, performer, producer, programmer, or group.

(b) This section does not require the original manufacturer or authorized licensees of software producers to disclose the contributing authors or programmers. As used in this section, the term "manufacturer" shall not include the manufacturer of the article's packaging, cover, box, jacket, or label itself.

History.
1973, c. 1279, s. 1; 1989, c. 589, s. 1; 2003-159, s. 3

§ 14-436. Recorded devices; civil action for damages

Any owner of an article as defined in this Article whose work is allegedly the subject of a violation of G.S. 14-433 or G.S. 14-434, shall have a cause of action in the courts of this State for all damages resulting from the violation, including actual, compensatory and incidental damages.

History.
1973, c. 1279, s. 1; 1989, c. 589, s. 1; 2003-159, s. 4

§ 14-437. Violation of Article; penalties

(a) Every individual act in contravention of the provisions of this Article shall constitute a Class 1 misdemeanor, except that the offense is a Class I felony with a maximum fine of one hundred fifty thousand dollars ($ 150,000) if (i) the offense involves at least 100 unauthorized articles during any 180-day period, or (ii) is a third or subsequent conviction for an offense that involves at least 26 unauthorized articles during any 180-day period.

(b) If a person is convicted of any violation under this Article, the court, in its judgment

of conviction, shall order the forfeiture and destruction or other disposition of:

(1) All infringing articles; and

(2) All implements, devices and equipment used or intended to be used in the manufacture of the infringing articles.

History.
1973, c. 1279, s. 1; 1989, c. 589, s. 1; 1993, c. 539, ss. 291, 1246; 1994, Ex. Sess., c. 24, s. 14(c); 2003-159, s. 5

§§ 14-438 through 14-440

Reserved for future codification purposes.

ARTICLE 58A.00
AUDIOVISUAL
RECORDINGS

§ 14-440.1. Unlawful operation of an audiovisual recording device

(a) **Definitions.** -- The following definitions apply to this section:

(1) "Audiovisual recording device" means a digital or analog video camera, or any other technology or device now known or later developed, capable of recording, copying, or transmitting a motion picture, or any part thereof, regardless of whether audiovisual recording is the sole or primary purpose of the device.

(2) "Motion picture theater" means a movie theater, screening room, or other venue that is being utilized primarily for the exhibition of a motion picture at the time of the offense.

(a1) **Misdemeanor Offense.** -- Any person who knowingly operates or attempts to operate a device capable of functioning as a digital or analog photographic camera for the purpose of recording, copying, or transmitting a part of a motion picture not greater than one image, without the written consent of the motion picture theater owner shall be guilty of a Class 1 misdemeanor.

(b) **Felony Offense.** -- Any person who knowingly operates or attempts to operate an audiovisual recording device in a motion picture theater to transmit, record, or otherwise make a copy of a motion picture, or any part thereof, without the written consent of the motion picture theater owner shall be guilty of a felony, punishable as provided in subsection (c) of this section.

(c) **Penalty.** -- A violation of subsection (b) of this section is punishable as follows:

(1) Unless the conduct is covered under some other provision of law providing greater punishment, any person convicted

of a violation of subsection (b) of this section is guilty of:

    a. A Class I felony, if the violation is a first offense under this section, with a minimum fine of two thousand five hundred dollars ($ 2,500).

    b. A Class I felony, if the violation is a second or subsequent offense under this section, with a minimum fine of five thousand dollars ($ 5,000).

(2) If a person is convicted of a violation of subsection (b) of this section, the court, in its judgment of conviction, shall order the forfeiture and destruction or other disposition of the following:

    a. All unauthorized copies of motion pictures or other audiovisual works, or any parts thereof.

    b. All implements, devices, and equipment used or intended to be used in connection with the offense.

(d) **Immunity of Certain Persons.** -- The owner or lessee of a motion picture theater, or the authorized agent or employee of the owner or lessee, who detains any person shall not be held civilly liable for claims arising out of such detention, when the detention is upon the premises of the motion picture theater or in a reasonable proximity thereto, is in a reasonable manner for a reasonable length of time, and, if in detaining the person, the owner, lessee, agent, or employee had, at the time of the detention, probable cause to believe that the person committed an offense under this section. If the person being detained by the owner, lessee, agent, or employee is a minor under the age of 18 years, the owner, lessee, agent, or employee shall call or notify, or make a reasonable effort to call or notify, the parent or guardian of the minor during the period of detention. An owner, lessee, agent, or employee who makes a reasonable effort to call or notify the parent or guardian of the minor shall not be held civilly liable for failing to notify the parent or guardian of the minor.

(e) **Authorized Activities.** -- This section does not prevent any lawfully authorized investigative, protective, law enforcement, or intelligence gathering employee or agent of a local, State, or federal government from operating any audiovisual recording device in a motion picture theater, as part of lawfully authorized investigative, protective, law enforcement, or intelligence gathering activities.

History.
2005-301, s. 1; 2007-463, s. 1; 2007-484, s. 43.7J

§§ 14-441, 14-442

Reserved for future codification purposes.

ARTICLE 59
PUBLIC INTOXICATION

§ 14-443. Definitions

As used in this Article:

(1) "Alcoholism" is the state of a person who habitually lacks self-control as to the use of alcoholic beverages, or uses alcoholic beverages to the extent that his health is substantially impaired or endangered or his social or economic function is substantially disrupted; and

(2) "Intoxicated" is the condition of a person whose mental or physical functioning is presently substantially impaired as a result of the use of alcohol; and

(3) A "public place" is a place which is open to the public, whether it is publicly or privately owned.

History.
1977, 2nd Sess., c. 1134, s. 1; 1981, c. 412, s. 4; c. 747, s. 66

§ 14-444. Intoxicated and disruptive in public

(a) It shall be unlawful for any person in a public place to be intoxicated and disruptive in any of the following ways:

(1) Blocking or otherwise interfering with traffic on a highway or public vehicular area, or

(2) Blocking or lying across or otherwise preventing or interfering with access to or passage across a sidewalk or entrance to a building, or

(3) Grabbing, shoving, pushing or fighting others or challenging others to fight, or

(4) Cursing or shouting at or otherwise rudely insulting others, or

(5) Begging for money or other property.

(b) Any person who violates this section shall be guilty of a Class 3 misdemeanor.

History.
1977, 2nd Sess., c. 1134, s. 1; 1993, c. 539, s. 292; 1994, Ex. Sess., c. 24, s. 14(c); 2015-247, s. 3(c)

§ 14-445. Defense of alcoholism

(a) It is a defense to a charge of being intoxicated and disruptive in a public place that the defendant suffers from alcoholism.

(b) The presiding judge at the trial of a defendant charged with being intoxicated and disruptive in public shall consider the defense of alcoholism even though the defendant does not raise the defense, and may request additional information on whether the defendant is suffering from alcoholism.

(c) Whenever any person charged with committing a misdemeanor under G.S. 14-444 enters a plea to the charge, the court may, without entering a judgment, defer further proceedings for up to 15 days to determine whether the person is suffering from alcoholism.

(d) If he believes it will be of value in making his determination, the district court judge may direct an alcoholism court counselor, if available, to conduct a prehearing review of the alleged alcoholic's drinking history in order to gather additional information as to whether the defendant is suffering from alcoholism.

History.
1977, 2nd Sess., c. 1134, s. 1; 1981, c. 519, s. 1

§ 14-446. Disposition of defendant acquitted because of alcoholism

If a defendant is found not guilty of being intoxicated and disruptive in a public place because he suffers from alcoholism, the court in which he was tried may retain jurisdiction over him for up to 15 days to determine whether he is a substance abuser and dangerous to himself or others as provided in G.S. 122C-281. The trial judge may make that determination at the time the defendant is found not guilty or he may require the defendant to return to court for the determination at some later time within the 15-day period.

History.
1977, 2nd Sess., c. 1134, s. 1; 1985, c. 589, s. 6

§ 14-447. No prosecution for public intoxication

(a) No person may be prosecuted solely for being intoxicated in a public place. A person who is intoxicated in a public place and is not disruptive may be assisted as provided in G.S. 122C-301.

(b) If, after arresting a person for being intoxicated and disruptive in a public place, the law-enforcement officer making the arrest determines that the person would benefit from the care of a shelter or health-care facility as provided by G.S. 122C-301, and that he would not likely be disruptive in such a facility, the officer may transport and release the person to the appropriate facility and issue him a citation for the offense of being intoxicated and disruptive in a public place. This authority to arrest and then issue a citation is granted as an exception to the requirements of G.S. 15A-501(2).

History.
1977, 2nd Sess., c. 1134, s. 1; 1981, c. 519, s. 2; 1985, c. 589, s. 7

§§ 14-448 through 14-452

Reserved for future codification purposes.

ARTICLE 60
COMPUTER-RELATED CRIME

§ 14-453. Definitions

As used in this Article, unless the context clearly requires otherwise, the following terms have the meanings specified:

(1) "Access" means to instruct, communicate with, cause input, cause output, cause data processing, or otherwise make use of any resources of a computer, computer system, or computer network.

(1a) "Authorization" means having the consent or permission of the owner, or of the person licensed or authorized by the owner to grant consent or permission to access a computer, computer system, or computer network in a manner not exceeding the consent or permission.

(1b) "Commercial electronic mail" means messages sent and received electronically consisting of commercial advertising material, the principal purpose of which is to promote the for-profit sale or lease of goods or services to the recipient.

(2) "Computer" means an internally programmed, automatic device that performs data processing or telephone switching.

(3) "Computer network" means the interconnection of communication systems with a computer through remote terminals, or a complex consisting of two or more interconnected computers or telephone switching equipment.

(4) "Computer program" means an ordered set of data that are coded instructions or statements that when executed by a computer cause the computer to process data.

(4a) "Computer services" means computer time or services, including data processing services, Internet services, electronic mail services, electronic message services, or information or data stored in connection with any of these services.

(5) "Computer software" means a set of computer programs, procedures and associated documentation concerned with the operation of a computer, computer system, or computer network.

(6) "Computer system" means at least one computer together with a set of related, connected, or unconnected peripheral devices.

(6a) "Data" means a representation of information, facts, knowledge, concepts, or instructions prepared in a formalized or other manner and intended for use in a computer, computer system, or computer network. Data may be embodied in any form including computer printouts, magnetic storage media, optical storage media, and punch cards, or may be stored internally in the memory of a computer.

(6b) "Electronic mail" means the same as the term is defined in G.S. 14-196.3(a) (2).

(6c) "Electronic mail service provider" means any person who (i) is an intermediary in sending or receiving electronic mail and (ii) provides to end users of electronic mail services the ability to send or receive electronic mail.

(7) "Financial instrument" includes any check, draft, money order, certificate of deposit, letter of credit, bill of exchange, credit card or marketable security, or any electronic data processing representation thereof.

(7a) "Government computer" means any computer, computer program, computer system, computer network, or any part thereof, that is owned, operated, or used by any State or local governmental entity.

(7b) "Internet chat room" means a computer service allowing two or more users to communicate with each other in real time.

(7c) "Profile" means (i) a configuration of user data required by a computer so that the user may access programs or services and have the desired functionality on that computer or (ii) a Web site user's personal page or section of a page made up of data, in text or graphical form, which displays significant, unique, or identifying information, including, but not limited to, listing acquaintances, interests, associations, activities, or personal statements.

(8) "Property" includes financial instruments, information, including electronically processed or produced data, and computer software and computer programs in either machine or human readable form, and any other tangible or intangible item of value.

(8a) "Resource" includes peripheral devices, computer software, computer programs, and data, and means to be a part of a computer, computer system, or computer network.

(9) "Services" includes computer time, data processing and storage functions.

(10) "Unsolicited" means not addressed to a recipient with whom the initiator has an existing business or personal relationship and not sent at the request of, or with the express consent of, the recipient.

History.
1979, c. 831, s. 1; 1993 (Reg. Sess., 1994), c. 764, s. 1; 1999-212, s. 2; 2000-125, s. 3; 2002-157, s. 1; 2009-551, s. 2; 2012-149, s. 2

§ 14-453.1. Exceptions

This Article does not apply to or prohibit:

(1) Any terms or conditions in a contract or license related to a computer, computer network, software, computer system, database, or telecommunication device; or

(2) Any software or hardware designed to allow a computer, computer network, software, computer system, database, information, or telecommunication service to operate in the ordinary course of a lawful business or that is designed to allow an owner or authorized holder of information to protect data, information, or rights in it.

History.
2002-157, s. 2

§ 14-453.2. Jurisdiction

Any offense under this Article committed by the use of electronic communication may be deemed to have been committed where the electronic communication was originally sent or where it was originally received in this State. "Electronic communication" means the same as the term is defined in G.S. 14-196.3(a).

History.
2002-157, s. 3

§ 14-454. Accessing computers

(a) It is unlawful to willfully, directly or indirectly, access or cause to be accessed any computer, computer program, computer system, computer network, or any part thereof, for the purpose of:

(1) Devising or executing any scheme or artifice to defraud, unless the object of the scheme or artifice is to obtain educational testing material, a false educational testing score, or a false academic or vocational grade, or

(2) Obtaining property or services other than educational testing material, a false educational testing score, or a false academic or vocational grade for a person, by means of false or fraudulent pretenses, representations or promises.

A violation of this subsection is a Class G felony if the fraudulent scheme or artifice results in damage of more than one thousand dollars ($ 1,000), or if the property or services obtained are worth more than one thousand dollars ($ 1,000). Any other violation of this subsection is a Class 1 misdemeanor.

(b) Any person who willfully and without authorization, directly or indirectly, accesses or causes to be accessed any computer, computer program, computer system, or computer network for any purpose other than those set forth in subsection (a) above, is guilty of a Class 1 misdemeanor.

(c) For the purpose of this section, the phrase "access or cause to be accessed" includes introducing, directly or indirectly, a computer program (including a self-replicating or a self-propagating computer program) into a computer, computer program, computer system, or computer network.

History.
1979, c. 831, s. 1; 1979, 2nd Sess., c. 1316, s. 19; 1981, cc. 63, 179; 1993, c. 539, s. 293; 1994, Ex. Sess., c. 24, s. 14(c); 1993 (Reg. Sess., 1994), c. 764, s. 1; 2000-125, s. 4

§ 14-454.1. Accessing government computers

(a) It is unlawful to willfully, directly or indirectly, access or cause to be accessed any government computer for the purpose of:

(1) Devising or executing any scheme or artifice to defraud, or

(2) Obtaining property or services by means of false or fraudulent pretenses, representations, or promises.

A violation of this subsection is a Class F felony.

(b) Any person who willfully and without authorization, directly or indirectly, accesses or causes to be accessed any government computer for any purpose other than those set forth in subsection (a) of this section is guilty of a Class H felony.

(c) Any person who willfully and without authorization, directly or indirectly, accesses or causes to be accessed any educational testing material or academic or vocational testing scores or grades that are in a government computer is guilty of a Class 1 misdemeanor.

(d) For the purpose of this section the phrase "access or cause to be accessed" includes introducing, directly or indirectly, a computer program (including a self-replicating or a self-propagating computer program) into a computer, computer program, computer system, or computer network.

History.
2002-157, s. 4

§ 14-455. Damaging computers, computer programs, computer systems, computer networks, and resources

(a) It is unlawful to willfully and without authorization alter, damage, or destroy a computer, computer program, computer system, computer network, or any part thereof. A violation of this subsection is a Class G felony if the damage caused by the alteration, damage, or destruction is more than one thousand dollars ($ 1,000). Any other violation of this subsection is a Class 1 misdemeanor.

(a1) It is unlawful to willfully and without authorization alter, damage, or destroy a government computer. A violation of this subsection is a Class F felony.

(b) This section applies to alteration, damage, or destruction effectuated by introducing, directly or indirectly, a computer program (including a self-replicating or a self-propagating computer program) into a computer, computer program, computer system, or computer network.

History.
1979, c. 831, s. 1; 1979, 2nd Sess., c. 1316, s. 20; 1981, cc. 63, 179; 1993, c. 539, s. 294; 1994, Ex. Sess., c. 24, s. 14(c); 1993 (Reg. Sess., 1994), c. 764, s. 1; 1995, c. 509, s. 12; 2000-125, s. 5; 2002-157, s. 5

§ 14-456. Denial of computer services to an authorized user

(a) Any person who willfully and without authorization denies or causes the denial of computer, computer program, computer system, or computer network services to an authorized user of the computer, computer program, computer system, or computer network services is guilty of a Class 1 misdemeanor.

(b) This section also applies to denial of services effectuated by introducing, directly or indirectly, a computer program (including a self-replicating or a self-propagating computer program) into a computer, computer program, computer system, or computer network.

History.
1979, c. 831, s. 1; 1993, c. 539, s. 295; 1994, Ex. Sess., c. 24, s. 14(c); 1993 (Reg. Sess., 1994), c. 764, s. 1; 2000-125, s. 6

§ 14-456.1. Denial of government computer services to an authorized user

(a) Any person who willfully and without authorization denies or causes the denial of government computer services is guilty of a Class H felony. For the purposes of this section, the term "government computer service" means any service provided or performed by a government computer as defined in G.S. 14-454.1.

(b) This section also applies to denial of services effectuated by introducing, directly or indirectly, a computer program (including a self-replicating or a self-propagating computer program) into a computer, computer program, computer system, or computer network.

History.
2002-157, s. 6

§ 14-457. Extortion

Any person who verbally or by a written or printed communication, maliciously threatens to commit an act described in G.S. 14-455 with the intent to extort money or any pecuniary advantage, or with the intent to compel any person to do or refrain from doing any act against his will, is guilty of a Class H felony.

History.
1979, c. 831, s. 1; 1979, 2nd Sess., c. 1316, s. 21; 1981, cc. 63, 179

§ 14-458. Computer trespass; penalty

(a) Except as otherwise made unlawful by this Article, it shall be unlawful for any person to use a computer or computer network without authority and with the intent to do any of the following:

(1) Temporarily or permanently remove, halt, or otherwise disable any computer data, computer programs, or computer software from a computer or computer network.

(2) Cause a computer to malfunction, regardless of how long the malfunction persists.

(3) Alter or erase any computer data, computer programs, or computer software.

(4) Cause physical injury to the property of another.

(5) Make or cause to be made an unauthorized copy, in any form, including, but not limited to, any printed or electronic form of computer data, computer programs, or computer software residing in, communicated by, or produced by a computer or computer network.

(6) Falsely identify with the intent to deceive or defraud the recipient or forge commercial electronic mail transmission information or other routing information in any manner in connection with the transmission of unsolicited bulk commercial electronic mail through or into the computer network of an electronic mail service provider or its subscribers.

For purposes of this subsection, a person is "without authority" when (i) the person has no right or permission of the owner to use a computer, or the person uses a computer in a manner exceeding the right or permission, or (ii) the person uses a computer or computer network, or the computer

services of an electronic mail service provider to transmit unsolicited bulk commercial electronic mail in contravention of the authority granted by or in violation of the policies set by the electronic mail service provider.

(b) Any person who violates this section shall be guilty of computer trespass, which offense shall be punishable as a Class 3 misdemeanor. If there is damage to the property of another and the damage is valued at less than two thousand five hundred dollars ($ 2,500) caused by the person's act in violation of this section, the offense shall be punished as a Class 1 misdemeanor. If there is damage to the property of another valued at two thousand five hundred dollars ($ 2,500) or more caused by the person's act in violation of this section, the offense shall be punished as a Class I felony.

(c) Any person whose property or person is injured by reason of a violation of this section may sue for and recover any damages sustained and the costs of the suit pursuant to G.S. 1-539.2A.

(d) It is not a violation of this section for a person to act pursuant to Chapter 36F of the General Statutes.

History.
1999-212, s. 3; 2000-125, s. 7; 2016-53, s. 2

§ 14-458.1. Cyber-bullying; penalty

(a) Except as otherwise made unlawful by this Article, it shall be unlawful for any person to use a computer or computer network to do any of the following:

(1) With the intent to intimidate or torment a minor:

a. Build a fake profile or Web site;

b. Pose as a minor in:

1. An Internet chat room;

2. An electronic mail message; or

3. An instant message;

c. Follow a minor online or into an Internet chat room; or

d. Post or encourage others to post on the Internet private, personal, or sexual information pertaining to a minor.

(2) With the intent to intimidate or torment a minor or the minor's parent or guardian:

a. Post a real or doctored image of a minor on the Internet;

b. Access, alter, or erase any computer network, computer data, computer program, or computer software, including breaking into a password protected account or stealing or otherwise accessing passwords; or

c. Use a computer system for repeated, continuing, or sustained electronic communications, including electronic mail or other transmissions, to a minor.

(3) Make any statement, whether true or false, intending to immediately provoke, and that is likely to provoke, any third party to stalk or harass a minor.

(4) Copy and disseminate, or cause to be made, an unauthorized copy of any data pertaining to a minor for the purpose of intimidating or tormenting that minor (in any form, including, but not limited to, any printed or electronic form of computer data, computer programs, or computer software residing in, communicated by, or produced by a computer or computer network).

(5) Sign up a minor for a pornographic Internet site with the intent to intimidate or torment the minor.

(6) Without authorization of the minor or the minor's parent or guardian, sign up a minor for electronic mailing lists or to receive junk electronic messages and instant messages, with the intent to intimidate or torment the minor.

(b) Any person who violates this section shall be guilty of cyber-bullying, which offense shall be punishable as a Class 1 misdemeanor if the defendant is 18 years of age or older at the time the offense is committed. If the defendant is under the age of 18 at the time the offense is committed, the offense shall be punishable as a Class 2 misdemeanor.

(c) Whenever any person pleads guilty to or is guilty of an offense under this section, and the offense was committed before the person attained the age of 18 years, the court may, without entering a judgment of guilt and with the consent of the defendant, defer further proceedings and place the defendant on probation upon such reasonable terms and conditions as the court may require. Upon fulfillment of the terms and conditions of the probation provided for in this subsection, the court shall discharge the defendant and dismiss the proceedings against the defendant. Discharge and dismissal under this subsection shall be without court adjudication of guilt and shall not be deemed a conviction for purposes of this section or for purposes of disqualifications or disabilities imposed by law upon conviction of a crime. Upon discharge and dismissal pursuant to this subsection, the person may apply for an order to expunge the complete record of the proceedings resulting in the dismissal and discharge, pursuant to the procedures and requirements set forth in G.S. 15A-146.

History.
2009-551, s. 1; 2012-149, s. 3

§ 14-458.2. Cyber-bullying of school employee by student; penalty

(a) The following definitions apply in this section:

(1) **School employee.** -- The term means any of the following:

a. An employee of a local board of education, a charter school authorized under G.S. 115C-218.5, a regional school created under G.S. 115C-238.62, a laboratory school created under G.S. 116-239.7, or a nonpublic school which has filed intent to operate under Part 1 or Part 2 of Article 39 of Chapter 115C of the General Statutes.

b. An independent contractor or an employee of an independent contractor of a local board of education, a charter school authorized under G.S. 115C-218.5, a regional school created under G.S. 115C-238.62, a laboratory school created under G.S. 116-239.7, or a nonpublic school which has filed intent to operate under Part 1 or Part 2 of Article 39 of Chapter 115C of the General Statutes, if the independent contractor carries out duties customarily performed by employees of the school.

(2) **Student.** -- A person who has been assigned to a school by a local board of education as provided in G.S. 115C-366 or has enrolled in a charter school authorized under G.S. 115C-218.5, a regional school created under G.S. 115C-238.62, a laboratory school created under G.S. 116-239.7, or a nonpublic school which has filed intent to operate under Part 1 or Part 2 of Article 39 of Chapter 115C of the General Statutes, or a person who has been suspended or expelled from any of those schools within the last year.

(b) Except as otherwise made unlawful by this Article, it shall be unlawful for any student to use a computer or computer network to do any of the following:

(1) With the intent to intimidate or torment a school employee, do any of the following:

a. Build a fake profile or Web site.

b. Post or encourage others to post on the Internet private, personal, or sexual information pertaining to a school employee.

c. Post a real or doctored image of the school employee on the Internet.

d. Access, alter, or erase any computer network, computer data, computer program, or computer software, including breaking into a password-protected account or stealing or otherwise accessing passwords.

e. Use a computer system for repeated, continuing, or sustained electronic communications, including electronic mail or other transmissions, to a school employee.

(2) Make any statement, whether true or false, intending to immediately provoke, and that is likely to provoke, any third party to stalk or harass a school employee.

(3) Copy and disseminate, or cause to be made, an unauthorized copy of any data pertaining to a school employee for the purpose of intimidating or tormenting that school employee (in any form, including, but not limited to, any printed or electronic form of computer data, computer programs, or computer software residing in, communicated by, or produced by a computer or computer network).

(4) Sign up a school employee for a pornographic Internet site with the intent to intimidate or torment the employee.

(5) Without authorization of the school employee, sign up a school employee for electronic mailing lists or to receive junk electronic messages and instant messages, with the intent to intimidate or torment the school employee.

(c) Any student who violates this section is guilty of cyber-bullying a school employee, which offense is punishable as a Class 2 misdemeanor.

(d) Whenever any student pleads guilty to or is guilty of an offense under this section, the court may, without entering a judgment of guilt and with the consent of the student, defer further proceedings and place the student on probation upon such reasonable terms and conditions as the court may require. Upon fulfillment of the terms and conditions of the probation provided for in this subsection, the court shall discharge the student and dismiss the proceedings against the student. Discharge and dismissal under this subsection shall be without court adjudication of guilt and shall not be deemed a conviction for purposes of this section or for purposes of disqualifications or disabilities imposed by law upon conviction of a crime. Upon discharge and dismissal pursuant to this subsection, the student may apply for an order to expunge the complete record of the proceedings resulting in the dismissal and discharge, pursuant to the procedures and requirements set forth in G.S. 15A-146.

(e) Whenever a complaint is received pursuant to Article 17 of Chapter 7B of the General Statutes based upon a student's violation of this section, the juvenile may, upon a finding of legal sufficiency pursuant to G.S. 7B-1706, enter into a diversion contract pursuant to G.S. 7B-1706.

History.
2012-149, s. 4; 2014-101, s. 7; 2016-94, s. 11.6(b); 2017-117, s. 2

N.C. Gen. Stat. § 14-459

Reserved for future codification purposes.

ARTICLE 61
TRAINS AND RAILROADS

§ 14-460. Riding on train unlawfully

If any person, with the intention of being transported free in violation of law, rides or attempts to ride on top of any car, coach, engine, or tender, on any railroad in this State, or on the drawheads between cars, or under cars, on truss rods, or trucks, or in any freight car, or on a platform of any baggage car, express car, or mail car on any train, he shall be guilty of a Class 3 misdemeanor.

History.
1998-128, s. 12

§ 14-461. Unauthorized manufacture or sale of switch-lock keys a misdemeanor

It shall be unlawful for any person to make, manufacture, sell, or give away to any other person any duplicate key to any lock used by any railroad company in this State on its switches or switch tracks, except upon the written order of that officer of such railroad company whose duty it is to distribute and issue switch-lock keys to the employees of such railroad company. Any person violating the provisions of this section shall be guilty of a Class 1 misdemeanor.

History.
1998-128, s. 12

CHAPTER 15
CRIMINAL PROCEDURE

ARTICLE 1
GENERAL PROVISIONS

§ 15-1. Statute of limitations for misdemeanors

(a) The crimes of deceit and malicious mischief, and the crime of petit larceny where the value of the property does not exceed five dollars ($ 5.00), and all misdemeanors except malicious misdemeanors, shall be charged within two years after the commission of the same, and not afterwards: Provided, that if any pleading shall be defective, so that no judgment can be given thereon, another prosecution may be instituted for the same offense, within one year after the first shall have been abandoned by the State.

(b) Notwithstanding subsection (a) of this section, the following misdemeanors shall be charged within 10 years of the commission of the crime:

    (1) G.S. 7B-301(b).
    (2) G.S. 14-27.33.
    (3) G.S. 14-202.2.
    (4) G.S. 14-318.2.
    (5) G.S. 14-318.6.

History.
1826, c. 11; R.C., c. 35, s. 8; Code, s. 1177; Rev., s. 3147; 1907, c. 408; C.S., s. 4512; 1943, c. 543; 2017-57, s. 17.8 .(a); 2017-212, s. 5.3; 2019-245, s. 2(a)

§§ 15-2, 15-3

Repealed by Session Laws 1973, c. 1286, s. 26.

§ 15-4. Accused entitled to counsel

Every person, accused of any crime whatsoever, shall be entitled to counsel in all matters which may be necessary for his defense.

History.
1777, c. 115, s. 85, P.R.; R.C., c. 35, s. 13; Code, s. 1182; Rev., s. 3150; C.S., s. 4515

§§ 15-4.1 through 15-5.1

Repealed by Session Laws 1969, c. 1013, s. 12.

§ 15-5.2

Repealed by Session Laws 1969, c. 1013, s. 6.

§§ 15-5.3, 15-5.4

Repealed by Session Laws 1969, c. 1013, s. 12.

§ 15-6. Imprisonment to be in county jail

No person over the age of 18 shall be imprisoned except in the common jail of the county, unless otherwise provided by law: Provided, that whenever the sheriff of any county shall be imprisoned, he may be imprisoned in the jail of any adjoining county. If the person being imprisoned is under the age of 18, that person shall be imprisoned in a detention facility approved by the Juvenile Justice Section of the Division of Adult Correction and Juvenile Justice to provide secure confinement and care for juveniles, or to a holdover facility as defined in G.S. 7B-1501(11).

History.
1797, c. 474, s. 3, P.R.; R.C., c. 35, s. 6; 1879, c. 12; Code, s. 1174; Rev., s. 3151; C.S., s. 4517; 1973, c. 1141, s. 1; 2020-83, s. 8(b)

§ 15-6.1. Changing place of confinement of prisoner committing offense

In all cases where a defendant has been convicted in a court inferior to the superior court and sentenced to a term in the county jail or to serve in some county institution other than under the supervision of the State Division of Adult Correction and Juvenile Justice of the Department of Public Safety, and such defendant is subsequently brought before such court for an offense committed prior to the expiration of the term to be served in such county institution, upon conviction, plea of guilty or nolo contendere, the judge shall have the power and authority to change the place of confinement of the prisoner and commit such defendant to work under the supervision of the Division of Adult Correction and Juvenile Justice of the Department of Public Safety. This provision shall apply whether or not the terms of the new sentence are to run concurrently with or consecutive to the remaining portion of the old sentence.

History.
1953, c. 778; 1957, c. 65, s. 11; 1967, c. 996, s. 16; 2011-145, s. 19.1(h); 2012-83, s. 20; 2017-186, s. 2(kk)

§ 15-6.2. Concurrent sentences for offenses of different grades or to be served in different places

When by a judgment of a court or by operation of law a prison sentence runs concurrently with any other sentence a prisoner shall not be required to serve any additional time in prison solely because the concurrent sentences are for different grades of offenses or that it is required that they be served in different places of confinement.

History.
1955, c. 57

§ 15-6.3. Credit for service of sentence while in another jurisdiction

When a person in actual confinement under sentence of another jurisdiction is brought for trial before a court of this State, the court may, upon sentencing, specifically impose a sentence to be concurrently served and direct that such person receive credit against the sentence imposed for all time subsequently served in the jurisdiction possessing physical custody of such person.

History.
1971, c. 828

§ 15-7. Postmortem examinations directed

In all cases of homicide, any officer prosecuting for the State may, at any time, direct a postmortem examination of the deceased to be made by one or more physicians to be summoned for the purpose; and the physicians shall be paid a reasonable compensation for such examination, the amount to be determined by the court and taxed in the costs, and if not collected out of the defendant the same shall be paid by the State.

History.
R.C., c. 35, s. 49; Code, s. 1214; Rev., s. 3152; C.S., s. 4518; 1973, c. 1141, s. 2

§ 15-8. Stolen property returned to owner

Upon the conviction of any person for robbing or stealing any money, goods, chattels, or other estate of any description whatever, the person from whom such goods, money, chattels or other estate were robbed or stolen shall be entitled to restitution thereof; and the court may award restitution of the articles so robbed or stolen, and make all such orders and issue such writs of restitution or otherwise as may be necessary for that purpose.

History.
21 Hen. VIII, c. 11; R.C., c. 35, s. 34; Code, s. 1201; Rev., s. 3153; C.S., s. 4519; 1943, c. 543

N.C. Gen. Stat. § 15-9

Repealed by Session Laws 1973, c. 1286, s. 26.

§ 15-10. Speedy trial or discharge on commitment for felony

When any person who has been committed for treason or felony, plainly and specially expressed in the warrant of commitment, upon his prayer in open court to be brought to his trial, shall not be indicted some time in the next term of the superior or criminal court ensuing such commitment, the judge of the court, upon notice in open court on the last day of the term, shall set at liberty such prisoner upon bail, unless it appear upon oath that the witnesses for the State could not be produced at the same term; and if such prisoner, upon his prayer as aforesaid, shall not be indicted and tried at the second term of the court, he shall be discharged from his imprisonment: Provided, the judge presiding may, in his discretion, refuse to discharge such person if the time between the first and second terms of the court be less than four months.

History.
1868-9, c. 116, s. 33; Code, s. 1658; Rev., s. 3155; 1913, c. 2; C.S., s. 4521

§ 15-10.1. Detainer; purpose; manner of use

Any person confined in the State prison system of North Carolina, subject to the authority and control of the Division of Adult Correction and Juvenile Justice of the Department of Public Safety, or any person confined in any other prison of North Carolina, may be held to account for any other charge pending against him only upon a written order from the clerk or judge of the court in which the charge originated upon a case regularly docketed, directing that such person be held to answer the charge pending in such court; and in no event shall the prison authorities hold any person to answer any charge upon a warrant or notice when the charge has not been regularly docketed in the court in which the warrant or charge has been issued: Provided, that this section shall not apply to any State agency exercising supervision over such person or prisoner by virtue of a judgment, order of court or statutory authority.

History.
1949, c. 303; 1953, c. 603; 1957, c. 349, s. 10; 1967, c. 996, s. 13; 2011-145, s. 19.1(h); 2012-83, s. 21; 2017-186, s. 2 (*ll*)

§ 15-10.2. Mandatory disposition of detainers -- request for final disposition of charges; continuance; information to be furnished prisoner

(a) Any prisoner serving a sentence or sentences within the State prison system who, during his term of imprisonment, shall have lodged against him a detainer to answer to any criminal charge pending against him in any court within the State, shall be brought to trial within eight months after he shall have caused to be sent to the district attorney of the court in which said criminal charge is pending, by registered mail, written notice of his place of confinement and request for a final disposition of the criminal charge against him; said request shall be accompanied by a certificate from the Secretary of Public Safety stating the term of the sentence or sentences under which the prisoner is being held, the date he was received, and the time remaining to be served; provided that, for good cause shown in open court, the prisoner or his counsel being present, the court may grant any necessary and reasonable continuance.

(b) The Secretary of Public Safety shall, upon request by the prisoner, inform the prisoner in writing of the source and contents of any charge for which a detainer shall have been lodged against such prisoner as shown by said detainer, and furnished the prisoner with the certificate referred to in subsection (a).

History.
1957, c. 1067, s. 1; 1967, c. 996, s. 15; 1973, c. 47, s. 2; c. 1262, s. 10; 2011-145, s. 19.1(i)

§ 15-10.3. Mandatory disposition of detainers -- procedure; return of prisoner after trial

The district attorney, upon receipt of the written notice and request for a final disposition as hereinbefore specified, shall make application to the court in which said charge is pending for a writ of habeas corpus ad prosequendum and the court upon such application shall issue such writ to the Secretary of Public Safety requiring the prisoner to be delivered to said court to answer the pending charge and to stand trial on said charge within the time hereinbefore provided; upon completion of said trial, the prisoner shall be returned to the State prison system to complete service of the sentence or sentences under which he was held at the time said writ was issued.

History.
1957, c. 1067, s. 2; 1967, c. 996, s. 15; 1973, c. 47, s. 2; c. 1262, s. 10; 2011-145, s. 19.1(i)

§ 15-10.4. Mandatory disposition of detainers -- exception as to prisoners who are mentally ill

The provisions of G.S. 15-10.2 and 15-10.3 shall not apply to any prisoner who has been transferred and assigned for observation or treatment to any unit of the prison system which is maintained for those prisoners who are mentally ill or are suffering from mental disorders.

History.
1957, c. 1067, s. 3

ARTICLE 2
RECORD AND DISPOSITION OF SEIZED, ETC., ARTICLES

§ 15-11. Sheriffs and police departments to maintain register of personal property confiscated, seized or found

Each sheriff and police department in this State is hereby required to keep and maintain a book or register, and it shall be the duty of each sheriff and police department to keep a record therein of all articles of personal property which may be seized or confiscated by him or it, or of which he or it may have become possessed in any way in the discharge of his duty. Said sheriffs and police departments shall cause to be kept in said registers a description of such property, the name of the person from whom it was seized, if such name be known, the date and place of its seizure, and, where the article was not taken from the person of a suspect or prisoner, a brief recital of the place and circumstances concerning the possession thereof by such sheriff and police department. Such sheriff and police department shall also keep in said register appropriate entries showing the manner, date, and to whom said articles are disposed of or delivered, and, if sold as hereinafter provided, a record showing the disposition of the proceeds arising from such sale.

History.
1939, c. 195, s. 1; 1973, c. 1141, s. 3

§ 15-11.1. Seizure, custody and disposition of articles; exceptions

(a) If a law-enforcement officer seizes property pursuant to lawful authority, he shall safely keep the property under the direction of the court or magistrate as long as necessary to assure that the property will be produced at and may be used as evidence in any trial. Upon application by the lawful owner or a person, firm or corporation entitled to possession or upon his own determination, the district attorney may release any property seized pursuant to his lawful authority if he determines that such property is no longer useful or necessary as evidence in a criminal trial and he is presented with satisfactory evidence of ownership. If the district attorney refuses to release such property, the lawful owner or a person, firm or corporation entitled to possession may make application to the court for return of the property. The court, after notice to all parties, including the defendant, and after hearing, may in its discretion order any or all of the property returned to the lawful owner or a person, firm or corporation entitled to possession. The court may enter such order as may be necessary to assure that the evidence will be available for use as evidence at the time of trial, and will otherwise protect the rights of all parties. Notwithstanding any other provision of law, photographs or other identification or analyses made of the property may be introduced at the time of the trial provided that the court determines that the introduction of such substitute evidence is not likely to substantially prejudice the rights of the defendant in the criminal trial.

(b) In the case of unknown or unapprehended defendants or of defendants willfully absent from the jurisdiction, the court shall determine whether an attorney should be appointed as guardian ad litem to represent and protect the interest of such unknown or absent defendants. Appointment shall be in accordance with rules adopted by the Office of Indigent Defense Services. The judicial findings concerning identification or value that are made at such hearing whereby property is returned to the lawful owner or a person, firm, or corporation entitled to possession, may be admissible into evidence at the trial. After final judgment all property lawfully seized by or otherwise coming into the possession of law-enforcement authorities shall be disposed of as the court or magistrate in its discretion orders, and may be forfeited and either sold or destroyed in accordance with due process of law.

(b1) Notwithstanding subsections (a) and (b) of this section or any other provision of law, if the property seized is a firearm and the district attorney determines the firearm is no longer necessary or useful as evidence in a criminal trial, the district attorney, after notice to all parties known or believed by the district attorney to have an ownership or a possessory interest in the firearm, including the defendant, shall apply to the court for an order of disposition of the firearm. The judge, after hearing, may order the disposition of the firearm in one of the following ways:

(1) By ordering the firearm returned to its rightful owner, when the rightful owner is someone other than the defendant and upon findings by the court (i) that the person, firm, or corporation determined by the court to be the rightful owner is entitled to possession of the firearm and (ii) that the person, firm, or corporation determined by the court to be the rightful owner of the firearm was unlawfully deprived of the same or had no knowledge or reasonable belief of the defendant's intention to use the firearm unlawfully.

(2) By ordering the firearm returned to the defendant, but only if the defendant is not convicted of any criminal offense in connection with the possession or use of the firearm, the defendant is the rightful owner of the firearm, and the defendant is not otherwise ineligible to possess such firearm.

(3) By ordering the firearm turned over to be destroyed by the sheriff of the county in which the firearm was seized or by his duly authorized agent if the firearm does not have a legible, unique identification number or is unsafe for use because of wear, damage, age, or modification. The sheriff shall maintain a record of the destruction of the firearm.

(4) By ordering the firearm turned over to a law enforcement agency in the county of trial for (i) the official use of the agency or (ii) sale, trade, or exchange by the agency to a federally licensed firearm dealer in accordance with all applicable State and federal firearm laws. The court may order a disposition of the firearm pursuant to this subdivision only if the firearm has a legible, unique identification number. If the law enforcement agency sells the firearm, then the proceeds of the sale shall be remitted to the appropriate county finance officer as provided by G.S. 115C-452 to be used to maintain free public schools. The receiving law enforcement agency shall maintain a record and inventory of all firearms received pursuant to this subdivision.

This subsection (b1) is not applicable to seizures pursuant to G.S. 113-137 of firearms used only in connection with a violation of Article 22 of Chapter 113 of the General Statutes or any local wildlife hunting ordinance.

(c) Any property, the forfeiture and disposition of which is specified in any general or special law, shall be disposed of in accordance therewith.

History.
1977, c. 613; 1979, c. 593; 1994, Ex. Sess., c. 16, s. 1; 2000-144, s. 27; 2005-287, s. 1; 2013-158, s. 1; 2014-115, s. 24.5

§ 15-11.2. Disposition of unclaimed firearms not confiscated or seized as trial evidence

(a) **Definition.** -- For purposes of this section, the term "unclaimed firearm" means a firearm that is found or received by a law enforcement agency and that remains unclaimed by the person who may be entitled to it for a period of 30 days after the publication of the notice required by subsection (b) of this section. The term does not include a firearm that is seized and disposed of pursuant to G.S. 15-11.1 or a firearm that is confiscated and disposed of pursuant to G.S. 14-269.1.

(b) **Published Notice of Unclaimed Firearm. --** When a law enforcement agency finds or receives a firearm and the firearm remains unclaimed for a period of 180 days, the agency shall publish at least one notice in a newspaper published in the county in which the agency is located. The notice shall include all of the following:

(1) A statement that the firearm is unclaimed and is in the custody of the law enforcement agency.

(2) A statement that the firearm may be sold or otherwise disposed of unless the firearm is claimed within 30 days of the date of the publication of the notice.

(3) A brief description of the firearm and any other information that the chief or head of the law enforcement agency may consider necessary or advisable to reasonably inform the public about the firearm.

(c) Repealed by Session Laws 2013-158, s. 2, effective September 1, 2013, and applicable to any firearm found or received by a local law enforcement agency on or after that date and to any judicial order for the disposition of any firearm on or after that date.

(d) **Disposition of Unclaimed Firearm. --** If the firearm remains unclaimed for a period of 30 days after the publication of the notice, then the head or chief of the law enforcement agency shall order the disposition of the firearm in one of the following ways:

(1) By having the firearm destroyed if the firearm does not have a legible, unique identification number or is unsafe for use because of wear, damage, age, or modification and will not be disposed of pursuant to subdivision (3) of this subsection. The head or chief of the law enforcement agency shall maintain a record of the destruction of the firearm.

(2) By sale, trade, or exchange by the agency to a federally licensed firearm dealer in accordance with all applicable State and federal firearm laws or by sale of the firearm at a public auction to persons licensed as firearms collectors, dealers, importers, or manufacturers. The head or chief of the law enforcement agency shall dispose of the firearm pursuant to this subdivision only if the firearm has a legible, unique identification number.

(3) By maintaining the firearm for training or experimental purposes or transferring the firearm to a museum or historical society.

(e) Repealed by Session Laws 2013-158, s. 2, effective September 1, 2013, and applicable to any firearm found or received by a local law enforcement agency on or after that date and to any judicial order for the disposition of any firearm on or after that date.

(f) **Disbursement of Proceeds of Sale. --** If the law enforcement agency sells the firearm pursuant to subdivision (2) of subsection (d) of this section, then the proceeds of the sale shall be retained by the law enforcement agency and used for law enforcement purposes. The receiving law enforcement agency shall maintain a record and inventory of all firearms received pursuant to this section, as well as the disposition of the firearm, including any funds received from a sale of a firearm or any firearms or other property received in exchange or trade of a firearm.

History.
2005-287, s. 2; 2013-158, s. 2; 2013-410, s. 17(a); 2014-115, s. 2

§ 15-12. Publication of notice of unclaimed property; advertisement and sale or donation of unclaimed bicycles

(a) Unless otherwise provided herein, whenever such articles in the possession of any sheriff or police department have remained unclaimed by the person who may be entitled thereto for a period of 180 days after such seizure, confiscation, or receipt thereof in any other manner, by such sheriff or police department, the said sheriff or police department in whose possession said articles are may cause to be published one time in some newspaper published in said county a notice to the effect that such articles are in the custody of such officer or department, and requiring all persons who may have or claim any interest therein to make and establish such claim or interest not later than 30 days from the date of the publication of such notice or in default thereof, such articles will be sold and disposed of. Such notice shall contain a brief description of the said articles and such other information as the said officer or department may consider necessary or advisable to reasonably inform the public as to the kind and nature of the article about which the notice relates.

(b) Notwithstanding subsection (a) of this section or Article 12 of Chapter 160A of the General Statutes, when bicycles which are in the possession of any sheriff or police department, as provided for in this Article, have remained unclaimed by the person who may be entitled thereto for a period of 60 days after such seizure, confiscation or receipt thereof, the said sheriff or police department who has possession of any such bicycle may proceed to advertise and sell such bicycles as provided by this Article, or may donate such bicycles to a charitable organization exempt under section 501(c) (3) of the Internal Revenue Code. If the bicycles are to be donated, the notice shall state that as the intended disposition if they are not claimed.

History.

1939, c. 195, s. 2; 1965, c. 807, s. 1; 1973, c. 1141, s. 4; 1997-180, s. 1

§ 15-13. Public sale 30 days after publication of notice

If said articles shall remain unclaimed or satisfactory evidence of ownership thereof not be presented to the sheriff or police department, as the case may be, for a period of 30 days after the publication of the notice provided for in G.S. 15-12, then the said sheriff or police department in whose custody such articles may be is hereby authorized and empowered to sell the same at public auction for cash to the highest bidder, either at the courthouse door of the county, the county law enforcement headquarters if the sale is conducted by the sheriff, or at the police headquarters of the municipality in which the said articles of property are located, and at such sale to deliver the same to the purchaser or purchasers thereof.

History.

1939, c. 195, s. 3; 1973, c. 1141, s. 5; 1991, c. 531, s. 2

§ 15-14. Notice of sale

Before any sale of said property is made under the provisions of this Article, however, the said sheriff or police department making the same shall first advertise the sale by publishing a notice thereof in some newspaper published in the said county at least one time not less than 10 days prior to the date of sale, and by posting a notice of the sale at the courthouse door and at three other public places in the said county. Said notice shall specify the time and place of sale, and contain a sufficient description of the articles of property to be sold. It shall not be required that the sale lay open for increase bids or objections, but it may be deemed closed when the purchaser at the sale pays the amount of the accepted bid.

History.

1939, c. 195, s. 4; 1973, c. 1141, s. 6

§ 15-14.1. Sale of property through electronic auction

In addition to selling property as authorized in G.S. 15-13, a sheriff or police department may sell property in his or its possession through an electronic auction service. The sheriff or police department shall comply with the publication and notice requirements provided in G.S. 15-12

through G.S. 15-14 prior to any sale under this section.

History.

2003-284, s. 18.6(c)

§ 15-15. Disbursement of proceeds of sale

From the proceeds realized from the sale of said property, the sheriff, police department or other officer making the same shall first pay the costs and expenses of the sale, and all other necessary expenses incident to a compliance with this Article, and any balance then remaining from the proceeds of said sale shall be paid within 30 days after the sale to the treasurer of the county board of education of the county in which such sale is made, for the benefit of the fund for maintaining the free public schools of such county.

History.

1939, c. 195, s. 5; 1973, c. 1141, s. 7

§ 15-16. Nonliability of officers

No sheriff, police department, or other officer shall be liable for any damages or claims on account of any such sale or disposition of such property, as provided in this Article.

History.

1939, c. 195, s. 6; 1973, c. 1141, s. 8

§ 15-17. Construction of Article

This Article shall not be construed to apply to the seizure and disposition of whiskey distilleries, game birds, and other property or articles which have been or may be seized, where the existing law now provides the method, manner, and extent of the disposition of such articles or of the proceeds derived from the sale thereof.

History.

1939, c. 195, s. 7

ARTICLE 3
WARRANTS

§§ 15-18 through 15-24

Repealed by Session Laws 1973, c. 1286, s. 26.

§ 15-24.1. Amendment of warrant to show ownership of property

Any criminal warrant may be amended in the superior court, before or during the trial, when there shall appear to be any variance between the allegations in the warrant and the evidence in setting forth the ownership of property if, in the opinion of the court, such amendment will not prejudice the defendant. This section shall be construed as enlarging and not limiting the conditions and situations under which a warrant may be amended.

History.
1965, c. 285

ARTICLE 4
SEARCH WARRANTS

N.C. Gen. Stat. § 15-25

Repealed by Session Laws 1973, c. 1286, s. 26.

§§ 15-25.1, 15-25.2

Repealed by Session Laws 1969, c. 869, s. 8.

§§ 15-26 through 15-27.1

Repealed by Session Laws 1973, c. 1286, s. 26.

ARTICLE 4A
ADMINISTRATIVE SEARCH
AND INSPECTION WARRANTS

§ 15-27.2. Warrants to conduct inspections authorized by law

(a) Notwithstanding the provisions of Article 11 of Chapter 15A, any official or employee of the State or of a unit of county or local government of North Carolina may, under the conditions specified in this section, obtain a warrant authorizing him to conduct a search or inspection of property if such a search or inspection is one that is elsewhere authorized by law, either with or without the consent of the person whose privacy would be thereby invaded, and is one for which such a warrant is constitutionally required.

(b) The warrant may be issued by any magistrate of the general court of justice, judge, clerk, or assistant or deputy clerk of any court of record whose territorial jurisdiction encompasses the property to be inspected.

(c) The issuing officer shall issue the warrant when he is satisfied the following conditions are met:

(1) The one seeking the warrant must establish under oath or affirmation that the property to be searched or inspected is to be searched or inspected as part of a legally authorized program of inspection which naturally includes that property, or

that there is probable cause for believing that there is a condition, object, activity or circumstance which legally justifies such a search or inspection of that property;

(2) An affidavit indicating the basis for the establishment of one of the grounds described in (1) above must be signed under oath or affirmation by the affiant;

(3) The issuing official must examine the affiant under oath or affirmation to verify the accuracy of the matters indicated by the statement in the affidavit;

(d) The warrant shall be validly issued only if it meets the following requirements:

(1) Except as provided in subsection (e), it must be signed by the issuing official and must bear the date and hour of its issuance above his signature with a notation that the warrant is valid for only 24 hours following its issuance;

(2) It must describe, either directly or by reference to the affidavit, the property where the search or inspection is to occur and be accurate enough in description so that the executor of the warrant and the owner or the possessor of the property can reasonably determine from it what person or property the warrant authorizes an inspection of;

(3) It must indicate the conditions, objects, activities or circumstances which the inspection is intended to check or reveal;

(4) It must be attached to the affidavit required to be made in order to obtain the warrant.

(e) Any warrant issued under this section for a search or inspection shall be valid for only 24 hours after its issuance, must be personally served upon the owner or possessor of the property between the hours of 8:00 A.M. and 8:00 P.M. and must be returned within 48 hours. If the warrant, however, was procured pursuant to an investigation authorized by G.S. 58-79-1, the warrant may be executed at any hour, is valid for 48 hours after its issuance, and must be returned without unnecessary delay after its execution or after the expiration of the 48 hour period if it is not executed. If the owner or possessor of the property is not present on the property at the time of the search or inspection and reasonable efforts to locate the owner or possessor have been made and have failed, the warrant or a copy thereof may be affixed to the property and shall have the same effect as if served personally upon the owner or possessor.

(f) No facts discovered or evidence obtained in a search or inspection conducted under authority of a warrant issued under this section shall be competent as evidence in any civil, criminal or administrative action, nor considered in imposing any civil, criminal, or administrative sanction against any person, nor as a basis for further seeking to obtain any warrant, if the warrant is invalid or if what is discovered or obtained is not a condition, object, activity or circumstance which it was the legal purpose of the search or inspection to discover; but this shall not prevent any such facts or evidence to be so used when the warrant issued is not constitutionally required in those circumstances.

(g) The warrants authorized under this section shall not be regarded as search warrants for the purposes of application of Article 11 of Chapter 15A of the General Statutes of North Carolina.

History.
1967, c. 1260; 1979, c. 729; 1983, c. 294, ss. 1, 2; c. 739, ss. 1, 2

ARTICLE 5
PEACE WARRANTS

§§ 15-28 through 15-38

Repealed by Session Laws 1973, c. 1286, ss. 11, 26.

ARTICLE 6
ARREST

§§ 15-39 through 15-42

Repealed by Session Laws 1973, c. 1286, s. 26.

§ 15-43. House broken open to prevent felony

All persons are authorized to break open and enter a house to prevent a felony about to be committed therein.

History.
1868-9, c. 178, subch. 1, s. 4; Code, s. 1127; Rev., s. 3179; C.S., s. 4545

§§ 15-44 through 15-47

Repealed by Session Laws 1973, c. 1286, s. 26.

ARTICLE 7
FUGITIVES FROM JUSTICE

N.C. Gen. Stat. § 15-48

Repealed by Session Laws 1997-80, s. 10 .

N.C. Gen. Stat. § 15-49

Repealed by Session Laws 1975, c. 166, s. 26.

§§ 15-50 through 15-52

Repealed by Session Laws 1973, c. 1286, s. 26.

§ 15-53. Governor may employ agents, and offer rewards

The Governor, on information made to the Governor of any person, whether the name of such person be known or unknown, having committed a felony or other infamous crime within the State, and of having fled out of the jurisdiction thereof, or who conceals himself or herself within the State to avoid arrest, or who, having been convicted, has escaped and cannot otherwise be apprehended, may either employ a special agent, with a sufficient escort, to pursue and apprehend such fugitive, or issue a proclamation, and therein offer a reward, not exceeding one hundred thousand dollars ($ 100,000), according to the nature of the case, as in the Governor's opinion may be sufficient for the purpose, to be paid to anyone who shall apprehend and deliver the fugitive to such person and at such place as in the proclamation shall be directed.

History.
1800, c. 561, P.R.; R.C., c. 35, s. 4; 1866, c. 28; 1868-9, c. 52; 1870-1, c. 15; 1871-2, c. 29; Code, s. 1169; 1891, c. 421; Rev., s. 3188; C.S., s. 4554; 1925, c. 275, s. 6; 1967, c. 165, s. 1; 2013-276, s. 1

§ 15-53.1. Governor may offer rewards for information leading to arrest and conviction

When it shall appear to the Governor, upon satisfactory information furnished to the Governor, that a felony or other infamous crime has been committed within the State, whether the name or names of the person or persons suspected of committing the said crime be known or unknown, the Governor may issue a proclamation and therein offer an award [reward] not exceeding one hundred thousand dollars ($ 100,000), according to the nature of the case as, in the Governor's opinion, may be sufficient for the purpose, to be paid to anyone who shall provide information leading to the arrest and conviction of such person or persons. The proclamation shall be upon such terms as the Governor may deem proper, but it shall identify the felony or felonies and the authority to whom the information is to be delivered and shall state such other terms as the Governor may require under which the reward is payable.

History.
1967, c. 165, s. 2; 2013-276, s. 2

§ 15-54. Officer entitled to reward

Any sheriff or other officer who shall make an arrest of any person charged with crime for whose apprehension a reward has been offered is entitled to such reward, and may sue for and recover the same in any court in this State having jurisdiction: Provided, that no reward shall be paid to any sheriff or other officer for any arrest made for a crime committed within the county of such sheriff or officer making such arrest.

History.
1913, c. 132; 1917, c. 8; C.S., s. 4555

ARTICLE 8
EXTRADITION

§§ 15-55 through 15-84

Transferred to G.S. 15A-721 to 15A-750 by Session Laws 1973, c. 1286, s. 16.

ARTICLE 9
PRELIMINARY EXAMINATION

§§ 15-85 through 15-101

Repealed by Session Laws 1973, c. 1286, s. 26.

ARTICLE 10
BAIL

§§ 15-102, 15-103

Repealed by Session Laws 1973, c. 1286, s. 26.

N.C. Gen. Stat. § 15-103.1

Repealed by Session Laws 1977, c. 711, s. 33.

N.C. Gen. Stat. § 15-103.2

Repealed by Session Laws 1975, c. 166, s. 26.

N.C. Gen. Stat. § 15-104

Repealed by Session Laws 1973, c. 1286, s. 26.

N.C. Gen. Stat. § 15-104.1

Repealed by Session Laws 1975, c. 166, s. 26.

§§ 15-105 through 15-107

Repealed by Session Laws 1973, c. 1286, s. 26.

N.C. Gen. Stat. § 15-107.1

Repealed by Session Laws 1975, c. 166, s. 26.

§§ 15-108, 15-109

Repealed by Session Laws 1973, c. 1286, s. 26.

ARTICLE 11
FORFEITURE OF BAIL

§§ 15-110 through 15-124

Repealed by Sessions Laws 1977, c. 711, s. 33.

ARTICLE 12
COMMITMENT TO PRISON

N.C. Gen. Stat. § 15-125

Repealed by Session Laws 1973, c. 1286, s. 26.

§ 15-126. Commitment to county jail

All persons committed to prison before conviction shall be committed to the jail of the county in which the examination is had, or to that of the county in which the offense is charged to have been committed: Provided, if the jails of these counties are unsafe, or injurious to the health of prisoners, the committing magistrate may commit to the jail of any other convenient county. And every sheriff or jailer to whose jail any person shall be committed by any court or magistrate of competent jurisdiction shall receive such prisoner and give a receipt for him, and be bound for his safekeeping as prescribed by law.

History.
1868-9, c. 178, subch. 2, s. 33; Code, s. 1164; Rev., s. 3231; C.S., s. 4598; 1973, c. 1286, s. 26; 1975, c. 166, s. 25

N.C. Gen. Stat. § 15-127

Repealed by Session Laws 1973, c. 1286, s. 26.

ARTICLE 13
VENUE

N.C. Gen. Stat. § 15-128

Repealed by Session Laws 1973, c. 1286, s. 26.

Chapter 15

§ 15-129. In offenses on waters dividing counties

When any offense is committed on any water, or watercourse whether at high or low water, which water or watercourse, or the sides or shores thereof, divides counties, such offense may be dealt with, inquired of, tried and determined, and punished at the discretion of the court, in either of the two counties which may be nearest to the place where the offense was committed.

History.

R.C., c. 35, s. 24; Code, s. 1193; Rev., s. 3234; C.S., s. 4601; 1973, c. 1286, s. 26; 1975, c. 166, s. 25

§ 15-130. Assault in one county, death in another

In all cases of felonious homicide when the assault has been made in one county within the State, and the person assaulted dies in any other county thereof, the offender shall be indicted and punished for the crime in the county wherein the assault was made.

History.

1831, c. 22, s. 1; R.C., c. 35, s. 27; Code, s. 1196; Rev., s. 3235; C.S., s. 4602

§ 15-131. Assault in this State, death in another

In all cases of felonious homicide, when the assault has been made within this State, and the person assaulted dies without the limits thereof, the offender shall be indicted and punished for the crime in the county where the assault was made, in the same manner, to all intents and purposes, as if the person assaulted had died within the limits of this State.

History.

1831, c. 22, s. 2; R.C., c. 35, s. 28; Code, s. 1197; Rev., s. 3236; C.S., s. 4603

§ 15-132. Person in this State injuring one in another

If any person, being in this State, unlawfully and willfully puts in motion a force from the effect of which any person is injured while in another state, the person so setting such force in motion shall be guilty of the same offense in this State as he would be if the effect had taken place within this State.

History.

1895, c. 169; Rev., s. 3237; C.S., s. 4604

§ 15-133. In county where death occurs

If a mortal wound is given or other violence or injury inflicted or poison is administered on the high seas or land, either within or without the limits of this State, by means whereof death ensues in any county thereof, the offense may be prosecuted and punished in the county where the death happens.

History.

1891, c. 68; Rev., s. 3238; C.S., s. 4605

§§ 15-134 through 15-136

Repealed by Session Laws 1973, c. 1286, s. 26.

ARTICLE 14
PRESENTMENT

§§ 15-137 through 15-139

Repealed by Session Laws 1973, c. 1286, s. 26.

ARTICLE 15
INDICTMENT

§§ 15-140 through 15-143

Repealed by Session Laws 1973, c. 1286, s. 26.

§ 15-144. Essentials of bill for homicide

In indictments for murder and manslaughter, it is not necessary to allege matter not required to be proved on the trial; but in the body of the indictment, after naming the person accused, and the county of his residence, the date of the offense, the averment "with force and arms," and the county of the alleged commission of the offense, as is now usual, it is sufficient in describing murder to allege that the accused person feloniously, willfully, and of his malice aforethought, did kill and murder (naming the person killed), and concluding as is now required by law; and it is sufficient in describing manslaughter to allege that the accused feloniously and willfully did kill and slay (naming the person killed), and concluding as aforesaid; and any bill of indictment containing the averments and allegations herein named shall be good and sufficient in law as an indictment for murder or manslaughter, as the case may be.

History.

1887, c. 58; Rev., s. 3245; C.S., s. 4614

§ 15-144.1. Essentials of bill for rape

(a) In indictments for rape it is not necessary to allege every matter required to be proved on the trial; but in the body of the indictment, after naming the person accused, the date of the offense, the county in which the offense of rape was allegedly committed, and the averment "with force and arms," it is sufficient in describing rape to allege that the accused person unlawfully, willfully, and feloniously did ravish and carnally know the victim, naming her, by force and against her will and concluding as required by law. Any bill of indictment containing the averments and allegations named in this section is good and sufficient in law as an indictment for rape in the first degree and will support a verdict of guilty of rape in the first degree, rape in the second degree, attempted rape, or assault on a female.

(b) If the victim is a female child under the age of 13 years, it is sufficient to allege that the accused unlawfully, willfully, and feloniously did carnally know and abuse a child under 13, naming her, and concluding as required by law. Any bill of indictment containing the averments and allegations named in this section is good and sufficient in law as an indictment for the rape of a female child under the age of 13 years and all lesser included offenses.

(c) If the victim is a person who has a mental disability or who is mentally incapacitated or physically helpless, it is sufficient to allege that the defendant unlawfully, willfully, and feloniously did carnally know and abuse a person who had a mental disability or who was mentally incapacitated or physically helpless, naming the victim, and concluding as required by law. Any bill of indictment containing the averments and allegations named in this section is good and sufficient in law for the rape of a person who has a mental disability or who is mentally incapacitated or physically helpless and all lesser included offenses.

History.
1977, c. 861, s. 1; 1979, c. 682, s. 10; 1983, c. 720, s. 1; 2002-159, s. 2(d); 2018-47, s. 4(i)

§ 15-144.2. Essentials of bill for sex offense

(a) In indictments for sex offense it is not necessary to allege every matter required to be proved on the trial; but in the body of the indictment, after naming the person accused, the date of the offense, the county in which the sex offense was allegedly committed, and the averment "with force and arms," it is sufficient in describing a sex offense to allege that the accused person unlawfully, willfully, and feloniously did engage in a sex offense with the victim, naming the victim, by force and against the will of the victim and concluding as required by law. Any bill of indictment containing the averments and allegations named in this section is good and sufficient in law as an indictment for a first degree sex offense and will support a verdict of guilty of a sex offense in the first degree, a sex offense in the second degree, an attempt to commit a sex offense, or an assault.

(b) If the victim is a person under the age of 13 years, it is sufficient to allege that the defendant unlawfully, willfully, and feloniously did engage in a sex offense with a child under the age of 13 years, naming the child, and concluding as required by law. Any bill of indictment containing the averments and allegations named in this section is good and sufficient in law as an indictment for a sex offense against a child under the age of 13 years and all lesser included offenses.

(c) If the victim is a person who has a mental disability or who is mentally incapacitated or physically helpless, it is sufficient to allege that the defendant unlawfully, willfully, and feloniously did engage in a sex offense with a person who had a mental disability or who was mentally incapacitated or physically helpless, naming the victim, and concluding as required by law. Any bill of indictment containing the averments and allegations named in this section is good and sufficient in law for a sex offense against a person who has a mental disability or who is mentally incapacitated or physically helpless and all lesser included offenses.

History.
1979, c. 682, s. 11; 1983, c. 720, ss. 2, 3; 2002-159, s. 2(e); 2018-47, s. 4(j)

§ 15-145. Form of bill for perjury

In every indictment for willful and corrupt perjury it is sufficient to set forth the substance of the offense charged upon the defendant, and by what court, or before whom, the oath was taken (averring such court or person to have competent authority to administer the same), together with the proper averments to falsify the matter wherein the perjury is assigned, without setting forth the bill, answer, information, indictment, declaration, or any part of any record or proceedings, either in law or equity, other than aforesaid, and without setting forth the commission or authority of the court or person before whom the perjury was committed. In indictments for perjury the following form shall be sufficient, to wit:

The jurors for the State, on their oath, present, that A.B., of

County, did unlawfully commit perjury upon the trial of an action in

court, in County, wherein was plaintiff and was

defendant, by falsely asserting, on oath (or solemn affirmation) (here set out

the statement or statements alleged to be false), knowing the said statement,

or statements, to be false, or being ignorant whether or not said statement

was true.

History.
1842, c. 49, s. 1; R.C., c. 35, s. 16; Code, s. 1185; 1889, c. 83; Rev., ss. 3246, 3247; C.S., s. 4615

§ 15-146. Bill for subornation of perjury

In every indictment for subornation of perjury, or for corrupt bargaining or contracting with others to commit willful and corrupt perjury, it is sufficient to set forth the substance of the offense charged upon the defendant, without setting forth the bill, answer, information, indictment, declaration or any part of any record or proceedings, and without setting forth the commission or authority of the court or person before whom the perjury was committed or was agreed or promised to be committed.

History.
1842, c. 49, s. 2; R.C., c. 35, s. 17; Code, s. 1186; Rev., s. 3248; C.S., s. 4616

N.C. Gen. Stat. § 15-147

Repealed by Session Laws 1973, c. 1286, s. 26.

§ 15-148. Manner of alleging joint ownership of property

In any indictment wherein it is necessary to state the ownership of any property whatsoever, whether real or personal, which belongs to, or is in the possession of, more than one person, whether such persons be partners in trade, joint tenants or tenants in common, it is sufficient to name one of such persons, and to state such property to belong to the person so named, and another or others as the case may be; and whenever, in any such indictment, it is necessary to mention, for any purpose whatsoever, any partners, joint tenants or tenants in common, it is sufficient to describe them in the manner aforesaid; and this provision shall extend to all joint-stock companies and trustees.

History.
R.C., c. 35, s. 19; Code, s. 1188; Rev., s. 3250; C.S., s. 4618

§ 15-149. Description in bill for larceny of money

In every indictment in which it is necessary to make any averment as to the larceny of any

money, or United States treasury note, or any note of any bank whatsoever, it is sufficient to describe such money, or treasury note, or bank note, simply as money, without specifying any particular coin, or treasury note, or bank note; and such allegation, so far as regards the description of the property, shall be sustained by proof of any amount of coin, or treasury note, or bank note, although the particular species of coin, of which such amount was composed, or the particular nature of the treasury note, or bank note, shall not be proven.

History.
1876-7, c. 68; Code, s. 1190; Rev., s. 3251; C.S., s. 4619

§ 15-150. Description in bill for embezzlement

In indictments for embezzlement, except when the offense relates to a chattel, it is sufficient to allege the embezzlement to be of money, without specifying any particular coin or valuable security; and such allegation, so far as regards the description of the property, shall be sustained if the offender shall be proved to have embezzled any amount, although the particular species of coin or valuable security of which such amount was composed shall not be proved.

History.
1871-2, c. 145, s. 2; Code, s. 1020; Rev., s. 3252; C.S., s. 4620

§ 15-151. Intent to defraud; larceny and receiving

In any case where an intent to defraud is required to constitute the offense of forgery, or any other offense whatever, it is sufficient to allege in the indictment an intent to defraud, without naming therein the particular person or body corporate intended to be defrauded; and on the trial of such indictment, it shall be sufficient, and shall not be deemed a variance, if there appear to be an intent to defraud the United States, or any state, county, city, town, or parish, or body corporate, or any public officer in his official capacity, or any copartnership or member thereof, or any particular person. The defendant may be charged in the same indictment in several counts with the separate offenses of receiving stolen goods, knowing them to be stolen, and larceny.

History.
1852, c. 87, s. 2; R.C., c. 35, ss. 21, 23; 1874-5, c. 62; Code, s. 1191; Rev., s. 3253; C.S., s. 4621

N.C. Gen. Stat. § 15-152

Repealed by Session Laws 1973, c. 1286, s. 26.

§ 15-153. Bill or warrant not quashed for informality

Every criminal proceeding by warrant, indictment, information, or impeachment is sufficient in form for all intents and purposes if it express the charge against the defendant in a plain, intelligible, and explicit manner; and the same shall not be quashed, nor the judgment thereon stayed, by reason of any informality or refinement, if in the bill or proceeding, sufficient matter appears to enable the court to proceed to judgment.

History.

37 Hen. VIII, c. 8; 1784, c. 210, s. 2, P.R.; 1811, c. 809, P.R.; R.C., c. 35, s. 14; Code, s. 1183; Rev., s. 3254; C.S., s. 4623

N.C. Gen. Stat. § 15-154

Repealed by Session Laws 1973, c. 1286, s. 26.

§ 15-155. Defects which do not vitiate

No judgment upon any indictment for felony or misdemeanor, whether after verdict, or by confession, or otherwise, shall be stayed or reversed for the want of the averment of any matter unnecessary to be proved, nor for omission of the words "as appears by the record," or of the words "with force and arms," nor for the insertion of the words "against the form of the statutes" instead of the words "against the form of the statute," or vice versa; nor for omission of the words "against the form of the statute" or "against the form of the statutes," nor for omitting to state the time at which the offense was committed in any case where time is not of the essence of the offense, nor for stating the time imperfectly, nor for stating the offense to have been committed on a day subsequent to the finding of the indictment, or on an impossible day, or on a day that never happened; nor for want of a proper and perfect venue, when the court shall appear by the indictment to have had jurisdiction of the offense.

History.

7 Hen. VIII, c. 8; R.C., c. 35, s. 20; Code, s. 1189; Rev., s. 3255; C.S., s. 4625

ARTICLE 15A
INVESTIGATION OF OFFENSES INVOLVING ABANDONMENT AND NONSUPPORT OF CHILDREN

§ 15-155.1. Reports to district attorneys of Work First Family Assistance and out-of-wedlock births

The Department of Health and Human Services by and through the Secretary of Health and Human Services shall promptly after June 19, 1959, make a report to each district attorney, setting out the names and addresses of all mothers who reside in his prosecutorial district as defined in G.S. 7A-60 and are recipients of assistance under the provisions of Part 2, Article 2, Chapter 108A of the General Statutes. Such report shall in some manner show the identity of the unwed mothers and shall set forth the number of children born to each said mother. Such a report shall also be made monthly thereafter setting out the names and addresses of all such mothers who reside in the district and who may have become recipients of assistance under the provisions of Part 2, Article 2, Chapter 108A of the General Statutes since the date of the last report.

History.

1959, c. 1210, s. 1; 1973, c. 47, s. 2; c. 476, s. 138; 1987 (Reg. Sess., 1988), c. 1037, s. 50; 1997-443, ss. 11A.118(a), 12.23

§ 15-155.2. District attorney to take action on report of Work First Family Assistance and children born out of wedlock

(a) Upon receipt of such reports as are provided for in G.S. 15-155.1, the district attorney of superior court may make an investigation to determine whether the mother of an out-of-wedlock child or who is a recipient of Work First Family Assistance, has abandoned, is willfully neglecting or is refusing to support and maintain the child within the meaning of G.S. 14-326 or 49-2 or is diverting any part of the funds received as Work First Family Assistance to any purpose other than for the support and maintenance of a child in violation of G.S. 108-76.1. In making this investigation the district attorney is authorized to call upon:

(1) Any county board of social services or the Department of Health and Human Services for personal, clerical or investigative assistance and for access to any records kept by either such board and relating to the matter under investigation and such boards are hereby directed to assist in all investigations hereunder and to furnish all records relating thereto when so requested by the district attorney;

(2) The board of county commissioners of any county within his district for legal or clerical assistance in making any investigation or investigations in such county and such boards are hereby authorized to furnish such assistance in their discretion; and

(3) The district attorney of any inferior court in his district for personal assistance

in making any investigation or investigations in the county in which the court is located and any district attorney so called upon is hereby authorized to furnish such assistance by and with the consent of the board of county commissioners of the county in which the court is located, which board shall provide and fix his compensation for assistance furnished.

(b) If following the investigation the district attorney has reasonable grounds to believe that a violation of G.S. 49-2, 14-326, 108-76.1 or any other criminal offense is being or has been committed, he shall send to the grand jury of the county in which he believes the offense is being or has been committed a bill of indictment charging the commission of the offense. Sole and exclusive jurisdiction of offenses discovered as a result of investigations under this section shall be vested in the superior court notwithstanding any other provisions of law, whether general, special or local. Provided nothing in this Article shall be construed to take from the inferior courts any authority or responsibility now vested in them by existing law or to compel the district attorney to again prosecute a crime that has been disposed of in the inferior courts.

(c) Repealed by Session Laws 1985, c. 589, s. 8.

History.
1959, c. 1210, s. 1; 1969, c. 982; 1973, c. 47, s. 2; c. 476, s. 138; 1985, c. 589, s. 8; 1997-443, ss. 11A.118(a), 12.24; 2013-198, s. 4

§ 15-155.3. Disclosure of information by district attorney or agent

No such district attorney, assistant district attorney, or any attorney-at-law especially appointed to assist the district attorney, or any agent or employee of the district attorney's office shall disclose any information, record, report, case history or any memorandum or document or any information contained therein, which may relate to or be connected with the mother or father of any child born out of wedlock, or any child born out of wedlock, unless in the opinion of the district attorney it is necessary or is required in the prosecution and performance of the district attorney's duties as set forth in the provisions of this Article.

History.
1959, c. 1210, s. 4; 1973, c. 47, s. 2; 2013-198, s. 5

ARTICLE 15B
PRETRIAL EXAMINATION OF WITNESSES AND EXHIBITS OF THE STATE

§§ 15-155.4, 15-155.5

Repealed by Session Laws 1973, c. 1286, s. 26.

ARTICLE 16
TRIAL BEFORE JUSTICE

§§ 15-156 through 15-158

Repealed by Session Laws 1973, c. 1286, s. 26.

N.C. Gen. Stat. § 15-159

Repealed by Session Laws 1977, c. 711, s. 33.

§§ 15-160, 15-161

Repealed by Session Laws 1973, c. 1286, s. 26.

ARTICLE 17
TRIAL IN SUPERIOR COURT

N.C. Gen. Stat. § 15-162

Repealed by Session Laws 1973, c. 1286, s. 26.

N.C. Gen. Stat. § 15-162.1

Repealed by Session Laws 1971, c. 1225.

§§ 15-163 through 15-165

Repealed by Session Laws 1967, c. 218, s. 4.

§ 15-166. Exclusion of bystanders in trial for rape and sex offenses

In the trial of cases for rape or sex offense or attempt to commit rape or attempt to commit a sex offense, the trial judge may, during the taking of the testimony of the prosecutrix, exclude from the courtroom all persons except the officers of the court, the defendant and those engaged in the trial of the case.

History.
1907, c. 21; C.S., s. 4636; 1973, c. 1141, s. 14; 1979, c. 682, s. 3; 1981, c. 682, s. 5

§ 15-167. Extension of session of court by trial judge

Whenever a trial for a felony is in progress on the last Friday of any session of court and it appears to the trial judge that it is unlikely that such trial can be completed before 5:00 P.M. on such Friday, the trial judge may extend the session as long as in his opinion it shall be necessary for the purposes of the case, but he may recess court on Friday or Saturday of such week to such time on the succeeding Sunday or Monday as, in his discretion, he deems wise. The trial judge, in his discretion, may exercise the same power in the trial of any other cause under the same circumstances, except civil actions begun after Thursday of the last week. The length of time such court shall remain in session each day shall be in the discretion of the trial judge. Whenever a trial judge continues a session pursuant to this section, he shall cause an order to such effect to be entered in the minutes, which order may be entered at such time as the judge directs, either before or after he has extended the session.

History.
1830, c. 22; R.C., c. 31, s. 16; C.C.P., s. 397; Code, s. 1229; 1893, c. 226; Rev., s. 3266; C.S., s. 4637; 1961, c. 181; 1973, c. 1141, s. 15

§ 15-168. Justification as defense to libel

Every defendant who is charged by indictment with the publication of a libel may prove on the trial for the same the truth of the facts alleged in the indictment; and if it shall appear to the satisfaction of the jury that the facts are true, the defendant shall be acquitted of the charge.

History.
R.C., c. 35, s. 26; Code, s. 1195; Rev., s. 3267; C.S., s. 4638

§ 15-169. Conviction of assault, when included in charge

On the trial of any person for any felony whatsoever, when the crime charged includes an assault against the person, it is lawful for the jury to acquit of the felony and to find a verdict of guilty of assault against the person indicted, if the evidence warrants such finding; and when such verdict is found the court shall have power to imprison the person so found guilty of an assault, for any term now allowed by law in cases of conviction when the indictment was originally for the assault of a like character.

History.
1885, c. 68; Rev., s. 3268; C.S., s. 4639; 1979, c. 682, s. 4

§ 15-170. Conviction for a less degree or an attempt

Upon the trial of any indictment the prisoner may be convicted of the crime charged therein or of a less degree of the same crime, or of an attempt to commit the crime so charged, or of an attempt to commit a less degree of the same crime.

History.
1891, c. 205, s. 2; Rev., s. 3269; C.S., s. 4640

N.C. Gen. Stat. § 15-171

Repealed by Session Laws 1953, c. 100.

§ 15-172. Verdict for murder in first or second degree

Nothing contained in the statute law dividing murder into degrees shall be construed to require any alteration or modification of the existing form of indictment for murder, but the jury before whom the offender is tried shall determine in their verdict whether the crime is murder in the first or second degree.

History.
1893, c. 85, s. 3; Rev., s. 3271; C.S., s. 4642

§ 15-173. Demurrer to the evidence

When on the trial of any criminal action in the superior or district court, the State has introduced its evidence and rested its case, the defendant may move to dismiss the action, or for judgment as in case of nonsuit. If the motion is allowed, judgment shall be entered accordingly; and such judgment shall have the force and effect of a verdict of "not guilty" as to such defendant. If the motion is refused and the defendant does not choose to introduce evidence, the case shall be submitted to the jury as in other cases, and the defendant may on appeal urge as ground for reversal, the trial court's denial of his motion without the necessity of the defendant's having taken exception to such denial.

If the defendant introduces evidence, he thereby waives any motion for dismissal or judgment as in case of nonsuit which he may have made prior to the introduction of his evidence and cannot urge such prior motion as ground for appeal. The defendant, however, may make such motion at the conclusion of all the evidence in the case, irrespective of whether or not he made a motion for dismissal or judgment as in case of nonsuit theretofore. If the motion is allowed, or shall be sustained on appeal, it shall in all cases have the force and effect of a verdict of "not guilty." If the motion is refused, the defendant may on appeal, after the jury has rendered its verdict, urge as ground for reversal the trial court's denial of his motion made at the close of all the evidence without the necessity of the defendant's having taken exception to such denial.

History.
1913, c. 73; Ex. Sess. 1913, c. 32; C.S., s. 4643; 1951, c. 1086, s. 1; 1973, c. 1141, s. 16

§§ 15-173.1, 15-174

Repealed by Session Laws 1977, c. 711, s. 33.

N.C. Gen. Stat. § 15-175

Repealed by Session Laws 1973, c. 1286, s. 26.

§ 15-176. Prisoner not to be tried in prison uniform

It shall be unlawful for any sheriff, jailer or other officer to require any person imprisoned in jail to appear in any court for trial dressed in the uniform or dress of a prisoner or convict, or in any uniform or apparel other than ordinary civilian's dress, or with shaven or clipped head. And no person charged with a criminal offense shall be tried in any court while dressed in the uniform or dress of a prisoner or convict, or in any uniform or apparel other than ordinary civilian's dress, or with head shaven or clipped by or under the direction and requirement of any sheriff, jailer or other officer, unless the head was shaven or clipped while such person was serving a term of imprisonment for the commission of a crime.

Any sheriff, jailer or other officer who violates the provisions of this section shall be guilty of a Class 1 misdemeanor.

History.
1915, c. 124; C.S., s. 4646; 1993, c. 539, s. 296; 1994, Ex. Sess., c. 24, s. 14(c)

§ 15-176.1. District attorney may argue for death penalty

In the trial of capital cases, the district attorney or other counsel appearing for the State may argue to the jury that a sentence of death should be imposed and that the jury should not recommend life imprisonment.

History.
1961, c. 890; 1973, c. 47, s. 2

N.C. Gen. Stat. § 15-176.2

Repealed by Session Laws 1973, c. 44, s. 1.

ARTICLE 17A
INFORMING JURY IN CASE INVOLVING DEATH PENALTY

§ 15-176.3. Informing and questioning potential jurors on consequences of guilty verdict

When a jury is being selected for a case in which the defendant is indicted for a crime for which the penalty is a sentence of death, the court, the defense, or the State may inform any person called to serve as a potential juror that the death penalty will be imposed upon the return of a verdict of guilty of that crime and may inquire of any person called to serve as a potential juror whether that person understands the consequences of a verdict of guilty of that crime.

History.
1973, c. 1286, s. 12

§ 15-176.4. Instruction to jury on consequences of guilty verdict

When a defendant is indicted for a crime for which the penalty is a sentence of death, the court, upon request by either party, shall instruct the jury that the death penalty will be imposed upon the return of a verdict of guilty of that crime.

History.
1973, c. 1286, s. 12

§ 15-176.5. Argument to jury on consequences of guilty verdict

When a case will be submitted to a jury on a charge for which the penalty is a sentence of death, either party in its argument to the jury may indicate the consequences of a verdict of guilty of that charge.

History.
1973, c. 1286, s. 12

§§ 15-176.6 through 15-176.8

Reserved for future codification purposes.

ARTICLE 17B
INFORMING JURY OF POSSIBLE PUNISHMENT UPON CONVICTION

§ 15-176.9. Loss of motor vehicle driver's license

When a case will be submitted to a jury on a charge for which the penalty involves the possibility of the loss of a motor vehicle driver's license, either party in its argument to the jury may indicate the consequences of a verdict of guilty of that charge.

History.
1973, c. 1286, s. 25

ARTICLE 18
APPEAL

§§ 15-177 through 15-178

Repealed by Session Laws 1973, c. 1141, s. 17.

§§ 15-179 through 15-186

Repealed by Session Laws 1977, c. 711, s. 33.

N.C. Gen. Stat. § 15-186.1

Repealed by Session Laws 1973, c. 44, s. 1.

ARTICLE 19
EXECUTION

§ 15-187. Death by administration of lethal drugs

Death by electrocution under sentence of law and death by the administration of lethal gas under sentence of law are abolished. Any person convicted of a criminal offense and sentenced to death shall be executed in accordance with G.S. 15-188 and the remainder of this Article. The warden of Central Prison may obtain and employ the drugs necessary to carry out the provisions of this Article, regardless of contrary provisions in Chapter 90 of the General Statutes.

History.
1909, ch. 443, s. 1; C.S., s. 4657; 1935, c. 294, s. 1; 1983, c. 678, ss. 1, 4; 1998-212, s. 17.22(a); 2015-198, s. 5

§ 15-188. Manner and place of execution

In accordance with G.S. 15-187, the mode of executing a death sentence must in every case be by administering to the convict or felon an intravenous injection of a substance or substances in a lethal quantity sufficient to cause death and until the person is dead, and that procedure shall be determined by the Secretary of the Department of Public Safety, who shall ensure compliance with the federal and State constitutions; and when any person, convict or felon shall be sentenced by any court of the State having competent jurisdiction to be so executed, the punishment shall only be inflicted within a permanent death chamber which the superintendent of the State penitentiary is hereby authorized and directed to provide within the walls of the North Carolina penitentiary at Raleigh, North Carolina. The superintendent of the State penitentiary shall also cause to be provided, in conformity with this Article, the necessary appliances for the infliction of the punishment of death and qualified personnel to set up and prepare the injection, administer the preinjections, insert the IV catheter, and to perform other tasks required for

this procedure in accordance with the requirements of this Article.

History.
1909, c. 443, s. 2; C.S., s. 4658; 1935, c. 294, s. 2; 1983, c. 678, s. 2; 1998-212, s. 17.22(b); 2012-136, s. 1; 2013-154, s. 3(a)

§ 15-188.1. Health care professional assistance

(a) Any assistance rendered with an execution under this Article by any licensed health care professional, including, but not limited to, physicians, nurses, and pharmacists, shall not be cause for any disciplinary or corrective measures by any board, commission, or other authority created by the State or governed by State law which oversees or regulates the practice of health care professionals, including, but not limited to, the North Carolina Medical Board, the North Carolina Board of Nursing, and the North Carolina Board of Pharmacy.

(b) The infliction of the punishment of death by administration of the required lethal substances under this Article shall not be construed to be the practice of medicine.

History.
2013-154, s. 1(a)

§ 15-189. Sentence of death; prisoner taken to penitentiary

Upon the sentence of death being pronounced against any person in the State of North Carolina convicted of a crime punishable by death, it shall be the duty of the judge pronouncing such death sentence to make the same in writing, which shall be filed in the papers in the case against such convicted person. The clerk of the superior court in which such death sentence is pronounced shall prepare a certified copy of said judgment or sentence of death, including therewith a copy of any notice or entries of appeal made in such case; if no entries or notice of appeal have been made or given in such case, a statement to the effect shall be included in the certificate of the clerk; it shall also be the duty of the district attorney, assistant district attorney, or attorney prosecuting in behalf of the State in the absence of the district attorney, to prepare and sign a certificate stating in substance that he prosecuted said case in behalf of the State and that notice or entries of appeal have or have not been made or given in said case, and further that he has examined a copy of said judgment or sentence of death certified by the clerk, including the copy of the notice or entries of appeal or statement to the effect that no appeal has been given, and to the best of his knowledge the same is correct; the certificate of said district attorney, or other prosecuting officer above named, shall be attached to the certified copy of said sentence of death, as prepared and certified by the clerk, and both certificates shall be transmitted by the clerk of the superior court in which said sentence of death is pronounced to the warden of the State penitentiary at Raleigh, North Carolina; at the same time and in the same manner, a duplicate original of said certificates shall be prepared by the clerk of the superior court and the district attorney, or other prosecuting officer above named, and the said duplicate original or said certificates shall be transmitted to the Attorney General of North Carolina. If notice of appeal is given or entries of appeal are made after the expiration of the term of superior court in which said sentence of death is pronounced, said certificates shall be prepared by the clerk of the superior court in which said sentence is pronounced and by the district attorney, or other prosecuting officer above named, prosecuting in behalf of the State, in the same manner and shall be transmitted as soon as possible to the warden of the State penitentiary at Raleigh, North Carolina, and to the Attorney General of North Carolina. The above certificates so prepared by the clerk of the superior court in which such sentence of death is pronounced and by the district attorney, or other prosecuting officer above named, shall be transmitted by the clerk of the superior court in which such sentence is pronounced to the warden of the State penitentiary at Raleigh, North Carolina, and to the Attorney General of North Carolina, not more than 20 or less than 10 days before the time fixed in the judgment of the court for the execution of the sentence; and in all cases where there is no appeal, said sentence of death shall not be carried out by the warden of the State penitentiary or by any of his deputies or agents until said certificates so prepared and transmitted by the clerk of the superior court in which said sentence of death is pronounced, and by the district attorney, or the prosecuting officer above named, have been received in the office of the warden of the State penitentiary at Raleigh, North Carolina. In all cases where there is no appeal from the sentence of death and in all cases where the sentence is pronounced against a prisoner convicted of the crime of rape it shall be the duty of the sheriff, together with at least one deputy, to convey to the penitentiary, at Raleigh, North Carolina, such condemned felon or convict forthwith upon the adjournment of the court in which the felon was tried, and deliver the convict or felon to the warden of the penitentiary.

History.

1909, c. 443, s. 3; C.S., s. 4659; 1951, c. 899, s. 1; 1973, c. 47, s. 2

§ 15-190. Person or persons to be designated by warden to execute sentence; supervision of execution; who shall be present

(a) Correction custody personnel or some other reliable person or persons to be named and designated by the warden from time to time shall cause the person, convict or felon against whom the death sentence has been so pronounced to be executed as provided by this Article and all amendments thereto. The execution shall be under the general supervision and control of the warden of the penitentiary, who shall from time to time, in writing, name and designate the correctional custody personnel or other reliable person or persons who shall cause the person, convict or felon against whom the death sentence has been pronounced to be executed as provided by this Article and all amendments thereto. At such execution there shall be present the warden or deputy warden or some person designated by the warden in the warden's place, and a licensed physician, or a medical professional other than a physician, to monitor the injection of the required lethal substances and certify the fact of the execution. If a licensed physician is not present at the execution, then a licensed physician shall be present on the premises and available to examine the body after the execution and pronounce the person dead. Four respectable citizens, two members of the victim's family, the counsel and any relatives of such person, convict or felon and a minister or member of the clergy or religious leader of the person's choosing may be present if they so desire. The identities, including the names, residential addresses, residential telephone numbers, and social security numbers, of witnesses or persons designated to carry out the execution shall be confidential and exempted from Chapter 132 of the General Statutes and are not subject to discovery or introduction as evidence in any proceeding. The Senior Resident Superior Court Judge for Wake County may order disclosure of names made confidential by this section after making findings that support a conclusion that disclosure is necessary to a proper administration of justice.

For purposes of this section, a "medical professional other than a physician" means a physician assistant, nurse practitioner, registered nurse, emergency medical technician, or emergency medical technician-paramedic who is licensed or credentialed by the licensing board, agency, or organization responsible for licensing or credentialing that profession.

(b) The warden shall report to the Joint Legislative Oversight Committee on Justice and Public Safety by April 1, 2014, and thereafter on October 1 of each year, on the status of the persons required by subsection (a) of this section to be named and designated by the warden to execute death sentences under this Article. The report shall confirm that the required persons are properly trained and ready to serve as an execution team. Alternatively, the Chairs of the Joint Legislative Oversight Committee on Justice and Public Safety may direct that the reports required under this subsection be made on other dates consistent with the Committee's schedule.

History.
1909, c. 443, s. 4; C.S., s. 4660; 1925, c. 123; 1935, c. 294, s. 3; 1983, c. 678, s. 3; 1997-70, s. 1; 2004-124, s. 17.6A; 2004-199, s. 52; 2004-203, s. 22; 2013-154, s. 4; 2015-198, s. 1; 2016-77, s. 8(a)

§ 15-191. Pending sentences unaffected

Nothing in G.S. 15-187, 15-188, and 15-190 shall be construed to alter in any manner the execution of the sentence of death imposed on account of any crime or crimes committed before July 1, 1935.

History.
1935, c. 294, s. 4

§ 15-192. Certificate filed with clerk

The warden, together with the licensed physician who was present on the premises to pronounce death as required by G.S. 15-190, shall certify the fact of the execution of the condemned person, convict or felon to the clerk of the superior court in which such sentence was pronounced, and the clerk shall file such certificate with the papers of the case and enter the same upon the records thereof.

History.
1909, c. 443, s. 5; C.S., s. 4661; 2015-198, s. 2

§ 15-193. Notice of reprieve or new trial

Should the condemned person, convict or felon be granted a reprieve by the Governor or obtain a writ of error, or a new trial be granted by the Supreme Court of the State of North Carolina, or should the execution of the sentence be stayed by any competent judicial tribunal or proceeding, notice of such reprieve, new trial, appeal, writ of error or stay of execution shall be served upon the warden or deputy warden of the penitentiary by the sheriff of Wake County, in case such condemned person is confined in the penitentiary, or upon any sheriff having the custody of any such condemned person, also upon the condemned person himself.

History.
1909, c. 443, s. 6; C.S., s. 4662

§ 15-194. Time for execution

(a) In sentencing a capital defendant to a death sentence pursuant to G.S. 15A-2000(b), the sentencing judge need not specify the date and time the execution is to be carried out by the Division of Adult Correction and Juvenile Justice of the Department of Public Safety. The Attorney General of North Carolina shall provide written notification to the Secretary of the Department of Public Safety of the occurrence of any of the following not more than 90 days from that occurrence:

(1) The United States Supreme Court has filed an opinion upholding the sentence of death following completion of the initial State and federal postconviction proceedings, if any;

(2) The mandate issued by the Supreme Court of North Carolina on direct appeal pursuant to N.C.R. App. P. 32(b) affirming the capital defendant's death sentence and the time for filing a petition for writ of certiorari to the United States Supreme Court has expired without a petition being filed;

(3) The capital defendant, if indigent, failed to timely seek the appointment of counsel pursuant to G.S. 7A-451(c), or failed to file a timely motion for appropriate relief as required by G.S. 15A-1415(a);

(4) The superior court denied the capital defendant's motion for appropriate relief, but the capital defendant failed to file a timely petition for writ of certiorari to the Supreme Court of North Carolina pursuant to N.C.R. App. P. 21(f);

(5) The Supreme Court of North Carolina denied the capital defendant's petition for writ of certiorari pursuant to N.C.R. App. P. 21(f), or, if certiorari was granted, upheld the capital defendant's death sentence, but the capital defendant failed to file a timely petition for writ of certiorari to the United States Supreme Court; or

(6) Following State postconviction proceedings, if any, the capital defendant failed to file a timely petition for writ of habeas corpus in the appropriate federal district court, or failed to timely appeal or petition an adverse habeas corpus decision to the United States Court of Appeals for the Fourth Circuit or the United States Supreme Court.

The Secretary of the Department of Public Safety shall immediately schedule a date for the execution of the original death sentence not less than 15 days or more than 120 days from the date of receiving written notification from the Attorney General under this section.

The Secretary shall send a certified copy of the document fixing the date to the clerk of superior court of the county in which the case was tried or, if venue was changed, in which the defendant was indicted. The certified copy shall be recorded in the minutes of the court. The Secretary shall also send certified copies to the capital defendant, the capital defendant's attorney, the district attorney who prosecuted the case, and the Attorney General of North Carolina.

(b) The Attorney General shall submit a written report to the Joint Legislative Oversight Committee on Justice and Public Safety by April 1, 2014, and thereafter on October 1 of each year, on the status of all pending postconviction capital cases. Alternatively, the Chairs of the Joint Legislative Oversight Committee on Justice and Public Safety may direct that the reports required under this subsection be made on other dates consistent with the Committee's schedule.

History.
1909, c. 443, s. 6; C.S., s. 4663; 1925, c. 55; 1951, c. 244, ss. 1, 2; 1973, c. 47, s. 2; 1981, c. 900; 1995 (Reg. Sess., 1996), c. 719, s. 5; 1997-289, s. 1; 1999-358, s. 2; 2011-145, s. 19.1(h), (i); 2013-154, s. 2; 2017-186, s. 2(mm)

§ 15-195. Prisoner taken to place of trial when new trial granted

Should a new trial be granted the condemned person, convict or felon against whom sentence of death has been pronounced, after he has been conveyed to the penitentiary, he shall be conveyed back to the place of trial by such correctional custody personnel as the warden of the penitentiary shall direct, their expenses to be paid as is now provided by law for the conveyance of convicts to the penitentiary.

History.
1909, c. 443, s. 7; C.S., s. 4664; 2016-77, s. 8(b)

N.C. Gen. Stat. § 15-196

Repealed by Session Laws 1989, c. 353, s. 3 .

ARTICLE 19A
CREDITS AGAINST THE SERVICE OF SENTENCES AND FOR ATTAINMENT OF PRISON PRIVILEGES

§ 15-196.1. Credits allowed

The minimum and maximum term of a sentence shall be credited with and diminished by the total amount of time a defendant has spent, committed to or in confinement in any State or local correctional, mental or other institution as a result of the charge that culminated in the sentence or the incident from which the charge arose. The credit provided shall be calculated from the date custody under the charge commenced and shall include credit for all time spent in custody pending trial, trial de novo, appeal, retrial, or pending parole, probation, or post-release supervision revocation hearing: Provided, however, the credit available herein shall not include any time that a defendant has spent in custody as a result of a pending charge while serving a sentence imposed for another offense.

History.
1973, c. 44, s. 1; 1977, c. 711, s. 16A; 1977, 2nd Sess., c. 1147, s. 30; 1997-237, s. 3; 2015-229, s. 1

§ 15-196.2. Allowance in cases of multiple sentences

In the event time creditable under this section shall have been spent in custody as the result of more than one pending charge, resulting in imprisonment for more than one offense, credit shall be allowed as herein provided. Consecutive sentences shall be considered as one sentence for the purpose of providing credit, and the creditable time shall not be multiplied by the number of consecutive offenses for which a defendant is imprisoned. Each concurrent sentence shall be credited with so much of the time as was spent in custody due to the offense resulting in the sentence. When both concurrent and consecutive sentences are imposed, both of the above rules shall obtain to the applicable extent.

Upon revocation of two or more consecutive sentences as a result of a probation violation, credit for time served on concurrent confinements in response to violation under G.S. 15A-1344(d2) shall be credited to only one sentence.

History.
1973, c. 44, s. 1; 2016-77, s. 5

§ 15-196.3. Effect of credit

Time creditable under this section shall reduce the minimum and maximum term of a sentence; and, irrespective of sentence, shall reduce the time required to attain privileges made available to inmates in the custody of the Division of Adult Correction and Juvenile Justice of the Department of Public Safety which are dependent, in whole or in part, upon the passage of a specific length of time in custody, including parole or post-release supervision consideration by the Post-Release Supervision and Parole

Commission. However, nothing in this section shall be construed as requiring an automatic award of privileges by virtue of the passage of time.

History.
1973, c. 44, s. 1; 1977, c. 711, s. 17; 1997-237, s. 4; 2011-145, s. 19.1(h); 2012-83, s. 22; 2017-186, s. 2(nn)

§ 15-196.4. Procedures for judicial award

Upon sentencing or activating a sentence, the judge presiding shall determine the credits to which the defendant is entitled and shall cause the clerk to transmit to the custodian of the defendant a statement of allowable credits. Upon committing a defendant upon the conclusion of an appeal, or a parole, probation, or post-release supervision revocation, the committing authority shall determine any credits allowable on account of these proceedings and shall cause to be transmitted, as in all other cases, a statement of the allowable credit to the custodian of the defendant. Upon reviewing a petition seeking credit not previously allowed, the court shall determine the credits due and forward an order setting forth the allowable credit to the custodian of the petitioner.

History.
1973, c. 44, s. 1; 1997-237, s. 5

ARTICLE 20
SUSPENSION OF SENTENCE AND PROBATION

§§ 15-197 through 15-200.1

Repealed by Session Laws 1977, c. 711, s. 33.

N.C. Gen. Stat. § 15-200.2

Repealed by Session Laws 1975, c. 309, s. 2.

§§ 15-201, 15-202

Repealed by Session Laws 1973, c. 1262, s. 10.

§ 15-203. Duties of the Secretary of Public Safety; appointment of probation officers; reports; requests for extradition

The Secretary of Public Safety, or the Secretary's designee, shall direct the work of the probation officers appointed under this Article. Notwithstanding any other provision of law, the Secretary of Public Safety shall have sole discretion to establish the minimum experience requirements to receive an appointment as a probation officer. The Office of State Human Resources shall work with the Secretary to establish position classifications for probation officers based on the experience requirements established by the Secretary. The Secretary, or the Secretary's designee, shall consult and cooperate with the courts and institutions in the development of methods and procedure in the administration of probation, and shall arrange conferences of probation officers and judges. The Secretary shall make an annual written report with statistical and other information to the Governor. The Secretary is authorized to present to the Governor written applications for requisitions for the return of probationers who have broken the terms of their probation, and are believed to be in another state, and the Secretary shall follow the procedure outlined for requests for extradition as set forth in G.S. 15A-743.

History.
1937, c. 132, s. 7; 1959, c. 127; 1963, c. 914, s. 2; 1973, c. 1262, s. 10; 2010-96, s. 2; 2011-145, s. 19.1(h), (i); 2012-83, s. 2; 2013-382, s. 9.1(c)

N.C. Gen. Stat. § 15-203.1

Repealed by Session Laws 1963, c. 914, s. 6.

§ 15-204. Assignment, compensation and oath of probation officers

Probation officers appointed under this Article shall be assigned to serve in such courts or districts or otherwise as the Secretary of Public Safety may determine. They shall be paid annual salaries to be fixed by the Department of Public Safety, and shall also be paid traveling and other necessary expenses incurred in the performance of their official duties as probation officers when such expense accounts have been authorized and approved by the Secretary of Public Safety.

Each person appointed as a probation officer shall take an oath of office before the judge of the court or courts in which he is to serve, which oath shall be as follows:

"I,, do solemnly and sincerely swear that I will be faithful and

bear true allegiance to the State of North Carolina, and to the constitutional

powers and authorities which are or may be established for the government

thereof; and that I will endeavor to support, maintain, and defend the

Constitution of said State, not inconsistent with the Constitution of the

United States, to the best of my knowledge and ability; so help me God,"

and shall be noted of record by the clerk of the court.

History.
1937, c. 132, s. 8; 1973, c. 1262, s. 10; 2011-145, s. 19.1(h), (i); 2012-83, s. 23

§ 15-205. Duties and powers of the probation officers

A probation officer shall investigate all cases referred to him for investigation by the judges of the courts or by the Secretary of Public Safety. Such officer shall keep informed concerning the conduct and condition of each person on probation under his supervision by visiting, requiring reports, and in other ways, and shall report thereon in writing as often as the court or the Secretary of Public Safety may require. Such officer shall use all practicable and suitable methods, not inconsistent with the conditions imposed by the court or the Secretary of Public Safety, to aid and encourage persons on probation to bring about improvement in their conduct and condition. Such officer shall keep detailed records of his work; shall make such reports in writing to the Secretary of Public Safety as he may require; and shall perform such other duties as the Secretary of Public Safety may require. A probation officer shall have, in the execution of his duties, the powers of arrest and, to the extent necessary for the performance of his duties, the same right to execute process as is now given, or that may hereafter be given by law, to the sheriffs of this State.

History.
1937, c. 132, s. 9; 1973, c. 1262, s. 10; 1975, c. 229, s. 1; 1977, c. 711, s. 18; 2011-145, s. 19.1(h), (i); 2013-101, s. 3

N.C. Gen. Stat. § 15-205.1

Repealed by Session Laws 1977, c. 711, s. 33.

§ 15-206. Cooperation with Division of Adult Correction and Juvenile Justice of the Department of Public Safety and officials of local units

It is hereby made the duty of every city, county, or State official or department to render all assistance and cooperation within the official's or the Department's fundamental power which may further the objects of this Article. The Division of Adult Correction and Juvenile Justice of the Department of Public Safety, the Secretary of Public Safety, and the probation officers are authorized to seek the cooperation of such officials and departments, and especially of the county superintendents of social services and of the Department of Health and Human Services.

History.
1937, c. 132, s. 10; 1961, c. 139, s. 2; 1969, c. 982; 1973, c. 476, s. 138; c. 1262, s. 10; 1997-443, s. 11A.118(a); 2011-145, ss. 19.1(h), (i); 2012-83, s. 24; 2017-186, s. 2(oo)

§ 15-207. Records treated as privileged information

All information and data obtained in the discharge of official duty by any probation officer shall be privileged information, shall not be receivable as evidence in any court, and shall not be disclosed directly or indirectly to any other than the judge or to others entitled under this Article to receive reports, unless and until otherwise ordered by a judge of the court or the Secretary of Public Safety.

History.
1937, c. 132, s. 11; 1973, c. 1262, s. 10; 2011-145, s. 19.1(i)

N.C. Gen. Stat. § 15-208

Repealed by Session Laws 1975, c. 138.

§ 15-209. Accommodations for probation offices

(a) The county commissioners in each county in which a probation office exists shall provide, in or near the courthouse, suitable office space for those probation officers assigned to the county who have probationary caseloads and their administrative support. This requirement does not include management staff of the Division of Adult Correction and Juvenile Justice of the Department of Public Safety, nonprobation staff, or other Division of Adult Correction and Juvenile Justice of the Department of Public Safety employees.

(b) If a county is unable to provide the space required under subsection (a) of this section for any reason, it may elect to request that the Division of Adult Correction and Juvenile Justice of the Department of Public Safety lease space for the probation office and receive reimbursement from the county for the leased space. If a county fails to reimburse the Division for such leased space, the Secretary of Public Safety may request that the Administrative Office of the Courts transfer the unpaid amount to the Division from the county's court and jail facility fee remittances.

History.
1937, c. 132, s. 13; 2009-451, s. 19.19; 2011-145, s. 19.1(h), (i); 2017-186, s. 2(pp)

ARTICLE 21
SEGREGATION OF YOUTHFUL OFFENDERS

§§ 15-210 through 15-216

Repealed by Session Laws 1967, c. 996, s. 17.

ARTICLE 22
REVIEW OF
CRIMINAL TRIALS

N.C. Gen. Stat. § 15-217

Repealed by Session Laws 1977, c. 711, s. 33.

N.C. Gen. Stat. § 15-217.1

Recodified as § 15A-1420(b1) by Session Laws 1995 (Regular Session, 1996), c. 719, s. 3.

§§ 15-218 through 15-222

Repealed by Session Laws 1977, c. 711, s. 33.

ARTICLE 23
EXPUNCTION OF RECORDS

§§ 15-223, 15-224

Recodified as §§ 15A-145 and 15A-146 by Session Laws 1985, c. 636, s. 1, effective July 5, 1985.

CHAPTER 15A
CRIMINAL
PROCEDURE ACT

DIVISION 01.
GENERAL

ARTICLE 1
DEFINITIONS AND
GENERAL PROVISIONS

§§ 15A-1 through 15A-100

Reserved for future codification purposes.

§ 15A-101. Definitions

Unless the context clearly requires otherwise, the following words have the listed meanings:

(1) **Appeal.** -- When used in a general context, the term "appeal" also includes appellate review upon writ of certiorari.

(1a) **Attorney of Record.** -- An attorney who, under Article 4 of this Chapter, Entry and Withdrawal of Attorney in Criminal Case, has entered a criminal proceeding and has not withdrawn.

(2) **Clerk.** -- Any clerk of superior court, acting clerk, or assistant or deputy clerk.

(3) **District Court.** -- The District Court Division of the General Court of Justice.

(4) **District Attorney.** -- The person elected and currently serving as district attorney in his prosecutorial district.

(4a) **Entry of Judgment.** -- Judgment is entered when sentence is pronounced. Prayer for judgment continued upon payment of costs, without more, does not constitute the entry of judgment.

(5) **Judicial Official.** -- A magistrate, clerk, judge, or justice of the General Court of Justice.

(6) **Officer.** -- Law-enforcement officer.

(7) **Prosecutor.** -- The district attorney, any assistant district attorney or any other attorney designated by the district attorney to act for the State or on behalf of the district attorney.

(8) **State.** -- The State of North Carolina, all land or water in respect to which the State of North Carolina has either exclusive or concurrent jurisdiction, and the airspace above that land or water. "Other state" means any state or territory of the United States, the District of Columbia or the Commonwealth of Puerto Rico.

(9) **Superior Court.** -- The Superior Court Division of the General Court of Justice.

(10) **Superior Court Judge.** -- A superior court judge who has jurisdiction pursuant to G.S. 7A-47.1 or G.S. 7A-48 in the district or set of districts as defined in G.S. 7A-41.1.

(11) **Vehicle.** -- Aircraft, watercraft, or landcraft or other conveyance.

History.
1973, c. 1286, s. 1; 1975, c. 166, s. 2; 1977, c. 711, s. 19; 1987 (Reg. Sess., 1988), c. 1037, s. 52; 1997-456, s. 27

§ 15A-101.1. Electronic technology in criminal process and procedure

As used in this Chapter, in Chapter 7A of the General Statutes, in Chapter 15 of the General Statutes, and in all other provisions of the General Statutes that deal with criminal process or procedure:

(1) "Copy" means all identical versions of a document created or existing in paper form, including the original and all other identical versions of the document in paper form.

(2) "Document" means any pleading, criminal process, subpoena, complaint, motion, application, notice, affidavit, commission, waiver, consent, dismissal, order, judgment, or other writing intended in a criminal or contempt proceeding to authorize or require an action, to record a decision or to communicate or record information. A document may be created and exist in paper form or in electronic form or in both forms. Each document shall contain the legible, printed name of the person who signed the document.

(3) "Electronic" means relating to technology having electrical, digital, magnetic, wireless, optical, electromagnetic, Internet, or similar capabilities.

(3a) "Electronic monitoring" or "electronically monitor" or "satellite-based monitoring" means monitoring with an electronic monitoring device that is not removed from a person's body, that is utilized by the supervising agency in conjunction with a Web-based computer system that actively monitors, identifies, tracks, and records a person's location at least once every minute 24 hours a day, that has a battery life of at least 48 hours without being recharged, that timely records and reports or records the person's presence near or within a crime scene or prohibited area or the person's departure from a specified geographic location, and that has incorporated into the software the ability to automatically compare crime scene data with locations of all persons being electronically monitored so as to provide any correlation daily or in real time. In areas of the State where lack of cellular coverage requires the use of an alternative device, the supervising agency shall use an alternative device that works in concert with the software and records location and tracking data for later download and crime scene comparison.

(4) "Electronic Repository" means an automated electronic repository for criminal process created and maintained pursuant to G.S. 15A-301.1.

(5) "Electronic signature" means any electronic method of signing a document that meets each of the following requirements:

    a. Identifies and authenticates a particular person as the signer of the document, is unique to the person using it, is capable of certification, and is under the sole control of the person using it.

    b. Is attached to or logically associated with the document in such a manner that if the document is altered in any way without authorization of the signer, the signature is invalidated.

    c. Indicates that person's intent to issue, enter or otherwise authenticate the document.

(6) "Entered" means signed and filed in the office of the clerk of superior court of the county in which the document is to be entered. A document may be entered in either paper form or electronic form.

(7) "Filing" or "filed" means:

    a. When the document is in paper form, delivering the original document to the office where the document is to be filed. Filing is complete when the original document is received in the office where the document is to be filed.

    b. When the document is in electronic form, creating and saving the document, or transmitting it, in such a way that it is unalterably retained in the electronic records of the office where the document is to be filed. A document is "unalterably retained" in an electronic record when it may not be edited or otherwise altered except by a person with authorization to do so. Filing is complete when the document has first been unalterably retained in the electronic records of the office where the document is to be filed.

(8) "Issued" applies to documents in either paper form or electronic form. A document that is first created in paper form is issued when it is signed. A document that is first created in electronic form is issued when it is signed, filed in the office of the clerk of superior court of the county for which it is to be issued, and retained in the Electronic Repository.

(9) "Original" means:

    a. A document first created and existing only in paper form, bearing the original signature of the person who signed it. The term also includes each copy in paper form that is printed through the facsimile transmission of the copy bearing the original signature of the person who signed it.

    b. A document existing in electronic form, including the electronic form of the document and any copy that is printed from the electronic form.

(10) "Signature" means any symbol, including, but not limited to, the name of an individual, which is executed by that individual, personally or through an authorized agent, with the intent to authenticate or to effect the issuance or entry of a document. The term includes an electronic signature. A document may be signed by the use of any manual, mechanical or electronic means that causes the individual's signature to appear in or on the document. Any party challenging the validity of a signature shall have the burden of pleading, producing evidence, and proving the following:

    a. The signature was not the act of the person whose signature it appears to be.

    b. If the signature is an electronic signature, the requirements of subdivision (5) of this section have not been met.

History.
2002-64, s. 1; 2011-245, s. 2(a); 2012-194, s. 6; 2021-47, s. 10(b)

ARTICLE 2
JURISDICTION

§§ 15A-102 through 15A-130

Reserved for future codification purposes.

ARTICLE 3
VENUE

§ 15A-131. Venue generally

(a) Venue for pretrial and trial proceedings in district court of cases within the original jurisdiction of the district court lies in the county where the charged offense occurred.

(b) Except for the probable cause hearing, venue for pretrial proceedings in cases within the original jurisdiction of the superior court lies in the superior court district or set of districts as defined in G.S. 7A-41.1 embracing the county where the venue for trial proceedings lies.

(c) Except as otherwise provided in this subsection, venue for probable cause hearings and trial proceedings in cases within the original jurisdiction of the superior court lies in the county where the charged offense occurred. Except as otherwise provided in this subsection, if the alleged offense is committed within the corporate limits of a municipality which is the seat of superior court and is located in more than one county, venue lies in the superior court which sits within that municipality, but upon timely objection of the defendant or the district attorney in the county in which the alleged offense occurred the case must be transferred to the county in which the alleged offense occurred. However, for charges brought by municipal law enforcement officers only, if the alleged offense is committed within the corporate limits of a municipality that extends into four or more counties, each of which is in a separate superior court district, offenses committed within the corporate limits of the municipality but in a superior court district other than the one for which the municipality is the seat of superior court shall be disposed of in the municipality with no allowance for objections by the defendant or the district attorney.

(d) Venue for misdemeanors appealed for trial de novo in superior court lies in the county where the misdemeanor was first tried.

(e) An offense occurs in a county if any act or omission constituting part of the offense occurs within the territorial limits of the county.

(f) For the purposes of this Article, pretrial proceedings are proceedings occurring after the initial appearance before the magistrate and prior to arraignment.

History.
1973, c. 1286, s. 1; 1975, 2nd Sess., c. 983, s. 134; 1983, c. 727; 1987 (Reg. Sess., 1988), c. 1037, s. 53; 2009-398, s. 3

§ 15A-132. Concurrent venue

(a) If acts or omissions constituting part of the commission of the charged offense occurred in more than one county, each county has concurrent venue.

(b) If charged offenses which may be joined in a single criminal pleading under G.S. 15A-926 occurred in more than one county, each county has concurrent venue as to all charged offenses.

(c) When counties have concurrent venue, the first county in which a criminal process is issued in the case becomes the county with exclusive venue.

History.
1973, c. 1286, s. 1

§ 15A-133. Waiver of venue; motion for change of venue; indictment may be returned in other county

(a) A waiver of venue must be in writing and signed by the defendant and the prosecutor indicating the consent of all parties to the waiver. The waiver must specify what stages of the proceedings are affected by the waiver, and the county to which venue is changed. If the venue is to be laid in a county in another prosecutorial district, the consent in writing of the prosecutor in that district must be filed with the clerks of both counties.

(b) Repealed by Session Laws 1989, c. 688, s. 2.

(c) Motions for change of venue by the defendant are made under G.S. 15A-957. If venue is laid in a county in another prosecutorial district by order of the judge ruling on the motion, no consent of any prosecutor is required.

(d) If venue is changed to a county in another prosecutorial district, whether upon waiver of venue or by order of a judge, the prosecutor of the prosecutorial district where the case originated must prosecute the case unless the prosecutor of the district to which venue has been changed consents to conduct the prosecution.

(e) If venue is changed, whether upon waiver of venue or by order of a judge, the grand jury in the county to which venue has been transferred has the power to return an indictment in the case. If an indictment has already been returned before the change of venue, no new indictment is necessary and prosecution may be had in the new county under the original indictment.

History.
1921, c. 12, ss. 1, 2; C.S., ss. 4606(a), 4606(b); 1973, c. 1286, s. 1; 1975, c. 166, s. 27; 1987 (Reg. Sess., 1988), c. 1037, s. 54; 1989, c. 688, s. 2

§ 15A-134. Offense occurring in part outside North Carolina

If a charged offense occurred in part in North Carolina and in part outside North Carolina, a person charged with that offense may be tried in this State if he has not been placed in jeopardy for the identical offense in another state.

History.
1973, c. 1286, s. 1

§ 15A-135. Allegation of venue conclusive in absence of timely motion

Allegations of venue in any criminal pleading become conclusive in the absence of a timely motion to dismiss for improper venue under G.S. 15A-952. A defendant may move to dismiss for improper venue upon trial de novo in superior court, provided he did not in the district court with benefit of counsel stipulate venue or expressly waive his right to contest venue.

History.

1973, c. 1286, s. 1

§ 15A-136. Venue for sexual offenses

If a person is transported by any means, with the intent to violate any of the provisions of Article 7B of Chapter 14 (§ 14-27.20 et seq.) of the General Statutes and the intent is followed by actual violation thereof, the defendant may be tried in the county where transportation was offered, solicited, begun, continued or ended.

History.

1979, c. 682, s. 2; 2015-181, ss. 19, 47

§§ 15A-137 through 15A-140

Reserved for future codification purposes.

ARTICLE 4
ENTRY AND WITHDRAWAL OF ATTORNEY IN CRIMINAL CASE

§ 15A-141. When entry of attorney in criminal proceeding occurs

An attorney enters a criminal proceeding when he:

(1) Files a written notice of entry with the clerk indicating an intent to represent a defendant in a specified criminal proceeding; or

(2) Appears in a criminal proceeding without limiting the extent of his representation; or

(3) Appears in a criminal proceeding for a limited purpose and indicates the extent of his representation by filing written notice thereof with the clerk; or

(4) Accepts assignment to represent an indigent defendant under the terms of Article 36 of Chapter 7A of the General Statutes; or

(5) Files a written waiver of arraignment, except that representation in this instance may not be limited pursuant to subdivision (3).

History.

1973, c. 1286, s. 1; 1975, 2nd Sess., c. 983, s. 135

§ 15A-142. Requirement that clerk record entry

The clerk must note each entry by an attorney in the records of the proceeding.

History.

1973, c. 1286, s. 1

§ 15A-143. Attorney making general entry obligated to represent defendant at all subsequent stages

An attorney who enters a criminal proceeding without limiting the extent of his representation pursuant to G.S. 15A-141(3) undertakes to represent the defendant for whom the entry is made at all subsequent stages of the case until entry of final judgment, at the trial stage. An attorney who appears for a limited purpose under the provisions of G.S. 15A-141(3) undertakes to represent the defendant only for that purpose and is deemed to have withdrawn from the proceedings, without the need for permission of the court, when that purpose is fulfilled.

History.

1973, c. 1286, s. 1; 1977, c. 1117

§ 15A-144. Withdrawal of attorney with permission of court

The court may allow an attorney to withdraw from a criminal proceeding upon a showing of good cause.

History.

1973, c. 1286, s. 1

ARTICLE 5
EXPUNCTION OF RECORDS

§ 15A-145. Expunction of records for first offenders under the age of 18 at the time of conviction of misdemeanor; expunction of certain other misdemeanors

(a) Whenever any person who has not previously been convicted of any felony, or misdemeanor other than a traffic violation, under the laws of the United States, the laws of this State or any other state, (i) pleads guilty to or is guilty of a misdemeanor other than a traffic violation, and the offense was committed before the person attained the age of 18 years, or (ii) pleads guilty to or is guilty of a misdemeanor possession of alcohol pursuant to G.S. 18B-302(b)(1), and the offense was committed before the person attained the age of 21 years, he may file a petition in the court of the county where he was convicted for expunction of the misdemeanor from his criminal record. The petition cannot be filed earlier than: (i) two years after the date of the conviction, or (ii) the completion of any period of probation, whichever occurs later, and the petition shall contain, but not be limited to, the following:

(1) An affidavit by the petitioner that he has been of good behavior for the two-year period since the date of conviction of the misdemeanor in question and has not been convicted of any felony, or misdemeanor other than a traffic violation, under the laws of the United States or the laws of this State or any other state.

(2) Verified affidavits of two persons who are not related to the petitioner or to each other by blood or marriage, that they know the character and reputation of the petitioner in the community in which he lives and that his character and reputation are good.

(3) A statement that the petition is a motion in the cause in the case wherein the petitioner was convicted.

(4) Repealed by Session Laws 2010-174, s. 2, effective October 1, 2010, and applicable to petitions for expunctions filed on or after that date.

(4a) An application on a form approved by the Administrative Office of the Courts requesting and authorizing a name-based State and national criminal record check by the Department of Public Safety using any information required by the Administrative Office of the Courts to identify the individual and a search of the confidential record of expunctions maintained by the Administrative Office of the Courts. The application shall be filed with the clerk of superior court. The clerk of superior court shall forward the application to the Department of Public Safety and to the Administrative Office of the Courts, which shall conduct the searches and report their findings to the court.

(5) An affidavit by the petitioner that no restitution orders or civil judgments representing amounts ordered for restitution entered against him are outstanding.

The petition shall be served upon the district attorney of the court wherein the case was tried resulting in conviction. The district attorney shall have 10 days thereafter in which to file any objection thereto and

shall be duly notified as to the date of the hearing of the petition.

The judge to whom the petition is presented is authorized to call upon a probation officer for any additional investigation or verification of the petitioner's conduct during the two-year period that he deems desirable.

(a1) Nothing in this section shall be interpreted to allow the expunction of any offense involving impaired driving as defined in G.S. 20-4.01(24a) or any offense requiring registration pursuant to Article 27A of Chapter 14 of the General Statutes, whether or not the person is currently required to register.

(b) If the court, after hearing, finds that the petitioner had remained of good behavior and been free of conviction of any felony or misdemeanor, other than a traffic violation, for two years from the date of conviction of the misdemeanor in question, the petitioner has no outstanding restitution orders or civil judgments representing amounts ordered for restitution entered against him, and (i) petitioner was not 18 years old at the time of the offense in question, or (ii) petitioner was not 21 years old at the time of the offense of possession of alcohol pursuant to G.S. 18B-302(b)(1), it shall order that such person be restored, in the contemplation of the law, to the status he occupied before such arrest or indictment or information.

(b1) No person as to whom such order has been entered shall be held thereafter under any provision of any laws to be guilty of perjury or otherwise giving a false statement by reason of his failure to recite or acknowledge such arrest, or indictment, information, or trial, or response to any inquiry made of him for any purpose. This subsection shall not apply to a sentencing hearing when the person has been convicted of a subsequent criminal offense.

(c) The court shall also order that the misdemeanor conviction, or a civil revocation of a drivers license as the result of a criminal charge, be expunged from the records of the court. The court shall direct all law-enforcement agencies, the Division of Adult Correction and Juvenile Justice of the Department of Public Safety, the Division of Motor Vehicles, and any other State or local government agencies identified by the petitioner as bearing record of the same to expunge their records of the petitioner's conviction or a civil revocation of a drivers license as the result of a criminal charge. This subsection does not apply to civil or criminal charges based upon the civil revocation, or to civil revocations under G.S. 20-16.2. The clerk shall notify State and local agencies of the court's order as provided in G.S. 15A-150. The clerk shall forward a certified copy of the order to the Division of Motor Vehicles for the expunction of a civil revocation provided the underlying criminal charge is also expunged. The civil revocation of a drivers license shall not be expunged prior to a final disposition of any pending civil or criminal charge based upon the civil revocation.

(d) The clerk shall notify State and local agencies of the court's order as provided in G.S. 15A-150.

(d1) Repealed by Session Laws 2012-191, s. 3, effective December 1, 2012.

(e) A person who files a petition for expunction of a criminal record under this section must pay the clerk of superior court a fee of one hundred seventy-five dollars ($ 175.00) at the time the petition is filed. Fees collected under this subsection are payable to the Administrative Office of the Courts. The clerk of superior court shall remit one hundred twenty-two dollars and fifty cents ($ 122.50) of each fee to the North Carolina Department of Public Safety for the costs of criminal record checks performed in connection with processing petitions for expunctions under this section. The remaining fifty-two dollars and fifty cents ($ 52.50) of each fee shall be retained by the Administrative Office of the Courts and used to pay the costs of processing petitions for expunctions under this section. This subsection does not apply to petitions filed by an indigent.

History.

1973, c. 47, s. 2; c. 748; 1975, c. 650, s. 5; 1977, c. 642, s. 1; c. 699, ss. 1, 2; 1979, c. 431, ss. 1, 2; 1985, c. 636, s. 1; 1999-406, s. 8; 2002-126, ss. 29A.5(a), (b); 2004-133, s. 1; 2005-276, s. 43.1(e); 2007-509, s. 1; 2008-187, s. 35; 2009-510, s. 4(a), (b); 2009-577, s. 10; 2010-174, ss. 2, 3; 2011-145, s. 19.1(h); 2012-191, s. 3; 2013-360, s. 18B.16(a); 2014-100, s. 17.1(o); 2015-150, s. 2; 2017-186, s. 2(qq); 2017-195, s. 1; 2021-115, s. 2

§ 15A-145.1. Expunction of records for first offenders under the age of 18 at the time of conviction of certain gang offenses

(a) Whenever any person who has not previously been convicted of any felony or misdemeanor other than a traffic violation under the laws of the United States or the laws of this State or any other state pleads guilty to or is guilty of (i) a Class H felony under Article 13A of Chapter 14 of the General Statutes or (ii) an enhanced offense under G.S. 14-50.22, or has been discharged and had the proceedings against the person dismissed pursuant to G.S. 14-50.29, and the offense was committed before the person attained the age of 18 years, the person may file a petition in the court of the county where the person was convicted for expunction of the offense from the person's criminal record. Except as provided in G.S. 14-50.29 upon discharge and dismissal, the petition cannot be filed earlier than (i) two years after the date of the conviction or (ii) the completion of any

period of probation, whichever occurs later. The petition shall contain, but not be limited to, the following:

(1) An affidavit by the petitioner that the petitioner has been of good behavior (i) during the period of probation since the decision to defer further proceedings on the offense in question pursuant to G.S. 14-50.29 or (ii) during the two-year period since the date of conviction of the offense in question, whichever applies, and has not been convicted of any felony or misdemeanor other than a traffic violation under the laws of the United States or the laws of this State or any other state.

(2) Verified affidavits of two persons who are not related to the petitioner or to each other by blood or marriage, that they know the character and reputation of the petitioner in the community in which the petitioner lives, and that the petitioner's character and reputation are good.

(3) If the petition is filed subsequent to conviction of the offense in question, a statement that the petition is a motion in the cause in the case wherein the petitioner was convicted.

(4) Repealed by Session Laws 2010-174, s. 4, effective October 1, 2010, and applicable to petitions for expunctions filed on or after that date.

(4a) An application on a form approved by the Administrative Office of the Courts requesting and authorizing a name-based State and national criminal record check by the Department of Public Safety using any information required by the Administrative Office of the Courts to identify the individual and a search of the confidential record of expunctions maintained by the Administrative Office of the Courts. The application shall be filed with the clerk of superior court. The clerk of superior court shall forward the application to the Department of Public Safety and to the Administrative Office of the Courts, which shall conduct the searches and report their findings to the court.

(5) An affidavit by the petitioner that no restitution orders or civil judgments representing amounts ordered for restitution entered against the petitioner are outstanding.

The petition shall be served upon the district attorney of the court wherein the case was tried resulting in conviction. The district attorney shall have 10 days thereafter in which to file any objection thereto and shall be duly notified as to the date of the hearing of the petition.

The judge to whom the petition is presented is authorized to call upon a probation officer for any additional investigation or verification of the petitioner's conduct during the probationary period or during the two-year period after conviction.

(b) If the court, after hearing, finds that (i) the petitioner was dismissed and the proceedings against the petitioner discharged pursuant to G.S. 14-50.29 and that the person had not yet attained 18 years of age at the time of the offense or (ii) the petitioner has remained of good behavior and been free of conviction of any felony or misdemeanor other than a traffic violation for two years from the date of conviction of the offense in question, the petitioner has no outstanding restitution orders or civil judgments representing amounts ordered for restitution entered against the petitioner, and the petitioner had not attained the age of 18 years at the time of the offense in question, it shall order that such person be restored, in the contemplation of the law, to the status occupied by the petitioner before such arrest or indictment or information, and that the record be expunged from the records of the court.

(b1) No person as to whom such order has been entered shall be held thereafter under any provision of any laws to be guilty of perjury or otherwise giving a false statement by reason of the person's failure to recite or acknowledge such arrest, or indictment or information, or trial, or response to any inquiry made of the person for any purpose. This subsection shall not apply to a sentencing hearing when the person has been convicted of a subsequent criminal offense.

(b2) The court shall also direct all law enforcement agencies, the Division of Adult Correction and Juvenile Justice of the Department of Public Safety, the Division of Motor Vehicles, and any other State or local government agencies identified by the petitioner as bearing record of the same to expunge their records of the petitioner's criminal charge and any conviction resulting from the charge. The clerk shall notify State and local agencies of the court's order as provided in G.S. 15A-150.

(c) This section is supplemental and in addition to existing law and shall not be construed so as to repeal any existing provision contained in the General Statutes of North Carolina.

(d) A person who files a petition for expunction of a criminal record under this section must pay the clerk of superior court a fee of one hundred seventy-five dollars ($ 175.00) at the time the petition is filed. Fees collected under this subsection are payable to the Administrative Office of the Courts. The clerk of superior court shall remit one hundred twenty-two dollars and fifty cents ($ 122.50) of each fee to the North Carolina Department of Public Safety for the costs of criminal record checks performed in connection with processing petitions for expunctions under this section. The remaining

fifty-two dollars and fifty cents ($ 52.50) of each fee shall be retained by the Administrative Office of the Courts and used to pay the costs of processing petitions for expunctions under this section. This subsection does not apply to petitions filed by an indigent.

History.
2009-577, s. 1; 2010-174, s. 4; 2011-145, s. 19.1(h); 2013-360, s. 18B.16(b); 2014-100, s. 17.1(o); 2017-186, s. 2(rr); 2017-195, s. 1

§ 15A-145.2. Expunction of records for first offenders not over 21 years of age at the time of the offense of certain drug offenses

(a) Whenever a person is discharged, and the proceedings against the person dismissed, pursuant to G.S. 90-96(a) or (a1), and the person was not over 21 years of age at the time of the offense, the person may apply to the court of the county where charged for an order to expunge from all official records, other than the confidential files retained under G.S. 15A-151, all recordation relating to the person's arrest, indictment or information, trial, finding of guilty, and dismissal and discharge pursuant to this section. The applicant shall attach to the petition the following:

(1) An affidavit by the petitioner that he or she has been of good behavior during the period of probation since the decision to defer further proceedings on the offense in question and has not been convicted of any felony or misdemeanor other than a traffic violation under the laws of the United States or the laws of this State or any other state;

(2) Verified affidavits by two persons who are not related to the petitioner or to each other by blood or marriage, that they know the character and reputation of the petitioner in the community in which he or she lives, and that the petitioner's character and reputation are good;

(3) Repealed by Session Laws 2010-174, s. 5, effective October 1, 2010, and applicable to petitions for expunctions filed on or after that date.

(3a) An application on a form approved by the Administrative Office of the Courts requesting and authorizing a name-based State and national criminal record check by the Department of Public Safety using any information required by the Administrative Office of the Courts to identify the individual and a search of the confidential record of expunctions maintained by the Administrative Office of the Courts. The application shall be filed with the clerk of superior court. The clerk of superior court shall forward the application to the Department of Public Safety and to the Administrative Office of the Courts, which shall conduct the searches and report their findings to the court.

The judge to whom the petition is presented is authorized to call upon a probation officer for any additional investigation or verification of the petitioner's conduct during the probationary period deemed desirable.

If the court determines, after hearing, that such person was discharged and the proceedings against him or her dismissed and that the person was not over 21 years of age at the time of the offense, it shall enter such order. The effect of such order shall be to restore such person in the contemplation of the law to the status the person occupied before such arrest or indictment or information.

(a1) No person as to whom such order was entered shall be held thereafter under any provision of any law to be guilty of perjury or otherwise giving a false statement by reason of the person's failures to recite or acknowledge such arrest, or indictment or information, or trial in response to any inquiry made of him or her for any purpose. This subsection shall not apply to a sentencing hearing when the person has been convicted of a subsequent criminal offense.

(a2) The court shall also order that all records of the proceeding be expunged from the records of the court and direct all law enforcement agencies, the Division of Adult Correction and Juvenile Justice, the Division of Motor Vehicles, and any other State and local government agencies identified by the petitioner as bearing records of the same to expunge their records of the proceeding. The clerk shall notify State and local agencies of the court's order as provided in G.S. 15A-150.

(b) Whenever any person is charged with a misdemeanor under Article 5 of Chapter 90 of the General Statutes by possessing a controlled substance included within Schedules I through VI of Article 5 of Chapter 90 of the General Statutes or a felony under G.S. 90-95(a)(3), upon dismissal by the State of the charges against the person, upon entry of a nolle prosequi, or upon a finding of not guilty or other adjudication of innocence, such person may apply to the court for an order to expunge from all official records all recordation relating to his or her arrest, indictment or information, or trial. If the court determines, after hearing, that such person was not over 21 years of age at the time the offense for which the person was charged occurred, it shall enter such order. The clerk shall notify State and local agencies of the court's order as provided in G.S. 15A-150. No person as to whom such order has been entered

shall be held thereafter under any provision of any law to be guilty of perjury or otherwise giving a false statement by reason of the person's failures to recite or acknowledge such arrest, or indictment or information, or trial in response to any inquiry made of him or her for any purpose.

(c) Whenever any person who has not previously been convicted of (i) any felony offense under any state or federal laws; (ii) any offense under Chapter 90 of the General Statutes; or (iii) an offense under any statute of the United States or any state relating to controlled substances included in any schedule of Chapter 90 of the General Statutes or to that paraphernalia included in Article 5B of Chapter 90 of the General Statutes, pleads guilty to or has been found guilty of a misdemeanor under Article 5 of Chapter 90 of the General Statutes by possessing a controlled substance included within Schedules I through VI of Chapter 90, or by possessing drug paraphernalia as prohibited by G.S. 90-113.22 or pleads guilty to or has been found guilty of a felony under G.S. 90-95(a)(3), the court may, upon application of the person not sooner than 12 months after conviction, order cancellation of the judgment of conviction and expunction of the records of the person's arrest, indictment or information, trial, and conviction. A conviction in which the judgment of conviction has been canceled and the records expunged pursuant to this subsection shall not be thereafter deemed a conviction for purposes of this subsection or for purposes of disqualifications or liabilities imposed by law upon conviction of a crime, except as provided in G.S. 15A-151.5. Cancellation and expunction under this subsection may occur only once with respect to any person. Disposition of a case under this subsection at the district court division of the General Court of Justice shall be final for the purpose of appeal.

The granting of an application filed under this subsection shall cause the issue of an order to expunge from all official records, other than the confidential files retained under G.S. 15A-151, all recordation relating to the petitioner's arrest, indictment or information, trial, finding of guilty, judgment of conviction, cancellation of the judgment, and expunction of records pursuant to this subsection.

The judge to whom the petition is presented is authorized to call upon a probation officer for additional investigation or verification of the petitioner's conduct since conviction. If the court determines that the petitioner was convicted of (i) a misdemeanor under Article 5 of Chapter 90 of the General Statutes for possessing a controlled substance included within Schedules I through VI of Article 5 of Chapter 90 of the General Statutes or for possessing drug paraphernalia as prohibited in G.S. 90-113.22 or (ii) a felony under G.S. 90-95(a)(3), that the petitioner has no disqualifying previous convictions as set forth in this subsection, that the petitioner was not over 21 years of age at the time of the offense, that the petitioner has been of good behavior since his or her conviction, that the petitioner has successfully completed a drug education program approved for this purpose by the Department of Health and Human Services, and that the petitioner has not been convicted of a felony or misdemeanor other than a traffic violation under the laws of this State at any time prior to or since the conviction for the offense in question, it shall enter an order of expunction of the petitioner's court record. The effect of such order shall be to restore the petitioner in the contemplation of the law to the status the petitioner occupied before arrest or indictment or information or conviction. No person as to whom such order was entered shall be held thereafter under any provision of any law to be guilty of perjury or otherwise giving a false statement by reason of the person's failures to recite or acknowledge such arrest, or indictment or information, or conviction, or trial in response to any inquiry made of him or her for any purpose. The judge may waive the condition that the petitioner attend the drug education school if the judge makes a specific finding that there was no drug education school within a reasonable distance of the defendant's residence or that there were specific extenuating circumstances which made it likely that the petitioner would not benefit from the program of instruction.

The court shall also order all law enforcement agencies, the Department of Public Safety, the Division of Motor Vehicles, and any other State or local agencies identified by the petitioner as bearing records of the conviction and records relating thereto to expunge their records of the conviction. The clerk shall notify State and local agencies of the court's order as provided in G.S. 15A-150.

(d) A person who files a petition for expunction of a criminal record under this section must pay the clerk of superior court a fee of one hundred seventy-five dollars ($ 175.00) at the time the petition is filed. Fees collected under this subsection are payable to the Administrative Office of the Courts. The clerk of superior court shall remit one hundred twenty-two dollars and fifty cents ($ 122.50) of each fee to the North Carolina Department of Public Safety for the costs of criminal record checks performed in connection with processing petitions for expunctions under this section. The remaining fifty-two dollars and fifty cents ($ 52.50) of each fee shall be retained by the Administrative Office of the Courts and used to pay the costs of processing petitions for expunctions under this

section. This subsection does not apply to petitions filed by an indigent.

History.

2009-577, s. 2; 2010-174, s. 5; 2011-145, s. 19.1(h); 2011-192, s. 5(b); 2011-412, s. 2.6(a); 2013-360, s. 18B.16(c); 2014-100, s. 17.1(o); 2017-186, s. 2(ss); 2017-195, s. 1

§ 15A-145.3. Expunction of records for first offenders not over 21 years of age at the time of the offense of certain toxic vapors offenses

(a) Whenever a person is discharged and the proceedings against the person dismissed under G.S. 90-113.14(a) or (a1), such person, if he or she was not over 21 years of age at the time of the offense, may apply to the court of the county where charged for an order to expunge from all official records, other than the confidential files retained under G.S. 15A-151, all recordation relating to the person's arrest, indictment or information, trial, finding of guilty, and dismissal and discharge pursuant to this section. The applicant shall attach to the petition the following:

(1) An affidavit by the petitioner that the petitioner has been of good behavior during the period of probation since the decision to defer further proceedings on the misdemeanor in question and has not been convicted of any felony or misdemeanor other than a traffic violation under the laws of the United States or the laws of this State or any other state;

(2) Verified affidavits by two persons who are not related to the petitioner or to each other by blood or marriage, that they know the character and reputation of the petitioner in the community in which the petitioner lives, and that his or her character and reputation are good;

(3) Repealed by Session Laws 2010-174, s. 6, effective October 1, 2010, and applicable to petitions for expunctions filed on or after that date.

(3a) An application on a form approved by the Administrative Office of the Courts requesting and authorizing a name-based State and national criminal record check by the Department of Public Safety using any information required by the Administrative Office of the Courts to identify the individual and a search of the confidential record of expunctions maintained by the Administrative Office of the Courts. The application shall be filed with the clerk of superior court. The clerk of superior court shall forward the application to the Department of Public Safety and to the Administrative Office of the Courts, which shall conduct the searches and report their findings to the court.

The judge to whom the petition is presented is authorized to call upon a probation officer for any additional investigation or verification of the petitioner's conduct during the probationary period deemed desirable.

If the court determines, after hearing, that such person was discharged and the proceedings against the person dismissed and that he or she was not over 21 years of age at the time of the offense, it shall enter such order. The effect of such order shall be to restore such person in the contemplation of the law to the status the person occupied before such arrest or indictment or information. No person as to whom such order was entered shall be held thereafter under any provision of any law to be guilty of perjury or otherwise giving a false statement by reason of the person's failures to recite or acknowledge such arrest, or indictment or information, or trial in response to any inquiry made of him or her for any purpose.

The court shall also order that all records of the proceeding be expunged from the records of the court and direct all law enforcement agencies bearing records of the same to expunge their records of the proceeding. The clerk shall notify State and local agencies of the court's order as provided in G.S. 15A-150.

(b) Whenever any person is charged with a misdemeanor under Article 5A of Chapter 90 of the General Statutes or possessing drug paraphernalia as prohibited by G.S. 90-113.22, upon dismissal by the State of the charges against the person or upon entry of a nolle prosequi or upon a finding of not guilty or other adjudication of innocence, such person may apply to the court for an order to expunge from all official records all recordation relating to the person's arrest, indictment or information, and trial. If the court determines, after hearing that such person was not over 21 years of age at the time the offense for which the person was charged occurred, it shall enter such order. The clerk shall notify State and local agencies of the court's order as provided in G.S. 15A-150.

(b1) No person as to whom such order has been entered shall be held thereafter under any provision of any law to be guilty of perjury or otherwise giving a false statement by reason of the person's failures to recite or acknowledge such arrest, or indictment or information, or trial in response to any inquiry made of him or her for any purpose. This subsection shall not apply to a sentencing hearing when the person has been convicted of a subsequent criminal offense.

(c) Whenever any person who has not previously been convicted of an offense under Article 5 or 5A of Chapter 90 of the General Statutes or under any statute of the United States or any state relating to controlled substances included in any schedule of Article 5 of Chapter 90 of the General Statutes or to that paraphernalia included in Article 5B of Chapter 90 of the General Statutes pleads guilty to or has been found guilty of a misdemeanor under Article 5A of Chapter 90 of the General Statutes, the court may, upon application of the person not sooner than 12 months after conviction, order cancellation of the judgment of conviction and expunction of the records of the person's arrest, indictment or information, trial, and conviction. A conviction in which the judgment of conviction has been cancelled and the records expunged pursuant to this subsection shall not be thereafter deemed a conviction for purposes of this subsection or for purposes of disqualifications or liabilities imposed by law upon conviction of a crime, except as provided in G.S. 15A-151.5. Cancellation and expunction under this subsection may occur only once with respect to any person. Disposition of a case under this subsection at the district court division of the General Court of Justice shall be final for the purpose of appeal.

The granting of an application filed under this subsection shall cause the issue of an order to expunge from all official records, other than the confidential files retained under G.S. 15A-151, all recordation relating to the person's arrest, indictment or information, trial, finding of guilty, judgment of conviction, cancellation of the judgment, and expunction of records pursuant to this subsection.

The judge to whom the petition is presented is authorized to call upon a probation officer for additional investigation or verification of the petitioner's conduct since conviction. If the court determines that the petitioner was convicted of a misdemeanor under Article 5A of Chapter 90 of the General Statutes, or for possessing drug paraphernalia as prohibited by G.S. 90-113.22, that the petitioner was not over 21 years of age at the time of the offense, that the petitioner has been of good behavior since his or her conviction, that the petitioner has successfully completed a drug education program approved for this purpose by the Department of Health and Human Services, and that the petitioner has not been convicted of a felony or misdemeanor other than a traffic violation under the laws of this State at any time prior to or since the conviction for the misdemeanor in question, it shall enter an order of expunction of the petitioner's court record. The effect of such order shall be to restore the petitioner in the contemplation of the law to the status he occupied before such arrest or indictment or information or conviction.

No person as to whom such order was entered shall be held thereafter under any provision of any law to be guilty of perjury or otherwise giving a false statement by reason of the person's failures to recite or acknowledge such arrest, or indictment or information, or conviction, or trial in response to any inquiry made of him or her for any purpose. The judge may waive the condition that the petitioner attend the drug education school if the judge makes a specific finding that there was no drug education school within a reasonable distance of the defendant's residence or that there were specific extenuating circumstances which made it likely that the petitioner would not benefit from the program of instruction.

The clerk shall notify State and local agencies of the court's order as provided in G.S. 15A-150.

(d) A person who files a petition for expunction of a criminal record under this section must pay the clerk of superior court a fee of one hundred seventy-five dollars ($ 175.00) at the time the petition is filed. Fees collected under this subsection are payable to the Administrative Office of the Courts. The clerk of superior court shall remit one hundred twenty-two dollars and fifty cents ($ 122.50) of each fee to the North Carolina Department of Public Safety for the costs of criminal record checks performed in connection with processing petitions for expunctions under this section. The remaining fifty-two dollars and fifty cents ($ 52.50) of each fee shall be retained by the Administrative Office of the Courts and used to pay the costs of processing petitions for expunctions under this section. This subsection does not apply to petitions filed by an indigent.

History.
2009-577, s. 3; 2010-174, s. 6; 2013-360, s. 18B.16(d); 2014-100, s. 17.1(o); 2017-195, s. 1

§ 15A-145.4. Expunction of records for first offenders who are under 18 years of age at the time of the commission of a nonviolent felony

(a) For purposes of this section, the term "nonviolent felony" means any felony except the following:

(1) A Class A through G felony.

(2) A felony that includes assault as an essential element of the offense.

(3) A felony that is an offense requiring registration pursuant to Article 27A of Chapter 14 of the General Statutes, whether or not the person is currently required to register.

(4) Repealed by Session Laws 2012-191, s. 2, effective December 1, 2012.

(5) Any felony offense under the following sex-related or stalking offenses: G.S.

14-27.25(b), 14-27.30(b), 14-190.7, 14-190.8, 14-202, 14-208.11A, 14-208.18, 14-277.3, 14-277.3A, 14-321.1.

(6) Any felony offense in Chapter 90 of the General Statutes where the offense involves methamphetamines, heroin, or possession with intent to sell or deliver or sell and deliver cocaine; except that if a prayer for judgment continued has been entered for an offense classified as either a Class G, H, or I felony, the prayer for judgment continued shall be subject to expunction under the procedures in this section.

(7) A felony offense under G.S. 14-12.12(b), 14-12.13, or 14-12.14, or any felony offense for which punishment was determined pursuant to G.S. 14-3(c).

(8) A felony offense under G.S. 14-401.16.

(9) Any felony offense in which a commercial motor vehicle was used in the commission of the offense.

(10) Any felony offense involving impaired driving as defined in G.S. 20-4.01(24a).

(b) Notwithstanding any other provision of law, if the person is convicted of more than one nonviolent felony in the same session of court and none of the nonviolent felonies are alleged to have occurred after the person had already been served with criminal process for the commission of a nonviolent felony, then the multiple nonviolent felony convictions shall be treated as one nonviolent felony conviction under this section, and the expunction order issued under this section shall provide that the multiple nonviolent felony convictions shall be expunged from the person's record in accordance with this section.

(c) Whenever any person who had not yet attained the age of 18 years at the time of the commission of the offense and has not previously been convicted of any felony or misdemeanor other than a traffic violation under the laws of the United States or the laws of this State or any other state pleads guilty to or is guilty of a nonviolent felony, the person may file a petition in the court of the county where the person was convicted for expunction of the nonviolent felony from the person's criminal record. The petition shall not be filed earlier than four years after the date of the conviction or when any active sentence, period of probation, and post-release supervision has been served, whichever occurs later. The person shall also perform at least 100 hours of community service, preferably related to the conviction, before filing a petition for expunction under this section. The petition shall contain the following:

(1) An affidavit by the petitioner that the petitioner has been of good moral character since the date of conviction of the nonviolent felony in question and has not been convicted of any other felony or any

misdemeanor other than a traffic violation under the laws of the United States or the laws of this State or any other state.

(2) Verified affidavits of two persons who are not related to the petitioner or to each other by blood or marriage, that they know the character and reputation of the petitioner in the community in which the petitioner lives and that the petitioner's character and reputation are good.

(3) A statement that the petition is a motion in the cause in the case wherein the petitioner was convicted.

(4) An application on a form approved by the Administrative Office of the Courts requesting and authorizing (i) a State and national criminal history record check by the Department of Public Safety using any information required by the Administrative Office of the Courts to identify the individual; (ii) a search by the Department of Public Safety for any outstanding warrants or pending criminal cases; and (iii) a search of the confidential record of expunctions maintained by the Administrative Office of the Courts. The application shall be filed with the clerk of superior court. The clerk of superior court shall forward the application to the Department of Public Safety and to the Administrative Office of the Courts, which shall conduct the searches and report their findings to the court.

(5) An affidavit by the petitioner that no restitution orders or civil judgments representing amounts ordered for restitution entered against the petitioner are outstanding.

(6) An affidavit by the petitioner that the petitioner has performed at least 100 hours of community service since the conviction for the nonviolent felony. The affidavit shall include a list of the community services performed, a list of the recipients of the services, and a detailed description of those services.

(7) An affidavit by the petitioner that the petitioner possesses a high school diploma, a high school graduation equivalency certificate, or a General Education Development degree.

The petition shall be served upon the district attorney of the court wherein the case was tried resulting in conviction. The district attorney shall have 30 days thereafter in which to file any objection thereto and shall be duly notified as to the date of the hearing of the petition. The district attorney shall make his or her best efforts to contact the victim, if any, to notify the victim of the request for expunction prior to the date of the hearing.

(d) The court in which the petition was filed shall take the following steps and shall consider the following issues in rendering a decision upon a petition for expunction of records of a nonviolent felony under this section:

(1) Call upon a probation officer for additional investigation or verification of the petitioner's conduct during the four-year period since the date of conviction of the nonviolent felony in question.

(2) Review the petitioner's juvenile record, ensuring that the petitioner's juvenile records remain separate from adult records and files and are withheld from public inspection as provided under Article 30 of Chapter 7B of the General Statutes.

(3) Review the amount of restitution made by the petitioner to the victim of the nonviolent felony to be expunged and give consideration to whether or not restitution was paid in full.

(4) Review any other information the court deems relevant, including, but not limited to, affidavits or other testimony provided by law enforcement officers, district attorneys, and victims of nonviolent felonies committed by the petitioner.

(e) The court may order that the person be restored, in the contemplation of the law, to the status the person occupied before the arrest or indictment or information if the court finds all of the following after a hearing:

(1) The petitioner has remained of good moral character and has been free of conviction of any felony or misdemeanor, other than a traffic violation, for four years from the date of conviction of the nonviolent felony in question or any active sentence, period of probation, or post-release supervision has been served, whichever is later.

(2) The petitioner has not previously been convicted of any felony or misdemeanor other than a traffic violation under the laws of the United States or the laws of this State or any other state.

(3) The petitioner has no outstanding warrants or pending criminal cases.

(4) The petitioner has no outstanding restitution orders or civil judgments representing amounts ordered for restitution entered against the petitioner.

(5) The petitioner was less than 18 years old at the time of the commission of the offense in question.

(6) The petitioner has performed at least 100 hours of community service since the time of the conviction and possesses a high school diploma, a high school graduation equivalency certificate, or a General Education Development degree.

(7) The search of the confidential records of expunctions conducted by the Administrative Office of the Courts shows that the

petitioner has not been previously granted an expunction.

(f) No person as to whom an order has been entered pursuant to subsection (e) of this section shall be held thereafter under any provision of any laws to be guilty of perjury or otherwise giving a false statement by reason of that person's failure to recite or acknowledge the arrest, indictment, information, trial, or conviction. This subsection shall not apply to a sentencing hearing when the person has been convicted of a subsequent criminal offense.

(f1) Persons required by State law to obtain a criminal history record check on a prospective employee shall not be deemed to have knowledge of any convictions expunged under this section.

(f2) Persons pursuing certification under the provisions of Article 1 of Chapter 17C or Article 2 of Chapter 17E of the General Statutes, however, shall disclose any and all felony convictions to the certifying Commission regardless of whether or not the felony convictions were expunged pursuant to the provisions of this section.

(f3) Persons requesting a disclosure statement be prepared by the North Carolina Sheriffs' Education and Training Standards Commission pursuant to Article 3 of Chapter 17E of the General Statutes, however, shall disclose any and all felony convictions to the North Carolina Sheriffs' Education and Training Standards Commission regardless of whether or not the felony convictions were expunged pursuant to the provisions of this section.

(g) The court shall also order that the nonviolent felony conviction be expunged from the records of the court and direct all law enforcement agencies bearing record of the same to expunge their records of the conviction. The clerk shall notify State and local agencies of the court's order as provided in G.S. 15A-150.

(h) Any other applicable State or local government agency shall expunge from its records entries made as a result of the conviction ordered expunged under this section. The agency shall also vacate any administrative actions taken against a person whose record is expunged under this section as a result of the charges or convictions expunged. A person whose administrative action has been vacated by an occupational licensing board pursuant to an expunction under this section may then reapply for licensure and must satisfy the board's then current education and preliminary licensing requirements in order to obtain licensure. This subsection shall not apply to the Department of Justice for DNA records and samples stored in the State DNA Database and the State DNA Databank.

(i) Any person eligible for expunction of a criminal record under this section shall be notified about the provisions of this section by the probation officer assigned to that person. If no probation officer is assigned, notification of the provisions of this section shall be provided by the court at the time of the conviction of the felony which is to be expunged under this section.

(j) A person who files a petition for expunction of a criminal record under this section must pay the clerk of superior court a fee of one hundred seventy-five dollars ($ 175.00) at the time the petition is filed. Fees collected under this subsection are payable to the Administrative Office of the Courts. The clerk of superior court shall remit one hundred twenty-two dollars and fifty cents ($ 122.50) of each fee to the North Carolina Department of Public Safety for the costs of criminal record checks performed in connection with processing petitions for expunctions under this section. The remaining fifty-two dollars and fifty cents ($ 52.50) of each fee shall be retained by the Administrative Office of the Courts and used to pay the costs of processing petitions for expunctions under this section. This subsection does not apply to petitions filed by an indigent.

History.
2011-278, s. 1; 2012-191, s. 2; 2013-53, s. 1; 2013-360, s. 18B.16(e); 2014-100, s. 17.1(o); 2015-150, s. 3; 2015-181, s. 44; 2017-195, s. 1; 2021-107, s. 7(b)

§ 15A-145.5. Expunction of certain misdemeanors and felonies; no age limitation*

(a) For purposes of this section, the term "nonviolent misdemeanor" or "nonviolent felony" means any misdemeanor or felony except the following:

(1) A Class A through G felony or a Class A1 misdemeanor.

(2) An offense that includes assault as an essential element of the offense.

(3) An offense requiring registration pursuant to Article 27A of Chapter 14 of the General Statutes, whether or not the person is currently required to register.

(4) Any of the following sex-related or stalking offenses: G.S. 14-27.25(b), 14-27.30(b), 14-190.7, 14-190.8, 14-190.9, 14-202, 14-208.11A, 14-208.18, 14-277.3, 14-277.3A, 14-321.1.

(5) Any felony offense in Chapter 90 of the General Statutes where the offense involves methamphetamines, heroin, or possession with intent to sell or deliver or sell and deliver cocaine.

(6) An offense under G.S. 14-12.12(b), 14-12.13, or 14-12.14, or any offense for which punishment was determined pursuant to G.S. 14-3(c).

(7) An offense under G.S. 14-401.16.

(7a) An offense under G.S. 14-54(a) or G.S. 14-54(a1).

(8) Any felony offense in which a commercial motor vehicle was used in the commission of the offense.

(8a) Repealed by Session Laws 2021-118, s. 1, effective December 1, 2021, and applicable to petitions filed on or after that date.

(9) Any offense that is an attempt to commit an offense described in subdivisions (1) through (8) of this subsection.

(a1) An offense involving impaired driving as defined in G.S. 20-4.01(24a) is not eligible for expunction.

(b) Notwithstanding any other provision of law, if the person is convicted of more than one nonviolent felony or nonviolent misdemeanor in the same session of court, then the multiple nonviolent felony or nonviolent misdemeanor convictions shall be treated as one nonviolent felony or nonviolent misdemeanor conviction under this section, and the expunction order issued under this section shall provide that the multiple nonviolent felony convictions or nonviolent misdemeanor convictions shall be expunged from the person's record in accordance with this section.

(c) A person may file a petition, in the court of the county where the person was convicted.

(1) For expunction of one or more nonviolent misdemeanor convictions, the petition shall not be filed earlier than one of the following:

　　a. For expunction of one nonviolent misdemeanor, five years after the date of the conviction or when any active sentence, period of probation, or post-release supervision has been served, whichever occurs later.

　　b. For expunction of more than one nonviolent misdemeanor, seven years after the date of the person's last conviction, other than a traffic offense not listed in the petition for expunction, or seven years after any active sentence, period of probation, or post-release supervision has been served, whichever occurs later.

(2) For expunction of up to three nonviolent felony convictions, the petition shall not be filed earlier than one of the following:

　　a. For expunction of one nonviolent felony, 10 years after the date of the conviction or 10 years after any active sentence, period of probation, or post-release supervision, related to the conviction listed in the petition, has been served, whichever occurs later.

　　b. For expunction of two or three nonviolent felonies, 20 years after the date of the most recent conviction listed in the petition, or 20 years after any active sentence, period of probation, or

post-release supervision, related to a conviction listed in the petition, has been served, whichever occurs later.

A person previously granted an expunction under this section is not eligible for relief under this section for any offense committed after the date of the previous order for expunction. Except as provided in subsections (c4) and (c5) of this section, a person previously granted an expunction under this section for one or more misdemeanors is not eligible for expunction of additional misdemeanors under this section and a person previously granted an expunction under this section for one or more felonies is not eligible for expunction of additional felonies under this section.

(c1) A petition filed pursuant to this section shall contain, but not be limited to, the following:

(1) An affidavit by the petitioner that the petitioner is of good moral character and has not been convicted of any other felony or misdemeanor, other than a traffic violation, under the laws of the United States or the laws of this State or any other state during the applicable five-year, seven-year, 10-year, or 20-year waiting period set forth in subsection (c) of this section.

(2) Verified affidavits of two persons who are not related to the petitioner or to each other by blood or marriage, that they know the character and reputation of the petitioner in the community in which the petitioner lives and that the petitioner's character and reputation are good.

(3) A statement that the petition is a motion in the cause in the case wherein the petitioner was convicted.

(4) An application on a form approved by the Administrative Office of the Courts requesting and authorizing a name-based State and national criminal history record check by the Department of Public Safety using any information required by the Administrative Office of the Courts to identify the individual, a search by the Department of Public Safety for any outstanding warrants on pending criminal cases, and a search of the confidential record of expunctions maintained by the Administrative Office of the Courts. The application shall be filed with the clerk of superior court. The clerk of superior court shall forward the application to the Department of Public Safety and to the Administrative Office of the Courts, which shall conduct the searches and report their findings to the court.

(5) An affidavit by the petitioner that no restitution orders or civil judgments

representing amounts ordered for restitution entered against the petitioner are outstanding.

(6) An affidavit by the petitioner providing information on any additional petitions the petitioner has submitted, or intends to submit, in other counties pursuant to subsection (c4) of this section seeking expunction of additional convictions.

(7) An acknowledgement by the petitioner that, except as provided in subsection (c5) of this section, the expunction of one nonviolent misdemeanor prior to the seven-year waiting period or one nonviolent felony prior to the 20-year waiting period will preclude the petitioner from expunging additional nonviolent misdemeanors or nonviolent felonies that might otherwise be eligible for expunction pursuant to sub-subdivision b. of subdivision (1) of subsection (c) of this section or sub-subdivision b. of subdivision (2) of subsection (c) of this section.

Upon filing of the petition, the petition shall be served upon the district attorney of the court wherein the case was tried resulting in conviction. The district attorney shall have 30 days thereafter in which to file any objection thereto and shall be duly notified as to the date of the hearing of the petition. Upon good cause shown, the court may grant the district attorney an additional 30 days to file objection to the petition. The district attorney shall make his or her best efforts to contact the victim, if any, to notify the victim of the request for expunction prior to the date of the hearing. Upon request by the victim, the victim has a right to be present at any hearing on the petition for expunction and the victim's views and concerns shall be considered by the court at such hearing.

The presiding judge is authorized to call upon a probation officer for any additional investigation or verification of the petitioner's conduct since the conviction. The court shall review any other information the court deems relevant, including, but not limited to, affidavits or other testimony provided by law enforcement officers, district attorneys, and victims of crimes committed by the petitioner.

(c2) The court, after hearing a petition for expunction of one or more nonviolent misdemeanors, shall order that the petitioner be restored, in the contemplation of the law, to the status the petitioner occupied before the arrest or indictment or information, except as provided in G.S. 15A-151.5, if the court finds all of the following:

(1) One of the following:

a. The petitioner has not previously been granted an expunction under this

section for one or more nonviolent misdemeanors.

b. Any previous expunction granted to the petitioner under this section for one or more nonviolent misdemeanors was granted pursuant to a petition filed prior to December 1, 2021.

(2) The petitioner is of good moral character.

(3) The petitioner has no outstanding warrants or pending criminal cases.

(4) The petitioner has no other felony or misdemeanor convictions, other than a traffic violation not listed in the petition for expunction, during the applicable five-year or seven-year waiting period set forth in subsection (c) of this section.

(5) The petitioner has no outstanding restitution orders or civil judgments representing amounts ordered for restitution entered against the petitioner.

(6) The petitioner meets one of the following criteria:

a. For a petition for expunction of one nonviolent misdemeanor, the petitioner has no convictions for any other felony or misdemeanor, other than a traffic offense.

b. For a petition for expunction of more than one nonviolent misdemeanor, the petitioner has no convictions for a misdemeanor or felony that is listed as an exception to the terms "nonviolent misdemeanor" or "nonviolent felony" as provided in subsection (a) of this section.

(7) The petitioner was convicted of an offense or offenses eligible for expunction under this section.

(8) The petitioner has completed the applicable five-year or seven-year waiting period set forth in subsection (c) of this section.

If the court denies the petition, the order shall include a finding as to the reason for the denial.

(c3) The court, after hearing a petition for expunction of one or up to three nonviolent felonies, may order that the petitioner be restored, in the contemplation of the law, to the status the petitioner occupied before the arrest or indictment or information, except as provided in G.S. 15A-151.5, if the court finds all of the following:

(1) One of the following:

a. The petitioner has not previously been granted an expunction under this section for one or more nonviolent felonies.

b. Any previous expunction granted to the petitioner under this section for a felony was granted pursuant to a petition filed prior to December 1, 2021.

(2) The petitioner is of good moral character.

(3) The petitioner has no outstanding warrants or pending criminal cases.

(4) If the petition is for the expunction of one felony, the petitioner has no misdemeanor convictions, other than a traffic violation not listed in the petition for expunction, in the five years preceding the petition, and no other felony convictions during the applicable 10-year waiting period set forth in subsection (c) of this section.

(4a) If the petition is for the expunction of two or three felonies, or if the petitioner has filed petitions in more than one county pursuant to subsection (c4) of this section, the petitioner has no misdemeanor convictions other than a traffic violation not listed in the petition for expunction in the five years preceding the petition, and no other felony convictions during the applicable 20-year waiting period set forth in subsection (c) of this section.

(4b) If the petition is for the expunction of two or three felonies, if the petitioner has filed petitions in more than one county pursuant to subsection (c4) of this section, or if the petition is filed pursuant to subsection (c5) of this section, the felony offenses were committed within the same 24-month period.

(5) The petitioner has no outstanding restitution orders or civil judgments representing amounts ordered for restitution entered against the petitioner.

(6) The petitioner has no convictions for a misdemeanor that is listed as an exception to the term "nonviolent misdemeanor" as provided in subsection (a) of this section or any other felony offense.

(7) The petitioner was convicted of an offense eligible for expunction under this section.

(8) The petitioner has completed the applicable 10-year or 20-year waiting period set forth in subsection (c) of this section.

If the court denies the petition, the order shall include a finding as to the reason for the denial.

(c4) A person petitioning for expunction of multiple convictions pursuant to sub-subdivision b. of subdivision (1) of subsection (c) of this section or sub-subdivision b. of subdivision (2) of subsection (c) of this section, where the convictions were obtained in more than one county, shall file a petition in each county of conviction. All petitions shall be filed within a 30-day period. The granting of one petition shall not preclude the granting of any other petition filed within the same 30-day period.

(c5) A person granted an expunction under this section of one or more nonviolent misdemeanors pursuant to a petition filed prior to December 1, 2021, may petition for the expunction of additional nonviolent misdemeanors if the offenses were committed prior to the date of the previous expunction. A person granted an expunction under this section of one nonviolent felony pursuant to a petition filed prior to December 1, 2021, may petition for the expunction of up to two additional nonviolent felonies if the offenses were committed prior to the date of the previous expunction and within the same 24-month period as the previously expunged felony.

(d) No person as to whom an order has been entered pursuant to subsection (c) of this section shall be held thereafter under any provision of any law to be guilty of perjury or otherwise giving a false statement by reason of that person's failure to recite or acknowledge the arrest, indictment, information, trial, or conviction. This subsection shall not apply to a sentencing hearing when the person has been convicted of a subsequent criminal offense.

(d1) Persons pursuing certification under the provisions of Article 1 of Chapter 17C or Article 2 of Chapter 17E of the General Statutes, however, shall disclose any and all convictions to the certifying Commission, regardless of whether or not the convictions were expunged pursuant to the provisions of this section.

(d2) Persons requesting a disclosure statement be prepared by the North Carolina Sheriffs' Education and Training Standards Commission pursuant to Article 3 of Chapter 17E of the General Statutes, however, shall disclose any and all felony convictions to the North Carolina Sheriffs' Education and Training Standards Commission regardless of whether or not the felony convictions were expunged pursuant to the provisions of this section.

(d3) Persons required by State law to obtain a criminal history record check on a prospective employee shall not be deemed to have knowledge of any convictions expunged under this section.

(e) The court shall also order that the conviction or convictions be expunged from the records of the court and direct all law enforcement agencies bearing record of the same to expunge their records of the conviction. The clerk shall notify State and local agencies of the court's order, as provided in G.S. 15A-150.

(f) Any other applicable State or local government agency shall expunge from its records entries made as a result of the conviction or convictions ordered expunged under this section upon receipt from the petitioner of an order entered pursuant to this section. The agency shall also vacate any administrative actions taken against a person whose record is expunged under this section as a result of the charges or convictions expunged. A person whose administrative action has been vacated by an occupational licensing board pursuant to an expunction under this section may then reapply for licensure and must satisfy the board's then current education and preliminary licensing requirements in order to obtain licensure. This subsection shall not apply to the Department of Justice for DNA records and samples stored in the State DNA Database and the State DNA Databank.

(g) A person who files a petition for expunction of a criminal record under this section must pay the clerk of superior court a fee of one hundred seventy-five dollars ($ 175.00) at the time the petition is filed. Fees collected under this subsection shall be deposited in the General Fund. This subsection does not apply to petitions filed by an indigent.

History.
2012-191, s. 1; 2013-53, s. 2; 2013-410, s. 4; 2014-100, s. 17.1(o); 2014-119, ss. 1(a), 11(a); 2015-150, s. 4; 2015-181, s. 43; 2017-195, s. 1; 2020-35, s. 4(a); 2021-107, s. 7(c); 2021-118, s. 1

* See Session Law 2021-167, included in frontmatter of this book, for 2021 amendment details.

§ 15A-145.6. Expunctions for certain defendants convicted of prostitution

(a) The following definitions apply in this section:

(1) **Prostitution offense.** -- A conviction for (i) violation of G.S. 14-204 or (ii) engaging in prostitution in violation of G.S. 14-204(7) for an offense that occurred prior to October 1, 2013.

(2) **Violent felony or violent misdemeanor.** -- A Class A through G felony or a Class A1 misdemeanor that includes assault as an essential element of the offense.

(b) A person who has been convicted of a prostitution offense may file a petition in the court of the county where the person was convicted for expunction of the prostitution offense from the person's criminal record provided that all the following criteria are met:

(1) The person has not previously been convicted of any violent felony or violent misdemeanor under the laws of the United States or the laws of this State or any other state.

(2) The person satisfies any one of the following criteria:

a. Repealed by Session Laws 2019-158, s. 4(a), effective December 1, 2019, and applicable to petitions filed on or after that date.

b. The person has no prior convictions for a prostitution offense and at least three years have passed since the

date of conviction or the completion of any active sentence, period of probation, and post-release supervision, whichever occurs later.

c. The person was discharged and the charge was dismissed upon completion of a conditional discharge under G.S. 14-204(b).

(c) The petition shall contain all of the following:

(1) An affidavit by the petitioner that the petitioner (i) has no prior conviction of a violent felony or violent misdemeanor, (ii) has been of good moral character since the date of conviction of the prostitution offense in question, and (iii) has not been convicted of any felony or misdemeanor under the laws of the United States or the laws of this State or any other state since the date of the conviction of the prostitution offense in question.

(2) Verified affidavits of two persons, who are not related to the petitioner or to each other by blood or marriage, that they know the character and reputation of the petitioner in the community in which the petitioner lives and that the petitioner's character and reputation are good.

(3) A statement that the petition is a motion in the cause in the case wherein the petitioner was convicted.

(4) An application on a form approved by the Administrative Office of the Courts requesting and authorizing (i) a State and national criminal history record check by the Department of Public Safety using any information required by the Administrative Office of the Courts to identify the individual; (ii) a search by the Department of Public Safety for any outstanding warrants or pending criminal cases; and (iii) a search of the confidential record of expunctions maintained by the Administrative Office of the Courts. The application shall be filed with the clerk of superior court. The clerk of superior court shall forward the application to the Department of Public Safety and to the Administrative Office of the Courts, which shall conduct the searches and report their findings to the court.

(5) An affidavit by the petitioner that no restitution orders or civil judgments representing amounts ordered for restitution entered against the petitioner are outstanding.

(d) The petition shall be served upon the district attorney of the court wherein the case was tried resulting in conviction. The district attorney shall have 30 days thereafter in which to file any objection thereto and shall be duly notified as to the date of the hearing of the petition.

(e) The court in which the petition was filed shall take the following steps and shall consider

Chapter 15A

the following issues in rendering a decision upon a petition for expunction of records of a prostitution offense under this section:

(1) Call upon a probation officer for additional investigation or verification of the petitioner's conduct during the period since the date of conviction of the prostitution offense in question.

(2) Review any other information the court deems relevant, including, but not limited to, affidavits or other testimony provided by law enforcement officers and district attorneys.

(f) The court shall order that the person be restored, in the contemplation of the law, to the status the person occupied before the arrest and indictment or information if the court finds all of the following after a hearing:

(1) The criteria set out in subsection (b) of this section are satisfied.

(2) The petitioner has remained of good moral character and has been free of conviction of any felony or misdemeanor, other than a traffic violation, since the date of conviction of the prostitution offense in question.

(3) The petitioner has no outstanding warrants or pending criminal cases.

(4) The petitioner has no outstanding restitution orders or civil judgments representing amounts ordered for restitution entered against the petitioner.

(5) The search of the confidential records of expunctions conducted by the Administrative Office of the Courts shows that the petitioner has not been previously granted an expunction, other than an expunction for a prostitution offense.

(g) No person as to whom an order has been entered pursuant to subsection (f) of this section shall be held thereafter under any provision of any laws to be guilty of perjury or otherwise giving a false statement by reason of that person's failure to recite or acknowledge the arrest, indictment, information, trial, or conviction. This subsection shall not apply to a sentencing hearing when the person has been convicted of a subsequent criminal offense.

(g1) Persons pursuing certification under the provisions of Article 1 of Chapter 17C or Article 2 of Chapter 17E of the General Statutes, however, shall disclose any and all prostitution convictions to the certifying Commission regardless of whether or not the prostitution convictions were expunged pursuant to the provisions of this section.

(g2) Persons requesting a disclosure statement be prepared by the North Carolina Sheriffs' Education and Training Standards Commission pursuant to Article 3 of Chapter 17E of the General Statutes, however, shall disclose any and all felony convictions to the North

Carolina Sheriffs' Education and Training Standards Commission regardless of whether or not the felony convictions were expunged pursuant to the provisions of this section.

(g3) Persons required by State law to obtain a criminal history record check on a prospective employee shall not be deemed to have knowledge of any convictions expunged under this section.

(h) The court shall also order that the conviction of the prostitution offense be expunged from the records of the court and direct all law enforcement agencies bearing record of the same to expunge their records of the conviction. The clerk shall notify State and local agencies of the court's order as provided in G.S. 15A-150.

(i) Any other applicable State or local government agency shall expunge from its records entries made as a result of the conviction ordered expunged under this section. The agency shall also reverse any administrative actions taken against a person whose record is expunged under this section as a result of the charges or convictions expunged. This subsection shall not apply to the Department of Justice for DNA records and samples stored in the State DNA Database and the State DNA Databank.

(j) Any person eligible for expunction of a criminal record under this section shall be notified about the provisions of this section by the probation officer assigned to that person. If no probation officer is assigned, notification of the provisions of this section shall be provided by the court at the time of the conviction of the prostitution offense which is to be expunged under this section.

History.
2013-368, s. 11; 2014-100, s. 17.1(o); 2017-195, s. 1; 2019-158, s. 4(a); 2021-107, s. 7(d)

§ 15A-145.7. Expunction of records for first offenders under 20 years of age at the time of the offense of certain offenses

(a) Whenever a person is discharged, and the proceedings against the person dismissed, pursuant to G.S. 14-277.8, and the person was under 20 years of age at the time of the offense, the person may apply to the court of the county where charged for an order to expunge from all official records, other than the confidential files retained under G.S. 15A-151, all recordation relating to the person's arrest, indictment or information, trial, finding of guilty, and dismissal and discharge pursuant to this section. The applicant shall attach to the petition the following:

(1) An affidavit by the petitioner that he or she has been of good behavior during the period of probation since the decision to defer further proceedings on the offense in

question and has not been convicted of any felony or misdemeanor other than a traffic violation under the laws of the United States or the laws of this State or any other state;

(2) Verified affidavits by two persons who are not related to the petitioner or to each other by blood or marriage, that they know the character and reputation of the petitioner in the community in which he or she lives, and that the petitioner's character and reputation are good;

(3) An application on a form approved by the Administrative Office of the Courts requesting and authorizing a name-based State and national criminal record check by the Department of Public Safety using any information required by the Administrative Office of the Courts to identify the individual and a search of the confidential record of expunctions maintained by the Administrative Office of the Courts. The application shall be filed with the clerk of superior court. The clerk of superior court shall forward the application to the Department of Public Safety and to the Administrative Office of the Courts, which shall conduct the searches and report their findings to the court.

The judge to whom the petition is presented is authorized to call upon a probation officer for any additional investigation or verification of the petitioner's conduct during the probationary period deemed desirable.

If the court determines, after hearing, that such person was discharged and the proceedings against him or her dismissed and that the person was under 20 years of age at the time of the offense, it shall enter such order. The effect of such order shall be to restore such person in the contemplation of the law to the status the person occupied before such arrest or indictment or information.

(b) No person as to whom such order was entered shall be held thereafter under any provision of any law to be guilty of perjury or otherwise giving a false statement by reason of the person's failures to recite or acknowledge such arrest, or indictment or information, or trial in response to any inquiry made of him or her for any purpose. This subsection shall not apply to a sentencing hearing when the person has been convicted of a subsequent criminal offense.

(c) The court shall also order that all records of the proceeding be expunged from the records of the court and direct all law enforcement agencies, the Division of Adult Correction and Juvenile Justice, the Division of Motor Vehicles, and any other State and local government agencies identified by the petitioner as bearing

records of the same to expunge their records of the proceeding. The clerk shall notify State and local agencies of the court's order as provided in G.S. 15A-150.

(d) A person who files a petition for expunction of a criminal record under this section must pay the clerk of superior court a fee of one hundred seventy-five dollars ($ 175.00) at the time the petition is filed. Fees collected under this subsection are payable to the Administrative Office of the Courts. The clerk of superior court shall remit one hundred twenty-two dollars and fifty cents ($ 122.50) of each fee to the North Carolina Department of Public Safety for the costs of criminal record checks performed in connection with processing petitions for expunctions under this section. The remaining fifty-two dollars and fifty cents ($ 52.50) of each fee shall be retained by the Administrative Office of the Courts and used to pay the costs of processing petitions for expunctions under this section. This subsection does not apply to petitions filed by an indigent.

History.
2018-72, s. 4

§ 15A-145.8. Expunction of records when charges are remanded to district court for juvenile adjudication

(a) Upon remand pursuant to G.S. 7B-2200.5(d), the court shall order expunction of all remanded charges. No person as to whom such an order has been entered shall be held thereafter under any provision of any law to be guilty of perjury, or to be guilty of otherwise giving a false statement or response to any inquiry made for any purpose, by reason of his or her failure to recite or acknowledge any expunged entries concerning apprehension or trial.

(b) The court shall also order the expunction of DNA records when the person's charges have been remanded to district court for juvenile adjudication and the person's DNA record or profile has been included in the State DNA Database and the person's DNA sample is stored in the State DNA Databank as a result of the charges that were remanded. The order of expungement shall include the name and address of the defendant and the defendant's attorney and shall direct the North Carolina State Crime Laboratory to send a letter documenting expungement as required by subsection (c) of this section.

(c) Upon receiving an order of expungement entered pursuant to subsection (b) of this section, the North Carolina State Crime Laboratory shall purge the DNA record and all other identifying information from the State DNA Database and the DNA sample stored in the State DNA Databank covered by the order, except that the order shall not apply to other offenses committed by the individual that qualify for inclusion in the State DNA Database and the State DNA Databank. A letter documenting expungement of the DNA record and destruction of the DNA sample shall be sent by the North Carolina State Crime Laboratory to the defendant and the defendant's attorney at the address specified by the court in the order of expungement.

(d) Upon order of expungement, the clerk shall send a certified copy of the expungement order to the defendant, the defendant's attorney, the Administrative Office of the Courts, and the State and local agencies listed in G.S. 15A-150(b). An agency receiving a certified copy of an order under this subsection shall delete any public records made as a result of the charges that have been remanded to district court for juvenile adjudication, in accordance with G.S. 15A-150. Any records related to the juvenile adjudication shall not be deleted but shall be maintained as confidential records pursuant to Article 30 of Chapter 7B of the General Statutes.

History.
2019-186, s. 11; 2019-243, s. 21(a).

§ 15A-145.8A. Expunction of records for offenders under the age of 18 at the time of commission of certain misdemeanors and felonies uponcompletion of the sentence.

(a) A person, the district attorney, or an attorney at the request of a person eligible for expunction under this section, may file, in the court of the county where the person was convicted, a petition for expunction from the person's criminal record of any misdemeanor or Class H or I felony not excluded by subsection (b) of this section if the offense was committed prior to December 1, 2019, and while the person was less than 18 years of age, but at least 16 years of age. The petition shall not be filed until (i) any active sentence, period of probation, and post-release supervision ordered for the offense has been served and (ii) the person has no restitution orders for the offense or outstanding civil judgments representing amounts ordered for restitution for the offense.

(b) An offense is not eligible for expunction under this section if it is (i) a violation of the motor vehicle laws under Chapter 20 of the General Statutes, including any offense involving impaired driving as defined in G.S. 20-4.01(24a) or (ii) an offense requiring registration pursuant to Article 27A of Chapter 14 of the General Statutes, whether or not the person is currently required to register.

(c) If the petition was not filed by the district attorney, the petition shall be served upon the

district attorney of the court wherein the case was tried resulting in conviction. The district attorney shall have 30 days thereafter in which to file any objection thereto and shall be duly notified as to the date of the hearing of the petition. The district attorney shall make his or her best efforts to contact the victim, if any, to notify the victim of the request for expunction prior to the date of the hearing. Upon request by the victim, the victim has a right to be present at any hearing on the petition for expunction and the victim's views and concerns shall be considered by the court at such hearing.

(d) If the court, after hearing, finds that (i) the offense was a misdemeanor or Class H or I felony eligible for expunction under this section, (ii) the offense was committed prior to December 1, 2019, and while the person was less than 18 years of age, but at least 16 years of age, (iii) any active sentence, period of probation, and post-release supervision ordered for the offense was completed, and (iv) the person has no restitution orders for the offense or outstanding civil judgments representing amounts ordered for restitution for the offense, the court shall order that the person be restored, in the contemplation of the law, to the status the person occupied before such arrest or indictment or information, and that the record be expunged from the records of the court. A person convicted of multiple offenses shall be eligible to have those convictions expunged pursuant to this section.

(e) Any petition for expunction under this section shall be on a form approved by the Administrative Office of the Courts and shall be filed with the clerk of superior court in the county where the person was convicted. Upon order of expunction, the clerk shall forward the order to the Administrative Office of the Courts.

(f) No person as to whom such order has been entered shall be held thereafter under any provision of any laws to be guilty of perjury or otherwise giving a false statement by reason of that person's failure to recite or acknowledge such arrest, or indictment, information, or trial, or response to any inquiry made of the person for any purpose.

(g) The court shall also order that the conviction be expunged from the records of the court. The court shall direct all law enforcement agencies, the Division of Adult Correction and Juvenile Justice of the Department of Public Safety, the Division of Motor Vehicles, and any other State or local government agencies identified by the petitioner as bearing record of the same to expunge their records of the petitioner's conviction. The clerk shall notify State and local agencies of the court's order as provided in G.S. 15A-150.

(h) A person who files a petition for expunction of a criminal record under this section must pay the clerk of superior court a fee of one hundred seventy-five dollars ($ 175.00) at the time the petition is filed. Fees collected under this subsection are payable to the Administrative Office of the Courts. The clerk of superior court shall remit one hundred twenty-two dollars and fifty cents ($ 122.50) of each fee to the North Carolina Department of Public Safety for the costs of criminal record checks performed in connection with processing petitions for expunctions under this section. The remaining fifty-two dollars and fifty cents ($ 52.50) of each fee shall be retained by the Administrative Office of the Courts and used to pay the costs of processing petitions for expunctions under this section. This subsection does not apply to petitions filed by an indigent.

History.
2020-35, s. 1(a); 2021-118, s. 2

§ 15A-145.9. Expunctions of certain offenses committed by human trafficking victims

(a) **Definition.** -- For purposes of this section, the following terms apply:

(1) **Nonviolent offense.** -- Any misdemeanor or felony except the following:

a. A Class A through G felony.

b. An offense that includes assault as an essential element of the offense.

c. An offense requiring registration pursuant to Article 27A of Chapter 14 of the General Statutes, whether or not the person is currently required to register.

d. Any of the following sex-related or stalking offenses: G.S. 14-27.25(b), 14-27.30(b), 14-190.7, 14-190.8, 14-190.9, 14-202, 14-208.11A, 14-208.18, 14-277.3A, or 14-321.1.

e. An offense under G.S. 14-12.12(b), 14-12.13, or 14-12.14, or any offense for which punishment was determined pursuant to G.S. 14-3(c).

f. An offense under G.S. 14-401.16.

g. A traffic offense.

h. Any offense that is an attempt to commit an offense described in subsubdivisions a. through g. of this subdivision.

(2) **Trafficking victim.** -- A person that meets the definition for the term "victim" set forth in G.S. 14-43.10 or a victim of a severe form of trafficking under the federal Trafficking Victims Protection Act (22 U.S.C. § 7102(13)).

(b) **Expunction Authorized.** -- A person who has been convicted of a nonviolent offense may file a petition in the court of the county where the person was convicted for expunction of the nonviolent offense from the person's

criminal record if the court finds that the person was coerced or deceived into committing the offense as a direct result of having been a trafficking victim.

(c) **Petition Requirements.** -- The petition shall contain all of the following:

(1) An affidavit by the petitioner that the petitioner is a victim of human trafficking and was coerced or deceived into committing the offense as a direct result of their status as a trafficking victim.

(2) A statement that the petition is a motion in the cause in the case wherein the petitioner was convicted.

(3) An application on a form approved by the Administrative Office of the Courts requesting and authorizing a search by the Department of Public Safety for any outstanding warrants. The application shall be filed with the clerk of superior court. The clerk of superior court shall forward the application to the Department of Public Safety, which shall conduct the search and report its findings to the court.

(4) An affidavit by the petitioner that no restitution orders or civil judgments representing amounts ordered for restitution entered against the petitioner are outstanding.

(d) **Service of Petition.** -- The petition shall be served upon the district attorney of the court wherein the case was tried resulting in conviction. The district attorney shall have 30 days thereafter in which to file any objection thereto and shall be duly notified as to the date of the hearing of the petition.

(e) **Issues for Consideration.** -- The court in which the petition was filed may take the following steps and may consider the following issues in rendering a decision upon a petition for expunction of records of an offense under this section:

(1) Call upon a probation officer for additional investigation or verification of the petitioner's conduct during the period since the date of conviction of the offense in question.

(2) Review any other information the court deems relevant, including, but not limited to, affidavits or other testimony provided by law enforcement officers, district attorneys, or licensed social workers.

(f) **Restoration of Status.** -- The court shall order that the person be restored, in the contemplation of the law, to the status the person occupied before the arrest or indictment or information if the court finds all of the following after a hearing:

(1) The criteria set out in subsection (b) of this section are satisfied.

(2) The petitioner has no outstanding warrants.

(3) The petitioner has no outstanding restitution orders or civil judgments representing amounts ordered for restitution entered against the petitioner.

(g) **Effect.** -- No person as to whom an order has been entered pursuant to subsection (f) of this section shall be held thereafter under any provision of any laws to be guilty of perjury or otherwise giving false statement by reason of that person's failure to recite or acknowledge the arrest, indictment, information, trial, or conviction. Persons required by State law to obtain a criminal history record check on a prospective employee shall not be deemed to have knowledge of any convictions expunged under this section.

(h) **Law Enforcement Certification.** -- Persons pursuing certification under the provisions of Article 1 of Chapter 17C of 17E of the General Statutes, however, shall disclose all convictions to the certifying Commission regardless of whether or not the convictions were expunged pursuant to the provisions of this section.

(i) **Records Expunged.** -- The court shall also order that the conviction of the offenses be expunged from the records of the court and direct all law enforcement agencies bearing record of the same to expunge their records of the conviction. The clerk shall notify State and local agencies of the court's order as provided in G.S. 15A-150.

(j) **Additional Records Expunged.** -- Any other applicable State or local government agency shall expunge from its records entries made as a result of the conviction ordered expunged under this section. The agency shall also reverse any administrative actions taken against a person whose record is expunged under this section as a result of the charges or convictions expunged. This subsection shall not apply to the Department of Justice for DNA records and samples stored in the State DNA Database and the State DNA Databank.

History.
2019-158, s. 4(b)

§ 15A-146. Expunction of records when charges are dismissed or there are findings of not guilty.

(a) **Dismissal of Single Charge.** -- If any person is charged with a crime, either a misdemeanor or a felony, or was charged with an infraction under G.S. 18B-302(i) prior to December 1, 1999, and the charge is dismissed, that person or the district attorney may petition the court of the county where the charge was brought for an order to expunge from all official records any entries relating to that person's apprehension or trial. Upon a finding that the sole

charge was dismissed, the court shall order the expunction.

(a1) **Multiple Dismissals.** -- If a person is charged with multiple offenses and any charges are dismissed, then that person or the district attorney may petition to have each of the dismissed charges expunged. If the court finds that all of the charges were dismissed, the court shall order the expunction. If the court finds that any charge resulted in a conviction on the day of the dismissal or had not yet reached final disposition, the court may order the expunction of any charge that was dismissed.

(a2) **Finding of Not Guilty.** -- If any person is charged with one or more crimes, either a misdemeanor or a felony, or an infraction under G.S. 18B-302(i) prior to December 1, 1999, and a finding of not guilty or not responsible is entered for any or all of the charges, that person or the district attorney may petition the court of the county where the charge was brought for an order to expunge from all official records any entries relating to apprehension or trial of that crime. Upon determining that a finding of not guilty or not responsible was entered and all related criminal charges have reached final disposition, the court shall order the expunction of any charges disposed by a finding of not guilty or not responsible.

(a3) **Effect of Expunction.** -- Except as provided in G.S. 15A-151.5(b)(5), no person as to whom an order has been entered by a court or by operation of law under this section shall be held thereafter under any provision of any law to be guilty of perjury, or to be guilty of otherwise giving a false statement or response to any inquiry made for any purpose, by reason of the person's failure to recite or acknowledge any expunged entries concerning apprehension or trial.

(a4) (Effective December 1, 2021) Dismissal, Not Guilty, or Not Responsible on or After December 1, 2021. If any person is charged with a crime, either a misdemeanor or a felony, or is charged with an infraction, the charges in the case are expunged by operation of law if all of the following apply:

(1) All charges in the case are disposed on or after December 1, 2021.

(2) All charges in the case are dismissed without leave, dismissed by the court, or result in a finding of not guilty or not responsible.

Notwithstanding the provisions of this subsection, no case with a felony charge that was dismissed pursuant to a plea agreement will be expunged pursuant to this subsection. Prior to December 1, 2021, the Administrative Office of the Courts shall develop and have in place procedures to automate the expunction of records pursuant to this subsection.

(a5) Notwithstanding the provisions of subsections (a), (a1), and (a2) of this section, an arresting agency may maintain investigative records related to a charge that has been expunged pursuant to this section.

(a6) **Hearing.** -- Except as otherwise specifically provided in this section, a court may grant a petition for expunction under this section without a hearing.

(b) The court may also order that the said entries, including civil revocations of drivers licenses as a result of the underlying charge, shall be expunged from the records of the court, and direct all law-enforcement agencies, the Division of Adult Correction and Juvenile Justice of the Department of Public Safety, the Division of Motor Vehicles, and any other State or local government agencies identified by the petitioner as bearing record of the same to expunge their records of the entries, including civil revocations of drivers licenses as a result of the underlying charge being expunged. This subsection does not apply to civil or criminal charges based upon the civil revocation, or to civil revocations under G.S. 20-16.2. The clerk shall notify State and local agencies of the court's order as provided in G.S. 15A-150. The clerk shall forward a certified copy of the order to the Division of Motor Vehicles for the expunction of a civil revocation provided the underlying criminal charge is also expunged. The civil revocation of a drivers license shall not be expunged prior to a final disposition of any pending civil or criminal charge based upon the civil revocation. The costs of expunging the records, as required under G.S. 15A-150, shall not be taxed against the petitioner.

(b1) Any person entitled to expungement under this section may also apply to the court for an order expunging DNA records when the person's case has been dismissed by the trial court and the person's DNA record or profile has been included in the State DNA Database and the person's DNA sample is stored in the State DNA Databank. A copy of the application for expungement of the DNA record or DNA sample shall be served on the district attorney for the judicial district in which the felony charges were brought not less than 20 days prior to the date of the hearing on the application. If the application for expungement is granted, a certified copy of the trial court's order dismissing the charges shall be attached to an order of expungement. The order of expungement shall include the name and address of the defendant and the defendant's attorney and shall direct the North Carolina State Crime Laboratory to send a letter documenting expungement as required by subsection (b2) of this section.

(b2) Upon receiving an order of expungement entered pursuant to subsection (b1) of this section, the North Carolina State Crime Laboratory shall purge the DNA record and all other identifying information from the State DNA Database and the DNA sample stored in the State DNA Databank covered by the order, except that the order shall not apply to other offenses committed by the individual that qualify for inclusion in the State DNA Database and the State DNA Databank. A letter documenting expungement of the DNA record and destruction of the DNA sample shall be sent by the North Carolina State Crime Laboratory to the defendant and the defendant's attorney at the address specified by the court in the order of expungement.

(c) Any petition required to be filed for expungement under this section shall be on a form approved by the Administrative Office of the Courts and be filed with the clerk of superior court. Excluding any expunction granted by operation of law pursuant to subsection (a4) of this section, upon order of expungement by a court, the clerk shall notify State and local agencies of the court's order as provided in G.S. 15A-150 and forward the petition to the Administrative Office of the Courts.

(d) A person charged with a crime that is dismissed pursuant to compliance with a deferred prosecution agreement or the terms of a conditional discharge and who files a petition for expunction of a criminal record under this section must pay the clerk of superior court a fee of one hundred seventy-five dollars ($ 175.00) at the time the petition is filed. Fees collected under this subsection are payable to the Administrative Office of the Courts. The clerk of superior court shall remit one hundred twenty-two dollars and fifty cents ($ 122.50) of each fee to the North Carolina Department of Public Safety for the costs of criminal record checks performed in connection with processing petitions for expunctions under this section. The remaining fifty-two dollars and fifty cents ($ 52.50) of each fee shall be retained by the Administrative Office of the Courts and used to pay the costs of processing petitions for expunctions under this section. This subsection does not apply to petitions filed by an indigent.

History.
1979, c. 61; 1985, c. 636, ss. 1-7; 1991, c. 326, s. 1; 1997-138, s. 1; 1999-406, s. 9; 2001-108, s. 2; 2001-282, s. 1; 2002-126, s. 29A.5(c); 2005-452, s. 1; 2007-509, s. 2; 2009-510, s. 5(a), (b); 2009-577, ss. 3.1, 8, 9; 2011-145, s. 19.1(h); 2012-191, s. 4; 2013-360, ss. 17.6(e), 18B.16(f); 2014-100, s. 17.1(o); 2014-119, s. 2(d); 2017-186, s. 2(tt); 2017-195, s. 1; 2020-35, s. 3(a)

§ 15A-147. Expunction of records when charges are dismissed or there are findings of not guilty as a result of identity theft or mistaken identity

(a) If any person is named in a charge for an infraction or a crime, either a misdemeanor or a felony, as a result of another person using the identifying information of the named person or mistaken identity and a finding of not guilty is entered, or the conviction is set aside, the named person may petition the court where the charge was last pending on a form approved by the Administrative Office of the Courts supplied by the clerk of court for an order to expunge from all official records any entries relating to the person's apprehension, charge, or trial. The court, after notice to the district attorney, shall hold a hearing on the petition and, upon finding that the person's identity was used without permission and the charges were dismissed or the person was found not guilty, the court shall order the expunction.

(a1) If any person is named in a charge for an infraction or a crime, either a misdemeanor or a felony, as a result of another person using the identifying information of the named person or mistaken identity, and the charge against the named person is dismissed, the prosecutor or other judicial officer who ordered the dismissal shall provide notice to the court of the dismissal, and the court shall order the expunction of all official records containing any entries relating to the person's apprehension, charge, or trial.

(a2) Any petition for expungement under this section shall be on a form approved by the Administrative Office of the Courts and be filed with the clerk of superior court. Upon order of expungement, the clerk shall forward the petition to the Administrative Office of the Courts.

(b) No person as to whom such an order has been entered under this section shall be held thereafter under any provision of any law to be guilty of perjury, or to be guilty of otherwise giving a false statement or response to any inquiry made for any purpose, by reason of the person's failure to recite or acknowledge any expunged entries concerning apprehension, charge, or trial.

(c) The court shall also order that the said entries shall be expunged from the records of the court and direct all law enforcement agencies, the Division of Adult Correction and Juvenile Justice of the Department of Public Safety, the Division of Motor Vehicles, or any other State or local government agencies identified by the petitioner, or the person eligible for automatic expungement under subsection (a1) of this section, as bearing record of the same to expunge their records of the entries. The clerk shall notify State and local agencies of the court's order as provided in G.S. 15A-150. The costs of expunging the records, as required under G.S. 15A-150, shall not be taxed against the petitioner.

(d) The Division of Motor Vehicles shall expunge from its records entries made as a result of the charge or conviction ordered expunged under this section. The Division of Motor Vehicles shall also reverse any administrative actions taken against a person whose record is expunged under this section as a result of the charges or convictions expunged, including the assessment of drivers license points and drivers license suspension or revocation. Notwithstanding any other provision of this Chapter, the Division of Motor Vehicles shall provide to the person whose motor vehicle record is expunged under this section a certified corrected driver history at no cost and shall reinstate at no cost any drivers license suspended or revoked as a result of a charge or conviction expunged under this section.

(e) The Division of Adult Correction and Juvenile Justice of the Department of Public Safety and any other applicable State or local government agency shall expunge its records as provided in G.S. 15A-150. The agency shall also reverse any administrative actions taken against a person whose record is expunged under this section as a result of the charges or convictions expunged. Notwithstanding any other provision of law, the normal fee for any reinstatement of a license or privilege resulting under this section shall be waived.

(f) Any insurance company that charged any additional premium based on insurance points assessed against a policyholder as a result of a charge or conviction that was expunged under this section shall refund those additional premiums to the policyholder upon notification of the expungement.

(g) For purposes of this section, the term "mistaken identity" means the erroneous arrest of a person for a crime as a result of misidentification by a witness or law enforcement, confusion on the part of a witness or law enforcement as to the identity of the person who committed the crime, misinformation provided to law enforcement as to the identity of the person who committed the crime, or some other mistake on the part of a witness or law enforcement as to the identity of the person who committed the crime.

History.
2001-108, s. 1; 2005-414, s. 8; 2009-510, s. 6; 2011-145, s. 19.1(h); 2015-202, s. 1; 2017-186, s. 2(uu); 2017-195, s. 1

§ 15A-148. Expunction of DNA records when charges are dismissed on appeal or pardon of innocence is granted

(a) Upon a motion by the defendant following the issuance of a final order by an appellate court reversing and dismissing a conviction of an offense for which a DNA analysis was done in accordance with Article 13 of Chapter 15A of the General Statutes, or upon receipt of a pardon of innocence with respect to any such offense, the court shall issue an order of expungement of the DNA record and samples in accordance with subsection (b) of this section. The order of expungement shall include the name and address of the defendant and the defendant's attorney and shall direct the North Carolina State Crime Laboratory to send a letter documenting expungement as required by subsection (b) of this section.

(b) When an order of expungement has been issued pursuant to subsection (a) of this section, the order of expungement, together with a certified copy of the final appellate court order reversing and dismissing the conviction or a certified copy of the instrument granting the pardon of innocence, shall be provided to the North Carolina State Crime Laboratory by the clerk of court. Upon receiving an order of expungement for an individual whose DNA record or profile has been included in the State DNA Database and whose DNA sample is stored in the State DNA Databank, the DNA profile shall be expunged and the DNA sample destroyed by the North Carolina State Crime Laboratory, except that the order shall not apply to other offenses committed by the individual that qualify for inclusion in the State DNA Database and the State DNA Databank. A letter documenting expungement of the DNA record and destruction of the DNA sample shall be sent by the North Carolina State Crime Laboratory to the defendant and the defendant's attorney at the address specified by the court in the order of expungement. The North Carolina State Crime Laboratory shall adopt procedures to comply with this subsection.

(c) Any petition for expungement under this section shall be on a form approved by the Administrative Office of the Courts and be filed with the clerk of superior court. Upon order of expungement, the clerk shall forward the petition to the Administrative Office of the Courts.

History.
2001-282, s. 2; 2013-360, s. 17.6(e); 2017-195, s. 1

§ 15A-149. Expunction of records when pardon of innocence is granted

(a) If any person is convicted of a crime and receives a pardon of innocence, the person may petition the court in which the person was convicted on a form approved by the Administrative Office of the Courts supplied by the clerk of court for an order to expunge from all official records any entries relating to the person's apprehension, charge, or trial. Upon receipt of the petition, the clerk of court shall verify that an attested copy of the warrant and return granting a pardon of innocence has been filed with the court in accordance with G.S. 147-25. Upon

verification by the clerk that the warrant and return have been filed, the court shall issue an order of expunction.

(b) The order of expunction shall include an instruction that any entries relating to the person's apprehension, charge, or trial shall be expunged from the records of the court and direct all law enforcement agencies, the Division of Adult Correction and Juvenile Justice of the Department of Public Safety, the Division of Motor Vehicles, or any other State or local government agencies identified by the petitioner as bearing record of the same to expunge their records of the entries. The clerk shall notify State and local agencies of the court's order as provided in G.S. 15A-150 and shall forward the petition to the Administrative Office of the Courts. The costs of expunging the records, as required under G.S. 15A-150, shall not be taxed against the petitioner.

(c) No person as to whom such an order has been entered under this section shall be held thereafter under any provision of any law to be guilty of perjury, or to be guilty of otherwise giving a false statement or response to any inquiry made for any purpose, by reason of the person's failure to recite or acknowledge any expunged entries concerning apprehension, charge, or trial.

History.
2005-319, s. 1; 2009-510, s. 7; 2011-145, s. 19.1(h); 2017-186, s. 2(vv); 2017-195, s. 1

§ 15A-150. Notification requirements

(a) **Notification to AOC.** -- The clerk of superior court in each county in North Carolina shall, as soon as practicable after each term of court, file with the Administrative Office of the Courts the petitions granted under this Article, any orders of expunction, and the names of the following:

(1) Persons granted an expunction under this Article.

(2), (3) Repealed by Session Laws 2015-40, s. 3, effective December 1, 2015, and applicable to conditional discharges granted on or after that date.

(4) Repealed by Session Laws 2010-174, s. 7, effective October 1, 2010.

(5) Repealed by Session Laws 2015-40, s. 3, effective December 1, 2015, and applicable to conditional discharges granted on or after that date.

(6) Persons granted a dismissal upon completion of a conditional discharge under G.S. 14-50.29, 14-204, 14-277.8, 14-313(f), 15A-1341(a4), 90-96, or 90-113.14.

(b) **Notification to Other State and Local Agencies.** -- Unless otherwise instructed by the Administrative Office of the Courts pursuant to an agreement entered into under subsection (e) of this section for the electronic or facsimile transmission of information, the clerk of superior court in each county in North Carolina shall send a certified copy of an order granting an expunction to a person named in subsection (a) of this section to (i) all of the agencies listed in this subsection and (ii) the person granted the expunction. Expunctions granted pursuant to G.S. 15A-146(a4) are excluded from all clerk of superior court notice provisions of this subsection. An agency receiving an order under this subsection shall purge from its records all entries made as a result of the charge or conviction ordered expunged, except as provided in G.S. 15A-151. The list of agencies is as follows:

(1) The sheriff, chief of police, or other arresting agency.

(2) When applicable, the Division of Motor Vehicles.

(3) Any State or local agency identified by the petition as bearing record of the offense that has been expunged.

(4) The Department of Public Safety, Combined Records Section.

(5) The State Bureau of Investigation.

(c) **Notification to FBI. --** The State Bureau of Investigation shall forward the order received under this section to the Federal Bureau of Investigation.

(d) **Notification to Private Entities. --** A State agency that receives a certified copy of an order under this section shall notify any private entity with which it has a licensing agreement for bulk extracts of data from the agency criminal record database to delete the record in question. The private entity shall notify any other entity to which it subsequently provides in a bulk extract data from the agency criminal database to delete the record in question from its database.

(e) The Director of the Administrative Office of the Courts may enter into an agreement with any of the State agencies listed in subsection (b) of this section for electronic or facsimile transmission of any information that must be provided under this section. The Administrative Office of the Courts also may provide notice to State and local agencies, in a manner and format determined by the Administrative Office of the Courts, of expunctions granted pursuant to G.S. 15A-146(a4).

History.
2009-510, s. 1; 2010-174, s. 7; 2011-145, s. 19.1(h); 2013-368, s. 12; 2014-100, s. 17.1 (eeee), (ffff), (gggg); 2014-115, s. 27(a); 2015-40, s. 3; 2015-247, s. 8; 2015-264, s. 5; 2017-195, s. 1; 2018-72, s. 5; 2020-35, s. 3(b); 2021-47, s. 15

§ 15A-151. Confidential agency files; exceptions to expunction

(a) The Administrative Office of the Courts shall maintain a confidential file for expungements containing the petitions granted under this Article and the names of those people for whom it received a notice under G.S. 15A-150. The information contained in the file may be disclosed only as follows:

(1) Upon request of a judge of the General Court of Justice of North Carolina for the purpose of ascertaining whether a person charged with an offense has been previously granted a discharge or an expunction.

(2) Upon request of a person requesting confirmation of the person's own discharge or expunction.

(3) To the General Court of Justice of North Carolina in response to a subpoena or other court order issued pursuant to a civil action under G.S. 15A-152.

(4) Upon request of State or local law enforcement, if the criminal record was expunged under this Chapter for employment purposes only.

(5) Upon the request of the North Carolina Criminal Justice Education and Training Standards Commission, if the criminal record was expunged under this Chapter for certification purposes only.

(6) Upon request of the North Carolina Sheriff's Standards Commission, if the criminal record was expunged under this Chapter for certification purposes only.

(7) To the district attorney in accordance with G.S. 15A-151.5.

(8) Upon request of the North Carolina Sheriffs' Education and Training Standards Commission, if the criminal record was expunged under this Chapter for purposes of preparing a disclosure statement in accordance with Article 3 of Chapter 17E of the General Statutes.

(9) For disclosure of records of previous dismissal pursuant to conditional discharge, upon joint request of the district attorney and the defendant in a pending proceeding for the purpose of determining eligibility for a conditional discharge. Any report disclosed in response to the joint request shall be delivered only to the clerk of superior court of the county in which the matter is pending. Upon receipt of the report from the Administrative Office of the Courts, the clerk shall provide a copy to the district attorney and to the defendant. The clerk shall otherwise maintain the information as a confidential record in the court file for the case.

(b) All agencies required under G.S. 15A-150 to expunge from records all entries made as a result of a charge or conviction ordered expunged who maintain a licensing agreement to provide record information to a private entity shall maintain a confidential file containing information verifying the expunction and subsequent notification to private entities as required by G.S. 15A-150(d). The information contained in the file shall be disclosed only to a person requesting confirmation of expunction of the record of the person's own discharge or expunction, as provided in G.S. 15A-152.

(c) The Division of Motor Vehicles shall not be required to expunge a record if the expunction of the record is expressly prohibited by the federal Commercial Motor Vehicle Safety Act of 1986, the federal Motor Carrier Safety Improvement Act of 1999, or regulations adopted pursuant to either act.

History.
2009-510, s. 1; 2010-174, s. 8; 2011-278, s. 2; 2012-191, s. 5; 2013-368, s. 13; 2015-40, s. 4; 2017-195, s. 1; 2020-35, s. 2(b); 2021-107, s. 6; 2021-118, s. 3

§ 15A-151.5. Prosecutor access to expunged files

(a) Notwithstanding any other provision of this Article, the Administrative Office of the Courts shall make all confidential files maintained under G.S. 15A-151 electronically available to all prosecutors of this State if the criminal record was expunged on or after July 1, 2018, under any of the following:

(1) G.S. 15A-145. Expunction of records for first offenders under the age of 18 at the time of conviction of misdemeanor; expunction of certain other misdemeanors.

(2) G.S. 15A-145.1. Expunction of records for first offenders under the age of 18 at the time of conviction of certain gang offenses.

(3) G.S. 15A-145.2. Expunction of records for first offenders not over 21 years of age at the time of the offense of certain drug offenses.

(4) G.S. 15A-145.3. Expunction of records for first offenders not over 21 years of age at the time of the offense of certain toxic vapors offenses.

(5) G.S. 15A-145.4. Expunction of records for first offenders who are under 18 years of age at the time of the commission of a nonviolent felony.

(6) G.S. 15A-145.5. Expunction of certain misdemeanors and felonies; no age limitation.

(7) G.S. 15A-145.6. Expunctions for certain defendants convicted of prostitution.

(7a) G.S. 15A-145.7. Expunction of records for first offenders under 20 years of age at the time of the offense of certain offenses.

(7b) G.S. 15A-145.8A. Expunction of records for offenders under the age of 18 at the time of commission of certain

misdemeanors and felonies upon completion of the sentence.

(7c) G.S. 15A-145.9. Expunction of records of certain offenses committed by human trafficking victims.

(8) G.S. 15A-146(a). Expunction of records when charges are dismissed.

(9) G.S. 15A-146(a1). Expunction of records when charges are dismissed.

(b) For any expungement granted on or after July 1, 2018, the record of a criminal conviction expunged under subdivisions (1) through (7b) of subsection (a) of this section may be considered a prior conviction and used for any of the following purposes:

(1) To calculate prior record level and prior conviction level if the named person is convicted of a subsequent criminal offense.

(2) To serve as a basis for indictment for a habitual offense pursuant to G.S. 14-7.1 or G.S. 14-7.26.

(3) When a conviction of a prior offense raises the offense level of a subsequent offense.

(4) To determine eligibility for relief under G.S. 90-96(a).

(5) When permissible in a criminal case under Rule 404(b) or Rule 609 of the North Carolina Rules of Evidence.

(c) For any expungement granted on or after July 1, 2018, the information maintained by the Administrative Office of the Courts, and made available under subsection (a) of this section, is prima facie evidence of the expunged conviction for the purposes provided in subsection (b) of this section and is admissible into evidence. The expungement of a conviction shall not serve as a basis to challenge a conviction or sentence entered before the expungement of that conviction.

(d) Notwithstanding any other provision of this Article, the Administrative Office of the Courts shall make all records of dismissals pursuant to conditional discharge maintained under G.S. 15A-151 electronically available to all prosecutors of this State.

History.
2017-195, s. 1; 2019-158, s. 4(c); 2020-35, s. 2(a); 2020-69, s. 8(a), (b); 2020-78, s. 10.1(a), (b); 2021-88, s. 3; 2021-118, s. 4

§ 15A-152. Civil liability for dissemination of certain criminal history information

(a) **Duty to Delete Record.** -- A private entity that holds itself out as being in the business of compiling and disseminating criminal history record information for compensation shall destroy and shall not disseminate any information in the possession of the entity with respect to which the entity has received a notice to delete the record in question. The private entity shall delete the record within the specified time and pursuant to the terms of the licensing agreement with the State agency. If the license does not specify a time for deletion, or if no license agreement exists between the private entity and state agency, the private entity shall delete the record within 10 business days of receiving notice to delete the record in question.

(b) **Dissemination of Information.** -- Unless the entity is regulated by the federal Fair Credit Reporting, Act 15 U.S.C. § 1681, et seq. or the Gramm-Leach-Bliley Act 15 U.S.C. §§ 6801-6809, a private entity described by subsection (a) of this section that is licensed to access a State agency's criminal history record database may disseminate that information only if, within the 90-day period preceding the date of dissemination, the entity originally obtained the information or received the information as an updated record information to its database. The private entity must notify the State agency from which it receives the information of any other entity to which it subsequently provides a bulk extract of the information.

(c) **Civil Liability.** -- A private entity subject to the provisions of this section that disseminates information in violation of this section is liable for any damages that are sustained as a result of the violation by the person who is the subject of that information. A person who prevails in an action brought under this section is also entitled to recover court costs and reasonable attorneys' fees. This subsection does not apply to an entity regulated by and subject to the civil liability remedies of the federal Fair Credit Reporting Act, 15 U.S.C. § 1681, et seq., or the Gramm Leach-Bliley Act, 15 U.S.C. 6801-6809, et seq.

(d) **Certificate of Verification.** -- Prior to filing an action under this section, a person who is the subject of a record that has been expunged may apply to the Administrative Office of the Courts for a certificate verifying that the person is the subject of a record that has been expunged and that notice of the expunction was made in accordance with G.S. 15A-150. The application must include a sworn affidavit attesting, under penalty of perjury, that the applicant is the person who was the subject of the record in question and identifying the specific case expunged. A notary or official taking an acknowledgment, oath, or affirmation of an applicant's affidavit under this subsection may not disclose the nature or content of the application, except as required in a court action related to the application. Unless made part of the record of a subsequent court proceeding, a certificate of verification and an application for the certificate are not public records under G.S. 132-1. The Administrative Office of the Courts may establish procedures pertaining to the application for and issuance of certificates of verification.

(e) **Notice of Record Removal.** -- Prior to filing an action under this section, a person who is the subject of a record that has been expunged may request a notice of record removal of the expunction and subsequent notification to private entities as required by G.S. 15A-150(d) from an agency required under G.S. 15A-150 to expunge that person's record who maintains a licensing agreement to provide record information to a private entity. The application must include a sworn affidavit attesting, under penalty of perjury, that the applicant is the person who was the subject of the record in question and identifying the specific case expunged. A notary or official taking an acknowledgment, oath, or affirmation of an applicant's affidavit under this subsection may not disclose the nature or content of the application, except as required in a court action related to the application. Unless made part of the record of a subsequent court proceeding, a notice of record removal and an application for the notice are not public records under G.S. 132-1. State and local agencies may establish procedures pertaining to the application for and issuance of notices of record removal.

History.
2009-510, s. 1; 2010-174, s. 9

§ 15A-153. Effect of expunction; prohibited practices by employers, educational institutions, agencies of State and local governments

(a) Purpose. The purpose of this section is to clear the public record of any entry of any arrest, criminal charge, or criminal conviction that has been expunged so that (i) the person who is entitled to and obtains the expunction may omit reference to the charges or convictions to potential employers and others and (ii) a records check for prior arrests and convictions will not disclose the expunged entries. Nothing in this section shall be construed to prohibit an employer from asking a job applicant about criminal charges or convictions that have not been expunged and are part of the public record.

(b) *[Nondisclosure Protected. --]* No person as to whom an order of expunction has been entered pursuant to this Article shall be held thereafter under any provision of any laws to be guilty of perjury or otherwise giving a false statement by reason of that person's failure to recite or acknowledge any expunged arrest, apprehension, charge, indictment, information, trial, or conviction in response to any inquiry made of him or her for any purpose other than as provided in subsection (e) of this section.

(c) Employer or Educational Institution Inquiry Regarding Disclosure of Expunged Arrest, Criminal Charge, or Conviction. An employer or educational institution shall not, in any application, interview, or otherwise, require an applicant for employment or admission to disclose information concerning any arrest, criminal charge, or criminal conviction of the applicant that has been expunged and shall not knowingly and willingly inquire about any arrest, charge, or conviction that they know to have been expunged. An applicant need not, in answer to any question concerning any arrest or criminal charge that has not resulted in a conviction, include a reference to or information concerning arrests, charges, or convictions that have been expunged. This subsection does not apply to State or local law enforcement agencies authorized pursuant to G.S. 15A-151 to obtain confidential information for employment purposes.

(d) State or Local Government Agency, Official, and Employee Inquiry Regarding Disclosure of Expunged Arrest, Criminal Charge, or Conviction. Agencies, officials, and employees of the State and local governments who request disclosure of information concerning any arrest, criminal charge, or criminal conviction of the applicant shall first advise the applicant that State law allows the applicant to not refer to any arrest, charge, or conviction that has been expunged. An applicant need not, in answer to any question concerning any arrest or criminal charge that has not resulted in a conviction, include a reference to or information concerning charges or convictions that have been expunged. Such application shall not be denied solely because of the applicant's refusal or failure to disclose information concerning any arrest, criminal charge, or criminal conviction of the applicant that has been expunged.

(e) *[Exceptions. --]* The provisions of subsection (d) of this section do not apply to any applicant or licensee seeking or holding any certification issued by the North Carolina Criminal Justice Education and Training Standards Commission pursuant to Article 1 of Chapter 17C of the General Statutes or the North Carolina Sheriffs Education and Training Standards Commission pursuant to Article 2 of Chapter 17E of the General Statutes:

(1) Convictions expunged pursuant to G.S. 15A-145.4. -- Persons pursuing certification under the provisions of Article 1 of Chapter 17C or Article 2 of Chapter 17E of the General Statutes shall disclose any and all felony convictions to the certifying Commission regardless of whether or not the felony convictions were expunged pursuant to the provisions of G.S. 15A-145.4.

(2) Convictions expunged pursuant to G.S. 15A-145.5. -- Persons pursuing certification under the provisions of Article 1 of Chapter 17C or Article 2 of Chapter 17E of the General Statutes shall disclose any

and all convictions to the certifying Commission regardless of whether or not the convictions were expunged pursuant to the provisions of G.S. 15A-145.5.

(e1) The provisions of subsection (d) of this section do not apply to any individual requesting a disclosure statement be prepared by the North Carolina Sheriffs' Education and Training Standards Commission pursuant to Article 3 of Chapter 17E of the General Statutes.

(f) (See note) Penalty for Violation. Upon investigation by the Commissioner of Labor or the Commissioner's authorized representative, any employer found to be in violation of subsection (c) of this section shall be issued a written warning for a first violation and shall be subject to a civil penalty of up to five hundred dollars ($ 500.00) for each additional violation occurring after receipt of the written warning. In determining the amount of any penalty ordered under authority of this section, the Commissioner shall give due consideration to the appropriateness of the penalty with respect to the size of the business of the person being charged, the gravity of the violation, the good faith of the person, and the record of previous violations. The determination of the amount of the penalty by the Commissioner shall be final, unless within 15 days after receipt of notice thereof by certified mail with return receipt, by signature confirmation as provided by the U.S. Postal Service, by a designated delivery service authorized pursuant to 26 U.S.C. § 7502(f)(2) with delivery receipt, or via hand delivery, the person charged with the violation takes exception to the determination in which event the final determination of the penalty shall be made in an administrative proceeding and in a judicial proceeding pursuant to Chapter 150B of the General Statutes, the Administrative Procedure Act. The Commissioner of Labor may adopt, modify, or revoke such rules as are necessary for carrying out the provisions of this subsection.

Nothing in this section shall be construed to create a private cause of action against any employer or its agents or employees, any educational institutions or their agents or employees, or any State or local government agencies, officials, or employees.

History.
2013-53, s. 3; 2021-107, s. 7(a)

§§ 15A-154 through 15A-159

Reserved for future codification purposes.

§ 15A-160. Reporting requirement

The Department of Public Safety, in conjunction with the Department of Justice and the

Administrative Office of the Courts, shall report jointly to the Chairs of the Joint Legislative Oversight Committee on Justice and Public Safety Oversight by September 1 of each year regarding expunctions. The report shall include all of the following information:

(1) The number and types of expunctions granted during the fiscal year in which the report is made.

(2) The number and type of expunctions granted each fiscal year for the five fiscal years preceding the date of the report.

(3) A full accounting of how the agencies have spent the receipts generated by the expunction fees received during the fiscal year in which the report is made and for the five preceding fiscal years.

History.
2013-360, s. 18B.16(h); 2015-241, s. 16B.5(a)

§§ 15A-161 through 15A-173

Reserved for future codification purposes.

ARTICLE 6
CERTIFICATE OF RELIEF

§ 15A-173.1. Definitions

The following definitions apply in this Article:

(1) **Collateral consequence. --** A collateral sanction or a disqualification.

(2) **Collateral sanction. --** A penalty, disability, or disadvantage, however denominated, imposed on an individual as a result of the individual's conviction of an offense which applies by operation of law, whether or not the penalty, disability, or disadvantage is included in the judgment or sentence. The term does not include imprisonment, probation, parole, post-release supervision, forfeiture, restitution, fine, assessment, or costs of prosecution.

(3) **Disqualification. --** A penalty, disability, or disadvantage, however denominated, that an administrative agency, governmental official, or court in a civil proceeding may impose on an individual on grounds relating to the individual's conviction of an offense.

(4) **District attorney. --** The office of the district attorney that prosecuted the offense giving rise to the collateral consequence from which relief is sought.

History.
2011-265, s. 1

§ 15A-173.2. Certificate of Relief

(a) An individual who is convicted of no more than (i) three Class H or I felonies and (ii) any misdemeanors may petition the court where the individual was convicted for a Certificate of Relief relieving collateral consequences as permitted by this Article. If the person is convicted of more than one Class H or I felony in the same session of court, then the multiple felony convictions shall be treated as one felony conviction under this section. Except as otherwise provided in this subsection, the petition shall be heard by the senior resident superior court judge if the convictions were in superior court, or the chief district court judge if the convictions were in district court. The senior resident superior court judge and chief district court judge in each district may delegate their authority to hold hearings and issue, modify, or revoke Certificates of Relief to judges, clerks, or magistrates in that district.

(b) Except as otherwise provided in G.S. 15A-173.3, the court may issue a Certificate of Relief if, after reviewing the petition, the individual's comprehensive criminal history as provided by the district attorney, any information provided by a victim under G.S. 15A-173.6 or the district attorney, and any other relevant evidence, it finds the individual has established by a preponderance of the evidence all of the following:

(1) Twelve months have passed since the individual has completed his or her sentence. For purposes of this subdivision, an individual has not completed his or her sentence until the individual has served all of the active time, if any, imposed for each offense and has also completed any period of probation, post-release supervision, and parole related to the offense that is required by State law or court order.

(2) The individual is engaged in, or seeking to engage in, a lawful occupation or activity, including employment, training, education, or rehabilitative programs, or the individual otherwise has a lawful source of support.

(3) The individual has complied with all requirements of the individual's sentence, including any terms of probation, that may include substance abuse treatment, anger management, and educational requirements.

(4) The individual is not in violation of the terms of any criminal sentence, or that any failure to comply is justified, excused, involuntary, or insubstantial.

(5) A criminal charge is not pending against the individual.

(6) Granting the petition would not pose an unreasonable risk to the safety or welfare of the public or any individual.

(c) The Certificate of Relief shall specify any restriction imposed and collateral sanction or disqualification from which relief has not been granted under G.S. 15A-173.4(a).

(d) Unless modified or revoked, a Certificate of Relief relieves all collateral sanctions, except those listed in G.S. 15A-173.3, those sanctions imposed by the North Carolina Constitution or federal law, and any others specifically excluded in the certificate. A Certificate of Relief does not automatically relieve a disqualification; however, an administrative agency, governmental official, or court in a civil proceeding shall consider a Certificate of Relief favorably in determining whether a conviction should result in disqualification.

(e) A Certificate of Relief issued under this Article does not result in the expunction of any criminal history record information, nor does it constitute a pardon.

(f) A Certificate of Relief is automatically revoked pursuant to G.S. 15A-173.4(b) if the individual is subsequently convicted of a felony or misdemeanor other than a traffic violation. The Administrative Office of the Courts shall provide the following declaration on the Petition and Order for a Certificate of Relief: "Any Certificate of Relief is automatically revoked for a subsequent conviction of a felony or misdemeanor other than a traffic violation in this State."

(g) The denial of a petition for a Certificate of Relief shall state the reasons for the denial, and the petitioner may file a subsequent petition 12 months from the denial and shall demonstrate that the petitioner has remedied the defects in the previous petition and has complied with any conditions for reapplication set by the court pursuant to G.S. 15A-173.4(a) in order to have the petition granted.

(h) A petitioner who files a petition under this section shall pay a one-time fee of fifty dollars ($ 50.00) to the clerk of superior court at the time of filing. Fees collected under this subsection shall be deposited in the General Fund. This subsection shall not apply to a petition filed by an indigent. The fee shall be waived by the clerk of superior court on a showing by the petitioner that the one-time fee was previously paid, even if in another county.

(i) Any person who is granted a Certificate of Relief under this Article shall notify any employer, landlord, or other party who has relied on the Certificate of Relief of any conviction, modification, or revocation subsequent to the Certificate of Relief within 10 days of the conviction, modification, or revocation.

History.
2011-265, s. 1; 2018-79, s. 1; 2018-145, s. 19; 2019-91, s. 1

§ 15A-173.3. Collateral sanctions not subject to order of limited relief or Certificate of Relief

A Certificate of Relief shall not be issued to relieve any of the following collateral sanctions:

(1) Requirements imposed by, and any statutory requirements or prohibitions imposed as a result of registration pursuant to, Article 27A of Chapter 14 of the General Statutes.

(2) Prohibitions on possession of firearms imposed by Articles 54A and 54B of Chapter 14 of the General Statutes.

(3) A motor vehicle license suspension, revocation, limitation, or ineligibility imposed pursuant to Chapter 20 of the General Statutes.

(4) Ineligibility for certification pursuant to Article 1 of Chapter 17C or 17E of the General Statutes.

(5) Ineligibility for employment as any of the following if the ineligibility is a sanction imposed by a statute or session law of North Carolina.

    a. A corrections or probation officer.

    b. A prosecutor or investigator in either the Department of Justice or in the office of a district attorney. For purposes of this subdivision, the term district attorney shall include any district attorney authorized pursuant to G.S. 7A-60.

History.
2011-265, s. 1

§ 15A-173.4. Issuance, modification, and revocation of Certificate of Relief by the court

(a) When a petition is filed under G.S. 15A-173.2, including a petition for enlargement of an existing Certificate of Relief, the court shall notify the district attorney at least three weeks before the hearing on the matter. The court may issue a Certificate of Relief subject to restriction, condition, or additional requirement. When issuing, denying, modifying, or revoking a Certificate of Relief, the court may impose conditions for reapplication.

(b) The court shall revoke a Certificate of Relief it issued if it finds by a preponderance of the evidence that the individual has a subsequent conviction for an offense in another jurisdiction that is deemed a felony or misdemeanor other than a traffic violation in this State. The court may modify or revoke a Certificate of Relief it issued if it finds by a preponderance of the evidence that the petitioner made a material misrepresentation in the petition for Certificate of Relief. A motion for modification or revocation of a Certificate of Relief may be initiated by the court on its own motion, or upon motion of the district attorney or the individual for whom the Certificate of Relief has been issued. The individual for whom the Certificate of Relief has been issued, and the district attorney, shall be given notice of the motion at least three weeks before any hearing on the matter.

(c) The district attorney shall have the right to appear and be heard at any proceeding relating to the issuance, modification, or revocation of the Certificate of Relief.

(d) The court is authorized to call upon a probation officer for any additional investigation or verification of the individual's conduct it reasonably believes necessary to its decision to issue, modify, or revoke a Certificate of Relief. If there are material disputed issues of fact or law, the individual and the district attorney may submit evidence and be heard on those issues.

(e) The issuance, modification, and revocation of Certificates of Relief shall be a public record.

History.
2011-265, s. 1; 2018-79, s. 2

§ 15A-173.5. Reliance on order or Certificate of Relief as evidence of due care

In a judicial or administrative proceeding alleging negligence, a Certificate of Relief is a bar to any action alleging lack of due care in hiring, retaining, licensing, leasing to, admitting to a school or program, or otherwise transacting business or engaging in activity with the individual to whom the Certificate of Relief was issued, if the person against whom the judicial or administrative proceeding is brought relied on the Certificate of Relief at the time of the alleged negligence.

History.
2011-265, s. 1; 2018-79, s. 3

§ 15A-173.6. Victim's rights

The victim of the underlying offense for which a Certificate of Relief is sought may appear and be heard, or may file a statement for consideration by the court, in a proceeding for issuance, modification, or revocation of the Certificate of Relief. Notification to the victim shall be made through the Victim Witness Coordinator in the office of the district attorney.

History.
2011-265, s. 1

§§ 15A-174 through 15A-200

Reserved for future codification purposes.

SUBCHAPTER 02. LAW-ENFORCEMENT AND INVESTIGATIVE PROCEDURES

ARTICLE 7

§§ 15A-201 through 15A-210

Reserved for future codification purposes.

ARTICLE 8 ELECTRONIC RECORDING OF INTERROGATIONS

§ 15A-211. Electronic recording of interrogations

(a) **Purpose.** -- The purpose of this Article is to require the creation of an electronic record of an entire custodial interrogation in order to eliminate disputes about interrogations, thereby improving prosecution of the guilty while affording protection to the innocent and increasing court efficiency.

(b) **Application.** -- The provisions of this Article shall apply to all custodial interrogations of juveniles in criminal investigations conducted at any place of detention. The provisions of this Article shall also apply to any custodial interrogation of any person in a criminal investigation conducted at any place of detention if the investigation is related to any of the following crimes: any Class A, B1, or B2 felony, and any Class C felony of rape, sex offense, or assault with a deadly weapon with intent to kill inflicting serious injury.

(c) **Definitions.** -- The following definitions apply in this Article:

(1) **Electronic recording.** -- An audio recording that is an authentic, accurate, unaltered record; or a visual recording that is an authentic, accurate, unaltered record. A visual and audio recording shall be simultaneously produced whenever reasonably feasible, provided that a defendant may not raise this as grounds for suppression of evidence.

(2) **In its entirety.** -- An uninterrupted record that begins with and includes a law enforcement officer's advice to the person in custody of that person's constitutional rights, ends when the interview has completely finished, and clearly shows both the interrogator and the person in custody throughout. If the record is a visual recording, the camera recording the custodial interrogation must be placed so that

the camera films both the interrogator and the suspect. Brief periods of recess, upon request by the person in custody or the law enforcement officer, do not constitute an "interruption" of the record. The record will reflect the starting time of the recess and the resumption of the interrogation.

(3) **Place of detention.** -- A jail, police or sheriff's station, correctional or detention facility, holding facility for prisoners, or other facility where persons are held in custody in connection with criminal charges.

(d) **Electronic Recording of Interrogations Required.** -- Any law enforcement officer conducting a custodial interrogation in an investigation of a juvenile shall make an electronic recording of the interrogation in its entirety. Any law enforcement officer conducting a custodial interrogation in an investigation relating to any of the following crimes shall make an electronic recording of the interrogation in its entirety: any Class A, B1, or B2 felony; and any Class C felony of rape, sex offense, or assault with a deadly weapon with intent to kill inflicting serious injury.

(e) **Admissibility of Electronic Recordings.** -- During the prosecution of any offense to which this Article applies, an oral, written, nonverbal, or sign language statement of a defendant made in the course of a custodial interrogation may be presented as evidence against the defendant if an electronic recording was made of the custodial interrogation in its entirety and the statement is otherwise admissible. If the court finds that the defendant was subjected to a custodial interrogation that was not electronically recorded in its entirety, any statements made by the defendant after that non-electronically recorded custodial interrogation, even if made during an interrogation that is otherwise in compliance with this section, may be questioned with regard to the voluntariness and reliability of the statement. The State may establish through clear and convincing evidence that the statement was both voluntary and reliable and that law enforcement officers had good cause for failing to electronically record the interrogation in its entirety. Good cause shall include, but not be limited to, the following:

(1) The accused refused to have the interrogation electronically recorded, and the refusal itself was electronically recorded.

(2) The failure to electronically record an interrogation in its entirety was the result of unforeseeable equipment failure, and obtaining replacement equipment was not feasible.

(f) **Remedies for Compliance or Noncompliance.** -- All of the following remedies shall be granted as relief for compliance or noncompliance with the requirements of this section:

(1) Failure to comply with any of the requirements of this section shall be considered by the court in adjudicating motions to suppress a statement of the defendant made during or after a custodial interrogation.

(2) Failure to comply with any of the requirements of this section shall be admissible in support of claims that the defendant's statement was involuntary or is unreliable, provided the evidence is otherwise admissible.

(3) When evidence of compliance or noncompliance with the requirements of this section has been presented at trial, the jury shall be instructed that it may consider credible evidence of compliance or noncompliance to determine whether the defendant's statement was voluntary and reliable.

(g) **Article Does Not Preclude Admission of Certain Statements.** -- Nothing in this Article precludes the admission of any of the following:

(1) A statement made by the accused in open court during trial, before a grand jury, or at a preliminary hearing.

(2) A spontaneous statement that is not made in response to a question.

(3) A statement made during arrest processing in response to a routine question.

(4) A statement made during a custodial interrogation that is conducted in another state by law enforcement officers of that state.

(5) A statement obtained by a federal law enforcement officer.

(6) A statement given at a time when the interrogators are unaware that the person is suspected of an offense to which this Article applies.

(7) A statement used only for impeachment purposes and not as substantive evidence.

(h) **Destruction or Modification of Recording After Appeals Exhausted.** -- The State shall not destroy or alter any electronic recording of a custodial interrogation of a defendant convicted of any offense related to the interrogation until one year after the completion of all State and federal appeals of the conviction, including the exhaustion of any appeal of any motion for appropriate relief or habeas corpus proceedings. Every electronic recording should be clearly identified and catalogued by law enforcement personnel.

History.
2007-434, s. 1; 2011-329, s. 2

§§ 15A-212 through 15A-219

Reserved for future codification purposes.

ARTICLE 8A
SBI AND STATE CRIME LABORATORY ACCESS TO VIEW AND ANALYZE RECORDINGS

§ 15A-220. SBI and State Crime Laboratory access to view and analyze recordings

Any State or local law enforcement agency that uses the services of the State Bureau of Investigation or the North Carolina State Crime Laboratory to analyze a recording covered by G.S. 132-1.4A shall, at no cost, provide access to a method to view and analyze the recording upon request of the State Bureau of Investigation or the North Carolina State Crime Laboratory.

History.
2016-88, s. 2(d)

ARTICLE 9
SEARCH AND SEIZURE BY CONSENT

§ 15A-221. General authorization; definition of "consent"

(a) **Authority to Search and Seize Pursuant to Consent.** -- Subject to the limitations in the other provisions of this Article, a law-enforcement officer may conduct a search and make seizures, without a search warrant or other authorization, if consent to the search is given.

(b) **Definition of "Consent".** -- As used in this Article, "consent" means a statement to the officer, made voluntarily and in accordance with the requirements of G.S. 15A-222, giving the officer permission to make a search.

History.
1973, c. 1286, s. 1

§ 15A-222. Person from whom effective consent may be obtained

The consent needed to justify a search and seizure under G.S. 15A-221 must be given:

(1) By the person to be searched;

(2) By the registered owner of a vehicle to be searched or by the person in apparent control of its operation and contents at the time the consent is given;

(3) By a person who by ownership or otherwise is reasonably apparently entitled to give or withhold consent to a search of premises.

History.
1973, c. 1286, s. 1

§ 15A-223. Permissible scope of consent search and seizure

(a) **Search Limited by Scope of Consent.** -- A search conducted pursuant to the provisions of this Article may not exceed, in duration or physical scope, the limits of the consent given.

(b) **Items Seizable as Result of Consent Search.** -- The things subject to seizure in the course of a search pursuant to this Article are the same as those specified in G.S. 15A-242. Upon completion of the search, the officer must make a list of the things seized, and must deliver a receipt embodying the list to the person who consented to the search and, if known, to the owner of the vehicle or premises searched.

History.
1973, c. 1286, s. 1

§§ 15A-224 through 15A-230

Reserved for future codification purposes.

ARTICLE 10
OTHER SEARCHES AND SEIZURES

§ 15A-231. Other searches and seizures

Constitutionally permissible searches and seizures which are not regulated by the General Statutes of North Carolina are not prohibited.

History.
1973, c. 1286, s. 1

§§ 15A-232 through 15A-240

Reserved for future codification purposes.

ARTICLE 11
SEARCH WARRANTS

§ 15A-241. Definition of search warrant

A search warrant is a court order and process directing a law-enforcement officer to search designated premises, vehicles, or persons for the purpose of seizing designated items and accounting for any items so obtained to the court which issued the warrant.

History.
1868-9, c. 178, subch. 3, s. 38; Code, s. 1171; Rev., s. 3163; C.S., s. 4529; 1941, c. 53; 1949, c. 1179; 1955, c. 7; 1965, c. 377; 1969, c. 869, s. 8; 1973, c. 1286, s. 1

§ 15A-242. Items subject to seizure under a search warrant

An item is subject to seizure pursuant to a search warrant if there is probable cause to believe that it:
(1) Is stolen or embezzled; or
(2) Is contraband or otherwise unlawfully possessed; or
(3) Has been used or is possessed for the purpose of being used to commit or conceal the commission of a crime; or
(4) Constitutes evidence of an offense or the identity of a person participating in an offense.

History.
1868-9, c. 178, subch. 3, s. 38; Code, s. 1171; Rev., s. 3163; C.S., s. 4529; 1941, c. 53; 1949, c. 1179; 1955, c. 7; 1965, c. 377; 1969, c. 869, s. 8; 1973, c. 1286, s. 1

§ 15A-243. Who may issue a search warrant

(a) A search warrant valid throughout the State may be issued by:
(1) A Justice of the Supreme Court.
(2) A judge of the Court of Appeals.
(3) A judge of the superior court.
(b) Other search warrants may be issued by:
(1) A judge of the district court as provided in G.S. 7A-291.
(2) A clerk as provided in G.S. 7A-180 and 7A-181.
(3) A magistrate as provided in G.S. 7A-273.

History.
1868-9, c. 178, subch. 3, s. 38; Code, s. 1171; Rev., s. 3163; C.S., s. 4529; 1941, c. 53; 1949, c. 1179; 1955, c. 7; 1965, c. 377; 1969, c. 869, s. 8; 1973, c. 1286, s. 1

§ 15A-244. Contents of the application for a search warrant

Each application for a search warrant must be made in writing upon oath or affirmation. All applications must contain:
(1) The name and title of the applicant; and
(2) A statement that there is probable cause to believe that items subject to seizure under G.S. 15A-242 may be found in

or upon a designated or described place, vehicle, or person; and
(3) Allegations of fact supporting the statement. The statements must be supported by one or more affidavits particularly setting forth the facts and circumstances establishing probable cause to believe that the items are in the places or in the possession of the individuals to be searched; and
(4) A request that the court issue a search warrant directing a search for and the seizure of the items in question.

History.
1973, c. 1286, s. 1

§ 15A-245. Basis for issuance of a search warrant; duty of the issuing official

(a) Before acting on the application, the issuing official may examine on oath the applicant or any other person who may possess pertinent information, but information other than that contained in the affidavit may not be considered by the issuing official in determining whether probable cause exists for the issuance of the warrant unless the information is either recorded or contemporaneously summarized in the record or on the face of the warrant by the issuing official. The information must be shown by one or both of the following:
(1) Affidavit.
(2) Oral testimony under oath or affirmation before the issuing official.
(3) Repealed by Session Laws 2021-47, s. 10(c), effective June 18, 2021, and applicable to proceedings occurring on or after that date.
(b) If the issuing official finds that the application meets the requirements of this Article and finds there is probable cause to believe that the search will discover items specified in the application which are subject to seizure under G.S. 15A-242, he must issue a search warrant in accordance with the requirements of this Article. The issuing official must retain a copy of the warrant and warrant application and must promptly file them with the clerk. If he does not so find, the official must deny the application.

History.
1973, c. 1286, s. 1; 2005-334, s. 1; 2021-47, s. 10(c)

§ 15A-246. Form and content of the search warrant

A search warrant must contain:
(1) The name and signature of the issuing official with the time and date of issuance above his signature; and

(2) The name of a specific officer or the classification of officers to whom the warrant is addressed; and

(3) The names of the applicant and of all persons whose affidavits or testimony were given in support of the application; and

(4) A designation sufficient to establish with reasonable certainty the premises, vehicles, or persons to be searched; and

(5) A description or a designation of the items constituting the object of the search and authorized to be seized.

History.
1868-9, c. 178, subch. 3, s. 39; Code, s. 1172; Rev., s. 3164; C.S., s. 4530; 1961, c. 1069; 1969, c. 869, s. 8; 1973, c. 1286, s. 1

§ 15A-247. Who may execute a search warrant

A search warrant may be executed by any law-enforcement officer acting within his territorial jurisdiction, whose investigative authority encompasses the crime or crimes involved.

History.
1868-9, c. 178, subch. 3, s. 38; Code, s. 1171; Rev., s. 3163; C.S., s. 4529; 1941, c. 53; 1949, c. 1179; 1955, c. 7; 1965, c. 377; 1969, c. 869, s. 8; 1973, c. 1286, s. 1

§ 15A-248. Time of execution of a search warrant

A search warrant must be executed within 48 hours from the time of issuance. Any warrant not executed within that time limit is void and must be marked "not executed" and returned without unnecessary delay to the clerk of the issuing court.

History.
1973, c. 1286, s. 1

§ 15A-249. Officer to give notice of identity and purpose

The officer executing a search warrant must, before entering the premises, give appropriate notice of his identity and purpose to the person to be searched, or the person in apparent control of the premises to be searched. If it is unclear whether anyone is present at the premises to be searched, he must give the notice in a manner likely to be heard by anyone who is present.

History.
1973, c. 1286, s. 1

N.C. Gen. Stat. § 15A-250

Reserved for future codification purposes.

§ 15A-251. Entry by force

An officer may break and enter any premises or vehicle when necessary to the execution of the warrant if:

(1) The officer has previously announced his identity and purpose as required by G.S. 15A-249 and reasonably believes either that admittance is being denied or unreasonably delayed or that the premises or vehicle is unoccupied; or

(2) The officer has probable cause to believe that the giving of notice would endanger the life or safety of any person.

History.
1973, c. 1286, s. 1

§ 15A-252. Service of a search warrant

Before undertaking any search or seizure pursuant to the warrant, the officer must read the warrant and give a copy of the warrant application and affidavit to the person to be searched, or the person in apparent control of the premises or vehicle to be searched. If no one in apparent and responsible control is occupying the premises or vehicle, the officer must leave a copy of the warrant affixed to the premises or vehicle.

History.
1973, c. 1286, s. 1

§ 15A-253. Scope of the search; seizure of items not named in the warrant

The scope of the search may be only such as is authorized by the warrant and is reasonably necessary to discover the items specified therein. Upon discovery of the items specified, the officer must take possession or custody of them. If in the course of the search the officer inadvertently discovers items not specified in the warrant which are subject to seizure under G.S. 15A-242, he may also take possession of the items so discovered.

History.
1973, c. 1286, s. 1

§ 15A-254. List of items seized

Upon seizing items pursuant to a search warrant, an officer must write and sign a receipt itemizing the items taken and containing the name of the court by which the warrant was issued. If the items were taken from a person, the receipt must be given to the person. If items are taken from a place or vehicle, the receipt must be given to the owner, or person in apparent control of the premises or vehicle if the person is present; or if he is not, the officer must leave the receipt in the premises or vehicle from which the items were taken.

History.
1973, c. 1286, s. 1

§ 15A-255. Frisk of persons present in premises or vehicle to be searched

An officer executing a warrant directing a search of premises or of a vehicle may, if the officer reasonably believes that his safety or the safety of others then present so requires, search for any dangerous weapons by an external patting of the clothing of those present. If in the course of such a frisk he feels an object which he reasonably believes to be a dangerous weapon, he may take possession of the object.

History.
1973, c. 1286, s. 1

§ 15A-256. Detention and search of persons present in private premises or vehicle to be searched

An officer executing a warrant directing a search of premises not generally open to the public or of a vehicle other than a common carrier may detain any person present for such time as is reasonably necessary to execute the warrant. If the search of such premises or vehicle and of any persons designated as objects of the search in the warrant fails to produce the items named in the warrant, the officer may then search any person present at the time of the officer's entry to the extent reasonably necessary to find property particularly described in the warrant which may be concealed upon the person, but no property of a different type from that particularly described in the warrant may be seized or may be the basis for prosecution of any person so searched. For the purpose of this section, all controlled substances are the same type of property.

History.
1973, c. 1286, s. 1

§ 15A-257. Return of the executed warrant

An officer who has executed a search warrant must, without unnecessary delay, return to the clerk of the issuing court the warrant together with a written inventory of items seized. The inventory, if any, and return must be signed and sworn to by the officer who executed the warrant.

History.
1973, c. 1286, s. 1

§ 15A-258. Disposition of seized property

Property seized shall be held in the custody of the person who applied for the warrant, or of the officer who executed it, or of the agency or department by which the officer is employed, or of any other law-enforcement agency or person for purposes of evaluation or analysis, upon condition that upon order of the court the items may be retained by the court or delivered to another court.

History.
1973, c. 1286, s. 1

§ 15A-259. Application of Article to all warrants; exception as to inspection warrants and special riot situations

The requirements of this Article apply to search warrants issued for any purpose, except that the contents of and procedure relating to inspection warrants are to be governed by the provisions of Article 4A of Chapter 15 and warrants to inspect vehicles in riot areas or approaching municipalities during emergencies are subject to the special procedures set out in G.S. 14-288.11. Nothing in this Article is intended to alter or affect the emergency search doctrine.

History.
1957, c. 496; 1969, c. 869, s. 8; 1971, c. 872, s. 4; 1973, c. 1286, s. 1

ARTICLE 12
PEN REGISTERS; TRAP AND TRACE DEVICES

§ 15A-260. Definitions

As used in this Article:

(1) "Electronic communication," "electronic communication service," and "wire communication" shall have the meaning as set forth in Section 2510 of Title 18 of the United States Code;

(2) "Pen register" means a device which records or decodes electronic or other impulses which identify numbers dialed or otherwise transmitted on the telephone line to which such device is attached, but the term does not include any device used by a provider or customer of a wire or electronic service for billing, or recording as an incident to billing, for communication services provided by the provider or any device

used by a provider or customer of a wire communication service for cost accounting or other like purposes in the ordinary course of its business, nor shall the term include any device which allows the listening or recording of communications transmitted on the telephone line to which the device is attached;

(3) "Trap and trace device" means a device which captures the incoming electronic or other impulses which identify the originating number of an instrument or device from which a wire or electronic communication was transmitted.

History.
1987 (Reg. Sess., 1988), c. 1104, s. 1

§ 15A-261. Prohibition and exceptions

(a) **In General.** -- Except as provided in subsection (b) of this section, no person may install or use a pen register or a trap and trace device without first obtaining a court order as provided in this Article.

(b) **Exception.** -- The prohibition of subsection (a) of this section does not apply to the use of a pen register or a trap and trace device by a provider of wire or electronic communication service:

(1) Relating to the operation, maintenance, or testing of a wire or electronic communication service or to the protection of the rights or property of the provider, or to the protection of users of that service from abuse of service or unlawful use of service; or

(2) To record the fact that a wire or electronic communication was initiated or completed in order to protect the provider, another provider furnishing service toward the completion of the wire communication, or a user of that service, from fraudulent, unlawful or abusive use of service; or

(3) With the consent of the user of that service.

(c) **Penalty.** -- A person who willfully and knowingly violates subsection (a) of this section is guilty of a Class 1 misdemeanor.

History.
1987 (Reg. Sess., 1988), c. 1104, s. 1; 1993, c. 539, s. 297; 1994, Ex. Sess., c. 24, s. 14(c)

§ 15A-262. Application for order for pen register or trap and trace device

(a) **Application.** -- A law enforcement officer may make an application for an order or an extension of an order under G.S. 15A-263 authorizing or approving the installation and use of a pen register or a trap and trace device, in writing under oath or affirmation, to a superior court judge.

(b) **Contents of Application.** -- An application under subsection (a) of this section shall include:

(1) The identity of the law enforcement officer making the application and the identity of the law enforcement agency conducting the investigation; and

(2) A certification by the applicant that the information likely to be obtained is relevant to an ongoing criminal investigation being conducted by that agency.

History.
1987 (Reg. Sess., 1988), c. 1104, s. 1

§ 15A-263. Issuance of order for pen register or trap and trace device

(a) **In General.** -- Following application made under G.S. 15A-262, a superior court judge may enter an ex parte order authorizing the installation and use of a pen register or a trap and trace device within the State if the judge finds:

(1) That there is reasonable suspicion to believe that a felony offense, or a Class A1 or Class 1 misdemeanor offense has been committed;

(2) That there are reasonable grounds to suspect that the person named or described in the affidavit committed the offense, if that person is known and can be named or described; and

(3) That the results of procedures involving pen registers or trap and trace devices will be of material aid in determining whether the person named in the affidavit committed the offense.

(b) **Contents of Order.** -- An order issued under this section:

(1) Shall specify:

a. The identity, if known, of the person to whom is leased or in whose name is listed the telephone line to which the pen register or trap and trace device is to be attached;

b. The identity, if known, of the person who is the subject of the criminal investigation;

c. The number and, if known, physical location of the telephone line to which the pen register or trap and trace device is to be attached and, in the case of a trap and trace device, the geographic limits of the trap and trace order; and

d. The offense to which the information likely to be obtained by the pen

Chapter 15A

register or trap and trace device relates; and

(2) Shall direct, upon request of the applicant, the furnishing of information, facilities, or technical assistance necessary to accomplish the installation of the pen register or trap and trace device under G.S. 15A-264.

(c) Time Period and Extension.

(1) An order issued under this section shall authorize the installation and use of a pen register or a trap and trace device for a period not to exceed 60 days.

(2) An extension of an order issued under this section may be granted, but only upon an application for an order under G.S. 15A-262 and upon the judicial finding required by subsection (a) of this section. The period of extension shall not exceed 60 days.

(d) **Nondisclosure of Existence of Pen Register or a Trap and Trace Device.** -- An order authorizing or approving the installation and use of a pen register or a trap and trace device shall direct that:

(1) The order be sealed until otherwise ordered by the judge; and

(2) The person owning or leasing the line to which the pen register or a trap and trace device is attached, or who has been ordered by the judge to provide assistance to the applicant, not disclose the existence of the pen register or trap and trace device or the existence of the investigation to the listed subscriber, or to any person, unless otherwise ordered by the judge.

The provisions of G.S. 15A-903 and 15A-904 shall apply to this Article.

History.
1987 (Reg. Sess., 1988), c. 1104, s. 1; 1997-80, s. 13

§ 15A-264. Assistance in installation and use of a pen register or a trap and trace device

(a) **Pen Registers.** -- Upon the request of a law enforcement officer authorized to install and use a pen register under this Article, a provider of wire or electronic communication service, a landlord, a custodian, or other person shall furnish the officer promptly with all information, facilities, or technical assistance necessary to accomplish the installation of the pen register unobtrusively and with a minimum of interference with the communication services, if the assistance is directed by a court order as provided in G.S. 15A-263(b)(2).

(b) **Trap and Trace Devices.** -- Upon the request of a law enforcement officer authorized to receive the results of a trap and trace device under this Article, a provider of a wire or

electronic communication service, a landlord, a custodian, or other person shall install the device immediately on the appropriate line and shall furnish the officer all additional information, facilities, or technical assistance, including installation and operation of the device unobtrusively and with a minimum of interference with the communication services, if the installation and assistance are directed by court order as provided in G.S. 15A-263(b)(2). Unless otherwise ordered by the judge, the results of the trap and trace device shall be furnished to the law enforcement officer designated in the court order at reasonable intervals during regular business hours for the duration of the order.

(c) **Compensation.** -- A provider of a wire or electronic communication service, a landlord, a custodian, or other person who furnishes facilities or technical assistance pursuant to this section shall be compensated for the reasonable expenses incurred in providing the facilities and assistance.

(d) **No Cause of Action Against a Provider Giving Information or Assistance Under this Article.** -- No cause of action shall be allowed in any court against any provider of a wire or electronic communication service, its officers, employees, agents, or other specified persons for providing information, facilities, or assistance in accordance with the terms of a court order under this Article.

(e) **Defense.** -- A good faith reliance on a court order or a statutory authorization is a complete defense against any civil or criminal action brought under this Article or any other law.

History.
1987 (Reg. Sess., 1988), c. 1104, s. 1

N.C. Gen. Stat. § 15A-265

Reserved for future codification purposes.

ARTICLE 13
DNA DATABASE AND DATABANK

§ 15A-266. Short title

This Article may be cited as the DNA Database and Databank Act of 1993.

History.
1993, c. 401, s. 1

§ 15A-266.1. Policy

It is the policy of the State to assist federal, State, and local criminal justice and law enforcement agencies in the identification, detection, or exclusion of individuals who are subjects of the investigation or prosecution of felonies or violent crimes against the person. Identification, detection, and exclusion are facilitated by the analysis of biological evidence that is often left by the perpetrator or is recovered from the crime scene. The analysis of biological evidence can also be used to identify missing persons and victims of mass disasters.

History.

1993, c. 401, s. 1; 2003-376, s. 1; 2009-203, s. 1

§ **15A-266.2. Definitions**

As used in this Article, unless another meaning is specified or the context clearly requires otherwise, the following terms have the meanings specified:

(1) "Arrestee" means any person arrested for an offense in G.S. 15A-266.3A(f) or (g).

(1a) "CODIS" means the FBI's national DNA identification index system that allows the storage and exchange of DNA records submitted by federal, State and local forensic DNA laboratories. The term "CODIS" is derived from Combined DNA Index System (NDIS) administered and operated by the Federal Bureau of Investigation.

(1b) "Conviction" includes a conviction by a jury or a court, a guilty plea, a plea of nolo contendere, or a finding of not guilty by reason of insanity or mental disease or defect.

(1c) "Crime Laboratory" [means] the North Carolina State Crime Laboratory of the Department of Justice.

(1d) "Criminal Justice Agency" means an agency or institution of a federal, State, or local government, other than the office of the public defender, that performs as part of its principal function, activities relating to the apprehension, investigation, prosecution, adjudication, incarceration, supervision, or rehabilitation of criminal offenders.

(1e) "Custodial Agency" means the governmental entity in possession of evidence collected as part of a criminal investigation or prosecution.

(2) "DNA" means deoxyribonucleic acid. DNA is located in the cells and provides an individual's personal genetic blueprint. DNA encodes genetic information that is the basis of human heredity and forensic identification.

(3) "DNA Record" means DNA identification information stored in the State DNA Database or CODIS for the purpose of generating investigative leads or supporting statistical interpretation of DNA test results. The DNA record is the result obtained from the DNA analysis. The DNA record is comprised of the characteristics of a DNA sample which are of value in establishing the identity of individuals. The results of all DNA identification analyses on an individual's DNA sample are also collectively referred to as the DNA profile of an individual.

(4) "DNA Sample" means blood, cheek swabs, or any biological sample containing cells provided by any person with respect to offenses covered by this Article or submitted to the State Crime Laboratory pursuant to this Article for analysis pursuant to a criminal investigation or storage or both.

(5) "FBI" means the Federal Bureau of Investigation.

(5a) "NDIS" means the National DNA Index System that is the national DNA database system of DNA records that meet federal quality assurance and privacy standards.

(6) Repealed by Session Laws 2013-360, s. 17.6(i), effective July 1, 2013.

(7) "State DNA Databank" means the repository of DNA samples collected under the provisions of this Article.

(8) "State DNA Database" means the Crime Laboratory's DNA identification record system to support law enforcement. It is administered by the Crime Laboratory and provides DNA records to the FBI for storage and maintenance in CODIS. The Crime Laboratory's DNA Database system is the collective capability provided by computer software and procedures administered by the Crime Laboratory to store and maintain DNA records related to: forensic casework; convicted offenders and arrestees required to provide a DNA sample under this Article; persons required to register as sex offenders under G.S. 14-208.7; unidentified persons or body parts; missing persons; relatives of missing persons; and anonymous DNA profiles used for forensic validation, forensic protocol development, or quality control purposes or establishment of a population statistics database for use by criminal justice agencies.

History.

1993, c. 401, s. 1; 2009-203, s. 2; 2010-94, s. 2; 2011-19, s. 5; 2013-360, s. 17.6(i); 2014-100, s. 17.1(cc)

§ **15A-266.3. Establishment of State DNA database and databank**

There is established under the administration of the Crime Laboratory, the State DNA Database and State DNA Databank. The Crime Laboratory shall provide DNA records to the FBI for the searching of DNA records nationwide and storage and maintenance by CODIS.

The State DNA Databank shall serve as the repository for DNA samples obtained pursuant to this Article. The State DNA Database shall be compatible with the procedures specified by the FBI, including use of comparable test procedures, laboratory and computer equipment, supplies and computer platform and software. The State DNA Database shall have the capability provided by computer software and procedures administered by the Crime Laboratory to store and maintain DNA records related to all of the following:

(1) Crime scene evidence and forensic casework.

(2) Arrestees, offenders, and persons found not guilty by reason of insanity, who are required to provide a DNA sample under this Article.

(3) Persons required to register as sex offenders under G.S. 14-208.7.

(4) Unidentified persons or body parts.

(5) Missing persons.

(6) Relatives of missing persons.

(7) Anonymous DNA profiles used for forensic validation, forensic protocol development, or quality control purposes or establishment of a population statistics database, for use by criminal justice agencies.

History.
1993, c. 401, s. 1; 2010-94, s. 3; 2013-360, s. 17.6(f)

§ 15A-266.3A. DNA sample required for DNA analysis upon arrest for certain offenses

(a) Unless a DNA sample has previously been obtained by lawful process and the DNA record stored in the State DNA Database, and that record and sample has not been expunged pursuant to any provision of law, a DNA sample for DNA analysis and testing shall be obtained from any person who is arrested for committing an offense described in subsection (f) or (g) of this section.

(b) The arresting law enforcement officer shall obtain, or cause to be obtained, a DNA sample from an arrested person at the time of arrest, or when fingerprinted. However, if the person is arrested without a warrant, then the DNA sample shall not be taken until a probable cause determination has been made pursuant to G.S. 15A-511(c)(1). The DNA sample shall be by cheek swab unless a court order authorizes that a DNA blood sample be obtained. If a DNA blood sample is taken, it shall comply with the requirements of G.S. 15A-266.6(b). The arresting law enforcement officer shall forward, or cause to be forwarded, the DNA sample to the appropriate laboratory for DNA analysis and testing.

(c) At the time a DNA sample is taken pursuant to this section, the person obtaining the DNA sample shall record, on a form promulgated by the Crime Laboratory, the date and time the sample was taken, the name of the person taking the DNA sample, the name and address of the person from whom the sample was taken, and the offense or offenses for which the person was arrested. This record shall be maintained in the case file and shall be available to the prosecuting district attorney for the purpose of completing the requirements of subsection (j) of this section.

(d) After taking a DNA sample from an arrested person required to provide a DNA sample pursuant to this section, the person taking the DNA sample shall provide the arrested person with a written notice of the procedures for seeking an expunction of the DNA sample pursuant to subsections (h), (i), (j), (k), and (l) of this section. The Department of Justice shall provide the written notice required by this subsection.

(e) The DNA record of identification characteristics resulting from the DNA testing and the DNA sample itself shall be stored and maintained by the Crime Laboratory in the State DNA Databank pursuant to this Article.

(f) This section applies to a person arrested for violating any one of the following offenses in Chapter 14 of the General Statutes:

(1) G.S. 14-16.6(b), Assault with a deadly weapon on executive, legislative, or court officer; and G.S. 14-16.6(c), Assault inflicting serious bodily injury on executive, legislative, or court officer.

(1a) G.S. 14-17, First and Second Degree Murder.

(2) G.S. 14-18, Manslaughter.

(2a) Any felony offense in Article 6A, Unborn Victims.

(3) Any offense in Article 7B, Rape and Other Sex Offenses.

(4) G.S. 14-28, Malicious castration; G.S. 14-29, Castration or other maiming without malice aforethought; G.S. 14-30, Malicious maiming; G.S. 14-30.1, Malicious throwing of corrosive acid or alkali; G.S. 14-31, Maliciously assaulting in a secret manner; G.S. 14-32, Felonious assault with deadly weapon with intent to kill or inflicting serious injury; G.S. 14-32.1(e), Aggravated assault or assault and battery on an individual with a disability; G.S. 14-32.2(a) when punishable pursuant to G.S. 14-32.2(b)(1), Patient abuse and neglect, intentional conduct proximately causes death; G.S. 14-32.3(a), Domestic abuse of disabled or elder adults resulting in injury; G.S. 14-32.4, Assault inflicting serious bodily injury or injury by strangulation; G.S. 14-33.2, Habitual misdemeanor

Chapter 15A

945

assault; G.S. 14-34.1, Discharging certain barreled weapons or a firearm into occupied property; G.S. 14-34.2, Assault with a firearm or other deadly weapon upon governmental officers or employees, company police officers, or campus police officers; G.S. 14-34.4, Adulterated or misbranded food, drugs, etc.; intent to cause serious injury or death; intent to extort; G.S. 14-34.5, Assault with a firearm on a law enforcement, probation, or parole officer or on a person employed at a State or local detention facility; G.S. 14-34.6, Assault or affray on a firefighter, an emergency medical technician, medical responder, emergency department nurse, or emergency department physician; G.S. 14-34.7, Assault inflicting serious injury on a law enforcement, probation, or parole officer or on a person employed at a State or local detention facility; G.S. 14-34.9, Discharging a firearm from within an enclosure; and G.S. 14-34.10, Discharge firearm within enclosure to incite fear.

(5) Any offense in Article 10, Kidnapping and Abduction, or Article 10A, Human Trafficking.

(5a) Any offense in Article 13, Malicious Injury or Damage by Use of Explosive or Incendiary Device or Material.

(6) G.S. 14-51, First and second degree burglary; G.S. 14-53, Breaking out of dwelling house burglary; G.S. 14-54(a1), Breaking or entering buildings with intent to terrorize or injure; G.S. 14-54.1, Breaking or entering a place of religious worship; and G.S. 14-57, Burglary with explosives.

(7) Any offense in Article 15, Arson.

(8) G.S. 14-87, Armed robbery; Common law robbery punishable pursuant to G.S. 14-87.1; and G.S. 14-88, Train robbery.

(8a) G.S. 14-163.1(a1), Assaulting a law enforcement agency animal, an assistance animal, or a search and rescue animal willfully killing the animal.

(9) Any offense which would require the person to register under the provisions of Article 27A of Chapter 14 of the General Statutes, Sex Offender and Public Protection Registration Programs.

(10) G.S. 14-196.3, Cyberstalking.

(10a) G.S. 14-202, Secretly peeping into room occupied by another person.

(10b) G.S. 14-258.2, Possession of dangerous weapon in prison resulting in bodily injury or escape; G.S. 14-258.3, Taking of hostage, etc., by prisoner; and G.S. 14-258.4, Malicious conduct by prisoner.

(11) G.S. 14-277.3A, Stalking.

(12) G.S. 14-288.9, Assault on emergency personnel with a dangerous weapon or substance.

(13) G.S. 14-288.21, Unlawful manufacture, assembly, possession, storage, transportation, sale, purchase, delivery, or acquisition of a nuclear, biological, or chemical weapon of mass destruction; exceptions; and G.S. 14-288.22, Unlawful use of a nuclear, biological, or chemical weapon of mass destruction.

(14) G.S. 14-318.4(a), Child abuse inflicting serious injury and G.S. 14-318.4(a3), Child abuse inflicting serious bodily injury.

(15) G.S. 14-360(a1), Cruelty to animals; maliciously kill by intentional deprivation of necessary sustenance; and G.S. 14-360(b), Cruelty to animals; maliciously torture, mutilate, maim, cruelly beat, disfigure, poison, or kill.

(16) G.S. 14-401.22(e), Attempt to conceal evidence of non-natural death by dismembering or destroying remains.

(g) This section also applies to a person arrested for attempting, solicitation of another to commit, conspiracy to commit, or aiding and abetting another to commit, any of the violations included in subsection (f) of this section.

(h) The Crime Laboratory shall remove a person's DNA record, and destroy any DNA biological samples that may have been retained, from the State DNA Database and DNA Databank if both of the following are determined pursuant to subsection (i) of this section:

(1) As to the charge, or all charges, resulting from the arrest upon which a DNA sample is required under this section, a court or the district attorney has taken action resulting in any one of the following:

a. The charge has been dismissed.

b. The person has been acquitted of the charge.

c. The defendant is convicted of a lesser-included misdemeanor offense that is not an offense included in subsection (f) or (g) of this section.

d. No charge was filed within the statute of limitations, if any.

e. No conviction has occurred, at least three years has passed since the date of arrest, and no active prosecution is occurring.

(2) The person's DNA record is not required to be in the State DNA Database under some other provision of law, or is not required to be in the State DNA Database based upon an offense from a different transaction or occurrence from the one which was the basis for the person's arrest.

(i) Prior to June 1, 2012, upon the occurrence of one of the events in sub-subdivision d. or e. of subdivision (1) of subsection (h) of this section, the defendant or the defendant's counsel shall provide the prosecuting district attorney with a signed request form, promulgated by the

Administrative Office of the Courts, requesting that the defendant's DNA record be expunged from the DNA Database and that any biological samples in the DNA Databank be destroyed. On or after June 1, 2012, upon the occurrence of one of the events in sub-subdivision d. or e. of subdivision (1) of subsection (h) of this section, no request form shall be required and the prosecuting district attorney shall initiate the procedure provided in subsection (j) of this section.

(j) Prior to June 1, 2012, within 30 days of the receipt of the form required by subsection (i) of this section or the occurrence of one of the events in sub-subdivision a., b., or c. of subdivision (1) of subsection (h) of this section; and on or after June 1, 2012, within 30 days of the occurrence of one of the events in subdivision (1) of subsection (h) of this section, the prosecuting district attorney shall determine if a DNA sample was taken pursuant to this section, and if so, shall do all of the following:

(1) Verify and indicate the facts of the qualifying event on a verification form promulgated by the Administrative Office of the Courts.

(2) Include the last known address of the defendant, as reflected in the court files, on the verification form.

(3) Sign the verification form or, if the defendant was acquitted or the charges were dismissed by the court, obtain the signature of a judge.

(4) Transmit the verification form to the Crime Laboratory.

(k) Within 90 days of receipt of the verification form, the Crime Laboratory shall do all of the following:

(1) Determine whether the requirement of subdivision (2) of subsection (h) of this section has been met.

(2) If the requirement has been met, remove the defendant's DNA record and samples as required by subsection (h) of this section.

(3) Mail to the defendant, at the address specified in the verification form, a notice doing either of the following:

a. Documenting expunction of the DNA record and destruction of the DNA sample.

b. Notifying the defendant that the DNA record and sample do not qualify for expunction pursuant to subsection (h) of this section.

(l) The defendant may file a motion with the court to review the denial of the defendant's request or the failure of either the district attorney or the Crime Laboratory to act within the prescribed time period.

(m) Any identification, warrant, probable cause to arrest, or arrest based upon a database match of the defendant's DNA sample which occurs after the expiration of the statutory periods prescribed for expunction of the defendant's DNA sample, shall be invalid and inadmissable in the prosecution of the defendant for any criminal offense.

(n) Notwithstanding subsection (h) of this section, the Crime Laboratory is not required to destroy or remove an item of physical evidence obtained from a sample if evidence relating to another person would thereby be destroyed.

(o) The Crime Laboratory shall adopt procedures to comply with this section.

History.

2010-94, s. 4; 2013-171, s. 9; 2013-360, s. 17.6(f), (j); 2015-181, s. 47; 2015-241, s. 17.3(a); 2018-47, s. 4(n)

§ 15A-266.4. DNA sample required for DNA analysis upon conviction or finding of not guilty by reason of insanity

(a) Unless a DNA sample has previously been obtained by lawful process and a record stored in the State DNA Database, and that record and sample have not been expunged pursuant to any provision of law, a person:

(1) Who is convicted of any of the crimes listed in subsection (b) of this section or who is found not guilty of any of these crimes by reason of insanity and committed to a mental health facility in accordance with G.S. 15A-1321, shall provide a DNA sample upon intake to jail, prison, or the mental health facility. In addition, every person convicted of any of these crimes, but who is not sentenced to a term of confinement, shall provide a DNA sample as a condition of the sentence.

(2) Who has been convicted and incarcerated as a result of a conviction of one or more of the crimes listed in subsection (b) of this section, or who was found not guilty of any of these crimes by reason of insanity and committed to a mental health facility in accordance with G.S. 15A-1321, shall provide a DNA sample before parole or release from the penal system or before release from the mental health facility.

(b) Crimes covered by this Article include all of the following:

(1) All felonies.

(2) G.S. 14-32.1 -- Assaults on individuals with a disability.

(3) Former G.S. 14-277.3 -- Stalking.

(4) Repealed by Session Laws 2010-94, s. 5, effective February 1, 2011.

(5) All offenses described in G.S. 15A-266.3A.

History.

1993, c. 401, s. 1; 2001-487, s. 46; 2003-376, s. 2; 2005-130, s. 2; 2009-58, s. 2; 2010-94, s. 5; 2018-47, s. 4(o)

§ 15A-266.5. Tests to be performed on DNA sample

(a) The tests to be performed on each DNA sample are:

(1) To analyze and type only the genetic markers that are used for identification purposes contained in or derived from the DNA.

(2) For law enforcement identification purposes.

(3) For research and administrative purposes, including:

a. Development of a population database when personal identifying information is removed.

b. To support identification research and protocol development of forensic DNA analysis methods.

c. For quality control purposes.

d. To assist in the recovery or identification of human remains from mass disasters or for other humanitarian purposes, including identification of missing persons.

(b) The DNA record of identification characteristics resulting from the DNA testing shall be stored and maintained by the Crime Laboratory in the State DNA Database. The DNA sample itself will be stored and maintained by the Crime Laboratory in the State DNA Databank.

(c) The Crime Laboratory shall report annually to the Joint Legislative Oversight Committee on Justice and Public Safety, on or before September 1, with information for the previous fiscal year, which shall include: a summary of the operations and expenditures relating to the DNA Database and DNA Databank; the number of DNA records from arrestees entered; the number of DNA records from arrestees that have been expunged; and the number of DNA arrestee matches or hits that occurred with an unknown sample, and how many of those have led to an arrest and conviction; and how many letters notifying defendants that a record and sample have been expunged, along with the number of days it took to complete the expunction and notification process, from the date of the receipt of the verification form from the State.

(d) The Department of Justice, in consultation with the Administrative Office of the Courts and the Conference of District Attorneys, shall study, develop, and recommend an automated procedure to facilitate the process of expunging DNA samples and records taken pursuant to G.S. 15A-266.3A, and shall report to the Joint Legislative Commission on Governmental Operations, the Joint Legislative Oversight Committee on Justice and Public Safety, and the Courts Commission, on or before February 1, 2011.

History.

1993, c. 401, s. 1; 2010-94, s. 6; 2011-291, s. 2.3; 2013-360, s. 17.6(f); 2015-241, s. 17.2

§ 15A-266.5A. Statewide sexual assault examination kit testing protocol

(a) **Legislative Intent.** -- The General Assembly finds that deoxyribonucleic acid (DNA) evidence is a powerful law enforcement tool that can identify unknown suspects, create case linkages, connect crimes to known perpetrators, and exonerate the innocent. Timely testing is vital to solve cases, punish offenders, bring justice to victims, and prevent future crimes. It is the intent of the General Assembly that every sexual assault examination kit reported to law enforcement in this State be tested and to eliminate the inventory of untested sexual assault examination kits located statewide. The purpose of this section is to address the manner in which sexual assault examination kits are processed and the protocol for testing the statewide inventory of untested sexual assault examination kits identified pursuant to the findings of the statewide audit completed pursuant to Section 17.7 of S.L. 2017-57.

(b) **Definitions.** -- The following definitions apply in this section:

(1) CODIS -- As defined in G.S. 15A-266.2.

(2) **Collecting agency.** -- Any agency, program, center, or other entity that collects a sexual assault examination kit.

(3) **Reported sexual assault examination kit.** -- A sexual assault examination kit collected from a person who consented to the collection of the sexual assault examination kit and has consented to participate in the criminal justice process by reporting the crime to law enforcement.

(4) **State DNA database.** -- As defined in G.S. 15A-266.2.

(5) **Unfounded sexual assault examination kit.** -- A reported sexual assault examination kit, whereupon completion of the investigation it was concluded by the investigating law enforcement agency, based on clear and convincing evidence, that a crime did not occur.

(6) **Unreported sexual assault examination kit.** -- A sexual assault examination kit collected from a person who consented to the collection of the sexual assault examination kit, but has not consented to participate in the criminal justice process.

(c) **Notification and Submission Requirements for Kits Completed On or**

Chapter 15A

After July 1, 2019. -- Any collecting agency that collects a sexual assault examination kit completed on or after July 1, 2019, shall preserve the kit according to guidelines established under G.S. 15A-268(a2) and notify the appropriate law enforcement agency as soon as practicable, but no later than 24 hours after the collection occurred. A law enforcement agency notified under this subsection shall do all of the following:

(1) Take custody of a sexual assault examination kit from the collecting agency that collected the kit within seven days of receiving notification. The law enforcement agency that takes custody of a kit under this subdivision shall retain and preserve the kit in accordance with the requirements of G.S. 15A-268.

(2) Submit a reported sexual assault examination kit to the State Crime Laboratory, or a laboratory approved by the State Crime Laboratory, not more than 45 days after taking custody of the reported sexual assault examination kit.

(3) Submit an unreported sexual assault examination kit to the Department of Public Safety not more than 45 days after taking custody of the unreported sexual assault examination kit. The Department of Public Safety shall store any kit it receives under this subdivision pursuant to the authority set forth in G.S. 143B-601(13).

(d) **Notification and Submission Requirements for Kits Completed On or Before January 1, 2018.** -- Any law enforcement agency that possesses a sexual assault examination kit completed on or before January 1, 2018, shall do the following:

(1) Establish a review team that may consist of prosecutors, active or retired law enforcement officers, sexual assault nurse examiners, victim advocacy groups, and representatives from a forensic laboratory. The review team required under this subdivision shall be established as soon as practicable, but no later than three months after the effective date of this section.

(2) Utilize the review team established under subdivision (1) of this subsection to survey the law enforcement agency's entire untested sexual assault examination kit inventory and conduct a case review to determine each sexual assault examination kit's testing priority. The survey and review required under this subdivision shall be completed as soon as practicable, but no later than six months after the effective date of this section. The review required under this subdivision shall consider each of the following factors in determining the submission priority of a sexual assault examination kit:

a. Investigative and evidentiary value for the individual case.

b. CODIS potential to link profiles and identify possible serial offenders.

c. Potential for victim participation in the investigation and prosecution.

d. Potential value for admission as evidence under Rule 404(b) of the North Carolina Rules of Evidence.

e. Age and health of victim.

f. Potential for exculpatory value for a convicted person.

g. Any other factor the review team deems to be relevant.

(3) Upon determination by the review team that a sexual assault examination kit is of priority status and not subject to subsection (e) of this section, the law enforcement agency shall notify the State Crime Laboratory, or a laboratory approved by the State Crime Laboratory, of the sexual assault examination kit and submit a request for testing of the sexual assault examination kit. The law enforcement agency shall continue the process set forth in subdivisions (2) and (3) of this subsection until all untested sexual assault examination kits eligible for submission within its inventory have been submitted for testing. The following untested sexual assault examinations kits are not eligible for submission for testing under this subdivision:

a. Unreported sexual assault examination kits. Unreported sexual assault examination kits shall be sent within 45 days of the review required under subdivision (2) of this subsection to the Department of Public of Safety for storage pursuant to the authority set forth in G.S. 143B-601(13).

b. Sexual assault examination kits that have been confirmed as unfounded sexual assault examination kits after a comprehensive case review by the law enforcement agency and complete review by the review team established under subdivision (1) of this subsection. The law enforcement agency shall track within the agency the number of sexual assault examination kits which are concluded to be unfounded along with a brief summary indicating the information and evidence supporting the determination of an unfounded sexual assault examination kit. If the law enforcement agency receives any information or evidence that creates investigative or evidentiary value for testing the unfounded sexual assault examination kit, the law enforcement agency shall send the unfounded sexual assault examination kit to the

State Crime Laboratory, or a laboratory approved by the State Crime Laboratory, as soon as practicable.

c. Sexual assault examination kits in which (i) a criminal prosecution has resulted in conviction, (ii) the convicted person does not seek DNA testing, and (iii) the convicted person's DNA profile is already in CODIS.

(e) **Submission Requirements for Other Kits.** -- Sexual assault examination kits that are not subject to the requirements of subsections (c) or (d) of this section shall be submitted to the State Crime Laboratory, or a laboratory approved by the State Crime Laboratory, as soon as practicable.

(f) **Testing Requirements for Accepted Kits.** -- As soon as practicable after receiving a written request for testing of a sexual assault examination kit subject to subsection (d) of this section, the State Crime Laboratory, or a laboratory approved by the State Crime Laboratory, shall notify the submitting law enforcement agency of the request's approval and provide shipment instructions for the sexual assault examination kit. The State Crime Laboratory, or a laboratory approved by the State Crime Laboratory, shall pursue DNA analysis of any sexual assault examination kit accepted from a law enforcement agency under this section to develop DNA profiles that are eligible for entry into CODIS and the State DNA Database pursuant to G.S. 15A-266.5 and G.S. 15A-266.7. The State CODIS System Administrator, or the Administrator's designee, shall enter a DNA profile developed under this subsection into the CODIS database pursuant to G.S. 15A-266.8 and into the State DNA Database, provided that the testing of the sexual assault examination kit resulted in an eligible DNA profile.

(g) **Lack of Compliance.** -- Lack of compliance with the requirements set forth in this section shall not result in any of the following:

(1) Constituting grounds upon which a person may challenge in any hearing, trial, or other court proceeding the validity of DNA evidence in any criminal or civil proceeding.

(2) Justification for the exclusion of evidence generated from a sexual assault examination kit.

(3) Providing a person who is accused or convicted of committing a crime against a victim a basis to request that the person's case be dismissed or conviction set aside, or providing a cause of action or civil claim.

(h) **Sexual Assault Response and Training.** -- The Department of Justice, the North Carolina Coalition Against Sexual Assault, the North Carolina Victims Assistance Network, and the Conference of District Attorneys shall jointly develop and provide response and training programs to law enforcement and their sexual assault examination kit review teams regarding sexual assault investigations, including victim interactions and kit collection, storage, tracking, and testing.

History.
2019-221, s. 2

§ 15A-266.6. Procedures for obtaining DNA sample for analysis; refusal to provide sample

(a) Each DNA sample provided pursuant to G.S. 15A-266.4 from persons who are incarcerated shall be obtained at the place of incarceration. DNA samples from persons who are not sentenced to a term of confinement shall be obtained immediately following sentencing. The sentencing court shall order any person not sentenced to a term of confinement, who has not previously provided a DNA sample pursuant to any provision of law requiring a sample and whose DNA record and sample have not been expunged pursuant to law, to report immediately following sentencing to the location designated by the sheriff. If the sample cannot be taken immediately, the sheriff shall inform the court of the date, time, and location at which the sample shall be taken, and the court shall enter that date, time, and location into its order. A copy of the court order indicating the date, time, and location the person is to appear to have a sample taken shall be given to the sheriff. If a person not sentenced to a term of confinement fails to appear immediately following sentencing or at the date, time, and location designated in the court order, the sheriff shall inform the court of the failure to appear and the court may issue an order to show cause pursuant to G.S. 5A-15 and may issue an order for arrest pursuant to G.S. 5A-16. The defendant shall continue to be subject to the court's order to provide a DNA sample until such time as his or her DNA sample is analyzed and a record is successfully entered into the State DNA Database.

(b) If, for any reason, the defendant provides a DNA blood sample instead of a cheek swab, only a correctional health nurse technician, physician, registered professional nurse, licensed practical nurse, laboratory technician, phlebotomist, or other health care worker with phlebotomy training shall draw the DNA blood sample to be submitted for analysis. No civil liability shall attach to any person authorized to draw blood by this section as a result of drawing blood from any person if the blood was drawn according to recognized medical procedures. No person shall be relieved from liability for negligence in obtaining a DNA sample by any method.

(c) The Crime Laboratory shall provide the materials, supplies, and postage prepaid envelopes necessary to obtain a DNA sample from a person required to provide a DNA sample pursuant to this Article and to forward the DNA sample to the appropriate laboratory for DNA analysis and testing. Any DNA sample obtained pursuant to this Article, other than a DNA sample obtained from a person who is incarcerated, shall be taken using the materials and supplies provided by the Crime Laboratory.

History.
1993, c. 401, s. 1; 2003-376, s. 3; 2010-94, s. 7; 2013-360, s. 17.6(f)

§ 15A-266.7. Procedures for conducting DNA analysis of DNA sample

(a) The Crime Laboratory shall:

(1) Adopt procedures to be used in the collection, security, submission, identification, analysis, and storage of DNA samples and typing results of DNA samples submitted under this Article. These procedures shall also include quality assurance guidelines to insure that DNA identification records meet audit standards for laboratories which submit DNA records to the State DNA Database.

(2) Adopt Quality Assurance Guidelines for DNA Testing Laboratories and DNA Databasing Laboratories that meet or exceed the quality assurance guidelines established for such laboratories by the CODIS unit of the Federal Bureau of Investigation.

(b) DNA samples shall be securely stored in the State DNA Databank. The typing results shall be securely stored in the State DNA Database.

(c) Records of testing shall be retained on file at the Crime Laboratory.

History.
1993, c. 401, s. 1; 2010-94, s. 8; 2013-360, s. 17.6(f)

§ 15A-266.8. DNA database exchange

(a) It shall be the duty of the Crime Laboratory to receive DNA samples, to store, to analyze or to contract out the DNA typing analysis to a qualified DNA laboratory that meets the guidelines as established by the Crime Laboratory, classify, and file the DNA record of identification characteristic profiles of DNA samples submitted pursuant to this Article and to make such information available as provided in this section. The Crime Laboratory may contract out DNA typing analysis to a qualified DNA laboratory that meets guidelines as established by the Crime Laboratory. The results of the DNA profile of individuals in the State Database shall

be made available to local, State, or federal law enforcement agencies, approved crime laboratories which serve these agencies, or the district attorney's office upon written or electronic request and in furtherance of an official investigation of a criminal offense. These records shall also be available upon receipt of a valid court order directing the Crime Laboratory to release these results to appropriate parties not listed above, when the court order is signed by a superior court judge after a hearing. The Crime Laboratory shall maintain a file of such court orders.

(b) The Crime Laboratory shall adopt rules governing the methods of obtaining information from the State Database and CODIS and procedures for verification of the identity and authority of the requester.

(c) The Crime Laboratory shall create a separate population database comprised of DNA samples obtained under this Article, after all personal identification is removed. Nothing shall prohibit the Crime Laboratory from sharing or disseminating population databases with other law enforcement agencies, crime laboratories that serve them, or other third parties the Crime Laboratory deems necessary to assist the Crime Laboratory with statistical analysis of the Crime Laboratory's population databases. The population database may be made available to and searched by other agencies participating in the CODIS system.

(d) A law enforcement agency that receives an actionable CODIS hit on a submitted DNA sample shall provide electronic notice to the State Crime Laboratory as follows:

(1) Detailing any arrest of a person made in connection with the CODIS hit, no later than 15 days after the arrest.

(2) Detailing any conviction of a person resulting from the CODIS hit, no later than 15 days from the date of conviction.

History.
1993, c. 401, s. 1; 2010-94, s. 9; 2013-360, s. 17.6(f); 2019-221, s. 3.

§ 15A-266.9. Cancellation of authority to exchange DNA records

The Crime Laboratory is authorized to revoke the right of a forensic DNA laboratory within the State to exchange DNA identification records with federal, State, or local criminal justice agencies if the required control and privacy standards specified by the Crime Laboratory for the State DNA Database are not met by these agencies.

History.
1993, c. 401, s. 1; 2013-360, s. 17.6(f)

N.C. Gen. Stat. § 15A-266.10

Repealed by Session Laws 2001-282, s. 3, effective October 1, 2001.

§ 15A-266.11. Unauthorized uses of DNA Databank; penalties

(a) Any person who has possession of, or access to, individually identifiable DNA information contained in the State DNA Database or Databank and who willfully discloses it in any manner to any person or agency not entitled to receive it is guilty of a Class H felony.

(b) Any person who, without authorization, willfully obtains individually identifiable DNA information from the State DNA Database or Databank is guilty of a Class H felony.

History.

1993, c. 401, s. 1; 1994, Ex. Sess., c. 14, s. 15; 2010-94, s. 10

§ 15A-266.12. Confidentiality of records

(a) All DNA profiles and samples submitted to the Crime Laboratory pursuant to this Article shall be treated as confidential and shall not be disclosed to or shared with any person or agency except as provided in G.S. 15A-266.8.

(b) Only DNA records and samples that directly relate to the identification of individuals shall be collected and stored. These records and samples shall solely be used as a part of the criminal justice system for the purpose of facilitating the personal identification of the perpetrator of a criminal offense; provided that in appropriate circumstances such records may be used to identify potential victims of mass disasters or missing persons.

(c) DNA records and DNA samples submitted to the Crime Laboratory pursuant to this Article are not a public record as defined by G.S. 132-1.

(d) In the case of a criminal proceeding, requests to access a person's DNA record shall be in accordance with the rules for criminal discovery as defined in G.S. 15A-902. The Crime Laboratory shall not be required to provide the State DNA Database for criminal discovery purposes.

(e) DNA records and DNA samples submitted to the Crime Laboratory may only be released for the following authorized purposes:

(1) For law enforcement identification purposes, including the identification of human remains, to federal, State, or local criminal justice agencies.

(2) For criminal defense and appeal purposes, to a defendant who shall have access to samples and analyses performed in connection with the case in which such defendant is charged or was convicted.

(3) If personally identifiable information is removed to local, State, or federal law enforcement agencies for forensic validation studies, forensic protocol development or quality control purposes, and for establishment or maintenance of a population statistics database.

(f) In order to maintain the computer system security of the Crime Laboratory DNA database program, the computer software and database structures used by the Crime Laboratory to implement this Article are confidential.

History.

1993, c. 401, s. 1; 2003-376, s. 4; 2010-94, s. 11; 2013-360, s. 17.6(f)

§ 15A-267. Access to DNA samples from crime scene

(a) A criminal defendant shall have access before trial to the following:

(1) Any DNA analyses performed in connection with the case in which the defendant is charged.

(2) Any biological material, that has not been DNA tested, that was collected from the crime scene, the defendant's residence, or the defendant's property.

(3) A complete inventory of all physical evidence collected in connection with the investigation.

(b) Access as provided for in subsection (a) of this section shall be governed by G.S. 15A-902 and G.S. 15A-952.

(c) Upon a defendant's motion made before trial in accordance with G.S. 15A-952, the court shall order the Crime Laboratory or any approved vendor that meets Crime Laboratory contracting standards to perform DNA testing and, if the data meets NDIS criteria, order the Crime Laboratory to search and/or upload to CODIS any profiles obtained from the testing upon a showing of all of the following:

(1) That the biological material is relevant to the investigation.

(2) That the biological material was not previously DNA tested or that more accurate testing procedures are now available that were not available at the time of previous testing and there is a reasonable possibility that the result would have been different.

(3) That the testing is material to the defendant's defense.

(d) The defendant shall be responsible for bearing the cost of any further testing and comparison of the biological materials, including any costs associated with the testing and comparison by the Crime Laboratory in accordance with this section, unless the court has determined the defendant is indigent, in which event the State shall bear the costs.

History.

2001-282, s. 4; 2007-539, s. 1; 2009-203, s. 3; 2013-360, s. 17.6(f)

§ 15A-268. Preservation of biological evidence

(a) As used in this section, the term "biological evidence" includes the contents of a sexual assault examination kit or any item that contains blood, semen, hair, saliva, skin tissue, fingerprints, or other identifiable human biological material that may reasonably be used to incriminate or exculpate any person in the criminal investigation, whether that material is catalogued separately on a slide or swab, in a test tube, or some other similar method, or is present on clothing, ligatures, bedding, other household materials, drinking cups, cigarettes, or any other item of evidence.

(a1) Notwithstanding any other provision of law and subject to subsection (b) of this section, a custodial agency shall preserve any physical evidence, regardless of the date of collection, that is reasonably likely to contain any biological evidence collected in the course of a criminal investigation or prosecution. Evidence shall be preserved in a manner reasonably calculated to prevent contamination or degradation of any biological evidence that might be present, subject to a continuous chain of custody, and securely retained with sufficient official documentation to locate the evidence.

(a2) The Crime Laboratory shall promulgate and publish minimum guidelines that meet the requirements for retention and preservation of biological evidence under subsection (a1) of this section. Guidelines shall be published no later than January 1, 2010, and shall be reviewed and updated biennially thereafter. Law enforcement agencies and the Conference of Clerks of Superior Court shall ensure the guidelines are distributed to all employees with responsibility for maintaining custody of evidence.

(a3) When physical evidence is offered or admitted into evidence in a criminal proceeding of the General Court of Justice, the presiding judge shall inquire of the State and defendant as to the identity of the collecting agency of the evidence and whether the evidence in question is reasonably likely to contain biological evidence and if that biological evidence is relevant to establishing the identity of the perpetrator in the case. If either party asserts that the evidence in question may have biological evidentiary value, and the court so finds, the court shall instruct that the evidence be so designated in the court's records and that the evidence be preserved pursuant to the requirements of this section.

(a4) If evidence has been designated by the court as biological evidence pursuant to subsection (a3) of this section, the clerk of superior court that takes custody of evidence pursuant to the rules of practice and procedure for the superior and district courts as adopted by the Supreme Court pursuant to G.S. 7A-34 shall preserve such evidence consistent with subsection (a1) of this section. Upon conclusion of the clerk's role as custodian, as provided in the applicable rules of practice, the clerk shall return such evidence to the collecting agency, as determined in subsection (a3) of this section, in a manner that ensures the chain of custody is maintained and documented.

(a5) The duty to preserve may not be waived knowingly and voluntarily by a defendant, without a court hearing, which may include any other hearing associated with the disposition of the case.

(a6) The evidence described by subsection (a1) of this section shall be preserved for the following period:

(1) For conviction resulting in a sentence of death, until execution.

(2) For conviction resulting in a sentence of life without parole, until the death of the convicted person.

(3) For conviction of any homicide, sex offense, assault, kidnapping, burglary, robbery, arson or burning, for which a Class B1-E felony punishment is imposed, the evidence shall be preserved during the period of incarceration and mandatory supervised release, including sex offender registration pursuant to Article 27A of Chapter 14 of the General Statutes, except in cases where the person convicted entered and was convicted on a plea of guilty, in which case the evidence shall be preserved for the earlier of three years from the date of conviction or until released.

(4) Biological evidence collected as part of a criminal investigation of any homicide or rape, in which no charges are filed, shall be preserved for the period of time that the crime remains unsolved.

(5) A custodial agency in custody of biological evidence unrelated to a criminal investigation or prosecution referenced by subdivision (1), (2), (3), or (4) of this subsection may dispose of the evidence in accordance with the rules of the agency.

(6) Notwithstanding the retention requirements in subdivisions (1) through (5) of this subsection, at any time after collection and prior to or at the time of disposition of the case at the trial court level, if the evidence collected as part of the criminal investigation is of a size, bulk, or physical character as to render retention impracticable or should be returned to its rightful owner, the State may petition the court for retention of samples of the biological evidence in lieu of the actual physical evidence.

After giving any defendant charged in connection with the case an opportunity to be heard, the court may order that the collecting agency take reasonable measures to remove or preserve for retention portions of evidence likely to contain biological evidence related to the offense through cuttings, swabs, or other means consistent with Crime Laboratory minimum guidelines in a quantity sufficient to permit DNA testing before returning or disposing of the evidence.

(a7) Upon written request by the defendant, the custodial agency shall prepare an inventory of biological evidence relevant to the defendant's case that is in the custodial agency's custody. If the evidence was destroyed through court order or other written directive, the custodial agency shall provide the defendant with a copy of the court order or written directive.

(b) The custodial agency required to preserve evidence pursuant to subsection (a1) of this section may dispose of the evidence prior to the expiration of the period of time described in subsection (a6) of this section if all of the following conditions are met:

(1) The custodial agency sent notice of its intent to dispose of the evidence to the district attorney in the county in which the conviction was obtained.

(1a) The custodial agency has determined that it has no duty to preserve the evidence under G.S. 15A-1471.

(2) The district attorney gave to each of the following persons written notification of the intent of the custodial agency to dispose of the evidence: any defendant convicted of a felony who is currently incarcerated in connection with the case, the defendant's counsel of record for that case, and the Office of Indigent Defense Services. The notice shall be consistent with the provisions of this section, and the district attorney shall send a copy of the notice to the custodial agency. Delivery of written notification from the district attorney to the defendant was effectuated by the district attorney transmitting the written notification to the superintendent of the correctional facility where the defendant was assigned at the time and the superintendent's personal delivery of the written notification to the defendant. Certification of delivery by the superintendent to the defendant in accordance with this subdivision was in accordance with subsection (c) of this section.

(3) The written notification from the district attorney specified the following:

a. That the custodial agency would destroy the evidence collected in connection with the case unless the custodial agency received a written request that the evidence not be destroyed.

b. The address of the custodial agency where the written request was to be sent.

c. That the written request from the defendant, or his or her representative, must be received by the custodial agency within 90 days of the date of receipt by the defendant of the district attorney's written notification.

d. That the written request must ask that the evidence not be destroyed or disposed of for one of the following reasons:

1. The case is currently on appeal.

2. The case is currently in post-conviction proceedings.

3. The defendant will file a motion for DNA testing pursuant to G.S. 15A-269 within 180 days of the postmark of the defendant's response to the district attorney's written notification of the custodial agency's intent to dispose of the evidence, unless a request for extension is requested by the defendant and agreed to by the custodial agency.

4. The case has been referred to the North Carolina Innocence Inquiry Commission pursuant to Article 92 of Chapter 15A of the General Statutes.

(4) The custodial agency did not receive a written request in compliance with the conditions set forth in sub-subdivision (3)d. of this subsection within 90 days of the date of receipt by the defendant of the district attorney's written notification.

(c) Upon receiving a written notification from a district attorney in accordance with subdivision (b)(3) of this section, the superintendent shall personally deliver the written notification to the defendant. Upon effectuating personal delivery on the defendant, the superintendent shall sign a sworn written certification that the written notification had been delivered to the defendant in compliance with this subsection indicating the date the delivery was made. The superintendent's certification shall be sent by the superintendent to the custodial agency that intends to dispose of the sample of evidence. The custodial agency may rely on the superintendent's certification as evidence of the date of receipt by the defendant of the district attorney's written notification.

(d) After a hearing held in response to a defendant's written request that the evidence not be destroyed in response to notice pursuant to subsection (b) of this section, the court may enter an order authorizing the custodial agency to dispose of the evidence if the court determines by the preponderance of the evidence that the evidence:

(1) Has no significant value for biological analysis and should be returned to its rightful owner, destroyed, used for training purposes, or otherwise disposed of as provided by law; or

(2) Repealed by Session Laws 2009-203, s. 4, effective December 1, 2009.

(3) May have value for biological analysis but is of a size, bulk, or physical character as to render retention impracticable or should be returned to its rightful owner.

(e) The court order allowing the disposition of the evidence pursuant to subdivision (d)(3) of this section shall require the custodial agency to return such evidence to the collecting agency. The collecting agency shall take reasonable measures to remove or preserve portions of evidence likely to contain biological evidence related to the offense through cuttings, swabs, or other means consistent with Crime Laboratory minimum guidelines in a quantity sufficient to permit DNA testing before returning or disposing of the evidence. The court may provide the defendant an opportunity to take reasonable measures to preserve the evidence.

(f) An order regarding the disposition of evidence pursuant to this section shall be a final and appealable order. The defendant shall have 30 days from the entry of the order to file notice of appeal. The custodial agency shall not dispose of the evidence while the appeal is pending.

(g) If an entity is asked to produce evidence that is required to be preserved under the provisions of this section and cannot produce the evidence, the chief evidence custodian of the custodial agency shall provide an affidavit in which he or she describes, under penalty of perjury, the efforts taken to locate the evidence and affirms that the evidence could not be located. If the evidence that is required to be preserved pursuant to this section has been destroyed, the court may conduct a hearing to determine whether obstruction of justice and contempt proceedings are in order. If the court finds the destruction violated the defendant's due process rights, the court shall order an appropriate remedy, which may include dismissal of charges.

(h) All records documenting the possession, control, storage, and destruction of evidence related to a criminal investigation or prosecution of an offense referenced in subdivision (1), (2), (3), or (4) of subsection (a6) of this section shall be retained.

(i) Whoever knowingly and intentionally destroys, alters, conceals, or tampers with evidence that is required to be preserved under this section, with the intent to impair the integrity of that evidence, prevent that evidence from being subjected to DNA testing, or prevent production or use of that evidence in an official proceeding, shall be punished as follows:

(1) If the evidence is for a noncapital crime, then a violation of this subsection is a Class I felony.

(2) If the evidence is for a crime of first degree murder, then a violation of this subsection is a Class H felony.

History.
2001-282, s. 4.; 2007-539, s. 2; 2009-203, s. 4; 2009-570, s. 30(a), (b); 2012-7, ss. 1 -3; 2013-360, s. 17.6(f); 2015-247, s. 10(a), (b)

§ 15A-269. Request for postconviction DNA testing

(a) A defendant may make a motion before the trial court that entered the judgment of conviction against the defendant for performance of DNA testing and, if testing complies with FBI requirements and the data meets NDIS criteria, profiles obtained from the testing shall be searched and/or uploaded to CODIS if the biological evidence meets all of the following conditions:

(1) Is material to the defendant's defense.

(2) Is related to the investigation or prosecution that resulted in the judgment.

(3) Meets either of the following conditions:

a. It was not DNA tested previously.

b. It was tested previously, but the requested DNA test would provide results that are significantly more accurate and probative of the identity of the perpetrator or accomplice or have a reasonable probability of contradicting prior test results.

(b) The court shall grant the motion for DNA testing and, if testing complies with FBI requirements, the run of any profiles obtained from the testing, upon its determination that:

(1) The conditions set forth in subdivisions (1), (2), and (3) of subsection (a) of this section have been met;

(2) If the DNA testing being requested had been conducted on the evidence, there exists a reasonable probability that the verdict would have been more favorable to the defendant; and

(3) The defendant has signed a sworn affidavit of innocence.

(b1) If the court orders DNA testing, such testing shall be conducted by a Crime Laboratory-approved testing facility, mutually agreed upon by the petitioner and the State and approved by the court. If the parties cannot agree, the court shall designate the testing facility and provide

Chapter 15A

the parties with reasonable opportunity to be heard on the issue.

(c) In accordance with rules adopted by the Office of Indigent Defense Services, the court shall appoint counsel for the person who brings a motion under this section if that person is indigent. If the petitioner has filed pro se, the court shall appoint counsel for the petitioner in accordance with rules adopted by the Office of Indigent Defense Services upon a showing that the DNA testing may be material to the petitioner's claim of wrongful conviction.

(d) The defendant shall be responsible for bearing the cost of any DNA testing ordered under this section unless the court determines the defendant is indigent, in which event the State shall bear the costs.

(e) DNA testing ordered by the court pursuant to this section shall be done as soon as practicable. However, if the court finds that a miscarriage of justice will otherwise occur and that DNA testing is necessary in the interests of justice, the court shall order a delay of the proceedings or execution of the sentence pending the DNA testing.

(f) Upon receipt of a motion for postconviction DNA testing, the custodial agency shall inventory the evidence pertaining to that case and provide the inventory list, as well as any documents, notes, logs, or reports relating to the items of physical evidence, to the prosecution, the petitioner, and the court.

(g) Upon receipt of a motion for postconviction DNA testing, the State shall, upon request, reactivate any victim services for the victim of the crime being investigated during the reinvestigation of the case and pendency of the proceedings.

(h) Nothing in this Article shall prohibit a convicted person and the State from consenting to and conducting postconviction DNA testing by agreement of the parties, without filing a motion for postconviction testing under this Article.

History.
2001-282, s. 4; 2007-539, s. 3; 2009-203, s. 5; 2011-326, s. 12(d); 2013-360, s. 17.6(k).

§ 15A-270. Post-test procedures

(a) Notwithstanding any other provision of law, upon receiving the results of the DNA testing conducted under G.S. 15A-269, the court shall conduct a hearing to evaluate the results and to determine if the results are unfavorable or favorable to the defendant.

(b) If the results of DNA testing conducted under this section are unfavorable to the defendant, the court shall dismiss the motion and, in the case of a defendant who is not indigent, shall assess the defendant for the cost of the testing.

(c) If the results of DNA testing conducted under this section are favorable to the defendant, the court shall enter any order that serves the interests of justice, including an order that does any of the following:

(1) Vacates and sets aside the judgment.

(2) Discharges the defendant, if the defendant is in custody.

(3) Resentences the defendant.

(4) Grants a new trial.

History.
2001-282, s. 4

§ 15A-270.1. Right to appeal denial of defendant's motion for DNA testing

The defendant may appeal an order denying the defendant's motion for DNA testing under this Article, including by an interlocutory appeal. The court shall appoint counsel in accordance with rules adopted by the Office of Indigent Defense Services upon a finding of indigency.

History.
2007-539, s. 4; 2009-203, s. 6; 2011-326, s. 12(e)

ARTICLE 14
NONTESTIMONIAL IDENTIFICATION

§ 15A-271. Authority to issue order

A nontestimonial identification order authorized by this Article may be issued by any judge upon request of a prosecutor. As used in this Article, "nontestimonial identification" means identification by fingerprints, palm prints, footprints, measurements, blood specimens, urine specimens, saliva samples, hair samples, or other reasonable physical examination, handwriting exemplars, voice samples, photographs, and lineups or similar identification procedures requiring the presence of a suspect.

History.
1973, c. 1286, s. 1; 1975, c. 166, s. 27

§ 15A-272. Time of application; additional investigative procedures not precluded

A request for a nontestimonial identification order may be made prior to the arrest of a suspect or after arrest and prior to trial. Nothing in this Article shall preclude such additional investigative procedures as are otherwise permitted by law.

History.
1973, c. 1286, s. 1

§ 15A-273. Basis for order

An order may issue only on an affidavit or affidavits sworn to before the judge and establishing the following grounds for the order:

(1) That there is probable cause to believe that a felony offense, or a Class A1 or Class 1 misdemeanor offense has been committed;

(2) That there are reasonable grounds to suspect that the person named or described in the affidavit committed the offense; and

(3) That the results of specific nontestimonial identification procedures will be of material aid in determining whether the person named in the affidavit committed the offense.

History.
1973, c. 1286, s. 1; 1997-80, s. 14

§ 15A-274. Issuance of order

Upon a showing that the grounds specified in G.S. 15A-273 exist, the judge may issue an order requiring the person named or described with reasonable certainty in the affidavit to appear at a designated time and place and to submit to designated nontestimonial identification procedures. Unless the nature of the evidence sought makes it likely that delay will adversely affect its probative value, or when it appears likely that the person named in the order may destroy, alter, or modify the evidence sought or may not appear, the order must be served at least 72 hours before the time designated for the nontestimonial identification procedure.

History.
1973, c. 1286, s. 1; 1977, c. 832, s. 1

§ 15A-275. Modification of order

At the request of a person ordered to appear, the judge may modify the order with respect to time and place of appearance whenever it appears reasonable under the circumstances to do so.

History.
1973, c. 1286, s. 1

§ 15A-276. Failure to appear

Any person who fails without adequate excuse to obey an order to appear served upon him pursuant to this Article may be held in contempt of the court which issued the order.

History.
1973, c. 1286, s. 1

§ 15A-277. Service of order

An order to appear pursuant to this Article may be served by a law-enforcement officer. The order must be served upon the person named or described in the affidavit by delivery of a copy to him personally. The order must be served at least 72 hours in advance of the time of compliance, unless the judge issuing the order has determined, in accordance with G.S. 15A-274, that delay will adversely affect the probative value of the evidence sought or when it appears likely that the person named in the order may destroy, alter, or modify the evidence sought, or may not appear.

History.
1973, c. 1286, s. 1; 1977, c. 832, s. 2

§ 15A-278. Contents of order

An order to appear must be signed by the judge and must state:

(1) That the presence of the person named or described in the affidavit is required for the purpose of permitting nontestimonial identification procedures in order to aid in the investigation of the offense specified therein;

(2) The time and place of the required appearance;

(3) The nontestimonial identification procedures to be conducted, the methods to be used, and the approximate length of time such procedures will require;

(4) The grounds to suspect that the person named or described in the affidavit committed the offense specified therein;

(5) That the person is entitled to be represented by counsel at the procedure, and to the appointment of counsel if he cannot afford to retain one;

(6) That the person will not be subjected to any interrogation or asked to make any statement during the period of his appearance except that required for voice identification;

(7) That the person may request the judge to make a reasonable modification of the order with respect to time and place of appearance, including a request to have any nontestimonial identification procedure other than a lineup conducted at his place of residence; and

(8) That the person, if he fails to appear, may be held in contempt of court.

History.
1973, c. 1286, s. 1

Chapter 15A

§ 15A-279. Implementation of order

(a) Nontestimonial identification procedures may be conducted by any law-enforcement officer or other person designated by the judge issuing the order. The extraction of any bodily fluid must be conducted by a qualified member of the health professions and the judge may require medical supervision for any other test ordered pursuant to this Article when he considers such supervision necessary.

(b) In conducting authorized identification procedures, no unreasonable or unnecessary force may be used.

(c) No person who appears under an order of appearance issued under this Article may be detained longer than is reasonably necessary to conduct the specified nontestimonial identification procedures, and in no event for longer than six hours, unless he is arrested for an offense.

(d) Any such person is entitled to have counsel present and must be advised prior to being subjected to any nontestimonial identification procedures of his right to have counsel present during any nontestimonial identification procedure and to the appointment of counsel if he cannot afford to retain counsel. Appointment of counsel shall be in accordance with rules adopted by the Office of Indigent Defense Services. No statement made during nontestimonial identification procedures by the subject of the procedures shall be admissible in any criminal proceeding against him, unless his counsel was present at the time the statement was made.

(e) Any person who resists compliance with the authorized nontestimonial identification procedures may be held in contempt of the court which issued the order pursuant to the provisions of G.S. 5A-12(a) and G.S. 5A-21(b).

(f) A nontestimonial identification order may not be issued against a person previously subject to a nontestimonial identification order unless it is based on different evidence which was not reasonably available when the previous order was issued.

(g) Resisting compliance with a nontestimonial identification order is not itself grounds for finding probable cause to arrest the suspect, but it may be considered with other evidence in making the determination whether probable cause exists.

History.
1973, c. 1286, s. 1; 1977, c. 711, s. 20; 2000-144, s. 28

§ 15A-280. Return

Within 90 days after the nontestimonial identification procedure, a return must be made to the judge who issued the order or to a judge designated in the order setting forth an inventory of the products of the nontestimonial identification procedures obtained from the person named in the affidavit. If, at the time of the return, probable cause does not exist to believe that the person has committed the offense named in the affidavit or any other offense, the person named in the affidavit is entitled to move that the authorized judge issue an order directing that the products and reports of the nontestimonial identification procedures, and all copies thereof, be destroyed. The motion must, except for good cause shown, be granted.

History.
1973, c. 1286, s. 1

§ 15A-281. Nontestimonial identification order at request of defendant

A person arrested for or charged with a felony offense, or a Class A1 or Class 1 misdemeanor offense may request that nontestimonial identification procedures be conducted upon himself. If it appears that the results of specific nontestimonial identification procedures will be of material aid in determining whether the defendant committed the offense, the judge to whom the request was directed must order the State to conduct the identification procedures.

History.
1973, c. 1286, s. 1; 1997-80, s. 15

§ 15A-282. Copy of results to person involved

A person who has been the subject of nontestimonial identification procedures or his attorney must be provided with a copy of any reports of test results as soon as the reports are available.

History.
1973, c. 1286, s. 1

§§ 15A-283 through 15A-284.49

Reserved for future codification purposes.

ARTICLE 14A
EYEWITNESS IDENTIFICATION REFORM ACT

§ 15A-284.50. Short title

This Article shall be called the "Eyewitness Identification Reform Act."

History.
2007-421, s. 1

§ 15A-284.51. Purpose

The purpose of this Article is to help solve crime, convict the guilty, and exonerate the innocent in criminal proceedings by improving procedures for eyewitness identification of suspects.

History.
2007-421, s. 1

§ 15A-284.52. Eyewitness identification reform

(a) **Definitions.** -- The following definitions apply in this Article:

(1) **Eyewitness.** -- A person, including a law enforcement officer, whose identification by sight of another person may be relevant in a criminal proceeding.

(2) **Filler.** -- A person or a photograph of a person who is not suspected of an offense and is included in a lineup.

(3) **Independent administrator.** -- A lineup administrator who is not participating in the investigation of the criminal offense and is unaware of which person in the lineup is the suspect.

(4) **Lineup.** -- A photo lineup or live lineup.

(5) **Lineup administrator.** -- The person who conducts a lineup.

(6) **Live lineup.** -- A procedure in which a group of people is displayed to an eyewitness for the purpose of determining if the eyewitness is able to identify the perpetrator of a crime.

(7) **Photo lineup.** -- A procedure in which an array of photographs is displayed to an eyewitness for the purpose of determining if the eyewitness is able to identify the perpetrator of a crime.

(8) **Show-up.** -- A procedure in which an eyewitness is presented with a single live suspect for the purpose of determining whether the eyewitness is able to identify the perpetrator of a crime.

(b) **Eyewitness Identification Procedures.** -- Lineups conducted by State, county, and other local law enforcement officers shall meet all of the following requirements:

(1) A lineup shall be conducted by an independent administrator or by an alternative method as provided by subsection (c) of this section.

(2) Individuals or photos shall be presented to witnesses sequentially, with each individual or photo presented to the witness separately, in a previously determined order, and removed after it is viewed before the next individual or photo is presented.

(3) Before a lineup, the eyewitness shall be instructed that:

a. The perpetrator might or might not be presented in the lineup,

b. The lineup administrator does not know the suspect's identity,

c. The eyewitness should not feel compelled to make an identification,

d. It is as important to exclude innocent persons as it is to identify the perpetrator, and

e. The investigation will continue whether or not an identification is made.

The eyewitness shall acknowledge the receipt of the instructions in writing. If the eyewitness refuses to sign, the lineup administrator shall note the refusal of the eyewitness to sign the acknowledgement and shall also sign the acknowledgement.

(4) In a photo lineup, the photograph of the suspect shall be contemporary and, to the extent practicable, shall resemble the suspect's appearance at the time of the offense.

(5) The lineup shall be composed so that the fillers generally resemble the eyewitness's description of the perpetrator, while ensuring that the suspect does not unduly stand out from the fillers. In addition:

a. All fillers selected shall resemble, as much as practicable, the eyewitness's description of the perpetrator in significant features, including any unique or unusual features.

b. At least five fillers shall be included in a photo lineup, in addition to the suspect.

c. At least five fillers shall be included in a live lineup, in addition to the suspect.

d. If the eyewitness has previously viewed a photo lineup or live lineup in connection with the identification of another person suspected of involvement in the offense, the fillers in the lineup in which the current suspect participates shall be different from the fillers used in any prior lineups.

(6) If there are multiple eyewitnesses, the suspect shall be placed in a different position in the lineup or photo array for each eyewitness.

(7) In a lineup, no writings or information concerning any previous arrest, indictment, or conviction of the suspect shall be visible or made known to the eyewitness.

(8) In a live lineup, any identifying actions, such as speech, gestures, or other

movements, shall be performed by all lineup participants.

(9) In a live lineup, all lineup participants must be out of view of the eyewitness prior to the lineup.

(10) Only one suspect shall be included in a lineup.

(11) Nothing shall be said to the eyewitness regarding the suspect's position in the lineup or regarding anything that might influence the eyewitness's identification.

(12) The lineup administrator shall seek and document a clear statement from the eyewitness, at the time of the identification and in the eyewitness's own words, as to the eyewitness's confidence level that the person identified in a given lineup is the perpetrator. The lineup administrator shall separate all witnesses in order to discourage witnesses from conferring with one another before or during the procedure. Each witness shall be given instructions regarding the identification procedures without other witnesses present.

(13) If the eyewitness identifies a person as the perpetrator, the eyewitness shall not be provided any information concerning the person before the lineup administrator obtains the eyewitness's confidence statement about the selection. There shall not be anyone present during the live lineup or photographic identification procedures who knows the suspect's identity, except the eyewitness and counsel as required by law.

(14) Unless it is not practical, a video record of live identification procedures shall be made. If a video record is not practical, the reasons shall be documented, and an audio record shall be made. If neither a video nor audio record are practical, the reasons shall be documented, and the lineup administrator shall make a written record of the lineup.

(15) Whether video, audio, or in writing, the record shall include all of the following information:

a. All identification and nonidentification results obtained during the identification procedure, signed by the eyewitness, including the eyewitness's confidence statement. If the eyewitness refuses to sign, the lineup administrator shall note the refusal of the eyewitness to sign the results and shall also sign the notation.

b. The names of all persons present at the lineup.

c. The date, time, and location of the lineup.

d. The words used by the eyewitness in any identification, including words

that describe the eyewitness's certainty of identification.

e. Whether it was a photo lineup or live lineup and how many photos or individuals were presented in the lineup.

f. The sources of all photographs or persons used.

g. In a photo lineup, the photographs themselves.

h. In a live lineup, a photo or other visual recording of the lineup that includes all persons who participated in the lineup.

(c) **Alternative Methods for Identification if Independent Administrator Is Not Used.** -- In lieu of using an independent administrator, a photo lineup eyewitness identification procedure may be conducted using an alternative method specified and approved by the North Carolina Criminal Justice Education and Training Standards Commission. Any alternative method shall be carefully structured to achieve neutral administration and to prevent the administrator from knowing which photograph is being presented to the eyewitness during the identification procedure. Alternative methods may include any of the following:

(1) Automated computer programs that can automatically administer the photo lineup directly to an eyewitness and prevent the administrator from seeing which photo the witness is viewing until after the procedure is completed.

(2) A procedure in which photographs are placed in folders, randomly numbered, and shuffled and then presented to an eyewitness such that the administrator cannot see or track which photograph is being presented to the witness until after the procedure is completed.

(3) Any other procedures that achieve neutral administration.

(c1) **Show-Up Procedures.** -- A show-up conducted by State, county, and other local law enforcement officers shall meet all of the following requirements:

(1) A show-up may only be conducted when a suspect matching the description of the perpetrator is located in close proximity in time and place to the crime, or there is reasonable belief that the perpetrator has changed his or her appearance in close time to the crime, and only if there are circumstances that require the immediate display of a suspect to an eyewitness.

(2) A show-up shall only be performed using a live suspect and shall not be conducted with a photograph.

(3) Investigators shall photograph a suspect at the time and place of the show-up to preserve a record of the appearance of the suspect at the time of the show-up procedure.

(4) Notwithstanding G.S. 7B-2103, an investigator shall photograph a juvenile suspect who is 10 years of age or older at the time and place of the show-up as required by this subsection if the juvenile is reported to have committed a nondivertible offense as set forth in G.S. 7B-1701 or common law robbery. Photographs of juveniles shall be retained or disposed of as required by G.S. 7B-2108, except that the law enforcement agency is required to make written certification to the court of the destruction of records under G.S. 7B-2108(6) only if a petition was filed. Photographs taken pursuant to this subdivision are not public records under Chapter 132 of the General Statutes and the photographs shall be (i) kept separate from the records of adults, (ii) withheld from public inspection, and (iii) examined only by order of the court, except that the following persons may examine it without an order of the court:

    a. The juvenile or the juvenile's attorney.

    b. The juvenile's parent or guardian.

    c. The prosecutor.

    d. Court counselors.

(c2) *(See Editor's note)* The North Carolina Criminal Justice Education and Training Standards Commission shall develop a policy regarding standard procedures for the conduct of show-ups in accordance with this section. The policy shall apply to all law enforcement agencies and shall address all of the following, in addition to the provisions of this section:

(1) Standard instructions for eyewitnesses.

(2) Confidence statements by the eyewitness, including information related to the eyewitness' vision, the circumstances of the events witnessed, and communications with other eyewitnesses, if any.

(3) Training of law enforcement officers specific to conducting show-ups.

(4) Any other matters deemed appropriate by the Commission.

(d) **Remedies. --** All of the following shall be available as consequences of compliance or noncompliance with the requirements of this section:

(1) Failure to comply with any of the requirements of this section shall be considered by the court in adjudicating motions to suppress eyewitness identification.

(2) Failure to comply with any of the requirements of this section shall be admissible in support of claims of eyewitness misidentification, as long as such evidence is otherwise admissible.

(3) When evidence of compliance or noncompliance with the requirements of this section has been presented at trial, the jury shall be instructed that it may consider credible evidence of compliance or noncompliance to determine the reliability of eyewitness identifications.

(e) Nothing in this section shall be construed to require a law enforcement officer while acting in his or her official capacity to be required to participate in a show-up as an eyewitness.

History.
2007-421, s. 1; 2015-212, s. 1; 2019-47, s. 2

§ 15A-284.53. Training of law enforcement officers

Pursuant to its authority under G.S. 17C-6 and G.S. 17E-4, the North Carolina Criminal Justice Education and Training Standards Commission and the North Carolina Sheriffs' Education and Training Standards Commission, in consultation with the Department of Justice, shall create educational materials and conduct training programs on how to conduct lineups and show-ups in compliance with this Article.

History.
2007-421, s. 1; 2015-212, s. 2

ARTICLE 15
URGENT NECESSITY

§ 15A-285. Non-law-enforcement actions when urgently necessary

When an officer reasonably believes that doing so is urgently necessary to save life, prevent serious bodily harm, or avert or control public catastrophe, the officer may take one or more of the following actions:

(1) Enter buildings, vehicles, and other premises.

(2) Limit or restrict the presence of persons in premises or areas.

(3) Exercise control over the property of others.

An action taken to enforce the law or to seize a person or evidence cannot be justified by authority of this section.

History.
1973, c. 1286, s. 1

ARTICLE 16
ELECTRONIC
SURVEILLANCE

§ 15A-286. Definitions

As used in this Article, unless the context requires otherwise:

(1) "Aggrieved person" means a person who was a party to any intercepted wire, oral, or electronic communication or a person against whom the interception was directed.

(2) "Attorney General" means the Attorney General of the State of North Carolina, unless otherwise specified.

(3) "Aural transfer" means a transfer containing the human voice at any point between and including the point of origin and the point of reception.

(4) "Chapter 119 of the United States Code" means Chapter 119 of Part I of Title 18, United States Code, being Public Law 90-351, the Omnibus Crime Control and Safe Streets Act of 1968, as amended by the Electronic Communications Privacy Act of 1986.

(5) "Communications common carrier" shall have the same meaning which is given the term "common carrier" by section 153(h) of Title 47 of the United States Code.

(6) "Contents" when used with respect to any wire, oral, or electronic communication means and includes any information concerning the substance, purport, or meaning of that communication.

(7) "Electronic, mechanical, or other device" means any device or apparatus which can be used to intercept a wire, oral, or electronic communication other than:

    a. Any telephone or telegraph instrument, equipment, or facility, or any component thereof:

        1. Furnished to the subscriber or user by a provider of wire or electronic communication service in the ordinary course of its business and being used by the subscriber or user in the ordinary course of its business or furnished by the subscriber or user for connection to the facilities of such service and used in the ordinary course of its business; or

        2. Being used by a provider of wire or electronic communication service in the ordinary course of its business or by an investigative or law enforcement officer in the ordinary course of the officer's duties.

    b. A hearing aid or similar device being used to correct subnormal hearing to not better than normal.

(8) "Electronic communication" means any transfer of signs, signals, writing, images, sounds, data, or intelligence of any nature transmitted in whole or in part by a wire, radio, electromagnetic, photoelectronic, or photooptical system that affects interstate or foreign commerce but does not include:

    a. Any wire or oral communication;

    b. Any communication made through a tone-only paging device; or

    c. Any communication from a tracking device (as defined in section 3117 of Title 18 of the United States Code).

(9) "Electronic communication service" means any service which provides to users thereof the ability to send or receive wire or electronic communications.

(10) "Electronic communication system" means any wire, radio, electronic, magnetic, photooptical, or photoelectronic facilities for the transmission of electronic communications, and any computer facilities or related electronic equipment for the storage of such communications.

(11) "Electronic surveillance" means the interception of wire, oral, or electronic communications as provided by this Article.

(12) "Electronic storage" means:

    a. Any temporary, intermediate storage of a wire or electronic communication incidental to the electronic transmission thereof; and

    b. Any storage of such communication by an electronic communication service for the purposes of backup protection of the communication.

(13) "Intercept" means the aural or other acquisition of the contents of any wire, oral, or electronic communication through the use of any electronic, mechanical, or other device.

(14) "Investigative or law enforcement officer" means any officer of the State of North Carolina or any political subdivision thereof, who is empowered by the laws of this State to conduct investigations of or to make arrests for offenses enumerated in G.S. 15A-290, and any attorney authorized by the laws of this State to prosecute or participate in the prosecution of those offenses, including the Attorney General of North Carolina.

(15) "Judge" means any judge of the trial divisions of the General Court of Justice.

(16) "Judicial review panel" means a three-judge body, composed of such judges as may be assigned by the Chief Justice of the Supreme Court of North Carolina, which shall review applications for electronic surveillance orders and may issue orders valid throughout the State authorizing such surveillance as provided by this Article, and which shall submit a report of its decision to the Chief Justice.

Chapter 15A

(17) "Oral communication" means any oral communication uttered by a person exhibiting an expectation that such communication is not subject to interception under circumstances justifying such expectation, but the term does not include any electronic communication.

(18) "Person" means any employee or agent of the United States or any state or any political subdivision thereof, and any individual, partnership, association, joint stock company, trust, or corporation.

(19) "Readily accessible to the general public" means, with respect to a radio communication, that the communication is not:

a. Scrambled or encrypted;

b. Transmitted using modulation techniques whose essential parameters have been withheld from the public with the intention of preserving the privacy of the communication;

c. Carried on a subcarrier or other signal subsidiary to a radio transmission;

d. Transmitted over a communications system provided by a common carrier, unless the communication is a tone-only paging system communication; or

e. Transmitted on frequencies allocated under Part 25, Subpart D, E, or F or Part 94 of the Rules of the Federal Communications Commission as provided by 18 U.S.C. § 2510(16)(E).

(20) "User" means any person or entity who:

a. Uses an electronic communications service; and

b. Is duly authorized by the provider of the service to engage in the use.

(21) "Wire communication" means any aural transfer made in whole or in part through the use of facilities for the transmission of communications by the aid of wire, cable, or other like connection between the point of origin and the point of reception (including the use of such connection in a switching station) furnished or operated by any person engaged in providing or operating such facilities for the transmission of interstate or foreign communications or communications affecting interstate or foreign commerce and the term includes any electronic storage of such communication.

History.
1995, c. 407, s. 1; 1997-435, s. 1

§ 15A-287. Interception and disclosure of wire, oral, or electronic communications prohibited

(a) Except as otherwise specifically provided in this Article, a person is guilty of a Class H felony if, without the consent of at least one party to the communication, the person:

(1) Willfully intercepts, endeavors to intercept, or procures any other person to intercept or endeavor to intercept, any wire, oral, or electronic communication.

(2) Willfully uses, endeavors to use, or procures any other person to use or endeavor to use any electronic, mechanical, or other device to intercept any oral communication when:

a. The device is affixed to, or otherwise transmits a signal through, a wire, cable, or other like connection used in wire communications; or

b. The device transmits communications by radio, or interferes with the transmission of such communications.

(3) Willfully discloses, or endeavors to disclose, to any other person the contents of any wire, oral, or electronic communication, knowing or having reason to know that the information was obtained through violation of this Article; or

(4) Willfully uses, or endeavors to use, the contents of any wire or oral communication, knowing or having reason to know that the information was obtained through the interception of a wire or oral communication in violation of this Article.

(b) It is not unlawful under this Article for any person to:

(1) Intercept or access an electronic communication made through an electronic communication system that is configured so that the electronic communication is readily accessible to the general public;

(2) Intercept any radio communication which is transmitted:

a. For use by the general public, or that relates to ships, aircraft, vehicles, or persons in distress;

b. By any governmental, law enforcement, civil defense, private land mobile, or public safety communication system, including police and fire, readily available to the general public;

c. By a station operating on any authorized band within the bands allocated to the amateur, citizens band, or general mobile radio services; or

d. By any marine or aeronautical communication system; or

(3) Intercept any communication in a manner otherwise allowed by Chapter 119 of the United States Code.

(c) It is not unlawful under this Article for an operator of a switchboard, or an officer, employee, or agent of a provider of electronic communication service, whose facilities are used in the transmission of a wire or electronic communication, to intercept, disclose, or use that communication in the normal course of employment while engaged in any activity that is a necessary incident to the rendition of his or her service or to the protection of the rights or property of the provider of that service, provided that a provider of wire or electronic communication service may not utilize service observing or random monitoring except for mechanical or service quality control checks.

(d) It is not unlawful under this Article for an officer, employee, or agent of the Federal Communications Commission, in the normal course of his employment and in discharge of the monitoring responsibilities exercised by the Commission in the enforcement of Chapter 5 of Title 47 of the United States Code, to intercept a wire or electronic communication, or oral communication transmitted by radio, or to disclose or use the information thereby obtained.

(e) Any person who, as a result of the person's official position or employment, has obtained knowledge of the contents of any wire, oral, or electronic communication lawfully intercepted pursuant to an electronic surveillance order or of the pendency or existence of or implementation of an electronic surveillance order who shall knowingly and willfully disclose such information for the purpose of hindering or thwarting any investigation or prosecution relating to the subject matter of the electronic surveillance order, except as is necessary for the proper and lawful performance of the duties of his position or employment or as shall be required or allowed by law, shall be guilty of a Class G felony.

(f) Any person who shall, knowingly or with gross negligence, divulge the existence of or contents of any electronic surveillance order in a way likely to hinder or thwart any investigation or prosecution relating to the subject matter of the electronic surveillance order or anyone who shall, knowingly or with gross negligence, release the contents of any wire, oral, or electronic communication intercepted under an electronic surveillance order, except as is necessary for the proper and lawful performance of the duties of his position or employment or as is required or allowed by law, shall be guilty of a Class 1 misdemeanor.

(g) Any public officer who shall violate subsection (a) or (d) of this section or who shall knowingly violate subsection (e) of this section shall be removed from any public office he may hold and shall thereafter be ineligible to hold any public office, whether elective or appointed.

History.
1995, c. 407, s. 1

§ 15A-288. Manufacture, distribution, possession, and advertising of wire, oral, or electronic communication intercepting devices prohibited

(a) Except as otherwise specifically provided in this Article, a person is guilty of a Class H felony if the person:

(1) Manufactures, assembles, possesses, purchases, or sells any electronic, mechanical, or other device, knowing or having reason to know that the design of the device renders it primarily useful for the purpose of the surreptitious interception of wire, oral, or electronic communications; or

(2) Places in any newspaper, magazine, handbill, or other publication, any advertisement of:

a. Any electronic, mechanical, or other device knowing or having reason to know that the design of the device renders it primarily useful for the purpose of the surreptitious interception of wire, oral, or electronic communications; or

b. Any other electronic, mechanical, or other device where the advertisement promotes the use of the device for the purpose of the surreptitious interception of wire, oral, or electronic communications.

(b) It is not unlawful under this section for the following persons to manufacture, assemble, possess, purchase, or sell any electronic, mechanical, or other device, knowing or having reason to know that the design of the device renders it primarily useful for the purpose of the surreptitious interception of wire, oral, or electronic communications:

(1) A communications common carrier or an officer, agent, or employee of, or a person under contract with, a communications common carrier, acting in the normal course of the communications common carrier's business, or

(2) An officer, agent, or employee of, or a person under contract with, the State, acting in the course of the activities of the State, and with the written authorization of the Attorney General.

(c) An officer, agent, or employee of, or a person whose normal and customary business is to design, manufacture, assemble, advertise and sell electronic, mechanical and other devices primarily useful for the purpose of the surreptitious interceptions of wire, oral, or electronic communications, exclusively for and restricted to State and federal investigative or law enforcement agencies and departments.

History.
1995, c. 407, s. 1

§ 15A-289. Confiscation of wire, oral, or electronic communication interception devices

Any electronic, mechanical, or other device used, sent, carried, manufactured, assembled, possessed, sold, or advertised in violation of G.S. 15A-288 may be seized and forfeited to this State.

History.
1995, c. 407, s. 1

§ 15A-290. Offenses for which orders for electronic surveillance may be granted

(a) Orders authorizing or approving the interception of wire, oral, or electronic communications may be granted, subject to the provisions of this Article and Chapter 119 of Title 18 of the United States Code, when the interception does any of the following:

(1) May provide or has provided evidence of the commission of, or any conspiracy to commit, any of the following:

a. Any of the drug-trafficking violations listed in G.S. 90-95(h).

b. A continuing criminal enterprise in violation of G.S. 90-95.1.

(2) May expedite the apprehension of persons indicted for the commission of, or any conspiracy to commit, an offense listed in subdivision (1) of this subsection.

(b) Orders authorizing or approving the interception of wire, oral, or electronic communications may be granted, subject to the provisions of this Article and Chapter 119 of Title 18 of the United States Code, when the interception may provide, or has provided, evidence of any offense that involves the commission of, or any conspiracy to commit, murder, kidnapping, hostage taking, robbery, extortion, bribery, rape, or any sexual offense, or when the interception may expedite the apprehension of persons indicted for the commission of these offenses.

(c) Orders authorizing or approving the interception of wire, oral, or electronic communications may be granted, subject to the provisions of this Article and Chapter 119 of Title 18 of the United States Code, when the interception may provide, or has provided, evidence of any of the following offenses, or any conspiracy to commit these offenses, or when the interception may expedite the apprehension of persons indicted for the commission of these offenses:

(1) Any felony offense against a minor, including any violation of G.S. 14-27.31 (Sexual activity by a substitute parent or custodian), G.S. 14-27.32 (Sexual activity with a student), G.S. 14-41 (Abduction of children), G.S. 14-43.11 (Human trafficking), G.S. 14-43.12 (Involuntary servitude), G.S. 14-43.13 (Sexual servitude), G.S. 14-190.16 (First degree sexual exploitation of a minor), G.S. 14-190.17 (Second degree sexual exploitation of a minor), G.S. 14-202.1 (Taking indecent liberties with children), G.S. 14-205.2(c) or (d) (Patronizing a prostitute who is a minor or has a mental disability), or G.S. 14-205.3(b) (Promoting prostitution of a minor or a person who has a mental disability).

(2) Any felony obstruction of a criminal investigation, including any violation of G.S. 14-221.1 (Altering, destroying, or stealing evidence of criminal conduct).

(3) Any felony offense involving interference with, or harassment or intimidation of, jurors or witnesses, including any violation of G.S. 14-225.2 or G.S. 14-226.

(4) Any felony offense involving assault or threats against any executive or legislative officer in violation of Article 5A of Chapter 14 of the General Statutes or assault with a firearm or other deadly weapon upon governmental officers or employees in violation of G.S. 14-34.2.

(5) Any offense involving the manufacture, assembly, possession, storage, transportation, sale, purchase, delivery, or acquisition of weapons of mass death or destruction in violation of G.S. 14-288.8 or the adulteration or misbranding of food, drugs, cosmetics, etc., with the intent to cause serious injury in violation of G.S. 14-34.4.

(d) When an investigative or law enforcement officer, while engaged in intercepting wire, oral, or electronic communications in the manner authorized, intercepts wire, electronic, or oral communications relating to offenses other than those specified in the order of authorization or approval, the contents of the communications and evidence derived from the communications may be disclosed or used as provided in G.S. 15A-294(a) and (b). The contents of the communications and any evidence derived from the communications may be used in accordance with G.S. 15A-294(c) when authorized or approved by a judicial review panel where the panel finds, on subsequent application made as soon as practicable, that the contents were otherwise intercepted in accordance with this Article or Chapter 119 of Title 18 of the United States Code.

(e) No otherwise privileged wire, oral, or electronic communication intercepted in accordance with, or in violation of, the provisions of this Article or Chapter 119 of Title 18 of the United States Code, shall lose its privileged character.

History.
1995, c. 407, s. 1; 2013-368, s. 6; 2015-181, s. 46; 2018-47, s. 4(k)

Chapter 15A

§ 15A-291. Application for electronic surveillance order; judicial review panel

(a) The Attorney General or the Attorney General's designee may, pursuant to the provisions of section 2516(2) of Chapter 119 of the United States Code, apply to a judicial review panel for an order authorizing or approving the interception of wire, oral, or electronic communications by investigative or law enforcement officers having responsibility for the investigation of the offenses as to which the application is made, and for such offenses and causes as are enumerated in G.S. 15A-290. A judicial review panel shall be composed of such judges as may be assigned by the Chief Justice of the Supreme Court of North Carolina or an Associate Justice acting as the Chief Justice's designee, which shall review applications for electronic surveillance orders and may issue orders valid throughout the State authorizing such surveillance as provided by this Article, and which shall submit a report of its decision to the Chief Justice. A judicial review panel may be appointed by the Chief Justice or an Associate Justice acting as the Chief Justice's designee upon the notification of the Attorney General's Office of the intent to apply for an electronic surveillance order.

(b) A judicial review panel is hereby authorized to grant orders valid throughout the State for the interception of wire, oral, or electronic communications. Applications for such orders may be made by the Attorney General or the Attorney General's designee. The Attorney General or the Attorney General's designee in applying for such orders, and a judicial review panel in granting such orders, shall comply with all procedural requirements of section 2518 of Chapter 119 of the United States Code. The Attorney General or the Attorney General's designee may make emergency applications as provided by section 2518 of Chapter 119 of the United States Code. In applying section 2518 the word "judge" in that section shall be construed to refer to the judicial review panel, unless the context otherwise indicates. The judicial review panel may stipulate any special conditions it feels necessary to assure compliance with the terms of this act.

(c) No judge who sits as a member of a judicial review panel shall preside at any trial or proceeding resulting from or in any manner related to information gained pursuant to a lawful electronic surveillance order issued by that panel.

(d) Each application for an order authorizing or approving the interception of a wire, oral, or electronic communication must be made in writing upon oath or affirmation to the judicial review panel. Each application must include the following information:

(1) The identity of the office requesting the application;

(2) A full and complete statement of the facts and circumstances relied upon by the applicant, to justify his belief that an order should be issued, including:

a. Details as to the particular offense that has been, or is being committed;

b. Except as provided in G.S. 15A-294(i), a particular description of the nature and location of the facilities from which or the place where the communication is to be intercepted;

c. A particular description of the type of communications sought to be intercepted; and

d. The identity of the person, if known, committing the offense and whose communications are to be intercepted;

(3) A full and complete statement as to whether or not other investigative procedures have been tried and failed or why they reasonably appear to be unlikely to succeed if tried or to be too dangerous;

(4) A statement of the period of time for which the interception is required to be maintained. If the nature of the investigation is such that the authorization for interception should not automatically terminate when the described type of communication has been obtained, a particular description of facts establishing probable cause to believe that additional communications of the same type will occur thereafter must be added;

(5) A full and complete statement of the facts concerning all previous applications known to the individual authorizing and making adjudication, made to a judicial review panel for authorization to intercept, or for approval of interceptions of wire, oral, or electronic communications involving any of the same persons, facilities, or places specified in the application, and the action taken by that judicial review panel on each such application; and

(6) Where the application is for the extension of an order, a statement setting forth the results thus far obtained from the interception, or a reasonable explanation of the failure to obtain such results.

(e) Before acting on the application, the judicial review panel may examine on oath the person requesting the application or any other person who may possess pertinent information, but information other than that contained in the affidavit may not be considered by the panel in determining whether probable cause exists for the issuance of the order unless the information is either recorded or contemporaneously summarized in the record or on the face of the order by the panel.

History.
1995, c. 407, s. 1; 1997-435, s. 2; 2005-207, s. 1

§ 15A-292. Request for application for electronic surveillance order

(a) The head of any municipal, county, or State law enforcement agency or any district attorney may submit a written request to the Attorney General that the Attorney General apply to a judicial review panel for an electronic surveillance order to be executed within the requesting agency's jurisdiction. The written requests shall be on a form approved by the Attorney General and shall provide sufficient information to form the basis for an application for an electronic surveillance order. The head of a law enforcement agency shall also submit a copy of the request to the district attorney, who shall review the request and forward it to the Attorney General along with any comments he may wish to include. The Attorney General is authorized to review the request and decide whether it is appropriate to submit an application to a judicial review panel for an electronic surveillance order. If a request for an application is deemed inappropriate, the Attorney General shall send a signed, written statement to the person submitting the request, and to the district attorney, summarizing the reasons for failing to make an application. If the Attorney General decides to submit an application to a judicial review panel, he shall so notify the requesting agency head, the district attorney, and the head of the local law enforcement agency which has the primary responsibility for enforcing the criminal laws in the location in which it is anticipated the majority of the surveillance will take place, if not the same as the requesting agency head, unless the Attorney General has probable cause to believe that the latter notifications should substantially jeopardize the success of the surveillance or the investigation in general. If a judicial review panel grants an electronic surveillance order, a copy of such order shall be sent to the requesting agency head and the district attorney, and a summary of the order shall be sent to the head of the local law enforcement agency with primary responsibility for enforcing the criminal laws in the jurisdiction where the majority of the surveillance will take place, if not the same as the requesting agency head, unless the judicial review panel finds probable cause to believe that the latter notifications would substantially jeopardize the success of the surveillance or the investigation.

(b) This Article does not limit the authority of the Attorney General to apply for electronic surveillance orders independent of, or contrary to, the requests of law enforcement agency heads, nor does it limit the discretion of the Attorney General in determining whether an application is appropriate under any given circumstances.

(c) The Chief Justice of the North Carolina Supreme Court shall receive a report concerning each decision of a judicial review panel.

History.
1995, c. 407, s. 1

§ 15A-293. Issuance of order for electronic surveillance; procedures for implementation

(a) Upon application by the Attorney General pursuant to the procedures in G.S. 15A-291, a judicial review panel may enter an ex parte order, as requested or as modified, authorizing the interception of wire, oral, or electronic communications, if the panel determines on the basis of the facts submitted by the applicant that:

(1) There is probable cause for belief that an individual is committing, has committed, or is about to commit an offense set out in G.S. 15A-290;

(2) There is probable cause for belief that particular communications concerning that offense will be obtained through such interception;

(3) Normal investigative procedures have been tried and have failed or reasonably appear to be unlikely to succeed if tried or to be too dangerous; and

(4) Except as provided in G.S. 15A-294(i), there is probable cause for belief that the facilities from which, or the place where, the wire, oral, or electronic communications are to be intercepted are being used, or are about to be used, in connection with the commission of such offense, or are leased to, listed in the name of, or commonly used by the individual described in subdivision (1) of this subsection.

(b) Each order authorizing the interception of any wire, oral, or electronic communications must specify:

(1) The identity of the person, if known, whose communications are to be intercepted;

(2) The nature and location of the communications facilities as to which, or the place where, authority to intercept is granted, and the means by which such interceptions may be made;

(3) A particular description of the type of communication sought to be intercepted and a statement of the particular offense to which it relates;

(4) The identity of the agency authorized to intercept the communications and of the person requesting the application; and

(5) The period of time during which such interception is authorized, including a statement as to whether or not the interception automatically terminates when the described communication has been first obtained.

(c) No order entered under this Article may authorize the interception of any wire, oral, or

Chapter 15A

electronic communication for any period longer than is necessary to achieve the objective of the authorization, nor in any event longer than 30 days. Such 30-day period begins on the earlier of the day on which the investigative or law enforcement officer first begins to conduct an interception under the order or 10 days after the order is entered. Extensions of an order may be granted, but only upon application for an extension made in accordance with G.S. 15A-291 and the panel making the findings required by subsection (a) of this section. The period of extension shall be no longer than the panel determines to be necessary to achieve the purpose for which it was granted and in no event for longer than 30 days. Every order and extension thereof must contain a provision that the authorization to intercept be executed as soon as practicable, be conducted in such a way as to minimize the interception of communications not otherwise subject to interception under this Article, and terminate upon attainment of the authorized objective, or in any event in 30 days, as is appropriate. In the event the intercepted communication is in a code or foreign language, and an expert in that foreign language or code is not reasonably available during the interception period, minimization may be accomplished as soon as practicable after the interception. An interception under this Article may be conducted in whole or in part by State or federal government personnel, or by an individual operating under a contract with the State or federal government, acting under the supervision of an investigative or law enforcement officer authorized to conduct the interception.

(d) Whenever an order authorizing interception is entered pursuant to this Article, the order may require reports to be made to the issuing judicial review panel showing that progress has been made toward achievement of the authorized objective and the need for continued interception. Such reports must be made at such intervals as the panel may require.

(1) The contents of any wire, oral, or electronic communication intercepted by any means authorized by this Article must be recorded on tape, wire, or electronic or other comparable device. The recording of the contents of any wire, electronic, or oral communication under this subsection must be done in such way as will protect the recording from editing or other alterations. Immediately upon the expiration of the period of the order, or extensions thereof, the recordings must be made available to the judicial review panel and sealed under its direction. Custody of the recordings is wherever the panel orders. They may not be destroyed except upon an order of the issuing panel and in any event must be kept for 10 years. Duplicate recordings may be made for use or disclosure pursuant to the provisions of G.S. 15A-294(a) and (b) for investigations. The contents of any wire, oral, or electronic communication or evidence derived therefrom may not be disclosed or used under G.S. 15A-294(c) unless they have been kept sealed.

(2) Applications made and orders granted under this Article must be sealed by the panel. Custody of the applications and orders may be disclosed only upon a showing of good cause before the issuing panel and may not be destroyed except on its order and in any event must be kept for 10 years.

(3) Any violation of the provisions of this subsection may be punished as for contempt.

(e) The State Bureau of Investigation shall own or control and may operate any equipment used to implement electronic surveillance orders issued by a judicial review panel and may operate or use, in implementing any electronic surveillance order, electronic surveillance equipment in which a local government or any of its agencies has a property interest.

(f) The Attorney General shall establish procedures for the use of electronic surveillance equipment in assisting local law enforcement agencies implementing electronic surveillance orders. The Attorney General shall supervise such assistance given to local law enforcement agencies and is authorized to conduct statewide training sessions for investigative and law enforcement officers regarding this Article.

History.
1995, c. 407, s. 1; 1997-435, s. 2.1; 2005-207, ss. 2, 3

§ 15A-294. Authorization for disclosure and use of intercepted wire, oral, or electronic communications

(a) Any investigative or law enforcement officer who, by any means authorized by this Article or Chapter 119 of the United States Code, has obtained knowledge of the contents of any wire, oral, or electronic communication, or evidence derived therefrom, may disclose such contents to another investigative or law enforcement officer to the extent that such disclosure is appropriate to the proper performance of the official duties of the officer making or receiving the disclosure.

(b) Any investigative or law enforcement officer, who by any means authorized by this Article or Chapter 119 of the United States Code, has obtained knowledge of the contents of any wire, oral, or electronic communication, or evidence derived therefrom, may use such contents to the extent such use is appropriate to the proper performance of the officers' official duties.

(c) Any person who has received, by any means authorized by this Article or Chapter 119 of the

United States Code, any information concerning a wire, oral, or electronic communication, or evidence derived therefrom, intercepted in accordance with the provisions of this Article, may disclose the contents of that communication or such derivative evidence while giving testimony under oath or affirmation in any proceeding in any court or before any grand jury in this State, or in any court of the United States or of any state, or in any federal or state grand jury proceeding.

(d) Within a reasonable time, but no later than 90 days after the filing of an application for an order or the termination of the period of an order or the extensions thereof, the issuing judicial review panel must cause to be served on the persons named in the order or the application and such other parties as the panel in its discretion may determine, an inventory that includes notice of:

(1) The fact of the entry of the order or the application;

(2) The date of the entry and the period of the authorized interception; and

(3) The fact that during the period wire, oral, or electronic communications were or were not intercepted.

(d1) The notification required pursuant to G.S. 15A-294(d) may be delayed if the judicial review panel has probable cause to believe that notification would substantially jeopardize the success of an electronic surveillance or a criminal investigation. Delay of notification shall be only by order of the judicial review panel. The period of delay shall be designated by the judicial review panel and may be extended from time to time until the jeopardy to the electronic surveillance or the criminal investigation dissipates.

(e) The issuing judicial review panel, upon the filing of a motion, may in its discretion, make available to such person or his counsel for inspection, such portions of the intercepted communications, applications, and orders as the panel determines to be required by law or in the interest of justice.

(f) The contents of any intercepted wire, oral, or electronic communication, or evidence derived therefrom, may not be received in evidence or otherwise disclosed in any trial, hearing, or other proceeding in any court of this State unless each party, not less than 20 working days before the trial, hearing, or other proceeding, has been furnished with a copy of the order and accompanying application, under which the interception was authorized.

(g) Any aggrieved person in any trial, hearing, or proceeding in or before any court, department, officer, agency, regulatory body, or other authority of this State, or a political subdivision thereof, may move to suppress the contents of any intercepted wire, oral, or electronic communication, or evidence derived therefrom, on the grounds that:

(1) The communication was unlawfully intercepted;

(2) The order of authorization under which it was intercepted is insufficient on its face; or

(3) The interception was not made in conformity with the order of authorization.

Such motion must be made before the trial, hearing, or proceeding unless there was no opportunity to make such motion or the person was not aware of the grounds of this motion. If the motion is granted, the contents of the intercepted wire, oral, or electronic communication, or evidence derived therefrom, must be treated as having been obtained in violation of this Article.

(h) In addition to any other right to appeal, the State may appeal:

(1) From an order granting a motion to suppress made under subdivision (1) of this subsection, if the district attorney certifies to the judge granting the motion that the appeal is not taken for purposes of delay. The appeal must be taken within 30 days after the date the order of suppression was entered and must be prosecuted as are other interlocutory appeals; or

(2) From an order denying an application for an order of authorization, and the appeal may be made ex parte and must be considered in camera and in preference to all other pending appeals.

(i) The requirements of G.S. 15A-293(b)(2) and G.S. 15A-293(a)(4) relating to the specification of the facilities from which, or the place where, the communication is to be intercepted do not apply if:

(1) In the case of an application with respect to the interception of an oral communication:

a. The application is by a State investigative or law enforcement officer and is approved by the Attorney General or his designee;

b. The application contains a full and complete statement as to why the specification is not practical and identifies the person committing the offense and whose communications are to be intercepted; and

c. The judicial review panel finds that the specification is not practical.

(2) In the case of an application with respect to a wire or electronic communication:

a. The application is by a State investigative or law enforcement officer and is approved by the Attorney General or his designee;

b. The application identifies the person believed to be committing the offense and whose communications are to be intercepted, and the applicant makes a showing that there is probable cause to believe that the person's actions could have the effect of thwarting interception from a specified facility;

c. The judicial review panel finds that the showing has been adequately made; and

d. The order authorizing or approving the interception is limited to interception only for such time as it is reasonable to presume that the person identified in the application is or was reasonably proximate to the instrument through which the communication will be or was transmitted.

(j) An interception of a communication under an order with respect to which the requirements of G.S. 15A-293(b)(2) and G.S. 15A-293(a)(4) do not apply by reason of subdivision (i)(1) of this section shall not begin until the place where the communication is to be intercepted is ascertained by the person implementing the interception order. A provider of wire or electronic communications service that has received an order as provided for in subdivision (i)(2) of this section may move the court to modify or quash the order on the grounds that its assistance with respect to the interception cannot be performed in a timely or reasonable fashion. The court, upon notice to the government, shall decide such a motion expeditiously.

History.
1995, c. 407, s. 1; 1997-435, s. 3; 2005-207, s. 4

§ 15A-295. Reports concerning intercepted wire, oral, or electronic communications

In January of each year, the Attorney General of this State must report to the Administrative Office of the United States Court the information required to be filed by section 2519 of Title 18 of the United States Code, as heretofore or hereafter amended, and file a copy of the report with the Administrative Office of the Courts of North Carolina.

History.
1995, c. 407, s. 1

§ 15A-296. Recovery of civil damages authorized

(a) Any person whose wire, oral, or electronic communication is intercepted, disclosed, or used in violation of this Article, has a civil cause of action against any person who intercepts, discloses, uses, or procures any other person to intercept, disclose, or use such communications, and is entitled to recover from any other person:

(1) Actual damages, but not less than liquidated damages, computed at the rate of one hundred dollars ($ 100.00) a day for each day of violation or one thousand dollars ($ 1,000), whichever is higher;

(2) Punitive damages; and

(3) A reasonable attorneys' fee and other litigation costs reasonably incurred.

(b) Good faith reliance on a court order or on a representation made by the Attorney General or a district attorney is a complete defense to any civil or criminal action brought under this Article.

History.
1995, c. 407, s. 1

§ 15A-297. Conformity to provisions of federal law

It is the intent of this Article to conform the requirements of all interceptions of wire, oral, or electronic communications conducted by investigative or law enforcement officers in this State to provisions of Chapter 119 of the United States Code, except where the context indicates a purpose to provide safeguards even more protective of individual privacy and constitutional rights.

History.
1995, c. 407, s. 1

§ 15A-298. Subpoena authority

The Director of the State Bureau of Investigation or the Director's designee may issue an administrative subpoena to a communications common carrier or an electronic communications service to compel production of business records if the records:

(1) Disclose information concerning local or long-distance toll records or subscriber information; and

(2) Are material to an active criminal investigation being conducted by the State Bureau of Investigation.

History.
1995, c. 407, s. 1; 1997-435, s. 4; 2014-100, s. 17.1(ee); 2015-276, s. 4

ARTICLE 16A
DISCONTINUATION OF TELECOMMUNICATIONS SERVICES

§ 15A-299. Discontinuation of telecommunications services used for unlawful purposes

(a) The legislature finds that some persons use telecommunications services to violate State or federal criminal law. The legislature further finds that some persons use telecommunications services or technology, such as call forwarding and cellular radio transmission, to avoid detection or arrest.

(b) A customer of a telecommunications company operating within the State may use telecommunications services only for lawful purposes.

(c) If a local, State, or federal law enforcement officer acting within the scope of the officer's duties obtains evidence that telecommunications services are being used or have been used by a customer or by the employee or agent of the customer to violate State or federal criminal law, the officer may request either the district attorney or the Attorney General as appropriate to apply to the district court of the county in which the suspected violation of State or federal criminal law occurred for an order requiring the telecommunications company to discontinue service to the customer. The court shall hold a hearing on the application as soon as possible, but no sooner than 48 hours after notice of the application for discontinuation of service is delivered to the address at which the telecommunications services are furnished or to the address to which bills for telecommunications services are mailed, according to the telecommunications company records. Notice must also be given to the registered agent for the service of process upon the telecommunications company at least 48 hours prior to the hearing. Notices required under this section shall be given pursuant to the provisions of Rule 4 of the North Carolina Rules of Civil Procedure. If the court finds clear and convincing evidence that the telecommunications services are being used or have been used to violate State or federal criminal law, the court may order the telecommunications company to discontinue such service immediately.

(d) Telecommunications services discontinued under this section may be reinstated only by court order, and call forwarding or message referrals, whether recorded or live, may not be provided until reinstatement of service is ordered by the court. The court may order reinstatement of telecommunications services if it finds that the customer is not likely to use the services to violate State or federal criminal law. The standard of proof shall be the same as that used for the disconnect order.

(e) A telecommunications company shall be held harmless from liability to any person when complying with any court order issued under this section.

History.
1997-372, s. 1

N.C. Gen. Stat. § 15A-300

Reserved for future codification purposes.

ARTICLE 16B
USE OF UNMANNED AIRCRAFT SYSTEMS

§ 15A-300.1. Restrictions on use of unmanned aircraft systems

(a) **Definitions.** -- The following definitions apply to this Article:

(1) **Manned aircraft.** -- An aircraft, as defined in G.S. 63-1, that is operated with a person in or on the aircraft.

(2) Repealed by Session Laws 2017-160, s. 1, effective December 1, 2017, and applicable to offenses committed on or after that date and acts occurring and causes of action arising on or after that date.

(3) **Unmanned aircraft.** -- An aircraft, as defined in G.S. 63-1, that is operated without the possibility of human intervention from within or on the aircraft.

(4) **Unmanned aircraft system.** -- An unmanned aircraft and associated elements, including communication links and components that control the unmanned aircraft that are required for the pilot in command to operate safely and efficiently in the national airspace system.

(b) **General Prohibitions.** -- Except as otherwise provided in this section, no person, entity, or State agency shall use an unmanned aircraft system to do any of the following:

(1) Conduct surveillance of:

a. A person or a dwelling occupied by a person and that dwelling's curtilage without the person's consent.

b. Private real property without the consent of the owner, easement holder, or lessee of the property.

(2) Photograph an individual, without the individual's consent, for the purpose of publishing or otherwise publicly disseminating the photograph. This subdivision shall not apply to newsgathering, newsworthy events, or events or places to which the general public is invited.

(c) **Law Enforcement Exceptions.** -- Notwithstanding the provisions of subsection (b) of this section, the use of unmanned aircraft systems by law enforcement agencies of the State or a political subdivision of the State is not prohibited in the following instances:

(1) To counter a high risk of a terrorist attack by a specific individual or organization if the United States Secretary of Homeland Security or the Secretary of the North Carolina Department of Public Safety

determines that credible intelligence indicates that such a risk exists.

(2) To conduct surveillance in an area that is within a law enforcement officer's plain view when the officer is in a location the officer has a legal right to be.

(3) If the law enforcement agency first obtains a search warrant authorizing the use of an unmanned aircraft system.

(4) If the law enforcement agency possesses reasonable suspicion that, under particular circumstances, swift action is needed to prevent imminent danger to life or serious damage to property, to forestall the imminent escape of a suspect or the destruction of evidence, to conduct pursuit of an escapee or suspect, or to facilitate the search for a missing person.

(5) To photograph gatherings to which the general public is invited on public or private land.

(c1) **Emergency Management Exception.** -- Notwithstanding the provisions of subsection (b) of this section, an emergency management agency, as defined in G.S. 166A-19.3, may use unmanned aircraft systems for all functions and activities related to emergency management, including incident command, area reconnaissance, search and rescue, preliminary damage assessment, hazard risk management, and floodplain mapping.

(d) Repealed by Session Laws 2017-160, s. 2, effective July 21, 2017.

(e) Any person who is the subject of unwarranted surveillance, or whose photograph is taken in violation of the provisions of this section, shall have a civil cause of action against the person, entity, or State agency that conducts the surveillance or that uses an unmanned aircraft system to photograph for the purpose of publishing or otherwise disseminating the photograph. In lieu of actual damages, the person whose photograph is taken may elect to recover five thousand dollars ($ 5,000) for each photograph or video that is published or otherwise disseminated, as well as reasonable costs and attorneys' fees and injunctive or other relief as determined by the court.

(f) Evidence obtained or collected in violation of this section is not admissible as evidence in a criminal prosecution in any court of law in this State except when obtained or collected under the objectively reasonable, good-faith belief that the actions were lawful.

History.
2014-100, s. 34.30(a); 2017-160, ss. 1 -3

§ 15A-300.2. Regulation of launch and recovery sites

(a) No unmanned aircraft system may be launched or recovered from any State or private property without consent.

(b) A unit of local government may adopt an ordinance to regulate the use of the local government's property for the launch or recovery of unmanned aircraft systems.

History.
2014-100, s. 34.30(a)

§ 15A-300.3. Use of an unmanned aircraft system near a confinement or correctional facility prohibited

(a) **Prohibition.** -- No person, entity, or State agency shall use an unmanned aircraft system within either a horizontal distance of 500 feet, or a vertical distance of 250 feet from any local confinement facility, as defined in G.S. 153A-217, or State or federal correctional facility. For the purpose of this section, horizontal distance shall extend outward from the furthest exterior building walls, perimeter fences, and permanent fixed perimeter, or from another boundary clearly marked with posted notices. Posted notices shall be conspicuously posted not more than 100 yards apart along a marked boundary and comply with Department of Transportation guidelines.

(b) **Exceptions.** -- Unless the use of the unmanned aircraft system is otherwise prohibited under State or federal law, the distance restrictions of subsection (a) of this section do not apply to any of the following:

(1) A person operating an unmanned aircraft system with written consent from the official in responsible charge of the facility.

(2) A law enforcement officer using an unmanned aircraft system in accordance with G.S. 15A-300.1(c).

(3) A public utility, as defined in G.S. 62-3(23), a provider, as defined in G.S. 146-29.2(a)(6), or a commercial entity, provided that the public utility, provider, or commercial entity complies with all of the following:

a. The unmanned aircraft system must not be used within either a horizontal distance of 150 feet, or within a vertical distance of 150 feet from any local confinement facility or State or federal correctional facility.

b. Notifies the official in responsible charge of the facility at least 24 hours prior to operating the unmanned aircraft system. A commercial entity operating in compliance with G.S.15A-300.1 and pursuant to the provisions of this subdivision is exempt from the 24-hour notice requirement.

c. Uses the unmanned aircraft system for the purpose of inspecting public utility or provider transmission lines, equipment, or communication infrastructure or for another purpose directly related to the business of the public utility, provider, or commercial entity.

d. Uses the unmanned aircraft system for commercial purposes pursuant to and in compliance with (i) Federal Aviation Administration regulations, authorizations, or exemptions and (ii) Article 10 of Chapter 63 of the General Statutes.

e. The person operating the unmanned aircraft system does not physically enter the prohibited space without an escort from the facility.

(4) An emergency management agency, as defined in G.S. 166A-19.3, emergency medical services personnel, firefighters, and law enforcement officers, when using an unmanned aircraft system in response to an emergency.

(c) **Penalty.** -- The following penalties apply for violations of this section:

(1) A person who uses an unmanned aircraft system (i) in violation of subsection (a) of this section or (ii) pursuant to an exception in subsection (b) of this section and who delivers, or attempts to deliver, a weapon to a local confinement facility or State or federal correctional facility is guilty of a Class H felony, which shall include a fine of one thousand five hundred dollars ($ 1,500). For purposes of this subdivision, the term "weapon" is as defined in G.S. 14-401.24(c).

(2) A person who uses an unmanned aircraft system (i) in violation of subsection (a) of this section or (ii) pursuant to an exception in subsection (b) of this section and who delivers, or attempts to deliver, contraband to a local confinement facility or State or federal correctional facility is guilty of a Class I felony, which shall include a fine of one thousand dollars ($ 1,000). For purposes of this subdivision, the term "contraband" includes controlled substances, as defined in G.S. 90-87, cigarettes, alcohol, and communication devices, but does not include weapons.

(3) A person who uses an unmanned aircraft system in violation of subsection (a) of this section for any other purpose is guilty of a Class 1 misdemeanor, which shall include a fine of five hundred dollars ($ 500.00).

(d) **Seizure, Forfeiture, and Disposition of Seized Property.** -- A law enforcement agency may seize an unmanned aircraft system and any attached property, weapons, and contraband used in violation of this section. An unmanned aircraft system used in violation of this section and seized by a law enforcement agency is subject to forfeiture and disposition pursuant to G.S. 18B-504. An innocent owner or holder of a security interest applying to the court for release of the unmanned aircraft system, in accordance with G.S. 18B-504(h), shall also provide proof of ownership or security interest and written certification that the unmanned aircraft system will not be returned to the person who was charged with the violation of subsection (a) of this section. The court shall forfeit and dispose of any other property, weapons, or contraband seized by a law enforcement agency in connection with a violation of this section pursuant to G.S. 18B-504, 14-269.1, 90-112, or any combination thereof.

History.
2017-179, s. 1

SUBCHAPTER 03. CRIMINAL PROCESS

ARTICLE 17 CRIMINAL PROCESS

§ 15A-301. Criminal process generally

(a) **Formal Requirements.** --

(1) A record of each criminal process issued in the trial division of the General Court of Justice must be maintained in the office of the clerk in either paper form or in electronic form in the Electronic Repository as provided in G.S. 15A-301.1.

(2) Criminal process, other than a citation, must be signed and dated by the justice, judge, magistrate, or clerk who issues it. The citation must be signed and dated by the law-enforcement officer who issues it.

(b) **To Whom Directed.** -- Warrants for arrest and orders for arrest must be directed to a particular officer, a class of officers, or a combination thereof, having authority and territorial jurisdiction to execute the process. A criminal summons must be directed to the person summoned to appear and must be delivered to and may be served by any law-enforcement officer having authority and territorial jurisdiction to make an arrest for the offense charged, except that in those instances where the defendant is called into a law-enforcement agency to receive a summons, any employee so designated by the agency's chief executive officer may serve a criminal summons at the agency's office. The citation must be directed to the person cited to appear.

(b1) *(For effective date, see note) Approval by District Attorney; school personnel.* -- Notwithstanding any other provision of law, no warrant for arrest, order for arrest, criminal summons, or other criminal process shall be issued by a magistrate against a school employee, as defined in G.S. 14-33(c)(6), for an offense that occurred while the school employee was in the process of discharging his or her duties of employment, without the prior written approval of the district attorney or the district attorney's designee. For purposes of this subsection, the term "district attorney" means the person elected to the office of district attorney. This subsection does not apply if the offense is a traffic offense or if the offense occurred in the presence of a sworn law enforcement officer. The district attorney may decline to accept the authority set forth in this subsection; in such case, the procedure and review authority shall be as set forth in subsection (b2) of this section.

(b2) *(For effective date, see note) Magistrate review; school personnel.* -- A district attorney may decline the authority provided under subsection (b1) of this section by transmitting a letter so indicating to the chief district court judge. Upon receipt of a letter from the district attorney declining the authority provided in subsection (b1) of this section, the chief district court judge shall appoint a magistrate or magistrates to review any application for a warrant for arrest, order for arrest, criminal summons, or other criminal process against a school employee, as defined in G.S. 14-33(c)(6), where the allegation is that the school employee committed a misdemeanor offense while discharging his or her duties of employment. The failure to comply with any of the requirements in this subsection shall not affect the validity of any warrant, order, summons, or other criminal process. The following exceptions apply to the requirements in this subsection:

(1) The offense is a traffic offense.

(2) The offense occurred in the presence of a sworn law enforcement officer.

(3) There is no appointed magistrate available to review the application.

(c) **Service.** --

(1) A law-enforcement officer or other employee designated as provided in subsection (b) receiving for service or execution a criminal process that was first created and exists only in paper form must note thereon the date and time of its receipt. A law enforcement officer receiving a copy of a criminal process that was printed in paper form as provided in G.S. 15A-301.1 shall cause the date of receipt to be recorded as provided in that section. Upon execution or service, a copy of the process must be delivered to the person arrested or served.

(2) A corporation may be served with criminal summons as provided in G.S. 15A-773.

(d) **Return.** --

(1) The officer or other employee designated as provided in subsection (b) who serves or executes a criminal process that was first created and exists only in paper form must enter the date and time of the service or execution on the process and return it to the clerk of court in the county in which issued. The officer or other employee designated as provided in subsection (b) of this section who serves or executes a copy of a criminal process that was printed in paper form as provided in G.S. 15A-301.1 shall promptly cause the date of the service or execution to be recorded as provided in that section.

(2) If criminal process that was created and exists only in paper form is not served or executed within a number of days indicated below, it must be returned to the clerk of court in the county in which it was issued, with a reason for the failure of service or execution noted thereon.

    a. Warrant for arrest -- 180 days.

    b. Order for arrest -- 180 days.

    c. Criminal summons -- 90 days or the date the defendant is directed to appear, whichever is earlier.

(3) Failure to return the process to the clerk as required by subdivision (2) of this subsection does not invalidate the process, nor does it invalidate service or execution made after the period specified in subdivision (2).

(4) The clerk to which return of a criminal process that was created and exists only in paper form is made may redeliver the process to a law-enforcement officer or other employee designated as provided in subsection (b) for further attempts at service. If the process is a criminal summons, he may reissue it only upon endorsement of a new designated time and date of appearance.

(e) **Copies to Be Made by Clerk.** --

(1) The clerk may make a certified copy of any criminal process that was created and exists only in paper form filed in his office pursuant to subsection (a) when the original process has been lost or when the process has been returned pursuant to subdivision (d)(2). The copy may be executed as effectively as the original process whether or not the original has been redelivered as provided in G.S. 15A-301(d)(4).

(2) When criminal process is returned to the clerk pursuant to subdivision (d)(1) and it appears that the appropriate venue is in another county, the clerk must make and

retain a certified copy of the process and transmit the original process to the clerk in the appropriate county.

(3) Upon request of a defendant, the clerk must make and furnish to him without charge one copy of every criminal process filed against him.

(4) Nothing in this section prevents the making and retention of uncertified copies of process for information purposes under G.S. 15A-401(a)(2) or for any other lawful purpose.

(f) **Protection of Process Server.** -- An officer or other employee designated as provided in subsection (b), and serving process as provided in subsection (b), receiving under this section or under G.S. 15A-301.1 criminal process which is complete and regular on its face may serve the process in accordance with its terms and need not inquire into its regularity or continued validity, nor does he incur criminal or civil liability for its due service.

(g) **Recall of Process -- Authority.** -- A criminal process that has not been served on the defendant, other than a citation, shall be recalled by a judicial official or by a person authorized to act on behalf of a judicial official as follows:

(1) A warrant or criminal summons shall be recalled by the issuing judicial official when that official determines that probable cause did not exist for its issuance.

(2) Any criminal process other than a warrant or criminal summons may be recalled for good cause by any judicial official of the trial division in which it was issued. Good cause includes, without limitation, the fact that:

a. A copy of the process has been served on the defendant.

b. All charges on which the process is based have been disposed.

c. The person named as the defendant in the process is not the person who committed the charged offense.

d. It has been determined that grounds for the issuance of an order for arrest did not exist, no longer exist or have been satisfied.

(3) The disposition of all charges on which a process is based shall effect the recall, without further action by the court, of that process and of all other outstanding process issued in connection with the charges, including all orders for arrest issued for the defendant's failure to appear to answer the charges.

When the process was first created and exists only in paper form, the recall shall promptly be communicated by any reasonable means to each law enforcement agency known to be in possession of the original or a copy of the process, and each agency shall promptly return the process to the court, unserved. When the process is in the Electronic Repository, the recall shall promptly be entered in the Electronic Repository, and no further copies of the process shall be printed in paper form. The recall shall also be communicated by any reasonable means to each agency that is known to be in possession of a copy of the process in paper form and that does not have remote electronic access to the Electronic Repository.

History.
1868-9, c. 178, subch. 3, s. 4; Code, s. 1135; Rev., s. 3159; C.S., s. 4525; 1957, c. 346; 1969, c. 44, s. 28; 1973, c. 1286, s. 1; 1975, 2nd Sess., c. 983, ss. 136, 137; 1979, c. 725, ss. 1-3; 1989, c. 262, s. 3; 2002-64, s. 3; 2012-149, s. 5

§ 15A-301.1. Electronic Repository

(a) The Administrative Office of the Courts shall create and maintain, in cooperation with State and local law enforcement agencies, an automated electronic repository for criminal process (hereinafter referred to as the Electronic Repository), which shall comprise a secure system of electronic data entry, storage, and retrieval that provides for creating, signing, issuing, entering, filing, and retaining criminal process in electronic form, and that provides for the following with regard to criminal process in electronic form:

(1) Tracking criminal process.

(2) Accessing criminal process through remote electronic means by all authorized judicial officials and employees and all authorized law enforcement officers and agencies that have compatible electronic access capacity.

(3) Printing any criminal process in paper form by any authorized judicial official or employee or any authorized law enforcement officer or agency.

The Administrative Office of the Courts shall assure that all electronic signatures effected through use of the system meet the requirements of G.S. 15A-101.1(5).

(b) Any criminal process may be created, signed, and issued in electronic form, filed electronically in the office of a clerk of superior court, and retained in electronic form in the Electronic Repository.

(c) Any process that was first created, signed, and issued in paper form may subsequently be filed in electronic form and entered in the Electronic Repository by the judicial official who issued the process or by any person authorized to enter it on behalf of the judicial official. All copies of the process in paper form are then

Chapter 15A

subject to the provisions of subsections (i) and (k) of this section.

(d) Any criminal process in the Electronic Repository shall be part of the official records of the clerk of superior court of the county for which it was issued and shall be maintained in the office of that clerk as required by G.S. 15A-301(a).

(e) Any criminal process in the Electronic Repository may, at any time and at any place in this State, be printed in paper form and delivered to a law enforcement agency or officer by any judicial official, law enforcement officer, or other authorized person.

(f) When printed in paper form pursuant to subsection (e) of this section, any copy of a criminal process in the Electronic Repository confers the same authority and has the same force and effect for all other purposes as the original of a criminal process that was created and exists only in paper form.

(g) Service of any criminal process in the Electronic Repository may be effected by delivering to the person to be served a copy of the process that was printed in paper form pursuant to subsection (e) of this section.

(h) The tracking information specified in subsection (i) of this section shall promptly be entered in the Electronic Repository when one or both of the following occurs:

(1) A process is first created, signed, and issued in paper form and subsequently entered in electronic form in the Electronic Repository as provided in subsection (c) of this section.

(2) A copy of a process in the Electronic Repository is printed in paper form pursuant to subsection (e) of this section.

(i) The following tracking information shall be entered in the Electronic Repository in accordance with subsections (c) and (h) of this section:

(1) The date and time when the process was printed in paper form.

(2) The name of the law enforcement agency by or for which the process was printed in paper form.

(3) If available, the name and identification number of the law enforcement officer to whom any copy of the process was delivered.

(j) The service requirements set forth in subsection (k) of this section shall apply to:

(1) Each copy of a criminal process that is first created in paper form and subsequently entered into the Electronic Repository as provided in subsection (c) of this section.

(2) Each copy of a criminal process in the Electronic Repository that is printed in paper form pursuant to subsection (e) of this section.

(k) **Service Requirements for Process Entered in the Electronic Repository. --** The copy of the process shall be served not later than 24 hours after it has been printed. The date, time, and place of service shall promptly be recorded in the Electronic Repository and shall be part of the official records of the court. If the process is not served within 24 hours, that fact shall promptly be recorded in the Electronic Repository and all copies of the process in paper form shall be destroyed. The process may again be printed in paper form at later times and at the same or other places. Subsection (f) of this section applies to each successively printed copy of the process. When service of the warrant is no longer being actively pursued, that fact shall be promptly recorded in the Electronic Repository.

(l) A law enforcement officer or agency that does not have compatible remote access to the Electronic Repository shall promptly communicate, by any reasonable means, the information required by subsection (k) of this section to the clerk of superior court of the county in which the process was issued or to any other person authorized to enter information into the Electronic Repository, and the information shall promptly be entered in the Electronic Repository.

(m) Failure to enter any information as required by subsection (i) or (k) of this section does not invalidate the process, nor does it invalidate service or execution made after the period specified in subsection (k) of this section.

(n) A warrant created and existing only in paper form is returned within the meaning of G.S. 132-1.4(k) when it is returned as provided in G.S. 15A-301(d). A warrant that exists only in electronic form in the Electronic Repository is returned within the meaning of G.S. 132-1.4(k), when it has been served or when service of the warrant is no longer being actively pursued, as either fact is entered in the Electronic Repository pursuant to subsection (k) of this section.

(o) At the time an individual is taken into custody, the custodial law enforcement agency shall attempt to identify all outstanding warrants against that individual and notify the appropriate law enforcement agencies of the location of the individual.

(p) Prior to the entry of any order of the court in a criminal case, the court shall attempt to identify all outstanding warrants against that individual, if in custody, and notify the appropriate law enforcement agencies of the location of the individual.

History.
2002-64, s. 2; 2015-48, s. 1; 2017-101, s. 1

§ 15A-302. Citation

(a) **Definition.** -- A citation is a directive, issued by a law enforcement officer or other person authorized by statute, that a person appear in court and answer a misdemeanor or infraction charge or charges.

(b) **When Issued.** -- An officer may issue a citation to any person who he has probable cause to believe has committed a misdemeanor or infraction.

(c) **Contents.** -- The citation must:

(1) Identify the crime charged, including the date, and where material, identify the property and other persons involved,

(2) Contain the name and address of the person cited, or other identification if that cannot be ascertained,

(3) Identify the officer issuing the citation, and

(4) Cite the person to whom issued to appear in a designated court, at a designated time and date.

(d) **Service.** -- A copy of the citation shall be delivered to the person cited who may sign a receipt on the original which shall thereafter be filed with the clerk by the officer. If the cited person refuses to sign, the officer shall certify delivery of the citation by signing the original, which shall thereafter be filed with the clerk. Failure of the person cited to sign the citation shall not constitute grounds for his arrest or the requirement that he post a bond. When a citation is issued for a parking offense, a copy shall be delivered to the operator of a vehicle who is present at the time of service, or shall be delivered to the registered owner of the vehicle if the operator is not present by affixing a copy of the citation to the vehicle in a conspicuous place.

(e) **Dismissal by Prosecutor.** -- If the prosecutor finds that no crime or infraction is charged in the citation, or that there is insufficient evidence to warrant prosecution, he may dismiss the charge and so notify the person cited. An appropriate entry must be made in the records of the clerk. It is not necessary to enter the dismissal in open court or to obtain consent of the judge.

(f) **Citation No Bar to Criminal Summons or Warrant.** -- If the offense is a misdemeanor, a criminal summons or a warrant may issue notwithstanding the prior issuance of a citation for the same offense. If a defendant fails to appear in court as directed by a citation that charges the defendant with a misdemeanor, an order for arrest for failure to appear may be issued by a judicial official.

(g) **Preparation of Form.** -- The form and content of the citation is as prescribed by the Administrative Officer of the Courts. The form of citation used for violation of the motor vehicle laws must contain a notice that the driving privilege of the person cited may be revoked for failure to appear as cited, and must be prepared as provided in G.S. 7A-148(b).

History.

1973, c. 1286, s. 1; 1975, c. 166, ss. 3, 27; 1983, c. 327, s. 4; 1985, c. 385; c. 764, s. 4; 1989, c. 243, s. 1; 2003-15, s. 1

§ 15A-303. Criminal summons

(a) **Definition.** -- A criminal summons consists of a statement of the crime or infraction of which the person to be summoned is accused, and an order directing that the person so accused appear and answer to the charges made against him. It is based upon a showing of probable cause supported by oath or affirmation.

(b) **Statement of the Crime or Infraction.** -- The criminal summons must contain a statement of the crime or infraction of which the person summoned is accused. No criminal summons is invalid because of any technicality of pleading if the statement is sufficient to identify the crime or infraction.

(c) **Showing of Probable Cause; Record.** -- The showing of probable cause for the issuance of a criminal summons, and the record thereof, is the same as provided in G.S. 15A-304(d) for the issuance of a warrant for arrest.

(d) **Order to Appear.** -- The summons must order the person named to appear in a designated court at a designated time and date and answer to the charges made against him and advise him that he may be held in contempt of court for failure to appear. Except for cause noted in the criminal summons by the issuing official, an appearance date may not be set more than one month following the issuance or reissuance of the criminal summons.

(e) **Enforcement.** --

(1) If the offense charged is a criminal offense, a warrant for arrest, based upon the same or another showing of probable cause, may be issued by the same or another issuing official, notwithstanding the prior issuance of a criminal summons.

(2) If the offense charged is a criminal offense, an order for arrest, as provided in G.S. 15A-305, may issue for the arrest of any person who fails to appear as directed in a duly executed criminal summons.

(3) A person served with criminal summons who willfully fails to appear as directed may be punished for contempt as provided in G.S. 5A-11.

(4) Repealed by Session Laws 1975, c. 166, s. 4.

(f) **Who May Issue.** -- A criminal summons, valid throughout the State, may be issued by any person authorized to issue warrants for arrest.

History.
1973, c. 1286, s. 1; 1975, c. 166, ss. 4, 5; 1975, 2nd Sess., c. 983, s. 138; 1983, c. 294, s. 3; 1985, c. 764, s. 5

§ 15A-304. Warrant for arrest

(a) **Definition.** -- A warrant for arrest consists of a statement of the crime of which the person to be arrested is accused, and an order directing that the person so accused be arrested and held to answer to the charges made against him. It is based upon a showing of probable cause supported by oath or affirmation.

(b) **When Issued.** --

(1) **Generally.** -- A warrant for arrest may be issued, instead of or subsequent to a criminal summons, when it appears to the judicial official that the person named should be taken into custody. Circumstances to be considered in determining whether the person should be taken into custody may include, but are not limited to, failure to appear when previously summoned, facts making it apparent that a person summoned will fail to appear, danger that the person accused will escape, danger that there may be injury to person or property, or the seriousness of the offense.

(2) Repealed by Session Laws 2018-40, s. 7.1. See editor's note for effective date and applicability.

(3) **When Citizen-initiated.** -- If the finding of probable cause pursuant to subsection (d) of this section is based solely upon an affidavit or oral testimony under oath or affirmation of a person who is not a sworn law enforcement officer, the issuing official shall not issue a warrant for arrest and instead shall issue a criminal summons, unless one of the following circumstances exists:

a. There is corroborating testimony of the facts establishing probable cause from a sworn law enforcement officer or at least one disinterested witness.

b. The official finds that obtaining investigation of the alleged offense by a law enforcement agency would constitute a substantial burden for the complainant.

c. The official finds substantial evidence of one or more of the circumstances listed in subdivision (1) of this subsection.

(c) **Statement of the Crime.** -- The warrant must contain a statement of the crime of which the person to be arrested is accused. No warrant for arrest, nor any arrest made pursuant thereto, is invalid because of any technicality of pleading if the statement is sufficient to identify the crime.

(d) **Showing of Probable Cause.** -- A judicial official may issue a warrant for arrest only when he is supplied with sufficient information, supported by oath or affirmation, to make an independent judgment that there is probable cause to believe that a crime has been committed and that the person to be arrested committed it. The information must be shown by one or both of the following:

(1) Affidavit.

(2) Oral testimony under oath or affirmation before the issuing official.

(3) Repealed by Session Laws 2021-47, s. 10(d), effective June 18, 2021, and applicable to proceedings occurring on or after that date.

If the information is insufficient to show probable cause, the warrant may not be issued. A judicial official shall not refuse to issue a warrant for the arrest of a person solely because a prior warrant has been issued for the arrest of another person involved in the same matter.

(e) **Order for Arrest.** -- The order for arrest must direct that a law-enforcement officer take the defendant into custody and bring him without unnecessary delay before a judicial official to answer to the charges made against him.

(f) **Who May Issue.** -- A warrant for arrest, valid throughout the State, may be issued by:

(1) A Justice of the Supreme Court.

(2) A judge of the Court of Appeals.

(3) A judge of the superior court.

(4) A judge of the district court, as provided in G.S. 7A-291.

(5) A clerk, as provided in G.S. 7A-180 and 7A-181.

(6) A magistrate, as provided in G.S. 7A-273.

History.
1868-9, c. 178, subch. 3, ss. 1-3; Code, ss. 1132-1134; 1901, c. 668; Rev., ss. 3156-3158; C.S., ss. 4522-4524; 1955, c. 332; 1969, c. 44, s. 27; c. 1062, s. 1; 1973, c. 1286, s. 1; 1997-268, s. 2; 2004-186, s. 15.1; 2017-176, s. 5(a); 2018-40, s. 7.1; 2021-47, s. 10(d)

§ 15A-305. Order for arrest

(a) **Definition.** -- As used in this section, an order for arrest is an order issued by a justice, judge, clerk, or magistrate that a law-enforcement officer take a named person into custody.

(b) **When Issued.** -- An order for arrest may be issued when:

(1) A grand jury has returned a true bill of indictment against a defendant who is not in custody and who has not been released from custody pursuant to Article 26 of this Chapter, Bail, to answer to the charges in the bill of indictment.

Chapter 15A

(2) A defendant who has been arrested and released from custody pursuant to Article 26 of this Chapter, Bail, fails to appear as required.

(3) The defendant has failed to appear as required by a duly executed criminal summons issued pursuant to G.S. 15A-303 that charged the defendant with a criminal offense, or a citation issued by a law enforcement officer or other person authorized by statute pursuant to G.S. 15A-302 that charged the defendant with a misdemeanor.

(4) A defendant has violated the conditions of probation.

(5) In any criminal proceeding in which the defendant has become subject to the jurisdiction of the court, it becomes necessary to take the defendant into custody.

(6) It is authorized by G.S. 15A-803 in connection with material witness proceedings.

(7) The common-law writ of capias has heretofore been issuable.

(8) When a defendant fails to appear as required in a show cause order issued in a criminal proceeding.

(9) It is authorized by G.S. 5A-16 in connection with contempt proceedings.

(c) **Statement of Cause and Order; Copy of Indictment. --**

(1) The process must state the cause for its issuance and order an officer described in G.S. 15A-301(b) to take the person named therein into custody and bring him before the court. If the defendant is to be held without bail, the order must so provide.

(2) When the order is issued pursuant to subdivision (b)(1), a copy of the bill of indictment must be attached to each copy of the order for arrest.

(d) **Who May Issue. --** An order for arrest, valid throughout the State, may be issued by any person authorized to issue warrants for arrest.

History.
1973, c. 1286, s. 1; 1975, c. 166, s. 6; 1977, c. 711, s. 21; 2003-15, s. 2; 2021-47, s. 6(a)

§§ 15A-306 through 15A-310

Reserved for future codification purposes.

ARTICLE 18
IDENTIFICATION DOCUMENTS

§ 15A-311. Consulate documents not acceptable as identification

(a) The following documents are not acceptable for use in determining a person's actual identity or residency by a justice, judge, clerk, magistrate, law enforcement officer, or other government official:

(1) A matricula consular or other similar document, other than a valid passport, issued by a consulate or embassy of another country.

(2) An identity document issued or created by any person, organization, county, city, or other local authority, except where expressly authorized to be used for this purpose by the General Assembly.

(b) No local government or law enforcement agency may establish, by policy or ordinance, the acceptability of any of the documents described in subsection (a) of this section as a form of identification to be used to determine the identity or residency of any person. Any local government policy or ordinance that contradicts this section is hereby repealed.

(c) Notwithstanding subsection (a) of this section, documents described in subdivision (2) of subsection (a) of this section may be used by a law enforcement officer to assist in determining the identity or residency of a person when they are the only documents providing an indication of identity or residency available to the law enforcement officer at the time.

History.
2015-264, s. 36.3; 2015-294, s. 11

ARTICLE 19

§§ 15A-354 through 15A-400

Reserved for future codification purposes.

SUBCHAPTER 04.
ARREST

ARTICLE 20
ARREST

§ 15A-401. Arrest by law-enforcement officer

(a) **Arrest by Officer Pursuant to a Warrant. --**

(1) **Warrant in Possession of Officer.** -- An officer having a warrant for arrest in his possession may arrest the person named or described therein at any time and at any place within the officer's territorial jurisdiction.

(2) **Warrant Not in Possession of Officer.** -- An officer who has knowledge that a warrant for arrest has been issued and has not been executed, but who does not have the warrant in his possession, may arrest the person named therein at any time. The officer must inform the person arrested that the warrant has been issued and serve the warrant upon him as soon as possible. This subdivision applies even though the arrest process has been returned to the clerk under G.S. 15A-301.

(b) **Arrest by Officer Without a Warrant.** --

(1) **Offense in Presence of Officer.** -- An officer may arrest without a warrant any person who the officer has probable cause to believe has committed a criminal offense, or has violated a pretrial release order entered under G.S. 15A-534 or G.S. 15A-534.1(a)(2), in the officer's presence.

(2) **Offense Out of Presence of Officer.** -- An officer may arrest without a warrant any person who the officer has probable cause to believe:

a. Has committed a felony; or

b. Has committed a misdemeanor, and:

1. Will not be apprehended unless immediately arrested, or

2. May cause physical injury to himself or others, or damage to property unless immediately arrested; or

c. Has committed a misdemeanor under G.S. 14-72.1, 14-134.3, 20-138.1, or 20-138.2; or

d. Has committed a misdemeanor under G.S. 14-33(a), 14-33(c)(1), 14-33(c)(2), or 14-34 when the offense was committed by a person with whom the alleged victim has a personal relationship as defined in G.S. 50B-1; or

e. Has committed a misdemeanor under G.S. 50B-4.1(a); or

f. Has violated a pretrial release order entered under G.S. 15A-534 or G.S. 15A-534.1(a)(2).

(3) Repealed by Session Laws 1991, c. 150.

(4) A law enforcement officer may detain an individual arrested for violation of an order limiting freedom of movement or access issued pursuant to G.S. 130A-475 or G.S. 130A-145 in the area designated by the State Health Director or local health director pursuant to such order. The person may be detained in such area until the initial appearance before a judicial official pursuant to G.S. 15A-511 and G.S. 15A-534.5.

(c) **How Arrest Made.** --

(1) An arrest is complete when:

a. The person submits to the control of the arresting officer who has indicated his intention to arrest, or

b. The arresting officer, with intent to make an arrest, takes a person into custody by the use of physical force.

(2) Upon making an arrest, a law-enforcement officer must:

a. Identify himself as a law-enforcement officer unless his identity is otherwise apparent,

b. Inform the arrested person that he is under arrest, and

c. As promptly as is reasonable under the circumstances, inform the arrested person of the cause of the arrest, unless the cause appears to be evident.

(d) **Use of Force in Arrest.** --

(1) Subject to the provisions of subdivision (2), a law-enforcement officer is justified in using force upon another person when and to the extent that he reasonably believes it necessary:

a. To prevent the escape from custody or to effect an arrest of a person who he reasonably believes has committed a criminal offense, unless he knows that the arrest is unauthorized; or

b. To defend himself or a third person from what he reasonably believes to be the use or imminent use of physical force while effecting or attempting to effect an arrest or while preventing or attempting to prevent an escape.

(2) A law-enforcement officer is justified in using deadly physical force upon another person for a purpose specified in subdivision (1) of this subsection only when it is or appears to be reasonably necessary thereby:

a. To defend himself or a third person from what he reasonably believes to be the use or imminent use of deadly physical force;

b. To effect an arrest or to prevent the escape from custody of a person who he reasonably believes is attempting to escape by means of a deadly weapon, or who by his conduct or any other means indicates that he presents an imminent threat of death or serious physical injury to others unless apprehended without delay; or

c. To prevent the escape of a person from custody imposed upon him as a result of conviction for a felony.

Nothing in this subdivision constitutes justification for willful, malicious or criminally negligent conduct by any person which injures or endangers any person or property, nor shall it be construed to excuse or justify the use of unreasonable or excessive force.

Chapter 15A

(d1) **Duty to Intervene and Report Excessive Use of Force.** -- A law enforcement officer, while in the line of duty, who observes another law enforcement officer use force against another person that the observing officer reasonably believes exceeds the amount of force authorized by subsection (d) of this section and who possesses a reasonable opportunity to intervene, shall, if it is safe to do so, attempt to intervene to prevent the use of excessive force. Additionally, the observing officer shall, within a reasonable period of time not to exceed 72 hours thereafter, report what the officer reasonably believes to be an unauthorized use of force to a superior law enforcement officer within the agency of the observing officer, even if the observing officer did not have a reasonable opportunity to intervene. If the head of the law enforcement agency of the observing officer was involved or present during what the observing officer reasonably believes to be unauthorized use of force, the observing officer shall make the report to the highest ranking law enforcement officer of that officer's agency who was not involved in or present during the use of force.

(e) **Entry on Private Premises or Vehicle; Use of Force.** --

(1) A law-enforcement officer may enter private premises or a vehicle to effect an arrest when:

a. The officer has in his possession a warrant or order or a copy of the warrant or order for the arrest of a person, provided that an officer may utilize a copy of a warrant or order only if the original warrant or order is in the possession of a member of a law enforcement agency located in the county where the officer is employed and the officer verifies with the agency that the warrant is current and valid; or the officer is authorized to arrest a person without a warrant or order having been issued,

b. The officer has reasonable cause to believe the person to be arrested is present, and

c. The officer has given, or made reasonable effort to give, notice of his authority and purpose to an occupant thereof, unless there is reasonable cause to believe that the giving of such notice would present a clear danger to human life.

(2) The law-enforcement officer may use force to enter the premises or vehicle if he reasonably believes that admittance is being denied or unreasonably delayed, or if he is authorized under subsection (e)(1)c to enter without giving notice of his authority and purpose.

(f) **Use of Deadly Weapon or Deadly Force to Resist Arrest.** --

(1) A person is not justified in using a deadly weapon or deadly force to resist an arrest by a law-enforcement officer using reasonable force, when the person knows or has reason to know that the officer is a law-enforcement officer and that the officer is effecting or attempting to effect an arrest.

(2) The fact that the arrest was not authorized under this section is no defense to an otherwise valid criminal charge arising out of the use of such deadly weapon or deadly force.

(3) Nothing contained in this subsection (f) shall be construed to excuse or justify the unreasonable or excessive force by an officer in effecting an arrest. Nothing contained in this subsection (f) shall be construed to bar or limit any civil action arising out of an arrest not authorized by this Article.

(g) **Care of minor children.** -- When a law enforcement officer arrests an adult who is supervising minor children who are present at the time of the arrest, the minor children must be placed with a responsible adult approved by a parent or guardian of the minor children. If it is not possible to place the minor children with a responsible adult approved by a parent or guardian within a reasonable period of time, the law enforcement officer shall contact the county department of social services.

History.
1868-9, c. 178, subch. 1, ss. 3, 5; Code, ss. 1126, 1128; Rev., ss. 3178, 3180; C.S., ss. 4544, 4546; 1955, c. 58; 1973, c. 1286, s. 1; 1979, c. 561, s. 3; c. 725, s. 4; 1983, c. 762, s. 1; 1985, c. 548; 1991, c. 150, s. 1; 1995, c. 506, s. 10; 1997-456, s. 3; 1999-23, s. 7; 1999-399, s. 1; 2002-179, s. 14; 2004-186, s. 13.1; 2009-544, s. 2; 2011-245, s. 1; 2021-137, s. 1(a); 2021-138, s. 16(a)

§ 15A-402. Territorial jurisdiction of officers to make arrests

(a) **Territorial Jurisdiction of State Officers.** -- Law-enforcement officers of the State of North Carolina may arrest persons at any place within the State.

(b) **Territorial Jurisdiction of County and City Officers.** -- Law-enforcement officers of cities and counties may arrest persons within their particular cities or counties and on any property and rights-of-way owned by the city or county outside its limits.

(c) **City Officers, Outside Territory.** -- Law-enforcement officers of cities may arrest persons at any point which is one mile or less from the nearest point in the boundary of such city. Law enforcement officers of cities may transport a person in custody to or from any

Chapter 15A

place within the State for the purpose of that person attending criminal court proceedings. While engaged in the transportation of persons for the purpose of attending criminal court proceedings, law enforcement officers of cities may arrest persons at any place within the State for offenses occurring in connection with and incident to the transportation of persons in custody.

(d) **County and City Officers, Immediate and Continuous Flight.** -- Law-enforcement officers of cities and counties may arrest persons outside the territory described in subsections (b) and (c) when the person arrested has committed a criminal offense within that territory, for which the officer could have arrested the person within that territory, and the arrest is made during such person's immediate and continuous flight from that territory.

(e) **County Officers, Outside Territory, for Felonies.** -- Law-enforcement officers of counties may arrest persons at any place in the State of North Carolina when the arrest is based upon a felony committed within the territory described in subsection (b). For purposes of this subsection, law enforcement officers of counties shall include all officers of consolidated county-city law enforcement agencies.

(f) **Campus Police Officers, Immediate and Continuous Flight.** -- A campus police officer: (i) appointed by a campus law-enforcement agency established pursuant to G.S. 116-40.5(a); (ii) appointed by a campus law enforcement agency established under G.S. 115D-21.1(a); or (iii) commissioned by the Attorney General pursuant to Chapter 74E or Chapter 74G of the General Statutes and employed by a college or university which is licensed, or exempted from licensure, by G.S. 116-15 may arrest a person outside his territorial jurisdiction when the person arrested has committed a criminal offense within the territorial jurisdiction, for which the officer could have arrested the person within that territory, and the arrest is made during such person's immediate and continuous flight from that territory.

History.
1935, c. 204; 1973, c. 1286, s. 1; 1987, c. 671, s. 3; 1989, c. 518, s. 4; 1991 (Reg. Sess., 1992), c. 1043, s. 3; 1995, c. 206, s. 1; 1999-68, s. 2; 2005-231, s. 7; 2007-45, s. 1

§ 15A-403. Arrest by officers from other states

(a) Any law-enforcement officer of a state contiguous to the State of North Carolina who enters this State in fresh pursuit and continues within this State in such fresh pursuit of a person who is in immediate and continuous flight from the commission of a criminal offense, has the same authority to arrest and hold in custody such person on the ground that he has committed a criminal offense in another state which is a criminal offense under the laws of the State of North Carolina as law-enforcement officers of this State have to arrest and hold in custody a person on the ground that he has committed a criminal offense in this State.

(b) If an arrest is made in this State by a law-enforcement officer of another state in accordance with the provisions of subsection (a), he must, without unnecessary delay, take the person arrested before a judicial official of this State, who must conduct a hearing for the purpose of determining the lawfulness of the arrest. If the judicial official determines that the arrest was lawful, he must commit the person arrested to await a reasonable time for the issuance of an extradition warrant by the Governor of this State or release him pursuant to Article 26 of this Chapter, Bail. If the judicial official determines that the arrest was unlawful, he must discharge the person arrested.

(c) This section applies only to law-enforcement officers of a state which by its laws has made similar provision for the arrest and custody of persons closely pursued within its territory.

History.
1973, c. 1286, s. 1

§ 15A-404. Detention of offenders by private persons

(a) **No Arrest; Detention Permitted.** -- No private person may arrest another person except as provided in G.S. 15A-405. A private person may detain another person as provided in this section.

(b) **When Detention Permitted.** -- A private person may detain another person when he has probable cause to believe that the person detained has committed in his presence:

(1) A felony,

(2) A breach of the peace,

(3) A crime involving physical injury to another person, or

(4) A crime involving theft or destruction of property.

(c) **Manner of Detention.** -- The detention must be in a reasonable manner considering the offense involved and the circumstances of the detention.

(d) **Period of Detention.** -- The detention may be no longer than the time required for the earliest of the following:

(1) The determination that no offense has been committed.

(2) Surrender of the person detained to a law-enforcement officer as provided in subsection (e).

(e) **Surrender to Officer.** -- A private person who detains another must immediately notify a law-enforcement officer and must, unless he releases the person earlier as required by subsection (d), surrender the person detained to the law-enforcement officer.

History.
1973, c. 1286, s. 1

§ 15A-405. Assistance to law-enforcement officers by private persons to effect arrest or prevent escape; benefits for private persons

(a) **Assistance upon Request; Authority.** -- Private persons may assist law-enforcement officers in effecting arrests and preventing escapes from custody when requested to do so by the officer. When so requested, a private person has the same authority to effect an arrest or prevent escape from custody as the officer making the request. He does not incur civil or criminal liability for an invalid arrest unless he knows the arrest to be invalid. Nothing in this subsection constitutes justification for willful, malicious or criminally negligent conduct by such person which injures or endangers any person or property, nor shall it be construed to excuse or justify the use of unreasonable or excessive force.

(b) **Benefits to Private Persons.** -- A private person assisting a law-enforcement officer pursuant to subsection (a) is:

(1) Repealed by Session Laws 1989, c. 290, s. 1.

(2) Entitled to the same benefits as a "law-enforcement officer" as that term is defined in G.S. 143-166.2, the Public Safety Employees' Death Benefit Act; and

(3) To be treated as an employee of the employer of the law-enforcement officer within the meaning of G.S. 97-2(2) (Workers' Compensation Act).

The Governor and the Council of State are authorized to allocate funds from the Contingency and Emergency Fund for the payment of benefits under subdivision (3) when no other source is available for the payment of such benefits and when they determine that such allocation is necessary and appropriate.

History.
1868-9, c. 178, subch. 1, s. 2; Code, s. 1125; Rev., s. 3181; C.S., s. 4547; 1973, c. 1286, s. 1; 1979, c. 714, s. 2; 1989, c. 290, s. 1; 2018-5, s. 35.29(b)

§ 15A-406. Assistance by federal officers

(a) For purposes of this section, "federal law enforcement officer" means any of the following persons who are employed as full-time law enforcement officers by the federal government and who are authorized to carry firearms in the performance of their duties:

(1) United States Secret Service special agents;

(2) Federal Bureau of Investigation special agents;

(3) Bureau of Alcohol, Tobacco and Firearms special agents;

(4) United States Naval Investigative Service special agents;

(5) Drug Enforcement Administration special agents;

(6) United States Customs Service officers;

(7) United States Postal Service inspectors;

(8) Internal Revenue Service special agents;

(9) United States Marshals Service marshals and deputies;

(10) United States Forest Service officers;

(11) National Park Service officers;

(12) United States Fish and Wildlife Service officers;

(13) Immigration and Naturalization Service officers;

(14) Tennessee Valley Authority officers; and

(15) Veterans Administration police officers.

(b) A federal law enforcement officer is authorized under the following circumstances to enforce criminal laws anywhere within the State:

(1) If the federal law enforcement officer is asked by the head of a state or local law enforcement agency, or his designee, to provide temporary assistance and the request is within the scope of the state or local law enforcement agency's subject matter and territorial jurisdiction; or

(2) If the federal law enforcement officer is asked by a state or local law enforcement officer to provide temporary assistance when at the time of the request the state or local law enforcement officer is acting within the scope of his subject matter and territorial jurisdiction.

(c) A federal law enforcement officer shall have the same powers as those invested by statute or common law in a North Carolina law enforcement officer, and shall have the same legal immunity from personal civil liability as a North Carolina law enforcement officer, while acting pursuant to this section.

(d) A federal law enforcement officer who acts pursuant to this section shall not be considered an officer, employee, or agent of any state or local law enforcement agency.

(e) For purposes of the Federal Tort Claims Act, a federal law enforcement officer acts within the scope of his office or employment while acting pursuant to this section.

(f) Nothing in this section shall be construed to expand the authority of federal officers to initiate or conduct an independent investigation into violation of North Carolina law.

History.

1991, c. 262, s. 1; 1991 (Reg. Sess., 1992), c. 1030, s. 8; 1993 (Reg. Sess., 1994), c. 571, s. 1; 2001-257, s. 1; 2003-36, s. 1

§§ 15A-407 through 15A-409

Reserved for future codification purposes.

ARTICLE 21

§§ 15A-410 through 15A-453

Reserved for future codification purposes.

ARTICLE 22

§§ 15A-454 through 15A-500

Reserved for future codification purposes.

SUBCHAPTER 05. CUSTODY

ARTICLE 23
POLICE PROCESSING AND DUTIES UPON ARREST

§ 15A-501. Police processing and duties upon arrest generally

Upon the arrest of a person, with or without a warrant, but not necessarily in the order hereinafter listed, a law-enforcement officer:

(1) Must inform the person arrested of the charge against him or the cause for his arrest.

(2) Must, with respect to any person arrested without a warrant and, for purpose of setting bail, with respect to any person arrested upon a warrant or order for arrest, take the person arrested before a judicial official without unnecessary delay.

(3) May, prior to taking the person before a judicial official, take the person arrested to some other place if the person so requests.

(4) May, prior to taking the person before a judicial official, take the person arrested

to some other place if such action is reasonably necessary for the purpose of having that person identified.

(5) Must without unnecessary delay advise the person arrested of his right to communicate with counsel and friends and must allow him reasonable time and reasonable opportunity to do so.

(6) Must make available to the State on a timely basis all materials and information acquired in the course of all felony investigations. This responsibility is a continuing affirmative duty.

History.

1868-9, c. 178, subch. 1, s. 7; Code, s. 1130; Rev., s. 3182; C.S., s. 4548; 1937, c. 257, ss. 1, 2; 1955, c. 889; 1969, c. 296; 1973, c. 1286, s. 1; 1975, c. 166, ss. 7, 8; 2004-154, s. 11

§ 15A-502. Photographs and fingerprints

(a) A person charged with the commission of a felony or a misdemeanor may be photographed and his fingerprints may be taken for law-enforcement records only when he has been:

(1) Arrested or committed to a detention facility, or

(2) Committed to imprisonment upon conviction of a crime, or

(3) Convicted of a felony.

(a1) It shall be the duty of the arresting law-enforcement agency to cause a person charged with the commission of a felony to be fingerprinted and to forward those fingerprints to the State Bureau of Investigation.

(a2) It shall be the duty of the arresting law enforcement agency to cause a person charged with the commission of any of the following misdemeanors to be fingerprinted and to forward those fingerprints to the State Bureau of Investigation:

(1) G.S. 14-134.3 (Domestic criminal trespass), G.S. 15A-1382.1 (Offense that involved domestic violence), or G.S. 50B 4.1 (Violation of a valid protective order).

(2) G.S. 20-138.1 (Impaired driving), G.S. 20-138.2 (Impaired driving in commercial vehicle), G.S. 20-138.2A (Operating a commercial vehicle after consuming alcohol), and G.S. 20-138.2B (Operating various school, child care, EMS, firefighting, or law enforcement vehicles after consuming alcohol).

(3) G.S. 90-95(a)(3)(Possession of a controlled substance).

(a3) It shall be the duty of the arresting law enforcement agency to cause a person charged with a crime to provide to the magistrate as much of the following information as possible for the person arrested:

(1) Name including first, last, middle, maiden, and nickname or alias.

(2) Address including street, city, and state.

(3) Drivers license number and state of issuance.

(4) Date of birth.

(5) Sex.

(6) Race.

(7) Social Security number.

(8) Relationship to the alleged victim and whether it is a "personal relationship" as defined by G.S. 50B-1(b).

(a4) It shall be the duty of the arresting law enforcement agency to cause a person who has been charged with a misdemeanor offense of assault, stalking, or communicating a threat and held under G.S. 15A 534.1 to be fingerprinted and to forward those fingerprints to the State Bureau of Investigation.

(a5) It shall be the duty of the magistrate to enter into the court information system all information provided by the arresting law enforcement agency on the person arrested.

(a6) If the person cannot be identified by a valid form of identification, it shall be the duty of the arresting law-enforcement agency to cause a person charged with the commission of:

(1) Any offense involving impaired driving, as defined in G.S. 20-4.01(24a), or

(2) Driving while license revoked if the revocation is for an Impaired Driving License Revocation as defined in G.S. 20-28.2 to be fingerprinted and photographed.

(b) This section does not authorize the taking of photographs or fingerprints when the offense charged is a Class 2 or 3 misdemeanor under Chapter 20 of the General Statutes, "Motor Vehicles." Notwithstanding the prohibition in this subsection, a photograph may be taken of a person who operates a motor vehicle on a street or highway if:

(1) The person is cited by a law enforcement officer for a motor vehicle moving violation, and

(2) The person does not produce a valid drivers license upon the request of a law enforcement officer, and

(3) The law enforcement officer has a reasonable suspicion concerning the true identity of the person.

As used in this subsection, the phrase "motor vehicle moving violation" does not include the offenses listed in the third paragraph of G.S. 20-16(c) for which no points are assessed, nor does it include equipment violations specified in Part 9 of Article 3 of Chapter 20 of the General Statutes.

(b1) Any photograph authorized by subsection (b) of this section and taken by a law enforcement officer or agency:

(1) Shall only be taken of the operator of the motor vehicle, and only from the neck up.

(2) Shall be taken at either the location where the citation is issued, or at the jail if an arrest is made.

(3) Shall be retained by the law enforcement officer or agency until the final disposition of the case.

(4) Shall not be used for any purpose other than to confirm the identity of the alleged offender.

(5) Shall be destroyed by the law enforcement officer or agency upon a final disposition of the charge.

(c) This section does not authorize the taking of photographs or fingerprints of a juvenile alleged to be delinquent except under Article 21 of Chapter 7B of the General Statutes.

(d) This section does not prevent the taking of photographs, moving pictures, video or sound recordings, fingerprints, or the like to show a condition of intoxication or for other evidentiary use.

(e) Fingerprints or photographs taken pursuant to subsection (a), (a1), or (a2) of this section may be forwarded to the State Bureau of Investigation, the Federal Bureau of Investigation, or other law-enforcement agencies.

(f) If a person is charged with an offense for which fingerprints are required pursuant to this section but the person is not arrested for that offense, the court before which the charge is pending shall order the defendant to submit to fingerprinting by the Sheriff or other appropriate law enforcement agency at the earliest practical opportunity. If the person fails to appear for fingerprinting as ordered by the court, the Sheriff or other designated agency shall so inform the court, and the court may initiate proceedings for criminal contempt against the person pursuant to G.S. 5A-15, including issue of an order for arrest pursuant to G.S. 5A-16, if necessary. The defendant shall continue to be subject to the court's order to provide fingerprints until submitted.

History.

1973, c. 1286, s. 1; 1977, c. 711, s. 22; 1979, c. 850; 1981, c. 862, s. 3; 1993, c. 539, s. 298; 1994, Ex. Sess., c. 24, s. 14(c); 1996, 2nd Ex. Sess., c. 18, s. 23.2(b); 1998-202, s. 13(f); 2007-370, s. 1; 2007-534, s. 1; 2015-195, s. 11(h); 2015-267, s. 2(a), (b); 2017-176, s. 4(a); 2019-243, s. 6

§ 15A-502.1. DNA sample upon arrest

A DNA sample shall be obtained from any person arrested for an offense designated under G.S. 15A-266.3A, in accordance with the provisions contained in Article 13 of Chapter 15A of the General Statutes.

History.

2010-94, s. 12

§ 15A-503. Police assistance to persons arrested while unconscious or semiconscious

(a) Whenever a law-enforcement officer arrests a person who is unconscious, semiconscious, or otherwise apparently suffering from some disabling condition, and who is unable to provide information on the causes of the condition, the officer should make a reasonable effort to determine if the person arrested is wearing a bracelet or necklace containing the Medic Alert Foundation's emergency alert symbol to indicate that the person suffers from diabetes, epilepsy, a cardiac condition, or any other form of illness which would cause a loss of consciousness. If such a symbol is found indicating that the person being arrested suffers from one of those conditions, the officer must make a reasonable effort to have appropriate medical care provided.

(b) Failure of a law-enforcement officer to make a reasonable effort to discover an emergency alert symbol, as required by this section, does not by itself establish negligence of the officer, but may be considered along with other evidence to determine if the officer took reasonable precautions to ascertain the emergency medical needs of the person in his custody.

(c) A person who is provided medical care under the provisions of this section is liable for the reasonable costs of that care unless he is indigent.

(d) Repealed by Session Laws 1975, c. 818, s. 1.

History.
1975, c. 306, s. 1; c. 818, s. 1

§ 15A-504. Return of released person

(a) Upon a magistrate's finding under G.S. 15A-511(c)(2) of no probable cause for a warrantless arrest, a law-enforcement officer may return the person previously arrested and any other person accompanying him to the scene of the arrest.

(b) No officer acting pursuant to this section may be held to answer in any civil or criminal action for injury to any person or damage to any property when damage results, whether directly or indirectly, from the actions of the person so released or transported.

(c) Nothing in this section shall be construed to supersede the provisions of G.S. 122C-301.

History.
1981, c. 928; 1987, c. 282, s. 3

§ 15A-505. Notification of parent and school

(a) A law enforcement officer who charges a minor with a criminal offense shall notify the minor's parent or guardian of the charge, as soon as practicable, in person or by telephone. If the minor is taken into custody, the law enforcement officer or the officer's immediate superior shall notify a parent or guardian in writing that the minor is in custody within 24 hours of the minor's arrest. If the parent or guardian of the minor cannot be found, then the officer or the officer's immediate superior shall notify the minor's next-of-kin of the minor's arrest as soon as practicable.

(b) The notification provided for by subsection (a) of this section shall not be required if:

(1) The minor is emancipated;

(2) The minor is not taken into custody and has been charged with a motor vehicle moving violation for which three or fewer points are assessed under G.S. 20-16(c), except an offense involving impaired driving, as defined in G.S. 20-4.01(24a); or

(3) The minor has been charged with a motor vehicle offense that is not a moving violation.

(c) A law enforcement officer who charges a person with a criminal offense that is a felony, except for a criminal offense under Chapter 20 of the General Statutes, shall notify the principal of any school the person attends of the charge as soon as practicable but at least within five days. The notification may be made in person or by telephone. If the person is taken into custody, the law enforcement officer or the officer's immediate supervisor shall notify the principal of any school the person attends. This notification shall be in writing and shall be made within five days of the person's arrest. If a principal receives notification under this subsection, a representative from the district attorney's office shall notify that principal of the final disposition at the trial court level. This notification shall be in writing and shall be made within five days of the disposition. As used in this subsection, the term "school" means any public or private school in the State that is authorized under Chapter 115C of the General Statutes.

History.
1983, c. 681, s. 1; 1994, Ex. Sess., c. 26, s. 1; 1997-443, s. 8.29(g)

§§ 15A-506 through 15A-510

Reserved for future codification purposes.

ARTICLE 24
INITIAL APPEARANCE

§ 15A-511. Initial appearance

(a) **Appearance before Magistrate. --**

(1) A law-enforcement officer making an arrest with or without a warrant must take the arrested person without unnecessary delay before a magistrate as provided in G.S. 15A-501.

(2) The magistrate must proceed in accordance with this section, except in those cases in which he has the power to determine the matter pursuant to G.S. 7A-273. In those cases, if the arrest has been without a warrant, the magistrate must prepare a magistrate's order containing a statement of the crime with which the defendant is charged.

(3) If the defendant brought before a magistrate is so unruly as to disrupt and impede the proceedings, becomes unconscious, is grossly intoxicated, or is otherwise unable to understand the procedural rights afforded him by the initial appearance, upon order of the magistrate he may be confined or otherwise secured. If this is done, the magistrate's order must provide for an initial appearance within a reasonable time so as to make certain that the defendant has an opportunity to exercise his rights under this Chapter.

(a1) Repealed by Session Laws 2021-47, s. 10(e), effective June 18, 2021, and applicable to proceedings occurring on or after that date.

(b) **Statement by the Magistrate.** -- The magistrate must inform the defendant of:

(1) The charges against him;

(2) His right to communicate with counsel and friends; and

(3) The general circumstances under which he may secure release under the provisions of Article 26, Bail.

(c) **Procedure When Arrest Is without Warrant; Magistrate's Order.** -- If the person has been arrested, for a crime, without a warrant:

(1) The magistrate must determine whether there is probable cause to believe that a crime has been committed and that the person arrested committed it, and in the manner provided by G.S. 15A-304(d).

(2) If the magistrate determines that there is no probable cause the person must be released.

(3) If the magistrate determines that there is probable cause, he must issue a magistrate's order:

    a. Containing a statement of the crime of which the person is accused in the same manner as is provided in G.S. 15A-304(c) for a warrant for arrest, and

    b. Containing a finding that the defendant has been arrested without a warrant and that there is probable cause for his detention.

(4) Following the issuance of the magistrate's order, the magistrate must proceed in accordance with subsection (e) and must file the order with any supporting affidavits and records in the office of the clerk.

(d) **Procedure When Arrest Is Pursuant to Warrant.** -- If the arrest is made pursuant to a warrant, the magistrate must proceed in accordance with subsection (e).

(e) **Commitment or Bail.** -- If the person arrested is not released pursuant to subsection (c), the magistrate must release him in accordance with Article 26 of this Chapter, Bail, or commit him to an appropriate detention facility pursuant to G.S. 15A-521 pending further proceedings in the case.

(f) **Powers Not Limited to Magistrate.** -- Any judge, justice, or clerk of the General Court of Justice may also conduct an initial appearance as provided in this section.

History.
1868-9, c. 178, subch. 1, s. 7; Code, s. 1130; Rev., s. 3182; C.S., s. 4548; 1973, c. 1286, s. 1; 1975, c. 166, ss. 9-11; 1975, 2nd Sess., c. 983, s. 141; 1997-268, s. 1; 2021-47, s. 10(e)

§§ 15A-512 through 15A-520

Reserved for future codification purposes.

ARTICLE 25
COMMITMENT

§ 15A-521. Commitment to detention facility pending trial

(a) **Commitment.** -- Every person charged with a crime and held in custody who has not been released pursuant to Article 26 of this Chapter, Bail, must be committed by a written order of the judicial official who conducted the initial appearance as provided in Article 24 to an appropriate detention facility as provided in this section. If the person being committed by written order is under the age of 18, that person must be committed to a detention facility approved by the Juvenile Justice Section of the Division of Adult Correction and Juvenile Justice to provide secure confinement and care for juveniles, or to a holdover facility as defined in G.S. 7B-1501(11). If the person being committed reaches the age of 18 years while held in custody, the person shall be transported by personnel of the Juvenile Justice Section of the Division, or personnel approved by the Juvenile Justice Section, to the custody of the sheriff of the county where the charges arose.

(b) Order of Commitment; Modification. -- The order of commitment must:

(1) State the name of the person charged or identify him if his name cannot be ascertained.

(2) Specify the offense charged.

(3) Designate the place of confinement.

(4) If release is authorized pursuant to Article 26 of this Chapter, Bail, state the conditions of release. If a separate order stating the conditions has been entered, the commitment may make reference to that order, a copy of which must be attached to the commitment.

(5) Subject to the provisions of subdivision (4), direct, as appropriate, that the defendant be:

a. Produced before a district court judge pursuant to Article 29 of this Chapter, First Appearance before District Court Judge,

b. Produced before a district court judge for a probable cause hearing as provided in Article 30 of this Chapter, Probable-Cause Hearing,

c. Produced for trial in the district or superior court, or

d. Held for other specified purposes.

(6) State the name and office of the judicial official making the order and be signed by that judicial official.

The order of commitment may be modified or continued by the same or another judicial official by supplemental order.

(c) Copies and Use of Order, Receipt of Prisoner. --

(1) The order of commitment must be delivered to a law-enforcement officer, who must deliver the order and the prisoner to the detention facility named therein.

(2) The jailer or personnel of the Juvenile Justice Section must receive the prisoner and the order of commitment, and note on the order of commitment the time and date of receipt. As used in this subdivision, "jailer" includes any person having control of a detention facility and "personnel of the Juvenile Justice Section" includes personnel approved by the Juvenile Justice Section.

(3) Upon releasing the prisoner pursuant to the terms of the order, or upon delivering the prisoner to the court, the jailer or personnel of the Juvenile Justice Section must note the time and date on the order and return it to the clerk. Personnel of the Juvenile Justice Section, or personnel approved by the Juvenile Justice Section, shall transport the person under the age of 18 from the juvenile detention facility or holdover facility to court and shall transfer the person back to the juvenile detention facility or holdover facility.

(4) Repealed by Session Laws 1975, 2nd Sess., c. 983, s. 142.

(d) Commitment of Witnesses. -- If a court directs detention of a material witness pursuant to G.S. 15A-803, the court must enter an order in the manner provided in this section, except that the order must:

(1) State the reason for the detention in lieu of the description of the offense charged, and

(2) Direct that the witness be brought before the appropriate court when his testimony is required.

History.

1868-9, c. 178, subch. 3, ss. 24, 32; Code, ss. 1155, 1163; Rev., ss. 3230, 3232; C.S., ss. 4597, 4599; 1973, c. 1286, s. 1; 1975, 2nd Sess., c. 983, s. 142; 2020-83, s. 8(c)

§§ 15A-522 through 15A-530

Reserved for future codification purposes.

ARTICLE 26
BAIL

PART 1
GENERAL PROVISIONS

§ 15A-531. Definitions

As used in this Article the following definitions apply unless the context clearly requires otherwise:

(1) "Accommodation bondsman" means a natural person who has reached the age of 18 years and is a bona fide resident of this State and who, aside from love and affection and release of the person concerned, receives no consideration for action as surety and who endorses the bail bond after providing satisfactory evidences of ownership, value, and marketability of real or personal property to the extent necessary to reasonably satisfy the official taking bond that such real or personal property will in all respects be sufficient to assure that the full principal sum of the bond will be realized in the event of breach of the conditions thereof. "Consideration" as used in this subdivision does not include the legal rights of a surety against a defendant by reason of breach of the conditions of a bail bond nor does it include collateral furnished to and securing the surety so long as the value of the surety's rights in the collateral do not exceed the defendant's liability to the surety by reason of a breach in the conditions of said bail bond.

(2) "Address of record" means:

a. For a defendant or an accommodation bondsman, the address entered on the bail bond under G.S. 15A-544.2, or any later address filed by that person with the clerk of superior court.

b. For an insurance company, the address of the insurance company as it appears on the power of appointment of the company's bail agent registered with the clerk of superior court under G.S. 58-71-140.

c. For a bail agent, the address shown on the bail agent's license from the Department of Insurance registered with the clerk of superior court under G.S. 58-71-140.

d. For a professional bondsman, the address shown on that bondsman's license from the Department of Insurance, as registered with the clerk of superior court under G.S. 58-71-140.

(3) "Bail agent" means any person who is licensed by the Commissioner as a surety bondsman under Article 71 of Chapter 58 of the General Statutes, is appointed by an insurance company by power of attorney to execute or countersign bail bonds for the insurance company in connection with judicial proceedings, and receives or is promised consideration for doing so.

(4) "Bail bond" means an undertaking by the defendant to appear in court as required upon penalty of forfeiting bail to the State in a stated amount. Bail bonds include an unsecured appearance bond, an appearance bond secured by a cash deposit of the full amount of the bond, an appearance bond secured by a mortgage under G.S. 58-74-5, and an appearance bond secured by at least one solvent surety. A bail bond signed by any surety, as defined in G.S. 15A-531(8)a. and b., is considered the same as a cash deposit for all purposes in this Article. Cash bonds set in child support contempt proceedings shall not be satisfied in any manner other than the deposit of cash.

(5) "Defendant" means a person obligated to appear in court as required upon penalty of forfeiting bail under a bail bond.

(5a) **House arrest with electronic monitoring.** -- Pretrial release in which the offender is required to remain at his or her residence unless the court authorizes the offender to leave for the purpose of employment, counseling, a course of study, or vocational training. The offender shall be required to wear a device which permits the supervising agency to electronically monitor the offender's compliance with the condition.

(6) "Insurance company" means any domestic, foreign, or alien surety company which has qualified under Chapter 58 of the General Statutes generally to transact surety business and specifically to transact bail bond business in this State.

(7) "Professional bondsman" means any person who is approved and licensed by the Commissioner of Insurance under Article 71 of Chapter 58 of the General Statutes and who pledges cash or approved securities with the Commissioner as security for bail bonds written in connection with a judicial proceeding and receives or is promised money or other things of value therefor.

(8) "Surety" means:

a. The insurance company, when a bail bond is executed by a bail agent on behalf of an insurance company.

b. The professional bondsman, when a bail bond is executed by a professional bondsman or by a runner on behalf of a professional bondsman.

c. The accommodation bondsman, when a bail bond is executed by an accommodation bondsman.

History.
1973, c. 1286, s. 1; 1975, c. 166, s. 12; 1995, c. 290, s. 1; c. 503, s. 1; 2000-133, s. 1; 2009-547, s. 2; 2013-139, s. 1

§ 15A-532. Persons authorized to determine conditions for release.

Judicial officials may determine conditions for release of persons in proceedings over which they are presiding, in accordance with this Article.

History.
1973, c. 1286, s. 1; 1993, c. 30, s. 1; 2021-47, s. 10(f)

§ 15A-533. Right to pretrial release in capital and noncapital cases

(a) A defendant charged with any crime, whether capital or noncapital, who is alleged to have committed this crime while still residing in or subsequent to his escape or during an unauthorized absence from involuntary commitment in a mental health facility designated or licensed by the Department of Health and Human Services, and whose commitment is determined to be still valid by the judge or judicial officer authorized to determine pretrial release to be valid, has no right to pretrial release. In lieu of pretrial release, however, the individual shall be returned to the treatment facility in which he was residing at the time of the alleged crime or from which he escaped or absented himself for continuation of his treatment pending the additional proceedings on the criminal offense.

(b) A defendant charged with a noncapital offense must have conditions of pretrial release determined, in accordance with G.S. 15A-534.

(c) A judge may determine in his discretion whether a defendant charged with a capital offense may be released before trial. If he determines release is warranted, the judge must authorize release of the defendant in accordance with G.S. 15A-534.

(d) There shall be a rebuttable presumption that no condition of release will reasonably assure the appearance of the person as required and the safety of the community if a judicial official finds the following:

(1) There is reasonable cause to believe that the person committed an offense involving trafficking in a controlled substance;

(2) The drug trafficking offense was committed while the person was on pretrial release for another offense; and

(3) The person has been previously convicted of a Class A through E felony or an offense involving trafficking in a controlled substance and not more than five years has elapsed since the date of conviction or the person's release from prison for the offense, whichever is later.

(e) There shall be a rebuttable presumption that no condition of release will reasonably assure the appearance of the person as required and the safety of the community, if a judicial official finds all of the following:

(1) There is reasonable cause to believe that the person committed an offense for the benefit of, at the direction of, or in association with, any criminal gang, as defined in G.S. 14-50.16A(1).

(2) The offense described in subdivision (1) of this subsection was committed while the person was on pretrial release for another offense.

(3) The person (i) has been previously convicted of an offense described in G.S. 14-50.16 through G.S. 14-50.20 or (ii) has been convicted of a criminal offense and received an enhanced sentence for that offense pursuant to G.S. 15A-1340.16E, and not more than five years has elapsed since the date of conviction or the person's release for the offense, whichever is later.

(f) There shall be a rebuttable presumption that no condition of release will reasonably assure the appearance of the person as required and the safety of the community, if a judicial official finds there is reasonable cause to believe that the person committed a felony or Class A1 misdemeanor offense involving the illegal use, possession, or discharge of a firearm; and the judicial official also finds any of the following:

(1) The offense was committed while the person was on pretrial release for another

felony or Class A1 misdemeanor offense involving the illegal use, possession, or discharge of a firearm.

(2) The person has previously been convicted of a felony or Class A1 misdemeanor offense involving the illegal use, possession, or discharge of a firearm and not more than five years have elapsed since the date of conviction or the person's release for the offense, whichever is later.

(g) Persons who are considered for bond under the provisions of subsections (d), (e), and (f) of this section may only be released by a district or superior court judge upon a finding that there is a reasonable assurance that the person will appear and release does not pose an unreasonable risk of harm to the community.

History.

1973, c. 1286, s. 1; 1981, c. 936, s. 2; 1997-443, s. 11A.118(a); 1998-208, s. 1; 2008-214, s. 4; 2013-298, s. 1; 2017-194, s. 19

§ 15A-534. Procedure for determining conditions of pretrial release

(a) In determining conditions of pretrial release a judicial official must impose at least one of the following conditions:

(1) Release the defendant on his written promise to appear.

(2) Release the defendant upon his execution of an unsecured appearance bond in an amount specified by the judicial official.

(3) Place the defendant in the custody of a designated person or organization agreeing to supervise him.

(4) Require the execution of an appearance bond in a specified amount secured by a cash deposit of the full amount of the bond, by a mortgage pursuant to G.S. 58-74-5, or by at least one solvent surety.

(5) House arrest with electronic monitoring.

If condition (5) is imposed, the defendant must execute a secured appearance bond under subdivision (4) of this subsection. If condition (3) is imposed, however, the defendant may elect to execute an appearance bond under subdivision (4). If the defendant is required to provide fingerprints pursuant to G.S. 15A-502(a1), (a2), (a4), or (a6), or a DNA sample pursuant to G.S. 15A-266.3A or G.S. 15A-266.4, and (i) the fingerprints or DNA sample have not yet been taken or (ii) the defendant has refused to provide the fingerprints or DNA sample, the judicial official shall make the collection of the fingerprints or DNA sample a condition of pretrial release. The judicial official may also place restrictions on the travel, associations, conduct, or place of abode of the defendant as conditions of pretrial release. The judicial official may include as a condition of pretrial release that the defendant abstain from alcohol consumption, as verified by the use of a continuous alcohol monitoring system, of a type approved by the Division of Adult Correction and Juvenile Justice of the Department of Public Safety, and that any violation of this condition be reported by the monitoring provider to the district attorney.

(b) The judicial official in granting pretrial release must impose condition (1), (2), or (3) in subsection (a) above unless he determines that such release will not reasonably assure the appearance of the defendant as required; will pose a danger of injury to any person; or is likely to result in destruction of evidence, subornation of perjury, or intimidation of potential witnesses. Upon making the determination, the judicial official must then impose condition (4) or (5) in subsection (a) above instead of condition (1), (2), or (3), and must record the reasons for so doing in writing to the extent provided in the policies or requirements issued by the senior resident superior court judge pursuant to G.S. 15A-535(a).

(c) In determining which conditions of release to impose, the judicial official must, on the basis of available information, take into account the nature and circumstances of the offense charged; the weight of the evidence against the defendant; the defendant's family ties, employment, financial resources, character, and mental condition; whether the defendant is intoxicated to such a degree that he would be endangered by being released without supervision; the length of his residence in the community; his record of convictions; his history of flight to avoid prosecution or failure to appear at court proceedings; and any other evidence relevant to the issue of pretrial release.

(d) The judicial official authorizing pretrial release under this section must issue an appropriate order containing a statement of the conditions imposed, if any; inform the defendant in writing of the penalties applicable to violations of the conditions of his release; and advise him that his arrest will be ordered immediately upon any violation. The order of release must be filed with the clerk and a copy given the defendant and any surety, or the agent thereof who is executing the bond for the defendant's release pursuant to that order.

(d1) When conditions of pretrial release are being imposed on a defendant who has failed on one or more prior occasions to appear to answer one or more of the charges to which the conditions apply, the judicial official shall at a minimum impose the conditions of pretrial release that are recommended in any order for the arrest of the defendant that was issued for the defendant's most recent failure to appear.

If no conditions are recommended in that order for arrest, the judicial official shall require the execution of a secured appearance bond in an amount at least double the amount of the most recent previous secured or unsecured bond for the charges or, if no bond has yet been required for the charges, in the amount of at least one thousand dollars ($ 1,000). The judicial official shall also impose such restrictions on the travel, associations, conduct, or place of abode of the defendant as will assure that the defendant will not again fail to appear. The judicial official shall indicate on the release order that the defendant was arrested or surrendered after failing to appear as required under a prior release order. If the information available to the judicial official indicates that the defendant has failed on two or more prior occasions to appear to answer the charges, the judicial official shall indicate that fact on the release order.

(d2) When conditions of pretrial release are being determined for a defendant who is charged with a felony offense and the defendant is currently on probation for a prior offense, a judicial official shall determine whether the defendant poses a danger to the public prior to imposing conditions of pretrial release and must record that determination in writing. This subsection shall apply to any judicial official authorized to determine or review the defendant's eligibility for release under any proceeding authorized by this Chapter.

(1) If the judicial official determines that the defendant poses a danger to the public, the judicial official must impose condition (4) or (5) in subsection (a) of this section instead of condition (1), (2), or (3).

(2) If the judicial official finds that the defendant does not pose a danger to the public, then conditions of pretrial release shall be imposed as otherwise provided in this Article.

(3) If there is insufficient information to determine whether the defendant poses a danger to the public, then the defendant shall be retained in custody until a determination of pretrial release conditions is made pursuant to this subdivision. The judicial official that orders that the defendant be retained in custody shall set forth, in writing, the following at the time that the order is entered:

a. The defendant is being held pursuant to this subdivision.

b. The basis for the judicial official's decision that additional information is needed to determine whether the defendant poses a danger to the public and the nature of the necessary information.

c. A date, within 96 hours of the time of arrest, when the defendant shall be brought before a judge for a first appearance pursuant to Article 29 of this Chapter. If the necessary information is provided to the court at any time prior to the first appearance, the first available judicial official shall set the conditions of pretrial release. The judge who reviews the defendant's eligibility for release at the first appearance shall determine the conditions of pretrial release as provided in this Article.

(d3) When conditions of pretrial release are being determined for a defendant who is charged with an offense and the defendant is currently on pretrial release for a prior offense, the judicial official may require the execution of a secured appearance bond in an amount at least double the amount of the most recent previous secured or unsecured bond for the charges or, if no bond has yet been required for the charges, in the amount of at least one thousand dollars ($ 1,000).

(e) A magistrate or a clerk may modify his pretrial release order at any time prior to the first appearance before the district court judge. At or after such first appearance, except when the conditions of pretrial release have been reviewed by the superior court pursuant to G.S. 15A-539, a district court judge may modify a pretrial release order of the magistrate or clerk or any pretrial release order entered by him at any time prior to:

(1) In a misdemeanor case tried in the district court, the noting of an appeal; and

(2) In a case in the original trial jurisdiction of the superior court, the binding of the defendant over to superior court after the holding, or waiver, of a probable-cause hearing.

After a case is before the superior court, a superior court judge may modify the pretrial release order of a magistrate, clerk, or district court judge, or any such order entered by him, at any time prior to the time set out in G.S. 15A-536(a).

(f) For good cause shown any judge may at any time revoke an order of pretrial release. Upon application of any defendant whose order of pretrial release has been revoked, the judge must set new conditions of pretrial release in accordance with this Article.

(g) In imposing conditions of pretrial release and in modifying and revoking orders of release under this section, the judicial official must take into account all evidence available to him which he considers reliable and is not strictly bound by the rules of evidence applicable to criminal trials.

(h) A bail bond posted pursuant to this section is effective and binding upon the obligor throughout all stages of the proceeding in the trial division of the General Court of Justice until the entry of judgment in the district court from which no appeal is taken or the entry of judgment in the superior court. The obligation of an obligor, however, is terminated at an earlier time if:

(1) A judge authorized to do so releases the obligor from his bond; or

(2) The principal is surrendered by a surety in accordance with G.S. 15A-540; or

(3) The proceeding is terminated by voluntary dismissal by the State before forfeiture is ordered under G.S. 15A-544.3; or

(4) Prayer for judgment has been continued indefinitely in the district court; or

(5) The court has placed the defendant on probation pursuant to a deferred prosecution or conditional discharge.

(i) Repealed by Session Laws 2012-146, s. 1(b), effective December 1, 2012.

History.
1973, c. 1286, s. 1; 1975, c. 166, s. 13; 1977, 2nd Sess., c. 1134, s. 5; 1987, c. 481, s. 1; 1989, c. 259; 2001-487, s. 46.5(b); 2009-412, s. 1; 2009-547, ss. 3, 4, 4.1; 2010-94, s. 12.1; 2010-96, s. 3; 2011-191, s. 5; 2012-146, s. 1(a), (b); 2013-298, s. 2; 2015-195, s. 11(n); 2015-247, s. 9(a); 2016-107, s. 1; 2017-186, s. 2(ww).

§ 15A-534.1. Crimes of domestic violence; bail and pretrial release

(a) In all cases in which the defendant is charged with assault on, stalking, communicating a threat to, or committing a felony provided in Articles 7B, 8, 10, or 15 of Chapter 14 of the General Statutes upon a spouse or former spouse, a person with whom the defendant lives or has lived as if married, or a person with whom the defendant is or has been in a dating relationship as defined in G.S. 50B-1(b)(6), with domestic criminal trespass, or with violation of an order entered pursuant to Chapter 50B, Domestic Violence, of the General Statutes, the judicial official who determines the conditions of pretrial release shall be a judge. The judge shall direct a law enforcement officer or a district attorney to provide a criminal history report for the defendant and shall consider the criminal history when setting conditions of release. After setting conditions of release, the judge shall return the report to the providing agency or department. No judge shall unreasonably delay the determination of conditions of pretrial release for the purpose of reviewing the defendant's criminal history report. The following provisions shall apply in addition to the provisions of G.S. 15A-534:

(1) Upon a determination by the judge that the immediate release of the defendant will pose a danger of injury to the alleged victim or to any other person or is likely to result in intimidation of the alleged victim

and upon a determination that the execution of an appearance bond as required by G.S. 15A-534 will not reasonably assure that such injury or intimidation will not occur, a judge may retain the defendant in custody for a reasonable period of time while determining the conditions of pretrial release.

(2) A judge may impose the following conditions on pretrial release:

a. That the defendant stay away from the home, school, business or place of employment of the alleged victim.

b. That the defendant refrain from assaulting, beating, molesting, or wounding the alleged victim.

c. That the defendant refrain from removing, damaging or injuring specifically identified property.

d. That the defendant may visit his or her child or children at times and places provided by the terms of any existing order entered by a judge.

e. That the defendant abstain from alcohol consumption, as verified by the use of a continuous alcohol monitoring system, of a type approved by the Division of Adult Correction and Juvenile Justice of the Department of Public Safety, and that any violation of this condition be reported by the monitoring provider to the district attorney.

The conditions set forth above may be imposed in addition to requiring that the defendant execute a secured appearance bond.

(3) Should the defendant be mentally ill and dangerous to himself or others or a substance abuser and dangerous to himself or others, the provisions of Article 5 of Chapter 122C of the General Statutes shall apply.

(b) A defendant may be retained in custody not more than 48 hours from the time of arrest without a determination being made under this section by a judge. If a judge has not acted pursuant to this section within 48 hours of arrest, the magistrate shall act under the provisions of this section.

History.

1979, c. 561, s. 4; 1989, c. 290, s. 2; 1995, c. 527, s. 3; 2001-518, s. 2; 2007-14, s. 1; 2010-135, s. 1; 2012-146, s. 2; 2015-62, s. 4(c); 2015-181, s. 47; 2017-186, s. 2(xx).

§ 15A-534.2. Detention of impaired drivers

(a) A judicial official conducting an initial appearance for an offense involving impaired driving, as defined in G.S. 20-4.01(24a), must follow the procedure in G.S. 15A-511 except as modified by this section. This section may not be interpreted to impede a defendant's right to communicate with counsel and friends.

(b) If at the time of the initial appearance the judicial official finds by clear and convincing evidence that the impairment of the defendant's physical or mental faculties presents a danger, if he is released, of physical injury to himself or others or damage to property, the judicial official must order that the defendant be held in custody and inform the defendant that he will be held in custody until one of the requirements of subsection (c) is met; provided, however, that the judicial official must at this time determine the appropriate conditions of pretrial release in accordance with G.S. 15A-534.

(c) A defendant subject to detention under this section has the right to pretrial release under G.S. 15A-534 when the judicial official determines either that:

(1) The defendant's physical and mental faculties are no longer impaired to the extent that he presents a danger of physical injury to himself or others or of damage to property if he is released; or

(2) A sober, responsible adult is willing and able to assume responsibility for the defendant until his physical and mental faculties are no longer impaired. If the defendant is released to the custody of another, the judicial official may impose any other condition of pretrial release authorized by G.S. 15A-534, including a requirement that the defendant execute a secured appearance bond.

The defendant may be denied pretrial release under this section for a period no longer than 24 hours, and after such detention may be released only upon meeting the conditions of pretrial release set in accordance with G.S. 15A-534. If the defendant is detained for 24 hours, a judicial official must immediately determine the appropriate conditions of pretrial release in accordance with G.S. 15A-534.

(d) In making his determination whether a defendant detained under this section remains impaired, the judicial official may request that the defendant submit to periodic tests to determine his alcohol concentration. Instruments acceptable for making preliminary breath tests under G.S. 20-16.3 may be used for this purpose as well as instruments for making evidentiary chemical analyses. Unless there is evidence that the defendant is still impaired from a combination of alcohol and some other impairing substance or condition, a judicial official must determine that a defendant with an alcohol concentration less than 0.05 is no longer impaired. The results of any periodic test to determine alcohol concentration may not be introduced in evidence:

(1) Against the defendant by the State in any criminal, civil, or administrative proceeding arising out of an offense involving impaired driving; or

(2) For any purpose in any proceeding if the test was not performed by a method approved by the Commission for Public Health under G.S. 20-139.1 and by a person licensed to administer the test by the Department of Health and Human Services.

The fact that a defendant refused to comply with a judicial official's request that he submit to a chemical analysis may not be admitted into evidence in any criminal action, administrative proceeding, or a civil action to review a decision reached by an administrative agency in which the defendant is a party.

History.
1983, c. 435, s. 4; 1997-443, s. 11A.118(a); 2007-182, s. 2

§ 15A-534.3. Detention for communicable diseases

If a judicial official conducting an initial appearance or first appearance hearing finds probable cause that an individual had a nonsexual exposure to the defendant in a manner that poses a significant risk of transmission of the AIDS virus or Hepatitis B by such defendant, the judicial official shall order the defendant to be detained for a reasonable period of time, not to exceed 24 hours, for investigation by public health officials and for testing for AIDS virus infection and Hepatitis B infection if required by public health officials pursuant to G.S. 130A-144 and G.S. 130A-148.

History.
1989, c. 499, s. 1; 2009-501, s. 1

§ 15A-534.4. Sex offenses and crimes of violence against child victims: bail and pretrial release

(a) In all cases in which the defendant is charged with felonious or misdemeanor child abuse, with taking indecent liberties with a minor in violation of G.S. 14-202.1, with rape or any other sex offense in violation of Article 7B, Chapter 14 of the General Statutes, against a minor victim, with incest with a minor in violation of G.S. 14-178, with kidnapping, abduction, or felonious restraint involving a minor victim, with a violation of G.S. 14-320.1, with assault or any other crime of violence against a minor victim, or with communicating a threat against a minor victim, in addition to the provisions of G.S. 15A-534 a judicial official shall impose the following conditions on pretrial release:

(1) That the defendant stay away from the home, temporary residence, school, business, or place of employment of the alleged victim.

(2) That the defendant refrain from communicating or attempting to communicate, directly or indirectly, with the victim, except under circumstances specified in an order entered by a judge with knowledge of the pending charges.

(3) That the defendant refrain from assaulting, beating, intimidating, stalking, threatening, or harming the alleged victim.

The conditions set forth above shall be imposed in addition to any other conditions that the judicial official may impose on pretrial release.

(b) Notwithstanding the provisions of subsection (a) of this section, upon request of the defendant, the judicial official may waive one or more of the conditions required by subdivisions (1) and (2) of subsection (a) of this section if the judicial official makes written findings of fact that it is not in the best interest of the alleged victim that the condition be imposed on the defendant.

History.
1993 (Reg. Sess., 1994), c. 723, s. 5; 2007-172, s. 1; 2015-181, s. 47

§ 15A-534.5. Detention to protect public health

If a judicial official conducting an initial appearance finds by clear and convincing evidence that a person arrested for violation of an order limiting freedom of movement or access issued pursuant to G.S. 130A-475 or G.S. 130A-145 poses a threat to the health and safety of others, the judicial official shall deny pretrial release and shall order the person to be confined in an area or facility designated by the judicial official. Such pretrial confinement shall terminate when a judicial official determines that the confined person does not pose a threat to the health and safety of others. These determinations shall be made only after the State Health Director or local health director has made recommendations to the court.

History.
2002-179, s. 15

§ 15A-534.6. Bail in cases of manufacture of methamphetamine

In all cases in which the defendant is charged with any violation of G.S. 90-95(b)(1a) or G.S. 90-95(d1)(2)b., in determining bond and other conditions of release, the magistrate, judge, or court shall consider any evidence that the person is in any manner dependent upon methamphetamine or has a pattern of regular illegal use of methamphetamine. A rebuttable presumption that no conditions of release on bond would assure the safety of the community or any person therein shall arise if the State shows by clear and convincing evidence both:

(1) The person was arrested for a violation of G.S. 90-95(b)(1a) or G.S. 90-95(d1)(2) b., relating to the manufacture of methamphetamine or possession of an immediate precursor chemical with knowledge or reasonable cause to know that the chemical will be used to manufacture methamphetamine.

(2) The person is in any manner dependent upon methamphetamine or has a pattern of regular illegal use of methamphetamine, and the violation referred to in subdivision (1) of this section was committed or attempted in order to maintain or facilitate the dependence or pattern of illegal use in any manner.

History.
2005-434, s. 6; 2007-484, s. 4

§ 15A-534.7. Communicating a threat of mass violence; bail and pretrial release

(a) In all cases in which the defendant is charged with communicating a threat of mass violence on educational property in violation of G.S. 14-277.6 or communicating a threat of mass violence at a place of religious worship in violation of G.S. 14-277.7, except as provided in subsection (b) of this section, the judicial official who determines the conditions of pretrial release shall be a judge. The judge shall direct a law enforcement officer or a district attorney to provide a criminal history report for the defendant and shall consider the criminal history when setting conditions of release. After setting conditions of release, the judge shall return the report to the providing agency or department. No judge shall unreasonably delay the determination of conditions of pretrial release for the purpose of reviewing the defendant's criminal history report. The following provisions shall apply in addition to the provisions of G.S. 15A-534:

(1) Upon a determination by the judge that the immediate release of the defendant will pose a danger of injury to persons and upon a determination that the execution of an appearance bond as required by G.S. 15A-534 will not reasonably assure that such injury will not occur, a judge may retain the defendant in custody for a reasonable period of time while determining the conditions of pretrial release.

(2) A judge may impose the following conditions on pretrial release:

a. That the defendant stay away from the educational property or place

of religious worship against which the threat was communicated.

b. That the defendant stay away from any other educational property or place of religious worship unless permission to be present is granted by the person in control of the property.

The conditions set forth in this subdivision may be imposed in addition to requiring that the defendant execute a secured appearance bond.

(3) Should the defendant be mentally ill and dangerous to himself or herself or others or a substance abuser and dangerous to himself or herself or others, the provisions of Article 5 of Chapter 122C of the General Statutes shall apply.

(b) A defendant may be retained in custody not more than 48 hours from the time of arrest without a determination being made under this section by a judge. If a judge has not acted pursuant to this section within 48 hours of arrest, the magistrate shall act under the provisions of this section.

History.
2018-72, s. 6

§ 15A-535. Issuance of policies on pretrial release

(a) Subject to the provisions of this Article, the senior resident superior court judge for each district or set of districts as defined in G.S. 7A-41.1(a) in consultation with the chief district court judge or judges of all the district court districts in which are located any of the counties in the senior resident superior court judge's district or set of districts, must devise and issue recommended policies to be followed within each of those counties in determining whether, and upon what conditions, a defendant may be released before trial and may include in such policies, or issue separately, a requirement that each judicial official who imposes condition (4) or (5) in G.S. 15A-534(a) must record the reasons for doing so in writing.

(b) In any county in which there is a pretrial release program, the senior resident superior court judge may, after consultation with the chief district court judge, order that defendants accepted by such program for supervision shall, with their consent, be released by judicial officials to supervision of such programs, and subject to its rules and regulations, in lieu of releasing the defendants on conditions (1), (2), or (3) of G.S. 15A-534(a).

History.
1973, c. 1286, s. 1; 1975, c. 791, s. 1; 1987, c. 481, s. 2; 1987 (Reg. Sess., 1988), c. 1037, s. 55; 2009-547, s. 5

Chapter 15A

§ 15A-536. Release after conviction in the superior court

(a) A defendant whose guilt has been established in the superior court and is either awaiting sentence or has filed an appeal from the judgment entered may be ordered released upon conditions in accordance with the provisions of this Article.

(b) If release is ordered, the judge must impose the conditions set out in G.S. 15A-534(a) which will reasonably assure the presence of the defendant when required and provide adequate protection to persons and the community. If no single condition gives the assurance, the judge may impose the condition in G.S. 15A-534(a)(3) in addition to any other condition and may also, or in lieu of the condition in G.S. 15A-534(a)(3), place restrictions on the travel, associations, conduct, or place of abode of the defendant.

(c) In determining what conditions of release to impose, the judge must, on the basis of available information, consider the appropriate factors set out in G.S. 15A-534(c).

(d) A judge authorizing release of a defendant under this section must issue an appropriate order containing a statement of the conditions imposed, if any; inform the defendant in writing of the penalties applicable to violations of the conditions of his release; and advise him that his arrest will be ordered immediately upon any such violation. The order of release must be filed with the clerk and a copy given the defendant.

(e) An order of release may be modified or revoked by any superior court judge who has ordered the release of a defendant under this section or, if that judge is absent from the superior court district or set of districts as defined in G.S. 7A-41.1, by any other superior court judge. If the defendant is placed in custody as the result of a revocation or modification of an order of release, the defendant is entitled to an immediate hearing on whether he is again entitled to release and, if so, upon what conditions.

(f) In imposing conditions of release and in modifying and revoking orders of release under this section, the judge must take into account all evidence available to him which he considers reliable and is not strictly bound by the rules of evidence applicable to criminal trials.

History.
1973, c. 1286, s. 1; 1987 (Reg. Sess., 1988), c. 1037, s. 56

§ 15A-537. Persons authorized to effect release

(a) Following any authorization of release of any person in accordance with the provisions of this Article, any judicial official must effect the release of that person upon satisfying himself that the conditions of release have been met.

In the absence of a judicial official, any law-enforcement officer or custodial official having the person in custody must effect the release upon satisfying himself that the conditions of release have been met, but law-enforcement and custodial agencies may administratively direct which officers or officials are authorized to effect release under this section. Satisfying oneself whether conditions of release are met includes determining if sureties are sufficiently solvent to meet the bond obligation, but no judicial official, officer, or custodial official may be held civilly liable for actions taken in good faith under this section.

(b) Upon release of the person in question, the person effecting release must file any bond, deposit, or mortgage and other papers pertaining to the release with the clerk of the court in which release was authorized.

(c) For the limited purposes of this section, any law-enforcement officer or custodial official may administer oaths to sureties and take other actions necessary in carrying out the duties imposed by this section. Any surety bond so taken is to be regarded in every respect as any other bail bond.

History.
1973, c. 1286, s. 1; 1977, c. 711, s. 23

§ 15A-538. Modification of order on motion of person detained; substitution of surety

(a) A person who is detained or objects to the conditions required for his release which were imposed or allowed to stand by order of a district court judge may apply in writing to a superior court judge to modify the order.

(b) The power to modify an order includes the power to substitute sureties upon any bond. Substitution or addition of acceptable sureties may be made at the request of any obligor on a bond or, in the interests of justice, at the request of a prosecutor under the provisions of G.S. 15A-539.

History.
1973, c. 1286, s. 1; 1975, c. 166, s. 27

§ 15A-539. Modification upon motion of prosecutor

(a) A prosecutor may at any time apply to an appropriate district court judge or superior court judge for modification or revocation of an order of release under this Article.

(b) A district or superior court judge may, upon motion of the State or upon the judge's own motion, and for good cause shown, conduct a hearing into the source of money or property to be posted for any defendant who is about to be released on a secured appearance bond. The court may refuse to accept offered money or property as security for the appearance bond that, because of its source, will not reasonably assure the appearance of the person as required. The State shall have the burden of proving, by a preponderance of the evidence, the facts supporting the court's decision to refuse to accept the offered money or property as security for the bond.

(c) Nothing in this section shall affect the legal rights of any surety on a bail bond, bonding company, or a professional bondsman.

History.
1973, c. 1286, s. 1; 1975, c. 166, s. 27; 2005-375, s. 1

§ 15A-540. Surrender of a defendant by a surety; setting new conditions of release

(a) **Going Off the Bond Before Breach.** -- Before there has been a breach of the conditions of a bail bond, the surety may surrender the defendant as provided in G.S. 58-71-20. Upon application by the surety after such surrender, the clerk must exonerate the surety from the bond.

(b) **Surrender After Breach of Condition.** -- After there has been a breach of the conditions of a bail bond, a surety may surrender the defendant as provided in this subsection. A surety may arrest the defendant for the purpose of returning the defendant to the sheriff. After arresting a defendant, the surety may surrender the defendant to the sheriff of the county in which the defendant is bonded to appear or to the sheriff where the defendant was bonded. Alternatively, a surety may surrender a defendant who is already in the custody of any sheriff by appearing in person and informing the sheriff that the surety wishes to surrender the defendant. Before surrendering a defendant to a sheriff, the surety must provide the sheriff with a copy of the bail bond, forfeiture, or release order. Upon surrender of the defendant, the sheriff shall provide a receipt to the surety.

(c) **New Conditions of Pretrial Release.** -- When a defendant is surrendered by a surety under subsection (b) of this section, the sheriff shall without unnecessary delay take the defendant before a judicial official, along with a copy of the undertaking received from the surety and a copy of the receipt provided to the surety. The judicial official shall then determine whether the defendant is again entitled to release and, if so, upon what conditions.

(d) A surety may utilize the services and assistance of any surety bondsman, professional bondsman, or runner licensed under G.S. 58-71-40 to effect the arrest or surrender of a defendant under subsection (a) or (b) of this section.

History.
1973, c. 1286, s. 1; 1995, c. 290, s. 2; 2000-133, s. 2; 2001-487, s. 46.5(a); 2013-139, s. 2; 2014-120, s. 12(b)

§ 15A-541. Persons prohibited from becoming surety

(a) No sheriff, deputy sheriff, other law-enforcement officer, judicial official, attorney, parole officer, probation officer, jailer, assistant jailer, employee of the General Court of Justice, other public employee assigned to duties relating to the administration of criminal justice, or spouse of any such person may in any case become surety on a bail bond for any person other than a member of his immediate family. In addition no person covered by this section may act as agent for any bonding company or professional bondsman. No such person may have an interest, directly or indirectly, in the financial affairs of any firm or corporation whose principal business is acting as bondsman.

(b) A violation of this section is a Class 2 misdemeanor.

History.
1973, c. 1286, s. 1; 1993, c. 539, s. 299; 1994, Ex. Sess., c. 24, s. 14(c)

§ 15A-542. False qualification by surety

(a) No person may sign an appearance bond as surety knowing or having reason to know that he does not own sufficient property over and above his exemption allowed by law to enable him to pay the bond should it be ordered forfeited.

(b) A violation of this section is a Class 2 misdemeanor.

History.
1973, c. 1286, s. 1; 1993, c. 539, s. 300; 1994, Ex. Sess., c. 24, s. 14(c)

§ 15A-543. Penalties for failure to appear

(a) In addition to forfeiture imposed under Part 2 of this Article, any person released pursuant to this Article who willfully fails to appear before any court or judicial official as required is subject to the criminal penalties set out in this section.

(b) A violation of this section is a Class I felony if:

(1) The violator was released in connection with a felony charge against him; or

(2) The violator was released under the provisions of G.S. 15A-536.

(c) If, except as provided in subsection (b) above, a violator was released in connection with a misdemeanor charge against him, a violation of this section is a Class 2 misdemeanor.

History.

1973, c. 1286, s. 1; 1983, c. 294, s. 4; 1993, c. 539, s. 301; 1994, Ex. Sess., c. 14, s. 16; c. 24, s. 14(c); 2000-133, s. 3

N.C. Gen. Stat. § 15A-544

Repealed by Session Laws 2000-133, s. 4, effective January 1, 2001.

PART 2
BAIL BOND FORFEITURE

§ 15A-544.1. Forfeiture jurisdiction

By executing a bail bond the defendant and each surety submit to the jurisdiction of the court and irrevocably consent to be bound by any notice given in compliance with this Part. The liability of the defendant and each surety may be enforced as provided in this Part, without the necessity of an independent action.

History.
2000-133, s. 6

§ 15A-544.2. Identifying information on bond

(a) The following information shall be entered on each bail bond executed under Part 1 of this Article:

(1) The name and mailing address of the defendant.

(2) The name and mailing address of any accommodation bondsman executing the bond as surety.

(3) The name and license number of any professional bondsman executing the bond as surety and the name and license number of the runner executing the bail bond on behalf of the professional bondsman.

(4) The name of any insurance company executing the bond as surety, and the name, license number, and power of appointment number of the bail agent executing the bail bond on behalf of the insurance company.

(b) If a defendant is released upon execution of a bail bond that does not contain all the information required by subsection (a) of this section, the defendant's order of pretrial release may be revoked as provided in G.S. 15A-534(f).

History.
2000-133, s. 6

§ 15A-544.3. Entry of forfeiture

(a) If a defendant who was released under Part 1 of this Article upon execution of a bail bond fails on any occasion to appear before the court as required, the court shall enter a forfeiture for the amount of that bail bond in favor of the State against the defendant and against each surety on the bail bond.

(b) The forfeiture shall contain the following information:

(1) The name and address of record of the defendant.

(2) The file number of each case in which the defendant's appearance is secured by the bail bond.

(3) The amount of the bail bond.

(4) The date on which the bail bond was executed.

(5) The name and address of record of each surety on the bail bond.

(6) The name, address of record, license number, and power of appointment number of any bail agent who executed the bail bond on behalf of an insurance company.

(7) The date on which the forfeiture is entered.

(8) The date on which the forfeiture will become a final judgment under G.S. 15A-544.6 if not set aside before that date.

(9) The following notice: "TO THE DEFENDANT AND EACH SURETY NAMED ABOVE: The defendant named above has failed to appear as required before the court in the case identified above. A forfeiture for the amount of the bail bond shown above was entered in favor of the State against the defendant and each surety named above on the date of forfeiture shown above. This forfeiture will be set aside if, on or before the final judgment date shown above, satisfactory evidence is presented to the court that one of the following events has occurred: (i) the defendant's failure to appear has been stricken by the court in which the defendant was required to appear and any order for arrest that was issued for that failure to appear is recalled, (ii) all charges for which the defendant was bonded to appear have been finally disposed by the court other than by the State's taking a voluntary dismissal with leave, (iii) the defendant has been surrendered by a surety or bail agent to a sheriff of this State as provided by law, (iv) the defendant has been served with an Order for Arrest for the Failure to Appear on the criminal charge in the case in question as evidenced by a copy of an official court record, including an electronic record, (v) the defendant died before or within the period between the forfeiture and the final judgment as demonstrated by the presentation of a death certificate, (vi) the defendant was incarcerated in a unit of the Division of Adult Correction and Juvenile Justice of the Department of Public Safety and is serving a sentence or in a unit of the

Federal Bureau of Prisons located within the borders of the State at the time of the failure to appear as evidenced by a copy of an official court record or a copy of a document from the Division of Adult Correction and Juvenile Justice of the Department of Public Safety or Federal Bureau of Prisons, or (vii) the defendant was incarcerated in a local, state, or federal detention center, jail, or prison located anywhere within the borders of the United States at the time of the failure to appear, and the district attorney for the county in which the charges are pending was notified of the defendant's incarceration while the defendant was still incarcerated and the defendant remains incarcerated for a period of 10 days following the district attorney's receipt of notice, as evidenced by a copy of the written notice served on the district attorney via hand delivery or certified mail and written documentation of date upon which the defendant was released from incarceration, if the defendant was released prior to the time the motion to set aside was filed. The forfeiture will not be set aside for any other reason. If this forfeiture is not set aside on or before the final judgment date shown above, and if no motion to set it aside is pending on that date, the forfeiture will become a final judgment on that date. The final judgment will be enforceable by execution against the defendant and any accommodation bondsman and professional bondsman on the bond. The final judgment will also be reported to the Department of Insurance. Further, no surety will be allowed to execute any bail bond in the above county until the final judgment is satisfied in full."

History.
2000-133, s. 6; 2007-105, s. 2; 2011-145, s. 19.1(h); 2012-83, s. 25; 2017-186, s. 2(yy)

§ 15A-544.4. Notice of forfeiture

(a) The court shall give notice of the entry of forfeiture by mailing a copy of the forfeiture to the defendant and to each surety whose name appears on the bail bond.

(b) The notice shall be sent by first-class mail to the defendant and to each surety named on the bond at the surety's address of record.

(c) If a bail agent on behalf of an insurance company executed the bond, the court shall also provide a copy of the forfeiture to the bail agent, but failure to provide notice to the bail agent shall not affect the validity of any notice given to the insurance company.

(d) Notice given under this section is effective when the notice is mailed.

(e) Notice under this section shall be mailed not later than the 30th day after the date on which the defendant fails to appear as required and a call and fail is ordered. If notice under this section is not given within the prescribed time, the forfeiture shall not become a final judgment and shall not be enforced or reported to the Department of Insurance.

History.
2000-133, s. 6; 2009-550, s. 1

§ 15A-544.5. Setting aside forfeiture

(a) **Relief Exclusive.** -- There shall be no relief from a forfeiture except as provided in this section. The reasons for relief are those specified in subsection (b) of this section. The procedures for obtaining relief are those specified in subsections (c) and (d) of this section. Subsections (f), (g), and (h) of this section apply regardless of the reason for relief given or the procedure followed.

(b) **Reasons for Set Aside.** -- Except as provided by subsection (f) of this section, a forfeiture shall be set aside for any one of the following reasons, and none other:

(1) The defendant's failure to appear has been set aside by the court and any order for arrest issued for that failure to appear has been recalled, as evidenced by a copy of an official court record, including an electronic record.

(2) All charges for which the defendant was bonded to appear have been finally disposed by the court other than by the State's taking dismissal with leave, as evidenced by a copy of an official court record, including an electronic record.

(3) The defendant has been surrendered by a surety on the bail bond as provided by G.S. 15A-540, as evidenced by the sheriff's receipt provided for in that section.

(4) The defendant has been served with an Order for Arrest for the Failure to Appear on the criminal charge in the case in question as evidenced by a copy of an official court record, including an electronic record.

(5) The defendant died before or within the period between the forfeiture and the final judgment as demonstrated by the presentation of a death certificate.

(6) The defendant was incarcerated in a unit of the Division of Adult Correction and Juvenile Justice of the Department of Public Safety and is serving a sentence or in a unit of the Federal Bureau of Prisons located within the borders of the State at the time of the failure to appear as evidenced by a copy of an official court record or a copy of a document from the Division of Adult Correction and Juvenile Justice of

Chapter 15A

999

the Department of Public Safety or Federal Bureau of Prisons, including an electronic record.

(7) The defendant was incarcerated in a local, state, or federal detention center, jail, or prison located anywhere within the borders of the United States at the time of the failure to appear, or any time between the failure to appear and the final judgment date, and the district attorney for the county in which the charges are pending was notified of the defendant's incarceration while the defendant was still incarcerated and the defendant remains incarcerated for a period of 10 days following the district attorney's receipt of notice, as evidenced by a copy of the written notice served on the district attorney via hand delivery or certified mail and written documentation of date upon which the defendant was released from incarceration, if the defendant was released prior to the time the motion to set aside was filed.

(c) **Procedure When Failure to Appear Is Stricken.** -- If the court before which a defendant's appearance was secured by a bail bond enters an order striking the defendant's failure to appear and recalling any order for arrest issued for that failure to appear, that court may simultaneously enter an order setting aside any forfeiture of that bail bond. When an order setting aside a forfeiture is entered, the defendant's further appearances shall continue to be secured by that bail bond unless the court orders otherwise.

(d) **Motion Procedure.** -- If a forfeiture is not set aside under subsection (c) of this section, the only procedure for setting it aside is as follows:

(1) At any time before the expiration of 150 days after the date on which notice was given under G.S. 15A-544.4, any of the following parties on a bail bond may make a written motion that the forfeiture be set aside:

    a. The defendant.

    b. Any surety.

    c. A professional bondsman or a runner acting on behalf of a professional bondsman.

    d. A bail agent acting on behalf of an insurance company.

The written motion shall state the reason for the motion and attach to the motion the evidence specified in subsection (b) of this section.

(2) The motion shall be filed in the office of the clerk of superior court of the county in which the forfeiture was entered. The moving party shall, under G.S. 1A-1, Rule 5, serve a copy of the motion on the district attorney for that county and on the attorney for the county board of education.

(3) Either the district attorney or the county board of education may object to the motion by filing a written objection in the office of the clerk and serving a copy on the moving party.

(4) If neither the district attorney nor the attorney for the board of education has filed a written objection to the motion by the twentieth day after a copy of the motion is served by the moving party pursuant to Rule 5 of the Rules of Civil Procedure, the clerk shall enter an order setting aside the forfeiture, regardless of the basis for relief asserted in the motion, the evidence attached, or the absence of either.

(5) If either the district attorney or the county board of education files a written objection to the motion, then not more than 30 days after the objection is filed a hearing on the motion and objection shall be held in the county, in the trial division in which the defendant was bonded to appear.

(6) If at the hearing the court allows the motion, the court shall enter an order setting aside the forfeiture.

(7) If at the hearing the court does not enter an order setting aside the forfeiture, the forfeiture shall become a final judgment of forfeiture on the later of:

    a. The date of the hearing.

    b. The date of final judgment specified in G.S. 15A-544.6.

(8) If at the hearing the court determines that the motion to set aside was not signed or that the documentation required to be attached pursuant to subdivision (1) of this subsection is fraudulent or was not attached to the motion at the time the motion was filed, the court may order monetary sanctions against the surety filing the motion, unless the court also finds that the failure to sign the motion or attach the required documentation was unintentional. A motion for sanctions and notice of the hearing thereof shall be served on the surety not later than 10 days before the time specified for the hearing. If the court concludes that a sanction should be ordered, in addition to ordering the denial of the motion to set aside, sanctions shall be imposed as follows: (i) twenty-five percent (25%) of the bond amount for failure to sign the motion; (ii) fifty percent (50%) of the bond amount for failure to attach the required documentation; and (iii) not less than one hundred percent (100%) of the bond amount for the filing of fraudulent documentation. Sanctions awarded under this subdivision shall be docketed by the clerk of superior court as a civil judgment as provided in G.S. 1-234. The clerk of superior court shall remit the clear proceeds of the sanction to the

Chapter 15A

county finance officer as provided in G.S. 115C-452. This subdivision shall not limit the criminal prosecution of any individual involved in the creation or filing of any fraudulent documentation.

(e) **Only One Motion Per Forfeiture.** -- No more than one motion to set aside a specific forfeiture may be considered by the court.

(f) **Set Aside Prohibited in Certain Circumstances.** -- No forfeiture of a bond may be set aside for any reason in any case in which the surety or the bail agent had actual notice before executing a bail bond that the defendant had already failed to appear on two or more prior occasions in the case for which the bond was executed. Actual notice as required by this subsection shall only occur if two or more failures to appear are indicated on the defendant's release order by a judicial official. The judicial official shall indicate on the release order when it is the defendant's second or subsequent failure to appear in the case for which the bond was executed.

(g) **No Final Judgment After Forfeiture Is Set Aside.** -- If a forfeiture is set aside under this section, the forfeiture shall not thereafter ever become a final judgment of forfeiture or be enforced or reported to the Department of Insurance.

(h) **Appeal.** -- An order on a motion to set aside a forfeiture is a final order or judgment of the trial court for purposes of appeal. Appeal is the same as provided for appeals in civil actions. When notice of appeal is properly filed, the court may stay the effectiveness of the order on any conditions the court considers appropriate.

History.
2000-133, s. 6; 2007-105, s. 1; 2009-437, ss. 1, 1.1, 2; 2011-145, s. 19.1(h); 2011-377, ss. 6 -8; 2011-412, s. 4.2(a) -(c); 2012-83, s. 26; 2013-139, ss. 3, 4; 2017-186, s. 2(zz); 2018-120, s. 6.1(a)

§ 15A-544.6. Final judgment of forfeiture

A forfeiture entered under G.S. 15A-544.3 becomes a final judgment of forfeiture without further action by the court and may be enforced under G.S. 15A-544.7, on the one hundred fiftieth day after notice is given under G.S. 15A-544.4, if:

(1) No order setting aside the forfeiture under G.S. 15A-544.5 is entered on or before that date; and

(2) No motion to set aside the forfeiture is pending on that date.

History.
2000-133, s. 6

§ 15A-544.7. Docketing and enforcement of final judgment of forfeiture

(a) **Final Judgment Docketed As Civil Judgment.** -- When a forfeiture has become a final judgment under this Part, the clerk of superior court, under G.S. 1-234, shall docket the judgment as a civil judgment against the defendant and against each surety named in the judgment.

(b) **Judgment Lien.** -- When a final judgment of forfeiture is docketed, the judgment shall become a lien on the real property of the defendant and of each surety named in the judgment, as provided in G.S. 1-234.

(c) **Execution; Copy to Commissioner of Insurance.** -- After docketing a final judgment under this section, the clerk shall:

(1) Issue execution on the judgment against the defendant and against each accommodation bondsman and professional bondsman named in the judgment and shall remit the clear proceeds to the county finance officer as provided in G.S. 115C-452.

(2) If an insurance company or professional bondsman is named in the judgment, send the Commissioner of Insurance a notice of the judgment, showing the date on which the judgment was docketed.

(d) **Sureties, Professional Bail Bondsmen, Bail Agents, and Runners May Not Execute Bonds in County.** -- After a final judgment is docketed as provided in this section, no surety named in the judgment shall become a surety on any bail bond in the county in which the judgment is docketed until the judgment is satisfied in full. In addition, no professional bail bondsman, bail agent, or runner whose name appears on a bond posted in that person's licensed capacity for which a final judgment of forfeiture has been entered shall sign any bond in any licensed capacity statewide until the judgment is satisfied in full.

History.
2000-133, s. 6; 2006-188, s. 2; 2016-107, s. 2

§ 15A-544.8. Relief from final judgment of forfeiture

(a) **Relief Exclusive.** -- There is no relief from a final judgment of forfeiture except as provided in this section.

(b) **Reasons.** -- The court may grant the defendant or any surety named in the judgment relief from the judgment, for the following reasons, and none other:

(1) The person seeking relief was not given notice as provided in G.S. 15A-544.4.

(2) Other extraordinary circumstances exist that the court, in its discretion, determines should entitle that person to relief.

(c) **Procedure.** -- The procedure for obtaining relief from a final judgment under this section is as follows:

(1) At any time before the expiration of three years after the date on which a judgment of forfeiture became final, any of the following parties named in the judgment may make a written motion for relief under this section:

a. The defendant.

b. Any surety.

c. A professional bondsman or a runner acting on behalf of a professional bondsman.

d. A bail agent acting on behalf of an insurance company.

The written motion shall state the reasons for the motion and set forth the evidence in support of each reason.

(2) The motion shall be filed in the office of the clerk of superior court of the county in which the final judgment was, entered. The moving party shall, under G.S. 1A-1, Rule 5, serve a copy of the motion on the district attorney for that county and on the attorney for the county board of education.

(3) A hearing on the motion shall be scheduled within a reasonable time in the trial division in which the defendant was bonded to appear.

(4) At the hearing the court may grant the party any relief from the judgment that the court considers appropriate, including the refund of all or a part of any money paid to satisfy the judgment.

(d) **Only One Motion.** -- No more than one motion by any party for relief under this section may be considered by the court.

(e) **Finality of Judgment as to Other Parties Not Affected.** -- The finality of a final judgment of forfeiture shall not be affected, as to any party to the judgment, by the filing of a motion by, or the granting of relief to, any other party.

(f) **Appeal.** -- An order on a motion for relief from a final judgment of forfeiture is a final order or judgment of the trial court for purposes of appeal. Appeal is the same as provided for appeals in civil actions. When notice of appeal is properly filed, the court may stay the effectiveness of the order on any conditions it considers appropriate.

History.
2000-133, s. 6; 2011-377, ss. 9, 10; 2013-139, s. 5

N.C. Gen. Stat. § 15A-545

Reserved for future codification purposes.

PART 3
OTHER PROVISIONS

§ 15A-546. Contempt

Nothing in this Article is intended to interfere with or prevent the exercise by the court of its contempt powers.

History.
1973, c. 1286, s. 1

§ 15A-547. Right to habeas corpus

Nothing in this Article is intended to abridge the right of habeas corpus.

History.
1973, c. 1286, s. 1

§ 15A-547.1. Remit bail bond if defendant sentenced to community or intermediate punishment

If a defendant is convicted and sentenced to community punishment or intermediate punishment and no appeal is pending, then the court shall remit the bail bond to the obligor in accordance with the provisions of this Article and shall not require that the bail bond continue to be posted while the defendant serves his or her sentence.

History.
1995, c. 290, s. 4

§§ 15A-547.2 through 15A-547.6

Reserved for future codification purposes.

ARTICLE 27

§§ 15A-548 through 15A-574

Reserved for future codification purposes.

ARTICLE 28

§§ 15A-575 through 15A-600

Reserved for future codification purposes.

SUBCHAPTER 06.
PRELIMINARY
PROCEEDINGS

ARTICLE 29
FIRST APPEARANCE BEFORE DISTRICT COURT JUDGE

§ 15A-601. First appearance before a district court judge; consolidation of first appearance before magistrate and before district court judge; first appearance before clerk of superior court; use of two-way audio and video transmission

(a) Any defendant charged in a magistrate's order under G.S. 15A-511 or criminal process under Article 17 of this Chapter, Criminal Process, with a crime in the original jurisdiction of the superior court must be brought before a district court judge in the district court district as defined in G.S. 7A-133 in which the crime is charged to have been committed. This first appearance before a district court judge is not a critical stage of the proceedings against the defendant.

Any defendant charged in a magistrate's order under G.S. 15A-511 or criminal process under Article 17 of this Chapter, Criminal Process, with a misdemeanor offense and held in custody must be brought before a district court judge in the district court district as defined in G.S. 7A-133 in which the crime is charged to have been committed. This first appearance before a district court judge is not a critical stage of the proceedings against the defendant.

(a1) Repealed by Session Laws 2021-47, s. 10(g), effective June 18, 2021, and applicable to proceedings occurring on or after that date.

(a2) Repealed by Session Laws 2021-47, s. 10(g), effective June 18, 2021, and applicable to proceedings occurring on or after that date.

(b) When a district court judge conducts an initial appearance as provided in G.S. 15A-511, the judge may consolidate those proceedings and the proceedings under this Article.

(c) Unless the defendant is released pursuant to Article 26 of this Chapter, Bail, first appearance before a district court judge must be held within 72 hours after the defendant is taken into custody or at the first regular session of the district court in the county, whichever occurs first. If the defendant is not taken into custody, or is released pursuant to Article 26 of this Chapter, Bail, within 72 hours after being taken into custody, first appearance must be held at the next session of district court held in the county. This subsection does not apply to a defendant whose first appearance before a district court judge has been set in a criminal summons pursuant to G.S. 15A-303(d).

(d) Upon motion of the defendant, the first appearance before a district court judge may be continued to a time certain. The defendant may not waive the holding of the first appearance before a district court judge but he need not appear personally if he is represented by counsel at the proceeding.

(e) The clerk of the superior court in the county in which the defendant is taken into custody may conduct a first appearance as provided in this Article if a district court judge is not available in the county within 72 hours after the defendant is taken into custody. A magistrate may conduct the first appearance if the clerk is not available. The clerk or magistrate, in conducting a first appearance, shall proceed under this Article as would a district court judge.

History.

1973, c. 1286, s. 1; 1975, 2nd Sess., c. 983, ss. 139, 140; 1979, c. 651; 1987 (Reg. Sess., 1988), c. 1037, s. 58; 1993, c. 30, s. 2; 2021-47, s. 10(g); 2021-138, s. 14(a)

§ 15A-602. Warning of right against self-incrimination

Except when he is accompanied by his counsel, the judge must inform the defendant of his right to remain silent and that anything he says may be used against him.

History.
1973, c. 1286, s. 1

§ 15A-603. Assuring defendant's right to counsel

(a) The judge must determine whether the defendant has retained counsel or, if indigent, has been assigned counsel.

(b) If the defendant is not represented by counsel, the judge must inform the defendant that he has important legal rights which may be waived unless asserted in a timely and proper manner and that counsel may be of assistance to the defendant in advising him and acting in his behalf. The judge must inform the defendant of his right to be represented by counsel and that he will be furnished counsel if he is indigent. The judge shall also advise the defendant that if he is convicted and placed on probation, payment of the expense of counsel assigned to represent him may be made a condition of probation, and that if he is acquitted, he will have no obligation to pay the expense of assigned counsel.

(c) If the defendant asserts that he is indigent and desires counsel, the judge must proceed in accordance with the provisions of Article 36 of Chapter 7A of the General Statutes.

(d) If the defendant is found not to be indigent and indicates that he desires to be represented

1003

by counsel, the judge must inform him that he should obtain counsel promptly.

(e) If the defendant desires to waive representation by counsel, the waiver must be in writing in accordance with the provisions of Article 36 of Chapter 7A of the General Statutes except as otherwise provided in this Article.

History.
1973, c. 1286, s. 1; 1981, c. 409, s. 1

§ 15A-604. Determination of sufficiency of charge

(a) The judge must examine each criminal process or magistrate's order and determine whether each charge against the defendant charges a criminal offense within the original jurisdiction of the superior court.

(b) If the judge determines that the process or order fails to charge a criminal offense within the original jurisdiction of the superior court, he must notify the prosecutor and take further appropriate action, including one or more of the following:

(1) Dismiss the charge.

(2) Permit the State to amend the statement of the crime in the process or order.

(3) Continue the proceedings, for not more than 24 hours, to permit the State to initiate new charges.

(4) With the consent of the prosecutor, set the case for trial in the district court if the charge is found to be within the original jurisdiction of the district court.

History.
1973, c. 1286, s. 1; 1975, c. 166, s. 27

§ 15A-605. Additional proceedings at first appearance before judge

The judge must:

(1) Inform the defendant of the charges against him;

(2) Determine that the defendant or his counsel has been furnished a copy of the process or order; and

(3) Determine or review the defendant's eligibility for release under Article 26 of this Chapter, Bail.

History.
1973, c. 1286, s. 1

§ 15A-606. Demand or waiver of probable-cause hearing

(a) The judge must schedule a probable-cause hearing unless the defendant waives in writing his right to such hearing. A defendant represented by counsel, or who desires to be represented by counsel, may not before the date of the scheduled hearing waive his right to a probable-cause hearing without the written consent of the defendant and his counsel.

(b) Evidence of a demand or waiver of a probable-cause hearing may not be admitted at trial.

(c) If the defendant waives a probable-cause hearing, the district court judge must bind the defendant over to the superior court for further proceedings in accordance with this Chapter.

(d) If the defendant does not waive a probable-cause hearing, the district court judge must schedule a hearing not later than 15 working days following the initial appearance before the district court judge; if no session of the district court is scheduled in the county within 15 working days, the hearing must be scheduled for the first day of the next session. The hearing may not be scheduled sooner than five working days following such initial appearance without the consent of the defendant and the prosecutor.

(e) If an unrepresented defendant is not indigent and has indicated his desire to be represented by counsel, the district court judge must inform him that he has a choice of appearing without counsel at the probable-cause hearing or of securing the attendance of counsel to represent him at the hearing. The judge must further inform him that the judge presiding at the hearing will not continue the hearing because of the absence of counsel except for extraordinary cause.

(f) Upon a showing of good cause, a scheduled probable-cause hearing may be continued by the district court upon timely motion of the defendant or the State. Except for extraordinary cause, a motion is not timely unless made at least 48 hours prior to the time set for the probable-cause hearing.

(g) If after the first appearance before a district court judge a defendant with consent of counsel desires to waive his right to a probable-cause hearing, he may do so in writing filed with the court signed by defendant and his counsel. Upon waiver the defendant must be bound over to the superior court.

History.
1973, c. 1286, s. 1; 1975, c. 166, s. 27

§§ 15A-607 through 15A-610

Reserved for future codification purposes.

ARTICLE 30
PROBABLE-CAUSE HEARING

§ 15A-611. Probable-cause hearing procedure

(a) At the probable-cause hearing:

(1) A prosecutor must represent the State.

(2) The defendant may be represented by counsel.

(3) The defendant may testify as a witness in his own behalf and call and examine other witnesses, and produce other evidence in his behalf.

(4) Each witness must testify under oath or affirmation and is subject to cross-examination.

(b) The State must by nonhearsay evidence, or by evidence that satisfies an exception to the hearsay rule, show that there is probable cause to believe that the offense charged has been committed and that there is probable cause to believe that the defendant committed it, except:

(1) A report or copy of a report made by a physicist, chemist, firearms identification expert, fingerprint technician, or an expert or technician in some other scientific, professional, or medical field, concerning the results of an examination, comparison, or test performed by him in connection with the case in issue, when stated by such person in a report made by him, is admissible in evidence.

(2) If there is no serious contest, reliable hearsay is admissible to prove value, ownership of property, possession of property in another than the defendant, lack of consent of the owner, possessor, or custodian of property to its taking or to the breaking or entering of premises, chain of custody, authenticity of signatures, and the existence and text of a particular ordinance or regulation of a governmental unit or agency.

The district court judge is not required to exclude evidence on the ground that it was acquired by unlawful means.

(c) If a defendant appears at a probable-cause hearing without counsel, the judge must determine whether counsel has been waived. If he determines that counsel has been waived, he may proceed without counsel. If he determines that counsel has not been waived, except in a situation covered by G.S. 15A-606(e) he must take appropriate action to secure the defendant's right to counsel.

(d) A probable-cause hearing may not be held if an information in superior court is filed upon waiver of indictment before the date set for the hearing.

History.
1973, c. 1286, s. 1; 1975, c. 166, s. 27

§ 15A-612. Disposition of charge on probable-cause hearing

(a) At the conclusion of a probable-cause hearing the judge must take one of the following actions:

(1) If he finds that the defendant probably committed the offense charged, or a lesser included offense of such offense within the original jurisdiction of the superior court, he must bind the defendant over to a superior court for further proceedings in accordance with this Chapter. The judge must note his findings in the case records.

(2) If he finds no probable cause as to the offense charged but probable cause with respect to a lesser included offense within the original jurisdiction of the district court, he may set the case for trial in the district court in accordance with the terms of G.S. 15A-613. In the absence of a new pleading, the judge may not set a case for trial in the district court on any offense which is not lesser included.

(3) If he finds no probable cause pursuant to subdivisions (1) or (2) as to any charge, he must dismiss the proceedings in question.

(b) No finding made by a judge under this section precludes the State from instituting a subsequent prosecution for the same offense.

History.
1973, c. 1286, s. 1; 1975, c. 166, s. 14

§ 15A-613. Setting offense for trial in district court

If an offense set for trial in the district court under the terms of G.S. 15A-604(b)(4) or any provision of G.S. 15A-612 is a lesser included offense of the charge before the court on a pleading, the judge may:

(1) Accept a plea of guilty or no contest, with the consent of the prosecutor; or

(2) Proceed to try the offense immediately, with the consent of both the defendant and the prosecutor.

Otherwise, the judge must enter an appropriate order for subsequent calendaring of the case for trial in the district court. The trial so ordered may not be earlier than five working days nor later than 15 working days from the date of the order. The judge must note in the case records the new offense with which the defendant is charged, has been tried, or to which he entered a plea of guilty or no contest.

History.
1973, c. 1286, s. 1; 1975, c. 166, s. 27

§ 15A-614. Review of eligibility for pretrial release

Upon binding a defendant in custody over to the superior court for trial or upon entering an order for subsequent calendaring of the case of such a defendant for trial in the district court, the judge must again review the eligibility of the defendant for release under Article 26 of this Chapter, Bail.

History.
1973, c. 1286, s. 1

§ 15A-615. Testing of certain persons for sexually transmitted infections

(a) After a finding of probable cause pursuant to the provisions of Article 30 of Chapter 15A of the General Statutes or indictment for an offense that involves nonconsensual vaginal, anal, or oral intercourse; an offense that involves vaginal, anal, or oral intercourse with a child 12 years old or less; or an offense under G.S. 14-202.1 that involves vaginal, anal, or oral intercourse with a child less than 16 years old; the victim or the parent, guardian, or guardian ad litem of a minor victim may request that a defendant be tested for the following sexually transmitted infections:

    (1) Chlamydia;
    (2) Gonorrhea;
    (3) Hepatitis B;
    (3a) Herpes;
    (4) HIV; and
    (5) Syphilis.

In the case of herpes, the defendant, pursuant to the provisions of this section, shall be examined for oral and genital herpetic lesions and, if a suggestive but nondiagnostic lesion is present, a culture for herpes shall be performed.

(b) Upon a request under subsection (a) of this section, the district attorney shall petition the court on behalf of the victim for an order requiring the defendant to be tested. Upon finding that there is probable cause to believe that the alleged sexual contact involved in the offense would pose a significant risk of transmission of a sexually transmitted infection listed in subsection (a) of this section, the court shall order the defendant to submit to testing for these infections. A defendant ordered to be tested under this section shall be tested not later than 48 hours after the date of the court order. A test for HIV ordered pursuant to this section shall use the HIV-RNA Detection Test for determining HIV infection.

(c) If the defendant is in the custody of the Division of Adult Correction and Juvenile Justice of the Department of Public Safety, the defendant shall be tested by the Division of Adult

Correction and Juvenile Justice of the Department of Public Safety. If the defendant is not in the custody of the Division of Adult Correction and Juvenile Justice of the Department of Public Safety, the defendant shall be tested by the local health department. The Division of Adult Correction and Juvenile Justice of the Department of Public Safety shall inform the local health director of all test results. The local health director shall ensure that the victim is informed of the results of the tests and counseled appropriately. The agency conducting the tests shall inform the defendant of the results of the tests and ensure that the defendant is counseled appropriately. The results of the tests shall not be admissible as evidence in any criminal proceeding.

History.
1993, c. 489, s. 1; 1994, Ex. Sess., c. 8, s. 1; 2006-226, s. 10; 2006-264, s. 33(a); 2007-403, s. 1; 2011-145, s. 19.1(h); 2017-186, s. 2(aaa)

§§ 15A-616 through 15A-620

Reserved for future codification purposes.

ARTICLE 31
THE GRAND JURY AND ITS PROCEEDINGS

§ 15A-621. "Grand jury" defined

A grand jury is a body consisting of not less than 12 nor more than 18 persons, impaneled by a superior court and constituting a part of such court.

History.
1973, c. 1286, s. 1

§ 15A-622. Formation and organization of grand juries; other preliminary matters

(a) The mode of selecting grand jurors and of drawing and impaneling grand jurors is governed by this Article and Chapter 9 of the General Statutes, Jurors. Challenges to the panel from which grand jurors were drawn are governed by the procedure in G.S. 15A-1211.

(b) To impanel a new grand jury, the presiding judge must direct that the names of all persons returned as jurors be separately placed in a container. The clerk must draw out the names of 18 persons to serve as grand jurors. Of these 18, the first nine drawn serve until the first session of court at which criminal cases are heard held in the county after the following January 1, and thereafter until their replacements are selected and sworn. The next nine serve until the first session of court at which criminal cases are heard held in the county after the following July 1, and thereafter until their replacements are selected and sworn. If this formula results in any term likely to be shorter than two months or longer than 15 months, the presiding judge impaneling the grand jury may modify the terms. Thereafter, beginning with the first session of superior court at which criminal cases are heard held in the county following January 1 and July 1 of each year, nine new grand jurors must be selected in the manner provided above to replace the jurors whose terms have expired. All new grand jurors so selected serve until the first session of court at which criminal cases are heard held after January 1 or July 1 which most nearly results in a 12-month term, and thereafter until their replacements are selected and sworn. If a vacancy occurs in the membership of the grand jury, the superior court judge next convening the jury or next holding a session of court at which criminal cases are heard in the county may order that a new juror be drawn in the manner provided above to fill the vacancy.

The senior resident superior court judge of the district may impanel a second grand jury in any county of the district to serve concurrently with the first. The second grand jury shall be impaneled as provided in the first paragraph of this subsection. The court shall continue to have two grand juries until the senior resident superior court judge orders the second grand jury to terminate.

In any county the senior resident superior court judge, if he finds that grand jury service is placing a disproportionate burden on grand jurors and their employers, may fix the term of service of a grand juror at six months rather than 12 months. In doing so, he shall prescribe procedures, consistent with this section, for replacement of half of the jurors of the grand jury or grand juries approximately every three months.

(c) Neither the grand jury panel nor any individual grand juror may be challenged, but a superior court judge may:

(1) At any time before new grand jurors are sworn, discharge them, or discharge the grand jury, and cause new grand jurors or a new grand jury to be drawn if he finds that jurors have not been selected in accordance with law or that the grand jury is illegally constituted; or

(2) At any time after a grand juror is drawn, refuse to swear him, or discharge him after he has been sworn, upon a finding that he is disqualified from service, incapable of performing his duties, or guilty of misconduct in the performance of his duties so as to impair the proper functioning of the grand jury.

(d) The presiding judge may excuse a grand juror from service of the balance of his term, upon his own motion or upon the juror's request for good cause shown. The foreman may excuse individual jurors from attending particular sessions of the grand jury, except that he may not excuse more than two jurors for any one session.

(e) After the impaneling of a new grand jury, or the impaneling of nine new jurors under the terms of this section, the presiding judge must appoint one of the grand jurors as foreman and may appoint another to act as foreman during any absence or disability of the foreman. Unless removed for cause by a superior court judge, the foreman serves until his successor is appointed and sworn.

(f) The foreman and other new grand jurors must take the oath prescribed in G.S. 11-11. After new grand jurors have been sworn, the presiding judge may give the grand jurors written or oral instructions relating to the performance of their duties. At subsequent sessions of court, the presiding judge is not required to give any additional instructions to the grand jurors.

(g) At any time when a grand jury is in recess, a superior court judge may, upon application of the prosecutor or upon his own motion, order the grand jury reconvened for the purpose of dealing with a matter requiring grand jury action.

(h) A written petition for convening of grand jury under this section may be filed by the district attorney, the district attorney's designated assistant, or a special prosecutor requested pursuant to G.S. 114-11.6, with the approval of a committee of at least three members of the North Carolina Conference of District Attorneys, and with the concurrence of the Attorney General, with the Clerk of the North Carolina Supreme Court. The Chief Justice shall appoint a panel of three judges to determine whether to order the grand jury convened. A grand jury under this section may be convened if the three-judge panel determines that:

(1) The petition alleges the commission of or a conspiracy to commit a violation of G.S. 90-95(h) or G.S. 90-95.1, any part of which violation or conspiracy occurred in the county where the grand jury sits, and that persons named in the petition have knowledge related to the identity of the perpetrators of those crimes but will not divulge that knowledge voluntarily or that such persons request that they be allowed to testify before the grand jury; and

(2) The affidavit sets forth facts that establish probable cause to believe that the crimes specified in the petition have been committed and reasonable grounds to suspect that the persons named in the petition have knowledge related to the identity of the perpetrators of those crimes.

The affidavit shall be based upon personal knowledge or, if the source of the information and basis for the belief are stated, upon information and belief. The panel's order convening the grand jury as an investigative grand jury shall direct the grand jury to investigate the crimes and persons named in the petition, and shall be filed with the Clerk of the North Carolina Supreme Court. A grand jury so convened retains all powers, duties, and responsibilities of a grand jury under this Article. The contents of the petition and the affidavit shall not be disclosed. Upon receiving a petition under this subsection, the Chief Justice shall appoint a panel to determine whether the grand jury should be convened as an investigative grand jury.

A grand jury authorized by this subsection may be convened from an existing grand jury or grand juries authorized by subsection (b) of this section or may be convened as an additional grand jury to an existing grand jury or grand juries. Notwithstanding subsection (b) of this section, grand jurors impaneled pursuant to this subsection shall serve for a period of 12 months, and, if an additional grand jury is convened, 18 persons shall be selected to constitute that grand jury. At any time for cause shown, the presiding superior court judge may excuse a juror temporarily or permanently, and in the latter event the court may impanel another person in place of the juror excused.

(i) An investigative grand jury may be convened pursuant to subsection (h) of this section if the petition alleges the commission of, attempt to commit or solicitation to commit, or a conspiracy to commit a violation of G.S. 14-43.11 (human trafficking), G.S. 14-43.12 (involuntary servitude), or G.S. 14-43.13 (sexual servitude).

(j) Any grand juror who serves the full term of service under subsection (b) or subsection (h) of this section shall not be required to serve again as a grand juror or as a juror for a period of six years.

History.

1779, c. 157, s. 11, P.R.; R.C., c. 31, s. 33; 1879, c. 12; Code, ss. 404, 1742; Rev., ss. 1969, 1971; C.S., ss. 2333, 2336; 1929, c. 228; 1967, c. 218, s. 1; 1973, c. 1286, s. 1; 1975, c. 166, s. 27; 1977, c. 711, s. 24; 1979, c. 177, s. 1; 1981, c. 440, s. 1; 1985 (Reg. Sess., 1986), c. 843, ss. 2, 6; 1987 (Reg. Sess., 1988), c. 1040, ss. 1, 3; 1989 (Reg. Sess., 1990), c. 1039, s. 4; 1991, c. 686, ss. 1, 3; 1995, c. 362, s. 1; 2013-148, s. 3; 2013-368, s. 21

§ 15A-623. Grand jury proceedings and operation in general

(a) The finding of an indictment, the return of a presentment, and every other affirmative official action or decision of the grand jury requires the concurrence of at least 12 members of the grand jury.

(b) The foreman presides over all hearings and has the power to administer oaths or affirmations to all witnesses.

(c) The foreman must indicate on each bill of indictment or presentment the witness or witnesses sworn and examined before the grand jury. Failure to comply with this provision does not vitiate a bill of indictment or presentment.

(d) During the deliberations and voting of a grand jury, only the grand jurors may be present in the grand jury room. During its other proceedings, the following persons, in addition to a witness being examined, may, as the occasion requires, also be present:

(1) An interpreter, if needed.

(2) A law-enforcement officer holding a witness in custody.

Any person other than a witness who is permitted in the grand jury room must first take an oath before the grand jury that he will keep secret all matters before it within his knowledge.

(e) Grand jury proceedings are secret and, except as expressly provided in this Article, members of the grand jury and all persons present during its sessions shall keep its secrets and refrain from disclosing anything which transpires during any of its sessions.

(f) The presiding judge may direct that a bill of indictment be kept secret until the defendant is arrested or appears before the court. The clerk must seal the bill of indictment and no person including a witness may disclose the finding of the bill of indictment, or the proceedings leading to the finding, except when necessary for the issuance and execution of an order of arrest.

(g) Any grand juror or other person authorized to attend sessions of the grand jury and bound to keep its secrets who discloses, other than to his attorney, matters occurring before the grand jury other than in accordance with the provisions of this section is in contempt of court and subject to proceedings in accordance with law.

(h) If a grand jury is convened pursuant to G.S. 15A-622(h), notwithstanding subsection (d) of this section, a prosecutor shall be present to examine witnesses, and a court reporter shall be present and record the examination of witnesses. The record shall be transcribed. If the prosecutor determines that it is necessary to compel testimony from the witness, he may grant use immunity to the witness. The grant of use immunity shall be given to the witness in writing by the prosecutor and shall be signed by the prosecutor. The written grant of use immunity shall also be read into the record by the prosecutor and shall include an explanation of use immunity as provided in G.S. 15A-1051. A witness shall have the right to leave the grand jury room to consult with his counsel at reasonable intervals and for a reasonable period of time upon the request of the witness. Notwithstanding subsection (e) of this section, the record of the examination of witnesses shall be made available to the examining prosecutor, and he may disclose contents of the record to other investigative or law-enforcement officers, the witness or his attorney to the extent that the disclosure is appropriate to the proper performance of his official duties. The record of the examination of a witness may be used in a trial to the extent that it is relevant and otherwise admissible. Further disclosure of grand jury proceedings convened pursuant to this act may be made upon written order of a superior court judge if the judge determines disclosure is essential:

(1) To prosecute a witness who appeared before the grand jury for contempt or perjury; or

(2) To protect a defendant's constitutional rights or statutory rights to discovery pursuant to G.S. 15A-903.

Upon the convening of the investigative grand jury pursuant to approval by the three-judge panel, the district attorney shall subpoena the witnesses. The subpoena shall be served by the investigative grand jury officer, who shall be appointed by the court. The name of the person subpoenaed and the issuance and service of the subpoena shall not be disclosed, except that a witness so subpoenaed may divulge that information. The presiding superior court judge shall hear any matter concerning the investigative grand jury in camera to the extent necessary to prevent disclosure of its existence. The court reporter for the investigative grand jury shall be present and record and transcribe the in camera proceeding. The transcription of any in camera proceeding and a copy of all subpoenas and other process shall be returned to the Chief Justice or to such member of the three-judge panel as the Chief Justice may designate, to be filed with the Clerk of the North Carolina Supreme Court. The subpoena shall otherwise be subject to the provisions of G.S. 15A-801 and Article 43 of Chapter 15A. When an investigative grand jury has completed its investigation of the crimes alleged in the petition, the investigative functions of the grand jury shall be dissolved and such investigation shall cease. The District Attorney shall file a notice of dissolution of the investigative functions of the grand jury with the Clerk of the North Carolina Supreme Court.

History.
1973, c. 1286, s. 1; 1985 (Reg. Sess., 1986), c. 843, ss. 3, 6; 1987 (Reg. Sess., 1988), c. 1040, ss. 1, 4; 1989 (Reg. Sess., 1990), c. 1039, s. 4; 1991, c. 686, ss. 2, 3

§ 15A-624. Grand jury the judge of facts; judge the source of legal advice

(a) The grand jury is the exclusive judge of the facts with respect to any matter before it.

(b) The legal advisor of the grand jury is the presiding or convening judge.

History.
1973, c. 1286, s. 1

N.C. Gen. Stat. § 15A-625

Reserved for future codification purposes.

§ 15A-626. Who may call witnesses before grand jury; no right to appear without consent of prosecutor or judge

(a) Except as provided in this section, no person has a right to call a witness or appear as a witness in a grand jury proceeding.

(b) In proceedings upon bills of indictment submitted by the prosecutor to the grand jury, the clerk must call as witnesses the persons whose names are listed on the bills by the prosecutor. If the grand jury desires to hear any witness not named on the bill under consideration, it must through its foreman request the prosecutor to call the witness. The prosecutor in his discretion may call, or refuse to call, the witness.

(c) In considering any matter before it a grand jury may swear and hear the testimony of a member of the grand jury.

(d) Any person not called as a witness who desires to testify before the grand jury concerning a criminal matter which may properly be considered by the grand jury must apply to the district attorney or to a superior court judge. The judge or the district attorney in his discretion may call the witness to appear before the grand jury.

(e) An official who is required or authorized to call a witness before the grand jury does so by issuing a subpoena for the witness or by causing one to be issued. If the official is assured that the witness will appear when requested without issuance of a subpoena, he may call the witness simply by notifying him of the time and place his presence is requested before the grand jury.

History.
1973, c. 1286, s. 1; 1975, c. 166, s. 27

§ 15A-627. Submission of bill of indictment to grand jury by prosecutor

(a) When a defendant has been bound over for trial in the superior court upon any charge in the original jurisdiction of such court, the prosecutor, unless he dismisses the charge under the terms of Article 50 of this Chapter, Voluntary Dismissal by the State, or proceeds upon a bill of information, must submit a bill of indictment charging the offense to the grand jury for its consideration.

(b) A prosecutor may submit a bill of indictment charging an offense within the original jurisdiction of the superior court.

History.

1973, c. 1286, s. 1; 1975, c. 166, s. 27

§ 15A-628. Functions of grand jury; record to be kept by clerk

(a) A grand jury:

(1) Must return a bill submitted to it by the prosecutor as a true bill of indictment if it finds from the evidence probable cause for the charge made.

(2) Must return a bill submitted to it by the prosecutor as not a true bill of indictment if it fails to find probable cause for the charge made. Upon returning a bill of indictment as not a true bill, the grand jury may request the prosecutor to submit a bill of indictment as to a lesser included or related offense.

(3) May return the bill to the court with an indication that the grand jury has not been able to act upon it because of the unavailability of witnesses.

(4) May investigate any offense as to which no bill of indictment has been submitted to it by the prosecutor and issue a presentment accusing a named person or named persons with one or more criminal offenses if it has found probable cause for the charges made. An investigation may be initiated upon the concurrence of 12 members of the grand jury itself or upon the request of the presiding or convening judge or the prosecutor.

(5) Must inspect the jail and may inspect other county offices or agencies and must report the results of its inspections to the court.

(b) In proceeding under subsection (a), the grand jury may consider any offense which may be prosecuted in the courts of the county, or in the courts of the superior court district or set of districts as defined in G.S. 7A-41.1 when there has been a waiver of venue in accordance with Article 3 of this Chapter, Venue.

(c) Bills of indictment submitted by the prosecutor to the grand jury, whether found to be true bills or not, must be returned by the foreman of the grand jury to the presiding judge in open court. Presentments must also be returned by the foreman of the grand jury to the presiding judge in open court.

(d) The clerk must keep a permanent record of all matters returned by the grand jury to the judge under the provisions of this section.

History.

1973, c. 1286, s. 1; 1975, c. 166, s. 27; 1987 (Reg. Sess., 1988), c. 1037, s. 59

§ 15A-629. Procedure upon finding of not a true bill; release of defendant, etc.; institution of new charge

(a) Upon the return of a bill of indictment as not a true bill, the presiding judge must immediately examine the case records to determine if the defendant is in custody or subject to bail or conditions of pretrial release. If so, except as provided in subsection (b), the judge must immediately order release from custody, exoneration of bail, or release from conditions of pretrial release, as the case may be.

(b) Upon the return of a bill of indictment as not a true bill but with a request that the prosecutor submit a bill of indictment to a lesser included or related offense, the judge may defer the action required in subsection (a) for a reasonable period, not to extend past the end of that session of superior court, to allow the institution of the new charge.

History.

1973, c. 1286, s. 1; 1975, c. 166, s. 27

§ 15A-630. Notice to defendant of true bill of indictment

Upon the return of a bill of indictment as a true bill the presiding judge must immediately cause notice of the indictment to be mailed or otherwise given to the defendant unless he is then represented by counsel of record. The notice must inform the defendant of the time limitations upon his right to discovery under Article 48 of this Chapter, Discovery in the Superior Court, and a copy of the indictment must be attached to the notice. If the judge directs that the indictment be sealed as provided in G.S. 15A-623(f), he may defer the giving of notice under this section for a reasonable length of time.

History.

1973, c. 1286, s. 1; 1975, 2nd Sess., c. 983, s. 143

§ 15A-631. Grand jury venue

In the General Court of Justice, the place for returning a presentment or indictment is a matter of venue and not jurisdiction. A grand jury shall have venue to present or indict in any case where the county in which it is sitting has venue for trial pursuant to the laws relating to trial venue.

History.
1985, c. 553, s. 1

§§ 15A-632 through 15A-640

Reserved for future codification purposes.

ARTICLE 32
INDICTMENT
AND RELATED
INSTRUMENTS

§ 15A-641. Indictment and related instruments; definitions of indictment, information, and presentment

(a) Any indictment is a written accusation by a grand jury, filed with a superior court, charging a person with the commission of one or more criminal offenses.

(b) An information is a written accusation by a prosecutor, filed with a superior court, charging a person represented by counsel with the commission of one or more criminal offenses.

(c) A presentment is a written accusation by a grand jury, made on its own motion and filed with a superior court, charging a person, or two or more persons jointly, with the commission of one or more criminal offenses. A presentment does not institute criminal proceedings against any person, but the district attorney is obligated to investigate the factual background of every presentment returned in his district and to submit bills of indictment to the grand jury dealing with the subject matter of any presentments when it is appropriate to do so.

History.
1797, c. 474, s. 3, P.R.; R.C., c. 35, s. 6; 1879, c. 12; Code, s. 1175; Rev., s. 3240; C.S., s. 4607; 1973, c. 1286, s. 1; 1975, c. 166, s. 27

§ 15A-642. Prosecutions originating in superior court to be upon indictment or information; waiver of indictment

(a) Prosecutions originating in the superior court must be upon pleadings as provided in Article 49 of this Chapter, Pleadings and Joinder.

(b) Indictment may not be waived in a capital case or in a case in which the defendant is not represented by counsel.

(c) Waiver of indictment must be in writing and signed by the defendant and his attorney.

The waiver must be attached to or executed upon the bill of information.

History.
1907, c. 71; C.S., s. 4610; 1951, c. 726, ss. 1, 2; 1971, c. 377, s. 30.1; 1973, c. 1286, s. 1

§ 15A-643. Joinder of offenses and defendants and consolidation of indictments and informations

The rules with respect to joinder of offenses and defendants and the consolidation of charges in indictments and informations are provided in Article 49 of this Chapter, Pleadings and Joinder.

History.
1917, c. 168; C.S., s. 4622; 1921, c. 100; 1973, c. 1286, s. 1

§ 15A-644. Form and content of indictment, information or presentment

(a) An indictment must contain:
    (1) The name of the superior court in which it is filed;
    (2) The title of the action;
    (3) Criminal charges pleaded as provided in Article 49 of this Chapter, Pleadings and Joinder;
    (4) The signature of the prosecutor, but its omission is not a fatal defect; and
    (5) The signature of the foreman or acting foreman of the grand jury attesting the concurrence of 12 or more grand jurors in the finding of a true bill of indictment.

(b) An information must contain everything required of an indictment in subsection (a) except that the accusation is that of the prosecutor and the provisions of subdivision (a)(5) do not apply. The information must also contain or have attached the waiver of indictment pursuant to G.S. 15A-642(c).

(c) A presentment must contain everything required of an indictment in subsection (a) except that the provisions of subdivisions (a)(4) and (5) do not apply and the foreman must by his signature attest the concurrence of 12 or more grand jurors in the presentment.

History.
1973, c. 1286, s. 1; 1975, c. 166, s. 27

§ 15A-644.1. Filing of information when plea of guilty or no contest in district court to Class H or I felony

A defendant who pleads guilty or no contest in district court pursuant to G.S. 7A-272(c)(1) shall enter that plea to an information complying with G.S. 15A-644(b), except it shall contain the name of the district court in which it is filed.

History.
1995 (Reg. Sess., 1996), c. 725, s. 3

§ 15A-645. Allegations of previous convictions

Trial upon indictments and informations involving allegation of previous convictions is subject to the provisions of G.S. 15A-928.

History.
1973, c. 1286, s. 1

§ 15A-646. Superseding indictments and informations

If at any time before entry of a plea of guilty to an indictment or information, or commencement of a trial thereof, another indictment or information is filed in the same court charging the defendant with an offense charged or attempted to be charged in the first instrument, the first one is, with respect to the offense, superseded by the second and, upon the defendant's arraignment upon the second indictment or information, the count of the first instrument charging the offense must be dismissed by the superior court judge. The first instrument is not, however, superseded with respect to any count contained therein which charged an offense not charged in the second indictment or information.

History.
1973, c. 1286, s. 1

ARTICLE 33

§§ 15A-647 through 15A-673

Reserved for future codification purposes.

ARTICLE 34

§§ 15A-674 through 15A-700

Reserved for future codification purposes.

SUBCHAPTER 07.
SPEEDY TRIAL; ATTENDANCE OF DEFENDANTS

ARTICLE 35
SPEEDY TRIAL

§§ 15A-701 through 15A-710

Repealed by Session Laws 1989, c. 688, s. 1.

ARTICLE 36
SPECIAL CRIMINAL PROCESS FOR ATTENDANCE OF DEFENDANTS

§ 15A-711. Securing attendance of criminal defendants confined in institutions within the State; requiring prosecutor to proceed

(a) When a criminal defendant is confined in a penal or other institution under the control of the State or any of its subdivisions and his presence is required for trial, the prosecutor may make written request to the custodian of the institution for temporary release of the defendant to the custody of an appropriate law-enforcement officer who must produce him at the trial. The period of the temporary release may not exceed 60 days. The request of the prosecutor is sufficient authorization for the release, and must be honored, except as otherwise provided in this section.

(b) If the defendant whose presence is sought is confined pursuant to another criminal proceeding in a different prosecutorial district as defined in G.S. 7A-60, the defendant and the prosecutor prosecuting the other criminal action must be given reasonable notice and opportunity to object to the temporary release. Objections must be heard by a superior court judge having authority to act in criminal cases in the superior court district or set of districts as defined in G.S. 7A-41.1 in which the defendant is confined, and he must make appropriate orders as to the precedence of the actions.

(c) A defendant who is confined in an institution in this State pursuant to a criminal proceeding and who has other criminal charges pending against him may, by written request filed with the clerk of the court where the other charges are pending, require the prosecutor prosecuting such charges to proceed pursuant to this section. A copy of the request must be served upon the prosecutor in the manner provided by the Rules of Civil Procedure, G.S. 1A-1, Rule 5(b). If the prosecutor does not proceed pursuant to subsection (a) within six months from the date the request is filed with the clerk, the charges must be dismissed.

(d) **Detainer. --**
(1) When a criminal defendant is imprisoned in this State pursuant to prior criminal proceedings, the clerk upon request of the prosecutor, must transmit to the custodian of the institution in which he is imprisoned, a copy of the charges filed against

the defendant and a detainer directing that the prisoner be held to answer to the charges made against him. The detainer must contain a notice of the prisoner's right to proceed pursuant to G.S. 15A-711(c).

(2) Upon receipt of the charges and the detainer, the custodian must immediately inform the prisoner of its receipt and furnish him copies of the charges and the detainer, must explain to him his right to proceed pursuant to G.S. 15A-711(c).

(3) The custodian must notify the clerk who transmitted the detainer of the defendant's impending release at least 30 days prior to the date of release. The notice must be given immediately if the detainer is received less than 30 days prior to the date of release. The clerk must direct the sheriff to take custody of the defendant and produce him for trial. The custodian must release the defendant to the custody of the sheriff, but may not hold the defendant in confinement beyond the date on which he is eligible for release.

(4) A detainer may be withdrawn upon request of the prosecutor, and the clerk must notify the custodian, who must notify the defendant.

History.
1949, c. 303; 1953, c. 603; 1957, c. 349, s. 10; c. 1067, ss. 1, 2; 1967, c. 996, ss. 13, 15; 1973, c. 1286, s. 1; 1975, c. 166, s. 27; 1979, c. 107, s. 1; 1987 (Reg. Sess., 1988), c. 1037, s. 61; 1989, c. 688, s. 3

§§ 15A-712 through 15A-720

Reserved for future codification purposes.

ARTICLE 37
UNIFORM CRIMINAL EXTRADITION ACT

§ 15A-721. Definitions

Where appearing in this Article the term "Governor" includes any person performing the functions of Governor by authority of the law of this State. The term "executive authority" includes the Governor, and any person performing the functions of governor in a state other than this State. The term "state," referring to a state other than this State, includes any other state or territory, organized or unorganized, of the United States of America.

History.
1937, c. 273, s. 1; 1973, c. 1286, s. 16

§ 15A-722. Duty of Governor as to fugitives from justice of other states

Subject to the provisions of this Article, the provisions of the Constitution of the United States controlling, and any and all acts of Congress enacted in pursuance thereof, it is the duty of the Governor of this State to have arrested and delivered up to the executive authority of any other state of the United States any person charged in that state with treason, felony or other crime, who has fled from justice and is found in this State.

History.
1937, c. 273, s. 2; 1973, c. 1286, s. 16

§ 15A-723. Form of demand for extradition

No demand for the extradition of a person charged with crime in another state shall be recognized by the Governor unless in writing alleging, except in cases arising under G.S. 15A-726, that the accused was present in the demanding state at the time of the commission of the alleged crime, and that thereafter he fled from the state, and accompanied by a copy of an indictment found or by information supported by affidavit in the state having jurisdiction of the crime, or by a copy of an affidavit made before a magistrate there, together with a copy of any warrant which was issued thereupon; or by a copy of a judgment of conviction or of a sentence imposed in execution thereof, together with a statement by the executive authority of the demanding state that the person claimed has escaped from confinement or has broken the terms of his bail, probation or parole. The indictment, information, or affidavit made before the magistrate must substantially charge the person demanded with having committed a crime under the law of that state; and the copy of indictment, information, affidavit, judgment of conviction or sentence must be authenticated by the executive authority making the demand.

History.
1937, c. 273, s. 3; 1973, c. 1286, s. 16

§ 15A-724. Governor may cause investigation to be made

When a demand shall be made upon the Governor of this State by the executive authority of another state for the surrender of a person so charged with crime, the Governor may call upon the Attorney General or any prosecuting officer in this State to investigate or assist in investigating the demand, and to report to him the situation and circumstances of the person so demanded, and whether he ought to be surrendered.

History.
1937, c. 273, s. 4; 1973, c. 1286, s. 16

§ 15A-725. Extradition of persons imprisoned or awaiting trial in another state or who have left the demanding state under compulsion

When it is desired to have returned to this State a person charged in this State with a crime, and such person is imprisoned or is held under criminal proceedings then pending against him in another state, the Governor of this State may agree with the executive authority of such other state for the extradition of such person before the conclusion of such proceedings or his term of sentence in such other state, upon condition that such person be returned to such other state at the expense of this State as soon as the prosecution in this State is terminated.

The Governor of this State may also surrender on demand of the executive authority of any other state any person in this State who is charged in the manner provided in G.S. 15A-743 with having violated the laws of the state whose executive authority is making the demand, even though such person left the demanding state involuntarily.

History.
1937, c. 273, s. 5; 1973, c. 1286, s. 16

§ 15A-726. Extradition of persons not present in demanding state at time of commission of crime

The Governor of this State may also surrender, on demand of the executive authority of any other state, any person in this State charged in such other state in the manner provided in G.S. 15A-723 with committing an act in this State, or in a third state, intentionally resulting in a crime in the state whose executive authority is making the demand, and the provisions of this Article, not otherwise inconsistent, shall apply to such cases, even though the accused was not in that state at the time of the commission of the crime, and has not fled therefrom.

History.
1937, c. 273, s. 6; 1973, c. 1286, s. 16

§ 15A-727. Issue of Governor's warrant of arrest; its recitals

If the Governor decides that the demand should be complied with, he shall sign a warrant of arrest, which shall be sealed with the State seal, and be directed to any peace officer or other person whom he may think fit to entrust with the execution thereof. The warrant must substantially recite the facts necessary to the validity of its issuance.

History.
1937, c. 273, s. 7; 1973, c. 1286, s. 16

§ 15A-728. Manner and place of execution of warrant

Such warrant shall authorize the peace officer or other person to whom directed to arrest the accused at any time and any place where he may be found within the State, and to command the aid of all peace officers or other persons in the execution of the warrant, and to deliver the accused, subject to the provisions of this Article, to the duly authorized agent of the demanding state.

History.
1937, c. 273, s. 8; 1973, c. 1286, s. 16

§ 15A-729. Authority of arresting officer

Every such peace officer or other person empowered to make the arrest shall have the same authority, in arresting the accused, to command assistance therein as peace officers have by law in the execution of any criminal process directed to them, with like penalties against those who refuse their assistance.

History.
1937, c. 273, s. 9; 1973, c. 1286, s. 16

§ 15A-730. Rights of accused person; application for writ of habeas corpus

No person arrested upon such warrant shall be delivered over to the agent whom the executive authority demanding him shall have appointed to receive him unless he shall first be taken forthwith before a judge of a court of record in this State, who shall inform him of the demand made for his surrender and of the crime with which he is charged, and that he has the right to demand and procure legal counsel; and if the prisoner or his counsel shall state that he or they desire to test the legality of his arrest, the judge of such court of record shall fix a reasonable time to be allowed him within which to apply for a writ of habeas corpus. When such writ is applied for, notice thereof, and of the time and place of hearing thereon, shall be given to the prosecuting officer of the county in which the arrest is made and in which the accused is in custody, and to the said agent of the demanding state.

History.
1937, c. 273, s. 10; 1973, c. 1286, s. 16

§ 15A-731. Penalty for noncompliance with G.S. 15A-730

Any officer who shall deliver to the agent for extradition of the demanding state a person in his custody under the Governor's warrant, in willful disobedience to G.S. 15A-730, shall be guilty of a Class 2 misdemeanor.

History.
1937, c. 273, s. 11; 1973, c. 1286, s. 16; 1993, c. 539, s. 302; 1994, Ex. Sess., c. 24, s. 14(c)

§ 15A-732. Confinement in jail when necessary

The officer or person executing the Governor's warrant of arrest, or the agent of the demanding state to whom the prisoner may have been delivered, may, when necessary, confine the prisoner in the jail of any county or city through which he may pass; and the keeper of such jail must receive and safely keep the prisoner until the officer or person having charge of him is ready to proceed on his route, such officer or person being chargeable with the expense of keeping.

The officer or agent of a demanding state to whom a prisoner may have been delivered following extradition proceedings in another state, or to whom a prisoner may have been delivered after waiving extradition in such other state, and who is passing through this State with such a prisoner for the purpose of immediately returning such prisoner to the demanding state may, when necessary, confine the prisoner in the jail of any county or city through which he may pass; and the keeper of such jail must receive and safely keep the prisoner until the officer or agent having charge of him is ready to proceed on his route, such officer or agent, however, being chargeable with the expense of keeping: Provided, however, that such officer or agent shall produce and show to the keeper of such jail satisfactory written evidence of the fact that he is actually transporting such prisoner to the demanding state after a requisition by the executive authority of such demanding state. Such prisoner shall not be entitled to demand a new requisition while in this State.

History.
1937, c. 273, s. 12; 1973, c. 1286, s. 16

§ 15A-733. Arrest prior to requisition

Whenever any person within this State shall be charged on the oath of any credible person before any judge or magistrate of this State with the commission of any crime in any other state and, except in cases arising under G.S. 15A-726, with having fled from justice, or with having been convicted of a crime in that state and having escaped from confinement, or having broken the terms of his bail, probation or parole, or whenever complaint shall have been made before any judge or magistrate in this State, setting forth on the affidavit of any credible person in another state that a crime has been committed in such other state, and that the accused has been charged in such state with the commission of the crime, and, except in cases arising under G.S. 15A-726, has fled from justice, or with having been convicted of a crime in that state and having escaped from confinement, or having broken the terms of his bail, probation or parole, and is believed to be in this State, the judge or magistrate shall issue a warrant directed to any peace officer commanding him to apprehend the person named therein, wherever he may be found in this State, and to bring him before the same or any other judge, magistrate or court who or which may be available in or convenient of access to the place where the arrest may be made, to answer the charge or complaint and affidavit, and a certified copy of the sworn charge or complaint and affidavit upon which the warrant is issued shall be attached to the warrant.

History.
1937, c. 273, s. 13; 1973, c. 1286, s. 16

§ 15A-734. Arrest without a warrant

The arrest of a person may be lawfully made also by any peace officer or a private person, without a warrant, upon reasonable information that the accused stands charged in the courts of a state with a crime punishable by death or imprisonment for a term exceeding one year, but when so arrested the accused must be taken before a judge or magistrate with all practicable speed, and complaint must be made against him under oath setting forth the ground for the arrest as in G.S. 15A-733; and thereafter his answer shall be heard as if he had been arrested on a warrant.

History.
1937, c. 273, s. 14; 1973, c. 1286, s. 16

§ 15A-735. Commitment to await requisition; bail

If from the examination before the judge or magistrate it appears that the person held is the person charged with having committed the crime alleged and, except in cases arising under G.S. 15A-726, that he has fled from justice, the judge or magistrate must, by a warrant reciting the accusation, commit him to the county jail for such a time, not exceeding 30 days and specified in the warrant, as will enable the arrest of the accused to be made under a warrant of the Governor on a requisition of the executive authority of the state having jurisdiction of the offense, unless the accused give bail as provided in G.S. 15A-736, or until he shall be legally discharged.

History.
1937, c. 273, s. 15; 1973, c. 1286, s. 16

§ 15A-736. Bail in certain cases; conditions of bond

Unless the offense with which the prisoner is charged is shown to be an offense punishable by death or life imprisonment under the laws of the state in which it was committed, a judge or magistrate in this State may admit the person arrested to bail by bond, with sufficient sureties, and in such sum as he deems proper, conditioned for his appearance before him at a time specified in such bond, and for his surrender, to be arrested upon the warrant of the Governor of this State.

History.
1937, c. 273, s. 16; 1973, c. 1286, s. 16

N.C. Gen. Stat. § 15A-736.1

Recodified as G.S. 15A-534.6 by Session Laws 2007-484, s. 4, effective August 30, 2007.

§ 15A-737. Extension of time of commitment; adjournment

If the accused is not arrested under warrant of the Governor by the expiration of the time specified in the warrant or bond, a judge or magistrate may discharge him or may recommit him for a further period not to exceed 60 days, or a judge or magistrate may again take bail for his appearance and surrender, as provided in G.S. 15A-736, but within a period not to exceed 60 days after the date of such new bond.

History.
1937, c. 273, s. 17; 1973, c. 1286, s. 16

§ 15A-738. Forfeiture of bail

If the prisoner is admitted to bail and fails to appear and surrender himself according to the conditions of his bond, the judge, or magistrate by proper order, shall declare the bond forfeited and order his immediate arrest without warrant if he be within this State. Recovery may be

had on such bond in the name of the State as in the case of other bonds given by the accused in criminal proceedings within this State.

History.
1937, c. 273, s. 18; 1973, c. 1286, s. 16

§ 15A-739. Persons under criminal prosecution in this State at time of requisition

If a criminal prosecution has been instituted against such person under the laws of this State and is still pending, the Governor, in his discretion, either may surrender him on demand of the executive authority of another state or hold him until he has been tried and discharged or convicted and punished in this State.

History.
1937, c. 273, s. 19; 1973, c. 1286, s. 16

§ 15A-740. Guilt or innocence of accused, when inquired into

The guilt or innocence of the accused as to the crime of which he is charged may not be inquired into by the Governor or in any proceeding after the demand for extradition accompanied by a charge of crime in legal form as above provided shall have been presented to the Governor, except as it may be involved in identifying the person held as the person charged with the crime.

History.
1937, c. 273, s. 20; 1973, c. 1286, s. 16

§ 15A-741. Governor may recall warrant or issue alias

The Governor may recall his warrant of arrest or may issue another warrant whenever he deems proper.

History.
1937, c. 273, s. 21; 1973, c. 1286, s. 16

§ 15A-742. Fugitives from this State; duty of governors

Whenever the Governor of this State shall demand a person charged with a crime or with escaping from confinement or breaking the terms of his bail, probation or parole in this State from the executive authority of any other state, or from the chief justice or an associate justice of the Supreme Court of the District of Columbia authorized to receive such demand under the laws of the United States, he shall issue a warrant under the seal of this State, to some agent, commanding him to receive the person so charged if delivered to him and convey him to the proper officer of the county in this State in which the offense was committed.

History.
1937, c. 273, s. 22; 1973, c. 1286, s. 16

§ 15A-743. Application for issuance of requisition; by whom made; contents

(a) When the return to this State of a person charged with crime in this State is required, the prosecuting attorney shall present to the Governor his written application for a requisition for the return of the person charged, in which application shall be stated the name of the person so charged, the crime charged against him, the approximate time, place and circumstances of its commission, the state in which he is believed to be, including the location of the accused therein, at the time the application is made and certifying that, in the opinion of the said prosecuting attorney, the ends of justice require the arrest and return of the accused to this State for trial and that the proceeding is not instituted to enforce a private claim.

(b) When the return to this State is required of a person who has been convicted of a crime in this State and has escaped from confinement or broken the terms of his bail, probation, post-release supervision, or parole, the prosecuting attorney of the county in which the offense was committed, the Post-Release Supervision and Parole Commission, the Director of Prisons, the Director of Community Corrections, or sheriff of the county from which escape was made, shall present to the Governor a written application for a requisition for the return of such person, in which application shall be stated the name of the person, the crime of which he was convicted, the circumstances of his escape from confinement or of the breach of the terms of his bail, probation or parole, the state in which he is believed to be, including the location of the person therein at the time application is made.

(c) The application shall be verified by affidavit, shall be executed in duplicate and shall be accompanied by two certified copies of the indictment returned, or information and affidavit filed, or of the complaint made to the judge or magistrate, stating the offense with which the accused is charged, or of the judgment of conviction or of the sentence. The prosecuting officer, parole board, warden or sheriff may also attach such further affidavits and other documents in duplicate as he shall deem proper to be submitted with such application. A copy of all papers shall be forwarded with the Governor's requisition.

History.
1937, c. 273, s. 23; 1973, c. 1286, s. 16; 1975, c. 132; 1993, c. 83, s. 1; 2016-77, s. 6

§ 15A-744. Costs and expenses

Subject to the requirements and restrictions set forth in this section, if the crime is a felony or if a person convicted in this State of a misdemeanor has broken the terms of his probation or parole, reimbursements for expenses shall be paid out of the State treasury on the certificate of the Governor. In all other cases, such expenses or reimbursements shall be paid out of the county treasury of the county wherein the crime is alleged to have been committed according to such regulations as the board of county commissioners may promulgate. In all cases, the expenses, for which repayment or reimbursement may be claimed, shall consist of the reasonable and necessary travel expense and subsistence costs of the extradition agent or fugitive officer, as well as the fugitive, together with such legal fees as were paid to the officials of the state on whose governor the requisition is made. The person or persons designated to return the fugitive shall not be allowed, paid or reimbursed for any expenses in connection with any requisition or extradition proceeding unless the expenses are itemized, the statement of same be sworn to under oath, and shall not then be paid or reimbursed unless a receipt is obtained showing the amount, the purpose for which said item or sum was expended, the place, date and to whom paid, and said receipt or receipts attached to said sworn statement and filed with the Governor. The Governor shall have the authority, upon investigation, to increase or decrease any item or expenses shown in said sworn statement, or to include items of expenses omitted by mistake or inadvertence. The decision or determination of the Governor as to the correct amount to be paid for such expenses or reimbursements shall be final. When it is deemed necessary for more than one agent, extradition agent, fugitive officer or person, to be designated to return a fugitive from another state to this State, the district attorney or prosecuting officer shall file with his written application to the Governor of this State an affidavit setting forth in detail the grounds or reasons why it is necessary to have more than one extradition agent, fugitive officer or person to be so designated. Among other things, and not by way of limitation, the affidavit shall set forth whether or not the alleged fugitive is a dangerous person, his previous criminal record if any, and any record of said fugitive on file with the Federal Bureau of Investigation or with the prison authorities of this State. As a further ground or reason for more than one extradition agent or fugitive officer to be designated, it may be shown in said affidavit the number of fugitives to be returned to this State and any other grounds or reasons for which more than one extradition agent or fugitive officer is desired. If the Governor finds or determines from his own investigation and from the information made available to him that more than one extradition agent or fugitive officer is necessary for the return of a fugitive or fugitives to this State, he may designate more than one extradition agent or fugitive officer for such purpose. All travel for which expenses or reimbursements are paid or allowed under this section shall be by the nearest, direct, convenient route of travel. If the extradition agent or agents or person or persons designated to return a fugitive or fugitives from another state to this State shall elect to travel by automobile, a sum not exceeding seven cents (7 cent(s)) per mile may be allowed in lieu of all travel expense, and which shall be paid upon a basis of mileage for the complete trip. The Governor may promulgate executive orders, rules and regulations governing travel, forms of statements, receipts or any other matter or objective provided for in this section. The Governor may delegate any or all of the duties, powers and responsibilities conferred upon him by this section to any executive agent or executive clerk on his staff or in his office, and such executive agent or executive clerk, when properly authorized, may perform any or all of the duties, powers and responsibilities conferred upon the Governor. Provided that if the fugitive from justice is an alleged felon, and he be returned without the service of extradition papers by the sheriff or the agent of the sheriff of the county in which the felony was alleged to have been committed, the expense of said return shall be borne by the State of North Carolina under the rules and regulations made and promulgated by the Governor of North Carolina or the executive agent or the executive clerk to whom the said Governor may have delegated his duties under this section.

History.
1937, c. 273, s. 24; 1953, c. 1203; 1955, c. 289; 1973, c. 1286, s. 16; 1975, c. 166, s. 27; 1981, c. 859, s. 13.9

§ 15A-745. Immunity from service of process in certain civil actions

A person brought into this State by, or after waiver of, extradition based on a criminal charge shall not be subject to service of personal process in civil actions arising out of the same facts as the criminal proceedings to answer which he is being or has been returned until he has been convicted in the criminal proceeding or, if acquitted, until he has had reasonable opportunity to return to the state from which he was extradited.

History.
1937, c. 273, s. 25; 1973, c. 1286, s. 16

§ 15A-746. Written waiver of extradition proceedings

Any person arrested in this State charged with having committed any crime in another state or alleged to have escaped from confinement, or broken the terms of his bail, probation or parole may waive the issuance and service of the warrant provided for in G.S. 15A-727 and 15A-728 and all other procedure incidental to extradition proceedings, by executing or subscribing in the presence of a judge of any court of record within this State or a clerk of the superior court a writing which states that he consents to return to the demanding state: Provided, however, that before such waiver shall be executed or subscribed by such person it shall be the duty of such judge or clerk of superior court to inform such person of his rights to the issuance and service of a warrant of extradition and to obtain a writ of habeas corpus as provided for in G.S. 15A-730.

If and when such consent has been duly executed it shall forthwith be forwarded to the office of the Governor of this State and filed therein. The judge or clerk of superior court shall direct the officer having such person in custody to deliver forthwith such person to the duly accredited agent or agents of the demanding state, and shall deliver or cause to be delivered to such agent or agents a copy of such consent: Provided, however, that nothing in this section shall be deemed to limit the rights of the accused person to return voluntarily and without formality to the demanding state, nor shall this waiver procedure be deemed to be an exclusive procedure or to limit the powers, rights or duties of the officers of the demanding state or of this State.

History.
1937, c. 273, s. 25a; 1959, c. 271; 1973, c. 1286, s. 16

§ 15A-747. Nonwaiver by this State

Nothing in this Article contained shall be deemed to constitute a waiver by this State of its right, power or privilege to try such demanded person for crime committed within this State, or of its right, power or privilege to regain custody of such person by extradition proceedings or otherwise for the purpose of trial, sentence or punishment for any crime committed within this State, nor shall any proceedings had under this Article which result in, or fail to result in, extradition be deemed a waiver by this State of any of its rights, privileges or jurisdiction in any way whatsoever.

History.
1937, c. 273, s. 25b; 1973, c. 1286, s. 16

§ 15A-748. No right of asylum; no immunity from other criminal prosecution while in this State

After a person has been brought back to this State by, or after waiver of, extradition proceedings, he may be tried in this State for other crimes which he may be charged with having committed here as well as that specified in the requisition for his extradition.

History.

1937, c. 273, s. 26; 1973, c. 1286, s. 16

§ 15A-749. Interpretation

The provisions of this Article shall be so interpreted and construed as to effectuate its general purposes to make uniform the law of those states which enact it.

History.

1937, c. 273, s. 27; 1973, c. 1286, s. 16

§ 15A-750. Short title

This Article may be cited as the Uniform Criminal Extradition Act.

History.

1937, c. 273, s. 30; 1973, c. 1286, s. 16

§§ 15A-751 through 15A-760

Reserved for future codification purposes.

ARTICLE 38
INTERSTATE AGREEMENT ON DETAINERS

§ 15A-761. Agreement on Detainers entered into; form and contents

This Agreement on Detainers is hereby enacted into law and entered into by this State with all other jurisdictions legally joining therein in the form substantially as follows: The contracting states solemnly agree:

Article I

The party states find that charges outstanding against a prisoner, detainers based on untried indictments, informations or complaints, and difficulties in securing speedy trial of persons already incarcerated in other jurisdictions, produce uncertainties which obstruct programs of prisoner treatment and rehabilitation. Accordingly, it is the policy of the party states and the purpose of this agreement to encourage the expeditious and orderly disposition of such charges and determination of the proper status of any and all detainers based on untried indictments, informations or complaints. The party states also find that proceedings with reference to such charges and detainers, when emanating from another jurisdiction, cannot properly be had in the absence of cooperative procedures. It is the further purpose of this agreement to provide such cooperative procedures.

Article II

As used in this agreement:

(a) "State" shall mean a state of the United States; the United States of America; a territory or possession of the United States; the District of Columbia; the Commonwealth of Puerto Rico.

(b) "Sending state" shall mean a state in which a prisoner is incarcerated at the time that he initiates a request for final disposition pursuant to Article III hereof or at the time that a request for custody or availability is initiated pursuant to Article IV hereof.

(c) "Receiving state" shall mean the state in which trial is to be had on an indictment, information or complaint pursuant to Article III or Article IV hereof.

Article III

(a) Whenever a person has entered upon a term of imprisonment in a penal or correctional institution of a party state, and whenever during the continuance of the term of imprisonment there is pending in any other party state any untried indictment, information or complaint on the basis of which a detainer has been lodged against the prisoner, he shall be brought to trial within 180 days after he shall have caused to be delivered to the prosecuting officer and the appropriate court of the prosecuting officer's jurisdiction written notice of the place of his imprisonment and his request for a final disposition to be made of the indictment, information or complaint: Provided that for good cause shown in open court, the prisoner or his counsel being present, the court having jurisdiction of the matter may grant any necessary or reasonable continuance. The request of the prisoner shall be accompanied by a certificate of the appropriate official having custody of the prisoner, stating the term of commitment under which the prisoner is being held, the time already served, the time remaining to be served on the sentence, the amount of good time earned, the time of parole eligibility of the prisoner, and any decisions of the state parole agency relating to the prisoner.

(b) The written notice and request for final disposition referred to in paragraph (a) hereof shall be given or sent by the prisoner to the warden, commissioner of corrections or other official having custody of him, who shall promptly forward it together with the certificate to the appropriate prosecuting official and court by registered or certified mail, return receipt requested.

(c) The warden, commissioner of corrections or other official having custody of the prisoner shall promptly inform him of the source and contents of any detainer lodged against him and shall also inform him of his right to make a request for final disposition of the indictment, information or complaint on which the detainer is based.

(d) Any request for final disposition made by a prisoner pursuant to paragraph (a) hereof shall operate as a request for final disposition of all untried indictments, informations or complaints on the basis of which detainers have been lodged against the prisoner from the state to whose prosecuting official the request for final disposition is specifically directed. The warden, commissioner of corrections or other official having custody of the prisoner shall forthwith notify all appropriate prosecuting officers and courts in the several jurisdictions within the state to which the prisoner's request for final disposition is being sent of the proceeding being initiated by the prisoner. Any notification sent pursuant to this paragraph shall be accompanied by copies of the prisoner's written notice, request and the certificate. If trial is not had on any indictment, information or complaint contemplated hereby prior to the return of the prisoner to the original place of imprisonment, such indictment, information or complaint shall not be of any further force or effect, and the court shall enter an order dismissing the same with prejudice.

(e) Any request for final disposition made by a prisoner pursuant to paragraph (a) hereof shall also be deemed to be a waiver of extradition with respect to any charge or proceeding contemplated thereby or included therein by reason of paragraph (d) hereof, and a waiver of extradition to the receiving state to serve any sentence there imposed upon him, after completion of his term of imprisonment in the sending state. The request for final disposition shall also constitute a consent by the prisoner to the production of his body in any court where his presence may be required in order to effectuate the purposes of this agreement and a further consent voluntarily to be returned to the original place of imprisonment in accordance with the provisions of this agreement. Nothing in this paragraph shall prevent the imposition of a concurrent sentence if otherwise permitted by law.

(f) Escape from custody by the prisoner subsequent to his execution of the request for final disposition referred to in paragraph (a) hereof shall void the request.

Article IV

(a) The appropriate officer of the jurisdiction in which an untried indictment, information or complaint is pending shall be entitled to have a prisoner against whom he has lodged a detainer and who is serving a term of imprisonment in any party state made available in accordance with Article V(a) hereof upon presentation of a written request for temporary custody or availability to the appropriate authorities of the state in which the prisoner is incarcerated: Provided that the court having jurisdiction of such indictment, information or complaint shall have duly approved, recorded and transmitted the request: And provided further that there shall be a period of 30 days after receipt by the appropriate authorities before the request be honored, within which period the governor of the sending state may disapprove the request for temporary custody or availability, either upon his own motion or upon motion of the prisoner.

(b) Upon receipt of the officer's written request as provided in paragraph (a) hereof, the appropriate authorities having the prisoner in custody shall furnish the officer with a certificate stating the term of commitment under which the prisoner is being held, the time already served, the time remaining to be served on the sentence, the amount of good time earned, the time of parole eligibility of the prisoner, and any decisions of the state parole agency relating to the prisoner. Said authorities simultaneously shall furnish all other officers and appropriate courts in the receiving state who have lodged detainers against the prisoner with similar certificates and with notices informing them of the request for custody or availability and of the reasons therefor.

(c) In respect of any proceeding made possible by this Article, trial shall be commenced within 120 days of the arrival of the prisoner in the receiving state, but for good cause shown in open court, the prisoner or his counsel being present, the court having jurisdiction of the matter may grant any necessary or reasonable continuance.

(d) Nothing contained in this Article shall be construed to deprive any prisoner of any right which he may have to contest the legality of his delivery as provided in paragraph (a) hereof, but such delivery may not be opposed or denied on the ground that the executive authority of the sending state has not affirmatively consented to or ordered such delivery.

(e) If trial is not had on any indictment, information or complaint contemplated hereby prior to the prisoner's being returned to the original place of imprisonment pursuant to Article V(e) hereof, such indictment, information or complaint shall not be of any further force or effect, and the court shall enter an order dismissing the same with prejudice.

Article V

(a) In response to a request made under Article III or Article IV hereof, the appropriate authority in a sending state shall offer to deliver temporary custody of such prisoner to the appropriate authority in the state where such indictment, information or complaint is pending against such person in order that speedy and efficient prosecution may be had. If the request for final disposition is made by the prisoner, the offer of temporary custody shall accompany the written notice provided for in Article III of this agreement. In the case of a federal prisoner, the appropriate authority in the receiving state shall be entitled to temporary custody as provided by this agreement or to the prisoner's presence in federal custody at the place for trial, whichever custodial arrangement may be approved by the custodian.

(b) The officer or other representative of a state accepting an offer of temporary custody shall present the following upon demand:

    (1) Proper identification and evidence of his authority to act for the state into whose temporary custody the prisoner is to be given.

    (2) A duly certified copy of the indictment, information or complaint on the basis of which the detainer has been lodged and on the basis of which the request for temporary custody of the prisoner has been made.

(c) If the appropriate authority shall refuse or fail to accept temporary custody of said person, or in the event that an action on the indictment, information or complaint on the basis of which the detainer has been lodged is not brought to trial within the period provided in Article III or Article IV hereof, the appropriate court of the jurisdiction where the indictment, information or complaint has been pending shall enter an order dismissing the same with prejudice, and any detainer based thereon shall cease to be of any force or effect.

(d) The temporary custody referred to in this agreement shall be only for the purpose of permitting prosecution on the charge or charges contained in one or more untried indictments, informations or complaints which form the basis of the detainer or detainers or for prosecution on any other charge or charges arising out of the same transaction. Except for his attendance at court and while being transported to or from any place at which his presence may be required, the prisoner shall be held in a suitable jail or other facility regularly used for persons awaiting prosecution.

(e) At the earliest practicable time consonant with the purposes of this agreement, the prisoner shall be returned to the sending state.

(f) During the continuance of temporary custody or while the prisoner is otherwise being made available for trial as required by this agreement, time being served on the sentence shall continue to run but good time shall be earned by the prisoner only if, and to the extent that, the law and practice of the jurisdiction which imposed the sentence may allow.

(g) For all purposes other than that for which temporary custody as provided in this agreement is exercised, the prisoner shall be deemed to remain in the custody of and subject to the jurisdiction of the sending state and any escape from temporary custody may be dealt with in the same manner as an escape from the original place of imprisonment or in any other manner permitted by law.

(h) From the time that a party state receives custody of a prisoner pursuant to this agreement until such prisoner is returned to the territory and custody of the sending state, the state in which the one or more untried indictments, informations or complaints are pending or in which trial is being had shall be responsible for the prisoner and shall also pay all costs of transporting, caring for, keeping and returning the prisoner. The provisions of this paragraph shall govern unless the states concerned shall have entered into a supplementary agreement providing for a different allocation of costs and responsibilities as between or among themselves. Nothing herein contained shall be construed to alter or affect any internal relationship among the departments, agencies and officers of and in the government of a party state, or between a party state and its subdivisions, as to the payment of costs, or responsibilities therefor.

Article VI

(a) In determining the duration and expiration dates of the time periods provided in Articles III and IV of this agreement, the running of said time periods shall be tolled whenever and for as long as the prisoner is unable to stand trial, as determined by the court having jurisdiction of the matter.

(b) No provision of this agreement, and no remedy made available by this agreement, shall apply to any person who is adjudged to be mentally ill.

Article VII

Each state party to this agreement shall designate an officer who, acting jointly with like officers of other party states, shall promulgate rules and regulations to carry out more effectively the terms and provisions of this agreement, and who shall provide, within and without the state, information necessary to the effective operation of this agreement.

Article VIII

This agreement shall enter into full force and effect as to a party state when such state has enacted the same into law. A state party to this agreement may withdraw herefrom by enacting a statute repealing the same. However, the withdrawal of any state shall not affect the status of any proceedings already initiated by inmates or by state officers at the time such withdrawal takes effect, nor shall it affect their rights in respect thereof.

Article IX

This agreement shall be liberally construed so as to effectuate its purposes. The provisions of this agreement shall be severable and if any phrase, clause, sentence or provision of this agreement is declared to be contrary to the constitution of any party state or of the United States or the applicability thereof to any government, agency, person or circumstance is held invalid, the validity of the remainder of this agreement and the applicability thereof to any government, agency, person or circumstance shall not be affected thereby. If this agreement shall be held contrary to the constitution of any state party hereto, the agreement shall remain in full force and effect as to the remaining states and in full force and effect as to the state affected as to all severable matters.

History.
1965, c. 295, s. 1; 1973, c. 1286, s. 22

§ 15A-762. Meaning of "appropriate court."

The phrase "appropriate court" as used in the Agreement on Detainers shall, with reference to the courts of this State, mean court of record with criminal jurisdiction.

History.
1965, c. 295, s. 2; 1973, c. 1286, s. 22

§ 15A-763. Cooperation in enforcement

All courts, departments, agencies, officers and employees of this State and its political subdivisions are hereby directed to enforce the Agreement on Detainers and to cooperate with one another and with other party states in enforcing the agreement and effectuating its purpose.

History.
1965, c. 295, s. 3; 1973, c. 1286, s. 22

§ 15A-764. Escape from temporary custody

Any prisoner released to temporary custody under the provisions of the Agreement on Detainers from a place of imprisonment in North Carolina who shall escape or attempt to escape from such temporary custody, whether within or without the borders of this State, shall be dealt with in the same manner as if the escape or attempt to escape were from the original place of imprisonment.

History.
1965, c. 295, s. 4; 1973, c. 1286, s. 22

§ 15A-765. Authority and duty of official in charge of institution

It shall be lawful and mandatory upon the warden or other official in charge of a penal or correctional institution in this State to give over the person of any inmate thereof whenever so required by the operation of the Agreement on Detainers.

History.
1965, c. 295, s. 5; 1973, c. 1286, s. 22

§ 15A-766. Designation of central administrator of and information agent for agreement

The Governor is hereby authorized and empowered to designate the officer who shall serve as central administrator of and information agent for the Agreement on Detainers, pursuant to the provisions of Article VII of the agreement.

History.
1965, c. 295, s. 6; 1973, c. 1286, s. 22

§ 15A-767. Distribution of copies of Article

Copies of this Article shall, upon its approval, be transmitted to the governor of each state, the Attorney General and the Administrator of General Services of the United States, and the Council of State Governments.

History.
1965, c. 295, s. 7; 1973, c. 1286, s. 22

§§ 15A-768 through 15A-770

Reserved for future codification purposes.

ARTICLE 39
OTHER SPECIAL PROCESS FOR ATTENDANCE OF DEFENDANTS

§ 15A-771. Securing attendance of defendants confined in federal prisons

(a) A defendant against whom a criminal action is pending in this State, and who is confined in a federal prison or custody either within or outside the State, may, with the consent of the Attorney General of the United States, be produced in such court for the purpose of criminal prosecution, pursuant to the provisions of:

(1) Section 4085 of Title 18 of the United States Code; or

(2) Subsection (b) of this section.

(b) When such a defendant is in federal custody as specified in subsection (a), a superior court may, upon application of the prosecutor, issue a certificate, addressed to the Attorney General of the United States, certifying the charges and the court in which they are pending, and that attendance of the defendant in such court for the purpose of criminal prosecution thereon is necessary in the interest of justice, and requesting the Attorney General of the United States to cause such defendant to be produced in such court, under custody of a federal public servant, upon a designated date and for a period of time necessary to complete the prosecution. Upon issuing such a certificate, the court may deliver it, or cause or authorize it to be delivered, together with a certified copy of the charges upon which it is based, to the Attorney General of the United States or to his representative authorized to entertain the request.

History.
1973, c. 1286, s. 1; 1975, c. 166, s. 27

§ 15A-772. Securing attendance of defendants who are outside the United States

(a) When a criminal action for an offense committed in this State is pending in a criminal court of this State against a defendant who is in a foreign country with which the United States has an extradition treaty, and when the offense charged is one which is declared in such treaty to be an extraditable one, the prosecutor may make an application to the Governor, requesting him to make an application to the President of the United States to institute extradition proceedings for the return of the defendant to this country and State for the purpose of prosecution of such action. The prosecutor's application must comply with rules, regulations, and guidelines established by the Governor for such applications and must be accompanied by all the charges, affidavits, and other documents required thereby.

(b) Upon receipt of the prosecutor's application, the Governor, if satisfied that the defendant is in the foreign country in question, that the offense charged is an extraditable one pursuant to the treaty in question, and that there are no factors or impediments which in law preclude such an extradition, may in his discretion make an application, addressed to the Secretary of State of the United States, requesting that the President of the United States institute extradition proceedings for the return of the defendant from such foreign country. The Governor's application must comply with applicable treaties and acts of Congress and with rules, regulations, and guidelines established by the Secretary of State for such applications and must be accompanied by all the charges, affidavits, and other documents required thereby.

(c) The provisions of this section apply equally to extradition or attempted extradition of a person who is a fugitive following the entry of a judgment of conviction against him in a criminal court of this State.

History.
1973, c. 1286, s. 1; 1975, c. 166, s. 27

§ 15A-773. Securing attendance of organizations; appearance

(a) The court attendance of an organization for purposes of commencing or prosecuting a criminal action against it may be accomplished by:

(1) Issuance and service of a criminal summons; or

(2) Issuance of an information and waiver of indictment by an authorized officer or agent of the organization and by counsel for the organization, as provided in G.S. 15A-642(c); or

(3) Service of the notice of the indictment, as provided in G.S. 15A-630.

The criminal summons or notice of indictment must be directed to the organization, and must be served by delivery to an officer, director, managing or general agent, cashier or assistant cashier of the organization, or to any other agent of the organization authorized by appointment or by law to receive service of process.

(b) At all stages of a criminal action, an organization may appear by counsel or agent having authority to transact the business of the organization.

(c) For purposes of this section, "organization" means corporation, unincorporated association, partnership, body politic, consortium, or other group, entity, or organization.

History.
1973, c. 1286, s. 1; 1977, c. 557

ARTICLE 40

§§ 15A-774 through 15A-786

Reserved for future codification purposes.

ARTICLE 41

§§ 15A-787 through 15A-800

Reserved for future codification purposes.

SUBCHAPTER 08.
ATTENDANCE OF WITNESSES; DEPOSITIONS

ARTICLE 42
ATTENDANCE OF WITNESSES GENERALLY

§ 15A-801. Subpoena for witness

The presence of a person as a witness in a criminal proceeding may be obtained by subpoena, which must be issued and served in the manner provided in Rule 45 of the Rules of Civil Procedure, G.S. 1A-1, except that subdivision (2) of subsection (b) of the rule does not apply to subpoenas issued under this section.

History.
1973, c. 1286, s. 1; 1975, c. 166, s. 15; 2003-276, s. 2

§ 15A-802. Subpoena for the production of documentary evidence

The production of records, books, papers, documents, or tangible things in a criminal proceeding may be obtained by subpoena which must be issued and served in the manner provided in Rule 45 of the Rules of Civil Procedure, G.S. 1A-1, except that subdivision (2) of subsection (b) of the rule does not apply to subpoenas issued under this section.

History.
1973, c. 1286, s. 1; 1975, c. 166, s. 15; 2003-276, s. 3

§ 15A-803. Attendance of witnesses

(a) **Material Witness Order Authorized.** -- A judge may issue an order assuring the attendance of a material witness at a criminal proceeding. This material witness order may be issued when there are reasonable grounds to believe that the person whom the State or a defendant desires to call as a witness in a pending criminal proceeding possesses information material to the determination of the proceeding and may not be amenable or responsive to a subpoena at a time when his attendance will be sought.

(b) **When Order Issued.** -- A material witness order may be issued by a judge of superior court at any time after the initiation of criminal proceedings. A judge of district court may issue a material witness order only at the time that a defendant is bound over to superior court at a probable-cause hearing.

(c) **How Long Effective.** -- A material witness order remains in effect during the period indicated in the order by the issuing judge unless it is sooner modified or vacated by a judge of superior court. In no event may a material witness order which provides for incarceration of the material witness be issued for a period longer than 20 days, but upon review a superior court judge in his discretion may renew an order one or more times for periods not to exceed five days each.

(d) **Procedure.** -- A material witness order may be obtained upon motion supported by affidavit showing cause for its issuance. The witness must be given reasonable notice, opportunity to be heard and present evidence, and the right of representation by counsel at a hearing on the motion. Counsel for a material witness may be appointed and compensated in the same manner as counsel for an indigent defendant. Appointment of counsel shall be in accordance with rules adopted by the Office of Indigent Defense Services. The order must be based on findings of fact supporting its issuance.

(e) **Order.** -- If the court makes a material witness order:

(1) It may direct release of the witness in the same manner that a defendant may be released under G.S. 15A-534.

(2) It may direct the detention of the witness.

(f) **Modification or Vacation.** -- A material witness order may be modified or vacated by a judge of superior court upon a showing of new or changed facts or circumstances by the witness, the State, or any defendant.

(g) **Securing Attendance or Custody of Material Witness.** -- The witness may be required to attend the hearing by subpoena, or if the court considers it necessary, by order for arrest. An order for arrest also may be issued if it becomes necessary to take the witness into custody after issuance of a material witness order.

History.
1973, c. 1286, s. 1; 2000-144, s. 29

§ 15A-804. Voluntary protective custody

(a) Upon request of a witness, a judge of superior court may determine whether he is a material witness, and may order his protective custody. The order may provide for confinement, custody in other than a penal institution, release to the custody of a law-enforcement officer or other person, or other provisions appropriate to the circumstances.

(b) A person having custody of the witness may not release him without his consent unless directed to do so by a superior court judge, or unless the order so provides.

(c) The issuance of either a material witness order or an order for voluntary protective custody does not preclude the issuance of the other order.

(d) An order for voluntary protective custody may be modified or vacated as appropriate by a superior court judge upon the request of the witness or upon the court's own motion.

History.
1973, c. 1286, s. 1

§ 15A-805. Securing attendance of witnesses confined in institutions within the State

(a) Upon motion of the State or any defendant, the judge of a court in which a criminal proceeding is pending must, for good cause shown, enter an order requiring that any person confined in an institution in this State be produced and compelled to attend as a witness in the action or proceeding.

(b) If the witness is confined pursuant to another pending criminal proceeding, and the judge determines that the production of the witness would result in an unreasonable interference with the conduct of the prior proceeding, he may deny the order. If an order for production is issued, a judge or justice of the appellate division of the General Court of Justice may, upon application of a defendant or prosecutor in the other district for good cause shown, vacate the order for production.

(c) The costs of production of the witness are assessed as are other witness fees.

History.
1973, c. 1286, s. 1; 1975, c. 166, s. 27

§§ 15A-806 through 15A-810

Reserved for future codification purposes.

ARTICLE 43
UNIFORM ACT TO SECURE ATTENDANCE OF WITNESSES FROM WITHOUT A STATE IN CRIMINAL PROCEEDINGS

§ 15A-811. Definitions

The word "state" shall include any territory of the United States and District of Columbia.

The word "summons" shall include a subpoena, order or other notice requiring the appearance of a witness.

"Witness" as used in this Article shall include a person whose testimony is desired in any proceeding or investigation by a grand jury or in a criminal action, prosecution or proceeding.

History.
1937, c. 217, s. 1; 1973, c. 1286, s. 9

§ 15A-812. Summoning witness in this State to testify in another state

If a judge of a court of record in any state which by its laws has made provision for commanding persons within that state to attend and testify in this State certifies, under the seal of such court, that there is a criminal prosecution pending in such court, or that a grand jury investigation has commenced or is about to commence, that a person being within this State is a material witness in such prosecution, or grand jury investigation, and that his presence will be required for a specified number of days, upon presentation of such certificate to any judge of a court of record in the county in which such person is, such judge shall fix a time and place for a hearing, and shall make an order directing the witness to appear at a time and place certain for the hearing.

If at a hearing the judge determines that the witness is material and necessary, that it will not cause undue hardship to the witness to be compelled to attend and testify in the prosecution or a grand jury investigation in the other state, and that the laws of the state in which the prosecution is pending, or grand jury investigation has commenced or is about to commence, and of any other state through which the witness may be required to pass by ordinary course of travel, will give to him protection from arrest and the service of civil and criminal process, he shall issue a summons, with a copy of the certificate attached, directing the witness to attend and testify in the court where the prosecution is pending, or where a grand jury investigation has commenced or is about to commence, at a time and place specified in the summons. In any such hearing the certificate shall be prima facie evidence of all the facts stated therein.

If said certificate recommends that the witness be taken into immediate custody and delivered to an officer of the requesting state to assure his attendance in the requesting state, such judge may, in lieu of notification of the hearing, direct that such witness be forthwith brought before him for said hearing; and the judge at the hearing, being satisfied of the desirability of such custody and delivery, for which determination the certificate shall be prima facie proof of such desirability may, in lieu of issuing subpoena or summons, order that said witness be forthwith taken into custody and delivered to an officer of the requesting state.

Chapter 15A

1025

If the witness, who is summoned as above provided, after being paid or tendered by some properly authorized person the sum of ten cents (10 cent(s)) a mile for each mile by the ordinary traveled route to and from the court where the prosecution is pending and five dollars ($ 5.00) for each day that he is required to travel and attend as a witness, fails without good cause to attend and testify as directed in the summons, he shall be punished in the manner provided for the punishment of any witness who disobeys a summons issued from a court of record in this State.

History.
1937, c. 217, s. 2; 1973, c. 1286, s. 9

§ 15A-813. Witness from another state summoned to testify in this State

If a person in any state which by its laws has made provision for commanding persons within its borders to attend and testify in criminal prosecutions, or grand jury investigations commenced or about to commence in this State, is a material witness in a prosecution pending in a court of record in this State, or in a grand jury investigation which has commenced or is about to commence, a judge of such court may issue a certificate under the seal of the court, stating these facts and specifying the number of days the witness will be required. Said certificate may include a recommendation that the witness be taken into immediate custody and delivered to an officer of this State to assure his attendance in this State. This certificate shall be presented to a judge of a court of record in the county in which the witness is found.

If the witness is summoned to attend and testify in this State he shall be compensated at the rate allowed to State officers and employees by subdivisions (1) and (2) of G.S. 138-6(a) for each mile by the ordinary traveled route to and from the court where the prosecution is pending, and five dollars ($ 5.00) for each day that he is required to travel and attend as a witness. A witness who has appeared in accordance with the provisions of the summons shall not be required to remain within this State a longer period of time than the period mentioned in the certificate unless otherwise ordered by the court. If such a witness is required to appear more than one day, he is also entitled to reimbursement for actual expenses incurred for lodging and meals, not to exceed the maximum currently authorized for State employees when traveling in the State. If such witness, after coming into this State, fails without good cause to attend and testify as directed in the summons, he shall be punished in the manner provided for the punishment of any witness who disobeys a summons issued from a court of record in this State.

History.
1937, c. 217, s. 3; 1973, c. 1286, s. 9; 1998-212, s. 16.25(b)

§ 15A-814. Exemption from arrest and service of process

If a person comes into this State in obedience to a summons directing him to attend and testify in this State he shall not, while in this State pursuant to such summons, be subject to arrest or the service of process, civil or criminal, in connection with matters which arose before his entrance into this State under the summons.

If a person passes through this State while going to another state in obedience to a summons to attend and testify in that state, or while returning therefrom, he shall not while so passing through this State be subject to arrest or the service of process, civil or criminal, in connection with matters which arose before his entrance into this State under the summons.

History.
1937, c. 217, s. 4; 1973, c. 1286, s. 9

§ 15A-815. Uniformity of interpretation

This Article shall be so interpreted and construed as to effectuate its general purpose to make uniform the law of the states which enact it.

History.
1937, c. 217, s. 5; 1973, c. 1286, s. 9

§ 15A-816. Title of Article

This Article may be cited as "Uniform Act to Secure the Attendance of Witnesses from without a State in Criminal Proceedings."

History.
1937, c. 217, s. 6; 1973, c. 1286, s. 9

§§ 15A-817 through 15A-820

Reserved for future codification purposes.

ARTICLE 44
SECURING ATTENDANCE OF PRISONERS AS WITNESSES

§ 15A-821. Securing attendance of prisoner in this State as witness in proceeding outside the State

(a) If a judge of a court of general jurisdiction in any other state, which by its laws has made provision for commanding a prisoner within that state to attend and testify in this State, certifies under the seal of that court that there is a criminal prosecution pending in the court or that a grand jury investigation has commenced, and that a person confined in an institution under the control of the Division of Adult Correction and Juvenile Justice of the Department of Public Safety of North Carolina, other than a person confined as criminally insane, is a material witness in the prosecution or investigation and that his presence is required for a specified number of days, upon presentment of the certificate to a superior court judge in the superior court district or set of districts as defined in G.S. 7A-41.1 where the person is confined, upon notice to the Attorney General, the judge must fix a time and place for a hearing and order the person having custody of the prisoner to produce him at the hearing.

(b) If at the hearing the judge determines that the prisoner is a material and necessary witness in the requesting state, the judge must order that the prisoner attend in the court where the prosecution or investigation is pending, upon such terms and conditions as the judge prescribes, including among other things, provision for the return of the prisoner at the conclusion of his testimony, proper safeguard for his custody, and proper financial reimbursement or other payment, including payment in advance, by the demanding jurisdiction for all expenses incurred in the production and return of the prisoner.

(c) The Attorney General may, as agent for the State of North Carolina, enter into such agreements with the demanding jurisdiction as necessary to ensure proper compliance with the order of the court.

History.
1973, c. 1286, s. 1; 1987 (Reg. Sess., 1988), c. 1037, s. 62; 2011-145, s. 19.1(h); 2012-83, s. 27; 2017-186, s. 2(bbb).

§ 15A-822. Securing attendance of prisoner outside the State as witness in proceeding in the State

(a) When
(1) A criminal action or proceeding is pending in a court of this State, and
(2) There is reasonable cause to believe that a person confined in a correctional institution or prison of another state, other than a person confined as mentally ill, possesses information material to such criminal action or proceeding, and
(3) The attendance of the person as a witness in such proceeding is desired by a party thereto, and
(4) The state in which such person is confined possesses a statute equivalent to G.S. 15A-821, the court in which such proceeding is pending may issue a certificate under the seal of the court, certifying all such facts and certifying that the attendance of the person as a witness in such court is required for a specified number of days.

(b) The certificate may be issued upon application of either the State or a defendant setting forth the facts specified in subsection (a).

(c) Upon issuing such a certificate, the court may cause it to be delivered to a court of such other state which is authorized to initiate or undertake action for the delivery of such prisoners to this State as witnesses.

History.
1973, c. 1286, s. 1

§ 15A-823. Securing attendance of prisoner in federal institution as witness in proceeding in the State

(a) When
(1) A criminal proceeding is pending in a court of this State; and
(2) There is reasonable cause to believe that a person confined in a federal prison or other federal custody, either within or outside this State, possesses information material to such criminal proceeding; and
(3) His attendance as a witness in such action or proceeding is desired by a party thereto, the court may issue a certificate, known as a writ of habeas corpus ad testificandum, addressed to the Attorney General of the United States certifying all such facts and requesting the Attorney General of the United States to cause the attendance of such person as a witness in such court for a specified number of days under custody of a federal public servant.

(b) The certificate may be issued upon application of either the State or a defendant, setting forth the facts specified in subsection (a).

(c) Upon issuing the certificate, the court may cause it to be delivered to the Attorney General of the United States or to his representative authorized to entertain the request.

History.
1973, c. 1286, s. 1

DIVISION 08A
RIGHTS OF CRIME VICTIMS AND WITNESSES

ARTICLE 45
FAIR TREATMENT FOR CERTAIN VICTIMS AND WITNESSES

§ 15A-824. Definitions

The following definitions apply in this Article:

(1) **Crime. --** A felony or serious misdemeanor as determined in the sole discretion of the district attorney, except those included in Article 46 of this Chapter, or an act by a juvenile as provided in Article 20A of Chapter 7B of the General Statutes.

(2) **Family member. --** A spouse, child, parent, guardian, legal custodian, sibling, or grandparent of the victim. The term does not include the accused.

(3) **Victim. --** A person against whom there is probable cause to believe a crime has been committed.

(4) **Witness. --** A person who has been or is expected to be summoned to testify for the prosecution in a criminal action concerning a felony, or who by reason of having relevant information is subject to being called or is likely to be called as a witness for the prosecution in such an action, whether or not an action or proceeding has been commenced.

History.
1985 (Reg. Sess., 1986), c. 998, s. 1; 1989, c. 596, s. 1; 1998-212, s. 19.4(a), (b); 2019-216, s. 1(a)

§ 15A-825. Treatment due victims and witnesses

(a) To the extent reasonably possible and subject to available resources, the employees of law enforcement agencies, the prosecutorial system, the judicial system, and the correctional system should make a reasonable effort to assure that each victim and witness within their jurisdiction:

(1) Is provided information regarding immediate medical assistance when needed and is not detained for an unreasonable length of time before having such assistance administered.

(2) Is provided information about available protection from harm and threats of harm arising out of cooperation with law enforcement and prosecution efforts, and receives such protection.

(2a) Is provided information that testimony as to one's home address is not relevant in every case, and that the victim or witness may request the district attorney to object to that line of questioning when appropriate.

(3) Has any stolen or other personal property expeditiously returned by law enforcement agencies when it is no longer needed as evidence, and the property's return would not impede an investigation or prosecution of the case. When feasible, all such property, except weapons, currency, contraband, property subject to evidentiary analysis, and property whose ownership is disputed, should be photographed and returned to the owner within a reasonable period of time of being recovered by law enforcement officials.

(4) Is provided appropriate employer intercession services to seek the employer's cooperation with the criminal justice system and minimize the employee's loss of pay and other benefits resulting from such cooperation whenever possible.

(5) Is provided, whenever practical, a secure waiting area during court proceedings that does not place the victim or witness in close proximity to defendants and families or friends of defendants.

(6) Is informed of the procedures to be followed to apply for and receive any appropriate witness fees or victim compensation.

(6a) Is informed of the right to be present throughout the entire trial of the defendant, subject to the right of the court to sequester witnesses.

(7) Is given the opportunity to be present during the final disposition of the case or is informed of the final disposition of the case, if the victim or witness has requested to be present or be informed.

(8) Is notified, whenever possible, that a court proceeding to which the victim or witness has been subpoenaed will not occur as scheduled.

(9) Is given the opportunity to prepare a victim impact statement for consideration by the court.

(9a) Prior to trial, is provided information about plea bargaining procedures and is informed that the district attorney may recommend a plea bargain to the court.

(10) Is informed that civil remedies may be available and that statutes of limitation apply in civil cases.

(11) Upon the victim's written request, is notified before a proceeding is held at which the release of the offender from custody is considered, if the crime for which the offender was placed in custody is a Class G or more serious felony.

(12) Upon the victim's written request, is notified if the offender escapes from custody or is released from custody, if the crime for which the offender was placed in custody is a Class G or more serious felony.

(13) Has family members of a homicide victim offered all the guarantees in this section, except those in subdivision (1).

(b) Nothing in this section shall be construed to create a cause of action for failure to comply with the requirements described in this section.

History.
1985 (Reg. Sess., 1986), c. 998, s. 1; 1989, c. 596, s. 2; 2019-216, s. 1(b).

§ 15A-826. District attorney legal assistants

In addition to providing administrative and legal support to the district attorney's office, district attorney legal assistants are responsible for coordinating efforts within the law-enforcement and judicial systems to assure that each victim and witness is treated in accordance with this Article.

History.
1985 (Reg. Sess., 1986), c. 998, s. 1; 1997-443, s. 18.7(e); 2015-241, s. 18A.8(c)

§ 15A-827. Scope

This Article does not create any civil or criminal liability on the part of the State of North Carolina or any criminal justice agency, employee, or volunteer.

History.
1985 (Reg. Sess., 1986), c. 998, s. 1

§§ 15A-828, 15A-829

Reserved for future codification purposes.

ARTICLE 46
CRIME VICTIMS' RIGHTS ACT

§ 15A-830. Definitions

(a) The following definitions apply in this Article:

(1) **Accused.** -- A person who has been arrested and charged with committing a crime covered by this Article.

(2) **Arresting law enforcement agency.** -- The law enforcement agency that makes the arrest of an accused.

(2a) **Court proceeding.** -- A critical stage of the post-arrest process heard by a judge in open court involving a plea that disposes of the case or the conviction, sentencing, or release of the accused, including the hearings described in G.S. 15A-837. The term does not include the preliminary proceedings described in Article 29 of Chapter 15A of the General Statutes. If it is known by law enforcement and the district attorney's office that (i) the defendant and the victim have a personal relationship as defined in G.S. 50B-1(b) and (ii) the hearing

may result in the defendant's release, efforts will be made to contact the victim.

(3) **Custodial agency.** -- The agency that has legal custody of an accused or defendant arising from a charge or conviction of a crime covered by this Article including, but not limited to, local jails or detention facilities, regional jails or detention facilities, facilities designated under G.S. 122C-252 for the custody and treatment of involuntary clients, or the Division of Adult Correction and Juvenile Justice of the Department of Public Safety.

(3a) **Family member.** -- A spouse, child, parent, guardian, legal custodian, sibling, or grandparent of the victim. The term does not include the accused.

(3b) **Felony property crime.** -- An act which constitutes a felony violation of one of the following:

a. Subchapter IV of Chapter 14 of the General Statutes.

b. Subchapter V of Chapter 14 of the General Statutes.

(4) **Investigating law enforcement agency.** -- The law enforcement agency with primary responsibility for investigating the crime committed against the victim.

(5) **Law enforcement agency.** -- An arresting law enforcement agency, a custodial agency, or an investigating law enforcement agency.

(6) Repealed by Session Laws 2019-216, s. 2, effective August 31, 2019, and applicable to offenses and acts of delinquency committed on or after that date.

(6a) **Offense against the person.** -- An offense against or involving the person of the victim which constitutes a violation of one of the following:

a. Subchapter III of Chapter 14 of the General Statutes.

b. Subchapter VII of Chapter 14 of the General Statutes.

c. Article 39 of Chapter 14 of the General Statutes.

d. Chapter 20 of the General Statutes, if an element of the offense involves impairment of the defendant, or injury or death to the victim.

e. A valid protective order under G.S. 50B-4.1, including, but not limited to, G.S. 14-134.3 and G.S. 14-269.8.

f. Article 35 of Chapter 14 of the General Statutes, if the elements of the offense involve communicating a threat or stalking.

g. An offense that triggers the enumerated victims' rights, as required by the North Carolina Constitution.

(7) **Victim.** -- A person against whom there is probable cause to believe an offense

against the person or a felony property crime has been committed.

(b) If the victim is a minor or is legally incapacitated, a parent, guardian, or legal custodian may assert the victim's rights under this Article. The accused may not assert the victim's rights. If the victim is deceased, then a family member, in the order set forth in the definition contained in this section, may assert the victim's rights under this Article, with the following limitations:

(1) The guardian or legal custodian of a deceased minor has priority over a family member.

(2) The right contained in G.S. 15A-834 may only be exercised by the personal representative of the victim's estate.

(c) An individual entitled to exercise the victim's rights as the appropriate family member in accordance with this section may designate any family member to act on behalf of the victim.

(d) An individual who, in the determination of the district attorney, would not act in the best interests of the victim shall not be entitled to assert or exercise the victim's rights. An individual may petition the court to review this determination by the district attorney.

History.
1998-212, s. 19.4(c); 2001-433, s. 1; 2001-487, s. 120; 2001-518, s. 2A; 2006-247, s. 20(e); 2007-116, s. 2; 2007-547, s. 2; 2009-58, s. 3; 2011-145, s. 19.1(h); 2014-115, s. 2.1(a); 2017-186, s. 2(ccc); 2019-216, s. 2

§ 15A-830.5. Victim's rights

(a) A victim of crime shall be treated with dignity and respect by the criminal justice system.

(b) A victim has the following rights:

(1) The right, upon request, to reasonable, accurate, and timely notice of court proceedings of the accused.

(2) The right, upon request, to be present at court proceedings of the accused.

(3) The right to be reasonably heard at court proceedings involving a plea that disposes of the case or the conviction, sentencing, or release of the accused.

(4) The right to receive restitution in a reasonably timely manner, when ordered by the court.

(5) The right to be given information about the crime, how the criminal justice system works, the rights of victims, and the availability of services for victims.

(6) The right, upon request, to receive information about the conviction or final disposition and sentence of the accused.

(7) The right, upon request, to receive notification of escape, release, proposed parole or pardon of the accused, or notice of a reprieve or commutation of the accused's sentence.

(8) The right to present the victim's views and concerns in writing to the Governor or agency considering any action that could result in the release of the accused, prior to such action becoming effective.

(9) The right to reasonably confer with the district attorney's office.

(c) This Article does not create a claim for damages against the State, any county or municipality, or any State or county agencies, instrumentalities, officers, or employees.

History.
2019-216, s. 3

§ 15A-831. Responsibilities of law enforcement agency

(a) As soon as practicable but within 72 hours after identifying a victim covered by this Article, the investigating law enforcement agency shall provide the victim with at least the following information in writing, on a form created by the Conference of District Attorneys:

(1) The availability of medical services, if needed.

(2) The availability of crime victims' compensation funds under Chapter 15B of the General Statutes and the address and telephone number of the agency responsible for dispensing the funds.

(3) The address and telephone number of the district attorney's office that will be responsible for prosecuting the victim's case.

(4) The name and telephone number of an investigating law enforcement agency employee whom the victim may contact if the victim has not been notified of an arrest in the victim's case within six months after the crime was reported to the law enforcement agency.

(5) Information about an accused's opportunity for pretrial release.

(6) The name and telephone number of an investigating law enforcement agency employee whom the victim may contact to find out whether the accused has been released from custody.

(7) The informational sheet described in G.S. 50B-3(c1), if there was a personal relationship, as defined in G.S. 50B-1(b), with the accused.

(8) A list of each right enumerated under G.S. 15A-830.5(b).

(9) Information about any other rights afforded to victims by law.

(b) Within 72 hours after the arrest of a person believed to have committed a crime covered by this Article, the arresting law enforcement

Chapter 15A

agency shall inform the investigating law enforcement agency of the arrest. Following receipt of this information, the investigating law enforcement agency shall notify the victim of the arrest within an additional 72 hours.

(c) Within 72 hours after receiving notification from the arresting law enforcement agency that the accused has been arrested, the investigating law enforcement agency shall also forward to the district attorney's office that will be responsible for prosecuting the case the defendant's name and the victim's name, address, and telephone number or other contact information, unless the victim refuses to disclose any or all of the information, in which case, the investigating law enforcement agency shall so inform the district attorney's office.

(d) Upon receiving the information in subsection (a) of this section, the victim shall, on a form created by the Conference of District Attorneys and provided by the investigating law enforcement agency, indicate whether the victim wishes to receive any further notices from the investigating law enforcement agency on the status of the accused during the pretrial process. If the victim elects to receive further notices during the pretrial process, the victim shall return the form to the investigating law enforcement agency within 10 business days of receipt of the form. The victim shall be responsible for notifying the investigating law enforcement agency of any changes in the victim's name, address, and telephone number.

(e) Upon receiving a form from the victim pursuant to subsection (d) of this section, the investigating law enforcement agency shall promptly share the form with the district attorney's office to facilitate compliance with the victim's preferences on notification.

History.
1998-212, s. 19.4(c); 2001-433, s. 2; 2001-487, s. 120; 2008-4, s. 1; 2019-216, s. 4

§ 15A-831.1. Polygraph examinations of victims of sexual assaults

(a) A criminal or juvenile justice agency shall not require a person claiming to be a victim of sexual assault or claiming to be a witness regarding the sexual assault of another person to submit to a polygraph or similar examination as a precondition to the agency conducting an investigation into the matter.

(b) An agency wishing to perform a polygraph examination of a person claiming to be a victim or witness of sexual assault shall inform the person of the following:

(1) That taking the polygraph examination is voluntary.

(2) That the results of the examination are not admissible in court.

(3) That the person's decision to submit to or refuse a polygraph examination will not be the sole basis for a decision by the agency not to investigate the matter.

(c) An agency which declines to investigate an alleged case of sexual assault following a decision by a person claiming to be a victim not to submit to a polygraph examination shall provide to that person, in writing, the reasons why the agency did not pursue the investigation at the request of the person.

History.
2007-294, s. 1

§ 15A-832. Responsibilities of the district attorney's office

(a) Within 21 days after the arrest of the accused, but not less than 24 hours before the accused's first scheduled probable-cause hearing, the district attorney's office shall provide to the victim a pamphlet or other written material that explains in a clear and concise manner the following:

(1) The victim's rights under this Article, including the right to reasonably confer with the district attorney's office about the disposition of the case and the right to provide a victim impact statement.

(2) The responsibilities of the district attorney's office under this Article.

(3) The victim's eligibility for compensation under the Crime Victims Compensation Act and the deadlines by which the victim must file a claim for compensation.

(4) The steps generally taken by the district attorney's office when prosecuting a crime.

(5) Suggestions on what the victim should do if threatened or intimidated by the accused or someone acting on the accused's behalf.

(6) The name and telephone number of a victim and witness assistant in the district attorney's office whom the victim may contact for further information.

(b) Upon receiving the information in subsection (a) of this section, the victim shall, on a form provided by the district attorney's office, indicate whether the victim wishes to receive notices of some, all, or none of the trial and posttrial proceedings involving the accused. If the victim elects to receive notices, the victim shall be responsible for notifying the district attorney's office or any other department or agency that has a responsibility under this Article of any changes in the victim's address and telephone number or other contact information. The victim may alter the request for notification at any time by notifying the district attorney's office and completing the form provided by the district attorney's office.

(c) The district attorney's office shall notify a victim of the date, time, and place of all court proceedings of the type that the victim has elected to receive notice, except as provided in G.S. 15A-835(b)(2) and G.S. 15A-837(a)(2). All notices required to be given by the district attorney's office shall be reasonable, accurate, and timely. The notices shall be given in a manner that is reasonably calculated to be received by the victim prior to the date of the court proceeding. The district attorney's office may provide the required notification electronically or by telephone, unless the victim requests otherwise. The notifications required by this section shall be documented by the district attorney's office.

(d) Whenever practical, the district attorney's office shall provide a secure waiting area during court proceedings that does not place the victim in close proximity to the defendant or the defendant's family.

(e) Repealed by Session Laws 2019-216, s. 5, effective August 31, 2019, and applicable to offenses and acts of delinquency committed on or after that date.

(f) The district attorney's office shall offer the victim the opportunity to reasonably confer with an attorney from the district attorney's office to obtain the views of the victim about, at a minimum, dismissal, plea or negotiations, sentencing, and any pretrial diversion programs.

(g) At the sentencing hearing, the prosecuting attorney shall submit to the court a copy of a form containing the identifying information set forth in G.S. 15A-831(c) about any victim's electing to receive further notices under this Article. The clerk of superior court shall include the form with the final judgment and commitment, or judgment suspending sentence, transmitted to the Division of Adult Correction and Juvenile Justice of the Department of Public Safety or other agency receiving custody of the defendant and shall be maintained by the custodial agency as a confidential file.

(h) When a person is a victim of a human trafficking offense and is entitled to benefits and services pursuant to G.S. 14-43.11(d), the district attorney's office shall so notify the Office of the Attorney General and Legal Aid of North Carolina, Inc., in addition to providing services under this Article.

(i) The district attorney's office shall make every effort to ensure that a victim's personal information is not disclosed unless otherwise required by law. The district attorney's office shall inform the victim that personal information such as the victim's telephone number, home address, and bank account number are not relevant in every case and that the victim may request the district attorney to object to that line of questioning when appropriate.

(j) The responsibilities of the district attorney's office extend to a victim of an act of delinquency if the juvenile's case is transferred to criminal court.

History.
1998-212, s. 19.4(c); 2001-433, s. 3; 2001-487, s. 120; 2007-547, s. 3; 2011-145, s. 19.1(h); 2017-186, s. 2(ddd); 2019-216, s. 5; 2019-243, s. 21.5(a)

§ 15A-832.1. Responsibilities of judicial officials

(a) In issuing a pleading as provided in G.S. 15A-921, for any misdemeanor offense against the person based on testimony or evidence from a complaining witness rather than from a law enforcement officer, a judicial official shall record the defendant's name and the victim's name, address, and telephone number electronically or on a form separate from the pleading and developed by the Administrative Office of the Courts for the purpose of recording that information, unless the victim refuses to disclose any or all of the information, in which case the judicial official shall so indicate.

(b) A judicial official issuing a pleading for any misdemeanor offense against the person based on testimony or evidence from a complaining witness rather than from a law enforcement officer shall deliver the court's copy of the warrant and the victim-identifying information to the office of the clerk of superior court by the close of the next business day. Within 72 hours, the office of the clerk of superior court shall forward to the district attorney's office the victim-identifying information set forth in subsection (a) of this section.

(c) The judge, in any court proceeding subject to this Article, shall inquire as to whether the victim is present and wishes to be heard. If the victim is present and wishes to be heard, the court shall grant the victim an opportunity to be reasonably heard. The right to be reasonably heard may be exercised, at the victim's discretion, through an oral statement, submission of a written statement, or submission of an audio or video statement.

(d) A judge notified by the clerk of court that a victim has filed a motion alleging a violation of the rights provided in this Article shall review the motion. The judge involved in the criminal proceeding that gave rise to the rights in question may, on the judge's own motion, recuse himself or herself if justice requires it and report the recusal to the Administrative Office of the Courts. The judge, or a judge appointed by the Administrative Office of the Courts in the event of recusal, shall dispose of the motion or set the motion for hearing as required by G.S. 15A-834.5.

(e) The court shall make every effort to provide a secure waiting area during court proceedings that does not place the victim in close proximity to the defendant or the defendant's family.

History.
2001-433, s. 4; 2001-487, s. 120; 2019-216, s. 6

§ 15A-833. Evidence of victim impact

(a) A victim has the right to offer admissible evidence of the impact of the crime, which shall be considered by the court or jury in sentencing the defendant. The evidence may include the following:

(1) A description of the nature and extent of any physical, psychological, or emotional injury suffered by the victim as a result of the offense committed by the defendant.

(2) An explanation of any economic or property loss suffered by the victim as a result of the offense committed by the defendant.

(3) A request for restitution and an indication of whether the victim has applied for or received compensation under the Crime Victims Compensation Act.

(b) No victim shall be required to offer evidence of the impact of the crime. No inference or conclusion shall be drawn from a victim's decision not to offer evidence of the impact of the crime. At the victim's request and with the consent of the defendant, a representative of the district attorney's office or a law enforcement officer may proffer evidence of the impact of the crime to the court.

History.
1998-212, s. 19.4(c); 2001-433, s. 5; 2001-487, s. 120

§ 15A-834. Restitution

A victim has the right to receive restitution as ordered by the court pursuant to Article 81C of Chapter 15A of the General Statutes.

History.
1998-212, s. 19.4(c)

§ 15A-834.5. Enforcement of the rights of a victim

(a) A victim may assert the rights provided in this Article pursuant to Section 37 of Article I of the North Carolina Constitution. In no event shall any underlying proceeding be subject to undue delay for the enforcement provided in this section. The procedure by which a victim may assert the rights provided under this Article shall be by motion to the court of jurisdiction. For the purposes of this section, the term

"victim" includes the following individuals acting on behalf of the victim:

(1) The victim's attorney.

(2) The prosecutor, at the request of the victim.

(3) A parent, guardian, or legal custodian, if the victim is a minor or is legally incapacitated, as provided in G.S. 15A-830.

(4) A family member, if the victim is deceased, as provided in G.S. 15A-830.

(b) A victim may allege a violation of the rights provided in this Article by filing a motion with the office of the clerk of superior court. The motion must be filed within the same criminal proceeding giving rise to the rights in question.

(c) If the motion involves an allegation that the district attorney failed to comply with the rights of a victim provided by this Article, the victim must first file a written complaint with the district attorney's office, to afford the district attorney's office an opportunity to resolve the issue stated in the written complaint in a timely manner.

(d) If the motion involves an allegation that a law enforcement agency failed to comply with the rights of a victim provided by this Article, the victim must first file a written complaint with that agency, to afford the agency an opportunity to resolve the issue stated in the written complaint in a timely manner.

(e) A victim has the right to consult with an attorney regarding an alleged violation of the rights provided in this Article, but the victim does not have the right to counsel provided by the State.

(f) The Administrative Office of the Courts shall create a form to serve as the motion and enable a victim to allege a violation of the rights provided in this Article. The form will indicate what specific right has allegedly been violated. The form will also provide the victim the opportunity to describe the substance of the alleged violation in detail. If the motion involves an allegation that the district attorney failed to comply with the rights of a victim provided in this Article, the victim must attach a copy of the written complaint that was previously filed with the district attorney as required by subsection (c) of this section. If the motion involves an allegation that a law enforcement agency failed to comply with the rights of a victim provided in this Article, the victim must attach a copy of the written complaint that was previously filed with that law enforcement agency as required by subsection (d) of this section.

(g) The clerk of superior court of each county shall provide the form created by the Administrative Office of the Courts to enable a victim to allege a violation of the rights provided in this Article. No fees shall be assessed for the filing of this motion. A copy of the motion required in subsection (b) of this section shall be given to the prosecutor if other than the elected District Attorney, the elected District Attorney, and the judge involved in the criminal proceeding that gave rise to the rights in question. If the motion involves an allegation that a law enforcement agency failed to comply with the rights of a victim provided by this Article, a copy of the motion required in subsection (b) of this section shall also be provided to the head of the law enforcement agency referenced in the motion.

(h) The judge shall review the motion and dispose of it or set it for hearing in a timely manner. Review may include conferring with the victim, the prosecutor if other than the District Attorney, and the District Attorney in order to inquire as to compliance with this Article. If the motion involves an allegation that a law enforcement agency failed to comply with the rights of a victim provided by this Article, the judge may confer with the head of that law enforcement agency as part of the review. At the conclusion of the review, the judge shall dispose of the motion or set the motion for hearing.

(i) If the judge fails to review the motion and dispose of it or set it for hearing in a timely manner, a victim may petition the North Carolina Court of Appeals for a writ of mandamus. The petition shall be filed without unreasonable delay. The court for good cause shown may shorten the time for filing a response.

(j) The failure or inability of any person to provide a right or service under this Article, including a service provided through the Statewide Automated Victim Assistance and Notification System established by the Governor's Crime Commission, may not be used by a defendant in a criminal case, by an inmate, by any other accused, or by any victim or any family member of a victim, as a ground for relief in any criminal or civil proceeding, except as provided in Section 37 of Article I of the North Carolina Constitution.

History.
2019-216, s. 7

§ 15A-835. Posttrial responsibilities

(a) Within 30 days after the final court proceeding in the case, the district attorney's office shall notify the victim, in writing, of:

(1) The final disposition of the case.

(2) The crimes of which the defendant was convicted.

(3) The defendant's right to appeal, if any.

(4) The telephone number of offices to contact in the event of nonpayment of restitution by the defendant.

(b) Upon a defendant's giving notice of appeal to the Court of Appeals or the Supreme Court, the district attorney's office shall forward to the Attorney General's office the defendant's name

and the victim's name, address, and telephone number. Upon receipt of this information, and thereafter as the circumstances require, the Attorney General's office shall provide the victim with the following:

(1) A clear and concise explanation of how the appellate process works, including information about possible actions that may be taken by the appellate court.

(2) Notice of the date, time, and place of any appellate proceedings involving the defendant. Notice shall be given in a manner that is reasonably calculated to be received by the victim prior to the date of the proceedings.

(3) The final disposition of an appeal.

(b1) Although the victim does not have a right to be heard, the victim is permitted to be present at any appellate proceeding that is an open hearing.

(c) If the defendant has been released on bail pending the outcome of the appeal, the agency that has custody of the defendant shall notify the investigating law enforcement agency as soon as practicable, and within 72 hours of receipt of the notification the investigating law enforcement agency shall notify the victim that the defendant has been released.

(d) If the defendant's conviction is overturned, and the district attorney's office decides to retry the case or the case is remanded to superior court for a new trial, the victim shall be entitled to the same rights under this Article as if the first trial did not take place.

(e) Repealed by Session Laws 2001-302, s. 1.

History.
1998-212, s. 19.4(c); 2001-302, s. 1; 2001-433, s. 6; 2001-487, s. 120; 2019-216, s. 7.5

§ 15A-836. Responsibilities of agency with custody of defendant

(a) When a form is included with the final judgment and commitment pursuant to G.S. 15A-832(g), or when the victim has otherwise filed a written request for notification with the custodial agency, the custodial agency shall notify the victim of:

(1) The projected date by which the defendant can be released from custody. The calculation of the release date shall be as exact as possible, including earned time and disciplinary credits if the sentence of imprisonment exceeds 90 days.

(2) An inmate's assignment to a minimum custody unit and the address of the unit. This notification shall include notice that the inmate's minimum custody status may lead to the inmate's participation in one or more community-based programs

Chapter 15A

such as work release or supervised leaves in the community.

(3) The victim's right to submit any concerns to the agency with custody and the procedure for submitting such concerns.

(4) The defendant's escape from custody, within 72 hours, except that if a victim has notified the agency in writing that the defendant has issued a specific threat against the victim, the agency shall notify the victim as soon as possible and within 24 hours at the latest.

(5) The defendant's capture, within 24 hours.

(6) The date the defendant is scheduled to be released from the facility. Whenever practical, notice shall be given 60 days before release. In no event shall notice be given less than seven days before release.

(7) The defendant's death.

(8) The procedure for alleging a failure of the custodial agency to notify the victim as required by this section.

(b) Notifications required in this section shall be provided within 60 days of the date the custodial agency takes custody of the defendant or within 60 days of the event requiring notification, or as otherwise specified in subsection (a) of this section.

History.
1998-212, s. 19.4(c); 2001-433, s. 7; 2001-487, s. 120; 2019-216, s. 8

§ 15A-837. Responsibilities of Section of Community Corrections of the Division of Adult Correction and Juvenile Justice

(a) The Section of Community Corrections of the Division of Adult Correction and Juvenile Justice shall notify the victim of:

(1) The defendant's regular conditions of probation or post-release supervision, special or added conditions, supervision requirements, and any subsequent changes.

(2) The date and location of any hearing to determine whether the defendant's supervision should be revoked, continued, modified, or terminated.

(3) The final disposition of any hearing referred to in subdivision (2) of this subsection.

(4) Any restitution modification.

(5) The defendant's movement into or out of any intermediate sanction as defined in G.S. 15A-1340.11(6).

(6) The defendant's absconding supervision, within 72 hours.

(7) The capture of a defendant described in subdivision (6) of this subsection, within 72 hours.

(8) The date when the defendant is terminated or discharged.

(9) The defendant's death.

(b) Notifications required in this section shall be provided within 30 days of the event requiring notification, or as otherwise specified in subsection (a) of this section.

History.
1998-212, s. 19.4(c); 2001-433, s. 8; 2001-487, ss. 47(a), 120; 2011-145, s. 19.1(k); 2017-186, s. 2(eee)

§ 15A-838. Notice of commuted sentence or pardon

The Governor's Clemency Office shall notify a victim when it is considering commuting the defendant's sentence or pardoning the defendant. The Governor's Clemency Office shall also give notice that the victim has the right to present a written statement to be considered by the Office before the defendant's sentence is commuted or the defendant is pardoned. The Governor's Clemency Office shall notify the victim of its decision. Notice shall be given in a manner that is reasonably calculated to allow for a timely response to the commutation or pardon decision.

History.
1998-212, s. 19.4(c)

§ 15A-839. No money damages

This Article, including the provision of a service pursuant to this Article through the Statewide Automated Victim Assistance and Notification System established by the Governor's Crime Commission, does not create a claim for damages against the State, a county, or a municipality, or any of its agencies, instrumentalities, officers, or employees.

History.
1998-212, s. 19.4(c); 1999-169, s. 1

§§ 15A-840, 15A-841

Repealed by Session Laws 2019-216, s. 9, effective August 31, 2019, and applicable to offenses and acts of delinquency committed on or after that date.

History.
G.S. 15A-840: 1998-212, s. 19.4(c); 1999-169, s. 2; repealed by 2019-216, s. 9, effective August 31, 2019. G.S. 15A-841: 1998-212, s. 19.4(c); repealed by 2019-216, s. 9, effective August 31, 2019

§§ 15A-842 through 15A-849

Reserved for future codification purposes.

ARTICLE 47

§§ 15A-850 through 15A-900

Reserved for future codification purposes.

SUBCHAPTER 09.
PRETRIAL PROCEDURE

ARTICLE 48
DISCOVERY IN THE SUPERIOR COURT

§ 15A-901. Application of Article

This Article applies to cases within the original jurisdiction of the superior court.

History.
1973, c. 1286, s. 1

§ 15A-902. Discovery procedure

(a) A party seeking discovery under this Article must, before filing any motion before a judge, request in writing that the other party comply voluntarily with the discovery request. A written request is not required if the parties agree in writing to voluntarily comply with the provisions of Article 48 of Chapter 15A of the General Statutes. Upon receiving a negative or unsatisfactory response, or upon the passage of seven days following the receipt of the request without response, the party requesting discovery may file a motion for discovery under the provisions of this Article concerning any matter as to which voluntary discovery was not made pursuant to request.

(b) To the extent that discovery authorized in this Article is voluntarily made in response to a request or written agreement, the discovery is deemed to have been made under an order of the court for the purposes of this Article.

(c) A motion for discovery under this Article must be heard before a superior court judge.

(d) If a defendant is represented by counsel, the defendant may as a matter of right request voluntary discovery from the State under subsection (a) of this section not later than the tenth working day after either the probable-cause hearing or the date the defendant waives the hearing. If a defendant is not represented by counsel, or is indicted or consents to the filing of a bill of information before the defendant has been afforded or waived a probable-cause hearing, the defendant may as a matter of right request voluntary discovery from the State under

subsection (a) of this section not later than the tenth working day after the later of:

(1) The defendant's consent to be tried upon a bill of information, or the service of notice upon the defendant that a true bill of indictment has been found by the grand jury, or

(2) The appointment of counsel.

For the purposes of this subsection a defendant is represented by counsel only if counsel was retained by or appointed for the defendant prior to or during a probable-cause hearing or prior to execution by the defendant of a waiver of a probable-cause hearing.

(e) The State may as a matter of right request voluntary discovery from the defendant, when authorized under this Article, at any time not later than the tenth working day after disclosure by the State with respect to the category of discovery in question.

(f) A motion for discovery made at any time prior to trial may be entertained if the parties so stipulate or if the judge for good cause shown determines that the motion should be allowed in whole or in part.

History.
1973, c. 1286, s. 1; 2004-154, s. 3

§ 15A-903. Disclosure of evidence by the State -- Information subject to disclosure

(a) Upon motion of the defendant, the court must order:

(1) The State to make available to the defendant the complete files of all law enforcement agencies, investigatory agencies, and prosecutors' offices involved in the investigation of the crimes committed or the prosecution of the defendant.

    a. The term "file" includes the defendant's statements, the codefendants' statements, witness statements, investigating officers' notes, results of tests and examinations, or any other matter or evidence obtained during the investigation of the offenses alleged to have been committed by the defendant. When any matter or evidence is submitted for testing or examination, in addition to any test or examination results, all other data, calculations, or writings of any kind shall be made available to the defendant, including, but not limited to, preliminary test or screening results and bench notes.

    b. The term "prosecutor's office" refers to the office of the prosecuting attorney.

    b1. The term "investigatory agency" includes any public or private entity that obtains information on behalf of a law enforcement agency or prosecutor's office in connection with the investigation of the crimes committed or the prosecution of the defendant.

c. Oral statements shall be in written or recorded form, except that oral statements made by a witness to a prosecuting attorney outside the presence of a law enforcement officer or investigatorial assistant shall not be required to be in written or recorded form unless there is significantly new or different information in the oral statement from a prior statement made by the witness.

d. The defendant shall have the right to inspect and copy or photograph any materials contained therein and, under appropriate safeguards, to inspect, examine, and test any physical evidence or sample contained therein.

(2) The prosecuting attorney to give notice to the defendant of any expert witnesses that the State reasonably expects to call as a witness at trial. Each such witness shall prepare, and the State shall furnish to the defendant, a report of the results of any examinations or tests conducted by the expert. The State shall also furnish to the defendant the expert's curriculum vitae, the expert's opinion, and the underlying basis for that opinion. The State shall give the notice and furnish the materials required by this subsection within a reasonable time prior to trial, as specified by the court. Standardized fee scales shall be developed by the Administrative Office of the Courts and Indigent Defense Services for all expert witnesses and private investigators who are compensated with State funds.

(3) The prosecuting attorney to give the defendant, at the beginning of jury selection, a written list of the names of all other witnesses whom the State reasonably expects to call during the trial. Names of witnesses shall not be subject to disclosure if the prosecuting attorney certifies in writing and under seal to the court that to do so may subject the witnesses or others to physical or substantial economic harm or coercion, or that there is other particularized, compelling need not to disclose. If there are witnesses that the State did not reasonably expect to call at the time of the provision of the witness list, and as a result are not listed, the court upon a good faith showing shall allow the witnesses to be called. Additionally, in the interest of justice, the court may in its discretion permit any undisclosed witness to testify.

(b) If the State voluntarily provides disclosure under G.S. 15A-902(a), the disclosure shall

be to the same extent as required by subsection (a) of this section.

(c) On a timely basis, law enforcement and investigatory agencies shall make available to the prosecutor's office a complete copy of the complete files related to the investigation of the crimes committed or the prosecution of the defendant for compliance with this section and any disclosure under G.S. 15A-902(a). Investigatory agencies that obtain information and materials listed in subdivision (1) of subsection (a) of this section shall ensure that such information and materials are fully disclosed to the prosecutor's office on a timely basis for disclosure to the defendant.

(d) Any person who willfully omits or misrepresents evidence or information required to be disclosed pursuant to subdivision (1) of subsection (a) of this section, or required to be provided to the prosecutor's office pursuant to subsection (c) of this section, shall be guilty of a Class H felony. Any person who willfully omits or misrepresents evidence or information required to be disclosed pursuant to any other provision of this section shall be guilty of a Class 1 misdemeanor.

History.
1973, c. 1286, s. 1; 1975, c. 166, s. 27; 1983, c. 759, ss. 1-3; 1983, Ex. Sess., c. 6, s. 1; 2001-282, s. 5; 2004-154, s. 4; 2007-183, s. 1; 2007-377, s. 1; 2007-393, s. 1; 2011-19, s. 9; 2011-250, s. 1

§ 15A-904. Disclosure by the State -- Certain information not subject to disclosure

(a) The State is not required to disclose written materials drafted by the prosecuting attorney or the prosecuting attorney's legal staff for their own use at trial, including witness examinations, voir dire questions, opening statements, and closing arguments. Disclosure is also not required of legal research or of records, correspondence, reports, memoranda, or trial preparation interview notes prepared by the prosecuting attorney or by members of the prosecuting attorney's legal staff to the extent they contain the opinions, theories, strategies, or conclusions of the prosecuting attorney or the prosecuting attorney's legal staff.

(a1) The State is not required to disclose the identity of a confidential informant unless the disclosure is otherwise required by law.

(a2) The State is not required to provide any personal identifying information of a witness beyond that witness's name, address, date of birth, and published phone number, unless the court determines upon motion of the defendant that such additional information is necessary to accurately identify and locate the witness.

(a3) The State is not required to disclose the identity of any individual providing information about a crime or criminal conduct to a Crime Stoppers organization under promise or assurance of anonymity unless ordered by the court. For purposes of this Article, a Crime Stoppers organization or similarly named entity means a private, nonprofit North Carolina corporation governed by a civilian volunteer board of directors that is operated on a local or statewide level that (i) offers anonymity to persons providing information to the organization, (ii) accepts and expends donations for cash rewards to persons who report to the organization information about alleged criminal activity and that the organization forwards to the appropriate law enforcement agency, and (iii) is established as a cooperative alliance between the news media, the community, and law enforcement officials.

(a4) The State is not required to disclose the Victim Impact Statement or its contents unless otherwise required by law. For purposes of this Chapter, a Victim Impact Statement is a document submitted by the victim or the victim's family to the State pursuant to the Victims' Rights Amendment.

(b) Nothing in this section prohibits the State from making voluntary disclosures in the interest of justice nor prohibits a court from finding that the protections of this section have been waived.

(c) This section shall have no effect on the State's duty to comply with federal or State constitutional disclosure requirements.

History.
1973, c. 1286, s. 1; 1975, c. 166, s. 27; 2004-154, s. 5; 2007-377, s. 2; 2011-250, s. 2

§ 15A-905. Disclosure of evidence by the defendant -- Information subject to disclosure

(a) **Documents and Tangible Objects.** -- If the court grants any relief sought by the defendant under G.S. 15A-903, the court must, upon motion of the State, order the defendant to permit the State to inspect and copy or photograph books, papers, documents, photographs, motion pictures, mechanical or electronic recordings, tangible objects, or copies or portions thereof which are within the possession, custody, or control of the defendant and which the defendant intends to introduce in evidence at the trial.

(b) **Reports of Examinations and Tests.** -- If the court grants any relief sought by the defendant under G.S. 15A-903, the court must, upon motion of the State, order the defendant to permit the State to inspect and copy or photograph results or reports of physical or mental examinations or of tests, measurements or experiments made in connection with the case, or copies thereof, within the possession and control of the defendant which the defendant intends to

introduce in evidence at the trial or which were prepared by a witness whom the defendant intends to call at the trial, when the results or reports relate to his testimony. In addition, upon motion of the State, the court must order the defendant to permit the State to inspect, examine, and test, subject to appropriate safeguards, any physical evidence or a sample of it available to the defendant if the defendant intends to offer such evidence, or tests or experiments made in connection with such evidence, as an exhibit or evidence in the case.

(c) **Notice of Defenses, Expert Witnesses, and Witness Lists.** -- If the court grants any relief sought by the defendant under G.S. 15A-903, or if disclosure is voluntarily made by the State pursuant to G.S. 15A-902(a), the court must, upon motion of the State, order the defendant to:

(1) Give notice to the State of the intent to offer at trial a defense of alibi, duress, entrapment, insanity, mental infirmity, diminished capacity, self-defense, accident, automatism, involuntary intoxication, or voluntary intoxication. Notice of defense as described in this subdivision is inadmissible against the defendant. Notice of defense must be given within 20 working days after the date the case is set for trial pursuant to G.S. 7A-49.4, or such other later time as set by the court.

a. As to the defense of alibi, the court may order, upon motion by the State, the disclosure of the identity of alibi witnesses no later than two weeks before trial. If disclosure is ordered, upon a showing of good cause, the court shall order the State to disclose any rebuttal alibi witnesses no later than one week before trial. If the parties agree, the court may specify different time periods for this exchange so long as the exchange occurs within a reasonable time prior to trial.

b. As to only the defenses of duress, entrapment, insanity, automatism, or involuntary intoxication, notice by the defendant shall contain specific information as to the nature and extent of the defense.

(2) Give notice to the State of any expert witnesses that the defendant reasonably expects to call as a witness at trial. Each such witness shall prepare, and the defendant shall furnish to the State, a report of the results of the examinations or tests conducted by the expert. The defendant shall also furnish to the State the expert's curriculum vitae, the expert's opinion, and the underlying basis for that opinion. The defendant shall give the notice and furnish the materials required by this subdivision

within a reasonable time prior to trial, as specified by the court. Standardized fee scales shall be developed by the Administrative Office of the Courts and Indigent Defense Services for all expert witnesses and private investigators who are compensated with State funds.

(3) Give the State, at the beginning of jury selection, a written list of the names of all other witnesses whom the defendant reasonably expects to call during the trial. Names of witnesses shall not be subject to disclosure if the defendant certifies in writing and under seal to the court that to do so may subject the witnesses or others to physical or substantial economic harm or coercion, or that there is other particularized, compelling need not to disclose. If there are witnesses that the defendant did not reasonably expect to call at the time of the provision of the witness list, and as a result are not listed, the court upon a good faith showing shall allow the witnesses to be called. Additionally, in the interest of justice, the court may in its discretion permit any undisclosed witness to testify.

(d) If the defendant voluntarily provides discovery under G.S. 15A-902(a), the disclosure shall be to the same extent as required by subsection (c) of this section.

History.
1973, c. 1286, s. 1; 1975, c. 166, s. 27; 2004-154, s. 6; 2011-250, s. 3

§ 15A-906. Disclosure of evidence by the defendant -- Certain evidence not subject to disclosure

Except as provided in G.S. 15A-905(b) this Article does not authorize the discovery or inspection of reports, memoranda, or other internal defense documents made by the defendant or his attorneys or agents in connection with the investigation or defense of the case, or of statements made by the defendant, or by prosecution or defense witnesses, or by prospective prosecution witnesses or defense witnesses, to the defendant, his agents, or attorneys.

History.
1973, c. 1286, s. 1

§ 15A-907. Continuing duty to disclose

If a party, who is required to give or who voluntarily gives discovery pursuant to this Article, discovers prior to or during trial additional evidence or witnesses, or decides to use additional evidence or witnesses, and the evidence or witness is or may be subject to discovery or inspection under this Article, the party must promptly notify the attorney for the other party of the existence of the additional evidence or witnesses.

History.
1973, c. 1286, s. 1; 1975, c. 166, s. 16; 2004-154, s. 7

§ 15A-908. Regulation of discovery -- Protective orders

(a) Upon written motion of a party and a finding of good cause, which may include, but is not limited to a finding that there is a substantial risk to any person of physical harm, intimidation, bribery, economic reprisals, or unnecessary annoyance or embarrassment, the court may at any time order that discovery or inspection be denied, restricted, or deferred, or may make other appropriate orders. A party may apply ex parte for a protective order and, if an ex parte order is granted, the opposing party shall receive notice that the order was entered, but without disclosure of the subject matter of the order.

(b) The court may permit a party seeking relief under subsection (a) to submit supporting affidavits or statements to the court for in camera inspection. If thereafter the court enters an order granting relief under subsection (a), the material submitted in camera must be sealed and preserved in the records of the court to be made available to the appellate court in the event of an appeal.

History.
1973, c. 1286, s. 1; 1983, Ex. Sess., c. 6, s. 2; 2004-154, s. 8

§ 15A-909. Regulation of discovery -- Time, place, and manner of discovery and inspection

An order of the court granting relief under this Article must specify the time, place, and manner of making the discovery and inspection permitted and may prescribe appropriate terms and conditions.

History.
1973, c. 1286, s. 1

§ 15A-910. Regulation of discovery -- Failure to comply

(a) If at any time during the course of the proceedings the court determines that a party has failed to comply with this Article or with an order issued pursuant to this Article, the court in addition to exercising its contempt powers may

　　(1) Order the party to permit the discovery or inspection, or

　　(2) Grant a continuance or recess, or

(3) Prohibit the party from introducing evidence not disclosed, or

(3a) Declare a mistrial, or

(3b) Dismiss the charge, with or without prejudice, or

(4) Enter other appropriate orders.

(b) Prior to finding any sanctions appropriate, the court shall consider both the materiality of the subject matter and the totality of the circumstances surrounding an alleged failure to comply with this Article or an order issued pursuant to this Article.

(c) For purposes of determining whether to impose personal sanctions for untimely disclosure of law enforcement and investigatory agencies' files, courts and State agencies shall presume that prosecuting attorneys and their staffs have acted in good faith if they have made a reasonably diligent inquiry of those agencies under G.S. 15A-903(c) and disclosed the responsive materials.

(d) If the court imposes any sanction, it must make specific findings justifying the imposed sanction.

History.
1973, c. 1286, s. 1; 1975, c. 166, s. 17; 1983, Ex. Sess., c. 6, s. 3; 2004-154, s. 9; 2011-250, s. 4

§§ 15A-911 through 15A-920

Reserved for future codification purposes.

ARTICLE 49
PLEADINGS AND JOINDER

§ 15A-921. Pleadings in criminal cases

Subject to the provisions of this Article, the following may serve as pleadings of the State in criminal cases:

(1) Citation.

(2) Criminal summons.

(3) Warrant for arrest.

(4) Magistrate's order pursuant to G.S. 15A-511 after arrest without warrant.

(5) Statement of charges.

(6) Information.

(7) Indictment.

History.
1973, c. 1286, s. 1; 1975, c. 166, s. 18

§ 15A-922. Use of pleadings in misdemeanor cases generally

(a) **Process as Pleadings. --** The citation, criminal summons, warrant for arrest, or magistrate's order serves as the pleading of the State for a misdemeanor prosecuted in the district

court, unless the prosecutor files a statement of charges, or there is objection to trial on a citation. When a statement of charges is filed it supersedes all previous pleadings of the State and constitutes the pleading of the State.

(b) Statement of Charges.

(1) A statement of charges is a criminal pleading which charges a misdemeanor. It must be signed by the prosecutor who files it.

(2) Upon appropriate motion, a defendant is entitled to a period of at least three working days for the preparation of his defense after a statement of charges is filed, or the time the defendant is first notified of the statement of charges, whichever is later, unless the judge finds that the statement of charges makes no material change in the pleadings and that no additional time is necessary.

(3) If the judge rules that the pleadings charging a misdemeanor are insufficient and a prosecutor is permitted to file a statement of charges pursuant to subsection (e), the order of the judge must allow the prosecutor three working days, unless the judge determines that a longer period is justified, in which to file the statement of charges, and must provide that the charges will be dismissed if the statement of charges is not filed within the period allowed.

(c) **Objection to Trial on Citation. --** A defendant charged in a citation with a criminal offense may by appropriate motion require that the offense be charged in a new pleading. The prosecutor must then file a statement of charges unless it appears that a criminal summons or a warrant for arrest should be secured in order to insure the attendance of the defendant, and in addition serve as the new pleading.

(d) **Statement of Charges upon Determination of Prosecutor. --** The prosecutor may file a statement of charges upon his own determination at any time prior to arraignment in the district court. It may charge the same offenses as the citation, criminal summons, warrant for arrest, or magistrate's order or additional or different offenses.

(e) **Objection to Sufficiency of Criminal Summons; Warrant for Arrest or Magistrate's Order as Pleading. --** If the defendant by appropriate motion objects to the sufficiency of a criminal summons, warrant for arrest, or magistrate's order as a pleading, at the time of or after arraignment in the district court or upon trial de novo in the superior court, and the judge rules that the pleading is insufficient, the prosecutor may file a statement of charges, but a statement of charges filed pursuant to this authorization may not change the nature of the offense.

(f) **Amendment of Pleadings prior to or after Final Judgment. --** A statement of charges, criminal summons, warrant for arrest, citation, or magistrate's order may be amended at any time prior to or after final judgment when the amendment does not change the nature of the offense charged.

(g) **Pleadings When Misdemeanor Prosecution Initiated in Superior Court.** -- When the prosecution of a misdemeanor is initiated in the superior court as permitted by G.S. 7A-271, the prosecution must be upon information or indictment.

(h) **Allegations in Superior Court of Prior Convictions.** -- When charges in the district court involve allegations of prior convictions and there is an appeal to the superior court for trial de novo, a statement of charges must be filed in the superior court to charge the offense in the manner provided in G.S. 15A-928.

History.
1973, c. 1286, s. 1; 1975, c. 166, s. 27; 1979, c. 770; 1985, c. 689, s. 6

§ 15A-923. Use of pleadings in felony cases and misdemeanor cases initiated in the superior court division

(a) **Prosecution on Information or Indictment.** -- The pleading in felony cases and misdemeanor cases initiated in the superior court division must be a bill of indictment, unless there is a waiver of the bill of indictment as provided in G.S. 15A-642. If there is a waiver, the pleading must be an information. A presentment by the grand jury may not serve as the pleading in a criminal case.

(b) **Form of Information or Indictment.** -- An information and a bill of indictment charge the crime or crimes in the same manner. An information has entered upon it or attached to it the defendant's written waiver of a bill of indictment. The bill of indictment has entered upon it the finding of the grand jury that it is a true bill.

(c) **Waiver of Indictment.** -- The defendant may waive a bill of indictment as provided in G.S. 15A-642.

(d) **Amendment of Information.** -- An information may be amended only with the consent of the defendant.

(e) **No Amendment of Indictment.** -- A bill of indictment may not be amended.

History.
1973, c. 1286, s. 1

§ 15A-924. Contents of pleadings; duplicity; alleging and proving previous convictions; failure to charge crime; surplusage

(a) A criminal pleading must contain:

(1) The name or other identification of the defendant but the name of the defendant need not be repeated in each count unless required for clarity.

(2) A separate count addressed to each offense charged, but allegations in one count may be incorporated by reference in another count.

(3) A statement or cross reference in each count indicating that the offense charged therein was committed in a designated county.

(4) A statement or cross reference in each count indicating that the offense charged was committed on, or on or about, a designated date, or during a designated period of time. Error as to a date or its omission is not ground for dismissal of the charges or for reversal of a conviction if time was not of the essence with respect to the charge and the error or omission did not mislead the defendant to his prejudice.

(5) A plain and concise factual statement in each count which, without allegations of an evidentiary nature, asserts facts supporting every element of a criminal offense and the defendant's commission thereof with sufficient precision clearly to apprise the defendant or defendants of the conduct which is the subject of the accusation. When the pleading is a criminal summons, warrant for arrest, or magistrate's order, or statement of charges based thereon, both the statement of the crime and any information showing probable cause which was considered by the judicial official and which has been furnished to the defendant must be used in determining whether the pleading is sufficient to meet the foregoing requirement.

(6) For each count a citation of any applicable statute, rule, regulation, ordinance, or other provision of law alleged therein to have been violated. Error in the citation or its omission is not ground for dismissal of the charges or for reversal of a conviction.

(7) A statement that the State intends to use one or more aggravating factors under G.S. 15A-1340.16(d)(20), with a plain and concise factual statement indicating the factor or factors it intends to use under the authority of that subdivision.

(b) If any count of an indictment or information charges more than one offense, the defendant may by timely filing of a motion require the State to elect and state a single offense alleged in the count upon which the State will proceed to trial. A count may be dismissed for duplicity if the State fails to make timely election.

(c) In trials in superior court, allegations of previous convictions are subject to the provisions of G.S. 15A-928.

(d) In alleging and proving a prior conviction, it is sufficient to state that the defendant was at a certain time and place convicted of the previous offense, without otherwise fully alleging all the elements. A duly certified transcript of the record of a prior conviction is, upon proof of the identity of the person of the defendant, sufficient evidence of a prior conviction. If the surname of a defendant charged is identical to the surname of a defendant previously convicted and there is identity with respect to one given name, or two initials, or two initials corresponding with the first letters of given names, between the two defendants, and there is no evidence that would indicate the two defendants are not one and the same, the identity of name is prima facie evidence that the two defendants are the same person.

(e) Upon motion of a defendant under G.S. 15A-952(b) the court must dismiss the charges contained in a pleading which fails to charge the defendant with a crime in the manner required by subsection (a), unless the failure is with regard to a matter as to which an amendment is allowable.

(f) Upon motion of a defendant under G.S. 15A-952(b) the court may strike inflammatory or prejudicial surplusage from the pleading.

History.
1973, c. 1286, s. 1; 1975, c. 642, s. 2; 1989, c. 290, s. 3; 2005-145, s. 3

§ 15A-925. Bill of particulars

(a) Upon motion of a defendant under G.S. 15A-952, the court in which a charge is pending may order the State to file a bill of particulars with the court and to serve a copy upon the defendant.

(b) A motion for a bill of particulars must request and specify items of factual information desired by the defendant which pertain to the charge and which are not recited in the pleading, and must allege that the defendant cannot adequately prepare or conduct his defense without such information.

(c) If any or all of the items of information requested are necessary to enable the defendant adequately to prepare or conduct his defense, the court must order the State to file and serve a bill of particulars. Nothing contained in this section authorizes an order for a bill of particulars which requires the State to recite matters of evidence.

(d) The bill of particulars must be filed with the court and must recite every item of information required in the order. A copy must be served upon the defendant, or his attorney. The proceedings are stayed pending the filing and service.

(e) A bill of particulars may not supply an omission or cure a defect in a criminal pleading. The evidence of the State, as to those matters within the scope of the motion, is limited to the items set out in the bill of particulars. The court may permit amendment of a bill of particulars at any time prior to trial.

History.
1973, c. 1286, s. 1

§ 15A-926. Joinder of offenses and defendants

(a) **Joinder of Offenses.** -- Two or more offenses may be joined in one pleading or for trial when the offenses, whether felonies or misdemeanors or both, are based on the same act or transaction or on a series of acts or transactions connected together or constituting parts of a single scheme or plan. Each offense must be stated in a separate count as required by G.S. 15A-924.

(b) Separate Pleadings for Each Defendant and Joinder of Defendants for Trial.

(1) Each defendant must be charged in a separate pleading.

(2) Upon written motion of the prosecutor, charges against two or more defendants may be joined for trial:

a. When each of the defendants is charged with accountability for each offense; or

b. When, even if all of the defendants are not charged with accountability for each offense, the several offenses charged:

1. Were part of a common scheme or plan; or

2. Were part of the same act or transaction; or

3. Were so closely connected in time, place, and occasion that it would be difficult to separate proof of one charge from proof of the others.

(c) Failure to Join Related Offenses.

(1) When a defendant has been charged with two or more offenses joinable under subsection (a) his timely motion to join them for trial must be granted unless the court determines that because the prosecutor does not have sufficient evidence to warrant trying some of the offenses at that time or if, for some other reason, the ends of justice would be defeated if the motion were granted. A defendant's failure to make this motion constitutes a waiver of any right of joinder of offenses joinable

under subsection (a) with which the defendant knew he was charged.

(2) A defendant who has been tried for one offense may thereafter move to dismiss a charge of a joinable offense. The motion to dismiss must be made prior to the second trial, and must be granted unless

    a. A motion for joinder of these offenses was previously denied, or

    b. The court finds that the right of joinder has been waived, or

    c. The court finds that because the prosecutor did not have sufficient evidence to warrant trying this offense at the time of the first trial, or because of some other reason, the ends of justice would be defeated if the motion were granted.

(3) The right to joinder under this subsection is not applicable when the defendant has pleaded guilty or no contest to the previous charge.

History.
1973, c. 1286, s. 1; 1975, c. 166, ss. 19, 27

§ 15A-927. Severance of offenses; objection to joinder of defendants for trial

(a) Timeliness of Motion; Waiver; Double Jeopardy.

(1) A defendant's motion for severance of offenses must be made before trial as provided in G.S. 15A-952, except as provided in G.S. 15A-953, and except that a motion for severance may be made before or at the close of the State's evidence if based upon a ground not previously known. Any right to severance is waived if the motion is not made at the appropriate time.

(2) If a defendant's pretrial motion for severance is overruled, he may renew the motion on the same grounds before or at the close of all the evidence. Any right to severance is waived by failure to renew the motion.

(3) Unless consented to by the defendant, a motion by the prosecutor for severance of offenses may be granted only prior to trial.

(4) If a motion for severance of offenses is granted during the trial, a motion by the defendant for a mistrial must be granted.

(b) **Severance of Offenses.** -- The court, on motion of the prosecutor or on motion of the defendant, must grant a severance of offenses whenever:

(1) If before trial, it is found necessary to promote a fair determination of the defendant's guilt or innocence of each offense; or

(2) If during trial, upon motion of the defendant or motion of the prosecutor with the consent of the defendant, it is found

necessary to achieve a fair determination of the defendant's guilt or innocence of each offense. The court must consider whether, in view of the number of offenses charged and the complexity of the evidence to be offered, the trier of fact will be able to distinguish the evidence and apply the law intelligently as to each offense.

(c) Objection to Joinder of Charges against Multiple Defendants for Trial; Severance.

(1) When a defendant objects to joinder of charges against two or more defendants for trial because an out-of-court statement of a codefendant makes reference to him but is not admissible against him, the court must require the prosecutor to select one of the following courses:

    a. A joint trial at which the statement is not admitted into evidence; or

    b. A joint trial at which the statement is admitted into evidence only after all references to the moving defendant have been effectively deleted so that the statement will not prejudice him; or

    c. A separate trial of the objecting defendant.

(2) The court, on motion of the prosecutor, or on motion of the defendant other than under subdivision (1) above must deny a joinder for trial or grant a severance of defendants whenever:

    a. If before trial, it is found necessary to protect a defendant's right to a speedy trial, or it is found necessary to promote a fair determination of the guilt or innocence of one or more defendants; or

    b. If during trial, upon motion of the defendant whose trial is to be severed, or motion of the prosecutor with the consent of the defendant whose trial is to be severed, it is found necessary to achieve a fair determination of the guilt or innocence of that defendant.

(3) The court may order the prosecutor to disclose, out of the presence of the jurors, any statements made by the defendants which he intends to introduce in evidence at the trial when that information would assist the court in ruling on an objection to joinder of defendants for trial or a motion for severance of defendants.

(d) **Failure to Prove Grounds for Joinder of Defendants for Trial.** -- If a defendant moves for severance at the conclusion of the State's case or of all the evidence, and there is not sufficient evidence to support the allegation upon which the moving defendant was joined for trial with the other defendant or defendants, the court must grant a severance if, in view of this lack of evidence, severance is found necessary to achieve a fair determination of that defendant's guilt or innocence.

(e) **Severance on Motion of Court.** -- The court may order a severance of offenses before trial or deny the joinder of defendants for trial if a severance or denial of joinder could be obtained on motion of a defendant or the prosecutor.

History.
1973, c. 1286, s. 1; 1975, c. 166, s. 27

§ 15A-928. Allegation and proof of previous convictions in superior court

(a) When the fact that the defendant has been previously convicted of an offense raises an offense of lower grade to one of higher grade and thereby becomes an element of the latter, an indictment or information for the higher offense may not allege the previous conviction. If a reference to a previous conviction is contained in the statutory name or title of the offense, the name or title may not be used in the indictment or information, but an improvised name or title must be used which labels and distinguishes the offense without reference to a previous conviction.

(b) An indictment or information for the offense must be accompanied by a special indictment or information, filed with the principal pleading, charging that the defendant was previously convicted of a specified offense. At the prosecutor's option, the special indictment or information may be incorporated in the principal indictment as a separate count. Except as provided in subsection (c) below, the State may not refer to the special indictment or information during the trial nor adduce any evidence concerning the previous conviction alleged therein.

(c) After commencement of the trial and before the close of the State's case, the judge in the absence of the jury must arraign the defendant upon the special indictment or information, and must advise him that he may admit the previous conviction alleged, deny it, or remain silent. Depending upon the defendant's response, the trial of the case must then proceed as follows:

(1) If the defendant admits the previous conviction, that element of the offense charged in the indictment or information is established, no evidence in support thereof may be adduced by the State, and the judge must submit the case to the jury without reference thereto and as if the fact of such previous conviction were not an element of the offense. The court may not submit to the jury any lesser included offense which is distinguished from the offense charged solely by the fact that a previous conviction is not an element thereof.

(2) If the defendant denies the previous conviction or remains silent, the State may prove that element of the offense charged before the jury as a part of its case. This section applies only to proof of a prior conviction when it is an element of the crime charged, and does not prohibit the State from introducing proof of prior convictions when otherwise permitted under the rules of evidence.

(d) When a misdemeanor is tried de novo in superior court in which the fact of a previous conviction is an element of the offense affecting punishment, the State must replace the pleading in the case with superseding statements of charges separately alleging the substantive offense and the fact of any prior conviction, in accordance with the provisions of this section relating to indictments and informations. Any jury trial in superior court on the misdemeanor must be held in accordance with the provisions of subsections (b) and (c).

(e) Nothing contained in this section precludes the State from proving a prior conviction before a grand jury or relieves the State from the obligation or necessity of so doing in order to submit a legally sufficient case.

History.
1973, c. 1286, s. 1; 1975, c. 166, s. 27

§§ 15A-929, 15A-930

Reserved for future codification purposes.

ARTICLE 50
VOLUNTARY DISMISSAL

§ 15A-931. Voluntary dismissal of criminal charges by the State

(a) Except as provided in G.S. 20-138.4, the prosecutor may dismiss any charges stated in a criminal pleading including those deferred for prosecution by entering an oral dismissal in open court before or during the trial, or by filing a written dismissal with the clerk at any time. The clerk must record the dismissal entered by the prosecutor and note in the case file whether a jury has been impaneled or evidence has been introduced.

(a1) Unless the defendant or the defendant's attorney has been notified otherwise by the prosecutor, a written dismissal of the charges against the defendant filed by the prosecutor shall be served in the same manner prescribed for motions under G.S. 15A-951. In addition, the written dismissal shall also be served on the chief officer of the custodial facility when the record reflects that the defendant is in custody.

Chapter 15A

(b) No statute of limitations is tolled by charges which have been dismissed pursuant to this section.

History.
1973, c. 1286, s. 1; 1975, c. 166, s. 27; 1983, c. 435, s. 5; 1991, c. 109, s. 1; 1997-228, s. 1

§15A-932. Dismissal with leave when defendant fails to appear and cannot be readily found or pursuant to a deferred prosecution agreement

(a) The prosecutor may enter a dismissal with leave for nonappearance when a defendant:

(1) Cannot be readily found to be served with an order for arrest after the grand jury had indicted him; or

(2) Fails to appear at a criminal proceeding at which his attendance is required, and the prosecutor believes the defendant cannot be readily found.

(a1) The prosecutor may enter a dismissal with leave pursuant to a deferred prosecution agreement entered into in accordance with the provisions of Article 82 of this Chapter.

(b) Dismissal with leave for nonappearance or pursuant to a deferred prosecution agreement results in removal of the case from the docket of the court, but all process outstanding retains its validity, and all necessary actions to apprehend the defendant, investigate the case, or otherwise further its prosecution may be taken, including the issuance of nontestimonial identification orders, search warrants, new process, initiation of extradition proceedings, and the like.

(c) The prosecutor may enter the dismissal with leave for nonappearance or pursuant to a deferred prosecution agreement orally in open court or by filing the dismissal in writing with the clerk. If the dismissal for nonappearance or pursuant to a deferred prosecution agreement is entered orally, the clerk must note the nature of the dismissal in the case records.

(d) Upon apprehension of the defendant, or in the discretion of the prosecutor when he believes apprehension is imminent, the prosecutor may reinstitute the proceedings by filing written notice with the clerk.

(d1) If the proceeding was dismissed pursuant to subdivision (2) of subsection (a) of this section and charged only offenses for which written appearance, waiver of trial or hearing, and plea of guilty or admission of responsibility are permitted pursuant to G.S. 7A-148(a), and the defendant later tenders to the court that waiver and payment in full of all applicable fines, costs, and fees, the clerk shall accept said waiver and payment without need for a written reinstatement from the prosecutor. Upon disposition of the case pursuant to this subsection, the clerk shall recall any outstanding criminal process in the case pursuant to G.S. 15A-301(g)(2)b.

(e) If the defendant fails to comply with the terms of a deferred prosecution agreement, the prosecutor may reinstitute the proceedings by filing written notice with the clerk.

History.
1977, c. 777, s. 1; 1985, c. 250; 1994, Ex. Sess., c. 2, s. 1; 2011-145, s. 31.23B; 2011-192, s. 7(o); 2011-391, s. 63(a); 2011-411, s. 1

§§15A-933 through 15A-940

Reserved for future codification purposes.

ARTICLE 51
ARRAIGNMENT

§15A-941. Arraignment before judge only upon written request; entry of not guilty plea if not arraigned.

(a) Arraignment consists of bringing a defendant before a judge having jurisdiction to try the offense, advising him of the charges pending against him, and directing him to plead. The prosecutor must read the charges or fairly summarize them to the defendant. If the defendant fails to plead, the court must record that fact, and the defendant must be tried as if he had pleaded not guilty.

(b) Repealed by Session Laws 2021-47, s. 10(h), effective June 18, 2021, and applicable to proceedings occurring on or after that date.

(c) Repealed by Session Laws 2021-47, s. 10(h), effective June 18, 2021, and applicable to proceedings occurring on or after that date.

(d) A defendant will be arraigned in accordance with this section only if the defendant files a written request with the clerk of superior court for an arraignment not later than 21 days after service of the bill of indictment. If a bill of indictment is not required to be served pursuant to G.S. 15A-630, then the written request for arraignment must be filed not later than 21 days from the date of the return of the indictment as a true bill. Upon the return of the indictment as a true bill, the court must immediately cause notice of the 21-day time limit within which the defendant may request an arraignment to be mailed or otherwise given to the defendant and to the defendant's counsel of record, if any. If the defendant does not file a written request for arraignment, then the court shall enter a not guilty plea on behalf of the defendant.

(e) Nothing in this section shall prevent the district attorney from calendaring cases for administrative purposes.

Chapter 15A

History.

1973, c. 1286, s. 1; 1975, c. 166, s. 27; 1993, c. 30, s. 3; 1995 (Reg. Sess., 1996), c. 725, s. 7; 2021-47, s. 10(h)

§ 15A-942. Right to counsel

If the defendant appears at the arraignment without counsel, the court must inform the defendant of his right to counsel, must accord the defendant opportunity to exercise that right, and must take any action necessary to effectuate the right. If the defendant does not file a written request for arraignment, the court, in addition to entering a plea of not guilty on behalf of the defendant, shall also verify that the defendant is aware of the right to counsel, that the defendant has been given the opportunity to exercise that right, and must take any action necessary to effectuate that right on behalf of the defendant.

History.

1777, c. 115, s. 85, P.R.; R.C., c. 35, s. 13; Code, s. 1182; Rev., s. 3150; C.S., s. 4515; 1973, c. 1286, s. 1; 1995 (Reg. Sess., 1996), c. 725, s. 8

§ 15A-943. Arraignment in superior court -- Required calendaring

(a) In counties in which there are regularly scheduled 20 or more weeks of trial sessions of superior court at which criminal cases are heard, and in other counties the Chief Justice designates, the prosecutor must calendar arraignments in the superior court on at least the first day of every other week in which criminal cases are heard. No cases in which the presence of a jury is required may be calendared for the day or portion of a day during which arraignments are calendared.

(b) When a defendant pleads not guilty at an arraignment required by subsection (a), he may not be tried without his consent in the week in which he is arraigned.

(c) Notwithstanding the provisions of subsection (a) of this section, in any county where as many as three simultaneous sessions of superior court, whether criminal, civil, or mixed, are regularly scheduled, the prosecutor may calendar arraignments in any of the criminal or mixed sessions, at least every other week, upon any day or days of a session, and jury cases may be calendared for trial in any other court at which criminal cases may be heard, upon such days.

History.

1973, c. 1286, s. 1; 1975, c. 166, s. 27; c. 471

§ 15A-944. Arraignment in superior court -- Optional calendaring

In counties other than those described in G.S. 15A-943 the prosecutor may, but is not required to, calendar arraignments in the manner described in that section.

History.

1973, c. 1286, s. 1; 1975, c. 166, s. 27

§ 15A-945. Waiver of arraignment

A defendant who is represented by counsel and who wishes to plead not guilty may waive arraignment prior to the day for which arraignment is calendared by filing a written plea, signed by the defendant and his counsel.

History.

1973, c. 1286, s. 1

§§ 15A-946 through 15A-950

Reserved for future codification purposes.

ARTICLE 52
MOTIONS PRACTICE

§ 15A-951. Motions in general; definition, service, and filing

(a) A motion must:

    (1) Unless made during a hearing or trial, be in writing;

    (2) State the grounds of the motion; and

    (3) Set forth the relief or order sought.

(b) Each written motion must be served upon the attorney of record for the opposing party or upon the defendant if he is not represented by counsel. Service upon the attorney or upon a party shall be made as provided in G.S. 1A-1, Rule 5.

(c) All written motions must be filed with the court. Proof of service must be made by filing with the court a certificate of service as provided in G.S. 1A-1, Rule 5(b1).

History.

1973, c. 1286, s. 1; 1975, c. 166, s. 27; 2021-47, s. 16(a)

§ 15A-952. Pretrial motions; time for filing; sanction for failure to file; motion hearing date

(a) Any defense, objection, or request which is capable of being determined without the trial of the general issue may be raised before trial by motion.

(b) Except as provided in subsection (d), when the following motions are made in superior court they must be made within the time limitations stated in subsection (c) unless the court permits filing at a later time:

(1) Motions to continue.

(2) Motions for a change of venue under G.S. 15A-957.

(3) Motions for a special venire under G.S. 9-12 or G.S. 15A-958.

(4) Motions to dismiss under G.S. 15A-955.

(5) Motions to dismiss for improper venue.

(6) Motions addressed to the pleadings, including:

a. Motions to dismiss for failure to plead under G.S. 15A-924(e).

b. Motions to strike under G.S. 15A-924(f).

c. Motions for bills of particulars under G.S. 15A-924(b) or G.S. 15A-925.

d. Motions for severance of offenses, to the extent required by G.S. 15A-927.

e. Motions for joinder of related offenses under G.S. 15A-926(c).

(c) Unless otherwise provided, the motions listed in subsection (b) must be made at or before the time of arraignment if a written request is filed for arraignment and if arraignment is held prior to the session of court for which the trial is calendared. If arraignment is to be held at the session for which trial is calendared, the motions must be filed on or before five o'clock P.M. on the Wednesday prior to the session when trial of the case begins.

If a written request for arraignment is not filed, then any motion listed in subsection (b) of this section must be filed not later than 21 days from the date of the return of the bill of indictment as a true bill.

(d) Motions concerning jurisdiction of the court or the failure of the pleading to charge an offense may be made at any time.

(e) Failure to file the motions in subsection (b) within the time required constitutes a waiver of the motion. The court may grant relief from any waiver except failure to move to dismiss for improper venue.

(f) When a motion is made before trial, the court in its discretion may hear the motion before trial, on the date set for arraignment, on the date set for trial before a jury is impaneled, or during trial.

(g) In superior or district court, the judge shall consider at least the following factors in determining whether to grant a continuance:

(1) Whether the failure to grant a continuance would be likely to result in a miscarriage of justice;

(2) Whether the case taken as a whole is so unusual and so complex, due to the number of defendants or the nature of the prosecution or otherwise, that more time is needed for adequate preparation; and

(3) Whether the case involves physical or sexual child abuse when a victim or witness is under 16 years of age, and whether further delay would have an adverse impact on the well-being of the child.

(4) Good cause for granting a continuance shall include those instances when the defendant, a witness, or counsel of record has an obligation of service to the State of North Carolina.

any service in carrying out any duties Assembly, or service on Commission or any other board, commission, or authority as an appointee of the Governor, the Lieutenant Governor, or the General Assembly.

A continuance requested to fulfill an obligation of service by carrying out any duties as a member of the General Assembly, or service on the Rules Review Commission or any other board, commission, or authority as an appointee of the Governor, the Lieutenant Governor, or the General Assembly, must be granted.

History.

1973, c. 1286, s. 1; 1989, c. 688, s. 5; 1995 (Reg. Sess., 1996), c. 725, s. 9; 1997-34, s. 12; 2019-243, s. 30(b); 2020-72, s. 2(b)

§ 15A-953. Motions practice in district court

In misdemeanor prosecutions in the district court motions should ordinarily be made upon arraignment or during the course of trial, as appropriate. A written motion may be made prior to trial in district court. With the consent of other parties and the district court judge, a motion may be heard before trial. Upon trial de novo in superior court, motions are subject to the provisions of G.S. 15A-952, and except as provided in G.S. 15A-135, no motion in superior court is prejudiced by any ruling upon, or a failure to make timely motion on, the subject in district court.

History.

1973, c. 1286, s. 1

§ 15A-954. Motion to dismiss -- Grounds applicable to all criminal pleadings; dismissal of proceedings upon death of defendant

(a) The court on motion of the defendant must dismiss the charges stated in a criminal pleading if it determines that:

(1) The statute alleged to have been violated is unconstitutional on its face or as applied to the defendant.

(2) The statute of limitations has run.

(3) The defendant has been denied a speedy trial as required by the Constitution

of the United States and the Constitution of North Carolina.

(4) The defendant's constitutional rights have been flagrantly violated and there is such irreparable prejudice to the defendant's preparation of his case that there is no remedy but to dismiss the prosecution.

(5) The defendant has previously been placed in jeopardy of the same offense.

(6) The defendant has previously been charged with the same offense in another North Carolina court of competent jurisdiction, and the criminal pleading charging the offense is still pending and valid.

(7) An issue of fact or law essential to a successful prosecution has been previously adjudicated in favor of the defendant in a prior action between the parties.

(8) The court has no jurisdiction of the offense charged.

(9) The defendant has been granted immunity by law from prosecution.

(10) The pleading fails to charge an offense as provided in G.S. 15A-924(e).

(b) Upon suggestion to the court that the defendant has died, the court upon determining that the defendant is dead must dismiss the charges.

(c) A motion to dismiss for the reasons set out in subsection (a) may be made at any time.

History.
1973, c. 1286, s. 1

§ 15A-955. Motion to dismiss -- Grounds applicable to indictments

The court on motion of the defendant may dismiss an indictment if it determines that:

(1) There is ground for a challenge to the array,

(2) The requisite number of qualified grand jurors did not concur in finding the indictment, or

(3) All of the witnesses before the grand jury on the bill of indictment were incompetent to testify.

History.
1973, c. 1286, s. 1

§ 15A-956. Deferral of ruling on motion to dismiss when charge to be reinstituted

If a motion to dismiss is made at arraignment or trial, upon motion of the prosecutor the court may recess the proceedings for a period of time requested by the prosecutor, not to exceed 24 hours, prior to ruling upon the motion.

History.
1973, c. 1286, s. 1; 1975, c. 166, s. 27

§ 15A-957. Motion for change of venue

If, upon motion of the defendant, the court determines that there exists in the county in which the prosecution is pending so great a prejudice against the defendant that he cannot obtain a fair and impartial trial, the court must either:

(1) Transfer the proceeding to another county in the prosecutorial district as defined in G.S. 7A-60 or to another county in an adjoining prosecutorial district as defined in G.S. 7A-60, or

(2) Order a special venire under the terms of G.S. 15A-958.

The procedure for change of venue is in accordance with the provisions of Article 3 of this Chapter, Venue.

History.
1973, c. 1286, s. 1; 1987 (Reg. Sess., 1988), c. 1037, s. 63

§ 15A-958. Motion for a special venire from another county

Upon motion of the defendant or the State, or on its own motion, a court may issue an order for a special venire of jurors from another county if in its discretion it determines the action to be necessary to insure a fair trial. The procedure for securing this special venire is governed by G.S. 9-12.

History.
1973, c. 1286, s. 1

§ 15A-959. Notice of defense of insanity; pretrial determination of insanity

(a) If a defendant intends to raise the defense of insanity, the defendant must file a notice of the defendant's intention to rely on the defense of insanity as provided in G.S. 15A-905(c) and, if the case is not subject to that section, within a reasonable time prior to trial. The court may for cause shown allow late filing of the notice or grant additional time to the parties to prepare for trial or make other appropriate orders.

(b) In cases not subject to the requirements of G.S. 15A-905(c), if a defendant intends to introduce expert testimony relating to a mental disease, defect, or other condition bearing upon the issue of whether the defendant had the mental state required for the offense charged, the defendant must within a reasonable time prior to trial file a notice of that intention. The court may for cause shown allow late filing of the notice or grant additional time to the parties to prepare for trial or make other appropriate orders.

(c) Upon motion of the defendant and with the consent of the State the court may conduct a hearing prior to the trial with regard to the defense of insanity at the time of the offense. If the court determines that the defendant has a valid defense of insanity with regard to any criminal charge, it may dismiss that charge, with prejudice, upon making a finding to that effect. The court's denial of relief under this subsection is without prejudice to the defendant's right to rely on the defense at trial. If the motion is denied, no reference to the hearing may be made at the trial, and recorded testimony or evidence taken at the hearing is not admissible as evidence at the trial.

History.
1973, c. 1286, s. 1; 1977, c. 711, s. 25; 2004-154, s. 10

§§ 15A-960 through 15A-970

Reserved for future codification purposes.

ARTICLE 53
MOTION TO SUPPRESS EVIDENCE

§ 15A-971. Definitions

As used in this Article the following definitions apply unless the context clearly requires otherwise:

(1) **Evidence. --** When referring to matter in the possession of or available to a prosecutor, any tangible property or potential testimony which may be offered in evidence in a criminal action.

(2) **Potential Testimony. --** Information or factual knowledge of a person who is or may be available as a witness.

History.
1973, c. 1286, s. 1; 1975, c. 166, s. 27

§ 15A-972. Motion to suppress evidence before trial in superior court in general

When an indictment has been returned or an information has been filed in the superior court, or a defendant has been bound over for trial in superior court, a defendant who is aggrieved may move to suppress evidence in accordance with the terms of this Article.

History.
1973, c. 1286, s. 1

§ 15A-973. Motion to suppress evidence in district court

In misdemeanor prosecutions in the district court, motions to suppress evidence should ordinarily be made during the course of the trial. A motion to suppress may be made prior to trial. With the consent of the prosecutor and the district court judge, the motion may be heard prior to trial.

History.
1973, c. 1286, s. 1; 1975, c. 166, s. 27

§ 15A-974. Exclusion or suppression of unlawfully obtained evidence

(a) Upon timely motion, evidence must be suppressed if:

(1) Its exclusion is required by the Constitution of the United States or the Constitution of the State of North Carolina; or

(2) It is obtained as a result of a substantial violation of the provisions of this Chapter. In determining whether a violation is substantial, the court must consider all the circumstances, including:

a. The importance of the particular interest violated;

b. The extent of the deviation from lawful conduct;

c. The extent to which the violation was willful;

d. The extent to which exclusion will tend to deter future violations of this Chapter.

Evidence shall not be suppressed under this subdivision if the person committing the violation of the provision or provisions under this Chapter acted under the objectively reasonable, good faith belief that the actions were lawful.

(b) The court, in making a determination whether or not evidence shall be suppressed under this section, shall make findings of fact and conclusions of law which shall be included in the record, pursuant to G.S. 15A-977(f).

History.
1973, c. 1286, s. 1; 2011-6, s. 1

§ 15A-975. Motion to suppress evidence in superior court prior to trial and during trial

(a) In superior court, the defendant may move to suppress evidence only prior to trial unless the defendant did not have reasonable opportunity to make the motion before trial or unless a motion to suppress is allowed during trial under subsection (b) or (c).

(b) A motion to suppress may be made for the first time during trial when the State has failed to notify the defendant's counsel or, if he has none, the defendant, sooner than 20 working days before trial, of its intention to use the evidence, and the evidence is:

(1) Evidence of a statement made by a defendant;

(2) Evidence obtained by virtue of a search without a search warrant; or

(3) Evidence obtained as a result of search with a search warrant when the defendant was not present at the time of the execution of the search warrant.

(c) If, after a pretrial determination and denial of the motion, the judge is satisfied, upon a showing by the defendant, that additional pertinent facts have been discovered by the defendant which he could not have discovered with reasonable diligence before the determination of the motion, he may permit the defendant to renew the motion before the trial or, if not possible because of the time of discovery of alleged new facts, during trial.

When a misdemeanor is appealed by the defendant for trial de novo in superior court, the State need not give the notice required by this section.

History.
1973, c. 1286, s. 1

§ 15A-976. Timing of pretrial suppression motion and hearing

(a) A motion to suppress evidence in superior court may be made at any time prior to trial except as provided in subsection (b).

(b) If the State gives notice not later than 20 working days before trial of its intention to use evidence and if the evidence is of a type listed in G.S. 15A-975(b), the defendant may move to suppress the evidence only if its motion is made not later than 10 working days following receipt of the notice from the State.

(c) When the motion is made before trial, the judge in his discretion may hear the motion before trial, on the date set for arraignment, on the date set for trial before a jury is impaneled, or during trial. He may rule on the motion before trial or reserve judgment until trial.

History.
1973, c. 1286, s. 1

§ 15A-977. Motion to suppress evidence in superior court; procedure

(a) A motion to suppress evidence in superior court made before trial must be in writing and a copy of the motion must be served upon the State. The motion must state the grounds upon which it is made. The motion must be accompanied by an affidavit containing facts supporting the motion. The affidavit may be based upon personal knowledge, or upon information and belief, if the source of the information and the basis for the belief are stated. The State may file an answer denying or admitting any of the allegations. A copy of the answer must be served on the defendant's counsel, or on the defendant if he has no counsel.

(b) The judge must summarily grant the motion to suppress evidence if:

(1) The motion complies with the requirements of subsection (a), it states grounds which require exclusion of the evidence, and the State concedes the truth of allegations of fact which support the motion; or

(2) The State stipulates that the evidence sought to be suppressed will not be offered in evidence in any criminal action or proceeding against the defendant.

(c) The judge may summarily deny the motion to suppress evidence if:

(1) The motion does not allege a legal basis for the motion; or

(2) The affidavit does not as a matter of law support the ground alleged.

(d) If the motion is not determined summarily the judge must make the determination after a hearing and finding of facts. Testimony at the hearing must be under oath.

(e) A motion to suppress made during trial may be made in writing or orally and may be determined in the same manner as when made before trial. The hearing, if held, must be out of the presence of the jury.

(f) The judge must set forth in the record his findings of facts and conclusions of law.

History.
1973, c. 1286, s. 1

§ 15A-978. Motion to suppress evidence in superior court or district court; challenge of probable cause supporting search on grounds of truthfulness; when identity of informant must be disclosed

(a) A defendant may contest the validity of a search warrant and the admissibility of evidence obtained thereunder by contesting the truthfulness of the testimony showing probable cause for its issuance. The defendant may contest the truthfulness of the testimony by cross-examination or by offering evidence. For the purposes of this section, truthful testimony is testimony which reports in good faith the circumstances relied on to establish probable cause.

(b) In any proceeding on a motion to suppress evidence pursuant to this section in which the truthfulness of the testimony presented to establish probable cause is contested and the testimony includes a report of information furnished by an informant whose identity is not disclosed in the testimony, the defendant is entitled to be informed of the informant's identity unless:

(1) The evidence sought to be suppressed was seized by authority of a search warrant or incident to an arrest with warrant; or

(2) There is corroboration of the informant's existence independent of the testimony in question.

The provisions of subdivisions (b)(1) and (b)(2) do not apply to situations in which disclosure of an informant's identity is required by controlling constitutional decisions.

(c) This section does not limit the right of a defendant to contest the truthfulness of testimony offered in support of a search made without a warrant.

History.
1973, c. 1286, s. 1

§ 15A-979. Motion to suppress evidence in superior and district court; orders of suppression; effects of orders and of failure to make motion

(a) Upon granting a motion to suppress evidence the judge must order that the evidence in question be excluded in the criminal action pending against the defendant. When the order is based upon the ground of an unlawful search and seizure and excludes tangible property unlawfully taken from the defendant's possession, and when the property is not contraband or otherwise subject to lawful retention by the State or another, the judge must order that the property be restored to the defendant at the conclusion of the trial including all appeals.

(b) An order finally denying a motion to suppress evidence may be reviewed upon an appeal from a judgment of conviction, including a judgment entered upon a plea of guilty.

(c) An order by the superior court granting a motion to suppress prior to trial is appealable to the appellate division of the General Court of Justice prior to trial upon certificate by the prosecutor to the judge who granted the motion that the appeal is not taken for the purpose of delay and that the evidence is essential to the case. The appeal is to the appellate court that would have jurisdiction if the defendant were found guilty of the charge and received the maximum punishment. If there are multiple charges affected by a motion to suppress, the ruling is appealable to the court with jurisdiction over the offense carrying the highest punishment.

(d) A motion to suppress evidence made pursuant to this Article is the exclusive method of challenging the admissibility of evidence upon the grounds specified in G.S. 15A-974.

History.
1973, c. 1286, s. 1; 1975, c. 166, s. 27; 1979, c. 723

§ 15A-980. Right to suppress use of certain prior convictions obtained in violation of right to counsel

(a) A defendant has the right to suppress the use of a prior conviction that was obtained in violation of his right to counsel if its use by the State is to impeach the defendant or if its use will:

(1) Increase the degree of crime of which the defendant would be guilty; or

(2) Result in a sentence of imprisonment that otherwise would not be imposed; or

(3) Result in a lengthened sentence of imprisonment.

(b) A defendant who has grounds to suppress the use of a conviction in evidence at a trial or other proceeding as set forth in (a) must do so by motion made in accordance with the procedure in this Article. A defendant waives his right to suppress use of a prior conviction if he does not move to suppress it.

(c) When a defendant has moved to suppress use of a prior conviction under the terms of subsection (a), he has the burden of proving by the preponderance of the evidence that the conviction was obtained in violation of his right to counsel. To prevail, he must prove that at the time of the conviction he was indigent, had no counsel, and had not waived his right to counsel. If the defendant proves that a prior conviction was obtained in violation of his right to counsel, the judge must suppress use of the conviction at trial or in any other proceeding if its use will contravene the provisions of subsection (a).

History.
1983, c. 513, s. 1

ARTICLE 54

§§ 15A-981 through 15A-990

Reserved for future codification purposes.

ARTICLE 55

§§ 15A-991 through 15A-1000

Reserved for future codification purposes.

SUBCHAPTER 10.
GENERAL TRIAL PROCEDURE

ARTICLE 56
INCAPACITY TO PROCEED

§ 15A-1001. No proceedings when defendant mentally incapacitated; exception

(a) No person may be tried, convicted, sentenced, or punished for a crime when by reason of mental illness or defect he is unable to understand the nature and object of the proceedings against him, to comprehend his own situation in reference to the proceedings, or to assist in his defense in a rational or reasonable manner. This condition is hereinafter referred to as "incapacity to proceed."

(b) This section does not prevent the court from going forward with any motions which can be handled by counsel without the assistance of the defendant.

History.
1973, c. 1286, s. 1

§ 15A-1002. Determination of incapacity to proceed; evidence; temporary commitment; temporary orders

(a) The question of the capacity of the defendant to proceed may be raised at any time on motion by the prosecutor, the defendant, the defense counsel, or the court. The motion shall detail the specific conduct that leads the moving party to question the defendant's capacity to proceed.

(b) (1) When the capacity of the defendant to proceed is questioned, the court shall hold a hearing to determine the defendant's capacity to proceed. If an examination is ordered pursuant to subdivision (1a) or (2) of this subsection, the hearing shall be held after the examination. Reasonable notice shall be given to the defendant and prosecutor, and the State and the defendant may introduce evidence.

(1a) In the case of a defendant charged with a misdemeanor or felony, the court may appoint one or more impartial medical experts, including forensic evaluators approved under rules of the Commission for Mental Health, Developmental Disabilities, and Substance Abuse Services, to examine the defendant and return a written report describing the present state of the defendant's mental health. Reports so prepared are admissible at the hearing. The court may call any expert so appointed to testify at the hearing with or without the request of either party.

(2) At any time in the case of a defendant charged with a felony, the court may order the defendant to a State facility for the mentally ill for observation and treatment for the period, not to exceed 60 days, necessary to determine the defendant's capacity to proceed. If a defendant is ordered to a State facility without first having an examination pursuant to subsection (b)(1a) of this section, the judge shall make a finding that an examination pursuant to this subsection would be more appropriate to determine the defendant's capacity. The sheriff shall return the defendant to the county when notified that the evaluation has been completed. The director of the facility shall direct his report on defendant's condition to the defense attorney and to the clerk of superior court, who shall bring it to the attention of the court. The report is admissible at the hearing.

(3) Repealed by Session Laws 1989, c. 486, s. 1.

(4) A presiding district or superior court judge of this State who orders an examination pursuant to subdivision (1a) or (2) of this subsection shall order the release of relevant confidential information to the examiner, including, but not limited to, the warrant or indictment, arrest records, the law enforcement incident report, the defendant's criminal record, jail records, any prior medical and mental health records of the defendant, and any school records of the defendant after providing the defendant with reasonable notice and an opportunity to be heard and then determining that the information is relevant and necessary to the hearing of the matter before the court and unavailable from any other source. This subdivision shall not be construed to relieve any court of its duty to conduct hearings and make findings required under relevant federal law before ordering the release of any private medical or mental health information or records related to substance abuse or HIV status or treatment. The records may be surrendered to the court for in camera review if surrender is necessary to make the required determinations. The records shall be withheld from public inspection and, except as provided in this subdivision, may be examined only by order of the court.

(b1) The order of the court shall contain findings of fact to support its determination of the defendant's capacity to proceed. The parties may stipulate that the defendant is capable of proceeding but shall not be allowed to stipulate that the defendant lacks capacity to proceed. If the court concludes that the defendant lacks capacity to proceed, proceedings for involuntary civil commitment under Chapter 122C of the General Statutes may be instituted on the basis of the report in either the county where the criminal proceedings are pending or, if the defendant is hospitalized, in the county in which the defendant is hospitalized.

(b2) Reports made to the court pursuant to this section shall be completed and provided to the court as follows:

(1) The report in a case of a defendant charged with a misdemeanor shall be completed and provided to the court no later than 10 days following the completion of the examination for a defendant who was in custody at the time the examination order was entered and no later than 20 days following the completion of the examination for a defendant who was not in custody at the time the examination order was entered.

(2) The report in the case of a defendant charged with a felony shall be completed and provided to the court no later than 30 days following the completion of the examination.

(3) In cases where the defendant challenges the determination made by the court-ordered examiner or the State facility and the court orders an independent psychiatric examination, that examination and report to the court must be completed within 60 days of the entry of the order by the court.

The court may, for good cause shown, extend the time for the provision of the report to the court for up to 30 additional days. The court may renew an extension of time for an additional 30 days upon request of the State or the defendant prior to the expiration of the previous extension. In no case shall the court grant extensions totaling more than 120 days beyond the time periods otherwise provided in this subsection.

(c) The court may make appropriate temporary orders for the confinement or security of the defendant pending the hearing or ruling of the court on the question of the capacity of the defendant to proceed.

(d) Any report made to the court pursuant to this section shall be forwarded to the clerk of superior court in a sealed envelope addressed to the attention of a presiding judge, with a covering statement to the clerk of the fact of the examination of the defendant and any conclusion as to whether the defendant has or lacks capacity to proceed. If the defendant is being held in the custody of the sheriff, the clerk shall send a copy of the covering statement to the sheriff. The sheriff and any persons employed by the sheriff shall maintain the copy of the covering statement as a confidential record. A copy of the full report shall be forwarded to defense counsel or to the defendant if he is not represented by counsel. If the question of the defendant's capacity to proceed is raised at any time, a copy of the full report must be forwarded to the district attorney, as provided in G.S. 122C-54(b). Until such report becomes a public record, the full report to the court shall be kept under such conditions as are directed by the court, and its contents shall not be revealed except the report and the relevant confidential information previously ordered released under subdivision (b)(4) of this section shall be released as follows: (i) to clinicians at the program where the defendant is receiving capacity restoration; (ii) to clinicians designated by the Secretary of Health and Human Services, and (iii) as directed by the court. Any report made to the court pursuant to this section shall not be a public record unless introduced into evidence.

History.
1973, c. 1286, s. 1; 1975, c. 166, ss. 20, 27; 1977, cc. 25, 860; 1979, 2nd Sess., c. 1313; 1985, c. 588; c. 589, s. 9; 1989, c. 486, s. 1; 1991, c. 636, s. 19(b); 1995, c. 299, s. 1; 1995 (Reg. Sess., 1996), c. 742, ss. 13, 14; 2013-18, s. 1; 2017-147, s. 1

§ 15A-1003. Referral of incapable defendant for civil commitment proceedings

(a) When a defendant is found to be incapable of proceeding, the presiding judge, upon such additional hearing, if any, as he determines to be necessary, shall determine whether there are reasonable grounds to believe the defendant meets the criteria for involuntary commitment under Part 7 of Article 5 of Chapter 122C of the General Statutes. If the presiding judge finds reasonable grounds to believe that the defendant meets the criteria, he shall make findings of fact and issue a custody order in the same manner, upon the same grounds and with the same effect as an order issued by a clerk or magistrate pursuant to G.S. 122C-261. Proceedings thereafter are in accordance with Part 7 of Article 5 of Chapter 122C of the General Statutes. If the defendant was charged with a violent crime, including a crime involving assault with a deadly weapon, the judge's custody order shall require a law-enforcement officer to take the defendant directly to a 24-hour facility as described in G.S. 122C-252; and the order must indicate that the defendant was charged with a violent crime and that he was found incapable of proceeding.

(b) The court may make appropriate orders for the temporary detention of the defendant pending that proceeding.

(c) Evidence used at the hearing with regard to capacity to proceed is admissible in the involuntary civil commitment proceedings.

History.
1973, c. 1286, s. 1; 1975, c. 166, s. 20; 1983, c. 380, s. 1; 1985, c. 589, s. 10; 1987, c. 596, s. 5

§ 15A-1004. Orders for safeguarding of defendant and return for trial

(a) When a defendant is found to be incapable of proceeding, the trial court must make appropriate orders to safeguard the defendant and to ensure his return for trial in the event that he subsequently becomes capable of proceeding.

(b) If the defendant is not placed in the custody of a hospital or other institution in a proceeding for involuntary civil commitment, appropriate orders may include any of the procedures, orders, and conditions provided in Article 26 of this Chapter, Bail, specifically including the power to place the defendant in the custody of a designated person or organization agreeing to supervise him.

(c) If the defendant is placed in the custody of a hospital or other institution in a proceeding for involuntary civil commitment, the orders must provide for reporting to the clerk if the defendant is to be released from the custody of the hospital or institution. The original or supplemental orders may make provisions as in subsection (b) in the event that the defendant is released. The court shall also order that the defendant shall be examined to determine whether the defendant has the capacity to proceed prior to release from custody. A report of the examination shall be provided pursuant to G.S. 15A-1002. If the defendant was charged with a violent crime, including a crime involving assault with a deadly weapon, and that charge has not been dismissed, the order must require that if the defendant is to be released from the custody of the hospital or other institution, he is to be released only to the custody of a specified law enforcement agency. If the original or supplemental orders do not specify to whom the respondent shall be released, the hospital or other institution may release the defendant to whomever it thinks appropriate.

(d) If the defendant is placed in the custody of a hospital or institution pursuant to proceedings for involuntary civil commitment, or if the defendant is placed in the custody of another person pursuant to subsection (b), the orders of the trial court must require that the hospital, institution, or individual report the condition of the defendant to the clerk at the same times that reports on the condition of the defendant-respondent are required under Part 7 of Article 5 of Chapter 122C of the General Statutes, or more frequently if the court requires, and immediately if the defendant gains capacity to proceed. The order must also require the report to state the likelihood of the defendant's gaining capacity to proceed, to the extent that the hospital, institution, or individual is capable of making such a judgment.

(e) The orders must require and provide for the return of the defendant to stand trial in the event that he gains capacity to proceed, unless the charges have been dismissed pursuant to G.S. 15A-1008, and may also provide for the confinement or pretrial release of the defendant in that event.

(f) The orders of the court may be amended or supplemented from time to time as changed conditions require.

History.
1973, c. 1286, s. 1; 1975, c. 166, s. 20; 1983, c. 380, s. 2; c. 460, s. 2; 1985, c. 589, s. 11; 2013-18, s. 2

§ 15A-1005. Reporting to court with regard to defendants incapable of proceeding

The clerk of the court in which the criminal proceeding is pending must keep a docket of defendants who have been determined to be incapable of proceeding. The clerk must submit the docket to the senior resident superior court judge in his district at least semiannually.

History.
1973, c. 1286, s. 1

§ 15A-1006. Return of defendant for trial upon gaining capacity

If a defendant who has been determined to be incapable of proceeding, and who is in the custody of an institution or an individual, has been determined by the institution or individual having custody to have gained capacity to proceed, the individual or institution shall provide written notification to the clerk in the county in which the criminal proceeding is pending. The clerk shall provide written notification to the district attorney, the defendant's attorney, and the sheriff. The sheriff shall return the defendant to the county for a supplemental hearing pursuant to G.S. 15A-1007, if conducted, and trial and hold the defendant for a supplemental hearing and trial, subject to the orders of the court entered pursuant to G.S. 15A-1004.

History.
1973, c. 1286, s. 1; 2013-18, s. 3

§ 15A-1007. Supplemental hearings

(a) When it has been reported to the court that a defendant has gained capacity to proceed, or when the defendant has been determined by the individual or institution having custody of him to have gained capacity and has been returned for trial, in accordance with G.S. 15A-1004(e) and G.S. 15A-1006, the clerk shall notify the district attorney. Upon receiving the notification, the district attorney shall calendar the matter for hearing at the next available term of court but no later than 30 days after receiving the notification. The court may hold a supplemental hearing to determine whether the defendant has capacity to proceed. The court may take any action at the supplemental hearing that it could have taken at an original hearing to determine the capacity of the defendant to proceed.

(b) The court may hold a supplemental hearing any time upon its own determination that a hearing is appropriate or necessary to inquire into the condition of the defendant.

(c) The court must hold a supplemental hearing if it appears that any of the conditions for dismissal of the charges have been met.

(d) If the court determines in a supplemental hearing that a defendant has gained the capacity to proceed, the case shall be calendared for trial at the earliest practicable time. Continuances that extend beyond 60 days after initial calendaring of the trial shall be granted only in extraordinary circumstances when necessary for the proper administration of justice, and the court shall issue a written order stating the grounds for granting the continuance.

History.
1973, c. 1286, s. 1; 2013-18, s. 4

§ 15A-1008. Dismissal of charges

(a) When a defendant lacks capacity to proceed, the court shall dismiss the charges upon the earliest of the following occurrences:

(1) When it appears to the satisfaction of the court that the defendant will not gain capacity to proceed.

(2) When as a result of incarceration, involuntary commitment to an inpatient facility, or other court-ordered confinement, the defendant has been substantially deprived of his liberty for a period of time equal to or in excess of the maximum term of imprisonment permissible for prior record Level VI for felonies or prior conviction Level III for misdemeanors for the most serious offense charged.

(3) Upon the expiration of a period of five years from the date of determination of incapacity to proceed in the case of misdemeanor charges and a period of 10 years in the case of felony charges.

(b) A dismissal entered pursuant to subdivision (2) of subsection (a) of this section shall be without leave.

(c) A dismissal entered pursuant to subdivision (1) or (3) of subsection (a) of this section shall be issued without prejudice to the refiling of the charges. Upon the defendant becoming capable of proceeding, the prosecutor may reinstitute proceedings dismissed pursuant to subdivision (1) or (3) of subsection (a) of this section by filing written notice with the clerk, with the

defendant, and with the defendant's attorney of record.

(d) Dismissal of criminal charges pursuant to this section shall be upon motion of the prosecutor or the defendant or upon the court's own motion.

History.
1973, c. 1286, s. 1; 2013-18, s. 5

N.C. Gen. Stat. § 15A-1009

Repealed by Session Laws 2013-18, s. 6, effective December 1, 2013.

History.
1983, c. 460, s. 1; repealed by 2013-18, s. 6, effective December 1, 2013

N.C. Gen. Stat. § 15A-1010

Reserved for future codification purposes.

ARTICLE 57
PLEAS

§ 15A-1011. Pleas in district and superior courts; waiver of appearance

(a) A defendant may plead not guilty, guilty, or no contest "(nolo contendere)." A plea may be received only from the defendant himself in open court except in any of the following circumstances:

(1) The defendant is a corporation, in which case the plea may be entered by counsel or a corporate officer.

(2) There is a waiver of arraignment and a filing of a written plea of not guilty under G.S. 15A-945.

(3) In misdemeanor cases when there is a written waiver of appearance submitted with the approval of the presiding judge.

(4) Written pleas for the types of offenses specified in G.S. 7A-273(2) and G.S. 7A-273(2a) are authorized under G.S. 7A-148(a).

(5) The defendant executes a waiver and plea of not guilty as provided in G.S. 15A-1011(d).

(6) The defendant, before a magistrate or clerk of court, enters a written appearance, waiver of trial and plea of guilty and at the same time makes restitution in a case wherein the sole allegation is a violation of G.S. 14-107, the check is in an amount provided in G.S. 7A-273(8), and the warrant does not charge a fourth or subsequent violation of this statute.

(b) A defendant may plead no contest only with the consent of the prosecutor and the presiding judge.

(c) Upon entry of a plea of guilty or no contest or after conviction on a plea of not guilty, the defendant may request permission to enter a plea of guilty or no contest as to other crimes with which he is charged in the same or another prosecutorial district as defined in G.S. 7A-60. A defendant may not enter any plea to crimes charged in another prosecutorial district as defined in G.S. 7A-60 unless the district attorney of that district consents in writing to the entry of such plea. The prosecutor or his representative may appear in person or by filing an affidavit as to the nature of the evidence gathered as to these other crimes. Entry of a plea under this subsection constitutes a waiver of venue. A superior court is granted jurisdiction to accept the plea, upon an appropriate indictment or information, even though the case may otherwise be within the exclusive original jurisdiction of the district court. A district court may accept pleas under this section only in cases within the original jurisdiction of the district court and in cases within the concurrent jurisdiction of the district and superior courts pursuant to G.S. 7A-272(c).

(d) A defendant may execute a written waiver of appearance and plead not guilty and designate legal counsel to appear in his behalf in the following circumstances:

(1) The defendant agrees in writing to waive the right to testify in person and waives the right to face his accusers in person and agrees to be bound by the decision of the court as in any other case of adjudication of guilty and entry of judgment, subject to the right of appeal as in any other case; and

(2) The defendant submits in writing circumstances to justify the request and submits in writing a request to proceed under this section; and

(3) The judge allows the absence of the defendant because of distance, infirmity or other good cause.

(e) In the event the judge shall permit the procedure set forth in the foregoing subsection (d), the State may offer evidence and the defendant may offer evidence, with right of cross-examination of witnesses, and the other procedures, including the right of the prosecutor to dismiss the charges, shall be the same as in any other criminal case, except for the absence of defendant.

History.
1973, c. 1286, s. 1; 1975, c. 166, s. 27; c. 626, s. 1; 1983, c. 586, s. 3; 1987, c. 355, s. 4; 1987 (Reg. Sess., 1988), c. 1037, s. 64; 1995 (Reg. Sess., 1996), c. 725, s. 5; 2021-47, s. 7(a)

§ 15A-1012. Aid of counsel; time for deliberation

(a) A defendant may not be called upon to plead until he has had an opportunity to retain counsel or, if he is eligible for assignment of counsel, until counsel has been assigned or waived in accordance with Article 36 of Chapter 7A of the General Statutes.

(b) In cases in the original jurisdiction of the superior court a defendant who has waived counsel may not plead within less than seven days following the date he was arrested or was otherwise informed of the charge.

History.
1973, c. 1286, s. 1

§§ 15A-1013 through 15A-1020

Reserved for future codification purposes.

ARTICLE 58
PROCEDURES RELATING TO GUILTY PLEAS IN SUPERIOR COURT

§ 15A-1021. Plea conference; improper pressure prohibited; submission of arrangement to judge; restitution and reparation as part of plea arrangement agreement, etc

(a) In superior court, the prosecution and the defense may discuss the possibility that, upon the defendant's entry of a plea of guilty or no contest to one or more offenses, the prosecutor will not charge, will dismiss, or will move for the dismissal of other charges, or will recommend or not oppose a particular sentence. If the defendant is represented by counsel in the discussions the defendant need not be present. The trial judge may participate in the discussions.

(b) No person representing the State or any of its political subdivisions may bring improper pressure upon a defendant to induce a plea of guilty or no contest.

(c) If the parties have reached a proposed plea arrangement in which the prosecutor has agreed to recommend a particular sentence, they may, with the permission of the trial judge, advise the judge of the terms of the arrangement and the reasons therefor in advance of the time for tender of the plea. The proposed plea arrangement may include a provision for the defendant to make restitution or reparation to an aggrieved party or parties for the damage or loss caused by the offense or offenses committed by the defendant. The judge may indicate to the parties whether he will concur in the proposed disposition. The judge may withdraw his concurrence if he learns of information not consistent with the representations made to him.

(d) When restitution or reparation by the defendant is a part of the plea arrangement agreement, if the judge concurs in the proposed disposition he may order that restitution or reparation be made as a condition of special probation pursuant to the provisions of G.S. 15A-1351, or probation pursuant to the provisions of G.S. 15A-1343(d). If an active sentence is imposed the court may recommend that the defendant make restitution or reparation out of any earnings gained by the defendant if he is granted work release privileges under the provisions of G.S. 148-33.1, or that restitution or reparation be imposed as a condition of parole in accordance with the provisions of G.S. 148-57.1. The order or recommendation providing for restitution or reparation shall be in accordance with the applicable provisions of G.S. 15A-1343(d) and Article 81C of this Chapter.

If the offense is one in which there is evidence of physical, mental or sexual abuse of a minor, the court should encourage the minor and the minor's parents or custodians to participate in rehabilitative treatment and the plea agreement may include a provision that the defendant will be ordered to pay for such treatment.

When restitution or reparation is recommended as part of a plea arrangement that results in an active sentence, the sentencing court shall enter as a part of the commitment that restitution or reparation is recommended as part of the plea arrangement. The Administrative Office of the Courts shall prepare and distribute forms which provide for ample space to make restitution or reparation recommendations incident to commitments.

History.
1973, c. 1286, s. 1; 1975, c. 117; c. 166, s. 27; 1977, c. 614, ss. 3, 4; 1977, 2nd Sess., c. 1147, s. 1; 1979, c. 760, s. 3; 1985, c. 474, s. 2; 1987, c. 598, s. 3; 1997-80, s. 2; 1998-212, s. 19.4(e)

§ 15A-1022. Advising defendant of consequences of guilty plea; informed choice; factual basis for plea; admission of guilt not required

(a) Except in the case of corporations or in misdemeanor cases in which there is a waiver of appearance under G.S. 15A-1011(a)(3), a superior court judge may not accept a plea of guilty or no contest from the defendant without first addressing him personally and:

    (1) Informing him that he has a right to remain silent and that any statement he makes may be used against him;

    (2) Determining that he understands the nature of the charge;

    (3) Informing him that he has a right to plead not guilty;

    (4) Informing him that by his plea he waives his right to trial by jury and his right to be confronted by the witnesses against him;

    (5) Determining that the defendant, if represented by counsel, is satisfied with his representation;

    (6) Informing him of the maximum possible sentence on the charge for the class of offense for which the defendant is being sentenced, including that possible from consecutive sentences, and of the mandatory minimum sentence, if any, on the charge; and

    (7) Informing him that if he is not a citizen of the United States of America, a plea of guilty or no contest may result in deportation, the exclusion from admission to this country, or the denial of naturalization under federal law.

(b) By inquiring of the prosecutor and defense counsel and the defendant personally, the judge must determine whether there were any prior plea discussions, whether the parties have entered into any arrangement with respect to the plea and the terms thereof, and whether any improper pressure was exerted in violation of G.S. 15A-1021(b). The judge may not accept a plea of guilty or no contest from a defendant without first determining that the plea is a product of informed choice.

(c) The judge may not accept a plea of guilty or no contest without first determining that there is a factual basis for the plea. This determination may be based upon information including but not limited to:

    (1) A statement of the facts by the prosecutor.

    (2) A written statement of the defendant.

    (3) An examination of the presentence report.

    (4) Sworn testimony, which may include reliable hearsay.

    (5) A statement of facts by the defense counsel.

(d) The judge may accept the defendant's plea of no contest even though the defendant does not admit that he is in fact guilty if the judge is nevertheless satisfied that there is a factual basis for the plea. The judge must advise the defendant that if he pleads no contest he will be treated as guilty whether or not he admits guilt.

History.
1973, c. 1286, s. 1; 1975, c. 166, s. 27; 1989, c. 280; 1993, c. 538, s. 10; 1994, Ex. Sess., c. 24, s. 14(b)

§ 15A-1022.1. Procedure in accepting admissions of the existence of aggravating factors in felonies

(a) Before accepting a plea of guilty or no contest to a felony, the court shall determine whether the State intends to seek a sentence in the aggravated range. If the State does intend to seek an aggravated sentence, the court shall determine which factors the State seeks to establish. The court shall determine whether the State seeks a finding that a prior record level point should be found under G.S. 15A-1340.14(b)(7). The court shall also determine whether the State has provided the notice to the defendant required by G.S. 15A-1340.16(a6) or whether the defendant has waived his or her right to such notice.

(b) In all cases in which a defendant admits to the existence of an aggravating factor or to a finding that a prior record level point should be found under G.S. 15A-1340.14(b)(7), the court shall comply with the provisions of G.S. 15A-1022(a). In addition, the court shall address the defendant personally and advise the defendant that:

    (1) He or she is entitled to have a jury determine the existence of any aggravating factors or points under G.S. 15A-1340.14(b)(7); and

    (2) He or she has the right to prove the existence of any mitigating factors at a sentencing hearing before the sentencing judge.

(c) Before accepting an admission to the existence of an aggravating factor or a prior record level point under G.S. 15A-1340.14(b)(7), the court shall determine that there is a factual basis for the admission, and that the admission is the result of an informed choice by the defendant. The court may base its determination on the factors specified in G.S. 15A-1022(c), as well as any other appropriate information.

(d) A defendant may admit to the existence of an aggravating factor or to the existence of a prior record level point under G.S. 15A-1340.14(b)(7) before or after the trial of the underlying felony.

(e) The procedures specified in this Article for the handling of pleas of guilty are applicable to the handling of admissions to aggravating factors and prior record points under G.S. 15A-1340.14(b)(7), unless the context clearly indicates that they are inappropriate.

History.
2005-145, s. 4

§ 15A-1023. Action by judge in plea arrangements relating to sentence; no approval required when arrangement does not relate to sentence

(a) If the parties have agreed upon a plea arrangement pursuant to G.S. 15A-1021 in which the prosecutor has agreed to recommend a particular sentence, they must disclose the substance of their agreement to the judge at the time the defendant is called upon to plead.

(b) Before accepting a plea pursuant to a plea arrangement in which the prosecutor has agreed to recommend a particular sentence, the judge must advise the parties whether he approves the arrangement and will dispose of the case accordingly. If the judge rejects the arrangement, he must so inform the parties, refuse to accept the defendant's plea of guilty or no contest, and advise the defendant personally that neither the State nor the defendant is bound by the rejected arrangement. The judge must advise the parties of the reasons he rejected the arrangement and afford them an opportunity to modify the arrangement accordingly. Upon rejection of the plea arrangement by the judge the defendant is entitled to a continuance until the next session of court. A decision by the judge disapproving a plea arrangement is not subject to appeal. If a judge rejects a plea arrangement disclosed, in open court, pursuant to subsection (a) of this section, then the judge shall order that the rejection be noted on the plea transcript and shall order that the plea transcript with the notation of the rejection be made a part of the record.

(c) If the parties have entered a plea arrangement relating to the disposition of charges in which the prosecutor has not agreed to make any recommendations concerning sentence, the substance of the arrangement must be disclosed to the judge at the time the defendant is called upon to plead. The judge must accept the plea if he determines that the plea is the product of the informed choice of the defendant and that there is a factual basis for the plea.

History.
1973, c. 1286, s. 1; 1975, c. 166, s. 27; 1977, c. 186; 2009-179, s. 1

§ 15A-1024. Withdrawal of guilty plea when sentence not in accord with plea arrangement

If at the time of sentencing, the judge for any reason determines to impose a sentence other than provided for in a plea arrangement between the parties, the judge must inform the defendant of that fact and inform the defendant that he may withdraw his plea. Upon withdrawal, the defendant is entitled to a continuance until the next session of court.

History.
1973, c. 1286, s. 1

§ 15A-1025. Plea discussion and arrangement inadmissible

The fact that the defendant or his counsel and the prosecutor engaged in plea discussions or made a plea arrangement may not be received in evidence against or in favor of the defendant in any criminal or civil action or administrative proceedings.

History.
1973, c. 1286, s. 1; 1975, c. 166, s. 27

§ 15A-1026. Record of proceedings

A verbatim record of the proceedings at which the defendant enters a plea of guilty or no contest and of any preliminary consideration of a plea arrangement by the judge pursuant to G.S. 15A-1021(c) must be made and preserved. This record must include the judge's advice to the defendant, and his inquiries of the defendant, defense counsel, and the prosecutor, and any responses. If the plea arrangement has been reduced to writing, it must be made a part of the record; otherwise the judge must require that the terms of the arrangement be stated for the record and that the assent of the defendant, his counsel, and the prosecutor be recorded. If the judge rejects the plea arrangement under G.S. 15A-1023(b), then the rejection of the plea arrangement must also be made part of the record pursuant to G.S. 15A-1023(b).

History.
1973, c. 1286, s. 1; 1975, c. 166, s. 27; 1975, 2nd Sess., c. 983, s. 144; 2009-179, s. 2

§ 15A-1027. Limitation on collateral attack on conviction

Noncompliance with the procedures of this Article may not be a basis for review of a conviction after the appeal period for the conviction has expired.

History.
1973, c. 1286, s. 1; 1975, c. 166, s. 21; 1989, c. 290, s. 4

§§ 15A-1028, 15A-1029

Reserved for future codification purposes.

ARTICLE 58A
PROCEDURES RELATING TO FELONY GUILTY PLEAS IN DISTRICT COURT

§ 15A-1029.1. Transfer of case from superior court to district court to accept guilty and no contest pleas for certain felony offenses

(a) With the consent of both the prosecutor and the defendant, the presiding superior court judge may order a transfer of the defendant's case to the district court for the purpose of allowing the defendant to enter a plea of guilty or no contest to a Class H or I felony.

(b) The provisions of Article 58 of this Chapter apply to a case transferred under this section from superior court to district court in the same manner as if the plea were entered in superior court. Appeals that are authorized in these matters are to the appellate division.

History.
1995 (Reg. Sess., 1996), c. 725, s. 6

N.C. Gen. Stat. § 15A-1030

Reserved for future codification purposes.

ARTICLE 59
MAINTENANCE OF ORDER IN THE COURTROOM

§ 15A-1031. Custody and restraint of defendant and witnesses

A trial judge may order a defendant or witness subjected to physical restraint in the courtroom when the judge finds the restraint to be reasonably necessary to maintain order, prevent the defendant's escape, or provide for the safety of persons. If the judge orders a defendant or witness restrained, he must:

    (1) Enter in the record out of the presence of the jury and in the presence of the person to be restrained and his counsel, if any, the reasons for his action; and

    (2) Give the restrained person an opportunity to object; and

    (3) Unless the defendant or his attorney objects, instruct the jurors that the restraint is not to be considered in weighing evidence or determining the issue of guilt.

If the restrained person controverts the stated reasons for restraint, the judge must conduct a hearing and make findings of fact.

History.
1977, c. 711, s. 1

§ 15A-1032. Removal of disruptive defendant

(a) A trial judge, after warning a defendant whose conduct is disrupting his trial, may order the defendant removed from the trial if he continues conduct which is so disruptive that the trial cannot proceed in an orderly manner. When practicable, the judge's warning and order for removal must be issued out of the presence of the jury.

(b) If the judge orders a defendant removed from the courtroom, he must:

(1) Enter in the record the reasons for his action; and

(2) Instruct the jurors that the removal is not to be considered in weighing evidence or determining the issue of guilt.

A defendant removed from the courtroom must be given the opportunity of learning of the trial proceedings through his counsel at reasonable intervals as directed by the court and must be given opportunity to return to the courtroom during the trial upon assurance of his good behavior.

History.
1977, c. 711, s. 1

§ 15A-1033. Removal of disruptive witnesses and spectators

The judge in his discretion may order any person other than a defendant removed from a courtroom when his conduct disrupts the conduct of the trial.

History.
1977, c. 711, s. 1

§ 15A-1034. Controlling access to the courtroom

(a) The presiding judge may impose reasonable limitations on access to the courtroom when necessary to ensure the orderliness of courtroom proceedings or the safety of persons present.

(b) The judge may order that all persons entering or any person present and choosing to remain in the courtroom be searched for weapons or devices that could be used to disrupt or impede the proceedings and may require that belongings carried by persons entering the courtroom be inspected. An order under this subsection must be entered on the record.

History.
1977, c. 711, s. 1

§ 15A-1035. Other powers

In addition to the use of the powers provided in this Article, a presiding judge may maintain courtroom order through the use of his contempt powers as provided in Chapter 5A, Contempt, and through the use of other inherent powers of the court.

History.
1977, c. 711, s. 1

§§ 15A-1036 through 15A-1039

Reserved for future codification purposes.

ARTICLE 60

§§ 15A-1040 through 15A-1050

Reserved for future codification purposes.

ARTICLE 61
GRANTING OF IMMUNITY TO WITNESSES

§ 15A-1051. Immunity; general provisions

(a) A witness who asserts his privilege against self-incrimination in a hearing or proceeding in court or before a grand jury of North Carolina may be ordered to testify or produce other information as provided in this Article. He may not thereafter be excused from testifying or producing other information on the ground that his testimony or other information required of him may tend to incriminate him. Except as provided in G.S. 15A-623(h), no testimony or other information so compelled, or any information directly or indirectly derived from the testimony or other information, may be used against the witness in a criminal case, except a prosecution for perjury or contempt arising from a failure to comply with an order of the court. In the event of a prosecution of the witness he shall be entitled to a record of his testimony.

(b) An order to testify or produce other information authorized by this Article may be issued prior to the witness's assertion of his privilege against self-incrimination, but the order is not effective until the witness asserts his privilege against self-incrimination and the person presiding over the inquiry communicates the order to him.

(c) As used in this Article, "other information" includes any book, paper, document, record, recordation, tangible object, or other material.

History.
1973, c. 1286, s. 1; 1985 (Reg. Sess., 1986), c. 843, ss. 4, 6; 1987 (Reg. Sess., 1988), c. 1040, s. 1; 1989 (Reg. Sess., 1990), c. 1039, s. 4; 1991, c. 636, s. 3

§ 15A-1052. Grant of immunity in court proceedings

(a) When the testimony or other information is to be presented to a court of the trial division of the General Court of Justice, the order to the witness to testify or produce other information must be issued by a superior court judge, upon application of the district attorney:

(1) Be in writing and filed with the permanent records of the case; or

(2) If orally made in open court, recorded and transcribed and made a part of the permanent records of the case.

(b) The application may be made whenever, in the judgment of the district attorney, the witness has asserted or is likely to assert his privilege against self-incrimination and his testimony or other information is or will be necessary to the public interest. Before making application to the judge, the district attorney must inform the Attorney General, or a deputy or assistant attorney general designated by him, of the circumstances and his intent to make an application.

(c) In a jury trial the judge must inform the jury of the grant of immunity and the order to testify prior to the testimony of the witness under the grant of immunity. During the charge to the jury, the judge must instruct the jury as in the case of interested witnesses.

History.
1973, c. 1286, s. 1; 1975, c. 166, s. 27

§ 15A-1053. Grant of immunity before grand jury

(a) When the testimony or other information is to be presented to a grand jury, the order to the witness to testify or produce other information must be issued by the presiding or convening superior court judge, upon application of the district attorney. The order of a superior court judge under this section must be in writing and filed as a part of the permanent records of the court.

(b) The application may be made when the district attorney has been informed by the foreman of the grand jury that the witness has asserted his privilege against self-incrimination and the district attorney determines that the testimony or other information is necessary to the public interest. Before making application to the judge, the district attorney must inform the Attorney General, or a deputy or assistant attorney general designated by him, of the circumstances and his intent to make an application.

History.
1973, c. 1286, s. 1; 1975, c. 166, s. 27

§ 15A-1054. Charge reductions or sentence concessions in consideration of truthful testimony

(a) Whether or not a grant of immunity is conferred under this Article, a prosecutor, when the interest of justice requires, may exercise his discretion not to try any suspect for offenses believed to have been committed within the prosecutorial district as defined in G.S. 7A-60, to agree to charge reductions, or to agree to recommend sentence concessions, upon the understanding or agreement that the suspect will provide truthful testimony in one or more criminal proceedings.

(b) Recommendations as to sentence concessions must be made to the trial judge by the prosecutor in accordance with the provisions of Article 58 of this Chapter, Procedure[s] Relating to Guilty Pleas in Superior Court.

(c) When a prosecutor enters into any arrangement authorized by this section, written notice fully disclosing the terms of the arrangement must be provided to defense counsel, or to the defendant if not represented by counsel, against whom such testimony is to be offered, a reasonable time prior to any proceeding in which the person with whom the arrangement is made is expected to testify. Upon motion of the defendant or his counsel on grounds of surprise or for other good cause or when the interests of justice require, the court must grant a recess.

History.
1973, c. 1286, s. 1; 1975, c. 166, s. 27; 1987 (Reg. Sess., 1988), c. 1037, s. 65

§ 15A-1055. Evidence of grant of immunity or testimonial arrangement may be fully developed; impact may be argued to the jury

(a) Notwithstanding any other rule of evidence to the contrary, any party may examine a witness testifying under a grant of immunity or pursuant to an arrangement under G.S. 15A-1054 with respect to that grant of immunity or arrangement. A party may also introduce evidence or examine other witnesses in corroboration or contradiction of testimony or evidence previously elicited by himself or another party concerning the grant of immunity or arrangement.

(b) A party may argue to the jury with respect to the impact of a grant of immunity or an arrangement under G.S. 15A-1054 upon the credibility of a witness.

History.
1973, c. 1286, s. 1

§§ 15A-1056 through 15A-1060

Reserved for future codification purposes.

ARTICLE 62
MISTRIAL

§ 15A-1061. Mistrial for prejudice to defendant

Upon motion of a defendant or with his concurrence the judge may declare a mistrial at any time during the trial. The judge must declare a mistrial upon the defendant's motion if there occurs during the trial an error or legal defect in the proceedings, or conduct inside or outside the courtroom, resulting in substantial and irreparable prejudice to the defendant's case. If there are two or more defendants, the mistrial may not be declared as to a defendant who does not make or join in the motion.

History.
1977, c. 711, s. 1

§ 15A-1062. Mistrial for prejudice to the State

Upon motion of the State, the judge may declare a mistrial if there occurs during the trial, either inside or outside the courtroom, misconduct resulting in substantial and irreparable prejudice to the State's case and the misconduct was by a juror or the defendant, his lawyer, or someone acting at the behest of the defendant or his lawyer. If there are two or more defendants, the mistrial may not be declared as to a defendant who does not join in the motion of the State if:

(1) Neither he, his lawyer, nor a person acting at his or his lawyer's behest participated in the misconduct; or

(2) The State's case is not substantially and irreparably prejudiced as to him.

History.
1977, c. 711, s. 1

§ 15A-1063. Mistrial for impossibility of proceeding

Upon motion of a party or upon his own motion, a judge may declare a mistrial if:

(1) It is impossible for the trial to proceed in conformity with law; or

(2) It appears there is no reasonable probability of the jury's agreement upon a verdict.

History.
1977, c. 711, s. 1

§ 15A-1064. Mistrial; finding of facts required

Before granting a mistrial, the judge must make finding of facts with respect to the grounds for the mistrial and insert the findings in the record of the case.

History.
1977, c. 711, s. 1

§ 15A-1065. Procedure following mistrial

When a mistrial is ordered, the judge must direct that the case be retained for trial or such other proceedings as may be proper.

History.
1977, c. 711, s. 1

§§ 15A-1066 through 15A-1070

Reserved for future codification purposes.

ARTICLE 63

§§ 15A-1071 through 15A-1080

Reserved for future codification purposes.

ARTICLE 64

§§ 15A-1081 through 15A-1100

Reserved for future codification purposes.

SUBCHAPTER 11.
TRIAL PROCEDURE IN DISTRICT COURT

ARTICLE 65
IN GENERAL

§ 15A-1101. Applicability of superior court procedure

Trial procedure in the district court is in accordance with the provisions of Subchapter XII, Trial in Superior Court, except for provisions:

(1) Relating to jury trial.

(2) Requiring recordation of proceedings unless they specify their applicability to the district court.

(3) That specify their applicability to superior court.

History.
1977, c. 711, s. 1

§§ 15A-1102 through 15A-1110

Reserved for future codification purposes.

ARTICLE 66
PROCEDURE FOR HEARING AND DISPOSITION OF INFRACTIONS

§ 15A-1111. General procedure for disposition of infractions

The procedure for the disposition of an infraction, as defined in G.S. 14-3.1, is as provided in this Article. If a question of procedure is not governed by this Article, the procedures applicable to the conduct of pretrial and trial proceedings for misdemeanors in district court are applicable unless the procedure is clearly inapplicable to the hearing of an infraction.

History.
1985, c. 764, s. 3

§ 15A-1112. Venue

Venue for the conduct of infraction hearings lies in any county where any act or omission constituting part of the alleged infraction occurred.

History.
1985, c. 764, s. 3

§ 15A-1113. Prehearing procedure

(a) **Process.** -- A law enforcement officer may issue a citation for an infraction in accordance with the provisions of G.S. 15A-302. A judicial official may issue a summons for an infraction in accordance with the provisions of G.S. 15A-303.

(b) **Detention of Person Charged.** -- A law enforcement officer who has probable cause to believe a person has committed an infraction may detain the person for a reasonable period in order to issue and serve him a citation.

(c) **Appearance Bond May Be Required.** -- A person charged with an infraction may not be required to post an appearance bond if:

(1) He is licensed to drive by a state that subscribes to the nonresident violator compact as defined in Article 1B of Chapter 20 of the General Statutes, the infraction charged is subject to the provisions of that compact, and he executes a personal recognizance as defined by that compact.

(2) He is a resident of North Carolina.

Any other person charged with an infraction may be required to post a bond to secure his appearance and a charging officer may require such a person charged to accompany him to a judicial official's office to allow the official to determine if a bond is necessary to secure the person's court appearance, and if so, what kind of bond is to be used. If the judicial official finds that the person is unable to post a secured bond, he must allow the person to be released on execution of an unsecured bond. The provisions of Article 26 of this Chapter relating to issuance and forfeiture of bail bonds are applicable to bonds required pursuant to this subsection.

(d) **Territorial Jurisdiction.** -- A law enforcement officer's territorial jurisdiction to charge a person with an infraction is the same as his jurisdiction to arrest specified in G.S. 15A-402.

(e) **Use of Same Process for Two Offenses.** -- A person may be charged with a criminal offense and an infraction in the same pleading.

History.
1985, c. 764, s. 3; 1985 (Reg. Sess., 1986), c. 852, s. 12

§ 15A-1114. Hearing procedure for infractions

(a) **Jurisdiction.** -- Jurisdiction for the adjudication and disposition of infractions is as specified in G.S. 7A-253 and G.S. 7A-271(d).

(b) **No Trial by Jury.** -- In adjudicatory hearings for infractions, no party has a right to a trial by jury in district court.

(c) **Infractions Heard in Civil or Criminal Session.** -- A district court judge may conduct proceedings relating to traffic infractions in a civil or criminal session of court, unless the infraction is joined with a criminal offense arising out of the same transaction or occurrence. In such a case, the criminal offense and the infraction must be heard at a session in which criminal matters may be heard.

(d) **Pleas.** -- A person charged with an infraction may admit or deny responsibility for the infraction. The plea must be made by the person charged in open court, unless he submits a written waiver of appearance which is approved by the presiding judge, or, if authorized by G.S. 7A-146, he waives his right to a hearing and admits responsibility for the infraction in writing and pays the specified penalty and costs.

(e) **Duty of District Attorney.** -- The district attorney is responsible for ensuring that infractions are calendared and prosecuted efficiently.

(f) **Burden of Proof.** -- The State must prove beyond a reasonable doubt that the person charged is responsible for the infraction unless the person admits responsibility.

(g) **Recording Not Necessary.** -- The State does not have to record the proceedings at infraction hearings. With the approval of the court, a party may, at his expense, record any proceeding.

Chapter 15A

History.

1985, c. 764, s. 3

§ 15A-1115. Review of infractions originally disposed of in superior court

(a) Repealed by Session Laws 2013-385, s. 1, effective December 1, 2013.

(b) **Review of Infractions Originally Disposed of in Superior Court.** -- If the superior court disposes of an infraction pursuant to its jurisdiction in G.S. 7A-271(d), appeal from that judgment is as provided for criminal actions in the superior court.

History.

1985, c. 764, s. 3; 1985 (Reg. Sess., 1986), c. 852, s. 10; 2013-385, s. 1

§ 15A-1116. Enforcement of sanctions

(a) Use of Contempt or Fine Collection Procedures: Notification of DMV. -- If the person does not comply with a sanction ordered by the court, the court may proceed in accordance with Chapter 5A of the General Statutes. If the person fails to pay a penalty or costs, the court may proceed in accordance with Article 84 of this Chapter. If the infraction is a motor vehicle infraction, the court must report a failure to pay the applicable penalty and costs to the Division of Motor Vehicles as specified in G.S. 20-24.2.

(b) **No Order for Arrest.** -- If a person served with a citation for an infraction fails to appear to answer the charge, the court may issue a criminal summons to secure the person's appearance, but an order for arrest may not be used in such cases.

History.

1985, c. 764, s. 3; 1985 (Reg. Sess., 1986), c. 852, ss. 1, 2, 15

N.C. Gen. Stat. § 15A-1117

Recodified as § 20-24.2 by Session Laws 1985 (Reg. Sess., 1986), c. 852, s. 3.

§ 15A-1118. Costs

Costs assessed for an infraction are as specified in G.S. 7A-304.

History.

1985, c. 764, s. 3

ARTICLE 67 TO 70

§§ 15A-1119 through 15A-1200

Reserved for future codification purposes.

SUBCHAPTER 12.
TRIAL PROCEDURE IN SUPERIOR COURT

ARTICLE 71
RIGHT TO TRIAL BY JURY

§ 15A-1201. Right to trial by jury; waiver of jury trial; procedure for waiver

(a) **Right to Jury Trial.** -- In all criminal cases the defendant has the right to be tried by a jury of 12 whose verdict must be unanimous. In the district court the judge is the finder of fact in criminal cases, but the defendant has the right to appeal for trial de novo in superior court as provided in G.S. 15A-1431. In superior court all criminal trials in which the defendant enters a plea of not guilty must be tried before a jury, unless the defendant waives the right to a jury trial, as provided in subsection (b) of this section.

(b) **Waiver of Right to Jury Trial.** -- A defendant accused of any criminal offense for which the State is not seeking a sentence of death in superior court may, knowingly and voluntarily, in writing or on the record in the court and with the consent of the trial judge, waive the right to trial by jury. When a defendant waives the right to trial by jury under this section, the jury is dispensed with as provided by law, and the whole matter of law and fact, to include all factors referred to in G.S. 20-179 and subsections (a1) and (a3) of G.S. 15A-1340.16, shall be heard and judgment given by the court. If a motion for joinder of co-defendants is allowed, there shall be a jury trial unless all defendants waive the right to trial by jury, or the court, in its discretion, severs the case.

(c) A defendant seeking to waive the right to trial by jury under subsection (b) of this section shall give notice of intent to waive a jury trial by any of the following methods:

(1) Stipulation, which may be conditioned on each party's consent to the trial judge, signed by both the State and the defendant and served on the counsel for any co-defendants.

(2) Filing a written notice of intent to waive a jury trial with the court and serving on the State and counsel for any co-defendants within the earliest of (i) 10 working days after arraignment, (ii) 10 working days after service of a calendar setting under G.S. 7A-49.4(b), or (iii) 10 working days after the setting of a definite trial date under G.S. 7A-49.4(c).

(3) Giving notice of intent to waive a jury trial on the record in open court by the earlier of (i) the time of arraignment or (ii)

the calling of the calendar under G.S. 7A-49.4(b) or G.S. 7A-49.4(c).

(d) **Judicial Consent to Jury Waiver. --** Upon notice of waiver by the defense pursuant to subsection (c) of this section, the State shall schedule the matter to be heard in open court to determine whether the judge agrees to hear the case without a jury. The decision to grant or deny the defendant's request for a bench trial shall be made by the judge who will actually preside over the trial. Before consenting to a defendant's waiver of the right to a trial by jury, the trial judge shall do all of the following:

(1) Address the defendant personally and determine whether the defendant fully understands and appreciates the consequences of the defendant's decision to waive the right to trial by jury.

(2) Determine whether the State objects to the waiver and, if so, why. Consider the arguments presented by both the State and the defendant regarding the defendant's waiver of a jury trial.

(e) **Revocation of Waiver. --** Once waiver of a jury trial has been made and consented to by the trial judge pursuant to subsection (d) of this section, the defendant may revoke the waiver one time as of right within 10 business days of the defendant's initial notice pursuant to subsection (c) of this section if the defendant does so in open court with the State present or in writing to both the State and the judge. In all other circumstances, the defendant may only revoke the waiver of trial by jury upon the trial judge finding the revocation would not cause unreasonable hardship or delay to the State. Once a revocation has been granted pursuant to this subsection, the decision is final and binding.

(f) **Suppression of Evidence. --** In the event that a defendant who has waived the right to trial by jury pursuant to this section makes a motion to suppress evidence under Article 53 of this Chapter, the court shall make written findings of fact and conclusions of law.

History.
1977, c. 711, s. 1; 2013-300, s. 4; 2015-289, s. 1

§§ 15A-1202 through 15A-1210

Reserved for future codification purposes.

ARTICLE 72
SELECTING AND IMPANELING THE JURY

§ 15A-1211. Selection procedure generally; role of judge; challenge to the panel; authority of judge to excuse jurors

(a) The provisions of Chapter 9 of the General Statutes, Jurors, pertinent to criminal cases apply except when this Chapter specifically provides a different procedure.

(b) The trial judge must decide all challenges to the panel and all questions concerning the competency of jurors.

(c) The State or the defendant may challenge the jury panel. A challenge to the panel:

(1) May be made only on the ground that the jurors were not selected or drawn according to law.

(2) Must be in writing.

(3) Must specify the facts constituting the ground of challenge.

(4) Must be made and decided before any juror is examined.

If a challenge to the panel is sustained, the judge must discharge the panel.

(d) The judge may excuse a juror without challenge by any party if he determines that grounds for challenge for cause are present.

History.
1977, c. 711, s. 1

§ 15A-1212. Grounds for challenge for cause

A challenge for cause to an individual juror may be made by any party on the ground that the juror:

(1) Does not have the qualifications required by G.S. 9-3.

(2) Is incapable by reason of mental or physical infirmity of rendering jury service.

(3) Has been or is a party, a witness, a grand juror, a trial juror, or otherwise has participated in civil or criminal proceedings involving a transaction which relates to the charge against the defendant.

(4) Has been or is a party adverse to the defendant in a civil action, or has complained against or been accused by him in a criminal prosecution.

(5) Is related by blood or marriage within the sixth degree to the defendant or the victim of the crime.

(6) Has formed or expressed an opinion as to the guilt or innocence of the defendant. It is improper for a party to elicit whether the opinion formed is favorable or adverse to the defendant.

(7) Is presently charged with a felony.

(8) As a matter of conscience, regardless of the facts and circumstances, would be unable to render a verdict with respect to the charge in accordance with the law of North Carolina.

(9) For any other cause is unable to render a fair and impartial verdict.

Chapter 15A

History.
1977, c. 711, s. 1

§ 15A-1213. Informing prospective jurors of case

Prior to selection of jurors, the judge must identify the parties and their counsel and briefly inform the prospective jurors, as to each defendant, of the charge, the date of the alleged offense, the name of any victim alleged in the pleading, the defendant's plea to the charge, and any affirmative defense of which the defendant has given pretrial notice as required by Article 52, Motions Practice. The judge may not read the pleadings to the jury.

History.
1977, c. 711, s. 1

§ 15A-1214. Selection of jurors; procedure

(a) The clerk, under the supervision of the presiding judge, must call jurors from the panel by a system of random selection which precludes advance knowledge of the identity of the next juror to be called. When a juror is called and he is assigned to the jury box, he retains the seat assigned until excused.

(b) The judge must inform the prospective jurors of the case in accordance with G.S. 15A-1213. He may briefly question prospective jurors individually or as a group concerning general fitness and competency to determine whether there is cause why they should not serve as jurors in the case.

(c) The prosecutor and the defense counsel, or the defendant if not represented by counsel, may personally question prospective jurors individually concerning their fitness and competency to serve as jurors in the case to determine whether there is a basis for a challenge for cause or whether to exercise a peremptory challenge. The prosecution or defense is not foreclosed from asking a question merely because the court has previously asked the same or similar question.

(d) The prosecutor must conduct his examination of the first 12 jurors seated and make his challenges for cause and exercise his peremptory challenges. If the judge allows a challenge for cause, or if a peremptory challenge is exercised, the clerk must immediately call a replacement into the box. When the prosecutor is satisfied with the 12 in the box, they must then be tendered to the defendant. Until the prosecutor indicates his satisfaction, he may make a challenge for cause or exercise a peremptory challenge to strike any juror, whether an original or replacement juror.

(e) Each defendant must then conduct his examination of the jurors tendered him, making his challenges for cause and his peremptory challenges. If a juror is excused, no replacement may be called until all defendants have indicated satisfaction with those remaining, at which time the clerk must call replacements for the jurors excused. The judge in his discretion must determine order of examination among multiple defendants.

(f) Upon the calling of replacement jurors, the prosecutor must examine the replacement jurors and indicate satisfaction with a completed panel of 12 before the replacement jurors are tendered to a defendant. Only replacement jurors may be examined and challenged. This procedure is repeated until all parties have accepted 12 jurors.

(g) If at any time after a juror has been accepted by a party, and before the jury is impaneled, it is discovered that the juror has made an incorrect statement during voir dire or that some other good reason exists:

(1) The judge may examine, or permit counsel to examine, the juror to determine whether there is a basis for challenge for cause.

(2) If the judge determines there is a basis for challenge for cause, he must excuse the juror or sustain any challenge for cause that has been made.

(3) If the judge determines there is no basis for challenge for cause, any party who has not exhausted his peremptory challenges may challenge the juror.

Any replacement juror called is subject to examination, challenge for cause, and peremptory challenge as any other unaccepted juror.

(h) In order for a defendant to seek reversal of the case on appeal on the ground that the judge refused to allow a challenge made for cause, he must have:

(1) Exhausted the peremptory challenges available to him;

(2) Renewed his challenge as provided in subsection (i) of this section; and

(3) Had his renewal motion denied as to the juror in question.

(i) A party who has exhausted his peremptory challenges may move orally or in writing to renew a challenge for cause previously denied if the party either:

(1) Had peremptorily challenged the juror; or

(2) States in the motion that he would have challenged that juror peremptorily had his challenges not been exhausted.

The judge may reconsider his denial of the challenge for cause, reconsidering facts and arguments previously adduced or taking cognizance of additional facts and arguments presented. If upon reconsideration the judge determines that the juror should have been excused for cause, he must allow the party an additional peremptory challenge.

(j) In capital cases the trial judge for good cause shown may direct that jurors be selected one at a time, in which case each juror must first be passed by the State. These jurors may be sequestered before and after selection.

History.
1977, c. 711, s. 1

§ 15A-1215. Alternate jurors

(a) The judge may permit the seating of one or more alternate jurors. Alternate jurors must be sworn and seated near the jury with equal opportunity to see and hear the proceedings. They must attend the trial at all times with the jury, and obey all orders and admonitions of the judge. When the jurors are ordered kept together, the alternate jurors must be kept with them. The court should ensure that the alternate jurors do not discuss the case with anyone until that alternate replaces a juror or is discharged. If at any time prior to a verdict being rendered, any juror dies, becomes incapacitated or disqualified, or is discharged for any other reason, an alternate juror becomes a juror, in the order in which selected, and serves in all respects as those selected on the regular trial panel. If an alternate juror replaces a juror after deliberations have begun, the court must instruct the jury to begin its deliberations anew. In no event shall more than 12 jurors participate in the jury's deliberations. Alternate jurors receive the same compensation as other jurors and, unless they become jurors, must be discharged in the same manner and at the same time as the original jury.

(b) In all criminal actions in which one or more defendants is to be tried for a capital offense, or enter a plea of guilty to a capital offense, the presiding judge shall provide for the selection of at least two alternate jurors, or more as he deems appropriate. The alternate jurors shall be retained during the deliberations of the jury on the issue of guilt or innocence under such restrictions, regulations and instructions as the presiding judge shall direct. In case of sequestration of a jury during deliberations in a capital case, alternates shall be sequestered in the same manner as is the trial jury, but such alternates shall also be sequestered from the trial jury. In no event shall more than 12 jurors participate in the jury's deliberations.

History.
1977, c. 711, s. 1; 1979, c. 711, s. 1; 2021-94, s. 1

§ 15A-1216. Impaneling jury

After all jurors, including alternate jurors, have been selected, the clerk
impanels the jury by instructing them as follows: "Members of the jury, you
have been sworn and are now impaneled to try the issue in the case of State of
North Carolina versus. You will sit together, hear the evidence, and
render your verdict accordingly."

History.
1977, c. 711, s. 1

§ 15A-1217. Number of peremptory challenges

(a) Capital cases.
(1) Each defendant is allowed 14 challenges.
(2) The State is allowed 14 challenges for each defendant.
(b) Noncapital cases.
(1) Each defendant is allowed six challenges.
(2) The State is allowed six challenges for each defendant.
(c) Each party is entitled to one peremptory challenge for each alternate juror in addition to any unused challenges.

History.
1977, c. 711, s. 1

§§ 15A-1218 through 15A-1220

Reserved for future codification purposes.

ARTICLE 73
CRIMINAL JURY TRIAL IN SUPERIOR COURT

§ 15A-1221. Order of proceedings in jury trial; reading of indictment prohibited

(a) The order of a jury trial, in general, is as follows:
(1) Repealed by Session Laws 1995 (Regular Session 1996), c. 725, s. 10.
(1a) Unless the defendant has filed a written request for an arraignment, the court must enter a not guilty plea on behalf of the defendant in accordance with G.S. 15A-941. If a defendant does file a written request for an arraignment, then the defendant must be arraigned and must have his or her plea recorded out of the presence of the prospective jurors in accordance with G.S. 15A-941.

(2) The judge must inform the prospective jurors of the case in accordance with G.S. 15A-1213.

(3) The jury must be sworn, selected and impaneled in accordance with Article 72, Selecting and Impaneling the Jury.

(4) Each party must be given the opportunity to make a brief opening statement, but the defendant may reserve his opening statement.

(5) The State must offer evidence.

(6) The defendant may offer evidence and, if he has reserved his opening statement, may precede his evidence with that statement.

(7) The State and the defendant may then offer successive rebuttals as provided in G.S. 15A-1226.

(8) At the conclusion of the evidence, the parties may make arguments to the jury in accordance with the provisions of G.S. 15A-1230.

(9) The judge must deliver a charge to the jury in accordance with the provisions of G.S. 15A-1231 and 15A-1232.

(10) The jury must retire to deliberate.

(b) At no time during the selection of the jury or during trial may any person read the indictment to the prospective jurors or to the jury.

History.
1977, c. 711, s. 1; 1977, 2nd Sess., c. 1147, s. 2; 1995 (Reg. Sess., 1996), c. 725, s. 10; 2021-94, s. 2

§ 15A-1222. Expression of opinion prohibited

The judge may not express during any stage of the trial, any opinion in the presence of the jury on any question of fact to be decided by the jury.

History.
1977, c. 711, s. 1

§ 15A-1223. Disqualification of judge

(a) A judge on his own motion may disqualify himself from presiding over a criminal trial or other criminal proceeding.

(b) A judge, on motion of the State or the defendant, must disqualify himself from presiding over a criminal trial or other criminal proceeding if he is:

(1) Prejudiced against the moving party or in favor of the adverse party; or

(2) Repealed by Session Laws 1983 (Regular Session, 1984), c. 1037, s. 6.

(3) Closely related to the defendant by blood or marriage; or

(4) For any other reason unable to perform the duties required of him in an impartial manner.

(c) A motion to disqualify must be in writing and must be accompanied by one or more affidavits setting forth facts relied upon to show the grounds for disqualification.

(d) A motion to disqualify a judge must be filed no less than five days before the time the case is called for trial unless good cause is shown for failure to file within that time. Good cause includes the discovery of facts constituting grounds for disqualification less than five days before the case is called for trial.

(e) A judge must disqualify himself from presiding over a criminal trial or proceeding if he is a witness for or against one of the parties in the case.

History.
1977, c. 711, s. 1; 1983 (Reg. Sess., 1984), c. 1037, s. 6

§ 15A-1224. Death or disability of trial judge

(a) If by reason of sickness or other disability a judge before whom the defendant is being tried is unable to continue presiding over the trial without the necessity of a continuance, he may in his discretion order a mistrial.

(b) If by reason of absence, death, sickness, or other disability, the judge before whom the defendant is being or has been tried is unable to perform the duties required of him before entry of judgment, and has not ordered a mistrial, any other judge assigned to the court may perform those duties, but if the other judge is satisfied that he cannot perform those duties because he did not preside at an earlier stage of the proceedings or for any other reason, he must order a mistrial.

History.
1977, c. 711, s. 1

§ 15A-1225. Exclusion of witnesses

Upon motion of a party the judge may order all or some of the witnesses other than the defendant to remain outside of the courtroom until called to testify, except when a minor child is called as a witness the parent or guardian may be present while the child is testifying even though his parent or guardian is to be called subsequently.

History.
1977, c. 711, s. 1

§ 15A-1225.1. Child witnesses; remote testimony

(a) *Definitions:*

Chapter 15A

(1) **Child.** -- For the purposes of this section, a minor who is under the age of 16 years old at the time of the testimony.

(2) **Criminal proceeding.** -- Any hearing or trial in a prosecution of a person charged with violating a criminal law of this State, and any hearing or proceeding conducted under Subchapter II of Chapter 7B of the General Statutes where a juvenile is alleged to have committed an offense that would be a criminal offense if committed by an adult.

(3) **Remote testimony.** -- A method by which a child witness testifies in a criminal proceeding outside of the physical presence of the defendant.

(b) **Remote Testimony Authorized.** -- In a criminal proceeding, a child witness who has been found competent to testify may testify, under oath or affirmation, other than in an open forum when the court determines:

(1) That the child witness would suffer serious emotional distress, not by the open forum in general, but by testifying in the defendant's presence, and

(2) That the child's ability to communicate with the trier of fact would be impaired.

(c) **Hearing Procedure.** -- Upon motion of a party or the court's own motion, and for good cause shown, the court shall hold an evidentiary hearing to determine whether to allow remote testimony. Hearings in the superior court division, and hearings conducted under Subchapter II of Chapter 7B of the General Statutes, shall be recorded. The presence of the child witness is not required at the hearing unless ordered by the presiding judge.

(d) **Order.** -- An order allowing or disallowing the use of remote testimony shall state the findings of fact and conclusions of law that support the court's determination. An order allowing the use of remote testimony shall do the following:

(1) State the method by which the child is to testify.

(2) List any individual or category of individuals allowed to be in, or required to be excluded from, the presence of the child during the testimony.

(3) State any special conditions necessary to facilitate the cross-examination of the child.

(4) State any condition or limitation upon the participation of individuals in the child's presence during his or her testimony.

(5) State any other condition necessary for taking or presenting the testimony.

(e) **Testimony.** -- The method used for remote testimony shall allow the judge, jury, and defendant or juvenile respondent to observe the demeanor of the child as the child testifies in a similar manner as if the child were in the open forum. The court shall ensure that the defense counsel, except a pro se defendant, is physically present where the child testifies, has a full and fair opportunity for cross-examination of the child witness, and has the ability to communicate privately with the defendant or juvenile respondent during the remote testimony. Nothing in this section shall be construed to limit the provisions of G.S. 15A-1225.

(f) **Nonexclusive Procedure and Standard.** -- Nothing in this section shall:

(1) Prohibit the use or application of any other method or procedure authorized or required by statute, common law, or rule for the introduction into evidence of the statements or testimony of a child in a criminal or noncriminal proceeding.

(2) Be construed to require a court, in noncriminal proceedings, to apply the standard set forth in subsection (b) of this section, or to deviate from a standard or standards authorized by statute, common law, or rule, for allowing the use of remote testimony in noncriminal proceedings.

(g) This section does not apply if the defendant is an attorney pro se, unless the defendant has a court-appointed attorney assisting the defendant in the defense, in which case only the court-appointed attorney shall be permitted in the room with the child during the child's testimony.

History.
2009-356, s. 1

§ 15A-1225.2. Witnesses with an intellectual or developmental disability; remote testimony

(a) **Definitions.** -- The following definitions apply to this section:

(1) The definitions set out in G.S. 122C-3.

(2) **Remote testimony.** -- A method by which a witness testifies outside of an open forum and outside of the physical presence of a party or parties.

(b) **Remote Testimony Authorized.** -- An individual with an intellectual or developmental disability who is competent to testify may testify by remote testimony in a prosecution of a person charged with violating a criminal law of this State and in any hearing or proceeding conducted under Subchapter II of Chapter 7B of the General Statutes where a juvenile is alleged to have committed an offense that would be a criminal offense if committed by an adult if the court determines by clear and convincing evidence that the witness would suffer serious emotional distress from testifying in the presence of the defendant and that the ability of the

Chapter 15A

witness to communicate with the trier of fact would be impaired by testifying in the presence of the defendant.

(c) **Hearing Procedure.** -- Upon motion of a party or the court's own motion, and for good cause shown, the court shall hold an evidentiary hearing to determine whether to allow remote testimony. The hearing shall be recorded unless recordation is waived by all parties. The presence of the witness is not required at the hearing unless so ordered by the presiding judge.

(d) **Order.** -- An order allowing or disallowing the use of remote testimony shall state the findings and conclusions of law that support the court's determination. An order allowing the use of remote testimony also shall do all of the following:

(1) State the method by which the witness is to testify.

(2) List any individual or category of individuals allowed to be in or required to be excluded from the presence of the witness during testimony.

(3) State any special conditions necessary to facilitate the cross-examination of the witness.

(4) State any condition or limitation upon the participation of individuals in the presence of the witness during the testimony.

(5) State any other conditions necessary for taking or presenting testimony.

(e) **Testimony.** -- The method of remote testimony shall allow the trier of fact and all parties to observe the demeanor of the witness as the witness testifies in a similar manner as if the witness were testifying in the open forum. The court shall ensure that the counsel for all parties, except a pro se defendant, is physically present where the witness testifies and has a full and fair opportunity for examination and cross-examination of the witness. The court shall ensure that the defendant or juvenile respondent has the ability to communicate privately with defense counsel during the remote testimony. A party may waive the right to have counsel physically present where the witness testifies. Nothing in this section limits the provisions of G.S. 15A-1225.

(f) **Nonexclusive Procedure and Standard.** -- Nothing in this section prohibits the use or application of any other method or procedure authorized or required by law for the introduction into evidence of statements or testimony of an individual with an intellectual or developmental disability.

History.
2009-514, s. 2; 2018-47, s. 3(b)

§ 15A-1225.3. Forensic analyst remote testimony

(a) **Definitions.** -- The following definitions apply to this section:

(1) **Criminal proceeding.** -- Any hearing or trial in a prosecution of a person charged with violating a criminal law of this State and any hearing or proceeding conducted under Subchapter II of Chapter 7B of the General Statutes where a juvenile is alleged to have committed an offense that would be a criminal offense if committed by an adult.

(2) **Remote testimony.** -- A method by which a forensic analyst testifies from a location other than the location where the hearing or trial is being conducted and outside the physical presence of a party or parties.

(b) **Remote Testimony Authorized.** -- In any criminal proceeding, the testimony of an analyst regarding the results of forensic testing admissible pursuant to G.S. 8-58.20, and reported by that analyst, shall be permitted by remote testimony if all of the following occur:

(1) The State has provided a copy of the report to the attorney of record for the defendant, or to the defendant if that person has no attorney, as required by G.S. 8-58.20(d). For purposes of this subdivision, "report" means the full laboratory report package provided to the district attorney.

(2) The State notifies the attorney of record for the defendant, or the defendant if that person has no attorney, at least 15 business days before the proceeding at which the evidence would be used of its intention to introduce the testimony regarding the results of forensic testing into evidence using remote testimony.

(3) The defendant's attorney of record, or the defendant if that person has no attorney, fails to file a written objection with the court, with a copy to the State, at least five business days before the proceeding at which the testimony will be presented that the defendant objects to the introduction of the remote testimony.

If the defendant's attorney of record, or the defendant if that person has no attorney, fails to file a written objection as provided in this subsection, then the objection shall be deemed waived and the analyst shall be allowed to testify by remote testimony.

(c) **Testimony.** -- The method used for remote testimony authorized by this section shall allow the trier of fact and all parties to observe the demeanor of the analyst as the analyst testifies in a similar manner as if the analyst were testifying in the location where the hearing or trial is being conducted. The court shall ensure that the defendant's attorney, or the defendant if that person has no attorney, has a full and fair opportunity for examination and cross-examination of the analyst.

(d) Nothing in this section shall preclude the right of any party to call any witness.

History.
2014-119, s. 8(a); 2015-173, s. 2

§ 15A-1226. Rebuttal evidence; additional evidence

(a) Each party has the right to introduce rebuttal evidence concerning matters elicited in the evidence in chief of another party. The judge may permit a party to offer new evidence during rebuttal which could have been offered in the party's case in chief or during a previous rebuttal, but if new evidence is allowed, the other party must be permitted further rebuttal.

(b) The judge in his discretion may permit any party to introduce additional evidence at any time prior to verdict.

History.
1977, c. 711, s. 1

§ 15A-1227. Motion for dismissal

(a) A motion for dismissal for insufficiency of the evidence to sustain a conviction may be made at the following times:

(1) Upon close of the State's evidence.

(2) Upon close of all the evidence.

(3) After return of a verdict of guilty and before entry of judgment.

(4) After discharge of the jury without a verdict and before the end of the session.

(b) Failure to make the motion at the close of the State's evidence or after all the evidence is not a bar to making the motion at a later time as provided in subsection (a).

(c) The judge must rule on a motion to dismiss for insufficiency of the evidence before the trial may proceed.

(d) The sufficiency of all evidence introduced in a criminal case is reviewable on appeal without regard to whether a motion has been made during trial, as provided in G.S. 15A-1446(d) (5).

History.
1977, c. 711, s. 1

§ 15A-1228. Notes by the jury

Except where the judge, on the judge's own motion or the motion of any party, directs otherwise, jurors may make notes and take them into the jury room during their deliberations.

History.
1977, c. 711, s. 1; 1993, c. 498, s. 1

§ 15A-1229. View by jury

(a) The trial judge in his discretion may permit a jury view. If a view is ordered, the judge must order the jury to be conducted to the place in question in the custody of an officer. The officer must be instructed to permit no person to communicate with the jury on any subject connected with the trial, except as provided in subsection (b), nor to do so himself, and to return the jurors to the courtroom without unnecessary delay or at a specified time. The judge, prosecutor, and counsel for the defendant must be present at the view by the jury. The defendant is entitled to be present at the view by the jury.

(b) A judge in his discretion may permit a witness under oath to testify at the site of the jury view and point out objects and physical characteristics material to his testimony. The testimony must be recorded.

History.
1977, c. 711, s. 1

§ 15A-1230. Limitations on argument to the jury

(a) During a closing argument to the jury an attorney may not become abusive, inject his personal experiences, express his personal belief as to the truth or falsity of the evidence or as to the guilt or innocence of the defendant, or make arguments on the basis of matters outside the record except for matters concerning which the court may take judicial notice. An attorney may, however, on the basis of his analysis of the evidence, argue any position or conclusion with respect to a matter in issue.

(b) Length, number, and order of arguments allotted to the parties are governed by G.S. 7A-97.

History.
1977, c. 711, s. 1; 2010-96, s. 4

§ 15A-1231. Jury instructions

(a) At the close of the evidence or at an earlier time directed by the judge, any party may tender written instructions. A party tendering instructions must furnish copies to the other parties at the time he tenders them to the judge.

(b) Before the arguments to the jury, the judge must hold a recorded conference on instructions out of the presence of the jury. At the conference the judge must inform the parties of the offenses, lesser included offenses, and affirmative defenses on which he will charge the jury and must inform them of what, if any, parts of tendered instructions will be given. A party is also entitled to be informed, upon request, whether the judge intends to include other

Chapter 15A

particular instructions in his charge to the jury. The failure of the judge to comply fully with the provisions of this subsection does not constitute grounds for appeal unless his failure, not corrected prior to the end of the trial, materially prejudiced the case of the defendant.

(c) After the arguments are completed, the judge must instruct the jury in accordance with G.S. 15A-1232.

(d) All instructions given and tendered instructions which have been refused become a part of the record. Failure to object to an erroneous instruction or to the erroneous failure to give an instruction does not constitute a waiver of the right to appeal on that error in accordance with G.S. 15A-1446(d)(13).

History.
1977, c. 711, s. 1; 1983, c. 635

§ 15A-1232. Jury instructions; explanation of law; opinion prohibited

In instructing the jury, the judge shall not express an opinion as to whether or not a fact has been proved and shall not be required to state, summarize or recapitulate the evidence, or to explain the application of the law to the evidence.

History.
1977, c. 711, s. 1; 1985, c. 537, s. 1

§ 15A-1233. Review of testimony; use of evidence by the jury

(a) If the jury after retiring for deliberation requests a review of certain testimony or other evidence, the jurors must be conducted to the courtroom. The judge in his discretion, after notice to the prosecutor and defendant, may direct that requested parts of the testimony be read to the jury and may permit the jury to reexamine in open court the requested materials admitted into evidence. In his discretion the judge may also have the jury review other evidence relating to the same factual issue so as not to give undue prominence to the evidence requested.

(b) Upon request by the jury and with consent of all parties, the judge may in his discretion permit the jury to take to the jury room exhibits and writings which have been received in evidence. If the judge permits the jury to take to the jury room requested exhibits and writings, he may have the jury take additional material or first review other evidence relating to the same issue so as not to give undue prominence to the exhibits or writings taken to the jury room. If the judge permits an exhibit to be taken to the jury room, he must, upon request, instruct the jury not to conduct any experiments with the exhibit.

History.
1977, c. 711, s. 1

§ 15A-1234. Additional instructions

(a) After the jury retires for deliberation, the judge may give appropriate additional instructions to:

(1) Respond to an inquiry of the jury made in open court; or

(2) Correct or withdraw an erroneous instruction; or

(3) Clarify an ambiguous instruction; or

(4) Instruct the jury on a point of law which should have been covered in the original instructions.

(b) At any time the judge gives additional instructions, he may also give or repeat other instructions to avoid giving undue prominence to the additional instructions.

(c) Before the judge gives additional instructions, he must inform the parties generally of the instructions he intends to give and afford them an opportunity to be heard. The parties upon request must be permitted additional argument to the jury if the additional instructions change, by restriction or enlargement, the permissible verdicts of the jury. Otherwise, the allowance of additional argument is within the discretion of the judge.

(d) All additional instructions must be given in open court and must be made a part of the record.

History.
1977, c. 711, s. 1

§ 15A-1235. Length of deliberations; deadlocked jury

(a) Before the jury retires for deliberation, the judge must give an instruction which informs the jury that in order to return a verdict, all 12 jurors must agree to a verdict of guilty or not guilty.

(b) Before the jury retires for deliberation, the judge may give an instruction which informs the jury that:

(1) Jurors have a duty to consult with one another and to deliberate with a view to reaching an agreement, if it can be done without violence to individual judgment;

(2) Each juror must decide the case for himself, but only after an impartial consideration of the evidence with his fellow jurors;

(3) In the course of deliberations, a juror should not hesitate to reexamine his own views and change his opinion if convinced it is erroneous; and

(4) No juror should surrender his honest conviction as to the weight or effect of the evidence solely because of the opinion of his

fellow jurors, or for the mere purpose of returning a verdict.

(c) If it appears to the judge that the jury has been unable to agree, the judge may require the jury to continue its deliberations and may give or repeat the instructions provided in subsections (a) and (b). The judge may not require or threaten to require the jury to deliberate for an unreasonable length of time or for unreasonable intervals.

(d) If it appears that there is no reasonable possibility of agreement, the judge may declare a mistrial and discharge the jury.

History.
1977, c. 711, s. 1

§ 15A-1236. Admonitions to jurors; regulation and separation of jurors

(a) The judge at appropriate times must admonish the jurors that it is their duty:

(1) Not to talk among themselves about the case except in the jury room after their deliberations have begun;

(2) Not to talk to anyone else, or to allow anyone else to talk with them or in their presence about the case and that they must report to the judge immediately the attempt of anyone to communicate with them about the case;

(3) Not to form an opinion about the guilt or innocence of the defendant, or express any opinion about the case until they begin their deliberations;

(4) To avoid reading, watching, or listening to accounts of the trial; and

(5) Not to talk during trial to parties, witnesses, or counsel.

The judge may also admonish them with respect to other matters which he considers appropriate.

(b) The judge in his discretion may direct that the jurors be sequestered.

(c) If the jurors are committed to the charge of an officer, he must be sworn by the clerk to keep the jurors together and not to permit any person to speak or otherwise communicate with them on any subject connected with the trial nor to do so himself, and to return the jurors to the courtroom as directed by the judge.

History.
1977, c. 711, s. 1; 1977, 2nd Sess., c. 1147, s. 3

§ 15A-1237. Verdict

(a) The verdict must be in writing, signed by the foreman, and made a part of the record of the case.

(b) The verdict must be unanimous, and must be returned by the jury in open court.

(c) If the jurors find the defendant not guilty on the ground that he was insane at the time of the commission of the offense charged, their verdict must so state.

(d) If there are two or more defendants, the jury must return a separate verdict with respect to each defendant. If the jury agrees upon a verdict for one defendant but not another, it must return that verdict upon which it agrees.

(e) If there are two or more offenses for which the jury could return a verdict, it may return a verdict with respect to any offense, including a lesser included offense on which the judge charged, as to which it agrees.

History.
1977, c. 711, s. 1

§ 15A-1238. Polling the jury

Upon the motion of any party made after a verdict has been returned and before the jury has dispersed, the jury must be polled. The judge may also upon his own motion require the polling of the jury. The poll may be conducted by the judge or by the clerk by asking each juror individually whether the verdict announced is his verdict. If upon the poll there is not unanimous concurrence, the jury must be directed to retire for further deliberations.

History.
1977, c. 711, s. 1

§ 15A-1239. Judicial comment on verdict

The trial judge may not comment upon the verdict of a jury in open court in the presence or hearing of any member of the jury panel. If he does so, any defendant whose case is calendared for that session of court is entitled, upon motion, to a continuance of his case to a time when all members of the entire jury panel are no longer serving.

History.
1977, c. 711, s. 1

§ 15A-1240. Impeachment of the verdict

(a) Upon an inquiry into the validity of a verdict, no evidence may be received to show the effect of any statement, conduct, event, or condition upon the mind of a juror or concerning the mental processes by which the verdict was determined.

(b) The limitations in subsection (a) do not bar evidence concerning whether the verdict was reached by lot.

(c) After the jury has dispersed, the testimony of a juror may be received to impeach the verdict of the jury on which he served, subject to the limitations in subsection (a), only when it concerns:

> (1) Matters not in evidence which came to the attention of one or more jurors under circumstances which would violate the defendant's constitutional right to confront the witnesses against him; or
>
> (2) Bribery, intimidation, or attempted bribery or intimidation of a juror.

History.
1977, c. 711, s. 1

§ 15A-1241. Record of proceedings

(a) The trial judge must require that the reporter make a true, complete, and accurate record of all statements from the bench and all other proceedings except:

> (1) Selection of the jury in noncapital cases;
>
> (2) Opening statements and final arguments of counsel to the jury; and
>
> (3) Arguments of counsel on questions of law.

(b) Upon motion of any party or on the judge's own motion, proceedings excepted under subdivisions (1) and (2) of subsection (a) must be recorded. The motion for recordation of jury arguments must be made before the commencement of any argument and if one argument is recorded all must be. Upon suggestion of improper argument, when no recordation has been requested or ordered, the judge in his discretion may require the remainder to be recorded.

(c) When a party makes an objection to unrecorded statements or other conduct in the presence of the jury, upon motion of either party the judge must reconstruct for the record, as accurately as possible, the matter to which objection was made.

(d) The trial judge may review the accuracy of the reporter's record of the proceedings, but may not make substantive changes in the transcript concerning his charge, rulings, and comments without notice to the State, the defense, and the reporter. When any correction of a transcript is ordered made by a judge, each party is entitled to receive, upon request, a copy of the transcript indicating the text as submitted by the reporter and as changed by the judge. Upon motion of any party, the judge must afford the parties a hearing upon any change ordered by the judge.

History.
1977, c. 711, s. 1

§ 15A-1242. Defendant's election to represent himself at trial

A defendant may be permitted at his election to proceed in the trial of his case without the assistance of counsel only after the trial judge makes thorough inquiry and is satisfied that the defendant:

> (1) Has been clearly advised of his right to the assistance of counsel, including his right to the assignment of counsel when he is so entitled;
>
> (2) Understands and appreciates the consequences of this decision; and
>
> (3) Comprehends the nature of the charges and proceedings and the range of permissible punishments.

History.
1977, c. 711, s. 1

§ 15A-1243. Standby counsel for defendant representing himself

When a defendant has elected to proceed without the assistance of counsel, the trial judge in his discretion may determine that standby counsel should be appointed to assist the defendant when called upon and to bring to the judge's attention matters favorable to the defendant upon which the judge should rule upon his own motion. Appointment and compensation of standby counsel shall be in accordance with rules adopted by the Office of Indigent Defense Services.

History.
1977, c. 711, s. 1; 2000-144, s. 30

§§ 15A-1244 through 15A-1250

Reserved for future codification purposes.

ARTICLE 74 TO 77

§§ 15A-1251 through 15A-1300

Reserved for future codification purposes.

SUBCHAPTER 13. DISPOSITION OF DEFENDANTS

ARTICLE 78 ORDER OF COMMITMENT TO IMPRISONMENT

§ 15A-1301. Order of commitment to imprisonment when not otherwise specified

When a judicial official orders that a defendant be imprisoned he must issue an appropriate written commitment order. When the commitment is to a sentence of imprisonment, the commitment must include the identification and class of the offense or offenses for which the defendant was convicted and, if the sentences are consecutive, the maximum sentence allowed by law upon conviction of each offense for the punishment range used to impose the sentence for the class of offense and prior record or conviction level, and, if the sentences are concurrent or consolidated, the longest of the maximum sentences allowed by law for the classes of offense and prior record or conviction levels upon conviction of any of the offenses. If the person sentenced to imprisonment is under the age of 18, the person must be committed to a detention facility approved by the Juvenile Justice Section of the Division of Adult Correction and Juvenile Justice to provide secure confinement and care for juveniles. If the person is under the age of 18, the person may be temporarily confined in a holdover facility as defined in G.S. 7B-1501(11) until the person can be transferred to a juvenile detention facility. Personnel of the Juvenile Justice Section or personnel approved by the Juvenile Justice Section shall transport the person to the juvenile detention facility or the holdover facility.

History.
1977, c. 711, s. 1; 1977, 2nd Sess., c. 1147, s. 4; 1993, c. 538, s. 11; 1994, Ex. Sess., c. 24, s. 14(b); 2020-83, s. 8(d)

§§ 15A-1302 through 15A-1310

Reserved for future codification purposes.

ARTICLE 79

§§ 15A-1311 through 15A-1320

Reserved for future codification purposes.

ARTICLE 80
DEFENDANTS FOUND NOT GUILTY BY REASON OF INSANITY

§ 15A-1321. Automatic civil commitment of defendants found not guilty by reason of insanity

(a) When a defendant charged with a crime, wherein it is not alleged that the defendant inflicted or attempted to inflict serious physical injury or death, is found not guilty by reason of insanity by verdict or upon motion pursuant to

G.S. 15A-959(c), the presiding judge shall enter an order finding that the defendant has been found not guilty by reason of insanity of a crime and committing the defendant to a State 24-hour facility designated pursuant to G.S. 122C-252. The court order shall also grant custody of the defendant to a law enforcement officer who shall take the defendant directly to that facility. Proceedings thereafter are in accordance with Part 7 of Article 5 of Chapter 122C of the General Statutes.

(b) When a defendant charged with a crime, wherein it is alleged that the defendant inflicted or attempted to inflict serious physical injury or death, is found not guilty by reason of insanity, by verdict, or upon motion pursuant to G.S. 15A-959(c), notwithstanding any other provision of law, the presiding judge shall enter an order finding that the defendant has been found not guilty by reason of insanity of a crime and committing the defendant to a Forensic Unit operated by the Department of Health and Human Services, where the defendant shall reside until the defendant's release in accordance with Chapter 122C of the General Statutes. The court order shall also grant custody of the defendant to a law enforcement officer who shall take the defendant directly to the facility. Proceedings not inconsistent with this section shall thereafter be in accordance with Part 7 of Article 5 of Chapter 122C of the General Statutes.

History.
1977, c. 711, s. 1; 1983, c. 380, s. 3; 1985, c. 589, s. 10; 1987, c. 596, s. 6; 1991, c. 37, s. 1; 1998-212, s. 12.35B(a)

§ 15A-1322. Temporary restraint

If the judge finds that there are reasonable grounds to believe that the defendant-respondent is mentally ill, as defined in G.S. 122C-3, and is dangerous to himself or others, and the judge determines upon appropriate findings of fact that it is appropriate to proceed under the provisions of this Article, he may order that the respondent be held under appropriate restraint pending proceedings under G.S. 15A-1321.

History.
1977, c. 711, s. 1; 1985, c. 589, s. 12

§§ 15A-1323 through 15A-1330

Reserved for future codification purposes.

ARTICLE 81
GENERAL SENTENCING PROVISIONS

Chapter 15A

§ 15A-1331. Authorized sentences; conviction

(a) The criminal judgment entered against a person in either district or superior court shall be consistent with the provisions of Article 81B of this Chapter and contain a sentence disposition consistent with that Article, unless the offense for which his guilt has been established is not covered by that Article.

(b) For the purpose of imposing sentence, a person has been convicted when he has been adjudged guilty or has entered a plea of guilty or no contest.

History.

1977, c. 711, s. 1; 1993, c. 538, s. 12; 1994, Ex. Sess., c. 24, s. 14(b)

N.C. Gen. Stat. § 15A-1331A

Recodified as G.S. 15A-1331.1 by Session Laws 2012-194, s. 45(a), effective July 17, 2012.

§ 15A-1331.1. Forfeiture of licensing privileges after conviction of a felony

(a) The following definitions apply in this section:

(1) **Licensing agency. --** Any department, division, agency, officer, board, or other unit of State or local government that issues licenses for licensing privileges.

(2) **Licensing privilege. --** The privilege of an individual to be authorized to engage in an activity as evidenced by the following licenses: regular and commercial drivers licenses, occupational licenses, hunting licenses and permits, and fishing licenses and permits.

(3) **Occupational license. --** A licensure, permission, certification, or similar authorization required by statute or rule to practice an occupation or business. The term does not include a tax license issued under Chapter 105 of the General Statutes, Article 7 of Chapter 153A of the General Statutes, or Article 9 of Chapter 160A of the General Statutes.

(b) Upon conviction of a felony, an individual automatically forfeits the individual's licensing privileges for the full term of the period the individual is placed on probation by the sentencing court at the time of conviction for the offense, if:

(1) The individual is offered a suspended sentence on condition the individual accepts probation and the individual refuses probation, or

(2) The individual's probation is revoked or suspended, and the judge makes findings in the judgment that the individual failed to make reasonable efforts to comply with the conditions of probation.

(c) Whenever an individual's licensing privileges are forfeited under this section, the judge shall make findings in the judgment of the licensing privileges held by the individual known to the court at that time, the drivers license number and social security number of the individual, and the beginning and ending date of the period of time of the forfeiture. The terms and conditions of the forfeiture shall be transmitted by the clerk of court to the Division of Motor Vehicles, in accordance with G.S. 20-24 and to the licensing agencies specified by the judge in the judgment. A licensing agency, upon receiving notice from the clerk of court, shall require the individual whose licensing privileges were forfeited to surrender the forfeited license issued by the agency and shall not reissue a license to that individual during the period of forfeiture as stated in the notice. Licensing agencies are authorized to establish procedures to implement this section.

(d) Notwithstanding any other provision of this section, the court may order that an individual whose licensing privileges are forfeited under this section be granted a limited driving privilege in accordance with the provisions of G.S. 20-179.3.

History.

1994, Ex. Sess., c. 20, ss. 1, 5; 2012-194, s. 45(a)

§ 15A-1331.2. Prayer for judgment continued for a period of time that exceeds 12 months is an improper disposition of a Class B1, B2, C, D, or E felony

The court shall not dispose of any criminal action that is a Class B1, B2, C, D, or E felony by ordering a prayer for judgment continued that exceeds 12 months. If the court orders a prayer for judgment continued in any criminal action that is a Class B1, B2, C, D, or E felony, the court shall include as a condition that the State shall pray judgment within a specific period of time not to exceed 12 months. At the time the State prays judgment, or 12 months from the date of the prayer for judgment continued order, whichever is earlier, the court shall enter a final judgment unless the court finds that it is in the interest of justice to continue the order for prayer for judgment continued. If the court continues the order for prayer for judgment continued, the order shall be continued for a specific period of time not to exceed 12 months. The court shall not continue a prayer for judgment continued order for more than one additional 12-month period.

History.

2012-149, s. 11; 2012-194, s. 45(e)

§ 15A-1332. Presentence reports

(a) **Presentence Reports Generally.** -- To obtain a presentence report, the court may order either a presentence investigation as provided in subsection (b) or a presentence commitment for study as provided in subsection (c).

(b) **Presentence Investigation.** -- The court may order a probation officer to make a presentence investigation of any defendant. The court may order the investigation only after conviction unless the defendant moves for an earlier presentence investigation. A motion for an earlier presentence investigation may be addressed only to the judge of the session of court for which the defendant's case is calendared or, if the case has not been calendared, to a resident superior court judge if the case is in the jurisdiction of the superior court or to the chief district court judge if the case is in the jurisdiction of the district court. When the court orders a presentence investigation, the probation officer must promptly investigate all circumstances relevant to sentencing and submit either a written report or an oral report either on the record or with defense counsel and the prosecutor present. The report may include sentence recommendations only if such recommendations are requested by the court.

(c) **Presentence Commitment for Study.** -- When the court desires more detailed information as a basis for determining the sentence to be imposed than can be provided by a presentence investigation, the court may commit a defendant to the Division of Adult Correction and Juvenile Justice of the Department of Public Safety for study for the shortest period necessary to complete the study, not to exceed 90 days, if that defendant has been charged with or convicted of any felony or a Class A1 or Class 1 misdemeanor crime or crimes for which he may be imprisoned for more than six months and if he consents. The period of commitment must end when the study is completed, and may not exceed 90 days. The Division must conduct a complete study of a defendant committed to it under this subsection, inquiring into such matters as the defendant's previous delinquency or criminal experience, his social background, his capabilities, his mental, emotional and physical health, and the availability of resources or programs appropriate to the defendant. Upon completion of the study or the end of the 90-day period, whichever occurs first, the Division of Adult Correction and Juvenile Justice of the Department of Public Safety must release the defendant to the sheriff of the county in which his case is docketed. The Division must forward the study to the clerk in that county, including whatever recommendations the Division believes will be helpful to a proper resolution of the case. When a defendant is returned from a presentence commitment for study, the conditions of pretrial release which obtained for the defendant before the commitment continue until judgment is entered, unless the conditions are modified under the provisions of G.S. 15A-534(e).

History.
1977, c. 711, s. 1; 1981, c. 377, s. 1; 1993, c. 538, s. 13; 1994, Ex. Sess., c. 24, s. 14(b); 1995, c. 507, s. 19.5(e); 2011-145, s. 19.1(h); 2017-186, s. 2(fff)

§ 15A-1333. Availability of presentence report

(a) **Presentence Reports and Sentencing Services Information Not Public Records.** -- A written presentence report, the record of an oral presentence report, and information obtained in the preparation of a sentencing plan by a sentencing services program under Article 61 of Chapter 7A are not public records and may not be made available to any person except as provided in this section.

(b) **Access to Reports.** -- The defendant, his counsel, the prosecutor, or the court may have access at any reasonable time to a written presentence report or to any record of an oral presentence report. Access to a sentencing plan and information obtained in the preparation of a sentencing plan shall be in accordance with the comprehensive sentencing services program plan developed pursuant to G.S. 7A-774.

(c) **Expunging Reports.** -- On motion of the defendant, the court in its discretion may order a written presentence report, the record of an oral presentence report, or a sentencing plan expunged from the court record.

History.
1977, c. 711, s. 1; 2000-67, s. 15.9(c)

§ 15A-1334. The sentencing hearing

(a) **Time of Hearing.** -- Unless the defendant waives the hearing, the court must hold a hearing on the sentence. Either the defendant or the State may, upon a showing which the judge determines to be good cause, obtain a continuance of the sentencing hearing.

(b) **Proceeding at Hearing.** -- The defendant at the hearing may make a statement in his own behalf. The defendant and prosecutor may present witnesses and arguments on facts relevant to the sentencing decision and may cross-examine the other party's witnesses. No person other than the defendant, his counsel, the prosecutor, and one making a presentence report may comment to the court on sentencing unless called as a witness by the defendant, the prosecutor, or the court. Formal rules of evidence do not apply at the hearing.

(c) **Sentence Hearing in Other District. --** The judge who orders a presentence report may, in his discretion, direct that the sentencing hearing be held before him in another county or another district court district as defined in G.S. 7A-133 or superior court district or set of districts as defined in G.S. 7A-41.1, as the case may be, during or after the session in which the defendant was convicted. If sentence is imposed in a county other than the one where the defendant was convicted, the clerk of the county where sentence is imposed must forward the records of the sentencing proceeding to the clerk of the county of conviction.

(d) **Sentencing in Capital Cases. --** Sentencing in capital cases is governed by Article 100 of this Chapter.

(e) **Procedure Applicable when Certain Prior Convictions May Be Used. --** The procedure in G.S. 15A-980 governs if the State seeks to use a prior conviction in a sentencing hearing.

History.
1977, c. 711, s. 1; 1983, c. 513, s. 3; 1987 (Reg. Sess., 1988), c. 1037, s. 66

§ 15A-1335. Resentencing after appellate review

When a conviction or sentence imposed in superior court has been set aside on direct review or collateral attack, the court may not impose a new sentence for the same offense, or for a different offense based on the same conduct, which is more severe than the prior sentence less the portion of the prior sentence previously served. This section shall not apply when a defendant, on direct review or collateral attack, succeeds in having a plea of guilty vacated.

History.
1977, c. 711, s. 1; 2013-385, s. 3

§ 15A-1336. Compliance with criminal case firearm notification requirements of the federal Violence Against Women Act

The Administrative Office of the Courts, in cooperation with the North Carolina Coalition Against Domestic Violence and the North Carolina Governor's Crime Commission, shall develop a form to comply with the criminal case firearm notification requirements of the Violence Against Women Act of 2005.

History.
2007-294, s. 2

§§ 15A-1337 through 15A-1340

Reserved for future codification purposes.

ARTICLE 81A
SENTENCING PERSONS CONVICTED OF FELONIES

§§ 15A-1340.1 through 15A-1340.7

Repealed by Session Laws 1993, c. 538, s. 14

§§ 15A-1340.8, 15A-1340.9

Reserved for future codification purposes.

ARTICLE 81B
STRUCTURED SENTENCING OF PERSONS CONVICTED OF CRIMES

PART 1
GENERAL PROVISIONS

§ 15A-1340.10. Applicability of structured sentencing

This Article applies to criminal offenses in North Carolina, other than impaired driving under G.S. 20-138.1 and failure to comply with control measures under G.S. 130A-25, that occur on or after October 1, 1994. This Article does not apply to violent habitual felons sentenced under Article 2B of Chapter 14 of the General Statutes.

History.
1993, c. 538, s. 1; 1994, Ex. Sess., c. 22, s. 35; c. 24, s. 14(a), (b); 1993 (Reg. Sess., 1994), c. 767, s. 17

§ 15A-1340.11. Definitions

The following definitions apply in this Article:

(1) **Active punishment. --** A sentence in a criminal case that requires an offender to serve a sentence of imprisonment and is not suspended. Special probation, as defined in G.S. 15A-1351, is not an active punishment.

(2) **Community punishment. --** A sentence in a criminal case that does not include an active punishment or assignment to a drug treatment court, or special probation as defined in G.S. 15A-1351(a). It may include any one or more of the conditions set forth in G.S. 15A-1343(a1).

(3) Repealed by Session Laws 2011-192, s. 1(h), effective December 1, 2011.

(3a) **Drug treatment court program.** -- Program to which offenders are required, as a condition of probation, to comply with the rules adopted for the program as provided for in Article 62 of Chapter 7A of the General Statutes and to report on a regular basis for a specified time to participate in:

    a. Court supervision.

    b. Drug screening or testing.

    c. Drug or alcohol treatment programs.

(4) Repealed by Session Laws 1997-57, s. 2.

(4a) **House arrest with electronic monitoring.** -- Probation in which the offender is required to remain at his or her residence. The court, in the sentencing order, may authorize the offender to leave the offender's residence for employment, counseling, a course of study, vocational training, or other specific purposes and may modify that authorization. The probation officer may authorize the offender to leave the offender's residence for specific purposes not authorized in the court order upon approval of the probation officer's supervisor. The offender shall be required to wear a device which permits the supervising agency to monitor the offender's compliance with the condition.

(5) Repealed by Session Laws 2011-192, s. 1(i), effective December 1, 2011.

(6) **Intermediate punishment.** -- A sentence in a criminal case that places an offender on supervised probation. It may include drug treatment court, special probation as defined in G.S. 15A-1351(a), and one or more of the conditions set forth in G.S. 15A-1343(a1).

(7) **Prior conviction.** -- A person has a prior conviction when, on the date a criminal judgment is entered, the person being sentenced has been previously convicted of a crime:

    a. In the district court, and the person has not given notice of appeal and the time for appeal has expired; or

    b. In the superior court, regardless of whether the conviction is on appeal to the appellate division; or

    c. In the courts of the United States, another state, the Armed Forces of the United States, or another country, regardless of whether the offense would be a crime if it occurred in North Carolina,

regardless of whether the crime was committed before or after the effective date of this Article.

(8) Repealed by Session Laws 2011-192, s. 1(j), effective December 1, 2011.

History.

1993, c. 538, s. 1; 1994, Ex. Sess., c. 14, s. 17; c. 24, s. 14(b); 1997-57, s. 2; 1997-80, s. 6; 1999-306, s. 2; 2004-128, s. 3; 2009-372, s. 5; 2009-547, s. 6; 2011-183, s. 17; 2011-192, s. 1(a), (b), (h)-(j).

§ 15A-1340.12. Purposes of sentencing

The primary purposes of sentencing a person convicted of a crime are to impose a punishment commensurate with the injury the offense has caused, taking into account factors that may diminish or increase the offender's culpability; to protect the public by restraining offenders; to assist the offender toward rehabilitation and restoration to the community as a lawful citizen; and to provide a general deterrent to criminal behavior.

History.

1993, c. 538, s. 1; 1994, Ex. Sess., c. 24, s. 14(b)

PART 2
FELONY SENTENCING

§ 15A-1340.13. Procedure and incidents of sentence of imprisonment for felonies

(a) **Application to Felonies Only.** -- This Part applies to sentences imposed for felony convictions.

(b) **Procedure Generally; Requirements of Judgment; Kinds of Sentences.** -- Before imposing a sentence, the court shall determine the prior record level for the offender pursuant to G.S. 15A-1340.14. The sentence shall contain a sentence disposition specified for the class of offense and prior record level, and its minimum term of imprisonment shall be within the range specified for the class of offense and prior record level, unless applicable statutes require or authorize another minimum sentence of imprisonment. The kinds of sentence dispositions are active punishment, intermediate punishment, and community punishment.

(c) **Minimum and Maximum Term.** -- The judgment of the court shall contain a minimum term of imprisonment that is consistent with the class of offense for which the sentence is being imposed and with the prior record level for the offender. The maximum term of imprisonment applicable to each minimum term of imprisonment is, unless otherwise provided, as specified in G.S. 15A-1340.17. The maximum term shall be specified in the judgment of the court.

(d) **Service of Minimum Required; Earned Time Authorization.** -- An offender sentenced to an active punishment shall serve the minimum term imposed, except as provided in G.S. 15A-1340.18. The maximum term may be reduced to, but not below, the minimum term by earned time credits awarded to an offender by the Division of Adult Correction and Juvenile Justice of the Department of Public Safety or the custodian of the local confinement facility, pursuant to rules adopted in accordance with law.

(e) **Deviation from Sentence Ranges for Aggravation and Mitigation; No Sentence Dispositional Deviation Allowed.** -- The court may deviate from the presumptive range of minimum sentences of imprisonment specified for a class of offense and prior record level if it finds, pursuant to G.S. 15A-1340.16, that aggravating or mitigating circumstances support such a deviation. The amount of the deviation is in the court's discretion, subject to the limits specified in the class of offense and prior record level for mitigated and aggravated punishment. Deviations for aggravated or mitigated punishment are allowed only in the ranges of minimum and maximum sentences of imprisonment, and not in the sentence dispositions specified for the class of offense and prior record level, unless a statute specifically authorizes a sentence dispositional deviation.

(f) **Suspension of Sentence.** -- Unless otherwise provided, the court shall not suspend the sentence of imprisonment if the class of offense and prior record level do not permit community or intermediate punishment as a sentence disposition. The court shall suspend the sentence of imprisonment if the class of offense and prior record level require community or intermediate punishment as a sentence disposition. The court may suspend the sentence of imprisonment if the class of offense and prior record level authorize, but do not require, active punishment as a sentence disposition.

(g) **Dispositional Deviation for Extraordinary Mitigation.** -- Except as provided in subsection (h) of this section, the court may impose an intermediate punishment for a class of offense and prior record level that requires the imposition of an active punishment if it finds in writing all of the following:

(1) That extraordinary mitigating factors of a kind significantly greater than in the normal case are present.

(2) Those factors substantially outweigh any factors in aggravation.

(3) It would be a manifest injustice to impose an active punishment in the case.

The court shall consider evidence of extraordinary mitigating factors, but the decision to find any such factors, or to impose an intermediate punishment is in the discretion of the court. The extraordinary mitigating factors which the court finds shall be specified in its judgment.

(h) **Exceptions When Extraordinary Mitigation Shall Not Be Used.** -- The court shall not impose an intermediate sanction pursuant to subsection (g) of this section if:

(1) The offense is a Class A or Class B1 felony;

(2) The offense is a drug trafficking offense under G.S. 90-95(h) or a drug trafficking conspiracy offense under G.S. 90-95(i); or

(3) The defendant has five or more points as determined by G.S. 15A-1340.14.

History.
1993, c. 538, s. 1; 1994, Ex. Sess., c. 14, ss. 18, 18.1, 19; c. 22, s. 9; c. 24, s. 14(b); 1995, c. 375, s. 1; 2011-145, s. 19.1(h); 2011-192, s. 5(d); 2017-186, s. 2(ggg)

§ 15A-1340.14. Prior record level for felony sentencing

(a) **Generally.** -- The prior record level of a felony offender is determined by calculating the sum of the points assigned to each of the offender's prior convictions that the court, or with respect to subdivision (b)(7) of this section, the jury, finds to have been proved in accordance with this section.

(b) **Points.** -- Points are assigned as follows:

(1) For each prior felony Class A conviction, 10 points.

(1a) For each prior felony Class B1 conviction, 9 points.

(2) For each prior felony Class B2, C, or D conviction, 6 points.

(3) For each prior felony Class E, F, or G conviction, 4 points.

(4) For each prior felony Class H or I conviction, 2 points.

(5) For each prior misdemeanor conviction as defined in this subsection, 1 point. For purposes of this subsection, misdemeanor is defined as any Class A1 and Class 1 nontraffic misdemeanor offense, impaired driving (G.S. 20-138.1), impaired driving in a commercial vehicle (G.S. 20-138.2), and misdemeanor death by vehicle (G.S. 20-141.4(a2)), but not any other misdemeanor traffic offense under Chapter 20 of the General Statutes.

(6) If all the elements of the present offense are included in any prior offense for which the offender was convicted, whether or not the prior offense or offenses were used in determining prior record level, 1 point.

(7) If the offense was committed while the offender was on supervised or unsupervised probation, parole, or post-release supervision, or while the offender was serving a sentence of imprisonment, or while the offender was on escape from a correctional institution while serving a sentence of imprisonment, 1 point.

For purposes of determining prior record points under this subsection, a conviction for a first degree rape or a first degree sexual offense committed prior to the effective date of this subsection shall be treated as a felony Class B1 conviction, and a conviction for any other felony Class B offense committed prior to the effective date of this subsection shall be treated as a felony Class B2 conviction. G.S. 15A-1340.16(a5) specifies the procedure to be used to determine if a point exists under subdivision (7) of this subsection. The State must provide a defendant with written notice of its intent to prove the existence of the prior record point under subdivision (7) of this subsection as required by G.S. 15A-1340.16(a6).

(c) **Prior Record Levels for Felony Sentencing.** -- The prior record levels for felony sentencing are:

(1) Level I -- Not more than 1 point.

(2) Level II -- At least 2, but not more than 5 points.

(3) Level III -- At least 6, but not more than 9 points.

(4) Level IV -- At least 10, but not more than 13 points.

(5) Level V -- At least 14, but not more than 17 points.

(6) Level VI -- At least 18 points.

In determining the prior record level, the classification of a prior offense is the classification assigned to that offense at the time the offense for which the offender is being sentenced is committed.

(d) **Multiple Prior Convictions Obtained in One Court Week.** -- For purposes of determining the prior record level, if an offender is convicted of more than one offense in a single superior court during one calendar week, only the conviction for the offense with the highest point total is used. If an offender is convicted of more than one offense in a single session of district court, only one of the convictions is used.

(e) **Classification of Prior Convictions From Other Jurisdictions.** -- Except as otherwise provided in this subsection, a conviction occurring in a jurisdiction other than North Carolina is classified as a Class I felony if the jurisdiction in which the offense occurred classifies the offense as a felony, or is classified as a Class 3 misdemeanor if the jurisdiction in which the offense occurred classifies the offense as a misdemeanor. If the offender proves by the preponderance of the evidence that an offense classified as a felony in the other jurisdiction is substantially similar to an offense that is a misdemeanor in North Carolina, the conviction is treated as that class of misdemeanor for assigning prior record level points.

If the State proves by the preponderance of the evidence that an offense classified as either a misdemeanor or a felony in the other jurisdiction is substantially similar to an offense in North Carolina that is classified as a Class I felony or higher, the conviction is treated as that class of felony for assigning prior record level points. If the State proves by the preponderance of the evidence that an offense classified as a misdemeanor in the other jurisdiction is substantially similar to an offense classified as a Class A1 or Class 1 misdemeanor in North Carolina, the conviction is treated as a Class A1 or Class 1 misdemeanor for assigning prior record level points.

(f) **Proof of Prior Convictions.** -- A prior conviction shall be proved by any of the following methods:

(1) Stipulation of the parties.

(2) An original or copy of the court record of the prior conviction.

(3) A copy of records maintained by the Department of Public Safety, the Division of Motor Vehicles, or of the Administrative Office of the Courts.

(4) Any other method found by the court to be reliable.

The State bears the burden of proving, by a preponderance of the evidence, that a prior conviction exists and that the offender before the court is the same person as the offender named in the prior conviction. The original or a copy of the court records or a copy of the records maintained by the Department of Public Safety, the Division of Motor Vehicles, or of the Administrative Office of the Courts, bearing the same name as that by which the offender is charged, is prima facie evidence that the offender named is the same person as the offender before the court, and that the facts set out in the record are true. For purposes of this subsection, "a copy" includes a paper writing containing a reproduction of a record maintained electronically on a computer or other data processing equipment, and a document produced by a facsimile machine. The prosecutor shall make all feasible efforts to obtain and present to the court the offender's full record. Evidence presented by either party at trial may be utilized to prove prior convictions. Suppression of prior convictions is pursuant to G.S. 15A-980. If a motion is made pursuant to that section during the sentencing stage of the criminal action, the court may grant a continuance of the sentencing hearing. If asked by the defendant in compliance with G.S. 15A-903, the prosecutor shall furnish the defendant's prior criminal record to the defendant within a reasonable time sufficient to allow the defendant to determine

Chapter 15A

if the record available to the prosecutor is accurate. Upon request of a sentencing services program established pursuant to Article 61 of Chapter 7A of the General Statutes, the district attorney shall provide any information the district attorney has about the criminal record of a person for whom the program has been requested to provide a sentencing plan pursuant to G.S. 7A-773.1.

History.
1993, c. 538, s. 1; 1994, Ex. Sess., c. 22, s. 10; c. 24, s. 14(b); 1993 (Reg. Sess., 1994), c. 767, ss. 11-13; 1995, c. 507, s. 19.5(f); 1995 (Reg. Sess., 1996), c. 742, s. 15; 1997-80, s. 7; 1997-486, s. 1; 1999-306, s. 3; 1999-408, s. 3; 2005-145, s. 2; 2009-555, s. 1; 2014-100, s. 17.1(q)

§ 15A-1340.15. Multiple convictions

(a) **Consecutive Sentences.** -- This Article does not prohibit the imposition of consecutive sentences. Unless otherwise specified by the court, all sentences of imprisonment run concurrently with any other sentences of imprisonment.

(b) **Consolidation of Sentences.** -- If an offender is convicted of more than one offense at the same time, the court may consolidate the offenses for judgment and impose a single judgment for the consolidated offenses. The judgment shall contain a sentence disposition specified for the class of offense and prior record level of the most serious offense, and its minimum sentence of imprisonment shall be within the ranges specified for that class of offense and prior record level, unless applicable statutes require or authorize another minimum sentence of imprisonment.

History.
1993, c. 538, s. 1; 1994, Ex. Sess., c. 24, s. 14(b)

§ 15A-1340.16. Aggravated and mitigated sentences

(a) **Generally, Burden of Proof.** -- The court shall consider evidence of aggravating or mitigating factors present in the offense that make an aggravated or mitigated sentence appropriate, but the decision to depart from the presumptive range is in the discretion of the court. The State bears the burden of proving beyond a reasonable doubt that an aggravating factor exists, and the offender bears the burden of proving by a preponderance of the evidence that a mitigating factor exists.

(a1) **Jury to Determine Aggravating Factors; Jury Procedure if Trial Bifurcated.** -- The defendant may admit to the existence of an aggravating factor, and the factor so admitted shall be treated as though it were found by a jury pursuant to the procedures in this subsection. Admissions of the existence of an aggravating factor must be consistent with the provisions of G.S. 15A-1022.1. If the defendant does not so admit, only a jury may determine if an aggravating factor is present in an offense. The jury impaneled for the trial of the felony may, in the same trial, also determine if one or more aggravating factors is present, unless the court determines that the interests of justice require that a separate sentencing proceeding be used to make that determination. If the court determines that a separate proceeding is required, the proceeding shall be conducted by the trial judge before the trial jury as soon as practicable after the guilty verdict is returned. If at any time prior to rendering a decision to the court regarding whether one or more aggravating factors exist, any juror dies, becomes incapacitated or disqualified, or is discharged for any reason, an alternate juror shall become a part of the jury and serve in all respects as those selected on the regular trial panel. An alternate juror shall become a part of the jury in the order in which the juror was selected. If an alternate juror replaces a juror after deliberations have begun, the court must instruct the jury to begin its deliberations anew. In no event shall more than 12 jurors participate in the jury's deliberations. If the trial jury is unable to reconvene for a hearing on the issue of whether one or more aggravating factors exist after having determined the guilt of the accused, the trial judge shall impanel a new jury to determine the issue. A jury selected to determine whether one or more aggravating factors exist shall be selected in the same manner as juries are selected for the trial of criminal cases.

(a2) **Procedure if Defendant Admits Aggravating Factor Only.** -- If the defendant admits that an aggravating factor exists, but pleads not guilty to the underlying felony, a jury shall be impaneled to dispose of the felony charge. In that case, evidence that relates solely to the establishment of an aggravating factor shall not be admitted in the felony trial.

(a3) **Procedure if Defendant Pleads Guilty to the Felony Only.** -- If the defendant pleads guilty to the felony, but contests the existence of one or more aggravating factors, a jury shall be impaneled to determine if the aggravating factor or factors exist.

(a4) **Pleading of Aggravating Factors.** -- Aggravating factors set forth in subsection (d) of this section need not be included in an indictment or other charging instrument. Any aggravating factor alleged under subdivision (d)(20) of this section shall be included in an

Chapter 15A

indictment or other charging instrument, as specified in G.S. 15A-924.

(a5) **Procedure to Determine Prior Record Level Points Not Involving Prior Convictions.** -- If the State seeks to establish the existence of a prior record level point under G.S. 15A-1340.14(b)(7), the jury shall determine whether the point should be assessed using the procedures specified in subsections (a1) through (a3) of this section. The State need not allege in an indictment or other pleading that it intends to establish the point.

(a6) **Notice of Intent to Use Aggravating Factors or Prior Record Level Points.** -- The State must provide a defendant with written notice of its intent to prove the existence of one or more aggravating factors under subsection (d) of this section or a prior record level point under G.S. 15A-1340.14(b)(7) at least 30 days before trial or the entry of a guilty or no contest plea. A defendant may waive the right to receive such notice. The notice shall list all the aggravating factors the State seeks to establish.

(a7) **Procedure When Jury Trial Waived.** -- If a defendant waives the right to a jury trial under G.S. 15A-1201, the trial judge shall make all findings that are conferred upon the jury under the provisions of this section.

(b) **When Aggravated or Mitigated Sentence Allowed.** -- If the jury, or with respect to an aggravating factor under G.S. 15A-1340.16(d)(12a) or (18a), the court, finds that aggravating factors exist or the court finds that mitigating factors exist, the court may depart from the presumptive range of sentences specified in G.S. 15A-1340.17(c)(2). If aggravating factors are present and the court determines they are sufficient to outweigh any mitigating factors that are present, it may impose a sentence that is permitted by the aggravated range described in G.S. 15A-1340.17(c)(4). If the court finds that mitigating factors are present and are sufficient to outweigh any aggravating factors that are present, it may impose a sentence that is permitted by the mitigated range described in G.S. 15A-1340.17(c)(3).

(c) **Written Findings; When Required.** -- The court shall make findings of the aggravating and mitigating factors present in the offense only if, in its discretion, it departs from the presumptive range of sentences specified in G.S. 15A-1340.17(c)(2). If the jury finds factors in aggravation, the court shall ensure that those findings are entered in the court's determination of sentencing factors form or any comparable document used to record the findings of sentencing factors. Findings shall be in writing. The requirement to make findings in order to depart from the presumptive range applies regardless of whether the sentence of imprisonment is activated or suspended.

(d) **Aggravating Factors.** -- The following are aggravating factors:

(1) The defendant induced others to participate in the commission of the offense or occupied a position of leadership or dominance of other participants.

(2) The defendant joined with more than one other person in committing the offense and was not charged with committing a conspiracy.

(2a) The offense was committed for the benefit of, or at the direction of, any criminal gang as defined by G.S. 14-50.16A(1), with the specific intent to promote, further, or assist in any criminal conduct by gang members, and the defendant was not charged with committing a conspiracy.

(3) The offense was committed for the purpose of avoiding or preventing a lawful arrest or effecting an escape from custody.

(4) The defendant was hired or paid to commit the offense.

(5) The offense was committed to disrupt or hinder the lawful exercise of any governmental function or the enforcement of laws.

(6) The offense was committed against or proximately caused serious injury to a present or former law enforcement officer, employee of the Division of Adult Correction and Juvenile Justice of the Department of Public Safety, jailer, fireman, emergency medical technician, ambulance attendant, social worker, justice or judge, clerk or assistant or deputy clerk of court, magistrate, prosecutor, juror, or witness against the defendant, while engaged in the performance of that person's official duties or because of the exercise of that person's official duties.

(6a) The offense was committed against or proximately caused serious harm as defined in G.S. 14-163.1 or death to a law enforcement agency animal, an assistance animal, or a search and rescue animal as defined in G.S. 14-163.1, while engaged in the performance of the animal's official duties.

(7) The offense was especially heinous, atrocious, or cruel.

(8) The defendant knowingly created a great risk of death to more than one person by means of a weapon or device which would normally be hazardous to the lives of more than one person.

(9) The defendant held public elected or appointed office or public employment at the time of the offense and the offense directly related to the conduct of the office or employment.

Chapter 15A

(9a) The defendant is a firefighter or rescue squad worker, and the offense is directly related to service as a firefighter or rescue squad worker.

(10) The defendant was armed with or used a deadly weapon at the time of the crime.

(11) The victim was very young, or very old, or mentally or physically infirm, or handicapped.

(12) The defendant committed the offense while on pretrial release on another charge.

(12a) The defendant has, during the 10-year period prior to the commission of the offense for which the defendant is being sentenced, been found by a court of this State to be in willful violation of the conditions of probation imposed pursuant to a suspended sentence or been found by the Post-Release Supervision and Parole Commission to be in willful violation of a condition of parole or post-release supervision imposed pursuant to release from incarceration.

(13) The defendant involved a person under the age of 16 in the commission of the crime.

(13a) The defendant committed an offense and knew or reasonably should have known that a person under the age of 18 who was not involved in the commission of the offense was in a position to see or hear the offense.

(14) The offense involved an attempted or actual taking of property of great monetary value or damage causing great monetary loss, or the offense involved an unusually large quantity of contraband.

(15) The defendant took advantage of a position of trust or confidence, including a domestic relationship, to commit the offense.

(16) The offense involved the sale or delivery of a controlled substance to a minor.

(16a) The offense is the manufacture of methamphetamine and was committed where a person under the age of 18 lives, was present, or was otherwise endangered by exposure to the drug, its ingredients, its by-products, or its waste.

(16b) The offense is the manufacture of methamphetamine and was committed in a dwelling that is one of four or more contiguous dwellings.

(17) The offense for which the defendant stands convicted was committed against a victim because of the victim's race, color, religion, nationality, or country of origin.

(18) The defendant does not support the defendant's family.

(18a) The defendant has previously been adjudicated delinquent for an offense that would be a Class A, B1, B2, C, D, or E felony if committed by an adult.

(19) The serious injury inflicted upon the victim is permanent and debilitating.

(19a) The offense is a violation of G.S. 14-43.11 (human trafficking), G.S. 14-43.12 (involuntary servitude), or G.S. 14-43.13 (sexual servitude) and involved multiple victims.

(19b) The offense is a violation of G.S. 14-43.11 (human trafficking), G.S. 14-43.12 (involuntary servitude), or G.S. 14-43.13 (sexual servitude), and the victim suffered serious injury as a result of the offense.

(20) Any other aggravating factor reasonably related to the purposes of sentencing.

Evidence necessary to prove an element of the offense shall not be used to prove any factor in aggravation, and the same item of evidence shall not be used to prove more than one factor in aggravation. Evidence necessary to establish that an enhanced sentence is required under G.S. 15A-1340.16A may not be used to prove any factor in aggravation.

The judge shall not consider as an aggravating factor the fact that the defendant exercised the right to a jury trial.

Notwithstanding the provisions of subsection (a1) of this section, the determination that an aggravating factor under G.S. 15A-1340.16(d)(18a) is present in a case shall be made by the court, and not by the jury. That determination shall be made in the sentencing hearing.

(e) **Mitigating Factors. --** The following are mitigating factors:

(1) The defendant committed the offense under duress, coercion, threat, or compulsion that was insufficient to constitute a defense but significantly reduced the defendant's culpability.

(2) The defendant was a passive participant or played a minor role in the commission of the offense.

(3) The defendant was suffering from a mental or physical condition that was insufficient to constitute a defense but significantly reduced the defendant's culpability for the offense.

(4) The defendant's age, immaturity, or limited mental capacity at the time of commission of the offense significantly reduced the defendant's culpability for the offense.

(5) The defendant has made substantial or full restitution to the victim.

(6) The victim was more than 16 years of age and was a voluntary participant in the defendant's conduct or consented to it.

(7) The defendant aided in the apprehension of another felon or testified truthfully

on behalf of the prosecution in another prosecution of a felony.

(8) The defendant acted under strong provocation, or the relationship between the defendant and the victim was otherwise extenuating.

(9) The defendant could not reasonably foresee that the defendant's conduct would cause or threaten serious bodily harm or fear, or the defendant exercised caution to avoid such consequences.

(10) The defendant reasonably believed that the defendant's conduct was legal.

(11) Prior to arrest or at an early stage of the criminal process, the defendant voluntarily acknowledged wrongdoing in connection with the offense to a law enforcement officer.

(12) The defendant has been a person of good character or has had a good reputation in the community in which the defendant lives.

(13) The defendant is a minor and has reliable supervision available.

(14) The defendant has been honorably discharged from the Armed Forces of the United States.

(15) The defendant has accepted responsibility for the defendant's criminal conduct.

(16) The defendant has entered and is currently involved in or has successfully completed a drug treatment program or an alcohol treatment program subsequent to arrest and prior to trial.

(17) The defendant supports the defendant's family.

(18) The defendant has a support system in the community.

(19) The defendant has a positive employment history or is gainfully employed.

(20) The defendant has a good treatment prognosis, and a workable treatment plan is available.

(21) Any other mitigating factor reasonably related to the purposes of sentences.

(f) **Notice to State Treasurer of Finding.** -- If the court determines that an aggravating factor under subdivision (9) of subsection (d) of this section has been proven, the court shall notify the State Treasurer of the fact of the conviction as well as the finding of the aggravating factor. The indictment charging the defendant with the underlying offense must include notice that the State seeks to prove the defendant acted in accordance with subdivision (9) of subsection (d) of this section and that the State will seek to prove that as an aggravating factor.

History.
1993, c. 538, s. 1; 1994, Ex. Sess., c. 7, s. 6; c. 22, s. 22; c. 24, s. 14(b); 1995, c. 509, s. 13; 1997-443, ss. 19.25(w), 19.25(ee); 2003-378, s. 6; 2004-178, s. 2; 2004-186, s. 8.1; 2005-101, s. 1; 2005-145, s. 1; 2005-434, s. 4; 2007-80, s. 2; 2008-129, ss. 1, 2; 2009-460, s. 2; 2011-145, s. 19.1(h); 2011-183, s. 18; 2012-193, s. 9, 10; 2013-284, s. 2(b); 2013-368, s. 14; 2015-62, s. 4(a); 2015-264, s. 6; 2015-289, s. 3; 2017-186, s. 2(hhh); 2017-194, s. 17; 2021-94, s. 3

§ 15A-1340.16A. Enhanced sentence if defendant is convicted of a Class A, B1, B2, C, D, or E felony and the defendant used, displayed, orthreatened to use or display a firearm or deadly weapon during the commission of the felony

(a), (b) Repealed by Session Laws 2003-378, s. 2, effective August 1, 2003.

(c) If a person is convicted of a felony and it is found as provided in this section that: (i) the person committed the felony by using, displaying, or threatening the use or display of a firearm or deadly weapon and (ii) the person actually possessed the firearm or deadly weapon about his or her person, then the person shall have the minimum term of imprisonment to which the person is sentenced for that felony increased as follows:

(1) If the felony is a Class A, B1, B2, C, D, or E felony, the minimum term of imprisonment to which the person is sentenced for that felony shall be increased by 72 months. The maximum term of imprisonment shall be the maximum term that corresponds to the minimum term after it is increased by 72 months, as specified in G.S. 15A-1340.17(e) and (e1).

(2) If the felony is a Class F or G felony, the minimum term of imprisonment to which the person is sentenced for that felony shall be increased by 36 months. The maximum term of imprisonment shall be the maximum term that corresponds to the minimum term after it is increased by 36 months, as specified in G.S. 15A-1340.17(d).

(3) If the felony is a Class H or I felony, the minimum term of imprisonment to which the person is sentenced for that felony shall be increased by 12 months. The maximum term of imprisonment shall be the maximum term that corresponds to the minimum term after it is increased by 12 months, as specified in G.S. 15A-1340.17(d).

(d) An indictment or information for the felony shall allege in that indictment or information the facts set out in subsection (c) of this section. The pleading is sufficient if it alleges that the defendant committed the felony by using, displaying, or threatening the use or display of a firearm or deadly weapon and the defendant actually possessed the firearm or deadly weapon about the defendant's person. One pleading is sufficient for all felonies that are tried at a single trial.

(e) The State shall prove the issues set out in subsection (c) of this section beyond a reasonable doubt during the same trial in which the defendant is tried for the felony unless the defendant pleads guilty or no contest to the issues. If the defendant pleads guilty or no contest to the felony but pleads not guilty to the issues set out in subsection (c) of this section, then a jury shall be impaneled to determine the issues.

(f) Subsection (c) of this section does not apply if the evidence of the use, display, or threatened use or display of the firearm or deadly weapon is needed to prove an element of the felony or if the person is not sentenced to an active term of imprisonment.

History.
1994, Ex. Sess., c. 22, s. 20; 2003-378, s. 2; 2008-214, s. 5; 2013-369, s. 5

§ 15A-1340.16B. Life imprisonment without parole for a second or subsequent conviction of a Class B1 felony if the victim was 13 years of age or younger and there are no mitigating factors

(a) If a person is convicted of a Class B1 felony and it is found as provided in this section that: (i) the person committed the felony against a victim who was 13 years of age or younger at the time of the offense and (ii) the person has one or more prior convictions of a Class B1 felony, then the person shall be sentenced to life imprisonment without parole.

(b), (c) Repealed by Session Laws 2003-378, s. 3, effective August 1, 2003.

(d) An indictment or information for the Class B1 felony shall allege in that indictment or information or in a separate indictment or information the facts set out in subsection (a) of this section. The pleading is sufficient if it alleges that the defendant committed the felony against a victim who was 13 years of age or younger at the time of the felony and that the defendant had one or more prior convictions of a Class B1 felony. One pleading is sufficient for all Class B1 felonies that are tried at a single trial.

(e) The State shall prove the issues set out in subsection (a) of this section beyond a reasonable doubt during the same trial in which the defendant is tried for the felony unless the defendant pleads guilty or no contest to the issues. The issues shall be presented in the same manner as provided in G.S. 15A-928(c).

If the defendant pleads guilty or no contest to the felony but pleads not guilty to the issues set out in subsection (a) of this section, then a jury shall be impaneled to determine the issues.

(f) Subsection (a) of this section does not apply if there are mitigating factors present under G.S. 15A-1340.16(e).

History.
1998-212, s. 17.16(a); 2003-378, s. 3

§ 15A-1340.16C. Enhanced sentence if defendant is convicted of a felony and the defendant was wearing or had in his or her immediate possession a bullet-proof vest during the commission of the felony

(a) If a person is convicted of a felony and it is found as provided in this section that the person wore or had in his or her immediate possession a bullet-proof vest at the time of the felony, then the person is guilty of a felony that is one class higher than the underlying felony for which the person was convicted.

(b) Repealed by Session Laws 2003-378, s. 4, effective August 1, 2003.

(b1) This section does not apply to law enforcement officers, unless the State proves beyond a reasonable doubt, pursuant to subsection (d) of this section, both of the following:

(1) That the law enforcement officer was not performing or attempting to perform a law enforcement function.

(2) That the law enforcement officer knowingly wore or had in his or her immediate possession a bulletproof vest at the time of the commission of the felony for the purpose of aiding the law enforcement officer in the commission of the felony.

(c) An indictment or information for the felony shall allege in that indictment or information or in a separate indictment or information the facts set out in subsection (a) of this section. The pleading is sufficient if it alleges that the defendant committed the felony while wearing or having in the defendant's immediate possession a bulletproof vest. One pleading is sufficient for all felonies that are tried at a single trial.

(d) The State shall prove the issue set out in subsection (a) of this section beyond a reasonable doubt during the same trial in which the defendant is tried for the felony unless the defendant pleads guilty or no contest to that issue. If the defendant pleads guilty or no contest to the felony but pleads not guilty to the issue set out in subsection (a) of this section, then a jury shall be impaneled to determine that issue.

(e) Subsection (a) of this section does not apply if the evidence that the person wore or had in the person's immediate possession a bulletproof vest is needed to prove an element of the felony.

History.
1999-263, s. 1; 2003-378, s. 4

§ 15A-1340.16D. Manufacturing methamphetamine; enhanced sentence

(a) If a person is convicted of the offense of manufacture of methamphetamine under G.S. 90-95(b)(1a) and it is found as provided in this section that a law enforcement officer, probation officer, parole officer, emergency medical services employee, or a firefighter suffered serious injury while discharging or attempting to discharge his or her official duties and that the injury was directly caused by one of the hazards associated with the manufacture of methamphetamine, then the person shall have the minimum term of imprisonment to which the person is sentenced for that felony increased by 24 months. The maximum term of imprisonment shall be the maximum term that corresponds to the minimum term after it is increased by 24 months, as specified in G.S. 15A-1340.17(e) and (e1).

(a1) If a person is convicted of the offense of manufacture of methamphetamine under G.S. 90-95(b)(1a) and it is found as provided in this section that:

(1) A minor under 18 years of age resided on the property used for the manufacture of methamphetamine, or was present at a location where methamphetamine was being manufactured, then the person shall have the minimum term of imprisonment to which the person is sentenced for that felony increased by 24 months. The maximum term of imprisonment shall be the maximum term that corresponds to the minimum term after it is increased by 24 months, as specified in G.S. 15A-1340.17(e) and (e1).

(2) A disabled or elder adult resided on the property used for the manufacture of methamphetamine, or was present at a location where methamphetamine was being manufactured, then the person shall have the minimum term of imprisonment to which the person is sentenced for that felony increased by 24 months. The maximum term of imprisonment shall be the maximum term that corresponds to the minimum term after it is increased by 24 months, as specified in G.S. 15A-1340.17(e) and (e1).

(3) A minor and a disabled or elder adult resided on the property, or were present at a location where methamphetamine was being manufactured, then the person shall have the minimum term of imprisonment to which the person is sentenced for that felony increased by 48 months. The maximum term of imprisonment shall be the maximum term that corresponds to the minimum term after it is increased by 48 months, as specified in G.S. 15A-1340.17(e) and (e1).

(a2) For the purposes of this section, the terms "disabled adult" and "elder adult" shall be defined as set forth in G.S. 14-32.3(d).

(a3) The penalties set forth in this section are cumulative. The minimum sentence shall be increased by the sum of the number of months for convictions under subsections (a) and (a1) of this section, and the maximum term of imprisonment shall be the maximum term that corresponds to the total number of months, as specified in G.S. 15A-1340.17(e) and (e1).

(b) An indictment or information for the offense of manufacture of methamphetamine under G.S. 90-95(b)(1a) shall allege in that indictment or information the facts set out in subsection (a) or (a1) of this section. The pleading is sufficient if it alleges any or all of the following:

(1) The defendant committed the offense of manufacture of methamphetamine and that as a result of the offense a law enforcement officer, probation officer, parole officer, emergency medical services employee, or firefighter suffered serious injury while discharging or attempting to discharge his or her official duties.

(2) The defendant committed the offense of manufacture of methamphetamine and that a minor resided on the property used for manufacturing the methamphetamine, or was present at a location where methamphetamine was being manufactured.

(3) The defendant committed the offense of manufacture of methamphetamine and that a disabled or elder adult resided on the property used for manufacturing the methamphetamine, or was present at a location where methamphetamine was being manufactured.

(4) The defendant committed the offense of manufacture of methamphetamine and that a minor and a disabled or elder adult resided on the property used for manufacturing the methamphetamine, or were present at a location where methamphetamine was being manufactured.

One pleading is sufficient for all felonies that are tried at a single trial.

(c) The State shall prove the issue or issues set out in subsection (b) of this section beyond a reasonable doubt during the same trial in

Chapter 15A

which the defendant is tried for the offense of manufacture of methamphetamine unless the defendant pleads guilty or no contest to the issue. If the defendant pleads guilty or no contest to the offense of manufacture of methamphetamine but pleads not guilty to the issue or issues set out in subsection (b) of this section, then a jury shall be impaneled to determine the issue.

(d) This section does not apply if the offense is packaging or repackaging methamphetamine, or labeling or relabeling the methamphetamine container.

History.

2004-178, s. 8; 2013-124, s. 2

§ 15A-1340.16E. Enhanced sentence for offenses committed by criminal gang members as a part of criminal gang activity

(a) Except as otherwise provided in subsection (b) of this section, if a person is convicted of any felony other than a Class A, B1, or B2 felony, and it is found that the offense was committed as part of criminal gang activity as defined in G.S. 14-50.16A(2), then the person shall be sentenced at a felony class level one class higher than the principal felony for which the person was convicted.

(b) If subsection (a) of this section applies and the person is found to be a criminal gang leader or organizer as defined in G.S. 14-50.16A(3), the person shall be sentenced at a felony class level two classes higher than the principal felony for which the person was convicted.

(c) No defendant sentenced pursuant to this section shall be sentenced at a level higher than a Class C felony. Any sentence imposed under this section shall run consecutively with and shall commence at the expiration of any sentence being served by the person sentenced under this section.

(d) An indictment or information for the felony shall allege in that indictment or information the facts that qualify the offense for an enhancement under this section. One pleading is sufficient for all felonies that are tried at a single trial.

(e) The State shall prove the issues set out under subsection (a) or (b) of this section beyond a reasonable doubt. The issues shall be proven and found in the same manner as provided for aggravating factors in G.S. 15A-1340.16(a1), (a2), or (a3) as applicable.

(f) This section shall not apply to any gang offense included under Article 13A of Chapter 14 of the General Statutes.

History.

2017-194, s. 5

§ 15A-1340.17. Punishment limits for each class of offense and prior record level

(a) **Offense Classification; Default Classifications. --** The offense classification is as specified in the offense for which the sentence is being imposed. If the offense is a felony for which there is no classification, it is a Class I felony.

(b) **Fines. --** Any judgment that includes a sentence of imprisonment may also include a fine. If a community punishment is authorized, the judgment may consist of a fine only. Additionally, when the defendant is other than an individual, the judgment may consist of a fine only. Unless otherwise provided, the amount of the fine is in the discretion of the court.

(c) **Punishments for Each Class of Offense and Prior Record Level; Punishment Chart Described. --** The authorized punishment for each class of offense and prior record level is as specified in the chart below. Prior record levels are indicated by the Roman numerals placed horizontally on the top of the chart. Classes of offense are indicated by the letters placed vertically on the left side of the chart. Each cell on the chart contains the following components:

(1) A sentence disposition or dispositions: "C" indicates that a community punishment is authorized; "I" indicates that an intermediate punishment is authorized; "A" indicates that an active punishment is authorized; and "Life Imprisonment Without Parole" indicates that the defendant shall be imprisoned for the remainder of the prisoner's natural life.

(2) A presumptive range of minimum durations, if the sentence of imprisonment is neither aggravated or mitigated; any minimum term of imprisonment in that range is permitted unless the court finds pursuant to G.S. 15A-1340.16 that an aggravated or mitigated sentence is appropriate. The presumptive range is the middle of the three ranges in the cell.

(3) A mitigated range of minimum durations if the court finds pursuant to G.S. 15A-1340.16 that a mitigated sentence of imprisonment is justified; in such a case, any minimum term of imprisonment in the mitigated range is permitted. The mitigated range is the lower of the three ranges in the cell.

(4) An aggravated range of minimum durations if the court finds pursuant to G.S. 15A-1340.16 that an aggravated sentence of imprisonment is justified; in such a case, any minimum term of imprisonment in the aggravated range is permitted. The aggravated range is the higher of the three ranges in the cell.

PRIOR RECORD LEVEL

	I 0-1 Pt	II 2-5 Pts	III 6-9 Pts	IV 10-13 Pts	V 14-17 Pts	VI 18+ Pts	DISPOSITION
	A	A	A	A	A	A	DISPOSITION
	240-300	276-345	317-397	365-456	Life Imprisonment Without Parole		Aggravated
B1	192-240	221-276	254-317	292-365	336-420	386-483	PRESUMPTIVE
	144-192	166-221	190-254	219-292	252-336	290-386	Mitigated
	A	A	A	A	A	A	DISPOSITION
	157-196	180-225	207-258	238-297	273-342	314-393	Aggravated
B2	125-157	144-180	165-207	190-238	219-273	251-314	PRESUMPTIVE
	94-125	108-144	124-165	143-190	164-219	189-251	Mitigated
	A	A	A	A	A	A	DISPOSITION
	73-92	83-104	96-120	110-138	127-159	146-182	Aggravated
C	58-73	67-83	77-96	88-110	101-127	117-146	PRESUMPTIVE
	44-58	50-67	58-77	66-88	76-101	87-117	Mitigated
	A	A	A	A	A	A	DISPOSITION
	64-80	73-92	84-105	97-121	111-139	128-160	Aggravated
D	51-64	59-73	67-84	78-97	89-111	103-128	PRESUMPTIVE
	38-51	44-59	51-67	58-78	67-89	77-103	Mitigated
	I/A	I/A	A	A	A	A	DISPOSITION
	25-31	29-36	33-41	38-48	44-55	50-63	Aggravated
E	20-25	23-29	26-33	30-38	35-44	40-50	PRESUMPTIVE
	15-20	17-23	20-26	23-30	26-35	30-40	Mitigated
	I/A	I/A	I/A	A	A	A	DISPOSITION
	16-20	19-23	21-27	25-31	28-36	33-41	Aggravated
F	13-16	15-19	17-21	20-25	23-28	26-33	PRESUMPTIVE
	10-13	11-15	13-17	15-20	17-23	20-26	Mitigated
	I/A	I/A	I/A	I/A	A	A	DISPOSITION
	13-16	14-18	17-21	19-24	22-27	25-31	Aggravated
G	10-13	12-14	13-17	15-19	17-22	20-25	PRESUMPTIVE
	8-10	9-12	10-13	11-15	13-17	15-20	Mitigated
	C/I/A	I/A	I/A	I/A	I/A	A	DISPOSITION
	6-8	8-10	10-12	11-14	15-19	20-25	Aggravated
H	5-6	6-8	8-10	9-11	12-15	16-20	PRESUMPTIVE
	4-5	4-6	6-8	7-9	9-12	12-16	Mitigated
	C	C/I	I	I/A	I/A	I/A	DISPOSITION
	6-8	6-8	6-8	8-10	9-11	10-12	Aggravated
I	4-6	4-6	5-6	6-8	7-9	8-10	PRESUMPTIVE
	3-4	3-4	4-5	4-6	5-7	6-8	Mitigated

Chapter 15A

(d) **Maximum Sentences Specified for Class F through Class I Felonies.** -- Unless provided otherwise in a statute establishing a punishment for a specific crime, for each minimum term of imprisonment in the chart in subsection (c) of this section, expressed in months, the corresponding maximum term of imprisonment, also expressed in months, is as specified in the table below for Class F through Class I felonies. The first figure in each cell in the table is the minimum term and the second is the maximum term.

3-13	4-14	5-15	6-17	7-18	8-19	9-20	10-21
11-23	12-24	13-25	14-26	15-27	16-29	17-30	18-31
19-32	20-33	21-35	22-36	23-37	24-38	25-39	26-41
27-42	28-43	29-44	30-45	31-47	32-48	33-49	34-50
35-51	36-53	37-54	38-55	39-56	40-57	41-59	42-60
43-61	44-62	45-63	46-65	47-66	48-67	49-68	

(e) Maximum Sentences Specified for Class B1 through Class E Felonies for Minimum Terms up to 339 Months. Unless provided otherwise in a statute establishing a punishment for a specific crime, for each minimum term of imprisonment in the chart in subsection (c) of this section, expressed in months, the corresponding maximum term of imprisonment, also expressed in months, is as specified in the table below for Class B1 through Class E felonies. The first figure in each cell of the table is the minimum term and the second is the maximum term.

15-30	16-32	17-33	18-34	19-35	20-36	21-38	22-39
23-40	24-41	25-42	26-44	27-45	28-46	29-47	30-48
31-50	32-51	33-52	34-53	35-54	36-56	37-57	38-58
39-59	40-60	41-62	42-63	43-64	44-65	45-66	46-68
47-69	48-70	49-71	50-72	51-74	52-75	53-76	54-77
55-78	56-80	57-81	58-82	59-83	60-84	61-86	62-87
63-88	64-89	65-90	66-92	67-93	68-94	69-95	70-96
71-98	72-99	73-100	74-101	75-102	76-104	77-105	78-106
79-107	80-108	81-110	82-111	83-112	84-113	85-114	86-116
87-117	88-118	89-119	90-120	91-122	92-123	93-124	94-125
95-126	96-128	97-129	98-130	99-131	100-132	101-134	102-135
103-136	104-137	105-138	106-140	107-141	108-142	109-143	110-144
111-146	112-147	113-148	114-149	115-150	116-152	117-153	118-154
119-155	120-156	121-158	122-159	123-160	124-161	125-162	126-164
127-165	128-166	129-167	130-168	131-170	132-171	133-172	134-173
135-174	136-176	137-177	138-178	139-179	140-180	141-182	142-183
143-184	144-185	145-186	146-188	147-189	148-190	149-191	150-192
151-194	152-195	153-196	154-197	155-198	156-200	157-201	158-202
159-203	160-204	161-206	162-207	163-208	164-209	165-210	166-212
167-213	168-214	169-215	170-216	171-218	172-219	173-220	174-221
175-222	176-224	177-225	178-226	179-227	180-228	181-230	182-231
183-232	184-233	185-234	186-236	187-237	188-238	189-239	190-240
191-242	192-243	193-244	194-245	195-246	196-248	197-249	198-250
199-251	200-252	201-254	202-255	203-256	204-257	205-258	206-260
207-261	208-262	209-263	210-264	211-266	212-267	213-268	214-269
215-270	216-272	217-273	218-274	219-275	220-276	221-278	222-279
223-280	224-281	225-282	226-284	227-285	228-286	229-287	230-288
231-290	232-291	233-292	234-293	235-294	236-296	237-297	238-298
239-299	240-300	241-302	242-303	243-304	244-305	245-306	246-308
247-309	248-310	249-311	250-312	251-314	252-315	253-316	254-317

255-318	256-320	257-321	258-322	259-323	260-324	261-326	262-327
263-328	264-329	265-330	266-332	267-333	268-334	269-335	270-336
271-338	272-339	273-340	274-341	275-342	276-344	277-345	278-346
279-347	280-348	281-350	282-351	283-352	284-353	285-354	286-356
287-357	288-358	289-359	290-360	291-362	292-363	293-364	294-365
295-366	296-368	297-369	298-370	299-371	300-372	301-374	302-375
303-376	304-377	305-378	306-380	307-381	308-382	309-383	310-384
311-386	312-387	313-388	314-389	315-390	316-392	317-393	318-394
319-395	320-396	321-398	322-399	323-400	324-401	325-402	326-404
327-405	328-406	329-407	330-408	331-410	332-411	333-412	334-413
335-414	336-416	337-417	338-418	339-419			

(e1) **Maximum Sentences Specified for Class B1 through Class E Felonies for Minimum Terms of 340 Months or More.** -- Unless provided otherwise in a statute establishing a punishment for a specific crime, when the minimum sentence is 340 months or more, the corresponding maximum term of imprisonment shall be equal to the sum of the minimum term of imprisonment and twenty percent (20%) of the minimum term of imprisonment, rounded to the next highest month, plus 12 additional months.

(f) **Maximum Sentences Specified for Class B1 Through Class E Sex Offenses.** -- Unless provided otherwise in a statute establishing a punishment for a specific crime, for offenders sentenced for a Class B1 through E felony that is a reportable conviction subject to the registration requirement of Article 27A of Chapter 14 of the General Statutes, the maximum term of imprisonment shall be equal to the sum of the minimum term of imprisonment and twenty percent (20%) of the minimum term of imprisonment, rounded to the next highest month, plus 60 additional months.

History.
1993, c. 538, s. 1; 1994, Ex. Sess., c. 14, ss. 20, 21; c. 22, s. 7; c. 24, s. 14(b); 1995, c. 507, s. 19.5 (*l*); 1997-80, s. 3; 2009-555, s. 2; 2009-556, s. 1; 2011-192, s. 2(e) -(g); 2011-307, s. 1; 2011-412, s. 2.4(a); 2013-101, s. 6; 2013-410, s. 3(b)

§ **15A-1340.18. Advanced supervised release**

(a) **Definitions.** -- For the purposes of this section, the following definitions apply:
(1) "Advanced supervised release" or "ASR" means release from prison and placement on post-release supervision under this section if an eligible defendant is sentenced to active time.
(2) "Eligible defendant" means a defendant convicted and sentenced based upon any of the following felony classes and prior record levels:
a. Class D, Prior Record Level I-III.
b. Class E, Prior Record Level I-IV.
c. Class F, Prior Record Level I-V.
d. Class G, Prior Record Level I-VI.
e. Class H, Prior Record Level I-VI.
(3) "Risk reduction incentive" is a sentencing condition which, upon successful completion during incarceration, results in a prisoner being placed on ASR.

(b) The Division of Adult Correction and Juvenile Justice of the Department of Public Safety is authorized to create risk reduction incentives consisting of treatment, education, and rehabilitative programs. The incentives shall be designed to reduce the likelihood that the prisoner who receives the incentive will reoffend.

(c) When imposing an active sentence for an eligible defendant, the court, in its discretion and without objection from the prosecutor, may order that the Department of Correction admit the defendant to the ASR program. The Department of Correction shall admit to the ASR program only those defendants for which ASR is ordered in the sentencing judgment.

(d) The court shall impose a sentence calculated pursuant to Article 81B of the General Statutes. The ASR date shall be the shortest mitigated sentence for the offense at the offender's prior record level. If the court utilizes the mitigated range in sentencing the defendant, then the ASR date shall be eighty percent (80%) of the minimum sentence imposed.

(e) The defendant shall be notified at sentencing that if the defendant completes the risk reduction incentives as identified by the Department, then he or she will be released on the ASR date, as determined by the Department pursuant to the provisions of subsection (d) of this section. If the Department determines that the defendant is unable to complete the incentives by the ASR date, through no fault of the defendant, then the defendant shall be released at the ASR date.

(f) Termination from the risk reduction incentive program shall result in the nullification of the ASR date, and the defendant's release date shall be calculated based upon the adjudged sentence. A prisoner who has completed the risk reduction incentives prior to the ASR date may have the ASR date nullified due to noncompliance with Division rules or regulations.

(g) A defendant released on the ASR date is subject to post-release supervision under this Article. Notwithstanding the provisions in G.S. 15A-1368.3(c), if the defendant has been returned to prison for three, three-month periods of confinement, a subsequent violation shall result in the defendant returning to prison to serve the time remaining on the maximum imposed term, and is ineligible for further post-release supervision regardless of the amount of time remaining to be served.

(h) The Division shall adopt policies and procedures for the assessment to occur at diagnostic processing, for documentation of the inmate's progress, and for termination from the incentive program due to a lack of progress or a pattern of noncompliance in the program or with other Division rules or regulations.

History.
2011-145, s. 19.1(h); 2011-192, s. 5(c); 2011-412, ss. 2.7, 2.8; 2017-186, s. 2(iii)

N.C. Gen. Stat. § 15A-1340.19

Reserved for future codification purposes.

PART 2A
SENTENCING FOR MINORS SUBJECT TO LIFE IMPRISONMENT WITHOUT PAROLE.

§ 15A-1340.19A. Applicability

Notwithstanding the provisions of G.S. 14-17, a defendant who is convicted of first degree murder, and who was under the age of 18 at the time of the offense, shall be sentenced in accordance with this Part. For the purposes of this Part, "life imprisonment with parole" shall mean that the defendant shall serve a minimum of 25 years imprisonment prior to becoming eligible for parole.

History.
2012-148, s. 1

§ 15A-1340.19B. Penalty determination

(a) In determining a sentence under this Part, the court shall do one of the following:

(1) If the sole basis for conviction of a count or each count of first degree murder was the felony murder rule, then the court shall sentence the defendant to life imprisonment with parole.

(2) If the court does not sentence the defendant pursuant to subdivision (1) of this subsection, then the court shall conduct a hearing to determine whether the defendant should be sentenced to life imprisonment without parole, as set forth in G.S. 14-17, or a lesser sentence of life imprisonment with parole.

(b) The hearing under subdivision (2) of subsection (a) of this section shall be conducted by the trial judge as soon as practicable after the guilty verdict is returned. The State and the defendant shall not be required to resubmit evidence presented during the guilt determination phase of the case. Evidence, including evidence in rebuttal, may be presented as to any matter that the court deems relevant to sentencing, and any evidence which the court deems to have probative value may be received.

(c) The defendant or the defendant's counsel may submit mitigating circumstances to the court, including, but not limited to, the following factors:

(1) Age at the time of the offense.

(2) Immaturity.

(3) Ability to appreciate the risks and consequences of the conduct.

(4) Intellectual capacity.

(5) Prior record.

(6) Mental health.

(7) Familial or peer pressure exerted upon the defendant.

(8) Likelihood that the defendant would benefit from rehabilitation in confinement.

(9) Any other mitigating factor or circumstance.

(d) The State and the defendant or the defendant's counsel shall be permitted to present argument for or against the sentence of life imprisonment with parole. The defendant or the defendant's counsel shall have the right to the last argument.

(e) The provisions of Article 58 of Chapter 15A of the General Statutes apply to proceedings under this Part.

History.
2012-148, s. 1

§ 15A-1340.19C. Sentencing; assignment for resentencing

(a) The court shall consider any mitigating factors in determining whether, based upon all the circumstances of the offense and the particular circumstances of the defendant, the defendant should be sentenced to life imprisonment with parole instead of life imprisonment without parole. The order adjudging the sentence shall include findings on the absence or presence of any mitigating factors and such other findings as the court deems appropriate to include in the order.

(b) All motions for appropriate relief filed in superior court seeking resentencing under the provisions of this Part may be heard and determined in the trial division by any judge (i) who is empowered to act in criminal matters in the superior court district or set of districts as defined in G.S. 7A-41.1, in which the judgment was entered and (ii) who is assigned pursuant to this section to review the motion for appropriate relief and take the appropriate administrative action to dispense with the motion.

(c) The judge who presided at the trial of the defendant is empowered to act upon the motion for appropriate relief even though the judge is in another district or even though the judge's commission has expired; however, if the judge who presided at the trial is still unavailable to act, the senior resident superior court judge shall assign a judge who is empowered to act under subsection (b) of this section.

(d) All motions for appropriate relief filed in superior court seeking resentencing under the provisions of this Part shall, when filed, be referred to the senior resident superior court judge, who shall assign the motion as provided by this section for review and administrative action, including, as may be appropriate, dismissal, calendaring for hearing, entry of a scheduling order for subsequent events in the case, or other appropriate actions.

History.
2012-148, s. 1

§ 15A-1340.19D. Incidents of parole

(a) Except as otherwise provided in this section, a defendant sentenced to life imprisonment with parole shall be subject to the conditions and procedures set forth in Article 85 of Chapter 15A of the General Statutes, including the notification requirement in G.S. 15A-1371(b)(3).

(b) The term of parole for a person released from imprisonment from a sentence of life imprisonment with parole shall be five years and may not be terminated earlier by the Post-Release Supervision and Parole Commission.

(c) A defendant sentenced to life imprisonment with parole who is paroled, and then violates a condition of parole and is returned to prison to serve the life sentence, shall not be eligible for parole for five years from the date of the return to confinement.

(d) Life imprisonment with parole under this Part means that unless the defendant receives parole, the defendant shall remain imprisoned for the defendant's natural life.

History.
2012-148, s. 1

PART 3
MISDEMEANOR SENTENCING

§ 15A-1340.20. Procedure and incidents of sentence of imprisonment for misdemeanors

(a) **Application to Misdemeanors Only.** -- This Part applies to sentences imposed for misdemeanor convictions.

(b) **Procedure Generally; Term of Imprisonment.** -- A sentence imposed for a misdemeanor shall contain a sentence disposition specified for the class of offense and prior conviction level, and any sentence of imprisonment shall be within the range specified for the class of offense and prior conviction level, unless applicable statutes require otherwise. The kinds of sentence dispositions are active punishment, intermediate punishment, and community punishment. Except for the work and earned time credits authorized by G.S. 162-60, or earned time credits authorized by G.S. 15A-1355(c), if applicable, an offender whose sentence of imprisonment is activated shall serve each day of the term imposed.

(c) **Suspension of Sentence.** -- Unless otherwise provided, the court shall suspend a sentence of imprisonment if the class of offense and prior conviction level requires community or intermediate punishment as a sentence disposition.

(c1) **Active Punishment Exception.** -- The court may impose an active punishment for a class of offense and prior conviction level that does not otherwise authorize the imposition of an active punishment if the term of imprisonment is equal to or less than the total amount of time the offender has already spent committed to or in confinement in any State or local correctional, mental, or other institution as a result of the charge that culminated in the sentence.

(d) **Earned Time Authorization.** -- An offender sentenced to a term of imprisonment that is activated is eligible to receive earned time credit for misdemeanant offenders awarded by the Division of Adult Correction and Juvenile Justice of the Department of Public Safety or the custodian of a local confinement facility, pursuant to rules adopted in accordance with law and pursuant to G.S. 162-60. These rules and statute combined shall not award misdemeanant offenders more than four days of earned time credit per month of incarceration.

History.
1993, c. 538, s. 1; 1994, Ex. Sess., c. 24, s. 14(b); 1993 (Reg. Sess., 1994), c. 767, s. 1; 1997-79, s. 1; 2011-145, s. 19.1(h); 2017-186, s. 2(jjj)

§ 15A-1340.21. Prior conviction level for misdemeanor sentencing

(a) **Generally.** -- The prior conviction level of a misdemeanor offender is determined by calculating the number of the offender's prior convictions that the court finds to have been proven in accordance with this section.

(b) **Prior Conviction Levels for Misdemeanor Sentencing.** -- The prior conviction levels for misdemeanor sentencing are:

(1) Level I -- 0 prior convictions.

(2) Level II -- At least 1, but not more than 4 prior convictions.

(3) Level III -- At least 5 prior convictions.

In determining the prior conviction level, a prior offense may be included if it is either a felony or a misdemeanor at the time the offense for which the offender is being sentenced is committed.

(c) **Proof of Prior Convictions.** -- A prior conviction shall be proved by any of the following methods:

(1) Stipulation of the parties.

(2) An original or copy of the court record of the prior conviction.

(3) A copy of records maintained by the Department of Public Safety, the Division of Motor Vehicles, or of the Administrative Office of the Courts.

(4) Any other method found by the court to be reliable.

The State bears the burden of proving, by a preponderance of the evidence, that a prior conviction exists and that the offender before the court is the same person as the offender named in the prior conviction. The original or a copy of the court records or a copy of the records maintained by the Department of Public Safety, the Division of Motor Vehicles, or of the Administrative Office of the Courts, bearing the same name as that by which the offender is charged, is prima facie evidence that the offender named is the same person as the offender before the court, and that the facts set out in the record are true. For purposes of this subsection, "copy" includes a paper writing containing a reproduction of a record maintained electronically on a computer or other data processing equipment, and a document produced by a facsimile machine. Evidence presented by either party at trial may be utilized to prove prior convictions. Suppression of prior convictions is pursuant to G.S. 15A-980. If a motion is made pursuant to that section during the sentencing stage of the criminal action, the court may grant a continuance of the sentencing hearing.

(d) **Multiple Prior Convictions Obtained in One Court Week.** -- For purposes of this section, if an offender is convicted of more than one offense in a single session of district court, or in a single week of superior court or of a court in another jurisdiction, only one of the convictions may be used to determine the prior conviction level.

History.

1993, c. 538, s. 1; 1994, Ex. Sess., c. 24, s. 14(b); 1993 (Reg. Sess., 1994), c. 767, s. 13.1; 1997-80, s. 8; 2014-100, s. 17.1(q)

§ 15A-1340.22. Multiple convictions

(a) **Limits on Consecutive Sentences.** -- If the court elects to impose consecutive sentences for two or more misdemeanors and the most serious misdemeanor is classified in Class A1, Class 1, or Class 2, the cumulative length of the sentences of imprisonment shall not exceed twice the maximum sentence authorized for the class and prior conviction level of the most serious offense. Consecutive sentences shall not be imposed if all convictions are for Class 3 misdemeanors.

(b) **Consolidation of Sentences.** -- If an offender is convicted of more than one offense at the same session of court, the court may consolidate the offenses for judgment and impose a single judgment for the consolidated offenses. Any sentence imposed shall be consistent with the appropriate prior conviction level of the most serious offense.

History.

1993, c. 538, s. 1; 1994, Ex. Sess., c. 24, s. 14(b); 1995 (Reg. Sess., 1996), c. 742, s. 16

§ 15A-1340.23. Punishment limits for each class of offense and prior conviction level

(a) **Offense Classification; Default Classifications.** -- The offense classification is as specified in the offense for which the sentence is being imposed. If the offense is a misdemeanor for which there is no classification, it is as classified in G.S. 14-3.

(b) **Fines.** -- Any judgment that includes a sentence of imprisonment may also include a fine. Additionally, when the defendant is other than an individual, the judgment may consist of a fine only. If a community punishment is authorized, the judgment may consist of a fine only. Unless otherwise provided for a specific offense, the maximum fine that may be imposed is two hundred dollars ($ 200.00) for a Class 3 misdemeanor and one thousand dollars ($ 1,000) for a Class 2 misdemeanor. The amount of the fine for a Class 1 misdemeanor and a Class A1 misdemeanor is in the discretion of the court.

(c) **Punishment for Each Class of Offense and Prior Conviction Level; Punishment Chart Described.** -- Unless otherwise provided for a specific offense, the authorized punishment for each class of offense and prior conviction level is as specified in the chart below. Prior conviction levels are indicated by the Roman numerals placed horizontally on the top of the chart. Classes of offenses are indicated by the Arabic numbers placed vertically on the left side of the chart. Each grid on the chart contains the following components:

(1) A sentence disposition or dispositions: "C" indicates that a community punishment is authorized; "I" indicates that an intermediate punishment is authorized; and "A" indicates that an active punishment is authorized; and

(2) A range of durations for the sentence of imprisonment: any sentence within the duration specified is permitted.

MISDEMEANOR OFFENSE	PRIOR CONVICTION LEVELS		
	LEVEL I	LEVEL II	LEVEL III
CLASS	No Prior Convictions	One to Four Prior Convictions	Five or More Prior Convictions
A1	1-60 days C/I/A	1-75 days C/I/A	1-150 days C/I/A
1	1-45 days C	1-45 days C/I/A	1-120 days C/I/A
2	1-30 days C	1-45 days C/I	1-60 days C/I/A
3	1-10 days C	1-15 days C	1-20 days C/I/A.
		if one to three prior convictions	
		1-15 days C/I if four prior convictions	

(d) **Fine Only for Certain Class 3 Misdemeanors.** -- Unless otherwise provided for a specific offense, the judgment for a person convicted of a Class 3 misdemeanor who has no more than three prior convictions shall consist only of a fine.

History.
1993, c. 538, s. 1; 1994, Ex. Sess., c. 24, s. 14(b); 1995, c. 507, s. 19.5(g); 2013-360, s. 18B.13(a)

§§ 15A-1340.24 through 15A-1340.33

Reserved for future codification purposes.

ARTICLE 81C
RESTITUTION

§ 15A-1340.34. Restitution generally

(a) When sentencing a defendant convicted of a criminal offense, the court shall determine whether the defendant shall be ordered to make restitution to any victim of the offense in question. For purposes of this Article, the term "victim" means a person directly and proximately harmed as a result of the defendant's commission of the criminal offense.

(b) If the defendant is being sentenced for an offense for which the victim is entitled to restitution under Article 46 of this Chapter, the court shall, in addition to any penalty authorized by law, require that the defendant make restitution to the victim or the victim's estate for any injuries or damages arising directly and proximately out of the offense committed by the defendant. If the defendant is placed on probation or post-release supervision, any restitution ordered under this subsection shall be a condition of probation as provided in G.S. 15A-1343(d) or a condition of post-release supervision as provided in G.S. 148-57.1.

(c) When subsection (b) of this section does not apply, the court may, in addition to any other penalty authorized by law, require that the defendant make restitution to the victim or the victim's estate for any injuries or damages arising directly and proximately out of the offense committed by the defendant.

History.
1998-212, s. 19.4(d)

§ 15A-1340.35. Basis for restitution

(a) In determining the amount of restitution, the court shall consider the following:

(1) In the case of an offense resulting in bodily injury to a victim:

a. The cost of necessary medical and related professional services and devices or equipment relating to physical, psychiatric, and psychological care required by the victim;

b. The cost of necessary physical and occupational therapy and rehabilitation required by the victim; and

Chapter 15A

c. Income lost by the victim as a result of the offense.

(2) In the case of an offense resulting in the damage, loss, or destruction of property of a victim of the offense:

a. Return of the property to the owner of the property or someone designated by the owner; or

b. If return of the property under sub-subdivision (2)a. of this subsection is impossible, impracticable, or inadequate:

1. The value of the property on the date of the damage, loss, or destruction; or

2. The value of the property on the date of sentencing, less the value of any part of the property that is returned.

(3) Any measure of restitution specifically provided by law for the offense committed by the defendant.

(4) In the case of an offense resulting in bodily injury that results in the death of the victim, the cost of the victim's necessary funeral and related services, in addition to the items set out in subdivisions (1), (2), and (3) of this subsection.

(b) The court may require that the victim or the victim's estate provide admissible evidence that documents the costs claimed by the victim or the victim's estate under this section. Any such documentation shall be shared with the defendant before the sentencing hearing.

History.
1998-212, s. 19.4(d)

§ 15A-1340.36. Determination of restitution

(a) In determining the amount of restitution to be made, the court shall take into consideration the resources of the defendant including all real and personal property owned by the defendant and the income derived from the property, the defendant's ability to earn, the defendant's obligation to support dependents, and any other matters that pertain to the defendant's ability to make restitution, but the court is not required to make findings of fact or conclusions of law on these matters. The amount of restitution must be limited to that supported by the record, and the court may order partial restitution when it appears that the damage or loss caused by the offense is greater than that which the defendant is able to pay. If the court orders partial restitution, the court shall state on the record the reasons for such an order.

(b) The court may require the defendant to make full restitution no later than a certain date or, if the circumstances warrant, may allow the defendant to make restitution in installments over a specified time period.

(c) When an active sentence is imposed, the court shall consider whether it should recommend to the Secretary of Public Safety that restitution be made by the defendant out of any earnings gained by the defendant if the defendant is granted work-release privileges, as provided in G.S. 148-33.2. The court shall also consider whether it should recommend to the Post-Release Supervision and Parole Commission that restitution by the defendant be made a condition of any parole or post-release supervision granted the defendant, as provided in G.S. 148-57.1.

History.
1998-212, s. 19.4(d); 2011-145, s. 19.1(i)

§ 15A-1340.37. Effect of restitution order; beneficiaries

(a) An order providing for restitution does not abridge the right of a victim or the victim's estate to bring a civil action against the defendant for damages arising out of the offense committed by the defendant. Any amount paid by the defendant under the terms of a restitution order under this Article shall be credited against any judgment rendered against the defendant in favor of the same victim in a civil action arising out of the criminal offense committed by the defendant.

(b) The court may order the defendant to make restitution to a person other than the victim, or to any organization, corporation, or association, including the Crime Victims Compensation Fund, that provided assistance to the victim following the commission of the offense by the defendant and is subrogated to the rights of the victim. Restitution shall be made to the victim or the victim's estate before it is made to any other person, organization, corporation, or association under this subsection.

(c) No government agency shall benefit by way of restitution except for particular damage or loss to it over and above its normal operating costs and except that the State may receive restitution for the total amount of a judgment authorized by G.S. 7A-455(b).

(d) Repealed by Session Laws 2016-78, s. 6.4, effective December 1, 2016.

History.
1998-212, s. 19.4(d); 2016-78, s. 6.4

§ 15A-1340.38. Enforcement of certain orders for restitution

(a) In addition to the provisions of G.S. 15A-1340.36, when an order for restitution under G.S. 15A-1340.34(b) requires the defendant to pay restitution in an amount in excess of two hundred fifty dollars ($ 250.00) to a victim, the order may be enforced in the same manner as a civil judgment, subject to the provisions of this section.

(b) The order for restitution under G.S. 15A-1340.34(b) shall be docketed and indexed in the county of the original conviction in the same manner as a civil judgment pursuant to G.S. 1-233, et seq., and may be docketed in any other county pursuant to G.S. 1-234. The judgment may be collected in the same manner as a civil judgment unless the order to pay restitution is a condition of probation. If the order to pay restitution is a condition of probation, the judgment may only be executed upon in accordance with subsection (c) of this section.

(c) If the defendant is ordered to pay restitution under G.S. 15A-1340.34(b) as a condition of probation, a judgment docketed under this section may be collected in the same manner as a civil judgment. However, the docketed judgment for restitution may not be executed upon the property of the defendant until the date of notification to the clerk of superior court in the county of the original conviction that the judge presiding at the probation termination or revocation hearing has made a finding that restitution in a sum certain remains due and payable, that the defendant's probation has been terminated or revoked, and that the remaining balance of restitution owing may be collected by execution on the judgment. The clerk shall then enter upon the judgment docket the amount that remains due and payable on the judgment, together with amounts equal to the standard fees for docketing, copying, certifying, and mailing, as appropriate, and shall collect any other fees or charges incurred as in the enforcement of other civil judgments, including accrued interest. However, no interest shall accrue on the judgment until the entry of an order terminating or revoking probation and finding the amount remaining due and payable, at which time interest shall begin to accrue at the legal rate pursuant to G.S. 24-5. The interest shall be applicable to the amount determined at the termination or revocation hearing to be then due and payable. The clerk shall notify the victim by first-class mail at the victim's last known address that the judgment may be executed upon, together with the amount of the judgment. Until the clerk receives notification of termination or revocation of probation and the amount that remains due and payable on the order of restitution, the clerk shall not be required to update the judgment docket to reflect partial payments on the order of restitution as a condition of probation. The stay of execution under this subsection shall not apply to property of the defendant after the transfer or conveyance of the property to another person. When the criminal order of restitution has been paid in full, the civil judgment indexed under this section shall be deemed satisfied and the judgment shall be cancelled. Payment satisfying the civil judgment shall also be credited against the order of restitution.

(d) An appeal of the conviction upon which the order of restitution is based shall stay execution on the judgment until the appeal is completed. If the conviction is overturned, the judgment shall be cancelled.

History.
1998-212, s. 19.4(d)

§ 15A-1340.39. Remission of restitution, notice, and hearing required

(a) **Notice and Hearing Required.** -- No court may remit all or part of an order of restitution entered pursuant to G.S. 15A-1340.34 without providing notice and an opportunity to be heard to the district attorney and the victim, victim's estate, or any other entity to which the order directs restitution to be paid. The court shall provide notice to the district attorney and the victim, the victim's estate, or other entity of (i) the date and time of the hearing and (ii) the right to be heard and make an objection to the remission of all or part of the order of restitution, at least 15 days prior to hearing. Notice shall be made to the victim, victim's estate, or other entity by first-class mail to the address provided for receipt of funds paid pursuant to the order of restitution.

(b) **Ruling; Criteria.** -- If the court finds that the remission of the order is warranted and serves the interests of justice, the court may remit the order of restitution.

(c) **Civil Action Not Abridged.** -- The remission of an order of restitution, pursuant to this section, does not abridge the right of a victim or the victim's estate to bring a civil action against the defendant for damages arising out of the offense committed by the defendant.

History.
2017-16, s. 1

§§ 15A-1340.40 through 15A-1340.49

Reserved for future codification purposes.

ARTICLE 81D
PERMANENT NO CONTACT ORDER AGAINST CONVICTED SEX OFFENDER

§ 15A-1340.50. Permanent no contact order prohibiting future contact by convicted sex offender with crime victim

(a) The following definitions apply in this Article:

(1) **Permanent no contact order. --** A permanent injunction that prohibits any contact by a defendant with the victim of the sex offense for which the defendant is convicted. The duration of the injunction is the lifetime of the defendant.

(2) **Sex offense. --** Any criminal offense that requires registration under Article 27A of Chapter 14 of the General Statutes.

(3) **Victim. --** The person against whom the sex offense was committed.

(b) When sentencing a defendant convicted of a sex offense, the judge, at the request of the district attorney, shall determine whether to issue a permanent no contact order. The judge shall order the defendant to show cause why a permanent no contact order shall not be issued and shall hold a show cause hearing as part of the sentencing procedures for the defendant.

(c) The victim shall have a right to be heard at the show cause hearing.

(d) The judge sentencing the defendant is the trier of fact regarding the show cause hearing.

(e) At the conclusion of the show cause hearing the judge shall enter a finding for or against the defendant. If the judge determines that reasonable grounds exist for the victim to fear any future contact with the defendant, the judge shall issue the permanent no contact order. The judge shall enter written findings of fact and the grounds on which the permanent no contact order is issued. The no contact order shall be incorporated into the judgment imposing the sentence on the defendant for the conviction of the sex offense.

(f) The court may grant one or more of the following forms of relief in a permanent no contact order under this Article:

(1) Order the defendant not to threaten, visit, assault, molest, or otherwise interfere with the victim.

(2) Order the defendant not to follow the victim, including at the victim's workplace.

(3) Order the defendant not to harass the victim.

(4) Order the defendant not to abuse or injure the victim.

(5) Order the defendant not to contact the victim by telephone, written communication, or electronic means.

(6) Order the defendant to refrain from entering or remaining present at the victim's residence, school, place of employment, or other specified places at times when the victim is present.

(7) Order other relief deemed necessary and appropriate by the court.

(g) A permanent no contact order entered pursuant to this Article shall be enforced by all North Carolina law enforcement agencies without further order of the court. A law enforcement officer shall arrest and take a person into custody, with or without a warrant or other process, if the officer has probable cause to believe that the person knowingly has violated a permanent no contact order. A person who knowingly violates a permanent no contact order is guilty of a Class A1 misdemeanor.

(h) At any time after the issuance of the order, the State, at the request of the victim, or the defendant may make a motion to rescind the permanent no contact order. If the court determines that reasonable grounds for the victim to fear any future contact with the defendant no longer exist, the court may rescind the permanent no contact order.

(i) The remedy provided by this Article is not exclusive but is in addition to other remedies provided under law.

History.
2009-380, s. 1

ARTICLE 82
PROBATION

§ 15A-1341. Probation generally

(a) **Use of Probation. --** Unless specifically prohibited, a person who has been convicted of any criminal offense may be placed on probation as provided by this Article if the class of offense of which the person is convicted and the person's prior record or conviction level under Article 81B of this Chapter authorizes a community or intermediate punishment as a type of sentence disposition or if the person is convicted of impaired driving under G.S. 20-138.1. The provisions of subsections (a1), (a2), (a4), and (a5) of this section do not apply and a person is not eligible for deferred prosecution or a conditional discharge under those subsections if the person is being placed on probation under this Article for a conviction of impaired driving under G.S. 20-138.1.

(a1) **Deferred Prosecution. --** A person who has been charged with a Class H or I felony or a misdemeanor may be placed on probation as provided in this Article on motion of the defendant and the prosecutor if the court finds each of the following facts:

(1) Prosecution has been deferred by the prosecutor pursuant to written agreement with the defendant, with the approval of the court, for the purpose of allowing the defendant to demonstrate his good conduct.

(2) Each known victim of the crime has been notified of the motion for probation by subpoena or certified mail and has been given an opportunity to be heard.

(3) The defendant has not been convicted of any felony or of any misdemeanor involving moral turpitude.

(4) The defendant has not previously been placed on probation and so states under oath.

(5) The defendant is unlikely to commit another offense other than a Class 3 misdemeanor.

(a2) **Deferred Prosecution for Purpose of Drug Treatment Court Program.** -- A defendant eligible for a Drug Treatment Court Program pursuant to Article 62 of Chapter 7A of the General Statutes may be placed on probation if the court finds that prosecution has been deferred by the prosecutor, with the approval of the court, pursuant to a written agreement with the defendant, for the purpose of allowing the defendant to participate in and successfully complete the Drug Treatment Court Program.

(a3) **Conditional Discharge for Prostitution.** -- A defendant for whom the court orders a conditional discharge pursuant to G.S. 14-204(b) may be placed on probation as provided in this Article.

(a4) **Conditional Discharge.** -- Whenever a person pleads guilty to or is found guilty of a Class H or I felony or a misdemeanor, the court may, on joint motion of the defendant and the prosecutor, and without entering a judgment of guilt and with the consent of the person, defer further proceedings and place the person on probation as provided in this Article for the purpose of allowing the defendant to demonstrate the defendant's good conduct if the court finds each of the following facts:

(1) Each known victim of the crime has been notified of the motion for probation by subpoena or certified mail and has been given an opportunity to be heard.

(2) The defendant has not been convicted of any felony or of any misdemeanor involving moral turpitude.

(3) The defendant has not previously been placed on probation and so states under oath.

(4) The defendant is unlikely to commit another offense other than a Class 3 misdemeanor.

(a5) **Conditional Discharge for Purpose of Drug Treatment Court Program.** -- When a defendant is eligible for a Drug Treatment Court Program pursuant to Article 62 of Chapter 7A of the General Statutes, the court may, without entering a judgment of guilt and with the consent of the defendant, defer further proceedings and place the defendant on probation for the purpose of allowing the defendant to participate in and successfully complete the Drug Treatment Court Program.

(a6) **Compliance With Terms of Conditional Discharge.** -- Upon violation of a term

or condition of a conditional discharge granted pursuant to this section, the court may enter an adjudication of guilt and proceed as otherwise provided. Upon fulfillment of the terms and conditions of a conditional discharge granted pursuant to this section, any plea or finding of guilty previously entered shall be withdrawn and the court shall discharge the person and dismiss the proceedings against the person.

(b) **Supervised and Unsupervised Probation.** -- The court may place a person on supervised or unsupervised probation. A person on unsupervised probation is subject to all incidents of probation except supervision by or assignment to a probation officer.

(c) Repealed by Session Laws 1995, c. 429, s. 1.

(d) **Search of Sex Offender Registration Information Required When Placing a Defendant on Probation.** -- When the court places a defendant on probation, the probation officer assigned to the defendant shall conduct a search of the defendant's name or other identifying information against the registration information regarding sex offenders compiled by the Department of Public Safety in accordance with Article 27A of Chapter 14 of the General Statutes. The probation officer may conduct the search using the Internet site maintained by the Department of Public Safety.

(e) **Review of Defendant's Juvenile Record.** -- The probation officer assigned to a defendant may examine and obtain copies of the defendant's juvenile record in a manner consistent with G.S. 7B-3000(b) and (e1).

History.
1977, c. 711, s. 1; 1977, 2nd Sess., c. 1147, ss. 4A, 5; 1981, c. 377, ss. 2, 3; 1993, c. 538, s. 15; 1994, Ex. Sess., c. 24, s. 14(b); 1995, c. 429, s. 1; 1999-298, s. 1; 2006-247, s. 14; 2009-372, s. 4; 2013-368, s. 7; 2014-100, s. 17.1(dd); 2014-119, s. 2(a); 2015-150, s. 1

§ 15A-1342. Incidents of probation

(a) **Period.** -- The court may place a convicted offender on probation for the appropriate period as specified in G.S. 15A-1343.2(d), not to exceed a maximum of five years. The court may place a defendant as to whom prosecution has been deferred or who receives a conditional discharge on probation for a maximum of two years. The probation remains conditional and subject to revocation during the period of probation imposed, unless terminated as provided in subsection (b) or G.S. 15A-1341(c).

Extension. -- In addition to G.S. 15A-1344, the court with the consent of the defendant may extend the period of probation beyond the original period (i) for the purpose of allowing the defendant to complete a program of restitution, or (ii) to allow the defendant to continue medical

Chapter 15A

or psychiatric treatment ordered as a condition of the probation. The period of extension shall not exceed three years beyond the original period of probation. The special extension authorized herein may be ordered only in the last six months of the original period of probation. Any probationary judgment form provided to a defendant on supervised probation shall state that probation may be extended pursuant to this subsection.

(a1) **Supervision of Defendants on Deferred Prosecution or Conditional Discharge.** -- The Section of Community Corrections of the Division of Adult Correction and Juvenile Justice of the Department of Public Safety may be ordered by the court to supervise an offender's compliance with the terms of a conditional discharge or deferred prosecution agreement. Violations of the terms of the agreement or conditional discharge shall be reported to the court as provided in this Article and to the district attorney in the district in which the agreement was entered.

(b) **Early Termination.** -- The court may terminate a period of probation and discharge the defendant at any time earlier than that provided in subsection (a) if warranted by the conduct of the defendant and the ends of justice.

(c) **Conditions; Suspended Sentence.** -- When the court places a convicted offender on probation, it must determine conditions of probation as provided in G.S. 15A-1343. In addition, it must impose a suspended sentence of imprisonment, determined as provided in Article 83, Imprisonment, which may be activated upon violation of conditions of probation.

(d) **Mandatory Review of Probation.** -- Each probation officer must bring the cases of each probationer assigned to him before a court with jurisdiction to review the probation when the probationer has served three years of a probationary period greater than three years. The probation officer must give reasonable notice to the probationer, and the probationer may appear. The court must review the case file of a probationer so brought before it and determine whether to terminate his probation.

(e) **Out-of-State Supervision.** -- Supervised probationers are subject to out-of-State supervision under the provisions of Article 4B of Chapter 148 of the General Statutes.

(f) **Appeal from Judgment of Probation.** -- A defendant may seek post-trial relief from a judgment which includes probation notwithstanding the authority of the court to modify or revoke the probation.

(g) **Invalid Conditions; Timing of Objection.** -- The regular conditions of probation imposed pursuant to G.S. 15A-1343(b) are in every circumstance valid conditions of probation. A court may not revoke probation for violation of an invalid condition imposed pursuant to G.S.

15A-1343(b1). The failure of a defendant to object to a condition of probation imposed pursuant to G.S. 15A-1343(b1) at the time such a condition is imposed does not constitute a waiver of the right to object at a later time to the condition.

(h) **Limitation on Jurisdiction to Alter or Revoke Unsupervised Probation.** -- In the judgment placing a person on unsupervised probation, the judge may limit jurisdiction to alter or revoke the sentence under G.S. 15A-1344. When jurisdiction to alter or revoke is limited, the effect is as provided in G.S. 15A-1344(b).

(i) **Immunity from Prosecution upon Compliance.** -- Upon the expiration or early termination as provided in subsection (b) of a period of probation imposed after deferral of prosecution and before conviction or a conditional discharge, the defendant shall be immune from prosecution of the charges deferred or discharged and dismissed.

(j) **Immunity for Injury to Defendant Performing Community Service.** -- Immunity from liability for injury to a defendant performing community service shall be as set forth in G.S. 143B-708(d).

History.
1977, c. 711, s. 1; 1977, 2nd Sess., c. 1147, ss. 6, 7; 1981, c. 377, ss. 4-6; 1983, c. 435, s. 5.1; c. 561, s. 7; 1985 (Reg. Sess., 1986), c. 960, s. 1; 1993, c. 84, s. 1; 1993 (Reg. Sess., 1994), c. 767, s. 6; 1995, c. 330, s. 1; 2008-129, s. 3; 2009-372, s. 10; 2010-96, s. 5; 2011-145, s. 19.1(h), (k), (ee); 2013-368, s. 8; 2014-119, s. 2(e); 2015-40, s. 5; 2017-186, s. 2(kkk)

§ 15A-1343. Conditions of probation

(a) **In General.** -- The court may impose conditions of probation reasonably necessary to insure that the defendant will lead a law-abiding life or to assist him to do so.

(a1) **Community and Intermediate Probation Conditions.** -- In addition to any conditions a court may be authorized to impose pursuant to G.S. 15A-1343(b1), the court may include any one or more of the following conditions as part of a community or intermediate punishment:

(1) House arrest with electronic monitoring.

(2) Perform community service and pay the fee prescribed by law for this supervision.

(3) Submission to a period or periods of confinement in a local confinement facility for a total of no more than six days per month during any three separate months during the period of probation. The six days per month confinement provided for in this subdivision may only be imposed as two-day or three-day consecutive periods. When

a defendant is on probation for multiple judgments, confinement periods imposed under this subdivision shall run concurrently and may total no more than six days per month. If the person being ordered to a period or periods of confinement is under the age of 18, that person must be confined in a detention facility approved by the Juvenile Justice Section of the Division of Adult Correction and Juvenile Justice to provide secure confinement and care for juveniles or to a holdover facility as defined in G.S. 7B-1501(11). If the person being ordered to a period or periods of confinement reaches the age of 18 years while in confinement, the person may be transported by personnel of the Juvenile Justice Section of the Division, or personnel approved by the Juvenile Justice Section, to the custody of the sheriff of the applicable local confinement facility.

(4) Substance abuse assessment, monitoring, or treatment.

(4a) Abstain from alcohol consumption and submit to continuous alcohol monitoring when alcohol dependency or chronic abuse has been identified by a substance abuse assessment.

(5) Participation in an educational or vocational skills development program, including an evidence-based program.

(6) Submission to satellite-based monitoring, pursuant to Part 5 of Article 27A of Chapter 14 of the General Statutes, if the defendant is described by G.S. 14-208.40(a) (2), and based on the Division of Adult Correction and Juvenile Justice's risk assessment program requires the highest possible level of supervision and monitoring.

(b) **Regular Conditions.** -- As regular conditions of probation, a defendant must:

(1) Commit no criminal offense in any jurisdiction.

(2) Remain within the jurisdiction of the court unless granted written permission to leave by the court or his probation officer.

(3) Report as directed by the court or his probation officer to the officer at reasonable times and places and in a reasonable manner, permit the officer to visit him at reasonable times, answer all reasonable inquiries by the officer and obtain prior approval from the officer for, any change in address or employment.

(3a) Not abscond by willfully avoiding supervision or by willfully making the defendant's whereabouts unknown to the supervising probation officer, if the defendant is placed on supervised probation.

(4) Satisfy child support and other family obligations as required by the court. If the court requires the payment of child support, the amount of the payments shall be determined as provided in G.S. 50-13.4(c).

(5) Possess no firearm, explosive device or other deadly weapon listed in G.S. 14-269 without the written permission of the court.

(6) Pay a supervision fee as specified in subsection (c1).

(7) Remain gainfully and suitably employed or faithfully pursue a course of study or of vocational training that will equip him for suitable employment. A defendant pursuing a course of study or of vocational training shall abide by all of the rules of the institution providing the education or training, and the probation officer shall forward a copy of the probation judgment to that institution and request to be notified of any violations of institutional rules by the defendant.

(8) Notify the probation officer if he fails to obtain or retain satisfactory employment.

(9) Pay the costs of court, any fine ordered by the court, and make restitution or reparation as provided in subsection (d).

(10) Pay the State of North Carolina for the costs of appointed counsel, public defender, or appellate defender to represent him in the case(s) for which he was placed on probation.

(11) Repealed by Session Laws 2011-62, s. 1, as amended by Session Laws 2011-412, s. 2.2, effective December 1, 2011, and applicable to offenses committed on or after December 1, 2011.

(12) Attend and complete an abuser treatment program if (i) the court finds the defendant is responsible for acts of domestic violence and (ii) there is a program, approved by the Domestic Violence Commission, reasonably available to the defendant, unless the court finds that such would not be in the best interests of justice. A defendant attending an abuser treatment program shall abide by all of the rules of the program.

a. If the defendant is placed on supervised probation, the following procedures apply:

1. The probation officer shall forward a copy of the judgment, including all conditions of probation, to the abuser treatment program.

2. The program shall notify the probation officer if the defendant fails to participate in the program or if the defendant is discharged from the program for violating any of the program rules.

3. If the defendant fails to participate in the program or is

discharged from the program for failure to comply with the program or its rules, the probation officer shall file a violation report with the court and notify the district attorney of such noncompliance.

b. If the defendant is placed on unsupervised probation, the following procedures apply:

1. The defendant shall be required to notify the district attorney and the abuser treatment program of their choice of program within 10 days of the judgment if the program has not previously been selected.

2. The district attorney shall forward a copy of the judgment, including all conditions of probation, to the abuser treatment program.

3. If the defendant fails to participate in the program or is discharged from the program for failure to comply with the program or its rules, the program shall notify the district attorney of such noncompliance.

(13) Submit at reasonable times to warrantless searches by a probation officer of the probationer's person and of the probationer's vehicle and premises while the probationer is present, for purposes directly related to the probation supervision, but the probationer may not be required to submit to any other search that would otherwise be unlawful.

(14) Submit to warrantless searches by a law enforcement officer of the probationer's person and of the probationer's vehicle, upon a reasonable suspicion that the probationer is engaged in criminal activity or is in possession of a firearm, explosive device, or other deadly weapon listed in G.S. 14-269 without written permission of the court.

(15) Not use, possess, or control any illegal drug or controlled substance unless it has been prescribed for him or her by a licensed physician and is in the original container with the prescription number affixed on it; not knowingly associate with any known or previously convicted users, possessors, or sellers of any such illegal drugs or controlled substances; and not knowingly be present at or frequent any place where such illegal drugs or controlled substances are sold, kept, or used.

(16) Supply a breath, urine, or blood specimen for analysis of the possible presence of prohibited drugs or alcohol when instructed by the defendant's probation officer for purposes directly related to the probation supervision. If the results of the analysis are positive, the probationer may be required to reimburse the Division of Adult Correction and Juvenile Justice of the Department of Public Safety for the actual costs of drug or alcohol screening and testing.

(17) Waive all rights relating to extradition proceedings if taken into custody outside of this State for failing to comply with the conditions imposed by the court upon a felony conviction.

(18) Submit to the taking of digitized photographs, including photographs of the probationer's face, scars, marks, and tattoos, to be included in the probationer's records.

In addition to these regular conditions of probation, a defendant required to serve an active term of imprisonment as a condition of special probation pursuant to G.S. 15A-1344(e) or G.S. 15A-1351(a) shall, as additional regular conditions of probation, obey the rules and regulations of the Division of Adult Correction and Juvenile Justice of the Department of Public Safety governing the conduct of inmates while imprisoned and report to a probation officer in the State of North Carolina within 72 hours of his discharge from the active term of imprisonment.

Regular conditions of probation apply to each defendant placed on supervised probation unless the presiding judge specifically exempts the defendant from one or more of the conditions in open court and in the judgment of the court. It is not necessary for the presiding judge to state each regular condition of probation in open court, but the conditions must be set forth in the judgment of the court.

Defendants placed on unsupervised probation are subject to the provisions of this subsection, except that defendants placed on unsupervised probation are not subject to the regular conditions contained in subdivisions (2), (3), (6), (8), (13), (14), (15), (16) and (17) of this subsection.

(b1) **Special Conditions. --** In addition to the regular conditions of probation specified in subsection (b), the court may, as a condition of probation, require that during the probation the defendant comply with one or more of the following special conditions:

(1) Undergo available medical or psychiatric treatment and remain in a specified institution if required for that purpose. Notwithstanding the provisions of G.S. 15A-1344(e) or any other provision of law, the defendant may be required to participate in such treatment for its duration regardless of the length of the suspended sentence imposed.

(2) Attend or reside in a facility providing rehabilitation, counseling, treatment, social skills, or employment training, instruction, recreation, or residence for persons on probation.

(2a) Repealed by Session Laws 2002, ch. 126, s. 17.18, effective August 15, 2002.

(2b) Participate in and successfully complete a Drug Treatment Court Program pursuant to Article 62 of Chapter 7A of the General Statutes.

(2c) Abstain from alcohol consumption and submit to continuous alcohol monitoring when alcohol dependency or chronic abuse has been identified by a substance abuse assessment.

(3) Submit to imprisonment required for special probation under G.S. 15A-1351(a) or G.S. 15A-1344(e).

(3a) Repealed by Session Laws 1997-57, s. 3.

(3b) Repealed by Session Laws 2011-192, s. 1(g), effective December 1, 2011.

(3c) Remain at his or her residence. The court, in the sentencing order, may authorize the offender to leave the offender's residence for employment, counseling, a course of study, vocational training, or other specific purposes and may modify that authorization. The probation officer may authorize the offender to leave the offender's residence for specific purposes not authorized in the court order upon approval of the probation officer's supervisor. The offender shall be required to wear a device which permits the supervising agency to monitor the offender's compliance with the condition electronically and to pay a fee for the device as specified in subsection (c2) of this section.

(4) Surrender his or her driver's license to the clerk of superior court, and not operate a motor vehicle for a period specified by the court.

(5) Compensate the Department of Environmental Quality or the North Carolina Wildlife Resources Commission, as the case may be, for the replacement costs of any marine and estuarine resources or any wildlife resources which were taken, injured, removed, harmfully altered, damaged or destroyed as a result of a criminal offense of which the defendant was convicted. If any investigation is required by officers or agents of the Department of Environmental Quality or the Wildlife Resources Commission in determining the extent of the destruction of resources involved, the court may include compensation of the agency for investigative costs as a condition of probation. The court may also include, as a condition of probation, compensation of an

agency for any reward paid for information leading to the arrest and conviction of the offender. This subdivision does not apply in any case governed by G.S. 143-215.3(a)(7).

(6) Perform community or reparation service under the supervision of the Section of Community Corrections of the Division of Adult Correction and Juvenile Justice and pay the fee required by G.S. 143B-708.

(7), (8) Repealed by Session Laws 2009-372, s. 9(b), effective December 1, 2009, and applicable to offenses committed on or after that date.

(8a) Purchase the least expensive annual statewide license or combination of licenses to hunt, trap, or fish listed in G.S. 113-270.2, 113-270.3, 113-270.5, 113-271, 113-272, and 113-272.2 that would be required to engage lawfully in the specific activity or activities in which the defendant was engaged and which constitute the basis of the offense or offenses of which he was convicted.

(9) If the offense is one in which there is evidence of physical, mental or sexual abuse of a minor, the court should encourage the minor and the minor's parents or custodians to participate in rehabilitative treatment and may order the defendant to pay the cost of such treatment.

(9a) Repealed by Session Laws 2004-186, s. 1.1, effective December 1, 2004, and applicable to offenses committed on or after that date.

(9b) Any or all of the following conditions relating to criminal gangs as defined in G.S. 14-50.16A(1):

a. Not knowingly associate with any known criminal gang members and not knowingly be present at or frequent any place or location where criminal gangs gather or where criminal gang activity is known to occur.

b. Not wear clothes, jewelry, signs, symbols, or any paraphernalia readily identifiable as associated with or used by a criminal gang.

c. Not initiate or participate in any contact with any individual who was or may be a witness against or victim of the defendant or the defendant's criminal gang.

(9c) Participate in any Project Safe Neighborhood activities as directed by the probation officer.

(10) Satisfy any other conditions determined by the court to be reasonably related to his rehabilitation.

(b2) **Special Conditions of Probation for Sex Offenders and Persons Convicted of Offenses Involving Physical, Mental, or Sexual Abuse of a Minor.** -- As special conditions of probation, a defendant who has been convicted of an offense which is a reportable conviction as defined in G.S. 14-208.6(4), or which involves the physical, mental, or sexual abuse of a minor, must:

(1) Register as required by G.S. 14-208.7 if the offense is a reportable conviction as defined by G.S. 14-208.6(4).

(2) Participate in such evaluation and treatment as is necessary to complete a prescribed course of psychiatric, psychological, or other rehabilitative treatment as ordered by the court.

(3) Not communicate with, be in the presence of, or found in or on the premises of the victim of the offense.

(4) Not reside in a household with any minor child if the offense is one in which there is evidence of sexual abuse of a minor.

(5) Not reside in a household with any minor child if the offense is one in which there is evidence of physical or mental abuse of a minor, unless the court expressly finds that it is unlikely that the defendant's harmful or abusive conduct will recur and that it would be in the minor child's best interest to allow the probationer to reside in the same household with a minor child.

(6) Satisfy any other conditions determined by the court to be reasonably related to his rehabilitation.

(7) Submit to satellite-based monitoring pursuant to Part 5 of Article 27A of Chapter 14 of the General Statutes, if the defendant is described by G.S. 14-208.40(a)(1), and the Division of Adult Correction and Juvenile Justice of the Department of Public Safety, based on the Division's risk assessment program, recommends that the defendant submit to the highest possible level of supervision and monitoring.

(8) Submit to satellite-based monitoring pursuant to Part 5 of Article 27A of Chapter 14 of the General Statutes, if the defendant is in the category described by G.S. 14-208.40(a)(2), and the Division of Adult Correction and Juvenile Justice of the Department of Public Safety, based on the Division's risk assessment program, recommends that the defendant submit to the highest possible level of supervision and monitoring.

(9) Submit at reasonable times to warrantless searches by a probation officer of the probationer's person and of the probationer's vehicle and premises while the probationer is present, for purposes specified by the court and reasonably related to the probation supervision, but the probationer may not be required to submit to any other search that would otherwise be unlawful. For purposes of this subdivision, warrantless searches of the probationer's computer or other electronic mechanism which may contain electronic data shall be considered reasonably related to the probation supervision. Whenever the warrantless search consists of testing for the presence of illegal drugs, the probationer may also be required to reimburse the Division of Adult Correction and Juvenile Justice of the Department of Public Safety for the actual cost of drug screening and drug testing, if the results are positive.

Defendants subject to the provisions of this subsection shall not be placed on unsupervised probation.

(b3) **Screening and Assessing for Chemical Dependency.** -- A defendant ordered to submit to a period of residential treatment in the Drug Alcohol Recovery Treatment program (DART) or the Black Mountain Substance Abuse Treatment Center for Women operated by the Division of Adult Correction and Juvenile Justice of the Department of Public Safety must undergo a screening to determine chemical dependency. If the screening indicates the defendant is chemically dependent, the court shall order an assessment to determine the appropriate level of treatment. The assessment may be conducted either before or after the court imposes the condition, but participation in the program shall be based on the results of the assessment.

(b4) **Intermediate Conditions.** -- The following conditions of probation apply to each defendant subject to intermediate punishment:

(1) If required in the discretion of the defendant's probation officer, perform community service under the supervision of the Section of Community Corrections of the Division of Adult Correction and Juvenile Justice and pay the fee required by G.S. 143B-708.

(2) Not use, possess, or control alcohol.

(3) Remain within the county of residence unless granted written permission to leave by the court or the defendant's probation officer.

(4) Participate in any evaluation, counseling, treatment, or educational program as directed by the probation officer, keeping all appointments and abiding by the rules, regulations, and direction of each program.

These conditions apply to each defendant subject to intermediate punishment unless the court specifically exempts the defendant from one or more of the conditions in its judgment or order. It is not necessary for the presiding judge to state each of these conditions in open court, but the conditions must be set forth in the judgment or order of the court.

(c) **Statement of Conditions.** -- A defendant released on supervised probation must be given a written statement explicitly setting forth the conditions on which the defendant is being released. If any modification of the terms of that probation is subsequently made, the defendant must be given a written statement setting forth the modifications.

Upon entry of an order of supervised probation by the court, a defendant shall submit to the Division of Adult Correction and Juvenile Justice for filing with the clerk of superior court a signed document stating that:

    (1) The defendant will comply with the conditions that have been imposed by the court.

    (2) If the defendant fails to comply with the conditions imposed by the court and is taken into custody outside of this State, the defendant waives all rights relating to extradition proceedings if the defendant was convicted of a felony.

(c1) **Supervision Fee.** -- Any person placed on supervised probation pursuant to subsection (a) of this section shall pay a supervision fee of forty dollars ($ 40.00) per month, unless exempted by the court. The court may exempt a person from paying the fee only for good cause and upon motion of the person placed on supervised probation. No person shall be required to pay more than one supervision fee per month. The court may require that the fee be paid in advance or in a lump sum or sums, and a probation officer may require payment by such methods if he is authorized by subsection (g) to determine the payment schedule. Supervision fees must be paid to the clerk of court for the county in which the judgment was entered, the deferred prosecution agreement was filed, or the conditional discharge was ordered. Fees collected under this subsection shall be transmitted to the State for deposit into the State's General Fund.

(c2) **Electronic Monitoring Device Fees.** -- Any person placed on house arrest with electronic monitoring under subsection (a1) or (b1) of this section shall pay a fee of ninety dollars ($ 90.00) for the electronic monitoring device and a daily fee in an amount that reflects the actual cost of providing the electronic monitoring. The court may exempt a person from paying the fees only for good cause and upon motion of the person placed on house arrest with electronic monitoring. The court may require that the fees be paid in advance or in a lump sum or sums, and a probation officer may require payment by those methods if the officer is authorized by subsection (g) of this section to determine the payment schedule. The fees must be paid to the clerk of court for the county in which the judgment was entered, the deferred prosecution agreement was filed, or the conditional discharge was ordered. Fees collected under this subsection for the electronic

monitoring device shall be transmitted to the State for deposit into the State's General Fund. The daily fees collected under this subsection shall be remitted to the Department of Public Safety to cover the costs of providing the electronic monitoring.

(d) **Restitution as a Condition of Probation.** -- As a condition of probation, a defendant may be required to make restitution or reparation to an aggrieved party or parties who shall be named by the court for the damage or loss caused by the defendant arising out of the offense or offenses committed by the defendant. When restitution or reparation is a condition imposed, the court shall take into consideration the factors set out in G.S. 15A-1340.35 and G.S. 15A-1340.36. As used herein, "reparation" shall include but not be limited to the performing of community services, volunteer work, or doing such other acts or things as shall aid the defendant in his rehabilitation. As used herein "aggrieved party" includes individuals, firms, corporations, associations, other organizations, and government agencies, whether federal, State or local, including the Crime Victims Compensation Fund established by G.S. 15B-23. A government agency may benefit by way of reparation even though the agency was not a party to the crime provided that when reparation is ordered, community service work shall be rendered only after approval has been granted by the owner or person in charge of the property or premises where the work will be done.

(e) **Costs of Court and Appointed Counsel.** -- Unless the court finds there are extenuating circumstances, any person placed upon supervised or unsupervised probation under the terms set forth by the court shall, as a condition of probation, be required to pay all court costs and all fees and costs for appointed counsel, public defender, or counsel employed by or under contract with the Office of Indigent Defense Services in the case in which the person was convicted. The fees and costs for appointed counsel, public defender, or other counsel services shall be determined in accordance with rules adopted by the Office of Indigent Defense Services. The court shall determine the amount of those costs and fees to be repaid and the method of payment.

(f) Repealed by Session Laws 1983, c. 561, s. 5.

(g) **Probation Officer May Determine Payment Schedules and May Transfer Low-Risk Misdemeanants to Unsupervised Probation.** -- If a person placed on supervised probation is required as a condition of that probation to pay any moneys to the clerk of superior court, the court may delegate to a probation officer the responsibility to determine the payment schedule. The court may also authorize the probation officer to transfer the person to unsupervised probation after all the moneys are paid to the clerk. If the probation officer transfers a person to unsupervised probation, he must notify the clerk of that action. In addition, a probation officer may transfer a misdemeanant from supervised to unsupervised probation if the misdemeanant is not subject to any special conditions and was placed on probation solely for the collection of court-ordered payments, and the risk assessment shows the misdemeanant to be a low-risk offender; however, such a transfer to unsupervised probation does not relieve the misdemeanant of the obligation to continue making court-ordered payments under the terms of the misdemeanant's probation.

History.
1977, c. 711, s. 1; 1977, 2nd Sess., c. 1147, ss. 8-10; 1979, c. 662, s. 1; c. 801, s. 3; c. 830, s. 12; 1981, c. 530, ss. 1, 2; 1983, c. 135, s. 1; c. 561, ss. 1-6; c. 567, s. 2; c. 712, s. 1; 1983 (Reg. Sess., 1984), c. 972, ss. 1, 2; 1985, c. 474, ss. 1, 7, 8; 1985 (Reg. Sess., 1986), c. 859, ss. 1, 2; 1987, c. 282, s. 33; c. 397, s. 1; c. 579, ss. 1, 2; c. 598, s. 1; c. 819, s. 32; c. 830, s. 17; 1989, c. 529, s. 5; c. 727, s. 218(4); 1989 (Reg. Sess., 1990), c. 1010, s. 1; c. 1034, s. 1; 1991 (Reg. Sess., 1992), c. 1000, s. 1; 1993, c. 538, s. 16; 1994, Ex. Sess., c. 9, s. 1; c. 24, s. 14(b); 1996, 2nd Ex. Sess., c. 18, s. 20.14(c); 1997-57, s. 3; 1997-443, ss. 11A.119(a), 19.11(a); 1998-212, ss. 17.21(a), 19.4(f); 1999-298, s. 2; 2000-125, s. 8; 2000-144, s. 31; 2002-105, s. 3; 2002-126, ss. 17.18(a), 29A.2(a); 2003-141, s. 1; 2004-186, s. 1.1; 2005-250, s. 4; 2005-276, ss. 17.29, 43.1(f), 43.2(a); 2006-247, s. 15(b); 2007-213, s. 7; 2009-275, s. 1; 2009-372, s. 9(a) -(c); 2009-547, s. 7; 2010-31, s. 19.3(a); 2010-96, s. 28(a), (b); 2011-62, ss. 1, 2; 2011-145, s. 19.1(h), (k); 2011-192, s. 1(c), (g), 4(a); 2011-254, ss. 1, 2; 2011-412, ss. 2.1, 2.2, 2.3(a), 2.5; 2012-39, s. 1; 2012-146, ss. 3 -5; 2012-188, s. 3; 2013-101, s. 1; 2013-123, s. 1; 2013-360, s. 16C.16(a); 2013-363, s. 6.7(a), (c); 2013-380, s. 2; 2014-119, s. 2(f); 2015-241, s. 14.30(u); 2016-77, s. 1; 2017-186, ss. 2(lll), 3(a); 2017-194, s. 18; 2020-83, s. 8(e); 2021-138, s. 18(j).

N.C. Gen. Stat. § 15A-1343.1

Repealed by Session Laws 2002-126, s. 17.18, effective August 15, 2002.

§ 15A-1343.2. Special probation rules for persons sentenced under Article 81B

(a) **Applicability.** -- This section applies only to persons sentenced under Article 81B of this Chapter.

(b) **Purposes of Probation for Community and Intermediate Punishments.** -- The Division of Adult Correction and Juvenile Justice of the Department of Public Safety shall develop a plan to handle offenders sentenced to community and intermediate punishments. The probation program designed to handle

these offenders shall have the following principal purposes: to hold offenders accountable for making restitution, to ensure compliance with the court's judgment, to effectively rehabilitate offenders by directing them to specialized treatment or education programs, and to protect the public safety.

(b1) **Departmental Risk Assessment by Validated Instrument Required.** -- As part of the probation program developed by the Division of Adult Correction and Juvenile Justice of the Department of Public Safety pursuant to subsection (b) of this section, the Division of Adult Correction and Juvenile Justice of the Department of Public Safety shall use a validated instrument to assess each probationer for risk of reoffending and shall place a probationer in a supervision level based on the probationer's risk of reoffending and criminogenic needs.

(c) **Probation Caseload Goals.** -- It is the goal of the General Assembly that, subject to the availability of funds, caseloads for probation officers supervising persons who are determined to be high or moderate risk of rearrest as determined by the Division's validated risk assessment should not exceed an average of 60 offenders per officer.

(d) **Lengths of Probation Terms Under Structured Sentencing.** -- Unless the court makes specific findings that longer or shorter periods of probation are necessary, the length of the original period of probation for offenders sentenced under Article 81B shall be as follows:

(1) For misdemeanants sentenced to community punishment, not less than six nor more than 18 months;

(2) For misdemeanants sentenced to intermediate punishment, not less than 12 nor more than 24 months;

(3) For felons sentenced to community punishment, not less than 12 nor more than 30 months; and

(4) For felons sentenced to intermediate punishment, not less than 18 nor more than 36 months.

If the court finds at the time of sentencing that a longer period of probation is necessary, that period may not exceed a maximum of five years, as specified in G.S. 15A-1342 and G.S. 15A-1351.

Extension. -- The court may with the consent of the offender extend the original period of the probation if necessary to complete a program of restitution or to complete medical or psychiatric treatment ordered as a condition of probation. This extension may be for no more than three years, and may only be ordered in the last six months of the original period of probation.

(e) **Delegation to Probation Officer in Community Punishment.** -- Unless the presiding judge specifically finds in the judgment of the court that delegation is not appropriate, the Section of Community Corrections of the Division of Adult Correction and Juvenile Justice of the Department of Public Safety may require an offender sentenced to community punishment to do any of the following:

(1) Perform up to 20 hours of community service, and pay the fee prescribed by law for this supervision.

(2) Report to the offender's probation officer on a frequency to be determined by the officer.

(3) Submit to substance abuse assessment, monitoring or treatment.

(4) Submit to house arrest with electronic monitoring.

(5) Submit to a period or periods of confinement in a local confinement facility for a total of no more than six days per month during any three separate months during the period of probation. The six days per month confinement provided for in this subdivision may only be imposed as two-day or three-day consecutive periods. When a defendant is on probation for multiple judgments, confinement periods imposed under this subdivision shall run concurrently and may total no more than six days per month. If the person being ordered to a period or periods of confinement is under the age of 18, that person must be confined in a detention facility approved by the Juvenile Justice Section of the Division of Adult Correction and Juvenile Justice to provide secure confinement and care for juveniles or to a holdover facility as defined in G.S. 7B-1501(11). If the person being ordered to a period or periods of confinement reaches the age of 18 years while in confinement, the person may be transported by personnel of the Juvenile Justice Section of the Division, or personnel approved by the Juvenile Justice Section, to the custody of the sheriff of the applicable local confinement facility.

(6) Submit to a curfew which requires the offender to remain in a specified place for a specified period each day and wear a device that permits the offender's compliance with the condition to be monitored electronically.

(7) Participate in an educational or vocational skills development program, including an evidence-based program.

If the Section imposes any of the above requirements, then it may subsequently reduce or remove those same requirements.

The probation officer may exercise authority delegated to him or her by the court pursuant to subsection (e) of this section after administrative review and approval by a Chief Probation Officer. The offender may file a motion with the court to review the action taken by the probation officer. The offender shall be given notice of the right to seek such a court review. However, the offender shall have no right of review if he or she has signed a written waiver of rights as required by this subsection. The Section may exercise any authority delegated to it under this subsection only if it first determines that the offender has failed to comply with one or more of the conditions of probation imposed by the court or the offender is determined to be high risk based on the results of the risk assessment in G.S. 15A-1343.2, except that the condition at subdivision (5) of this subsection may not be imposed unless the Section determines that the offender failed to comply with one or more of the conditions imposed by the court. Nothing in this section shall be construed to limit the availability of the procedures authorized under G.S. 15A-1345.

The Division shall adopt guidelines and procedures to implement the requirements of this section, which shall include a supervisor's approval prior to exercise of the delegation of authority authorized by this section. Prior to imposing confinement pursuant to subdivision (5) of this subsection, the probationer must first be presented with a violation report, with the alleged violations noted and advised of the right (i) to a hearing before the court on the alleged violation, with the right to present relevant oral and written evidence; (ii) to have counsel at the hearing, and that one will be appointed if the probationer is indigent; (iii) to request witnesses who have relevant information concerning the alleged violations; and (iv) to examine any witnesses or evidence. The probationer may be confined for the period designated on the violation report upon the execution of a waiver of rights signed by the probationer and by two officers acting as witnesses. Those two witnesses shall be the probation officer and another officer to be designated by the Chief of the Community Corrections Section in written Division policy.

(f) **Delegation to Probation Officer in Intermediate Punishments.** -- Unless the presiding judge specifically finds in the judgment of the court that delegation is not appropriate, the Section of Community Corrections of the Division of Adult Correction and Juvenile Justice of the Department of Public Safety may require an offender sentenced to intermediate punishment to do any of the following:

(1) Perform up to 50 hours of community service, and pay the fee prescribed by law for this supervision.

Chapter 15A

(2) Submit to a curfew which requires the offender to remain in a specified place for a specified period each day and wear a device that permits the offender's compliance with the condition to be monitored electronically.

(3) Submit to substance abuse assessment, monitoring or treatment, including continuous alcohol monitoring when abstinence from alcohol consumption has been specified as a term of probation.

(4) Participate in an educational or vocational skills development program, including an evidence-based program.

(5) Submit to satellite-based monitoring pursuant to Part 5 of Article 27A of Chapter 14 of the General Statutes, if the defendant is described by G.S. 14-208.40(a)(2), and based on the Division of Adult Correction and Juvenile Justice's risk assessment program requires the highest possible level of supervision and monitoring.

(6) Submit to a period or periods of confinement in a local confinement facility for a total of no more than six days per month during any three separate months during the period of probation. The six days per month confinement provided for in this subdivision may only be imposed as two-day or three-day consecutive periods. When a defendant is on probation for multiple judgments, confinement periods imposed under this subdivision shall run concurrently and may total no more than six days per month. If the person being ordered to a period or periods of confinement is under the age of 18, that person must be confined in a detention facility approved by the Juvenile Justice Section of the Division of Adult Correction and Juvenile Justice to provide secure confinement and care for juveniles or to a holdover facility as defined in G.S. 7B-1501(11). If the person being ordered to a period or periods of confinement reaches the age of 18 years while in confinement, the person may be transported by personnel of the Juvenile Justice Section of the Division, or personnel approved by the Juvenile Justice Section, to the custody of the sheriff of the applicable local confinement facility.

(7) Submit to house arrest with electronic monitoring.

(8) Report to the offender's probation officer on a frequency to be determined by the officer.

If the Section imposes any of the above requirements, then it may subsequently reduce or remove those same requirements.

The probation officer may exercise authority delegated to him or her by the court pursuant to subsection (f) of this section after administrative review and approval by a Chief Probation Officer. The offender may file a motion with the court to review the action taken by the probation officer. The offender shall be given notice of the right to seek such a court review. However, the offender shall have no right of review if he or she has signed a written waiver of rights as required by this subsection. The Section may exercise any authority delegated to it under this subsection only if it first determines that the offender has failed to comply with one or more of the conditions of probation imposed by the court or the offender is determined to be high risk based on the results of the risk assessment in G.S. 15A-1343.2, except that the condition at subdivision (6) of this subsection may not be imposed unless the Section determines that the offender failed to comply with one or more of the conditions imposed by the court. Nothing in this section shall be construed to limit the availability of the procedures authorized under G.S. 15A-1345.

The Division shall adopt guidelines and procedures to implement the requirements of this section, which shall include a supervisor's approval prior to exercise of the delegation of authority authorized by this section. Prior to imposing confinement pursuant to subdivision (6) of this subsection, the probationer must first be presented with a violation report, with the alleged violations noted and advised of the right (i) to a hearing before the court on the alleged violation, with the right to present relevant oral and written evidence; (ii) to have counsel at the hearing, and that one will be appointed if the probationer is indigent; (iii) to request witnesses who have relevant information concerning the alleged violations; and (iv) to examine any witnesses or evidence. The probationer may be confined for the period designated on the violation report upon the execution of a waiver of rights signed by the probationer and by two officers acting as witnesses. Those two witnesses shall be the probation officer and another officer to be designated by the Chief of the Community Corrections Section in written Division policy.

(f1) **Mandatory Condition of Satellite-Based Monitoring for Some Sex Offenders.** -- Notwithstanding any other provision of this section, the court shall impose satellite-based monitoring pursuant to Part 5 of Article 27A of Chapter 14 of the General Statutes as a condition of probation on any offender who is described by G.S. 14-208.40(a)(1), and based on the Division of Adult Correction and Juvenile Justice's risk assessment program requires the highest possible level of supervision and monitoring.

(g) Repealed by Session Laws 1993 (Reg. Sess., 1994), c. 19, s. 3.

(h) **Definitions.** -- For purposes of this section, the definitions in G.S. 15A-1340.11 apply.

History.
1993, c. 538, s. 17.1; 1994, Ex. Sess., c. 14, s. 22; c. 19, s. 3; c. 24, s. 14(b); 1993 (Reg. Sess., 1994), c. 767, s. 8; 1997-57, s. 4; 2001-487, s. 47(b); 2006-247, ss. 15(c), 15(d); 2011-145, s. 19.1(h), (k); 2011-192, s. 1(d) -(f), (k); 2011-412, s. 2.3(b), (c); 2012-146, s. 6; 2012-188, s. 1(a), (b); 2017-186, s. 2(mmm); 2020-83, s. 8(f), (g); 2021-138, s. 18(k).

§ 15A-1343.3. Division of Adult Correction and Juvenile Justice of the Department of Public Safety to establish regulations for continuous alcohol monitoring systems; payment of fees; authority to terminate monitoring

(a) The Division of Adult Correction and Juvenile Justice of the Department of Public Safety shall establish regulations for continuous alcohol monitoring systems that are authorized for use by the courts as evidence that an offender on probation has abstained from the use of alcohol for a specified period of time. A "continuous alcohol monitoring system" is a device that is worn by a person that can detect, monitor, record, and report the amount of alcohol within the wearer's system over a continuous 24-hour daily basis. The regulations shall include the procedures for supervision of the offender, collection and monitoring of the results, and the transmission of the data to the court for consideration by the court. All courts, including those using continuous alcohol monitoring systems prior to July 4, 2007, shall comply with the regulations established by the Division pursuant to this section.

The Secretary, or the Secretary's designee, shall approve continuous alcohol monitoring systems for use by the courts prior to their use by a court as evidence of alcohol abstinence, or their use as a condition of probation. The Secretary shall not unreasonably withhold approval of a continuous alcohol monitoring system and shall consult with the Division of Purchase and Contract in the Department of Administration to ensure that potential vendors are not discriminated against.

(b) Any fees or costs paid by an offender on probation in order to comply with continuous alcohol monitoring shall be paid directly to the monitoring provider. A monitoring provider shall not terminate the provision of continuous alcohol monitoring for nonpayment of fees unless authorized by the court.

History.
2007-165, s. 6; 2011-145, s. 19.1(h); 2012-146, s. 7; 2017-186, s. 2(nnn)

§ 15A-1344. Response to violations; alteration and revocation

(a) **Authority to Alter or Revoke.** -- Except as provided in subsection (a1) or (b), probation may be reduced, terminated, continued, extended, modified, or revoked by any judge entitled to sit in the court which imposed probation and who is resident or presiding in the district court district as defined in G.S. 7A-133 or superior court district or set of districts as defined in G.S. 7A-41.1, as the case may be, where the sentence of probation was imposed, where the probationer violates probation, or where the probationer resides. Upon a finding that an offender sentenced to community punishment under Article 81B has violated one or more conditions of probation, the court's authority to modify the probation judgment includes the authority to require the offender to comply with conditions of probation that would otherwise make the sentence an intermediate punishment. The court may only revoke probation for a violation of a condition of probation under G.S. 15A-1343(b)(1) or G.S. 15A-1343(b)(3a), except as provided in G.S. 15A-1344(d2). Imprisonment may be imposed pursuant to G.S. 15A-1344(d2) for a violation of a requirement other than G.S. 15A-1343(b)(1) or G.S. 15A-1343(b)(3a). The district attorney of the prosecutorial district as defined in G.S. 7A-60 in which probation was imposed must be given reasonable notice of any hearing to affect probation substantially.

(a1) **Authority to Supervise Probation in Drug Treatment Court.** -- Jurisdiction to supervise, modify, and revoke probation imposed in cases in which the offender is required to participate in a drug treatment court or a therapeutic court is as provided in G.S. 7A-272(e) and G.S. 7A-271(f). Proceedings to modify or revoke probation in these cases must be held in the county in which the drug treatment court or therapeutic court is located.

(b) **Limits on Jurisdiction to Alter or Revoke Unsupervised Probation.** -- If the sentencing judge has entered an order to limit jurisdiction to consider a sentence of unsupervised probation under G.S. 15A-1342(h), a sentence of unsupervised probation may be reduced, terminated, continued, extended, modified, or revoked only by the sentencing judge or, if the sentencing judge is no longer on the bench, by a presiding judge in the court where the defendant was sentenced.

(b1) **Service of Notice of Hearing on Violation of Unsupervised Probation.** --

(1) Notice of a hearing in response to a violation of unsupervised probation shall be given either by personal delivery to the person to be notified or by depositing the notice in the United States mail in an envelope

with postage prepaid, addressed to the person at the last known address available to the preparer of the notice and reasonably believed to provide actual notice to the offender. The notice shall be mailed at least 10 days prior to any hearing and shall state the nature of the violation.

(2) If notice is given by depositing the notice in the United States mail, pursuant to subdivision (1) of this subsection, and the defendant does not appear at the hearing, the court may do either of the following:

a. Terminate the probation and enter appropriate orders for the enforcement of any outstanding monetary obligations as otherwise provided by law.

b. Provide for other notice to the person as authorized by this Chapter for further proceedings and action authorized by Article 82 of Chapter 15A of the General Statutes for a violation of a condition of probation.

If the person is present at the hearing, the court may take any further action authorized by Article 82 of Chapter 15A of the General Statutes for a violation of a condition of probation.

(c) **Procedure on Altering or Revoking Probation; Returning Probationer to District Where Sentenced. --** When a judge reduces, terminates, extends, modifies, or revokes probation outside the county where the judgment was entered, the clerk must send a copy of the order and any other records to the court where probation was originally imposed. A court on its own motion may return the probationer to the district court district as defined in G.S. 7A-133 or superior court district or set of districts as defined in G.S. 7A-41.1, as the case may be, where probation was imposed or where the probationer resides for reduction, termination, continuation, extension, modification, or revocation of probation. In cases where the probation is revoked in a county other than the county of original conviction the clerk in that county must issue a commitment order and must file the order revoking probation and the commitment order, which will constitute sufficient permanent record of the proceeding in that court, and must send a certified copy of the order revoking probation, the commitment order, and all other records pertaining thereto to the county of original conviction to be filed with the original records. The clerk in the county other than the county of original conviction must issue the formal commitment to the Division of Adult Correction and Juvenile Justice of the Department of Public Safety.

(d) **Extension and Modification; Response to Violations. --** At any time prior to the expiration or termination of the probation period or in accordance with subsection

(f) of this section, the court may after notice and hearing and for good cause shown extend the period of probation up to the maximum allowed under G.S. 15A-1342(a) and may modify the conditions of probation. A hearing extending or modifying probation may be held in the absence of a defendant who fails to appear for the hearing after a reasonable effort to notify the defendant. If a probationer violates a condition of probation at any time prior to the expiration or termination of the period of probation, the court, in accordance with the provisions of G.S. 15A-1345, may continue the defendant on probation, with or without modifying the conditions, may place the defendant on special probation as provided in subsection (e), or, if continuation, modification, or special probation is not appropriate, may revoke the probation and activate the suspended sentence imposed at the time of initial sentencing, if any, or may order that charges as to which prosecution has been deferred be brought to trial; provided that probation may not be revoked solely for conviction of a Class 3 misdemeanor. The court, before activating a sentence to imprisonment established when the defendant was placed on probation, may reduce the sentence, but the reduction shall be consistent with subsection (d1) of this section. A sentence activated upon revocation of probation commences on the day probation is revoked and runs concurrently with any other period of probation, parole, or imprisonment to which the defendant is subject during that period unless the revoking judge specifies that it is to run consecutively with the other period.

(d1) **Reduction of Initial Sentence. --** If the court elects to reduce the sentence of imprisonment for a felony, it shall not deviate from the range of minimum durations established in Article 81B of this Chapter for the class of offense and prior record level used in determining the initial sentence. If the presumptive range is used for the initial suspended sentence, the reduced sentence shall be within the presumptive range. If the mitigated range is used for the initial suspended sentence, the reduced sentence shall be within the mitigated range. If the aggravated range is used for the initial suspended sentence, the reduced sentence shall be within the aggravated range. If the court elects to reduce the sentence for a misdemeanor, it shall not deviate from the range of durations established in Article 81B for the class of offense and prior conviction level used in determining the initial sentence.

(d2) **Confinement in Response to Violation. --** When a defendant under supervision for a felony conviction has violated a condition of probation other than G.S. 15A-1343(b)(1) or G.S. 15A-1343(b)(3a), the court may impose a period of confinement of 90 consecutive days to be served in the custody of the Division of Adult

Correction and Juvenile Justice of the Department of Public Safety. The court may not revoke probation unless the defendant has previously received a total of two periods of confinement under this subsection. A defendant may receive only two periods of confinement under this subsection. The 90-day term of confinement ordered under this subsection for a felony shall not be reduced by credit for time already served in the case. Any such credit shall instead be applied to the suspended sentence. However, if the time remaining on the maximum imposed sentence on a defendant under supervision for a felony conviction is 90 days or less, then the term of confinement is for the remaining period of the sentence. Confinement under this section shall be credited pursuant to G.S. 15-196.1.

When a defendant under supervision for a misdemeanor conviction sentenced pursuant to Article 81B of Chapter 15A of the General Statutes has violated a condition of probation other than G.S. 15A-1343(b)(1) or G.S. 15A-1343(b)(3a), the court may impose a period of confinement pursuant to G.S. 15A-1343(a1)(3). If the person being ordered to a period of confinement is under the age of 18, that person must be confined in a detention facility approved by the Juvenile Justice Section of the Division of Adult Correction and Juvenile Justice to provide secure confinement and care for juveniles or to a holdover facility as defined in G.S. 7B-1501(11). If the person being ordered to a period of confinement reaches the age of 18 years while in confinement, the person may be transported by personnel of the Juvenile Justice Section of the Division, or personnel approved by the Juvenile Justice Section, to the custody of the sheriff of the applicable local confinement facility. The court may not revoke probation unless the defendant has previously received at least two periods of confinement for violating a condition of probation other than G.S. 15A-1343(b)(1) or G.S. 15A-1343(b)(3a). Those periods of confinement may have been imposed pursuant to G.S. 15A-1343(a1)(3), 15A-1343.2(e)(5), or 15A-1343.2(f)(6). The second period of confinement must have been imposed for a violation that occurred after the defendant served the first period of confinement. Confinement under this section shall be credited pursuant to G.S. 15-196.1.

When a defendant under supervision for a misdemeanor conviction not sentenced pursuant to Article 81B of Chapter 15A of the General Statutes has violated a condition of probation other than G.S. 15A-1343(b)(1) or G.S. 15A-1343(b)(3a), the court may impose a period of confinement of up to 90 consecutive days to be served where the defendant would have served an active sentence. The court may not revoke probation unless the defendant has previously received a total of two periods of confinement under this subsection. A defendant may receive only two periods of confinement under this subsection. Confinement under this section shall be credited pursuant to G.S. 15-196.1.

The period of confinement imposed under this subsection on a defendant who is on probation for multiple offenses shall run concurrently on all cases related to the violation. Confinement shall be immediate unless otherwise specified by the court.

(e) **Special Probation in Response to Violation.** -- When a defendant has violated a condition of probation, the court may modify the probation to place the defendant on special probation as provided in this subsection. In placing the defendant on special probation, the court may continue or modify the conditions of probation and in addition require that the defendant submit to a period or periods of imprisonment, either continuous or noncontinuous, at whatever time or intervals within the period of probation the court determines. In addition to any other conditions of probation which the court may impose, the court shall impose, when imposing a period or periods of imprisonment as a condition of special probation, the condition that the defendant obey the rules and regulations of the Division of Adult Correction and Juvenile Justice of the Department of Public Safety governing conduct of inmates, and this condition shall apply to the defendant whether or not the court imposes it as a part of the written order. If imprisonment is for continuous periods, the confinement may be in either the custody of the Division of Adult Correction and Juvenile Justice of the Department of Public Safety or a local confinement facility. Noncontinuous periods of imprisonment under special probation may only be served in a designated local confinement or treatment facility. If the person being ordered to a period or periods of imprisonment, either continuous or noncontinuous, is under the age of 18, that person must be imprisoned in a detention facility approved by the Juvenile Justice Section of the Division of Adult Correction and Juvenile Justice to provide secure confinement and care for juveniles or to a holdover facility as defined in G.S. 7B-1501(11). If the person being ordered to a period or periods of imprisonment reaches the age of 18 years while imprisoned, the person may be transported by personnel of the Juvenile Justice Section of the Division, or personnel approved by the Juvenile Justice Section, to the custody of the sheriff of the applicable local confinement facility.

Except for probationary sentences for impaired driving under G.S. 20-138.1, the total of all periods of confinement imposed as an incident of special probation, but not including an activated suspended sentence, may not exceed one-fourth the maximum sentence of imprisonment imposed for the offense. For probationary sentences for impaired driving under G.S.

Chapter 15A

20-138.1, the total of all periods of confinement imposed as an incident of special probation, but not including an activated suspended sentence, shall not exceed one-fourth the maximum penalty allowed by law. No confinement other than an activated suspended sentence may be required beyond the period of probation or beyond two years of the time the special probation is imposed, whichever comes first.

(e1) **Criminal Contempt in Response to Violation. --** If a defendant willfully violates a condition of probation, the court may hold the defendant in criminal contempt as provided in Article 1 of Chapter 5A of the General Statutes. A finding of criminal contempt by the court shall not revoke the probation. If the offender serves a sentence for contempt in a local confinement facility, the Division of Adult Correction and Juvenile Justice of the Department of Public Safety shall pay for the confinement at the standard rate set by the General Assembly pursuant to G.S. 148-32.1(a) regardless of whether the offender would be eligible under the terms of that subsection.

(e2) Repealed by Session Laws 2021-138, s. 18(l), effective December 1, 2021, and applicable to satellite-based monitoring determinations on or after that date.

(f) **Extension, Modification, or Revocation after Period of Probation. --** The court may extend, modify, or revoke probation after the expiration of the period of probation if all of the following apply:

(1) Before the expiration of the period of probation the State has filed a written violation report with the clerk indicating its intent to conduct a hearing on one or more violations of one or more conditions of probation.

(2) The court finds that the probationer did violate one or more conditions of probation prior to the expiration of the period of probation.

(3) The court finds for good cause shown and stated that the probation should be extended, modified, or revoked.

(4) If the court opts to extend the period of probation, the court may extend the period of probation up to the maximum allowed under G.S. 15A-1342(a).

(g) Repealed by Session Laws 2011-62, s. 3, as amended by Session Laws 2011-412, s. 2.2, effective December 1, 2011, and applicable to persons placed on probation on or after December 1, 2011.

History.

1977, c. 711, s. 1; 1977, 2nd Sess., c. 1147, ss. 11, 11A, 13A; 1979, c. 749, ss. 1-3; 1981, c. 377, s. 7; 1983, c. 536; 1987, (Reg. Sess., 1988), c. 1037, ss. 67, 68; 1993, c. 538, s. 18; 1994, Ex. Sess., c. 19, s. 2; c. 24, s. 14(b); 1993 (Reg. Sess., 1994), c. 767, s. 9; c. 769, s. 21.7(a); 1998-212, s. 17.21(c); 2003-151, s. 1; 2006-247, s. 15(e); 2008-129, s. 4; 2008-187, s. 46; 2009-372, s. 11(a), (b); 2009-411, s. 1; 2009-452, ss. 3, 4; 2009-516, ss. 9, 10(a), (b); 2010-96, s. 26(c); 2010-97, s. 13; 2011-62, s. 3; 2011-145, s. 19.1(h); 2011-192, s. 4(b), (c); 2011-412, ss. 2.2, 2.3(d), 2.5; 2012-83, s. 28; 2012-188, s. 2; 2012-194, s. 7; 2013-101, s. 4; 2014-100, s. 16C.8(a); 2015-191, s. 1; 2017-186, ss. 2(ooo), 3(a); 2020-83, s. 8(h), (i); 2021-138, s. 18 (l)

§ 15A-1344.1. Procedure to insure payment of child support

(a) When the court requires, as a condition of supervised or unsupervised probation, that a defendant support his children, the court may order at any time that support payments be made to the State Child Support Collection and Disbursement Unit for remittance to the party entitled to receive the payments. For child support orders initially entered on or after January 1, 1994, the immediate income withholding provisions of G.S. 110-136.5(c1) apply. If child support is to be paid through income withholding, the payments shall be made in accordance with G.S. 110-139(f).

(b) After entry of such an order by the court, the clerk of court shall maintain records listing the amount of payments, the date payments are required to be made, and the names and addresses of the parties affected by the order.

(c) The parties affected by the order shall inform the clerk of court and the State Child Support Collection and Disbursement Unit of any change of address or of other condition that may affect the administration of the order. The court may provide in the order that a defendant failing to inform the court and the State Child Support Collection and Disbursement Unit of a change of address within reasonable period of time may be held in violation of probation.

(d) When a defendant in a non-IV-D case, as defined in G.S. 110-129, fails to make required payments of child support and is in arrears, upon notification by the State Child Support Collection and Disbursement Unit the clerk of superior court may mail by regular mail to the last known address of the defendant a notice of delinquency that sets out the amount of child support currently due and that demands immediate payment of the amount. Failure to receive the delinquency notice is not a defense in any probation violation hearing or other proceeding thereafter. If the arrearage is not paid in full within 21 days after the mailing of the delinquency notice, or is not paid within 30 days after the defendant becomes delinquent if the clerk has elected not to send a delinquency notice, the clerk shall certify the amount due to the district attorney and probation officer, who shall initiate proceedings for revocation of probation pursuant to Article 82 of Chapter 15A or make a motion in the criminal case for income withholding pursuant to G.S. 110-136.5 or both.

When a defendant in a IV-D case, as defined in G.S. 110-129, fails to make required payments of child support and is in arrears, at the request of the IV-D obligee the clerk shall certify the amount due to the district attorney and probation officer, who shall initiate proceedings for revocation of probation pursuant to Article 82 of Chapter 15A or make a motion in the criminal case for income withholding pursuant to G.S. 110-136.5 or both.

History.
1983, c. 567, s. 1; 1983 (Reg. Sess., 1984), c. 1100, ss. 1, 2; 1985 (Reg. Sess., 1986), c. 949, s. 7; 1993, c. 517, s. 4; 1999-293, ss. 10, 23

§ 15A-1345. Arrest and hearing on probation violation

(a) **Arrest for Violation of Probation. --** A probationer is subject to arrest for violation of conditions of probation by a law-enforcement officer or probation officer upon either an order for arrest issued by the court or upon the written request of a probation officer, accompanied by a written statement signed by the probation officer that the probationer has violated specified conditions of his probation. However, a probation revocation hearing under subsection (e) may be held without first arresting the probationer.

(a1) **Suspension of Public Assistance Benefits for Probation Violators Who Avoid Arrest. --** The court may order the suspension of any public assistance benefits that are being received by a probationer for whom the court has issued an order for arrest for violation of the conditions of probation but who is absconding or otherwise willfully avoiding arrest. The suspension of benefits shall continue until such time as the probationer surrenders to or is otherwise brought under the jurisdiction of the court. For purposes of this section, the term "public assistance benefits" includes unemployment benefits, Medicaid or other medical assistance benefits, Work First Family Assistance, food and nutrition benefits, any other programs of public assistance under Article 2 of Chapter 108A of the General Statutes, and any other financial assistance of any kind being paid to the probationer from State or federal funds. Nothing in this subsection shall be construed to suspend, or in any way affect the eligibility for, any public assistance benefits that are being received by or for the benefit of a family member of a probation violator.

(b) **Bail Following Arrest for Probation Violation. --** If at any time during the period of probation the probationer is arrested for a violation of any of the conditions of probation,

he must be taken without unnecessary delay before a judicial official to have conditions of release pending a revocation hearing set in the same manner as provided in G.S. 15A-534.

(b1) If the probationer is arrested for a violation of any of the conditions of probation and (i) has a pending charge for a felony offense or (ii) has been convicted of an offense at any time that requires registration under Article 27A of Chapter 14 of the General Statutes or an offense that would have required registration but for the effective date of the law establishing the Sex Offender and Public Protection Registration Program, the judicial official shall determine whether the probationer poses a danger to the public prior to imposing conditions of release and must record that determination in writing.

(1) If the judicial official determines that the probationer poses a danger to the public, the probationer shall be denied release pending a revocation hearing.

(2) If the judicial official finds that the defendant does not pose a danger to the public, then conditions of release shall be imposed as otherwise provided in Article 26 of this Chapter.

(3) If there is insufficient information to determine whether the defendant poses a danger to the public, then the defendant shall be retained in custody for not more than seven days from the date of the arrest in order for the judicial official, or a subsequent reviewing judicial official, to obtain sufficient information to determine whether the defendant poses a danger to the public.

(4) If the defendant has been held seven days from the date of arrest pursuant to subdivision (3) of this subsection, and the court has been unable to obtain sufficient information to determine whether the defendant poses a danger to the public, then the defendant shall be brought before any judicial official, who shall record that fact in writing and shall impose conditions of pretrial release as otherwise provided in this section.

(c) **When Preliminary Hearing on Probation Violation Required. --** Unless the hearing required by subsection (e) is first held or the probationer waives the hearing, a preliminary hearing on probation violation must be held within seven working days of an arrest of a probationer to determine whether there is probable cause to believe that he violated a condition of probation. Otherwise, the probationer must be released seven working days after his arrest to continue on probation pending a hearing, unless the probationer has been denied release pursuant to subdivision (1) of subsection (b1) of this section, in which case the probationer shall be held until the revocation hearing date.

(d) **Procedure for Preliminary Hearing on Probation Violation.** -- The preliminary hearing on probation violation must be conducted by a judge who is sitting in the county where the probationer was arrested or where the alleged violation occurred. If no judge is sitting in the county where the hearing would otherwise be held, the hearing may be held anywhere in the district court district as defined in G.S. 7A-133 or superior court district or set of districts as defined in G.S. 7A-41.1, as the case may be. The State must give the probationer notice of the hearing and its purpose, including a statement of the violations alleged. At the hearing the probationer may appear and speak in his own behalf, may present relevant information, and may, on request, personally question adverse informants unless the court finds good cause for not allowing confrontation. Formal rules of evidence do not apply at the hearing. If probable cause is found or if the probable cause hearing is waived, the probationer may be held for a revocation hearing, subject to release under the provisions of subsection (b). If the hearing is held and probable cause is not found, the probationer must be released to continue on probation.

(e) **Revocation Hearing.** -- Before revoking or extending probation, the court must, unless the probationer waives the hearing, hold a hearing to determine whether to revoke or extend probation and must make findings to support the decision and a summary record of the proceedings. The State must give the probationer notice of the hearing and its purpose, including a statement of the violations alleged. The notice, unless waived by the probationer, must be given at least 24 hours before the hearing. At the hearing, evidence against the probationer must be disclosed to him, and the probationer may appear and speak in his own behalf, may present relevant information, and may confront and cross-examine adverse witnesses unless the court finds good cause for not allowing confrontation. The probationer is entitled to be represented by counsel at the hearing and, if indigent, to have counsel appointed in accordance with rules adopted by the Office of Indigent Defense Services. Formal rules of evidence do not apply at the hearing, but the record or recollection of evidence or testimony introduced at the preliminary hearing on probation violation are inadmissible as evidence at the revocation hearing. When the violation alleged is the nonpayment of fine or costs, the issues and procedures at the hearing include those specified in G.S. 15A-1364 for response to nonpayment of fine.

History.
1977, c. 711, s. 1; 1977, 2nd Sess., c. 1147, ss. 12, 13; 1979, c. 749, s. 4; 1979, 2nd Sess., c. 1316, s. 39; 1987

(Reg. Sess., 1988), c. 1037, s. 69; 2008-117, s. 19; 2009-412, s. 2; 2011-326, s. 12(c); 2012-170, s. 1

§ 15A-1346. Commencement of probation; multiple sentence

(a) **Commencement of Probation.** -- Except as provided in subsection (b), a period of probation commences on the day it is imposed and runs concurrently with any other period of probation, parole, or imprisonment to which the defendant is subject during that period.

(b) **Consecutive and Concurrent Sentences.** -- If a period of probation is being imposed at the same time a period of imprisonment is being imposed or if it is being imposed on a person already subject to an undischarged term of imprisonment, the period of probation may run either concurrently or consecutively with the term of imprisonment, as determined by the court. If not specified, it runs concurrently.

History.
1977, c. 711, s. 1

§ 15A-1347. Appeal from revocation of probation or imposition of special probation upon violation; consequences of waiver of hearing

(a) Except as provided in subsection (b) of this section, when a district court judge, as a result of a finding of a violation of probation, activates a sentence or imposes special probation, the defendant may appeal to the superior court for a de novo revocation hearing. At the hearing the probationer has all rights and the court has all authority they have in a revocation hearing held before the superior court in the first instance. Appeals from lower courts to the superior courts from judgments revoking probation may be heard in term or out of term, in the county or out of the county by the resident superior court judge of the district or the superior court judge assigned to hold the courts of the district, or a judge of the superior court commissioned to hold court in the district, or a special superior court judge residing in the district. When the defendant appeals to the superior court because a district court has found he violated probation and has activated his sentence or imposed special probation, and the superior court, after a de novo revocation hearing, orders that the defendant continue on probation under the same or modified conditions, the superior court is considered the court that originally imposed probation with regard to future revocation proceedings and other purposes of this Article. When a superior court judge, as a result of a finding of a violation of probation, activates a sentence or imposes special probation, either in the first instance or upon a de novo hearing after appeal from a district court, the defendant may appeal under G.S. 7A-27.

(b) If a defendant waives a revocation hearing, the finding of a violation of probation, activation of sentence, or imposition of special probation may not be appealed to the superior court.

(c) If a defendant appeals an activation of a sentence as a result of a finding of a violation of probation by the district or superior court and is released pursuant to Article 26 of Chapter 15A of the General Statutes, probation supervision will continue under the same conditions until the expiration of the period of probation or disposition of the appeal, whichever comes first.

History.

1977, c. 711, s. 1; 1977, 2nd Sess., c. 1147, s. 14; 2013-385, s. 2; 2015-247, s. 4; 2016-77, s. 7

§§ 15A-1348 through 15A-1350

Reserved for future codification purposes.

ARTICLE 83
IMPRISONMENT

§ 15A-1351. Sentence of imprisonment; incidents; special probation

(a) The judge may sentence to special probation a defendant convicted of a criminal offense other than impaired driving under G.S. 20-138.1, if based on the defendant's prior record or conviction level as found pursuant to Article 81B of this Chapter, an intermediate punishment is authorized for the class of offense of which the defendant has been convicted. A defendant convicted of impaired driving under G.S. 20-138.1 may also be sentenced to special probation. Under a sentence of special probation, the court may suspend the term of imprisonment and place the defendant on probation as provided in Article 82, Probation, and in addition require that the defendant submit to a period or periods of imprisonment in the custody of the Division of Adult Correction and Juvenile Justice of the Department of Public Safety or a designated local confinement or treatment facility at whatever time or intervals within the period of probation, consecutive or nonconsecutive, the court determines, as provided in this subsection. For probationary sentences for misdemeanors, including impaired driving under G.S. 20-138.1, all imprisonment under this subsection shall be in a designated local confinement or treatment facility. If the person being ordered to a period or periods of imprisonment is under the age of 18, that person must be imprisoned in a detention facility

approved by the Juvenile Justice Section of the Division of Adult Correction and Juvenile Justice to provide secure confinement and care for juveniles or to a holdover facility as defined in G.S. 7B-1501(11). If the person being ordered to a period or periods of imprisonment reaches the age of 18 years while imprisoned, the person may be transported by personnel of the Juvenile Justice Section of the Division, or personnel approved by the Juvenile Justice Section, to the custody of the sheriff of the applicable local confinement facility. In addition to any other conditions of probation which the court may impose, the court shall impose, when imposing a period or periods of imprisonment as a condition of special probation, the condition that the defendant obey the Rules and Regulations of the Division of Adult Correction and Juvenile Justice of the Department of Public Safety governing conduct of inmates, and this condition shall apply to the defendant whether or not the court imposes it as a part of the written order. Except for probationary sentences for misdemeanors, including impaired driving under G.S. 20-138.1, if imprisonment is for continuous periods, the confinement may be in the custody of either the Division of Adult Correction and Juvenile Justice of the Department of Public Safety or a local confinement facility. Noncontinuous periods of imprisonment under special probation may only be served in a designated local confinement or treatment facility. If the person being ordered continuous or noncontinuous periods of imprisonment is under the age of 18, that person must be imprisoned in a detention facility approved by the Juvenile Justice Section of the Division of Adult Correction and Juvenile Justice to provide secure confinement and care for juveniles or to a holdover facility as defined in G.S. 7B-1501(11). If the person being ordered to a period or periods of imprisonment reaches the age of 18 years while imprisoned, the person may be transported by personnel of the Juvenile Justice Section of the Division, or personnel approved by the Juvenile Justice Section, to the custody of the sheriff of the applicable local confinement facility. Except for probationary sentences of impaired driving under G.S. 20-138.1, the total of all periods of confinement imposed as an incident of special probation, but not including an activated suspended sentence, may not exceed one-fourth the maximum sentence of imprisonment imposed for the offense, and no confinement other than an activated suspended sentence may be required beyond two years of conviction. For probationary sentences for impaired driving under G.S. 20-138.1, the total of all periods of confinement imposed as an incident of special probation, but not including an activated suspended sentence, shall not exceed one-fourth the maximum penalty allowed by law. In imposing a sentence of special probation, the judge may credit any time spent committed or confined, as a result of the charge, to either the suspended sentence or to the imprisonment required for special probation. The original period of probation, including the period of imprisonment required for special probation, shall be as specified in G.S. 15A-1343.2(d), but may not exceed a maximum of five years, except as provided by G.S. 15A-1342(a). The court may revoke, modify, or terminate special probation as otherwise provided for probationary sentences.

(b) Sentencing of a person convicted of a felony or of a misdemeanor other than impaired driving under G.S. 20-138.1 that occurred on or after the effective date of Article 81B is subject to that Article. For persons convicted of impaired driving under G.S. 20-138.1, a sentence to imprisonment must impose a maximum term and may impose a minimum term. The impaired driving judgment may state the minimum term or may state that a term constitutes both the minimum and maximum terms. If the impaired driving judgment states no minimum term, the defendant becomes eligible for parole in accordance with G.S. 15A-1371(a).

(c) Repealed by Session Laws 1979, c. 749, s. 7.

(d), (e) Repealed by Session Laws 1993, c. 538, s. 19.

(f) **Work Release. --** When sentencing a person convicted of a felony, the sentencing court may recommend that the sentenced offender be granted work release as authorized in G.S. 148-33.1. When sentencing a person convicted of a misdemeanor, the sentencing court may recommend or, with the consent of the person sentenced, order that the sentenced offender be granted work release as authorized in G.S. 148-33.1.

(g) **Credit. --** Credit towards a sentence to imprisonment is as provided in Article 19A of Chapter 15 of the General Statutes.

(h) Repealed by Session Laws 2003-141, s. 2, effective December 1, 2003.

History.

1977, c. 711, s. 1; 1977, 2nd Sess., c. 1147, ss. 15-17; 1979, c. 749, ss. 5-7; c. 760, s. 4; 1985 (Reg. Sess., 1986), c. 1014, s. 201(a); 1987, c. 738, s. 111(e); 1993, c. 84, s. 2; c. 538, s. 19; 1994, Ex. Sess., c. 24, s. 14(b); 1993 (Reg. Sess., 1994), c. 767, ss. 7, 10; 1998-212, s. 17.21(b); 2003-141, s. 2; 2003-151, s. 2; 2011-145, s. 19.1(h); 2014-100, s. 16C.1(a); 2017-186, s. 2(ppp); 2020-83, s. 8(j).

§ 15A-1352. Commitment to Division of Adult Correction and Juvenile Justice of the Department of Public Safety or local confinement facility

(a) Except as provided in subsection (f) of this section, a person sentenced to imprisonment for a misdemeanor under this Article or for nonpayment of a fine for conviction of a misdemeanor under Article 84 of this Chapter shall be committed for the term designated by the court to the Statewide Misdemeanant Confinement Program as provided in G.S. 148-32.1 or, if the period is for 90 days or less, to a local confinement facility, except as provided for in G.S. 148-32.1(b).

If a person is sentenced to imprisonment for a misdemeanor under this Article or for nonpayment of a fine under Article 84 of this Chapter, the sentencing judge may make a finding of fact as to whether the person would be suitable for placement in a county satellite jail/work release unit operated pursuant to G.S. 153A-230.3. If the sentencing judge makes a finding of fact that the person would be suitable for placement in a county satellite jail/work release unit and the person meets the requirements listed in G.S. 153A-230.3(a)(1), then the custodian of the local confinement facility may transfer the misdemeanant to a county satellite jail/work release unit.

If the person sentenced to imprisonment is under the age of 18, the person must be committed to a detention facility approved by the Juvenile Justice Section of the Division of Adult Correction and Juvenile Justice to provide secure confinement and care for juveniles. Personnel of the Juvenile Justice Section of the Division or personnel approved by the Juvenile Justice Section shall transport the person to the detention facility. If the person sentenced to imprisonment reaches the age of 18 years while imprisoned, the person may be transported by personnel of the Juvenile Justice Section of the Division, or personnel approved by the Juvenile Justice Section, to the custody of the sheriff of the applicable local confinement facility.

(b) A person sentenced to imprisonment for a felony under this Article or for nonpayment of a fine for conviction of a felony under Article 84 of this Chapter shall be committed for the term designated by the court to the custody of the Division of Adult Correction and Juvenile Justice of the Department of Public Safety.

(c) Repealed by Session Laws 2014-100, s. 16C.1(b), effective October 1, 2014. See Editor's note for applicability.

(d) Notwithstanding any other provision of law, when the sentencing court, with the consent of the person sentenced, orders that a person convicted of a misdemeanor be granted work release, the court may commit the person to a specific prison facility or local confinement facility or satellite jail/work release unit within the county of the sentencing court in order to facilitate the work release arrangement. When appropriate to facilitate the work release arrangement, the sentencing court may, with the consent of the sheriff or board of commissioners, commit the person to a specific local confinement facility or satellite jail/work release unit in another county.

(e) Repealed by Session Laws 2014-100, s. 16C.1(b), effective October 1, 2014. See Editor's note for applicability.

(f) A person sentenced to imprisonment of any duration for impaired driving under G.S. 20-138.1, other than imprisonment required as a condition of special probation under G.S. 15A-1351(a) or G.S. 15A-1344(e), shall be committed to the Statewide Misdemeanant Confinement Program established under G.S. 148-32.1.

If the person sentenced to imprisonment is under the age of 18, the person must be committed to a detention facility approved by the Juvenile Justice Section of the Division of Adult Correction and Juvenile Justice to provide secure confinement and care for juveniles. Personnel of the Juvenile Justice Section or personnel approved by the Juvenile Justice Section shall transport the person to the detention facility. If the person sentenced to imprisonment reaches the age of 18 years while imprisoned, the person may be transported by personnel of the Juvenile Justice Section of the Division, or personnel approved by the Juvenile Justice Section, to the custody of the sheriff of the applicable local confinement facility.

History.
1977, c. 711, s. 1; 1977, 2nd Sess., c. 1147, s. 18; 1979, c. 456, s. 1; c. 787, ss. 1, 2; 1985 (Reg. Sess., 1986), c. 1014, s. 201(b); 1987, c. 207, s. 3; 1989, c. 761, s. 6; 1991, Ex. Sess., c. 486, s. 1; c. 8, s. 1; 1993, c. 538, s. 37; 1994, Ex. Sess., c. 24, s. 14(b); 2011-145, s. 19.1(h); 2011-192, s. 7(b) -(c); 2014-100, s. 16C.1(b); 2017-186, s. 2(qqq); 2020-83, s. 8(k)

§ 15A-1353. Order of commitment when imprisonment imposed; release pending appeal

(a) When a sentence includes a term or terms of imprisonment, the court must issue an order of commitment setting forth the judgment. Unless otherwise specified in the order of commitment, the date of the order is the date service of the sentence is to begin.

If a female defendant is convicted of a nonviolent crime and the court is provided medical evidence from a licensed physician that the defendant is pregnant or the court otherwise determines that the defendant is pregnant, the court may specify in the order that the date of service of the sentence is not to begin until at least six weeks after the birth of the child or other termination of the pregnancy unless the defendant requests to serve her term as the court would otherwise order. The court may impose reasonable conditions upon defendant during such waiting period to insure that

defendant will return to begin service of the sentence.

If the court sentences a defendant pursuant to G.S. 15A-1351(a), the period during which that defendant is awaiting imprisonment shall be considered part of the probationary sentence and such defendant shall be subject to all incidents and conditions of probation.

(b) There must be included in the commitment, or in a separate order referred to in the commitment, any provisions with regard to release under Article 26, Bail, if an appeal is taken, and the conditions of the release. If the commitment has been entered before appeal or the setting of the conditions for release, appropriate copies of those documents must be forwarded to the agency having custody of the defendant.

(c) Unless a later time is directed in the order of commitment, or the defendant has been released from custody pursuant to Article 26, Bail, or the defendant is appealing from a judgment of the district court to the superior court for a trial de novo, the sheriff must cause the defendant to be placed in the custody of the agency specified in the judgment on the day service of sentence is to begin or as soon thereafter as practicable.

(d) A certified copy of the order of commitment, together with any separate order providing for release of the defendant pending appeal, must be delivered to the custodian of the confinement facility.

(e) When a defendant has been committed pursuant to this section:

(1) If appeal has been entered and conditions of release have been set as provided in Article 26, Bail, the agency having custody of the defendant may effect his release in the manner provided in G.S. 15A-537; or

(2) If appeal is entered and the conditions of release are not set until after the order of commitment has been issued, and the defendant has been placed in the custody of the agency directed therein, appropriate copies of the conditions of release must be certified by the clerk and forwarded to the agency, which then may effect his release in the manner provided in G.S. 15A-537.

(f) When the sentencing court, with the consent of the person sentenced, orders that a person convicted of a misdemeanor be granted work release, the following provisions must be included in the commitment, or in a separate order referred to in the commitment:

(1) The date work release is to begin;

(2) The prison or local confinement facility to which the offender is to be committed;

(3) A provision that work release terminates the date the offender loses his job or violates the conditions of the work-release plan established by the Division of Adult

Correction and Juvenile Justice of the Department of Public Safety; and

(4) A determination whether the earnings of the offender are to be disbursed by the Division of Adult Correction and Juvenile Justice of the Department of Public Safety or the clerk of the sentencing court in the manner that the court in its order directs.

History.
1977, c. 711, s. 1; 1979, c. 758, s. 1; 1983, c. 389; 1985 (Reg. Sess., 1986), c. 1014, s. 201(c); 2011-145, s. 19.1(h); 2017-186, s. 2(rrr)

§ 15A-1354. Concurrent and consecutive terms of imprisonment

(a) **Authority of Court.** -- When multiple sentences of imprisonment are imposed on a person at the same time or when a term of imprisonment is imposed on a person who is already subject to an undischarged term of imprisonment, including a term of imprisonment in another jurisdiction, the sentences may run either concurrently or consecutively, as determined by the court. If not specified or not required by statute to run consecutively, sentences shall run concurrently.

(b) **Effect of Consecutive Terms.** -- In determining the effect of consecutive sentences imposed under authority of this Article and the manner in which they will be served, the Division of Adult Correction and Juvenile Justice of the Department of Public Safety must treat the defendant as though he has been committed for a single term with the following incidents:

(1) The maximum prison sentence consists of the total of the maximum terms of the consecutive sentences, less 12 months for each of the second and subsequent sentences imposed for Class B through Class E felonies, or less 60 months for each second or subsequent Class B1 through E felony for which the sentence was established pursuant to G.S. 15A-1340.17(f), and less nine months for each of the second and subsequent sentences imposed for Class F through Class I felonies; and

(2) The minimum term consists of the total of the minimum terms of the consecutive sentences.

History.
1977, c. 711, s. 1; 1979, c. 760, s. 4; 1979, 2nd Sess., c. 1316, s. 40; 1985, c. 21; 1994, Ex. Sess., c. 14, s. 23; 2011-145, s. 19.1(h); 2011-192, s. 2(i); 2011-307, s. 3; 2017-186, s. 2(sss)

§ 15A-1355. Calculation of terms of imprisonment

(a) **Commencement of Sentence.** -- The commencement date of a sentence of imprisonment under authority of this Article is as provided in G.S. 15A-1353(a), except when the sentence is a consecutive sentence. When it is a consecutive sentence, it commences to run when the State has custody of the defendant following completion of the prior sentence.

(b) Repealed by Session Laws 1977, 2nd Sess., c. 1147, s. 19.

(c) **Earned Time; Credit for Good Behavior for Impaired Drivers.** -- Persons convicted of felonies or misdemeanors under Article 81B of this Chapter may, consistent with rules of the Division of Adult Correction and Juvenile Justice of the Department of Public Safety, earn credit which may be used to reduce their maximum terms of imprisonment as provided in G.S. 15A-1340.13(d) for felony sentences and in G.S. 15A-1340.20(d) for misdemeanor sentences.

For sentences of imprisonment imposed for convictions of impaired driving under G.S. 20-138.1, the Division of Adult Correction and Juvenile Justice of the Department of Public Safety may give credit toward service of the maximum term and any minimum term of imprisonment and toward eligibility for parole for allowances of time as provided in rules and regulations made under G.S. 148-11 and 148-13.

(d) **Earned Time Credit for Medically and Physically Unfit Inmates.** -- Inmates in the custody of the Division of Adult Correction and Juvenile Justice of the Department of Public Safety who suffer from medical conditions or physical disabilities that prevent their assignment to work release or other rehabilitative activities may, consistent with rules of the Division of Adult Correction and Juvenile Justice of the Department of Public Safety, earn credit based upon good behavior or other criteria determined by the Division that may be used to reduce their maximum term of imprisonment as provided in G.S. 15A-1340.13(d) for felony sentences and in G.S. 15A-1340.20(d) for misdemeanor sentences.

History.
1977, c. 711, s. 1; 1977, 2nd Sess., c. 1147, s. 19; 1979, c. 749, s. 8; c. 760, s. 4; 1981, c. 571; c. 1127, s. 84; 1983, c. 560, § 1; 1993, c. 538, s. 20; 1994, Ex. Sess., c. 24, s. 14(b); 2001-424, s. 25.1(a); 2002-126, s. 17.19(d); 2002-159, s. 77; 2011-145, s. 19.1(h); 2017-186, s. 2(ttt)

§§ 15A-1356 through 15A-1360

Reserved for future codification purposes.

ARTICLE 84
FINES

§ 15A-1361. Authorized fines and penalties

A person who has been convicted of a criminal offense may be ordered to pay a fine as provided by law. A person who has been found responsible for an infraction may be ordered to pay a penalty as provided by law. Unless the context clearly requires otherwise, references in this Article to fines also include penalties.

History.
1977, c. 711, s. 1; 1985, c. 764, s. 6

§ 15A-1362. Imposition of fines

(a) **General Criteria. --** In determining the method of payment of a fine, the court should consider the burden that payment will impose in view of the financial resources of the defendant.

(b) **Installment or Delayed Payments. --** When a defendant is ordered to pay a fine, the court may provide for the payment to be made within a specified period of time or in specified installments. If no such provision is made a part of the sentence, the fine is payable forthwith.

(c) **Nonpayment. --** When a defendant is ordered, other than as a condition of probation, to pay a fine, costs, or both, the court may impose at the same time a sentence to be served in the event that the fine is not paid. The court also may impose an order that the defendant appear, if he fails to make the required payment, at a specified time to show cause why he should not be imprisoned.

History.
1977, c. 711, s. 1

§ 15A-1363. Remission of a fine or costs

A defendant who has been required to pay a fine or costs, including a requirement to pay fine or costs as a condition of probation, or a prosecutor, may at any time petition the sentencing court for a remission or revocation of the fine or costs or any unpaid portion of it. If it appears to the satisfaction of the court that the circumstances which warranted the imposition of the fine or costs no longer exist, that it would otherwise be unjust to require payment, or that the proper administration of justice requires resolution of the case, the court may remit or revoke the fine or costs or the unpaid portion in whole or in part or may modify the method of payment.

History.
1977, c. 711, s. 1

§ 15A-1364. Response to nonpayment

(a) **Response to Default. --** When a defendant who has been required to pay a fine or costs or both defaults in payment or in any installment, the court, upon the motion of the prosecutor or upon its own motion, may require the defendant to appear and show cause why he should not be imprisoned or may rely upon a conditional show cause order entered under G.S. 15A-1362(c). If the defendant fails to appear, an order for his arrest may be issued.

(b) **Imprisonment; Criteria. --** Following a requirement to show cause under subsection (a), unless the defendant shows inability to comply and that his nonpayment was not attributable to a failure on his part to make a good faith effort to obtain the necessary funds for payment, the court may order the suspended sentence, if any, activated, or, if the law provides no term of imprisonment for the offense for which the defendant was convicted or if no suspended sentence was imposed, the court may order the defendant imprisoned for a term not to exceed 30 days. The court, before activating a sentence of imprisonment, may reduce the sentence. The court may provide in its order that payment or satisfaction at any time of the fine and costs imposed by the court will entitle the defendant to his release from the imprisonment or, after entering the order, may at any time reduce the sentence for good cause shown, including payment or satisfaction of the fine.

(c) **Modification of Fine or Costs. --** If it appears that the default in the payment of a fine or costs is not attributable to failure on the defendant's part to make a good faith effort to obtain the necessary funds for payment, the court may enter an order:

(1) Allowing the defendant additional time for payment; or

(2) Reducing the amount of the fine or costs or of each installment; or

(3) Revoking the fine or costs or the unpaid portion in whole or in part.

(d) **Organizations. --** When an organization is required to pay a fine or costs or both, it is the duty of the person or persons authorized to make disbursement of the assets of the organization to make payment from assets of the organization, and a failure to do so constitutes contempt of court.

History.
1977, c. 711, s. 1

§ 15A-1365. Judgment for fines docketed; lien and execution

When a defendant has defaulted in payment of a fine or costs, the judge may order that the judgment be docketed. Upon being docketed, the judgment becomes a lien on the real estate of the defendant in the same manner as do judgments in civil actions. Executions on docketed judgments may be stayed only when an appeal is taken and security is given as required in civil cases. If the judgment is affirmed on appeal to the appellate division, the clerk of the superior court, on receipt of the certificate from the appellate division, must issue execution on the judgment. The clerk may not issue an execution, however, if the fine or costs were imposed for an offense other than trafficking in controlled substances or conspiring to traffic in controlled substances under G.S. 90-95(h) and (i), respectively, and the defendant elects to serve the suspended sentence, if any, or serve a term of 30 days, if no suspended sentence was imposed.

History.
1977, c. 711, s. 1; 1985, c. 411

§§ 15A-1366, 15A-1367

Reserved for future codification purposes.

ARTICLE 84A
POST-RELEASE SUPERVISION

§ 15A-1368. Definitions and administration

(a) The following words have the listed meaning in this Article:

(1) **Post-release supervision or supervision.** -- The time for which a sentenced prisoner is released from prison before the termination of his maximum prison term, controlled by the rules and conditions of this Article. Purposes of post-release supervision include all or any of the following: to monitor and control the prisoner in the community, to assist the prisoner in reintegrating into society, to collect restitution and other court indebtedness from the prisoner, and to continue the prisoner's treatment or education.

(2) **Supervisee.** -- A person released from incarceration and in the custody of the Division of Adult Correction and Juvenile Justice of the Department of Public Safety and Post-Release Supervision and Parole Commission on post-release supervision.

(3) **Commission.** -- The Post-Release Supervision and Parole Commission, whose general authority is described in G.S. 143B-720.

(4) **Minimum imposed term.** -- The minimum term of imprisonment imposed on an individual prisoner by a court judgment, as described in G.S. 15A-1340.13(c). When a prisoner is serving consecutive imprisonment terms, the minimum imposed term, for purposes of this Article, is the sum of all minimum terms imposed in the court judgment.

(5) **Maximum imposed term.** -- The maximum term of imprisonment imposed on an individual prisoner by a court judgment,

as described in G.S. 15A-1340.13(c). When a prisoner is serving consecutive prison terms, the maximum imposed term, for purposes of this Article, is the sum of all maximum terms imposed in the court judgment or judgments, less 12 months for each of the second and subsequent sentences imposed for Class B through Class E felonies, or less 60 months for each second or subsequent Class B1 through E felony for which the sentence was established pursuant to G.S. 15A-1340.17(f), and less nine months for each of the second and subsequent sentences imposed for Class F through Class I felonies.

(b) **Administration.** -- The Post-Release Supervision and Parole Commission, as authorized in Chapter 143 of the General Statutes, shall administer post-release supervision as provided in this Article.

History.
1993, c. 538, s. 20.1; 1994, Ex. Sess., c. 14, ss. 24, 25; c. 24, s. 14(b); 1997-237, s. 2; 2011-145, s. 19.1(h); 2011-192, s. 2(h); 2011-307, s. 4; 2017-186, s. 2(uuu)

§ 15A-1368.1. Applicability of Article 84A

This Article applies to all felons sentenced to an active punishment under Article 81B of this Chapter or G.S. 90-95(h), but does not apply to felons in Class A and Class B1 sentenced to life imprisonment without parole. Prisoners subject to Articles 85 and 85A of this Chapter are excluded from this Article's coverage.

History.
1993, c. 538, s. 20.1; 1994, Ex. Sess., c. 14, s. 26; c. 22, s. 8; c. 24, s. 14(b); 2011-192, s. 2(a); 2012-188, s. 6

§ 15A-1368.2. Post-release supervision eligibility and procedure

(a) Except as otherwise provided in this subsection, a prisoner to whom this Article applies shall be released from prison for post-release supervision on the date equivalent to his maximum imposed prison term less 12 months in the case of Class B1 through E felons and less nine months in the case of Class F through I felons, less any earned time awarded by the Division of Adult Correction and Juvenile Justice of the Department of Public Safety or the custodian of a local confinement facility under G.S. 15A-1340.13(d). A prisoner whose maximum sentence is established pursuant to G.S. 15A-1340.17(f) shall be released from prison for post-release supervision on the date equivalent to his or her maximum imposed prison term less 60 months, less any earned time awarded by the Division of Adult Correction and Juvenile Justice of the Department of Public Safety or the custodian of a local confinement facility under G.S. 15A-1340.13(d). If a prisoner has not been awarded any earned time, the prisoner shall be released for post-release supervision on the date equivalent to his maximum prison term less 12 months for Class B1 through E felons and less nine months for Class F through I felons.

(b) A prisoner shall not refuse post-release supervision. Willful refusal to accept post-release supervision or to comply with the terms of post-release supervision by a prisoner whose offense requiring post-release supervision is a reportable conviction subject to the registration requirement of Article 27A of Chapter 14 of the General Statutes, is punishable as contempt of court under G.S. 5A-11 and may result in imprisonment under G.S. 5A-12. Furthermore, any period of time during which a prisoner whose offense requiring post-release supervision is a reportable conviction subject to the registration requirement of Article 27A of Chapter 14 of the General Statutes is not in fact released pursuant to subsection (a) of this section due to the prisoner's resistance to that release shall toll the running of the period of supervised release imposed by subsection (c) of this section. For purposes of this subsection and the provisions of G.S. 5A-11, "willful refusal to accept post-release supervision or to comply with the terms of post-release supervision" includes, but is not limited to, knowingly violating the terms of post-release supervision in order to be returned to prison to serve out the remainder of the prisoner's sentence. Notwithstanding any other provision of law, a prisoner punished for the offense of contempt of court under this subsection is not eligible for credit for time served against the sentence for which the prisoner is subject to post-release supervision. Punishment by contempt for willful refusal to accept post-release supervision or to comply with the terms of post-release supervision does not preclude the application of any other sanction provided by law for the same conduct.

(c) A supervisee's period of post-release supervision shall be for a period of 12 months in the case of Class B1 through E felons and nine months in the case of Class F through I felons, unless the offense is an offense for which registration is required pursuant to Article 27A of Chapter 14 of the General Statutes. For offenses subject to the registration requirement of Article 27A of Chapter 14 of the General Statutes, the period of post-release supervision is five years. The conditions of post-release supervision are as authorized in G.S. 15A-1368.5.

(c1) Notwithstanding subsection (c) of this section, a person required to submit to satellite-based monitoring pursuant to G.S. 15A-1368.4(b1)(6) shall continue to participate in satellite-based monitoring beyond the period of post-release supervision until the Commission releases the person from that requirement pursuant to G.S. 14-208.43.

(d) A supervisee's period of post-release supervision may be reduced while the supervisee is under supervision by earned time awarded by the Division of Adult Correction and Juvenile Justice of the Department of Public Safety, pursuant to rules adopted in accordance with law. A supervisee is eligible to receive earned time credit toward the period of supervision for compliance with reintegrative conditions described in G.S. 15A-1368.5.

(e) Repealed by Session Laws 1997-237, s. 7.

(f) When a supervisee completes the period of post-release supervision, the sentence or sentences from which the supervisee was placed on post-release supervision are terminated.

History.
1993, c. 538, s. 20.1; 1994, Ex. Sess., c. 24, s. 14(b); 1993 (Reg. Sess., 1994), c. 767, s. 4; 1996, 2nd Ex. Sess., c. 18, s. 20.14(a); 1997-237, s. 7; 2006-247, s. 15(f); 2011-145, s. 19.1(h); 2011-192, s. 2(b); 2011-307, ss. 2, 5; 2017-186, s. 2(vvv)

§ 15A-1368.3. Incidents of post-release supervision

(a) **Conditionality. --** Post-release supervision is conditional and subject to revocation.

(b) **Modification. --** The Commission may for good cause shown modify the conditions of post-release supervision at any time before the termination of the supervision period.

(c) **Effect of Violation. --** If the supervisee violates a condition, described in G.S. 15A-1368.4, at any time before the termination of the supervision period, the Commission may continue the supervisee on the existing supervision, with or without modifying the conditions, or if continuation or modification is not appropriate, may revoke post-release supervision as provided in G.S. 15A-1368.6 and reimprison the supervisee for a term consistent with the following requirements:

(1) Supervisees who were convicted of an offense for which registration is required under Article 27A of Chapter 14 of the General Statutes and supervisees whose supervision is revoked for a violation of the required controlling condition under G.S. 15A-1368.4(b) or for absconding in violation of G.S. 15A-1368.4(e)(7a) will be returned to prison up to the time remaining on their maximum imposed terms. All other supervisees will be returned to prison for three months and may be returned for three months on each of two subsequent violations, after which supervisees who were Class B1 through E felons may be returned to prison up to the time remaining on their

maximum imposed terms. Reimprisonment for a violation under this subdivision tolls the running of the period of supervised release, except that a supervisee shall not be rereleased on post-release supervision if the supervisee has served all the time remaining on the supervisee's maximum imposed term.

(2) The supervisee shall not receive any credit for days on post-release supervision against the maximum term of imprisonment imposed by the court under G.S. 15A-1340.13.

(3) Pursuant to Article 19A of Chapter 15, the Division of Adult Correction and Juvenile Justice of the Department of Public Safety shall award a prisoner credit against any term of reimprisonment for all time spent in custody as a result of revocation proceedings under G.S. 15A-1368.6, unless as a result of a violation of the conditions, the supervisee is returned to prison for a three-month period. The three-month period shall not be reduced by credit for time already served. Any such credit shall be applied toward the maximum prison term.

(4) The prisoner is eligible to receive earned time credit against the maximum prison term as provided in G.S. 15A-1340.13(d) for time served in prison after the revocation.

(d) **Re-Release After Revocation of Post-Release Supervision.** -- A prisoner who has been reimprisoned prior to completing a post-release supervision period may again be released on post-release supervision by the Commission subject to the provisions which govern initial release.

(e) **Timing of Revocation.** -- The Commission may revoke post-release supervision for violation of a condition during the period of supervision. The Commission may also revoke post-release supervision following a period of supervision if:

(1) Before the expiration of the period of post-release supervision, the Commission has recorded its intent to conduct a revocation hearing; and

(2) The Commission finds that every reasonable effort has been made to notify the supervisee and conduct the hearing earlier. Prima facie evidence of reasonable effort to notify is the issuance of a temporary or conditional revocation order, as provided in G.S. 15A-1376, that goes unserved.

History.
1993, c. 538, s. 20.1; 1994, Ex. Sess., c. 14, s. 27; c. 24, s. 14(b); 1993 (Reg. Sess., 1994), c. 767, s. 5; 2011-145, s. 19.1(h); 2011-192, s. 2(d); 2012-188, s. 4; 2016-77, s. 2; 2017-186, s. 2(www)

§ 15A-1368.4. Conditions of post-release supervision

(a) **In General.** -- Conditions of post-release supervision may be reintegrative in nature or designed to control the supervisee's behavior and to enforce compliance with law or judicial order. A supervisee may have his supervision period revoked for any violation of a controlling condition or for repeated violation of a reintegrative condition. Compliance with reintegrative conditions may entitle a supervisee to earned time credits as described in G.S. 15A-1368.2(d).

(b) **Required Condition.** -- The Commission shall provide as an express condition of every release that the supervisee not commit another crime during the period for which the supervisee remains subject to revocation. A supervisee's failure to comply with this controlling condition is a supervision violation for which the supervisee may face revocation as provided in G.S. 15A-1368.3.

(b1) **Additional Required Conditions for Sex Offenders and Persons Convicted of Offenses Involving Physical, Mental, or Sexual Abuse of a Minor.** -- In addition to the required condition set forth in subsection (b) of this section, for a supervisee who has been convicted of an offense which is a reportable conviction as defined in G.S. 14-208.6(4), or which involves the physical, mental, or sexual abuse of a minor, controlling conditions, violations of which may result in revocation of post-release supervision, are:

(1) Register as required by G.S. 14-208.7 if the offense is a reportable conviction as defined by G.S. 14-208.6(4).

(2) Participate in such evaluation and treatment as is necessary to complete a prescribed course of psychiatric, psychological, or other rehabilitative treatment as ordered by the Commission.

(3) Not communicate with, be in the presence of, or found in or on the premises of the victim of the offense.

(4) Not reside in a household with any minor child if the offense is one in which there is evidence of sexual abuse of a minor.

(5) Not reside in a household with any minor child if the offense is one in which there is evidence of physical or mental abuse of a minor, unless a court of competent jurisdiction expressly finds that it is unlikely that the defendant's harmful or abusive conduct will recur and that it would be in the child's best interest to allow the supervisee to reside in the same household with a minor child.

(6) Submit to satellite-based monitoring pursuant to Part 5 of Article 27A of Chapter 14 of the General Statutes, if the offense is a reportable conviction as defined

by G.S. 14-208.6(4), the supervisee is in the category described by G.S. 14-208.40(a)(1), and based on the Division of Adult Correction and Juvenile Justice's risk assessment program requires the highest possible level of supervision and monitoring.

(7) Submit to satellite-based monitoring pursuant to Part 5 of Article 27A of Chapter 14 of the General Statutes, if the offense is a reportable conviction as defined by G.S. 14-208.6(4), the supervisee is in the category described by G.S. 14-208.40(a)(2), and based on the Division of Adult Correction and Juvenile Justice's risk assessment program requires the highest possible level of supervision and monitoring.

(8) Submit at reasonable times to warrantless searches by a post-release supervision officer of the supervisee's person and of the supervisee's vehicle and premises while the supervisee is present, for purposes reasonably related to the post-release supervision, but the supervisee may not be required to submit to any other search that would otherwise be unlawful. For purposes of this subdivision, warrantless searches of the supervisee's computer or other electronic mechanism which may contain electronic data shall be considered reasonably related to the post-release supervision. Whenever the warrantless search consists of testing for the presence of illegal drugs, the supervisee may also be required to reimburse the Division of Adult Correction and Juvenile Justice of the Department of Public Safety for the actual cost of drug screening and drug testing, if the results are positive.

(c) **Discretionary Conditions.** -- The Commission, in consultation with the Section of Community Corrections of the Division of Adult Correction and Juvenile Justice, may impose conditions on a supervisee it believes reasonably necessary to ensure that the supervisee will lead a law-abiding life or to assist the supervisee to do so. The Commission may also impose a condition of community service on a supervisee who was a Class F through I felon and who has failed to fully satisfy any order for restitution, reparation, or costs imposed against the supervisee as part of the supervisee's sentence; however, the Commission shall not impose such a condition of community service if the Commission determines, upon inquiry, that the supervisee has the financial resources to satisfy the order.

(c1) Repealed by Session Laws 2013-196, s. 2, effective June 26, 2013.

(d) **Reintegrative Conditions.** -- Appropriate reintegrative conditions, for which a supervisee may receive earned time credits against the length of the supervision period, and

repeated violation that may result in revocation of post-release supervision, are:

(1) Work faithfully at suitable employment or faithfully pursue a course of study or vocational training that will equip the supervisee for suitable employment.

(2) Undergo available medical or psychiatric treatment and remain in a specified institution if required for that purpose.

(3) Attend or reside in a facility providing rehabilitation, instruction, recreation, or residence for persons on post-release supervision.

(4) Support the supervisee's dependents and meet other family responsibilities.

(5) In the case of a supervisee who attended a basic skills program during incarceration, continue attending a basic skills program in pursuit of an adult high school equivalency diploma or adult high school diploma.

(6) Satisfy other conditions reasonably related to reintegration into society.

(e) **Controlling Conditions.** -- Appropriate controlling conditions, violation of which may result in revocation of post-release supervision, are:

(1) Not use, possess, or control any illegal drug or controlled substance unless it has been prescribed for the supervisee by a licensed physician and is in the original container with the prescription number affixed on it; not knowingly associate with any known or previously convicted users, possessors, or sellers of any such illegal drugs or controlled substances; and not knowingly be present at or frequent any place where such illegal drugs or controlled substances are sold, kept, or used.

(2) Comply with a court order to pay the costs of reintegrative treatment for a minor and a minor's parents or custodians where the offense involved evidence of physical, mental, or sexual abuse of a minor.

(3) Comply with a court order to pay court costs and costs for appointed counsel or public defender in the case for which the supervisee was convicted.

(4) Not possess a firearm, destructive device, or other dangerous weapon unless granted written permission by the Commission or a post-release supervision officer.

(5) Report to a post-release supervision officer at reasonable times and in a reasonable manner, as directed by the Commission or a post-release supervision officer.

(6) Permit a post-release supervision officer to visit at reasonable times at the supervisee's home or elsewhere.

(7) Remain within the geographic limits fixed by the Commission unless granted written permission to leave by the

Commission or the post-release supervision officer.

(7a) Not to abscond, by willfully avoiding supervision or by willfully making the supervisee's whereabouts unknown to the supervising probation officer.

(8) Answer all reasonable inquiries by the post-release supervision officer and obtain prior approval from the post-release supervision officer for any change in address or employment.

(9) Promptly notify the post-release supervision officer of any change in address or employment.

(10) Submit at reasonable times to searches of the supervisee's person by a post-release supervision officer for purposes reasonably related to the post-release supervision. The Commission shall not require as a condition of post-release supervision that the supervisee submit to any other searches that would otherwise be unlawful. Whenever the search consists of testing for the presence of illegal drugs, the supervisee may also be required to reimburse the Division of Adult Correction and Juvenile Justice of the Department of Public Safety for the actual cost of drug testing and drug screening, if the results are positive.

(11) Make restitution or reparation to an aggrieved party as provided in G.S. 148-57.1.

(12) Comply with an order from a court of competent jurisdiction regarding the payment of an obligation of the supervisee in connection with any judgment rendered by the court.

(13) Remain in one or more specified places for a specified period or periods each day, and wear a device that permits the defendant's compliance with the condition to be monitored electronically and pay a fee of ninety dollars ($ 90.00) for the electronic monitoring device and a daily fee in an amount that reflects the actual cost of providing the electronic monitoring. The Commission may exempt a person from paying the fees only for a good cause. Fees collected under this subsection for the electronic monitoring device shall be transmitted to the State for deposit in the State's General Fund. The daily fees collected under this subsection shall be remitted to the Department of Public Safety to cover the costs of providing the electronic monitoring.

(14) Repealed by Session Laws 2013-101, s. 1, effective June 12, 2013.

(e1) **Prohibited Conditions.** -- The Commission shall not impose community service as a condition of post-release supervision.

(f) **Required Supervision Fee.** -- The Commission shall require as a condition of post-release supervision that the supervisee pay a supervision fee of forty dollars ($ 40.00) per month. The Commission may exempt a supervisee from this condition only if it finds that requiring payment of the fee is an undue economic burden. The fee shall be paid to the clerk of superior court of the county in which the supervisee was convicted. The clerk shall transmit any money collected pursuant to this subsection to the State to be deposited in the State's General Fund. In no event shall a supervisee be required to pay more than one supervision fee per month.

History.

1993, c. 538, s. 20.1; 1994, Ex. Sess., c. 24, s. 14(b); 1996, 2nd Ex. Sess., c. 18, s. 20.14(b); 1997-57, s. 6; 1997-237, s. 6; 2001-487, s. 47(c); 2002-126, s. 29A.2(b); 2006-247, s. 15(g); 2007-213, s. 9; 2010-31, s. 19.3(b); 2011-145, s. 19.1(h), (k); 2011-192, s. 2(c); 2013-101, s. 2; 2013-196, s. 1; 2013-363, s. 6.7(b); 2014-115, s. 28(a); 2017-186, s. 2(xxx); 2021-138, s. 18(m)

§ 15A-1368.5. Commencement of post-release supervision; multiple sentences

A period of post-release supervision begins on the day the prisoner is released from imprisonment. Periods of post-release supervision run concurrently with any federal or State prison, jail, probation, or parole terms to which the prisoner is subject during the period, only if the jurisdiction which sentenced the prisoner to prison, jail, probation, or parole permits concurrent crediting of supervision time.

History.

1993, c. 538, s. 20.1; 1994, Ex. Sess., c. 24, s. 14(b)

§ 15A-1368.6. Arrest and hearing on post-release supervision violation

(a) **Arrest for Violation of Post-Release Supervision.** -- A supervisee is subject to arrest by a law enforcement officer or a post-release supervision officer for violation of conditions of post-release supervision only upon issuance of an order of temporary or conditional revocation of post-release supervision by the Commission. However, a post-release supervision revocation hearing under subsection (e) of this section may be held without first arresting the supervisee.

(b) **When and Where Preliminary Hearing on Post-Release Supervision Violation Required.** -- Unless the hearing required by subsection (e) of this section is first held or a continuance is requested by the supervisee, a preliminary hearing on supervision violation shall be held reasonably near the place of the alleged violation or arrest and within seven working days of the arrest of a supervisee to determine whether there is probable cause to believe that the supervisee violated a condition of post-release supervision. The preliminary hearing for violations of post-release supervision may be conducted by videoconference. Otherwise, the supervisee shall be released seven working days after arrest to continue on supervision pending a hearing. If the supervisee is not within the State, the preliminary hearing is as prescribed by G.S. 148-65.1A.

(b1) **Bail Following Arrest for Violation of Post-Release Supervision if Releasee Is a Sex Offender.** -- Notwithstanding subsection (b) of this section, if the releasee has been convicted of an offense that requires registration under Article 27A of Chapter 14 of the General Statutes and is arrested for a violation in accordance with this section, the releasee shall be detained without bond until the preliminary hearing is conducted.

(c) **Officers to Conduct Preliminary Hearing.** -- The preliminary hearing on post-release supervision violation shall be conducted by a judicial official, or by a hearing officer designated by the Commission. A person employed by the Division of Adult Correction and Juvenile Justice of the Department of Public Safety shall not serve as a hearing officer at a hearing provided by this section unless that person is a member of the Commission, or is employed solely as a hearing officer.

(d) **Procedure for Preliminary Hearing.** -- The Division of Adult Correction and Juvenile Justice of the Department of Public Safety shall give the supervisee notice of the preliminary hearing and its purpose, including a statement of the violations alleged. At the hearing, the supervisee may appear and speak in the supervisee's own behalf, may present relevant information, and may, on request, personally question witnesses and adverse informants, unless the hearing officer finds good cause for not allowing confrontation. If the person holding the hearing determines there is probable cause to believe the supervisee violated conditions of supervision, the hearing officer shall summarize the reasons for the determination and the evidence relied on. Formal rules of evidence do not apply at the hearing. If probable cause is found, the supervisee may be held in the custody of the Division of Adult Correction and Juvenile Justice of the Department of Public Safety to serve the appropriate term of imprisonment, subject to the outcome of a revocation hearing under subsection (e) of this section.

(e) **Revocation Hearing.** -- Before finally revoking post-release supervision, the Commission shall, unless the supervisee waived the hearing or the time limit, provide a hearing within 45 days of the supervisee's reconfinement to determine whether to revoke supervision finally. For purposes of this subsection, the 45-day period begins when the preliminary hearing required by subsection (b) of this section is held or waived, or upon the passage of seven working days after arrest, whichever is sooner. The revocation hearing for violations of post-release supervision may be conducted by videoconference. The Commission shall adopt rules governing the hearing.

History.
1993, c. 538, s. 20.1; 1994, Ex. Sess., c. 24, s. 14(b); 1996, 2nd Ex. Sess., c. 18, s. 20.15(b); 1997-237, s. 1; 2000-189, s. 1; 2008-117, s. 20; 2011-145, s. 19.1(h); 2016-77, s. 4(b); 2017-186, s. 2(yyy).

ARTICLE 84B
MEDICAL RELEASE OF INMATES

§ 15A-1369. Definitions

For purposes of this Article, the term:

(1) "Commission" means the Post-Release Supervision and Parole Commission.

(2) "Division" means the Division of Adult Correction and Juvenile Justice of the Department of Public Safety.

(3) "Geriatric" describes an inmate who is 65 years of age or older and suffers from chronic infirmity, illness, or disease related to aging that has progressed such that the inmate is incapacitated to the extent that he or she does not pose a public safety risk.

(4) "Inmate" means any person sentenced to the custody of the Division of Adult Correction and Juvenile Justice of the Department of Public Safety.

(5) "Medical release" means a program enabling the Commission to release inmates who are permanently and totally disabled, terminally ill, or geriatric.

(6) "Medical release plan" means a comprehensive written medical and psychosocial care plan that is specific to the inmate and includes, at a minimum:

a. The proposed course of treatment;

b. The proposed site for treatment and post-treatment care;

c. Documentation that medical providers qualified to provide the medical services identified in the medical release plan are prepared to provide those services; and

d. The financial program in place to cover the cost of this plan for the duration of the medical release, which shall include eligibility for enrollment in commercial insurance, Medicare, or Medicaid or access to other adequate financial resources for the duration of the medical release.

(7) "Permanently and totally disabled" describes an inmate who, as determined by a licensed physician, suffers from permanent and irreversible physical incapacitation as a result of an existing physical or medical condition that was unknown at the time of sentencing or, since the time of sentencing, has progressed to render the inmate permanently and totally disabled, such that the inmate does not pose a public safety risk.

(8) "Terminally ill" describes an inmate who, as determined by a licensed physician, has an incurable condition caused by illness or disease that was unknown at the time of sentencing or, since the time of sentencing, has progressed to render the inmate terminally ill, and that will likely produce death within six months, and that is so debilitating such that the inmate does not pose a public safety risk.

History.
2008-2, s. 1; 2011-145, s. 19.1(h); 2017-186, s. 2(zzz)

§ 15A-1369.1. Authority to release

The Commission shall establish a medical release program to be administered by the Division. The Commission shall prescribe when and under what conditions an inmate may be released for medical release, consistent with the provisions of G.S. 15A-1369.4. The Commission may adopt rules to implement the medical release program.

History.
2008-2, s. 1; 2011-145, s. 19.1(h)

§ 15A-1369.2. Eligibility

(a) Except as otherwise provided in this section, notwithstanding any other provision of law, an inmate is eligible to be considered for medical release if the Division determines that the inmate is:

(1) Diagnosed as permanently and totally disabled, terminally ill, or geriatric under the procedure described in G.S. 15A-1369.3(b)(1); and

(2) Incapacitated to the extent that the inmate does not pose a public safety risk.

(b) Persons convicted of a capital felony or a Class A, B1, or B2 felony and persons convicted of an offense that requires registration under Article 27A of Chapter 14 of the General Statutes shall not be eligible for release under this Article.

History.
2008-2, s. 1; 2011-145, s. 19.1(h)

§ 15A-1369.3. Procedure for medical release

(a) The Commission shall consider an inmate for medical release upon referral by the Division. The Division may base its referral upon either a request or petition for release filed by the inmate, the inmate's attorney, or the inmate's next of kin or upon a recommendation from within the Division.

(b) The referral shall include an assessment of the inmate's medical and psychosocial condition and the risk the inmate poses to society, as follows:

(1) The Division medical director, or a designee of the director who is a licensed physician, shall review the case of each inmate who meets the eligibility requirements for medical release set forth in G.S. 15A-1369.2. Any physician who examines an inmate being considered for medical release shall prepare a written diagnosis that includes:

a. A description of any and all terminal conditions, physical incapacities, and chronic conditions; and

b. A prognosis concerning the likelihood of recovery from any and all terminal conditions, physical incapacities, and chronic conditions.

(2) The Division shall make an assessment of the risk for violence and recidivism that the inmate poses to society. In order to make this assessment, the Division may consider such factors as the inmate's medical condition, the severity of the offense for which the inmate is incarcerated, the inmate's prison record, and the release plan.

(c) If the Division determines that the inmate meets the criteria for release, the Division shall forward its referral and medical release plan for the inmate to the Commission. The Division shall complete the risk assessment and forward its referral and medical release plan within 45 days of receiving a request, petition, or recommendation for release.

(d) The Commission shall make a determination of whether to grant medical release within 15 days of receiving a referral from the Division for release of a terminally ill inmate and within 20 days of receiving a referral from the Division for release of a permanently and totally disabled inmate or a geriatric inmate. In making the determination, the Commission shall make an independent assessment of the risk for violence and recidivism that the inmate poses to society. The Commission also shall provide the victim or victims of the inmate or the victims' family or families with an opportunity to be heard.

(e) A denial of medical release by the Commission shall not affect an inmate's eligibility for any other form of parole or release under applicable law.

(f) If the Division determines that an inmate should not be considered for release under this Article or the Commission denies medical release under this Article, the inmate may not reapply or be reconsidered unless there is a demonstrated change in the inmate's medical condition.

History.
2008-2, s. 1; 2011-145, s. 19.1(h)

§ 15A-1369.4. Conditions of medical release

(a) The Commission shall set reasonable conditions upon an inmate's medical release that shall apply through the date upon which the inmate's sentence would have expired. These conditions shall include:

(1) That the released inmate's care be consistent with the care specified in the medical release plan as approved by the Commission;

(2) That the released inmate shall cooperate with and comply with the prescribed medical release plan and with reasonable requirements of medical providers to whom the released inmate is to be referred to continued treatment;

(3) That the released inmate shall be subject to supervision by the Section of Community Corrections of the Division of Adult Correction and Juvenile Justice and shall permit officers from the Division to visit the inmate at reasonable times at the inmate's home or elsewhere;

(4) That the released inmate shall comply with any conditions of release set by the Commission; and

(5) That the Commission shall receive periodic assessments from the inmate's treating physician.

(b) The Commission shall promptly order an inmate returned to the custody of the Division to await a revocation hearing if the Commission receives credible information that an inmate has failed to comply with any reasonable condition set upon the inmate's release. If the Commission subsequently revokes an inmate's medical release for failure to comply with conditions of release, the inmate shall resume serving the balance of the sentence with credit given only for the duration of the inmate's medical release served in compliance with all reasonable conditions set forth pursuant to subsection (a) of this section. Revocation of an inmate's medical release for violating a condition of release shall not preclude an inmate's eligibility for any other form of parole or release provided by law but may be used as a factor in determining eligibility for that parole or release.

History.
2008-2, s. 1; 2011-145, s. 19.1(h), (k); 2017-186, s. 2 (aaaa)

§ 15A-1369.5. Change in medical status

(a) If a periodic medical assessment reveals that an inmate released on medical release has improved so that the inmate would not be eligible for medical release if being considered at that time, the Commission shall order the inmate returned to the custody of the Division to await a revocation hearing. In determining whether to revoke medical release, the Commission shall consider the most recent medical assessment of the inmate and a risk assessment of the inmate conducted pursuant to G.S. 15A-1369.3(b)(2). If the Commission revokes the inmate's medical release, the inmate shall resume serving the balance of the sentence with credit given for the duration of the medical release.

(b) Revocation of an inmate's medical release due to a change in the inmate's medical condition shall not preclude an inmate's eligibility for medical release in the future or for any other form of parole or release provided by law.

History.
2008-2, s. 1; 2011-145, s. 19.1(h)

N.C. Gen. Stat. § 15A-1370

Reserved for future codification purposes.

ARTICLE 85
PAROLE

§ 15A-1370.1. Applicability of Article 85

This Article is applicable to all prisoners serving sentences of imprisonment for convictions of impaired driving under G.S. 20-138.1. This Article does not apply to a prisoner serving a sentence of life imprisonment without parole. A prisoner serving a sentence of life imprisonment without parole shall not be eligible for parole at any time.

History.
1979, c. 760, s. 4; 1979, 2nd Sess., c. 1316, s. 41; 1981, c. 662, s. 3; 1993, c. 538, s. 21; 1994, Ex. Sess., c. 21, s. 2; c. 22, ss. 33, 34; c. 24, s. 14(b)

§ 15A-1371. Parole eligibility, consideration, and refusal

(a) **Eligibility.** -- Unless his sentence includes a minimum sentence, a prisoner serving a term of imprisonment for a conviction of impaired driving under G.S. 20-138.1 other than one included in a sentence of special probation imposed under authority of this Subchapter is eligible for release on parole at any time. A prisoner whose sentence includes a minimum term of imprisonment imposed under authority of this Subchapter is eligible for release on parole only upon completion of the service of that minimum term or one fifth of the maximum penalty allowed by law for the offense for which the prisoner is sentenced, whichever is less, less any credit allowed under G.S. 15A-1355(c) and Article 19A of Chapter 15 of the General Statutes. A prisoner sentenced under the Fair Sentencing Act for a Class D through Class J felony, who meets the criteria established pursuant to this section, is eligible for parole consideration after completion of the service of at least 20 years imprisonment less any credit allowed under applicable State law.

(a1) Repealed by Session Laws 1994, Ex. Sess., c. 21, s. 3.

(b) (1), (2) Repealed by Session Laws 1993, c. 538, s. 22.

(3) Whenever the Post-Release Supervision and Parole Commission will be considering for parole a prisoner serving a sentence of life imprisonment the Commission must notify, at least 30 days in advance of considering the parole, by first class mail at the last known address:

a. The prisoner;

b. The district attorney of the district where the prisoner was convicted;

c. The head of the law enforcement agency that arrested the prisoner and the sheriff of the county where the crime occurred;

d. Any of the victim's immediate family members who have requested in writing to be notified; and

e. Repealed by Session Laws 1993, c. 538, s. 22.

f. As many newspapers of general circulation and other media in the county where the defendant was convicted and if different, in the county where the prisoner was charged, as reasonable. The Commission may elect to use electronic means rather than the mail to notify the media under this subsubdivision if such notification would be more timely and cost-effective.

The Post-Release Supervision and Parole Commission must consider any information provided by any such parties before consideration of parole. The Commission must also give the district attorney, the head of the law enforcement agency who has requested in writing to be notified, the victim, any member of the victim's immediate family who has requested to be notified, and as many newspapers of general circulation and other media in the county or counties designated in sub-subdivision f. of this section as reasonable, written notice of its decision within 10 days of that decision. The Commission may elect to use electronic means rather than the mail to notify the media under this paragraph if such notification would be more timely and cost-effective. The Parole Commission shall not, however, include the name of any victim in its notification to the newspapers and other media.

(c) Repealed by Session Laws 1993, c. 538, s. 22.

(d) **Criteria.** -- The Post-Release Supervision and Parole Commission may refuse to release on parole a prisoner it is considering for parole if it believes:

(1) There is a substantial risk that he will not conform to reasonable conditions of parole; or

(2) His release at that time would unduly depreciate the seriousness of his crime or promote disrespect for law; or

(3) His continued correctional treatment, medical care, or vocational or other training in the institution will substantially enhance his capacity to lead a law-abiding life if he is released at a later date; or

(4) There is a substantial risk that he would engage in further criminal conduct.

(e) **Refusal of Parole.** -- A prisoner who has been granted parole may elect to refuse parole and to serve the remainder of his term of imprisonment.

(f) Repealed by Session Laws 1993, c. 538, s. 22.

(g) Notwithstanding the provisions of subsection (a), a prisoner serving a sentence of not less than 30 days nor as great as 18 months for impaired driving may be released on parole when he completes service of one-third of his maximum sentence unless the Post-Release Supervision and Parole Commission finds in writing that:

(1) There is a substantial risk that he will not conform to reasonable conditions of parole; or

(2) His release at that time would unduly depreciate the seriousness of his crime or promote disrespect for law; or

(3) His continued correctional treatment, medical care, or vocational or other training in the institution will substantially enhance his capacity to lead a law-abiding life if he is released at a later date; or

(4) There is a substantial risk that he would engage in further criminal conduct.

If a prisoner is released on parole by operation of this subsection, the term of parole is the unserved portion of the sentence to imprisonment, and the conditions of parole, unless otherwise specified by the Post-Release Supervision and Parole Commission, are those authorized in G.S. 15A-1374(b)(4) through (10).

In order that the Post-Release Supervision and Parole Commission may have an adequate opportunity to make a determination whether parole under this section should be denied, no prisoner eligible for parole under this subsection shall be released from confinement prior to the fifth full working day after he shall have been placed in the custody of the Secretary of Public Safety or the custodian of a local confinement facility.

(h) **Community Service Parole.** -- Notwithstanding the provisions of any other subsection herein, prisoners serving sentences for impaired driving shall be eligible for community service parole after serving the minimum sentence required by G.S. 20-179, in the discretion of the Post-Release Supervision and Parole Commission.

Community service parole is early parole for the purpose of participation in community service under the supervision of the Section of Community Corrections of the Division of Adult Correction and Juvenile Justice. A parolee who is paroled under this subsection must perform as a condition of parole community service in an amount and over a period of time to be determined by the Post-Release Supervision and Parole Commission. However, the total amount of community service shall not exceed an amount equal to 32 hours for each month of active service remaining in his minimum sentence. The Post-Release Supervision and Parole Commission may grant early parole under this section without requiring the performance of community service if it determines that such performance is inappropriate to a particular case.

The probation/parole officer and the judicial services coordinator shall develop a program of community service for the parolee. The coordinator shall report any willful failure to perform community service work to the probation/parole officer. Parole may be revoked for any parolee who willfully fails to perform community service work as directed by the Section of Community Corrections of the Division of Adult Correction and Juvenile Justice. The provisions of G.S. 15A-1376 shall apply to this violation of a condition of parole.

Community service parole eligibility shall be available to a prisoner:

(1) Who is serving an active sentence the term of which exceeds six months; and

(2) Who, in the opinion of the Post-Release Supervision and Parole Commission, is unlikely to engage in further criminal conduct; and

(3) Who agrees to complete service of his sentence as herein specified; and

(4) Who has served one-half of his minimum sentence, at least 10 days if sentenced to Level One punishment or at least seven days if sentenced to Level Two punishment, whichever is longer.

In computing the service requirements of subdivision (4) of this subsection, credit shall be given for good time and gain time credit earned pursuant to G.S. 148-13 but only after a person has served at least 10 days if sentenced to Level One punishment or at least seven days if sentenced to Level Two punishment. Nothing herein is intended to create or shall be construed to create a right or entitlement to community service parole in any prisoner.

(i) The fee required by G.S. 143B-708 shall be paid by all persons who participate in the Community Service Parole Program.

(j) The Post-Release Supervision and Parole Commission may terminate a prisoner's community service parole before the expiration of the term of imprisonment where doing so will not endanger the public, unduly depreciate the seriousness of the crime, or promote disrespect for the law.

History.
1977, c. 711, s. 1; 1977, 2nd Sess., c. 1147, ss. 19A-22; 1979, c. 749, ss. 9, 10; 1979, 2nd Sess., c. 1316, s. 42; 1981, c. 63, s. 1; c. 179, s. 14; 1983 (Reg. Sess., 1984), c. 1098, s. 1; 1985, c. 453, ss. 1, 2; 1985 (Reg. Sess., 1986), c. 960, s. 2; c. 1012, ss. 2, 5; 1987, c. 47; c. 783, s. 7; 1989, c. 1, ss. 3, 4; 1991, c. 217, s. 3; c. 288, s. 2; 1993, c. 538, s. 22; 1994, Ex. Sess., c. 21, s. 3; c. 24, s. 14(b); c. 25, ss. 1, 2; 2002-126, s. 29A.1(a); 2006-264, s. 34; 2008-133, s. 1; 2009-372, s. 13(a), (b); 2009-451, s. 19.26(a), (d); 2009-575, s. 16A; 2010-107, s. 1; 2011-145, s. 19.1(i), (k); 2013-348, s. 3; 2013-368, s. 20; 2015-228, s. 1; 2017-186, s. 2 (bbbb)

§ 15A-1372. Length and effect of parole term

(a) **Term of Parole.** -- The term of parole for any person released from imprisonment may be no greater than one year.

(b) Repealed by Session Laws 1993, c. 538, s. 23.

(c) **Termination of Sentence.** -- When a parolee completes his period of parole, the sentence or sentences from which he was paroled are terminated.

(d) Repealed by Session Laws 1993, c. 538, s. 23.

History.
1977, c. 711, s. 1; 1981, c. 642; 1989, c. 1, s. 8; 1989 (Reg. Sess., 1990), c. 1031, s. 3; 1991, c. 217, s. 1; 1993, c. 538, s. 23; 1994, Ex. Sess., c. 21, s. 4; c. 24, s. 14(b)

§ 15A-1373. Incidents of parole

(a) **Conditionality of Parole.** -- Unless terminated sooner as provided in subsection (b), parole remains conditional and subject to revocation.

(b) **Early Termination.** -- The Post-Release Supervision and Parole Commission may terminate a period of parole and discharge the parolee at any time after the expiration of one year of successful parole if warranted by the conduct of the parolee and the ends of justice.

(c) **Modification of Conditions.** -- The Post-Release Supervision and Parole Commission may for good cause shown modify the conditions of parole at any time prior to the expiration or termination of the period for which the parole remains conditional.

(d) **Effect of Violation.** -- If the parolee violates a condition at any time prior to the expiration or termination of the period, the Commission may continue him on the existing parole, with or without modifying the conditions, or, if continuation or modification is not appropriate, may revoke the parole as provided in G.S. 15A-1376 and reimprison the parolee for a term consistent with the following requirements:

(1) The time the parolee was at liberty on parole and in compliance with all terms and conditions of that parole shall be credited on a day-for-day basis against the maximum term of imprisonment imposed by the court under G.S. 15A-1351, except that the parolee shall receive no credit for the last six months of his parole.

(2) The prisoner must be given credit against the term of reimprisonment for all time spent in custody as a result of revocation proceedings under G.S. 15A-1376.

(e) **Re-parole.** -- A prisoner who has been reimprisoned following parole may be re-paroled by the Post-Release Supervision and Parole Commission subject to the provisions which govern initial parole. In the event that a defendant serves the final six months of his maximum imprisonment as a result of being recommitted for violation of parole, he may not be required to serve a further period on parole.

(f) **Timing of Revocation.** -- The Post-Release Supervision and Parole Commission may revoke parole for violation of a condition during the period of parole. The Commission also may revoke following the period of parole if:

(1) Before the expiration of the period of parole, the Commission has recorded its intent to conduct a revocation hearing, and

(2) The Commission finds that every reasonable effort has been made to notify the parolee and conduct the hearing earlier.

History.
1977, c. 711, s. 1; 1979, c. 927; 1991, c. 217, s. 2; 1993, c. 538, s. 38; 1994, Ex. Sess., c. 24, s. 14(b)

§ 15A-1374. Conditions of parole

(a) **In General.** -- The Post-Release Supervision and Parole Commission may in its discretion impose conditions of parole it believes reasonably necessary to insure that the parolee will lead a law-abiding life or to assist him to do so. The Commission must provide as an express condition of every parole that the parolee not commit another crime during the period for which the parole remains subject to revocation. When the Commission releases a person on parole, it must give him a written statement of the conditions on which he is being released.

(a1) **Required Conditions for Certain Offenders.** -- A person serving a term of imprisonment for an impaired driving offense sentenced pursuant to G.S. 20-179 that:

(1) Has completed any recommended treatment or training program required by G.S. 20-179(p)(3); and

(2) Is not being paroled to a residential treatment program;

shall, as a condition of parole, receive community service parole pursuant to G.S. 15A-1371(h), or be required to comply with subdivision (b)(8a) of this section.

(b) **Appropriate Conditions.** -- As conditions of parole, the Commission may require that the parolee comply with one or more of the following conditions:

(1) Work faithfully at suitable employment or faithfully pursue a course of study or vocational training that will equip him for suitable employment.

(2) Undergo available medical or psychiatric treatment and remain in a specified institution if required for that purpose.

(3) Attend or reside in a facility providing rehabilitation, instruction, recreation, or residence for persons on parole.

(4) Support his dependents and meet other family responsibilities.

(5) Refrain from possessing a firearm, destructive device, or other dangerous weapon unless granted written permission by the Commission or the parole officer.

(6) Report to a parole officer at reasonable times and in a reasonable manner, as directed by the Commission or the parole officer.

(7) Permit the parole officer to visit him at reasonable times at his home or elsewhere.

(8) Remain within the geographic limits fixed by the Commission unless granted written permission to leave by the Commission or the parole officer.

(8a) Remain in one or more specified places for a specified period or periods each day and wear a device that permits the defendant's compliance with the condition to be monitored electronically.

(8b) Remain alcohol free, and prove such abstinence through evaluation by a continuous alcohol monitoring system of a type approved by the Division of Adult Correction and Juvenile Justice of the Department of Public Safety.

(9) Answer all reasonable inquiries by the parole officer and obtain prior approval from the parole officer for any change in address or employment.

(10) Promptly notify the parole officer of any change in address or employment.

(11) Submit at reasonable times to warrantless searches by a parole officer of the parolee's person and of the parolee's vehicle and premises while the parolee is present, for purposes reasonably related to the parole supervision. The Commission may not require as a condition of parole that the parolee submit to any other searches that would otherwise be unlawful. If the parolee has been convicted of an offense which is a reportable conviction as defined in G.S. 14-208.6(4), or which involves the physical, mental, or sexual abuse of a minor, warrantless searches of the parolee's computer or other electronic mechanism which may contain electronic data shall be considered reasonably related to the parole supervision. Whenever the search consists of testing for the presence of illegal drugs, the parolee may also be required to reimburse the Division of Adult Correction and Juvenile Justice of the Department of Public Safety for the actual cost of drug testing and drug screening, if the results are positive.

(11a) Make restitution or reparation to an aggrieved party as provided in G.S. 148-57.1.

(11b) Comply with an order from a court of competent jurisdiction regarding the payment of an obligation of the parolee in connection with any judgment rendered by the court.

(11c) In the case of a parolee who was attending a basic skills program during incarceration, continue attending a basic skills program in pursuit of an adult high school equivalency diploma or adult high school diploma.

(12) Satisfy other conditions reasonably related to his rehabilitation.

(b1) **Mandatory Satellite-Based Monitoring Required as Condition of Parole for Certain Offenders.** -- If a parolee is in a category described by G.S. 14-208.40(a)(1) or G.S. 14-208.40(a)(2) and based on the Division of Adult Correction and Juvenile Justice's risk assessment program requires the highest possible level of supervision and monitoring, the Commission must require as a condition of parole that the parolee submit to satellite-based monitoring pursuant to Part 5 of Article 27A of Chapter 14 of the General Statutes.

(c) **Supervision Fee.** -- The Commission must require as a condition of parole that the parolee pay a supervision fee of forty dollars ($ 40.00) per month. The Commission may exempt a parolee from this condition of parole only if it finds that requiring him to pay the fee will constitute an undue economic burden. The fee must be paid to the clerk of superior court of the county in which the parolee was convicted. The clerk must transmit any money collected pursuant to this subsection to the State to be deposited in the general fund of the State. In no event shall a person released on parole be required to pay more than one supervision fee per month.

(d) Any fees or costs paid by the parolee in order to comply with the imposition of subdivision (8b) of subsection (b) of this section shall be paid to the clerk of court for the county in which the parolee was convicted. Fees or costs collected under this subsection shall be transmitted to the entity providing the continuous alcohol monitoring system.

History.
1977, c. 711, s. 1; 1979, c. 749, s. 11; 1983, c. 562; 1985, c. 474, s. 6; 1987, c. 579, s. 3; c. 830, s. 17; 1989 (Reg. Sess., 1990), c. 1034, s. 2; 1991, c. 54, s. 1; 1991 (Reg. Sess., 1992), c. 1000, s. 2; 1993, c. 538, s. 39; 1994, Ex. Sess., c. 24, s. 14(b); 2002-126, s. 29A.2(c); 2006-247, s. 15(h); 2006-253, s. 27; 2007-165, ss. 4, 5; 2007-213, s. 8; 2010-31, s. 19.3(c); 2011-145, s. 19.1(h); 2014-115, s. 28(b); 2017-186, s. 2 (cccc); 2021-138, s. 18(n)

§ 15A-1375. Commencement of parole; multiple sentences

A period of parole commences on the day the prisoner is released from imprisonment. Periods of parole run concurrently with any federal or State prison, jail, probation, or parole term to which the defendant is subject during the period.

History.
1977, c. 711, s. 1

§ 15A-1376. Arrest and hearing on parole violation

(a) **Arrest for Violation of Parole.** -- A parolee is subject to arrest by a law-enforcement officer or a parole officer for violation of conditions of parole only upon the issuance of an order of temporary or conditional revocation of parole by the Post-Release Supervision and Parole Commission. However, a parole revocation hearing under subsection (e) may be held without first arresting the parolee.

(b) **When and Where Preliminary Hearing on Parole Violation Required.** -- Unless the hearing required by subsection (e) is first held or a continuance is requested by the parolee, a preliminary hearing on parole violation must be held reasonably near the place of the alleged violation or arrest and within seven working days of the arrest of a parolee to determine whether there is probable cause to believe that he violated a condition of parole. The preliminary hearing for violations of parole may be conducted by videoconference. Otherwise, the parolee must be released seven working days after his arrest to continue on parole pending a hearing. If the parolee is not within the State, his preliminary hearing is as prescribed by G.S. 148-65.1A.

(c) **Officers to Conduct Hearing.** -- The preliminary hearing on parole violation must be conducted by a judicial official, or by a hearing officer designated by the Post-Release Supervision and Parole Commission. No person employed by the Division of Adult Correction and Juvenile Justice of the Department of Public Safety may serve as a hearing officer at a hearing provided in this section unless he is a member of the Post-Release Supervision and Parole Commission or is employed solely as a hearing officer.

(d) **Procedure for Preliminary Hearing on Parole Violation.** -- The Division of Adult Correction and Juvenile Justice of the Department of Public Safety must give the parolee notice of the preliminary hearing and its purpose, including a statement of the violations alleged. At the hearing, the parolee may appear and speak in his own behalf, may present relevant information, and may, on request, personally question witnesses and adverse informants, unless the hearing officer finds good cause for not allowing confrontation. If the person holding the hearing determines there is probable cause to believe the parolee violated his parole, he must summarize the reasons for his determination and the evidence he relied on. Formal rules of evidence do not apply at the hearing. If probable cause is found, the parolee may be held in the custody of the Division of Adult Correction and Juvenile Justice of the Department of Public Safety to serve the appropriate term of imprisonment, subject to the outcome of a revocation hearing under subsection (e).

(e) **Revocation Hearing.** -- Before finally revoking parole, the Post-Release Supervision and Parole Commission must, unless the parolee waived the hearing or the time limit, provide a hearing within 45 days of the parolee's reconfinement to determine whether to revoke parole finally. The revocation hearing may be conducted by videoconference. The Post-Release Supervision and Parole Commission must adopt rules governing the hearing.

History.
1977, c. 711, s. 1; 1977, 2nd Sess., c. 1147, ss. 23-26; 1987, c. 827, s. 1; 1993, c. 538, s. 40; 1994, Ex. Sess., c. 24, s. 14(b); 1996, 2nd Ex. Sess., c. 18, s. 20.15(a); 2000-189, s. 2; 2011-145, s. 19.1(h); 2016-77, s. 4(c); 2017-186, s. 2 (dddd)

N.C. Gen. Stat. § 15A-1377

Repealed by Session Laws 1977, 2nd Sess., c. 1147, s. 27.

§§ 15A-1378 through 15A-1380

Reserved for future codification purposes.

ARTICLE 85A
PAROLE OF CERTAIN CONVICTED FELONS

§§ 15A-1380.1 through 15A-1380.4

Repealed by Session Laws 1993, c. 538, s. 24.

ARTICLE 85B
REVIEW OF SENTENCES OF LIFE IMPRISONMENT WITHOUT PAROLE

N.C. Gen. Stat. § 15A-1380.5

Repealed by Session Laws 1998-212, s. 19.4(q), effective December 1, 1998, and applicable to offenses committed on or after that date.

ARTICLE 86
REPORTS OF DISPOSITIONS OF CRIMINAL CASES

§ 15A-1381. Disposition defined

As used in this Article, the term "disposition" means any action which results in termination or indeterminate suspension of the prosecution of a criminal charge. A disposition may be any one of the following actions:

(1) A finding of no probable cause pursuant to G.S. 15A-511(c)(2);

(2) An order of dismissal pursuant to G.S. 15A-604;

(3) A finding of no probable cause pursuant to G.S. 15A-612(a)(3);

(4) A return of not a true bill pursuant to G.S. 15A-629;

(5) Repealed by Session Laws 1989, c. 688, s. 4.

(6) Dismissal pursuant to G.S. 15A-931 or 15A-932;

(7) Dismissal pursuant to G.S. 15A-954, 15A-955 or 15A-959;

(8) Finding of a defendant's incapacity to proceed pursuant to G.S. 15A-1002 or dismissal of charges pursuant to G.S. 15A-1008;

(9) Entry of a plea of guilty or no contest pursuant to G.S. 15A-1011, without regard to the sentence imposed upon the plea, and even though prayer for judgment on the plea be continued;

(10) Dismissal pursuant to G.S. 15A-1227;

(11) Return of verdict pursuant to G.S. 15A-1237, without regard to the sentence imposed upon such verdict and even though prayer for judgment on such verdict be continued.

History.
1981, c. 862, s. 1; 1989, c. 688, s. 4

§ 15A-1382. Reports of disposition; fingerprints

(a) When the defendant is fingerprinted pursuant to G.S. 15A-502 prior to the disposition of the case, a report of the disposition of the charges shall be made to the State Bureau of Investigation on a form supplied by the State Bureau of Investigation within 60 days following disposition.

(b) When a defendant is found guilty of any felony, regardless of the class of felony, a report of the disposition of the charges shall be made to the State Bureau of Investigation on a form supplied by the State Bureau of Investigation within 60 days following disposition. If a convicted felon was not fingerprinted pursuant to G.S. 15A-502 prior to the disposition of the case, his fingerprints shall be taken and submitted to the State Bureau of Investigation along with the report of the disposition of the charges on forms supplied by the State Bureau of Investigation.

History.
1981, c. 862, s. 1

§ 15A-1382.1. Reports of disposition; domestic violence; child abuse; sentencing

(a) When a defendant is found guilty of an offense involving assault, communicating a threat, or any of the acts as defined in G.S. 50B-1(a), the presiding judge shall determine whether the defendant and victim had a personal relationship. If the judge determines that there was a personal relationship between the defendant and the victim, then the judge shall indicate on the form reflecting the judgment that the case involved domestic violence. The clerk of court shall insure that the official record of the defendant's conviction includes the court's determination, so that any inquiry into the defendant's criminal record will reflect that the offense involved domestic violence.

(a1) When a defendant is found guilty of an offense involving child abuse or is found guilty of an offense involving assault or any of the acts as defined in G.S. 50B-1(a) and the offense was committed against a minor, then the judge shall indicate on the form reflecting the judgment that the case involved child abuse. The clerk of court shall ensure that the official record of the defendant's conviction includes the court's determination, so that any inquiry into the defendant's criminal record will reflect that the offense involved child abuse.

(b) Repealed by Session Laws 2012-39, s. 2, effective December 1, 2012, and applicable to defendants placed on probation on or after that date.

(c) The following definitions apply to this section:

(1) "An offense involving assault" includes any offense where an assault occurred, whether or not the conviction is for an offense under Article 8 of Chapter 14 of the General Statutes.

(2) "Inquiry" shall include any lawful review of the criminal records of persons convicted of an offense in this State, whether by law enforcement personnel or by private individuals.

(3) "Personal relationship" is as defined in G.S. 50B-1(b).

History.
2004-186, s. 11.1; 2012-39, s. 2; 2013-35, s. 2; 2013-123, s. 2

§ 15A-1382.2. Sentencing court to include in judgment whether firearm was used

When a person is found guilty of a felony offense, the presiding judge shall determine whether the defendant used or displayed a firearm while committing the felony. If the judge determines that the defendant used or displayed a firearm while committing the felony, the sentencing court shall include that fact when entering the judgment that imposes the sentence for the felony conviction.

History.
2013-369, s. 27

§ 15A-1383. Plans for implementation of Article; punishment for failure to comply; modification of plan

(a) On January 1, 1982, or on the first day of the month following the date on which any superior court district becomes effective under G.S. 7A-41, each senior resident superior court judge shall file a plan with the Director of the State Bureau of Investigation for the implementation of the provisions of this Article. The plan shall be entered as an order of the court on that date. In drawing up the plan, the senior resident superior court judge may consult with any public official having authority within his district or set of districts as defined in G.S. 7A-41.1(a) and with any other persons as he may deem appropriate. Upon the request of the senior resident superior court judge, the State Bureau of Investigation shall provide such technical assistance in the preparation of the plan as the judge desires.

(b) A person who is charged by the plan with a duty to make reports who fails to make such reports as required by the plan is punishable for civil contempt under Article 2 of Chapter 5A of the General Statutes.

(c) When the senior resident superior court judge modifies, alters or amends a plan under this Article, the order making such modification, alteration or amendment shall be filed with the Director of the State Bureau of Investigation within 10 days of its entry.

(d) Plans prepared under this Article are not "rules" within the meaning of Chapter 150B of the General Statutes.

History.
1981, c. 862, s. 1; 1987 (Reg. Sess., 1988), c. 1037, s. 70; 1989, c. 770, s. 4; 2010-96, s. 6

§§ 15A-1384 through 15A-1390

Reserved for future codification purposes.

ARTICLE 87

§§ 15A-1391 through 15A-1400

Reserved for future codification purposes.

SUBCHAPTER 14.
CORRECTION OF ERRORS AND APPEAL

ARTICLE 88
POST-TRIAL MOTIONS AND APPEAL

§ 15A-1401. Post-trial motions and appeal

Relief from errors committed in criminal trials and proceedings and other post-trial relief may be sought by:

(1) Motion for appropriate relief, as provided in Article 89.

(1a) Motion for innocence claim inquiry as provided in Article 92 of Chapter 15A of the General Statutes.

(2) Appeal and trial de novo in misdemeanor cases, as provided in Article 90.

(3) Appeal, as provided in Article 91.

History.
1977, c. 711, s. 1; 2006-184, s. 2; 2010-171, s. 5

§§ 15A-1402 through 15A-1410

Reserved for future codification purposes.

ARTICLE 89
MOTION FOR APPROPRIATE RELIEF AND OTHER POST-TRIAL RELIEF

§ 15A-1411. Motion for appropriate relief

(a) Relief from errors committed in the trial division, or other post-trial relief, may be sought by a motion for appropriate relief. Procedure for the making of the motion is as set out in G.S. 15A-1420.

(b) A motion for appropriate relief, whether made before or after the entry of judgment, is a motion in the original cause and not a new proceeding.

(c) The relief formerly available by motion in arrest of judgment, motion to set aside the verdict, motion for new trial, post-conviction proceedings, *coram nobis* and all other post-trial motions is available by motion for appropriate relief. The availability of relief by motion for appropriate relief is not a bar to relief by writ of habeas corpus.

(d) A claim of factual innocence asserted through the North Carolina Innocence Inquiry Commission does not constitute a motion for appropriate relief and does not impact rights or relief provided for in this Article.

History.
1977, c. 711, s. 1; 2006-184, s. 4; 2010-171, s. 5

§ 15A-1412. Provisions of Article procedural

The provision in this Article for the right to seek relief by motion for appropriate relief is procedural and is not determinative of the question of whether the moving party is entitled to the relief sought or to other appropriate relief.

History.
1977, c. 711, s. 1

§ 15A-1413. Trial judges empowered to act; assignment of motions for appropriate relief

(a) A motion for appropriate relief made pursuant to G.S. 15A-1415 may be heard and determined in the trial division by any judge who (i) is empowered to act in criminal matters in the district court district as defined in G.S. 7A-133 or superior court district or set of districts as defined in G.S. 7A-41.1, as the case may be, in which the judgment was entered and (ii) is assigned pursuant to this section to review the motion for appropriate relief and take the appropriate administrative action to dispense with the motion.

(b) The judge who presided at the trial is empowered to act upon a motion for appropriate relief made pursuant to G.S. 15A-1414. The judge may act even though the judge is in another district or even though the judge's commission has expired; however, if the judge who presided at the trial is still unavailable to act, the senior resident superior court judge or the chief district court judge, as appropriate, shall assign a judge who is empowered to act under subsection (a) of this section.

(c) Repealed by Session Laws 2012-168, s. 2(a), effective December 1, 2012.

(d) All motions for appropriate relief filed in superior court shall, when filed, be referred to the senior resident superior court judge, who shall assign the motion as provided by this section for review and administrative action, including, as may be appropriate, dismissal, calendaring for hearing, entry of a scheduling order for subsequent events in the case, including disclosure of expert witness information described in G.S. 15A-903(a)(2) and G.S. 15A-905(c)(2) for expert witnesses reasonably expected to be called at a hearing on the motion, or other appropriate actions.

All motions for appropriate relief filed in district court shall, when filed, be referred to the chief district court judge, who shall assign the motion as provided by this section for review and administrative action, including, as may be appropriate, dismissal, calendaring for hearing, entry of a scheduling order for subsequent events in the case, or other appropriate actions.

(e) The assignment of a motion for appropriate relief filed under G.S. 15A-1415 is in the discretion of the senior resident superior court judge or chief district court judge as appropriate.

History.
1977, c. 711, s. 1; 1987 (Reg. Sess., 1988), c. 1037, s. 71; 2012-168, s. 2(a); 2017-176, s. 1(a)

§ 15A-1414. Motion by defendant for appropriate relief made within 10 days after verdict

(a) After the verdict but not more than 10 days after entry of judgment, the defendant by motion may seek appropriate relief for any error committed during or prior to the trial.

(b) Unless included in G.S. 15A-1415, all errors, including but not limited to the following, must be asserted within 10 days after entry of judgment:

(1) Any error of law, including the following:

a. The court erroneously failed to dismiss the charge prior to trial pursuant to G.S. 15A-954.

b. The court's ruling was contrary to law with regard to motions made before or during the trial, or with regard to the admission or exclusion of evidence.

c. The evidence, at the close of all the evidence, was insufficient to justify submission of the case to the jury, whether or not a motion so asserting was made before verdict.

d. The court erroneously instructed the jury.

(2) The verdict is contrary to the weight of the evidence.

(3) For any other cause the defendant did not receive a fair and impartial trial.

(4) The sentence imposed on the defendant is not supported by evidence introduced at the trial and sentencing hearing. This motion must be addressed to the sentencing judge.

(c) The motion may be made and acted upon in the trial court whether or not notice of appeal has been given.

History.
1977, c. 711, s. 1; 1979, c. 760, s. 3; 1981, c. 179, s. 6

§ 15A-1415. Grounds for appropriate relief which may be asserted by defendant after verdict; limitation as to time

(a) At any time after verdict, a noncapital defendant by motion may seek appropriate relief upon any of the grounds enumerated in this section. In a capital case, a postconviction motion for appropriate relief shall be filed within 120 days from the latest of the following:

(1) The court's judgment has been filed, but the defendant failed to perfect a timely appeal;

(2) The mandate issued by a court of the appellate division on direct appeal pursuant to N.C.R. App. P. 32(b) and the time for filing a petition for writ of certiorari to the United States Supreme Court has expired without a petition being filed;

(3) The United States Supreme Court denied a timely petition for writ of certiorari

of the decision on direct appeal by the Supreme Court of North Carolina;

(4) Following the denial of discretionary review by the Supreme Court of North Carolina, the United States Supreme Court denied a timely petition for writ of certiorari seeking review of the decision on direct appeal by the North Carolina Court of Appeals;

(5) The United States Supreme Court granted the defendant's or the State's timely petition for writ of certiorari of the decision on direct appeal by the Supreme Court of North Carolina or North Carolina Court of Appeals, but subsequently left the defendant's conviction and sentence undisturbed; or

(6) The appointment of postconviction counsel for an indigent capital defendant.

(b) The following are the only grounds which the defendant may assert by a motion for appropriate relief made more than 10 days after entry of judgment:

(1) The acts charged in the criminal pleading did not at the time they were committed constitute a violation of criminal law.

(2) The trial court lacked jurisdiction over the person of the defendant or over the subject matter.

(3) The conviction was obtained in violation of the Constitution of the United States or the Constitution of North Carolina.

(4) The defendant was convicted or sentenced under a statute that was in violation of the Constitution of the United States or the Constitution of North Carolina.

(5) The conduct for which the defendant was prosecuted was protected by the Constitution of the United States or the Constitution of North Carolina.

(6) Repealed by Session Laws 1995 (Regular Session, 1996), c. 719, s. 1, effective June 21, 1996.

(7) There has been a significant change in law, either substantive or procedural, applied in the proceedings leading to the defendant's conviction or sentence, and retroactive application of the changed legal standard is required.

(8) The sentence imposed was unauthorized at the time imposed, contained a type of sentence disposition or a term of imprisonment not authorized for the particular class of offense and prior record or conviction level was illegally imposed, or is otherwise invalid as a matter of law. However, a motion for appropriate relief on the grounds that the sentence imposed on the defendant is not supported by evidence introduced at the trial and sentencing hearing must be made before the sentencing judge.

(9) The defendant is in confinement and is entitled to release because his sentence has been fully served.

(10) The defendant was convicted of a nonviolent offense as defined in G.S. 15A-145.9; the defendant's participation in the offense was a result of having been a victim of human trafficking under G.S. 14-43.11, sexual servitude under G.S. 14-43.13, or the federal Trafficking Victims Protection Act (22 U.S.C. § 7102(13)); and the defendant seeks to have the conviction vacated.

(c) Notwithstanding the time limitations herein, a defendant at any time after verdict may by a motion for appropriate relief, raise the ground that evidence is available which was unknown or unavailable to the defendant at the time of trial, which could not with due diligence have been discovered or made available at that time, including recanted testimony, and which has a direct and material bearing upon the defendant's eligibility for the death penalty or the defendant's guilt or innocence. A motion based upon such newly discovered evidence must be filed within a reasonable time of its discovery.

(d) For good cause shown, the defendant may be granted an extension of time to file the motion for appropriate relief. The presumptive length of an extension of time under this subsection is up to 30 days, but can be longer if the court finds extraordinary circumstances.

(e) Where a defendant alleges ineffective assistance of prior trial or appellate counsel as a ground for the illegality of his conviction or sentence, he shall be deemed to waive the attorney-client privilege with respect to both oral and written communications between such counsel and the defendant to the extent the defendant's prior counsel reasonably believes such communications are necessary to defend against the allegations of ineffectiveness. This waiver of the attorney-client privilege shall be automatic upon the filing of the motion for appropriate relief alleging ineffective assistance of prior counsel, and the superior court need not enter an order waiving the privilege.

(f) In the case of a defendant who is represented by counsel in postconviction proceedings in superior court, the defendant's prior trial or appellate counsel shall make available to the defendant's counsel their complete files relating to the case of the defendant. The State, to the extent allowed by law, shall make available to the defendant's counsel the complete files of all law enforcement and prosecutorial agencies involved in the investigation of the crimes committed or the prosecution of the defendant. If the State has a reasonable belief that allowing inspection of any portion of the files by counsel for the defendant would not be in the interest of justice, the State may submit for inspection by the court those portions of the files so identified. If upon examination of the files, the court finds that the files could not assist the defendant in investigating, preparing, or presenting a motion for appropriate relief, the court in its discretion may allow the State to withhold that portion of the files.

(g) The defendant may file amendments to a motion for appropriate relief at least 30 days prior to the commencement of a hearing on the merits of the claims asserted in the motion or at any time before the date for the hearing has been set, whichever is later. Where the defendant has filed an amendment to a motion for appropriate relief, the State shall, upon request, be granted a continuance of 30 days before the date of hearing. After such hearing has begun, the defendant may file amendments only to conform the motion to evidence adduced at the hearing, or to raise claims based on such evidence.

History.
1977, c. 711, s. 1; 1981, c. 179, s. 7; 1993, c. 538, s. 25; 1994, Ex. Sess., c. 24, s. 14(b); 1995 (Reg. Sess., 1996), c. 719, s. 1; 2009-517, s. 2; 2013-368, s. 9; 2019-158, s. 5(a)

§ 15A-1416. Motion by the State for appropriate relief

(a) After the verdict but not more than 10 days after entry of judgment, the State by motion may seek appropriate relief for any error which it may assert upon appeal.

(b) At any time after verdict the State may make a motion for appropriate relief for:

(1) The imposition of sentence when prayer for judgment has been continued and grounds for the imposition of sentence are asserted.

(2) The initiation of any proceeding authorized under Article 82, Probation; Article 83, Imprisonment; and Article 84, Fines, with regard to the modification of sentences. The procedural provisions of those Articles are controlling.

History.
1977, c. 711, s. 1

§ 15A-1416.1. Motion by the defendant to vacate a nonviolent offense conviction for human trafficking victim

(a) A motion for appropriate relief seeking to vacate a conviction for a nonviolent offense based on the grounds set out in G.S. 15A-1415(b)(10) shall be filed in the court where the conviction occurred. The motion may be filed at any time following the entry of a verdict or finding of guilty. Any motion for appropriate relief filed under this section shall state why the facts giving rise to this motion were not presented to the trial court and shall be made with due diligence after the defendant has ceased to be a victim of such trafficking or has sought services for victims of such offenses, subject to reasonable concerns for the safety of the defendant, family members of the defendant, or other victims of such trafficking that may be jeopardized by the bringing of such motion or for other reasons consistent with the purpose of this section. The motion shall be contemporaneously served upon the district attorney in the prosecutorial district in which the conviction was entered. The district attorney shall have 30 days thereafter in which to file any objection thereto and shall be duly notified as to the date of the hearing of the motion.

(b) The court may grant the motion if, in the discretion of the court, the defendant has demonstrated, by the preponderance of the evidence, that the violation was a direct result of the defendant having been a victim of human trafficking or sexual servitude and that the offense would not have been committed but for the defendant having been a victim of human trafficking or sexual servitude. Evidence of such may include any of the following documents listed in subdivisions (1) through (4) of this subsection; alternatively, the court may consider such other evidence as it deems of sufficient credibility and probative value in determining whether the defendant is a trafficking victim:

(1) Certified records of federal or State court proceedings which demonstrate that the defendant was a victim of a person charged with an offense under G.S. 14-43.11, G.S. 14-43.13, or under 22 U.S.C. Chapter 78.

(2) Certified records of "approval notices" or "enforcement certifications" generated from federal immigration proceedings available to such victims.

(3) A sworn statement from a trained professional staff of a victim services organization, an attorney, a member of the clergy, or a medical or other professional from whom the defendant has sought assistance in addressing the trauma associated with being trafficked.

(4) A sworn statement or affidavit from a federal, State, or local law enforcement officer who investigated the violation of G.S. 14-43.11, G.S. 14-43.13, or the federal Trafficking Victims Protection Act, as stated within the defendant's motion.

(c) If the court grants a motion under this section, the court must vacate the conviction and may take such additional action as is appropriate in the circumstances.

(d) A previous or subsequent conviction shall not affect a person's eligibility for relief under this section.

Chapter 15A

1137

History.
2013-368, s. 10; 2019-158, s. 6(a)

§ 15A-1417. Relief available

(a) The following relief is available when the court grants a motion for appropriate relief:

(1) New trial on all or any of the charges.

(2) Dismissal of all or any of the charges.

(3) The relief sought by the State pursuant to G.S. 15A-1416.

(3a) For claims of factual innocence, referral to the North Carolina Innocence Inquiry Commission established by Article 92 of Chapter 15A of the General Statutes.

(4) Any other appropriate relief.

(b) When relief is granted in the trial court and the offense is divided into degrees or necessarily includes lesser offenses, and the court is of the opinion that the evidence does not sustain the verdict but is sufficient to sustain a finding of guilty of a lesser degree or of a lesser offense necessarily included in the one charged, the court may, with consent of the State, accept a plea of guilty to the lesser degree or lesser offense.

(c) If resentencing is required, the trial division may enter an appropriate sentence. If a motion is granted in the appellate division and resentencing is required, the case must be remanded to the trial division for entry of a new sentence.

History.
1977, c. 711, s. 1; 2006-184, s. 3; 2010-171, s. 5

§ 15A-1418. Motion for appropriate relief in the appellate division

(a) When a case is in the appellate division for review, a motion for appropriate relief based upon grounds set out in G.S. 15A-1415 must be made in the appellate division. For the purpose of this section a case is in the appellate division when the jurisdiction of the trial court has been divested as provided in G.S. 15A-1448, or when a petition for a writ of certiorari has been granted. When a petition for a writ of certiorari has been filed but not granted, a copy or written statement of any motion made in the trial court, and of any disposition of the motion, must be filed in the appellate division.

(b) When a motion for appropriate relief is made in the appellate division, the appellate court must decide whether the motion may be determined on the basis of the materials before it, whether it is necessary to remand the case to the trial division for taking evidence or conducting other proceedings, or, for claims of factual innocence, whether to refer the case for further investigation to the North Carolina Innocence Inquiry Commission established by Article 92

of Chapter 15A of the General Statutes. If the appellate court does not remand the case for proceedings on the motion, it may determine the motion in conjunction with the appeal and enter its ruling on the motion with its determination of the case.

(c) The order of remand must provide that the time periods for perfecting or proceeding with the appeal are tolled, and direct that the order of the trial division with regard to the motion be transmitted to the appellate division so that it may proceed with the appeal or enter an appropriate order terminating it.

History.
1977, c. 711, s. 1; 2006-184, s. 5; 2010-171, s. 5

§ 15A-1419. When motion for appropriate relief denied

(a) The following are grounds for the denial of a motion for appropriate relief, including motions filed in capital cases:

(1) Upon a previous motion made pursuant to this Article, the defendant was in a position to adequately raise the ground or issue underlying the present motion but did not do so. This subdivision does not apply when the previous motion was made within 10 days after entry of judgment or the previous motion was made during the pendency of the direct appeal.

(2) The ground or issue underlying the motion was previously determined on the merits upon an appeal from the judgment or upon a previous motion or proceeding in the courts of this State or a federal court, unless since the time of such previous determination there has been a retroactively effective change in the law controlling such issue.

(3) Upon a previous appeal the defendant was in a position to adequately raise the ground or issue underlying the present motion but did not do so.

(4) The defendant failed to file a timely motion for appropriate relief as required by G.S. 15A-1415(a).

(b) The court shall deny the motion under any of the circumstances specified in this section, unless the defendant can demonstrate:

(1) Good cause for excusing the grounds for denial listed in subsection (a) of this section and can demonstrate actual prejudice resulting from the defendant's claim; or

(2) That failure to consider the defendant's claim will result in a fundamental miscarriage of justice.

(c) For the purposes of subsection (b) of this section, good cause may only be shown if the defendant establishes by a preponderance of the evidence that his failure to raise the claim or file a timely motion was:

(1) The result of State action in violation of the United States Constitution or the North Carolina Constitution including ineffective assistance of trial or appellate counsel;

(2) The result of the recognition of a new federal or State right which is retroactively applicable; or

(3) Based on a factual predicate that could not have been discovered through the exercise of reasonable diligence in time to present the claim on a previous State or federal postconviction review.

A trial attorney's ignorance of a claim, inadvertence, or tactical decision to withhold a claim may not constitute good cause, nor may a claim of ineffective assistance of prior postconviction counsel constitute good cause.

(d) For the purposes of subsection (b) of this section, actual prejudice may only be shown if the defendant establishes by a preponderance of the evidence that an error during the trial or sentencing worked to the defendant's actual and substantial disadvantage, raising a reasonable probability, viewing the record as a whole, that a different result would have occurred but for the error.

(e) For the purposes of subsection (b) of this section, a fundamental miscarriage of justice only results if:

(1) The defendant establishes that more likely than not, but for the error, no reasonable fact finder would have found the defendant guilty of the underlying offense; or

(2) The defendant establishes by clear and convincing evidence that, but for the error, no reasonable fact finder would have found the defendant eligible for the death penalty.

A defendant raising a claim of newly discovered evidence of factual innocence or ineligibility for the death penalty, otherwise barred by the provisions of subsection (a) of this section or G.S. 15A-1415(c), may only show a fundamental miscarriage of justice by proving by clear and convincing evidence that, in light of the new evidence, if credible, no reasonable juror would have found the defendant guilty beyond a reasonable doubt or eligible for the death penalty.

History.
1977, c. 711, s. 1; 1995 (Reg. Sess., 1996), c. 719, s. 2

§ 15A-1420. Motion for appropriate relief; procedure

(a) **Form, Service, Filing. --**

(1) A motion for appropriate relief must:

a. Be made in writing unless it is made:

1. In open court;
2. Before the judge who presided at trial;
3. Before the end of the session if made in superior court; and
4. Within 10 days after entry of judgment;

b. State the grounds for the motion;

c. Set forth the relief sought;

c1. If the motion for appropriate relief is being made in superior court and is being made by an attorney, the attorney must certify in writing that there is a sound legal basis for the motion and that it is being made in good faith; and that the attorney has notified both the district attorney's office and the attorney who initially represented the defendant of the motion; and further, that the attorney has reviewed the trial transcript or made a good-faith determination that the nature of the relief sought in the motion does not require that the trial transcript be read in its entirety. In the event that the trial transcript is unavailable, instead of certifying that the attorney has read the trial transcript, the attorney shall set forth in writing what efforts were undertaken to locate the transcript; and

d. Be timely filed.

(2) A written motion for appropriate relief must be served in the manner provided in G.S. 15A-951(b). When a motion for appropriate relief is permitted to be made orally the court must determine whether the matter may be heard immediately or at a later time. If the opposing party, or his counsel if he is represented, is not present, the court must provide for the giving of adequate notice of the motion and the date of hearing to the opposing party, or his counsel if he is represented by counsel.

(3) A written motion for appropriate relief must be filed in the manner provided in G.S. 15A-951(c).

(4) An oral or written motion for appropriate relief may not be granted in district court without the signature of the district attorney, indicating that the State has had an opportunity to consent or object to the motion. However, the court may grant a motion for appropriate relief without the district attorney's signature 10 business days after the district attorney has been notified in open court of the motion, or served with the motion pursuant to G.S. 15A-951(c).

(5) An oral or written motion for appropriate relief made in superior court and made by an attorney may not be granted by the court unless the attorney has complied

with the requirements of sub-subdivision c1. of subdivision (1) of this subsection.

(b) **Supporting Affidavits. --**

(1) A motion for appropriate relief made after the entry of judgment must be supported by affidavit or other documentary evidence if based upon the existence or occurrence of facts which are not ascertainable from the records and any transcript of the case or which are not within the knowledge of the judge who hears the motion.

(2) The opposing party may file affidavits or other documentary evidence.

(b1) **Filing Motion With Clerk. --**

(1) The proceeding shall be commenced by filing with the clerk of superior court of the district wherein the defendant was indicted a motion, with service on the district attorney in noncapital cases, and service on both the district attorney and Attorney General in capital cases.

(2) The clerk, upon receipt of the motion, shall place the motion on the criminal docket. When a motion is placed on the criminal docket, the clerk shall promptly bring the motion, or a copy of the motion, to the attention of the senior resident superior court judge or chief district court judge, as appropriate, for assignment to the appropriate judge pursuant to G.S. 15A-1413.

(3) The judge assigned to the motion shall conduct an initial review of the motion. If the judge determines that all of the claims alleged in the motion are frivolous, the judge shall deny the motion. If the motion presents sufficient information to warrant a hearing or the interests of justice so require, the judge shall appoint counsel for an indigent defendant who is not represented by counsel. Counsel so appointed shall review the motion filed by the petitioner and either adopt the motion or file an amended motion. After postconviction counsel files an initial or amended motion, or a determination is made that the petitioner is proceeding without counsel, the judge may direct the State to file an answer. Should the State contend that as a matter of law the defendant is not entitled to the relief sought, the State may request leave to file a limited answer so alleging.

(b2) Repealed by Session Laws 2013-385, s. 3.1, effective December 1, 2013.

(b3) Repealed by Session Laws 2013-385, s. 3.1, effective December 1, 2013.

(c) **Hearings, Showing of Prejudice; Findings. --**

(1) Any party is entitled to a hearing on questions of law or fact arising from the motion and any supporting or opposing information presented unless the court determines that the motion is without merit.

The court must determine, on the basis of these materials and the requirements of this subsection, whether an evidentiary hearing is required to resolve questions of fact. Upon the motion of either party, the judge may direct the attorneys for the parties to appear before him for a conference on any prehearing matter in the case.

(2) An evidentiary hearing is not required when the motion is made in the trial court pursuant to G.S. 15A-1414, but the court may hold an evidentiary hearing if it is appropriate to resolve questions of fact.

(3) The court must determine the motion without an evidentiary hearing when the motion and supporting and opposing information present only questions of law. The defendant has no right to be present at such a hearing where only questions of law are to be argued.

(4) If the court cannot rule upon the motion without the hearing of evidence, it must conduct a hearing for the taking of evidence, and must make findings of fact. The defendant has a right to be present at the evidentiary hearing and to be represented by counsel. A waiver of the right to be present must be in writing.

(5) If an evidentiary hearing is held, the moving party has the burden of proving by a preponderance of the evidence every fact essential to support the motion.

(6) A defendant who seeks relief by motion for appropriate relief must show the existence of the asserted ground for relief. Relief must be denied unless prejudice appears, in accordance with G.S. 15A-1443.

(7) The court must rule upon the motion and enter its order accordingly. When the motion is based upon an asserted violation of the rights of the defendant under the Constitution or laws or treaties of the United States, the court must make and enter conclusions of law and a statement of the reasons for its determination to the extent required, when taken with other records and transcripts in the case, to indicate whether the defendant has had a full and fair hearing on the merits of the grounds so asserted.

(d) **Action on Court's Own Motion. --** At any time that a defendant would be entitled to relief by motion for appropriate relief, the court may grant such relief upon its own motion. The court must cause appropriate notice to be given to the parties.

(e) Nothing in this section shall prevent the parties to the action from entering into an agreement for appropriate relief, including an agreement as to any aspect, procedural or otherwise, of a motion for appropriate relief.

History.
1965, c. 352, s. 1; 1973, c. 47, s. 2; 1977, c. 711, s. 1; 1995 (Reg. Sess., 1996), c. 719, ss. 3, 4; 2006-253, s. 30; 2009-517, s. 1; 2012-168, s. 2(b); 2013-385, s. 3.1; 2017-176, s. 1(b)

§ 15A-1421. Indigent defendants

The provisions of Chapter 7A of the General Statutes with regard to the appointment of counsel for indigent defendants are applicable to proceedings under this Article. The court also may make appropriate orders relieving indigent defendants of all or a portion of the costs of the proceedings.

History.
1977, c. 711, s. 1

§ 15A-1422. Review upon appeal

(a) The making of a motion for appropriate relief is not a prerequisite for asserting an error upon appeal.

(b) The grant or denial of relief sought pursuant to G.S. 15A-1414 is subject to appellate review only in an appeal regularly taken.

(c) The court's ruling on a motion for appropriate relief pursuant to G.S. 15A-1415 is subject to review:

(1) If the time for appeal from the conviction has not expired, by appeal.

(2) If an appeal is pending when the ruling is entered, in that appeal.

(3) If the time for appeal has expired and no appeal is pending, by writ of certiorari.

(d) There is no right to appeal from the denial of a motion for appropriate relief when the movant is entitled to a trial de novo upon appeal.

(e) When an error asserted upon appeal has also been the subject of a motion for appropriate relief, denial of the motion has no effect on the right to assert error upon appeal.

(f) Decisions of the Court of Appeals on motions for appropriate relief that embrace matter set forth in G.S. 15A-1415(b) are final and not subject to further review by appeal, certification, writ, motion, or otherwise.

History.
1977, c. 711, s. 1; 1981, c. 470, s. 3

§§ 15A-1423 through 15A-1430

Reserved for future codification purposes.

ARTICLE 90
APPEALS FROM MAGISTRATES AND DISTRICT COURT JUDGES

§ 15A-1431. Appeals by defendants from magistrate and district court judge; trial de novo

(a) A defendant convicted before a magistrate may appeal for trial de novo before a district court judge without a jury.

(b) A defendant convicted in the district court before the judge may appeal to the superior court for trial de novo with a jury as provided by law. Upon the docketing in the superior court of an appeal from a judgment imposed pursuant to a plea arrangement between the State and the defendant, the jurisdiction of the superior court over any misdemeanor dismissed, reduced, or modified pursuant to that plea arrangement shall be the same as was had by the district court prior to the plea arrangement.

(c) Within 10 days of entry of judgment, notice of appeal may be given orally in open court or in writing to the clerk. Within 10 days of entry of judgment, the defendant may withdraw his appeal and comply with the judgment. Upon expiration of the 10-day period, if an appeal has been entered and not withdrawn, the clerk must transfer the case to the appropriate court.

(d) A defendant convicted by a magistrate or district court judge is not barred from appeal because of compliance with the judgment, but notice of appeal after compliance must be given by the defendant in person to the magistrate or judge who heard the case or, if he is not available, notice must be given:

(1) Before a magistrate in the county, in the case of appeals from the magistrate; or

(2) During an open session of district court in the district court district as defined in G.S. 7A-133, in the case of appeals from district court.

The magistrate or district court judge must review the case and fix conditions of pretrial release as appropriate. If a defendant has paid a fine or costs and then appeals, the amount paid must be remitted to the defendant, but the judge, clerk or magistrate to whom notice of appeal is given may order the remission delayed pending the determination of the appeal.

(e) Any order of pretrial release remains in effect pending appeal by the defendant unless the judge modifies the order.

(f) Repealed by Session Laws 2005-339, s. 1, effective August 26, 2005.

(f1) Appeal pursuant to this section stays the execution of all portions of the judgment, including all of the following:

(1) Payment of costs.

(2) Payment of a fine.

(3) Probation or special probation.

(4) Active punishment.

Pursuant to subsection (e) of this section, however, the judge may order any appropriate condition of pretrial release, including confinement in a local confinement facility, pending the trial de novo in superior court.

(g) The defendant may withdraw his appeal at any time prior to calendaring of the case for trial de novo. The case is then automatically remanded to the court from which the appeal was taken, for execution of the judgment.

(h) The defendant may withdraw his appeal after the calendaring of the case for trial de novo only by consent of the court, and with the attachment of costs of that court, unless the costs or any part of the costs are remitted by the court. The case may then be remanded by order of the court to the court from which the appeal was taken for execution of the judgment with any additional court costs that attached and that have not been remitted.

History.
1977, c. 711, s. 1; 1979, c. 758, p. 2; 1979, 2nd Sess., c. 1328, s. 1; 1987 (Reg. Sess., 1988), c. 1037, s. 72; 1991, c. 63, s. 1; 2005-339, s. 1

§ 15A-1432. Appeals by State from district court judge

(a) Unless the rule against double jeopardy prohibits further prosecution, the State may appeal from the district court judge to the superior court:

(1) When there has been a decision or judgment dismissing criminal charges as to one or more counts.

(2) Upon the granting of a motion for a new trial on the ground of newly discovered or newly available evidence but only on questions of law.

(b) When the State appeals pursuant to subsection (a) the appeal is by written motion specifying the basis of the appeal made within 10 days after the entry of the judgment in the district court. The motion must be filed with the clerk and a copy served upon the defendant.

(c) The motion may be heard by any judge of superior court having authority for the trial of criminal cases in the district. The State and the defendant are entitled to file briefs and are entitled to adequate time for their preparation, consonant with the expeditious handling of the appeal.

(d) If the superior court finds that a judgment, ruling, or order dismissing criminal charges in the district court was in error, it must reinstate the charges and remand the matter to district court for further proceedings. The defendant may appeal this order to the appellate division as in the case of other orders of the superior court, including by an interlocutory appeal if the defendant, or his attorney, certifies to the superior court judge who entered the order that the appeal is not taken for the purpose of delay and if the judge finds the cause is appropriately justiciable in the appellate division as an interlocutory matter.

(e) If the superior court finds that the order of the district court was correct, it must enter an order affirming the judgment of the district court. The State may appeal the order of the superior court to the appellate division upon certificate by the district attorney to the judge who affirmed the judgment that the appeal is not taken for the purpose of delay.

History.
1977, c. 711, s. 1; 1987, c. 398

§§ 15A-1433 through 15A-1440

Reserved for future codification purposes.

ARTICLE 91
APPEAL TO APPELLATE DIVISION

§ 15A-1441. Correction of errors by appellate division

Errors of law may be corrected upon appellate review as provided in this Article, except that review of capital cases shall be given priority on direct appeal and in State postconviction proceedings.

History.
1977, c. 711, s. 1; 1995 (Reg. Sess., 1996), c. 719, s. 6

§ 15A-1442. Grounds for correction of error by appellate division

The following constitute grounds for correction of errors by the appellate division.

(1) **Lack of Jurisdiction. --**
a. The trial court lacked jurisdiction over the offense.
b. The trial court did not have jurisdiction over the person of the defendant.

(2) **Error in the Criminal Pleading.**
-- Failure to charge a crime, in that:
a. The criminal pleading charged acts which at the time they were committed did not constitute a violation of criminal law; or
b. The pleading fails to state essential elements of an alleged violation as required by G.S. 15A-924(a)(5).

(3) **Insufficiency of the Evidence. --** The evidence was insufficient as a matter of law.

(4) **Errors in Procedure. --**

a. There has been a denial of pretrial motions or relief to which the defendant is entitled, so as to affect the defendant's preparation or presentation of his defense, to his prejudice.

b. There has been a denial of a trial motion or relief to which the defendant is entitled, to his prejudice.

c. There has been error in the admission or exclusion of evidence, to the prejudice of the defendant.

d. There has been error in the judge's instructions to the jury, to the prejudice of the defendant.

e. There has been a denial of a post-trial motion or relief to which the defendant is entitled, to his prejudice. This provision is subject to the provisions of G.S. 15A-1422.

(5) **Constitutionally Invalid Procedure or Statute; Prosecution for Constitutionally Protected Conduct. --**

a. The conviction was obtained by a violation of the Constitution of the United States or of the Constitution of North Carolina.

b. The defendant was convicted under a statute that is in violation of the Constitution of the United States or the Constitution of North Carolina.

c. The conduct for which the defendant was prosecuted was protected by the Constitution of the United States or the Constitution of North Carolina.

(5a) **Insufficient Basis for Sentence.** -- The sentence imposed on the defendant is not supported by evidence introduced at the trial and sentencing hearing.

(5b) **Violation of Sentencing Structure. --** The sentence imposed:

a. Results from an incorrect finding of the defendant's prior record level under G.S. 15A-1340.14 or the defendant's prior conviction level under G.S. 15A-1340.21;

b. Contains a type of sentence disposition that is not authorized by G.S. 15A-1340.17 or G.S. 15A-1340.23 for the defendant's class of offense and prior record or conviction level; or

c. Contains a term of imprisonment that is for a duration not authorized by G.S. 15A-1340.17 or G.S. 15A-1340.23 for the defendant's class or offense and prior record or conviction level.

(6) **Other Errors of Law. --** Any other error of law was committed by the trial court to the prejudice of the defendant.

History.

1977, c. 711, s. 1; 1979, c. 760, s. 3; 1979, (2nd Sess.) c. 1316, s. 47; 1981, c. 63, s. 1; 1981, c. 179, s. 14; 1993, c. 538, s. 26; 1994, Ex. Sess., c. 24, s. 14(b)

§ 15A-1443. Existence and showing of prejudice

(a) A defendant is prejudiced by errors relating to rights arising other than under the Constitution of the United States when there is a reasonable possibility that, had the error in question not been committed, a different result would have been reached at the trial out of which the appeal arises. The burden of showing such prejudice under this subsection is upon the defendant. Prejudice also exists in any instance in which it is deemed to exist as a matter of law or error is deemed reversible per se.

(b) A violation of the defendant's rights under the Constitution of the United States is prejudicial unless the appellate court finds that it was harmless beyond a reasonable doubt. The burden is upon the State to demonstrate, beyond a reasonable doubt, that the error was harmless.

(c) A defendant is not prejudiced by the granting of relief which he has sought or by error resulting from his own conduct.

History.

1977, c. 711, s. 1

§ 15A-1444. When defendant may appeal; certiorari

(a) A defendant who has entered a plea of not guilty to a criminal charge, and who has been found guilty of a crime, is entitled to appeal as a matter of right when final judgment has been entered.

(a1) A defendant who has been found guilty, or entered a plea of guilty or no contest to a felony, is entitled to appeal as a matter of right the issue of whether his or her sentence is supported by evidence introduced at the trial and sentencing hearing only if the minimum sentence of imprisonment does not fall within the presumptive range for the defendant's prior record or conviction level and class of offense. Otherwise, the defendant is not entitled to appeal this issue as a matter of right but may petition the appellate division for review of this issue by writ of certiorari.

(a2) A defendant who has entered a plea of guilty or no contest to a felony or misdemeanor in superior court is entitled to appeal as a matter of right the issue of whether the sentence imposed:

(1) Results from an incorrect finding of the defendant's prior record level under G.S. 15A-1340.14 or the defendant's prior conviction level under G.S. 15A-1340.21;

Chapter 15A

(2) Contains a type of sentence disposition that is not authorized by G.S. 15A-1340.17 or G.S. 15A-1340.23 for the defendant's class of offense and prior record or conviction level; or

(3) Contains a term of imprisonment that is for a duration not authorized by G.S. 15A-1340.17 or G.S. 15A-1340.23 for the defendant's class of offense and prior record or conviction level.

(b) Procedures for appeal from the magistrate to the district court are as provided in Article 90, Appeals from Magistrates and from District Court Judges.

(c) Procedures for appeal from the district court to the superior court are as provided in Article 90, Appeals from Magistrates and from District Court Judges.

(d) Procedures for appeal to the appellate division are as provided in this Article, the rules of the appellate division, and Chapter 7A of the General Statutes. The appeal must be perfected and conducted in accordance with the requirements of those provisions.

(e) Except as provided in subsections (a1) and (a2) of this section and G.S. 15A-979, and except when a motion to withdraw a plea of guilty or no contest has been denied, the defendant is not entitled to appellate review as a matter of right when he has entered a plea of guilty or no contest to a criminal charge in the superior court, but he may petition the appellate division for review by writ of certiorari. If an indigent defendant petitions the appellate division for a writ of certiorari, the presiding superior court judge may in his discretion order the preparation of the record and transcript of the proceedings at the expense of the State.

(f) The ruling of the court upon a motion for appropriate relief is subject to review upon appeal or by writ of certiorari as provided in G.S. 15A-1422.

(g) Review by writ of certiorari is available when provided for by this Chapter, by other rules of law, or by rule of the appellate division.

History.
1977, c. 711, s. 1; 1979, c. 760, s. 3; 1981, c. 179, ss. 8, 9; 1993, c. 538, s. 27; 1994, Ex. Sess., c. 24, s. 14(b); 1997-80, s. 4

§ 15A-1445. Appeal by the State

(a) Unless the rule against double jeopardy prohibits further prosecution, the State may appeal from the superior court to the appellate division:

(1) When there has been a decision or judgment dismissing criminal charges as to one or more counts.

(2) Upon the granting of a motion for a new trial on the ground of newly discovered

or newly available evidence but only on questions of law.

(3) When the State alleges that the sentence imposed:

a. Results from an incorrect determination of the defendant's prior record level under G.S. 15A-1340.14 or the defendant's prior conviction level under G.S. 15A-1340.21;

b. Contains a type of sentence disposition that is not authorized by G.S. 15A-1340.17 or G.S. 15A-1340.23 for the defendant's class of offense and prior record or conviction level;

c. Contains a term of imprisonment that is for a duration not authorized by G.S. 15A-1340.17 or G.S. 15A-1340.23 for the defendant's class of offense and prior record or conviction level; or

d. Imposes an intermediate punishment pursuant to G.S. 15A-1340.13(g) based on findings of extraordinary mitigating circumstances that are not supported by evidence or are insufficient as a matter of law to support the dispositional deviation.

(b) The State may appeal an order by the superior court granting a motion to suppress as provided in G.S. 15A-979.

History.
1977, c. 711, s. 1; 1993, c. 538, s. 28; 1994, Ex. Sess., c. 14, s. 28

§ 15A-1446. Requisites for preserving the right to appellate review

(a) Except as provided in subsection (d), error may not be asserted upon appellate review unless the error has been brought to the attention of the trial court by appropriate and timely objection or motion. No particular form is required in order to preserve the right to assert the alleged error upon appeal if the motion or objection clearly presented the alleged error to the trial court. Formal exceptions are not required, but when evidence is excluded a record must be made in the manner provided in G.S. 1A-1, Rule 43(c), in order to assert upon appeal error in the exclusion of that evidence.

(b) Failure to make an appropriate and timely motion or objection constitutes a waiver of the right to assert the alleged error upon appeal, but the appellate court may review such errors affecting substantial rights in the interest of justice if it determines it appropriate to do so.

(c) The making of post-trial motions is not a prerequisite to the assertion of error on appeal.

(d) Errors based upon any of the following grounds, which are asserted to have occurred, may be the subject of appellate review even though no objection, exception or motion has been made in the trial division.

(1) Lack of jurisdiction of the trial court over the offense of which the defendant was convicted.

(2) Lack of jurisdiction of the trial court over the person of the defendant.

(3) The criminal pleading charged acts which, at the time they were committed, did not constitute a violation of criminal law.

(4) The pleading fails to state essential elements of an alleged violation, as required by G.S. 15A-924(a)(5).

(5) The evidence was insufficient as a matter of law.

(6) The defendant was convicted under a statute that is in violation of the Constitution of the United States or the Constitution of North Carolina.

(7) Repealed by Session Laws 1977, 2nd Sess., c. 1147, s. 28.

(8) The conduct for which the defendant was prosecuted was protected by the Constitution of the United States or the Constitution of North Carolina.

(9) Subsequent admission of evidence from a witness when there has been an improperly overruled objection to the admission of evidence on the ground that the witness is for a specified reason incompetent or not qualified or disqualified.

(10) Subsequent admission of evidence involving a specified line of questioning when there has been an improperly overruled objection to the admission of evidence involving that line of questioning.

(11) Questions propounded to a witness by the court or a juror.

(12) Rulings and orders of the court, not directed to the admissibility of evidence during trial, when there has been no opportunity to make an objection or motion.

(13) Error of law in the charge to the jury.

(14) The court has expressed to the jury an opinion as to whether a fact is fully or sufficiently proved.

(15) The defendant was not present at any proceeding at which his presence was required.

(16) Error occurred in the entry of the plea.

(17) The form of the verdict was erroneous.

(18) The sentence imposed was unauthorized at the time imposed, exceeded the maximum authorized by law, was illegally imposed, or is otherwise invalid as a matter of law.

(19) A significant change in law, either substantive or procedural, applies to the proceedings leading to the defendant's conviction or sentence, and retroactive application of the changed legal standard is required.

History.
1977, c. 711, s. 1; 1977, 2nd Sess., c. 1147, s. 28; 1983 (Reg. Sess., 1984), c. 1037, s. 1

§ 15A-1447. Relief available upon appeal

(a) If the appellate court finds that there has been reversible error which denied the defendant a fair trial conducted in accordance with law, it must grant the defendant a new trial.

(b) If the appellate court finds that the facts charged in a pleading were not at the time charged a crime, the judgment must be reversed and the charge must be dismissed.

(c) If the appellate court finds that the evidence with regard to a charge is insufficient as a matter of law, the judgment must be reversed and the charge must be dismissed unless there is evidence to support a lesser included offense. In that case the court may remand for trial on the lesser offense.

(d) If the appellate court affirms only some of the charges, or if it finds error relating only to the sentence, it may direct the return of the case to the trial court for the imposition of an appropriate sentence.

(e) If the appellate court affirms one or more of the charges, but not all of them, and makes a finding that the sentence is sustained by the charge or charges which are affirmed and is appropriate, the court may affirm the sentence.

(f) If the appellate court finds that there is an error with regard to the sentence which may be corrected without returning the case to the trial division for that purpose, it may direct the entry of the appropriate sentence.

(g) If the appellate court finds that there has been reversible error and the rule against double jeopardy prohibits further prosecution, it must dismiss the charges with prejudice.

History.
1977, c. 711, s. 1

§ 15A-1448. Procedures for taking appeal

(a) **Time for Entry of Appeal; Jurisdiction over the Case. --**

(1) A case remains open for the taking of an appeal to the appellate division for the period provided in the rules of appellate procedure for giving notice of appeal.

(2) When a motion for appropriate relief is made under G.S. 15A-1414 or G.S. 15A-1416(a), the case remains open for the taking of an appeal until the court has ruled on the motion. The time for taking an appeal as provided in subsection (b) shall begin to run immediately upon the entry of an order under G.S. 15A-1420(c)(7), and the

case shall remain open for the taking of an appeal until the expiration of that time.

(3) The jurisdiction of the trial court with regard to the case is divested, except as to actions authorized by G.S. 15A-1453, when notice of appeal has been given and the period described in (1) and (2) has expired.

(4) Repealed by Session Laws 1987, c. 624.

(5) The right to appeal is not waived by withdrawal of an appeal if the appeal is re-entered within the time specified in (1) and (2).

(6) The right to appeal is not waived by compliance with all or a portion of the judgment imposed. If the defendant appeals, the court may enter appropriate orders remitting any fines or costs which have been paid. The court may delay the remission pending the determination of the appeal.

(b) **How and When Appeal of Right Taken.** -- Notice of appeal shall be given within the time, in the manner and with the effect provided in the rules of appellate procedure.

(c) **Certiorari.** -- Petitions for writs of certiorari are governed by rules of the appellate division.

History.
1977, c. 711, s. 1; 1977, 2nd Sess., c. 1147, s. 29; 1987, c. 624; 1989, c. 377, s. 5

§ 15A-1449. Security for costs not required

In criminal cases no security for costs is required upon appeal to the appellate division.

History.
1977, c. 711, s. 1

§ 15A-1450. Withdrawal of appeal

An appeal may be withdrawn by filing with the clerk of superior court a written notice of the withdrawal, signed by the defendant and, if he has counsel, his attorney. The clerk must forward a copy of the notice to the clerk of the appellate division in which the case is pending. The appellate division may enter an appropriate order with regard to the costs of the appeal.

History.
1977, c. 711, s. 1

§ 15A-1451. Stay of sentence; bail; no stay when State appeals

(a) When a defendant has given notice of appeal:

(1) Payment of costs is stayed.

(2) Payment of a fine is stayed.

(3) Confinement is stayed only when the defendant has been released pursuant to Article 26, Bail.

(4) Probation or special probation is stayed.

(b) The effect of dismissal of charges is not stayed by an appeal by the State, and the defendant is free from such charges unless they are subsequently reinstated as a result of the determination upon appeal.

History.
1977, c. 711, s. 1

§ 15A-1452. Execution of sentence upon determination of appeal; compliance with directive of appellate court

(a) If an appeal is withdrawn for a judgment that imposed an active sentence or imposed only monetary obligations without probation, the clerk of superior court must enter an order reflecting that fact and directing compliance with the judgment.

(a1) If an appeal is withdrawn for a judgment that imposed a suspended sentence, the clerk of superior court shall notify the district attorney who shall calendar a review hearing as required in subsection (d) of this section.

(b) If the appellate division affirms in whole or in part, a judgment that imposed an active sentence or imposed only monetary obligations without probation, the clerk of superior court must file the directive of the appellate division and order compliance with its terms.

(b1) If the appellate division affirms a judgment that imposed a suspended sentence, the clerk of superior court shall file the directive of the appellate division and bring the matter to the attention of the district attorney, who shall calendar a review hearing as provided in subsection (d) of this section.

(c) If the appellate division orders a new trial or directs other relief or proceedings, the clerk must file the directive of the appellate court and bring the directive to the attention of the district attorney or the court for compliance with the directive.

(d) When notified by the clerk as provided in this section, the district attorney shall calendar a hearing in superior court for review of the judgment imposed. The defendant shall be entitled to be present and represented by counsel to the same extent as in the original sentencing hearing.

(1) At the review hearing, the court shall enter an order directing compliance with the judgment either as imposed or as modified as provided in this subsection. The defendant's period of probation shall commence as of the date of the court's order.

(2) If the defendant's ability to comply with any date or period of time specified in the original judgment has become impractical or impossible due to the pendency of the appeal, the court may modify those dates in order to give effect to the original judgment as closely as possible.

(3) The court shall not modify the judgment other than to adjust dates or periods for compliance as provided in subdivision (2) of this subsection, unless the court otherwise complies with the procedures for modification of probation in G.S. 15A-1344.

History.
1977, c. 711, s. 1; 2019-243, s. 7(a)

§ 15A-1453. Ancillary actions during appeal

(a) While an appeal is pending in the appellate division, the court in which the defendant was convicted has continuing authority to act with regard to the defendant's release pursuant to Article 26, Bail.

(b) The appropriate court of the appellate division may direct that additional steps be taken in the trial court while the appeal is pending, including but not limited to:

(1) Appointment of counsel.

(2) Hearings with regard to matters relating to the appeal.

(3) Taking evidence or conducting other proceedings relating to motions for appropriate relief made in the appellate division, as provided in G.S. 15A-1418.

History.
1977, c. 711, s. 1

§§ 15A-1454 through 15A-1459

Reserved for future codification purposes.

ARTICLE 92
NORTH CAROLINA INNOCENCE INQUIRY COMMISSION

§ 15A-1460. Definitions

The following definitions apply in this Article:

(1) "Claim of factual innocence" means a claim on behalf of a living person convicted of a felony in the General Court of Justice of the State of North Carolina, asserting the complete innocence of any criminal responsibility for the felony for which the person was convicted and for any other reduced level of criminal responsibility relating to the crime, and for which there is some credible, verifiable evidence of innocence that has not previously been presented at trial or considered at a hearing granted through postconviction relief.

(1a) "Claimant" means a person asserting that he or she is completely innocent of any criminal responsibility for a felony crime upon which the person was convicted and for any other reduced level of criminal responsibility relating to the crime.

(2) "Commission" means the North Carolina Innocence Inquiry Commission established by this Article.

(3) "Director" means the Director of the North Carolina Innocence Inquiry Commission.

(3a) "Formal inquiry" means the stage of an investigation when the Commission has entered into a signed agreement with the original claimant and the Commission has made efforts to notify the victim.

(4) "Victim" means the victim of the crime, or if the victim of the crime is deceased, the next of kin of the victim.

History.
2006-184, s. 1; 2010-171, s. 5; 2012-7, s. 4; 2016-73, s. 1

§ 15A-1461. Purpose of Article

This Article establishes an extraordinary procedure to investigate and determine credible claims of factual innocence that shall require an individual to voluntarily waive rights and privileges as described in this Article.

History.
2006-184, s. 1; 2010-171, s. 5

§ 15A-1462. Commission established

(a) There is established the North Carolina Innocence Inquiry Commission. The North Carolina Innocence Inquiry Commission shall be an independent commission under the Administrative Office of the Courts for administrative purposes.

(b) The Administrative Office of the Courts shall provide administrative support to the Commission as needed. The Director of the Administrative Office of the Courts shall not reduce or modify the budget of the Commission or use funds appropriated to the Commission without the approval of the Commission. The Administrative Office of the Courts shall conduct an annual audit of the Commission.

History.
2006-184, s. 1; 2010-171, s. 5; 2015-241, s. 18A.16

§ 15A-1463. Membership; chair; meetings; quorum

(a) The Commission shall consist of eight voting members as follows:

> (1) One shall be a superior court judge.
> (2) One shall be a prosecuting attorney.
> (3) One shall be a victim advocate.
> (4) One shall be engaged in the practice of criminal defense law.
> (5) One shall be a public member who is not an attorney and who is not an officer or employee of the Judicial Department.
> (6) One shall be a sheriff holding office at the time of his or her appointment.
> (7) The vocations of the two remaining appointed voting members shall be at the discretion of the Chief Justice.

The Chief Justice of the North Carolina Supreme Court shall make the initial appointment for members identified in subdivisions (4) through (6) of this subsection. The Chief Judge of the Court of Appeals shall make the initial appointment for members identified in subdivisions (1) through (3) of this subsection. After an appointee has served his or her first three-year term, the subsequent appointment shall be by the Chief Justice or Chief Judge who did not make the previous appointment. Thereafter, the Chief Justice or Chief Judge shall rotate the appointing power, except for the two discretionary appointments identified by subdivision (7) of this subsection which shall be appointed by the Chief Justice.

(b) The appointing authority shall also appoint alternate Commission members for the Commission members he or she has appointed to serve in the event of scheduling conflicts, conflicts of interest, disability, or other disqualification arising in a particular case. The alternate members shall have the same qualifications for appointment as the original member. In making the appointments, the appointing authority shall make a good faith effort to appoint members with different perspectives of the justice system. The appointing authority shall also consider geographical location, gender, and racial diversity in making the appointments.

(c) The superior court judge who is appointed as a member under subsection (a) of this section shall serve as Chair of the Commission. The Commission shall have its initial meeting no later than January 31, 2007, at the call of the Chair. The Commission shall meet a minimum of once every six months and may also meet more often at the call of the Chair. The Commission shall meet at such time and place as designated by the Chair. Notice of the meetings shall be given at such time and manner as provided by the rules of the Commission. A majority of the members shall constitute a quorum. All Commission votes shall be by majority vote.

History.
2006-184, s. 1; 2010-171, s. 5

§ 15A-1464. Terms of members; compensation; expenses

(a) Of the initial members, two appointments shall be for one-year terms, three appointments shall be for two-year terms, and three appointments shall be for three-year terms. Thereafter, all terms shall be for three years. Members of the Commission shall serve no more than two consecutive three-year terms plus any initial term of less than three years. Unless provided otherwise by this act, all terms of members shall begin on January 1 and end on December 31.

Members serving by virtue of elective or appointive office, except for the sheriff, may serve only so long as the officeholders hold those respective offices. The Chief Justice may remove members, with cause. Vacancies occurring before the expiration of a term shall be filled in the manner provided for the members first appointed.

(b) The Commission members shall receive no salary for serving. All Commission members shall receive necessary subsistence and travel expenses in accordance with the provisions of G.S. 138-5 and G.S. 138-6, as applicable.

History.
2006-184, s. 1; 2010-171, s. 5

§ 15A-1465. Director and other staff

(a) The Commission shall employ a Director. The Director shall report to the Director of the Administrative Office of the Courts, who shall consult with the Commission chair. The Director shall be an attorney licensed to practice in North Carolina at the time of appointment and at all times during service as Director. The Director shall assist the Commission in developing rules and standards for cases accepted for review, coordinate investigation of cases accepted for review, maintain records for all case investigations, prepare reports outlining Commission investigations and recommendations to the trial court, and apply for and accept on behalf of the Commission any funds that may become available from government grants, private gifts, donations, or devises from any source.

(b) Subject to the approval of the Chair, the Director shall employ such other staff and shall contract for services as is necessary to assist the Commission in the performance of its duties, and as funds permit.

(c) The Commission may, with the approval of the Legislative Services Commission, meet in the State Legislative Building or the Legislative Office Building, or may meet in an area provided by the Director of the Administrative Office of the Courts. The Director of the Administrative Office of the Courts shall provide office space for the Commission and the Commission staff.

History.
2006-184, s. 1; 2010-171, s. 5; 2011-284, s. 11; 2016-73, s. 2

§ 15A-1466. Duties

The Commission shall have the following duties and powers:

(1) To establish the criteria and screening process to be used to determine which cases shall be accepted for review.

(2) To conduct inquiries into claims of factual innocence, with priority to be given to those cases in which the convicted person is currently incarcerated solely for the crime for which he or she claims factual innocence.

(3) To coordinate the investigation of cases accepted for review.

(4) To maintain records for all case investigations.

(5) To prepare written reports outlining Commission investigations and recommendations to the trial court at the completion of each inquiry.

(6) To apply for and accept any funds that may become available for the Commission's work from government grants, private gifts, donations, or devises from any source.

History.
2006-184, s. 1; 2010-171, s. 5; 2011-284, s. 12

§ 15A-1467. Claims of innocence; waiver of convicted person's procedural safeguards and privileges; formal inquiry; notification of the crime victim

(a) A claim of factual innocence for any conviction may be referred to the Commission by any court, a State or local agency, or a claimant's counsel. A claim of factual innocence for convictions of homicide pursuant to Article 6 of Chapter 14 of the General Statutes, robbery pursuant to Article 17 of Chapter 14 of the General Statutes, any offense requiring registration pursuant to Article 27A of Chapter 14 of the General Statutes, and any Class A through E felony may be made directly by the claimant. The Commission shall not consider a claim of factual innocence if the convicted person is deceased. A claimant who received notice pursuant to subsection (c1) of this section and did not make a claim of factual innocence shall be barred from investigation of a claim of factual innocence by the Commission absent a showing of good cause and approval of the Commission Chair. The determination of whether to grant a formal inquiry regarding any other claim of factual innocence is in the discretion of the Commission. The Commission may informally screen and dismiss a case summarily at its discretion.

(b) No formal inquiry into a claim of innocence shall be made by the Commission unless the Director or the Director's designee first obtains a signed agreement from the convicted person in which the convicted person waives his or her procedural safeguards and privileges, agrees to cooperate with the Commission, and agrees to provide full disclosure regarding all inquiry requirements of the Commission. The waiver under this subsection does not apply to matters unrelated to a convicted person's claim of innocence. The convicted person shall have the right to advice of counsel prior to the execution of the agreement and, if a formal inquiry is granted, throughout the formal inquiry. If counsel represents the convicted person, then the convicted person's counsel must be present at the signing of the agreement. If counsel does not represent the convicted person, the Commission Chair shall determine the convicted person's indigency status and, if appropriate, enter an order for the appointment of counsel by Indigent Defense Services for the purpose of advising on the agreement. If the convicted person has requested a specific attorney with knowledge of the case, the Director shall inform Indigent Defense Services of that request for their consideration.

(b1) Forensic testing and claimant interviews shall not be conducted by the Commission prior to obtaining a signed agreement from the convicted person.

(c) If a formal inquiry regarding a claim of factual innocence is granted, the Director shall use all due diligence to notify the victim in the case and explain the inquiry process. The Commission shall give the victim notice that the victim has the right to present his or her views and concerns throughout the Commission's investigation.

(c1) Absent a showing of good cause and approval of the Commission chair, if a formal inquiry regarding a claim of factual innocence is granted, the Commission shall use all due diligence to notify each codefendant of the claim that an investigation will be conducted and that if the codefendant wishes to also file a claim, they must do so within 60 days from receipt of the notice or their claim may be barred from future investigation by the Commission.

(c2) If a formal inquiry regarding a claim of factual innocence is granted, the Director shall provide a confidential case status update for each case in formal inquiry to (i) the District Attorney and (ii) the convicted person, or counsel, if any, at least once every six months. If there is no defense counsel, the update shall be provided to the District Attorney, the convicted person, and referring counsel, if any. The case status update shall include a summary of the actions taken since the last update and the results of any forensic testing that has been conducted.

(d) The Commission may use any measure provided in Chapter 15A of the General Statutes and the Rules of Civil Procedure as set out in G.S. 1A-1 to obtain information necessary to its inquiry. The Commission may also do any of the following: issue process to compel the attendance of witnesses and the production of evidence, administer oaths, petition the Superior Court of Wake County or of the original jurisdiction for enforcement of process or for other relief, and prescribe its own rules of procedure. All challenges with regard to the Commission's authority or the Commission's access to evidence shall be heard by the Commission Chair in the Chair's judicial capacity, including any in camera review required by G.S. 15A-908.

(e) While performing duties for the Commission, the Director or the Director's designee may serve subpoenas or other process issued by the Commission throughout the State in the same manner and with the same effect as an officer authorized to serve process of the General Court of Justice.

(f) All State discovery and disclosure statutes in effect at the time of formal inquiry shall be enforceable as if the convicted person were currently being tried for the charge for which the convicted person is claiming innocence.

(g) If, at any point during an inquiry, the convicted person refuses to comply with requests of the Commission or is otherwise deemed to be uncooperative by the Commission, the Commission shall discontinue the inquiry.

History.
2006-184, s. 1; 2010-171, s. 5; 2012-7, s. 5; 2016-73, s. 3

§ 15A-1468. Commission proceedings

(a) At the completion of a formal inquiry, all relevant evidence shall be presented to the full Commission in a public hearing. Any public hearing held in accordance with this section shall be subject to the Commission's rules of operation. The Commission's rules of operation shall not exclude the district attorney or defense counsel from any portion of the hearing.

(a1) The Commission may compel the testimony of any witness. If a witness asserts his or her privilege against self-incrimination in a proceeding under this Article, the Commission chair, in the chair's judicial capacity, may order the witness to testify or produce other information if the chair first determines that the witness's testimony will likely be material to the investigation and necessary to reach a correct factual determination in the case at hand. However, the Commission chair shall not order the witness to testify or produce other information that would incriminate the witness in the prosecution of any offense other than an offense for which the witness is granted immunity under this subsection. The order shall prevent a prosecutor from using the compelled testimony, or evidence derived therefrom, to prosecute the witness for previous false statements made under oath by the witness in prior proceedings. The prosecutor has a right to be heard by the Commission chair prior to the chair issuing the order. Once granted, the immunity shall apply throughout all proceedings conducted pursuant to this Article. The limited immunity granted under this section shall not prohibit prosecution of statements made under oath that are unrelated to the Commission's formal inquiry, false statements made under oath during proceedings under this Article, or prosecution for any other crimes.

(a2) The Innocence Inquiry Commission shall include, as part of its rules of operation, the holding of a prehearing conference to be held at least 10 days prior to any proceedings of the full Commission. Only the following persons shall be notified and authorized to attend the prehearing conference: the District Attorney, or the District Attorney's designee, of the district where the claimant was convicted of the felony upon which the claim of factual innocence is based; the claimant's counsel, if any; the Chair of the Commission; the Executive Director of the Commission; and any Commission staff designated by the Director. The District Attorney, or designee, shall be provided (i) an opportunity to inspect any evidence that may be presented to the Commission that has not previously been presented to any judicial officer or body and (ii) any information that the District Attorney, or the District Attorney's designee, deems relevant to the proceedings. At least 72 hours prior to any Commission proceedings, the District Attorney or designee is authorized to provide the Commission with a written statement, which shall be part of the record.

(b) The Director shall use all due diligence to notify the victim at least 30 days prior to any proceedings of the full Commission held in regard to the victim's case. The Commission shall notify the victim that the victim is permitted to attend proceedings otherwise closed to the public, subject to any limitations imposed by this Article. If the victim plans to attend proceedings otherwise closed to the public, the victim shall notify the Commission at least 10 days in advance of the proceedings of the victim's intent to attend.

(c) After hearing the evidence, the full Commission shall vote to establish further case disposition as provided by this subsection. All eight voting members of the Commission shall participate in that vote.

Except in cases where the convicted person entered and was convicted on a plea of guilty, if five or more of the eight voting members of the Commission conclude there is sufficient evidence of factual innocence to merit judicial review, the case shall be referred to the senior resident superior court judge in the district of original jurisdiction by filing with the clerk of court the opinion of the Commission with supporting findings of fact, as well as the record in support of such opinion, with service on the convicted person or the convicted person's counsel, if any, and the district attorney in noncapital cases or service on both the district attorney and Attorney General in capital cases. In cases where the convicted person entered and was convicted on a plea of guilty, if all of the eight voting members of the Commission conclude there is sufficient evidence of factual innocence to merit judicial review, the case shall be referred to the senior resident superior court judge in the district of original jurisdiction.

If less than five of the eight voting members of the Commission, or in cases where the convicted person entered and was convicted on a guilty plea less than all of the eight voting members of the Commission, conclude there is sufficient evidence of factual innocence to merit judicial review, the Commission shall conclude there is insufficient evidence of factual innocence to merit judicial review. The Commission shall document that opinion, along with supporting findings of fact, and file those documents and supporting materials with the clerk of superior court in the district of original jurisdiction, with a copy to the convicted person or the convicted person's counsel, if any, the district attorney and the senior resident superior court judge.

The Director of the Commission shall use all due diligence to notify immediately the victim of the Commission's conclusion in a case.

(d) Evidence of criminal acts, professional misconduct, or other wrongdoing disclosed through formal inquiry or Commission proceedings shall be referred to the appropriate authority. Evidence favorable to the convicted person disclosed through formal inquiry or Commission proceedings shall be disclosed to the convicted person and the convicted person's counsel, if the convicted person has counsel.

(e) All proceedings of the Commission shall be recorded and transcribed as part of the record. All Commission member votes shall be recorded in the record. The supporting records for the Commission's conclusion that there is sufficient evidence of factual innocence to merit judicial review, including all files and materials considered by the Commission and a full transcript of the hearing before the Commission, shall become public when filed with the superior court as required in subsection (c) of this section. Commission records for conclusions of insufficient evidence of factual innocence to merit judicial review shall remain confidential, except as provided in subsection (d) of this section.

(f) At any point in the formal inquiry regarding a claim of factual innocence, the District Attorney and the convicted person or the convicted person's counsel may agree that there is sufficient evidence of factual innocence to merit judicial review by the three-judge panel and bypass the eight-member panel. The Director and the Chair of the Commission shall be notified in writing of any such agreement.

(g) Except as otherwise provided in this section, all files and records not filed with the clerk of superior court or presented at the Commission hearings are confidential and exempt from the public record. If the Commission concludes there is sufficient evidence of factual innocence to merit judicial review, the Commission shall make a copy of the entire file available to the district attorney and defense counsel. Upon availability, the Commission shall provide the district attorney and defense counsel a copy of the uncertified and certified transcript of the Commission's proceedings. Absent a judicial finding of malicious conduct, the Commission and Commission staff shall not be civilly liable for acting in compliance with this subsection.

(h) With respect to the evidence presented to the three-judge panel, the district attorney and defense counsel may determine which evidence, if any, will be presented to the three-judge panel.

History.
2006-184, s. 1; 2009-360, s. 1; 2010-171, s. 5; 2012-7, ss. 6, 7; 2016-73, s. 4

§ 15A-1469. Postcommission three-judge panel

(a) If the Commission concludes or the district attorney and the convicted person's counsel agree pursuant to G.S. 15A-1468(f), there is sufficient evidence of factual innocence to merit judicial review, the Chair of the Commission shall request the Chief Justice to appoint a three-judge panel, not to include any trial judge that has had substantial previous involvement in the case, and issue commissions to the members of the three-judge panel to convene a special session of the superior court of the original jurisdiction to hear evidence relevant to the Commission's recommendation. The senior judge of the panel shall preside. The Chief Justice shall appoint the three-judge panel within 20 days of the filing of the

Chapter 15A

Commission's opinion finding sufficient evidence of factual innocence to merit judicial review.

(a1) If the Commission concludes that there is credible evidence of prosecutorial misconduct in the case, the Chair of the Commission may request the Attorney General to appoint a special prosecutor to represent the State in lieu of the district attorney of the district of conviction or the district attorney's designee. The request for the special prosecutor shall be made within 20 days of the filing of the Commission's opinion finding sufficient evidence of innocence to merit judicial review.

Upon receipt of a request under this subsection to appoint a special prosecutor, the Attorney General may temporarily assign a district attorney, assistant district attorney, or other qualified attorney, to represent the State at the hearing before the three-judge panel. However, the Attorney General shall not appoint as special prosecutor any attorney who prosecuted or assisted with the prosecution in the trial of the convicted person, or is a prosecuting attorney in the district where the convicted person was tried. The appointment shall be made no later than 20 days after the receipt of the request.

(b) The senior resident superior court judge in the district of original jurisdiction shall enter an order setting the case for hearing at the special session of superior court for which the three judge panel is commissioned and shall require the State to file a response to the Commission's opinion within 90 days of the date of the order. Such response, at the time of original filing or through amendment at any time before or during the proceedings, may include joining the defense in a motion to dismiss the charges with prejudice on the basis of innocence.

(b1) The Commission's entire file, including files obtained from other agencies, shall be unencumbered by protective orders when transferred to the district attorney and defense counsel pursuant to G.S. 15A-1468(g), unless either of the following apply:

(1) The district attorney and defense counsel have consented to a protective order over a portion of the file.

(2) The district attorney and defense counsel have been given an opportunity to be heard by the senior judge of the three-judge panel before a protective order is issued.

(c) The district attorney of the district of conviction, or the district attorney's designee, shall represent the State at the hearing before the three-judge panel, except as otherwise provided by this section.

(d) The three-judge panel shall conduct an evidentiary hearing. At the hearing, the court, and the defense and prosecution through the court, may compel the testimony of any witness, including the convicted person. All credible, verifiable evidence relevant to the case, even if considered by a jury or judge in a prior proceeding, may be presented during the hearing. The convicted person may not assert any privilege or prevent a witness from testifying. The convicted person has a right to be present at the evidentiary hearing and to be represented by counsel. A waiver of the right to be present shall be in writing.

(e) The senior resident superior court judge in the district of original jurisdiction shall determine the convicted person's indigency status and, if appropriate, enter an order for the appointment of counsel by Indigent Defense Services. If the convicted person has requested a specific attorney with knowledge of the case, the Director shall inform Indigent Defense Services of that request for their consideration. The court may also enter an order relieving an indigent convicted person of all or a portion of the costs of the proceedings.

(f) The clerk of court shall provide written notification to the victim 30 days prior to any case-related hearings.

(g) Upon the motion of either party, the senior judge of the panel may direct the attorneys for the parties to appear before him or her for a conference on any matter in the case.

(h) The three-judge panel shall rule as to whether the convicted person has proved by clear and convincing evidence that the convicted person is innocent of the charges. Such a determination shall require a unanimous vote. If the vote is unanimous, the panel shall enter dismissal of all or any of the charges. If the vote is not unanimous, the panel shall deny relief.

(i) A person who is determined by the three-judge panel to be innocent of all charges and against whom the charges are dismissed pursuant to this section is eligible for compensation under Article 8 of Chapter 148 of the General Statutes without obtaining a pardon of innocence from the Governor.

History.
2006-184, s. 1; 2010-171, ss. 1, 5; 2012-7, s. 8; 2016-73, s. 5; 2019-243, s. 22(a)

§ 15A-1470. No right to further review of decision by Commission or three-judge panel; convicted person retains right to other postconviction relief

(a) Unless otherwise authorized by this Article, the decisions of the Commission and of the three-judge panel are final and are not subject to further review by appeal, certification, writ, motion, or otherwise.

(b) A claim of factual innocence asserted through the Innocence Inquiry Commission shall not adversely affect the convicted person's rights to other postconviction relief.

History.
2006-184, s. 1; 2010-171, s. 5

§ 15A-1471. Preservation of files and evidence; production of files and evidence; forensic and DNA testing

(a) Upon receiving written notice from the Commission of a Commission inquiry, the State shall preserve all files and evidence subject to disclosure under G.S. 15A-903. Once the Commission provides written notice to the State that the Commission's inquiry is complete, the duty to preserve under this section shall cease; however, other preservation requirements may be applicable.

(b) The Commission is entitled to a copy of all records preserved under subsection (a) of this section, including access to inspect and examine all physical evidence.

(c) Upon request of the Commission, the State shall transfer custody of physical evidence to the Commission's Director, or the Director's designee, for forensic and DNA testing. The Commission shall preserve evidence in a manner reasonably calculated to prevent contamination or degradation of any biological evidence that might be present, while subject to a continuous chain of custody and securely retained with sufficient official documentation to locate the evidence. At or prior to the completion of the Commission's inquiry, the Commission shall return all remaining evidence.

(d) The Commission shall have the right to subject physical evidence to forensic and DNA testing, including consumption of biological material, as necessary for the Commission's inquiry. If testing complies with FBI requirements and the data meets NDIS criteria, profiles obtained from the testing shall be searched and uploaded to CODIS. The Commission shall incur all costs associated with ensuring compliance with FBI requirements and NDIS criteria.

History.
2012-7, s. 10

§§ 15A-1472 through 15A-1474

Reserved for future codification purposes.

§ 15A-1475. Reports

Beginning January 1, 2008, and annually thereafter, the North Carolina Innocence Inquiry Commission shall report on its activities to the Joint Legislative Oversight Committee on Justice and Public Safety and the State Judicial Council. The report may contain recommendations of any needed legislative changes related to the activities of the Commission. The report shall recommend the funding needed by the Commission, the district attorneys, and the State Bureau of Investigation in order to meet their responsibilities under S.L. 2006-184. Recommendations concerning the district attorneys or the State Bureau of Investigation shall only be made after consultations with the North Carolina Conference of District Attorneys and the Director of the State Bureau of Investigation.

History.
2006-184, s. 9; 2011-291, s. 2.4; 2014-100, ss. 17.1(p), 18B.1(f)

ARTICLE 93 TO 99

§§ 15A-1476 through 15A-1999

Reserved for future codification purposes.

SUBCHAPTER 15. CAPITAL PUNISHMENT

ARTICLE 100 CAPITAL PUNISHMENT

§ 15A-2000. Sentence of death or life imprisonment for capital felonies; further proceedings to determine sentence

(a) **Separate Proceedings on Issue of Penalty. --**

(1) Except as provided in G.S. 15A-2004, upon conviction or adjudication of guilt of a defendant of a capital felony in which the State has given notice of its intent to seek the death penalty, the court shall conduct a separate sentencing proceeding to determine whether the defendant should be sentenced to death or life imprisonment. A capital felony is one which may be punishable by death.

(2) The proceeding shall be conducted by the trial judge before the trial jury as soon as practicable after the guilty verdict is returned. If prior to the time that the trial jury begins its deliberations on the issue of penalty, any juror dies, becomes incapacitated or disqualified, or is discharged for any reason, an alternate juror shall become a part of the jury and serve in all respects as those selected on the regular trial panel. An alternate juror shall become a part of the jury in the order in which the alternate juror was selected. If the trial jury is unable to reconvene for a hearing on the issue of penalty after having determined the guilt of the accused, the trial judge shall impanel a

new jury to determine the issue of the punishment. If the defendant pleads guilty, the sentencing proceeding shall be conducted before a jury impaneled for that purpose. A jury selected for the purpose of determining punishment in a capital case shall be selected in the same manner as juries are selected for the trial of capital cases.

(3) In the proceeding there shall not be any requirement to resubmit evidence presented during the guilt determination phase of the case, unless a new jury is impaneled, but all such evidence is competent for the jury's consideration in passing on punishment. Evidence may be presented as to any matter that the court deems relevant to sentence, and may include matters relating to any of the aggravating or mitigating circumstances enumerated in subsections (e) and (f) of this section. Any evidence which the court deems to have probative value may be received.

(4) The State and the defendant or his counsel shall be permitted to present argument for or against sentence of death. The defendant or defendant's counsel shall have the right to the last argument.

(b) **Sentence Recommendation by the Jury.** -- Instructions determined by the trial judge to be warranted by the evidence shall be given by the court in its charge to the jury prior to its deliberation in determining sentence. The court shall give appropriate instructions in those cases in which evidence of the defendant's intellectual disability requires the consideration by the jury of the provisions of G.S. 15A-2005. In all cases in which the death penalty may be authorized, the judge shall include in the judge's instructions to the jury that it must consider any aggravating circumstance or circumstances or mitigating circumstance or circumstances from the lists provided in subsections (e) and (f) of this section which may be supported by the evidence, and shall furnish to the jury a written list of issues relating to such aggravating or mitigating circumstance or circumstances.

After hearing the evidence, argument of counsel, and instructions of the court, the jury shall deliberate and render a sentence recommendation to the court, based upon all of the following matters:

(1) Whether any sufficient aggravating circumstance or circumstances as enumerated in subsection (e) of this section exist.

(2) Whether any sufficient mitigating circumstance or circumstances as enumerated in subsection (f) of this section, which outweigh the aggravating circumstance or circumstances found, exist.

(3) Based on these considerations, whether the defendant should be sentenced

to death or to imprisonment in the State's prison for life.

The sentence recommendation must be agreed upon by a unanimous vote of the 12 jurors. Upon delivery of the sentence recommendation by the foreman of the jury, the jury shall be individually polled to establish whether each juror concurs and agrees to the sentence recommendation returned.

If the jury cannot, within a reasonable time, unanimously agree to its sentence recommendation, the judge shall impose a sentence of life imprisonment. The judge shall in no instance impose the death penalty when the jury cannot agree unanimously to its sentence recommendation.

(c) **Findings in Support of Sentence of Death.** -- When the jury recommends a sentence of death, the foreman of the jury shall sign a writing on behalf of the jury that shows all of the following:

(1) The statutory aggravating circumstance or circumstances which the jury finds beyond a reasonable doubt.

(2) That the statutory aggravating circumstance or circumstances found by the jury are sufficiently substantial to call for the imposition of the death penalty.

(3) That the mitigating circumstance or circumstances are insufficient to outweigh the aggravating circumstance or circumstances found.

(d) **Review of Judgment and Sentence.** --

(1) The judgment of conviction and sentence of death shall be subject to automatic review by the Supreme Court of North Carolina pursuant to procedures established by the Rules of Appellate Procedure. In its review, the Supreme Court shall consider the punishment imposed as well as any errors assigned on appeal.

(2) The sentence of death shall be overturned and a sentence of life imprisonment imposed in lieu thereof by the Supreme Court upon a finding that the record does not support the jury's findings of any aggravating circumstance or circumstances upon which the sentencing court based its sentence of death, or upon a finding that the sentence of death was imposed under the influence of passion, prejudice, or any other arbitrary factor, or upon a finding that the sentence of death is excessive or disproportionate to the penalty imposed in similar cases, considering both the crime and the defendant. The Supreme Court may suspend consideration of death penalty cases until such time as the court determines it is prepared to make the comparisons required under this section.

(3) If the sentence of death and the judgment of the trial court are reversed on appeal for error in the post-verdict sentencing proceeding, the Supreme Court shall order that a new sentencing hearing be conducted in conformity with the procedures of this Article.

(e) **Aggravating Circumstances.** -- Aggravating circumstances which may be considered are limited to the following:

(1) The capital felony was committed by a person lawfully incarcerated.

(2) The defendant had been previously convicted of another capital felony or had been previously adjudicated delinquent in a juvenile proceeding for committing an offense that would be a capital felony if committed by an adult.

(3) The defendant had been previously convicted of a felony involving the use or threat of violence to the person or had been previously adjudicated delinquent in a juvenile proceeding for committing an offense that would be a Class A, B1, B2, C, D, or E felony involving the use or threat of violence to the person if the offense had been committed by an adult.

(4) The capital felony was committed for the purpose of avoiding or preventing a lawful arrest or effecting an escape from custody.

(5) The capital felony was committed while the defendant was engaged, or was an aider or abettor, in the commission of, or an attempt to commit, or flight after committing or attempting to commit, any homicide, robbery, rape or a sex offense, arson, burglary, kidnapping, or aircraft piracy or the unlawful throwing, placing, or discharging of a destructive device or bomb.

(6) The capital felony was committed for pecuniary gain.

(7) The capital felony was committed to disrupt or hinder the lawful exercise of any governmental function or the enforcement of laws.

(8) The capital felony was committed against a law-enforcement officer, employee of the Division of Adult Correction and Juvenile Justice of the Department of Public Safety, jailer, fireman, judge or justice, former judge or justice, prosecutor or former prosecutor, juror or former juror, or witness or former witness against the defendant, while engaged in the performance of his official duties or because of the exercise of his official duty.

(9) The capital felony was especially heinous, atrocious, or cruel.

(10) The defendant knowingly created a great risk of death to more than one person by means of a weapon or device which would normally be hazardous to the lives of more than one person.

(11) The murder for which the defendant stands convicted was part of a course of conduct in which the defendant engaged and which included the commission by the defendant of other crimes of violence against another person or persons.

(f) **Mitigating Circumstances.** -- Mitigating circumstances which may be considered include, but are not limited to, the following:

(1) The defendant has no significant history of prior criminal activity.

(2) The capital felony was committed while the defendant was under the influence of mental or emotional disturbance.

(3) The victim was a voluntary participant in the defendant's homicidal conduct or consented to the homicidal act.

(4) The defendant was an accomplice in or accessory to the capital felony committed by another person and the defendant's participation was relatively minor.

(5) The defendant acted under duress or under the domination of another person.

(6) The capacity of the defendant to appreciate the criminality of the defendant's conduct or to conform that conduct to the requirements of law was impaired.

(7) The age of the defendant at the time of the crime.

(8) The defendant aided in the apprehension of another capital felon or testified truthfully on behalf of the prosecution in another prosecution of a felony.

(9) Any other circumstance arising from the evidence which the jury deems to have mitigating value.

History.
1977, c. 406, s. 2; 1979, c. 565, s. 1; c. 682, s. 9; 1981, c. 652, s. 1; 1994, Ex. Sess., c. 7, s. 5; 1995, c. 509, s. 14; 2001-81, s. 1; 2001-346, s. 2; 2011-145, s. 19.1(h); 2017-186, s. 2 (eeee); 2018-47, s. 5

§ 15A-2001. Capital offenses; plea of guilty

(a) Any defendant who has been indicted for an offense punishable by death may enter a plea of guilty at any time after the indictment.

(b) If the defendant enters a guilty plea to first degree murder and the State has not given notice of intent to seek the death penalty as provided in G.S. 15A-2004 or the State has agreed to accept a sentence of life imprisonment where it initially gave notice of intent to seek the death penalty, then the court shall sentence the person to life imprisonment. The defendant may plead guilty to first degree murder and the State may agree to accept a sentence of life imprisonment, even if evidence of an aggravating circumstance exists.

(c) If the defendant enters a guilty plea to first degree murder and the State has given notice of its intent to seek the death penalty, then the court may sentence the defendant to life imprisonment or to death pursuant to the procedures of G.S. 15A-2000. Before sentencing the defendant in a case in which the State has given notice of its intent to seek the death penalty, the presiding judge shall impanel a jury for the limited purpose of hearing evidence and determining a sentence recommendation as to the appropriate sentence pursuant to G.S. 15A-2000. The jury's sentence recommendation in cases where the defendant pleads guilty and the State has given notice of its intent to seek the death penalty shall be determined under the same procedure of G.S. 15A-2000 applicable to defendants who have been tried and found guilty by a jury.

History.
1977, c. 406, s. 2; 2001-81, s. 2

§ 15A-2002. Capital offenses; jury verdict and sentence

If the recommendation of the jury is that the defendant be sentenced to death, the judge shall impose a sentence of death in accordance with the provisions of Chapter 15, Article 19 of the General Statutes. If the recommendation of the jury is that the defendant be imprisoned for life in the State's prison, the judge shall impose a sentence of imprisonment for life in the State's prison, without parole.

The judge shall instruct the jury, in words substantially equivalent to those of this section, that a sentence of life imprisonment means a sentence of life without parole.

History.
1977, c. 406, s. 2; 1993, c. 538, s. 29; 1994, Ex. Sess., c. 21, s. 5; c. 24, s. 14(b)

§ 15A-2003. Disability of trial judge

In the event that the trial judge shall become disabled or unable to conduct the sentencing proceeding provided in this Article, the Chief Justice shall designate a judge to conduct such proceeding.

History.
1977, c. 406, s. 2

§ 15A-2004. Prosecutorial discretion

(a) The State, in its discretion, may elect to try a defendant capitally or noncapitally for first degree murder, even if evidence of an

aggravating circumstance exists. The State may agree to accept a sentence of life imprisonment for a defendant at any point in the prosecution of a capital felony, even if evidence of an aggravating circumstance exists.

(b) A sentence of death may not be imposed upon a defendant convicted of a capital felony unless the State has given notice of its intent to seek the death penalty. Notice of intent to seek the death penalty shall be given to the defendant and filed with the court on or before the date of the pretrial conference in capital cases required by Rule 24 of the General Rules of Practice for the Superior and District Courts, or the arraignment, whichever is later. A court may discipline or sanction the State for failure to comply with the time requirements in Rule 24, but shall not declare a case as noncapital as a consequence of such failure. In addition to any discipline or sanctions the court may impose, the court shall continue the case for a sufficient time so that the defendant is not prejudiced by any delays in holding the hearing required by Rule 24.

(c) If the State has not given notice of its intent to seek the death penalty prior to trial, the trial shall be conducted as a noncapital proceeding, and the court, upon adjudication of the defendant's guilt of first degree murder, shall impose a sentence of life imprisonment.

(d) Notwithstanding any other provision of Article 100 of Chapter 15A of the General Statutes, the State may agree to accept a sentence of life imprisonment for a defendant upon remand from the Supreme Court of North Carolina of a capital case for resentencing or upon an order of resentencing by a court in a State or federal post-conviction proceeding. If the State exercises its discretion and does agree to accept a sentence of life imprisonment for the defendant, then the court shall impose a sentence of life imprisonment.

History.
2001-81, s. 3; 2012-136, s. 2

§ 15A-2005. Intellectual disability; death sentence prohibited

(a) (1) The following definitions apply in this section:

a. **Intellectual disability.** -- A condition marked by significantly subaverage general intellectual functioning, existing concurrently with significant limitations in adaptive functioning, both of which were manifested before the age of 18.

b. **Significant limitations in adaptive functioning.** -- Significant limitations in two or more of the following adaptive skill areas: communication, self-care, home living, social skills, community use, self-direction, health and safety, functional academics, leisure skills and work skills.

c. **Significantly subaverage general intellectual functioning.** -- An intelligence quotient of 70 or below.

(2) The defendant has the burden of proving significantly subaverage general intellectual functioning, significant limitations in adaptive functioning, and that intellectual disability was manifested before the age of 18. An intelligence quotient of 70 or below on an individually administered, scientifically recognized standardized intelligence quotient test administered by a licensed psychiatrist or psychologist is evidence of significantly subaverage general intellectual functioning; however, it is not sufficient, without evidence of significant limitations in adaptive functioning and without evidence of manifestation before the age of 18, to establish that the defendant has an intellectual disability. An intelligence quotient of 70, as described in this subdivision, is approximate and a higher score resulting from the application of the standard error of measurement to an intelligence quotient of 70 shall not preclude the defendant from being able to present additional evidence of intellectual disability, including testimony regarding adaptive deficits. Accepted clinical standards for diagnosing significant limitations in intellectual functioning and adaptive behavior shall be applied in the determination of intellectual disability.

(b) Notwithstanding any provision of law to the contrary, no defendant with an intellectual disability shall be sentenced to death.

(c) Upon motion of the defendant, supported by appropriate affidavits, the court may order a pretrial hearing to determine if the defendant has an intellectual disability. The court shall order such a hearing with the consent of the State. The defendant has the burden of production and persuasion to demonstrate intellectual disability by clear and convincing evidence. If the court determines that the defendant has an intellectual disability, the court shall declare the case noncapital, and the State may not seek the death penalty against the defendant.

(d) The pretrial determination of the court shall not preclude the defendant from raising any legal defense during the trial.

(e) If the court does not find that the defendant has an intellectual disability in the pretrial proceeding, upon the introduction of evidence raising the issue of intellectual disability during the sentencing hearing, the court shall submit a special issue to the jury as to whether the defendant has an intellectual disability as defined in this section. This special issue shall be considered and answered by the jury prior to the consideration of aggravating or mitigating factors and the determination of sentence. If the jury determines that the defendant has an intellectual disability, the court shall declare the case noncapital and the defendant shall be sentenced to life imprisonment.

(f) The defendant has the burden of production and persuasion to demonstrate intellectual disability to the jury by a preponderance of the evidence.

(g) If the jury determines that the defendant does not have an intellectual disability as defined by this section, the jury may consider any evidence of intellectual disability presented during the sentencing hearing when determining aggravating or mitigating factors and the defendant's sentence.

(h) The provisions of this section do not preclude the sentencing of an offender with an intellectual disability to any other sentence authorized by G.S. 14-17 for the crime of murder in the first degree.

History.
2001-346, s. 1; 2015-247, s. 5

N.C. Gen. Stat. § 15A-2006

Expired pursuant to Session Laws 2001-346, s. 3, effective October 1, 2002.

§§ 15A-2007 through 15A-2009

Reserved for future codification purposes.

ARTICLE 101
NORTH CAROLINA RACIAL JUSTICE ACT

§§ 15A-2010 through 15A-2012

Repealed by Session Laws 2013-154, s. 5(a), effective June 19, 2013.

History.
§ 15A-2010: 2009-464, s. 1; repealed by 2013-154, s. 5(a), effective June 19, 2013; § 15A-2011: 2009-464, s. 1; 2012-136, s. 3, repealed by 2013-154, s. 5(a), effective June 19, 2013; § 15A-2012: 2009-464, s. 1; repealed by 2012-136, s. 4, effective July 2, 2012

CHAPTER 15B
VICTIMS COMPENSATION

ARTICLE 1
CRIME VICTIMS COMPENSATION ACT

§ 15B-1. Short title

This Article may be cited as the "North Carolina Crime Victims Compensation Act."

History.
1983, c. 832, s. 1; 1991, c. 301, s. 1; 2004-159, s. 1

§ 15B-2. Definitions

As used in this Article, the following definitions apply, unless the context requires otherwise:

(1) **Allowable expense. --** Reasonable charges incurred for reasonably needed products, services, and accommodations, including those for medical care, rehabilitation, medically-related property, and other remedial treatment and care. Reasonably needed services include (i) counseling for immediate family members of children under the age of 18 who are victims of rape, sexual assault, or domestic violence and (ii) family counseling and grief counseling for immediate family members of homicide victims. The cumulative total for counseling services provided to immediate family members shall not exceed three thousand dollars ($ 3,000) per family.

Allowable expense includes a total charge not in excess of five thousand dollars ($ 5,000) for expenses related to funeral, cremation, and burial, including transportation of a body, but excluding expenses for flowers, gravestone, and other items not directly related to the funeral service.

Allowable expense for medical care, counseling, rehabilitation, medically-related property, and other remedial treatment and care of a victim shall be limited to sixty-six and two-thirds percent (66 2/3%) of the amount usually charged by the provider for the treatment or care. By accepting the compensation paid as allowable expense pursuant to this subdivision, the provider agrees that the compensation is payment in full for the treatment or care and shall not charge or otherwise hold a claimant financially responsible for the cost of services in addition to the amount of allowable expense.

(2) **Claimant. --** Any of the following persons who claims an award of compensation under this Article:

a. A victim;

b. A dependent of a deceased victim;

c. A third person who is not a collateral source and who provided benefit to the victim or his family other than in the course or scope of his employment, business, or profession;

d. A person who is authorized to act on behalf of a victim, a dependent, or a third person described in sub-subdivision c. of this subdivision;

e. A person who was convicted of a first offense under G.S. 14-204 and whose participation in the offense was a result of having been a trafficking victim under G.S. 14-43.11 or G.S. 14-43.13 or a victim of a severe form of trafficking under the federal Trafficking Victims Protection Act (22 U.S.C. § 7102(13)).

The claimant, however, may not be the offender or an accomplice of the offender who committed the criminally injurious conduct, except as provided in sub-subdivision e. of this subdivision.

(3) **Collateral source. --** A source of benefits or advantages for economic loss otherwise compensable that the victim or claimant has received or that is readily available to the victim or the claimant from any of the following sources:

a. The offender.

b. The government of the United States or any of its agencies, a state or any of its political subdivisions, or an instrumentality of two or more states.

c. Social Security, Medicare, or Medicaid.

d. State-required, temporary, nonoccupational disability insurance.

e. Worker's compensation.

f. Wage continuation programs of any employer.

g. Proceeds of a contract of insurance payable to the victim for loss that the victim sustained because of the criminally injurious conduct.

h. A contract providing prepaid hospital and other health care services, or benefits for disability.

i. A contract of insurance that will pay for expenses directly related to a funeral, cremation, and burial, including transportation of a body.

j. A charitable gift or donation by a third party, including a charity care write-off of expenses by a medical provider, regardless of whether the gift or donation is subsequently rescinded.

(4) **Commission.** -- The Crime Victims Compensation Commission established by G.S. 15B-3.

(4a) **Consumer reporting agency.** -- As defined in G.S. 75-61(4).

(4b) **Credit report.** -- As defined in G.S. 75-61(3).

(5) **Criminally injurious conduct.** -- Conduct that by its nature poses a substantial threat of personal injury or death, and is punishable by fine or imprisonment or death, or would be so punishable but for the fact that the person engaging in the conduct lacked the capacity to commit the crime under the laws of this State. Criminally injurious conduct includes conduct that amounts to an offense involving impaired driving as defined in G.S. 20-4.01(24a), and conduct that amounts to a violation of G.S. 20-166 if the victim was a pedestrian or was operating a vehicle moved solely by human power or a mobility impairment device. For purposes of this Article, a mobility impairment device is a device that is designed for and intended to be used as a means of transportation for a person with a mobility impairment, is suitable for use both inside and outside a building, and whose maximum speed does not exceed 12 miles per hour when the device is being operated by a person with a mobility impairment. Criminally injurious conduct does not include conduct arising out of the ownership, maintenance, or use of a motor vehicle when the conduct is punishable only as a violation of other provisions of Chapter 20 of the General Statutes. Criminally injurious conduct shall also include an act of terrorism, as defined in 18 U.S.C. § 2331, that is committed outside of the United States against a citizen of this State.

(6) **Dependent.** -- An individual wholly or substantially dependent upon the victim for care and support and includes a child of the victim born after his death.

(7) **Dependent's economic loss.** -- Loss after a victim's death of contributions of things of economic value to his dependents, not including services they would have received from the victim if he had not suffered the fatal injury, less expenses of the dependents avoided by reason of the victim's death. Dependent's economic loss will be limited to a 26-week period commencing from the date of the injury, and compensation shall not exceed three hundred dollars ($ 300.00) per week.

(8) **Dependent's replacement service loss.** -- Loss reasonably incurred by dependents after a victim's death in obtaining ordinary and necessary services in lieu of those the victim would have performed for their benefit if he had not suffered the fatal injury, less expenses of the dependents avoided by reason of the victim's death and not subtracted in calculating dependent's economic loss.

Dependent's replacement service loss will be limited to a 26-week period commencing from the date of the injury and compensation shall not exceed two hundred dollars ($ 200.00) per week.

(9) **Director.** -- The Director of the Commission appointed under G.S. 15B-3(g).

(10) **Economic loss.** -- Economic detriment consisting only of allowable expense, work loss, replacement services loss, and household support loss. If criminally injurious conduct causes death, economic loss includes a dependent's economic loss and a dependent's replacement service loss. Noneconomic detriment is not economic loss, but economic loss may be caused by pain and suffering or physical impairment.

(10a) **Household support loss.** -- The loss of support that a victim would have received from the victim's spouse for the purpose of maintaining a home or residence for the victim and the victim's dependents. A victim may be compensated fifty dollars ($ 50.00) per week for each dependent child. Compensation for household support loss shall not exceed three hundred dollars ($ 300.00) per week and shall be limited to 26 weeks commencing from the date of the injury. A victim may receive only one compensation for household support loss. Household support loss is only available to an unemployed victim whose spouse is the offender who committed the criminally injurious conduct that is the basis of the victim's claim under this act.

(11) **Noneconomic detriment.** -- Pain, suffering, inconvenience, physical impairment, or other nonpecuniary damage.

(12) **Replacement services loss.** -- Expenses reasonably incurred in obtaining ordinary and necessary services in lieu of those the injured person would have performed, not for income but for the benefit of himself or his family, if he had not been injured.

Replacement service loss will be limited to a 26-week period commencing from the date of the injury, and compensation may not exceed two hundred dollars ($ 200.00) per week.

(12a) **Substantial evidence.** -- Relevant evidence that a reasonable mind might accept as adequate to support a conclusion.

(13) **Victim.** -- A person who suffers personal injury or death proximately caused by criminally injurious conduct.

Chapter 15B

(14) **Work loss.** -- Loss of income from work that the injured person would have performed if he had not been injured and expenses reasonably incurred by him to obtain services in lieu of those he would have performed for income, reduced by any income from substitute work actually performed by him, or by income he would have earned in available appropriate substitute work that he was capable of performing but unreasonably failed to undertake.

Compensation for work loss will be limited to 26 weeks commencing from the date of the injury, and compensation shall not exceed three hundred dollars ($ 300.00) per week. A claim for work loss will be paid only upon proof that the injured person was gainfully employed at the time of the criminally injurious conduct and, by physician's certificate, that the injured person was unable to work.

History.
1983, c. 832, s. 1; 1987, c. 819, ss. 1-8; 1989, c. 322, s. 1; c. 679, s. 1; 1991, c. 301, s. 1; 1997-227, ss. 1, 2; 1998-212, s. 19.4(l); 2004-124, s. 18.1; 2004-159, s. 1; 2006-183, ss. 1, 2; 2009-355, s. 5; 2011-267, s. 1; 2013-368, s. 15; 2017-57, s. 16.6(a)

§ 15B-3. Crime Victims Compensation Commission

(a) There is established the Crime Victims Compensation Commission of the Department of Public Safety, consisting of seven members as follows:

(1) One member to be appointed by the Governor;

(2) One member to be appointed by the General Assembly upon the recommendation of the President Pro Tempore of the Senate under G.S. 120-121;

(3) One member to be appointed by the General Assembly upon the recommendation of the Speaker of the House of Representatives under G.S. 120-121;

(4) The Attorney General or the Attorney General's designee;

(5) The Secretary of the Department of Public Safety or the Secretary's designee; and

(6) Two members to be appointed by the Secretary of the Department of Public Safety.

(b) Members shall serve terms of four years. A member shall continue to serve until his successor is duly appointed, but a holdover under this provision does not affect the expiration date of the succeeding term.

(c) In case of a vacancy on the Commission before the expiration of a member's term, a successor shall be appointed within 30 days of the vacancy for the remainder of the unexpired term by the appropriate official pursuant to subsection (a). Vacancies in legislative appointments shall be filled under G.S. 120-122.

(d) The Commission shall elect one of its members as chairman to serve until the expiration of his term.

(e) A majority of the Commission constitutes a quorum to transact business.

(f) Members shall receive compensation and reimbursement for expenses as provided in G.S. 138-5.

(g) The Commission shall name a Director upon the recommendation of the Secretary of Public Safety. The Director shall serve at the pleasure of the Commission. The Department of Public Safety shall provide for the compensation of the Director and shall provide professional and clerical staff necessary for the work of the Commission.

History.
1983, c. 832, s. 1; 1987, c. 819, ss. 9, 10; 1991, c. 301, s. 1; 1995, c. 490, s. 14; 1999-269, s. 1; 2004-159, s. 1; 2011-145, s. 19.1(g)

§ 15B-4. Award of compensation

(a) Subject to the limitations in G.S. 15B-22, compensation for criminally injurious conduct shall be awarded to a claimant if substantial evidence establishes that the requirements for an award have been met. Compensation shall only be paid for economic loss and not for noneconomic detriment. The Commission shall follow the rules of liability applicable to civil tort law in North Carolina.

(b) Compensation shall only be awarded for criminally injurious conduct that occurs or is attempted in this State except that criminally injurious conduct that occurs or is attempted against a resident of this State while in another state which does not have a victims compensation program of any type may be a basis of compensation.

History.
1983, c. 832, s. 1; 1987, c. 819, s. 11; 1989, c. 322, s. 2; 1991, c. 301, s. 1; 2004-159, s. 1; 2006-183, s. 3

§ 15B-5. Attorney General to represent State

The Attorney General shall represent the interest of the State when:

(1) A decision of the Commission is appealed to the courts; and

(2) When the State is sued or when it brings or enters a lawsuit pursuant to this Article.

History.
1983, c. 832, s. 1; 1991, c. 301, s. 1; 2004-159, s. 1

§ 15B-6. Powers of the Commission and Director

(a) In addition to powers authorized by this Article and Chapter 150B, the Commission may:

(1) Adopt rules in accordance with Part 3, Article 1 of Chapter 143B and Article 2A of Chapter 150B of the General Statutes necessary to carry out the purposes of this Article;

(2) Establish general policies and guidelines for awarding compensation and provide guidance to the staff assigned by the Secretary of the Department of Public Safety to administer the program;

(3) Accept for any lawful purpose and functions under this Article any and all donations, both real and personal, and grants of money from any governmental unit or public agency, or from any institution, person, firm, or corporation, and may deposit the same to the Crime Victims Compensation Fund.

(b) The Director shall have the following authority:

(1) With the consent of the district attorney, to request that law enforcement officers employed by the State or any political subdivision provide copies of any information or data gathered in the investigation of criminally injurious conduct that is the basis of any claim to enable the Director or Commission to determine whether, and the extent to which, a claimant qualifies for an award of compensation;

(2) With the consent of the district attorney, to request that prosecuting attorneys, law enforcement officers, and State agencies conduct investigations and provide information necessary to enable the Director or Commission to determine whether, and the extent to which, a claimant qualifies for an award of compensation; and

(3) To require the claimant to supplement the application for an award of compensation with any reasonably available medical or psychological reports pertaining to the injury for which the award of compensation is claimed.

Information obtained pursuant to this subsection is subject to the same privilege against public disclosure that may be asserted by the providing source.

History.
1983, c. 832, s. 1; 1987, c. 819, s. 12; 1989, c. 679, s. 2; 1991, c. 301, s. 1; 2000-189, s. 3; 2004-159, s. 1; 2011-145, s. 19.1(g)

§ 15B-7. Filing of application for compensation award; contents

(a) A claim for an award of compensation is commenced by filing an application for an award with the Director. The application shall be in a form prescribed by the Commission and shall contain the following information:

(1) The name and address of the victim of the criminally injurious conduct, the name and address of the claimant, and the relationship of the claimant to the victim;

(2) If the victim is deceased, the name and address of each dependent of the victim and the extent to which each is dependent upon the victim for care and support;

(3) The nature of the criminally injurious conduct that is the basis for the claim and the date on which the conduct occurred;

(4) The law-enforcement agency or officer to whom the criminally injurious conduct was reported and the date on which it was reported;

(5) The nature and extent of the injuries that the victim sustained from the criminally injurious conduct for which compensation is sought, the name and address of any person who gave medical treatment to the victim for the injuries, the name and address of any hospital or similar institution where the victim received medical treatment for the injuries, and whether the victim died as a result of the injuries;

(6) The total amount of the economic loss that the victim, a dependent, or the claimant sustained as a result of the criminally injurious conduct, without regard to the financial limitations set forth in G.S. 15B-11(f) and (g).

(7) The amount of benefits or advantages that the victim, a dependent, or other claimant has received or is entitled to receive from any collateral source for economic loss that resulted from the criminally injurious conduct, and the name of each collateral source;

(8) Whether the claimant is the spouse, parent, child, brother, or sister of the offender, or is similarly related to an accomplice of the offender who committed the criminally injurious conduct;

(9) A release authorizing the Commission and the Commission's staff to obtain any report, document, or information that relates to the determination of the claim for an award of compensation;

(10) Any additional relevant information that the Commission may require. The Commission may require the claimant to submit, with the application, materials to substantiate the facts that are stated in the application.

(b) A person who knowingly and willfully presents or attempts to present a false or fraudulent application, or a State officer or employee who knowingly and willfully participates or assists in the preparation or presentation of a false or fraudulent application is guilty of a Class 1 misdemeanor if the application is for a claim of not more than four hundred dollars ($ 400.00). If the application is for a claim of more than four hundred dollars ($ 400.00), the person is guilty of a Class I felony.

History.
1983, c. 832, s. 1; 1987, c. 819, s. 13; 1991, c. 301, s. 1; 1993, c. 539, s. 303; 1994, Ex. Sess., c. 24, s. 14(c); 2004-159, s. 1

§ 15B-8. Procedure for filing application

(a) The Director shall establish procedures for screening, filing, recording, investigating, and processing applications for an award of compensation. The Director shall also establish the procedures and methods for processing follow-up claims for compensation. The procedures and methods established by the Director under this subsection shall conform to any rules adopted by the Commission.

(b) Repealed by Session Laws 1987, c. 819, s. 14.

History.
1983, c. 832, s. 1; 1987, c. 819, s. 14; 1991, c. 301, s. 1; 2004-159, s. 1

§ 15B-8.1. Privilege and records of the Commission

(a) In a proceeding under this Article, the privileges set forth in G.S. 8-53, 8-53.3, 8-53.4, 8-53.7, 8-53.8, and 8-56 do not apply to communications or records concerning the physical, mental or emotional condition of the claimant or victim if that condition is relevant to a claim for compensation.

(b) All medical information relating to the mental, physical, or emotional condition of a victim or claimant and all law enforcement records and information and any juvenile records shall be held confidential by the Commission and Director. All personal information, as that term is defined in 18 U.S.C. § 2725(3), of victims and claimants and all information concerning the disposition of claims for compensation, except for the total amount awarded a victim or claimant, shall be held confidential by the Commission and Director. Except for information held confidential under this subsection, the records of the Division shall be open to public inspection.

History.
1989, c. 679, s. 3; 2004-159, s. 1; 2011-267, s. 2

N.C. Gen. Stat. § 15B-9

Repealed by Session Laws 1987, c. 819, s. 15.

§ 15B-10. Awarding claims

(a) The Director shall decide the award of compensation for an initial claim or follow-up claim when the claim does not exceed twelve thousand five hundred dollars ($ 12,500) and does not include future economic loss. The Director shall report all awards under this subsection to the Commission.

(b) The Director shall recommend the award of compensation for an initial claim or follow-up claim when the claim exceeds twelve thousand five hundred dollars ($ 12,500) or involves future economic loss. The Commission shall decide the award of compensation for a claim based on a review of written evidence submitted to the Commission by the Director.

(c) In reporting a decision under subsection (a) or recommending a decision under subsection (b), the Director shall submit to the Commission documentation to establish the economic loss of the claimant by substantial evidence.

(d) The Director shall send each claimant a written statement of a decision made under subsection (a) or (b) that gives the reasons for the decision. A claimant who is dissatisfied with a decision may commence a contested case under Article 3 of Chapter 150B of the General Statutes.

History.
1983, c. 832, s. 1; 1987, c. 819, s. 16; 1991, c. 301, s. 1; 1999-269, s. 2; 2004-159, s. 1; 2009-354, s. 3

§ 15B-11. Grounds for denial of claim or reduction of award

(a) An award of compensation shall be denied if:

(1) The claimant fails to file an application for an award within two years after the date of the criminally injurious conduct that caused the injury or death for which the claimant seeks the award;

(2) The economic loss is incurred after one year from the date of the criminally injurious conduct that caused the injury or death for which the victim seeks the award, except in the case where the victim for whom compensation is sought was 10 years old or younger at the time the injury occurred. In that case an award of compensation will be denied if the economic loss is incurred after two years from the date of the criminally injurious conduct that caused the injury or death for which the victim seeks the award;

(3) The criminally injurious conduct was not reported to a law enforcement officer or agency within 72 hours of its occurrence, and there was no good cause for the delay;

(4) The award would benefit the offender or the offender's accomplice, unless a determination is made that the interests of justice require that an award be approved in a particular case;

(5) The criminally injurious conduct occurred while the victim was confined in any State, county, or city prison, correctional, youth services, or juvenile facility, or local confinement facility, or half-way house, group home, or similar facility; or

(6) The victim was participating in a felony at or about the time that the victim's injury occurred.

(b) A claim may be denied or an award of compensation may be reduced if:

(1) The victim was participating in a nontraffic misdemeanor at or about the time that the victim's injury occurred; or

(2) The claimant or a victim through whom the claimant claims engaged in contributory misconduct.

(b1) The Commission or Director, whichever has the authority to decide a claim under G.S. 15B-10, shall exercise discretion in determining whether to deny a claim under subsection (b) of this section. In exercising discretion, the Commission or Director shall consider whether any proximate cause exists between the injury and the misdemeanor or contributory misconduct, when applicable. The Director or Commission shall deny claims upon a finding that there was contributory misconduct that is a proximate cause of becoming a victim. However, contributory misconduct that is not a proximate cause of becoming a victim shall not lead to an automatic denial of a claim.

(c) A claim may be denied, an award of compensation may be reduced, and a claim that has already been decided may be reconsidered upon finding that the claimant or victim, without good cause, has not fully cooperated with appropriate law enforcement agencies or in the prosecution of criminal cases with regard to the criminally injurious conduct that is the basis for the award.

(c1) A claim may be denied upon a finding that the claimant has been convicted of any felony classified as a Class A, B1, B2, C, D, or E felony under the laws of the State of North Carolina and that such felony was committed within 3 years of the time the victim's injury occurred.

(d) After reaching a decision to approve an award of compensation, but before notifying the claimant, the Director shall require the claimant to submit current information as to collateral sources on forms prescribed by the Commission.

An award that has been approved shall nevertheless be denied or reduced to the extent that the economic loss upon which the claim is based is or will be recouped from a collateral source. If an award is reduced or a claim is denied because of the expected recoupment of all or part of the economic loss of the claimant from a collateral source, the amount of the award or the denial of the claim shall be conditioned upon the claimant's economic loss being recouped by the collateral source. If it is thereafter determined that the claimant will not receive all or part of the expected recoupment, the claim shall be reopened and an award shall be approved in an amount equal to the amount of expected recoupment that it is determined the claimant will not receive from the collateral source, subject to the limitations set forth in subsections (f) and (g).

(e) Repealed by Session Laws 1998-212, s. 19.4(m), effective December 1, 1998.

(f) Repealed by Session Laws 2011-267, s. 3, effective July 1, 2011.

(g) Compensation payable to a victim and to all other claimants sustaining economic loss because of injury to, or the death of, that victim may not exceed thirty thousand dollars ($ 30,000) in the aggregate in addition to allowable funeral, cremation, and burial expenses.

(h) The right to reconsider or reopen a claim does not affect the finality of its decision for the purpose of judicial review.

History.
1983, c. 832, s. 1; 1987, c. 819, ss. 17-21; 1989 (Reg. Sess., 1990), c. 898, s. 1; c. 1066, s. 131; 1991, c. 301, s. 1; 1994, Ex. Sess., c. 3, s. 1; 1997-227, s. 3; 1998-212, s. 19.4(m); 1999-269, s. 3; 2004-159, s. 1; 2006-183, ss. 4, 5; 2009-354, s. 4; 2011-267, s. 3; 2011-326, s. 3

§ 15B-12. Evidence in contested cases

(a) Except as provided in this section, evidence in a contested case shall be taken in accordance with Article 3 of Chapter 150B of the General Statutes.

(b) In a proceeding under this Article, the privileges set forth in G.S. 8-53, 8-53.3, 8-53.4, 8-53.7, 8-53.8, and 8-56 do not apply to communications or records concerning the physical, mental or emotional condition of the claimant or victim if that condition is relevant to a claim for compensation.

(c) If the mental, physical, or emotional condition of a victim or claimant is material to a claim for an award of compensation, the administrative law judge may order the victim or claimant to submit to a mental or physical examination by a physician or psychologist, and may order an autopsy of a deceased victim. The order may be made for good cause shown and upon notice to the person to be examined and to the claimant. The order shall specify the time, place, manner, conditions, and scope of the examination or autopsy and the person by whom it is to be made, and shall require the person who performs the examination or autopsy to file with the administrative law judge a detailed written report of the examination or autopsy. The report shall set out the findings, including the results of all tests made, diagnosis, prognosis, and other conclusions, and reports of earlier examinations of the same conditions. On request of the person examined, the administrative law judge shall furnish him a copy of the report. If the victim is deceased, the administrative law judge on request, shall furnish the claimant a copy of the report.

(d) The administrative law judge may request that law-enforcement officers employed by the State or any political subdivision thereof provide it with copies of any information or data gathered in the investigation of the criminally injurious conduct that is the basis of any claim to enable it to determine whether, and the extent to which, a claimant qualifies for an award of compensation. The administrative law judge may also request that prosecuting attorneys, law-enforcement officers, and State agencies conduct investigations and provide information necessary to enable the administrative law judge to determine whether, and the extent to which, a claimant qualifies for an award of compensation. Information obtained pursuant to this subsection is subject to the same privilege against public disclosure that may be asserted by the providing source.

(e) The administrative law judge may require the claimant to supplement the application for an award of compensation with any reasonably available medical or psychological reports relating to the injury for which the award of compensation is claimed.

(f) The administrative law judge may not request the victim or the claimant to supply any evidence that would not be admissible at a trial under G.S. 8C-1, Rule 412.

(g) Notwithstanding any provision to the contrary relating to the confidentiality of juvenile records, the administrative law judge shall have access to the records of juvenile proceedings which bear upon an application for compensation, but to the extent possible, it shall maintain the confidentiality of those records.

(h) The administrative law judge may exclude from a hearing of any matter at issue all persons, except those engaged in the hearing, during the taking of medical information and law-enforcement investigative records and information as evidence.

(i) Except for information held confidential by the administrative law judge, the official record in a contested case under this Article is open to public inspection.

History.
1983, c. 832, s. 1; 1987, c. 819, s. 22; 1989, c. 679, ss. 4, 5; 1991, c. 301, s. 1; 2004-159, s. 1

N.C. Gen. Stat. § 15B-13

Repealed by Session Laws 1987, c. 819, s. 23.

§ 15B-14. Effect of prosecution or conviction of offender

(a) An award of compensation may be approved whether or not any person is prosecuted or convicted for committing the conduct that is the basis of the award. Proof of conviction of a person whose conduct gave rise to a claim is conclusive evidence that the crime was committed, unless an application for rehearing, an appeal of the conviction, or a writ of certiorari is pending, or a rehearing or new trial has been ordered.

(b) Upon a request of the Attorney General, the proceedings in a claim for an award of compensation shall be suspended pending disposition of a criminal prosecution that has been commenced or is imminent.

(c) In making an award, any specific statement of loss to a victim that a trial court has included in its judgment in the case may be considered.

History.
1983, c. 832, s. 1; 1987, c. 819, s. 24; 1991, c. 301, s. 1; 2004-159, s. 1; 2011-267, s. 4

§ 15B-15. Clerks of court to be notified

The Director shall notify in writing the clerk of superior court of the county in which the offense occurred of any award made from the Crime Victims Compensation Fund to the victim. The clerk shall place the notice in the case file of any defendant charged with the offense that gave rise to the award to the victim.

History.
1983, c. 832, s. 1; 1987, c. 819, s. 25; 1991, c. 301, s. 1; 2004-159, s. 1

§ 15B-16. Manner of payment; non-assignability and exemptions

(a) The Director shall pay award payments directly to the service provider on behalf of the claimant. Eligible out-of-pocket costs borne by the claimant shall be paid directly to the victim only if such costs can be documented and verified.

(b) Upon request of the claimant, future economic loss, other than allowable expense, may be commuted to a lump sum only on a finding that:

(1) The award in a lump sum will promote the interests of the claimant; or

(2) The present value of all future economic loss other than allowable expense does not exceed one thousand dollars ($ 1,000).

(c) An award for future economic loss payable in installments may be made only for a period as to which future economic loss can reasonably be determined. An award for future economic loss payable in installments may be reconsidered and modified upon a finding that a material and substantial change of circumstances has occurred.

(d) An order on reconsideration of an award may not require refund of amounts previously paid unless the award was obtained by fraud.

(e) The Director, even after an award made by the Commission, may negotiate with any service provider in order to obtain a reduction of the amount claimed by the provider in exchange for a full release of any claim against a claimant.

History.
1983, c. 832, s. 1; 1987, c. 819, s. 26; 1989, c. 679, s. 6; 1991, c. 301, s. 1; 2004-159, s. 1

§ 15B-17. Award not subject to taxation or execution

(a) An award is exempt from taxation.

(b) An award is not subject to execution, attachment, garnishment, or other process, except that, upon receipt of an award by a claimant, the part of the award that is for allowable expense is not exempt from such an action by a creditor to the extent that he provides products, services, or accommodations the costs of which are included in the award, and the part of the award that is for work loss is not exempt from such an action to secure payment of alimony, maintenance, or child support.

History.
1983, c. 832, s. 1; 1991, c. 301, s. 1; 2004-159, s. 1

§ 15B-18. Subrogation by State

(a) If compensation is awarded, the Crime Victims Compensation Fund is subrogated to all the claimant's rights to receive or recover benefits or advantages for economic loss from a source that is, or if readily available to the victim or claimant would be, a collateral source, to the extent of the compensation awarded.

(b) The Crime Victims Compensation Fund is an eligible recipient for restitution under G.S. 15A-1021, 15A-1343, 148-33.1, 148-33.2, 148-57.1, and any other applicable statutes.

(c) As a prerequisite to bringing an action to recover damages related to criminally injurious conduct for which compensation is claimed or awarded, the claimant shall give the Commission prior written notice of the proposed action. After receiving the notice the Commission shall immediately notify the Attorney General who shall promptly:

(1) Join in the action as a party plaintiff to recover compensation awarded;

(2) Require that the claimant bring the action in his individual name as a trustee in behalf of the State to recover compensation awarded; or

(3) Reserve its rights and do neither in the proposed action. If, as requested by the Attorney General, the claimant brings the action as trustee and recovers compensation awarded from the Crime Victims Compensation Fund, he may deduct from the compensation recovered in behalf of the State the reasonable expenses, including attorney fees, allocable by the court for that recovery.

(d) If a judgment or verdict separately indicates economic loss and noneconomic detriment, payments on the judgment shall be allocated between them in proportion to the amounts indicated. In an action in a court of this State arising out of criminally injurious conduct, the judge, on timely motion, shall direct the jury to return a special verdict, indicating separately the awards for noneconomic detriment, punitive damages, and economic loss.

(e) Any funds recovered by the Crime Victims Compensation Fund pursuant to this section shall be paid to the general fund.

(f) The Director may pursue any claim of the Crime Victim's Compensation Fund or the Commission set forth in this Article. At the request of the Director, or otherwise, the Attorney General is authorized to assert the rights of the Crime Victim's Compensation Fund or Commission before any administrative or judicial tribunal for purposes of enforcing a claim or right set forth in this Article.

History.
1983, c. 832, s. 1; 1987, c. 819, s. 27; 1989, c. 679, s. 6; 1991, c. 301, s. 1; 2004-159, s. 1

§ 15B-19. Subrogation by collateral sources prohibited

Subrogation rights that a collateral source may have may not extend to a recovery from a claimant of all or any part of an award made under this Article. A collateral source may not apply in the name of a claimant or otherwise for an award of compensation based upon injury to a claimant to whose rights the collateral source may be subrogated.

History.
1983, c. 832, s. 1; 1991, c. 301, s. 1; 2004-159, s. 1

§ 15B-20. Publicity

Law enforcement agencies responsible for investigating offenses committed in the State may provide information to victims of those offenses and to their dependents concerning the existence of the Crime Victims Compensation Fund and the source of applications for compensation from the Fund.

History.

1983, c. 832, s. 1; 1987, c. 819, s. 28; 1991, c. 301, s. 1; 2004-159, s. 1

§ 15B-21. Annual report

The Commission shall, by March 15 each year, prepare and transmit to the chairs of the Joint Legislative Oversight Committee on Justice and Public Safety and to the chairs of the House and Senate Appropriations Committees on Justice and Public Safety a report of its activities in the prior fiscal year and the current fiscal year to date. The report shall include:

(1) The number of claims filed;

(2) The number of awards made;

(2a) The number of pending cases by year received;

(3) The amount of each award;

(4) A statistical summary of claims denied and awards made;

(5) The administrative costs of the Commission, including the compensation of commissioners;

(6) The current unencumbered balance of the North Carolina Crime Victims Compensation Fund;

(7) The amount of funds carried over from the prior fiscal year;

(8) The amount of funds received in the prior fiscal year from the Division of Adult Correction and Juvenile Justice of the Department of Public Safety and from the compensation fund established pursuant to the Victims Crime Act of 1984, 42 U.S.C. § 10601, et seq.; and

(9) The amount of funds expected to be received in the current fiscal year, as well as the amount actually received in the current fiscal year on the date of the report, from the Division of Adult Correction and Juvenile Justice of the Department of Public Safety and from the compensation fund established pursuant to the Victims Crime Act of 1984, 42 U.S.C. § 10601, et seq.

The Attorney General and State Auditor shall assist the Commission in the preparation of the report required by this section.

History.

1983, c. 832, s. 1; 1987, c. 819, s. 29; 1991, c. 301, s. 1; 1999-237, s. 20.2; 2001-424, s. 26.5; 2004-159, s. 1;

2011-145, s. 19.1(h); 2015-241, s. 16A.2; 2017-186, s. 2 (ffff)

§ 15B-22. Disbursements

If compensation awarded under this Article cannot be paid due to insufficient funds in the Crime Victims Compensation Fund, payment shall be delayed until sufficient funds are available and no further awards of compensation shall be made until sufficient funds are available.

History.

1983, c. 832, s. 1; 1987, c. 819, s. 31; 1991, c. 301, s. 1; 2004-159, s. 1

§ 15B-23. Crime Victims Compensation Fund

There is established the Crime Victims Compensation Fund. Revenue in the Crime Victims Compensation Fund includes amounts credited to the Fund under G.S. 148-2 and other funds. Any surplus in the Crime Victims Compensation Fund shall not revert. The Crime Victims Compensation Fund shall be kept on deposit with the State Treasurer, as in the case of other State funds, and may be invested by the State Treasurer in any lawful security for the investment of State money. The Crime Victims Compensation Fund is subject to the oversight of the State Auditor pursuant to Article 5A of Chapter 147 of the General Statutes.

History.

1987, c. 819, s. 30; 1993 (Reg. Sess., 1994), c. 769, s. 21.5(b); 2004-159, s. 1

§ 15B-24. Requiring defendant to pay restitution encouraged

Pursuant to a Court's power to require restitution as a condition of probation, parole or work-release privileges, a Court may require a defendant to pay restitution to a victim, regardless of whether the victim receives compensation from the Crime Victims Compensation Fund, or to the Fund. It is the intent of the General Assembly that a victim's receipt of compensation from the Fund shall not discourage a Court from considering, where appropriate, payment of restitution by the defendant and alternatives to incarceration of the defendant.

History.

1987, c. 819, s. 33; 2004-159, s. 1

§ 15B-25. Compensation limits

This Article shall not be construed to create a right to receive compensation. Compensation payable under Chapter 15B shall only be available to the extent that the General Assembly appropriates funds that purpose.

History.
1987, c. 819, s. 36; 2004-159, s. 1

§ 15B-26. Crime victims credit protection

(a) A creditor that is owed money for services provided to a victim as a result of the criminally injurious conduct inflicted on the victim shall not communicate any information about the debt to a consumer reporting agency during the pendency of an application for an award filed pursuant to G.S. 15B-7 or during the pendency of an appeal from a decision related to such an application.

(b) The victim bears the burden of notifying the creditor that the debt is subject to subsection (a) of this section.

(c) A creditor may request monthly verification from the Commission that the application or appeal is still pending, and the Commission shall provide this verification.

History.
2009-355, s. 6

§§ 15B-27 through 15B-29

Reserved for future codification purposes.

ARTICLE 2
THE CRIME VICTIMS FINANCIAL RECOVERY ASSISTANCE ACT

§ 15B-30. Declaration of policy and purpose

The General Assembly of North Carolina hereby declares as a matter of public policy that:

(1) No person who commits a crime should thereafter gain monetary profit as the result of committing the crime.

(2) Victims of crime have a special relationship to any profit from the crime committed against them, including the personal belongings and memorabilia of a convicted felon whose criminal actions and resulting notoriety enhance the value of those belongings and memorabilia.

(3) To the extent profit from crime would not have been realized but for an offender's commission of illegal acts, an offender does not have an equitable interest in the profit and allowing the offender to retain the profit would result in the offender's unjust enrichment.

The General Assembly finds that the State has a compelling interest in ensuring that persons convicted of crimes do not profit from those crimes, and that victims of crime are compensated by those who have harmed them.

The General Assembly further finds that crime victims have difficulty satisfying restitution orders or civil judgments entered against their offenders because the victims often lack the expertise and resources to identify or locate assets that an offender may have.

In order to carry out this public policy and to satisfy these compelling interests, the General Assembly has enacted the provisions of this Article providing a mechanism by which crime victims are notified of the existence of an offender's assets and are authorized to bring an action to recover those assets.

History.
2004-159, s. 2

§ 15B-31. Definitions

The following definitions apply in this Article:

(1) **Commission.** -- The Crime Victims Compensation Commission established under G.S. 15B-3.

(2) **Convicted.** -- A finding or verdict of guilty by a jury or by entry of a plea of guilty or no contest, or a finding of not guilty by reason of insanity.

(3) **Crime memorabilia.** -- Any tangible property belonging to or that belonged to an offender prior to conviction, the value of which is increased by the notoriety gained from the conviction of a felony.

(4) **Earned income.** -- Income derived from one's own labor or through active participation in a business, as distinguished from income including dividends or investments.

(5) **Eligible person.** -- Any of the following:

a. A victim of the crime for which the offender was convicted.

b. A surviving spouse, parent, or child of a deceased victim of the crime for which the offender was convicted.

c. Any other person dependent for the person's principal support upon a deceased victim of the crime for which the offender was convicted.

However, "eligible person" does not include the offender or an accomplice to the offender.

(6) **Felony.** -- An offense defined as a felony by any North Carolina or United States statute that was committed in North Carolina and that resulted in physical or emotional injury, or death, to another person.

Chapter 15B

(7) **Funds of an offender.** -- All funds and property received from any source by an offender, excluding child support and earned income, where the offender:

    a. Is an inmate serving a sentence with the Division of Adult Correction and Juvenile Justice of the Department of Public Safety or a prisoner confined at a local correctional facility or federal correctional institute, and includes funds that a superintendent, sheriff, or municipal official receives on behalf of an inmate or prisoner and deposits in an inmate account to the credit of the inmate or deposits in a prisoner account to the credit of the prisoner; or

    b. Is not an inmate or prisoner but who is serving a sentence of probation, conditional discharge, or post-release supervision.

(8) **Offender.** -- A person who has been convicted of a felony or that person's legal representative or assignee.

(9) **Profit from crime.** -- Any income, assets, or property obtained through or generated from the commission of a crime for which the offender was convicted, including any income, assets, or property generated from the sale of crime memorabilia or obtained through the use of unique knowledge obtained during the commission of, or in preparation for the commission of the crime, as well as any gain from the sale, conversion, or exchange of the income, assets, or property. "Profit from crime" does not include voluntary donations or contributions to an offender used to assist in the appeal of a conviction, provided the donation or contribution is not given in exchange for something of material value.

(10) **Victim.** -- Any natural person who suffers physical or emotional injury, or the threat of physical or emotional injury, as the result of the commission of a felony.

History.
2004-159, s. 2; 2011-145, s. 19.1(h); 2017-186, s. 2 (gggg)

§ 15B-32. Notice of contract or agreement to pay

(a) **Notice to Commission.** --

    (1) Every person, firm, corporation, partnership, association, or other legal entity, or representative of a person, firm, corporation, partnership, association, or entity that knowingly contracts for, pays, or agrees to pay to an offender (i) profit from crime or (ii) funds of an offender where the value or aggregate value of the payment or payments exceeds ten thousand dollars ($ 10,000) shall submit to the Commission a copy of the contract or reduce to writing the terms of any oral agreement or obligation to pay as soon as practicable after discovering the payment or intended payment constitutes profit from crime or funds of an offender.

    (2) Whenever the payment or obligation to pay involves funds of an offender that a superintendent, sheriff, or municipal officer (i) receives or will receive on behalf of an inmate serving a sentence with the Division of Adult Correction and Juvenile Justice of the Department of Public Safety or a prisoner confined at a local correctional facility, (ii) deposits or will deposit in an inmate account to the credit of an inmate or prisoner, and (iii) the value of such funds exceeds or will exceed ten thousand dollars ($ 10,000), the State or subdivision of the State shall also give written notice to the Commission.

    (3) Whenever the State or a subdivision of the State makes a payment or has an obligation to pay funds of an offender and the value of such funds exceeds or will exceed ten thousand dollars ($ 10,000), the State or subdivision of the State shall also give written notice to the Commission.

    (4) In all other instances where the payment or obligation to pay involves funds of an offender and the value or aggregate value of the funds exceeds or will exceed ten thousand dollars ($ 10,000), the offender who receives or will receive the funds shall give written notice to the Commission.

(b) **Notice to Eligible Persons.** -- The Commission shall, upon receipt of a notice of a contract, an agreement to pay, or payment of profit from crime or funds of an offender, notify in writing by certified mail, return receipt requested, all known eligible persons where the eligible persons' names and addresses are known to the Commission. The Commission may, in its discretion, provide for additional notice as it deems necessary.

History.
2004-159, s. 2; 2011-145, s. 19.1(h); 2017-186, s. 2 (hhhh)

§ 15B-33. Penalties

(a) **Assessment and Civil Penalty for Failure to Give Notice.** -- Any person or entity, other than the State, a subdivision of the State, or a person who is a superintendent, sheriff, or municipal official, who willfully fails to give notice as required by G.S. 15B-32 is subject to an assessment of up to the amount of the payment or obligation to pay and a civil penalty of up to one thousand dollars ($ 1,000) or ten percent (10%) of the payment or obligation to pay, whichever is greater.

(b) **Notice and Opportunity to Be Heard Required.** -- After providing notice and opportunity to be heard in accordance with the provisions of Chapter 150B of the General Statutes, the Commission may order the respondent to pay the assessment and civil penalty imposed by this section.

(c) **Failure to Pay.** -- If a respondent fails to pay the assessment and civil penalty imposed by this section within sixty (60) days of being ordered to pay, the assessment and civil penalty may be recovered from the respondent by an action brought by the attorney general, upon the request of the Commission, in any court of competent jurisdiction.

(d) **Establishment of Escrow Account; Notice to Eligible Persons.** -- The Commission shall deposit the assessment in an escrow account pending the expiration of the three-year statute of limitations authorized by G.S. 15B-34 to preserve the funds to satisfy a civil judgment in favor of an eligible person to whom the failure to give notice relates. The Commission shall notify any eligible person who may have a claim against the offender of the existence of the funds being held in escrow. The notice shall instruct the eligible person that the person may have a right to commence a civil action against the offender as well as any other information deemed necessary by the Commission.

(e) **Satisfaction of Judgment from Escrow Account.** -- Upon an eligible person's presentation to the Commission of a civil judgment for damages arising out of the offense for which the offender was convicted, the Commission shall satisfy up to one hundred percent (100%) of that judgment, including costs and disbursements as taxed by the clerk of the court, with the escrowed fund obtained pursuant to this section, but in no event shall the amount of all judgments, costs, and disbursements satisfied from the escrowed funds exceed the amount in escrow. If more than one eligible person indicates to the Commission that the eligible person intends to commence or has commenced a civil action against the offender, the Commission shall delay satisfying any judgment, costs, and disbursements until the claims of all eligible persons are reduced to judgment. If the aggregate of all judgments, costs, and disbursement obtained exceeds the amount of escrowed funds, the amount used to partially satisfy each judgment shall be reduced to a pro rata share.

(f) **Return of Unclaimed Escrowed Funds.** -- After the expiration of the three-year statute of limitations period established in G.S. 15B-34, the Commission shall review all judgments that have been satisfied from the escrowed funds. In the event no claim was filed prior to the expiration of the three-year statute

of limitations, the Commission shall return the escrowed amount to the respondent. In the event a claim or claims are pending at the expiration of the statute of limitations, the funds shall remain escrowed until the final determination of all claims to allow the Commission to satisfy any judgment which may be obtained by the eligible person after which time any remaining escrowed amount shall be returned to the respondent.

(g) **Remittance of Proceeds from Civil Penalty.** -- The Commission shall remit the clear proceeds of the civil penalty of up to one thousand dollars ($ 1,000) or ten percent (10%) of the payment or obligation to pay, whichever is greater, assessed under this section to the Civil Penalty and Forfeiture Fund in accordance with G.S. 115C-457.2.

History.
2004-159, s. 2

§ 15B-34. Civil action to recover profits or funds; responsibilities of the Commission

(a) **Civil Action.** -- Notwithstanding any inconsistent provision of law with respect to the timely bringing of an action, an eligible person may, within three years of the discovery of any profit from crime or funds of an offender, bring a civil action in a court of competent jurisdiction against an offender for damages arising out of the offense for which the offender was convicted.

(b) **Notice by Eligible Persons.** -- Upon filing an action under subsection (a) of this section, the eligible person shall give notice to the Commission of the filing by delivering a copy of the summons and complaint to the Commission. The eligible person may also give notice to the Commission prior to filing the action so as to allow the Commission to apply for any appropriate provisional remedies, which are otherwise authorized to be invoked prior to the commencement of an action.

(c) **Responsibilities of Commission.** -- Upon receipt of a copy of a summons and complaint, or upon receipt of notice from the eligible person prior to filing an action, the Commission shall immediately take action to:

(1) Notify all other known eligible persons of the filing of the civil action by certified mail, return receipt requested, where the eligible persons' names and addresses are known to the Commission.

(2) Provide, in its discretion, for additional notice as it deems necessary.

(3) Avoid the wasting of the assets identified in the complaint as the profit from crime or funds of an offender in any manner consistent with subsection (d) of this section.

(d) **Standing; Authority to Avoid Wasting of Assets. --** The Commission has standing and, acting on its own behalf or on behalf of all eligible persons, shall have the right to apply for any and all provisional remedies that are also otherwise available to the plaintiff in the civil action brought under subsection (a) of this section, including attachment, injunction, constructive trust, and receivership. On a motion for a provisional remedy, the moving party shall state whether any other provisional remedy has previously been sought in the same action against the same defendant. The court may require the moving party to elect between those remedies to which it would otherwise be entitled.

History.
2004-159, s. 2

§ 15B-35. Subrogation by the Crime Victims Compensation Fund

Claims on profit from crime or funds of an offender are subject to subrogation by the Crime Victims Compensation Fund pursuant to G.S. 15B-18.

History.
2004-159, s. 2

§ 15B-36. Conviction overturned or pardon issued

If profit from crime is subject to a provisional remedy on behalf of eligible persons and the conviction for the criminal offense from which profit from crime is realized is reversed, vacated, or set aside, or if the offender has been granted an unconditional pardon of innocence for the criminal offense, those funds shall be returned to the rightful owner.

History.
2004-159, s. 2

§ 15B-37. Evasive action void

Any action taken by an offender, whether by way of execution of a power of attorney, creation of corporate entities, or otherwise, to defeat the purpose of this Article shall be void as against the public policy of this State.

History.
2004-159, s. 2

CHAPTER 15C
ADDRESS CONFIDENTIALITY PROGRAM

§ 15C-1. Purpose

The purpose of this Chapter is to enable the State and the agencies of North Carolina to respond to requests for public records without disclosing the location of a victim of domestic violence, sexual offense, stalking, or human trafficking; to enable interagency cooperation in providing address confidentiality for victims of domestic violence, sexual offense, stalking, or human trafficking; and to enable the State and its agencies to accept a program participant's use of an address designated by the Office of the Attorney General as a substitute address.

History.
2002-171, s. 1; 2007-547, s. 4

§ 15C-2. Definitions

The following definitions apply in this Chapter:

(1) **Actual address or address.** -- A residential, work, or school street address as specified on the individual's application to be a program participant under this Chapter.

(2) **Address Confidentiality Program or Program.** -- A program in the Office of the Attorney General to protect the confidentiality of the address of a relocated victim of domestic violence, sexual offense, or stalking to prevent the victim's assailants or potential assailants from finding the victim through public records.

(3) **Agency of North Carolina or agency.** -- Includes every elected or appointed State or local public office, public officer, or official; institution, board, commission, bureau, council, department, authority, or other unit of government of the State or of any local government; or unit, special district, or other political subdivision of State or local government.

(4) **Application assistant.** -- An employee of an agency or nonprofit organization who provides counseling, referral, shelter, or other specialized services to victims of domestic violence, sexual offense, stalking, or human trafficking and who has been designated by the Attorney General to assist individuals with applications to participate in the Address Confidentiality Program.

(5) **Attorney General.** -- Office of the Attorney General.

(6) **Person.** -- Any individual, corporation, limited liability company, partnership, trust, estate, or other association or any state, the United States, or any subdivision thereof.

(7) **Program participant.** -- An individual accepted into the Address Confidentiality Program in accordance with this Chapter.

(8) **Public record.** -- A public record as defined in Chapter 132 of the General Statutes.

(9) **Substitute address.** -- An address designated by the Attorney General under the Address Confidentiality Program.

(10) **Victim of domestic violence.** -- An individual against whom domestic violence, as described in G.S. 50B-1, has been committed.

(11) **Victim of a sexual offense.** -- An individual against whom a sexual offense, as described in Article 7B of Chapter 14 of the General Statutes, has been committed.

(12) **Victim of stalking.** -- An individual against whom stalking, as described in former G.S. 14-277.3 for acts occurring before December 1, 2008, or G.S. 14-277.3A for acts occurring on or after December 1, 2008, has been committed.

(13) **Victim of human trafficking.** -- An individual against whom human trafficking, as described in G.S. 14-43.11, has been committed.

History.
2002-171, s. 1; 2007-547, s. 5; 2009-58, s. 4; 2015-181, s. 47

§ 15C-3. Address Confidentiality Program

The General Assembly establishes the Address Confidentiality Program in the Office of the Attorney General to protect the confidentiality of the address of a relocated victim of domestic violence, sexual offense, stalking, or human trafficking to prevent the victim's assailants or potential assailants from finding the victim through public records. Under this Program, the Attorney General shall designate a substitute address for a program participant and act as the agent of the program participant for purposes of service of process and receiving and forwarding first-class mail or certified or registered mail. The Attorney General shall not be required to forward any mail other than first-class mail or certified or registered mail to the program participant. The Attorney General shall not be required to track or otherwise maintain records of any mail received on behalf of a program participant unless the mail is certified or registered mail.

History.
2002-171, s. 1; 2007-547, s. 6

§ 15C-4. Filing and certification of applications; authorization card

(a) An individual who wants to participate in the Address Confidentiality Program shall file an application with the Attorney General with the assistance of an application assistant. Any of the following individuals may apply to the Attorney General to have an address designated by the Attorney General to serve as the substitute address of the individual:

(1) An adult individual.

(2) A parent or guardian acting on behalf of a minor when the minor resides with the individual.

(3) A guardian acting on behalf of an incapacitated individual.

(b) The application shall be dated, signed, and verified by the applicant and shall be signed by the application assistant who assisted in the preparation of the application.

(c) The application shall contain all of the following:

(1) A statement by the applicant that the applicant is a victim of domestic violence, sexual offense, stalking, or human trafficking and that the applicant fears for the applicant's safety or the safety of the applicant's child.

(2) Evidence that the applicant is a victim of domestic violence, sexual offense, stalking, or human trafficking. This evidence may include any of the following:

a. Law enforcement, court, or other federal or state agency records or files.

b. Documentation from a domestic violence program if the applicant is alleged to be a victim of domestic violence.

c. Documentation from a religious, medical, or other professional from whom the applicant has sought assistance in dealing with the alleged domestic violence, sexual offense, or stalking.

d. Documentation submitted to support a victim of human trafficking's application for federal assistance or benefits under federal human trafficking laws.

(3) A statement by the applicant that disclosure of the applicant's address would endanger the applicant's safety or the safety of the applicant's child.

(4) A statement by the applicant that the applicant has or will confidentially relocate in North Carolina.

(5) A designation of the Attorney General as an agent for the applicant for purposes of service of process and the receipt of first-class mail or certified or registered mail.

(6) The mailing address and telephone number where the applicant can be contacted by the Attorney General.

(7) The address that the applicant requests not to be disclosed by the Attorney General that directly relates to the increased risk of domestic violence, sexual offense, or stalking.

(8) A statement as to whether there is any existing court order or court action involving the applicant related to divorce proceedings, child support, child custody, or child visitation and the court that issued the order or has jurisdiction over the action.

(9) A statement by the applicant that to the best of the applicant's knowledge, the information contained in the application is true.

(10) A recommendation of an application assistant that the applicant have an address designated by the Attorney General to serve as the substitute address of the applicant.

(d) Upon the filing of a properly completed application, the Attorney General shall certify the applicant as a program participant. Upon certification, the Attorney General shall issue an Address Confidentiality Program authorization card to the program participant. The Address Confidentiality Program authorization card shall remain valid for so long as the program participant remains certified under the Program.

(e) Applicants shall be certified for four years following the date of filing unless the certification is withdrawn or canceled prior to the end of the four-year period. A program participant may withdraw the certification by filing a request for withdrawal acknowledged before a notary with the Attorney General. A certification may be renewed by filing an application containing the information required by G.S. 15C-3 with the Attorney General at least 30 days prior to expiration of the current certification.

History.
2002-171, s. 1; 2007-547, s. 7

§ 15C-5. Change of name, address, or telephone number

(a) A program participant shall notify the Attorney General within 30 days after the program participant has obtained a legal name change by providing the Attorney General a certified copy of any judgment or order evidencing the change or any other documentation the

Attorney General deems to be sufficient evidence of the name change. If the program participant fails to notify the Attorney General of a name change in the manner provided in this subsection, the Attorney General shall cancel the certification of the program participant in the Program.

(b) A program participant shall notify the Attorney General of a change in address or telephone number from the address or telephone number listed for the program participant on the application at least seven days before the change occurs. If the program participant fails to notify the Attorney General of a change in address or telephone number in the manner provided in this subsection, the Attorney General shall cancel the certification of the program participant in the Program.

History.
2002-171, s. 1

§ 15C-6. Falsifying application information

An applicant who falsely attests in an application that disclosure of the applicant's address would endanger the applicant's safety or the safety of the applicant's child or who knowingly provides false information when applying for certification or renewal shall lose certification in the Program. The Attorney General shall investigate violations of this section. Upon finding that a violation has occurred, the Attorney General shall assess a civil penalty against the applicant not to exceed five hundred dollars ($ 500.00).

History.
2002-171, s. 1

§ 15C-7. Certification cancellation; records

(a) The Attorney General shall cancel the certification of a program participant under any of the following circumstances:

(1) The program participant files a request for withdrawal of the certification pursuant to G.S. 15C-4.

(2) The program participant fails to notify the Attorney General of a change in the program participant's name, address, or telephone number listed on the application pursuant to G.S. 15C-5.

(3) The program participant submitted false information in applying for certification to the Program in violation of G.S. 15C-6.

(4) Mail forwarded to the program participant by the Attorney General is returned as undeliverable.

(b) The provisions of Article 3 of Chapter 150B of the General Statutes shall not apply

to any cancellation of certification by the Attorney General pursuant to subsection (a) of this section.

(c) The Attorney General shall send notice of cancellation to the program participant. Notice of cancellation shall set out the reasons for cancellation. The program participant shall have 30 days to appeal the cancellation decision under procedures developed by the Attorney General.

(d) Any records or documents pertaining to a program participant shall be maintained in accordance with The General Schedule for State Agencies as established by the Department of Natural and Cultural Resources.

(e) An individual who ceases to be a program participant is responsible for notifying persons who use the substitute address designated by the Attorney General as the program participant's address that the designated substitute address is no longer the individual's address.

History.
2002-171, s. 1; 2015-241, s. 14.30(s)

§ 15C-8. Address use by State or local agencies

(a) The program participant, and not the Attorney General, is responsible for requesting that agencies of North Carolina use the address designated by the Attorney General as the substitute address of the program participant.

(b) Except as otherwise provided in this section, when a program participant submits a current and valid Address Confidentiality Program authorization card to an agency of North Carolina, the agency shall accept the address designation by the Attorney General on the authorization card as the program participant's substitute address when creating a new public record.

(c) An agency may request a waiver from the requirements of the Address Confidentiality Program by submitting a waiver request to the Attorney General. The agency's waiver request shall be in writing and include an explanation of why the agency cannot meet its statutory or administrative obligations by possessing or using the substitute address and an affirmation that, if the Attorney General accepts the waiver, the agency will only use the program participant's actual address for those statutory or administrative purposes.

(d) The Attorney General's acceptance or denial of an agency's waiver request shall be made in writing and include a statement of specific reasons for acceptance or denial. Acceptance or denial of an agency's waiver request is not subject to further review.

(e) A board of elections shall use the actual address of a program participant for all election-related purposes and shall keep the address confidential from the public under the provisions of G.S. 163-82.10(e). Use of the actual address on letters placed in the United States mail by a board of elections shall not be considered a breach of confidentiality. The substitute address designation provided by the Attorney General shall not be used as an address for voter registration or verification purposes.

(f) For purposes of levying and collecting property taxes on motor vehicles pursuant to Article 22A of Chapter 105 of the General Statutes, the Attorney General shall issue to the county, city, or town assessor or tax collector a list containing the names and actual addresses of program participants residing in that county, city, or town. This list shall be used only for the purposes of listing, appraising, or assessing taxes on motor vehicles and collecting property taxes on motor vehicles in the county, city, or town. The county, city, or town assessor or tax collector or any current or former officer, employee, or agent of any county, city, or town, who in the course of service to or employment by the county, city, or town has access to the name and actual address of a program participant, shall not disclose this information to any other person.

(g) The substitute address designated by the Attorney General shall not be used for purposes of listing, appraising, or assessing taxes on property and collecting taxes on property under the provisions of Subchapter II of Chapter 105 of the General Statutes.

(h) The substitute address designated by the Attorney General shall not be used as an address by any register of deeds on recorded documents or for the purpose of indexing land registered under Article 4 of Chapter 43 of the General Statutes in the index of registered instruments pursuant to G.S. 161-22.

(i) A local school administrative unit shall use the actual address of a program participant for any purpose related to admission or assignment pursuant to Article 25 of Chapter 115C of the General Statutes and shall keep the actual address confidential from the public under the provisions of this Article. The substitute address designated by the Attorney General shall not be used as an address for admission or assignment purposes. For purposes of student records created under Chapter 115C of the General Statutes, the substitute address designated by the Attorney General shall be used.

(j) Except as otherwise provided in this section, a program participant's actual address and telephone number maintained by an agency of North Carolina is not a public record within the meaning of Chapter 132 of the General Statutes. A program participant's actual address or telephone number maintained by the Attorney General or disclosed by the Attorney General pursuant to this Chapter is not a public record within the meaning of Chapter 132 of the General Statutes.

History.
2002-171, s. 1; 2017-6, s. 3; 2018-146, ss. 3.1(a), (b), 6.1

§ 15C-9. Disclosure of address prohibited

(a) The Attorney General is prohibited from disclosing any address or telephone number of a program participant other than the substitute address designated by the Attorney General, except under the following circumstances:

(1) The information is requested by a federal, state, or local law enforcement agency for official use only.

(2) The information is required by direction of a court order. However, any person to whom a program participant's address or telephone number has been disclosed shall not disclose the address or telephone number to any other person unless permitted to do so by order of the court.

(3) Upon request by an agency to verify the participation of a specific program participant when the verification is for official use only.

(4) Upon request by an agency, in the manner provided for by G.S. 15C-8.

(5) The program participant is required to disclose the program participant's actual address as part of a registration required by Article 27A of Chapter 14 of the General Statutes.

(b) The Attorney General shall provide immediate notification of disclosure to a program participant when disclosure is made pursuant to subdivision (2) or (4) of subsection (a) of this section.

(c) If, at the time of application, an applicant is subject to a court order related to divorce proceedings, child support, child custody, or child visitation, the Attorney General shall notify the court that issued the order of the certification of the program participant in the Address Confidentiality Program and the substitute address designated by the Attorney General. If, at the time of application, an applicant is involved in a court action related to divorce proceedings, child support, child custody, or child visitation, the Attorney General shall notify the court having jurisdiction over the action of the certification of the applicant in the Address Confidentiality Program and the substitute address designated by the Attorney General.

(d) No person shall knowingly and intentionally obtain a program participant's actual address or telephone number from the Attorney General or an agency knowing that the person is not authorized to obtain the address information.

Chapter 15C

(e) No employee of the Attorney General or an agency shall knowingly and intentionally disclose a program participant's actual address or telephone number to a person known to the employee to be prohibited from receiving the program participant's actual address or telephone number, unless the disclosure is permissible by law. This subsection only applies when an employee obtains a program participant's actual address or telephone number during the course of the employee's official duties and, at the time of disclosure, the employee has specific knowledge that the actual address or telephone number disclosed belongs to a program participant.

(f) Any person who knowingly and intentionally obtains or discloses information in violation of this Chapter shall be guilty of a Class 1 misdemeanor and assessed a fine not to exceed two thousand five hundred dollars ($ 2,500).

History.
2002-171, s. 1

§ 15C-10. Assistance for program applicants

(a) The Attorney General shall designate agencies of North Carolina and nonprofit organizations that provide counseling and shelter services to victims of domestic violence, sexual offense, stalking, or human trafficking to assist individuals applying to be program participants. Any assistance and counseling rendered by the Office of the Attorney General or its designee to applicants shall in no way be construed as legal advice.

(b) The Attorney General, upon receiving notification pursuant to G.S. 15A-832(h), shall, within 96 hours of receiving the notification, issue the victim a letter of certification of eligibility or other relevant document entitling the person to have access to State benefits and services.

History.
2002-171, s. 1; 2007-547, s. 8

§ 15C-11. Limited liability

The State, agencies of North Carolina, and their officers, officials, employees, and agents, both past and present, in their official and individual capacities, shall be immune and held harmless from any liability in any action brought by or on behalf of any person injured or harmed by the actions or inactions of these entities and individuals in implementing this Chapter. However, if an employee's actions resulting in harm were not within the course and scope of the employee's duties, then that employee may be subject to suit as an individual to the extent permitted by the laws of the State of North Carolina.

History.
2002-159, s. 28.5; 2002-171, s. 1

§ 15C-12. Rule-making authority

The Attorney General is authorized to adopt any rules deemed necessary to carry out the provisions of this Chapter.

History.
2002-171, s. 1

§ 15C-13. Additional time for action

Whenever the laws of this State provide a program participant a legal right to act within a prescribed period of 10 days or less after the service of a notice or other paper upon the program participant, and the notice or paper is served upon the program participant by mail pursuant to this Chapter, five days shall be added to the prescribed period.

History.
2002-171, s. 1

CHAPTER 17
HABEAS CORPUS

ARTICLE 1
CONSTITUTIONAL PROVISIONS

§ 17-1. Remedy without delay for restraint of liberty

Every person restrained of his liberty is entitled to a remedy to inquire into the lawfulness thereof, and to remove the same, if unlawful; and such remedy ought not to be denied or delayed.

History.
Const., art. 1, s. 18; Rev., s. 1819; C.S., s. 2203

§ 17-2. Habeas corpus not to be suspended

The privileges of the writ of habeas corpus shall not be suspended.

History.
Const., art. 1, s. 21; Rev., s. 1820; C.S., s. 2204

ARTICLE 2
APPLICATION

§ 17-3. Who may prosecute writ

Every person imprisoned or restrained of his liberty within this State, for any criminal or supposed criminal matter, or on any pretense whatsoever, except in cases specified in G.S. 17-4, may prosecute a writ of habeas corpus, according to the provisions of this Chapter, to inquire into the cause of such imprisonment or restraint, and, if illegal, to be delivered therefrom.

History.
1868-9, c. 116, s. 1; Code, s. 1623; Rev., s. 1821; C.S., s. 2205

§ 17-4. When application denied

Application to prosecute the writ shall be denied in the following cases:

(1) Where the persons are committed or detained by virtue of process issued by a court of the United States, or a judge thereof, in cases where such courts or judges have exclusive jurisdiction under the laws of the United States, or have acquired exclusive jurisdiction by the commencement of suits in such courts.

(2) Where persons are committed or detained by virtue of the final order, judgment or decree of a competent tribunal of civil or criminal jurisdiction, or by virtue of an execution issued upon such final order, judgment or decree.

(3) Where any person has willfully neglected, for the space of two whole sessions after his imprisonment, to apply for the writ to the superior court of the county in which he may be imprisoned, such person shall not have a habeas corpus in vacation time for his enlargement.

(4) Where no probable ground for relief is shown in the application.

History.
1868-9, c. 116, s. 2; Code, s. 1624; Rev., s. 1822; C.S., s. 2206; 1971, c. 528, s. 1

§ 17-5. By whom application is made

Application for the writ may be made either by the party for whose relief it is intended or by any person in his behalf.

History.
1868-9, c. 116, s. 3; Code, s. 1625; Rev., s. 1823; C.S., s. 2207

§ 17-6. To judge of appellate division or superior court in writing

Application for the writ shall be made in writing, signed by the applicant --

(1) To any one of the justices or judges of the appellate division.

(2) To any one of the superior court judges, either during a session or in vacation.

History.
1868-9, c. 116, s. 4; Code, s. 1626; Rev., s. 1824; C.S., s. 2208; 1969, c. 44, s. 41; 1971, c. 528, s. 2

§ 17-7. Contents of application

The application must state, in substance, as follows:

(1) That the party, in whose behalf the writ is applied for, is imprisoned or restrained of his liberty, the place where, and the officer or person by whom he is imprisoned or restrained, naming both parties, if their names are known, or describing them if they are not known.

(2) The cause or pretense of such imprisonment or restraint, according to the knowledge or belief of the applicant.

(3) If the imprisonment is by virtue of any warrant or other process, a copy thereof shall be annexed, or it shall be made to appear that a copy thereof has

been demanded and refused, or that for some sufficient reason a demand for such copy could not be made.

(4) If the imprisonment or restraint is alleged to be illegal, the application must state in what the alleged illegality consists; and that the legality of the imprisonment or restraint has not been already adjudged, upon a prior writ of habeas corpus, to the knowledge or belief of the applicant.

(5) The facts set forth in the application must be verified by the oath of the applicant, or by that of some other credible witness, which oath may be administered by any person authorized by law to take affidavits.

History.
1868-9, c. 116, s. 5; Code, s. 1627; Rev., s. 1825; C.S., s. 2209

§ 17-8. Issuance of writ without application

When the appellate division or superior court division, or any judge of either division, has evidence from any judicial proceeding before such court or judge that any person within this State is illegally imprisoned or restrained of his liberty, it is the duty of said court or judge to issue a writ of habeas corpus for his relief, although no application be made for such writ.

History.
1868-9, c. 116, s. 10; Code, s. 1632; Rev., s. 1826; C.S., s. 2210; 1969, c. 44, s. 42

ARTICLE 3
WRIT

§ 17-9. Writ granted without delay

Any court or judge empowered to grant the writ, to whom such applications may be presented, shall grant the writ without delay, unless it appear from the application itself or from the documents annexed that the person applying or for whose benefit it is intended is, by this Chapter, prohibited from prosecuting the writ.

History.
1868-9, c. 116, s. 6; Code, s. 1628; Rev., s. 1827; C.S., s. 2211

§ 17-10. Penalty for refusal to grant

If any judge authorized by this Chapter to grant writs of habeas corpus refuses to grant such writ when legally applied for, every such judge shall forfeit to the party aggrieved two thousand five hundred dollars ($ 2,500).

History.
1868-9, c. 116, s. 9; Code, s. 1631; Rev., s. 1828; C.S., s. 2212

§ 17-11. Sufficiency of writ; defects of form immaterial

No writ of habeas corpus shall be disobeyed on account of any defect of form. It shall be sufficient --

(1) If the person having the custody of the party imprisoned or restrained be designated either by his name of office, if he have any, or by his own name, or, if both such names be unknown or uncertain, he may be described by an assumed appellation, and anyone who may be served with the writ shall be deemed the person to whom it is directed, although it may be directed to him by a wrong name, or description, or to another person.

(2) If the person who is directed to be produced be designated by name, or if his name be uncertain or unknown, he may be described by an assumed appellation or in any other way, so as to designate the person intended.

History.
1868-9, c. 116, ss. 7, 8; Code, ss. 1629, 1630; Rev., s. 1829; C.S., s. 2213

§ 17-12. Service of writ

The writ of habeas corpus may be served by any qualified elector of this State thereto authorized by the court or judge allowing the same. It may be served by delivering the writ, or a copy thereof, to the person to whom it is directed; or, if such person cannot be found, by leaving it, or a copy, at the jail, or other place in which the party for whose relief it is intended is confined, with some under officer or other person of proper age; or, if none such can be found, or if the person attempting to serve the writ be refused admittance, by affixing a copy thereof in some conspicuous place on the outside, either of the dwelling house of the party to whom the writ is directed or of the place where the party is confined for whose relief it is sued out.

History.
1868-9, c. 116, s. 32; Code, s. 1657; Rev., s. 1833; C.S., s. 2214

ARTICLE 4
RETURN

§ 17-13. When writ returnable

Writs of habeas corpus may be made returnable at a certain time, or forthwith, as the case may require. If the writ be returnable at a certain time, such return shall be made and the party shall be produced at the time and place specified therein.

History.

1868-9, c. 116, s. 31; Code, s. 1656; Rev., s. 1830; C.S., s. 2215

§ 17-14. Contents of return; verification

The person or officer on whom the writ is served must make a return thereto in writing, and, except where such person is a sworn public officer and makes his return in his official capacity, it must be verified by his oath. The return must state plainly and unequivocally --

(1) Whether he has or has not the party in his custody or under his power or restraint.

(2) If he has the party in his custody or power, or under his restraint, the authority and the cause of such imprisonment or restraint, setting forth the same at large.

(3) If the party is detained by virtue of any writ, warrant, or other written authority, a copy thereof shall be annexed to the return; and the original shall be produced and exhibited on the return of the writ to the court or judge before whom the same is returnable.

(4) If the person or officer upon whom such writ is served has had the party in his power or custody, or under his restraint, at any time prior or subsequent to the date of the writ, but has transferred such custody or restraint to another, the return shall state particularly to whom, at what time, for what cause and by what authority such transfer took place.

History.

1868-9, c. 116, s. 11; Code, s. 1633; Rev., s. 1831; C.S., s. 2216

§ 17-15. Production of body if required

If the writ requires it, the officer or person on whom the same has been served shall also produce the body of the party in his custody or power, according to the command of the writ, except in the case of the sickness of such party, as hereinafter provided.

History.

1868-9, c. 116, s. 14; Code, s. 1636; Rev., s. 1832; C.S., s. 2217

ARTICLE 5
ENFORCEMENT OF WRIT

§ 17-16. Attachment for failure to obey

If the person or officer on whom any writ of habeas corpus has been duly served refuses or neglects to obey the same, by producing the body of the party named or described therein, and by making a full and explicit return thereto, within the time required, and no sufficient excuse is shown for such refusal or neglect, it is the duty of the court or judge before whom the writ has been made returnable, upon due proof of the service thereof, forthwith to issue an attachment against such person or officer, directed to the sheriff of any county within this State, and commanding him forthwith to apprehend such person or officer and bring him immediately before such court or judge. On being so brought such person or officer shall be committed to close custody in the jail of the county where such court or judge may be, without being allowed the liberties thereof, until such person or officer make return to such writ and comply with any order that may be made by such court or judge in relation to the party for whose relief the writ has been issued.

History.

1868-9, c. 116, s. 15; Code, s. 1637; Rev., s. 1834; C.S., s. 2218

§ 17-17. Liability of judge refusing attachment

If any judge willfully refuses to grant the writ of attachment, as provided for in G.S. 17-16, he shall be liable to impeachment, and moreover shall forfeit to the party aggrieved twenty-five hundred dollars ($ 2,500).

History.

1870-1, c. 221, s. 2; Code, s. 1638; Rev., s. 1835; C.S., s. 2219

§ 17-18. Attachment against sheriff to be directed to coroner; procedure

If a sheriff has neglected to return the writ agreeably to the command thereof, the attachment against him may be directed to the coroner or to any other person to be designated therein, who shall have power to execute the same, and such sheriff, upon being brought up, may be committed to the jail of any county other than his own.

History.

1868-9, c. 116, s. 16; Code, s. 1639; Rev., s. 1836; C.S., s. 2220

§ 17-19. Precept to bring up party detained

The court or judge by whom any such attachment may be issued may also at the same time, or afterwards, direct a precept to any sheriff, coroner, or other person to be designated therein, commanding him to bring forthwith before such court or judge the party, wherever to be found, for whose benefit the writ of habeas corpus has been granted.

History.
1868-9, c. 116, s. 17; Code, s. 1640; Rev., s. 1837; C.S., s. 2221

§ 17-20. Liability of judge refusing precept

If any judge refuses to grant the precept provided for in G.S. 17-19, he shall be liable to impeachment, and moreover shall forfeit to the party aggrieved twenty-five hundred dollars ($ 2,500).

History.
1870-1, c. 221, s. 3; Code, s. 1641; Rev., s. 1838; C.S., s. 2222

§ 17-21. Liability of judge conniving at insufficient return

If any judge grants the attachment, or the precept, and gives the officer or other person charged with the execution of the same verbal or written instructions not to execute the same, or to make any evasive or insufficient return, or any return other than that provided by law; or shall connive at the failing to make any return or any evasive or insufficient return, or any return other than that provided by law, he shall be liable to impeachment, and moreover shall forfeit to the party aggrieved twenty-five hundred dollars ($ 2,500).

History.
1870-1, c. 221, s. 4; Code, s. 1642; Rev., s. 1839; C.S., s. 2223

§ 17-22. Power of county to aid service

In the execution of any such attachment, precept or writ, the sheriff, coroner, or other person to whom it may be directed, may call to his aid the power of the county, as in other cases.

History.
1868-9, c. 116, s. 18; Code, s. 1643; Rev., s. 1840; C.S., s. 2224

§ 17-23. Obedience to order of discharge compelled

Obedience to a judgment or order for the discharge of a prisoner or person restrained of his liberty, pursuant to the provisions of this Chapter, may be enforced by the court or judge by attachment in the same manner and with the same effect as for a neglect to make return to a writ of habeas corpus; and the person found guilty of such disobedience shall forfeit to the party aggrieved two thousand five hundred dollars ($ 2,500), besides any special damages which such party may have sustained.

History.
1868-9, c. 116, s. 24; Code, s. 1649; Rev., s. 1841; C.S., s. 2225

§ 17-24. No civil liability for obedience

No officer or other person shall be liable to any civil action for obeying a judgment or order of discharge upon writ of habeas corpus.

History.
1868-9, c. 116, s. 25; Code, s. 1650; Rev., s. 1842; C.S., s. 2226

§ 17-25. Recommittal after discharge; penalty

If any person shall knowingly again imprison or detain one who has been set at large upon any writ of habeas corpus, for the same cause, other than by the legal process or order of the court wherein he is bound by recognizance to appear, or of any other court having jurisdiction in the case, he shall be guilty of a Class 1 misdemeanor.

History.
1868-9, c. 116, s. 26; Code, s. 1651; Rev., s. 3581; C.S., s. 2227; 1993, c. 539, s. 306; 1994, Ex. Sess., c. 24, s. 14(c)

§ 17-26. Disobedience to writ or refusing copy of process; penalty

If any person to whom a writ of habeas corpus is directed shall neglect or refuse to make due return thereto, or to bring the body of the party detained according to the command of the writ without delay, or shall not, within six hours after demand made therefor, deliver a copy of the commitment or cause of detainer, such person shall, upon conviction on indictment, be fined one thousand dollars ($ 1,000), or imprisoned not exceeding 12 months, and if such person be an officer, shall moreover be removed from office.

History.
1868-9, c. 116, s. 27; Code, s. 1652; Rev., s. 3597; C.S., s. 2228

§ 17-27. Penalty for false return

If any person shall make a false return to a writ of habeas corpus, he shall be guilty of a Class 1 misdemeanor.

History.
1868-9, c. 116, s. 28; Code, s. 1653; Rev., s. 3582; C.S., s. 2229; 1993, c. 539, s. 307; 1994, Ex. Sess., c. 24, s. 14(c)

§ 17-28. Penalty for concealing party entitled to writ

If anyone having in his custody, or under his power, any party who, by law, would be entitled to a writ of habeas corpus, or for whose relief such writ shall have been issued, shall, with intent to elude the service of such writ, or to avoid the effect thereof, transfer the party to the custody, or put him under the power or control, of another, or shall conceal or change the place of his confinement, or shall knowingly aid or abet another in so doing, he shall be guilty of a Class 1 misdemeanor.

History.
1868-9, c. 116, ss. 29, 30; Code, ss. 1654, 1655; Rev., s. 3583; C.S., s. 2230; 1993, c. 539, s. 308; 1994, Ex. Sess., c. 24, s. 14(c)

ARTICLE 6
PROCEEDINGS AND JUDGMENT

§ 17-29. Notice to interested parties

When it appears from the return to the writ that the party named therein is in custody on any process, or by reason of any claim of right, under which any other person has an interest in continuing his imprisonment or restraint, no order shall be made for his discharge until it appears that the person so interested, or his attorney, if he have one, has had reasonable notice of the time and place at which such writ is returnable.

History.
1868-9, c. 116, s. 12; 1870-1, c. 221, s. 1; Code, s. 1634; Rev., s. 1843; C.S., s. 2231

§ 17-30. Notice to district attorney

When it appears from the return that such party is detained upon any criminal accusation, the court or judge may, if he thinks proper, make no order for the discharge of such party until sufficient notice of the time and place at which the writ has been returned, or is made returnable, is given to the district attorney of

the district in which the person prosecuting the writ is detained.

History.
1868-9, c. 116, s. 13; Code, s. 1635; Rev., s. 1844; C.S., s. 2232; 1973, c. 47, s. 2

§ 17-31. Subpoenas to witnesses

Any party to a proceeding on a writ of habeas corpus may procure the attendance of witnesses at the hearing, by subpoena, to be issued by the clerk of any superior court, under the same rules, regulations and penalties prescribed by law in other cases.

History.
1868-9, c. 116, s. 34; Code, s. 1659; Rev., s. 1845; C.S., s. 2233

§ 17-32. Proceedings on return; facts examined; summary hearing of issues

The court or judge before whom the party is brought on a writ of habeas corpus shall, immediately after the return thereof, examine into the facts contained in such return, and into the cause of the confinement or restraint of such party, whether the same has been upon commitment for any criminal or supposed criminal matter or not; and if issue be taken upon the material facts in the return, or other facts are alleged to show that the imprisonment or detention is illegal, or that the party imprisoned is entitled to his discharge, the court or judge shall proceed, in a summary way, to hear the allegations and proofs on both sides, and to do what to justice appertains in delivering, bailing or remanding such party.

History.
1868-9, c. 116, s. 19; Code, s. 1644; Rev., s. 1846; C.S., s. 2234

§ 17-33. When party discharged

If no legal cause is shown for such imprisonment or restraint, or for the continuance thereof, the court or judge shall discharge the party from the custody or restraint under which he is held. But if it appears on the return to the writ that the party is in custody by virtue of civil process from any court legally constituted, or issued by any officer in the course of judicial proceedings before him, authorized by law, such party can be discharged only in one of the following cases:

(1) Where the jurisdiction of such court or officer has been exceeded, either as to matter, place, sum or person.

(2) Where, though the original imprisonment was lawful, yet by some act, omission

or event, which has taken place afterwards, the party has become entitled to be discharged.

(3) Where the process is defective in some matter of substance required by law, rendering such process void.

(4) Where the process, though in proper form, has been issued in a case not allowed by law.

(5) Where the person, having the custody of the party under such process, is not the person empowered by law to detain him.

(6) Where the process is not authorized by any judgment, order or decree of any court, nor by any provision of law.

History.
1868-9, c. 116, s. 20; Code, s. 1645; Rev., s. 1847; C.S., s. 2235

§ 17-34. When party remanded

It is the duty of the court or judge forthwith to remand the party, if it appears that he is detained in custody, either --

(1) By virtue of process issued by any court or judge of the United States, in a case where such court or judge has exclusive jurisdiction.

(2) By virtue of the final judgment or decree of any competent court of civil or criminal jurisdiction, or of any execution issued upon such judgment or decree.

(3) For any contempt specially and plainly charged in the commitment by some court, officer or body having authority to commit for the contempt so charged.

(4) That the time during which such party may be legally detained has not expired.

History.
1868-9, c. 116, s. 21; Code, s. 1646; Rev., s. 1848; C.S., s. 2236

§ 17-35. When the party bailed or remanded

If it appears that the party has been legally committed for any criminal offense, or if it appears by the testimony offered with the return of the writ, or upon the hearing thereof, that the party is guilty of such an offense, although the commitment is irregular, the court or judge shall proceed to let such party to bail, if the case is bailable and good bail is offered; if not, the court or judge shall forthwith remand such party to the custody or place him under the restraint from which he was taken, if the person or officer, under whose custody or restraint he was, is legally entitled thereto; if not so entitled, the court or judge shall commit such party to

the custody of the officer or person legally entitled thereto.

History.
1868-9, c. 116, s. 22; Code, s. 1647; Rev., s. 1849; C.S., s. 2237

§ 17-36. Party held in execution not to be discharged

When a writ of habeas corpus cum causa issues and the sheriff or other officer to whom it is directed returns upon the same that the prisoner is condemned, by judgment given against him, and held in custody by virtue of an execution issued against him, the prisoner shall not be let to bail but shall be presently remanded, where he shall remain until discharged in due course of law.

History.
2 Hen. V, c. 2; R.C., c. 31, s. 111; Code, s. 937; Rev., s. 1850; C.S., s. 2238

§ 17-37. When party ill, cause determined in his absence

When, from the illness or infirmity of the person directed to be produced by a writ of habeas corpus, such person cannot, without danger, be brought before the court or judge where the writ is made returnable, the party in whose custody he is may state the fact in his return to the writ; and if the court or judge is satisfied of the truth of the allegation, and the return is otherwise sufficient, the court or judge shall proceed to decide on such return and to dispose of the matter in the same manner as if the body had been produced.

History.
1868-9, c. 116, s. 23; Code, s. 1648; Rev., s. 1851; C.S., s. 2239

§ 17-38. No second committal after discharge; penalty

No person who has been set at large upon any writ of habeas corpus shall be again imprisoned or detained for the same cause by any person whatsoever other than by the legal order or process of the court wherein he shall be bound by recognizance to appear or of any other court having jurisdiction in the case, under the penalty of two thousand five hundred dollars ($ 2,500) to the party aggrieved thereby.

History.
1868-9, c. 116, s. 26; Code, s. 1651; Rev., s. 1852; C.S., s. 2240

ARTICLE 7
HABEAS CORPUS FOR CUSTODY OF CHILDREN IN CERTAIN CASES

§§ 17-39 through 17-40

Repealed by Session Laws 1967, c. 1153, s. 1.

ARTICLE 8
HABEAS CORPUS AD TESTIFICANDUM

§ 17-41. Authority to issue the writ

Every court of record has power, upon the application of any party to any suit or proceeding, civil or criminal, pending in such court, to issue a writ of habeas corpus, for the purpose of bringing before the said court any prisoner who may be detained in any jail or prison within the State, for any cause, except a prisoner under sentence for a capital felony, to be examined as a witness in such suit or proceeding in behalf of the party making the application.

Such writ of habeas corpus may be issued by any magistrate or clerk of the superior court, upon application as provided in this section, to bring any person confined in the jail or prison of the same county where such magistrate or clerk may reside, to be examined as a witness before such magistrate or clerk.

In cases where the testimony of any prisoner is needed in a proceeding before a magistrate, or a clerk, and such person is confined in a county in which such magistrate or clerk does not reside, application for habeas corpus to testify may be made to any justice or judge of the General Court of Justice.

History.
1868-9, c. 116, ss. 37, 38; Code, ss. 1663, 1664; Rev., ss. 1855, 1856; C.S., s. 2243; 1969, c. 44, s. 43; 1971, c. 528, s. 3

§ 17-42. Contents of application

The application for the writ shall be made by the party to the suit or proceeding in which the writ is required, or by his agent or attorney. It must be verified by the applicant; and shall state --

(1) The title and nature of the suit or proceeding in regard to which the testimony of such prisoner is desired.

(2) That the testimony of such prisoner is material and necessary to such party on the trial or hearing of such suit or proceeding, as he is advised by counsel and verily believes.

History.
1868-9, c. 116, s. 39; Code, s. 1665; Rev., s. 1857; C.S., s. 2244

§ 17-43. Service of writ

The writ of habeas corpus to testify shall be served by the same person, and in like manner in all respects, and enforced by the court or officer issuing the same as prescribed in this Chapter for the service and enforcement of the writ of habeas corpus cum causa.

History.
1868-9, c. 116, s. 40; Code, s. 1666; Rev., s. 1858; C.S., s. 2245

§ 17-44. Applicant to pay expenses and give bond to return

The service of the writ shall not be complete, however, unless the applicant for the same tenders to the person in whose custody the prisoner may be, if such person is a sheriff, coroner, or marshal, the fees and expenses allowed by law for bringing such prisoner, nor unless he also gives bond, with sufficient security, to such sheriff, coroner, or marshal, as the case may be, conditioned that such applicant will pay the charges of carrying back such prisoner.

History.
1868-9, c. 116, s. 41; Code, s. 1667; Rev., s. 1859; C.S., s. 2246; 1971, c. 528, s. 4

§ 17-45. Duty of officer to whom writ delivered or on whom served

It is the duty of the officer to whom the writ is delivered or upon whom it is served, whether such writ is directed to him or not, upon payment or tender of the charges allowed by law, and the delivery or tender of the bond herein prescribed, to obey and return such writ according to the exigency thereof upon pain, on refusal or neglect, to forfeit to the party on whose application the same has been issued the sum of five hundred dollars ($ 500.00).

History.
1868-9, c. 116, s. 42; Code, s. 1668; Rev., s. 1860; C.S., s. 2247

§ 17-46. Prisoner to be remanded

After having testified, the prisoner shall be remanded to the prison from which he was taken.

History.
1868-9, c. 116, s. 43; Code, s. 1669; Rev., s. 1861; C.S., s. 2248

Chapter 17

CHAPTER 17C
NORTH CAROLINA CRIMINAL JUSTICE EDUCATION AND TRAINING STANDARDS COMMISSION

ARTICLE 1
GENERAL

§ 17C-1. Findings and policy

The General Assembly finds that the administration of criminal justice is of statewide concern, and that proper administration is important to the health, safety and welfare of the people of the State and is of such nature as to require education and training of a professional nature. It is in the public interest that such education and training be made available to persons who seek to become criminal justice officers, persons who are serving as such officers in a temporary or probationary capacity, and persons already in regular service.

History.
1971, c. 963, s. 1; 1979, c. 763, s. 1

§ 17C-2. Definitions

Unless the context clearly otherwise requires, the following definitions apply in this Article:

(1) **Commission.** -- The North Carolina Criminal Justice Education and Training Standards Commission.

(2) **Criminal justice agencies.** -- The State and local law-enforcement agencies, the State correctional agencies, other correctional agencies maintained by local governments, and the juvenile justice agencies, but shall not include deputy sheriffs, special deputy sheriffs, sheriffs' jailers, or other sheriffs' department personnel governed by the provisions of Chapter 17E of these General Statutes.

(3) **Criminal justice officers.** -- The administrative and subordinate personnel of all the departments, agencies, units or entities comprising the criminal justice agencies who are sworn law-enforcement officers, both State and local, with the power of arrest; State correctional officers; State probation/parole officers; State probation/parole officers-surveillance; officers, supervisory and administrative personnel of local confinement facilities; State juvenile justice officers; chief court counselors; and juvenile court counselors.

(3a) **Critical incident.** -- An incident involving any use of force by a law-enforcement officer that results in death or serious bodily injury to a person.

(4) **Entry level.** -- The initial appointment or employment of any person by a criminal justice agency, or any appointment or employment of a person previously employed by a criminal justice agency who has not been employed by a criminal justice agency for the 12-month period preceding this appointment or employment, or any appointment or employment of a previously certified criminal justice officer to a position which requires a different type of certification.

History.
1971, c. 963, s. 2; 1979, c. 763, s. 1; 1983, c. 558, s. 2; c. 745, s. 2; 1989, c. 757, s. 1; 1989 (Reg. Sess., 1990), c. 1024, s. 4(a); 1997-503, s. 2; 2001-490, s. 1.1; 2018-5, s. 17.1(a); 2021-138, s. 3(a)

§ 17C-3. North Carolina Criminal Justice Education and Training Standards Commission established; members; terms; vacancies

(a) There is established the North Carolina Criminal Justice Education and Training Standards Commission, hereinafter called "the Commission." The Commission shall be composed of 34 members as follows:

(1) **Police Chiefs.** -- Three police chiefs selected by the North Carolina Association of Chiefs of Police and one police chief appointed by the Governor.

(2) **Police Officers.** -- Three police officials appointed by the North Carolina Police Executives Association and two criminal justice officers certified by the Commission as selected by the North Carolina Law-Enforcement Officers' Association.

(3) **Departments.** -- The Attorney General of the State of North Carolina; the Secretary of Public Safety; the Director of the State Bureau of Investigation, the Commander of the State Highway Patrol, and the President of the North Carolina Community Colleges System.

(3a) Repealed by Session Laws 2001-490, s. 1.2, effective June 30, 2001.

(4) **At-large Groups.** -- One individual representing and appointed by each of the following organizations: one mayor selected by the League of Municipalities; one law-enforcement training officer selected by the North Carolina Law-Enforcement Training Officers' Association; one criminal

justice professional selected by the North Carolina Criminal Justice Association; one sworn law-enforcement officer selected by the North State Law-Enforcement Officers' Association; one member selected by the North Carolina Law-Enforcement Women's Association; and one District Attorney selected by the North Carolina Association of District Attorneys.

(5) **Citizens and Others.** -- The President of The University of North Carolina; the Dean of the School of Government at the University of North Carolina at Chapel Hill; and two citizens, one of whom shall be selected by the Governor and one of whom shall be selected by the Attorney General. The General Assembly shall appoint four persons, two upon the recommendation of the Speaker of the House of Representatives and two upon the recommendation of the President Pro Tempore of the Senate. Appointments by the General Assembly shall be made in accordance with G.S. 120-122. Appointments by the General Assembly shall be for two-year terms to conclude on June 30th in odd-numbered years.

(6) **Adult Correction and Juvenile Justice.** -- Four correctional officers in management positions employed by the Division of Adult Correction and Juvenile Justice of the Department of Public Safety shall be appointed, two from the Section of Community Corrections upon the recommendation of the Speaker of the House of Representatives and two from the Section of Prisons upon the recommendation of the President Pro Tempore of the Senate. Appointments by the General Assembly shall be made in accordance with G.S. 120-122. Appointments by the General Assembly shall serve two-year terms to conclude on June 30th in odd-numbered years or until the appointee no longer serves in a management position with the Division of Adult Correction and Juvenile Justice, whichever occurs first. The Governor shall appoint one correctional officer employed by the Division of Adult Correction and Juvenile Justice of the Department of Public Safety and assigned to the Office of Staff Development and Training, and one juvenile justice officer employed by the Juvenile Justice Section of the Division of Adult Correction and Juvenile Justice. The Governor's appointments shall serve three-year terms or until the appointee is no longer assigned to the Office of Staff Development and Training or is no longer a juvenile justice officer, whichever occurs first.

(b) The members shall be appointed for staggered terms. The initial appointments shall be made prior to September 1, 1983, and the appointees shall hold office until July 1 of the year in which their respective terms expire and until their successors are appointed and qualified as provided hereafter:

For the terms of one year: one member from subdivision (1) of subsection (a) of this section, serving as a police chief; three members from subdivision (2) of subsection (a) of this section, one serving as a police official, and two criminal justice officers; one member from subdivision (4) of subsection (a) of this section, appointed by the North Carolina Law-Enforcement Training Officers' Association; and two members from subdivision (5) of subsection (a) of this section, one appointed by the Governor and one appointed by the Attorney General.

For the terms of two years: one member from subdivision (1) of subsection (a) of this section, serving as a police chief; one member from subdivision (2) of subsection (a) of this section, serving as a police official; and two members from subdivision (4) of subsection (a) of this section, one appointed by the League of Municipalities and one appointed by the North Carolina Association of District Attorneys.

For the terms of three years: two members from subdivision (1) of subsection (a) of this section, one police chief appointed by the North Carolina Association of Chiefs of Police and one police chief appointed by the Governor; one member from subdivision (2) of subsection (a) of this section, serving as a police official; and three members from subdivision (4) of subsection (a) of this section, one appointed by the North Carolina Law-Enforcement Women's Association, one appointed by the North Carolina Criminal Justice Association, and one appointed by the North State Law-Enforcement Officers' Association.

Thereafter, as the term of each member expires, his successor shall be appointed for a term of three years. Notwithstanding the appointments for a term of years, each member shall serve at the will of the appointing authority.

The Attorney General, the President of The University of North Carolina, the Dean of the School of Government at the University of North Carolina at Chapel Hill, the President of the North Carolina Community Colleges System, the Director of the State Bureau of Investigation, the Commander of the State Highway Patrol, and the Secretary of Public Safety shall be continuing members of the Commission during their tenure. These members of the Commission shall serve ex officio and shall perform their duties on the Commission in addition to the other duties of their offices. The ex officio members may elect to serve personally at any or all meetings of the Commission or may designate, in writing, one member of their respective office, department, university or agency to represent and vote for them on the Commission at all meetings the ex officio members are unable to attend.

Vacancies in the Commission occurring for any reason shall be filled, for the unexpired term, by the authority making the original appointment of the person causing the vacancy. A vacancy may be created by removal of a Commission member by majority vote of the Commission for misconduct, incompetence, or neglect of duty. A Commission member may be removed only pursuant to a hearing, after notice, at which the member subject to removal has an opportunity to be heard.

History.
1971, c. 963, s. 3; 1977, c. 70, ss. 29, 30; 1979, c. 763, s. 1; 1981 (Reg. Sess., 1982), c. 1191, s. 31; 1983, c. 558, s. 3; c. 618, ss. 1, 2; c. 807, ss. 1, 2; 1987, c. 282, s. 4; 1989, c. 757, s. 2; 1995, c. 490, s. 15; 1997-443, s. 11A.118(a); 1998-202, s. 4(c); 2000-137, s. 4(d); 2000-140, s. 38.1(a); 2001-487, s. 5; 2001-490, s. 1.2; 2006-264, s. 29(c), (d); 2011-145, s. 19.1(g) -(k), (m); 2012-83, s. 29; 2015-49, s. 2; 2017-186, s. 2 (iiii)

§ 17C-4. Compensation

(a) Members of the Commission who are State officers or employees shall receive no compensation for serving on the Commission, but may be reimbursed for their expenses in accordance with G.S. 138-6. Members of the Commission who are full-time salaried public officers or employees other than State officers or employees shall receive no compensation for serving on the Commission, but may be reimbursed for their expenses in accordance with G.S. 138-5(b). All other members of the Commission may receive compensation and reimbursement for expenses in accordance with G.S. 138-5.

(b) The Chairman of the Commission may appoint such ad hoc members of the Commission's standing and select committees as are necessary to carry out the business of the Commission, and such service shall be reimbursed as provided in G.S. 17C-4(a), subject to the approval of the Attorney General.

History.
1971, c. 963, s. 4; 1979, c. 763, s. 1; 1989, c. 757, s. 3

§ 17C-5. Chairman; vice-chairman; other officers; meetings; reports

(a) The Commission shall elect one of the members of the Commission as Chairman at the first regular meeting after July 1 of each year. The ex officio members shall not be eligible for election as Chairman.

(b) The Commission shall select a vice-chairman and such other officers and committee chairmen from among its members as it deems desirable at the first regular meeting of the Commission after its creation and at the first regular meeting after July 1 of each year thereafter. Nothing in this subsection, however, shall prevent the creation or abolition of committees or offices of the Commission, other than the office of vice-chairman, as the need may arise at any time during the year.

(c) The Commission shall hold at least four regular meetings per year upon the call of the chairman. Special meetings shall be held upon the call of the chairman or the vice-chairman, or upon the written request of five members of the Commission. Such special meetings must be held within 30 days.

(d) The Commission shall present regular and special reports and recommendations to the Attorney General or the General Assembly, or both, as the need may arise or as the Attorney General or General Assembly may request.

History.
1971, c. 963, s. 5; 1979, c. 763, s. 1; 1983, c. 807, s. 3

§ 17C-6. Powers of Commission

(a) In addition to powers conferred upon the Commission elsewhere in this Article, the Commission shall have the following powers, which shall be enforceable through its rules and regulations, certification procedures, or the provisions of G.S. 17C-10:

(1) Promulgate rules and regulations for the administration of this Article, which rules may require (i) the submission by any criminal justice agency of information with respect to the employment, education, retention, and training of its criminal justice officers, and (ii) the submission by any criminal justice training school of information with respect to its criminal justice training programs that are required by this Article.

(2) Establish minimum educational and training standards that must be met in order to qualify for entry level employment and retention as a criminal justice officer in temporary or probationary status or in a permanent position. The standards for entry level employment shall include all of the following:

　　a. Education and training in response to, and investigation of, domestic violence cases, as well as training in investigation for evidence-based prosecutions.

　　b. Education and training on juvenile justice issues, including (i) the handling and processing of juvenile matters for referrals, diversion, arrests, and detention; (ii) best practices for handling incidents involving juveniles; (iii) adolescent development and psychology;

and (iv) promoting relationship building with youth as a key to delinquency prevention.

c. Education and training to develop knowledge and increase awareness of effective mental health and wellness strategies for criminal justice officers.

(3) Certify and recertify, suspend, revoke, or deny, pursuant to the standards that it has established for the purpose, persons as qualified under the provisions of this Article to be employed at entry level and retained as criminal justice officers.

(4) Establish minimum standards for the certification of criminal justice training schools and programs or courses of instruction that are required by this Article.

(5) Certify and recertify, suspend, revoke, or deny, pursuant to the standards that it has established for the purpose, criminal justice training schools and programs or courses of instruction that are required by this Article.

(6) Establish minimum standards and levels of education and experience for all criminal justice instructors and school directors who participate in programs or courses of instruction that are required by this Article.

(7) Certify and recertify, suspend, revoke, or deny, pursuant to the standards that it has established for the purpose, criminal justice instructors and school directors who participate in programs or courses of instruction that are required by this Article or are required and approved by their respective criminal justice agency to include those certified under Chapter 17E or an educational institution accredited by the Commission.

(8) Investigate and make such evaluations as may be necessary to determine if criminal justice agencies, schools, and individuals are complying with the provisions of this Article.

(9) Adopt and amend bylaws, consistent with law, for its internal management and control.

(10) Enter into contracts incident to the administration of its authority pursuant to this Article.

(11) Establish minimum standards and levels of training for certification and periodic recertification of operators of and instructors for training programs in radio microwave, laser, and other electronic speed-measuring instruments.

(12) Certify and recertify, suspend, revoke, or deny, pursuant to the standards that it has established, operators and instructors for training programs for each approved type of radio microwave, laser, and other electronic speed-measuring instruments.

(13) In conjunction with the Secretary of Public Safety, approve use of specific models and types of radio microwave, laser, and other speed-measuring instruments and establish the procedures for operation of each approved instrument and standards for calibration and testing for accuracy of each approved instrument.

(13a) Expired effective September 30, 2007.

(14) Establish minimum standards for in-service training for criminal justice officers. In-service training standards for sworn law enforcement officers shall include all of the following training topics:

a. Response to, and investigation of, domestic violence cases, as well as training investigation for evidence-based prosecutions.

b. Juvenile justice issues, including (i) the handling and processing of juvenile matters for referrals, diversion, arrests, and detention; (ii) best practices for handling incidents involving juveniles; (iii) adolescent development and psychology; and (iv) promoting relationship building with youth as a key to delinquency prevention.

c. Ethics.

d. Mental health for criminal justice officers.

e. Community policing.

f. Minority sensitivity.

g. Use of force.

h. The duty to intervene and report.

(15) Establish minimum standards and levels of training for certification of instructors for the domestic violence training and juvenile justice training required by subdivisions (2) and (14) of this subsection.

(16) Establish standards and guidelines for the annual firearms certification of qualified retired law enforcement officers, as defined in G.S. 14-415.10(4b), to efficiently implement the provisions of G.S. 14-415.25. The standards shall provide for the courses, qualifications, and the issuance of the annual firearms qualification certification. The Commission may adopt any rules necessary to effect the provisions of this section, and may charge a reasonable fee to applicants for the costs incurred in compliance with this subdivision.

(17) Establish minimum educational and training standards for employment and continuing education for criminal justice officers concerning:

a. Recognizing and appropriately interacting with persons who are deaf or hard of hearing.

b. Drivers license and vehicle registration identifiers of persons who are deaf or hard of hearing, as authorized by G.S. 20-7(q2), including that those identifiers are optional.

(18) Monitor compliance with G.S. 20-185.1(d).

(19) Establish minimum standards and levels of training for certification of diversion investigators and diversion supervisors, as defined in G.S. 90-113.74(i). As part of these minimum standards, the Commission shall require that certified diversion investigators receive training in the following:

a. Definition of drug diversion.

b. Categories of drugs most subject to diversion and misuse.

c. Methods used to divert drugs.

d. Proper investigation of drug diversion cases.

e. Appropriate use of the controlled substances reporting system to investigate drug diversion cases.

f. Requests of prescriptions and records related to prescriptions pursuant to G.S. 90-107.1, including best practices for working with pharmacies in a manner that minimizes disruption of customer service and pharmacy operations.

g. Data privacy and security provisions of the Health Insurance Portability and Accountability Act of 1996 (HIPAA) and other pertinent federal and State laws governing privacy and security of confidential data and records.

h. Proper handling of confidential data and records from any source.

i. Criminal and civil penalties under federal and State law for improperly accessing, handling, or disclosing confidential prescription data or other confidential data or records.

(20) Certify and recertify at least once every three years, suspend, revoke, or deny, pursuant to the standards that it has established for the purpose, persons as qualified to be employed at entry level and retained as diversion investigators and diversion supervisors, as defined in G.S. 90-113.74(i).

(21) Search the National Decertification Index (NDI) maintained by the International Association of Directors of Law Enforcement Standards and Training (IADLEST) using the name of every applicant for certification or applicant for lateral transfer, and any other personal identifying information necessary to complete the search, and shall utilize any record of conviction of a criminal offense received as a result of the search during the application and lateral transfer process to determine if the applicant has any record that would disqualify the applicant for certification.

(b) The Commission shall have the following powers, which shall be advisory in nature and for which the Commission is not authorized to undertake any enforcement actions:

(1) Identify types of criminal justice positions, other than entry level positions, for which advanced or specialized training and education are appropriate, and establish minimum standards for the certification of persons as being qualified for those positions on the basis of specified education, training, and experience; provided, that compliance with these minimum standards shall be discretionary on the part of criminal justice agencies with respect to their criminal justice officers;

(2) Certify, pursuant to the standards that it has established for the purpose, criminal justice officers for those criminal justice agencies that elect to comply with the minimum education, training, and experience standards established by the Commission for positions for which advanced or specialized training, education, and experience are appropriate;

(3) Consult and cooperate with counties, municipalities, agencies of this State, other governmental agencies, and with universities, colleges, junior colleges, and other institutions concerning the development of criminal justice training schools and programs or courses of instruction;

(4) Study and make reports and recommendations concerning criminal justice education and training in North Carolina;

(5) Conduct and stimulate research by public and private agencies which shall be designed to improve education and training in the administration of criminal justice;

(6) Study, obtain data, statistics, and information and make reports concerning the recruitment, selection, education, retention, and training of persons serving criminal justice agencies in this State; to make recommendations for improvement in methods of recruitment, selection, education, retention, and training of persons serving criminal justice agencies;

(7) Make recommendations concerning any matters within its purview pursuant to this Article;

(8) Appoint such advisory committees as it may deem necessary;

(9) Do such things as may be necessary and incidental to the administration of its authority pursuant to this Article;

(10) Formulate basic plans for and promote the development and improvement of a comprehensive system of education and training for the officers and employees of

Chapter 17C

criminal justice agencies consistent with its rules and regulations;

(11) Maintain liaison among local, State and federal agencies with respect to criminal justice education and training;

(12) Promote the planning and development of a systematic career development program for criminal justice professionals.

(c) All decisions and rules and regulations heretofore made by the North Carolina Criminal Justice Training and Standards Council and the North Carolina Criminal Justice Education and Training System Council shall remain in full force and effect unless and until repealed or suspended by action of the North Carolina Criminal Justice Education and Training Standards Commission established herein. The present Councils are terminated on December 31, 1979, and their power, duties and responsibilities vest in the North Carolina Criminal Justice Education and Training Standards Commission effective January 1, 1980.

(d) The standards established by the Commission pursuant to G.S. 17C-6(a)(11) and 17C-6(a)(12) and by the Commission and the Secretary of Public Safety pursuant to G.S. 17C-6(a)(13) shall not be less stringent than standards established by the U.S. Department of Transportation, National Highway Traffic Safety Administration, National Bureau of Standards, or the Federal Communications Commission.

History.
1971, c. 963, s. 6; 1975, c. 372, s. 2; 1979, c. 763, s. 1; 1979, 2nd Sess., c. 1184, ss. 1, 2; 1989, c. 757, s. 4; 1994, Ex. Sess., c. 18, s. 2; 1995, c. 509, s. 14.1; 2000-140, s. 38.1(b); 2002-159, s. 29; 2003-280, s. 3; 2004-186, ss. 2.1, 2.3, 2.5; 2005-27, ss. 1, 2; 2007-427, s. 2; 2009-546, s. 2; 2011-145, s. 19.1(g); 2016-94, s. 18.2; 2017-57, s. 16D.4(bb); 2017-191, s. 2; 2018-5, ss. 17.1(a), 35.25(d); 2018-44, s. 14(a); 2018-142, s. 23(b); 2021-136, s. 1(a); 2021-137, s. 2(a); 2021-138, ss. 7(a), 11(a), 15(a)

§ 17C-7. Functions of the Department of Justice

(a) The Attorney General shall provide such staff assistance as the Commission shall require in the performance of its duties.

(b) The Attorney General shall have legal custody of all books, papers, documents, or other records and property of the Commission.

(c) Any papers, documents, or other records which become the property of the Commission that are placed in the criminal justice officer's personnel file maintained by the Commission shall be subject to the same disclosure requirements as set forth in Chapters 126, 153A, and 160A of the General Statutes regarding the privacy of personnel records.

History.
1979, c. 763, s. 1; 1989, c. 757, s. 5

§ 17C-8. System established

The North Carolina Criminal Justice Education and Training Standards Commission shall establish a North Carolina Criminal Justice Education and Training System. The system shall be a cooperative arrangement among criminal justice agencies, both State and local, and criminal justice education and training schools, both public and private, to provide education and training to the officers and employees of the criminal justice agencies of the State of North Carolina and its local governments. Members of the system shall include the North Carolina Justice Academy as well as such other public or private agencies or institutions within the State, that are engaged in criminal justice education and training, and desire to be affiliated with the system for the purpose of achieving greater coordination of criminal justice education and training efforts in North Carolina.

History.
1979, c. 763, s. 1

§ 17C-9. Criminal Justice Standards Division of the Department of Justice established; appointment of director; duties

(a) There is hereby established, within the Department of Justice, the Criminal Justice Standards Division, hereinafter called "the Division," which shall be organized and staffed in accordance with applicable laws and regulations and within the limits of authorized appropriations.

(b) The Attorney General shall appoint a director for the Division chosen from a list of three nominees submitted to him by the Commission who shall be responsible to and serve at the pleasure of the Attorney General and the Commission.

(c) The Division shall administer such programs as are assigned to it by the Commission. The Division shall also administer such additional related programs as may be assigned to it by the Attorney General or the General Assembly. Administrative duties and responsibilities shall include, but are not limited to, the following:

(1) Administering any and all programs assigned to the Division by the Commission and reporting any violations of or deviations from the rules and regulations of the Commission as the Commission may require;

(2) Compiling data, developing reports, identifying needs and performing research

Chapter 17C

relevant to beneficial improvement of the criminal justice agencies;

(3) Developing new and revising existing programs for adoption consideration by the Commission;

(4) Monitoring and evaluating programs of the Commission;

(5) Providing technical assistance to relevant agencies of the criminal justice system to aid them in the discharge of program participation and responsibilities;

(6) Disseminating information on Commission programs to concerned agencies and/or individuals;

(7) Taking such other actions as may be deemed necessary or appropriate to carry out its assigned duties and responsibilities;

(8) The director may divulge any information in the Division's personnel file of a criminal justice officer or applicant for certification to the head of the criminal justice agency employing the officer or considering the applicant for employment when the director deems it necessary and essential to the retention or employment of said officer or applicant. The information may be divulged whether or not such information was contained in a personnel file maintained by a State or by a local government agency.

History.
1979, c. 763, s. 1; 1983, c. 807, s. 4

§ 17C-10. Required standards

(a) Criminal justice officers shall not be required to meet any requirement of subsections (b) and (c) of this section as a condition of continued employment, nor shall failure of any such criminal justice officer to fulfill such requirements make him ineligible for any promotional examination for which he is otherwise eligible if the criminal justice officer held a permanent appointment prior to June 1, 1986, and is an officer, supervisor or administrator of a local confinement facility; prior to March 15, 1973, and is a sworn law enforcement officer with power of arrest; prior to January 1, 1974, and is a State adult correctional officer; prior to July 1, 1975, and is a State probation/parole officer; prior to July 1, 1974, and is a State youth services officer; prior to January 15, 1980, and is a State probation/parole intake officer, prior to April 1, 1983, and is a State parole case analyst; prior to December 14, 1983, and is a State probation/parole officer-surveillance; or prior to February 1, 1987, and is a State probation/parole intensive officer.

The legislature finds, and it is declared to be the policy of this Article, that such criminal justice officers have satisfied such entry level requirements by their experience. It is the intent of the Chapter that all criminal justice officers employed at the entry level after the Commission has adopted the required standards shall meet the requirements of this Article. All criminal justice officers who are exempted from the required entry level standards by this subsection shall be subject thereafter to the requirements of subsections (b) and (c) of this section as well as the requirements of G.S. 17C-6(a) in order to retain certification.

If any criminal justice officer exempted from the required standards by this provision fails to serve as a criminal justice officer for a 12-month period, said officer shall be required to comply with the required entry level standards established by the Commission pursuant to the authority otherwise granted in this section and in G.S. 17C-6(a).

(b) The Commission shall provide, by regulation, for a period of probationary employment and certification for criminal justice officers. The Commission may prescribe such training requirements as are required for the award of either probationary or permanent certification of officers, in addition to the pre-employment requirements authorized in G.S. 17C-6(a). Any criminal justice officer appointed on a temporary or probationary basis who does not comply with the training provisions of this Article is not authorized to exercise the powers of a criminal justice officer to include the power of arrest. If, however, a criminal justice officer has enrolled in a Commission-approved preparatory program of training that concludes later than the end of the officer's probationary period, and the Commission does not require such training to be completed prior to the award of probationary certification, the Commission may extend, for good cause shown, the probationary period for a period not to exceed six months.

Upon separation of a criminal justice officer from a criminal justice agency within the prescribed period of temporary or probationary appointment, the officer's probationary certification shall be terminated by the Commission. Upon the reappointment to the same agency or appointment to another criminal justice agency of an officer who has separated from an agency within the probationary period, the officer shall be charged with the cumulative amount of time served during his initial or subsequent appointments and allowed the remainder of the probationary period to complete the Commission's requirements. Upon reappointment to the same agency or appointment to another agency of an officer who has separated from an agency within the probationary period and who has remained out of service for more than one year after the date of separation, the officer shall be allowed another probationary period to satisfy the Commission's requirements.

(c) In addition to the requirements of subsection (b) of this section, the Commission, by rules and regulations, shall fix other qualifications for the employment, training, and retention of criminal justice officers including minimum age, education, physical and mental standards, citizenship, good moral character, experience, and such other matters as relate to the competence and reliability of persons to assume and discharge the responsibilities of criminal justice officers, and the Commission shall prescribe the means for presenting evidence of fulfillment of these requirements.

Where minimum educational standards are not met, yet the individual shows potential and a willingness to achieve the standards by extra study, they may be waived by the Commission for the reasonable amount of time it will take to achieve the standards required. Such an educational waiver shall not exceed 12 months.

(d) The Commission may issue a certificate evidencing satisfaction of the requirements of subsections (b) and (c) of this section to any applicant who presents such evidence as may be required by its rules and regulations of satisfactory completion of a program or course of instruction in another jurisdiction equivalent in content and quality to that required by the Commission for approved criminal justice education and training programs in this State.

History.
1971, c. 963, s. 1; 1979, c. 763, s. 1; 1981, c. 8; c. 400; 1983, c. 745, s. 3; 1989, c. 757, s. 6; 2018-5, s. 17.1(a); 2021-136, s. 1(c); 2021-138, s. 7(c)

§ 17C-10.1. Certification of military service members and veterans with law enforcement training and experience

(a) Notwithstanding any other provision of law, the Commission shall waive an applicant's completion of the Commission-accredited training course and issue probationary certification to a current or honorably discharged former military police officer provided the Commission, upon evaluating the individual applicant's combined training and experience pursuant to G.S. 93B-15.1(a), determines that the applicant's combined training and experience is substantially equivalent to or exceeds the minimum expectations for employment as a law enforcement officer and the applicant satisfies all of the following conditions:

(1) Successfully completed a military police training program and been awarded a military police occupational specialty rating.

(2) Performed military police officer duties in any of the branches of military service, active or reserve, or the National Guard for not less than two of the five years

preceding the date of the application for certification as a law enforcement officer.

(3) Meets the minimum standards for law enforcement officers as set out in 12 NCAC 9B.0101 and 12 NCAC 9B.0111.

(b) An applicant certified pursuant to subsection (a) of this section must successfully complete the employing agency's in-service firearms training and qualification program prior to employment and shall serve a one-year period of probation. During the one-year period of probation, the applicant must successfully complete the Legal Unit and 24 hours of training in the service of civil process in a Commission-accredited Basic Law Enforcement Training Course and successfully pass the State Comprehensive Examination in its entirety.

(c) The Commission shall issue certification to a current or honorably discharged former military police officer whose combined training and experience is not substantially equivalent to or does not exceed the minimum expectations for employment as a law enforcement officer if the applicant meets all of the following requirements:

(1) Successfully completed a formal military basic training program and been awarded a military police occupational specialty rating.

(2) Engaged in the active practice of military police officer duties in any of the branches of military service, active or reserve, or the National Guard for not less than two of the five years preceding the date of the application for certification as a law enforcement officer.

(3) Meets the minimum standards for law enforcement officers as set out in 12 NCAC 9B.0101 and 12 NCAC 9B.0111.

(4) Successfully completes the Legal Unit and 24 hours of training in the service of civil process in a Commission-accredited Basic Law Enforcement Training Course.

(5) Successfully completes any supplementary high-liability training as deemed necessary by the Commission, not to exceed an additional 180 hours.

(6) Obtains a passing grade on the State Comprehensive Basic Law Enforcement Training (BLET) Exam.

(d) Members of the Air/Army National Guard and Military Reserve Components who have performed as a military police officer for not less than 1,040 hours during the five years preceding the date of application shall be deemed to satisfy the requirements of subdivision (2) of subsection (a) and subdivision (2) of subsection (c) of this section.

(e) An applicant who, after completing the required training in subsection (a) or (c) of this section, fails to obtain a passing score on not more than two of the units of the comprehensive exam may be retested in the units the applicant failed. An applicant who fails three or more of the units must enroll in and successfully complete a subsequent offering of the Basic Law Enforcement Training Course in its entirety in order to be eligible to be certified.

(f) An active duty military police officer who obtains certification under this section may retain the certification for the duration of active duty provided the officer continues to serve in a military police capacity and complies with any in-service training requirements as may be required by the Commission. An active duty member who is unable to complete annual in-service requirements due to deployment or overseas assignment shall have 12 months from the time the officer returns to the United States in which to complete any required in-service training. The officer shall retain the certification for a period of one year following separation from active duty.

(g) As used in this section, the following terms mean:

(1) **Branches of military service. --** The United States Armed Forces: Air Force; Army; Marine; Navy; active, reserve, Air/ Army National Guard components; and the Coast Guard.

(2) **Combined training. --** Basic military training, basic military police training, in-service or advanced military police training and, any other military training courses that may be applicable to the performance of law enforcement duties.

(3) **Military police. --** All law enforcement occupational classifications in the various branches of the Armed Forces, including Military Police Officer, Security Forces Specialist, Master-at-Arms, Maritime Enforcement Specialist, Boarding Officer, and Security forces.

(h) The Commission shall adopt rules to implement the provisions of this section.

History.
2015-49, s. 1; 2015-264, s. 37(a)

§ 17C-11. Compliance; enforcement

(a) Any criminal justice officer who the Commission determines does not comply with this Article or any rules adopted under this Article shall not exercise the powers of a criminal justice officer and shall not exercise the power of arrest unless the Commission waives that certification or deficiency. The Commission shall enforce this section by the entry of appropriate orders effective upon service on either the criminal justice agency or the criminal justice officer.

(a1) Any criminal justice training school, program, or course of instruction that the Commission determines does not comply with this Article, or any rules adopted under this Article, shall not continue to offer programs or courses of instruction unless the Commission waives that certification or deficiency. Any criminal justice instructor, school director, commission certified operator, and any commission certified instructor, who the Commission determines does not comply with this Article, or any rules adopted under this Article, shall not act as an instructor, school director, or operator unless the Commission waives that certification or deficiency. The Commission shall enforce this section by the entry of appropriate orders effective upon service on the criminal justice training school or the individual holding commission certification.

(b) Any person who desires to appeal the proposed denial, suspension, or revocation of any certification authorized to be issued by the Commission shall file a written appeal with the Commission not later than 30 days following notice of denial, suspension, or revocation.

(c) The Commission may appear in its own name and apply to courts having jurisdiction for injunctions to prevent violations of this Article or of rules issued pursuant thereto; specifically, the performance of criminal justice officer functions by officers or individuals who are not in compliance with the standards and requirements of G.S. 17C-6(a) and G.S. 17C-10. A single act of performance of a criminal justice officer function by an officer or individual who is performing such function in violation of this Article is sufficient, if shown, to invoke the injunctive relief of this section.

History.
1979, c. 763, s. 1; 1989, c. 757, s. 7; 2001-490, s. 1.3; 2009-546, s. 3; 2018-5, s. 17.1(a)

§ 17C-12. Grants under the supervision of Commission and the State; donations and appropriations

(a) The Commission may accept for any of its purposes and functions under this Article any and all donations, both real and personal, and grants of money from any governmental unit or public agency, or from any institution, person, firm or corporation, and may receive, utilize and dispose of the same. Any arrangements pursuant to this section shall be detailed in an annual report of the Commission. Such report shall include the identity of the donor, the nature of the transaction, and the conditions, if any. Any money received by the Commission pursuant to this section shall be deposited in the State Treasury to the account of the Commission.

(b) The Commission may authorize the reimbursement to each political subdivision of the State not exceeding sixty percent (60%) of the salary and of the allowable tuition, living and travel expenses incurred by the officers in attendance at approved training programs, providing said political subdivisions do in fact adhere to the selection and training standards established by the Commission.

(c) The Commission by rules and regulations, shall provide for administration of the grant program authorized by this section. In promulgating such rules, the Commission shall promote the most efficient and economical program of criminal justice training, including the maximum utilization of existing facilities and programs for the purpose of avoiding duplication.

(d) The Commission may provide grants as a reimbursement for actual expenses incurred by the State or political subdivision thereof for the provisions of training programs of officers from other jurisdictions within the State.

History.
1971, c. 963, ss. 8, 9; 1979, c. 763, s. 1; 2018-5, s. 17.1(a)

§ 17C-13. Pardons; expunctions

(a) When a person presents competent evidence that he has been granted an unconditional pardon for a crime in this State, any other state, or the United States, the Commission may not deny, suspend, or revoke that person's certification based solely on the commission of that crime or for an alleged lack of good moral character due to the commission of that crime.

(b) Notwithstanding G.S. 15A-145.4 or G.S. 15A-145.5, the Commission may gain access to a person's felony conviction records, including those maintained by the Administrative Office of the Courts in its confidential files containing the names of persons granted expunctions. The Commission may deny, suspend, or revoke a person's certification based solely on that person's felony conviction, whether or not that conviction was expunged.

History.
1989, c. 757, s. 8; 2011-278, s. 3; 2012-191, s. 6

§ 17C-14. Database of law enforcement officer certification suspensions and revocations

The Commission shall develop and maintain a statewide database accessible to the public on its website that contains all revocations and suspensions of law enforcement officer certifications by the Commission.

History.
2021-138, s. 1(a)

§ 17C-15. Database for law enforcement officer critical incident information

(a) The Division shall develop and maintain a statewide database for use by law enforcement agencies that tracks all critical incident data of law enforcement officers in North Carolina.

(b) All law enforcement agencies in the State that employ personnel certified by the Commission shall provide any information requested by the Division to maintain the database required by subsection (a) of this section.

(c) Information collected under this section that is confidential under State or federal law shall remain confidential.

(d) A law enforcement officer who is reported to the Division as having been involved in a critical incident who disputes being involved in a critical incident has a right, prior to being placed in the database, to request a hearing in superior court for a determination of whether the officer's involvement was properly placed in the database.

History.
2021-138, s. 3(b)

§ 17C-16. Requirement to report material relevant to testimony

(a) Any person who is certified by the Commission or has received a conditional offer of employment and who has been notified that the person may not be called to testify at trial based on bias, interest, or lack of credibility shall report and provide a copy of that notification to the Criminal Justice Standards Division within 30 days of receiving the notification, except as provided in subsection (h) of this section. This requirement shall only apply if the person is notified by one of the following methods:

(1) In writing by a superior court judge, district court judge, federal judge, district attorney, assistant district attorney, United States attorney, assistant United States attorney, or the person's agency head.

(2) In open court by a superior court judge, district court judge, or federal judge, and documented in a written order.

(b) The report to the Division shall be in writing and shall state who notified the person that the person may not be called to testify at trial. A person required to report to the Division under subsection (a) of this section shall make the same report to the person's agency head within 30 days of being notified that the person may not be called to testify at trial. An agency head who receives a report that a person in the agency has been notified that they may not be called to testify at trial shall also report the notification to the Division in writing within 30 days of the agency head's receipt of that report.

(c) A superior court judge, district court judge, federal judge, district attorney, assistant district attorney, United States attorney, or assistant United States attorney who notifies a person that they may not be called to testify at trial as provided in subsection (a) of this section shall report that notification to the Division and provide a copy of the written document or order within 30 days of notifying the person that they may not be called to testify at trial.

(d) If the Division transfers to another agency the certification of any person required to report to the Division pursuant to subsection (a) of this section, the Division shall provide written notification to both the head of the new agency and the elected district attorney in the prosecutorial district where the agency is located that the person has been previously notified that the person may not be called to testify at trial. If the new agency receiving notification pursuant to this subsection is a State agency, the Division shall notify the elected district attorney in every prosecutorial district of the State.

(e) If any person required to report to the Division pursuant to subsection (a) of this section is subsequently informed in writing that that notification has been rescinded, the person shall provide the Division a copy of that document. The provisions of subsection (d) of this section do not apply if the person required to report pursuant to subsection (a) of this section is subsequently informed in writing that the notification has been rescinded.

(f) No later than March 1 each year, the Commission shall report to the Joint Legislative Oversight Committee on Justice and Public Safety regarding the number of individuals for whom the Division received a report required by subsection (a) of this section during the previous calendar year. The report shall include information for each case on whether a final agency decision has been entered pursuant to Chapter 150B of the General Statutes and what action, if any, has been taken against each certification. The report shall not include the name or any other identifying information of any person required to report pursuant to subsection (a) of this section.

(g) The reports and notifications received by the Division pursuant to this section shall not be public record.

(h) Any person who has received a notification that may meet the reporting requirement provided in subsection (a) of this section may apply for a hearing in superior court for a judicial determination of whether or not the person received a notification that the person may not be called to testify at trial based on bias, interest, or lack of credibility. This hearing is limited to reviewing whether (i) a person who is certified by the Commission or has received a conditional offer of employment, (ii) has been notified in writing by a superior court judge, district court judge, federal judge, district attorney, assistant district attorney, United States attorney, or assistant United States attorney; or notified in open court by a superior court judge, district court judge, or federal judge, and documented in a written order, and (iii) that notification states that the person may not be called to testify at trial based on bias, interest, or lack of credibility, not matters of law or admissibility. The person must provide notice of the hearing to the Division. One extension of 15 days will be added to the 30-day reporting requirement provided in subsection (a) of this section if notice of a hearing is received.

History.
2021-137, s. 3(a); 2021-138, s. 4(a)

ARTICLE 2
NORTH CAROLINA CRIMINAL JUSTICE FELLOWS PROGRAM

§ 17C-20. Definitions

As used in this Article, the following definitions apply:

(1) **Commission.** -- The North Carolina Criminal Justice Education and Training Standards Commission.

(2) **Committee.** -- The North Carolina Criminal Justice Fellows Committee.

(3) **Community college.** -- As defined in G.S. 115D-2(2).

(4) **Division.** -- The Criminal Justice Standards Division of the North Carolina Department of Justice.

(5) **Eligible county.** -- A county with a population of less than 125,000 according to the latest federal decennial census or a county designated as a development tier one area pursuant to G.S. 143B-437.08, or both.

(6) **Eligible criminal justice professions.** -- State and local sworn law enforcement officers, State correctional officers, other correctional officers maintained by local governments and juvenile justice agencies, sworn sheriffs and deputy sheriffs, detention officers, and telecommunicators under the direct supervision of a law enforcement agency.

(7) **Program.** -- The North Carolina Criminal Justice Fellows Program.

(8) **Recipient.** -- An individual selected by the Committee to receive a forgivable loan under the Program.

History.
2018-5, s. 17.1(b); 2020-78, s. 11.1(a)

§ 17C-21. North Carolina Criminal Justice Fellows Committee established; membership

(a) **Committee Established. --** There is established the North Carolina Criminal Justice Fellows Committee. The Committee shall be a Special Committee of the North Carolina Criminal Justice Education and Training Standards Commission, as defined in the Commission's bylaws. The Committee shall determine program and forgivable loan recipient selection criteria, selection procedures, and shall select the recipients to receive forgivable loans under the North Carolina Criminal Justice Fellows Program in accordance with the requirements of this Article.

(b) **Membership. --** The Committee shall consist of 10 members who shall be appointed as follows:

(1) The chair of the Commission shall appoint eight members of the Commission to the Committee as follows:

a. Three at-large members.

b. Two sworn law enforcement officers.

c. Two correctional officers.

d. The ex officio member representing the President of The North Carolina Community College System.

(2) The chair of the North Carolina Sheriffs' Education and Training Standards Commission shall appoint two members of the North Carolina Sheriffs' Education and Training Standards Commission to the Committee.

(c) **Terms of Office. --** Appointments to the Committee shall be for two-year terms, commencing July 1, 2018.

(d) **Chair; Meetings. --** The chair of the Commission shall call the first meeting of the Committee. The Committee members shall elect a chair and a vice-chair from the membership of the Committee pursuant to the Commission's bylaws to serve one-year terms. The Committee shall meet regularly at times and places deemed necessary by the chair or, in the absence of the chair, by the vice-chair.

(e) **Expenses. --** Committee members shall receive per diem, subsistence, and travel allowances in accordance with G.S. 138-5 or G.S. 138-6, as appropriate.

(f) **Vacancies. --** Except as otherwise provided, if a vacancy occurs in the membership of the Committee, the appointing authority shall appoint another person meeting the same qualifications to serve for the balance of the unexpired term.

History.
2018-5, s. 17.1(b)

§ 17C-22. North Carolina Criminal Justice Fellows Program established; administration

(a) **Program. --** There is established the North Carolina Criminal Justice Fellows Program to be administered by the Committee with the assistance of the Division. The purpose of the Program is to increase the number of criminal justice professionals by providing forgivable loans to exceptional individuals to obtain Applied Associate Degrees in Criminal Justice or other Committee-approved related fields of study as preparation to enter a criminal justice profession.

(b) **Program Administrator. --** The Director of the Division shall select a member of the Division staff, with the consent of the Committee, to serve as the Program administrator. The Program administrator will be responsible for all administrative duties and oversight of the Program as established by the Committee. The Program administrator will conduct recruitment efforts to include the following:

(1) Target eligible counties.

(2) Target high school graduates who, due to economic circumstances, are displaced, unemployed, or underemployed.

(3) Target high school seniors who demonstrate an interest in becoming criminal justice professionals.

(4) Engage with criminal justice professionals and leaders in eligible counties for input in the Program.

(5) Attend high school career days, job fairs, and other activities in eligible counties to recruit qualified individuals into the Program.

(c) **Awards of Forgivable Loans. --** The Program shall provide forgivable loans of up to three thousand one hundred fifty-two dollars ($ 3,152.00) per year for up to two years to selected individuals. The funds from the forgivable loans may be used for tuition, fees, and the cost of books. The Committee may determine the maximum amount of loan proceeds that may be applied to community college fees and course textbooks. The number of forgivable loans awarded annually shall not exceed 100 and the total number of recipients in the Program each year shall not exceed 200. The Committee shall select recipients no later than June 1 of each year.

(d) **Eligibility Criteria. --** An applicant must be domiciled in an eligible county at the time of application, a resident for tuition purposes as defined in G.S. 116-143.1(a)(2), a high school graduate or a high school senior who will graduate from high school by the end of the current academic year, and demonstrate the intent upon completion of the Program to be employed as a criminal justice professional in an eligible county. An applicant who has been convicted of any of the following is ineligible to receive a forgivable loan:

   (1) A felony.

   (2) A crime for which the punishment could have been imprisonment for more than two years.

   (3) A crime or unlawful act defined as a Class B misdemeanor within the five-year period prior to the date of application.

   (4) Four or more crimes or unlawful acts defined as Class A misdemeanors, except the trainee may be enrolled if the last conviction date occurred more than two years prior to the date of application.

   (5) A combination of four or more Class A misdemeanors or Class B misdemeanors regardless of the date of conviction.

(e) **Application Process.** -- The Committee may specify required application materials, including a certified State and local background check for applicants who are at least 18 years of age. Application materials and Committee deliberations are confidential and are not a public record as defined in G.S. 132-1. The Committee shall publish application, award, and notification deadlines and provide written notification to applicants regarding the outcome of the Committee's deliberations.

(f) **Award of Forgivable Loan.** -- The Committee shall adopt standards for awarding forgivable loans based on measures the Committee deems appropriate, including the following, and the selection of recipients by the Committee shall be final:

   (1) Scholastic Profile as determined by SAT or ACT scores, grade point average, and class rank when available.

   (2) Potential for excellence in an eligible criminal justice profession.

   (3) School and community service.

   (4) At least two references.

   (5) Demonstrated writing ability.

(g) **Administration of Forgivable Loan Awards.** -- Upon the naming of recipients by the Committee, the Division shall perform all administrative functions necessary to implement this Article, which functions shall include dissemination of information, disbursement, receipt, liaison with participating community colleges, determination of the acceptability of service repayment agreements, and all other functions necessary for the execution, payment, and enforcement of promissory notes required under this Article.

(h) **Recipient Obligations.** -- A recipient must become and remain a full-time student at a North Carolina community college in an Applied Associate Degree in Criminal Justice or in a Committee-approved related field of study at all times during each of the recipient's two academic years of community college study and pursue continuously studies that will qualify the recipient to be employed in an eligible criminal justice profession upon graduation. The recipient must maintain a minimum cumulative 2.0 GPA throughout the course of study and also maintain appropriate credit hours for each semester to obtain an Applied Associate Degree in Criminal Justice or Committee-approved field of study within two years. The recipient must also accept employment in an eligible county as a criminal justice professional for at least four out of five years following graduation. The Committee may adopt additional recipient obligations it deems appropriate.

(i) **Annual Report.** -- The Program administrator, in coordination with the Committee, shall report no later than January 1, 2020, and annually thereafter, to the Joint Legislative Oversight Committee on Justice and Public Safety regarding the following:

   (1) The number of forgivable loans awarded for each academic year disaggregated to include geographic and other demographic information.

   (2) Aggregated student performance, retention, and graduation rates.

   (3) Employment subsequent to completion of the Program broken down by eligible county and eligible criminal justice profession.

   (4) Forgiveness, termination, default, and repayment rates.

   (5) Retention rates of recipients within eligible criminal justice professions disaggregated by eligible county.

History.

2018-5, s. 17.1(b)

§ 17C-23. Terms of forgivable loans; receipt and disbursement of funds; default

(a) **Forgivable Loans.** -- All forgivable loans shall be evidenced by notes made payable to the Program that bear interest at a rate not to exceed ten percent (10%) per year as set by the Committee and beginning on the first day of September after the completion of the Program or 60 days after termination of the forgivable loan, whichever is earlier. The forgivable loan may be terminated upon the recipient's withdrawal from school, by the recipient's failure to meet the standards set by the Committee, or by the recipient's default based on conditions set by the Committee. The Committee may only disburse funds to the community college where the recipient is enrolled and may not disburse funds directly to a recipient.

(b) **Forgiveness.** -- The Committee shall forgive the loan and any interest accrued on the loan if, within five years after obtaining an Applied Associate Degree in Criminal Justice or

Chapter 17C

Committee-approved field of study, the recipient is employed on a full-time basis for a period of at least four years in an eligible county in an eligible criminal justice profession. The recipient shall provide the Committee within 60 days of completion of the Program verification of the recipient's intent to seek employment as a criminal justice professional in an eligible county. The recipient shall provide verification of employment to the Committee each year until the obligation is satisfied. The Committee shall also forgive the loan if it finds that it is impossible for the recipient to meet the terms of the loan, after or before graduation, due to death or permanent disability of the recipient.

(c) **Extension.** -- The Committee may extend repayment of the loan for up to two years on a year-to-year basis for each year if (i) the recipient is on active duty with the Armed Forces of the United States or (ii) the Committee, in its sole discretion, determines that circumstances warrant an extension.

(d) **Repayment.** -- If the recipient notifies the Committee that the recipient intends to forego forgiveness of the loan after completion of the Program, the Committee shall provide the recipient with the conditions of repayment and the recipient will have 60 days to begin repayment of all funds distributed, including interest. The recipient will have up to 60 months to repay all funds distributed, including interest.

(e) **Default.** -- The Committee shall determine the events that constitute a default during the Program, including, but not limited to, failure by the recipient to comply with the obligations set out in G.S. 17C-22(h). In the event of default during the Program, the Committee may declare the entire unpaid amount of indebtedness evidenced by the note, including interest, immediately due and payable. A default shall preclude further participation by the recipient in the Program. Upon default, the Committee shall notify the recipient, in writing, by certified mail, return receipt requested, addressed to the recipient at the last address on file with the Committee. Refusal or nondelivery at that address will be deemed delivered after seven days. The Committee may allow a recipient who is in default to repay all funds distributed, including interest. If the Committee approves repayment, the recipient will receive the conditions of repayment and will have 60 days to begin repayment of all funds distributed, including interest. The recipient will have up to 60 months to repay all funds distributed, including interest.

History.
2018-5, s. 17.1(b)

CHAPTER 17D
NORTH CAROLINA
JUSTICE ACADEMY

§ 17D-1. Definitions

As used in this Chapter, unless the context otherwise requires:

(1) "Academy" means the North Carolina Justice Academy.

(2) "Academy property" means property that is owned or leased in whole or in part by the State of North Carolina and which is subject to the general management and control of the Department of Justice and is located in Salemburg, North Carolina, or at any other locations within the State which are dedicated to the use of the North Carolina Justice Academy subsequent to this Chapter being enacted.

(3) "The Commission" means the North Carolina Criminal Justice Education and Training Standards Commission.

(4) "Criminal justice agencies" means the State and local law enforcement agencies, the State and local police traffic service agencies, the State correctional agencies, the jails and other correctional agencies maintained by local governments, the courts of the State and the juvenile justice agencies.

(5) "Criminal justice personnel" means any person who serves or assists any State or local agency engaged in crime prevention, crime reduction, crime investigation, training or educating of persons employed by criminal justice agencies, or enforcement of the criminal law; or any person employed by a criminal justice agency.

(6) "Department" means the Department of Justice.

History.
1973, c. 749; 1977, c. 831, s. 1; 1979, c. 763, s. 2; 1997-456, s. 27

§ 17D-2. Academy established; duties

(a) The North Carolina Department of Justice shall establish a North Carolina Justice Academy.

(b) The Department of Justice shall employ the staff of the academy and direct its operations.

(c) Duties of the academy. The North Carolina Justice Academy shall have, but is not limited to, the following functions:

(1) It may provide training programs for criminal justice personnel.

(2) It may provide technical assistance upon request to criminal justice agencies to aid them in the discharge of their responsibilities.

(3) It may develop, publish, and distribute educational and training materials.

(4) It may take such other actions as may be deemed necessary or appropriate to carry out its assigned duties and responsibilities.

History.
1973, c. 749; 1979, c. 763, s. 2

§ 17D-3. Donations

The Department of Justice may accept for any of its purposes and functions under this Article any and all donations, both real and personal, and grants of money from any governmental unit or public agency, or from any institution, person, firm or corporation. Any arrangements pursuant to this section shall be detailed in an annual report of the academy. Such reports shall include the identity of the donor, the nature of the transaction, and the conditions, if any. Any money received by the Department of Justice pursuant to this section shall be deposited in the State Treasury to the account of the academy. All moneys involved shall be subject to audit by the State Auditor.

History.
1979, c. 763, s. 2

§ 17D-4. Application of State highway and motor vehicles laws at the academy; authority of Department of Justice to regulate traffic, etc

(a) Except as otherwise provided in this section, all of the provisions of Chapter 20 of the General Statutes relating to the use of highways of the State and the operation of vehicles thereon are applicable to all streets, alleys, driveways, and parking lots on academy property. Nothing in this section modifies any rights of ownership or control of academy property, now or hereafter vested in the State of North Carolina ex rel., Department of Justice.

(b) The Department of Justice may by ordinance prohibit, regulate, divert, control, and limit pedestrian or vehicular traffic and the parking of vehicles and other modes of conveyance on the campus. In fixing speed limits, the Department of Justice is not subject to G.S. 20-141(f) or (g), but may fix any speed limit reasonable and safe under the circumstances as conclusively determined by the Department of Justice. The Department of Justice may not regulate traffic on streets open to the public as of right, except as specifically provided in this section.

Chapter 17D

(c) The Department of Justice may by ordinance provide for the registration of vehicles maintained or operated on the campus by any student, faculty member, or employee of the academy and may fix fees for such registration. The ordinance may make it unlawful for any person to operate an unregistered vehicle on the campus when the vehicle is required by the ordinance to be registered.

(d) The Department of Justice may by ordinance set aside parking lots on the campus for use by students, faculty, and employees of the academy and members of the general public attending schools, conferences, or meetings at the academy, visiting or making use of any academy facilities, or attending to official business with the academy. The Department of Justice may issue permits to park in these lots and may charge a fee therefor. The Department of Justice may also by ordinance make it unlawful for any person to park a vehicle in any lot or other parking facility without procuring the requisite permit and displaying it on the vehicle.

(e) The Department of Justice may by ordinance provide for the issuance of stickers, decals, permits or other indicia representing the registration of vehicles or the eligibility of vehicles to park on the campus and may by ordinance prohibit the forgery, counterfeiting, unauthorized transfer, or unauthorized use of such stickers, decals, permits or other indicia.

(f) Violation of an ordinance adopted under any portion of this section is a Class 3 misdemeanor. An ordinance may provide that certain acts prohibited thereby shall not be enforced by criminal sanctions, and in such cases a person committing any such act shall not be guilty of a misdemeanor.

(g) An ordinance adopted under this section may provide that a violation will subject the offender to a civil penalty. Penalties may be graduated according to the seriousness of the offense or the number of prior offenses committed by the person charged. The Department of Justice may establish procedure for the collection of these penalties and may enforce the penalties by civil action in the nature of debt. The Department of Justice may also provide for appropriate administrative sanctions if an offender does not pay a validly due penalty or has committed repeated offenses. Appropriate administrative sanctions include, but are not limited to, revocation of parking permits, termination of vehicle registration, and termination or suspension of enrollment in or employment by the academy.

(h) An ordinance adopted under this section may provide that any vehicle illegally parked may be removed to a storage area, in which case the person so removing the vehicle shall be deemed a legal possessor within the meaning of G.S. 44A-2(d).

(i) Evidence that a vehicle was found parked or unattended in violation of a council ordinance is prima facie evidence that the vehicle was parked by:

(1) The person holding an academy parking permit for the vehicle;

(2) If no academy parking permit has been issued for the vehicle, the person in whose name the vehicle is registered with the academy pursuant to subsection (c); or

(3) If no academy parking permit has been issued for the vehicle and the vehicle is not registered with the academy, the person in whose name it is registered with the North Carolina Department of Motor Vehicles or the corresponding agency of another state or nation.

The rule of evidence established by this subsection applies only in civil, criminal, or administrative actions or proceedings concerning violations of ordinances of the Department of Justice. G.S. 20-162.1 does not apply to such actions or proceedings.

(j) The Department of Justice shall cause to be posted appropriate notice to the public of applicable traffic and parking restrictions.

(k) All ordinances adopted under this section shall be filed in the offices of the North Carolina Attorney General and the Secretary of State. The Department of Justice shall provide for printing and distributing copies of its traffic and parking ordinances.

(l) All moneys received pursuant to this section shall be State funds as defined in G.S. 143C-1-1.

History.
1977, c. 831, s. 2; 1979, c. 763, s. 2; 1993, c. 539, s. 309; 1994, Ex. Sess., c. 24, s. 14(c); 2006-203, s. 12

CHAPTER 17E
NORTH CAROLINA SHERIFFS' EDUCATION AND TRAINING STANDARDS COMMISSION

ARTICLE 1.
GENERAL

§ 17E-1. Findings and policy

The General Assembly finds and declares that the office of sheriff, the office of deputy sheriff and the other officers and employees of the sheriff of a county are unique among all of the law-enforcement offices of North Carolina. The administration of criminal justice has been declared by Article 1 of Chapter 17C of the General Statutes to be of statewide concern to the people of the State. The sheriff is the only officer of local government required by the Constitution. The sheriff, in addition to his criminal justice responsibilities, is the only officer who is also responsible for the courts of the State, and acting as their bailiff and marshall. The sheriff administers and executes criminal and civil justice and acts as the ex officio detention officer.

The deputy sheriff has been held by the Supreme Court of this State to hold an office of special trust and confidence, acting in the name of and with powers coterminous with his principal, the elected sheriff.

The offices of sheriff and deputy sheriff are therefore of special concern to the public health, safety, welfare and morals of the people of the State. The training and educational needs of such officers therefore require particularized and differential treatment from those of the criminal justice officers certified under Article 1 of Chapter 17C of the General Statutes.

History.
1983, c. 558, s. 1; 1995, c. 103, s. 1

§ 17E-2. Definitions

Unless the context clearly requires otherwise, the following definitions apply to this Chapter:

(1) "Commission" means the North Carolina Sheriffs' Education and Training Standards Commission.

(1a) "Critical incident" means an incident involving any use of force by a law enforcement officer that results in death or serious bodily injury to a person.

(2) "Office" or "department" means the sheriff of a county, his deputies, his employees and such equipment, space, provisions and quarters as are supplied for their use.

(3) "Justice officer" means:

a. A person who, through the special trust and confidence of the sheriff, has taken the oath of office prescribed by Chapter 11 of the General Statutes as a peace officer in the office of the sheriff. This term includes "deputy sheriffs", "reserve deputy sheriffs", and "special deputy sheriffs", but does not include clerical and support personnel not required to take an oath. The term "special deputy" means a person who, through appointment by the sheriff, becomes an unpaid criminal justice officer to perform a specific act directed by the sheriff; or

b. A person who, through the special trust and confidence of the sheriff, has been appointed as a detention officer by the sheriff; or

c. A person who is either the administrator or other custodial personnel of district confinement facilities as defined in G.S. 153A-219; however, nothing in this Chapter transfers any supervisory or administrative control over employees of district confinement facilities to the office of the sheriff; or

d. A person who, through the special trust and confidence of the sheriff, is under the direct supervision and control of the sheriff and serves as a telecommunicator, or who is presented to the Commission for appointment as a telecommunicator by an employing entity other than the sheriff for the purpose of obtaining certification from the Commission as a telecommunicator.

History.
1983, c. 558, s. 1; c. 745, s. 1; 1991, c. 265, s. 1; 1995, c. 103, s. 2; 1997-443, s. 20.11(b); 2021-107, s. 3(a); 2021-138, s. 3(c)

§ 17E-3. North Carolina Sheriffs' Education and Training Standards Commission established; members; terms; vacancies

(a) There is hereby established the North Carolina Sheriffs' Education and Training Standards Commission. The Commission shall be composed of 17 members as follows:

(1) **Sheriffs. --** Twelve sheriffs appointed by the North Carolina Sheriffs' Association, 10 representing each of the Commission

Districts established in this section, and two appointed at large in such manner as shall be prescribed by the Constitution or bylaws of the Association.

(2) **Appointees of the General Assembly.** -- One person appointed by the Speaker of the House of Representatives pursuant to G.S. 120-121 and one person appointed by the General Assembly upon the recommendation of the President Pro Tempore of the Senate pursuant to G.S. 120-121.

(3) **County Commissioners.** -- One county commissioner appointed by the Governor as recommended from three nominees from the North Carolina Association of County Commissioners.

(4) **Others.** -- The President of the Community Colleges System or the President's designee and the Dean of the School of Government at the University of North Carolina at Chapel Hill or the Dean's designee shall be ex officio, nonvoting members of the Commission.

(b) **Terms.** -- Members shall be appointed for staggered terms. Beginning September 1, 1995, sheriffs representing Commission Districts 3, 6, and 9 shall be appointed to three-year terms; sheriffs representing Commission Districts 1, 4, and 7 shall be appointed to one-year terms; sheriffs representing Commission Districts 2, 5, 8, and 10 and the two at-large sheriffs, shall be appointed to two-year terms. The appointee of the House of Representatives shall serve a term of two years. The appointee of the Senate shall serve a term of two years. The county commissioner appointed by the North Carolina Association of County Commissioners shall serve a term of two years. After the initial terms established herein have expired, all sheriffs appointed to the Commission shall be appointed to terms of three years.

If an individual ceases to be a sheriff then his seat on the Commission becomes vacated upon his ceasing to be qualified to hold that seat. Any individual appointed or designated to serve on this Commission shall serve until his successor is appointed and qualified.

(c) **Vacancies.** -- If any vacancy occurs in the membership of the Commission, the appointing authority shall appoint another person to fill the unexpired term of the vacating member.

(d) **Compensation.** -- None of the members of the Commission shall receive compensation for serving on the Commission. However, if the North Carolina Department of Justice has funds available, then members of the Commission who are State officers or employees may be reimbursed for their expenses in accordance with G.S. 138-6; members of the Commission who are full-time salaried public officers or employees other than State officers or employees may be reimbursed for their expenses in accordance with G.S. 138-5(b). All other members of the Commission may receive compensation and reimbursement for expenses in accordance with G.S. 138-5.

(e) **Officers.** -- The chairman shall be elected from among the membership. The Commission shall select its other officers from among the membership as it deems necessary. All officers serve for one year, or until successors are qualified.

(f) **Removal.** -- The Commission may remove a member for misfeasance, malfeasance, nonfeasance or neglect of duty.

(g) The Commission has power to adopt its own rules of procedure. The Commission shall meet no less than four times a year. It shall also meet on the call of the chairman or vice-chairman, or any four members of the Commission.

(h) The Commission may appoint any resident of the State to an adjunct or special committee created or appointed by it to study or make recommendations or reports on any subject matter related to its duties or the office of sheriff.

(i) Members of the Commission shall have the authority to designate, in writing, one member of his office to represent them and, if the member possesses voting authority, vote for them on the Commission at all meetings the voting member is unable to attend. This voting authority shall extend to all matters brought before the Commission which require a vote, to include the entry of final agency decisions and the adoption of administrative rules.

(j) The State is divided into 10 Commission Districts established for the appointment of members of the North Carolina Sheriffs' Education and Training Standards Commission as follows:

District 1: The Counties of Bertie, Camden, Chowan, Currituck, Gates, Hertford, Pasquotank, Perquimans, Tyrrell, and Washington.

District 2: The Counties of Caswell, Edgecombe, Franklin, Granville, Halifax, Nash, Northampton, Person, Vance, and Warren.

District 3: The Counties of Beaufort, Craven, Dare, Duplin, Hyde, Jones, Lenoir, Martin, Pamlico, and Pitt.

District 4: The Counties of Chatham, Durham, Greene, Harnett, Johnston, Lee, Orange, Wake, Wayne, and Wilson.

District 5: The Counties of Alleghany, Alexander, Ashe, Catawba, Gaston, Lincoln, Surry, Watauga, Wilkes, and Yadkin.

District 6: The Counties of Alamance, Davidson, Davie, Forsyth, Guilford, Iredell, Randolph, Rockingham, Rowan, and Stokes.

District 7: The Counties of Bladen, Brunswick, Carteret, Columbus, Cumberland, New

Hanover, Onslow, Pender, Robeson, and Sampson.

District 8: The Counties of Anson, Cabarrus, Hoke, Mecklenburg, Montgomery, Moore, Richmond, Scotland, Stanly, and Union.

District 9: The Counties of Avery, Burke, Caldwell, Cleveland, Madison, McDowell, Mitchell, Polk, Rutherford, and Yancey.

District 10: The Counties of Buncombe, Cherokee, Clay, Graham, Haywood, Henderson, Jackson, Macon, Swain, and Transylvania.

History.

1983, c. 558, s. 1; 1991 (Reg. Sess., 1992), c. 1005, ss. 1, 2; 1993 (Reg. Sess., 1994), c. 562, s. 1; c. 767, s. 33; 1995, c. 103, s. 3; c. 490, s. 48; 2006-264, s. 29(e)

§ 17E-4. Powers and duties of the Commission

(a) The Commission shall have the following powers, duties, and responsibilities, which are enforceable through its rules and regulations, certification procedures, or the provisions of G.S. 17E-8 and G.S. 17E-9:

(1) Promulgate rules and regulations for the administration of this Chapter, which rules may require (i) the submission by any agency of information with respect to the employment, education, and training of its justice officers, and (ii) the submission by any training school of information with respect to its programs that are required by this Chapter;

(2) Establish minimum educational and training standards that may be met in order to qualify for entry level employment as an officer in temporary or probationary status or in a permanent position. The standards for entry level employment of officers shall include all of the following:

   a. Training in response to, and investigation of, domestic violence cases, as well as training in investigation for evidence-based prosecutions. For purposes of the domestic violence training requirement, the term "officers" shall include justice officers as defined in G.S. 17E-2(3)a., except that the term shall not include "special deputy sheriffs" as defined in G.S. 17E-2(3)a.

   b. Training on juvenile justice issues, including (i) the handling and processing of juvenile matters for referrals, diversion, arrests, and detention; (ii) best practices for handling incidents involving juveniles; (iii) adolescent development and psychology; and (iv) promoting relationship building with youth as a key to delinquency prevention.

   c. Education and training to develop knowledge and increase awareness of effective mental health and wellness strategies for justice officers.

(3) Certify, pursuant to the standards that it may establish for the purpose, persons as qualified under the provisions of this Chapter who may be employed at entry level as officers;

(4) Establish minimum standards for the certification of training schools and programs or courses of instruction that are required by this Chapter;

(5) Certify, pursuant to the standards that it has established for the purpose, training schools and programs or courses of instruction that are required by this Chapter;

(6) Establish standards and levels of education or equivalent experience for teachers who participate in programs or courses of instruction that are required by this Chapter;

(7) Certify, pursuant to the standards that it has established for the purpose, teachers who participate in programs or courses of instruction that are required by this Chapter;

(8) Investigate and make such evaluations as may be necessary to determine if agencies are complying with the provision[s] of this Chapter;

(9) Adopt and amend bylaws, consistent with law, for its internal management and control;

(10) Enter into contracts incident to the administration of its authority pursuant to this Chapter;

(11) Establish minimum standards for in-service training for justice officers. In-service training standards for sworn law enforcement officers shall include all of the following training topics:

   a. Response to, and investigation of, domestic violence cases, as well as training in investigation for evidence-based prosecutions. For purposes of the domestic violence training requirement, the term "justice officer" shall include those defined in G.S. 17E-2(3)a., except that the term shall not include "special deputy sheriffs" as defined in G.S. 17E-2(3)a.

   b. Juvenile justice issues, including (i) the handling and processing of juvenile matters for referrals, diversion, arrests, and detention; (ii) best practices for handling incidents involving juveniles; (iii) adolescent development and psychology; and (iv) promoting relationship building with youth as a key to delinquency prevention.

Chapter 17E

c. Training to develop knowledge and increase awareness of effective mental health and wellness strategies for justice officers. The standards established shall include two hours of training on this issue every three years.

d. Ethics.

e. Mental health for justice officers.

f. Community policing.

g. Minority sensitivity.

h. Use of force.

i. The duty to intervene and report.

(12) Establish minimum standards and levels of training for certification of instructors for the domestic violence training and juvenile justice training required by subdivisions (2) and (11) of this subsection.

(13) Establish minimum educational and training standards for employment and continuing education for officers concerning:

a. Recognizing and appropriately interacting with persons who are deaf or hard of hearing.

b. Drivers license and vehicle registration identifiers of persons who are deaf or hard of hearing, as authorized by G.S. 20-7(q2), including that those identifiers are optional.

(14) Monitor compliance with G.S. 20-185.1(d).

(15) Establish minimum standards and levels of training for certification of diversion investigators and diversion supervisors, as defined in G.S. 90-113.74(i). As part of these minimum standards, the Commission shall require that certified diversion investigators receive training in the following:

a. Definition of drug diversion.

b. Categories of drugs most subject to diversion and misuse.

c. Methods used to divert drugs.

d. Proper investigation of drug diversion cases.

e. Appropriate use of the controlled substances reporting system to investigate drug diversion cases.

f. Requests of prescriptions and records related to prescriptions pursuant to G.S. 90-107.1, including best practices for working with pharmacies in a manner that minimizes disruption of customer service and pharmacy operations.

g. Data privacy and security provisions of the Health Insurance Portability and Accountability Act of 1996 (HIPAA) and other pertinent federal and State laws governing privacy and security of confidential data and records.

h. Proper handling of confidential data and records from any source.

i. Criminal and civil penalties under federal and State law for improperly accessing, handling, or disclosing confidential prescription data or other confidential data or records.

(16) Certify and recertify at least once every three years, suspend, revoke, or deny, pursuant to the standards that it has established for the purpose, persons as qualified to be employed at entry level and retained as diversion investigators and diversion supervisors, as defined in G.S. 90-113.74(i).

(17) Search the National Decertification Index (NDI) maintained by the International Association of Directors of Law Enforcement Standards and Training (IADLEST) using the name of every applicant for certification or applicant for lateral transfer, and any other personal identifying information necessary to complete the search, and shall utilize any record of conviction of a criminal offense received as a result of the search during the application and lateral transfer process to determine if the applicant has any record that would disqualify the applicant for certification.

The Commission may certify, and no additional certification shall be required from it, programs, courses and teachers certified by the North Carolina Criminal Justice Education and Training Standards Commission. Where the Commission determines that a program, course, instructor or teacher is required for an area which is unique to the office of sheriff, the Commission may certify such program, course, instructor, or teacher under such standards and procedures as it may establish.

(b) [Recodified as G.S. 17E-4.1.]

History.

1983, c. 558, s. 1; 1991, c. 265, s. 2; 1995, c. 103, ss. 4, 5; 2004-186, ss. 2.7, 2.9, 2.10, 2.12; 2017-57, s. 16D.4(cc); 2017-191, s. 3; 2018-5, s. 35.25(e); 2018-44, s. 14(b); 2018-142, s. 23(b); 2021-107, s. 3(a), (c); 2021-136, s. 1(b); 2021-137, s. 2(b); 2021-138, ss. 7(b), 11(b), 15(b)

§ 17E-5. Functions of the Department of Justice

(a) The Attorney General shall provide such staff assistance as the Commission shall require and direct in the performance of its duties.

(b) The Attorney General shall have legal custody of all books, papers, documents, or other records and property of the Commission.

History.
1983, c. 558, s. 1

§ 17E-6. Justice Officers' Standards Division established; appointment of director; duties

(a) There is hereby established, within the Department of Justice, the Justice Officers' Standards Division hereinafter called "the Division," which shall be organized and staffed in accordance with applicable laws and regulations and within the limits of authorized appropriations.

(b) The Attorney General shall appoint a director for the Division chosen from a list of nominees submitted to him by the Commission who shall be responsible to and serve at the pleasure of the Attorney General and the Commission.

(c) The Division shall administer such programs as are assigned to it by the Commission. Administrative duties and responsibilities shall include, but are not limited to, the following:

(1) Administering any and all programs assigned to the Division by the Commission and reporting any violations of or deviations from the rules and regulations of the Commission as the Commission may require;

(2) Compiling data, developing reports, identifying needs and performing research relevant to improvement of the agencies;

(3) Developing new and revising existing programs for adoption consideration by the Commission;

(4) Monitoring and evaluating programs of the Commission;

(5) Providing technical assistance to agencies of the justice system to aid them in the discharge of program participation and responsibilities;

(6) Disseminating information on Commission programs to concerned agencies or individuals;

(7) Taking such other actions as may be deemed necessary or appropriate to carry out its assigned duties and responsibilities;

(8) The director may divulge any information in the Division's personnel file of a justice officer or applicant for certification to the head of the department employing the officer or considering the applicant for employment when the director deems it necessary and essential to the retention or employment of said officer or applicant. The information may be divulged whether or not such information was contained in a personnel file maintained by a State or by a local government agency.

History.
1983, c. 558, s. 1; 1995, c. 103, s. 6

ARTICLE 12.
JUSTICE OFFIFCERS

§ 17E-7. Required standards

(a) Justice officers, other than those set forth in subsection (c1) of this section, shall not be required to meet any requirements of subsections (b) and (c) of this section as a condition of continued employment, nor shall failure of a justice officer to fulfill such requirements make him ineligible for any promotional examination for which he is otherwise eligible if the officer held an appointment prior to July 1, 1983, and is a sworn law-enforcement officer with power of arrest. The legislature finds, and it is hereby declared to be the policy of this Chapter, that such officers have satisfied such requirements by their experience. It is the intent of the Chapter that all justice officers employed at the entry level after the Commission has adopted the required standards shall meet the requirements of this Chapter. All justice officers who are exempted from the required entry level standards by this subsection are subject to the requirements of subsections (b) and (c) of this section as well as the requirements of G.S. 17E-4(a) in order to retain certification.

(b) The Commission shall provide, by regulation, that no person may be appointed as a justice officer at entry level, except on a temporary or probationary basis, unless such person has satisfactorily completed an initial preparatory program of training at a school certified by the Commission or has been exempted from that requirement by the Commission pursuant to this Chapter. Upon separation of a justice officer from a sheriff's department within the temporary or probationary period of appointment, the probationary certification shall be terminated by the Commission. Upon the reappointment to the same department or appointment to another department of an officer who has separated from a department within the probationary period, the officer shall be charged with the amount of time served during his initial appointment and allowed the remainder of the probationary period to complete the basic training requirement. Upon the reappointment to the same department or appointment to another department of an officer who has separated from a department within the probationary period and who has remained out of service for more than one year from the date of separation, the officer shall be allowed another probationary period to complete such training as the Commission shall require by rule for an officer returning to service.

(c) In addition to the requirements of subsection (b) of this section, the Commission, by rules and regulations, may fix other qualifications for the employment and retention of justice officers including minimum age, education, physical and mental standards, citizenship, good moral character, experience, and such other matters as relate to the competence and reliability of persons to assume and discharge the responsibilities of the office. The Commission shall prescribe the means for presenting evidence of fulfillment of these requirements. The Commission shall require the administration of a psychological screening examination, including a face-to-face, in-person interview conducted by a licensed psychologist, to determine the justice officer's psychological suitability to properly fulfill the responsibilities of the justice officer. If face-to-face, in-person is not practicable, the face-to-face evaluation can be virtual as long as both the audio and video allow for a professional clinical evaluation in a clinical environment. The psychological screening examination shall be given (i) prior to the initial certification or (ii) prior to the criminal justice officer performing any action requiring certification by the Commission.

Where minimum educational standards are not met, yet the individual shows potential and a willingness to achieve the standards by extra study, they may be waived by the Commission for the reasonable amount of time it will take to achieve the standards required. Upon petition from a sheriff, the Commission may grant a waiver of any provisions of this section (17E-7) for any justice officer serving that sheriff.

(c1) Any justice officer appointed as a telecommunicator at the entry level after March 1, 1998, shall meet all requirements of this Chapter. Any person employed in the capacity of a telecommunicator as defined by the Commission on or before March 1, 1998, shall not be required to meet any entry-level requirements as a condition of continued employment but shall be reported to the Commission for certification. All justice officers who are exempted from the required entry-level standards by this subsection are subject to the requirements of subsections (b) and (c) of this section as well as the requirements of G.S. 17E-4(a) in order to retain certification.

(c2) Effective July 1, 2022, any person employed as a telecommunicator by a municipal police agency shall meet all the requirements for telecommunicators as set forth in this Chapter.

(d) The Commission may issue a certificate evidencing satisfaction of the requirements of subsections (b), (c), and (c1) of this section to any applicant who presents such evidence as may be required by its rules and regulations of satisfactory completion of a program or course of instruction in another jurisdiction.

History.

1983, c. 558, s. 1; 1987, c. 783, s. 8; 1991, c. 265, s. 3; 1995, c. 103, s. 7; 1997-443, s. 20.11(c); 2019-200, s. 12; 2021-34, s. 1; 2021-107, s. 3(b); 2021-136, s. 1(d); 2021-138, s. 7(d)

§ 17E-8. Special requirements; authorizations

(a) Nothing in this Chapter shall be construed as a condition precedent to the taking of the oath of office or the exercise of the powers, duties or privileges of the offices of sheriff or justice officer.

(b) Any sheriff or justice officer, who has taken the oath of office, or person who has received a special deputation for the purpose from the sheriff, acts validly, and his arrests, executions, levies and sales are valid, without regard to whether he has complied with this Chapter or the rules or regulations adopted under this Chapter, unless he has been ordered to cease and desist from such actions by the court, or pursuant to G.S. 17E-9.

History.

1983, c. 558, s. 1; 1995, c. 103, s. 8

§ 17E-9. Compliance; enforcement

(a) Any justice officer who the Commission determines does not comply with this Chapter or any rules adopted under this Chapter shall not exercise the powers of a justice officer and shall not exercise the power of arrest unless the Commission waives that certification or deficiency. The Commission shall enforce this section by the entry of appropriate orders effective upon service on either the department or the justice officer.

(b) Any person who desires to appeal the proposed denial, suspension, or revocation of any certification authorized to be issued by the Commission shall file a written appeal with the Commission not later than 30 days following notice of denial, suspension, or revocation.

(c) The Commission may appear in its own name and apply to courts having jurisdiction for injunctions to prevent violations of this Chapter or of rules issued pursuant thereto; specifically, the performance of justice officer functions by officers or individuals who are not in compliance with the standards and requirements of this Chapter or of rules issued pursuant thereto. A single act of performance of a justice officer function by an officer or individual who is performing such function in violation of this Chapter is sufficient, if shown, to invoke the injunctive relief of this section.

History.
1983, c. 558, s. 1; 1995, c. 103, s. 9; 2001-490, s. 1.4

§ 17E-10. Donations to the Commission; grants and appropriations

(a) The Commission may accept for any of its purposes and functions under this Chapter any and all donations, both real and personal, and grants of money from any governmental unit or public agency, or from any institution, person, firm or corporation, and may receive, utilize and dispose of same. Any arrangement pursuant to this section shall be detailed in a biennial report of the Commission to the General Assembly. Such report shall include the identity of the donor, the nature of the transaction, and the conditions, if any. Any money received by the Commission pursuant to this section shall be deposited in the State Treasury to the account of the Commission.

(b) The Commission may authorize grants pursuant to this section and consistent with the powers conferred upon the Commission under G.S. 17E-6.

(c) The Commission in providing for the administration of the grant program authorized by this section shall promote the most efficient and economical program of criminal justice education and training, including the maximum utilization of existing facilities and programs for the purpose of avoiding duplication.

(d) The Commission may provide grants as a reimbursement for actual expenses incurred by the State or any political subdivision thereof for the provision of training programs providing said political subdivisions and State law-enforcement agencies do adhere to the selection and training standards established by the Commission.

History.
1983, c. 558, s. 1; 1991 (Reg. Sess., 1992), c. 1030, s. 9

§ 17E-11. Application and construction of Chapter

(a) Nothing in this Article shall apply to the sheriff elected by the people.

(b) Nothing in this Article shall be construed as modifying the character of a sheriff from an elective office, or as modifying the character of the office of deputy sheriff from an appointive office.

(c) If a justice officer, or a criminal justice officer as defined in G.S. 17C-2(c), becomes sheriff, the justice officer is not required to maintain certification for the period served as sheriff.

The Commission shall reinstate certification upon the conclusion of the period of service as sheriff and in conformance with the rules of the Commission for the application for certification.

History.
1983, c. 558, s. 1; 1991, c. 265, s. 4; 2021-107, ss. 3(b), 4

§ 17E-12. Pardons; expunctions

(a) When a person presents competent evidence that the person has been granted an unconditional pardon of innocence for a crime in this State, any other state, or the United States, the Commission may not deny, suspend, or revoke that person's certification based solely on the commission of that crime or for alleged lack of good moral character due to the commission of that crime.

(b) Notwithstanding G.S. 15A-145.4 or G.S. 15A-145.5, the Commission may gain access to a person's felony conviction records, including those maintained by the Administrative Office of the Courts in its confidential files containing the names of persons granted expunctions. The Commission may deny, suspend, or revoke a person's certification based solely on that person's felony conviction, whether or not that conviction was expunged.

History.
1995, c. 103, s. 10; 2011-278, s. 4; 2012-191, s. 7; 2021-107, s. 3(b)

§ 17E-14. Database of justice officer certification suspensions and revocations

The Commission shall develop and maintain a statewide database accessible to the public on its website that contains all revocations and suspensions of justice officer certifications by the Commission.

History.
2021-138, s. 1(b)

EDITOR'S NOTE. —
Session Laws 2021-138, s. 1(c), made this section effective October 1, 2021.
Session Laws 2021-138, s. 22(a), is a severability clause.

§ 17E-15. Database for justice officer critical incident information

(a) The Division shall develop and maintain a statewide database for use by law enforcement agencies that tracks all critical incident data of justice officers in North Carolina.

Chapter 17E

(b) All law enforcement agencies in the State that employ personnel certified by the Commission shall provide any information requested by the Commission to maintain the database required by subsection (a) of this section.

(c) Information collected under this section that is confidential under State or federal law shall remain confidential.

(d) A justice officer who is reported to the Division as having been involved in a critical incident who disputes being involved in a critical incident has a right, prior to being placed in the database, to request a hearing in superior court for a determination of whether the officer's involvement was properly placed in the database.

History
2021-138, s. 3(d)

EDITOR'S NOTE. —
Session Laws 2021-138, s. 3(e), made this section, as added by Session Laws 2021-138, s. 3(d), effective October 1, 2021, and applicable to critical incidents on or after that date.

Session Laws 2021-138, s. 22(a), is a severability clause.

§ 17E-16. Requirement to report material relevant to testimony

(a) Any person who is certified by the Commission or has received a conditional offer of employment and who has been notified that the person may not be called to testify at trial based on bias, interest, or lack of credibility shall report and provide a copy of that notification to the Justice Officers' Standards Division within 30 days of receiving the notification, except as provided in subsection (h) of this section. This requirement shall only apply if the person is notified by one of the following methods:

(1) In writing by a superior court judge, district court judge, federal judge, district attorney, assistant district attorney, United States attorney, assistant United States attorney, or the person's agency head.

(2) In open court by a superior court judge, district court judge, or federal judge, and documented in a written order.

(b) The report to the Division shall be in writing and shall state who notified the person that the person may not be called to testify at trial. A person required to report to the Division under subsection (a) of this section shall make the same report to the person's agency head within 30 days of being notified that the person may not be called to testify at trial. An agency head who receives a report that a person in the agency has been notified that they

may not be called to testify at trial shall also report the notification to the Division in writing within 30 days of the agency head's receipt of that report.

(c) A superior court judge, district court judge, federal judge, district attorney, assistant district attorney, United States attorney, or assistant United States attorney who notifies a person that they may not be called to testify at trial as provided in subsection (a) of this section shall report that notification to the Division and provide a copy of the written document or order within 30 days of notifying the person that they may not be called to testify at trial.

(d) If the Division transfers to another agency the certification of any person required to report to the Division pursuant to subsection (a) of this section, the Division shall provide written notification to both the head of the new agency and the elected district attorney in the prosecutorial district where the agency is located that the person has been previously notified that the person may not be called to testify at trial. If the new agency receiving notification pursuant to this subsection is a State agency, the Division shall notify the elected district attorney in every prosecutorial district of the State.

(e) If any person required to report to the Division pursuant to subsection (a) of this section is subsequently informed in writing that that notification has been rescinded, the person shall provide the Division a copy of that document. The provisions of subsection (d) of this section do not apply if the person required to report pursuant to subsection (a) of this section is subsequently informed in writing that the notification has been rescinded.

(f) No later than March 1 each year, the Commission shall report to the Joint Legislative Oversight Committee on Justice and Public Safety regarding the number of individuals for whom the Division received a report required by subsection (a) of this section during the previous calendar year. The report shall include information for each case on whether a final agency decision has been entered pursuant to Chapter 150B of the General Statutes and what action, if any, has been taken against each certification. The report shall not include the name or any other identifying information of any person required to report pursuant to subsection (a) of this section.

(g) The reports and notifications received by the Division pursuant to this section shall not be public record.

(h) Any person who has received a notification that may meet the reporting requirement provided in subsection (a) of this section may apply for a hearing in superior court for a judicial determination of whether or not the person received a notification that the person may not be called to testify at trial based on bias, interest, or lack of credibility. This hearing is limited to reviewing whether (i) a person who is certified by the Commission or has received a conditional offer of employment, (ii) has been notified in writing by a superior court judge, district court judge, federal judge, district attorney, assistant district attorney, United States attorney, or assistant United States attorney; or notified in open court by a superior court judge, district court judge, or federal judge, and documented in a written order, and (iii) that notification states that the person may not be called to testify at trial based on bias, interest, or lack of credibility, not matters of law or admissibility. The person must provide notice of the hearing to the Division. One extension of 15 days will be added to the 30-day reporting requirement provided in subsection (a) of this section if notice of a hearing is received.

History.
2021-137, s. 3(b)

EDITOR'S NOTE. —
Session Laws 2021-137, s. 3(c), made this section, as added by Session Laws 2021-137, s. 3(b), effective October 1, 2021, and applicable to notifications received prior to, on, or after that date by persons required to report pursuant to this act.

ARTICLE 12.
SHERIFFS

§ 17E-25. Disclosure of convictions and expungements for the office of sheriff

(a) Each individual filing, or intending to file, a notice of candidacy for election or any individual prior to appointment to fill a vacancy to the office of sheriff shall request the Commission to prepare a disclosure statement verifying that individual has no prior felony convictions or expungements of felony convictions. The individual shall provide such information as required by the Commission for the completion of the disclosure statement, including any evidence that the individual has been granted an unconditional pardon of innocence for a felony crime in this State, any other state, or the United States.

(b) Upon the request of an individual filing, or intending to file, a notice of candidacy for election as sheriff or any individual prior to appointment to fill a vacancy to the office of sheriff, the Commission shall prepare a disclosure statement verifying that the individual has no prior felony convictions or expungements for felony convictions. The disclosure statement shall be in a format as determined by the Commission but shall include at least all of the following:

(1) Name of the individual.

(2) Date the disclosure statement was prepared.

(3) County of residence of the individual.

(4) A statement that the individual has no prior felony convictions or expungements for felony convictions, if in fact the individual has no prior felony convictions or expungements for felony convictions.

(c) In preparing the disclosure statement, the Commission shall do at least all of the following:

(1) Conduct a criminal history record check of State and national databases to determine if the individual has a record of a felony conviction.

(2) Contact the Administrative Office of the Courts and request confirmation of whether or not the individual has previously received an expunction of a felony record.

(3) Determine if the individual has ever been convicted of a felony in violation of Section 2 of Article VII of the North Carolina Constitution.

(d) Any request for a disclosure statement, any supporting documentation used in the preparation of any disclosure statement, and any disclosure statement prepared by the Commission in accordance with this section is confidential and not a public record under Chapter 132 of the General Statutes.

History.
2021-107, s. 5

EDITOR'S NOTE. —
Session Laws 2021-107, s. 5, enacted the sections in this Article as G.S. 17E-20 through 17E-30. The sections were renumbered as G.S. 17E-25 through 17E-35 at the direction of the Revisor of Statutes.

Session Laws 2021-107, s. 10, made this Article, as added by Session Laws 2021-107, s. 5, effective October 1, 2021, and applicable to elections and appointments to the office of sheriff on or after that date.

§§ 17E-26 through 17E-29

Reserved for future codification purposes.

§ 17E-30. Expunction records access

Notwithstanding G.S. 15A-145.4 or G.S. 15A-145.5, the Commission may gain access to an individual's felony conviction records, including those maintained by the Administrative Office of the Courts in its confidential files containing the names of persons granted expunctions for the purposes of this Article.

History.
2021-107, s. 5

§§ 17E-31 through 17E-34

Reserved for future codification purposes.

§ 17E-35. Expiration of disclosure of convictions and expungements for the office of sheriff

Any disclosure statement prepared by the Commission shall be valid for the purpose of filing in accordance with G.S. 163-106, 162-5, or 162-5.1 for 90 days after issuance.

History.
2021-107, s. 5

CHAPTER 17F
LAW-ENFORCEMENT

§17F-10. Development of law enforcement early warning system

(a) Every agency in the State that employs personnel certified by the North Carolina Criminal Justice Education and Training Standards Commission or the North Carolina Sheriffs' Education and Training Standards Commission shall develop and implement an early warning system to document and track the actions and behaviors of law enforcement officers for the purpose of intervening and improving performance. The early warning system required by this section shall include information, at a minimum, regarding the following:

(1) Instances of the discharge of a firearm.

(2) Instances of use of force.

(3) Vehicle collisions.

(4) Citizen complaints.

(b) Information collected under this section that is confidential under State or federal law shall remain confidential.

(c) For purposes of this section, "law enforcement officer" means any sworn law enforcement officers with the power of arrest, both State and local.

History.
2021-138, s. 8(a)

CHAPTER 18B
REGULATION OF ALCOHOLIC BEVERAGES

ARTICLE 1
GENERAL PROVISIONS

§ 18B-100. Purpose of Chapter

This Chapter is intended to establish a uniform system of control over the sale, purchase, transportation, manufacture, consumption, and possession of alcoholic beverages in North Carolina, and to provide procedures to insure the proper administration of the ABC laws under a uniform system throughout the State. This Chapter shall be liberally construed to the end that the sale, purchase, transportation, manufacture, consumption, and possession of alcoholic beverages shall be prohibited except as authorized in this Chapter. If any provision of this Chapter, or its application to any person or circumstance, is determined by a court or other authority of competent jurisdiction to be invalid or unconstitutional, such provision shall be stricken and the remaining provisions shall be construed in accordance with the intent of the General Assembly to further limit rather than expand commerce in alcoholic beverages, and with respect to malt beverages, unfortified wine, and fortified wine, the remaining provisions shall be construed to enhance strict regulatory control over taxation, distribution, and sale of alcoholic beverages through the three-tier regulatory system and the franchise laws imposed by this Chapter.

Except as provided in this Chapter, local ordinances establishing different rules on the manufacture, sale, purchase, transportation, possession, consumption, or other use of alcoholic beverages, or requiring additional permits or fees, are prohibited.

History.
1937, c. 49, s. 1; 1971, c. 872, s. 1; 1981, c. 412, s. 2; 2019-18, s. 1

§ 18B-101. Definitions

As used in this Chapter, unless the context requires otherwise:

(1) "ABC law" or "ABC laws" means any statute or statutes in this Chapter or in Article 2C of Chapter 105, and the rules issued by the Commission under the authority of this Chapter.

(2) "ABC permit" or "permits" means any written or printed authorization issued by the Commission pursuant to the provisions of this Chapter, other than a purchase-transportation permit. Unless the context clearly requires otherwise, as in the provisions concerning applications for permits, "ABC permit" or "permit" means a presently valid permit.

(3) "ABC system" means a local board, all ABC stores operated by a local board, and the designated ABC law enforcement officers employed pursuant to G.S. 18B-501.

(4) "Alcoholic beverage" means any beverage containing at least one-half of one percent (0.5%) alcohol by volume, including malt beverages, unfortified wine, fortified wine, spirituous liquor, mixed beverages, and any alcohol consumable.

(4a) "Alcohol consumable" means any manufactured and packaged ice cream, ice pop, gum-based, or gelatin-based food product containing at least one-half of one percent (0.5%) alcohol by volume.

(5) "ALE Division" means the Alcohol Law Enforcement Division of the Department of Public Safety.

(5a) "Antique spirituous liquor" means spirituous liquor that has not been in production or bottled in the last 20 years, is in the original manufacturer's unopened container, is not owned by a distillery, and is not otherwise available for purchase by an ABC Board except through the special order process pursuant to G.S. 18B-1001(20).

(5b) "Antique spirituous liquor seller" means a person who sells antique spirituous liquor to an ABC Board.

(5c) "Bailment surcharge" means the charge imposed on each case of liquor shipped from a Commission warehouse as provided in G.S. 18B-208. This bailment surcharge is in addition to the bailment charge imposed by G.S. 18B-804(b)(2).

(6) "Commission" means the North Carolina Alcoholic Beverage Control Commission established under G.S. 18B-200.

(6a) "Finance officer" means the local board employee, other than a general manager, who is responsible for keeping the accounts of the local board, receiving and depositing receipts, disbursing funds, and any other duties assigned by the local board or Commission.

(7) "Fortified wine" means any wine or alcohol consumable containing more than sixteen percent (16%) and no more than twenty-four percent (24%) alcohol by volume, made by fermentation from grapes, fruits, berries, rice, or honey; or by the addition of pure cane, beet, or dextrose sugar; or by the addition of pure brandy from the

same type of grape, fruit, berry, rice, or honey that is contained in the base wine and produced in accordance with the regulations of the United States.

(7a) "General manager" means the local board employee who is responsible for the oversight of daily operations of the ABC system and any other duties assigned by the local board or Commission. The board may designate only one employee to be the general manager.

(7b) "Historic ABC establishment" means a restaurant or hotel that meets all of the following requirements:

a. Is on the national register of historic places or located within a State historic district.

b. Is a property designed to attract local, State, national, and international tourists located on a State Route (SR) and with a property line located within 1.5 miles of the intersection of a designated North Carolina scenic byway as defined in G.S. 136-18(31).

c. Is located within 15 miles of a national scenic highway.

d. Is located in a county in which the on-premises sale of malt beverages or unfortified wine is authorized in two or more cities in the county.

(7c) "Keg" means a portable container designed to hold and dispense 7.75 gallons or more of malt beverage.

(8) "Local board" means a city or county ABC board, or local board created pursuant to the provisions of G.S. 18B-703. A local board is an independent local political subdivision of the State. Nothing in this Chapter shall be construed as constituting a local board the agency of a city or county or of the Commission.

(8a) "Lottery law" or "lottery laws" means any provision of Chapter 18C of the General Statutes and the rules issued by the Lottery Commission under the authority of Chapter 18C of the General Statutes.

(9) "Malt beverage" means beer, lager, malt liquor, ale, porter, and any other brewed or fermented beverage or alcohol consumable except unfortified or fortified wine as defined by this Chapter, containing at least one-half of one percent (0.5%), and not more than fifteen percent (15%), alcohol by volume. Any malt beverage containing more than six percent (6%) alcohol by volume shall bear a label clearly indicating the alcohol content of the malt beverage.

(10) "Mixed beverage" means either of the following:

a. A drink composed in whole or in part of spirituous liquor and served in a quantity less than the quantity contained in a closed package.

b. A premixed cocktail served from a closed package containing only one serving.

(11) "Nontaxpaid alcoholic beverage" means any alcoholic beverage upon which the taxes imposed by the United States, this State, or any other territorial jurisdiction in which the alcoholic beverage was purchased have not been paid.

(12) "Person" means an individual, firm, partnership, association, corporation, limited liability company, other organization or group, or other combination of individuals acting as a unit.

(12a) "Premises" means a fixed permanent establishment, including all areas inside or outside the licensed establishment, where the permittee has control through a lease, deed, or other legal process.

(12b) "Powdered alcohol" means any powder or crystalline substance capable of being converted into a liquid alcoholic beverage fit for human consumption.

(13) "Sale" means any transfer, trade, exchange, or barter, in any manner or by any means, for consideration.

(13a) *(See note)* "Special ABC area" means an area that meets the following requirements:

Either:

a. The area has fewer than 500 permanent residents, and the area:

1. Is located in a county that borders another state, that has at least one city that has approved the operation of an ABC store, and in which the sale of unfortified wine and malt beverages is permitted countywide or in one city; and

2. Contains more than 500 contiguous acres made up of privately-owned land and land owned by an association or a club that is exempt from income tax on its membership income under Article 4 of Chapter 105 of the General Statutes, has more than 200 members, was created for municipal and recreational purposes, and, for three or more years, has levied assessments or dues and provided municipal services; or

b. The area has more than 500 permanent residents, and the area:

1. Is located in a county:

Chapter 18B

I. Where ABC stores have heretofore been established but in which the sale of mixed beverages has not been approved;

II. That borders on a county that has approved the sale of alcoholic beverages county-wide and contains an international airport; and

III. Borders on a county where ABC stores have heretofore been established by petition pursuant to law; and

2. Contains more than 500 contiguous acres made up of privately-owned land and land owned by an association or a club that is exempt from income tax on its membership income under Article 4 of Chapter 105 of the General Statutes, has more than 200 members, was created for municipal and recreational purposes, and, for three or more years, has levied assessments or dues and provided municipal services; or

c. The area is an area of a county where the following requirements are met:

1. The county borders on the Atlantic Ocean and has a seaport supporting oceangoing vessels;

2. ABC stores have been established in the county and the sale of mixed beverages is allowed in six or more municipalities;

3. The population of the county, according to the 2000 census, exceeds 52,000;

4. The tourism economy of the county is made up of more than 3,000 tourism-related jobs; and

5. Tourism expenditures within the county exceed two hundred million dollars ($ 200,000,000) annually.

(14) "Spirituous liquor" or "liquor" means distilled spirits or ethyl alcohol, and any alcohol consumable containing distilled spirits or ethyl alcohol, including spirits of wine, whiskey, rum, brandy, gin and all other distilled spirits and mixtures of cordials, liqueur, and premixed cocktails, in closed containers regardless of their dilution.

(14a) "Tourism ABC establishment" means a restaurant or hotel that meets both of the following requirements:

a. Is located on property, a property line of which is located within 1.5 miles of the end of an entrance or exit ramp of a junction on a national scenic parkway designed to attract local, State, national, and international tourists between the State line and Milepost 469, provided that the Eastern Band of Cherokee Indians tribal alcoholic beverage control commission established under G.S. 18B-112 shall have exclusive authority to issue permits pursuant to this subdivision between Milepost 460 and the southern terminus of the national scenic byway at Milepost 469 for any restaurant or hotel that is located wholly on Indian Country lands.

b. Is located in a county in which the on-premises or off-premises sale of malt beverages or unfortified wine is authorized in at least one city.

(14b) "Tourism resort" means:

a. Any restaurant and lodging facility, whether public or private, owned and operated as a resort property offering food, beverage, lodging, and meeting facilities to travelers and tourists and featuring one or more golf courses and two or more tennis courts along with other recreational and sporting activities, or

b. Any restaurant, whether public or private, owned and operated as a resort property offering food and beverage to travelers and tourists and featuring an equestrian center and two or more tennis courts along with other recreational and sporting activities.

Receipts from sporting and recreational activities of a tourism resort shall be at least twenty-five percent (25%) of total gross receipts. Receipts from the sale of alcoholic beverages shall not exceed fifty percent (50%) of total gross receipts. A tourism resort open to the public shall advertise at least quarterly in a regional or national travel or sports industry publication, or in the State travel guide published by the North Carolina Department of Commerce.

(15) "Unfortified wine" means any wine or alcohol consumable containing sixteen percent (16%) or less alcohol by volume made by fermentation from grapes, fruits, berries, rice, or honey; or by the addition of pure cane, beet, or dextrose sugar; or by the addition of pure brandy from the same type of grape, fruit, berry, rice, or honey that is contained in the base wine and produced in accordance with the regulations of the United States.

History.

1981, c. 412, s. 2; 1981 (Reg. Sess., 1982), c. 1262, s. 2; c. 1285, s. 1; 1983, c. 435, s. 41; 1985, c. 69; 1987, c. 443, s. 1; 1989, c. 629, s. 1; 1989 (Reg. Sess., 1990), c. 1024, s. 5; 1991 (Reg. Sess., 1992), c. 920, ss. 1, 10; 1993, c. 415, ss. 1, 2; 1995, c. 466, s. 1; 1997-443, s. 16.27(b); 1999-461, s. 1; 1999-462, ss. 1, 13; 2001-515, s. 1; 2004-135, s. 1; 2004-203, s. 23; 2005-276, s. 31.1(x); 2005-277, s. 1; 2005-344, s. 10.1(a); 2005-392, s. 1; 2005-435, s. 25(a); 2006-253, s. 2; 2006-264, s. 95; 2010-122, s. 1; 2011-145, s. 19.1(g), (gg); 2014-100, s. 17.1(xxx); 2015-98, ss. 1(a), 2(a), 3(b); 2019-182, s. 12; 2019-203, s. 5; 2021-150, s. 27.1

§ 18B-102. Manufacture, sale, etc., forbidden except as expressly authorized

(a) **General Prohibition.** -- It shall be unlawful for any person to manufacture, sell, transport, import, deliver, furnish, purchase, consume, or possess any alcoholic beverages except as authorized by the ABC law.

(a1) **Powdered Alcohol Prohibition.** -- It shall be unlawful for any person to manufacture, sell, transport, import, deliver, furnish, purchase, consume, or possess powdered alcohol.

(b) **Violation a Class 1 Misdemeanor.** -- Unless a different punishment is otherwise expressly stated, any person who violates any provision of this Chapter shall be guilty of a Class 1 misdemeanor. In addition the court may impose the provisions of G.S. 18B-202 and of G.S. 18B-503, 18B-504, and 18B-505.

History.

1923, c. 1, s. 1; C.S., s. 3411(a); 1937, c. 49, s. 24; c. 411; 1939, c. 158, s. 501; 1941, c. 339, ss. 1, 3, 4; 1945, c. 780; c. 903, ss. 1, 3, 10; 1971, c. 872, s. 1; 1973, c. 476, s. 193; c. 1014; 1975, c. 329; c. 411, s. 2; 1977, 2nd Sess., c. 1138, s. 1; 1979, c. 683, s. 1; 1981, c. 412, s. 2; 1989, c. 800, s. 1; 1993, c. 539, s. 310; 1994, Ex. Sess., c. 14, s. 29; c. 24, s. 14(c); 2015-98, s. 2(b)

§ 18B-102.1. Direct shipments from out-of-state prohibited

(a) It is unlawful for any person who is an out-of-state retail or wholesale dealer in the business of selling alcoholic beverages to ship or cause to be shipped any alcoholic beverage directly to any North Carolina resident who does not hold a valid wholesaler's permit under Article 11 of this Chapter.

(b) The Commission shall mail a notice by certified mail ordering a person who violates the provisions of subsection (a) of this section to cease and desist any shipments of alcoholic beverages to North Carolina residents. If the offender cannot produce a receipt or otherwise show that applicable State taxes have been paid on the shipped alcohol within 30 days after

this notice has been deposited by certified mail addressed to the out-of-state retail or wholesale dealer either at the address shown on the shipment or the last known address of that dealer in any legal registry, such as a registry with the Secretary of State for incorporation of a business, or within 30 days after personal service of the notice on the out-of-state retail or wholesale dealer, it shall be presumptive evidence of his intent to ship alcoholic beverages directly to a North Carolina resident who does not hold a valid wholesaler's permit issued by the Commission.

(c) This section shall not apply to producers of beverage alcohol holding a basic permit from the Bureau of Alcohol, Tobacco and Firearms.

(d) Upon determination by the Commission that a holder of a basic permit from the Bureau of Alcohol, Tobacco and Firearms has made an illegal shipment to consumers in North Carolina, the Commission shall notify the Bureau of Alcohol, Tobacco and Firearms in writing and by certified mail and request the Bureau to take appropriate action.

(e) Whoever violates the provisions of this section shall be guilty of a Class I felony and shall pay a fine of not more than ten thousand dollars ($ 10,000).

History.

1997-348, s. 1

§ 18B-103. Exemptions

All of the following activities shall be permitted:

(1) The use of ethyl alcohol for scientific, chemical, pharmaceutical, mechanical, and industrial purposes.

(2) The use of ethyl alcohol by persons authorized to obtain it tax free, as provided by federal law.

(3) The use of ethyl alcohol in the manufacture and preparation of any product unfit for use as a beverage.

(4) The use of alcoholic beverages by licensed physicians, druggists, or dental surgeons for medicinal or pharmaceutical purposes; or the use of alcoholic beverages by medical facilities established and maintained for the treatment of patients addicted to the use of alcohol or drugs.

(5) The use of grain alcohol by college, university or State laboratories, and by manufacturers of medicine, for compounding, mixing, or preserving medicines or medical preparations, or for surgical purposes.

(5a) The manufacture, possession, and consumption of alcoholic beverages for the purpose of conducting scientific, chemical, pharmaceutical, mechanical, industrial, and educational research in connection with teaching, research, or extension programs conducted by, or under the supervision of, an instructor at an accredited community college, public or private college or university, or an extension agent in connection with educational programs and activities offered by the North Carolina CooperativeExtension Service.

(6) The manufacture, importation, and possession of denatured alcohol produced and used as provided by federal law.

(7) The manufacture or sale of cider or vinegar.

(8) The possession and use of unfortified wine or fortified wine for sacramental purpose by any organized church or ordained minister, including in public school buildings when the use of those buildings is approved by the local school board.

(9) The possession and use of alcohol acquired for controlled-drinking programs as authorized under G.S. 20-139.1(g).

(10) The use of spirituous liquor in the manufacture of flavors or flavoring extracts that are unfit for beverage use.

(11) Under the direct supervision of an instructor during a culinary class that is part of an established culinary curriculum at an accredited college or university, the delivery to or possession or consumption by a student who is less than 21 years of age, when the student is required to taste or imbibe the alcoholic beverage during a culinary class conducted pursuant to the curriculum.

(12) The trade or exchange of lawfully purchased spirituous liquor if all of the following requirements are met:

a. The transaction only involves the trade or exchange of lawfully purchased spirituous liquor for other lawfully purchased spirituous liquor.

b. The trade or exchange is only between individuals, for personal use only, and not for resale.

c. The spirituous liquor to be traded or exchanged is or has been approved by the Commission for sale in this State and is not unfit for human consumption.

d. The spirituous liquor is not an antique spirituous liquor as that term is defined in G.S. 18B-101(5a).

History.
1923, c. 1, ss. 4, 19, 20; C.S., s. 3411(d), (s), (t); 1935, c. 1141; 1971, c. 872, s. 1; c. 1233; 1981, c. 412, s. 2; c. 747, s. 36; 1981 (Reg. Sess., 1982), c. 1262, s. 3; 1983, c. 435, s. 6; 1985, c. 566, s. 2; 1993, c. 127, s. 1; 2004-199, s. 8; 2009-539, s. 1; 2021-150, s. 23.1

§ 18B-104. Administrative penalties

(a) **Penalties.** -- For any violation of the ABC laws, the Commission may take any of the following actions against a permittee:

(1) Suspend the permittee's permit for a specified period of time not longer than three years.

(2) Revoke the permittee's permit.

(3) For all violations not listed in subdivision (3a) of this subsection, fine the permittee up to five hundred dollars ($ 500.00) for the first violation, up to seven hundred fifty dollars ($ 750.00) for the second violation within three years, and up to one thousand dollars ($ 1,000) for the third violation within three years of the first violation.

(3a) If the violations involve acts of violence, controlled substances, or prostitution occurring on the licensed premises, fine the permittee up to seven hundred fifty dollars ($ 750.00) for the first violation, up to one thousand dollars ($ 1,000) for a second violation within three years, and up to one thousand two hundred fifty dollars ($ 1,250) for a third violation within three years of the first violation. Additionally, the Commission may impose conditions on the operating hours of the business for violations listed in this subdivision.

(4) Suspend the permittee's permit under subdivision (1) [of this subsection] and impose a fine under subdivision (3) or (3a) [of this subsection].

(b) **Compromise.** -- In any case in which the Commission is entitled to suspend or revoke a permit, the Commission may accept from the permittee an offer in compromise to pay a penalty of not more than five thousand dollars ($ 5,000). The Commission may either accept a compromise or revoke a permit, but not both. The Commission may accept a compromise and suspend the permit in the same case.

(b1) **Compromise for Certain Egregious Violations.** -- In any case in which there are two or more violations within three years in which the Commission is entitled to suspend or revoke a permit, the Commission may accept from the permittee an offer in compromise to pay a penalty of not more than ten thousand dollars ($ 10,000) if the violations involve any of the following acts:

(1) Acts of violence occurring on the licensed premises.

(2) The permittee or the permittee's agent or employee knowingly allowing any violation of the controlled substances or prostitution statutes on the licensed premises.

The Commission may also impose conditions on the operating hours of the business as part of a compromise pursuant to this

Chapter 18B

subsection. The Commission may either accept a compromise or revoke a permit, but not both. The Commission may accept a compromise and suspend the permit in the same case.

(c) **Fines and Penalties to Treasurer.** -- The clear proceeds of fines and penalties assessed pursuant to this section shall be remitted to the Civil Penalty and Forfeiture Fund in accordance with G.S. 115C-457.2.

(d) **Effect on Licenses.** -- Suspension or revocation of a permit includes automatic suspension or revocation of any related State or local revenue license.

(e) **Effect on Other Permits.** -- Unless some other disposition is ordered by the Commission, revocation or suspension of a permit under subsection (a) includes automatic revocation or suspension, respectively, of any other ABC permit held by the same permittee for the same establishment.

History.
1939, c. 158, s. 514; 1943, c. 400, s. 6; 1945, c. 903, s. 1; 1947, c. 1098, ss. 2, 3; 1949, c. 974, ss. 7, 14; 1953, c. 1207, ss. 2-5; 1957, cc. 1048, 1440; 1963, c. 426, ss. 4, 5, 10, 12; c. 460, s. 1; 1971, c. 872, s. 1; 1973, c. 476, s. 193; 1977, c. 669, s. 1; 1981, c. 412, s. 2; 1998-215, s. 27; 2019-49, s. 1

§ 18B-105. Advertising

(a) **General Rule.** -- No person shall advertise alcoholic beverages in this State except in compliance with the rules of the Commission.

(b) **Rule-making Authority.** -- The Commission shall have the authority to adopt rules to:

(1) Prohibit or regulate advertising of alcoholic beverages by permittees in newspapers, pamphlets, and other print media;

(2) Prohibit or regulate advertising by on-premises permittees of brands or prices of alcoholic beverages via newspapers, radio, television, and other mass media;

(3) Prohibit deceptive or misleading advertising of alcoholic beverages;

(4) Require all advertisements of alcoholic beverages to disclose fully the identity of the advertiser and of the product being advertised;

(5) Prohibit advertisements of alcoholic beverages on the premises of a permittee, or regulate the size, number, and appearance of those advertisements;

(6) Prohibit or regulate advertisement of prices of alcoholic beverages on the premises of a permittee;

(7) Prohibit or regulate alcoholic beverage advertisements on billboards;

(8) Prohibit alcoholic beverage advertisements on outdoor signs, or regulate the nature, size, number, and appearance of those advertisements;

(9) Prohibit or regulate advertising of alcoholic beverages by mail;

(10) Prohibit or regulate contests, games, or other promotions which serve or tend to serve as advertisement for a specific brand or brands of alcoholic beverages; and

(11) Prohibit or regulate any advertising of alcoholic beverages which is contrary to the public interest.

History.
1923, c. 1, s. 3; C.S., s. 3411(c); 1933, cc. 216, 229; 1945, c. 903, s. 1; 1947, c. 1098, ss. 2, 3; 1957, c. 1048; 1963, c. 426, s. 10; c. 460, s. 1; 1971, c. 872, s. 1; 1981, c. 412, s. 2

§ 18B-106. Alcoholic beverages for use on oceangoing ships

(a) **Delivery Permitted.** -- Alcoholic beverages for use outside the United States on oceangoing vessels shall be delivered as follows:

(1) Spirituous liquor may be imported into this State under United States customs bonds, held in United States customs bonded warehouses, and transferred between those warehouses. Spirituous liquors may only be released from customs bonds for delivery to an officer or agent of an oceangoing vessel who has obtained a permit from the Commission for that purpose.

(2) Malt beverages, unfortified wine, and fortified wine may be sold and delivered by any wholesaler or retailer licensed in this State to an officer or agent of an oceangoing vessel. The Commission may require the officer or agent to obtain a permit before purchasing alcoholic beverages under this subdivision.

(b) **Definition.** -- "Oceangoing vessel" means a ship which plies the high seas in interstate or foreign commerce, in the transport of freight or passengers, or both, for hire exclusively.

(c) **Rules.** -- The Commission may issue rules relating to applications for permits and otherwise regulate the importation, sale, and delivery of alcoholic beverages under this section to insure that those beverages are used only on oceangoing vessels outside the United States.

History.
1981, c. 412, s. 2

§ 18B-107. Alcoholic beverages for use in air commerce

(a) **Purchase and Storage.** -- The Commission may issue permits authorizing air carriers offering regularly scheduled or chartered flights in foreign, interstate, or intrastate commerce to

Chapter 18B

purchase malt beverages, unfortified wine, and fortified wine from any wholesaler or retailer licensed in this State, and to transport those alcoholic beverages. The Commission may also authorize air carriers to store, at facilities approved by the Commission, alcoholic beverages to be sold or served pursuant to subsection (b).

(b) **Sale.** -- Air carriers may sell and serve alcoholic beverages anywhere in this State to passengers while in transit aboard any aircraft. At airports which service airplanes boarding at least 150,000 passengers annually, air carriers may serve complimentary alcoholic beverages to their passengers in air carrier passenger rooms approved by the Commission. Alcoholic beverages may not be sold in such a room unless a permit has been issued under Article 10 authorizing sale there.

History.
1981, c. 412, s. 2

§ 18B-108. Sales on trains

Alcoholic beverages may be sold on railroad trains in this State upon compliance with Article 2C of Chapter 105 of the General Statutes. Malt beverages, unfortified wine, and fortified wine may be sold and delivered by any wholesaler or retailer licensed in this State to an officer or agent of a rail line that carries at least 60,000 passengers annually.

History.
1981, c. 412, s. 2; c. 747, s. 37; 1985, c. 114, s. 5; 2000-140, s. 39; 2006-227, s. 8

§ 18B-109. Direct shipment of alcoholic beverages into State

(a) **General Prohibition.** -- Except as provided in G.S. 18B-1001.1, no person shall have any alcoholic beverage mailed or shipped to him from outside this State unless he has the appropriate ABC permit.

(b) **Armed Forces Installation and Indian Country Lands.** -- No person shall have malt beverages or unfortified wine shipped directly from a point outside this State to an installation of the Armed Forces of the United States within this State if those alcoholic beverages are for resale on the installation or to the Eastern Band of Cherokee Indians for resale on Indian Country lands within this State under the jurisdiction of the Eastern Band of Cherokee Indians.

(c) **Wine Shipper Permittees.** -- It is unlawful for a wine shipper permittee to ship any wines except in compliance with this Chapter and Articles 2C and 5 of Chapter 105 of the General Statutes.

(d) **On-Premises Purchases.** -- A person who purchases wine while visiting the premises of a winery, whether located within or outside the State, may authorize the winery to ship by common carrier, or may personally ship by common carrier, the purchased wine directly to addresses in the State in amounts that can be personally transported in accordance with the laws of this State and of the state in which the winery is located. A winery shipping wine pursuant to this subsection is not required to have a wine shipper permit.

History.
1923, c. 1, s. 2; C.S., s. 3411(b); 1971, c. 872, s. 1; 1975, c. 654, s. 4; 1981, c. 412, s. 2; 2003-402, s. 4; 2011-183, s. 19; 2011-333, s. 1

§ 18B-110. Emergency

When the Governor finds that an emergency, as that term is defined in G.S. 166A-19.3, exists anywhere in this State, the Governor may

    (1) Order the closing of all ABC stores; and

    (2) Order the cessation of all sales, transportation, manufacture, and bottling of alcoholic beverages.

The Governor's order shall apply in those portions of the State designated in the order, for the duration of the state of emergency. Any order by the Governor under this section shall be directed to the Chairman of the Commission and to the Secretary of Public Safety.

History.
1969, c. 869, ss. 4, 5; 1971, c. 872, s. 1; 1977, c. 70, s. 21; 1977, 2nd Sess., c. 1138, s. 16; 1981, c. 412, s. 2; 2011-145, s. 19.1(g); 2012-12, s. 2(cc)

§ 18B-111. Nontaxpaid alcoholic beverages

No person may possess, transport, or sell nontaxpaid alcoholic beverages except as authorized by the ABC law.

History.
1981 (Reg. Sess., 1982), c. 1262, s. 4

§ 18B-112. Tribal alcoholic beverage control

(a) **Application of This Chapter.** -- The Eastern Band of Cherokee Indians, a federally recognized Indian tribe and sovereign nation, shall be exempt from the provisions of this Chapter, except for those made applicable by this section. The Eastern Band of Cherokee Indians tribe shall adopt by ordinance the provisions of this Chapter which are made applicable to the tribe by this section, and such ordinance shall be approved by the Secretary of the United States Department of the Interior and published in the Federal Register accordingly.

The Eastern Band of Cherokee Indians shall hold lawful tribal elections as set out in G.S. 18B-600(a), and if the result of such election authorizes the activity upon which a vote was held, the activity shall be deemed authorized by this section. For the purposes of this section, the tribal alcoholic beverage control commission shall possess the same powers and authority conveyed upon the North Carolina Alcoholic Beverage Control Commission by any section of this Chapter made applicable to the tribe by this section.

(b) **Compliance Required.** -- The Eastern Band of Cherokee Indians shall comply with the following provisions of this Chapter to the extent they apply to or can be made applicable to the tribe:

(1) **The following provisions of Article 1.** -- General Provisions.

a. G.S. 18B-101(4), (7), (7c), (9), (10), (11), (12), (12a), (13), (14)(14a), (14b), and (15).

b. G.S. 18B-102.1.

c. G.S. 18B-104.

d. G.S. 18B-105, except that this section shall not apply to any establishment where gaming is permitted under a State compact and pursuant to federal law.

e. G.S. 18B-109(b).

f. G.S. 18B-110.

g. G.S. 18B-111.

h. G.S. 18B-112.

(2) **Article 1A.** -- Compensation for Injury Caused by Sales to Underage Persons, to the extent it applies to retail establishments or the tribal alcoholic beverage control commission if it operates ABC stores, or any other permitted establishment, at retail pursuant to the provisions of this section.

(3) **Article 3.** -- Sale, Possession, and Consumption, except for G.S. 18B-309.

(4) **Article 4.** -- Transportation.

(5) **Article 5.** -- Enforcement, except for G.S. 18B-500 and G.S. 18B-501.

(5a) **Article 6.** -- Elections, compliance with only G.S. 18B-603(f) and (g) are required.

(6) **Article 9.** -- Issuance of Permits, except for G.S. 18B-902(g) and (h) and G.S. 18B-906.

(7) **Article 10.** -- Retail Activity.

(8) **Article 11.** -- Commercial Activity, as clarified by the following:

a. The tribal alcoholic beverage control commission may issue commercial activity permits to any qualifying applicant that establishes a commercial business wholly on Indian Country lands and shall have sole enforcement authority over any permittee receiving a permit from the tribal alcoholic beverage control commission only to the extent the regulated conduct occurs on Indian Country lands.

b. The Eastern Band of Cherokee Indians shall recognize any permit issued by the North Carolina Alcoholic Beverage Control Commission allowing commercial activity in the same manner as if such permit was issued by the tribal alcoholic beverage control commission. The North Carolina Alcoholic Beverage Control Commission shall recognize any commercial activity permit issued by the tribal alcoholic beverage commission in the same manner as if the permit were issued by the North Carolina Alcoholic Beverage Control Commission.

c. The North Carolina Alcoholic Beverage Control Commission shall retain exclusive enforcement authority over all permits it issues to commercial activity permittees for violations of its rules or this Chapter.

Any provision of Articles 12 and 13 of this Chapter which has not been made applicable to the Eastern Band of Cherokee Indians by this section shall act as a bar to engaging in any activity authorized by that Article or section.

(b1) In accordance with G.S. 18B-1004(c), the Eastern Band of Cherokee Indians tribe may adopt an ordinance allowing for the sale of malt beverages, unfortified wine, fortified wine, and mixed beverages beginning at 10:00 A.M. on Sunday pursuant to the licensed premises' permit issued under the authority of G.S. 18B-112(d).

(c) **Alcoholic Beverages Which May Be Sold.** -- No alcoholic beverage may be sold on Indian Country lands under the jurisdiction of the Eastern Band of Cherokee Indians pursuant to this section which has not been approved for sale in this State by the North Carolina Alcoholic Beverage Control Commission.

(d) **Establishment of a Tribal Commission.** -- In accordance with the provisions of 18 U.S.C. § 1161, the Eastern Band of Cherokee Indians is authorized to establish a tribal alcoholic beverage control commission to regulate the purchase, possession, consumption, sale, and delivery of alcoholic beverages on any land designated as Indian Country pursuant to 18 U.S.C. § 1151 under the jurisdiction of the Eastern Band of Cherokee Indians. The tribal commission shall have exclusive authority to issue ABC permits to retail and commercial establishments located wholly on Indian Country lands under the jurisdiction of the Eastern Band of Cherokee Indians and to regulate the

Chapter 18B

purchase, possession, consumption, sale, and delivery of alcoholic beverages at permitted outlets and premises. Permits issued by the tribal commission pursuant to this section shall be deemed issued by the State for the purposes of sales and delivery of beer and wine by wholesalers to the retail outlets located on Indian Country lands. The fees generated by the tribal alcoholic beverage control commission for the issuance of retail permits may be retained by the Eastern Band of Cherokee Indians to offset costs of operating the tribal alcoholic beverage control commission.

(e) **Establishment of Rules.** -- The tribal alcoholic beverage control commission shall adopt the rules of the North Carolina Alcoholic Beverage Control Commission regulating retail outlet activity.

(f) **Authority of the North Carolina Alcoholic Beverage Control Commission.** -- The North Carolina Alcoholic Beverage Control Commission shall have the authority to enter into agreements with the tribal alcoholic beverage control commission to provide for the sale, delivery, and distribution of spirituous liquor to the tribal alcoholic beverage control commission. The tribal alcoholic beverage control commission shall purchase spirituous liquor for resale by the tribal alcoholic beverage control commission exclusively from the North Carolina Alcoholic Beverage Control Commission at the same price and on the same basis that such spirits are purchased by local boards. To the extent there is a conflict between the tribal alcoholic beverage control commission's authority or purpose and the North Carolina Alcoholic Beverage Control Commission's authority or purpose, the North Carolina Alcoholic Beverage Control Commission shall prevail.

(g) **Discrimination.** -- The tribal alcoholic beverage control commission shall not discriminate against non-Indians in the application of the tribal ABC law. Non-Indians shall be entitled to apply for and receive ABC permits in the same manner as an Indian on Indian Country lands under the jurisdiction of the Eastern Band of Cherokee Indians.

(h) **Resolution of Contested Cases.** -- If the tribal alcoholic beverage control commission levies a fine or suspends or revokes a permit pursuant to the provisions of G.S. 18B-104 for a violation of the provisions applicable to the Eastern Band of Cherokee Indians in this section, the permittee shall have the right of appeal of an agency final decision of the tribal commission to the tribal courts. Any further appeal shall be to the appellate courts of the tribe. All fines paid to the tribal commission in satisfaction of any penalty assessed by the tribal commission may be retained by the Eastern Band of Cherokee Indians to offset costs of operating the tribal alcoholic beverage control commission.

(i) **Failure to Comply With Laws of This State.** -- If the Eastern Band of Cherokee Indians fails to adopt the provisions of this Chapter, made applicable to the tribe by this section, by ordinance; fails to amend tribal ordinances to comply with amendments to the provisions of this Chapter, made applicable to the tribe by this section, within six months of passage of such amendments; or fails to comply with the provisions of this Chapter, made applicable to the tribe by this section, as required by 18 U.S.C. § 1161, the North Carolina Alcoholic Beverage Control Commission is authorized to terminate and prohibit future delivery of any alcoholic beverages from any person to the tribal alcoholic beverage control commission until the Eastern Band of Cherokee Indians complies with the provisions of this Chapter made applicable to the tribe by this section and 18 U.S.C. § 1161.

(j) **Conflict of Laws.** -- If any provision of this section or its application conflicts with federal law, the conflict of laws shall be resolved in favor of the federal law unless compliance with the federal law abrogates a right reserved to the State under the Constitution of the United States.

History.
2011-333, s. 3; 2015-98, s. 3(a); 2017-87, s. 4(d); 2019-182, s. 14(c)

ARTICLE 1A
COMPENSATION FOR INJURY CAUSED BY SALES TO UNDERAGE PERSONS

§ 18B-120. Definitions

As used in this Article:

(1) "Aggrieved party" means a person who sustains an injury as a consequence of the actions of the underage person, but does not include the underage person or a person who aided or abetted in the sale or furnishing to the underage person.

(2) "Injury" includes, but is not limited to, personal injury, property loss, loss of means of support, or death. Damages for death shall be determined under the provisions of G.S. 28A-18-2(b). Nothing in G.S. 28A-18-2(a) or subdivision (1) of this section shall be interpreted to preclude recovery under this Article for loss of support or death on account of injury to or death of the underage person or a person who aided or abetted in the sale or furnishing to the underage person.

(3) "Underage person" means a person who is less than the age legally required for purchase of the alcoholic beverage in question.

(4) "Vehicle" shall have the same meaning as prescribed by G.S. 20-4.01(49).

History.
1983, c. 435, s. 37

§ 18B-121. Claim for relief created for sale to underage person

An aggrieved party has a claim for relief for damages against a permittee or local Alcoholic Beverage Control Board if:

(1) The permittee or his agent or employee or the local board or its agent or employee negligently sold or furnished an alcoholic beverage to an underage person; and

(2) The consumption of the alcoholic beverage that was sold or furnished to an underage person caused or contributed to, in whole or in part, an underage driver's being subject to an impairing substance within the meaning of G.S. 20-138.1 at the time of the injury; and

(3) The injury that resulted was proximately caused by the underage driver's negligent operation of a vehicle while so impaired.

History.
1983, c. 435, s. 37

§ 18B-122. Burden of proof and admissibility of evidence

The plaintiff shall have the burden of proving that the sale or furnishing of the alcoholic beverage to the underage person, as defined, was, under the circumstances, negligent. Proof of the sale or furnishing of the alcoholic beverage to an underage person, as defined, without request for identification shall be admissible as evidence of negligence. Proof of good practices (including but not limited to, instruction of employees as to laws regarding the sale of alcoholic beverages, training of employees, enforcement techniques, admonishment to patrons concerning laws regarding the purchase or furnishing of alcoholic beverages, or detention of a person's identification documents in accordance with G.S. 18B-129 and inquiry about the age or degree of intoxication of the person), evidence that an underage person misrepresented his age, or that the sale or furnishing was made under duress is admissible as evidence that the permittee was not negligent.

History.
1983, c. 435, s. 37

§ 18B-123. Limitation on damages

The total amount of damages that may be awarded to all aggrieved parties pursuant to any claims for relief under this Article is limited to no more than five hundred thousand dollars ($ 500,000) per occurrence. When all claims arising out of an occurrence exceed five hundred thousand dollars ($ 500,000), each claim shall abate in the proportion it bears to the total of all claims.

History.
1983, c. 435, s. 37

§ 18B-124. Joint and several liability

The liability of the negligent driver or owner of the vehicle that caused the injury and the permittee or ABC board which sold or furnished the alcoholic beverage shall be joint and several, with right of contribution but not indemnification.

History.
1983, c. 435, s. 37

§ 18B-125. Exceptions

This Article does not create a claim for relief against the following:

(1) One who holds only a brown bagging permit, a special occasions permit, or a limited special occasions permit;

(2) One who holds only a special one-time permit under G.S. 18B-1002;

(3) One who holds only permits listed in G.S. 18B-1100;

(4) One who holds any combination of the permits listed in this section.

History.
1983, c. 435, s. 37

§ 18B-126. Statute of limitations

The statute of limitations is as provided in G.S. 1-54.

History.
1983, c. 435, s. 37

§ 18B-127. Duty of clerk of superior court

When execution on a judgment on a cause of action under G.S. 18B-121 is returned unsatisfied, in whole or in part, the clerk of superior court to whom such return is made shall transmit to the Commission certified copies of the judgment, the execution and return and any other proceedings upon the judgment.

History.
1983, c. 435, s. 37

§ 18B-128. Common-law rights not abridged

The creation of any claim for relief by this Article may not be interpreted to abrogate or abridge any claims for relief under the common law, but this Article does not authorize double recovery for the same injury.

History.
1983, c. 435, s. 37

§ 18B-129. No liability for refusal to sell or for holding documents

(a) No permittee or his agent or employee may be held liable for damages resulting from the refusal to sell or furnish an alcoholic beverage to a person who fails to show proper identification as described in G.S. 18B-302(d), or who appears to be an underage person.

(b) No permittee or his agent or employee may be held civilly liable if the permittee or his agent or employee holds a customer's identification documents for a reasonable length of time in a good faith attempt to determine whether the customer is of legal age to purchase an alcoholic beverage, provided the permittee or his agent or employee informs the customer of the reason for his actions.

History.
1983, c. 435, s. 37

ARTICLE 3
SALE, POSSESSION, AND CONSUMPTION

§ 18B-300. Purchase, possession and consumption of malt beverages and unfortified wine

(a) **Generally.** -- Except as otherwise provided in this Chapter, the purchase, consumption, and possession of malt beverages and unfortified wine by individuals 21 years old and older for their own use is permitted without restriction.

(a1) **Consumption on Premises During Time of Permit Revocation or Suspension.** -- It shall be unlawful to consume or for a permittee or his agent or employee to allow the consumption of malt beverages or unfortified wine on the premises of any business during the period of time that any on-premises permit issued to the business authorizing the sale and consumption of malt beverages or unfortified wine has been suspended or revoked by the Commission. The prohibition in this subsection does not apply to the premises upon which the business was located at the time the permit was suspended or revoked if the business ceases to operate in that location and the owner of the

property is not the permittee, provided that the permittee is not engaged in any other business or other activity on the premises during the period of suspension or revocation.

(b) **Consumption at Off-Premises Establishment.** -- It shall be unlawful to consume, or for a permittee to allow the consumption of, malt beverages or unfortified wine on any premises having only an off-premises permit for the kind of alcoholic beverage being consumed.

(c) **Local Ordinance.** -- A city or county may by ordinance:

(1) Regulate or prohibit the consumption of malt beverages and unfortified wine on the public streets in that city or county by persons who are not occupants of motor vehicles and on property owned, occupied, or controlled by that city or county;

(2) Regulate or prohibit the possession of open containers of malt beverages and unfortified wine on public streets in that city or county by persons who are not occupants of motor vehicles and on property owned, occupied, or controlled by that city or county; and

(3) Regulate or prohibit the possession of malt beverages and unfortified wine on public streets, alleys, or parking lots which are temporarily closed to regular traffic for special events.

For the purposes of this subsection, an open container means a container whose seal has been broken or a container other than the manufacturer's unopened original container. As provided by G.S. 18B-102(a), possession or consumption of alcoholic beverages is unlawful except as authorized by the ABC law.

History.
1939, c. 158, s. 503; 1971, c. 872, s. 1; 1973, c. 1452, ss. 1-3; 1977, c. 176, ss. 2, 3; c. 693; 1979, c. 19, s. 2; c. 445, s. 4; c. 893, s. 11; 1981, c. 412, s. 2; 1983, c. 435, s. 32; 1985, c. 141, s. 1; 1995, c. 144, s. 1; c. 366, s. 2; 2001-79, s. 1; 2013-392, s. 1

§ 18B-301. Possession and consumption of fortified wine and spirituous liquor

(a) **Possession at Home.** -- It shall be lawful, without an ABC permit, for any person at least 21 years old to possess for lawful purposes any amount of fortified wine and spirituous liquor at his home or a temporary residence, such as a hotel room.

(b) **Possession on Other Property.** -- It shall be lawful, without an ABC permit, for a person to possess for his personal use and the use of his guests not more than eight liters of fortified wine or spirituous liquor, or eight liters of the two combined, at the following places:

Chapter 18B

(1) The residence of any other person with that person's consent;

(2) Any other property not primarily used for commercial purposes and not open to the public at the time the alcoholic beverage is possessed, if the owner or other person in charge of the property consents to that possession and consumption;

(3) An establishment with a brown-bagging permit as defined in G.S. 18B-1001(7).

(c) **Special Occasions.** -- It shall be lawful for a person to possess, without a permit and not for sale, any amount of fortified wine or spirituous liquor for a private party, private reception, or private special occasion, at the following places:

(1) His home or a temporary residence, such as a hotel room;

(2) Any other property not primarily used for commercial purposes, which is under his exclusive control and supervision, and which is not open to the public during the event;

(3) The licensed premises of any business for which the Commission has issued a special occasions permit under G.S. 18B-1001(8), if he is the host of that private function and has the permission of the permittee.

(d) **Consumption.** -- It shall be lawful for a person to consume fortified wine and spirituous liquor in any place where it is lawful for him to possess those alcoholic beverages under subsections (a) through (c).

(e) **Incident to Sale.** -- It shall be lawful to possess fortified wine and spirituous liquor at any place, such as an ABC store, where possession is a necessary incident to lawful sale. Consumption at such a place shall be unlawful unless the establishment has a permit authorizing consumption on the premises as well as sale.

(f) **Unlawful Possession or Use.** -- As illustration, but not limitation, of the general prohibition stated in G.S. 18B-102(a), it shall be unlawful for:

(1) Any person to consume fortified wine, spirituous liquor, or mixed beverages or to offer such beverages to another person at any of the following places:

  a. Unless a consumer tasting authorized by G.S. 18B-1114.7 is being conducted, on the premises of an ABC store.

  b. Upon any property used or occupied by a local board.

  c. On any public road, street, highway, or sidewalk, unless a consumer tasting authorized by G.S. 18B-1114.7 is being conducted.

(2) Any person to display publicly at an athletic contest fortified wine, spirituous liquor, or mixed beverages;

(3) Any person to permit any fortified wine, spirituous liquor, or mixed beverages to be possessed or consumed upon any premises not authorized by this Chapter;

(4) Any person to possess or consume any fortified wine, spirituous liquor, or mixed beverages upon any premises where such possession or consumption is not authorized by law, or where the person has been forbidden to possess or consume that beverage by the owner or other person in charge of the premises;

(5) Any person to possess on any of the premises described in subsections (a) through (c) a greater amount of fortified wine or spirituous liquor than authorized by this Chapter;

(6) Any permittee, other than a mixed beverage or culinary permittee, to possess spirituous liquor or mixed beverages on his licensed premises.

(7) Any person to possess on his person or consume malt beverages or unfortified wine upon any property owned or leased by a local board of education and used by the local board of education for school purposes. Provided, however, the prohibition in G.S. 18B-102(a) and this subdivision shall not apply on property owned by a local board of education which was leased for 99 years or more to a nonprofit auditorium authority created prior to 1991 whose governing board is appointed by a city board of aldermen, a county board of commissioners, or a local school board.

History.

1905, c. 498, ss. 6-8; Rev., ss. 3526, 3534; C.S., s. 3371; 1937, c. 49, ss. 12, 16, 22; c. 411; 1955, c. 999; 1967, c. 222, ss. 1, 8; c. 1256, s. 3; 1969, c. 1018; 1971, c. 872, s. 1; 1973, c. 1226; 1977, c. 176, s. 1; 1977, 2nd Sess., c. 1138, ss. 8-12, 18; 1979, c. 384, s. 3; c. 609, s. 2; c. 718; c. 893, s. 10; 1981, c. 412, s. 2; c. 747, s. 39; 1983, c. 917, s. 1; 1985, c. 566, s. 1; 1991, c. 459, s. 1; 1993, c. 508, s. 1; 1995, c. 372, s. 1; 2017-87, s. 2(a); 2019-182, s. 6(b)

§ 18B-302. Sale to or purchase by underage persons

(a) **Sale.** -- It is unlawful for any person to do any of the following:

(1) Sell malt beverages or unfortified wine to anyone less than 21 years old.

(2) Sell fortified wine, spirituous liquor, or mixed beverages to anyone less than 21 years old.

Chapter 18B

(a1) **Give.** -- It is unlawful for any person to do any of the following:

(1) Give malt beverages or unfortified wine to anyone less than 21 years old.

(2) Give fortified wine, spirituous liquor, or mixed beverages to anyone less than 21 years old.

(b) **Purchase, Possession, or Consumption.** -- It is unlawful for a person less than 21 years old to do any of the following:

(1) Purchase, attempt to purchase, or possess malt beverages or unfortified wine.

(2) Purchase, attempt to purchase, or possess fortified wine, spirituous liquor, or mixed beverages.

(3) Consume any alcoholic beverage.

(c) **Aider and Abettor.** --

(1) **By Underage Person.** -- Any person who is under the lawful age to purchase and who aids or abets another in violation of subsection (a), (a1), or (b) of this section is guilty of a Class 2 misdemeanor.

(2) **By Person over Lawful Age.** -- Any person who is over the lawful age to purchase and who aids or abets another in violation of subsection (a), (a1), or (b) of this section is guilty of a Class 1 misdemeanor.

(d) **Defense.** -- It is a defense to a violation of subsection (a) of this section if the seller does any of the following:

(1) Shows that the purchaser produced a driver's license, a special identification card issued under G.S. 20-37.7 or issued by the state agency of any other state authorized to issue similar official state special identification cards for that state, a military identification card, or a passport, showing the purchaser's age to be at least the required age for purchase and bearing a physical description of the person named on the card reasonably describing the purchaser.

(2) Produces evidence of other facts that reasonably indicated at the time of sale that the purchaser was at least the required age.

(3) Shows that at the time of purchase, the purchaser utilized a biometric identification system that demonstrated (i) the purchaser's age to be at least the required age for the purchase and (ii) the purchaser had previously registered with the seller or seller's agent a drivers license, a special identification card issued under G.S. 20-37.7 or issued by the state agency of any other state authorized to issue similar official state special identification cards for that state, a military identification card, or a passport showing the purchaser's date of birth and bearing a physical description of the person named on the document.

(e) **Fraudulent Use of Identification.** -- It is unlawful for any person to enter or attempt to enter a place where alcoholic beverages are sold or consumed, or to obtain or attempt to obtain alcoholic beverages, or to obtain or attempt to obtain permission to purchase alcoholic beverages, in violation of subsection (b) of this section, by using or attempting to use any of the following:

(1) A fraudulent or altered drivers license.

(2) A fraudulent or altered identification document other than a drivers license.

(3) A drivers license issued to another person.

(4) An identification document other than a drivers license issued to another person.

(5) Any other form or means of identification that indicates or symbolizes that the person is not prohibited from purchasing or possessing alcoholic beverages under this section.

(f) **Allowing Use of Identification.** -- It is unlawful for any person to permit the use of the person's drivers license or any other form of identification of any kind issued or given to the person by any other person who violates or attempts to violate subsection (b) of this section.

(g) **Conviction Report Sent to Division of Motor Vehicles.** -- The court shall file a conviction report with the Division of Motor Vehicles indicating the name of the person convicted and any other information requested by the Division if the person is convicted of any of the following:

(1) A violation of subsection (e) or (f) of this section.

(2) A violation of subsection (c) of this section.

(3) A violation of subsection (b) of this section, if the violation occurred while the person was purchasing or attempting to purchase an alcoholic beverage.

(4) A violation of subsection (a1) of this section.

Upon receipt of a conviction report, the Division shall revoke the person's license as required by G.S. 20-17.3.

(h) **Handling in Course of Employment.** -- Nothing in this section prohibits an underage person from selling, transporting, possessing, or dispensing alcoholic beverages in the course of employment, if the employment of the person for that purpose is lawful under applicable youth employment statutes and Commission rules.

(i) **Purchase, Possession, or Consumption by 19 or 20-Year Old.** -- A violation of subdivision (b)(1) or (b)(3) of this section by a person who is 19 or 20 years old is a Class 3 misdemeanor.

(j) **Screening Test.** -- Notwithstanding any other provisions of law, a law enforcement officer may require any person the officer has probable cause to believe is less than 21 years old and has consumed alcohol to submit to an

Chapter 18B

alcohol screening test using a device approved by the Department of Health and Human Services. The results of any screening device administered in accordance with the rules of the Department of Health and Human Services are admissible in any court or administrative proceeding. A refusal to submit to an alcohol screening test is admissible in any court or administrative proceeding.

(k) **Exception.** -- Notwithstanding the provisions in this section, it is not unlawful for a person less than 21 years old to consume unfortified wine or fortified wine during participation in an exempted activity under G.S. 18B-103(4), (8), or (11).

History.
1933, c. 216, s. 8; 1959, c. 745, s. 1; 1967, c. 222, s. 3; 1969, c. 998; 1971, c. 872, s. 1; 1973, c. 27; 1977, 2nd Sess., c. 1138, s. 2; 1979, c. 683, s. 2; 1981, c. 412, s. 2; c. 747, ss. 40, 41; 1983, c. 435, ss. 32, 35; c. 740, ss. 1, 2; Ex. Sess., c. 5; 1985, c. 141, ss. 2-3; 1993, c. 539, s. 311; 1994, Ex. Sess., c. 24, s. 14(c); 1999-406, s. 7; 2001-461, ss. 2, 3; 2001-487, s. 42(b); 2005-350, s. 6(a); 2006-253, s. 26; 2007-537, s. 1; 2015-264, s. 7; 2021-88, s. 4(a); 2021-150, s. 10.1(a)

§ 18B-302.1. Penalties for certain offenses related to underage persons

(a) A violation of G.S. 18B-302(a) or (a1) is a Class 1 misdemeanor. Notwithstanding the provisions of G.S. 15A-1340.23, if the court imposes a sentence that does not include an active punishment, the court must include among the conditions of probation a requirement that the person pay a fine of at least two hundred fifty dollars ($ 250.00) as authorized by G.S. 15A-1343(b)(9) and a requirement that the person complete at least 25 hours of community service, as authorized by G.S. 15A-1343(b1)(6). If the person has a previous conviction of this offense in the four years immediately preceding the date of the current offense, and the court imposes a sentence that does not include an active punishment, the court must include among the conditions of probation a requirement that the person pay a fine of at least five hundred dollars ($ 500.00) as authorized by G.S. 15A-1343(b)(9) and a requirement that the person complete at least 150 hours of community service, as authorized by G.S. 15A-1343(b1)(6).

(b) A violation of G.S. 18B-302(c)(2) is a Class 1 misdemeanor. Notwithstanding the provisions of G.S. 15A-1340.23, if the court imposes a sentence that does not include an active punishment, the court must include among the conditions of probation a requirement that the person pay a fine of at least five hundred dollars ($ 500.00) as authorized by G.S. 15A-1343(b) (9) and a requirement that the person complete at least 25 hours of community service, as

authorized by G.S. 15A-1343(b1)(6). If the person has a previous conviction of this offense in the four years immediately preceding the date of the current offense, and the court imposes a sentence that does not include an active punishment, the court must include among the conditions of probation a requirement that the person pay a fine of at least one thousand dollars ($ 1,000) as authorized by G.S. 15A-1343(b)(9) and a requirement that the person complete at least 150 hours of community service, as authorized by G.S. 15A-1343(b1)(6).

(c) In addition to the punishments imposed under this section, the court may impose the provisions of G.S. 18B-202 and of G.S. 18B-503, 18B-504, and 18B-505.

History.
1999-433, s. 1; 2007-537, s. 2

§ 18B-302.2. Medical treatment; limited immunity

(a) **Limited Immunity for Samaritan.** -- Notwithstanding any other provision of law, a person under the age of 21 shall not be prosecuted for a violation of G.S. 18B-302 for the possession or consumption of alcoholic beverages if all of the following requirements and conditions are met:

(1) The person sought medical assistance for an individual experiencing an alcohol-related overdose by contacting the 911 system, a law enforcement officer, or emergency medical services personnel.

(1a) The person acted in good faith when seeking medical assistance, upon a reasonable belief that he or she was the first to call for assistance.

(2) The person provided his or her own name to the 911 system or to a law enforcement officer upon arrival.

(3) Repealed by Session Laws 2015-94, s. 2, effective August 1, 2015, and applicable to offenses committed on or after that date.

(4) The person did not seek the medical assistance during the course of the execution of an arrest warrant, search warrant, or other lawful search.

(5) The evidence for prosecution of a violation of G.S. 18B-302 for the possession or consumption of alcoholic beverages was obtained as a result of the person seeking medical assistance for the alcohol-related overdose.

(b) **Limited Immunity for Overdose Victim.** -- The immunity described in subsection (a) of this section shall extend to the person who needed medical assistance if the requirements in subdivisions (1), (1a), (4), and (5) of subsection (a) are satisfied.

(c) Probation or Release. -- A person shall not be subject to arrest or revocation of pretrial release, probation, parole, or post-release if the arrest or revocation is based on an offense for which the person is immune from prosecution under subsection (a) or (b) of this section. The arrest of a person for an offense for which subsection (a) or (b) of this section may provide the person with immunity will not itself be deemed to be a commission of a new criminal offense in violation of a condition of the person's pretrial release, condition of probation, or condition of parole or post-release.

(d) Civil Liability for Arrest or Charges. -- In addition to any other applicable immunity or limitation on civil liability, a law enforcement officer who, acting in good faith, arrests or charges a person who is thereafter determined to be entitled to immunity under this section shall not be subject to civil liability for the arrest or filing of charges.

History.
2013-23, s. 3; 2015-94, s. 2

§ 18B-303. Amounts of alcoholic beverages that may be purchased

(a) Purchases Allowed. -- Without a permit, a person may purchase at one time:

(1) Not more than 80 liters of malt beverages, except draft malt beverages in kegs for off-premises consumption. For purchase of a keg or kegs of malt beverages for off-premises consumption, the permit required by G.S. 18B-403.1(a) must first be obtained;

(2) Any amount of draft malt beverages by a permittee in kegs for on-premise consumption;

(3) Not more than 50 liters of unfortified wine;

(4) Not more than eight liters of either fortified wine or spirituous liquor, or eight liters of the two combined.

(b) Unlawful Purchase. -- Except as provided in subsections (c) and (d) of this section, and in Article 11 of this Chapter, it shall be unlawful for any person to purchase, or for any person to sell, an amount of alcoholic beverages greater than that stated in subsection (a).

(c) Greater Amounts. -- Amounts of alcoholic beverages greater than those listed in subdivisions (a)(3) and (a)(4) may be purchased with a purchase-transportation permit under G.S. 18B-403.

(d) Mixed Beverage Permittee Exception. -- A mixed beverage permittee, or an employee of a mixed beverage permittee, may purchase and transport any amount of fortified wine or spirituous liquor for use by the mixed beverage permittee without obtaining a purchase-transportation permit under G.S. 18B-403. An employee of a local board may transport to a mixed beverage permittee any amount of fortified wine or spirituous liquor purchased by the mixed beverage permittee without obtaining a purchase-transportation permit under G.S. 18B-403. An independent contractor employed pursuant to G.S. 18B-701(a)(1), by either a mixed beverage permittee or a local board, shall not be considered an employee of a mixed beverage permittee or a local board for purposes of this subsection.

History.
1905, c. 498, ss. 6-8; Rev., ss. 3526, 3534; C.S., s. 3371; 1937, c. 49, ss. 12, 16, 22; c. 411; 1955, c. 999; 1967, c. 222, ss. 1, 8; c. 1256, s. 3; 1969, c. 1018; 1971, c. 872, s. 1; 1973, c. 1226; 1977, c. 176, s. 1; 1977, 2nd Sess., c. 1138, ss. 8-12, 18; 1979, c. 384, s. 3; c. 609, s. 2; c. 718; c. 893, s. 10; 1981, c. 412, s. 2; 1989, c. 553, s. 1; 1993, c. 508, s. 2; 2001-262, s. 5; 2006-253, s. 3.2; 2019-182, s. 23(a)

§ 18B-304. Sale and possession for sale

(a) Offense. -- It shall be unlawful for any person to sell any alcoholic beverage, or possess any alcoholic beverage for sale, without first obtaining the applicable ABC permit and revenue licenses.

(b) Prima Facie Evidence. -- Possession of the following amounts of alcoholic beverages, without a permit authorizing that possession, shall be prima facie evidence that the possessor is possessing those alcoholic beverages for sale:

(1) More than 80 liters of malt beverages, other than draft malt beverages in kegs;

(2) More than eight liters of spirituous liquor; or

(3) Any amount of nontaxpaid alcoholic beverages.

History.
1913, c. 44, s. 2; 1915, c. 97, s. 8; 1923, c. 1, ss. 2, 6, 10; C.S., ss. 3379, 3411(b), (f), (j); 1937, c. 49, ss. 13, 15; 1945, c. 635; 1949, c. 1251, s. 2; 1951, c. 850; 1955, c. 560; 1957, c. 984; c. 1235, s. 1; 1963, c. 932; 1967, c. 222, ss. 4, 6; 1969, c. 789; 1971, c. 872, s. 1; 1975, c. 654, s. 4; 1977, c. 176, ss. 1-3; 1981, c. 412, s. 2; c. 747, s. 42; 1989, c. 553, s. 2; 1993, c. 508, s. 3

§ 18B-305. Other prohibited sales

(a) Sale to Intoxicated Person. -- It shall be unlawful for a permittee or his employee or for an ABC store employee to knowingly sell or give alcoholic beverages to any person who is intoxicated.

(b) Discretion for Seller. -- Any person authorized to sell alcoholic beverages under this Chapter may, in his discretion, refuse to sell to anyone. It shall be unlawful for any person to knowingly buy alcoholic beverages for someone

Chapter 18B

who has been refused the right to purchase under this subsection.

(c) Notwithstanding subsection (b) of this section, no permittee may refuse to sell alcoholic beverages to a person solely based on that person's race, religion, color, national origin, sex, or disability.

History.
1937, c. 49, ss. 11, 15; c. 411; 1971, c. 872, s. 1; 1977, 2nd Sess., c. 1138, s. 5; 1981, c. 412, s. 2; 1999-462, s. 5

§ 18B-306. Making wines and malt beverages for private use

(a) **Authority.** -- An individual may make, possess, and transport wines and malt beverages for the individual's own use, the use of the individual's family and guests, or the use at organized affairs, exhibitions, or competitions. For purposes of this section, the term "organized affairs, exhibitions, or competitions" includes homemaker's contests, tastings, and judgings.

(b) **Selling Prohibited.** -- Wines and malt beverages made pursuant to this section may not be sold or offered for sale.

(c) **Kits.** -- Wine kits and malt beverage kits may be sold in this State.

(d) **Permit.** -- No ABC permit is required to make wines or malt beverages pursuant to this section.

History.
1971, c. 872, s. 1; 1973, c. 1218; 1981, c. 412, s. 2; c. 747, s. 43; 1985, c. 114, s. 6; 2017-87, s. 10

§ 18B-307. Manufacturing offenses

(a) **Offenses.** -- It shall be unlawful for any person, except as authorized by this Chapter, to:

(1) Sell or possess equipment or ingredients intended for use in the manufacture of any alcoholic beverage, except equipment and ingredients provided under a Brew on Premises permit or a Winemaking on Premises permit; or

(2) Knowingly allow real or personal property owned or possessed by him to be used by another person for the manufacture of any alcoholic beverage, except pursuant to a Brew on Premises permit or a Winemaking on Premises permit.

(b) **Unlawful Manufacturing.** -- Except as provided in G.S. 18B-306, it shall be unlawful for any person to manufacture any alcoholic beverage, except at an establishment with a Brew on Premises permit or a Winemaking on Premises permit, without first obtaining the applicable ABC permit and revenue licenses.

(c) **Second Offense of Manufacturing.** -- A second offense of unlawful manufacturing of alcoholic beverage shall be a Class I felony.

History.
1905, c. 498, s. 2; Rev., s. 3533; 1923, c. 1, ss. 4, 6, 26; C.S., ss. 3407, 3411(d), (f), (z); 1937, c. 49, s. 13; 1945, c. 635; 1951, c. 850; 1955, c. 560; 1957, c. 984; c. 1235, s. 1; 1969, c. 789; 1971, c. 872, s. 1; 1979, c. 699, s. 1; 1981, c. 412, s. 2; c. 747, s. 44; 1997-467, s. 1; 2006-222, s. 2.2; 2006-227, s. 2

§ 18B-308. Sale and consumption at bingo games

It shall be unlawful to sell or consume, or for the owner or other person in charge of the premises to allow the sale or consumption of, any alcoholic beverage in any room while a bingo game is being conducted in that room under Part 2 of Article 37 of Chapter 14 of the General Statutes.

History.
1905, c. 498, ss. 6-8; Rev., ss. 3526, 3534; C.S., s. 3371; 1937, c. 49, ss. 12, 16, 22; c. 411; 1955, c. 999; 1967, c. 222, ss. 1, 8; c. 1256, s. 3; 1969, c. 1018; 1971, c. 872, s. 1; 1973, c. 1226; 1977, c. 176, s. 1; 1977, 2nd Sess., c. 1138, ss. 8-12, 18; 1979, c. 384, s. 3; c. 609, s. 2; c. 718; c. 893, s. 10; 1981, c. 412, s. 2; 1983, c. 896, s. 4; 2018-100, s. 5(c).

§ 18B-309. Alcoholic beverage sales in Urban Redevelopment Areas

(a) A food business as defined in G.S. 18B-1000(3), a retail business as defined in G.S. 18B-1000(7), or an eating establishment as defined in G.S. 18B-1000(2) that holds an ABC permit under this Chapter and is located in a part of a city that has been designated as an Urban Redevelopment Area under Article 22 of Chapter 160A of the General Statutes shall not have alcoholic beverage sales in excess of fifty percent (50%) of the business's total annual sales. The city council, or its designee, shall file a certified copy of the official action and original documents, including a map or similar information, designating the area as an Urban Redevelopment Area. The Commission shall make this information available to any permittee who makes a request for this information to the Commission.

(b) Upon request of a city, the Commission shall investigate the total annual alcohol sales and total sales of a business as defined in this section. The Commission shall report the results of such an investigation to the city council, and the report shall contain only the percentage of annual alcohol sales in proportion to the business's total annual sales. A city may request an investigation of a particular business by the Commission only once in each calendar year.

Chapter 18B

1225

These audits may be conducted by the Commission only upon the request of the city council.

(c) Businesses covered by this section shall maintain full and accurate monthly records of their finances, separately indicating each of the following:

(1) Amounts expended by the business for the purchase of alcoholic beverages and the quantity of alcoholic beverages purchased;

(2) Amounts collected from the sale of alcoholic beverages sold; and

(3) Amounts collected from the sale of food, nonalcoholic beverages, and all other items sold by the business.

Records of purchases of alcoholic beverages and sales of alcoholic beverages shall be filed separate and apart from all other records maintained on the premises, and all records related to alcoholic beverages, including original invoices, shall be maintained on the premises for three years and shall be open for inspection and audit pursuant to G.S. 18B-502.

History.
1999-322, s. 1; 2001-515, s. 3(a)

ARTICLE 4
TRANSPORTATION

§ 18B-400. Amounts that may be transported

A person may transport at one time the same amount of alcoholic beverages that he is allowed to buy under G.S. 18B-303(a). Greater amounts of fortified wine, unfortified wine and spirituous liquor may be transported with a purchase-transportation permit under G.S. 18B-403. The Commission may also authorize a distillery representative, in the course of his business, to transport and possess up to 10 gallons of spirituous liquor.

History.
1923, c. 1, s. 25; C.S., s. 3411(y); 1937, c. 49, ss. 14, 16; c. 411; 1967, c. 222, ss. 1, 7; c. 1256, s. 3; 1969, c. 598, ss. 2, 3; c. 1018; 1971, c. 872, s. 1; 1977, c. 176, s. 1; c. 586; 1979, c. 607, s. 1; 1981, c. 412, s. 2; 1985, c. 757, s. 163

§ 18B-401. Manner of transportation

(a) **Opened Containers.** -- Except as authorized by a common carrier vehicle permit under G.S. 18B-1001(23), it shall be unlawful for a person to transport fortified wine or spirituous liquor in the passenger area of a motor vehicle in other than the manufacturer's unopened original container. It shall be unlawful for a person who is driving a motor vehicle on a highway or public vehicular area to consume in

the passenger area of that vehicle any malt beverage or unfortified wine. Violation of this subsection shall constitute a Class 3 misdemeanor.

(b) **Taxis.** -- It shall be unlawful for a person operating a for-hire passenger vehicle as defined in G.S. 20-4.01(27)f., to transport fortified wine or spirituous liquor unless the vehicle is transporting a paying passenger who owns the alcoholic beverage being transported. Not more than eight liters of fortified wine or spirituous liquor, or combination of the two, may be transported by each passenger. A violation of this subsection shall not be grounds for suspension of the driver's license for illegal transportation of intoxicating liquors under G.S. 20-16(a)(8).

(c) **Definitions.** -- The definitions in Chapter 20 of the General Statutes apply in interpreting this section. If the seal on a container of alcoholic beverages has been broken, it is opened within the meaning of this section. For purposes of this section, "passenger area of a motor vehicle" means the area designed to seat the driver and passengers and any area within the reach of a seated driver or passenger, including the glove compartment. In the case of a station wagon, hatchback or similar vehicle, the area behind the last upright back seat shall not be considered part of the passenger area.

History.
1923, c. 1, s. 25; C.S., s. 3411(y); 1937, c. 49, ss. 14, 16; c. 411; 1967, c. 222, ss. 1, 7; c. 1256, s. 3; 1969, c. 598, ss. 2, 3; c. 1018; 1971, c. 872, s. 1; 1977, c. 176, s. 1; c. 586; 1979, c. 607, s. 1; 1981, c. 412, s. 2; c. 747, s. 45; 1983, c. 435, s. 7; 1989, c. 553, s. 3; 1993, c. 508, s. 4; c. 539, s. 312; 1994, Ex. Sess., c. 24, s. 14(c); 2017-102, s. 5.2(b); 2021-150, s. 28.3

§ 18B-402. Alcoholic beverages purchased out-of-State

A person may bring into North Carolina alcoholic beverages purchased legally outside the jurisdiction of this State in the same amounts that may be legally transported within the State under G.S. 18B-400 or G.S. 18B-403, except that no more than four liters of spirituous liquor purchased outside this State may be brought into this State.

History.
1923, c. 1, s. 25; C.S., s. 3411(y); 1937, c. 49, ss. 14, 16; c. 411; 1967, c. 222, ss. 1, 7; c. 1256, s. 3; 1969, c. 598, ss. 2, 3; c. 1018; 1971, c. 872, s. 1; 1977, c. 176, s. 1; c. 586; 1979, c. 607, s. 1; 1981, c. 412, s. 2; 1981 (Reg. Sess., 1982), c. 1262, s. 5

§ 18B-403. Purchase-transportation permit

(a) **Amounts.** -- With a purchase-transportation permit, a person may purchase and transport an amount of alcoholic beverages greater than the amount specified in G.S. 18B-303(a). A permit authorizes the holder to transport from the place of purchase to the destination within North Carolina indicated on the permit at one time the following amount of alcoholic beverages:

(1) A maximum of 100 liters of unfortified wine.

(2) A maximum of 40 liters of either fortified wine or spirituous liquor, or 40 liters of the two combined.

(3) The amount of fortified wine or spirituous liquors specified on the purchase-transportation permit for transportation to a mixed beverage permittee by an independent contractor employed pursuant to G.S. 18B-701(a)(1).

(b) **Issuance of Permit.** -- A purchase-transportation permit may be issued by any of the following:

(1) The local board chairman.

(2) A member of the local board.

(3) The general manager or supervisor of the local board.

(4) Any employee of an ABC store, if the employee is authorized to issue permits by the local board chairman.

(5) For spirituous liquor sold by the distillery only, the owner, or an employee designated by the owner, of a distillery authorized to sell spirituous liquor under G.S. 18B-1105.

(c) **Disqualifications.** -- A purchase-transportation permit shall not be issued to a person who meets any of the following:

(1) Is not sufficiently identified or known to the issuer.

(2) Is known or shown to be an alcoholic or bootlegger.

(3) Has been convicted within the previous three years of an offense involving the sale, possession, or transportation of non-taxpaid alcoholic beverages.

(4) Has been convicted within the previous three years of an offense involving the sale of alcoholic beverages without a permit.

(d) **Form.** -- A purchase-transportation permit shall be issued on a printed form adopted by the Commission. The Commission shall adopt rules specifying the content of the permit form.

(e) **Restrictions on Permit.** -- A purchase may be made only from the store or distillery named on the permit. One copy of the permit shall be kept by the issuing person, one by the purchaser, and one by the store or distillery from which the purchase is made. The purchaser shall display his copy of the permit to any law-enforcement officer upon request. A permit for the purchase and transportation of spirituous liquor may be issued only by an authorized agent of the local board for the jurisdiction in which the purchase will be made or in accordance with subdivision (5) of subsection (b) of this section.

(f) **Time.** -- A purchase-transportation permit is valid only until 9:30 P.M. on the date of purchase, which date shall be stated on the permit.

(g) **Special Occasion Purchase-Transportation Permit.** -- When a person holds a special occasion for which a permit under G.S. 18B-1001(8) or (9) is required, the purchase-transportation permit issued to him may provide for the storage at and transportation to and from the site of the special occasion of unfortified wine, fortified wine, and spirituous liquor for a period of no more than 48 hours before and after the special occasion. The purchase-transportation permit authorizes that person to transport only the amounts of those alcoholic beverages authorized by subsection (a). The Commission may adopt rules to govern issuance of these extended purchase-transportation permits.

History.

1969, c. 617, s. 1; 1971, c. 872, s. 1; 1973, c. 94; c. 819, s. 1; 1975, ss. 1-4; 1977, c. 176, ss. 1, 2, 4; 1979, c. 19, ss. 3, 4; c. 286, s. 1; c. 445, ss. 1, 3; c. 1076, ss. 1, 2, 3; 1981, c. 412, s. 2; 1981 (Reg. Sess., 1982), c. 1262, ss. 6-8; 1983, c. 457, s. 1; 2019-182, ss. 5(a), 23(b)

§ 18B-403.1. Purchase-transportation permit for keg or kegs of malt beverages

(a) **Purchase-Transportation.** -- A person who is not a permittee may purchase and transport for off-premises consumption a keg or kegs as defined in G.S. 18B-101(7c) after obtaining a purchase-transportation permit. Failure to obtain a purchase-transportation permit according to this section is a violation of G.S. 18B-303(b).

(b) **Issuance.** -- A person holding a permit (permittee) pursuant to G.S. 18B-1001(2) shall issue a purchase-transportation permit for a keg or kegs of malt beverage to a purchaser. A copy of the purchase-transportation permit shall be maintained by the permittee for 90 days. Upon request by any person, the permittee shall maintain the permit for a requested period in excess of 90 days.

(c) **Form.** -- A purchase-transportation permit shall be issued on a printed form adopted and provided by the Commission. The Commission shall adopt rules specifying the content of the permit form.

(d) **Restrictions on Permit.** -- A purchase may be made only from the store named on the permit. One copy of the permit shall be kept by the purchaser and one by the permittee from whom the purchase is made. The purchaser

Chapter 18B

shall display his copy of the permit to any law enforcement officer upon request.

(e) **Violation.** -- The first violation of this section by a permittee shall result in a warning to the permittee.

History.
2006-253, s. 3.1; 2010-122, s. 1

§ 18B-404. Additional provisions for purchase and transportation by mixed beverage permittees

(a) **Designated Employee.** -- A mixed beverages permittee may designate an employee to purchase and transport spirituous liquor as authorized by the permittee's permit.

(b) **Issuance.** -- If mixed beverages sales have been approved for an establishment under G.S. 18B-603(d1) or under G.S. 18B-603(e), or for an establishment located in a township in which mixed beverages have been approved the purchase-transportation permit for that establishment may be issued by the local board of any city located in the same county as the establishment, provided the city has approved the sale of mixed beverages. Otherwise a licensed establishment may obtain a mixed beverages purchase-transportation permit only from the local board for the jurisdiction in which it is located. If there is no ABC store within the establishment's jurisdiction, then the mixed beverages permittee shall obtain a mixed beverages purchase-transportation permit from the nearest and most convenient ABC store.

(c) **Designated Store.** -- A local board may designate a store within its system to make sales to mixed beverages permittees.

(d) **Size of Bottles.** -- A purchase-transportation permit for a mixed beverages permittee shall authorize the purchase and transportation only of 355 milliliter or larger containers. A purchase-transportation permit for a mixed beverages permittee who is also a guest room cabinet permittee may authorize the purchase and transportation of containers in sizes approved by the Commission.

(e) **Electronic Payment.** -- A local board shall accept electronic payments for any spirituous liquor purchased by a mixed beverages permittee. A local board may not charge a fee for accepting electronic payments under this subsection. For purposes of this subsection, the term "electronic payment" means payment by debit card or by electronic funds transfer as defined in G.S. 105-228.90, but does not include payment by charge card or credit card.

(f) **(Effective July 1, 2022)** A local board shall offer delivery service to mixed beverage permittees. In providing delivery of purchased products to mixed beverage permittees, the local board may use its employees or contract with one or more independent contractors and may charge a fee to the permittee. A local board in a Tier 1 or Tier 2 county, as defined in G.S. 143B-472.35(a2)(18), may request an exemption to this requirement from the ABC Commission. The Commission shall grant the request if the local board can show evidence of unreasonable hardship or difficulty incurred by implementing delivery service.

History.
1981, c. 412, s. 2; c. 747, ss. 46, 47; 1987, c. 136, s. 3; 1991, c. 459, s. 10; c. 565, ss. 5, 7; 1991 (Reg. Sess., 1992), c. 920, s. 2; 1999-462, s. 4; 2003-218, s. 3; 2019-182, s. 17(a); 2021-150, s. 30.1

§ 18B-405. Transportation by permittee

The holder of a permit for the retail sale of malt beverages, unfortified wine, or fortified wine may transport in the course of his business any amount of the alcoholic beverage he is authorized to sell, without a purchase-transportation permit or a commercial transportation permit under G.S. 18B-1115.

History.
1923, c. 1, s. 15; C.S., s. 3411(o); 1939, c. 158, s. 503; 1971, c. 872, s. 1; 1975, c. 411, s. 7; 1977, c. 70, s. 20; c. 176, s. 7; 1979, c. 286, s. 5; 1981, c. 412, s. 2; 1987, c. 136, s. 4

§ 18B-406. Unlawful transportation

It shall be unlawful to transport a greater amount of alcoholic beverage than permitted by this Article, unless the transportation is authorized under Article 11.

History.
1981, c. 412, s. 2

ARTICLE 5
LAW ENFORCEMENT

§ 18B-500. Alcohol law-enforcement agents

(a) **Appointment.** -- The Secretary of Public Safety shall appoint and supervise the Director of the Division of Alcohol Law Enforcement of the Department of Public Safety. The Director of the Division of Alcohol Law Enforcement of the Department of Public Safety may appoint and supervise a sufficient number of assistants who shall be competent and qualified to do the work of the Division. The Director is responsible for making all hiring and personnel decisions of the Division. Notwithstanding the provisions of this Chapter or Chapter 143A of the General Statutes, the Director may hire or fire personnel and transfer personnel within the Division. The

Director may also appoint a regular employee of the Commission as an ALE agent, provided the employee was employed by the ABC Commission and serving as an ALE agent on January 1, 2019. Alcohol law-enforcement agents shall be designated as "alcohol law-enforcement agents." Persons serving as reserve alcohol law-enforcement agents are considered employees of the Division for workers' compensation purposes while performing duties assigned or approved by the Director of the Division or the Director's designee.

(b) **Subject Matter Jurisdiction.** -- After taking the oath prescribed for a peace officer, an alcohol law-enforcement agent shall have authority to arrest and take other investigatory and enforcement actions for any criminal offense:

(1) Occurring, encountered, or otherwise discovered on the premises of, or elsewhere when the conduct relates to, a location under application for or holding a permit issued by the North Carolina Alcoholic Beverage Control Commission or the North Carolina Education Lottery Commission.

(2) Encountered or otherwise discovered while investigating or enforcing matters for the North Carolina Alcoholic Beverage Control Commission or the North Carolina Education Lottery Commission or encountered or otherwise discovered while investigating or enforcing the provisions of this Chapter, Chapter 18C of the General Statutes, G.S. 14-313, or Parts 1 and 2 of Article 37 of Chapter 14 of the General Statutes.

(3) Encountered or otherwise discovered while carrying out any duty or function assigned to the Division by law.

(4) Occurring in an agent's presence.

(5) When assisting another law enforcement agency.

(b1) **Authority.** -- Alcohol law-enforcement agents have authority as peace officers to execute criminal process, respond to and take enforcement action for any crime of violence or breach of the peace, and any additional duties as may from time to time be directed by the Governor or the Secretary of Public Safety when needed for security purposes at a public event or to protect persons or property because of a disaster or state of emergency.

(b2) **Primary Responsibilities.** -- The primary responsibilities of an alcohol law-enforcement agent are the enforcement of this Chapter, Chapter 18C of the General Statutes, G.S. 14-313, and Parts 1 and 2 of Article 37 of Chapter 14 of the General Statutes.

(c) **Territorial Jurisdiction.** -- An alcohol law-enforcement agent is a State officer with jurisdiction throughout the State.

(d) **Service of Commission Orders.** -- Alcohol law-enforcement agents may serve and execute notices, orders, or demands issued by the Alcoholic Beverage Control Commission or the North Carolina State Lottery Commission for the surrender of permits or relating to any administrative proceeding. While serving and executing such notices, orders, or demands, alcohol law-enforcement agents shall have all the power and authority possessed by law-enforcement officers when executing an arrest warrant.

(e) **Discharge.** -- Alcohol law-enforcement agents are subject to the discharge provisions of G.S. 18B-202.

(f) Repealed by Session Laws 1995, c. 507, s. 6.2(a).

(g) **Shifting of Personnel From One District to Another.** -- The Director of the Alcohol Law Enforcement Division may, from time to time, shift the forces from one district to another or consolidate more than one district force at any point for special purposes. Whenever an agent of the Alcohol Law Enforcement Division is transferred from one district to another for the convenience of the State or for reasons other than the request of the agent, the Department shall be responsible for transporting the household goods, furniture, and personal apparel of the agent and members of the agent's household.

History.
1939, c. 158, s. 514; 1943, c. 400, s. 6; 1949, c. 974, ss. 11, 14; c. 1251, s. 4; 1951, c. 1056, s. 1; c. 1186, ss. 1, 2; 1953, c. 1207, ss. 2-4; 1957, c. 1440; 1961, c. 645; 1963, c. 426, ss. 1, 2, 4, 5, 12; 1967, c. 868; 1971, c. 872, s. 1; 1977, c. 70, s. 17; 1981, c. 412, s. 2; 1983, c. 629, s. 1; c. 768, ss. 25.1, 25.2; 1995, c. 466, s. 2; c. 507, s. 6.2(a); 2005-276, ss. 31.1(y), 31.1(z); 2005-344, ss. 10.1(b), 10.1(c); 2006-264, s. 35; 2011-145, s. 19.1(z); 2011-391, s. 43(j); 2012-83, s. 3; 2014-100, s. 17.1(www); 2018-5, s. 16B.3(b); 2019-203, s. 4

§ 18B-501. Local ABC officers

(a) **Appointment.** -- Except as provided in subsection (f), each local board shall hire one or more ABC enforcement officers. Local ABC enforcement officers shall be designated as "ABC Officers". The local board may designate one officer as the chief ABC officer for that board.

(b) **Subject Matter Jurisdiction.** -- After taking the oath prescribed for a peace officer, a local ABC officer may arrest and take other investigatory and enforcement actions for any criminal offense; however, the primary responsibility of a local ABC officer is enforcement of the ABC laws and Article 5 of Chapter 90 (The Controlled Substances Act).

(c) **Territorial Jurisdiction.** -- A local ABC officer has jurisdiction anywhere in the county in which he is employed except that a city ABC officer's territorial jurisdiction is subject to any limitation included in any local act governing

Chapter 18B

that city ABC system. A local ABC officer may pursue outside his normal territorial jurisdiction anyone who commits an offense within that jurisdiction, as provided in G.S. 15A-402(d).

(d) **Assisting Other Local Agencies.** -- The local ABC officers employed by a local board shall constitute a "law-enforcement agency" for purposes of G.S. 160A-288, and a local board shall have the same authority as a city or county governing body to approve cooperation between law-enforcement agencies under that section.

(e) **Assisting State and Federal Enforcement.** -- A local ABC officer may assist State and federal law-enforcement agencies in the investigation of criminal offenses in North Carolina, under the following conditions:

(1) The local board employing the officer has adopted a resolution approving such assistance and stating the conditions under which it may be provided;

(2) The State or federal agency has made a written request for assistance from that local board, either for a particular investigation or for any investigation that might require assistance within a certain period of time;

(3) The local ABC officer is supervised by someone in the requesting agency; and

(4) As soon as practical after the assistance begins, an acknowledgement of the action is placed in the records of the local board.

A local ABC officer shall have territorial jurisdiction throughout North Carolina while assisting a State or federal agency under this section. While providing that assistance the officer shall continue to be considered an employee of the local board for purposes of salary, worker's compensation, and other benefits, unless a different arrangement is negotiated between the local board and the requesting agency.

(f) **Contracts with Other Agencies.** -- Instead of hiring local ABC officers, a local board may contract to pay its enforcement funds to a sheriff's department, city police department, or other local law-enforcement agency for enforcement of the ABC laws within the law-enforcement agency's territorial jurisdiction. Enforcement agreements may be made with more than one agency at the same time. When such a contract for enforcement exists, the designated officers of the contracting law-enforcement agency shall have the same authority to inspect under G.S. 18B-502 that an ABC officer employed by that local board would have. An agency contracted to provide ABC law enforcement shall designate no more than five officers to conduct inspections pursuant to this section and G.S. 18B-502. If a city located in two or more counties approves the sale of some

type of alcoholic beverage pursuant to the provisions of G.S. 18B-600(e4), and there are no local ABC boards established in the city and one of the counties in which the city is located, the local ABC board of any county in which the city is located may enter into an enforcement agreement with the city's police department for enforcement of the ABC laws within the entire city, including that portion of the city located in the county of the ABC board entering into the enforcement agreement.

(f1) **Accountability; Enforcement Reports.** -- To ensure accountability to the appointing authority and the Commission, every local board's ABC officers and those law enforcement agencies subject to an enforcement agreement entered into pursuant to subsection (f) of this section shall report to the local board, by the fifth business day of each month, on a form developed by the Commission, the following:

(1) The number of arrests made for ABC law, Controlled Substance Act, or other violations, by category, at ABC permitted outlets.

(2) The number of arrests made for ABC law, Controlled Substance Act, or other violations, by category, at other locations.

(3) The number of agencies assisted with ABC law or controlled substance related matters.

(4) The number of alcohol education and responsible server programs presented.

The local board shall submit a copy of the enforcement report to the appointing authority and the Commission not later than five business days after receipt of the enforcement report by the local board. The Commission shall publish this information, by local board and enforcement agency, on a public Internet Web site maintained by the Commission.

(g) **Discharge.** -- Local ABC officers and the designated officers of agencies which contract with local boards for enforcement of the ABC laws are subject to the discharge and ineligibility provisions of G.S. 18B-202.

History.
1949, c. 1251, s. 4; 1961, c. 645; 1963, c. 426, s. 2; 1967, c. 868; 1971, c. 872, s. 1; 1973, c. 29; 1977, c. 908; 1981, c. 412, s. 2; 1993, c. 193, s. 2; 1995, c. 466, ss. 3, 4; 2010-122, ss. 5, 6, 7(a)

§ 18B-502. Inspection of licensed premises

(a) **Authority.** -- To procure evidence of violations of the ABC law, alcohol law-enforcement agents, employees of the Commission, local ABC officers, and officers of local law-enforcement agencies that have contracted to provide ABC enforcement under G.S. 18B-501(f) shall have authority to investigate the operation of each licensed premises for which an ABC permit has been issued, to make inspections that include viewing the entire premises, and to examine the books and records of the permittee. The inspection authorized by this section may be made at any time it reasonably appears that someone is on the premises. Alcohol law-enforcement agents are also authorized to be on the premises to the extent necessary to enforce the provisions of Article 68 of Chapter 143 of the General Statutes. For purposes of this subsection, the phrase "licensed premises for which an ABC permit has been issued" includes a social district authorized under G.S. 18B-904.1 and an extended area authorized under G.S. 18B-904(h).

(b) **Interference with Inspection.** -- Refusal by a permittee or by any employee of a permittee to permit officers to enter the premises to make an inspection authorized by subsection (a) shall be cause for revocation, suspension or other action against the permit of the permittee as provided in G.S. 18B-104. It shall be a Class 2 misdemeanor for any person to resist or obstruct an officer attempting to make a lawful inspection under this section.

History.
1939, c. 158, s. 514; 1943, c. 400, s. 6; 1949, c. 974, ss. 11, 14; c. 1251, s. 4; 1951, c. 1056, s. 1; c. 1186, ss. 1, 2; 1953, c. 1207, ss. 2-4; 1957, c. 1440; 1961, c. 645; 1963, c. 426, ss. 1, 2, 4, 5, 12; 1967, c. 868; 1971, c. 872, s. 1; 1977, c. 70, s. 17; 1981, c. 412, s. 2; 1993, c. 539, s. 313; 1994, Ex. Sess., c. 24, s. 14(c); 1998-212, s. 19.11(f); 2021-150, s. 22.1

§ 18B-503. Disposition of seized alcoholic beverages

(a) **Storage.** -- A law-enforcement officer who seizes alcoholic beverages as evidence of an ABC law violation shall provide for the storage of those alcoholic beverages until the commencement of the trial or administrative hearing relating to the violation, unless some other disposition is authorized under this section.

(b) **Disposition Before Trial.** -- After giving notice to each defendant, to any other known owner, and to the Commission, a judge may order any of the following dispositions of alcoholic beverages seized as evidence of an ABC law violation:

(1) The destruction of any malt beverages except that amount needed for evidence at trial.

(2) The sale of any alcoholic beverages other than malt beverages or nontaxpaid alcoholic beverages, and other than any alcoholic beverages needed for evidence at trial, if the trial is likely to be delayed for more than 90 days, or if the quantity or nature of the alcoholic beverages is such that storage is impractical or unduly expensive.

(3) The destruction of the alcoholic beverages if storage or sale is not practical.

(4) Continued storage of the alcoholic beverages.

(c) **Disposition After Trial.** -- After the criminal charge is resolved, a judge may order the following dispositions of seized alcoholic beverages:

(1) If the owner or possessor of the alcoholic beverages is found guilty of a criminal charge relating to those alcoholic beverages, the judge may order the sale or destruction of any alcoholic beverages that were held until trial.

(2) If the owner or possessor of the alcoholic beverages is found not guilty, or if charges are dismissed or otherwise resolved in favor of the owner or possessor, the judge shall order the alcoholic beverages returned to that owner or possessor, except as provided in subdivision (3).

(3) If the owner or possessor of the alcoholic beverages is found not guilty, or if charges are otherwise resolved in favor of the owner or possessor, but possession of the alcoholic beverages by that owner or possessor would be unlawful, the judge shall order the alcoholic beverages either sold or destroyed.

(4) If ownership of the alcoholic beverages remains uncertain after trial or after the charges have been dismissed, the judge may order the alcoholic beverages held, or the alcoholic beverages sold and the proceeds held, for a specified time, until ownership of the alcoholic beverages can be determined.

(d) **Holding for Administrative Hearings.** -- If alcoholic beverages used as evidence in a criminal proceeding are also needed as evidence at an administrative hearing, a judge shall not order any of the dispositions set out in subsection (c), but shall order the alcoholic beverages held for the administrative hearing and for a determination of final disposition by the Commission. The Commission may, before or after an administrative hearing, order any of the dispositions authorized under subsections (b) and (c). If no related criminal proceeding has commenced, the Commission shall not order sale or destruction of alcoholic beverages until notice has been given to the district attorney for the district where the alcoholic beverages were seized or any violation of ABC laws related to the seizure of the alcoholic beverages is likely to be prosecuted.

(e) **Sale Procedure.** -- The sale of unfortified wine or fortified wine shall be by public auction unless those wines would likely become spoiled

Chapter 18B

or lose value in the time required to arrange a public auction. If spoilage or loss of value is likely, the judge ordering the sale or the Commission may authorize sale at the prevailing wholesale price, as determined by the Commission, to one or more persons holding the appropriate retail wine permits in the county in which the wine was seized, or in a neighboring county if there are no such persons in the county in which the wine was seized. Spirituous liquor may be sold only to the local ABC board serving the city or county in which the liquor was seized, or, if there is no local board for that city or county, to the nearest local board. The sale price shall be at least ten percent (10%) less than the price the local board would pay for the same liquor bought through the State warehouse.

(f) **Sale Proceeds.** -- An agency selling alcoholic beverages seized under the provisions of this Chapter shall keep the proceeds in a separate account until some other disposition is ordered by a judge or the Commission. In a criminal proceeding, if the owner or possessor of the alcoholic beverages is found guilty of a violation relating to seizure of the alcoholic beverages, if the owner or possessor is found not guilty or the charge is dismissed or otherwise resolved in favor of the owner or possessor, but the possession of the alcoholic beverages by that owner or possessor would be unlawful, or if the ownership of the alcoholic beverages cannot be determined, the proceeds from the sale of those alcoholic beverages shall be paid to the school fund of the county in which the alcoholic beverages were seized. If the owner or possessor of alcoholic beverages seized for violation of the ABC laws is found not guilty of criminal charges relating to the seizure of those beverages or the charge is dismissed or otherwise resolved in favor of the owner or possessor, and if possession of the alcoholic beverages by that owner or possessor was lawful when the beverages were seized, the proceeds from the sale of those alcoholic beverages shall be paid to the owner or possessor. The agency making the sale may deduct and retain from the amount to be placed in the county school fund the costs of storing the seized alcoholic beverages and of conducting the sale, but may not deduct those costs from the amount to be turned over to an owner or possessor of the alcoholic beverages.

(g) **Court Action by Owner.** -- Any person who claims any of the following resulting from the seizure of alcoholic beverages may bring an action in the superior court of the county in which the alcoholic beverages were seized:

(1) To be the owner of alcoholic beverages that are wrongfully held.

(2) To be the owner of alcoholic beverages that are needed as evidence in another proceeding.

(3) To be entitled to proceeds from a sale of seized alcoholic beverages.

(4) To be entitled to restitution for alcoholic beverages wrongfully destroyed.

History.
1923, c. 1, s. 12; C.S., s. 3411(l); 1939, c. 12; 1941, c. 310; 1957, c. 1235, s. 3; 1971, c. 872, s. 1; 1981, c. 412, s. 2; 1993, c. 415, s. 5

§ 18B-504. Forfeiture

(a) **Property Subject to Forfeiture.** -- The following kinds of property shall be subject to forfeiture:

(1) Motor vehicles, boats, airplanes, and all other conveyances used to transport nontaxpaid alcoholic beverages in violation of the ABC laws;

(2) Containers for alcoholic beverages which are manufactured, possessed, sold, or transported in violation of the ABC laws; and

(3) Equipment or ingredients used in the manufacture of alcoholic beverages in violation of the ABC laws.

(b) **Exemption for Forfeiture.** -- Property which may be possessed lawfully shall not be subject to forfeiture when it was used unlawfully by someone other than the owner of the property and the owner did not consent to the unlawful use.

(c) **Seizure of Property.** -- If property subject to forfeiture has not already been seized as part of an arrest or search, a law-enforcement officer may apply to a judge for an order authorizing seizure of that property. An order for seizure may be issued only after criminal process has been issued for an ABC law violation in connection with that property. The order shall describe the property to be seized and shall state the facts establishing probable cause to believe that the property is subject to forfeiture.

(d) **Custody until Trial.** -- A law-enforcement officer seizing property subject to forfeiture shall provide for its safe storage until trial. The officer may destroy stills and perishable materials seized under subdivision (a)(3), if storage is impractical and if the absence of the property will not be likely to adversely affect the defendant's right to defend against the charge that is the basis for the forfeiture. If the officer having custody of the property is satisfied that it will be returned at the time of trial, he may return the property to the owner upon receiving a bond for the value of the property, signed by sufficient sureties. If the property is not returned at the time of trial, the full amount of the bond shall be forfeited to the court. Property which it is unlawful to possess may not be returned to the owner.

(e) **Disposition after Trial.** -- The presiding judge in a criminal proceeding for violation of

ABC laws may take the following actions after resolution of a charge against the owner or possessor of property subject to forfeiture under this section:

(1) If the owner or possessor of the property is found guilty of an ABC offense, the judge may order the property forfeited.

(2) If the owner or possessor of the property is found not guilty, or if the charge is dismissed or otherwise resolved in favor of the owner or possessor, the judge shall order the property returned to the owner or possessor.

(3) If ownership of the property remains uncertain after trial, the judge may order the property held for a specified time to determine ownership. If the judge finds that ownership cannot be determined with reasonable effort, the judge shall order the property forfeited.

(4) Regardless of the disposition of the charge, if the property is something that may not be possessed lawfully, the judge shall order it forfeited.

(5) If the property is also needed as evidence at an administrative hearing, the judge shall provide that the order does not go into effect until the Commission determines that the property is no longer needed for the administrative proceeding.

(f) **Disposition of Forfeited Property.** -- A judge ordering forfeiture of property may order any one of the following dispositions:

(1) Sale at public auction;

(2) Sale at auction after notice to certain named individuals or groups, if only a limited number of people would have use for that property;

(3) Delivery to a named State or local law-enforcement agency, if the property is not suited for sale, with preference to be given in the following order, to: the agency that seized the property, the ALE Division, the Commission, the local board of the jurisdiction in which the property was seized, and the Department of Justice; or

(4) Destruction, if possession of the property would be unlawful and it could not be used or is not wanted for law enforcement, or if sale or other disposition is not practical.

(g) **Proceeds of Sale.** -- If forfeited property is sold, the proceeds of that sale shall be paid to the school fund of the county in which the property was seized, except as provided in subsection (h). Before placing the proceeds in the school fund the agency making the sale may deduct and retain the costs of storing the property and conducting the sale.

(h) **Innocent Parties.** -- At any time before forfeiture is ordered, an owner of seized property or a holder of a security interest in seized property, other than the defendant, may apply to protect his interest in the property. The application may be made to any judge who has jurisdiction to try the offense with which the property is associated. If the judge finds that the property owner or holder of a security interest did not consent to the unlawful use of the property, and that the property may be possessed lawfully by the owner or holder, the judge may order:

(1) That the property be returned to the owner, if it is not needed as evidence at trial;

(2) That the property be returned to the owner following trial or other resolution of the case; or

(3) That, if the property is sold following trial, a specified sum be paid from the proceeds of that sale to the holder of the security interest.

(i) **Defendant Unavailable.** -- When property is seized for forfeiture, but the owner is unknown, the district attorney may seek forfeiture under this section by an action in rem against the property. If the owner is known and has been charged with an offense, but is unavailable for trial, the district attorney may seek forfeiture either by an action in rem against the property or by motion in the criminal action.

(j) **When No Charge is Made.** -- Any owner of property seized for forfeiture may apply to a judge to have the property returned to him if no criminal charge has been made in connection with that property within a reasonable time after seizure. The judge may not order the return of the property if possession by the owner would be unlawful.

History.
1923, c. 1, s. 6; C.S., s. 3411(f); 1927, c. 18; 1945, c. 635; 1951, c. 850; 1955, c. 560; 1957, c. 1235, s. 1; 1969, c. 789; 1971, c. 872, s. 1; 1977, c. 854, s. 2; 1981, c. 412, s. 2; c. 747, s. 48; 1993, c. 415, s. 6; 2011-145, s. 19.1(q); 2014-100, s. 17.1(xxx); 2019-203, s. 9(a)

§ 18B-505. Restitution

When a person is convicted of a violation of the ABC laws, the court may order him to make restitution to any law-enforcement agency for reasonable expenditures made in purchasing alcoholic beverages from him or his agent as part of an investigation leading to his conviction.

History.
1981, c. 412, s. 2

ARTICLE 8
OPERATION OF ABC STORES

§ 18B-800. Sale of alcoholic beverages in ABC stores

(a) **Spirituous Liquor.** -- Except as provided in Articles 10 and 11 of this Chapter, spirituous liquor may be sold only in ABC stores operated by local boards. For purposes of this subsection, the term "sold only in ABC stores operated by local boards" includes online orders placed in accordance with subsection (c3) of this section.

(b) **Fortified Wine.** -- In addition to spirituous liquor, ABC stores may sell fortified wine. ABC stores may also sell wine products, irrespective of alcohol content by volume, which were classified as fortified wine by the ABC Commission prior to July 7, 2004.

(c) **Commission Approval.** -- No ABC store may sell any alcoholic beverage which has not been approved by the Commission for sale in this State.

(c1) **Special Orders of Special Items.** -- Through the process established by rule of the Commission for special orders of spirituous liquor that are on the special item list approved by the Commission, ABC stores shall allow the purchase of individual bottles of spirituous liquor. ABC stores may sell in store any bottles it receives from a special item case in excess of what was purchased by the requesting customer. Bottles purchased pursuant to this subsection may be affixed with personalized labeling by the manufacturer, distiller, broker, or supplier of spirituous liquor. The personalized labeling shall comply with any other labeling requirements set by law. The personalized labeling shall not cover any portion of the manufacturer's original label. For purposes of this subsection, the term "personalized labeling" means the inclusion of any of the following on the label:

(1) The name of the purchaser of the bottle or the name of any individual, business entity, club, ABC Board, or ABC store on whose behalf the bottle is purchased.

(2) "Bottled for," "distilled for," "in honor of," or other similar language.

(3) Dates, locations, occasions, and other similar information.

(c2) **Orders of Eligible Distillery Products by Mixed Beverages Permittees.** -- A local board shall fulfill an order by a mixed beverages permittee for individual bottles or cases of spirituous liquor produced by an eligible distillery that are listed as a regular code item for sale in the State. If a local board cannot fulfill an order of a mixed beverages permittee for individual bottles or cases of spirituous liquor produced by an eligible distillery that are listed as a regular code item for sale in the State because the product ordered is not in the local board's stock inventory or the order cannot otherwise be fulfilled within the time period requested by the permittee, the local board shall notify the Commission within 48 hours of the request for the order and request authorization

for direct shipment. The Commission shall then determine if the eligible distillery desires to directly ship the ordered product directly to the local board, and if so the Commission shall authorize the eligible distillery to ship the spirituous liquor ordered to the local board for the fulfillment of the mixed beverages permittee's order. Merchandise authorized to be shipped by direct shipment under this subsection shall be consigned by the State ABC warehouse to the distiller's account in care of the local board. The local board shall acknowledge receipt of the merchandise on the shipping documents and forward them to the State ABC warehouse for processing through the accounting system as though the merchandise were shipped from the State ABC warehouse. As used in this subsection, an "eligible distillery" is a distillery (i) that sells, to consumers at the distillery, to exporters, to local boards, and to private or public agencies or establishments of other states or nations, fewer than 10,000 proof gallons of in-house brand spirituous liquors distilled or produced and manufactured by it at the permit holder's distillery per year, and (ii) that is either the holder of a distillery permit pursuant to G.S. 18B-1105 or is a business located outside the State that is licensed or permitted to manufacture spirituous liquor in the jurisdiction where the business is located and whose products are lawfully sold in this State.

(c3) **Online Orders.** -- An ABC store may accept an online order, including payment, for alcoholic beverages sold in its store. An order placed online pursuant to this subsection shall be picked up in person at the store by the individual who placed the order. An order placed online pursuant to this subsection shall include the name and unique identifier number of the individual placing the order, who shall be at least 21 years of age as shown on the form of identification authorized pursuant to G.S. 18B-302(d)(1) and otherwise legally authorized to purchase alcoholic beverages. An employee of the ABC store shall confirm that the online order is picked up in person at the store by the individual who placed the order by verifying the individual's identification that conforms to the identifying information contained in the online order.

(c4) **Refrigerated Beverages.** -- ABC stores may sell alcoholic beverages authorized for sale under this section in a refrigerated unit. For purposes of this subsection, the term "refrigerated unit" means a refrigerated merchandiser or other appliance that is artificially kept cool and suitable to be used to store food and drink.

(d) Expired.

(e) Each ABC store shall display spirits which are distilled or produced in North Carolina in an area dedicated solely to North Carolina products.

History.
1981, c. 412, s. 2; 1985, c. 59, s. 1; 1989, c. 800, s. 21;
2004-135, s. 4; 2010-31, s. 14.12(a); 2015-98, s. 4(f);
2017-87, s. 1(c); 2019-182, s. 3(a); 2021-117, s. 12(a);
2021-150, ss. 1.1, 1.2, 2.1, 15.1

ARTICLE 10
RETAIL ACTIVITY

§ 18B-1000. Definitions concerning establishments

The following requirements and definitions shall apply to this Chapter:

(1) **Community theatre.** -- An establishment owned and operated by a bona fide nonprofit organization that is engaged solely in the business of sponsoring or presenting amateur or professional theatrical events to the public. A permit issued for a community theatre is valid only during regularly scheduled theatrical events sponsored by such nonprofit organization.

(1a) **Congressionally chartered veterans organizations.** -- An establishment that is organized as a federally chartered, nonprofit veterans organization, and is operated solely for patriotic or fraternal purposes.

(1b) **Convention center.** -- An establishment that meets either of the following requirements:

a. A publicly owned or operated establishment that is engaged in the business of sponsoring or hosting conventions and similar large gatherings, including auditoriums, armories, civic centers, convention centers, and coliseums.

b. A privately owned facility located in a city that has a population of at least 200,000 but not more than 250,000 by the 2000 federal census and is located in a county that has previously authorized the issuance of mixed beverage permits by referendum. To qualify as a convention center under this subdivision, the facility shall meet each of the following requirements:

1. The facility shall be certified by the appropriate local official as being consistent with the city's redevelopment plan for the area in which the facility is located.

2. The facility shall contain at least 7,500 square feet of floor space that is available for public use and shall be used exclusively for banquets, receptions, meetings, and similar gatherings.

3. The facility's annual gross receipts from the sale of alcoholic beverages shall be less than fifty percent (50%) of the gross receipts paid to all providers at permitted functions for food, nonalcoholic beverages, alcoholic beverages, service, and facility usage fees (excluding receipts or charges for entertainment and ancillary services not directly related to providing food and beverage service). The person to whom a permit has been issued for a privately owned facility shall be required to maintain copies of all contracts and invoices for items supplied by providers for a period of three years from the date of the event.

A permit issued for a convention center shall be valid only for those parts of the building used for conventions, banquets, receptions, and other events, and only during scheduled activities.

(1c) **Cooking school.** -- An establishment substantially engaged in the business of operating a school in which cooking techniques are taught for a fee.

(2) **Eating establishment.** -- An establishment engaged in the business of regularly and customarily selling food, primarily to be eaten on the premises. Eating establishments shall include businesses that are referred to as restaurants, cafeterias, or cafes, but that do not qualify under subdivision (6) [of this section]. Eating establishments shall also include lunchstands, grills, snack bars, fast-food businesses, and other establishments, such as drugstores, which have a lunch counter or other section where food is sold to be eaten on the premises.

(3) **Food business.** -- An establishment engaged in the business of regularly and customarily selling food, primarily to be eaten off the premises. Food businesses shall include grocery stores, convenience stores, and other establishments, such as variety stores or drugstores, where food is regularly sold, and shall also include establishments engaged primarily in selling unfortified or fortified wine or both, for consumption off the premises.

(4) **Hotel.** -- An establishment substantially engaged in the business of furnishing lodging. A hotel shall have a restaurant either on or closely associated with the premises. The restaurant and hotel need not be owned or operated by the same person.

(4a) **Multi-tenant establishment.** -- A building or structure, or multiple buildings and structures on the same property,

Chapter 18B

or within the same planned development project that may be subject to a common declaration of restrictive covenants administered by a common property owners' association, and under common ownership, control or property owners' association governance, that contain or contains multiple businesses that sell food, goods, services, or a combination of food, goods, and services, and that include or are connected by common areas. For purposes of this Chapter, "common areas" shall include portions of a building or structure and outdoor areas that are used jointly by multiple businesses on a property or within a planned development project, whether such areas are under common ownership or are subject to cross-access easements for use by multiple businesses. A shopping mall is not a multi-tenant establishment if more than fifty percent (50%) of the shopping mall's common areas, measured in acreage or square footage, are enclosed and air-conditioned. Any outdoor common area not used as a parking field that is associated with a shopping mall shall be deemed appropriate for a Common Area Entertainment Permit as allowed in this Chapter.

(4e) **Private bar.** -- An establishment that is organized and operated as a for-profit entity and that is not open to the general public but is open only to the members of the organization and their bona fide guests for the purpose of allowing its members and their guests to socialize and engage in recreation.

(5) **Private club.** -- An establishment that qualifies under Section 501(c) of the Internal Revenue Code, as amended, 26 U.S.C. § 501(c), and that has been in operation for a minimum of 12 months prior to application for an ABC permit.

(5a) **Qualified facility.** -- A facility that has any of the following permits:

a. On-premises malt beverage.
b. On-premises unfortified wine.
c. On-premises fortified wine.
d. Mixed beverages.

(5b) **Residential private club.** -- A private club that is located in a privately owned, primarily residential and recreational development.

(6) **Restaurant.** -- An establishment substantially engaged in the business of preparing and serving meals. To qualify as a restaurant, an establishment's gross receipts from food and nonalcoholic beverages shall be not less than thirty percent (30%) of the total gross receipts from food, nonalcoholic beverages, and alcoholic beverages sold for on-premises consumption. A restaurant shall also have a kitchen and an inside dining area with seating for at least 36 people. If the restaurant is located on an 18-hole golf course, the premises shall include the parking lot and the playing area of the golf course, including the teeing areas, greens, fairways, roughs, hazards, and cart paths.

(7) **Retail business.** -- An establishment engaged in any retail business, regardless of whether food is sold on the premises.

(7a) **Sports and entertainment venue.** -- Stadiums, ballparks, and other similar facilities with a permanently constructed seating capacity of 3,000 or more which are not located on the campus of a school, college, or university.

(8) **Sports club.** -- An establishment that meets either of the following requirements:

a. The establishment is substantially engaged in the business of providing equine boarding, training, and coaching services, and the establishment offers on-site dining, lodging, and meeting facilities and hosts horse trials and other events sanctioned or endorsed by the United States Equestrian Federation, Inc.; or

b. The establishment is substantially engaged in the business of providing an 18-hole golf course, two or more tennis courts, or both.

The sports club can either be open to the general public or to members and their guests. To qualify as a sports club, an establishment's gross receipts for club activities shall be greater than its gross receipts for alcoholic beverages. The premises of a sports club substantially engaged in the business of providing an 18-hole golf course shall include the parking lot and the playing area of the golf course, including the teeing areas, greens, fairways, roughs, hazards, and cart paths. This provision does not prohibit a sports club from operating a restaurant. Receipts for food shall be included in with the club activity fee.

(9) Recodified as subdivision (1a) by Session Laws 2019-177, s. 4.1.

(10) **Wine producer.** -- A farming establishment of at least five acres committed to the production of grapes, berries, or other fruits for the manufacture of unfortified wine.

History.
1905, c. 498, ss. 6-8; Rev., ss. 3526, 3534; C.S., s. 3371; 1937, c. 49, ss. 12, 16, 22; c. 411; 1955, c. 999; 1967, c. 222, ss. 1, 8; c. 1256, s. 3; 1969, c. 1018; 1971, c. 872, s. 1; 1973, c. 1226; 1977, c. 176, s. 1; 1981, c. 412, s. 2; 1981 (Reg. Sess., 1982), c. 1262, s. 15; 1983, c. 583,

s. 1; c. 896, s. 5; 1987, c. 307, s. 1; c. 391, s. 1; 1993, c. 415, ss. 14, 15; 1993 (Reg. Sess., 1994), c. 579, s. 1; 1995, c. 466, s. 8; c. 509, s. 15; 2001-262, s. 7; 2001-487, s. 49(d); 2002-188, s. 1; 2003-135, s. 1; 2009-539, s. 4; 2013-392, s. 2; 2018-100, s. 4(a); 2019-13, s. 3; 2019-49, s. 5; 2019-177, s. 4.1; 2019-182, s. 19(a); 2021-150, s. 17.1

§ 18B-1001. Kinds of ABC permits; places eligible

When the issuance of the permit is lawful in the jurisdiction in which the premises are located, the Commission may issue the following kinds of permits:

(1) **On-Premises Malt Beverage Permit.** -- An on-premises malt beverage permit authorizes (i) the retail sale of malt beverages for consumption on the premises, (ii) the retail sale of malt beverages in the manufacturer's original container for consumption off the premises, and (iii) the retail sale of malt beverages in a cleaned and sanitized container that is filled or refilled and sealed for consumption off the premises and that identifies the permittee and the date the container was filled or refilled. The permit also authorizes the permittee to transfer malt beverages, not more than four times per calendar year, to another on-premises malt beverage permittee that is under common ownership or control as the transferor. Except as authorized by this subdivision, transfers of malt beverages by on-premises malt beverage permittees, purchases of malt beverages by a retail permittee from another retail permittee for the purpose of resale, and sales of malt beverages by a retail permittee to another retail permittee for the purpose of resale are unlawful. In addition, a particular brand of malt beverages may be transferred only if both the transferor and transferee are located within the territory designated between the brewery and the wholesaler on file with the Commission. Prior to or contemporaneous with any such transfer, the transferor shall notify each wholesaler who distributes the transferred product of the transfer. The notice shall be in writing or verifiable electronic format and shall identify the transferor and transferee, the date of the transfer, quantity, and items transferred. It also authorizes the holder of the permit to ship malt beverages in closed containers to individual purchasers inside and outside the State. The permit may be issued for any of the following:

   a. Restaurants.
   b. Hotels.
   c. Eating establishments.
   d. Food businesses.
   e. Retail businesses.
   f. Private clubs.
   g. Convention centers.
   h. Community theatres.
   i. Breweries as authorized by subdivisions (7) and (8) of G.S. 18B-1104(a).
   j. Sports and entertainment venues.
   k. Private bars.
   l. The holder of a distillery permit authorized under G.S. 18B-1105.

(2) **Off-Premises Malt Beverage Permit.** -- An off-premises malt beverage permit authorizes (i) the retail sale of malt beverages in the manufacturer's original container for consumption off the premises, (ii) the retail sale of malt beverages in a cleaned and sanitized container that is filled or refilled and sealed for consumption off the premises and that identifies the permittee and the date the container was filled or refilled, and (iii) the holder of the permit to ship malt beverages in closed containers to individual purchasers inside and outside the State. The permit also authorizes the permittee to transfer malt beverages, not more than four times per calendar year, to another off-premises malt beverage permittee that is under common ownership or control as the transferor. Except as authorized by this subdivision, transfers of malt beverages by off-premises malt beverage permittees, purchases of malt beverages by a retail permittee from another retail permittee for the purpose of resale, and sales of malt beverages by a retail permittee to another retail permittee for the purpose of resale are unlawful. In addition, a particular brand of malt beverages may be transferred only if both the transferor and transferee are located within the territory designated between the brewery and the wholesaler on file with the Commission. Prior to or contemporaneous with any such transfer, the transferor shall notify each wholesaler who distributes the transferred product of the transfer. The notice shall be in writing or verifiable electronic format and shall identify the transferor and transferee, the date of the transfer, quantity, and items transferred. The permit may be issued for any of the following:

   a. Restaurants.
   b. Hotels.
   c. Eating establishments.
   d. Food businesses.
   e. Retail businesses.
   f. The holder of a brewing, distillation, and fermentation course authorization under G.S. 18B-1114.6. A school obtaining a permit under this subdivision is authorized to sell malt beverages manufactured during its brewing,

Chapter 18B

distillation, and fermentation program at one noncampus location in a county where the permittee holds and offers classes on a regular full-time basis in a facility owned by the permittee.

(3) **On-Premises Unfortified Wine Permit.** -- An on-premises unfortified wine permit authorizes (i) the retail sale of unfortified wine for consumption on the premises, either alone or mixed with other beverages, (ii) the retail sale of unfortified wine in the manufacturer's original container for consumption off the premises, and (iii) the retail sale of unfortified wine dispensed from a tap connected to a pressurized container utilizing carbon dioxide or similar gas into a cleaned and sanitized container that is filled or refilled and sealed for consumption off the premises and that identifies the permittee and the date the container was filled or refilled. The permit also authorizes the permittee to transfer unfortified wine, not more than four times per calendar year, to another on-premises unfortified wine permittee that is under common ownership or control as the transferor. Except as authorized by this subdivision, transfers of wine by on-premises unfortified wine permittees, purchases of wine by a retail permittee from another retail permittee for the purpose of resale, and sale of wine by a retail permittee to another retail permittee for the purpose of resale are unlawful. In addition, a particular brand of wine may be transferred only if both the transferor and transferee are located within the territory designated between the winery and the wholesaler on file with the Commission. Prior to or contemporaneous with any such transfer, the transferor shall notify each wholesaler who distributes the transferred product of the transfer. The notice shall be in writing or verifiable electronic format and shall identify the transferor and transferee, the date of the transfer, quantity, and items transferred. The holder of the permit is authorized to ship unfortified wine in closed containers to individual purchasers inside and outside the State. Orders received by a winery by telephone, Internet, mail, facsimile, or other off-premises means of communication shall be shipped pursuant to a wine shipper permit and not pursuant to this subdivision. The permit may be issued for any of the following:

    a. Restaurants.
    b. Hotels.
    c. Eating establishments.
    d. Private clubs.
    e. Convention centers.
    f. Cooking schools.

    g. Community theatres.
    h. Wineries.
    i. Wine producers.
    j. Retail businesses.
    k. Sports and entertainment venues.
    l. Private bars.
    m. The holder of a distillery permit authorized under G.S. 18B-1105.

(4) **Off-Premises Unfortified Wine Permit.** -- An off-premises unfortified wine permit authorizes (i) the retail sale of unfortified wine in the manufacturer's original container for consumption off the premises, (ii) the retail sale of unfortified wine dispensed from a tap connected to a pressurized container utilizing carbon dioxide or similar gas into a cleaned and sanitized container that is filled or refilled and sealed for consumption off the premises and that identifies the permittee and the date the container was filled or refilled, and (iii) the holder of the permit to ship unfortified wine in closed containers to individual purchasers inside and outside the State. The permit may be issued for retail businesses. The permit also authorizes the permittee to transfer unfortified wine, not more than four times per calendar year, to another off-premises unfortified wine permittee that is under common ownership or control as the transferor. Except as authorized by this subdivision, transfers of wine by off-premises unfortified wine permittees, purchases of wine by a retail permittee from another retail permittee for the purpose of resale, and sale of wine by a retail permittee to another retail permittee for the purpose of resale are unlawful. In addition, a particular brand of wine may be transferred only if both the transferor and transferee are located within the territory designated between the winery and the wholesaler on file with the Commission. Prior to or contemporaneous with any such transfer, the transferor shall notify each wholesaler who distributes the transferred product of the transfer. The notice shall be in writing or verifiable electronic format and shall identify the transferor and transferee, the date of the transfer, quantity, and items transferred. The permit may also be issued to the holder of a viticulture/enology course authorization under G.S. 18B-1114.4. A school obtaining a permit under this subdivision is authorized to sell wines manufactured during its viticulture/enology program at one non-campus location in a county where the permittee holds and offers classes on a regular full-time basis in a facility owned by the permittee. The permit may also be issued for a winery or a wine producer for sale of its own unfortified

Chapter 18B

wine during hours when the winery or wine producer's premises is open to the public, subject to any local ordinance adopted pursuant to G.S. 18B-1004(d) concerning hours for the retail sale of unfortified wine. A winery obtaining a permit under this subdivision is authorized to sell wine manufactured by the winery at one additional location in the county under the same conditions specified in G.S. 18B-1101(5) for the sale of wine at the winery; provided, however, that no other alcohol sales shall be authorized at the additional location. Orders received by a winery by telephone, Internet, mail, facsimile, or other off-premises means of communication shall be shipped pursuant to a wine shipper permit and not pursuant to this subdivision.

(5) **On-Premises Fortified Wine Permit.** -- An on-premises fortified wine permit authorizes the retail sale of fortified wine for consumption on the premises, either alone or mixed with other beverages, and the retail sale of fortified wine in the manufacturer's original container for consumption off the premises. The permit also authorizes the permittee to transfer fortified wine, not more than four times per calendar year, to another on-premises fortified wine permittee that is under common ownership or control as the transferor. Except as authorized by this subdivision, transfers of wine by on-premises fortified wine permittees, purchases of wine by a retail permittee from another retail permittee for the purpose of resale, and sale of wine by a retail permittee to another retail permittee for the purpose of resale are unlawful. In addition, a particular brand of wine may be transferred only if both the transferor and transferee are located within the territory designated between the winery and the wholesaler on file with the Commission. Prior to or contemporaneous with any such transfer, the transferor shall notify each wholesaler who distributes the transferred product of the transfer. The notice shall be in writing or verifiable electronic format and shall identify the transferor and transferee, the date of the transfer, quantity, and items transferred. The holder of the permit is authorized to ship fortified wine in closed containers to individual purchasers inside and outside the State. Orders received by a winery by telephone, Internet, mail, facsimile, or other off-premises means of communication shall be shipped pursuant to a wine shipper permit and not pursuant to this subdivision. The permit may be issued for any of the following:

    a. Restaurants.
    b. Hotels.
    c. Private clubs.

    d. Community theatres.
    e. Wineries.
    f. Convention centers.
    g. Private bars.
    h. The holder of a distillery permit authorized under G.S. 18B-1105.
    i. Sports and entertainment venues.

(6) **Off-Premises Fortified Wine Permit.** -- An off-premises fortified wine permit authorizes the retail sale of fortified wine in the manufacturer's original container for consumption off the premises and it authorizes the holder of the permit to ship fortified wine in closed containers to individual purchasers inside and outside the State. The permit may be issued for food businesses. The permit may also be issued for a winery for sale of its own fortified wine. Orders received by a winery by telephone, Internet, mail, facsimile, or other off-premises means of communication shall be shipped pursuant to a wine shipper permit and not pursuant to this subdivision. The permit also authorizes the permittee to transfer fortified wine, not more than four times per calendar year, to another off-premises fortified wine permittee that is under common ownership or control as the transferor. Except as authorized by this subdivision, transfers of wine by off-premises fortified wine permittees, purchases of wine by a retail permittee from another retail permittee for the purpose of resale, and sale of wine by a retail permittee to another retail permittee for the purpose of resale are unlawful. In addition, a particular brand of wine may be transferred only if both the transferor and transferee are located within the territory designated between the winery and the wholesaler on file with the Commission. Prior to or contemporaneous with any such transfer, the transferor shall notify each wholesaler who distributes the transferred product of the transfer. The notice shall be in writing or verifiable electronic format and shall identify the transferor and transferee, the date of the transfer, quantity, and items transferred.

(7) **Brown-Bagging Permit.** -- A brown-bagging permit authorizes each individual patron of an establishment, with the permission of the permittee, to bring up to eight liters of fortified wine or spirituous liquor, or eight liters of the two combined, onto the premises and to consume those alcoholic beverages on the premises. The permit may be issued for any of the following:

    a. Restaurants.
    b. Hotels.
    c. Private clubs.
    d. Community theatres.

e. Congressionally chartered veterans organizations.

f. Private bars.

(8) **Special Occasion Permit.** -- A special occasion permit authorizes the host of a reception, party or other special occasion, with the permission of the permittee, to bring fortified wine and spirituous liquor onto the premises of the business and to serve the same to his guests. The permit may be issued for any of the following:

a. Restaurants.

b. Hotels.

c. Eating establishments.

d. Private clubs.

e. Convention centers.

f. Private bars.

g. Sports and entertainment venues.

(9) **Limited Special Occasion Permit.** -- A limited special occasion permit authorizes the permittee to bring fortified wine and spirituous liquor onto the premises of a business, with the permission of the owner of that property, and to serve those alcoholic beverages to the permittee's guests at a reception, party, or other special occasion being held there. The permit may be issued to any individual other than the owner or possessor of the premises. An applicant for a limited special occasion permit shall have the written permission of the owner or possessor of the property on which the special occasion is to be held.

(10) **Mixed Beverages Permit.** -- A mixed beverages permit authorizes the retail sale of mixed beverages for consumption on the premises. The permit also authorizes a mixed beverages permittee (i) to obtain a purchase-transportation permit under G.S. 18B-403 and 18B-404, (ii) to obtain an antique spirituous liquor permit under subdivision (20) of this section, and (iii) to use for culinary purposes spirituous liquor lawfully purchased for use in mixed beverages. The permit may be issued for any of the following:

a. Restaurants.

b. Hotels.

c. Private clubs.

d. Convention centers.

e. Community theatres.

f. Nonprofit organizations.

g. Political organizations.

h. Sports and entertainment venues.

i. Private bars.

j. The holder of a distillery permit authorized under G.S. 18B-1105.

(11) **Culinary Permit.** -- A culinary permit authorizes a permittee to possess up to 12 liters of either fortified wine or spirituous liquor, or 12 liters of the two combined, in the kitchen of a business and to use those alcoholic beverages for culinary purposes. The permit may be issued for either of the following:

a. Restaurants;

b. Hotels;

c. Cooking schools.

A culinary permit may also be issued to a catering service to allow the possession of the amount of fortified wine and spirituous liquor stated above at the business location of that service and at the cooking site. The permit shall also authorize the caterer to transport those alcoholic beverages to and from the business location and the cooking site, and use them in cooking.

(12) **Mixed Beverages Catering Permit.** -- A mixed beverages catering permit authorizes a hotel or a restaurant that has a mixed beverages permit to bring spirituous liquor onto the premises where the hotel or restaurant is catering food for an event and to serve the liquor to guests at the event.

(13) **Guest Room Cabinet Permit.** -- A guest room cabinet permit authorizes a guest room cabinet permittee to sell to its room guests, from securely locked cabinets, malt beverages, unfortified wine, fortified wine, and spirituous liquor. A permittee shall designate and maintain at least ten percent (10%) of the permittee's guest rooms as rooms that do not have a guest room cabinet. A permittee may dispense alcoholic beverages from a guest room cabinet only in accordance with written policies and procedures filed with and approved by the Commission. A permittee shall provide a reasonable number of vending machines, coolers, or similar machines on premises for the sale of soft drinks to hotel guests.

A guest room cabinet permit may be issued to any of the following:

a. A hotel (i) holding a mixed beverages permit and (ii) located in a county subject to G.S. 18B-600(f).

b. A hotel (i) holding a mixed beverages permit and (ii) located in a county that has a population in excess of 150,000 by the last federal census.

c. A private club (i) holding a mixed beverages permit, (ii) having management contracts for the rental of living units, and (iii) located in a county defined in G.S. 18B-101(13a)b.2.

d. An 18-hole golf course (i) holding a mixed beverages permit or located in a county where ABC stores have heretofore been established but in which the sale of mixed beverages has not been approved, (ii) having management contracts for the rental of living units, and (iii) located in a county that has a population in excess of 20,000 people by the last federal census.

(14) **Brew on Premises Permit. --** A permit may be issued to a business, located in a jurisdiction where the sale of malt beverages is allowed, where individual customers who are 21 years old or older may purchase ingredients and rent the equipment, time, and space to brew malt beverages for personal use in amounts set forth in 27 C.F.R. § 25.205. The customer must do all of the following:

a. Select a recipe and kettle.

b. Weigh out the proper ingredients and add them to the kettle.

c. Transfer the wort to the fermenter.

d. Add the yeast.

e. Place the ingredients in a fermentation room.

f. Filter, carbonate, and bottle the malt beverage.

A permittee may transfer the ingredients from the fermentation room to the cold room and may assist the customer in all the steps involved in brewing a malt beverage except adding the yeast. A malt beverage produced under this subdivision may not contain more than six percent (6%) alcohol by volume.

(15) **Wine-Tasting Permit. --** A wine-tasting permit authorizes wine tastings on a premises holding a retail permit, by the retail permit holder or his employee. A wine tasting consists of the offering of a sample of one or more unfortified wine products, in amounts of no more than one ounce for each sample, without charge, to customers of the business. Any person pouring wine at a wine tasting shall be at least 21 years of age.

a. Representatives of the winery, which produced the wine, the wine producer, a wholesaler, or a wholesaler's employee may assist with the tasting. Assisting with a wine tasting includes:

1. Pouring samples for customers.

2. Checking the identification of patrons being served at the wine tasting.

b. When a representative of the winery that produced the wine, the wine producer, a wine wholesaler, or a wine wholesaler's employee assists in a wine tasting conducted by a retail permit holder:

1. The retail permit holder shall designate an employee to actively supervise the wine tasting.

2. A retail permit holder's employee shall not supervise more than three wine-tasting areas.

3. No more than six wines may be tasted at any one tasting area.

4. The wine tasting shall not last longer than four hours from the time designated as the starting time by the retail permit holder.

c. The retail permit holder shall be solely liable for any violations of this Chapter occurring in connection with the wine tasting. The Commission shall adopt rules to assure that the tastings are limited to samplings and not a subterfuge for the unlawful sale or distribution of wine, and that the tastings are not used by industry members for unlawful inducements to retail permit holders. Except for purposes of this subsection, the holder of a wine-tasting permit shall not be construed to hold a permit for the on-premises sale or consumption of alcoholic beverages. Any food business is eligible for a wine-tasting permit.

(16) **Wine Shop Permit. --** A wine shop permit authorizes (i) the retail sale of malt beverages, unfortified wine, and fortified wine in the manufacturer's original container for consumption off the premises, (ii) the retail sale of malt beverages or unfortified wine dispensed from a tap connected to a pressurized container utilizing carbon dioxide or similar gas in a cleaned and sanitized container that is filled or refilled and sealed for consumption off the premises and that identifies the permittee and the date the container was filled or refilled, and (iii) wine tastings on the premises conducted and supervised by the permittee in accordance with subdivision (15) of this section. It also authorizes the holder of the permit to ship malt beverages, unfortified wine, and fortified wine in closed containers to individual purchasers inside and outside the State. The permit may be issued for retail businesses whose primary purpose is selling malt beverages and wine for consumption off the premises and

regularly and customarily educating consumers through tastings, classes, and seminars about the selection, serving, and storing of wine. The holder of the permit is authorized to sell unfortified wine for consumption on the premises, provided that the sale of wine for consumption on the premises does not exceed forty percent (40%) of the establishment's total sales for any 30-day period. The holder of a wine-tasting permit not engaged in the preparation or sale of food on the premises is not subject to Part 6 of Article 8 of Chapter 130A of the General Statutes.

(17) **Winemaking on Premises Permit.** -- A permit may be issued to a business, located in a jurisdiction where the sale of unfortified wine is allowed, where individual customers who are 21 years old or older may purchase ingredients and rent the equipment, time, and space to make unfortified wine for personal use in amounts set forth in 27 C.F.R. § 24.75. Except for wine produced for testing equipment or recipes and samples pursuant to this subdivision, the permit holder shall not engage in the actual production or manufacture of wine. Samples may be consumed on the premises only by a person who has a nonrefundable contract to ferment at the premises, and the samples may not exceed one ounce per sample. All wine produced at a winemaking on premises facility shall be removed from the premises by the customer and may only be used for home consumption and the personal use of the customer.

(18) **Malt Beverage Tasting Permit.** -- A malt beverage tasting permit authorizes malt beverage tastings on a premises holding a retail permit by the retail permit holder or his employee. A representative of the brewery whose beverages are being featured at the tasting shall be present at the tasting unless the wholesaler or a wholesaler's employee determines that no representative of the brewery needs to be present. A malt beverage tasting consists of the offering of a sample of one or more malt beverage products, in amounts of no more than two ounces for each sample, without charge, to customers of the business. Any persons pouring malt beverage at a malt beverage tasting shall be at least 21 years of age.

a. Representatives of the brewery which produced the malt beverage, a wholesaler, or a wholesaler's employee may assist with the tasting. Assisting with a malt beverage tasting includes:

1. Pouring samples for customers.

2. Checking the identification of patrons being served at the malt beverage tasting.

b. When a representative of the brewery that produced the malt beverage, a malt beverage wholesaler, or a malt beverage wholesaler's employee assists in a malt beverage tasting conducted by a retail permit holder:

1. The retail permit holder shall designate an employee to actively supervise the malt beverage tasting.

2. A retail permit holder's employee shall not supervise more than three malt beverage tasting areas.

3. No more than four malt beverages may be tasted at any one tasting area.

4. The malt beverage tasting shall not last longer than four hours from the time designated as the starting time by the retail permit holder.

c. The retail permit holder shall be solely liable for any violations of this Chapter occurring in connection with the malt beverage tasting. The Commission shall adopt rules to assure that the tastings are limited to samplings and not a subterfuge for the unlawful sale or distribution of malt beverages, and that the tastings are not used by industry members for unlawful inducements to retail permit holders. Except for purposes of this subdivision, the holder of a malt beverage tasting permit shall not be construed to hold a permit for the on-premises sale or consumption of alcoholic beverages. Any food business is eligible for a malt beverage tasting permit.

(19) **Spirituous liquor tasting permit.** -- The holder of any distillery permit authorized by G.S. 18B-1105 may conduct a consumer tasting event on the premises of the distillery subject to the following conditions:

a. Any person pouring spirituous liquor at a tasting shall be an employee of the distillery and at least 21 years of age.

b. The person pouring the spirituous liquor shall be responsible for checking the identification of patrons being served at the tasting.

c. Each consumer is limited to tasting samples of 0.25 ounce of each spirituous liquor which total no more than 1.5 ounces of spirituous liquor in any calendar day.

d. The consumer shall not be charged for any spirituous liquor tasting sample.

e. The spirituous liquor used in the consumer tasting event shall be distilled or produced at the distillery where the event is being held by the permit holder conducting the event.

f. A consumer tasting event shall not be allowed when the sale of spirituous liquor is otherwise prohibited.

g. Tasting samples are not to be offered to, or allowed to be consumed by, any person under the legal age for consuming spirituous liquor.

h. Consumer tasting events authorized under this subdivision may be conducted on any part of the licensed premises of the distillery, except as prohibited by federal law.

The distillery permit holder shall be solely liable for any violations of this Chapter occurring in connection with the tasting. The Commission shall adopt rules to assure that the tastings are limited to samplings and not a subterfuge for the unlawful sale or distribution of spirituous liquor and that the tastings are not used by industry members for unlawful inducements to retail permit holders.

(20) **Antique spirituous liquor permit.** -- A permit under this subdivision may be issued to a holder of a mixed beverages permit issued under subdivision (10) of this section. Notwithstanding any law to the contrary, the permit holder may sell at retail antique spirituous liquor for use in mixed beverages for consumption on premises. The acquisition of antique spirituous liquor on or after September 1, 2015, shall be in accordance with the process established by rule of the Commission for special orders of spirituous liquor that is not on the list approved by the Commission.

(21) **Common Area Entertainment Permit.** -- A permit under this subdivision may be issued to the owner or property owners' association of a multi-tenant establishment that has at least two tenants that hold a permit issued under subdivision (1), (3), (5), or (10) of this section. A common area entertainment permit authorizes a customer of a multi-tenant establishment tenant holding a permit issued under subdivision (1), (3), (5), or (10) of this section to exit that licensed premises with an open container of the alcoholic beverage sold by the tenant holding the permit and consume the alcoholic beverage within the confines of any indoor or outdoor common area on the premises of the multi-tenant establishment designated by the owner or property owners' association of the multi-tenant establishment for consumption of alcoholic beverages. Additionally, a permit issued under this subdivision is subject to all of the following conditions:

a. The owner or property owners' association of the multi-tenant establishment shall designate the common area in which alcoholic beverages may be consumed. Additionally, the owner or property owners' association of the multi-tenant establishment shall post signs in conspicuous locations on the multi-tenant establishment property indicating which common area is the designated common area. The owner or property owners' association of the multi-tenant establishment shall submit to the Commission for review and approval (i) a plat of the multi-tenant establishment property for a designated outdoor common area with the common area designated for alcohol consumption clearly marked or (ii) a detailed map of the relevant building on the multi-tenant establishment property for a designated indoor common area with the common area designated for alcohol consumption clearly marked. The Commission shall reject any plat or map submitted under this sub-subdivision that does not meet the requirements of this subdivision or any rule adopted by the Commission. The owner or property owners' association of the multi-tenant establishment shall submit a plat or map as required under this sub-subdivision for each renewal of the permit issued under this subdivision and at least 10 days prior to making any adjustments to the designated common area.

b. Alcoholic beverages sold for consumption in a designated common area shall be dispensed only in a container that clearly identifies the licensed premises from which the beverage was purchased. The amount of alcoholic beverage dispensed into a container under this sub-subdivision shall not exceed 16 fluid ounces.

c. A customer is not allowed to possess or consume more than one alcoholic beverage at a time while within the designated common area.

d. Alcoholic beverages may only be consumed within the designated common area during the hours in which the alcoholic beverage may be sold under G.S. 18B-1004, and the owner or property owners' association of the multi-tenant establishment may further limit the days and times in which an alcoholic beverage may be consumed in a designated common area. The owner or property owners' association of the multi-tenant establishment shall post signs in conspicuous locations on the multi-tenant establishment property indicating the days and times in which a person may consume an alcoholic beverage in a designated common area.

e. A customer in the designated common area shall dispose of any alcoholic beverage in his or her possession prior to exiting the designated common area unless the customer is entering a licensed premises that allows the customer to enter with the alcoholic beverage. A customer is not allowed to exit a designated common area with any alcoholic beverage he or she was consuming within the area except to enter a licensed premises that allows the customer to enter with the alcoholic beverage.

f. A customer is not allowed to bring and consume within the designated common area alcoholic beverages not purchased from a tenant of the multi-tenant establishment holding an applicable permit.

g. Any additional conditions imposed by the Commission. Any additional conditions imposed by the Commission shall be posted on the Commission's Web site.

(22) **Airport Central Storage Permit.** -- A permit under this subdivision may be issued to the owner of a bonded storage warehouse that meets the federal Transportation Security Administration (TSA) security standards (49 C.F.R. §§ 1542.1 through 1542.307). This permit authorizes the permittee to contract with retail permittees holding permits issued pursuant to G.S. 18B-1001(1), (3), (5), and (10) with one or more retail locations at airports which service airplanes boarding at least 150,000 passengers annually to do the following: (i) store at a central receiving facility located on or within 5 miles of the airport property and outside the retail permittee's licensed premises alcoholic beverages to be sold or served at the retail permittee's airport locations as approved by the Commission and (ii) transport alcoholic beverages from the central receiving facility to the retail permittee's premises or support locations within the airport terminal pursuant to subsections (d) and (e) of G.S. 18B-1115. Alcoholic beverages stored pursuant to this subdivision shall be the property of the retail permittee. The portion of the airport central storage permitted premises where the retail permittee's alcoholic beverages are stored shall be deemed an extension of the retail permittee's permitted premises for storage only and subject to inspection pursuant to G.S. 18B-503.

(23) **Common Carrier Vehicle Permit.** -- Notwithstanding the results of any local election, a permit under this subdivision may be issued to a business primarily engaged in this State in the intrastate operation of common carriers of passengers and operating under a certificate of authority issued by the North Carolina Utilities Commission. A common carrier vehicle permit authorizes the sale or service of malt beverages, unfortified wine, fortified wine, and mixed beverages in the passenger area of a common carrier of passengers for consumption by passengers in the passenger area during journeys of 75 miles or longer that do not terminate within 10 miles of the origin of the journey. The permit issued to the business shall cover all common

carriers of passengers owned by the business. The permit or a copy of the permit shall be prominently displayed on each common carrier of passengers on which alcoholic beverages are served or sold. Notwithstanding G.S. 18B-101(12a), the passenger area of a permittee's common carrier of passengers constitutes the premises for the permit. This permit shall not allow consumption of alcohol on a common carrier of passengers by any employee of the permittee. A permittee may not sell or serve alcoholic beverages to a passenger between the hours of 2:00 A.M. and 7:00 A.M., and a passenger may not be allowed to consume alcoholic beverages between the hours of 2:30 A.M. and 7:00 A.M. Notwithstanding G.S. 18B-1004(c) or any local ordinance, alcoholic beverages may not be sold or consumed before 10:00 A.M. on Sundays. For purposes of this subdivision, a common carrier of passengers has the same meaning as in G.S. 20-4.01(27)d.

History.
1945, c. 903, s. 1; 1947, c. 1098, ss. 2, 3; 1949, c. 974, s. 1; 1957, cc. 1048, 1448; 1963, c. 426, ss. 10, 12; c. 460, s. 1; 1971, c. 872, s. 1; 1973, c. 476, s. 128; 1975, c. 586, s. 1; c. 654, ss. 1, 2; c. 722, s. 1; 1977, c. 70, s. 19; c. 182, s. 1; c. 669, ss. 1, 2; c. 676, ss. 1, 2; c. 911; 1979, c. 348, ss. 2, 3; c. 683, ss. 5, 6, 11, 12; 1981, c. 412, s. 2; 1981 (Reg. Sess., 1982), c. 1262, ss. 16, 17, 22; 1983, c. 457, s. 3; c. 583, ss. 2-5; 1985, c. 89, ss. 1-3; c. 596, s. 1; 1987, c. 391, s. 2; c. 434, s. 1; 1989, c. 800, ss. 11, 12; 1991, c. 459, ss. 5, 6; c. 565, ss. 1, 7; c. 669, s. 1; 1991 (Reg. Sess., 1992), c. 920, s. 7; 1993, c. 508, s. 5; 1995, c. 466, s. 10; c. 509, ss. 16 -18; 1997-443, s. 16.28; 1997-467, s. 3; 2001-262, s. 1; 2001-487, s. 49(a); 2003-402, s. 5; 2005-350, ss. 1, 2(a); 2006-222, s. 2.1; 2006-227, ss. 1, 9; 2006-264, s. 35.3; 2009-377, s. 2; 2009-539, s. 3; 2010-31, s. 14.12(c); 2011-73, ss. 3, 4; 2011-107, s. 1; 2011-333, ss. 4, 5; 2013-76, s. 1; 2014-115, s. 28.2(a); 2014-120, s. 17(c); 2015-98, ss. 1(b), 1(d), 5(a), 8; 2017-87, ss. 5(a), 7, 16(d); 2018-100, s. 4(b); 2019-49, s. 6; 2019-182, ss. 1(a), 10, 19(b), 22; 2021-117, s. 12(b); 2021-150, ss. 9.2(a), 19.1, 28.1

§ 18B-1001.1. Authorization of wine shipper permit

(a) A winery holding a federal basic wine manufacturing permit located within or outside of the State may apply to the Commission for issuance of a wine shipper permit that shall authorize the shipment of brands of fortified and unfortified wines identified in the application. The applicant shall not be required to pay an application fee for the wine shipper permit. A wine shipper permittee may amend the brands of wines identified in the permit application but shall file any amendment with the Commission. Any winery that applies for a wine shipper permit shall notify in writing any wholesalers that have been authorized to distribute the winery's brands within the State that an application has been filed for a wine shipper permit. A wine shipper permittee may sell and ship not more than two cases of wine per month to any person in North Carolina to whom alcoholic beverages may be lawfully sold. All sales and shipments shall be for personal use only and not for resale. A case of wine shall mean any combination of packages containing not more than nine liters of wine.

(b) A wine shipper permittee that ships to addresses in the State more than 1,000 cases of wine in a calendar year must appoint at least one wholesaler to offer and sell the products of the wine shipper permittee under Article 12 of this Chapter if the wine shipper permittee is contacted by a wholesaler that wishes to sell the products of the wine shipper permittee. This provision shall not be construed to require the wine shipper permittee to appoint the wholesaler that originally contacted the wine shipper permittee. Wine purchased by a resident of the State at the premises of the wine shipper permittee and shipped to an address in the State under G.S. 18B-109(d) shall not be included in calculating the total of 1,000 cases per year.

(c) A wine shipper permittee may contract with the holder of a wine shipper packager permit for the packaging and shipment of wine pursuant to this section. The direct shipment of wine by wine shipper or wine shipper packager permittees pursuant to this section shall be made by approved common carrier only. Each common carrier shall apply to the Commission for approval to provide common carriage of wines shipped by holders of permits issued pursuant to this section.

Each common carrier making deliveries pursuant to this section shall:

(1) Require the recipient, upon delivery, to demonstrate that the recipient is at least 21 years of age by providing a form of identification specified in G.S. 18B-302(d)(1).

(2) Require the recipient to sign an electronic or paper form or other acknowledgment of receipt as approved by the Commission.

(3) Refuse delivery when the proposed recipient appears to be under the age of 21 years and refuses to present valid identification as required by subdivision (1) of this subsection.

(4) Submit any other information that the Commission shall require.

All wine shipper and wine shipper packager permittees shipping wines pursuant to this section shall affix a notice in 26-point type or larger to the outside of each package of wine shipped within or to the State in a conspicuous location stating: "CONTAINS ALCOHOLIC BEVERAGES; SIGNATURE OF PERSON AGED 21 YEARS OR OLDER REQUIRED FOR DELIVERY". Any delivery of wines to a person under 21 years of age by a common carrier shall constitute a violation of G.S. 18B-302(a)(1) by the common carrier. The common carrier and the wine shipper or wine shipper packager permittee shall be liable only for their independent acts.

(d) A wine shipper permittee shall be subject to jurisdiction of the North Carolina courts by virtue of applying for a wine shipper permit and shall comply with any audit or other compliance requirements of the Commission and the Department of Revenue.

History.
2003-402, s. 2; 2004-203, s. 26(a); 2005-380, s. 2; 2006-227, s. 4

§ 18B-1001.2. Additional wine shipping requirements

(a) A wine shipper permittee shall:

(1) Compile and submit to the Commission quarterly a summary indicating all wine products shipped, including brand and price of each product, date of each shipment, quantity of each shipment, and amount of excise and sales tax remitted to the Department of Revenue. The report shall include all wine products shipped on the permittee's behalf under contract with a wine shipper packager.

(2) Register with the Department of Revenue as a wine shipper permittee and provide any additional information required by the Department.

(b) The Commission may adopt rules to carry out the provisions of this section and other related provisions governing the direct shipping of wine.

History.
2003-402, s. 3; 2006-227, s. 5

§ 18B-1001.3. Authorization of wine shipper packager permit

The holder of a wine shipper packager permit may provide services for the warehousing, packaging, and shipment of wine on behalf of a winery holding a wine shipper permit. A wine shipper packager permit authorizes the holder to receive, in closed containers, wine produced by and belonging to a wine shipper permittee and to place the unopened wine in containers

or packaging materials as a service to the wine shipper permittee in connection with the marketing and sale of its wine products. A wine shipper packager may package and return wine products to the wine shipper permittee or, on behalf of the wine shipper permittee, may package and ship wine products in closed containers to individual purchasers inside and outside this State in accordance with the provisions of G.S. 18B-1001.1. The permit may be issued to a USDA-approved company specializing in warehousing and contract packaging.

History.
2006-227, s. 6

§ 18B-1001.4. Authorization of delivery service permit

(a) **Authorization.** -- The holder of a delivery service permit, or the permit holder's employee or independent contractor, may deliver malt beverages, unfortified wine, or fortified wine on behalf of a retailer holding a permit issued pursuant to subdivisions (1) through (6) and (16) of G.S. 18B-1001 to a location designated by the purchaser. A delivery service permittee may also facilitate delivery through technology services that connect consumers and licensed retailers through the use of the Internet, mobile applications, and other similar technology.

(b) **Training and Payment.** -- Prior to making any deliveries, each individual delivering alcoholic beverages pursuant to a delivery service permit shall successfully complete a course approved by the Commission related to the delivery of alcoholic beverages. Upon receipt of a proposed training program from a holder of a delivery service permit, the Commission shall have 15 business days to approve, deny, or request modifications to the proposed training program. An individual delivering alcoholic beverages pursuant to a delivery service permit shall not handle or possess funds used to purchase an alcoholic beverage that is to be delivered, but may facilitate the sales transaction in a manner that does not involve taking possession of funds.

(c) **Age of Recipient and Notice.** -- An individual may only deliver alcoholic beverages pursuant to a delivery service permit to an individual who is at least 21 years of age and who immediately takes actual possession of the alcoholic beverages purchased. A delivery of alcoholic beverages in a package that obscures the manufacturer's original packaging shall have affixed to the outside of the package a notice in 26-point type or larger stating: "CONTAINS ALCOHOLIC BEVERAGES; AGE VERIFICATION REQUIRED."

(d) **Limitations.** -- A delivery service permittee shall deliver alcoholic beverages only within

Chapter 18B

the time allowed for lawful sales and consumption in the jurisdiction where the delivery is located. No delivery shall be made to any jurisdiction within the State that has not authorized the sale of the purchased alcoholic beverages. A delivery service permittee shall not deliver alcoholic beverages to the premises of another licensed retailer or more than 50 miles from the retailer's licensed premises. Only alcoholic beverages purchased for personal consumption and from a licensed retailer's existing inventory located on the retailer's premises may be delivered pursuant to a delivery service permit.

(e) **Scope and Construction.** -- A delivery service permit is not required for a common carrier lawfully transporting or shipping alcoholic beverages. Nothing in this section shall be construed as exempting the delivery of alcoholic beverages pursuant to a delivery service permit from the requirements set forth in Article 4 of Chapter 18B of the General Statutes. Nothing in this section shall be construed to require a technology services company to obtain a delivery service permit if the company does not employ or contract with delivery drivers, but rather provides software or an application that connects consumers and licensed retailers for the delivery of alcoholic beverages from the licensed retailer. Nothing in this section shall be construed to require a retailer that holds a permit issued pursuant to subdivisions (1) through (6) and (16) of G.S. 18B-1001 to obtain a delivery service permit in order for employees of the retail permittee to deliver malt beverages, unfortified wine, or fortified wine to a location designated by the purchaser, however, the other provisions of this section apply to the retailer.

(f) **Penalties for Violations in Residence Halls.** -- Notwithstanding G.S. 18B-104, if a delivery service permittee commits a violation of this Chapter when delivering to a residence hall located on the premises of an institution of higher education the delivery service permittee shall be subject to a fine of up to one thousand dollars ($ 1,000) for the first violation, up to one thousand five hundred dollars ($ 1,500) for a second violation within three years of the first violation, and up to two thousand dollars ($ 2,000) for a third or subsequent violation within three years of the first violation. In any case in which there are two or more violations within three years by a delivery service permittee when delivering to a residence hall on the premises of an institution of higher education in which the Commission is entitled to suspend or revoke a permit, the Commission may accept from the permittee an offer in compromise to pay a penalty of not more than ten thousand dollars ($ 10,000). The Commission may either accept a compromise or revoke a permit, but not both. The Commission may accept a compromise and suspend the permit in the same case.

History.
2019-182, s. 20(a); 2021-150, s. 26.1

§ 18B-1002. Special one-time permits

(a) **Kinds of Permits.** -- In addition to the other permits authorized by this Chapter, the Commission may issue permits for the following activities:

(1) A permit may be issued to a person who acquires ownership or possession of alcoholic beverages through bankruptcy, inheritance, foreclosure, judicial sale, or other special occurrence, and who does not already have a permit authorizing the sale of that kind of alcoholic beverage. The permit may authorize the sale or other disposition of the alcoholic beverages in a manner prescribed by the Commission.

(2) A permit may be issued to a nonprofit organization to allow the retail sale of malt beverages, unfortified wine, fortified wine, or mixed beverages, or to allow brown-bagging, at a single fund-raising event of that organization. A permit for this purpose shall not be issued for the sale of any kind of alcoholic beverage in a jurisdiction where the sale of that alcoholic beverage is not lawful.

(3) A permit may be issued to a permittee who is going out of business to authorize the sale or other disposition of his alcoholic beverages stock in a manner that would not otherwise be authorized under his permit.

(4) A permit may be issued to a collector of wine, decorative decanters of spirituous liquor, or antique spirituous liquor authorizing that person to bring into the State, transport, or possess as a collector, a greater amount of those alcoholic beverages than is otherwise authorized by this Chapter, or to sell those alcoholic beverages in a manner prescribed by the Commission.

(5) A permit may be issued to a unit of local government, or to a nonprofit organization or a political organization to serve wine, malt beverages, and spirituous liquor at a ticketed event held to allow the unit of local government or organization to raise funds. For purposes of this subdivision "nonprofit organization" means an organization that is exempt from taxation under Section 501(c)(3), 501(c)(4), 501(c)(6), 501(c)(8), 501(c)(10), 501(c)(19), or 501(d) of the Internal Revenue Code or is exempt under similar provisions of the General Statutes as a bona fide nonprofit charitable, civic, religious, fraternal, patriotic, or veterans' organization or as a nonprofit volunteer fire department, or as a nonprofit volunteer rescue squad or a bona fide homeowners' or property owners' association. For purposes

Chapter 18B

1247

of this subdivision "political organization" means an organization covered by the provisions of G.S. 163-96(a)(1) or (2) or a campaign organization established by or for a person who is a candidate who has filed a notice of candidacy, paid the filing fees or filed the required petition, and been certified as a candidate. The issuance of this permit shall also allow the issuance of a purchase-transportation permit under G.S. 18B-403 and 18B-404 and the use for culinary purposes of spirituous liquor lawfully purchased for use in mixed beverages. The issuance of this permit shall also allow a nonprofit organization to offer alcoholic beverages in the manufacturer's original closed container as a prize in a raffle or sell alcoholic beverages in the manufacturer's original closed container at auction at the ticketed event to allow the nonprofit organization to raise funds.

(6) A permit may be issued to a professional sports organization to allow the retail sale of malt beverages, unfortified wine, fortified wine, or mixed beverages for consumption on the premises at a professional sporting event held at a stadium (i) with a seating capacity of at least 40,000 people and (ii) that is owned or leased by a constituent institution of The University of North Carolina located in a county with a population of at least 900,000 people according to the most recent federal decennial census. The issuance of this permit also allows the issuance of a purchase-transportation permit under G.S. 18B-403 and G.S. 18B-404. For purposes of this subdivision, the term "professional sports organization" means an organization that is a member of an association or league of professional sports organizations that (i) has 6 or more members, (ii) has total combined revenues from all members that exceeds ten million dollars ($ 10,000,000) per year, and (iii) governs the conduct of its members and regulates the contests and exhibitions in which its member organizations regularly engage.

(b) **Intent.** -- Permits under this section are to be issued only for the limited circumstances listed in subsection (a) of this section and not as substitutes for other permits required by this Chapter.

(c) **Conditions of Permit.** -- A permit issued under this section shall be valid only for the single transaction or the kind of activity specified in the permit and shall be subject to any conditions the Commission may impose as to the time, place and manner of the authorized activity.

(d) **Administrative Procedure.** -- Denial or revocation of a permit under this section shall not entitle the applicant or permittee to a hearing under Chapter 150B.

History.
1977, c. 854, s. 1; 1981, c. 412, s. 2; 1987, c. 434, s. 2; c. 827, s. 1; 1989, c. 130; c. 800, ss. 13, 14; 2001-262, s. 9; 2008-159, s. 1; 2017-6, s. 3; 2017-87, s. 3(b); 2018-100, s. 5(e); 2018-145, s. 13(a); 2018-146, ss. 3.1(a), (b), 6.1

§ 18B-1002.1. Special auction permit

(a) **Permit Authorized.** -- A permit may be issued upon application to an auction firm or auctioneer licensed by the North Carolina Auctioneers Commission pursuant to Chapter 85B of the General Statutes to allow the licensed auction firm or auctioneer to sell at auction items described in G.S. 18B-1002(a)(4). An auction held under this section may receive competing bids that are in person or by telephone, fax, or online.

(b) **Conditions of Permit.** -- A permit issued under this section is valid only for the auction specified in the permit. Any sales under this permit are subject to the purchase restrictions in G.S. 18B-303.

(c) **Administrative Procedure.** -- Denial or revocation of a permit under this section does not entitle the applicant or permittee to a hearing under Chapter 150B of the General Statutes.

History.
2017-87, s. 3(c)

§ 18B-1003. Responsibilities of permittee

(a) **Premises.** -- For purposes of this Chapter, a permittee shall be responsible for the entire premises for which the permit is issued. The permittee shall keep the premises clean, well-lighted and orderly.

(b) **Employees.** -- For purposes of this Chapter, a permittee shall be responsible for the actions of all employees of the business for which the permit is issued. Each holder of a salesman's permit shall be responsible for all sales and deliveries made by his helpers.

(c) **Certain Employees Prohibited.** -- A permittee shall not knowingly employ in the sale or distribution of alcoholic beverages any person who has been:

(1) Convicted of a felony within three years;

(2) Convicted of a felony more than three years previously and has not had his citizenship restored;

(3) Convicted of an alcoholic beverage offense within two years; or

(4) Convicted of a misdemeanor controlled substances offense within two years; [or]

(5) A past permit holder under Chapter 18B of the General Statutes whose permit had been revoked within the last 18 months and who had been the permit holder at the location where the person would be employed.

For purposes of this subsection, "conviction" has the same meaning as in G.S. 18B-900(b). To avoid undue hardship, the Commission may, in its discretion, exempt persons on a case-by-case basis from this subsection.

(c1) **Posting Human Trafficking Hotline.** -- All permittees shall prominently display on the premises in a place that is clearly conspicuous and visible to employees a public awareness sign created and provided by the North Carolina Human Trafficking Commission that contains the National Human Trafficking Resource hotline information.

(d) **Financial Responsibility.** -- A permittee shall pay all judgments rendered against him under the provisions of Article 1A of this Chapter. When the Commission is informed, under the provisions of G.S. 18B-127 that there is an outstanding unsatisfied judgment against a permittee, the Commission shall suspend all of the permittee's permits. Notice and hearing are not required for a suspension under this subsection, and the suspension shall become effective immediately upon the Commission's receipt of the report. The suspension shall remain in effect until the permittee demonstrates that he has satisfied the judgment by payment in full. Nothing in this section relieves the permittee of the obligation to pay any applicable fees as a precondition of the reinstatement of his permit.

History.
1981, c. 412, s. 2; 1983, c. 435, s. 40; 2006-253, s. 28; 2017-57, s. 17.4(b); 2017-197, s. 5.8; 2018-97, s. 5.4

§ 18B-1004. Hours for sale and consumption

(a) **Hours.** -- Except as otherwise provided in this section, it shall be unlawful to sell malt beverages, unfortified wine, fortified wine, or mixed beverages between the hours of 2:00 A.M. and 7:00 A.M., or to consume any of those alcoholic beverages between the hours of 2:30 A.M. and 7:00 A.M., in any place that has been issued a permit under G.S. 18B-1001 or G.S. 18B-1105.

(b) Repealed by Session Laws 1991, c. 689, s. 310, effective August 1, 1991.

(c) **Sunday Hours.** -- Except as authorized pursuant to G.S. 18B-112(b1), 153A-145.7, or 160A-205.3, it shall be unlawful to sell or consume alcoholic beverages on any licensed premises from the time at which sale or consumption must cease on Sunday morning until 12:00 Noon on that day.

(d) **Local Option.** -- A city may adopt an ordinance prohibiting in the city the retail sale of malt beverages, unfortified wine, and fortified wine during any or all of the hours from 12:00 Noon on Sunday until 7:00 A.M. on the following Monday. A county may adopt an ordinance prohibiting, in the parts of the county outside any city, the retail sale of malt beverages, unfortified wine, and fortified wine during any or all of the hours from 12:00 Noon on Sunday until 7:00 A.M. on the following Monday. Neither a city nor a county, however, may prohibit those sales in establishments having brown-bagging or mixed beverages permits.

(e) This section does not prohibit at any time the wholesale delivery and sale of unfortified wine, fortified wine, and malt beverages to retailers issued permits pursuant to G.S. 18B-1001 or G.S. 18B-1002(a)(2) or (5).

History.
1943, c. 339, ss. 1-3; 1949, c. 974, s. 12; 1951, c. 997, s. 1; 1953, c. 675, s. 4; 1963, c. 426, ss. 7-9, 12; 1969, c. 1131; 1971, c. 872, s. 1; 1973, cc. 56, 153; 1979, c. 286, s. 3; 1981, c. 412, s. 2; 1987, c. 35; c. 308; 1991, c. 689, s. 310; 1993, c. 243, ss. 1, 2; c. 415, s. 16; 2017-87, s. 4(a); 2021-150, s. 12.1

§ 18B-1005. Conduct on licensed premises

(a) **Certain Conduct.** -- It shall be unlawful for a permittee or his agent or employee to knowingly allow any of the following kinds of conduct to occur on his licensed premises:

(1) Any violation of this Chapter;

(2) Any fighting or other disorderly conduct that can be prevented without undue danger to the permittee, his employees or patrons; or

(3) Any violation of the controlled substances, gambling, or prostitution statutes, or any other unlawful acts.

(4) through (6) Repealed by Session Laws 2003-382, s. 1, effective August 1, 2003.

(b) **Supervision.** -- It shall be unlawful for a permittee to fail to superintend in person or through a manager the business for which a permit is issued.

History.
1943, c. 400, s. 6; 1945, c. 708, s. 6; c. 903, s. 1; 1947, c. 1098, ss. 2, 3; 1949, c. 974, ss. 13, 15; c. 1251, s. 3; 1957, c. 1048; 1959, c. 745, s. 2; 1963, c. 426, ss. 6, 10, 12; c. 460, s. 1; 1971, c. 872, s. 1; 1973, c. 30; c. 1295; c. 1452, s. 4; 1977, c. 176, ss. 1-3; 1981, c. 412, s. 2; 1981 (Reg. Sess., 1982), c. 1262, ss. 18, 19; 2003-382, s. 1

Chapter 18B

§ 18B-1005.1. Sexually explicit conduct on licensed premises

(a) It shall be unlawful for a permittee or his agent or employee to knowingly allow or engage in any of the following kinds of conduct on his licensed premises:

(1) Any conduct or entertainment by any person whose genitals are exposed or who is wearing transparent clothing that reveals the genitals;

(2) Any conduct or entertainment that includes or simulates sexual intercourse, masturbation, sodomy, bestiality, oral copulation, flagellation, or any act that includes or simulates the penetration, however slight, by any object into the genital or anal opening of a person's body; or

(3) Any conduct or entertainment that includes the fondling of the breasts, buttocks, anus, vulva, or genitals.

(b) **Supervision. --** It shall be unlawful for a permittee to fail to superintend in person or through a manager the business for which a permit is issued.

(c) **Exception. --** This section does not apply to persons operating theaters, concert halls, art centers, museums, or similar establishments that are primarily devoted to the arts or theatrical performances, when the performances that are presented are expressing matters of serious literary, artistic, scientific, or political value.

History.
2003-382, s. 2

§ 18B-1006. Miscellaneous provisions on permits

(a) **School and College Campuses. --** No permit for the sale of alcoholic beverages shall be issued to a business on the campus or property of a public school, college, or university. This subsection shall not apply to the following:

(1) A regional facility as defined by G.S. 160A-480.2 operated by a facility authority under Part 4 of Article 20 of Chapter 160A of the General Statutes.

(2) Property owned by a local board of education and leased for 99 years or more to a nonprofit auditorium authority created prior to 1991 whose governing board is appointed by a city governing board, a county board of commissioners, or a local school board.

(3) A hotel.

(4) A nonprofit alumni organization.

(5) Restaurants, eating establishments, food businesses, or retail businesses on the property defined by G.S. 116-198.33(4).

(6) Any golf courses owned or leased by the public college or university and open to the public for use.

(7) The sale of malt beverages, unfortified wine, or fortified wine at the following:

a. Performing arts centers located on property owned or leased by the public college or university.

b. Any stadiums that support a NASCAR-sanctioned one-fourth mile asphalt flat oval short track, that are owned or leased by the public college or university.

(8) Special one-time permits as described in G.S. 18B-1002(a)(5) for the Loudermilk Center for Excellence facility at the University of North Carolina at Chapel Hill.

(9) Special one-time permits described in G.S. 18B-1002(a)(6).

(10) A stadium, athletic facility, or arena on the campus or property of a public college or university, if the Board of Trustees of the public college or university has voted to allow the issuance of permits for use at that stadium, athletic facility, or arena. If a Board of Trustees votes to allow the issuance of permits in accordance with this subdivision, the Board of Trustees shall provide written notice to the Commission that it has voted to allow the issuance of permits. For purposes of this subdivision, the term "public college or university" does not include a community college. Any permit described in G.S. 18B-1001, 18B-1002(a)(2), or 18B-1002(a)(5) may be issued pursuant to this subdivision to applicants meeting the requirements for the requested permit. Notwithstanding the issuance of a mixed beverages permit pursuant to G.S. 18B-1001(10), this subdivision does not authorize the sale of mixed beverages when the stadium, athletic facility, or arena is being used for a sports event sponsored by the public college or university. This subdivision does not apply to any sales authorized under subdivisions (1) through (8) of this subsection. For purposes of this subdivision, the premises of a stadium, athletic facility, or arena shall include any area that meets all of the following requirements:

a. Is within 500 feet of the furthest exterior building wall, perimeter fence, or permanent fixed perimeter.

b. Is designated by the stadium, athletic facility, or arena in a map or written description that clearly defines the boundary of the area, and that map or written description is included in the permit application.

c. Can be designated in a manner that enables the stadium, athletic facility, or arena to ensure compliance with the provisions of this Chapter.

(b) **Lockers at Clubs. --** A private club or congressionally-chartered veterans organization

Chapter 18B

which has been issued a brown-bagging permit may, but is not required to, provide lockers for its members to store their alcoholic beverages. If lockers are provided, however, they shall not be shared but shall be for individual members. Each locker and each bottle of alcoholic beverages on the premises shall be labelled with the name of the member to whom it belongs. No more than eight liters each of malt beverages or unfortified wine may be stored by a member at one time. No more than eight liters of either fortified wine or spirituous liquor, or eight liters of the two combined, may be stored by a member at one time.

(c) **Wine Sales.** -- Holders of retail or wholesale permits for the sale of unfortified or fortified wine may buy and sell only wines on the Commission's approved list. The Commission may authorize the importation and purchase of wines not on the approved list by permittees and others. An authorization shall state the kind and amount of wine that may be imported and purchased and the time within which the transaction shall be completed.

(d) **Unlawful Possession or Consumption.** -- It shall be unlawful for a permittee to possess or consume, or allow any other person to possess or consume, on the licensed premises, any fortified wine or spirituous liquor, the possession or consumption of which is not authorized either by the permits issued to him for the premises or by any other provision of the ABC law.

(e) **Facsimile Permit.** -- It shall be unlawful for any person to produce or possess any false or facsimile permit, or for a permittee to display any false or facsimile permit on his licensed premises.

(f) **Failure to Surrender Permit.** -- It shall be unlawful for any person to refuse to surrender any permit to the Commission upon lawful demand of the Commission or its agents.

(g) **Restrictions on Sales at Cooking Schools.** -- Retail sales of food or alcoholic beverages to be consumed on the premises of a cooking school are restricted to bona fide enrolled students of that school. Violation of this subsection is a ground for administrative action under G.S. 18B-104.

(h) **Purchase Restrictions.** -- A retail permittee may purchase malt beverages, unfortified wine, or fortified wine only from a wholesaler who maintains a place of business in this State and has the proper permit.

(i) **Tour Boats.** -- The Commission may issue permits to boats that conduct regularly scheduled tours upon the rivers or waterways of this State under the following conditions:

(1) A boat shall offer food and non-alcoholic beverages for sale on each tour.

(2) A boat's gross receipts from sales of alcoholic beverages shall be no more than twenty-five percent (25%) of its total gross receipts.

(3) A boat may hold the permits listed in G.S. 18B-1001(1), (3), (5), (7), and (10), but no off-premises sales may be made pursuant to those permits;

(4) A boat shall have a home port in an area where issuance of any of the permits listed in subdivision (3) is legal, and all passengers shall enter the boat at the home port or at other ports listed on a preannounced itinerary. The boat's permits are valid during tours that leave and return to the boat's home port, and apply regardless of whether the boat crosses into an area where sales are not legal, if the boat docks only at a port listed on the preannounced itinerary, except in an emergency; and

(5) A boat conducting tours along the intracoastal waterway and navigable waterways that enters into the intracoastal waterway, pursuant to a preannounced itinerary that includes visits to two or more cities, may serve alcoholic beverages pursuant to ABC permits issued according to the jurisdiction of its home port in the following manner:

a. While on tour, alcoholic beverages may be served to passengers;

b. While docked in any other port alcoholic beverages may be served only to tour passengers;

c. During special city-sponsored events and festivals, in which case the boat may open its galley and bars at dockside to the general public and sell those alcoholic beverages that are lawful in the jurisdiction in which it is docked. Any sales in this manner shall be in accordance with the requirements of any ordinances of the jurisdiction in which the boat is docked.

(6) Liquor purchased for resale in mixed beverages may be purchased only from the local board for the jurisdiction of the boat's home port.

(j) **Recreation Districts.** -- Notwithstanding the provisions of Article 6 of this Chapter, the Commission may issue permits for the sale of malt beverages, unfortified wine, fortified wine, and mixed beverages to qualified businesses in a recreation district.

A "recreation district" is an area that meets any of the following requirements:

(1) An area that is located in a county that has not approved the issuance of permits, has at least two cities that have approved the sale of malt beverages, wine, and the operation of an ABC store, and contains a facility of at least 450 acres where five or more public auto racing events are held each year.

(2) An area that is located in a county that borders a county which has held

elections pursuant to G.S. 18B-600(f) and borders on another state and which (i) contains a facility of at least 225 acres where four or more public auto racing events are held each year or (ii) contains a facility of at least 140 acres where 80 or more motor sports events are held each year.

(3) A recreation district includes the area within a half-mile radius of a racing facility that meets the requirements of subdivision (1) or (2) of this subsection.

(4) Repealed by Session Laws 2004-203, s. 27, effective August 17, 2004.

(k) **Residential Private Club and Sports Club Permits.** -- The Commission may issue the permits listed in G.S. 18B-1001, without approval at an election, to a residential private club or a sports club, except if the sale of mixed beverages is not lawful within a jurisdiction and that locality has voted against the sale of mixed beverages in a referendum conducted on or after September 1, 2001. If the issuance of permits is prohibited by the exception in the previous sentence, the Commission may renew existing permits and may continue to issue permits for a business location that had previously held permits under this subsection. No permit may be issued to any residential private club or sports club that practices discrimination on the basis of race, gender or ethnicity.

The mixed beverages purchase-transportation permit authorized by G.S. 18B-404(b) shall be issued by a local board operating a store located in the county.

(*l*) Repealed by Session Laws 2004-203, s. 65, effective August 17, 2004.

(m) **Interstate Interchange Economic Development Zones.** --

(1) The Commission may issue permits listed in G.S. 18B-1001(10), without approval at an election, to qualified establishments defined in G.S. 18B-1000(4), (6), and (8) located within one mile of an interstate highway interchange located in a county that:

a. Has approved the sale of malt beverages, unfortified wine, and fortified wine, but not mixed beverages;

b. Operates ABC stores;

c. Borders on another state; and

d. Lies north and east of the Roanoke River.

(2) The Commission may issue permits listed in G.S. 18B-1001(1), (3), (5), and (10) to qualified establishments defined in G.S. 18B-1000(4), (6), and (8) and may issue permits listed in G.S. 18B-1001(2) and (4) to qualified establishments defined in G.S. 18B-1000(3) in any county that qualifies for issuance of permits pursuant to G.S. 18B-1006(k). These permits may be issued without approval at an election and shall

be issued only to qualified establishments that meet all of the following requirements:

a. Located within one mile of any interstate highway interchange in that county;

b. Located within one mile of an establishment issued a permit under G.S. 18B-1006(k); and

c. Is, or is located within one-quarter mile of, a hotel with 70 or more rooms.

(3) Repealed by Session Laws 2004-203, s. 28, effective August 17, 2004.

(n) **National Historic Landmark District.** -- The Commission may issue permits listed in G.S. 18B-1001(10), without approval at an election, to qualified establishments defined in G.S. 18B-1000(4) and (6) located within a National Historical Landmark as defined in 16 U.S.C. § 470a(a)(1)(B) located in a county that meets all of the following requirements:

(1) Has approved the sale of malt beverages and unfortified wine but not mixed beverages.

(2) Has at least one city that has approved the operation of an ABC store and the sale of mixed beverages.

(3) Has at least 150,000 population based on the last federal census.

(n1) **State Boundary Certification.** -- The Commission may issue permits listed in G.S. 18B-1001(2) and (4), without approval at an election, to qualified establishments defined in G.S. 18B-1000(7) that meet all of the following requirements:

(1) The establishment is located in a county that borders on another state.

(2) The location of the establishment was reclassified from out-of-state to North Carolina as a result of a State boundary certification.

(3) The establishment was licensed or permitted by the previous state of record to sell malt beverages and unfortified wine.

(n2) **Event Centers.** -- The Commission may issue permits listed in G.S. 18B-1001(10) and (12), without approval at an election, to qualified establishments defined in G.S. 18B-1000(4) and (6) that meet all of the following requirements:

(1) The establishment is located in a county that has more than two man-made lakes.

(2) The establishment is located in a county that has approved the sale of malt beverages and unfortified wine but not mixed beverages.

(3) The establishment is open to the public and includes on its premises a hotel with accommodations for 20 or more overnight guests, agritourism activities as defined in G.S. 99E-30, and firearm sports.

(o) Expired.

(p) The Commission shall issue a special occasion permit under G.S. 18B-1001(8) to a mixed beverage permittee in a sports facility occupied by a major league professional sports team with suites available for sale or lease to patrons of the facility to authorize patrons to make available alcoholic beverages in those suites as if the patron were a host of a reception, party or other special occasion. If the patron occupying the suite so desires, alcoholic beverages by self-service may be made available to any person at least 21 years of age possessing a valid ticket to the event authorizing that person to occupy the suite. At no event may the patron make available a quantity of alcoholic beverages in excess of the amount a person is allowed to buy under G.S. 18B-303(a). A mixed beverage permittee who holds a permit shall provide mixed beverage tax paid spirituous liquor for resale by the container in approved sizes of no larger than 750 milliliters to the host or patron of the suite. This subsection does not authorize any person possessing a valid ticket to an event at the facility to bring alcoholic beverages onto the premises and consume those alcoholic beverages on the premises, or to remove those beverages from the suite.

(q) The hours for sales and consumption of alcoholic beverages on the premises of a permittee who meets the requirements of G.S. 18B-1009 shall be one hour earlier than permitted by G.S. 18B-1004(c).

History.
1981, c. 412, s. 2; 1981 (Reg. Sess., 1982), c. 1262, s. 23; 1985, c. 114, s. 2; c. 301; 1987, c. 515; c. 760; 1989, c. 360; c. 770, s. 49; c. 800, s. 18; 1991, c. 340, s. 1; c. 459, s. 7; 1991 (Reg. Sess., 1992), c. 920, s. 12; 1993, c. 415, ss. 17 -19; c. 508, s. 6; 1995, c. 224, s. 1; c. 372, s. 2; c. 458, s. 8; c. 466, ss. 11 -12; 1997-182, s. 3; 1997-395, s. 1; 1997-443, s. 16.27(a); 1999-462, ss. 2, 10, 12, 14; 2001-130, ss. 1, 1.4; 2004-199, s. 10; 2004-203, ss. 27, 28, 65; 2005-327, ss. 1, 2, 4; 2006-227, s. 7; 2006-264, s. 100; 2007-323, s. 6.25; 2013-394, s. 5(b); 2013-410, s. 27.9; 2014-120, s. 14; 2016-23, s. 8; 2018-145, s. 13(b); 2019-52, s. 1; 2021-150, ss. 3.1, 31.1.

§ 18B-1006.1. Additional requirement for certain permittees to recycle beverage containers

Holders of on-premises malt beverage permits, on-premises unfortified wine permits, on-premises fortified wine permits, and mixed beverages permits shall separate, store, and provide for the collection for recycling of all recyclable beverage containers of all beverages sold at retail on the premises. A permittee has satisfied the requirements of this section if it implements a recycling program that meets the minimum standards of the model recycling program developed by the Commission pursuant

to G.S. 130A-309.14(m). Failure to comply with the requirements of this section shall not be grounds for revocation of a permit. A conviction for violation of this section shall not constitute an alcoholic beverage offense within the meaning of G.S. 18B-900(a)(4).

History.
2005-348, s. 1; 2007-402, s. 2(a); 2008-187, s. 35.5

§ 18B-1007. Additional requirements for mixed beverages permittees

(a) **Purchases.** -- A mixed beverages permittee may purchase spirituous liquor for resale as mixed beverages and a guest room cabinet permittee may purchase spirituous liquor for resale from a guest room cabinet only at an ABC store designated by a local board and only with a purchase-transportation permit issued by that local board under G.S. 18B-403 and 18B-404.

(b) **Handling Bottles.** -- It shall be unlawful for a mixed beverages permittee or the permittee's agent or employee to do any of the following:

(1) Store any other spirituous liquor with liquor possessed for resale in mixed beverages or from a guest room cabinet.

(2) Refill any spirituous liquor container having a mixed beverages tax stamp with any other alcoholic beverage, or add to the contents of such a container any other alcoholic beverage.

(3) Transfer from one container to another a mixed beverages tax stamp.

(4) Possess any container of spirituous liquor not bearing a mixed beverages tax stamp, except for containers being brought onto the premises by the host of a private function under a special occasion permit.

(c) **Price List.** -- Each mixed beverages permittee shall have available for its customers the printed prices of the most common or popular mixed beverages offered for sale by the permittee. Violation of this subsection shall not be a criminal offense, but shall be punishable under G.S. 18B-104.

(d) When a temporary mixed beverages permit has been issued to a new permittee for the continuation of a business at the same location, the permittee going out of business may sell existing mixed beverages inventory to the new permittee, and the Commission may request that the local ABC board restamp the inventory with the mixed beverages tax stamp assigned by the local board to the new mixed beverages permittee.

History.
1981, c. 412, s. 2; c. 746, s. 2; 1981 (Reg. Sess., 1982), c. 1262, s. 20; 1989, c. 800, s. 15; 1991, c. 565, ss. 6, 7; 1991 (Reg. Sess., 1992), c. 920, s. 8; 1995, c. 466, s. 13

§ 18B-1008. Rules concerning retail permits

The Commission is authorized to use broad discretion in further defining the kinds of places eligible for permits under this Article. The rules may state the kind and amount of food that shall be sold to qualify in each category, the relationship between food sales and other receipts, the size of the establishment required for each category, the kinds of facilities needed to qualify, the kinds of activities at which alcoholic beverages may not be sold, and any other matters which are necessary to determine which businesses are bona fide establishments of the kinds listed in G.S. 18B-1000. Rules concerning private clubs may also include requirements that the club have a membership committee to review all applications for membership, that the club charge membership dues substantially greater than what would be paid by a one-time or casual user, that the club restrict use by non-members, and that the club provide facilities or activities other than those directly related to the use of alcoholic beverages.

History.
1981, c. 412, s. 2; 2009-381, s. 1

§ 18B-1009. In-stand sales

(a) Nothing in this Chapter shall be construed to prohibit a retail permittee from selling for consumption, malt beverages in the seating areas of stadiums, ballparks, and other similar public places with a seating capacity of 3,000 or more during professional sporting events, provided that:

(1) The seating areas are designated as part of the retail permittee's licensed premises;

(2) The retail permittee has notified the Commission, in writing, of its intent to sell malt beverages in the seating areas at sporting events;

(3) Service of food and nonalcoholic beverages is available in the seating areas;

(4) The retail permittee has certified to the Commission that it has trained its employees:

    a. To identify underage persons and intoxicated persons; and

    b. To refuse to sell malt beverages to those persons as required by G.S. 18B-305; and

(5) The employees do not verbally shout or hawk the sale of malt beverages.

(b) The North Carolina Alcoholic Beverage Control Commission shall adopt rules for the suspension of alcohol sales in the latter portion of professional sporting events in order to protect public safety at these events.

History.
1997-167, s. 1; 2000-140, s. 93.1(a); 2001-424, s. 12.2(b); 2013-83, ss. 1, 2

§ 18B-1010. Sale and delivery of more than one drink at a time to a single patron

(a) Except as otherwise provided in this section, the holder of an on-premises malt beverage permit, on-premises unfortified wine permit, on-premises fortified wine permit, or mixed beverages permit issued under G.S. 18B-1001 may sell and deliver alcoholic beverage drinks to a single patron with the following limitations:

(1) Not more than two alcoholic beverage drinks at one time if the alcoholic beverage drinks are any of the following:

    a. A malt beverage.

    b. Unfortified wine.

    c. Fortified wine.

(2) Not more than one alcoholic beverage at one time if an alcoholic beverage drink is a mixed beverage or contains spirituous liquor.

(b) Repealed by Session Laws 2021-150, s. 11.1(a), effective September 10, 2021, and applicable to the sale and delivery of alcoholic beverages on or after that date.

History.
2019-182, s. 13(a); 2021-150, s. 11.1(a)

§ 18B-1011. Retail permittee off-site airport storage

(a) Permittees holding permits issued pursuant to G.S. 18B-1001(1), (3), (5), and (10) for premises located within airport terminals may contract with an airport central storage permittee for storage at the airport central storage permittee's licensed premises of the permittee's alcoholic beverages to be sold at the retail permittee's airport locations as authorized by the Commission. The permittee may contract with the airport central storage permittee to transport the retail permittee's alcoholic beverages from the airport central storage facility to the retail permittee's premises or support location.

(b) The location where the retail permittee's alcoholic beverages are stored on the airport central storage permittee's premises shall be deemed an extension of the retail permittee's licensed premises for purposes of this Chapter.

History.
2021-150, s. 19.4

CHAPTER 19
OFFENSES AGAINST
PUBLIC MORALS

ARTICLE 1
ABATEMENT OF NUISANCES

§ 19-1. What are nuisances under this Chapter

(a) The erection, establishment, continuance, maintenance, use, ownership or leasing of any building or place for the purpose of assignation, prostitution, gambling, illegal possession or sale of alcoholic beverages, illegal possession or sale of controlled substances as defined in the North Carolina Controlled Substances Act, or illegal possession or sale of obscene or lewd matter, as defined in this Chapter, shall constitute a nuisance. The activity sought to be abated need not be the sole purpose of the building or place in order for it to constitute a nuisance under this Chapter.

(b) The erection, establishment, continuance, maintenance, use, ownership or leasing of any building or place wherein or whereon are carried on, conducted, or permitted repeated acts which create and constitute a breach of the peace shall constitute a nuisance.

(b1) The erection, establishment, continuance, maintenance, use, ownership or leasing of any building or place wherein or whereon are carried on, conducted, or permitted repeated activities or conditions which violate a local ordinance regulating sexually oriented businesses so as to contribute to adverse secondary impacts shall constitute a nuisance.

(b2) The erection, establishment, continuance, maintenance, use, ownership, or leasing of any building or place for the purpose of carrying on, conducting, or engaging in any activities in violation of G.S. 14-72.7.

(c) The building, place, vehicle, or the ground itself, in or upon which a nuisance as defined in subsection (a), (b), or (b1) of this section is carried on, and the furniture, fixtures, and contents, are also declared a nuisance, and shall be enjoined and abated as hereinafter provided.

(d) No nuisance action under this Article may be brought against a place or business which is subject to regulation under Chapter 18B of the General Statutes when the basis for the action constitutes a violation of laws or regulations under that Chapter pertaining to the possession or sale of alcoholic beverages.

History.
Pub. Loc. 1913, c. 761, s. 25; 1919, c. 288; C.S., s. 3180; 1949, c. 1164; 1967, c. 142; 1971, c. 655; 1977, c. 819, ss. 1, 2; 1981, c. 412, s. 4; c. 747, s. 66; 1998-46, s. 7; 1999-371, s. 1; 2007-178, s. 3; 2013-229, s. 1

§ 19-1.1. Definitions

As used in this Chapter relating to illegal possession or sale of obscene matter or to the other conduct prohibited in G.S. 19-1(a), the following definitions shall apply:

(1) "Breach of the peace" means repeated acts that disturb the public order including, but not limited to, homicide, assault, affray, communicating threats, unlawful possession of dangerous or deadly weapons, and discharging firearms.

(1a) "Knowledge" or "knowledge of such nuisance" means having knowledge of the contents and character of the patently offensive sexual conduct which appears in the lewd matter, or knowledge of the acts of lewdness. With regard to nuisances involving assignation, prostitution, gambling, the illegal possession or sale of alcoholic beverages, the illegal possession or sale of controlled substances as defined in the North Carolina Controlled Substances Act, or repeated acts which create and constitute a breach of the peace, evidence that the defendant knew or by the exercise of due diligence should have known of the acts or conduct constitutes proof of knowledge.

(2) "Lewd matter" is synonymous with "obscene matter" and means any matter:

  a. Which the average person, applying contemporary community standards, would find, when considered as a whole, appeals to the prurient interest; and

  b. Which depicts patently offensive representations of:

    1. Ultimate sexual acts, normal or perverted, actual or simulated;

    2. Masturbation, excretory functions, or lewd exhibition of the genitals or genital area;

    3. Masochism or sadism; or

    4. Sexual acts with a child or animal.

    Nothing herein contained is intended to include or proscribe any writing or written material, nor to include or proscribe any matter which, when considered as a whole, and in the context in which it is used, possesses serious literary, artistic, political, educational, or scientific value.

(3) "Lewdness" is synonymous with obscenity and shall mean the act of selling,

Chapter 19

exhibiting or possessing for sale or exhibition lewd matter.

(4) "Matter" means a motion picture film or a publication or both.

(5) "Motion picture film" shall include any:

    a. Film or plate negative;

    b. Film or plate positive;

    c. Film designed to be projected on a screen for exhibition;

    d. Films, glass slides or transparencies, either in negative or positive form, designed for exhibition by projection on a screen;

    e. Video tape, compact disc, digital video disc, or any other medium used to electronically reproduce images on a screen.

(6) "Person" means any individual, partnership, firm, association, corporation, or other legal entity.

(7) "Place" includes, but is not limited to, any building, structure or places, or any separate part or portion thereof, whether permanent or not, or the ground itself.

(7a) "Preserving the status quo" as used in G.S. 19-2.3 means returning conditions to the last actual, peaceable, lawful, and noncontested status which preceded the pending controversy and not allow the nuisance to continue.

(7b) "Prostitution" means offering in any manner or receiving of the body in return for a fee, for acts of vaginal intercourse, anal intercourse, fellatio, cunnilingus, masturbation, or physical contact with a person's genitals, pubic area, buttocks, or breasts, or other acts of sexual conduct offered or received for pay and sexual gratification.

(8) "Publication" shall include any book, magazine, pamphlet, illustration, photograph, picture, sound recording, or a motion picture film which is offered for sale or exhibited in a coin-operated machine.

(9) "Sale of obscene or lewd matter" means a passing of title or right of possession from a seller to a buyer for valuable consideration, and shall include, but is not limited to, any lease or rental arrangement or other transaction wherein or whereby any valuable consideration is received for the use of, or transfer or possession of, lewd matter.

(10) "Sale" as the term relates to proscribed acts other than sale of obscene or lewd matter shall have the same meaning as the term is defined in Chapter 18B and Chapter 90 of the General Statutes prohibiting the illegal sale of alcoholic beverages and controlled substances respectively.

(11) "Used for profit" shall mean any use of real or personal property to produce income in any manner, including, but not limited to, any commercial or business activities, or selling, leasing, or otherwise providing goods and services for profit.

History.

1977, c. 819, s. 3; 1981, c. 412, s. 4; c. 747, s. 66; 1999-371, s. 2

§ 19-1.2. Types of nuisances

The following are declared to be nuisances wherein obscene or lewd matter or other conduct prohibited in G.S. 19-1(a) is involved:

(1) Any and every place in the State where lewd films are publicly exhibited as a predominant and regular course of business, or possessed for the purpose of such exhibition;

(2) Any and every place in the State where a lewd film is publicly and repeatedly exhibited, or possessed for the purpose of such exhibition;

(3) Any and every lewd film which is publicly exhibited, or possessed for such purpose at a place which is a nuisance under this Article;

(4) Any and every place of business in the State in which lewd publications constitute a principal or substantial part of the stock in trade;

(5) Any and every lewd publication possessed at a place which is a nuisance under this Article;

(6) Every place which, as a regular course of business, is used for the purposes of lewdness, assignation, gambling, the illegal possession or sale of alcoholic beverages, the illegal possession or sale of controlled substances as defined in the North Carolina Controlled Substances Act, or prostitution, and every such place in or upon which acts of lewdness, assignation, gambling, the illegal possession or sale of alcoholic beverages, the illegal possession or sale of controlled substances as defined in the North Carolina Controlled Substances Act, or prostitution, are held or occur.

History.

1977, c. 819, s. 3; 1981, c. 412, s. 4; c. 747, s. 66; 1999-371, s. 3

§ 19-1.3. Personal property as a nuisance; knowledge of nuisance

The following are also declared to be nuisances, as personal property used in conducting and maintaining a nuisance under this Chapter:

(1) All moneys paid as admission price to the exhibition of any lewd film found to be a nuisance;

(2) All valuable consideration received for the sale of any lewd publication which is found to be a nuisance;

(3) All money or other valuable consideration, vehicles, conveyances, or other property received or used in gambling, prostitution, the illegal sale of alcoholic beverages or the illegal sale of substances proscribed under the North Carolina Controlled Substances Act, as well as the furniture and movable contents of a place used in connection with such prohibited conduct.

From and after service of a copy of the notice of hearing of the application for a preliminary injunction, provided for in G.S. 19-2.4 upon the place, or its manager, or acting manager, or person then in charge, all such parties are deemed to have knowledge of the contents of the restraining order and the use of the place occurring thereafter. Where the circumstantial proof warrants a determination that a person had knowledge of the nuisance prior to such service of process, the court may make such finding.

History.
1977, c. 819, s. 3; 1981, c. 412, s. 4; c. 747, s. 66; 1999-371, s. 4

§ 19-1.4. Liability of successive owners for continuing nuisance

After notice of a temporary restraining order, preliminary injunction, or permanent injunction, every successive owner of property who neglects to abate a continuing nuisance upon, or in the use of such property, created by a former owner, is liable therefor in the same manner as the one who first created it.

History.
1977, c. 819, s. 3

§ 19-1.5. Abatement does not preclude action

The abatement of a nuisance does not prejudice the right of any person to recover damages for its past existence.

History.
1977, c. 819, s. 3

N.C. Gen. Stat. § 19-2

Repealed by Session Laws 1977, c. 819, s. 4.

§ 19-2.1. Action for abatement; injunction

Wherever a nuisance is kept, maintained, or exists, as defined in this Article, the Attorney General, district attorney, county, municipality, or any private citizen of the county may maintain a civil action in the name of the State of North Carolina to abate a nuisance under this Chapter, perpetually to enjoin all persons from maintaining the same, and to enjoin the use of any structure or thing adjudged to be a nuisance under this Chapter; provided, however, that no private citizen may maintain such action where the alleged nuisance involves the illegal possession or sale of obscene or lewd matter.

Upon request from the Attorney General, district attorney, county or municipality, including the sheriff or chief of police of any county or municipality, the Alcohol Law Enforcement Division of the Department of Public Safety or any other law enforcement agency with jurisdiction may investigate alleged public nuisances and make recommendations regarding actions to abate the public nuisances.

If an action is instituted by a private person, the complainant shall execute a bond prior to the issuance of a restraining order or a temporary injunction, with good and sufficient surety to be approved by the court or clerk thereof, in the sum of not less than one thousand dollars ($ 1,000), to secure to the party enjoined the damages he may sustain if such action is wrongfully brought, not prosecuted to final judgment, or is dismissed, or is not maintained, or if it is finally decided that the temporary restraining order or preliminary injunction ought not to have been granted. The party enjoined shall have recourse against said bond for all damages suffered, including damages to his property, person, or character and including reasonable attorney's fees incurred by him in making defense to said action. No bond shall be required of the prosecuting attorney, the Attorney General, county, or municipality, and no action shall be maintained against any public official or public entity, their employees, or agents for investigating or maintaining an action for abatement of a nuisance under the provisions of this Chapter.

History.
1977, c. 819, s. 4; 1995, c. 528, s. 1; 1999-371, s. 5; 2011-145, s. 19.1(g), (n); 2014-100, s. 17.1(xxx); 2019-203, s. 9(a)

§ 19-2.2. Pleadings; jurisdiction; venue; application for preliminary injunction

The action, provided for in this Chapter, shall be brought in the superior court of the county in which the property is located. Such action shall be commenced by the filing of a verified complaint alleging the facts constituting the nuisance. After the filing of said complaint, application for a preliminary injunction may be made to the court in which the action is filed which court shall grant a hearing within 10 days after the filing of said application.

History.
1977, c. 819, s. 4

§ 19-2.3. Temporary order restraining removal of personal property from premises; service; punishment

Where such application for a preliminary injunction is made, the court may, on application of the complainant showing good cause, issue an ex parte temporary restraining order in accordance with G.S. 1A-1, Rule 65(b), preserving the status quo and restraining the defendant and all other persons from removing or in any manner interfering with any evidence specifically described, or in any manner removing or interfering with the personal property and contents of the place where such nuisance is alleged to exist, until the decision of the court granting or refusing such preliminary injunction and until further order of the court thereon. Nothing herein shall be interpreted to allow the prior restraint of the distribution of any matter or the sale of the stock in trade, but an inventory and full accounting of all business transactions involving alleged obscene or lewd matter thereafter shall be required. The inventory provisions provided by this section shall not apply to nuisances occurring at a private dwelling place unless the court finds the private dwelling place is used for profit.

Any person, firm, or corporation enjoined pursuant to this section may file with the court a motion to dissolve any temporary restraining order. Such a motion shall be heard within 24 hours of the time a copy of the motion is served on the complaining party, or on the next day the superior courts are open in the district, whichever is later. At such hearing the complaining party shall have the burden of showing why the restraining order should be continued.

In the event a temporary restraining order is issued, it may be served in accordance with the provisions of G.S. 1A-1, Rule 4, or may be served by handing to and leaving a copy of such order with any person in charge of such place or residing therein, or by posting a copy thereof in a conspicuous place at or upon one or more of the principal doors or entrances to such place, or by such service under said Rule 4, delivery and posting. The officer serving such temporary restraining order shall forthwith enter upon the property and make and return into court an inventory of the personal property and contents situated in and used in conducting or maintaining such nuisance.

Any violation of such temporary restraining order is a contempt of court, and where such order is posted, mutilation or removal thereof,

while the same remains in force, is a contempt of court, provided such posted order contains therein a notice to that effect.

History.
1977, c. 819, s. 4; 1999-371, s. 6

§ 19-2.4. Notice of hearing on preliminary injunction; consolidation

A copy of the complaint, together with a notice of the time and place of the hearing of the application for a preliminary injunction, shall be served upon the defendant at least five days before such hearing. The place may also be served by posting such papers in the same manner as is provided for in G.S. 19-2.3 in the case of a temporary restraining order. If the hearing is then continued at the instance of any defendant, the temporary restraining order may be continued as a matter of course until the hearing.

Before or after the commencement of the hearing of an application for a preliminary injunction, the court, on application of either of the parties or on its own motion, may order the trial of the action on the merits to be advanced and consolidated with the hearing on the application for the preliminary injunction; provided, however, the defendant shall be entitled to a jury trial if requested.

History.
1977, c. 819, s. 4

§ 19-2.5. Hearing on the preliminary injunction; issuance

If upon hearing, the allegations of the complaint are sustained to the satisfaction of the court, the court shall issue a preliminary injunction restraining the defendant and any other person from continuing the nuisance and effectually enjoining its use thereafter for the purpose of conducting any such nuisance. The court may, in its discretion, order the closure of the property pending trial on the merits.

History.
1977, c. 819, s. 4; 1999-371, s. 7

§ 19-3. Priority of action; evidence

(a) The action provided for in this Chapter shall be set down for trial at the first term of the court and shall have precedence over all other cases except crimes, election contests, or injunctions.

(b) In such action, an admission or finding of guilt of any person under the criminal laws against lewdness, assignation, prostitution, gambling, breaches of the peace, the illegal possession or sale of alcoholic beverages, or the illegal possession or sale of substances proscribed by the North Carolina Controlled Substances Act, at any such place, is admissible for the purpose of proving the existence of said nuisance, and is evidence of such nuisance and of knowledge of, and of acquiescence and participation therein, on the part of the person charged with maintaining said nuisance.

(c) At all hearings upon the merits, evidence of the general reputation of the building or place constituting the alleged nuisance, of the inmates thereof, and of those resorting thereto, is admissible for the purpose of proving the existence of such nuisance.

History.

Pub. Loc. 1913, c. 761, s. 27; 1919, c. 288; C.S., s. 3182; 1971, c. 528, s. 6; 1973, c. 47, s. 2; 1977, c. 819, s. 5; 1981, c. 412, s. 4; c. 747, s. 66; 1999-371, s. 8

§ 19-4. Violation of injunction; punishment

In case of the violation of any injunction granted under the provisions of this Chapter, the court, or, in vacation, a judge thereof, may summarily try and punish the offender. A party found guilty of contempt under the provisions of this section shall be punished by a fine of not less than two hundred ($ 200.00) or more than one thousand dollars ($ 1,000), or by imprisonment in the county jail not less than three or more than six months, or by both fine and imprisonment.

History.

Pub. Loc. 1913, c. 761, s. 28; 1919, c. 288; C.S., s. 3183

§ 19-5. Content of final judgment and order

If the existence of a nuisance is admitted or established in an action as provided for in this Chapter an order of abatement shall be entered as a part of the judgment in the case, which judgment and order shall perpetually enjoin the defendant and any other person from further maintaining the nuisance at the place complained of, and the defendant from maintaining such nuisance elsewhere within the jurisdiction of this State. Lewd matter, illegal alcoholic beverages, gambling paraphernalia, or substances proscribed under the North Carolina Controlled Substances Act shall be destroyed and not be sold.

Such order may also require the effectual closing of the place against its use thereafter for the purpose of conducting any such nuisance.

The provisions of this Article, relating to the closing of a place with respect to obscene or lewd matter, shall not apply in any order of the court to any theatre or motion picture establishment which does not, in the regular, predominant, and ordinary course of its business, show or demonstrate lewd films or motion pictures, as defined in this Article, but any such establishment may be permanently enjoined from showing such film judicially determined to be obscene hereunder and such film or motion picture shall be destroyed and all proceeds and moneys received therefrom, after the issuance of a preliminary injunction, forfeited.

History.

Pub. Loc. 1913, c. 761, s. 29; 1919, c. 288; C.S., s. 3184; 1977, c. 819, s. 6; 1981, c. 412, s. 4; c. 747, s. 66

§ 19-6. Civil penalty; forfeiture; accounting; lien as to expenses of abatement; invalidation of lease

Lewd matter is contraband, and there are no property rights therein. All personal property, including all money and other considerations, declared to be a nuisance under the provisions of G.S. 19-1.3 and other sections of this Article, are subject to forfeiture to the local government and are recoverable as damages in the county wherein such matter is sold, exhibited or otherwise used. Such property including moneys may be traced to and shall be recoverable from persons who, under G.S. 19-2.4, have knowledge of the nuisance at the time such moneys are received by them.

Upon judgment against the defendant or defendants in legal proceedings brought pursuant to this Article, an accounting shall be made by such defendant or defendants of all moneys received by them which have been declared to be a nuisance under this Article. An amount equal to the sum of all moneys estimated to have been taken in as gross income from such unlawful commercial activity shall be forfeited to the general funds of the city and county governments wherein such activity took place, to be shared equally, as a forfeiture of the fruits of an unlawful enterprise, and as partial restitution for damages done to the public welfare; provided, however, that no provision of this Article shall authorize the recovery of any moneys or gross income received from the sale of any book, magazine, or exhibition of any motion picture prior to the issuance of a preliminary injunction. Where the action is brought pursuant to this Article, special injury need not be proven, and the costs of abatement are a lien on both the real and personal property used in maintaining the nuisance. Costs of abatement include, but are not limited to, reasonable attorney's fees and court costs.

Upon the filing of the action, the plaintiff may file a notice of lis pendens in the official records of the county where the property is located.

If it is judicially found after an adversary hearing pursuant to this Article that a tenant or occupant of a building or tenement, under a lawful title, uses such place for the purposes of lewdness, assignation, prostitution, gambling, sale or possession of illegal alcoholic beverages or substances proscribed under the North Carolina Controlled Substances Act, or repeated acts which create and constitute a breach of the peace, such use makes void the lease or other title under which he holds, at the option of the owner, and, without any act of the owner, causes the right of possession to revert and vest in such owner.

The clear proceeds of civil penalties and forfeitures provided for in this section, except for penalties and properties that accrue to local governments instead of the State, shall be remitted to the Civil Penalty and Forfeiture Fund in accordance with G.S. 115C-457.2.

History.
Pub. Loc. 1913, c. 761, s. 30; 1919, c. 288; C.S., s. 3185; 1977, c. 819, s. 7; 1981, c. 412, s. 4; c. 747, s. 66; 1998-215, s. 106; 1999-371, s. 9

§ 19-6.1. Forfeiture of real property

In all actions where a preliminary injunction, permanent injunction, or an order of abatement is issued pursuant to this Article in which the nuisance consists of or includes at least two prior occurrences within five years of the manufacture, possession with intent to sell, or sale of controlled substances as defined by the North Carolina Controlled Substances Act, two prior occurrences of the possession of any controlled substance included within Schedule I or II of that Act, or two prior convictions within five years of violation of G.S. 14-72.7, the real property on which the nuisance exists or is maintained is subject to forfeiture in accordance with this section. In the case of the two prior convictions of G.S. 14-72.7, the convictions shall not arise out of the same transaction or occurrence.

If all of the owners of the property are defendants in the action, the plaintiff, other than a plaintiff who is a private citizen, may request forfeiture of the real property as part of the relief sought. If forfeiture is requested, and if jurisdiction over all defendant owners is established, upon judgment against the defendant or defendants, the court shall order forfeiture as follows:

(1) If the court finds by clear and convincing evidence that all the owners either (i) have participated in maintaining the nuisance on the property, or (ii) prior to the action had written notice from the plaintiff, or any governmental agent or entity authorized to bring an action pursuant to this Chapter, that the nuisance existed or was maintained on the property and have not made good faith efforts to stop the nuisance from occurring or recurring, the court shall order that the property be forfeited;

(2) If the court finds that one or more of the owners did not participate in maintaining the nuisance on the property or did not have written notice from the plaintiff prior to the action that the nuisance existed or was maintained on the property, the court shall not order forfeiture of the property immediately upon judgment. However, if after judgment and an order directing the defendants to abate the nuisance, the nuisance either continues, begins again, or otherwise recurs within five years of the order and the defendants have not made good faith efforts to abate the nuisance, the plaintiff may petition the court for forfeiture. Upon such petition, the defendant owner or owners shall be given notice and an opportunity to appear and be heard at a hearing to determine the continuation or recurrence of the nuisance. If, in this hearing (i) the plaintiff establishes by clear and convincing evidence that the nuisance, with the owner's or owners' knowledge, has either continued, begun again, or otherwise recurred, and (ii) the defendants fail to establish that they have made and are continuing to make good faith efforts to abate the nuisance, the court shall order that the property be forfeited.

For the purposes of this section, factors which may evidence good faith by the defendant to abate the nuisance include but are not limited to (i) cooperation with law enforcement authorities to abate the nuisance; (ii) lease restrictions prohibiting the illegal possession or sale of narcotic drugs and an action to evict a tenant for any violations of the lease provision; (iii) a criminal record check of prospective tenants; and (iv) reference checks of prior residency of prospective tenants.

Upon an order of forfeiture, title to the property shall vest in the school board of the county in which the property is located. If at the time of forfeiture the property is subject to a lien or security interest of a person not participating in the maintenance of the nuisance, the school board shall either (i) pay an amount to that person satisfying the lien or security interest; or (ii) sell the property and satisfy the lien or security interest from the proceeds of the sale. If the property is not subject to any lien or security interest at the time of forfeiture, the school board may hold, maintain, lease, sell, or otherwise dispose of the property as it sees fit.

Upon the filing of the action, the plaintiff may file a notice of lis pendens in the official records of the county where the property is located. If the plaintiff files a notice of lis pendens, any person purchasing or obtaining an interest in the property thereafter shall be considered to have notice of the alleged nuisance, and shall forfeit his interest in the property upon a judgment of forfeiture in favor of the plaintiff.

If in the same action in which real property is forfeited the court finds that a tenant or occupant of the property participated in or maintained the nuisance, the lease or other title under which the tenant or occupant holds is void, and the right of possession vests in the new owner. Upon forfeiture, the rights of innocent tenants occupying separate units of the property who were not involved in the nuisance at the time the action was filed shall be in accordance with any relevant lease provisions in effect at the time or, in the absence of relevant lease provisions, in accordance with the law applying to other tenants or occupants of property that is sold, foreclosed upon, or otherwise obtained by new owners.

History.
1995, c. 528, s. 2; 1999-371, s. 10; 2007-178, s. 4

§ 19-7. How order of abatement may be canceled

If the owner appears and pays all cost of the proceeding and files a bond, with sureties to be approved by the clerk, in the full value of the property, to be ascertained by the court, or, in vacation, by the clerk of the superior court, conditioned that he will immediately abate said nuisance, and prevent the same from being established or kept within a period of one year thereafter, the court may, if satisfied of his good faith, order the premises closed under the order of abatement to be delivered to said owner, and said order of abatement canceled so far as same may relate to said property; and if the proceeding be a civil action, and said bond be given and costs therein paid before judgment and order of abatement, the action shall be thereby abated as to said building only. The release of the property under the provisions of this section shall not release it from any judgment, lien, penalty, or liability to which it may be subject by law.

History.
Pub. Loc. 1913, c. 761, s. 31; 1919, c. 288; C.S., s. 3186

§ 19-8. Costs

The prevailing party shall be entitled to his costs. The court shall tax as part of the costs in any action brought hereunder such fee for the attorney prosecuting or defending the action or proceedings as may in the court's discretion be reasonable remuneration for the services performed by such attorney.

History.
Pub. Loc. 1913, c. 761, s. 32; 1919, c. 288; C.S., s. 3187; 1977, c. 819, s. 8

§ 19-8.1. Immunity

The provisions of any criminal statutes with respect to the exhibition of, or the possession with the intent to exhibit, any obscene film shall not apply to a motion picture projectionist, usher, or ticket taker acting within the scope of his employment, provided that such projectionist, usher, or ticket taker: (i) Has no financial interest in the place wherein he is so employed, and (ii) freely and willingly gives testimony regarding such employment in any judicial proceedings brought under this Chapter, including pretrial discovery proceedings incident thereto, when and if such is requested, and upon being granted immunity by the trial judge sitting in such matters.

History.
1977, c. 819, s. 9

§ 19-8.2. Right of entry

Authorized representatives of the Commission for Public Health, any local health department or the Department of Health and Human Services, upon presenting appropriate credentials to the owner, operator, or agent in charge of a place described in G.S. 19-1.2, are authorized to enter without delay and at any reasonable time any such place in order to inspect and investigate during the regular hours of operation of such place.

History.
1977, c. 819, s. 9; 1997-443, s. 11A.118(a); 2007-182, s. 2

§ 19-8.3. Severability

If any section, subsection, sentence, or clause of this Article is adjudged to be unconstitutional or invalid, such adjudication shall not affect the validity of the remaining portion of this Article. It is hereby declared that this Article would have been passed, and each section, sentence, or clause thereof, irrespective of the fact that any one or more sections, subsections, sentences or clauses might be adjudged to be unconstitutional, or for any other reason invalid.

History.
1977, c. 819, s. 10

§ 19-8.4. Human trafficking public awareness sign

The owner, operator, or agent in charge of a business described in G.S. 19-1.2 shall

Chapter 19

prominently display on the premises in a place that is clearly conspicuous and visible to employees and the public a public awareness sign created and provided by the North Carolina Human Trafficking Commission that contains the

National Human Trafficking Resource hotline information.

History.
2017-57, s. 17.4(c); 2017-197, s. 5.8

CHAPTER 19A
PROTECTION OF ANIMALS

ARTICLE 3
ANIMAL WELFARE ACT

§ 19A-20. Title of Article

This Article may be cited as the Animal Welfare Act.

History.
1977, 2nd Sess., c. 1217, s. 1

§ 19A-21. Purposes

The purposes of this Article are (i) to protect the owners of dogs and cats from the theft of such pets; (ii) to prevent the sale or use of stolen pets; (iii) to insure that animals, as items of commerce, are provided humane care and treatment by regulating the transportation, sale, purchase, housing, care, handling and treatment of such animals by persons or organizations engaged in transporting, buying, or selling them for such use; (iv) to insure that animals confined in pet shops, kennels, animal shelters and auction markets are provided humane care and treatment; (v) to prohibit the sale, trade or adoption of those animals which show physical signs of infection, communicable disease, or congenital abnormalities, unless veterinary care is assured subsequent to sale, trade or adoption.

History.
1977, 2nd Sess., c. 1217, s. 2

§ 19A-22. Animal Welfare Section in Animal Health Division of Department of Agriculture and Consumer Services created; Director

There is hereby created within the Animal Health Division of the North Carolina Department of Agriculture and Consumer Services, a new section thereof, to be known as the Animal Welfare Section of said division.

The Commissioner of Agriculture is hereby authorized to appoint a Director of said section whose duties and authority shall be determined by the Commissioner subject to the approval of the Board of Agriculture and subject to the provisions of this Article.

History.
1977, 2nd Sess., c. 1217, s. 3; 1997-261, s. 1

§ 19A-23. Definitions

For the purposes of this Article, the following terms, when used in the Article or the rules or orders made pursuant thereto, shall be construed respectively to mean:

(1) "Adequate feed" means the provision at suitable intervals, not to exceed 24 hours, of a quantity of wholesome foodstuff suitable for the species and age, sufficient to maintain a reasonable level of nutrition in each animal. Such foodstuff shall be served in a receptacle, dish, or container.

(2) "Adequate water" means a constant access to a supply of clean, fresh, potable water provided in a sanitary manner or provided at suitable intervals for the species and not to exceed 24 hours at any interval.

(3) "Ambient temperature" means the temperature surrounding the animal.

(4) "Animal" means any domestic dog (Canis familiaris), or domestic cat (Felis domestica).

(5) "Animal shelter" means a facility which is used to house or contain seized, stray, homeless, quarantined, abandoned or unwanted animals and which is under contract with, owned, operated, or maintained by a county, city, town, or other municipality, or by a duly incorporated humane society, animal welfare society, society for the prevention of cruelty to animals, or other nonprofit organization devoted to the welfare, protection, rehabilitation, or humane treatment of animals.

(5a) "Approved foster care provider" means an individual, nonprofit corporation, or association that cares for stray animals that has been favorably assessed by the operator of the animal shelter through the application of written standards.

(5b) "Approved rescue organization" means a nonprofit corporation or association that cares for stray animals that has been favorably assessed by the operator of the animal shelter through the application of written standards.

(5c) "Boarding kennel" means a facility or establishment which regularly offers to the public the service of boarding dogs or cats or both for a fee. Such a facility or establishment may, in addition to providing shelter, food and water, offer grooming or other services for dogs and/or cats.

(6) "Commissioner" means the Commissioner of Agriculture of the State of North Carolina.

(7) "Dealer" means any person who sells, exchanges, or donates, or offers to sell, exchange, or donate animals to another dealer, pet shop, or research facility;

provided, however, that an individual who breeds and raises on his own premises no more than the offspring of five canine or feline females per year, unless bred and raised specifically for research purposes shall not be considered to be a dealer for the purposes of this Article.

(8) "Director" means the Director of the Animal Welfare Section of the Animal Health Division of the Department of Agriculture and Consumer Services.

(9) "Euthanasia" means the humane destruction of an animal accomplished by a method that involves rapid unconsciousness and immediate death or by a method that involves anesthesia, produced by an agent which causes painless loss of consciousness, and death during such loss of consciousness.

(10) "Housing facility" means any room, building, or area used to contain a primary enclosure or enclosures.

(11) "Person" means any individual, partnership, firm, joint-stock company, corporation, association, trust, estate, or other legal entity.

(12) "Pet shop" means a person or establishment that acquires for the purposes of resale animals bred by others whether as owner, agent, or on consignment, and that sells, trades or offers to sell or trade such animals to the general public at retail or wholesale.

(13) "Primary enclosure" means any structure used to immediately restrict an animal or animals to a limited amount of space, such as a room, pen, cage compartment or hutch.

(14) "Public auction" means any place or location where dogs or cats are sold at auction to the highest bidder regardless of whether such dogs or cats are offered as individuals, as a group, or by weight.

(15) "Research facility" means any place, laboratory, or institution at which scientific tests, experiments, or investigations involving the use of living animals are carried out, conducted, or attempted.

(16) "Sanitize" means to make physically clean and to remove and destroy to a practical minimum, agents injurious to health.

History.

1977, 2nd Sess., c. 1217, s. 4; 1979, c. 734, s. 1; 1987, c. 827, s. 61; 1997-261, s. 2; 2005-276, s. 11.5(a); 2013-377, s. 1

§ 19A-24. Powers of Board of Agriculture

(a) The Board of Agriculture shall:

(1) Establish standards for the care of animals at animal shelters, boarding kennels, pet shops, and public auctions. A boarding kennel that offers dog day care services and has a ratio of dogs to employees or supervisors, or both employees and supervisors, of not more than 10 to one, shall not as to such services be subject to any regulations that restrict the number of dogs that are permitted within any primary enclosure.

(2) Prescribe the manner in which animals may be transported to and from registered or licensed premises.

(3) Require licensees and holders of certificates to keep records of the purchase and sale of animals and to identify animals at their establishments.

(4) Adopt rules to implement this Article, including federal regulations promulgated under Title 7, Chapter 54, of the United States Code.

(5) Adopt rules on the euthanasia of animals in the possession or custody of any person required to obtain a certificate of registration under this Article. An animal shall only be put to death by a method and delivery of method approved by the American Veterinary Medical Association, the Humane Society of the United States, or the American Humane Association. The Department shall establish rules for the euthanasia process using any one or combination of methods and standards prescribed by the three aforementioned organizations. The rules shall address the equipment, the process, and the separation of animals, in addition to the animals' age and condition. If the gas method of euthanasia is approved, rules shall require (i) that only commercially compressed carbon monoxide gas is approved for use, and (ii) that the gas must be delivered in a commercially manufactured chamber that allows for the individual separation of animals. Rules shall also mandate training for any person who participates in the euthanasia process.

(b) In addition to rules on the euthanasia of animals adopted pursuant to subdivision (5) of subsection (a) of this section, the Board of Agriculture shall adopt rules for the certification of euthanasia technicians. The rules may provide for:

(1) Written and practical examinations for persons who perform euthanasia.

(2) Issuance of certification to persons who have successfully completed both training and examinations to become a euthanasia technician.

(3) Recertification of euthanasia technicians on a periodic basis.

(4) Standards and procedures for the approval of persons who conduct training of euthanasia technicians.

(5) Approval of materials for use in euthanasia technician training.

(6) Minimum certification criteria for persons seeking to become euthanasia technicians including, but not limited to: age; previous related experience; criminal record; and other qualifications that are related to an applicant's fitness to perform euthanasia.

(7) Denial, suspension, or revocation of certification of euthanasia technicians who:

    a. Violate any provision of this Article or rules adopted pursuant to this Article;

    b. Have been convicted of or entered a plea of guilty or nolo contendere to:

        1. Any felony;

        2. Any misdemeanor or infraction involving animal abuse or neglect; or

        3. Any other offense related to animal euthanasia, the duties or responsibilities of a euthanasia technician, or a euthanasia technician's fitness for certification;

    c. Make any false statement, give false information, or omit material information in connection with an application for certification or for renewal or reinstatement of certification as a euthanasia technician; or

    d. Otherwise are or become ineligible for certification.

(8) Provision of the names of persons who perform euthanasia at animal shelters and for the animal shelter to notify the Department when those persons are no longer affiliated, employed, or serving as a volunteer with the shelter.

(9) Certified euthanasia technicians to notify the Department when they are no longer employed by or are serving as a volunteer at an animal shelter.

(10) The duties, responsibilities, and standards of conduct for certified euthanasia technicians.

(c) Regardless of the extent to which the Board exercises its authority under subsection (b) of this section, the Department may deny, revoke, or suspend the certification of a euthanasia technician who has been convicted of or entered a plea of guilty or nolo contendere to a felony involving the illegal use, possession, sale, manufacture, distribution, or transportation of a controlled substance, drug, or narcotic.

(d) Persons seeking certification as euthanasia technicians, or a renewal of such certification, shall provide the Department a fingerprint card in a format acceptable to the Department, a form signed by the person consenting to a criminal record check and the use of the person's fingerprints, and such other identifying information as may be required by the State or national data banks. The Department may deny certification to persons who refuse to provide the fingerprint card or consent to the criminal background check. Fees required by the Department of Public Safety for conducting the criminal background check shall be collected by the Department and remitted to the Department of Public Safety along with the fingerprint card and consent form.

History.
1977, 2nd Sess., c. 1217, s. 5; 1987, c. 827, s. 62; 2004-199, s. 12; 2005-276, s. 11.5(b); 2005-345, s. 22; 2008-198, s. 2(a); 2010-127, ss. 2, 3; 2014-100, s. 17.1(o)

§ 19A-25. Employees; investigations; right of entry

For the enforcement of the provisions of this Article, the Director is authorized, subject to the approval of the Commissioner to appoint employees as are necessary in order to carry out and enforce the provisions of this Article, and to assign them interchangeably with other employees of the Animal Health Division. The Director shall cause the investigation of all reports of violations of the provisions of this Article, and the rules adopted pursuant to the provisions hereof; provided further, that if any person shall deny the Director or his representative admittance to his property, either person shall be entitled to secure from any superior court judge a court order granting such admittance.

History.
1977, 2nd Sess., c. 1217, s. 6; 1987, c. 827, s. 63

§ 19A-26. Certificate of registration required for animal shelter

No person shall operate an animal shelter unless a certificate of registration for such animal shelter shall have been granted by the Director. Application for such certificate shall be made in the manner provided by the Director. No fee shall be required for such application or certificate. Certificates of registration shall be valid for a period of one year or until suspended or revoked and may be renewed for like periods upon application in the manner provided.

History.
1977, 2nd Sess., c. 1217, s. 7; 1987, c. 827, s. 64

§ 19A-27. License required for operation of pet shop

No person shall operate a pet shop unless a license to operate such establishment shall have been granted by the Director. Application for such license shall be made in the manner provided by the Director. The license shall be for the fiscal year and the license fee shall be seventy-five dollars ($ 75.00) for each license period or part thereof beginning with the first day of the fiscal year.

History.
1977, 2nd Sess., c. 1217, s. 8; 1987, c. 827, s. 65; 1989, c. 544, s. 17; 2011-145, s. 31.5(a).

§ 19A-28. License required for public auction or boarding kennel

No person shall operate a public auction or a boarding kennel unless a license to operate such establishment shall have been granted by the Director. Application for such license shall be made in the manner provided by the Director. The license period shall be the fiscal year and the license fee shall be seventy-five dollars ($ 75.00) for each license period or part thereof beginning with the first day of the fiscal year.

History.
1977, 2nd Sess., c. 1217, s. 9; 1987, c. 827, s. 65; 1989, c. 544, s. 18; 2011-145, s. 31.5(b).

§ 19A-29. License required for dealer

No person shall be a dealer unless a license to deal shall have been granted by the Director to such person. Application for such license shall be in the manner provided by the Director. The license period shall be the fiscal year and the license fee shall be seventy-five dollars ($ 75.00) for each license period or part thereof, beginning with the first day of the fiscal year.

History.
1977, 2nd Sess., c. 1217, s. 10; 1987, c. 827, s. 66; 1989, c. 544, s. 19; 2011-145, s. 31.5(c).

§ 19A-30. Refusal, suspension or revocation of certificate or license

The Director may refuse to issue or renew or may suspend or revoke a certificate of registration for any animal shelter or a license for any public auction, kennel, pet shop, or dealer, if after an impartial investigation as provided in this Article he determines that any one or more of the following grounds apply:

(1) Material misstatement in the application for the original certificate of registration or license or in the application for any renewal under this Article;

(2) Willful disregard or violation of this Article or any rules issued pursuant thereto;

(3) Failure to provide adequate housing facilities and/or primary enclosures for the purposes of this Article, or if the feeding, watering, sanitizing and housing practices at the animal shelter, public auction, pet shop, or kennel are not consistent with the intent of this Article or the rules adopted under this Article;

(4) Allowing one's license under this Article to be used by an unlicensed person;

(5) Conviction of any crime an essential element of which is misstatement, fraud, or dishonesty, or conviction of any felony;

(6) Making substantial misrepresentations or false promises of a character likely to influence, persuade, or induce in connection with the business of a public auction, commercial kennel, pet shop, or dealer;

(7) Pursuing a continued course of misrepresentation of or making false promises through advertising, salesmen, agents, or otherwise in connection with the business to be licensed;

(8) Failure to possess the necessary qualifications or to meet the requirements of this Article for the issuance or holding of a certificate of registration or license.

The Director shall, before refusing to issue or renew and before suspension or revocation of a certificate of registration or a license, give to the applicant or holder thereof a written notice containing a statement indicating in what respects the applicant or holder has failed to satisfy the requirements for the holding of a certificate of registration or a license. If a certificate of registration or a license is suspended or revoked under the provisions hereof, the holder shall have five days from such suspension or revocation to surrender all certificates of registration or licenses issued thereunder to the Director or his authorized representative.

A person to whom a certificate of registration or a license is denied, suspended, or revoked by the Director may contest the action by filing a petition under G.S. 150B-23 within five days after the denial, suspension, or revocation.

Any licensee whose license is revoked under the provisions of this Article shall not be eligible to apply for a new license hereunder until one year has elapsed from the date of the order revoking said license or if an appeal is taken from said order of revocation, one year from the date of the order or final judgment sustaining said revocation. Any person who has been an officer, agent, or employee of a licensee whose license has been revoked or suspended and who is responsible for or participated in the violation upon which the order of suspension or revocation was based, shall not be licensed within the period during which the order of suspension or revocation is in effect.

History.
1977, 2nd Sess., c. 1217, s. 11; 1987, c. 827, s. 67

§ 19A-31. License not transferable; change in management, etc., of business or operation

A license is not transferable. When there is a transfer of ownership, management, or operation of a business of a licensee hereunder, the new owner, manager, or operator, as the case may be, whether it be an individual, firm, partnership, corporation, or other entity shall have 10 days from such sale or transfer to secure a new license from the Director to operate said business. A licensee shall promptly notify the Director of any change in the name, address, management, or substantial control of his business or operation.

History.
1977, 2nd Sess., c. 1217, s. 12

§ 19A-32. Procedure for review of Director's decisions

A denial, suspension, or revocation of a certificate or license under this Article shall be made in accordance with Chapter 150B of the General Statutes.

History.
1977, 2nd Sess., c. 1217, s. 13; 1987, c. 827, s. 68

§ 19A-32.1. Minimum holding period for animals in animal shelters; public viewing of animals in animal shelters; disposition of animals

(a) Except as otherwise provided in this section, all animals received by an animal shelter or by an agent of an animal shelter shall be held for a minimum holding period of 72 hours, or for any longer minimum period established by a board of county commissioners, prior to being euthanized or otherwise disposed of.

(b) Before an animal may be euthanized or otherwise disposed of, it shall be made available for adoption under procedures that enable members of the public to inspect the animal, except in the following cases:

(1) The animal has been found by the operator of the shelter to be unadoptable due to injury or defects of health or temperament.

(2) The animal is seriously ill or injured, in which case the animal may be euthanized before the expiration of the minimum holding period if the manager of the animal shelter determines, in writing, that it is appropriate to do so. The writing shall include the reason for the determination.

(3) The animal is being held as evidence in a pending criminal case.

(c) Except as otherwise provided in this subsection, a person who comes to an animal shelter attempting to locate a lost pet is entitled to view every animal held at the shelter, subject to rules providing for such viewing during at least four hours a day, three days a week. If the shelter is housing animals that must be kept apart from the general public for health reasons, public safety concerns, or in order to preserve evidence for criminal proceedings, the shelter shall make reasonable arrangements that allow pet owners to determine whether their lost pets are among those animals.

(d) During the minimum holding period, an animal shelter may place an animal it is holding into foster care by transferring possession of the animal to an approved foster care provider, an approved rescue organization, or the person who found the animal. If an animal shelter transfers possession of an animal under this subsection, at least one photograph depicting the head and face of the animal shall be displayed at the shelter in a conspicuous location that is available to the general public during hours of operation, and that photograph shall remain posted until the animal is disposed of as provided in subsection (f) of this section.

(e) If a shelter places an animal in foster care, the shelter may, in writing, appoint the person or organization possessing the animal to be an agent of the shelter. After the expiration of the minimum holding period, the shelter may (i) direct the agent possessing the animal to return it to the shelter, (ii) allow the agent to adopt the animal consistent with the shelter's adoption policies, or (iii) extend the period of time that the agent holds the animal on behalf of the shelter. A shelter may terminate an agency created under this subsection at any time by directing the agent to deliver the animal to the shelter. The local government or organization operating the shelter, as principal in the agency relationship, shall not be liable to reimburse the agent for the costs of care of the animal and shall not be liable to the owner of the animal for harm to the animal caused by the agent, absent a written contract providing otherwise.

(f) An animal that is surrendered to an animal shelter by the animal's owner and not reclaimed by that owner during the minimum holding period may be disposed of in one of the following manners:

(1) Returned to the owner.

(2) Adopted as a pet by a new owner.

(3) Euthanized by a procedure approved by rules adopted by the Department of Agriculture and Consumer Services or, in the absence of such rules, by a procedure approved by the American Veterinary Medical Association, the Humane Society of the United States, or the American Humane Association.

(g) An animal that is surrendered to an animal shelter by the animal's owner may be disposed of before the expiration of the minimum holding period in a manner authorized under subsection (f) of this section if the owner provides to the shelter (i) some proof of ownership of the animal and (ii) a signed written consent to the disposition of the animal before the expiration of the minimum holding period.

(h) If the owner of a dog surrenders the dog to an animal shelter, the owner shall state in writing whether the dog has bitten any individual within the 10 days preceding the date of surrender.

(i) **An animal shelter shall require every person to whom an animal is released to present one of the following valid forms of government-issued photographic identification:**

(i) a drivers license, (ii) a special identification card issued under G.S. 20-37.7, (iii) a military identification card, or (iv) a passport. Upon presentation of the required photographic identification, the shelter shall document the name of the person, the type of photographic identification presented by the person, and the photographic identification number.

(j) Animal shelters shall maintain a record of all animals impounded at the shelter, shall retain those records for a period of at least three years from the date of impoundment, and shall make those records available for inspection during regular inspections pursuant to this Article or upon the request of a representative of the Animal Welfare Section. These records shall contain, at a minimum:

(1) The date of impoundment.

(2) The length of impoundment.

(3) The disposition of each animal, including the name and address of any person to whom the animal is released, any institution that person represents, and the identifying information required under subsection (i) of this section.

(4) Other information required by rules adopted by the Board of Agriculture.

History.
2013-377, s. 2

§ 19A-33. Penalty for operation of pet shop, kennel or auction without license

Operation of a pet shop, kennel, or public auction without a currently valid license shall constitute a Class 3 misdemeanor subject only to a penalty of not less than five dollars ($ 5.00) nor more than twenty-five dollars ($ 25.00), and each day of operation shall constitute a separate offense.

History.
1977, 2nd Sess., c. 1217, s. 14; 1993, c. 539, s. 315; 1994, Ex. Sess., c. 24, s. 14(c)

§ 19A-34. Penalty for acting as dealer without license; disposition of animals in custody of unlicensed dealer

Acting as a dealer in animals as defined in this Article without a currently valid dealer's license shall constitute a Class 2 misdemeanor. Continued illegal operation after conviction shall constitute a separate offense. Animals found in possession or custody of an unlicensed dealer shall be subject to immediate seizure and impoundment and upon conviction of such unlicensed dealer shall become subject to sale or euthanasia in the discretion of the Director.

History.
1977, 2nd Sess., c. 1217, s. 15; 1993, c. 539, s. 316; 1994, Ex. Sess., c. 24, s. 14(c)

§ 19A-35. Penalty for failure to adequately care for animals; disposition of animals

Failure of any person licensed or registered under this Article to adequately house, feed, and water animals in his possession or custody shall constitute a Class 3 misdemeanor, and such person shall be subject to a fine of not less than five dollars ($ 5.00) per animal or more than a total of one thousand dollars ($ 1,000). Such animals shall be subject to seizure and impoundment and upon conviction may be sold or euthanized at the discretion of the Director and such failure shall also constitute grounds for revocation of license after public hearing.

History.
1977, 2nd Sess., c. 1217, s. 16; 1999-408, s. 4

§ 19A-36. Penalty for violation of Article by dog warden

Violation of any provision of this Article which relates to the seizing, impoundment, and custody of an animal by a dog warden shall constitute a Class 3 misdemeanor and the person convicted thereof shall be subject to a fine of not less than fifty dollars ($ 50.00) and not more than one hundred dollars ($ 100.00), and each animal handled in violation shall constitute a separate offense.

History.
1977, 2nd Sess., c. 1217, s. 17; 1993, c. 539, s. 317; 1994, Ex. Sess., c. 24, s. 14(c)

§ 19A-37. Application of Article

This Article shall not apply to a place or establishment which is operated under the immediate supervision of a duly licensed veterinarian as a hospital where animals are harbored, boarded, and cared for incidental to the treatment, prevention, or alleviation of disease processes during the routine practice of the profession of veterinary medicine. This Article shall not apply to any dealer, pet shop, public auction, commercial kennel or research facility during the period such dealer or research facility is in the possession of a valid license or registration granted by the Secretary of Agriculture pursuant to Title 7, Chapter 54, of the United States Code. This Article shall not apply to any individual who occasionally boards an animal on a noncommercial basis, although such individual may receive nominal sums to cover the cost of such boarding.

History.
1977, 2nd Sess., c. 1217, s. 18; 1987, c. 827, s. 69

§ 19A-38. Use of license fees

All license fees collected shall be used in enforcing and administering this Article.

History.
1977, 2nd Sess., c. 1217, s. 19

§ 19A-39. Article inapplicable to establishments for training hunting dogs

Nothing in this Article shall apply to those kennels or establishments operated primarily for the purpose of boarding or training hunting dogs.

History.
1977, 2nd Sess., c. 1217, s. 21; 1979, c. 734, s. 2

§ 19A-40. Civil Penalties

The Director may assess a civil penalty of not more than five thousand dollars ($ 5,000) against any person who violates a provision of this Article or any rule promulgated thereunder. In determining the amount of the penalty, the Director shall consider the degree and extent of harm caused by the violation. The clear proceeds of civil penalties assessed pursuant to this section shall be remitted to the Civil Penalty and Forfeiture Fund in accordance with G.S. 115C-457.2.

History.
1995, c. 516, s. 6; 1998-215, s. 3

§ 19A-41. Legal representation by the Attorney General

It shall be the duty of the Attorney General to represent the Commissioner of Agriculture and the Department of Agriculture and Consumer Services, or to designate some member of his staff to represent the Commissioner and the Department, in all actions or proceedings in connection with this Article.

History.
2005-276, s. 11.5(c)

ARTICLE 4
ANIMAL CRUELTY INVESTIGATORS

§ 19A-45. Appointment of animal cruelty investigators; term of office; removal; badge; oath; bond

(a) The board of county commissioners is authorized to appoint one or more animal cruelty investigators to serve without any compensation or other employee benefits in his county. In making these appointments, the board may consider persons nominated by any society incorporated under North Carolina law for the prevention of cruelty to animals. Prior to making any such appointment, the board of county commissioners is authorized to enter into an agreement whereby any necessary expenses of caring for seized animals not collectable pursuant to G.S. 19A-47 may be paid by the animal cruelty investigator or by any society incorporated under North Carolina law for the prevention of cruelty to animals that is willing to bear such expense.

(b) Animal cruelty investigators shall serve a one-year term subject to removal for cause by the board of county commissioners. Animal cruelty investigators shall, while in the performance of their official duties, wear in plain view a badge of a design approved by the board identifying them as animal cruelty investigators, and provided at no cost to the county.

(c) Animal cruelty investigators shall take and subscribe the oath of office required of public officials. The oath shall be filed with the clerk of superior court. Animal cruelty investigators shall not be required to post any bond.

(d) Upon approval by the board of county commissioners, the animal cruelty investigator or investigators may be reimbursed for all necessary and actual expenses, to be paid by the county.

History.
1979, c. 808, s. 1

§ 19A-46. Powers; magistrate's order; execution of order; petition; notice to owner

(a) Whenever any animal is being cruelly treated as defined in G.S. 19A-1(2), an animal cruelty investigator may file with a magistrate a sworn complaint requesting an order allowing the investigator to provide suitable care for and take immediate custody of the animal. The magistrate shall issue the order only when he finds probable cause to believe that the animal is being cruelly treated and that it is necessary for the investigator to immediately take custody of it. Any magistrate's order issued under this section shall be valid for only 24 hours after its issuance. After he executes the order, the animal cruelty investigator shall return it with a written inventory of the animals seized to the clerk of court in the county where the order was issued.

(b) The animal cruelty investigator may request a law-enforcement officer or animal control officer to accompany him to help him seize the animal. An investigator may forcibly enter any premises or vehicle when necessary to execute the order only if he reasonably believes that the premises or vehicle is unoccupied by any person and that the animal is on the premises or in the vehicle. Forcible entry shall be used only when the animal cruelty investigator is accompanied by a law-enforcement officer. In any case, he must give notice of his identity and purpose to anyone who may be present before entering said premises. Forcible entry shall only be used during the daylight hours.

(c) When he has taken custody of such an animal, the animal cruelty investigator shall file a complaint pursuant to Article 1 of this Chapter as soon as possible. When he seizes the animal, he shall leave with the owner, if known, or affixed to the premises or vehicle a copy of the magistrate's order and a written notice of a description of the animal, the place where the animal will be taken, the reason for taking the animal, and the investigator's intent to file a complaint in district court requesting custody of the animal pursuant to Article 1 of this Chapter.

(d) Notwithstanding the provisions of G.S. 7A-305(c), any person who commences a proceeding under this Article or Article 1 of this Chapter shall not be required to pay any court costs or fees prior to a final judicial determination as provided in G.S. 19A-4, at which time those costs shall be paid pursuant to the provisions of G.S. 6-18.

(e) Any judicial order authorizing forcible entry shall be issued by a district court judge.

History.
1979, c. 808, s. 1

§ 19A-47. Care of seized animals

The investigator must take any animal he seizes directly to some safe and secure place and provide suitable care for it. The necessary expenses of caring for seized animals, including necessary veterinary care, shall be a charge against the animal's owner and a lien on the animal to be enforced as provided by G.S. 44A-4.

History.
1979, c. 808, s. 1

§ 19A-48. Interference unlawful

It shall be a Class 1 misdemeanor, to interfere with an animal cruelty investigator in the performance of his official duties.

History.
1979, c. 808, s. 1; 1993, c. 539, s. 318; 1994, Ex. Sess., c. 24, s. 14(c)

§ 19A-49. Educational requirements

Each animal cruelty investigator at his own expense must attend annually a course of at least six hours instruction offered by the North Carolina Humane Federation or some other agency. The course shall be designed to give the investigator expertise in the investigation of complaints relating to the care and treatment of animals. Failure to attend a course approved by the board of county commissioners shall be cause for removal from office.

History.
1979, c. 808, s. 1

ARTICLE 6
CARE OF ANIMAL SUBJECTED TO ILLEGAL TREATMENT

§ 19A-70. Care of animal subjected to illegal treatment

(a) In every arrest under any provision of Article 47 of Chapter 14 of the General Statutes or under G.S. 67-4.3 or upon the commencement of an action under Article 1 of this Chapter by a county or municipality, by a county-approved animal cruelty investigator, by other county or municipal official, or by an organization operating a county or municipal shelter under contract, if an animal shelter takes custody of an animal, the operator of the shelter may file a petition with the court requesting that the defendant be ordered to deposit funds in an amount sufficient to secure payment of all the reasonable expenses expected to be incurred by the animal shelter in caring for and providing for the animal pending the disposition of the litigation. For purposes of this section, "reasonable expenses" includes the cost of providing food, water, shelter, and care, including medical care, for at least 30 days.

(b) Upon receipt of a petition, the court shall set a hearing on the petition to determine the need to care for and provide for the animal pending the disposition of the litigation. The hearing shall be conducted no less than 10 and no more than 15 business days after the petition is filed. The operator of the animal shelter shall mail written notice of the hearing and a copy of the petition to the defendant at the address contained in the criminal charges or the complaint or summons by which a civil action was initiated. If the defendant is in a local detention facility at the time the petition is filed, the operator of the animal shelter shall also provide notice to the custodian of the detention facility.

(c) The court shall set the amount of funds necessary for 30 days' care after taking into consideration all of the facts and circumstances of the case, including the need to care for and provide for the animal pending the disposition of the litigation, the recommendation of the operator of the animal shelter, the estimated cost of caring for and providing for the animal, and the defendant's ability to pay. If the court determines that the defendant is unable to deposit funds, the court may consider issuing an order under subsection (f) of this section.

Any order for funds to be deposited pursuant to this section shall state that if the operator of the animal shelter files an affidavit with the clerk of superior court, at least two business days prior to the expiration of a 30-day period, stating that, to the best of the affiant's knowledge, the case against the defendant has not yet been resolved, the order shall be automatically renewed every 30 days until the case is resolved.

(d) If the court orders that funds be deposited, the amount of funds necessary for 30 days shall be posted with the clerk of superior court. The defendant shall also deposit the same amount with the clerk of superior court every 30 days thereafter until the litigation is resolved, unless the defendant requests a hearing no less than five business days prior to the expiration of a 30-day period. If the defendant fails to deposit the funds within five business days of the initial hearing, or five business days of the expiration of a 30-day period, the animal is forfeited by operation of law. If funds have been deposited in accordance with this section, the operator of the animal shelter may draw from the funds the actual costs incurred in caring for the animal.

In the event of forfeiture, the animal shelter may determine whether the animal is suitable for adoption and whether adoption can be arranged for the animal. The animal may not be adopted by the defendant or by any person residing in the defendant's household. If the adopted animal is a dog used for fighting, the animal shelter shall notify any persons adopting the dog of the liability provisions for owners of dangerous dogs under Article 1A of Chapter 67 of the General Statutes. If no adoption can be arranged after the forfeiture, or the animal is unsuitable for adoption, the shelter shall humanely euthanize the animal.

(e) The deposit of funds shall not prevent the animal shelter from disposing of the animal prior to the expiration of the 30-day period covered by the deposit if the court makes a final determination of the charges or claims against the defendant. Upon determination, the defendant is entitled to a refund for any portion of the deposit not incurred as expenses by the animal shelter. A person who is acquitted of all criminal charges or not found to have committed animal cruelty in a civil action under Article 1 of this Chapter is entitled to a refund of the deposit remaining after any draws from the deposit in accordance with subsection (d) of this section.

(f) Pursuant to subsection (c) of this section, the court may order a defendant to provide necessary food, water, shelter, and care, including any necessary medical care, for any animal that is the basis of the charges or claims against the defendant without the removal of the animal from the existing location and until the charges or claims against the defendant are adjudicated. If the court issues such an order, the court shall provide for an animal control officer or other law enforcement officer to make regular visits to the location to ensure that the animal is receiving necessary food, water, shelter, and care, including any necessary medical care, and to impound the animal if it is not receiving those necessities.

History.
2005-383, s. 1; 2006-113, s. 2.1

CHAPTER 20
MOTOR VEHICLES

ARTICLE 1
DIVISION OF MOTOR VEHICLES

§ 20-1. Division of Motor Vehicles established

The Division of Motor Vehicles of the Department of Transportation is established. This Chapter sets out the powers and duties of the Division.

History.
1941, c. 36, s. 1; 1949, c. 1167; 1973, c. 476, s. 193; 1975, c. 716, s. 5; c. 863; 1987, c. 827, s. 2; c. 847, s. 1; 1995 (Reg. Sess., 1996), c. 756, s. 1

§ 20-2. Commissioner of Motor Vehicles; rules

(a) **Commissioner and Assistants.** -- The Division of Motor Vehicles shall be administered by the Commissioner of Motor Vehicles, who shall be appointed by and serve at the pleasure of the Secretary of the Department of Transportation. The Commissioner shall be paid an annual salary to be fixed by the Governor and allowed traveling expenses as allowed by law.

In any action, proceeding, or matter of any kind, to which the Commissioner of Motor Vehicles is a party or in which he may have an interest, all pleadings, legal notices, proof of claim, warrants for collection, certificates of tax liability, executions, and other legal documents, may be signed and verified on behalf of the Commissioner of Motor Vehicles by the Assistant Commissioner of Motor Vehicles or by any director or assistant director of any section of the Division of Motor Vehicles or by any other agent or employee of the Division so authorized by the Commissioner of Motor Vehicles.

(b) **Rules.** -- The Commissioner may adopt rules to implement this Chapter. Chapter 150B of the General Statutes governs the adoption of rules by the Commissioner.

History.
1941, c. 36, s. 2; 1945, c. 527; 1955, c. 472; 1975, c. 716, s. 5; 1983, c. 717, s. 5; 1983 (Reg. Sess., 1984), c. 1034, s. 164; 1991, c. 477, s. 4; 2012-142, s. 25.1 (b)

§ 20-3. Organization of Division

The Commissioner, subject to the approval of the Secretary of the Department of Transportation, shall organize and administer the Division in such manner as he may deem necessary to conduct the work of the Division.

History.
1941, c. 36, s. 3; 1975, c. 716, s. 5

§ 20-3.1. Purchase of additional airplanes

The Division of Motor Vehicles shall not purchase additional airplanes without the express authorization of the General Assembly.

History.
1963, c. 911, s. 1 1/2; 1971, c. 198; 1975, c. 716, s. 5

N.C. Gen. Stat. § 20-4

Repealed by Session Laws 2002-190, s. 4, effective January 1, 2003.

§ 20-4.01. Definitions

Unless the context requires otherwise, the following definitions apply throughout this Chapter to the defined words and phrases and their cognates:

(1) **Airbag.** -- A motor vehicle inflatable occupant restraint system device that is part of a supplemental restraint system.

(1a) **Alcohol.** -- Any substance containing any form of alcohol, including ethanol, methanol, propanol, and isopropanol.

(1b) **Alcohol Concentration.** -- The concentration of alcohol in a person, expressed either as:

a. Grams of alcohol per 100 milliliters of blood; or

b. Grams of alcohol per 210 liters of breath.

The results of a defendant's alcohol concentration determined by a chemical analysis of the defendant's breath or blood shall be reported to the hundredths. Any result between hundredths shall be reported to the next lower hundredth.

(1c) **All-Terrain Vehicle or ATV.** -- A motorized vehicle 50 inches or less in width that is designed to travel on three or more low-pressure tires and manufactured for off-highway use. The terms "all-terrain vehicle" or "ATV" do not include a golf cart or a utility vehicle, as defined in this section, or a riding lawn mower.

(1d) **Business District.** -- The territory prescribed as such by ordinance of the Board of Transportation.

(2) **Canceled.** -- As applied to drivers' licenses and permits, a declaration that a license or permit which was issued through error or fraud, or to which G.S. 20-15(a) applies, is void and terminated.

(2a) **Class A Motor Vehicle.** -- A combination of motor vehicles that meets either of the following descriptions:

a. Has a combined GVWR of at least 26,001 pounds and includes as part of the combination a towed unit that has a GVWR of at least 10,001 pounds.

b. Has a combined GVWR of less than 26,001 pounds and includes as part of the combination a towed unit that has a GVWR of at least 10,001 pounds.

(2b) **Class B Motor Vehicle.** -- Any of the following:

a. A single motor vehicle that has a GVWR of at least 26,001 pounds.

b. A combination of motor vehicles that includes as part of the combination a towing unit that has a GVWR of at least 26,001 pounds and a towed unit that has a GVWR of less than 10,001 pounds.

(2c) **Class C Motor Vehicle.** -- Any of the following:

a. A single motor vehicle not included in Class B.

b. A combination of motor vehicles not included in Class A or Class B.

(3) Repealed by Session Laws 1979, c. 667, s. 1.

(3a) **Chemical Analysis.** -- A test or tests of the breath, blood, or other bodily fluid or substance of a person to determine the person's alcohol concentration or presence of an impairing substance, performed in accordance with G.S. 20-139.1, including duplicate or sequential analyses.

(3b) **Chemical Analyst.** -- A person granted a permit by the Department of Health and Human Services under G.S. 20-139.1 to perform chemical analyses.

(3c) **Commercial Drivers License (CDL).** -- A license issued by a state to an individual who resides in the state that authorizes the individual to drive a class of commercial motor vehicle. A "nonresident commercial drivers license (NRCDL)" is issued by a state to an individual who resides in a foreign jurisdiction.

(3d) **Commercial Motor Vehicle.** -- Any of the following motor vehicles that are designed or used to transport passengers or property:

a. A Class A motor vehicle that has a combined GVWR of at least 26,001 pounds and includes as part of the combination a towed unit that has a GVWR of at least 10,001 pounds.

b. A Class B motor vehicle.

c. A Class C motor vehicle that meets either of the following descriptions:

1. Is designed to transport 16 or more passengers, including the driver.

2. Is transporting hazardous materials and is required to be placarded in accordance with 49 C.F.R. Part 172, Subpart F.

d. Repealed by Session Laws 1999, c. 330, s. 9, effective December 1, 1999.

(4) **Commissioner.** -- The Commissioner of Motor Vehicles.

(4a) **Conviction.** -- A conviction for an offense committed in North Carolina or another state:

a. In-State. When referring to an offense committed in North Carolina, the term means any of the following:

1. A final conviction of a criminal offense, including a no contest plea.

2. A determination that a person is responsible for an infraction, including a no contest plea.

3. An unvacated forfeiture of cash in the full amount of a bond required by Article 26 of Chapter 15A of the General Statutes.

4. A third or subsequent prayer for judgment continued within any five-year period.

5. Any prayer for judgment continued if the offender holds a commercial drivers license or if the offense occurs in a commercial motor vehicle.

b. Out-of-State. When referring to an offense committed outside North Carolina, the term means any of the following:

1. An unvacated adjudication of guilt.

2. A determination that a person has violated or failed to comply with the law in a court of original jurisdiction or an authorized administrative tribunal.

3. An unvacated forfeiture of bail or collateral deposited to secure the person's appearance in court.

4. A violation of a condition of release without bail, regardless of whether or not the penalty is rebated, suspended, or probated.

5. A final conviction of a criminal offense, including a no contest plea.

6. Any prayer for judgment continued, including any payment of a fine or court costs, if the offender holds a commercial drivers license or if the offense occurs in a commercial motor vehicle.

(4b) **Counterfeit supplemental restraint system component.** -- A replacement supplemental restraint system component, including an airbag, that displays a mark identical to, or substantially similar to, the genuine mark of a motor vehicle manufacturer or a supplier of parts to the manufacturer of a motor vehicle, without authorization from the manufacturer or supplier.

(4c) **Crash.** -- Any event that results in injury or property damage attributable directly to the motion of a motor vehicle or its load. The terms collision, accident, and crash and their cognates are synonymous.

(5) **Dealer.** -- Every person engaged in the business of buying, selling, distributing, or exchanging motor vehicles, trailers, or semitrailers in this State, and having an established place of business in this State.

The terms "motor vehicle dealer," "new motor vehicle dealer," and "used motor vehicle dealer" as used in Article 12 of this Chapter have the meaning set forth in G.S. 20-286.

(5a) **Dedicated natural gas vehicle.** -- A four-wheeled motor vehicle that meets each of the following requirements:

a. Is made by a manufacturer primarily for use on public streets, roads, and highways and meets National Highway Traffic Safety Administration standards included in 49 C.F.R. § 571.

b. Has not been modified from original manufacturer specifications with regard to power train or any manner of powering the vehicle.

c. Is powered solely by natural gas.

d. Is rated at not more than 8,500 pounds unloaded gross vehicle weight.

e. Has a maximum speed capability of at least 65 miles per hour.

(5b) **Disqualification.** -- A withdrawal of the privilege to drive a commercial motor vehicle.

(6) **Division.** -- The Division of Motor Vehicles acting directly or through its duly authorized officers and agents.

(7) **Driver.** -- The operator of a vehicle, as defined in subdivision (25). The terms "driver" and "operator" and their cognates are synonymous.

(7a) **Electric Assisted Bicycle.** -- A bicycle with two or three wheels that is equipped with a seat or saddle for use by the rider, fully operable pedals for human propulsion, and an electric motor of no more than 750 watts, whose maximum speed on a level surface when powered solely by such a motor is no greater than 20 miles per hour.

(7b) **Electric Personal Assistive Mobility Device.** -- A self-balancing nontandem two-wheeled device, designed to transport one person, with a propulsion system that limits the maximum speed of the device to 15 miles per hour or less.

(7c) **Employer.** -- Any person who owns or leases a commercial motor vehicle or assigns a person to drive a commercial motor vehicle and would be subject to the alcohol and controlled substance testing provisions of 49 C.F.R. § 382 and also includes any consortium or third-party administrator administering the alcohol and controlled substance testing program on behalf of owner-operators subject to the provisions of 49 C.F.R. § 382.

(8) **Essential Parts.** -- All integral and body parts of a vehicle of any type required to be registered hereunder, the removal, alteration, or substitution of which would tend to conceal the identity of the vehicle or substantially alter its appearance, model, type, or mode of operation.

(9) **Established Place of Business.** -- Except as provided in G.S. 20-286, the place actually occupied by a dealer or manufacturer at which a permanent business of bargaining, trading, and selling motor vehicles is or will be carried on and at which the books, records, and files necessary and incident to the conduct of the business of automobile dealers or manufacturers shall be kept and maintained.

(10) **Explosives.** -- Any chemical compound or mechanical mixture that is commonly used or intended for the purpose of producing an explosion and which contains any oxidizing and combustive units or other ingredients in such proportions, quantities, or packing that an ignition by fire, by friction, by concussion, by percussion, or by detonator of any part of the compound or mixture may cause such a sudden generation of highly heated gases that the resultant gaseous pressures are capable of producing destructible effects on contiguous objects or of destroying life or limb.

(11) **Farm Tractor.** -- Every motor vehicle designed and used primarily as a farm implement for drawing plows, mowing machines, and other implements of husbandry.

(11a) **For-Hire Motor Carrier.** -- A person who transports passengers or property by motor vehicle for compensation.

(12) **Foreign Vehicle.** -- Every vehicle of a type required to be registered hereunder brought into this State from another state, territory, or country, other than in the ordinary course of business, by or through a manufacturer or dealer and not registered in this State.

(12a) **Fuel cell electric vehicle.** -- A four-wheeled motor vehicle that does not have the ability to be propelled by a gasoline engine and that meets each of the following requirements:

    a. Is made by a manufacturer primarily for use on public streets, roads, and highways and meets National Highway Traffic Safety Administration standards included in 49 C.F.R. § 571.

    b. Has not been modified from original manufacturer specifications with regard to power train or any manner of powering the vehicle.

    c. Uses hydrogen and a fuel cell to produce electricity on board to power an electric motor to propel the vehicle.

    d. Is rated at not more than 8,500 pounds unloaded gross vehicle weight.

    e. Has a maximum speed capability of at least 65 miles per hour.

(12b) **Golf Cart.** -- A vehicle designed and manufactured for operation on a golf course for sporting or recreational purposes and that is not capable of exceeding speeds of 20 miles per hour.

(12c) **Gross Combination Weight Rating (GCWR).** -- Defined in 49 C.F.R. § 390.5.

(12d) **Gross Combined Weight (GCW).** -- The total weight of a combination (articulated) motor vehicle, including passengers, fuel, cargo, and attachments.

(12e) **Gross Vehicle Weight (GVW).** -- The total weight of a vehicle, including passengers, fuel, cargo, and attachments.

(12f) **Gross Vehicle Weight Rating (GVWR).** -- The value specified by the manufacturer as the maximum loaded weight a vehicle is capable of safely hauling. The GVWR of a combination vehicle is the GVWR of the power unit plus the GVWR of the towed unit or units. When a vehicle is determined by an enforcement officer to be structurally altered in any way from the manufacturer's original design in an attempt to increase the hauling capacity of the vehicle, the GVWR of that vehicle shall be deemed to be the greater of the license weight or the total weight of the vehicle or combination of vehicles for the purpose of enforcing this Chapter. For the purpose of classification of commercial drivers license and skills testing, the manufacturer's GVWR shall be used.

(12g) **Hazardous Materials.** -- Any material that has been designated as hazardous under 49 U.S.C. § 5103 and is required to be placarded under Subpart F of Part 172 of Title 49 of the Code of Federal Regulations, or any quantity of a material listed as a select agent or toxin under Part 73 of Title 42 of the Code of Federal Regulations.

(12h) **High-Mobility Multipurpose Wheeled Vehicle (HMMWV).** -- A four-wheel drive vehicle produced for military or government use and commonly referred to as a "HMMWV" or "Humvee".

(13) **Highway.** -- The entire width between property or right-of-way lines of every way or place of whatever nature, when any part thereof is open to the use of the public as a matter of right for the purposes of vehicular traffic. The terms "highway" and "street" and their cognates are synonymous.

(14) **House Trailer.** -- Any trailer or semitrailer designed and equipped to provide living or sleeping facilities and drawn by a motor vehicle. This term shall not include a manufactured home as defined in subdivision (18a) of this section.

(14a) **Impairing Substance.** -- Alcohol, controlled substance under Chapter 90 of the General Statutes, any other drug or psychoactive substance capable of impairing a person's physical or mental faculties, or any combination of these substances.

(15) **Implement of Husbandry.** -- Every vehicle which is designed for agricultural purposes and used exclusively in the conduct of agricultural operations.

(15a) **Inoperable Vehicle.** -- A motor vehicle that is substantially disassembled and for this reason is mechanically unfit or unsafe to be operated or moved upon a public street, highway, or public vehicular area.

(16) **Intersection.** -- The area embraced within the prolongation of the lateral curblines or, if none, then the lateral edge of roadway lines of two or more highways which join one another at any angle whether or not one such highway crosses the other.

Where a highway includes two roadways 30 feet or more apart, then every crossing of each roadway of such divided highway by an intersecting highway shall be regarded as a separate intersection. In the event that such intersecting highway also includes two roadways 30 feet or more apart, then every crossing of two roadways of such highways shall be regarded as a separate intersection.

(17) **License.** -- Any driver's license or any other license or permit to operate a motor vehicle issued under or granted by the laws of this State including:

    a. Any temporary license or learner's permit;

    b. The privilege of any person to drive a motor vehicle whether or not such person holds a valid license; and

    c. Any nonresident's operating privilege.

Chapter 20

(18) **Local Authorities.** -- Every county, municipality, or other territorial district with a local board or body having authority to adopt local police regulations under the Constitution and laws of this State.

(18a) **Manufactured Home.** -- Defined in G.S. 143-143.9(6).

(19) **Manufacturer.** -- Every person, resident, or nonresident of this State, who manufactures or assembles motor vehicles.

(20) **Manufacturer's Certificate.** -- A certification on a form approved by the Division, signed by the manufacturer, indicating the name of the person or dealer to whom the therein-described vehicle is transferred, the date of transfer and that such vehicle is the first transfer of such vehicle in ordinary trade and commerce. The description of the vehicle shall include the make, model, year, type of body, identification number or numbers, and such other information as the Division may require.

(21) **Metal Tire.** -- Every tire the surface of which in contact with the highway is wholly or partly of metal or other hard, nonresilient material.

(21a) Repealed by Session Laws 2016-90, s. 13(a), effective December 1, 2016, and applicable to offenses committed on or after that date.

(21b) **Motor Carrier.** -- A for-hire motor carrier or a private motor carrier.

(22) **Motorcycle.** -- A type of passenger vehicle as defined in G.S. 20-4.01(27).

(23) **Motor Vehicle.** -- Every vehicle which is self-propelled and every vehicle designed to run upon the highways which is pulled by a self-propelled vehicle. Except as specifically provided otherwise, this term shall not include mopeds or electric assisted bicycles.

(23a) **Nonfunctional airbag.** -- A replacement airbag that meets any of the following criteria:

a. The airbag was previously deployed or damaged.

b. The airbag has an electric fault that is detected by the vehicle's airbag diagnostic systems when the installation procedure is completed and the vehicle is returned to the customer who requested the work to be performed or when ownership is intended to be transferred.

c. The airbag includes a part or object, including a supplemental restraint system component that is installed in a motor vehicle to mislead the owner or operator of the motor vehicle into believing that a functional airbag has been installed.

d. The airbag is subject to the prohibitions of 49 U.S.C. § 30120(j).

(24) **Nonresident.** -- Any person whose legal residence is in some state, territory, or jurisdiction other than North Carolina or in a foreign country.

(24a) **Offense Involving Impaired Driving.** -- Any of the following offenses:

a. Impaired driving under G.S. 20-138.1.

b. Any offense set forth under G.S. 20-141.4 when conviction is based upon impaired driving or a substantially similar offense under previous law.

c. First or second degree murder under G.S. 14-17 or involuntary manslaughter under G.S. 14-18 when conviction is based upon impaired driving or a substantially similar offense under previous law.

d. An offense committed in another jurisdiction which prohibits substantially similar conduct prohibited by the offenses in this subsection.

e. A repealed or superseded offense substantially similar to impaired driving, including offenses under former G.S. 20-138 or G.S. 20-139.

f. Impaired driving in a commercial motor vehicle under G.S. 20-138.2, except that convictions of impaired driving under G.S. 20-138.1 and G.S. 20-138.2 arising out of the same transaction shall be considered a single conviction of an offense involving impaired driving for any purpose under this Chapter.

g. Habitual impaired driving under G.S. 20-138.5.

A conviction under former G.S. 20-140(c) is not an offense involving impaired driving.

(24b) **On-track equipment.** -- Any railcar, rolling stock, equipment, vehicle, or other device that is operated on stationary rails.

(25) **Operator.** -- A person in actual physical control of a vehicle which is in motion or which has the engine running. The terms "operator" and "driver" and their cognates are synonymous.

(25a) **Out of Service Order.** -- A declaration that a driver, a commercial motor vehicle, or a motor carrier operation is out-of-service.

(26) **Owner.** -- A person holding the legal title to a vehicle, or in the event a vehicle is the subject of a chattel mortgage or an agreement for the conditional sale or lease thereof or other like agreement, with the right of purchase upon performance

of the conditions stated in the agreement, and with the immediate right of possession vested in the mortgagor, conditional vendee or lessee, said mortgagor, conditional vendee or lessee shall be deemed the owner for the purpose of this Chapter. For the purposes of this Chapter, the lessee of a vehicle owned by the government of the United States shall be considered the owner of said vehicle.

(27) **Passenger Vehicles. --**

a. **Ambulances. --** Vehicles equipped for transporting wounded, injured, or sick persons.

b. **Autocycle. --** A three-wheeled motorcycle that has a steering wheel, pedals, seat safety belts for each occupant, antilock brakes, completely or partially enclosed seating that does not require the operator to straddle or sit astride, and is otherwise manufactured to comply with federal safety requirements for motorcycles.

c. **Child care vehicles. --** Vehicles under the direction and control of a child care facility, as defined in G.S. 110-86(3), and driven by an owner, employee, or agent of the child care facility for the primary purpose of transporting children to and from the child care facility, or to and from a place for participation in an event or activity in connection with the child care facility.

d. **Common carriers of passengers. --** Vehicles operated under a certificate of authority issued by the Utilities Commission for operation on the highways of this State between fixed termini or over a regular route for the transportation of persons for compensation.

e. **Excursion passenger vehicles. --** Vehicles transporting persons on sight-seeing or travel tours.

f. **For-hire passenger vehicles. --** Vehicles transporting persons for compensation. This classification shall not include the following:

1. Vehicles operated as ambulances.

2. Vehicles operated by the owner where the costs of operation are shared by the passengers.

3. Vehicles operated pursuant to a ridesharing arrangement as defined in G.S. 136-44.21.

4. Vehicles transporting students for the public school system under contract with the State Board of Education.

5. Vehicles leased to the United States of America or any of its agencies on a nonprofit basis.

6. Vehicles used for human service.

7. Vehicles used for volunteer transportation.

8. Vehicles operated in a TNC service, excluding vehicles operated in connection with a brokering transportation network company, regulated under Article 10A of Chapter 20 of the General Statutes.

g. **Low-speed vehicle. --** A four-wheeled electric vehicle whose top speed is greater than 20 miles per hour but less than 25 miles per hour.

g1. **Mini-truck. --** A motor vehicle designed, used, or maintained primarily for the transportation of property and having four wheels, an engine displacement of 660cc or less, an overall length of 130 inches or less, an overall height of 78 inches or less, and an overall width of 60 inches or less.

g2. **Modified utility vehicle. --** A motor vehicle that (i) is manufactured or upfitted by a licensed manufacturer, dealer, or person or business otherwise engaged in vehicle manufacturing or modification for off-road use with equipment required by G.S. 20-121.1(2a), except a vehicle identification number, and (ii) has four wheels, an overall length of 110 inches or greater, an overall width of 58 inches or greater, an overall height of 60 inches or greater, a maximum speed capability of 40 miles per hour or greater, and does not require an operator or passenger to straddle a seat. "Modified utility vehicle" does not include an all-terrain vehicle, golf cart, or utility vehicle, as defined in this section, or a riding lawn mower.

h. **Motorcycles. --** Vehicles having a saddle for the use of the rider and designed to travel on not more than three wheels in contact with the ground, including autocycles, motor scooters, and motor-driven bicycles, but excluding tractors and utility vehicles equipped with an additional form of device designed to transport property, three-wheeled vehicles while being used by law-enforcement agencies, electric assisted bicycles, and mopeds as defined in sub-subdivision d1. of this subdivision.

i. **Motor-driven bicycle. --** A vehicle with two or three wheels, a steering handle, one or two saddle seats, pedals, and a motor that cannot propel the vehicle at a speed greater than 20 miles per hour on a level surface. This term shall not include an electric assisted bicycle as defined in subdivision (7a) of this section.

j. **Moped.** -- A vehicle, other than a motor-driven bicycle or electric assisted bicycle, that has two or three wheels, no external shifting device, a motor that does not exceed 50 cubic centimeters piston displacement and cannot propel the vehicle at a speed greater than 30 miles per hour on a level surface. The motor may be powered by electricity, alternative fuel, motor fuel, or a combination of each.

k. **Motor home or house car.** -- A vehicular unit, designed to provide temporary living quarters, built into as an integral part, or permanently attached to, a self-propelled motor vehicle chassis or van. The vehicle must provide at least four of the following facilities: cooking, refrigeration or icebox, self-contained toilet, heating or air conditioning, a portable water supply system including a faucet and sink, separate 110-125 volt electrical power supply, or an LP gas supply.

l. **Private passenger vehicles.** -- All other passenger vehicles not included in the above definitions.

m. **School activity bus.** -- A vehicle, generally painted a different color from a school bus, whose primary purpose is to transport school students and others to or from a place for participation in an event other than regular classroom work. The term includes a public, private, or parochial vehicle that meets this description.

n. **School bus.** -- A vehicle whose primary purpose is to transport school students over an established route to and from school for the regularly scheduled school day, that is equipped with alternately flashing red lights on the front and rear and a mechanical stop signal, that is painted primarily yellow below the roofline, and that bears the plainly visible words "School Bus" on the front and rear. The term includes a public, private, or parochial vehicle that meets this description.

o. **U-drive-it passenger vehicles.** -- Passenger vehicles included in the definition of U-drive-it vehicles set forth in this section.

(28) **Person.** -- Every individual, firm, partnership, association, corporation, governmental agency, or combination thereof of whatsoever form or character.

(28a) **Personal delivery device.** -- An electrically powered device intended for transporting cargo that is equipped with automated driving technology that enables device operation with or without the remote support and supervision of a human and that does not exceed (i) a weight of 500 pounds, excluding cargo, (ii) a length of 40 inches, and (iii) a width of 30 inches.

(28b) **Plug-in electric vehicle.** -- A four-wheeled motor vehicle that does not have the ability to be propelled by a gasoline engine and that meets each of the following requirements:

a. Is made by a manufacturer primarily for use on public streets, roads, and highways and meets National Highway Traffic Safety Administration standards included in 49 C.F.R. § 571.

b. Has not been modified from original manufacturer specifications with regard to power train or any manner of powering the vehicle.

c. Is rated at not more than 8,500 pounds unloaded gross vehicle weight.

d. Has a maximum speed capability of at least 65 miles per hour.

e. Draws electricity from a battery that has all of the following characteristics:

1. A capacity of not less than four kilowatt hours.

2. Capable of being recharged from an external source of electricity.

(29) **Pneumatic Tire.** -- Every tire in which compressed air is designed to support the load.

(29a) **Private Motor Carrier.** -- A person who transports passengers or property by motor vehicle in interstate commerce and is not a for-hire motor carrier.

(30) **Private Road or Driveway.** -- Every road or driveway not open to the use of the public as a matter of right for the purpose of vehicular traffic.

(31) **Property-Hauling Vehicles.** --

a. Vehicles used for the transportation of property.

b., c. Repealed by Session Laws 1995 (Regular Session, 1996), c. 756, s. 4.

d. **Semitrailers.** -- Vehicles without motive power designed for carrying property or persons and for being drawn by a motor vehicle, and so constructed that part of their weight or their load rests upon or is carried by the pulling vehicle.

e. **Trailers.** -- Vehicles without motive power designed for carrying property or persons wholly on their own structure and to be drawn by a motor vehicle, including "pole trailers" or a pair of wheels used primarily to balance a load rather than for purposes of transportation.

f. Repealed by Session Laws 1995 (Regular Session, 1996), c. 756, s. 4.

(31a) **Provisional Licensee.** -- A person under the age of 18 years.

(32) **Public Vehicular Area.** -- Any area within the State of North Carolina that meets one or more of the following requirements:

a. The area is used by the public for vehicular traffic at any time, including by way of illustration and not limitation any drive, driveway, road, roadway, street, alley, or parking lot upon the grounds and premises of any of the following:

1. Any public or private hospital, college, university, school, orphanage, church, or any of the institutions, parks or other facilities maintained and supported by the State of North Carolina or any of its subdivisions.

2. Any service station, drive-in theater, supermarket, store, restaurant, or office building, or any other business, residential, or municipal establishment providing parking space whether the business or establishment is open or closed.

3. Any property owned by the United States and subject to the jurisdiction of the State of North Carolina. (The inclusion of property owned by the United States in this definition shall not limit assimilation of North Carolina law when applicable under the provisions of Title 18, United States Code, section 13).

b. The area is a beach area used by the public for vehicular traffic.

c. The area is a road used by vehicular traffic within or leading to a gated or non-gated subdivision or community, whether or not the subdivision or community roads have been offered for dedication to the public.

d. The area is a portion of private property used by vehicular traffic and designated by the private property owner as a public vehicular area in accordance with G.S. 20-219.4.

(32a) **Ramp Meter.** -- A traffic control device that consists of a circular red and circular green display placed at a point along an interchange entrance ramp.

(32b) **Recreational Vehicle.** -- A vehicular type unit primarily designed as temporary living quarters for recreational, camping, or travel use that either has its own motive power or is mounted on, or towed by, another vehicle. The basic entities are camping trailer, fifth-wheel travel trailer, motor home, travel trailer, and truck camper. This term shall not include a manufactured home as defined in G.S. 143-143.9(6). The basic entities are defined as follows:

a. **Camping trailer.** -- A vehicular portable unit mounted on wheels and constructed with collapsible partial side walls that fold for towing by another vehicle and unfold at the campsite to provide temporary living quarters for recreational, camping, or travel use.

b. **Fifth-wheel trailer.** -- A vehicular unit mounted on wheels designed to provide temporary living quarters for recreational, camping, or travel use, of a size and weight that does not require a special highway movement permit and designed to be towed by a motorized vehicle that contains a towing mechanism that is mounted above or forward of the tow vehicle's rear axle.

c. **Motor home.** -- As defined in G.S. 20-4.01(27)k.

d. **Travel trailer.** -- A vehicular unit mounted on wheels, designed to provide temporary living quarters for recreational, camping, or travel use, and of a size or weight that does not require a special highway movement permit when towed by a motorized vehicle.

e. **Truck camper.** -- A portable unit that is constructed to provide temporary living quarters for recreational, camping, or travel use, consisting of a roof, floor, and sides and is designed to be loaded onto and unloaded from the bed of a pickup truck.

(32c) **Regular Drivers License.** -- A license to drive a commercial motor vehicle that is exempt from the commercial drivers license requirements or a noncommercial motor vehicle.

(33) a. Flood Vehicle. -- A motor vehicle that has been submerged or partially submerged in water to the extent that damage to the body, engine, transmission, or differential has occurred.

b. Non-U.S.A. Vehicle. -- A motor vehicle manufactured outside of the United States and not intended by the manufacturer for sale in the United States.

c. **Reconstructed Vehicle.** -- A motor vehicle of a type required to be registered hereunder that has been materially altered from original construction due to removal, addition or substitution of new or used essential parts; and includes glider kits and custom assembled vehicles.

d. **Salvage Motor Vehicle.** -- Any motor vehicle damaged by collision or other occurrence to the extent that the cost of repairs to the vehicle and rendering the vehicle safe for use on the public streets and highways would exceed seventy-five percent (75%) of its fair retail market value, whether or not the motor vehicle has been declared a total loss by an insurer. Repairs shall include the cost of parts and labor. Fair market retail values shall be as found in the NADA Pricing Guide Book or other publications approved by the Commissioner.

e. **Salvage Rebuilt Vehicle.** -- A salvage vehicle that has been rebuilt for title and registration.

f. **Junk Vehicle.** -- A motor vehicle which is incapable of operation or use upon the highways and has no resale value except as a source of parts or scrap, and shall not be titled or registered.

(33a) **Relevant Time after the Driving.** -- Any time after the driving in which the driver still has in his body alcohol consumed before or during the driving.

(33b) **Reportable Crash.** -- A crash involving a motor vehicle that results in one or more of the following:

a. Death or injury of a human being.

b. Total property damage of one thousand dollars ($ 1,000) or more, or property damage of any amount to a vehicle seized pursuant to G. S. 20-28.3.

(33c) **Reserve components of the Armed Forces of the United States.** -- The organizations listed in Title 10 United States Code, section 10101, which specifically includes the Army and Air National Guard.

(34) **Resident.** -- Any person who resides within this State for other than a temporary or transitory purpose for more than six months shall be presumed to be a resident of this State; but absence from the State for more than six months shall raise no presumption that the person is not a resident of this State.

(35) **Residential District.** -- The territory prescribed as such by ordinance of the Department of Transportation.

(36) **Revocation or Suspension.** -- Termination of a licensee's or permittee's privilege to drive or termination of the registration of a vehicle for a period of time stated in an order of revocation or suspension.

The terms "revocation" or "suspension" or a combination of both terms shall be used synonymously.

(37) **Road Tractors.** -- Vehicles designed and used for drawing other vehicles upon the highway and not so constructed as to carry any part of the load, either independently or as a part of the weight of the vehicle so drawn.

(38) **Roadway.** -- That portion of a highway improved, designed, or ordinarily used for vehicular travel, exclusive of the shoulder. In the event a highway includes two or more separate roadways the term "roadway" as used herein shall refer to any such roadway separately but not to all such roadways collectively.

(39) **Safety Zone.** -- Traffic island or other space officially set aside within a highway for the exclusive use of pedestrians and which is so plainly marked or indicated by proper signs as to be plainly visible at all times while set apart as a safety zone.

(40) **Security Agreement.** -- Written agreement which reserves or creates a security interest.

(41) **Security Interest.** -- An interest in a vehicle reserved or created by agreement and which secures payments or performance of an obligation. The term includes but is not limited to the interest of a chattel mortgagee, the interest of a vendor under a conditional sales contract, the interest of a trustee under a chattel deed of trust, and the interest of a lessor under a lease intended as security. A security interest is "perfected" when it is valid against third parties generally.

(41a) **Serious Traffic Violation.** -- A conviction of one of the following offenses when operating a commercial or other motor vehicle:

a. Excessive speeding, involving a single charge of any speed 15 miles per hour or more above the posted speed limit.

b. Careless and reckless driving.

c. A violation of any State or local law relating to motor vehicle traffic control, other than a parking violation, arising in connection with a fatal accident.

d. Improper or erratic lane changes.

e. Following the vehicle ahead too closely.

f. Driving a commercial motor vehicle without obtaining a commercial drivers license.

g. Driving a commercial motor vehicle without a commercial drivers license in the driver's possession.

h. Driving a commercial motor vehicle without the proper class of commercial drivers license or endorsements for the specific vehicle group being operated or for the passenger or type of cargo being transported.

i. Unlawful use of a mobile telephone under G.S. 20-137.4A or Part 390 or Part 392 of Title 49 of the Code of Federal Regulations while operating a commercial motor vehicle.

(42) **Solid Tire.** -- Every tire of rubber or other resilient material which does not depend upon compressed air for the support of the load.

(43) **Specially Constructed Vehicles.** -- Motor vehicles required to be registered under this Chapter and that fit within one of the following categories:

a. **Replica vehicle.** -- A vehicle, excluding motorcycles, that when assembled replicates an earlier year, make, and model vehicle.

b. **Street rod vehicle.** -- A vehicle, excluding motorcycles, manufactured prior to 1949 that has been materially altered or has a body constructed from nonoriginal materials.

c. **Custom-built vehicle.** -- A vehicle, including motorcycles, reconstructed or assembled by a nonmanufacturer from new or used parts that has an exterior that does not replicate or resemble any other manufactured vehicle. This category also includes any motorcycle that was originally sold unassembled and manufactured from a kit or that has been materially altered or that has a body constructed from nonoriginal materials.

(44) **Special Mobile Equipment.** -- Defined in G.S. 105-164.3.

(44a) **Specialty Vehicles.** -- Vehicles of a type required to be registered under this Chapter that are modified from their original construction for an educational, emergency services, or public safety use.

(45) **State.** -- A state, territory, or possession of the United States, District of Columbia, Commonwealth of Puerto Rico, a province of Canada, or the Sovereign Nation of the Eastern Band of the Cherokee Indians with tribal lands, as defined in 18 U.S.C. § 1151, located within the boundaries of the State of North Carolina. For provisions in this Chapter that apply to commercial drivers licenses, "state" means a state of the United States and the District of Columbia.

(46) **Street.** -- A highway, as defined in subdivision (13). The terms "highway" and "street" and their cognates are synonymous.

(46a) **Supplemental restraint system.** -- A passive inflatable motor vehicle occupant crash protection system designed for use in conjunction with a seat belt assembly as defined in 49 C.F.R. § 571.209, and includes one or more airbags and all components required to ensure that an airbag works as designed by the vehicle manufacturer, including both of the following:

a. The airbag operates as designed in the event of a crash.

b. The airbag is designed in accordance with federal motor vehicle safety standards for the specific make, model, and year of the motor vehicle in which it is or will be installed.

(47) **Suspension.** -- Termination of a licensee's or permittee's privilege to drive or termination of the registration of a vehicle for a period of time stated in an order of revocation or suspension. The terms "revocation" or "suspension" or a combination of both terms shall be used synonymously.

(48) **Truck Tractors.** -- Vehicles designed and used primarily for drawing other vehicles and not so constructed as to carry any load independent of the vehicle so drawn.

(48a) *(Effective until December 31, 2024)* U-drive-it vehicles. -- The following vehicles that are either rented to a person, to be operated by that person, or loaned by a franchised motor vehicle dealer, with or without charge, to a customer of that dealer who is having a vehicle serviced or repaired by the dealer:

a. A private passenger vehicle other than the following:

1. A private passenger vehicle of nine-passenger capacity or less that is rented for a term of one year or more.

2. A private passenger vehicle that is rented to public school authorities for driver-training instruction.

b. A property-hauling vehicle under 7,000 pounds that does not haul products for hire and that is rented for a term of less than one year.

c. Motorcycles.

(48a) *(Effective December 31, 2024)* U-drive-it vehicles. -- The following vehicles that are rented to a person, to be operated by that person:

a. A private passenger vehicle other than the following:

1. A private passenger vehicle of nine-passenger capacity or less that is rented for a term of one year or more.

2. A private passenger vehicle that is rented to public school authorities for driver-training instruction.

b. A property-hauling vehicle under 7,000 pounds that does not haul products for hire and that is rented for a term of less than one year.

c. Motorcycles.

(48b) **Under the Influence of an Impairing Substance. --** The state of a person having his physical or mental faculties, or both, appreciably impaired by an impairing substance.

(48c) **Utility Vehicle. --** A motor vehicle that is (i) designed for off-road use and (ii) used for general maintenance, security, agricultural, or horticultural purposes. "Utility vehicle" does not include an all-terrain vehicle or golf cart, as defined in this section, or a riding lawn mower.

(49) **Vehicle. --** Every device in, upon, or by which any person or property is or may be transported or drawn upon a highway, excepting devices moved by human power or used exclusively upon fixed rails or tracks; provided, that for the purposes of this Chapter bicycles and electric assisted bicycles shall be deemed vehicles and every rider of a bicycle or an electric assisted bicycle upon a highway shall be subject to the provisions of this Chapter applicable to the driver of a vehicle except those which by their nature can have no application. This term shall not include a device which is designed for and intended to be used as a means of transportation for a person with a mobility impairment, or who uses the device for mobility enhancement, is suitable for use both inside and outside a building, including on sidewalks, and is limited by design to 15 miles per hour when the device is being operated by a person with a mobility impairment, or who uses the device for mobility enhancement. This term shall not include (i) an electric personal assistive mobility device as defined in subdivision (7b) of this section or (ii) a personal delivery device as defined by this section. Unless the context requires otherwise, and except as provided under G.S. 20-109.2, 47-20.6, or 47-20.7, a manufactured home shall be deemed a vehicle.

(50) **Wreckers. --** Vehicles with permanently attached cranes used to move other vehicles; provided, that said wreckers shall be equipped with adequate brakes for units being towed.

History.
1973, c. 1330, s. 1; 1975, cc. 94, 208; c. 716, s. 5; c. 743; c. 859, s. 1; 1977, c. 313; c. 464, s. 34; 1979, c. 39; c. 423, s. 1; c. 574, ss. 1-4; c. 667, s. 1; c. 680; 1981, c. 606, s. 3; c. 792, s. 2; 1983, c. 435, s. 8; 1983 (Reg. Sess., 1984), c. 1101, ss. 1-3; 1985, c. 509, s. 6; 1987, c. 607, s. 2; c. 658, s. 1; 1987 (Reg. Sess., 1988), c. 1069; c. 1105,

s. 1; c. 1112, ss. 1-3; 1989, c. 455, ss. 1, 2; c. 727, s. 219(1); c. 771, ss. 1, 18; 1991, c. 449, s. 2; c. 726, ss. 1 -4; 1991 (Reg. Sess., 1992), c. 1015, s. 1; 1993 (Reg. Sess., 1994), c. 761, s. 22; 1995, c. 191, s. 1; 1995 (Reg. Sess., 1996), c. 756, ss. 2-4; 1997-379, s. 5.1; 1997-443, s. 11A.8; 1997-456, s. 27; 1998-149, s. 1; 1998-182, ss. 1, 1.1, 26; 1998-217, s. 62(e); 1999-330, s. 9; 1999-337, s. 28(c) -(e); 1999-406, s. 14; 1999-452, ss. 1 -5; 2000-155, s. 9; 2000-173, s. 10(c); 2001-212, s. 2; 2001-341, ss. 1, 2; 2001-356, ss. 1, 2; 2001-441, s. 1; 2001-487, ss. 50(a), 51; 2002-72, s. 19(b); 2002-98, ss. 1 -3; 2003-397, s. 1; 2005-282, s. 1; 2005-349, ss. 1 -3; 2006-253, s. 8; 2007-56, s. 4; 2007-382, ss. 2, 3; 2007-455, s. 1; 2007-493, s. 1; 2008-156, s. 1; 2009-274, s. 1; 2009-405, ss. 1, 4; 2009-416, ss. 1, 2; 2010-129, s. 1; 2011-95, s. 1; 2011-206, s. 1; 2013-410, s. 47.5; 2014-58, s. 10(a), (c), (d); 2014-115, s. 28.3; 2015-125, s. 1; 2015-163, s. 1; 2015-232, s. 1.1(a); 2015-237, s. 2; 2016-59, s. 1; 2016-90, ss. 12.5(a), 13(a); 2016-94, s. 35.20(a); 2017-69, s. 2.1(a); 2017-102, s. 5.2(a), (b); 2018-27, s. 4.5(b); 2018-42, s. 3(b); 2019-34, s. 1; 2019-36, s. 1; 2019-155, s. 1; 2019-227, s. 1(a), (b); 2020-40, s. 1; 2020-51, s. 1(b); 2020-73, s. 1; 2021-33, s. 1

§ 20-4.02. Quadrennial adjustment of certain fees and rates

(a) **Adjustment for Inflation. --** Beginning July 1, 2020, and every four years thereafter, the Division shall adjust the fees and rates imposed pursuant to the statutes listed in this subsection for inflation in accordance with the Consumer Price Index computed by the Bureau of Labor Statistics. The adjustment for per transaction rates in subdivision (8a) of this subsection shall be rounded to the nearest cent and all other adjustments under this subsection shall be rounded to the nearest twenty-five cents (25 cent(s)):

(1) G.S. 20-7.

(2) G.S. 20-11.

(3) G.S. 20-14.

(4) G.S. 20-16.

(5) G.S. 20-26.

(6) G.S. 20-37.15.

(7) G.S. 20-37.16.

(8) G.S. 20-42(b).

(8a) G.S. 20-63(h), with respect to the per transaction rates set in that subsection.

(9) G.S. 20-85(a)(1) through (10).

(10) G.S. 20-85.1.

(11) G.S. 20-87, except for the additional fee set forth in G.S. 20-87(6) for private motorcycles.

(12) G.S. 20-88.

(13) G.S. 20-289.

(14) G.S. 20-385.

(15) G.S. 44A-4(b)(1).

(b) **Computation. --** In determining the rate of inflation to use when making an adjustment pursuant to subsection (a) of this section, the Division shall base the rate on the percent change in the annual Consumer Price Index over the preceding four-year period.

(c) **Rules.** -- The provisions of Chapter 150B of the General Statutes shall not apply to the inflation adjustment required by this section.

(d) **Consultation and Publication.** -- At least 90 days prior to making an adjustment pursuant to subsection (a) of this section, and notwithstanding any provision of G.S. 12-3.1 to the contrary, the Division shall (i) consult with the Joint Legislative Commission on Governmental Operations, (ii) provide a report to the chairs of the Senate Appropriations Committee on Department of Transportation and the House of Representatives Appropriations Committee on Transportation, and (iii) publish notice of the fees that will be in effect in the offices of the Division and on the Division's Web site.

(e) **Effective Date.** -- Any adjustment to fees or rates under this section applicable to a motor vehicle sold or leased by a motor vehicle dealer, as defined in G.S. 20-286(11), is only applicable to a motor vehicle sale or lease made on or after the effective date of the fee or rate adjustment regardless of the date of submission of a title and registration application for the motor vehicle to the Division. No adjustment to fees or rates under this section applies to a motor vehicle sale or lease made prior to the effective date of the fee or rate adjustment.

History.
2015-241, s. 29.30(s); 2016-120, s. 1; 2018-42, s. 8

§ 20-4.03. Administrative hearing fees

(a) **Authorization.** -- The Division is authorized to charge a fee to any person who requests an administrative hearing before the Division in accordance with this Chapter.

(b) **Requirements for Requesting a Hearing.** -- Any request for an administrative hearing before the Division must be in writing and accompanied by the total applicable administrative hearing fee charged by the Division. An administrative hearing shall not be granted by the Division unless the administrative hearing request complies with the requirements of this subsection. Notwithstanding any provision of this Chapter to the contrary, any pending revocation, suspension, civil penalty assessment, or other adverse action shall not be stayed upon receipt of an administrative hearing request unless the request complies with the requirements of this subsection.

(c) **Report.** -- Beginning October 1, 2018, and quarterly thereafter, the Division shall submit a report to the Fiscal Research Division of the General Assembly detailing all of the following for each month of the applicable quarter and for each type of administrative hearing:

(1) The total number of administrative hearings.

(2) The total amount of revenue collected.

(3) The total number of fee waivers granted.

(4) The counties where the administrative hearings were held.

(5) The average amount of time required to conduct an administrative hearing, with the time required of hearing officers and the time required of administrative personnel listed separately.

History.
2017-57, s. 34.32(b); 2017-197, s. 7.3(a); 2018-5, s. 34.23(d)

ARTICLE 1A
RECIPROCITY AGREEMENTS AS TO REGISTRATION AND LICENSING

§ 20-4.1. Declaration of policy

It is the policy of this State to promote and encourage the fullest possible use of its highway system by authorizing the making and execution of motor vehicle reciprocal registration agreements, arrangements and declarations with other states, provinces, territories and countries with respect to vehicles registered in this and such other states, provinces, territories and countries thus contributing to the economic and social development and growth of this State.

History.
1961, c. 642, s. 1

§ 20-4.2. Definitions

As used in this Article:

(1) "Commercial vehicle" means any vehicle which is operated in furtherance of any commercial enterprise.

(2) "Commissioner" means the Commissioner of Motor Vehicles of North Carolina.

(3) "Division" means the Division of Motor Vehicles of North Carolina.

(4) "Jurisdiction" means and includes a state, district, territory or possession of the United States, a foreign country and a state or province of a foreign country.

(5) "Properly registered," as applied to place of registration, means:

a. The jurisdiction where the person registering the vehicle has his legal residence, or

b. In the case of a commercial vehicle, including a leased vehicle, the jurisdiction in which it is registered if the commercial enterprise in which such vehicle is used has a place of business therein, and, if the vehicle is most frequently dispatched, garaged, serviced, maintained, operated or otherwise controlled in or from such place of business, and, the vehicle has been assigned to such place of business, or

c. In the case of a commercial vehicle, including leased vehicles, the jurisdiction where, because of an agreement or arrangement between two or more jurisdictions, or pursuant to a declaration, the vehicle has been registered as required by said jurisdiction.

d. In case of doubt or dispute as to the proper place of registration of a vehicle, the Division shall make the final determination, but in making such determination, may confer with departments of the other jurisdictions affected.

History.
1961, c. 642, s. 1; 1975, c. 716, s. 5; 1979, c. 470, s. 2

§ 20-4.3. Commissioner may make reciprocity agreements, arrangements or declarations

The Commissioner of Motor Vehicles shall have the authority to execute or make agreements, arrangements or declarations to carry out the provisions of this Article.

History.
1961, c. 642, s. 1

§ 20-4.4. Authority for reciprocity agreements; provisions; reciprocity standards

(a) The Commissioner may enter into an agreement or arrangement for interstate or intrastate operations with the duly authorized representatives of another jurisdiction, granting to vehicles or to owners of vehicles which are properly registered or licensed in such jurisdiction and for which evidence of compliance is supplied, benefits, privileges and exemptions from the payment, wholly or partially, of any taxes, fees, or other charges imposed upon such vehicles or owners with respect to the operation or ownership of such vehicles under the laws of this State. Such an agreement or arrangement shall provide that vehicles properly registered or licensed in this State when operated upon highways of such other jurisdiction shall receive exemptions, benefits and privileges of a similar kind or to a similar degree as are extended to vehicles properly registered or licensed in such

jurisdiction when operated in this State. Each such agreement or arrangement shall, in the judgment of the Commissioner, be in the best interest of this State and the citizens thereof and shall be fair and equitable to this State and the citizens thereof, and all of the same shall be determined on the basis and recognition of the benefits which accrue to the economy of this State from the uninterrupted flow of commerce.

(b) When the Commissioner enters into a reciprocal registration agreement or arrangement with another jurisdiction which has a motor vehicle tax, license or fee which is not subject to waiver by a reciprocity agreement, the Commissioner is empowered and authorized to provide as a condition of the agreement or arrangement that owners of vehicles licensed in such other jurisdiction shall pay some equalizing tax or fee to the Division. The failure of any owner or operator of a vehicle to pay the taxes or fees provided in the agreement or arrangement shall prohibit them from receiving any benefits therefrom and they shall be required to register their vehicles and pay taxes as if there was no agreement or arrangement.

History.
1961, c. 642, s. 1; 1971, c. 588; 1975, c. 716, s. 5

§ 20-4.5. Base-state registration reciprocity

An agreement or arrangement entered into, or a declaration issued under the authority of this Article may contain provisions authorizing the registration or licensing in another jurisdiction of vehicles located in or operated from a base in such other jurisdiction which vehicles otherwise would be required to be registered or licensed in some other state; and in such event the exemptions, benefits and privileges extended by such agreement, arrangement or declaration shall apply to such vehicles, when properly licensed or registered in such base jurisdiction.

History.
1961, c. 642, s. 1

N.C. Gen. Stat. § 20-4.6

Repealed by Session Laws 1997-122, s. 1.

§ 20-4.7. Extension of reciprocal privileges to lessees authorized

An agreement or arrangement entered into, or a declaration issued under the authority of this Article, may contain provisions under which a leased vehicle properly registered by the lessor thereof may be entitled, subject to terms and conditions stated therein, to the exemptions, benefits and privileges extended by such agreement, arrangement or declaration.

History.
1961, c. 642, s. 1

§ 20-4.8. Automatic reciprocity, when

On and after July 1, 1961, if no agreement, arrangement or declaration is in effect with respect to another jurisdiction as authorized by this Article, any vehicle properly registered or licensed in such other jurisdiction and for which evidence of compliance supplied shall receive, when operated in this State, the same exemptions, benefits and privileges granted by such other jurisdiction to vehicles properly registered in this State. Reciprocity extended under this section shall apply to commercial vehicles only when engaged exclusively in interstate operations.

History.
1961, c. 642, s. 1

§ 20-4.9. Suspension of reciprocity benefits

Agreements, arrangements or declarations made under the authority of this Article may include provisions authorizing the Division to suspend or cancel the exemptions, benefits or privileges granted thereunder to a vehicle which is in violation of any of the conditions or terms of such agreements, arrangements or declarations or is in violation of the laws of this State relating to motor vehicles or rules and regulations lawfully promulgated thereunder.

History.
1961, c. 642, s. 1; 1975, c. 716, s. 5

§ 20-4.10. Agreements to be written, filed and available for distribution

All agreements, arrangements or declarations or amendments thereto shall be in writing and shall be filed in the office of the Commissioner. Copies thereof shall be made available by the Commissioner upon request and upon payment of a fee therefor in an amount necessary to defray the costs of reproduction thereof.

History.
1961, c. 642, s. 1

§ 20-4.11. Reciprocity agreements in effect at time of Article

All reciprocity registration agreements, arrangements and declarations relating to vehicles in force and effect July 1, 1961, shall continue in force and effect until specifically

amended or revoked as provided by law or by such agreements or arrangements.

History.
1961, c. 642, s. 1

§ 20-4.12. Article part of and supplemental to motor vehicle registration law

This Article shall be, and construed as, a part of and supplemental to the motor vehicle registration law of this State.

History.
1961, c. 642, s. 1

§§ 20-4.13 through 20-4.17

Reserved for future codification purposes.

ARTICLE 1B
RECIPROCAL PROVISIONS AS TO ARREST OF NONRESIDENTS

§ 20-4.18. Definitions

Unless the context otherwise requires, the following words and phrases, for the purpose of this Article, shall have the following meanings:

(1) **Citation.** -- Any citation, summons, ticket, or other document issued by a law-enforcement officer for the violation of a traffic law, ordinance, rule or regulation.

(2) **Collateral or Bond.** -- Any cash or other security deposited to secure an appearance following a citation by a law-enforcement officer.

(3) Repealed by Session Laws 1979, c. 667, s. 2.

(4) **Nonresident.** -- A person who holds a license issued by a reciprocating state.

(5) **Personal Recognizance.** -- An agreement by a nonresident to comply with the terms of the citation issued to the nonresident.

(6) **Reciprocating State.** -- Any state or other jurisdiction which extends by its laws to residents of North Carolina substantially the rights and privileges provided by this Article.

(7) **State.** -- The State of North Carolina.

History.
1973, c. 736; 1979, c. 667, s. 2; 1981, c. 508; 1999-452, s. 6

§ 20-4.19. Issuance of citation to nonresident; officer to report noncompliance

(a) Notwithstanding other provisions of this Chapter, a law-enforcement officer observing a violation of this Chapter or other traffic regulation by a nonresident shall issue a citation as appropriate and shall not, subject to the provisions of subsection (b) of this section, require such nonresident to post collateral or bond to secure appearance for trial, but shall accept such nonresident's personal recognizance; provided, however, that the nonresident shall have the right upon request to post collateral or bond in a manner provided by law and in such case the provisions of this Article shall not apply.

(b) A nonresident may be required to post collateral or bond to secure appearance for trial if the offense is one which would result in the suspension or revocation of a person's license under the laws of this State.

(c) Upon the failure of the nonresident to comply with the citation, the clerk of court shall report the noncompliance to the Division. The report of noncompliance shall clearly identify the nonresident; describe the violation, specifying the section of the statute, code, or ordinance violated; indicate the location and date of offense; and identify the vehicle involved.

History.
1973, c. 736; 1975, c. 716, s. 5; 1991, c. 682, s. 1; 1999-452, s. 7

§ 20-4.20. Division to transmit report to reciprocating state; suspension of license for noncompliance with citation issued by reciprocating state

(a) Upon receipt of a report of noncompliance, the Division shall transmit a certified copy of such report to the official in charge of the issuance of licenses in the reciprocating state in which the nonresident resides or by which he is licensed.

(b) When the licensing authority of a reciprocating state reports that a person holding a North Carolina license has failed to comply with a citation issued in such state, the Commissioner shall forthwith suspend such person's license. The order of suspension shall indicate the reason for the order, and shall notify the person that his license shall remain suspended until he has furnished evidence satisfactory to the Commissioner that he has complied with the terms of the citation which was the basis for the suspension order by appearing before the tribunal to which he was cited and complying with any order entered by said tribunal.

(c) A copy of any suspension order issued hereunder may be furnished to the licensing authority of the reciprocating state.

(d) The Commissioner shall maintain a current listing of reciprocating states hereunder. Such lists shall from time to time be disseminated among the appropriate departments, divisions, bureaus, and agencies of this State; the principal law-enforcement officers of the several counties, cities, and towns of this State; and the licensing authorities in reciprocating states.

(e) The Commissioner shall have the authority to execute or make agreements, arrangements, or declarations to carry out the provisions of this Article.

History.
1973, c. 736; 1975, c. 716, s. 5; 1979, c. 104

ARTICLE 1C
DRIVERS LICENSE COMPACT

§ 20-4.21. Title of Article

This Article is the Drivers License Compact and may be cited by that name.

History.
1993, c. 533, s. 1

§ 20-4.22. Commissioner may make reciprocity agreements, arrangements, or declarations

The Commissioner may execute or make agreements, arrangements, or declarations to implement this Article.

History.
1993, c. 533, s. 1

§ 20-4.23. Legislative findings and policy

(a) **Findings.** -- The General Assembly and the states that are members of the Drivers License Compact find that:

(1) The safety of their streets and highways is materially affected by the degree of compliance with state laws and local ordinances relating to the operation of motor vehicles.

(2) The violation of a law or an ordinance relating to the operation of a motor vehicle is evidence that the violator engages in conduct that is likely to endanger the safety of persons and property.

(3) The continuance in force of a license to drive is predicated upon compliance with laws and ordinances relating to the operation of motor vehicles in whichever jurisdiction the vehicle is operated.

(b) **Policy.** -- It is the policy of the General Assembly and of each of the states that is a member of the Drivers License Compact to:

(1) Promote compliance with the laws, ordinances, and administrative rules and regulations of a member state relating to the operation of motor vehicles.

(2) Make the reciprocal recognition of licenses to drive and the eligibility for a license to drive more just and equitable by making consideration of overall compliance with motor vehicle laws, ordinances, and administrative rules and regulations a condition precedent to the continuance or issuance of any license that authorizes the holder of the license to operate a motor vehicle in a member state.

History.
1993, c. 533, s. 1

§ 20-4.24. Reports of convictions; effect of reports

(a) **Reports.** -- A state that is a member of the Drivers License Compact shall report to another member state of the compact a conviction for any of the following:

(1) Manslaughter or negligent homicide resulting from the operation of a motor vehicle.

(2) Driving a motor vehicle while impaired.

(3) A felony in the commission of which a motor vehicle was used.

(4) Failure to stop and render aid in the event of a motor vehicle accident resulting in the death or personal injury of another.

If the laws of a member state do not describe the listed violations in precisely the words used in this subsection, the member state shall construe the descriptions to apply to offenses of the member state that are substantially similar to the ones described.

A state that is a member of the Drivers License Compact shall report to another member state of the compact a conviction for any other offense or any other information concerning convictions that the member states agree to report.

(b) **Effect.** -- A state that is a member of the Drivers License Compact shall treat a report of a conviction received from another member state of the compact as a report of the conduct that resulted in the conviction. For a conviction required to be reported under subsection (a), a member state shall give the same effect to the report as if the conviction had occurred in that state. For a conviction that is not required to be reported under subsection (a), a member state shall give the effect to the report that is required by the laws of that state. G.S. 20-23 governs the effect in this State of convictions that are not required to be reported under subsection (a).

History.
1993, c. 533, s. 1

§ 20-4.25. Review of license status in other states upon application for license in member state

Upon application for a license to drive, the licensing authority of a state that is a member of the Drivers License Compact must determine if the applicant has ever held, or currently holds, a license to drive issued by another member state. The licensing authority of the member state where the application is made may not issue the applicant a license to drive if:

(1) The applicant has held a license, but it has been revoked for a violation and the revocation period has not ended. If the revocation period is for more than one year and it has been at least one year since the license was revoked, the licensing authority may allow the applicant to apply for a new license if the laws of the licensing authority's state permit the application.

(2) The applicant currently holds a license to drive issued by another member state and does not surrender that license.

History.
1993, c. 533, s. 1

§ 20-4.26. Effect on other laws or agreements

Except as expressly required by the provisions of this Article, this Article does not affect the right of a member state to the Drivers License Compact to apply any of its other laws relating to licenses to drive to any person or circumstance, nor does it invalidate or prevent any driver license agreement or other cooperative arrangement between a member state and a state that is not a member.

History.
1993, c. 533, s. 1

§ 20-4.27. Effect on other State driver license laws

To the extent that this Article conflicts with general driver licensing provisions in this Chapter, this Article prevails. Where this Article is silent, the general driver licensing provisions apply.

History.
1993, c. 533, s. 1

§ 20-4.28. Administration and exchange of information

Chapter 20

The head of the licensing authority of each member state is the administrator of the Drivers License Compact for that state. The administrators, acting jointly, have the power to formulate all necessary procedures for the exchange of information under this compact. The administrator of each member state shall furnish to the administrator of each other member state any information or documents reasonably necessary to facilitate the administration of this compact.

History.
1993, c. 533, s. 1

§ 20-4.29. Withdrawal from Drivers License Compact

A member state may withdraw from the Drivers License Compact. A withdrawal may not become effective until at least six months after the heads of all other member states have received notice of the withdrawal. Withdrawal does not affect the validity or applicability by the licensing authorities of states remaining members of the compact of a report of a conviction occurring prior to the withdrawal.

History.
1993, c. 533, s. 1

§ 20-4.30. Construction and severability

This Article shall be liberally construed to effectuate its purposes. The provisions of this Article are severable; if any part of this Article is declared to be invalid by a court, the invalidity does not affect other parts of this Article that can be given effect without the invalid provision. If the Drivers License Compact is declared invalid by a court in a member state, the compact remains in full force and effect in the remaining member states and in full force and effect for all severable matters in that member state.

History.
1993, c. 533, s. 1

ARTICLE 2
UNIFORM DRIVER'S LICENSE ACT

§ 20-5. Title of Article

This Article may be cited as the Uniform Driver's License Act.

History.
1935, c. 52, s. 31

N.C. Gen. Stat. § 20-6

Repealed by Session Laws 1973, c. 1330, s. 39.

§ 20-7. Issuance and renewal of drivers licenses

(a) **License Required.** -- To drive a motor vehicle on a highway, a person must be licensed by the Division under this Article or Article 2C of this Chapter to drive the vehicle and must carry the license while driving the vehicle. The Division issues regular drivers licenses under this Article and issues commercial drivers licenses under Article 2C.

A license authorizes the holder of the license to drive any vehicle included in the class of the license and any vehicle included in a lesser class of license, except a vehicle for which an endorsement is required. To drive a vehicle for which an endorsement is required, a person must obtain both a license and an endorsement for the vehicle. A regular drivers license is considered a lesser class of license than its commercial counterpart.

The classes of regular drivers licenses and the motor vehicles that can be driven with each class of license are:

(1) **Class A.** -- A Class A license authorizes the holder to drive any of the following:

a. A Class A motor vehicle that is exempt under G.S. 20-37.16 from the commercial drivers license requirements.

b. A Class A motor vehicle that has a combined GVWR of less than 26,001 pounds and includes as part of the combination a towed unit that has a GVWR of at least 10,001 pounds.

(2) **Class B.** -- A Class B license authorizes the holder to drive any Class B motor vehicle that is exempt under G.S. 20-37.16 from the commercial drivers license requirements.

(3) **Class C.** -- A Class C license authorizes the holder to drive any of the following:

a. A Class C motor vehicle that is not a commercial motor vehicle.

b. When operated by a volunteer member of a fire department, a rescue squad, or an emergency medical service (EMS) in the performance of duty, a Class A or Class B fire-fighting, rescue, or EMS motor vehicle or a combination of these vehicles.

c. A combination of noncommercial motor vehicles that have a GVWR of more than 10,000 pounds but less than 26,001 pounds. This sub-subdivision does not apply to a Class C license holder less than 18 years of age.

The Commissioner may assign a unique motor vehicle to a class that is different from the class in which it would otherwise belong.

A person holding a commercial drivers license issued by another jurisdiction must apply for a transfer and obtain a North Carolina issued commercial drivers license within 30 days of becoming a resident. Any other new resident of North Carolina who has a drivers license issued by another jurisdiction must obtain a license from the Division within 60 days after becoming a resident.

(a1) **Motorcycles and Mopeds.** -- To drive a motorcycle, a person shall have one of the following:

(1) A full provisional license with a motorcycle learner's permit.

(2) A regular drivers license with a motorcycle learner's permit.

(3) A full provisional license with a motorcycle endorsement.

(4) A regular drivers license with a motorcycle endorsement.

Subsection (a2) of this section sets forth the requirements for a motorcycle learner's permit. To obtain a motorcycle endorsement, a person shall pay the fee set in subsection (i) of this section. In addition, to obtain an endorsement, a person age 18 or older shall demonstrate competence to drive a motorcycle by passing a knowledge test concerning motorcycles, and by passing a road test or providing proof of successful completion of one of the following:

(1) The North Carolina Motorcycle Safety Education Program Basic Rider Course or Experienced Rider Course.

(2) Any course approved by the Commissioner consistent with the instruction provided through the Motorcycle Safety Instruction Program established under G.S. 115D-72.

A person less than 18 years of age shall demonstrate competence to drive a motorcycle by passing a knowledge test concerning motorcycles and providing proof of successful completion of one of the following:

(1) Repealed by Session Laws 2012-85, s. 1, effective July 1, 2012.

(2) The North Carolina Motorcycle Safety Education Program Basic Rider Course or Experienced Rider Course.

(3) Any course approved by the Commissioner consistent with the instruction provided through the Motorcycle Safety Instruction Program established under G.S. 115D-72.

A person less than 18 years of age with a motorcycle endorsement may not drive a motorcycle with a passenger.

Neither a drivers license nor a motorcycle endorsement is required to drive a moped.

(a2) **Motorcycle Learner's Permit.** -- The following persons are eligible for a motorcycle learner's permit:

(1) A person who is at least 16 years old but less than 18 years old and has a full provisional license issued by the Division.

(2) A person who is at least 18 years old and has a license issued by the Division.

To obtain a motorcycle learner's permit, an applicant shall pass a vision test, a road sign test, and a knowledge test specified by the Division. An applicant who is less than 18 years old shall successfully complete the North Carolina Motorcycle Safety Education Program Basic Rider Course or any course approved by the Commissioner consistent with the instruction provided through the Motorcycle Safety Instruction Program established under G.S. 115D-72. A motorcycle learner's permit expires twelve months after it is issued and may be renewed for one additional six-month period. The holder of a motorcycle learner's permit may not drive a motorcycle with a passenger. The fee for a motorcycle learner's permit is the amount set in G.S. 20-7(*l*) for a learner's permit.

(a3) **Autocycles.** -- For purposes of this section, the term "motorcycle" shall not include autocycles. To drive an autocycle, a person shall have a regular drivers license.

(b) Repealed by Session Laws 1993, c. 368, s. 1, c. 533, s. 12.

(b1) **Application.** -- To obtain an identification card, learners permit, or drivers license from the Division, a person shall complete an application form provided by the Division, present at least two forms of identification approved by the Commissioner, be a resident of this State, and, except for an identification card, demonstrate his or her physical and mental ability to drive safely a motor vehicle included in the class of license for which the person has applied. At least one of the forms of identification shall indicate the applicant's residence address. The Division may copy the identification presented or hold it for a brief period of time to verify its authenticity. To obtain an endorsement, a person shall demonstrate his or her physical and mental ability to drive safely the type of motor vehicle for which the endorsement is required.

The application form shall request all of the following information, and it shall contain the disclosures concerning the request for an applicant's social security number required by section 7 of the federal Privacy Act of 1974, Pub. L. No. 93-579:

(1) The applicant's full name.

(2) The applicant's mailing address and residence address.

(3) A physical description of the applicant, including the applicant's sex, height, eye color, and hair color.

(4) The applicant's date of birth.

(5) The applicant's valid social security number.

(6) The applicant's signature.

The Division shall not issue an identification card, learners permit, or drivers license to an applicant who fails to provide the applicant's valid social security number.

(b2) **Disclosure of Social Security Number.** -- The social security number of an applicant is not a public record. The Division may not disclose an applicant's social security number except as allowed under federal law. A violation of the disclosure restrictions is punishable as provided in 42 U.S.C. § 408, and amendments to that law.

In accordance with 42 U.S.C. 405 and 42 U.S.C. 666, and amendments thereto, the Division may disclose a social security number obtained under subsection (b1) of this section only as follows:

(1) For the purpose of administering the drivers license laws.

(2) To the Department of Health and Human Services, Child Support Enforcement Program for the purpose of establishing paternity or child support or enforcing a child support order.

(3) To the Department of Revenue for the purpose of verifying taxpayer identity.

(4) To the Office of Indigent Defense Services of the Judicial Department for the purpose of verifying the identity of a represented client and enforcing a court order to pay for the legal services rendered.

(5) To each county jury commission for the purpose of verifying the identity of deceased persons whose names should be removed from jury lists.

(6) To the State Chief Information Officer for the purposes of G.S. 143B-1385.

(7) To the Department of Commerce, Division of Employment Security, for the purpose of verifying employer and claimant identity.

(8) To the Judicial Department for the purpose of administering the criminal and motor vehicle laws.

(b3) The Division shall adopt rules implementing the provisions of subsection (b1) of this section with respect to proof of residency in this State. Those rules shall ensure that applicants submit verified or verifiable residency and address information that can be reasonably considered to be valid and that is provided on any of the following:

(1) A document issued by an agency of the United States or by the government of another nation.

(2) A document issued by another state.

(3) A document issued by the State of North Carolina, or a political subdivision of this State. This includes an agency or instrumentality of this State.

(4) A preprinted bank or other corporate statement.

(5) A preprinted business letterhead.

(6) Any other document deemed reliable by the Division.

(b4) Examples of documents that are reasonably reliable indicators of residency include, but are not limited to, any of the following:

(1) A pay stub with the payee's address.

(2) A utility bill showing the address of the applicant-payor.

(3) A contract for an apartment, house, modular unit, or manufactured home with a North Carolina address signed by the applicant.

(4) A receipt for personal property taxes paid.

(5) A receipt for real property taxes paid to a North Carolina locality.

(6) A current automobile insurance policy issued to the applicant and showing the applicant's address.

(7) A monthly or quarterly financial statement from a North Carolina regulated financial institution.

(8), (9) Repealed by Session Laws 2015-294, s. 12, effective October 1, 2015, and applicable to contracts entered into on or after that date.

(b5) The Division rules adopted pursuant to subsection (b3) of this section shall also provide that if an applicant cannot produce any documentation specified in subsection (b3) or (b4) of this section, the applicant, or in the case of a minor applicant a parent or legal guardian of the applicant, may complete an affidavit, on a form provided by the Division and sworn to before an official of the Division, indicating the applicant's current residence address. The affidavit shall contain the provisions of G.S. 20-15(a) and G.S. 20-17(a)(5) and shall indicate the civil and criminal penalties for completing a false affidavit.

(c) **Tests.** -- To demonstrate physical and mental ability, a person must pass an examination. The examination may include road tests, vision tests, oral tests, and, in the case of literate applicants, written tests, as the Division may require. The tests must ensure that an applicant recognizes the handicapped international symbol of access, as defined in G.S. 20-37.5. The Division may not require a person who applies to renew a license that has not expired to take a written test or a road test unless one or more of the following applies:

(1) The person has been convicted of a traffic violation since the person's license was last issued.

(2) The applicant suffers from a mental or physical condition that impairs the person's ability to drive a motor vehicle.

The Division shall require sign and symbol testing upon initial issuance of a license. The Division shall require vision testing as a part of required in-person, in-office renewals of a license.

The Division may not require a person who is at least 60 years old to parallel park a motor vehicle as part of a road test. A person shall not use an autocycle to complete a road test under this subsection.

(c1) **Insurance.** -- The Division may not issue a drivers license to a person until the person has furnished proof of financial responsibility. Proof of financial responsibility shall be in one of the following forms:

(1) A written certificate or electronically-transmitted facsimile thereof from any insurance carrier duly authorized to do business in this State certifying that there is in effect a nonfleet private passenger motor vehicle liability policy for the benefit of the person required to furnish proof of financial responsibility. The certificate or facsimile shall state the effective date and expiration date of the nonfleet private passenger motor vehicle liability policy and shall state the date that the certificate or facsimile is issued. The certificate or facsimile shall remain effective proof of financial responsibility for a period of 30 consecutive days following the date the certificate or facsimile is issued but shall not in and of itself constitute a binder or policy of insurance.

(2) A binder for or policy of nonfleet private passenger motor vehicle liability insurance under which the applicant is insured, provided that the binder or policy states the effective date and expiration date of the nonfleet private passenger motor vehicle liability policy.

The preceding provisions of this subsection do not apply to applicants who do not own currently registered motor vehicles and who do not operate nonfleet private passenger motor vehicles that are owned by other persons and that are not insured under commercial motor vehicle liability insurance policies. In such cases, the applicant shall sign a written certificate to that effect. Such certificate shall be furnished by the Division and may be incorporated into the license application form. Any material misrepresentation made by such person on such certificate shall be grounds for suspension of that person's license for a period of 90 days.

For the purpose of this subsection, the term "nonfleet private passenger motor vehicle" has the definition ascribed to it in Article 40 of General Statute Chapter 58.

The Commissioner may require that certificates required by this subsection be on a form approved by the Commissioner.

The requirement of furnishing proof of financial responsibility does not apply to a person who applies for a renewal of his or her drivers license.

Nothing in this subsection precludes any person from showing proof of financial responsibility in any other manner authorized by Articles 9A and 13 of this Chapter.

(d) Repealed by Session Laws 1993, c. 368, s. 1.

(e) **Restrictions.** -- The Division may impose any restriction it finds advisable on a drivers license. It is unlawful for the holder of a restricted license to operate a motor vehicle without complying with the restriction and is the equivalent of operating a motor vehicle without a license. If any applicant shall suffer from any physical or mental disability or disease that affects his or her operation of a motor vehicle, the Division may require to be filed with it a certificate of the applicant's condition signed by a medical authority of the applicant's community designated by the Division. The Division may, in its discretion, require the certificate to be completed and submitted after a license or renewal has been issued based on the applicant's performance during a road test administered by the Division. Upon submission, the certificate shall be reviewed in accordance with the procedure set forth in G.S. 20-9(g)(3). This certificate shall in all cases be treated as confidential and subject to release under G.S. 20-9(g)(4)h. Nothing in this subsection shall be construed to prevent the Division from refusing to issue a license, either restricted or unrestricted, to any person deemed to be incapable of safely operating a motor vehicle based on information observed or received by the Division, including observations during a road test and medical information submitted about the applicant. An applicant may seek review pursuant to G.S. 20-9(g)(4) of a licensing decision made on the basis of a physical or mental disability or disease. This subsection does not prohibit deaf persons from operating motor vehicles who in every other way meet the requirements of this section.

(f) **Duration and Renewal of Licenses.** -- Drivers licenses shall be issued and renewed pursuant to the provisions of this subsection:

(1) **Duration of license for persons under age 18.** -- A full provisional license issued to a person under the age of 18 expires 60 days following the person's twenty-first birthday.

(2) **Duration of original license for persons at least 18 years of age or older.** -- A drivers license issued to a person at least 18 years old but less than 66 years old expires on the birthday of the

licensee in the eighth year after issuance. A drivers license issued to a person at least 66 years old expires on the birthday of the licensee in the fifth year after issuance. A commercial drivers license expires on the birthday of the licensee in the fifth year after issuance. A commercial drivers license that has a vehicles carrying passengers (P) and school bus (S) endorsement issued pursuant to G.S. 20-37.16 expires on the birthday of the licensee in the third year after issuance, if the licensee is certified to drive a school bus in North Carolina.

(2a) **Duration of renewed licenses.** -- A renewed drivers license that was issued by the Division to a person at least 18 years old but less than 66 years old expires eight years after the expiration date of the license that is renewed. A renewed drivers license that was issued by the Division to a person at least 66 years old expires five years after the expiration date of the license that is renewed. A renewed commercial drivers license expires five years after the expiration date of the license that is renewed.

(3) **Duration of license for certain other drivers.** -- The durations listed in subdivisions (1), (2) and (2a) of this subsection are valid unless the Division determines that a license of shorter duration should be issued when the applicant holds valid documentation issued by, or under the authority of, the United States government that demonstrates the applicant's legal presence of limited duration in the United States. In no event shall a license of limited duration expire later than the expiration of the authorization for the applicant's legal presence in the United States. A drivers license issued to an H-2A worker expires three years after the date of issuance of the H-2A worker's visa; provided, if at any time during that three-year period an H-2A worker's visa duration is not extended by United States Citizenship and Immigration Services, the license expires on the date the H-2A worker's visa expires. For purposes of this subdivision, the term "H-2A worker" means a foreign worker who holds a valid H-2A visa pursuant to the Immigration and Nationality Act (8 U.S.C. § 1101(a)(15)(H)(ii)(a)) and who is legally residing in this State.

(3a) **When to renew.** -- A person may apply to the Division to renew a license during the 180-day period before the license expires. The Division may not accept an application for renewal made before the 180-day period begins.

(3b) Renewal for certain members of the Armed Forces of the United States and reserve components of the Armed Forces of the United States.

a. The Division may renew a drivers license, without limitation on the period of time before the license expires, if the person applying for renewal is a member of the Armed Forces of the United States or of a reserve component of the Armed Forces of the United States and provides orders that place the member on active duty and duty station outside this State.

b. A person who is a member of a reserve component of the Armed Forces of the United States whose license bears an expiration date that occurred while the person was on active duty outside this State shall be considered to have a valid license until 60 days after the date of release from active duty upon showing proof of the release date, unless the license was rescinded, revoked, or otherwise invalidated under some other provision of law. Notwithstanding the provisions of this subsubdivision, no license shall be considered valid more than 18 months after the date of expiration.

(4) **Renewal by mail.** -- The Division may renew by mail a drivers license issued by the Division to a person who meets any of the following descriptions:

a. Is a member of the Armed Forces of the United States or a reserve component of the Armed Forces of the United States serving on active duty and is stationed outside this State.

b. Is a resident of this State and has been residing outside the State for at least 30 continuous days.

When renewing a license by mail, the Division may waive the examination that would otherwise be required for the renewal and may impose any conditions it finds advisable. A license renewed by mail is a temporary license that expires 60 days after the person to whom it is issued returns to this State.

(5) **License to be sent by mail.** -- The Division shall issue to the applicant a temporary driving certificate valid for 60 days, unless the applicant is applying for renewal by mail under subdivision (4) of this subsection. The temporary driving certificate shall be valid for driving purposes and shall not be valid for identification purposes, except when conducting business with the Division and not otherwise prohibited by federal law. The Division shall produce the applicant's drivers license at a central location and send it to the applicant by first-class mail at the residence address

provided by the applicant, unless the applicant is ineligible for mail delivery by the United States Postal Service at the applicant's residence. If the United States Postal Service documents that it does not deliver to the residential address provided by the applicant, and the Division has verified the applicant's residential address by other means, the Division may mail the drivers license to the post office box provided by the applicant. Applicants whose only mailing address prior to July 1, 2008, was a post office box in this State may continue to receive their license at that post office box, provided the applicant's residential address has been verified by the Division.

(6) **Remote renewal or conversion. --** Subject to the following requirements and limitations, the Division may offer remote renewal of a drivers license or remote conversion of a full provisional license issued by the Division:

a. **Requirements. --** To be eligible for remote renewal or conversion under this subdivision, a person must meet all of the following requirements:

1. The license holder possesses either (i) a valid Class C drivers license or (ii) a valid full provisional license and is at least 18 years old at the time of the remote conversion.

2. The license holder's current license includes no restrictions other than a restriction for corrective lenses.

3. The license holder attests, in a manner designated by the Division, that (i) the license holder is a resident of the State and currently resides at the address on the license to be renewed or converted, (ii) the license holder's name as it appears on the license to be renewed or converted has not changed, and (iii) all other information required by the Division for an in-person renewal under this Article has been provided completely and truthfully. If the license holder does not currently reside at the address on the license to be renewed or converted, the license holder may comply with the address requirement of this sub-sub-subdivision by providing the address at which the license holder resides at the time of the remote renewal or conversion request.

4. For a remote renewal, the most recent renewal was an in-person renewal and not a remote renewal under this subdivision.

5. The license holder is otherwise eligible for renewal or conversion under this subsection.

b. **Waiver of requirements. --** When renewing or converting a drivers license pursuant to this subdivision, the Division may waive the examination and photograph that would otherwise be required for the renewal or conversion.

c. **Duration of remote renewal or conversion. --** A drivers license issued to a person by remote renewal or conversion under this subdivision expires according to the following schedule:

1. For a person at least 18 years old but less than 66 years old, on the birthday of the licensee in the eighth year after issuance.

2. For a person at least 66 years old, on the birthday of the licensee in the fifth year after issuance.

d. **Rules. --** The Division shall adopt rules to implement this subdivision.

e. **Federal law. --** Nothing in this subdivision shall be construed to supersede any more restrictive provisions for renewal or conversion of drivers licenses prescribed by federal law or regulation.

f. **Definition. --** For purposes of this subdivision, "remote renewal or conversion" means renewal of a drivers license or conversion of a full provisional license by mail, telephone, electronic device, or other secure means approved by the Commissioner.

(6a) **(Effective October 1, 2021) Remote conversion for active duty military. --** The Division shall offer remote conversion to the holder of a full provisional license issued under G.S. 20-11 to a resident of this State if the provisional license holder is deployed out-of-state as a member of the Armed Forces of the United States. The Division shall adopt rules to implement this subdivision.

(g) Repealed by Session Laws 1979, c. 667, s. 6.

(h) Repealed by Session Laws 1979, c. 113, s. 1.

(i) **Fees. --** The fee for a regular drivers license is the amount set in the following table multiplied by the number of years in the period for which the license is issued:

Class of Regular License	Fee For Each Year
Class A	$ 5.00
Class B	$ 5.00
Class C	$ 5.00

The fee for a motorcycle endorsement is two dollars and thirty cents ($ 2.30) for each year of the period for which the endorsement is issued. The appropriate fee shall be paid before a person receives a regular drivers license or an endorsement.

(i1) **Restoration Fee.** -- Any person whose drivers license has been revoked pursuant to the provisions of this Chapter, other than G.S. 20-17(a)(2) shall pay a restoration fee of sixty five dollars ($ 65.00). A person whose drivers license has been revoked under G.S. 20-17(a)(2) shall pay a restoration fee of one hundred thirty dollars ($ 130.00). The fee shall be paid to the Division prior to the issuance to such person of a new drivers license or the restoration of the drivers license. The restoration fee shall be paid to the Division in addition to any and all fees which may be provided by law. This restoration fee shall not be required from any licensee whose license was revoked or voluntarily surrendered for medical or health reasons whether or not a medical evaluation was conducted pursuant to this Chapter. The sixty five dollar ($ 65.00) fee, and the first one hundred five dollars ($ 105.00) of the one hundred thirty dollar ($ 130.00) fee, shall be deposited in the Highway Fund. Twenty five dollars ($ 25.00) of the one hundred thirty dollar ($ 130.00) fee shall be used to fund a statewide chemical alcohol testing program administered by the Forensic Tests for Alcohol Branch of the Chronic Disease and Injury Section of the Department of Health and Human Services. Notwithstanding any other provision of law, a restoration fee assessed pursuant to this subsection may be waived by the Division when (i) the restoration fee remains unpaid for more than 10 years from the date of assessment and (ii) the person responsible for payment of the restoration fee has been issued a drivers license by the Division after the effective date of the revocation for which the restoration fee is owed. The Office of State Budget and Management shall annually report to the General Assembly the amount of fees deposited in the General Fund and transferred to the Forensic Tests for Alcohol Branch of the Chronic Disease and Injury Section of the Department of Health and Human Services under this subsection.

(j) **Highway Fund.** -- The fees collected under this section and G.S. 20-14 shall be placed in the Highway Fund.

(j1) [Maintenance of Organ Donor Registry Internet Site.] The Division of Motor Vehicles shall retain a portion of five cents ($ 0.05) collected for the issuance of each drivers license and duplicate license to offset the actual cost of developing and maintaining the online Organ Donor Internet site established pursuant to G.S. 20-43.2. The remainder of the five cents ($ 0.05) shall be credited to the License to Give Trust Fund established under G.S. 20-7.4 and shall be used for the purposes authorized under G.S. 20-7.4 and G.S. 20-7.5.

(k) Repealed by Session Laws 1991, c. 726, s. 5.

(*l*) **Learner's Permit.** -- A person who is at least 18 years old may obtain a learner's permit. A learner's permit authorizes the permit holder to drive a specified type or class of motor vehicle while in possession of the permit. A learner's permit is valid for a period of 18 months after it is issued. The fee for a learner's permit is twenty dollars ($ 20.00). A learner's permit may be renewed, or a second learner's permit may be issued, for an additional period of 18 months. The permit holder must, while operating a motor vehicle over the highways, be accompanied by a person who is licensed to operate the motor vehicle being driven and is seated beside the permit holder.

(*l* -1) Repealed by Session Laws 1991, c. 726, s. 5.

(m) **Instruction Permit.** -- The Division upon receiving proper application may in its discretion issue a restricted instruction permit effective for a school year or a lesser period to any of the following applicants:

(1) An applicant who is less than 18 years old and is enrolled in a drivers education program that is approved by the State Superintendent of Public Instruction and is offered at a public high school, a nonpublic secondary school, or a licensed drivers training school.

(2) A restricted instruction permit authorizes the holder of the permit to drive a specified type or class of motor vehicle when in possession of the permit, subject to any restrictions imposed by the Division. The restrictions the Division may impose on a permit include restrictions to designated areas and highways and restrictions prohibiting operation except when an approved instructor is occupying a seat beside the permittee. A restricted instruction permit is not required to have a distinguishing number or a picture of the person to whom the permit is issued.

(n) **Format.** -- A drivers license issued by the Division must be tamperproof and must contain all of the following information:

(1) An identification of this State as the issuer of the license.

(2) The license holder's full name.

(3) The license holder's residence address.

(4) A color photograph of the license holder applied to material that is measured by the industry standard of security and durability and is resistant to tampering and reproduction.

(5) A physical description of the license holder, including sex, height, eye color, and hair color.

(6) The license holder's date of birth.

(7) An identifying number for the license holder assigned by the Division. The identifying number may not be the license holder's social security number.

(8) Each class of motor vehicle the license holder is authorized to drive and any endorsements or restrictions that apply.

(9) The license holder's signature.

(10) The date the license was issued and the date the license expires.

The Commissioner shall ensure that applicants 21 years old or older are issued drivers licenses and special identification cards that are printed in a horizontal format. The Commissioner shall ensure that applicants under the age of 21 are issued drivers licenses and special identification cards that are printed in a vertical format, that distinguishes them from the horizontal format, for ease of identification of individuals under age 21 by members of industries that regulate controlled products that are sale restricted by age and law enforcement officers enforcing these laws.

At the request of an applicant for a drivers license, a license issued to the applicant must contain the applicant's race, which shall be designated with the letters "AI" for an applicant who is American Indian.

(o) Repealed by Session Laws 1991, c. 726, s. 5.

(p) The Division must give the clerk of superior court in each county at least 50 copies of the driver license handbook free of charge. The clerk must give a copy to a person who requests it.

(q) **Active Duty Military Designation.** -- The Division shall develop a military designation for drivers licenses that may, upon request, be granted to North Carolina residents on active duty and to their spouses and dependent children. A drivers license with a military designation on it may be renewed by mail no more than two times during the license holder's lifetime. A license renewed by mail under this subsection is a permanent license and does not expire when the license holder returns to the State. A drivers license with a military designation on it issued to a person on active duty may be renewed up to one year prior to its expiration upon presentation of military or Department of Defense credentials.

(q1) **Veteran Military Designation.** -- The Division shall develop a military designation for drivers licenses and identification cards that may, upon request, be granted to North Carolina residents who are honorably discharged from military service in the Armed Forces of the United States. An applicant requesting this designation must produce a Form DD-214 showing the applicant has been honorably discharged from the Armed Forces of the United States.

(q2) **Deaf or Hard of Hearing Designation.** -- The Division shall develop, in consultation with the Department of Public Safety, the State Highway Patrol, the Division of Services for the Deaf and Hard of Hearing, and pursuant to this subsection, a drivers license designation that may, upon request, be granted to a person who is deaf or hard of hearing. The Division shall comply with the following requirements applicable to the designation:

(1) At the request of a person who is deaf or hard of hearing, the Division shall place a unique symbol on the front of the person's license. The unique symbol placed on the license shall not include any further descriptor. The Division shall record the designation in the electronic record associated with the person's drivers license.

(2) At the request of a person who is deaf or hard of hearing, the Division shall enter the drivers license symbol and a descriptor into the electronic record of any motor vehicle registered in the same name of the deaf or hard of hearing person.

(3) For the purposes of this subsection, a person shall be considered to be deaf or hard of hearing if they provide verification or documentation substantiating their hearing loss that is recommended by the Division of Services for the Deaf and the Hard of Hearing as acceptable. The Division of Motor Vehicles shall consult with the Division of Services for the Deaf and the Hard of Hearing to identify acceptable forms of verification that do not result in undue burden to the person requesting the designation of hearing loss. Acceptable documentation shall include any of the following:

a. Documentation of certification or examination by a medical, health, or audiology professional showing evidence of hearing loss.

b. Affidavit executed by the person, their parent, or guardian attesting to the person's hearing loss.

c. Documentation deemed by the Division of Motor Vehicles to qualify as satisfactory proof of the person's hearing loss.

(4) Nothing in this subsection shall be construed as authorizing the issuance of a drivers license to a person ineligible under G.S. 20-9.

(5) Nothing in this subsection shall be construed as prohibiting the issuance of a drivers license to a person otherwise eligible under the law.

(6) Any individual who chooses to register or not to register shall not be deemed to have waived any protections under the law.

(7) Information collected under this subsection shall only be available to law

Chapter 20

enforcement and only for the purpose of ensuring mutually safe interactions between law enforcement and persons who are deaf or hard of hearing. It shall not be accessed or used for any other purpose.

(8) The right to make the decision for inclusion or removal of the designation from the database is entirely voluntary and shall only be made by the person who holds the drivers license associated with the designation.

(9) The Division, in conjunction with the Department of Health and Human Services, shall develop a process for removal of the designation authorized by this subsection that is available online, by mail, or in person.

(r) **Waiver of Vision Test.** -- The following license holders shall be exempt from any required eye exam when renewing a drivers license by mail under either subsection (f) of this section or subsection (q) of this section if, at the time of renewal, the license holder is serving in a combat zone or a qualified hazardous duty zone:

(1) A member of the Armed Forces of the United States.

(2) A member of a reserve component of the Armed Forces of the United States.

(s) Notwithstanding the requirements of subsection (b1) of this section that an applicant present a valid social security number, the Division shall issue a drivers license of limited duration, under subsection (f) of this section, to an applicant present in the United States who holds valid documentation issued by, or under the authority of, the United States government that demonstrates the applicant's legal presence of limited duration in the United States if the applicant presents that valid documentation and meets all other requirements for a license of limited duration. Notwithstanding the requirements of subsection (n) of this section addressing background colors and borders, a drivers license of limited duration issued under this section shall bear a distinguishing mark or other designation on the face of the license clearly denoting the limited duration of the license.

(t) **Use of Bioptic Telescopic Lenses.** --

(1) An applicant using bioptic telescopic lenses shall be eligible for a regular Class C drivers license under this section if the applicant meets all of the following:

a. Demonstrates a visual acuity of at least 20/200 in one or both eyes and a field of 70 degrees horizontal vision with or without corrective carrier lenses, or if the person has vision in one eye only, the person demonstrates a field of at least 40 degrees temporal and 30 degrees nasal horizontal vision.

b. Demonstrates a visual acuity of at least 20/70 in one or both eyes with the bioptic telescopic lenses and without the use of field expanders.

c. Provides a report of examination by an ophthalmologist or optometrist, on a form prescribed by the Division, for the Division to determine if all field of vision requirements are met or additional testing is needed.

d. Successfully passes a road test administered by the Division. This requirement is waived if the applicant is a new resident of North Carolina who has a valid drivers license issued by another jurisdiction that requires a road test.

e. Meets all other criteria for licensure.

(2) In addition to the requirements listed in subdivision (1) of this subsection, the Division shall require an applicant using bioptic telescopic lenses to successfully complete a behind-the-wheel training and assessment program prescribed by the Division. This requirement is waived if the applicant has successfully completed a behind-the-wheel training and assessment program as a condition of licensure in another jurisdiction.

(3) Applicants using bioptic telescopic lenses shall be eligible for a limited learner's permit or provisional drivers license issued pursuant to G.S. 20-11, provided the requirements of this subsection are met and any other required testing or documentation is completed and submitted with the application.

(4) Applicants issued a regular Class C drivers license, limited learner's permit, or provisional drivers license shall be subject to the following restrictions on the license issued:

a. The license or permit holder shall not be eligible for any endorsements.

b. The license or permit shall permit the operation of motor vehicles only during the period beginning one-half hour after sunrise and ending one-half hour before sunset.

(5) Applicants issued a regular Class C drivers license may drive motor vehicles between the period beginning one-half hour before sunset and ending one-half hour after sunrise if the applicant meets the following requirements:

a. Demonstrates a visual acuity of at least 20/40 in one or both eyes with the bioptic telescopic lenses and without the use of field expanders.

b. Provides a report of examination by an ophthalmologist or optometrist in accordance with sub-subdivision c. of subdivision (1) of this subsection that does not recommend restricting the applicant to driving a motor vehicle only during the period beginning one-half hour after sunrise and ending one-half hour before sunset.

History.
1935, c. 52, s. 2; 1943, c. 649, s. 1; c. 787, s. 1; 1947, c. 1067, s. 10; 1949, c. 583, ss. 9, 10; c. 826, ss. 1, 2; 1951, c. 542, ss. 1, 2; c. 1196, ss. 1-3; 1953, cc. 839, 1284, 1311; 1955, c. 1187, ss. 2-6; 1957, c. 1225; 1963, cc. 754, 1007, 1022; 1965, c. 410, s. 5; 1967, c. 509; 1969, c. 183; c. 783, s. 1; c. 865; 1971, c. 158; 1973, cc. 73, 705; c. 1057, ss. 1, 3; 1975, c. 162, s. 1; c. 295; c. 296, ss. 1, 2; c. 684; c. 716, s. 5; c. 841; c. 875, s. 4; c. 879, s. 46; 1977, c. 6; c. 340, s. 3; c. 354, s. 1; c. 865, ss. 1, 3; 1979, c. 37, s. 1; c. 113; c. 178, s. 2; c. 667, ss. 3-11, 41; c. 678, ss. 1-3; c. 801, ss. 5, 6; 1981, c. 42; c. 690, ss. 8-10; c. 792, s. 3; 1981 (Reg. Sess., 1982), c. 1257, s. 1; 1983, c. 443, s. 1; 1985, c. 141, s. 4; c. 682, ss. 1, 2; 1987, c. 869, ss. 10, 11; 1989, c. 436, ss. 1, 2; c. 771, s. 5; c. 786, s. 4; 1991, c. 478, s. 1; c. 689, s. 325; c. 726, s. 5; 1991 (Reg. Sess., 1992), c. 1007, s. 27; c. 1030, s. 10; 1993, c. 368, s. 1; c. 533, ss. 2, 3, 12; 1993 (Reg. Sess., 1994), c. 595, ss. 1, 2; c. 750, s. 1; c. 761, s. 1.1; 1995 (Reg. Sess., 1996), c. 675, s. 1; 1997-16, ss. 5, 8, 9; 1997-122, ss. 2, 3; 1997-377, s. 1; 1997-433, s. 4; 1997-443, ss. 11A.122, 32.20; 1997-456, s. 32, 33; 1998-17, s. 1; 1998-149, s. 2; 2000-120, ss. 14, 15; 2000-140, s. 93.1(a); 2001-424, ss. 12.2(b), 27.10A(a)-(d); 2001-513, s. 32(a); 2003-152, ss. 1, 2; 2003-284, s. 36.1; 2004-189, s. 5(a), (c); 2004-203, s. 2; 2005-276, s. 44.1(a), (q); 2005-349, s. 4; 2006-257, ss. 1, 2; 2006-264, s. 35.2; 2007-56, ss. 1 -3; 2007-249, s. 1; 2007-350, s. 1; 2007-512, s. 5; 2008-202, ss. 2, 3; 2008-217, s. 1; 2008-221, s. 1; 2009-274, ss. 2, 3; 2009-451, s. 9.5(a); 2009-492, ss. 1, 2; 2010-130, s. 1; 2010-131, ss. 1, 2; 2010-132, s. 1; 2011-35, ss. 1, 2; 2011-183, ss. 21, 127(a); 2011-326, s. 28; 2011-381, s. 2; 2012-78, s. 1; 2012-85, ss. 1, 2; 2012-142, s. 9.16; 2012-145, s. 2.2; 2013-195, s. 2; 2013-231, s. 1; 2013-360, s. 7.10(a); 2014-58, s. 5; 2014-100, s. 34.8(a); 2014-115, s. 56.8(c); 2015-163, s. 2; 2015-238, s. 2.1; 2015-241, ss. 7A.4(b), 29.30(a), 29.30(a1), 29.36; 2015-294, s. 12; 2016-75, s. 1; 2016-90, ss. 6(a), 8(a), 9(a); 2017-191, s. 1; 2018-74, s. 10(a); 2018-145, s. 14; 2019-199, s. 7(a); 2019-227, s. 3(a), (b); 2021-78, s. 12(a); 2021-89, s. 1

N.C. Gen. Stat. § 20-7.01

Repealed by Session Laws 1979, c. 667, s. 43.

§ 20-7.1. Notice of change of address or name

(a) **Address.** -- A person whose address changes from the address stated on a drivers license must notify the Division of the change within 60 days after the change occurs. If the person's address changed because the person moved, the person must obtain a duplicate

license within that time limit stating the new address. A person who does not move but whose address changes due to governmental action may not be charged with violating this subsection. A person who has provided an e-mail or electronic address to the Division pursuant to G.S. 20-48(a) shall notify the Division of any change or discontinuance of that e-mail or electronic address within 30 days after the change or discontinuance.

(b) **Name.** -- A person whose name changes from the name stated on a drivers license must notify the Division of the change within 60 days after the change occurs and obtain a duplicate drivers license stating the new name.

(c) **Fee.** -- G.S. 20-14 sets the fee for a duplicate license.

History.
1975, c. 223, s. 1; 1979, c. 970; 1983, c. 521, s. 1; 1997-122, s. 4; 2016-90, s. 10(a)

N.C. Gen. Stat. § 20-7.2

Repealed by Session Laws 1987, c. 581, s. 2.

§ 20-7.3. Availability of organ, eye, and tissue donor cards at motor vehicle offices

The Division shall make organ, eye, and tissue donor cards available to interested individuals in each office authorized to issue drivers licenses or special identification cards. The Division shall obtain donor cards from qualified organ, eye, or tissue procurement organizations or tissue banks, as defined in G.S. 130A-412.4(31). The Division shall offer organ donation information and a donor card to each applicant for a drivers license. The organ donation information shall include the following:

(1) A statement informing the individual that federally designated organ procurement organizations and eye banks have read-only access to the Department-operated Organ Donor Registry Internet site (hereafter "Donor Registry") listing those individuals who have stated to the Division of Motor Vehicles the individual's intent to be an organ donor and have an organ donation symbol on the individual's drivers license or special identification card.

(2) The type of information that will be made available on the Donor Registry.

History.
2001-481, s. 3; 2004-189, s. 3; 2007-538, s. 7

§ 20-7.4. License to Give Trust Fund established

(a) There is established the License to Give Trust Fund. Revenue in the Fund includes amounts credited by the Division as required by law, and other funds. Any surplus in the Fund shall not revert but shall be used for the purposes stated in this section. The Fund shall be kept on deposit with the State Treasurer, as in the case of other State Funds, and may be invested by the State Treasurer in any lawful securities for investment of State funds. The License to Give Trust Fund is subject to oversight by the State Auditor pursuant to Article 5A of Chapter 147 of the General Statutes.

(b) The purposes for which funds may be expended by the License to Give Trust Fund Commission from the License to Give Trust Fund are as follows:

(1) As grants-in-aid for initiatives that educate about and promote organ and tissue donation and health care decision making at life's end.

(2) Expenses of the License to Give Trust Fund Commission as authorized in G.S. 20-7.5.

History.
2004-189, s. 4(a); 2015-241, s. 27.8(a); 2015-276, s. 6.5

§ 20-7.5. License to Give Trust Fund Commission established

(a) There is established the License to Give Trust Fund Commission. The Commission shall be located in the Department of Administration for budgetary and administrative purposes only. The Commission may allocate funds from the License to Give Trust Fund for the purposes authorized in G.S. 20-7.4. The Commission shall have 15 members, appointed as follows:

(1) Four members by the General Assembly, upon the recommendation of the President Pro Tempore of the Senate:

a. One representative of Carolina Donor Services.

b. One representative of LifeShare of The Carolinas.

c. Two members who have demonstrated an interest in organ and tissue donation and education.

(2) Four members by the General Assembly, upon the recommendation of the Speaker of the House of Representatives:

a. One representative of The North Carolina Eye Bank, Inc.

b. One representative of The Carolinas Center for Hospice and End-of-Life Care.

c. Two members who have demonstrated an interest in promoting advance care planning education.

(3) Seven members by the Governor:

a. Three members representing organ, tissue, and eye recipients, families of recipients, or families of donors. Of

these three, one each from the mountain, heartland, and coastal regions of the State.

b. One member who is a transplant physician licensed to practice medicine in this State.

c. One member who has demonstrated an interest in organ and tissue donation and education.

d. One member who has demonstrated an interest in promoting advance care planning education.

e. A representative of the North Carolina Department of Transportation.

(b) The Commission shall elect from its membership a chair and a vice-chair for two-year terms. The Secretary of Administration shall provide meeting facilities for the Commission as required by the Chair.

(c) The members of the Commission shall receive per diem and necessary travel and subsistence expenses in accordance with G.S. 138-5 and G.S. 138-6, as applicable. Per diem, subsistence, and travel expenses of the members shall be paid from the License to Give Trust Fund.

(d) The members of the Commission shall comply with G.S. 14-234 prohibiting conflicts of interest. In addition to the restrictions imposed under G.S. 14-234, a member shall not vote on, participate in the deliberations of, or otherwise attempt through his or her official capacity to influence the vote on allocations of moneys from the License to Give Trust Fund to a nonprofit entity of which the member is an officer, director, or employee, or to a governmental entity of which the member is an employee or a member of the governing board. A violation of this subsection is a Class 1 misdemeanor.

History.
2004-189, s. 4(b)

§ 20-7.6. Powers and duties of the License to Give Trust Fund Commission

The License to Give Trust Fund Commission has the following powers and duties:

(1) Establish general policies and guidelines for awarding grants-in-aid to nonprofit entities to conduct education and awareness activities on organ and tissue donation and advance care planning.

(2) Accept gifts or grants from other sources to further the purposes of the License to Give Trust Fund. Such gifts or grants shall be transmitted to the State Treasurer for credit to the Fund.

(3) Hire staff or contract for other expertise for the administration of the Fund. Expenses related to staffing shall be paid from the License to Give Trust Fund.

History.

2004-189, s. 4(b); 2015-241, s. 27.8(b); 2015-276, s. 6.5

§ 20-8. Persons exempt from license

The following are exempt from license hereunder:

(1) Any person while operating a motor vehicle the property of and in the service of the Armed Forces of the United States. This shall not be construed to exempt any operators of the United States Civilian Conservation Corps motor vehicles;

(2) Any person while driving or operating any road machine, farm tractor, or implement of husbandry temporarily operated or moved on a highway;

(3) A nonresident who is at least 16 years of age who has in his immediate possession a valid driver's license issued to him in his home state or country if the nonresident is operating a motor vehicle in this State in accordance with the license restrictions and vehicle classifications that would be applicable to him under the laws and regulations of his home state or country if he were driving in his home state or country. This exemption specifically applies to nonresident military spouses, regardless of their employment status, who are temporarily residing in North Carolina due to the active duty military orders of a spouse.

(4) to (6) Repealed by Session Laws 1979, c. 667, s. 13.

(7) Any person who is at least 16 years of age and while operating a moped.

History.

1935, c. 52, s. 3; 1963, c. 1175; 1973, c. 1017; 1975, c. 859, s. 2; 1979, c. 574, s. 7; c. 667, s. 13; 1983, c. 436; 2009-274, s. 4

§ 20-9. What persons shall not be licensed

(a) To obtain a regular drivers license, a person must have reached the minimum age set in the following table for the class of license sought:

Class of Regular License	Minimum Age
Class A	18
Class B	18
Class C	16

G.S. 20-37.13 sets the age qualifications for a commercial drivers license.

(b) The Division shall not issue a drivers license to any person whose license has been suspended or revoked during the period for which the license was suspended or revoked.

(b1) The Division shall not issue a drivers license to any person whose permit or license has been suspended or revoked under G.S.

20-13.2(c1) during the suspension or revocation period, unless the Division has restored the person's permit or license under G.S. 20-13.2(c1).

(c) The Division shall not issue a drivers license to any person who is an habitual drunkard or is an habitual user of narcotic drugs or barbiturates, whether or not the use is in accordance with the prescription of a physician.

(d) Repealed by Session Laws 2012-194, s. 8, effective July 17, 2012.

(e) The Division shall not issue a drivers license to any person when in the opinion of the Division the person is unable to exercise reasonable and ordinary control over a motor vehicle while operating the vehicle upon the highways, nor shall a license be issued to any person who is unable to understand highway warnings or direction signs.

(f) The Division shall not issue a drivers license to any person whose license or driving privilege is in a state of cancellation, suspension, or revocation in any jurisdiction, if the acts or things upon which the cancellation, suspension, or revocation in the other jurisdiction was based would constitute lawful grounds for cancellation, suspension, or revocation in this State had those acts or things been done or committed in this State. However, any such cancellation shall not prohibit issuance for a period in excess of 18 months.

(g) The Division may issue a restricted or unrestricted drivers license under the following conditions to an otherwise eligible applicant suffering from a physical or mental disability or disease that affects his or her ability to exercise reasonable and ordinary control of a motor vehicle:

(1) The applicant submits to the Division a certificate in the form prescribed in subdivision (2) of this subsection. The Division may request the certificate at the applicant's initial application, at any time following the issuance of the license, or at the initial application and any time following the issuance of the license. Until a license issued under this subdivision expires, is cancelled, or is revoked, the license continues in force as long as the licensee presents to the Division a certificate in the form prescribed in subdivision (2) of this subsection at the intervals determined by the Division to be in the best interests of public safety.

(2) The Division may request a signed certificate from a health care provider duly licensed to practice medicine in the United States that the applicant or licensee has submitted to a physical examination by the health care provider. The certificate shall be devised by the Commissioner with the advice of qualified experts in the field of diagnosing and treating physical and mental disabilities and diseases as the

Commissioner may select to assist him or her and shall be designed to elicit the maximum medical information necessary to aid in determining whether or not it would be a hazard to public safety to permit the applicant or licensee to operate a motor vehicle, including, if such is the fact, the examining provider's statement that the applicant or licensee is under medication and treatment and that the applicant's or licensee's physical or mental disability or disease is controlled. The certificate shall contain a waiver of privilege and the recommendation of the examining provider to the Commissioner as to whether a license should be issued to the applicant or licensee and whether the applicant or licensee can safely operate a motor vehicle.

(3) The Commissioner is not bound by the recommendation of the examining health care provider but shall give fair consideration to the recommendation in exercising his or her discretion in making licensing decisions, the criterion being whether or not, upon all the evidence, it appears that it is safe to permit the applicant or licensee to operate a motor vehicle. The burden of proof of this fact is upon the applicant or licensee. In deciding whether to issue, restrict, cancel, or deny a license, the Commissioner may be guided by the opinion of experts in the field of diagnosing and treating the specific physical or mental disability or disease suffered by an applicant or licensee and the experts may be compensated for their services on an equitable basis. The Commissioner may also take into consideration any other factors which bear on the issue of public safety.

(4) Whenever a license is restricted, cancelled, or denied by the Commissioner on the basis of a physical or mental disability or disease, the action may be reviewed by a reviewing board upon written request of the applicant or licensee filed with the Division within 10 days after receipt of notice given in accordance with G.S. 20-48 of the action taken. The reviewing board shall consist of the Commissioner or the Commissioner's authorized representative and at least two medical professionals selected by the Commissioner and duly licensed to practice medicine by the appropriate licensing authority in the State. The medical professionals selected by the Commissioner may be compensated for their services on an equitable basis, including reimbursement for ordinary and necessary travel expenses. The Commissioner or the Commissioner's authorized representative, plus any two medical professionals selected by the Commissioner, shall constitute a quorum. The procedure for hearings authorized by this section shall be as follows:

a. Applicants shall be afforded an opportunity for hearing, after reasonable notice of not less than 10 days, before the review board established by this subdivision. The notice shall be in writing and shall be delivered to the applicant in person or sent by certified mail, with return receipt requested. The notice shall state the time, place, and subject of the hearing. If a hearing is requested under this subdivision to contest a restriction placed on a license under subdivision (3) of this subsection, the restriction shall be stayed unless the Division determines there is an imminent threat to public safety if continued unrestricted driving is permitted. No stay shall be granted if a hearing is requested under this subdivision to contest a denial or cancellation of a license under subdivision (3) of this subsection. Nothing in this sub-subdivision authorizes the stay of a restriction placed on a license pursuant to another provision of law.

b. The review board may compel the attendance of witnesses and the production of such books, records, and papers as it desires at a hearing authorized by this section. Upon request of an applicant or licensee, a subpoena to compel the attendance of any witness or a subpoena duces tecum to compel the production of any books, records, or papers shall be issued by the board. Subpoenas shall be directed to the sheriff of the county where the witness resides or is found and shall be served and returned in the same manner as a subpoena in a criminal case. Fees of the sheriff and witnesses shall be the same as that allowed in the district court in cases before that court and shall be paid in the same manner as other expenses of the Division of Motor Vehicles are paid. In any case of disobedience or neglect of any subpoena served on any person, or the refusal of any witness to testify to any matters regarding which the witness may be lawfully interrogated, the district court or superior court where the disobedience, neglect, or refusal occurs, or any judge thereof, on application by the board, shall compel obedience or punish as for contempt.

c. A hearing may be continued upon motion of the applicant or licensee for good cause shown with approval of the board or upon order of the board.

d. The board shall pass upon the admissibility of evidence at a hearing but the applicant or licensee affected may at the time object to the board's ruling, and, if evidence offered by an applicant or licensee is rejected, the party may proffer the evidence, and the proffer shall be made a part of the record. The board shall not be bound by common law or statutory rules of evidence which prevail in courts of law or equity and may admit and give probative value to evidence which possesses probative value commonly accepted by reasonably prudent persons in the conduct of their affairs. It may exclude incompetent, immaterial, irrelevant, and unduly repetitious evidence. Uncontested facts may be stipulated by agreement between an applicant or licensee and the board, and evidence relating to stipulated facts may be excluded. All evidence, including records and documents in the possession of the Division of Motor Vehicles or the board, of which the board desires to avail itself shall be made a part of the record. Documentary evidence may be received in the form of copies or excerpts, or by incorporation by reference. The board shall prepare an official record, which shall include testimony and exhibits. A record of the testimony and other evidence submitted shall be taken, but it shall not be necessary to transcribe shorthand notes or electronic recordings unless requested for purposes of court review.

e. Every decision and order adverse to an applicant or licensee shall be in writing or stated in the record and shall be accompanied by findings of fact and conclusions of law. The findings of fact shall consist of a concise statement of the board's conclusions on each contested issue of fact. The applicant or licensee shall be notified of the board's decision in person or by registered mail with return receipt requested. A copy of the board's decision with accompanying findings and conclusions shall be delivered or mailed upon request to the applicant's or licensee's attorney of record or to the applicant or licensee, if he or she has no attorney.

f. Actions of the reviewing board are subject to judicial review as provided under Chapter 150B of the General Statutes.

g. Repealed by Session Laws 1977, c. 840.

h. All records and evidence collected and compiled by the Division and the reviewing board shall not be considered public records within the meaning of Chapter 132 of the General Statutes and may be made available to the public only upon an order of a court of competent jurisdiction. An applicant or licensee may obtain, without a court order, a copy of records and evidence collected and compiled under this subdivision about the applicant or licensee by submitting a written request to the Division, signing any release forms required by the Division, and remitting the required fee set by the Division. All information furnished by, about, or on behalf of an applicant or licensee under this section shall be without prejudice and shall be for the use of the Division, the reviewing board, or the court in administering this section and shall not be used in any manner as evidence, or for any other purposes in any trial, civil or criminal. The prohibition on release and use under this sub-subdivision applies without regard to who authored or produced the information collected, compiled, and used by the Division under this subdivision.

(h) The Division shall not issue a drivers license to an applicant who currently holds a license to drive issued by another state unless the applicant surrenders the license.

(i) The Division shall not issue a drivers license to an applicant who has resided in this State for less than 12 months until the Division has searched the National Sex Offender Public Registry to determine if the person is currently registered as a sex offender in another state. The following applies in this subsection:

(1) If the Division finds that the person is currently registered as a sex offender in another state, the Division shall not issue a drivers license to the person until the person submits proof of registration pursuant to Article 27A of Chapter 14 of the General Statutes issued by the sheriff of the county where the person resides.

(2) If the person does not appear on the National Sex Offender Public Registry, the Division shall issue a drivers license but shall require the person to sign an affidavit acknowledging that the person has been notified that if the person is a sex offender, then the person is required to register pursuant to Article 27A of Chapter 14 of the General Statutes.

(3) If the Division is unable to access all states' information contained in the National Sex Offender Public Registry, but the person is otherwise qualified to obtain

Chapter 20

a drivers license, then the Division shall issue the drivers license but shall first require the person to sign an affidavit stating that: (i) the person does not appear on the National Sex Offender Public Registry and (ii) acknowledging that the person has been notified that if the person is a sex offender, then the person is required to register pursuant to Article 27A of Chapter 14 of the General Statutes. The Division shall search the National Sex Offender Public Registry for the person within a reasonable time after access to the Registry is restored. If the person does appear in the National Sex Offender Public Registry, the person is in violation of G.S. 20-30, and the Division shall immediately revoke the drivers license and shall promptly notify the sheriff of the county where the person resides of the offense.

(4) Any person denied a license or whose license has been revoked by the Division pursuant to this subsection has a right to file a petition within 30 days thereafter for a hearing in the matter in the superior court of the county where the person resides, or to petition the resident judge of the district or judge holding the court of that district, or special or emergency judge holding a court in the district, and the court or judge is hereby vested with jurisdiction. The court or judge shall set the matter for hearing upon 30 days' written notice to the Division. At the hearing, the court or judge shall take testimony and examine the facts of the case and shall determine whether the petitioner is entitled to a license under this subsection and whether the petitioner is in violation of G.S. 20-30.

History.
1935, c. 52, s. 4; 1951, c. 542, s. 3; 1953, c. 773; 1955, c. 118, s. 7; 1967, cc. 961, 966; 1971, c. 152; c. 528, s. 11; 1973, cc. 135, 441; c. 476, s. 128; c. 1331, s. 3; 1975, c. 716, s. 5; 1979, c. 667, ss. 14, 41; 1983, c. 545; 1987, c. 827, s. 1; 1989, c. 771, s. 7; 1991, c. 726, s. 6; 1993, c. 368, s. 2; c. 533, s. 4; 1999-243, s. 4; 1999-452, s. 8; 2003-14, s. 1; 2006-247, s. 19(c); 2007-182, s. 2; 2012-194, s. 8; 2016-94, s. 35.20(c); 2018-74, s. 10(b); 2018-142, s. 3(a)

§ 20-9.1. Physicians, psychologists, and other medical providers providing medical information on drivers with physical or mental disabilities or diseases

(a) Notwithstanding G.S. 8-53 for physicians and G.S. 8-53.3 for psychologists, or any other law relating to confidentiality of communications between physicians, psychologists, or other medical providers and their patients, a physician, psychologist, or other medical

provider duly licensed in the State of North Carolina may disclose after consultation with the patient to the Commissioner information about a patient who has a physical or mental disability or disease that the physician, psychologist, or other medical provider believes may affect the patient's ability to safely operate a motor vehicle. This information shall be limited to the patient's name, address, date of birth, and diagnosis.

(b) The information provided to the Commissioner pursuant to subsection (a) of this section shall be confidential and shall be used only for the purpose of determining the qualifications of the patient to operate a motor vehicle.

(c) A physician, psychologist, or other medical provider disclosing or not disclosing information pursuant to this section, or conducting an evaluation and making a recommendation to the Division regarding a person's ability to safely operate a motor vehicle, is immune from any civil or criminal liability that might otherwise be incurred or imposed based on the action taken provided that the physician, psychologist, or other medical provider was acting in good faith and without malice. In any proceeding involving liability, good faith and lack of malice are presumed.

History.
1997-464, s. 1; 2016-94, s. 35.20(d)

§ 20-9.2. Selective service system registration requirements

(a) Any male United States citizen or immigrant who is at least 18 years of age but less than 26 years of age shall be registered in compliance with the requirements of the Military Selective Service Act, 50 U.S.C. § 453 (1948), when applying for the issuance, renewal, or duplication of a drivers license, commercial drivers license, or identification card.

(b) The Division shall forward in an electronic format the necessary personal information of the applicants identified in subsection (a) of this section required for registration to the Selective Service System. An application for the issuance, renewal, or duplication of a drivers license, commercial drivers license, or identification card constitutes an affirmation that the applicant has already registered with the Selective Service System or that he authorizes the Division to forward the necessary information to the Selective Service System for registration. The Division shall notify the applicant that his application for the issuance, renewal, or duplication of a drivers license, commercial drivers license, or identification card serves as his consent to be registered with the Selective Service System pursuant to this section.

(c) This section does not apply to special identification cards issued pursuant to G.S. 20-37.7(d)(5) or (6).

History.
2002-162, s. 1; 2014-111, s. 14

§ 20-9.3. Notification of requirements for sex offender registration

The Division shall provide notice to each person who applies for the issuance of a drivers license, learner's permit, or instruction permit to operate a motor vehicle, and to each person who applies for an identification card, that if the person is a sex offender, then the person is required to register pursuant to Article 27A of Chapter 14 of the General Statutes.

History.
2006-247, s. 19(b)

§ 20-10. Age limits for drivers of public passenger-carrying vehicles

It shall be unlawful for any person, whether licensed under this Article or not, who is under the age of 18 years to drive a motor vehicle while in use as a public passenger-carrying vehicle. For purposes of this section, an ambulance when operated for the purpose of transporting persons who are sick, injured, or otherwise incapacitated shall not be treated as a public passenger-carrying vehicle.

No person 14 years of age or under, whether licensed under this Article or not, shall operate any road machine, farm tractor or motor driven implement of husbandry on any highway within this State. Provided any person may operate a road machine, farm tractor, or motor driven implement of husbandry upon a highway adjacent to or running in front of the land upon which such person lives when said person is actually engaged in farming operations.

History.
1935, c. 52, s. 5; 1951, c. 764; 1967, c. 343, s. 4; 1971, c. 1231, s. 1

§ 20-10.1. Mopeds

It shall be unlawful for any person who is under the age of 16 years to operate a moped as defined in G.S. 20-4.01(27)j. upon any highway or public vehicular area of this State.

History.
1979, c. 574, s. 8; 2002-72, s. 6; 2016-90, s. 13(b); 2017-102, s. 5.2(b)

§ 20-11. Issuance of limited learner's permit and provisional drivers license to person who is less than 18 years old

(a) **Process.** -- Safe driving requires instruction in driving and experience. To ensure that a person who is less than 18 years old has both instruction and experience before obtaining a drivers license, driving privileges are granted first on a limited basis and are then expanded in accordance with the following process:

(1) **Level 1.** -- Driving with a limited learner's permit.

(2) **Level 2.** -- Driving with a limited provisional license.

(3) **Level 3.** -- Driving with a full provisional license.

A permit or license issued under this section must indicate the level of driving privileges granted by the permit or license.

(b) **Level 1.** -- A person who is at least 15 years old but less than 18 years old may obtain a limited learner's permit if the person meets all of the following requirements:

(1) Passes a course of driver education prescribed in G.S. 115C-215 or a course of driver instruction at a licensed commercial driver training school.

(2) Passes a written test administered by the Division.

(3) Has a driving eligibility certificate or a high school diploma or its equivalent.

(c) **Level 1 Restrictions.** -- A limited learner's permit authorizes the permit holder to drive a specified type or class of motor vehicle only under the following conditions:

(1) The permit holder must be in possession of the permit.

(2) A supervising driver must be seated beside the permit holder in the front seat of the vehicle when it is in motion. No person other than the supervising driver can be in the front seat.

(3) For the first six months after issuance, the permit holder may drive only between the hours of 5:00 a.m. and 9:00 p.m.

(4) After the first six months after issuance, the permit holder may drive at any time.

(5) Every person occupying the vehicle being driven by the permit holder must have a safety belt properly fastened about his or her body, or be restrained by a child passenger restraint system as provided in G.S. 20-137.1(a), when the vehicle is in motion.

(6) The permit holder shall not use a mobile telephone or other additional technology associated with a mobile telephone while operating the motor vehicle on a public street or highway or public vehicular area.

(d) **Level 2.** -- A person who is at least 16 years old but less than 18 years old may obtain a limited provisional license if the person meets all of the following requirements:

(1) *(Effective May 24, 2021 until December 31, 2022)* Has held a limited learner's permit issued by the Division for at least six months.

(1) *(Effective December 31, 2022)* Has held a limited learner's permit issued by the Division for at least 12 months.

(2) Has not been convicted of a motor vehicle moving violation or seat belt infraction or a violation of G.S. 20-137.3 during the preceding six months.

(3) Passes a road test administered by the Division.

(4) Has a driving eligibility certificate or a high school diploma or its equivalent.

(5) Has completed a driving log, on a form approved by the Division, detailing a minimum of 60 hours as the operator of a motor vehicle of a class for which the driver has been issued a limited learner's permit. The log must show at least 10 hours of the required driving occurred during nighttime hours. No more than 10 hours of driving per week may be counted toward the 60-hour requirement. The driving log must be signed by the supervising driver and submitted to the Division at the time the applicant seeks to obtain a limited provisional license. If the Division has cause to believe that a driving log has been falsified, the limited learner's permit holder shall be required to complete a new driving log with the same requirements and shall not be eligible to obtain a limited provisional license for six months.

(e) **Level 2 Restrictions.** -- A limited provisional license authorizes the license holder to drive a specified type or class of motor vehicle only under the following conditions:

(1) The license holder shall be in possession of the license.

(2) The license holder may drive without supervision in any of the following circumstances:

a. From 5:00 a.m. to 9:00 p.m.

b. When driving directly to or from work.

c. When driving directly to or from an activity of a volunteer fire department, volunteer rescue squad, or volunteer emergency medical service, if the driver is a member of the organization.

(3) The license holder may drive with supervision at any time. When the license holder is driving with supervision, the supervising driver shall be seated beside the license holder in the front seat of the vehicle when it is in motion. The supervising driver need not be the only other occupant of the front seat, but shall be the person seated next to the license holder.

(4) When the license holder is driving the vehicle and is not accompanied by the supervising driver, there may be no more than one passenger under 21 years of age in the vehicle. This limit does not apply to passengers who are members of the license holder's immediate family or whose primary residence is the same household as the license holder. However, if a family member or member of the same household as the license holder who is younger than 21 years of age is a passenger in the vehicle, no other passengers under 21 years of age, who are not members of the license holder's immediate family or members of the license holder's household, may be in the vehicle.

(5) Every person occupying the vehicle being driven by the license holder shall have a safety belt properly fastened about his or her body, or be restrained by a child passenger restraint system as provided in G.S. 20-137.1(a), when the vehicle is in motion.

(6) The license holder shall not use a mobile telephone or other additional technology associated with a mobile telephone while operating the vehicle on a public street or highway or public vehicular area.

(f) **Level 3.** -- A person who is at least 16 years old but less than 18 years old may obtain a full provisional license if the person meets all of the following requirements:

(1) Has held a limited provisional license issued by the Division for at least six months.

(2) Has not been convicted of a motor vehicle moving violation or seat belt infraction or a violation of G.S. 20-137.3 during the preceding six months.

(3) Has a driving eligibility certificate or a high school diploma or its equivalent.

(4) Has completed a driving log, on a form approved by the Division, detailing a minimum of 12 hours as the operator of a motor vehicle of a class for which the driver is licensed. The log must show at least six hours of the required driving occurred during nighttime hours. The driving log must be signed by the supervising driver for any hours driven outside the provisions of subdivision (e)(2) of this section and submitted to the Division at the time the applicant seeks to obtain a full provisional license. If the Division has cause to believe that a driving log has been falsified, the limited provisional licensee shall be required to complete a new driving log with the same

Chapter 20

requirements and shall not be eligible to obtain a full provisional license for six months.

A person who meets these requirements may obtain a full provisional license by mail.

(g) **Level 3 Restrictions.** -- The restrictions on Level 1 and Level 2 drivers concerning time of driving, supervision, and passenger limitations do not apply to a full provisional license. However, the prohibition against operating a motor vehicle while using a mobile telephone under G.S. 20-137.3(b) shall apply to a full provisional license.

(h) **Exception for Persons 16 to 18 Who Have an Unrestricted Out-of-State License.** -- A person who is at least 16 years old but less than 18 years old, who was a resident of another state and has an unrestricted drivers license issued by that state, and who becomes a resident of this State may obtain one of the following upon the submission of a driving eligibility certificate or a high school diploma or its equivalent:

(1) A temporary permit, if the person has not completed a drivers education program that meets the requirements of the Superintendent of Public Instruction but is currently enrolled in a drivers education program that meets these requirements. A temporary permit is valid for the period specified in the permit and authorizes the holder of the permit to drive a specified type or class of motor vehicle when in possession of the permit, subject to any restrictions imposed by the Division concerning time of driving, supervision, and passenger limitations. The period must end within 10 days after the expected completion date of the drivers education program in which the applicant is enrolled.

(2) A full provisional license, if the person has completed a drivers education program that meets the requirements of the Superintendent of Public Instruction, has held the license issued by the other state for at least 12 months, and has not been convicted during the preceding six months of a motor vehicle moving violation, a seat belt infraction, or an offense committed in another jurisdiction that would be a motor vehicle moving violation or seat belt infraction if committed in this State.

(2a) A full provisional license, if the person has completed a drivers education program that meets the requirements of the Superintendent of Public Instruction, has held both a learner's permit and a restricted license from another state for at least six months each, the Commissioner finds that the requirements for the learner's permit and restricted license are comparable to

the requirements for a learner's permit and restricted license in this State, and the person has not been convicted during the preceding six months of a motor vehicle moving violation, a seat belt infraction, or an offense committed in another jurisdiction that would be a moving violation or a seat belt infraction if committed in this State.

(3) A limited provisional license, if the person has completed a drivers education program that meets the requirements of the Superintendent of Public Instruction but either did not hold the license issued by the other state for at least 12 months or was convicted during the preceding six months of a motor vehicle moving violation, a seat belt infraction, or an offense committed in another jurisdiction that would be a motor vehicle moving violation or seat belt infraction if committed in this State.

(h1) **Exception for Persons 16 to 18 Who Have an Out-of-State Restricted License.** -- A person who is at least 16 years old but less than 18 years old, who was a resident of another state and has a restricted drivers license issued by that state, and who becomes a resident of this State may obtain one of the following:

(1) A limited provisional license, if the person has completed a drivers education program that meets the requirements of the Superintendent of Public Instruction, held the restricted license issued by the other state for at least 12 months, and whose parent or guardian certifies that the person has not been convicted during the preceding six months of a motor vehicle moving violation, a seat belt infraction, or an offense committed in another jurisdiction that would be a motor vehicle moving violation or seat belt infraction if committed in this State.

(2) A limited learners permit, if the person has completed a drivers education program that meets the requirements of the Superintendent of Public Instruction but either did not hold the restricted license issued by the other state for at least 12 months or was convicted during the preceding six months of a motor vehicle moving violation, a seat belt infraction, or an offense committed in another jurisdiction that would be a motor vehicle moving violation or seat belt infraction if committed in this State. A person who qualifies for a limited learners permit under this subdivision and whose parent or guardian certifies that the person has not been convicted of a moving violation in the preceding six months shall be deemed to have held a limited learners permit in this State for each month the person held a restricted license in another state.

(h2) **Exception for Persons Age 15 Who Have an Out-of-State Unrestricted or Restricted License.** -- A person who is age 15, who was a resident of another state, has an unrestricted or restricted drivers license issued by that state, and who becomes a resident of this State may obtain a limited learners permit if the person has completed a drivers education program that meets the requirements of the Superintendent of Public Instruction. A person who qualifies for a limited learners permit under this subsection and whose parent or guardian certifies that the person has not been convicted of a moving violation in the preceding six months shall be deemed to have held a limited learners permit in this State for each month the person held an unrestricted or restricted license in another state.

(h3) **Exception for Persons Less Than Age 18 Who Have a Federally Issued Unrestricted or Restricted License.** -- A person who is less than age 18, who has an unrestricted or restricted drivers license issued by the federal government, and who becomes a resident of this State may obtain a limited provisional license or a provisional license if the person has completed a drivers education program substantially equivalent to the drivers education program that meets the requirements of the Superintendent of Public Instruction. A person who qualifies for a limited provisional license or a provisional license under this subsection and whose parent or guardian certifies that the person has not been convicted of a moving violation in the preceding six months shall be deemed to have held a limited provisional license or a provisional license in this State for each month the person held an unrestricted or restricted license issued by the federal government.

(i) **Application.** -- An application for a permit or license authorized by this section must be signed by both the applicant and another person. That person must be:

(1) The applicant's parent or guardian;

(2) A person approved by the applicant's parent or guardian; or

(3) A person approved by the Division.

(4) With respect to minors in the legal custody of the county department of social services, any of the following:

a. A guardian ad litem or attorney advocate appointed to advocate for the minor under G.S. 7B-601.

b. The director of the county department of social services or the director's designee.

c. If no person listed in subsubdivision a. or b. of this subdivision is available, the court with continuing jurisdiction over the minor's placement under G.S. 7B-1000(b).

(j) **Duration and Fee.** -- A limited learner's permit expires on the eighteenth birthday of the permit holder. A limited provisional license expires on the eighteenth birthday of the license holder. A limited learner's permit or limited provisional license issued under this section that expires on a weekend or State holiday shall remain valid through the fifth regular State business day following the date of expiration. A full provisional license expires on the date set under G.S. 20-7(f). The fee for a limited learner's permit or a limited provisional license is twenty dollars ($ 20.00). The fee for a full provisional license is the amount set under G.S. 20-7(i).

(k) **Supervising Driver.** -- A supervising driver shall be a parent, grandparent, or guardian of the permit holder or license holder or a responsible person approved by the parent or guardian or the Division. A supervising driver shall be a licensed driver who has been licensed for at least five years. At least one supervising driver shall sign the application for a permit or license.

(*l*) **Violations.** -- It is unlawful for the holder of a limited learner's permit, a temporary permit, or a limited provisional license to drive a motor vehicle in violation of the restrictions that apply to the permit or license. Failure to comply with a restriction concerning the time of driving or the presence of a supervising driver in the vehicle constitutes operating a motor vehicle without a license. Failure to comply with the restriction regarding the use of a mobile telephone while operating a motor vehicle is an infraction punishable by a fine of twenty-five dollars ($ 25.00). Failure to comply with any other restriction, including seating and passenger limitations, is an infraction punishable by a monetary penalty as provided in G.S. 20-176. Failure to comply with the provisions of subsections (e) and (g) of this section shall not constitute negligence per se or contributory negligence by the driver or passenger in any action for the recovery of damages arising out of the operation, ownership or maintenance of a motor vehicle. Any evidence of failure to comply with the provisions of subdivisions (1), (2), (3), (4), and (5) of subsection (e) of this section shall not be admissible in any criminal or civil trial, action, or proceeding except in an action based on a violation of this section. No drivers license points or insurance surcharge shall be assessed for failure to comply with seating and occupancy limitations in subsection (e) of this section. No drivers license points or insurance surcharge shall be assessed for failure to comply with subsection (e) or (g) of this section regarding the use of a mobile telephone while operating a motor vehicle.

(m) **Insurance Status.** -- The holder of a limited learner's permit is not considered a licensed driver for the purpose of determining the inexperienced operator premium surcharge under automobile insurance policies.

(n) **Driving Eligibility Certificate.** -- A person who desires to obtain a permit or license issued under this section must have a high school diploma or its equivalent or must have a driving eligibility certificate. A driving eligibility certificate must meet the following conditions:

(1) The person who is required to sign the certificate under subdivision (4) of this subsection must show that he or she has determined that one of the following requirements is met:

a. The person is currently enrolled in school and is making progress toward obtaining a high school diploma or its equivalent.

b. A substantial hardship would be placed on the person or the person's family if the person does not receive a certificate.

c. The person cannot make progress toward obtaining a high school diploma or its equivalent.

(1a) The person who is required to sign the certificate under subdivision (4) of this subsection also must show that one of the following requirements is met:

a. The person who seeks a permit or license issued under this section is not subject to subsection (n1) of this section.

b. The person who seeks a permit or license issued under this section is subject to subsection (n1) of this section and is eligible for the certificate under that subsection.

(2) It must be on a form approved by the Division.

(3) It must be dated within 30 days of the date the person applies for a permit or license issuable under this section.

(4) It must be signed by the applicable person named below:

a. The principal, or the principal's designee, of the public school in which the person is enrolled.

b. The administrator, or the administrator's designee, of the nonpublic school in which the person is enrolled.

c. The person who provides the academic instruction in the home school in which the person is enrolled.

c1. The person who provides the academic instruction in the home in accordance with an educational program found by a court, prior to July 1, 1998, to comply with the compulsory attendance law.

d. The designee of the board of directors of the charter school in which the person is enrolled.

e. The president, or the president's designee, of the community college in which the person is enrolled.

Notwithstanding any other law, the decision concerning whether a driving eligibility certificate was properly issued or improperly denied shall be appealed only as provided under the rules adopted in accordance with G.S. 115C-12(28), 115D-5(a3), or 115C-566, whichever is applicable, and may not be appealed under this Chapter.

(n1) Lose Control; Lose License.

(1) The following definitions apply in this subsection:

a. **Applicable State entity.** -- The State Board of Education for public schools and charter schools, the State Board of Community Colleges for community colleges, or the Secretary of Administration for nonpublic schools and home schools.

b. **Certificate.** -- A driving eligibility certificate that meets the conditions of subsection (n) of this section.

c. **Disciplinary action.** -- An expulsion, a suspension for more than 10 consecutive days, or an assignment to an alternative educational setting for more than 10 consecutive days.

d. **Enumerated student conduct.** -- One of the following behaviors that results in disciplinary action:

1. The possession or sale of an alcoholic beverage or an illegal controlled substance on school property.

2. The bringing, possession, or use on school property of a weapon or firearm that resulted in disciplinary action under G.S. 115C-390.10 or that could have resulted in that disciplinary action if the conduct had occurred in a public school.

3. The physical assault on a teacher or other school personnel on school property.

e. **School.** -- A public school, charter school, community college, nonpublic school, or home school.

f. **School administrator.** -- The person who is required to sign certificates under subdivision (4) of subsection (n) of this section.

g. **School property.** -- The physical premises of the school, school buses or other vehicles under the school's control or contract and that are used to transport students, and school-sponsored curricular or extracurricular activities that occur on or off the physical premises of the school.

h. **Student.** -- A person who desires to obtain a permit or license issued under this section.

(2) Any student who was subject to disciplinary action for enumerated student conduct that occurred either after the first day of July before the school year in which the student enrolled in the eighth grade or after the student's fourteenth birthday, whichever event occurred first, is subject to this subsection.

(3) A student who is subject to this subsection is eligible for a certificate when the school administrator determines that the student has exhausted all administrative appeals connected to the disciplinary action and that one of the following conditions is met:

a. The enumerated student conduct occurred before the student reached the age of 15, and the student is now at least 16 years old.

b. The enumerated student conduct occurred after the student reached the age of 15, and it is at least one year after the date the student exhausted all administrative appeals connected to the disciplinary action.

c. The student needs the certificate in order to drive to and from school, a drug or alcohol treatment counseling program, as appropriate, or a mental health treatment program, and no other transportation is available.

(4) A student whose permit or license is denied or revoked due to ineligibility for a certificate under this subsection may otherwise be eligible for a certificate if, after six months from the date of the ineligibility, the school administrator determines that one of the following conditions is met:

a. The student has returned to school or has been placed in an alternative educational setting, and has displayed exemplary student behavior, as defined by the applicable State entity.

b. The disciplinary action was for the possession or sale of an alcoholic beverage or an illegal controlled substance on school property, and the student subsequently attended and successfully completed, as defined by the applicable State entity, a drug or alcohol treatment counseling program, as appropriate.

History.
1935, c. 52, s. 6; 1953, c. 355; 1955, c. 1187, s. 8; 1963, c. 968, ss. 2, 2A; 1965, c. 410, s. 3; c. 1171; 1967, c. 694; 1969, c. 37; 1973, c. 191, ss. 1, 2; c. 664, ss. 1, 2; 1975, c. 79; c. 716, s. 5; 1979, c. 101; c. 667, ss. 15, 16, 41; 1981 (Reg. Sess., 1982), c. 1257, s. 2; 1989 (Reg. Sess.,

1990), c. 1021, s. 11; 1991, c. 689, s. 326; 1993, c. 539, s. 319; 1994, Ex. Sess., c. 24, s. 14(c); 1997-16, s. 1; 1997-443, s. 32.20; 1997-507, s. 1; 1998-149, ss. 2.1, 2.2, 2.3, 2.4, 2.5; 1998-212, s. 9.21(c); 1999-243, ss. 1, 2; 1999-276, s. 1; 1999-387, s. 4; 1999-452, s. 9; 2001-194, s. 1; 2001-487, s. 51.5(a); 2002-73, ss. 1, 2; 2002-159, s. 30; 2005-276, s. 44.1(b); 2006-177, ss. 2 -7; 2011-145, s. 28.37(d); 2011-282, s. 15; 2011-381, s. 3; 2011-385, ss. 1 -3; 2011-412, s. 3.2; 2015-135, s. 4.2; 2015-241, s. 29.30(b); 2021-24, s. 1; 2021-134, s. 12

N.C. Gen. Stat. § 20-11.1

Repealed by Session Laws 1965, c. 410, s. 4.

N.C. Gen. Stat. § 20-12

Repealed by Session Laws 1997-16, s. 6.

§ 20-12.1. Impaired supervision or instruction

(a) It is unlawful for a person to serve as a supervising driver under G.S. 20-7(*l*) or G.S. 20-11 or as an approved instructor under G.S. 20-7(m) in any of the following circumstances:

(1) While under the influence of an impairing substance.

(2) After having consumed sufficient alcohol to have, at any relevant time after the driving, an alcohol concentration of 0.08 or more.

(b) An offense under this section is an implied-consent offense under G.S. 20-16.2.

History.
1977, c. 116, ss. 1, 2; 1981, c. 412, s. 4; c. 747, s. 66; 1983, c. 435, s. 9; 1993, c. 285, s. 2; 1997-16, s. 7; 1997-443, s. 32.20

§ 20-13. Suspension of license of provisional licensee

(a) The Division may suspend, with or without a preliminary hearing, the operator's license of a provisional licensee upon receipt of notice of the licensee's conviction of a motor vehicle moving violation, in accordance with subsection (b), if the offense was committed while the person was still a provisional licensee. As used in this section, the phrase "motor vehicle moving violation" does not include the offenses listed in the third paragraph of G.S. 20-16(c) for which no points are assessed, nor does it include equipment violations specified in Part 9 of Article 3 of this Chapter. However, if the Division revokes without a preliminary hearing and the person whose license is being revoked requests a hearing before the effective date of the revocation, the licensee retains his license unless it is revoked under some other provision of the law, until the hearing is held, the person withdraws his request, or he fails to appear at a scheduled hearing.

(b) The Division may suspend the license of a provisional licensee as follows:

(1) For the first motor vehicle moving violation, the Division may not suspend the license of the provisional licensee.

(2) For conviction of a second motor vehicle moving violation committed within 12 months of the date the first offense was committed, the Division may suspend the licensee's license for up to 30 days.

(3) For conviction of a third motor vehicle moving violation committed within 12 months of the date the first offense was committed, the Division may suspend the licensee's license for up to 90 days.

(4) For conviction of a fourth motor vehicle moving violation committed within 12 months of the date the first offense was committed, the Division may suspend the licensee's license for up to six months.

The Division may, in lieu of suspension and with the written consent of the licensee, place the licensee on probation for a period of not more than 12 months on such terms and conditions as the Division sees fit to impose.

If the Division suspends the provisional licensee's license for at least 90 days without a preliminary hearing, the parent, guardian or other person standing in loco parentis of the provisional licensee may request a hearing to determine if the provisional licensee's license should be restored on a probationary status. The Division may wait until one-half the period of suspension has expired to hold the hearing. The Division may place the licensee on probation for up to 12 months on such terms and conditions as the Division sees fit to impose, if the licensee consents in writing to the terms and conditions of probation.

(c) In the event of conviction of two or more motor vehicle moving offenses committed on a single occasion, a licensee shall be charged, for purposes of this section, with only one moving offense, except as otherwise provided.

(d) The suspension provided for in this section is in addition to any other remedies which the Division may have against a licensee under other provisions of law; however, when the license of any person is suspended under this section and at the same time is also suspended under other provisions of law, the suspensions run concurrently.

(e) Repealed by Session Laws 1987, c. 869, s. 14, effective January 1, 1988.

History.
1963, c. 968, s. 1; 1965, c. 897; 1967, c. 295, s. 1; 1971, c. 120, ss. 1, 2; 1973, c. 439; 1975, c. 716, s. 5; 1979,

c. 555, s. 1; 1983, c. 538, ss. 1, 2; 1983 (Reg. Sess., 1984), c. 1101, s. 3; 1987, c. 744, ss. 3, 4; c. 869, s. 14

N.C. Gen. Stat. § 20-13.1

Repealed by Session Laws 1979, c. 555, s. 2.

§ 20-13.2. Grounds for revoking provisional license

(a) The Division must revoke the license of a person convicted of violating the provisions of G.S. 20-138.3 upon receipt of a record of the licensee's conviction.

(b) If a person is convicted of an offense involving impaired driving and the offense occurs while he is less than 21 years old, his license must be revoked under this section in addition to any other revocation required or authorized by law.

(c) If a person willfully refuses to submit to a chemical analysis pursuant to G.S. 20-16.2 while he is less than 21 years old, his license must be revoked under this section, in addition to any other revocation required or authorized by law. A revocation order entered under authority of this subsection becomes effective at the same time as a revocation order issued under G.S. 20-16.2 for the same willful refusal.

(c1) Upon receipt of notification from the proper school authority that a person no longer meets the requirements for a driving eligibility certificate under G.S. 20-11(n), the Division must expeditiously notify the person that his or her permit or license is revoked effective on the tenth calendar day after the mailing of the revocation notice. The Division must revoke the permit or license of that person on the tenth calendar day after the mailing of the revocation notice. Notwithstanding subsection (d) of this section, the length of revocation must last for the following periods:

(1) If the revocation is because of ineligibility for a driving eligibility certificate under G.S. 20-11(n)(1), then the revocation shall last until the person's eighteenth birthday.

(2) If the revocation is because of ineligibility for a driving eligibility certificate under G.S. 20-11(n1), then the revocation shall be for a period of one year.

For a person whose permit or license was revoked due to ineligibility for a driving eligibility certificate under G.S. 20-11(n)(1), the Division must restore a person's permit or license before the person's eighteenth birthday, if the person submits to the Division one of the following:

(1) A high school diploma or its equivalent.

(2) A driving eligibility certificate as required under G.S. 20-11(n).

If the Division restores a permit or license that was revoked due to ineligibility for a driving eligibility certificate under G.S. 20-11(n)(1), any record of revocation or suspension shall be expunged by the Division from the person's driving record. The Division shall not expunge a suspension or revocation record if a person has had a prior expunction from the person's driving record for any reason.

For a person whose permit or license was revoked due to ineligibility for a driving eligibility certificate under G.S. 20-11(n1), the Division shall restore a person's permit or license before the end of the revocation period, if the person submits to the Division a driving eligibility certificate as required under G.S. 20-11(n).

Notwithstanding any other law, the decision concerning whether a driving eligibility certificate was properly issued or improperly denied shall be appealed only as provided under the rules adopted in accordance with G.S. 115C-12(28), 115D-5(a3), or 115C-566, whichever is applicable, and may not be appealed under this Chapter.

(c2) The Division must revoke the permit or license of a person under the age of 18 upon receiving a record of the person's conviction for malicious use of an explosive or incendiary device to damage property (G.S. 14-49(b) and (b1)); conspiracy to injure or damage by use of an explosive or incendiary device (G.S. 14-50); making a false report concerning a destructive device in a public building (G.S. 14-69.1(c)); perpetrating a hoax concerning a destructive device in a public building (G.S. 14-69.2(c)); possessing or carrying a dynamite cartridge, bomb, grenade, mine, or powerful explosive on educational property (G.S. 14-269.2(b1)); or causing, encouraging, or aiding a minor to possess or carry a dynamite cartridge, bomb, grenade, mine, or powerful explosive on educational property (G.S. 14-269.2(c1)).

(d) The length of revocation under this section shall be one year. Revocations under this section run concurrently with any other revocations.

(e) Before the Division restores a driver's license that has been suspended or revoked under any provision of this Article, other than G.S. 20-24.1, the person seeking to have his driver's license restored shall submit to the Division proof that he has notified his insurance agent or company of his seeking the restoration and that he is financially responsible. Proof of financial responsibility shall be in one of the following forms:

(1) A written certificate or electronically-transmitted facsimile thereof from any insurance carrier duly authorized to do business in this State certifying that there is in effect a nonfleet private passenger motor vehicle liability policy for the benefit of the person required to furnish proof of financial responsibility. The certificate or facsimile shall state the effective date and expiration date of the nonfleet private passenger motor vehicle liability policy and shall state the date that the certificate or facsimile is issued. The certificate or facsimile shall remain effective proof of financial responsibility for a period of 30 consecutive days following the date the certificate or facsimile is issued but shall not in and of itself constitute a binder or policy of insurance or

(2) A binder for or policy of nonfleet private passenger motor vehicle liability insurance under which the applicant is insured, provided that the binder or policy states the effective date and expiration date of the nonfleet private passenger motor vehicle liability policy.

The preceding provisions of this subsection do not apply to applicants who do not own currently registered motor vehicles and who do not operate nonfleet private passenger motor vehicles that are owned by other persons and that are not insured under commercial motor vehicle liability insurance policies. In such cases, the applicant shall sign a written certificate to that effect. Such certificate shall be furnished by the Division and may be incorporated into the restoration application form. Any material misrepresentation made by such person on such certificate shall be grounds for suspension of that person's license for a period of 90 days.

For the purposes of this subsection, the term "nonfleet private passenger motor vehicle" has the definition ascribed to it in Article 40 of General Statute Chapter 58.

The Commissioner may require that certificates required by this subsection be on a form approved by the Commissioner. The financial responsibility required by this subsection shall be kept in effect for not less than three years after the date that the license is restored. Failure to maintain financial responsibility as required by this subsection shall be grounds for suspending the restored driver's license for a period of thirty (30) days. Nothing in this subsection precludes any person from showing proof of financial responsibility in any other manner authorized by Articles 9A and 13 of this Chapter.

History.
1983, c. 435, s. 33; 1987, c. 869, s. 12; 1989, c. 436, s. 3; 1993, c. 285, s. 8; 1995, c. 506, ss. 3, 4, 5; 1997-507, s. 2; 1999-243, s. 3; 1999-257, s. 4; 2013-133, s. 1

§ 20-13.3. Immediate civil license revocation for provisional licensees charged with certain offenses

(a) **Definitions.** -- As used in this section, the following words and phrases have the following meanings:

(1) **Clerk.** -- As defined in G.S. 15A-101(2).

(2) **Criminal moving violation.** -- A violation of Part 9 or 10 of Article 3 of this Chapter which is punishable as a misdemeanor or a felony offense. This term does not include the offenses listed in the third paragraph of G.S. 20-16(c) for which no points are assessed, nor does it include equipment violations specified in Part 9 of Article 3 of this Chapter.

(3) **Judicial official.** -- As defined in G.S. 15A-101(5).

(4) **Provisional licensee.** -- A person under the age of 18 who has a limited learner's permit, a limited provisional license, or a full provisional license issued pursuant to G.S. 20-11.

(5) **Revocation report.** -- A sworn statement by a law enforcement officer containing facts indicating that the conditions of subsection (b) of this section have been met.

(b) **Revocations for Provisional Licensees Charged With Criminal Moving Violation.** -- A provisional licensee's permit or license is subject to revocation under this section if a law enforcement officer has reasonable grounds to believe that the provisional licensee has committed a criminal moving violation, the provisional licensee is charged with that offense, and the provisional licensee is not subject to a civil revocation pursuant to G.S. 20-16.5.

(c) **Duty of Law Enforcement Officers to Notify Provisional Licensee and Report to Judicial Officials.** -- If a provisional licensee's permit or license is subject to revocation under this section, the law enforcement officer must execute a revocation report. It is the specific duty of the law enforcement officer to make sure that the report is expeditiously filed with a judicial official as required by this section. If no initial appearance is required on the underlying criminal moving violation at the time of the issuance of the charge, the law enforcement officer must verbally notify the provisional licensee that the provisional licensee's permit or license is subject to revocation pursuant to this section and must provide the provisional licensee with a written form containing notice of the process for revocation and hearing under this section.

(c1) **Which Judicial Official Must Receive Report.** -- The judicial official with whom the revocation report must be filed is:

(1) The judicial official conducting the initial appearance on the underlying criminal moving violation.

(2) The clerk of superior court in the county in which the underlying criminal charge has been brought if no initial appearance is required.

(d) **Procedure If Report Filed With Judicial Official When Provisional Licensee Is Present.** -- If an initial appearance is required, the law enforcement officer must file the revocation report with the judicial official conducting the initial appearance on the underlying criminal moving violation. If a properly executed revocation report concerning a provisional licensee is filed with a judicial official when the person is present before that official, the judicial official shall, after completing any other proceedings involving the provisional licensee, determine whether there is probable cause to believe that the conditions of subsection (b) of this section have been met. If the judicial official determines there is such probable cause, the judicial official shall enter an order revoking the provisional licensee's permit or license. In addition to setting it out in the order, the judicial official shall personally inform the provisional licensee of the right to a hearing as specified in subsection (d2) of this section and that the provisional licensee's permit or license remains revoked pending the hearing. The period of revocation is for 30 days and begins at the time the revocation order is issued and continues for 30 additional calendar days. The judicial official shall give the provisional licensee a copy of the revocation order, which shall include the beginning date of the revocation and shall clearly state the final day of the revocation period and the date on which the provisional licensee's permit or license will again become valid. The provisional licensee shall not be required to surrender the provisional licensee's permit or license; however, the provisional licensee shall not be authorized to drive at any time or for any purpose during the period of revocation.

(d1) **Procedure If Report Filed With Clerk of Court When Provisional Licensee Not Present.** -- When a clerk receives a properly executed report under subdivision (2) of subsection (c1) of this section and the provisional licensee named in the revocation report is not present before the clerk, the clerk shall determine whether there is probable cause to believe that the conditions of subsection (b) of this section have been met. If the clerk determines there is such probable cause, the clerk shall mail to the provisional licensee a revocation order by first-class mail. The order shall inform the provisional licensee that the period of revocation is for 30 days, that the revocation becomes effective on the fourth day after the order is deposited in the United States mail and continues for 30 additional calendar days, of the right to a hearing as specified in subsection (d2) of this section, and that the revocation remains in effect pending the hearing. The provisional licensee shall not be required to surrender the provisional licensee's permit or license; however, the provisional licensee shall not be authorized to drive at any time or for any purpose during the period of revocation.

(d2) **Hearing Before Magistrate or Judge If Provisional Licensee Contests Validity of Revocation.** -- A provisional licensee whose permit or license is revoked under this section may request in writing a hearing to contest the validity of the revocation. The request may be made at the time of the person's initial appearance, or within 10 days of the effective date of the revocation to the clerk or a magistrate designated by the clerk, and may specifically request that the hearing be conducted by a district court judge. The Administrative Office of the Courts must develop a hearing request form for any provisional licensee requesting a hearing. Unless a district court judge is requested, the hearing must be conducted within the county by a magistrate assigned by the chief district court judge to conduct such hearings. If the provisional licensee requests that a district court judge hold the hearing, the hearing must be conducted within the district court district as defined in G.S. 7A-133 by a district court judge assigned to conduct such hearings. The revocation remains in effect pending the hearing, but the hearing must be held within three working days following the request if the hearing is before a magistrate or within ten working days if the hearing is before a district court judge. The request for the hearing must specify the grounds upon which the validity of the revocation is challenged, and the hearing must be limited to the grounds specified in the request. A witness may submit his evidence by affidavit unless he is subpoenaed to appear. Any person who appears and testifies is subject to questioning by the judicial official conducting the hearing, and the judicial official may adjourn the hearing to seek additional evidence if the judicial official is not satisfied with the accuracy or completeness of evidence. The provisional licensee contesting the validity of the revocation may, but is not required to, testify in his own behalf. Unless contested by the person requesting the hearing, the judicial official may accept as true any matter stated in the revocation report. If any relevant condition under subsection (b) of this section is contested, the judicial official must find by the greater weight of the evidence that the condition was met in order to sustain the revocation. At the conclusion of the hearing, the judicial official must enter an order sustaining or rescinding the revocation. The judicial official's findings are without prejudice to the provisional licensee contesting the revocation and to any other potential party as to any other proceedings, civil or criminal, that may involve

facts bearing upon the conditions in subsection (b) of this section considered by the judicial official. The decision of the judicial official is final and may not be appealed in the General Court of Justice. If the hearing is not held and completed within three working days of the written request for a hearing before a magistrate or within ten working days of the written request for a hearing before a district court judge, the judicial official must enter an order rescinding the revocation, unless the provisional licensee contesting the revocation contributed to the delay in completing the hearing. If the provisional licensee requesting the hearing fails to appear at the hearing or any rescheduling thereof after having been properly notified, the provisional licensee forfeits the right to a hearing.

(e) **Report to Division.** -- The clerk shall notify the Division of the issuance of a revocation order pursuant to this section within two business days of the issuance of the revocation order. The notification shall identify the person whose provisional license has been revoked and specify the beginning and end date of the revocation period.

(f) **Effect of Revocations.** -- A revocation under this section revokes a provisional licensee's privilege to drive in North Carolina. Revocations under this section are independent of and run concurrently with any other revocations, except for a revocation pursuant to G.S. 20-16.5. Any civil revocation issued pursuant to G.S. 20-16.5 for the same underlying conduct as a revocation under this section shall have the effect of terminating a revocation pursuant to this section. No court imposing a period of revocation following conviction for an offense involving impaired driving may give credit for any period of revocation imposed under this section. A person whose license is revoked pursuant to this section is not eligible to receive a limited driving privilege.

(g) **Designation of Proceedings.** -- Proceedings under this section are civil actions and must be identified by the caption "In the Matter of " and filed as directed by the Administrative Office of the Courts.

(h) No drivers license points or insurance surcharge shall be assessed for a revocation pursuant to this section. Possession of a drivers license revoked pursuant to this section shall not be a violation of G.S. 20-30.

(i) The Administrative Office of the Courts shall adopt forms to implement this section.

History.
2011-385, s. 4; 2011-412, s. 3.2; 2012-168, s. 3

§ 20-14. Duplicate licenses

A person may obtain a duplicate of a license issued by the Division by paying a fee of thirteen dollars ($ 13.00) and giving the Division satisfactory proof that any of the following has occurred:

(1) The person's license has been lost or destroyed.

(2) It is necessary to change the name or address on the license.

(3) Because of age, the person is entitled to a license with a different color photographic background or a different color border.

(4) The Division revoked the person's license, the revocation period has expired, and the period for which the license was issued has not expired.

History.
1935, c. 52, s. 9; 1943, c. 649, s. 2; 1969, c. 783, s. 2; 1975, c. 716, s. 5; 1979, c. 667, s. 41; 1981, c. 690, s. 11; 1983, c. 443, s. 3; 1991, c. 682, s. 2; c. 689, s. 327; 1991 (Reg. Sess., 1992), c. 1007, s. 28; 1995 (Reg. Sess., 1996), c. 675, s. 2; 2004-189, s. 5(b); 2005-276, s. 44.1(c); 2015-241, s. 29.30(c)

§ 20-15. Authority of Division to cancel license or endorsement

(a) The Division shall have authority to cancel any driver's license upon determining any of the following:

(1) The licensee was not entitled to the issuance of the license under this Chapter.

(2) The licensee failed to give the required or correct information on the license application or committed fraud in making the application.

(3) The licensee is no longer authorized under federal law to be legally present in the United States.

(4) The licensee suffers from a physical or mental disability or disease that affects his or her ability to safely operate a motor vehicle, as determined by the applicable State or federal law, rule, or regulation.

(5) The licensee has failed to submit the certificate required under G.S. 20-7(e) and G.S. 20-9(g).

(b) Upon such cancellation, the licensee must surrender the license so cancelled to the Division.

(c) Any person whose license is canceled under this section for failure to give the required or correct information, or for committing fraud, in an application for a commercial drivers license shall be prohibited from reapplying for a commercial drivers license for a period of 60 days from the date of cancellation.

(d) The Division shall have authority to revoke an H endorsement of a commercial drivers license holder if the person with the endorsement is determined by the federal Transportation Security Administration to constitute

a security threat, as specified in 49 C.F.R. § 1572.5(d)(4).

History.
1935, c. 52, s. 10; 1943, c. 649, s. 3; 1975, c. 716, s. 5; 1979, c. 667, s. 41; 2005-349, s. 5; 2007-56, s. 5; 2016-94, s. 35.20(e)

§ 20-15.1. Revocations when licensing privileges forfeited

The Division shall revoke the license of a person whose licensing privileges have been forfeited under G.S. 15A-1331.1, 50-13.12, and 110-142.2. If a revocation period set by this Chapter is longer than the revocation period resulting from the forfeiture of licensing privileges, the revocation period in this Chapter applies.

History.
1994, Ex. Sess., c. 20, s. 2; 1995, c. 538, s. 2(a); 2012-194, s. 45(b)

§ 20-16. Authority of Division to suspend license

(a) The Division shall have authority to suspend the license of any operator with or without a preliminary hearing upon a showing by its records or other satisfactory evidence that the licensee:

(1) through (4) Repealed by Session Laws 1979, c. 36;

(5) Has, under the provisions of subsection (c) of this section, within a three-year period, accumulated 12 or more points, or eight or more points in the three-year period immediately following the reinstatement of a license which has been suspended or revoked because of a conviction for one or more traffic offenses;

(6) Has made or permitted an unlawful or fraudulent use of such license or a learner's permit, or has displayed or represented as his own, a license or learner's permit not issued to him;

(7) Has committed an offense in another state, which if committed in this State would be grounds for suspension or revocation;

(8) Has been convicted of illegal transportation of alcoholic beverages;

(8a) Has been convicted of impaired instruction under G.S. 20-12.1;

(8b) Has violated on a military installation a regulation of that installation prohibiting conduct substantially similar to conduct that constitutes impaired driving under G.S. 20-138.1 and, as a result of that violation, has had his privilege to drive on that installation revoked or suspended after an administrative hearing authorized by the commanding officer of the installation and that commanding officer has general court martial jurisdiction;

(9) Has, within a period of 12 months, been convicted of (i) two or more charges of speeding in excess of 55 and not more than 80 miles per hour, (ii) one or more charges of reckless driving and one or more charges of speeding in excess of 55 and not more than 80 miles per hour, or (iii) one or more charges of aggressive driving and one or more charges of speeding in excess of 55 and not more than 80 miles per hour;

(10) Has been convicted of operating a motor vehicle at a speed in excess of 75 miles per hour on a public road or highway where the maximum speed is less than 70 miles per hour;

(10a) Has been convicted of operating a motor vehicle at a speed in excess of 80 miles per hour on a public highway where the maximum speed is 70 miles per hour; or

(11) Has been sentenced by a court of record and all or a part of the sentence has been suspended and a condition of suspension of the sentence is that the operator not operate a motor vehicle for a period of time.

However, if the Division revokes without a preliminary hearing and the person whose license is being revoked requests a hearing before the effective date of the revocation, the licensee retains his license unless it is revoked under some other provision of the law, until the hearing is held, the person withdraws his request, or he fails to appear at a scheduled hearing.

(b) Pending an appeal from a conviction of any violation of the motor vehicle laws of this State, no driver's license shall be suspended by the Division of Motor Vehicles because of such conviction or because of evidence of the commission of the offense for which the conviction has been had.

(c) The Division shall maintain a record of convictions of every person licensed or required to be licensed under the provisions of this Article as an operator and shall enter therein records of all convictions of such persons for any violation of the motor vehicle laws of this State and shall assign to the record of such person, as of the date of commission of the offense, a number of points for every such conviction in accordance with the following schedule of convictions and points, except that points shall not be assessed for convictions resulting in suspensions or revocations under other provisions of laws: Further, any points heretofore charged for violation of the motor vehicle inspection laws shall not be considered by the Division of Motor Vehicles as a basis for suspension or revocation of driver's license:

Schedule of Point Values

Passing stopped school bus	5
Aggressive driving	5
Reckless driving	4
Hit and run, property damage only	4
Following too close	4
Driving on wrong side of road	4
Illegal passing	4
Failure to yield right-of-way to pedestrian pursuant to G.S. 20-158(b)(2)b	4
Failure to yield right-of-way to bicycle, motor scooter, or motorcycle	4
Running through stop sign	3
Speeding in excess of 55 miles per hour	3
Failing to yield right-of-way	3
Running through red light	3
No driver's license or license expired more than one year	3
Failure to stop for siren	3
Driving through safety zone	3
No liability insurance	3
Failure to report accident where such report is required	3
Speeding in a school zone in excess of the posted school zone speed limit	3
Failure to properly restrain a child in a restraint or seat belt	2
All other moving violations	2
Littering pursuant to G.S. 14-399 when the littering involves the use of a motor vehicle	1

Schedule of Point Values for Violations While Operating a Commercial Motor Vehicle

Passing stopped school bus	8
Rail-highway crossing violation	6
Careless and reckless driving in violation of G.S. 20-140(f)	6
Speeding in violation of G.S. 20-141(j3)	6
Aggressive driving	6
Reckless driving	5
Hit and run, property damage only	5
Following too close	5
Driving on wrong side of road	5
Illegal passing	5
Failure to yield right-of-way to pedestrian pursuant to G.S. 20-158(b)(2)b	5
Failure to yield right-of-way to bicycle, motor scooter, or motorcycle	5
Running through stop sign	4
Speeding in excess of 55 miles per hour	4
Failing to yield right-of-way	4
Running through red light	4
No driver's license or license expired more than one year	4
Failure to stop for siren	4
Driving through safety zone	4
No liability insurance	4

Failure to report accident where such
report is required.. 4

Speeding in a school zone in excess of the
posted school zone speed limit.................... 4

Possessing alcoholic beverages in the
passenger area of a commercial motor
vehicle 4

All other moving violations............................ 3

Littering pursuant to G.S. 14-399 when
the littering involves the use of a motor
vehicle 1

The above provisions of this subsection shall only apply to violations and convictions which take place within the State of North Carolina. The Schedule of Point Values for Violations While Operating a Commercial Motor Vehicle shall not apply to any commercial motor vehicle known as an "aerial lift truck" having a hydraulic arm and bucket station, and to any commercial motor vehicle known as a "line truck" having a hydraulic lift for cable, if the vehicle is owned, operated by or under contract to a public utility, electric or telephone membership corporation or municipality and used in connection with installation, restoration or maintenance of utility services.

No points shall be assessed for conviction of the following offenses:

Overloads
Over length
Over width
Over height
Illegal parking
Carrying concealed weapon
Improper plates
Improper registration
Improper muffler
Improper display of license plates or dealers' tags
Unlawful display of emblems and insignia
Failure to display current inspection certificate.

In case of the conviction of a licensee of two or more traffic offenses committed on a single occasion, such licensee shall be assessed points for one offense only and if the offenses involved have a different point value, such licensee shall be assessed for the offense having the greater point value.

Upon the restoration of the license or driving privilege of such person whose license or driving privilege has been suspended or revoked because of conviction for a traffic offense, any points that might previously have been accumulated in the driver's record shall be cancelled.

Whenever any licensee accumulates as many as seven points or accumulates as many as four points during a three-year period immediately following reinstatement of his license after a period of suspension or revocation, the Division

may request the licensee to attend a conference regarding such licensee's driving record. The Division may also afford any licensee who has accumulated as many as seven points or any licensee who has accumulated as many as four points within a three-year period immediately following reinstatement of his license after a period of suspension or revocation an opportunity to attend a driver improvement clinic operated by the Division and, upon the successful completion of the course taken at the clinic, three points shall be deducted from the licensee's conviction record; provided, that only one deduction of points shall be made on behalf of any licensee within any five-year period.

When a license is suspended under the point system provided for herein, the first such suspension shall be for not more than 60 days; the second such suspension shall not exceed six months and any subsequent suspension shall not exceed one year.

Whenever the driver's license of any person is subject to suspension under this subsection and at the same time also subject to suspension or revocation under other provisions of laws, such suspensions or revocations shall run concurrently.

In the discretion of the Division, a period of probation not to exceed one year may be substituted for suspension or for any unexpired period of suspension under subsections (a)(1) through (a)(10a) of this section. Any violation of probation during the probation period shall result in a suspension for the unexpired remainder of the suspension period. Any accumulation of three or more points under this subsection during a period of probation shall constitute a violation of the condition of probation.

(d) Upon suspending the license of any person as authorized in this section, the Division shall immediately notify the licensee in writing and upon his request shall afford him an opportunity for a hearing, not to exceed 60 days after receipt of the request, unless a preliminary hearing was held before his license was suspended. Upon such hearing the duly authorized agents of the Division may administer oaths and may issue subpoenas for the attendance of witnesses and the production of relevant books and papers and may require a reexamination of the licensee. Upon such hearing the Division shall either rescind its order of suspension, or good cause appearing therefor, may extend the suspension of such license. Provided further upon such hearing, preliminary or otherwise, involving subsections (a)(1) through

(a) (10a) of this section, the Division may for good cause appearing in its discretion substitute a period of probation not to exceed one year for the suspension or for any unexpired period of suspension. Probation shall mean any written agreement between

Chapter 20

1315

the suspended driver and a duly authorized representative of the Division and such period of probation shall not exceed one year, and any violation of the probation agreement during the probation period shall result in a suspension for the unexpired remainder of the suspension period. The authorized agents of the Division shall have the same powers in connection with a preliminary hearing prior to suspension as this subsection provided in connection with hearings held after suspension. These agents shall also have the authority to take possession of a surrendered license on behalf of the Division if the suspension is upheld and the licensee requests that the suspension begin immediately.

(e) The Division may conduct driver improvement clinics for the benefit of those who have been convicted of one or more violations of this Chapter. Each driver attending a driver improvement clinic shall pay a fee of sixty-five dollars ($ 65.00).

(e1) Notwithstanding any other provision of this Chapter, if the Division suspends the license of an operator pursuant to subdivisions (a)(9), (a)(10), or (a)(10a) of this section, upon the first suspension only, a district court judge may allow the licensee a limited driving privilege or license for a period not to exceed 12 months, provided he has not been convicted of any other motor vehicle moving violation within the previous 12 months. The limited driving privilege shall be issued in the same manner and under the terms and conditions prescribed in G.S. 20-16.1(b)(1), (2), (3), (4), and (5).

(e2) If the Division revokes a person's drivers license pursuant to G.S. 20-17(a)(16), a judge may allow the licensee a limited driving privilege for a period not to exceed the period of revocation. The limited driving privilege shall be issued in the same manner and under the terms and conditions prescribed in G.S. 20-16.1(b)(1), (2), (3), (4), (5), and (g).

History.
1935, c. 52, s. 11; 1947, c. 893, ss. 1, 2; c. 1067, s. 13; 1949, c. 373, ss. 1, 2; c. 1032, s. 2; 1953, c. 450; 1955, c. 1152, s. 15; c. 1187, ss. 9-12; 1957, c. 499, s. 1; 1959, c. 1242, ss. 1-2; 1961, c. 460, ss. 1, 2(a); 1963, c. 1115; 1965, c. 130; 1967, c. 16; 1971, c. 234, ss. 1, 2; c. 793, ss. 1, 2; c. 1198, ss. 1, 2; 1973, c. 17, ss. 1, 2; 1975, c. 716, s. 5; 1977, c. 902, s. 1; 1979, c. 36; c. 667, ss. 18, 41; 1981, c. 412, s. 4; c. 747, ss. 33, 66; 1981 (Reg. Sess., 1982), c. 1256; 1983, c. 435, s. 10; c. 538, ss. 3-5; c. 798; 1983 (Reg. Sess., 1984), c. 1101, s. 4; 1987, c. 744, ss. 1, 2; 1987 (Reg. Sess., 1988), c. 1037, s. 75; 1989, c. 784, s. 9; 1991, c. 682, s. 3; 1999-330, s. 7; 1999-452, s. 10; 2000-109, s. 7(d); 2000-117, s. 2; 2000-155, s. 10; 2001-352, s. 2; 2004-172, s. 3; 2004-193, ss. 2, 3; 2005-276, s. 44.1(d); 2015-241, s. 29.30(d)

§ 20-16.01. Double penalties for offenses committed while operating a commercial motor vehicle

Any person who commits an offense for which points may be assessed pursuant to the Schedule of Point Values for Violations While Operating a Commercial Motor Vehicle as provided in G.S. 20-16(c) may be assessed double the amount of any fine or penalty authorized by statute.

History.
1999-330, s. 8

§ 20-16.1. Mandatory suspension of driver's license upon conviction of excessive speeding; limited driving permits for first offenders

(a) Notwithstanding any other provisions of this Article, the Division shall suspend for a period of 30 days the license of any driver without preliminary hearing on receiving a record of the driver's conviction of either (i) exceeding by more than 15 miles per hour the speed limit, either within or outside the corporate limits of a municipality, if the person was also driving at a speed in excess of 55 miles per hour at the time of the offense, or (ii) driving at a speed in excess of 80 miles per hour at the time of the offense.

(b) (1) Upon a first conviction only of violating subsection (a), the trial judge may when feasible allow a limited driving privilege or license to the person convicted for proper purposes reasonably connected with the health, education and welfare of the person convicted and his family. For purposes of determining whether conviction is a first conviction, no prior offense occurring more than seven years before the date of the current offense shall be considered. The judge may impose upon such limited driving privilege any restrictions as in his discretion are deemed advisable including, but not limited to, conditions of days, hours, types of vehicles, routes, geographical boundaries and specific purposes for which limited driving privilege is allowed. Any such limited driving privilege allowed and restrictions imposed thereon shall be specifically recorded in a written judgment which shall be as near as practical to that hereinafter set forth and shall be signed by the trial judge and shall be affixed with the seal of the court and shall be made a part of the records of the said court. A copy of said judgment shall be transmitted to the Division of Motor Vehicles along with any driver's license in the possession of the person convicted and a notice of the conviction. Such permit issued hereunder shall be valid for 30 days from the date of issuance by trial court. Such permit shall constitute a valid license to operate motor vehicles of the class or type that would be allowed by the person's license if it were not currently revoked upon the streets and highways of this or any other state in accordance with the restrictions noted thereon and shall be subject to all provisions of law relating to driver's license, not by their nature, rendered inapplicable.

(2) The judgment issued by the trial judge as herein permitted shall as near as practical be in form and content as follows:

This cause coming on to be heard and being heard before the Honorable, Judge presiding, and it appearing to the court that the defendant, _____, has been convicted of the offense of excessive speeding in violation of G.S. 20-16.1(a), and it further appearing to the court that the defendant should be issued a restrictive driving license and is entitled to the issuance of a restrictive driving privilege under and by the authority of G.S. 20-16.1(b);

Now, therefore, it is ordered, adjudged and decreed that the defendant be allowed to operate a motor vehicle under the following conditions and under no other circumstances.

Name:_____
Race:_____ Sex: _____
Height:_____ Weight:_____
Color of Hair:____ Color of Eyes: _____
Birth Date:_____
Driver's License Number: _____
Signature of Licensee: _____
Conditions of Restriction: _____
Type of Vehicle: _____
Geographic Restrictions: _____
Hours of Restriction: _____
Other Restrictions:_____

This limited license shall be effective from_____to_____subject to further orders as the court in its discretion may deem necessary and proper.

This the_____day of_____,_____

_____
(Judge Presiding)

(3) Upon conviction of such offense outside the jurisdiction of this State the person so convicted may apply to a district court judge of the district or set of districts as defined in G.S. 7A-41.1(a) in which he resides for limited driving privileges hereinbefore defined. Upon such application the judge shall have the authority to issue such limited driving privileges in the same manner as if he were the trial judge.

(4) Any violation of the restrictive driving privileges as set forth in the judgment of the trial judge allowing such privileges shall constitute the offense of driving while

license has been suspended as set forth in G.S. 20-28. Whenever a person is charged with operating a motor vehicle in violation of the restrictions, the limited driving privilege shall be suspended pending the final disposition of the charge.

(5) This section is supplemental and in addition to existing law and shall not be construed so as to repeal any existing provision contained in the General Statutes of North Carolina.

(c) Upon conviction of a similar second or subsequent offense which offense occurs within one year of the first or prior offense, the license of such operator shall be suspended for 60 days, provided such first or prior offense occurs subsequent to July 1, 1953.

(d) Notwithstanding any other provisions of this Article, the Division shall suspend for a period of 60 days the license of any driver without preliminary hearing on receiving a record of such driver's conviction of having violated the laws against speeding described in subsection (a) and of having violated the laws against reckless driving on the same occasion as the speeding offense occurred.

(e) The provisions of this section shall not prevent the suspension or revocation of a license for a longer period of time where the same may be authorized by other provisions of law.

(f) Repealed by Session Laws 1987, c. 869, s. 14.

(g) Any judge granting limited driving privileges under this section shall, prior to granting such privileges, be furnished proof and be satisfied that the person being granted such privileges is financially responsible. Proof of financial responsibility shall be in one of the following forms:

(1) A written certificate or electronically-transmitted facsimile thereof from any insurance carrier duly authorized to do business in this State certifying that there is in effect a nonfleet private passenger motor vehicle liability policy for the benefit of the person required to furnish proof of financial responsibility. The certificate or facsimile shall state the effective date and expiration date of the nonfleet private passenger motor vehicle liability policy and shall state the date that the certificate or facsimile is issued. The certificate or facsimile shall remain effective proof of financial responsibility for a period of 30 consecutive days following the date the certificate or facsimile is issued but shall not in and of itself constitute a binder or policy of insurance or

(2) A binder for or policy of nonfleet private passenger motor vehicle liability insurance under which the applicant is insured, provided that the binder or policy states the effective date and expiration

date of the nonfleet private passenger motor vehicle liability policy.

The preceding provisions of this subsection do not apply to applicants who do not own currently registered motor vehicles and who do not operate nonfleet private passenger motor vehicles that are owned by other persons and that are not insured under commercial motor vehicle liability insurance policies. In such cases, the applicant shall sign a written certificate to that effect. Such certificate shall be furnished by the Division. Any material misrepresentation made by such person on such certificate shall be grounds for suspension of that person's license for a period of 90 days.

For the purpose of this subsection "nonfleet private passenger motor vehicle" has the definition ascribed to it in Article 40 of General Statute Chapter 58.

The Commissioner may require that certificates required by this subsection be on a form approved by the Commissioner. Such granting of limited driving privileges shall be conditioned upon the maintenance of such financial responsibility during the period of the limited driving privilege. Nothing in this subsection precludes any person from showing proof of financial responsibility in any other manner authorized by Articles 9A and 13 of this Chapter.

History.
1953, c. 1223; 1955, c. 1187, s. 15; 1959, c. 1264, s. 4; 1965, c. 133; 1975, c. 716, s. 5; c. 763; 1979, c. 667, ss. 19, 41; 1983, c. 77; 1987, c. 869, ss. 13, 14; 1989, c. 436, s. 4; 770, s. 57; 1995 (Reg. Sess., 1996), c. 652, s. 2; 1999-456, s. 59; 2004-199, s. 13(a)

§ 20-16.2. Implied consent to chemical analysis; mandatory revocation of license in event of refusal; right of driver to request analysis

(a) **Basis for Officer to Require Chemical Analysis; Notification of Rights.** -- Any person who drives a vehicle on a highway or public vehicular area thereby gives consent to a chemical analysis if charged with an implied-consent offense. Any law enforcement officer who has reasonable grounds to believe that the person charged has committed the implied-consent offense may obtain a chemical analysis of the person.

Before any type of chemical analysis is administered the person charged shall be taken before a chemical analyst authorized to administer a test of a person's breath or a law enforcement officer who is authorized to administer chemical analysis of the breath, who shall inform the person orally and also give the person a notice in writing that:

(1) You have been charged with an implied-consent offense. Under the implied-consent law, you can refuse any test, but your drivers license will be revoked for one year and could be revoked for a longer period of time under certain circumstances, and an officer can compel you to be tested under other laws.

(2) Repealed by Session Laws 2006-253, s. 15, effective December 1, 2006, and applicable to offenses committed on or after that date.

(3) The test results, or the fact of your refusal, will be admissible in evidence at trial.

(4) Your driving privilege will be revoked immediately for at least 30 days if you refuse any test or the test result is 0.08 or more, 0.04 or more if you were driving a commercial vehicle, or 0.01 or more if you are under the age of 21.

(5) After you are released, you may seek your own test in addition to this test.

(6) You may call an attorney for advice and select a witness to view the testing procedures remaining after the witness arrives, but the testing may not be delayed for these purposes longer than 30 minutes from the time you are notified of these rights. You must take the test at the end of 30 minutes even if you have not contacted an attorney or your witness has not arrived.

(a1) **Meaning of Terms.** -- Under this section, an "implied-consent offense" is an offense involving impaired driving, a violation of G.S. 20-141.4(a2), or an alcohol-related offense made subject to the procedures of this section. A person is "charged" with an offense if the person is arrested for it or if criminal process for the offense has been issued.

(b) **Unconscious Person May Be Tested.** -- If a law enforcement officer has reasonable grounds to believe that a person has committed an implied-consent offense, and the person is unconscious or otherwise in a condition that makes the person incapable of refusal, the law enforcement officer may direct the taking of a blood sample or may direct the administration of any other chemical analysis that may be effectively performed. In this instance the notification of rights set out in subsection (a) and the request required by subsection (c) are not necessary.

(c) **Request to Submit to Chemical Analysis.** -- A law enforcement officer or chemical analyst shall designate the type of test or tests to be given and may request the person charged to submit to the type of chemical analysis designated. If the person charged willfully refuses to submit to that chemical analysis, none may be given under the provisions of this section, but the refusal does not preclude testing under other applicable procedures of law.

(c1) Procedure for Reporting Results and Refusal to Division. -- Whenever a person refuses to submit to a chemical analysis, a person has an alcohol concentration of 0.15 or more, or a person's drivers license has an alcohol concentration restriction and the results of the chemical analysis establish a violation of the restriction, the law enforcement officer and the chemical analyst shall without unnecessary delay go before an official authorized to administer oaths and execute an affidavit(s) stating that:

(1) The person was charged with an implied-consent offense or had an alcohol concentration restriction on the drivers license;

(2) A law enforcement officer had reasonable grounds to believe that the person had committed an implied-consent offense or violated the alcohol concentration restriction on the drivers license;

(3) Whether the implied-consent offense charged involved death or critical injury to another person, if the person willfully refused to submit to chemical analysis;

(4) The person was notified of the rights in subsection (a); and

(5) The results of any tests given or that the person willfully refused to submit to a chemical analysis.

If the person's drivers license has an alcohol concentration restriction, pursuant to G.S. 20-19(c3), and an officer has reasonable grounds to believe the person has violated a provision of that restriction other than violation of the alcohol concentration level, the officer and chemical analyst shall complete the applicable sections of the affidavit and indicate the restriction which was violated. The officer shall immediately mail the affidavit(s) to the Division. If the officer is also the chemical analyst who has notified the person of the rights under subsection (a), the officer may perform alone the duties of this subsection.

(d) Consequences of Refusal; Right to Hearing before Division; Issues. -- Upon receipt of a properly executed affidavit required by subsection (c1), the Division shall expeditiously notify the person charged that the person's license to drive is revoked for 12 months, effective on the thirtieth calendar day after the mailing of the revocation order unless, before the effective date of the order, the person requests in writing a hearing before the Division. Except for the time referred to in G.S. 20-16.5, if the person shows to the satisfaction of the Division that his or her license was surrendered to the court, and remained in the court's possession, then the Division shall credit the amount

of time for which the license was in the possession of the court against the 12-month revocation period required by this subsection. If the person properly requests a hearing, the person retains his or her license, unless it is revoked under some other provision of law, until the hearing is held, the person withdraws the request, or the person fails to appear at a scheduled hearing. The hearing officer may subpoena any witnesses or documents that the hearing officer deems necessary. The person may request the hearing officer to subpoena the charging officer, the chemical analyst, or both to appear at the hearing if the person makes the request in writing at least three days before the hearing. The person may subpoena any other witness whom the person deems necessary, and the provisions of G.S. 1A-1, Rule 45, apply to the issuance and service of all subpoenas issued under the authority of this section. The hearing officer is authorized to administer oaths to witnesses appearing at the hearing. The hearing shall be conducted in the county where the charge was brought, and shall be limited to consideration of whether:

(1) The person was charged with an implied-consent offense or the driver had an alcohol concentration restriction on the drivers license pursuant to G.S. 20-19;

(2) A law enforcement officer had reasonable grounds to believe that the person had committed an implied-consent offense or violated the alcohol concentration restriction on the drivers license;

(3) The implied-consent offense charged involved death or critical injury to another person, if this allegation is in the affidavit;

(4) The person was notified of the person's rights as required by subsection (a); and

(5) The person willfully refused to submit to a chemical analysis.

If the Division finds that the conditions specified in this subsection are met, it shall order the revocation sustained. If the Division finds that any of the conditions (1), (2), (4), or (5) is not met, it shall rescind the revocation. If it finds that condition (3) is alleged in the affidavit but is not met, it shall order the revocation sustained if that is the only condition that is not met; in this instance subsection (d1) does not apply to that revocation. If the revocation is sustained, the person shall surrender his or her license immediately upon notification by the Division.

(d1) Consequences of Refusal in Case Involving Death or Critical Injury. -- If the refusal occurred in a case involving death or critical injury to another person, no limited driving privilege may be issued. The 12-month revocation begins only after all other periods of revocation have terminated unless the person's license is revoked under G.S. 20-28, 20-28.1, 20-19(d), or 20-19(e). If the revocation is based on those sections, the revocation under this subsection begins at the time and in the manner specified in subsection (d) for revocations under this section. However, the person's eligibility for a hearing to determine if the revocation under those sections should be rescinded is postponed for one year from the date on which the person would otherwise have been eligible for the hearing. If the person's driver's license is again revoked while the 12-month revocation under this subsection is in effect, that revocation, whether imposed by a court or by the Division, may only take effect after the period of revocation under this subsection has terminated.

(e) **Right to Hearing in Superior Court.** -- If the revocation for a willful refusal is sustained after the hearing, the person whose license has been revoked has the right to file a petition in the superior court district or set of districts defined in G.S. 7A-41.1, where the charges were made, within 30 days thereafter for a hearing on the record. The superior court review shall be limited to whether there is sufficient evidence in the record to support the Commissioner's findings of fact and whether the conclusions of law are supported by the findings of fact and whether the Commissioner committed an error of law in revoking the license.

(e1) **Limited Driving Privilege after Six Months in Certain Instances.** -- A person whose driver's license has been revoked under this section may apply for and a judge authorized to do so by this subsection may issue a limited driving privilege if:

(1) At the time of the refusal the person held either a valid drivers license or a license that had been expired for less than one year;

(2) At the time of the refusal, the person had not within the preceding seven years been convicted of an offense involving impaired driving;

(3) At the time of the refusal, the person had not in the preceding seven years willfully refused to submit to a chemical analysis under this section;

(4) The implied consent offense charged did not involve death or critical injury to another person;

(5) The underlying charge for which the defendant was requested to submit to a chemical analysis has been finally disposed of:

a. Other than by conviction; or

b. By a conviction of impaired driving under G.S. 20-138.1, at a punishment level authorizing issuance of a limited driving privilege under G.S. 20-179.3(b), and the defendant has

complied with at least one of the mandatory conditions of probation listed for the punishment level under which the defendant was sentenced;

(6) Subsequent to the refusal the person has had no unresolved pending charges for or additional convictions of an offense involving impaired driving;

(7) The person's license has been revoked for at least six months for the refusal; and

(8) The person has obtained a substance abuse assessment from a mental health facility and successfully completed any recommended training or treatment program.

Except as modified in this subsection, the provisions of G.S. 20-179.3 relating to the procedure for application and conduct of the hearing and the restrictions required or authorized to be included in the limited driving privilege apply to applications under this subsection. If the case was finally disposed of in the district court, the hearing shall be conducted in the district court district as defined in G.S. 7A-133 in which the refusal occurred by a district court judge. If the case was finally disposed of in the superior court, the hearing shall be conducted in the superior court district or set of districts as defined in G.S. 7A-41.1 in which the refusal occurred by a superior court judge. A limited driving privilege issued under this section authorizes a person to drive if the person's license is revoked solely under this section or solely under this section and G.S. 20-17(2). If the person's license is revoked for any other reason, the limited driving privilege is invalid.

(f) **Notice to Other States as to Nonresidents.** -- When it has been finally determined under the procedures of this section that a nonresident's privilege to drive a motor vehicle in this State has been revoked, the Division shall give information in writing of the action taken to the motor vehicle administrator of the state of the person's residence and of any state in which the person has a license.

(g) Repealed by Session Laws 1973, c. 914.

(h) Repealed by Session Laws 1979, c. 423, s. 2.

(i) **Right to Chemical Analysis before Arrest or Charge.** -- A person stopped or questioned by a law enforcement officer who is investigating whether the person may have committed an implied consent offense may request the administration of a chemical analysis before any arrest or other charge is made for the offense. Upon this request, the officer shall afford the person the opportunity to have a chemical analysis of his or her breath, if available, in accordance with the procedures required by G.S. 20-139.1(b). The request constitutes the person's consent to be transported by the law enforcement officer to the place where the chemical analysis is to be administered. Before the chemical analysis is made, the person shall confirm the request in writing and shall be notified:

(1) That the test results will be admissible in evidence and may be used against you in any implied consent offense that may arise;

(2) Your driving privilege will be revoked immediately for at least 30 days if the test result is 0.08 or more, 0.04 or more if you were driving a commercial vehicle, or 0.01 or more if you are under the age of 21.

(3) That if you fail to comply fully with the test procedures, the officer may charge you with any offense for which the officer has probable cause, and if you are charged with an implied consent offense, your refusal to submit to the testing required as a result of that charge would result in revocation of your driving privilege. The results of the chemical analysis are admissible in evidence in any proceeding in which they are relevant.

History.
1963, c. 966, s. 1; 1965, c. 1165; 1969, c. 1074, s. 1; 1971, c. 619, ss. 3-6; 1973, c. 206, ss. 1, 2; cc. 824, 914; 1975, c. 716, s. 5; 1977, c. 812; 1979, c. 423, s. 2; 1979, 2nd Sess., c. 1160; 1981, c. 412, s. 4; c. 747, s. 66; 1983, c. 87; c. 435, s. 11; 1983 (Reg. Sess., 1984), c. 1101, ss. 5-8; 1987, c. 797, s. 3; 1987 (Reg. Sess., 1988), c. 1037, ss. 76, 77; c. 1112; 1989, c. 771, ss. 13, 14, 18; 1991, c. 689, s. 233.1(c); 1993, c. 285, ss. 3, 4; 1995, c. 163, s. 1; 1997-379, ss. 3.1 -3.3; 1998-182, s. 28; 1999-406, ss. 1, 10; 2000-155, s. 5; 2006-253, s. 15; 2007-493, ss. 25, 27; 2011-119, s. 1; 2021-134, s. 9(a)

§ 20-16.3. Alcohol screening tests required of certain drivers; approval of test devices and manner of use by Department of Health and Human Services; use of test results or refusal

(a) **When Alcohol Screening Test May Be Required; Not an Arrest. --** A law-enforcement officer may require the driver of a vehicle to submit to an alcohol screening test within a relevant time after the driving if the officer has:

(1) Reasonable grounds to believe that the driver has consumed alcohol and has:

    a. Committed a moving traffic violation; or

    b. Been involved in an accident or collision; or

(2) An articulable and reasonable suspicion that the driver has committed an implied-consent offense under G.S. 20-16.2, and the driver has been lawfully stopped for a driver's license check or otherwise

lawfully stopped or lawfully encountered by the officer in the course of the performance of the officer's duties.

Requiring a driver to submit to an alcohol screening test in accordance with this section does not in itself constitute an arrest.

(b) **Approval of Screening Devices and Manner of Use. --** The Department of Health and Human Services is directed to examine and approve devices suitable for use by law-enforcement officers in making on-the-scene tests of drivers for alcohol concentration. For each alcohol screening device or class of devices approved, the Department must adopt regulations governing the manner of use of the device. For any alcohol screening device that tests the breath of a driver, the Department is directed to specify in its regulations the shortest feasible minimum waiting period that does not produce an unacceptably high number of false positive test results.

(c) **Tests Must Be Made with Approved Devices and in Approved Manner. --** No screening test for alcohol concentration is a valid one under this section unless the device used is one approved by the Department and the screening test is conducted in accordance with the applicable regulations of the Department as to the manner of its use.

(d) **Use of Screening Test Results or Refusal by Officer. --** The fact that a driver showed a positive or negative result on an alcohol screening test, but not the actual alcohol concentration result, or a driver's refusal to submit may be used by a law-enforcement officer, is admissible in a court, or may also be used by an administrative agency in determining if there are reasonable grounds for believing:

(1) That the driver has committed an implied-consent offense under G.S. 20-16.2; and

(2) That the driver had consumed alcohol and that the driver had in his or her body previously consumed alcohol, but not to prove a particular alcohol concentration. Negative results on the alcohol screening test may be used in factually appropriate cases by the officer, a court, or an administrative agency in determining whether a person's alleged impairment is caused by an impairing substance other than alcohol.

History.
1973, c. 312, s. 1; c. 476, s. 128; 1981, c. 412, s. 4; c. 747, s. 66; 1983, c. 435, s. 12; 2006-253, s. 7

§ 20-16.3A. Checking stations and roadblocks

(a) A law-enforcement agency may conduct checking stations to determine compliance with the provisions of this Chapter. If the agency is conducting a checking station for the purposes of determining compliance with this Chapter, it must:

(1) Repealed by Session Laws 2006-253, s. 4, effective December 1, 2006, and applicable to offenses committed on or after that date.

(2) Designate in advance the pattern both for stopping vehicles and for requesting drivers that are stopped to produce drivers license, registration, or insurance information.

(2a) Operate under a written policy that provides guidelines for the pattern, which need not be in writing. The policy may be either the agency's own policy, or if the agency does not have a written policy, it may be the policy of another law enforcement agency, and may include contingency provisions for altering either pattern if actual traffic conditions are different from those anticipated, but no individual officer may be given discretion as to which vehicle is stopped or, of the vehicles stopped, which driver is requested to produce drivers license, registration, or insurance information. If officers of a law enforcement agency are operating under another agency's policy, it must be stated in writing.

(3) Advise the public that an authorized checking station is being operated by having, at a minimum, one law enforcement vehicle with its blue light in operation during the conducting of the checking station.

(a1) A pattern designated by a law enforcement agency pursuant to subsection (a) of this section shall not be based on a particular vehicle type, except that the pattern may designate any type of commercial motor vehicle as defined in G.S. 20-4.01(3d). The provisions of this subsection shall apply to this Chapter only and are not to be construed to restrict any other type of checkpoint or roadblock which is lawful and meets the requirements of subsection (c) of this section.

(b) An officer who determines there is a reasonable suspicion that an occupant has violated a provision of this Chapter, or any other provision of law, may detain the driver to further investigate in accordance with law. The operator of any vehicle stopped at a checking station established under this subsection may be requested to submit to an alcohol screening test under G.S. 20-16.3 if during the course of the stop the officer determines the driver had previously consumed alcohol or has an open container of alcoholic beverage in the vehicle. The officer so requesting shall consider the results of any alcohol screening test or the driver's refusal in determining if there is reasonable suspicion to investigate further.

(c) Law enforcement agencies may conduct any type of checking station or roadblock as long as it is established and operated in accordance with the provisions of the United States Constitution and the Constitution of North Carolina.

(d) The placement of checkpoints should be random or statistically indicated, and agencies shall avoid placing checkpoints repeatedly in the same location or proximity. This subsection shall not be grounds for a motion to suppress or a defense to any offense arising out of the operation of a checking station.

History.
1983, c. 435, s. 22; 2006-253, s. 4; 2011-216, s. 1

N.C. Gen. Stat. § 20-16.4

Repealed by Session Laws 1989, c. 691, s. 4.

§ 20-16.5. Immediate civil license revocation for certain persons charged with implied-consent offenses

(a) **Definitions.** -- As used in this section the following words and phrases have the following meanings:

(1) **Law Enforcement Officer.** -- As described in G.S. 20-16.2(a1).

(2) **Clerk.** -- As defined in G.S. 15A-101(2).

(3) **Judicial Official.** -- As defined in G.S. 15A-101(5).

(4) **Revocation Report.** -- A sworn statement by a law enforcement officer and a chemical analyst containing facts indicating that the conditions of subsection (b) have been met, and whether the person has a pending offense for which the person's license had been or is revoked under this section. When one chemical analyst analyzes a person's blood and another chemical analyst informs a person of his rights and responsibilities under G.S. 20-16.2, the report must include the statements of both analysts.

(5) **Surrender of a Driver's License.** -- The act of turning over to a court or a law-enforcement officer the person's most recent, valid driver's license or learner's permit issued by the Division or by a similar agency in another jurisdiction, or a limited driving privilege issued by a North Carolina court. A person who is validly licensed but who is unable to locate his license card may file an affidavit with the clerk setting out facts that indicate that he is unable to locate his license card and that he is validly licensed; the filing of the affidavit constitutes a surrender of the person's license.

(b) **Revocations for Persons Who Refuse Chemical Analyses or Who Are Charged With Certain Implied-Consent Offenses.** -- A person's driver's license is subject to revocation under this section if:

(1) A law enforcement officer has reasonable grounds to believe that the person has committed an offense subject to the implied-consent provisions of G.S. 20-16.2;

(2) The person is charged with that offense as provided in G.S. 20-16.2(a);

(3) The law enforcement officer and the chemical analyst comply with the procedures of G.S. 20-16.2 and G.S. 20-139.1 in requiring the person's submission to or procuring a chemical analysis; and

(4) The person:

a. Willfully refuses to submit to the chemical analysis;

b. Has an alcohol concentration of 0.08 or more within a relevant time after the driving;

c. Has an alcohol concentration of 0.04 or more at any relevant time after the driving of a commercial motor vehicle; or

d. Has any alcohol concentration at any relevant time after the driving and the person is under 21 years of age.

(b1) **Precharge Test Results as Basis for Revocation.** -- Notwithstanding the provisions of subsection (b), a person's driver's license is subject to revocation under this section if:

(1) The person requests a precharge chemical analysis pursuant to G.S. 20-16.2(i); and

(2) The person has:

a. An alcohol concentration of 0.08 or more at any relevant time after driving;

b. An alcohol concentration of 0.04 or more at any relevant time after driving a commercial motor vehicle; or

c. Any alcohol concentration at any relevant time after driving and the person is under 21 years of age; and

(3) The person is charged with an implied-consent offense.

(c) **Duty of Law Enforcement Officers and Chemical Analysts to Report to Judicial Officials.** -- If a person's driver's license is subject to revocation under this section, the law enforcement officer and the chemical analyst must execute a revocation report. If the person has refused to submit to a chemical analysis, a copy of the affidavit to be submitted to the Division under G.S. 20-16.2(c) may be substituted for the revocation report if it contains the information required by this section. It is the specific duty of the law enforcement officer to make sure that the report is expeditiously filed with a judicial official as required by this section.

(d) **Which Judicial Official Must Receive Report.** -- The judicial official with whom the revocation report must be filed is:

(1) The judicial official conducting the initial appearance on the underlying criminal charge if:

a. No revocation report has previously been filed; and

b. At the time of the initial appearance the results of the chemical analysis, if administered, or the reports indicating a refusal, are available.

(2) A judicial official conducting any other proceeding relating to the underlying criminal charge at which the person is present, if no report has previously been filed.

(3) The clerk of superior court in the county in which the underlying criminal charge has been brought if subdivisions (1) and (2) are not applicable at the time the law enforcement officer must file the report.

(e) **Procedure if Report Filed with Judicial Official When Person Is Present.** -- If a properly executed revocation report concerning a person is filed with a judicial official when the person is present before that official, the judicial official shall, after completing any other proceedings involving the person, determine whether there is probable cause to believe that each of the conditions of subsection (b) has been met. If he determines that there is such probable cause, he shall enter an order revoking the person's driver's license for the period required in this subsection. The judicial official shall order the person to surrender his license and if necessary may order a law-enforcement officer to seize the license. The judicial official shall give the person a copy of the revocation order. In addition to setting it out in the order the judicial official shall personally inform the person of his right to a hearing as specified in subsection (g), and that his license remains revoked pending the hearing. The revocation under this subsection begins at the time the revocation order is issued and continues until the person's license has been surrendered for the period specified in this subsection, and the person has paid the applicable costs. The period of revocation is 30 days, if there are no pending offenses for which the person's license had been or is revoked under this section. If at the time of the current offense, the person has one or more pending offenses for which his license had been or is revoked under this section, the revocation shall remain in effect until a final judgment, including all appeals, has been entered for the current offense and for all pending offenses. In no event, may the period of revocation under this subsection be less than 30 days. If within five working days of the effective date of the order, the person does not surrender his license or demonstrate that he is not currently licensed, the clerk shall immediately issue a pick-up order. The pick-up order shall be issued to a member of a local law-enforcement agency if the law enforcement officer was employed by the agency at the time of the charge and the person resides in or is present in the agency's territorial jurisdiction. In all other cases, the pick-up order shall be issued to an officer or inspector of the Division. A pick-up order issued pursuant to this section is to be served in accordance with G.S. 20-29 as if the order had been issued by the Division.

(f) **Procedure if Report Filed with Clerk of Court When Person Not Present.** -- When a clerk receives a properly executed report under subdivision (d)(3) and the person named in the revocation report is not present before the clerk, the clerk shall determine whether there is probable cause to believe that each of the conditions of subsection (b) has been met. For purposes of this subsection, a properly executed report under subdivision (d)(3) may include a sworn statement by the law enforcement officer along with an affidavit received directly by the Clerk from the chemical analyst. If he determines that there is such probable cause, he shall mail to the person a revocation order by first-class mail. The order shall direct that the person on or before the effective date of the order either surrender his license to the clerk or appear before the clerk and demonstrate that he is not currently licensed, and the order shall inform the person of the time and effective date of the revocation and of its duration, of his right to a hearing as specified in subsection (g), and that the revocation remains in effect pending the hearing. Revocation orders mailed under this subsection become effective on the fourth day after the order is deposited in the United States mail. If within five working days of the effective date of the order, the person does not surrender his license to the clerk or appear before the clerk to demonstrate that he is not currently licensed, the clerk shall immediately issue a pick-up order. The pick-up order shall be issued and served in the same manner as specified in subsection (e) for pick-up orders issued pursuant to that subsection. A revocation under this subsection begins at the date specified in the order and continues until the person's license has been revoked for the period specified in this subsection and the person has paid the applicable costs. If the person has no pending offenses for which his license had been or is revoked under this section, the period of revocation under this subsection is:

(1) Thirty days from the time the person surrenders his license to the court, if the surrender occurs within five working days of the effective date of the order; or

(2) Thirty days after the person appears before the clerk and demonstrates that he is not currently licensed to drive, if the appearance occurs within five working days of the effective date of the revocation order; or

(3) Forty-five days from the time:

a. The person's drivers license is picked up by a law-enforcement officer following service of a pick-up order; or

b. The person demonstrates to a law-enforcement officer who has a pick-up order for his license that he is not currently licensed; or

c. The person's drivers license is surrendered to the court if the surrender occurs more than five working days after the effective date of the revocation order; or

d. The person appears before the clerk to demonstrate that he is not currently licensed, if he appears more than five working days after the effective date of the revocation order.

If at the time of the current offense, the person has one or more pending offenses for which his license had been or is revoked under this section, the revocation shall remain in effect until a final judgment, including all appeals, has been entered for the current offense and for all pending offenses. In no event may the period of revocation for the current offense be less than the applicable period of revocation in subdivision (1), (2), or (3) of this subsection. When a pick-up order is issued, it shall inform the person of his right to a hearing as specified in subsection (g), and that the revocation remains in effect pending the hearing. An officer serving a pick-up order under this subsection shall return the order to the court indicating the date it was served or that he was unable to serve the order. If the license was surrendered, the officer serving the order shall deposit it with the clerk within three days of the surrender.

(g) **Hearing before Magistrate or Judge if Person Contests Validity of Revocation.** -- A person whose license is revoked under this section may request in writing a hearing to contest the validity of the revocation. The request may be made at the time of the person's initial appearance, or within 10 days of the effective date of the revocation to the clerk or a magistrate designated by the clerk, and may specifically request that the hearing be conducted by a district court judge. The Administrative Office of the Courts must develop a hearing request form for any person requesting a hearing. Unless a district court judge is requested, the hearing must be conducted within the county by a magistrate assigned by the chief district court judge to conduct such hearings. If the person requests that a district court judge hold the hearing, the hearing must be conducted within the district court district as defined in G.S. 7A-133 by a district court judge assigned to conduct such hearings. The revocation remains in effect pending the hearing, but the hearing must be held within three working days following the request if the hearing is before a magistrate or within five working days if the hearing is before a district court judge. The request for the hearing must specify the grounds upon which the validity of the revocation is challenged and the hearing must be limited to the grounds specified in the request. A witness may submit his evidence by affidavit unless he is subpoenaed to appear. Any person who appears and testifies is subject to questioning by the judicial official conducting the hearing, and the judicial official may adjourn the hearing to seek additional evidence if he is not satisfied with the accuracy or completeness of evidence. The person contesting the validity of the revocation may, but is not required to, testify in his own behalf. Unless contested by the person requesting the hearing, the judicial official may accept as true any matter stated in the revocation report. If any relevant condition under subsection (b) is contested, the judicial official must find by the greater weight of the evidence that the condition was met in order to sustain the revocation. At the conclusion of the hearing the judicial official must enter an order sustaining or rescinding the revocation. The judicial official's findings are without prejudice to the person contesting the revocation and to any other potential party as to any other proceedings, civil or criminal, that may involve facts bearing upon the conditions in subsection (b) considered by the judicial official. The decision of the judicial official is final and may not be appealed in the General Court of Justice. If the hearing is not held and completed within three working days of the written request for a hearing before a magistrate or within five working days of the written request for a hearing before a district court judge, the judicial official must enter an order rescinding the revocation, unless the person contesting the revocation contributed to the delay in completing the hearing. If the person requesting the hearing fails to appear at the hearing or any rescheduling thereof after having been properly notified, he forfeits his right to a hearing.

(h) **Return of License.** -- After the applicable period of revocation under this section, or if the magistrate or judge orders the revocation rescinded, the person whose license was revoked may apply to the clerk for return of his surrendered license. Unless the clerk finds that the person is not eligible to use the surrendered license, he must return it if:

(1) The applicable period of revocation has passed and the person has tendered payment for the costs under subsection (j); or

(2) The magistrate or judge has ordered the revocation rescinded.

If the license has expired, he may return it to the person with a caution that it is no longer valid. Otherwise, if the person is not eligible to use the license and the license was issued by the Division or in another state, the clerk must mail it to the Division. If the person has surrendered his copy of a limited driving privilege and he is no longer eligible to use it, the clerk must make a record that he has withheld the limited driving privilege and forward that record to the clerk in the county in which the limited driving privilege was issued for filing in the case file. If the person's license is revoked under this section and under another section of this Chapter, the clerk must surrender the license to the Division if the revocation under this section can terminate before the other revocation; in such cases, the costs required by subsection (j) must still be paid before the revocation under this section is terminated.

(i) **Effect of Revocations.** -- A revocation under this section revokes a person's privilege to drive in North Carolina whatever the source of his authorization to drive. Revocations under this section are independent of and run concurrently with any other revocations. No court imposing a period of revocation following conviction of an offense involving impaired driving may give credit for any period of revocation imposed under this section. A person whose license is revoked pursuant to this section is not eligible to receive a limited driving privilege except as specifically authorized by G.S. 20-16.5(p).

(j) **Costs.** -- Unless the magistrate or judge orders the revocation rescinded, a person whose license is revoked under this section must pay a fee of one hundred dollars ($ 100.00) as costs for the action before the person's license may be returned under subsection (h) of this section. Fifty percent (50%) of the costs collected under this section shall be credited to the General Fund. Twenty-five percent (25%) of the costs collected under this section shall be used to fund a statewide chemical alcohol testing program administered by the Injury Control Section of the Department of Health and Human Services. The remaining twenty-five percent (25%) of the costs collected under this section shall be remitted to the county for the sole purpose of reimbursing the county for jail expenses incurred due to enforcement of the impaired driving laws.

(k) **Report to Division.** -- Except as provided below, the clerk shall mail a report to the Division:

Chapter 20

1325

(1) If the license is revoked indefinitely, within 10 working days of the revocation of the license; and

(2) In all cases, within 10 working days of the return of a license under this section or of the termination of a revocation of the driving privilege of a person not currently licensed.

The report shall identify the person whose license has been revoked, specify the date on which his license was revoked, and indicate whether the license has been returned. The report must also provide, if applicable, whether the license is revoked indefinitely. No report need be made to the Division, however, if there was a surrender of the driver's license issued by the Division, a 30-day minimum revocation was imposed, and the license was properly returned to the person under subsection (h) within five working days after the 30-day period had elapsed.

(*l*) **Restoration Fee for Unlicensed Persons.** -- If a person whose license is revoked under this section has no valid license, he must pay the restoration fee required by G.S. 20-7 before he may apply for a license from the Division.

(m) **Modification of Revocation Order.** -- Any judicial official presiding over a proceeding under this section may issue a modified order if he determines that an inappropriate order has been issued.

(n) **Exception for Revoked Licenses.** -- Notwithstanding any other provision of this section, if the judicial official required to issue a revocation order under this section determines that the person whose license is subject to revocation under subsection (b):

(1) Has a currently revoked driver's license;

(2) Has no limited driving privilege; and

(3) Will not become eligible for restoration of his license or for a limited driving privilege during the period of revocation required by this section,

the judicial official need not issue a revocation order under this section. In this event the judicial official must file in the records of the civil proceeding a copy of any documentary evidence and set out in writing all other evidence on which he relies in making his determination.

(o) **Designation of Proceedings.** -- Proceedings under this section are civil actions, and must be identified by the caption "In the Matter of " and filed as directed by the Administrative Office of the Courts.

(p) **Limited Driving Privilege.** -- A person whose drivers license has been revoked for a specified period of 30 or 45 days under this section may apply for a limited driving privilege if:

(1) At the time of the alleged offense the person held either a valid drivers license or a license that had been expired for less than one year;

(2) Does not have an unresolved pending charge involving impaired driving except the charge for which the license is currently revoked under this section or additional convictions of an offense involving impaired driving since being charged for the violation for which the license is currently revoked under this section;

(3) The person's license has been revoked for at least 10 days if the revocation is for 30 days or 30 days if the revocation is for 45 days; and

(4) The person has obtained a substance abuse assessment from a mental health facility and registers for and agrees to participate in any recommended training or treatment program.

A person whose license has been indefinitely revoked under this section may, after completion of 30 days under subsection (e) or the applicable period of time under subdivision (1), (2), or (3) of subsection (f), apply for a limited driving privilege. In the case of an indefinite revocation, a judge of the division in which the current offense is pending may issue the limited driving privilege only if the privilege is necessary to overcome undue hardship and the person meets the eligibility requirements of G.S. 20-179.3, except that the requirements in G.S. 20-179.3(b)(1)c. and G.S. 20-179.3(e) shall not apply. Except as modified in this subsection, the provisions of G.S. 20-179.3 relating to the procedure for application and conduct of the hearing and the restrictions required or authorized to be included in the limited driving privilege apply to applications under this subsection. Any district court judge authorized to hold court in the judicial district is authorized to issue such a limited driving privilege. A limited driving privilege issued under this section authorizes a person to drive if the person's license is revoked solely under this section. If the person's license is revoked for any other reason, the limited driving privilege is invalid.

History.
1983, c. 435, s. 14; 1983 (Reg. Sess., 1984), c. 1101, ss. 11-17; 1985, c. 690, ss. 1, 2; 1987 (Reg. Sess., 1988), c. 1037, s. 80, c. 1112; 1989, c. 771, ss. 15, 16, 18; 1991, c. 689, s. 233.1(a); 1993, c. 285, ss. 5, 6; 1997-379, ss. 3.4 -3.8; 1997-443, s. 11A.9; 1997-486, ss. 2 -6; 1998-182, ss. 29, 30; 1999-406, s. 13; 2000-140, s. 103A; 2000-155, s. 15; 2001-487, ss. 6, 7; 2003-104, s. 1; 2007-323, s. 30.10(e); 2007-493, s. 17

Chapter 20

§ 20-17. Mandatory revocation of license by Division

(a) The Division shall forthwith revoke the license of any driver upon receiving a record of the driver's conviction for any of the following offenses:

(1) Manslaughter (or negligent homicide) resulting from the operation of a motor vehicle.

(2) Either of the following impaired driving offenses:

a. Impaired driving under G.S. 20-138.1.

b. Impaired driving under G.S. 20-138.2, if the driver's alcohol concentration level was .06 or higher. For the purposes of this sub-subdivision, the driver's alcohol concentration level result, obtained by chemical analysis, shall be conclusive and is not subject to modification by any party, with or without approval by the court.

(3) Any felony in the commission of which a motor vehicle is used.

(4) Failure to stop and render aid in violation of G.S. 20-166(a) or (b).

(5) Perjury or the making of a false affidavit or statement under oath to the Division under this Article or under any other law relating to the ownership of motor vehicles.

(6) Conviction, within a period of 12 months, of (i) two charges of reckless driving, (ii) two charges of aggressive driving, or (iii) one or more charges of reckless driving and one or more charges of aggressive driving.

(7) Conviction upon one charge of aggressive driving or reckless driving while engaged in the illegal transportation of intoxicants for the purpose of sale.

(8) Conviction of using a false or fictitious name or giving a false or fictitious address in any application for a drivers license, or learner's permit, or any renewal or duplicate thereof, or knowingly making a false statement or knowingly concealing a material fact or otherwise committing a fraud in any such application or procuring or knowingly permitting or allowing another to commit any of the foregoing acts.

(9) Any offense set forth under G.S. 20-141.4.

(10) Repealed by Session Laws 1997-443, s. 19.26(b).

(11) Conviction of assault with a motor vehicle.

(12) A second or subsequent conviction of transporting an open container of alcoholic beverage under G.S. 20-138.7.

(13) A second or subsequent conviction, as defined in G.S. 20-138.2A(d), of driving a commercial motor vehicle after consuming alcohol under G.S. 20-138.2A.

(14) A conviction of driving a school bus, school activity bus, or child care vehicle after consuming alcohol under G.S. 20-138.2B.

(15) A conviction of malicious use of an explosive or incendiary device to damage property (G.S. 14-49(b) and (b1)); making a false report concerning a destructive device in a public building (G.S. 14-69.1(c)); perpetrating a hoax concerning a destructive device in a public building (G.S. 14-69.2(c)); possessing or carrying a dynamite cartridge, bomb, grenade, mine, or powerful explosive on educational property (G.S. 14-269.2(b1)); or causing, encouraging, or aiding a minor to possess or carry a dynamite cartridge, bomb, grenade, mine, or powerful explosive on educational property (G.S. 14-269.2(c1)).

(16) A second or subsequent conviction of larceny of motor fuel under G.S. 14-72.5. A conviction for violating G.S. 14-72.5 is a second or subsequent conviction if at the time of the current offense the person has a previous conviction under G.S. 14-72.5 that occurred in the seven years immediately preceding the date of the current offense.

(17) A third or subsequent conviction of operating a private passenger automobile with prohibited modifications on any highway or public vehicular area under G.S. 20-135.4(d). A conviction for violating G.S. 20-135.4(d) is a third or subsequent conviction if at the time of the current infraction the person has two or more previous convictions under G.S. 20-135.4 that occurred in the 12 months immediately preceding the date of the current infraction.

(b) On the basis of information provided by the child support enforcement agency or the clerk of court, the Division shall:

(1) Ensure that no license or right to operate a motor vehicle under this Chapter is renewed or issued to an obligor who is delinquent in making child support payments when a court of record has issued a revocation order pursuant to G.S. 110-142.2 or G.S. 50-13.12. The obligor shall not be entitled to any other hearing before the Division as a result of the revocation of his license pursuant to G.S. 110-142.2 or G.S. 50-13.12; or

(2) Revoke the drivers license of any person who has willfully failed to complete court-ordered community service and a court has issued a revocation order. This revocation shall continue until the Division receives certification from the clerk of court that the person has completed the court-ordered community service. No person

whose drivers license is revoked pursuant to this subdivision shall be entitled to any other hearing before the Division as a result of this revocation.

History.
1935, c. 52, s. 12; 1947, c. 1067, s. 14; 1967, c. 1098, s. 2; 1971, c. 619, s. 7; 1973, c. 18, s. 1; c. 1081, s. 3; c. 1330, s. 2; 1975, c. 716, s. 5; c. 831; 1979, c. 667, ss. 20, 41; 1981, c. 412, s. 4; c. 747, s. 66; 1983, c. 435, s. 15; 1989, c. 771, s. 11; 1991, c. 726, s. 7; 1993 (Reg. Sess., 1994), c. 761, s. 1; 1995, c. 506, s. 7; c. 538, s. 2(b); 1997-234, s. 3; 1997-443, s. 19.26(b); 1998-182, s. 18; 1999-257, s. 4.1; 2001-352, s. 3; 2001-487, s. 52; 2004-193, ss. 4, 5; 2006-253, s. 22.2; 2007-493, s. 2; 2021-128, s. 2

§ 20-17.1. Revocation of license of mental incompetents, alcoholics and habitual users of narcotic drugs

(a) The Commissioner, upon receipt of notice that any person has been legally adjudicated incompetent or has been involuntarily committed to an institution for the treatment of alcoholism or drug addiction, shall forthwith make inquiry into the facts for the purpose of determining whether such person is competent to operate a motor vehicle. If a person has been adjudicated incompetent under Chapter 35A of the General Statutes, in making an inquiry into the facts, the Commissioner shall consider the clerk of court's recommendation regarding whether the incompetent person should be allowed to retain his or her driving privilege. Unless the Commissioner is satisfied that such person is competent to operate a motor vehicle with safety to persons and property, he shall revoke such person's driving privilege. Provided that if such person requests, in writing, a hearing, he shall retain his license until after the hearing, and if the revocation is sustained after such hearing, the person whose driving privilege has been revoked under the provisions of this section, shall have the right to a review by the review board as provided in G.S. 20-9(g)(4) upon written request filed with the Division.

(b) If any person shall be adjudicated as incompetent or is involuntarily committed for the treatment of alcoholism or drug addiction, the clerk of the court in which any such adjudication is made shall forthwith send a certified copy of abstract thereof to the Commissioner.

(c) Repealed by Session Laws 1973, c. 475, s. 3 1/2.

(d) It is the intent of this section that the provisions herein shall be carried out by the Commissioner of Motor Vehicles for the safety of the motoring public. The Commissioner shall have authority to make such agreements as are necessary with the persons in charge of every institution of any nature for the care and treatment of alcoholics or habitual users of narcotic drugs, to effectively carry out the duty hereby imposed and the person in charge of the institutions described above shall cooperate with and assist the Commissioner of Motor Vehicles.

(e) Notwithstanding the provisions of G.S. 8-53, 8-53.2, and Article 3 of Chapter 122C of the General Statutes, the person or persons in charge of any institution as set out in subsection (a) hereinabove shall furnish such information as may be required for the effective enforcement of this section. Information furnished to the Division of Motor Vehicles as provided herein shall be confidential and the Commissioner of Motor Vehicles shall be subject to the same penalties and is granted the same protection as is the department, institution or individual furnishing such information. No criminal or civil action may be brought against any person or agency who shall provide or submit to the Commissioner of Motor Vehicles or his authorized agents the information as required herein.

(f) Revocations under this section may be reviewed as provided in G.S. 20-9(g)(4).

History.
1947, c. 1006, s. 9; 1953, c. 1300, s. 36; 1955, c. 1187, s. 16; 1969, c. 186, s. 1; c. 1125; 1971, c. 208, ss. 1, 1 1/2; c. 401, s. 1; c. 767; 1973, c. 475, s. 3 1/2; c. 1362; 1975, c. 716, s. 5; 1983, c. 768, s. 3; 1987, c. 720, s. 1; 2008-182, s. 1

§ 20-17.1A. Restoration of license for person adjudicated to be restored to competency

If otherwise eligible under G.S. 20-7 and any other applicable provision of law, the Division shall restore the drivers license of a person adjudicated to be restored to competency under G.S. 35A-1130 upon receiving notice from the clerk of court in which the adjudication is made. Nothing in this section shall be construed as requiring the Division to restore the drivers license of a person if (i) the person's drivers license was revoked because of a conviction or other act requiring revocation and (ii) the person has not met the requirements set forth in this Article for restoration of the person's drivers license.

History.
2015-165, s. 1

N.C. Gen. Stat. § 20-17.2

Repealed by Session Laws 2006-253, s. 25, effective December 1, 2006, and applicable to offenses committed on or after that date.

§ 20-17.3. Revocation for underage purchasers of alcohol

The Division shall revoke for one year the driver's license of any person who has been convicted of violating any of the following:

    (1) G.S. 18B-302(c), (e), or (f).

    (2) G.S. 18B-302(b), if the violation occurred while the person was purchasing or attempting to purchase an alcoholic beverage.

    (3) G.S. 18B-302(a1).

If the person's license is currently suspended or revoked, then the revocation under this section shall begin at the termination of that revocation. A person whose license is revoked under this section for a violation of G.S. 18B-302(a1) or G.S. 18B-302(c) shall be eligible for a limited driving privilege under G.S. 20-179.3.

History.
1983, c. 435, s. 36; 2007-537, s. 3

§ 20-17.4. Disqualification to drive a commercial motor vehicle

(a) **One Year.** -- Any of the following disqualifies a person from driving a commercial motor vehicle for one year if committed by a person holding a commercial drivers license, or, when applicable, committed while operating a commercial motor vehicle by a person who does not hold a commercial drivers license:

    (1) A first conviction of G.S. 20-138.1, driving while impaired, for a holder of a commercial drivers license that occurred while the person was driving a motor vehicle that is not a commercial motor vehicle.

    (2) A first conviction of G.S. 20-138.2, driving a commercial motor vehicle while impaired.

    (3) A first conviction of G.S. 20-166, hit and run.

    (4) A first conviction of a felony in the commission of which a commercial motor vehicle was used or the first conviction of a felony in which any motor vehicle is used by a holder of a commercial drivers license.

    (5) Refusal to submit to a chemical test when charged with an implied-consent offense, as defined in G.S. 20-16.2.

    (6) A second or subsequent conviction, as defined in G.S. 20-138.2A(d), of driving a commercial motor vehicle after consuming alcohol under G.S. 20-138.2A.

    (7) A civil license revocation under G.S. 20-16.5, or a substantially similar revocation obtained in another jurisdiction, arising out of a charge that occurred while the person was either operating a commercial motor vehicle or while the person was holding a commercial drivers license.

    (8) A first conviction of vehicular homicide under G.S. 20-141.4 or vehicular manslaughter under G.S. 14-18 occurring while the person was operating a commercial motor vehicle.

    (9) Driving a commercial motor vehicle during a period when the person's commercial drivers license is revoked, suspended, cancelled, or the driver is otherwise disqualified from operating a commercial motor vehicle.

(a1) **Ten-Day Disqualification.** -- A person who is convicted for a first offense of driving a commercial motor vehicle after consuming alcohol under G.S. 20-138.2A is disqualified from driving a commercial motor vehicle for 10 days.

(b) **Modified Life.** -- A person who has been disqualified from driving a commercial motor vehicle for a conviction or refusal described in subsection (a) who, as the result of a separate incident, is subsequently convicted of an offense or commits an act requiring disqualification under subsection (a) is disqualified for life. The Division may adopt guidelines, including conditions, under which a disqualification for life under this subsection may be reduced to 10 years.

(b1) **Life Without Reduction.** -- A person is disqualified from driving a commercial motor vehicle for life, without the possibility of reinstatement after 10 years, if that person is convicted of a third or subsequent violation of G.S. 20-138.2, a fourth or subsequent violation of G.S. 20-138.2A, or if the person refuses to submit to a chemical test a third time when charged with an implied-consent offense, as defined in G.S. 20-16.2, that occurred while the person was driving a commercial motor vehicle.

(c) **Life.** -- A person is disqualified from driving a commercial motor vehicle for life if that person either uses a commercial motor vehicle in the commission of any felony involving the manufacture, distribution, or dispensing of a controlled substance, or possession with intent to manufacture, distribute, or dispense a controlled substance or is the holder of a commercial drivers license at the time of the commission of any such felony.

(c1) **Life.** -- A person shall be disqualified from driving a commercial motor vehicle for life, without the possibility of reinstatement, if that person has had a commercial drivers license reinstated in the past and is convicted of another major disqualifying offense as defined in 49 C.F.R. § 383.51(b).

(d) **Less Than a Year.** -- A person is disqualified from driving a commercial motor vehicle for 60 days if that person is convicted of two serious traffic violations, or 120 days if convicted of three or more serious traffic violations, arising from separate incidents occurring within a three-year period, committed in a commercial motor vehicle or while holding a commercial drivers license. This disqualification shall be in addition to, and shall be served at the end of, any other prior disqualification. For purposes of this subsection, a "serious violation" includes violations of G.S. 20-140(f) and G.S. 20-141(j3).

(e) **Three Years.** -- A person is disqualified from driving a commercial motor vehicle for three years if that person is convicted of an offense or commits an act requiring disqualification under subsection (a) and the offense or act occurred while the person was transporting a hazardous material that required the motor vehicle driven to be placarded.

(f) **Revocation Period.** -- A person is disqualified from driving a commercial motor vehicle for the period during which the person's regular or commercial drivers license is revoked, suspended, or cancelled.

(g) **Violation of Out-of-Service Order.** -- Any person holding a commercial learner's permit or commercial drivers license or required to have a commercial learner's permit or commercial drivers license convicted for violating an out-of-service order, except as described in subsection (h) of this section, shall be disqualified as follows:

(1) A person is disqualified from driving a commercial vehicle for a period of no less than 180 days and no more than one year if convicted of a first violation of an out-of-service order while operating a commercial motor vehicle.

(2) A person is disqualified for a period of no less than two years and no more than five years if convicted of a second violation of an out-of-service order while operating a commercial motor vehicle during any 10-year period, arising from separate incidents.

(3) A person is disqualified for a period of no less than three years and no more than five years if convicted of a third or subsequent violation of an out-of-service order while operating a commercial motor vehicle during any 10-year period, arising from separate incidents.

(h) **Violation of Out-of-Service Order; Special Rule for Hazardous Materials and Passenger Offenses.** -- Any person holding a commercial learner's permit or commercial drivers license or required to have a commercial learner's permit or commercial drivers license convicted for violating an out-of-service order while transporting hazardous materials, as defined in 49 C.F.R. § 383.5, or while operating a commercial vehicle designed or used to transport 16 or more passengers, including the driver, shall be disqualified as follows:

(1) A person is disqualified for a period of no less than 180 days and no more than two years if convicted of a first violation of an out-of-service order while operating a commercial motor vehicle.

(2) A person is disqualified for a period of no less than three years and no more than five years if convicted of a second or subsequent violation of an out-of-service order while operating a commercial motor vehicle during any 10-year period, arising from separate incidents.

(3) A person is disqualified for a period of no less than three years and no more than five years if convicted of a third or subsequent violation of an out-of-service order while operating a commercial motor vehicle during any 10-year period arising from separate incidents.

(i) **Disqualification for Out-of-State Violations.** -- The Division shall withdraw the privilege to operate a commercial vehicle of any resident of this State or person transferring to this State upon receiving notice of the person's conviction or Administrative Per Se Notice in another state for an offense that, if committed in this State, would be grounds for disqualification, even if the offense occurred in another jurisdiction prior to being licensed in this State where no action had been taken at that time in the other jurisdiction. The period of disqualification shall be the same as if the offense occurred in this State.

(j) **Disqualification of Persons Without Commercial Drivers Licenses.** -- Any person convicted of an offense that requires disqualification under this section, but who does not hold a commercial drivers license, shall be disqualified from operating a commercial vehicle in the same manner as if the person held a valid commercial drivers license.

(k) **Disqualification for Railroad Grade Crossing Offenses.** -- Any person convicted of a violation of G.S. 20-142.1 through G.S. 20-142.5, when the driver is operating a commercial motor vehicle, shall be disqualified from driving a commercial motor vehicle as follows:

(1) A person is disqualified for a period of 60 days if convicted of a first violation of a railroad grade crossing offense listed in this subsection.

(2) A person is disqualified for a period of 120 days if convicted during any three-year period of a second violation of any combination of railroad grade crossing offenses listed in this subsection.

(3) A person is disqualified for a period of one year if convicted during any three-year period of a third or subsequent violation of any combination of railroad grade crossing offenses listed in this subsection.

(*l*) **Disqualification for Testing Positive in a Drug or Alcohol Test.** -- Upon receipt of notice of a positive drug or alcohol test, or of refusal to participate in a drug or alcohol test, pursuant to G.S. 20-37.19(c), the Division must disqualify a CDL holder from operating a commercial motor vehicle for a minimum of 30 days and until receipt of proof of successful completion of assessment and treatment by a substance abuse professional in accordance with 49 C.F.R. § 382.503.

(m) **Disqualifications of Drivers Who Are Determined to Constitute an Imminent Hazard.** -- The Division shall withdraw the privilege to operate a commercial motor vehicle for any resident of this State for a period of 30 days in accordance with 49 C.F.R. § 383.52.

(n) **Disqualification for Conviction of Criminal Offense That Requires Registration Under the Sex Offender and Public Protection Registration Programs.** -- Effective December 1, 2009, except as otherwise provided by this subsection, a person convicted of a violation that requires registration under Article 27A of Chapter 14 of the General Statutes is disqualified from driving a commercial motor vehicle that requires a commercial drivers license with a P or S endorsement for the period of time during which the person is required to maintain registration under Article 27A of Chapter 14 of the General Statutes. If a person who is registered pursuant to Article 27A of Chapter 14 of the General Statutes on December 1, 2009, also has a valid commercial drivers license with a P or S endorsement that was issued on or before December 1, 2009, then the person is not disqualified under this subsection until that license expires, provided the person does not commit a subsequent offense that requires registration under Article 27A of Chapter 14 of the General Statutes.

(o) **Disqualification for Passing Stopped School Bus.** -- Any person whose drivers license is revoked under G.S. 20-217 is disqualified from driving a commercial motor vehicle for the period of time in which the person's drivers license remains revoked under G.S. 20-217.

History.
1989, c. 771, s. 3; 1991, c. 726, s. 8; 1993, c. 533, s. 5; 1998-149, s. 3; 1998-182, s. 19; 2000-109, s. 7(e); 2002-72, s. 7; 2003-397, s. 2; 2005-156, s. 2; 2005-349, s. 6; 2007-492, s. 1; 2008-175, s. 1; 2009-416, s. 3; 2009-491, s. 2; 2013-293, s. 3; 2016-90, s. 6(c), (d)

§ 20-17.5. Effect of disqualification

(a) **When No Accompanying Revocation.** -- A person who is disqualified as the result of a conviction that requires disqualification but not revocation may keep any regular Class C drivers license the person had at the time of the offense resulting in disqualification. If the person had a Class A or Class B regular drivers license or a commercial drivers license when the offense occurred, all of the following apply:

(1) The person must give the license to the court that convicts the person or, if the

person is not present when convicted, to the Division.

(2) The person may apply for a regular Class C drivers license.

(b) **When Revocation and Disqualification.** -- When a person is disqualified as the result of a conviction that requires both disqualification and revocation, all of the following apply:

(1) The person must give any drivers license the person has to the court that convicts the person or, if the person is not present when convicted, to the Division.

(2) The person may obtain limited driving privileges to drive a noncommercial motor vehicle during the revocation period to the extent the law would allow limited driving privileges if the person had been driving a noncommercial motor vehicle when the offense occurred. The same procedure, eligibility requirements, and mandatory conditions apply to limited driving privileges authorized by this subdivision that would apply if the person had been driving a noncommercial motor vehicle when the offense occurred.

(3) If the disqualification period is longer than the revocation period, the person may apply for a regular Class C drivers license at the end of the revocation period.

(c) **Refusal to Take Chemical Test.** -- When a person is disqualified for refusing to take a chemical test, all of the following apply:

(1) The person must give any license the person has to a court, a law enforcement officer, or the Division, in accordance with G.S. 20-16.2 and G.S. 20-16.5.

(2) The person may obtain limited driving privileges to drive a noncommercial motor vehicle during the period the person's license is revoked for the refusal that disqualified the person to the extent the law would allow limited driving privileges if the person had been driving a noncommercial motor vehicle at the time of the refusal. The same procedure, eligibility requirements, and mandatory conditions apply to limited driving privileges authorized by this subdivision that would apply if the person had been driving a noncommercial motor vehicle at the time of the refusal.

(3) If the disqualification period is longer than the revocation period, the person may apply for a regular Class C drivers license at the end of the revocation period.

(d) **Obtaining Class C Regular License.** -- A person who is authorized by this section to apply for a regular Class C drivers license and who meets all of the following criteria may obtain a regular Class C drivers license without taking a test:

(1) The person must have had a Class A or Class B regular drivers license or a

commercial drivers license when the person was disqualified.

(2) The person's license must have been issued by the Division.

(3) The person's license must not have expired by the date the person applies for a regular Class C drivers license.

Upon application and payment of the fee set in G.S. 20-14 for a duplicate license, the Division shall issue a person who meets these criteria a regular Class C drivers license. The license shall include the same endorsements and restrictions as the former Class A regular, Class B regular, or commercial drivers license, to the extent they apply to a regular Class C drivers license. A regular Class C drivers license issued to a person who meets these criteria expires the same day as the license it replaces.

G.S. 20-7 governs the issuance of a regular Class C drivers license to a person who is authorized by this section to apply for a regular Class C drivers license but who does not meet the listed criteria. In accordance with that statute, the Division may require the person to take a test and the person must pay the license fee.

(e) **Restoration Fee.** -- A person who is disqualified must pay the restoration fee set in G.S. 20-7(i1) the first time any of the following events occurs as a result of the same disqualification:

(1) The Division reinstates a Class A regular drivers license, a Class B regular drivers license, or a commercial drivers license the person had at the time of the disqualification by issuing the person a duplicate license.

(2) The Division issues a Class A regular drivers license, a Class B regular drivers license, or a commercial drivers license to the person.

(3) If the person's license was revoked because of the conviction or act requiring disqualification, the Division issues a regular Class C drivers license to the person.

The restoration fee does not apply the second time any of these events occurs as a result of the same disqualification.

History.
1991, c. 726, s. 9

§ 20-17.6. Restoration of a license after a conviction of driving while impaired or driving while less than 21 years old after consuming alcohol or drugs

(a) **Scope.** -- This section applies to a person whose license was revoked as a result of a conviction of any of the following offenses:

(1) G.S. 20-138.1, driving while impaired (DWI).

(2) G.S. 20-138.2, commercial DWI.

(3) G.S. 20-138.3, driving while less than 21 years old after consuming alcohol or drugs.

(4) G.S. 20-138.2A, driving a commercial motor vehicle with an alcohol concentration of greater than 0.00 and less than 0.04, if the person's drivers license was revoked under G.S. 20-17(a)(13).

(5) G.S. 20-138.2B, driving a school bus, a school activity bus, or a child care vehicle with an alcohol concentration of greater than 0.00, if the person's drivers license was revoked under G.S. 20-17(a)(14).

(b) **Requirement for Restoring License.** -- The Division must receive a certificate of completion for a person who is subject to this section before the Division can restore that person's license. The revocation period for a person who is subject to this section is extended until the Division receives the certificate of completion.

(c) **Certificate of Completion.** -- To obtain a certificate of completion, a person must have a substance abuse assessment and, depending on the results of the assessment, must complete either an alcohol and drug education traffic (ADET) school or a substance abuse treatment program. The substance abuse assessment must be conducted by one of the entities authorized by the Department of Health and Human Services to conduct assessments. G.S. 122C-142.1 describes the procedure for obtaining a certificate of completion.

(d) **Notice of Requirement.** -- When a court reports to the Division a conviction of a person who is subject to this section, the Division must send the person written notice of the requirements of this section and of the consequences of failing to comply with these requirements. The notification must include a statement that the person may contact the local area mental health, developmental disabilities, and substance abuse program for a list of agencies and entities in the person's area that are authorized to make a substance abuse assessment and provide the education or treatment needed to obtain a certificate of completion.

(e) **Effect on Limited Driving Privileges.** -- A person who is subject to this section is not eligible for limited driving privileges if the revocation period for the offense that caused the person to become subject to this section has ended and the person's license remains revoked only because the Division has not obtained a certificate of completion for that person. The issuance of limited driving privileges during the revocation period for the offense that caused the person to become subject to this section is governed by the statutes that apply to that offense.

History.

1995, c. 496, ss. 1, 11, 12; 1997-443, s. 11A.118(a); 1998-182, s. 20

§ 20-17.7. Commercial motor vehicle out-of-service fines authorized

The Secretary of Public Safety may adopt rules implementing fines for violation of out-of-service criteria as defined in 49 C.F.R. § 390.5. These fines may not exceed the schedule of fines adopted by the Commercial Motor Vehicle Safety Alliance that is in effect on the date of the violations.

History.

1999-330, s. 1; 2002-159, s. 31.5(b); 2002-190, s. 3; 2011-145, s. 19.1(g)

§ 20-17.8. Restoration of a license after certain driving while impaired convictions; ignition interlock

(a) **Scope.** -- This section applies to a person whose license was revoked as a result of a conviction of driving while impaired, G.S. 20-138.1, and:

(1) The person had an alcohol concentration of 0.15 or more;

(2) The person has been convicted of another offense involving impaired driving, which offense occurred within seven years immediately preceding the date of the offense for which the person's license has been revoked; or

(3) The person was sentenced pursuant to G.S. 20-179(f3).

For purposes of subdivision (1) of this subsection, the results of a chemical analysis, as shown by an affidavit or affidavits executed pursuant to G.S. 20-16.2(c1), shall be used by the Division to determine that person's alcohol concentration.

(a1) **Additional Scope.** -- This section applies to a person whose license was revoked as a result of a conviction of habitual impaired driving, G.S. 20-138.5.

(b) **Ignition Interlock Required.** -- Except as provided in subsection (*l*) of this section, when the Division restores the license of a person who is subject to this section, in addition to any other restriction or condition, it shall require the person to agree to and shall indicate on the person's drivers license the following restrictions for the period designated in subsection (c):

(1) A restriction that the person may operate only a vehicle that is equipped with a functioning ignition interlock system of a type approved by the Commissioner. The Commissioner shall not unreasonably withhold approval of an ignition interlock

system and shall consult with the Division of Purchase and Contract in the Department of Administration to ensure that potential vendors are not discriminated against.

(2) A requirement that the person personally activate the ignition interlock system before driving the motor vehicle.

(3) An alcohol concentration restriction as follows:

a. If the ignition interlock system is required pursuant only to subdivision (a)(1) of this section, a requirement that the person not drive with an alcohol concentration of 0.04 or greater;

b. If the ignition interlock system is required pursuant to subdivision (a)(2) or (a)(3) of this section, or subsection (a1) of this section, a requirement that the person not drive with an alcohol concentration of greater than 0.00; or

c. If the ignition interlock system is required pursuant to subdivision (a)(1) of this section, and the person has also been convicted, based on the same set of circumstances, of: (i) driving while impaired in a commercial vehicle, G.S. 20-138.2, (ii) driving while less than 21 years old after consuming alcohol or drugs, G.S. 20-138.3, (iii) a violation of G.S. 20-141.4, or (iv) manslaughter or negligent homicide resulting from the operation of a motor vehicle when the offense involved impaired driving, a requirement that the person not drive with an alcohol concentration of greater than 0.00.

(c) **Length of Requirement.** -- The requirements of subsection (b) shall remain in effect for:

(1) One year from the date of restoration if the original revocation period was one year;

(2) Three years from the date of restoration if the original revocation period was four years; or

(3) Seven years from the date of restoration if the original revocation was a permanent revocation.

(c1) **Vehicles Subject to Requirement.** -- A person subject to this section shall have all registered vehicles owned by that person equipped with a functioning ignition interlock system of a type approved by the Commissioner. The Commissioner shall not issue a license to a person subject to this section until presented with proof of the installation of an ignition interlock system in all registered vehicles owned by the person. In order to avoid an undue financial hardship, a person subject to this section may seek a waiver from the Division for any vehicle registered to that person that is relied upon by another member of that person's family for transportation and that the vehicle is not in the possession of the person subject to this section. The Division shall determine such waiver on a case-by-case basis following an assessment of financial hardship to the person subject to this restriction. The Commissioner shall cancel the drivers license of any person subject to this section for registration of a motor vehicle owned by the person without an installed ignition interlock system or removal of the ignition interlock system from a motor vehicle owned by the person, other than when changing ignition interlock providers or upon sale of the vehicle.

(d) **Effect of Limited Driving Privileges.** -- If the person was eligible for and received a limited driving privilege under G.S. 20-179.3, with the ignition interlock requirement contained in G.S. 20-179.3(g5), the period of time for which that limited driving privilege was held shall be applied towards the requirements of subsection (c).

(e) **Notice of Requirement.** -- When a court reports to the Division a conviction of a person who is subject to this section, the Division must send the person written notice of the requirements of this section and of the consequences of failing to comply with these requirements. The notification must include a statement that the person may contact the Division for information on obtaining and having installed an ignition interlock system of a type approved by the Commissioner.

(f) **Effect of Violation of Restriction.** -- A person subject to this section who violates any of the restrictions of this section commits the offense of driving while license revoked for impaired driving under G.S. 20-28(a1) and is subject to punishment and license revocation as provided in that section. If a law enforcement officer has reasonable grounds to believe that a person subject to this section has consumed alcohol while driving or has driven while he has remaining in his body any alcohol previously consumed, the suspected offense of driving while license is revoked is an alcohol-related offense subject to the implied-consent provisions of G.S. 20-16.2. If a person subject to this section is charged with driving while license revoked by violating a condition of subsection (b) of this section, and a judicial official determines that there is probable cause for the charge, the person's license is suspended pending the resolution of the case, and the judicial official must require the person to surrender the license. The judicial official must also notify the person that he is not entitled to drive until his case is resolved. An alcohol concentration report from the ignition interlock system shall not be admissible as evidence of driving while license revoked, nor shall it be admissible in an administrative revocation proceeding as provided in subsection

(g) of this section, unless the person operated a vehicle when the ignition interlock system indicated an alcohol concentration in violation of the restriction placed upon the person by subdivision (b)(3) of this section.

(g) **Effect of Violation of Restriction When Driving While License Revoked Not Charged.** -- A person subject to this section who violates any of the restrictions of this section, but is not charged or convicted of driving while license revoked pursuant to G.S. 20-28(a), shall have the person's license revoked by the Division for a period of one year.

(h) **Beginning of Revocation Period.** -- If the original period of revocation was imposed pursuant to G.S. 20-19(d) or (e), any remaining period of the original revocation, prior to its reduction, shall be reinstated and the revocation required by subsection (f) or (g) of this section begins after all other periods of revocation have terminated.

(i) **Notification of Revocation.** -- If the person's license has not already been surrendered to the court, the Division must expeditiously notify the person that the person's license to drive is revoked pursuant to subsection (f) or (g) of this section effective on the thirtieth calendar day after the mailing of the revocation order.

(j) **Right to Hearing Before Division; Issues.** -- If the person's license is revoked pursuant to subsection (g) of this section, before the effective date of the order issued under subsection (i) of this section, the person may request in writing a hearing before the Division. Except for the time referred to in G.S. 20-16.5, if the person shows to the satisfaction of the Division that the person's license was surrendered to the court and remained in the court's possession, then the Division shall credit the amount of time for which the license was in the possession of the court against the revocation period required by subsection (g) of this section. If the person properly requests a hearing, the person retains the person's license, unless it is revoked under some other provision of law, until the hearing is held, the person withdraws the request, or the person fails to appear at a scheduled hearing. The hearing officer may subpoena any witnesses or documents that the hearing officer deems necessary. The person may request the hearing officer to subpoena the charging officer, the chemical analyst, or both to appear at the hearing if the person makes the request in writing at least three days before the hearing. The person may subpoena any other witness whom the person deems necessary, and the provisions of G.S. 1A-1, Rule 45, apply to the issuance and service of all subpoenas issued under the authority of this section. The hearing officer is authorized to administer oaths to witnesses appearing at the hearing. The hearing must be conducted in the county where the charge was brought, except when the evidence of the violation is an alcohol concentration report from an ignition interlock system, the hearing may be conducted in the county where the person resides. The hearing must be limited to consideration of whether:

(1) The drivers license of the person had an ignition interlock requirement; and

(2) The person:

a. Was driving a vehicle that was not equipped with a functioning ignition interlock system; or

b. Did not personally activate the ignition interlock system before driving the vehicle; or

c. Drove the vehicle in violation of an applicable alcohol concentration restriction prescribed by subdivision (b)(3) of this section.

If the Division finds that the conditions specified in this subsection are met, it must order the revocation sustained. If the Division finds that the condition of subdivision (1) is not met, or that none of the conditions of subdivision (2) are met, it must rescind the revocation. If the revocation is sustained, the person must surrender the person's license immediately upon notification by the Division. If the revocation is sustained, the person may appeal the decision of the Division pursuant to G.S. 20-25.

(k) **Restoration After Violation.** -- When the Division restores the license of a person whose license was revoked pursuant to subsection (f) or (g) of this section and the revocation occurred prior to completion of time period required by subsection (c) of this section, in addition to any other restriction or condition, it shall require the person to comply with the conditions of subsection (b) of this section until the person has complied with those conditions for the cumulative period of time as set forth in subsection (c) of this section. The period of time for which the person successfully complied with subsection (b) of this section prior to revocation pursuant to subsection (f) or (g) of this section shall be applied towards the requirements of subsection (c) of this section.

(*l*) **Medical Exception to Requirement.** -- A person subject to this section solely for the reason set forth in subdivision (a)(1) of this section and who has a medically diagnosed physical condition that makes the person incapable of personally activating an ignition interlock system may request an exception to the requirements of this section from the Division. The Division shall not issue an exception to this section unless the person has submitted to a physical examination by two or more physicians or surgeons duly licensed to practice

medicine in this State or in any other state of the United States and unless such examining physicians or surgeons have completed and signed a certificate in the form prescribed by the Division. Such certificate shall be devised by the Commissioner with the advice of those qualified experts in the field of diagnosing and treating physical disorders that the Commissioner may select and shall be designed to elicit the maximum medical information necessary to aid in determining whether or not the person is capable of personally activating an ignition interlock system. The certificate shall contain a waiver of privilege and the recommendation of the examining physician to the Commissioner as to whether the person is capable of personally activating an ignition interlock system.

The Commissioner is not bound by the recommendations of the examining physicians but shall give fair consideration to such recommendations in acting upon the request for medical exception, the criterion being whether or not, upon all the evidence, it appears that the person is in fact incapable of personally activating an ignition interlock system. The burden of proof of such fact is upon the person seeking the exception.

Whenever an exception is denied by the Commissioner, such denial may be reviewed by a reviewing board upon written request of the person seeking the exception filed with the Division within 10 days after receipt of such denial. The composition, procedures, and review of the reviewing board shall be as provided in G.S. 20-9(g)(4). This subsection shall not apply to persons subject to an ignition interlock requirement under this section for the reasons set forth in subdivision (a)(2) or (a)(3) of this section.

History.
1999-406, s. 3; 2000-155, ss. 1 -3; 2001-487, s. 8; 2006-253, ss. 22.3, 22.4; 2007-493, ss. 5, 10, 28; 2009-369, ss. 5, 6; 2011-191, s. 3; 2013-348, s. 1; 2014-108, s. 1(a); 2014-115, s. 61.5; 2015-186, s. 4; 2015-264, s. 86; 2017-176, s. 2(b); 2021-134, s. 9(b)

§ 20-17.8A. Tampering with ignition interlock systems

Any person who tampers with, circumvents, or attempts to circumvent an ignition interlock device required to be installed on a motor vehicle pursuant to judicial order, statute, or as may be otherwise required as a condition for an individual to operate a motor vehicle, for the purpose of avoiding or altering testing on the ignition interlock device in the operation or attempted operation of a vehicle, or altering the testing results received or results in the process of being received on the ignition interlock device, is guilty of a Class 1 misdemeanor. Each act of tampering, circumvention, or attempted circumvention under this statute shall constitute a separate violation.

History.
2011-381, s. 1

§ 20-17.9. Revocation of commercial drivers license with a P or S endorsement upon conviction of certain offenses

The Division shall revoke the commercial drivers license with a P or S endorsement of any person convicted of any offense on or after December 1, 2009, that requires registration under Article 27A of Chapter 14 of the General Statutes. The person may apply for the issuance of a new commercial drivers license pursuant to this Chapter, but, pursuant to G.S. 20-17.4, shall remain disqualified from obtaining a commercial drivers license with a P or S endorsement for the period of time during which the person is required to maintain registration.

History.
2009-491, s. 3

§ 20-18. Conviction of offenses described in § 20-181 not ground for suspension or revocation

Conviction of offenses described in G.S. 20-181 shall not be cause for the suspension or revocation of driver's license under the terms of this Article.

History.
1939, c. 351, s. 2; 1955, c. 913, s. 1; 1979, c. 667, s. 41

§ 20-19. Period of suspension or revocation; conditions of restoration

(a) When a license is suspended under subdivision (8) or (9) of G.S. 20-16(a), the period of suspension shall be in the discretion of the Division and for such time as it deems best for public safety but shall not exceed six months.

(b) When a license is suspended under subdivision (10) of G.S. 20-16(a), the period of suspension shall be in the discretion of the Division and for such time as it deems best for public safety but shall not exceed a period of 12 months.

(c) When a license is suspended under any other provision of this Article which does not specifically provide a period of suspension, the period of suspension shall be not more than one year.

(c1) When a license is revoked under subdivision (2) of G.S. 20-17, and the period of revocation is not determined by subsection (d) or (e) of this section, the period of revocation is one year.

(c2) When a license is suspended under G.S. 20-17(a)(14), the period of revocation for a first

conviction shall be for 10 days. For a second or subsequent conviction as defined in G.S. 20-138.2B(d), the period of revocation shall be one year.

(c3) **Restriction; Revocations.** -- When the Division restores a person's drivers license which was revoked pursuant to G.S. 20-13.2(a), G.S. 20-23 when the offense involved impaired driving, G.S. 20-23.2, subdivision (2) of G.S. 20-17(a), subdivision (1) or (9) of G.S. 20-17(a) when the offense involved impaired driving, G.S. 20-138.5(d), or this subsection, in addition to any other restriction or condition, it shall place the applicable restriction on the person's drivers license as follows:

(1) For the first restoration of a drivers license for a person convicted of driving while impaired, G.S. 20-138.1, or a drivers license revoked pursuant to G.S. 20-23 or G.S. 20-23.2 when the offense for which the person's license was revoked prohibits substantially similar conduct which if committed in this State would result in a conviction of driving while impaired under G.S. 20-138.1, that the person not operate a vehicle with an alcohol concentration of 0.04 or more at any relevant time after the driving;

(2) For the second or subsequent restoration of a drivers license for a person convicted of driving while impaired, G.S. 20-138.1, or a drivers license revoked pursuant to G.S. 20-23 or G.S. 20-23.2 when the offense for which the person's license was revoked prohibits substantially similar conduct which if committed in this State would result in a conviction of driving while impaired under G.S. 20-138.1, that the person not operate a vehicle with an alcohol concentration greater than 0.00 at any relevant time after the driving;

(3) For any restoration of a drivers license for a person convicted of driving while impaired in a commercial motor vehicle, G.S. 20-138.2, habitual impaired driving, G.S. 20-138.5, driving while less than 21 years old after consuming alcohol or drugs, G.S. 20-138.3, felony death by vehicle, G.S. 20-141.4(a1), manslaughter or negligent homicide resulting from the operation of a motor vehicle when the offense involved impaired driving, or a revocation under this subsection, that the person not operate a vehicle with an alcohol concentration of greater than 0.00 at any relevant time after the driving;

(4) For any restoration of a drivers license revoked pursuant to G.S. 20-23 or G.S. 20-23.2 when the offense for which the person's license was revoked prohibits substantially similar conduct which if committed in this State would result in a

conviction of driving while impaired in a commercial motor vehicle, G.S. 20-138.2, driving while less than 21 years old after consuming alcohol or drugs, G.S. 20-138.3, a violation of G.S. 20-141.4, or manslaughter or negligent homicide resulting from the operation of a motor vehicle when the offense involved impaired driving, that the person not operate vehicle with an alcohol concentration of greater than 0.00 at any relevant time after the driving.

In addition, the person seeking restoration of a license must agree to submit to a chemical analysis in accordance with G.S. 20-16.2 at the request of a law enforcement officer who has reasonable grounds to believe the person is operating a motor vehicle on a highway or public vehicular area in violation of the restriction specified in this subsection. The person must also agree that, when requested by a law enforcement officer, the person will agree to be transported by the law enforcement officer to the place where chemical analysis is to be administered.

The restrictions placed on a license under this subsection shall be in effect (i) seven years from the date of restoration if the person's license was permanently revoked, (ii) until the person's twenty-first birthday if the revocation was for a conviction under G.S. 20-138.3, and (iii) three years in all other cases.

A law enforcement officer who has reasonable grounds to believe that a person has violated a restriction placed on the person's drivers license shall complete an affidavit pursuant to G.S. 20-16.2(c1). On the basis of information reported pursuant to G.S. 20-16.2, the Division shall revoke the drivers license of any person who violates a condition of reinstatement imposed under this subsection. An alcohol concentration report from an ignition interlock system shall not be used as the basis for revocation under this subsection. A violation of a restriction imposed under this subsection or the willful refusal to submit to a chemical analysis shall result in a one-year revocation. If the period of revocation was imposed pursuant to subsection (d) or (e), or G.S. 20-138.5(d), any remaining period of the original revocation, prior to its reduction, shall be reinstated and the one-year revocation begins after all other periods of revocation have terminated.

(c4) **Applicable Procedures.** -- When a person has violated a condition of restoration by refusing a chemical analysis, the notice and hearing procedures of G.S. 20-16.2 apply. When a person has submitted to a chemical analysis and the results show a violation of the alcohol concentration restriction, the notification and hearing procedures of this section apply.

(c5) **Right to Hearing Before Division; Issues.** -- Upon receipt of a properly executed affidavit required by G.S. 20-16.2(c1), the Division must expeditiously notify the person charged that the person's license to drive is revoked for the period of time specified in this section, effective on the thirtieth calendar day after the mailing of the revocation order unless, before the effective date of the order, the person requests in writing a hearing before the Division. Except for the time referred to in G.S. 20-16.5, if the person shows to the satisfaction of the Division that the person's license was surrendered to the court and remained in the court's possession, then the Division shall credit the amount of time for which the license was in the possession of the court against the revocation period required by this section. If the person properly requests a hearing, the person retains the person's license, unless it is revoked under some other provision of law, until the hearing is held, the person withdraws the request, or the person fails to appear at a scheduled hearing. The hearing officer may subpoena any witnesses or documents that the hearing officer deems necessary. The person may request the hearing officer to subpoena the charging officer, the chemical analyst, or both to appear at the hearing if the person makes the request in writing at least three days before the hearing. The person may subpoena any other witness whom the person deems necessary, and the provisions of G.S. 1A-1, Rule 45, apply to the issuance and service of all subpoenas issued under the authority of this section. The hearing officer is authorized to administer oaths to witnesses appearing at the hearing. The hearing must be conducted in the county where the charge was brought, and must be limited to consideration of whether:

(1) The charging officer had reasonable grounds to believe that the person had violated the alcohol concentration restriction;

(2) The person was notified of the person's rights as required by G.S. 20-16.2(a);

(3) The drivers license of the person had an alcohol concentration restriction; and

(4) The person submitted to a chemical analysis upon the request of the charging officer, and the analysis revealed an alcohol concentration in excess of the restriction on the person's drivers license.

If the Division finds that the conditions specified in this subsection are met, it must order the revocation sustained. If the Division finds that any of the conditions (1), (2), (3), or (4) is not met, it must rescind the revocation. If the revocation is sustained, the person must surrender the person's license immediately upon notification by the Division.

Chapter 20

(c6) **Appeal to Court.** -- There is no right to appeal the decision of the Division. However, if the person properly requested a hearing before the Division under subsection (c5) and the Division held such a hearing, the person may within 30 days of the date the Division's decision is mailed to the person, petition the superior court of the county in which the hearing took place for discretionary review on the record of the revocation. The superior court may stay the imposition of the revocation only if the court finds that the person is likely to succeed on the merits of the case and will suffer irreparable harm if such a stay is not granted. The stay shall not exceed 30 days. The reviewing court shall review the record only and shall be limited to determining if the Division hearing officer followed proper procedures and if the hearing officer made sufficient findings of fact to support the revocation. There shall be no further appeal.

(d) When a person's license is revoked under (i) G.S. 20-17(a)(2) and the person has another offense involving impaired driving for which he has been convicted, which offense occurred within three years immediately preceding the date of the offense for which his license is being revoked, or (ii) G.S. 20-17(a)(9) due to a violation of G.S. 20-141.4(a3), the period of revocation is four years, and this period may be reduced only as provided in this section. The Division may conditionally restore the person's license after it has been revoked for at least two years under this subsection if he provides the Division with satisfactory proof that:

(1) He has not in the period of revocation been convicted in North Carolina or any other state or federal jurisdiction of a motor vehicle offense, an alcoholic beverage control law offense, a drug law offense, or any other criminal offense involving the possession or consumption of alcohol or drugs; and

(2) He is not currently an excessive user of alcohol, drugs, or prescription drugs, or unlawfully using any controlled substance. The person may voluntarily submit themselves to continuous alcohol monitoring for the purpose of proving abstinence from alcohol consumption during a period of revocation immediately prior to the restoration consideration.

a. Monitoring periods of 120 days or longer shall be accepted by the Division as evidence of abstinence if the Division receives sufficient documentation that reflects that the person abstained from alcohol use during the monitoring period.

b. The continuous alcohol monitoring system shall be a system approved under G.S. 15A-1343.3.

c. The Division may establish guidelines for the acceptance of evidence of abstinence under this subdivision.

If the Division restores the person's license, it may place reasonable conditions or restrictions on the person for the duration of the original revocation period.

(e) When a person's license is revoked under (i) G.S. 20-17(a)(2) and the person has two or more previous offenses involving impaired driving for which the person has been convicted, and the most recent offense occurred within the five years immediately preceding the date of the offense for which the person's license is being revoked, (ii) G.S. 20-17(a)(2) and the person was sentenced pursuant to G.S. 20-179(f3) for the offense resulting in the revocation, or (iii) G.S. 20-17(a)(9) due to a violation of G.S. 20-141.4(a4), the revocation is permanent.

(e1) Notwithstanding subsection (e) of this section, the Division may conditionally restore the license of a person to whom subsection (e) applies after it has been revoked for at least three years under subsection (e) if the person provides the Division with satisfactory proof of all of the following:

(1) In the three years immediately preceding the person's application for a restored license, the person has not been convicted in North Carolina or in any other state or federal court of a motor vehicle offense, an alcohol beverage control law offense, a drug law offense, or any criminal offense involving the consumption of alcohol or drugs.

(2) The person is not currently an excessive user of alcohol, drugs, or prescription drugs, or unlawfully using any controlled substance. The person may voluntarily submit themselves to continuous alcohol monitoring for the purpose of proving abstinence from alcohol consumption during a period of revocation immediately prior to the restoration consideration.

a. Monitoring periods of 120 days or longer shall be accepted by the Division as evidence of abstinence if the Division receives sufficient documentation that reflects that the person abstained from alcohol use during the monitoring period.

b. The continuous alcohol monitoring system shall be a system approved under G.S. 15A-1343.3.

c. The Division may establish guidelines for the acceptance of evidence of abstinence under this subdivision.

(e2) Notwithstanding subsection (e) of this section, the Division may conditionally restore the license of a person to whom subsection (e) applies after it has been revoked for at least 24 months under G.S. 20-17(a)(2) if the person provides the Division with satisfactory proof of all of the following:

(1) The person has not consumed any alcohol for the 12 months preceding the restoration while being monitored by a continuous alcohol monitoring device of a type approved by the Division of Adult Correction and Juvenile Justice of the Department of Public Safety.

(2) The person has not in the period of revocation been convicted in North Carolina or any other state or federal jurisdiction of a motor vehicle offense, an alcoholic beverage control law offense, a drug law offense, or any other criminal offense involving the possession or consumption of alcohol or drugs.

(3) The person is not currently an excessive user of drugs or prescription drugs.

(4) The person is not unlawfully using any controlled substance.

(e3) If the Division restores a person's license under subsection (e1), (e2), or (e4) of this section, it may place reasonable conditions or restrictions on the person for any period up to five years from the date of restoration.

(e4) When a person's license is revoked under G.S. 20-138.5(d), the Division may conditionally restore the license of that person after it has been revoked for at least 10 years after the completion of any sentence imposed by the court, if the person provides the Division with satisfactory proof of all of the following:

(1) In the 10 years immediately preceding the person's application for a restored license, the person has not been convicted in North Carolina or in any other state or federal court of a motor vehicle offense, an alcohol beverage control law offense, a drug law offense, or any other criminal offense.

(2) The person is not currently a user of alcohol, unlawfully using any controlled substance, or an excessive user of prescription drugs.

(f) When a license is revoked under any other provision of this Article which does not specifically provide a period of revocation, the period of revocation shall be one year.

(g) When a license is suspended under subdivision (11) of G.S. 20-16(a), the period of suspension shall be for a period of time not in excess of the period of nonoperation imposed by the court as a condition of the suspended sentence; further, in such case, it shall not be necessary to comply with the Motor Vehicle Safety and Financial Responsibility Act in order to have such license returned at the expiration of the suspension period.

(g1) When a license is revoked under subdivision (12) of G.S. 20-17, the period of revocation is six months for conviction of a second offense and one year for conviction of a third or subsequent offense.

(g2) When a license is revoked under G.S. 20-17(a)(16), the period of revocation is 90 days for a second conviction and six months for a third or subsequent conviction. The term "second or subsequent conviction" shall have the same meaning as found in G.S. 20-17(a)(16).

(h) Repealed by Session Laws 1983, c. 435, s. 17.

(i) *(For applicability, see Editor's note)* When a person's license is revoked under G.S. 20-17(a)(1) or G.S. 20-17(a)(9), and the offense is one involving impaired driving and a fatality, the revocation is permanent. The Division may, however, conditionally restore the person's license after it has been revoked for at least five years under this subsection if he provides the Division with satisfactory proof that:

(1) In the five years immediately preceding the person's application for a restored license, he has not been convicted in North Carolina or in any other state or federal court of a motor vehicle offense, an alcohol beverage control law offense, a drug law offense, or any criminal offense involving the consumption of alcohol or drugs; and

(2) He is not currently an excessive user of alcohol or drugs.

If the Division restores the person's license, it may place reasonable conditions or restrictions on the person for any period up to seven years from the date of restoration.

(j) The Division is authorized to issue amended revocation orders issued under subsections (d) and (e), if necessary because convictions do not respectively occur in the same order as offenses for which the license may be revoked under those subsections.

(k) Before the Division restores a driver's license that has been suspended or revoked under G.S. 20-138.5(d), or under any provision of this Article, other than G.S. 20-24.1, the person seeking to have his driver's license restored shall submit to the Division proof that he has notified his insurance agent or company of his seeking the restoration and that he is financially responsible. Proof of financial responsibility shall be in one of the following forms:

(1) A written certificate or electronically-transmitted facsimile thereof from any insurance carrier duly authorized to do business in this State certifying that there is in effect a nonfleet private passenger motor vehicle liability policy for the benefit of the person required to furnish proof of financial responsibility. The certificate or facsimile shall state the effective date and expiration date of the nonfleet private passenger motor vehicle liability policy and shall state the date that the certificate or facsimile is issued. The certificate or facsimile shall

remain effective proof of financial responsibility for a period of 30 consecutive days following the date the certificate or facsimile is issued but shall not in and of itself constitute a binder or policy of insurance or

(2) A binder for or policy of nonfleet private passenger motor vehicle liability insurance under which the applicant is insured, provided that the binder or policy states the effective date and expiration date of the nonfleet private passenger motor vehicle liability policy.

The preceding provisions of this subsection do not apply to applicants who do not own currently registered motor vehicles and who do not operate nonfleet private passenger motor vehicles that are owned by other persons and that are not insured under commercial motor vehicle liability insurance policies. In such cases, the applicant shall sign a written certificate to that effect. Such certificate shall be furnished by the Division and may be incorporated into the restoration application form. Any material misrepresentation made by such person on such certificate shall be grounds for suspension of that person's license for a period of 90 days.

For the purposes of this subsection, the term "nonfleet private passenger motor vehicle" has the definition ascribed to it in Article 40 of General Statute Chapter 58.

The Commissioner may require that certificates required by this subsection be on a form approved by the Commissioner. The financial responsibility required by this subsection shall be kept in effect for not less than three years after the date that the license is restored. Failure to maintain financial responsibility as required by this subsection shall be grounds for suspending the restored driver's license for a period of thirty (30) days. Nothing in this subsection precludes any person from showing proof of financial responsibility in any other manner authorized by Articles 9A and 13 of this Chapter.

History.
1935, c. 52, s. 13; 1947, c. 1067, s. 15; 1951, c. 1202, ss. 2-4; 1953, c. 1138; 1955, c. 1187, ss. 13, 17, 18; 1957, c. 499, s. 2; c. 515, s. 1; 1959, c. 1264, s. 11A; 1969, c. 242; 1971, c. 619, ss. 8-10; 1973, c. 1445, ss. 1-4; 1975, c. 716, s. 5; 1979, c. 903, ss. 4-6; 1981, c. 412, s. 4; c. 747, ss. 34, 66; 1983, c. 435, s. 17; 1983 (Reg. Sess., 1984), c. 1101, s. 18; 1987, c. 869, s. 12; 1987 (Reg. Sess., 1988), c. 1112; 1989, c. 436, s. 5; c. 771, s. 18; 1995, c. 506, s. 8; 1998-182, s. 21; 1999-406, s. 2; 1999-452, ss. 11, 12; 2000-140, ss. 3, 4; 2000-155, s. 6; 2001-352, s. 4; 2007-165, ss. 1(a), (b); 2007-493, ss. 11-14; 2008-187, s. 9; 2009-99, s. 1; 2009-369, ss. 1-4; 2009-500, ss. 1, 2; 2011-145, s. 19.1(h); 2011-191, s. 2;

2014-115, s. 61.5; 2017-176, s. 2(b); 2017-186, s. 2 (jjjj); 2021-128, s. 3; 2021-134, s. 9(c)

N.C. Gen. Stat. § 20-20

Repealed by Session Laws 1981, c. 938, s. 5.

§ 20-20.1. Limited driving privilege for certain revocations

(a) **Definitions.** -- The following definitions apply in this section:

(1) **Limited driving privilege.** -- A judgment issued by a court authorizing a person with a revoked drivers license to drive under specified terms and conditions.

(2) **Nonstandard working hours.** -- Anytime other than 6:00 A.M. until 8:00 P.M. on Monday through Friday.

(3) **Standard working hours.** -- Anytime from 6:00 A.M. until 8:00 P.M. on Monday through Friday.

(4) **Underlying offense.** -- The offense for which a person's drivers license was revoked when the person was charged under G.S. 20-28(a), driving with a revoked license, or under G.S. 20-28.1, committing a motor vehicle moving offense while driving with a revoked license.

(b) **Eligibility.** -- A person is eligible to apply for a limited driving privilege under this section if all of the following conditions apply:

(1) The person's license is currently revoked under G.S. 20-28(a) or G.S. 20-28.1.

(2) The person has complied with the revocation for the period required in subsection (c) of this section immediately preceding the date the person files a petition for a limited driving privilege under this section.

(3) The person's underlying offense is not an offense involving impaired driving and, if the person's license is revoked under G.S. 20-28.1 for committing a motor vehicle moving offense while driving with a revoked license, the moving offense is not an offense involving impaired driving.

(4) The revocation period for the underlying offense has expired.

(5) The revocation under G.S. 20-28(a) or G.S. 20-28.1 is the only revocation in effect.

(6) The person is not eligible to receive a limited driving privilege under any other law.

(7) The person has not held a limited driving privilege issued under this section at anytime during the three years prior to the date the person files the current petition.

(8) The person has no pending charges for any motor vehicle offense in this or in any other state and has no unpaid motor

Chapter 20

vehicle fines or penalties in this or in any other state.

(9) The person's drivers license issued by another state has not been revoked by that state.

(10) G.S. 20-9(e) or G.S. 20-9(f) does not prohibit the Division from issuing the person a license.

(c) **Compliance Period.** -- The following table sets out the period during which a person must comply with a revocation under G.S. 20-28(a) or G.S. 20-28.1 to be eligible for a limited driving privilege under this section:

Revocation Period	Compliance Period
1 Year	90 Days
2 Years	1 Year
Permanent	2 Years

(d) **Petition.** -- A person may apply for a limited driving privilege under this section by filing a petition. A petition filed under this section is separate from the action that resulted in the initial revocation and is a civil action. A petition must be filed in district court in the county of the person's residence as reflected by the Division's records or, if the Division's records are inaccurate, in the county of the person's actual residence. A person must attach to a petition a copy of the person's motor vehicle record. A petition must include a sworn statement that the person filing the petition is eligible for a limited driving privilege under this section.

A court, for good cause shown, may issue a limited driving privilege to an eligible person in accordance with this section. The costs required under G.S. 7A-305(a) and G.S. 20-20.2 apply to a petition filed under this section. The clerk of court for the court that issues a limited driving privilege under this section must send a copy of the limited driving privilege to the Division.

(e) **Scope of Privilege.** -- A limited driving privilege restricts the person to essential driving related to one or more of the purposes listed in this subsection. Any driving that is not related to the purposes authorized in this subsection is unlawful even though done at times and upon routes that may be authorized by the privilege. Except as otherwise provided, all driving must be for a purpose and done within the restrictions specified in the privilege.

The permissible purposes for a limited driving privilege are:

(1) Travel to and from the person's place of employment and in the course of employment.

(2) Travel necessary for maintenance of the person's household.

(3) Travel to provide emergency medical care for the person or for an immediate family member of the person who resides in the same household with the person. Driving related to emergency medical care is authorized at anytime and without restriction as to routes.

(f) **Employment Driving in Standard Working Hours.** -- The court may authorize driving for employment-related purposes during standard working hours without specifying times and routes for the driving. If the person is required to drive for essential employment-related purposes only during standard working hours, the limited driving privilege must prohibit driving during nonstandard working hours unless the driving is for emergency medical care or for authorized household maintenance. The limited driving privilege must state the name and address of the person's employer and may, in the discretion of the court, include other information and restrictions applicable to employment-related driving.

(g) **Employment Driving in Nonstandard Working Hours.** -- If a person is required to drive during nonstandard working hours for an essential employment-related purpose and the person provides documentation of that fact to the court, the court may authorize the person to drive for that purpose during those hours. If the person is self-employed, the documentation must be attached to or made a part of the limited driving privilege. If the person is employed by another, the limited driving privilege must state the name and address of the person's employer and may, in the discretion of the court, include other information and restrictions applicable to employment-related driving. If the court determines that it is necessary for the person to drive during nonstandard working hours for an employment-related purpose, the court may authorize the person to drive subject to these limitations:

(1) If the person is required to drive to and from a specific place of employment at regular times, the limited driving privilege must specify the general times and routes by which the person may drive to and from work and must restrict driving to those times and routes.

(2) If the person is required to drive to and from work at a specific place but is unable to specify the times during which the driving will occur, the limited driving privilege must specify the general routes by which the person may drive to and from work and must restrict driving to those general routes.

(3) If the person is required to drive to and from work at regular times but is unable to specify the places at which work is to be performed, the limited driving privilege must specify the general times and geographic boundaries within which the person may drive and must restrict driving to those times and boundaries.

Chapter 20

(4) If the person can specify neither the times nor places in which the person will be driving to and from work, the limited driving privilege must specify the geographic boundaries within which the person may drive and must restrict driving to those boundaries.

(h) **Household Maintenance.** -- A limited driving privilege may allow driving for maintenance of the household only during standard working hours. The court, at its discretion, may impose additional restrictions on driving for the maintenance of the household.

(i) **Restrictions.** -- A limited driving privilege that is not authorized by this section or that does not contain the restrictions required by law is invalid. A limited driving privilege issued under this section is subject to the following conditions:

(1) **Financial responsibility.** -- A person applying for a limited driving privilege under this section must provide the court proof of financial responsibility acceptable under G.S. 20-16.1(g) and must maintain the financial responsibility during the period of the limited driving privilege.

(2) **Alcohol restrictions.** -- A person who received a limited driving privilege under this section may not consume alcohol while driving or drive at anytime while the person has remaining in the person's body any alcohol or controlled substance previously consumed, unless the controlled substance was lawfully obtained and taken in therapeutically appropriate amounts.

(3) **Others.** -- The court may impose any other reasonable restrictions or conditions necessary to achieve the purposes of this section.

(j) **Term and Reinstatement.** -- The term of a limited driving privilege issued under this section is the shorter of one year or the length of time remaining in the revocation period imposed under G.S. 20-28(a) or G.S. 20-28.1. When the term of the limited driving privilege expires, the Division must reinstate the person's license if the person meets all of the conditions listed in this subsection. The Division may impose restrictions or conditions on the new license in accordance with G.S. 20-7(e). The conditions are:

(1) Payment of the restoration fee as required under G.S. 20-7(i1).

(2) Providing proof of financial responsibility as required under G.S. 20-7(c1).

(3) Providing the proof required for reinstatement of a license under G.S. 20-28(c1).

(k) **Modification.** -- A court may modify or revoke a person's limited driving privilege issued under this section upon a showing that the circumstances have changed sufficiently to justify modification or revocation. If the judge who issued the privilege is not presiding in the court in which the privilege was issued, a presiding judge in that court may modify or revoke the privilege. The judge must indicate in the order of modification or revocation the reasons for the order or make specific findings indicating the reason for the order and enter those findings in the record of the case. When a court issues an order of modification or revocation, the clerk of court must send a copy of the order to the Division.

(*l*) **Effect of Violation.** -- A violation of a limited driving privilege issued under this section constitutes the offense of driving while license revoked under G.S. 20-28. When a person is charged with operating a motor vehicle in violation of the limited driving privilege, the limited driving privilege is suspended pending the final disposition of the charge.

History.
2007-293, s. 1; 2007-323, s. 30.11(d); 2007-345, s. 9.1(c); 2008-118, s. 2.9(b)

§ 20-20.2. Processing fee for limited driving privilege

Upon the issuance of a limited driving privilege by a court under this Chapter, the applicant or petitioner must pay, in addition to any other costs associated with obtaining the privilege, a processing fee of one hundred dollars ($ 100.00). The applicant or petitioner shall pay this fee to the clerk of superior court in the county in which the limited driving privilege is issued. The fee must be remitted to the State Treasurer and used for support of the General Court of Justice. The failure to pay this fee shall render the privilege invalid.

History.
2007-323, s. 30.11(b); 2007-345, s. 9.1(b)

§ 20-21. No operation under foreign license during suspension or revocation in this State

Any resident or nonresident whose driver's license or right or privilege to operate a motor vehicle in this State has been suspended or revoked as provided in this Article shall not operate a motor vehicle in this State under a license, permit or registration issued by another jurisdiction or otherwise during such suspension, or after such revocation until a new license is obtained when and as permitted under this Article.

History.
1935, c. 52, s. 15; 1979, c. 667, s. 41

§ 20-22. Suspending privileges of nonresidents and reporting convictions

(a) The privilege of driving a motor vehicle on the highways of this State given to a nonresident hereunder shall be subject to suspension or revocation by the Division in like manner and for like cause as a driver's license issued hereunder may be suspended or revoked.

(b) The Division is further authorized, upon receiving a record of the conviction in this State of a nonresident driver of a motor vehicle of any offense under the motor vehicle laws of this State, to forward a certified copy of such record to the motor vehicle administrator in the state wherein the person so convicted is a resident.

History.
1935, c. 52, s. 16; 1975, c. 716, s. 5; 1979, c. 667, s. 41

§ 20-23. Revoking resident's license upon conviction in another state

The Division may revoke the license of any resident of this State upon receiving notice of the person's conviction in another state of an offense set forth in G.S. 20-26(a).

History.
1935, c. 52, s. 17; 1971, c. 486, s. 2; 1975, c. 716, s. 5; 1979, c. 667, s. 22; 1993, c. 533, s. 6

§ 20-23.1. Suspending or revoking operating privilege of person not holding license

In any case where the Division would be authorized to suspend or revoke the license of a person but such person does not hold a license, the Division is authorized to suspend or revoke the operating privilege of such a person in like manner as it could suspend or revoke his license if such person held a driver's license, and the provisions of this Chapter governing suspensions, revocations, issuance of a license, and driving after license suspended or revoked, shall apply in the discretion of the Division in the same manner as if the license has been suspended or revoked.

History.
1955, c. 1187, s. 19; 1969, c. 186, s. 2; 1975, c. 716, s. 5; 1979, c. 667, s. 41

§ 20-23.2. Suspension of license for conviction of offense involving impaired driving in federal court

Upon receipt of notice of conviction in any court of the federal government of an offense involving impaired driving, the Division is authorized to revoke the driving privilege of the person convicted in the same manner as if the conviction had occurred in a court of this State.

History.
1969, c. 988; 1971, c. 619, s. 11; 1975, c. 716, s. 5; 1979, c. 903, s. 12; 1981, c. 412, s. 4; c. 747, s. 66; 1983, c. 435, s. 18

§ 20-24. When court or child support enforcement agency to forward license to Division and report convictions, child support delinquencies, and prayers for judgment continued

(a) **License.** -- A court that convicts a person of an offense that requires revocation of the person's drivers license or revokes a person's drivers license pursuant to G.S. 50-13.12 shall require the person to give the court any regular or commercial drivers license issued to that person. A court that convicts a person of an offense that requires disqualification of the person but would not require revocation of a regular drivers license issued to that person shall require the person to give the court any Class A or Class B regular drivers license and any commercial drivers license issued to that person.

The clerk of court in a non-IV-D case, and the child support enforcement agency in a IV-D case, shall accept a drivers license required to be given to the court under this subsection. A clerk of court or the child support enforcement agency who receives a drivers license shall give the person whose license is received a copy of a dated receipt for the license. The receipt must be on a form approved by the Commissioner. A revocation or disqualification for which a license is received under this subsection is effective as of the date on the receipt for the license.

The clerk of court or the child support enforcement agency shall notify the Division of a license received under this subsection either by forwarding to the Division the license, a record of the conviction for which the license was received, a copy of the court order revoking the license for failure to pay child support for which the license was received, and the original dated receipt for the license or by electronically sending to the Division the information on the license, the record of conviction or court order revoking the license for failure to pay child support, and the receipt given for the license. The clerk of court or the child support enforcement agency must forward the required items unless the Commissioner has given the clerk of court or the child support enforcement agency approval to notify the Division electronically. If the clerk of court or the child support enforcement agency notifies the Division electronically, the clerk of court or the child support enforcement agency must destroy a license received after sending to the Division the required information. The clerk of court or the child support enforcement agency shall notify the Division within 30 days after entry of the conviction or court order revoking the license for failure to pay child support for which the license was received.

(b) **Convictions, Court Orders of Drivers License Revocations, and PJCs.** -- The clerk of court shall send the Division a record of any of the following:

(1) A conviction of a violation of a law regulating the operation of a vehicle.

(2) A conviction for which the convicted person is placed on probation and a condition of probation is that the person not drive a motor vehicle for a period of time, stating the period of time for which the condition applies.

(3) A conviction of a felony in the commission of which a motor vehicle is used, when the judgment includes a finding that a motor vehicle was used in the commission of the felony.

(4) A conviction that requires revocation of the drivers license of the person convicted and is not otherwise reported under subdivision (1).

(4a) A court order revoking drivers license pursuant to G.S. 50-13.12.

(5) An order entering prayer for judgment continued in a case involving an alleged violation of a law regulating the operation of a vehicle.

The child support enforcement agency shall send the Division a record of any court order revoking drivers license pursuant to G.S. 110-142.2(a)(1).

With the approval of the Commissioner, the clerk of court or the child support enforcement agency may forward a record of conviction, court order revoking drivers license, or prayer for judgment continued to the Division by electronic data processing means.

(b1) In any case in which the Division, for any reason, does not receive a record of a conviction or a prayer for judgment continued until more than one year after the date it is entered, the Division may, in its discretion, substitute a period of probation for all or any part of a revocation or disqualification required because of the conviction or prayer for judgment continued.

(c) Repealed by Session Laws 1991, c. 726, s. 10.

(d) **Scope.** -- This Article governs drivers license revocation and disqualification. A drivers license may not be revoked and a person may not be disqualified except in accordance with this Article.

(e) **Special Information.** -- A judgment for a conviction for an offense for which special information is required under this subsection shall, when appropriate, include a finding of the special information. The convictions for which special information is required and the specific information required is as follows:

(1) **Homicide.** -- If a conviction of homicide involves impaired driving, the judgment must indicate that fact.

(2) G.S. 20-138.1, Driving While Impaired. -- If a conviction under G.S. 20-138.1 involves a commercial motor vehicle, the judgment must indicate that fact. If a conviction under G.S. 20-138.1 involves a commercial motor vehicle that was transporting a hazardous substance required to be placarded, the judgment must indicate that fact.

(3) G.S. 20-138.2, Driving Commercial Motor Vehicle While Impaired. -- If the commercial motor vehicle involved in an offense under G.S. 20-138.2 was transporting a hazardous material required to be placarded, a judgment for that offense must indicate that fact.

(4) G.S. 20-166, Hit and Run. -- If a conviction under G.S. 20-166 involves a commercial motor vehicle, the judgment must indicate that fact. If a conviction under G.S. 20-166 involves a commercial motor vehicle that was transporting a hazardous substance required to be placarded, the judgment must indicate that fact.

(5) **Felony Using Commercial Motor Vehicle.** -- If a conviction of a felony in which a commercial motor vehicle was used involves the manufacture, distribution, or dispensing of a controlled substance, or possession with intent to manufacture, distribute, or dispense a controlled substance, the judgment must indicate that fact. If a commercial motor vehicle used in a felony was transporting a hazardous substance required to be placarded, the judgment for that felony must indicate that fact.

History.

1935, c. 52, s. 18; 1949, c. 373, ss. 3, 4; 1955, c. 1187, s. 14; 1959, c. 47; 1965, c. 38; 1973, c. 19; 1975, cc. 46, 445; c. 716, s. 5; c. 871, s. 1; 1979, c. 667, s. 41; 1981, c. 416; c. 839; 1983, c. 294, s. 5; c. 435, s. 19; 1985, c. 764, s. 18; 1985 (Reg. Sess., 1986), c. 852, s. 17; 1987, c. 581, s. 1; c. 658, s. 2; 1989, c. 771, s. 10; 1991, c. 726, s. 10; 1993, c. 533, s. 7; 1995, c. 538, s. 2(c)

§ 20-24.1. Revocation for failure to appear or pay fine, penalty or costs for motor vehicle offenses

(a) The Division must revoke the driver's license of a person upon receipt of notice from a court that the person was charged with a motor vehicle offense and he:

(1) failed to appear, after being notified to do so, when the case was called for a trial or hearing; or

(2) failed to pay a fine, penalty, or court costs ordered by the court.

Revocation orders entered under the authority of this section are effective on the sixtieth day after the order is mailed or personally delivered to the person.

(b) A license revoked under this section remains revoked until the person whose license has been revoked:

(1) disposes of the charge in the trial division in which he failed to appear when the case was last called for trial or hearing; or

(2) demonstrates to the court that he is not the person charged with the offense; or

(3) pays the penalty, fine, or costs ordered by the court; or

(4) demonstrates to the court that his failure to pay the penalty, fine, or costs was not willful and that he is making a good faith effort to pay or that the penalty, fine, or costs should be remitted.

Upon receipt of notice from the court that the person has satisfied the conditions of this subsection applicable to his case, the Division must restore the person's license as provided in subsection (c). In addition, if the person whose license is revoked is not a resident of this State, the Division may notify the driver licensing agency in the person's state of residence that the person's license to drive in this State has been revoked.

(b1) A defendant must be afforded an opportunity for a trial or a hearing within a reasonable time of the defendant's appearance. Upon motion of a defendant, the court must order that a hearing or a trial be heard within a reasonable time.

(c) If the person satisfies the conditions of subsection (b) that are applicable to his case before the effective date of the revocation order, the revocation order and any entries on his driving record relating to it shall be deleted and the person does not have to pay the restoration fee set by G.S. 20-7(i1). For all other revocation orders issued pursuant to this section, G.S. 50-13.12 or G.S. 110-142.2, the person must pay the restoration fee and satisfy any other applicable requirements of this Article before the person may be relicensed.

(d) To facilitate the prompt return of licenses and to prevent unjustified charges of driving while license revoked, the clerk of court, upon request, must give the person a copy of the notice it sends to the Division to indicate that the person has complied with the conditions of subsection (b) applicable to his case. If the person complies with the condition before the effective date of the revocation, the notice must indicate that the person is eligible to drive if he is otherwise validly licensed.

(e) As used in this section and in G.S. 20-24.2, the word offense includes crimes and infractions created by this Chapter.

(f) If a license is revoked under subdivision (2) of subsection (a) of this section, and for no other reason, the person subject to the order may apply to the court for a limited driving privilege valid for up to one year or until any fine, penalty, or court costs ordered by the court are paid. The court may grant the limited driving privilege in the same manner and under the terms and conditions prescribed in G.S. 20-16.1. A person is eligible to apply for a limited driving privilege under this subsection only if the person has not had a limited driving privilege granted under this subsection within the three years prior to application.

History.
1985, c. 764, s. 19; 1985 (Reg. Sess., 1986), c. 852, ss. 4-6, 9, 17; 1987, c. 581, s. 4; 1991, c. 682, s. 4; 1993, c. 313, s. 1; 1995, c. 538, s. 2(d); 2020-77, s. 6.5(a)

§ 20-24.2. Court to report failure to appear or pay fine, penalty or costs

(a) The court must report to the Division the name of any person charged with a motor vehicle offense under this Chapter who:

(1) Fails to appear to answer the charge as scheduled, unless within 20 days after the scheduled appearance, he either appears in court to answer the charge or disposes of the charge pursuant to G.S. 7A-146; or

(2) Fails to pay a fine, penalty, or costs within 40 days of the date specified in the court's judgment.

(b) The reporting requirement of this section and the revocation mandated by G.S. 20-24.1 do not apply to offenses in which an order of forfeiture of a cash bond is entered and reported to the Division pursuant to G.S. 20-24. If an order is sent to the Division by the clerk through clerical mistake or other inadvertence, the clerk's office that sent the report of noncompliance must withdraw the report and send notice to the Division which shall correct its records accordingly.

History.
1985, c. 764, s. 3; 1985 (Reg. Sess., 1986), c. 852, ss. 3, 17; 1987, c. 581, s. 3; 1991, c. 682, s. 5; 2015-247, s. 1(b)

§ 20-25. Right of appeal to court

Any person denied a license or whose license has been canceled, suspended or revoked by the Division, except where such cancellation is mandatory under the provisions of this Article, shall have a right to file a petition within 30 days thereafter for a hearing in the matter in the superior court of the county wherein such person shall reside, or to the resident judge of the district or judge holding the court of that district, or special or emergency judge holding a court in such district in which the violation was committed, and such court or judge is hereby vested with jurisdiction and it shall be its or his duty to set the matter for hearing upon 30 days' written notice to the Division, and thereupon to take testimony and examine into the facts of the case, and to determine whether the petitioner is entitled to a license or is subject to suspension, cancellation or revocation of license under the provisions of this Article. Provided, a judge of the district court shall have limited jurisdiction under this section to sign and enter a temporary restraining order only.

History.

1935, c. 52, s. 19; 1975, c. 716, s. 5; 1987, c. 659, s. 1

§ 20-26. Records; copies furnished; charge

(a) The Division shall keep a record of all applications for a drivers license, all tests given an applicant for a drivers license, all applications for a drivers license that are denied, all drivers licenses issued, renewed, cancelled, or revoked, all disqualifications, all convictions affecting a drivers license, and all prayers for judgment continued that may lead to a license revocation. When the Division cancels or revokes a commercial drivers license or disqualifies a person, the Division shall update its records to reflect that action within 10 days after the cancellation, revocation, or disqualification becomes effective. When a person who is not a resident of this State is convicted of an offense or commits an act requiring revocation of the person's commercial drivers license or disqualification of the person, the Division shall notify the licensing authority of the person's state of residence.

The Division shall keep records of convictions occurring outside North Carolina for the offenses of exceeding a stated speed limit of 55 miles per hour or more by more than 15 miles per hour, driving while license suspended or revoked, careless and reckless driving, engaging in prearranged speed competition, engaging willfully in speed competition, hit-and-run driving resulting in damage to property, unlawfully passing a stopped school bus, illegal transportation of alcoholic beverages, and the offenses included in G.S. 20-17. The Division shall also keep records of convictions occurring outside North Carolina for any serious traffic violation that involves a commercial motor vehicle and is not otherwise required to be kept under this subsection.

(b) The Division shall furnish certified copies of license records required to be kept by subsection (a) of this section to State, county, municipal and court officials of this State for official use only, without charge. A certified copy of a driver's records kept pursuant to subsection (a) may be sent by the Police Information Network. In addition to the uses authorized by G.S. 8-35.1, a copy certified under the authority of this section is admissible as prima facie evidence of the status of the person's license. The Attorney General and the Commissioner of Motor Vehicles are authorized to promulgate such rules and regulations as may be necessary to implement the provision of this subsection.

(b1) The registered or declared weight set forth on the vehicle registration card or a certified copy of the Division record sent by the Department of Public Safety or otherwise is admissible in any judicial or administrative proceeding and shall be prima facie evidence of the registered or declared weight.

(c) The Division shall furnish copies of license records required to be kept by subsection (a) of this section in accordance with G.S. 20-43.1 to other persons for uses other than official upon prepayment of the following fees:

(1) Limited extract copy of license record, for period up to three years ... $ 10.00

(2) Complete extract copy of license record 10.00

(3) Certified true copy of complete license record ....14.00.

All fees received by the Division under this subsection shall be credited to the Highway Fund.

(d) The charge for records provided pursuant to this section shall not be subject to the provisions of Chapter 132 of the General Statutes.

(e) In the event of a mistake on the part of any person in ordering license records under subsection (c) of this section, the Commissioner may refund or credit to that person up to sixty-five percent (65%) of the amount paid for the license records.

(f) On and after July 1, 1988, the Division shall expeditiously furnish to insurance agents, insurance companies, and to insurance support organizations as defined in G.S. 58-39-15(12), for the purpose of rating nonfleet private passenger motor vehicle insurance policies, through electronic data processing means or otherwise, copies of or information pertaining to license records that are required to be kept pursuant to subsection (a) of this section.

History.

1935, c. 52, s. 20; 1961, c. 307; 1969, c. 783, s. 3; 1971, c. 486, s. 1; 1975, c. 716, s. 5; 1979, c. 667, s. 23; c. 903, ss. 9, 10; 1981, c. 145, s. 1; c. 412, s. 4; c. 690, s. 13; c. 747, s. 66; 1983, c. 435, s. 20; c. 761, s. 149; 1987, c. 869, s. 16; 1987 (Reg. Sess., 1988), c. 1112, ss. 14, 17; 1989, c. 771, ss. 9, 17, 18; 1991, c. 689, s. 330; c. 726, s. 11; 1997-443, s. 32.25(b); 2005-276, s. 44.1(e); 2014-100, s. 17.1(q); 2015-241, s. 29.30(e)

§ 20-27. Availability of records

(a) All records of the Division pertaining to application and to drivers' licenses, except the confidential medical report referred to in G.S. 20-7, of the current or previous five years shall be open to public inspection in accordance with G.S. 20-43.1, at any reasonable time during office hours and copies shall be provided pursuant to the provisions of G.S. 20-26.

(b) All records of the Division pertaining to chemical tests as provided in G.S. 20-16.2 shall be available to the courts as provided in G.S. 20-26(b).

History.

1935, c. 52, s. 21; 1975, c. 716, s. 5; 1979, c. 667, s. 24; c. 903, s. 11; 1981, c. 145, s. 2; 1997-443, s. 32.25(c)

§ 20-27.1. Unlawful for sex offender to drive commercial passenger vehicle or school bus without appropriate commercial license or while disqualified

A person who drives a commercial passenger vehicle or a school bus and who does not have a valid commercial drivers license with a P or S endorsement because the person was convicted of a violation that requires registration under Article 27A of Chapter 14 of the General Statutes is guilty of a Class F felony.

History.
2009-491, s. 4

§ 20-28. Unlawful to drive while license revoked, after notification, or while disqualified

(a) **Driving While License Revoked.** -- Except as provided in subsections (a1) or (a2) of this section, any person whose drivers license has been revoked who drives any motor vehicle upon the highways of the State while the license is revoked is guilty of a Class 3 misdemeanor.

(a1) **Driving While License Revoked for Impaired Driving.** -- Any person whose drivers license has been revoked for an impaired driving revocation as defined in G.S. 20-28.2(a) and who drives any motor vehicle upon the highways of the State is guilty of a Class 1 misdemeanor. Upon conviction, the person's license shall be revoked for an additional period of one year for the first offense, two years for the second offense, and permanently for a third or subsequent offense.

If the person's license was originally revoked for an impaired driving revocation, the court may order as a condition of probation that the offender abstain from alcohol consumption and verify compliance by use of a continuous alcohol monitoring system, of a type approved by the Division of Adult Correction and Juvenile Justice of the Department of Public Safety, for a minimum period of 90 days.

The restoree of a revoked drivers license who operates a motor vehicle upon the highways of the State without maintaining financial responsibility as provided by law shall be punished as for driving without a license.

(a2) **Driving Without Reclaiming License.** -- A person convicted under subsection (a) or (a1) of this section shall be punished as if the person had been convicted of driving without a license under G.S. 20-35 if the person demonstrates to the court that either of the following is true:

(1) At the time of the offense, the person's license was revoked solely under G.S. 20-16.5 and one of the following applies:

a. The offense occurred more than 45 days after the effective date of a revocation order issued under G.S. 20-16.5(f) and the period of revocation was 45 days as provided under subdivision (3) of that subsection; or

b. The offense occurred more than 30 days after the effective date of the revocation order issued under any other provision of G.S. 20-16.5.

(2) At the time of the offense the person had met the requirements of G.S. 50-13.12, or G.S. 110-142.2 and was eligible for reinstatement of the person's drivers license privilege as provided therein.

In addition, a person punished under this subsection shall be treated for drivers license and insurance rating purposes as if the person had been convicted of driving without a license under G.S. 20-35, and the conviction report sent to the Division must indicate that the person is to be so treated.

(a3) **Driving After Notification or Failure to Appear.** -- A person shall be guilty of a Class 1 misdemeanor if:

(1) The person operates a motor vehicle upon a highway while that person's license is revoked for an impaired drivers license revocation after the Division has sent notification in accordance with G.S. 20-48; or

(2) The person fails to appear for two years from the date of the charge after being charged with an implied-consent offense.

Upon conviction, the person's drivers license shall be revoked for an additional period of one year for the first offense, two years for the second offense, and permanently for a third or subsequent offense. The restoree of a revoked drivers license who operates a motor vehicle upon the highways of the State without maintaining financial responsibility as provided by law shall be punished as for driving without a license.

(b) Repealed by Session Laws 1993 (Reg. Sess., 1994), c. 761, s. 3.

(c) **When Person May Apply for License.** -- A person whose license has been revoked may apply for a license as follows:

(1) If revoked under subsection (a1) of this section for one year, the person may apply for a license after 90 days.

(2) If punished under subsection (a2) of this section and the original revocation was pursuant to G.S. 20-16.5, in order to obtain reinstatement of a drivers license, the person must obtain a substance abuse assessment and show proof of financial responsibility to the Division. If the assessment recommends education or treatment, the person must complete the education or treatment within the time limits specified by the Division.

(3) If revoked under subsection (a3) of this section for one year, the person may apply for a license after one year.

(4) If revoked under this section for two years, the person may apply for a license after one year.

(5) If revoked under this section permanently, the person may apply for a license after three years.

(c1) Upon the filing of an application the Division may, with or without a hearing, issue a new license upon satisfactory proof that the former licensee has not been convicted of a moving violation under this Chapter or the laws of another state, a violation of any provision of the alcoholic beverage laws of this State or another state, or a violation of any provisions of the drug laws of this State or another state when any of these violations occurred during the revocation period. For purposes of this subsection, a violation of subsection (a) of this section shall not be considered a moving violation.

(c2) The Division may impose any restrictions or conditions on the new license that the Division considers appropriate for the balance of the revocation period. When the revocation period is permanent, the restrictions and conditions imposed by the Division may not exceed three years.

(c3) A person whose license is revoked for violation of subsection (a1) of this section where the person's license was originally revoked for an impaired driving revocation, or a person whose license is revoked for a violation of subsection (a3) of this section, may only have the license conditionally restored by the Division pursuant to the provisions of subsection (c4) of this section.

(c4) For a conditional restoration under subsection (c3) of this section, the Division shall require at a minimum that the driver obtain a substance abuse assessment prior to issuance of a license and show proof of financial

responsibility. If the substance abuse assessment recommends education or treatment, the person must complete the education or treatment within the time limits specified. If the assessment determines that the person abuses alcohol, the Division shall require the person to install and use an ignition interlock system on any vehicles that are to be driven by that person for the period of time that the conditional restoration is active.

(c5) For licenses conditionally restored pursuant to subsections (c3) and (c4) of this section, the Division shall cancel the license and impose the remaining revocation period if any of the following occur:

(1) The person violates any condition of the restoration.

(2) The person is convicted of any moving offense in this or another state.

(3) The person is convicted for a violation of the alcoholic beverage or controlled substance laws of this or any other state.

(d) **Driving While Disqualified.** -- A person who was convicted of a violation that disqualified the person and required the person's drivers license to be revoked who drives a motor vehicle during the revocation period is punishable as provided in subsection (a1) of this section. A person who has been disqualified who drives a commercial motor vehicle during the disqualification period is guilty of a Class 1 misdemeanor and is disqualified for an additional period as follows:

(1) For a first offense of driving while disqualified, a person is disqualified for a period equal to the period for which the person was disqualified when the offense occurred.

(2) For a second offense of driving while disqualified, a person is disqualified for a period equal to two times the period for which the person was disqualified when the offense occurred.

(3) For a third offense of driving while disqualified, a person is disqualified for life.

The Division may reduce a disqualification for life under this subsection to 10 years in accordance with the guidelines adopted under G.S. 20-17.4(b). A person who drives a commercial motor vehicle while the person is disqualified and the person's drivers license is revoked is punishable for both driving while the person's license was revoked and driving while disqualified.

History.
1935, c. 52, s. 22; 1945, c. 635; 1947, c. 1067, s. 16; 1955, c. 1020, s. 1; c. 1152, s. 18; c. 1187, s. 20; 1957, c. 1046; 1959, c. 515; 1967, c. 447; 1973, c. 47, s. 2; cc. 71, 1132; 1975, c. 716, s. 5; 1979, c 377, ss. 1, 2; c. 667, s. 41; 1981, c. 412, s. 4; c. 747, s. 66; 1983, c. 51; 1983

(Reg. Sess., 1984), c. 1101, s. 18A; 1989, c. 771, s. 4; 1991, c. 509, s. 2; c. 726, s. 12; 1993, c. 539, ss. 320 -322; 1994, Ex. Sess., c. 24, s. 14(c); 1993 (Reg. Sess., 1994), c. 761, ss. 2, 3; 1995, c. 538, s. 2(e), (f); 2002-159, s. 6; 2006-253, s. 22.1; 2007-493, ss. 4, 19; 2012-146, s. 8; 2013-360, s. 18B.14(f); 2015-186, s. 2; 2015-264, ss. 38(a), 86; 2017-186, s. 2 (kkkk)

§ 20-28.1. Conviction of moving offense committed while driving during period of suspension or revocation of license

(a) Upon receipt of notice of conviction of any person of a motor vehicle moving offense, such offense having been committed while such person's driving privilege was in a state of suspension or revocation, the Division shall revoke such person's driving privilege for an additional period of time as set forth in subsection (b) hereof. For purposes of this section a violation of G.S. 20-7(a), 20-24.1, or 20-28(a) or (a2) shall not be considered a "motor vehicle moving offense" unless the offense occurred in a commercial motor vehicle or the person held a commercial drivers license at the time of the offense.

(b) When a driving privilege is subject to revocation under this section, the additional period of revocation shall be as follows:

(1) A first such revocation shall be for one year;

(2) A second such revocation shall be for two years; and

(3) A third or subsequent such revocation shall be permanent.

(c) A person whose license has been revoked under this section for one year may apply for a license after 90 days. A person whose license has been revoked under this section for two years may apply for a license after 12 months. A person whose license has been revoked under this section permanently may apply for a license after three years. Upon the filing of an application, the Division may, with or without a hearing, issue a new license upon satisfactory proof that the former licensee has not been convicted of a moving violation under this Chapter or the laws of another state, or a violation of any provision of the alcoholic beverage laws of this State or another state, or a violation of any provision of the drug laws of this State or another state when any of these violations occurred during the revocation period. The Division may impose any restrictions or conditions on the new license that the Division considers appropriate for the balance of the revocation period. When the revocation period is permanent, the restrictions and conditions imposed by the Division may not exceed three years.

(d) Repealed by Session Laws 1979, c. 378, s. 2.

History.
1965, c. 286; 1969, c. 348; 1971, c. 163; 1973, c. 47, s. 2; 1975, c. 716, s. 5; 1979, c. 378, ss. 1, 2; 1981, c. 412, s. 4; c. 747, s. 66; 1991, c. 509, s. 1; c. 682, s. 6; c. 726, s. 22.1; 2015-186, s. 3; 2015-264, s. 86

§ 20-28.2. Forfeiture of motor vehicle for impaired driving after impaired driving license revocation; forfeiture for felony speeding to elude arrest

(a) **Meaning of "Impaired Driving License Revocation".** -- The revocation of a person's drivers license is an impaired driving license revocation if the revocation is pursuant to:

(1) G.S. 20-13.2, 20-16(a)(8b), 20-16.2, 20-16.5, 20-17(a)(2), 20-17(a)(12), or 20-138.5; or

(2) G.S. 20-16(a)(7), 20-17(a)(1), 20-17(a)(3), 20-17(a)(9), or 20-17(a)(11), if the offense involves impaired driving; or

(3) The laws of another state and the offense for which the person's license is revoked prohibits substantially similar conduct which if committed in this State would result in a revocation listed in subdivisions (1) or (2).

(a1) **Definitions.** -- As used in this section and in G.S. 20-28.3, 20-28.4, 20-28.5, 20-28.7, 20-28.8, 20-28.9, 20-54.1, and 20-141.5, the following terms mean:

(1) **Fair Market Value.** -- The value of the seized motor vehicle, as determined in accordance with the schedule of values adopted by the Commissioner pursuant to G.S. 105-187.3.

(1a) **Impaired Driving Acknowledgment.** -- A written document acknowledging that:

a. The motor vehicle was operated by a person charged with an offense involving impaired driving, and:

1. That person's drivers license was revoked as a result of a prior impaired drivers license revocation; or

2. That person did not have a valid drivers license, and did not have liability insurance.

b. If the motor vehicle is again operated by this particular person, and the person is charged with an offense involving impaired driving, then the vehicle is subject to impoundment and forfeiture if (i) the offense occurs while that person's drivers license is revoked, or (ii) the offense occurs while the person has no valid drivers license, and has no liability insurance.

c. A lack of knowledge or consent to the operation will not be a defense in

Chapter 20

the future, unless the motor vehicle owner has taken all reasonable precautions to prevent the use of the motor vehicle by this particular person and immediately reports, upon discovery, any unauthorized use to the appropriate law enforcement agency.

(2) **Innocent Owner.** -- A motor vehicle owner:

a. Who, if the offense resulting in seizure was an impaired driving offense, did not know and had no reason to know that (i) the defendant's drivers license was revoked, or (ii) that the defendant did not have a valid drivers license, and that the defendant had no liability insurance; or

b. Who, if the offense resulting in seizure was an impaired driving offense, knew that (i) the defendant's drivers license was revoked, or (ii) that the defendant had no valid drivers license, and that the defendant had no liability insurance, but the defendant drove the vehicle without the person's expressed or implied permission, and the owner files a police report for unauthorized use of the motor vehicle and agrees to prosecute the unauthorized operator of the motor vehicle, or who, if the offense resulting in seizure was a felony speeding to elude arrest offense, did not give the defendant express or implied permission to drive the vehicle, and the owner files a police report for unauthorized use of the motor vehicle and agrees to prosecute the unauthorized operator of the motor vehicle; or

c. Whose vehicle was reported stolen; or

d. Repealed by Session Laws 1999-406, s. 17.

e. Who is (i) a rental car company as defined in G.S. 66-201(a) and the vehicle was driven by a person who is not listed as an authorized driver on the rental agreement as defined in G.S. 66-201; or (ii) a rental car company as defined in G.S. 66-201(a) and the vehicle was driven by a person who is listed as an authorized driver on the rental agreement as defined in G.S. 66-201 and if the offense resulting in seizure was an impaired driving offense, the rental car company has no actual knowledge of the revocation of the renter's drivers' license at the time the rental agreement is entered, or if the offense resulting in seizure was a felony speeding to elude arrest offense, the rental agreement expressly

prohibits use of the vehicle while committing a felony; or

f. Who is in the business of leasing motor vehicles, who holds legal title to the motor vehicle as a lessor at the time of seizure and, if the offense resulting in seizure was an impaired driving offense, who has no actual knowledge of the revocation of the lessee's drivers license at the time the lease is entered.

(2a) **Insurance Company.** -- Any insurance company that has coverage on or is otherwise liable for repairs or damages to the motor vehicle at the time of the seizure.

(2b) **Insurance Proceeds.** -- Proceeds paid under an insurance policy for damage to a seized motor vehicle less any payments actually paid to valid lienholders and for towing and storage costs incurred for the motor vehicle after the time the motor vehicle became subject to seizure.

(3) **Lienholder.** -- A person who holds a perfected security interest in a motor vehicle at the time of seizure.

(3a) **Motor Vehicle Owner.** -- A person in whose name a registration card or certificate of title for a motor vehicle is issued at the time of seizure.

(4) **Order of Forfeiture.** -- An order by the court which terminates the rights and ownership interest of a motor vehicle owner in a motor vehicle and any insurance proceeds or proceeds of sale in accordance with G.S. 20-28.2.

(5) Repealed by Session Laws 1998-182, s. 2.

(6) **Registered Owner.** -- A person in whose name a registration card for a motor vehicle is issued at the time of seizure.

(7) Repealed by Session Laws 1998-182, s. 2.

(8) **Speeding to Elude Arrest Acknowledgment.** -- A written document acknowledging that:

a. The motor vehicle was operated by a person charged with felony speeding to elude arrest pursuant to G.S. 20-141.5(b) or (b1).

b. If the motor vehicle is again operated by this particular person and the person is charged with felony speeding to elude arrest pursuant to G.S. 20-141.5(b) or (b1), then the vehicle is subject to impoundment and forfeiture.

c. A lack of knowledge or consent to the operation will not be a defense in the future unless the motor vehicle owner has taken all reasonable precautions to prevent the use of the motor vehicle by this particular person and immediately reports upon discovery

Chapter 20

any unauthorized use to the appropriate law enforcement agency.

(9) **State Surplus Property Agency.** -- The Department of Administration.

(b) **When Motor Vehicle Becomes Property Subject to Order of Forfeiture; Impaired Driving and Prior Revocation.** -- A judge may determine whether the vehicle driven by an impaired driver at the time of the offense becomes subject to an order of forfeiture. The determination may be made at any of the following times:

(1) A sentencing hearing for the underlying offense involving impaired driving.

(2) A separate hearing after conviction of the defendant.

(3) A forfeiture hearing held at least 60 days after the defendant failed to appear at the scheduled trial for the underlying offense, and the defendant's order of arrest for failing to appear has not been set aside.

The vehicle shall become subject to an order of forfeiture if the greater weight of the evidence shows that the defendant is guilty of an offense involving impaired driving, and that the defendant's license was revoked pursuant to an impaired driving license revocation as defined in subsection (a) of this section.

(b1) **When a Motor Vehicle Becomes Property Subject to Order of Forfeiture; No License and No Insurance.** -- A judge may determine whether the vehicle driven by an impaired driver at the time of the offense becomes subject to an order of forfeiture. The determination may be made at any of the following times:

(1) A sentencing hearing for the underlying offense involving impaired driving.

(2) A separate hearing after conviction of the defendant.

(3) A forfeiture hearing held at least 60 days after the defendant failed to appear at the scheduled trial for the underlying offense, and the defendant's order of arrest for failing to appear has not been set aside.

The vehicle shall become subject to an order of forfeiture if the greater weight of the evidence shows that the defendant is guilty of an offense involving impaired driving, and: (i) the defendant was driving without a valid drivers license, and (ii) the defendant was not covered by an automobile liability policy.

(b2) **When a Motor Vehicle Becomes Property Subject to Order of Forfeiture; Felony Speeding to Elude Arrest.** -- A judge may determine whether the vehicle driven at the time of the offense becomes subject to an order of forfeiture. The determination may be made at any of the following times:

(1) A sentencing hearing for the underlying felony speeding to elude arrest offense.

(2) A separate hearing after conviction of the defendant.

(3) A forfeiture hearing held at least 60 days after the defendant failed to appear at the scheduled trial for the underlying offense, and the defendant's order of arrest for failing to appear has not been set aside.

The vehicle shall become subject to an order of forfeiture if the greater weight of the evidence shows that the defendant is guilty of felony speeding to elude arrest pursuant to G.S. 20-141.5(b) or (b1).

(c) **Duty of Prosecutor to Notify Possible Innocent Parties.** -- In any case in which a prosecutor determines that a motor vehicle driven by a defendant may be subject to forfeiture under this section and the motor vehicle has not been permanently released to a nondefendant vehicle owner pursuant to G.S. 20-28.3(e1), a defendant owner pursuant to G.S. 20-28.3(e2), or a lienholder, pursuant to G.S. 20-28.3(e3), the prosecutor shall notify the defendant, each motor vehicle owner, and each lienholder that the motor vehicle may be subject to forfeiture and that the defendant, motor vehicle owner, or the lienholder may intervene to protect that person's interest. The notice may be served by any means reasonably likely to provide actual notice, and shall be served at least 10 days before the hearing at which an order of forfeiture may be entered.

(c1) **Motor Vehicles Involved in Accidents.** -- If a motor vehicle subject to forfeiture was damaged while the defendant operator was committing the underlying offense resulting in seizure, or was damaged incident to the seizure of the motor vehicle, the Division shall determine the name of any insurance companies that are the insurers of record with the Division for the motor vehicle at the time of the seizure or that may otherwise be liable for repair to the motor vehicle. In any case where a seized motor vehicle was involved in an accident, the Division shall notify the insurance companies that the claim for insurance proceeds for damage to the seized motor vehicle shall be paid to the clerk of superior court of the county where the motor vehicle driver was charged to be held and disbursed pursuant to further orders of the court. Any insurance company that receives written or other actual notice of seizure pursuant to this section shall not be relieved of any legal obligation under any contract of insurance unless the claim for property damage to the seized motor vehicle minus the policy owner's deductible is paid directly to the clerk of court. The insurance company paying insurance proceeds to the clerk of court pursuant to this section shall be immune from suit by the motor vehicle owner for any damages alleged to have occurred as a result of the motor vehicle seizure. The proceeds shall be held by the clerk.

Chapter 20

The clerk shall disburse the insurance proceeds pursuant to further orders of the court.

(d) **Forfeiture Hearing.** -- Unless a motor vehicle that has been seized pursuant to G.S. 20-28.3 has been permanently released to an innocent owner pursuant to G.S. 20-28.3(e1), a defendant owner pursuant to G.S. 20-28.3(e2), or to a lienholder pursuant to G.S. 20-28.3(e3), the court shall conduct a hearing on the forfeiture of the motor vehicle. The hearing may be held at the sentencing hearing on the underlying offense resulting in seizure, at a separate hearing after conviction of the defendant, or at a separate forfeiture hearing held not less than 60 days after the defendant failed to appear at the scheduled trial for the underlying offense and the defendant's order of arrest for failing to appear has not been set aside. If at the forfeiture hearing, the judge determines that the motor vehicle is subject to forfeiture pursuant to this section and proper notice of the hearing has been given, the judge shall order the motor vehicle forfeited. If at the sentencing hearing or at a forfeiture hearing, the judge determines that the motor vehicle is subject to forfeiture pursuant to this section and proper notice of the hearing has been given, the judge shall order the motor vehicle forfeited unless another motor vehicle owner establishes, by the greater weight of the evidence, that such motor vehicle owner is an innocent owner as defined in this section, in which case the trial judge shall order the motor vehicle released to the innocent owner pursuant to the provisions of subsection (e) of this section. In any case where the motor vehicle is ordered forfeited, the judge shall:

(1) a. Authorize the sale of the motor vehicle at public sale or allow the county board of education to retain the motor vehicle for its own use pursuant to G.S. 20-28.5; or

b. Order the motor vehicle released to a lienholder pursuant to the provisions of subsection (f) of this section; and

(2) a. Order any proceeds of sale or insurance proceeds held by the clerk of court to be disbursed to the county board of education; and

b. Order any outstanding insurance claims be assigned to the county board of education in the event the motor vehicle has been damaged in an accident incident to the seizure of the motor vehicle.

If the judge determines that the motor vehicle is subject to forfeiture pursuant to this section, but that notice as required by subsection (c) has not been given, the judge shall continue the forfeiture proceeding until adequate notice has been given. In no circumstance shall the sentencing of the defendant be delayed as a result of the failure of the prosecutor to give adequate notice.

(e) **Release of Vehicle to Innocent Motor Vehicle Owner.** -- At a forfeiture hearing, if a nondefendant motor vehicle owner establishes by the greater weight of the evidence that: (i) the motor vehicle was being driven by a person who was not the only motor vehicle owner or had no ownership interest in the motor vehicle at the time of the underlying offense and (ii) the petitioner is an "innocent owner", as defined by this section, a judge shall order the motor vehicle released to that owner, conditioned upon payment of all towing and storage charges incurred as a result of the seizure and impoundment of the motor vehicle.

Release to an innocent owner shall only be ordered upon satisfactory proof of:

(1) The identity of the person as a motor vehicle owner;

(2) The existence of financial responsibility to the extent required by Article 13 of this Chapter or by the laws of the state in which the vehicle is registered; and

(3) Repealed by Session Laws 1998-182, s. 2, effective December 1, 1998.

(4) The execution of:

a. An impaired driving acknowledgment as defined in subdivision (a1)(1a) of this section if the seizure was for an offense involving impaired driving; or

b. A speeding to elude arrest acknowledgment as defined in subdivision (a1)(8) of this section if the seizure was for violation of G.S. 20-141.5(b) or (b1).

If the nondefendant owner is a lessor, the release shall also be conditioned upon the lessor agreeing not to sell, give, or otherwise transfer possession of the forfeited motor vehicle to the defendant or any person acting on the defendant's behalf. A lessor who refuses to sell, give, or transfer possession of a seized motor vehicle to the defendant or any person acting on the behalf of the defendant shall not be liable for damages arising out of the refusal.

No motor vehicle subject to forfeiture under this section shall be released to a nondefendant motor vehicle owner if the records of the Division indicate the motor vehicle owner had previously signed an impaired driving acknowledgment or a speeding to elude arrest acknowledgment, as required by this section, and the same person was operating the motor vehicle at the time of the current seizure unless the innocent owner shows by the greater weight of the evidence that the motor vehicle

Chapter 20

owner has taken all reasonable precautions to prevent the use of the motor vehicle by this particular person and immediately reports, upon discovery, any unauthorized use to the appropriate law enforcement agency. A determination by the court at the forfeiture hearing held pursuant to subsection (d) of this section that the petitioner is not an innocent owner is a final judgment and is immediately appealable to the Court of Appeals.

(f) **Release to Lienholder.** -- At a forfeiture hearing, the trial judge shall order a forfeited motor vehicle released to the lienholder upon payment of all towing and storage charges incurred as a result of the seizure of the motor vehicle if the judge determines, by the greater weight of the evidence, that:

(1) The lienholder's interest has been perfected and appears on the title to the forfeited vehicle;

(2) The lienholder agrees not to sell, give, or otherwise transfer possession of the forfeited motor vehicle to the defendant or to the motor vehicle owner who owned the motor vehicle immediately prior to forfeiture, or any person acting on the defendant's or motor vehicle owner's behalf;

(3) The forfeited motor vehicle had not previously been released to the lienholder;

(4) The owner is in default under the terms of the security instrument evidencing the interest of the lienholder and as a consequence of the default the lienholder is entitled to possession of the motor vehicle; and

(5) The lienholder agrees to sell the motor vehicle in accordance with the terms of its agreement and pursuant to the provisions of Part 6 of Article 9 of Chapter 25 of the General Statutes. Upon the sale of the motor vehicle, the lienholder will pay to the clerk of court of the county in which the vehicle was forfeited all proceeds from the sale, less the amount of the lien in favor of the lienholder, and any towing and storage costs paid by the lienholder.

A lienholder who refuses to sell, give, or transfer possession of a forfeited motor vehicle to the defendant, the vehicle owner who owned the motor vehicle immediately prior to forfeiture, or any person acting on the behalf of the defendant or motor vehicle owner shall not be liable for damages arising out of such refusal. The defendant, the motor vehicle owner who owned the motor vehicle immediately prior to forfeiture, and any person acting on the defendant's or motor vehicle owner's behalf are prohibited from purchasing the motor vehicle at any sale conducted by the lienholder.

(g) Repealed by Session Laws 1998-182, s. 2, effective December 1, 1998.

(h) Any order issued pursuant to this section authorizing the release of a seized vehicle shall require the payment of all towing and storage charges incurred as a result of the seizure and impoundment of the motor vehicle. This requirement shall not be waived.

History.
1983, c. 435, s. 21; 1983 (Reg. Sess., 1984), c. 1101, s. 19; 1989 (Reg. Sess., 1990), c. 1024, s. 6; 1997-379, s. 1.1; 1997-456, s. 30; 1998-182, s. 2; 1999-406, ss. 11, 12, 17; 2000-169, s. 28; 2001-362, s. 7; 2006-253, s. 31; 2007-493, ss. 7, 8, 21; 2013-243, s. 1; 2013-410, s. 18(a); 2015-241, s. 27.3(a)

§ 20-28.3. Seizure, impoundment, forfeiture of motor vehicles for offenses involving impaired driving while license revoked or without license and insurance, and for felony speeding to elude arrest

(a) **Motor Vehicles Subject to Seizure for Impaired Driving Offenses.** -- A motor vehicle that is driven by a person who is charged with an offense involving impaired driving is subject to seizure if:

(1) At the time of the violation, the drivers license of the person driving the motor vehicle was revoked as a result of a prior impaired driving license revocation as defined in G.S. 20-28.2(a); or

(2) At the time of the violation:

a. The person was driving without a valid drivers license, and

b. The driver was not covered by an automobile liability policy.

For the purposes of this subsection, a person who has a complete defense, pursuant to G.S. 20-35, to a charge of driving without a drivers license, shall be considered to have had a valid drivers license at the time of the violation.

(a1) **Motor Vehicles Subject to Seizure for Felony Speeding to Elude Arrest.** -- A motor vehicle is subject to seizure if it is driven by a person who is charged with the offense of felony speeding to elude arrest pursuant to G.S. 20-141.5(b) or (b1).

(b) **Duty of Officer.** -- If the charging officer has probable cause to believe that a motor vehicle driven by the defendant may be subject to forfeiture under this section, the officer shall seize the motor vehicle and have it impounded. If the officer determines prior to seizure that the motor vehicle had been reported stolen, the officer shall not seize the motor vehicle pursuant to this section. If the officer determines prior to seizure that the motor vehicle was a rental vehicle driven by a person not listed as an authorized driver on the rental contract, the

Chapter 20

officer shall not seize the motor vehicle pursuant to this section, but shall make a reasonable effort to notify the owner of the rental vehicle that the vehicle was stopped and that the driver of the vehicle was not listed as an authorized driver on the rental contract. Probable cause may be based on the officer's personal knowledge, reliable information conveyed by another officer, records of the Division, or other reliable sources. The seizing officer shall notify the Division as soon as practical but no later than 24 hours after seizure of the motor vehicle of the seizure in accordance with procedures established by the Division.

(b1) **Written Notification of Impoundment. --** Within 48 hours of receipt within regular business hours of the notice of seizure, the Division shall issue written notification of impoundment to any lienholder of record and to any motor vehicle owner who was not operating the motor vehicle at the time of the offense. A notice of seizure received outside regular business hours shall be considered to have been received at the start of the next business day. The notification of impoundment shall be sent by first-class mail to the most recent address contained in the Division's records. If the motor vehicle is registered in another state, notice shall be sent to the address shown on the records of the state where the motor vehicle is registered. This written notification shall provide notice that the motor vehicle has been seized, state the reason for the seizure and the procedure for requesting release of the motor vehicle. Additionally, if the motor vehicle was damaged while the operator was committing an offense resulting in seizure or incident to the seizure, the Division shall issue written notification of the seizure to the owner's insurance company of record and to any other insurance companies that may be insuring other motor vehicles involved in the accident. The Division shall prohibit title to a seized motor vehicle from being transferred by a motor vehicle owner unless authorized by court order.

(b2) **Additional Notification to Lienholders. --** In addition to providing written notification pursuant to subsection (b1) of this section, within eight hours of receipt within regular business hours of the notice of seizure, the Division shall notify by facsimile any lienholder of record that has provided the Division with a designated facsimile number for notification of impoundment. The facsimile notification of impoundment shall state that the vehicle has been seized, state the reason for the seizure, and notify the lienholder of the additional written notification that will be provided pursuant to subsection (b1) of this section. The Division shall establish procedures to allow a lienholder to provide one designated facsimile number for notification of impoundment for any vehicle for which the lienholder is a lienholder of record

and shall maintain a centralized database of the provided facsimile numbers. The lienholder must provide a facsimile number at which the Division may give notification of impoundment at anytime.

(c) **Review by Magistrate. --** Upon determining that there is probable cause for seizing a motor vehicle, the seizing officer shall present to a magistrate within the county where the driver was charged an affidavit of impoundment setting forth the basis upon which the motor vehicle has been or will be seized for forfeiture. The magistrate shall review the affidavit of impoundment and if the magistrate determines the requirements of this section have been met, shall order the motor vehicle held. The magistrate may request additional information and may hear from the defendant if the defendant is present. If the magistrate determines the requirements of this section have not been met, the magistrate shall order the motor vehicle released to a motor vehicle owner upon payment of towing and storage fees. If the motor vehicle has not yet been seized, and the magistrate determines that seizure is appropriate, the magistrate shall issue an order of seizure of the motor vehicle. The magistrate shall provide a copy of the order of seizure to the clerk of court. The clerk shall provide copies of the order of seizure to the district attorney and the attorney for the county board of education.

(c1) **Effecting an Order of Seizure. --** An order of seizure shall be valid anywhere in the State. Any officer with territorial jurisdiction and who has subject matter jurisdiction for violations of this Chapter may use such force as may be reasonable to seize the motor vehicle and to enter upon the property of the defendant to accomplish the seizure. An officer who has probable cause to believe the motor vehicle is concealed or stored on private property of a person other than the defendant may obtain a search warrant to enter upon that property for the purpose of seizing the motor vehicle.

(d) **Custody of Motor Vehicle. --** Unless the motor vehicle is towed pursuant to a statewide or regional contract, or a contract with the county board of education, the seized motor vehicle shall be towed by a commercial towing company designated by the law enforcement agency that seized the motor vehicle. Seized motor vehicles not towed pursuant to a statewide or regional contract or a contract with a county board of education shall be retrieved from the commercial towing company within a reasonable time, not to exceed 10 business days, by the county board of education or their agent who must pay towing and storage fees to the commercial towing company when the motor vehicle is retrieved. If either a statewide or regional contractor, or the county board of education, chooses to contract for local towing services, all towing companies on the towing list for each law enforcement agency with jurisdiction within the county shall be given written notice and an opportunity to submit proposals prior to a contract for local towing services being awarded. The seized motor vehicle is under the constructive possession of the county board of education for the county in which the operator of the vehicle is charged at the time the vehicle is delivered to a location designated by the county board of education or delivered to its agent pending release or sale, or in the event a statewide or regional contract is in place, under the constructive possession of the State Surplus Property Agency on behalf of the State at the time the vehicle is delivered to a location designated by the State Surplus Property Agency or delivered to its agent pending release or sale. Absent a statewide or regional contract that provides otherwise, each county board of education may elect to have seized motor vehicles stored on property owned or leased by the county board of education and charge a reasonable fee for storage, not to exceed ten dollars ($ 10.00) per calendar day. In the alternative, the county board of education may contract with a commercial towing and storage facility or other private entity for the towing, storage, and disposal of seized motor vehicles, and a storage fee of not more than ten dollars ($ 10.00) per calendar day may be charged. Except for gross negligence or intentional misconduct, neither the State Surplus Property Agency, the county board of education, nor any of their employees, shall be liable to the owner or lienholder for damage to or loss of the motor vehicle or its contents, or to the owner of personal property in a seized vehicle, during the time the motor vehicle is being towed or stored pursuant to this subsection.

(e) **Release of Motor Vehicle Pending Trial.** -- A motor vehicle owner, other than the driver at the time of the underlying offense resulting in the seizure, may apply to the clerk of superior court in the county where the charges are pending for pretrial release of the motor vehicle.

The clerk shall release the motor vehicle to a nondefendant motor vehicle owner conditioned upon payment of all towing and storage charges incurred as a result of seizure and impoundment of the motor vehicle under the following conditions:

(1) The motor vehicle has been seized for not less than 24 hours;

(2) Repealed by Session Laws 1998-182, s. 3, effective December 1, 1998.

(3) A bond in an amount equal to the fair market value of the motor vehicle as defined by G.S. 20-28.2 has been executed and is secured by a cash deposit in the full amount of the bond, by a recordable deed of trust to real property in the full amount of the bond, by a bail bond under G.S. 58-71-1(2), or by at least one solvent surety, payable to the county school fund and conditioned on return of the motor vehicle, in substantially the same condition as it was at the time of seizure and without any new or additional liens or encumbrances, on the day of any hearing scheduled and noticed by the district attorney under G.S. 20-28.2(c), unless the motor vehicle has been permanently released;

(4) Execution of either:

    a. An impaired driving acknowledgment as described in G.S. 20-28.2(a1) (1a) if the seizure was for an offense involving impaired driving; or

    b. A speeding to elude arrest acknowledgment as defined in G.S. 20-28.2(a1)(8) if the seizure was for violation of G.S. 20-141.5(b) or (b1).

(5) A check of the records of the Division indicates that the requesting motor vehicle owner has not previously executed an acknowledgment naming the operator of the seized motor vehicle; and

(6) A bond posted to secure the release of this motor vehicle under this subsection has not been previously ordered forfeited under G.S. 20-28.5.

In the event a nondefendant motor vehicle owner who obtains temporary possession of a seized motor vehicle pursuant to this subsection does not return the motor vehicle on the day of the forfeiture hearing as noticed by the district attorney under G.S. 20-28.2(c) or otherwise violates a condition of pretrial release of the seized motor vehicle as set forth in this subsection, the bond posted shall be ordered forfeited and an order of seizure shall be issued by the court. Additionally, a nondefendant motor vehicle owner or lienholder who willfully violates any condition of pretrial release may be held in civil or criminal contempt.

(e1) **Pretrial Release of Motor Vehicle to Innocent Owner.** -- A nondefendant motor vehicle owner may file a petition with the clerk of court seeking a pretrial determination that the petitioner is an innocent owner. The clerk shall consider the petition and make a determination as soon as may be feasible. At any proceeding conducted pursuant to this subsection, the clerk is not required to determine the issue of forfeiture, only the issue of whether the petitioner is an innocent owner. If the clerk determines that the petitioner is an innocent owner, the clerk shall release the motor vehicle to the petitioner subject to the same conditions as if the petitioner were an innocent owner under G.S. 20-28.2(e). The clerk shall send a copy of the order authorizing or

Chapter 20

denying release of the vehicle to the district attorney and the attorney for the county board of education. An order issued under this subsection finding that the petitioner failed to establish that the petitioner is an innocent owner may be reconsidered by the court as part of the forfeiture hearing conducted pursuant to G.S. 20-28.2(d).

(e2) **Pretrial Release of Motor Vehicle to Defendant Owner. --**

(1) If the seizure was for an offense involving impaired driving, a defendant motor vehicle owner may file a petition with the clerk of court seeking a pretrial determination that the defendant's license was not revoked pursuant to an impaired driving license revocation as defined in G.S. 20-28.2(a). The clerk shall schedule a hearing before a judge of the division in which the underlying criminal charge is pending for a hearing to be held within 10 business days or as soon thereafter as may be feasible. Notice of the hearing shall be given to the defendant, the district attorney, and the attorney for the county board of education. The clerk shall forward a copy of the petition to the district attorney for the district attorney's review. If, based on available information, the district attorney determines that the defendant's motor vehicle is not subject to forfeiture, the district attorney may note the State's consent to the release of the motor vehicle on the petition and return the petition to the clerk of court who shall enter an order releasing the motor vehicle to the defendant upon payment of all towing and storage charges incurred as a result of the seizure and impoundment of the motor vehicle, subject to the satisfactory proof of the identity of the defendant as a motor vehicle owner and the existence of financial responsibility to the extent required by Article 13 of this Chapter, and no hearing shall be held. The clerk shall send a copy of the order of release to the attorney for the county board of education. At any pretrial hearing conducted pursuant to this subdivision, the court is not required to determine the issue of the underlying offense of impaired driving only the existence of a prior drivers license revocation as an impaired driving license revocation. Accordingly, the State shall not be required to prove the underlying offense of impaired driving. An order issued under this subdivision finding that the defendant failed to establish that the defendant's license was not revoked pursuant to an impaired driving license revocation as defined in G.S. 20-28.2(a) may be reconsidered by the court as part of the forfeiture hearing conducted pursuant to G.S. 20-28.2(d).

(2) If the seizure was for a felony speeding to elude arrest offense, a defendant motor vehicle owner may apply to the clerk of superior court in the county where the charges are pending for pretrial release of the motor vehicle. The clerk shall release the motor vehicle to the defendant motor vehicle owner conditioned upon payment of all towing and storage charges incurred as a result of seizure and impoundment of the motor vehicle under the following conditions:

a. The motor vehicle has been seized for not less than 24 hours;

b. A bond in an amount equal to the fair market value of the motor vehicle as defined by G.S. 20-28.2 has been executed and is secured by a cash deposit in the full amount of the bond, by a recordable deed of trust to real property in the full amount of the bond, by a bail bond under G.S. 58-71-1(2), or by at least one solvent surety, payable to the county school fund and conditioned on return of the motor vehicle, in substantially the same condition as it was at the time of seizure and without any new or additional liens or encumbrances, on the day of any hearing scheduled and noticed by the district attorney under G.S. 20-28.2(c), unless the motor vehicle has been permanently released;

c. A bond posted to secure the release of this motor vehicle under this subdivision has not been previously ordered forfeited under G.S. 20-28.5.

In the event a defendant motor vehicle owner who obtains temporary possession of a seized motor vehicle pursuant to this subdivision does not return the motor vehicle on the day of the forfeiture hearing as noticed by the district attorney under G.S. 20-28.2(c) or otherwise violates a condition of pretrial release of the seized motor vehicle as set forth in this subdivision, the bond posted shall be ordered forfeited, and an order of seizure shall be issued by the court. Additionally, a defendant motor vehicle owner who willfully violates any condition of pretrial release may be held in civil or criminal contempt.

(e3) **Pretrial Release of Motor Vehicle to Lienholder. --**

(1) A lienholder may file a petition with the clerk of court requesting the court to order pretrial release of a seized motor vehicle. The lienholder shall serve a copy of the petition on all interested parties which shall include the registered owner, the titled

owner, the district attorney, and the county board of education attorney. Upon 10 days' prior notice of the date, time, and location of the hearing sent by the lienholder to all interested parties, a judge, after a hearing, shall order a seized motor vehicle released to the lienholder conditioned upon payment of all towing and storage costs incurred as a result of the seizure and impoundment of the motor vehicle if the judge determines, by the greater weight of the evidence, that:

a. Default on the obligation secured by the motor vehicle has occurred;

b. As a consequence of default, the lienholder is entitled to possession of the motor vehicle;

c. The lienholder agrees to sell the motor vehicle in accordance with the terms of its agreement and pursuant to the provisions of Part 6 of Article 9 of Chapter 25 of the General Statutes. Upon sale of the motor vehicle, the lienholder will pay to the clerk of court of the county in which the driver was charged all proceeds from the sale, less the amount of the lien in favor of the lienholder, and any towing and storage costs paid by the lienholder;

d. The lienholder agrees not to sell, give, or otherwise transfer possession of the seized motor vehicle while the motor vehicle is subject to forfeiture, or the forfeited motor vehicle after the forfeiture hearing, to the defendant or the motor vehicle owner; and

e. The seized motor vehicle while the motor vehicle is subject to forfeiture, or the forfeited motor vehicle after the forfeiture hearing, had not previously been released to the lienholder as a result of a prior seizure involving the same defendant or motor vehicle owner.

(2) The clerk of superior court may order a seized vehicle released to the lienholder conditioned upon payment of all towing and storage costs incurred as a result of the seizure and impoundment of the motor vehicle at any time when all interested parties have, in writing, waived any rights that they may have to notice and a hearing, and the lienholder has agreed to the provision of subdivision (1)d. above. A lienholder who refuses to sell, give, or transfer possession of a seized motor vehicle while the motor vehicle is subject to forfeiture, or a forfeited motor vehicle after the forfeiture hearing, to:

a. The defendant;

b. The motor vehicle owner who owned the motor vehicle immediately prior to seizure pending the forfeiture

hearing, or to forfeiture after the forfeiture hearing; or

c. Any person acting on the behalf of the defendant or the motor vehicle owner,

shall not be liable for damages arising out of such refusal. However, any subsequent violation of the conditions of release by the lienholder shall be punishable by civil or criminal contempt.

(f), (g) Repealed by Session Laws 1998-182, s. 3, effective December 1, 1998.

(h) **Insurance Proceeds. --** In the event a motor vehicle is damaged incident to the conduct of the defendant which gave rise to the defendant's arrest and seizure of the motor vehicle pursuant to this section, the county board of education, or its authorized designee, is authorized to negotiate the county board of education's interest with the insurance company and to compromise and accept settlement of any claim for damages. Property insurance proceeds accruing to the defendant, or other owner of the seized motor vehicle, shall be paid by the responsible insurance company directly to the clerk of superior court in the county where the motor vehicle driver was charged. If the motor vehicle is declared a total loss by the insurance company liable for the damages to the motor vehicle, the clerk of superior court, upon application of the county board of education, shall enter an order that the motor vehicle be released to the insurance company upon payment into the court of all insurance proceeds for damage to the motor vehicle after payment of towing and storage costs and all valid liens. The clerk of superior court shall provide the Division with a certified copy of the order entered pursuant to this subsection, and the Division shall transfer title to the insurance company or to such other person or entity as may be designated by the insurance company. Insurance proceeds paid to the clerk of court pursuant to this subsection shall be subject to forfeiture pursuant to G.S. 20-28.5 and shall be disbursed pursuant to further orders of the court. An affected motor vehicle owner or lienholder who objects to any agreed upon settlement under this subsection may file an independent claim with the insurance company for any additional monies believed owed. Notwithstanding any other provisions in this Chapter, nothing in this section or G.S. 20-28.2 shall require an insurance company to make payments in excess of those required pursuant to its policy of insurance on the seized motor vehicle.

(i) **Expedited Sale of Seized Motor Vehicles in Certain Cases. --** In order to avoid additional liability for towing and storage costs pending resolution of the criminal proceedings of the defendant, the State Surplus Property

Chapter 20

Agency or county board of education may, after expiration of 90 days from the date of seizure, sell any motor vehicle having a fair market value of one thousand five hundred dollars ($ 1,500) or less. The county board of education may also sell a motor vehicle, regardless of the fair market value, any time the outstanding towing and storage costs exceed eighty-five percent (85%) of the fair market value of the vehicle, or with the consent of all the motor vehicle owners. Any sale conducted pursuant to this subsection shall be conducted in accordance with the provisions of G.S. 20-28.5(a) or G.S. 20-28.5(a1), as applicable, and the proceeds of the sale, after the payment of outstanding towing and storage costs or reimbursement of towing and storage costs paid by a person other than the defendant, shall be deposited with the clerk of superior court. If an order of forfeiture is entered by the court, the court shall order the proceeds held by the clerk to be disbursed as provided in G.S. 20-28.5(b). If the court determines that the motor vehicle is not subject to forfeiture, the court shall order the proceeds held by the clerk to be disbursed first to pay the sale, towing, and storage costs, second to pay outstanding liens on the motor vehicle, and the balance to be paid to the motor vehicle owners.

(j) **Retrieval of Certain Personal Property.** -- At reasonable times, the entity charged with storing the motor vehicle may permit owners of personal property not affixed to the motor vehicle to retrieve those items from the motor vehicle, provided satisfactory proof of ownership of the motor vehicle or the items of personal property is presented to the storing entity.

(k) **County Board of Education Right to Appear and Participate in Proceedings.** -- The attorney for the county board of education shall be given notice of all proceedings regarding offenses related to a motor vehicle subject to forfeiture under this section. However, the notice requirement under this subsection does not apply to proceedings conducted under G.S. 20-28.3(e1). The attorney for the county board of education shall also have the right to appear and to be heard on all issues relating to the seizure, possession, release, forfeiture, sale, and other matters related to the seized vehicle under this section. With the prior consent of the county board of education, the district attorney may delegate to the attorney for the county board of education any or all of the duties of the district attorney under this section. Clerks of superior court, law enforcement agencies, and all other agencies with information relevant to the seizure, impoundment, release, or forfeiture of motor vehicles are authorized and directed to provide county boards of education with access to that information and to do so by electronic means when existing technology makes this type of transmission possible.

(*l*) **Payment of Fees Upon Conviction.** -- If the driver of a motor vehicle seized pursuant to this section is convicted of the underlying offense resulting in the seizure of a motor vehicle pursuant to this section, the defendant shall be ordered to pay as restitution to the county board of education, the motor vehicle owner, or the lienholder the cost paid or owing for the towing, storage, and sale of the motor vehicle to the extent the costs were not covered by the proceeds from the forfeiture and sale of the motor vehicle. If the underlying offense resulting in the seizure is felony speeding to elude arrest pursuant to G.S. 20-141.5(b) or (b1) and the defendant's conviction is for misdemeanor speeding to elude arrest pursuant to G.S. 20-141.5(a), whether or not the reduced charge is by plea agreement, the defendant shall be ordered to pay as restitution to the county board of education, the motor vehicle owner, or the lienholder the cost paid or owing for the towing and storage of the motor vehicle. In addition, a civil judgment for the costs under this section in favor of the party to whom the restitution is owed shall be docketed by the clerk of superior court. If the defendant is sentenced to an active term of imprisonment, the civil judgment shall become effective and be docketed when the defendant's conviction becomes final. If the defendant is placed on probation, the civil judgment in the amount found by a judge during the probation revocation or termination hearing to be due shall become effective and be docketed by the clerk when the defendant's probation is revoked or terminated.

(m) **Trial Priority.** -- District court trials of offenses involving forfeitures of motor vehicles pursuant to G.S. 20-28.2 shall be scheduled on the arresting officer's next court date or within 30 days of the offense, whichever comes first.

Once scheduled, the case shall not be continued unless all of the following conditions are met:

(1) A written motion for continuance is filed with notice given to the opposing party prior to the motion being heard.

(2) The judge makes a finding of a "compelling reason" for the continuance.

(3) The motion and finding are attached to the court case record.

Upon a determination of guilt, the issue of vehicle forfeiture shall be heard by the judge immediately, or as soon thereafter as feasible, and the judge shall issue the appropriate orders pursuant to G.S. 20-28.2(d).

Should a defendant appeal the conviction to superior court, any party who has not previously been heard on a petition for pretrial release under subsection (e1) or (e3) of this section or any party whose motor vehicle has not been the subject of a forfeiture hearing held pursuant to G.S. 20-28.2(d) may be heard on a petition for pretrial release pursuant to subsection (e1) or (e3) of this section. The provisions of subsection (e) of this section shall also apply to seized motor vehicles pending trial in superior court. Where a motor vehicle was released pursuant to subsection (e) of this section pending trial in district court, the release of the motor vehicle continues, and the terms and conditions of the original bond remain the same as those required for the initial release of the motor vehicle under subsection (e) of this section, pending the resolution of the underlying offense involving impaired driving in superior court.

(n) Any order issued pursuant to this section authorizing the release of a seized vehicle shall require the payment of all towing and storage charges incurred as a result of the seizure and impoundment of the motor vehicle. This requirement shall not be waived.

History.
1997-379, s. 1.2; 1997-456, s. 31; 1998-182, s. 3; 1998-217, s. 62(a)-(c); 2000-169, s. 29; 2001-362, ss. 1, 2, 3, 4, 5, 6; 2001-487, s. 9; 2006-253, s. 32; 2013-243, s. 2; 2015-241, s. 27.3(b)

§ 20-28.4. Release of impounded motor vehicles by judge

(a) **Release Upon Conclusion of Trial. --** If the driver of a motor vehicle seized pursuant to G.S. 20-28.3:

(1) Is subsequently not convicted of the underlying offense resulting in seizure due to dismissal or a finding of not guilty; or

(2) The judge at a forfeiture hearing conducted pursuant to G.S. 20-28.2(d) finds that the criteria for forfeiture have not otherwise been met; and

(3) The vehicle has not previously been released to a lienholder pursuant to G.S. 20-28.3(e3),

the seized motor vehicle or insurance proceeds held by the clerk of court pursuant to G.S. 20-28.2(c1) or G.S. 20-28.3(h) shall be released to the motor vehicle owner conditioned upon payment of towing and storage costs. The court shall not waive the payment of towing and storage costs. The court shall include in its order notice to the owner of the seized motor vehicle still being held, that within 30 days of the date of the court's order, the owner must make payment of the outstanding towing and storage costs for the motor vehicle and retrieve the motor vehicle, or give notice to Division of Motor Vehicles requesting a judicial hearing on the validity of any mechanics' lien on the motor vehicle for towing and storage costs.

(b) Notwithstanding G.S. 44A-2(d), if the owner of the seized motor vehicle does not obtain release of the vehicle within 30 days from the date of the court's order, the possessor of the seized motor vehicle has a mechanics' lien on the seized motor vehicle for the full amount of the towing and storage charges incurred since the motor vehicle was seized and may dispose of the seized motor vehicle pursuant to Article 1 of Chapter 44A of the General Statutes. Notice of the right to a judicial hearing on the validity of the mechanics' lien given to the owner of the motor vehicle in open court in accordance with subsection (a) of this section or delivery to the owner of the vehicle of a copy of the court's order entered in accordance with subsection (a) of this section shall satisfy the notice requirement of G.S. 44A-4(b).

History.
1997-379, s. 1.3; 1998-182, s. 4; 2001-362, s. 8; 2004-128, s. 4; 2013-243, s. 3

§ 20-28.5. Forfeiture of impounded motor vehicle or funds

(a) **Sale of Vehicle in Possession of County Board of Education. --** A motor vehicle in the possession or constructive possession of a county board of education ordered forfeited and sold or a seized motor vehicle authorized to be sold pursuant to G.S. 20-28.3(i), shall be sold at a public sale conducted in accordance with the provisions of Article 12 of Chapter 160A of the General Statutes, applicable to sales authorized pursuant to G.S. 160A-266(a)(2), (3), or (4), subject to the notice requirements of this subsection, and shall be conducted by the county board of education or a person acting on its behalf. Notice of sale, including the date, time, location, and manner of sale, shall be given by first-class mail to all motor vehicle owners of the vehicle to be sold at the address shown by the records of the Division. Written notice of sale shall also be given to all lienholders on file with the Division. Notice of sale shall be given to the Division in accordance with the procedures established by the Division. Notices required to be given under this subsection shall be mailed at least 10 days prior to the date of sale. A lienholder shall be permitted to purchase the motor vehicle at any such sale by bidding in the amount of its lien, if that should be the highest bid, without being required to tender any additional funds, other than the towing and storage fees. The county board of education, or its agent, shall not sell, give, or otherwise transfer possession of the forfeited motor vehicle to the defendant, the motor vehicle owner who owned the motor vehicle immediately prior to forfeiture, or any person acting on the defendant's or motor vehicle owner's behalf.

(a1) **Sale of Vehicle in Possession of the State Surplus Property Agency. --** A motor vehicle in the possession or constructive possession of the State Surplus Property Agency ordered forfeited and sold or a seized motor vehicle authorized to be sold pursuant to G.S. 20-28.3(i) shall be sold at a public sale conducted in accordance with the provisions of Article 3A of Chapter 143 of the General Statutes, subject to the notice requirements of this subsection, and shall be conducted by the State Surplus Property Agency or a person acting on its behalf. Notice of sale, including the date, time, location, and manner of sale, shall be given by first-class mail to all motor vehicle owners of the vehicle to be sold at the address shown by the records of the Division. Written notice of sale shall also be given to all lienholders on file with the Division. Notice of sale shall be given to the Division in accordance with the procedures established by the State Surplus Property Agency. Notices required to be given under this subsection shall be mailed at least 10 days prior to the date of sale. A lienholder shall be permitted to purchase the motor vehicle at any such sale by bidding in the amount of its lien, if that should be the highest bid, without being required to tender any additional funds, other than the towing and storage fees. The State Surplus Property Agency, or its agent, shall not sell, give, or otherwise transfer possession of the forfeited motor vehicle to the defendant, the motor vehicle owner who owned the motor vehicle immediately prior to forfeiture, or any person acting on the defendant's or motor vehicle owner's behalf.

(b) **Proceeds of Sale. --** Proceeds of any sale conducted under this section, G.S. 20-28.2(f)(5), or G.S. 20-28.3(e3)(3), shall first be applied to all costs incurred by the State Surplus Property Agency or county board of education and then to satisfy towing and storage costs. The balance of the proceeds of sale, if any, shall be used to satisfy any other existing liens of record that were properly recorded prior to the date of initial seizure of the vehicle. Any remaining balance shall be paid to the county school fund in the county in which the motor vehicle was ordered forfeited. If there is more than one school board in the county, then the net proceeds of sale, after reimbursement to the county board of education of reasonable administrative costs incurred in connection with the forfeiture and sale of the motor vehicle, shall be distributed in the same manner as fines and other forfeitures. The sale of a motor vehicle pursuant to this section shall be deemed to extinguish all existing liens on the motor vehicle and the motor vehicle shall be transferred free and clear of any liens.

(c) **Retention of Motor Vehicle. --** A board of education may, at its option, retain any forfeited motor vehicle for its use upon payment of towing and storage costs. If the motor vehicle

is retained, any valid lien of record at the time of the initial seizure of the motor vehicle shall be satisfied by the county board of education relieving the motor vehicle owner of all liability for the obligation secured by the motor vehicle. If there is more than one school board in the county, and the motor vehicle is retained by a board of education, then the fair market value of the motor vehicle, less the costs for towing, storage, reasonable administrative costs, and liens paid, shall be used to determine and pay the share due each of the school boards in the same manner as fines and other forfeitures.

(d) Repealed by Session Laws 1998-182, s. 5, effective December 1, 1998.

(e) **Order of Forfeiture; Appeals. --** An order of forfeiture is stayed pending appeal of a conviction for an offense that is the basis for the order. When the conviction of an offense that is the basis for an order of forfeiture is appealed from district court, the issue of forfeiture shall be heard in superior court de novo. Appeal from a final order of forfeiture shall be to the Court of Appeals.

History.
1997-379, s. 1.4; 1998-182, s. 5; 1998-217, s. 62(d); 1999-456, s. 11; 2015-241, s. 27.3(c)

N.C. Gen. Stat. § 20-28.6

Repealed by Session Laws 1998-182, s. 6, effective December 1, 1998, and applicable to offenses committed, contracts entered, and motor vehicles seized on or after that date.

§ 20-28.7. Responsibility of Division of Motor Vehicles

The Division shall establish procedures by rule to provide for the orderly seizure, forfeiture, sale, and transfer of motor vehicles pursuant to the provisions of G.S. 20-28.2, 20-28.3, 20-28.4, and 20-28.5.

History.
1997-379, s. 1.6; 1998-182, s. 7

§ 20-28.8. Reports to the Division

In any case in which a vehicle has been seized pursuant to G.S. 20-28.3, in addition to any other information that must be reported pursuant to this Chapter, the clerk of superior court shall report to the Division by electronic means the execution of an impaired driving acknowledgment as defined in G.S. 20-28.2(a1)(1a), a speeding to elude arrest acknowledgment as defined in G.S. 20-28.2(a1)(8), the entry of an order of forfeiture as defined in G.S. 20-28.2(a1)(4), and the entry of an order of release as defined in G.S. 20-28.3 and G.S. 20-28.4. Each report shall include any of the following information that has not previously been reported to the Division in the case: the name, address, and drivers license number of the defendant; the name, address, and drivers license number of the nondefendant motor vehicle owner, if known; and the make, model, year, vehicle identification number, state of registration, and vehicle registration plate number of the seized vehicle, if known.

History.
1998-182, s. 8; 2013-243, s. 4

§ 20-28.9. Authority for the State Surplus Property Agency to administer a statewide or regional towing, storage, and sales program for vehicles forfeited

(a) The State Surplus Property Agency is authorized to enter into a contract for a statewide service or contracts for regional services to tow, store, process, maintain, and sell motor vehicles seized pursuant to G.S. 20-28.3. All motor vehicles seized under G.S. 20-28.3 shall be subject to contracts entered into pursuant to this section. Contracts shall be let by the State Surplus Property Agency in accordance with the provisions of Article 3 of Chapter 143 of the General Statutes. All contracts shall ensure the safety of the motor vehicles while held and any funds arising from the sale of any seized motor vehicle. The contract shall require the contractor to maintain and make available to the agency a computerized up-to-date inventory of all motor vehicles held under the contract, together with an accounting of all accrued charges, the status of the vehicle, and the county school fund to which the proceeds of sale are to be paid. The contract shall provide that the contractor shall pay the towing and storage charges owed on a seized vehicle to a commercial towing company at the time the seized vehicle is obtained from the commercial towing company, with the contractor being reimbursed this expense when the vehicle is released or sold. The State Surplus Property Agency shall not enter into any contract under this section under which the State will be obligated to pay a deficiency arising from the sale of any forfeited motor vehicle.

(b) The State Surplus Property Agency, through its contractor or contractors designated in accordance with subsection (a) of this section, may charge a reasonable fee for storage not to exceed ten dollars ($ 10.00) per calendar day for the storage of seized vehicles pursuant to G.S. 20-28.3.

(c) Repealed by Session Laws 2015-241, s. 27.3(d), effective July 1, 2015.

History.
1998-182, s. 8; 2014-115, s. 2.2; 2015-241, s. 27.3(d); 2015-264, s. 38.3(a)

§ 20-29. Surrender of license

Any person operating or in charge of a motor vehicle, when requested by an officer in uniform, or, in the event of accident in which the vehicle which he is operating or in charge of shall be involved, when requested by any other person, who shall refuse to write his name for the purpose of identification or to give his name and address and the name and address of the owner of such vehicle, or who shall give a false name or address, or who shall refuse, on demand of such officer or such other person, to produce his license and exhibit same to such officer or such other person for the purpose of examination, or who shall refuse to surrender his license on demand of the Division, or fail to produce same when requested by a court of this State, shall be guilty of a Class 2 misdemeanor. Pickup notices for drivers' licenses or revocation or suspension of license notices and orders or demands issued by the Division for the surrender of such licenses may be served and executed by patrolmen or other peace officers or may be served in accordance with G.S. 20-48. Patrolmen and peace officers, while serving and executing such notices, orders and demands, shall have all the power and authority possessed by peace officers when serving the executing warrants charging violations of the criminal laws of the State.

History.
1935, c. 52, s. 23; 1949, c. 583, s. 7; 1975, c. 716, s. 5; 1979, c. 667, s. 25; 1981, c. 938, s. 1; 1993, c. 539, s. 323; 1994, Ex. Sess., c. 24, s. 14(c)

§ 20-29.1. Commissioner may require reexamination; issuance of limited or restricted licenses

The Commissioner of Motor Vehicles, having good and sufficient cause to believe that a licensed operator is incompetent or otherwise not qualified to be licensed, may, upon written notice of at least five days to such licensee, require him to submit to a reexamination to determine his competency to operate a motor vehicle. Upon the conclusion of such examination, the Commissioner shall take such action as may be appropriate, and may suspend or revoke the license of such person or permit him to retain such license, or may issue a license subject to restrictions or upon failure of such reexamination may cancel the license of such person until he passes a reexamination. Refusal or neglect of the licensee to submit to such reexamination shall be grounds for the cancellation of the license of the person failing to be reexamined, and the license so canceled shall remain canceled until such person satisfactorily complies with the reexamination requirements of the Commissioner. The Commissioner may, in his discretion and upon the written application of any person qualified to receive a driver's license, issue to such person a driver's license restricting or limiting the licensee to the operation of a single prescribed motor vehicle or to the operation of a particular class or type of motor vehicle. Such a limitation or restriction shall be noted on the face of the license, and it shall be unlawful for the holder of such limited or restricted license to operate any motor vehicle or class of motor vehicle not specified by such restricted or limited license, and the operation by such licensee of motor vehicles not specified by such license shall be deemed the equivalent of operating a motor vehicle without any driver's license. Any such restricted or limited licensee may at any time surrender such restricted or limited license and apply for and receive an unrestricted driver's license upon meeting the requirements therefor.

History.
1943, c. 787, s. 2; 1949, c. 1121; 1971, c. 546; 1979, c. 667, ss. 26, 41

§ 20-30. Violations of license, learner's permit, or special identification card provisions

It shall be unlawful for any person to commit any of the following acts:

(1) To display or cause to be displayed or to have in possession a driver's license, learner's permit, or special identification card, knowing the same to be fictitious or to have been canceled, revoked, suspended or altered.

(2) To counterfeit, sell, lend to, or knowingly permit the use of, by one not entitled thereto, a driver's license, learner's permit, or special identification card.

(3) To display or to represent as one's own a drivers license, learner's permit, or special identification card not issued to the person so displaying same.

(4) To fail or refuse to surrender to the Division upon demand any driver's license, learner's permit, or special identification card that has been suspended, canceled or revoked as provided by law.

(5) To use a false or fictitious name or give a false or fictitious address in any application for a driver's license, learner's permit, or special identification card, or any renewal or duplicate thereof, or knowingly to make a false statement or knowingly conceal a material fact or otherwise commit a fraud in any such application, or for any person to procure, or knowingly permit or allow another to commit any of the foregoing acts. Any license, learner's permit, or special identification card procured as aforesaid shall be void from the issuance

thereof, and any moneys paid therefor shall be forfeited to the State. Any person violating the provisions of this subdivision shall be guilty of a Class 1 misdemeanor.

(6) To make a color photocopy or otherwise make a color reproduction of a drivers license, learner's permit, or special identification card, unless such color photocopy or other color reproduction was authorized by the Commissioner or is made to comply with G.S. 163-230.2. It shall be lawful to make a black and white photocopy of a drivers license, learner's permit, or special identification card or otherwise make a black and white reproduction of a drivers license, learner's permit, or special identification card. This subdivision does not apply to: (i) a lender that is licensed or otherwise authorized to engage in the lending business in this State; (ii) a licensed motor vehicle dealer creating, storing, or receiving, in the ordinary course of business, a color image of a drivers license, learner's permit, or special identification card of a borrower or loan applicant; or (iii) a federally insured depository institution or its affiliates creating, storing, or receiving, in the ordinary course of business, a color image of a drivers license, learner's permit, or special identification card of a consumer.

(7) To sell or offer for sale any reproduction or facsimile or simulation of a driver's license, learner's permit, or special identification card. The provisions of this subdivision shall not apply to agents or employees of the Division while acting in the course and scope of their employment. Any person, firm or corporation violating the provisions of this subsection shall be guilty of a Class I felony.

(8) To possess more than one commercial drivers license or to possess a commercial drivers license and a regular drivers license. Any commercial drivers license other than the one most recently issued is subject to immediate seizure by any law enforcement officer or judicial official. Any regular drivers license possessed at the same time as a commercial drivers license is subject to immediate seizure by any law enforcement officer or judicial official.

(9) To present, display, or use a drivers license, learner's permit, or special identification card that contains a false or fictitious name in the commission or attempted commission of a felony. Any person violating the provisions of this subdivision shall be guilty of a Class I felony.

History.
1935, c. 52, s. 24; 1951, c. 542, s. 4; 1967, c. 1098, s. 1; 1973, c. 18, s. 2; 1975, c. 716, s. 5; 1979, c. 415;

Chapter 20

c. 667, ss. 27, 41; 1979, 2nd Sess., c. 1316, s. 22; 1989, c. 771, s. 8; 1991, c. 726, s. 13; 1991 (Reg. Sess., 1992), c. 1007, s. 29; 1993, c. 539, s. 1247; 1994, Ex. Sess., c. 24, s. 14(c); 1999-299, s. 1; 2001-461, s. 1.1; 2001-487, s. 50(b); 2011-381, s. 4; 2019-239, s. 1.3(c); 2021-134, s. 3

§ 20-31. Making false affidavits perjury

Any person who shall make any false affidavit, or shall knowingly swear or affirm falsely, to any matter or thing required by the terms of this Article to be sworn to or affirmed shall be guilty of a Class I felony.

History.
1935, c. 52, s. 25; 1993, c. 539, s. 1249; 1994, Ex. Sess., c. 24, s. 14(c)

§ 20-32. Unlawful to permit unlicensed minor to drive motor vehicle

It shall be unlawful for any person to cause or knowingly permit any minor under the age of 18 years to drive a motor vehicle upon a highway as an operator, unless such minor shall have first obtained a license to so drive a motor vehicle under the provisions of this Article.

History.
1935, c. 52, s. 26; 1973, c. 684

N.C. Gen. Stat. § 20-33

Repealed by Session Laws 1979, c. 667, s. 28.

§ 20-34. Unlawful to permit violations of this Article

No person shall authorize or knowingly permit a motor vehicle owned by him or under his control to be driven by any person who has no legal right to do so or in violation of any of the provisions of this Article.

History.
1935, c. 52, s. 28

§ 20-34.1. Violations for wrongful issuance of a drivers license or a special identification card

(a) An employee of the Division or of an agent of the Division who does any of the following commits a Class I felony:

(1) Charges or accepts any money or other thing of value, except the required fee, for the issuance of a drivers license or a special identification card.

(2) Knowing it is false, accepts false proof of identification submitted for a drivers license or a special identification card.

(3) Knowing it is false, enters false information concerning a drivers license or a special identification card in the records of the Division.

(b) **Defenses Precluded. --** The fact that the Division does not issue a license or a special identification card after an employee or an agent of the Division charges or accepts money or another thing of value for its issuance is not a defense to a criminal action under this section. It is not a defense to a criminal action under this section to show that the person who received or was intended to receive the license or special identification card was eligible for it.

(c) **Dismissal. --** An employee of the Division who violates this section shall be dismissed from employment and may not hold any public office or public employment in this State for five years after the violation. If a person who violates this section is an employee of the agent of the Division, the Division shall cancel the contract of the agent unless the agent dismisses that person. A person dismissed by an agent because of a violation of this section may not hold any public office or public employment in this State for five years after the violation.

History.
1951, c. 211; 1975, c. 716, s. 5; 1979, c. 667, s. 41; 1993, c. 533, s. 8; c. 539, s. 1250; 1994, Ex. Sess., c. 14, s. 30; c. 24, s. 14(c)

§ 20-35. Penalties for violating Article; defense to driving without a license

(a) **Penalty. --** Except as otherwise provided in subsection (a1) or (a2) of this section, a violation of this Article is a Class 2 misdemeanor unless a statute in the Article sets a different punishment for the violation. If a statute in this Article sets a different punishment for a violation of the Article, the different punishment applies.

(a1) The following offenses are Class 3 misdemeanors:

(1) Failure to obtain a license before driving a motor vehicle, in violation of G.S. 20-7(a).

(2) Failure to comply with license restrictions, in violation of G.S. 20-7(e).

(3) Permitting a motor vehicle owned by the person to be operated by an unlicensed person, in violation of G.S. 20-34.

(a2) A person who does any of the following is responsible for an infraction:

(1) Fails to carry a valid license while driving a motor vehicle, in violation of G.S. 20-7(a).

(2) Operates a motor vehicle with an expired license, in violation of G.S. 20-7(f).

(3) Fails to notify the Division of an address change for a drivers license within 60

days after the change occurs, in violation of G.S. 20-7.1.

(b) Repealed by Session Laws 1993 (Reg. Sess., 1994), c. 761, s. 4.

(c) **Defenses. --** A person may not be found responsible for failing to carry a regular drivers license if, when tried for that offense, the person produces in court a regular drivers license issued to the person that was valid when the person was charged with the offense. A person may not be found responsible for driving a motor vehicle with an expired drivers license if, when tried for that offense, the person shows all the following:

(1) That, at the time of the offense, the person had an expired license.

(2) The person renewed the expired license within 30 days after it expired and now has a drivers license.

(3) The person could not have been charged with driving without a license if the person had the renewed license when charged with the offense.

(d) **Defense for Deployed Member of the Armed Forces of the United States. --** A person may not be found responsible for driving a motor vehicle with an expired drivers license if, when tried for that offense, the person provides verifiable written proof of deployment and establishes the following:

(1) The person was deployed as a member of the Armed Forces of the United States when the drivers license expired.

(2) The person obtained a renewed drivers license within 30 days after returning from deployment.

History.
1935, c. 52, s. 29; 1991, c. 726, s. 14; 1993, c. 539, s. 324; 1994, Ex. Sess., c. 24, s. 14(c); 1993 (Reg. Sess., 1994), c. 761, s. 4; 2013-360, s. 18B.14(g); 2013-385, s. 4; 2021-89, s. 2(a)

§ 20-36. Ten-year-old convictions not considered

Except for offenses occurring in a commercial motor vehicle, offenses by the holder of a commercial drivers license involving a noncommercial motor vehicle, or a second failure to submit to a chemical test when charged with an implied-consent offense, as defined in G.S. 20-16.2, that occurred while the person was driving a commercial motor vehicle, no conviction of any other violation of the motor vehicle laws shall be considered by the Division in determining whether any person's driving privilege shall be suspended or revoked or in determining the appropriate period of suspension or revocation after 10 years has elapsed from the date of that conviction.

History.
1971, c. 15; 1975, c. 716, s. 5; 1998-182, s. 22; 2005-349, s. 7; 2009-416, s. 4

§ 20-37. Limitations on issuance of licenses

There shall be no driver's license issued within this State other than that provided for in this Article, nor shall there be any other examination required: Provided, however, that cities and towns shall have the power to license, regulate and control drivers and operators of taxicabs within the city or town limits and to regulate and control operators of taxicabs operating between the city or town to points, not incorporated, within a radius of five miles of said city or town.

History.
1935, c. 52, s. 34; 1943, c. 639, s. 2; 1979, c. 667, s. 41

§ 20-37.01. Drivers License Technology Fund

The Drivers License Technology Fund is established in the Department of Transportation as a nonreverting, interest-bearing special revenue account. The revenue in the Fund at the end of a fiscal year does not revert, and earnings on the Fund shall be credited to the Fund annually. All money collected by the Commissioner pursuant to G.S. 20-37.02 shall be remitted to the State Treasurer and held in the Fund. Money held in the Fund shall be used to supplement funds otherwise available to the Division for information technology and office automation needs. The Commissioner shall report by February 1 and August 1 of each year to the Joint Legislative Commission on Governmental Operations, the chairs of the Senate and House of Representatives Appropriation Committees, and the chairs of the Senate and House of Representatives Appropriations Subcommittees on Transportation on all money collected and deposited in the Fund and on the proposed expenditure of funds collected during the preceding six months.

History.
2001-461, s. 4; 2001-487, s. 42(c)

§ 20-37.02. Verification of drivers license information

(a) The Commissioner shall establish and operate an electronic system that can be used to verify drivers licenses and identification cards issued by the Division and the dates of birth on these documents in order to facilitate access to drivers license information by retailers and persons holding ABC permits to prevent the utilization of fictitious identification for the purpose of underage purchases of certain age-restricted products or to commit certain crimes.

(b) The electronic system established and operated by the Commissioner pursuant to subsection (a) of this section shall allow a retailer, as defined in G.S. 105-164.3(229), a person who holds an ABC permit, as defined in G.S. 18B-101(2), or an agent of the retailer or a person holding an ABC permit, to verify the validity of a drivers license or identification card issued by the Division and the date of birth of the person issued the drivers license or identification card. The Commissioner shall make drivers license and identification card information available in a read-only format, and the information to be made available shall not exceed the information contained on the face of the drivers license. The Division shall not keep a record of the inquiry. The retailer or a person holding an ABC permit may retain such information as is necessary to provide evidence that the person's drivers license or identification card was validated or that the person's age was verified. A retailer or permittee shall agree to comply with the requirements of this section prior to using the system.

(c) Except for purposes allowed in this section, a person using the electronic system established in accordance with subsection (a) of this section shall not collect or retain any information obtained through the use of the electronic system, nor transfer or make accessible to a third party any information obtained through an inquiry permitted under this section. A violation of the provisions of this subsection shall be punished as a Class 2 misdemeanor.

(d) A retailer or permittee using the electronic system established pursuant to this section shall be responsible for the costs of the equipment and communication lines approved by the Division needed by the retailer or permittee to access the system.

(e) The establishment and operation of an electronic system pursuant to this section may be funded through grants received from the State, the federal government, a private entity, or any other funding source made available to the Drivers License Technology Fund. All funds obtained through grants to the Fund shall be remitted to the State Treasurer to be held in the Drivers License Technology Fund established in G.S. 20-37.01.

History.
2001-461, s. 4

ARTICLE 2A
AFFLICTED, DISABLED OR
HANDICAPPED PERSONS

N.C. Gen. Stat. § 20-37.1

Repealed by Session Laws 1989, c. 157, s. 1.

§§ 20-37.2 through 20-37.4

Repealed by Session Laws 1991, c. 411, s. 5.

§ 20-37.5. Definitions

Unless the context requires otherwise, the following definitions apply throughout this Article to the defined words and phrases and their cognates:

(1) "Distinguishing license plate" means a license plate that displays the International Symbol of Access using the same color, size of plate, and size of letters or numbers as a regular plate.

(1a) Guardian. -- Any of the following:
a. **Custodian.** -- As defined in G.S. 7B-101(8).
b. **General guardian.** -- As defined in G.S. 35A-1202(7).
c. **Guardian of the person.** -- As defined in G.S. 35A-1202(10).

(2) "Handicapped" shall mean a person with a mobility impairment who, as determined by a licensed physician:
a. Cannot walk 200 feet without stopping to rest;
b. Cannot walk without the use of, or assistance from, a brace, cane, crutch, another person, prosthetic device, wheelchair, or other assistive device;
c. Is restricted by lung disease to such an extent that the person's forced (respiratory) expiratory volume of one second, when measured by spirometry, is less than one liter, or the arterial oxygen tension is less than 60 mm/hg on room air at rest;
d. Uses portable oxygen;
e. Has a cardiac condition to the extent that the person's functional limitations are classified in severity as Class III or Class IV according to standards set by the American Heart Association;
f. Is severely limited in their ability to walk due to an arthritic, neurological, or orthopedic condition; or
g. Is totally blind or whose vision with glasses is so defective as to prevent the performance of ordinary activity for which eyesight is essential, as certified by a licensed ophthalmologist, optometrist, or the Division of Services for the Blind.

(3) "International Symbol of Access" means the symbol adopted by Rehabilitation International in 1969 at its Eleventh

World Congress on Rehabilitation of the Disabled.

(4) "Removable windshield placard" means a two-sided, hooked placard which includes on each side:

    a. The International Symbol of Access, which is at least three inches in height, centered on the placard, and is white on a blue shield;

    b. An identification number;

    c. An expiration date that is visible from at least 20 feet and the month and year of expiration; and

    d. The seal or other identification of the issuing authority.

History.

1967, c. 296, s. 5; 1977, c. 340, s. 1; 1991, c. 411, s. 1; 2009-493, s. 1; 2019-213, s. 1(a)

§ 20-37.6. Parking privileges for handicapped drivers and passengers

(a) **General Parking.** -- Any vehicle that is driven by or is transporting a person who is handicapped and that displays a distinguishing license plate, a removable windshield placard, or a temporary removable windshield placard may be parked for unlimited periods in parking zones restricted as to the length of time parking is permitted. This provision has no application to those zones or during times in which the stopping, parking, or standing of all vehicles is prohibited or which are reserved for special types of vehicles. Any qualifying vehicle may park in spaces designated as restricted to vehicles driven by or transporting the handicapped.

(b) **Distinguishing License Plates.** -- If the registered owner of a vehicle is handicapped or the registered owner certifies that the registered owner is the guardian or parent of a handicapped person, the registered owner may apply for and display a distinguishing license plate. This license plate shall be issued for the normal fee applicable to standard license plates. Any vehicle owner who qualifies for a distinguishing license plate shall be notified by the Division at the time the plate is issued that the applicant is also eligible to receive one removable windshield placard and, upon request, shall be issued a placard at that time. A vehicle with a distinguishing license plate may be lawfully used when a handicapped person is not a driver or passenger so long as the vehicle is not using handicapped privileges including parking in a space designated with a sign pursuant to subsection (d) of this section.

(c) **Distinguishing Placards.** -- A handicapped person may apply for the issuance of a removable windshield placard or a temporary removable windshield placard. Upon request, one additional placard may be issued to applicants who do not have a distinguishing license plate. Any organization which, as determined and certified by the State Vocational Rehabilitation Agency, regularly transports handicapped persons may also apply. These organizations may receive one removable windshield placard for each transporting vehicle. When the removable windshield or temporary removable windshield placard is properly displayed, all parking rights and privileges extended to vehicles displaying a distinguishing license plate issued pursuant to subsection (b) shall apply. The removable windshield placard or the temporary removable windshield placard shall be displayed so that it may be viewed from the front and rear of the vehicle by hanging it from the front windshield rearview mirror of a vehicle using a parking space allowed for handicapped persons. When there is no inside rearview mirror, or when the placard cannot reasonably be hung from the rearview mirror by the handicapped person, the placard shall be displayed on the driver's side of the dashboard. A removable windshield placard placed on a motorized wheelchair or similar vehicle shall be displayed in a clearly visible location. The Division shall establish procedures for the issuance of the placards and may charge a fee sufficient to pay the actual cost of issuance, but in no event less than five dollars ($ 5.00) per placard. The Division shall issue a placard registration card with each placard issued to a handicapped person. The registration card shall bear the name of the person to whom the placard is issued, the person's address, the placard number, and an expiration date. The registration card shall be in the vehicle in which the placard is being used, and the person to whom the placard is issued shall be the operator or a passenger in the vehicle in which the placard is displayed.

(c1) **Application and Renewal; Medical Certification.** -- The initial application for a distinguishing license plate, removable windshield placard, or temporary removable windshield placard shall be accompanied by a certification of a licensed physician, a licensed ophthalmologist, a licensed optometrist, a licensed physician assistant, a licensed nurse practitioner, or the Division of Services for the Blind that the applicant or person in the applicant's custody or care is handicapped or by a disability determination by the United States Department of Veterans Affairs that the applicant or person in the applicant's custody or care is handicapped. For an initial application for a temporary removable windshield placard only, the certification that the applicant is handicapped may be made by a licensed certified nurse midwife. The application for a temporary removable windshield placard shall contain additional certification to include the period of time the certifying authority determines the applicant will have the disability. Distinguishing license plates shall be renewed annually, but subsequent applications shall not require a medical certification that the applicant is handicapped, except that a registered owner that certified pursuant to subsection (b) of this section that the registered owner is the guardian or parent of a handicapped person must recertify every five years. Removable windshield placards shall be renewed every five years, and, except for a person certified as totally and permanently disabled at the time of the initial application or a prior renewal under this subsection, the renewal shall require a medical recertification that the person is handicapped; provided that a medical certification shall not be required to renew any placard that expires after the person to whom it is issued is 80 years of age. Temporary removable windshield placards shall expire no later than six months after issuance.

(c2) **Existing Placards; Expiration; Exchange for New Placards.** -- All existing placards shall expire on January 1, 1992. No person shall be convicted of parking in violation of this Article by reason of an expired placard if the defendant produces in court, at the time of trial on the illegal parking charge, an expired placard and a renewed placard issued within 30 days of the expiration date of the expired placard and which would have been a defense to the charge had it been issued prior to the time of the alleged offense. Existing placards issued on or after July 1, 1989, may be exchanged without charge for the new placards.

(c3) It shall be unlawful to sell a distinguishing license plate, a removable windshield placard, or a temporary removable windshield placard issued pursuant to this section. A violation of this subsection shall be a Class 2 misdemeanor and may be punished pursuant to G.S. 20-176(c) and (c1).

(d) **Designation of Parking Spaces.** -- Designation of parking spaces for handicapped persons on streets and public vehicular areas shall comply with G.S. 136-30. A sign designating a parking space for handicapped persons shall state the maximum penalty for parking in the space in violation of the law. For purposes of this section, a parking space designated for handicapped persons includes clearly marked access aisles, and all provisions, restrictions, and penalties applicable to parking in spaces designated for handicapped persons also apply to clearly marked access aisles.

(d1) Repealed by Session Laws 1991, c. 530, s. 4.

(e) **Enforcement of Handicapped Parking Privileges.** -- It shall be unlawful:

(1) To park or leave standing any vehicle in a space designated with a sign pursuant to subsection (d) of this section for handicapped persons when the vehicle does not display the distinguishing license plate, removable windshield placard, temporary removable windshield placard as provided in this section, a disabled veteran registration plate issued under G.S. 20-79.4, or a partially disabled veteran registration plate issued under G.S. 20-79.4;

(2) For any person not qualifying for the rights and privileges extended to handicapped persons under this section to exercise or attempt to exercise such rights or privileges by the unauthorized use of a distinguishing license plate, removable windshield placard, or temporary removable windshield placard issued pursuant to the provisions of this section;

(3) To park or leave standing any vehicle so as to obstruct a curb ramp or curb cut for handicapped persons as provided for by the North Carolina Building Code or as designated in G.S. 136-44.14;

(4) For those responsible for designating parking spaces for the handicapped to erect or otherwise use signs not conforming to G.S. 20-37.6(d) for this purpose.

This section is enforceable in all public vehicular areas.

(f) **Penalties for Violation.** --

(1) A violation of G.S. 20-37.6(e)(1), (2) or (3) is an infraction which carries a penalty of at least one hundred dollars ($ 100.00) but not more than two hundred fifty dollars ($ 250.00) and whenever evidence shall be presented in any court of the fact that any automobile, truck, or other vehicle was found to be parked in a properly designated handicapped parking space in violation of the provisions of this section, it shall be prima facie evidence in any court in the State of North Carolina that the vehicle was parked and left in the space by the person, firm, or corporation in whose name the vehicle is registered and licensed according to the records of the Division. No evidence tendered or presented under this authorization shall be admissible or competent in any respect in any court or tribunal except in cases concerned solely with a violation of this section.

(2) A violation of G.S. 20-37.6(e)(4) is an infraction which carries a penalty of at least one hundred dollars ($ 100.00) but not more than two hundred fifty dollars ($ 250.00) and whenever evidence shall be presented in any court of the fact that a nonconforming sign is being used it shall be prima facie evidence in any court in the State of North Carolina that the person, firm, or corporation with ownership of the property where the nonconforming sign is located is responsible for violation

of this section. Building inspectors and others responsible for North Carolina State Building Code violations specified in G.S. 143-138(h) where such signs are required by the Handicapped Section of the North Carolina State Building Code, may cause a citation to be issued for this violation and may also initiate any appropriate action or proceeding to correct such violation.

(3) A law-enforcement officer, including a company police officer commissioned by the Attorney General under Chapter 74E of the General Statutes, or a campus police officer commissioned by the Attorney General under Chapter 74G of the General Statutes, may cause a vehicle parked in violation of this section to be towed. The officer is a legal possessor as provided in G.S. 20-161(d) (2). The officer shall not be held to answer in any civil or criminal action to any owner, lienholder or other person legally entitled to the possession of any motor vehicle removed from a space pursuant to this section, except where the motor vehicle is willfully, maliciously, or negligently damaged in the removal from the space to a place of storage.

(4) Notwithstanding any other provision of the General Statutes, the provisions of this section relative to handicapped parking shall be enforced by State, county, city and other municipal authorities in their respective jurisdictions whether on public or private property in the same manner as is used to enforce other parking laws and ordinances by said agencies.

History.
1971, c. 374, s. 1; 1973, cc. 126, 1384; 1977, c. 340, s. 2; 1979, c. 632; 1981, c. 682, s. 7; 1983, c. 326, ss. 1, 2; 1985, c. 249; c. 586; c. 764, s. 24; 1985 (Reg. Sess., 1986), c. 852, s. 17; 1987, c. 843; 1989, c. 760, s. 3; 1989 (Reg. Sess., 1990), c. 1052, ss. 1-3.1; 1991, c. 411, s. 2; c. 530, s. 4; c. 672, s. 5; c. 726, s. 23; c. 761, s. 5; 1991 (Reg. Sess., 1992), c. 1007, s. 30; c. 1043, s. 4; 1993, c. 373, s. 1; 1994, Ex. Sess., c. 14, s. 31; 1999-265, s. 1; 2005-231, s. 11; 2009-493, s. 2; 2015-22, s. 1; 2015-29, s. 1; 2016-25, ss. 1, 2; 2017-111, s. 1; 2018-77, s. 4; 2019-199, s. 8; 2019-213, s. 1(b).

§ 20-37.6A. Parking privileges for out-of-state handicapped drivers and passengers

Any vehicle displaying an out-of-State handicapped license plate, placard, or other evidence of handicap issued by the appropriate authority of the appropriate jurisdiction may park in any space reserved for the handicapped pursuant to G.S. 20-37.6.

History.
1981, c. 48; 1991, c. 411, s. 3; 1991 (Reg. Sess., 1992), c. 1007, s. 31

ARTICLE 2B
SPECIAL IDENTIFICATION CARDS FOR NONOPERATORS

§ 20-37.7. Special identification card

(a) **Eligibility.** -- A person who is a resident of this State is eligible for a special identification card.

(b) **Application.** -- To obtain a special identification card from the Division, a person must complete the application form used to obtain a drivers license.

(b1) **Search National Sex Offender Public Registry.** -- The Division shall not issue a special identification card to an applicant who has resided in this State for less than 12 months until the Division has searched the National Sex Offender Public Registry to determine if the person is currently registered as a sex offender in another state. The following applies in this subsection:

(1) If the Division finds that the person is currently registered as a sex offender in another state, the Division shall not issue a special identification card to the person until the person submits proof of registration pursuant to Article 27A of Chapter 14 of the General Statutes issued by the sheriff of the county where the person resides.

(2) If the person does not appear on the National Sex Offender Public Registry, the Division shall issue a special identification card but shall require the person to sign an affidavit acknowledging that the person has been notified that if the person is a sex offender, then the person is required to register pursuant to Article 27A of Chapter 14 of the General Statutes.

(3) If the Division is unable to access all states' information contained in the National Sex Offender Public Registry, but the person is otherwise qualified to obtain a special identification card, then the Division shall issue the card but shall first require the person to sign an affidavit stating that: (i) the person does not appear on the National Sex Offender Public Registry and (ii) acknowledging that the person has been notified that if the person is a sex offender, then the person is required to register pursuant to Article 27A of Chapter 14 of the General Statutes. The Division shall search the National Sex Offender Public Registry for the person within a reasonable time after access to the Registry is restored. If the person does appear in the National Sex Offender Public Registry, the person is in violation of G.S. 20-37.8, and the Division shall promptly notify the sheriff of the

county where the person resides of the offense.

(4) Any person denied a special identification card by the Division pursuant to this subsection has a right to file a petition within 30 days thereafter for a hearing in the matter in the superior court of the county where the person resides, or to petition the resident judge of the district or judge holding the court of that district, or special or emergency judge holding a court in the district, and the court or judge is hereby vested with jurisdiction. The court or judge shall set the matter for hearing upon 30 days' written notice to the Division. At the hearing, the court or judge shall take testimony and examine the facts of the case and shall determine whether the petitioner is entitled to a special identification card under this subsection and whether the petitioner is in violation of G.S. 20-37.8.

(c) **Format.** -- A special identification card shall include a color photograph of the special identification card holder and shall be similar in size, shape, and design to a drivers license, but shall clearly state that it does not entitle the person to whom it is issued to operate a motor vehicle. A special identification card issued to an applicant must have the same background color that a drivers license issued to the applicant would have.

(d) **Expiration and Fee.** -- A special identification card issued to a person for the first time under this section expires when a drivers license issued on the same day to that person would expire. A special identification card renewed under this section expires when a drivers license renewed by the card holder on the same day would expire. The Division shall offer renewal of a special identification card in person and online on the Division's Web site.

The fee for a special identification card is the same as the fee set in G.S. 20-14 for a duplicate license. The fee does not apply to a special identification card issued to a resident of this State as follows:

(1) The applicant is legally blind.

(2) The applicant is at least 17 years old.

(3) The applicant has been issued a drivers license but the drivers license is cancelled under G.S. 20-15, in accordance with G.S. 20-9(e) and (g), as a result of a physical or mental disability or disease.

(4) The applicant is homeless. To obtain a special identification card without paying a fee, a homeless person must present a letter to the Division from the director of a facility that provides care or shelter to homeless persons verifying that the person is homeless.

(5), (6) Repealed by Session Laws 2018-144, s. 1.3(a), effective December 19, 2018.

(7) The applicant has a developmental disability. To obtain a special identification card without paying a fee pursuant to this subdivision, an applicant must present a letter from his or her primary care provider certifying that the applicant has a developmental disability. For purposes of this subdivision, the term "developmental disability" has the same meaning as in G.S. 122C-3.

(d1) For a person who has a physician's letter certifying that a severe disability causes the person to be homebound, the Division shall adopt rules allowing for application for or renewal of a special photo identification card under this section by means other than a personal appearance.

(d2) Notwithstanding subsection (b) of this section, for a person whose valid drivers license, permit, or endorsement, is required to be seized or surrendered due to cancellation, disqualification, suspension, or revocation under applicable State law, the Division shall issue a special identification card to that person without application, if eligible to receive a special identification card, upon receipt by the Division of the seized or surrendered document. The Division shall issue and mail, via first-class mail to that person's address on file, a special identification card pursuant to this subsection at no charge.

(e) **Offense.** -- Any fraud or misrepresentation in the application for or use of a special identification card issued under this section is a Class 2 misdemeanor.

(f) **Records.** -- The Division shall maintain a record of all recipients of a special identification card.

(g) **No State Liability.** -- The fact of issuance of a special identification card pursuant to this section shall not place upon the State of North Carolina or any agency thereof any liability for the misuse thereof and the acceptance thereof as valid identification is a matter left entirely to the discretion of any person to whom such card is presented.

(h) **Advertising.** -- The Division may utilize the various communications media throughout the State to inform North Carolina residents of the provisions of this section.

History.
1973, c. 438, s. 1; 1975, c. 716, s. 5; 1979, c. 469, c. 667, s. 30; 1981, c. 673, ss. 1, 2; c. 690, s. 12; 1981 (Reg. Sess., 1982), c. 1257, s. 3; 1983, c. 443, s. 2; 1983 (Reg. Sess., 1984), c. 1062, s. 7; 1985, c. 141, s. 5; 1991, c. 689, s. 328; 1993, c. 368, s. 3; c. 490, ss. 1, 2; c. 539, s. 325; c. 553, s. 77; 1994, Ex. Sess., c. 24, s. 14(c); 1993 (Reg. Sess., 1994), c. 750, s. 2; 2006-247, s. 19(d); 2009-493, s. 3; 2013-233, ss. 1, 2; 2013-381, s. 3.1; 2016-80, s. 1; 2017-6, s. 3; 2018-142, s. 3(b); 2018-144, s. 1.3(a); 2020-17, s. 9

Chapter 20

§ 20-37.8. Fraudulent use prohibited

(a) It shall be unlawful for any person to use a false or fictitious name or give a false or fictitious address in any application for a special identification card or knowingly to make a false statement or knowingly conceal a material fact or otherwise commit a fraud in any such application or to obtain or possess more than one such card for a fraudulent purpose or knowingly to permit or allow another to commit any of the foregoing acts.

(b) It shall be unlawful for any person to present, display, or use a special identification card which contains a false or fictitious name in the commission or attempted commission of a felony.

(c) A violation of subsection (a) of this section shall constitute a Class 2 misdemeanor. A violation of subsection (b) of this section shall constitute a Class I felony.

History.
1979, c. 603, s. 1; 1993, c. 539, s. 326; 1994, Ex. Sess., c. 24, s. 14(c); 1999-299, s. 2

§ 20-37.9. Notice of change of address or name

(a) **Address.** -- A person whose address changes from the address stated on a special identification card must notify the Division of the change within 60 days after the change occurs. If the person's address changed because the person moved, the person must obtain a new special identification card within that time limit stating the new address. A person who does not move but whose address changes due to governmental action may not be charged with violating this subsection.

(b) **Name.** -- A person whose name changes from the name stated on a special identification card must notify the Division of the change within 60 days after the change occurs and obtain a new special identification card stating the new name.

(c) **Fee.** -- G.S. 20-37.7 sets the fee for a special identification card.

History.
1981, c. 521, s. 2; 1991, c. 689, s. 329; 1997-122, s. 6

ARTICLE 2C
COMMERCIAL DRIVER LICENSE

§ 20-37.10. Title of Article

This Article may be cited as the Commercial Driver License Act.

History.
1989, c. 771, s. 2

§ 20-37.11. Purpose

The purpose of this Article is to implement the federal Commercial Motor Vehicle Safety Act of 1986, 49 U.S.C. Chapter 36, and reduce or prevent commercial motor vehicle accidents, fatalities, and injuries by:

    (1) Permitting commercial drivers to hold one license;

    (2) Disqualifying commercial drivers who have committed certain serious traffic violations, or other specified offenses; and

    (3) Strengthening commercial driver licensing and testing standards.

To the extent that this Article conflicts with general driver licensing provisions, this Article prevails. Where this Article is silent, the general driver licensing provisions apply.

History.
1989, c. 771, s. 2

§ 20-37.12. Commercial drivers license required

(a) On or after April 1, 1992, no person shall operate a commercial motor vehicle on the highways of this State unless he has first been issued and is in immediate possession of a commercial drivers license with applicable endorsements valid for the vehicle he is driving; provided, a person may operate a commercial motor vehicle after being issued and while in possession of a commercial driver learner's permit and while accompanied by the holder of a commercial drivers license valid for the vehicle being driven.

(b) The out-of-service criteria as referred to in 49 C.F.R. Subchapter B apply to a person who drives a commercial motor vehicle. No person shall drive a commercial motor vehicle on the highways of this State in violation of an out-of-service order.

(c) Repealed by Session Laws 1991, c. 726, s. 15.

(d) Any person who is not a resident of this State, who has been issued a commercial drivers license by his state of residence, or who holds any license recognized by the federal government that grants the privilege of driving a commercial motor vehicle, who has that license in his immediate possession, whose privilege to drive any motor vehicle is not suspended, revoked, or cancelled, and who has not been disqualified from driving a commercial motor vehicle shall be permitted without further examination or licensure by the Division to drive a commercial motor vehicle in this State.

(e) G.S. 20-7 sets the time period in which a new resident of North Carolina must obtain a license from the Division. The Commissioner may establish by rule the conditions under which the test requirements for a commercial drivers license may be waived for a new resident who is licensed in another state.

(f) A person shall not be convicted of failing to carry a commercial drivers license if, by the date the person is required to appear in court for the violation, the person produces to the court a commercial drivers license issued to the person that was valid on the date of the offense.

History.

1989, c. 771, s. 2; 1991, c. 726, s. 15; 1997-122, s. 5; 1998-149, s. 4; 2003-397, s. 3; 2009-416, s. 5

§ 20-37.13. Commercial drivers license qualification standards

(a) No person shall be issued a commercial drivers license unless the person meets all of the following requirements:

(1) Is a resident of this State.

(2) Is 21 years of age.

(3) Has passed a knowledge test and a skills test for driving a commercial motor vehicle that comply with minimum federal standards established by federal regulation enumerated in 49 C.F.R., Part 383, Subparts F, G, and H.

(4) Has satisfied all other requirements of the Commercial Motor Vehicle Safety Act in addition to other requirements of this Chapter or federal regulation.

(5) Has held a commercial learner's permit for a minimum of 14 days.

For the purpose of skills testing and determining commercial drivers license classification, only the manufacturer's GVWR shall be used.

The tests shall be prescribed and conducted by the Division. Provided, a person who is at least 18 years of age may be issued a commercial drivers license if the person is exempt from, or not subject to, the age requirements of the federal Motor Carrier Safety Regulations contained in 49 C.F.R., Part 391, as adopted by the Division.

(b) The Division may permit a person, including an agency of this or another state, an employer, a private driver training facility, or an agency of local government, to administer the skills test specified by this section, provided:

(1) The test is the same as that administered by the Division; and

(2) The third party has entered into an agreement with the Division which complies with the requirements of 49 C.F.R. § 383.75. The Division may charge a fee to applicants for third-party testing authority in order to investigate the applicants'

qualifications and to monitor their program as required by federal law.

(b1) The Division shall allow a third party to administer a skills test for driving a commercial motor vehicle pursuant to subsection (b) of this section any day of the week.

(c) Prior to October 1, 1992, the Division may waive the skills test for applicants licensed at the time they apply for a commercial drivers license if:

(1) For an application submitted by April 1, 1992, the applicant has not, and certifies that he or she has not, at any time during the two years immediately preceding the date of application done any of the following and for an application submitted after April 1, 1992, the applicant has not, and certifies that he or she has not, at any time during the two years preceding April 1, 1992:

a. Had more than one drivers license, except during the 10-day period beginning on the date he or she is issued a drivers license, or unless, prior to December 31, 1989, he or she was required to have more than one license by a State law enacted prior to June 1, 1986;

b. Had any drivers license or driving privilege suspended, revoked, or cancelled;

c. Had any convictions involving any kind of motor vehicle for the offenses listed in G.S. 20-17 or had any convictions for the offenses listed in G.S. 20-17.4;

d. Been convicted of a violation of State or local laws relating to motor vehicle traffic control, other than a parking violation, which violation arose in connection with any reportable traffic accident; or

e. Refused to take a chemical test when charged with an implied consent offense, as defined in G.S. 20-16.2; and

(2) The applicant certifies, and provides satisfactory evidence, that he or she is regularly employed in a job requiring the operation of a commercial motor vehicle, and he or she either:

a. Has previously taken and successfully completed a skills test that was administered by a state with a classified licensing and testing system and the test was behind the wheel in a vehicle representative of the class and, if applicable, the type of commercial motor vehicle for which the applicant seeks to be licensed; or

b. Has operated for the relevant two-year period under subpart (1)a. of this subsection, a vehicle representative of the class and, if applicable, the type of commercial motor vehicle for which the applicant seeks to be licensed.

(c1) The Division may waive the skills test for any qualified military applicant at the time the applicant applies for a commercial drivers license if the applicant is currently licensed at the time of application and meets all of the following:

(1) The applicant has passed all required written knowledge exams.

(2) The applicant has not, and certifies that the applicant has not, at any time during the two years immediately preceding the date of application done any of the following:

a. Had any drivers license or driving privilege suspended, revoked, or cancelled.

b. Had any convictions involving any kind of motor vehicle for the offenses listed in G.S. 20-17 or had any convictions for the offenses listed in G.S. 20-17.4.

c. Been convicted of a violation of military, State, or local laws relating to motor vehicle traffic control, other than a parking violation, which violation arose in connection with any reportable traffic accident.

d. Refused to take a chemical test when charged with an implied consent offense, as defined in G.S. 20-16.2.

e. Had more than one drivers license, except for a drivers license issued by the military.

(3) The applicant certifies, and provides satisfactory evidence on the date of application, that the applicant is a retired, discharged, or current member of an active or reserve component of the Armed Forces of the United States and is regularly employed or was regularly employed within the one-year period immediately preceding the date of application in a military position requiring the operation of a commercial motor vehicle, and the applicant meets either of the following requirements:

a. Repealed by Session Laws 2013-201, s. 1, effective June 26, 2013.

b. Has operated for the two-year period immediately preceding the date of application a vehicle representative of the class and, if applicable, the type of commercial motor vehicle for which the applicant seeks to be licensed, and has taken and successfully completed a skills test administered by the military.

c. For an applicant who is a retired or discharged member of an active or reserve component of the Armed Forces of the United States, the applicant (i) has operated for the two-year period immediately preceding the date of retirement or discharge a vehicle representative of the class and, if applicable, the type of commercial motor vehicle for which the applicant seeks to be licensed, and has taken and successfully completed a skills test administered by the military, (ii) has retired or received either an honorable or general discharge, and (iii) has retired or been discharged from the Armed Forces within the one-year period immediately preceding the date of application.

(c2) The one-year period referenced in subdivision (3) of subsection (c1) of this section applies unless a different period is provided by federal law. An applicant may provide his or her Form DD 214, "Certificate of Release or Discharge from Active Duty," and his or her drivers license issued by the military, to satisfy the certification required by subdivision (3) of subsection (c1) of this section. An applicant who is retired or discharged must provide a drivers license issued by the military that was valid at the time of his or her retirement or discharge when using the process in this subsection to satisfy the certification required by subdivision (3) of subsection (c1) of this section.

(c3) The Division may waive the knowledge and skills test for a qualified military applicant who has been issued a military license that authorizes the holder to operate a motor vehicle representative of the class and endorsements for which the applicant seeks to be licensed. The applicant must certify and provide satisfactory evidence on the date of application that the applicant meets all of the following requirements:

(1) The applicant is a current or former member of an active or reserve component of the Armed Forces of the United States and was issued a military license that authorized the applicant to operate a vehicle that is representative of the class and type of commercial motor vehicle for which the applicant seeks to be licensed and whose military occupational specialty or rating are eligible for waiver, as allowed by the Federal Motor Carrier Safety Administration.

(2) The applicant is or was, within the year prior to the date of application, regularly employed in a military position requiring operation of a motor vehicle representative of the class of commercial motor vehicle for which the applicant seeks to be licensed.

(3) The applicant meets the qualifications listed in subdivision (2) of subsection (c1) of this section.

(d) A commercial drivers license or learner's permit shall not be issued to a person while the person is subject to a disqualification from driving a commercial motor vehicle, or while the person's drivers license is suspended, revoked, or cancelled in any state; nor shall a commercial drivers license be issued unless the person who has applied for the license first surrenders all other drivers licenses issued by the Division or by another state. If a person surrenders a drivers license issued by another state, the Division must return the license to the issuing state for cancellation.

(e) A commercial learner's permit may be issued to an individual who holds a regular Class C drivers license and has passed the knowledge test for the class and type of commercial motor vehicle the individual will be driving. The permit is valid for a period not to exceed 180 days. The fee for a commercial driver learner's permit is the same as the fee set by G.S. 20-7 for a regular learner's permit.

(f) Notwithstanding subsection (e) of this section, a commercial driver learner's permit with a P or S endorsement shall not be issued to any person who is required to register under Article 27A of Chapter 14 of the General Statutes.

(g) The issuance of a commercial driver learner's permit is a precondition to the initial issuance of a commercial drivers license. The issuance of a commercial driver learner's permit is also a precondition to the upgrade of a commercial drivers license if the upgrade requires a skills test.

(h) The Division shall promptly notify any driver who fails to meet the medical certification requirements in accordance with 49 C.F.R. § 383.71. The Division shall give the driver 60 days to provide the required documentation. If the driver fails to provide the required commercial drivers license medical certification documentation within the period allowed, the Division shall automatically downgrade a commercial drivers license to a class C regular drivers license.

History.
1989, c. 771, s. 2; 1991, c. 726, s. 16; 1991 (Reg. Sess., 1992), c. 916, s. 1; 2005-349, s. 8; 2009-274, s. 4; 2009-491, s. 5; 2009-494, s. 1; 2011-183, s. 22; 2013-195, s. 1; 2013-201, s. 1; 2014-115, s. 28.5(a), (b); 2015-115, s. 1; 2016-90, s. 6(b); 2018-74, s. 9(a)

§ 20-37.13A. Medical qualifications standards; waiver for intrastate drivers

(a) **Medical Qualifications Standards Applicable to Commercial Drivers.** -- All commercial drivers license holders and applicants for commercial drivers licenses must meet the medical qualifications standards set forth in 49 C.F.R. § 391.41. As allowed under G.S. 20-9(g) (4)h., the Division may release information it deems necessary to any other State or federal government agency for purposes of determining an individual's ability to safely operate a commercial motor vehicle or to obtain a commercial drivers license.

(b) **Intrastate Medical Waiver.** -- Any person unable to meet the standards in 49 C.F.R. § 391.41, as adopted by the Division, may apply for a medical waiver that, if approved, will authorize intrastate operation of a commercial motor vehicle. Applications for the medical waiver must be submitted to the Division in writing. Waivers may be granted for no more than two years.

(c) **Intrastate Operation Subject to Waiver.** -- Any person granted an intrastate commercial drivers license medical waiver is permitted to maintain a commercial drivers license and operate a commercial motor vehicle in intrastate commerce subject to the following conditions:

(1) The commercial drivers license must display a restriction to signify it is only valid for intrastate operation.

(2) The holder of the license must submit to medical recertification at intervals set by the Division.

(3) The holder of the license must timely submit all documentation required by the Division.

(4) Failure to meet any condition within the time period allowed will result in an automatic downgrade of the license holder's commercial drivers license to a Class C regular drivers license.

History.
2016-90, s. 6(e); 2018-74, s. 10(c)

§ 20-37.14. Nonresident commercial driver license

The Division may issue a nonresident commercial driver license (NRCDL) to a resident of a foreign jurisdiction if the United States Secretary of Transportation has determined that the commercial motor vehicle testing and licensing standards in the foreign jurisdiction do not meet the testing standards established in 49 C.F.R., Part 383. The word "Nonresident" must appear on the face of the NRCDL. An applicant must surrender any NRCDL issued by another state. Prior to issuing a NRCDL, the Division shall establish the practical capability of revoking, suspending, or cancelling the NRCDL and disqualifying that person with the same conditions applicable to the commercial driver license issued to a resident of this State.

History.
1989, c. 771, s. 2

§ 20-37.14A. Prohibit issuance or renewal of certain categories of commercial drivers licenses to sex offenders

(a) Effective December 1, 2009, the Division shall not issue or renew a commercial drivers license with a P or S endorsement to any person who is required to register under Article 27A of Chapter 14 of the General Statutes.

(b) The Division shall not issue a commercial drivers license with a P or S endorsement to an applicant until the Division has searched both the statewide registry and the National Sex Offender Public Registry to determine if the person is currently registered as a sex offender in North Carolina or another state.

(1) If the Division finds that the person is currently registered as a sex offender in either North Carolina or another state, the Division, in compliance with subsection (a) of this section, shall not issue a commercial drivers license with a P or S endorsement to the person.

(2) If the Division is unable to access either the statewide registry or all of the states' information contained in the National Sex Offender Public Registry, but the person is otherwise qualified to obtain a commercial drivers license with a P or S endorsement, then the Division shall issue the commercial drivers license with the P or S endorsement but shall first require the person to sign an affidavit stating that the person does not appear on either the statewide registry or the National Sex Offender Public Registry. The Division shall search the statewide registry and the National Sex Offender Public Registry for the person within a reasonable time after access to the statewide registry or the National Sex Offender Public Registry is restored. If the person does appear in either registry, the person is in violation of this section, and the Division shall immediately cancel the commercial drivers license and shall promptly notify the sheriff of the county where the person resides of the offense.

(3) Any person denied a commercial license with a P or S endorsement or who is disqualified from driving a commercial motor vehicle that requires a commercial drivers license with a P or S endorsement by the Division pursuant to this subsection shall have a right to file a petition within 30 days thereafter for a hearing in the matter, in the superior court of the county where the person resides, or to the resident judge of the district or judge holding the court of that district, or special or emergency judge holding a court in such district. The court or judge is vested with jurisdiction to hear the petition, and it shall be the duty of the judge or court to set the matter for hearing upon 30 days' written notice to the Division, and thereupon to take testimony and examine into the facts of the case and to determine whether the petitioner is entitled to a commercial drivers license with a P or S endorsement under the provisions of this subsection.

(c) Any person who makes a false affidavit, or who knowingly swears or affirms falsely, to any matter or thing required by the terms of this section to be affirmed to or sworn is guilty of a Class I felony.

History.
2009-491, s. 6

§ 20-37.15. Application for commercial drivers license

(a) An application for a commercial drivers license must include the information required by G.S. 20-7 for a regular drivers license and a consent to release driving record information.

(a1) The application must be accompanied by a nonrefundable application fee of forty dollars ($ 40.00). This fee does not apply in any of the following circumstances:

(1) When an individual surrenders a commercial driver learner's permit issued by the Division when submitting the application.

(2) When the application is to renew a commercial drivers license issued by the Division.

This fee shall entitle the applicant to three attempts to pass the written knowledge test without payment of a new fee. No application fee shall be charged to an applicant eligible for a waiver under G.S. 20-37.13(c).

(b) When the holder of a commercial drivers license changes his name or residence address, an application for a duplicate shall be made as provided in G.S. 20-7.1 and a fee paid as provided in G.S. 20-14.

History.
1989, c. 771, s. 2; 1991, c. 726, s. 17; 1993 (Reg. Sess., 1994), c. 750, s. 3; 2005-276, s. 44.1(f); 2015-241, s. 29.30(f)

§ 20-37.16. Content of license; classifications and endorsements; fees

(a) A commercial drivers license must be marked "Commercial Drivers License" or "CDL" and must contain the information required by G.S. 20-7 for a regular drivers license.

(b) The classes of commercial drivers licenses are:

(1) Class A CDL -- A Class A commercial drivers license authorizes the holder to drive any Class A motor vehicle.

(2) Class B CDL -- A Class B commercial drivers license authorizes the holder to drive any Class B motor vehicle.

(3) Class C CDL -- A Class C commercial drivers license authorizes the holder to drive any Class C motor vehicle.

(c) **Endorsements. --** The endorsements required to drive certain motor vehicles are as follows:

Endorsement Vehicles That Can Be Driven

H Vehicles, regardless of size or class, except tank vehicles, when transporting hazardous materials that require the vehicle to be placarded
M Motorcycles
N Tank vehicles not carrying hazardous materials
P Vehicles carrying passengers
S School bus
T Double trailers
X Tank vehicles carrying hazardous materials.

To qualify for any of the above endorsements, an applicant shall pass a knowledge test. To obtain an H or an X endorsement, an applicant must take a test. This requirement applies when a person first obtains an H or an X endorsement and each time a person renews an H or an X endorsement. An applicant who has an H or an X endorsement issued by another state who applies for an H or an X endorsement must take a test unless the person has passed a test that covers the information set out in 49 C.F.R. § 383.121 within the preceding two years. For purposes of this subsection, the term "motorcycle" shall not include autocycles. Autocycles shall be subject to the requirements under this section for motor vehicles.

(c1) Expired.

(c2) **Expiration of H and X Endorsements. --** Hazardous materials endorsements shall be renewed every five years or less so that individuals subject to a Transportation Security Administration security screening required pursuant to 49 C.F.R. § 383.141 may receive the screening and be authorized to renew the endorsements of H or X to transport hazardous materials. Notwithstanding G.S. 20-7(f), a commercial drivers license that contains an H or X endorsement as defined in subsection (c) of this section shall expire on the date of expiration of the licensee's security threat assessment conducted by the Transportation Security Administration of the United States Department of Homeland Security. When the commercial drivers license also contains an S endorsement and the licensee is certified to drive a school bus in this State, the commercial drivers license shall expire as provided in G.S. 20-7(f). The H and X endorsements on a commercial drivers license shall expire when the commercial drivers license expires.

(d) The fee for a Class A, B, or C commercial drivers license is twenty dollars ($ 20.00) for each year of the period for which the license is issued. The fee for each endorsement is four dollars ($ 4.00) for each year of the period for which the endorsement is issued. The fees required under this section do not apply to employees of the Driver License Section of the Division who are designated by the Commissioner.

(e) The requirements for a commercial drivers license do not apply to vehicles used for personal use such as recreational vehicles. A commercial drivers license is also waived for the following classes of vehicles as permitted by regulation of the United States Department of Transportation:

(1) Vehicles owned or operated by the Department of Defense, including the National Guard, while they are driven by active duty military personnel, or members of the National Guard when on active duty, in the pursuit of military purposes.

(2) Any vehicle when used as firefighting or emergency equipment for the purpose of preserving life or property or to execute governmental functions, including, but not limited to, necessary maintenance, training, or required operation for official business of the department.

(3) A farm vehicle that meets all of the following criteria:

a. Is controlled and operated by the farmer or the farmer's employee and used exclusively for farm use.

b. Is used to transport either agricultural products, farm machinery, or farm supplies, both to or from a farm.

c. Is not used in the operations of a for-hire motor carrier.

d. Is used within 150 miles of the farmer's farm.

A farm vehicle includes a forestry vehicle that meets the listed criteria when applied to the forestry operation.

(f) For the purposes of this section, the term "school bus" has the same meaning as in 49 C.F.R. § 383.5.

History.
1989, c. 771, s. 2; 1991, c. 726, s. 18; 1993, c. 368, s. 4; 1993 (Reg. Sess., 1994), c. 750, ss. 4, 6; 1995 (Reg. Sess., 1996), c. 695, s. 1; c. 756, s. 5; 1998-149, s. 5; 2003-397, ss. 4, 5; 2005-276, s. 44.1(g); 2005-349, s. 9; 2011-228, s. 1; 2012-85, s. 3; 2015-163, s. 3; 2015-241, s. 29.30(g); 2018-74, s. 15

Chapter 20

§ 20-37.17. Record check and notification of license issuance

Before issuing a commercial driver license, the Division shall obtain driving record information from the Commercial Driver License Information System (CDLIS), the National Driver Register, and from each state in which the person has been licensed.

Within 10 days after issuing a commercial driver license, the Division shall notify CDLIS of the issuance of the commercial driver license, providing all information necessary to ensure identification of the person.

History.
1989, c. 771, s. 2

§ 20-37.18. Notification required by driver

(a) Any driver holding a commercial driver license issued by this State who is convicted of violating any State law or local ordinance relating to motor vehicle traffic control in any other state, other than parking violations, shall notify the Division in the manner specified by the Division within 30 days of the date of the conviction.

(b) Any driver holding a commercial driver license issued by this State who is convicted of violating any State law or local ordinance relating to motor vehicle traffic control in this or any other state, other than parking violations, shall notify his employer in writing of the conviction within 30 days of the date of conviction.

(c) Any driver whose commercial driver license is suspended, revoked, or cancelled by any state, or who loses the privilege to drive a commercial motor vehicle in any state for any period, including being disqualified from driving a commercial motor vehicle, or who is subject to an out-of-service order, shall notify his employer of that fact before the end of the business day following the day the driver received notice of that fact.

(d) Any person who applies to be a commercial motor vehicle driver shall provide the employer, at the time of the application, with the following information for the 10 years preceding the date of application:

(1) A list of the names and addresses of the applicant's previous employers for which the applicant was a driver of a commercial motor vehicle;

(2) The dates between which the applicant drove for each employer; and

(3) The reason for leaving that employer.

The applicant shall certify that all information furnished is true and complete. Any employer may require an applicant to provide additional information.

History.
1989, c. 771, s. 2

§ 20-37.19. Employer responsibilities

(a) Each employer shall require the applicant to provide the information specified in G.S. 20-37.18(c).

(b) No employer shall knowingly allow, permit, or authorize a driver to drive a commercial motor vehicle during any period:

(1) In which the driver has had his commercial driver license suspended, revoked, or cancelled by any state, is currently disqualified from driving a commercial vehicle, or is subject to an out-of-service order in any state; or

(2) In which the driver has more than one driver license; [or]

(3) In which the driver, the commercial motor vehicle being operated, or the motor carrier operation, is subject to an out-of-service order.

(c) The employer of any employee or applicant who tests positive or of any employee who refuses to participate in a drug or alcohol test required under 49 C.F.R. Part 382 and 49 C.F.R. Part 655 must notify the Division in writing within five business days following the employer's receipt of confirmation of a positive drug or alcohol test or of the employee's refusal to participate in the test. The notification must include the driver's name, address, drivers license number, social security number, and results of the drug or alcohol test or documentation from the employer of the refusal by the employee to take the test.

History.
1989, c. 771, s. 2; 2005-156, s. 1; 2007-492, s. 2; 2009-416, s. 6

§ 20-37.20. Notification of traffic convictions

(a) **Out-of-state Resident.** -- Within 10 days after receiving a report of the conviction of any nonresident holder of a commercial driver license for any violation of State law or local ordinance relating to motor vehicle traffic control, other than parking violations, committed in a commercial vehicle, the Division shall notify the driver licensing authority in the licensing state of the conviction.

(b) **Foreign Diplomat.** -- The Division must notify the United States Department of State within 15 days after it receives one or more of the following reports for a holder of a drivers license issued by the United States Department of State:

(1) A report of a conviction for a violation of State law or local ordinance relating

to motor vehicle traffic control, other than parking violations.

(2) A report of a civil revocation order.

History.
1989, c. 771, s. 2; 2001-498, s. 7; 2002-159, s. 31; 2006-209, s. 7

§ 20-37.20A. Driving record notation for testing positive in a drug or alcohol test

Upon receipt of notice pursuant to G.S. 20-37.19(c) of positive result in an alcohol or drug test of a person holding a commercial drivers license, and subject to any appeal of the disqualification pursuant to G.S. 20-37.20B, the Division shall place a notation on the driving record of the driver. A notation of a disqualification pursuant to G.S. 20-17.4(*l*) shall be retained on the record of a person for a period of three years following the end of any disqualification of that person.

History.
2005-156, s. 3; 2008-175, s. 2

§ 20-37.20B. Appeal of disqualification for testing positive in a drug or alcohol test

Following receipt of notice pursuant to G.S. 20-37.19(c) of a positive test in an alcohol or drug test, the Division shall notify the driver of the pending disqualification of the driver to operate a commercial vehicle and the driver's right to a hearing if requested within 20 days of the date of the notice. If the Division receives no request for a hearing, the disqualification shall become effective at the end of the 20-day period. If the driver requests a hearing, the disqualification shall be stayed pending outcome of the hearing. The hearing shall take place at the offices of the Division of Motor Vehicles in Raleigh. The hearing shall be limited to issues of testing procedure and protocol. A copy of a positive test result accompanied by certification by the testing officer of the accuracy of the laboratory protocols that resulted in the test result shall be prima facie evidence of a confirmed positive test result. The decision of the Division hearing officer may be appealed in accordance with the procedure of G.S. 20-19(c6).

History.
2005-156, s. 4

§ 20-37.21. Penalties

(a) Any person who drives a commercial motor vehicle in violation of G.S. 20-37.12 shall be guilty of a Class 3 misdemeanor and, upon conviction, shall be fined not less than two hundred fifty dollars ($ 250.00) for a first offense and not less than five hundred dollars ($ 500.00) for a second or subsequent offense. In addition, the person shall be subject to a civil penalty pursuant to the provisions of 49 C.F.R. § 383.53(b).

(b) Any person who violates G.S. 20-37.18 shall have committed an infraction and, upon being found responsible, shall pay a penalty of not less than one hundred dollars ($ 100.00) nor more than five hundred dollars ($ 500.00).

(c) Any employer who violates G.S. 20-37.19 shall have committed an infraction and, upon being found responsible, shall pay a penalty of not less than five hundred dollars ($ 500.00) nor more than one thousand dollars ($ 1,000). In addition, upon conviction, the employer shall be subject to a civil penalty of not less than two thousand seven hundred fifty dollars ($ 2,750) nor more than eleven thousand dollars ($ 11,000).

(d) An employer who knowingly allows, requires, permits, or otherwise authorizes an employee to violate any railroad grade requirements contained in G.S. 20-142.1 through G.S. 20-142.5 shall pay a civil penalty of not more than ten thousand dollars ($ 10,000).

History.
1989, c. 771, s. 2; 1993, c. 539, s. 327; 1994, Ex. Sess., c. 24, s. 14(c); 2005-349, s. 10; 2009-416, s. 7

§ 20-37.22. Rule making authority

The Division may adopt any rules necessary to carry out the provisions of this Article.

History.
1989, c. 771, s. 2

§ 20-37.23. Authority to enter agreements

The Commissioner shall have the authority to execute or make agreements, arrangements, or declarations to carry out the provisions of this Article.

History.
1989, c. 771, s. 2

N.C. Gen. Stat. § 20-38

Repealed by Session Laws 1973, c. 1330, s. 39.

ARTICLE 2D
IMPLIED-CONSENT OFFENSE PROCEDURES

§ 20-38.1. Applicability

The procedures set forth in this Article shall be followed for the investigation and processing of an implied-consent offense as defined in G.S.

Chapter 20

20-16.2. The trial procedures shall apply to any implied-consent offense litigated in the District Court Division.

History.
2006-253, s. 5

§ 20-38.2. Investigation

A law enforcement officer who is investigating an implied-consent offense or a vehicle crash that occurred in the officer's territorial jurisdiction is authorized to investigate and seek evidence of the driver's impairment anywhere in-state or out-of-state, and to make arrests at any place within the State.

History.
2006-253, s. 5

§ 20-38.3. Police processing duties

Upon the arrest of a person, with or without a warrant, but not necessarily in the order listed, a law enforcement officer:

(1) Shall inform the person arrested of the charges or a cause for the arrest.

(2) May take the person arrested to any place within the State for one or more chemical analyses at the request of any law enforcement officer and for any evaluation by a law enforcement officer, medical professional, or other person to determine the extent or cause of the person's impairment.

(3) May take the person arrested to some other place within the State for the purpose of having the person identified, to complete a crash report, or for any other lawful purpose.

(4) May take photographs and fingerprints in accordance with G.S. 15A-502.

(5) Shall take the person arrested before a judicial official for an initial appearance after completion of all investigatory procedures, crash reports, chemical analyses, and other procedures provided for in this section.

History.
2006-253, s. 5

§ 20-38.4. Initial appearance

(a) **Appearance Before a Magistrate. --** Except as modified in this Article, a magistrate shall follow the procedures set forth in Article 24 of Chapter 15A of the General Statutes.

(1) A magistrate may hold an initial appearance at any place within the county and shall, to the extent practicable, be available at locations other than the courthouse when it will expedite the initial appearance.

(2) In determining whether there is probable cause to believe a person is impaired, the magistrate may review all alcohol screening tests, chemical analyses, receive testimony from any law enforcement officer concerning impairment and the circumstances of the arrest, and observe the person arrested.

(3) If there is a finding of probable cause, the magistrate shall consider whether the person is impaired to the extent that the provisions of G.S. 15A-534.2 should be imposed.

(4) The magistrate shall also:

a. Inform the person in writing of the established procedure to have others appear at the jail to observe his condition or to administer an additional chemical analysis if the person is unable to make bond; and

b. Require the person who is unable to make bond to list all persons he wishes to contact and telephone numbers on a form that sets forth the procedure for contacting the persons listed. A copy of this form shall be filed with the case file.

(b) The Administrative Office of the Courts shall adopt forms to implement this Article.

History.
2006-253, s. 5

§ 20-38.5. Facilities

(a) The Chief District Court Judge, the Department of Health and Human Services, the district attorney, and the sheriff shall:

(1) Establish a written procedure for attorneys and witnesses to have access to the chemical analysis room.

(2) Approve the location of written notice of implied-consent rights in the chemical analysis room in accordance with G.S. 20-16.2.

(3) Approve a procedure for access to a person arrested for an implied-consent offense by family and friends or a qualified person contacted by the arrested person to obtain blood or urine when the arrested person is held in custody and unable to obtain pretrial release from jail.

(b) Signs shall be posted explaining to the public the procedure for obtaining access to the room where the chemical analysis of the breath is administered and to any person arrested for an implied-consent offense. The initial signs shall be provided by the Department of Transportation, without costs. The signs shall thereafter be maintained by the county for all county buildings and the county courthouse.

(c) If the instrument for performing a chemical analysis of the breath is located in a State or municipal building, then the head of the highway patrol for the county, the chief of police for the city or that person's designee shall be substituted for the sheriff when determining signs and access to the chemical analysis room. The signs shall be maintained by the owner of the building. When a breath testing instrument is in a motor vehicle or at a temporary location, the Department of Health and Human Services shall alone perform the functions listed in subdivisions (a)(1) and (a)(2) of this section.

History.
2006-253, s. 5

§ 20-38.6. Motions and district court procedure

(a) The defendant may move to suppress evidence or dismiss charges only prior to trial, except the defendant may move to dismiss the charges for insufficient evidence at the close of the State's evidence and at the close of all of the evidence without prior notice. If, during the course of the trial, the defendant discovers facts not previously known, a motion to suppress or dismiss may be made during the trial.

(b) Upon a motion to suppress or dismiss the charges, other than at the close of the State's evidence or at the close of all the evidence, the State shall be granted reasonable time to procure witnesses or evidence and to conduct research required to defend against the motion.

(c) The judge shall summarily grant the motion to suppress evidence if the State stipulates that the evidence sought to be suppressed will not be offered in evidence in any criminal action or proceeding against the defendant.

(d) The judge may summarily deny the motion to suppress evidence if the defendant failed to make the motion pretrial when all material facts were known to the defendant.

(e) If the motion is not determined summarily, the judge shall make the determination after a hearing and finding of facts. Testimony at the hearing shall be under oath.

(f) The judge shall set forth in writing the findings of fact and conclusions of law and preliminarily indicate whether the motion should be granted or denied. If the judge preliminarily indicates the motion should be granted, the judge shall not enter a final judgment on the motion until after the State has appealed to superior court or has indicated it does not intend to appeal.

History.
2006-253, s. 5

§ 20-38.7. Appeal to superior court

(a) The State may appeal to superior court any district court preliminary determination granting a motion to suppress or dismiss. If there is a dispute about the findings of fact, the superior court shall not be bound by the findings of the district court but shall determine the matter de novo. Any further appeal shall be governed by Article 90 of Chapter 15A of the General Statutes.

(b) The defendant may not appeal a denial of a pretrial motion to suppress or to dismiss but may appeal upon conviction as provided by law.

(c) Notwithstanding the provisions of G.S. 15A-1431, for any implied-consent offense that is first tried in district court and that is appealed to superior court by the defendant for a trial de novo as a result of a conviction, when an appeal is withdrawn or a case is remanded back to district court, the sentence imposed by the district court is vacated and the district court shall hold a new sentencing hearing and shall consider any new convictions unless one of the following conditions is met:

(1) If the appeal is withdrawn pursuant to G.S. 15A-1431(c), the prosecutor has certified to the clerk, in writing, that the prosecutor has no new sentencing factors to offer the court.

(2) If the appeal is withdrawn and remanded pursuant to G.S. 15A-1431(g), the prosecutor has certified to the clerk, in writing, that the prosecutor has no new sentencing factors to offer the court.

(3) If the appeal is withdrawn and remanded pursuant to G.S. 15A-1431(h), the prosecutor has certified to the clerk, in writing, that the prosecutor consents to the withdrawal and remand and has no new sentencing factors to offer the court.

(d) Following a new sentencing hearing in district court pursuant to subsection (c) of this section, a defendant has a right of appeal to the superior court only if:

(1) The sentence is based upon additional facts considered by the district court that were not considered in the previously vacated sentence, and

(2) The defendant would be entitled to a jury determination of those facts pursuant to G.S. 20-179.

A defendant who has a right of appeal under this subsection, gives notice of appeal, and subsequently withdraws the appeal shall have the sentence imposed by the district court reinstated by the district court as a final judgment that is not subject to further appeal.

History.
2006-253, s. 5; 2007-493, s. 9; 2008-187, s. 10; 2015-150, s. 5; 2015-264, s. 39(a)

ARTICLE 3
MOTOR VEHICLE ACT
OF 1937

PART 1
GENERAL PROVISIONS

N.C. Gen. Stat. § 20-38.100

Reserved for future codification purposes.

PART 2
AUTHORITY AND DUTIES
OF COMMISSIONER
AND DIVISION

§ 20-39. Administering and enforcing laws; rules and regulations; agents, etc.; seal; fees

(a) The Commissioner is hereby vested with the power and is charged with the duty of administering and enforcing the provisions of this Article and of all laws regulating the operation of vehicles or the use of the highways, the enforcement or administration of which is now or hereafter vested in the Division.

(b) The Commissioner is hereby authorized to adopt and enforce such rules and regulations as may be necessary to carry out the provisions of this Article and any other laws the enforcement and administration of which are vested in the Division.

(c) The Commissioner is authorized to designate and appoint such agents, field deputies, and clerks as may be necessary to carry out the provisions of this Article.

(d) The Commissioner shall adopt an official seal for the use of the Division.

(e) The Commissioner is authorized to cooperate with and provide assistance to the Environmental Management Commission, or appropriate local government officials, and to develop, adopt, and ensure enforcement of necessary rules and regulations, regarding programs of motor vehicle emissions inspection/maintenance required for areas in which ambient air pollutant concentrations exceed National Ambient Air Quality Standards. The Commissioner is further authorized to allow offices of the Division that provide vehicle titling and registration services and commission contractors of the Division under G.S. 20-63 to serve, upon agreement with the Wildlife Resources Commission, as vessel agents under G.S. 75A-5.2.

(f) The Commissioner is authorized to charge and collect the following fees for the verification of equipment to be used on motor vehicles or to be sold in North Carolina, when that approval is required pursuant to this Chapter:

(1) When a federal standard has been established, the fee shall be equal to the cost of verifying compliance with the applicable federal standard; or

(2) When no federal standard has been established, the fee shall be equal to the cost of verifying compliance with the applicable State standard. Any motor vehicle manufacturer or distributor who is required to certify his products under the National Traffic and Motor Vehicle Safety Act of 1966, as from time to time amended, may satisfy the provisions of this section by submitting an annual written certification to the Commissioner attesting to the compliance of his vehicles with applicable federal requirements. Failure to comply with the certification requirement or failure to meet the federal standards will subject the manufacturer or distributor to the fee requirements of this subsection.

(g), (h) Repealed by Session Laws 2001-424, s. 6.14(e), effective September 26, 2001.

(i) Notwithstanding the requirements of G.S. 20-7.1 and G.S. 20-67(a), the Commissioner may correct the address records of drivers license and registration plate holders as shown in the files of the Division to that shown on notices and renewal cards returned to the Division with new addresses provided by the United States Postal Service.

History.

1937, c. 407, s. 4; 1975, c. 716, s. 5; 1979, 2nd Sess., c. 1180, s. 1; 1983, c. 223; c. 629, s. 2; c. 768, ss. 25.1, 25.2; 1985, c. 767, ss. 1, 2; 1987, c. 552; 1991, c. 53, s. 1; c. 654, s. 1; 1993, c. 539, s. 328; 1994, Ex. Sess., c. 24, s. 14(c); 1995, c. 507, s. 6.2(b); 1996, 2nd Ex. Sess., c. 18, s. 23(a); 1997-256, s. 8; 1997-347, s. 4; 1997-401, s. 4; 1997-418, s. 3; 1997-443, s. 20.10(a), (b); 2001-424, ss. 6.14(e), 6.14(f); 2015-241, s. 29.38

§ 20-39.1. Publicly owned vehicles to be marked; private license plates on publicly owned vehicles

(a) Except as otherwise provided in this section, the executive head of every department of State government and every county, institution, or agency of the State shall mark every motor vehicle owned by the State, county, institution, or agency with a statement that the vehicle belongs to the State, county, institution, or agency. The requirements of this subsection are complied with if:

(1) The vehicle has imprinted on the license plate, above the license number, the words "State Owned" and the vehicle

has affixed to the front the words "State Owned";

(2) In the case of a county, the vehicle has painted or affixed on its side a circle not less than eight inches in diameter showing a replica of the seal of the county; or

(3) In the case of vehicles assigned to members of the Council of State, the vehicle has imprinted on the license plate the license number assigned to the appropriate member of the Council of State pursuant to G.S. 20-79.5(a); a member of the Council of State shall not be assessed any registration fee if the member elects to have a State-owned motor vehicle assigned to the member designated by the official plate number.

(b) A motor vehicle used by any State or county officer or official for transporting, apprehending, or arresting persons charged with violations of the laws of the United States or the laws of this State is not required to be marked as provided in subsection (a) of this section. The Commissioner may lawfully provide private license plates to local, State, or federal departments or agencies for use on publicly owned or leased vehicles used for those purposes. Private license plates issued under this subsection shall be issued on an annual basis and the records of issuance shall be maintained in accordance with the provisions of G.S. 20-56.

(c) A motor vehicle used by a county for transporting day or residential facility clients of area mental health, developmental disabilities, and substance abuse authorities established under Article 4 of Chapter 122C of the General Statutes is not required to be marked as provided in subsection (a) of this section. The Commissioner may lawfully provide private license plates to counties for use on publicly owned or leased vehicles used for that purpose. Private license plates issued under this subsection shall be issued on an annual basis and the records of issuance shall be maintained in accordance with the provisions of G.S. 20-56.

(c1) A motor vehicle used by the Department of Agriculture and Consumer Services exclusively for Meat and Poultry compliance officers to conduct inspections is not required to be marked as provided in subsection (a) of this section. The Commissioner may lawfully provide private license plates to the Department of Agriculture and Consumer Services for use on publicly owned or leased vehicles used for this purpose. Private license plates issued under this subsection shall be issued on an annual basis and the records of issuance shall be maintained in accordance with the provisions of G.S. 20-56.

(d) For purposes of this section, the term "private license plate" refers to a license plate that would normally be issued to a private party and therefore lacks any markings indicating that it

has been assigned to a publicly owned vehicle. "Confidential" license plates are a specialized form of private license plate for which a confidential registration has been authorized under subsection (e) of this section. "Fictitious" license plates are a specialized form of private license plate for which a fictitious registration has been issued under subsection (f) or (g) of this section.

(e) Upon approval and request of the Director of the State Bureau of Investigation, the Commissioner shall issue confidential license plates to local, State, or federal law enforcement agencies, the Department of Public Safety, agents of the Internal Revenue Service, and agents of the Department of Defense in accordance with the provisions of this subsection. Applicants in these categories shall provide satisfactory evidence to the Director of the State Bureau of Investigation of the following:

(1) The confidential license plate requested is to be used on a publicly owned or leased vehicle that is primarily used for transporting, apprehending, or arresting persons charged with violations of the laws of the United States or the State of North Carolina;

(2) The use of a confidential license plate is necessary to protect the personal safety of an officer or for placement on a vehicle used primarily for surveillance or undercover operations; and

(3) The application contains an original signature of the head of the requesting agency or department or, in the case of a federal agency, the signature of the senior ranking officer for that agency in this State.

Confidential license plates issued under this subsection shall be issued on an annual basis and the Division shall maintain a separate registration file for vehicles bearing confidential license plates. That file shall be confidential for the use of the Division and is not a public record within the meaning of Chapter 132 of the General Statutes. Upon the annual renewal of the registration of a vehicle for which a confidential status has been established under this section, the registration shall lose its confidential status unless the agency or department supplies the Director of the State Bureau of Investigation with information demonstrating that an officer's personal safety remains at risk or that the vehicle is still primarily used for surveillance or undercover operations at the time of renewal.

(f) The Commissioner may to the extent necessary provide law enforcement officers of the Division on special undercover assignments with motor vehicle operator's licenses and motor vehicle license plates under assumed names, using false or fictitious addresses. The Commissioner shall be responsible for the request for issuance and use of such licenses and license plates, and may direct the immediate return of any license or license plate issued pursuant to this subsection.

(g) The Commissioner may, upon the request of the Director of the State Bureau of Investigation and to the extent necessary, lawfully provide local, State, and federal law enforcement officers on special undercover assignments and to agents of the Department of Defense with motor vehicle drivers licenses and motor vehicle license plates under assumed names, using false or fictitious addresses. Fictitious license plates shall only be used on publicly owned or leased vehicles. A request for fictitious licenses and license plates by a local, State or federal law enforcement agency or department or by the Department of Defense shall be made in writing to the Director of the State Bureau of Investigation and shall contain an original signature of the head of the requesting agency or department or, in the case of a federal agency, the signature of the senior ranking officer for that agency in this State.

Prior to the issuance of any fictitious license or license plate, the Director of the State Bureau of Investigation shall make a specific written finding that the request is justified and necessary. The Director shall maintain a record of all such licenses, license plates, assumed names, false or fictitious addresses, and law enforcement officers using the licenses or license plates. That record shall be confidential and is not a public record within the meaning of Chapter 132 of the General Statutes. The Director shall request the immediate return of any license or registration that is no longer necessary.

Licenses and license plates provided under this subsection shall expire six months after initial issuance unless the Director of the State Bureau of Investigation has approved an extension in writing. The head of the local, State, or federal law enforcement agency or the Department of Defense shall be responsible for the use of the licenses and license plates and shall return them immediately to the Director for cancellation upon either (i) their expiration, (ii) request of the Director of the State Bureau of Investigation, or (iii) request of the Commissioner. Failure to return a license or license plate issued pursuant to this subsection shall be punished as a Class 2 misdemeanor. At no time shall the number of valid licenses issued under this subsection exceed two hundred nor shall the number of valid license plates issued under this subsection exceed one hundred twenty-five unless the Director determines that exceptional circumstances justify exceeding those amounts. However, fictitious licenses and license plates issued to special agents of the State Bureau of Investigation, State alcohol law enforcement agents, and the Department of Defense shall not be counted against the limitation on the total number of fictitious licenses and plates established by this subsection and shall be renewable annually.

(h) No private, confidential, or fictitious license plates issued under this section shall be used on privately owned vehicles under any circumstances.

(i) The Commissioner shall administer the issuance of private plates for publicly owned vehicles under the provisions of this section to ensure strict compliance with those provisions. The Division shall report to the Joint Legislative Commission on Governmental Operations by January 1 and July 1 of each year on the total number of private plates issued to each agency, and the total number of fictitious licenses and plates issued by the Division.

History.
2001-424, s. 6.14(a); 2001-424, s. 6.14(b); 2001-487, ss. 53, 54; 2003-152, ss. 3, 4; 2003- 284, ss. 6.5(a), (b); 2004-124, s. 6.5(a), (b); 2005-276, s. 6.18(a); 2011-145, s. 19.1(g); 2017-108, s. 10

§ 20-40. Offices of Division

The Commissioner shall maintain an office in Wake County, North Carolina, or a surrounding county, and in such places in the State as the Commissioner deems necessary to properly carry out the provisions of this Article.

History.
1937, c. 407, s. 5; 2018-5, s. 34.24(c)

§ 20-41. Commissioner to provide forms required

The Commissioner shall provide suitable forms for applications, certificates of title and registration cards, registration number plates and all other forms requisite for the purpose of this Article, and shall prepay all transportation charges thereon.

History.
1937, c. 407, s. 6

§ 20-42. Authority to administer oaths and certify copies of records

(a) Officers and employees of the Division designated by the Commissioner are, for the purpose of administering the motor vehicle laws, authorized to administer oaths and acknowledge signatures, and shall charge for the acknowledgment of signatures a fee according to the following schedule:

(1) One signature............................. $ 2.00
(2) Two signatures............................. 3.00

(3) Three or more signatures 4.00

Funds received under the provisions of this subsection shall be used to defray a part of the costs of distribution of license plates, registration certificates and certificates of title issued by the Division.

(b) The Commissioner and officers of the Division designated by the Commissioner may prepare under the seal of the Division and deliver upon request a certified copy of any document of the Division for a fee. The fee for a document, other than an accident report under G.S. 20-166.1, is thirteen dollars ($ 13.00). The fee for an accident report is five dollars ($ 5.00). A certified copy shall be admissible in any proceeding in any court in like manner as the original thereof, without further certification. The certification fee does not apply to a document furnished for official use to a judicial official or to an official of the federal government, a state government, or a local government.

History.
1937, c. 407, s. 7; 1955, c. 480; 1961, c. 861, s. 1; 1967, c. 691, s. 41; c. 1172; 1971, c. 749; 1975, c. 716, s. 5; 1977, c. 785; 1979, c. 801, s. 7; 1981, c. 690, ss. 22, 23; 1991, c. 689, s. 331; 1995, c. 191, s. 8; 2005-276, s. 44.1(h); 2015-241, s. 29.30(h)

§ 20-43. Records of Division

(a) All records of the Division, other than those declared by law to be confidential for the use of the Division, shall be open to public inspection during office hours in accordance with G.S. 20-43.1. A signature recorded in any format by the Division for a drivers license or a special identification card is confidential and shall not be released except for law enforcement purposes or to the State Chief Information Officer for purposes of G.S. 143B-1385 or the State Board of Elections in connection with its official duties under Chapter 163 of the General Statutes. A photographic image recorded in any format by the Division for a drivers license or a special identification card is confidential and shall not be released except for law enforcement purposes or to the State Chief Information Officer for the purposes of G.S. 143B-1385 or the State Board of Elections in connection with its official duties under Chapter 163 of the General Statutes.

(b) The Commissioner, upon receipt of notification from another state or foreign country that a certificate of title issued by the Division has been surrendered by the owner in conformity with the laws of such other state or foreign country, may cancel and destroy such record of certificate of title.

History.
1937, c. 407, s. 8; 1947, c. 219, s. 1; 1971, c. 1070, s. 1; 1975, c. 716, s. 5; 1995, c. 195, s. 1; 1997-443, s.

32.25(d); 2013-360, s. 7.10(b); 2014-115, s. 56.8(d); 2015-241, s. 7A.4(c); 2016-94, s. 24.1; 2017-6, s. 3; 2018-146, ss. 3.1(a), (b), 6.1

§ 20-43.1. Disclosure of personal information in motor vehicle records

(a) The Division shall disclose personal information contained in motor vehicle records in accordance with the federal Driver's Privacy Protection Act of 1994, as amended, 18 U.S.C. §§ 2721, et seq.

(b) As authorized in 18 U.S.C. § 2721, the Division shall not disclose personal information for the purposes specified in 18 U.S.C. § 2721(b)(11).

(c) The Division shall not disclose personal information for the purposes specified in 18 U.S.C. § 2721(b)(12) unless the Division receives prior written permission from the person about whom the information is requested.

(d) As authorized in 18 U.S.C. § 2721, the Division may disclose personal information to federally designated organ procurement organizations and eye banks operating in this State for the purpose of identifying individuals who have indicated an intent to be an organ donor. Personal information authorized under this subsection is limited to the individual's first, middle, and last name, date of birth, address, sex, county of residence, and drivers license number. Employees of the Division who provide access to or disclosure of information in good-faith compliance with this subsection are not liable in damages for access to or disclosure of the information.

(e) As authorized in 18 U.S.C. § 2721, the Division may also provide copies of partial crash report data collected pursuant to G.S. 20-166.1, partial driver license data kept pursuant to G.S. 20-26(a), and partial vehicle registration application data collected pursuant to G.S. 20-52 in bulk form to persons, private companies, or other entities, for uses other than official, upon payment of a fee of three cents (3 cent(s)) per individual record. The Division shall not furnish such data except upon execution by the recipient of a written agreement to comply with the Driver's Privacy Protection Act of 1994, as amended, 18 U.S.C. §§ 2721, et seq. The information released to persons, private companies, or other entities, for uses other than official, pursuant to this subsection, shall not be a public record pursuant to Chapter 132 of the General Statutes.

(f) E-mail addresses or other electronic addresses provided to the Division are personal information for purposes of this section and shall only be disclosed in accordance with this section.

History.
1997-443, s. 32.25(a); 1999-237, s. 27.9(b); 2004-189, s. 2; 2011-145, s. 31.29; 2016-90, s. 10(b)

§ 20-43.2. Internet access to organ donation records by organ procurement organizations

(a) The Department of Transportation, Division of Motor Vehicles, shall establish and maintain a statewide, online Organ Donor Registry Internet site (hereafter "Donor Registry"). The purpose of the Donor Registry is to enable federally designated organ procurement organizations and eye banks to have access 24 hours per day, seven days per week to obtain relevant information on the Donor Registry to determine, at or near death of the donor or a prospective donor, whether the donor or prospective donor has made, amended, or revoked an anatomical gift through a symbol on the donor's or prospective donor's drivers license, special identification card, or other manner. The data available on the Donor Registry shall be limited to the individual's first, middle, and last name, date of birth, address, sex, county of residence, and drivers license number. The Division of Motor Vehicles shall ensure that only federally designated organ procurement organizations and eye banks operating in this State have access to the Donor Registry in read-only format. The Division of Motor Vehicles shall enable federally designated organ procurement organizations and eye banks operating in this State to have online access in read-only format to the Donor Registry through a unique identifier and password issued to the organ procurement organization or eye bank by the Division of Motor Vehicles. Employees of the Division who provide access to or disclosure of information in good-faith compliance with this section are not liable in damages for access to or disclosure of the information.

(b) When accessing and using information obtained from the Donor Registry, federally designated organ procurement organizations and eye banks shall comply with the requirements of Part 3A of Article 16 of Chapter 130A of the General Statutes.

(c) Personally identifiable information on a donor registry about a donor or prospective donor may not be used or disclosed without the express consent of the donor, prospective donor, or person that made the anatomical gift for any purpose other than to determine, at or near death of the donor or prospective donor, whether the donor or prospective donor has made, amended, or revoked an anatomical gift.

(d) This section does not prohibit any person from creating or maintaining a donor registry that is not established by or under contract with the State. Any such registry must comply with subsections (b) and (c) of this section.

History.
2004-189, s. 1; 2007-538, s. 2

§ 20-43.3. Authorization for the collection of data to enforce the Federal Motor Carrier Safety Administration's Performance and Registration Information Systems Management (PRISM) program

The Division is authorized to collect and maintain necessary motor carrier or commercial motor vehicle data in a manner that complies with the information system established by the United States Secretary of Transportation under 49 U.S.C. § 31106.

History.
2019-196, s. 1

§ 20-43.4. Current list of licensed drivers to be provided to jury commissions

(a) The Commissioner of Motor Vehicles shall provide to each county jury commission an alphabetical list of all persons that the Commissioner has determined are residents of the county, who will be 18 years of age or older as of the first day of January of the following year, and licensed to drive a motor vehicle as of July 1 of each odd-numbered year, provided that if an annual master jury list is being prepared under G.S. 9-2(a), the list to be provided to the county jury commission shall be updated and provided annually.

(b) The list shall include those persons whose license to drive has been suspended, and those former licensees whose license has been canceled, except that the list shall not include the name of any formerly licensed driver whose license is expired and has not been renewed for eight years or more. The list shall contain the address and zip code of each driver, plus the driver's date of birth, sex, social security number, and drivers license number, and may be in either printed or computerized form, as requested by each county. Before providing the list to the county jury commission, the Commissioner shall have computer-matched the list with the voter registration list of the State Board of Elections to eliminate duplicates. The Commissioner shall also remove from the list the names of those residents of the county who are (i) issued a drivers license of limited duration under G.S. 20-7(s), (ii) issued a drivers license of regular duration under G.S. 20-7(f) and who hold a valid permanent resident card issued by the United States, or (iii) who are recently deceased, which names shall be supplied to the Commissioner by the State Registrar under G.S. 130A-121(b). The Commissioner shall include in the list provided to the county jury commission names of registered voters who do not have drivers licenses, and shall indicate the licensed or formerly licensed drivers who are also registered voters, the licensed or formerly licensed drivers who are not registered voters, and the registered voters who are not licensed or formerly licensed drivers.

(c) The list so provided shall be used solely for jury selection and election records purposes and no other. Information provided by the Commissioner to county jury commissions and the State Board of Elections under this section shall remain confidential, shall continue to be subject to the disclosure restriction provisions of G.S. 20-43.1, and shall not be a public record for purposes of Chapter 132 of the General Statutes.

History.
1981, c. 720, s. 2; 1983, c. 197, ss. 1, 1.1; c. 754; c. 768, s. 25.3; 2003-226, s. 7(c); 2007-512, s. 3; 2012-180, s. 11.5; 2017-6, s. 3; 2018-146, ss. 3.1(a), (b), 6.1

§ 20-44. Authority to grant or refuse applications

The Division shall examine and determine the genuineness, regularity and legality of every application for registration of a vehicle and for a certificate of title therefor, and of any other application lawfully made in the Division, and may in all cases make investigation as may be deemed necessary or require additional information, and shall reject any such application if not satisfied of the genuineness, regularity, or legality thereof or the truth of any statement contained therein, or for any other reason, when authorized by law.

History.
1937, c. 407, s. 9; 1975, c. 716, s. 5

§ 20-45. Seizure of documents and plates

(a) The Division is authorized to take possession of any certificate of title, registration card, permit, license, or registration plate issued by it upon expiration, revocation, cancellation, or suspension thereof, or which is fictitious, or which has been unlawfully or erroneously issued, or which has been unlawfully used.

(b) The Division may give notice to the owner, licensee or lessee of its authority to take possession of any certificate of title, registration card, permit, license, or registration plate issued by it and require that person to surrender it to the Commissioner or the Commissioner's officers or agents. Any person who fails to surrender the certificate of title, registration card, permit, license, or registration plate or any duplicate thereof, upon personal service of notice or within 10 days after receipt of notice by mail as provided in G.S. 20-48, shall be guilty of a Class 2 misdemeanor.

(c) Any sworn law enforcement officer with jurisdiction, including a member of the State Highway Patrol, is authorized to seize the certificate of title, registration card, permit, license, or registration plate, if the officer has electronic or other notification from the Division that the item has been revoked or cancelled, or otherwise has probable cause to believe that the item has been revoked or cancelled under any law or statute, including G.S. 20-311. If a criminal proceeding relating to a certificate of title, registration card, permit, or license is pending, the law enforcement officer in possession of that item shall retain the item pending the entry of a final judgment by a court with jurisdiction. If there is no criminal proceeding pending, the law enforcement officer shall deliver the item to the Division.

(d) Any law enforcement officer who seizes a registration plate pursuant to this section shall report the seizure to the Division within 48 hours of the seizure and shall return the registration plate, but not a fictitious registration plate, to the Division within 10 business days of the seizure.

History.
1937, c. 407, s. 10; 1975, c. 716, s. 5; 1981, c. 938, s. 2; 1993, c. 539, s. 329; 1994, Ex. Sess., c. 24, s. 14(c); 2005-357, s. 1; 2006-105, ss. 2.1, 2.2; 2006-264, s. 98.1; 2017-102, s. 6

N.C. Gen. Stat. § 20-46

Repealed by Session Laws 1979, c. 99.

§ 20-47. Division may summon witnesses and take testimony

(a) The Commissioner and officers of the Division designated by him shall have authority to summon witnesses to give testimony under oath or to give written deposition upon any matter under the jurisdiction of the Division. Such summons may require the production of relevant books, papers, or records.

(b) Every such summons shall be served at least five days before the return date, either by personal service made by any person over 18 years of age or by registered mail, but return acknowledgment is required to prove such latter service. Failure to obey such a summons so served shall constitute a Class 2 misdemeanor. The fees for the attendance and travel of witnesses shall be the same as for witnesses before the superior court.

(c) The superior court shall have jurisdiction, upon application by the Commissioner, to enforce all lawful orders of the Commissioner under this section.

History.
1937, c. 407, s. 12; 1975, c. 716, s. 5; 1993, c. 539, s. 330; 1994, Ex. Sess., c. 24, s. 14(c)

§ 20-48. Giving of notice

(a) Whenever the Division is authorized or required to give any notice under this Chapter or other law regulating the operation of vehicles, unless a different method of giving such notice is otherwise expressly prescribed, such notice shall be given either by personal delivery thereof to the person to be so notified or by deposit in the United States mail of such notice in an envelope with postage prepaid, addressed to such person at his address as shown by the records of the Division. The giving of notice by mail is complete upon the expiration of four days after such deposit of such notice. In lieu of providing notice by personal delivery or United States mail, the Division may give notice under this Chapter by e-mail or other electronic means if the person to be notified has consented to receiving notices via electronic means and has provided the Division an e-mail address or other like electronic address for receiving the notices. Proof of the giving of notice in any such manner pursuant to this section may be made by a notation in the records of the Division that the notice was sent to a particular address, physical or electronic, and the purpose of the notice. A certified copy of the Division's records may be sent by the Police Information Network, facsimile, or other electronic means. A copy of the Division's records sent under the authority of this section is admissible as evidence in any court or administrative agency and is sufficient evidence to discharge the burden of the person presenting the record that notice was sent to the person named in the record, at the physical or electronic address indicated in the record, and for the purpose indicated in the record. There is no requirement that the actual notice or letter be produced.

(a1) A person may consent to receive any notice under this Chapter by electronic delivery by completing a written or electronic authorization for this method of delivery. The authorization must advise the person that all of the following apply to consent to electronic delivery of a notice:

(1) Consent is effective until it is revoked in accordance with the procedure set by the Division.

(2) At the option of the Division, electronic delivery may be the only method of delivery.

(3) A notice sent by electronic delivery to an e-mail or electronic address is considered to have been received even if the person to whom it is sent does not receive it.

(a2) A person who consents to electronic notification pursuant to this section shall notify the Division of any change or discontinuance of any e-mail or electronic address provided to the Division in accordance with the provisions of this section and G.S. 20-7.1(a). Upon the failure of a person to notify the Division of any change or discontinuance of an electronic notification pursuant to this section, any notices sent to the original or discontinued electronic address shall be deemed to have been received by the person and a copy of the Division's records sent under the authority of this section is sufficient evidence that notice was sent to the person named in the record, at the physical or electronic address indicated in the record, and for the purpose indicated in the record.

(b) Notwithstanding any other provision of this Chapter at any time notice is now required by registered mail with return receipt requested, certified mail with return receipt requested may be used in lieu thereof and shall constitute valid notice to the same extent and degree as notice by registered mail with return receipt requested.

(c) The Commissioner shall appoint such agents of the Division as may be needed to serve revocation notices required by this Chapter. The fee for service of a revocation notice by personal delivery shall be fifty dollars ($ 50.00).

History.
1937, c. 407, s. 13; 1955, c. 1187, s. 21; 1971, c. 1231, s. 1; 1975, c. 326, s. 3; c. 716, s. 5; 1983, c. 761, s. 148; 1985, c. 479, s. 171; 2006-253, s. 21; 2016-90, s. 10(c)

§ 20-49. Police authority of Division

The Commissioner and such officers and inspectors of the Division as he shall designate and all members of the Highway Patrol and law enforcement officers of the Department of Public Safety shall have the power:

(1) Of peace officers for the purpose of enforcing the provisions of this Article and of any other law regulating the operation of vehicles or the use of the highways.

(2) To make arrests upon view and without warrant for any violation committed in their presence of any of the provisions of this Article or other laws regulating the operation of vehicles or the use of the highways.

(3) At all time to direct all traffic in conformance with law, and in the event of a fire or other emergency or to expedite traffic or to insure safety, to direct traffic as conditions may require, notwithstanding the provisions of law.

(4) When on duty, upon reasonable belief that any vehicle is being operated in violation of any provision of this Article or of any other law regulating the operation of vehicles to require the driver thereof to stop and exhibit his driver's license and the registration card issued for the vehicle, and submit to an inspection of such vehicle, the

Chapter 20

registration plates and registration card thereon or to an inspection and test of the equipment of such vehicle.

(5) To inspect any vehicle of a type required to be registered hereunder in any public garage or repair shop or in any place where such vehicles are held for sale or wrecking, for the purpose of locating stolen vehicles and investigating the title and registration thereof.

(6) To serve all warrants relating to the enforcement of the laws regulating the operation of vehicles or the use of the highways.

(7) To investigate traffic accidents and secure testimony of witnesses or of persons involved.

(8) To investigate reported thefts of motor vehicles, trailers and semitrailers and make arrest for thefts thereof.

(9) For the purpose of determining compliance with the provisions of this Chapter, to inspect all files and records of the persons hereinafter designated and required to be kept under the provisions of this Chapter or of the registrations of the Division:

    a. Persons dealing in or selling and buying new, used or junked motor vehicles and motor vehicle parts; and

    b. Persons operating garages or other places where motor vehicles are repaired, dismantled, or stored.

History.
1937, c. 407, s. 14; 1955, c. 554, s. 1; 1975, c. 716, s. 5; 1979, c. 93; 2002-159, s. 31.5(b); 2002-190, s. 5; 2011-145, s. 19.1(g)

§ 20-49.1. Supplemental police authority of Division officers

(a) In addition to the law enforcement authority granted in G.S. 20-49 or elsewhere, the Commissioner and the officers and inspectors of the Division whom the Commissioner designates have the authority to enforce criminal laws under any of the following circumstances:

(1) When they have probable cause to believe that a person has committed a criminal act in their presence and at the time of the violation they are engaged in the enforcement of laws otherwise within their jurisdiction.

(2) When they are asked to provide temporary assistance by the head of a State or local law enforcement agency or his designee and the request is within the scope of the agency's subject matter jurisdiction.

While acting pursuant to this subsection, the Division officers shall have the same powers vested in law enforcement officers by statute or common law. When acting pursuant to subdivision (2) of this subsection, the

Division officers shall not be considered an officer, employee, or agent of the State or local law enforcement agency or designee asking for temporary assistance. Nothing in this section shall be construed to expand the Division officers' authority to initiate or conduct an independent investigation into violations of criminal laws outside the scope of their subject matter or territorial jurisdiction.

(b) In addition to the law enforcement authority granted in G.S. 20-49 or elsewhere, the Commissioner and the officers and inspectors of the Division whom the Commissioner designates have the authority to investigate drivers license fraud and identity thefts related to drivers license fraud and to make arrests for these offenses.

History.
2004-148, s. 1

§ 20-49.2. Supplemental authority of State Highway Patrol Motor Carrier Enforcement officers

In addition to law enforcement authority granted in G.S. 20-49 or elsewhere, all sworn Motor Carrier Enforcement officers of the State Highway Patrol shall have the authority to enforce criminal laws under the following circumstances:

(1) When they have probable cause to believe that a person has committed a criminal act in their presence and at the time of the violation they are engaged in the enforcement of laws otherwise within their jurisdiction.

(2) When they are asked to provide temporary assistance by the head of a State or local law enforcement agency or his designee and the request is within the scope of the agency's subject matter jurisdiction.

While acting pursuant to this section, they shall have the same powers invested in law enforcement officers by statute or common law. When acting pursuant to subdivision (2) of this section, they shall not be considered an officer, employee, or agent for the State or local law enforcement agency or designee asking for temporary assistance. Nothing in this statute shall be construed to expand their authority to initiate or conduct an independent investigation into violations of criminal laws outside the scope of their subject matter or territorial jurisdiction.

History.
2004-148, s. 2

§ 20-49.3. Bureau of License and Theft; custody of seized vehicles

(a) **Vehicles Seized by the Division of Motor Vehicles. --** Notwithstanding any other provision of law, the Division of Motor Vehicles, Bureau of License and Theft, may retain any vehicle seized by the Division of Motor Vehicles, Bureau of License and Theft, in the course of any investigation authorized by the provisions of G.S. 20-49 or G.S. 20-49.1 and forfeited to the Division by a court of competent jurisdiction.

(b) **Vehicles Seized by the United States Government. --** Notwithstanding any other provision of law, the Division may accept custody and ownership of any vehicle seized by the United States Government, forfeited by a court of competent jurisdiction, and turned over to the Division.

(c) **Use of Vehicles. --** All vehicles forfeited to, or accepted by, the Division pursuant to this section shall be used by the Bureau of License and Theft to conduct undercover operations and inspection station compliance checks throughout the State.

(d) **Disposition of Seized Vehicles. --** Upon determination by the Commissioner of Motor Vehicles that a vehicle transferred pursuant to the provisions of this section is of no further use to the agency for use in official investigations, the vehicle shall be sold as surplus property in the same manner as other vehicles owned by the law enforcement agency and the proceeds from the sale after deducting the cost of sale shall be paid to the treasurer or proper officer authorized to receive fines and forfeitures to be used for the school fund of the county in the county in which the vehicle was seized, provided, that any vehicle transferred to any law enforcement agency under the provisions of this Article that has been modified to increase speed shall be used in the performance of official duties only and not for resale, transfer, or disposition other than as junk. The Division shall also reimburse the appropriate county school fund for any diminution in value of any vehicle seized under subsection (a) of this section during its period of use by the Division. Any vehicle seized outside of this State shall be sold as surplus property in the same manner as other vehicles owned by the law enforcement agency and the proceeds from the sale after deducting the cost of sale shall be paid to the treasurer and placed in the Civil Fines and Forfeitures Fund established pursuant to G.S. 115C-457.1.

History.
2009-495, s. 1

PART 3
REGISTRATION AND CERTIFICATES OF TITLES OF MOTOR VEHICLES

§ 20-50. Owner to secure registration and certificate of title; temporary registration markers

(a) A vehicle intended to be operated upon any highway of this State must be registered with the Division in accordance with G.S. 20-52, and the owner of the vehicle must comply with G.S. 20-52 before operating the vehicle. A vehicle that is leased to an individual who is a resident of this State is a vehicle intended to be operated upon a highway of this State.

The Commissioner of Motor Vehicles or the Commissioner's duly authorized agent is empowered to grant a special one-way trip permit to move a vehicle without license upon good cause being shown. When the owner of a vehicle leases the vehicle to a carrier of passengers or property and the vehicle is actually used by the carrier in the operation of its business, the license plates may be obtained by the lessee, upon written consent of the owner, after the certificate of title has been obtained by the owner. When the owner of a vehicle leases the vehicle to a farmer and the vehicle is actually used by the farmer in the operation of a farm, the license plates may be obtained by the farmer at the applicable farmer rate, upon written consent of the owner, after the certificate of title has been obtained by the owner. The lessee shall make application on an appropriate form furnished by the Division and file such evidence of the lease as the Division may require.

(b) The Division may issue a temporary license plate for a vehicle. A temporary license plate is valid for the period set by the Division. The period may not be less than 10 days nor more than 60 days.

A person may obtain a temporary license plate for a vehicle by filing an application with the Division and paying the required fee. An application must be filed on a form provided by the Division.

The fee for a temporary license plate that is valid for 10 days is ten dollars ($ 10.00). The fee for a temporary license plate that is valid for more than 10 days is the amount that would be required with an application for a license plate for the vehicle. If a person obtains for a vehicle a temporary license plate that is valid for more than 10 days and files an application for a license plate for that vehicle before the temporary license plate expires, the person is not required to pay the fee that would otherwise be required for the license plate.

A temporary license plate is subject to the following limitations and conditions:

(1) It may be issued only upon proper proof that the applicant has met the applicable financial responsibility requirements.

(2) It expires on midnight of the day set for expiration.

(3) It may be used only on the vehicle for which issued and may not be transferred, loaned, or assigned to another.

(4) If it is lost or stolen, the person who applied for it must notify the Division.

(5) It may not be issued by a dealer.

(6) The provisions of G.S. 20-63, 20-71, 20-110 and 20-111 that apply to license plates apply to temporary license plates insofar as possible.

History.

1937, c. 407, s. 15; 1943, c. 648; 1945, c. 956, s. 3; 1947, c. 219, s. 2; 1953, c. 831, s. 3; 1957, c. 246, s. 2; 1961, c. 360, s. 1; 1963, c. 552, s. 1; 1973, c. 919; 1975, c. 462; c. 716, s. 5; c. 767, s. 1; 1995, c. 394, s. 1; 1999-438, s. 26; 2005-276, s. 44.1(i); 2015-241, s. 29.35(b)

N.C. Gen. Stat. § 20-50.1

Repealed by Session Laws 1979, c. 574, s. 5.

N.C. Gen. Stat. § 20-50.2

Repealed by Session Laws 1991, c. 624, s. 4.

N.C. Gen. Stat. § 20-50.3

Repealed by Session Laws 2005-294, s. 10, effective July 1, 2013, and applicable to combined tax and registration notices issued on or after that date. See Editor's note.

History.

1991, c. 624, s. 5; 1991 (Reg. Sess., 1992), c. 961, s. 11; 2005-294, s. 10; 2006-259, s. 31.5; 2007-527, s. 22(b); 2008-134, s. 65; 2011-330, s. 42(a); 2012-79, s. 3.6; 2013-414, s. 70(d); repealed by 2005-294, s. 10, effective July 1, 2013

§ 20-50.4. Division to refuse to register vehicles on which county and municipal taxes and fees are not paid and when there is a failure to meet court-ordered child support obligations

(a) **Property Taxes Paid with Registration.** -- The Division shall refuse to register a vehicle on which county and municipal taxes and fees have not been paid.

(b) **Delinquent Child Support Obligations.** -- Upon receiving a report from a child support enforcement agency that sanctions pursuant to G.S. 110-142.2(a)(3) have been imposed, the Division shall refuse to register a vehicle for the owner named in the report until the Division receives certification pursuant to G.S. 110-142.2 that the payments are no longer considered delinquent.

History.

1991, c. 624, s. 5; 1995, c. 538, s. 2(g); 1995 (Reg. Sess., 1996), c. 741, ss. 1, 2; 2005-294, s. 11; 2006-259, s. 31.5; 2007-527, s. 22(b); 2008-134, s. 65; 2011-330, s. 42(a); 2012-79, s. 3.6; 2013-414, s. 70(d)

§ 20-51. Exempt from registration

The following shall be exempt from the requirement of registration and certificate of title:

(1) Any such vehicle driven or moved upon a highway in conformance with the provisions of this Article relating to manufacturers, dealers, or nonresidents.

(2) Any such vehicle which is driven or moved upon a highway only for the purpose of crossing such highway from one property to another.

(3) Any implement of husbandry, farm tractor, road construction or maintenance machinery or other vehicle which is not self-propelled that was designed for use in work off the highway and which is operated on the highway for the purpose of going to and from such nonhighway projects.

(4) Any vehicle owned and operated by the government of the United States.

(5) Farm tractors equipped with rubber tires or semitrailers when attached thereto and when used by a farmer, his tenant, agent, or employee in transporting his own farm implements, farm supplies, or farm products from place to place on the same farm, from one farm to another, from farm to market, or from market to farm. This exemption shall extend also to any tractor, implement of husbandry, and trailer or semitrailer while on any trip within a radius of 10 miles from the point of loading, provided that the vehicle does not exceed a speed of 35 miles per hour. This section shall not be construed as granting any exemption to farm tractors, implements of husbandry, and trailers or semitrailers which are operated on a for-hire basis, whether money or some other thing of value is paid or given for the use of such tractors, implements of husbandry, and trailers or semitrailers.

(6) Any trailer or semitrailer attached to and drawn by a properly licensed motor vehicle when used by a farmer, his tenant, agent, or employee in transporting unginned cotton, peanuts, soybeans, corn, hay, tobacco, silage, cucumbers, potatoes, all vegetables, fruits, greenhouse and nursery plants and flowers, Christmas trees, livestock, live poultry, animal waste, pesticides, seeds, fertilizers or chemicals purchased or owned by the farmer or tenant for personal use in implementing husbandry, irrigation pipes, loaders, or equipment owned by the farmer or tenant

from place to place on the same farm, from one farm to another, from farm to gin, from farm to dryer, or from farm to market, and when not operated on a for-hire basis. The term "transporting" as used herein shall include the actual hauling of said products and all unloaded travel in connection therewith.

(7) Those small farm trailers known generally as tobacco-handling trailers, tobacco trucks or tobacco trailers when used by a farmer, his tenant, agent or employee, when transporting or otherwise handling tobacco in connection with the pulling, tying or curing thereof.

(8) Any vehicle which is driven or moved upon a highway only for the purpose of crossing or traveling upon such highway from one side to the other provided the owner or lessee of the vehicle owns the fee or a leasehold in all the land along both sides of the highway at the place or crossing.

(9) Repealed by Session Laws 2014-114, s. 2, effective July 1, 2015, and applicable to offenses committed on or after that date.

(10) Devices which are designed for towing private passenger motor vehicles or vehicles not exceeding 5,000 pounds gross weight. These devices are known generally as "tow dollies." A tow dolly is a two-wheeled device without motive power designed for towing disabled motor vehicles and is drawn by a motor vehicle in the same manner as a trailer.

(11) Devices generally called converter gear or dollies consisting of a tongue attached to either a single or tandem axle upon which is mounted a fifth wheel and which is used to convert a semitrailer to a full trailer for the purpose of being drawn behind a truck tractor and semitrailer.

(12) Motorized wheelchairs or similar vehicles not exceeding 1,000 pounds gross weight when used for pedestrian purposes by a handicapped person with a mobility impairment as defined in G.S. 20-37.5.

(13) Any vehicle registered in another state and operated temporarily within this State by a public utility, a governmental or cooperative provider of utility services, or a contractor for one of these entities for the purpose of restoring utility services in an emergency outage.

(14) Electric personal assistive mobility devices as defined in G.S. 20-4.01(7b).

(15) Any vehicle that meets all of the following:

     a. Is designed for use in work off the highway.

     b. Is used for agricultural quarantine programs under the supervision of the Department of Agriculture and Consumer Services.

     c. Is driven or moved on the highway for the purpose of going to and from nonhighway projects.

     d. Is identified in a manner approved by the Division of Motor Vehicles.

     e. Is operated by a person who possesses an identification card issued by the Department of Agriculture and Consumer Services.

(16) A vehicle that meets all of the following conditions is exempt from the requirement of registration and certificate of title. The provisions of G.S. 105-449.117 continue to apply to the vehicle and to the person in whose name the vehicle would be registered.

     a. Is an agricultural spreader vehicle. An "agricultural spreader vehicle" is a vehicle that is designed for off-highway use on a farm to spread feed, fertilizer, seed, lime, or other agricultural products.

     b. Is driven on the highway only for the purpose of going from the location of its supply source for fertilizer or other products to and from a farm.

     c. Does not exceed a speed of 45 miles per hour.

     d. Does not drive outside a radius of 50 miles from the location of its supply source for fertilizer and other products.

     e. Is driven by a person who has a license appropriate for the class of the vehicle.

     f. Is insured under a motor vehicle liability policy in the amount required under G.S. 20-309.

     g. Displays a valid federal safety inspection decal if the vehicle has a gross vehicle weight rating of at least 10,001 pounds.

(17) A header trailer when transported to or from a dealer, or after a sale or repairs, to the farm or another dealership.

History.
1937, c. 407, s. 16; 1943, c. 500; 1949, c. 429; 1951, c. 705, s. 2; 1953, c. 826, ss. 2, 3; c. 1316, s. 1; 1961, cc. 334, 817; 1963, c. 145; 1965, c. 1146; 1971, c. 107; 1973, cc. 478, 757, 964; 1979, c. 574, s. 6; 1981 (Reg. Sess., 1982), c. 1286; 1983, cc. 288, 732; 1987, c. 608; 1989, c. 157, s. 2; 1991, c. 411, s. 4; 1995, c. 50, s. 4; 1999-281, s. 2; 2002-98, s. 4; 2002-150, s. 1; 2006-135, s. 2; 2007-194, s. 1; 2007-527, s. 41; 2012-78, ss. 2, 3; 2014-114, s. 2; 2015-263, s. 7; 2016-90, s. 13(i)

§ 20-52. Application for registration and certificate of title

(a) An owner of a vehicle subject to registration must apply to the Division for a certificate of title, a registration plate, and a registration card for the vehicle. To apply, an owner must complete an application provided by the Division. The application shall contain a preprinted option that co-owners may use to title the vehicle as a joint tenancy with right of survivorship. The co-owners' designation of a joint tenancy with right of survivorship on the application shall be valid notwithstanding whether this designation appears on the assignment of title. The application must request all of the following information and may request other information the Division considers necessary:

(1) The owner's name.

(1a) If the owner is an individual, the following information:

a. The owner's mailing address and residence address.

b. One of the following at the option of the applicant:

1. The owner's North Carolina drivers license number or North Carolina special identification card number.

2. The owner's home state drivers license number or home state special identification card number and valid active duty military identification card number or military dependent identification card number if the owner is a person or the spouse or dependent child of a person on active duty in the Armed Forces of the United States who is stationed in this State or deployed outside this State from a home base in this State. The owner's inability to provide a photocopy or reproduction of a military or military dependent identification card pursuant to any prohibition of the United States government or any agency thereof against the making of such photocopy or reproduction shall not operate to prevent the owner from making an application for registration and certificate of title pursuant to this subdivision.

3. The owner's home state drivers license number or home state special identification card number and proof of enrollment in a school in this State if the owner is a permanent resident of another state but is currently enrolled in a school in this State.

4. The owner's home state drivers license number or home state special identification card number if the owner provides a signed affidavit certifying that the owner intends to principally garage the

vehicle in this State and provides the address where the vehicle is or will be principally garaged. For purposes of this section, "principally garage" means the vehicle is garaged for six or more months of the year on property in this State which is owned, leased, or otherwise lawfully occupied by the owner of the vehicle.

5. The owner's home state drivers license number or home state special identification card number, provided that the application is made pursuant to a court authorized sale or a sale authorized by G.S. 44A-4 for the purpose of issuing a title to be registered in another state or country.

6. The co-owner's home state drivers license number or home state special identification card number if at least one co-owner provides a North Carolina drivers license number or North Carolina special identification number.

7. The owner's home state drivers license number or special identification card number if the application is for a motor home or house car, as defined in G.S. 20-4.01(27) k., or for a house trailer, as defined in G.S. 20-4.01(14).

(1b) If the owner is a firm, partnership, a corporation, or another entity, the address of the entity.

(2) A description of the vehicle, including the following:

a. The make, model, type of body, and vehicle identification number of the vehicle.

b. Whether the vehicle is new or used and, if a new vehicle, the date the manufacturer or dealer sold the vehicle to the owner and the date the manufacturer or dealer delivered the vehicle to the owner.

(3) A statement of the owner's title and of all liens upon the vehicle, including the names and addresses of all lienholders in the order of their priority, and the date and nature of each lien.

(4) -- (6) Repealed by Session Laws 2017-69, s. 2(a), effective July 1, 2017.

(7) A statement that the owner has proof of financial responsibility, as required by Article 9A or Article 13 of this Chapter.

(a1) An owner who would otherwise be capable of attaining a drivers license or special identification card from this State or any other state, except for a medical or physical condition that can be documented to, and verified by, the Division, shall be issued a registration plate and certificate of title if the owner provides a signed affidavit certifying that the owner intends to principally garage the vehicle in this State and provides the address where the vehicle is or will be principally garaged.

(b) When such application refers to a new vehicle purchased from a manufacturer or dealer, such application shall be accompanied with a manufacturer's certificate of origin that is properly assigned to the applicant. If the new vehicle is acquired from a dealer or person located in another jurisdiction other than a manufacturer, the application shall be accompanied with such evidence of ownership as is required by the laws of that jurisdiction duly assigned by the disposer to the purchaser, or, if no such evidence of ownership be required by the laws of such other jurisdiction, a notarized bill of sale from the disposer.

(c) Unless otherwise prohibited by federal law, an application for a certificate of title, salvage certificate of title, a registration plate, a registration card, and any other document required by the Division to be submitted with the application and requiring a signature may be submitted to the Division with an electronic signature in accordance with Article 40 of Chapter 66 of the General Statutes. The required notarization of any electronic signature on any application or document submitted to the Division pursuant to this subsection may be performed electronically in accordance with Article 2 of Chapter 10B of the General Statutes. The Division will not certify or approve a specific electronic process or vendor. Any entity offering an electronic signature process assumes all responsibility and liability for the accuracy of the signature. The Division shall be held harmless from any liability to a claim arising from applications submitted with an inaccurate electronic signature pursuant to this subsection.

History.
1937, c. 407, s. 17; 1961, c. 835, ss. 2, 3; 1975, c. 716, s. 5; 1991, c. 183, s. 2; 1993 (Reg. Sess., 1994), c. 750, s. 5; 2007-164, s. 4; 2007-209, ss. 1, 2; 2007-443, s. 6; 2007-481, ss. 4 -7; 2008-124, s. 4.1; 2009-274, s. 4; 2015-270, s. 1; 2016-90, s. 10.5(a); 2017-69, s. 2(a), (b); 2017-102, s. 5.2(b); 2019-153, s. 1

§ 20-52.1. Manufacturer's certificate of transfer of new motor vehicle

(a) Any manufacturer transferring a new motor vehicle to another shall, at the time of the transfer, supply the transferee with a manufacturer's certificate of origin assigned to the transferee.

(b) Any dealer transferring a new vehicle to another dealer shall, at the time of transfer,

give such transferee the proper manufacturer's certificate assigned to the transferee.

(c) Upon sale of a new vehicle by a dealer to a consumer-purchaser, the dealer shall execute in the presence of a person authorized to administer oaths an assignment of the manufacturer's certificate of origin for the vehicle, including in such assignment the name and address of the transferee and no title to a new motor vehicle acquired by a dealer under the provisions of subsections (a) and (b) of this section shall pass or vest until such assignment is executed and the motor vehicle delivered to the transferee.

Any dealer transferring title to, or an interest in, a new vehicle shall deliver the manufacturer's certificate of origin duly assigned in accordance with the foregoing provision to the transferee at the time of delivering the vehicle, except that where a security interest is obtained in the motor vehicle from the transferee in payment of the purchase price or otherwise, the transferor shall deliver the manufacturer's certificate of origin to the lienholder and the lienholder shall forthwith forward the manufacturer's certificate of origin together with the transferee's application for certificate of title and necessary fees to the Division. Any person who delivers or accepts a manufacturer's certificate of origin assigned in blank shall be guilty of a Class 2 misdemeanor, unless done in accordance with subsection (d) of this section.

(d) When a manufacturer's statement of origin or an existing certificate of title on a motor vehicle is unavailable, a motor vehicle dealer licensed under Article 12 of this Chapter may also transfer title to a vehicle to another by certifying in writing in a sworn statement to the Division signed by the dealer principal, general manager, general sales manager, controller, owner, or other manager of the dealership that, to the best of the signatory's knowledge and information as of the date of sworn certification, all prior perfected liens on the vehicle that are known or reasonably ascertainable by the signatory have been paid and that the motor vehicle dealer, despite having used reasonable diligence, is unable to obtain the vehicle's statement of origin or certificate of title. For purposes of this subsection, a dealer may certify that the dealer is unable to obtain the vehicle's statement of origin or certificate of title because the statement of origin or certificate of title was either (i) not delivered to the dealer or (ii) lost or misplaced. The Division is authorized to require any information it deems necessary for the transfer of the vehicle and shall develop a form for this purpose. The knowing and intentional filing of a false sworn certification with the Division pursuant to this subsection shall constitute a Class H felony. A dealer principal, owner, or manager who is not a signatory of the sworn certification under this subsection may only be charged for a criminal violation for filing a false certification under this subsection by another dealership employee if the dealer principal, owner, or manager had actual knowledge of the falsity of the sworn certification at the time the sworn certification was submitted to the Division. The dealer shall hold harmless and indemnify the consumer-purchaser from any damages arising from the use of the procedure authorized by this subsection. No person shall have a cause of action against the Division or Division contractors arising from the transfer of a vehicle by a sworn certification pursuant to this section.

History.
1961, c. 835, s. 4; 1967, c. 863; 1975, c. 716, s. 5; 1993, c. 539, s. 331; 1994, Ex. Sess., c. 24, s. 14(c); 2000-182, s. 1; 2018-42, s. 2(a); 2018-145, s. 4; 2019-181, s. 5(a); 2020-51, s. 3(a)

§ 20-52.2. Unregisterable certificate of title

(a) Notwithstanding the provisions of G.S. 20-52, the Division is directed to create and issue an unregisterable certificate of title. An owner of an eligible vehicle may apply for an unregisterable certificate of title by submitting an application on a form provided by the Division.

(b) The Division may determine the color, content, and format of an unregisterable certificate of title, provided that:

    (1) An unregisterable certificate of title shall be distinct in color from other types of vehicle titles.

    (2) An unregisterable certificate of title shall contain a notice that the vehicle described thereon is no longer able to be registered for highway use in this State. The notice shall also contain a statement that the unregisterable certificate of title is solely intended for proof of ownership and use in transferring the vehicle for parts only, destruction, or recycling.

(c) Vehicles meeting the requirements of G.S. 20-109.1A are eligible for issuance of an unregisterable certificate of title.

(d) A vehicle issued an unregisterable certificate of title under this section is no longer eligible for titling or registration for highway use, provided that the Division may rescind the issuance of an unregisterable certificate of title if it determines the title was issued in error.

History.
2021-126, s. 1

§ 20-53. Application for specially constructed, reconstructed, or foreign vehicle

(a) In the event the vehicle to be registered is a specially constructed, reconstructed, or foreign vehicle, such fact shall be stated in the application, and with reference to every foreign vehicle which has been registered outside of this State, the owner shall surrender to the Division all registration cards, certificates of title or notarized copies of original titles on vehicles 35 model years old and older, or other evidence of such foreign registration as may be in his possession or under his control, except as provided in subsection (b) hereof. After initial review, the Division shall return to the owner any original titles presented on vehicles 35 model years old and older appropriately marked indicating that the title has been previously submitted.

(b) Where, in the course of interstate operation of a vehicle registered in another state, it is desirable to retain registration of said vehicle in such other state, such applicant need not surrender, but shall submit for inspection said evidence of such foreign registration, and the Division in its discretion, and upon a proper showing, shall register said vehicle in this State but shall not issue a certificate of title for such vehicle.

(c), (d) Repealed by Session Laws 1965, c. 734, s. 2.

(e) No title shall be issued to an initial applicant for (i) out-of-state vehicles that are 1980 model year or older or (ii) a specially constructed vehicle prior to the completion of a vehicle verification conducted by the License and Theft Bureau of the Division of Motor Vehicles. These verifications shall be conducted as soon as practical. For an out-of-state vehicle that is 1980 model year or older, this inspection shall consist of verifying the public vehicle identification number to ensure that it matches the vehicle and ownership documents. No covert vehicle identification numbers are to be examined on an out-of-state vehicle 1980 model year or older unless the inspector develops probable cause to believe that the ownership documents or public vehicle identification number presented does not match the vehicle being examined. However, upon such application and the submission of any required documentation, the Division shall be authorized to register the vehicle pending the completion of the verification of the vehicle. The registration shall be valid for one year but shall not be renewed unless and until the vehicle examination has been completed.

If an inspection and verification is not conducted by the License and Theft Bureau of the Division of Motor Vehicles within 15 days after receiving a request for such and the inspector has no probable cause to believe that the ownership documents or public vehicle identification number presented does not match the vehicle being examined, the vehicle shall be deemed to have satisfied all inspection and verification requirements and title shall issue to the owner within 15 days thereafter. If an inspection and verification is timely performed and the vehicle passes the inspection and verification, title shall issue to the owner within 15 days of the date of the inspection.

(f) If a vehicle owner desires a vehicle title classification change, he or she may, upon proper application, be eligible for a reclassification.

History.
1937, c. 407, s. 18; 1949, c. 675; 1953, c. 853; 1957, c. 1355; 1965, c. 734, s. 2; 1975, c. 716, s. 5; 2009-405, s. 5; 2013-349, s. 1; 2016-90, s. 11(a)

§ 20-53.1. Specially constructed vehicle certificate of title and registration

(a) Specially constructed vehicles shall be titled in the following manner:

(1) Replica vehicles shall be titled as the year, make, and model of the vehicle intended to be replicated. A label of "Replica" shall be applied to the title and registration card. All replica vehicle titles shall be labeled "Specially Constructed Vehicle."

(2) The model year of a street rod vehicle shall continue to be recognized as the manufacturer's assigned model year. The manufacturer's name shall continue to be used as the make with a label of "Street Rod" applied to the title and registration card. All street rod vehicle titles shall be labeled "Specially Constructed Vehicle."

(3) Custom-built vehicles shall be titled and registered showing the make as "Custom-built," and the year the vehicle was built shall be the vehicle model year. All custom-built vehicle titles shall be labeled "Specially Constructed Vehicle."

(b) Inoperable vehicles may be titled, but no registration may be issued until such time as the License and Theft Bureau inspects the vehicle to ensure it is substantially assembled. Once a vehicle has been verified as substantially assembled pursuant to an inspection by the License and Theft Bureau, the Commissioner shall title the vehicle by classifying it in the proper category and collecting all highway use taxes applicable to the value of the car at the time the vehicle is retitled to a proper classification, as described in this section.

(c) Motor vehicle certificates of title and registration cards issued pursuant to this section shall be labeled in accordance with this section. As used in this section, "labeled" means that the title and registration card shall contain a designation that discloses if the vehicle is classified as any of the following:

(1) Specially constructed vehicle.
(2) Inoperable vehicle.

History.
2009-405, s. 2

N.C. Gen. Stat. § 20-53.2

Reserved for future codification purposes.

§ 20-53.3. Appeal of specially constructed vehicle classification determination to Vehicle Classification Review Committee

(a) Any person aggrieved by the Division's determination of the appropriate vehicle classification for a specially constructed vehicle may request review of that determination by the Vehicle Classification Review Committee. This review shall be initiated by completing a Vehicle Classification Review Request and returning the request to the Division. The Vehicle Classification Review Request shall be made on a form provided by the Division. The decision of the Review Committee may be appealed to the Commissioner of Motor Vehicles.

(b) The Vehicle Classification Review Committee shall consist of five members as follows:

(1) Two members shall be personnel of the License and Theft Bureau of the Division of Motor Vehicles appointed by the Commissioner.

(2) One member shall be a member of the public with expertise in antique or specially constructed vehicles appointed by the Commissioner from a list of nominees provided by the Antique Automobile Club of America.

(3) One member shall be a member of the public with expertise in antique or specially constructed vehicles appointed by the Commissioner from a list of nominees provided by the Specialty Equipment Market Association.

(4) One member shall be a member of the public with expertise in antique or specially constructed vehicles appointed by the Commissioner from a list of nominees provided by the National Corvette Restorers Society.

(c) Members of the Vehicle Classification Review Committee shall serve staggered two-year terms. Initial appointments shall be made on or before October 1, 2009. The initial appointment of one of the members from the License and Theft Bureau and the member nominated by the Antique Automobile Club of America shall be for one year. The initial appointments of the remaining members shall be for two years. At the expiration of these initial terms, appointments shall be for two years. A member of the Committee may be removed at any time by unanimous vote of the remaining four members. Vacancies shall be filled in the manner set out in subsection (b) of this section.

History.
2009-405, s. 6

§ 20-53.4. Registration of mopeds; certificate of title

(a) **Registration.** -- Mopeds shall be registered with the Division. The owner of the moped shall pay the same base fee and be issued the same type of registration card and plate issued for a motorcycle. In order to be registered with the Division and operated upon a highway or public vehicular area, a moped must meet the following requirements:

(1) The moped has a manufacturer's certificate of origin.

(2) The moped was designed and manufactured for use on highways or public vehicular areas.

(b) **Certificate of Title.** -- Notwithstanding G.S. 20-52 and G.S. 20-57, the owner of a moped is not required to apply for, and the Division is not required to issue, a certificate of title.

History.
2014-114, s. 1; 2015-125, s. 9

§ 20-53.5. Titling and registration of HMMWV

(a) **Registration and Certificate of Title.** -- The Division shall register and issue a certificate of title for an HMMWV if all of the following conditions are met:

(1) The applicant for the title and registration of the HMMWV has provided to the Division a sworn affidavit from a manufacturer, motor vehicle dealer, or seller of the HMMWV certifying that the vehicle complies with all applicable federal motor vehicle safety standards for vehicles designed for highway use.

(2) The vehicle has a vehicle identification number that matches the vehicle ownership documents. If the vehicle does not have a vehicle identification number, the Division shall assign one to the vehicle prior to registration. The existence of a valid vehicle identification number for the vehicle shall be verified by the License and Theft Bureau of the Division prior to its registration and titling.

(b) **Applicability of This Chapter.** -- All provisions of this Chapter shall apply to an HMMWV, including the provisions of Article 3A and Article 9A of this Chapter, to the same extent they would apply to any other registered motor vehicle.

(c) **Fees.** -- The vehicle registration fees applicable to property-hauling vehicles shall apply to the registration of an HMMWV.

(d) **No Liability for Operations.** -- Neither the State nor its commission contract agents shall be liable for any injury or damages resulting from the operation of an HMMWV registered or titled pursuant to this section.

History.
2017-69, s. 2.1(b)

§ 20-54. Authority for refusing registration or certificate of title

The Division shall refuse registration or issuance of a certificate of title or any transfer of registration upon any of the following grounds:

(1) The application contains a false or fraudulent statement, the applicant has failed to furnish required information or reasonable additional information requested by the Division, or the applicant is not entitled to the issuance of a certificate of title or registration of the vehicle under this Article.

(2) The vehicle is mechanically unfit or unsafe to be operated or moved upon the highways.

(3) The Division has reasonable ground to believe that the vehicle is a stolen or embezzled vehicle, or that the granting of registration or the issuance of a certificate of title would constitute a fraud against the rightful owner or another person who has a valid lien against the vehicle.

(4) The registration of the vehicle stands suspended or revoked for any reason as provided in the motor vehicle laws of this State, except in such cases to abide by the ignition interlock installation requirements of G.S. 20-17.8.

(5) The required fee has not been paid, including any additional registration fees or taxes due pursuant to G.S. 20-91(c).

(6) The vehicle is not in compliance with the inspection requirements of Part 2 of Article 3A of this Chapter or a civil penalty assessed as a result of the failure of the vehicle to comply with that Part has not been paid.

(7) The Division has been notified that the motor vehicle has been seized by a law enforcement officer and is subject to forfeiture pursuant to G.S. 20-28.2, et seq., or any other statute. However, the Division shall not prevent the renewal of existing registration prior to an order of forfeiture.

(8) The vehicle is a golf cart or utility vehicle.

(9) The applicant motor carrier is subject to an order issued by the Federal Motor Carrier Safety Administration or the Division. The Division shall deny registration of a vehicle of a motor carrier if the applicant

Chapter 20

fails to disclose material information required, or if the applicant has made a materially false statement on the application, or if the applicant has applied as a subterfuge for the real party in interest who has been issued a federal out-of-service order, or if the applicant's business is operated, managed, or otherwise controlled by or affiliated with a person who is ineligible for registration, including the applicant entity, a relative, family member, corporate officer, or shareholder. The Division shall deny registration for a vehicle that has been assigned for safety to a commercial motor carrier who has been prohibited from operating by the Federal Motor Carrier Safety Administration or a carrier whose business is operated, managed, or otherwise controlled by or affiliated with a person who is ineligible for registration, including the owner, a relative, family member, corporate officer, or shareholder.

(10) The North Carolina Turnpike Authority has notified the Division that the owner of the vehicle has not paid the amount of tolls, fees, and civil penalties the owner owes the Authority for use of a Turnpike project.

(11) The Division has been notified (i) pursuant to G.S. 20-217(g2) that the owner of the vehicle has failed to pay any fine imposed pursuant to G.S. 20-217 or (ii) pursuant to G.S. 153A-246(b)(14) that the owner of the vehicle has failed to pay a civil penalty due under G.S. 153A-246.

(12) The owner of the vehicle has failed to pay any penalty or fee imposed pursuant to G.S. 20-311.

(13) The Division has been notified by the State Highway Patrol that the owner of the vehicle has failed to pay any civil penalty and fees imposed by the State Highway Patrol for a violation of Part 9 of Article 3 of this Chapter.

History.
1937, c. 407, s. 19; 1975, c. 716, s. 5; 1993 (Reg. Sess., 1994), c. 754, s. 7; 1998-182, s. 9; 2001-356, s. 3; 2002-152, s. 1; 2007-164, s. 5; 2008-225, s. 7; 2009-319, s. 1; 2013-293, s. 4; 2015-241, s. 29.31(b); 2016-87, s. 4; 2017-188, s. 3; 2019-196, s. 2

§ 20-54.1. Forfeiture of right of registration

(a) Upon receipt of notice of conviction of a violation of an offense involving impaired driving while the person's license is revoked as a result of a prior impaired driving license revocation as defined in G.S. 20-28.2, the Division shall revoke the registration of all motor vehicles registered in the convicted person's name and shall not register a motor vehicle in the convicted person's name until the convicted person's license is restored, except in such cases to abide by the ignition interlock installation requirements of G.S. 20-17.8. Upon receipt of notice of revocation of registration from the Division, the convicted person shall surrender the registration on all motor vehicles registered in the convicted person's name to the Division within 10 days of the date of the notice.

(a1) Upon receipt of notice of conviction of a felony speeding to elude arrest offense under G.S. 20-141.5(b) or (b1), the Division shall revoke the registration of all motor vehicles registered in the convicted person's name and shall not register a motor vehicle in the convicted person's name until the convicted person's license is restored. Upon receipt of notice of revocation of registration from the Division, the convicted person shall surrender the registration on all motor vehicles registered in the convicted person's name to the Division within 10 days of the date of the notice.

(b) Upon receipt of a notice of conviction under subsection (a) or (a1) of this section, the Division shall revoke the registration of the motor vehicle seized, and the owner shall not be allowed to register the motor vehicle seized until the convicted operator's drivers license has been restored. The Division shall not revoke the registration of the owner of the seized motor vehicle if the owner is determined to be an innocent owner. The Division shall revoke the owner's registration only after the owner is given an opportunity for a hearing to demonstrate that the owner is an innocent owner as defined in G.S. 20-28.2. Upon receipt of notice of revocation of registration from the Division, the owner shall surrender the registration on the motor vehicle seized to the Division within 10 days of the date of the notice.

History.
1998-182, s. 10; 2007-164, s. 6; 2013-243, s. 5

§ 20-55. Examination of registration records and index of seized, stolen, and recovered vehicles

The Division, upon receiving application for any transfer of registration or for original registration of a vehicle, other than a new vehicle sold by a North Carolina dealer, shall first check the engine and serial numbers shown in the application with its record of registered motor vehicles, and against the index of seized, stolen and recovered motor vehicles required to be maintained by this Article.

History.
1937, c. 407, s. 20; 1971, c. 1070, s. 2; 1975, c. 716, s. 5; 1998-182, s. 11

§ 20-56. Registration indexes

(a) The Division shall file each application received, and when satisfied as to the genuineness and regularity thereof, and that the applicant is entitled to register such vehicle and to the issuance of a certificate of title, shall register the vehicle therein described and keep a record thereof as follows:

(1) Under a distinctive registration number assigned to the vehicle;

(2) Alphabetically, under the name of the owner;

(3) Under the motor number or any other identifying number of the vehicle; and

(4) In the discretion of the Division, in any other manner it may deem advisable.

(b) Repealed by Session Laws 2001, c. 424, s. 6.14(g), effective September 26, 2001.

History.
1937, c. 407, s. 20 1/2; 1949, c. 583, s. 5; 1971, c. 1070, s. 3; 1975, c. 716, s. 5; 1991, c. 53, s. 2; 2001-424, s. 6.14(g)

§ 20-57. Division to issue certificate of title and registration card

(a) The Division upon registering a vehicle shall issue a registration card and a certificate of title as separate documents.

(b) The registration card shall be delivered to the owner and shall contain upon the face thereof the name and address of the owner, the registration number assigned to the vehicle, and a description of the vehicle as determined by the Commissioner, provided that if there are more than two owners the Division may show only two owners on the registration card and indicate that additional owners exist by placing after the names listed "et al." An owner may obtain a copy of a registration card issued in the owner's name by applying to the Division for a copy and paying the fee set in G.S. 20-85.

(c) Every such registration card shall at all times be carried in the vehicle to which it refers or in the vehicle to which transfer is being effected, as provided by G.S. 20-64 at the time of its operation, and such registration card shall be displayed upon demand of any peace officer or any officer of the Division: Provided, however, any person charged with failing to so carry such registration card shall not be convicted if he produces in court a registration card theretofore issued to him and valid at the time of his arrest: Provided further, that in case of a transfer of a license plate from one vehicle to another under the provisions of G.S. 20-72, evidence of application for transfer shall be carried in the vehicle in lieu of the registration card.

(d) The certificate of title shall contain upon the face thereof the identical information required upon the face of the registration card except the abbreviation "et al." if such appears and in addition thereto the name of all owners, the date of issuance and all liens or encumbrances disclosed in the application for title. All such liens or encumbrances shall be shown in the order of their priority, according to the information contained in such application.

(e) The certificate of title shall contain upon the reverse side an assignment of title or interest and warranty by registered owner or registered dealer. The purchaser's application for North Carolina certificate of title shall be made on a form prescribed by the Commissioner and shall include a space for notation of liens and encumbrances on the vehicle at the time of transfer.

(f) Certificates of title upon which liens or encumbrances are shown shall be delivered or mailed by the Division to the holder of the first lien or encumbrance.

(g) Certificates of title shall bear thereon the seal of the Division.

(h) Certificates of title need not be renewed annually, but shall remain valid until canceled by the Division for cause or upon a transfer of any interest shown therein.

History.
1937, c. 407, s. 21; 1943, c. 715; 1961, c. 360, s. 2; c. 835, s. 5; 1963, c. 552, s. 2; 1973, c. 72; c. 764, ss. 1-3; c. 1118; 1975, c. 716, s. 5; 1979, c. 139; 1981, c. 690, s. 20; 1983, c. 252; 1991, c. 193, s. 7; 2016-90, s. 12(a); 2019-227, s. 2

§ 20-58. Perfection by indication of security interest on certificate of title

(a) Except as provided in G.S. 20-58.8, a security interest in a vehicle of a type for which a certificate of title is required shall be perfected only as hereinafter provided:

(1) If the vehicle is not registered in this State, the application for notation of a security interest shall be the application for certificate of title provided for in G.S. 20-52.

(2) If the vehicle is registered in this State, the application for notation of a security interest shall be in the form prescribed by the Division, signed by the debtor, and contain the date of application of each security interest, and name and address of the secured party from whom information concerning the security interest may be obtained. The application may be signed by electronic signature by the debtor without notarization, provided the application is submitted by a licensed or regulated lender in this State having a lienholder identification number issued by the Division. The application must be accompanied by the existing certificate of title unless in the possession of a prior secured party or in

the event the manufacturer's statement of origin or existing certificate of title (i) was not delivered to the dealer or (ii) was lost or misplaced on the date the dealer sells or transfers the motor vehicle. If there is an existing certificate of title issued by this or any other jurisdiction in the possession of a prior secured party, the application for notation of the security interest shall in addition contain the name and address of such prior secured party. An application for notation of a security interest may be signed by the secured party instead of the debtor when the application is accompanied by documentary evidence of the applicant's security interest in that motor vehicle signed by the debtor and by affidavit of the applicant stating the reason the debtor did not sign the application. An application for a notation of a security interest submitted to the Division signed by the secured party instead of the debtor does not require documentary evidence of the applicant's security interest in that motor vehicle signed by the debtor, provided the application is submitted by a licensed or regulated lender in this State having a lienholder identification number issued by the Division. In the event the certificate cannot be obtained for recordation of the security interest, when title remains in the name of the debtor, the Division shall cancel the certificate and issue a new certificate of title listing all the respective security interests. Neither the Division nor its commission contractors shall be liable for any cause of action arising from a notation of security interest placed on a certificate of title pursuant to applications submitted to the Division fraudulently or erroneously by a licensed or regulated lender in this State having a lienholder identification number issued by the Division. Any entity offering an electronic signature process for applications submitted pursuant to this subdivision assumes all responsibility and liability for the accuracy of the signature. The Division and its commission contractors shall be held harmless from any liability to a claim arising from applications submitted with an inaccurate electronic signature pursuant to this subdivision.

(3) If the application for notation of security interest is made in order to continue the perfection of a security interest perfected in another jurisdiction, it may be signed by the secured party instead of the debtor. Such application shall be accompanied by documentary evidence of a perfected security interest. No such application shall be valid unless an application for a certificate of title has been made in North Carolina. The security interest perfected herein shall be subject to the provisions set forth in G.S. 20-58.5.

(b) If a manufacturer's statement of origin or an existing certificate of title on a motor vehicle was (i) not delivered to the dealer or (ii) was lost or misplaced on or prior to the date the dealer sells or transfers the motor vehicle, a first lienholder or his designee may file a notarized copy of an instrument creating and evidencing a security interest in the motor vehicle with the Division of Motor Vehicles. A filing pursuant to this subsection shall constitute constructive notice to all persons of the security interest in the motor vehicle described in the filing. The constructive notice shall be effective on the date of the security agreement if the filing is made within 20 days after the date of the security agreement. The constructive notice shall date from the date of the filing with the Division if it is made more than 20 days after the date of the security agreement. The notation of a security interest created under this subsection shall automatically expire 60 days after the date of the creation of the security interest, or upon perfection of the security interest as provided in subsection (a) of this section, whichever occurs first. A security interest notation made under this subsection and then later perfected under subsection (a) of this section shall be presumed to have been perfected on the date of the earlier filing. The Division may charge a fee not to exceed ten dollars ($ 10.00) for each notation of security interest filed pursuant to this subsection. The fee shall be credited to the Highway Fund. It shall constitute a Class H felony for a person to knowingly and intentionally file a false notice with the Division pursuant to this subsection. A dealer principal, owner, or manager of a motor vehicle dealership who is not a signatory of the notice required under this subsection may only be charged for a criminal violation for filing a false notice with the Division under this subsection by another dealership employee if the dealer principal, owner, or manager had actual knowledge of the falsity of the filing at the time the filing was submitted to the Division.

(c) An application for the notation of a security interest pursuant to subsection (a) of this section on a certificate of title for a manufactured home shall state the maturity date of the secured obligation. The Division shall include the stated maturity date for the certificate of title, including the notation of the maturity date on the certificate of title, in its public records and in any reports regarding the certificate of title provided to third parties. For the purposes of this subsection, the maturity date of the security interest is defined in G.S. 45-36.24.

History.
1937, c. 407, s. 22; 1955, c. 554, s. 2; 1961, c. 835, s. 6; 1969, c. 838, s. 1; 1975, c. 716, s. 5; 1979, c. 145, ss. 1,

2; c. 199; 2000-182, s. 2; 2016-59, s. 2; 2018-42, s. 2(b); 2018-145, s. 4; 2021-134, s. 7(a)

§ 20-58.1. Duty of the Division upon receipt of application for notation of security interest

(a) Upon receipt of an application for notation of security interest, the required fee and accompanying documents required by G.S. 20-58, the Division, if it finds the application and accompanying documents in order, shall either endorse upon the certificate of title or issue a new certificate of title containing, the name and address of each secured party, and the date of perfection of each security interest as determined by the Division. The Division shall deliver or mail the certificate to the first secured party named in it and shall also notify the new secured party that his security interest has been noted upon the certificate of title.

(b) If the certificate of title is in the possession of some prior secured party, the Division, when satisfied that the application is in order, shall procure the certificate of title from the secured party in whose possession it is being held, for the sole purpose of noting the new security interest. Upon request of the Division, a secured party in possession of a certificate of title shall forthwith deliver or mail the certificate of title to the Division. Such delivery of the certificate does not affect the rights of any secured party under his security agreement.

History.
1961, c. 835, s. 6; 1969, c. 838, s. 1; 1975, c. 716, s. 5; 1979, c. 145, s. 3

§ 20-58.2. Date of perfection

If the application for notation of security interest with the required fee is delivered to the Division within 20 days after the date of the security agreement, the security interest is perfected as of the date of the execution of the security agreement. Otherwise, the security interest is perfected as of the date of delivery of the application to the Division.

History.
1961, c. 835, s. 6; 1969, c. 838, s. 1; 1975, c. 716, s. 5; 1991, c. 414, s. 1

§ 20-58.3. Notation of assignment of security interest on certificate of title

An assignee of a security interest may have the certificate of title endorsed or issued with the assignee named as the secured party, upon delivering to the Division on a form prescribed by the Division, with the required fee, an assignment by the secured party named in the certificate together with the certificate of title. The assignment must contain the address of the assignee from which information concerning the security interest may be obtained. If the certificate of title is in the possession of some other secured party the procedure prescribed by G.S. 20-58.1(b) shall be followed.

History.
1961, c. 835, s. 6; 1969, c. 838, s. 1; 1975, c. 716, s. 5

§ 20-58.3A. Automatic expiration of security interest in manufactured home; renewal of security interests in manufactured homes

(a) For the purposes of this section, the term "secured party" means the secured party named on a certificate of title for a manufactured home and those parties that succeed to the rights of the secured party as a secured creditor by assignment or otherwise. The term "borrower" means the homeowner or the debtor on the obligation secured by the security interest noted on the certificate of title for a manufactured home.

(b) With the exception of a security interest in a manufactured home perfected pursuant to G.S. 20-58(c), unless satisfied pursuant to G.S. 20-58.4 or G.S. 20-109.2, the perfection of a security interest in a manufactured home that is perfected by a notation on the certificate of title shall automatically expire 30 years after the date of the issuance of the original certificate of title containing the notation of the security interest, unless a different maturity date is stated on the title.

(c) Unless satisfied pursuant to G.S. 20-58.4 or G.S. 20-109.2, the perfection of a security interest in a manufactured home perfected by a notation on the certificate of title pursuant to G.S. 20-58(c) shall automatically expire as follows:

(1) If the perfection of the security interest has not been renewed as provided in this section, on the earlier of (i) 90 days after the maturity date stated on the application for the security interest or (ii) 15 years plus 180 days after the date of issuance of the original certificate of title containing the notation of the security interest.

(2) If the perfection of the security interest has been renewed as provided in this section, on the earlier of (i) 10 years after the date of the renewal of the perfection of the security interest, (ii) 90 days after the original maturity date of the security interest, if the original maturity date has not been extended, or (iii) 90 days after any extended maturity date stated on the application of renewal.

(d) Prior to the date that perfection of a secured party's security interest in a

Chapter 20

manufactured home automatically expires pursuant to subsection (b) or (c) of this section, the secured party may deliver to the Division an application for renewal of the perfection of the secured party's security interest. The application for the renewal of the perfection of the secured party's security interest shall be in a form prescribed by the Division. Nothing in this section shall be construed to extend the maturity date of the secured obligation unless an agreement in writing has been executed by the borrower extending the original maturity date. The application for renewal of the perfection of the secured party's security interest shall contain all of the following:

(1) The secured party's signature.

(2) The existing certificate of title, unless it is in the possession of a prior secured party.

(3) An affirmative statement of any agreement executed by the borrower to extend the maturity date.

(4) If the application is submitted by the assignee or successor in interest of the secured party listed on the certificate of title, documentary evidence that the applicant is the assignee or successor in interest of the secured party listed on the certificate of title.

(5) The name and address of the party from whom information concerning the security interest may be obtained.

(6) Any other information requested by the Division.

(e) Upon receipt of the application for renewal of the perfection of the secured party's security interest, the Division shall do one of the following:

(1) If the existing certificate of title is included with the application for renewal, the Division shall issue a new certificate of title bearing the original or extended maturity date of the security interest.

(2) If the existing certificate of title is in the possession of a prior secured party, the Division, if satisfied as to the genuineness and regularity of the application for renewal, may request the certificate of title from the party in possession for the purpose of notating the original or extended maturity date of the security interest. Once the notations have been made, the Division shall return the certificate of title to the possession of the secured party.

(3) If the existing certificate of title is not obtained upon request, the Division shall cancel the existing certificate of title and issue a new certificate of title. The new certificate of title shall list all known security interests and shall bear notation that shows the original or extended maturity date of the security interest.

(f) An application for the renewal of a secured party's security interest pursuant to this section shall be effective to renew the perfection of the security interest as of the date the application is delivered to the Division. Each renewed security interest shall retain its original date of perfection and the perfection shall thereafter expire on the earlier to occur of (i) 10 years after the date of renewal of the perfection of the security interest, (ii) 90 days after the original maturity date of the security interest, if the original maturity date has not been extended, or (iii) 90 days after any extended maturity date stated on the application of renewal. Perfection of a security interest in a manufactured home may be renewed more than once pursuant to this section.

(g) The Division shall not be subject to a claim under Article 31 of Chapter 143 of the General Statutes and a commission contractor of the Division shall not be subject to a claim or cause of action related to the renewal of the perfection of a security interest or the failure to acknowledge or give effect to an expired perfection of a security interest on a certificate of title for a manufactured home pursuant to this section if the claim is based on reliance by the Division, or a commission contractor of the Division, on any application for renewal submitted to the Division, or a commission contractor of the Division, by a third party pursuant to this section or based on the automatic expiration of a perfection of a security interest pursuant to this section.

History.
2016-59, s. 3; 2018-74, s. 16.3(b); 2021-134, s. 6.2

§ 20-58.4. Release of security interest

(a) Upon the satisfaction or other discharge of a security interest in a vehicle for which the certificate of title is in the possession of the secured party, the secured party shall, within the earlier of 10 days after demand or 30 days from the date of satisfaction, execute a release of his security interest, in the space provided therefor on the certificate or as the Division prescribes, and mail or deliver the certificate and release to the next secured party named therein, or if none, to the owner or other person authorized to receive the certificate for the owner.

(a1) Upon the satisfaction or other discharge of a security interest in a vehicle for which the certificate of title data is notated by a lien through electronic means pursuant to G.S. 20-58.4A, the secured party shall, within seven business days from the date of satisfaction, send electronic notice of the release of the security interest to the Division through the electronic lien release system established pursuant to G.S. 20-58.4A. The electronic notice of the release of the security interest sent to the Division by the secured party shall direct that a physical certificate of title be mailed or delivered to the address noted by the secured party providing notice of the satisfaction or other discharge of the security interest. Upon receipt by the Division of an electronic notice of the release of the security interest, the Division shall mail or deliver a certificate of title to the address noted by the secured party within three business days.

(b) Upon the satisfaction or other discharge of a security interest in a vehicle for which the certificate of title is in the possession of a prior secured party, the secured party whose security interest is satisfied shall within 10 days execute a release of his security interest in such form as the Division prescribes and mail or deliver the same to the owner or other person authorized to receive the same for the owner.

(c) An owner, upon securing the release of any security interest in a vehicle shown upon the certificate of title issued therefor, may exhibit the documents evidencing such release, signed by the person or persons making such release, and the certificate of title to the Division, or a commission contractor of the Division, which shall, when satisfied as to the genuineness of the release, issue to the owner either a new certificate of title in proper form or an endorsement or rider attached thereto showing the release of the security interest.

(d) If an owner exhibits documents evidencing the release of a security interest as provided in subsection (c) of this section but is unable to furnish the certificate of title to the Division, or a commission contractor of the Division, because it is in possession of a prior secured party, the Division, when satisfied as to the genuineness of the release, shall procure the certificate of title from the person in possession thereof for the sole purpose of noting thereon the release of the subsequent security interest, following which the Division shall return the certificate of title to the person from whom it was obtained and notify the owner that the release has been noted on the certificate of title.

(e) If it is impossible for the owner to secure from the secured party the release contemplated by this section, the owner may exhibit to the Division such evidence as may be available showing satisfaction or other discharge of the debt secured, together with a sworn affidavit by the owner that the debt has been satisfied.

(e1) If the vehicle is a manufactured home, the owner may proceed in accordance with subsection (e) of this section or may, in the alternative, provide the Division with a sworn affidavit by the owner stating that the debt has been satisfied and that either:

(1) After diligent inquiry, the owner has been unable to determine the identity or the current location of the secured creditor or its successor in interest; or

(2) The secured creditor has not responded within 30 days to a written request from the owner to release the secured creditor's security interest.

For purposes of this subsection, the term "owner" shall mean any of the following: (i) the owner of the manufactured home; (ii) the owner of real property on which the manufactured home is affixed; or (iii) a title insurance company as insurer of an insured owner of real property on which the manufactured home is affixed.

(e2) The Division shall treat either of the methods employed by the owner pursuant to subsection (e) or subsection (e1) of this section as a proper release for purposes of this section when satisfied as to the genuineness, truth and sufficiency thereof. Before cancelling a security interest under this section, the Division shall send notice to the last known address of the secured party. If the secured party files an objection within 15 days after notice was sent, the security interest shall not be cancelled.

(f) The Division shall not be subject to a claim under Article 31 of Chapter 143 of the General Statutes and a commission contractor of the Division shall not be subject to a claim or cause of action related to the release of the perfection of a security interest on a certificate of title for a manufactured home pursuant to this section if the claim is based on reliance by the Division, or a commission contractor of the Division, on any release, affidavit, notation of the certificate of title, or documents evidencing the release or satisfaction of a security interest submitted to the Division, or a commission contractor of the Division, by a third party pursuant to this section.

History.
1961, c. 835, s. 6; 1969, c. 838, s. 1; 1975, c. 716, s. 5; 2011-318, s. 1; 2015-270, s. 2; 2016-59, s. 4; 2018-74, s. 16.3(a); 2021-134, s. 6.3

§ 20-58.4A. Electronic lien system

(a) **Implementation.** -- No later than January 1, 2015, the Division shall implement a statewide electronic lien system to process the notification, release, and maintenance of security interests and certificate of title data where a lien is notated, through electronic means instead of paper documents otherwise required by this Chapter. The Division may contract with a qualified vendor or vendors to develop and implement this statewide electronic lien system, or the Division may develop and make available to qualified service providers a well-defined set of information services that will enable secure access to the data and internal application components necessary to facilitate the creation of an electronic lien system.

(b) **Minimum Standards for a Vendor Implemented System.** -- When contracting with a qualified vendor or vendors to implement the system required in subsection (a) of this section, the Division shall set the following minimum standards:

(1) The Division shall issue a competitive request for proposal to assess the qualifications of any vendor or vendors responsible for the establishment and ongoing support of the statewide electronic lien system. The Division may also reserve the right to receive input regarding specifications for the electronic lien system from parties that do not respond to a request for proposal to establish and operate an electronic lien system.

(2) Any contract entered into with a vendor or vendors shall include no costs or charges payable by the Division to the vendor or vendors. The vendor or vendors shall reimburse the Division for documented reasonable implementation costs directly associated with the establishment and ongoing support of the statewide electronic lien system.

(3) Upon implementation of the electronic lien system pursuant to subsection (a) of this section, the qualified vendor or vendors may charge participating lienholders or their agents a per-transaction fee for each lien notification. The per-transaction lien notification fee shall be consistent with market pricing in an amount not to exceed three dollars and fifty cents ($ 3.50) for costs associated with the development and ongoing administration of the electronic lien system. The qualified vendor or vendors shall not charge lienholders or their agents any additional fee for lien releases, assignments, or transfers. To recover their costs, participating lienholders or their agents may charge the borrower of a motor vehicle loan or the lessee of an automotive lease an amount equal to the transaction fee per lien notification plus a fee in an amount not to exceed three dollars ($ 3.00) for each electronic transaction where a lien is notated.

(4) A qualified vendor or vendors may also serve as a service provider to lienholders, if all of the following conditions are met:

a. The contract with the vendor must include provisions specifically prohibiting the vendor from using information concerning vehicle titles for marketing or business solicitation purposes.

b. The contract with the vendor must include an acknowledgment by the vendor that it is required to enter into agreements to exchange electronic lien data with any service providers who offer electronic lien and title services in the State and who have been approved by the Division for participation in the system and with service providers who are not qualified vendors.

c. The Division must periodically monitor fees charged by a qualified vendor also serving as a service provider to lienholders and providing services as a qualified vendor to other service providers to ensure the vendor is not engaged in predatory pricing.

(c) **Minimum Standards for Division-Developed System.** -- If the Division chooses to develop an interface to enable service provider access to data to facilitate the creation of an electronic lien system, then the Division shall do so for a cost not to exceed two hundred fifty thousand dollars ($ 250,000) and set the following minimum standards:

(1) The Division shall establish qualifications for third-party service providers offering electronic lien services and establish a qualification process that will vet applications developed by service providers for compliance with defined security and architecture standards as follows:

a. Qualifications shall be posted within 60 days of the effective date of this section.

b. Interested service providers shall respond by providing qualifications within 30 days of posting.

c. The Division shall notify service providers of their approval.

d. Within 30 days of approval, each qualified service provider shall remit payment in an amount equal to the development costs as a fraction of the number of qualified service providers participating in the electronic lien services.

e. If there is a service provider who later wishes to participate but did not apply or pay the initial development costs, then that provider may apply to participate if the provider meets all qualifications and pays the same amount in development costs as other participating service providers.

(2) Each qualified service provider shall remit to the Division an annual fee not to exceed three thousand dollars ($ 3,000) on a date prescribed by the Division to be used for the operation and maintenance of the electronic lien system.

(3) Any contract entered into with a service provider shall include no costs or

charges payable by the Division to the service provider.

(4) Upon implementation of the electronic lien system pursuant to subsection (a) of this section, the service provider may charge participating lienholders or their agents a per-transaction fee consistent with market pricing.

(5) The contract with the service provider must include provisions specifically prohibiting the service provider from using information concerning vehicle titles for marketing or business solicitation purposes.

(d) Qualified vendors and service providers shall have experience in directly providing electronic lien and title solutions to State motor vehicle departments or agencies.

(e) Notwithstanding any requirement in this Chapter that a lien on a motor vehicle shall be noted on the face of the certificate of title, if there are one or more liens or encumbrances on the motor vehicle or mobile home, the Division may electronically transmit the lien to the first lienholder and notify the first lienholder of any additional liens. Subsequent lien satisfactions may be electronically transmitted to the Division and shall include the name and address of the person satisfying the lien.

(f) When electronic transmission of liens and lien satisfactions is used, a certificate of title need not be issued until the last lien is satisfied and a clear certificate of title is issued to the owner of the vehicle.

(g) When a vehicle is subject to an electronic lien, the certificate of title for the vehicle shall be considered to be physically held by the lienholder for purposes of compliance with State or federal odometer disclosure requirements.

(h) A duly certified copy of the Division's electronic record of the lien shall be admissible in any civil, criminal, or administrative proceeding in this State as evidence of the existence of the lien.

(i) **Mandatory Participation.** -- All individuals and lienholders who conduct at least five transactions annually shall utilize the electronic lien system implemented in subsection (a) of this section to record information concerning the perfection and release of a security interest in a vehicle.

(j) **Effect of Electronic Notice or Release.** -- An electronic notice or release of a security interest made through the electronic system implemented pursuant to subsection (a) of this section shall have the same force and effect as a notice or release on a paper document provided under G.S. 20-58 through G.S. 20-58.8.

(k) Nothing in this section shall preclude the Division from collecting a title fee for the preparation and issuance of a title.

(*l*) The Division may convert an existing paper title to an electronic lien upon request of a primary lienholder. The Division or a party contracting with the Division under this section is authorized to collect a fee not to exceed three dollars ($ 3.00) for each conversion.

History.
2013-341, s. 1; 2014-100, s. 34.7(a); 2014-115, s. 29(a), (b); 2015-264, s. 40; 2018-42, s. 1; 2021-134, s. 8(a)

§ 20-58.5. Duration of security interest in favor of corporations which dissolve or become inactive

Any security interest recorded in favor of a corporation which, since the recording of such security interest, has dissolved or become inactive for any reason, and which remains of record as a security interest of such corporation for a period of more than three years from the date of such dissolution or becoming inactive, shall become null and void and of no further force and effect.

History.
1961, c. 835, s. 6; 1969, c. 838, s. 1; 1979, c. 145, s. 4

§ 20-58.6. Duty of secured party to disclose information

A secured party named in a certificate of title shall, upon written request of the Division, the owner or another secured party named on the certificate, disclose information when called upon by such person, within 10 days after his lien shall have been paid and satisfied, and any person convicted under this section shall be fined not more than fifty dollars ($ 50.00) or imprisoned not more than 30 days.

History.
1937, c. 407, s. 23; 1975, c. 716, s. 5

§ 20-58.7. Cancellation of certificate

The cancellation of a certificate of title shall not, in and of itself, affect the validity of a security interest noted on it.

History.
1961, c. 835, s. 6; 1969, c. 838, s. 1

§ 20-58.8. Applicability of §§ 20-58 to 20-58.8; use of term "lien"

(a) Repealed by Session Laws 2000, c. 169, s. 30, effective July 1, 2001.

(b) The provisions of G.S. 20-58 through 20-58.8 inclusive shall not apply to or affect:

(1) A lien given by statute or rule of law for storage of a motor vehicle or to a supplier of services or materials for a vehicle;

(2) A lien arising by virtue of a statute in favor of the United States, this State or any political subdivision of this State; or

(3) A security interest in a vehicle created by a manufacturer or by a dealer in new or used vehicles who holds the vehicle in his inventory.

(c) When the term "lien" is used in other sections of this Chapter, or has been used prior to October 1, 1969, with reference to transactions governed by G.S. 20-58 through 20-58.8, to describe contractual agreements creating security interests in personal property, the term "lien" shall be construed to refer to a "security interest" as the term is used in G.S. 20-58 through 20-58.8 and the Uniform Commercial Code.

History.
1961, c. 835, s. 6; 1969, c. 838, s. 1; 2000-169, s. 30

N.C. Gen. Stat. § 20-58.9

Repealed by Session Laws 1969, c. 838, s. 3.

§ 20-58.10. Effective date of §§ 20-58 to 20-58.9

The provisions of G.S. 20-58 through 20-58.9 inclusive shall be effective and relate to the perfecting and giving notice of security interests entered into on and after January 1, 1962.

History.
1961, c. 835, s. 6

§ 20-59. Unlawful for lienor who holds certificate of title not to surrender same when lien satisfied

It shall be unlawful and constitute a Class 3 misdemeanor for a lienor who holds a certificate of title as provided in this Article to refuse or fail to surrender such certificate of title to the person legally entitled thereto, when called upon by such person, within 10 days after his lien shall have been paid and satisfied.

History.
1937, c. 407, s. 23; 1993, c. 539, s. 332; 1994, Ex. Sess., c. 24, s. 14(c)

§ 20-60. Owner after transfer not liable for negligent operation

The owner of a motor vehicle who has made a bona fide sale or transfer of his title or interest, and who has delivered possession of such vehicle and the certificate of title thereto properly endorsed to the purchaser or transferee, shall not be liable for any damages thereafter resulting from negligent operation of such vehicle by another.

History.
1937, c. 407, s. 24

§ 20-61. Owner dismantling or wrecking vehicle to return evidence of registration

Except as permitted under G.S. 20-62.1, any owner dismantling or wrecking any vehicle shall forward to the Division the certificate of title, registration card and other proof of ownership, and the registration plates last issued for such vehicle, unless such plates are to be transferred to another vehicle of the same owner. In that event, the plates shall be retained and preserved by the owner for transfer to such other vehicle. No person, firm or corporation shall dismantle or wreck any motor vehicle without first complying with the requirements of this section. The Commissioner upon receipt of certificate of title and notice from the owner thereof that a vehicle has been junked or dismantled may cancel and destroy such record of certificate of title.

History.
1937, c. 407, s. 25; 1947, c. 219, s. 3; 1961, c. 360, s. 3; 1975, c. 716, s. 5; 2007-505, s. 2

N.C. Gen. Stat. § 20-62

Repealed by Session Laws 1993, c. 533, s. 9.

§ 20-62.1. Purchase of vehicles for purposes of scrap or parts only

(a) **Records for Scrap or Parts.** -- A secondary metals recycler, as defined in G.S. 66-420(8), and a salvage yard, as defined in G.S. 20-137.7(6), purchasing motor vehicles solely for the purposes of dismantling or wrecking such motor vehicles for the recovery of scrap metal or for the sale of parts only, shall comply with the provisions of G.S. 20-61 and subsection (a1) of this section, provided, however, that a secondary metals recycler or salvage yard may purchase a motor vehicle without a certificate of title, if the motor vehicle is 10 model years old or older and the secondary metals recycler or salvage yard comply with the following requirements:

(1) Maintain a record on a form, or in a format, as approved by the Division of Motor Vehicles (DMV) of all purchase transactions of motor vehicles. The following information shall be maintained for transactions of motor vehicles:

a. The name, address, and contact information of the secondary metals recycler or salvage yard.

b. The name, initials, or other identification of the individual entering the information.

c. The date of the transaction.

d. A description of the motor vehicle, including the year, make, and model to the extent practicable.

e. The vehicle identification number (VIN) of the vehicle.

f. The amount of consideration given for the motor vehicle.

g. A written statement signed by the seller or the seller's agent certifying that (i) the seller or the seller's agent has the lawful right to sell and dispose of the motor vehicle, (ii) the motor vehicle is at least 10 model years old, and (iii) the motor vehicle is not subject to any security interest or lien.

g1. A written statement that the motor vehicle will be scrapped or crushed for disposal or dismantled for parts only.

h. The name, address, and drivers license number of the person from whom the motor vehicle is being purchased.

i. A photocopy or electronic scan of a valid drivers license or identification card issued by the DMV of the seller of the motor vehicle, or seller's agent, to the secondary metals recycler or salvage yard, or in lieu thereof, any other identification card containing a photograph of the seller as issued by any state or federal agency of the United States: provided, that if the buyer has a copy of the seller's photo identification on file, the buyer may reference the identification that is on file, without making a separate photocopy for each transaction. If seller has no identification as described in this sub-subdivision, the secondary metals recycler or salvage yard shall not complete the transaction.

(1a) Verify with the DMV whether or not the motor vehicle has been reported stolen. The DMV shall develop a method to allow a person subject to this section to verify, at the time of the transaction, through the use of the Internet, that the vehicle has not been reported stolen, and that also allows for the DMV's response to be printed and retained by the person making the request. One of the following shall apply following the DMV response:

a. If the Division of Motor Vehicles confirms that the motor vehicle has been reported stolen, the secondary metals recycler or salvage yard shall not complete the transaction and shall notify the DMV of the current location of the vehicle and the identifying information of the person attempting to transfer the vehicle.

b. If the Division of Motor Vehicles confirms that the motor vehicle has not

been stolen, the secondary metals recycler or salvage yard may proceed with the transaction and shall not be held criminally or civilly liable if the motor vehicle later turns out to be a stolen vehicle, unless the secondary metals recycler had knowledge that the motor vehicle was a stolen vehicle.

c. If the Division of Motor Vehicles has not received information from a federal, State, or local department or independent source that a vehicle has been stolen and reports pursuant to this section that a vehicle is not stolen, any person damaged does not have a cause of action against the Division.

(2) Maintain the information required under subdivision (1) of this subsection, and the record confirming that the vehicle was not stolen, required under subdivision (1a) of this subsection, for not less than two years from the date of the purchase of the motor vehicle.

(a1) **Reporting Requirement.** -- Within 72 hours of each day's close of business, a secondary metals recycler or salvage yard purchasing a motor vehicle under this section shall submit to the National Motor Vehicle Title Information System (NMVTIS) such information contained in subdivision (1) of subsection (a) of this section, along with any other information or statement pertaining to the intended disposition of the motor vehicle, as may be required. The information shall be in a format that will satisfy the requirement for reporting information in accordance with rules adopted by the United States Department of Justice in 28 C.F.R. § 25.56. A secondary metals recycler or salvage yard may comply with this subsection by reporting the information required by this subsection to a third-party consolidator as long as the third-party consolidator reports the information to the NMVTIS in compliance with the provisions of this subsection.

(b) **Inspection of Motor Vehicles and Records.** -- At any time it appears a secondary metals recycler, salvage yard, or any other person involved in secondary metals operations is open for business, a law enforcement officer shall have the right to inspect the following:

(1) Any and all motor vehicles in the possession of the secondary metals recycler, the salvage yard, or any other person involved in secondary metals operations.

(2) Any records required to be maintained under subsection (a) of this section.

(b1) **Availability of Information.** -- The information obtained by the Division of Motor Vehicles pursuant to this section shall be made available to law enforcement agencies only. The information submitted pursuant to this section is confidential and shall not be considered a public record as that term is defined in G.S. 132-1.

(c) **Violations.** -- Any person who knowingly and willfully violates any of the provisions of this section, or any person who falsifies the statement required under subsection (a)(1)g. of this section, shall be guilty of a Class I felony and shall pay a minimum fine of one thousand dollars ($ 1,000). The court may order a defendant seller under this subsection to make restitution to the secondary metals recycler or salvage yard or lien holder for any damage or loss caused by the defendant seller arising out of an offense committed by the defendant seller.

(d) **Confiscation of Vehicle or Tools Used in Illegal Sale.** -- Any motor vehicle used to transport another motor vehicle illegally sold under this section may be seized by law enforcement and is subject to forfeiture by the court, provided, however, that no vehicle used by any person in the transaction of a sale of regulated metals is subject to forfeiture unless it appears that the owner or other person in charge of the motor vehicle is a consenting party or privy to the commission of a crime, and a forfeiture of the vehicle encumbered by a bona fide security interest is subject to the interest of the secured party who had no knowledge of or consented to the act.

Whenever property is forfeited under this subsection by order of the court, the law enforcement agency having custody of the property shall sell any forfeited property which is not required to be destroyed by law and which is not harmful to the public, provided that the proceeds are remitted to the Civil Fines and Forfeitures Fund established pursuant to G.S. 115C-457.1.

(e) **Exemptions.** -- As used in this section, the term "motor vehicle" shall not include motor vehicles which have been mechanically flattened, crushed, baled, or logged and sold for purposes of scrap metal only.

(f) **Preemption.** -- No local government shall enact any local law or ordinance with regards to the regulation of the sale of motor vehicles to secondary metals recyclers or salvage yards.

History.
2007-505, s. 1; 2012-46, s. 30; 2013-323, s. 2; 2013-410, s. 28(a)

§ 20-63. Registration plates furnished by Division; requirements; replacement of regular plates with First in Flight plates, First in Freedom plates, or National/State Mottos plates; surrender and reissuance; displaying; preservation and cleaning; alteration or concealment of numbers; commission contracts for issuance

(a) The Division upon registering a vehicle shall issue to the owner one registration plate for a motorcycle, trailer or semitrailer and for every other motor vehicle. Registration plates issued by the Division under this Article shall be and remain the property of the State, and it shall be lawful for the Commissioner or his duly authorized agents to summarily take possession of any plate or plates which he has reason to believe is being illegally used, and to keep in his possession such plate or plates pending investigation and legal disposition of the same. Whenever the Commissioner finds that any registration plate issued for any vehicle pursuant to the provisions of this Article has become illegible or is in such a condition that the numbers thereon may not be readily distinguished, he may require that such registration plate, and its companion when there are two registration plates, be surrendered to the Division. When said registration plate or plates are so surrendered to the Division, a new registration plate or plates shall be issued in lieu thereof without charge. The owner of any vehicle who receives notice to surrender illegible plate or plates on which the numbers are not readily distinguishable and who willfully refuses to surrender said plates to the Division shall be guilty of a Class 2 misdemeanor.

(b) Every license plate must display the registration number assigned to the vehicle for which it is issued, the name of the State of North Carolina, which may be abbreviated, and the year number for which it is issued or the date of expiration. A plate issued for a commercial vehicle, as defined in G.S. 20-4.2(1), and weighing 26,001 pounds or more, must bear the word "commercial," unless the plate is a special registration plate authorized in G.S. 20-79.4 or the commercial vehicle is a trailer or is licensed for 6,000 pounds or less. The plate issued for vehicles licensed for 7,000 pounds through 26,000 pounds must bear the word "weighted," unless the plate is a special registration plate authorized in G.S. 20-79.4.

A registration plate issued by the Division for a private passenger vehicle or for a private hauler vehicle licensed for 6,000 pounds or less shall be, at the option of the owner, either (i) a "First in Flight" plate, (ii) a "First in Freedom" plate, or (iii) a "National/State Mottos" plate. A "First in Flight" plate shall have the words "First in Flight" printed at the top of the plate above all other letters and numerals. The background of the "First in Flight" plate shall depict the Wright Brothers biplane flying over Kitty Hawk Beach, with the plane flying slightly upward and to the right. A "First in Freedom" plate shall have the words "First in Freedom" printed at the top of the plate above all other letters and numerals. The background of the "First in Freedom" plate may include an image chosen by the Division that is representative of the Mecklenburg Declaration of 1775 or the Halifax Resolves of 1776. A "National/State Mottos" plate shall have in words the motto of the United States "In God We Trust" printed at the top of the plate above all other letters and numerals and have in words the State motto "To Be Rather Than To Seem". The background of the "National/State Mottos" plate shall include an image chosen by the Division that is representative of the American Flag.

(b1) The following special registration plates do not have to be a "First in Flight" plate, "First in Freedom" plate, or "National/State Mottos" plate as provided in subsection (b) of this section. The design of the plates that are not "First in Flight" plates, "First in Freedom" plates, or "National/State Mottos" plate must be developed in accordance with G.S. 20-79.4(a3). For special plates authorized in G.S. 20-79.7 on or after July 1, 2013, the Division may not issue the plate on a background under this subsection unless it receives the required number of applications set forth in G.S. 20-79.3A(a).

(1) AIDS Awareness -- Expired July 1, 2016.

(2) Alpha Phi Alpha.

(3) **ARTS NC.**

(4) Back Country Horsemen of North Carolina -- Expired July 1, 2016.

(5) Battle of Kings Mountain.

(6) Big Rock Blue Marlin Tournament.

(7) Blue Ridge Parkway Foundation.

(8) Buddy Pelletier Surfing Foundation.

(9) Carolina Panthers.

(10) Carolina Raptor Center -- Expired July 1, 2016.

(11) Carolinas Credit Union Foundation -- Expired July 1, 2016.

(12) Choose Life.

(13) Coastal Land Trust.

(14) Colorectal Cancer Awareness.

(15) Core Sound Waterfowl Museum and Heritage Center.

(16) Donate Life.

(17) Ducks Unlimited.

(18) Farmland Preservation -- Expired July 1, 2016.

(19) First in Forestry.

(20) Fox Hunting -- Expired July 1, 2016.

(21) Friends of the Appalachian Trail.

(22) Friends of the Great Smoky Mountains National Park.

(23) Guilford Battleground Company.

(24) Home Care and Hospice.

(25) Hospice Care -- Expired July 1, 2016.

(26) In God We Trust.

(27) Kappa Alpha Psi Fraternity.

(28) Keeping The Lights On.

(29) Lung Cancer Research -- Expired July 1, 2016.

(30) Mountains-to-Sea Trail, Inc.

(31) National Wild Turkey Federation.

(32) Native Brook Trout.

(33) NC Civil War -- Expired July 1, 2016.

(34) NC Coastal Federation.

(35) NC Horse Council.

(36) NC Mining -- Expired July 1, 2016.

(37) NC State Parks.

(38) NC Surveyors.

(39) NC Tennis Foundation.

(40) NC Trout Unlimited.

(41) North Carolina Aquarium Society.

(42) North Carolina Green Industry Council -- Expired July 1, 2016.

(43) North Carolina Sheriffs' Association.

(44) North Carolina State Flag -- Expired July 1, 2016.

(45) North Carolina Wildlife Habitat Foundation.

(46) North Carolina Zoological Society.

(47) Order of the Long Leaf Pine.

(48) Pisgah Conservancy.

(49) POW/MIA Bring Them Home.

(50) Red Drum -- Expired July 1, 2016.

(51) Rocky Mountain Elk Foundation.

(52) Save the Honey Bee (SB).

(53) S.T.A.R. -- Expired July 1, 2016.

(54) Stock Car Racing Theme.

(55) Support Our Troops.

(56) Travel and Tourism -- Expired July 1, 2016.

(57) United States Service Academy.

(58) US Equine Rescue League -- Expired July 1, 2016.

(c) Such registration plate and the required numerals thereon, except the year number for which issued, shall be of sufficient size to be plainly readable from a distance of 100 feet during daylight.

(d) Registration plates issued for a motor vehicle other than a motorcycle, trailer, or semi-trailer shall be attached thereto, one in the front and the other in the rear: Provided, that when only one registration plate is issued for a motor vehicle other than a truck-tractor, said registration plate shall be attached to the rear of the motor vehicle. The registration plate issued for a truck-tractor shall be attached to the front thereof. Provided further, that when only one registration plate is issued for a motor vehicle and this motor vehicle is transporting a substance that may adhere to the plate so as to cover or discolor the plate or if the motor vehicle has a mechanical loading device that may damage the plate, the registration plate may be attached to the front of the motor vehicle.

Any motor vehicle of the age of 35 years or more from the date of manufacture may bear the license plates of the year of manufacture instead of the current registration plates, if the current registration plates are maintained within the vehicle and produced upon the request of any person.

The Division shall provide registered owners of motorcycles and property hauling motorcycle trailers attached to the rear of motorcycles with suitably reduced size registration plates, approximately four by seven inches in size, that are issued on a multiyear basis in accordance with G.S. 20-88(c), or on an annual basis as otherwise provided in this Chapter.

(e) **Preservation and Cleaning of Registration Plates.** -- It shall be the duty of each and every registered owner of a motor vehicle to keep the registration plates assigned to such motor vehicle reasonably clean and free from dust and dirt, and such registered owner, or any person in his employ, or who operates such motor vehicle by his authority, shall, upon the request of any proper officer, immediately clean such registration plates so that the numbers thereon may be readily distinguished, and any person who shall neglect or refuse to so clean a registration plate, after having been requested to do so, shall be guilty of a Class 3 misdemeanor.

(f) **Operating with False Numbers.** -- Any person who shall willfully operate a motor vehicle with a registration plate which has been repainted or altered or forged shall be guilty of a Class 2 misdemeanor.

(g) **Alteration, Disguise, or Concealment of Numbers.** -- Any operator of a motor vehicle who shall willfully mutilate, bend, twist, cover or cause to be covered or partially covered by any bumper, light, spare tire, tire rack, strap, or other device, or who shall paint, enamel, emboss, stamp, print, perforate, or alter or add to or cut off any part or portion of a registration plate or the figures or letters thereon, or who shall place or deposit or cause to be placed or deposited any oil, grease, or other substance upon such registration plates for the purpose of making dust adhere thereto, or who shall deface, disfigure, change, or attempt to change any letter or figure thereon, or who shall display a number plate in other than a horizontal upright position, shall be guilty of a Class 2 misdemeanor. Any operator of a motor vehicle who shall willfully cover or cause to be covered any part or portion of a registration plate or the figures or letters thereon by any device designed or intended to prevent or interfere with the taking of a clear photograph of a registration plate by a traffic control or toll collection system using cameras commits an infraction and shall be penalized under G.S. 14-3.1. Any operator of a motor vehicle who shall otherwise intentionally cover any number or registration renewal sticker on a registration plate with any material that makes the number or registration renewal sticker illegible commits an infraction and shall be penalized under G.S. 14-3.1. Any operator of a motor vehicle who covers any registration plate with any frame or transparent,

clear, or color-tinted cover that makes a number or letter included in the vehicle's registration, the State name on the plate, or a number or month on the registration renewal sticker on the plate illegible commits an infraction and shall be penalized under G.S. 14-3.1.

(h) **Commission Contracts for Issuance of Plates and Certificates.** -- All registration plates, registration certificates, and certificates of title issued by the Division, outside of those issued from the office of the Division located in Wake, Cumberland, or Mecklenburg Counties and those issued and handled through the United States mail, shall be issued insofar as practicable and possible through commission contracts entered into by the Division for the issuance of the plates and certificates in localities throughout North Carolina, including military installations within this State, with persons, firms, corporations or governmental subdivisions of the State of North Carolina. The Division shall make a reasonable effort in every locality, except as noted above, to enter into a commission contract for the issuance of the plates and certificates and a record of these efforts shall be maintained in the Division. In the event the Division is unsuccessful in making commission contracts, it shall issue the plates and certificates through the regular employees of the Division. Whenever registration plates, registration certificates, and certificates of title are issued by the Division through commission contract arrangements, the Division shall provide proper supervision of the distribution. Nothing contained in this subsection allows or permits the operation of fewer outlets in any county in this State than are now being operated.

The terms of a commission contract entered under this subsection shall specify the duration of the contract and either include or incorporate by reference standards by which the Division may supervise and evaluate the performance of the commission contractor. The duration of an initial commission contract may not exceed eight years and the duration of a renewal commission contract may not exceed two years. The Division may award monetary performance bonuses, not to exceed an aggregate total of ninety thousand dollars ($ 90,000) annually, to commission contractors based on their performance.

The amount of compensation payable to a commission contractor is determined on a per transaction basis. The collection of the highway use tax and the removal of an inspection stop are each considered a separate transaction for which one dollar and fifty-six cents ($ 1.56) compensation shall be paid. The issuance of a limited registration "T" sticker and the collection of property tax are each considered a separate transaction for which compensation at the rate of one dollar and thirty cents ($ 1.30) and one dollar and eight cents ($ 1.08) respectively, shall be paid by counties and municipalities as a cost of the combined motor vehicle registration renewal and property tax collection system. The performance at the same time of one or more of the transactions below is considered a single transaction for which one dollar and seventy-five cents ($ 1.75) compensation shall be paid:

(1) Issuance of a registration plate, a registration card, a registration sticker, or a certificate of title.

(2) Issuance of a handicapped placard or handicapped identification card.

(3) Acceptance of an application for a personalized registration plate.

(4) Acceptance of a surrendered registration plate, registration card, or registration renewal sticker, or acceptance of an affidavit stating why a person cannot surrender a registration plate, registration card, or registration renewal sticker.

(5) Cancellation of a title because the vehicle has been junked.

(6) Acceptance of an application for, or issuance of, a refund for a fee or a tax, other than the highway use tax.

(7) Receipt of the civil penalty imposed by G.S. 20-311 for a lapse in financial responsibility or receipt of the restoration fee imposed by that statute.

(8) Acceptance of a notice of failure to maintain financial responsibility for a motor vehicle.

(8a) Collection of civil penalties imposed for violations of G.S. 20-183.8A.

(8b), (9) Repealed by Session Laws 2013-372, s. 2(a), effective July 1, 2013.

(10) Acceptance of a temporary lien filing.

(11) Conversion of an existing paper title to an electronic lien upon request of a primary lienholder.

(h1) Commission contracts entered into by the Division under this subsection shall also provide for the payment of an additional one dollar ($ 1.00) of compensation to commission contract agents for any transaction assessed a fee under subdivision (a)(1), (a)(2), (a)(3), (a)(7), (a)(8), or (a)(9) of G.S. 20-85.

(h2) Upon the closing of the only contract license plate agency in a county, the Division shall as soon as practicable designate a temporary location for the issuance of all registration plates, registration certificates, and certificates of title issued by the Division for that county. The designation shall be posted at the former agency location for not less than 30 days and shall include the street address and telephone number of the temporary location. A former contract agent shall allow the posting of this required notice at the former location for a period of not less than 30 days. A failure to comply with the posting requirements of this section by a former contract agent shall be a Class 3 misdemeanor.

(i) **Electronic Applications and Collections.** -- The Division shall accept electronic applications for the issuance of registration plates, registration certificates, salvage certificates of title, and certificates of title, and is authorized to electronically collect fees from online motor vehicle registration vendors under contract with the Division.

(j) The Division shall contract with at least two online motor vehicle registration vendors which may enter into contracts with motor vehicle dealers to complete and file Division required documents for the issuance of a certificate of title, registration plate, or registration card or a duplicate certificate of title, registration plate, or registration card for a motor vehicle, upon purchase or sale of a vehicle. Vendors under contract with the Division pursuant to this subsection may also enter into contracts with used motor vehicle dealers whose primary business is the sale of salvage vehicles on behalf of insurers to complete and file documents required by the Division for the issuance of a salvage certificate of title.

(k) Commission contract agents are authorized to enter into contracts with online motor vehicle registration vendors which are under contract with the Division to complete and file Division required documents for the issuance of a certificate of title, registration plate, or registration card or a duplicate certificate of title, registration plate, or registration card for a motor vehicle.

History.
1937, c. 407, s. 27; 1943, c. 726; 1951, c. 102, ss. 1-3; 1955, c. 119, s. 1; 1961, c. 360, s. 4; c. 861, s. 2; 1963, c. 552, s. 6; c. 1071; 1965, c. 1088; 1969, c. 1140; 1971, c. 945; 1973, c. 629; 1975, c. 716, s. 5; 1979, c. 470, s. 1; c. 604, s. 1; c. 917, s. 4; 1981, c. 750; c. 859, s. 76; 1983, c. 253, ss. 1-3; 1985, c. 257; 1991 (Reg. Sess., 1992), c. 1007, s. 32; 1993, c. 539, ss. 333 -336; 1994, Ex. Sess., c. 24, s. 14(c); 1997-36, s. 1; 1997-443, s. 32.7(a); 1997-461, s. 1; 1998-160, s. 3; 1998-212, ss. 15.4(a), 27.6(a); 1999-452, ss. 13, 14; 2000-182, s. 3; 2001-424, s. 27.21; 2001-487, s. 50(c); 2002-159, s. 31.1; 2003-424, s. 1; 2004-77, s. 1; 2004-79, s. 1; 2004-131, s. 1; 2004-185, s. 1; 2005-216, s. 1; 2006-209, s. 1; 2006-213, s. 4; 2007-243, s. 1; 2007-400, s. 1; 2007-483, s. 1; 2007-488, ss. 2 -5; 2008-225, s. 8; 2009-445, s. 24(b1); 2009-456, s. 1; 2010-96, s. 40(a); 2010-132, ss. 2, 3; 2011-382, s. 4; 2011-392, ss. 1, 1.1; 2012-79, s. 1.12(a); 2013-87, s. 1; 2013-372, s. 2(a); 2013-376, s. 9(a), (b), (d); 2014-3, s. 13.2; 2014-96, s. 2; 2014-100, ss. 8.11(e), 34.7(b), 34.28(a); 2015-241, ss. 29.32(a), 29.40(a); 2015-264, s. 40.6(a); 2015-286, s. 3.5(a); 2016-120, s. 2; 2017-107, s. 1; 2017-114, s. 1; 2018-5, s. 34.27(a); 2018-74, ss. 12(a), 16.10; 2018-77, s. 2(a); 2019-153, s. 2; 2019-213, s. 2(a); 2019-231, s. 4.18(a)

Chapter 20

§ 20-63.01. Bonds required for commission contractors

(a) A guaranty bond is required for each commission contractor that is not a governmental subdivision of this State that is granted a contract to issue license plates or conduct business pursuant to G.S. 20-63. Provided, however, a commission contractor that is unable to secure a bond may, with the consent of the Division, provide an alternative to a guaranty bond, as provided in subsection (c) of this section.

The Division may revoke, with cause, a contract with a commission contractor that fails to maintain a bond or an alternative to a bond, pursuant to this section.

(b) (1) When application is made for a contract or contract renewal, the applicant shall file a guaranty bond with the clerk of the superior court and/or the register of deeds of the county in which the commission contractor will be located. The bond shall be in favor of the Division. The bond shall be executed by the applicant as principal and by a bonding company authorized to do business in this State. The bond shall be conditioned to provide indemnification to the Division for a loss of revenue for any reason, including bankruptcy, employee embezzlement or theft, foreclosure, or ceasing to operate.

(2) The bond shall be in an amount determined by the Division to be adequate to provide indemnification to the Division under the terms of the bond. The bond amount shall be at least one hundred thousand dollars ($ 100,000).

(3) The bond shall remain in force and effect until cancelled by the guarantor. The guarantor may cancel the bond upon 30 days' notice to the Division. Cancellation of the bond shall not affect any liability incurred or accrued prior to the termination of the notice period.

(4) The Division may be able to negotiate bonds for contractors who qualify for bonds as a group under favorable rates or circumstances. If so, the Division may require those contractors who can qualify for the group bond to obtain their bond as part of a group of contractors. The Division may deduct the premiums for any bonds it may be able to negotiate at group rates from the commissioned contractors' compensation.

(c) An applicant that is unable to secure a bond may seek a waiver of the guaranty bond from the Division and approval of one of the guaranty bond alternatives set forth in this subsection. With the approval of the Division, an applicant may file with the clerk of the superior court and/or the register of deeds of the county in which the commission contractor will be located, in lieu of a bond:

(1) An assignment of a savings account in an amount equal to the bond required (i) that is in a form acceptable to the Division; (ii) that is executed by the applicant; (iii) that is executed by a federally insured depository institution or a trust institution authorized to do business in this State; and (iv) for which access to the account in favor of the State of North Carolina is subject to the same conditions as for a bond in subsection (b) of this section.

(2) A certificate of deposit (i) that is executed by a federally insured depository institution or a trust institution authorized to do business in this State; (ii) that is either payable to the State of North Carolina, unrestrictively endorsed to the Division of Motor Vehicles; in the case of a negotiable certificate of deposit, is unrestrictively endorsed to the Division of Motor Vehicles; or in the case of a nonnegotiable certificate of deposit, is assigned to the Division of Motor Vehicles in a form satisfactory to the Division; and (iii) for which access to the certificate of deposit in favor of the State of North Carolina is subject to the same conditions as for a bond in subsection (b) of this section.

History.
2007-488, s. 1; 2017-25, s. 1(b)

§ 20-63.02. Advisory committee of commission contractors

(a) **Committee and Duties. --** An advisory committee is established and is designated the License Plate Agent (LPA) Advisory Committee. The Division and the LPA Advisory Committee are directed to work together to ensure excellent and efficient customer service with respect to vehicle titling and registration services provided through commission contracts awarded under G.S. 20-63. As part of this effort, the Division and the Committee must periodically review all forms and instructions used in the vehicle titling and registration process to ensure that they are readily understandable and not duplicative. The Committee must meet at least quarterly.

(b) **Membership and Terms. --** The LPA Advisory Committee consists of persons who are on the staff of the Division of Motor Vehicles and six persons appointed by the North Carolina Association of Motor Vehicle Registration Contractors. The Commissioner determines the number of Division staff persons to appoint to the Committee and designates the chair of the Committee. Members of the Committee appointed by the Commissioner serve ex officio. Members of the Committee appointed by the Association serve two-year terms beginning on

July 1 of an odd-numbered year. A member who serves for a specific term continues to serve after the expiration of the member's term until a successor is appointed.

(c) **Expenses.** -- Members of the LPA Advisory Committee are allowed the per diem, subsistence, and travel allowances established under G.S. 138-5 for service on State boards and commissions.

History.
2013-372, s. 1(a)

§ 20-63.1. Division shall cause plates to be reflectorized

(a) **Registration Plate Standards.** -- The Division of Motor Vehicles is hereby authorized to cause vehicle license plates for 1968 and future years to be completely treated with reflectorized materials designed to increase visibility and legibility of license plates at night. The Division of Motor Vehicles shall develop standards for reflectivity that use the most current technology available while maintaining a competitive bid process.

(b) **Registration Plate Mandatory Replacement.** -- All registration plates shall be replaced every seven years.

History.
1967, c. 8; 1975, c. 716, s. 5; 2019-227, s. 5(a)

§ 20-64. Transfer of registration plates to another vehicle

(a) Except as otherwise provided in this Article, registration plates shall be retained by the owner thereof upon disposition of the vehicle to which assigned, and may be assigned to another vehicle, belonging to such owner and of a like vehicle category within the meaning of G.S. 20-87 and 20-88, upon proper application to the Division and payment of a transfer fee and such additional fees as may be due because the vehicle to which the plates are to be assigned requires a greater registration fee than that vehicle to which the license plates were last assigned. In cases where the plate is assigned to another vehicle belonging to such owner, and is not of a like vehicle category within the meaning of G.S. 20-87 and 20-88, the owner shall surrender the plate to the Division and receive therefor a plate of the proper category, and the unexpired portion of the fee originally paid by the owner for the plate so surrendered shall be a credit toward the fee charged for the new plate of the proper category. Provided, that the owner shall not be entitled to a cash refund when the registration fee for the vehicle to which the plates are to be assigned is less than the registration fee for that vehicle to which

the license plates were last assigned. An owner assigning or transferring plates to another vehicle as provided herein shall be subject to the same assessments and penalties for use of the plates on another vehicle or for improper use of the plates, as he could have been for the use of the plates on the vehicle to which last assigned. Provided, however, that upon compliance with the requirements of this section, the registration plates of vehicles owned by and registered in the name of a corporation may be transferred and assigned to a like vehicle category within the meaning of G.S. 20-87 and 20-88, upon the showing that the vehicle to which the transfer and assignment is to be made is owned by a corporation which is a wholly owned subsidiary of the corporation applying for such transfer and assignment.

(b) Upon a change of the name of a corporation or a change of the name under which a proprietorship or partnership is doing business, the corporation, partnership or proprietorship shall forthwith apply for correction of the certificate of title of all vehicles owned by such corporation, partnership or proprietorship so as to correctly reflect the name of the corporation or the name under which the proprietorship or partnership is doing business, and pay the fees required by law.

(c) Upon a change in the composition of a partnership, ownership of vehicles belonging to such partnership shall not be deemed to have changed so long as one partner of the predecessor partnership remains a partner in the reconstituted partnership, but the reconstituted partnership shall forthwith apply for correction of the certificate of title of all vehicles owned by such partnership so as to correctly reflect the composition of the partnership and the name under which it is doing business, if any, and pay the fees required by law.

(d) When a proprietorship or partnership is incorporated, the corporation shall retain license plates assigned to vehicles belonging to it and may use the same, provided the corporation applies for and obtains transfers of the certificates of title of all vehicles and pays the fees required by law.

(e) Upon death of the owner of a registered vehicle, such registration shall continue in force as a valid registration until the end of the year for which the license is issued unless ownership of the vehicle passes or is transferred to any person other than the surviving spouse before the end of the year.

(f) The owner or transferor of a registered vehicle who surrenders the registration plate to the division may secure a refund for the unexpired portion of such plate prorated on a monthly basis, beginning the first day of the month following surrender of the plate to the division, provided the annual fee of such surrendered plate is sixty dollars ($ 60.00) or more. This refund may not exceed one half of the annual license fee. No refund shall be made unless the owner or transferor furnishes proof of financial responsibility on the registered vehicle effective until the date of the surrender of the plate. Proof of financial responsibility shall be furnished in a manner prescribed by the Commissioner.

(g) The Commissioner of Motor Vehicles shall have the power to make such rules and regulations as he may deem necessary for the administration of transfers of license plates and vehicles under this Article.

History.

1937, c. 407, s. 28; 1945, c. 576, s. 1; 1947, c. 914, s. 1; 1951, c. 188; c. 819, s. 1; 1961, c. 360, s. 5; 1963, cc. 1067, 1190; 1967, c. 995; 1973, c. 1134; 1975, c. 716, s. 5; 1981, c. 227; 2004-167, s. 1; 2004-199, s. 59; 2007-491, s. 5

N.C. Gen. Stat. § 20-64.1

Repealed by Session Laws 1995 (Regular Session, 1996), c. 756, s. 6.

N.C. Gen. Stat. § 20-64.2

Repealed by Session Laws 2010-132, s. 4, effective December 1, 2010.

History.

1957, c. 402; 1975, c. 716, s. 5

N.C. Gen. Stat. § 20-65

Repealed by Session Laws 1979, 2nd Session, c. 1280, s. 1.

§ 20-66. Renewal of vehicle registration

(a) **Annual Renewal.** -- The registration of a vehicle must be renewed annually. In accordance with G.S. 105-330.5(b), upon receiving written consent from the owner of the vehicle, the Division may send any required notice of renewal electronically to an e-mail address provided by the owner of the vehicle. To renew the registration of a vehicle, the owner of the vehicle must file an application with the Division and pay the required registration fee. The Division may receive and grant an application for renewal of registration at any time before the registration expires.

(b) **Method of Renewal.** -- When the Division renews the registration of a vehicle, it must issue a new registration card for the vehicle and either a new registration plate or a registration renewal sticker. The Division may renew a registration plate for any type of vehicle by means of a renewal sticker.

(b1) Repealed by Session Laws 1993, c. 467, s. 2.

(c) **Renewal Stickers.** -- A single registration renewal sticker issued by the Division must be displayed on the registration plate that it renews in the place prescribed by the Commissioner and must indicate the period for which it is valid. Except where physical differences between a registration renewal sticker and a registration plate render a provision of this Chapter inapplicable, the provisions of this Chapter relating to registration plates apply to registration renewal stickers.

(d), (e) Repealed by Session Laws 1993 (Reg. Sess., 1994), c. 761, § 5.

(f) Repealed by Session Laws 1993, c. 467, s. 2.

(g) **When Renewal Sticker Expires.** -- The registration of a vehicle that is renewed by means of a registration renewal sticker expires at midnight on the last day of the month designated on the sticker. It is lawful, however, to operate the vehicle on a highway until midnight on the fifteenth day of the month following the month in which the sticker expired.

The Division may vary the expiration dates of registration renewal stickers issued for a type of vehicle so that an approximately equal number expires at the end of each month, quarter, or other period consisting of one or more months. When the Division implements registration renewal for a type of vehicle by means of a renewal sticker, it may issue a registration renewal sticker that expires at the end of any monthly interval.

(g1) **Expiration of Registration by Other Means.** -- The registration of a vehicle renewed by means of a new registration plate expires at midnight on the last day of the year in which the registration plate was issued. It is lawful, however, to operate the vehicle on a highway through midnight February 15 of the following year.

(h) Repealed by Session Laws 2004-167, s. 3, as amended by Session Laws 2004-199, s. 59, effective January 1, 2006.

(i) **Property Tax Consolidation.** -- When the Division receives an application under subsection (a) for the renewal of registration before the current registration expires, the Division shall grant the application if it is made for the purpose of consolidating the property taxes payable by the applicant on classified motor vehicles, as defined in G.S. 105-330. The registration fee for a motor vehicle whose registration cycle is changed under this subsection shall be reduced by a prorated amount. The prorated amount is one-twelfth of the registration fee in effect when the motor vehicle's registration was last renewed multiplied by the number of full months remaining in the motor vehicle's current registration cycle, rounded to the nearest multiple of twenty-five cents (25 cent(s)).

(j) **Inspection Prior to Renewal of Registration.** -- The Division shall not renew the registration of a vehicle unless it has a current safety or emissions inspection.

(k) Repealed by Session Laws 2008-190, s. 1, effective October 1, 2008.

History.
1937, c. 407, s. 30; 1955, c. 554, s. 3; 1973, c. 1389, s. 1; 1975, c. 716, s. 5; 1977, c. 337; 1979, 2nd Sess., c. 1280, ss. 2, 3; 1981 (Reg. Sess., 1982), c. 1258, s. 1; 1985 (Reg. Sess., 1986), c. 982, s. 24; 1991, c. 624, ss. 6, 7; c. 672, s. 7; c. 726, s. 23; 1993, c. 467, s. 2; 1993 (Reg. Sess., 1994), c. 761, s. 5; 2004-167, ss. 2, 3; 2004-199, s. 59; 2007-503, s. 1; 2008-190, s. 1; 2014-108, s. 2(a); 2015-108, s. 2; 2016-90, s. 7(a); 2017-96, s. 1

N.C. Gen. Stat. § 20-66.1

Repealed by Session Laws 1973, c. 1389, s. 2.

§ 20-67. Notice of change of address or name

(a) **Address.** -- A person whose address changes from the address stated on a certificate of title or registration card must notify the Division of the change within 60 days after the change occurs. The person may obtain a duplicate certificate of title or registration card stating the new address but is not required to do so. A person who does not move but whose address changes due to governmental action may not be charged with violating this subsection.

(b) **Name.** -- A person whose name changes from the name stated on a certificate of title or registration card must notify the Division of the change within 60 days after the change occurs. The person may obtain a duplicate certificate of title or registration card but is not required to do so.

(c) **Fee.** -- G.S. 20-85 sets the fee for a duplicate certificate of title or registration card.

History.
1937, c. 407, s. 31; 1955, c. 554, s. 4; 1975, c. 716, s. 5; 1979, c. 106; 1997-122, s. 7

§ 20-68. Replacement of lost or damaged certificates, cards and plates

(a) In the event any registration card or registration plate is lost, mutilated, or becomes illegible, the owner or legal representative of the owner of the vehicle for which the same was issued, as shown by the records of the Division, shall immediately make application for and may obtain a duplicate or a substitute or a new registration under a new registration number, as determined to be most advisable by the Division, upon the applicant's furnishing under oath information satisfactory to the Division and payment of required fee.

(b) If a certificate of title is lost, stolen, mutilated, destroyed or becomes illegible, the first lienholder or, if none, the owner or legal representative of the owner named in the certificate, as shown by the records of the Division, shall promptly make application for and may obtain a duplicate upon furnishing information satisfactory to the Division. It shall be mailed to the first lienholder named in it or, if none, to the owner. The Division shall not issue a new certificate of title upon application made on a duplicate until 15 days after receipt of the application. A person recovering an original certificate of title for which a duplicate has been issued shall promptly surrender the original certificate to the Division.

History.
1937, c. 407, s. 32; 1961, c. 360, s. 7; c. 835, s. 7; 1975, c. 716, s. 5

§ 20-69. Division authorized to assign new engine number

The owner of a motor vehicle upon which the engine number or serial number has become illegible or has been removed or obliterated shall immediately make application to the Division for a new engine or serial number for such motor vehicle. The Division, when satisfied that the applicant is the lawful owner of the vehicle referred to in such application is hereby authorized to assign a new engine or serial number thereto, and shall require that such number, together with the name of this State, or a symbol indicating this State, be stamped upon the engine, or in the event such number is a serial number, then upon such portion of the motor vehicle as shall be designated by the Division.

History.
1937, c. 407, s. 33; 1975, c. 716, s. 5

§ 20-70. Division to be notified when another engine is installed or body changed

(a) Whenever a motor vehicle registered hereunder is altered by the installation of another engine in place of an engine, the number of which is shown in the registration records, or the installation of another body in place of a body, the owner of such motor vehicle shall immediately give notice to the Division in writing on a form prepared by it, which shall state the number of the former engine and the number of the newly installed engine, the registration number of the motor vehicle, the name of the owner and any other information which the Division may require. Whenever another engine has been substituted as provided in this section, and the notice given as required hereunder, the Division shall insert the number of the newly installed engine upon the registration card and certificate of title issued for such motor vehicle.

(b) Whenever a new engine or serial number has been assigned to and stamped upon a motor vehicle as provided in G.S. 20-69, or whenever a new engine has been installed or body changed as provided in this section, the Division shall require the owner to surrender to the Division the registration card and certificate of title previously issued for said vehicle. The Division shall also require the owner to make application for a duplicate registration card and a duplicate certificate of title showing the new motor or serial number thereon or new style of body, and upon receipt of such application and fee, as for any other duplicate title, the Division shall issue to said owner a duplicate registration and a duplicate certificate of title showing thereon the new number in place of the original number or the new style of body.

(c) The notification and registration requirements contained in subsections (a) and (b) of this section regarding an engine change shall be required only if the motor vehicle into which a new engine is installed uses an engine number as the sole means to identify the vehicle.

History.
1937, c. 407, s. 34; 1943, c. 726; 1975, c. 716, s. 5; 2009-405, s. 3

§ 20-71. Altering or forging certificate of title, registration card or application, a felony; reproducing or possessing blank certificate of title

(a) Any person who, with fraudulent intent, shall alter any certificate of title, registration card issued by the Division, or any application for a certificate of title or registration card, or forge or counterfeit any certificate of title or registration card purported to have been issued by the Division under the provisions of this Article, or who, with fraudulent intent, shall alter, falsify or forge any assignment thereof, or who shall hold or use any such certificate, registration card, or application, or assignment, knowing the same to have been altered, forged or falsified, shall be guilty of a felony and upon conviction thereof shall be punished in the discretion of the court.

(b) It shall be unlawful for any person with fraudulent intent to reproduce or possess a blank North Carolina certificate of title or facsimile thereof. Any person, firm or corporation violating the provisions of this section shall be guilty of a Class I felony.

History.
1937, c. 407, s. 35; 1959, c. 1264, s. 2; 1971, c. 99; 1975, c. 716, s. 5; 1979, c. 499; 1993, c. 539, s. 1251; 1994, Ex. Sess., c. 24, s. 14(c)

§ 20-71.1. Registration evidence of ownership; ownership evidence of defendant's responsibility for conduct of operation

(a) In all actions to recover damages for injury to the person or to property or for the death of a person, arising out of an accident or collision involving a motor vehicle, proof of ownership of such motor vehicle at the time of such accident or collision shall be prima facie evidence that said motor vehicle was being operated and used with the authority, consent, and knowledge of the owner in the very transaction out of which said injury or cause of action arose.

(b) Proof of the registration of a motor vehicle in the name of any person, firm, or corporation, shall for the purpose of any such action, be prima facie evidence of ownership and that such motor vehicle was then being operated by and under the control of a person for whose conduct the owner was legally responsible, for the owner's benefit, and within the course and scope of his employment.

History.
1951, c. 494; 1961, c. 975

PART 3A
SALVAGE TITLES

§ 20-71.2. Declaration of purpose

The titling of salvage motor vehicles constitutes a problem in North Carolina because members of the public are sometimes misled into believing a motor vehicle has not been damaged by collision, fire, flood, accident, or other cause or that the vehicle has not been altered, rebuilt, or modified to such an extent that it impairs or changes the original components of the motor vehicle. It is therefore in the public interest that the Commissioner of Motor Vehicles issue rules to give public notice of the titling of such vehicles and to carry out the provisions of this Part of the motor vehicle laws of North Carolina.

History.
1987, c. 607, s. 1

§ 20-71.3. Salvage and other vehicles -- titles and registration cards to be branded

(a) Motor vehicle certificates of title and registration cards issued pursuant to G.S. 20-57 shall be branded in accordance with this section.

As used in this section, "branded" means that the title and registration card shall contain a designation that discloses if the vehicle is classified as any of the following:

(1) Salvage Motor Vehicle.

(2) Salvage Rebuilt Vehicle.

(3) Reconstructed Vehicle.

(4) Flood Vehicle.

(5) Non-U.S.A. Vehicle.

(6) Any other classification authorized by law.

(a1) Any motor vehicle that is declared a total loss by an insurance company licensed and approved to conduct business in North Carolina, in addition to the designations noted in subsection (a) of this section, shall:

(1) Have the title and registration card marked "TOTAL LOSS CLAIM".

(2) Have a tamperproof permanent marker inserted into the doorjamb of that vehicle by the Division, at the time of the final inspection of the reconstructed vehicle, that states "TOTAL LOSS CLAIM VEHICLE". Should that vehicle be later reconstructed, repaired, or rebuilt, a permanent tamperproof marker shall be inserted in the doorjamb of the reconstructed, repaired, or rebuilt vehicle.

(b) Any motor vehicle up to and including six model years old damaged by collision or other occurrence, that is to be retitled in this State, shall be subject to preliminary and final inspections by the Enforcement Section of the Division. For purposes of this section, the term "six model years" shall be calculated by counting the model year of the vehicle's manufacture as the first model year and the current calendar year as the final model year.

These inspections serve as antitheft measures and do not certify the safety or roadworthiness of a vehicle.

(c) The Division shall not retitle a vehicle described in subsection (b) of this section that has not undergone the preliminary and final inspections required by that subsection.

(d) Any motor vehicle up to and including six model years old that has been inspected pursuant to subsection (b) of this section may be retitled with an unbranded title based upon a title application by the rebuilder with a supporting affidavit disclosing all of the following:

(1) The parts used or replaced.

(2) The major components replaced.

(3) The hours of labor and the hourly labor rate.

(4) The total cost of repair.

(5) The existence, if applicable, of the doorjamb "TOTAL LOSS CLAIM VEHICLE" marker.

The unbranded title shall be issued only if the cost of repairs, including parts and labor, does not exceed seventy-five percent (75%) of its fair market retail value.

(e) Any motor vehicle more than six model years old damaged by collision or other occurrence that is to be retitled by the State may be retitled, without inspection, with an unbranded title based upon a title application by the rebuilder with a supporting affidavit disclosing all of the following:

(1) The parts used or replaced.

(2) The major components replaced.

(3) The hours of labor and the hourly labor rate.

(4) The total cost of repair.

(5) The existence, if applicable, of the doorjamb "TOTAL LOSS CLAIM VEHICLE" marker.

(6) The cost to replace the air bag restraint system.

The unbranded title shall be issued only if the cost of repairs, including parts and labor and excluding the cost to replace the air bag restraint system, does not exceed seventy-five percent (75%) of its fair market retail value.

(f) The Division shall maintain the affidavits required by this section and make them available for review and copying by persons researching the salvage and repair history of the vehicle.

(g) Any motor vehicle that has been branded in another state shall be branded with the nearest applicable brand specified in this section, except that no junk vehicle or vehicle that has been branded junk in another state shall be titled or registered.

(h) A branded title for a salvage motor vehicle damaged by collision or other occurrence shall be issued as follows:

(1) For motor vehicles up to and including six model years old, a branded title shall be issued if the cost of repairs, including parts and labor, exceeds seventy-five percent (75%) of its fair market value at the time of the collision or other occurrence.

(2) For motor vehicles more than six model years old, a branded title shall be issued if the cost of repairs, including parts and labor and excluding the cost to replace the air bag restraint system, exceeds seventy-five percent (75%) of its fair market value at the time of the collision or other occurrence.

(i) Once the Division has issued a branded title for a motor vehicle all subsequent titles for that motor vehicle shall continue to reflect the branding.

(j) The Division shall prepare necessary forms and doorjamb marker specifications and may adopt rules required to carry out the provisions of this Part.

Chapter 20

History.

1987, c. 607, s. 1; 1987 (Reg. Sess., 1988), c. 1105, s. 2; 1989, c. 455, ss. 2, 3; 1989 (Reg. Sess., 1990), c. 916, s. 1; 1997-443, s. 32.26; 1998-212, s. 27.8(a); 2003-258, s. 1

§ 20-71.4. Failure to disclose damage to a vehicle shall be a misdemeanor

(a) It shall be unlawful for any transferor of a motor vehicle to do any of the following:

(1) Transfer a motor vehicle up to and including five model years old when the transferor has knowledge that the vehicle has been involved in a collision or other occurrence to the extent that the cost of repairing that vehicle, excluding the cost to replace the air bag restraint system, exceeds twenty-five percent (25%) of its fair market retail value at the time of the collision or other occurrence, without disclosing that fact in writing to the transferee prior to the transfer of the vehicle.

(2) Transfer a motor vehicle when the transferor has knowledge that the vehicle is, or was, a flood vehicle, a reconstructed vehicle, or a salvage motor vehicle, without disclosing that fact in writing to the transferee prior to the transfer of the vehicle.

(3) Transfer a motor vehicle when the transferor has knowledge that a counterfeit supplemental restraint system, or a nonfunctional airbag, or no airbag has been installed in the vehicle. For purposes of this subdivision, in the event the owners of a franchised motor vehicle dealer, as defined in G.S. 20-286(8b), have no actual knowledge that a counterfeit supplemental restraint system component or nonfunctional air bag has been installed in a vehicle, knowledge by any other person shall not be imputed to the franchised motor vehicle dealer or its owners, and the franchised motor vehicle dealer or its owners shall not be deemed to have committed an unlawful act under this subdivision.

(a1) For purposes of this section, the term "five model years" shall be calculated by counting the model year of the vehicle's manufacture as the first model year and the current calendar year as the final model year. Failure to disclose any of the information required under subsection (a) of this section that is within the knowledge of the transferor will also result in civil liability under G.S. 20-348. The Commissioner may prepare forms to carry out the provisions of this section.

(b) It shall be unlawful for any person to remove the title or supporting documents to any motor vehicle from the State of North Carolina with the intent to conceal damage (or damage which has been repaired) occurring as a result of a collision or other occurrence.

(c) It shall be unlawful for any person to remove, tamper with, alter, or conceal the "TOTAL LOSS CLAIM VEHICLE" tamperproof permanent marker that is affixed to the doorjamb of any total loss claim vehicle. It shall be unlawful for any person to reconstruct a total loss claim vehicle and not include or affix a "TOTAL LOSS CLAIM VEHICLE" tamperproof permanent marker to the doorjamb of the rebuilt vehicle. Violation of this subsection shall constitute a Class I felony, punishable by a fine of not less than five thousand dollars ($ 5,000) for each offense.

(d) Violation of subsections (a) and (b) of this section shall constitute a Class 2 misdemeanor.

(e) The provisions of this section shall not apply to a State agency that assists the United States Department of Defense with purchasing, transferring, or titling a vehicle to another State agency, a unit of local government, a volunteer fire department, or a volunteer rescue squad.

History.

1987, c. 607, s. 1; 1987 (Reg. Sess., 1988), c. 1105, s. 3; 1989, c. 455, s. 4; 1989 (Reg. Sess., 1990), c. 916, s. 2; 1993, c. 539, s. 337; 1994, Ex. Sess., c. 24, s. 14(c); 1998-212, s. 27.8(b); 2003-258, s. 2; 2009-550, s. 2(a); 2019-155, s. 2

PART 4
TRANSFER OF TITLE OR INTEREST

§ 20-72. Transfer by owner

(a) Whenever the owner of a registered vehicle transfers or assigns his title or interests thereto, he shall remove the license plates. The registration card and plates shall be forwarded to the Division unless the plates are to be transferred to another vehicle as provided in G.S. 20-64. If they are to be transferred to and used with another vehicle, then the endorsed registration card and the plates shall be retained and preserved by the owner. If such registration plates are to be transferred to and used with another vehicle, then the owner shall make application to the Division for assignment of the registration plates to such other vehicle under the provisions of G.S. 20-64. Such application shall be made within 20 days after the date on which such plates are last used on the vehicle to which theretofore assigned.

(b) In order to assign or transfer title or interest in any motor vehicle registered under the provisions of this Article, the owner shall execute in the presence of a person authorized to administer oaths an assignment and warranty of title on the reverse of the certificate of title in form approved by the Division, including in such assignment the name and address of the transferee; and no title to any motor vehicle shall pass or vest until such assignment is executed and the motor vehicle delivered to the transferee. The provisions of this section shall not apply to any foreclosure or repossession under a chattel mortgage or conditional sales contract or any judicial sale. The provisions of this subsection shall not apply to (i) any transfer to an insurer pursuant to G.S. 20-109.1(b)(2) or (ii) any transfer to a used motor vehicle dealer pursuant to G.S. 20-109.1(e1). The provisions of this subsection requiring that an assignment and warranty of title be executed in the presence of a person authorized to administer oaths shall not apply to any transfer of title to or from an insurer pursuant to G.S. 20-109.1.

When a manufacturer's statement of origin or an existing certificate of title on a motor vehicle is unavailable, a motor vehicle dealer licensed under Article 12 of this Chapter may also transfer title to a vehicle to another by certifying in writing in a sworn statement to the Division that is signed by the dealer principal, general manager, general sales manager, controller, owner, or other manager of the dealership that, to the best of the signatory's knowledge and information as of the date of the sworn certification, all prior perfected liens on the vehicle that are known or reasonably ascertainable by the signatory have been paid and that the motor vehicle dealer, despite having used reasonable diligence, was unable to obtain the vehicle's statement of origin or certificate of title. For purposes of this subsection, a dealer may certify that the dealer is unable to obtain the vehicle's statement of origin or certificate of title if the statement of origin or certificate of title has either (i) not been delivered to the dealer or (ii) has been lost or misplaced. The Division is authorized to request any information it deems necessary to transfer the vehicle and shall develop a form for this purpose. The knowing and intentional filing of a false sworn certification with the Division pursuant to this subsection shall constitute a Class H felony. A dealer principal, owner, or manager of a motor vehicle dealership who is not a signatory of the sworn certification required under this subsection may only be charged for a criminal violation for filing a false certification under this subsection by another dealership employee if the dealer principal, owner, or manager had actual knowledge of the falsity of the sworn certification at the time the sworn certification was submitted to the Division.

Any person transferring title or interest in a motor vehicle shall deliver the certificate of title duly assigned in accordance with the foregoing provision to the transferee at the time of delivering the vehicle, except when a certificate of title is unavailable as provided in this subsection or in G.S. 20-72.1, and except that where a security interest is obtained in the motor vehicle from the transferee in payment of the purchase price or otherwise, the transferor shall deliver the certificate of title to the lienholder and the lienholder shall forward the certificate of title together with the transferee's application for new title and necessary fees to the Division within 20 days. If the title to a vehicle is unavailable and the dealer transfers the vehicle on a sworn certification pursuant to this section or G.S. 20-52.1, and the title is subsequently received or found by the dealer, the dealer shall retain a copy for its records and submit the title to the Division. Any person who delivers or accepts a certificate of title assigned in blank shall be guilty of a Class 2 misdemeanor. No person shall have a cause of action against the Division or Division contractors arising from the transfer of a vehicle by a sworn certification pursuant to this section.

The title to a salvage vehicle shall be forwarded to the Division as provided in G.S. 20-109.1, except with respect to the title of any salvage vehicle transferred pursuant to G.S. 20-109.1(b)(2) or G.S. 20-109.1(e1).

(c) When the Division finds that any person other than the registered owner of a vehicle has in his possession a certificate of title to the vehicle on which there appears an endorsement of an assignment of title but there does not appear in the assignment any designation to show the name and address of the assignee or transferee, the Division shall be authorized and empowered to seize and hold said certificate of title until the assignor whose name appears in the assignment appears before the Division to complete the execution of the assignment or until evidence satisfactory to the Division is presented to the Division to show the name and address of the transferee.

History.
1937, c. 407, s. 36; 1947, c. 219, ss. 4, 5; 1955, c. 554, ss. 5, 6; 1961, c. 360, s. 8; c. 835, s. 8; 1963, c. 552, ss. 3, 4; 1971, c. 678; 1973, c. 1095, s. 2; 1975, c. 716, s. 5; 1993, c. 539, s. 338; 1994, Ex. Sess., c. 24, s. 14(c); 2000-182, s. 4; 2013-400, s. 2; 2018-42, s. 2(c); 2018-145, s. 4; 2019-153, s. 3; 2019-181, s. 5(b); 2020-51, s. 3(b)

§ 20-72.1. Transfer by owner when a certificate of title is unavailable; consumer remedies

(a) Notwithstanding any other provision in this Article, when a manufacturer's statement of origin or an existing certificate of title on a motor vehicle is unavailable, a motor vehicle dealer licensed under Article 12 of this Chapter shall deliver the manufacturer's statement of origin or certificate of title to the Division within 20 days of receipt of the title, but no later than 60 days following the later of the date of the sale or transfer of the vehicle or the date of the creation of a security interest in the vehicle pursuant to G.S. 20-58(b). The dealer may offer the vehicle for sale provided that the purchaser is given written notice prior to sale that the dealer is not in possession of the manufacturer's statement of origin or certificate of title and that the purchaser may be entitled to liquidated damages pursuant to subsection (b) of this section if the dealer fails to deliver the manufacturer's statement of origin or certificate of title to the Division in accordance with this subsection. For purposes of this subsection, a vehicle's manufacturer's statement of origin or existing certificate of title shall be considered unavailable under either of the following circumstances:

(1) The manufacturer's statement of origin or certificate of title has not been actually delivered to the dealer on or prior to the date the dealer sold or transferred the vehicle.

(2) The manufacturer's statement of origin or certificate of title was lost or misplaced on or prior to the date the dealer sold or transferred the vehicle.

(b) In any case where a dealer fails to deliver the manufacturer's statement of origin or certificate of title to the Division within the 60-day time period allowed in subsection (a) of this section, the vehicle purchaser may elect to receive liquidated damages from the dealer in the amount of five percent (5%) of the vehicle purchase price, not to exceed one thousand dollars ($ 1,000), provided that the dealer receives written demand for liquidated damages from the purchaser within 10 days after the expiration of the 60-day period provided in subsection (a) of this section. The liquidated damages provided in this subsection shall be payable by the dealer within 30 days after the receipt of the purchaser's written demand. Nothing in this section shall be construed to limit any other civil remedies or consumer protections available to the vehicle purchaser. Nothing in this section shall be construed to prohibit a motor vehicle dealer who pays liquidated damages or other valuable consideration to a vehicle purchaser or lessee from obtaining a release from the purchaser or lessee for any other damages or liability arising out of or related to the sale or lease of the vehicle.

(c) Notwithstanding any other provision in this Article, a motor vehicle dealer licensed under Article 12 of this Chapter may sell or transfer a motor vehicle when a manufacturer's statement of origin or an existing certificate of title on the motor vehicle is unavailable and the motor vehicle is sold or transferred to a current lessee of the motor vehicle regardless of whether the payment of any residual amount

or payoff amount for the vehicle has been made to the lessor who holds legal title to the motor vehicle at the time of the sale or transfer. The vehicle purchaser notice requirement in subsection (a) of this section, liquidated damages requirements in subsections (a) and (b) of this section, and sworn certification requirements of G.S. 20-52.1(d) and G.S. 20-72(b) shall not be applicable when a motor vehicle is sold or transferred to the current lessee of the motor vehicle.

History.
2018-42, s. 2(d); 2018-145, s. 4; 2019-181, s. 5(c)

§ 20-73. New owner must get new certificate of title

(a) **Time Limit.** -- A person to whom a vehicle is transferred, whether by purchase or otherwise, must apply to the Division for a new certificate of title. An application for a certificate of title must be submitted within 28 days after the vehicle is transferred. A person who must follow the procedure in G.S. 20-76 to get a certificate of title and who applies for a title within the required 20-day time limit or who transfers title to a vehicle pursuant to a sworn certificate pursuant to G.S. 20-52.1(d) is considered to have complied with this section even when the Division issues a certificate of title to the person after the time limit has elapsed.

A person may apply directly for a certificate of title or may allow another person, such as the person from whom the vehicle is transferred or a person who has a lien on the vehicle, to apply for a certificate of title on that person's behalf. A person to whom a vehicle is transferred is responsible for getting a certificate of title within the time limit regardless of whether the person allowed another to apply for a certificate of title on the person's behalf.

(b) **Exceptions.** -- This section does not apply to any of the following:

(1) A dealer or an insurance company to whom a vehicle is transferred when the transfer meets the requirements of G.S. 20-75.

(2) A State agency that assists the United States Department of Defense with purchasing, transferring, or titling a vehicle to another State agency, a unit of local government, a volunteer fire department, or a volunteer rescue squad.

(c) **Penalties.** -- A person to whom a vehicle is transferred who fails to apply for a certificate of title within the required time is subject to a civil penalty of twenty dollars ($ 20.00) and is guilty of a Class 2 misdemeanor. A person who undertakes to apply for a certificate of title on behalf of another person and who fails to apply for a title within the required time is subject to a civil penalty of twenty dollars ($ 20.00).

Chapter 20

When a person to whom a vehicle is transferred fails to obtain a title within the required time because a person who undertook to apply for the certificate of title did not do so within the required time, the Division may impose a civil penalty only on the person who undertook to apply for the title. Civil penalties collected under this subsection shall be credited to the Highway Fund.

History.
1937, c. 407, s. 37; 1939, c. 275; 1947, c. 219, s. 6; 1961, c. 360, s. 9; 1975, c. 716, s. 5; 1991, c. 689, s. 332; 1993, c. 539, s. 339; 1994, Ex. Sess., c. 24, s. 14(c); 2005-276, s. 44.1(j); 2009-81, s. 1; 2009-550, s. 2(b); 2015-241, s. 29.30(i); 2018-42, s. 2(g); 2018-145, s. 4

§ 20-74. Penalty for making false statement about transfer of vehicle

A dealer or another person who, in an application required by this Division, knowingly makes a false statement about the date a vehicle was sold or acquired shall be guilty of a Class 3 misdemeanor.

History.
1937, c. 407, s. 38; 1939, c. 275; 1961, c. 360, s. 10; 1975, c. 716, s. 5; 1979, c. 801, s. 8; 1981, c. 690, s. 21; 1991, c. 689, s. 333; 1993, c. 539, s. 340; 1994, Ex. Sess., c. 24, s. 14(c)

§ 20-75. When transferee is a charitable organization, dealer, or insurance company

A transferee of a vehicle registered under this Article is not required to register the vehicle or forward the certificate of title to the Division as provided in G.S. 20-73 when the transferee is any of the following:

(1) A dealer who is licensed under Article 12 of this Chapter and who holds the vehicle for resale.

(2) An insurance company taking the vehicle for sale or disposal for salvage purposes where the title is taken or requested as a part of a bona fide claim settlement transaction and only for the purpose of resale.

(3) A charitable organization operating under section 501(c)(3) of the Internal Revenue Code (26 U.S.C. § 501(c)(3)) and the vehicle was donated to the charitable organization solely for purposes of resale by the charitable organization.

To assign or transfer title or interest in the vehicle, the charitable organization or dealer shall execute, in the presence of a person authorized to administer oaths, a reassignment and warranty of title on the reverse of the certificate of title in the form approved by the Division,

which shall include the name and address of the transferee. To assign or transfer title or interest in the vehicle, the insurance company shall execute a reassignment and warranty of title on the reverse of the certificate of title in the form approved by the Division, which shall include the name and address of the transferee. The title to the vehicle shall not pass or vest until the reassignment is executed and the motor vehicle delivered to the transferee.

The dealer transferring title or interest in a motor vehicle shall deliver the certificate of title duly assigned in accordance with the foregoing provision to the transferee at the time of delivering the vehicle, except:

(1) Where a security interest in the motor vehicle is obtained from the transferee in payment of the purchase price or otherwise, the dealer shall deliver the certificate of title to the lienholder and the lienholder shall forward the certificate of title together with the transferee's application for new certificate of title and necessary fees to the Division within 20 days; or

(2) Where the transferee has the option of cancelling the transfer of the vehicle within 10 days of delivery of the vehicle, the dealer shall deliver the certificate of title to the transferee at the end of that period. Delivery need not be made if the contract for sale has been rescinded in writing by all parties to the contract.

Any person who delivers or accepts a certificate of title assigned in blank shall be guilty of a Class 2 misdemeanor.

The title to a salvage vehicle shall be forwarded to the Division as provided in G.S. 20-109.1, except with respect to the title of any salvage vehicle transferred pursuant to G.S. 20-109.1(b)(2) or G.S. 20-109.1(e1).

History.
1937, c. 407, s. 39; 1961, c. 835, s. 9; 1963, c. 552, s. 5; 1967, c. 760; 1973, c. 1095, s. 3; 1975, c. 716, s. 5; 1993, c. 440, s. 12; c. 539, s. 341; 1994, Ex. Sess., c. 24, s. 14(c); 1997-327, s. 2.1; 2013-400, s. 3; 2018-43, s. 2; 2019-153, s. 4

§ 20-75.1. Conditional delivery of motor vehicles

Notwithstanding G.S. 20-52.1, 20-72, and 20-75, nothing contained in those sections prohibits a dealer from entering into a contract with any purchaser for the sale of a vehicle and delivering the vehicle to the purchaser under terms by which the dealer's obligation to execute the manufacturer's certificate of origin or the certificate of title is conditioned on the purchaser obtaining financing for the purchase of the vehicle. Liability, collision, and comprehensive insurance on a vehicle sold and delivered

Chapter 20

conditioned on the purchaser obtaining financing for the purchaser of the vehicle shall be covered by the dealer's insurance policy until such financing is finally approved and execution of the manufacturer's certificate of origin or execution of the certificate of title. Upon final approval and execution of the manufacturer's certificate of origin or the certificate of title, and upon the purchaser having liability insurance on another vehicle, the delivered vehicle shall be covered by the purchaser's insurance policy beginning at the time of final financial approval and execution of the manufacturer's certificate of origin or the certificate of title. The dealer shall notify the insurance agency servicing the purchaser's insurance policy or the purchaser's insurer of the purchase on the day of, or if the insurance agency or insurer is not open for business, on the next business day following approval of the purchaser's financing and execution of the manufacturer's certificate of origin or the certificate of title. This subsection is in addition to any other provisions of law or insurance policies and does not repeal or supersede those provisions.

History.
1993, c. 328, s. 1

§ 20-76. Title lost or unlawfully detained; bond as condition to issuance of new certificate

(a) Whenever the applicant for the registration of a vehicle or a new certificate of title thereto is unable to present a certificate of title thereto by reason of the same being lost or unlawfully detained by one in possession, or the same is otherwise not available, the Division is hereby authorized to receive such application and to examine into the circumstances of the case, and may require the filing of affidavits or other information; and when the Division is satisfied that the applicant is entitled thereto and that G.S. 20-72 has been complied with, it is hereby authorized to register such vehicle and issue a new registration card, registration plate or plates and certificates of title to the person entitled thereto, upon payment of proper fees.

(b) Whenever the applicant for a new certificate of title is unable to satisfy the Division that he is entitled thereto as provided in subsection (a) of this section, the applicant may nevertheless obtain issuance of a new certificate of title by filing a bond with the Division as a condition to the issuance thereof. The bond shall be in the form prescribed by the Division and shall be executed by the applicant. It shall be accompanied by the deposit of cash with the Division, be executed as surety by a person, firm or corporation authorized to conduct a surety business in this State or be in the nature of a real estate bond as

described in G.S. 20-279.24(a). The bond shall be in an amount equal to one and one-half times the value of the vehicle as determined by the Division and conditioned to indemnify any prior owner or lienholder, any subsequent purchaser of the vehicle or person acquiring any security interest therein, and their respective successors in interest, against any expense, loss or damage, reason of the issuance of the certificate of title to the vehicle or on account of any defect in or undisclosed security interest in the right, title and interest of the applicant in and to the vehicle. Any person damaged by issuance of the certificate of title shall have a right of action to recover on the bond for any breach of its conditions, but the aggregate liability of the surety to all persons shall not exceed the amount of the bond. The bond, and any deposit accompanying it, shall be returned at the end of three years or prior thereto if the vehicle is no longer registered in this State and the currently valid certificate of title is surrendered to the Division, unless the Division has been notified of the pendency of an action to recover on the bond.

(c) Whenever an applicant for the registration of a moped is unable to present a manufacturer's certificate of origin for the moped, the applicant must submit an affidavit stating why the applicant does not have the manufacturer's certificate of origin and attesting that the applicant is entitled to registration. Upon receipt of the application and accompanying affidavit, the Division shall issue the applicant a registration card and plate. The Division may not require the applicant to post a bond as required under subsection (b) of this section. A person damaged by issuance of the registration card does not have a right of action against the Division.

History.
1937, c. 407, s. 40; 1947, c. 219, s. 7; 1961, c. 360, s. 11; c. 835, s. 10; 1975, c. 716, s. 5; 2014-114, s. 3

§ 20-77. Transfer by operation of law; sale under mechanic's or storage lien; unclaimed vehicles

(a) Whenever the title or interest of an owner in or to a vehicle shall pass to another by operation of law, as upon order in bankruptcy, execution sale, repossession upon default in performing the terms of a lease or executory sales contract, or otherwise than by voluntary transfer, the transferee shall secure a new certificate of title upon proper application, payment of the fees provided by law, and presentation of the last certificate of title, if available and such instruments or documents of authority or certified copies thereof as may be sufficient or required by law to evidence or effect a transfer of interest in or to chattels in such cases.

(b) In the event of transfer as upon inheritance or devise, the Division shall, upon a receipt of a certified copy of a will, letters of administration and/or a certificate from the clerk of the superior court showing that the motor vehicle registered in the name of the decedent owner has been assigned to the owner's surviving spouse as part of the spousal year's allowance, transfer both title and license as otherwise provided for transfers. If a decedent dies intestate and no administrator has qualified or the clerk of superior court has not issued a certificate of assignment as part of the spousal year's allowance, or if a decedent dies testate with a small estate and leaving a purported will, which, in the opinion of the clerk of superior court, does not justify the expense of probate and administration and probate and administration is not demanded by any interested party entitled by law to demand same, and provided that the purported will is filed in the public records of the office of the clerk of the superior court, the Division may upon affidavit executed by all heirs effect such transfer. The affidavit shall state the name of the decedent, date of death, that the decedent died intestate or testate and no administration is pending or expected, that all debts have been paid or that the proceeds from the transfer will be used for that purpose, the names, ages and relationship of all heirs and devisees (if there be a purported will), and the name and address of the transferee of the title. A surviving spouse may execute the affidavit and transfer the interest of the decedent's minor or incompetent children where such minor or incompetent does not have a guardian. A transfer under this subsection shall not affect the validity nor be in prejudice of any creditor's lien.

(c) **Mechanic's or Storage Lien.** -- In any case where a vehicle is sold under a mechanic's or storage lien, or abandoned property, the Division shall be given a 20-day notice as provided in G.S. 20-114.

(d) An operator of a place of business for garaging, repairing, parking or storing vehicles for the public in which a vehicle remains unclaimed for 10 days, or the landowners upon whose property a motor vehicle has been abandoned for more than 30 days, shall, within five days after the expiration of that period, report the vehicle as unclaimed to the Division. Failure to make the report shall constitute a Class 3 misdemeanor. Persons who are required to make this report and who fail to do so within the time period specified may collect other charges due but may not collect storage charges for the period of time between when they were required to make this report and when they actually did send the report to the Division by certified mail.

Any vehicle which remains unclaimed after report is made to the Division may be sold by the operator or landowner in accordance with the provisions relating to the enforcement of liens and the application of proceeds of sale of Article 1 of Chapter 44A. The Division shall make all forms required by the Division to effectuate a sale under this subsection available on the Division's Web site, and the Division shall allow for the electronic submission of these forms. Any form required by the Division to effectuate a sale under this subsection that requires a signature may be submitted with an electronic signature in accordance with Article 40 of Chapter 66 of the General Statutes.

(e) Any person, who shall sell a vehicle to satisfy a mechanic's or storage lien or any person who shall sell a vehicle as upon order in bankruptcy, execution sale, repossession upon default in performing the terms of a lease or executory sales contract, or otherwise by operation of law, shall remove any license plates attached thereto and return them to the Division.

History.
1937, c. 407, s. 41; 1943, c. 726; 1945, cc. 289, 714; 1955, c. 296, s. 1; 1959, c. 1264, s. 3; 1961, c. 360, ss. 12, 13; 1967, c. 562, s. 8; 1971, cc. 230, 512, 876; 1973, c. 1386, ss. 1, 2; c. 1446, s. 21; 1975, c. 438, s. 2; c. 716, s. 5; 1993, c. 539, s. 342; 1994, Ex. Sess., c. 24, s. 14(c); 1995 (Reg. Sess., 1996), c. 635, s. 1; 2003-336, s. 1; 2011-284, s. 14; 2017-57, s. 34.41(a)

§ 20-78. When Division to transfer registration and issue new certificate; recordation

(a) The Division, upon receipt of a properly endorsed certificate of title, application for transfer thereof and payment of all proper fees, shall issue a new certificate of title as upon an original registration. The Division, upon receipt of an application for transfer of registration plates, together with payment of all proper fees, shall issue a new registration card transferring and assigning the registration plates and numbers thereon as upon an original assignment of registration plates. The Division, upon receipt of an application for transfer thereof and payment of all proper fees, but without receipt of a properly endorsed certificate of title, shall issue a salvage certificate of title pursuant to G.S. 20-109.1(b)(2) or G.S. 20-109.1(e1).

(b) The Division shall maintain a record of certificates of title issued by the Division for a period of 20 years. After 20 years, the Division shall maintain a record of the last two owners.

The Commissioner is hereby authorized and empowered to provide for the photographic or photostatic recording of certificate of title records in such manner as he may deem expedient. The photographic or photostatic copies herein authorized shall be sufficient as evidence in tracing of titles of the motor vehicles designated therein, and shall also be admitted in evidence in all actions and proceedings to the same extent that the originals would have been admitted.

History.

1937, c. 407, s. 42; 1943, c. 726; 1947, c. 219, s. 8; 1961, c. 360, s. 14; 1971, c. 1070, s. 4; 1975, c. 716, s. 5; 1999-452, s. 15; 2013-400, s. 4

§ 20-78.1. Terminal rental adjustment clauses; vehicle leases that are not sales or security interests

Notwithstanding any other provision of law, a lease transaction does not create a sale or security interest in a motor vehicle or trailer merely because the lease contains a terminal rental adjustment clause that provides that the rental price is permitted or required to be adjusted up or down by reference to the amount of money realized upon the sale or other disposition of the motor vehicle or trailer.

History.

2011-223, s. 1

PART 5
ISSUANCE OF SPECIAL PLATES

§ 20-79. Dealer license plates

(a) **How to Get a Dealer Plate.** -- The Division may issue a person licensed under Article 12 of this Chapter the appropriate classification of dealer license plate. A person eligible for a dealer license plate may obtain one by filing an application with the Division and paying the required fee. An application must be filed on a form provided by the Division. The required fee is the amount set by G.S. 20-87(7).

(b) **Number of Plates.** -- A dealer who was licensed under Article 12 of this Chapter for the previous 12-month period ending December 31 may obtain the number of dealer license plates allowed by the following table; the number allowed is based on the number of motor vehicles the dealer sold during the relevant 12-month period and the average number of qualifying sales representatives the dealer employed during that same 12-month period:

Vehicles Sold In Relevant 12-Month Period	Maximum Number of Plates
Fewer than 12	3
At least 12 but less than 25	6
At least 25 but less than 37	7
At least 37 but less than 49	8
49 or more	At least 8, but no more than 5 times the average number of qualifying sales representatives employed by the dealer during the relevant 12-month period.

A dealer who was not licensed under Article 12 of this Chapter for part or all of the previous 12-month period ending December 31 may obtain the number of dealer license plates that equals four times the number of qualifying sales representatives employed by the dealer on the date the dealer files the application. A "qualifying sales representative" is a sales representative who works for the dealer at least 25 hours a week on a regular basis and is compensated by the dealer for this work.

A dealer who sold fewer than 49 motor vehicles the previous 12-month period ending December 31 but has sold at least that number since January 1 may apply for additional dealer license plates at any time. The maximum number of dealer license plates the dealer may obtain is the number the dealer could have obtained if the dealer had sold at least 49 motor vehicles in the previous 12-month period ending December 31.

A dealer who applies for a dealer license plate must certify to the Division the number of motor vehicles the dealer sold in the relevant period. Making a material misstatement in an application for a dealer license plate is grounds for the denial, suspension, or revocation of a dealer's license under G.S. 20-294.

A dealer engaged in the alteration and sale of specialty vehicles may apply for up to two dealer plates in addition to the number of dealer plates that the dealer would otherwise be entitled to under this section.

This subsection does not apply to manufacturers licensed under Article 12 of this Chapter.

(c) **Form and Duration.** -- A dealer license plate is subject to G.S. 20-63, except for the requirement that the plate display the registration number of a motor vehicle and the requirement that the plate be a "First in Flight" plate, a "First in Freedom" plate, or a "National/State Mottos" plate. A dealer license plate must have a distinguishing symbol identifying the plate as a dealer license plate. The symbol may vary depending upon the classification of dealer license plate issued. The Division must provide suitably reduced sized license plates for motorcycle dealers and manufacturers.

A dealer license plate is issued for a period of one year. The Division shall vary the expiration dates of dealer registration renewals so that an approximately equal number expires at the end of each month, quarter, or other period consisting of one or more months. A dealer license plate may be transferred from one vehicle to another. When the Division issues a dealer plate, it may issue a registration that expires at the end of any monthly interval. When one of the following occurs, a dealer must surrender to the Division all dealer license plates issued to the dealer:

    (1) The dealer surrenders the license issued to the dealer under Article 12 of this Chapter.

    (2) The Division suspends or revokes the license issued to the dealer under Article 12 of this Chapter.

    (3) The Division rescinds the dealer license plates because of a violation of the restrictions on the use of a dealer license plate.

To obtain a dealer license plate after it has been surrendered, the dealer must file a new application for a dealer license plate and pay the required fee for the plate.

(c1) **Dealer Plate Mandatory Replacement.** -- Notwithstanding G.S. 20-63.1, registration plates issued under this section shall be replaced every three years.

(d) **(Effective until December 31, 2024) Restrictions on Use.** -- A dealer license plate may be displayed only on a motor vehicle that meets all of the following requirements:

    (1) Is part of the inventory of the dealer.

    (2) Is not consigned to the dealer.

    (3) Is covered by liability insurance that meets the requirements of Article 9A of this Chapter.

    (4) Is not used by the dealer in another business in which the dealer is engaged.

    (5) Is driven on a highway by a person who meets one of the following descriptions:

        a. Has a demonstration permit to test-drive the motor vehicle and carries the demonstration permit while driving the motor vehicle.

        b. Is an officer or sales representative of the dealer and is driving the vehicle for a business purpose of the dealer.

        c. Is an employee of the dealer and is driving the vehicle in the course of employment.

        d. Is an employee of the dealer or of a contractor of the dealer and is driving the vehicle within a 20-mile radius of a place where the vehicle is being repaired or otherwise prepared for sale.

        e. Is an employee of the dealer or of a contractor of the dealer and is transporting the vehicle to or from a vehicle auction or to the dealer's established salesroom.

        f. Is an officer, sales representative, or other employee of an independent or franchised motor vehicle dealer or is an immediate family member of an officer, sales representative, or other employee of an independent or franchised motor vehicle dealer.

    (6) A copy of the registration card for the dealer plate issued to the dealer is carried by the person operating the motor vehicle or, if the person is operating the motor vehicle in this State, the registration card is maintained on file at the dealer's address listed on the registration card, and the registration card must be able to be produced within 24 hours upon request of any law enforcement officer.

A dealer may issue a demonstration permit for a motor vehicle to a person licensed to drive that type of motor vehicle. A demonstration permit authorizes each person named in the permit to drive the motor vehicle described in the permit for up to 96 hours after the time the permit is issued. A dealer may, for good cause, renew a demonstration permit for one additional 96-hour period. A franchised motor vehicle dealer is not prohibited from using a demonstration permit pursuant to this subsection by reason of the dealer's receipt of incentive or warranty compensation or other reimbursement or consideration from a manufacturer, factory branch, distributor, distributor branch or from a third-party warranty, maintenance, or service contract company relating to the use of the vehicle as a demonstrator or service loaner.

A dealer may not lend, rent, lease, or otherwise place a dealer license plate at the disposal of a person except as authorized by this subsection.

(d) **(Effective December 31, 2024) Restrictions on Use.** -- A dealer license plate may be displayed only on a motor vehicle that meets all of the following requirements:

    (1) Is part of the inventory of the dealer.

    (2) Is not consigned to the dealer.

    (3) Is covered by liability insurance that meets the requirements of Article 9A of this Chapter.

    (4) Is not used by the dealer in another business in which the dealer is engaged.

    (5) Is driven on a highway by a person who meets one of the following descriptions:

Chapter 20

a. Has a demonstration permit to test-drive the motor vehicle and carries the demonstration permit while driving the motor vehicle.

b. Is an officer or sales representative of the dealer and is driving the vehicle for a business purpose of the dealer.

c. Is an employee of the dealer and is driving the vehicle in the course of employment.

d. Is an employee of the dealer or of a contractor of the dealer and is driving the vehicle within a 20-mile radius of a place where the vehicle is being repaired or otherwise prepared for sale.

e. Is an employee of the dealer or of a contractor of the dealer and is transporting the vehicle to or from a vehicle auction or to the dealer's established salesroom.

f. Is an officer, sales representative, or other employee of an independent or franchised motor vehicle dealer or is an immediate family member of an officer, sales representative, or other employee of an independent or franchised motor vehicle dealer.

(6) A copy of the registration card for the dealer plate issued to the dealer is carried by the person operating the motor vehicle or, if the person is operating the motor vehicle in this State, the registration card is maintained on file at the dealer's address listed on the registration card, and the registration card must be able to be produced within 24 hours upon request of any law enforcement officer.

A dealer may issue a demonstration permit for a motor vehicle to a person licensed to drive that type of motor vehicle. A demonstration permit authorizes each person named in the permit to drive the motor vehicle described in the permit for up to 96 hours after the time the permit is issued. A dealer may, for good cause, renew a demonstration permit for one additional 96-hour period.

A dealer may not lend, rent, lease, or otherwise place a dealer license plate at the disposal of a person except as authorized by this subsection.

(e) **Sanctions.** -- The following sanctions apply when a motor vehicle displaying a dealer license plate is driven in violation of the restrictions on the use of the plate:

(1) The individual driving the motor vehicle is responsible for an infraction and is subject to a penalty of one hundred dollars ($ 100.00).

(2) The dealer to whom the plate is issued is subject to a civil penalty imposed

by the Division of two hundred fifty dollars ($ 250.00).

(3) The Division may rescind all dealer license plates issued to the dealer whose plate was displayed on the motor vehicle.

A penalty imposed under subdivision (1) of this subsection is payable to the county where the infraction occurred, as required by G.S. 14-3.1. A civil penalty imposed under subdivision (2) of this subsection shall be credited to the Highway Fund as nontax revenue.

(f) **Transfer of Dealer Registration.** -- No change in the name of a firm, partnership or corporation, nor the taking in of a new partner, nor the withdrawal of one or more of the firm, shall be considered a new business; but if any one or more of the partners remain in the firm, or if there is change in ownership of less than a majority of the stock, if a corporation, the business shall be regarded as continuing and the dealers' plates originally issued may continue to be used.

(g) **Penalties.** -- The clear proceeds of all civil penalties, civil forfeitures, and civil fines that are collected by the Department of Transportation pursuant to this section shall be remitted to the Civil Penalty and Forfeiture Fund in accordance with G.S. 115C-457.2.

(h) **Definition.** -- For purposes of this section, the term "dealer" means a person who is licensed under Article 12 of this Chapter.

History.
1937, c. 407, s. 43; 1947, c. 220, s. 2; 1949, c. 583, s. 3; 1951, c. 985, s. 2; 1959, c. 1264, s. 3.5; 1961, c. 360, s. 15; 1975, c. 716, s. 5; 1979, c. 239; c. 612, s. 1; 1985, c. 764, s. 21; 1985 (Reg. Sess., 1986), c. 852, s. 17; 1989, c. 770, s. 74.1(a); 1993, c. 321, s. 169.4; c. 440, s. 2; c. 539, s. 343; 1993 (Reg. Sess., 1994), c. 697, ss. 1, 2; c. 761, s. 6; 1994, Ex. Sess., c. 24, s. 14(c); 1997-335, s. 1; 2001-212, s. 1; 2004-167, s. 4; 2004-199, s. 59; 2005-276, s. 6.37(q); 2007-291, s. 1; 2007-481, s. 1; 2010-132, s. 5; 2011-318, s. 2; 2014-100, s. 34.28(b); 2015-232, s. 1.4(a); 2015-264, s. 42(b); 2016-90, s. 13.5; 2018-5, s. 34.27(b); 2018-27, s. 4.5(c); 2018-42, s. 3(c); 2020-51, s. 1(c); 2021-134, s. 4

§ 20-79.01. Special sports event temporary license plates

(a) **Application.** -- A dealer who is licensed under Article 12 of this Chapter and who agrees to loan to another for use at a special sports event a vehicle that could display a dealer license plate if driven by an officer or employee of the dealer may obtain a temporary special sports event license plate for that vehicle by filing an application with the Division and paying the required fee. A "special sports event" is a sports event that is held no more than once a year and is open to the public. An application

Chapter 20

must be filed on a form provided by the Division and contain the information required by the Division. The fee for a temporary special sports event license plate is five dollars ($ 5.00).

(b) **Form and Duration.** -- A temporary special sports event license plate must state on the plate the date it was issued, the date it expires, and the make, model, and serial number of the vehicle for which it is issued. A temporary special sports event license plate may be issued for no more than 45 days. The dealer to whom the plate is issued must destroy the plate on or before the date it expires.

(c) **Restrictions on Use.** -- A temporary special sports event license plate may be displayed only on the vehicle for which it is issued. A vehicle displaying a temporary special sports event license plate may be driven by anyone who is licensed to drive the type of vehicle for which the plate is issued and may be driven for any purpose.

History.
1993, c. 440, s. 13

§ 20-79.02. Loaner/Dealer "LD" license plate for franchised dealer loaner vehicles

(a) **Application; Fee.** -- A franchised motor vehicle dealer, as defined in G.S. 20-286(8b) and licensed in accordance with Article 12 of this Chapter, who agrees to loan, with or without charge, a new motor vehicle owned by the dealer to a customer of the dealer who is having his or her vehicle serviced by the dealer, may obtain a Loaner/Dealer "LD" license plate for the vehicle by filing an application with the Division and paying the required fee. Receipt by a franchised motor vehicle dealer of compensation or other consideration from a manufacturer, distributor, manufacturer branch, distributor branch, third-party warranty, maintenance or service contract company, or other third-party source related to a vehicle, including, but not limited to, incentive compensation or reimbursement for maintenance, repairs, or other work performed on the vehicle, does not prevent the franchised motor vehicle dealer from receiving an LD license plate for the vehicle. An application must be filed on a form provided by the Division and contain the information required by the Division. The annual fee for an LD license plate is two hundred dollars ($ 200.00) per 12 calendar months.

(b) **Number of Plates.** -- There is no limit on the number of LD license plates that a franchised motor vehicle dealer may be issued, provided that the applicable annual fee for each plate is paid.

(c) **Form and Duration.** -- An LD license plate is subject to G.S. 20-63, except for the requirement that the plate display the registration number of a motor vehicle and the requirement that the plate be a "First in Flight" plate, "First in Freedom" plate, or a "National/State Mottos" plate. An LD license plate must have a distinguishing symbol identifying the plate as an LD license plate. Subject to the limitations in this section, an LD license plate may continue in existence perpetually and may be transferred to other vehicles in the dealer's loaner fleet when the vehicle on which the LD license plate is displayed has been sold or leased to a third party or otherwise removed from the dealer's loaner fleet.

(d) **Restrictions on Use.** -- The following restrictions apply with regard to the use and display of an LD license plate:

(1) An LD license plate may be displayed only on a motor vehicle that meets all of the following requirements:

a. Is part of the inventory of a franchised motor vehicle dealer.

b. Is not consigned to the franchised motor vehicle dealer or affiliate.

c. Is covered by liability insurance that meets the requirements of Article 9A of this Chapter; provided, however, that nothing herein prevents or prohibits a franchised motor vehicle dealer from contractually shifting the risk of loss and insurance requirements contained in Article 9A of this Chapter to an individual or entity to which a vehicle is loaned.

d. Is not used by the franchised motor vehicle dealer in another business in which the dealer is engaged.

e. Is driven on a highway by a customer of the franchised motor vehicle dealer who is having a vehicle serviced or repaired by the dealer.

(2) The person operating the motor vehicle must carry a copy of the assignment by the franchised motor vehicle dealer and a copy of the registration card for the LD license plate issued to the franchised motor vehicle dealer, or, if the person is operating the motor vehicle in this State, the registration card must be maintained on file at the franchised motor vehicle dealer's address listed on the registration card, and the registration card must be able to be produced within 24 hours upon request of a law enforcement officer.

(3) A vehicle displaying an LD license plate may be driven only by a person who is licensed to drive the type of motor vehicle for which the plate is issued.

(4) An LD license plate may be displayed only on the motor vehicle for which it has been assigned by the franchised motor vehicle dealer.

Chapter 20

(5) The franchised motor vehicle dealer to whom an LD license plate is issued is responsible for completing and maintaining documentation prescribed by the Division relating to the assignment of each motor vehicle on which an LD license plate is displayed to a customer of the franchised dealer.

(e) **Penalties.** -- A driver of a motor vehicle or a franchised motor vehicle dealer who violates a restriction on the use or display of an LD license plate as set out in subsection (d) of this section is subject to the penalties listed in this subsection. The clear proceeds of all civil penalties, civil forfeitures, and civil fines that are collected pursuant to this section shall be remitted to the Civil Penalty and Forfeiture Fund in accordance with G.S. 115C-457.2. The penalties are as follows:

(1) The driver of the motor vehicle who violates a restriction on the use or display of an LD license plate is responsible for an infraction and is subject to a penalty of one hundred dollars ($ 100.00).

(2) A franchised motor vehicle dealer to whom the plate is issued who violates a restriction on the use or display of an LD license plate is subject to an infraction and is subject to a penalty of two hundred fifty dollars ($ 250.00). The Division may rescind all LD license plates issued to the franchised motor vehicle dealer for knowing repeated violations of subsection (d) of this section.

(f) **Transfer of Dealer Registration.** -- A change in the name of a firm, partnership, or corporation is not considered a new business, and the franchised motor vehicle dealer's LD license plates may continue to be used.

(g) **Applicability.** -- Prior to January 1, 2025, a new motor vehicle dealer may, but is not required to, display an LD license plate on a service loaner vehicle. Beginning on or after January 1, 2025, a new motor vehicle dealer shall display an LD license plate on any new motor vehicle placed into service as a loaner vehicle if either of the following circumstances exists:

(1) The new motor vehicle dealer is receiving incentive or warranty compensation from a manufacturer, factory branch, distributor, or distributor branch for the use of the vehicle as a service loaner.

(2) The new motor vehicle dealer is receiving a fee or other compensation from the dealer's customers for the use of the vehicle as a service loaner.

History.
2015-232, s. 1.3(a); 2018-5, s. 34.27(c); 2018-27, s. 4.5(a); 2018-42, s. 3(a); 2020-51, s. 1(a)

§ 20-79.1. Use of temporary registration plates or markers by purchasers of motor vehicles in lieu of dealers' plates

(a) The Division may, subject to the limitations and conditions hereinafter set forth, deliver temporary registration plates or markers designed by said Division to a dealer duly registered under the provisions of this Article who applies for at least 25 such plates or markers and who encloses with the application a fee of one dollar ($ 1.00) for each plate or marker for which application is made. The application shall be made upon a form prescribed and furnished by the Division. The Division shall provide methods for physical and electronic application submission and payment. Any electronic application submitted to the Division under this subsection may include a method for electronic signature by the dealer. Dealers, subject to the limitations and conditions hereinafter set forth, may issue temporary registration plates or markers to owners of vehicles, provided that owners comply with the pertinent provisions of this section.

(b) Every dealer who has made application for temporary registration plates or markers shall maintain in permanent form a record of all temporary registration plates or markers delivered to him, and shall also maintain in permanent form a record of all temporary registration plates or markers issued by him, and in addition thereto, shall maintain in permanent form a record of any other information pertaining to the receipt or the issuance of temporary registration plates or markers that the Division may require. Each record shall be kept for a period of at least one year from the date of entry of such record. Every dealer shall allow full and free access to such records during regular business hours, to duly authorized representatives of the Division and to peace officers.

(c) Every dealer who issues temporary registration plates or markers shall also issue a temporary registration certificate upon a form furnished by the Division and deliver it with the registration plate or marker to the owner.

(d) A dealer shall:

(1) Not issue, assign, transfer, or deliver temporary registration plates or markers to anyone other than a bona fide purchaser or owner of a vehicle which he has sold.

(2) Not issue a temporary registration plate or marker without first obtaining from the purchaser or owner a written application for titling and registration of the vehicle and the applicable fees.

(3) Within 20 days of the issuance of a temporary registration plate or marker, mail or deliver the application and fees to the Division or deliver the application and fees to a local license agency for processing.

Delivery need not be made if the contract for sale has been rescinded by all parties to the contract.

(4) Not deliver a temporary registration plate to anyone purchasing a vehicle that has an unexpired registration plate that is to be transferred to the purchaser.

(5) Not lend to anyone, or use on any vehicle that he may own, any temporary registration plates or markers.

A dealer may issue temporary markers, without obtaining the written application for titling and registration or collecting the applicable fees, to nonresidents for the purpose of removing the vehicle from the State.

(e) Every dealer who issues temporary plates or markers shall write clearly and indelibly on the face of the temporary registration plate or marker:

(1) The dates of issuance and expiration;

(2) The make, motor number, and serial numbers of the vehicle; and

(3) Any other information that the Division may require.

It shall be unlawful for any person to issue a temporary registration plate or marker containing any misstatement of fact or to knowingly write any false information on the face of the plate or marker.

(f) If the Division finds that the provisions of this section or the directions of the Division are not being complied with by the dealer, the Division may suspend, after a hearing, the right of a dealer to issue temporary registration plates or markers. Nothing in this section shall be deemed to require a dealer to collect or receive property taxes from any person.

(g) Every person to whom temporary registration plates or markers have been issued shall permanently destroy such temporary registration plates or markers immediately upon receiving the limited registration plates or the annual registration plates from the Division: Provided, that if the limited registration plates or the annual registration plates are not received within 30 days of the issuance of the temporary registration plates or markers, the owner shall, notwithstanding, immediately upon the expiration of such 30-day period, permanently destroy the temporary registration plates or markers.

(h) Temporary registration plates or markers shall expire and become void upon the receipt of the limited registration plates or the annual registration plates from the Division, or upon the rescission of a contract to purchase a motor vehicle, or upon the expiration of 30 days from the date of issuance, depending upon whichever event shall first occur. No refund or credit or fees paid by dealers to the Division for temporary registration plates or markers shall be allowed, except in the event that the Division discontinues the issuance of temporary registration plates or markers or unless the dealer discontinues business. In this event the unissued registration plates or markers with the unissued registration certificates shall be returned to the Division and the dealer may petition for a refund. Upon the expiration of the 30 days from the date of issuance, a second 30-day temporary registration plate or marker may be issued by the dealer upon showing the vehicle has been sold or leased, and that the dealer, having used reasonable diligence, is unable to obtain the vehicle's statement of origin or certificate of title so that the lien may be perfected. For purposes of this subsection, a dealer shall be considered unable to obtain the vehicle's statement of origin or certificate of title if the statement of origin or certificate of title either (i) has not been delivered to the dealer or (ii) was lost or misplaced.

(i) A temporary registration plate or marker may be used on the vehicle for which issued only and may not be transferred, loaned, or assigned to another. In the event a temporary registration plate or marker or temporary registration certificate is lost or stolen, the owner shall permanently destroy the remaining plate or marker or certificate and no operation of the vehicle for which the lost or stolen registration certificate, registration plate or marker has been issued shall be made on the highways until the regular license plate is received and attached thereto.

(j) The Commissioner of Motor Vehicles shall have the power to make such rules and regulations, not inconsistent herewith, as he shall deem necessary for the purpose of carrying out the provisions of this section.

(k) The provisions of G.S. 20-63, 20-71, 20-110 and 20-111 shall apply in like manner to temporary registration plates or markers as is applicable to nontemporary plates.

(l) The Division is authorized to enter into agreements to utilize commission contractors under contract with the Division under G.S. 20-63(h) to distribute temporary registration plates to dealers as provided in this section. The Division must provide compensation to commission contractors for distributing temporary registration plates at the transaction rate established for issuing registration documents in G.S. 20-63(h)(1). The Division must provide commission contractors with any forms, equipment, and supplies necessary for distributing temporary registration plates and provide appropriate guidance and supervision of the distribution. If the Division enters into agreements with commission contractors under this subsection, the Division shall make every effort to enter into agreements with commission contractors across all geographic regions of the State in order to make temporary registration plates accessible to all dealers.

Chapter 20

History.

1957, c. 246, s. 1; 1963, c. 552, s. 8; 1975, c. 716, s. 5; 1985, c. 95; c. 263; 1997-327, ss. 1, 2; 2000-182, s. 5; 2007-471, s. 1; 2009-445, s. 25(a); 2010-95, s. 22(d); 2013-414, s. 70(c); 2018-42, ss. 2(e), 4; 2018-145, s. 4; 2019-181, s. 5(d); 2020-77, ss. 2, 4(a)

§ 20-79.1A. Limited registration plates

(a) **Eligibility.** -- A limited registration plate is issuable to any of the following:

(1) A person who applies, either directly or through a dealer licensed under Article 12 of this Chapter, for a title to a motor vehicle and a registration plate for the vehicle and who submits payment for the applicable title and registration fees but does not submit payment for any municipal corporation property taxes on the vehicle. A person who submits payment for municipal corporation property taxes receives an annual registration plate.

(2) A person who applies for a plate for a vehicle that was previously registered with the Division but whose registration has not been current for at least a year because the plate for the vehicle was surrendered or the vehicle's registration expired over a year ago.

(b) **Form and Authorization.** -- A limited registration plate must be clearly and visibly designated as "temporary." The plate expires on the last day of the second month following the date of application of the limited registration plate. The plate may be used only on the vehicle for which it is issued and may not be transferred, loaned, or assigned to another. If the plate is lost or stolen, the vehicle for which the plate was issued may not be operated on a highway until a replacement limited registration plate or a regular license plate is received and attached to the vehicle.

(c) **Registration Certificate.** -- The Division is not required to issue a registration certificate for a limited registration plate. A combined tax and registration notice issued under G.S. 105-330.5 serves as the registration certificate for the plate.

History.

2007-471, s. 2; 2009-445, ss. 24(b), 25(a); 2010-95, ss. 22(c), (d); 2013-414, s. 70(b), (c); 2014-3, s. 14.24

§ 20-79.2. Transporter plates

(a) **Who Can Get a Plate.** -- The Division may issue a transporter plate authorizing the limited operation of a motor vehicle in the circumstances listed in this subsection. A person who receives a transporter plate must have proof of financial responsibility that meets the requirements of Article 9A of this Chapter. The person to whom a transporter plate may be issued and the circumstances in which the vehicle bearing the plate may be operated are as follows:

(1) To a business or a dealer to facilitate the manufacture, construction, rebuilding, or delivery of new or used truck cabs or bodies between manufacturer, dealer, seller, or purchaser.

(2) To a financial institution that has a recorded lien on a motor vehicle to repossess the motor vehicle.

(3) To a dealer or repair facility to pick up and deliver a motor vehicle that is to be repaired, is to undergo a safety or emissions inspection, or is to otherwise be prepared for sale by a dealer, to road-test the vehicle, if it is repaired or inspected within a 20-mile radius of the place where it is repaired or inspected, and to deliver the vehicle to the dealer. A repair facility may not receive more than two transporter plates for this purpose.

(4) To a business that has at least 10 registered vehicles to move a motor vehicle that is owned by the business and is a replaced vehicle offered for sale.

(5) To a dealer or a business that contracts with a dealer and has a business privilege license to take a motor vehicle either to or from a motor vehicle auction where the vehicle will be or was offered for sale. The title to the vehicle, a bill of sale, or written authorization from the dealer or auction must be inside the vehicle when the vehicle is operated with a transporter plate.

(6) To a business or dealer to road-test a repaired truck whose GVWR is at least 15,000 pounds when the test is performed within a 10-mile radius of the place where the truck was repaired and the truck is owned by a person who has a fleet of at least five trucks whose GVWRs are at least 15,000 pounds and who maintains the place where the truck was repaired.

(7) To a business or dealer to move a mobile office, a mobile classroom, or a mobile or manufactured home, or to transport a newly manufactured travel trailer, fifth-wheel trailer, or camping trailer between a manufacturer and a dealer. Any transporter plate used under this subdivision may not be used on the power unit.

(8) To a business to drive a motor vehicle that is registered in this State and is at least 35 years old to and from a parade or another public event and to drive the motor vehicle in that event. A person who owns one of these motor vehicles is considered to be in the business of collecting those vehicles.

(9) To a dealer to drive a motor vehicle that is part of the inventory of a dealer to and from a motor vehicle trade show or exhibition or to, during, and from a parade in which the motor vehicle is used.

(10) To drive special mobile equipment in any of the following circumstances:

a. From the manufacturer of the equipment to a facility of a dealer.

b. From one facility of a dealer to another facility of a dealer.

c. From a dealer to the person who buys the equipment from the dealer.

(b) **How to Get a Plate.** -- A business or a dealer may obtain a transporter plate by filing an application with the Division and paying the required fee. An application must be on a form provided by the Division and contain the information required by the Division. The fee for a transporter plate is one-half the fee set in G.S. 20-87(5) for a passenger motor vehicle of not more than 15 passengers.

(b1) **Number of Plates.** -- The total number of Dealer-Transporter or dealer plates issued to a dealer may not exceed the total number of plates that can be issued to the dealer under G.S. 20-79(b). Transporter plates issued to a dealer shall bear the words "Dealer-Transporter." This subsection does not apply to a person who is not a dealer.

(b2) **Sanctions.** -- The following sanctions apply when a motor vehicle displaying a "Dealer-Transporter" or "Transporter" license plate is driven in violation of the restrictions on the use of the plate or of the requirement to have proof of financial responsibility:

(1) The individual driving the motor vehicle is responsible for an infraction and is subject to a penalty of one hundred dollars ($ 100.00).

(2) The dealer or business to whom the plate is issued is subject to a civil penalty imposed by the Division of two hundred fifty dollars ($ 250.00) per occurrence.

(3) The Division may rescind all dealer license plates, dealer transporter plates, or transporter plates issued to the dealer or business whose plate was displayed on the motor vehicle.

(4) A person who sells, rents, leases, or otherwise provides a transporter plate to another person in exchange for the money or any other thing of value is guilty of a Class I felony. A conviction for a violation of this subdivision is considered a felony involving moral turpitude for purposes of G.S. 20-294.

A penalty imposed under subdivision (1) of this subsection is payable to the county where the infraction occurred, as required by G.S. 14-3.1. A civil penalty imposed under subdivision (2) of this subsection shall be credited to the Highway Fund as nontax revenue. A law enforcement officer having probable cause to believe that a transporter plate is being used in violation of this section may seize the plate.

(c) **Form, Duration, and Transfer.** -- A transporter plate is subject to G.S. 20-63, except for the requirement that the plate display the registration number of a motor vehicle and the requirement that the plate be a "First in Flight" plate, a "First in Freedom" plate, or a "National/State Mottos" plate. A transporter plate shall have a distinguishing symbol identifying the plate as a transporter plate. The symbol may vary depending upon the classification of transporter plate issued. A transporter plate is issued for a period of one year. The Division shall vary the expiration dates of transporter registration renewals so that an approximately equal number expires at the end of each month, quarter, or other period consisting of one or more months. When the Division issues a transporter plate, it may issue a registration that expires at the end of any monthly interval. During the year for which it is issued, a business or dealer may transfer a transporter plate from one vehicle to another as long as the vehicle is driven only for a purpose authorized by subsection (a) of this section. The Division must rescind a transporter plate that is displayed on a motor vehicle driven for a purpose that is not authorized by subsection (a) of this section.

(d) **County.** -- A county may obtain one transporter plate, without paying a fee, by filing an application with the Division on a form to be provided by the Division. A transporter plate issued pursuant to this subsection may only be used to transport motor vehicles as part of a program established by the county to receive donated motor vehicles and make them available to low-income individuals.

If a motor vehicle is operated on the highways of this State using a transporter plate authorized by this section, all of the following requirements shall be met:

(1) The driver of the vehicle shall have in his or her possession the certificate of title for the motor vehicle, which has been properly reassigned by the previous owner to the county or the affected donor program.

(2) The vehicle shall be covered by liability insurance that meets the requirements of Article 9A of this Chapter.

The form and duration of the transporter plate shall be as provided in subsection (c) of this section.

(e) Any vehicle being operated on the highways of this State using a transporter plate shall have proof of financial responsibility that meets the requirement of Article 9A of this Chapter.

History.

1961, c. 360, s. 21; 1969, c. 600, s. 1; 1975, c. 222; 1979, c. 473, ss. 1, 2; c. 627, ss. 1-3; 1981, c. 727, ss. 1, 2; 1983, c. 426; 1987, c. 520; 1993, c. 440, s. 4; 1995, c. 50, s. 1; 1997-335, s. 2; 2001-147, s. 1; 2010-132, s. 6; 2014-100, s. 34.28(c); 2018-5, s. 34.27(d)

N.C. Gen. Stat. § 20-79.3

Repealed by Session Laws 1993, c. 440, s. 5.

§ 20-79.3A. Requirements to establish a special registration plate

(a) **Minimum Number of Paid Applications.** -- An applicant under this section is a person, organization, or other legal entity seeking authorization to establish a special registration plate for a motor vehicle or a motorcycle. An applicant must obtain the minimum number of paid applications from potential purchasers before submitting a Special Registration Plate Development Application to the Division. A "paid application" means an application completed by a potential purchaser and submitted to the applicant requesting purchase of the special registration plate being proposed by the applicant plus payment of the proposed additional fee amount. The minimum number of paid applications is as follows:

(1) 300 for a special registration plate on a standard background described in G.S. 20-63(b).

(2) 500 for a special registration plate on a background authorized under G.S. 20-63(b1).

(b) **Application.** -- An applicant must submit all of the items listed in this subsection to the Division by February 15 in order for a bill authorizing the special registration plate to be considered for approval during the legislative session being held that year. The Division shall consider an application received after February 15 for approval in the legislative session that begins in the year following the submission date. The application items must include:

(1) A completed Special Registration Plate Development Application.

(2) A fee equal to number of paid applications received by the applicant, which shall be no less than the minimum number of paid applications required under subsection (a) of this section, multiplied by the proposed additional fee amount stated on the Special Registration Plate Development Application submitted by the applicant.

(c) **Report to General Assembly.** -- On or before March 15 of each year, the Division shall submit to the Chairs of the House and Senate Transportation Committees, the Chairs of the House and Senate Finance Committees, and the Legislative Analysis Division of the General Assembly a report that identifies each applicant that has applied for a special registration plate to be authorized in the legislative session being held that year and indicates whether the applicant met the requirements of this section. If an applicant meets the requirements of this section, then a bill may be considered during the legislative session being held that year to authorize a special registration plate for the applicant that submitted the application.

(d) **Legislative Approval.** -- If a special registration plate requested under this section is approved by law, the applicant must submit all of the following items to the Division no later than 60 days after the act approving the plate becomes law. If the applicant fails to timely submit the items required under this subsection, the authorization for the special registration plate shall expire in accordance with G.S. 20-79.8(a1). The items to be submitted are:

(1) The final artwork for the plate. The Division must review the artwork to ensure it complies with the standardized format established by G.S. 20-79.4(a3).

(2) A list of purchasers who submitted to the applicant a paid application for the special registration plate and any additional fees submitted by potential purchasers to the applicant after submission of the Special Registration Plate Development Application.

(e) **Legislative Disapproval.** -- If the special registration plate is not authorized in the legislative session in which the authorization was sought, the Division shall refund to the applicant the fee submitted under subdivision (2) of subsection (b) of this section.

(f) **Issuance.** -- Within 180 days after receipt of the requester's design and the minimum number of paid applications, the Division shall issue the special registration plate.

History.

2014-96, s. 3(a); 2018-142, s. 4(a)

§ 20-79.4. Special registration plates

(a) **General.** -- Upon application and payment of the required registration fees, a person may obtain from the Division a special registration plate for a motor vehicle registered in that person's name if the person qualifies for the registration plate. A holder of a special registration plate who becomes ineligible for the plate, for whatever reason, must return the special plate within 30 days. A special registration plate may not be issued for a vehicle registered under the International Registration Plan. A special registration plate may be issued for a commercial vehicle that is not registered under the International Registration Plan. A special registration plate may not be developed using a name or logo for which a trademark has been issued unless the holder of the trademark licenses, without charge, the State to use the name or logo on the special registration plate.

(a1) **Qualifying for a Special Plate.** -- In order to qualify for a special plate, an applicant shall meet all of the qualifications set out in this section. The Division of Motor Vehicles shall verify the qualifications of an individual to whom any special plate is issued to ensure only qualified applicants receive the requested special plates.

(a2) **Special Plates Based Upon Military Service.** -- The Department of Military and Veterans Affairs shall be responsible for verifying and maintaining all verification documentation for all special plates that are based upon military service. The Department shall not issue a special plate that is based on military service unless the application is accompanied by a motor vehicle registration (MVR) verification form signed by the Secretary of Military and Veterans Affairs, or the Secretary's designee, showing that the Department of Military and Veterans Affairs has verified the applicant's credentials and qualifications to hold the special plate applied for. The following shall apply to special plates issued under this subsection:

(1) Unless a qualifying condition exists requiring annual verification, no additional verification shall be required to renew a special registration plate either in person or through an online service.

(2) If the Department of Military and Veterans Affairs determines a special registration plate has been issued due to an error on the part of the Division of Motor Vehicles, the plate shall be recalled and canceled.

(3) If the Department of Military and Veterans Affairs determines a special registration plate has been issued to an applicant who falsified documents or has fraudulently applied for the special registration plate, the Division of Motor Vehicles shall revoke the special plate and take appropriate enforcement action.

(4) The surviving spouse of a person who had a special plate issued under the terms of this subsection may continue to renew the plate so long as the surviving spouse does not remarry. This is a qualifying condition requiring verification under subdivision (1) of this subsection.

(a3) The Division shall develop, in consultation with the State Highway Patrol and the Division of Adult Correction and Juvenile Justice, a standardized format for special license plates. The format shall allow for the name of the State and the license plate number to be reflective and to contrast with the background so it may be easily read by the human eye and by cameras installed along roadways as part of tolling and speed enforcement. A designated segment of the plate shall be set aside for unique design representing various groups and interests. Nothing in this subsection shall be construed to require the recall of existing special license plates.

(b) **Types.** -- The Division shall issue the following types of special registration plates:

(1) **82nd Airborne Division Association Member.** -- Issuable to a member of the 82nd Airborne Division Association, Inc. The plate shall bear the insignia of the 82nd Airborne Division Association, Inc. The Division may not issue the plate authorized by this subdivision unless it receives at least 300 applications for the plate.

(2) **Administrative Officer of the Courts.** -- Issuable to the Director of the Administrative Office of the Courts. The plate shall bear the phrase "J-20".

(3) **AIDS Awareness.** -- Expired July 1, 2016.

(4) **Air Medal Recipient.** -- Issuable to the recipient of the Air Medal. The plate shall bear the emblem of the Air Medal and the words "Air Medal".

(5) **Alpha Kappa Alpha Sorority.** -- Issuable to the registered owner of a motor vehicle. The plate shall bear the sorority's symbol and name. The Division may not issue the plate authorized by this subdivision unless it receives at least 300 applications for the plate.

(6) **Alpha Phi Alpha Fraternity.** -- Issuable to a member or supporter of the Alpha Phi Alpha Fraternity in accordance with G.S. 20-81.12. The plate shall bear the fraternity's symbol and name.

(7) **ALS Research.** -- Issuable to a registered owner of a motor vehicle in accordance with G.S. 20-81.12. The plate shall bear a picture of a baseball and the phrase "Cure ALS."

(8) **Alternative Fuel Vehicles.** -- Expired July 1, 2016.

(9) **Amateur Radio Operator.** -- Issuable to an amateur radio operator who holds an unexpired and unrevoked amateur radio license issued by the Federal Communications Commission and who asserts to the Division that a portable transceiver is carried in the vehicle. The plate shall bear the phrase "Amateur Radio". The plate shall bear the operator's official amateur radio call letters, or call letters with numerical or letter suffixes so that an owner of more than one vehicle may have the call letters on each.

(10) **American Legion.** -- Issuable to a member of the American Legion. The plate shall bear the words "American Legion"

and the emblem of the American Legion. The Division may not issue the plate authorized by this subdivision unless it receives at least 300 applications for the plate.

(11) **American Red Cross.** -- Expired July 1, 2016.

(12) **Animal Lovers.** -- Issuable to the registered owner of a motor vehicle in accordance with G.S. 20-81.12. The plate may bear a picture of a dog and cat and the phrase "I Care."

(13) **ARC of North Carolina.** -- Expired July 1, 2016.

(14) **Armed Forces Expeditionary Medal Recipient.** -- Expired July 1, 2016.

(15) **Arthritis Foundation.** -- Expired July 1, 2016.

(16) **ARTS NC.** -- Issuable to the registered owner of a motor vehicle in accordance with G.S. 20-81.12. The plate shall bear the phrase "The Creative State" with a logo designed by ARTS North Carolina, Inc.

(17) **Audubon North Carolina.** -- Expired July 1, 2016.

(18) **Autism Society of North Carolina.** -- Issuable to the registered owner of a motor vehicle in accordance with G.S. 20-81.12. The plate shall bear the phrase "Autism Society of North Carolina", and the logo of the Autism Society.

(19) **Aviation Maintenance Technician.** -- Expired July 1, 2016.

(20) **Back Country Horsemen of North Carolina.** -- Expired July 1, 2016.

(21) **Battle of Kings Mountain.** -- Issuable to the registered owner of a motor vehicle in accordance with G.S. 20-81.12. The plate shall bear the phrase "Battle of Kings Mountain" with a representation of Kings Mountain on it. The plate authorized by this subdivision is not subject to the provisions of G.S. 20-79.3A or G.S. 20-79.8.

(22) **Be Active NC.** -- Expired July 1, 2016.

(23) **Big Rock Blue Marlin Tournament.** -- Issuable to the registered owner of a motor vehicle in accordance with G.S. 20-81.12. The plate shall bear the words "Big Rock Blue Marlin Tournament" and include a representation of a blue marlin.

(24) **Blue Knights.** -- Expired July 1, 2016.

(25) **Boy Scouts of America.** -- Expired July 1, 2016.

(26) **Brain Injury Awareness.** -- Expired July 1, 2016.

(27) **Breast Cancer Awareness.** -- Issuable to the registered owner of a motor vehicle. The plate shall bear the phrase "Early Detection Saves Lives" and a representation of a pink ribbon. The Division

must receive 300 or more applications for the plate before it may be developed.

(28) **Breast Cancer Earlier Detection.** -- Expired July 1, 2016.

(29) **Brenner Children's Hospital.** -- Expired July 1, 2016.

(30) **Bronze Star Recipient.** -- Issuable to a recipient of the Bronze Star. The plate shall bear the emblem of the Bronze Star and the words "Bronze Star".

(31) **Bronze Star Valor Recipient.** -- Issuable to a recipient of the Bronze Star Medal for valor in combat. The plate shall bear the emblem of the Bronze Star with a "Combat V" emblem and the words "Bronze Star." To be eligible for this plate, the applicant must provide documentation that the medal was issued for valor in combat.

(32) **Buddy Pelletier Surfing Foundation.** -- Issuable to the registered owner of a motor vehicle in accordance with G.S. 20-81.12. The plate shall bear the words "Buddy Pelletier Surfing Foundation" and bear the logo of the Foundation.

(33) **Buffalo Soldiers.** -- Expired July 1, 2016.

(34) **Carolina Panthers.** -- Issuable to the registered owner of a motor vehicle in accordance with G.S. 20-81.12. The plate shall bear the phrase "Keep Pounding", the logo of the Carolina Panthers, and the letters "CP". The Division shall not develop a plate under this subdivision without a license to use copyrighted or registered words, symbols, trademarks, or designs associated with the plate. The Division shall not pay a royalty for the license to use the copyrighted or registered words, symbols, trademarks, or designs associated with the plate. The plate authorized by this subdivision is not subject to the provisions of G.S. 20-79.3A or G.S. 20-79.8.

(35) **Carolina Raptor Center.** -- Expired July 1, 2016.

(36) **Carolina Regional Volleyball Association.** -- Expired July 1, 2016.

(37) **Carolina's Aviation Museum.** -- Expired July 1, 2016.

(38) **Carolinas Credit Union Foundation.** -- Expired July 1, 2016.

(39) **Carolinas Golf Association.** -- Issuable to the registered owner of a motor vehicle in accordance with G.S. 20-81.12. The plate shall bear the phrase "Carolinas Golf Association" and an emblem of the Carolinas Golf Association.

(40) **Celebrate Adoption.** -- Expired July 1, 2016.

(41) **Charlotte Checkers.** -- Expired July 1, 2016.

(42) **Childhood Cancer Awareness.** -- Expired July 1, 2016.

Chapter 20

(43) **Choose Life.** -- Issuable to a registered owner of a motor vehicle in accordance with G.S. 20-81.12. The plate shall bear the phrase "Choose Life."

(44) **Civic Club.** -- Issuable to a member of a nationally recognized civic organization whose member clubs in the State are exempt from State corporate income tax under G.S. 105-130.11(a)(5). Examples of these clubs include Jaycees, Kiwanis, Optimist, Rotary, Ruritan, and Shrine. The plate shall bear a word or phrase identifying the civic club and the emblem of the civic club. A person may obtain from the Division a special registration plate under this subdivision for the registered owner of a motor vehicle or a motorcycle. The registration fees and the restrictions on the issuance of a specialized registration plate for a motorcycle are the same as for any motor vehicle. The Division may not issue a civic club plate authorized by this subdivision unless it receives at least 300 applications for that civic club plate.

(45) **Civil Air Patrol Member.** -- Issuable to an active member of the North Carolina Wing of the Civil Air Patrol. The plate shall bear the phrase "Civil Air Patrol". A plate issued to an officer member shall begin with the number "201" and the number shall reflect the seniority of the member; a plate issued to an enlisted member, a senior member, or a cadet member shall begin with the number "501".

(46) **Class D Citizen's Radio Station Operator.** -- Issuable to a Class D citizen's radio station operator. For an operator who has been issued Class D citizen's radio station call letters by the Federal Communications Commission, the plate shall bear the operator's official Class D citizen's radio station call letters. For an operator who has not been issued Class D citizen's radio station call letters by the Federal Communications Commission, the plate shall bear the phrase "Citizen's Band Radio".

(47) **Clerk of Superior Court.** -- Expired July 1, 2016.

(48) **Coast Guard Auxiliary Member.** -- Issuable to an active member of the United States Coast Guard Auxiliary. The plate shall bear the phrase "Coast Guard Auxiliary".

(49) **Coastal Conservation Association.** -- Expired July 1, 2016.

(50) **Coastal Land Trust.** -- Issuable to the registered owner of a motor vehicle in accordance with G.S. 20-81.12. The plate shall bear the phrase "Coastal Land Trust" with a logo designed by the North Carolina Coastal Land Trust.

(51) **Cold War Veteran.** -- Expired July 1, 2016.

(52) **Collegiate Insignia Plate.** -- Issuable to the registered owner of a motor vehicle in accordance with G.S. 20-81.12. The plate may bear a phrase or an insignia representing a public or private college or university.

(53) **Colorectal Cancer Awareness.** -- Issuable to the registered owner of a motor vehicle in accordance with G.S. 20-81.12. The plate shall bear (i) the phrase "It Takes a Warrior to Battle Cancer!" across the top of the plate, (ii) a symbol on the left side of the plate of a blue ribbon with two wings that are colored blue, grey, and black, (iii) the phrase "Blue Ribbon Warrior" above the symbol, (iv) the phrase "Colorectal Cancer Awareness" below the symbol, and (v) the letters "CC" on the right side of the plate. The plate authorized under this subdivision is not subject to G.S. 20-79.3A(c) or the deadline set forth in G.S. 20-79.3A(b).

(54) **Combat Infantry Badge Recipient.** -- Expired July 1, 2016.

(55) **Combat Veteran.** -- Expired July 1, 2016.

(56) **Commercial Fishing.** -- Expired July 1, 2016.

(57) **Concerned Bikers Association/ ABATE of North Carolina.** -- Expired July 1, 2016.

(58) **Corvette Club.** -- Expired July 1, 2016.

(59) **County Commissioner.** -- Issuable to a county commissioner of a county in this State. The plate shall bear the words "County Commissioner" followed first by a number representing the commissioner's county and then by a letter or number that distinguishes plates issued to county commissioners of the same county. The number of a county shall be the order of the county in an alphabetical list of counties that assigns number one to the first county in the list and a letter or number to distinguish different cars owned by the county commissioners in that county. The plate authorized by this subdivision is not subject to the provisions of G.S. 20-79.3A or G.S. 20-79.8.

(60) **Crystal Coast.** -- Expired July 1, 2016.

(61) **Daniel Stowe Botanical Garden.** -- Expired July 1, 2016.

(62) **Daughters of the American Revolution.** -- Expired July 1, 2016.

(63) **Delta Sigma Theta Sorority.** -- Issuable to the registered owner of a motor vehicle. The plate shall bear the sorority's name and symbol. The Division must receive 300 or more applications for the plate before it may be developed.

(64) **Disabled Veteran.** -- Issuable to a veteran of the Armed Forces of the United States who suffered a 100% service-connected disability. A person may obtain from the Division a special registration plate under this subdivision for the registered owner of a motor vehicle or a motorcycle.

(65) **Distinguished Flying Cross.** -- Issuable to a recipient of the Distinguished Flying Cross. The plate shall bear the emblem of the Distinguished Flying Cross and the words "Distinguished Flying Cross".

(66) **District Attorney.** -- Issuable to a North Carolina or United States District Attorney. The plate issuable to a North Carolina district attorney shall bear the letters "DA" followed by a number that represents the prosecutorial district the district attorney serves. The plate for a United States attorney shall bear the phrase "U.S. Attorney" followed by a number that represents the district the attorney serves, with 1 being the Eastern District, 2 being the Middle District, and 3 being the Western District.

(67) **Donate Life.** -- Issuable to the registered owner of a motor vehicle in accordance with G.S. 20-81.12. The plate shall bear the phrase "Donate Life" with a logo designed by Donate Life North Carolina.

(68) **Don't Tread on Me.** -- Expired July 1, 2016.

(69) **Ducks Unlimited.** -- Issuable to the registered owner of a motor vehicle in accordance with G.S. 20-81.12. The plate shall bear the logo of Ducks Unlimited, Inc., and shall bear the words: "Ducks Unlimited".

(70) **E-911 Telecommunicator.** -- Expired July 1, 2016.

(71) **Eagle Scout.** -- Issuable to a young man who has been certified as an Eagle Scout by the Boy Scouts of America, or to his parents or guardians. The plate shall bear the insignia of the Boy Scouts of America and shall bear the words "Eagle Scout". The Division may not issue the plate authorized by this subdivision unless it receives at least 300 applications for the plate.

(72) **Eastern Band of Cherokee Indians.** -- Issuable to a member of the Eastern Band of Cherokee Indians who presents to the Division a tribal identification card. The plate may bear a phrase or emblem representing the Eastern Band of Cherokee Indians. The plate authorized by this subdivision is not subject to the provisions of G.S. 20-79.3A.

(73) **El Pueblo.** -- Expired July 1, 2016.

(74) **Emergency Medical Technician.** -- Expired July 1, 2016.

(75) **Farmland Preservation.** -- Expired July 1, 2016.

(76) **Fire Department or Rescue Squad Member.** -- Issuable to an active regular member or volunteer member of a fire department, rescue squad, or both a fire department and rescue squad. The plate shall bear the words "Firefighter", "Rescue Squad", or "Firefighter-Rescue Squad".

(77) **First in Forestry.** -- Issuable to the registered owner of a motor vehicle. The plate shall bear the words "First in Forestry". The Division may not issue the plate authorized by this subdivision unless it receives at least 300 applications for the plate.

(78) **First in Turf.** -- Expired July 1, 2016.

(79) **First Tee.** -- Expired July 1, 2016.

(80) **Flag of the United States of America.** -- Expired July 1, 2016.

(81) **Fox Hunting.** -- Expired July 1, 2016.

(82) **Fraternal Order of Police.** -- The plate authorized by this subdivision shall bear a representation of the Fraternal Order of Police emblem containing the letters "FOP". The Division must receive 300 applications for the plate before it may be developed. The plate is issuable to one of the following:

a. A person who presents proof of active membership in the State Lodge, Fraternal Order of Police for the year in which the license plate is sought.

b. The surviving spouse of a person who was a member of the State Lodge, Fraternal Order of Police, so long as the surviving spouse continues to renew the plate and does not remarry.

(83) **Future Farmers of America.** -- Expired July 1, 2016.

(84) **Girl Scout Gold Award recipient.** -- Expired July 1, 2016.

(85) **Girl Scouts.** -- Expired July 1, 2016.

(86) **Gold Star Lapel Button.** -- Issuable to the recipient of the Gold Star lapel button. The plate shall bear the emblem of the Gold Star lapel button and the words "Gold Star".

(87) **Goodness Grows.** -- Expired July 1, 2016.

(88) **Greensboro Symphony Guild.** -- Expired July 1, 2016.

(89) **Greyhound Friends of North Carolina.** -- Expired July 1, 2016.

(90) **Guilford Battleground Company.** -- Issuable to the registered owner of a motor vehicle in accordance with G.S. 20-81.12. The plate shall bear the phrase "Revolutionary" used by the Guilford Battleground Company and an image that depicts General Nathaniel Greene.

(91) **Harley Owners' Group.** -- Issuable to the registered owner of a motor vehicle

in accordance with G.S. 20-81.12. The plate shall be designed in consultation with and approved by the Harley-Davidson Motor Company, Inc., and shall bear the words and trademark of the "Harley Owners' Group".

(92) **High Point Furniture Market 100th Anniversary.** -- Expired July 1, 2016.

(93) **High School Insignia Plate.** -- Issuable to the registered owner of a motor vehicle in accordance with G.S. 20-81.12. The plate may bear a phrase or an insignia representing a public high school in North Carolina.

(94) **Historic Vehicle Owner.** -- Issuable for a motor vehicle that is at least 30 years old measured from the date of manufacture. The plate for an historic vehicle shall bear the word "Antique" unless the vehicle is a model year 1943 or older. The plate for a vehicle that is a model year 1943 or older shall bear the word "Antique" or the words "Horseless Carriage", at the option of the vehicle owner.

(95) **Historical Attraction Plate.** -- Issuable to the registered owner of a motor vehicle in accordance with G.S. 20-81.12. The plate may bear a phrase or an insignia representing a publicly owned or nonprofit historical attraction located in North Carolina.

(96) **Hollerin'.** -- Expired July 1, 2016.

(97) **Home Care and Hospice.** -- Issuable to the registered owner of a motor vehicle in accordance with G.S. 20-81.12. The plate shall bear the phrase "Home Care and Hospice" and the letters "HH" on the right side of the plate.

(98) **Home of American Golf.** -- Expired July 1, 2016.

(99) **HOMES4NC Plate.** -- Issuable to the registered owner of a motor vehicle in accordance with G.S. 20-81.12. The plate shall bear "HOMES4NC", the logo of the North Carolina Association of Realtors Housing Opportunity Foundation, and shall be developed in conjunction with that organization. The Division may not issue the plate authorized by this subdivision unless it receives at least 300 applications for the plate.

(100) **Honorary Plate.** -- Issuable to a member of the Honorary Consular Corps, who has been certified by the U. S. State Department, the plate shall bear the words "Honorary Consular Corps" and a distinguishing number based on the order of issuance.

(101) **Hospice Care.** -- Expired July 1, 2016.

(102) **I.B.P.O.E.W.** -- Expired July 1, 2016.

(103) **I Support Teachers.** -- Expired July 1, 2016.

(104) **In God We Trust.** -- Issuable to the registered owner of a motor vehicle in accordance with G.S. 20-81.12. The plate shall bear the phrase "In God We Trust."

(105) **International Association of Fire Fighters.** -- The plate authorized by this subdivision shall bear the logo of the International Association of Fire Fighters. The Division may not issue the plate unless it receives at least 300 applications for the plate. The plate is issuable to one of the following in accordance with G.S. 20-81.12:

    a. A person who presents proof of active membership in the International Association of Fire Fighters for the year in which the license plate is sought.

    b. The surviving spouse of a person who was a member of the International Association of Fire Fighters, so long as the surviving spouse continues to renew the plate and does not remarry.

(106) **Jaycees.** -- Expired July 1, 2016.

(107) **Judge or Justice.** -- Issuable to a sitting or retired judge or justice in accordance with G.S. 20-79.6.

(108) **Juvenile Diabetes Research Foundation.** -- Issuable to the registered owner of a motor vehicle in accordance with G.S. 20-81.12. The plate shall bear the phrase "Juvenile Diabetes Research" and the "sneaker" logo of the nonprofit group Juvenile Diabetes Research Foundation International, Inc.

(109) **Kappa Alpha Order.** -- Expired July 1, 2016.

(110) **Kappa Alpha Psi Fraternity.** -- Issuable to the registered owner of a motor vehicle who is a member of the Kappa Alpha Psi Fraternity. The plate shall bear the fraternity's symbol and name. The Division may not issue the plate authorized by this subdivision unless it receives at least 300 applications for the plate.

(111) **Keeping The Lights On.** -- Issuable to a registered owner of a motor vehicle in accordance with G.S. 20-81.12. The plate shall have a background of mountains to the coast and bear a picture of a line worker on a utility pole on the left and the phrase "Keeping The Lights On" at the top of the registration plate.

(112) **Kick Cancer for Kids.** -- Issuable to the registered owner of a motor vehicle in accordance with G.S. 20-81.12. The plate shall bear the words "Kick Cancer for Kids" and a representation of a gold ribbon with children's handprints surrounding the ribbon.

Chapter 20

(113) **Kids First.** -- Issuable to the registered owner of a motor vehicle in accordance with G.S. 20-81.12. The plate may bear the phrase "Kids First" and a logo of children's hands.

(114) **Legion of Merit.** -- Issuable to a recipient of the Legion of Merit award. The plate shall bear the emblem and name of the Legion of Merit decoration.

(115) **Legion of Valor.** -- Issuable to a recipient of one of the following military decorations: the Congressional Medal of Honor, the Distinguished Service Cross, the Navy Cross, the Air Force Cross, or the Coast Guard Cross. The plate shall bear the emblem and name of the recipient's decoration.

(116) **Legislator.** -- Issuable to a member of the North Carolina General Assembly. The plate shall bear "The Great Seal of the State of North Carolina" and, as appropriate, the word "Senate" or "House" followed by the Senator's or Representative's assigned seat number.

(117) **Leukemia & Lymphoma Society.** -- Expired July 1, 2016.

(118) **Lifetime Sportsman.** -- Expired July 1, 2016.

(119) **Litter Prevention.** -- Issuable to the registered owner of a motor vehicle in accordance with G.S. 20-81.12. The plate may bear a phrase and picture appropriate to the subject of litter prevention in North Carolina.

(120) **Lung Cancer Research.** -- Expired July 1, 2016.

(121) **Maggie Valley Trout Festival.** -- Expired July 1, 2016.

(122) **Magistrate.** -- Issuable to a current or retired North Carolina magistrate. A plate issued to a current magistrate shall bear the letters "MJ" followed by a number indicating the district court district the magistrate serves, then by a hyphen, and then by a number indicating the seniority of the magistrate. The Division shall use the number "9" to designate District Court Districts 9 and 9B. A plate issued to a retired magistrate shall bear the phrase "Magistrate, Retired", the letters "MJX" followed by a hyphen and the number that indicates the district court district the magistrate served, followed by a letter based on the order of issuance of the plates.

(123) **March of Dimes.** -- Expired July 1, 2016.

(124) **Marine Corps League.** -- Issuable to a member of the Marine Corps League. The plate shall bear the words "Marine Corps League" or the letters "MCL" and the emblem of the Marine Corps League. The Division may not issue the plate authorized by this subdivision unless it receives at least 150 applications for the plate.

(125) **Marshal.** -- Issuable to a United States Marshal. The plate shall bear the phrase "U.S. Marshal" followed by a number that represents the district the Marshal serves, with 1 being the Eastern District, 2 being the Middle District, and 3 being the Western District.

(126) **Mayor.** -- Expired July 1, 2016.

(127) **Military Reservist.** -- Issuable to a member of a reserve component of the Armed Forces of the United States. The plate shall bear the name and insignia of the appropriate reserve component. Plates shall be numbered sequentially for members of a component with the numbers 1 through 5000 reserved for officers, without regard to rank.

(128) **Military Retiree.** -- Issuable to an individual who has retired from the Armed Forces of the United States. The plate shall bear the word "Retired" and the name and insignia of the branch of service from which the individual retired.

(129) **Military Veteran.** -- Issuable to an individual who served honorably in the Armed Forces of the United States. The plate shall bear the words "U.S. Military Veteran" and the name and insignia of the branch of service in which the individual served. The plate authorized by this subdivision is not subject to the provisions of G.S. 20-79.3A or G.S. 20-79.8.

(130) **Military Wartime Veteran.** -- Issuable to either a member or veteran of the Armed Forces of the United States who served during a period of war who received a campaign or expeditionary ribbon or medal for their service. If the person is a veteran of the Armed Forces of the United States, then the veteran must be separated from the Armed Forces of the United States under honorable conditions. The plate shall bear a word or phrase identifying the period of war and a replica of the campaign badge or medal awarded for that war. The Division may not issue the plate authorized by this subdivision unless it receives a total of 300 applications for all periods of war, combined, to be represented on this plate. A "period of war" is any of the following:

a. World War I, meaning the period beginning April 16, 1917, and ending November 11, 1918.

b. World War II, meaning the period beginning December 7, 1941, and ending December 31, 1946.

c. The Korean Conflict, meaning the period beginning June 27, 1950, and ending January 31, 1955.

Chapter 20

d. The Vietnam Era, meaning the period beginning August 5, 1964, and ending May 7, 1975.

e. Desert Storm, meaning the period beginning August 2, 1990, and ending April 11, 1991.

f. Operation Enduring Freedom, meaning the period beginning October 24, 2001, and ending at a date to be determined.

g. Operation Iraqi Freedom, meaning the period beginning March 19, 2003, and ending at a date to be determined.

h. Any other campaign, expedition, or engagement for which the United States Department of Defense authorizes a campaign badge or medal.

(131) **Mission Foundation.** -- Expired July 1, 2016.

(132) **Morehead Planetarium.** -- Expired July 1, 2016.

(133) **Morgan Horse Club.** -- Expired July 1, 2016.

(134) **Mothers Against Drunk Driving.** -- Expired July 1, 2016.

(135) **Mountains-to-Sea Trail.** -- Issuable to the registered owner of a motor vehicle in accordance with G.S. 20-81.12. The plate shall bear the phrase "Mountains-to-Sea Trail" with a background designed by the Friends of the Mountains-to-Sea Trail, Inc.

(136) **Municipal Council.** -- Expired July 1, 2016.

(137) **Municipality Plate.** -- Expired July 1, 2016.

(138) **National Defense Service Medal.** -- Expired July 1, 2016.

(139) **National Guard Member.** -- Issuable to an active or a retired member of the North Carolina National Guard. The plate shall bear the phrase "National Guard". A plate issued to an active member shall bear a number that reflects the seniority of the member; a plate issued to a commissioned officer shall begin with the number "1"; a plate issued to a noncommissioned officer with a rank of E7, E8, or E9 shall begin with the number "1601"; a plate issued to an enlisted member with a rank of E6 or below shall begin with the number "3001". The plate issued to a retired or separated member shall indicate the member's retired status.

(140) **National Kidney Foundation.** -- Expired July 1, 2016.

(141) **National Law Enforcement Officers Memorial.** -- Expired July 1, 2016.

(142) **National Multiple Sclerosis Society.** -- Issuable to the registered owner of a motor vehicle in accordance with G.S. 20-81.12. The plate shall have the logo of the National Multiple Sclerosis Society and the telephone number "1-800-FIGHT MS" on the plate.

(143) **National Rifle Association.** -- Issuable to the registered owner of a motor vehicle. The plate shall bear a phrase or insignia representing the National Rifle Association of America. The Division must receive 300 or more applications for the plate before it may be developed.

(144) **National Wild Turkey Federation.** -- Issuable to the registered owner of a motor vehicle. The plate shall bear the design of a strutting wild turkey and dogwood blossoms and the words "Working For The Wild Turkey." The Division must receive 300 or more applications for the plate before it may be developed.

(145) **Native American.** -- Issuable to the registered owner of a motor vehicle in accordance with G.S. 20-81.12. The plate may bear a phrase or an insignia representing Native Americans. The Division must receive 300 or more applications for the plate before it may be developed.

(146) **Native Brook Trout.** -- Issuable to the registered owner of a motor vehicle in accordance with G.S. 20-81.12. The plate shall bear the phrase "Native Brook Trout" with a picture of a brook trout native to North Carolina in the background.

(147) **NC Agribusiness.** -- Expired July 1, 2016.

(148) **NCAMC/NCACC Clerk.** -- Expired July 1, 2016.

(149) **NC Beekeepers.** -- Expired July 1, 2016.

(150) **NC Children's Promise.** -- Expired July 1, 2016.

(151) **NC Civil War.** -- Expired July 1, 2016.

(152) **NC Coastal Federation.** -- Issuable to the registered owner of a motor vehicle in accordance with G.S. 20-81.12. The plate shall bear a phrase used by the North Carolina Coastal Federation and an image that depicts the coastal area of the State.

(153) **NC FIRST Robotics.** -- Expired July 1, 2016.

(154) **NC Fisheries Association.** -- Expired July 1, 2016.

(155) **NC Horse Council.** -- Issuable to the registered owner of a motor vehicle in accordance with G.S. 20-81.12. The plate shall bear the phrase "NC Horse Council" and a logo designed by the North Carolina Horse Council, Inc.

(156) **NC Mining.** -- Expired July 1, 2016.

(157) **NCSC.** -- Expired July 1, 2016.

(158) **NC Surveyors.** -- Issuable to the registered owner of a motor vehicle in

accordance with G.S. 20-81.12. The plate shall bear the phrase "Following In Their Footsteps", a picture representing a surveyor, and the letters "PS" on the right side of the plate.

(159) **NC Tennis Foundation.** -- Issuable to the registered owner of a motor vehicle in accordance with G.S. 20-81.12. The plate shall bear the phrase "Play Tennis" and the image of an implement of the tennis sport.

(160) **NC Trout Unlimited.** -- Issuable to the registered owner of a motor vehicle in accordance with G.S. 20-81.12. The plate shall bear the phrase "Back the Brookie" and an image that depicts a North Carolina brook trout.

(161) **NC Veterinary Medical Association.** -- Expired July 1, 2016.

(162) **NC Victim Assistance Network.** -- Expired July 1, 2016.

(163) **NC Wildlife Federation.** -- Expired July 1, 2016.

(164) **NC Youth Soccer Association.** -- Expired July 1, 2016.

(165) **North Carolina 4-H Development Fund.** -- Expired July 1, 2016.

(166) **North Carolina Bluegrass Association.** -- Expired July 1, 2016.

(167) **North Carolina Cattlemen's Association.** -- Expired July 1, 2016.

(168) **North Carolina Emergency Management Association.** -- Expired July 1, 2016.

(169) **North Carolina Green Industry Council.** -- Expired July 1, 2016.

(170) **North Carolina Libraries.** -- Expired July 1, 2016.

(171) **North Carolina Master Gardener.** -- Issuable to the registered owner of a motor vehicle in accordance with G.S. 20-81.12. The plate shall bear the letters "MG" with a logo representing the North Carolina Master Gardeners.

(172) **North Carolina Paddle Festival.** -- Expired July 1, 2016.

(173) **North Carolina Sheriffs' Association.** -- Issuable to the registered owner of a motor vehicle in accordance with G.S. 20-81.12. The plate may bear a phrase and logo selected by the North Carolina Sheriffs' Association, Inc.

(174) **North Carolina State Flag.** -- Expired July 1, 2016.

(175) **North Carolina Wildlife Habitat Foundation.** -- Issuable to the owner of a motor vehicle in accordance with G.S. 20-81.12. The plate shall bear the logo of the North Carolina Wildlife Habitat Foundation on the left side. The numbers or other writing on the plate shall be black and the border shall be black. The plate shall be developed by the Division in consultation with and approved by the North Carolina Wildlife Habitat Foundation. The Division may not issue the plate authorized by this subdivision unless it receives at least 300 applications for the plate.

(176) **Nurses.** -- Issuable to the registered owner of a motor vehicle in accordance with G.S. 20-81.12. The plate shall bear the phrase "First in Nursing" and a representation relating to nursing.

(177) **Olympic Games.** -- Issuable to the registered owner of a motor vehicle in accordance with G.S. 20-81.12. The plate may bear a phrase or insignia representing the Olympic Games.

(178) **Omega Psi Phi Fraternity.** -- Issuable to the registered owner of a motor vehicle in accordance with G.S. 20-81.12. The plate shall bear the fraternity's symbol and name.

(179) **Operation Coming Home.** -- Expired July 1, 2016.

(180) **Order of the Eastern Star Prince Hall Affiliated.** -- Issuable to an active member of the Order of the Eastern Star Prince Hall Affiliated in accordance with G.S. 20-81.12. The plate shall bear the Order of the Eastern Star Prince Hall Affiliated logo.

(181) **Order of the Long Leaf Pine.** -- Issuable to a person who has received the award of membership in the Order of the Long Leaf Pine from the Governor. The plate shall bear the phrase "Order of the Long Leaf Pine."

(182) **Outer Banks Preservation Association.** -- Expired July 1, 2016.

(183) **Pamlico-Tar River Foundation.** -- Expired July 1, 2016.

(184) **Pancreatic Cancer Awareness.** -- Expired July 1, 2016.

(185) **Paramedics.** -- Expired July 1, 2016.

(186) **Partially Disabled Veteran.** -- Issuable to a veteran of the Armed Forces of the United States who suffered a service connected disability of less than 100%. A person may obtain from the Division a special registration plate under this subdivision for the registered owner of a motor vehicle or a motorcycle.

(187) **Pearl Harbor Survivor.** -- Issuable to a veteran of the Armed Forces of the United States who was present at and survived the attack on Pearl Harbor on December 7, 1941. The plate will bear the phrase "Pearl Harbor Survivor" and the insignia of the Pearl Harbor Survivors' Association.

(188) **P.E.O. Sisterhood.** -- Expired July 1, 2016.

(189) **Personalized.** -- Issuable to the registered owner of a motor vehicle. The plate will bear the letters or letters and numbers requested by the owner. The Division may refuse to issue a plate with a letter combination that is offensive to good taste and decency. The Division may not issue a plate that duplicates another plate.

(190) **Piedmont Airlines.** -- This plate is issuable to the registered owner of a motor vehicle in accordance with G.S. 20-81.12. The plate authorized by this subdivision shall bear the phrase "PA" and the Piedmont Speed Bird logo.

(191) **Pisgah Conservancy.** -- Issuable to the registered owner of a motor vehicle in accordance with G.S. 20-81.12. The plate shall bear (i) the phrase "The Pisgah Conservancy", (ii) a representation of Looking Glass Rock and rhododendron flowers, and (iii) a background of a blue sky.

(192) **POW/MIA.** -- Expired July 1, 2016.

(193) **POW/MIA Bring Them Home.** -- The plate shall have the phrase "POW/MIA Bring Them Home" with artwork submitted by Rolling Thunder, Inc., Chapter #1 North Carolina and reviewed by the Division to ensure compliance with G.S. 20-79.4(a3). A person may obtain from the Division a special registration plate under this subdivision for the registered owner of a motor vehicle or a motorcycle. The division may not issue a plate authorized under this subdivision until it receives at least 350 applications for the plate. Applications for motor vehicle special registration plates and motorcycle special registration plates received by the Division each count towards the minimum number of applications necessary to issue a plate under this subdivision.

(194) **Prince Hall Mason.** -- This plate is issuable to the registered owner of a motor vehicle in accordance with G.S. 20-81.12. The plate shall bear the phrase "Prince Hall Mason" and a picture of the Masonic symbol.

(195) **Prisoner of War.** -- Issuable to a member or veteran member of the Armed Forces of the United States who has been captured and held prisoner by forces hostile to the United States while serving in the Armed Forces of the United States.

(196) **Professional Engineer.** -- Expired July 1, 2016.

(197) **Professional Sports Fan.** -- Issuable to the registered owner of a motor vehicle. The plate shall bear the logo of a professional sports team located in North Carolina. The Division shall receive 300 or more applications for a professional sports fan plate before a plate may be issued.

(198) **Prostate Cancer Awareness.** -- Expired July 1, 2016.

(199) **Purple Heart Recipient.** -- Issuable to a recipient of the Purple Heart award. The plate shall bear the phrase "Purple Heart Veteran, Combat Wounded." A person may obtain from the Division a special registration plate under this subdivision for the registered owner of a motor vehicle or a motorcycle. A motorcycle plate issued under this subdivision shall bear a depiction of the Purple Heart Medal and the phrase "Purple Heart Veteran, Combat Wounded."

(200) **Red Drum.** -- Expired July 1, 2016.

(201) **Red Hat Society.** -- Expired July 1, 2016.

(202) **Register of Deeds.** -- Issuable to a register of deeds of a county of this State. The plate shall bear the words "Register of Deeds" and the letter "R" followed by a number representing the county of the register of deeds. The number of a county shall be the order of the county in an alphabetical list of counties that assigns number one to the first county in the list. A plate issued to a retired register of deeds shall bear the phrase "Register of Deeds, Retired," followed by a number that indicates the county where the register of deeds served and a designation indicating the retired status of the register of deeds. For purposes of this subdivision, a "retired register of deeds" is a person (i) with at least 10 years of service as a register of deeds of a county of this State and (ii) who no longer holds that office for any reason other than removal under G.S. 161-27.

(203) **Relay for Life.** -- Expired July 1, 2016.

(204) **Retired Law Enforcement Officers.** -- The plate authorized by this subdivision shall bear the phrase "Retired Law Enforcement Officer" and a representation of a law enforcement badge. The Division must receive 300 or more applications for the plate before it may be developed. The plate is issuable to one of the following:

    a. A retired law enforcement officer presenting to the Division, along with the application for the plate, a copy of the officer's retired identification card or letter of retirement.

    b. The surviving spouse of a person who had a retired law enforcement officer plate at the time of death so long as the surviving spouse continues to renew the plate and does not remarry.

(205) **Retired Legislator.** -- Issuable to a retired member of the North Carolina General Assembly in accordance with G.S. 20-81.12. A person who has served in the

Chapter 20

North Carolina General Assembly is a retired member for purposes of this subdivision. The plate shall bear "The Great Seal of the State of North Carolina" and, as appropriate, the phrase "Retired Senate Member" or "Retired House Member" followed by a number representing the retired member's district with the letters "RM". If more than one retired member is from the same district, then the number shall be followed by a letter from A through Z. The plates shall be issued in the order applications are received.

(206) **Retired State Highway Patrol.** -- The plate authorized by this subdivision shall bear the phrase "SHP, Retired." The Division may not issue the plate authorized by this subdivision unless it receives at least 300 applications for the plate. The plate is issuable to one of the following:

a. An individual who has retired from the North Carolina State Highway Patrol, presenting to the Division, along with the application for the plate, a copy of the retiree's retired identification card or letter of retirement.

b. The surviving spouse of a person who had retired from the State Highway Patrol who, along with the application for the plate, presents a copy of the deceased retiree's identification card or letter of retirement and certifies in writing that the retiree is deceased and that the applicant is not remarried.

(207) **RiverLink.** -- Expired July 1, 2016.

(208) **Rocky Mountain Elk Foundation.** -- Issuable to the registered owner of a motor vehicle in accordance with G.S. 20-81.12. The plate shall bear the phrase "Rocky Mountain Elk Foundation" and a logo approved by the Rocky Mountain Elk Foundation, Inc.

(209) **Ronald McDonald House.** -- Issuable to the registered owner of a motor vehicle in accordance with G.S. 20-81.12. The plate shall bear the phrase "House and Hands" with the words "Ronald McDonald House Charities" below the emblem and the letters "RH".

(210) **Save the Honey Bee (HB).** -- Issuable to the registered owner of a motor vehicle in accordance with G.S. 20-81.12. The plate shall bear the phrase "Save the Honey Bee", a picture representing a honey bee, and the letters "HB" on the right side of the plate.

(211) **Save the Honey Bee (SB).** -- Issuable to the registered owner of a motor vehicle in accordance with G.S. 20-81.12. The plate shall bear the phrase "Save the Honey Bee", a picture representing a honey bee on a blue flower inside of a hexagon, a honeycomb background, and the letters "SB" on the right side of the plate.

(212) **Save the Sea Turtles.** -- Issuable to the registered owner of a motor vehicle in accordance with G.S. 20-81.12. The plate may bear the phrase "Save the Sea Turtles" and a representation related to sea turtles.

(213) **Scenic Rivers.** -- Expired July 1, 2016.

(214) **School Board.** -- Expired July 1, 2016.

(215) **School Technology.** -- Expired July 1, 2016.

(216) **SCUBA.** -- Issuable to the registered owner of a motor vehicle in accordance with G.S. 20-81.12. The plate shall bear the phrase "SCUBA" and a logo of the Diver Down Flag.

(217) **Shag Dancing.** -- Issuable to the registered owner of a motor vehicle in accordance with G.S. 20-81.12. The plate may bear the phrase "I'd Rather Be Shaggin'" and a picture representing shag dancing.

(218) **Share the Road.** -- Issuable to the registered owner of a motor vehicle in accordance with G.S. 20-81.12. The plate shall bear a representation of a bicycle and the phrase "Share the Road".

(219) **Sheriff.** -- Issuable to a current sheriff or to a retired sheriff who served as sheriff for at least 10 years before retiring. A plate issued to a current sheriff shall bear the word "Sheriff" and the letter "S" followed by a number that indicates the county the sheriff serves. A plate issued to a retired sheriff shall bear the phrase "Sheriff, Retired", the letter "S" followed by a number that indicates the county the sheriff served, and the letter "X" indicating the sheriff's retired status.

(220) **Sigma Gamma Rho Sorority.** -- Expired July 1, 2016.

(221) **Silver Star Recipient.** -- Issuable to a recipient of the Silver Star. The plate shall bear the emblem of the Silver Star and the words "Silver Star".

(222) **Silver Star Recipient/Disabled Veteran.** -- Issuable to a recipient of the Silver Star who is also a veteran of the Armed Forces of the United States who suffered a one hundred percent (100%) service-connected disability. The plate shall bear the emblem of the Silver Star laid over the universal symbol for the handicapped and the words "Silver Star." For the purposes of a fee for this plate, it shall be treated as a one hundred percent (100%) Disabled Veteran plate.

(223) **Sneads Ferry Shrimp Festival.** -- Expired July 1, 2016.

Chapter 20

(224) **Soil and Water Conservation.** -- Expired July 1, 2016.

(225) **Special Forces Association.** -- Expired July 1, 2016.

(226) **Special Olympics.** -- Expired July 1, 2016.

(227) **Sport Fishing.** -- Expired July 1, 2016.

(228) **Square Dance Clubs.** -- Issuable to a member of a recognized square dance organization exempt from corporate income tax under G.S. 105-130.11(a)(5). The plate shall bear a word or phrase identifying the club and the emblem of the club. The Division shall not issue a dance club plate authorized by this subdivision unless it receives at least 300 applications for that dance club plate.

(229) S.T.A.R. -- Expired July 1, 2016.

(230) **State Attraction.** -- Issuable to the registered owner of a motor vehicle in accordance with G.S. 20-81.12. The plate may bear a phrase or an insignia representing a publicly owned or nonprofit State or federal attraction located in North Carolina.

(231) **State Government Official.** -- Issuable to elected and appointed members of State government in accordance with G.S. 20-79.5.

(232) **Stock Car Racing Theme.** -- Issuable to the registered owner of a motor vehicle pursuant to G.S. 20-81.12. This is a series of plates bearing an emblem, seal, other symbol or design displaying themes of professional stock car auto racing, or professional stock car auto racing drivers. The Division shall not develop any plate in the series without a license to use copyrighted or registered words, symbols, trademarks, or designs associated with the plate. The plate shall be designed in consultation with and approved by the person authorized to provide the State with the license to use the words, symbols, trademarks, or designs associated with the plate. The Division shall not pay a royalty for the license to use the copyrighted or registered words, symbols, trademarks, or designs associated with the plate.

(233) **Street Rod Owner.** -- Expired July 1, 2016.

(234) **Support NC Education.** -- Expired July 1, 2016.

(235) **Support Our Troops.** -- Issuable to the registered owner of a motor vehicle in accordance with G.S. 20-81.12. The plate shall bear a picture of a soldier and a child and shall bear the words: "Support Our Troops".

(236) **Support Soccer.** -- Issuable to the registered owner of a motor vehicle in accordance with G.S. 20-81.12. The plate shall bear the phrase "Support Soccer" and a logo designed by the North Carolina Soccer Hall of Fame, Inc.

(237) **Surveyor Plate.** -- Issuable to the registered owner of a motor vehicle in accordance with G.S. 20-81.12. The plate shall bear the words "Following In Their Footsteps" and shall bear a picture of a transit.

(238) **Sustainable Fisheries.** -- Expired July 1, 2016.

(239) **Sweet Potato.** -- Expired July 1, 2016.

(240) **Tarheel Classic Thunderbird Club.** -- Expired July 1, 2016.

(241) **Toastmasters Club.** -- Expired July 1, 2016.

(242) **Tobacco Heritage.** -- Issuable to the registered owner of a motor vehicle. The plate shall bear a picture of a tobacco leaf and plow. The Division may not issue the plate authorized by this subdivision unless it receives at least 300 applications for the plate.

(243) **Topsail Island Shoreline Protection.** -- Expired July 1, 2016.

(244) **Town of Oak Island.** -- Expired July 1, 2016.

(245) **Transportation Personnel.** -- Issuable to various members of the Divisions of the Department of Transportation. The plate shall bear the letters "DOT" followed by a number from 1 to 85, as designated by the Governor.

(246) **Travel and Tourism.** -- Expired July 1, 2016.

(247) **Turtle Rescue Team.** -- Expired July 1, 2016.

(248) **United States Service Academy.** -- Issuable to a graduate of one of the service academies, upon furnishing to the Division proof of graduation. The plate shall bear the name of the specific service academy with an emblem that designates the specific service academy being represented. The Division, with the cooperation of each service academy, shall develop a special plate for each of the service academies. The Division must receive a combined total of 600 or more applications for all the plates authorized by this subdivision before a specific service academy plate may be developed. The plates authorized by this subdivision are not subject to the provisions of G.S. 20-79.3A or G.S. 20-79.8.

(249) **University Health Systems of Eastern Carolina.** -- Expired July 1, 2016.

(250) **US Equine Rescue League.** -- Expired July 1, 2016.

(251) U.S. Navy Submarine Veteran. -- Issuable to a veteran of the United States Navy Submarine Service. The plate shall bear the phrase "United States Navy Submarine Veteran" and shall bear a

representation of the Submarine Service Qualification insignia overlaid upon a representation of the State of North Carolina. The Division may not issue the plate authorized by this subdivision unless it receives at least 150 applications for the plate.

(252) U.S. Representative. -- Issuable to a United States Representative for North Carolina. The plate shall bear the phrase "U.S. House" and shall be issued on the basis of Congressional district numbers.

(253) U.S. Senator. -- Issuable to a United States Senator for North Carolina. The plates shall bear the phrase "U.S. Senate" and shall be issued on the basis of seniority represented by the numbers 1 and 2.

(254) **USA Triathlon.** -- Expired July 1, 2016.

(255) **USO of NC.** -- Expired July 1, 2016.

(256) **The V Foundation for Cancer Research.** -- Issuable to the registered owner of a motor vehicle in accordance with G.S. 20-81.12. The plate shall bear a phrase and insignia representing The V Foundation for Cancer Research.

(257) **Veterans of Foreign Wars.** -- Issuable to a member or a supporter of the Veterans of Foreign Wars. The plate shall bear the words "Veterans of Foreign Wars" or "VFW" and the emblem of the VFW. The Division may not issue the plate authorized by this subdivision unless it receives at least 300 applications for the plate.

(258) **Victory Junction Gang Camp.** -- Expired July 1, 2016.

(259) **Vietnam Veterans of America.** -- Expired July 1, 2016.

(260) **Volunteers in Law Enforcement.** -- Expired July 1, 2016.

(261) **Watermelon.** -- Issuable to the registered owner of a motor vehicle. The plate shall bear a picture representing a slice of watermelon. The Division may not issue the plate authorized by this subdivision unless it receives at least 300 applications for the plate.

(262) **Wildlife Resources.** -- Issuable to the registered owner of a motor vehicle in accordance with G.S. 20-81.12. The plate shall bear a picture representing a native wildlife species occurring in North Carolina.

(263) **Wrightsville Beach.** -- Issuable to a registered owner of a motor vehicle in accordance with G.S. 20-81.12. The plate shall bear the Town of Wrightsville Beach logo followed by the four assigned or personalized characters ending with the suffix WB.

(264) **YMCA.** -- Expired July 1, 2016.

(265) **Zeta Phi Beta Sorority.** -- Issuable to the registered owner of a motor vehicle in accordance with G.S. 20-81.12. The plate shall bear the sorority's name and symbol.

(c) Repealed by Session Laws 1991 (Regular Session, 1992), c. 1042, s. 1.

History.
1991, c. 672, s. 2; c. 726, s. 23; 1991 (Reg. Sess., 1992), c. 1042, s. 1; 1993, c. 543, s. 2; 1995, c. 326, ss. 1 -3; c. 433, ss. 1, 4.1; 1997-156, s. 1; 1997-158, s. 1; 1997-339, s. 1; 1997-427, s. 1; 1997-461, ss. 2 -4; 1997-477, s. 1; 1997-484, ss. 1 -3; 1998-155, s. 1; 1998-160, ss. 1, 2; 1998-163, ss. 3 -5; 1999-220, s. 3.1; 1999-277, s. 1; 1999-314, s. 1; 1999-403, s. 1; 1999-450, s. 1; 1999-452, s. 16; 2000-159, ss. 1, 2; 2001-40, s. 1; 2001-483, s. 1; 2001-498, ss. 1(a), 1(b), 2; 2002-134, ss. 1 -4; 2002-159, s. 68; 2003-10, s. 1; 2003-11, s. 1; 2003-68, s. 1; 2003-424, s. 2; 2004-131, s. 2; 2004-182, s. 1; 2004-185, s. 2; 2004-200, s. 1; 2005-216, ss. 2, 3; 2006-209, ss. 2, 7; 2007-400, s. 2; 2007-470, s. 1; 2007-483, ss. 2, 8(d); 2007-522, s. 1; 2009-121, s. 1; 2009-274, s. 4; 2009-376, s. 1; 2010-39, s. 1; 2011-145, ss. 2; 19.1(h); 2011-183, s. 23; 2011-392, ss. 2, 3; 2012-194, ss. 45.7, 57; 2013-376, ss. 1, 2, 9(e); 2013-414, s. 57(a); 2014-100, s. 8.11(b); 2015-241, ss. 24.1(m), 14.30(s), 29.40(b), (f), (g), (i), (j), (*l*)-(o), (q); 2015-264, s. 40.6(b); 2015-268, s. 7.3(a); 2017-100, s. 1; 2017-107, ss. 2, 5; 2017-114, ss. 2, 5; 2017-186, s. 2 (*llll*); 2018-7, ss. 1(a), 1(c); 2018-74, ss. 11(a), 11(d), 11(e), 12(b), 14(a); 2018-77, ss. 1(a), 2(b), 3.5(a), (d); 2019-213, s. 2(b); 2019-231, s. 4.15(a); 2021-134, s. 4.5(a)

§ 20-79.5. Special registration plates for elected and appointed State government officials

(a) **Plates.** -- The State government officials listed in this section are eligible for a special registration plate under G.S. 20-79.4. The plate shall bear the number designated in the following table for the position held by the official.

Position	Number on Plate
Governor	1
Lieutenant Governor	2
Speaker of the House of Representatives	3
President Pro Tempore of the Senate	4
Secretary of State	5
State Auditor	6
State Treasurer	7
Superintendent of Public Instruction	8
Attorney General	9
Commissioner of Agriculture	10
Commissioner of Labor	11
Commissioner of Insurance	12
Speaker Pro Tempore of the House	13
Legislative Services Officer	14
Secretary of Administration	15

Chapter 20

Position	Number on Plate
Secretary of Environmental Quality	16
Secretary of Revenue	17
Secretary of Health and Human Services	18
Secretary of Commerce	19
Secretary of Public Safety	20
Secretary of Natural and Cultural Resources	21
Secretary of Military and Veterans Affairs	22
Governor's Staff	23-29
State Budget Officer	30
Director of the Office of State Human Resources	31
Chair of the State Board of Education	32
President of the U.N.C. System	33
President of the Community Colleges System	34
State Board Member, Commission Member, or State Employee Not Named in List	35-43
Alcoholic Beverage Control Commission	44-46
Assistant Commissioners of Agriculture	47-48
Deputy Secretary of State	49
Deputy State Treasurer	50
Assistant State Treasurer	51
Deputy Commissioner for the Department of Labor	52
Chief Deputy for the Department of Insurance	53
Assistant Commissioner of Insurance	54
Deputies and Assistant to the Attorney General	55-65
Board of Economic Development Nonlegislative Member	66-88
State Ports Authority Nonlegislative Member	89-96
Utilities Commission Member	97-103
State Board Member, Commission Member, or State Employee Not Named in List	104
Post-Release Supervision and Parole Commission Member	105-107
State Board Member, Commission Member, or State Employee Not Named in List	108-200

(b) **Designation.** -- When the table in subsection (a) designates a range of numbers for certain officials, the number given an official in that group shall be assigned. The Governor shall assign a number for members of the Governor's staff, nonlegislative members of the Board of Economic Development, nonlegislative members of the State Ports Authority, members of State boards and commissions, and for State employees. The Attorney General shall assign a number for the Attorney General's deputies and assistants.

The first number assigned to the Alcoholic Beverage Control Commission is reserved for the Chair of that Commission. The remaining numbers shall be assigned to the Alcoholic Beverage Control Commission members on the basis of seniority. The first number assigned to the Utilities Commission is reserved for the Chair of that Commission. The remaining numbers shall be assigned to the Utilities Commission members on the basis of seniority. The first number assigned to the Post-Release Supervision and Parole Commission is reserved for the Chair of that Commission. The remaining numbers shall be assigned to the Post-Release Supervision and Parole Commission members on the basis of seniority.

History.
1991, c. 672, s. 2; c. 726, s. 23; 1991 (Reg. Sess., 1992), c. 959, s. 1; 1996, 2nd Ex. Sess., c. 18, s. 8(a); 1997-443, ss. 11A.118(a), 11A.119(a); 2000-137, s. 4.(e); 2006-203, s. 14; 2007-483, s. 3(a); 2011-145, s. 19.1(g), (i), (m); 2012-83, s. 4; 2013-382, s. 9.1(c); 2015-241, ss. 24.1(n), 14.30(t), (v); 2015-268, s. 7.3(a)

§ 20-79.6. Special registration plates for members of the judiciary

(a) **Supreme Court.** -- A special plate issued to a Justice of the North Carolina Supreme Court shall bear the words "Supreme Court" and the Great Seal of North Carolina and a number from 1 through 7. The Chief Justice of the Supreme Court of North Carolina shall be issued the plate bearing the number 1 and the remaining plates shall be issued to the Associate Justices on the basis of seniority.

Special plates issued to retired members of the Supreme Court shall bear a number indicating the member's position of seniority at the time of retirement followed by the letter "X" to indicate the member's retired status.

(a1) **Court of Appeals.** -- A special plate issued to a Judge of the North Carolina Court of Appeals shall bear the words "Court of Appeals" and the Great Seal of North Carolina and a number beginning with the number 1. The Chief Judge of the North Carolina Court of Appeals shall be issued a plate with the number 1 and the remaining plates shall be issued to the

Chapter 20

1443

Associate Judges with the numbers assigned on the basis of seniority.

Special plates issued to retired members of the Court of Appeals shall bear a number indicating the member's position of seniority at the time of retirement followed by the letter "X" to indicate the member's retired status.

(b) **Superior Court.** -- A special plate issued to a resident superior court judge shall bear the letter "J" followed by a number indicative of the judicial district the judge serves. The number issued to the senior resident superior court judge shall be the numerical designation of the judge's judicial district, as defined in G.S. 7A-41.1(a)(1). If a district has more than one regular resident superior court judge, a special plate for a resident superior court judge of that district shall bear the number issued to the senior resident superior court judge followed by a hyphen and a letter of the alphabet beginning with the letter "A" to indicate the judge's seniority.

For any grouping of districts having the same numerical designation, other than districts where there are two or more resident superior court judges, the number issued to the senior resident superior court judge shall be the number the districts in the set have in common. A special plate issued to the other regular resident superior court judges of the set of districts shall bear the number issued to the senior resident superior court judge followed by a hyphen and a letter of the alphabet beginning with the letter "A" to indicate the judge's seniority among all of the regular resident superior court judges of the set of districts. The letter assigned to a resident superior court judge will not necessarily correspond with the letter designation of the district the judge serves.

Where there are two or more regular resident superior court judges for the district or set of districts, the registration plate with the letter "A" shall be issued to the judge who, from among all the regular resident superior court judges of the district or set of districts, has the most continuous service as a regular resident superior court judge; provided if two or more judges are of equal service, the oldest of those judges shall receive the next letter registration plate. Thereafter, registration plates shall be issued based on seniority within the district or set of districts.

A special judge, emergency judge, or retired judge of the superior court shall be issued a special plate bearing the letter "J" followed by a number designated by the Administrative Office of the Courts with the approval of the Chief Justice of the Supreme Court of North Carolina. The plate for a retired judge shall have the letter "X" after the designated number to indicate the judge's retired status.

(c) **District Court.** -- A special plate issued to a North Carolina district court judge shall bear the letter "J" followed by a number. For the chief judge of the district court district, the number shall be equal to the sum of the numerical designation of the district court district the chief judge serves, plus 100. The number for all other judges of the district courts serving within the same district court district shall be the same number as appears on the special plate issued to the chief district judge followed by a letter of the alphabet beginning with the letter "A" to indicate the judge's seniority. A retired district court judge shall be issued a similar plate except that the numerical designation shall be followed by the letter "X" to indicate the judge's retired status.

(d) **United States.** -- A special plate issued to a Justice of the United States Supreme Court, a Judge of the United States Circuit Court of Appeals, or a District Judge of the United States District Court residing in North Carolina shall bear the words "U.S. J" followed by a number beginning with "1". The number shall reflect the judge's seniority based on continuous service as a United States Judge as designated by the Secretary of State. A judge who has retired or taken senior status shall be issued a similar plate except that the number shall be based on the date of the judge's retirement or assumption of senior status and shall follow the numerical designation of active justices and judges.

History.
1991, c. 672, s. 2; c. 726, s. 23; 1999-403, s. 5; 1999-456, s. 67.1

§ 20-79.7. Fees for special registration plates and distribution of the fees

(a) **Free of Charge.** -- Upon request, and except for the special registration plate listed in subdivision (2) of this subsection, the Division shall annually provide and issue free of charge a single special registration plate listed in this subsection to a person qualified to receive the plate in accordance with G.S. 20-79.4(a2). For the special registration plate listed in subdivision (2) of this subsection, and upon request, the Division shall annually provide and issue free of charge a single registration plate for both a motor vehicle and a motorcycle to a person qualified to receive each plate in accordance with G.S. 20-79.4(a2). This subsection does not apply to a special registration plate issued for a vehicle that has a registered weight greater than 6,000 pounds. The regular motor vehicle registration fees in G.S. 20-88 apply if the registered weight of the vehicle is greater than 6,000 pounds:

(1) A Legion of Valor registration plate to a recipient of the Legion of Valor award.

(2) A 100% Disabled Veteran registration plate to a 100% disabled veteran.

(3) An Ex-Prisoner of War registration plate to an ex-prisoner of war.

(4) A Bronze Star Valor registration plate to a recipient of the Bronze Star Medal for valor in combat award.

(5) A Silver Star registration plate to a recipient of the Silver Star award.

(a1) **Fees.** -- All other special registration plates are subject to the regular motor vehicle registration fee in G.S. 20-87 or G.S. 20-88 plus an additional fee in the following amount:

Special Plate	Additional Fee Amount
Alpha Phi Alpha Fraternity	$ 30.00
ALS Research	$ 30.00
American Red Cross	Expired July 1, 2016
Animal Lovers	$ 30.00
Arthritis Foundation	Expired July 1, 2016
ARTS NC	$ 30.00
Back Country Horsemen of NC	Expired July 1, 2016
Big Rock Blue Marlin Tournament	$ 30.00
Boy Scouts of America	Expired July 1, 2016
Brenner Children's Hospital	Expired July 1, 2016
Carolina Panthers	$ 30.00
Carolina Raptor Center	Expired July 1, 2016
Carolinas Credit Union Foundation	Expired July 1, 2016
Carolinas Golf Association	$ 30.00
Coastal Conservation Association	Expired July 1, 2016
Coastal Land Trust	$ 30.00
Colorectal Cancer Awareness	$ 30.00
Crystal Coast	Expired July 1, 2016
Daniel Stowe Botanical Garden	Expired July 1, 2016
El Pueblo	Expired July 1, 2016
Farmland Preservation	Expired July 1, 2016
First in Forestry	$ 30.00
First Tee	Expired July 1, 2016
Girl Scouts	Expired July 1, 2016
Greensboro Symphony Guild	Expired July 1, 2016
Historical Attraction	$ 30.00
Home Care and Hospice	$ 30.00
Home of American Golf	Expired July 1, 2016
HOMES4NC	$ 30.00
Hospice Care	Expired July 1, 2016
In God We Trust	$ 30.00
Keeping the Lights On	$ 30.00
Kick Cancer for Kids	$ 30.00
Maggie Valley Trout Festival	Expired July 1, 2016
Morehead Planetarium	Expired July 1, 2016
Morgan Horse Club	Expired July 1, 2016
Mountains-to-Sea Trail	$ 30.00
Municipality Plate	Expired July 1, 2016
NC Civil War	Expired July 1, 2016
NC Coastal Federation	$ 30.00
NC FIRST Robotics	Expired July 1, 2016
NCSC	Expired July 1, 2016
NC Veterinary Medical Association	Expired July 1, 2016
National Kidney Foundation	Expired July 1, 2016
National Law Enforcement Officers Memorial	Expired July 1, 2016
Native Brook Trout	$ 30.00
North Carolina 4-H Development Fund	Expired July 1, 2016
North Carolina Bluegrass Association	Expired July 1, 2016
North Carolina Cattlemen's Association	Expired July 1, 2016
North Carolina Emergency Management	Expired July 1, 2016

Special Plate	Additional Fee Amount
Association	
North Carolina Green Industry Council	Expired July 1, 2016
North Carolina Libraries	Expired July 1, 2016
North Carolina Paddle Festival	Expired July 1, 2016
North Carolina Sheriffs' Association	$ 30.00
Operation Coming Home	Expired July 1, 2016
Outer Banks Preservation Association	Expired July 1, 2016
Pamlico-Tar River Foundation	Expired July 1, 2016
Pancreatic Cancer Awareness	Expired July 1, 2016
P.E.O. Sisterhood	Expired July 1, 2016
Personalized	$ 30.00
Pisgah Conservancy	$ 30.00
Red Drum	Expired July 1, 2016
Retired Legislator	$ 30.00
RiverLink	Expired July 1, 2016
Ronald McDonald House	$ 30.00
Share the Road	$ 30.00
S.T.A.R.	Expired July 1, 2016
State Attraction	$ 30.00
Stock Car Racing Theme	$ 30.00
Support NC Education	Expired July 1, 2016
Support Our Troops	$ 30.00
Sustainable Fisheries	Expired July 1, 2016
Toastmasters Club	Expired July 1, 2016
Topsail Island Shoreline Protection	Expired July 1, 2016
Travel and Tourism	Expired July 1, 2016
Turtle Rescue Team	Expired July 1, 2016
United States Service Academy	$ 30.00
Wildlife Resources	$ 30.00
Volunteers in Law Enforcement	Expired July 1, 2016
YMCA	Expired July 1, 2016
AIDS Awareness	Expired July 1, 2016
Buffalo Soldiers	Expired July 1, 2016
Charlotte Checkers	Expired July 1, 2016
Choose Life	$ 25.00
Collegiate Insignia	$ 25.00
First in Turf	Expired July 1, 2016
Goodness Grows	Expired July 1, 2016
High School Insignia	$ 25.00
I.B.P.O.E.W.	Expired July 1, 2016
Kids First	$ 25.00
National Multiple Sclerosis Society	$ 25.00
National Wild Turkey Federation	$ 25.00
NC Agribusiness	Expired July 1, 2016
NC Children's Promise	Expired July 1, 2016
NC Surveyors	$ 25.00
Nurses	$ 25.00
Olympic Games	$ 25.00
Professional Engineer	Expired July 1, 2016
Rocky Mountain Elk Foundation	$ 25.00
Special Olympics	Expired July 1, 2016
Support Soccer	$ 25.00
Surveyor Plate	$ 25.00
The V Foundation for Cancer Research Division	$ 25.00
University Health Systems of Eastern Carolina	Expired July 1, 2016

Special Plate	Additional Fee Amount
ALS Association, Jim "Catfish" Hunter Chapter	Expired July 1, 2016
ARC of North Carolina	Expired July 1, 2016
Audubon North Carolina	Expired July 1, 2016
Autism Society of North Carolina	$ 20.00
Battle of Kings Mountain	$ 20.00
Be Active NC	Expired July 1, 2016
Brain Injury Awareness	Expired July 1, 2016
Breast Cancer Earlier Detection	Expired July 1, 2016
Buddy Pelletier Surfing Foundation	$ 20.00
Concerned Bikers Association/ABATE of North Carolina	Expired July 1, 2016
Daughters of the American Revolution	Expired July 1, 2016
Donate Life	$ 20.00
Ducks Unlimited	$ 20.00
Fraternal Order of Police	$ 20.00
Greyhound Friends of North Carolina	Expired July 1, 2016
Guilford Battleground Company	$ 20.00
Harley Owners' Group	$ 20.00
International Association of Fire Fighters	$ 20.00
I Support Teachers	Expired July 1, 2016
Jaycees	Expired July 1, 2016
Juvenile Diabetes Research Foundation	$ 20.00
Kappa Alpha Order	Expired July 1, 2016
Litter Prevention	$ 20.00
March of Dimes	Expired July 1, 2016
Mission Foundation	Expired July 1, 2016
Native American	$ 20.00
NC Fisheries Association	Expired July 1, 2016
NC Horse Council	$ 20.00
NC Mining	Expired July 1, 2016
NC Tennis Foundation	$ 20.00
NC Trout Unlimited	$ 20.00
NC Victim Assistance	Expired July 1, 2016
NC Wildlife Federation	Expired July 1, 2016
NC Wildlife Habitat Foundation	$ 20.00
NC Youth Soccer Association	Expired July 1, 2016
North Carolina Master Gardener	$ 20.00
Omega Psi Phi Fraternity	$ 20.00
Order of the Eastern Star Prince Hall Affiliated	$ 20.00
Order of the Long Leaf Pine	$ 20.00
Piedmont Airlines	$ 20.00
POW/MIA Bring Them Home	$ 20.00
Prince Hall Mason	$ 20.00
Save the Sea Turtles	$ 20.00
Scenic Rivers	Expired July 1, 2016
School Technology	Expired July 1, 2016
SCUBA	$ 20.00
Soil and Water Conservation	Expired July 1, 2016
Special Forces Association	Expired July 1, 2016
US Equine Rescue League	Expired July 1, 2016
USO of NC	Expired July 1, 2016
Wrightsville Beach	$ 20.00
Zeta Phi Beta Sorority	$ 20.00
Carolina Regional Volleyball Association	Expired July 1, 2016

Chapter 20

Special Plate	Additional Fee Amount
Carolina's Aviation Museum	Expired July 1, 2016
Leukemia & Lymphoma Society	Expired July 1, 2016
Lung Cancer Research	Expired July 1, 2016
NC Beekeepers	Expired July 1, 2016
Save the Honey Bee (HB)	$ 15.00
Save the Honey Bee (SB)	$ 15.00
Shag Dancing	$ 15.00
Active Member of the National Guard	None
Bronze Star Combat Recipient	None
Bronze Star Recipient	None
Combat Veteran	Expired July 1, 2016
100% Disabled Veteran	None
Eastern Band of Cherokee Indians	None
Ex-Prisoner of War	None
Gold Star Lapel Button	None
Legion of Merit	None
Legion of Valor	None
Military Veteran	None
Military Wartime Veteran	None
Partially Disabled Veteran	None
Pearl Harbor Survivor	None
Purple Heart Recipient	None
Silver Star Recipient	None
All Other Special Plates	$ 10.00.

(b) **Distribution of Fees.** -- The Special Registration Plate Account and the Collegiate and Cultural Attraction Plate Account are established within the Highway Fund. The Division must credit the additional fee imposed for the special registration plates listed in subsection (a1) of this section among the Special Registration Plate Account (SRPA), the Collegiate and Cultural Attraction Plate Account (CCAPA), the Clean Water Management Trust Fund (CWMTF), which is established under G.S. 143B-135.234, and the Parks and Recreation Trust Fund, which is established under G.S. 143B-135.56, as follows:

Special Plate	SRPA	CCAPA	NHTF	PRTF
AIDS Awareness -- Expired July 1, 2016				
Alpha Phi Alpha Fraternity	$10	$20	0	0
ALS Association, Jim "Catfish" Hunter Chapter -- Expired July 1, 2016				
ALS Research	$10	$20	0	0
American Red Cross -- Expired July 1, 2016				
Animal Lovers	$10	$20	0	0
ARC of North Carolina -- Expired July 1, 2016				
Arthritis Foundation -- Expired July 1, 2016				
ARTS NC	$10	$20	0	0
Audubon North Carolina -- Expired July 1, 2016				
Autism Society of North Carolina	$10	$10	0	0
Back Country Horsemen of NC -- Expired July 1, 2016				
Battle of Kings Mountain	$10	$10	0	0
Be Active NC -- Expired July 1, 2016				
Big Rock Blue Marlin Tournament	$10	$20	0	0
Boy Scouts of America -- Expired July 1, 2016				
Brain Injury Awareness -- Expired July 1, 2016				
Breast Cancer Earlier Detection -- Expired July 1, 2016				
Brenner Children's Hospital -- Expired July 1, 2016				
Buddy Pelletier Surfing Foundation	$10	$10	0	0

Special Plate	SRPA	CCAPA	NHTF	PRTF
Buffalo Soldiers -- Expired July 1, 2016				
Carolina Panthers	$10	$20	0	0
Carolina Raptor Center -- Expired July 1, 2016				
Carolina Regional Volleyball Association -- Expired July 1, 2016				
Carolina's Aviation Museum -- Expired July 1, 2016				
Carolinas Credit Union Foundation -- Expired July 1, 2016				
Carolinas Golf Association	$10	$20	0	0
Charlotte Checkers -- Expired July 1, 2016				
Choose Life	$10	$15	0	0
Coastal Conservation Association -- Expired July 1, 2016				
Coastal Land Trust	$10	$20	0	0
Colorectal Cancer Awareness	$10	$20	0	0
Concerned Bikers Association / ABATE of North Carolina -- Expired July 1, 2016				
Crystal Coast -- Expired July 1, 2016				
Daniel Stowe Botanical Gardens -- Expired July 1, 2016				
Daughters of the American Revolution -- Expired July 1, 2016				
Donate Life	$10	$10	0	0
Ducks Unlimited	$10	$10	0	0
El Pueblo -- Expired July 1, 2016				
Farmland Preservation -- Expired July 1, 2016				
First in Forestry	$10	$10	$10	0
First in Turf -- Expired July 1, 2016				
First Tee -- Expired July 1, 2016				
Fraternal Order of Police	$10	$10	0	0
Girl Scouts -- Expired July 1, 2016				
Goodness Grows -- Expired July 1, 2016				
Greensboro Symphony Guild -- Expired July 1, 2016				
Greyhound Friends of North Carolina -- Expired July 1, 2016				
Guilford Battleground Company	$10	$10	0	0
Harley Owners' Group	$10	$10	0	0
High School Insignia	$10	$15	0	0
Historical Attraction	$10	$20	0	0
Home Care and Hospice	$10	$20	0	0
Home of American Golf -- Expired July 1, 2016				
HOMES4NC	$10	$20	0	0
Hospice Care -- Expired July 1, 2016				
I.B.P.O.E.W. -- Expired July 1, 2016				
In God We Trust	$10	$20	0	0
In-State Collegiate Insignia	$10	$15	0	0
International Association of Fire Fighters	$10	$10	0	0
I Support Teachers -- Expired July 1, 2016				
Jaycees -- Expired July 1, 2016				
Juvenile Diabetes Research Foundation	$10	$10	0	0
Kappa Alpha Order -- Expired July 1, 2016				
Keeping The Lights On	$10	$20	0	0
Kick Cancer for Kids	$10	$20	0	0
Kids First	$10	$15	0	0
Leukemia & Lymphoma Society -- Expired July 1, 2016				
Litter Prevention	$10	$10	0	0
Lung Cancer Research -- Expired July 1, 2016				
Maggie Valley Trout Festival -- Expired July 1, 2016				
March of Dimes -- Expired July 1, 2016				
Mission Foundation -- Expired July 1, 2016				
Morgan Horse Club -- Expired July 1, 2016				

Chapter 20

Special Plate	SRPA	CCAPA	NHTF	PRTF
Morehead Planetarium -- Expired July 1, 2016				
Mountains-to-Sea Trail	$10	$20	0	0
Municipality Plate -- Expired July 1, 2016				
National Kidney Foundation -- Expired July 1, 2016				
National Law Enforcement Officers Memorial -- Expired July 1, 2016				
National Multiple Sclerosis Society	$10	$15	0	0
National Wild Turkey Federation	$10	$15	0	0
Native American	$10	$10	0	0
NC Agribusiness -- Expired July 1, 2016				
NC Beekeepers -- Expired July 1, 2016				
NC Children's Promise -- Expired July 1, 2016				
NC Civil War -- Expired July 1, 2016				
NC Coastal Federation	$10	$20	0	0
NC 4-H Development Fund -- Expired July 1, 2016				
NC FIRST Robotics -- Expired July 1, 2016				
NC Fisheries Association -- Expired July 1, 2016				
NC Horse Council	$10	$10	0	0
NC Mining -- Expired July 1, 2016				
NCSC -- Expired July 1, 2016				
NC Surveyors	$10	$15	0	0
NC Tennis Foundation	$10	$10	0	0
NC Trout Unlimited	$10	$10	0	0
NC Veterinary Medical Association -- Expired July 1, 2016				
NC Victim Assistance -- Expired July 1, 2016				
NC Wildlife Federation -- Expired July 1, 2016				
NC Wildlife Habitat Foundation	$10	$10	0	0
NC Youth Soccer Association -- Expired July 1, 2016				
North Carolina Bluegrass Association -- Expired July 1, 2016				
North Carolina Cattlemen's Association -- Expired July 1, 2016				
North Carolina Emergency Management Association -- Expired July 1, 2016				
North Carolina Green Industry Council -- Expired July 1, 2016				
North Carolina Libraries -- Expired July 1, 2016				
North Carolina Master Gardener	$10	$10	0	0
North Carolina Paddle Festival -- Expired July 1, 2016				
North Carolina Sheriffs' Association	$10	$20	0	0
Nurses	$10	$15	0	0
Olympic Games	$10	$15	0	0
Omega Psi Phi Fraternity	$10	$10	0	0
Operation Coming Home -- Expired July 1, 2016				
Order of the Eastern Star Prince Hall Affiliated	$10	$10	0	0
Order of the Long Leaf Pine	$10	$10	0	0
Out-of-state Collegiate Insignia	$10	0	$15	0
Outer Banks Preservation Association -- Expired July 1, 2016				
Pamlico-Tar River Foundation -- Expired July 1, 2016				
Pancreatic Cancer Awareness -- Expired July 1, 2016				
P.E.O. Sisterhood -- Expired July 1, 2016				
Personalized	$10	0	$15	$5
Piedmont Airlines	$10	$10	0	0
Pisgah Conservancy	$10	$20	0	0
POW/MIA Bring Them Home	$10	$10	0	0
Prince Hall Mason	$10	$10	0	0
Professional Engineer -- Expired July 1, 2016				
Retired Legislator	$10	$20	0	0

Chapter 20

Special Plate	SRPA	CCAPA	NHTF	PRTF
RiverLink -- Expired July 1, 2016				
Rocky Mountain Elk Foundation	$10	$15	0	0
Ronald McDonald House	$10	$20	0	0
Save the Honey Bee (HB)	$10	$5	0	0
Save the Honey Bee (SB)	$10	$5	0	0
Save the Sea Turtles	$10	$10	0	0
Scenic Rivers -- Expired July 1, 2016				
School Technology -- Expired July 1, 2016				
SCUBA	$10	$10	0	0
Shag Dancing	$10	$5	0	0
Share the Road	$10	$20	0	0
Sneads Ferry Shrimp Festival -- Expired July 1, 2016				
Soil and Water Conservation -- Expired July 1, 2016				
Special Forces Association -- Expired July 1, 2016				
Special Olympics -- Expired July 1, 2016				
S.T.A.R. -- Expired July 1, 2016				
State Attraction	$10	$20	0	0
Stock Car Racing Theme	$10	$20	0	0
Support NC Education -- Expired July 1, 2016				
Support Our Troops	$10	$20	0	0
Support Soccer	$10	$15	0	0
Surveyor Plate	$10	$15	0	0
Sustainable Fisheries -- Expired July 1, 2016				
The V Foundation for Cancer Research	$10	$15	0	0
Toastmasters Club -- Expired July 1, 2016				
Topsail Island Shoreline Protection -- Expired July 1, 2016				
Travel and Tourism -- Expired July 1, 2016				
Turtle Rescue Team -- Expired July 1, 2016				
University Health Systems of Eastern Carolina -- Expired July 1, 2016				
United States Service Academy	$10	$20	0	0
US Equine Rescue League -- Expired July 1, 2016				
USO of NC -- Expired July 1, 2016				
Volunteers in Law Enforcement -- Expired July 1, 2016				
Wildlife Resources	$10	$20	0	0
Wrightsville Beach	$10	$10	0	0
YMCA -- Expired July 1, 2016				
Zeta Phi Beta Sorority	$10	$10	0	0
All other Special Plates	$10	0	0	0

(c) **Use of Funds in Special Registration Plate Account. --**

(1) The Division shall deduct the costs of special registration plates, including the costs of issuing, handling, and advertising the availability of the special plates, from the Special Registration Plate Account.

(2) From the funds remaining in the Special Registration Plate Account after the deductions in accordance with subdivision (1) of this subsection, there is annually appropriated from the Special Registration Plate Account the sum of one million three hundred thousand dollars ($ 1,300,000) to provide operating assistance for the Visitor Centers:

a. on U.S. Highway 17 in Camden County, ninety-two thousand eight hundred fifty-seven dollars ($ 92,857);

b. on U.S. Highway 17 in Brunswick County, ninety-two thousand eight hundred fifty-seven dollars ($ 92,857);

c. on U.S. Highway 441 in Macon County, ninety-two thousand eight hundred fifty-seven dollars ($ 92,857);

d. in Watauga County, ninety-two thousand eight hundred fifty-seven dollars ($ 92,857);

e. on U.S. Highway 29 in Caswell County, ninety-two thousand eight hundred fifty-seven dollars ($ 92,857);

f. on U.S. Highway 70 in Carteret County, ninety-two thousand eight hundred fifty-seven dollars ($ 92,857);

g. on U.S. Highway 64 in Tyrrell County, ninety-two thousand eight hundred fifty-seven dollars ($ 92,857);

h. at the intersection of U.S. Highway 701 and N.C. 904 in Columbus County, ninety-two thousand eight hundred fifty-seven dollars ($ 92,857);

i. on U.S. Highway 221 in McDowell County, ninety-two thousand eight hundred fifty-seven dollars ($ 92,857);

j. on Staton Road in Transylvania County, ninety-two thousand eight hundred fifty-seven dollars ($ 92,857);

k. in the Town of Fair Bluff, Columbus County, near the intersection of U.S. Highway 76 and N.C. 904, ninety-two thousand eight hundred fifty-seven dollars ($ 92,857);

l. on U.S. Highway 421 in Wilkes County, ninety-two thousand eight hundred fifty-seven dollars ($ 92,857); and

m. at the intersection of Interstate 73 and Interstate 74 in Randolph County, ninety-two thousand eight hundred fifty-eight dollars ($ 92,858) each, for two centers.

(3) The Division shall transfer fifty percent (50%) of the remaining revenue in the Special Registration Plate Account quarterly, and funds are hereby appropriated to the Department of Transportation to be used solely for the purpose of beautification of highways. These funds shall be administered by the Department of Transportation for beautification purposes not inconsistent with good landscaping and engineering principles. The Division shall transfer the remaining revenue in the Special Registration Plate Account quarterly to the Highway Fund to be used for the Roadside Vegetation Management Program.

History.
1967, c. 413; 1971, c. 42; 1973, c. 507, s. 5; c. 1262, s. 86; 1975, c. 716, s. 5; 1977, c. 464, s. 3; c. 771, s. 4; 1979, c. 126, ss. 1, 2; 1981 (Reg. Sess., 1982), c. 1258, s. 6; 1983, c. 848; 1985, c. 766; 1987, c. 252; c. 738, s. 140; c. 830, ss. 113(a), 116(a)-(c); 1989, c. 751, s. 7(1); c. 774, s. 1; 1989 (Reg. Sess., 1990), c. 814, s. 31; 1991, c. 672, s. 3; c. 726, s. 23; 1991 (Reg. Sess., 1992), c. 959, s. 2; c. 1042, s. 2; c. 1044, ss. 33, 34; 1993, c. 321, s. 169.3(a); c. 543, s. 3; 1995, c. 163, s. 2; c. 324, s. 18.7(a); c. 433, ss. 2, 3; c. 507, s. 18.17(a); 1996, 2nd Ex. Sess., c. 18, s. 19.11(e); 1997-443, s. 11A.118(a); 1997-477, ss. 2, 3; 1997-484, ss. 4, 5; 1998-163, s. 1; 1999-277, ss. 2, 3; 1999-403, ss. 2, 3; 1999-450, ss. 2, 3; 2000-159, ss. 3, 4; 2001-414, s. 32; 2001-498, ss. 3(a), 3(b), 4(a), 4(b); 2002-134, ss. 5, 6; 2003-11, ss. 2, 3; 2003-68, ss. 2, 3; 2003-424, ss. 3, 4; 2004-124, s. 30.3A; 2004-131, ss. 3, 4; 2004-185, ss. 3, 4; 2004-200, ss. 2, 3; 2005-216, ss. 4, 5; 2005-276, s. 28.16; 2006-209, ss. 3, 4, 7; 2007-323, s. 27.20(b); 2007-345, s. 10.1; 2007-400, ss. 3, 4; 2007-483, ss. 4, 5, 8(a), (b); 2009-228, s. 1; 2010-31, ss. 11.4(i), (j), 28.11; 2010-132, s. 7; 2011-145, s. 28.30(b); 2011-392, ss. 4, 5, 5.1; 2012-79, s. 1.12(b); 2013-360, ss. 14.3(c), 34.22; 2013-376, ss. 3, 4, 9(c), (d); 2013-414, s. 57(b), (c); 2014-100, s. 8.11(d); 2015-241,

ss. 14.30(dd), 29.30B(a), 29.36A, 29.40(c), (h), (j), (n); 2017-100, s. 2; 2017-107, s. 3; 2017-114, s. 3; 2018-7, s. 1(b); 2018-74, ss. 11(b), (e), 12(c)-(e), 13, 14(b); 2018-77, ss. 1(b), 2(c)-(e), 3.5(b); 2019-32, s. 1(c); 2019-213, s. 2(c)

§ 20-79.8. Expiration of special registration plate authorization

(a) **Expiration of Plates Authorized Prior to October 1, 2014.** -- A special registration plate authorized after July 1, 2011, and before October 1, 2014, pursuant to G.S. 20-79.4 shall expire, as a matter of law, on July 1 of the second calendar year following the year in which the special plate was authorized if the number of required applications for the authorized special plate has not been received by the Division. The Division shall not accept applications for nor advertise any special registration plate that has expired pursuant to this section.

(a1) **Expiration of Plates Authorized On or After October 1, 2014.** -- A special registration plate authorized on or after October 1, 2014, pursuant to G.S. 20-79.4, shall expire as a matter of law upon an applicant's failure to submit to the Division all of the items required under G.S. 20-79.3A(d) within 60 days of the act approving the special registration plate becoming law. The Division shall not accept applications for nor advertise any special registration plate that has expired pursuant to this section.

(b) **Notification.** -- The Division shall notify the Revisor of Statutes in writing, not later than August 1 of each year, which special registration plate authorizations have expired as a matter of law pursuant to subsection (a) of this section. The Division shall publish a copy of the written notification sent to the Revisor of Statutes pursuant to this subsection on a Web site maintained by the Division or the Department of Transportation.

(c) **Revisor of Statutes Responsibilities.** -- Upon notification of expiration of the authorization for any special registration plate by the Division pursuant to this section, the Revisor of Statutes shall verify that the authorization for each special registration plate listed has expired and shall notate the expiration in the applicable statutes. If an authorization for a special registration plate listed in G.S. 20-79.4 expires, the Revisor of Statutes shall revise the subdivision referring to the special registration plate to leave the name of the special registration plate authorized and the date the special registration plate's authorization expired. If an authorization for a special registration plate listed in G.S. 20-79.4 expires, the Revisor of Statutes shall also make corresponding changes to reflect the expiration of the special registration plate's authorization, if applicable, in G.S. 20-63(b), 20-79.7, and 20-81.12.

History.
2011-392, s. 8; 2014-96, s. 6

§§ 20-80 through 20-81.2

Repealed by Session Laws 1991, c. 672, s. 1, as amended by Session Laws 1991, c. 726, s. 23.

N.C. Gen. Stat. § 20-81.3

Recodified as § 20-79.7 by Session Laws 1991, c. 672, s. 3, as amended by Session Laws 1991, c. 726, s. 23.

§§ 20-81.4 through 20-81.11

Repealed by Session Laws 1991, c. 672, s. 1, as amended by Session Laws 1991, c. 726, s. 23.

§ 20-81.12. Collegiate insignia plates and certain other special plates

(a) **AIDS Awareness.** -- Expired July 1, 2016.

(b) **Alpha Phi Alpha Fraternity.** -- The Division shall transfer quarterly the money in the Collegiate and Cultural Attraction Plate Account derived from the sale of the Alpha Phi Alpha Fraternity plates to the Education Consortium of North Carolina, Inc., for scholarships for the benefit of African-American males attending accredited North Carolina colleges and universities.

(b1) **ALS Research.** -- The Division shall transfer quarterly the money in the Collegiate and Cultural Attraction Plate Account derived from the sale of ALS Research plates to The ALS Association of North Carolina Chapter to support ALS research.

(b2) **American Red Cross.** -- Expired July 1, 2016.

(b3) **Animal Lovers Plates.** -- The Division must receive 300 or more applications before an animal lovers plate may be developed. The Division shall transfer quarterly the money in the Collegiate and Cultural Attraction Plate Account derived from the sale of the animal lovers plate to the Spay/Neuter Account established in G.S. 19A-62.

(b4) **ARC of North Carolina.** -- Expired July 1, 2016.

(b5) **Arthritis Foundation.** -- Expired July 1, 2016.

(b6) **ARTS NC.** -- The Division must receive 300 or more applications for the ARTS NC plate before the plate may be developed. The Division must transfer quarterly the money in the Collegiate and Cultural Attraction Plate Account derived from the sale of ARTSNC plates to ARTS North Carolina, Inc., to provide funding to promote the arts in North Carolina.

(b7) **Audubon North Carolina Plates.** -- Expired July 1, 2016.

(b8) **Autism Society of North Carolina.** -- The Division must receive 300 or more applications for an Autism Society of North Carolina plate before the plate may be developed. The Division must transfer quarterly the money in the Collegiate and Cultural Attraction Plate Account derived from the sale of Autism Society of North Carolina plates to the Autism Society of North Carolina, Inc., for support services to individuals with autism and their families.

(b9) **Back Country Horsemen of North Carolina.** -- Expired July 1, 2016.

(b10) **Battle of Kings Mountain.** -- The Division shall transfer quarterly the money in the Collegiate and Cultural Attraction Plate Account derived from the sale of "Battle of Kings Mountain" plates by transferring fifty percent (50%) to the Kings Mountain Tourism Development Authority and fifty percent (50%) to Kings Mountain Gateway Trails, Inc., to be used to develop tourism to the area and provide safe and adequate trails for visitors to the park.

(b11) **Battleship North Carolina.** -- The Division must receive 300 or more applications for the "Battleship North Carolina" plate before the plate may be developed. The Division must transfer quarterly the money in the Collegiate and Cultural Attraction Plate Account derived from the sale of "Battleship North Carolina" plates to the U.S.S. North Carolina Battleship Commission to provide funding for information and education about the role of the Battleship U.S.S. North Carolina in history and for administrative and operating costs of the U.S.S. North Carolina Battleship Commission.

(b12) **Be Active NC.** -- Expired July 1, 2016.

(b13) **Big Rock Blue Marlin Tournament.** -- The Division shall transfer quarterly the money in the Collegiate and Cultural Attraction Plate Account derived from the sale of Big Rock Blue Marlin Tournament plates to the Big Rock Blue Marlin Tournament to be used to fund charities in North Carolina.

(b14) **Boy Scouts of America.** -- Expired July 1, 2016.

(b15) **Brain Injury Awareness.** -- Expired July 1, 2016.

(b16) **Breast Cancer Earlier Detection.** -- Expired July 1, 2016.

(b17) **Brenner Children's Hospital.** -- Expired July 1, 2016.

(b18) **Buddy Pelletier Surfing Foundation.** -- The Division must receive 300 or more applications for the Buddy Pelletier Surfing Foundation plate before the plate may be developed. The Division shall transfer quarterly the money in the Collegiate and Cultural Attraction Plate Account derived from the sale of the Buddy Pelletier Surfing Foundation to the Foundation to fund the Foundation's scholastic and humanitarian aid programs.

(b19) **Buffalo Soldiers.** -- Expired July 1, 2016.

(b20) **Carolina Panthers.** -- The Division shall transfer quarterly one-half of the money in the Collegiate and Cultural Attraction Plate Account derived from the sale of Carolina Panthers plates to the Keep Pounding Fund of the Carolinas Healthcare Foundation, Inc., to be used to support cancer research at the Carolinas Medical Center, and shall transfer quarterly one-half of the money in the Collegiate and Cultural Attraction Plate Account derived from the sale of the Carolina Panthers plates to the Carolina Panthers Charities Fund of the Foundation for the Carolinas to be used to create new athletic opportunities for children, support their educational needs, and promote healthy lifestyles for families.

(b21) **Carolina Raptor Center.** -- Expired July 1, 2016.

(b22) **Carolina Regional Volleyball Association.** -- Expired July 1, 2016.

(b23) **Carolina's Aviation Museum.** -- Expired July 1, 2016.

(b24) **Carolinas Credit Union Foundation.** -- Expired July 1, 2016.

(b25) **Carolinas Golf Association.** -- The Division must receive 300 or more applications for the "Carolinas Golf Association" plate before the plate may be developed. The Division shall transfer quarterly the money in the Collegiate and Cultural Attraction Plate Account derived from the sale of "Carolinas Golf Association" plates to the Carolinas Golf Association to be used to promote amateur golf in North Carolina.

(b26) **Charlotte Checkers.** -- Expired July 1, 2016.

(b27) **Choose Life.** -- The Division must receive 300 or more applications for a "Choose Life" plate before the plate may be developed. The Division shall transfer quarterly the money in the Collegiate and Cultural Attraction Plate Account derived from the sale of "Choose Life" plates to the Carolina Pregnancy Care Fellowship, which shall distribute the money annually to nongovernmental, not-for-profit agencies that provide pregnancy services that are limited to counseling and/or meeting the physical needs of pregnant women. Funds received pursuant to this section shall not be distributed to any agency, organization, business, or other entity that provides, promotes, counsels, or refers for abortion and shall not be distributed to any entity that charges women for services received.

(b28) **Coastal Conservation Association.** -- Expired July 1, 2016.

(b29) **Coastal Land Trust.** -- The Division must receive 300 or more applications for the "Coastal Land Trust" plate before the plate may be developed. The Division shall transfer quarterly the money in the Collegiate and Cultural Attraction Plate Account derived from the sale of the "Coastal Land Trust" plates to the North Carolina Coastal Land Trust to be used to acquire open space and natural areas, to ensure conservation education, to promote good land stewardship, to set aside lands for conservation, and for other administrative and operating costs.

(b30) **Collegiate Insignia Plates.** -- Except for a collegiate insignia plate for a public military college or university, the Division must receive 300 or more applications for a collegiate insignia license plate for a college or university before a collegiate license plate may be developed. For a collegiate insignia license plate for a public military college or university, the Division must receive 100 or more applications before a collegiate license plate may be developed. The color, design, and material for the plate must be approved by both the Division and the alumni or alumnae association of the appropriate college or university. The Division must transfer quarterly the money in the Collegiate and Cultural Attraction Plate Account derived from the sale of in-State collegiate insignia plates to the Board of Governors of The University of North Carolina for in-State, public colleges and universities and to the respective board of trustees for in-State, private colleges and universities in proportion to the number of collegiate plates sold representing that institution for use for academic enhancement.

(b31) **Colorectal Cancer Awareness.** -- The Division must receive 300 or more applications for a Colorectal Cancer Awareness plate before the plate may be developed. The Division shall transfer quarterly the money in the Collegiate and Cultural Attraction Plate Account derived from the sale of Colorectal Cancer Awareness plates to the Colon Cancer Coalition to be used to promote prevention and early detection of colorectal cancer and to provide support to persons affected.

(b32) **Concerned Bikers Association/ABATE of North Carolina.** -- Expired July 1, 2016.

(b33) **Crystal Coast.** -- Expired July 1, 2016.

(b34) **Daniel Stowe Botanical Garden.** -- Expired July 1, 2016.

(b35) **Daughters of the American Revolution.** -- Expired July 1, 2016.

(b36) **Donate Life.** -- The Division must receive 300 or more applications for the "Donate Life" plate before the plate may be developed. The Division must transfer quarterly the money in the Collegiate and Cultural Attraction Plate Account derived from the sale of "Donate Life" plates to Donate Life North Carolina to be divided equally among Donate Life North Carolina and each of the transplant centers in North Carolina to include Bowman Gray Medical Center, Carolinas Medical Center, Duke University,

East Carolina University, and the University of North Carolina at Chapel Hill. The transplant centers shall use all of the proceeds received from this plate to provide funding for expenses incurred by needy families, recipients, and expenses related to organ donation.

(b37) **Ducks Unlimited Plates.** -- The Division must receive 300 or more applications for a Ducks Unlimited plate and receive any necessary licenses from Ducks Unlimited, Inc., for use of their logo before the plate may be developed. The Division shall transfer quarterly the money in the Collegiate and Cultural Attraction Plate Account derived from the sale of Ducks Unlimited plates to the Wildlife Resources Commission to be used to support the conservation programs of Ducks Unlimited, Inc., in this State.

(b38) **El Pueblo.** -- Expired July 1, 2016.

(b39) **Farmland Preservation.** -- Expired July 1, 2016.

(b40) **First in Forestry.** -- The Division must receive 300 or more applications for the First in Forestry plate before the plate may be developed. The Division shall transfer quarterly one-half of the money in the Collegiate and Cultural Attraction Plate Account derived from the sale of the First in Forestry plates to the North Carolina Forest Service of the Department of Agriculture and Consumer Services for a State forests and forestry education program and shall transfer quarterly one-half of the money in the Collegiate and Cultural Attraction Plate Account derived from the sale of the First in Forestry plates to the Forest Education and Conservation Foundation for their programs.

(b41) **First in Turf.** -- Expired July 1, 2016.

(b42) **First Tee.** -- Expired July 1, 2016.

(b43) **Fraternal Order of Police.** -- The Division shall transfer quarterly the money in the Collegiate and Cultural Attraction Plate Account derived from the sale of Fraternal Order of Police plates to The North Carolina Fraternal Order of Police to support the State Lodge.

(b44) **Girl Scouts.** -- Expired July 1, 2016.

(b45) **Goodness Grows Plates.** -- Expired July 1, 2016.

(b46) **Greensboro Symphony Guild.** -- Expired July 1, 2016.

(b47) **Greyhound Friends of North Carolina.** -- Expired July 1, 2016.

(b48) **Guilford Battleground Company.** -- The Division must receive 300 or more applications for a Guilford Battleground Company plate before the plate may be developed. The Division shall transfer quarterly the money in the Collegiate and Cultural Attraction Plate Account derived from the sale of Guilford Battleground Company plates to the Guilford Battleground Company for its programs.

(b49) **Harley Owners' Group.** -- The Division must receive 300 or more applications for a Harley Owners' Group plate before the plate may be developed. The Division shall transfer quarterly the money in the Collegiate and Cultural Attraction Plate Account derived from the sale of Harley Owners' Group plates to the State Board of Community Colleges to support the motorcycle safety instruction program established pursuant to G.S. 115D-72.

(b50) **High School Insignia Plate.** -- The Division must receive 300 or more applications for a high school insignia plate for a public high school in North Carolina before a high school insignia plate may be issued for that school. The Division must transfer quarterly the money in the Collegiate and Cultural Attraction Plate Account derived from the sale of high school insignia plates to the Department of Public Instruction to be deposited into the State Aid to Local School Administrative Units account. The Division must also send the Department of Public Instruction information as to the number of plates sold representing a particular high school. The Department of Public Instruction must annually transfer the money in the State Aid to Local School Administrative Units account that is derived from the sale of the high school insignia plates to the high schools which have a high school insignia plate in proportion to the number of high school insignia plates sold representing that school. The high school must use the money for academic enhancement.

(b51) **Historical Attraction Plates.** -- The Division must receive 300 or more applications for an historical attraction plate representing a publicly owned or nonprofit historical attraction located in North Carolina and listed below before the plate may be developed. The Division must transfer quarterly the money in the Collegiate and Cultural Attraction Plate Account derived from the sale of historical attraction plates to the organizations named below in proportion to the number of historical attraction plates sold representing that organization:

(1) **Historical Attraction Within Historic District.** -- The revenue derived from the special plate shall be transferred quarterly to the appropriate Historic Preservation Commission, or entity designated as the Historic Preservation Commission, and used to maintain property in the historic district in which the attraction is located. As used in this subdivision, the term "historic district" means a district created under G.S. 160A-400.4.

(2) **Nonprofit Historical Attraction.** -- The revenue derived from the special plate shall be transferred quarterly to the nonprofit corporation that is responsible for maintaining the attraction for which the plate is issued and used to develop and operate the attraction.

(3) **State Historic Site.** -- The revenue derived from the special plate shall be

Chapter 20

transferred quarterly to the Department of
Natural and Cultural Resources and used
to develop and operate the site for which
the plate is issued. As used in this subdivision, the term "State historic site" has the
same meaning as in G.S. 121-2(11).

(b52) **Home Care and Hospice.** -- The Division must receive 300 or more applications
for the Home Care and Hospice plate before
the plate may be developed. The Division must
transfer quarterly the money in the Collegiate
and Cultural Attraction Plate Account derived
from the sale of Home Care and Hospice plates
to The Association for Home and Hospice Care
of North Carolina for its educational programs
in support of home care and hospice care in
North Carolina.

(b53) **Home of American Golf.** -- Expired
July 1, 2016.

(b54) HOMES4NC. -- The Division must re-
ceive 300 or more applications for the HOME-
S4NC plate before the plate may be developed.
The Division shall transfer quarterly the money
in the Collegiate and Cultural Attraction Plate
Account derived from the sale of the HOME-
S4NC plates to the NCAR Housing Opportunity
Foundation to promote safe, decent, and afford-
able housing for all in North Carolina.

(b55) **Hospice Care.** -- Expired July 1, 2016.

(b56) I.B.P.O.E.W. -- Expired July 1, 2016.

(b57) **I Support Teachers Plates.** -- Expired
July 1, 2016.

(b58) **In God We Trust.** -- The Division must
receive 300 or more applications for the In God
We Trust plate before the plate may be developed. The Division shall transfer quarterly the
money in the Collegiate and Cultural Attraction
Plate Account derived from the sale of the In
God We Trust plates to the Department of Public Safety to be deposited into The N.C. National
Guard Soldiers and Airmen Assistance Fund of
The Minuteman Partnership to help provide assistance to the families of North Carolina National Guardsmen who have been activated and
deployed in federal service.

(b59) **International Association of Fire
Fighters.** -- The Division shall transfer quarterly the money in the Collegiate and Cultural
Attraction Plate Account derived from the sale
of "International Association of Fire Fighters"
plates to the Professional Firefighters of North
Carolina Charitable Fund.

(b60) **Jaycees.** -- Expired July 1, 2016.

(b61) **Juvenile Diabetes Research Foundation.** -- The Division must receive 300 or more
applications for the Juvenile Diabetes Research
Foundation plate before the plate may be developed. The Division must transfer quarterly the
money in the Collegiate and Cultural Attraction
Plate Account derived from the sale of Juvenile
Diabetes Research Foundation plates to the Tri-
angle Eastern North Carolina Chapter of the

Juvenile Diabetes Research Foundation International, Inc., to provide funding for research to
cure diabetes. The Foundation must distribute
the amount it receives to all Juvenile Diabetes
Research Foundation, Inc., chapters located in
the State in equal shares.

(b62) **Kappa Alpha Order.** -- Expired July 1,
2016.

(b63) **Keeping The Lights On.** -- The Division shall transfer quarterly the money in
the Collegiate and Cultural Attraction Plate
Account derived from the sale of Keeping The
Lights On plates to the UNC Jaycee Burn Center.

(b64) **Kick Cancer for Kids.** -- The Division
shall transfer quarterly the money in the Collegiate and Cultural Attraction Plate Account
derived from the sale of Kick Cancer for Kids
plates as follows:

(1) Fifty percent (50%) to The Children's
Oncology Group Foundation to be used to
provide support for the mission and goals of
the Foundation.

(2) Fifty percent (50%) to Riley's Army,
Inc., to be used to provide support to children with cancer and their families.

(b65) **Kids First Plates.** -- The Division must
receive 300 or more applications for a Kids First
plate before the plate may be developed. The
Division shall transfer quarterly the money in
the Collegiate and Cultural Attraction Plate Account derived from the sale of Kids First plates
to the North CarolinaChildren's Trust Fund established in G.S. 7B-1302.

(b66) **Leukemia & Lymphoma Society.** --
Expired July 1, 2016.

(b67) **Litter Prevention Plates.** -- The Division must receive 300 or more applications for
a Litter Prevention plate before the plate may
be developed. The Division shall transfer quarterly the money in the Collegiate and Cultural
Attraction Plate Account derived from the sale
of the litter prevention plates to the Litter Prevention Account created pursuant to G.S. 136-
125.1.

(b68) **Lung Cancer Research.** -- Expired
July 1, 2016.

(b69) **Maggie Valley Trout Festival.** -- Expired July 1, 2016.

(b70) **March of Dimes Plates.** -- Expired
July 1, 2016.

(b71) **Mission Foundation.** -- Expired
July 1, 2016.

(b72) **Morehead Planetarium.** -- Expired
July 1, 2016.

(b73) **Morgan Horse Club.** -- Expired July 1,
2016.

(b74) **Mountains-to-Sea Trail.** -- The Division must receive 300 or more applications for
the "Mountains-to-Sea Trail" plate before the
plate may be developed. The Division shall
transfer quarterly the money in the Collegiate

Chapter 20

and Cultural Attraction Plate Account derived from the sale of "Mountains-to-Sea Trail" plates to the Friends of the Mountains-to-Sea Trail, Inc., to be used to fund trail projects and related administrative and operating expenses.

(b75) **Municipality Plate.** -- Expired July 1, 2016.

(b76) **National Kidney Foundation.** -- Expired July 1, 2016.

(b77) **National Law Enforcement Officers Memorial.** -- Expired July 1, 2016.

(b78) **National Multiple Sclerosis Society.** -- The Division must receive 300 or more applications for the National Multiple Sclerosis Society plate before the plate may be developed. The Division shall transfer quarterly the money in the Collegiate and Cultural Attraction Plate Account derived from the sale of the National Multiple Sclerosis Society plates to the National Multiple Sclerosis Society for its public awareness programs.

(b79) **National Wild Turkey Federation.** -- The Division must receive 300 or more applications for the National Wild Turkey Federation plate before the plate may be developed. The Division shall transfer quarterly the money in the Collegiate and Cultural Attraction Plate Account derived from the sale of the National Wild Turkey Federation plates to the North Carolina State Chapter of the National Wild Turkey Federation for special projects to benefit the public.

(b80) **Native American.** -- The Division must receive 300 or more applications for the "Native American" plate before the plate may be developed. The Division shall transfer quarterly the money in the Collegiate and Cultural Attraction Plate Account derived from the sale of "Native American" plates to the Native American College Fund for scholarships to be awarded to Native American students from North Carolina.

(b81) **Native Brook Trout.** -- The Division must receive 300 or more applications for the Native Brook Trout plate before the plate may be developed. The Division must transfer quarterly the money in the Collegiate and Cultural Attraction Plate Account derived from the sale of Native Brook Trout plates to the North Carolina Wildlife Resources Commission to be used to fund public access to and habitat protection of brook trout waters.

(b82) **NC Agribusiness.** -- Expired July 1, 2016.

(b83) **NC Beekeepers.** -- Expired July 1, 2016.

(b84) **NC Children's Promise.** -- Expired July 1, 2016.

(b85) **NC Civil War.** -- Expired July 1, 2016.

(b86) **NC Coastal Federation.** -- The Division must receive 300 or more applications for a NC Coastal Federation plate before the plate may be developed. The Division shall transfer quarterly the money in the Collegiate and

Cultural Attraction Plate Account derived from the sale of NC Coastal Federation plates to the North Carolina Coastal Federation, Inc.

(b87) **NC FIRST Robotics.** -- Expired July 1, 2016.

(b88) **NC Fisheries Association.** -- Expired July 1, 2016.

(b89) **NC Horse Council.** -- The Division must receive 300 or more applications for the "NC Horse Council" plate before the plate may be developed. The Division shall transfer quarterly the money in the Collegiate and Cultural Attraction Plate Account derived from the sale of "NC Horse Council" plates to the North Carolina Horse Council, Inc., to promote and enhance the equine industry in North Carolina.

(b90) **NC Mining.** -- Expired July 1, 2016.

(b91) **NCSC.** -- Expired July 1, 2016.

(b92) **NCSurveyors.** -- The applicable requirements of G.S. 20-79.3A shall be met before the NCSurveyors plate may be developed. The Division shall transfer quarterly the money in the Collegiate and Cultural Attraction Plate Account derived from the sale of NCSurveyors plates to the North Carolina Society of Surveyors Education Foundation, Inc., to be used to grant financial assistance to those persons genuinely interested in pursuing or continuing to pursue a formal education in the field of surveying.

(b93) **NC Tennis Foundation.** -- The Division must receive 300 or more applications for the NC Tennis Foundation plate before the plate may be developed. The Division must transfer quarterly the money in the Collegiate and Cultural Attraction Plate Account derived from the sale of NC Tennis Foundation plates to the North Carolina Tennis Foundation, Inc., to provide funding for development and growth of tennis as a sport in North Carolina.

(b94) **NC Trout Unlimited.** -- The Division must receive 300 or more applications for an NC Trout Unlimited plate before the plate may be developed. The Division shall transfer quarterly the money in the Collegiate and Cultural Attraction Plate Account derived from the sale of NC Trout Unlimited plates to North Carolina Trout Unlimited for its programs.

(b95) **NC Veterinary Medical Association.** -- Expired July 1, 2016.

(b96) **NC Victim Assistance Network.** -- Expired July 1, 2016.

(b97) **NC Wildlife Federation.** -- Expired July 1, 2016.

(b98) **NC Youth Soccer Association.** -- Expired July 1, 2016.

(b99) **North Carolina 4-H Development Fund.** -- Expired July 1, 2016.

(b100) **North Carolina Bluegrass Association.** -- Expired July 1, 2016.

(b101) **North Carolina Cattlemen's Association.** -- Expired July 1, 2016.

Chapter 20

(b102) **North Carolina Emergency Management Association.** -- Expired July 1, 2016.

(b103) **North Carolina Green Industry Council.** -- Expired July 1, 2016.

(b104) **North Carolina Libraries.** -- Expired July 1, 2016.

(b105) **North Carolina Master Gardener.** -- The Division must receive 300 or more applications for the "North Carolina Master Gardener" plate before the plate may be developed. The Division shall transfer quarterly the money in the Collegiate and Cultural Attraction Plate Account derived from the sale of "North Carolina Master Gardener" plates to the Master Gardener's Endowment Fund maintained by the Agricultural Foundation of North Carolina State University to be used for educational programs by trained volunteers who work in partnership with their county Cooperative Extension offices to extend information in consumer horticulture.

(b106) **North Carolina Paddle Festival.** -- Expired July 1, 2016.

(b107) **North Carolina Sheriffs' Association.** -- The applicable requirements of G.S. 20-79.3A shall be met before the North Carolina Sheriffs' Association plate may be developed. The Division shall transfer quarterly the money in the Collegiate and Cultural Attraction Plate Account derived from the sale of North Carolina Sheriffs' Association plates to the North Carolina Sheriffs' Association, Inc., to support the operating expenses of the North Carolina Sheriffs' Association.

(b108) **North Carolina Wildlife Habitat Foundation.** -- The Division must receive 300 or more applications for the North Carolina Wildlife Habitat Foundation plate before the plate may be developed. The Division shall transfer quarterly the money in the Collegiate and Cultural Attraction Plate Account derived from the sale of the North Carolina Wildlife Habitat Foundation plates to the North Carolina Wildlife Habitat Foundation for its programs.

(b109) **Nurses.** -- The Division must receive 300 or more applications for a Nurses plate before the plate may be developed. The Division shall transfer quarterly the money in the Collegiate and Cultural Attraction Plate Account derived from the sale of Nurses plates to the NC Foundation for Nursing for nursing scholarships for citizens of North Carolina to be awarded annually.

(b110) **Olympic Games.** -- The Division may not issue an Olympic Games special plate unless it receives 300 or more applications for the plate and the U.S. Olympic Committee licenses, without charge, the State to develop a plate bearing the Olympic Games symbol and name. The Division must transfer quarterly the money in the Collegiate and Cultural Attraction Plate Account derived from the sale of Olympic Games plates to North Carolina Amateur Sports, which will allocate the funds as follows:

(1) Sixty-seven percent (67%) to the U.S. Olympic Committee to assist in training Olympic athletes.

(2) Thirty-three percent (33%) to North Carolina Amateur Sports to assist with administration of the State Games of North Carolina.

(3) Repealed by Session Laws 2013-376, s. 7, effective July 29, 2013.

(b111) **Omega Psi Phi Fraternity Plates.** -- The Division must receive 300 or more applications for an Omega Psi Phi Fraternity plate and receive any necessary licenses, without charge, from Omega Psi Phi Fraternity, Incorporated, before the plate may be developed. The Division must transfer quarterly the money in the Collegiate and Cultural Attraction Plate Account derived from the sale of Omega Psi Phi Fraternity plates to the Carolina Uplift Foundation, Inc., for youth activity and scholarship programs.

(b112) **Operation Coming Home.** -- Expired July 1, 2016.

(b113) **Order of the Eastern Star Prince Hall Affiliated.** -- The Division shall transfer quarterly the money in the Collegiate and Cultural Attraction Plate Account derived from the sale of "Order of the Eastern Star Prince Hall Affiliated" plates to The Most Worshipful Prince Hall Grand Lodge of Free and Accepted Masons of North Carolina and Jurisdiction, Inc.

(b114) **Order of the Long Leaf Pine.** -- The Order of the Long Leaf Pine plate is not subject to the provisions of G.S. 20-79.3A or G.S. 20-79.8, including the minimum number of applications required under G.S. 20-63(b1). The Division shall transfer quarterly the money in the Collegiate and Cultural Attraction Plate Account derived from the sale of Order of the Long Leaf Pine plates to the General Fund.

(b115) **Outer Banks Preservation Association.** -- Expired July 1, 2016.

(b116) **Pamlico-Tar River Foundation.** -- Expired July 1, 2016.

(b117) **Pancreatic Cancer Awareness.** -- Expired July 1, 2016.

(b118) **P.E.O. Sisterhood.** -- Expired July 1, 2016.

(b119) **Phi Beta Sigma Fraternity.** -- The Division must receive 300 or more applications for the "Phi Beta Sigma Fraternity" plate before the plate may be developed. The Division shall transfer quarterly the money in the Collegiate and Cultural Attraction Plate Account derived from the sale of "Phi Beta Sigma Fraternity" plates to the Phi Beta Sigma Fraternity, Inc., to provide funding for scholarships, education, and professional development, or similar programs. None of the proceeds from this special plate may be distributed to any board member as compensation or as an honorarium.

(b120) **Piedmont Airlines.** -- The Division must receive 300 or more applications for a "Piedmont Airlines" plate before the plate may be developed. The Division must transfer quarterly the money in the Collegiate and Cultural Attraction Plate Account derived from the sale of "Piedmont Airlines" plates to Piedmont Silver Eagles Charitable Funds, Inc., to be used for scholarships and family assistance for Piedmont Airlines employees and their families, including surviving spouses and dependents, suffering economic hardship.

(b121) **Pisgah Conservancy.** -- The applicable requirements of G.S. 20-79.3A shall be met before the Pisgah Conservancy plate may be developed. The Division shall transfer quarterly the money in the Collegiate and Cultural Attraction Plate Account derived from the sale of Pisgah Conservancy plates to The Pisgah Conservancy to be used to provide support for the mission and goals of the Conservancy.

(b122) **POW/MIA Bring Them Home.** -- The Division shall transfer quarterly the money in the Collegiate and Cultural Attraction Plate Account derived from the sale of POW/MIA Bring Them Home plates to Rolling Thunder, Inc., Chapter #1 North Carolina.

(b123) **Prince Hall Mason.** -- The Division must receive 300 or more applications for a Prince Hall Mason plate before the plate may be developed. The Division must transfer quarterly the money in the Collegiate and Cultural Attraction Plate Account derived from the sale of Prince Hall Mason plates to The Most Worshipful Prince Hall Grand Lodge of Free and Accepted Masons of North Carolina and Jurisdiction, Inc., to be used for scholarships, family assistance, and other charitable causes.

(b124) **Professional Engineer.** -- Expired July 1, 2016.

(b125) **Red Drum.** -- Expired July 1, 2016.

(b126) **Retired Legislator.** -- The Division shall transfer quarterly the money in the Collegiate and Cultural Attraction Plate Account derived from the sale of Retired Legislator plates to the State Capitol Foundation, Inc., to be used to provide support for the mission and goals of the foundation.

(b127) **RiverLink.** -- Expired July 1, 2016.

(b128) **Rocky Mountain Elk Foundation.** -- The Division must receive 300 or more applications for a Rocky Mountain Elk Foundation plate before the plate may be developed. The Division must transfer quarterly the money in the Collegiate and Cultural Attraction Account derived from the sale of Rocky Mountain Elk Foundation plates to Rocky Mountain Elk Foundation, Inc.

(b129) **Ronald McDonald House.** -- The Division must receive 300 or more applications for the "Ronald McDonald House" plate before the plate may be developed. The Division shall transfer quarterly the money in the Collegiate and Cultural Attraction Plate Account derived from the sale of "Ronald McDonald House" plates to Ronald McDonald House Charities of North Carolina, Inc., to be used for Ronald McDonald Houses located within North Carolina and related administrative and operating expenses.

(b130) **Save the Honey Bee (HB).** -- The applicable requirements of G.S. 20-79.3A shall be met before the Save the Honey Bee plate may be developed. The Division shall transfer quarterly the money in the Collegiate and Cultural Attraction Plate Account derived from the sale of Save the Honey Bee plates to the North Carolina State University Apiculture Program.

(b131) **Save the Honey Bee (SB).** -- The applicable requirements of G.S. 20-79.3A shall be met before the Save the Honey Bee plate may be developed. The Division shall transfer quarterly one-half of the money in the Collegiate and Cultural Attraction Plate Account derived from the sale of Save the Honey Bee plates to the Grandfather Mountain Stewardship Foundation to be used to support the Honey Bee Haven and honey bee educational programs and shall transfer one-half of the money in the Collegiate and Cultural Attraction Plate Account derived from the sale of Save the Honey Bee plates to the North Carolina State University Apiculture Program to be used to support work on honey bee biology and apicultural science.

(b132) **Save the Sea Turtles.** -- The Division must receive 300 or more applications for a Save the Sea Turtles plate before the plate may be developed. The Division must transfer quarterly the money in the Collegiate and Cultural Attraction Plate Account derived from the sale of Save the Sea Turtles plates to The Karen Beasley Sea Turtle Rescue and Rehabilitation Center.

(b133) **Scenic Rivers Plates.** -- Expired July 1, 2016.

(b134) **School Technology Plates.** -- Expired July 1, 2016.

(b135) **SCUBA.** -- The Division must receive 300 or more applications for the SCUBA plate before the plate may be developed. The Division shall transfer quarterly the money in the Collegiate and Cultural Plate Account derived for the sale of the SCUBA plates to the Division of Marine Fisheries for the purpose of developing the State's artificial reefs.

(b136) **Shag Dancing.** -- The Division must receive 300 or more applications for the Shag Dancing plate before the plate may be developed. The Division shall transfer quarterly the money in the Collegiate and Cultural Attraction Plate Account derived from the sale of Shag Dancing plates to the Hall of Fame Foundation.

Chapter 20

(b137) **Share the Road.** -- The Division must receive 300 or more applications for the Share the Road plate before the plate may be developed. The Division shall transfer quarterly the money in the Collegiate and Cultural Attraction Plate Account derived from the sale of the Share the Road plates to the Department of Transportation, Division of Bicycle and Pedestrian Transportation, for its programs.

(b138) **Soil and Water Conservation Plates.** -- Expired July 1, 2016.

(b139) **Special Forces Association.** -- Expired July 1, 2016.

(b140) **Special Olympics Plates.** -- Expired July 1, 2016.

(b141) **S.T.A.R.** -- Expired July 1, 2016.

(b142) **State Attraction Plates.** -- The Division must receive 300 or more applications for a State attraction plate before the plate may be developed. The Division must transfer quarterly the money in the Collegiate and Cultural Attraction Plate Account derived from the sale of State attraction plates to the organizations named below in proportion to the number of State attraction plates sold representing that organization:

(1) **Aurora Fossil Museum.** -- The revenue derived from the special plate shall be transferred quarterly to the Aurora Fossil Museum Foundation, Inc., to be used for educational programs, for enhancing collections, and for operating expenses of the Aurora Fossil Museum.

(2) **Blue Ridge Parkway Foundation.** -- The revenue derived from the special plate shall be transferred quarterly to Blue Ridge Parkway Foundation for use in promoting and preserving the Blue Ridge Parkway as a scenic attraction in North Carolina. A person may obtain from the Division a special registration plate under this subdivision for the registered owner of a motor vehicle or a motorcycle. The registration fees and the restrictions on the issuance of a specialized registration plate for a motorcycle are the same as for any motor vehicle. The Division must receive a minimum of 300 applications to develop a special registration plate for a motorcycle.

(3) **Friends of the Appalachian Trail.** -- The revenue derived from the special plate shall be transferred quarterly to The Appalachian Trail Conference to be used for educational materials, preservation programs, trail maintenance, trailway and viewshed acquisitions, trailway and viewshed easement acquisitions, capital improvements for the portions of the Appalachian Trail and connecting trails that are located in North Carolina, and related administrative and operating expenses.

(4) **Friends of the Great Smoky Mountains National Park.** -- The revenue derived from the special plate shall be transferred quarterly to the Friends of the Great Smoky Mountains National Park, Inc., to be used for educational materials, preservation programs, capital improvements for the portion of the Great Smoky Mountains National Park that is located in North Carolina, and operating expenses of the Great Smoky Mountains National Park.

(5) **The North Carolina Aquariums.** -- The revenue derived from the special plate shall be transferred quarterly to the North Carolina Aquarium Society, Inc., for its programs in support of the North Carolina Aquariums.

(6) **The North Carolina Arboretum.** -- The revenue derived from the special plate shall be transferred quarterly to The North Carolina Arboretum Society and used to help the Society obtain grants for the North Carolina Arboretum and for capital improvements to the North Carolina Arboretum.

(7) **The North Carolina Maritime Museum.** -- The revenue derived from the special plate shall be transferred quarterly to Friends of the Museum, North Carolina Maritime Museum, Inc., to be used for educational programs and conservation programs and for operating expenses of the North Carolina Maritime Museum.

(8) **The North Carolina Museum of Natural Sciences.** -- The revenue derived from the special plate shall be transferred quarterly to the Friends of the North Carolina State Museum of Natural Sciences for its programs in support of the museum.

(9) **North Carolina State Parks.** -- The revenue derived from the special plate shall be transferred quarterly to Friends of State Parks, Inc., for its educational, conservation, and other programs in support of the operations of the State Parks System established in Part 32 of Article 7 [Article 2] of Chapter 143B of the General Statutes.

(10) **The North Carolina Transportation Museum.** -- The revenue derived from the special plate shall be transferred quarterly to the North Carolina Transportation Museum Foundation to be used for educational programs and conservation programs and for operating expenses of the North Carolina Transportation Museum.

(11) **The North Carolina Zoological Society.** -- The revenue derived from the special plate shall be transferred quarterly to The North Carolina Zoological Society, Incorporated, to be used for educational programs and conservation programs at

Chapter 20

the North Carolina Zoo at Asheboro and for operating expenses of the North Carolina Zoo at Asheboro.

(12) **"Old Baldy," Bald Head Island Lighthouse.** -- The revenue derived from the special plate shall be transferred quarterly to the Old Baldy Foundation, Inc., for its programs in support of the Bald Head Island Lighthouse.

(13) U.S.S. North Carolina Battleship Commission. -- The revenue derived from the special plate shall be transferred quarterly to the U.S.S. North Carolina Battleship Commission to be used for educational programs and preservation programs on the U.S.S. North Carolina (BB-55) and for operating expenses of the U.S.S. North Carolina Battleship Commission.

(b143) **Stock Car Racing Theme.** -- The Division may issue any plate in this series without a minimum number of applications if the person providing the State with the license to use the words, logos, trademarks, or designs associated with the plate produces the plate for the State without a minimum order quantity.

The cost of the Stock Car Racing Theme plate shall include all costs to produce blank plates for issuance by the Division. Notwithstanding G.S. 66-58(b), the Division or the Division of Adult Correction and Juvenile Justice of the Department of Public Safety may contract for the production of the blank plates in this series to be issued by the Division, provided the plates meet or exceed the State's specifications including durability and retroreflectivity, and provided the plates are manufactured using high-quality embossable aluminum. The cost of the blank plates to the State shall be substantially equivalent to the price paid to the Division of Adult Correction and Juvenile Justice of the Department of Public Safety for license tags, as provided in G.S. 66-58(b)(15).

The Division shall transfer quarterly the money in the Collegiate and Cultural Attraction Plate Account derived from the sale of Stock Car Racing Theme plates to the North Carolina Motorsports Foundation, Inc.; except that the Division shall transfer quarterly the money in the Collegiate and Cultural Attraction Plate Account derived from the sale of Charlotte Motor Speedway plates to Speedway Children's Charities.

(b144) **Support NC Education.** -- Expired July 1, 2016.

(b145) **Support Our Troops.** -- The Division must receive 300 or more applications for a Support Our Troops plate before the plate may be developed. The Division shall transfer quarterly the money in the Collegiate and Cultural Attraction Plate Account derived from the sale of Support Our Troops plates to NC Support Our Troops, Inc., to be used to provide support and assistance to the troops and their families.

(b146) **Support Soccer.** -- The Division must receive 300 or more applications for the "Support Soccer" plate before the plate may be developed. The Division shall transfer quarterly the money in the Collegiate and Cultural Attraction Plate Account derived from the sale of "Support Soccer" plates to the North Carolina Soccer Hall of Fame, Inc., to provide funding to promote the sport of soccer in North Carolina.

(b147) **Surveyor Plate.** -- The Division must receive 300 or more applications for a Surveyor plate before the plate may be developed. The Division shall transfer quarterly the money in the Collegiate and Cultural Attraction Plate Account derived from the sale of Surveyor plates to The North Carolina Society of Surveyors Education Foundation, Inc., for public educational programs.

(b148) **Sustainable Fisheries.** -- Expired July 1, 2016.

(b149) **Toastmasters Club.** -- Expired July 1, 2016.

(b150) **Topsail Island Shoreline Protection.** -- Expired July 1, 2016.

(b151) **Travel and Tourism.** -- Expired July 1, 2016.

(b152) **Turtle Rescue Team.** -- Expired July 1, 2016.

(b153) **United States Service Academy.** -- The Division must transfer quarterly the money in the Collegiate and Cultural Attraction Plate Account derived from the sale of United States Service Academy plates to the United Services Organization of North Carolina to support its mission to lead the way to enriching the lives of America's military in North Carolina.

(b154) **University Health Systems of Eastern Carolina.** -- Expired July 1, 2016.

(b155) **US Equine Rescue League.** -- Expired July 1, 2016.

(b156) **USO of NC.** -- Expired July 1, 2016.

(b157) **The V Foundation for Cancer Research.** -- The Division must receive 300 or more applications for a V Foundation plate before the plate may be developed. The Division shall transfer quarterly the money in the Collegiate and Cultural Attraction Plate Account derived from the sale of V Foundation plates to The V Foundation for Cancer Research to fund cancer research grants.

(b158) **Volunteers in Law Enforcement.** -- Expired July 1, 2016.

(b159) **Wildlife Resources Plates.** -- The Division must receive 300 or more applications for a wildlife resources plate with a picture representing a particular native wildlife species occurring in North Carolina before the plate may be developed. The Division must transfer quarterly the money in the Collegiate and Cultural Attraction Plate Account derived from the sale of wildlife resources plates to the Wildlife Conservation Account established by G.S. 143-247.2.

(b160) **Wrightsville Beach.** -- The Division shall transfer quarterly the money in the Collegiate and Cultural Attraction Plate Account derived from the sale of Wrightsville Beach plates to the Town of Wrightsville Beach to help fund the Town's continuing efforts to maintain and improve recreational opportunities for residents and visitors of Wrightsville Beach.

(b161) **YMCA.** -- Expired July 1, 2016.

(b162) **Zeta Phi Beta Sorority.** -- The Division must receive 300 or more applications for a Zeta Phi Beta Sorority plate before the plate may be developed. The Division shall transfer quarterly the money in the Collegiate and Cultural Attraction Plate Account derived from the sale of Zeta Phi Beta Sorority plates to the Zeta Phi Beta Sorority Education Foundation, through the Raleigh office, for the benefit of undergraduate scholarships in this State.

(c) **General.** -- An application for a special license plate named in this section may be made at any time during the year. If the application is made to replace an existing current valid plate, the special plate must be issued with the appropriate decals attached. No refund shall be made to the applicant for any unused portion remaining on the original plate. The request for a special license plate named in this section may be combined with a request that the plate be a personalized license plate.

(c1) In accordance with G.S. 143C-1-2, the transfers mandated in this section are appropriations made by law.

(d) through (g) Repealed by Session Laws 1991 (Regular Session, 1992), c. 1042, s. 3.

History.

1991, c. 758, s. 1; 1991 (Reg. Sess., 1992), c. 1007, s. 33; c. 1042, s. 3; 1993, c. 543, s. 5; 1995, c. 433, s. 4; 1997-427, s. 2; 1997-477, s. 4; 1997-484, s. 6; 1999-277, s. 4; 1999-403, s. 4; 1999-450, s. 4; 2000-159, ss. 5, 6; 2000-163, s. 3; 2001-498, ss. 6(a), 6(b); 2002-134, s. 7; 2003-11, s. 4; 2003-68, s. 4; 2003-424, ss. 5, 6; 2004-131, s. 5; 2004-185, s. 5; 2004-200, s. 4; 2005-216, ss. 6, 7; 2005-435, s. 40; 2006-209, ss. 5, 6, 7; 2007-323, s. 27.2(a); 2007-345, s. 10.1; 2007-400, ss. 5, 6; 2007-483, ss. 6(a), 7, 8(c); 2010-31, s. 11.4(m); 2010-95, s. 35; 2011-145, ss. 19.1(g), (h), 13.25(*ll*); 2011-392, ss. 6, 7; 2013-155, s. 2; 2013-360, s. 14.3B; 2013-376, ss. 5-8; 2013-414, s. 57(d); 2014-100, s. 8.11(c); 2015-241, ss. 14.30(dd1), 15.4(a), 29.40(d), (j), (k), (n), (p); 2017-100, s. 3; 2017-107, s. 4; 2017-114, s. 4; 2017-186, ss. 2 (mmmm), 3(a); 2018-74, ss. 11(c), (e), 12(f), 14(c), 14.5; 2018-77, ss. 2(f), 3, 3.5(c); 2019-213, s. 2(d)

N.C. Gen. Stat. § 20-82

Repealed by Session Laws 1995, c. 163, s. 3.

PART 6
VEHICLES OF NONRESIDENTS OF STATE; PERMANENT PLATES; HIGHWAY PATROL

§ 20-83. Registration by nonresidents

(a) When a resident carrier of this State interchanges a properly licensed trailer or semi-trailer with another carrier who is a resident of another state, and adequate records are on file in his office to verify such interchanges, the North Carolina licensed carrier may use the trailer licensed in such other state the same as if it is his own during the time the nonresident carrier is using the North Carolina licensed trailer.

(b) Motor vehicles duly registered in a state or territory which are not allowed exemptions by the Commissioner, as provided for in the preceding paragraph, desiring to make occasional trips into or through the State of North Carolina, or operate in this State for a period not exceeding 30 days, may be permitted the same use and privileges of the highways of this State as provided for similar vehicles regularly licensed in this State, by procuring from the Commissioner trip licenses upon forms and under rules and regulations to be adopted by the Commissioner, good for use for a period of 30 days upon the payment of a fee in compensation for said privilege equivalent to one tenth of the annual fee which would be chargeable against said vehicle if regularly licensed in this State: Provided that only one such permit allowed by this section shall be issued for the use of the same vehicle within the same registration year. Provided, however, that nothing in this provision shall prevent the extension of the privileges of the use of the roads of this State to vehicles of other states under the reciprocity provisions provided by law: Provided further, that nothing herein contained shall prevent the owners of vehicles from other states from licensing such vehicles in the State of North Carolina under the same terms and the same fees as like vehicles are licensed by owners resident in this State.

(c) Every nonresident, including any foreign corporation carrying on business within this State and owning and operating in such business any motor vehicle, trailer or semitrailer within this State, shall be required to register each such vehicle and pay the same fees therefor as is required with reference to like vehicles owned by residents of this State.

History.

1937, c. 407, s. 47; 1941, cc. 99, 365; 1957, c. 681, s. 1; 1961, c. 642, s. 4; 1967, c. 1090

§ 20-84. Permanent registration plates; State Highway Patrol

(a) **General.** -- The Division may issue a permanent registration plate for a motor vehicle owned by one of the entities authorized to have a permanent registration plate in this section. To obtain a permanent registration plate, an authorized representative of the entity must provide proof of ownership, provide proof of financial responsibility as required by G.S. 20-309, and pay a fee of six dollars ($ 6.00). A permanent plate issued under this section may be transferred as provided in G.S. 20-78 to a replacement vehicle of the same classification. A permanent registration plate issued under this section must be a distinctive color and bear the word "permanent". In addition, a permanent registration plate issued under subdivision (b) (1) of this section must have distinctive color and design that is readily distinguishable from all other permanent registration plates issued under this section. Every eligible entity that receives a permanent registration plate under this section shall ensure that the permanent registration plate is registered under a single name. That single name shall be the full legal name of the eligible entity.

(b) **Permanent Registration Plates.** -- The Division may issue permanent plates for the following motor vehicles:

(1) A motor vehicle owned by the State or one of its agencies.

(2) A motor vehicle owned by a county, city or town.

(3) A motor vehicle owned by a board of education.

(3a) A motor vehicle that is owned and exclusively operated by a nonprofit corporation authorized under G.S. 115C-218.5 to operate a charter school and identified by a permanent decal or painted marking disclosing the name of the nonprofit corporation. The motor vehicle shall only be used for student transportation and official charter school related activities.

(4) Repealed by Session Laws 2012-159, s. 1, effective July 1, 2012.

(5) A motor vehicle owned by the civil air patrol.

(6) A motor vehicle owned by an incorporated emergency rescue squad.

(7) through (9) Repealed by Session Laws 2012-159, s. 1, effective July 1, 2012.

(10) A motor vehicle owned by a rural fire department, agency, or association.

(11) Repealed by Session Laws 2012-159, s. 1, effective July 1, 2012.

(12) A motor vehicle owned by a local chapter of the American National Red Cross and used for emergency or disaster work.

(13) through (16) Repealed by Session Laws 2012-159, s. 1, effective July 1, 2012.

(17) A motor vehicle owned by a community college. A community college vehicle purchased with State equipment funds shall be issued a permanent registration plate with the same distinctive color and design as a permanent registration plate issued under subdivision (1) of this subsection.

(18) A motor vehicle that is owned and operated by a sanitary district created under Part 2 of Article 2 of Chapter 130A of the General Statutes.

(19) Any motor vehicle owned by a federally recognized tribe.

(20) A motor vehicle owned by a public transportation service provider that is a designated recipient or direct recipient of Federal Transit Administration formula grant funds pursuant to 49 U.S.C. § 5311 or 49 U.S.C. § 5307.

(c) **State Highway Patrol.** -- In lieu of all other registration requirements, the Commissioner shall each year assign to the State Highway Patrol, upon payment of six dollars ($ 6.00) per registration plate, a sufficient number of regular registration plates of the same letter prefix and in numerical sequence beginning with number 100 to meet the requirements of the State Highway Patrol for use on Division vehicles assigned to the State Highway Patrol. The commander of the Patrol shall, when such plates are assigned, issue to each member of the State Highway Patrol a registration plate for use upon the Division vehicle assigned to the member pursuant to G.S. 20-190 and assign a registration plate to each Division service vehicle operated by the Patrol. An index of such assignments of registration plates shall be kept at each State Highway Patrol radio station and a copy of it shall be furnished to the registration division of the Division. Information as to the individual assignments of the registration plates shall be made available to the public upon request to the same extent and in the same manner as regular registration information. The commander, when necessary, may reassign registration plates provided that the reassignment shall appear upon the index required under this subsection within 20 days after the reassignment.

(d) **Revocation.** -- The Division may revoke all permanent registration plates issued to eligible entities for vehicles that are 90 days or more past due for a vehicle inspection, as required by G.S. 20-183.4C. This subsection does not limit or restrict the authority of the Division to revoke permanent registration plates pursuant to other applicable law.

History.
1937, c. 407, s. 48; 1939, c. 275; 1949, c. 583, s. 1; 1951, c. 388; 1953, c. 1264; 1955, cc. 368, 382; 1967, c. 284;

1969, c. 800; 1971, c. 460, s. 1; 1975, c. 548; c. 716, s. 5; 1977, c. 370, s. 1; 1979, c. 801, s. 9; 1981 (Reg. Sess., 1982), c. 1159; 1983, c. 593, ss. 1, 2; 1987 (Reg. Sess., 1988), c. 885; 1991 (Reg. Sess., 1992), c. 1030, s. 11; 1997-443, s. 11A.118(a); 1999-220, s. 3; 2000-159, s. 7; 2012-159, s. 1; 2014-101, s. 6.6(a); 2014-108, s. 3(a); 2015-241, s. 29.40(r); 2016-94, s. 35.16

N.C. Gen. Stat. § 20-84.1

Repealed by Session Laws 1999-220, s. 4, effective July 1, 1999.

PART 6A
RENTAL VEHICLES

§ 20-84.2. Definition; reciprocity; Commissioner's powers

(a) The term rental vehicle when used herein shall mean and include any motor vehicle which is rented or leased to another by its owner for a period of not more than 30 days solely for the transportation of the lessee or the private hauling of the lessee's personal property.

(b) Rental vehicles owned or operated by any nonresident person engaged in the business of leasing such vehicles for use in intrastate or interstate commerce shall be extended full reciprocity and exempted from registration fees only in instances where:

(1) Such person has validly licensed all rental vehicles owned by him in the state wherein the owner actually resides; provided, that such state affords equal recognition, either in fact or in law to such vehicles licensed in the State of North Carolina and operating similarly within the owner's state of residence; and further provided, that such person is not engaged in this State in the business of leasing rental vehicles; or where

(2) Such person operates vehicles which are a part of a common fleet of vehicles which are easily identifiable as a part of such fleet and such person has validly licensed in the State of North Carolina a percentage of the total number of vehicles in each weight classification in such fleet which represents the percentage of total miles travelled in North Carolina by all vehicles in each weight classification of such fleet to total miles travelled in all jurisdictions in which such fleet is operated by all vehicles in each weight classification of such fleet.

(c) The Commissioner of Motor Vehicles requires such person to submit under oath such information as is deemed necessary for fairly administering this section. The Commissioner's determination, after hearing, as to the number of vehicles in each weight classification to be licensed in North Carolina shall be final.

Any person who licenses vehicles under subsection (b)(2) above shall keep and preserve for three years the mileage records on which the percentage of the total fleet is determined. Upon request these records shall be submitted or made available to the Commissioner of Motor Vehicles for audit or review, or the owner or operator shall pay reasonable costs of an audit by the duly appointed representative of the Commissioner at the place where the records are kept.

If the Commissioner determines that the person licensing vehicles under subsection (b)(2) above should have licensed more vehicles in North Carolina or that such person's records are insufficient for proper determination the Commissioner may deny that person the right or any further benefits under this subsection until the correct number of vehicles have been licensed, and all taxes determined by the Commissioner to be due have been paid.

(d) Upon payment by the owner of the prescribed fee, the Division shall issue registration certificates and plates for the percentage of vehicles determined by the Commissioner. Thereafter, all rental vehicles properly identified and licensed in any state, territory, province, country or the District of Columbia, and belonging to such owner, shall be permitted to operate in this State on an interstate or intrastate basis.

History.
1959, c. 1066; 1971, c. 808; 1973, c. 1446, s. 23; 1975, c. 716, s. 5

PART 7
TITLE AND REGISTRATION FEES

§ 20-85. Schedule of fees

(a) The following fees are imposed concerning a certificate of title, a registration card, or a registration plate for a motor vehicle. These fees are payable to the Division and are in addition to the tax imposed by Article 5A of Chapter 105 of the General Statutes:

(1) Each application for certificate of title .... $ 52.00
(2) Each application for duplicate or corrected certificate of title...................... 20.00
(3) Each application of repossessor for certificate of title................................. 20.00
(4) Each transfer of registration..... 20.00
(5) Each set of replacement registration plates 20.00

(6) Each application for duplicate registration card.. 20.00

(7) Each application for recording supplementary lien.. 20.00

(8) Each application for renewing a security interest on a certificate of title or removing a lien or security interest from a certificate of title................................. 20.00

(9) Each application for certificate of title for a motor vehicle transferred to a manufacturer, as defined in G.S. 20-286, or a motor vehicle retailer for the purpose of resale 20.00

(10) Each application for a salvage certificate of title made by an insurer pursuant to G.S. 20-109.1 or by a used motor vehicle dealer pursuant to G.S. 20-109.1(e1) 20.00

(11) Each set of replacement Stock Car Racing Theme plates issued under G.S. 20-79.4 ....25.00.

(a1) *(Effective until June 30, 2031)* One dollar ($ 1.00) of the fee imposed for any transaction assessed a fee under subdivision (a)(1), (a)(2), (a)(3), (a)(7), (a)(8), or (a)(9) of this section shall be credited to the North Carolina Highway Fund. The Division shall use the fees derived from transactions with commission contract agents for the payment of compensation to commission contract agents. An additional twenty cents (20 cent(s)) of the fee imposed for any transaction assessed a fee under subdivision (a)(1) of this section shall be credited to the Mercury Pollution Prevention Fund in the Department of Environmental Quality.

(a1) *(Effective June 30, 2031)* One dollar ($ 1.00) of the fee imposed for any transaction assessed a fee under subdivision (a)(1), (a)(2), (a)(3), (a)(7), (a)(8), or (a)(9) of this section shall be credited to the North Carolina Highway Fund. The Division shall use the fees derived from transactions with commission contract agents for the payment of compensation to commission contract agents.

(a2) From the fees collected under subdivisions (a)(1) through (a)(9) of this section, the Department shall annually credit the sum of four hundred thousand dollars ($ 400,000) to the Reserve for Visitor Centers in the Highway Fund.

(b) Except as otherwise provided in subsections (a1) and (a2) of this section, the fees collected under subdivisions (a)(1) through (a)(9) of this section shall be credited to the North Carolina Highway Trust Fund. The fees collected under subdivision (a)(10) of this section shall be credited to the Highway Fund.

(c) The Division shall not collect a fee for a certificate of title for a motor vehicle entitled to a permanent registration plate under G.S. 20-84.

History.
1937, c. 407, s. 49; 1943, c. 648; 1947, c. 219, s. 9; 1955, c. 554, s. 4; 1961, c. 360, s. 19; c. 835, s. 11; 1975, c. 430; c. 716, s. 5; c. 727; c. 875, s. 4; c. 879, s. 46; 1979, c. 801, s. 11; 1981, c. 690, s. 19; 1989, c. 692, s. 2.1; c. 700, s. 1; c. 770, s. 74.11; 1991, c. 193, s. 8; 1993, c. 467, s. 5; 1995, c. 50, s. 2; c. 390, s. 34; c. 509, s. 135.2(i), (j); 1999-220, s. 2; 2004-77, s. 2; 2004-185, s. 6; 2005-276, s. 44.1(k); 2005-384, s. 2; 2006-255, s. 5; 2006-264, s. 35.5; 2007-142, s. 8; 2011-145, ss. 28.30(a), 31.11; 2011-391, s. 54; 2013-183, s. 2.1; 2013-360, s. 34.16(b); 2013-400, s. 5; 2015-241, ss. 14.30(u), 29.30(j); 2016-59, s. 5; 2016-94, ss. 14.1(a), 35.3(a); 2017-57, s. 34.37(a); 2019-153, s. 5; 2020-74, s. 7(c)

§ 20-85.1. Registration by mail; one-day title service; fees

(a) The owner of a vehicle registered in North Carolina may renew that vehicle registration by mail.

(b) The Commissioner and the employees of the Division designated by the Commissioner may prepare and deliver upon request a certificate of title, charging a fee of ninety-eight dollars ($ 98.00) for one-day title service, in lieu of the title fee required by G.S. 20-85(a). The fee for one-day title service must be paid by cash or by certified check. This fee shall be credited to the Highway Trust Fund.

(c) Repealed by Session Laws 2010-132, s. 8, effective December 1, 2010, and applicable to offenses committed on or after that date.

History.
1983, c. 50, s. 1; 1989, c. 692, s. 2.2; c. 700, s. 1; 1991, c. 689, s. 324; 2005-276, s. 44.1 (*l*); 2010-132, s. 8; 2015-241, s. 29.30(k)

§ 20-86. Penalty for engaging in a "for-hire" business without proper license plates

Any person, firm or corporation engaged in the business of transporting persons or property for compensation, except as otherwise provided in this Article, shall, before engaging in such business, pay the license fees prescribed by this Article and secure the license plates provided for vehicles operated for hire. Any person, firm or corporation operating vehicles for hire without having paid the tax prescribed or using private plates on such vehicles shall be liable for an additional tax of twenty-five dollars ($ 25.00) for each vehicle in addition to the normal fees provided in this Article; provided, that when the vehicle subject to for-hire license has attached thereto a trailer or semitrailer, each unit in the combination, including the tractor, trailer and/or semitrailer, shall be subject to the additional tax as herein prescribed; provided, further that the additional tax herein provided shall not apply to trailers having a gross weight of 3,000 pounds or less.

Chapter 20

History.
1937, c. 407, s. 50; 1965, c. 659

§ 20-86.1. International Registration Plan

(a) The registration fees required under this Article may be proportioned for vehicles which qualify and are licensed under the provisions of the International Registration Plan.

(b) Notwithstanding any other provisions of this Chapter, the Commissioner is hereby authorized to promulgate and enforce such rules and regulations as may be necessary to carry out the provisions of any agreement entered pursuant to the International Registration Plan.

History.
1975, c. 767, s. 2; 1981, c. 859, s. 77; c. 1127, s. 53

§ 20-87. Passenger vehicle registration fees

These fees shall be paid to the Division annually for the registration and licensing of passenger vehicles, according to the following classifications and schedules:

(1) **For-Hire Passenger Vehicles.** -- The fee for a for-hire passenger vehicle with a capacity of 15 passengers or less is one hundred dollars ($ 100.00). The fee for a for-hire passenger vehicle with a capacity of more than 15 passengers is one dollar and eighty cents ($ 1.80) per hundred pounds of empty weight of the vehicle.

(2) **U-Drive-It Vehicles.** -- U-drive-it vehicles shall pay the following tax:

Motorcycles:

1-passenger capacity	$ 23.00
2-passenger capacity	30.00
3-passenger capacity	34.00

Automobiles:

15 or fewer passengers	$ 66.00
Buses: 16 or more passengers	$ 2.60 per hundred pounds of empty weight

Trucks under 7,000 pounds that do not haul products for hire:

4,000 pounds	$ 54.00
5,000 pounds	$ 66.00
6,000 pounds	$ 80.00.

(3) Repealed by Session Laws 1981, c. 976, s. 3.

(4) **Limousine Vehicles.** -- For-hire passenger vehicles on call or demand which do not solicit passengers indiscriminately for hire between points along streets or highways, shall be taxed at the same rate as for-hire passenger vehicles under G.S. 20-87(1) but shall be issued appropriate registration plates to distinguish such vehicles from taxicabs.

(5) **Private Passenger Vehicles.** -- There shall be paid to the Division annually, as of the first day of January, for the registration and licensing of private passenger vehicles, fees according to the following classifications and schedules:

Private passenger vehicles of not more than fifteen passengers	$ 36.00
Private passenger vehicles over fifteen passengers	40.00

Provided, that a fee of only one dollar and thirty cents ($ 1.30) shall be charged for any vehicle given by the federal government to any veteran on account of any disability suffered during war so long as such vehicle is owned by the original donee or other veteran entitled to receive such gift under Title 38, section 252, United States Code Annotated.

(6) **Private Motorcycles.** -- The base fee on private passenger motorcycles shall be twenty dollars ($ 20.00); except that when a motorcycle is equipped with an additional form of device designed to transport persons or property, the base fee shall be thirty dollars ($ 30.00). An additional fee of four dollars ($ 4.00) is imposed on each private motorcycle registered under this subdivision in addition to the base fee. The revenue from the additional fee, in addition to any other funds appropriated for this purpose, shall be used to fund the Motorcycle Safety Instruction Program created in G.S. 115D-72.

(7) **Dealer License Plates.** -- The fee for a dealer license plate is the regular fee for each of the first five plates issued to the same dealer and is one-half the regular fee for each additional dealer license plate issued to the same dealer. The "regular fee" is the fee set in subdivision (5) of this section for a private passenger motor vehicle of not more than 15 passengers.

(8) **Driveaway Companies.** -- Any person engaged in the business of driving new motor vehicles from the place of manufacture to the place of sale in this State for compensation shall pay a fee of one-half of the amount that would otherwise be payable under this section for each set of plates.

(9) **House Trailers.** -- In lieu of other registration and license fees levied on house trailers under this section or G.S. 20-88, the registration and license fee on house

Chapter 20

trailers shall be fourteen dollars ($ 14.00) for the license year or any portion thereof.

(10) **Special Mobile Equipment.** -- The fee for special mobile equipment for the license year or any part of the license year is two times the fee in subdivision (5) for a private passenger motor vehicle of not more than 15 passengers.

(11) Any vehicle fee determined under this section according to the weight of the vehicle shall be increased by the sum of four dollars ($ 4.00) to arrive at the total fee.

(12) **Low-Speed Vehicles, Mini-Trucks, and Modified Utility Vehicles.** -- The fee for a low-speed vehicle, mini-truck, or modified utility vehicle is the same as the fee for private passenger vehicles of not more than 15 passengers. However, the fee for any low-speed vehicle, mini-truck, or modified utility vehicle that is offered for rent shall be the same as the fee for a U-drive-it automobile.

(13) **Additional fee for certain electric vehicles.** -- At the time of an initial registration or registration renewal, the owner of a plug-in electric vehicle that is not a low-speed vehicle and that does not rely on a nonelectric source of power shall pay a fee in the amount of one hundred thirty dollars ($ 130.00) in addition to any other required registration fees.

History.
1937, c. 407, s. 51; 1939, c. 275; 1943, c. 648; 1945, c. 564, s. 1; c. 576, s. 2; 1947, c. 220, s. 3; c. 1019, ss. 1-3; 1949, c. 127; 1951, c. 819, ss. 1, 2; 1953, c. 478; c. 826, s. 4; 1955, c. 1313, s. 2; 1957, c. 1340, s. 3; 1961, c. 1172, s. 1a; 1965, c. 927; 1967, c. 1136; 1969, c. 600, ss. 3-11; 1971, c. 952; 1973, c. 107; 1975, c. 716, s. 5; 1981, c. 976, ss. 1-4; 1981 (Reg. Sess., 1982), c. 1255; 1983, c. 713, s. 61; c. 761, ss. 142, 143, 145; 1985, c. 454, s. 2; 1987, c. 333; 1989, c. 755, ss. 2, 4; c. 770, ss. 74.2, 74.3; 1989 (Reg. Sess., 1990), c. 830, s. 1; 1991 (Reg. Sess., 1992), c. 1015, s. 2; 1993, c. 320, s. 5; c. 440, s. 7; 1995 (Reg. Sess., 1996), c. 756, s. 7; 1999-438, s. 27; 1999-452, s. 17; 2001-356, s. 4; 2001-414, s. 31; 2002-72, s. 8; 2004-167, s. 5; 2004-199, s. 59; 2005-276, s. 44.1(m); 2013-360, s. 34.21(a); 2015-237, s. 3; 2015-241, s. 29.30 (*l*); 2019-34, s. 2; 2020-40, s. 2

§ 20-87.1. Interchange of passenger buses with nonresident common carriers of passengers

When a resident common carrier of passengers of this State interchanges a properly licensed bus with another common carrier of passengers who is a resident of another state, and adequate records are on file in its office to verify such interchanges, the North Carolina licensed common carrier of passengers may use the bus licensed in such other state the same as if it is its own during the time the nonresident carrier is using the North Carolina licensed bus.

History.
1971, c. 871, s. 1; 1975, c. 716, s. 5; 1981, c. 976, s. 5

§ 20-88. Property-hauling vehicles

(a) **Determination of Weight.** -- For the purpose of licensing, the weight of self-propelled property-carrying vehicles shall be the empty weight and heaviest load to be transported, as declared by the owner or operator; provided, that any determination of weight shall be made only in units of 1,000 pounds or major fraction thereof, weights of over 500 pounds counted as 1,000 and weights of 500 pounds or less disregarded. The declared gross weight of self-propelled property-carrying vehicles operated in conjunction with trailers or semitrailers shall include the empty weight of the vehicles to be operated in the combination and the heaviest load to be transported by such combination at any time during the registration period, except that the gross weight of a trailer or semitrailer is not required to be included when the operation is to be in conjunction with a self-propelled property-carrying vehicle which is licensed for 6,000 pounds or less gross weight and the gross weight of such combination does not exceed 9,000 pounds, except wreckers as defined under G.S. 20-4.01(50). Those property-hauling vehicles registered for 4,000 pounds shall be permitted a tolerance of 500 pounds above the weight permitted under the table of weights and rates appearing in subsection (b) of this section.

(b) The following fees are imposed on the annual registration of self-propelled property-hauling vehicles; the fees are based on the type of vehicle and its weight:

SCHEDULE OF WEIGHTS AND RATES

Rates Per Hundred Pound Gross Weight

Farmer Rate	
Not over 4,000 pounds	$ 0.38
4,001 to 9,000 pounds inclusive	.52
9,001 to 13,000 pounds inclusive	.65
13,001 to 17,000 pounds inclusive	.88
Over 17,000 pounds	1.00

Chapter 20

Rates Per Hundred Pound Gross Weight	
General Rate	
Not over 4,000 pounds	0.77
4,001 to 9,000 pounds inclusive	1.05
9,001 to 13,000 pounds inclusive	1.30
13,001 to 17,000 pounds inclusive	1.77
Over 17,000 pounds	2.00

(1) The minimum fee for a vehicle licensed under this subsection is thirty dollars ($ 30.00) at the farmer rate and thirty-six dollars ($ 36.00) at the general rate.

(2) The term "farmer" as used in this subsection means any person engaged in the raising and growing of farm products on a farm in North Carolina not less than 10 acres in area, and who does not engage in the business of buying products for resale.

(3) License plates issued at the farmer rate shall be placed upon trucks and truck-tractors that are operated for the primary purpose of carrying or transporting the applicant's farm products, raised or produced on the applicant's farm, and farm supplies. The license plates shall not be used on a vehicle operated in hauling for hire.

(4) "Farm products" means any food crop, livestock, poultry, dairy products, flower bulbs, or other nursery products and other agricultural products designed to be used for food purposes, including in the term "farm products" also cotton, tobacco, logs, bark, pulpwood, tannic acid wood and other forest products grown, produced, or processed by the farmer.

(5) The Division shall issue necessary rules and regulations providing for the recall, transfer, exchange or cancellation of "farmer" plates, when vehicle bearing such plates shall be sold or transferred.

(5a) Notwithstanding any other provision of this Chapter, license plates issued pursuant to this subsection at the farmer rate may be purchased for any three-month period at one fourth of the annual fee.

(6) There shall be paid to the Division annually the following fees for "wreckers" as defined under G.S. 20-4.01(50): a wrecker fully equipped weighing 7,000 pounds or less, ninety-eight dollars ($ 98.00); wreckers weighing in excess of 7,000 pounds shall pay one hundred ninety-two dollars ($ 192.00). Fees to be prorated monthly. Provided, further, that nothing herein shall prohibit a licensed dealer from using a dealer's license plate to tow a vehicle for a customer.

(c) The fee for a semitrailer or trailer is twenty-five dollars ($ 25.00) for each year or part of a year. The fee is payable each year. Upon the application of the owner of a semitrailer or trailer, the Division may issue a multiyear plate and registration card for the semitrailer or trailer for a fee of ninety-eight dollars ($ 98.00). A multiyear plate and registration card for a semitrailer or trailer are valid until the owner transfers the semitrailer or trailer to another person or surrenders the plate and registration card to the Division. A multiyear plate may not be transferred to another vehicle.

The Division shall issue a multiyear semitrailer or trailer plate in a different color than an annual semitrailer or trailer plate and shall include the word "multiyear" on the plate. The Division may not issue a multiyear plate for a house trailer.

(d) Rates on trucks, trailers and semitrailers wholly or partially equipped with solid tires shall be double the above schedule.

(e) Repealed by Session Laws 1981, c. 976, s. 6.

(f) Repealed by Session Laws 1995, c. 163, s. 6.

(g) Repealed by Session Laws 1969, c. 600, s. 17.

(h) Repealed by Session Laws 1979, c. 419.

(i) Any vehicle fee determined under this section according to the weight of the vehicle shall be increased by the sum of four dollars ($ 4.00) to arrive at the total fee.

(j) No heavy vehicle subject to the use tax imposed by Section 4481 of the Internal Revenue Code of 1954 (26 U.S.C. 4481) may be registered or licensed pursuant to G.S. 20-88 without proof of payment of the use tax imposed by that law. The proof of payment shall be on a form prescribed by the United States Secretary of Treasury pursuant to the provisions of 23 U.S.C. 141(d).

(k) A person may not drive a vehicle on a highway if the vehicle's gross weight exceeds its declared gross weight. A vehicle driven in violation of this subsection is subject to the axle-group weight penalties set in G.S. 20-118(e). The penalties apply to the amount by which the vehicle's gross weight exceeds its declared weight.

(*l*) The Division shall issue permanent truck and truck-tractor plates to Class A and Class B Motor Vehicles and shall include the word "permanent" on the plate. The permanent registration plates issued pursuant to this section shall be subject to annual registration fees set in this section. The Division shall issue the necessary rules providing for the recall, transfer, exchange, or cancellation of permanent plates issued pursuant to this section.

(m) Any vehicle weighing greater than the gross weight limits found in G.S. 20-118(b)(3), as authorized by G.S. 20-118(c)(12), (c)(14), and (c)(15), must be registered for the maximum weight allowed for the vehicle configuration as listed in G.S. 20-118(b). A vehicle driven in violation of this subsection is subject to the axle group penalties set out in G.S. 20-118(e). The penalties apply to the amount by which the vehicle's maximum gross weight as listed in G.S. 20-118(b) exceeds its declared weight.

History.
1937, c. 407, s. 52; 1939, c. 275; 1941, cc. 36, 227; 1943, c. 648; 1945, c. 569, s. 1; c. 575, s. 1; c. 576, s. 3; c. 956, ss. 1, 2; 1949, cc. 355, 361; 1951, c. 583; c. 819, ss. 1, 2; 1953, c. 568; c. 694, s. 1; c. 1122; 1955, c. 554, s. 8; 1957, c. 681, s. 2; c. 1215; 1959, c. 571; 1961, c. 685; 1963, c. 501; c. 702, ss. 2, 3; 1967, c. 1095, ss. 1, 2; 1969, c. 600, ss. 12-17; c. 1056, s. 1; 1973, c. 154, ss. 1, 2; c. 291; 1975, c. 716, s. 5; 1977, c. 638; 1979, c. 419; c. 631; 1981, c. 67; c. 690, ss. 29, 30; c. 976, s. 6; 1983, c. 43; c. 190, s. 1; c. 761, s. 144; c. 768, s. 4; 1991 (Reg. Sess., 1992), c. 947, s. 1; 1993, c. 467, s. 4; c. 543, s. 1; 1995, c. 109, s. 1; c. 163, s. 6; 1995 (Reg. Sess., 1996), c. 756, s. 8; 1997-466, s. 1; 2004-167, ss. 6, 7; 2004-199, s. 59; 2005-276, s. 44.1(n); 2008-221, s. 2; 2012-78, s. 4; 2013-92, s. 1; 2015-241, s. 29.30(o)

§ 20-88.01. Revocation of registration for failure to register for or comply with road tax or pay civil penalty for buying or selling non-tax-paid fuel

(a) **Road Tax.** -- The Secretary of Revenue may notify the Commissioner of those motor vehicles that are registered or are required to be registered under Article 36B of Chapter 105 and whose owners or lessees, as appropriate, are not in compliance with Article 36B, 36C, or 36D of Chapter 105. When notified, the Commissioner shall withhold or revoke the registration plate for the vehicle.

(b) **Non-tax-paid Fuel.** -- The Secretary of Revenue may notify the Commissioner of those motor vehicles for which a civil penalty imposed under G.S. 105-449.118 has not been paid. When notified, the Commissioner shall withhold or revoke the registration plate of the vehicle.

History.
1983, c. 713, s. 54; 1989, c. 692, s. 6.1; c. 770, s. 74.5; 1991, c. 613, s. 4; 1995, c. 390, s. 11

§ 20-88.02. Registration of logging vehicles

Upon receipt of an application on a form prescribed by it, the Division shall register trucks and tractor trucks used exclusively in connection with logging operations, as provided in section 4483(e) of the Internal Revenue Code and 26 C.F.R. § 41.4483-6 for the collection of the federal heavy vehicle use tax. For the purposes of this section, "logging" shall mean the harvesting of timber and transportation from a forested site to places of sale.

Fees for the registration of vehicles under this section shall be the same as those ordinarily charged for the type of vehicle being registered.

History.
1985, c. 458, s. 1; 2010-132, s. 9

§ 20-88.03. Late fee; motor vehicle registration

(a) **Late Fee.** -- In addition to the applicable fees required under this Article for the registration of a motor vehicle and any interest assessed under G.S. 105-330.4, the Division shall charge a late fee according to the following schedule to a person who pays the applicable registration fee required under this Article after the registration expires:

(1) If the registration has been expired for less than one month, a late fee of fifteen dollars ($ 15.00).

(2) If the registration has been expired for one month or greater, but less than two months, a late fee of twenty dollars ($ 20.00).

(3) If the registration has been expired for two months or greater, a late fee of twenty-five dollars ($ 25.00).

(a1) **(Effective October 1, 2021) Waiver.** -- The Division shall waive the late fee assessed under subsection (a) of this section against a person who establishes the following:

(1) The person was deployed as a member of the Armed Forces of the United States when the registration expired.

(2) The person obtained a renewed registration within 30 days after the deployment ended.

(b) **Proceeds.** -- The clear proceeds of any late fee charged under this section shall be remitted to the Civil Penalty and Forfeiture Fund in accordance with G.S. 115C-457.2. The clear proceeds of the late fee charged under this section shall be used to provide a dedicated source of revenue for the drivers education program administered by the Department of Public Instruction in accordance with G.S. 115C-215.

(c) **Construction.** -- For purposes of this section, payment by mail of a registration fee required under this Article is considered to be made on the date shown on the postmark stamped by the United States Postal Service. If payment by mail is not postmarked or does not show the date of mailing, the payment is considered to be made on the date the Division receives the payment.

(d) **Grace Period Inapplicable.** -- The 15-day grace period provided in G.S. 20-66(g) shall

Chapter 20

not apply to any late fee assessed under this section.

(e) **Surrender of Registration Plate. --** Nothing in this section shall be construed as requiring the Division to assess a late fee under this section if, on or prior to the date the registration expires, the owner surrenders to the Division the registration plate issued for the vehicle.

History.
2015-241, s. 29.30(m); 2015-268, s. 8.2(a); 2016-94, s. 35.13; 2017-57, s. 5.4(d); 2021-89, s. 3

§ 20-88.1. Driver education

(a) through (b1) Repealed by Session Laws 2011-145, s. 28.37(c), effective July 1, 2011.

(c) Repealed by Session Laws 2014-100, s. 8.15(a), effective July 1, 2015.

(d) The Division shall prepare a driver license handbook that explains the traffic laws of the State and shall periodically revise the handbook to reflect changes in these laws. The Division, in consultation with the State Highway Patrol, the North Carolina Sheriff's Association, and the North Carolina Association of Chiefs of Police, shall include in the driver license handbook a description of law enforcement procedures during traffic stops and the actions that a motorist should take during a traffic stop, including appropriate interactions with law enforcement officers. At the request of the Department of Public Instruction, the Division shall provide free copies of the handbook to that Department for use in the program of driver education offered at public high schools.

History.
1957, c. 682, s. 1; 1965, c. 410, s. 1; 1975, c. 431; c. 716, s. 5; 1977, c. 340, s. 4; c. 1002; 1983, c. 761, s. 141; 1985 (Reg. Sess., 1986), c. 982, s. 25; 1991, c. 689, s. 32(a); 1993 (Reg. Sess., 1994), c. 761, s. 7; 1997-16, s. 3; 1997-443, s. 32.20; 2011-145, s. 28.37(c); 2014-100, s. 8.15(a); 2017-95, s. 1

N.C. Gen. Stat. § 20-89

Repealed by Session Laws 1981, c. 976, s. 7.

N.C. Gen. Stat. § 20-90

Repealed by Session Laws 1981, c. 976, s. 8.

§ 20-91. Audit of vehicle registrations under the International Registration Plan

(a) Repealed by Session Laws 1995 (Regular Session, 1996), c. 756, s. 9.

(b) The Department of Revenue may audit a person who registers or is required to register a vehicle under the International Registration Plan to determine if the person has paid the registration fees due under this Article. A person who registers a vehicle under the International Registration Plan must keep any records used to determine the information when registering the vehicle. The records must be kept for three years after the date of the registration to which the records apply. The Department of Revenue may examine these records during business hours. If the records are not located in North Carolina and an auditor must travel to the location of the records, the registrant shall reimburse North Carolina for per diem and travel expense incurred in the performance of the audit. If more than one registrant is audited on the same out-of-state trip, the per diem and travel expense may be prorated.

The Secretary of Revenue may enter into reciprocal audit agreements with other agencies of this State or agencies of another jurisdiction for the purpose of conducting joint audits of any registrant subject to audit under this section.

(c) If an audit is conducted and it becomes necessary to assess the registrant for deficiencies in registration fees or taxes due based on the audit, the assessment will be determined based on the schedule of rates prescribed for that registration year, adding thereto and as a part thereof an amount equal to five percent (5%) of the tax to be collected. If, during an audit, it is determined that:

(1) A registrant failed or refused to make acceptable records available for audit as provided by law; or

(2) A registrant misrepresented, falsified or concealed records, then all plates and cab cards shall be deemed to have been issued erroneously and are subject to cancellation. The Commissioner, based on information provided by the Department of Revenue audit, may assess the registrant for an additional percentage up to one hundred percent (100%) North Carolina registration fees at the rate prescribed for that registration year, adding thereto and as a part thereof an amount equal to five percent (5%) of the tax to be collected. The Commissioner may cancel all registration and reciprocal privileges.

As a result of an audit, no assessment shall be issued and no claim for refund shall be allowed which is in an amount of less than ten dollars ($ 10.00).

The results of any audit conducted under this section shall be provided to the Division. The notice of any assessments shall be sent by the Division to the registrant by registered or certified mail at the address of the registrant as it appears in the records of the Division of Motor Vehicles in Raleigh. The notice, when sent in accordance with the requirements indicated above, will be sufficient regardless of whether or not it was ever received.

The failure of any registrant to pay any additional registration fees or tax within 30 days after the billing date, shall constitute cause for revocation of registration license plates, cab cards and reciprocal privileges, or shall constitute cause for the denial of registration of a vehicle registered through the International Registration Plan or a vehicle no longer registered through the International Registration Plan.

(d) Repealed by Session Laws 1995 (Regular Session, 1996), c. 756, s. 9.

History.
1937, c. 407, s. 55; 1939, c. 275; 1941, c. 36; 1943, c. 726; 1945, c. 575, s. 3; 1947, c. 914, s. 2; 1951, c. 190, s. 1; c. 819, s. 1; 1955, c. 1313, s. 2; 1967, c. 1079, s. 2; 1975, c. 716, s. 5; c. 767, s. 3; 1981, c. 859, s. 78; c. 976, s. 9; c. 1127, s. 53; 1995 (Reg. Sess., 1996), c. 756, s. 9; 2005-435, s. 22; 2007-164, s. 7; 2007-484, s. 41.5

§§ 20-91.1, 20-91.2

Repealed by Session Laws 2007-491, s. 2, effective January 1, 2008.

N.C. Gen. Stat. § 20-92

Repealed by Session Laws 1995 (Regular Session, 1996), c. 756, s. 10.

N.C. Gen. Stat. § 20-93

Repealed by Session Laws 1981, c. 976, s. 10.

§ 20-94. Partial payments

In the purchase of licenses, where the gross amount of the license fee to any one owner amounts to more than four hundred dollars ($ 400.00), half of such payment may, if the Commissioner is satisfied of the financial responsibility of such owner, be deferred until six months from the month of renewal in any calendar year upon the execution to the Commissioner of a draft upon any bank or trust company upon forms to be provided by the Commissioner in an amount equivalent to one half of such fee, plus a carrying charge of three percent (3%) of the deferred portion of the license fee: Provided, that any person using any tag so purchased after the first day of six months from the month of renewal in any such year without having first provided for the payment of such draft, shall be guilty of a Class 2 misdemeanor. No further license plates shall be issued to any person executing such a draft after the due date of any such draft so long as such draft or any portion thereof remains unpaid. Any such draft being dishonored and not paid shall be subject to the

penalties prescribed in G.S. 20-178 and shall be immediately turned over by the Commissioner to his duly authorized agents and/or the State Highway Patrol, to the end that this provision may be enforced. When the owner of the vehicles for which a draft has been given sells or transfers ownership to all vehicles covered by the draft, such draft shall become payable immediately, and such vehicles shall not be transferred by the Division until the draft has been paid. Any one owner whose gross license fee amounts to more than two hundred dollars ($ 200.00) but not more than four hundred dollars ($ 400.00) may also be permitted to sign a draft in accordance with the foregoing provisions of this section provided such owner makes application for the draft during the month of renewal.

History.
1937, c. 407, s. 58; 1943, c. 726; 1945, c. 49, ss. 1, 2; 1947, c. 219, s. 10; 1953, c. 192; 1967, c. 712; 1975, c. 716, s. 5; 1979, c. 801, s. 12; 1987 (Reg. Sess., 1988), c. 938; 1989, c. 661; 1993, c. 539, s. 344; 1994, Ex. Sess., c. 24, s. 14(c)2004-167, s. 8; 2004-199, s. 59

§ 20-95. Prorated fee for license plate issued for other than a year

(a) **Calendar-Year Plate.** -- The fee for a calendar-year license plate issued on or after April 1 of a year is a percentage of the annual fee determined in accordance with the following table:

Date Plate Issued	Percentage of Annual Fee
April 1 through June 30	75%
July 1 through September 30	50
October 1 through December 31	25.

(a1) **Plate With Renewal Sticker.** -- The fee for a license plate whose registration is renewed by means of a registration renewal sticker for a period of other than 12 months is a prorated amount of the annual fee. The prorated amount is one-twelfth of the annual fee multiplied by the number of full months in the period beginning the date the renewal sticker becomes effective until the date the renewal sticker expires, rounded to the nearest dollar.

(b) **Scope.** -- This section does not apply to license plates issued pursuant to G.S. 20-79.1, 20-79.2, 20-84, 20-84.1, 20-87(9) or (10), and 20-88(c).

History.
1937, c. 407, s. 59; 1947, c. 914, s. 3; 1979, c. 476; 1991, c. 672, s. 6; c. 726, s. 23; 1993, c. 440, s. 6; 1993 (Reg. Sess., 1994), c. 761, s. 8

Chapter 20

§ 20-96. Detaining property-hauling vehicles or vehicles regulated by the Motor Carrier Safety Regulation Unit until fines or penalties and taxes are collected

(a) **Authority to Detain Vehicles.** -- A law enforcement officer may seize and detain the following property-hauling vehicles operating on the highways of the State:

(1) A property-hauling vehicle with an overload in violation of G.S. 20-88(k) and G.S. 20-118.

(2) A property-hauling vehicle that does not have a proper registration plate as required under G.S. 20-118.3.

(3) A property-hauling vehicle that is owned by a person liable for any overload penalties or assessments due and unpaid for more than 30 days.

(4) A property-hauling vehicle that is owned by a person liable for any taxes or penalties under Article 36B of Chapter 105 of the General Statutes.

(5) Any commercial vehicle operating under the authority of a motor carrier when the motor carrier has been assessed a fine pursuant to G.S. 20-17.7 and that fine has not been paid.

(6) A property-hauling vehicle operating in violation of G.S. 20-119.

The officer may detain the vehicle until the delinquent fines or penalties and taxes are paid and, in the case of a vehicle that does not have the proper registration plate, until the proper registration plate is secured.

(b) **Storage; Liability.** -- When necessary, an officer who detains a vehicle under this section may have the vehicle stored. The motor carrier under whose authority the vehicle is being operated or the owner of a vehicle that is detained or stored under this section is responsible for the care of any property being hauled by the vehicle and for any storage charges. The State shall not be liable for damage to the vehicle or loss of the property being hauled.

(c) The authority of a law enforcement officer to seize a motor vehicle pursuant to subsection (a) of this section shall not be affected by the statutes of limitations set out in Chapter 1 of the North Carolina General Statutes.

History.
1937, c. 407, s. 60; 1943, c. 726; 1949, c. 583, s. 8; c. 1207, s. 41/2; c. 1253; 1951, c. 1013, ss. 1-3; 1953, c. 694, ss. 2, 3; 1955, c. 554, s. 9; 1957, c. 65, s. 11; 1959, c. 1264, s. 5; 1973, c. 507, s. 5; 1985, c. 116, ss. 1-3; 1993, c. 539, s. 345; 1994, Ex. Sess., c. 24, s. 14(c); 1995, c. 109, s. 2; 1999-452, s. 18; 2000-67, s. 25.11; 2005-361, s. 1; 2010-129, s. 2

§ 20-97. Taxes credited to Highway Fund; municipal vehicle taxes

(a) **State Taxes to Highway Fund.** -- All taxes levied under this Article are compensatory taxes for the use and privileges of the public highways of this State. The taxes collected shall be credited to the State Highway Fund. Except as provided in this section, no county or municipality shall levy any license or privilege tax upon any motor vehicle licensed by the State.

(b) Repealed by Session Laws 2015-241, s. 29.27A(a), effective July 1, 2016.

(b1) **Municipal Vehicle Tax.** -- A city or town may levy an annual municipal vehicle tax upon any vehicle resident in the city or town. The aggregate annual municipal vehicle tax levied, including any annual municipal vehicle tax authorized by local legislation, may not exceed thirty dollars ($ 30.00) per vehicle. A city or town may use the net proceeds from the municipal vehicle tax as follows:

(1) **General purpose.** -- Not more than five dollars ($ 5.00) of the tax levied may be used for any lawful purpose.

(2) **Public transportation.** -- Not more than five dollars ($ 5.00) of the tax levied may be used for financing, constructing, operating, and maintaining local public transportation systems. This subdivision only applies to a city or town that operates a public transportation system as defined in G.S. 105-550.

(3) **Public streets.** -- The remainder of the tax levied may be used for maintaining, repairing, constructing, reconstructing, widening, or improving public streets in the city or town that do not form a part of the State highway system.

(c) Repealed by Session Laws 2015-241, s. 29.27A(a), effective July 1, 2016.

(d) **Municipal Taxi Tax.** -- Cities and towns may levy a tax of not more than fifteen dollars ($ 15.00) per year upon each vehicle operated in the city or town as a taxicab. The proceeds of the tax may be used for any lawful purpose.

(e) **No Additional Local Tax.** -- No county, city or town may impose a franchise tax, license tax, or other fee upon a motor carrier unless the tax is authorized by this section.

History.
1937, c. 407, s. 61; 1941, c. 36; 1943, c. 639, ss. 3, 4; 1975, c. 716, s. 5; 1977, c. 433, s. 1; c. 880, s. 1; 1979, c. 173, s. 1; c. 216, s. 1; c. 217; c. 248, s. 1; c. 398; c. 400, s. 1; c. 458; c. 530, s. 1; c. 790; 1979, 2nd Sess., c. 1152; c. 1153, s. 1; c. 1155, s. 1; c. 1189; c. 1308, s. 1; 1981, cc. 74, 129, 210, 228, 310, 311, 312, 315, 368, 370, s. 10; c. 415, s. 10; cc. 857, 858, 991; 1981 (Reg. Sess., 1982), cc. 1202, 1250; 1983, cc. 9, 75; c. 106, s. 1; c. 188, ss. 1, 2; 1993, c. 321, s. 146, c. 479, s. 4; c. 456, s. 1; 1997-417, s. 2; 2009-166, s. 2(b); 2015-241, s. 29.27A(a)

§§ 20-98, 20-99

Repealed by Session Laws 2007-491, s. 2, effective January 1, 2008.

§ 20-100. Vehicles junked or destroyed by fire or collision

Upon satisfactory proof to the Commissioner that any motor vehicle, duly licensed, has been completely destroyed by fire or collision, or has been junked and completely dismantled so that the same can no longer be operated as a motor vehicle, the owner of such vehicle may be allowed on the purchase of a new license for another vehicle a credit equivalent to the unexpired proportion of the cost of the original license, dating from the first day of the next month after the date of such destruction.

History.
1937, c. 407, s. 64; 1939, c. 369, s. 1

§ 20-101. Certain business vehicles to be marked

(a) A motor vehicle that is subject to 49 C.F.R. Part 390, the federal motor carrier safety regulations, shall be marked as required by that Part.

(b) A motor vehicle with a gross vehicle weight rating of more than 26,000 pounds that is used in intrastate commerce shall have (i) the name of the owner and (ii) the motor carrier's identification number preceded by the letters "USDOT" and followed by the letters "NC" printed on each side of the vehicle in letters not less than three inches in height. The provisions of this subsection shall not apply if any of the following are true:

(1) The motor vehicle is subject to 49 C.F.R. Part 390.

(2) The motor vehicle is of a type listed in 49 C.F.R. 390.3(f).

(3) The motor vehicle is licensed at the farmer rate under G.S. 20-88.

(c) A motor vehicle that is subject to regulation by the North Carolina Utilities Commission shall be marked as required by that Commission and as otherwise required by this section.

(d) A motor vehicle equipped to tow or transport another motor vehicle, hired for the purpose of towing or transporting another motor vehicle, shall have the name and address of the registered owner of the vehicle, and the name of the business or person being hired if different, printed on each side of the vehicle in letters not less than three inches in height. This subsection shall not apply to motor vehicles subject to 49 C.F.R. Part 390.

History.
1937, c. 407, s. 65; 1951, c. 819, s. 1; 1967, c. 1132; 1985, c. 132; 1995 (Reg. Sess., 1996), c. 756, s. 12; 2000-67, s. 25.8; 2001-487, s. 50(d); 2007-404, s. 1; 2009-376, s. 3; 2012-41, s. 1; 2017-108, s. 15

§ 20-101.1. Conspicuous disclosure of dealer administrative fees.

(a) A motor vehicle dealer shall not charge an administrative, origination, documentary, procurement, or other similar administrative fee related to the sale or lease of a motor vehicle, whether or not that fee relates to costs or charges that the dealer is required to pay to third parties or is attributable to the dealer's internal overhead or profit, unless the dealer complies with all of the following requirements:

(1) The dealer shall post a conspicuous notice in the sales or finance area of the dealership measuring at least 24 inches on each side informing customers that a fee regulated by this section may or will be charged and the amount of the fee.

(2) The fact that the dealer charges a fee regulated by this section and the amount of the fee shall be disclosed whenever the dealer engages in the price advertising of vehicles.

(3) The amount of a fee regulated by this section shall be separately identified on the customer's buyer's order, purchase order, or bill of sale.

(b) Nothing contained in this section or elsewhere under the law of this State shall be deemed to prohibit a dealer from, in the dealer's discretion, deciding not to charge an administrative, origination, documentary, procurement, or other similar administrative fee or reducing the amount of the fee in certain cases, as the dealer may deem appropriate.

(c) Notwithstanding the terms of any contract, franchise, novation, or agreement, it shall be unlawful for any manufacturer, manufacturer branch, distributor, or distributor branch to prevent, attempt to prevent, prohibit, coerce, or attempt to coerce, any new motor vehicle dealer located in this State from charging any administrative, origination, documentary, procurement, or other similar administrative fee related to the sale or lease of a motor vehicle. It shall further be unlawful for any manufacturer, manufacturer branch, distributor, or distributor branch, notwithstanding the terms of any contract, franchise, novation, or agreement, to prevent or prohibit any new motor vehicle dealer in this State from participating in any program relating to the sale of motor vehicles or reduce the amount of compensation to be paid to any dealer in this State, based upon the dealer's willingness to refrain from charging or reduce the amount of any administrative, origination, documentary, procurement, or other similar administrative fee related to the sale or lease of a motor vehicle.

(d) This section does not apply to a dealer fee related to the online registration of a motor vehicle when the dealer fee is separately stated on the buyer's order, purchase order, retail installment sales agreement, lease, or bill of sale.

History.
2001-487, s. 123.5; 2001-492, s. 1; 2014-108, s. 4(a)

§ 20-101.2. Conspicuous disclosure of dealer finance yield charges

(a) A motor vehicle dealer shall not charge a fee or receive a commission or other compensation for providing, procuring, or arranging financing for the retail purchase or lease of a motor vehicle, unless the dealer complies with both of the following requirements:

(1) The dealer shall post a conspicuous notice in the sales or finance area of the dealership measuring at least 24 inches on each side informing customers that the dealer may receive a fee, commission, or other compensation for providing, procuring, or arranging financing for the retail purchase or lease of a motor vehicle, for which the customer may be responsible.

(2) The dealer shall disclose conspicuously on the purchase order or buyer's order, or on a separate form provided to the purchaser at or prior to the closing on the sale of the vehicle, that the dealer may receive a fee, commission, or other compensation for providing, procuring, or arranging financing for the retail purchase or lease of a motor vehicle, for which the customer may be responsible.

(b) Nothing contained in this section or elsewhere under the law of this State shall be deemed to require that a motor vehicle dealer disclose to any actual or potential purchaser the dealer's contractual arrangements with any finance company, bank, leasing company, or other lender or financial institution, or the amount of markup, profit, or compensation that the dealer will receive in any particular transaction or series of transactions from the charging of such fees.

History.
2001-487, s. 123.5; 2001-492, s. 2

§ 20-101.3. Conspicuous disclosure of dealer shop and other service-related fees

(a) **Requirement.** -- A motor vehicle dealer shall not charge shop fees in conjunction with service work performed by the dealer, or other discretionary fees relating to environmental

or regulatory compliance, record retention, or other costs incurred by the dealer in conjunction with service work performed by the dealer, whether or not the fees are attributable to or include the dealer's internal overhead or profit, unless the dealer complies with both of the following requirements:

(1) The dealer shall post a conspicuous notice in the service area of the dealership measuring at least 24 inches on each side informing customers that fees regulated by this section may or will be charged and that customers should inquire of dealership personnel if they would like to know the type and amount or basis of the fees charged by the dealer.

(2) The total amount of all fees regulated by this section shall be disclosed on the customer's repair order or repair invoice. Nothing in this subdivision shall be construed as requiring a dealer to list separately each fee charged by the dealer.

(b) **Discretion.** -- Notwithstanding any provision of law to the contrary, a dealer is not required to charge a shop or other service-related fee regulated under this section and may reduce the amount of any or all fees charged.

(c) Notwithstanding any other section of this Chapter, the fees covered by this section shall not be considered a warranty expense and are not subject to the compensation requirements of G.S. 20-305.1.

History.
2017-148, s. 5

PART 8
ANTI-THEFT AND ENFORCEMENT PROVISIONS

§ 20-102. Report of stolen and recovered motor vehicles

Every sheriff, chief of police, or peace officer upon receiving reliable information that any vehicle registered hereunder has been stolen shall report such theft to the Division. Any said officer upon receiving information that any vehicle, which he has previously reported as stolen, has been recovered, shall report the fact of such recovery to the Division.

History.
1937, c. 407, s. 66; 1975, c. 716, s. 5; 2005-182, s. 4

§ 20-102.1. False report of theft or conversion a misdemeanor

A person who knowingly makes to a peace officer or to the Division a false report of the theft or conversion of a motor vehicle shall be guilty of a Class 2 misdemeanor.

History.
1963, c. 1083; 1975, c. 716, s. 5; 1993, c. 539, s. 346; 1994, Ex. Sess., c. 24, s. 14(c)

§ 20-102.2. Report of failure to return hired motor vehicles

Every sheriff, chief of police, or peace officer, upon receiving a vehicle theft report, warrant, or other reliable information that any rental, for-hire, or leased vehicle registered pursuant to this Chapter has not been returned as set forth in G.S. 14-167, shall report the failure to the National Crime Information Center. Any officer upon receiving information concerning the recovery of a vehicle that the officer previously reported as not having been returned shall report the recovery to the National Crime Information Center. The officer shall also attempt to notify the reporting party of the location and condition of the recovered vehicle by telephone, if the telephone number of the reporting party is available or readily accessible.

History.
2005-182, s. 5

§ 20-103. Reports by owners of stolen and recovered vehicles

The owner, or person having a lien or encumbrance upon a registered vehicle which has been stolen or embezzled, may notify the Division of such theft or embezzlement, but in the event of an embezzlement may make such report only after having procured the issuance of a warrant for the arrest of the person charged with such embezzlement. Every owner or other person who has given any such notice must notify the Division of the recovery of such vehicle.

History.
1937, c. 407, s. 67; 1975, c. 716, s. 5

§ 20-104. Action by Division on report of stolen or embezzled vehicles

(a) The Division, upon receiving a report of a stolen or embezzled vehicle as hereinbefore provided, shall file and appropriately index the same and shall immediately suspend the registration of the vehicle so reported, and shall not transfer the registration of the same until such time as it is notified in writing that such vehicle has been recovered.

(b) The Division shall at least once each month compile and maintain at its headquarters office a list of all vehicles which have been stolen or embezzled or recovered as reported

to it during the preceding month, and such lists shall be open to inspection by any peace officer or other persons interested in any such vehicle.

History.
1937, c. 407, s. 68; 1975, c. 716, s. 5

N.C. Gen. Stat. § 20-105

Repealed by Session Laws 1973, c. 1330, s. 39.

Section 20-106. Receiving or transferring stolen vehicles

Recodified as G.S. 14-71.2 by Session Laws 2019-186, s. 1(c), effective December 1, 2019, and applicable to offenses committed on or after that date.

History.
1937, c. 407, s. 70; 1979, c. 760, s. 5; 1979, 2nd Sess., c. 1316, s. 47; 1981, c. 63, s. 1; c. 179, s. 14; 1993, c. 539, s. 1252; 1994, Ex. Sess., c. 24, s. 14(c).

§ 20-106.1. Fraud in connection with rental of motor vehicles

Any person with the intent to defraud the owner of any motor vehicle or a person in lawful possession thereof, who obtains possession of said vehicle by agreeing in writing to pay a rental for the use of said vehicle, and further agreeing in writing that the said vehicle shall be returned to a certain place, or at a certain time, and who willfully fails and refuses to return the same to the place and at the time specified, or who secretes, converts, sells or attempts to sell the same or any part thereof shall be guilty of a Class I felony.

History.
1961, c. 1067; 1993, c. 539, s. 1253; 1994, Ex. Sess., c. 24, s. 14(c)

§ 20-106.2. Sublease and loan assumption arranging regulated

(a) As used in this section:

(1) "Buyer" means a purchaser of a motor vehicle under the terms of a retail installment contract. "Buyer" shall include any co-buyer on the retail installment contract.

(2) "Lease" means an agreement between a lessor and lessee whereby the lessee obtains the possession and use of a motor vehicle for the period of time, for the purposes, and for the consideration set forth in the agreement whether or not the agreement includes an option to purchase the motor vehicle; provided, however, "lease" shall not include a residential rental agreement of

Chapter 20

a manufactured home which is subject to Chapter 42 of the General Statutes.

(3) "Lessor" means any person who in the regular course of business or as a part of regular business activity leases motor vehicles under motor vehicle lease agreements, purchases motor vehicle lease agreements, or any sales finance company that purchases motor vehicle lease agreements.

(4) "Lessee" means a person who obtains possession and use of a motor vehicle through a motor vehicle lease agreement. "Lessee" shall include any co-lessee listed on the motor vehicle lease agreement.

(5) "Person" means an individual, partnership, corporation, association or any other group however organized.

(6) "Security interest" means an interest in personal property that secures performance of an obligation.

(7) "Secured party" means a lender, seller, or other person in whose favor there is a security interest, including a person to whom accounts or retail installment sales contracts have been sold.

(8) "Sublease" means an agreement whether written or oral:

a. To transfer to a third party possession of a motor vehicle which is and will, while in that third party's possession, remain the subject of a security interest which secures performance of a retail installment contract or consumer loan; or

b. To transfer or assign to a third party any of the buyer's rights, interests, or obligations under the retail installment contract or consumer loan; or

c. To transfer to a third party possession of a motor vehicle which is and will, while in the third party's possession, remain the subject of a motor vehicle lease agreement; or

d. To transfer or assign to a third party any of the lessee's or buyer's rights, interests, or obligations under the motor vehicle lease agreement.

(9) "Sublease arranger" means a person who engages in the business of inducing by any means buyers and lessees to enter into subleases as sublessors and inducing third parties to enter into subleases as sublessees, however such contracts may be called. "Sublease arranger" does not include the publisher, owner, agent or employee of a newspaper, periodical, radio station, television station, cable-television system or other advertising medium which disseminates any advertisement or promotion of any act governed by this section.

(10) "Third party" means a person other than the buyer or the lessee of the vehicle.

(11) "Transfer" means to transfer possession of a motor vehicle by means of a sale, loan assumption, lease, sublease, or lease assignment.

(b) A sublease arranger commits an offense if the sublease arranger arranges a sublease of a motor vehicle and:

(1) Does not first obtain written authorization for the sublease from the vehicle's secured party or lessor; or

(2) Accepts a fee without having first obtained written authorization for the sublease from the vehicle's secured party or lessor; or

(3) Does not disclose the location of the vehicle on the request of the vehicle's buyer, lessee, secured party, or lessor; or

(4) Does not provide to the third party new, accurate disclosures under the Consumer Credit Protection Act, 15 U.S.C. Section 1601, et seq.; or

(5) Does not provide oral and written notice to the buyer or lessee that he will not be released from liability; or

(6) Does not ensure that all rights under warranties and service contracts regarding the motor vehicle transfer to the third party, unless a pro rata rebate for any unexpired coverage is applied to reduce the third party's cost under the sublease; or

(7) Does not take reasonable steps to ensure that the third party is financially able to assume the payment obligations of the buyer or lessee according to the terms of the lease agreement, retail installment contract, or consumer loan.

(c) It is not a defense to prosecution under subsection (b) of this section that the motor vehicle's buyer or lessee, secured party or lessor has violated a contract creating a security interest or lease in the motor vehicle, nor may any sublease arranger shift to the lessee, buyer or third party the arranger's duty under subdivision (b)(1) or (b)(2) to obtain prior written authorization for formation of a sublease.

(d) An offense under subdivision (b)(1) or (b)(2) of this section is a Class I felony.

(e) All other offenses under subsection (b) of this section are Class 1 misdemeanors. Each failure to disclose the location of the vehicle under subdivision (b)(3) shall constitute a separate offense.

(f) Any buyer, lessee, sublessee, secured party or lessor injured or damaged by reason of any act in violation of this section, whether or not there is a conviction for the violation, may file a civil action to recover damages based on the violation with the following available remedies:

(1) Three times the amount of any actual damages or fifteen hundred dollars ($ 1500), whichever is greater;

(2) Equitable relief, including a temporary restraining order, a preliminary or

permanent injunction, or restitution of money or property;

(3) Reasonable attorney fees and costs; and

(4) Any other relief which the court deems just.

The rights and remedies provided by this section are in addition to any other rights and remedies provided by law.

(g) This section and G.S. 14-114 and G.S. 14-115 are mutually exclusive and prosecution under those sections shall not preclude criminal prosecution or civil action under this section.

History.
1989 (Reg. Sess., 1990), c. 1011; 1993, c. 539, ss. 347, 1254; 1994, Ex. Sess., c. 24, s. 14(c)

§ 20-107. Injuring or tampering with vehicle

(a) Any person who either individually or in association with one or more other persons willfully injures or tampers with any vehicles or breaks or removes any part or parts of or from a vehicle without the consent of the owner is guilty of a Class 2 misdemeanor.

(b) Any person who with intent to steal, commit any malicious mischief, injury or other crime, climbs into or upon a vehicle, whether it is in motion or at rest, or with like intent attempts to manipulate any of the levers, starting mechanism, brakes, or other mechanism or device of a vehicle while the same is at rest and unattended or with like intent sets in motion any vehicle while the same is at rest and unattended, is guilty of a Class 2 misdemeanor.

History.
1937, c. 407, s. 71; 1965, c. 621, s. 1; 1993, c. 539, s. 348; 1994, Ex. Sess., c. 24, s. 14(c)

§ 20-108. Vehicles or component parts of vehicles without manufacturer's numbers

(a) Any person who knowingly buys, receives, disposes of, sells, offers for sale, conceals, or has in his possession any motor vehicle, or engine or transmission or component part which has been stolen or removed from a motor vehicle and from which the manufacturer's serial or engine number or other distinguishing number or identification mark or number placed thereon under assignment from the Division has been removed, defaced, covered, altered, or destroyed for the purpose of concealing or misrepresenting the identity of said motor vehicle or engine or transmission or component part is guilty of a Class 2 misdemeanor.

(b) The Commissioner and such officers and inspectors of the Division of Motor Vehicles as he has designated may take and possess any motor vehicle or component part if its engine number, vehicle identification number, or manufacturer's serial number has been altered, changed, or obliterated or if such officer has probable cause to believe that the driver or person in charge of the motor vehicle or component part has violated subsection (a) above. Any officer who so takes possession of a motor vehicle or component part shall immediately notify the Division of Motor Vehicles and the rightful owner, if known. The notification shall contain a description of the motor vehicle or component part and any other facts that may assist in locating or establishing the rightful ownership thereof or in prosecuting any person for a violation of the provisions of this Article.

(c) Within 15 days after seizure of a motor vehicle or component part pursuant to this section, the Division shall send notice by certified mail to the person from whom the property was seized and to all claimants to the property whose interest or title is in the registration records in the Division of Motor Vehicles that the Division has taken custody of the motor vehicle or component part. The notice shall also contain the following information:

(1) The name and address of the person or persons from whom the motor vehicle or component part was seized;

(2) A statement that the motor vehicle or component part has been seized for investigation as provided in this section and that the motor vehicle or component part will be released to the rightful owner:

a. Upon a determination that the identification number has not been altered, changed, or obliterated; or

b. Upon presentation of satisfactory evidence of the ownership of the motor vehicle or component part if no other person claims an interest in it within 30 days of the date the notice is mailed. Otherwise, a hearing regarding the disposition of the motor vehicle or component part may take place in a court having jurisdiction.

(3) The name and address of the officer to whom evidence of ownership of the motor vehicle or component part may be presented; and

(4) A copy statement of the text contained in this section.

(d) Whenever a motor vehicle or component part comes into the custody of an officer, the Division of Motor Vehicles may commence a civil action in the District Court in the county in which the motor vehicle or component part was seized to determine whether the motor vehicle or component part should be destroyed, sold, converted to the use of the Division or otherwise disposed of by an order of the court. The Division shall give notice of the commencement of such an action to the person from whom the motor vehicle or component part was seized and all claimants to the property whose interest or title is in the registration records of the Division of Motor Vehicles. Notice shall be by certified mail sent within 10 days after the filing of the action. In addition, any possessor of a motor vehicle or component part described in this section may commence a civil action under the provisions of this section, to which the Division of Motor Vehicles may be made a party, to provide for the proper disposition of the motor vehicle or component part.

(e) Nothing in this section shall preclude the Division of Motor Vehicles from returning a seized motor vehicle or component part to the owner following presentation of satisfactory evidence of ownership, and, if determined necessary, requiring the owner to obtain an assignment of an identification number for the motor vehicle or component part from the Division of Motor Vehicles.

(f) No court order providing for disposition shall be issued unless the person from whom the motor vehicle or component was seized and all claimants to the property whose interest or title is in the registration records in the Division of Motor Vehicles are provided a postseizure hearing by the court having jurisdiction. Ten days' notice of the postseizure hearing shall be given by certified mail to the person from whom the motor vehicle was seized and all claimants to the property whose interest or title is in the registration records in the Division of Motor Vehicles. If such motor vehicle or component part has been held or identified as evidence in a pending civil or criminal action or proceeding, no final disposition of such motor vehicle or component part shall be ordered without prior notice to the parties in said proceeding.

(g) At a hearing held pursuant to any action filed by the Division to determine the disposition of any motor vehicle or component part seized pursuant to this section, the court shall consider the following:

(1) If the evidence reveals either that the motor vehicle or component part identification number has not been altered, changed or obliterated or that the identification number has been altered, changed, or obliterated but satisfactory evidence of ownership has been presented, the motor vehicle or component part shall be returned to the person entitled to it. If ownership cannot be established, nothing in this section shall preclude the return of said motor vehicle or component part to a good faith purchaser following the presentation of satisfactory evidence of ownership thereof and, if necessary, upon the good faith purchaser's obtaining an assigned number from the

Division of Motor Vehicles and posting a reasonable bond for a period of three years. The amount of the bond shall be set by the court.

(2) If the evidence reveals that the motor vehicle or component part identification number has been altered, changed, or obliterated and satisfactory evidence of ownership has not been presented, the motor vehicle or component part shall be destroyed, sold, converted to the use of the Division of Motor Vehicles or otherwise disposed of, as provided for by order of the court.

(h) At the hearing, the Division shall have the burden of establishing, by a preponderance of the evidence, that the motor vehicle or component part has been stolen or that its identification number has been altered, changed, or obliterated.

(i) At the hearing any claimant to the motor vehicle or component part shall have the burden of providing satisfactory evidence of ownership.

(j) An officer taking into custody a motor vehicle or component part under the provisions of this section is authorized to obtain necessary removal and storage services, but shall incur no personal liability for such services. The person or company so employed shall be entitled to reasonable compensation as a claimant under (e), and shall not be deemed an unlawful possessor under (a).

History.
1937, c. 407, s. 72; 1965, c. 621, s. 2; 1973, c. 1149, ss. 1, 2; 1975, c. 716, s. 5; 1983, c. 592; 1985, c. 764, s. 22; 1985 (Reg. Sess., 1986), c. 852, s. 17; 1993, c. 539, s. 349; 1994, Ex. Sess., c. 24, s. 14(c)

§ 20-109. Altering or changing engine or other numbers

(a) It shall be unlawful and constitute a felony for:

(1) Any person to willfully deface, destroy, remove, cover, or alter the manufacturer's serial number, transmission number, or engine number; or

(2) Any vehicle owner to knowingly permit the defacing, removal, destroying, covering, or alteration of the serial number, transmission number, or engine number; or

(3) Any person except a licensed vehicle manufacturer as authorized by law to place or stamp any serial number, transmission number, or engine number upon a vehicle, other than one assigned thereto by the Division; or

(4) Any vehicle owner to knowingly permit the placing or stamping of any serial number or motor number upon a motor vehicle, except such numbers as assigned thereto by the Division.

A violation of this subsection shall be punishable as a Class I felony.

(b) It shall be unlawful and constitute a felony for:

(1) Any person, with intent to conceal or misrepresent the true identity of the vehicle, to deface, destroy, remove, cover, alter, or use any serial or motor number assigned to a vehicle by the Division; or

(2) Any vehicle owner, with intent to conceal or misrepresent the true identity of the vehicle, to permit the defacing, destruction, removal, covering, alteration, or use of a serial or motor number assigned to a vehicle by the Division; or

(3) Any vehicle owner, with the intent to conceal or misrepresent the true identity of a vehicle, to permit the defacing, destruction, removal, covering, alteration, use, gift, or sale of any manufacturer's serial number, serial number plate, or any part or parts of a vehicle containing the serial number or portions of the serial number.

A violation of this subsection shall be punishable as a Class I felony.

History.
1937, c. 407, s. 73; 1943, c. 726; 1953, c. 216; 1965, c. 621, s. 3; 1967, c. 449; 1973, c. 1089; 1975, c. 716, s. 5; 1979, c. 760, s. 5; 1979, 2nd Sess., c. 1316, s. 47; 1981, c. 63, s. 1;; 1987, c. 512; 1993, c. 539, s. 1255; 1994, Ex. Sess., c. 24, s. 14(c)

§ 20-109.1. Surrender of titles to salvage vehicles

(a) **Option to Keep Title.** -- When a vehicle is damaged to the extent that it becomes a salvage vehicle and the owner submits a claim for the damages to an insurer, the insurer must determine whether the owner wants to keep the vehicle after payment of the claim. If the owner does not want to keep the vehicle after payment of the claim, the procedures in subsection (b) of this section apply. If the owner wants to keep the vehicle after payment of the claim, the procedures in subsection (c) of this section apply.

(b) **Transfer to Insurer.** --

(1) If a salvage vehicle owner does not want to keep the vehicle, the owner must assign the vehicle's certificate of title to the insurer when the insurer pays the claim. The insurer must send the assigned title to the Division within 10 days after receiving it from the vehicle owner. The Division must then send the insurer a form to use to transfer title to the vehicle from the insurer to a person who buys the vehicle from the insurer. If the insurer sells the vehicle, the insurer must complete the form and give it to the buyer. If the buyer rebuilds

the vehicle, the buyer may apply for a new certificate of title to the vehicle.

(2) If a salvage vehicle owner fails to assign and deliver the vehicle's certificate of title to the insurer within 30 days of the payment of the claim in accordance with subdivision (b)(1) of this section, the insurer, without surrendering the certificate of title, may, at any time thereafter, request that the Division send the insurer a form to use to transfer title to the vehicle from the insurer to a person who buys the vehicle from the insurer. The request shall be made on a form prescribed by the Division and shall be accompanied by proof of payment of the claim and proof of notice sent to the owner and any lienholder requesting the vehicle's certificate of title. If the records of the Division indicate there is an outstanding lien against the vehicle immediately before the payment of the claim and if the payment was made to a lienholder or to a lienholder and the owner jointly, the proof of payment shall include evidence that funds were paid to the first lienholder shown on the records of the Division. The notice must be sent by the insurer at least 30 days prior to requesting the Division send the insurer a form to use to transfer title and must be sent by certified mail or by another commercially available delivery service providing proof of delivery to the address on record with the Division. Upon the Division's receipt of such request, the vehicle's certificate of title is deemed to be assigned to the insurer. Notwithstanding any outstanding liens against the vehicle, the Division must send the insurer a form to use to transfer title to the vehicle from the insurer to a person who buys the vehicle from the insurer. The Division's issuance of the form extinguishes all existing liens on the motor vehicle. If the insurer sells the vehicle, the insurer must complete the form and give it to the buyer. In such a sale by the insurer, the motor vehicle shall be transferred free and clear of any liens. If the buyer rebuilds the vehicle, the buyer may apply for a new certificate of title to the vehicle.

(3) Notwithstanding any other provision of law, with respect to a vehicle described in this subsection, the following shall be exempt from the requirements of notarization, including exemption from the notarization of electronic signature requirements of G.S. 20-52(c):

a. The transfer of ownership on the certificate of title.

b. Any power of attorney required in connection with the transfer of ownership to the insurer.

c. Any required odometer disclosure statement.

d. The application for a salvage certificate of title.

e. The transfer of ownership on the salvage certificate of title issued.

f. Any statement pursuant to subdivision (2) of subsection (b) of this section.

g. Any statement on the salvage certificate of title issued.

(c) **Owner Keeps Vehicle. --** If a salvage vehicle owner wants to keep the vehicle, the insurer must give the owner an owner-retained salvage form. The owner must complete the form and give it to the insurer when the insurer pays the claim. The owner's signature on the owner-retained salvage form must be notarized. The insurer must send the completed form to the Division within 10 days after receiving it from the vehicle owner. The Division must then note in its vehicle registration records that the vehicle listed on the form is a salvage vehicle.

(d) **Theft Claim on Salvage Vehicle. --** An insurer that pays a theft loss claim on a vehicle and, upon recovery of the vehicle, determines that the vehicle has been damaged to the extent that it is a salvage vehicle must send the vehicle's certificate of title to the Division within 10 days after making the determination. The Division and the insurer must then follow the procedures set in subdivision (1) of subsection (b) of this section.

(e) **Out-of-State Vehicle. --** A person who acquires a salvage vehicle that is registered in a state that does not require surrender of the vehicle's certificate of title must send the title to the Division within 10 days after the vehicle enters this State. The Division and the person must then follow the procedures set in subdivision (1) of subsection (b) of this section.

(e1) **Owner or Lienholder Abandons Vehicle. --** If an insurer requests a used motor vehicle dealer, the primary business of which is the sale of salvage vehicles on behalf of insurers, to take possession of a salvage vehicle that is the subject of an insurance claim and subsequently the insurer does not take ownership of the vehicle, the insurer may direct the used motor vehicle dealer to release the vehicle to the owner or lienholder. The insurer shall provide the used motor vehicle dealer a release statement authorizing the used motor vehicle dealer to release the vehicle to the vehicle's owner or lienholder.

Upon receiving a release statement from an insurer, the used motor vehicle dealer shall send notice to the owner and any lienholder of the vehicle informing the owner or lienholder that the vehicle is available for pick up. The notice shall include an invoice for any outstanding charges owed to the used motor vehicle dealer.

The notice shall inform the owner and any lienholder that the owner or lienholder has 30 days from the date of the notice, and upon payment of applicable charges owed to the used motor vehicle dealer, to pick up the vehicle from the used motor vehicle dealer. Notice under this subsection must be sent by certified mail or by another commercially available delivery service providing proof of delivery to the address on record with the Division.

If the owner or any lienholder of the vehicle does not pick up the vehicle within 30 days after notice was sent to the owner and any lienholder in accordance with this subsection, the vehicle shall be considered abandoned, the vehicle's certificate of title is deemed to be assigned to the used motor vehicle dealer, and the used motor vehicle dealer, without surrendering the certificate of title, may request that the Division send the used motor vehicle dealer a form to use to transfer title to the vehicle from the used motor vehicle dealer to a person who buys the vehicle from the used motor vehicle dealer. The request shall be accompanied by a copy of the notice required by this subsection and proof of delivery of the notice required by this subsection sent to the owner and any lienholder. Notwithstanding any outstanding liens against the vehicle, the Division must send the used motor vehicle dealer a form to use to transfer title to the vehicle from the used motor vehicle dealer to a person who buys the vehicle from the used motor vehicle dealer. The Division's issuance of the form extinguishes all existing liens on the motor vehicle. If the used motor vehicle dealer sells the vehicle, the used motor vehicle dealer must complete the form and give it to the buyer. In such a sale by the used motor vehicle dealer, the motor vehicle shall be transferred free and clear of any liens. If the buyer rebuilds the vehicle, the buyer may apply for a new certificate of title.

(f) **Sanctions. --** Violation of this section is a Class 1 misdemeanor. In addition to this criminal sanction, a person who violates this section is subject to a civil penalty of up to one hundred dollars ($ 100.00), to be imposed in the discretion of the Commissioner.

(g) **Fee. --** G.S. 20-85 sets the fee for issuing a salvage certificate of title.

(h) **Claims. --** The Division shall not be subject to a claim under Article 31 of Chapter 143 of the General Statutes related to the cancellation of a title pursuant to this section if the claim is based on reliance by the Division on any proof of payment or proof of notice submitted to the Division by a third party pursuant to subdivision (b)(2) or subsection (e1) of this section.

History.
1973, c. 1095, s. 1; 1975, c. 716, s. 5; c. 799; 1983, c. 713, s. 94; 1989, c. 455, s. 5; 1993, c. 539, s. 350; 1994,

Ex. Sess., c. 24, s. 14(c); 1995, c. 50, s. 3; c. 517, s. 33.1; 2013-400, s. 1; 2019-153, s. 6

§ 20-109.1A. Application for unregisterable certificate of title

(a) If an insurance company is unable to obtain the properly endorsed title, certificate of ownership, or other evidence of ownership to a vehicle registered in another state, the company, or its agent or contractor, may apply to the Division for an unregisterable certificate of title in the name of the insurance company if all of the following conditions are met:

(1) The vehicle has been declared a total loss.

(2) The occurrence that damaged the vehicle occurred within the boundaries of this State.

(3) The vehicle has remained within this State continuously since the occurrence of the loss.

(4) The owner of the vehicle has accepted an offer of an amount in settlement of the total loss from the insurance company.

(5) The insurance company, or its agent or contractor, has made a written request for the title from the vehicle owner and any lienholders of record at the addresses contained in the records of the state of registration. The written request must be delivered by certified United States Postal Service mail or by another commercially available delivery service providing proof of delivery.

(6) The owner and lienholder have failed to deliver the title for more than 30 days from the receipt of the written request, or the written request has been returned as undeliverable.

(b) An application for an unregisterable certificate of title under this section shall be made on a form provided by the Division, and the Division may require a notarized affidavit attesting under penalty of perjury that the conditions of subsection (a) of this section have been met. The form shall be accompanied by (i) evidence of a total loss payment in the form of either a copy of a claims check or a screenshot from the insurance company's claim system showing a payment was made and (ii) evidence of delivery of notice to the vehicle owner. Any company, agent, or contractor that has applied for an unregisterable certificate of title under this section shall maintain a record of any supporting documentation for a period of three years. The fee for an unregisterable certificate of title pursuant to this section shall be twenty-one dollars and fifty cents ($ 21.50).

(c) If an out-of-state registered vehicle has been damaged in this State and an insurance company, its agent, or its contractor takes possession of the vehicle with the permission of the owner, the company's agent or contractor taking possession of the vehicle shall have a towing and storage lien on the vehicle for any amount actually accrued in the possession, towing, and storage of the vehicle. This lien is superior to any other liens on the vehicle. If the insurance company subsequently denies coverage or otherwise fails to reach a settlement with the owner, the company, or its agent or contractor may make written demand that the owner or lienholder retake possession of the vehicle upon payment of any towing or storage fees accrued by the agent or contractor. If the owner or lienholder fails to satisfy the lien and take possession of the vehicle within 14 calendar days of the written demand, the agent or contractor may apply for an unregisterable certificate of title in the name of the agent or contractor for purposes of selling the vehicle to recoup any towing or storage fees accrued by the agent or contractor. The application shall be on a notarized form provided by the Division attesting by the applicant that the requirements of this section have been completed. Included with this form shall be evidence of delivery of notice to the vehicle owner. The written demand required by this subsection must be delivered by United States Postal Service mail or by another commercially available delivery service providing proof of delivery.

(d) Any vehicle that has been issued an unregisterable certificate of title under this section may only be sold for parts, scrap, or recycling.

(e) Any owner, lienholder, or subsequent purchaser harmed as a result of an unregisterable certificate of title being issued pursuant to this section, or harmed by the sale of any such vehicle following issuance of the same, shall have no cause of action against the Division, and the Division shall not be liable to any such persons in any matter related to actions taken under this section.

History.
2021-126, s. 2

§ 20-109.2. Surrender of title to manufactured home

(a) **Surrender of Title.** -- If a certificate of title has been issued for a manufactured home, the owner listed on the title has the title, and the manufactured home qualifies as real property as defined in G.S. 105-273(13), the owner listed on the title shall submit an affidavit to the Division that the manufactured home meets this definition and surrender the certificate of title to the Division.

(a1) **Surrender When Title Not Available.** -- If a certificate of title has been issued for a manufactured home, no issued title is available, and the manufactured home qualifies as real property as defined in G.S. 105-273(13), the owner listed on the title shall be deemed to have surrendered the title to the Division if the owner of the real property on which the manufactured home is affixed (i) submits an affidavit to the Division that the manufactured home meets the definition of real property under G.S. 105-273(13) and in compliance with subsection (b) of this section and (ii) submits a tax record showing the manufactured home listed for ad valorem taxes as real property pursuant to Article 17 of Chapter 105 of the General Statutes in the name of the record owner of the real property on which the manufactured home is affixed.

(b) **Affidavit.** -- The affidavit must be in a form approved by the Commissioner and shall include or provide for all of the following information:

(1) The manufacturer and, if applicable, the model name of the manufactured home affixed to real property upon which cancellation is sought.

(2) The vehicle identification number and serial number of the manufactured home affixed to real property upon which cancellation is sought.

(3) The legal description of the real property on which the manufactured home is affixed, stating that the owner of the manufactured home also owns the real property or that the owner of the manufactured home has entered into a lease with a primary term of at least 20 years for the real property on which the manufactured home is affixed with a copy of the lease or a memorandum thereof pursuant to G.S. 47-18 attached to the affidavit, if not previously recorded.

(4) A description of any security interests in the manufactured home affixed to real property upon which cancellation is sought.

(5) A section for the Division's notation or statement that either the procedure in subsection (a) of this section for surrendering the title has been surrendered and the title has been cancelled by the Division or the affiant submits this affidavit pursuant to subsection (a1) of this section to have the title deemed surrendered by the owner listed on the certificate of title.

(6) An affirmative statement that the affiant is (i) the record owner of the real property on which the manufactured home is affixed and the lease for the manufactured home does not include a provision allowing the owner listed on the certificate of title to dispose of the manufactured home prior to the end of the primary term of the lease or (ii) is the owner of the manufactured home and either owns the real property on which the manufactured home is

affixed or has entered into a lease with a primary term of at least 20 years for the real property on which the manufactured home is affixed.

(7) The affiant affirms that he or she has sent notice of this cancellation by hand delivery or by first-class mail to the last known address of the owner listed on the certificate of title prior to filing this affidavit with the Division.

(c) **Cancellation.** -- Upon compliance with the procedures in subsection (a) or (a1) of this section for surrender of title, the Division shall rescind and cancel the certificate of title. If a security interest has been recorded on the certificate of title and not released by the secured party, the Division may not cancel the title without written consent from all secured parties. After canceling the title, the Division shall return the original of the affidavit to the affiant, or to the secured party having the first recorded security interest, with the Division's notation or statement that the title has been surrendered and has been cancelled by the Division. The affiant or secured party shall file the affidavit returned by the Division with the office of the register of deeds of the county where the real property is located. The Division may charge five dollars ($ 5.00) for a cancellation of a title under this section.

(d) **Application for Title After Cancellation.** -- If the owner of a manufactured home whose certificate of title has been cancelled under this section subsequently seeks to separate the manufactured home from the real property, the owner may apply for a new certificate of title. The owner must submit to the Division an affidavit containing the same information set out in subsection (b) of this section, verification that the manufactured home has been removed from the real property, verification of the identity of the current owner of the real property upon which the manufactured home was located, and written consent of any affected owners of recorded mortgages, deeds of trust, or security interests in the real property where the manufactured home was placed. Upon receipt of this information, together with a title application and required fee, the Division shall issue a new title for the manufactured home in the name of the current owner of the real property upon which the manufactured home was located.

(e) **Sanctions.** -- Any person who violates this section is subject to a civil penalty of up to one hundred dollars ($ 100.00), to be imposed in the discretion of the Commissioner.

(f) **No Right of Action.** -- A person damaged by the cancellation of a certificate of title pursuant to subsection (a1) of this section does not have a right of action against the Division or a commission contractor of the Division.

History.
2001-506, s. 2; 2003-400, s. 1; 2013-79, s. 1; 2016-59, s. 6; 2021-134, s. 6.1

§ 20-109.3. Disposition of vehicles abandoned by charitable organizations

(a) If a charitable organization operating under section 501(c)(3) of the Internal Revenue Code (26 U.S.C. § 501(c)(3)) requests a licensed used motor vehicle dealer, whose primary business is the sale of salvage vehicles on behalf of insurers or charitable organizations, to take possession of a donated vehicle that is currently titled in this State, and the vehicle title is not provided to the used motor vehicle dealer at the time of donation or within 10 days of the donation, then the following provisions apply:

(1) The used motor vehicle dealer receiving the vehicle on behalf of the charitable organization shall send notice to the last registered owner and any reasonably ascertainable lienholders of the vehicle informing the owner or lienholder that the vehicle has been donated to the named charitable organization. The notice shall set forth the current location of the vehicle, the name of the charitable organization to which the vehicle was donated, and the name of the vehicle donor. The notice shall inform the owner or lienholder that, if the owner or lienholder objects to the donation of the vehicle, the owner or lienholder has 30 days from the date of the notice to provide proof of ownership and reclaim the vehicle from the used motor vehicle dealer at no charge. Notice under this subdivision must be sent by certified mail or by another commercially available delivery service providing proof of delivery to the address on record with the Division.

(2) If the owner or any lienholder of the vehicle receives notice but fails to object to the donation and pick up the vehicle within 30 days, any claim to the vehicle by the owner or lienholder is considered abandoned, the certificate of title to the vehicle is deemed to be transferred to the charitable organization by the owner, and the lien is deemed to be extinguished. The charitable organization, or the used motor vehicle dealer acting on its behalf through a power of attorney, may then execute an application for duplicate title with transfer upon payment of any applicable fees. The application for duplicate title with transfer shall be accompanied by a copy of the written donation statement, a copy of the notice required by subdivision (1) of this subsection, and proof of delivery of the notice sent to the owner and any lienholder. If the application is being executed by the used motor vehicle dealer on behalf of the charitable organization, a copy of the power of attorney shall also be submitted with the application.

(3) Upon receipt of an application for duplicate title with transfer, any additional documentation required under subdivision (2) of this subsection and payment of required fees, the Division shall issue a title to the donated vehicle in the name of the charitable organization and mail the title, free and clear of any liens, to the used motor vehicle dealer possessing the vehicle.

(4) If the notice required under subdivision (1) of this subsection is not received or is returned as undeliverable, the used motor vehicle dealer may file a special proceeding to obtain an order allowing the vehicle to be sold. In such a proceeding, the used motor vehicle dealer may include more than one vehicle.

(5) If the donated vehicle is not currently titled in this State, does not appear in the Division's records, or the owner and any lienholders are not otherwise reasonably ascertainable for any reason, the used motor vehicle dealer may institute a civil action in the county where the vehicle is being held for authorization to sell that vehicle as salvage on behalf of the charitable organization. In such a proceeding, the used motor vehicle dealer may include more than one vehicle. If the court enters an order authorizing the sale of the vehicle, upon proper application and payment of the appropriate taxes and fees, the Division shall issue a salvage branded title to the person who purchases the vehicle at a subsequent sale.

(b) No person shall have a cause of action against the Division or Division contractors arising from the issuance of a title pursuant to this section, and the Division and Division contractors shall not be held liable for any damages arising from the transfer or subsequent operation of any vehicle titled or sold pursuant to this section.

History.
2018-43, s. 1

§ 20-110. When registration shall be rescinded

(a) The Division shall rescind and cancel the registration of any vehicle which the Division shall determine is unsafe or unfit to be operated or is not equipped as required by law.

(b) The Division shall rescind and cancel the registration of any vehicle whenever the person to whom the registration card or registration number plates therefor have been issued shall make or permit to be made any unlawful use of the said card or plates or permit the use thereof by a person not entitled thereto.

(c) Repealed by Session Laws 1993, c. 440, s. 8.

(d) The Division shall rescind and cancel the certificate of title to any vehicle which has been erroneously issued or fraudulently obtained or is unlawfully detained by anyone not entitled to possession.

(e) and (f) Repealed by Session Laws 1993, c. 440, s. 8.

(g) The Division shall rescind and cancel the registration plates issued to a carrier of passengers or property which has been secured by such carrier as provided under G.S. 20-50 when the license is being used on a vehicle other than the one for which it was issued or which is being used by the lessor-owner after the lease with such lessee has been terminated.

(h) The Division may rescind and cancel the registration or certificate of title on any vehicle on the grounds that the application therefor contains any false or fraudulent statement or that the holder of the certificate was not entitled to the issuance of a certificate of title or registration.

(i) The Division may rescind and cancel the registration or certificate of title of any vehicle when the Division has reasonable grounds to believe that the vehicle is a stolen or embezzled vehicle, or that the granting of registration or the issuance of certificate of title constituted a fraud against the rightful owner or person having a valid lien upon such vehicle.

(j) The Division may rescind and cancel the registration or certificate of title of any vehicle on the grounds that the registration of the vehicle stands suspended or revoked under the motor vehicle laws of this State.

(k) The Division shall rescind and cancel a certificate of title when the Division finds that such certificate has been used in connection with the registration or sale of a vehicle other than the vehicle for which the certificate was issued.

(l) The Division may rescind and cancel the registration and certificate of title of a vehicle when presented with evidence, such as a sworn statement, that the vehicle has been transferred to a person who has failed to get a new certificate of title for the vehicle as required by G.S. 20-73. A person may submit evidence to the Division by mail.

(m) The Division shall rescind and cancel the registration of vehicles of a motor carrier that is the subject of an order issued by the Federal Motor Carrier Safety Administration or the Division.

(n) The Division shall rescind and cancel the registration of a vehicle of a motor carrier if the applicant fails to disclose material information

required, or if the applicant has made a materially false statement on the application, or if the applicant has applied as a subterfuge for the real party in interest who has been issued a federal out-of-service order, or if the applicant's business is operated, managed, or otherwise controlled by or affiliated with a person who is ineligible for registration, including the applicant entity, a relative, family member, corporate officer, or shareholder. The Division shall rescind and cancel the registration for a vehicle that has been assigned for safety to a commercial motor carrier who has been prohibited from operating by the Federal Motor Carrier Safety Administration or a carrier whose business is operated, managed, or otherwise controlled by or affiliated with a person who is ineligible for registration, including the owner, a relative, family member, corporate officer, or shareholder.

History.
1937, c. 407, s. 74; 1945, c. 576, s. 5; 1947, c. 220, s. 4; 1951, c. 985, s. 1; 1953, c. 831, s. 4; 1955, c. 294, s. 1; c. 554, s. 11; 1975, c. 716, s. 5; 1981, c. 976, s. 11; 1991, c. 183, s. 1; 1993, c. 440, s. 8; 2002-152, s. 2; 2019-196, s. 3

§ 20-111. Violation of registration provisions

It shall be unlawful for any person to commit any of the following acts:

(1) To drive a vehicle on a highway, or knowingly permit a vehicle owned by that person to be driven on a highway, when the vehicle is not registered with the Division in accordance with this Article or does not display a current registration plate. Violation of this subdivision is a Class 3 misdemeanor.

(2) To display or cause or permit to be displayed or to have in possession any registration card, certificate of title or registration number plate knowing the same to be fictitious or to have been canceled, revoked, suspended or altered, or to willfully display an expired license or registration plate on a vehicle knowing the same to be expired. Violation of this subdivision is a Class 3 misdemeanor.

(3) The giving, lending, or borrowing of a license plate for the purpose of using same on some motor vehicle other than that for which issued shall make the giver, lender, or borrower guilty of a Class 3 misdemeanor. Where license plate is found being improperly used, such plate or plates shall be revoked or canceled, and new license plates must be purchased before further operation of the motor vehicle.

(4) To fail or refuse to surrender to the Division, upon demand, any title certificate,

registration card or registration number plate which has been suspended, canceled or revoked as in this Article provided. Service of the demand shall be in accordance with G.S. 20-48.

(5) To use a false or fictitious name or address in any application for the registration of any vehicle or for a certificate of title or for any renewal or duplicate thereof, or knowingly to make a false statement or knowingly to conceal a material fact or otherwise commit a fraud in any such application. A violation of this subdivision shall constitute a Class 1 misdemeanor.

(6) To give, lend, sell or obtain a certificate of title for the purpose of such certificate being used for any purpose other than the registration, sale, or other use in connection with the vehicle for which the certificate was issued. Any person violating the provisions of this subdivision shall be guilty of a Class 2 misdemeanor.

History.
1937, c. 407, s. 75; 1943, c. 592, s. 2; 1945, c. 576, s. 6; c. 635; 1949, c. 360; 1955, c. 294, s. 2; 1961, c. 360, s. 20; 1975, c. 716, s. 5; 1981, c. 938, s. 3; 1993, c. 440, s. 9; c. 539, ss. 351 -353; 1994, Ex. Sess., c. 24, s. 14(c); 2013-360, s. 18B.14(i)

§ 20-112. Making false affidavit perjury

Any person who shall knowingly make any false affidavit or shall knowingly swear or affirm falsely to any matter or thing required by the terms of this Article to be sworn or affirmed to shall be guilty of a Class I felony.

History.
1937, c. 407, s. 76; 1993, c. 539, s. 1256; 1994, Ex. Sess., c. 24, s. 14(c)

N.C. Gen. Stat. § 20-113

Repealed by Session Laws 1995 (Regular Session, 1996), c. 756, s. 13.

§ 20-114. Duty of officers; manner of enforcement

(a) For the purpose of enforcing the provisions of this Article, it is hereby made the duty of every police officer of any incorporated city or village, and every sheriff, deputy sheriff, and all other lawful officers of any county to arrest within the limits of their jurisdiction any person known personally to any such officer, or upon the sworn information of a creditable witness, to have violated any of the provisions of this Article, and to immediately bring such offender before any magistrate or officer having jurisdiction, and any such person so arrested shall have the right of immediate trial, and all other rights given to any person arrested for having committed a misdemeanor. Every officer herein named who shall neglect or refuse to carry out the duties imposed by this Chapter shall be liable on his official bond for such neglect or refusal as provided by law in like cases.

(b) It shall be the duty of all sheriffs, police officers, deputy sheriffs, deputy police officers, and all other officers within the State to cooperate with and render all assistance in their power to the officers herein provided for, and nothing in this Article shall be construed as relieving said sheriffs, police officers, deputy sheriffs, deputy police officers, and other officers of the duties imposed on them by this Chapter.

(c) It shall also be the duty of every law enforcement officer to make immediate report to the Commissioner of all motor vehicles reported to the officer as abandoned or that are seized by the officer for being used for illegal transportation of alcoholic beverages or other unlawful purposes, or seized and are subject to forfeiture pursuant to G.S. 20-28.2, et seq., or any other statute, and no motor vehicle shall be sold by any sheriff, police or peace officer, or by any person, firm or corporation claiming a mechanic's or storage lien, or under judicial proceedings, until notice on a form approved by the Commissioner shall have been given the Commissioner at least 20 days before the date of such sale.

History.
1937, c. 407, s. 78; 1943, c. 726; 1967, c. 862; 1971, c. 528, s. 13; 1981, c. 412, s. 4; c. 747, s. 66; 1998-182, s. 12

§ 20-114.1. Willful failure to obey law-enforcement or traffic-control officer; firemen as traffic-control officers; appointment, etc., of traffic-control officers

(a) No person shall willfully fail or refuse to comply with any lawful order or direction of any law-enforcement officer or traffic-control officer invested by law with authority to direct, control or regulate traffic, which order or direction related to the control of traffic.

(b) In addition to other law enforcement or traffic control officers, uniformed regular and volunteer firemen and uniformed regular and volunteer members of a rescue squad may direct traffic and enforce traffic laws and ordinances at the scene of or in connection with fires, accidents, or other hazards in connection with their duties as firemen or rescue squad members. Except as herein provided, firemen and members of rescue squads shall not be considered law enforcement or traffic control officers.

(b1) Any member of a rural volunteer fire department or volunteer rescue squad who receives no compensation for services shall not be liable in civil damages for any acts or omissions relating to the direction of traffic or enforcement of traffic laws or ordinances at the scene of or in connection with a fire, accident, or other hazard unless such acts or omissions amount to gross negligence, wanton conduct, or intentional wrongdoing.

(c) The chief of police of a local or county police department or the sheriff of any county is authorized to appoint traffic-control officers, who shall have attained the age of 18 years and who are hereby authorized to direct, control, or regulate traffic within their respective jurisdictions at times and places specifically designated in writing by the police chief or the sheriff. A traffic-control officer, when exercising this authority, must be attired in a distinguishing uniform or jacket indicating that he is a traffic-control officer and must possess a valid authorization card issued by the police chief or sheriff who appointed him. Unless an earlier expiration date is specified, an authorization card shall expire two years from the date of its issuance. In order to be appointed as a traffic-control officer, a person shall have received at least three hours of training in directing, controlling, or regulating traffic under the supervision of a law-enforcement officer. A traffic-control officer shall be subject to the rules and regulations of the respective local or county police department or sheriff's office as well as the lawful command of any other law-enforcement officer. The appointing police chief or sheriff shall have the right to revoke the appointment of any traffic-control officer at any time with or without cause. The appointing police chief or sheriff shall not be held liable for any act or omission of a traffic-control officer. A traffic-control officer shall not be deemed to be an agent or employee of the respective local or county police department or of the sheriff's office, nor shall he be considered a law-enforcement officer except as provided herein. A traffic-control officer shall not have nor shall he exercise the power of arrest.

(d) No police chief or sheriff who is authorized to appoint traffic-control officers under subsection (c) of this section shall appoint any person to direct, control, or regulate traffic unless there is indemnity against liability of the traffic-control officer for wrongful death, bodily injury, or property damage that is proximately caused by the negligence of the traffic-control officer while acting within the scope of his duties as a traffic-control officer. Such indemnity shall provide a minimum of twenty-five thousand dollars ($ 25,000) for the death of or bodily injury to one person in any one accident, fifty thousand dollars ($ 50,000) for the death of or bodily injury to two or more persons in any one accident, and ten thousand dollars ($ 10,000) for injury to or

destruction of property of others in any one accident.

History.
1961, c. 879; 1969, c. 59; 1983, c. 483, ss. 1-3; 1987, c. 146, ss. 1, 3

N.C. Gen. Stat. § 20-114.3

Repealed by Session Laws 2007-433, s. 3(a), (b), effective October 1, 2007.

PART 9
THE SIZE, WEIGHT, CONSTRUCTION AND EQUIPMENT OF VEHICLES

§ 20-115. Scope and effect of regulations in this Part

It shall be unlawful for any person to drive or move or for the owner to cause or knowingly permit to be driven or moved on any highway any vehicle or vehicles of a size or weight exceeding the limitations stated in this Part, or any vehicle or vehicles which are not so constructed or equipped as required in this Part, or the rules and regulations of the Department of Transportation adopted pursuant to this Part and the maximum size and weight of vehicles specified in this Part shall be lawful throughout this State, and local authorities shall have no power or authority to alter the limitations except as express authority may be granted in this Article.

History.
1937, c. 407, s. 79; 1973, c. 507, s. 5; 1977, c. 464, s. 34; 1985 (Reg. Sess., 1986), c. 852, s. 8; 2015-264, s. 8(a)

§ 20-115.1. Limitations on tandem trailers and semitrailers on certain North Carolina highways

(a) Motor vehicle combinations consisting of a truck tractor and two trailing units may be operated in North Carolina only on highways of the interstate system (except those exempted by the United States Secretary of Transportation pursuant to 49 USC 2311(i)) and on those sections of the federal-aid primary system designated by the United States Secretary of Transportation. No trailer or semitrailer operated in this combination shall exceed 28 feet in length; Provided, however, a 1982 or older year model trailer or semitrailer of up to 28 1/2 feet in length may operate in a combination permitted by this section for trailers or semitrailers which are 28 feet in length.

(b) Motor vehicle combinations consisting of a semitrailer of not more than 53 feet in length and a truck tractor may be operated on all primary highway routes of North Carolina provided the motor vehicle combination meets the requirements of this subsection. The Department may, at any time, prohibit motor vehicle combinations on portions of any route on the State highway system. If the Department prohibits a motor vehicle combination on any route, it shall submit a written report to the Joint Legislative Transportation Oversight Committee within six months of the prohibition clearly documenting through traffic engineering studies that the operation of a motor vehicle combination on that route cannot be safely accommodated and that the route does not have sufficient capacity to handle the vehicle combination. To operate on a primary highway route, a motor vehicle combination described in this subsection must meet all of the following requirements:

(1) The motor vehicle combination must comply with the weight requirements in G.S. 20-118.

(2) A semitrailer in excess of 48 feet in length must meet one or more of the following conditions:

(a) The distance between the kingpin of the trailer and the rearmost axle, or a point midway between the two rear axles, if the two rear axles are a tandem axle, does not exceed 41 feet.

(b) The semitrailer is used exclusively or primarily to transport vehicles in connection with motorsports competition events, and the distance between the kingpin of the trailer and the rearmost axle, or a point midway between the two rear axles, if the two rear axles are a tandem axle, does not exceed 46 feet.

(3) A semitrailer in excess of 48 feet must be equipped with a rear underride guard of substantial construction consisting of a continuous lateral beam extending to within four inches of the lateral extremities of the semitrailer and located not more than 30 inches from the surface as measured with the vehicle empty and on a level surface.

(c) Motor vehicles with a width not exceeding 102 inches may be operated on the interstate highways (except those exempted by the United States Secretary of Transportation pursuant to 49 USC 2316(e)) and other qualifying federal-aid highways designated by the United States Secretary of Transportation, with traffic lanes designed to be a width of 12 feet or more and any other qualifying federal-aid primary system highway designated by the United States Secretary of Transportation if the Secretary has determined that the designation is consistent with highway safety.

(d) Notwithstanding the provisions of subsections (a) and (b) of this section which limit the length of trailers which may be used in motor vehicle combinations in this State on highways of the interstate system (except those exempted by the United States Secretary of Transportation pursuant to 49 USC 2311(i)) and on those sections of the federal-aid primary system designated by the United States Secretary of Transportation, there is no limitation of the length of the truck tractor which may be used in motor vehicle combinations on these highways and therefore, in compliance with Section 411(b) of the Surface Transportation Act of 1982, there is no overall length limitation for motor vehicle combinations regulated by this section.

(e) The length and width limitations in this section are subject to exceptions and exclusions for safety devices and specialized equipment as provided for in 49 USC 2311(d)(h) and Section 416 of the Surface Transportation Act of 1982 as amended (49 USC 2316).

(f) Motor vehicle combinations operating pursuant to this section shall have reasonable access between (i) highways on the interstate system (except those exempted by the United States Secretary of Transportation pursuant to 49 USC 2311(i) and 49 USC 2316(e)) and other qualifying federal-aid highways as designated by the United States Secretary of Transportation and (ii) terminals, facilities for food, fuel, repairs, and rest and points of loading and unloading by household goods carriers and by any truck tractor-semitrailer combination in which the semitrailer has a length not to exceed 28 1/2 feet and a width not to exceed 102 inches as provided in subsection (c) of this section and which generally operates as part of a vehicle combination described in subsection (a) of this section. The North Carolina Department of Transportation may, on streets and highways on the State highway system, and any municipality may, on streets and highways on the municipal street system, impose reasonable restrictions based on safety considerations on any truck tractor-semitrailer combination in which the semitrailer has a length not to exceed 28 1/2 feet and which generally operates as part of a vehicle combination described in subsection (a) of this section. "Reasonable access" to facilities for food, fuel, repairs and rest shall be deemed to be those facilities which are located within three road miles of the interstate or designated highway. The Department of Transportation is authorized to promulgate rules and regulations providing for "reasonable access." The Department may approve reasonable access routes for one particular type of STAA (Surface Transportation Assistance Act) dimensioned vehicle when significant, substantial differences in their operating characteristics exist.

(g) Under certain conditions, and after consultation with the Joint Legislative Commission on Governmental Operations, the North Carolina Department of Transportation may designate State highway system roads in addition to those highways designated by the United States Secretary of Transportation for use by the vehicle combinations authorized in this section. Such designations by the Department shall only be made under the following conditions:

(1) A determination of the public convenience and need for such designation;

(2) A traffic engineering study which clearly shows the road proposed to be designated can safely accommodate and has sufficient capacity to handle these vehicle combinations; and

(3) A public hearing is held or the opportunity for a public hearing is provided in each county through which the designated highway passes, after two weeks notice posted at the courthouse and published in a newspaper of general circulation in each county through which the designated State highway system road passes, and consideration is given to the comments received prior to the designation.

(4) The Department may designate routes for one particular type of STAA (Surface Transportation Assistance Act) dimensioned vehicle when significant, substantial differences in their operating characteristics exist.

The Department may not designate any portion of the State highway system that has been deleted or exempted by the United States Secretary of Transportation based on safety considerations. For the purpose of this section, any highway designated by the Department shall be deemed to be the same as a federal-aid primary highway designated by the United States Secretary of Transportation pursuant to 49 USC 2311 and 49 USC 2316, and the vehicle combinations authorized in this section shall be permitted to operate on such highway.

(h) Any owner of a semitrailer less than 50 feet in length in violation of subsections (a) or (b) is responsible for an infraction and is subject to a penalty of one hundred dollars ($ 100.00). Any owner of a semitrailer 50 feet or greater in length in violation of subsection (b) is responsible for an infraction and subject to a penalty of two hundred dollars ($ 200.00).

(i) Any driver of a vehicle with a semitrailer less than 50 feet in length violating subsections (a) or (b) of this section is guilty of a Class 3 misdemeanor punishable only by a fine of one hundred dollars ($ 100.00). Any driver of a vehicle with a semitrailer 50 feet or more in length violating subsection (b) of this section is guilty of a Class 3 misdemeanor

punishable only by a fine of two hundred dollars ($ 200.00).

(j) Notwithstanding any other provision of this section, a manufacturer of trailer frames, with a permit issued pursuant to G.S. 20-119, is authorized to transport the trailer frame to another location within three miles of the first place of manufacture to the location of completion on any public street or highway if the width of the trailer frame does not exceed 14 feet and oversize markings and safety flags are used during transport. Trailer frames transported pursuant to this subsection shall not exceed 7,000 pounds, and the vehicle towing the trailer frame shall have a towing capacity greater than 10,000 pounds and necessary towing equipment. The transport of trailer frames under this subsection shall only be done during daylight hours.

History.
1983, c. 898, s. 1; 1985, c. 423, ss. 1-7; 1989, c. 790, ss. 1, 3, 3.1; 1993, c. 533, s. 10; c. 539, s. 354; 1994, Ex. Sess., c. 24, s. 14(c); 1998-149, s. 6; 2007-77, ss. 2, 3; 2008-160, s. 1; 2008-221, ss. 3, 4

§ 20-116. Size of vehicles and loads

(a) The total outside width of any vehicle or the load thereon shall not exceed 102 inches, except as otherwise provided in this section. When hogsheads of tobacco are being transported, a tolerance of six inches is allowed. When sheet or bale tobacco is being transported the load must not exceed a width of 114 inches at the top of the load and the bottom of the load at the truck bed must not exceed the width of 102 inches inclusive of allowance for load shifting or settling. Vehicles (other than passenger buses) that do not exceed the overall width of 102 inches and otherwise provided in this section may be operated in accordance with G.S. 20-115.1(c), (f), and (g).

(b) No passenger-type vehicle or recreational vehicle shall be operated on any highway with any load carried thereon extending beyond the line of the fenders on the left side of such vehicle nor extending more than six inches beyond the line of the fenders on the right side thereof.

(c) No vehicle, unladen or with load, shall exceed a height of 13 feet, six inches. Provided, however, that neither the State of North Carolina nor any agency or subdivision thereof, nor any person, firm or corporation, shall be required to raise, alter, construct or reconstruct any underpass, wire, pole, trestle, or other structure to permit the passage of any vehicle having a height, unladen or with load, in excess of 12 feet, six inches. Provided further, that the operator or owner of any vehicle having an overall height, whether unladen or with load, in excess of 12 feet, six inches, shall be liable for damage to any structure caused by such vehicle having a height in excess of 12 feet, six inches.

(d) **Maximum Length.** -- The following maximum lengths apply to vehicles. A truck-tractor and semitrailer shall be regarded as two vehicles for the purpose of determining lawful length and license taxes.

(1) Except as otherwise provided in this subsection, a single vehicle having two or more axles shall not exceed 40 feet in length overall of dimensions inclusive of front and rear bumpers.

(2) Trucks transporting unprocessed cotton from farm to gin, or unprocessed sage from farm to market shall not exceed 50 feet in length overall of dimensions inclusive of front and rear bumpers.

(3) Recreational vehicles shall not exceed 45 feet in length overall, excluding bumpers and mirrors.

(4) Vehicles owned or leased by State, local, or federal government, when used for official law enforcement or emergency management purposes, shall not exceed 45 feet in length overall, excluding bumpers and mirrors.

(e) Except as provided by G.S. 20-115.1, no combination of vehicles coupled together shall consist of more than two units and no such combination of vehicles shall exceed a total length of 60 feet inclusive of front and rear bumpers, subject to the following exceptions: Motor vehicle combinations of one semitrailer of not more than 53 feet in length and a truck tractor (power unit) may exceed the 60-foot maximum length. Said maximum overall length limitation shall not apply to vehicles operated in the daytime when transporting poles, pipe, machinery or other objects of a structural nature which cannot readily be dismembered, nor to such vehicles transporting such objects operated at nighttime by a public utility when required for emergency repair of public service facilities or properties, provided the trailer length does not exceed 53 feet in length, but in respect to such night transportation every such vehicle and the load thereon shall be equipped with a sufficient number of clearance lamps on both sides and marker lamps upon the extreme ends of said projecting load to clearly mark the dimensions of such load: Provided that vehicles designed and used exclusively for the transportation of motor vehicles shall be permitted an overhang tolerance front or rear not to exceed five feet. Provided, that wreckers may tow a truck, combination tractor and trailer, trailer, or any other disabled vehicle or combination of vehicles to a place for repair, parking, or storage within 50 miles of the point where the vehicle was disabled and may tow a truck, tractor, or other replacement vehicle to the site of the disabled vehicle. Provided further, that the said limitation that no combination of vehicles coupled together shall consist of more than two units shall not apply to trailers not exceeding three in number drawn by a motor vehicle used by municipalities for the removal of domestic and commercial refuse and street rubbish, but such combination of vehicles shall not exceed a total length of 50 feet inclusive of front and rear bumpers. Provided further, that the said limitation that no combination of vehicles coupled together shall consist of more than two units shall not apply to a combination of vehicles coupled together by a saddle mount device used to transport motor vehicles in a driveway service when no more than three saddle mounts are used and provided further, that equipment used in said combination is approved by the safety regulations of the Federal Highway Administration and the safety rules of the Department of Public Safety.

(f) The load upon any vehicle operated alone, or the load upon the front vehicle of a combination of vehicles, shall not extend more than three feet beyond the foremost part of the vehicle. Under this subsection "load" shall include the boom on a self-propelled vehicle.

A utility pole carried by a self-propelled pole carrier may extend beyond the front overhang limit set in this subsection if the pole cannot be dismembered, the pole is less than 80 feet in length and does not extend more than 10 feet beyond the front bumper of the vehicle, and either of the following circumstances apply:

(1) It is daytime and the front of the extending load of poles is marked by a flag of the type required by G.S. 20-117 for certain rear overhangs.

(2) It is nighttime, operation of the vehicle is required to make emergency repairs to utility service, and the front of the extending load of poles is marked by a light of the type required by G.S. 20-117 for certain rear overhangs.

As used in this subsection, a "self-propelled pole carrier" is a vehicle designed to carry a pole on the side of the vehicle at a height of at least five feet when measured from the bottom of the brace used to carry the pole. A self-propelled pole carrier may not tow another vehicle when carrying a pole that extends beyond the front overhang limit set in this subsection.

(g) (1) No vehicle shall be driven or moved on any highway unless the vehicle is constructed and loaded to prevent any of its load from falling, blowing, dropping, sifting, leaking, or otherwise escaping therefrom, and the vehicle shall not contain any holes, cracks, or openings through which any of its load may escape. However, sand may be dropped for the purpose of securing traction, or water or other substance may be sprinkled, dumped, or spread on a roadway in cleaning or maintaining the roadway. For purposes of this subsection, the terms "load" and "leaking" do not include water accumulated from precipitation.

(2) A truck, trailer, or other vehicle licensed for more than 7,500 pounds gross vehicle weight that is loaded with rock, gravel, stone, or any other similar substance, other than sand, that could fall, blow, leak, sift, or drop shall not be driven or moved on any highway unless:

a. The height of the load against all four walls does not extend above a horizontal line six inches below their tops when loaded at the loading point; and

b. The load is securely covered by tarpaulin or some other suitable covering to prevent any of its load from falling, dropping, sifting, leaking, blowing, or otherwise escaping therefrom.

(3) A truck, trailer, or other vehicle licensed for 7,500 pounds or less gross vehicle weight and loaded with rock, gravel, stone, or any other similar substance that could fall, blow, leak, or sift, or licensed for any gross vehicle weight and loaded with sand, shall not be driven or moved on any highway unless:

a. The height of the load against all four walls does not extend above a horizontal line six inches below the top when loaded at the loading point;

b. The load is securely covered by tarpaulin or some other suitable covering; or

c. The vehicle is constructed to prevent any of its load from falling, dropping, sifting, leaking, blowing, or otherwise escaping therefrom.

(4) This section shall not be applicable to or in any manner restrict the transportation of seed cotton, poultry or livestock, or silage or other feed grain used in the feeding of poultry or livestock.

(h) Whenever there exist two highways of the State highway system of approximately the same distance between two or more points, the Department of Transportation may, when in the opinion of the Department of Transportation, based upon engineering and traffic investigation, safety will be promoted or the public interest will be served, designate one of the highways the "truck route" between those points, and to prohibit the use of the other highway by heavy trucks or other vehicles of a gross vehicle weight or axle load limit in excess of a designated maximum. In such instances the highways selected for heavy vehicle traffic shall be designated as "truck routes" by signs conspicuously posted, and the highways upon which heavy vehicle traffic is prohibited shall likewise be designated by signs conspicuously posted

showing the maximum gross vehicle weight or axle load limits authorized for those highways. The operation of any vehicle whose gross vehicle weight or axle load exceeds the maximum limits shown on signs over the posted highway shall constitute a Class 2 misdemeanor: Provided, that nothing in this subsection shall prohibit a truck or other motor vehicle whose gross vehicle weight or axle load exceeds that prescribed for those highways from using them when its destination is located solely upon that highway, road or street: Provided, further, that nothing in this subsection shall prohibit passenger vehicles or other light vehicles from using any highways designated for heavy truck traffic.

(i) Repealed by Session Laws 1973, c. 1330, s. 39.

(j) Nothing in this section shall be construed to prevent the operation of self-propelled grain combines or other self-propelled farm equipment with or without implements, not exceeding 25 feet in width on any highway, unless the operation violates a provision of this subsection. Farm equipment includes a vehicle that is designed exclusively to transport compressed seed cotton from a farm to a gin and has a self-loading bed. Combines or equipment which exceed 10 feet in width may be operated only if they meet all of the conditions listed in this subsection. A violation of one or more of these conditions does not constitute negligence per se.

(1) The equipment may only be operated during daylight hours.

(2) The equipment must display a red flag on front and rear ends or a flashing warning light. The flags or lights shall be attached to the equipment as to be visible from both directions at all times while being operated on the public highway for not less than 300 feet.

(3) Equipment covered by this section, which by necessity must travel more than 10 miles or where by nature of the terrain or obstacles the flags or lights referred to in subdivision (2) of this subsection are not visible from both directions for 300 feet at any point along the proposed route, must be preceded at a distance of 300 feet and followed at a distance of 300 feet by a flagman in a vehicle having mounted thereon an appropriate warning light or flag. No flagman in a vehicle shall be required pursuant to this subdivision if the equipment is being moved under its own power or on a trailer from any field to another field, or from the normal place of storage of the vehicle to any field, for no more than ten miles and if visible from both directions for 300 feet at any point along the proposed route.

(4) Every piece of equipment so operated shall operate to the right of the center line unless the combined width of the traveling

Chapter 20

lane and the accessible shoulder is less than the width of the equipment.

(5) Repealed by Session Laws 2008-221, s. 6, effective September 1, 2008.

(6) When the equipment is causing a delay in traffic, the operator of the equipment shall move the equipment off the paved portion of the highway at the nearest practical location until the vehicles following the equipment have passed.

(7) The equipment shall be operated in the designed transport position that minimizes equipment width. No removal of equipment or appurtenances is required under this subdivision.

(8) Equipment covered by this subsection shall not be operated on a highway or section of highway that is a fully controlled access highway or is a part of the National System of Interstate and Defense Highways without authorization from the North Carolina Department of Transportation. The Department shall develop an authorization process and approve routes under the following conditions:

a. Persons shall submit an application to the Department requesting authorization to operate equipment covered by this subsection on a particular route that is part of a highway or section of highway that is a fully controlled access highway or is a part of the National System of Interstate and Defense Highways.

b. The Department shall have a period of 30 days from receipt of a complete application to approve or reject the application. A complete application shall be deemed approved if the Department does not take action within 30 days of receipt by the Department; such a route may then be used by the original applicant.

c. The Department shall approve an application upon a showing that the route is necessary to accomplish one or more of the following:

1. Prevent farming operations from traveling more than five miles longer than the requested route during the normal course of business.

2. Prevent excess traffic delays on local or secondary roads.

3. Allow farm equipment access due to dimension restrictions on local or secondary roads.

d. For applications that do not meet the requirements of sub-subdivision c. of this subdivision, the Department may also approve an application upon review of relevant safety factors.

e. The Department may consult with the North Carolina State Highway Patrol, the North Carolina Department of Agriculture and Consumer Services, or other parties concerning an application.

f. Any approved route may be subject to any of the following additional conditions:

1. A requirement that the subject equipment be followed by a flag vehicle with flashing lights that shall be operated at all times on the route so as to be visible from a distance of at least 300 feet.

2. Restrictions on maximum and minimum speeds of the equipment.

3. Restrictions on the maximum dimensions of the equipment.

4. Restrictions on the time of day that the equipment may be operated on the approved route.

g. The Department shall publish all approved routes, including any conditions on the routes' use, and shall notify appropriate State and local law enforcement officers of any approved route.

h. Once approved for use and published by the Department, a route may be used by any person who adheres to the route, including any conditions on the route's use imposed by the Department.

i. The Department may revise published routes as road conditions on the routes change.

(k) Nothing in this section shall be construed to prevent the operation of passenger buses having an overall width of 102 inches, exclusive of safety equipment, upon the highways of this State which are 20 feet or wider and that are designated as the State primary system, or as municipal streets, when, and not until, the federal law and regulations thereunder permit the operation of passenger buses having a width of 102 inches or wider on the National System of Interstate and Defense Highways.

(l) Nothing in this section shall be construed to prevent the operation of passenger buses that are owned and operated by units of local government, operated as a single vehicle only and having an overall length of 45 feet or less, on public streets or highways. The Department of Transportation may prevent the operation of buses that are authorized under this subsection if the operation of such buses on a street or highway presents a hazard to passengers of the buses or to the motoring public.

(m) Notwithstanding subsection (a) of this section, a boat or boat trailer with an outside

Chapter 20

width of less than 120 inches may be towed without a permit. The towing of a boat or boat trailer 102 inches to 114 inches in width may take place on any day of the week, including weekends and holidays, and may take place at night. The towing of a boat or boat trailer 114 inches to 120 inches in width may take place on any day of the week, including weekends and holidays from sun up to sun down. A boat or boat trailer in excess of 102 inches but less than 120 inches must be equipped with a minimum of two operable amber lamps on the widest point of the boat and the boat trailer such that the dimensions of the boat and the boat trailer are clearly marked and visible.

(n) Vehicle combinations used in connection with motorsports competition events that include a cab or other motorized vehicle unit with living quarters, and an attached enclosed specialty trailer, the combination of which does not exceed 90 feet in length, may be operated on the highways of this State, provided that such operation takes place for one or more of the following purposes:

(1) Driving to or from a motorsports competition event.

(2) For trips conducted for the purpose of purchasing fuel or conducting repairs or other maintenance on the competition vehicle.

(3) For other activities related to motorsports purposes, including, but not limited to, performance testing of the competition vehicle.

The Department of Transportation may prohibit combinations authorized by this subsection from specific routes, pursuant to G.S. 20-115.1(b).

(o) Any vehicle carrying baled hay from place to place on the same farm, from one farm to another, from farm to market, or from market to farm that does not exceed 12 feet in width may be operated on the highways of this State. Vehicles carrying baled hay that exceed 10 feet in width may only be operated under the following conditions:

(1) The vehicle may only be operated during daylight hours.

(2) The vehicle shall display a red flag or a flashing warning light on both the rear and front ends. The flags or lights shall be attached to the equipment as to be visible from both directions at all times while being operated on the public highway for not less than 300 feet.

(p) Notwithstanding any provision of this section to the contrary, the following may operate on the highways of this State without an oversize permit for the purpose of Department snow removal and snow removal training operations:

(1) Truck supporting snow plows with blades not exceeding 12 feet in width. A truck operated pursuant to this subdivision shall have adequate illumination when the plow is in the up and the down positions; visible signal lights; and a plow that is angled so that the minimum width is exposed to oncoming traffic during periods of travel between assignments.

(2) Motor graders not exceeding 102 inches in width, measured from the outside edge of the tires. A motor grader operated pursuant to this subdivision shall have adequate illumination when the moldboard is in the up and down positions; visible signal lights; and a moldboard that is angled not to exceed 102 inches during periods of travel between assignments.

History.
1937, c. 246; c. 407, s. 80; 1943, c. 213, s. 1; 1945, c. 242, s. 1; 1947, c. 844; 1951, c. 495, s. 1; c. 733; 1953, cc. 682, 1107; 1955, c. 296, s. 2; c. 729; 1957, c. 65, s. 11; cc. 493, 1183, 1190; 1959, c. 559; 1963, c. 356, s. 1; c. 610, ss. 1, 2; c. 702, s. 4; c. 1027, s. 1; 1965, c. 471; 1967, c. 24, s. 4; c. 710; 1969, cc. 128, 880; 1971, cc. 128, 680, 688, 1079; 1973, c. 507, s. 5; c. 546; c. 1330, s. 39; 1975, c. 148, ss. 1-5; c. 716, s. 5; 1977, c. 464, s. 34; 1979, cc. 21, 218; 1981, c. 169, s. 1; 1983, c. 724, s. 2; 1985, c. 587; 1987, c. 272; 1989, c. 277, s. 1; c. 790, s. 2; 1991, c. 112, s. 1; c. 449, ss. 1, 2.1; 1993, c. 539, s. 355; 1994, Ex. Sess., c. 24, s. 14(c); 1995 (Reg. Sess., 1996), c. 573, s. 1; c. 756, s. 14; 1998-149, s. 7; 1999-438, s. 28; 2000-185, s. 2; 2001-341, ss. 3, 4; 2001-512, s. 2; 2002-72, s. 19(c); 2002-159, s. 31.5(b); 2002-190, s. 2; 2003-383, s. 8; 2005-248, s. 2; 2007-77, s. 1; 2007-194, ss. 2, 3; 2007-484, s. 5; 2007-499, s. 1; 2008-221, ss. 5, 6; 2008-229, s. 1; 2009-7, s. 1; 2009-127, s. 1; 2009-128, s. 1; 2011-145, s. 19.1(g); 2012-33, s. 1; 2012-78, s. 5; 2013-413, s. 59.2(f); 2014-115, s. 17; 2015-263, ss. 5, 6(a); 2015-264, s. 41; 2015-286, s. 1.8(a)

§ 20-117. Flag or light at end of load

(a) **General Provisions.** -- Whenever the load on any vehicle shall extend more than four feet beyond the rear of the bed or body thereof, there shall be displayed at the end of such load, in such position as to be clearly visible at all times from the rear of such load, a red or orange flag not less than 18 inches both in length and width, except that from sunset to sunrise there shall be displayed at the end of any such load a red or amber light plainly visible under normal atmospheric conditions at least 200 feet from the rear of such vehicle. At no time shall a load extend more than 14 feet beyond the rear of the bed or body of the vehicle, with the exception of vehicles transporting forestry products or utility poles.

(b) **Commercial Motor Vehicles.** -- A commercial motor vehicle, or a motor vehicle with a GVWR of 10,001 pounds or more that is engaged in commerce, that is being used to tow a

Chapter 20

load or that has a load that protrudes from the rear or sides of the vehicle shall comply with the provisions of 49 C.F.R. Part 393.

History.
1937, c. 407, s. 81; 1985, c. 455; 1997-178, s. 1; 2005-361, s. 2; 2009-376, s. 4

§ 20-117.1. Requirements for mirrors and fuel container

(a) **Rear-Vision Mirrors.** -- Every bus, truck, and truck tractor with a GVWR of 10,001 pounds or more shall be equipped with two rear-vision mirrors, one at each side, firmly attached to the outside of the motor vehicle, and located as to reflect to the driver a view of the highway to the rear and along both sides of the vehicle. Only one outside mirror shall be required, on the driver's side, on trucks which are so constructed that the driver also has a view to the rear by means of an interior mirror. In driveaway-towaway operations, a driven vehicle shall have at least one mirror furnishing a clear view to the rear, and if the interior mirror does not provide the clear view, an additional mirror shall be attached to the left side of the driven vehicle to provide the clear view to the rear.

(b) **Fuel Container Not to Project.** -- No part of any fuel tank or container or intake pipe shall project beyond the sides of the motor vehicle.

History.
1949, c. 1207, s. 1; 1951, c. 819, s. 1; 1955, c. 1157, ss. 1, 4; 1991, c. 113, s. 1; c. 761, s. 6

§ 20-118. Weight of vehicles and load

(a) For the purposes of this section, the following definitions apply:

(1), (2) Repealed by Session Laws 2018-142, s. 5(b), effective December 14, 2018.

(3) **Axle group.** -- Any two or more consecutive axles on a vehicle or combination of vehicles.

(4) **Gross weight.** -- The weight of any single axle, tandem axle, or axle group of a vehicle or combination of vehicles plus the weight of any load thereon.

(5) **Light-traffic roads.** -- Any highway on the State Highway System, excepting routes designated I, U.S. or N.C., posted by the Department of Transportation to limit the axle weight below the statutory limits.

(6) **Single axle weight.** -- The gross weight transmitted by all wheels whose centers may be included between two parallel transverse vertical planes 40 inches apart, extending across the full width of the vehicle.

(7) **Tandem axle weight.** -- The gross weight transmitted to the road by two or more consecutive axles whose centers may be included between parallel vertical planes spaced more than 40 inches and not more than 96 inches apart, extending across the full width of the vehicle.

(b) The following weight limitations apply to vehicles operating on the highways of the State:

(1) The single-axle weight of a vehicle or combination of vehicles shall not exceed 20,000 pounds.

(2) The tandem-axle weight of a vehicle or combination of vehicles shall not exceed 38,000 pounds.

(3) The gross weight imposed upon the highway by any axle group of a vehicle or combination of vehicles shall not exceed the maximum weight given for the respective distance between the first and last axle of the group of axles measured longitudinally to the nearest foot as set forth in the following table:

Distance Between Axles*	Maximum Weight in Pounds for any Group of Two or More Consecutive Axles					
	2 Axles	3 Axles	4 Axles	5 Axles	6 Axles	7 Axles
4	38000					
5	38000					
6	38000					
7	38000					
8 or less	38000	38000				
more than 8	38000	42000				
9	39000	42500				
10	40000	43500				
11		44000				
12		45000	50000			
13		45500	50500			
14		46500	51500			
15		47000	52000			
16		48000	52500	58000		

Chapter 20

Distance Between Axles*	Maximum Weight in Pounds for any Group of Two or More Consecutive Axles					
	2 Axles	3 Axles	4 Axles	5 Axles	6 Axles	7 Axles
17		48500	53500	58500		
18		49500	54000	59000		
19		50000	54500	60000		
20		51000	55500	60500	66000	
21		51500	56000	61000	66500	
22		52500	56500	61500	67000	
23		53000	57500	62500	68000	
24		54000	58000	63000	68500	74000
25		54500	58500	63500	69000	74500
26		55500	59500	64000	69500	75000
27		56000	60000	65000	70000	75500
28		57000	60500	65500	71000	76500
29		57500	61500	66000	71500	77000
30		58500	62000	66500	72000	77500
31		59000	62500	67500	72500	78000
32		60000	63500	68000	73000	78500
33			64000	68500	74000	79000
34			64500	69000	74500	80000
35			65500	70000	75000	
36			66000**	70500	75500	
37			66500**	71000	76000	
38			67500**	72000	77000	
39			68000	72500	77500	
40			68500	73000	78000	
41			69500	73500	78500	
42			70000	74000	79000	
43			70500	75000	80000	
44			71500	75500		
45			72000	76000		
46			72500	76500		
47			73500	77500		
48			74000	78000		
49			74500	78500		
50			75500	79000		
51			76000	80000		
52			76500			
53			77500			
54			78000			
55			78500			
56			79500			
57			80000			

*Distance in Feet Between the Extremes of any Group of Two or More Consecutive Axles.
**See exception in subdivision (c)(1) of this section.

(4) The Department of Transportation may establish light-traffic roads and further restrict the axle weight limit on such light-traffic roads lower than the statutory limits. The Department of Transportation has the authority to designate any highway on the State Highway System, excluding routes designated by I, U.S. and N.C., as a light-traffic road when in the opinion of the Department of Transportation, the road is inadequate to carry and will be injuriously affected by vehicles using the road carrying the maximum axle weight.

All such roads so designated shall be conspicuously posted as light-traffic roads and the maximum axle weight authorized shall be displayed on proper signs erected thereon.

(c) **Exceptions.** -- The following exceptions apply to subsections (b) and (e) of this section:

(1) Two consecutive sets of tandem axles may carry a gross weight of 34,000 pounds each without penalty provided the overall distance between the first and last axles of the consecutive sets of tandem axles is 36 feet or more.

Chapter 20

(2) When a vehicle is operated in violation of subdivision (b)(1), (b)(2), or (b)(3) of this section, but the gross weight of the vehicle or combination of vehicles does not exceed that permitted by subdivision (b)(3) of this section, the owner of the vehicle shall be permitted to shift the load within the vehicle, without penalty, from one axle to another to comply with the weight limits in the following cases:

a. Where the single-axle load exceeds the statutory limits, but does not exceed 21,000 pounds.

b. Where the vehicle or combination of vehicles has tandem axles, but the tandem-axle weight does not exceed 40,000 pounds.

(3) When a vehicle is operated in violation of subdivision (b)(4) of this section, the owner of the vehicle shall be permitted, without penalty, to shift the load within the vehicle from one axle to another to comply with the weight limits where the single-axle weight does not exceed the posted limit by 2,500 pounds.

(4) A truck or other motor vehicle shall be exempt from the light-traffic road limitations provided for pursuant to subdivision (b)(4) of this section, when transporting supplies, material, or equipment necessary to carry out a farming operation engaged in the production of meats and agricultural crops and livestock or poultry by-products or a business engaged in the harvest or processing of seafood when the destination of the vehicle and load is located solely upon a light-traffic road.

(5) The light-traffic road limitations provided for pursuant to subdivision (b)(4) of this section do not apply to a vehicle while that vehicle is transporting only the following from its point of origin on a light-traffic road to either one of the two nearest highways that is not a light-traffic road. If that vehicle's point of origin is a non-light-traffic road and that road is blocked by light-traffic roads from all directions and is not contiguous with other non-light-traffic roads, then the road at point of origin is treated as a light-traffic road for purposes of this subdivision:

a. Processed or unprocessed seafood transported from boats or any other point of origin to a processing plant or a point of further distribution.

b. Meats, live poultry, or agricultural crop products transported from a farm to a processing plant or market.

c. Forest products originating and transported from a farm or from woodlands to market without interruption or delay for further packaging

or processing after initiating transport.

d. Livestock or live poultry transported from their point of origin to a processing plant or market.

e. Livestock by-products or poultry by-products transported from their point of origin to a rendering plant.

f. Recyclable material transported from its point of origin to a scrap-processing facility for processing. As used in this subpart, the terms "recyclable material" and "processing" have the same meaning as in G.S. 130A-290(a).

g. Garbage collected by the vehicle from residences or garbage dumpsters if the vehicle is fully enclosed and is designed specifically for collecting, compacting, and hauling garbage from residences or from garbage dumpsters. As used in this subpart, the term "garbage" does not include hazardous waste as defined in G.S. 130A-290(a), spent nuclear fuel regulated under G.S. 20-167.1, low-level radioactive waste as defined in G.S. 104E-5, or radioactive material as defined in G.S. 104E-5.

h. Treated sludge collected from a wastewater treatment facility.

i. Apples when transported from the orchard to the first processing or packing point.

j. Trees grown as Christmas trees from the field, farm, stand, or grove, and other forest products, including chips and bark, to a processing point.

k. Water, fertilizer, pesticides, seeds, fuel, and animal waste transported to or from a farm by a farm vehicle as defined in G.S. 20-37.16(e)(3).

(6) A truck or other motor vehicle shall be exempt from the light-traffic road limitations provided by subdivision (b)(4) of this section when the motor vehicles are owned, operated by or under contract to a public utility, electric or telephone membership corporation or municipality and are used in connection with installation, restoration, or emergency maintenance of utility services.

(7) A wrecker may tow any disabled truck or other motor vehicle or combination of vehicles to a place for repairs, parking, or storage within 50 miles from the point that the vehicle was disabled and may tow a truck, tractor, or other replacement vehicle to the site of the disabled vehicle without being in violation of this section provided that the wrecker and towed vehicle or combination of vehicles otherwise meet all requirements of this section.

(8) A firefighting vehicle operated by any member of a municipal or rural fire

Chapter 20

department in the performance of the member's duties, regardless of whether members of that fire department are paid or voluntary, and any vehicle of a voluntary lifesaving organization, when operated by a member of that organization while answering an official call, shall be exempt from the light-traffic road limitations provided by subdivision (b)(4) of this section.

(9) Repealed by Session Laws 1993 (Reg. Sess., 1994), c. 761, s. 12.

(10) Fully enclosed motor vehicles designed specifically for collecting, compacting, and hauling garbage from residences or from garbage dumpsters shall, when operating for those purposes, be allowed a single axle weight not to exceed 23,500 pounds on the steering axle on vehicles equipped with a boom, or on the rear axle on vehicles loaded from the rear. This exemption does not apply to vehicles operating on interstate highways, vehicles transporting hazardous waste as defined in G.S. 130A-290(a)(8), spent nuclear fuel regulated under G.S. 20-167.1, low-level radioactive waste as defined in G.S. 104E-5(9a), or radioactive material as defined in G.S. 104E-5(14).

(11) A truck or other motor vehicle shall be exempt for light-traffic road limitations issued under subdivision (b)(4) of this section when transporting heating fuel for on-premises use at a destination located on the light-traffic road.

(12) Subsections (b) and (e) of this section do not apply to a vehicle or vehicle combination that meets all of the conditions set out below:

　　a. Is transporting any of the following items within 150 miles of the point of origination:

　　　1. Agriculture, dairy, and crop products transported from a farm or holding facility to a processing plant, feed mill, or market.

　　　2. Water, fertilizer, pesticides, seeds, fuel, or animal waste transported to or from a farm.

　　　3. Meats, livestock, or live poultry transported from the farm where they were raised to a processing plant or market.

　　　3a. Feed or feed ingredients that are used in the feeding of poultry or livestock and transported from a storage facility, holding facility, or mill to a farm.

　　　4. Forest products originating and transported from a farm or woodlands to market with delay interruption or delay for further

packaging or processing after initiating transport.

　　　5. Wood residuals, including wood chips, sawdust, mulch, or tree bark from any site.

　　　6. Raw logs to market.

　　　7. Trees grown as Christmas trees from field, farm, stand, or grove to a processing point.

　　b. Repealed by Session Laws 1993 (Reg. Sess., 1994), c. 761, s. 13.

　　b1. Does not operate on an interstate highway or exceed any posted bridge weight limits during transportation or hauling of agricultural products.

　　c. Meets any of the following vehicle configurations:

　　　1. Does not exceed a single-axle weight of 22,000 pounds, a tandem-axle weight of 42,000 pounds, or a gross weight of 90,000 pounds.

　　　2. Consists of a five or more axle combination vehicle that does not exceed a single-axle weight of 26,000 pounds, a tandem-axle weight of 44,000 pounds and a gross weight of 90,000 pounds, with a length of at least 48 feet between the center of axle one and the center of the last axle of the vehicle and a minimum of 11 feet between the center of axle one and the center of axle two of the vehicle.

　　　3. Consists of a two-axle vehicle that does not exceed a gross weight of 37,000 pounds and a single-axle weight of no more than 27,000 pounds, with a length of at least 14 feet between the center of axle one and the center of axle two of the vehicle.

　　d. Repealed by Session Laws 2012-78, s. 6, effective June 26, 2012.

(13) Vehicles specifically designed for fire fighting that are owned by a municipal or rural fire department. This exception does not apply to vehicles operating on interstate highways.

(14) Subsections (b) and (e) of this section do not apply to a vehicle that meets all of the conditions below, but all other enforcement provisions of this Article remain applicable:

　　a. Is hauling aggregates from a distribution yard or a State-permitted production site located within a North Carolina county contiguous to the North Carolina State border to a destination in another state adjacent to that county as verified by a weight ticket in the driver's possession and available for inspection by enforcement personnel.

b. Does not operate on an interstate highway or exceed any posted bridge weight limits.

c. Does not exceed 69,850 pounds gross vehicle weight and 53,850 pounds per axle grouping for tri-axle vehicles. For purposes of this subsection, a tri-axle vehicle is a single power unit vehicle with a three consecutive axle group on which the respective distance between any two consecutive axles of the group, measured longitudinally center to center to the nearest foot, does not exceed eight feet. For purposes of this subsection, the tolerance provisions of subsection (h) of this section do not apply, and vehicles must be licensed in accordance with G.S. 20-88.

d. Repealed by Session Laws 2001-487, s. 10, effective December 16, 2001.

e. Repealed by Session Laws 2012-78, s. 6, effective June 26, 2012.

(15) Subsections (b) and (e) of this section do not apply to a vehicle or vehicle combination that meets all of the conditions below, but all other enforcement provisions of this Article remain applicable:

a. Is transporting bulk soil, bulk rock, sand, sand rock, or asphalt millings from a site that does not have a certified scale for weighing the vehicle.

b. Does not operate on an interstate highway, a posted light-traffic road, except as provided by subdivision (c) (5) of this section, or exceed any posted bridge weight limits.

c. Does not exceed a maximum gross weight 4,000 pounds in excess of what is allowed in subsection (b) of this section.

d. Does not exceed a single-axle weight of more than 22,000 pounds and a tandem-axle weight of more than 42,000 pounds.

e. Repealed by Session Laws 2012-78, s. 6, effective June 26, 2012.

(16) Subsections (b) and (e) of this section do not apply to a vehicle or vehicle combination that meets all of the conditions below, but all other enforcement provisions of this Article remain applicable:

a. Is hauling unhardened ready-mixed concrete.

b. Does not operate on an interstate highway or a posted light-traffic road, or exceed any posted bridge weight limits.

c. Has a single steer axle weight of no more than 22,000 pounds and a

tandem-axle weight of no more than 46,000 pounds.

d. Does not exceed a maximum gross weight of 66,000 pounds on a three-axle vehicle with a length of at least 21 feet between the center of axle one and the center of axle three of the vehicle.

e. Does not exceed a maximum gross weight of 72,600 pounds on a four-axle vehicle with a length of at least 36 feet between the center of axle one and the center of axle four. The four-axle vehicle shall have a maximum gross weight of 66,000 pounds on axles one, two, and three with a length of at least 21 feet between the center of axle one and the center of axle three.

For purposes of this subdivision, no additional weight allowances in this section apply for the gross weight, single-axle weight, and tandem-axle weight, and the tolerance allowed by subsection (h) of this section does not apply.

(17) Subsections (b) and (e) of this section do not apply to a truck owned, operated by, or under contract to a public utility, electric or telephone membership corporation, or municipality that meets all of the conditions listed below, but all other enforcement provisions of this Article remain applicable:

a. Is being used in connection with the installation, restoration, or maintenance of utility services within a North Carolina county located in whole or in part west of Interstate 77, and the terrain, road widths, and other naturally occurring conditions prevent the safe navigation and operation of a truck having more than a single axle or using a trailer.

b. Does not operate on an interstate highway.

c. Does not exceed a single-axle weight of more than 28,000 pounds.

d. Does not exceed a maximum gross weight in excess of 48,000 pounds.

(18) Subsections (b) and (e) of this section do not apply to a vehicle or vehicle combination that meets all of the conditions set out below:

a. Is transporting metal commodities or construction equipment.

b. Does not operate on an interstate highway, a posted light traffic road, or exceed any posted bridge weight limit.

c. Does not exceed a single-axle weight of 22,000 pounds, a tandem-axle weight of 42,000 pounds, or a gross weight of 90,000 pounds.

(19) Any additional weight allowance authorized by 23 U.S.C. § 127, and applicable

to all interstate highways, also applies to all State roads, unless the road is a posted road or posted bridge, or unless specifically prohibited by State law or a Department ordinance applicable to a specific road.

(d) The Department of Transportation is authorized to abrogate certain exceptions. The exceptions provided for in subdivisions (c)(4) and (c)(5) of this section as applied to any light-traffic road may be abrogated by the Department of Transportation upon a determination of the Department of Transportation that undue damage to the light-traffic road is resulting from vehicles exempted by subdivisions (c)(4) and (c)(5) of this section. In those cases where the exemption to the light-traffic roads are abrogated by the Department of Transportation, the Department shall post the road to indicate no exemptions.

(e) **Penalties. --**

(1) Except as provided in subdivision (2) of this subsection, for each violation of the single-axle or tandem-axle weight limits set in subdivision (b)(1), (b)(2), or (b)(4) of this section or axle weights authorized by special permit according to G.S. 20-119(a), the Department of Public Safety shall assess a civil penalty against the owner or registrant of the vehicle in accordance with the following schedule: for the first 1,000 pounds or any part thereof, four cents (4 cent(s)) per pound; for the next 1,000 pounds or any part thereof, six cents (6 cent(s)) per pound; and for each additional pound, ten cents (10 cent(s)) per pound. These penalties apply separately to each weight limit violated. In all cases of violation of the weight limitation, the penalty shall be computed and assessed on each pound of weight in excess of the maximum permitted.

(2) The penalty for a violation of the single-axle or tandem-axle weight limits by a vehicle that is transporting an item listed in subdivision (c)(5) of this section is one-half of the amount it would otherwise be under subdivision (1) of this subsection.

(3) If an axle-group weight of a vehicle exceeds the weight limit set in subdivision (b)(3) of this section plus any tolerance allowed in subsection (h) of this section or axle-group weights or gross weights authorized by special permit under G.S. 20-119(a), the Department of Public Safety shall assess a civil penalty against the owner or registrant of the motor vehicle. The penalty shall be assessed on the number of pounds by which the axle-group weight exceeds the limit set in subdivision (b)(3) of this section, or by a special permit issued pursuant to G.S. 20-119, as follows: for the first 2,000 pounds or any part thereof, two cents (2)

per pound; for the next 3,000 pounds or any part thereof, four cents (4) per pound; for each pound in excess of 5,000 pounds, ten cents (10) per pound. Tolerance pounds in excess of the limit set in subdivision (b)(3) of this section are subject to the penalty if the vehicle exceeds the tolerance allowed in subsection (h) of this section. These penalties apply separately to each axle-group weight limit violated. Notwithstanding any provision to the contrary, a vehicle with a special permit that is subject to additional penalties under this subsection based on a violation of any of the permit restrictions set out in G.S. 20-119(d1) shall be assessed a civil penalty, not to exceed ten thousand dollars ($ 10,000), based on the number of pounds by which the axle-group weight exceeds the limit set in subdivision (b)(3) of this section.

(4) The penalty for a violation of an axle-group weight limit by a vehicle that is transporting an item listed in subdivision (c)(5) of this section is one-half of the amount it would otherwise be under subdivision (3) of this subsection.

(5) A violation of a weight limit in this section or of a permitted weight under G.S. 20-119 is not punishable under G.S. 20-176.

(6) The penalty for violating the gross weight or axle-group weight by a dump truck or dump trailer vehicle transporting bulk soil, bulk rock, sand, sand rock, or asphalt millings intrastate from a site that does not have a certified scale for weighing the vehicle is one-half of the amount it otherwise would be under subdivisions (1) and (3) of this subsection.

(7) The clear proceeds of all civil penalties, civil forfeitures, and civil fines that are collected by the Department of Transportation pursuant to this section shall be remitted to the Civil Penalty and Forfeiture Fund in accordance with G.S. 115C-457.2.

(f) Repealed by Session Laws 1993 (Reg. Sess., 1994), c. 761, s. 15.

(g) This section does not permit the gross weight of any vehicle or combination in excess of the safe load carrying capacity established by the Department of Transportation on any bridge pursuant to G.S. 136-72.

(h) **Tolerance. --** A vehicle may exceed maximum and the inner axle-group weight limitations set forth in subdivision (b)(3) of this section by a tolerance of ten percent (10%). This exception does not authorize a vehicle to exceed either the single-axle or tandem-axle weight limitations set forth in subdivisions (b)(1) and (b)(2) of this section, or the maximum gross weight limit of 80,000 pounds. This exception does not apply to a vehicle exceeding posted bridge weight limitations as posted under G.S. 136-72 or to vehicles operating on interstate highways. The tolerance allowed under this subsection does not authorize the weight of a vehicle to exceed the weight for which that vehicle is licensed under G.S. 20-88. No tolerance on the single-axle weight or the tandem-axle weight provided for in subdivisions (b)(1) and (b)(2) of this section shall be granted administratively or otherwise. The Department of Transportation shall report back to the Transportation Oversight Committee and to the General Assembly on the effects of the tolerance granted under this section, any abuses of this tolerance, and any suggested revisions to this section by that Department on or before May 1, 1998.

(i) Repealed by Session Laws 1993 (Reg. Sess., 1994), c. 761, s. 16.

(j) Repealed by Session Laws 1987, c. 392.

(k) A vehicle which is equipped with a self-loading bed and which is designed and used exclusively to transport compressed seed cotton from the farm to a cotton gin, or sage to market, may operate on the highways of the State, except interstate highways, with a tandem-axle weight not exceeding 50,000 pounds. Such vehicles are exempt from light-traffic road limitations only from point of origin on the light-traffic road to the nearest State-maintained road which is not posted to prohibit the transportation of statutory load limits. This exemption does not apply to restricted, posted bridge structures.

(l) A vehicle or vehicle combination that hauls unhardened ready-mixed concrete may be weighed with weigh in motion scales, but the vehicle or vehicle combination must be weighed static, allowing the drum to come to a complete stop.

History.
1937, c. 407, s. 82; 1943, c. 213, s. 2; cc. 726, 784; 1945, c. 242, s. 2; c. 569, s. 2; c. 576, s. 7; 1947, c. 1079; 1949, c. 1207, s. 2; 1951, c. 495, s. 2; c. 942, s. 1; c. 1013, ss. 5, 6, 8; 1953, cc. 214, 1092; 1959, c. 872; c. 1264, s. 6; 1963, c. 159; c. 610, ss. 3-5; c. 702, s. 5; 1965, cc. 483, 1044; 1969, c. 537; 1973, c. 507, s. 5; c. 1449, ss. 1, 2; 1975, c. 325; c. 373, s. 2; c. 716, s. 5; c. 735; c. 736, ss. 1-3; 1977, c. 461; c. 464, s. 34; 1977, 2nd Sess., c. 1178; 1981, c. 690, ss. 27, 28; c. 726; c. 1127, s. 53.1; 1983, c. 407; c. 724, s. 1; 1983 (Reg. Sess., 1984), c. 1116, ss. 105-109; 1985, c. 54; c. 274; 1987, c. 392; c. 707, ss. 1-4; 1991, c. 202, s. 1; 1991 (Reg. Sess., 1992), c. 905, s. 1; 1993, c. 426, ss. 1, 2; c. 470, s. 1; c. 533, s. 11; 1993 (Reg. Sess., 1994), c. 761, ss. 10-16; 1995, c. 109, s. 3; c. 163, s. 4; c. 332, ss. 1 -3; c. 509, s. 135.1(b); 1995 (Reg. Sess., 1996), c. 756, s. 29; 1997-354, s. 1; 1997-373, s. 1; 1997-466, s. 2; 1998-149, ss. 8, 9, 9.1; 1998-177, s. 1; 1999-452, s. 23; 2000-57, s. 1; 2001-487, ss. 10, 50(e); 2002-126, s. 26.16(a); 2004-145, ss. 1, 2; 2005-248, s. 1; 2005-276, s. 6.37(o); 2005-361, s. 3; 2006-135, s. 1; 2006-264, s. 37; 2008-221, ss. 7, 8, 9; 2009-127, s. 2; 2009-376, ss. 6, 16(a), 16(b); 2009-531, s. 1; 2010-129, s. 3; 2010-132, s. 10; 2011-71, s. 1; 2011-145, s. 19.1(g); 2011-200, s. 1; 2012-78, ss. 6, 13; 2013-120, s. 1; 2013-134, s. 1; 2015-263, s. 9(a); 2016-90, s. 2.1(a); 2018-74, s. 16.5; 2018-142, s. 5(b)

§ 20-118.1. Officers may weigh vehicles and require overloads to be removed

A law enforcement officer may stop and weigh a vehicle to determine if the vehicle's weight is in compliance with the vehicle's declared gross weight and the weight limits set in this Part. The officer may require the driver of the vehicle to drive to a scale located within five miles of where the officer stopped the vehicle.

Any person operating a vehicle or a combination of vehicles having a GVWR of 10,001 pounds or more or any vehicle transporting hazardous materials that is required to be placarded under 49 C.F.R. § 171-180 must enter a permanent weigh station or temporary inspection or weigh site as directed by duly erected signs or an electronic transponder for the purpose of being electronically screened for compliance, or weighed, or inspected.

If the vehicle's weight exceeds the amount allowable, the officer may detain the vehicle until the overload has been removed. Any property removed from a vehicle because the vehicle was overloaded is the responsibility of the owner or operator of the vehicle. The State is not liable for damage to or loss of the removed property.

Failure to permit a vehicle to be weighed or to remove an overload is a misdemeanor of the Class set in G.S. 20-176. An officer must weigh a vehicle with a scale that has been approved by the Department of Agriculture and Consumer Services.

A privately owned noncommercial horse trailer constructed to transport four or fewer horses shall not be required to stop at any permanent weigh station in the State while transporting horses, unless the driver of the vehicle hauling the trailer is directed to stop by a law enforcement officer. A 'privately owned noncommercial horse trailer' means a trailer used solely for the occasional transportation of horses and not for compensation or in furtherance of a commercial enterprise.

History.
1927, c. 148, s. 37; 1949, c. 1207, s. 3; 1951, c. 1013, s. 4; 1979, c. 436, ss. 1, 2; 1981 (Reg. Sess., 1982), c. 1259, s. 2; 1993, c. 539, s. 356; 1994, Ex. Sess., c. 24, s. 14(c); 1995, c. 109, s. 4; 1997-261, s. 109; 2001-487, s. 50(f); 2003-338, s. 1

§ 20-118.2. Authority to fix higher weight limitations at reduced speeds for certain vehicles

The Department of Transportation is hereby authorized and empowered to fix higher weight limitations at reduced speeds for vehicles used in transporting property when the point of origin or destination of the motor vehicles is located upon any light traffic highway, county road, farm-to-market road, or any other roads of the secondary system only and/or to the extent only that the motor vehicle is necessarily using said highway in transporting the property from the bona fide point of origin of the property being transported or to the bona fide point of destination of said property and such weights may be different from the weight of those vehicles otherwise using such roads.

History.
1951, c. 1013, s. 7A; 1957, c. 65, s. 11; 1973, c. 507, s. 5; 1977, c. 464, s. 34

§ 20-118.3. Vehicle or combination of vehicles operated without registration plate subject to civil penalty

Any vehicle or combination of vehicles being operated upon the highway of this State either by a resident or nonresident without having been issued therefor a registration plate by the appropriate jurisdiction shall be subject to a civil penalty equal to the North Carolina annual fee for the gross weight of the vehicle and in addition thereto the license fee applicable for the remainder of the current registration year, provided a nonresident shall pay the North Carolina license fee or furnish satisfactory proof of payment of required registration fee to its base jurisdiction. The civil penalties provided for in this section shall not be enforceable through criminal sanctions and the provisions of G.S. 20-176 shall not apply to this section.

History.
1981 Reg. Sess., 1982, c. 1259, s. 1

§ 20-118.4. Firefighting equipment exempt from size and weight restrictions while transporting or moving heavy equipment for emergency response and preparedness and fire prevention; permits

(a) **Exemption From Weight and Size Restrictions.** -- Any overweight or oversize vehicle owned and operated by a State or local government or cooperating federal agency is exempt from the weight and size restrictions of this Chapter and implementing rules while it is actively engaged in (i) a response to a fire under the authority of a forest ranger pursuant to G.S. 106-899(a); (ii) a county request for forest protection assistance pursuant to G.S. 106-906; (iii) a request for assistance under a state of emergency declared pursuant to G.S. 166A-19.20 or G.S. 166A-19.22, and any other applicable statutes and provisions of common

law; (iv) a request for assistance under a disaster declared pursuant to G.S. 166A-19.21; or (v) performance of other required duties for emergency preparedness and fire prevention, when the vehicle meets the following conditions:

(1) The vehicle weight does not exceed the manufacturer's GVWR or 90,000 pounds gross weight, whichever is less.

(2) The tri-axle grouping weight does not exceed 50,000 pounds, tandem axle weight does not exceed 42,000 pounds, and the single axle weight does not exceed 22,000 pounds.

(3) A vehicle/vehicle combination does not exceed 12 feet in width and a total overall vehicle combination length of 75 feet from bumper to bumper.

(b) **Marking, Lighting, and Bridge Requirements.** -- Vehicle/vehicle combinations subject to an exemption or permit under this section shall not be exempt from the requirement of a yellow banner on the front and rear measuring a total length of seven feet by 18 inches bearing the legend "Oversize Load" in 10 inch black letters 1.5 inches wide, and red or orange flags measuring 18 inches square to be displayed on all sides at the widest point of load. In addition, when operating between sunset and sunrise, flashing amber lights shall be displayed on each side of the load at the widest point. Vehicle/vehicle combinations subject to an exemption or permit under this section shall not exceed posted bridge limits without prior approval from the Department of Transportation.

(c) Definition of "Response." -- A response lasts from the time an overweight or oversize vehicle is requested until the vehicle is returned to its base location and restored to a state of readiness for another response.

(c1) Definition of "Preparedness and Fire Prevention." -- Movement of equipment for the purpose of hazardous fuel reduction, training, equipment maintenance, pre-suppression fire line installation, fire prevention programs, and equipment staging. In order to qualify for the exception in subsection (a) of this section, equipment must remain configured during movement for one or more of these purposes.

(d) **Discretionary Annual or Single Trip Permit for Emergency Response by a Commercial Vehicle.** -- The Department of Transportation may, in its discretion, issue an annual or single trip special use permit waiving the weight and size restrictions of this Chapter and implementing rules for a commercial overweight or oversize vehicle actively engaged in a response to a fire or a request for assistance from a person authorized to direct emergency operations. The Department of Transportation may condition the permit with safety measures that do not unreasonably delay a response. The

Department of Transportation may issue the single trip special use permit upon verbal communication, provided the requestor submits appropriate documentation and fees on the next business day.

(e) **No Liability for Issuance of Permit Under This Section.** -- The action of issuing a permit by the Department of Transportation under this section is a governmental function and does not subject the Department of Transportation to liability for injury to a person or damage to property as a result of the activity.

History.
2007-290, s. 1; 2012-12, s. 2(g); 2012-78, s. 7

§ 20-119. Special permits for vehicles of excessive size or weight; fees

(a) The Department of Transportation may, in its discretion, upon application, for good cause being shown therefor, issue a special permit in writing authorizing the applicant to operate or move a vehicle of a size or weight exceeding a maximum specified in this Article upon any highway under the jurisdiction and for the maintenance of which the body granting the permit is responsible. However, the Department is not authorized to issue any permit to operate or move over the State highways twin trailers, commonly referred to as double bottom trailers. Every such permit shall be carried in the vehicle to which it refers and shall be open to inspection by any peace officer. The authorities in any incorporated city or town may grant permits in writing and for good cause shown, authorizing the applicant to move a vehicle over the streets of such city or town, the size or weight exceeding the maximum expressed in this Article. The Department of Transportation shall issue rules to implement this section.

(a1) Where permitted by the posted road and bridge limits, the Department may issue a single trip permit for a vehicle or vehicle combination responding to an emergency event that could result in severe damage, injury, or loss of life or property resulting from any natural or man-made emergency as determined by either the Secretary of Public Safety or the Secretary of Transportation or their designees. A permit issued under this subsection may allow for travel from a specific origin to destination and return 24 hours a day, seven days a week, including holidays. Permits issued under this subsection shall include a requirement for banners, flags, and other safety devices, as determined by the Department, and a requirement for a law enforcement escort or a vehicle being operated by a certified escort vehicle operator if traveling between sunset and sunrise. To obtain authorization to travel during restricted times, application shall be made with any

required documentation to the proper officials as designated by the Department. If an emergency permit is issued under this subsection, the requestor shall contact the Department of Transportation's central permit office on the next business day to complete any further documentation and pay the applicable fees.

(b) Upon the issuance of a special permit for an oversize or overweight vehicle by the Department of Transportation in accordance with this section, the applicant shall pay to the Department for a single trip permit a fee of twelve dollars ($ 12.00) for each dimension over lawful dimensions, including height, length, width, and weight up to 132,000 pounds. For overweight vehicles, the applicant shall pay to the Department for a single trip permit in addition to the fee imposed by the previous sentence a fee of three dollars ($ 3.00) per 1,000 pounds over 132,000 pounds.

Upon the issuance of an annual permit for a single vehicle, the applicant shall pay a fee in accordance with the following schedule:

Commodity:	Annual Fee:
Annual Permit to Move House Trailers or Trailer Frames	$ 200.00
Annual Permit to Move Other Commodities	$ 100.00

In addition to the fees set out in this subsection, applications for permits that require an engineering study for pavement or structures or other special conditions or considerations shall be accompanied by a nonrefundable application fee of one hundred dollars ($ 100.00).

This subsection does not apply to farm equipment or machinery being used at the time for agricultural purposes, nor to the moving of a house as provided for by the license and permit requirements of Article 16 of this Chapter. Fees will not be assessed for permits for oversize and overweight vehicles issued to any agency of the United States Government or the State of North Carolina, its agencies, institutions, subdivisions, or municipalities if the vehicle is registered in the name of the agency.

(b1) Neither the Department nor the Board may require review or renewal of annual permits, with or without fee, more than once per calendar year.

(b2) The Department shall issue single trip permits for the transport and delivery of a manufactured or modular home with a maximum width of 16 feet and a gutter edge that does not exceed three inches from the manufacturer to an authorized dealership within this State, for delivery of a manufactured or modular home by a manufacturer and authorized dealer or their transporters to a location within this State, and for transport and delivery of a manufactured or modular home by a homeowner from one location to another within this State. The Department shall promulgate rules that set the days allowed for transport and delivery, times of day transport or delivery may occur, the display and use of banners and escort vehicles for public safety purposes, and any other reasonable rules as are necessary to promote public safety and commerce. For the purposes of this subsection, manufactured home and modular home shall have the same meanings as those terms are defined in G.S. 105-164.3.

(b3) For a special permit issued under this section for the transport and delivery of cargo, containers, or other equipment, the Department may allow travel after sunset if the Department determines it will be safe and expedite traffic flow. The Department shall not include a term or condition prohibiting travel after sunset for any permitted shipments going to or from international ports. Nothing in this subsection precludes the Department from restricting movements it determines to be unsafe.

(c) Nothing in this section shall require the Department of Transportation to issue any permit for any load.

(d) For each violation of any of the terms or conditions of a special permit issued or where a permit is required but not obtained under this section the Department of Public Safety shall assess a civil penalty for each violation against the registered owner of the vehicle as follows:

(1) A fine of one thousand five hundred dollars ($ 1,500) for operating without the proper number of certified escorts as determined by the actual loaded weight or size of the vehicle combination.

(1a) A fine of five hundred dollars ($ 500.00) for any of the following: operating without the issuance of a permit, moving a load off the route specified in the permit, falsifying information to obtain a permit, or failing to comply with dimension restrictions of a permit.

(2) A fine of two hundred fifty dollars ($ 250.00) for moving loads beyond the distance allowances of an annual permit covering the movement of house trailers from the retailer's premises or for operating in violation of time of travel restrictions.

(3) A fine of one hundred dollars ($ 100.00) for any other violation of the permit conditions or requirements imposed by applicable regulations.

The Department of Transportation may refuse to issue additional permits or suspend existing permits if there are repeated violations of subdivision (1), (1a), or (2) of this subsection.

(d1) In addition to the penalties assessed under subsection (d) of this section, the Department of Public Safety shall assess a civil penalty, not to exceed ten thousand dollars ($ 10,000), in accordance with G.S. 20-118(e)(1) and (e)(3) against the registered owner of the vehicle for any of the following:

(1) Operating without the issuance of a required permit.

(2) Operating off permitted route of travel.

(3) Failing to comply with travel restrictions of the permit.

(4) Operating without the proper vehicle registration or license for the class of vehicle being operated.

A violation of this subsection constitutes operating a vehicle without a special permit.

(e) It is the intent of the General Assembly that the permit fees provided in G.S. 20-119 shall be adjusted periodically to assure that the revenue generated by the fees is equal to the cost to the Department of administering the Oversize/Overweight Permit Unit Program within the Division of Highways. At least every two years, the Department shall review and compare the revenue generated by the permit fees and the cost of administering the program, and shall report to the Joint Legislative Transportation Oversight Committee created in G.S.120-70.50 its recommendations for adjustments to the permit fees to bring the revenues and the costs into alignment.

(f) The Department of Transportation shall issue rules to establish an escort driver training and certification program for escort vehicles accompanying oversize/overweight loads. Any driver operating a vehicle escorting an oversize/overweight load shall meet any training requirements and obtain certification under the rules issued pursuant to this subsection. These rules may provide for reciprocity with other states having similar escort certification programs. Certification credentials for the driver of an escort vehicle shall be carried in the vehicle and be readily available for inspection by law enforcement personnel. The escort and training certification requirements of this subsection shall not apply to the transportation of agricultural machinery until October 1, 2004. The Department of Transportation shall develop and implement an in-house training program for agricultural machinery escorts by September 1, 2004.

(g) The Department of Transportation shall issue annual overwidth permits for the following:

(1) A vehicle carrying agricultural equipment or machinery from the dealer to the farm or from the farm to the dealer that does not exceed 14 feet in width. A permit issued under this subdivision is valid for unlimited movement without escorts on all State highways where the overwidth vehicle does not exceed posted bridge and load limits.

(2) A boat or boat trailer whose outside width equals or exceeds 120 inches. A permit issued under this subdivision must restrict a vehicle's towing of the boat or boat trailer to daylight hours only.

(h) No law enforcement officer shall issue a citation to a person for a violation of this section if the officer is able to determine by electronic means that the person has a permit valid at the time of the violation but does not have the permit in his or her possession. Any person issued a citation pursuant to this section who does not have the permit in his or her possession at the time of the issuance of the citation shall not be responsible for a violation, and the Department of Public Safety may not impose any fines under this section if the person submits evidence to the Department of the existence of a permit valid at the time of the violation within 30 days of the date of the violation.

(i) One, two, or three steel coils, transported on the same vehicle, shall be considered a nondivisible load for purposes of permit issuance pursuant to this section.

History.

1937, c. 407, s. 83; 1957, c. 65, s. 11; 1959, c. 1129; 1973, c. 507, s. 5; 1977, c. 464, s. 34; 1981, c. 690, ss. 31, 32; c. 736, ss. 1, 2; 1989, c. 54; 1991, c. 604, ss. 1, 2; c. 689, s. 334; 1993, c. 539, s. 357; 1994, Ex. Sess., c. 24, s. 14(c); 2000-109, ss. 7(a), 7(f), 7(g); 2001-424, s. 27.10; 2003-383, s. 7; 2004-124, s. 30.3E(a), (b); 2004-145, s. 3; 2005-361, s. 4; 2007-290, s. 2; 2008-160, s. 2; 2008-229, s. 2; 2009-376, ss. 7, 8; 2011-145, s. 19.1(g); 2011-358, s. 1; 2016-90, s. 2.1(b); 2017-97, s. 1

§ 20-119.1. Use of excess overweight and oversize fees

Funds generated by overweight and oversize permit fees in excess of the cost of administering the program, as determined pursuant to G.S. 20-119(e), shall be used for highway and bridge maintenance required as a result of damages caused from overweight or oversize loads.

History.

2005-276, s. 28.5

§ 20-120. Operation of flat trucks on State highways regulated; trucks hauling leaf tobacco in barrels or hogsheads

It shall be unlawful for any person, firm or corporation to operate, or have operated on any public highway in the State any open, flat truck loaded with logs, cotton bales, boxes or other load piled on said truck, without having the said load securely fastened on said truck.

It shall be unlawful for any firm, person or corporation to operate or permit to be operated on any highway of this State a truck or trucks on which leaf tobacco in barrels or hogsheads is carried unless each section or tier of such barrels or hogsheads are reasonably securely fastened to such truck or trucks by metal chains or wire cables, or manila or hemp ropes of not less than five-eighths inch in diameter, to hold said barrels or hogsheads in place under any ordinary traffic or road condition: Provided that the provisions of this paragraph shall not apply to any truck or trucks on which the hogsheads or barrels of tobacco are arranged in a single layer, tier, or plane, it being the intent of this paragraph to require the use of metal chains or wire cables only when barrels or hogsheads of tobacco are stacked or piled one upon the other on a truck or trucks. Nothing in this paragraph shall apply to trucks engaged in transporting hogsheads or barrels of tobacco between factories and storage houses of the same company unless such hogsheads or barrels are placed upon the truck in tiers. In the event the hogsheads or barrels of tobacco are placed upon the truck in tiers same shall be securely fastened to the said truck as hereinbefore provided in this paragraph.

Any person violating the provisions of this section shall be guilty of a Class 2 misdemeanor.

History.

1939, c. 114; 1947, c. 1094; 1953, c. 240; 1993, c. 539, s. 358; 1994, Ex. Sess., c. 24, s. 14(c)

§ 20-121. When authorities may restrict right to use highways

The Department of Transportation or local authorities may prohibit the operation of vehicles upon or impose restrictions as to the weight thereof, for a total period not to exceed 90 days in any one calendar year, when operated upon any highway under the jurisdiction of and for the maintenance of which the body adopting the ordinance is responsible, whenever any said highway by reason of deterioration, rain, snow or other climatic conditions will be damaged unless the use of vehicles thereon is prohibited or the permissible weights thereof reduced. The local authority enacting any such ordinance shall erect, or cause to be erected and maintained, signs designating the provisions of the ordinance at each end of that portion of any highway to which the ordinance is applicable, and the ordinance shall not be effective until or unless such signs are erected and maintained.

History.

1937, c. 407, s. 84; 1957, c. 65, s. 11; 1973, c. 507, s. 5; 1977, c. 464, s. 34

§ 20-121.1. Operation of a low-speed vehicle, mini-truck, or modified utility vehicle on certain roadways.

The operation of a low-speed vehicle, mini-truck, or modified utility vehicle is authorized with the following restrictions:

(1) A low-speed vehicle may be operated only on streets and highways where the posted speed limit is 35 miles per hour or less. A mini-truck or modified utility vehicle may be operated only on streets and highways where the posted speed limit is 55 miles per hour or less; provided, a modified utility vehicle may not be operated on any street or highway having four or more travel lanes unless the posted speed limit is 35 miles per hour or less. This subdivision does not prohibit a low-speed vehicle, mini-truck, or modified utility vehicle from crossing a road or street at an intersection where the road or street being crossed has a posted speed limit of more than 35 miles per hour.

(2) A low-speed vehicle or mini-truck shall be equipped with headlamps, stop lamps, turn signal lamps, tail lamps, reflex reflectors, parking brakes, rearview mirrors, windshields, windshield wipers, speedometer, seat belts, and a vehicle identification number. Any such required equipment shall be maintained in proper working order.

(2a) A modified utility vehicle shall be equipped with headlamps, stop lamps, turn signal lamps, tail lamps, reflex reflectors, parking brakes, rearview mirrors, a speedometer, seat belts, and a vehicle identification number. Any such required equipment shall be maintained in proper working order. If a modified utility vehicle does not have a vehicle identification number, upon application by the owner, the Division shall assign a vehicle identification number to the modified utility vehicle prior to registration. The operator of and all passengers on a modified utility vehicle that is not equipped with a windshield and windshield wipers shall wear a safety helmet, with a retention strap properly secured, that complies with Federal Motor Vehicle Safety Standard (FMVSS) 218.

(3) A low-speed vehicle, mini-truck, or modified utility vehicle shall be registered and insured in accordance with G.S. 20-50 and G.S. 20-309.

(4) Notwithstanding the provisions of any other subdivision of this section, the Department of Transportation may prohibit the operation of low-speed vehicles, mini-trucks, or modified utility vehicles on any road or highway if it determines that the prohibition is necessary in the interest of safety.

(5) Low-speed vehicles must comply with the safety standards in 49 C.F.R. § 571.500.

(6) Regardless of age, a mini-truck shall not qualify as an antique vehicle or historic vehicle as described in G.S. 20-79.4(b).

History.
2001-356, s. 5; 2019-34, s. 3; 2020-40, s. 3; 2021-33, s. 2

§ 20-122. Restrictions as to tire equipment

(a) No vehicle will be allowed to move on any public highway unless equipped with tires of rubber or other resilient material which depend upon compressed air, for support of a load, except by special permission of the Department of Transportation which may grant such special permits upon a showing of necessity. This subsection shall have no application to the movement of farm vehicles on highways.

(b) No tire on a vehicle moved on a highway shall have on its periphery any block, stud, flange, cleat or spike or any other protuberance of any material other than rubber which projects beyond the tread of the traction surface of the tire, except that it shall be permissible to use farm machinery with tires having protuberances which will not injure the highway and except, also, that it shall be permissible to use tire chains of reasonable proportions upon any vehicle when required for safety because of snow, ice or other conditions tending to cause a vehicle to slide or skid. It shall be permissible to use upon any vehicle for increased safety, regular and snow tires with studs which project beyond the tread of the traction surface of the tire not more than one sixteenth of an inch when compressed.

(c) The Department of Transportation or local authorities in their respective jurisdictions may, in their discretion, issue special permits authorizing the operation upon a highway of traction engines or tractors having movable tracks with transverse corrugation upon the periphery of such movable tracks or farm tractors or other farm machinery.

(d) It shall not be unlawful to drive farm tractors on dirt roads from farm to farm: Provided, in doing so they do not damage said dirt roads or interfere with traffic.

History.
1937, c. 407, s. 85; 1939, c. 266; 1957, c. 65, s. 11; 1965, c. 435; 1973, c. 507, s. 5; 1977, c. 464, s. 34; 1979, c. 515

§ 20-122.1. Motor vehicles to be equipped with safe tires

(a) Every motor vehicle subject to safety equipment inspection in this State and operated on the streets and highways of this State shall be equipped with tires which are safe for the operation of the motor vehicle and which do not expose the public to needless hazard. Tires shall be considered unsafe if cut so as to expose tire cord, cracked so as to expose tire cord, or worn so as to expose tire cord or there is a visible tread separation or chunking or the tire has less than two thirty-seconds inch tread depth at two or more locations around the circumference of the tire in two adjacent major tread grooves, or if the tread wear indicators are in contact with the roadway at two or more locations around the circumference of the tire in two adjacent major tread grooves: Provided, the two thirty-seconds tread depth requirements of this section shall not apply to dual wheel trailers. For the purpose of this section, the following definitions shall apply:

(1) "Chunking" -- separation of the tread from the carcass in particles which may range from very small size to several square inches in area.

(2) "Cord" -- strands forming a ply in a tire.

(3) "Tread" -- portion of tire which comes in contact with road.

(4) "Tread depth" -- the distance from the base of the tread design to the top of the tread.

(a1) Any motor vehicle that has a GVWR of at least 10,001 pounds or more and is operated on the streets or highways of this State shall be equipped with tires that are safe for the operation of the vehicle and do not expose the public to needless hazard. A tire is unsafe if any of the following applies:

(1) It is cut, cracked, or worn so as to expose tire cord.

(2) There is a visible tread separation or chunking.

(3) The steering axle tire has less than four thirty-seconds inch tread depth at any location around the circumference of the tire on any major tread groove.

(4) Any nonsteering axle tire has less than two thirty-seconds inch tread depth around the circumference of the tire in any major tread groove.

(5) The tread wear indicators are in contact with the roadway at any location around the circumference of the tire on any major tread groove.

(b) The driver of any vehicle who is charged with a violation of this section shall be allowed 15 calendar days within which to bring the tires of such vehicle in conformance with the requirements of this section. It shall be a defense to any such charge that the person arrested produce in court, or submit to the prosecuting attorney prior to trial, a certificate from an official safety inspection equipment station showing that within 15 calendar days after such arrest, the tires on such vehicle had been made to conform with the requirements of this section or that such vehicle had been sold, destroyed, or permanently removed from the highways. Violation of this section shall not constitute negligence per se.

History.
1969, c. 378, s. 1; c. 1256; 1985, c. 93, ss. 1, 2; 2009-376, s. 5

§ 20-123. Trailers and towed vehicles

(a) The limitations in G.S. 20-116 on combination vehicles do not prohibit the towing of farm trailers not exceeding three in number nor exceeding a total length of 50 feet during the period from one-half hour before sunrise until one-half hour after sunset when a red flag of at least 12 inches square is prominently displayed on the last vehicle. The towing of farm trailers and equipment allowed by this subsection does not apply to interstate or federal numbered highways.

(b) No trailer or semitrailer or other towed vehicle shall be operated over the highways of the State unless such trailer or semitrailer or other towed vehicle be firmly attached to the rear of the towing unit, and unless so equipped that it will not snake, but will travel in the path of the vehicle drawing such trailer or semitrailer or other towed vehicle, which equipment shall at all times be kept in good condition.

(c) In addition to the requirements of subsections (a) and (b) of this section, the towed vehicle shall be attached to the towing unit by means of safety chains or cables which shall be of sufficient strength to hold the gross weight of the towed vehicle in the event the primary towing device fails or becomes disconnected while being operated on the highways of this State if the primary towing attachment is a ball hitch. Trailers and semitrailers having locking pins or bolts in the towing attachment to prevent disconnection, and the locking pins or bolts are of sufficient strength and condition to hold the gross weight of the towed vehicle, need not be equipped with safety chains or cables unless their operation is subject to the requirements of the Federal Motor Carrier Safety Regulations. Semitrailers in combinations of vehicles that are equipped with fifth wheel assemblies that include locking devices need not be equipped with safety chains or cables.

History.
1937, c. 407, s. 86; 1955, c. 296, s. 3; 1963, c. 356, s. 2; c. 1027, s. 2; 1965, c. 966; 1971, c. 639; 1973, c. 507, s. 5; 1975, c. 716, s. 5; 1977, c. 464, s. 34; 1981 (Reg. Sess., 1982), c. 1195; 1993, c. 71, s. 1; 1995 (Reg. Sess., 1996), c. 756, s. 15

Chapter 20

§ 20-123.1. Steering mechanism

The steering mechanism of every self-propelled motor vehicle operated on the highway shall be maintained in good working order, sufficient to enable the operator to control the vehicle's movements and to maneuver it safely.

History.
1957, c. 1038, s. 3

§ 20-123.2. Speedometer

(a) Every self-propelled motor vehicle when operated on the highway shall be equipped with a speedometer which shall be maintained in good working order.

(b) Any person violating this section shall have committed an infraction and may be ordered to pay a penalty of not more than twenty-five dollars ($ 25.00). No drivers license points, insurance points or premium surcharge shall be assessed on or imputed to any party on account of a violation of this section.

History.
1989 (Reg. Sess., 1990), c. 822, s. 2

§ 20-124. Brakes

(a) Every motor vehicle when operated upon a highway shall be equipped with brakes adequate to control the movement of and to stop such vehicle or vehicles, and such brakes shall be maintained in good working order and shall conform to regulations provided in this section.

(b) Repealed by Session Laws 1973, c. 1330, s. 39.

(c) Every motor vehicle when operated on a highway shall be equipped with brakes adequate to control the movement of and to stop and hold such vehicle, and shall have all originally equipped brakes in good working order, including two separate means of applying the brakes. If these two separate means of applying the brakes are connected in any way, they shall be so constructed that failure of any one part of the operating mechanism shall not leave the motor vehicle without brakes.

(d) Every motorcycle and every motor-driven cycle when operated upon a highway shall be equipped with at least one brake which may be operated by hand or foot. For purposes of this section, the term "motorcycle" shall not include autocycles. Autocycles shall be subject to the requirements under this section for motor vehicles.

(e) Motor trucks and tractor-trucks with semitrailers attached shall be capable of stopping on a dry, hard, approximately level highway free from loose material at a speed of 20 miles per hour within the following distances: Thirty feet with both hand and service brake applied simultaneously and 50 feet when either is applied separately, except that vehicles maintained and operated permanently for the transportation of property and which were registered in this or any other state or district prior to August, 1929, shall be capable of stopping on a dry, hard, approximately level highway free from loose material at a speed of 20 miles per hour within a distance of 50 feet with both hand and service brake applied simultaneously, and within a distance of 75 feet when either applied separately.

(e1) Every motor truck and truck-tractor with semitrailer attached, shall be equipped with brakes acting on all wheels, except trucks and truck-tractors having three or more axles need not have brakes on the front wheels if manufactured prior to July 25, 1980. However, such trucks and truck-tractors must be capable of complying with the performance requirements of G.S. 20-124(e).

(f) Every semitrailer, or trailer, or separate vehicle, attached by a drawbar or coupling to a towing vehicle, and having a gross weight of two tons, and all house trailers of 1,000 pounds gross weight or more, shall be equipped with brakes controlled or operated by the driver of the towing vehicle, which shall conform to the specifications set forth in subsection (e) of this section and shall be of a type approved by the Commissioner.

It shall be unlawful for any person or corporation engaged in the business of selling house trailers at wholesale or retail to sell or offer for sale any house trailer which is not equipped with the brakes required by this subsection.

This subsection shall not apply to house trailers being used as dwellings, or to house trailers not intended to be used or towed on public highways and roads. This subsection shall not apply to house trailers with a manufacturer's certificate of origin dated prior to December 31, 1974.

(g) The provisions of this section shall not apply to a trailer when used by a farmer, a farmer's tenant, agent, or employee if the trailer is exempt from registration by the provisions of G.S. 20-51. This exemption does not apply to trailers that are equipped with brakes from the manufacturer and that are manufactured after October 1, 2009.

(h) From and after July 1, 1955, no person shall sell or offer for sale for use in motor vehicle brake systems in this State any hydraulic brake fluid of a type and brand other than those approved by the Commissioner of Motor Vehicles. From and after January 1, 1970, no person shall sell or offer for sale in motor vehicle brake systems any brake lining of a type or brand other than those approved by the Commissioner of Motor Vehicles. Violation of the provisions of this subsection shall constitute a Class 2 misdemeanor.

History.
1937, c. 407, s. 87; 1953, c. 1316, s. 2; 1955, c. 1275; 1959, c. 990; 1965, c. 1031; 1967, c. 1188; 1969, cc. 787, 866; 1973, c. 1203; c. 1330, s. 39; 1993, c. 539, s. 359; 1994, Ex. Sess., c. 24, s. 14(c); 2009-376, ss. 10, 11; 2015-163, s. 4

§ 20-125. Horns and warning devices

(a) Every motor vehicle when operated upon a highway shall be equipped with a horn in good working order capable of emitting sound audible under normal conditions from a distance of not less than 200 feet, and it shall be unlawful, except as otherwise provided in this section, for any vehicle to be equipped with or for any person to use upon a vehicle any siren, compression or spark plug whistle or for any person at any time to use a horn otherwise than as a reasonable warning or to make any unnecessary or unreasonable loud or harsh sound by means of a horn or other warning device. All such horns and warning devices shall be maintained in good working order and shall conform to regulation not inconsistent with this section to be promulgated by the Commissioner.

(b) Every vehicle owned or operated by a police department or by the Department of Public Safety including the State Highway Patrol or by the Wildlife Resources Commission or the Division of Marine Fisheries of the Department of Environmental Quality, or by the Division of Parks and Recreation of the Department of Natural and Cultural Resources, or by the North Carolina Forest Service of the Department of Agriculture and Consumer Services, and used exclusively for law enforcement, firefighting, or other emergency response purposes, or by the Division of Emergency Management, or by a fire department, either municipal or rural, or by a fire patrol, whether such fire department or patrol be a paid organization or a voluntary association, vehicles used by an organ procurement organization or agency for the recovery and transportation of human tissues and organs for transplantation, and every ambulance or emergency medical service emergency support vehicle used for answering emergency calls, shall be equipped with special lights, bells, sirens, horns or exhaust whistles of a type approved by the Commissioner of Motor Vehicles.

The operators of all such vehicles so equipped are hereby authorized to use such equipment at all times while engaged in the performance of their duties and services, both within their respective corporate limits and beyond.

In addition to the use of special equipment authorized and required by this subsection, the chief and assistant chiefs of any police department or of any fire department, whether the same be municipal or rural, paid or voluntary, county fire marshals, assistant fire marshals, transplant coordinators, and emergency management coordinators, are hereby authorized to use such special equipment on privately owned vehicles operated by them while actually engaged in the performance of their official or semiofficial duties or services either within or beyond their respective corporate limits.

And vehicles driven by law enforcement officers of the North Carolina Division of Motor Vehicles shall be equipped with a bell, siren, or exhaust whistle of a type approved by the Commissioner, and all vehicles owned and operated by the State Bureau of Investigation for the use of its agents and officers in the performance of their official duties may be equipped with special lights, bells, sirens, horns or exhaust whistles of a type approved by the Commissioner of Motor Vehicles.

Every vehicle used or operated for law enforcement purposes by the sheriff or any salaried deputy sheriff or salaried rural policeman of any county, whether owned by the county or not, may be, but is not required to be, equipped with special lights, bells, sirens, horns or exhaust whistles of a type approved by the Commissioner of Motor Vehicles. Such special equipment shall not be operated or activated by any person except by a law enforcement officer while actively engaged in performing law enforcement duties.

In addition to the use of special equipment authorized and required by this subsection, the chief and assistant chiefs of each emergency rescue squad which is recognized or sponsored by any municipality or civil preparedness agency, are hereby authorized to use such special equipment on privately owned vehicles operated by them while actually engaged in their official or semiofficial duties or services either within or beyond the corporate limits of the municipality which recognizes or sponsors such organization.

(c) Repealed by Session Laws 1979, c. 653, s. 2.

History.
1937, c. 407, s. 88; 1951, cc. 392, 1161; 1955, c. 1224; 1959, c. 166, s. 1; c. 494; c. 1170, s. 1; c. 1209; 1965, c. 257; 1975, c. 588; c. 734, s. 15; 1977, c. 52, s. 1; c. 438, s. 1; 1979, c. 653, s. 2; 1981, c. 964, s. 19; 1983, c. 32, s. 2; c. 768, s. 5; 1987, c. 266; 1989, c. 537; 1989 (Reg. Sess., 1990), c. 1020, s. 1; 1993 (Reg. Sess., 1994), c. 719, s. 2; 2011-145, s. 19.1(g); 2013-415, s. 1(a); 2015-241, s. 14.30(ee)

§ 20-125.1. Directional signals

(a) It shall be unlawful for the owner of any motor vehicle of a changed model or series designation indicating that it was manufactured or assembled after July 1, 1953, to register such vehicle or cause it to be registered in this State, or to obtain, or cause to be obtained in this State registration plates therefor, unless such vehicle is equipped with a mechanical or electrical signal device by which the operator of the vehicle may indicate to the operator of another vehicle, approaching from either the front or rear and within a distance of 200 feet, his intention to turn from a direct line. Such signal device must be of a type approved by the Commissioner of Motor Vehicles.

(b) It shall be unlawful for any dealer to sell or deliver in this State any motor vehicle of a changed model or series designation indicating that it was manufactured or assembled after July 1, 1953, if he knows or has reasonable cause to believe that the purchaser of such vehicle intends to register it or cause it to be registered in this State or to resell it to any other person for registration in and use upon the highways of this State, unless such motor vehicle is equipped with a mechanical or electrical signal device by which the operator of the vehicle may indicate to the operator of another vehicle, approaching from either of the front or rear or within a distance of 200 feet, his intention to turn from a direct line. Such signal device must be of a type approved by the Commissioner of Motor Vehicles: Provided that in the case of any motor vehicle manufactured or assembled after July 1, 1953, the signal device with which such motor vehicle is equipped shall be presumed prima facie to have been approved by the Commissioner of Motor Vehicles. Irrespective of the date of manufacture of any motor vehicle a certificate from the Commissioner of Motor Vehicles to the effect that a particular type of signal device has been approved by his Division shall be admissible in evidence in all the courts of this State.

(c) Trailers satisfying the following conditions are not required to be equipped with a directional signal device:

(1) The trailer and load does not obscure the directional signals of the towing vehicle from the view of a driver approaching from the rear and within a distance of 200 feet;

(2) The gross weight of the trailer and load does not exceed 4,000 pounds.

(d) Nothing in this section shall apply to motorcycles. For purposes of this section, the term "motorcycle" shall not include autocycles. Autocycles shall be subject to the requirements under this section for motor vehicles.

History.
1953, c. 481; 1957, c. 488, s. 1; 1963, c. 524; 1969, c. 622; 1975, c. 716, s. 5; 2015-163, s. 5

§ 20-126. Mirrors

(a) No person shall drive a motor vehicle on the streets or highways of this State unless equipped with an inside rearview mirror of a type approved by the Commissioner, which provides the driver with a clear, undistorted, and reasonably unobstructed view of the highway to the rear of such vehicle; provided, a vehicle so constructed or loaded as to make such inside rearview mirror ineffective may be operated if equipped with a mirror of a type to be approved by the Commissioner located so as to reflect to the driver a view of the highway to the rear of such vehicle. A violation of this subsection shall not constitute negligence per se in civil actions. Farm tractors, self-propelled implements of husbandry and construction equipment and all self-propelled vehicles not subject to registration under this Chapter are exempt from the provisions of this section. Provided that pickup trucks equipped with an outside rearview mirror approved by the Commissioner shall be exempt from the inside rearview mirror provision of this section. Any inside mirror installed in any motor vehicle by its manufacturer shall be deemed to comply with the provisions of this subsection.

(b) It shall be unlawful for any person to operate upon the highways of this State any vehicle manufactured, assembled or first sold on or after January 1, 1966 and registered in this State unless such vehicle is equipped with at least one outside mirror mounted on the driver's side of the vehicle. Mirrors herein required shall be of a type approved by the Commissioner.

(c) No person shall operate a motorcycle upon the streets or highways of this State unless such motorcycle is equipped with a rearview mirror so mounted as to provide the operator with a clear, undistorted and unobstructed view of at least 200 feet to the rear of the motorcycle. No motorcycle shall be registered in this State after January 1, 1968, unless such motorcycle is equipped with a rearview mirror as described in this section. Violation of the provisions of this subsection shall not be considered negligence per se or contributory negligence per se in any civil action.

History.
1937, c. 407, s. 89; 1965, c. 368; 1967, c. 282, s. 1; c. 674, s. 2; c. 1139; 2002-159, ss. 22(a), 22(b)

§ 20-127. Windows and windshield wipers

(a) **Windshield Wipers.** -- A vehicle that is operated on a highway and has a windshield shall have a windshield wiper to clear rain or other substances from the windshield in front of the driver of the vehicle and the windshield wiper shall be in good working order. If a vehicle has more than one windshield wiper to clear substances from the windshield, all the windshield wipers shall be in good working order.

(b) **Window Tinting Restrictions.** -- A window of a vehicle that is operated on a highway or a public vehicular area shall comply with this subsection. The windshield of the vehicle may be tinted only along the top of the windshield and the tinting may not extend more than five inches below the top of the windshield or below the AS1 line of the windshield, whichever measurement is longer. Provided, however, an untinted clear film which does not obstruct vision but which reduces or eliminates ultraviolet radiation from entering a vehicle may be applied to the windshield. Any other window of the vehicle may be tinted in accordance with the following restrictions:

(1) The total light transmission of the tinted window shall be at least thirty-five percent (35%). A vehicle window that, by use of a light meter approved by the Commissioner, measures a total light transmission of more than thirty-two percent (32%) is conclusively presumed to meet this restriction.

(2) The light reflectance of the tinted window shall be twenty percent (20%) or less.

(3) Tinted film or another material used to tint the window shall be nonreflective and shall not be red, yellow, or amber.

(b1) Notwithstanding subsection (b) of this section, a window of a vehicle that is operated on a public street or highway and which is subject to the provisions of Part 393 of Title 49 of the Code of Federal Regulations shall comply with the provisions of that Part.

(c) **Tinting Exceptions.** -- The window tinting restrictions in subsection (b) of this section apply without exception to the windshield of a vehicle. The window tinting restrictions in subdivisions (b)(1) and (b)(2) of this section do not apply to any of the following vehicle windows:

(1) A window of an excursion passenger vehicle, as defined in G.S. 20-4.01(27).

(2), (3) Repealed by Session Laws 2012-78, s. 8, effective December 1, 2012. For applicability, see Editor's notes.

(4) A window of a motor home, as defined in G.S. 20-4.01(27)k.

(5) A window of an ambulance, as defined in G.S. 20-4.01(27)a.

(6) The rear window of a property-hauling vehicle, as defined in G.S. 20-4.01(31).

(7) A window of a limousine.

(8) A window of a law enforcement vehicle.

(9) A window of a multipurpose vehicle that is behind the driver of the vehicle. A multipurpose vehicle is a passenger vehicle that is designed to carry 10 or fewer passengers and either is constructed on a truck chassis or has special features designed for occasional off-road operation. A minivan and a pickup truck are multipurpose vehicles.

(10) A window of a vehicle that is registered in another state and meets the requirements of the state in which it is registered.

(11) A window of a vehicle for which the Division has issued a medical exception permit under subsection (f) of this section.

(d) **Violations.** -- A person who does any of the following commits a Class 3 misdemeanor:

(1) Applies tinting to the window of a vehicle that is subject to a safety inspection in this State and the resulting tinted window does not meet the window tinting restrictions set in this section.

(2) Drives on a highway or a public vehicular area a vehicle that has a window that does not meet the window tinting restrictions set in this section.

(e) **Defense.** -- It is a defense to a charge of driving a vehicle with an unlawfully tinted window that the tinting was removed within 15 days after the charge and the window now meets the window tinting restrictions. To assert this defense, the person charged shall produce in court, or submit to the prosecuting attorney before trial, a certificate from the Division of Motor Vehicles or the Highway Patrol showing that the window complies with the restrictions.

(f) **Medical Exception.** -- A person who suffers from a medical condition that causes the person to be photosensitive to visible light may obtain a medical exception permit. To obtain a permit, an applicant shall apply in writing to the Drivers Medical Evaluation Program and have his or her doctor complete the required medical evaluation form provided by the Division. The permit shall be valid for five years from the date of issue, unless a shorter time is directed by the Drivers Medical Evaluation Program. The renewal shall require a medical recertification that the person continues to suffer from a medical condition requiring tinting.

A person may receive no more than two medical exception permits that are valid at any one time. A permit issued under this subsection shall specify the vehicle to which it applies, the windows that may be tinted, and the permitted levels of tinting. The permit shall be carried in the vehicle to which it applies when the vehicle is driven on a highway.

The Division shall give a person who receives a medical exception permit a sticker to place on the lower left-hand corner of the rear window of the vehicle to which it applies. The sticker shall be designed to give prospective purchasers of the vehicle notice that the windows of the vehicle do not meet the requirements of G.S. 20-127(b), and shall be placed between the window and the tinting when the tinting is installed. The Division shall adopt rules regarding the specifications of the medical exception sticker. Failure to display the sticker is an infraction punishable by a two hundred dollar ($ 200.00) fine.

History.
1937, c. 407, s. 90; 1953, c. 1254; 1955, c. 1157, s. 2; 1959, c. 1264, s. 7; 1967, c. 1077; 1985, c. 789; 1985 (Reg. Sess., 1986), c. 997; 1987, c. 567; 1987 (Reg. Sess., 1988), c. 1082, ss. 7-8.1; 1989, c. 770, s. 66; 1991 (Reg. Sess., 1992), c. 1007, s. 34; 1993, c. 539, s. 360; 1994, Ex. Sess., c. 24, s. 14(c); 1993 (Reg. Sess., 1994), c. 683, s. 1; c. 754, s. 4; 1995, c. 14, s. 1; c. 473, s. 1; 2000-75, s. 1; 2012-78, s. 8; 2013-360, s. 18B.14(j); 2015-163, s. 13; 2017-102, s. 5.2(b)

§ 20-128. Exhaust system and emissions control devices

(a) No person shall drive a motor vehicle on a highway unless such motor vehicle is equipped with a muffler, or other exhaust system of the type installed at the time of manufacture, in good working order and in constant operation to prevent excessive or unusual noise, annoying smoke and smoke screens.

(b) It shall be unlawful to use a "muffler cutout" on any motor vehicle upon a highway.

(c) No motor vehicle registered in this State that was manufactured after model year 1967 shall be operated in this State unless it is equipped with emissions control devices that were installed on the vehicle at the time the vehicle was manufactured and these devices are properly connected.

(d) The requirements of subsection (c) of this section shall not apply if the emissions control devices have been removed for the purpose of converting the motor vehicle to operate on natural or liquefied petroleum gas or other modifications have been made in order to reduce air pollution and these modifications are approved by the Department of Environmental Quality.

History.
1937, c. 407, s. 91; 1971, c. 455, s. 1; 1983, c. 132; 1989, c. 727, s. 9; 1997-443, s. 11A.119(a); 2000-134, s. 6; 2015-241, s. 14.30(u)

§ 20-128.1. Control of visible emissions

(a) It shall be a violation of this Article:

(1) For any gasoline-powered motor vehicle registered and operated in this State to emit visible air contaminants under any mode of operation for longer than five consecutive seconds.

(2) For any diesel-powered motor vehicle registered and operated in this State to emit for longer than five consecutive seconds under any mode of operation visible air contaminants which are equal to or darker than the shade or density designated as No. 1 on the Ringelmann Chart or are equal to or darker than a shade or density of twenty percent (20%) opacity.

(b) Any person charged with a violation of this section shall be allowed 30 days within which to make the necessary repairs or modification to bring the motor vehicle into conformity with the standards of this section and to have the motor vehicle inspected and approved by the agency issuing the notice of violation. Any person who, within 30 days of receipt of a notice of violation, and prior to inspection and approval by the agency issuing the notice, receives additional notice or notices of violation, may exhibit a certificate of inspection and approval from the agency issuing the first notice in lieu of inspection and approval by the agencies issuing the subsequent notices.

(c) The provisions of this section shall be enforceable by all persons designated in G.S. 20-49; by all law-enforcement officers of this State within their respective jurisdictions; by the personnel of local air pollution control agencies within their respective jurisdictions; and by personnel of State air pollution control agencies throughout the State.

(d) Any person who fails to comply with the provisions of this section shall be subject to the penalties provided in G.S. 20-176.

History.
1971, c. 1167, s. 10

§ 20-128.2. Motor vehicle emission standards

(a) The rules and regulations promulgated pursuant to G.S. 143-215.107(a)(6) shall be implemented when the Environmental Management Commission certifies to the Commissioner of Motor Vehicles that the ambient air quality in an area will be improved by the implementation of a motor vehicle inspection/maintenance program within a specified county or group of counties, as necessary to effect attainment or preclude violations of the National Ambient Air Quality Standards for carbon monoxide or ozone; provided the Environmental Management Commission may prescribe different vehicle emission limits for different areas as may be necessary and appropriate to meet the stated purposes of this section.

(b) Repealed by Session Laws 1993 (Reg. Sess., 1994), c. 754, s. 5.

History.
1979, 2nd Sess., c. 1180, s. 2; 1989, c. 391, s. 1; 1993 (Reg. Sess., 1994), c. 754, s. 5

§ 20-129. Required lighting equipment of vehicles

(a) **When Vehicles Must Be Equipped. --** Every vehicle upon a highway within this State shall be equipped with lighted headlamps and rear lamps as required for different classes of vehicles, and subject to exemption with reference to lights on parked vehicles as declared in G.S. 20-134:

(1) During the period from sunset to sunrise,

(2) When there is not sufficient light to render clearly discernible any person on the highway at a distance of 400 feet ahead, or

(3) Repealed by Session Laws 1989 (Reg. Sess., 1990), c. 822, s. 1.

(4) At any other time when windshield wipers are in use as a result of smoke, fog, rain, sleet, or snow, or when inclement weather or environmental factors severely reduce the ability to clearly discern persons and vehicles on the street and highway at a distance of 500 feet ahead, provided, however, the provisions of this subdivision shall not apply to instances when windshield wipers are used intermittently in misting rain, sleet, or snow. Any person violating this subdivision during the period from October 1, 1990, through December 31, 1991, shall be given a warning of the violation only. Thereafter, any person violating this subdivision shall have committed an infraction and shall pay a fine of five dollars ($ 5.00) and shall not be assessed court costs. No drivers license points, insurance points or premium surcharge shall be assessed on account of violation of this subdivision and no negligence or liability shall be assessed on or imputed to any party on account of a violation of this subdivision. The Commissioner of Motor Vehicles and the Superintendent of Public Instruction shall incorporate into driver education programs and driver licensing programs instruction designed to encourage compliance with this subdivision as an important means of reducing accidents by making vehicles more discernible during periods of limited visibility.

(b) **Headlamps on Motor Vehicles.** -- Every self-propelled motor vehicle other than motorcycles, road machinery, and farm tractors shall be equipped with at least two headlamps, all in good operating condition with at least one on each side of the front of the motor vehicle. Headlamps shall comply with the requirements and limitations set forth in G.S. 20-131 or 20-132.

(c) **Headlamps on Motorcycles.** -- Every motorcycle shall be equipped with at least one and not more than two headlamps which shall comply with the requirements and limitations set forth in G.S. 20-131 or 20-132. The headlamps on a motorcycle shall be lighted at all times while the motorcycle is in operation on highways or public vehicular areas. For purposes of this section, the term "motorcycle" shall not include autocycles. Autocycles shall be subject to the requirements under this section for motor vehicles.

(d) **Rear Lamps.** -- Every motor vehicle, and every trailer or semitrailer attached to a motor vehicle and every vehicle which is being drawn at the end of a combination of vehicles, shall have all originally equipped rear lamps or the equivalent in good working order, which lamps shall exhibit a red light plainly visible under normal atmospheric conditions from a distance of 500 feet to the rear of such vehicle. One rear lamp or a separate lamp shall be so constructed and placed that the number plate carried on the rear of such vehicle shall under like conditions be illuminated by a white light as to be read from a distance of 50 feet to the rear of such vehicle. Every trailer or semitrailer shall carry at the rear, in addition to the originally equipped lamps, a red reflector of the type which has been approved by the Commissioner and which is so located as to height and is so maintained as to be visible for at least 500 feet when opposed by a motor vehicle displaying lawful undimmed lights at night on an unlighted highway.

Notwithstanding the provisions of the first paragraph of this subsection, it shall not be necessary for a trailer weighing less than 4,000 pounds, or a trailer described in G.S. 20-51(6) weighing less than 6,500 pounds, to carry or be equipped with a rear lamp, provided such vehicle is equipped with and carries at the rear two red reflectors of a diameter of not less than three inches, such reflectors to be approved by the Commissioner, and which are so designed and located as to height and are maintained so that each reflector is visible for at least 500 feet when approached by a motor vehicle displaying lawful undimmed headlights at night on an unlighted highway.

The rear lamps of a motorcycle shall be lighted at all times while the motorcycle is in operation on highways or public vehicular areas.

(e) **Lamps on Bicycles.** -- Every bicycle shall be equipped with a reflex mirror on the rear and both of the following when operated at night on any public street, public vehicular area, or public greenway:

(1) A lighted lamp on the front thereof, visible under normal atmospheric conditions from a distance of at least 300 feet in front of such bicycle.

(2) A lamp on the rear, exhibiting a red light visible under like conditions from a distance of at least 300 feet to the rear of such bicycle, or the operator must wear clothing or a vest that is bright and visible from a distance of at least 300 feet to the rear of the bicycle.

(f) **Lights on Other Vehicles.** -- All vehicles not heretofore in this section required to be equipped with specified lighted lamps shall carry on the left side one or more lighted lamps or lanterns projecting a white light, visible under normal atmospheric conditions from a distance of not less than 500 feet to the front of such vehicle and visible under like conditions from a distance of not less than 500 feet to the rear of such vehicle, or in lieu of said lights shall be equipped with reflectors of a type which is approved by the Commissioner. Farm tractors operated on a highway at night must be equipped with at least one white lamp visible at a distance of 500 feet from the front of the tractor and with at least one red lamp visible at a distance of 500 feet to the rear of the tractor. Two red reflectors each having a diameter of at least four inches may be used on the rear of the tractor in lieu of the red lamp.

(g) No person shall sell or operate on the highways of the State any motor vehicle manufactured after December 31, 1955, and on or before December 31, 1970, unless it shall be equipped with a stop lamp on the rear of the vehicle. No person shall sell or operate on the highways of the State any motor vehicle, manufactured after December 31, 1970, unless it shall be equipped with stop lamps, one on each side of the rear of the vehicle. No person shall sell or operate on the highways of the State any motorcycle or motor-driven cycle, manufactured after December 31, 1955, unless it shall be equipped with a stop lamp on the rear of the motorcycle or motor-driven cycle. The stop lamps shall emit, reflect, or display a red or amber light visible from a distance of not less than 100 feet to the rear in normal sunlight, and shall be actuated upon application of the service (foot) brake. The stop lamps may be incorporated into a unit with one or more other rear lamps.

(h) **Backup Lamps.** -- Every motor vehicle originally equipped with white backup lamps shall have those lamps in operating condition.

History.
1937, c. 407, s. 92; 1939, c. 275; 1947, c. 526; 1955, c. 1157, ss. 3-5, 8; 1957, c. 1038, s. 1; 1967, cc. 1076, 1213; 1969, c. 389; 1973, c. 531, ss. 1, 2; 1979, c. 175; 1981, c. 549, s. 1; 1985, c. 66; 1987, c. 611; 1989 (Reg. Sess., 1990), c. 822, s. 1; 1991, c. 18, s. 1; 1999-281, s. 1; 2015-31, s. 1; 2015-163, s. 6; 2015-241, s. 29.36B(a); 2016-90, s. 5.1(a); 2017-211, s. 12(a)

§ 20-129.1. Additional lighting equipment required on certain vehicles

In addition to other equipment required by this Chapter, the following vehicles shall be equipped as follows:

(1) On every bus or truck, whatever its size, there shall be the following:

On the rear, two reflectors, one at each side, and two stop lamps, one at each side.

(2) On every bus or truck 80 inches or more in overall width, in addition to the requirements in subdivision (1):

On the front, two clearance lamps, one at each side.

On the rear, two clearance lamps, one at each side.

On each side, two side marker lamps, one at or near the front and one at or near the rear.

On each side, two reflectors, one at or near the front and one at or near the rear.

(3) On every truck tractor:

On the front, two clearance lamps, one at each side.

On the rear, two stop lamps, one at each side.

(4) On every trailer or semitrailer having a gross weight of 4,000 pounds or more:

On the front, two clearance lamps, one at each side.

On each side, two side marker lamps, one at or near the front and one at or near the rear.

On each side, two reflectors, one at or near the front and one at or near the rear.

On the rear, two clearance lamps, one at each side, also two reflectors, one at each side, and two stop lamps, one at each side.

(5) On every pole trailer having a gross weight of 4,000 pounds or more:

On each side, one side marker lamp and one clearance lamp which may be in combination, to show to the front, side and rear.

On the rear of the pole trailer or load, two reflectors, one at each side.

(6) On every trailer, semitrailer or pole trailer having a gross weight of less than 4,000 pounds:

On the rear, two reflectors, one on each side. If any trailer or semitrailer is so loaded or is of such dimensions as to obscure the stoplight on the towing vehicle, then such vehicle shall also be equipped with two stop lamps, one at each side.

(7) Front clearance lamps and those marker lamps and reflectors mounted on the front or on the side near the front of a vehicle shall display or reflect an amber color.

(8) Rear clearance lamps and those marker lamps and reflectors mounted on the rear or on the sides near the rear of a vehicle shall display or reflect a red color.

(9) Stop lamps (and/or brake reflectors) on the rear of a motor vehicle shall be constructed so that the light emitted, reflected, or displayed is red, except that a motor vehicle originally manufactured with amber stop lamps may emit, reflect, or display an amber light. The light illuminating the license plate shall be white. All other lights shall be white, amber, yellow, clear or red.

(10) On every trailer and semitrailer which is 30 feet or more in length and has a gross weight of 4,000 pounds or more, one combination marker lamp showing amber and mounted on the bottom side rail at or near the center of each side of the trailer.

History.
1955, c. 1157, s. 4; 1969, c. 387; 1983, c. 245; 1987, c. 363, s. 1; 2000-159, s. 10; 2015-31, s. 2

§ 20-129.2. Lighting equipment for mobile homes

Notwithstanding the provisions of G.S. 20-129 and 20-129.1, the lighting equipment required to be provided and equipped on a house trailer, mobile home, modular home, or structural component thereof shall be as designated by the Commissioner of Motor Vehicles and from time to time promulgated by regulation of the Division.

History.
1975, c. 716, s. 5; c. 833, s. 1

§ 20-130. Additional permissible light on vehicle

(a) **Spot Lamps.** -- Any motor vehicle may be equipped with not to exceed two spot lamps, except that a motorcycle shall not be equipped with more than one spot lamp, and every lighted spot lamp shall be so aimed and used upon approaching another vehicle that no part of the beam will be directed to the left of the center of the highway nor more than 100 feet ahead of the vehicle. No spot lamps shall be used on the rear of any vehicle. For purposes of this section, the term "motorcycle" shall not include autocycles. Autocycles shall be subject to the requirements under this section for motor vehicles.

(b) **Auxiliary Driving Lamps.** -- Any motor vehicle may be equipped with not to exceed two auxiliary driving lamps mounted on the front, and every such auxiliary driving lamp or lamps shall meet the requirements and limitations set forth in G.S. 20-131, subsection (c).

(c) **Restrictions on Lamps.** -- Any device, other than headlamps, spot lamps, or auxiliary driving lamps, which projects a beam of light of an intensity greater than 25 candlepower, shall be so directed that no part of the beam will

strike the level of the surface on which the vehicle stands at a distance of more than 50 feet from the vehicle.

(d) **Electronically Modulated Headlamps.** -- Nothing contained in this Chapter shall prohibit the use of electronically modulated headlamps on motorcycles, law-enforcement and fire department vehicles, county fire marshals and Emergency Management coordinators, public and private ambulances, and rescue squad emergency service vehicles, provided such headlamps and light modulator are of a type or kind which have been approved by the Commissioner of Motor Vehicles.

(e) **High Mounted Flashing Deceleration Lamps.** -- Public transit vehicles may be equipped with amber, high mounted, flashing deceleration lamps on the rear of the vehicle.

(f) **Light Bar Lighting Device.** -- Notwithstanding any provision of this section to the contrary, and excluding vehicles described in subsection (d) of this section, and excluding vehicles listed in G.S. 20-130.1(b), no person shall drive a motor vehicle on the highways of this State while using a light bar lighting device. This subsection does not apply to or otherwise restrict use of a light bar lighting device with strobing lights. For purposes of this subsection, the term "light bar lighting device" means a bar-shaped lighting device comprised of multiple lamps capable of projecting a beam of light at an intensity greater than that set forth in subsection (c) of this section.

History.
1937, c. 407, s. 93; 1977, c. 104; 1989, c. 770, s. 7; 2004-82, s. 1; 2015-163, s. 7; 2017-112, s. 1

§ 20-130.1. Use of red or blue lights on vehicles prohibited; exceptions

(a) It is unlawful for any person to install or activate or operate a red light in or on any vehicle in this State. As used in this subsection, unless the context requires otherwise, "red light" means an operable red light not sealed in the manufacturer's original package which: (i) is designed for use by an emergency vehicle or is similar in appearance to a red light designed for use by an emergency vehicle; and (ii) can be operated by use of the vehicle's battery, vehicle's electrical system, or a dry cell battery. As used in this subsection, the term "red light" shall also mean any red light installed on a vehicle after initial manufacture of the vehicle.

(b) The provisions of subsection (a) of this section do not apply to the following:
(1) A police vehicle.
(2) A highway patrol vehicle.
(3) A vehicle owned by the Wildlife Resources Commission and operated

exclusively for law enforcement, firefighting, or other emergency response purposes.

(4) An ambulance.

(5) A vehicle used by an organ procurement organization or agency for the recovery and transportation of blood, human tissues, or organs for transplantation.

(6) A fire-fighting vehicle.

(7) A school bus.

(8) A vehicle operated by any member of a municipal or rural fire department in the performance of his duties, regardless of whether members of that fire department are paid or voluntary.

(9) A vehicle of a voluntary lifesaving organization (including the private vehicles of the members of such an organization) that has been officially approved by the local police authorities and which is manned or operated by members of that organization while answering an official call.

(10) A vehicle operated by medical doctors or anesthetists in emergencies.

(11) A motor vehicle used in law enforcement by the sheriff, or any salaried rural policeman in any county, regardless of whether or not the county owns the vehicle.

(11a) A vehicle operated by the State Fire Marshal or his representatives in the performance of their duties, whether or not the State owns the vehicle.

(12) A vehicle operated by any county fire marshal, assistant fire marshal, or emergency management coordinator in the performance of his duties, regardless of whether or not the county owns the vehicle.

(13) A light required by the Federal Highway Administration.

(14) A vehicle operated by a transplant coordinator who is an employee of an organ procurement organization or agency when the transplant coordinator is responding to a call to recover or transport human tissues or organs for transplantation.

(15) A vehicle operated by an emergency medical service as an emergency support vehicle.

(16) A State emergency management vehicle.

(17) An Incident Management Assistance Patrol vehicle operated by the Department of Transportation, when using rear-facing red lights while stopped for the purpose of providing assistance or incident management.

(18) A vehicle operated by the Division of Marine Fisheries of the Department of Environmental Quality or the Division of Parks and Recreation of the Department of Natural and Cultural Resources that is used for law enforcement, firefighting, or other emergency response purpose.

(19) A vehicle operated by the North Carolina Forest Service of the Department of Agriculture and Consumer Services that is used for law enforcement, firefighting, or other emergency response purpose.

(20) A vehicle operated by official members or Teams of REACT International, Inc., that is used to provide additional manpower authorized by law enforcement, firefighting, or other emergency response entities.

(c) It is unlawful for any person to possess a blue light or to install, activate, or operate a blue light in or on any vehicle in this State, except for a publicly owned vehicle used for law enforcement purposes or any other vehicle when used by law enforcement officers in the performance of their official duties. As used in this subsection, unless the context requires otherwise, "blue light" means any blue light installed on a vehicle after initial manufacture of the vehicle; or an operable blue light which:

(1) Is not (i) being installed on, held in inventory for the purpose of being installed on, or held in inventory for the purpose of sale for installation on a vehicle on which it may be lawfully operated or (ii) installed on a vehicle which is used solely for the purpose of demonstrating the blue light for sale to law enforcement personnel;

(1a) Is designed for use by an emergency vehicle, or is similar in appearance to a blue light designed for use by an emergency vehicle; and

(2) Can be operated by use of the vehicle's battery, the vehicle's electrical system, or a dry cell battery.

(c1) The provisions of subsection (c) of this section do not apply to the possession and installation of an inoperable blue light on a vehicle that is inspected by and registered with the Department of Motor Vehicles as a specially constructed vehicle and that is used primarily for participation in shows, exhibitions, parades, or holiday/weekend activities, and not for general daily transportation. For purposes of this subsection, "inoperable blue light" means a blue-colored lamp housing or cover that does not contain a lamp or other mechanism having the ability to produce or emit illumination.

(d) Repealed by Session Laws 1999-249, s. 1.

(e) Violation of subsection (a) or (c) of this section is a Class 1 misdemeanor.

History.
1943, c. 726; 1947, c. 1032; 1953, c. 354; 1955, c. 528; 1957, c. 65, s. 11; 1959, c. 166, s. 2; c. 1170, s. 2; 1967, c. 651, s. 1; 1971, c. 1214; 1977, c. 52, s. 2; c. 438, s. 2; 1979, c. 653, s. 1; c. 887; 1983, c. 32, s. 1; c. 768, s. 6; 1985 (Reg. Sess., 1986), c. 1027, s. 50; 1989, c. 537, s. 2; 1989 (Reg. Sess., 1990), c. 1020, s. 2; 1991, c. 263, s. 1; 1993, c. 539, s. 361; 1994, Ex. Sess., c. 24, s. 14(c);

1993 (Reg. Sess., 1994), c. 719, s. 1; 1995, c. 168, s. 1; 1995 (Reg. Sess., 1996), c. 756, s. 16; 1999-249, s. 1; 2005-152, s. 1; 2009-526, s. 1; 2009-550, s. 3; 2010-132, s. 11; 2013-415, s. 1(b); 2015-241, s. 14.30(ff); 2015-276, s. 2

§ 20-130.2. Use of amber lights on certain vehicles; limited use

(a) All wreckers operated on the highways of the State shall be equipped with an amber-colored flashing light which shall be so mounted and located as to be clearly visible in all directions from a distance of 500 feet, which light shall be activated when at the scene of an accident or recovery operation and when towing a vehicle which has a total outside width exceeding 96 inches or which exceeds the width of the towing vehicle. It shall be lawful to equip any other vehicle with a similar warning light including, but not by way of limitation, maintenance or construction vehicles or equipment of the Department of Transportation engaged in performing maintenance or construction work on the roads, maintenance or construction vehicles of any person, firm or corporation, Radio Emergency Associated Citizens Team (REACT) vehicles, and any other vehicles required to contain a warning light.

(b) Except as otherwise permitted under this Article, it shall be unlawful for any vehicle to operate a flashing or strobing amber light while in motion on a street or highway unless one of the following conditions apply:

(1) A law enforcement vehicle when in route to an emergency or when engaged in the chase or apprehension of violators of the law or of persons charged with or suspected of any violation.

(2) A fire, rescue, first responder, or emergency response vehicle in route to an emergency situation, when traveling in response to a fire alarm or responding to any other incident warranting the use of emergency lights and siren.

(3) When any vehicle, or vehicle's load exceeds a width of 102 inches, including oversize loads in accordance with G.S. 20-116.

(4) When the use of flashing or strobing lights is required by the Department of Transportation.

(5) When the vehicle must travel 15 miles per hour or more below the posted speed limit for safety reasons or is otherwise impeding traffic which could cause a danger to the public, in performing the vehicle's intended service, including waste management vehicles, utility vehicles, school buses, farm equipment, mail delivery vehicles, or any vehicle being used in a work zone.

(6) During a state of emergency declared by the Governor.

History.
1967, c. 651, s. 2; 1973, c. 507, s. 5; 1977, c. 464, s. 34; 1979, c. 1; c. 765; 1981, c. 390; 1991, c. 44, s. 1; 2019-157, s. 3

§ 20-130.3. Use of white or clear lights on rear of vehicles prohibited; exceptions

It shall be unlawful for any person to willfully drive a motor vehicle in forward motion upon the highways of this State displaying white or clear lights on the rear of said vehicle. The provisions of this section shall not apply to the white light required by G.S. 20-129(d) or so-called backup lights lighted only when said vehicle is in reverse gear or backing. Violation of this section does not constitute negligence per se in any civil action.

History.
1973, c. 1071

§ 20-131. Requirements as to headlamps and auxiliary driving lamps

(a) The headlamps of motor vehicles shall be so constructed, arranged, and adjusted that, except as provided in subsection (c) of this section, they will at all times mentioned in G.S. 20-129, and under normal atmospheric conditions and on a level road, produce a driving light sufficient to render clearly discernible a person 200 feet ahead, but any person operating a motor vehicle upon the highways, when meeting another vehicle, shall so control the lights of the vehicle operated by him by shifting, depressing, deflecting, tilting, or dimming the headlight beams in such manner as shall not project a glaring or dazzling light to persons within a distance of 500 feet in front of such headlamp. Every new motor vehicle, other than a motorcycle or motor-driven cycle, registered in this State after January 1, 1956, which has multiple-beam road-lighting equipment shall be equipped with a beam indicator, which shall be lighted whenever the uppermost distribution of light from the headlamps is in use, and shall not otherwise be lighted. Said indicator shall be so designed and located that when lighted it will be readily visible without glare to the driver of the vehicle so equipped. For purposes of this section, the term "motorcycle" shall not include autocycles. Autocycles shall be subject to the requirements under this section for motor vehicles.

(b) Headlamps shall be deemed to comply with the foregoing provisions prohibiting glaring and dazzling lights if none of the main bright portion of the headlamp beams rises above a horizontal plane passing through the lamp centers parallel to the level road upon which the loaded vehicle stands, and in no case higher than 42 inches, 75 feet ahead of the vehicle.

(c) Whenever a motor vehicle is being operated upon a highway, or portion thereof, which is sufficiently lighted to reveal a person on the highway at a distance of 200 feet ahead of the vehicle, it shall be permissible to dim the headlamps or to tilt the beams downward or to substitute therefor the light from an auxiliary driving lamp or pair of such lamps, subject to the restrictions as to tilted beams and auxiliary driving lamps set forth in this section.

(d) Whenever a motor vehicle meets another vehicle on any highway it shall be permissible to tilt the beams of the headlamps downward or to substitute therefor the light from an auxiliary driving lamp or pair of such lamps subject to the requirement that the tilted headlamps or auxiliary lamp or lamps shall give sufficient illumination under normal atmospheric conditions and on a level road to render clearly discernible a person 75 feet ahead, but shall not project a glaring or dazzling light to persons in front of the vehicle: Provided, that at all times required in G.S. 20-129 at least two lights shall be displayed on the front of and on opposite sides of every motor vehicle other than a motorcycle, road roller, road machinery, or farm tractor.

(e) No city or town shall enact an ordinance in conflict with this section.

History.
1937, c. 407, s. 94; 1939, c. 351, s. 1; 1955, c. 1157, ss. 6, 7; 2015-163, s. 8

§ 20-132. Acetylene lights

Motor vehicles eligible for a Historic Vehicle Owner special registration plate under G.S. 20-79.4 may be equipped with two acetylene headlamps of approximately equal candlepower when equipped with clear plane-glass fronts, bright six-inch spherical mirrors, and standard acetylene five-eighths foot burners not more and not less and which do not project a glaring or dazzling light into the eyes of approaching drivers.

History.
1937, c. 407, s. 95; 1995, c. 379, s. 18.1

§ 20-133. Enforcement of provisions

(a) The Commissioner is authorized to designate, furnish instructions to and to supervise official stations for adjusting headlamps and auxiliary driving lamps to conform with the provisions of G.S. 20-129. When headlamps and auxiliary driving lamps have been adjusted in conformity with the instructions issued by the Commissioner, a certificate of adjustment shall be issued to the driver of the motor vehicle on forms issued in duplicate by the Commissioner

and showing date of issue, registration number of the motor vehicle, owner's name, make of vehicle and official designation of the adjusting station.

(b) The driver of any motor vehicle equipped with approved headlamps, auxiliary driving lamps, rear lamps or signal lamps, who is arrested upon a charge that such lamps are improperly adjusted or are equipped with bulbs of a candlepower not approved for use therewith, shall be allowed 48 hours within which to bring such lamps into conformance with the requirements of this Article. It shall be a defense to any such charge that the person arrested produce in court or submit to the prosecuting attorney a certificate from an official adjusting station showing that within 48 hours after such arrest such lamps have been made to conform with the requirements of this Article.

History.
1937, c. 407, s. 96

§ 20-134. Lights on parked vehicles

(a) Whenever a vehicle is parked or stopped upon a highway, whether attended or unattended during the times mentioned in G.S. 20-129, there shall be displayed upon such vehicle one or more lamps projecting a white or amber light visible under normal atmospheric conditions from a distance of 500 feet to the front of such vehicle, and projecting a red light visible under like conditions from a distance of 500 feet to the rear, except that local authorities may provide by ordinance that no lights need be displayed upon any such vehicle when parked in accordance with local ordinances upon a highway where there is sufficient light to reveal any person within a distance of 200 feet upon such highway.

(b) A motor vehicle operated on a highway by a rural letter carrier or by a newspaper delivery person shall be equipped and operated with flashing amber lights at any time the vehicle is being used in the delivery of mail or newspapers, regardless of whether the vehicle is attended or unattended.

History.
1937, c. 407, s. 97; 1959, c. 1264, s. 9; 1995 (Reg. Sess., 1996), c. 715, s. 1

§ 20-135. Safety glass

(a) It shall be unlawful to operate knowingly, on any public highway or street in this State, any motor vehicle which is registered in the State of North Carolina and which shall have been manufactured or assembled on or after January 1, 1936, unless such motor vehicle be equipped with safety glass wherever glass is used in doors, windows, windshields, wings or partitions; or for a dealer to sell a motor vehicle manufactured or assembled on or after January 1, 1936, for operation upon the said highways or streets unless it be so equipped. The provisions of this Article shall not apply to any motor vehicle if such motor vehicle shall have been registered previously in another state by the owner while the owner was a bona fide resident of said other state.

(b) The term "safety glass" as used in this Article shall be construed as meaning glass so treated or combined with other materials as to reduce, in comparison with ordinary sheet glass or plate glass, the likelihood of injury to persons by glass when the glass is cracked or broken.

(c) The Division of Motor Vehicles shall approve and maintain a list of the approved types of glass, conforming to the specifications and requirements for safety glass as set forth in this Article, and in accordance with standards recognized by the United States Bureau of Standards, and shall not issue a license for or relicense any motor vehicle subject to the provisions of this Article unless such motor vehicle be equipped as herein provided with such approved type of glass.

(d) Repealed by Session Laws 1985, c. 764, s. 26.

History.
1937, c. 407, s. 98; 1941, c. 36; 1975, c. 716, s. 5; 1985, c. 764, s. 26; 1985 (Reg. Sess., 1986), c. 852, s. 17

N.C. Gen. Stat. § 20-135.1

Repealed by Session Laws 1995 (Regular Session, 1996), c. 756, s. 30.

§ 20-135.2. Safety belts and anchorages

(a) Every new motor vehicle registered in this State and manufactured, assembled, or sold after January 1, 1964, shall, at the time of registration, be equipped with at least two sets of seat safety belts for the front seat of the motor vehicle. Such seat safety belts shall be of such construction, design, and strength to support a loop load strength of not less than 5,000 pounds for each belt, and must be of a type approved by the Commissioner.

This subsection shall not apply to passenger motor vehicles having a seating capacity in the front seat of less than two passengers.

(b) After July 1, 1962, no seat safety belt shall be sold for use in connection with the operation of a motor vehicle on any highway of this State unless it shall be constructed and installed as to have a loop strength through the complete attachment of not less than 5,000 pounds and the buckle or closing device shall be of such construction and design that after it has received

the aforesaid loop belt load it can be released with one hand with a pull of less than 45 pounds.

(c) The provisions of this section shall apply only to passenger vehicles of nine-passenger capacity or less, except motorcycles.

(d) For purposes of this section, the term "motorcycle" shall not include autocycles. Every autocycle registered in this State shall be equipped with seat safety belts for the front seats of the autocycle. The seat safety belts shall meet the same construction, design, and strength requirements under this section for seat safety belts in motor vehicles.

History.
1961, c. 1076; 1963, c. 288; 2015-163, s. 9

§ 20-135.2A. (See Editor's note) Seat belt use mandatory

(a) Except as otherwise provided in G.S. 20-137.1, each occupant of a motor vehicle manufactured with seat belts shall have a seatbelt properly fastened about his or her body at all times when the vehicle is in forward motion on a street or highway in this State.

(b) Repealed by Session Laws 2006-140, s. 1, effective December 1, 2006.

(c) This section shall not apply to any of the following:

(1) A driver or occupant of a noncommercial motor vehicle with a medical or physical condition that prevents appropriate restraint by a safety belt or with a professionally certified mental phobia against the wearing of vehicle restraints.

(2) A motor vehicle operated by a rural letter carrier of the United States Postal Service while performing duties as a rural letter carrier and a motor vehicle operated by a newspaper delivery person while actually engaged in delivery of newspapers along the person's specified route.

(3) A driver or passenger frequently stopping and leaving the vehicle or delivering property from the vehicle if the speed of the vehicle between stops does not exceed 20 miles per hour.

(4) Any vehicle registered and licensed as a property-carrying vehicle in accordance with G.S. 20-88, while being used for agricultural purposes in intrastate commerce.

(5) A motor vehicle not required to be equipped with seat safety belts under federal law.

(6) Any occupant of a motor home, as defined in G.S. 20-4.01(27)k, other than the driver and front seat passengers.

(7) Any occupant, while in the custody of a law enforcement officer, being transported in the backseat of a law enforcement vehicle.

(8) A passenger of a residential garbage or recycling truck while the truck is operating during collection rounds.

(d) Evidence of failure to wear a seat belt shall not be admissible in any criminal or civil trial, action, or proceeding except in an action based on a violation of this section or as justification for the stop of a vehicle or detention of a vehicle operator and passengers.

(d1) Failure of a rear seat occupant of a vehicle to wear a seat belt shall not be justification for the stop of a vehicle.

(e) Any driver or front seat passenger who fails to wear a seat belt as required by this section shall have committed an infraction and shall pay a penalty of twenty-five dollars and fifty cents ($ 25.50) plus the following court costs: the General Court of Justice fee provided for in G.S. 7A-304(a)(4), the telephone facilities fee provided for in G.S. 7A-304(a)(2a), and the law enforcement training and certification fee provided for in G.S. 7A-304(a)(3b). Any rear seat occupant of a vehicle who fails to wear a seat belt as required by this section shall have committed an infraction and shall pay a penalty of ten dollars ($ 10.00) and no court costs. Court costs assessed under this section are for the support of the General Court of Justice and shall be remitted to the State Treasurer. Conviction of an infraction under this section has no other consequence.

(f) No drivers license points or insurance surcharge shall be assessed on account of violation of this section.

(g) The Commissioner of Motor Vehicles and the Department of Public Instruction shall incorporate in driver education programs and driver licensing programs instructions designed to encourage compliance with this section as an important means of reducing the severity of injury to the users of restraint devices and on the requirements and penalties specified in this law.

(h) Repealed by Session Laws 1999-183, s. 3, effective October 1, 1999.

History.
1985, c. 222, s. 1; 1987, c. 623; 1991, c. 448, s. 1; 1994, Ex. Sess., c. 5, s. 1; 1997-16, s. 2; 1997-443, s. 32.20; 1999-183, ss. 1 -3; 2002-126, s. 29A.3(a); 2005-276, s. 43.1(g); 2006-66, s. 21.11; 2006-140, s. 1; 2006-221, s. 21(a); 2007-289, s. 1; 2007-404, s. 2; 2009-376, s. 12; 2009-451, s. 15.20(j); 2017-102, s. 5.2(b)

§ 20-135.2B. Transporting children under 16 years of age in open bed or open cargo area of a vehicle prohibited; exceptions

(a) The operator of a vehicle having an open bed or open cargo area shall ensure that no child under 16 years of age is transported in the bed or cargo area of that vehicle. An open bed or open cargo area is a bed or cargo area without permanent overhead restraining construction.

(b) Subsection (a) of this section does not apply in any of the following circumstances:

(1) An adult is present in the bed or cargo area of the vehicle and is supervising the child.

(2) The child is secured or restrained by a seat belt manufactured in compliance with Federal Motor Vehicle Safety Standard No. 208, installed to support a load strength of not less than 5,000 pounds for each belt, and of a type approved by the Commissioner.

(3) An emergency situation exists.

(4) The vehicle is being operated in a parade.

(5) The vehicle is being operated in an agricultural enterprise, including providing transportation to and from the principal place of the agricultural enterprise.

(6) Repealed by Session Laws 2008-216, s. 1, effective October 1, 2008.

(c) Any person violating this section shall have committed an infraction and shall pay a penalty of not more than twenty-five dollars ($ 25.00), even if more than one child less than 16 years of age is riding in the open bed or open cargo area of a vehicle. A person found responsible for a violation of this section may not be assessed court costs.

(d) No drivers license points or insurance surcharge shall be assessed on account of violation of this section. A violation of this section shall not constitute negligence per se.

History.
1993 (Reg. Sess., 1994), c. 672, s. 1; 1995, c. 163, s. 7; 1999-183, s. 4; 2008-216, s. 1

§ 20-135.3. Seat belt anchorages for rear seats of motor vehicles

(a) Every new motor vehicle registered in this State and manufactured, assembled or sold after July 1, 1966, shall be equipped with sufficient anchorage units at the attachment points for attaching at least two sets of seat safety belts for the rear seat of the motor vehicle. Such anchorage units at the attachment points shall be of such construction, design, and strength to support a loop load strength of not less than 5,000 pounds for each belt.

(b) The provisions of this section shall apply to passenger vehicles of nine-passenger capacity or less, except motorcycles.

(c) For purposes of this section, the term "motorcycle" shall not include autocycles. Every autocycle registered in this State shall be equipped with sufficient anchorage units at the attachment points for attaching seat safety belts for the rear seats of the autocycle. The anchorage unit shall meet the same construction, design, and strength requirements under this section for anchorage units in motor vehicles.

History.
1965, c. 372; 2015-163, s. 10; 2016-90, s. 12.5(c)

§ 20-135.4. Certain automobile safety standards

(a) **Definitions.** -- For the purposes of this section, the term "private passenger automobile" means a four-wheeled motor vehicle designed principally for carrying passengers on public roads and highways.

(b), (c) Repealed by Session Laws 1975, c. 856.

(d) **Prohibited Modifications.** -- A private passenger automobile shall not be operated upon any highway or public vehicular area if, by alteration of the suspension, frame, or chassis, the height of the front fender is 4 or more inches greater than the height of the rear fender. For the purposes of this subsection, the height of the fender shall be a vertical measurement from and perpendicular to the ground, through the centerline of the wheel, and to the bottom of the fender.

On or after January 1, 1975, no self-propelled passenger vehicle that has been so altered, modified or changed shall be operated upon any highway or public vehicular area without the prior written approval of the Commissioner.

History.
1971, c. 485; 1973, cc. 58, 1082; 1975, c. 856; 2021-128, s. 1

§ 20-136. Smoke screens

(a) It shall be unlawful for any person or persons to drive, operate, equip or be in the possession of any automobile or other motor vehicle containing, or in any manner provided with, a mechanical machine or device designed, used or capable of being used for the purpose of discharging, creating or causing, in any manner, to be discharged or emitted, either from itself or from the automobile or other motor vehicle to which attached, any unusual amount of smoke, gas or other substance not necessary to the actual propulsion, care and keep of said vehicle, and the possession by any person or persons of any such device, whether the same is attached to any such motor vehicle, or detached therefrom, shall be prima facie evidence of the guilt of such person or persons of a violation of this section.

(b) Any person or persons violating the provisions of this section shall be guilty of a Class I felony.

History.
1937, c. 407, s. 99; 1993, c. 539, s. 1257; 1994, Ex. Sess., c. 24, s. 14(c)

§ 20-136.1. Location of television, computer, or video players, monitors, and screens

No person shall drive any motor vehicle upon a public street or highway or public vehicular area while viewing any television, computer, or video player which is located in the motor vehicle at any point forward of the back of the driver's seat, and which is visible to the driver while operating the motor vehicle. This section does not apply to the use of global positioning systems; turn-by-turn navigation displays or similar navigation devices; factory-installed or aftermarket global positioning systems or wireless communications devices used to transmit or receive data as part of a digital dispatch system; equipment that displays audio system information, functions, or controls, or weather, traffic, and safety information; vehicle safety or equipment information; or image displays that enhance the driver's view in any direction, inside or outside of the vehicle. The provisions of this section shall not apply to law enforcement or emergency personnel while in the performance of their official duties, or to the operator of a vehicle that is lawfully parked or stopped.

History.
1949, c. 583, s. 4; 2009-376, s. 13

§ 20-136.2. Counterfeit supplemental restraint system components and nonfunctional airbags

(a) It shall be unlawful for any person, firm, or corporation to knowingly import, manufacture, sell, offer for sale, distribute, install or reinstall a counterfeit supplemental restraint system or nonfunctional airbag in any motor vehicle, or other component device that causes a motor vehicle to fail to meet federal motor vehicle safety standards as provided in 49 C.F.R. § 571.208. Any person, firm, or corporation violating this section shall be guilty of a Class 1 misdemeanor, and violation constitutes an unfair and deceptive trade practice under G.S. 75-1.1. If a violation of this section contributes to a person's physical injury or death, the person, firm, or corporation violating this section shall be guilty of a Class H felony. For purposes of this section, in the event that a franchised motor vehicle dealer, as defined in G.S. 20-286(8b) or its owners, have no actual knowledge that a counterfeit supplemental restraint system component, nonfunctional airbag, or other component device has been imported, manufactured, sold, offered for sale, installed, or reinstalled in lieu of a supplemental restraint system component at the franchised motor vehicle dealer's place of business or elsewhere, knowledge by any other person shall not be imputed to the franchised motor vehicle dealer or its owners, and the franchised motor vehicle dealer or its owners shall not be deemed to have committed an unlawful act under this section and shall not have any criminal liability under this section.

(b) Nothing in this section is intended to prohibit automotive dealers, repair professionals, recyclers, original equipment manufacturers, or contractors from disposing of counterfeit supplemental restraint system components or nonfunctional airbags in accordance with federal and State law.

History.
2003-258, s. 3; 2019-155, s. 3

N.C. Gen. Stat. § 20-137

Repealed by Session Laws 1995, c. 379, s. 18.2.

§ 20-137.1. Child restraint systems required

(a) Every driver who is transporting one or more passengers of less than 16 years of age shall have all such passengers properly secured in a child passenger restraint system or seat belt which meets federal standards applicable at the time of its manufacture.

(a1) A child less than eight years of age and less than 80 pounds in weight shall be properly secured in a weight-appropriate child passenger restraint system. In vehicles equipped with an active passenger-side front air bag, if the vehicle has a rear seat, a child less than five years of age and less than 40 pounds in weight shall be properly secured in a rear seat, unless the child restraint system is designed for use with air bags. If no seating position equipped with a lap and shoulder belt to properly secure the weight-appropriate child passenger restraint system is available, a child less than eight years of age and between 40 and 80 pounds may be restrained by a properly fitted lap belt only.

(b) The provisions of this section shall not apply: (i) to ambulances or other emergency vehicles; (ii) if all seating positions equipped with child passenger restraint systems or seat belts are occupied; or (iii) to vehicles which are not required by federal law or regulation to be equipped with seat belts.

(c) Any driver found responsible for a violation of this section may be punished by a penalty not to exceed twenty-five dollars ($ 25.00), even when more than one child less than 16 years of age was not properly secured in a restraint system. No driver charged under this section for failure to have a child under eight years of age properly secured in a restraint system shall be convicted if he produces at the time of his trial proof satisfactory to the court that he has subsequently acquired an approved

child passenger restraint system for a vehicle in which the child is normally transported.

(d) A violation of this section shall have all of the following consequences:

(1) Two drivers license points shall be assessed pursuant to G.S. 20-16.

(2) No insurance points shall be assessed.

(3) The violation shall not constitute negligence per se or contributory negligence per se.

(4) The violation shall not be evidence of negligence or contributory negligence.

History.
1981, c. 804, ss. 1, 4, 5; 1985, c. 218; 1993 (Reg. Sess., 1994), c. 748, s. 1; 1999-183, ss. 6, 7; 2000-117, s. 1; 2004-191, ss. 1, 2; 2007-6, s. 1

§ 20-137.2. Operation of vehicles resembling law-enforcement vehicles unlawful; punishment

(a) It is unlawful for any person other than a law-enforcement officer of the State or of any county, municipality, or other political subdivision thereof, with the intent to impersonate a law-enforcement officer, to operate any vehicle, which by its coloration, insignia, lettering, and blue or red light resembles a vehicle owned, possessed, or operated by any law-enforcement agency.

(b) Violation of subsection (a) of this section is a Class 1 misdemeanor.

History.
1979, c. 567, s. 1; 1993, c. 539, s. 362; 1994, Ex. Sess., c. 24, s. 14(c)

§ 20-137.3. Unlawful use of a mobile phone by persons under 18 years of age

(a) **Definitions.** -- The following definitions apply in this section:

(1) **Additional technology.** -- Any technology that provides access to digital media including, but not limited to, a camera, music, the Internet, or games. The term does not include electronic mail or text messaging.

(2) **Mobile telephone.** -- A device used by subscribers and other users of wireless telephone service to access the service. The term includes: (i) a device with which a user engages in a call using at least one hand, and (ii) a device that has an internal feature or function, or that is equipped with an attachment or addition, whether or not permanently part of the mobile telephone, by which a user engages in a call without the use of either hand, whether or not the use of either hand is necessary to activate, deactivate, or initiate a function of such telephone.

(3) **Wireless telephone service.** -- A service that is a two-way real-time voice telecommunications service that is interconnected to a public switched telephone network and is provided by a commercial mobile radio service, as such term is defined by 47 C.F.R. § 20.3.

(b) **Offense.** -- Except as otherwise provided in this section, no person under the age of 18 years shall operate a motor vehicle on a public street or highway or public vehicular area while using a mobile telephone or any additional technology associated with a mobile telephone while the vehicle is in motion. This prohibition shall not apply to the use of a mobile telephone or additional technology in a stationary vehicle.

(c) **Seizure.** -- The provisions of this section shall not be construed as authorizing the seizure or forfeiture of a mobile telephone, unless otherwise provided by law.

(d) **Exceptions.** -- The provisions of subsection (b) of this section shall not apply if the use of a mobile telephone is for the sole purpose of communicating with:

(1) Any of the following regarding an emergency situation: an emergency response operator; a hospital, physician's office, or health clinic; a public or privately owned ambulance company or service; a fire department; or a law enforcement agency.

(2) The motor vehicle operator's parent, legal guardian or spouse.

(e) **Penalty.** -- Any person violating this section shall have committed an infraction and shall pay a fine of twenty-five dollars ($ 25.00). This offense is an offense for which a defendant may waive the right to a hearing or trial and admit responsibility for the infraction pursuant to G.S. 7A-148. No drivers license points, insurance surcharge, or court costs shall be assessed as a result of a violation of this section.

History.
2006-177, s. 1; 2009-135, s. 1

§ 20-137.4. Unlawful use of a mobile phone

(a) **Definitions.** -- For purposes of this section, the following terms shall mean:

(1) **Additional technology.** -- As defined in G.S. 20-137.3(a)(1).

(2) **Emergency situation.** -- Circumstances such as medical concerns, unsafe road conditions, matters of public safety, or mechanical problems that create a risk of harm for the operator or passengers of a school bus.

(3) **Mobile telephone.** -- As defined in G.S. 20-137.3(a)(2).

(4) **School bus.** -- As defined in G.S. 20-4.01(27)n. The term also includes any

school activity bus as defined in G.S. 20-4.01(27)m. and any vehicle transporting public, private, or parochial school students for compensation.

(b) **Offense.** -- Except as otherwise provided in this section, no person shall operate a school bus on a public street or highway or public vehicular area while using a mobile telephone or any additional technology associated with a mobile telephone while the school bus is in motion. This prohibition shall not apply to the use of a mobile telephone or additional technology associated with a mobile telephone in a stationary school bus.

(c) **Seizure.** -- The provisions of this section shall not be construed as authorizing the seizure or forfeiture of a mobile telephone or additional technology, unless otherwise provided by law.

(d) **Exceptions.** -- The provisions of subsection (b) of this section shall not apply to the use of a mobile telephone or additional technology associated with a mobile telephone for the sole purpose of communicating in an emergency situation.

(e) **Local Ordinances.** -- No local government may pass any ordinance regulating the use of mobile telephones or additional technology associated with a mobile telephone by operators of school buses.

(f) **Penalty.** -- A violation of this section shall be a Class 2 misdemeanor and shall be punishable by a fine of not less than one hundred dollars ($ 100.00). No drivers license points or insurance surcharge shall be assessed as a result of a violation of this section. Failure to comply with the provisions of this section shall not constitute negligence per se or contributory negligence by the operator in any action for the recovery of damages arising out of the operation, ownership, or maintenance of a school bus.

History.
2007-261, s. 1; 2017-102, s. 5.2(b)

§ 20-137.4A. Unlawful use of mobile telephone for text messaging or electronic mail

(a) **Offense.** -- It shall be unlawful for any person to operate a vehicle on a public street or highway or public vehicular area while using a mobile telephone to:

(1) Manually enter multiple letters or text in the device as a means of communicating with another person; or

(2) Read any electronic mail or text message transmitted to the device or stored within the device, provided that this prohibition shall not apply to any name or number stored in the device nor to any caller identification information.

Chapter 20

(a1) Motor Carrier Offense. -- It shall be unlawful for any person to operate a commercial motor vehicle subject to Part 390 or 392 of Title 49 of the Code of Federal Regulations on a public street or highway or public vehicular area while using a mobile telephone or other electronic device in violation of those Parts. Nothing in this subsection shall be construed to prohibit the use of hands-free technology.

(b) Exceptions. -- The provisions of this section shall not apply to:

(1) The operator of a vehicle that is lawfully parked or stopped.

(2) Any of the following while in the performance of their official duties: a law enforcement officer; a member of a fire department; or the operator of a public or private ambulance.

(3) The use of factory-installed or aftermarket global positioning systems (GPS) or wireless communications devices used to transmit or receive data as part of a digital dispatch system.

(4) The use of voice operated technology.

(c) Penalty. -- A violation of this section while operating a school bus, as defined in G.S. 20-137.4(a)(4), shall be a Class 2 misdemeanor and shall be punishable by a fine of not less than one hundred dollars ($ 100.00). Any other violation of this section shall be an infraction and shall be punishable by a fine of one hundred dollars ($ 100.00) and the costs of court.

No drivers license points or insurance surcharge shall be assessed as a result of a violation of this section. Failure to comply with the provisions of this section shall not constitute negligence per se or contributory negligence per se by the operator in any action for the recovery of damages arising out of the operation, ownership, or maintenance of a vehicle.

History.
2009-135, s. 2; 2012-78, s. 9

§ 20-137.5. Child passenger safety technician; limitation of liability

(a) The following definitions apply in this section:

(1) **Certified child passenger safety technician. --** A certified child passenger safety technician is an individual who has successfully completed the U.S. Department of Transportation National Highway Traffic Safety Administration's (NHTSA) National Standardized Child Passenger Safety Certification Training Program and who maintains a current child passenger safety technician or technician instructor certification through the current certifying body for the National Child Passenger Safety Training Program as designated by the National Highway Traffic Safety Administration.

(2) **Sponsoring organization. --** A sponsoring organization is a person or organization other than a manufacturer of or employee or agent of a manufacturer of child safety seats that:

a. Offers or arranges for the public a nonprofit child safety seat educational program, checkup event, or checking station program utilizing certified child passenger safety technicians; or

b. Owns property upon which a nonprofit child safety seat educational program, checkup event, or checking station program for the public occurs utilizing certified child passenger safety technicians.

(b) Limitation of Liability. -- Except as provided in subsection (c) of this section, a certified child passenger safety technician or sponsoring organization shall not be liable to any person as a result of any act or omission that occurs solely in the inspection, installation, or adjustment of a child safety seat or in providing education regarding the installation or adjustment of a child safety seat if:

(1) The service is provided without fee or charge other than reimbursement for expenses, and

(2) The child passenger safety technician or sponsoring organization acts in good faith and within the scope of training for which the technician is currently certified.

(c) Exceptions. -- The limitation on liability shall not apply under any of the following conditions:

(1) The act or omission of the certified child passenger safety technician or sponsoring organization constitutes willful or wanton misconduct or gross negligence.

(2) The inspection, installation, or adjustment of a child safety seat or education provided regarding the installation or adjustment of a child safety seat is in conjunction with the for-profit sale of a child safety seat.

History.
2008-178, s. 1

PART 9A
ABANDONED AND DERELICT MOTOR VEHICLES

§ 20-137.6. Declaration of purpose

Abandoned and derelict motor vehicles constitute a hazard to the health and welfare of the people of the State in that such vehicles can harbor noxious diseases, furnish shelter and breeding places for vermin, and present physical dangers to the safety and well-being of children and other citizens. It is therefore in the public interest that the present accumulation of abandoned and derelict motor vehicles be eliminated and that the future abandonment of such vehicles be prevented.

History.
1973, c. 720, s. 1

§ 20-137.7. Definitions of words and phrases

The following words and phrases when used in this Part shall for the purpose of this Part have the meaning respectively prescribed to them in this Part, except in those instances where the context clearly indicates a different meaning:

(1) "Abandoned vehicle" means a motor vehicle that has remained illegally on private or public property for a period of more than 10 days without the consent of the owner or person in control of the property.

(2) "Demolisher" means any person, firm or corporation whose business is to convert a motor vehicle into processed scrap or scrap metal or otherwise to wreck, or dismantle, such a vehicle.

(3) "Department" means the North Carolina Department of Transportation.

(4) "Derelict vehicle" means a motor vehicle:

a. Whose certificate of registration has expired and the registered and legal owner no longer resides at the address listed on the last certificate of registration on record with the North Carolina Department of Transportation; or

b. Whose major parts have been removed so as to render the vehicle inoperable and incapable of passing inspection as required under existing standards; or

c. Whose manufacturer's serial plates, vehicle identification numbers, license number plates and any other means of identification have been removed so as to nullify efforts to locate or identify the registered and legal owner; or

d. Whose registered and legal owner of record disclaims ownership or releases his rights thereto; or

e. Which is more than 12 years old and does not bear a current license as required by the Department.

(5) "Officer" means any law-enforcement officer of the State, of any county or of any municipality including county sanitation officers.

(6) "Salvage yard" means a business or a person who possesses five or more derelict vehicles, regularly engages in buying and selling used vehicle parts.

(7) "Secretary" means the Secretary of the North Carolina Department of Transportation.

(8) "Tag" means any type of notice affixed to an abandoned or derelict motor vehicle advising the owner or the person in possession that the same has been declared an abandoned or derelict vehicle and will be treated as such, which tag shall be of sufficient size as to be easily discernible and contain such information as the Secretary deems necessary to enforce this Part.

(9) "Vehicle" means every device in, upon, or by which any person or property is or may be transported or drawn upon a highway by mechanical means.

(10) "Vehicle recycling" means the process whereby discarded vehicles (abandoned, derelict or wrecked) are collected and then processed by shredding, bailing or shearing to produce processed scrap iron and steel which is then remelted by steel mills and foundries to make raw materials which are subsequently used to manufacture new metal-based products for the consumer.

History.
1973, c. 720, s. 1

§ 20-137.8. Secretary may adopt rules and regulations

The Secretary is hereby vested with the power and is charged with the duties of administering the provisions of this Part and is authorized to adopt such rules and regulations as may be necessary to carry out the provisions thereof.

History.
1973, c. 720, s. 1

§ 20-137.9. Removal from private property

Any abandoned or any derelict vehicle in this State shall be subject to be removed from public or private property provided not objected to by the owner of the private property after notice as hereinafter provided and disposed of in accordance with the provisions of this Part, provided, that all abandoned motor vehicles left on any right-of-way of any road or highway in this State may be removed in accordance with G.S. 20-161.

History.
1973, c. 720, s. 1

§ 20-137.10. Abandoned and derelict vehicles to be tagged; determination of value

(a) When any vehicle is derelict or abandoned in this State, the Secretary shall cause a tag to be placed on the vehicle which shall be notice to the owner, the person in possession of the vehicle, or any lienholder that the same is considered to have been derelict or abandoned and is subject to forfeiture to the State.

(b) Repealed by Session Laws 1975, c. 438, s. 3.

(c) The tag shall serve as the only notice that if the vehicle is not removed within five days from the date reflected on the tag, it will be removed to a designated place to be sold. After the vehicle is removed, the Secretary shall give notice in writing to the person in whose name the vehicle was last registered at the last address reflected in the Department's records and to any lienholder of record that the vehicle is being held, designating the place where the vehicle is being held and that if it is not redeemed within 10 days from the date of the notice by paying all costs of removal and storage the same shall be sold for recycling purposes. The proceeds of the sale shall be deposited in the highway fund established for the purpose of administering the provisions of this Part.

(d) If the value of the vehicle is determined to be more than one hundred dollars ($ 100.00), and if the identity of the last registered owner cannot be determined or if the registration contains no address for the owner, or if it is impossible to determine with reasonable certainty the identification and addresses of any lienholders, notice by one publication in a newspaper of general circulation in the area where the vehicle was located shall be sufficient to meet all requirements of notice pursuant to this Part. The notice of publication may contain multiple listings of vehicles. Five days after date of publication the advertised vehicles may be sold. The proceeds of such sale shall be deposited in the highway fund established for the purpose of administering the provisions of this Part.

(d1) If the value of the vehicle is determined to be less than one hundred dollars ($ 100.00), and if the identity of the last registered owner cannot be determined or if the registration contains no address for the owner, or if it is impossible to determine with reasonable certainty the identification and addresses of any lienholders, no notice in addition to that required by subsection (a) hereof shall be required prior to sale.

(e) All officers, as defined in this Part, are given the authority to appraise or determine the value of derelict or abandoned vehicles as defined in this Part.

History.
1973, c. 720, s. 1; 1975, c. 438, s. 3

§ 20-137.11. Title to vest in State

Title to all vehicles sold or disposed of in accordance with this Part shall vest in the State. All manufacturers' serial number plates and any other identification numbers for all vehicles sold to any person other than a demolisher shall at the time of the sale be turned in to the Department for destruction. Any demolisher purchasing or acquiring any vehicle hereunder shall, under oath, state to the Department that the vehicles purchased or acquired by it have been shredded or recycled.

The Secretary shall remove and destroy all departmental records relating to such vehicles in such method and manner as he may prescribe.

History.
1973, c. 720, s. 1

§ 20-137.12. Secretary may contract for disposal

The Secretary is hereby authorized to contract with any federal, other state, county or municipal authority or private enterprise for tagging, collection, storage, transportation or any other services necessary to prepare derelict or abandoned vehicles for recycling or other methods of disposal. Publicly owned properties, when available, shall be provided as temporary collecting areas for the vehicles defined herein. The Secretary shall have full authority to sell such derelict or abandoned vehicles. If the Secretary deems it more advisable and practical, in addition, he is authorized to contract with private enterprise for the purchase of such vehicles for recycling.

History.
1973, c. 720, s. 1

§ 20-137.13. No liability for removal

No agent or employee of any federal, State, county or municipal government, no person or occupant of the premises from which any derelict or abandoned vehicle shall be removed, nor any person or firm contracting for the removal of or disposition of any such vehicle shall be held criminally or civilly liable in any way arising out of or caused by carrying out or enforcing any provisions of this Part.

History.
1973, c. 720, s. 1

§ 20-137.14. Enclosed, antique, registered and certain other vehicles exempt

The provisions of this Part shall not apply to vehicles located on used car lots, in private garages, enclosed parking lots, or on any other parking area on private property which is not visible from any public street or highway, nor to motor vehicles classified as antiques and registered under the laws of the State of North Carolina, those not required by law to be registered, or those in possession of a salvage yard as defined in G.S. 20-137.7, unless that vehicle presents some safety or health hazard or constitutes a nuisance.

History.
1973, c. 720, s. 1

PART 10
OPERATION OF VEHICLES AND RULES OF THE ROAD

N.C. Gen. Stat. § 20-138

Repealed by Session Laws 1983, c. 435, s. 23.

§ 20-138.1. Impaired driving

(a) **Offense.** -- A person commits the offense of impaired driving if he drives any vehicle upon any highway, any street, or any public vehicular area within this State:

    (1) While under the influence of an impairing substance; or

    (2) After having consumed sufficient alcohol that he has, at any relevant time after the driving, an alcohol concentration of 0.08 or more. The results of a chemical analysis shall be deemed sufficient evidence to prove a person's alcohol concentration; or

    (3) With any amount of a Schedule I controlled substance, as listed in G.S. 90-89, or its metabolites in his blood or urine.

(a1) A person who has submitted to a chemical analysis of a blood sample, pursuant to G.S. 20-139.1(d), may use the result in rebuttal as evidence that the person did not have, at a relevant time after driving, an alcohol concentration of 0.08 or more.

(b) **Defense Precluded.** -- The fact that a person charged with violating this section is or has been legally entitled to use alcohol or a drug is not a defense to a charge under this section.

(b1) **Defense Allowed.** -- Nothing in this section shall preclude a person from asserting that a chemical analysis result is inadmissible pursuant to G.S. 20-139.1(b2).

(c) **Pleading.** -- In any prosecution for impaired driving, the pleading is sufficient if it states the time and place of the alleged offense in the usual form and charges that the defendant drove a vehicle on a highway or public vehicular area while subject to an impairing substance.

(d) **Sentencing Hearing and Punishment.** -- Impaired driving as defined in this section is a misdemeanor. Upon conviction of a defendant of impaired driving, the presiding judge shall hold a sentencing hearing and impose punishment in accordance with G.S. 20-179.

(e) **Exception.** -- Notwithstanding the definition of "vehicle" pursuant to G.S. 20-4.01(49), for purposes of this section the word "vehicle" does not include a horse.

History.
1983, c. 435, s. 24; 1989, c. 711, s. 2; 1993, c. 285, s. 1; 2006-253, s. 9

§ 20-138.2. Impaired driving in commercial vehicle

(a) **Offense.** -- A person commits the offense of impaired driving in a commercial motor vehicle if he drives a commercial motor vehicle upon any highway, any street, or any public vehicular area within the State:

    (1) While under the influence of an impairing substance; or

    (2) After having consumed sufficient alcohol that he has, at any relevant time after the driving, an alcohol concentration of 0.04 or more. The results of a chemical analysis shall be deemed sufficient evidence to prove a person's alcohol concentration; or

    (3) With any amount of a Schedule I controlled substance, as listed in G.S. 90-89, or its metabolites in his blood or urine.

(a1) A person who has submitted to a chemical analysis of a blood sample, pursuant to G.S. 20-139.1(d), may use the result in rebuttal as evidence that the person did not have, at a relevant time after driving, an alcohol concentration of 0.04 or more.

(a2) In order to prove the gross vehicle weight rating of a vehicle as defined in G.S. 20-4.01(12f), the opinion of a person who observed the vehicle as to the weight, the testimony of the gross vehicle weight rating affixed to the vehicle, the registered or declared weight shown on the Division's records pursuant to G.S. 20-26(b1), the gross vehicle weight rating as determined from the vehicle identification number, the listed gross weight publications from the manufacturer of the vehicle, or any other description or evidence shall be admissible.

(b) **Defense Precluded.** -- The fact that a person charged with violating this section is or has been legally entitled to use alcohol or a drug is not a defense to a charge under this section.

(b1) **Defense Allowed.** -- Nothing in this section shall preclude a person from asserting that a chemical analysis result is inadmissible pursuant to G.S. 20-139.1(b2).

(c) **Pleading.** -- To charge a violation of this section, the pleading is sufficient if it states the time and place of the alleged offense in the usual form and charges the defendant drove a commercial motor vehicle on a highway, street, or public vehicular area while subject to an impairing substance.

(d) **Implied Consent Offense.** -- An offense under this section is an implied consent offense subject to the provisions of G.S. 20-16.2.

(e) **Punishment.** -- The offense in this section is a misdemeanor and any defendant convicted under this section shall be sentenced under G.S. 20-179. This offense is not a lesser included offense of impaired driving under G.S. 20-138.1, and if a person is convicted under this section and of an offense involving impaired driving under G.S. 20-138.1 arising out of the same transaction, the aggregate punishment imposed by the Court may not exceed the maximum punishment applicable to the offense involving impaired driving under G.S. 20-138.1.

(f) Repealed by Session Laws 1991, c. 726, s. 19.

(g) **Chemical Analysis Provisions.** -- The provisions of G.S. 20-139.1 shall apply to the offense of impaired driving in a commercial motor vehicle.

History.
1989, c. 771, s. 12; 1991, c. 726, s. 19; 1993, c. 539, s. 363; 1994, Ex. Sess., c. 24, s. 14(c); 1998-182, s. 24; 2006-253, s. 10; 2010-129, s. 1

§ 20-138.2A. Operating a commercial vehicle after consuming alcohol

(a) **Offense.** -- A person commits the offense of operating a commercial motor vehicle after consuming alcohol if the person drives a commercial motor vehicle, as defined in G.S. 20-4.01(3d)a. and b., upon any highway, any street, or any public vehicular area within the State while consuming alcohol or while alcohol remains in the person's body.

(b) **Implied-Consent Offense.** -- An offense under this section is an implied-consent offense subject to the provisions of G.S. 20-16.2. The provisions of G.S. 20-139.1 shall apply to an offense committed under this section.

(b1) **Odor Insufficient.** -- The odor of an alcoholic beverage on the breath of the driver is insufficient evidence by itself to prove beyond a reasonable doubt that alcohol was remaining in the driver's body in violation of this section unless the driver was offered an alcohol screening test or chemical analysis and refused to provide all required samples of breath or blood for analysis.

(b2) **Alcohol Screening Test.** -- Notwithstanding any other provision of law, an alcohol

screening test may be administered to a driver suspected of violation of subsection (a) of this section, and the results of an alcohol screening test or the driver's refusal to submit may be used by a law enforcement officer, a court, or an administrative agency in determining if alcohol was present in the driver's body. No alcohol screening tests are valid under this section unless the device used is one approved by the Department of Health and Human Services, and the screening test is conducted in accordance with the applicable regulations of the Department as to its manner and use.

(c) **Punishment.** -- Except as otherwise provided in this subsection, a violation of the offense described in subsection (a) of this section is a Class 3 misdemeanor and, notwithstanding G.S. 15A-1340.23, is punishable by a penalty of one hundred dollars ($ 100.00). A second or subsequent violation of this section is a misdemeanor punishable under G.S. 20-179. This offense is a lesser included offense of impaired driving of a commercial vehicle under G.S. 20-138.2.

(d) **Second or Subsequent Conviction Defined.** -- A conviction for violating this offense is a second or subsequent conviction if at the time of the current offense the person has a previous conviction under this section, and the previous conviction occurred in the seven years immediately preceding the date of the current offense. This definition of second or subsequent conviction also applies to G.S. 20-17(a)(13) and G.S. 20-17.4(a)(6).

History.
1998-182, s. 23; 1999-406, s. 15; 2000-140, s. 5; 2000-155, s. 16; 2007-182, s. 2; 2008-187, s. 36(a)

§ 20-138.2B. Operating a school bus, school activity bus, child care vehicle, ambulance, other EMS vehicle, firefighting vehicle, or law enforcement vehicle after consuming alcohol

(a) **Offense.** -- A person commits the offense of operating a school bus, school activity bus, child care vehicle, ambulance, other emergency medical services vehicle, firefighting vehicle, or law enforcement vehicle after consuming alcohol if the person drives a school bus, school activity bus, child care vehicle, ambulance, other emergency medical services vehicle, firefighting vehicle, or law enforcement vehicle upon any highway, any street, or any public vehicular area within the State while consuming alcohol or while alcohol remains in the person's body. This section does not apply to law enforcement officers acting in the course of, and within the scope of, their official duties.

(b) **Implied-Consent Offense.** -- An offense under this section is an implied-consent offense subject to the provisions of G.S. 20-16.2. The provisions of G.S. 20-139.1 shall apply to an offense committed under this section.

(b1) **Odor Insufficient.** -- The odor of an alcoholic beverage on the breath of the driver is insufficient evidence by itself to prove beyond a reasonable doubt that alcohol was remaining in the driver's body in violation of this section unless the driver was offered an alcohol screening test or chemical analysis and refused to provide all required samples of breath or blood for analysis.

(b2) **Alcohol Screening Test.** -- Notwithstanding any other provision of law, an alcohol screening test may be administered to a driver suspected of violation of subsection (a) of this section, and the results of an alcohol screening test or the driver's refusal to submit may be used by a law enforcement officer, a court, or an administrative agency in determining if alcohol was present in the driver's body. No alcohol screening tests are valid under this section unless the device used is one approved by the Department of Health and Human Services, and the screening test is conducted in accordance with the applicable regulations of the Department as to its manner and use.

(c) **Punishment.** -- Except as otherwise provided in this subsection, a violation of the offense described in subsection (a) of this section is a Class 3 misdemeanor and, notwithstanding G.S. 15A-1340.23, is punishable by a penalty of one hundred dollars ($ 100.00). A second or subsequent violation of this section is a misdemeanor punishable under G.S. 20-179. This offense is a lesser included offense of impaired driving of a commercial vehicle under G.S. 20-138.1.

(d) **Second or Subsequent Conviction Defined.** -- A conviction for violating this offense is a second or subsequent conviction if at the time of the current offense the person has a previous conviction under this section, and the previous conviction occurred in the seven years immediately preceding the date of the current offense. This definition of second or subsequent conviction also applies to G.S. 20-19(c2).

History.
1998-182, s. 27; 1999-406, s. 16; 2000-140, s. 6; 2000-155, s. 17; 2007-182, s. 2; 2008-187, s. 36(b); 2013-105, s. 1

§ 20-138.2C. Possession of alcoholic beverages while operating a commercial motor vehicle

A person commits the offense of operating a commercial motor vehicle while possessing alcoholic beverages if the person drives a commercial motor vehicle, as defined in G.S. 20-4.01(3d), upon any highway, any street, or any public vehicular area within the State while having an open or closed alcoholic beverage in the passenger area of the commercial motor vehicle. This section shall not apply to the driver of a commercial motor vehicle that is also an excursion passenger vehicle, a for-hire passenger vehicle, a common carrier of passengers, or a motor home, if the alcoholic beverage is in possession of a passenger or is in the passenger area of the vehicle.

History.
1999-330, s. 2

§ 20-138.3. Driving by person less than 21 years old after consuming alcohol or drugs

(a) **Offense.** -- It is unlawful for a person less than 21 years old to drive a motor vehicle on a highway or public vehicular area while consuming alcohol or at any time while he has remaining in his body any alcohol or controlled substance previously consumed, but a person less than 21 years old does not violate this section if he drives with a controlled substance in his body which was lawfully obtained and taken in therapeutically appropriate amounts.

(b) **Subject to Implied-Consent Law.** -- An offense under this section is an alcohol-related offense subject to the implied-consent provisions of G.S. 20-16.2.

(b1) **Odor Insufficient.** -- The odor of an alcoholic beverage on the breath of the driver is insufficient evidence by itself to prove beyond a reasonable doubt that alcohol was remaining in the driver's body in violation of this section unless the driver was offered an alcohol screening test or chemical analysis and refused to provide all required samples of breath or blood for analysis.

(b2) **Alcohol Screening Test.** -- Notwithstanding any other provision of law, an alcohol screening test may be administered to a driver suspected of violation of subsection (a) of this section, and the results of an alcohol screening test or the driver's refusal to submit may be used by a law enforcement officer, a court, or an administrative agency in determining if alcohol was present in the driver's body. No alcohol screening tests are valid under this section unless the device used is one approved by the Department of Health and Human Services, and the screening test is conducted in accordance with the applicable regulations of the Department as to its manner and use.

(c) **Punishment; Effect When Impaired Driving Offense Also Charged.** -- The offense in this section is a Class 2 misdemeanor. It is not, in any circumstances, a lesser included offense of impaired driving under G.S. 20-138.1, but if a person is convicted under this section

Chapter 20

and of an offense involving impaired driving arising out of the same transaction, the aggregate punishment imposed by the court may not exceed the maximum applicable to the offense involving impaired driving, and any minimum punishment applicable shall be imposed.

(d) **Limited Driving Privilege.** -- A person who is convicted of violating subsection (a) of this section and whose drivers license is revoked solely based on that conviction may apply for a limited driving privilege as provided in G.S. 20-179.3. This subsection shall apply only if the person meets both of the following requirements:

(1) Is 18, 19, or 20 years old on the date of the offense.

(2) Has not previously been convicted of a violation of this section.

The judge may issue the limited driving privilege only if the person meets the eligibility requirements of G.S. 20-179.3, other than the requirement in G.S. 20-179.3(b)(1) c. G.S. 20-179.3(e) shall not apply. All other terms, conditions, and restrictions provided for in G.S. 20-179.3 shall apply. G.S. 20-179.3, rather than this subsection, governs the issuance of a limited driving privilege to a person who is convicted of violating subsection (a) of this section and of driving while impaired as a result of the same transaction.

History.
1983, c. 435, s. 34; 1985 (Reg. Sess., 1986), c. 852, s. 11; 1993, c. 539, s. 364; 1994, Ex. Sess., c. 24, s. 14(c); 1995, c. 506, s. 6; 1997-379, ss. 4, 5.2; 2000-140, s. 7; 2000-155, s. 18; 2006-253, s. 11

§ 20-138.4. Requirement that prosecutor explain reduction or dismissal of charge in implied-consent case

(a) Any prosecutor shall enter detailed facts in the record of any case subject to the implied-consent law or involving driving while license revoked for impaired driving as defined in G.S. 20-28.2 explaining orally in open court and in writing the reasons for his action if he:

(1) Enters a voluntary dismissal; or

(2) Accepts a plea of guilty or no contest to a lesser included offense; or

(3) Substitutes another charge, by statement of charges or otherwise, if the substitute charge carries a lesser mandatory minimum punishment or is not a case subject to the implied-consent law; or

(4) Otherwise takes a discretionary action that effectively dismisses or reduces the original charge in a case subject to the implied-consent law.

General explanations such as "interests of justice" or "insufficient evidence" are not sufficiently detailed to meet the requirements of this section.

(b) The written explanation shall be signed by the prosecutor taking the action on a form approved by the Administrative Office of the Courts and shall contain, at a minimum:

(1) The alcohol concentration or the fact that the driver refused.

(2) A list of all prior convictions of implied-consent offenses or driving while license revoked.

(3) Whether the driver had a valid drivers license or privilege to drive in this State as indicated by the Division's records.

(4) A statement that a check of the database of the Administrative Office of the Courts revealed whether any other charges against the defendant were pending.

(5) The elements that the prosecutor believes in good faith can be proved, and a list of those elements that the prosecutor cannot prove and why.

(6) The name and agency of the charging officer and whether the officer is available.

(7) Any reason why the charges are dismissed.

(c) *(See Editor's note on effective date)* A copy of the form required in subsection (b) of this section shall be sent to the head of the law enforcement agency that employed the charging officer, to the district attorney who employs the prosecutor, and filed in the court file. The Administrative Office of the Courts shall electronically record this data in its database and make it available upon request.

History.
1983, c. 435, s. 25; 1987 (Reg. Sess., 1988), c. 1112; 1989, c. 771, s. 18; 2006-253, s. 19; 2007-493, s. 16

§ 20-138.5. Habitual impaired driving

(a) A person commits the offense of habitual impaired driving if he drives while impaired as defined in G.S. 20-138.1 and has been convicted of three or more offenses involving impaired driving as defined in G.S. 20-4.01(24a) within 10 years of the date of this offense.

(b) A person convicted of violating this section shall be punished as a Class F felon and shall be sentenced to a minimum active term of not less than 12 months of imprisonment, which shall not be suspended. Sentences imposed under this subsection shall run consecutively with and shall commence at the expiration of any sentence being served.

(c) An offense under this section is an implied consent offense subject to the provisions of G.S. 20-16.2. The provisions of G.S. 20-139.1 shall apply to an offense committed under this section.

(d) A person convicted under this section shall have his license permanently revoked.

(e) If a person is convicted under this section, the motor vehicle that was driven by the defendant at the time the defendant committed the offense of impaired driving becomes property subject to forfeiture in accordance with the procedure set out in G.S. 20-28.2. In applying the procedure set out in that statute, an owner or a holder of a security interest is considered an innocent party with respect to a motor vehicle subject to forfeiture under this subsection if any of the following applies:

(1) The owner or holder of the security interest did not know and had no reason to know that the defendant had been convicted within the previous seven years of three or more offenses involving impaired driving.

(2) The defendant drove the motor vehicle without the consent of the owner or the holder of the security interest.

History.
1989 (Reg. Sess., 1990), c. 1039, s. 7; 1993, c. 539, s. 1258; 1994, Ex. Sess., c. 14, s. 32; c. 24, s. 14(c); 1993 (Reg. Sess., 1994), c. 761, s. 34.1; c. 767, s. 32; 1997-379, s. 6; 2006-253, ss. 12, 13

N.C. Gen. Stat. § 20-138.6

Reserved for future codification purposes.

§ 20-138.7. Transporting an open container of alcoholic beverage.

(a) **Offense.** -- No person shall drive a motor vehicle on a highway or the right-of-way of a highway:

(1) While there is an alcoholic beverage in the passenger area in other than the unopened manufacturer's original container; and

(2) While the driver is consuming alcohol or while alcohol remains in the driver's body.

(a1) **Offense.** -- No person shall possess an alcoholic beverage other than in the unopened manufacturer's original container, or consume an alcoholic beverage, in the passenger area of a motor vehicle while the motor vehicle is on a highway or the right-of-way of a highway. For purposes of this subsection, only the person who possesses or consumes an alcoholic beverage in violation of this subsection shall be charged with this offense.

(a2) **Exception.** -- It shall not be a violation of subsection (a1) of this section for a passenger to possess an alcoholic beverage other than in the unopened manufacturer's original container, or for a passenger to consume an alcoholic beverage, if the container is:

(1) In the passenger area of a motor vehicle that is designed, maintained, or used

primarily for the transportation of persons for compensation;

(2) In the living quarters of a motor home or house car as defined in G.S. 20-4.01(27) k.; or

(3) In a house trailer as defined in G.S. 20-4.01(14).

(a3) **Meaning of Terms.** -- Under this section, the term "motor vehicle" means any vehicle driven or drawn by mechanical power and manufactured primarily for use on public highways and includes mopeds.

(b) **Subject to Implied-Consent Law.** -- An offense under this section is an alcohol-related offense subject to the implied-consent provisions of G.S. 20-16.2.

(c) **Odor Insufficient.** -- The odor of an alcoholic beverage on the breath of the driver is insufficient evidence to prove beyond a reasonable doubt that alcohol was remaining in the driver's body in violation of this section, unless the driver was offered an alcohol screening test or chemical analysis and refused to provide all required samples of breath or blood for analysis.

(d) **Alcohol Screening Test.** -- Notwithstanding any other provision of law, an alcohol screening test may be administered to a driver suspected of violating subsection (a) of this section, and the results of an alcohol screening test or the driver's refusal to submit may be used by a law enforcement officer, a court, or an administrative agency in determining if alcohol was present in the driver's body. No alcohol screening tests are valid under this section unless the device used is one approved by the Commission for Public Health, and the screening test is conducted in accordance with the applicable regulations of the Commission as to the manner of its use.

(e) **Punishment; Effect When Impaired Driving Offense Also Charged.** -- Violation of subsection (a) of this section shall be a Class 3 misdemeanor for the first offense and shall be a Class 2 misdemeanor for a second or subsequent offense. Violation of subsection (a) of this section is not a lesser included offense of impaired driving under G.S. 20-138.1, but if a person is convicted under subsection (a) of this section and of an offense involving impaired driving arising out of the same transaction, the punishment imposed by the court shall not exceed the maximum applicable to the offense involving impaired driving, and any minimum applicable punishment shall be imposed. Violation of subsection (a1) of this section by the driver of the motor vehicle is a lesser-included offense of subsection (a) of this section. A violation of subsection (a) shall be considered a moving violation for purposes of G.S. 20-16(c).

Violation of subsection (a1) of this section shall be an infraction and shall not be considered a moving violation for purposes of G.S. 20-16(c).

(f) **Definitions.** -- If the seal on a container of alcoholic beverages has been broken, it is opened within the meaning of this section. For purposes of this section, "passenger area of a motor vehicle" means the area designed to seat the driver and passengers and any area within the reach of a seated driver or passenger, including the glove compartment. The area of the trunk or the area behind the last upright back seat of a station wagon, hatchback, or similar vehicle shall not be considered part of the passenger area. The term "alcoholic beverage" is as defined in G.S. 18B-101(4).

(g) **Pleading.** -- In any prosecution for a violation of subsection (a) of this section, the pleading is sufficient if it states the time and place of the alleged offense in the usual form and charges that the defendant drove a motor vehicle on a highway or the right-of-way of a highway with an open container of alcoholic beverage after drinking.

In any prosecution for a violation of subsection (a1) of this section, the pleading is sufficient if it states the time and place of the alleged offense in the usual form and charges that (i) the defendant possessed an open container of alcoholic beverage in the passenger area of a motor vehicle while the motor vehicle was on a highway or the right-of-way of a highway, or (ii) the defendant consumed an alcoholic beverage in the passenger area of a motor vehicle while the motor vehicle was on a highway or the right-of-way of a highway.

(h) **Limited Driving Privilege.** -- A person who is convicted of violating subsection (a) of this section and whose drivers license is revoked solely based on that conviction may apply for a limited driving privilege as provided for in G.S. 20-179.3. The judge may issue the limited driving privilege only if the driver meets the eligibility requirements of G.S. 20-179.3, other than the requirement in G.S. 20-179.3(b)(1)c. G.S. 20-179.3(e) shall not apply. All other terms, conditions, and restrictions provided for in G.S. 20-179.3 shall apply. G.S. 20-179.3, rather than this subsection, governs the issuance of a limited driving privilege to a person who is convicted of violating subsection (a) of this section and of driving while impaired as a result of the same transaction.

History.
1995, c. 506, s. 9; 2000-155, s. 4; 2002-25, s. 1; 2006-66, s. 21.7; 2007-182, s. 2; 2013-348, s. 4; 2017-102, s. 5.2(b)

N.C. Gen. Stat. § 20-139

Repealed by Session Laws 1983, c. 435, s. 23.

§ 20-139.1. Procedures governing chemical analyses; admissibility; evidentiary provisions; controlled-drinking programs

(a) **Chemical Analysis Admissible.** -- In any implied-consent offense under G.S. 20-16.2, a person's alcohol concentration or the presence of any other impairing substance in the person's body as shown by a chemical analysis is admissible in evidence. This section does not limit the introduction of other competent evidence as to a person's alcohol concentration or results of other tests showing the presence of an impairing substance, including other chemical tests.

(b) **Approval of Valid Test Methods; Licensing Chemical Analysts.** -- The results of a chemical analysis shall be deemed sufficient evidence to prove a person's alcohol concentration. A chemical analysis of the breath administered pursuant to the implied-consent law is admissible in any court or administrative hearing or proceeding if it meets both of the following requirements:

(1) It is performed in accordance with the rules of the Department of Health and Human Services.

(2) The person performing the analysis had, at the time of the analysis, a current permit issued by the Department of Health and Human Services authorizing the person to perform a test of the breath using the type of instrument employed.

For purposes of establishing compliance with subdivision (b)(1) of this section, the court or administrative agency shall take notice of the rules of the Department of Health and Human Services. For purposes of establishing compliance with subdivision (b)(2) of this section, the court or administrative agency shall take judicial notice of the list of permits issued to the person performing the analysis, the type of instrument on which the person is authorized to perform tests of the breath, and the date the permit was issued. The Department of Health and Human Services may ascertain the qualifications and competence of individuals to conduct particular chemical analyses and the methods for conducting chemical analyses. The Department may issue permits to conduct chemical analyses to individuals it finds qualified subject to periodic renewal, termination, and revocation of the permit in the Department's discretion.

(b1) **When Officer May Perform Chemical Analysis.** -- Any person possessing a current permit authorizing the person to perform chemical analysis may perform a chemical analysis.

(b2) **Breath Analysis Results Preventive Maintenance.** -- The Department of Health and Human Services shall perform preventive maintenance on breath-testing instruments used for chemical analysis. A court or administrative agency shall take judicial notice of the preventive maintenance records of the Department. Notwithstanding the provisions of subsection (b), the results of a chemical analysis of a person's breath performed in accordance with this section are not admissible in evidence if:

(1) The defendant objects to the introduction into evidence of the results of the chemical analysis of the defendant's breath; and

(2) The defendant demonstrates that, with respect to the instrument used to analyze the defendant's breath, preventive maintenance procedures required by the regulations of the Department of Health and Human Services had not been performed within the time limits prescribed by those regulations.

(b3) **Sequential Breath Tests Required.** -- The methods governing the administration of chemical analyses of the breath shall require the testing of at least duplicate sequential breath samples. The results of the chemical analysis of all breath samples are admissible if the test results from any two consecutively collected breath samples do not differ from each other by an alcohol concentration greater than 0.02. Only the lower of the two test results of the consecutively administered tests can be used to prove a particular alcohol concentration. A person's refusal to give the sequential breath samples necessary to constitute a valid chemical analysis is a refusal under G.S. 20-16.2(c).

A person's refusal to give the second or subsequent breath sample shall make the result of the first breath sample, or the result of the sample providing the lowest alcohol concentration if more than one breath sample is provided, admissible in any judicial or administrative hearing for any relevant purpose, including the establishment that a person had a particular alcohol concentration for conviction of an offense involving impaired driving.

(b4) Repealed by Session Laws 2006-253, s. 16, effective December 1, 2006, and applicable to offenses committed on or after that date.

(b5) **Subsequent Tests Allowed.** -- A person may be requested, pursuant to G.S. 20-16.2, to submit to a chemical analysis of the person's blood or other bodily fluid or substance in addition to or in lieu of a chemical analysis of the breath, in the discretion of a law enforcement officer; except that a person charged with a violation of G.S. 20-141.4 shall be requested, at any relevant time after the driving, to provide a blood sample in addition to or in lieu of a chemical analysis of the breath. However, if a breath sample shows an alcohol concentration of .08 or more, then requesting a blood sample shall be in the discretion of a law enforcement officer.

If a subsequent chemical analysis is requested pursuant to this subsection, the person shall again be advised of the implied consent rights in accordance with G.S. 20-16.2(a). A person's willful refusal to submit to a chemical analysis of the blood or other bodily fluid or substance is a willful refusal under G.S. 20-16.2. If a person willfully refuses to provide a blood sample under this subsection, and the person is charged with a violation of G.S. 20-141.4, then a law enforcement officer with probable cause to believe that the offense involved impaired driving or was an alcohol-related offense made subject to the procedures of G.S. 20-16.2 shall seek a warrant to obtain a blood sample. The failure to obtain a blood sample pursuant to this subsection shall not be grounds for the dismissal of a charge and is not an appealable issue.

(b6) The Department of Health and Human Services shall post on a Web page a list of all persons who have a permit authorizing them to perform chemical analyses, the types of analyses that they can perform, the instruments that each person is authorized to operate, the effective dates of the permits, and the records of preventive maintenance. A court or administrative agency shall take judicial notice of whether, at the time of the chemical analysis, the chemical analyst possessed a permit authorizing the chemical analyst to perform the chemical analysis administered and whether preventive maintenance had been performed on the breath-testing instrument in accordance with the Department's rules.

(c) **Blood and Urine for Chemical Analysis.** -- Notwithstanding any other provision of law, when a blood or urine test is specified as the type of chemical analysis by a law enforcement officer, a physician, registered nurse, emergency medical technician, or other qualified person shall withdraw the blood sample and obtain the urine sample, and no further authorization or approval is required. If the person withdrawing the blood or collecting the urine requests written confirmation of the law enforcement officer's request for the withdrawal of blood or collecting the urine, the officer shall furnish it before blood is withdrawn or urine collected. When blood is withdrawn or urine collected pursuant to a law enforcement officer's request, neither the person withdrawing the blood nor any hospital, laboratory, or other institution, person, firm, or corporation employing that person, or contracting for the service of withdrawing blood or collecting urine, may be held criminally or civilly liable by reason of withdrawing the blood or collecting the urine, except that there is no immunity from liability for negligent acts or omissions. A person requested to withdraw blood or collect urine pursuant to this subsection may refuse to do so only if it reasonably appears that the procedure cannot be performed without endangering the safety of the person collecting the sample or the safety of the person from whom the sample is being collected. If the officer requesting the blood or urine requests a written justification for the refusal, the medical provider who determined the sample could not be collected safely shall provide written justification at the time of the refusal.

(c1) **Admissibility. --** The results of a chemical analysis of blood or urine reported by the North Carolina State Crime Laboratory, the Charlotte, North Carolina, Police Department Laboratory, or any other laboratory approved for chemical analysis by the Department of Health and Human Services (DHHS), are admissible as evidence in all administrative hearings, and in any court, without further authentication and without the testimony of the analyst. For the purposes of this section, a "laboratory approved for chemical analysis" by the DHHS includes, but is not limited to, any hospital laboratory approved by DHHS pursuant to the program resulting from the federal Clinical Laboratory Improvement Amendments of 1988 (CLIA).

The results shall be certified by the person who performed the analysis. The provisions of this subsection may be utilized in any administrative hearing, but can only be utilized in cases tried in the district and superior court divisions, or in an adjudicatory hearing in juvenile court, if:

(1) The State notifies the defendant no later than 15 business days after receiving the report and at least 15 business days before the proceeding at which the evidence would be used of its intention to introduce the report into evidence under this subsection and provides a copy of the report to the defendant, and

(2) The defendant fails to file a written objection with the court, with a copy to the State, at least five business days before the proceeding at which the report would be used that the defendant objects to the introduction of the report into evidence.

If the defendant's attorney of record, or the defendant if that person has no attorney, fails to file a written objection as provided in this subsection, then the objection shall be deemed waived and the report shall be admitted into evidence without the testimony of the analyst. Upon filing a timely objection, the admissibility of the report shall be determined and governed by the appropriate rules of evidence.

If the proceeding at which the report would be introduced into evidence under this subsection is continued, the notice provided by the State, the written objection filed by the defendant, or the failure of the defendant to file a written objection shall remain effective at any subsequent calendaring of that proceeding.

The report containing the results of any blood or urine test may be transmitted electronically or via facsimile. A copy of the affidavit sent electronically or via facsimile shall be admissible in any court or administrative hearing without further authentication. A copy of the report shall be sent to the charging officer, the clerk of superior court in the county in which the criminal charges are pending, the Division of Motor Vehicles, and the Department of Health and Human Services.

Nothing in this subsection precludes the right of any party to call any witness or to introduce any evidence supporting or contradicting the evidence contained in the report.

(c2) Repealed by Session Laws 2013-194, s. 1, effective June 26, 2013.

(c3) **Procedure for Establishing Chain of Custody Without Calling Unnecessary Witnesses. --**

(1) For the purpose of establishing the chain of physical custody or control of blood or urine tested or analyzed to determine whether it contains alcohol, a controlled substance or its metabolite, or any impairing substance, a statement signed by each successive person in the chain of custody that the person delivered it to the other person indicated on or about the date stated is prima facie evidence that the person had custody and made the delivery as stated, without the necessity of a personal appearance in court by the person signing the statement.

(2) The statement shall contain a sufficient description of the material or its container so as to distinguish it as the particular item in question and shall state that the material was delivered in essentially the same condition as received. The statement may be placed on the same document as the report provided for in subsection (c1) or the affidavit provided for in subsection (e1) of this section, as applicable.

(3) The provisions of this subsection may be utilized in any administrative hearing, but can only be utilized in cases tried in the district and superior court divisions, or in an adjudicatory hearing in juvenile court, if:

a. The State notifies the defendant no later than 15 business days after receiving the statement and at least 15 business days before the proceeding at which the statement would be used of its intention to introduce the statement into evidence under this subsection and provides a copy of the statement to the defendant, and

b. The defendant fails to file a written notification with the court, with a copy to the State, at least five business days before the proceeding at which the statement would be used that the defendant objects to the introduction of the statement into evidence.

If the defendant's attorney of record, or the defendant if that person has no attorney, fails to file a written objection as provided in this subsection, then the objection shall be deemed waived and the statement shall be admitted into evidence without the necessity of a personal appearance by the person signing the statement. Upon filing a timely objection, the admissibility of the statement shall be determined and governed by the appropriate rules of evidence.

If the proceeding at which the statement would be introduced into evidence under this subsection is continued, the notice provided by the State, the written objection filed by the defendant, or the failure of the defendant to file a written objection shall remain effective at any subsequent calendaring of that proceeding.

(4) Nothing in this subsection precludes the right of any party to call any witness or to introduce any evidence supporting or contradicting the evidence contained in the statement.

(c4) Repealed by Session Laws 2013-194, s. 1, effective June 26, 2013.

(c5) The testimony of an analyst regarding the results of a chemical analysis of blood or urine admissible pursuant to subsection (c1) of this section, and reported by that analyst, shall be permitted by remote testimony, as defined in G.S. 15A-1225.3, in all administrative hearings, and in any court, if all of the following occur:

(1) The State has provided a copy of the report to the attorney of record for the defendant, or to the defendant if that person has no attorney, as required by subsections (c1) and (c3) of this section.

(2) The State notifies the attorney of record for the defendant or the defendant if that person has no attorney, at least 15 business days before the proceeding at which the evidence would be used of its intention to introduce the testimony regarding the chemical analysis into evidence using remote testimony.

(3) The defendant's attorney of record, or the defendant if that person has no attorney, fails to file a written objection with the court, with a copy to the State, at least five business days before the proceeding at which the testimony will be presented that the defendant objects to the introduction of the remote testimony.

If the defendant's attorney of record, or the defendant if that person has no attorney, fails to file a written objection as provided in this subsection, then the objection shall be deemed waived and the analyst shall be allowed to testify by remote testimony.

The method used for remote testimony authorized by this subsection shall allow the trier of fact and all parties to observe the demeanor of the analyst as the analyst testifies in a similar manner as if the analyst were testifying in the location where the hearing or trial is being conducted. The court shall ensure that the defendant's attorney, or the defendant if that person has no attorney, has a full and fair opportunity for examination and cross-examination of the analyst.

Nothing in this section shall preclude the right of any party to call any witness. Nothing in this subsection shall obligate the Administrative Office of the Courts or the State Crime Laboratory to incur expenses related to remote testimony absent an appropriation of funds for that purpose.

(d) **Right to Additional Test.** -- Nothing in this section shall be construed to prohibit a person from obtaining or attempting to obtain an additional chemical analysis. If the person is not released from custody after the initial appearance, the agency having custody of the person shall make reasonable efforts in a timely manner to assist the person in obtaining access to a telephone to arrange for any additional test and allow access to the person in accordance with the agreed procedure in G.S. 20-38.5. The failure or inability of the person who submitted to a chemical analysis to obtain any additional test or to withdraw blood does not preclude the admission of evidence relating to the chemical analysis.

(d1) **Right to Require Additional Tests.** -- If a person refuses to submit to any test or tests pursuant to this section, any law enforcement officer with probable cause may, without a court order, compel the person to provide blood or urine samples for analysis if the officer reasonably believes that the delay necessary to obtain a court order, under the circumstances, would result in the dissipation of the percentage of alcohol in the person's blood or urine.

(d2) Notwithstanding any other provision of law, when a blood or urine sample is requested under subsection (d1) of this section by a law enforcement officer, a physician, registered nurse, emergency medical technician, or other qualified person shall withdraw the blood and obtain the urine sample, and no further authorization or approval is required. If the person withdrawing the blood or collecting the urine requests written confirmation of the charging officer's request for the withdrawal of blood or obtaining urine, the officer shall furnish it before blood is withdrawn or urine obtained. A person requested to withdraw blood or collect urine pursuant to this subsection may refuse to do so only if it reasonably appears that the procedure cannot be performed without endangering the safety of the person collecting the sample or the safety of the person from whom the sample is being collected. If the officer requesting the blood or urine requests a written justification for the refusal, the medical provider who determined the sample could not be collected safely shall provide written justification at the time of the refusal.

(d3) When blood is withdrawn or urine collected pursuant to a law enforcement officer's request, neither the person withdrawing the blood nor any hospital, laboratory, or other institution, person, firm, or corporation employing that person, or contracting for the service of withdrawing blood, may be held criminally or civilly liable by reason of withdrawing that blood, except that there is no immunity from liability for negligent acts or omissions. The results of the analysis of blood or urine under this subsection shall be admissible if performed by the State Crime Laboratory or any other hospital or qualified laboratory.

(e) **Recording Results of Chemical Analysis of Breath. --** A person charged with an implied-consent offense who has not received, prior to a trial, a copy of the chemical analysis results the State intends to offer into evidence may request in writing a copy of the results. The failure to provide a copy prior to any trial shall be grounds for a continuance of the case but shall not be grounds to suppress the results of the chemical analysis or to dismiss the criminal charges.

(e1) **Use of Chemical Analyst's Affidavit in District Court. --** An affidavit by a chemical analyst sworn to and properly executed before an official authorized to administer oaths shall be admissible in evidence without further authentication and without the testimony of the analyst in any hearing or trial in the District Court Division of the General Court of Justice with respect to the following matters:

(1) The alcohol concentration or concentrations or the presence or absence of an impairing substance of a person given a chemical analysis and who is involved in the hearing or trial.

(2) The time of the collection of the blood, breath, or other bodily fluid or substance sample or samples for the chemical analysis.

(3) The type of chemical analysis administered and the procedures followed.

(4) The type and status of any permit issued by the Department of Health and Human Services that the analyst held on the date the analyst performed the chemical analysis in question.

(5) If the chemical analysis is performed on a breath-testing instrument for which regulations adopted pursuant to subsection (b) require preventive maintenance, the date the most recent preventive maintenance procedures were performed on the breath-testing instrument used, as shown on the maintenance records for that instrument.

The Department of Health and Human Services shall develop a form for use by chemical analysts in making this affidavit.

(e2) Except as governed by subsection (c1) or (c3) of this section, the State can only use the provisions of subsection (e1) of this section if:

(1) The State notifies the defendant no later than 15 business days after receiving the affidavit and at least 15 business days before the proceeding at which the affidavit would be used of its intention to introduce the affidavit into evidence under this subsection and provides a copy of the affidavit to the defendant, and

(2) The defendant fails to file a written notification with the court, with a copy to the State, at least five business days before the proceeding at which the affidavit would be used that the defendant objects to the introduction of the affidavit into evidence.

The failure to file a timely objection as provided in this subsection shall be deemed a waiver of the right to object to the admissibility of the affidavit, and the affidavit shall be admitted into evidence without the testimony of the analyst. Upon filing a timely objection, the admissibility of the report shall be determined and governed by the appropriate rules of evidence. The case shall be continued until the analyst can be present. The criminal case shall not be dismissed due to the failure of the analyst to appear, unless the analyst willfully fails to appear after being ordered to appear by the court. If the proceeding at which the affidavit would be introduced into evidence under this subsection is continued, the notice provided by the State, the written objection filed by the defendant, or the failure of the defendant to file a written objection shall remain effective at any subsequent calendaring of that proceeding.

Nothing in subsection (e1) or subsection (e2) of this section precludes the right of any party to call any witness or to introduce any evidence supporting or contradicting the evidence contained in the affidavit.

(f) **Evidence of Refusal Admissible. --** If any person charged with an implied-consent offense refuses to submit to a chemical analysis or to perform field sobriety tests at the request of an officer, evidence of that refusal is admissible in any criminal, civil, or administrative action against the person.

(g) **Controlled-Drinking Programs.** -- The Department of Health and Human Services may adopt rules concerning the ingestion of controlled amounts of alcohol by individuals submitting to chemical testing as a part of scientific, experimental, educational, or demonstration programs. These regulations shall prescribe procedures consistent with controlling federal law governing the acquisition, transportation, possession, storage, administration, and disposition of alcohol intended for use in the programs. Any person in charge of a controlled-drinking program who acquires alcohol under these regulations must keep records accounting for the disposition of all alcohol acquired, and the records must at all reasonable times be available for inspection upon the request of any federal, State, or local law-enforcement officer with jurisdiction over the laws relating to control of alcohol. A controlled-drinking program exclusively using lawfully purchased alcoholic beverages in places in which they may be lawfully possessed, however, need not comply with the record-keeping requirements of the regulations authorized by this subsection. All acts pursuant to the regulations reasonably done in furtherance of bona fide objectives of a controlled-drinking program authorized by the regulations are lawful notwithstanding the provisions of any other general or local statute, regulation, or ordinance controlling alcohol.

(h) **Disposition of Blood Evidence.** -- Notwithstanding any other provision of law, any blood or urine sample subject to chemical analysis for the presence of alcohol, a controlled substance or its metabolite, or any impairing substance pursuant to this section may be destroyed by the analyzing agency 12 months after the case is filed or after the case is concluded in the trial court and not under appeal, whichever is later, without further notice to the parties. However, if a Motion to Preserve the evidence has been filed by either party, the evidence shall remain in the custody of the analyzing agency or the agency that collected the sample until dispositive order of a court of competent jurisdiction is entered.

History.
1963, c. 966, s. 2; 1967, c. 123; 1969, c. 1074, s. 2; 1971, c. 619, ss. 12, 13; 1973, c. 476, s. 128; c. 1081, s. 2; c. 1331, s. 3; 1975, c. 405; 1979, 2nd Sess., c. 1089; 1981, c. 412, s. 4; c. 747, s. 66; 1983, c. 435, s. 26; 1983 (Reg. Sess., 1984), c. 1101, s. 20; 1989, c. 727, s. 219(2); 1991, c. 689, s. 233.1(b); 1993, c. 285, s. 7; 1997-379, ss. 5.3 -5.5; 1997-443, s. 11A.10; 1997-443, s. 11A.123; 1997-456, s. 34(b); 2000-155, s. 8; 2003-95, s. 1; 2003-104, s. 2; 2006-253, s. 16; 2007-115, ss. 5, 6;

2007-493, ss. 3, 18, 22, 23; 2009-473, ss. 3 -6; 2011-19, ss. 5, 8; 2011-119, s. 2; 2011-307, s. 9; 2012-168, s. 6; 2013-171, ss. 1, 4-6; 2013-194, s. 1; 2013-338, s. 1; 2014-119, s. 8(b); 2015-173, s. 3; 2015-276, s. 1; 2016-10, s. 1

§ 20-140. Reckless driving

(a) Any person who drives any vehicle upon a highway or any public vehicular area carelessly and heedlessly in willful or wanton disregard of the rights or safety of others shall be guilty of reckless driving.

(b) Any person who drives any vehicle upon a highway or any public vehicular area without due caution and circumspection and at a speed or in a manner so as to endanger or be likely to endanger any person or property shall be guilty of reckless driving.

(c) Repealed by Session Laws 1983, c. 435, s. 23.

(d) Reckless driving as defined in subsections (a) and (b) is a Class 2 misdemeanor.

(e) Repealed by Session Laws 1983, c. 435, s. 23.

(f) A person is guilty of the Class 2 misdemeanor of reckless driving if the person drives a commercial motor vehicle carrying a load that is subject to the permit requirements of G.S. 20-119 upon a highway or any public vehicular area either:

 (1) Carelessly and heedlessly in willful or wanton disregard of the rights or safety of others; or

 (2) Without due caution and circumspection and at a speed or in a manner so as to endanger or be likely to endanger any person or property.

History.
1937, c. 407, s. 102; 1957, c. 1368, s. 1; 1959, c. 1264, s. 8; 1973, c. 1330, s. 3; 1979, c. 903, ss. 7, 8; 1981, c. 412, s. 4; c. 466, s. 7; c. 747, s. 66; 1983, c. 435, s. 23; 1985, c. 764, s. 28; 1985 (Reg. Sess., 1986), c. 852, s. 17; 1993, c. 539, s. 365; 1994, Ex. Sess., c. 24, s. 14(c); 2000-109, s. 7(b)

N.C. Gen. Stat. § 20-140.1

Repealed by Session Laws 1973, c. 1330, s. 39.

§ 20-140.2. Overloaded or overcrowded vehicle

No person shall operate upon a highway or public vehicular area a motor vehicle which is so loaded or crowded with passengers or property, or both, as to obstruct the operator's view of the highway or public vehicular area, including intersections, or so as to impair or restrict otherwise the proper operation of the vehicle.

History.
1953, c. 1233; 1967, c. 674, s. 1; 1973, c. 1143, s. 2; c. 1330, s. 4

§ 20-140.3. Unlawful use of National System of Interstate and Defense Highways and other controlled-access highways

On those sections of highways which are or become a part of the National System of Interstate and Defense Highways and other controlled-access highways, it shall be unlawful for any person:

(1) To drive a vehicle over, upon, or across any curb, central dividing section or other separation or dividing line on said highways.

(2) To make a left turn or a semicircular or U-turn except through an opening provided for that purpose in the dividing curb, separation section, or line on said highways.

(3) To drive any vehicle except in the proper lane provided for that purpose and in the proper direction and to the right of the central dividing curb, separation section, or line on said highways.

(4) To drive a vehicle onto or from any controlled-access highway except at such entrances and exits as are established by public authority.

(5) To stop, park, or leave standing any vehicle, whether attended or unattended, on any part or portion of the right-of-way of said highways, except in the case of an emergency or as directed by a peace officer, or at designated parking areas.

(6) To fail to yield the right-of-way when entering the highway to any vehicle already travelling on the highway.

(7) Notwithstanding any other subdivision of this section, a law enforcement officer may cross the median of a divided highway when the officer has reasonable grounds to believe that a felony is being or has been committed, has personal knowledge that a vehicle is being operated at a speed or in a manner which is likely to endanger persons or property, or the officer has reasonable grounds to believe that the officer's presence is immediately required at a location which would necessitate crossing a median of a divided highway for this purpose. Fire department vehicles and public or private ambulances and rescue squad emergency service vehicles traveling in response to a fire alarm or other emergency call may cross the median of a divided highway when assistance is immediately required at a location which would necessitate the vehicle crossing a median of a divided highway for this purpose.

History.
1973, c. 1330, s. 5; 1977, c. 731, s. 1; 1999-330, s. 5

§ 20-140.4. Special provisions for motorcycles and mopeds

(a) No person shall operate a motorcycle or moped upon a highway or public vehicular area:

(1) When the number of persons upon or within such motorcycle or moped, including the operator, shall exceed the number of persons which it was designed to carry.

(2) Unless the operator and all passengers thereon wear on their heads, with a retention strap properly secured, safety helmets of a type that complies with Federal Motor Vehicle Safety Standard (FMVSS) 218. This subdivision shall not apply to an operator of, or any passengers within, an autocycle that has completely enclosed seating or is equipped with a roll bar or roll cage.

(b) Violation of any provision of this section shall not be considered negligence per se or contributory negligence per se in any civil action.

(c) Any person convicted of violating this section shall have committed an infraction and shall pay a penalty of twenty-five dollars and fifty cents ($ 25.50) plus the following court costs: the General Court of Justice fee provided for in G.S. 7A-304(a)(4), the telephone facilities fee provided for in G.S. 7A-304(a)(2a), and the law enforcement training and certification fee provided for in G.S. 7A-304(a)(3b). Conviction of an infraction under this section has no other consequence.

(d) No drivers license points or insurance surcharge shall be assessed on account of violation of this section.

History.
1973, c. 1330, s. 6; 1989, c. 711, s. 1; 2007-360, s. 7; 2009-451, s. 15.20(k); 2015-163, s. 11; 2016-90, s. 12.5(b); 2019-227, s. 6(a)

§ 20-140.5. Special mobile equipment may tow certain vehicles

Special mobile equipment may not tow any vehicle other than the following:

(1) A single passenger vehicle that can carry no more than nine passengers and is carrying no passengers.

(2) A single property-hauling vehicle that has a registered weight of 5,000 pounds or less, is carrying no passengers, and does not exceed its registered weight.

History.
1991 (Reg. Sess., 1992), c. 1015, s. 3; 1999-438, s. 29

§ 20-141. Speed restrictions

(a) No person shall drive a vehicle on a highway or in a public vehicular area at a speed greater than is reasonable and prudent under the conditions then existing.

(b) Except as otherwise provided in this Chapter, it shall be unlawful to operate a vehicle in excess of the following speeds:

(1) Thirty-five miles per hour inside municipal corporate limits for all vehicles.

(2) Fifty-five miles per hour outside municipal corporate limits for all vehicles except for school buses and school activity buses.

(c) Except while towing another vehicle, or when an advisory safe-speed sign indicates a slower speed, or as otherwise provided by law, it shall be unlawful to operate a passenger vehicle upon the interstate and primary highway system at less than the following speeds:

(1) Forty miles per hour in a speed zone of 55 miles per hour.

(2) Forty-five miles per hour in a speed zone of 60 miles per hour or greater.

These minimum speeds shall be effective only when appropriate signs are posted indicating the minimum speed.

(d) (1) Whenever the Department of Transportation determines on the basis of an engineering and traffic investigation that any speed allowed by subsection (b) is greater than is reasonable and safe under the conditions found to exist upon any part of a highway outside the corporate limits of a municipality or upon any part of a highway designated as part of the Interstate Highway System or any part of a controlled-access highway (either inside or outside the corporate limits of a municipality), the Department of Transportation shall determine and declare a reasonable and safe speed limit.

(2) Whenever the Department of Transportation determines on the basis of an engineering and traffic investigation that a higher maximum speed than those set forth in subsection (b) is reasonable and safe under the conditions found to exist upon any part of a highway designated as part of the Interstate Highway System or any part of a controlled-access highway (either inside or outside the corporate limits of a municipality) the Department of Transportation shall determine and declare a reasonable and safe speed limit. A speed limit set pursuant to this subsection may not exceed 70 miles per hour.

Speed limits set pursuant to this subsection are not effective until appropriate signs giving notice thereof are erected upon the parts of the highway affected.

(e) Local authorities, in their respective jurisdictions, may authorize by ordinance higher speeds or lower speeds than those set out in subsection (b) upon all streets which are not part of the State highway system; but no speed so fixed shall authorize a speed in excess of 55 miles per hour. Speed limits set pursuant to this subsection shall be effective when appropriate signs giving notice thereof are erected upon the part of the streets affected.

(e1) Local authorities within their respective jurisdictions may authorize, by ordinance, lower speed limits than those set in subsection (b) of this section on school property. If the lower speed limit is being set on the grounds of a public school, the local school administrative unit must request or consent to the lower speed limit. If the lower speed limit is being set on the grounds of a private school, the governing body of the school must request or consent to the lower speed limit. Speed limits established pursuant to this subsection shall become effective when appropriate signs giving notice of the speed limit are erected upon affected property. A person who drives a motor vehicle on school property at a speed greater than the speed limit set and posted under this subsection is responsible for an infraction and is required to pay a penalty of two hundred fifty dollars ($ 250.00).

(f) Whenever local authorities within their respective jurisdictions determine upon the basis of an engineering and traffic investigation that a higher maximum speed than those set forth in subsection (b) is reasonable and safe, or that any speed hereinbefore set forth is greater than is reasonable and safe, under the conditions found to exist upon any part of a street within the corporate limits of a municipality and which street is a part of the State highway system (except those highways designated as part of the interstate highway system or other controlled-access highway) said local authorities shall determine and declare a safe and reasonable speed limit. A speed limit set pursuant to this subsection may not exceed 55 miles per hour. Limits set pursuant to this subsection shall become effective when the Department of Transportation has passed a concurring ordinance and signs are erected giving notice of the authorized speed limit.

When local authorities annex a road on the State highway system, the speed limit posted on the road at the time the road was annexed shall remain in effect until both the Department and municipality pass concurrent ordinances to change the speed limit.

The Department of Transportation is authorized to raise or lower the statutory speed limit on all highways on the State highway system within municipalities which do not have a governing body to enact municipal ordinances as provided by law. The Department of Transportation shall determine a reasonable and safe speed limit in the same manner as is provided in G.S. 20-141(d)(1) and G.S. 20-141(d)(2) for changing the speed limits outside of municipalities, without action of the municipality.

(g) Whenever the Department of Transportation or local authorities within their respective jurisdictions determine on the basis of an engineering and traffic investigation that slow speeds on any part of a highway considerably impede the normal and reasonable movement of traffic, the Department of Transportation or such local authority may determine and declare a minimum speed below which no person shall operate a motor vehicle except when necessary for safe operation in compliance with law. Such minimum speed limit shall be effective when appropriate signs giving notice thereof are erected on said part of the highway. Provided, such minimum speed limit shall be effective as to those highways and streets within the corporate limits of a municipality which are on the State highway system only when ordinances adopting the minimum speed limit are passed and concurred in by both the Department of Transportation and the local authorities. The provisions of this subsection shall not apply to farm tractors and other motor vehicles operating at reasonable speeds for the type and nature of such vehicles.

(h) No person shall operate a motor vehicle on the highway at such a slow speed as to impede the normal and reasonable movement of traffic except when reduced speed is necessary for safe operation or in compliance with law; provided, this provision shall not apply to farm tractors and other motor vehicles operating at reasonable speeds for the type and nature of such vehicles.

(i) The Department of Transportation shall have authority to designate and appropriately mark certain highways of the State as truck routes.

(j) Repealed by Session Laws 1997, c. 443, s. 19.26(b).

(j1) A person who drives a vehicle on a highway at a speed that is either more than 15 miles per hour more than the speed limit established by law for the highway where the offense occurred or over 80 miles per hour is guilty of a Class 3 misdemeanor.

(j2) A person who drives a motor vehicle in a highway work zone at a speed greater than the speed limit set and posted under this section shall be required to pay a penalty of two hundred fifty dollars ($ 250.00). This penalty shall be imposed in addition to those penalties established in this Chapter. A "highway work zone" is the area between the first sign that informs motorists of the existence of a work zone on a highway and the last sign that informs motorists of the end of the work zone. The additional penalty imposed by this subsection applies only if signs are posted at the beginning and end of

any segment of the highway work zone stating the penalty for speeding in that segment of the work zone. The Secretary shall ensure that work zones shall only be posted with penalty signs if the Secretary determines, after engineering review, that the posting is necessary to ensure the safety of the traveling public due to a hazardous condition.

A law enforcement officer issuing a citation for a violation of this section while in a highway work zone shall indicate the vehicle speed and speed limit posted in the segment of the work zone, and determine whether the individual committed a violation of G.S. 20-141(j1). Upon an individual's conviction of a violation of this section while in a highway work zone, the clerk of court shall report that the vehicle was in a work zone at the time of the violation, the vehicle speed, and the speed limit of the work zone to the Division of Motor Vehicles.

(j3) A person is guilty of a Class 2 misdemeanor if the person drives a commercial motor vehicle carrying a load that is subject to the permit requirements of G.S. 20-119 upon a highway or any public vehicular area at a speed of 15 miles per hour or more above either:

   (1) The posted speed; or

   (2) The restricted speed, if any, of the permit, or if no permit was obtained, the speed that would be applicable to the load if a permit had been obtained.

(k) Repealed by Session Laws 1995 (Regular Session, 1996), c. 652, s. 1.

(l) Notwithstanding any other provision contained in G.S. 20-141 or any other statute or law of this State, including municipal charters, any speed limit on any portion of the public highways within the jurisdiction of this State shall be uniformly applicable to all types of motor vehicles using such portion of the highway, if on November 1, 1973, such portion of the highway had a speed limit which was uniformly applicable to all types of motor vehicles using it. Provided, however, that a lower speed limit may be established for any vehicle operating under a special permit because of any weight or dimension of such vehicle, including any load thereon. The requirement for a uniform speed limit hereunder shall not apply to any portion of the highway during such time as the condition of the highway, weather, an accident, or other condition creates a temporary hazard to the safety of traffic on such portion of the highway.

(m) The fact that the speed of a vehicle is lower than the foregoing limits shall not relieve the operator of a vehicle from the duty to decrease speed as may be necessary to avoid colliding with any person, vehicle or other conveyance on or entering the highway, and to avoid injury to any person or property.

(n) Notwithstanding any other provision contained in G.S. 20-141 or any other statute or law of this State, the failure of a motorist to stop his vehicle within the radius of its headlights or the range of his vision shall not be held negligence per se or contributory negligence per se.

(o) A violation of G.S. 20-123.2 shall be a lesser included offense in any violation of this section, and shall be subject to the following limitations and conditions:

(1) A violation of G.S. 20-123.2 shall be recorded in the driver's official record as "Improper equipment -- Speedometer."

(2) The lesser included offense under this subsection shall not apply to charges of speeding in excess of 25 miles per hour or more over the posted speed limit.

No drivers license points or insurance surcharge shall be assessed on account of a violation of this subsection.

(p) A driver charged with speeding in excess of 25 miles per hour over the posted speed limit shall be ineligible for a disposition of prayer for judgment continued.

History.
1937, c. 297, s. 2; c. 407, s. 103; 1939, c. 275; 1941, c. 347; 1947, c. 1067, s. 17; 1949, c. 947, s. 1; 1953, c. 1145; 1955, c. 398; c. 555, ss. 1, 2; c. 1042; 1957, c. 65, s. 11; c. 214; 1959, c. 640; c. 1264, s. 10; 1961, cc. 99, 1147; 1963, cc. 134, 456, 949; 1967, c. 106; 1971, c. 79, ss. 1-3; 1973, c. 507, s. 5; c. 1330, s. 7; 1975, c. 225; 1977, c. 367; c. 464, s. 34; c. 470; 1983, c. 131; 1985, c. 764, ss. 29, 30; 1985 (Reg. Sess., 1986), c. 852, s. 17; 1987, c. 164; 1991 (Reg. Sess., 1992), c. 818, s. 1; c. 1034, s. 1; 1993, c. 539, ss. 366, 367; 1994, Ex. Sess., c. 24, s. 14(c); 1995 (Reg. Sess., 1996), c. 652, s. 1; 1997-341, s. 1; 1997-443, s. 19.26(b); 1997-488, s. 1; 1999-330, s. 3; 2000-109, s. 7(c); 2003-110, s. 1; 2004-203, s. 70(a); 2005-349, s. 11; 2007-380, ss. 1, 2; 2009-234, ss. 1, 2; 2011-64, s. 2; 2012-194, s. 9; 2013-360, s. 18B.14(k).

§ 20-141.1. Speed limits in school zones

The Board of Transportation or local authorities within their respective jurisdictions may, by ordinance, set speed limits lower than those designated in G.S. 20-141 for areas adjacent to or near a public, private or parochial school. Limits set pursuant to this section shall become effective when signs are erected giving notice of the school zone, the authorized speed limit, and the days and hours when the lower limit is effective, or by erecting signs giving notice of the school zone, the authorized speed limit and which indicate the days and hours the lower limit is effective by an electronic flasher operated with a time clock. Limits set pursuant to this section may be enforced only on days when school is in session, and no speed limit below 20 miles per hour may be set under the authority of this section. A person who drives a motor vehicle in a school zone at a speed greater than the speed limit set and posted under this section is responsible for an infraction and is required to pay a penalty of two hundred fifty dollars ($ 250.00).

History.
1977, c. 902, s. 2; 1979, c. 613; 1997-341, s. 1.1; 2011-64, s. 1

§ 20-141.2. Prima facie rule of evidence as to operation of motor vehicle altered so as to increase potential speed

Proof of the operation upon any street or highway of North Carolina at a speed in excess of the limits provided by law of any motor vehicle when the motor, or any mechanical part or feature, or the design of the motor vehicle has been changed or altered so that there is a variation between such motor vehicle as changed or altered and the motor vehicle as constructed according to specification of the original motor vehicle manufacturer, with the result that the potential speed of such vehicle has been increased beyond that which existed prior to such change or alteration, or the proof of operation upon any street or highway of North Carolina at a speed in excess of the limits provided by law of any motor vehicle assembled from parts of two or more different makes of motor vehicles, whether or not any specially made or specially designed parts or appliances are included in the manufacture and assembly thereof, shall be prima facie evidence that such motor vehicle was operated at such time by the registered owner thereof.

History.
1953, c. 1220

§ 20-141.3. Unlawful racing on streets and highways

(a) It shall be unlawful for any person to operate a motor vehicle on a street or highway willfully in prearranged speed competition with another motor vehicle. Any person violating the provisions of this subsection shall be guilty of a Class 1 misdemeanor.

(b) It shall be unlawful for any person to operate a motor vehicle on a street or highway willfully in speed competition with another motor vehicle. Any person willfully violating the provisions of this subsection shall be guilty of a Class 2 misdemeanor.

(c) It shall be unlawful for any person to authorize or knowingly permit a motor vehicle owned by him or under his control to be operated on a public street, highway, or thoroughfare in prearranged speed competition with another motor vehicle, or to place or receive any bet, wager, or other thing of value from the outcome of any prearranged speed competition on any public street, highway, or thoroughfare. Any person violating the provisions of this subsection shall be guilty of a Class 1 misdemeanor.

(d) The Commissioner of Motor Vehicles shall revoke the driver's license or privilege to drive of every person convicted of violating the provisions of subsection (a) or subsection (c) of this section, said revocation to be for three years; provided any person whose license has been revoked under this section may apply for a new license after 18 months from revocation. Upon filing of such application the Division may issue a new license upon satisfactory proof that the former licensee has been of good behavior for the past 18 months and that his conduct and attitude are such as to entitle him to favorable consideration and upon such terms and conditions which the Division may see fit to impose for the balance of the three-year revocation period, which period shall be computed from the date of the original revocation.

(e) The Commissioner may suspend the driver's license or privilege to drive of every person convicted of violating the provisions of subsection (b) of this section. Such suspension shall be for a period of time within the discretion of the Commissioner, but not to exceed one year.

(f) All suspensions and revocations made pursuant to the provisions of this section shall be in the same form and manner and shall be subject to all procedures as now provided for suspensions and revocations made under the provisions of Article 2 of Chapter 20 of the General Statutes.

(g) When any officer of the law discovers that any person has operated or is operating a motor vehicle willfully in prearranged speed competition with another motor vehicle on a street or highway, he shall seize the motor vehicle and deliver the same to the sheriff of the county in which such offense is committed, or the same shall be placed under said sheriff's constructive possession if delivery of actual possession is impractical, and the vehicle shall be held by the sheriff pending the trial of the person or persons arrested for operating such motor vehicle in violation of subsection (a) of this section. The sheriff shall restore the seized motor vehicle to the owner upon execution by the owner of a good and valid bond, with sufficient sureties, in an amount double the value of the property, which bond shall be approved by said sheriff and shall be conditioned on the return of the motor vehicle to the custody of the sheriff on the day of trial of the person or persons accused. Upon the acquittal of the person charged with operating said motor vehicle willfully in prearranged speed competition with another motor vehicle, the sheriff shall return the motor vehicle to the owner thereof.

Notwithstanding the provisions for sale set out above, on petition by a lienholder, the court, in its discretion and upon such terms and conditions as it may prescribe, may allow reclamation of the vehicle by the lienholder. The lienholder shall file with the court an accounting of the proceeds of any subsequent sale of the vehicle and pay into the court any proceeds received in excess of the amount of the lien.

Upon conviction of the operator of said motor vehicle of a violation of subsection (a) of this section, the court shall order a sale at public auction of said motor vehicle and the officer making the sale, after deducting the expenses of keeping the motor vehicle, the fee for the seizure, and the costs of the sale, shall pay all liens, according to their priorities, which are established, by intervention or otherwise, at said hearing or in other proceeding brought for said purpose, as being bona fide, and shall pay the balance of the proceeds to the proper officer of the county who receives fines and forfeitures to be used for the school fund of the county. All liens against a motor vehicle sold under the provisions of this section shall be transferred from the motor vehicle to the proceeds of its sale. If, at the time of hearing, or other proceeding in which the matter is considered, the owner of the vehicle can establish to the satisfaction of the court that said motor vehicle was used in prearranged speed competition with another motor vehicle on a street or highway without the knowledge or consent of the owner, and that the owner had no reasonable grounds to believe that the motor vehicle would be used for such purpose, the court shall not order a sale of the vehicle but shall restore it to the owner, and the said owner shall, at his request, be entitled to a trial by jury upon such issues.

If the owner of said motor vehicle cannot be found, the taking of the same, with a description thereof, shall be advertised in some newspaper published in the city or county where taken, or, if there be no newspaper published in such city or county, in a newspaper having circulation in the county, once a week for two weeks and by handbills posted in three public places near the place of seizure, and if said owner shall not appear within 10 days after the last publication of the advertisement, the property shall be sold, or otherwise disposed of in the manner set forth in this section.

When any vehicle confiscated under the provisions of this section is found to be specially equipped or modified from its original manufactured condition so as to increase its speed, the court shall, prior to sale, order that the special equipment or modification be removed and destroyed and the vehicle restored to its original manufactured condition. However, if the court should find that such equipment and modifications are so extensive that it would be impractical to restore said vehicle to its original manufactured condition, then the court may order that the vehicle be turned over to such governmental agency or public official within the territorial jurisdiction of the court as the court shall see fit, to be used in the performance of official duties only, and not for resale, transfer, or disposition other than as junk: Provided, that nothing herein contained shall affect the rights of lienholders and other claimants to said vehicles as set out in this section.

History.
1955, c. 1156; 1957, c. 1358; 1961, c. 354; 1963, c. 318; 1967, c. 446; 1969, c. 186, s. 3; 1973, c. 1330, s. 8; 1975, c. 716, s. 5; 1979, c. 667, s. 31; 1993, c. 539, ss. 368 -370; 1994, Ex. Sess., c. 24, s. 14(c); 1995, c. 163, ss. 8, 9

§ 20-141.4. Felony and misdemeanor death by vehicle; felony serious injury by vehicle; aggravated offenses; repeat felony death by vehicle

(a) Repealed by Session Laws 1983, c. 435, s. 27.

(a1) **Felony Death by Vehicle.** -- A person commits the offense of felony death by vehicle if:

(1) The person unintentionally causes the death of another person,

(2) The person was engaged in the offense of impaired driving under G.S. 20-138.1 or G.S. 20-138.2, and

(3) The commission of the offense in subdivision (2) of this subsection is the proximate cause of the death.

(a2) **Misdemeanor Death by Vehicle.** -- A person commits the offense of misdemeanor death by vehicle if:

(1) The person unintentionally causes the death of another person,

(2) The person was engaged in the violation of any State law or local ordinance applying to the operation or use of a vehicle or to the regulation of traffic, other than impaired driving under G.S. 20-138.1, and

(3) The commission of the offense in subdivision (2) of this subsection is the proximate cause of the death.

(a3) **Felony Serious Injury by Vehicle.** -- A person commits the offense of felony serious injury by vehicle if:

(1) The person unintentionally causes serious injury to another person,

(2) The person was engaged in the offense of impaired driving under G.S. 20-138.1 or G.S. 20-138.2, and

(3) The commission of the offense in subdivision (2) of this subsection is the proximate cause of the serious injury.

(a4) **Aggravated Felony Serious Injury by Vehicle.** -- A person commits the offense of aggravated felony serious injury by vehicle if:

(1) The person unintentionally causes serious injury to another person,

(2) The person was engaged in the offense of impaired driving under G.S. 20-138.1 or G.S. 20-138.2,

(3) The commission of the offense in subdivision (2) of this subsection is the proximate cause of the serious injury, and

(4) The person has a previous conviction involving impaired driving, as defined in G.S. 20-4.01(24a), within seven years of the date of the offense.

(a5) **Aggravated Felony Death by Vehicle.** -- A person commits the offense of aggravated felony death by vehicle if:

(1) The person unintentionally causes the death of another person,

(2) The person was engaged in the offense of impaired driving under G.S. 20-138.1 or G.S. 20-138.2,

(3) The commission of the offense in subdivision (2) of this subsection is the proximate cause of the death, and

(4) The person has a previous conviction involving impaired driving, as defined in G.S. 20-4.01(24a), within seven years of the date of the offense.

(a6) **Repeat Felony Death by Vehicle Offender.** -- A person commits the offense of repeat felony death by vehicle if:

(1) The person commits an offense under subsection (a1) or subsection (a5) of this section; and

(2) The person has a previous conviction under:

a. Subsection (a1) of this section;

b. Subsection (a5) of this section; or

c. G.S. 14-17 or G.S. 14-18, and the basis of the conviction was the unintentional death of another person while engaged in the offense of impaired driving under G.S. 20-138.1 or G.S. 20-138.2.

The pleading and proof of previous convictions shall be in accordance with the provisions of G.S. 15A-928.

(b) **Punishments.** -- Unless the conduct is covered under some other provision of law providing greater punishment, the following classifications apply to the offenses set forth in this section:

(1) Repeat felony death by vehicle is a Class B2 felony.

(1a) Aggravated felony death by vehicle is a Class D felony. Notwithstanding the provisions of G.S. 15A-1340.17, the court shall sentence the defendant in the aggravated range of the appropriate Prior Record Level.

(2) Felony death by vehicle is a Class D felony. Notwithstanding the provisions of G.S. 15A-1340.17, intermediate punishment is authorized for a defendant who is a Prior Record Level I offender.

(3) Aggravated felony serious injury by vehicle is a Class E felony.

(4) Felony serious injury by vehicle is a Class F felony.

(5) Misdemeanor death by vehicle is a Class A1 misdemeanor.

(c) **No Double Prosecutions.** -- No person who has been placed in jeopardy upon a charge of death by vehicle may be prosecuted for the offense of manslaughter arising out of the same death; and no person who has been placed in jeopardy upon a charge of manslaughter may be prosecuted for death by vehicle arising out of the same death.

History.

1973, c. 1330, s. 9; 1983, c. 435, s. 27; 1993, c. 285, s. 10; c. 539, ss. 371, 1259; 1994, Ex. Sess., c. 24, s. 14(c); 2006-253, s. 14; 2007-493, s. 15; 2009-528, s. 1; 2012-165, s. 2, 3

§ 20-141.5. Speeding to elude arrest; seizure and sale of vehicles

(a) It shall be unlawful for any person to operate a motor vehicle on a street, highway, or public vehicular area while fleeing or attempting to elude a law enforcement officer who is in the lawful performance of his duties. Except as provided in subsection (b) of this section, violation of this section shall be a Class 1 misdemeanor.

(b) If two or more of the following aggravating factors are present at the time the violation occurs, violation of this section shall be a Class H felony.

(1) Speeding in excess of 15 miles per hour over the legal speed limit.

(2) Gross impairment of the person's faculties while driving due to:

    a. Consumption of an impairing substance; or

    b. A blood alcohol concentration of 0.14 or more within a relevant time after the driving.

(3) Reckless driving as proscribed by G.S. 20-140.

(4) Negligent driving leading to an accident causing:

    a. Property damage in excess of one thousand dollars ($ 1,000); or

    b. Personal injury.

(5) Driving when the person's drivers license is revoked.

(6) Driving in excess of the posted speed limit, during the days and hours when the posted limit is in effect, on school property or in an area designated as a school zone pursuant to G.S. 20-141.1, or in a highway work zone as defined in G.S. 20-141(j2).

(7) Passing a stopped school bus as proscribed by G.S. 20-217.

(8) Driving with a child under 12 years of age in the vehicle.

(b1) When a violation of subsection (a) of this section is the proximate cause of the death of any person, the person violating subsection (a) of this section shall be guilty of a Class H felony. When a violation of subsection (b) of this section is the proximate cause of the death of any person, the person violating subsection (b) of this section shall be guilty of a Class E felony.

(c) Whenever evidence is presented in any court or administrative hearing of the fact that a vehicle was operated in violation of this section, it shall be prima facie evidence that the vehicle was operated by the person in whose name the vehicle was registered at the time of the violation, according to the Division's records. If the vehicle is rented, then proof of that rental shall be prima facie evidence that the vehicle was operated by the renter of the vehicle at the time of the violation.

(d) The Division shall suspend, for up to one year, the drivers license of any person convicted of a misdemeanor under this section. The Division shall revoke, for two years, the drivers license of any person convicted of a felony under this section if the person was convicted on the basis of the presence of two of the aggravating factors listed in subsection (b) of this section. The Division shall revoke, for three years, the drivers license of any person convicted of a felony under this section if the person was convicted on the basis of the presence of three or more aggravating factors listed in subsection (b) of this section. In the case of a first felony conviction under this section where only two aggravating factors were present, the licensee may apply to the sentencing court for a limited driving privilege after a period of 12 months of revocation, provided the operator's license has not also been revoked or suspended under any other provision of law. A limited driving privilege issued under this subsection shall be valid for the period of revocation remaining in the same manner and under the terms and conditions prescribed in G.S. 20-16.1(b). If the person's license is revoked under any other statute, the limited driving privilege issued pursuant to this subsection is invalid.

(e) When the probable cause of the law enforcement officer is based on the prima facie evidence rule set forth in subsection (c) above, the officer shall make a reasonable effort to contact the registered owner of the vehicle prior to initiating criminal process.

(f) Each law enforcement agency shall adopt a policy applicable to the pursuit of fleeing or eluding motorists. Each policy adopted pursuant to this subsection shall specifically include factors to be considered by an officer in determining when to initiate or terminate a pursuit. The Attorney General shall develop a model policy or policies to be considered for use by law enforcement agencies.

(g) through (j) Repealed by Session Laws 2013-243, s. 6, effective December 1, 2013, and applicable to offenses committed on or after that date.

(k) If a person is convicted of a violation of subsection (b) or (b1) of this section, the motor vehicle that was driven by the defendant at the time the defendant committed the offense of felony speeding to elude arrest becomes property subject to forfeiture in accordance with the procedure set out in G.S. 20-28.2, 20-28.3, 20-28.4, and 20-28.5.

History.
1997-443, s. 19.26(a); 2005-341, s. 1; 2011-271, s. 1; 2013-243, ss. 6, 7

§ 20-141.6. Aggressive Driving

(a) Any person who operates a motor vehicle on a street, highway, or public vehicular area is guilty of aggressive driving if the person:

(1) Violates either G.S. 20-141 or G.S. 20-141.1, and

(2) Drives carelessly and heedlessly in willful or wanton disregard of the rights or safety of others.

(b) For the purposes of this section only, in order to prove a violation of subsection (a)(2), the State must show that the person committed two or more of the below specified offenses while in violation of subsection (a)(1):

(1) Running through a red light in violation of G.S. 20-158(b)(2) or (b)(3), or G.S. 20-158(c)(2) or (c)(3).

(2) Running through a stop sign in violation of G.S. 20-158(b)(1) or (c)(1).

(3) Illegal passing in violation of G.S. 20-149 or G.S. 20-150.

(4) Failing to yield right-of-way in violation of G.S. 20-155, 20-156, 20-158(b)(4) or (c)(4) or 20-158.1.

(5) Following too closely in violation of G.S. 20-152.

(c) A person convicted of aggressive driving is guilty of a Class 1 misdemeanor.

(d) The offense of reckless driving under G.S. 20-140 is a lesser-included offense of the offense set forth in this section.

History.
2004-193, s. 1

N.C. Gen. Stat. § 20-142

Repealed by Session Laws 1991, c. 368, s. 2.

§ 20-142.1. Obedience to railroad signal

(a) Whenever any person driving a vehicle approaches a railroad grade crossing under any of the circumstances stated in this section, the driver of the vehicle shall stop within 50 feet, but not less than 15 feet from the nearest rail of the railroad and shall not proceed until he can do so safely. These requirements apply when:

(1) A clearly visible electrical or mechanical signal device gives warning of the immediate approach of a railroad train or on-track equipment;

(2) A crossing gate is lowered or when a human flagman gives or continues to give a signal of the approach or passage of a railroad train or on-track equipment;

(3) A railroad train or on-track equipment approaching within approximately 1500 feet of the highway crossing emits a signal audible from that distance, and the railroad train or on-track equipment is an immediate hazard because of its speed or nearness to the crossing; or

(4) An approaching railroad train or on-track equipment is plainly visible and is in hazardous proximity to the crossing.

(b) No person shall drive any vehicle through, around, or under any crossing gate or barrier at a railroad crossing while the gate or barrier is closed or is being opened or closed, nor shall any pedestrian pass through, around, over, or under any crossing gate or barrier at a railroad crossing while the gate or barrier is closed or is being opened or closed.

(c) When stopping as required at a railroad crossing, the driver shall keep as far to the right of the highway as possible and shall not form two lanes of traffic unless the roadway is marked for four or more lanes of traffic.

(d) Any person who violates any provisions of this section shall be guilty of an infraction and punished in accordance with G.S. 20-176. Violation of this section shall not constitute negligence per se.

(e) An employer who knowingly allows, requires, permits, or otherwise authorizes a driver of a commercial motor vehicle to violate this section shall be guilty of an infraction. Such employer will also be subject to a civil penalty under G.S. 20-37.21.

History.
1991, c. 368, s. 1; 2005-349, s. 12; 2019-36, s. 2

§ 20-142.2. Vehicles stop at certain grade crossing

The Department of Transportation may designate particularly dangerous highway crossings of railroads and erect stop signs at those crossings. When a stop sign is erected at a highway crossing of a railroad, the driver of any vehicle shall stop within 50 feet but not less than 15 feet from the nearest rail of such grade crossing and shall proceed only upon exercising due care. Any person who violates this section shall be guilty of an infraction and punished in accordance with G.S. 20-176. Violation of this section shall not constitute negligence per se. An employer who knowingly allows, requires, permits, or otherwise authorizes a driver of a commercial motor vehicle to violate this section shall be guilty of an infraction. Such employer will also be subject to a civil penalty under G.S. 20-37.21.

History.
1991, c. 368, s. 1; 2005-349, s. 13

§ 20-142.3. Certain vehicles must stop at railroad grade crossing

(a) Before crossing at grade any track or tracks of a railroad, the driver of any school bus, any activity bus, any motor vehicle carrying passengers for compensation, any commercial motor vehicle listed in 49 C.F.R. § 392.10, and any motor vehicle with a capacity of 16 or more persons shall stop the vehicle within 50 feet but not less than 15 feet from the nearest rail of the railroad. While stopped, the driver shall listen and look in both directions along the track for any approaching train or on-track equipment and shall not proceed until the driver can do so safely. Upon proceeding, the driver of the vehicle shall cross the track in a gear that allows the driver to cross the track without changing gears and the driver shall not change gears while crossing the track or tracks.

(b) Except for school buses and activity buses, the provisions of this section shall not require the driver of a vehicle to stop:

(1) At railroad tracks used exclusively for industrial switching purposes within a business district.

(2) At a railroad grade crossing which a police officer or crossing flagman directs traffic to proceed.

(3) At a railroad grade crossing protected by a gate or flashing signal designed to stop traffic upon the approach of a train or on-track equipment, when the gate or flashing signal does not indicate the approach of a train or on-track equipment.

(4) At an abandoned railroad grade crossing which is marked with a sign indicating that the rail line is abandoned.

(5) At an industrial or spur line railroad grade crossing marked with a sign reading "Exempt" erected by or with the consent of the appropriate State or local authority.

(c) A person violating the provisions of this section shall be guilty of an infraction and punished in accordance with G.S. 20-176. Violation of this section shall not constitute negligence per se.

(d), (e) Repealed by Session Laws 2001-487, s. 50(g).

(f) An employer who knowingly allows, requires, permits, or otherwise authorizes a driver of a commercial motor vehicle to violate this section shall be guilty of an infraction. Such employer will also be subject to a civil penalty under G.S. 20-37.21.

History.
1991, c. 368, s. 1; 1999-274, ss. 1, 2; 2001-487, s. 50(g); 2005-349, s. 14; 2019-36, s. 3

§ 20-142.4. Moving heavy equipment at railroad grade crossing

(a) No person shall operate or move any crawler-type tractor, crane, or roller or any equipment or structure having a normal operating speed of five or less miles per hour upon or across any tracks at a railroad crossing without first complying with this section.

(b) Notice of any intended crossing described in subsection (a) of this section shall be given to a superintendent of the railroad and a reasonable time be given to the railroad to provide protection at the crossing.

(c) Before making any crossing described in subsection (a) of this section, the person operating or moving the vehicle or equipment shall:

(1) Stop the vehicle or equipment not less than 15 feet nor more than 50 feet from the nearest rail of the railroad;

(2) While stopped, shall listen and look both directions along the track for any approaching train or on-track equipment and for signals indicating the approach of a train or on-track equipment; and

(3) Shall not proceed until the crossing can be made safely.

(d) No crossing described in subsection (a) of this section shall be made when warning is given by automatic signal or crossing gates or a flagman or otherwise of the immediate approach of a railroad train or on-track equipment.

(e) Subsection (c) of this section shall not apply at any railroad crossing where State or local authorities have determined that trains are not operating during certain periods or seasons of the year and have erected an official sign carrying the legend "Exempt".

(f) Any person who violates any provision of this section shall be guilty of an infraction and punished in accordance with G.S. 20-176. Violation of this section shall not constitute negligence per se.

(g) An employer who knowingly allows, requires, permits, or otherwise authorizes a driver of a commercial motor vehicle to violate this section shall be guilty of an infraction. Such employer will also be subject to a civil penalty under G.S. 20-37.21.

History.

1991, c. 368, s. 1; 2005-349, s. 15; 2019-36, s. 4

§ 20-142.5. Stop when traffic obstructed

No driver shall enter an intersection or a marked crosswalk or drive onto any railroad grade crossing unless there is sufficient space on the other side of the intersection, crosswalk, or railroad grade crossing to accommodate the vehicle he is operating without obstructing the passage of other vehicles, pedestrians, or railroad trains or on-track equipment, notwithstanding the indication of any traffic control signal to proceed. Any person who violates any provision of this section shall be guilty of an infraction and punished in accordance with G.S. 20-176. Violation of this section shall not constitute negligence per se.

An employer who knowingly allows, requires, permits, or otherwise authorizes a driver of a commercial motor vehicle to violate this section shall be guilty of an infraction. Such employer will also be subject to a civil penalty under G.S. 20-37.21.

History.

1991, c. 368, s. 1; 2005-349, s. 16; 2019-36, s. 5

§§ 20-143, 20-143.1

Repealed by Session Laws 1991, c. 368, ss. 2, 3.

§ 20-144. Special speed limitation on bridges

It shall be unlawful to drive any vehicle upon any public bridge, causeway or viaduct at a speed which is greater than the maximum speed which can with safety to such structure be maintained thereon, when such structure is signposted as provided in this section.

The Department of Transportation, upon request from any local authorities, shall, or upon its own initiative may, conduct an investigation of any public bridge, causeway or viaduct, and if it shall thereupon find that such structure cannot with safety to itself withstand vehicles traveling at the speed otherwise permissible under this Article, the Division shall determine and declare the maximum speed of vehicles which such structure can withstand, and shall cause or permit suitable signs stating such maximum speed to be erected and maintained at a distance of 100 feet beyond each end of such structure. The findings and determination of the Department of Transportation shall be conclusive evidence of the maximum speed which can with safety to any such structure be maintained thereon.

History.

1937, c. 407, s. 106; 1957, c. 65, s. 11; 1973, c. 507, ss. 5, 21; 1975, c. 716, s. 5; 1977, c. 464, s. 34

§ 20-145. When speed limit not applicable

The speed limitations set forth in this Article shall not apply to vehicles when operated with due regard for safety under the direction of the police in the chase or apprehension of violators of the law or of persons charged with or suspected of any such violation, nor to fire department or fire patrol vehicles when traveling in response to a fire alarm, nor to public or private ambulances and rescue squad emergency service vehicles when traveling in emergencies, nor to vehicles operated by county fire marshals and civil preparedness coordinators when traveling in the performances of their duties, nor to any of the following when either operated by a law enforcement officer in the chase or apprehension of violators of the law or of persons charged with or suspected of any such violation, when traveling in response to a fire alarm, or for other emergency response purposes: (i) a vehicle operated by the Division of Marine Fisheries of the Department of Environmental Quality or the Division of Parks and Recreation of the Department of Natural and Cultural Resources or (ii) a vehicle operated by the North Carolina Forest Service of the Department of Agriculture and Consumer Services. This exemption shall not, however, protect the driver of any such vehicle from the consequence of a reckless disregard of the safety of others.

History.

1937, c. 407, s. 107; 1947, c. 987; 1971, c. 5; 1977, c. 52, s. 3; 1985, c. 454, s. 5; 2013-415, s. 1(c); 2015-241, s. 14.30(gg).

§ 20-146. Drive on right side of highway; exceptions

(a) Upon all highways of sufficient width a vehicle shall be driven upon the right half of the highway except as follows:

(1) When overtaking and passing another vehicle proceeding in the same direction under the rules governing such movement;

(2) When an obstruction exists making it necessary to drive to the left of the center of the highway; provided, any person so doing shall yield the right-of-way to all vehicles traveling in the proper direction upon the unobstructed portion of the highway within such distance as to constitute an immediate hazard;

(3) Upon a highway divided into three marked lanes for traffic under the rules applicable thereon; or

(4) Upon a highway designated and sign-posted for one-way traffic.

(a1) Self-propelled grain combines or other self-propelled farm equipment shall be operated to the right of the centerline except as provided in G.S. 20-116(j)(4).

(b) Upon all highways any vehicle proceeding at less than the legal maximum speed limit shall be driven in the right-hand lane then available for thru traffic, or as close as practicable to the right-hand curb or edge of the highway, except when overtaking and passing another vehicle proceeding in the same direction or when preparing for a left turn.

(c) Upon any highway having four or more lanes for moving traffic and providing for two-way movement of traffic, no vehicle shall be driven to the left of the centerline of the highway, except when authorized by official traffic-control devices designating certain lanes to the left side of the center of the highway for use by traffic not otherwise permitted to use such lanes or except as permitted under subsection (a)(2) hereof.

(d) Whenever any street has been divided into two or more clearly marked lanes for traffic, the following rules in addition to all others consistent herewith shall apply.

(1) A vehicle shall be driven as nearly as practicable entirely within a single lane and shall not be moved from such lane until the driver has first ascertained that such movement can be made with safety.

(2) Upon a street which is divided into three or more lanes and provides for the two-way movement of traffic, a vehicle shall not be driven in the center lane except when overtaking and passing another vehicle traveling in the same direction when such center lane is clear of traffic within a safe distance, or in the preparation for making a left turn or where such center lane is at the time allocated exclusively to traffic moving in the same direction that the vehicle is proceeding and such allocation is designated by official traffic-control device.

(3) Official traffic-control devices may be erected directing specified traffic to use a designated lane or designating those lanes to be used by traffic moving in a particular direction regardless of the center of the street and drivers of vehicles shall obey the direction of every such device.

(4) Official traffic-control devices may be installed prohibiting the changing of lanes on sections of streets, and drivers of vehicles shall obey the directions of every such device.

(e) Notwithstanding any other provisions of this section, when appropriate signs have been posted, it shall be unlawful for any person to operate a motor vehicle over and upon the inside lane, next to the median of any dual-lane highway at a speed less than the posted speed limit when the operation of said motor vehicle over and upon said inside lane shall impede the steady flow of traffic except when preparing for a left turn. "Appropriate signs" as used herein shall be construed as including "Slower Traffic Keep Right" or designations of similar import.

History.
1937, c. 407, s. 108; 1965, c. 678, s. 2; 1973, c. 1330, s. 3; 1975, c. 593; 1985, c. 764, s. 25; 1985 (Reg. Sess., 1986), c. 852, s. 17; 2001-487, s. 11; 2015-263, s. 6(b)

§ 20-146.1. Operation of motorcycles

(a) All motorcycles are entitled to full use of a lane and no motor vehicle shall be driven in such a manner as to deprive any motorcycle of the full use of a lane. This subsection shall not apply to motorcycles operated two abreast in a single lane.

(b) Motorcycles shall not be operated more than two abreast in a single lane. For purposes of this subsection, the term "motorcycle" shall not include autocycles. Autocycles shall not be operated more than one abreast in a single lane.

History.
1965, c. 909; 1973, c. 1330, s. 14; 1975, c. 786; 2015-163, s. 12

§ 20-146.2. Rush hour traffic lanes authorized

(a) **HOV Lanes. --** The Department of Transportation may designate one or more travel lanes as high occupancy vehicle (HOV) lanes on streets and highways on the State Highway System and cities may designate one or more travel lanes as high occupancy vehicle (HOV) lanes on streets on the Municipal Street System. HOV lanes shall be reserved for vehicles with a specified number of passengers as determined by the Department of Transportation or the city having jurisdiction over the street or highway. When HOV lanes have been designated, and have been appropriately marked with signs or other markers, they shall be reserved for privately or publicly operated buses, and automobiles or other vehicles containing the specified number of persons. Where access restrictions are applied on HOV lanes through designated signing and pavement markings, vehicles shall only cross into or out of an HOV lane at designated openings. A motor vehicle shall not travel in a designated HOV lane if the motor vehicle has more than three axles, regardless of the number of occupants. HOV lane restrictions shall not apply to any of the following:

(1) Motorcycles.

(2) Vehicles designed to transport 15 or more passengers, regardless of the actual number of occupants.

(3) Emergency vehicles. As used in this subdivision, the term "emergency vehicle" means any law enforcement, fire, police, or other government vehicle, and any public and privately owned ambulance or emergency service vehicle, when responding to an emergency.

(4) Plug-in electric vehicles as defined in G.S. 20-4.01(28b), regardless of the number of passengers in the vehicle. These vehicles must be able to travel at the posted speed limit while operating in the HOV lane.

(5) Dedicated natural gas vehicles as defined in G.S. 20-4.01(5a), regardless of the number of passengers in the vehicle. These vehicles must be able to travel at the posted speed limit while operating in the HOV lane.

(6) Fuel cell electric vehicles as defined in G.S. 20-4.01(12a), regardless of the number of passengers in the vehicle. These vehicles must be able to travel at the posted speed limit while operating in the HOV lane.

(a1) **Transitway Lanes.** -- The Department of Transportation may designate one or more travel lanes as a transitway on streets and highways on the State Highway System and cities may designate one or more travel lanes as a transitway on streets on the Municipal Street System. Transitways shall be reserved for public transportation vehicles as determined by the Department of Transportation or the city having jurisdiction over the street or highway. When transitways have been designated, and they have been appropriately marked with signs or other markers, they shall be reserved for privately or publicly operated transportation vehicles as determined by the Department or the city having jurisdiction.

(b) **Temporary Peak Traffic Shoulder Lanes.** -- The Department of Transportation may modify, upgrade, and designate shoulders of controlled access facilities and partially controlled access facilities as temporary travel lanes during peak traffic periods. When these shoulders have been appropriately marked, it shall be unlawful to use these shoulders for stopping or emergency parking. Emergency parking areas shall be designated at other appropriate areas, off these shoulders, when available.

(c) **Directional Flow Peak Traffic Lanes.** -- The Department of Transportation may designate travel lanes for the directional flow of peak traffic on streets and highways on the State Highway System and cities may designate travel lanes for the directional flow of peak traffic on streets on the Municipal Street System. These travel lanes may be designated

for time periods by the agency controlling the streets and highways.

History.
1987, c. 547, s. 1; 1999-350, s. 1; 2003-184, s. 5; 2011-95, s. 2; 2011-206, s. 2; 2012-194, s. 10; 2020-73, s. 4

§ 20-147. Keep to the right in crossing intersections or railroads

In crossing an intersection of highways or the intersection of a highway by a railroad right-of-way, the driver of a vehicle shall at all times cause such vehicle to travel on the right half of the highway unless such right side is obstructed or impassable.

History.
1937, c. 407, s. 109

§ 20-147.1. Passenger vehicle towing other vehicles to keep right

Whenever a noncommercial passenger vehicle as defined in G.S. 20-4.01(27)*l.* is towing another vehicle as defined in G.S. 20-4.01(49), the driver of the towing vehicle shall at all times cause that vehicle to travel on the right half of the highway, and upon any highway having four or more lanes for moving traffic and providing for two-way movement of traffic, the vehicle shall not be driven in the left-most lane of the right half of the highway except when overtaking and passing another vehicle proceeding in the same direction, when preparing for a left turn, or the right lanes are obstructed or impassable. These towing vehicles shall also comply with all signage for vehicles of three or more axles erected pursuant to G.S. 20-146(d)(3).

History.
2004-124, s. 30.6(a); 2004-199, s. 56; 2017-102, s. 5.2(b)

§ 20-148. Meeting of vehicles

Drivers of vehicles proceeding in opposite directions shall pass each other to the right, each giving to the other at least one half of the main-traveled portion of the roadway as nearly as possible.

History.
1937, c. 407, s. 110

§ 20-149. Overtaking a vehicle

(a) The driver of any such vehicle overtaking another vehicle proceeding in the same direction shall pass at least two feet to the left thereof, and shall not again drive to the right side of the highway until safely clear of such overtaken vehicle. This subsection shall not apply when the overtaking and passing is done pursuant to the provisions of G.S. 20-150(e) or G.S. 20-150.1.

(b) Except when overtaking and passing on the right is permitted, the driver of an overtaken vehicle shall give way to the right in favor of the overtaking vehicle while being lawfully overtaken on audible signal and shall not increase the speed of his vehicle until completely passed by the overtaking vehicle.

Failure to comply with this subsection:

(1) Is a Class 1 misdemeanor when the failure is the proximate cause of a collision resulting in serious bodily injury.

(2) Is a Class 2 misdemeanor when the failure is the proximate cause of a collision resulting in bodily injury or property damage.

(3) Is, in all other cases, an infraction.

History.
1937, c. 407, s. 111; 1955, c. 913, s. 3; 1959, c. 247; 1973, c. 1330, s. 15; 1995, c. 283, s. 1; 2016-90, s. 5.5(b)

§ 20-150. Limitations on privilege of overtaking and passing

(a) The driver of a vehicle shall not drive to the left side of the center of a highway, in overtaking and passing another vehicle proceeding in the same direction, unless such left side is clearly visible and is free of oncoming traffic for a sufficient distance ahead to permit such overtaking and passing to be made in safety.

(b) The driver of a vehicle shall not overtake and pass another vehicle proceeding in the same direction upon the crest of a grade or upon a curve in the highway where the driver's view along the highway is obstructed within a distance of 500 feet.

(c) The driver of a vehicle shall not overtake and pass any other vehicle proceeding in the same direction at any railway grade crossing nor at any intersection of highway unless permitted so to do by a traffic or police officer. For the purposes of this section the words "intersection of highway" shall be defined and limited to intersections designated and marked by the Department of Transportation by appropriate signs, and street intersections in cities and towns.

(d) The driver of a vehicle shall not drive to the left side of the centerline of a highway upon the crest of a grade or upon a curve in the highway where such centerline has been placed upon such highway by the Department of Transportation, and is visible.

(e) The driver of a vehicle shall not overtake and pass another on any portion of the highway which is marked by signs, markers or markings placed by the Department of Transportation stating or clearly indicating that passing should

not be attempted. The prohibition in this section shall not apply when the overtaking and passing is done in accordance with all of the following:

(1) The slower moving vehicle to be passed is a bicycle or a moped.

(2) The slower moving vehicle is proceeding in the same direction as the faster moving vehicle.

(3) The driver of the faster moving vehicle either (i) provides a minimum of four feet between the faster moving vehicle and the slower moving vehicle or (ii) completely enters the left lane of the highway.

(4) The operator of the slower moving vehicle is not (i) making a left turn or (ii) signaling in accordance with G.S. 20-154 that he or she intends to make a left turn.

(5) The driver of the faster moving vehicle complies with all other applicable requirements set forth in this section.

(e1) The driver of a vehicle shall not overtake and pass self-propelled farm equipment proceeding in the same direction when the farm equipment is (i) making a left turn or (ii) signaling that it intends to make a left turn.

(f) The foregoing limitations shall not apply upon a one-way street nor to the driver of a vehicle turning left in or from an alley, private road, or driveway.

History.
1937, c. 407, s. 112; 1955, c. 862; c. 913, s. 2; 1957, c. 65, s. 11; 1969, c. 13; 1973, c. 507, s. 5; c. 1330, s. 16; 1977, c. 464, s. 34; 1979, c. 472; 2016-90, s. 5.5(a); 2020-18, s. 2(a)

§ 20-150.1. When passing on the right is permitted

The driver of a vehicle may overtake and pass upon the right of another vehicle only under the following conditions:

(1) When the vehicle overtaken is in a lane designated for left turns;

(2) Upon a street or highway with unobstructed pavement of sufficient width which have been marked for two or more lanes of moving vehicles in each direction and are not occupied by parked vehicles;

(3) Upon a one-way street, or upon a highway on which traffic is restricted to one direction of movement when such street or highway is free from obstructions and is of sufficient width and is marked for two or more lanes of moving vehicles which are not occupied by parked vehicles;

(4) When driving in a lane designating a right turn on a red traffic signal light.

History.
1953, c. 679

N.C. Gen. Stat. § 20-151

Repealed by Session Laws 1995, c. 283, s. 2.

§ 20-152. Following too closely

(a) The driver of a motor vehicle shall not follow another vehicle more closely than is reasonable and prudent, having due regard for the speed of such vehicles and the traffic upon and the condition of the highway.

(b) The driver of any motor vehicle traveling upon a highway outside of a business or residential district and following another motor vehicle shall, whenever conditions permit, leave sufficient space so that an overtaking vehicle may enter and occupy such space without danger, except that this shall not prevent a motor vehicle from overtaking and passing another motor vehicle. This provision shall not apply to funeral processions.

(c) Subsections (a) and (b) of this section shall not apply to the driver of any non-leading commercial motor vehicle traveling in a platoon on any roadway where the Department of Transportation has by traffic ordinance authorized travel by platoon. For purposes of this subsection, the term "platoon" means a group of individual commercial motor vehicles traveling at close following distances in a unified manner through the use of an electronically interconnected braking system.

History.
1937, c. 407, s. 114; 1949, c. 1207, s. 4; 1973, c. 1330, s. 17; 2017-169, s. 1

§ 20-153. Turning at intersections

(a) **Right Turns. --** Both the approach for a right turn and a right turn shall be made as close as practicable to the right-hand curb or edge of the roadway.

(b) **Left Turns. --** The driver of a vehicle intending to turn left at any intersection shall approach the intersection in the extreme left-hand lane lawfully available to traffic moving in the direction of travel of that vehicle, and, after entering the intersection, the left turn shall be made so as to leave the intersection in a lane lawfully available to traffic moving in the direction upon the roadway being entered.

(c) Local authorities and the Department of Transportation, in their respective jurisdictions, may modify the foregoing method of turning at intersections by clearly indicating by buttons, markers, or other direction signs within an intersection the course to be followed by vehicles turning thereat, and it shall be unlawful for any driver to fail to turn in a manner as so directed.

History.
1937, c. 407, s. 115; 1955, c. 913, s. 5; 1973, c. 1330, s. 18; 1977, c. 464, s. 34; 1997-405, s. 1

§ 20-154. Signals on starting, stopping or turning

(a) The driver of any vehicle upon a highway or public vehicular area before starting, stopping or turning from a direct line shall first see that such movement can be made in safety, and if any pedestrian may be affected by such movement shall give a clearly audible signal by sounding the horn, and whenever the operation of any other vehicle may be affected by such movement, shall give a signal as required in this section, plainly visible to the driver of such other vehicle, of the intention to make such movement. The driver of a vehicle shall not back the same unless such movement can be made with safety and without interfering with other traffic.

(a1) A person who violates subsection (a) of this section and causes a motorcycle or bicycle operator to change travel lanes or leave that portion of any public street or highway designated as travel lanes shall be responsible for an infraction and shall be assessed a fine of not less than two hundred dollars ($ 200.00). A person who violates subsection (a) of this section that results in a crash causing property damage or personal injury to a motorcycle or bicycle operator or passenger shall be responsible for an infraction and shall be assessed a fine of not less than five hundred dollars ($ 500.00) unless subsection (a2) of this section applies.

(a2) A person who violates subsection (a) of this section and the violation results in a crash causing property damage in excess of five thousand dollars ($ 5,000) or a serious bodily injury as defined in G.S. 20-160.1(b) to a motorcycle or bicycle operator or passenger shall be responsible for an infraction and shall be assessed a fine of not less than seven hundred fifty dollars ($ 750.00). A violation of this subsection shall be treated as a failure to yield right-of-way to a motorcycle or bicycle, as applicable, for purposes of assessment of points under G.S. 20-16(c). In addition, the trial judge shall have the authority to order the license of any driver violating this subsection suspended for a period not to exceed 30 days. If a judge orders suspension of a person's drivers license pursuant to this subsection, the judge may allow the licensee a limited driving privilege for a period not to exceed the period of suspension. The limited driving privilege shall be issued in the same manner and under the terms and conditions prescribed in G.S. 20-16.1(b)(1), (2), (3), (4), (5), and G.S. 20-16.1(g).

(b) The signal herein required shall be given by means of the hand and arm in the manner

1549

herein specified, or by any mechanical or electrical signal device approved by the Division, except that when a vehicle is so constructed or loaded as to prevent the hand and arm signal from being visible, both to the front and rear, the signal shall be given by a device of a type which has been approved by the Division.

Except as otherwise provided in subsection (b1) of this section, whenever the signal is given the driver shall indicate his intention to start, stop, or turn by extending the hand and arm from and beyond the left side of the vehicle as hereinafter set forth.

Left turn -- hand and arm horizontal, forefinger pointing.

Right turn -- upper arm horizontal, forearm and hand pointed upward.

Stop -- upper arm horizontal, forearm and hand pointed downward.

All hand and arm signals shall be given from the left side of the vehicle and all signals shall be maintained or given continuously for the last 100 feet traveled prior to stopping or making a turn. Provided, that in all areas where the speed limit is 45 miles per hour or higher and the operator intends to turn from a direct line of travel, a signal of intention to turn from a direct line of travel shall be given continuously during the last 200 feet traveled before turning.

Any motor vehicle in use on a highway shall be equipped with, and required signal shall be given by, a signal lamp or lamps or mechanical signal device when the distance from the center of the top of the steering post to the left outside limit of the body, cab or load of such motor vehicle exceeds 24 inches, or when the distance from the center of the top of the steering post to the rear limit of the body or load thereof exceeds 14 feet. The latter measurement shall apply to any single vehicle, also to any combination of vehicles except combinations operated by farmers in hauling farm products.

(b1) Notwithstanding the requirement set forth in subsection (b) of this section that a driver signal a right turn by extending his or her hand and arm from beyond the left side of the vehicle, an operator of a bicycle may signal his or her intention to make a right turn by extending his or her hand and arm horizontally, with the forefinger pointing, from beyond the right side of the bicycle.

(c) No person shall operate over the highways of this State a right-hand-drive motor vehicle or a motor vehicle equipped with the steering mechanism on the right-hand side thereof unless said motor vehicle is equipped with mechanical or electrical signal devices by which the signals for left turns and right turns may be given. Such mechanical or electrical devices shall be approved by the Division.

(d) A violation of this section shall not constitute negligence per se.

History.

1937, c. 407, s. 116; 1949, c. 1016, s. 1; 1951, cc. 293, 360; 1955, c. 1157, s. 9; 1957, c. 488, s. 2; 1965, c. 768; 1973, c. 1330, s. 19; 1975, c. 716, s. 5; 1981, c. 599, s. 4; 1985, c. 96; 2011-361, s. 1; 2013-366, s. 5(a); 2016-90, s. 5.5(c)

§ 20-155. Right-of-way

(a) When two vehicles approach or enter an intersection from different highways at approximately the same time, the driver of the vehicle on the left shall yield the right-of-way to the vehicle on the right.

(b) The driver of a vehicle intending to turn to the left within an intersection or into an alley, private road, or driveway shall yield the right-of-way to any vehicle approaching from the opposite direction which is within the intersection or so close as to constitute an immediate hazard.

(c) The driver of any vehicle upon a highway within a business or residence district shall yield the right-of-way to a pedestrian crossing such highway within any clearly marked crosswalk, or any regular pedestrian crossing included in the prolongation of the lateral boundary lines of the adjacent sidewalk at the end of a block, except at intersections where the movement of traffic is being regulated by traffic officers or traffic direction devices.

(d) The driver of any vehicle approaching but not having entered a traffic circle shall yield the right-of-way to a vehicle already within such traffic circle.

History.

1937, c. 407, s. 117; 1949, c. 1016, s. 2; 1955, c. 913, ss. 6, 7; 1967, c. 1053; 1973, c. 1330, s. 20

§ 20-156. Exceptions to the right-of-way rule

(a) The driver of a vehicle about to enter or cross a highway from an alley, building entrance, private road, or driveway shall yield the right-of-way to all vehicles approaching on the highway to be entered.

(b) The driver of a vehicle upon the highway shall yield the right-of-way to police and fire department vehicles and public and private ambulances, vehicles used by an organ procurement organization or agency for the recovery or transportation of human tissues and organs for transplantation or a vehicle operated by a transplant coordinator who is an employee of an organ procurement organization or agency when the transplant coordinator is responding to a call to recover or transport human tissues or organs for transplantation, and to rescue squad emergency service vehicles and vehicles operated by county fire marshals and civil preparedness coordinators, and to a vehicle operated by the Division of Marine Fisheries of the Department of Environmental Quality or the Division of Parks and Recreation of the Department of Natural and Cultural Resources when used for law enforcement, firefighting, or other emergency response purpose, and to a vehicle operated by the North Carolina Forest Service of the Department of Agriculture and Consumer Services when used for a law enforcement, firefighting, or other emergency response purpose, when the operators of said vehicles are giving a warning signal by appropriate light and by bell, siren or exhaust whistle audible under normal conditions from a distance not less than 1,000 feet. When appropriate warning signals are being given, as provided in this subsection, an emergency vehicle may proceed through an intersection or other place when the emergency vehicle is facing a stop sign, a yield sign, or a traffic light which is emitting a flashing strobe signal or a beam of steady or flashing red light. This provision shall not operate to relieve the driver of a police or fire department vehicle, or a vehicle owned or operated by the Department of Environmental Quality, or the Department of Agriculture and Consumer Services, or public or private ambulance or vehicles used by an organ procurement organization or agency for the recovery or transportation of human tissues and organs for transplantation or a vehicle operated by a transplant coordinator who is an employee of an organ procurement organization or agency when the transplant coordinator is responding to a call to recover or transport human tissues or organs for transplantation, or rescue squad emergency service vehicle or county fire marshals or civil preparedness coordinators from the duty to drive with due regard for the safety of all persons using the highway, nor shall it protect the driver of any such vehicle or county fire marshal or civil preparedness coordinator from the consequence of any arbitrary exercise of such right-of-way.

History.
1937, c. 407, s. 118; 1971, cc. 78, 106; 1973, c. 1330, s. 21; 1977, c. 52, s. 4; c. 438, s. 3; 1985, c. 427; 1989, c. 537, s. 3; 2013-415, s. 1(d); 2015-241, s. 14.30(u), (hh)

§ 20-157. Approach of law enforcement, fire department or rescue squad vehicles or ambulances; driving over fire hose or blocking fire fighting equipment; parking, etc., near law enforcement, fire department, or rescue squad vehicle or ambulance

(a) Upon the approach of any law enforcement or fire department vehicle or public or private ambulance or rescue squad emergency service vehicle, or a vehicle operated by the Division of Marine Fisheries of the Department of Environmental Quality, or the Division of Parks and Recreation of the Department of Natural and Cultural Resources, or the North Carolina Forest Service of the Department of Agriculture and Consumer Services when traveling in response to a fire alarm or other emergency response purpose, giving warning signal by appropriate light and by audible bell, siren or exhaust whistle, audible under normal conditions from a distance not less than 1000 feet, the driver of every other vehicle shall immediately drive the same to a position as near as possible and parallel to the right-hand edge or curb, clear of any intersection of streets or highways, and shall stop and remain in such position unless otherwise directed by a law enforcement or traffic officer until the law enforcement or fire department vehicle, or the vehicle operated by the Division of Marine Fisheries of the Department of Environmental Quality, or the Division of Parks and Recreation of the Department of Natural and Cultural Resources, or the North Carolina Forest Service of the Department of Agriculture and Consumer Services, or the public or private ambulance or rescue squad emergency service vehicle shall have passed. Provided, however, this subsection shall not apply to vehicles traveling in the opposite direction of the vehicles herein enumerated when traveling on a four-lane limited access highway with a median divider dividing the highway for vehicles traveling in opposite directions, and provided further that the violation of this subsection shall be negligence per se. Violation of this subsection is a Class 2 misdemeanor.

(b) It shall be unlawful for the driver of any vehicle other than one on official business to follow any fire apparatus traveling in response to a fire alarm closer than one block or to drive into or park such vehicle within one block where fire apparatus has stopped in answer to a fire alarm.

(c) Outside of the corporate limits of any city or town it shall be unlawful for the driver of any vehicle other than one on official business to follow any fire apparatus traveling in response to a fire alarm closer than 400 feet or to drive into or park such vehicle within a space of 400 feet from where fire apparatus has stopped in answer to a fire alarm.

(d) It shall be unlawful to drive a motor vehicle over a fire hose or any other equipment that is being used at a fire at any time, or to block a fire-fighting apparatus or any other equipment from its source of supply regardless of its distance from the fire.

(e) It shall be unlawful for the driver of a vehicle, other than one on official business, to park and leave standing such vehicle within 100 feet of law enforcement or fire department vehicles, public or private ambulances, or rescue squad emergency vehicles which are engaged in the investigation of an accident or engaged in rendering assistance to victims of such accident.

(f) When an authorized emergency vehicle as described in subsection (a) of this section or any public service vehicle is parked or standing within 12 feet of a roadway and is giving a warning signal by appropriate light, the driver of every other approaching vehicle shall, as soon as it is safe and when not otherwise directed by an individual lawfully directing traffic, do one of the following:

(1) Move the vehicle into a lane that is not the lane nearest the parked or standing authorized emergency vehicle or public service vehicle and continue traveling in that lane until safely clear of the authorized emergency vehicle. This paragraph applies only if the roadway has at least two lanes for traffic proceeding in the direction of the approaching vehicle and if the approaching vehicle may change lanes safely and without interfering with any vehicular traffic.

(2) Slow the vehicle, maintaining a safe speed for traffic conditions, and operate the vehicle at a reduced speed and be prepared to stop until completely past the authorized emergency vehicle or public service vehicle. This paragraph applies only if the roadway has only one lane for traffic proceeding in the direction of the approaching vehicle or if the approaching vehicle may not change lanes safely and without interfering with any vehicular traffic.

For purposes of this section, "public service vehicle" means a vehicle that (i) is being used to assist motorists or law enforcement officers with wrecked or disabled vehicles, (ii) is being used to install, maintain, or restore utility service, including electric, cable, telephone, communications, and gas, (iii) is being used in the collection of refuse, solid waste, or recycling, or (iv) is a highway maintenance vehicle owned and operated by or contracted by the State or a local government and is operating an amber-colored flashing light authorized by G.S. 20-130.2. Violation of this subsection shall be negligence per se.

(g) Except as provided in subsections (a), (h), and (i) of this section, violation of this section shall be an infraction punishable by a fine of two hundred fifty dollars ($ 250.00).

(h) A person who violates this section and causes damage to property in the immediate area of the authorized emergency vehicle or public service vehicle in excess of five hundred dollars ($ 500.00), or causes injury to a law enforcement officer, a firefighter, an emergency vehicle operator, an Incident Management Assistance Patrol member, a public service vehicle operator, or any other emergency response person in the immediate area of the authorized emergency vehicle or public service vehicle is guilty of a Class 1 misdemeanor.

(i) A person who violates this section and causes serious injury or death to a law enforcement officer, a firefighter, an emergency vehicle operator, an Incident Management Assistance Patrol member, a public service vehicle operator, or any other emergency response person in the immediate area of the authorized emergency vehicle or public service vehicle is guilty of a Class F felony. The Division may suspend, for up to six months, the drivers license of any person convicted under this subsection. If the Division suspends a person's license under this subsection, a judge may allow the licensee a limited driving privilege for a period not to exceed the period of suspension, provided the person's license has not also been revoked or suspended under any other provision of law. The limited driving privilege shall be issued in the same manner and under the terms and conditions prescribed in G.S. 20-16.1(b).

History.
1937, c. 407, s. 119; 1955, cc. 173, 744; 1971, c. 366, ss. 1, 2; 1985, c. 764, s. 31; 1985 (Reg. Sess., 1986), c. 852, s. 17; 1993, c. 539, s. 372; 1994, Ex. Sess., c. 24, s. 14(c); 2001-331, s. 1; 2005-189, s. 1; 2006-259, s. 9; 2007-360, s. 1; 2010-132, s. 12; 2012-14, s. 1; 2013-415, s. 1(e); 2015-26, s. 3; 2015-241, s. 14.30(ii); 2019-157, s. 2

§ 20-157.1. Funeral processions

(a) As used in this section, a "funeral procession" means two or more vehicles accompanying the remains of a deceased person, or traveling to the church, chapel, or other location at which the funeral services are to be held, in which the lead vehicle is either a State or local law enforcement vehicle, other vehicle designated by a law enforcement officer or the funeral director, or the lead vehicle displays a flashing amber or purple light, sign, pennant, flag, or other insignia furnished by a funeral home indicating a funeral procession.

(b) Each vehicle in the funeral procession shall be operated with its headlights illuminated, if so equipped, and its hazard warning signal lamps illuminated, if so equipped.

(c) The operator of the lead vehicle in a funeral procession shall comply with all traffic-control signals, but when the lead vehicle in a funeral procession has progressed across an intersection in accordance with the traffic-control sign or signal, or when directed to do so by a law enforcement officer or a designee of a law enforcement officer or the funeral director, or when the lead vehicle is a law enforcement vehicle which progresses across the intersection while giving appropriate warning by light or siren, all vehicles in the funeral procession may proceed through the intersection without stopping, except that the operator of each vehicle shall exercise reasonable care towards any other vehicle or pedestrian on the highway. An operator of a vehicle that is not part of the funeral procession shall not join the funeral procession for the purpose of securing the right-of-way granted by this subsection.

(d) Operators of vehicles in a funeral procession shall drive on the right-hand side of the roadway and shall follow the vehicle ahead as closely as reasonable and prudent having due regard for speed and existing conditions.

(e) Operators of vehicles in a funeral procession shall yield the right-of-way to law enforcement vehicles, fire protection vehicles, rescue vehicles, ambulances, and other emergency vehicles giving appropriate warning signals by light or siren and shall yield the right-of-way when directed to do so by a law enforcement officer.

(f) Operators of vehicles in a funeral procession shall proceed at the posted minimum speed, except that the operator of such vehicle shall exercise reasonable care having due regard for speed and existing conditions.

(g) The operator of a vehicle proceeding in the opposite direction as a funeral procession may yield to the funeral procession. If the operator chooses to yield to the procession, the operator must do so by reducing speed, or by stopping completely off the roadway when meeting the procession or while the procession passes, so that operators of other vehicles proceeding in the opposite direction of the procession can continue to travel without leaving their lane of traffic.

(h) The operator of a vehicle proceeding in the same direction as a funeral procession shall not pass or attempt to pass the funeral procession, except that the operator of such a vehicle may pass a funeral procession when the highway has been marked for two or more lanes of moving traffic in the same direction of the funeral procession.

(i) An operator of a vehicle shall not knowingly drive between vehicles in a funeral procession by crossing their path unless directed to do so by a person authorized to direct traffic. When a funeral procession is proceeding through a steady or strobe-beam stoplight emitting a red light as permitted by subsection (c), an operator of a vehicle that is not in the funeral procession shall not enter the intersection knowing a funeral procession is in progress, even if facing a steady or strobe-beam stoplight emitting a green light, unless the operator can do so safely without crossing the path of the funeral procession.

(j) Nothing in this section shall be construed to prevent State or local law enforcement officers from escorting funeral processions in law enforcement vehicles.

(k) A violation of this section shall not constitute negligence per se.

(l) To the extent that a local government unit's ordinance is in direct conflict with any part of this statute, the ordinance shall control and prevail over the conflicting part.

(m) A violation of this section shall not be considered a moving violation for purposes of G.S. 58-36-65 or G.S. 58-36-75.

History.
1999-441, s. 1

§ 20-158. Vehicle control signs and signals

(a) The Department of Transportation, with reference to State highways, and local authorities, with reference to highways under their jurisdiction, are hereby authorized to control vehicles:

(1) At intersections, by erecting or installing stop signs requiring vehicles to come to a complete stop at the entrance to that portion of the intersection designated as the main traveled or through highway. Stop signs may also be erected at three or more entrances to an intersection.

(2) At appropriate places other than intersections, by erecting or installing stop signs requiring vehicles to come to a complete stop.

(3) At intersections and other appropriate places, by erecting or installing steady-beam traffic signals and other traffic control devices, signs, or signals. All steady-beam traffic signals emitting alternate red and green lights shall be arranged so that the red light in vertical-arranged signal faces shall appear above, and in horizontal-arranged signal faces shall appear to the left of all yellow and green lights.

(4) At intersections and other appropriate places, by erecting or installing flashing red or yellow lights.

(b) **Control of Vehicles at Intersections.** --

(1) When a stop sign has been erected or installed at an intersection, it shall be unlawful for the driver of any vehicle to fail to stop in obedience thereto and yield the right-of-way to vehicles operating on the designated main-traveled or through highway. When stop signs have been erected at three or more entrances to an intersection, the driver, after stopping in obedience thereto, may proceed with caution.

(2) a. When a traffic signal is emitting a steady red circular light controlling traffic approaching an intersection, an approaching vehicle facing the red light shall come to a stop and shall not enter the intersection. After coming to a complete stop and unless prohibited by an appropriate sign,

that approaching vehicle may make a right turn.

    b. Any vehicle that turns right under this subdivision shall yield the right-of-way to:

      1. Other traffic and pedestrians using the intersection; and

      2. Pedestrians who are moving towards the intersection, who are in reasonably close proximity to the intersection, and who are preparing to cross in front of the traffic that is required to stop at the red light.

    c. Failure to yield to a pedestrian under this subdivision shall be an infraction, and the court may assess a penalty of not more than five hundred dollars ($ 500.00) and not less than one hundred dollars ($ 100.00).

    d. Repealed by Session Laws 2014-58, s. 4, effective July 7, 2014.

    (2a) When a traffic signal is emitting a steady yellow circular light on a traffic signal controlling traffic approaching an intersection or a steady yellow arrow light on a traffic signal controlling traffic turning at an intersection, vehicles facing the yellow light are warned that the related green light is being terminated or a red light will be immediately forthcoming. When the traffic signal is emitting a steady green light, vehicles may proceed with due care through the intersection subject to the rights of pedestrians and other vehicles as may otherwise be provided by law.

    (3) When a flashing red light has been erected or installed at an intersection, approaching vehicles facing the red light shall stop and yield the right-of-way to vehicles in or approaching the intersection. The right to proceed shall be subject to the rules applicable to making a stop at a stop sign.

    (4) When a flashing yellow light has been erected or installed at an intersection, approaching vehicles facing the yellow flashing light may proceed through the intersection with caution, yielding the right-of-way to vehicles in or approaching the intersection.

    (5) When a stop sign, traffic signal, flashing light, or other traffic-control device authorized by subsection (a) of this section requires a vehicle to stop at an intersection, the driver shall stop (i) at an appropriately marked stop line, or if none, (ii) before entering a marked crosswalk, or if none, (iii) before entering the intersection at the point nearest the intersecting street where the driver has a view of approaching traffic on the intersecting street.

    (6) When a traffic signal is not illuminated due to a power outage or other malfunction, vehicles shall approach the intersection and proceed through the intersection as though such intersection is controlled by a stop sign on all approaches to the intersection. This subdivision shall not apply if the movement of traffic at the intersection is being directed by a law enforcement officer, another authorized person, or another type of traffic control device.

    (c) **Control of Vehicles at Places other than Intersections. --**

    (1) When a stop sign has been erected or installed at a place other than an intersection, it shall be unlawful for the driver of any vehicle to fail to stop in obedience thereto and yield the right-of-way to pedestrians and other vehicles.

    (2) When a traffic signal has been erected or installed at a place other than an intersection, and is emitting a steady red light, vehicles facing the red light shall come to a complete stop. When the traffic signal is emitting a steady yellow light, vehicles facing the light shall be warned that a red light will be immediately forthcoming and that vehicles may not proceed through such a red light. When the traffic signal is emitting a steady green light, vehicles may proceed subject to the rights of pedestrians and other vehicles as may otherwise be provided by law.

    (3) When a flashing red light has been erected or installed at a place other than an intersection, approaching vehicles facing the light shall stop and yield the right-of-way to pedestrians or other vehicles.

    (4) When a flashing yellow light has been erected or installed at a place other than an intersection, approaching vehicles facing the light may proceed with caution, yielding the right-of-way to pedestrians and other vehicles.

    (5) When a traffic signal, stop sign, or other traffic control device authorized by subsection (a) requires a vehicle to stop at a place other than an intersection, the driver shall stop at an appropriately marked stop line, or if none, before entering a marked crosswalk, or if none, before proceeding past the traffic control device.

    (6) When a ramp meter is displaying a circular red display, vehicles facing the red light must stop. When a ramp meter is displaying a circular green display, a vehicle may proceed for each lane of traffic facing the meter. When the display is dark or not emitting a red or green display, a vehicle may proceed without stopping. A violation of this subdivision is an infraction. No drivers license points or insurance surcharge shall be assessed as a result of a violation of this subdivision.

(d) No failure to stop as required by the provisions of this section shall be considered negligence or contributory negligence per se in any action at law for injury to person or property, but the facts relating to such failure to stop may be considered with the other facts in the case in determining whether a party was guilty of negligence or contributory negligence.

(e) **Defense.** -- It shall be a defense to a violation of sub-subdivision (b)(2)a. of this section if the operator of a motorcycle, as defined in G.S. 20-4.01(27)h., shows all of the following:

(1) The operator brought the motorcycle to a complete stop at the intersection or stop bar where a steady red light was being emitted in the direction of the operator.

(2) The intersection is controlled by a vehicle actuated traffic signal using an inductive loop to activate the traffic signal.

(3) No other vehicle that was entitled to have the right-of-way under applicable law was sitting at, traveling through, or approaching the intersection.

(4) No pedestrians were attempting to cross at or near the intersection.

(5) The motorcycle operator who received the citation waited a minimum of three minutes at the intersection or stop bar where the steady red light was being emitted in the direction of the operator before entering the intersection.

History.
1937, c. 407, s. 120; 1941, c. 83; 1949, c. 583, s. 2; 1955, c. 384, s. 1; c. 913, s. 7; 1957, c. 65, s. 11; 1973, c. 507, s. 5; c. 1191; c. 1330, s. 22; 1975, c. 1; 1977, c. 464, s. 34; 1979, c. 298, s. 1; 1989, c. 285; 2004-141, ss. 1, 2; 2004-172, ss. 2, 5; 2006-264, s. 6; 2007-260, s. 1; 2007-360, ss. 2, 3; 2014-58, ss. 4, 10(b); 2017-102, s. 5.2(b)

§ 20-158.1. Erection of "yield right-of-way" signs

The Department of Transportation, with reference to State highways, and cities and towns with reference to highways and streets under their jurisdiction, are authorized to designate main-traveled or through highways and streets by erecting at the entrance thereto from intersecting highways or streets, signs notifying drivers of vehicles to yield the right-of-way to drivers of vehicles approaching the intersection on the main-traveled or through highway. Notwithstanding any other provisions of this Chapter, except G.S. 20-156, whenever any such yield right-of-way signs have been so erected, it shall be unlawful for the driver of any vehicle to enter or cross such main-traveled or through highway or street unless he shall first slow down and yield right-of-way to any vehicle in movement on the main-traveled or through highway or street which is approaching so as to arrive

at the intersection at approximately the same time as the vehicle entering the main-traveled or through highway or street. No failure to so yield the right-of-way shall be considered negligence or contributory negligence per se in any action at law for injury to person or property, but the facts relating to such failure to yield the right-of-way may be considered with the other facts in the case in determining whether either party in such action was guilty of negligence or contributory negligence.

History.
1955, c. 295; 1957, c. 65, s. 11; 1973, c. 507, s. 5; c. 1330, s. 23; 1977, c. 464, s. 34

§ 20-158.2. Control of vehicles on Turnpike System

The North Carolina Turnpike Authority may control vehicles at appropriate places by erecting traffic control devices to collect tolls.

History.
2002-133, s. 2

§ 20-158.3. Emergency entry to controlled access roads

Any person, association, or other legal entity having responsibility for a controlled access system on a road that is a public vehicular area shall provide a means of immediate access to all emergency service vehicles, which shall include law enforcement, fire, rescue, ambulance, and first responder vehicles. This section shall not apply to any entity where federal regulations and requirements on its activities preempt application of State regulations or requirements.

History.
2007-455, s. 2

N.C. Gen. Stat. § 20-159

Repealed by Session Laws 1973, c. 1330, s. 39.

§ 20-160. Driving through safety zone or on sidewalks prohibited

(a) The driver of a vehicle shall not at any time drive through or over a safety zone.

(b) No person shall drive any motor vehicle upon a sidewalk or sidewalk area except upon a permanent or temporary driveway.

History.
1937, c. 407, s. 122; 1973, c. 1330, s. 24

§ 20-160.1. Failure to yield causing serious bodily injury; penalties

(a) Unless the conduct is covered under some other law providing greater punishment, a person who commits the offense of failure to yield while approaching or entering an intersection, turning at a stop or yield sign, entering a roadway, upon the approach of an emergency vehicle, or at highway construction or maintenance shall be punished under this section. When there is serious bodily injury but no death resulting from the violation, the violator shall be fined five hundred dollars ($ 500.00) and the violator's drivers license or commercial drivers license shall be suspended for 90 days.

(b) As used in this section, "serious bodily injury" means bodily injury that involves a substantial risk of death, extreme physical pain, protracted and obvious disfigurement, or protracted loss or impairment of the function of a bodily member, organ, or mental faculty.

History.
2004-172, s. 1

§ 20-161. Stopping on highway prohibited; warning signals; removal of vehicles from public highway

(a) No person shall park or leave standing any vehicle, whether attended or unattended, upon the main-traveled portion of any highway or highway bridge with the speed limit posted less than 45 miles per hour unless the vehicle is disabled to such an extent that it is impossible to avoid stopping and temporarily leaving the vehicle upon the paved or main traveled portion of the highway or highway bridge. This subsection shall not apply to a solid waste vehicle stopped on a highway while engaged in collecting garbage as defined in G.S. 20-118(c)(5)g. or recyclable material as defined in G.S. 130A-290(a)(26).

(a1) No person shall park or leave standing any vehicle, whether attended or unattended, upon the paved or main-traveled portion of any highway or highway bridge with the speed limit posted 45 miles per hour or greater unless the vehicle is disabled to such an extent that it is impossible to avoid stopping and temporarily leaving the vehicle upon the paved or main-traveled portion of the highway or highway bridge. This subsection shall not apply to a solid waste vehicle stopped on a highway while engaged in collecting garbage as defined in G.S. 20-118(c)(5)g. or recyclable material as defined in G.S. 130A-290(a)(26).

(b) No person shall park or leave standing any vehicle upon the shoulder of a public highway unless the vehicle can be clearly seen by approaching drivers from a distance of 200 feet in both directions and does not obstruct the normal movement of traffic.

(c) The operator of any truck, truck tractor, trailer or semitrailer which is disabled upon any portion of the highway shall display warning devices of a type and in a manner as required under the rules and regulations of the United States Department of Transportation as adopted by the Division of Motor Vehicles. Such warning devices shall be displayed as long as the vehicle is disabled.

(d) The owner of any vehicle parked or left standing in violation of law shall be deemed to have appointed any investigating law-enforcement officer his agent:

(1) For the purpose of removing the vehicle to the shoulder of the highway or to some other suitable place; and

(2) For the purpose of arranging for the transportation and safe storage of any vehicle which is interfering with the regular flow of traffic or which otherwise constitutes a hazard, in which case the officer shall be deemed a legal possessor of the vehicle within the meaning of G.S. 44A-2(d).

(e) When any vehicle is parked or left standing upon the right-of-way of a public highway, including rest areas, for a period of 24 hours or more, the owner shall be deemed to have appointed any investigating law-enforcement officer his agent for the purpose of arranging for the transportation and safe storage of such vehicle and such investigating law-enforcement officer shall be deemed a legal possessor of the motor vehicle within the meaning of that term as it appears in G.S. 44A-2(d).

(f) An investigating law enforcement officer, with the concurrence of the Department of Transportation, or the Department of Transportation, with the concurrence of an investigating law enforcement officer, may immediately remove or cause to be removed from the State highway system any wrecked, abandoned, disabled, unattended, burned, or partially dismantled vehicle, cargo, or other personal property interfering with the regular flow of traffic or which otherwise constitutes a hazard. In the event of a motor vehicle crash involving serious personal injury or death, no removal shall occur until the investigating law enforcement officer determines that adequate information has been obtained for preparation of a crash report. No state or local law enforcement officer, Department of Transportation employee, or person or firm contracting or assisting in the removal or disposition of any such vehicle, cargo, or other personal property shall be held criminally or civilly liable for any damage or economic injury related to carrying out or enforcing the provisions of this section.

(g) The owner shall be liable for any costs incurred in the removal, storage, and subsequent disposition of a vehicle, cargo, or other personal property under the authority of this section.

History.
1937, c. 407, s. 123; 1951, c. 1165, s. 1; 1971, c. 294, s. 1; 1973, c. 1330, s. 25; 1985, c. 454, s. 6; 2003-310, s. 1; 2007-360, ss. 4, 5; 2009-104, s. 1; 2010-132, ss. 13, 14, 15; 2015-231, s. 1

§ 20-161.1. Regulation of night parking on highways

No person parking or leaving standing a vehicle at night on a highway or on a side road entering into a highway shall permit the bright lights of said vehicle to continue burning when such lights face oncoming traffic.

History.
1953, c. 1052

N.C. Gen. Stat. § 20-161.2

Repealed by Session Laws 1983, c. 420, s. 1.

§ 20-162. Parking in front of private driveway, fire hydrant, fire station, intersection of curb lines or fire lane

(a) No person shall park a vehicle or permit it to stand, whether attended or unattended, upon a highway in front of a private driveway or within 15 feet in either direction of a fire hydrant or the entrance to a fire station, nor within 25 feet from the intersection of curb lines or if none, then within 15 feet of the intersection of property lines at an intersection of highways; provided, that local authorities may by ordinance decrease the distance within which a vehicle may park in either direction of a fire hydrant.

(b) No person shall park a vehicle or permit it to stand, whether attended or unattended, upon any public vehicular area, street, highway or roadway in any area designated as a fire lane. This prohibition includes designated fire lanes in shopping center or mall parking lots and all other public vehicular areas. Provided, however, persons loading or unloading supplies or merchandise may park temporarily in a fire lane located in a shopping center or mall parking lot as long as the vehicle is not left unattended. The prima facie rule of evidence created by G.S. 20-162.1 is applicable to prosecutions for violation of this section. The owner of a vehicle parked in violation of this subsection shall be deemed to have appointed any State, county or municipal law-enforcement officer as his agent for the purpose of arranging for the transportation and safe storage of such vehicle. No law-enforcement officer removing such a vehicle shall be held criminally or civilly liable in any

way for any acts or omissions arising out of or caused by carrying out or enforcing any provisions of this subsection, unless the conduct of the officer amounts to wanton misconduct or intentional wrongdoing.

History.
1937, c. 407, s. 124; 1939, c. 111; 1979, c. 552; 1981, c. 574, s. 1

§ 20-162.1. Prima facie rule of evidence for enforcement of parking regulations

(a) Whenever evidence shall be presented in any court of the fact that any automobile, truck, or other vehicle was found upon any street, alley or other public place contrary to and in violation of the provisions of any statute or of any municipal or Department of Transportation ordinance limiting the time during which any such vehicle may be parked or prohibiting or otherwise regulating the parking of any such vehicle, it shall be prima facie evidence in any court in the State of North Carolina that such vehicle was parked and left upon such street, alley or public way or place by the person, firm or corporation in whose name such vehicle is then registered and licensed according to the records of the department or agency of the State of North Carolina, by whatever name designated, which is empowered to register such vehicles and to issue licenses for their operation upon the streets and highways of this State; provided, that no evidence tendered or presented under the authorization contained in this section shall be admissible or competent in any respect in any court or tribunal, except in cases concerned solely with violation of statutes or ordinances limiting, prohibiting or otherwise regulating the parking of automobiles or other vehicles upon public streets, highways, or other public places.

Any person found responsible for an infraction pursuant to this section shall be subject to a penalty of not more than five dollars ($ 5.00).

(b) The prima facie rule of evidence established by subsection (a) shall not apply to the registered owner of a leased or rented vehicle parked in violation of law when the owner can furnish sworn evidence that the vehicle was, at the time of the parking violation, leased or rented, to another person or company. In those instances, the owner of the vehicle shall furnish sworn evidence to the courts within 30 days after notification of the violation in accordance with this subsection.

If the notification is given to the owner of the vehicle within 90 days after the date of the violation, the owner shall include in the sworn evidence the name and address of the person or company that leased or rented the vehicle. If notification is given to the owner of the vehicle after 90 days have elapsed from the date of the violation, the owner is not required to include the name or address of the lessee or renter of the vehicle in the sworn evidence.

History.
1953, c. 879, ss. 1, 1 1/2; c. 978; 1955, c. 566, s. 1; 1983, c. 753; 1985, c. 764, s. 32; 1985 (Reg. Sess., 1986), c. 852, s. 17; 1987, c. 736, s. 1; 1989, c. 243, s. 2; 2001-259, s. 1

§§ 20-162.2, 20-162.3

Transferred to §§ 20-219.2, 20-219.3 by Session Laws 1973, c. 1330, s. 36.

§ 20-163. Unattended motor vehicles

No person driving or in charge of a motor vehicle shall permit it to stand unattended on a public highway or public vehicular area without first stopping the engine, effectively setting the brake thereon and, when standing upon any grade, turning the front wheels to the curb or side of the highway.

History.
1937, c. 407, s. 125; 1973, c. 1330, s. 26

N.C. Gen. Stat. § 20-164

Repealed by Session Laws 1973, c. 1330, s. 39.

N.C. Gen. Stat. § 20-165

Repealed by Session Laws 1995, c. 379, s. 6.

§ 20-165.1. One-way traffic

In all cases where the Department of Transportation has heretofore, or may hereafter lawfully designate any highway or other separate roadway, under its jurisdiction for one-way traffic and shall erect appropriate signs giving notice thereof, it shall be unlawful for any person to willfully drive or operate any vehicle on said highway or roadway except in the direction so indicated by said signs.

History.
1957, c. 1177; 1973, c. 507, s. 5; c. 1330, s. 28; 1977, c. 464, s. 34

§ 20-166. Duty to stop in event of a crash; furnishing information or assistance to injured person, etc.; persons assisting exempt from civil liability

(a) The driver of any vehicle who knows or reasonably should know:

(1) That the vehicle which he or she is operating is involved in a crash; and

(2) That the crash has resulted in serious bodily injury, as defined in G.S. 14-32.4, or death to any person;

shall immediately stop his or her vehicle at the scene of the crash. The driver shall remain with the vehicle at the scene of the crash until a law-enforcement officer completes the investigation of the crash or authorizes the driver to leave and the vehicle to be removed, unless remaining at the scene places the driver or others at significant risk of injury.

Prior to the completion of the investigation of the crash by a law enforcement officer, or the consent of the officer to leave, the driver may not facilitate, allow, or agree to the removal of the vehicle from the scene for any purpose other than to call for a law enforcement officer, to call for medical assistance or medical treatment as set forth in subsection (b) of this section, or to remove oneself or others from significant risk of injury. If the driver does leave for a reason permitted by this subsection, then the driver must return with the vehicle to the accident scene within a reasonable period of time, unless otherwise instructed by a law enforcement officer. A willful violation of this subsection shall be punished as a Class F felony.

(a1) The driver of any vehicle who knows or reasonably should know:

(1) That the vehicle which he or she is operating is involved in a crash; and

(2) That the crash has resulted in injury;

shall immediately stop his or her vehicle at the scene of the crash. The driver shall remain with the vehicle at the scene of the crash until a law enforcement officer completes the investigation of the crash or authorizes the driver to leave and the vehicle to be removed, unless remaining at the scene places the driver or others at significant risk of injury.

Prior to the completion of the investigation of the crash by a law enforcement officer, or the consent of the officer to leave, the driver may not facilitate, allow, or agree to the removal of the vehicle from the scene for any purpose other than to call for a law enforcement officer, to call for medical assistance or medical treatment as set forth in subsection (b) of this section, or to remove oneself or others from significant risk of injury. If the driver does leave for a reason permitted by this subsection, then the driver must return with the vehicle to the crash scene within a reasonable period of time, unless otherwise instructed by a law enforcement officer. A willful violation of this subsection shall be punished as a Class H felony.

(b) In addition to complying with the requirements of subsections (a) and (a1) of this section, the driver as set forth in subsections (a) and (a1) shall give his or her name, address, driver's license number and the license plate number of the vehicle to the person struck or the driver or occupants of any vehicle collided with, provided that the person or persons are physically and mentally capable of receiving such information, and shall render to any person injured in such crash reasonable assistance, including the calling for medical assistance if it is apparent that such assistance is necessary or is requested by the injured person. A violation of this subsection is a Class 1 misdemeanor.

(c) The driver of any vehicle, when the driver knows or reasonably should know that the vehicle which the driver is operating is involved in a crash which results:

(1) Only in damage to property; or

(2) In injury or death to any person, but only if the operator of the vehicle did not know and did not have reason to know of the death or injury;

shall immediately stop the vehicle at the scene of the crash. If the crash is a reportable crash, the driver shall remain with the vehicle at the scene of the crash until a law enforcement officer completes the investigation of the crash or authorizes the driver to leave and the vehicle to be removed, unless remaining at the scene places the driver or others at significant risk of injury.

Prior to the completion of the investigation of the crash by a law enforcement officer, or the consent of the officer to leave, the driver may not facilitate, allow, or agree to the removal of the vehicle from the scene, for any purpose other than to call for a law enforcement officer, to call for medical assistance or medical treatment, or to remove oneself or others from significant risk of injury. If the driver does leave for a reason permitted by this subsection, then the driver must return with the vehicle to the accident scene within a reasonable period of time, unless otherwise instructed by a law enforcement officer. A willful violation of this subsection is a Class 1 misdemeanor.

(c1) In addition to complying with the requirement of subsection (c) of this section, the driver as set forth in subsection (c) shall give his or her name, address, driver's license number and the license plate number of his vehicle to the driver or occupants of any other vehicle involved in the crash or to any person whose property is damaged in the crash. If the damaged property is a parked and unattended vehicle and the name and location of the owner is not known to or readily ascertainable by the driver of the responsible vehicle, the driver shall furnish the information required by this subsection to the nearest available peace officer, or, in the alternative, and provided the driver thereafter within 48 hours fully complies with G.S. 20-166.1(c), shall immediately place a paper-writing containing the information in a conspicuous place upon or in the damaged vehicle. If the damaged property is a guardrail, utility pole, or other fixed object owned by the Department of Transportation, a public utility, or other public service corporation to which report cannot readily be made at the scene, it shall be sufficient if the responsible driver shall furnish the information required to the nearest peace officer or make written report thereof containing the information by U.S. certified mail, return receipt requested, to the North Carolina Division of Motor Vehicles within five days following the collision. A violation of this subsection is a Class 1 misdemeanor.

(c2) Notwithstanding subsections (a), (a1), and (c) of this section, if a crash occurs on a main lane, ramp, shoulder, median, or adjacent area of a highway, each vehicle shall be moved as soon as possible out of the travel lane and onto the shoulder or to a designated accident investigation site to complete the requirements of this section and minimize interference with traffic if all of the following apply:

(1) The crash has not resulted in injury or death to any person or the drivers did not know or have reason to know of any injury or death.

(2) Each vehicle can be normally and safely driven. For purposes of this subsection, a vehicle can be normally and safely driven if it does not require towing and can be operated under its own power and in its usual manner, without additional damage or hazard to the vehicle, other traffic, or the roadway.

(d) Any person who renders first aid or emergency assistance at the scene of a motor vehicle crash on any street or highway to any person injured as a result of the accident, shall not be liable in civil damages for any acts or omissions relating to the services rendered, unless the acts or omissions amount to wanton conduct or intentional wrongdoing.

(e) The Division of Motor Vehicles shall revoke the drivers license of a person convicted of violating subsection (a) or (a1) of this section for a period of one year, unless the court makes a finding that a longer period of revocation is appropriate under the circumstances of the case. If the court makes this finding, the Division of Motor Vehicles shall revoke that person's drivers license for two years. Upon a first conviction only for a violation of subsection (a1) of this section, a trial judge may allow limited driving privileges in the manner set forth in G.S. 20-179.3(b)(2) during any period of time during which the drivers license is revoked.

Chapter 20

History.

1937, c. 407, s. 128; 1939, c. 10, ss. 1, 1 1/2; 1943, c. 439; 1951, cc. 309, 794, 823; 1953, cc. 394, 793; c. 1340, s. 1; 1955, c. 913, s. 8; 1965, c. 176; 1967, c. 445; 1971, c. 958, s. 1; 1973, c. 507, s. 5; 1975, c. 716, s. 5; 1977, c. 464, s. 34; 1979, c. 667, s. 32; 1983, c. 912, s. 1; 1985, c. 324, ss. 1-4; 1993, c. 539, ss. 373 -375, 1260; 1994, Ex. Sess., c. 24, s. 14(c); 2003-310, s. 2; 2003-394, s. 1; 2005-460, s. 1; 2008-128, s. 1

§ 20-166.1. Reports and investigations required in event of accident

(a) **Notice of Accident. --** The driver of a vehicle involved in a reportable accident must immediately, by the quickest means of communication, notify the appropriate law enforcement agency of the accident. If the accident occurred in a city or town, the appropriate agency is the police department of the city or town. If the accident occurred outside a city or town, the appropriate agency is the State Highway Patrol or the sheriff's office or other qualified rural police of the county where the accident occurred.

(b) **Insurance Verification. --** When requested to do so by the Division, the driver of a vehicle involved in a reportable accident must furnish proof of financial responsibility.

(c) **Parked Vehicle. --** The driver of a motor vehicle that collides with another motor vehicle left parked or unattended on a highway of this State must report the collision to the owner of the parked or unattended motor vehicle. This requirement applies to an accident that is not a reportable accident as well as to one that is a reportable accident. The report may be made orally or in writing, must be made within 48 hours of the accident, and must include the following:

(1) The time, date, and place of the accident.

(2) The driver's name, address, and drivers license number.

(3) The registration plate number of the vehicle being operated by the driver at the time of the accident.

If the driver makes a written report to the owner of the parked or unattended vehicle and the report is not given to the owner at the scene of the accident, the report must be sent to the owner by certified mail, return receipt requested, and a copy of the report must be sent to the Division.

(d) Repealed by Session Laws 1995, c. 191, s. 2.

(e) **Investigation by Officer. --** The appropriate law enforcement agency must investigate a reportable accident. A law-enforcement officer who investigates a reportable accident, whether at the scene of the accident or by subsequent investigations and interviews, must make a written report of the accident within 24 hours of the accident and must forward it as required by this subsection. The report must contain information on financial responsibility for the vehicle driven by the person whom the officer identified as at fault for the accident.

If the officer writing the report is a member of the State Highway Patrol, the officer must forward the report to the Division. If the officer is not a member of the State Highway Patrol, the officer must forward the report to the local law enforcement agency for the area where the accident occurred. A local law enforcement agency that receives an accident report must forward it to the Division within 10 days after receiving the report. Upon request of the driver of the motor vehicle involved in the accident or the insurance agent or company identified by the driver under subsection (b) of this section, and notwithstanding any provision of Chapter 132 of the General Statutes to the contrary, the officer writing the report may forward an uncertified copy of the report to the insurance agent or company identified by the driver under subsection (b) of this section if evidence satisfactory to the officer is provided showing a certified copy of the report has been requested from the Division and the applicable fee set in G.S. 20-42 has been paid. Nothing in this section shall prohibit a law enforcement agency from providing to the public accident reports or portions of accident reports that are public records.

When a person injured in a reportable accident dies as a result of the accident within 12 months after the accident and the death was not reported in the original report, the law enforcement officer investigating the accident must file a supplemental report that includes the death.

(f) **Medical Personnel. --** A county medical examiner must report to the Division the death of any person in a reportable accident and the circumstances of the accident. The medical examiner must file the report within five days after the death. A hospital must notify the medical examiner of the county in which the accident occurred of the death within the hospital of any person who dies as a result of injuries apparently sustained in a reportable accident.

(g) Repealed by Session Laws 1987, c. 49.

(h) **Forms. --** The Division shall provide forms or procedures for submitting crash data to persons required to make reports under this section and the reports shall be made in a format approved by the Commissioner. The following information shall be included about a reportable crash:

(1) The cause of the crash.

(2) The conditions existing at the time of the crash.

(3) The persons and vehicles involved, except that the name and address of a minor child involved in a school bus crash who is a passenger on a school bus may only

be disclosed to (i) the local board of education, (ii) the State Board of Education, (iii) the parent or guardian of the child, (iv) an insurance company investigating a claim arising out of the crash, (v) an attorney representing a person involved in the crash, and (vi) law enforcement officials investigating the crash. As used in this subdivision, school bus also includes a school activity bus as defined by G.S. 20-4.01(27).

(4) Whether the vehicle has been seized and is subject to forfeiture under G.S. 20-28.2.

(i) **Effect of Report. --** A report of an accident made under this section by a person who is not a law enforcement officer is without prejudice, is for the use of the Division, and shall not be used in any manner as evidence, or for any other purpose in any trial, civil or criminal, arising out of the accident. Any other report of an accident made under this section may be used in any manner as evidence, or for any other purpose, in any trial, civil or criminal, as permitted under the rules of evidence. At the demand of a court, the Division must give the court a properly executed certificate stating that a particular accident report has or has not been filed with the Division solely to prove a compliance with this section.

The reports made by persons who are not law enforcement officers or medical examiners are not public records. The reports made by law enforcement officers and medical examiners are public records and are open to inspection by the general public at all reasonable times. The Division must give a certified copy of one of these reports to a member of the general public who requests a copy and pays the fee set in G.S. 20-42.

(j) **Statistics. --** The Division may periodically publish statistical information on motor vehicle accidents based on information in accident reports. The Division may conduct detailed research to determine more fully the cause and control of accidents and may conduct experimental field tests within areas of the State from time to time to prove the practicability of various ideas advanced in traffic control and accident prevention.

(k) **Punishment. --** A violation of any provision of this section is a misdemeanor of the Class set in G.S. 20-176.

History.
1953, c. 1340, s. 2; 1955, c. 913, s. 9; 1963, c. 1249; 1965, c. 577; 1971, c. 55; c. 763, s. 1; c. 958, ss. 2, 3; 1973, c. 1133, ss. 1, 2; c. 1330, s. 29; 1975, c. 307; c. 716, s. 5; 1979, c. 667, s. 33; 1981, c. 690, s. 14; 1983, c. 229, ss. 1, 2; 1985, c. 764, s. 33; 1985 (Reg. Sess., 1986), c. 852, s. 17; 1987, c. 49; 1993, c. 539, ss. 376, 377; 1994, Ex. Sess., c. 24, s. 14(c); 1995, c. 191, s. 2; 1998-182, s. 12.1; 1999-452, s. 19; 2012-147, s. 1; 2016-90, s. 13.8

§ 20-166.2. Duty of passenger to remain at the scene of an accident

(a) The passenger of any vehicle who knows or reasonably should know that the vehicle in which he or she is a passenger is involved in an accident or collision shall not willfully leave the scene of the accident by acting as the driver of a vehicle involved in the accident until a law enforcement officer completes the investigation of the accident or collision or authorizes the passenger to leave, unless remaining at the scene places the passenger or others at significant risk of injury.

Prior to the completion of the investigation of the accident by a law enforcement officer, or the consent of the officer to leave, the passenger may not facilitate, allow, or agree to the removal of the vehicle from the scene, for any purpose other than to call for a law enforcement officer, to call for medical assistance or medical treatment as set forth in subsection (b) of this section, or to remove oneself or others from a significant risk of injury. If the passenger does leave the scene of an accident by driving a vehicle involved in the accident for a reason permitted by this subsection, the passenger must return with the vehicle to the accident scene within a reasonable period of time, unless otherwise instructed by a law enforcement officer. A willful violation of this subsection is a Class H felony if the accident or collision is described in G.S. 20-166(a). A willful violation of this subsection is a Class 1 misdemeanor if the accident or collision is a reportable accident described in G.S. 20-166(c).

(b) In addition to complying with the requirement of subsection (a) of this section, the passenger shall give the passenger's name, address, drivers license number, and the license plate number of the vehicle in which the passenger was riding, if possible, to the person struck or the driver or occupants of any vehicle collided with, provided that the person or persons are physically and mentally capable of receiving the information, and shall render to any person injured in the accident or collision reasonable assistance, including the calling for medical assistance if it is apparent that such assistance is necessary or is requested by the injured person. A violation of this subsection is a Class 1 misdemeanor.

History.
2005-460, s. 2

§ 20-166.3. Limit storage duration for vehicle damaged as a result of a collision

(a) **Limited Duration of Storage. --** A motor vehicle that is towed and stored at the direction of a law enforcement agency following a collision may be held for evidence for not more than 20 days without a court order. Absent a court order, the vehicle must be released to the vehicle owner, insurer, or lien holder upon payment of the towing and storage fees.

(b) **Application.** -- This section shall not apply to a motor vehicle (i) seized as a result of a violation of law or (ii) abandoned by the owner.

History.
2015-188, s. 1

§ 20-167. Vehicles transporting explosives

Any person operating any vehicle transporting any explosive as a cargo or part of a cargo upon a highway shall at all times comply with the rules and regulations of the United States Department of Transportation as adopted by the Division of Motor Vehicles.

History.
1937, c. 407, s. 129; 1985, c. 454, s. 7

§ 20-167.1. Transportation of spent nuclear fuel

(a) No person, firm or corporation shall transport upon the highways of this State any spent nuclear fuel unless such person, firm, or corporation notifies the State Highway Patrol in advance of transporting the spent nuclear fuel.

(b) The provisions of this section shall apply whether or not the fuel is for delivery in North Carolina and whether or not the shipment originated in North Carolina.

(c) The Radiation Protection Commission is authorized to adopt, promulgate, amend, and repeal rules and regulations necessary to implement the provisions of this section.

(d) Any person, firm or corporation violating any provision of this section is guilty of a Class 3 misdemeanor and shall be punished only by a fine of not less than five hundred dollars ($ 500.00), and each unauthorized shipment shall constitute a separate offense.

History.
1977, c. 839, s. 1; 1985, c. 764, s. 33.1; 1985 (Reg. Sess., 1986), c. 852, s. 17; 1993, c. 539, s. 378; 1994, Ex. Sess., c. 24, s. 14(c)

§ 20-168. Drivers of State, county, and city vehicles subject to the provisions of this Article

(a) Subject to the exceptions in subsection (b), the provisions of this Article applicable to the drivers of vehicles upon the highways shall apply to the drivers of all vehicles owned or operated by the State or any political subdivision thereof.

(b) While actually engaged in maintenance or construction work on the highways, but not while traveling to or from such work, drivers of vehicles owned or operated by the State or any political subdivision thereof are exempt from all provisions of this Article except:

(1) G.S. 20-138.1. Impaired driving.

(2) Repealed by Session Laws 1983, c. 435, s. 28.

(3) G.S. 20-139.1. Procedures governing chemical analyses; admissibility; evidentiary provisions; controlled-drinking programs.

(4) G.S. 20-140. Reckless driving.

(5) Repealed by Session Laws 1983, c. 435, s. 38.

(6) G.S. 20-141. Speed restrictions.

(7) G.S. 20-141.3. Unlawful racing on streets and highways.

(8) G.S. 20-141.4. Felony and misdemeanor death by vehicle.

History.
1937, c. 407, s. 130; 1973, c. 1330, s. 30; 1981, c. 412, s. 4; c. 747, s. 66; 1983, c. 435, s. 28

§ 20-169. Powers of local authorities

Local authorities, except as expressly authorized by G.S. 20-141 and 20-158, shall have no power or authority to alter any speed limitations declared in this Article or to enact or enforce any rules or regulations contrary to the provisions of this Article, except that local authorities shall have power to provide by ordinances for any of the following:

(1) Regulating traffic by means of traffic or semaphores or other signaling devices on any portion of the highway where traffic is heavy or continuous.

(2) Prohibiting other than one-way traffic upon certain highways.

(3) Regulating the use of the highways by processions or assemblages.

(4) Regulating the speed of vehicles on highways in public parks.

(5) Authorizing law enforcement or fire department vehicles, ambulances, and rescue squad emergency service vehicles, equipped with a siren to preempt any traffic signals upon city streets within local authority boundaries or, with the approval of the Department of Transportation, on State highways within the boundaries of local authorities. The Department of Transportation shall respond to requests for approval within 60 days of receipt of a request.

Signs shall be erected giving notices of the special limits and regulations under subdivisions (1) through (4) of this section.

History.

1937, c. 407, s. 131; 1949, c. 947, s. 2; 1955, c. 384, s. 2; 1963, c. 559; 1973, c. 507, s. 5; 1979, c. 298, s. 2; 1991, c. 530, s. 5; 1999-310, s. 1

§ 20-170. This Article not to interfere with rights of owners of real property with reference thereto

Nothing in this Article shall be construed to prevent the owner of real property used by the public for purposes of vehicular travel by permission of the owner, and not as matter of right from prohibiting such use nor from requiring other or different or additional conditions than those specified in this Article or otherwise regulating such use as may seem best to such owner.

History.

1937, c. 407, s. 132

§ 20-171. Traffic laws apply to persons riding animals or driving animal-drawn vehicles

Every person riding an animal or driving any animal drawing a vehicle upon a highway shall be subject to the provisions of this Article applicable to the driver of a vehicle, except those provisions of the Article which by their nature can have no application.

History.

1939, c. 275

PART 10A
OPERATION OF BICYCLES

§ 20-171.1. Definitions

As used in this Part, except where the context clearly requires otherwise, the words and expressions defined in this section shall be held to have the meanings here given to them:

Bicycle. -- A nonmotorized vehicle with two or three wheels tandem, a steering handle, one or two saddle seats, and pedals by which the vehicle is propelled, or an electric assisted bicycle, as defined in G.S. 20-4.01(7a).

History.

1977, c. 1123, s. 1; 2016-90, s. 13(c)

§ 20-171.2. Bicycle racing

(a) Bicycle racing on the highways is prohibited except as authorized in this section.

(b) Bicycle racing on a highway shall not be unlawful when a racing event has been approved by State or local authorities on any highway under their respective jurisdictions.

Approval of bicycle highway racing events shall be granted only under conditions which assure reasonable safety for all race participants, spectators and other highway users, and which prevent unreasonable interference with traffic flow which would seriously inconvenience other highway users.

(c) By agreement with the approving authority, participants in an approved bicycle highway racing event may be exempted from compliance with any traffic laws otherwise applicable thereto, provided that traffic control is adequate to assure the safety of all highway users.

History.

1977, c. 1123, s. 1

§§ 20-171.3 through 20-171.5

Reserved for future codification purposes.

PART 10B
CHILD BICYCLE SAFETY ACT

§ 20-171.6. Short title

This Article shall be known and may be cited as the "Child Bicycle Safety Act."

History.

2001-268, s. 1

§ 20-171.7. Legislative findings and purpose

(a) The General Assembly finds and declares that:

(1) Disability and death of children resulting from injuries sustained in bicycling accidents are a serious threat to the public health, welfare, and safety of the people of this State, and the prevention of that disability and death is a goal of all North Carolinians.

(2) Head injuries are the leading cause of disability and death from bicycling accidents.

(3) The risk of head injury from bicycling accidents is significantly reduced for bicyclists who wear proper protective bicycle helmets; yet helmets are worn by fewer than five percent (5%) of child bicyclists nationwide.

(4) The risk of head injury or of any other injury to a small child who is a passenger on a bicycle operated by another person would be significantly reduced if any child passenger sat in a separate restraining seat.

(b) The purpose of this Article is to reduce the incidence of disability and death resulting from injuries incurred in bicycling accidents by requiring that while riding on a bicycle on the public roads, public bicycle paths, and other public rights-of-way of this State, all bicycle operators and passengers under the age of 16 years wear approved protective bicycle helmets; that all bicycle passengers who weigh less than 40 pounds or are less than 40 inches in height be seated in separate restraining seats; and that no person who is unable to maintain an erect, seated position shall be a passenger in a bicycle restraining seat, and all other bicycle passengers shall be seated on saddle seats.

History.
2001-268, s. 1

§ 20-171.8. Definitions

As used in this Article, the following terms have the following meanings:

(1) "Bicycle" means a human-powered vehicle with two wheels in tandem designed to transport, by the action of pedaling, one or more persons seated on one or more saddle seats on its frame. This term also includes a human-powered vehicle, designed to transport by the action of pedaling which has more than two wheels where the vehicle is used on a public roadway, public bicycle path, or other public right-of-way, but does not include a tricycle.

(2) "Operator" means a person who travels on a bicycle seated on a saddle seat from which that person is intended to and can pedal the bicycle.

(3) "Other public right-of-way" means any right-of-way other than a public roadway or public bicycle path that is under the jurisdiction and control of this State or a local political subdivision of the State and is designed for use and used by vehicular and/or pedestrian traffic.

(4) "Passenger" means a person who travels on a bicycle in any manner except as an operator.

(5) "Protective bicycle helmet" means a piece of headgear that meets or exceeds the impact standards for protective bicycle helmets set by the American National Standards Institute (ANSI) or the Snell Memorial Foundation.

(6) "Public bicycle path" means a right-of-way under the jurisdiction and control of this State or a local political subdivision of the State for use primarily by bicycles and pedestrians.

(7) "Public roadway" means a right-of-way under the jurisdiction and control of this State or a local political subdivision

of the State for use primarily by motor vehicles.

(8) "Restraining seat" means a seat separate from the saddle seat of the operator of the bicycle that is fastened securely to the frame of the bicycle and is adequately equipped to restrain the passenger in such seat and protect such passenger from the moving parts of the bicycle.

(9) "Tricycle" means a three-wheeled, human-powered vehicle designed for use as a toy by a single child under the age of six years, the seat of which is no more than two feet from ground level.

History.
2001-268, s. 1

§ 20-171.9. Requirements for helmet and restraining seat use

With regard to any bicycle used on a public roadway, public bicycle path, or other public right-of-way:

(a) It shall be unlawful for any parent or legal guardian of a person below the age of 16 to knowingly permit that person to operate or be a passenger on a bicycle unless at all times when the person is so engaged he or she wears a protective bicycle helmet of good fit fastened securely upon the head with the straps of the helmet.

(b) It shall be unlawful for any parent or legal guardian of a person below the age of 16 to knowingly permit that person to be a passenger on a bicycle unless all of the following conditions are met:

(1) The person is able to maintain an erect, seated position on the bicycle.

(2) Except as provided in subdivision (3) of this subsection, the person is properly seated alone on a saddle seat (as on a tandem bicycle).

(3) With respect to any person who weighs less than 40 pounds, or is less than 40 inches in height, the person can be and is properly seated in and adequately secured to a restraining seat.

(c) No negligence or liability shall be assessed on or imputed to any party on account of a violation of subsection (a) or (b) of this section.

(d) Violation of this section shall be an infraction. Except as provided in subsection (e) of this section, any parent or guardian found responsible for violation of this section may be ordered to pay a civil fine of up to ten dollars ($ 10.00), inclusive of all penalty assessments and court costs.

(e) In the case of a first conviction of this section, the court may waive the fine upon receipt of satisfactory proof that the person responsible for the infraction has purchased or otherwise obtained, as appropriate, a protective bicycle helmet or a restraining seat, and uses and intends to use it whenever required under this section.

History.
2001-268, s. 1

§§ 20-171.10 through 20-171.14

Reserved for future codification purposes.

PART 10C
OPERATION OF ALL-TERRAIN VEHICLES

§ 20-171.15. Age restrictions

(a) It is unlawful for any parent or legal guardian of a person less than eight years of age to knowingly permit that person to operate an all-terrain vehicle.

(b) Repealed by Session Laws 2015-286, s. 3.13(a), effective October 22, 2015.

(c) It is unlawful for any parent or legal guardian of a person less than 16 years of age to knowingly permit that person to operate an all-terrain vehicle in violation of the Age Restriction Warning Label affixed by the manufacturer as required by the applicable American National Standards Institute/Specialty Vehicle Institute of America (ANSI/SVIA) design standard.

(d) It is unlawful for any parent or legal guardian of a person less than 16 years of age to knowingly permit that person to operate an all-terrain vehicle unless the person is under the continuous visual supervision of a person 18 years of age or older while operating the all-terrain vehicle.

(e) Subsection (c) of this section does not apply to any parent or legal guardian of a person born on or before August 15, 1997, who permits that person to operate an all-terrain vehicle and who establishes proof that the parent or legal guardian owned the all-terrain vehicle prior to August 15, 2005.

History.
2005-282, s. 2; 2015-286, s. 3.13(a)

§ 20-171.16. Passengers

No operator of an all-terrain vehicle shall carry a passenger, except on those vehicles specifically designed by the manufacturer to carry passengers in addition to the operator.

History.
2005-282, s. 2

§ 20-171.17. Prohibited acts by sellers

No person shall knowingly sell or offer to sell an all-terrain vehicle:

(1) For use by a person under the age of eight years.

(2) In violation of the Age Restriction Warning Label affixed by the manufacturer as required by the applicable American National Standards Institute/Specialty Vehicle Institute of America (ANSI/SVIA) design standard for use by a person less than 16 years of age.

(3) Repealed by Session Laws 2015-286, s. 3.13(b), effective October 22, 2015.

History.
2005-282, s. 2; 2015-286, s. 3.13(b)

§ 20-171.18. Equipment requirements

Every all-terrain vehicle sold, offered for sale, or operated in this State shall meet the following equipment standards:

(1) It shall be equipped with a brake system maintained in good operating condition.

(2) It shall be equipped with an effective muffler system maintained in good working condition.

(3) It shall be equipped with a United States Forest Service qualified spark arrester maintained in good working condition.

History.
2005-282, s. 2

§ 20-171.19. Prohibited acts by owners and operators

(a) No person shall operate an all-terrain vehicle on a public street or highway or public vehicular area when such operation is otherwise permitted by law, unless the person wears eye protection and a safety helmet meeting United States Department of Transportation standards for motorcycle helmets.

(a1) No person under 18 years of age shall operate an all-terrain vehicle off a public street or highway or public vehicular area unless the person wears eye protection and a safety helmet meeting United States Department of Transportation standards for motorcycle helmets.

(a2) Notwithstanding subsection (a1) of this section, a person who is under 18 years of age and employed by a supplier of retail electric service, while engaged in power line inspection, may operate an all-terrain vehicle while wearing both of the following:

(1) Head protection equipped with a chin strap that conforms to the standards applicable to suppliers of retail electric service adopted by the Occupational Safety and Health Division of the North Carolina Department of Labor.

(2) Eye protection that conforms to the standards applicable to suppliers of retail electric service adopted by the Occupational Safety and Health Division of the North Carolina Department of Labor.

(b) No owner shall authorize an all-terrain vehicle to be operated contrary to this Part.

(c) No person shall operate an all-terrain vehicle while under the influence of alcohol, any controlled substance, or a prescription or non-prescription drug that impairs vision or motor coordination.

(d) No person shall operate an all-terrain vehicle in a careless or reckless manner so as to endanger or cause injury or damage to any person or property.

(e) Except as otherwise permitted by law, no person shall operate an all-terrain vehicle on any public street, road, or highway except for purposes of crossing that street, road, or highway.

(f) Except as otherwise permitted by law, no person shall operate an all-terrain vehicle at anytime on an interstate or limited-access highway.

(g) No person shall operate an all-terrain vehicle during the hours of darkness, from one-half hour after sunset to one-half hour before sunrise and at anytime when visibility is reduced due to insufficient light or atmospheric conditions, without displaying a lighted headlamp and taillamp, unless the use of lights is prohibited by other applicable laws.

History.
2005-282, s. 2; 2006-259, s. 10(a); 2011-68, s. 1; 2013-410, s. 4.2

§ 20-171.20. Safety training and certificate

Effective October 1, 2006, every all-terrain vehicle operator born on or after January 1, 1990, shall possess a safety certificate indicating successful completion of an all-terrain vehicle safety course sponsored or approved by the All-Terrain Vehicle Safety Institute or by another all-terrain vehicle safety course approved by the Commissioner of Insurance. The North Carolina Community College System is authorized to provide all-terrain vehicle safety training, approved by the Commissioner, to persons less than 18 years of age.

History.
2005-282, s. 2; 2007-433, s. 4

§ 20-171.21. Penalties

Any person violating any of the provisions of this Part shall be responsible for an infraction and may be subject to a penalty of not more than two hundred dollars ($ 200.00).

History.
2005-282, s. 2; 2008-187, s. 11

§ 20-171.22. Exceptions

(a) The provisions of this Part do not apply to any owner, operator, lessor, or renter of a farm or ranch, or that person's employees or immediate family or household members, when operating an all-terrain vehicle while engaged in farming operations.

(a1) Any person may operate an all-terrain vehicle or utility vehicle on a public street or highway while engaged in farming operations.

(b) The provisions of this Part do not apply to any person using an all-terrain vehicle for hunting or trapping purposes if the person is otherwise lawfully engaged in those activities.

(c) The provisions of G.S. 20-171.19(a1) do not apply to any person 16 years of age or older if the person is otherwise lawfully using the all-terrain vehicle on any ocean beach area where such vehicles are allowed by law. As used in this subsection, "ocean beach area" means the area adjacent to the ocean and ocean inlets that is subject to public trust rights. Natural indicators of the landward extent of the ocean beaches include, but are not limited to, the first line of stable, natural vegetation; the toe of the frontal dune; and the storm trash line.

History.
2005-282, s. 2; 2008-91, s. 1; 2011-68, s. 2; 2015-263, s. 8

§ 20-171.23. Motorized all-terrain vehicles of law enforcement officers and fire, rescue, and emergency medical services permitted on certain highways

(a) Law enforcement officers acting in the course and scope of their duties may operate motorized all-terrain vehicles owned or leased by the agency, or under the direct control of the incident commander, on: (i) public highways where the speed limit is 35 miles per hour or less; and (ii) nonfully controlled access highways with higher speeds for the purpose of traveling from a speed zone to an adjacent speed zone where the speed limit is 35 miles per hour or less.

(b) Fire, rescue, and emergency medical services personnel acting in the course and scope of their duties may operate motorized all-terrain vehicles and owned or leased by fire, rescue, or emergency medical services departments, or under the direct control of the incident commander, on: (i) public highways where the speed limit is 35 miles per hour or less; and (ii) nonfully controlled access highways with higher speeds for the purpose of traveling from a speed zone to an adjacent speed zone where the speed limit is 35 miles per hour or less.

(c) This Part and all other State laws governing the operation of all-terrain vehicles apply to the operation of all-terrain vehicles authorized by this section.

(d) An all-terrain vehicle operated pursuant to this section shall be equipped with operable front and rear lights and a horn.

(e) A person operating an all-terrain vehicle pursuant to this section shall observe posted speed limits and shall not exceed the manufacturer's recommended speed for the vehicle.

(f) A person operating an all-terrain vehicle pursuant to this section shall carry an official identification card or badge.

(g) For purposes of this section, the term "motorized all-terrain vehicle" has the same meaning as in G.S. 14-159.3, except that the term also includes utility vehicles, as defined in this Chapter.

History.
2007-433, s. 1; 2015-26, ss. 1, 2.1

§ 20-171.24. Motorized all-terrain vehicle use by municipal and county employees permitted on certain highways

(a) Municipal and county employees may operate motorized all-terrain vehicles owned or leased by the agency on: (i) public highways where the speed limit is 35 miles per hour or less; and (ii) nonfully controlled access highways with higher speeds for the purpose of traveling from a speed zone to an adjacent speed zone where the speed limit is 35 miles per hour or less.

(b) This Part and all other State laws governing the operation of all-terrain vehicles apply to the operation of all-terrain vehicles authorized by this section.

(c) An all-terrain vehicle operated pursuant to this section shall be equipped with operable front and rear lights and a horn.

(d) A person operating an all-terrain vehicle pursuant to this section shall observe posted speed limits and shall not exceed the manufacturer's recommended speed for the vehicle.

(e) A person operating an all-terrain vehicle pursuant to this section shall carry an official identification card or badge.

(e1) For purposes of this section, the term "motorized all-terrain vehicle" has the same meaning as in G.S. 14-159.3, except that the term also includes utility vehicles, as defined in this Chapter.

(f) Repealed by Session Laws 2015-26, s. 2, effective May 21, 2015.

History.
2007-433, s. 2; 2008-99, s. 1; 2010-19, s. 1; 2010-46, s. 1; 2014-32, s. 1; 2015-26, ss. 2, 2.1; 2017-102, s. 7

§ 20-171.25. Motorized all-terrain vehicle use by certain employees of natural gas utilities permitted on public highways and rights-of-way

(a) Natural gas utility employees and contractors engaged in pipeline safety, leak survey, and patrolling activities, acting in the course and scope of their employment, may operate motorized all-terrain vehicles owned or leased by the utility on public highways and rights-of-way only to the extent necessary to perform those activities.

(b) This Part and all other State laws governing the operation of all-terrain vehicles apply to the operation of all-terrain vehicles authorized by this section.

(c) An all-terrain vehicle operated pursuant to this section shall be equipped with operable front and rear lights and a horn.

(d) A person operating an all-terrain vehicle pursuant to this section shall observe posted speed limits and shall not exceed the manufacturer's recommended speed for the vehicle.

(e) A person operating an all-terrain vehicle pursuant to this section shall carry an official company identification card or badge.

History.
2008-156, s. 2

§ 20-171.26. Motorized all-terrain vehicle use by disabled sportsmen

(a) Persons qualified under the Disabled Sportsmen Program, pursuant to G.S. 113-296, are authorized to transverse public roadways using an all-terrain vehicle while engaging in licensed hunting or fishing activities. Use of the all-terrain vehicle shall be limited to driving across the roadway, in a perpendicular fashion, without travel in either direction along the roadway.

(b) This Part and all other State laws governing the operation of all-terrain vehicles apply to the operation of all-terrain vehicles authorized by this section.

(c) An all-terrain vehicle operated pursuant to this section shall be equipped with operable front and rear lights and a horn.

(d) A person operating an all-terrain vehicle pursuant to this section shall observe posted speed limits and shall not exceed the manufacturer's recommended speed for the vehicle.

(e) A person operating an all-terrain vehicle pursuant to this section shall carry evidence of

Chapter 20

membership in the Disabled Sportsmen Program and the appropriate license to engage in the hunting or fishing activity.

History.
2010-146, s. 1

PART 11
PEDESTRIANS' RIGHTS AND DUTIES

§ 20-172. Pedestrians subject to traffic-control signals

(a) The Board of Transportation, with reference to State highways, and local authorities, with reference to highways under their jurisdiction, are hereby authorized to erect or install, at intersections or other appropriate places, special pedestrian control signals exhibiting the words or symbols "WALK" or "DON'T WALK" as a part of a system of traffic-control signals or devices.

(b) Whenever special pedestrian-control signals are in place, such signals shall indicate as follows:

(1) **WALK. --** Pedestrians facing such signal may proceed across the highway in the direction of the signal and shall be given the right-of-way by the drivers of all vehicles.

(2) **DON'T WALK. --** No pedestrian shall start to cross the highway in the direction of such signal, but any pedestrian who has partially completed his crossing on the "WALK" signal shall proceed to a sidewalk or safety island while the "DON'T WALK" signal is showing.

(c) Where a system of traffic-control signals or devices does not include special pedestrian-control signals, pedestrians shall be subject to the vehicular traffic-control signals or devices as they apply to pedestrian traffic.

(d) At places without traffic-control signals or devices, pedestrians shall be accorded the privileges and shall be subject to the restrictions stated in Part 11 of this Article.

History.
1937, c. 407, s. 133; 1973, c. 507, s. 5; c. 1330, s. 31; 1987, c. 125

§ 20-173. Pedestrians' right-of-way at crosswalks

(a) Where traffic-control signals are not in place or in operation the driver of a vehicle shall yield the right-of-way, slowing down or stopping if need be to so yield, to a pedestrian crossing the roadway within any marked crosswalk or within any unmarked crosswalk at or near an

intersection, except as otherwise provided in Part 11 of this Article.

(b) Whenever any vehicle is stopped at a marked crosswalk or at any unmarked crosswalk at an intersection to permit a pedestrian to cross the roadway, the driver of any other vehicle approaching from the rear shall not overtake and pass such stopped vehicle.

(c) The driver of a vehicle emerging from or entering an alley, building entrance, private road, or driveway shall yield the right-of-way to any pedestrian, or person riding a bicycle, approaching on any sidewalk or walkway extending across such alley, building entrance, road, or driveway.

History.
1937, c. 407, s. 134; 1973, c. 1330, s. 32

§ 20-174. Crossing at other than crosswalks; walking along highway

(a) Every pedestrian crossing a roadway at any point other than within a marked crosswalk or within an unmarked crosswalk at an intersection shall yield the right-of-way to all vehicles upon the roadway.

(b) Any pedestrian crossing a roadway at a point where a pedestrian tunnel or overhead pedestrian crossing has been provided shall yield the right-of-way to all vehicles upon the roadway.

(c) Between adjacent intersections at which traffic-control signals are in operation pedestrians shall not cross at any place except in a marked crosswalk.

(d) Where sidewalks are provided, it shall be unlawful for any pedestrian to walk along and upon an adjacent roadway. Where sidewalks are not provided, any pedestrian walking along and upon a highway shall, when practicable, walk only on the extreme left of the roadway or its shoulder facing traffic which may approach from the opposite direction. Such pedestrian shall yield the right-of-way to approaching traffic.

(e) Notwithstanding the provisions of this section, every driver of a vehicle shall exercise due care to avoid colliding with any pedestrian upon any roadway, and shall give warning by sounding the horn when necessary, and shall exercise proper precaution upon observing any child or any confused or incapacitated person upon a roadway.

History.
1937, c. 407, s. 135; 1973, c. 1330, s. 33

§ 20-174.1. Standing, sitting or lying upon highways or streets prohibited

(a) No person shall willfully stand, sit, or lie upon the highway or street in such a manner as to impede the regular flow of traffic.

(b) Violation of this section is a Class 2 misdemeanor.

History.
1965, c. 137; 1969, c. 1012; 1993 (Reg. Sess., 1994), c. 761, s. 17

§ 20-174.2. Local ordinances; pedestrians gathering, picketing, or protesting on roads or highways

(a) A municipality or a county may adopt an ordinance regulating the time, place, and manner of gatherings, picket lines, or protests by pedestrians that occur on State roadways and State highways.

(b) Nothing in this section shall permit a municipality or a county to impose restrictions or prohibitions on the activities of any of the following persons who are engaged in construction or maintenance, or in making traffic or engineering surveys:

(1) Licensees, employees, or contractors of the Department of Transportation.

(2) Licensees, employees, or contractors of a municipality.

History.
2007-360, s. 6

§ 20-175. Pedestrians soliciting rides, employment, business or funds upon highways or streets

(a) No person shall stand in any portion of the State highways, except upon the shoulders thereof, for the purpose of soliciting a ride from the driver of any motor vehicle.

(b) No person shall stand or loiter in the main traveled portion, including the shoulders and median, of any State highway or street, excluding sidewalks, or stop any motor vehicle for the purpose of soliciting employment, business or contributions from the driver or occupant of any motor vehicle that impedes the normal movement of traffic on the public highways or streets: Provided that the provisions of this subsection shall not apply to licensees, employees or contractors of the Department of Transportation or of any municipality engaged in construction or maintenance or in making traffic or engineering surveys.

(c) Repealed by Session Laws 1973, c. 1330, s. 39.

(d) Local governments may enact ordinances restricting or prohibiting a person from standing on any street, highway, or right-of-way excluding sidewalks while soliciting, or attempting to solicit, any employment, business, or contributions from the driver or occupants of any vehicle. No local government may enact or enforce any ordinance that prohibits engaging in the distribution of newspapers on the non-traveled portion of any street or highway except when those distribution activities impede the normal movement of traffic on the street or highway. This subsection does not permit additional restrictions or prohibitions on the activities of licensees, employees, or contractors of the Department of Transportation or of any municipality engaged in construction or maintenance or in making traffic or engineering surveys except as provided in subsection (e) of this section.

(e) A local government shall have the authority to grant authorization for a person to stand in, on, or near a street or State roadway, within the local government's municipal corporate limits, to solicit a charitable contribution if the requirements of this subsection are met.

A person seeking authorization under this subsection to solicit charitable contributions shall file a written application with the local government. This application shall be filed not later than seven days before the date the solicitation event is to occur. If there are multiple events or one event occurring on more than one day, each event shall be subject to the application and permit requirements of this subsection for each day the event is to be held, to include the application fee.

The application must include:

(1) The date and time when the solicitation is to occur;

(2) Each location at which the solicitation is to occur; and

(3) The number of solicitors to be involved in the solicitation at each location.

This subsection does not prohibit a local government from charging a fee for a permit, but in no case shall the fee be greater than twenty-five dollars ($ 25.00) per day per event.

The applicant shall also furnish to the local government advance proof of liability insurance in the amount of at least two million dollars ($ 2,000,000) to cover damages that may arise from the solicitation. The insurance coverage must provide coverage for claims against any solicitor and agree to hold the local government harmless.

A local government, by acting under this section, does not waive, or limit, any immunity or create any new liability for the local government. The issuance of an authorization under this section and the conducting of the solicitation authorized are not considered governmental functions of the local government.

In the event the solicitation event or the solicitors shall create a nuisance, delay traffic, create threatening or hostile situations, any law enforcement officer with proper jurisdiction may order the solicitations to cease. Any individual failing to follow a law enforcement officer's lawful order to cease solicitation shall be guilty of a Class 2 misdemeanor.

History.
1937, c. 407, s. 136; 1965, c. 673; 1973, c. 507, s. 5; c. 1330, s. 39; 1977, c. 464, s. 34; 2005-310, s. 1; 2006-250, ss. 7(a), 7(b); 2008-223, s. 1

PART 11A
BLIND PEDESTRIANS --
WHITE CANES OR
GUIDE DOGS

§ 20-175.1. Public use of white canes by other than blind persons prohibited

It shall be unlawful for any person, except one who is wholly or partially blind, to carry or use on any street or highway, or in any other public place, a cane or walking stick which is white in color or white tipped with red.

History.
1949, c. 324, s. 1

§ 20-175.2. Right-of-way at crossings, intersections and traffic-control signal points; white cane or guide dog to serve as signal for the blind

At any street, road or highway crossing or intersection, where the movement of traffic is not regulated by a traffic officer or by traffic-control signals, any blind or partially blind pedestrian shall be entitled to the right-of-way at such crossing or intersection, if such blind or partially blind pedestrian shall extend before him at arm's length a cane white in color or white tipped with red, or if such person is accompanied by a guide dog. Upon receiving such a signal, all vehicles at or approaching such intersection or crossing shall come to a full stop, leaving a clear lane through which such pedestrian may pass, and such vehicle shall remain stationary until such blind or partially blind pedestrian has completed the passage of such crossing or intersection. At any street, road or highway crossing or intersection, where the movement of traffic is regulated by traffic-control signals, blind or partially blind pedestrians shall be entitled to the right-of-way if such person having such cane or accompanied by a guide dog shall be partly across such crossing or intersection at the time the traffic-control signals change, and all vehicles shall stop and remain stationary until such pedestrian has completed passage across the intersection or crossing.

History.
1949, c. 324, s. 2

§ 20-175.3. Rights and privileges of blind persons without white cane or guide dog

Nothing contained in this Part shall be construed to deprive any blind or partially blind person not carrying a cane white in color or white tipped with red, or being accompanied by a guide dog, of any of the rights and privileges conferred by law upon pedestrians crossing streets and highways, nor shall the failure of such blind or partially blind person to carry a cane white in color or white tipped with red, or to be accompanied by a guide dog, upon the streets, roads, highways or sidewalks of this State, be held to constitute or be evidence of contributory negligence by virtue of this Part.

History.
1949, c. 324, s. 3

N.C. Gen. Stat. § 20-175.4

Repealed by Session Laws 1973, c. 1330, s. 39.

PART 11B
PEDESTRIAN RIGHTS AND
DUTIES OF PERSONS WITH A
MOBILITY IMPAIRMENT

§ 20-175.5. Use of motorized wheelchairs or similar vehicles not exceeding 1000 pounds gross weight

While a person with a mobility impairment as defined in G.S. 20-37.5 operates a motorized wheelchair or similar vehicle not exceeding 1000 pounds gross weight in order to provide that person with the mobility of a pedestrian, that person is subject to all the laws, ordinances, regulations, rights and responsibilities which would otherwise apply to a pedestrian, but is not subject to Part 10 of this Article or any other law, ordinance or regulation otherwise applicable to motor vehicles.

History.
1991, c. 206, s. 1

PART 11C
ELECTRIC PERSONAL
ASSISTIVE MOBILITY
DEVICES

§ 20-175.6. Electric personal assistive mobility devices

(a) **Electric Personal Assistive Mobility Device.** -- As defined in G.S. 20-4.01(7b).

(b) **Exempt From Registration.** -- As provided in G.S. 20-51.

(c) **Use of Device.** -- An electric personal assistive mobility device may be operated on public highways with posted speeds of 25 miles per hour or less, sidewalks, and bicycle paths. A person operating an electric personal assistive mobility device on a sidewalk, roadway, or bicycle path shall yield the right-of-way to pedestrians and other human-powered devices. A person operating an electric personal assistive mobility device shall have all rights and duties of a pedestrian, including the rights and duties set forth in Part 11 of this Article.

(d) **Municipal Regulation.** -- For the purpose of assuring the safety of persons using highways and sidewalks, municipalities having jurisdiction over public streets, sidewalks, alleys, bridges, and other ways of public passage may by ordinance regulate the time, place, and manner of the operation of electric personal assistive mobility devices, but shall not prohibit their use.

History.
2002-98, s. 5; 2016-90, s. 13(d)

§§ 20-175.7 through 20-175.14

Reserved for future codification purposes.

PART 11D
PERSONAL DELIVERY DEVICES

§ 20-175.15. Definitions

The following definitions apply to this Part:

(1) **Agent.** -- A director, officer, employee, or other person authorized to act on behalf of a business entity.

(2) **Business entity.** -- A corporation, limited liability company, partnership, sole proprietorship, or other legal entity authorized to conduct business under the laws of this State.

(3) **Operator.** -- An agent who is 16 years of age or older and is charged with the responsibility of monitoring and operating a personal delivery device.

(4) **Pedestrian area.** -- A sidewalk, crosswalk, school crosswalk, school crossing zone, or safety zone.

(5) **Personal delivery device.** -- As defined in G.S. 20-4.01.

History.
2020-73, s. 2

§ 20-175.16. Personal delivery devices authorized; operation; equipment

(a) A business entity may operate a personal delivery device in a pedestrian area or on a highway, with the rights and duties applicable to a pedestrian under this Chapter, subject to the requirements and restrictions of this Part. Except as authorized in this Part, no person may operate a personal delivery device in a pedestrian area or on a highway in this State.

(b) Operation of a personal delivery device shall comply with all of the following:

(1) The personal delivery device shall be monitored by an operator who is able to exercise remote control over the navigation and operation of the personal delivery device.

(2) The personal delivery device may not be operated in a pedestrian area at a speed greater than 10 miles per hour.

(3) The personal delivery device may not be operated on a highway except as necessary to cross a highway or along a highway if a sidewalk is not provided or accessible. When operating along a highway under this subdivision, the following additional restrictions apply:

    a. The personal delivery device shall be operated on the shoulder or as close as practicable to the extreme right of the highway in the direction of authorized traffic movement and shall yield the right-of-way to all vehicles.

    b. The personal delivery device may not be operated on a highway at a speed greater than 20 miles per hour.

    c. The personal delivery device may not be operated on a highway with a speed limit greater than 35 miles per hour.

(4) The personal delivery device shall obey all traffic and pedestrian control devices and signs.

(5) The personal delivery device shall yield the right-of-way to all human pedestrians.

(6) The personal delivery device shall not unreasonably interfere with any vehicle or pedestrian.

(7) The personal delivery device shall not transport materials regulated under the Hazardous Materials Transportation Act (49 U.S.C. §§ 5101 -- 5128) that require placarding pursuant to Subpart F of 49 C.F.R. Part 172 (49 C.F.R. §§ 172.500 -- 172.560).

(c) A personal delivery device shall be equipped with all of the following:

(1) A marker that clearly states the name and contact information of the owner and a unique identification number.

(2) A braking system that enables the device to come to a controlled stop.

(3) When operated at night, lights on the front and rear of the personal delivery

device that are visible and recognizable under normal atmospheric conditions from at least 500 feet on all sides of the personal delivery device.

(d) A violation of this section is an infraction.

History.
2020-73, s. 2

§ 20-175.17. (Effective until December 1, 2022) Local regulation

For the purpose of assuring the safety of persons using highways and sidewalks, a local government having jurisdiction over public streets, sidewalks, alleys, bridges, and other ways of public passage may by ordinance regulate time and place of the operation of personal delivery devices, but shall not prohibit their use.

History.
2020-73, s. 2

§ 20-175.17. (Effective December 1, 2022) Local regulation

For the purpose of assuring the safety of persons using highways and sidewalks, a local government having jurisdiction over public streets, sidewalks, alleys, bridges, and other ways of public passage may by ordinance prohibit operation of personal delivery devices within its jurisdiction if the local government determines that the prohibition is necessary.

History.
2020-73, ss. 2, 3(a)

§ 20-175.18. Insurance

A business entity that operates a personal delivery device under this Part shall maintain an insurance policy that includes general liability coverage of not less than one hundred thousand dollars ($ 100,000) per claim for damages arising from the operation of the personal delivery device.

History.
2020-73, s. 2

PART 12
SENTENCING; PENALTIES

§ 20-176. Penalty for misdemeanor or infraction

(a) Violation of a provision of Part 9, 10, 10A, or 11 of this Article is an infraction unless the violation is specifically declared by law to be

a misdemeanor or felony. Except as otherwise provided in subsection (a1) of this section, violation of the remaining Parts of this Article is a misdemeanor unless the violation is specifically declared by law to be an infraction or a felony.

(a1) A person who does any of the following is responsible for an infraction:

(1) Fails to carry the registration card in the vehicle, in violation of G.S. 20-57(c).

(2) Repealed by Session Laws 2016-90, s. 12(b), effective December 1, 2016, and applicable to registration cards issued on or after that date.

(3) Fails to notify the Division of an address change for a vehicle registration card within 60 days after the change occurs, in violation of G.S. 20-67.

(b) Unless a specific penalty is otherwise provided by law, a person found responsible for an infraction contained in this Article may be ordered to pay a penalty of not more than one hundred dollars ($ 100.00).

(c) Unless a specific penalty is otherwise provided by law, a person convicted of a misdemeanor contained in this Article is guilty of a Class 2 misdemeanor. A punishment is specific for purposes of this subsection if it contains a quantitative limit on the term of imprisonment or the amount of fine a judge can impose.

(c1) Repealed by Session Laws 2014-100, s. 16C.1(c), effective October 1, 2014.

(c2) Repealed by Session Laws 2013-385, s. 5, effective December 1, 2013.

(d) For purposes of determining whether a violation of an offense contained in this Chapter constitutes negligence per se, crimes and infractions shall be treated identically.

History.
1937, c. 407, s. 137; 1951, c. 1013, s. 7; 1957, c. 1255; 1967, c. 674, s. 3; 1969, c. 378, s. 3; 1973, c. 1330, s. 34; 1975, c. 644; 1985, c. 764, s. 20; 1985 (Reg. Sess., 1986), c. 852, ss. 7, 17; c. 1014, s. 202; 1993, c. 539, s. 379; 1994, Ex. Sess., c. 24, s. 14(c); 2013-360, s. 18B.14(h); 2013-385, s. 5; 2014-100, s. 16C.1(c); 2016-90, s. 12(b)

§ 20-177. Penalty for felony

Any person who shall be convicted of a violation of any of the provisions of this Article herein or by the laws of this State declared to constitute a felony shall, unless a different penalty is prescribed herein or by the laws of this State, be punished as a Class I felon.

History.
1937, c. 407, s. 138; 1979, c. 760, s. 5; 1979, 2nd Sess., c. 1316, s. 47; 1981, c. 63, s. 1; c. 179, s. 14

§ 20-178. Penalty for bad check

When any person, firm, or corporation shall tender to the Division any uncertified check for payment of any tax, fee or other obligation due by him under the provisions of this Article, and the bank upon which such check shall be drawn shall refuse to pay it on account of insufficient funds of the drawer on deposit in such bank, and such check shall be returned to the Division, an additional tax shall be imposed by the Division upon such person, firm or corporation, which additional tax shall be equal to ten percent (10%) of the tax or fee in payment of which such check was tendered: Provided, that in no case shall the additional tax be less than ten dollars ($ 10.00); provided, further, that no additional tax shall be imposed if, at the time such check was presented for payment, the drawer had on deposit in any bank of this State funds sufficient to pay such check and by inadvertence failed to draw the check upon such bank, or upon the proper account therein. The additional tax imposed by this section shall not be waived or diminished by the Division.

History.
1937, c. 407, s. 139; 1953, c. 1144; 1975, c. 716, s. 5; 1981, c. 690, s. 24

§ 20-178.1. Payment and review of civil penalty imposed by Department of Public Safety

(a) **Procedure.** -- A person who is assessed a civil penalty under this Article by the Department of Public Safety must pay the penalty within 30 calendar days after the date the penalty was assessed or make a written request within this time limit to the Department for a Departmental review of the penalty. A person who does not submit a request for review within the required time waives the right to a review and hearing on the penalty.

(b) **Department Review.** -- Any person who denies liability for a penalty imposed by the Department may request an informal review by the Secretary of the Department or the Secretary's designee. The request must be made in writing and must contain sufficient information for the Secretary, or the Secretary's designee, to determine the specific basis upon which liability is being challenged. Upon receiving a request for informal review, the Secretary, or the Secretary's designee, shall review the record and determine whether the penalty was assessed in error. If, after reviewing the record, the Secretary, or the Secretary's designee, determines that the assessment or a portion thereof was not issued in error, the penalty must be paid within 30 days of the notice of decision.

(c) **Judicial Review.** -- Any person who is dissatisfied with the decision of the Secretary and who has paid the penalty in full within 30 days of the notice of decision, as required by subsection (b) of this section, may, within 60 days of the decision, bring an action for refund of the penalty against the Department in the Superior Court of Wake County or in the superior court of the county in which the civil penalty was assessed. The court shall review the Secretary's decision and shall make findings of fact and conclusions of law. The hearing shall be conducted by the court without a jury. In reviewing the case, the court shall not give deference to the prior decision of the Secretary. A superior court may award attorneys' fees to a prevailing plaintiff only upon a showing of bad faith on the part of the Department, and any order for attorneys' fees must be supported by findings of fact and conclusions of law.

(d) **Interest.** -- Interest accrues on a penalty that is overdue. A penalty is overdue if it is not paid within the time required by this section. Interest is payable on a penalty assessed in error from the date the penalty was paid. The interest rate set in G.S. 105-241.21 applies to interest payable under this section.

(e) The clear proceeds of all civil penalties assessed by the Department pursuant to this Article, minus any fees paid as interest, filing fees, attorneys' fees, or other necessary costs of court associated with the defense of penalties imposed by the Department pursuant to this Article shall be remitted to the Civil Penalty and Forfeiture Fund in accordance with G.S. 115C-457.2.

History.
2009-376, s. 2(a); 2011-145, s. 19.1(g)

§ 20-179. Sentencing hearing after conviction for impaired driving; determination of grossly aggravating and aggravating and mitigating factors; punishments

(a) **Sentencing Hearing Required.** -- After a conviction under G.S. 20-138.1, G.S. 20-138.2, a second or subsequent conviction under G.S. 20-138.2A, or a second or subsequent conviction under G.S. 20-138.2B, or when any of those offenses are remanded back to district court after an appeal to superior court, the judge shall hold a sentencing hearing to determine whether there are aggravating or mitigating factors that affect the sentence to be imposed. The following apply:

(1) The court shall consider evidence of aggravating or mitigating factors present in the offense that make an aggravated or mitigated sentence appropriate. The State bears the burden of proving beyond a

reasonable doubt that an aggravating factor exists, and the offender bears the burden of proving by a preponderance of the evidence that a mitigating factor exists.

(2) Before the hearing the prosecutor shall make all feasible efforts to secure the defendant's full record of traffic convictions, and shall present to the judge that record for consideration in the hearing. Upon request of the defendant, the prosecutor shall furnish the defendant or the defendant's attorney a copy of the defendant's record of traffic convictions at a reasonable time prior to the introduction of the record into evidence. In addition, the prosecutor shall present all other appropriate grossly aggravating and aggravating factors of which the prosecutor is aware, and the defendant or the defendant's attorney may present all appropriate mitigating factors. In every instance in which a valid chemical analysis is made of the defendant, the prosecutor shall present evidence of the resulting alcohol concentration.

(a1) **Jury Trial in Superior Court; Jury Procedure if Trial Bifurcated. --**

(1) **Notice. --** If the defendant appeals to superior court, and the State intends to use one or more aggravating factors under subsections (c) or (d) of this section, the State must provide the defendant with notice of its intent. The notice shall be provided no later than 10 days prior to trial and shall contain a plain and concise factual statement indicating the factor or factors it intends to use under the authority of subsections (c) and (d) of this section. The notice must list all the aggravating factors that the State seeks to establish.

(2) **Aggravating factors. --** The defendant may admit to the existence of an aggravating factor, and the factor so admitted shall be treated as though it were found by a jury pursuant to the procedures in this section. If the defendant does not so admit, only a jury may determine if an aggravating factor is present. The jury impaneled for the trial may, in the same trial, also determine if one or more aggravating factors is present, unless the court determines that the interests of justice require that a separate sentencing proceeding be used to make that determination. If the court determines that a separate proceeding is required, the proceeding shall be conducted by the trial judge before the trial jury as soon as practicable after the guilty verdict is returned. The State bears the burden of proving beyond a reasonable doubt that an aggravating factor exists, and the offender bears the burden of proving by a preponderance of the evidence that a mitigating factor exists.

(3) **Convening the jury. --** If at any time prior to rendering a decision to the court regarding whether one or more aggravating factors exist, any juror dies, becomes incapacitated or disqualified, or is discharged for any reason, an alternate juror shall become a part of the jury and serve in all respects as those selected on the regular trial panel. An alternate juror shall become a part of the jury in the order in which the juror was selected. If an alternate juror replaces a juror after deliberations have begun, the court must instruct the jury to begin its deliberations anew. In no event shall more than 12 jurors participate in the jury's deliberations. If the trial jury is unable to reconvene for a hearing on the issue of whether one or more aggravating factors exist after having determined the guilt of the accused, the trial judge shall impanel a new jury to determine the issue.

(4) **Jury selection. --** A jury selected to determine whether one or more aggravating factors exist shall be selected in the same manner as juries are selected for the trial of criminal cases.

(a2) **Jury Trial on Aggravating Factors in Superior Court. --**

(1) **Defendant admits aggravating factor only. --** If the defendant admits that an aggravating factor exists, but pleads not guilty to the underlying charge, a jury shall be impaneled to dispose of the charge only. In that case, evidence that relates solely to the establishment of an aggravating factor shall not be admitted in the trial.

(2) **Defendant pleads guilty to the charge only. --** If the defendant pleads guilty to the charge, but contests the existence of one or more aggravating factors, a jury shall be impaneled to determine if the aggravating factor or factors exist.

(a3) **Procedure When Jury Trial Waived. --** If a defendant waives the right to a jury trial under G.S. 15A-1201, the trial judge shall make all findings that are conferred upon the jury under the provisions of this section.

(b) Repealed by Session Laws 1983, c. 435, s. 29.

(c) **Determining Existence of Grossly Aggravating Factors. --** At the sentencing hearing, based upon the evidence presented at trial and in the hearing, the judge, or the jury in superior court, must first determine whether there are any grossly aggravating factors in the case. Whether a prior conviction exists under subdivision (1) of this subsection, or whether a conviction exists under subdivision (d)(5) of this section, shall be matters to be determined by the judge, and not the jury, in district or superior court. If the sentencing hearing is for a case remanded back to district court from superior court, the judge shall determine whether the defendant has been convicted of any offense that was not considered at the initial sentencing hearing and impose the appropriate sentence under this section. The judge must impose the Aggravated Level One punishment under subsection (f3) of this section if it is determined that three or more grossly aggravating factors apply. The judge must impose the Level One punishment under subsection (g) of this section if it is determined that the grossly aggravating factor in subdivision (4) of this subsection applies or two of the other grossly aggravating factors apply. If the judge does not find that the aggravating factor at subdivision (4) of this subsection applies, then the judge must impose the Level Two punishment under subsection (h) of this section if it is determined that only one of the other grossly aggravating factors applies. The grossly aggravating factors are:

(1) A prior conviction for an offense involving impaired driving if:

a. The conviction occurred within seven years before the date of the offense for which the defendant is being sentenced; or

b. The conviction occurs after the date of the offense for which the defendant is presently being sentenced, but prior to or contemporaneously with the present sentencing; or

c. The conviction occurred in district court; the case was appealed to superior court; the appeal has been withdrawn, or the case has been remanded back to district court; and a new sentencing hearing has not been held pursuant to G.S. 20-38.7.

Each prior conviction is a separate grossly aggravating factor.

(2) Driving by the defendant at the time of the offense while the defendant's driver's license was revoked pursuant to G.S. 20-28(a1).

(3) Serious injury to another person caused by the defendant's impaired driving at the time of the offense.

(4) Driving by the defendant while (i) a child under the age of 18 years, (ii) a person with the mental development of a child under the age of 18 years, or (iii) a person with a physical disability preventing unaided exit from the vehicle was in the vehicle at the time of the offense.

In imposing an Aggravated Level One, a Level One, or a Level Two punishment, the judge may consider the aggravating and mitigating factors in subsections (d) and (e) of this section in determining the appropriate sentence. If there are no grossly aggravating factors in the case, the judge must weigh all aggravating and mitigating

factors and impose punishment as required by subsection (f) of this section.

(c1) **Written Findings.** -- The court shall make findings of the aggravating and mitigating factors present in the offense. If the jury finds factors in aggravation, the court shall ensure that those findings are entered in the court's determination of sentencing factors form or any comparable document used to record the findings of sentencing factors. Findings shall be in writing.

(d) **Aggravating Factors to Be Weighed.** -- The judge, or the jury in superior court, shall determine before sentencing under subsection (f) of this section whether any of the aggravating factors listed below apply to the defendant. The judge shall weigh the seriousness of each aggravating factor in the light of the particular circumstances of the case. The factors are:

(1) Gross impairment of the defendant's faculties while driving or an alcohol concentration of 0.15 or more within a relevant time after the driving. For purposes of this subdivision, the results of a chemical analysis presented at trial or sentencing shall be sufficient to prove the person's alcohol concentration, shall be conclusive, and shall not be subject to modification by any party, with or without approval by the court.

(2) Especially reckless or dangerous driving.

(3) Negligent driving that led to a reportable accident.

(4) Driving by the defendant while the defendant's driver's license was revoked.

(5) Two or more prior convictions of a motor vehicle offense not involving impaired driving for which at least three points are assigned under G.S. 20-16 or for which the convicted person's license is subject to revocation, if the convictions occurred within five years of the date of the offense for which the defendant is being sentenced, or one or more prior convictions of an offense involving impaired driving that occurred more than seven years before the date of the offense for which the defendant is being sentenced.

(6) Conviction under G.S. 20-141.5 of speeding by the defendant while fleeing or attempting to elude apprehension.

(7) Conviction under G.S. 20-141 of speeding by the defendant by at least 30 miles per hour over the legal limit.

(8) Passing a stopped school bus in violation of G.S. 20-217.

(9) Any other factor that aggravates the seriousness of the offense.

Except for the factor in subdivision (5) of this subsection the conduct constituting the aggravating factor shall occur during the same transaction or occurrence as the impaired driving offense.

(e) **Mitigating Factors to Be Weighed. --** The judge shall also determine before sentencing under subsection (f) of this section whether any of the mitigating factors listed below apply to the defendant. The judge shall weigh the degree of mitigation of each factor in light of the particular circumstances of the case. The factors are:

(1) Slight impairment of the defendant's faculties resulting solely from alcohol, and an alcohol concentration that did not exceed 0.09 at any relevant time after the driving.

(2) Slight impairment of the defendant's faculties, resulting solely from alcohol, with no chemical analysis having been available to the defendant.

(3) Driving at the time of the offense that was safe and lawful except for the impairment of the defendant's faculties.

(4) A safe driving record, with the defendant's having no conviction for any motor vehicle offense for which at least four points are assigned under G.S. 20-16 or for which the person's license is subject to revocation within five years of the date of the offense for which the defendant is being sentenced.

(5) Impairment of the defendant's faculties caused primarily by a lawfully prescribed drug for an existing medical condition, and the amount of the drug taken was within the prescribed dosage.

(6) The defendant's voluntary submission to a mental health facility for assessment after being charged with the impaired driving offense for which the defendant is being sentenced, and, if recommended by the facility, voluntary participation in the recommended treatment.

(6a) Completion of a substance abuse assessment, compliance with its recommendations, and simultaneously maintaining 60 days of continuous abstinence from alcohol consumption, as proven by a continuous alcohol monitoring system. The continuous alcohol monitoring system shall be of a type approved by the Division of Adult Correction and Juvenile Justice of the Department of Public Safety.

(7) Any other factor that mitigates the seriousness of the offense.

Except for the factors in subdivisions (4), (6), (6a), and (7) of this subsection, the conduct constituting the mitigating factor shall occur during the same transaction or occurrence as the impaired driving offense.

(f) **Weighing the Aggravating and Mitigating Factors. --** If the judge or the jury in the sentencing hearing determines that there are no grossly aggravating factors, the judge shall weigh all aggravating and mitigating factors listed in subsections (d) and (e) of this section. If the judge determines that:

(1) The aggravating factors substantially outweigh any mitigating factors, the judge shall note in the judgment the factors found and the judge's finding that the defendant is subject to the Level Three punishment and impose a punishment within the limits defined in subsection (i) of this section.

(2) There are no aggravating and mitigating factors, or that aggravating factors are substantially counterbalanced by mitigating factors, the judge shall note in the judgment any factors found and the finding that the defendant is subject to the Level Four punishment and impose a punishment within the limits defined in subsection (j) of this section.

(3) The mitigating factors substantially outweigh any aggravating factors, the judge shall note in the judgment the factors found and the judge's finding that the defendant is subject to the Level Five punishment and impose a punishment within the limits defined in subsection (k) of this section.

It is not a mitigating factor that the driver of the vehicle was suffering from alcoholism, drug addiction, diminished capacity, or mental disease or defect. Evidence of these matters may be received in the sentencing hearing, however, for use by the judge in formulating terms and conditions of sentence after determining which punishment level shall be imposed.

(f1) **Aider and Abettor Punishment. --** Notwithstanding any other provisions of this section, a person convicted of impaired driving under G.S. 20-138.1 under the common law concept of aiding and abetting is subject to Level Five punishment. The judge need not make any findings of grossly aggravating, aggravating, or mitigating factors in such cases.

(f2) **Limit on Consolidation of Judgments. --** Except as provided in subsection (f1) of this section, in each charge of impaired driving for which there is a conviction the judge shall determine if the sentencing factors described in subsections (c), (d) and (e) of this section are applicable unless the impaired driving charge is consolidated with a charge carrying a greater punishment. Two or more impaired driving charges may not be consolidated for judgment.

(f3) **Aggravated Level One Punishment. --** A defendant subject to Aggravated Level One punishment may be fined up to ten thousand dollars ($ 10,000) and shall be sentenced to a term of imprisonment that includes a minimum term of not less than 12 months and a maximum term of not more than 36 months.

Chapter 20

Notwithstanding G.S. 15A-1371, a defendant sentenced to a term of imprisonment pursuant to this subsection shall not be eligible for parole. However, the defendant shall be released from the Statewide Misdemeanant Confinement Program on the date equivalent to the defendant's maximum imposed term of imprisonment less four months and shall be supervised by the Section of Community Supervision of the Division of Adult Correction and Juvenile Justice under and subject to the provisions of Article 84A of Chapter 15A of the General Statutes and shall also be required to abstain from alcohol consumption for the four-month period of supervision as verified by a continuous alcohol monitoring system. For purposes of revocation, violation of the requirement to abstain from alcohol or comply with the use of a continuous alcohol monitoring system shall be deemed a controlling condition under G.S. 15A-1368.4.

The term of imprisonment may be suspended only if a condition of special probation is imposed to require the defendant to serve a term of imprisonment of at least 120 days. If the defendant is placed on probation, the judge shall impose as requirements that the defendant (i) abstain from alcohol consumption for a minimum of 120 days to a maximum of the term of probation, as verified by a continuous alcohol monitoring system pursuant to subsection (h1) of this section, and (ii) obtain a substance abuse assessment and the education or treatment required by G.S. 20-17.6 for the restoration of a drivers license and as a condition of probation. The judge may impose any other lawful condition of probation.

(g) **Level One Punishment.** -- A defendant subject to Level One punishment may be fined up to four thousand dollars ($ 4,000) and shall be sentenced to a term of imprisonment that includes a minimum term of not less than 30 days and a maximum term of not more than 24 months. The term of imprisonment may be suspended only if a condition of special probation is imposed to require the defendant to serve a term of imprisonment of at least 30 days. A judge may reduce the minimum term of imprisonment required to a term of not less than 10 days if a condition of special probation is imposed to require that a defendant abstain from alcohol consumption and be monitored by a continuous alcohol monitoring system, of a type approved by the Division of Adult Correction and Juvenile Justice of the Department of Public Safety, for a period of not less than 120 days. If the defendant is monitored on an approved continuous alcohol monitoring system during the pretrial period, up to 60 days of pretrial monitoring may be credited against the 120-day monitoring requirement for probation. If the defendant is placed on probation, the judge shall impose a requirement that the defendant

obtain a substance abuse assessment and the education or treatment required by G.S. 20-17.6 for the restoration of a drivers license and as a condition of probation. The judge may impose any other lawful condition of probation.

(h) **Level Two Punishment.** -- A defendant subject to Level Two punishment may be fined up to two thousand dollars ($ 2,000) and shall be sentenced to a term of imprisonment that includes a minimum term of not less than seven days and a maximum term of not more than 12 months. The term of imprisonment may be suspended only if a condition of special probation is imposed to require the defendant to serve a term of imprisonment of at least seven days or to abstain from consuming alcohol for at least 90 consecutive days, as verified by a continuous alcohol monitoring system, of a type approved by the Division of Adult Correction and Juvenile Justice of the Department of Public Safety. If the defendant is subject to Level Two punishment based on a finding that the grossly aggravating factor in subdivision (1) or (2) of subsection (c) of this section applies, the conviction for a prior offense involving impaired driving occurred within five years before the date of the offense for which the defendant is being sentenced and the judge suspends all active terms of imprisonment and imposes abstention from alcohol as verified by a continuous alcohol monitory system, then the judge must also impose as an additional condition of special probation that the defendant must complete 240 hours of community service. If the defendant is monitored on an approved continuous alcohol monitoring system during the pretrial period, up to 60 days of pretrial monitoring may be credited against the 90-day monitoring requirement for probation. If the defendant is placed on probation, the judge shall impose a requirement that the defendant obtain a substance abuse assessment and the education or treatment required by G.S. 20-17.6 for the restoration of a drivers license and as a condition of probation. The judge may impose any other lawful condition of probation.

(h1) **Alcohol Abstinence as Condition of Probation for Level One and Level Two Punishments.** -- The judge may impose, as a condition of probation for defendants subject to Level One or Level Two punishments, that the defendant abstain from alcohol consumption for a minimum of 30 days, to a maximum of the term of probation, as verified by a continuous alcohol monitoring system. The defendant's abstinence from alcohol shall be verified by a continuous alcohol monitoring system of a type approved by the Division of Adult Correction and Juvenile Justice of the Department of Public Safety.

(h2) Repealed by Session Laws 2011-191, s. 1, effective December 1, 2011, and applicable to offenses committed on or after that date.

(h3) Repealed by Session Laws 2012-146, s. 9, effective December 1, 2012.

(i) **Level Three Punishment. --** A defendant subject to Level Three punishment may be fined up to one thousand dollars ($ 1,000) and shall be sentenced to a term of imprisonment that includes a minimum term of not less than 72 hours and a maximum term of not more than six months. The term of imprisonment may be suspended. However, the suspended sentence shall include the condition that the defendant:

(1) Be imprisoned for a term of at least 72 hours as a condition of special probation; or

(2) Perform community service for a term of at least 72 hours; or

(3) Repealed by Session Laws 2006-253, s. 23, effective December 1, 2006, and applicable to offenses committed on or after that date.

(4) Any combination of these conditions.

If the defendant is placed on probation, the judge shall impose a requirement that the defendant obtain a substance abuse assessment and the education or treatment required by G.S. 20-17.6 for the restoration of a drivers license and as a condition of probation. The judge may impose any other lawful condition of probation.

(j) **Level Four Punishment. --** A defendant subject to Level Four punishment may be fined up to five hundred dollars ($ 500.00) and shall be sentenced to a term of imprisonment that includes a minimum term of not less than 48 hours and a maximum term of not more than 120 days. The term of imprisonment may be suspended. However, the suspended sentence shall include the condition that the defendant:

(1) Be imprisoned for a term of 48 hours as a condition of special probation; or

(2) Perform community service for a term of 48 hours; or

(3) Repealed by Session Laws 2006-253, s. 23, effective December 1, 2006, and applicable to offenses committed on or after that date.

(4) Any combination of these conditions.

If the defendant is placed on probation, the judge shall impose a requirement that the defendant obtain a substance abuse assessment and the education or treatment required by G.S. 20-17.6 for the restoration of a drivers license and as a condition of probation. The judge may impose any other lawful condition of probation.

(k) **Level Five Punishment. --** A defendant subject to Level Five punishment may be fined up to two hundred dollars ($ 200.00) and shall be sentenced to a term of imprisonment that includes a minimum term of not less than 24 hours and a maximum term of not more than 60 days. The term of imprisonment may be

suspended. However, the suspended sentence shall include the condition that the defendant:

(1) Be imprisoned for a term of 24 hours as a condition of special probation; or

(2) Perform community service for a term of 24 hours; or

(3) Repealed by Session Laws 2006-253, s. 23, effective December 1, 2006, and applicable to offenses committed on or after that date.

(4) Any combination of these conditions.

If the defendant is placed on probation, the judge shall impose a requirement that the defendant obtain a substance abuse assessment and the education or treatment required by G.S. 20-17.6 for the restoration of a drivers license and as a condition of probation. The judge may impose any other lawful condition of probation.

(k1) **Credit for Inpatient Treatment. --** Pursuant to G.S. 15A-1351(a), the judge may order that a term of imprisonment imposed as a condition of special probation under any level of punishment be served as an inpatient in a facility operated or licensed by the State for the treatment of alcoholism or substance abuse where the defendant has been accepted for admission or commitment as an inpatient. The defendant shall bear the expense of any treatment unless the trial judge orders that the costs be absorbed by the State. The judge may impose restrictions on the defendant's ability to leave the premises of the treatment facility and require that the defendant follow the rules of the treatment facility. The judge may credit against the active sentence imposed on a defendant the time the defendant was an inpatient at the treatment facility, provided such treatment occurred after the commission of the offense for which the defendant is being sentenced. This section shall not be construed to limit the authority of the judge in sentencing under any other provisions of law.

(k2) **Probationary Requirement for Abstinence and Use of Continuous Alcohol Monitoring. --** The judge may order that as a condition of special probation for any level of offense under G.S. 20-179 the defendant abstain from alcohol consumption, as verified by a continuous alcohol monitoring system, of a type approved by the Division of Adult Correction and Juvenile Justice of the Department of Public Safety.

(k3) **Continuous Alcohol Monitoring During Probation. --** The court, in the sentencing order, may authorize probation officers to require defendants to submit to continuous alcohol monitoring for assessment purposes if the defendant has been required to abstain from alcohol consumption during the term of probation and the probation officer believes the defendant is consuming alcohol. The defendant shall bear the costs of the continuous alcohol monitoring system if the use of the system has been authorized by a judge in accordance with this subsection.

(k4) **Continuous Alcohol Monitoring Exception.** -- Notwithstanding the provisions of subsections (g), (h), (k2), and (k3) of this section, if the court finds, upon good cause shown, that the defendant should not be required to pay the costs of the continuous alcohol monitoring system, the court shall not impose the use of a continuous alcohol monitoring system unless the local governmental entity responsible for the incarceration of the defendant in the local confinement facility agrees to pay the costs of the system.

(*l*) Repealed by Session Laws 1989, c. 691.

(m) Repealed by Session Laws 1995, c. 496, s. 2.

(n) **Time Limits for Performance of Community Service.** -- If the judgment requires the defendant to perform a specified number of hours of community service, a minimum of 24 hours must be ordered.

(o) **Evidentiary Standards; Proof of Prior Convictions.** -- In the sentencing hearing, the State shall prove any grossly aggravating or aggravating factor beyond a reasonable doubt, and the defendant shall prove any mitigating factor by the greater weight of the evidence. Evidence adduced by either party at trial may be utilized in the sentencing hearing. Except as modified by this section, the procedure in G.S. 15A-1334(b) governs. The judge may accept any evidence as to the presence or absence of previous convictions that the judge finds reliable but shall give prima facie effect to convictions recorded by the Division or any other agency of the State of North Carolina. A copy of such conviction records transmitted by the police information network in general accordance with the procedure authorized by G.S. 20-26(b) is admissible in evidence without further authentication. If the judge decides to impose an active sentence of imprisonment that would not have been imposed but for a prior conviction of an offense, the judge shall afford the defendant an opportunity to introduce evidence that the prior conviction had been obtained in a case in which the defendant was indigent, had no counsel, and had not waived the right to counsel. If the defendant proves by the preponderance of the evidence all three above facts concerning the prior case, the conviction may not be used as a grossly aggravating or aggravating factor.

(p) **Limit on Amelioration of Punishment.** -- For active terms of imprisonment imposed under this section:

(1) The judge may not give credit to the defendant for the first 24 hours of time spent in incarceration pending trial.

(2) The defendant shall serve the mandatory minimum period of imprisonment and good or gain time credit may not be used to reduce that mandatory minimum period.

(3) The defendant may not be released on parole unless the defendant is otherwise eligible, has served the mandatory minimum period of imprisonment, and has obtained a substance abuse assessment and completed any recommended treatment or training program or is paroled into a residential treatment program.

With respect to the minimum or specific term of imprisonment imposed as a condition of special probation under this section, the judge may not give credit to the defendant for the first 24 hours of time spent in incarceration pending trial.

(q) Repealed by Session Laws 1991, c. 726, s. 20.

(r) **Supervised Probation Terminated.** -- Unless a judge in the judge's discretion determines that supervised probation is necessary, and includes in the record that the judge has received evidence and finds as a fact that supervised probation is necessary, and states in the judgment that supervised probation is necessary, a defendant convicted of an offense of impaired driving shall be placed on unsupervised probation if the defendant meets three conditions. These conditions are that the defendant (i) has not been convicted of an offense of impaired driving within the seven years preceding the date of this offense for which the defendant is sentenced, (ii) is being sentenced under subsections (i), (j), and (k) of this section, and (iii) has obtained any necessary substance abuse assessment and completed any recommended treatment or training program.

When a judge determines in accordance with the above procedures that a defendant should be placed on supervised probation, the judge shall authorize the probation officer to modify the defendant's probation by placing the defendant on unsupervised probation upon the completion by the defendant of the following conditions of the suspended sentence:

(1) Community service; or

(2) Repealed by Session Laws 1995 c. 496, s. 2.

(3) Payment of any fines, court costs, and fees; or

(4) Any combination of these conditions.

(s) **Method of Serving Sentence.** -- The judge in the judge's discretion may order a term of imprisonment to be served on weekends, even if the sentence cannot be served in consecutive sequence. However, if the defendant is ordered to a term of 48 hours or more, or has 48 hours or more remaining on a term of imprisonment, the defendant shall be required to serve 48 continuous hours of imprisonment to be given credit for time served. All of the following apply to a sentence served under this subsection:

(1) Credit for any jail time shall only be given hour for hour for time actually served. The jail shall maintain a log showing number of hours served.

(2) The defendant shall be refused entrance and shall be reported back to court if the defendant appears at the jail and has remaining in the defendant's body any alcohol as shown by an alcohol screening device or controlled substance previously consumed, unless lawfully obtained and taken in therapeutically appropriate amounts.

(3) If a defendant has been reported back to court under subdivision (2) of this subsection, the court shall hold a hearing. The defendant shall be ordered to serve the defendant's jail time immediately and shall not be eligible to serve jail time on weekends if the court determines that, at the time of entrance to the jail, at least one of the following apply:

    a. The defendant had previously consumed alcohol in the defendant's body as shown by an alcohol screening device.

    b. The defendant had a previously consumed controlled substance in the defendant's body.

It shall be a defense to an immediate service of sentence of jail time and ineligibility for weekend service of jail time if the court determines that alcohol or controlled substance was lawfully obtained and was taken in therapeutically appropriate amounts.

(t) Repealed by Session Laws 1995, c. 496, s. 2.

History.
1937, c. 407, s. 140; 1947, c. 1067, s. 18; 1967, c. 510; 1969, c. 50; c. 1283, ss. 1-5; 1971, c. 619, s. 16; c. 1133, s. 1; 1975, c. 716, s. 5; 1977, c. 125; 1977, 2nd Sess., c. 1222, s. 1; 1979, c. 453, ss. 1, 2; c. 903, ss. 1, 2; 1981, c. 466, ss. 4-6; 1983, c. 435, s. 29; 1983 (Reg. Sess., 1984), c. 1101, ss. 21-29, 36; 1985, c. 706, s. 1; 1985 (Reg. Sess., 1986), c. 1014, s. 201(d); 1987, c. 139; c. 352, s. 1; c. 797, ss. 1, 2; 1989, c. 548, ss. 1, 2; c. 691, ss. 1-3, 4.1; 1989 (Reg. Sess., 1990), c. 1031, ss. 1, 2; c. 1039, s. 6; 1991, c. 636, s. 19(b), (c); c. 726, ss. 20, 21; 1993, c. 285, s. 9; 1995, c. 191, s. 3; c. 496, ss. 2 -7; c. 506, ss. 11-13; 1997-379, ss. 2.1 -2.8; 1997-443, s. 19.26(c); 1998-182, ss. 25, 31-35; 2006-253, s. 23; 2007-165, ss. 2, 3; 2007-493, ss. 6, 20, 26; 2009-372, s. 14; 2010-97, s. 2; 2011-145, s. 19.1(h), (k); 2011-191, s. 1; 2011-329, s. 1; 2012-146, s. 9; 2012-194, s. 51.5; 2013-348, s. 2; 2014-100, s. 16C.1(d); 2015-186, s. 6; 2015-264, ss. 38(b), 86; 2015-289, s. 2; 2017-102, s. 7.1; 2017-186, s. 2 (nnnn); 2021-94, s. 4

§ 20-179.1. Presentence investigation of persons convicted of offense involving impaired driving

When a person has been convicted of an offense involving impaired driving, the trial judge may request a presentence investigation to determine whether the person convicted would benefit from treatment for habitual use of alcohol or drugs. If the person convicted objects, no presentence investigation may be ordered, but the judge retains his power to order suitable treatment as a condition of probation, and must do so when required by statute.

History.
1973, c. 612; 1981, c. 412, s. 4; c. 747, s. 66; 1983, c. 435, s. 29.

N.C. Gen. Stat. § 20-179.2

Repealed by Session Laws 1995, c. 496, s. 8 .

§ 20-179.3. Limited driving privilege

(a) **Definition of Limited Driving Privilege. --** A limited driving privilege is a judgment issued in the discretion of a court for good cause shown authorizing a person with a revoked driver's license to drive for essential purposes related to any of the following:

(1) The person's employment.

(2) The maintenance of the person's household.

(3) The person's education.

(4) The person's court-ordered treatment or assessment.

(5) Community service ordered as a condition of the person's probation.

(6) Emergency medical care.

(7) Religious worship.

(b) **Eligibility. --**

(1) A person convicted of the offense of impaired driving under G.S. 20-138.1 is eligible for a limited driving privilege if:

    a. At the time of the offense the person held either a valid driver's license or a license that had been expired for less than one year;

    b. At the time of the offense the person had not within the preceding seven years been convicted of an offense involving impaired driving;

    c. Punishment Level Three, Four, or Five was imposed for the offense of impaired driving;

    d. Subsequent to the offense the person has not been convicted of, or had an unresolved charge lodged against the person for, an offense involving impaired driving; and

    e. The person has obtained and filed with the court a substance abuse assessment of the type required by G.S. 20-17.6 for the restoration of a drivers license.

A person whose North Carolina driver's license is revoked because of a conviction in another jurisdiction substantially similar to impaired driving under G.S. 20-138.1 is eligible for a limited driving privilege if the person would be eligible for it had the conviction occurred in North Carolina. Eligibility for a limited driving privilege following a revocation under G.S. 20-16.2(d) is governed by G.S. 20-16.2(e1).

(2) Any person whose licensing privileges are forfeited pursuant to G.S. 15A-1331.1 is eligible for a limited driving privilege if the court finds that at the time of the forfeiture, the person held either a valid drivers license or a drivers license that had been expired for less than one year and

a. The person is supporting existing dependents or must have a drivers license to be gainfully employed; or

b. The person has an existing dependent who requires serious medical treatment and the defendant is the only person able to provide transportation to the dependent to the health care facility where the dependent can receive the needed medical treatment.

The limited driving privilege granted under this subdivision must restrict the person to essential driving related to the purposes listed above, and any driving that is not related to those purposes is unlawful even though done at times and upon routes that may be authorized by the privilege.

(c) **Privilege Not Effective until after Compliance with Court-Ordered Revocation.** -- A person convicted of an impaired driving offense may apply for a limited driving privilege at the time the judgment is entered. A person whose license is revoked because of a conviction in another jurisdiction substantially similar to impaired driving under G.S. 20-138.1 may apply for a limited driving privilege only after having completed at least 60 days of a court-imposed term of nonoperation of a motor vehicle, if the court in the other jurisdiction imposed such a term of nonoperation.

(c1) **Privilege Restrictions for High-Risk Drivers.** -- Notwithstanding any other provision of this section, any limited driving privilege issued to a person convicted of an impaired driving offense with an alcohol concentration of 0.15 or more at the time of the offense shall:

(1) Not become effective until at least 45 days after the final conviction under G.S. 20-138.1;

(2) Require the applicant to comply with the ignition interlock requirements of subsection (g5) of this section; and

(3) Restrict the applicant to driving only to and from the applicant's place of employment, the place the applicant is enrolled in school, the applicant's place of religious worship, any court ordered treatment or substance abuse education, and any ignition interlock service facility.

For purposes of this subsection, the results of a chemical analysis presented at trial or sentencing shall be sufficient to prove a person's alcohol concentration, shall be conclusive, and shall not be subject to modification by any party, with or without approval by the court.

(d) **Application for and Scheduling of Subsequent Hearing.** -- The application for a limited driving privilege made at any time after the day of sentencing must be filed with the clerk in duplicate, and no hearing scheduled may be held until a reasonable time after the clerk files a copy of the application with the district attorney's office. The hearing must be scheduled before:

(1) The presiding judge at the applicant's trial if that judge is assigned to a court in the district court district as defined in G.S. 7A-133 or superior court district or set of districts as defined in G.S. 7A-41.1, as the case may be, in which the conviction for impaired driving was imposed.

(2) The senior regular resident superior court judge of the superior court district or set of districts as defined in G.S. 7A-41.1 in which the conviction for impaired driving was imposed, if the presiding judge is not available within the district and the conviction was imposed in superior court.

(3) The chief district court judge of the district court district as defined in G.S. 7A-133 in which the conviction for impaired driving was imposed, if the presiding judge is not available within the district and the conviction was imposed in district court.

If the applicant was convicted of an offense in another jurisdiction, the hearing must be scheduled before the chief district court judge of the district court district as defined in G.S. 7A-133 in which he resides. G.S. 20-16.2(e1) governs the judge before whom a hearing is scheduled if the revocation was under G.S. 20-16.2(d). The hearing may be scheduled in any county within the district court district as defined in G.S. 7A-133 or superior court district or set of districts as defined in G.S. 7A-41.1, as the case may be.

(e) **Limited Basis for and Effect of Privilege.** -- A limited driving privilege issued under this section authorizes a person to drive if the person's license is revoked solely under G.S. 20-17(a)(2) or as a result of a conviction in another jurisdiction substantially similar to impaired

Chapter 20

1581

driving under G.S. 20-138.1; if the person's license is revoked under any other statute, the limited driving privilege is invalid.

(f) **Overall Provisions on Use of Privilege.** -- Every limited driving privilege must restrict the applicant to essential driving related to the purposes listed in subsection (a), and any driving that is not related to those purposes is unlawful even though done at times and upon routes that may be authorized by the privilege. If the privilege is granted, driving related to emergency medical care is authorized at any time and without restriction as to routes, but all other driving must be for a purpose and done within the restrictions specified in the privilege.

(f1) **Definition of "Standard Working Hours".** -- Under this section, "standard working hours" are 6:00 A.M. to 8:00 P.M. on Monday through Friday.

(g) **Driving for Work-Related Purposes in Standard Working Hours.** -- In a limited driving privilege, the court may authorize driving for work-related purposes during standard working hours without specifying the times and routes in which the driving must occur. If the applicant is not required to drive for essential work-related purposes except during standard working hours, the limited driving privilege must prohibit driving during nonstandard working hours unless the driving is for emergency medical care or is authorized by subsection (g2). The limited driving privilege must state the name and address of the applicant's place of work or employer, and may include other information and restrictions applicable to work-related driving in the discretion of the court.

(g1) **Driving for Work-Related Purposes in Nonstandard Hours.** -- If the applicant is required to drive during nonstandard working hours for an essential work-related purpose, the applicant must present documentation of that fact before the judge may authorize the applicant to drive for this purpose during those hours. If the applicant is self-employed, the documentation must be attached to or made a part of the limited driving privilege. If the judge determines that it is necessary for the applicant to drive during nonstandard hours for a work-related purpose, the judge may authorize the applicant to drive subject to these limitations:

(1) If the applicant is required to drive to and from a specific place of work at regular times, the limited driving privilege must specify the general times and routes in which the applicant will be driving to and from work, and restrict driving to those times and routes.

(2) If the applicant is required to drive to and from work at a specific place, but is unable to specify the times at which that driving will occur, the limited driving privilege must specify the general routes in which the applicant will be driving to and from work, and restrict the driving to those general routes.

(3) If the applicant is required to drive to and from work at regular times but is unable to specify the places at which work is to be performed, the limited driving privilege must specify the general times and geographic boundaries in which the applicant will be driving, and restrict driving to those times and within those boundaries.

(4) If the applicant can specify neither the times nor places in which the applicant will be driving to and from work, or if the applicant is required to drive during these nonstandard working hours as a condition of employment, the limited driving privilege must specify the geographic boundaries in which the applicant will drive and restrict driving to that within those boundaries.

The limited driving privilege must state the name and address of the applicant's place of work or employer, and may include other information and restrictions applicable to work-related driving, in the discretion of the court.

(g2) A limited driving privilege may not allow driving for maintenance of the household except during standard working hours, and the limited driving privilege may contain any additional restrictions on that driving, in the discretion of the court. The limited driving privilege must authorize driving essential to the completion of any community work assignments, course of instruction at an Alcohol and Drug Education Traffic School, or substance abuse assessment or treatment, to which the applicant is ordered by the court as a condition of probation for the impaired driving conviction. If this driving will occur during nonstandard working hours, the limited driving privilege must specify the same limitations required by subsection (g1) for work-related driving during those hours, and it must include or have attached to it the name and address of the Alcohol and Drug Education Traffic School, the community service coordinator, or mental health treatment facility to which the applicant is assigned. Driving for educational purposes other than the course of instruction at an Alcohol and Drug Education Traffic School is subject to the same limitations applicable to work related driving under subsections (g) and (g1). Driving to and from the applicant's place of religious worship is subject to the same limitations applicable to work-related driving under subsections (g) and (g1) of this section.

(g3) **Ignition Interlock Allowed.** -- A judge may include all of the following in a limited driving privilege order:

(1) A restriction that the applicant may operate only a designated motor vehicle.

(2) A requirement that the designated motor vehicle be equipped with a functioning ignition interlock system of a type approved by the Commissioner. The Commissioner shall not unreasonably withhold approval of an ignition interlock system and shall consult with the Division of Purchase and Contract in the Department of Administration to ensure that potential vendors are not discriminated against.

(3) A requirement that the applicant personally activate the ignition interlock system before driving the motor vehicle.

(g4) The restrictions set forth in subsection (g3) and (g5) of this section do not apply to a motor vehicle that meets all of the following requirements:

(1) Is owned by the applicant's employer.

(2) Is operated by the applicant solely for work-related purposes.

(3) Its owner has filed with the court a written document authorizing the applicant to drive the vehicle, for work-related purposes, under the authority of a limited driving privilege.

(g5) **Ignition Interlock Required. --** If a person's drivers license is revoked for a conviction of G.S. 20-138.1, and the person had an alcohol concentration of 0.15 or more, a judge shall include all of the following in a limited driving privilege order:

(1) A restriction that the applicant may operate only a designated motor vehicle.

(2) A requirement that the designated motor vehicle be equipped with a functioning ignition interlock system of a type approved by the Commissioner, which is set to prohibit driving with an alcohol concentration of greater than 0.00. The Commissioner shall not unreasonably withhold approval of an ignition interlock system and shall consult with the Division of Purchase and Contract in the Department of Administration to ensure that potential vendors are not discriminated against.

(3) A requirement that the applicant personally activate the ignition interlock system before driving the motor vehicle.

For purposes of this subsection, the results of a chemical analysis presented at trial or sentencing shall be sufficient to prove a person's alcohol concentration, shall be conclusive, and shall not be subject to modification by any party, with or without approval by the court.

(h) **Other Mandatory and Permissive Conditions or Restrictions. --** In all limited driving privileges the judge shall also include a restriction that the applicant not consume alcohol while driving or drive at any time while the applicant has remaining in the applicant's body any alcohol or controlled substance previously consumed, unless the controlled substance was lawfully obtained and taken in therapeutically appropriate amounts. The judge may impose any other reasonable restrictions or conditions necessary to achieve the purposes of this section.

(i) **Modification or Revocation of Privilege. --** A judge who issues a limited driving privilege is authorized to modify or revoke the limited driving privilege upon a showing that the circumstances have changed sufficiently to justify modification or revocation. If the judge who issued the privilege is not presiding in the court in which the privilege was issued, a presiding judge in that court may modify or revoke a privilege in accordance with this subsection. The judge must indicate in the order of modification or revocation the reasons for the order, or the judge must make specific findings indicating the reason for the order and those findings must be entered in the record of the case.

(j) **Effect of Violation of Restriction. --** A person holding a limited driving privilege who violates any of its restrictions commits the offense of driving while license is revoked for impaired driving under G.S. 20-28(a1) and is subject to punishment and license revocation as provided in that section. If a law-enforcement officer has reasonable grounds to believe that the person holding a limited driving privilege has consumed alcohol while driving or has driven while the person has remaining in the person's body any alcohol previously consumed, the suspected offense of driving while license is revoked is an alcohol-related offense subject to the implied-consent provisions of G.S. 20-16.2. If a person holding a limited driving privilege is charged with driving while license revoked by violating a restriction contained in the limited driving privilege, and a judicial official determines that there is probable cause for the charge, the limited driving privilege is suspended pending the resolution of the case, and the judicial official must require the person to surrender the limited driving privilege. The judicial official must also notify the person that the person is not entitled to drive until the case is resolved.

Notwithstanding any other provision of law, an alcohol screening test may be administered to a driver suspected of violating this section, and the results of an alcohol screening test or the driver's refusal to submit may be used by a law enforcement officer, a court, or an administrative agency in determining if alcohol was present in the driver's body. No alcohol screening tests are valid under this section unless the device used is one approved by the Department of Health and Human Services, and the screening test is conducted in accordance with the applicable regulations of the Department as to the manner of its use.

(j1) **Effect of Violation of Community Service Requirement. --** Section of Community

Chapter 20

Corrections of the Division of Adult Correction and Juvenile Justice staff shall report significant violations of the terms of a probation judgment related to community service to the court that ordered the community service. The court shall then conduct a hearing to determine if there was a willful failure to comply. The hearing may be held in the district where the requirement was imposed, where the alleged violation occurred, or where the probationer resides. If the court determines that there was a willful failure to pay the prescribed fee or to complete the work as ordered within the applicable time limits, the court shall revoke any limited driving privilege issued in the impaired driving case until community service requirements have been met. In addition, the court may take any further action authorized by Article 82 of Chapter 15A of the General Statutes for violation of a condition of probation.

(k) **Copy of Limited Driving Privilege to Division; Action Taken if Privilege Invalid.** -- The clerk of court or the child support enforcement agency must send a copy of any limited driving privilege issued in the county to the Division. A limited driving privilege that is not authorized by this section, G.S. 20-16.2(e1), 20-16.1, 50-13.12, or 110-142.2, or that does not contain the limitations required by law, is invalid. If the limited driving privilege is invalid on its face, the Division must immediately notify the court and the person holding the privilege that it considers the privilege void and that the Division records will not indicate that the person has a limited driving privilege.

(*l*) Any judge granting limited driving privileges under this section shall, prior to granting such privileges, be furnished proof and be satisfied that the person being granted such privileges is financially responsible. Proof of financial responsibility shall be in one of the following forms:

(1) A written certificate or electronically-transmitted facsimile thereof from any insurance carrier duly authorized to do business in this State certifying that there is in effect a nonfleet private passenger motor vehicle liability policy for the benefit of the person required to furnish proof of financial responsibility. The certificate or facsimile shall state the effective date and expiration date of the nonfleet private passenger motor vehicle liability policy and shall state the date that the certificate or facsimile is issued. The certificate or facsimile shall remain effective proof of financial responsibility for a period of 30 consecutive days following the date the certificate or facsimile is issued but shall not in and of itself constitute a binder or policy of insurance or

(2) A binder for or policy of nonfleet private passenger motor vehicle liability

insurance under which the applicant is insured, provided that the binder or policy states the effective date and expiration date of the nonfleet private passenger motor vehicle liability policy.

The preceding provisions of this subsection do not apply to applicants who do not own currently registered motor vehicles and who do not operate nonfleet private passenger motor vehicles that are owned by other persons and that are not insured under commercial motor vehicle liability insurance policies. In such cases, the applicant shall sign a written certificate to that effect. Such certificate shall be furnished by the Division. Any material misrepresentation made by such person on such certificate shall be grounds for suspension of that person's license for a period of 90 days.

For the purpose of this subsection "nonfleet private passenger motor vehicle" has the definition ascribed to it in Article 40 of General Statute Chapter 58.

The Commissioner may require that certificates required by this subsection be on a form approved by the Commissioner. Such granting of limited driving privileges shall be conditioned upon the maintenance of such financial responsibility during the period of the limited driving privilege. Nothing in this subsection precludes any person from showing proof of financial responsibility in any other manner authorized by Articles 9A and 13 of this Chapter.

History.
1983, c. 435, s. 31; 1983 (Reg. Sess., 1984), c. 1101, ss. 30-33; 1985, c. 706, s. 2; 1987, c. 869, s. 13; 1987 (Reg. Sess., 1988), c. 1037, s. 78; 1989, c. 436, s. 6; 1994, Ex. Sess., c. 20, s. 3; 1995, c. 506, ss. 1, 2; c. 538, s. 2(h); 1995 (Reg. Sess., 1996), c. 756, s. 31; 1997-379, s. 5.6; 1999-406, ss. 4 -6; 2000-155, ss. 7, 11-13; 2001-487, s. 55; 2007-182, s. 2; 2007-493, ss. 24, 29, 30; 2008-187, s. 36(c); 2009-372, s. 15; 2011-145, s. 19.1(k); 2012-194, s. 45(c); 2015-185, s. 2(a); 2015-186, s. 5; 2015-264, s. 86; 2017-186, s. 2 (oooo)

N.C. Gen. Stat. § 20-179.4

Repealed by Session Laws 2009-372, s. 16, effective December 1, 2009, and applicable to offenses committed on or after that date.

N.C. Gen. Stat. § 20-180

Repealed by Session Laws 1973, c. 1330, s. 39.

§ 20-181. Penalty for failure to dim, etc., beams of headlamps

Any person operating a motor vehicle on the highways of this State, who shall fail to shift, depress, deflect, tilt or dim the beams of the headlamps thereon whenever another vehicle is met on such highways or when following another vehicle at a distance of less than 200 feet, except when engaged in the act of overtaking and passing may, upon a determination of responsibility for the offense, be required to pay a penalty of not more than ten dollars ($ 10.00).

History.
1939, c. 351, s. 3; 1955, c. 913, s. 1; 1987, c. 581, s. 5

N.C. Gen. Stat. § 20-182

Repealed by Session Laws 1983, c. 912, s. 2.

§ 20-183. Duties and powers of law-enforcement officers; warning by local officers before stopping another vehicle on highway; warning tickets

(a) It shall be the duty of the law-enforcement officers of the State and of each county, city, or other municipality to see that the provisions of this Article are enforced within their respective jurisdictions, and any such officer shall have the power to arrest on sight or upon warrant any person found violating the provisions of this Article. Such officers within their respective jurisdictions shall have the power to stop any motor vehicle upon the highways of the State for the purpose of determining whether the same is being operated in violation of any of the provisions of this Article. Provided, that when any county, city, or other municipal law-enforcement officer operating a motor vehicle overtakes another vehicle on the highways of the State, outside of the corporate limits of cities and towns, for the purpose of stopping the same or apprehending the driver thereof, for a violation of any of the provisions of this Article, he shall, before stopping such other vehicle, sound a siren or activate a special light, bell, horn, or exhaust whistle approved for law-enforcement vehicles under the provisions of G.S. 20-125(b).

(b) In addition to other duties and powers heretofore existing, all law-enforcement officers charged with the duty of enforcing the motor vehicle laws are authorized to issue warning tickets to motorists for conduct constituting a potential hazard to the motoring public which does not amount to a definite, clear-cut, substantial violation of the motor vehicle laws. Each warning ticket issued shall contain information necessary to identify the offender, and shall be signed by the issuing officer. A copy of each warning ticket issued shall be delivered to the offender. Information from issued warning tickets shall be made available to the Drivers License Section of the Division of Motor Vehicles in a manner approved by the Commissioner but shall not be filed with or in any manner become a part of the offender's driving record. Warning tickets issued as well as the fact of issuance shall be privileged information and available only to authorized personnel of the Division for statistical and analytical purposes.

History.
1937, c. 407, s. 143; 1961, c. 793; 1965, cc. 537, 999; 1975, c. 716, s. 5; 1998-149, s. 9.2

ARTICLE 3A
SAFETY AND EMISSIONS INSPECTION PROGRAM

PART 1
SAFE USE OF STREETS AND HIGHWAYS

N.C. Gen. Stat. § 20-183.1

Repealed by Session Laws 1993 (Reg. Sess., 1994), c. 754, s. 3.

PART 2
SAFETY AND EMISSIONS INSPECTIONS OF CERTAIN VEHICLES

§ 20-183.2. Description of vehicles subject to safety or emissions inspection; definitions

(a) **Safety.** -- A motor vehicle is subject to a safety inspection in accordance with this Part if it meets all of the following requirements:

(1) It is subject to registration with the Division under Article 3 of this Chapter.

(2) It is not subject to inspection under 49 C.F.R. Part 396, the federal Motor Carrier Safety Regulations.

(3) It is not a trailer whose gross weight is less than 4,000 pounds or a house trailer.

(a1) **Safety Inspection Exceptions.** -- The following vehicles shall not be subject to a safety inspection pursuant to this Article:

(1) Historic vehicles, as described in G.S. 20-79.4(b)(90).

(2) Buses titled to a local board of education and subject to the school bus inspection requirements specified by the State Board of Education and G.S. 115C-248.

(b) **Emissions.** -- A motor vehicle is subject to an emissions inspection in accordance with this Part if it meets all of the following requirements:

(1) It is subject to registration with the Division under Article 3 of this Chapter, except for motor vehicles operated on a federal

Chapter 20

installation as provided in sub-subdivision e. of subdivision (5) of this subsection.

(2) It is not a trailer whose gross weight is less than 4,000 pounds, a house trailer, or a motorcycle.

(3) *(Effective until contingency met -- see note)* It is (i) a 1996 or later model and older than the three most recent model years or (ii) a 1996 or later model and has 70,000 miles or more on its odometer.

(3) *(Contingent effective date -- see note)* It is (i) a vehicle with a model year within 20 years of the current year and older than the three most recent model years or (ii) a vehicle with a model year within 20 years of the current year and has 70,000 miles or more on its odometer.

(4) Repealed by Session Laws 1999-328, s. 3.11, effective July 21, 1999.

(5) It meets any of the following descriptions:

　　a. It is required to be registered in an emissions county.

　　b. It is part of a fleet that is operated primarily in an emissions county.

　　c. It is offered for rent in an emissions county.

　　d. It is a used vehicle offered for sale by a dealer in an emissions county.

　　e. It is operated on a federal installation located in an emissions county and it is not a tactical military vehicle. Vehicles operated on a federal installation include those that are owned or leased by employees of the installation and are used to commute to the installation and those owned or operated by the federal agency that conducts business at the installation.

　　f. It is otherwise required by 40 C.F.R. Part 51 to be subject to an emissions inspection.

(6) It is not licensed at the farmer rate under G.S. 20-88(b).

(7) It is not a new motor vehicle, as defined in G.S. 20-286(10)a. and has been a used motor vehicle, as defined in G.S. 20-286(10)b., for 12 months or more. However, a motor vehicle that has been leased or rented, or offered for lease or rent, is subject to an emissions inspection when it either:

　　a. Has been leased or rented, or offered for lease or rent, for 12 months or more.

　　b. Is sold to a consumer-purchaser.

(8) It is not a privately owned, nonfleet motor home or house car, as defined in G.S. 20-4.01(27)k., that is built on a single chassis, has a gross vehicle weight of more than 10,000 pounds, and is designed primarily for recreational use.

(9) It is not a plug-in electric vehicle as defined in G.S. 20-4.01(28b).

(10) It is not a fuel cell electric vehicle as defined in G.S. 20-4.01(12a).

(c) **Definitions.** -- The following definitions apply in this Part:

(1) **Electronic inspection authorization.** -- An inspection authorization that is generated electronically through the electronic accounting system that creates a unique nonduplicating authorization number assigned to the vehicle's inspection receipt upon successful passage of an inspection. The term "electronic inspection authorization" shall include the term "inspection sticker" during the transition period to use of electronic inspection authorizations.

(2) **Emissions county.** -- A county listed in G.S. 143-215.107A(c) and certified to the Commissioner of Motor Vehicles as a county in which the implementation of a motor vehicle emissions inspection program will improve ambient air quality.

(3) **Federal installation.** -- An installation that is owned by, leased to, or otherwise regularly used as the place of business of a federal agency.

History.
1965, c. 734, s. 1; 1967, c. 692, s. 1; 1969, c. 179, s. 2; cc. 219, 386; 1973, c. 679, s. 2; 1975, c. 683; c. 716, s. 5; 1979, c. 77; 1989, c. 467; 1991, c. 394, s. 1; c. 761, s. 7; 1993 (Reg. Sess., 1994), c. 754, s. 1; 1995, c. 163, s. 10; 1997-29, s. 12; 1999-328, s. 3.11; 2000-134, ss. 7, 7.1, 9, 11; 2001-504, ss. 4, 5, 6, 10; 2004-167, s. 10; 2004-199, s. 59; 2006-255, s. 1; 2007-503, s. 2; 2008-172, s. 1; 2009-570, s. 33; 2011-95, s. 3; 2011-206, s. 3; 2012-199, s. 1; 2012-200, s. 12(b); 2013-410, s. 5; 2015-264, s. 9; 2017-10, s. 3.5(b); 2017-102, s. 5.2(b); 2020-73, s. 5

§ 20-183.3. Scope of safety inspection and emissions inspection

(a) **Safety.** -- A safety inspection of a motor vehicle consists of an inspection of the following equipment to determine if the vehicle has the equipment required by Part 9 of Article 3 of this Chapter and if the equipment is in a safe operating condition:

(1) Brakes, as required by G.S. 20-124.

(2) Lights, as required by G.S. 20-129 or G.S. 20-129.1.

(3) Horn, as required by G.S. 20-125(a).

(4) Steering mechanism, as required by G.S. 20-123.1.

(5) Windows and windshield wipers, as required by G.S. 20-127. To determine if a vehicle window meets the window tinting restrictions, a safety inspection mechanic must first determine, based on use of an automotive film check card or knowledge of

window tinting techniques, if after-factory tint has been applied to the window. If after-factory tint has been applied, the mechanic must use a light meter approved by the Commissioner to determine if the window meets the window tinting restrictions.

(6) Directional signals, as required by G.S. 20-125.1.

(7) Tires, as required by G.S. 20-122.1.

(8) Mirrors, as required by G.S. 20-126.

(9) Exhaust system and emissions control devices, as required by G.S. 20-128. For a vehicle that is subject to an emissions inspection in addition to a safety inspection, a visual inspection of the vehicle's emissions control devices is included in the emissions inspection rather than the safety inspection.

(b) Repealed by Laws 2000-134, s. 12, effective January 1, 2006.

(b1) **Emissions.** -- An emissions inspection of a motor vehicle consists of a visual inspection of the vehicle's emissions control devices to determine if the devices are present, are properly connected, and are the correct type for the vehicle and an analysis of data provided by the on-board diagnostic (OBD) equipment installed by the vehicle manufacturer to identify any deterioration or malfunction in the operation of the vehicle that violates standards for the model year of the vehicle set by the Environmental Management Commission. To pass an emissions inspection a vehicle must pass both the visual inspection and the OBD analysis. When an emissions inspection is performed on a vehicle, a safety inspection must be performed on the vehicle as well.

(c) **Reinspection After Failure.** -- The scope of a reinspection of a vehicle that has been repaired after failing an inspection is the same as the original inspection unless the vehicle is presented for reinspection within 60 days of failing the original inspection. If the vehicle is presented for reinspection within this time limit and the inspection the vehicle failed was a safety inspection, the reinspection is limited to an inspection of the equipment that failed the original inspection. If the vehicle is presented for reinspection within this time limit and the inspection the vehicle failed was an emissions inspection, the reinspection is limited to the portion of the inspection the vehicle failed and any other portion of the inspection that would be affected by repairs made to correct the failure.

History.
1965, c. 734, s. 1; 1969, c. 378, s. 2; 1971, c. 455, s. 2; c. 478, ss. 1, 2; 1979, 2nd Sess., c. 1180, s. 3; 1981 (Reg. Sess., 1982), c. 1261, s. 1; 1989, c. 391, s. 2; 1991, c. 654, s. 2; 1993 (Reg. Sess., 1994), c. 754, s. 1; 1995, c. 473, s. 2; 2000-134, ss. 8, 10, 12; 2001-504, s. 7; 2007-364, s. 1

§ 20-183.4. License required to perform safety inspection; qualifications for license

(a) **License Required.** -- A safety inspection must be performed by one of the following methods:

(1) At a station that has a safety inspection station license issued by the Division and by a mechanic who is employed by the station and has a safety inspection mechanic license issued by the Division.

(2) At a place of business of a person who has a safety self-inspector license issued by the Division and by an individual who has a safety inspection mechanic license issued by the Division.

(b) **Station Qualifications.** -- An applicant for a license as a safety inspection station must meet all of the following requirements:

(1) Have a place of business that has adequate facilities, space, and equipment to conduct a safety inspection. A place of business designated in a station license that has been suspended or revoked cannot be the designated place for any other license applicant during the period of the suspension or revocation, unless the Division finds that operation of the place of business as an inspection station during this period by the license applicant would not defeat the purpose of the suspension or revocation because the license applicant has no connection with the person whose license was suspended or revoked or because of another reason. A finding made by the Division under this subdivision must be set out in a written statement that includes the finding and the reason for the finding.

(2) Regularly employ at least one mechanic who has a safety inspection mechanic license.

(3) Designate the individual who will be responsible for the day-to-day operation of the station. The individual designated must be of good character and have a reputation for honesty.

(4) Have equipment and software approved by the Division to transfer information on safety inspections to the Division by electronic means. During the initial implementation of the electronic inspection process, the vendor selected by the Division shall provide the equipment and software at no cost to a station that holds a license on October 1, 2008.

(c) **Mechanic Qualifications.** -- An applicant for a license as a safety inspection mechanic must meet all of the following requirements:

(1) Have successfully completed an eight-hour course approved by the Division that

teaches students about the safety equipment a motor vehicle is required to have to pass a safety inspection and how to conduct a safety inspection using equipment to electronically transmit the vehicle information and inspection results.

(2) Have a drivers license.

(3) Be of good character and have a reputation for honesty.

(d) **Self-Inspector Qualifications.** -- An applicant for a license as a safety self-inspector must meet all of the following requirements:

(1) Operate a fleet of at least 10 vehicles that are subject to a safety inspection.

(2) Regularly employ or contract with an individual who has a safety inspection mechanic license and who will perform a safety inspection on the vehicles that are part of the self-inspector's fleet.

History.
1965, c. 734, s. 1; 1967, c. 692, s. 2; 1975, c. 716, s. 5; 1993 (Reg. Sess., 1994), c. 754, s. 1; 1997-29, s. 1; 2007-503, s. 3; 2008-190, s. 2

§ 20-183.4A. License required to perform emissions inspection; qualifications for license

(a) **License Required.** -- An emissions inspection must be performed by one of the following methods:

(1) At a station that has an emissions inspection station license issued by the Division and by a mechanic who is employed by the station and has an emissions inspection mechanic license issued by the Division.

(2) At a place of business of a person who has an emissions self-inspector license issued by the Division and by an individual who has an emissions inspection mechanic license.

(b) **Station Qualifications.** -- An applicant for a license as an emissions inspection station must meet all of the following requirements:

(1) Have a license as a safety inspection station.

(2) Repealed by Laws 2000-134, s. 15, effective January 1, 2006.

(2a) Have equipment to analyze data provided by the on-board diagnostic (OBD) equipment approved by the Environmental Management Commission.

(3) Have equipment and software to transfer information on emissions inspections to the Division by electronic means. During the initial implementation of the electronic inspection process, the vendor selected by the Division shall provide the software at no cost to a station that holds a license on October 1, 2008.

(4) Regularly employ at least one mechanic who has an emissions inspection mechanic license.

(c) **Mechanic Qualifications.** -- An applicant for a license as an emissions inspection mechanic must meet all of the following requirements:

(1) Have a license as a safety inspection mechanic.

(2) Repealed by Laws 2000-134, s. 15, effective January 1, 2006.

(2a) Have successfully completed an eight-hour course approved by the Division that teaches students about the causes and effects of the air pollution problem, the purpose of the emissions inspection program, the vehicle emission standards established by the United States Environmental Protection Agency, the emission control devices on vehicles, how to conduct an emissions inspection using equipment to analyze data provided by the on-board diagnostic (OBD) equipment approved by the Environmental Management Commission, and any other topic required by 40 C.F.R. § 51.367 to be included in the course. Successful completion requires a passing score on a written test and on a hands-on test in which the student is required to conduct an emissions inspection of a motor vehicle.

(d) **Self-Inspector Qualifications.** -- An applicant for a license as an emissions self-inspector must meet all of the following requirements:

(1) Have a license as a safety self-inspector.

(2) Operate a fleet of at least 10 vehicles that are subject to an emissions inspection.

(3) Repealed by Laws 2000-134, s. 15, effective January 1, 2006.

(3a) Have, or have a contract with a person who has, equipment to analyze data provided by the on-board diagnostic (OBD) equipment approved by the Environmental Management Commission.

(4) Regularly employ or contract with an individual who has an emissions inspection mechanic license and who will perform an emissions inspection on the vehicles that are part of the self-inspector's fleet.

History.
1993 (Reg. Sess., 1994), c. 754, s. 1; 2000-134, ss. 13, 14, 15; 2007-503, s. 4

§ 20-183.4B. Application for license; duration of license; renewal of mechanic license

(a) **Application.** -- An applicant for a license issued under this Part must complete an application form provided by the Division. The application must contain the applicant's name and address and any other information needed by the Division to determine whether the applicant is qualified for the license. The Division must review an application for a license to determine if the applicant qualifies for the license. If the applicant meets the qualifications, the Division must issue the license. If the applicant does not meet the qualifications, the Division must deny the application and notify the applicant in writing of the reason for the denial.

(b) **Duration of License.** -- A safety inspection mechanic license expires four years after the date it is issued. An emissions mechanic inspection license expires two years after the date it is issued. A safety inspection station license, an emissions inspection station license, and a self-inspector license are effective until surrendered by the license holder or suspended or revoked by the Division.

(c) **Renewal of Mechanic License.** -- A safety or an emissions inspection mechanic may apply to renew a license by filing an application with the Division on a form provided by the Division. To renew an emissions inspection mechanic license, an applicant must have successfully completed a four-hour emissions refresher course approved by the Division within nine months of applying for renewal. Successful completion requires a passing score on a written test and on a hands-on test in which the student is required to conduct an emissions inspection of a motor vehicle.

History.
1993 (Reg. Sess., 1994), c. 754, s. 1

§ 20-183.4C. When a vehicle must be inspected; 10-day temporary license plate

(a) **Inspection.** -- A vehicle that is subject to a safety inspection, an emissions inspection, or both must be inspected as follows:

(1) Except as otherwise provided in this subdivision, a new vehicle must be inspected before it is delivered to a purchaser at retail in this State. Upon purchase, a receipt approved by the Division must be provided to the new owner certifying compliance. An inspection is not required if the vehicle was previously inspected by an affiliated dealership, or between dealerships having common or interrelated ownership, and the inspection occurred either within 180 days from the date of sale or within 300 miles from the mileage recorded at the date of sale.

(1a) A new motor vehicle dealer who is also licensed pursuant to this Article may, notwithstanding subdivision (1) of this section, examine the safety and emissions control devices on a new motor vehicle and perform such services necessary to ensure the motor vehicle conforms to the required specifications established by the manufacturer and contained in its predelivery check list. The completion of the predelivery inspection procedure required or recommended by the manufacturer on a new motor vehicle shall constitute the inspection required by subdivision (1) of this section. For the purposes of this subdivision, the date of inspection shall be deemed to be the date of the sale of the motor vehicle to a purchaser.

(2) Except as otherwise provided in this subdivision, a used vehicle must be inspected before it is offered for sale at retail in this State by a dealer. Upon purchase, a receipt approved by the Division must be provided to the new owner certifying compliance. An inspection is not required if the vehicle was previously inspected by an affiliated dealership, or between dealerships having common or interrelated ownership, and the inspection occurred either within 180 days from the date of sale or within 300 miles from the mileage recorded at the date of sale.

(3) Repealed by Session Law 2007-503, s. 5, effective October 1, 2008.

(4) Except as authorized by the Commissioner for a single period of time not to exceed 12 months from the initial date of registration, a new or used vehicle acquired by a resident of this State from outside the State must be inspected before the vehicle is registered with the Division.

(5) Except as authorized by the Commissioner for a single period of time not to exceed 12 months from the initial date of registration, a vehicle owned by a new resident of this State who transfers the registration of the vehicle from the resident's former home state to this State must be inspected before the vehicle is registered with the Division.

(5a) Repealed by Session Law 2007-503, s. 5, effective October 1, 2008.

(6) A vehicle that has been inspected in accordance with this Part must be inspected by the last day of the month in which the registration on the vehicle expires.

(7) A vehicle that is required to be inspected in accordance with this Part may be inspected 90 days prior to midnight of the last day of the month as designated by the vehicle registration sticker.

(8) A new or used vehicle acquired from a retailer or a private sale in this State and registered with the Division with a new registration or a transferred registration must be inspected in accordance with this Part when the current registration expires

Chapter 20

unless it has received a passing inspection within the previous 12 months.

(9) Repealed by Session Laws 2010-97, s. 3, effective July 20, 2010.

(10) An unregistered vehicle may be registered with the Division in accordance with G.S. 20-50(b) for a period not to exceed 10 days prior to the vehicle receiving a passing inspection in accordance with this Part.

(11) A person who owns a vehicle located outside of this State when its emissions inspection becomes due may obtain an emissions inspection in the jurisdiction where the vehicle is located, in lieu of a North Carolina emissions inspection, as long as the inspection meets the requirements of 40 C.F.R. § 51.

(b) **Temporary License Plate.** -- The Division may issue a temporary license plate under and in accordance with G.S. 20-50(b) that is valid for 10 days to a person that authorizes the person to drive a vehicle whose inspection authorization or registration has expired.

(c) **Exemption.** -- The Division may issue a temporary exemption from the inspection requirements of this Article for any vehicle that has been determined by the Division to be principally garaged, as defined under G.S. 58-37-1(11), in this State and is primarily operated outside a county subject to emissions inspection requirements or outside of this State.

History.
1993 (Reg. Sess., 1994), c. 754, s. 1; 1997-29, s. 2; 2001-504, s. 11; 2007-481, s. 2; 2007-503, s. 5; 2008-190, s. 3; 2009-319, s. 2; 2010-97, s. 3; 2015-241, s. 29.35(a); 2018-42, s. 5; 2021-134, s. 10; 2021-147, s. 14

§ 20-183.4D. Procedure when a vehicle is inspected

(a) **Receipt.** -- When a safety inspection mechanic or an emissions inspection mechanic inspects a vehicle, the mechanic must give the person who brought the vehicle in for inspection an inspection receipt. The inspection receipt must state the date of the inspection, identify the mechanic performing the inspection, identify the station or self-inspector where the inspection was performed, and list the components of the inspection performed and indicate for each component whether the vehicle passed or failed. A vehicle that fails a component of an inspection may be repaired at any repair facility chosen by the owner or operator of the vehicle.

(b) **Electronic Inspection Authorization.** -- When a vehicle that is subject to a safety inspection only passes the safety inspection, the safety inspection mechanic who performed the inspection must issue an electronic inspection authorization to the vehicle at the place

designated by the Division. When a vehicle that is subject to both a safety inspection and an emissions inspection passes both inspections or passes the safety inspection and has a waiver for the emissions inspection, the emissions mechanic performing the inspection must issue an electronic inspection authorization to the vehicle at the place designated by the Division.

(c), (d) Repealed by Session Laws 2007-503, s. 6, effective October 1, 2008.

(e) **When Electronic Inspection Authorization Expires.** -- An electronic inspection authorization issued under this Part expires at midnight of the last day of the month designated by the vehicle registration sticker of the following year.

History.
1993 (Reg. Sess., 1994), c. 754, s. 1; 2007-503, s. 6

§ 20-183.5. When a vehicle that fails an emissions inspection may obtain a waiver from the inspection requirement

(a) **Requirements.** -- The Division may issue a waiver for a vehicle, excluding a vehicle owned or being held for retail sale by a motor vehicle dealer, that meets all of the following requirements:

(1) Fails an emissions inspection because it passes the visual inspection but fails the analysis of data provided by the on-board diagnostic (OBD) equipment.

(2) Has documented repairs costing at least the waiver amount made to the vehicle to correct the cause of the failure. The waiver amount is two hundred dollars ($ 200.00).

(3) Is reinspected and again fails the inspection because it passes the visual inspection but fails the analysis of data provided by the on-board diagnostic (OBD) equipment.

(4) Meets any other waiver criteria required by 40 C.F.R. § 51.360, or as designated by the Division.

(b) **Procedure.** -- To obtain a waiver, a person must contact a local enforcement office of the Division. Before issuing a waiver, an employee of the Division must review the inspection receipts issued for the inspections of the vehicle, review the documents establishing what repairs were made to the vehicle and at what cost, review any statement denying warranty coverage of the repairs made, and do a visual inspection of the vehicle, if appropriate, to determine if the documented repairs were made. The Division must issue a waiver if it determines that the vehicle qualifies for a waiver. A person to whom a waiver is issued must present the waiver to the self-inspector or inspection station performing the inspection to obtain an electronic inspection authorization.

(c) **Repairs.** -- The following repairs and their costs cannot be considered in determining whether the cost of repairs made to a vehicle equals or exceeds the waiver amount:

(1) Repairs covered by a warranty that applies to the vehicle.

(2) Repairs needed as a result of tampering with an emission control device of the vehicle.

(3) Repairs made by an individual who is not professionally engaged in the business of repairing vehicles.

(4) OBD diagnostics without corresponding repairs.

(d) **Electronic Inspection Authorization.** -- An electronic inspection authorization issued to a vehicle after the vehicle receives a waiver from the requirement of passing the emissions inspection expires at the same time it would if the vehicle had passed the emissions inspection.

History.
1965, c. 734, s. 1; 1993 (Reg. Sess., 1994), c. 754, s. 1; 2000-134, ss. 16, 17; 2007-503, s. 7

§ 20-183.5A. When a vehicle that fails a safety inspection because of missing emissions control devices may obtain a waiver

(a) **Requirements.** -- The Division may issue a waiver for a vehicle that meets all of the following requirements:

(1) Fails a safety inspection because it does not have one or more emissions control devices.

(2) Has documented repairs within the previous calendar year to replace missing emissions control devices costing at least the waiver amount made to the vehicle to correct the cause of the failure. The waiver amount is two hundred dollars ($ 200.00) if the vehicle is a 1996 or newer model.

(b) **Procedure.** -- To obtain a waiver, a person must contact a local enforcement office of the Division. Before issuing a waiver, an employee of the Division must review the inspection receipts issued for the inspections of the vehicle, review the documents establishing what repairs were made to the vehicle and at what cost, review any statement denying warranty coverage of the repairs made, and do a visual inspection of the vehicle, if appropriate, to determine if the documented repairs were made. The Division must issue a waiver if it determines that the vehicle qualifies for a waiver. A person to whom a waiver is issued must present the waiver to the self-inspector or inspection station performing the inspection to obtain an electronic inspection authorization.

(c) **Repairs.** -- The following repairs and their costs cannot be considered in determining whether the cost of repairs made to a vehicle equals or exceeds the waiver amount:

(1) Repairs covered by a warranty that applies to the vehicle.

(2) Repairs needed as a result of tampering with an emission control device of the vehicle.

(3) Repairs made by an individual who is not professionally engaged in the business of repairing vehicles.

(d) **Electronic Inspection Authorization Expiration.** -- An electronic inspection authorization issued to a vehicle after the vehicle receives a waiver from the requirement of passing the safety inspection expires at the same time it would if the vehicle had passed the safety inspection.

History.
2007-503, ss. 8, 9

N.C. Gen. Stat. § 20-183.6

Repealed by Session Laws 2007-503, s. 10, effective October 1, 2008, and applicable to offenses committed on or after that date.

§ 20-183.6A. Administration of program; duties of license holders

(a) **Division.** -- The Division is responsible for administering the safety inspection and the emissions inspection programs. In exercising this responsibility, the Division must:

(1) Conduct performance audits, record audits, and equipment audits of those licensed to perform inspections to ensure that inspections are performed properly.

(2) Ensure that Division personnel who audit license holders are knowledgeable about audit procedures and about the requirements of both the safety inspection and the emissions inspection programs.

(3) Perform an emissions inspection on a vehicle when requested to do so by a vehicle owner so the owner can compare the result of the inspection performed by the Division with the result of an inspection performed at an emissions inspection station.

(4) Investigate complaints about a person licensed to perform inspections and reports of irregularities in performing inspections.

(5) Establish written procedures for the issuance of electronic inspection authorizations to persons licensed to perform electronic inspection authorizations.

(6) Submit information and reports to the federal Environmental Protection Agency as required by 40 C.F.R. Part 51.

(b) **License Holders.** -- A person who is licensed by the Division under this Part must post the license at the place required by the Division and must keep a record of inspections performed. The inspection record must identify the vehicle that was inspected, indicate the type of inspection performed and the date of inspection, and contain any other information required by the Division. A self-inspector or an inspection station must send its records of inspections to the Division in the form and at the time required by the Division. An auditor of the Division may review the inspection records of a person licensed by the Division under this Part during normal business hours.

History.
1993 (Reg. Sess., 1994), c. 754, s. 1; 2007-503, s. 11

§ 20-183.7. Fees for performing an inspection and issuing an electronic inspection authorization to a vehicle; use of civil penalties

(a) **Fee Amount.** -- When a fee applies to an inspection of a vehicle or the issuance of an electronic inspection authorization, the fee must be collected. The following fees apply to an inspection of a vehicle and the issuance of an electronic inspection authorization:

Type	Inspection	Authorization
Safety Only	$ 12.75	$.85
Emissions and Safety	23.75	6.25

The fee for performing an inspection of a vehicle applies when an inspection is performed, regardless of whether the vehicle passes the inspection. The fee for an electronic inspection authorization applies when an electronic inspection authorization is issued to a vehicle. The fee for inspecting after-factory tinted windows shall be ten dollars ($ 10.00), and the fee applies only to an inspection performed with a light meter after a safety inspection mechanic determined that the window had after-factory tint. A safety inspection mechanic shall not inspect an after-factory tinted window of a vehicle for which the Division has issued a medical exception permit pursuant to G.S. 20-127(f).

A vehicle that is inspected at an inspection station and fails the inspection is entitled to be reinspected at the same station at any time within 60 days of the failed inspection without paying another inspection fee.

The inspection fee for an emissions and safety inspection set out in this subsection is the maximum amount that an inspection station or an inspection mechanic may charge for an emissions and safety inspection of a vehicle. An inspection station or an inspection mechanic may charge the maximum amount or any lesser amount for an emissions and safety inspection of a vehicle. The inspection fee for a safety only inspection set out in this subsection may not be increased or decreased. The authorization fees set out in this subsection may not be increased or decreased.

(b) **Self-Inspector.** -- The fee for an inspection does not apply to an inspection performed by a self-inspector. The fee for issuing an electronic inspection authorization to a vehicle applies to an inspection performed by a self-inspector.

(c) **Fee Distribution.** -- Fees collected for electronic inspection authorizations are payable to the Division of Motor Vehicles. The amount of each fee listed in the table below shall be credited to the Highway Fund, the Volunteer Rescue/EMS Fund established in G.S. 58-87-5, the Rescue Squad Workers' Relief Fund established in G.S. 58-88-5, and the Division of Air Quality of the Department of Environmental Quality:

Recipient	Safety Only Electronic Authorization	Emissions and Safety Electronic Authorization
Highway Fund	.55	5.30
Volunteer Rescue/EMS Fund	.18	.18
Rescue Squad Workers' Relief Fund	.12	.12
Division of Air Quality	.00	.65

(d) Repealed by Session Laws 2013-360, s. 34.15(c), effective July 1, 2013.

(d1) Repealed by Session Laws 2013-360, s. 34.15(b), effective June 30, 2014.

(d2) Repealed by Session Laws 2001-504, s. 3, effective July 1, 2007.

(e) **Civil Penalties.** -- Civil penalties collected under this Part shall be credited to the Highway Fund as nontax revenue.

(f) **Inspection Stations Required to Post Fee Information.** -- The Division shall approve the form and style of one or more standard signs to be used to display the information required by this subsection. The Division shall require that one or more of the standard signs be conspicuously posted at each inspection station in a manner reasonably calculated to make the information on the sign readily available to each person who presents a motor vehicle to the station for inspection. The sign shall include the following information:

(1) The maximum and minimum amounts of the inspection fee authorized by this section.

(2) The amount of the inspection fee charged by the inspection station and a statement that clearly indicates that the amount of the inspection fee is determined by the inspection station, that the inspection fee is retained by the inspection station to compensate the station for performing the inspection, and that the inspection fee is not paid to the State.

(3) The amount of the electronic inspection authorization fee, if the motor vehicle passes the inspection, a statement that the electronic inspection authorization fee is paid to the State, and a brief summary of the purposes for which the electronic inspection authorization fee is collected.

(4) The total fee to be charged if the motor vehicle passes the inspection.

(5) A statement that a vehicle that fails an inspection may be reinspected at the same station within 60 days of the inspection without payment of another inspection fee.

(g) **Information on Receipt.** -- The information set out in subdivisions (1) through (5) of subsection (f) of this section shall be set out in not smaller than 12 point type and shall be shown graphically in the form of a pie chart on the inspection receipt.

(h) Subsections (f) and (g) of this section apply only to inspection stations that perform both emissions and safety inspections.

History.
1965, c. 734, s. 1; 1969, c. 1242; 1973, c. 1480; 1975, c. 547; c. 716, s. 5; c. 875, s. 4; 1979, c. 688; 1979, 2nd Sess., c. 1180, ss. 5, 6; 1981, c. 690, s. 17; 1981 (Reg. Sess., 1982), c. 1261, s. 2; 1985, c. 415, ss. 1-6; 1985 (Reg. Sess., 1986), c. 1018, s. 8; 1987, c. 584, ss. 1-3; 1987 (Reg. Sess., 1988), c. 1062, ss. 3-5; 1989, c. 391, s. 3; c. 534, s. 3; 1989 (Reg. Sess., 1990), c. 1066, s. 33(b); 1991 (Reg. Sess., 1992), c. 943, s. 1; 1993, c. 385, s. 1; 1993 (Reg. Sess., 1994), c. 754, s. 1; 1995, c. 473, s. 3; 1995 (Reg. Sess., 1996), c. 743, s. 1; 1997-29, s. 4; 1997-443, s. 11A.123; 2000-75, s. 3; 2001-504, ss. 1 -3; 2006-230, s. 2; 2007-364, s. 2; 2007-503, s. 12; 2009-319, s. 3; 2010-96, s. 7; 2011-145, s. 6A.15; 2013-302, s. 1; 2013-360, s. 34.15(b), (c); 2015-241, s. 14.30(u)

§ 20-183.7A. Penalties applicable to license holders and suspension or revocation of license for safety violations

(a) **Kinds of Violations.** -- The civil penalty schedule established in this section applies to safety self-inspectors, safety inspection stations, and safety inspection mechanics. The schedule categorizes safety violations into serious (Type I), minor (Type II), and technical (Type III) violations. A serious violation is a violation of this Part or a rule adopted to implement this Part that directly affects the safety or emissions reduction benefits of the safety inspection program. A minor violation is a violation of this Part or a rule adopted to implement this Part that reflects negligence or carelessness in conducting a safety inspection or complying with the safety inspection requirements but does not directly affect the safety benefits or emission reduction benefits of the safety inspection program. A technical violation is a violation that is not a serious violation, a minor violation, or another type of offense under this Part.

(b) **Penalty Schedule.** -- The Division must take the following action for a violation:

(1) **Type I.** -- For a first or second Type I violation within three years by a safety self-inspector or a safety inspection station, assess a civil penalty of two hundred fifty dollars ($ 250.00) and suspend the license of the business for 180 days. For a third or subsequent Type I violation within three years by a safety self-inspector or a safety inspection station, assess a civil penalty of one thousand dollars ($ 1,000) and revoke the license of the business for two years. For a first or second Type I violation within seven years by a safety inspection mechanic, assess a civil penalty of one hundred dollars ($ 100.00) and suspend the mechanic's license for six months. For a third or subsequent Type I violation within seven years by a safety inspection mechanic, assess a civil penalty of two hundred fifty dollars ($ 250.00) and revoke the mechanic's license for two years.

(2) **Type II.** -- For a first or second Type II violation within three years by a safety self-inspector or a safety inspection station, assess a civil penalty of one hundred dollars ($ 100.00). For a third or subsequent Type II violation within three years by a safety self-inspector or a safety inspection station, assess a civil penalty of two hundred fifty dollars ($ 250.00) and suspend the license of the business for 90 days. For a first or second Type II violation within seven years by a safety inspection mechanic, assess a civil penalty of fifty dollars ($ 50.00). For a third or subsequent Type II violation within seven years by a safety inspection mechanic, assess a civil penalty of one hundred dollars ($ 100.00) and suspend the mechanic's license for 90 days.

(3) **Type III.** -- For a first or second Type III violation within seven years by a safety self-inspector, a safety inspection station, or a safety inspection mechanic, send a warning letter. For a third or subsequent Type III violation within seven years by the same safety license holder, assess a civil penalty of twenty-five dollars ($ 25.00).

(c) **Station or Self-Inspector Responsibility.** -- It is the responsibility of a safety inspection station and a safety self-inspector to supervise the safety inspection mechanics it employs. A violation by a safety inspection mechanic is considered a violation by the station or self-inspector for whom the mechanic is employed. The Division may stay a term of suspension for a first occurrence of a Type I violation for a station if the station agrees to follow the reasonable terms and conditions of the stay as determined by the Division. In determining whether to suspend a first occurrence violation for a station, the Division may consider the supervision provided by the station over the individual or individuals who committed the violation, action that has been taken to remedy future violations, or prior knowledge of the station as to the acts committed by the individual or individuals who committed the violation, or a combination of these factors. The monetary penalty shall not be stayed or reduced.

(d) **Multiple Violations in a Single Safety Inspection.** -- If a safety self-inspector, a safety inspection station, or a safety inspection mechanic commits two or more violations in the course of a single safety inspection, the Division shall take only the action specified for the most significant violation.

(d1) **Multiple Violations in Separate Safety Inspections.** -- In the case of two or more violations committed in separate safety inspections, considered at one time, the Division shall consider each violation as a separate occurrence and shall impose a separate penalty for each violation as a first, second, or third or subsequent violation as found in the applicable penalty schedule. The Division may in its discretion direct that any suspensions for the first, second, or third or subsequent violations run concurrently. If the Division does not direct that the suspensions run concurrently, they shall run consecutively. Nothing in this section shall prohibit or limit a reviewing court's ability to affirm, reverse, remand, or modify the Division's decisions, whether discretionary or otherwise, pursuant to Article 4 of Chapter 150B of the General Statutes.

(e) **Mechanic Training.** -- A safety inspection mechanic whose license has been suspended or revoked must retake the course required under G.S. 20-183.4 and successfully complete the course before the mechanic's license can be reinstated. Failure to successfully complete this course continues the period of suspension or revocation until the course is completed successfully.

History.

2001-504, s. 12; 2013-302, s. 2

§ 20-183.7B. Acts that are Type I, II, or III safety violations

(a) **Type I.** -- It is a Type I violation for a safety self-inspector, a safety inspection station, or a safety inspection mechanic to do any of the following:

(1) Issue a safety electronic inspection authorization to a vehicle without performing a safety inspection of vehicle.

(2) Issue a safety electronic inspection authorization to a vehicle after performing a safety inspection of the vehicle and determining that the vehicle did not pass the inspection.

(3) Allow a person who is not licensed as a safety inspection mechanic to perform a safety inspection for a self-inspector or at a safety station.

(4) Sell, issue, or otherwise give an electronic inspection authorization to another, other than as the result of a vehicle inspection in which the vehicle passed the inspection.

(5) Repealed by Session Laws 2013-302, s. 3, effective October 1, 2013, and applicable to violations occurring on or after that date.

(6) Perform a safety-only inspection on a vehicle that is subject to both a safety and an emissions inspection.

(7) Repealed by Session Laws 2013-302, s. 3, effective October 1, 2013, and applicable to violations occurring on or after that date.

(8) Conduct a safety inspection of a vehicle without driving the vehicle and without raising the vehicle and without opening the hood of the vehicle to check equipment located therein.

(9) Solicit or accept anything of value to pass a vehicle other than as provided in this Part.

(b) **Type II.** -- It is a Type II violation for a safety self-inspector, a safety inspection station, or a safety inspection mechanic to do any of the following:

(1) Issue a safety electronic inspection authorization to a vehicle without driving the vehicle and checking the vehicle's braking reaction, foot brake pedal reserve, and steering free play.

(2) Issue a safety electronic inspection authorization to a vehicle without raising the vehicle to free each wheel and checking the vehicle's tires, brake lines, parking brake cables, wheel drums, exhaust system, and the emissions equipment.

(3) Issue a safety electronic inspection authorization to a vehicle without raising the hood and checking the master cylinder, horn mounting, power steering, and emissions equipment.

(4) Conduct a safety inspection of a vehicle outside the designated inspection area.

(5) Issue a safety electronic inspection authorization to a vehicle with inoperative equipment, or with equipment that does not conform to the vehicle's original equipment or design specifications, or with equipment that is prohibited by any provision of law.

(6) Issue a safety electronic inspection authorization to a vehicle without performing a visual inspection of the vehicle's exhaust system.

(7) Issue a safety electronic inspection authorization to a vehicle without checking the exhaust system for leaks.

(8) Issue a safety electronic inspection authorization to a vehicle that is required to have any of the following emissions control devices but does not have the device:
  a. Catalytic converter.
  b. PCV valve.
  c. Thermostatic air control.
  d. Oxygen sensor.
  e. Unleaded gas restrictor.
  f. Gasoline tank cap or capless fuel system.
  g. Air injection system.
  h. Evaporative emissions system.
  i. Exhaust gas recirculation (EGR) valve.

(9) Issue a safety electronic inspection authorization to a vehicle after failing to inspect four or more of following:
  a. Emergency brake.
  b. Horn.
  c. Headlight high beam indicator.
  d. Inside rearview mirror.
  e. Outside rearview mirror.
  f. Turn signals.
  g. Parking lights.
  h. Headlights -- operation and lens.
  i. Headlights -- aim.
  j. Stoplights.
  k. Taillights.
  l. License plate lights.
  m. Windshield wiper.
  n. Windshield wiper blades.
  o. Window tint.

(10) Impose no fee for a safety inspection of a vehicle or the issuance of a safety electronic inspection authorization or impose a fee for one of these actions in an amount that differs from the amount set in G.S. 20-183.7.

(c) **Type III.** -- It is a Type III violation for a safety self-inspector, a safety inspection station, or a safety inspection mechanic to do any of the following:

(1) Fail to post a safety inspection station license issued by the Division.

(2) Fail to send information on safety inspections to the Division at the time or in the form required by the Division.

(3) Fail to post all safety information required by federal law and by the Division.

(4) Fail to put the required information on an inspection receipt in a legible manner using ink.

(5) Issue a receipt that is signed by a person other than the safety inspection mechanic.

(6) Repealed by Session Laws 2013-302, s. 3, effective October 1, 2013, and applicable to violations occurring on or after that date.

(7) Issue a safety electronic inspection authorization to a vehicle after having failed to inspect three or fewer of the following:
  a. Emergency brake.
  b. Horn.
  c. Headlight high beam indicator.
  d. Inside rearview mirror.
  e. Outside rearview mirror.
  f. Turn signals.
  g. Parking lights.
  h. Headlights -- operation and lens.
  i. Headlights -- aim.
  j. Stoplights.
  k. Taillights.
  l. License plate lights.
  m. Windshield wiper.
  n. Windshield wiper blades.
  o. Window tint.

(d) **Other Acts.** -- The lists in this section of the acts that are Type I, Type II, or Type III violations are not the only acts that are one of these types of violations. The Division may designate other acts that are a Type I, Type II, or Type III violation.

History.
2001-504, s. 12; 2007-503, s. 13; 2013-302, s. 3

§ 20-183.8. Infractions and criminal offenses for violations of inspection requirements

(a) **Infractions.** -- A person who does any of the following commits an infraction and, if found responsible, is liable for a penalty of up to fifty dollars ($ 50.00):

(1) Operates a motor vehicle that is subject to inspection under this Part on a highway or public vehicular area in the State when the vehicle has not been inspected in accordance with this Part, as evidenced by the vehicle's lack of a current electronic inspection authorization or otherwise.

(2) Allows an electronic inspection authorization to be issued to a vehicle owned or operated by that person, knowing that the

vehicle was not inspected before the electronic inspection authorization was issued or was not inspected properly.

(3) Issues an electronic inspection authorization on a vehicle, knowing or having reasonable grounds to know that an inspection of the vehicle was not performed or was performed improperly. A person who is cited for a civil penalty under G.S. 20-183.8B for an emissions violation involving the inspection of a vehicle may not be charged with an infraction under this subdivision based on that same vehicle.

(4) Alters the original certified configuration or data link connectors of a vehicle in such a way as to make an emissions inspection by analysis of data provided by on-board diagnostic (OBD) equipment inaccurate or impossible.

(b) **Defenses to Infractions.** -- Any of the following is a defense to a violation under subsection (a) of this section:

(1) The vehicle was continuously out of State for at least the 30 days preceding the date the electronic inspection authorization expired and a current electronic inspection authorization was obtained within 10 days after the vehicle came back to the State.

(2) The vehicle displays a dealer license plate or a transporter plate, the dealer repossessed the vehicle or otherwise acquired the vehicle within the last 10 days, and the vehicle is being driven from its place of acquisition to the dealer's place of business or to an inspection station.

(3) Repealed by Session Laws 1997-29, s. 5.

(4) The charged infraction is described in subdivision (a)(1) of this section, the vehicle is subject to a safety inspection or an emissions inspection and the vehicle owner establishes in court that the vehicle was inspected after the citation was issued and within 30 days of the expiration date of the inspection sticker that was on the vehicle or the electronic inspection authorization was issued to the vehicle when the citation was issued.

(b1) A person who performs a safety inspection without a license, as required under G.S. 20-183.4, or an emissions inspection without a license, as required under G.S. 20-183.4A, is guilty of a Class 3 misdemeanor.

(c) **Felony.** -- A person who does any of the following commits a Class I felony:

(1) Forges an inspection sticker or inspection receipt.

(2) Buys, sells, issues, or possesses a forged inspection sticker or electronic inspection authorization.

(3) Buys, sells, issues, or possesses an electronic inspection authorization other than as the result of either of the following:

a. Having a license as an inspection station, a self-inspector, or an inspection mechanic and obtaining the electronic inspection authorization from the Division through an electronic authorization vendor in the course of business.

b. A vehicle inspection in which the vehicle passed the inspection or for which the vehicle received a waiver.

(4) Solicits or accepts anything of value in order to pass a vehicle that fails a safety or emissions inspection.

(5) Fails a vehicle for any reason not authorized by law.

History.
1965, c. 734, s. 1; 1967, c. 692, s. 3; 1969, c. 179, s. 1; c. 620; 1973, cc. 909, 1322; 1975, c. 716, s. 5; 1979, 2nd Sess., c. 1180, s. 4; 1985, c. 764, s. 23; 1985 (Reg. Sess., 1986), c. 852, s. 17; 1993 (Reg. Sess., 1994), c. 754, s. 1; 1997-29, s. 5; 1999-452, s. 25; 2001-504, s. 13; 2007-503, s. 14; 2009-319, s. 5

§ 20-183.8A. Civil penalties against motorists for emissions violations; waiver

(a) **Civil Penalties.** -- The Division must assess a civil penalty against a person who owns or leases a vehicle that is subject to an inspection and who engages in any of the emissions violations set out in this subsection. As provided in G.S. 20-54, the registration of a vehicle may not be renewed until a penalty imposed under this subsection has been paid. The civil penalties and violations are as follows:

(1) Fifty dollars ($ 50.00) for failure to have the vehicle inspected within four months after it is required to be inspected under this Part.

(2) Two hundred fifty dollars ($ 250.00) for instructing or allowing a person to tamper with an emission control device of the vehicle so as to make the device inoperative or fail to work properly.

(3) Two hundred fifty dollars ($ 250.00) for incorrectly stating the vehicle's county of registration to avoid having an emissions inspection of the vehicle.

(b) **Waiver.** -- The Division must waive the civil penalty assessed under subdivision (a)(1) of this section against a person who establishes the following:

(1) The person was continuously out of the State on active military duty from the date the electronic authorization expired to the date the four-month grace period expired.

(2) No person operated the vehicle from the date the electronic authorization expired to the date the four-month grace period expired.

Chapter 20

(3) The person obtained a current electronic authorization within 30 days after returning to the State.

History.
1993 (Reg. Sess., 1994), c. 754, ss. 1, 8; 1998-212, s. 27.6(b); 2007-364, ss. 3, 4; 2007-503, s. 15; 2009-319, s. 4

§ 20-183.8B. Civil penalties against license holders and suspension or revocation of license for emissions violations

(a) **Kinds of Violations.** -- The civil penalty schedule established in this section applies to emissions self-inspectors, emissions inspection stations, and emissions inspection mechanics. The schedule categorizes emissions violations into serious (Type I), minor (Type II), and technical (Type III) violations.

A serious violation is a violation of this Part or a rule adopted to implement this Part that directly affects the emission reduction benefits of the emissions inspection program. A minor violation is a violation of this Part or a rule adopted to implement this Part that reflects negligence or carelessness in conducting an emissions inspection or complying with the emissions inspection requirements but does not directly affect the emission reduction benefits of the emissions inspection program. A technical violation is a violation that is not a serious violation, a minor violation, or another type of offense under this Part.

(b) **Penalty Schedule.** -- The Division must take the following action for a violation:

(1) **Type I.** -- For a first or second Type I violation by an emissions self-inspector or an emissions inspection station, assess a civil penalty of two hundred fifty dollars ($ 250.00) and suspend the license of the business for 180 days. For a third or subsequent Type I violation within three years by an emissions self-inspector or an emissions inspection station, assess a civil penalty of one thousand dollars ($ 1,000) and revoke the license of the business for two years.

For a first or second Type I violation by an emissions inspection mechanic, assess a civil penalty of one hundred dollars ($ 100.00) and suspend the mechanic's license for 180 days. For a third or subsequent Type I violation within seven years by an emissions inspection mechanic, assess a civil penalty of two hundred fifty dollars ($ 250.00) and revoke the mechanic's license for two years.

(2) **Type II.** -- For a first or second Type II violation by an emissions self-inspector or an emissions inspection station, assess a civil penalty of one hundred dollars ($ 100.00). For a third or subsequent Type II violation within three years by an emissions self-inspector or an emissions inspection station, assess a civil penalty of two hundred fifty dollars ($ 250.00) and suspend the license of the business for 90 days.

For a first or second Type II violation by an emissions inspection mechanic, assess a civil penalty of fifty dollars ($ 50.00). For a third or subsequent Type II violation within seven years by an emissions inspection mechanic, assess a civil penalty of one hundred dollars ($ 100.00) and suspend the mechanic's license for 90 days.

(3) **Type III.** -- For a first or second Type III violation by an emissions self-inspector, an emissions inspection station, or an emissions inspection mechanic, send a warning letter. For a third or subsequent Type III violation within three years by the same emissions license holder, assess a civil penalty of twenty-five dollars ($ 25.00).

(c) **Station or Self-Inspector Responsibility.** -- It is the responsibility of an emissions inspection station and an emissions self-inspector to supervise the emissions mechanics it employs. A violation by an emissions inspector mechanic is considered a violation by the station or self-inspector for whom the mechanic is employed. The Division may stay a term of suspension for a first occurrence of a Type I violation for a station if the station agrees to follow the reasonable terms and conditions of the stay as determined by the Division. In determining whether to suspend a first occurrence violation for a station, the Division may consider the supervision provided by the station over the individual or individuals who committed the violation, action that has been taken to remedy future violations, or prior knowledge of the station as to the acts committed by the individual or individuals who committed the violation, or a combination of these factors. The monetary penalty shall not be stayed or reduced.

(c1) **Multiple Violations in a Single Emissions Inspection.** -- If an emissions self-inspector, an emissions inspection station, or an emissions inspection mechanic commits two or more violations in the course of a single emissions inspection, the Division shall take only the action specified for the most significant violation.

(c2) **Multiple Violations in Separate Emissions Inspections.** -- In the case of two or more violations committed in separate emissions inspections, considered at one time, the Division shall consider each violation as a separate occurrence and shall impose a separate penalty for each violation as a first, second, or third or subsequent violation as found in the applicable penalty schedule. The Division may in its discretion direct that any suspensions for the first, second, or third or subsequent violations run concurrently. If the Division does not direct that the suspensions run concurrently, they shall run consecutively. Nothing in this section shall prohibit or limit a reviewing court's ability to affirm, reverse, remand, or modify the Division's decisions, whether discretionary or otherwise, pursuant to Article 4 of Chapter 150B of the General Statutes.

(d), (d1) Repealed by Session Laws 2013-302, s. 4, effective October 1, 2013, and applicable to violations occurring on or after that date.

(e) **Mechanic Training.** -- An emissions inspection mechanic whose license has been suspended or revoked must retake the course required under G.S. 20-183.4A and successfully complete the course before the mechanic's license can be reinstated. Failure to successfully complete this course continues the period of suspension or revocation until the course is completed successfully.

History.
1993 (Reg. Sess., 1994), c. 754, s. 1; 1997-29, s. 6; 2001-504, s. 14; 2013-302, s. 4.

§ 20-183.8C. Acts that are Type I, II, or III emissions violations

(a) **Type I.** -- It is a Type I violation for an emissions self-inspector, an emissions inspection station, or an emissions inspection mechanic to do any of the following:

(1) Issue an emissions electronic inspection authorization on a vehicle without performing an emissions inspection of the vehicle.

(1a) Issue an emissions electronic inspection authorization to a vehicle after performing an emissions inspection of the vehicle and determining that the vehicle did not pass the inspection.

(2) Use a test-defeating strategy when conducting an emissions inspection by changing the emission standards for a vehicle by incorrectly entering the vehicle type or model year, or using data provided by the on-board diagnostic (OBD) equipment of another vehicle to achieve a passing result.

(3) Allow a person who is not licensed as an emissions inspection mechanic to perform an emissions inspection for a self-inspector or at an emissions station.

(4) Sell, issue, or otherwise give an electronic inspection authorization to another other than as the result of a vehicle inspection in which the vehicle passed the inspection or for which the vehicle received a waiver.

(5) Repealed by Session Laws 2013-302, s. 5, effective October 1, 2013, and applicable to violations occurring on or after that date.

(6) Perform a safety-only inspection on a vehicle that is subject to both a safety and an emissions inspection.

(7) Repealed by Session Laws 2013-302, s. 5, effective October 1, 2013, and applicable to violations occurring on or after that date.

(b) **Type II.** -- It is a Type II violation for an emissions self-inspector, an emissions inspection station, or an emissions inspection mechanic to do any of the following:

(1) Use the identification code of another to gain access to an emissions analyzer or to equipment to analyze data provided by on-board diagnostic (OBD) equipment.

(2) Keep compliance documents in a manner that makes them easily accessible to individuals who are not inspection mechanics.

(3) Issue a safety electronic inspection authorization or an emissions electronic inspection authorization on a vehicle that is required to have one of the following emissions control devices but does not have it:
   a. Catalytic converter.
   b. PCV valve.
   c. Thermostatic air control.
   d. Oxygen sensor.
   e. Unleaded gas restrictor.
   f. Gasoline tank cap or capless fuel system.
   g. Air injection system.
   h. Evaporative emissions system.
   i. Exhaust gas recirculation (EGR) valve.

(4) Issue a safety electronic inspection authorization or an emissions electronic inspection authorization on a vehicle without performing a visual inspection of the vehicle's exhaust system and checking the exhaust system for leaks.

(5) Impose no fee for an emissions inspection of a vehicle or the issuance of an emissions electronic inspection authorization or impose a fee for one of these actions in an amount that differs from the amount set in G.S. 20-183.7.

(6) Issue an emissions electronic inspection authorization to a vehicle with a faulty Malfunction Indicator Lamp (MIL) or to a vehicle that has been made inoperable.

(c) **Type III.** -- It is a Type III violation for an emissions self-inspector, an emissions inspection station, or an emissions inspection mechanic to do any of the following:

(1) Fail to post an emissions license issued by the Division.

Chapter 20

(2) Fail to send information on emissions inspections to the Division at the time or in the form required by the Division.

(3) Fail to post emissions information required by federal law to be posted.

(4) Repealed by Session Laws 2007-503, s. 16, effective October 1, 2008.

(5) Fail to put the required information on an inspection receipt in a legible manner.

(6) Repealed by Session Laws 2007-503, s. 16, effective October 1, 2008.

(d) **Other Acts.** -- The lists in this section of the acts that are Type I, Type II, or Type III violations are not the only acts that are one of these types of violations. The Division may designate other acts that are a Type I, Type II, or Type III violation.

History.
1993 (Reg. Sess., 1994), c. 754, s. 1; 1995, c. 163, s. 11; 1997-29, s. 7; 1997-456, s. 35; 2000-134, ss. 18, 19; 2001-504, ss. 15, 16, 19; 2007-503, s. 16; 2013-302, s. 5

§ 20-183.8D. Suspension or revocation of license

(a) **Safety.** -- The Division may suspend or revoke a safety self-inspector license, a safety inspection station license, and a safety inspection mechanic license issued under this Part if the license holder fails to comply with this Part or a rule adopted by the Commissioner to implement this Part.

(b) **Emissions.** -- The Division may suspend or revoke an emissions self-inspector license, an emissions inspection station license, and an emissions inspection mechanic license issued under this Part for any of the following reasons:

(1) The suspension or revocation is imposed under G.S. 20-183.8B.

(2) Failure to pay a civil penalty imposed under G.S. 20-183.8B within 30 days after it is imposed.

History.
1993 (Reg. Sess., 1994), c. 754, s. 1; 1997-29, s. 8

N.C. Gen. Stat. § 20-183.8E

Recodified as § 20-183.8G at the direction of the Revisor of Statutes.

§ 20-183.8F. Requirements for giving license holders notice of violations and for taking summary action

(a) Repealed by Session Laws 2011-145, s. 28.23B(a), effective July 1, 2011.

(b) **Notice of Charges.** -- When the Division decides to charge an inspection station, a self-inspector, or a mechanic with a violation that could result in the suspension or revocation of the person's license, the Division must deliver a written statement of the charges to the affected license holder. The statement of charges must inform the license holder of the right to request a hearing, instruct the person on how to obtain a hearing, and inform the license holder of the effect of not requesting a hearing. The license holder has the right to a hearing before the license is suspended or revoked. G.S. 20-183.8G sets out the procedure for obtaining a hearing.

(c) **Exception for Summary Action.** -- The right granted by subsection (b) of this section to have a hearing before a license is suspended or revoked does not apply if the Division summarily suspends or revokes the license after a judge has reviewed and authorized the proposed action. A license issued to an inspection station, a self-inspector, or a mechanic is a substantial property interest that cannot be summarily suspended or revoked without judicial review.

(d) A notice or statement prepared pursuant to this section or an order of the Division that is directed to a mechanic may be served on the mechanic by delivering a copy of the notice, statement, or order to the station or to the place of business of the self-inspector where the mechanic is employed. Delivery under this section to any person may be made via certified mail or by hand delivery.

History.
1997-29, s. 9; 1999-328, s. 3.13; 2001-504, s. 17; 2011-145, s. 28.23B(a)

§ 20-183.8G. Administrative and judicial review

(a) **Right to Hearing.** -- A person who applies for a license or registration under this Part or who has a license or registration issued under this Part has the right to a hearing when any of the following occurs:

(1) The Division denies the person's application for a license or registration.

(2) The Division delivers to the person a written statement of charges of a violation that could result in the suspension or revocation of the person's license.

(3) The Division summarily suspends or revokes the person's license following review and authorization of the proposed adverse action by a judge.

(4) The Division assesses a civil penalty against the person.

(5) The Division issues a warning letter to the person.

(6) The Division cancels the person's registration.

(b) **Hearing After Statement of Charges.** -- When a license holder receives a statement of charges of a violation that could result in the

Chapter 20

suspension or revocation of the person's license, the person can obtain a hearing by making a request for a hearing. The person must make the request to the Division within 10 days after receiving the statement of the charges. A person who does not request a hearing within this time limit waives the right to a hearing.

The Division must hold a hearing requested under this subsection within 30 days after receiving the request, unless the matter is continued for good cause. The hearing must be held at the location designated by the Division. Suspension or revocation of the license is stayed until a decision is made following the hearing.

If a person does not request a hearing within the time allowed for making the request, the proposed suspension or revocation becomes effective the day after the time for making the request ends. If a person requests a hearing but does not attend the hearing, the proposed suspension or revocation becomes effective the day after the date set for the hearing.

(c) **Hearing After Summary Action.** -- When the Division summarily suspends a license issued under this Part after judicial review and authorization of the proposed action, the person whose license was suspended or revoked may obtain a hearing by filing with the Division a written request for a hearing. The request must be filed within 10 days after the person was notified of the summary action. The Division must hold a hearing requested under this subsection within 14 days after receiving the request.

(d) **All Other Hearings.** -- When this section gives a person the right to a hearing and subsection (b) or (c) of this section does not apply to the hearing, the person may obtain a hearing by filing with the Division a written request for a hearing. The request must be filed within 10 days after the person receives written notice of the action for which a hearing is requested. The Division must hold a hearing within 90 days after the Division receives the request, unless the matter is continued for good cause.

(e) **Review by Commissioner.** -- The Commissioner may conduct a hearing required under this section or may designate a person to conduct the hearing. When a person designated by the Commissioner holds a hearing and makes a decision, the person who requested the hearing has the right to request the Commissioner to review the decision. The procedure set by the Division governs the review by the Commissioner of a decision made by a person designated by the Commissioner.

(f) **Decision.** -- Upon the Commissioner's review of a decision made after a hearing on the imposition of a monetary penalty against a motorist for an emissions violation or on a Type I, II, or III violation by a license holder, the Commissioner must uphold any monetary penalty,

license suspension, license revocation, or warning required by G.S. 20-183.7A, G.S. 20-183.8A or G.S. 20-183.8B, respectively, if the decision is based on evidence presented at the hearing that supports the hearing officer's determination that the motorist or license holder committed the act for which the monetary penalty, license suspension, license revocation, or warning was imposed. Pursuant to the authority under G.S. 20-183.7A(c) and G.S. 20-183.8B(c), the Commissioner may order a suspension for a first occurrence Type I violation of a station to be stayed upon reasonable compliance terms to be determined by the Commissioner. Pursuant to the authority under G.S. 20-183.7A(d1) and G.S. 183.8B(c2), the Commissioner may order the suspensions against a license holder to run consecutively or concurrently. The Commissioner may uphold, dismiss, or modify a decision made after a hearing on any other action.

(g) **Judicial Review.** -- Article 4 of Chapter 150B of the General Statutes governs judicial review of an administrative decision made under this section.

History.
1993 (Reg. Sess., 1994), c. 754, s. 1; 1997-29, s. 10; 1999-328, s. 3.14; 1999-456, s. 69; 2009-550, s. 3.1; 2011-145, s. 28.23B(b); 2013-302, s. 6; 2014-58, s. 1

ARTICLE 3B
PERMANENT WEIGH STATIONS AND PORTABLE SCALES

§ 20-183.9. Establishment and maintenance of permanent weigh stations

The Department of Public Safety is hereby authorized, empowered and directed to equip and operate permanent weigh stations equipped to weigh vehicles using the streets and highways of this State to determine whether such vehicles are being operated in accordance with legislative enactments relating to weights of vehicles and their loads. The permanent weigh stations shall be established at such locations on the streets and highways in this State as will enable them to be used most advantageously in determining the weight of vehicles and their loads. The Department of Transportation shall be responsible for the maintenance and upkeep of all permanent weigh stations established pursuant to this section.

History.
1951, c. 988, s. 1; 1957, c. 65, s. 11; 1973, c. 507, s. 5; 1977, c. 464, ss. 34, 37; 1979, c. 76; 2002-159, s. 31.5(b); 2002-190, s. 7; 2004-124, s. 18.3(b); 2006-66, s. 21.8; 2011-145, s. 19.1(g)

§ 20-183.10. Operation of the permanent weigh stations by the Department of Public Safety, State Highway Patrol, uniformed personnel

The permanent weigh stations to be established pursuant to the provisions of this Article shall be operated by the Department of Public Safety, State Highway Patrol, who shall assign a sufficient number of sworn and nonsworn personnel to the various weigh stations. Sworn personnel of the State Highway Patrol shall supervise all nonsworn personnel assigned to weigh stations. The sworn and nonsworn personnel shall have authority to weigh vehicles and to assess civil penalties pursuant to Article 3, Part 9 of this Chapter and shall wear uniforms to be selected and furnished by the Department of Public Safety, State Highway Patrol. The uniformed sworn and nonsworn personnel assigned to the various permanent weigh stations shall weigh vehicles and complete various reports as may be necessary for recording violations relating to the weight of vehicles and their loads. The uniformed officers assigned to the various permanent weigh stations shall have the powers of peace officers for the purpose of enforcing the provisions of this Chapter and in making arrests, serving process, and appearing in court in all matters and things relating to the weight of vehicles and their loads.

History.
1951, c. 988, s. 2; 1975, c. 716, s. 5; 1977, c. 319; 2002-159, s. 31.5(b); 2002-190, s. 8; 2004-124, s. 18.3(c); 2011-145, s. 19.1(g), (p); 2015-241, s. 16A.7(j).

N.C. Gen. Stat. § 20-183.11

Repealed by Session Laws 1995, c. 109, s. 5.

N.C. Gen. Stat. § 20-183.12

Repealed by Session Laws 1995, c. 163, s. 12.

ARTICLE 3C
VEHICLE EQUIPMENT SAFETY COMPACT

§ 20-183.13. Compact enacted into law; form of Compact

The Vehicle Equipment Safety Compact is hereby enacted into law and entered into with all other jurisdictions legally joining therein in the form substantially as follows:

VEHICLE EQUIPMENT
SAFETY COMPACT
ARTICLE I.
Findings and Purposes.

(a) The party states find that:

(1) Accidents and deaths on their streets and highways present a very serious human and economic problem with a major deleterious effect on the public welfare.

(2) There is a vital need for the development of greater interjurisdictional cooperation to achieve the necessary uniformity in the laws, rules, regulations and codes relating to vehicle equipment, and to accomplish this by such means as will minimize the time between the development of demonstrably and scientifically sound safety features and their incorporation into vehicles.

(b) The purposes of this Compact are to:

(1) Promote uniformity in regulation of and standards for equipment.

(2) Secure uniformity of law and administrative practice in vehicular regulation and related safety standards to permit incorporation of desirable equipment changes in vehicles in the interest of greater traffic safety.

(3) To provide means for the encouragement and utilization of research which will facilitate the achievement of the foregoing purposes, with due regard for the findings set forth in subdivision (a) of this article.

(c) It is the intent of this Compact to emphasize performance requirements and not to determine the specific detail of engineering in the manufacture of vehicles or equipment except to the extent necessary for the meeting of such performance requirements.

ARTICLE II.
Definitions.

As used in this Compact:

(a) "Vehicle" means every device in, upon or by which any person or property is or may be transported or drawn upon a highway, excepting devices moved by human power or used exclusively upon stationary rails or tracks.

(b) "State" means a state, territory or possession of the United States, the District of Columbia, or the Commonwealth of Puerto Rico.

(c) "Equipment" means any part of a vehicle or any accessory for use thereon which affects the safety of operation of such vehicle or the safety of the occupants.

ARTICLE III.
The Commission.

(a) There is hereby created an agency of the party states to be known as the "Vehicle Equipment Safety Commission" hereinafter called the Commission. The Commission shall be composed of one commissioner from each party state who shall be appointed, serve and be subject to removal in accordance with the laws of the state which he represents. If authorized by the laws of his party state, a commissioner may provide for the discharge of his duties and the performance of his functions on the Commission, either for the duration of his membership or for any lesser period of time, by an alternate. No such alternate shall be entitled to serve unless notification of his identity and appointment shall have been given to the Commission in such form as the Commission may require. Each commissioner, and each alternate, when serving in the place and stead of a commissioner, shall be entitled to be reimbursed by the Commission for expenses actually incurred in attending Commission meetings or while engaged in the business of the Commission.

(b) The commissioners shall be entitled to one vote each on the Commission. No action of the Commission shall be binding unless taken at a meeting at which a majority of the total number of votes on the Commission are cast in favor thereof. Action of the Commission shall be only at a meeting at which a majority of the commissioners, or their alternates, are present.

(c) The Commission shall have a seal.

(d) The Commission shall elect annually, from among its members, a chairman, a vice-chairman and a treasurer. The Commission may appoint an Executive Director and fix his duties and compensation. Such Executive Director shall serve at the pleasure of the Commission, and together with the treasurer shall be bonded in such amount as the Commission shall determine. The Executive Director also shall serve as secretary. If there be no Executive Director, the Commission shall elect a secretary in addition to the other officers provided by this subdivision.

(e) Irrespective of the civil service, personnel or other merit system laws of any of the party states, the Executive Director with approval of the Commission, or the Commission if there be no Executive Director, shall appoint, remove or discharge such personnel as may be necessary for the performance of the Commission's functions, and shall fix the duties and compensation of such personnel.

(f) The Commission may establish and maintain independently or in conjunction with any one or more of the party states, a suitable retirement system for its full-time employees. Employees of the Commission shall be eligible for Social Security coverage in respect of old age and survivor's insurance provided that the Commission takes such steps as may be necessary pursuant to the laws of the United States, to participate in such program of insurance as a government agency or unit. The Commission may establish and maintain or participate in such additional programs of employee benefits as may be appropriate.

(g) The Commission may borrow, accept or contract for the services of personnel from any party state, the United States, or any subdivision or agency of the aforementioned governments, or from any agency of two or more of the party states or their subdivisions.

(h) The Commission may accept for any of its purposes and functions under this Compact any and all donations, and grants of money, equipment, supplies, materials, and services, conditional or otherwise, from any state, the United States, or any other governmental agency and may receive, utilize and dispose of the same.

(i) The Commission may establish and maintain such facilities as may be necessary for the transacting of its business. The Commission may acquire, hold, and convey real and personal property and any interest therein.

(j) The Commission shall adopt bylaws for the conduct of its business and shall have the power to amend and rescind these bylaws. The Commission shall publish its bylaws in convenient form and shall file a copy thereof and a copy of any amendment thereto, with the appropriate agency or officer in each of the party states. The bylaws shall provide for appropriate notice to the commissioners of all Commission meetings and hearings and the business to be transacted at such meetings or hearings. Such notice shall also be given to such agencies or officers of each party state as the laws of such party state may provide.

(k) The Commission annually shall make to the governor and legislature of each party state a report covering the activities of the Commission for the preceding year, and embodying such recommendations as may have been issued by the Commission. The Commission may make such additional reports as it may deem desirable.

ARTICLE IV.
Research and Testing.

The Commission shall have power to:

(a) Collect, correlate, analyze and evaluate information resulting or derivable from research and testing activities in equipment and related fields.

(b) Recommend and encourage the undertaking of research and testing in any aspect of equipment or related matters when, in its judgment, appropriate or sufficient research or testing has not been undertaken.

(c) Contract for such equipment research and testing as one or more governmental agencies may agree to have contracted for by the Commission, provided that such governmental agency or agencies shall make available the funds necessary for such research and testing.

(d) Recommend to the party states changes in law or policy with emphasis on uniformity of laws and administrative rules, regulations or codes which would promote effective governmental action or coordination in the prevention of equipment-related highway accidents or the mitigation of equipment-related highway safety problems.

ARTICLE V.
Vehicular Equipment.

(a) In the interest of vehicular and public safety, the Commission may study the need for or desirability of the establishment of or changes in performance requirements or restrictions for any item of equipment. As a result of such study, the Commission may publish a report relating to any item or items of equipment, and the issuance of such a report shall be a condition precedent to any proceedings or other action provided or authorized by this article. No less than 60 days after the publication of a report containing the results of such study, the Commission upon due notice shall hold a hearing or hearings at such place or places as it may determine.

(b) Following the hearing or hearings provided for in subdivision (a) of this article, and with due regard for standards recommended by appropriate professional and technical associations and agencies, the Commission may issue rules, regulations or codes embodying performance requirements or restrictions for any item or items of equipment covered in the report, which in the opinion of the Commission will be fair and equitable and effectuate the purposes of this Compact.

(c) Each party state obligates itself to give due consideration to any and all rules, regulations and codes issued by the Commission and hereby declares its policy and intent to be the promotion of uniformity in the laws of the several party states relating to equipment.

(d) The Commission shall send prompt notice of its action in issuing any rule, regulation or code pursuant to this article to the appropriate motor vehicle agency of each party state and such notice shall contain the complete text of the rule, regulation or code.

(e) If the constitution of a party state requires, or if its statutes provide, the approval of the legislature by appropriate resolution or act may be made a condition precedent to the taking effect in such party state of any rule, regulation or code. In such event, the commissioner of such party state shall submit any Commission rule, regulation or code to the legislature as promptly as may be in lieu of administrative acceptance or rejection thereof by the party state.

(f) Except as otherwise specifically provided in or pursuant to subdivisions (e) and (g) of this article, the appropriate motor vehicle agency of a party state shall in accordance with its constitution or procedural laws adopt the rule, regulation or code within six months of the sending of the notice, and, upon such adoption, the rule, regulation or code shall have the force and effect of law therein.

(g) The appropriate motor vehicle agency of a party state may decline to adopt a rule, regulation or code issued by the Commission pursuant to this article if such agency specifically finds, after public hearing on due notice, that a variation from the Commission's rule, regulation or code is necessary to the public safety, and incorporates in such finding the reasons upon which it is based. Any such finding shall be subject to review by such procedure for review of administrative determinations as may be applicable pursuant to the laws of the party state. Upon request, the Commission shall be furnished with a copy of the transcript of any hearings held pursuant to this subdivision.

ARTICLE VI.
Finance.

(a) The Commission shall submit to the executive head or designated officer or officers of each party state a budget of its estimated expenditures for such period as may be required by the laws of that party state for presentation to the legislature thereof.

(b) Each of the Commission's budgets of estimated expenditures shall contain specific recommendations of the amount or amounts to be appropriated by each of the party states. The total amount of appropriations under any such budget shall be apportioned among the party states as follows: one third in equal shares; and the remainder in proportion to the number of motor vehicles registered in each party state. In determining the number of such registrations, the Commission may employ such source or sources of information as, in its judgment present the most equitable and accurate comparisons among the party states. Each of the Commission's budgets of estimated expenditures and requests for appropriations shall indicate the source or sources used in obtaining information concerning vehicular registrations.

(c) The Commission shall not pledge the credit of any party state. The Commission may meet any of its obligations in whole or in part with funds available to it under Article III(h) of this Compact, provided that the Commission takes specific action setting aside such funds prior to incurring any obligation to be met in whole or in part in such manner. Except where the Commission makes use of funds available to it under Article III(h) hereof, the Commission shall not incur any obligation prior to the allotment of funds by the party states adequate to meet the same.

(d) The Commission shall keep accurate accounts of all receipts and disbursements. The receipts and disbursements of the Commission shall be subject to the audit and accounting

Chapter 20

procedures established under its rules. However, all receipts and disbursements of funds handled by the Commission shall be audited yearly by a qualified public accountant and the report of the audit shall be included in and become part of the annual reports of the Commission.

(e) The accounts of the Commission shall be open at any reasonable time for inspection by duly constituted officers of the party states and by any persons authorized by the Commission.

(f) Nothing contained herein shall be construed to prevent Commission compliance with laws relating to audit or inspection of accounts by or on behalf of any government contributing to the support of the Commission.

ARTICLE VII.
Conflict of Interest.

(a) The Commission shall adopt rules and regulations with respect to conflict of interest for the commissioners of the party states, and their alternates, if any, and for the staff of the Commission and contractors with the Commission to the end that no member or employee or contractor shall have a pecuniary or other incompatible interest in the manufacture, sale or distribution of motor vehicles or vehicular equipment or in any facility or enterprise employed by the Commission or on its behalf for testing, conduct of investigations or research. In addition to any penalty for violation of such rules and regulations as may be applicable under the laws of the violator's jurisdiction of residence, employment or business, any violation of a Commission rule or regulation adopted pursuant to this article shall require the immediate discharge of any violating employee and the immediate vacating of membership, or relinquishing of status as a member on the Commission by any commissioner or alternate. In the case of a contractor, any violation of any such rule or regulation shall make any contract of the violator with the Commission subject to cancellation by the Commission.

(b) Nothing contained in this article shall be deemed to prevent a contractor for the Commission from using any facilities subject to his control in the performance of the contract even though such facilities are not devoted solely to work of or done on behalf of the Commission; nor to prevent such a contractor from receiving remuneration or profit from the use of such facilities.

ARTICLE VIII.
Advisory and Technical Committees.

The Commission may establish such advisory and technical committees as it may deem necessary, membership on which may include private citizens and public officials, and may cooperate with and use the services of any such committees and the organizations which the members represent in furthering any of its activities.

ARTICLE IX.
Entry into Force and Withdrawal.

(a) This Compact shall enter into force when enacted into law by any six or more states. Thereafter, this Compact shall become effective as to any other state upon its enactment thereof.

(b) Any party state may withdraw from this Compact by enacting a statute repealing the same, but no such withdrawal shall take effect until one year after the executive head of the withdrawing state has given notice in writing of the withdrawal to the executive heads of all other party states. No withdrawal shall affect any liability already incurred by or chargeable to a party state prior to the time of such withdrawal.

ARTICLE X.
Construction and Severability.

This Compact shall be liberally construed so as to effectuate the purposes thereof. The provisions of this Compact shall be severable and if any phrase, clause, sentence or provision of this Compact is declared to be contrary to the Constitution of any state or of the United States or the applicability thereof to any government, agency, person or circumstance is held invalid, the validity of the remainder of this Compact and the applicability thereof to any government, agency, person or circumstance shall not be affected thereby. If this Compact shall be held contrary to the constitution of any state participating herein, the Compact shall remain in full force and effect as to the remaining party states and in full force and effect as to the state affected as to all severable matters.

History.
1963, c. 1167, s. 1

§ 20-183.14. Legislative findings

The General Assembly finds that:

(1) The public safety necessitates the continuous development, modernization and implementation of standards and requirements of law relating to vehicle equipment, in accordance with expert knowledge and opinion.

(2) The public safety further requires that such standards and requirements be uniform from jurisdiction to jurisdiction, except to the extent that specific and compelling evidence supports variation.

(3) The Division of Motor Vehicles, acting upon recommendations of the Vehicle Equipment Safety Commission and

pursuant to the Vehicle Equipment Safety Compact provides a just, equitable and orderly means of promoting the public safety in the manner and within the scope contemplated by this Article.

History.
1963, c. 1167, s. 2; 1975, c. 716, s. 5

§ 20-183.15. Approval of rules and regulations by General Assembly required

Pursuant to Article V(e) of the Vehicle Equipment Safety Compact, it is the intention of this State and it is hereby provided that no rule, regulation or code issued by the Vehicle Equipment Safety Commission in accordance with Article V of the Compact shall take effect until approved by act of the General Assembly.

History.
1963, c. 1167, s. 3

§ 20-183.16. Compact Commissioner

The Commissioner of this State on the Vehicle Equipment Safety Commission shall be the Secretary of Transportation or such other officer of the Department of Transportation as the Secretary may designate.

History.
1963, c. 1167, s. 4; 1975, c. 716, s. 5

§ 20-183.17. Cooperation of State agencies authorized

Within appropriations available therefor, the departments, agencies and officers of the government of this State may cooperate with and assist the Vehicle Equipment Safety Commission within the scope contemplated by Article III(h) of the Compact. The departments, agencies and officers of the government of this State are authorized generally to cooperate with said Commission.

History.
1963, c. 1167, s. 5

§ 20-183.18. Filing of documents

Filing of documents as required by Article III(j) of the Compact shall be with the Secretary of State.

History.
1963, c. 1167, s. 6

§ 20-183.19. Budget procedure

Pursuant to Article VI(a) of the Compact, the Vehicle Equipment Safety Commission shall submit its budgets to the Director of the Budget.

History.
1963, c. 1167, s. 7

§ 20-183.20. Inspection of financial records of Commission

Pursuant to Article VI(e) of the Compact, the operations of the Vehicle Equipment Safety Commission shall be subject to the oversight of the State Auditor pursuant to Article 5A of Chapter 147 of the General Statutes.

History.
1963, c. 1167, s. 8; 1983, c. 913, s. 6

§ 20-183.21. "Executive head" defined

The term "executive head" as used in Article IX(b) of the Compact shall, with reference to this State, mean the Governor.

History.
1963, c. 1167, s. 9

§§ 20-183.22 through 20-183.29

Reserved for future codification purposes.

ARTICLE 3D
AUTOMATIC LICENSE PLATE READER SYSTEMS.

§ 20-183.30. Definitions

The following definitions apply in this Article:

(1) **Automatic license plate reader system.** -- A system of one or more mobile or fixed automated high-speed cameras used in combination with computer algorithms to convert images of license plates into computer-readable data. This term shall not include a traffic control photographic system, as that term is defined in G.S. 160A-300.1(a), or an open road tolling system, as that term is defined in G.S. 136-89.210(3).

(2) **Law enforcement agency.** -- Any agency or officer of the State of North Carolina or any political subdivision thereof who is empowered by the laws of this State to conduct investigations or to make arrests and any attorney, including the Attorney General of North Carolina, authorized by the laws of this State to prosecute or

participate in the prosecution of those persons arrested or persons who may be subject to civil actions related to or concerning an arrest.

History.
2015-190, s. 1

§ 20-183.31. Regulation of use

(a) Any State or local law enforcement agency using an automatic license plate reader system must adopt a written policy governing its use before the automatic license plate reader system is operational. The policy shall address all of the following:

(1) Databases used to compare data obtained by the automatic license plate reader system.

(2) Data retention.

(3) Sharing of data with other law enforcement agencies.

(4) Training of automatic license plate reader system operators.

(5) Supervisory oversight of automatic license plate reader system use.

(6) Internal data security and access.

(7) Annual or more frequent auditing and reporting of automatic license plate reader system use and effectiveness to the head of the agency responsible for operating the system.

(8) Accessing data obtained by automatic license plate reader systems not operated by the law enforcement agency.

(9) Any other subjects related to automatic license plate reader system use by the agency.

(b) Data obtained by a law enforcement agency in accordance with this section or G.S. 20-183.32 shall be obtained, accessed, preserved, or disclosed only for law enforcement or criminal justice purposes.

(c) Any law enforcement agency using an automatic license plate reader system must keep maintenance and calibration schedules and records for the system on file.

History.
2015-190, s. 1

§ 20-183.32. Preservation and disclosure of records

(a) Captured plate data obtained by an automatic license plate reader system, operated by or on behalf of a law enforcement agency for law enforcement purposes, shall not be preserved for more than 90 days after the date the data is captured.

(b) Notwithstanding subsection (a) of this section, data obtained by an automatic license plate reader may be preserved for more than 90 days pursuant to any of the following:

(1) A preservation request under subsection (c) of this section.

(2) A search warrant issued pursuant to Article 11 of Chapter 15A of the General Statutes.

(3) A federal search warrant issued in compliance with the Federal Rules of Criminal Procedure.

(c) Upon the request of a law enforcement agency, the custodian of the captured plate data shall take all necessary steps to immediately preserve captured plate data in its possession. A requesting agency must specify in a written, sworn statement all of the following:

(1) The location of the particular camera or cameras for which captured plate data must be preserved and the particular license plate for which captured plate data must be preserved.

(2) The date or dates and time frames for which captured plate data must be preserved.

(3) Specific and articulable facts showing that there are reasonable grounds to believe that the captured plate data is relevant and material to an ongoing criminal or missing persons investigation or is needed to prove a violation of a motor carrier safety regulation.

(4) The case and identity of the parties involved in that case.

After one year from the date of the initial preservation request, the captured plate data obtained by an automatic license plate reader system shall be destroyed according to the custodian's own record or data retention policy, unless the custodian receives within that period another preservation request under this subsection, in which case the retention period established under this subsection shall reset.

(d) A law enforcement agency that uses an automatic license plate reader system in accordance with G.S. 20-183.31 shall update the system from the databases specified therein every 24 hours if such updates are available or as soon as practicable after such updates become available.

(e) Captured plate data obtained in accordance with this Article is confidential and not a public record as that term is defined in G.S. 132-1. Data shall not be disclosed except to a federal, State, or local law enforcement agency for a legitimate law enforcement or public safety purpose pursuant to a written request from the requesting agency. Written requests may be in electronic format. Nothing in this subsection shall be construed as requiring the disclosure of captured plate data if a law enforcement agency determines that disclosure will compromise

Chapter 20

an ongoing investigation. Captured plate data shall not be sold for any purpose.

History.
2015-190, s. 1

ARTICLE 4
STATE HIGHWAY PATROL

§ 20-184. Patrol under supervision of Department of Public Safety

The Secretary of Public Safety, under the direction of the Governor, shall have supervision, direction and control of the State Highway Patrol. The Secretary shall establish in the Department of Public Safety a State Highway Patrol Division, prescribe regulations governing the Division, and assign to the Division such duties as the Secretary may deem proper.

History.
1935, c. 324, s. 2; 1939, c. 387, s. 1; 1941, c. 36; 1975, c. 716, s. 5; 1977, c. 70, ss. 13, 14, 15; 2011-145, s. 19.1(g), (hh); 2015-241, s. 16A.7(i)

§ 20-185. Personnel; appointment; salaries

(a) The State Highway Patrol shall consist of a commanding officer, who shall be appointed by the Governor and whose rank shall be designated by the Governor, and such additional subordinate officers and members as the Secretary of Public Safety, with the approval of the Governor, shall direct. Members of the State Highway Patrol shall be appointed by the Secretary, with the approval of the Governor, and shall serve at the pleasure of the Governor and Secretary. The commanding officer, other officers and members of the State Highway Patrol shall be paid such salaries as may be established by the Division of Personnel of the Department of Administration. Notwithstanding any other provision of this Article, the number of supervisory personnel of the State Highway Patrol shall not exceed a number equal to twenty-one percent (21%) of the personnel actually serving as uniformed highway patrolmen. Nothing in the previous sentence is intended to require the demotion, reassignment or change in status of any member of the State Highway Patrol presently assigned in a supervisory capacity. If a reduction in the number of Highway Patrol personnel assigned in supervisory capacity is required in order for the State Highway Patrol to meet the mandatory maximum percentage of supervisory personnel as set out in the fourth sentence of this subsection, that reduction shall be achieved through normal attrition resulting from supervisory personnel resigning, retiring or voluntarily transferring from supervisory positions.

(a1) Applicants for employment as a State Trooper shall be at least 21 years of age and not more than 39 years of age as of the first day of patrol school. Highway Patrol enforcement personnel hired on or after July 1, 2013, shall retire not later than the end of the month in which their 62nd birthday falls.

(b) to (f) Repealed by Session Laws 1979, 2nd Session, c. 1272, s. 2.

(g), (h) Struck out by Session Laws 1961, c. 833, s. 6.2.

(i) Positions in the State Highway Patrol approved by the General Assembly in the first fiscal year of a biennium to be added in the second fiscal year of a biennium may not be filled before adjustments to the budget for the second fiscal year of the budget are enacted by the General Assembly. If a position to be added in the State Highway Patrol for the second fiscal year of the biennium requires training, no applicant may be trained to fill the position until the budget adjustments for the second fiscal year are enacted by the General Assembly.

History.
1929, c. 218, s. 1; 1931, c. 381; 1935, c. 324, s. 1; 1937, c. 313, s. 1; 1941, c. 36; 1947, c. 461, s. 1; 1953, c. 1195, s. 1; 1955, c. 372; 1957, c. 1394; 1959, cc. 370, 1320; 1961, c. 833, s. 6.2; 1973, c. 59; 1975, c. 61, ss. 1, 2; c. 716, s. 5; 1977, c. 70, ss. 6-8, 13; c. 329, ss. 1-3; cc. 749, 889; 1979, 2nd Sess., c. 1272, s. 2; 1989 (Reg. Sess., 1990), c. 1066, s. 133; 2011-145, s. 19.1(g), (p); 2013-289, s. 9; 2015-241, s. 16A.7(j)

§ 20-185.1. Trooper training; reimbursement

(a) **Trooper Training Reimbursement.** -- The training of State Troopers is a substantial investment of State resources that provides individuals with skills that are transferable to other law enforcement opportunities. The State may require an individual to agree in writing to reimburse a portion of the training costs incurred if the individual completes the training and becomes a State Trooper but does not remain a State Trooper for 36 months. The portion of the State's cost to be reimbursed is thirty-six thousand dollars ($ 36,000), less one thousand dollars ($ 1,000) for each month an individual served as a State Trooper and member of the State Highway Patrol.

(b) **Administration.** -- The Secretary of Public Safety shall perform all of the administrative functions necessary to implement the reimbursement agreements required by this section, including rule making, disseminating information, implementing contracts, and taking other necessary actions.

Chapter 20

(c) **Hardships.** -- No contract shall be enforced under this section if the Secretary finds that it is impossible for the individual to serve as a member of the State Highway Patrol due to death, health-related reasons, or other hardship.

(d) **Law Enforcement Agency Requirements.** -- If a State Trooper separates from the State Highway Patrol before 36 months of service following completion of the training program and the State Trooper is hired within six months of separation from the State Highway Patrol by a municipal law enforcement agency, a Sheriff's office, or a company police agency certified under Chapter 74E of the General Statutes, then that hiring entity is liable to the State in the amount of thirty-six thousand dollars ($ 36,000), to be paid in full within 90 days of the date the State Trooper is employed by the hiring entity. No hiring entity shall make any arrangement to circumvent any portion of this subsection.

History.
2018-5, s. 35.25(c); 2018-97, s. 8.1(a)

§ 20-186. Oath of office

Each member of the State Highway Patrol shall subscribe and file with the Secretary of Public Safety an oath of office for the faithful performance of his duties.

History.
1929, c. 218, s. 2; 1937, c. 339, s. 1; 1941, c. 36; 1977, c. 70, s. 9; 2011-145, s. 19.1(g)

§ 20-187. Orders and rules for organization and conduct

The Secretary of Public Safety is authorized and empowered to make all necessary orders, rules and regulations for the organization, assignment, and conduct of the members of the State Highway Patrol. Such orders, rules and regulations shall be subject to the approval of the Governor.

History.
1929, c. 218, ss. 1, 3; 1931, c. 381; 1933, c. 214, ss. 1, 2; 1939, c. 387, s. 2; 1941, c. 36; 1977, c. 70, s. 13; 2011-145, s. 19.1(g)

§ 20-187.1. Awards

(a) The patrol commander shall appoint an awards committee consisting of one troop commander, one troop executive officer, one district sergeant, one corporal, two troopers and one member of patrol headquarters staff. All committee members shall serve for a term of one year. The member from patrol headquarters staff shall serve as secretary to the committee and shall vote only in case of ties. The committee shall meet at such times and places designated by the patrol commander.

(b) The award to be granted under the provisions of this section shall be the North Carolina State Highway Patrol award of honor. The North Carolina State Highway Patrol award of honor is awarded in the name of the people of North Carolina and by the Governor to a person who, while a member of the North Carolina State Highway Patrol, distinguishes himself conspicuously by gallantry and intrepidity at the risk of personal safety and beyond the call of duty while engaged in the preservation of life and property. The deed performed must have been one of personal bravery and self-sacrifice so conspicuous as to clearly distinguish the individual above his colleagues and must have involved risk of life. Proof of the performance of the service will be required and each recommendation for the award of this decoration will be considered on the standard of extraordinary merit.

(c) Recipients of the awards hereinabove provided for will be entitled to receive a framed certificate of the award and an insignia designed to be worn as a part of the State Highway Patrol uniform.

(d) The awards committee shall review and investigate all reports of outstanding service and shall make recommendations to the patrol commander with respect thereto. The committee shall consider members of the Patrol for the awards created by this section when properly recommended by any individual having personal knowledge of an act, achievement or service believed to warrant the award of a decoration. No recommendation shall be made except by majority vote of all members of the committee. All recommendations of the committee shall be in writing and shall be forwarded to the patrol commander.

(e) Upon receipt of a recommendation of the committee, the patrol commander shall inquire into the facts of the matter and shall reduce his recommendation to writing. The patrol commander shall forward his recommendation, together with the recommendation of the committee, to the Secretary of Public Safety. The Secretary shall have final authority to approve or disapprove recommendations affecting the issuance of all awards except the award of honor. All recommendations for the award of honor shall be forwarded to the Governor for final approval or disapproval.

(f) The patrol commander shall, with the approval of the Secretary, establish all necessary rules and regulations to fully implement the provisions of this section and such rules and regulations shall include, but shall not be limited to, the following:

(1) Announcement of awards
(2) Presentation of awards
(3) Recording of awards
(4) Replacement of awards
(5) Authority to wear award insignias.

History.
1967, c. 1179; 1971, c. 848; 1977, c. 70, s. 13; 2011-145, s. 19.1(g)

§ 20-187.2. Badges and service side arms of deceased or retiring members of State, city, and county law enforcement agencies; weapons of active members

(a) Surviving spouses, or in the event such members die unsurvived by a spouse, surviving children of members of North Carolina State, city, and county law enforcement agencies killed in the line of duty or who are members of such agencies at the time of their deaths, and retiring members of such agencies shall receive upon request and at no cost to them, the badge worn or carried by such deceased or retiring member. The governing body of a law enforcement agency may, in its discretion, also award to a retiring member or surviving relatives as provided herein, upon request, the service side arm of such deceased or retiring members, at a price determined by such governing body, upon determining that the person receiving the weapon is not ineligible to own, possess, or receive a firearm under the provisions of State or federal law, or if the weapon has been rendered incapable of being fired. Governing body shall mean for county and local alcohol beverage control officers, the county or local board of alcoholic control; for all other law enforcement officers with jurisdiction limited to a municipality or town, the city or town council; for all other law enforcement officers with countywide jurisdiction, the board of county commissioners; for all State law enforcement officers, the head of the department.

(b) Active members of North Carolina State, city, and county law enforcement agencies, upon change of type of weapons, may purchase the weapon worn or carried by such member at a price which shall be the average yield to the State, city, or county from the sale of similar weapons during the preceding year.

(c) For purposes of this section, certified probation and parole officers shall be considered members of a North Carolina State law enforcement agency.

History.
1971, c. 669; 1973, c. 1424; 1975, c. 44; 1977, c. 548; 1979, c. 882; 1987, c. 122; 2013-369, s. 19; 2016-77, s. 9(b); 2021-116, s. 1.3

§ 20-187.3. Quotas prohibited

(a) The Secretary of Public Safety shall not make or permit to be made any order, rule, or regulation requiring the issuance of any minimum number of traffic citations, or ticket quotas, by any member or members of the State Highway Patrol. Pay and promotions of members of the Highway Patrol shall be based on their overall job performance and not on the basis of the volume of citations issued or arrests made. Members of the Highway Patrol shall be subject to the salary schedule established by the Secretary of Public Safety and shall receive longevity pay for service as applicable to other State employees generally.

(b) Repealed by Session Laws 2018-5, s. 35.25(b), effective July 1, 2018.

History.
1981, c. 429; 1983 (Reg. Sess., 1984), c. 1034, ss. 106, 107; c. 1116, s. 89; 2011-145, s. 19.1(g); 2012-142, s. 25.2C(d); 2013-382, s. 9.1(c); 2018-5, s. 35.25(b)

§ 20-187.4. Disposition of retired service animals

(a) Upon determination that any service animal is no longer fit or needed for public service, the State or unit of local government may transfer ownership of the animal at a price determined by the State or unit of local government and upon any other terms and conditions as the State or unit of local government deems appropriate, to any of the following individuals, if that individual agrees to accept ownership, care, and custody of the service animal:

(1) The officer or employee who had normal custody and control of the service animal during the service animal's public service to the State or unit of local government.

(2) A surviving spouse, or in the event such officer or employee dies unsurvived by a spouse, surviving children of the officer or employee killed in the line of duty who had normal custody and control of the service animal during the service animal's public service to the State or unit of local government.

(3) An organization or program dedicated to the assistance or support of service animals retired from public service.

(b) For purposes of this section, the following definitions apply:

(1) "Service animal." -- Any horse, dog, or other animal owned by the State or a unit of local government that performs law enforcement, public safety, or emergency service functions.

(2) "Unit of local government." -- As defined in G.S. 159-7(b)(15).

Chapter 20

History.
2016-101, s. 1

§ 20-187.5. Trademark authorization

The North Carolina Troopers Association is authorized to use all trademarks identifying the North Carolina State Highway Patrol held by the North Carolina Department of Public Safety or its Divisions. The use authorized under this section shall be limited to purposes that support the State Highway Patrol, employees of the State Highway Patrol, and the family members of the employees of the State Highway Patrol.

History.
2017-57, s. 16B.8(a)

§ 20-188. Duties of Highway Patrol

The State Highway Patrol shall be subject to such orders, rules and regulations as may be adopted by the Secretary of Public Safety, with the approval of the Governor, and shall regularly patrol the highways of the State and enforce all laws and regulations respecting travel and the use of vehicles upon the highways of the State and all laws for the protection of the highways of the State. To this end, the members of the Patrol are given the power and authority of peace officers for the service of any warrant or other process issuing from any of the courts of the State having criminal jurisdiction, and are likewise authorized to arrest without warrant any person who, in the presence of said officers, is engaged in the violation of any of the laws of the State regulating travel and the use of vehicles upon the highways, or of laws with respect to the protection of the highways, and they shall have jurisdiction anywhere within the State, irrespective of county lines. The State Highway Patrol shall enforce the provisions of G.S. 14-399.

The State Highway Patrol shall have full power and authority to perform such additional duties as peace officers as may from time to time be directed by the Governor, and such officers may at any time and without special authority, either upon their own motion or at the request of any sheriff or local police authority, arrest persons accused of highway robbery, bank robbery, murder, or other crimes of violence.

The Secretary of Public Safety shall direct the officers and members of the State Highway Patrol in the performance of such other duties as may be required for the enforcement of the motor vehicle laws of the State.

Members of the State Highway Patrol, in addition to the duties, power and authority hereinbefore given, shall have the authority throughout the State of North Carolina of any police officer in respect to making arrests for any crimes committed in their presence and shall have authority to make arrests for any crime committed on any highway.

Regardless of territorial jurisdiction, any member of the State Highway Patrol who initiates an investigation of an accident or collision may not relinquish responsibility for completing the investigation, or for filing criminal charges as appropriate, without clear assurance that another law-enforcement officer or agency has fully undertaken responsibility, and in such cases he shall render reasonable assistance to the succeeding officer or agency if requested.

The State Highway Patrol recognizes the need to utilize private wrecker services to remove vehicles from public roadways as part of its public safety responsibility. In order to assure that this public safety responsibility is accomplished, the Troop Commander shall include on the Highway Patrol's rotation wrecker list only those wrecker services which agree in writing to impose reasonable charges for work performed and present one bill to the owner or operator of any towed vehicle. Towing, storage, and related fees charged may not be greater than fees charged for the same service for non-rotation calls that provide the same service, labor, and conditions.

History.
1929, c. 218, s. 4; 1933, c. 214, ss. 1, 2; 1935, c. 324, s. 3; 1939, c. 387, s. 2; 1941, c. 36; 1945, c. 1048; 1947, c. 1067, s. 20; 1973, c. 689; 1975, c. 716, s. 5; 1977, c. 70, ss. 10, 13; c. 887, s. 3; 2009-461, s. 3; 2011-145, s. 19.1(g)

§ 20-189. Patrolmen assigned to Governor's office

The Secretary of Public Safety, at the request of the Governor, shall assign and attach two members of the State Highway Patrol to the office of the Governor, there to be assigned such duties and perform such services as the Governor may direct. The salary of the State Highway Patrol members so assigned to the office of the Governor shall be paid from appropriations made to the office of the Governor and shall be fixed in an amount to be determined by the Governor.

History.
1941, cc. 23, 36; 1965, c. 1159; 1977, c. 70, s. 13; 1983, c. 717, s. 6; 1985 (Reg. Sess., 1986), c. 955, ss. 2, 3; 2006-203, s. 15; 2011-145, s. 19.1(g); 2012-83, s. 30

§ 20-189.1. Lieutenant Governor Executive Protection Detail

(a) **Creation.** -- There is created within the Highway Patrol a Lieutenant Governor's

Executive Protection Detail. The Lieutenant Governor shall submit the names of three sworn members in good standing of the North Carolina Highway Patrol to the Commander, and the Commander shall assign those officers to serve in the Lieutenant Governor's Executive Protection Detail. The Lieutenant Governor is authorized to remove any members of the detail, with or without cause. If the Lieutenant Governor removes a member of the detail, the Lieutenant Governor shall submit to the Commander the name of an officer to replace the member who has been removed and the Commander shall assign the replacement. Members of the Lieutenant Governor's Executive Protection Detail shall continue to be employed by the North Carolina Highway Patrol subject to the laws, rules, and regulations of the Highway Patrol. The North Carolina Highway Patrol shall provide vehicles necessary for the carrying out of the Detail's duties under this Article.

(b) **Duties.** -- The members of the Lieutenant Governor's Executive Protection Detail shall protect the Lieutenant Governor and the Lieutenant Governor's immediate family and perform duties as assigned by the Lieutenant Governor relating to the protection of the Lieutenant Governor.

History.
2017-57, s. 16B.4(a)

§ 20-189.2. State Highway Patrol Security Detail

The Speaker of the House of Representatives and the President Pro Tempore of the Senate, while traveling within the State on State business, may request a security detail. The request shall be made to the commander of the State Highway Patrol. If the request is made at least 48 hours in advance, the commander shall provide the detail. If the request is made less than 48 hours in advance, the commander shall provide the detail unless doing so would otherwise impair the ability of the State Highway patrol to perform its lawful duties.

History.
2017-57, s. 16B.9

§ 20-190. Uniforms; motor vehicles and arms; expense incurred; color of vehicle

The Department of Public Safety shall adopt some distinguishing uniform for the members of said State Highway Patrol, and furnish each member of the Patrol with an adequate number of said uniforms and each member of said Patrol force when on duty shall be dressed in said uniform. The Department of Public Safety shall likewise furnish each member of the Patrol with a suitable motor vehicle, and necessary arms, and provide for all reasonable expense incurred by said Patrol while on duty, provided, that not less than eighty-three percent (83%) of the number of motor vehicles operated on the highways of the State by members of the State Highway Patrol shall be painted a uniform color of black and silver.

History.
1929, c. 218, s. 5; 1941, c. 36; 1955, c. 1132, ss. 1, 1 1/4, 1 3/4; 1957, c. 478, s. 1; c. 673, s. 1; 1961, c. 342; 1975, c. 716, s. 5; 1977, c. 70, s. 15; 1979, c. 229; 2011-145, s. 19.1(g)

§ 20-190.1. Patrol vehicles to have sirens; sounding siren

Every motor vehicle operated on the highways of the State by officers and members of the State Highway Patrol shall be equipped with a siren. Whenever any such officer or member operating any unmarked car shall overtake another vehicle on the highway after sunset of any day and before sunrise for the purpose of stopping the same or apprehending the driver thereof, he shall sound said siren before stopping such other vehicle.

History.
1957, c. 478, s. 1 1/2

§ 20-190.2. Signs showing highways patrolled by unmarked vehicles

The Department of Transportation shall erect or cause to be erected signs at all points where paved highways enter this State from adjacent states stating that the highways are patrolled by unmarked police vehicles.

History.
1957, c. 673, s. 2; 1973, c. 507, s. 5; 1977, c. 464, s. 34.

§ 20-190.3. Assignment of new highway patrol cars

All new highway patrol cars, whether marked or unmarked, placed in service after July 1, 1985, shall be assigned to all members of the Highway Patrol.

History.
1985, c. 757, s. 165; 1987, c. 738, s. 122; 1989, c. 752, s. 114

§ 20-191. Use of facilities

Office space and other equipment and facilities of the Division of Motor Vehicles, Department of Transportation, presently being used by the State Highway Patrol shall continue to

Chapter 20

be used by the Patrol, and joint use of space, equipment and facilities between any division of the Department of Transportation and the State Highway Patrol may continue, unless such arrangements are changed by agreements between the Secretary of Public Safety and the Secretary of Transportation.

History.

1929, c. 218, s. 6; 1937, c. 313, s. 1; 1941, c. 36; 1947, c. 461, s. 2; 1975, c. 716, s. 5; 1977, c. 70, s. 11; 2011-145, s. 19.1(g)

§ 20-192. Shifting of personnel from one district to another

The commanding officer of the State Highway Patrol under such rules and regulations as the Department of Public Safety may prescribe shall have authority from time to time to shift the forces from one district to another, or to consolidate more than one district force at any point for special purposes. Whenever a member of the State Highway Patrol is transferred from one point to another for the convenience of the State or otherwise than upon the request of the Highway Patrol member, the Department shall be responsible for transporting the household goods, furniture and personal apparel of the Highway Patrol member and members of the Highway Patrol member's household.

History.

1929, c. 218, s. 7; 1937, c. 313, s. 1; 1941, c. 36; 1947, c. 461, s. 3; 1951, c. 285; 1975, c. 716, s. 5; 1977, c. 70, s. 15; 2011-145, s. 19.1(g); 2012-83, s. 31

N.C. Gen. Stat. § 20-193

Repealed by Session Laws 1993 (Reg. Sess., 1994), c. 761, s. 18.

§ 20-194. Defense of members and other State law-enforcement officers in civil actions; payment of judgments

(a) Repealed by Session Laws 2011-145, s. 28.27(d), effective July 1, 2011.

(b) In the event that a member of the Highway Patrol or any other State law-enforcement officer is sued in a civil action as an individual for acts occurring while such member was alleged to be acting within the course and scope of his office, employment, service, agency or authority, which was alleged to be a proximate cause of the injury or damage complained of, the Attorney General is hereby authorized to defend such employee through the use of a member of his staff or, in his discretion, employ private counsel, subject to the provisions of Article 31A of Chapter 143 of the General Statutes and G.S. 147-17(a) through (c) and (d). Any judgment

rendered as a result of said civil action against such member of the Highway Patrol or other State law-enforcement officer, for acts alleged to be committed within the course and scope of his office, employment, service, agency or authority shall be paid as an expense of administration up to the limit provided in the Tort Claims Act.

(c) The coverage afforded under this Article shall be excess coverage over any commercial liability insurance up to the limit of the Tort Claims Act.

History.

1929, c. 218, s. 9; 1941, c. 36; 1957, c. 65, s. 11; 1973, c. 507, s. 5; c. 1323; 1975, c. 210; 1977, c. 70, s. 12; 2011-145, s. 28.27(d); 2017-57, s. 6.7(d)

§ 20-195. Cooperation between Patrol and local officers

The Secretary of Public Safety with the approval of the Governor, through the State Highway Patrol, shall encourage the cooperation between the Highway Patrol and the several municipal and county peace officers of the State for the enforcement of all traffic laws and the proper administration of the Uniform Drivers' License Law, and arrangements for compensation of special services rendered by such local officers out of the funds allotted to the State Highway Patrol may be made, subject to the approval of the Director of the Budget.

History.

1935, c. 324, s. 5; 1939, c. 387, s. 3; 1941, c. 36; 1977, c. 70, ss. 13, 14; 2011-145, s. 19.1(g), (p); 2015-241, s. 16A.7(j)

§ 20-196. Statewide radio system authorized; use of telephone lines in emergencies

The Secretary of Public Safety, through the State Highway Patrol is hereby authorized and directed to set up and maintain a statewide radio system, with adequate broadcasting stations so situate as to make the service available to all parts of the State for the purpose of maintaining radio contact with the members of the State Highway Patrol and other officers of the State, to the end that the traffic laws upon the highways may be more adequately enforced and that the criminal use of the highways may be prevented. The Secretary of Public Safety, through the State Highway Patrol, is hereby authorized to establish a plan of operation in accordance with Federal Communication Commission rules so that all certified law-enforcement officers within the State may use the law enforcement emergency frequency of 155.475MHz.

The Secretary of Public Safety is likewise authorized and empowered to arrange with the various telephone companies of the State for the use of their lines for emergency calls by the members of the State Highway Patrol, if it shall be found practicable to arrange apparatus for temporary contact with said telephone circuits along the highways of the State.

In order to make this service more generally useful, the various boards of county commissioners and the governing boards of the various cities and towns are hereby authorized and empowered to provide radio receiving sets in the offices and vehicles of their various officers, and such expenditures are declared to be a legal expenditure of any funds that may be available for police protection.

History.
1935, c. 324, s. 6; 1941, c. 36; 1957, c. 65, s. 11; 1973, c. 507, s. 5; 1975, c. 716, s. 5; 1977, c. 70, ss. 13, 14; c. 464, s. 34; 1983, c. 717, s. 7; 1987, c. 525; 2011-145, s. 19.1(g), (p); 2015-241, s. 16A.7(j)

N.C. Gen. Stat. § 20-196.1

Repealed by Session Laws 1998-212, s. 19.6(a), effective December 1, 1998.

§ 20-196.2. Use of aircraft to discover certain motor vehicle violations; declaration of policy.

The State Highway Patrol is hereby permitted the use of aircraft to discover violations of Part 10 of Article 3 of Chapter 20 of the General Statutes relating to operation of motor vehicles and rules of the road. It is hereby declared the public policy of North Carolina that the aircraft should be used primarily for accident prevention and should also be used incident to the issuance of warning citations in accordance with the provisions of G.S. 20-183.

History.
1967, c. 513; 1998-212, s. 19.6(b)

§ 20-196.3. Who may hold supervisory positions over sworn members of the Patrol

Notwithstanding any other provision of the General Statutes, only the following individuals may hold a supervisory position over sworn members of the Patrol:

(1) The Governor.
(2) The Secretary of Public Safety.
(3) A uniformed member of the North Carolina State Highway Patrol who has met all requirements for employment within the Patrol, including completion of the basic Patrol school.

History.
1975, c. 47; 1977, c. 70, s. 14.1; 2002-159, ss. 31.5(a), (b); 2002-190, s. 9; 2011-145, s. 19.1(g); 2013-289, s. 10; 2015-241, s. 16A.7(h)

§ 20-196.4. Oversized and hazardous shipment escort fee

(a) Every person, firm, corporation, or entity required by the North Carolina Department of Transportation or any federal agency or commission to have a law enforcement escort provided by the State Highway Patrol for the transport of any oversized load or hazardous shipment by road or rail shall pay to the Department of Public Safety a fee covering the full cost to administer, plan, and carry out the escort within this State.

(b) If the State Highway Patrol provides an escort to accompany the transport of oversized loads or hazardous shipments by road or rail at the request of any person, firm, corporation, or entity that is not required to have a law enforcement escort pursuant to subsection (a) of this section, then the requester shall pay to the Department of Public Safety a fee covering the full cost to administer, plan, and carry out the escort within this State.

(c) A fee established under this section is subject to G.S. 12-3.1. The full cost of an escort includes costs for vehicle or equipment maintenance required before or after an escort to ensure the visibility and safety of the law enforcement escort and the motoring public.

(d) All fees collected pursuant to this section shall be placed in a special Escort Fee Account. Revenue in the account is annually appropriated to the Department to reimburse the Department for its expenses in providing escorts under this section.

(e) Repealed by Session Laws 2010-129, s. 4, effective July 21, 2010.

History.
2002-126, s. 26.17(a); 2010-129, s. 4; 2011-145, s. 19.1(g)

§ 20-196.5. Report on gang prevention recommendations

The State Highway Patrol, in conjunction with the State Bureau of Investigation and the Governor's Crime Commission, shall develop recommendations concerning the establishment of priorities and needed improvements with respect to gang prevention and shall report those recommendations to the chairs of the House of Representatives and Senate Appropriations Committees on Justice and Public Safety and to the chairs of the Joint Legislative Oversight Committee on Justice and Public Safety on or before March 1 of each year.

Chapter 20

History.
2015-241, s. 16B.3(a)

ARTICLE 5
ENFORCEMENT OF COLLECTION OF JUDGMENTS AGAINST IRRESPONSIBLE DRIVERS OF MOTOR VEHICLES

§§ 20-197 through 20-211

Repealed by Session Laws 1947, c. 1006, s. 58.

ARTICLE 6
GIVING PUBLICITY TO HIGHWAY TRAFFIC LAWS THROUGH THE PUBLIC SCHOOLS

§§ 20-212 through 20-215

Repealed by Session Laws 1993 (Reg. Sess., 1994), c. 761, s. 19.

ARTICLE 6A
MOTOR CARRIERS OF MIGRATORY FARM WORKERS

§ 20-215.1. Definitions

The following definitions apply in this Article:

(1) **Migratory farm worker.** -- An individual who is employed in agriculture.

(2) **Motor carrier of migratory farm workers.** -- A person who for compensation transports at any one time in North Carolina five or more migratory farm workers to or from their employment by any motor vehicle, other than a passenger automobile or station wagon. The term does not include any of the following:

a. A migratory farm worker who is transporting his or her immediate family.

b. A carrier of passengers regulated by the North Carolina Utilities Commission or the United States Department of Transportation.

c. The transportation of migratory farm workers on a vehicle owned by a farmer when the migratory farm workers are employed or to be employed by the farmer to work on a farm owned or controlled by the farmer.

(3) Repealed by Session Laws 1973, c. 1330, s. 39.

History.
1961, c. 505, s. 1; 1973, c. 1330, s. 39; 1995 (Reg. Sess., 1996), c. 756, s. 17

§ 20-215.2. Power to regulate; rules and regulations establishing minimum standards

Notwithstanding any other provisions of this Chapter the North Carolina Division of Motor Vehicles, hereinafter referred to as "Division," is hereby vested with the power and duty to make and enforce reasonable rules and regulations applicable to motor carriers of migratory farm workers to and from their places of employment. The rules promulgated shall establish minimum standards:

(1) For the construction and equipment of such vehicles, including coupling devices, lighting equipment, exhaust systems, rear vision mirrors, brakes, steering mechanisms, tires, windshield wipers and warning devices.

(2) For the operation of such vehicles, including driving rules, distribution of passengers and load, maximum hours of service for drivers, minimum requirements of age and skill of drivers, physical conditions of drivers and permits, licenses or other credentials required of drivers.

(3) For the safety and comfort of passengers in such vehicles, including emergency kits, fire extinguishers, first-aid equipment, sidewalls, seating accommodations, tail gates or doors, rest and meal stops, maximum number of passengers, and safe means of ingress and egress.

History.
1961, c. 505, s. 2; 1975, c. 716, s. 5

N.C. Gen. Stat. § 20-215.3

Repealed by Session Laws 1985, c. 454, s. 8.

§ 20-215.4. Violation of regulations a misdemeanor

The violation of any rule or regulation promulgated by the Division hereunder by any person, firm or corporation shall be a Class 3 misdemeanor.

History.
1961, c. 505, s. 4; 1975, c. 716, s. 5; 1993, c. 539, s. 381; 1994, Ex. Sess., c. 24, s. 14(c)

§ 20-215.5. Duties and powers of law-enforcement officers

It shall be the duty of the law-enforcement officers of the State, and of each county, city or town, to enforce the rules promulgated hereunder in their respective jurisdictions; and such officers shall have the power to stop any motor vehicle upon the highways of this State for the purpose of determining whether or not such motor vehicle is being operated in violation of such rules.

History.
1961, c. 505, s. 5

ARTICLE 7
MISCELLANEOUS PROVISIONS RELATING TO MOTOR VEHICLES

§ 20-216. Passing horses or other draft animals

Any person operating a motor vehicle shall use reasonable care when approaching or passing a horse or other draft animal whether ridden or otherwise under control.

History.
1917, c. 140, s. 15; C.S., s. 2616; 1969, c. 401

§ 20-217. Motor vehicles to stop for properly marked and designated school buses in certain instances; evidence of identity of driver

(a) When a school bus is displaying its mechanical stop signal or flashing red lights and the bus is stopped for the purpose of receiving or discharging passengers, the driver of any other vehicle that approaches the school bus from any direction on the same street, highway, or public vehicular area shall bring that other vehicle to a full stop and shall remain stopped. The driver of the other vehicle shall not proceed to move, pass, or attempt to pass the school bus until after the mechanical stop signal has been withdrawn, the flashing red stoplights have been turned off, and the bus has started to move.

(b) For the purpose of this section, a school bus includes a public school bus transporting children or school personnel, a public school bus transporting senior citizens under G.S. 115C-243, or a privately owned bus transporting children. This section applies only in the event the school bus bears upon the front and rear a plainly visible sign containing the words "school bus."

(c) Notwithstanding subsection (a) of this section, the driver of a vehicle traveling in the opposite direction from the school bus, upon any road, highway or city street that has been divided into two roadways, so constructed as to separate vehicular traffic between the two roadways by an intervening space (including a center lane for left turns if the roadway consists of at least four more lanes) or by a physical barrier, need not stop upon meeting and passing any school bus that has stopped in the roadway across the dividing space or physical barrier.

(d) It shall be unlawful for any school bus driver to stop and receive or discharge passengers or for any principal or superintendent of any school, routing a school bus, to authorize the driver of any school bus to stop and receive or discharge passengers upon any roadway described by subsection (c) of this section where passengers would be required to cross the roadway to reach their destination or to board the bus; provided, that passengers may be discharged or received at points where pedestrians and vehicular traffic are controlled by adequate stop-and-go traffic signals.

(e) Except as provided in subsection (g) of this section, any person violating this section shall be guilty of a Class 1 misdemeanor and shall pay a minimum fine of five hundred dollars ($ 500.00). A person who violates subsection (a) of this section shall not receive a prayer for judgment continued under any circumstances.

(f) Expired.

(g) Any person who willfully violates subsection (a) of this section and strikes any person shall be guilty of a Class I felony and shall pay a minimum fine of one thousand two hundred fifty dollars ($ 1,250). Any person who willfully violates subsection (a) of this section and strikes any person, resulting in the death of that person, shall be guilty of a Class H felony and shall pay a minimum fine of two thousand five hundred dollars ($ 2,500).

(g1) The Division shall revoke, for a period of one year, the drivers license of a person convicted of a second misdemeanor violation under this section within a three-year period. The Division shall revoke, for a period of two years, the drivers license of a person convicted of a Class I felony violation under this section. The Division shall revoke, for a period of three years, the drivers license of a person convicted of a Class H felony violation under this section. The Division shall permanently revoke the drivers license of (i) a person convicted of a second felony violation under this section within any period of time and (ii) a person convicted of a third misdemeanor violation under this section within any period of time.

In the case of a first felony conviction under this section, the licensee may apply to the sentencing court for a limited driving privilege after a period of six months of revocation, provided the person's drivers license has not also been revoked or suspended under any other provision of law. A limited driving privilege issued under this subsection shall be valid for the period of revocation remaining in the same manner and under the terms and conditions prescribed in G.S. 20-16.1(b). If the person's drivers license is revoked or suspended under any other statute, the limited driving privilege issued pursuant to this subsection is invalid.

In the case of a permanent revocation of a person's drivers license for committing a third misdemeanor violation under this section within any period of time, the person may apply for a drivers license after two years. The Division may, with or without a hearing, issue a new drivers license upon satisfactory proof that the former licensee has not been convicted of a moving violation under this Chapter or the laws of another state. The Division may impose any restrictions or conditions on the new drivers license that the Division considers appropriate. Any conditions or restrictions imposed by the Division shall not exceed two years.

In the case of a permanent revocation of a person's drivers license for committing a second Class I felony violation under this section within any period of time, the person may apply for a drivers license after three years. The Division may, with or without a hearing, issue a new drivers license upon satisfactory proof that the former licensee has not been convicted of a moving violation under this Chapter or the laws of another state. The Division may impose any restrictions or conditions on the new drivers license that the Division considers appropriate. Any conditions or restrictions imposed by the Division shall not exceed three years.

Any person whose drivers license is revoked under this section is disqualified pursuant to G.S. 20-17.4 from driving a commercial motor vehicle for the period of time in which the person's drivers license remains revoked under this section.

(g2) Pursuant to G.S. 20-54, failure of a person to pay any fine or costs imposed pursuant to this section shall result in the Division withholding the registration renewal of a motor vehicle registered in that person's name. The clerk of superior court in the county in which the case was disposed shall notify the Division of any person who fails to pay a fine or costs imposed pursuant to this section within 40 days of the date specified in the court's judgment, as required by G.S. 20-24.2(a)(2). The Division shall continue to withhold the registration renewal of a motor vehicle until the clerk of superior court notifies the Division that the person has satisfied the conditions of G.S. 20-24.1(b) applicable to the person's case. The provisions of this subsection shall be in addition to any other actions the Division may take to enforce the payment of any fine imposed pursuant to this section.

(h) Automated school bus safety cameras, as defined in G.S. 115C-242.1, may be used to detect and prosecute violations of this section. Any photograph or video recorded by an automated school bus safety camera shall, if consistent with the North Carolina Rules of Evidence, be admissible as evidence in any proceeding alleging a violation of subsection (a) of this section. Failure to produce a photograph or video recorded by an automated school bus safety camera shall not preclude prosecution under this section.

History.
1925, c. 265; 1943, c. 767; 1947, c. 527; 1955, c. 1365; 1959, c. 909; 1965, c. 370; 1969, c. 952; 1971, c. 245, s. 1; 1973, c. 1330, s. 35; 1977, 2nd Sess., c. 1280, s. 4; 1979, 2nd Sess., c. 1323; 1983, c. 779, s. 1; 1985, c. 700, s. 1; 1991, c. 290, s. 1; 1993, c. 539, s. 382; 1994, Ex. Sess., c. 24, s. 14(c); 1998-149, s. 10; 2005-204, s. 1; 2006-160, s. 1; 2006-259, s. 11(a); 2007-382, s. 1; 2009-147, ss. 1, 2; 2013-293, s. 2; 2017-188, s. 4; 2019-243, s. 8

N.C. Gen. Stat. § 20-217.1

Repealed by Session Laws 1983, c. 779, s. 2.

§ 20-218. Standard qualifications for school bus drivers; speed limit for school buses and school activity buses

(a) **Qualifications.** -- No person shall drive a school bus over the highways or public vehicular areas of North Carolina while it is occupied by one or more child passengers unless the person furnishes to the superintendent of the schools of the county in which the bus shall be operated a certificate from any representative duly designated by the Commissioner and from the Director of Transportation or a designee of the Director in charge of school buses in the county showing that the person has been examined by them and is fit and competent to drive a school bus over the highways and public vehicular areas of the State. The driver of a school bus must be at least 18 years of age and hold a Class A, B, or C commercial drivers license and a school bus driver's certificate. The driver of a school activity bus must meet the same qualifications as a school bus driver or must have a license appropriate for the class of vehicle being driven.

(b) **Speed Limits.** -- It is unlawful to drive a school bus occupied by one or more child passengers over the highways or public vehicular areas of the State at a greater rate of speed than 45 miles per hour. It is unlawful to drive a school activity bus occupied by one or more child passengers over the highways or public vehicular areas of North Carolina at a greater rate of speed than 55 miles per hour.

(c) **Punishment.** -- A person who violates this section commits a Class 3 misdemeanor.

History.

1937, c. 397, ss. 1-3; 1941, c. 21; 1943, c. 440; 1945, c. 216; 1957, cc. 139, 595; 1971, c. 293; 1977, c. 791, ss. 1, 2; c. 1102; 1979, c. 31, ss. 1, 2; c. 667, s. 36; 1981, c. 30; 1987, c. 337, s. 1; 1989, c. 558, s. 1; c. 771, s. 6; 1991, c. 726, s. 22; 1993, c. 217, s. 1; 1993 (Reg. Sess., 1994), c. 761, s. 20; 2009-550, s. 3.2

N.C. Gen. Stat. § 20-218.1

Repealed by Session Laws 1993 (Reg. Sess., 1994), c. 761, s. 21.

§ 20-218.2. Speed limit for nonprofit activity buses

It is unlawful to drive an activity bus that is owned by a nonprofit organization and is transporting persons in connection with nonprofit activities over the highways or public vehicular areas of North Carolina at a greater rate of speed than 55 miles per hour. A person who violates this section commits a Class 3 misdemeanor.

History.

1969, c. 1000, s. 2; 1987, c. 337, s. 2; 1993 (Reg. Sess., 1994), c. 761, s. 23

N.C. Gen. Stat. § 20-219

Repealed by Session Laws 1993 (Reg. Sess., 1994), c. 761, s. 24.

N.C. Gen. Stat. § 20-219.1

Repealed by Session Laws 1971, c. 294, s. 2.

§ 20-219.2. Removal of unauthorized vehicles from private lots

(a) It shall be unlawful for any person other than the owner or lessee of a privately owned or leased parking space to park a motor or other vehicle in such private parking space without the express permission of the owner or lessee of such space if the private parking lot is clearly designated as such by legible signs no smaller than 24 inches by 24 inches prominently displayed at all entrances thereto, displaying the current name and current phone number of the towing and storage company, and, if individually owned or leased, the parking lot or spaces within the lot are clearly marked by signs setting forth the name of each individual lessee or owner. A vehicle parked in a privately owned parking space in violation of this section may be removed from such space upon the written request of the parking space owner or lessee to a place of storage and the registered owner of such motor vehicle shall become liable for removal and storage charges. Any person who removes

a vehicle pursuant to this section shall not be held liable for damages for the removal of the vehicle to the owner, lienholder or other person legally entitled to the possession of the vehicle removed; however, any person who intentionally or negligently damages a vehicle in the removal of such vehicle, or intentionally or negligently inflicts injury upon any person in the removal of such vehicle, may be held liable for damages. The provisions of this section shall not apply until 72 hours after the required signs are posted.

(a1) If any vehicle is removed pursuant to this section and there is a place of storage within 15 miles, the vehicle shall not be transported for storage more than 15 miles from the place of removal. For all other vehicles, the vehicle shall not be transported for storage more than 25 miles from the place of removal.

(a2) Any person who tows or stores a vehicle subject to this section shall inform the owner in writing at the time of retrieval of the vehicle that the owner has the right to pay the amount of the lien asserted, request immediate possession, and contest the lien for towing charges pursuant to the provisions of G.S. 44A-4.

(a3) Any person who tows or stores a vehicle subject to this section shall not require any person retrieving a vehicle to sign any waiver of rights or other similar document as a condition of the release of the person's vehicle, other than a form acknowledging the release and receipt of the vehicle.

(b) Any person violating any of the provisions of this section shall be guilty of an infraction and upon conviction shall be only penalized not less than one hundred fifty dollars ($ 150.00) in the discretion of the court.

(c) This section shall apply only to the Counties of Craven, Cumberland, Dare, Forsyth, Gaston, Guilford, Mecklenburg, New Hanover, Orange, Richmond, Robeson, Wake, Wilson and municipalities in those counties, and to the Cities of Durham, Jacksonville, Charlotte and Fayetteville.

(d) The provisions of this section shall not be interpreted to preempt the authority of any county or municipality to enact ordinances regulating towing from private lots, as authorized by general law.

History.

1969, cc. 173, 288; 1971, c. 986; 1973, c. 183; c. 981, s. 1; c. 1330, s. 36; 1975, c. 575; 1979, c. 380; 1979, 2nd Sess., c. 1119; 1981 (Reg. Sess., 1982), c. 1251, s. 3; 1989, c. 417; c. 644, s. 1; 1993, c. 539, s. 383; 1994, Ex. Sess., c. 24, s. 14(c); 2008-68, s. 1; 2010-134, s. 1; 2013-190, s. 1; 2013-241, s. 2

§ 20-219.3. Removal of unauthorized vehicles from gasoline service station premises

Chapter 20

(a) No motor vehicle shall be left for more than 48 hours upon the premises of any gasoline service station without the consent of the owner or operator of the service station.

(b) The registered owner of any motor vehicle left unattended upon the premises of a service station in violation of subsection (a) shall be given notice by the owner or operator of said station of said violation. The notice given shall be by certified mail return receipt requested addressed to the registered owner of the motor vehicle.

(c) Upon the expiration of 10 days from the return of the receipt showing that the notice was received by the addressee, such vehicle left on the premises of a service station in violation of this section may be removed from the station premises to a place of storage and the registered owner of such vehicle shall become liable for the reasonable removal and storage charges and the vehicle subject to the storage lien created by G.S. 44A-1 et seq. Any person who removes a vehicle pursuant to this section shall not be held liable for damages for the removal of the vehicle to the owner, lienholder or other person legally entitled to the possession of the vehicle removed; however, any person who intentionally or negligently damages a vehicle in the removal of such vehicle, or intentionally or negligently inflicts injury upon any person in the removal of such vehicle, may be held liable for damages.

(d) In the alternative, the station owner or operator may charge for storage, assert a lien, and dispose of the vehicle under the terms of G.S. 44A-4(b) through (g). The proceeds from the sale of the vehicle shall be disbursed as provided in G.S. 44A-5.

History.
1971, c. 1220; 1973, c. 1330, s. 36; 1989, c. 644, s. 2

§ 20-219.4. Public vehicular area designated

(a) Any area of private property used for vehicular traffic may be designated by the property owner as a public vehicular area by registering the area with the Department of Transportation and by erecting signs identifying the area as a public vehicular area in conformity with rules adopted by the Department of Transportation.

(b) The Department of Transportation shall serve as a registry for registrations of public vehicular areas permitted under this section. The Department shall adopt rules for registration requirements and procedures. The Department shall also adopt rules governing the size and locations of signs designating public vehicular areas by private property owners in accordance with this section. These rules shall ensure that signs erected pursuant to this provision shall be placed so as to provide reasonable notice to motorists.

(c) The Department shall charge a fee not to exceed five hundred dollars ($ 500.00) per registration request authorized by this section. The Department may also charge the reasonable cost for furnishing a certified copy of a registration when requested. Funds collected under this subsection shall be used to cover the cost of maintaining the registry.

History.
2001-441, s. 2

§ 20-219.5. Dealer liability for third-party motor vehicle history reports

A motor vehicle dealer, as defined in G.S. 20-286(11), and the dealer's owners, shareholders, officers, employees, and agents who, in conjunction with the actual or potential sale or lease of a motor vehicle, arrange to provide, provide, or otherwise make available to a vehicle purchaser, lessee, or other person any third-party motor vehicle history report, shall not be liable to the vehicle purchaser, lessee, or other person for any errors, omissions, or other inaccuracies contained in the third-party motor vehicle history report that are not based on information provided directly to the preparer of the third-party motor vehicle history report by that dealer. For purposes of this section, a "third-party motor vehicle history report" means any information prepared by a party other than the dealer, relating to any one or more of the following: vehicle ownership or titling history; liens on the vehicle; vehicle service, maintenance, or repair history; vehicle condition; or vehicle accident or collision history.

History.
2019-181, s. 2

§§ 20-219.5 through 20-219.8

Reserved for future codification purposes.

ARTICLE 7A
POST-TOWING PROCEDURES

§ 20-219.9. Definitions

As used in this Article, unless the context clearly requires otherwise:

(1) "Tow" in any of its forms includes to remove a vehicle by any means including towing and to store the vehicle;

(2) "Tower" means the person who towed the vehicle;

(3) "Towing fee" means the fee charged for towing and storing.

History.
1983, c. 420, s. 2

§ 20-219.10. Coverage of Article

(a) This Article applies to each towing of a vehicle that is carried out pursuant to G.S. 115C-46(d) or G.S. 143-340(19), or pursuant to the direction of a law-enforcement officer except:

(1) This Article applies to towings pursuant to G.S. 115D-21, 116-44.4, 116-229, 153A-132, 153A-132.2, 160A-303, and 160A-303.2 only insofar as specifically provided;

(2) This Article does not apply to a seizure of a vehicle under G.S. 14-86.1, 18B-504, 90-112, 113-137, 20-28.2, 20-28.3, or to any other seizure of a vehicle for evidence in a criminal proceeding or pursuant to any other statute providing for the forfeiture of a vehicle;

(3) This Article does not apply to a seizure of a vehicle pursuant to a levy under execution.

(b) A person who authorizes the towing of a vehicle covered by this Article, G.S. 115D-21, 116-44.4, 116-229, 153A-132, 153A-132.2, 160A-303 or 160A-303.2 is a legal possessor of the vehicle within the meaning of G.S. 44A-1(1).

History.
1983, c. 420, s. 2; 1989, c. 743, s. 3; 1997-379, s. 1.7

§ 20-219.11. Notice and probable cause hearing

(a) Whenever a vehicle with a valid registration plate or registration is towed as provided in G.S. 20-219.10, the authorizing person shall immediately notify the last known registered owner of the vehicle of the following:

(1) A description of the vehicle;

(2) The place where the vehicle is stored;

(3) The violation with which the owner is charged, if any;

(4) The procedure the owner must follow to have the vehicle returned to him; and

(5) The procedure the owner must follow to request a probable cause hearing on the towing.

If the vehicle has a North Carolina registration plate or registration, notice shall be given to the owner within 24 hours; if the vehicle is not registered in this State, notice shall be given to the owner within 72 hours. This notice shall, if feasible, be given by telephone. Whether or not the owner is reached by telephone, notice shall be mailed to his last known address unless he or his agent waives this notice in writing.

(b) Whenever a vehicle with neither a valid registration plate nor registration is towed as provided in G.S. 20-219.10, the authorizing person shall make reasonable efforts, including checking the vehicle identification number, to determine the last known registered owner of the vehicle and to notify him of the information listed in subsection (a). Unless the owner has otherwise been given notice, it is presumed that the authorizing person has not made reasonable efforts, as required under this subsection, unless notice that the vehicle would be towed was posted on the windshield or some other conspicuous place at least seven days before the towing actually occurred; except, no pretowing notice need be given if the vehicle impeded the flow of traffic or otherwise jeopardized the public welfare so that immediate towing was necessary.

(c) The owner or any other person entitled to claim possession of the vehicle may request in writing a hearing to determine if probable cause existed for the towing. The request shall be filed with the magistrate in the county where the vehicle was towed. If there is more than one magistrate's office in that county, the request may be filed with the magistrate in the warrant-issuing office in the county seat or in any other office designated to receive requests by the chief district court judge. The magistrate shall set the hearing within 72 hours of his receiving the request. The owner, the person who requested the hearing if someone other than the owner, the tower, and the person who authorized the towing shall be notified of the time and place of the hearing.

(d) The owner, the tower, the person who authorized the towing, and any other interested parties may present evidence at the hearing. The person authorizing the towing and the tower may submit an affidavit in lieu of appearing personally, but the affidavit does not preclude that person from also testifying.

(e) The only issue at this hearing is whether or not probable cause existed for the towing. If the magistrate finds that probable cause did exist, the tower's lien continues. If the magistrate finds that probable cause did not exist, the tower's lien is extinguished.

(f) Any aggrieved party may appeal the magistrate's decision to district court.

History.
1983, c. 420, s. 2

§ 20-219.12. Option to pay or post bond

At any stage in the proceedings, including before the probable cause hearing, the owner may obtain possession of his vehicle by:

(1) Paying the towing fee, or

(2) Posting a bond for double the amount of the towing fee.

History.

1983, c. 420, s. 2

§ 20-219.13. Hearing on lien

The tower may seek to enforce his lien or the owner may seek to contest the lien pursuant to Chapter 44A.

History.

1983, c. 420, s. 2

§ 20-219.14. Payment to tower guaranteed

Every agency whose law-enforcement officers act pursuant to this Article, G.S. 115D-21, 116-44.4, 116-229, 153A-132, or 160A-303 shall by contract or rules provide compensation to the tower if a court finds no probable cause existed for the towing.

History.

1983, c. 420, s. 2

§§ 20-219.15 through 20-219.19

Reserved for future codification purposes.

ARTICLE 7B
NOTIFICATION OF TOWING

§ 20-219.20. Requirement to give notice of vehicle towing

(a) Whenever a vehicle is towed at the request of a person other than the owner or operator of the vehicle, the tower shall provide the following information to the local law enforcement agency having jurisdiction through calling the 10-digit telephone number designated by the local law enforcement agency having jurisdiction prior to moving the vehicle:

(1) A description of the vehicle.

(2) The place from which the vehicle was towed.

(3) The place where the vehicle will be stored.

(4) The contact information for the person from whom the vehicle owner may retrieve the vehicle.

If the vehicle is impeding the flow of traffic or otherwise jeopardizing the public welfare so that immediate towing is necessary, the notice to the local law enforcement agency having jurisdiction may be provided by a tower within 30 minutes of moving the vehicle rather than prior to moving the vehicle. If a caller to a local law enforcement agency having jurisdiction can provide the information required under subdivisions (1) and (2) of this subsection, then a local

law enforcement agency having jurisdiction shall provide to the caller the information provided under subdivisions (3) and (4) of this subsection. The local law enforcement agency having jurisdiction shall preserve the information required under this subsection for a period of not less than 30 days from the date on which the tower provided the information to the local law enforcement agency having jurisdiction.

(b) This section shall not apply to vehicles that are towed at the direction of a law enforcement officer or to vehicles removed from a private lot where signs are posted in accordance with G.S. 20-219.2(a).

(c) Violation of this section shall constitute an infraction subject to a penalty of not more than one hundred dollars ($ 100.00).

History.

2013-241, s. 1

ARTICLE 8
HABITUAL OFFENDERS

§§ 20-220 through 20-231

Repealed by Session Laws 1977, c. 243, s. 1.

ARTICLE 8A
ISSUANCE OF NEW LICENSES TO PERSONS ADJUDGED HABITUAL OFFENDERS

N.C. Gen. Stat. § 20-231.1

Repealed by Session Laws 1993 (Reg. Sess.; 1994), c. 761, s. 25.

ARTICLE 9
MOTOR VEHICLE SAFETY AND FINANCIAL RESPONSIBILITY ACT

§§ 20-232 through 20-279

Repealed by Session Laws 1953, c. 1300, s. 35.

ARTICLE 9A
MOTOR VEHICLE SAFETY AND FINANCIAL RESPONSIBILITY ACT OF 1953

§ 20-279.1. Definitions

The following words and phrases, when used in this Article, shall, for the purposes of this Article, have the meanings respectively ascribed to them in this section, except in those instances where the context clearly indicates a different meaning:

(1) Repealed by Session Laws 1973, c. 1330, s. 39.

(2) Repealed by Session Laws 1991, c. 726, s. 20.

. (3) "Judgment": Any judgment which shall have become final by expiration without appeal of the time within which an appeal might have been perfected, or by final affirmation on appeal, rendered by a court of competent jurisdiction of any state or of the United States, upon a cause of action arising out of the ownership, maintenance or use of any motor vehicle, for damages, including damages for care and loss of services, because of bodily injury to or death of any person, or for damages because of injury to or destruction of property, including the loss of use thereof, or upon a cause of action on an agreement of settlement for such damages.

(4) to (6) Repealed by Session Laws 1973, c. 1330, s. 39.

(6a) **Motor vehicle.** -- This term includes mopeds, as that term is defined in G.S. 20-4.01.

(7) "Nonresident's operating privilege": The privilege conferred upon a nonresident by the laws of this State pertaining to the operation by him of a motor vehicle in this State.

(8) to (10) Repealed by Session Laws 1973, c. 1330, s. 39.

(11) "Proof of financial responsibility": Proof of ability to respond in damages for liability, on account of accidents occurring subsequent to the effective date of said proof, arising out of the ownership, maintenance or use of a motor vehicle, in the amount of thirty thousand dollars ($ 30,000) because of bodily injury to or death of one person in any one accident, and, subject to said limit for one person, in the amount of sixty thousand dollars ($ 60,000) because of bodily injury to or death of two or more persons in any one accident, and in the amount of twenty-five thousand dollars ($ 25,000) because of injury to or destruction of property of others in any one accident. Nothing contained herein shall prevent an insurer and an insured from entering into a contract, not affecting third parties, providing for a deductible as to property damage at a rate approved by the Commissioner of Insurance.

(12) Repealed by Session Laws 1973, c. 1330, s. 39.

History.
1953, c. 1300, s. 1; 1955, c. 1152, s. 3; c. 1355; 1967, c. 277, s. 1; 1971, c. 1205, s. 1; 1973, c. 745, s. 1; c. 1330, s. 39; 1979, c. 832, s. 1; 1991, c. 469, s. 1; c. 726, s. 20; 1999-228, s. 1; 2015-125, s. 2

§ 20-279.2. Commissioners to administer Article; appeal to court

(a) Except for G.S. 20-279.21(d1), the Commissioner shall administer and enforce the provisions of this Article and may make rules and regulations necessary for its administration and shall provide for hearings upon request of persons aggrieved by orders or acts of the Commissioner under the provisions of this Article. The Commissioner of Insurance shall administer and enforce the provisions of G.S. 20-279.21(d1) and may make rules and regulations necessary for its administration.

(b) Any person aggrieved by an order or act of the Commissioner of Motor Vehicles requiring a suspension or revocation of the person's license under the provisions of this Article, or requiring the posting of security as provided in this Article, or requiring the furnishing of proof of financial responsibility, may file a petition in the superior court of the county in which the petitioner resides for a review, and the commencement of the proceeding shall suspend the order or act of the Commissioner pending the final determination of the review. A copy of the petition shall be served upon the Commissioner, and the Commissioner shall have 20 days after service in which to file answer. The appeal shall be heard in said county by the judge holding court in said county or by the resident judge. At the hearing upon the petition the judge shall sit without the intervention of a jury and shall receive any evidence deemed by the judge to be relevant and proper. Except as otherwise provided in this section, upon the filing of the petition herein provided for, the procedure shall be the same as in civil actions.

The matter shall be heard de novo and the judge shall enter an order affirming the act or order of the Commissioner, or modifying same, including the amount of bond or security to be given by the petitioner. If the court is of the opinion that the petitioner was probably not guilty of negligence or that the negligence of the other party was probably the sole proximate cause of the collision, the judge shall reverse the act or order of the Commissioner. Either party may appeal from the order to the Supreme Court in the same manner as in other appeals from the superior court and the appeal shall have the effect of further staying the act or order of the Commissioner requiring a suspension or revocation of the petitioner's license.

No act, or order given or rendered in any proceeding hereunder shall be admitted or used in any other civil or criminal action.

History.
1953, c. 1300, s. 2; 2018-5, s. 34.26(a)

§ 20-279.3. Commissioner to furnish operating record

The Commissioner shall upon request furnish any person a certified abstract of the operating record of any person required to comply with the provisions of this Article, which abstract shall also fully designate the motor vehicle, if any, registered in the name of such person, and if there shall be no record of any conviction of such person of violating any law relating to the operation of a motor vehicle or of any injury or damage caused by such person, the Commissioner shall so certify.

History.
1953, c. 1300, s. 3

N.C. Gen. Stat. § 20-279.4

Repealed by Session Laws 1995, c. 191, s. 4.

§ 20-279.5. Security required unless evidence of insurance; when security determined; suspension; exceptions

(a) When the Division receives a report of a reportable accident under G.S. 20-166.1, the Commissioner must determine whether the owner or driver of a vehicle involved in the accident must file security under this Article and, if so, the amount of security the owner or driver must file. The Commissioner must make this determination at the end of 20 days after receiving the report.

(b) The Commissioner shall, within 60 days after the receipt of such report of a motor vehicle accident, suspend the license of each operator and each owner of a motor vehicle in any manner involved in such accident, and if such operator or owner is a nonresident the privilege of operating a motor vehicle within this State, unless such operator or owner, or both, shall deposit security in the sum so determined by the Commissioner; provided, notice of such suspension shall be sent by the Commissioner to such operator and owner not less than 10 days prior to the effective date of such suspension and shall state the amount required as security; provided further, the provisions of this Article requiring the deposit of security and the suspension of license for failure to deposit security shall not apply to an operator or owner who

would otherwise be required to deposit security in an amount not in excess of one hundred dollars ($ 100.00). Where erroneous information is given the Commissioner with respect to the matters set forth in subdivisions (1), (2) or (3) of subsection (c) of this section or with respect to the ownership or operation of the vehicle, the extent of damage and injuries, or any other matters which would have affected the Commissioner's action had the information been previously submitted, he shall take appropriate action as hereinbefore provided, within 60 days after receipt by him of correct information with respect to said matters. The Commissioner, upon request and in his discretion, may postpone the effective date of the suspension provided in this section by 15 days if, in his opinion, such extension would aid in accomplishing settlements of claims by persons involved in accidents.

(c) This section shall not apply under the conditions stated in G.S. 20-279.6 nor:

(1) To such operator or owner if such owner had in effect at the time of such accident an automobile liability policy with respect to the motor vehicle involved in such accident;

(2) To such operator, if not the owner of such motor vehicle, if there was in effect at the time of such accident a motor vehicle liability policy or bond with respect to his operation of motor vehicles not owned by him;

(3) To such operator or owner if the liability of such operator or owner for damages resulting from such accident is, in the judgment of the Commissioner, covered by any other form of liability insurance policy or bond or sinking fund or group assumption of liability;

(4) To any person qualifying as a self-insurer, nor to any operator for a self-insurer if, in the opinion of the Commissioner from the information furnished him, the operator at the time of the accident was probably operating the vehicle in the course of the operator's employment as an employee or officer of the self-insurer; nor

(5) To any employee of the United States government while operating a vehicle in its service and while acting within the scope of his employment, such operations being fully protected by the Federal Tort Claims Act of 1946, which affords ample security to all persons sustaining personal injuries or property damage through the negligence of such federal employee.

No such policy or bond shall be effective under this section unless issued by an insurance company or surety company authorized to do business in this State, except that if such motor vehicle was not registered in this State, or was a motor vehicle which was registered elsewhere than in this State at the effective date of the policy or bond, or the most recent renewal thereof, or if such operator not an owner was a nonresident of this State, such policy or bond shall not be effective under this section unless the insurance company or surety company if not authorized to do business in this State shall execute a power of attorney authorizing the Commissioner to accept service on its behalf of notice or process in any action upon such policy, or bond arising out of such accident, and unless said insurance company or surety company, if not authorized to do business in this State, is authorized to do business in the state or other jurisdiction where the motor vehicle is registered or, if such policy or bond is filed on behalf of an operator not an owner who was a nonresident of this State, unless said insurance company or surety company, if not authorized to do business in this State, is authorized to do business in the state or other jurisdiction of residence of such operator; provided, however, every such policy or bond is subject, if the accident has resulted in bodily injury or death, to a limit, exclusive of interest and cost, of not less than thirty thousand dollars ($ 30,000) because of bodily injury to or death of one person in any one accident and, subject to said limit for one person, to a limit of not less than sixty thousand dollars ($ 60,000) because of bodily injury to or death of two or more persons in any one accident, and, if the accident has resulted in injury to or destruction of property, to a limit of not less than twenty-five thousand dollars ($ 25,000) because of injury to or destruction of property of others in any one accident.

History.
1953, c. 1300, s. 5; 1955, cc. 138, 854; c. 855, s. 1; c. 1152, ss. 4-8; c. 1355; 1967, c. 277, s. 2; 1971, c. 763, s. 3; 1973, c. 745, s. 2; 1979, c. 832, s. 2; 1983, c. 691, s. 2; 1991, c. 469, s. 2; 1991 (Reg. Sess., 1992), c. 837, s. 10; 1995, c. 191, s. 5; 1999-228, s. 2

§ 20-279.6. Further exceptions to requirement of security

The requirements as to security and suspension in G.S. 20-279.5 shall not apply:

(1) To the operator or the owner of a motor vehicle involved in an accident wherein no injury or damage was caused to the person or property of anyone other than such operator or owner;

(2) To the operator or the owner of a motor vehicle legally parked at the time of the accident;

(3) To the owner of a motor vehicle if at the time of the accident the vehicle was being operated without his permission, express or implied, or was parked by a person who had been operating such motor vehicle without such permission;

(4) If, prior to the date that the Commissioner would otherwise suspend the license or the nonresident's operating privilege under G.S. 20-279.5, there shall be filed with the Commissioner evidence satisfactory to him that the person who would otherwise have to file security has been released from liability or been finally adjudicated not to be liable or has executed a duly acknowledged written agreement providing for the payment of an agreed amount, in installments or otherwise, with respect to all claims for injuries or damages resulting from the accident;

(5) If, prior to the date that the Commissioner would otherwise suspend the license or the nonresident's operating privilege under G.S. 20-279.5, there shall be filed with the Commissioner evidence satisfactory to him that the person who would otherwise be required to file security has in any manner settled the claims of the other persons involved in the accident and if the Commissioner determines that, considering the circumstances of the accident and the settlement, the purposes of this Article and of protection of operators and owners of other motor vehicles are best accomplished by not requiring the posting of security or the suspension of the license. For the purpose of administering this subdivision, the Commissioner may consider a settlement made by an insurance company as the equivalent of a settlement made directly by the insured; nor

(6) If, prior to the date that the Commissioner would otherwise suspend the license or the nonresident's operating privilege under G.S. 20-279.5, there shall be filed with the Commissioner evidence satisfactory to him that another person involved in the accident has been convicted by a court of competent jurisdiction of a crime involving the operation of a motor vehicle at the time of the accident, and if the Commissioner in his discretion determines, after considering the circumstances of the accident or the nature and the circumstances of the crime, that the purpose of this Article and of protection of operators and owners of other motor vehicles are best accomplished by not requiring the posting of security or the suspension of the license.

History.
1953, c. 1300, s. 6; 1955, c. 1152, ss. 9, 10

§ 20-279.6A. Minors

In determining whether or not any of the exceptions set forth in G.S. 20-279.6 have been satisfied, in the case of accidents involving minors, the Commissioner may accept, for the purpose of this Article only, as valid releases on account of claims for injuries to minors or damage to the property of minors releases which have been executed by the parent of the minor having custody of the minor or by the guardian of the minor if there be one. In the case of an emancipated minor, the Commissioner may accept a release signed by or a settlement agreed upon by the minor without the approval of the parents of the minor. If in the opinion of the Commissioner the circumstances of the accident, the nature and extent of the injuries or damage, or any other circumstances make it advisable for the best protection of the interest of the minor, the Commissioner may decline to accept such releases or settlements and may require the approval of the superior court.

History.
1955, c. 1152, s. 11

§ 20-279.7. Duration of suspension

The license and nonresident's operating privilege suspended as provided in G.S. 20-279.5 shall remain so suspended and shall not be renewed nor shall any such license be issued to such person until:

(1) Such person shall deposit or there shall be deposited on his behalf the security required under G.S. 20-279.5;

(2) One year shall have elapsed following the date of such suspension and evidence satisfactory to the Commissioner has been filed with him that during such period no action for damages arising out of the accident has been instituted; or

(3) Evidence satisfactory to the Commissioner has been filed with him of a release from liability, or a final adjudication of nonliability, or a duly acknowledged written agreement, in accordance with subdivision (4) of G.S. 20-279.6 or a settlement accepted by the Commissioner as provided in subdivision (5) of G.S. 20-279.6, or a conviction accepted by the Commissioner as provided in subdivision (6) of G.S. 20-279.6; provided, if there is a default in the payment of any installment or sum under a duly acknowledged written agreement, the Commissioner shall, upon notice of the default, immediately suspend the license or nonresident's operating privilege of the defaulting person and may not restore it until:

a. That person deposits and thereafter maintains security as required

under G.S. 20-279.5 in an amount determined by the Commissioner; or

b. That person files evidence satisfactory to the Commissioner of a new duly acknowledged written agreement or a settlement.

History.
1953, c. 1300, s. 7; 1955, c. 1152, s. 12; 1983, c. 610, s. 1

§ 20-279.7A. Forms to carry statement concerning perjury

A person who makes a false affidavit or falsely sworn or affirmed statement concerning information required to be submitted under this Article commits a Class I felony. The Division shall include a statement of this offense on a form that it provides under this Article and that must be completed under oath.

History.
1983, c. 610, s. 3; 1993 (Reg. Sess., 1994), c. 761, s. 26

§ 20-279.8. Application to nonresidents, unlicensed drivers, unregistered motor vehicles and accidents in other states

(a) In case the operator or the owner of a motor vehicle involved in an accident within this State has no license, or is a nonresident, he shall not be allowed a license until he has complied with the requirements of this Article to the same extent that it would be necessary if, at the time of the accident, he had held a license.

(b) When a nonresident's operating privilege is suspended pursuant to G.S. 20-279.5 or 20-279.7, the Commissioner shall transmit a certified copy of the record of such action to the official in charge of the issuance of licenses in the state in which such nonresident resides, if the law of such other state provides for action in relation thereto similar to that provided for in subsection (c) of this section.

(c) Upon receipt of such certification that the operating privilege of a resident of this State has been suspended or revoked in any such other state pursuant to a law providing for its suspension or revocation for failure to deposit security for the payment of judgments arising out of a motor vehicle accident, under circumstances which would require the Commissioner to suspend a nonresident's operating privilege had the accident occurred in this State the Commissioner shall suspend the license of such resident. Such suspension shall continue until such resident furnishes evidence of his compliance with the law of such other state relating to the deposit of such security.

History.
1953, c. 1300, s. 8

§ 20-279.9. Form and amount of security

The security required under this Article shall be in such form and in such amount as the Commissioner may require but in no case in excess of the limits specified in G.S. 20-279.5 in reference to the acceptable limits of a policy or bond. The person depositing security shall specify in writing the person or persons on whose behalf the deposit is made and, at any time while such deposit is in the custody of the Commissioner or State Treasurer, the person depositing it may, in writing, amend the specification of the person or persons on whose behalf the deposit is made to include an additional person or persons; provided, however, that a single deposit of security shall be applicable only on behalf of persons required to furnish security because of the same accident.

The Commissioner may reduce the amount of security ordered in any case if, in his judgment, the amount ordered is excessive. In case the security originally ordered has been deposited the excess deposited over the reduced amount ordered shall be returned to the depositor or his personal representative forthwith, notwithstanding the provisions of G.S. 20-279.10.

History.
1953, c. 1300, s. 9

§ 20-279.10. Custody, disposition and return of security; escheat

(a) Security deposited in compliance with the requirements of this Article shall be placed by the Commissioner in the custody of the State Treasurer and shall be applicable only to the payment of a judgment or judgments rendered against the person or persons on whose behalf the deposit was made, for damages arising out of the accident in question in an action at law, begun not later than one year after the date of such accident, or within one year after the date of deposit of any security under subdivision (3) of G.S. 20-279.7, or to the payment in settlement, agreed to by the depositor, of a claim or claims arising out of such accident. Such deposit or any balance thereof shall be returned to the depositor or his personal representative when evidence satisfactory to the Commissioner has been filed with him that there has been a release from liability, or a final adjudication of nonliability, or a duly acknowledged agreement, in accordance with subdivision (4) of G.S. 20-279.6, or a settlement accepted by the Commissioner as provided in subdivision (5) of G.S. 20-279.6, or a conviction accepted by the Commissioner as provided in subdivision (6) of G.S. 20-279.6, or whenever, after the expiration of one year from the date of the accident, or from the date of deposit of any security under subdivision (3) of G.S. 20-279.7, whichever is

later, the Commissioner shall be given reasonable evidence that there is no such action pending and no judgment rendered in such action left unpaid.

(b) One year from the deposit of any security under the terms of this Article, the Commissioner shall notify the depositor thereof by registered mail addressed to his last known address that the depositor is entitled to a refund of the security upon giving reasonable evidence that no action at law for damages arising out of the accident in question is pending or that no judgment rendered in any such action remains unpaid. If, at the end of three years from the date of deposit, no claim therefor has been received, the Division shall notify the depositor thereof by registered mail and shall cause a notice to be posted at the courthouse door of the county in which is located the last known address of the depositor for a period of 60 days. Such notice shall contain the name of the depositor, his last known address, the date, amount and nature of the deposit, and shall state the conditions under which the deposit will be refunded. If, at the end of two years from the date of posting of such notice, no claim for the deposit has been received, the Commissioner shall certify such fact together with the facts of notice to the State Treasurer. These deposits shall be turned over to the Escheat Fund of the Department of State Treasurer.

History.
1953, c. 1300, s. 10; 1955, c. 1152, s. 13; 1967, c. 1227; 1975, c. 716, s. 5; 1981, c. 531, s. 16

§ 20-279.11. Matters not to be evidence in civil suits

Neither the information on financial responsibility contained in an accident report, the action taken by the Commissioner pursuant to this Article, the findings, if any, of the Commissioner upon which the action is based, or the security filed as provided in this Article shall be referred to in any way, nor be any evidence of the negligence or due care of either party, at the trial of any action at law to recover damages.

History.
1953, c. 1300, s. 11; 1995, c. 191, s. 6

§ 20-279.12. Courts to report nonpayment of judgments

Whenever any person fails within 60 days to satisfy any judgment, upon the written request of the judgment creditor or his attorney it shall be the duty of the clerk of the court, or of the judge of a court which has no clerk, in which any such judgment is rendered within this State, to forward to the Commissioner immediately after the expiration of said 60 days, a certified copy of such judgment.

If the defendant named in any certified copy of a judgment reported to the Commissioner is a nonresident, the Commissioner shall transmit a certified copy of the judgment to the official in charge of the issuance of licenses and registration certificates of the state of which the defendant is a resident.

History.
1953, c. 1300, s. 12

§ 20-279.13. Suspension for nonpayment of judgment; exceptions

(a) The Commissioner, upon the receipt of a certified copy of a judgment, which has remained unsatisfied for a period of 60 days, shall forthwith suspend the license and any nonresident's operating privilege of any person against whom such judgment was rendered, except as hereinafter otherwise provided in this section and in G.S. 20-279.16.

(b) The Commissioner shall not, however, revoke or suspend the license of an owner or driver if the insurance carried by him was in a company which was authorized to transact business in this State and which subsequent to an accident involving the owner or operator and prior to settlement of the claim therefor went into liquidation, so that the owner or driver is thereby unable to satisfy the judgment arising out of the accident.

(c) If the judgment creditor consents in writing, in such form as the Commissioner may prescribe, that the judgment debtor be allowed license or nonresident's operating privilege, the same may be allowed by the Commissioner, in his discretion, for six months from the date of such consent and thereafter until such consent is revoked in writing notwithstanding default in the payment of such judgment, or of any installments thereof prescribed in G.S. 20-279.16.

History.
1953, c. 1300, s. 13; 1965, c. 926, s. 1; 1969, c. 186, s. 4; 1979, c. 667, s. 37

§ 20-279.14. Suspension to continue until judgments satisfied

Such license and nonresident's operating privilege shall remain so suspended and shall not be renewed, nor shall any such license be thereafter issued in the name of such person, including any such person not previously licensed, unless and until every such judgment:

(1) Is stayed, or

(2) Is satisfied in full, or

(3) Is subject to the exemptions stated in G.S. 20-279.13 or G.S. 20-279.16, or

(4) Is barred from enforcement by the statute of limitations pursuant to G.S. 1-47,

(5) Is discharged in bankruptcy.

History.
1953, c. 1300, s. 14; 1969, c. 186, s. 5; 1975, c. 301

§ 20-279.15. Payment sufficient to satisfy requirements

In addition to other methods of satisfaction provided by law, judgments herein referred to shall, for the purpose of this Article, be deemed satisfied:

(1) When thirty thousand dollars ($ 30,000) has been credited upon any judgment or judgments rendered in excess of that amount because of bodily injury to or death of one person as the result of any one accident; or

(2) When, subject to such limit of thirty thousand dollars ($ 30,000) because of bodily injury to or death of one person, the sum of sixty thousand dollars ($ 60,000) has been credited upon any judgment or judgments rendered in excess of that amount because of bodily injury to or death of two or more persons as the result of any one accident; or

(3) When twenty-five thousand dollars ($ 25,000) has been credited upon any judgment or judgments rendered in excess of that amount because of injury to or destruction of property of others as a result of any one accident;

Provided, however, payments made in settlement of any claims because of bodily injury, death or property damage arising from a motor vehicle accident shall be credited in reduction of the amounts provided for in this section.

History.
1953, c. 1300, s. 15; 1963, c. 1238; 1967, c. 277, s. 3; 1973, c. 745, s. 3; c. 889; 1979, c. 832, ss. 3-5; 1991, c. 469, s. 3; 1991 (Reg. Sess., 1992), c. 837, s. 10; 1999-228, s. 3

§ 20-279.16. Installment payment of judgments; default

(a) A judgment debtor upon due notice to the judgment creditor may apply to the court in which such judgment was rendered for the privilege of paying such judgment in installments and the court, in its discretion and without prejudice to any other legal remedies which the judgment creditor may have, may so order and fix the amounts and times of payment of the installments.

(b) The Commissioner shall not suspend a license or a nonresident's operating privilege, and shall restore any license or nonresident's operating privilege suspended following non-payment of a judgment, when the judgment debtor obtains such an order permitting the payment of such judgment in installments, and while the payment of any said installment is not in default.

(c) In the event the judgment debtor fails to pay any installment as specified by such order, then upon notice of such default, the Commissioner shall forthwith suspend the license or nonresident's operating privilege of the judgment debtor until such judgment is satisfied, as provided in this Article.

History.
1953, c. 1300, s. 16; 1969, c. 186, s. 6

N.C. Gen. Stat. § 20-279.17

Repealed by Session Laws 1967, c. 866.

§ 20-279.18. Alternate methods of giving proof

Proof of financial responsibility when required under this Article with respect to a motor vehicle or with respect to a person who is not the owner of a motor vehicle may be given by filing:

(1) A certificate of insurance as provided in G.S. 20-279.19 or 20-279.20; or

(2) A bond as provided in G.S. 20-279.24; or

(3) A certificate of deposit of money or securities as provided in G.S. 20-279.25; or

(4) A certificate of self-insurance, as provided in G.S. 20-279.33, supplemented by an agreement by the self-insurer that, with respect to accidents occurring while the certificate is in force, he will pay the same judgments and in the same amounts that an insurer would have been obligated to pay under an owner's motor vehicle liability policy if it had issued such a policy to said self-insurer.

History.
1953, c. 1300, s. 18

§ 20-279.19. Certificate of insurance as proof

Proof of financial responsibility may be furnished by filing with the Commissioner the written certificate of any insurance carrier duly authorized to do business in this State certifying that there is in effect a motor vehicle liability policy for the benefit of the person required to furnish proof of financial responsibility. Such certificate shall give the effective date of such motor vehicle liability policy, which date shall be the same as the effective date of the certificate, and shall designate by explicit description or by appropriate reference all motor vehicles covered thereby, unless the policy is issued to a person who is not the owner of a motor vehicle. The Commissioner may require that certificates filed pursuant to this section be on a form approved by the Commissioner.

History.
1953, c. 1300, s. 19; 1955, c. 1152, s. 16

§ 20-279.20. Certificate furnished by nonresident as proof

(a) The nonresident owner of a motor vehicle not registered in this State may give proof of financial responsibility by filing with the Commissioner a written certificate or certificates of an insurance carrier authorized to transact business in the state in which the motor vehicle or motor vehicles described in such certificate is registered, or if such nonresident does not own a motor vehicle, then in the state in which the insured resides, provided such certificate otherwise conforms to the provisions of this Article, and the Commissioner shall accept the same upon condition that said insurance carrier complies with the following provisions with respect to the policies so certified:

(1) Said insurance carrier shall execute a power of attorney authorizing the Commissioner to accept service on its behalf of notice or process in any action arising out of a motor vehicle accident in this State; and

(2) Said insurance carrier shall agree in writing that such policies shall be deemed to conform with the laws of this State relating to the terms of motor vehicle liability policies issued herein.

(b) If any insurance carrier not authorized to transact business in this State, which has qualified to furnish proof of financial responsibility, defaults in any said undertakings or agreements, the Commissioner shall not thereafter accept as proof any certificate of said carrier whether theretofore filed or thereafter tendered as proof, so long as such default continues.

(c) The Commissioner may require that certificates and powers filed pursuant to this section be on forms approved by the Commissioner.

History.
1953, c. 1300, s. 20; 1955, c. 1152, s. 17

§ 20-279.21. "Motor vehicle liability policy" defined

(a) A "motor vehicle liability policy" as said term is used in this Article shall mean an owner's or an operator's policy of liability insurance, certified as provided in G.S. 20-279.19 or 20-279.20 as proof of financial responsibility, and

Chapter 20

issued, except as otherwise provided in G.S. 20-279.20, by an insurance carrier duly authorized to transact business in this State, to or for the benefit of the person named therein as insured.

(b) Except as provided in G.S. 20-309(a2), such owner's policy of liability insurance:

(1) Shall designate by explicit description or by appropriate reference all motor vehicles with respect to which coverage is thereby to be granted;

(2) Shall insure the person named therein and any other person, as insured, using any such motor vehicle or motor vehicles with the express or implied permission of such named insured, or any other persons in lawful possession, against loss from the liability imposed by law for damages arising out of the ownership, maintenance or use of such motor vehicle or motor vehicles within the United States of America or the Dominion of Canada subject to limits exclusive of interest and costs, with respect to each such motor vehicle, as follows: thirty thousand dollars ($ 30,000) because of bodily injury to or death of one person in any one accident and, subject to said limit for one person, sixty thousand dollars ($ 60,000) because of bodily injury to or death of two or more persons in any one accident, and twenty-five thousand dollars ($ 25,000) because of injury to or destruction of property of others in any one accident; and

(3) No policy of bodily injury liability insurance, covering liability arising out of the ownership, maintenance, or use of any motor vehicle, shall be delivered or issued for delivery in this State with respect to any motor vehicle registered or principally garaged in this State unless coverage is provided therein or supplemental thereto, under provisions filed with and approved by the Commissioner of Insurance, for the protection of persons insured thereunder who are legally entitled to recover damages from owners or operators of uninsured motor vehicles and hit-and-run motor vehicles because of bodily injury, sickness or disease, including death, resulting therefrom. The limits of such uninsured motorist bodily injury coverage shall be equal to the highest limits of bodily injury liability coverage for any one vehicle insured under the policy; provided, however, that (i) the limits shall not exceed one million dollars ($ 1,000,000) per person and one million dollars ($ 1,000,000) per accident regardless of whether the highest limits of bodily injury liability coverage for any one vehicle insured under the policy exceed those limits and (ii) a named insured may purchase greater or lesser limits, except that the limits shall not be less than the bodily

injury liability limits required pursuant to subdivision (2) of this subsection, and in no event shall an insurer be required by this subdivision to sell uninsured motorist bodily injury coverage at limits that exceed one million dollars ($ 1,000,000) per person and one million dollars ($ 1,000,000) per accident. When the policy is issued and renewed, the insurer shall notify the named insured as provided in subsection (m) of this section. The provisions shall include coverage for the protection of persons insured under the policy who are legally entitled to recover damages from owners or operators of uninsured motor vehicles because of injury to or destruction of the property of such insured. The limits of such uninsured motorist property damage coverage shall be equal to the highest limits of property damage liability coverage for any one vehicle insured under the policy; provided, however, that (i) the limits shall not exceed one million dollars ($ 1,000,000) per accident regardless of whether the highest limits of property damage liability coverage for any one vehicle insured under the policy exceed those limits and (ii) a named insured may purchase lesser limits, except that the limits shall not be less than the property damage liability limits required pursuant to subdivision (2) of this subsection. When the policy is issued and renewed, the insurer shall notify the named insured as provided in subsection (m) of this section. For uninsured motorist property damage coverage, the limits purchased by the named insured shall be subject, for each insured, to an exclusion of the first one hundred dollars ($ 100.00) of such damages. The provision shall further provide that a written statement by the liability insurer, whose name appears on the certification of financial responsibility made by the owner of any vehicle involved in an accident with the insured, that the other motor vehicle was not covered by insurance at the time of the accident with the insured shall operate as a prima facie presumption that the operator of the other motor vehicle was uninsured at the time of the accident with the insured for the purposes of recovery under this provision of the insured's liability insurance policy.

If a person who is legally entitled to recover damages from the owner or operator of an uninsured motor vehicle is an insured under the uninsured motorist coverage of a policy that insures more than one motor vehicle, that person shall not be permitted to combine the uninsured motorist limit applicable to any one motor vehicle with the uninsured motorist limit applicable to any other motor vehicle to determine the total amount of uninsured motorist coverage available to that person. If a person who is legally entitled to recover damages from the owner or operator of an uninsured motor vehicle is an insured under the uninsured motorist coverage of more than one policy, that person may combine the highest applicable uninsured motorist limit available under each policy to determine the total amount of uninsured motorist coverage available to that person. The previous sentence shall apply only to insurance on nonfleet private passenger motor vehicles as described in G.S. 58-40-10(1) and (2).

In addition to the above requirements relating to uninsured motorist insurance, every policy of bodily injury liability insurance covering liability arising out of the ownership, maintenance or use of any motor vehicle, which policy is delivered or issued for delivery in this State, shall be subject to the following provisions which need not be contained therein.

a. A provision that the insurer shall be bound by a final judgment taken by the insured against an uninsured motorist if the insurer has been served with copy of summons, complaint or other process in the action against the uninsured motorist by registered or certified mail, return receipt requested, or in any manner provided by law; provided however, that the determination of whether a motorist is uninsured may be decided only by an action against the insurer alone. The insurer, upon being served as herein provided, shall be a party to the action between the insured and the uninsured motorist though not named in the caption of the pleadings and may defend the suit in the name of the uninsured motorist or in its own name. The insurer, upon being served with copy of summons, complaint or other pleading, shall have the time allowed by statute in which to answer, demur or otherwise plead (whether the pleading is verified or not) to the summons, complaint or other process served upon it. The consent of the insurer shall not be required for the initiation of suit by the insured against the uninsured motorist: Provided, however, no action shall be initiated by the insured until 60 days following the posting of notice to the insurer at the address shown on the policy or after personal delivery of the notice to the insurer or its agent setting forth the belief of the insured that the prospective defendant

or defendants are uninsured motorists. No default judgment shall be entered when the insurer has timely filed an answer or other pleading as required by law. The failure to post notice to the insurer 60 days in advance of the initiation of suit shall not be grounds for dismissal of the action, but shall automatically extend the time for the filing of an answer or other pleadings to 60 days after the time of service of the summons, complaint, or other process on the insurer.

b. Where the insured, under the uninsured motorist coverage, claims that he has sustained bodily injury as the result of collision between motor vehicles and asserts that the identity of the operator or owner of a vehicle (other than a vehicle in which the insured is a passenger) cannot be ascertained, the insured may institute an action directly against the insurer: Provided, in that event, the insured, or someone in his behalf, shall report the accident within 24 hours or as soon thereafter as may be practicable, to a police officer, peace officer, other judicial officer, or to the Commissioner of Motor Vehicles. The insured shall also within a reasonable time give notice to the insurer of his injury, the extent thereof, and shall set forth in the notice the time, date and place of the injury. Thereafter, on forms to be mailed by the insurer within 15 days following receipt of the notice of the accident to the insurer, the insured shall furnish to insurer any further reasonable information concerning the accident and the injury that the insurer requests. If the forms are not furnished within 15 days, the insured is deemed to have complied with the requirements for furnishing information to the insurer. Suit may not be instituted against the insurer in less than 60 days from the posting of the first notice of the injury or accident to the insurer at the address shown on the policy or after personal delivery of the notice to the insurer or its agent. The failure to post notice to the insurer 60 days before the initiation of the suit shall not be grounds for dismissal of the action, but shall automatically extend the time for filing of an answer or other pleadings to 60 days after the time of service of the summons, complaint, or other process on the insurer.

Provided under this section the term "uninsured motor vehicle" shall include, but not be limited to, an insured motor vehicle where the liability insurer thereof is unable to make payment with respect to the legal liability within the limits specified therein because of insolvency.

An insurer's insolvency protection shall be applicable only to accidents occurring during a policy period in which its insured's uninsured motorist coverage is in effect where the liability insurer of the tort-feasor becomes insolvent within three years after such an accident. Nothing herein shall be construed to prevent any insurer from affording insolvency protection under terms and conditions more favorable to the insured than is provided herein.

In the event of payment to any person under the coverage required by this section and subject to the terms and conditions of coverage, the insurer making payment shall, to the extent thereof, be entitled to the proceeds of any settlement for judgment resulting from the exercise of any limits of recovery of that person against any person or organization legally responsible for the bodily injury for which the payment is made, including the proceeds recoverable from the assets of the insolvent insurer.

For the purpose of this section, an "uninsured motor vehicle" shall be a motor vehicle as to which there is no bodily injury liability insurance and property damage liability insurance in at least the amounts specified in subsection (c) of G.S. 20-279.5, or there is that insurance but the insurance company writing the insurance denies coverage thereunder, or has become bankrupt, or there is no bond or deposit of money or securities as provided in G.S. 20-279.24 or 20-279.25 in lieu of the bodily injury and property damage liability insurance, or the owner of the motor vehicle has not qualified as a self-insurer under the provisions of G.S. 20-279.33, or a vehicle that is not subject to the provisions of the Motor Vehicle Safety and Financial Responsibility Act; but the term "uninsured motor vehicle" shall not include:

a. A motor vehicle owned by the named insured;

b. A motor vehicle that is owned or operated by a self-insurer within the meaning of any motor vehicle financial responsibility law, motor carrier law or any similar law;

c. A motor vehicle that is owned by the United States of America, Canada, a state, or any agency of any of the foregoing (excluding, however, political subdivisions thereof);

d. A land motor vehicle or trailer, if operated on rails or crawler-treads or while located for use as a residence or premises and not as a vehicle; or

e. A farm-type tractor or equipment designed for use principally off public roads, except while actually upon public roads.

For purposes of this section "persons insured" means the named insured and, while resident of the same household, the spouse of any named insured and relatives of either, while in a motor vehicle or otherwise, and any person who uses with the consent, expressed or implied, of the named insured, the motor vehicle to which the policy applies and a guest in the motor vehicle to which the policy applies or the personal representative of any of the above or any other person or persons in lawful possession of the motor vehicle.

Notwithstanding the provisions of this subsection, no policy of motor vehicle liability insurance applicable solely to commercial motor vehicles as defined in G.S. 20-4.01(3d) or applicable solely to fleet vehicles shall be required to provide uninsured motorist coverage. When determining whether a policy is applicable solely to fleet vehicles, the insurer may rely upon the number of vehicles reported by the insured at the time of the issuance of the policy for the policy term in question. In the event of a renewal of the policy, when determining whether a policy is applicable solely to fleet vehicles, the insurer may rely upon the number of vehicles reported by the insured at the time of the renewal of the policy for the policy term in question. Any motor vehicle liability policy that insures both commercial motor vehicles as defined in G.S. 20-4.01(3d) and noncommercial motor vehicles shall provide uninsured motorist coverage in accordance with the provisions of this subsection in amounts equal to the highest limits of bodily injury and property damage liability coverage for any one noncommercial motor vehicle insured under the policy, subject to the right of the insured to purchase greater or lesser uninsured motorist bodily injury coverage limits and lesser uninsured motorist property damage coverage limits as set forth in this subsection. For the purpose of the immediately preceding sentence, noncommercial motor vehicle shall mean any motor vehicle that is not a commercial motor vehicle as defined in G.S. 20-4.01(3d), but that is otherwise subject to the requirements of this subsection.

(4) Shall, in addition to the coverages set forth in subdivisions (2) and (3) of this subsection, provide underinsured motorist coverage, to be used only with a policy that is written at limits that exceed those prescribed by subdivision (2) of this subsection. The limits of such underinsured motorist bodily injury coverage shall be equal to the highest limits of bodily injury liability coverage for any one vehicle insured under the policy; provided, however, that (i) the limits shall not exceed one million dollars ($ 1,000,000) per person and one million dollars ($ 1,000,000) per accident regardless of whether the highest limits of bodily injury liability coverage for any one vehicle insured under the policy exceed those limits, (ii) a named insured may purchase greater or lesser limits, except that the limits shall exceed the bodily injury liability limits required pursuant to subdivision (2) of this subsection, and in no event shall an insurer be required by this subdivision to sell underinsured motorist bodily injury coverage at limits that exceed one million dollars ($ 1,000,000) per person and one million dollars ($ 1,000,000) per accident, and (iii) the limits shall be equal to the limits of uninsured motorist bodily injury coverage purchased pursuant to subdivision (3) of this subsection. When the policy is issued and renewed, the insurer shall notify the named insured as provided in subsection (m) of this section. An "uninsured motor vehicle," as described in subdivision (3) of this subsection, includes an "underinsured highway vehicle," which means a highway vehicle with respect to the ownership, maintenance, or use of which, the sum of the limits of liability under all bodily injury liability bonds and insurance policies applicable at the time of the accident is less than the applicable limits of underinsured motorist coverage for the vehicle involved in the accident and insured under

the owner's policy. For purposes of an underinsured motorist claim asserted by a person injured in an accident where more than one person is injured, a highway vehicle will also be an "underinsured highway vehicle" if the total amount actually paid to that person under all bodily injury liability bonds and insurance policies applicable at the time of the accident is less than the applicable limits of underinsured motorist coverage for the vehicle involved in the accident and insured under the owner's policy. Notwithstanding the immediately preceding sentence, a highway vehicle shall not be an "underinsured motor vehicle" for purposes of an underinsured motorist claim under an owner's policy insuring that vehicle unless the owner's policy insuring that vehicle provides underinsured motorist coverage with limits that are greater than that policy's bodily injury liability limits. For the purposes of this subdivision, the term "highway vehicle" means a land motor vehicle or trailer other than (i) a farm-type tractor or other vehicle designed for use principally off public roads and while not upon public roads, (ii) a vehicle operated on rails or crawler-treads, or (iii) a vehicle while located for use as a residence or premises. The provisions of subdivision (3) of this subsection shall apply to the coverage required by this subdivision. Underinsured motorist coverage is deemed to apply when, by reason of payment of judgment or settlement, all liability bonds or insurance policies providing coverage for bodily injury caused by the ownership, maintenance, or use of the underinsured highway vehicle have been exhausted. Exhaustion of that liability coverage for the purpose of any single liability claim presented for underinsured motorist coverage is deemed to occur when either (a) the limits of liability per claim have been paid upon the claim, or (b) by reason of multiple claims, the aggregate per occurrence limit of liability has been paid. Underinsured motorist coverage is deemed to apply to the first dollar of an underinsured motorist coverage claim beyond amounts paid to the claimant under the exhausted liability policy.

In any event, the limit of underinsured motorist coverage applicable to any claim is determined to be the difference between the amount paid to the claimant under the exhausted liability policy or policies and the limit of underinsured motorist coverage applicable to the motor vehicle involved in the accident. Furthermore, if a claimant is an insured under the underinsured motorist coverage on separate or additional policies, the limit of underinsured motorist coverage

Chapter 20

applicable to the claimant is the difference between the amount paid to the claimant under the exhausted liability policy or policies and the total limits of the claimant's underinsured motorist coverages as determined by combining the highest limit available under each policy; provided that this sentence shall apply only to insurance on nonfleet private passenger motor vehicles as described in G.S. 58-40-15(9) and (10). The underinsured motorist limits applicable to any one motor vehicle under a policy shall not be combined with or added to the limits applicable to any other motor vehicle under that policy.

An underinsured motorist insurer may at its option, upon a claim pursuant to underinsured motorist coverage, pay moneys without there having first been an exhaustion of the liability insurance policy covering the ownership, use, and maintenance of the underinsured highway vehicle. In the event of payment, the underinsured motorist insurer shall be either: (a) entitled to receive by assignment from the claimant any right or (b) subrogated to the claimant's right regarding any claim the claimant has or had against the owner, operator, or maintainer of the underinsured highway vehicle, provided that the amount of the insurer's right by subrogation or assignment shall not exceed payments made to the claimant by the insurer. No insurer shall exercise any right of subrogation or any right to approve settlement with the original owner, operator, or maintainer of the underinsured highway vehicle under a policy providing coverage against an underinsured motorist where the insurer has been provided with written notice before a settlement between its insured and the underinsured motorist and the insurer fails to advance a payment to the insured in an amount equal to the tentative settlement within 30 days following receipt of that notice. Further, the insurer shall have the right, at its election, to pursue its claim by assignment or subrogation in the name of the claimant, and the insurer shall not be denominated as a party in its own name except upon its own election. Assignment or subrogation as provided in this subdivision shall not, absent contrary agreement, operate to defeat the claimant's right to pursue recovery against the owner, operator, or maintainer of the underinsured highway vehicle for damages beyond those paid by the underinsured motorist insurer. The claimant and the underinsured motorist insurer may join their claims in a single suit without requiring that the insurer be named as a party. Any claimant who intends to pursue recovery

against the owner, operator, or maintainer of the underinsured highway vehicle for moneys beyond those paid by the underinsured motorist insurer shall before doing so give notice to the insurer and give the insurer, at its expense, the opportunity to participate in the prosecution of the claim. Upon the entry of judgment in a suit upon any such claim in which the underinsured motorist insurer and claimant are joined, payment upon the judgment, unless otherwise agreed to, shall be applied pro rata to the claimant's claim beyond payment by the insurer of the owner, operator or maintainer of the underinsured highway vehicle and the claim of the underinsured motorist insurer.

A party injured by the operation of an underinsured highway vehicle who institutes a suit for the recovery of moneys for those injuries and in such an amount that, if recovered, would support a claim under underinsured motorist coverage shall give notice of the initiation of the suit to the underinsured motorist insurer as well as to the insurer providing primary liability coverage upon the underinsured highway vehicle. Upon receipt of notice, the underinsured motorist insurer shall have the right to appear in defense of the claim without being named as a party therein, and without being named as a party may participate in the suit as fully as if it were a party. The underinsured motorist insurer may elect, but may not be compelled, to appear in the action in its own name and present therein a claim against other parties; provided that application is made to and approved by a presiding superior court judge, in any such suit, any insurer providing primary liability insurance on the underinsured highway vehicle may upon payment of all of its applicable limits of liability be released from further liability or obligation to participate in the defense of such proceeding. However, before approving any such application, the court shall be persuaded that the owner, operator, or maintainer of the underinsured highway vehicle against whom a claim has been made has been apprised of the nature of the proceeding and given his right to select counsel of his own choice to appear in the action on his separate behalf. If an underinsured motorist insurer, following the approval of the application, pays in settlement or partial or total satisfaction of judgment moneys to the claimant, the insurer shall be subrogated to or entitled to an assignment of the claimant's rights against the owner, operator, or maintainer of the underinsured highway vehicle and, provided that adequate notice of right of

Chapter 20

independent representation was given to the owner, operator, or maintainer, a finding of liability or the award of damages shall be res judicata between the underinsured motorist insurer and the owner, operator, or maintainer of underinsured highway vehicle.

As consideration for payment of policy limits by a liability insurer on behalf of the owner, operator, or maintainer of an underinsured motor vehicle, a party injured by an underinsured motor vehicle may execute a contractual covenant not to enforce against the owner, operator, or maintainer of the vehicle any judgment that exceeds the policy limits. A covenant not to enforce judgment shall not preclude the injured party from pursuing available underinsured motorist benefits, unless the terms of the covenant expressly provide otherwise, and shall not preclude an insurer providing underinsured motorist coverage from pursuing any right of subrogation.

Notwithstanding the provisions of this subsection, no policy of motor vehicle liability insurance applicable solely to commercial motor vehicles as defined in G.S. 20-4.01(3d) or applicable solely to fleet vehicles shall be required to provide underinsured motorist coverage. When determining whether a policy is applicable solely to fleet vehicles, the insurer may rely upon the number of vehicles reported by the insured at the time of the issuance of the policy for the policy term in question. In the event of a renewal of the policy, when determining whether a policy is applicable solely to fleet vehicles, the insurer may rely upon the number of vehicles reported by the insured at the time of the renewal of the policy for the policy term in question. Any motor vehicle liability policy that insures both commercial motor vehicles as defined in G.S. 20-4.01(3d) and noncommercial motor vehicles shall provide underinsured motorist coverage in accordance with the provisions of this subsection in an amount equal to the highest limits of bodily injury liability coverage for any one noncommercial motor vehicle insured under the policy, subject to the right of the insured to purchase greater or lesser underinsured motorist bodily injury liability coverage limits as set forth in this subsection. For the purpose of the immediately preceding sentence, noncommercial motor vehicle shall mean any motor vehicle that is not a commercial motor vehicle as defined in G.S. 20-4.01(3d), but that is otherwise subject to the requirements of this subsection.

(c) Such operator's policy of liability insurance shall insure the person named as insured therein against loss from the liability imposed upon him by law for damages arising out of the use by him of any motor vehicle not owned by him, and within 30 days following the date of its delivery to him of any motor vehicle owned by him, within the same territorial limits and subject to the same limits of liability as are set forth above with respect to an owner's policy of liability insurance.

(d) Such motor vehicle liability policy shall state the name and address of the named insured, the coverage afforded by the policy, the premium charged therefor, the policy period and the limits of liability, and shall contain an agreement or be endorsed that insurance is provided thereunder in accordance with the coverage defined in this Article as respects bodily injury and death or property damage, or both, and is subject to all the provisions of this Article.

(d1) Such motor vehicle liability policy shall provide an alternative method of determining the amount of property damage to a motor vehicle when liability for coverage for the claim is not in dispute. For a claim for property damage to a motor vehicle against an insurer, the policy shall provide that if:

(1) The claimant and the insurer fail to agree as to the difference in fair market value of the vehicle immediately before the accident and immediately after the accident; and

(2) The difference in the claimant's and the insurer's estimate of the diminution in fair market value is greater than two thousand dollars ($ 2,000) or twenty-five percent (25%) of the fair market retail value of the vehicle prior to the accident as determined by the latest edition of the National Automobile Dealers Association Pricing Guide Book or other publications approved by the Commissioner of Insurance, whichever is less, then on the written demand of either the claimant or the insurer, each shall select a competent and disinterested appraiser and notify the other of the appraiser selected within 20 days after the demand. The appraisers shall then appraise the loss. Should the appraisers fail to agree, they shall then select a competent and disinterested appraiser to serve as an umpire. If the appraisers cannot agree upon an umpire within 15 days, either the claimant or the insurer may request that a magistrate resident in the county where the insured motor vehicle is registered or the county where the accident occurred select the umpire. The appraisers shall then submit their differences to the umpire. The umpire then shall prepare a report determining the amount of the loss and shall file the report with the insurer and the claimant. The agreement of the two appraisers

Chapter 20

1633

or the report of the umpire, when filed with the insurer and the claimant, shall determine the amount of the damages. In preparing the report, the umpire shall not award damages that are higher or lower than the determinations of the appraisers. In no event shall appraisers or the umpire make any determination as to liability for damages or as to whether the policy provides coverage for claims asserted. The claimant or the insurer shall have 15 days from the filing of the report to reject the report and notify the other party of such rejection. If the report is not rejected within 15 days from the filing of the report, the report shall be binding upon both the claimant and the insurer. Each appraiser shall be paid by the party selecting the appraiser, and the expenses of appraisal and umpire shall be paid by the parties equally. For purposes of this section, "appraiser" and "umpire" shall mean a person licensed as a motor vehicle damage appraiser under G.S. 58-33-26 and G.S. 58-33-30 and who as a part of his or her regular employment is in the business of advising relative to the nature and amount of motor vehicle damage and the fair market value of damaged and undamaged motor vehicles.

(e) Uninsured or underinsured motorist coverage that is provided as part of a motor vehicle liability policy shall insure that portion of a loss uncompensated by any workers' compensation law and the amount of an employer's lien determined pursuant to G.S. 97-10.2(h) or (j). In no event shall this subsection be construed to require that coverage exceed the applicable uninsured or underinsured coverage limits of the motor vehicle policy or allow a recovery for damages already paid by workers' compensation. The policy need not insure a loss from any liability for damage to property owned by, rented to, in charge of or transported by the insured.

(f) Every motor vehicle liability policy shall be subject to the following provisions which need not be contained therein:

(1) Except as hereinafter provided, the liability of the insurance carrier with respect to the insurance required by this Article shall become absolute whenever injury or damage covered by said motor vehicle liability policy occurs; said policy may not be canceled or annulled as to such liability by any agreement between the insurance carrier and the insured after the occurrence of the injury or damage; no statement made by the insured or on his behalf and no violation of said policy shall defeat or void said policy. As to policies issued to insureds in this State under the assigned risk plan or through the North Carolina Motor Vehicle Reinsurance Facility, a default judgment

taken against such an insured shall not be used as a basis for obtaining judgment against the insurer unless counsel for the plaintiff has forwarded to the insurer, or to one of its agents, by registered or certified mail with return receipt requested, or served by any other method of service provided by law, a copy of summons, complaint, or other pleadings, filed in the action. The return receipt shall, upon its return to plaintiff's counsel, be filed with the clerk of court wherein the action is pending against the insured and shall be admissible in evidence as proof of notice to the insurer. The refusal of insurer or its agent to accept delivery of the registered mail, as provided in this section, shall not affect the validity of such notice and any insurer or agent of an insurer refusing to accept such registered mail shall be charged with the knowledge of the contents of such notice. When notice has been sent to an agent of the insurer such notice shall be notice to the insurer. The word "agent" as used in this subsection shall include, but shall not be limited to, any person designated by the insurer as its agent for the service of process, any person duly licensed by the insurer in the State as insurance agent, any general agent of the company in the State of North Carolina, and any employee of the company in a managerial or other responsible position, or the North Carolina Commissioner of Insurance; provided, where the return receipt is signed by an employee of the insurer or an employee of an agent for the insurer, shall be deemed for the purposes of this subsection to have been received. The term "agent" as used in this subsection shall not include a producer of record or broker, who forwards an application for insurance to the North Carolina Motor Vehicle Reinsurance Facility.

The insurer, upon receipt of summons, complaint or other process, shall be entitled, upon its motion, to intervene in the suit against its insured as a party defendant and to defend the same in the name of its insured. In the event of such intervention by an insurer it shall become a named party defendant. The insurer shall have 30 days from the signing of the return receipt acknowledging receipt of the summons, complaint or other pleading in which to file a motion to intervene, along with any responsive pleading, whether verified or not, which it may deem necessary to protect its interest: Provided, the court having jurisdiction over the matter may, upon motion duly made, extend the time for the filing of responsive pleading or continue the trial of the matter for the purpose of affording the insurer a reasonable time in which to file responsive pleading or defend the action. If, after receiving copy of the summons, complaint or other pleading, the insurer elects not to defend the action, if coverage is in fact provided by the policy, the insurer shall be bound to the extent of its policy limits to the judgment taken by default against the insured, and noncooperation of the insured shall not be a defense.

If the plaintiff initiating an action against the insured has complied with the provisions of this subsection, then, in such event, the insurer may not cancel or annul the policy as to such liability and the defense of noncooperation shall not be available to the insurer: Provided, however, nothing in this section shall be construed as depriving an insurer of its defenses that the policy was not in force at the time in question, that the operator was not an "insured" under policy provisions, or that the policy had been lawfully canceled at the time of the accident giving rise to the cause of action.

Provided further that the provisions of this subdivision shall not apply when the insured has delivered a copy of the summons, complaint or other pleadings served on him to his insurance carrier within the time provided by law for filing answer, demurrer or other pleadings.

(2) The satisfaction by the insured of a judgment for such injury or damage shall not be a condition precedent to the right or duty of the insurance carrier to make payment on account of such injury or damage;

(3) The insurance carrier shall have the right to settle any claim covered by the policy, and if such settlement is made in good faith, the amount thereof shall be deductible from the limits of liability specified in subdivision (2) of subsection (b) of this section;

(4) The policy, the written application therefor, if any, and any rider or endorsement which does not conflict with the provisions of the Article shall constitute the entire contract between the parties.

(g) Any policy which grants the coverage required for a motor vehicle liability policy may also grant any lawful coverage in excess of or in addition to the coverage specified for a motor vehicle liability policy and such excess or additional coverage shall not be subject to the provisions of this Article. With respect to a policy which grants such excess or additional coverage the term "motor vehicle liability policy" shall apply only to that part of the coverage which is required by this section.

(h) Any motor vehicle liability policy may provide that the insured shall reimburse the insurance carrier for any payment the insurance carrier would not have been obligated to make under the terms of the policy except for the provisions of this Article.

(i) Any motor vehicle liability policy may provide for the prorating of the insurance thereunder with other valid and collectible insurance.

(j) The requirements for a motor vehicle liability policy may be fulfilled by the policies of one or more insurance carriers which policies together meet such requirements.

(k) Any binder issued pending the issuance of a motor vehicle liability policy shall be deemed to fulfill the requirements for such a policy.

(l) A party injured by an uninsured motor vehicle covered under a policy in amounts less than those set forth in G.S. 20-279.5, may execute a contractual covenant not to enforce against the owner, operator, or maintainer of the uninsured vehicle any judgment that exceeds the liability policy limits, as consideration for payment of any applicable policy limits by the insurer where judgment exceeds the policy limits. A covenant not to enforce judgment shall not preclude the injured party from pursuing available uninsured motorist benefits, unless the terms of the covenant expressly provide otherwise, and shall not preclude an insurer providing uninsured motorist coverage from pursuing any right of subrogation.

(m) Every insurer that sells motor vehicle liability policies subject to the requirements of subdivisions (b)(3) and (b)(4) of this section shall, when issuing and renewing a policy, give reasonable notice to the named insured of all of the following:

(1) The named insured is required to purchase uninsured motorist bodily injury coverage, uninsured motorist property damage coverage, and, if applicable, underinsured motorist bodily injury coverage.

(2) The named insured's uninsured motorist bodily injury coverage limits shall be equal to the highest limits of bodily injury liability coverage for any one vehicle insured under the policy unless the insured elects to purchase greater or lesser limits for uninsured motorist bodily injury coverage.

(3) The named insured's uninsured motorist property damage coverage limits shall be equal to the highest limits of property damage liability coverage for any one vehicle insured under the policy unless the insured elects to purchase lesser limits for uninsured motorist property damage coverage.

(4) The named insured's underinsured motorist bodily injury coverage limits, if applicable, shall be equal to the highest limits of bodily injury liability coverage for any one vehicle insured under the policy unless the insured elects to purchase greater

Chapter 20

or lesser limits for underinsured motorist bodily injury coverage.

(5) The named insured may purchase uninsured motorist bodily injury coverage and, if applicable, underinsured motorist coverage with limits up to one million dollars ($ 1,000,000) per person and one million dollars ($ 1,000,000) per accident.

An insurer shall be deemed to have given reasonable notice if it includes the following or substantially similar language on the policy's original and renewal declarations pages or in a separate notice accompanying the original and renewal declarations pages in at least 12 point type:

NOTICE: YOU ARE REQUIRED TO PURCHASE UNINSURED MOTORIST BODILY INJURY COVERAGE, UNINSURED MOTORIST PROPERTY DAMAGE COVERAGE AND, IN SOME CASES, UNDERINSURED MOTORIST BODILY INJURY COVERAGE. THIS INSURANCE PROTECTS YOU AND YOUR FAMILY AGAINST INJURIES AND PROPERTY DAMAGE CAUSED BY THE NEGLIGENCE OF OTHER DRIVERS WHO MAY HAVE LIMITED OR ONLY MINIMUM COVERAGE OR EVEN NO LIABILITY INSURANCE. YOU MAY PURCHASE UNINSURED MOTORIST BODILY INJURY COVERAGE AND, IF APPLICABLE, UNDERINSURED MOTORIST COVERAGE WITH LIMITS UP TO ONE MILLION DOLLARS ($ 1,000,000) PER PERSON AND ONE MILLION DOLLARS ($ 1,000,000) PER ACCIDENT OR AT SUCH LESSER LIMITS YOU CHOOSE. YOU CANNOT PURCHASE COVERAGE FOR LESS THAN THE MINIMUM LIMITS FOR THE BODILY INJURY AND PROPERTY DAMAGE COVERAGE THAT ARE REQUIRED FOR YOUR OWN VEHICLE. IF YOU DO NOT CHOOSE A GREATER OR LESSER LIMIT FOR UNINSURED MOTORIST BODILY INJURY COVERAGE, A LESSER LIMIT FOR UNINSURED MOTORIST PROPERTY DAMAGE COVERAGE, AND/OR A GREATER OR LESSER LIMIT FOR UNDERINSURED MOTORIST BODILY INJURY COVERAGE, THEN THE LIMITS FOR THE UNINSURED MOTORIST BODILY INJURY COVERAGE AND, IF APPLICABLE, THE UNDERINSURED MOTORIST BODILY INJURY COVERAGE WILL BE THE SAME AS THE HIGHEST LIMITS FOR BODILY INJURY LIABILITY COVERAGE FOR ANY ONE OF YOUR OWN VEHICLES INSURED UNDER THE POLICY AND THE LIMITS FOR THE UNINSURED MOTORIST PROPERTY DAMAGE COVERAGE WILL BE THE SAME AS THE HIGHEST LIMITS FOR PROPERTY DAMAGE LIABILITY COVERAGE FOR ANY ONE OF YOUR OWN VEHICLES INSURED UNDER THE POLICY. IF YOU WISH TO PURCHASE UNINSURED MOTORIST AND, IF APPLICABLE, UNDERINSURED MOTORIST COVERAGE AT DIFFERENT LIMITS THAN THE LIMITS FOR YOUR OWN VEHICLE INSURED UNDER THE POLICY, THEN YOU SHOULD CONTACT YOUR INSURANCE COMPANY OR AGENT TO DISCUSS YOUR OPTIONS FOR OBTAINING DIFFERENT COVERAGE LIMITS. YOU SHOULD ALSO READ YOUR ENTIRE POLICY TO UNDERSTAND WHAT IS COVERED UNDER UNINSURED AND UNDERINSURED MOTORIST COVERAGES.

(n) Nothing in this section shall be construed to provide greater amounts of uninsured or underinsured motorist coverage in a liability policy than the insured has purchased from the insurer under this section.

(o) An insurer that fails to comply with subsection (d1) or (m) of this section is subject to a civil penalty under G.S. 58-2-70.

History.
1953, c. 1300, s. 21; 1955, c. 1355; 1961, c. 640; 1965, c. 156; c. 674, s. 1; c. 898; 1967, c. 277, s. 4; c. 854; c. 1159, s. 1; c. 1162, s. 1; c. 1186, s. 1; c. 1246, s. 1; 1971, c. 1205, s. 2; 1973, c. 745, s. 4; 1975, c. 326, ss. 1, 2; c. 716, s. 5; c. 866, ss. 1-4; 1979, cc. 190, 675; c. 832, ss. 6, 7; 1983, c. 777, ss. 1, 2; 1985, c. 666, s. 74; 1985 (Reg. Sess., 1986), c. 1027, ss. 41, 42; 1987, c. 529; 1987 (Reg. Sess., 1988), c. 975, s. 33; 1991, c. 469, s. 4; c. 636, s. 3; c. 646, ss. 1, 2; c. 761, s. 12.3; 1991 (Reg. Sess., 1992), c. 837, s. 9; 1997-396, ss. 2, 3; 1999-195, s. 1; 1999-228, s. 4; 2003-311, ss. 1, 2; 2008-124, ss. 1.1, 1.2; 2009-440, s. 1; 2009-561, s. 1; 2009-566, s. 28; 2015-135, s. 4.4; 2018-5, s. 34.26(b)

§ 20-279.22. Notice of cancellation or termination of certified policy

When an insurance carrier has certified a motor vehicle liability policy under G.S. 20-279.19 or a policy under G.S. 20-279.20, the insurance so certified shall not be canceled or terminated until at least 20 days after a notice of cancellation or termination of the insurance so certified shall be filed in the office of the Commissioner, except that such a policy subsequently procured and certified shall, on the effective date of its certification, terminate the insurance previously certified with respect to any motor vehicle designated in both certificates.

History.
1953, c. 1300, s. 22

§ 20-279.23. Article not to affect other policies

(a) This Article shall not be held to apply to or affect policies of automobile insurance against liability which may now or hereafter be required by any other law of this State, and such policies, if they contain an agreement or are endorsed to conform to the requirements of this Article, may be certified as proof of financial responsibility under this Article.

(b) This Article shall not be held to apply to or affect policies insuring solely the insured named in the policy against liability resulting from the maintenance or use by persons in the insured's employ or on his behalf of motor vehicles not owned by the insured.

History.
1953, c. 1300, s. 23

§ 20-279.24. Bond as proof

(a) Proof of financial responsibility may be furnished by filing with the Commissioner the bond of a surety company duly authorized to transact business in the State or a bond with at least two individual sureties each owning real estate within this State, and together having equities in such real estate over and above any encumbrances thereon equal in value to at least twice the amount of such bond, which real estate shall be scheduled in the bond which shall be approved by the clerk of the superior court of the county wherein the real estate is situated. Such bond shall be conditioned for payments in amounts and under the same circumstances as would be required in a motor vehicle liability policy, and shall not be cancellable except after 20 days' written notice to the Commissioner. A certificate of the county tax supervisor or person performing the duties of the tax supervisor, showing the assessed valuation of each tract or parcel of real estate for tax purposes shall accompany a bond with individual sureties and, upon acceptance and approval by the Commissioner, the execution of such bond shall be proved before the clerk of the superior court of the county or counties wherein the land or any part thereof lies, and such bond shall be recorded in the office of the register of deeds of such county or counties. Such bond shall constitute a lien upon the real estate therein described from and after filing for recordation to the same extent as in the case of ordinary mortgages and shall be regarded as the equivalent of a mortgage or deed of trust. In the event of default in the terms of the bond the Commissioner may foreclose the lien thereof by making public sale upon publishing notice thereof as provided by G.S. 45-21.17; provided, that any such sale shall be subject to the provisions for upset or increased bids and resales and the procedure therefor as set out in Part 2 of Article 2A of Chapter 45 of the General Statutes. The proceeds of such sale shall be applied by the Commissioner toward the discharge of liability upon the bond, any excess to be paid over to the surety whose property was sold. The Commissioner shall have power to so sell as much of the property of either or both sureties described in the bond as shall be deemed necessary to discharge the liability under the bond, and shall not be required to apportion or prorate the liability as between sureties.

If any surety is a married person, his or her spouse shall be required to execute the bond, but only for the purpose of releasing any dower or curtesy interest in the property described in the bond, and the signing of such bond shall constitute a conveyance of dower or curtesy interest, as well as the homestead exemption of the surety, for the purpose of the bond, and the execution of the bond shall be duly acknowledged as in the case of deeds of conveyance. The Commissioner may require a certificate of title of a duly licensed attorney which shall show all liens and encumbrances with respect to each parcel of real estate described in the bond and, if any parcel of such real estate has buildings or other improvements thereon, the Commissioner may, in his discretion, require the filing with him of a policy or policies of fire and other hazard insurance, with loss clauses payable to the Commissioner as his interest may appear. All costs and expenses in connection with furnishing such bond and the registration thereof, and the certificate of title, insurance and other necessary items of expense shall be borne by the principal obligor under the bond, except that the costs of foreclosure may be paid from the proceeds of sale.

(b) If such a judgment, rendered against the principal on such bond shall not be satisfied within 60 days after it has become final, the judgment creditor may, for his own use and benefit and at his sole expense, bring an action or actions in the name of the State against the company or persons executing such bond, including an action or proceeding to foreclose any lien that may exist upon the real estate of a person who has executed such bond.

History.
1953, c. 1300, s. 24; 1993, c. 553, s. 10

§ 20-279.25. Money or securities as proof

(a) Proof of financial responsibility may be evidenced by the certificate of the State Treasurer that the person named therein has deposited with him eighty-five thousand dollars ($ 85,000) in cash, or securities such as may legally be purchased by savings banks or for trust funds of a market value of eighty-five thousand

Chapter 20

dollars ($ 85,000). The State Treasurer shall not accept any such deposit and issue a certificate therefor and the Commissioner shall not accept such certificate unless accompanied by evidence that there are no unsatisfied judgments of any character against the depositor in the county where the depositor resides.

(b) Such deposit shall be held by the State Treasurer to satisfy, in accordance with the provisions of this Article, any execution on a judgment issued against such person making the deposit for damages, including damages for care and loss of services because of bodily injury to or death of any person, or for damages because of injury to or destruction of property, including the loss of use thereof, resulting from the ownership, maintenance, use or operation of a motor vehicle after such deposit was made. Money or securities so deposited shall not be subject to attachment, garnishment, or execution unless such attachment, garnishment, or execution shall arise out of a suit for damages as aforesaid.

History.

1953, c. 1300, s. 25; 1965, c. 358, s. 1; 1967, c. 277, s. 5; 1973, c. 745, s. 5; 1979, c. 832, s. 8; 1991, c. 469, s. 8; 1999-228, s. 5

§ 20-279.26. Owner may give proof for others

Whenever any person required to give proof of financial responsibility hereunder is or later becomes an operator in the employ of any owner, or is or later becomes a member of the immediate family or household of the owner, the Commissioner shall accept proof given by such owner in lieu of proof by such other person to permit such other person to operate a motor vehicle for which the owner has given proof as herein provided. The Commissioner shall designate the restrictions imposed by this section on the face of such person's license.

History.

1953, c. 1300, s. 26

§ 20-279.27. Substitution of proof

The Commissioner shall consent to the cancellation of any bond or certificate of insurance or the Commissioner shall direct and the State Treasurer shall return any money or securities to the person entitled thereto upon the substitution and acceptance of other adequate proof of financial responsibility pursuant to this Article.

History.

1953, c. 1300, s. 27

§ 20-279.28. Other proof may be required

Whenever any proof of financial responsibility filed under the provisions of this Article no longer fulfills the purposes for which required, the Commissioner shall for the purpose of this Article, require other proof as required by this Article, or whenever it appears that proof filed to cover any motor vehicle owned by a person does not cover all motor vehicles registered in the name of such person, the Commissioner shall require proof covering all such motor vehicles. The Commissioner shall suspend the license or the nonresident's operating privilege pending the filing of such other proof.

History.

1953, c. 1300, s. 28

§ 20-279.29. Duration of proof; when proof may be canceled or returned

The Commissioner shall upon request consent to the immediate cancellation of any bond or certificate of insurance, or the Commissioner shall direct and the State Treasurer shall return to the person entitled thereto any money or securities deposited pursuant to this Article as proof of financial responsibility, or the Commissioner shall waive the requirement of filing proof, in any of the following events:

(1) At any time after two years from the date such proof was required when, during the two-year period preceding the request, the Commissioner has not received record of a conviction or a forfeiture of bail which would require or permit the suspension or revocation of the license, registration or nonresident's operating privilege of the person by or for whom such proof was furnished; or

(2) In the event of the death of the person on whose behalf such proof was filed or the permanent incapacity of such person to operate a motor vehicle; or

(3) In the event the person who has given proof surrenders his license to the Commissioner.

Provided, however, that the Commissioner shall not consent to the cancellation of any bond or the return of any money or securities in the event any action for damages upon a liability covered by such proof is then pending or any judgment upon any such liability is then unsatisfied or in the event the person who has filed such bond or deposited such money or securities, has, within one year immediately preceding such request, been involved as an operator or owner in any motor vehicle accident resulting in injury or damage to the person or property of others. An affidavit of the applicant as to the nonexistence of such facts, or that he has been released from all of his liability, or has been finally adjudicated not to be liable, for such injury or damage, shall be sufficient evidence thereof in the absence of evidence to the contrary in the records of the Commissioner.

Whenever any person whose proof has been canceled or returned under subdivision (3) of this section applies for a license within a period of two years from the date proof was originally required, any such application shall be refused unless the applicant shall reestablish such proof for the remainder of such two-year period.

History.
1953, c. 1300, s. 29

§ 20-279.30. Surrender of license

Any person whose license shall have been suspended as herein provided, or whose policy of insurance or bond, when required under this Article, shall have been canceled or terminated, or who shall neglect to furnish other proof upon request of the Commissioner shall immediately return his license to the Commissioner. If any person shall fail to return to the Commissioner the license as provided herein, the Commissioner shall forthwith direct any peace officer to secure possession thereof and to return the same to the Commissioner.

History.
1953, c. 1300, s. 30

§ 20-279.31. Other violations; penalties

(a) The Commissioner shall suspend the license of a person who fails to report a reportable accident, as required by G.S. 20-166.1, until the Division receives a report and for an additional period set by the Commissioner. The additional period may not exceed 30 days.

(b) Any person who does any of the following commits a Class 1 misdemeanor:

(1) Gives information required in a report of a reportable accident, knowing or having reason to believe the information is false.

(2) Forges or without authority signs any evidence of proof of financial responsibility.

(3) Files or offers for filing any evidence of proof of financial responsibility, knowing or having reason to believe that it is forged or signed without authority.

(c) Any person willfully failing to return a license as required in G.S. 20-279.30 is guilty of a Class 3 misdemeanor.

(c1) Any person who makes a false affidavit or knowingly swears or affirms falsely to any matter under G.S. 20-279.5, 20-279.6, or 20-279.7 is guilty of a Class I felony.

(d) Any person who shall violate any provision of this Article for which no penalty is otherwise provided is guilty of a Class 2 misdemeanor.

History.
1953, c. 1300, s. 31; 1983, c. 610, s. 2; 1993, c. 539, ss. 384, 1261; 1994, Ex. Sess., c. 24, s. 14(c); 1995, c. 191, s. 7

§ 20-279.32. Exceptions

This Article does not apply to a motor vehicle registered under G.S. 20-382 by a for-hire motor carrier. This Article does not apply to any motor vehicle owned by the State of North Carolina, nor does it apply to the operator of a vehicle owned by the State of North Carolina who becomes involved in an accident while operating the state-owned vehicle if the Commissioner determines that the vehicle at the time of the accident was probably being operated in the course of the operator's employment as an employee or officer of the State. This Article does not apply to any motor vehicle owned by a county or municipality of the State of North Carolina, nor does it apply to the operator of a vehicle owned by a county or municipality of the State of North Carolina who becomes involved in an accident while operating such vehicle in the course of the operator's employment as an employee or officer of the county or municipality. This Article does not apply to the operator of a vehicle owned by a political subdivision, other than a county or municipality, of the State of North Carolina who becomes involved in an accident while operating such vehicle if the Commissioner determines that the vehicle at the time of the accident was probably being operated in the course of the operator's employment as an employee or officer of the subdivision providing that the Commissioner finds that the political subdivision has waived any immunity it has with respect to such accidents and has in force an insurance policy or other method of satisfying claims which may arise out of the accident. This Article does not apply to any motor vehicle owned by the federal government, nor does it apply to the operator of a motor vehicle owned by the federal government who becomes involved in an accident while operating the government-owned vehicle if the Commissioner determines that the vehicle at the time of the accident was probably being operated in the course of the operator's employment as an employee or officer of the federal government.

History.
1953, c. 1300, s. 32; 1955, c. 1152, s. 19; 1979, c. 667, s. 38; 1989, c. 485, s. 54; 1995 (Reg. Sess., 1996), c. 756, s. 18; 1999-330, s. 4.1

§ 20-279.32A. Exception of school bus drivers

The provisions of this Article shall not apply to school bus drivers with respect to accidents or collisions in which they are involved while operating school buses in the course of their employment.

History.
1955, c. 1282

§ 20-279.33. Self-insurers

(a) Any person in whose name more than 25 motor vehicles are registered may qualify as a self-insurer by obtaining a certificate of self-insurance issued by the Commissioner as provided in subsection (b) of this section. For the purpose of this Article, the State of North Carolina shall be considered a self-insurer.

(b) The Commissioner may, in his discretion, upon the application of such a person, issue a certificate of self-insurance when he is satisfied that such person is possessed and will continue to be possessed of ability to pay judgments obtained against such person.

(c) Upon not less than five days' notice and a hearing pursuant to such notice, the Commissioner may upon reasonable grounds cancel a certificate of self-insurance. Failure to pay any judgment within 30 days after such judgment shall have become final shall constitute a reasonable ground for the cancellation of a certificate of self-insurance.

History.
1953, c. 1300, s. 33

§ 20-279.33A. Religious organizations; self-insurance

(a) Notwithstanding any other provision of this Article or Article 13 of this Chapter, any recognized religious organization having established tenets or teachings and that has been in existence at all times since December 31, 1950, may qualify as a self-insurer by obtaining a certificate of self-insurance from the Commissioner as provided in subsection (c) of this section if the Commissioner determines that all of the following conditions are met:

(1) Members of the religious organization operate five or more vehicles that are registered in this State and are either owned or leased by them.

(2) Members of the religious organization hold a common belief in mutual financial assistance in time of need to the extent that they share in financial obligations of other members who would otherwise be unable to meet their obligations.

(3) The religious organization has met all of its insurance obligations for the five years preceding its application.

(4) The religious organization is financially solvent and not subject to any actions in bankruptcy, trusteeship, receivership, or any other court proceeding in which the financial solvency of the religious organization is in question.

(5) Neither the religious organization nor any of its participating members has any judgments arising out of the operation, maintenance, or use of a motor vehicle taken against them that have remained unsatisfied for more than 30 days after becoming final.

(6) There are no other factors that cause the Commissioner to believe that the religious organization and its participating members are not of sufficient financial ability to pay judgments against them.

(7) The religious organization and its participating members meet other requirements that the Commissioner by administrative rule prescribes.

(b) The Commissioner may, in the Commissioner's discretion, upon the application of a religious organization, issue a certificate of self-insurance when the Commissioner is satisfied that the religious organization is possessed and will continue to be possessed of an ability to pay any judgments that might be rendered against the religious organization. The certificate shall serve as evidence of insurance for the purposes of G.S. 20-7(c1), 20-13.2(e), 20-16.1, 20-19(k), and 20-179.3(*l*).

(c) A group issued a certificate of self-insurance under this section shall notify the Commissioner in writing if any person ceases to be a member of the group. The group shall notify the Commissioner within 10 days of the person's removal or departure from the group.

(d) The Commissioner may, at any time after the issuance of a certificate of self-insurance under this subsection, cancel the certificate by giving 30 days' written notice of cancellation to the religious organization whenever there is reason to believe that the religious organization to whom the certificate was issued is no longer qualified as a self-insurer under this section.

History.
2006-145, s. 5

N.C. Gen. Stat. § 20-279.34

Repealed by Session Laws 1993 (Reg. Sess., 1994), c. 761, s. 27.

§ 20-279.35. Supplemental to motor vehicle laws; repeal of laws in conflict

This Article shall in no respect be considered as a repeal of any of the motor vehicle laws of this State but shall be construed as supplemental thereto.

The "Motor Vehicle Safety and Responsibility Act" enacted by the 1947 Session of the General Assembly, being Chapter 1006 of the Session Laws of 1947 (G.S. 20-224 to 20-279), is hereby repealed except with respect to any accident or violation of the motor vehicle laws of this State occurring prior to January 1, 1954, or with respect to any judgment arising from such accident or violation, and as to such accidents, violations or judgments Chapter 1006 of the Session Laws of 1947 shall remain in full force and effect. Except as herein stated, all laws and clauses of laws in conflict with this Article are hereby repealed.

History.
1953, c. 1300, s. 35

§ 20-279.36. Past application of Article

This Article shall not apply with respect to any accident, or judgment arising therefrom, or violation of the motor vehicle laws of this State, occurring prior to January 1, 1954.

History.
1953, c. 1300, s. 37

§ 20-279.37. Article not to prevent other process

Nothing in this Article shall be construed as preventing the plaintiff in any action at law from relying for relief upon the other processes provided by law.

History.
1953, c. 1300, s. 38

§ 20-279.38. Uniformity of interpretation

This Article shall be so interpreted and construed as to effectuate its general purpose to make uniform the laws of those states which enact it.

History.
1953, c. 1300, s. 39

§ 20-279.39. Title of Article

This Article may be cited as the "Motor Vehicle Safety-Responsibility Act of 1953."

History.
1953, c. 1300, s. 41

ARTICLE 10
FINANCIAL RESPONSIBILITY OF TAXICAB OPERATORS

§ 20-280. Filing proof of financial responsibility with governing board of municipality or county

(a) Within 30 days after March 27, 1951, every person, firm or corporation engaging in the business of operating a taxicab or taxicabs within a municipality shall file with the governing board of the municipality in which such business is operated proof of financial responsibility as hereinafter defined.

No governing board of a municipality shall hereafter issue any certificate of convenience and necessity, franchise, license, permit or other privilege or authority to any person, firm or corporation authorizing such person, firm or corporation to engage in the business of operating a taxicab or taxicabs within the municipality unless such person, firm or corporation first files with said governing board proof of financial responsibility as hereinafter defined.

Within 30 days after the ratification of this section, every person, firm or corporation engaging in the business of operating a taxicab or taxicabs without the corporate limits of a municipality or municipalities, shall file with the board of county commissioners of the county in which such business is operated proof of financial responsibility as hereinafter defined.

No person, firm or corporation shall hereafter engage in the business of operating a taxicab or taxicabs without the corporate limits of a municipality or municipalities in any county unless such person, firm or corporation first files with the board of county commissioners of the county in which such business is operated proof of financial responsibility as hereinafter defined.

(b) As used in this section "proof of financial responsibility" shall mean a certificate of any insurance carrier duly authorized to do business in the State of North Carolina certifying that there is in effect a policy of liability insurance insuring the owner and operator of the taxicab business, his agents and employees while in the performance of their duties against loss from any liability imposed by law for damages including damages for care and loss of services because of bodily injury to or death of any person and injury to or destruction of property caused by accident and arising out of the ownership, use or operation of such taxicab or taxicabs, subject to limits (exclusive of interests and costs) with respect to each such motor vehicle as follows: one hundred thousand dollars ($ 100,000) because of bodily injury to or death of one person in any one accident and, subject to said limit for one person, three hundred thousand dollars ($ 300,000) because of bodily injury to or death of two or more persons in any one accident, and fifty thousand dollars ($ 50,000) because of injury to or destruction of property of others in any one accident.

Chapter 20

(c) Repealed by Session Laws 2017-137, s. 2.5, effective January 1, 2018.

History.
1951, c. 406; 1965, c. 350, s. 1; 1967, c. 277, s. 7; 1973, c. 745, s. 6; 1979, c. 832, ss. 9, 10; 1991, c. 469, s. 5; 1999-228, s. 6; 2017-137, s. 2.5; 2017-212, s. 1.3

ARTICLE 10A
TRANSPORTATION NETWORK COMPANIES

§ 20-280.1. Definitions

The following definitions apply in this Article:

(1) **Airport operator.** -- Any person with police powers that owns or operates an airport.

(2) **Brokering transportation network company.** -- A transportation network company, as defined by this section, that exclusively dispatches TNC drivers that operate either of the following:

a. For-hire passenger vehicles regulated under G.S. 160A-304.

b. For-hire passenger vehicles regulated under G.S. 62-260(f) and subject to the requirements for security for protection of the public and safety of operation established for regulated motor common carriers.

(3) **Prearranged transportation services.** -- Transportation services available by advance request excluding for-hire passenger vehicles soliciting passengers for immediate transportation. No minimum waiting period is required between the advance request and the provision of the transportation services.

(4) **TNC driver.** -- An individual that uses a passenger vehicle in connection with a transportation network company's online-enabled application or platform to connect with passengers in exchange for payment of a fee to the transportation network company.

(5) **TNC service.** -- Prearranged transportation service provided by a TNC driver in connection with a transportation network company. The TNC service begins when the TNC driver accepts a ride request on the transportation network company's online-enabled application or platform and ends at the later of the following:

a. The time that the driver completes the transaction on the online-enabled application or platform.

b. The time that all passengers exit the vehicle and complete unloading of the vehicle.

(6) **Transportation network company (TNC).** -- Any person that uses an online-enabled application or platform to connect passengers with TNC drivers who provide prearranged transportation services.

History.
2015-237, s. 1

§ 20-280.2. Permissible services and limitations

(a) A transportation network company holding a valid permit issued under this Article and continuously meeting the requirements of this Article may operate in the State. The transportation network company may charge a fee for the TNC service. The fee must meet the following requirements:

(1) The transportation network company's online-enabled application or platform must disclose the fee calculation method before a passenger makes a ride request.

(2) The transportation network company's online-enabled application or platform must provide the option for a passenger to receive an estimated fee before the passenger makes a ride request.

(3) The transportation network company must send an electronic receipt to the customer that includes the following:

a. The locations where the TNC service started and ended.

b. The total time and distance of the TNC service.

c. An itemization and calculation of the total fee paid.

(4) The fee must be paid electronically through the transportation network company's online-enabled application or platform. No cash may be exchanged for the TNC service.

(b) A TNC driver may provide TNC service for compensation in the State.

History.
2015-237, s. 1

§ 20-280.3. Permits

(a) Every transportation network company must obtain a permit from the Division before operating in the State. Every transportation network company must pay to the Division a nonrefundable application fee of five thousand dollars ($ 5,000).

(b) Every transportation network company must renew the permit annually and pay to the Division a nonrefundable renewal fee of five thousand dollars ($ 5,000).

Chapter 20

(c) The Division must prescribe the form of the application for a permit and renewal of a permit.

(d) The initial application and renewal application must require information sufficient to confirm compliance with this Article and include the following:

(1) Proof of insurance meeting the requirements of G.S. 20-280.4. This subdivision does not apply to brokering transportation network companies.

(2) Resident agent for service of process.

(3) Proof the transportation network company is registered with the Secretary of State to do business in the State if the transportation network company is a foreign corporation.

(4) Policy of nondiscrimination based on customers' geographic departure point or destination.

(5) Policy of nondiscrimination based on customers' race, color, national origin, religious belief or affiliation, sex, disability, or age.

(e) The Division may retain the fees collected under this section and use the funds for its operations.

History.
2015-237, s. 1

§ 20-280.4. Financial responsibility

(a) Except as provided in subsection (n) of this section, TNC drivers or transportation network companies must maintain primary automobile insurance that meets all of the following requirements:

(1) Recognizes that the driver is a TNC driver or uses a vehicle to transport passengers for compensation.

(2) The following automobile insurance requirements apply while a TNC driver is logged on to the transportation network company's online-enabled application or platform but is not providing TNC service:

a. Primary automobile liability insurance in the amount of at least fifty thousand dollars ($ 50,000) because of death of or bodily injury to one person in any one accident and, subject to said limit for one person, one hundred thousand dollars ($ 100,000) because of death of or bodily injury to two or more persons in any one accident, and at least twenty-five thousand dollars ($ 25,000) because of injury to or destruction of property of others in any one accident.

b. Combined uninsured and underinsured motorist coverage, with limits for combined uninsured and underinsured

motorist bodily injury coverage which at least equals the bodily injury liability limits of the policy, and which otherwise complies with the requirements of G.S. 20-279.21(b)(3) and (b)(4).

(3) The following automobile insurance requirements apply while a TNC driver is engaged in TNC service:

a. Primary automobile liability insurance in the amount of at least one million five hundred thousand dollars ($ 1,500,000) because of death of one or more persons, bodily injury to one or more persons, injury to or destruction of property of others, or any combination thereof, in any one accident.

b. Combined uninsured and underinsured motorist coverage, with limits for combined uninsured and underinsured motorist bodily injury coverage of at least one million dollars ($ 1,000,000), and which otherwise complies with the requirements of G.S. 20-279.21(b)(3) and (b)(4).

(4) The coverage requirements of subdivisions (2) and (3) of this subsection may be satisfied by any of the following:

a. Automobile insurance maintained by the TNC driver.

b. Automobile insurance maintained by the transportation network company.

c. Any combination of subsubdivisions a. and b. of this subdivision.

(b) If insurance maintained by the TNC driver under subsection (a) of this section has lapsed or does not provide the required coverage, insurance maintained by the transportation network company must provide the coverage required under subsection (a) of this section beginning with the first dollar of a claim and must provide the defense of the claim.

(c) Insurance coverage under an automobile insurance policy maintained by the transportation network company must not be dependent on a personal automobile insurer denying a claim.

(d) Insurance required by this section may be placed with an insurer licensed in the State or with a surplus lines insurer eligible to write policies in the State.

(e) Insurance satisfying the requirements of this section satisfies the financial responsibility requirement for a motor vehicle.

(f) A TNC driver must carry proof of coverage satisfying the requirements of this section at all times during use of a vehicle in connection with a transportation network company's online-enabled application or platform. In the event of an accident, a TNC driver must provide insurance coverage information directly to interested parties, automobile insurers, and investigating police officers, upon request. Upon such request, a TNC driver must also disclose to directly interested parties, automobile insurers, and investigating police officers whether the TNC driver was logged on or off of the transportation network company's online-enabled application or platform at the time of the accident.

(g) Before any vehicle is used in connection with a transportation network company's online-enabled application or platform, a TNC driver must notify both the insurer of the vehicle and any lienholder with an interest in the vehicle of the TNC driver's intent to use the vehicle in connection with a transportation network company's online-enabled application or platform.

(h) Transportation network companies must disclose in writing to potential TNC drivers the following before the TNC driver provides TNC service:

(1) The insurance coverage, including the types of coverage and the limits for each coverage, that the transportation network company provides while the TNC driver uses a private passenger vehicle in connection with a transportation network company's online-enabled application or platform.

(2) The TNC driver may not have any coverage under a personal automobile insurance policy while using the transportation network company's online-enabled application or platform.

(3) The following notice in a distinctive clause: "If the vehicle with which you provide transportation network company services has a lien against it, you must notify the lienholder prior to providing transportation network company services of your intent to provide transportation services with the vehicle. You may disclose to the lienholder all insurance coverage information provided to you by the transportation network company. If you fail to provide the required insurance coverage under the terms of your contract with the lienholder or show evidence to the lienholder of the coverage provided by the transportation network company, you may violate the terms of your contract."

(i) Insurers that write automobile insurance in the State may exclude coverage under the policy issued to an owner or operator of a personal vehicle for any loss that occurs while the driver is logged on to a transportation network company's online-enabled application or platform or while the driver provides TNC service. This right to exclude all coverage applies to any coverage included in an automobile insurance policy, including all of the following:

(1) Liability coverage for bodily injury and property damage.

(2) Personal injury protection coverage.

(3) Uninsured and underinsured motorist coverage.

(4) Medical payments coverage.

(5) Comprehensive physical damage coverage.

(6) Collision physical damage coverage.

(j) Automobile insurers that exclude the coverage described in subsection (i) of this section have no duty to defend or indemnify any claim expressly excluded. An automobile insurer that defends or indemnifies a claim against a driver that is excluded under the terms of its policy has a right of contribution against other insurers that provide automobile insurance to the same driver in satisfaction of the coverage requirements of this section.

(k) No insurer is required to sell a policy of insurance providing the coverage required by this section.

(l) Notwithstanding G.S. 58-37-35(b)(1)e., no insurance policy providing coverage required by this section is cedable to the North Carolina Reinsurance Facility due solely to the requirements of this section.

(m) In a claims coverage investigation or accident, a TNC driver, transportation network companies, any insurer potentially providing coverage under this section, and other directly involved parties must exchange the following information:

(1) Description of the coverage, exclusions, and limits provided under any insurance policy.

(2) Precise times that a TNC driver logged on and off of the transportation network company's online-enabled application or platform in the 12-hour period immediately preceding and in the 12-hour period immediately following the accident.

(3) Precise times that a TNC driver provided TNC service in the 12-hour period immediately preceding and in the 12-hour period immediately following the accident.

(n) This section does not apply to brokering transportation network companies.

History.
2015-237, s. 1

§ 20-280.5. Safety requirements

(a) The transportation network company must require TNC drivers have their vehicles inspected annually to meet State safety requirements. The Division may, by regulation, specify alternative inspections that are acceptable as equivalent inspections, such as an inspection performed in another state. This subsection does not apply to brokering transportation network companies.

(b) The transportation network company's online-enabled application or platform must provide the following information to customers after a ride request is accepted by a TNC driver:

(1) Photograph of the TNC driver.

(2) License plate number of the TNC driver's vehicle.

(3) Description of the TNC driver's vehicle.

(4) Approximate location of the TNC driver's vehicle displayed on a map.

(c) The transportation network company must maintain the following records:

(1) The record of each TNC service provided in this State for one year from the date the TNC service occurred.

(2) The record of each TNC driver, which includes a driver's name and current address of the driver the TNC has on record at the time the driver's relationship with the TNC ended, in this State for one year from the date the TNC driver terminated their relationship with the transportation network company.

(d) The transportation network company must require a TNC driver to display the license plate number of the TNC driver's vehicle in a location that is visible from the front of the vehicle at the time a TNC service begins and at all times during a TNC service. The vehicle's license plate number displayed pursuant to this subsection must be printed in a legible and contrasting font no smaller than three inches in height but is not required to be permanently mounted on the vehicle. A TNC driver is not required to obtain approval from the transportation network company or the Division for a license plate number display required by this subsection.

(e) Except as provided in subsection (f) of this section, a transportation network company must require a TNC driver to display consistent and distinctive signage or emblems, known as a trade dress, trademark, branding, or logo of the TNC, on the TNC driver's vehicle at all times when the TNC driver is active on the TNC digital platform or when providing any TNC service that reasonably assists customers to identify or verify a TNC driver responding to a ride request. TNC signage or emblems required by this subsection may include magnetic or removable signage or emblems, must be approved by the Division before use, and must meet all of the following requirements:

(1) Be readable during daylight hours at a distance of 50 feet.

(2) Include an illuminated TNC-provided sign displaying the TNC's proprietary trademark or logo that is clearly visible so as to be seen in darkness.

(f) A transportation network company may seek approval from the Division for technological identifiers as an alternative to the distinctive signage or emblems required by subsection (e) of this section. The Division may approve an alternative technological identifier if it reasonably assists customers to identify or verify a TNC driver responding to a ride request. If approved by the Division, the approved technological identifier must be used by a TNC driver at all times when the TNC driver is active on the TNC digital platform or when providing any TNC service.

History.
2015-237, s. 1; 2019-194, s. 2(a); 2020-3, s. 4.36(a)

§ 20-280.6. Background checks

(a) Prior to permitting an individual to act as a TNC driver, the transportation network company must do all of the following:

(1) Require the individual to submit an application to the transportation network company, including, at a minimum, the following:

a. Address.

b. Age.

c. Drivers license number.

d. Driving history.

e. Motor vehicle registration.

f. Automobile liability insurance information.

(2) Conduct, or have a third party conduct, a local and national criminal background check for each applicant, including, at a minimum, the following:

a. Multi-State/Multi-Jurisdiction Criminal Records Locator or other similar commercial nationwide database with validation (primary source search).

b. National Sex Offender Registry.

(3) Review, or have a third party review, a driving history research report for such individual.

(b) The transportation network company must confirm that every TNC driver continues to meet all the requirements of this section every five years starting from the date the TNC driver met all the requirements of this section.

(c) The transportation network company must not permit an individual to act as a TNC driver if any of the following apply:

(1) Has had more than three moving violations in the prior three-year period or one major violation in the prior three-year period, including attempting to evade the police, reckless driving, or driving on a suspended or revoked license.

(2) Has been convicted within the past seven years of driving under the influence of drugs or alcohol, fraud, sexual offenses, use of a motor vehicle to commit a felony, or

a crime involving property damage, theft, acts of violence, or acts of terror.

(3) Is a match in the National Sex Offender Registry.

(4) Does not possess a valid drivers license.

(5) Does not possess proof of registration for the motor vehicle to be used to provide TNC services.

(6) Does not possess proof of automobile liability insurance for the motor vehicle to be used to provide TNC services.

(7) Is not at least 19 years of age.

(d) This section does not apply to brokering transportation network companies.

History.
2015-237, s. 1

§ 20-280.7. Authority of Division

The Division may issue regulations to implement this Article.

History.
2015-237, s. 1

§ 20-280.8. Presumption that TNC drivers are independent contractors

A rebuttable presumption exists that a TNC driver is an independent contractor and not an employee. The presumption may be rebutted by application of the common law test for determining employment status.

History.
2015-237, s. 1

§ 20-280.9. Airport operators

(a) An airport operator is authorized to charge transportation network companies and TNC drivers a reasonable fee for their use of the airport's facility.

(b) An airport operator is authorized to require an identifying decal be displayed by TNC drivers.

(c) An airport operator is authorized to require the purchase and use of equipment or establish other appropriate mechanisms for monitoring and auditing compliance, including having a transportation network company provide data for purposes of monitoring and auditing compliance.

(d) An airport operator is authorized to designate a location where TNC drivers may stage on the airport operator's facility, drop off passengers, and pick up passengers.

History.
2015-237, s. 1

§ 20-280.10. Statewide regulation

(a) Notwithstanding any other provision of law and except as authorized by this Chapter, no county, city, airport operator, or other governmental agency is authorized to impose fees, require licenses, limit the operation of TNC services, or otherwise regulate TNC services. TNC services remain subject to all ordinances and local laws outside the scope of this Chapter, including parking and traffic regulation.

(b) Any contract provision or term of service in a transportation network company's contract with a State resident or person present in the State contrary to this Article is void as against public policy.

History.
2015-237, s. 1

ARTICLE 10B
PEER-TO-PEER VEHICLE SHARING

§ 20-280.15. Definitions

The following definitions apply in this Article:

(1) **Airport operator.** -- As defined in G.S. 20-280.1.

(2) **Peer-to-peer vehicle sharing.** -- The authorized use of a shared vehicle by an individual other than the shared vehicle owner through a peer-to-peer vehicle sharing program.

(3) **Peer-to-peer vehicle sharing program.** -- A business platform that connects shared vehicle owners with drivers to enable the sharing of vehicles for financial consideration.

(4) **Shared vehicle.** -- A vehicle that is available for sharing through a peer-to-peer vehicle sharing program.

(5) **Shared vehicle owner.** -- The registered owner of a shared vehicle that is made available for sharing through a peer-to-peer vehicle sharing program.

(6) **Vehicle sharing provider.** -- The person or entity that operates, facilitates, or administers the provision of personal vehicle sharing through a peer-to-peer vehicle sharing program.

History.
2019-199, s. 9(a)

§ 20-280.17. Airport operators

An airport operator may (i) charge peer-to-peer vehicle sharing programs a reasonable fee for the use of the airport's facility, (ii) require an identifying decal be displayed on all shared vehicles that operate on airport property, (iii) require the purchase and use of equipment or establish other appropriate mechanisms for monitoring and auditing compliance, including having a peer-to-peer vehicle sharing program provide data for purposes of monitoring and auditing compliance, and (iv) designate a location where shared vehicles may stage on the airport operator's facility.

History.
2019-199, s. 9(a)

ARTICLE 11
LIABILITY INSURANCE REQUIRED OF PERSONS ENGAGED IN RENTING MOTOR VEHICLES

§ 20-281. Liability insurance prerequisite to engaging in business; coverage of policy

From and after July 1, 1953, it shall be unlawful for any person, firm or corporation to engage in the business of renting or leasing motor vehicles to the public for operation by the rentee or lessee unless such person, firm or corporation has secured insurance for his own liability and that of his rentee or lessee, in such an amount as is hereinafter provided, from an insurance company duly licensed to sell motor vehicle liability insurance in this State. Each such motor vehicle leased or rented must be covered by a policy of liability insurance insuring the owner and rentee or lessee and their agents and employees while in the performance of their duties against loss from any liability imposed by law for damages including damages for care and loss of services because of bodily injury to or death of any person and injury to or destruction of property caused by accident arising out of the operation of such motor vehicle, subject to the following minimum limits: thirty thousand dollars ($ 30,000) because of bodily injury to or death of one person in any one accident, and sixty thousand dollars ($ 60,000) because of bodily injury to or death of two or more persons in any one accident, and twenty-five thousand dollars ($ 25,000) because of injury to or destruction of property of others in any one accident. Provided, however, that nothing in this Article shall prevent such operators from qualifying as self-insurers under terms and conditions to be prepared and prescribed by the Commissioner of Motor Vehicles or by giving bond with personal or corporate surety, as now provided by G.S. 20-279.24, in lieu of securing the insurance policy hereinbefore provided for.

History.
1953, c. 1017, s. 1; 1955, c. 1296; 1965, c. 349, s. 1; 1967, c. 277, s. 8; 1973, c. 745, s. 7; 1979, c. 832, s. 11; 1991, c. 469, s. 6; 1999-228, s. 7

§ 20-282. Cooperation in enforcement of Article

The provisions of this Article shall be enforced by the Commissioner of Motor Vehicles in cooperation with the Commissioner of Insurance, the North Carolina Automobile Rate Administrative Office and with all law-enforcement officers and agents and other agencies of the State and the political subdivisions thereof.

History.
1953, c. 1017, s. 2

§ 20-283. Compliance with Article prerequisite to issuance of license plates

No license plates shall be issued by the Division of Motor Vehicles to operate a motor vehicle, for lease or rent for operation by the rentee or lessee, until the applicant for such license plates demonstrates to the Commissioner of Motor Vehicles that he has complied with the provisions of this Article.

History.
1953, c. 1017, s. 3; 1975, c. 716, s. 5

§ 20-284. Violation a misdemeanor

Any person, firm or corporation violating the provisions of this Article shall be guilty of a Class 1 misdemeanor.

History.
1953, c. 1017, s. 4; 1993, c. 539, s. 385; 1994, Ex. Sess., c. 24, s. 14(c)

ARTICLE 12
MOTOR VEHICLE DEALERS AND MANUFACTURERS LICENSING LAW

§ 20-285. Regulation of motor vehicle distribution in public interest

The General Assembly finds and declares that the distribution of motor vehicles in the State of North Carolina vitally affects the general economy of the State and the public interest and public welfare, and in the exercise of its police power, it is necessary to regulate and license motor vehicle manufacturers, distributors, dealers, salesmen, and their representatives doing business in North Carolina, in order to prevent frauds, impositions and other abuses upon its citizens and to protect and preserve the investments and properties of the citizens of this State.

History.
1955, c. 1243, s. 1; 1983, c. 704, s. 1

§ 20-286. Definitions

The following definitions apply in this Article:

(1), (2) Repealed by Session Laws 1973, c. 1330, s. 39.

(2a) **Dealership facilities.** -- The real estate, buildings, fixtures and improvements devoted to the conduct of business under a franchise.

(2b) **Designated family member.** -- The spouse, child, grandchild, parent, brother, or sister of a dealer, who, in the case of a deceased dealer, is entitled to inherit the dealer's ownership interest in the dealership under the terms of the dealer's will; or who has otherwise been designated in writing by a deceased dealer to succeed him in the motor vehicle dealership; or who under the laws of intestate succession of this State is entitled to inherit the interest; or who, in the case of an incapacitated dealer, has been appointed by a court as the legal representative of the dealer's property. The term includes the appointed and qualified personal representative and testamentary trustee of a deceased dealer.

(3) **Distributor.** -- A person, resident or nonresident of this State, who sells or distributes new motor vehicles to new motor vehicle dealers in this State, maintains a distributor representative in this State, controls any person, resident or nonresident, who in whole or in part offers for sale, sells or distributes any new motor vehicle to any motor vehicle dealer in this State.

(4) **Distributor branch.** -- A branch office maintained by a distributor for the sale of new motor vehicles to new motor vehicle dealers, or for directing or supervising the distributor's representatives in this State.

(5) **Distributor representative.** -- A person employed by a distributor or a distributor branch for the purpose of selling or promoting the sale of new motor vehicles or otherwise conducting the business of the distributor or distributor branch.

(5a) **Established office.** -- An office that meets the following requirements:

a. Contains at least 96 square feet of floor space in a permanent enclosed building.

b. Is a place where the books, records, and files required by the Division under this Article are kept.

(6) **Established salesroom.** -- A salesroom that meets the following requirements:

a. Contains at least 96 square feet of floor space in a permanent enclosed building.

b. Displays, or is located immediately adjacent to, a sign having block letters not less than three inches in height on contrasting background, clearly and distinctly designating the trade name of the business.

c. Is a place at which a permanent business of bartering, trading, and selling motor vehicles will be carried on in good faith on an ongoing basis whereby the dealer can be contacted by the public at reasonable times.

d. Is a place where the books, records, and files required by the Division under this Article are kept.

The term includes the area contiguous to or located within 500 feet of the premises on which the salesroom is located. The term does not include a tent, a temporary stand, or other temporary quarters. The minimum area requirement does not apply to any place of business lawfully in existence and duly licensed on or before January 1, 1978.

(7) **Factory branch.** -- A branch office, maintained for the sale of new motor vehicles to new motor vehicle dealers, or for directing or supervising the factory branch's representatives in this State.

(8) **Factory representative.** -- A person employed by a manufacturer or a factory branch for the purpose of selling or promoting the sale of the manufacturer's motor vehicles or otherwise conducting the business of the manufacturer or factory branch.

(8a) **Franchise.** -- A written agreement or contract between any new motor vehicle manufacturer, and any new motor vehicle dealer which purports to fix the legal rights and liabilities of the parties to such agreement or contract, and pursuant to which the dealer purchases and resells the franchised product or leases or rents the dealership premises.

(8b) **Franchised motor vehicle dealer.** -- A dealer who holds a currently valid franchise as defined in G.S. 20-286(8a) with a manufacturer or distributor of new motor vehicles, trailers, or semitrailers.

(8c) **Good faith.** -- Honesty in fact and the observation of reasonable commercial standards of fair dealing as defined and interpreted in G.S. 25-1-201(b)(20).

(8d) **Independent motor vehicle dealer.** -- A dealer in used motor vehicles.

(8e) **Manufacturer.** -- A person, resident or nonresident, who manufactures or

Chapter 20

assembles new motor vehicles, or who imports new motor vehicles for distribution through a distributor, including any person who acts for and is under the control of the manufacturer or assembler in connection with the distribution of the motor vehicles. Additionally, the term "manufacturer" shall include the terms "distributor" and "factory branch."

(9) Repealed by Session Laws 1973, c. 1330, s. 39.

(10) **Motor vehicle. --** Any motor propelled vehicle, regardless of the size and type of motor or source of power, trailer or semitrailer, required to be registered under the laws of this State. This term does not include mopeds, as that term is defined in G.S. 20-4.01.

a. "New motor vehicle" means a motor vehicle that has never been the subject of a completed, successful, or conditional sale that was subsequently approved other than between new motor vehicle dealers, or between a manufacturer and a new motor vehicle dealer of the same franchise. For purposes of this subdivision, the use of a new motor vehicle by a new motor vehicle dealer for demonstration or service loaner purposes does not render the new motor vehicle a used motor vehicle, notwithstanding (i) the commencement of the manufacturer's original warranty as a result of the franchised dealer's use of the vehicle for demonstration or loaner purposes, or (ii) the dealer's receipt of incentive or warranty compensation or other reimbursement or consideration from a manufacturer, factory branch, distributor, distributor branch or from a third-party warranty, maintenance, or service contract company relating to the use of a vehicle as a demonstrator or service loaner.

b. "Used motor vehicle" means a motor vehicle other than a motor vehicle described in sub-subdivision a. of this subdivision.

c. The term "motor vehicle" does not include an electrically powered device that is equipped with automated driving technology that enables device operation with or without remote support and supervision of a human, and to which all of the following apply: (i) the device does not exceed a weight of 750 pounds, excluding cargo, (ii) the device does not exceed a length of 40 inches when not linked with other devices, and (iii) the device does not exceed a width of 36 inches. An electrically powered device that is equipped with automated driving technology that enables device operation with or without remote support and supervision of a human and that exceeds any of the dimensions set out in this subsubdivision is included in the term "motor vehicle" under this Article, and the device is subject to the provisions of Article 18 of this Chapter if it falls within the definition of "fully autonomous vehicle" under G.S. 20-400(3).

(11) **Motor vehicle dealer or dealer. --**

a. A person who does any of the following:

1. For commission, money, or other thing of value, buys, sells, leases at retail, or exchanges, whether outright or on conditional sale, bailment lease, chattel mortgage, or otherwise, five or more motor vehicles within any 12 consecutive months, regardless of who owns the motor vehicles.

2. On behalf of another and for commission, money, or other thing of value, arranges, offers, attempts to solicit, or attempts to negotiate the sale, purchase, or exchange of an interest in five or more motor vehicles within any 12 consecutive months, regardless of who owns the motor vehicles.

3. Engages, wholly or in part, in the business of selling, leasing at retail, new motor vehicles or new or used motor vehicles, or used motor vehicles only, whether or not the motor vehicles are owned by that person, and sells five or more motor vehicles within any 12 consecutive months.

4. Offers to sell, displays, or permits the display for sale for any form of compensation five or more motor vehicles within any 12 consecutive months.

5. Primarily engages in the leasing or renting of motor vehicles to others and sells or offers to sell those vehicles at retail.

6. For commission, money, or other thing of value, or on behalf of another person sharing ten percent (10%) or more common ownership, offers new vehicles as part of a subscription program. This sub-sub-subdivision shall not apply to any person providing a vehicle subscription or monthly rental program on or after January 1, 2025.

b. The term "motor vehicle dealer" or "dealer" does not include any of the following:

1. Receivers, trustees, administrators, executors, guardians, or other persons appointed by or acting under the judgment or order of any court.

2. Public officers while performing their official duties.

3. Persons disposing of motor vehicles acquired for their own use or the use of a family member, and actually so used, when the vehicles have been acquired and used in good faith and not for the purpose of avoiding the provisions of this Article.

4. Persons who sell motor vehicles as an incident to their principal business but who are not engaged primarily in the selling of motor vehicles. This category includes financial institutions who sell repossessed motor vehicles and insurance companies who sell motor vehicles to which they have taken title as an incident of payments made under policies of insurance, and auctioneers who sell motor vehicles for the owners or the heirs of the owners of those vehicles as part of an auction of other personal or real property or for the purpose of settling an estate or closing a business or who sell motor vehicles on behalf of a governmental entity, and who do not maintain a used car lot or building with one or more employed motor vehicle sales representatives.

5. Persons manufacturing, distributing or selling trailers and semitrailers weighing not more than 2,500 pounds unloaded weight.

6. A licensed real estate broker or salesman who sells a mobile home for the owner as an incident to the sale of land upon which the mobile home is located.

7. An employee of an organization arranging for the purchase or lease by the organization of vehicles for use in the organization's business.

8. Any publication, broadcast, or other communications media when engaged in the business of advertising, but not otherwise arranging for the sale of motor vehicles owned by others.

9. Any person dealing solely in the sale or lease of vehicles designed exclusively for off-road use.

10. Any real property owner who leases any interest in property for use by a dealer.

11. Any person acquiring any interest in a motor vehicle for a family member.

12. Any auctioneer licensed pursuant to Chapter 85B of the General Statutes employed to be an auctioneer of motor vehicles for a licensed motor vehicle dealer, while conducting an auction for that dealer.

13. Any charitable organization operating under section 501(c)(3) of the Internal Revenue Code (26 U.S.C. § 501(c)(3)) where the vehicle was donated to the charitable organization solely for purposes of resale by the charitable organization.

(12) **Motor vehicle sales representative or salesman.** -- A person who is employed as a sales representative by, or has an agreement with, a motor vehicle dealer or a wholesaler to sell or exchange motor vehicles.

(13) **New motor vehicle dealer.** -- A motor vehicle dealer who buys, sells or exchanges, or offers or attempts to negotiate a sale or exchange of an interest in, or who is engaged, wholly or in part, in the business of selling, new or new and used motor vehicles.

(13a) **Person.** -- Defined in G.S. 20-4.01.

(13b) **Relevant market area or trade area.** -- The area within a radius of 20 miles around an existing dealer or the area of responsibility defined in the franchise, whichever is greater; except that, where a manufacturer is seeking to establish an additional new motor vehicle dealer the relevant market area shall be as follows:

a. If the population in an area within a radius of 10 miles around the proposed site is 250,000 or more, the relevant market area shall be that area within the 10 mile radius; or

b. If the population in an area within a radius of 10 miles around the proposed site is less than 250,000, but the population in an area within a radius of 15 miles around the proposed site is 150,000 or more, the relevant market area shall be that area within the 15 mile radius; or

c. Except as defined in subparts a. and b., the relevant market area shall be the area within a radius of 20 miles around an existing dealer.

In determining population for this definition the most recent census by the U.S. Bureau of the Census or the most recent population update either from Claritas Inc. or other similar recognized source shall be accumulated for all census tracts either wholly or partially within the relevant market area. In accumulating population for this definition, block group and block level data shall be used to apportion the population of census tracts which are only partially within the relevant market area so that population outside of the applicable radius is not included in the count.

(14) Repealed by Session Laws 1973, c. 1330, s. 39.

(15) **Retail installment sale.** -- A sale of one or more motor vehicles to a buyer for the buyer's use and not for resale, in which the price thereof is payable in one or more installments over a period of time and in which the seller has either retained title to the goods or has taken or retained a security interest in the goods under a form of contract designated as a conditional sale, bailment lease, chattel mortgage or otherwise.

(15a) **Special tool or essential tool.** -- A tool designed and required by the manufacturer or distributor and not readily available from another source that is utilized for the purpose of performing service repairs on a motor vehicle sold by a manufacturer or distributor to its franchised new motor vehicle dealers in this State.

(16) **Used motor vehicle dealer.** -- A motor vehicle dealer who buys, sells or exchanges, or offers or attempts to negotiate a sale or exchange of an interest in, or who is engaged, wholly or in part, in the business of selling, used motor vehicles only.

(17) **Wholesaler.** -- A person who sells or distributes used motor vehicles to motor vehicle dealers in this State, has a sales representative in this State, or controls any person who in whole or in part offers for sale, sells, or distributes any used motor vehicle to a motor vehicle dealer in this State. The provisions of G.S. 20-302, 20-305.1, and 20-305.2 that apply to distributors also apply to wholesalers.

History.
1955, c. 1243, s. 2; 1967, c. 1126, s. 1; c. 1173; 1973, c. 1330, s. 39; 1977, c. 560, s. 1; 1983, c. 312; c. 704, ss. 2, 3, 21; 1987, c. 381; 1991, c. 527, s. 1; c. 662, s. 1; 1991 (Reg. Sess., 1992), c. 819, s. 23; 1993, c. 331, s. 1; 1995, c. 234, s. 1; 1997-456. s. 27; 2003-254, s. 1; 2003-265, s. 1; 2005-409, s. 7; 2007-484, s. 6; 2015-125, s. 8; 2015-209, s. 1; 2015-232, s. 1.2; 2015-264, s. 42(a); 2018-43, s. 3; 2019-125, s. 1; 2020-73, s. 6; 2021-33, s. 2.3; 2021-147, ss. 2(c), 10

§ 20-287. Licenses required; penalties

(a) **License Required.** -- It shall be unlawful for any new motor vehicle dealer, used motor vehicle dealer, motor vehicle sales representative, manufacturer, factory branch, factory representative, distributor, distributor branch, distributor representative, or wholesaler to engage in business in this State without first obtaining a license as provided in this Article. If any motor vehicle dealer acts as a motor vehicle sales representative, the dealer shall obtain a motor vehicle sales representative's license in addition to a motor vehicle dealer's license. The sales representative license shall show the name of each dealer or wholesaler employing the sales representative. An individual who has submitted an application to the Division for a sales representative license pursuant to G.S. 20-288(a) may engage in activities as a sales representative while the application is pending under the following conditions: (i) the sales representative applicant is actively and directly supervised by a licensed motor vehicle dealer or a licensed sales representative designated by the dealer, (ii) the applicant certifies in the application that the applicant has not been previously denied a sales representative license for any dealer by the Division on nonprocedural grounds, and (iii) the applicant has not been previously convicted of a felony. Any license issued by the Division to a motor vehicle dealer, manufacturer, factory branch, factory representative, distributor, distributor branch, distributor representative, or wholesaler under this Article may not be assigned, sold, or otherwise transferred to any other person or entity.

(b) **Civil Penalty for Violations by Licensee.** -- In addition to any other punishment or remedy under the law for any violation of this section, the Division may levy and collect a civil penalty, in an amount not to exceed one thousand dollars ($ 1,000) for each violation, against any person who has obtained a license pursuant to this section, or is an applicant for a license under this section, if it finds that the person has violated any of the provisions of G.S. 20-285 through G.S. 20-303, Article 15 of this Chapter, or any statute or rule adopted by the Division relating to the sale of vehicles, vehicle titling, or vehicle registration. If the Division finds that a sales representative applicant has violated any of these provisions, the penalty shall be assessed against the applicant unless the Division finds that a dealership owner, manager, or officer had knowledge of the violation before the application was submitted to the Division.

(c) **Civil Penalty for Violations by Person Without a License.** -- In addition to any other punishment or remedy under the law for any violation of this section, the Division may levy and collect a civil penalty, in an amount not to exceed five thousand dollars ($ 5,000) for each violation, against any person who is required to obtain a license under this section and has not obtained the license, if it finds that the person has violated any of the provisions of G.S. 20-285 through G.S. 20-303, Article 15 of this Chapter, or any statute or rule adopted by the Division relating to the sale of vehicles, vehicle titling, or vehicle registration.

History.

1955, c. 1243, s. 3; 1991, c. 662, s. 2; 2001-345, s. 1; 2005-99, s. 1; 2019-181, s. 1; 2021-134, s. 1.1

§ 20-288. Application for license; license requirements; expiration of license; bond

(a) A new motor vehicle dealer, motor vehicle sales representative, manufacturer, factory branch, factory representative, distributor, distributor branch, distributor representative, or wholesaler may obtain a license by filing an application with the Division. An application must be on a form provided by the Division and contain the information required by the Division. An application for a license must be accompanied by the required fee. The following requirements also apply to applicants under this section:

    (1) An application for a new motor vehicle dealer license must be accompanied by an application for a dealer license plate. In addition, the Division shall require each applicant for a new motor vehicle dealer license to certify on the application whether the applicant or any parent, subsidiary, affiliate, or any other entity related to the applicant is a manufacturer, factory branch, factory representative, distributor, distributor branch, or distributor representative. In the event the applicant indicates on the application that the applicant or any parent, subsidiary, affiliate, or any other entity related to the applicant is a manufacturer, factory branch, factory representative, distributor, distributor branch, or distributor representative, the Division shall not issue a motor vehicle dealer license to the applicant until both of the following conditions are satisfied:

        a. The applicant states on the application the specific exception or exceptions to the prohibition on the issuance of a motor vehicle dealer license to any manufacturer, factory branch, factory representative, distributor, distributor branch, or distributor representative for which the applicant contends it qualifies under G.S. 20-305.2(a).

        b. If the applicant does not currently hold a motor vehicle dealer license issued by the Division, the Commissioner determines, after an evidentiary hearing, that the applicant qualifies under one or more of the exceptions to the prohibition against the issuance of a motor vehicle dealer license to any manufacturer, factory branch, factory representative, distributor, distributor branch, or distributor representative provided in G.S. 20-305.2(a). The applicant shall bear the burden of proving the applicant's qualification for the exception or exceptions claimed.

    (2) Upon submission of a license application by a manufacturer, factory branch, factory representative, distributor, distributor branch, or distributor representative that has not previously been issued a license by the Division, the Division shall promptly publish notice of the license application in the North Carolina Register. The notice shall include the applicant's name, address, application date, and the names and titles of any individual listed on the application as an owner, partner, member, or officer of the applicant. The Division shall not approve or issue any license for a manufacturer, factory branch, factory representative, distributor, distributor branch, or distributor representative earlier than 15 days from the date the notice of the license or license renewal application was published in the North Carolina Register.

(a1) A used motor vehicle dealer may obtain a license by filing an application, as prescribed in subsection (a) of this section, and providing the following:

    (1) The required fee.

    (2) Proof that the applicant, within the last 12 months, has completed a 12-hour licensing course approved by the Division if the applicant is seeking an initial license and a six-hour course approved by the Division if the applicant is seeking a renewal license. The requirements of this subdivision do not apply to a used motor vehicle dealer the primary business of which is the sale of salvage vehicles on behalf of insurers or to a manufactured home dealer licensed under G.S. 143-143.11 who complies with the continuing education requirements of G.S. 143-143.11B. The requirement of this subdivision does not apply to persons age 62 or older as of July 1, 2002, who are seeking a renewal license. This subdivision also does not apply to an applicant who holds a license as a new motor vehicle dealer as defined in G.S. 20-286(13) and operates from an established showroom located in an area within a radius of 30 miles around

the location of the established showroom for which the applicant seeks a used motor vehicle dealer license. An applicant who also holds a license as a new motor vehicle dealer may designate a representative to complete the licensing course required by this subdivision.

(3) If the applicant is an individual, proof that the applicant is at least 18 years of age and proof that all salespersons employed by the dealer are at least 18 years of age.

(4) The application for a dealer license plate.

(5) A certification as to whether the applicant or any entity having any common ownership or affiliation with the applicant is a motor vehicle manufacturer, factory branch, factory representative, distributor, distributor branch, or distributor representative. In the event the applicant indicates on the application that the applicant or any parent, subsidiary, affiliate, or any other entity related to the applicant is a manufacturer, factory branch, factory representative, distributor, distributor branch, or distributor representative, the applicant shall be required to state whether the applicant contends it qualifies for a motor vehicle dealer's license in accordance with any of the exceptions to the prohibition on the issuance of a motor vehicle dealer's license to any manufacturer, factory branch, factory representative, distributor, distributor branch, or distributor representative, as provided in G.S. 20-305.2(a).

(b) The Division shall require in such application, or otherwise, information relating to matters set forth in G.S. 20-294 as grounds for the refusing of licenses, and to other pertinent matters commensurate with the safeguarding of the public interest, all of which shall be considered by the Division in determining the fitness of the applicant to engage in the business for which he seeks a license. The Division shall not require submission of an applicant's fingerprints to be used in performing a criminal history record check of an applicant for a license or license renewal.

(b1) The Division shall require in such license application and each application for renewal of license a certification that the applicant is familiar with the North Carolina Motor Vehicle Dealers and Manufacturers Licensing Law and with other North Carolina laws governing the conduct and operation of the business for which the license or license renewal is sought and that the applicant shall comply with the provisions of these laws, with the provisions of Article 12 of Chapter 20 of the General Statutes, and with other lawful regulations of the Division.

(c) All licenses that are granted shall be for a period of one year unless sooner revoked or suspended. The Division shall vary the expiration dates of all licenses that are granted so that an equal number of licenses expire at the end of each month, quarter, or other period consisting of one or more months to coincide with G.S. 20-79(c).

(d) To obtain a license as a wholesaler, an applicant who intends to sell or distribute self-propelled vehicles must have an established office in this State, and an applicant who intends to sell or distribute only trailers or semitrailers of more than 2,500 pounds unloaded weight must have a place of business in this State where the records required under this Article are kept.

To obtain a license as a motor vehicle dealer, an applicant who intends to deal in self-propelled vehicles must have an established salesroom in this State, and an applicant who intends to deal in only trailers or semitrailers of more than 2,500 pounds unloaded weight must have a place of business in this State where the records required under this Article are kept.

An applicant for a license as a manufacturer, a factory branch, a distributor, a distributor branch, a wholesaler, or a motor vehicle dealer must have a separate license for each established office, established salesroom, or other place of business in this State. An application for any of these licenses shall include a list of the applicant's places of business in this State.

(e) Each applicant approved by the Division for license as a motor vehicle dealer, manufacturer, factory branch, distributor, distributor branch, or wholesaler shall furnish a corporate surety bond or cash bond or fixed value equivalent of the bond. The amount of the bond for an applicant for a motor vehicle dealer's license is fifty thousand dollars ($ 50,000) for one established salesroom of the applicant and twenty-five thousand dollars ($ 25,000) for each of the applicant's additional established salesrooms. The amount of the bond for other applicants required to furnish a bond is fifty thousand dollars ($ 50,000) for one place of business of the applicant and twenty-five thousand dollars ($ 25,000) for each of the applicant's additional places of business.

A corporate surety bond shall be approved by the Commissioner as to form and shall be conditioned that the obligor will faithfully conform to and abide by the provisions of this Article and Article 15. A cash bond or fixed value equivalent thereof shall be approved by the Commissioner as to form and terms of deposits as will secure the ultimate beneficiaries of the bond; and such bond shall not be available for delivery to any person contrary to the rules of the Commissioner. Any purchaser of a motor vehicle, including a motor vehicle dealer, who shall have suffered any loss or damage by the failure of any license holder subject to this subsection to deliver free and clear title to any vehicle purchased from a license holder or any other act of a license holder subject to this subsection that constitutes a violation of this Article or Article 15 of this Chapter shall have the right to institute an action to recover against the license holder and the surety. Every license holder against whom an action is instituted shall notify the Commissioner of the action within 10 days after served with process. Except as provided by G.S. 20-288(f) and (g), a corporate surety bond shall remain in force and effect and may not be canceled by the surety unless the bonded person stops engaging in business or the person's license is denied, suspended, or revoked under G.S. 20-294. That cancellation may be had only upon 30 days' written notice to the Commissioner and shall not affect any liability incurred or accrued prior to the termination of such 30-day period. This subsection does not apply to a license holder who deals only in trailers having an empty weight of 4,000 pounds or less. This subsection does not apply to manufacturers of, or dealers in, mobile or manufactured homes who furnish a corporate surety bond, cash bond, or fixed value equivalent thereof, pursuant to G.S. 143-143.12.

(f) A corporate surety bond furnished pursuant to this section or renewal thereof may also be canceled by the surety prior to the next premium anniversary date without the prior written consent of the license holder for the following reasons:

(1) Nonpayment of premium in accordance with the terms for issuance of the surety bond; or

(2) An act or omission by the license holder or his representative that constitutes substantial and material misrepresentation or nondisclosure of a material fact in obtaining the surety bond or renewing the bond.

Any cancellation permitted by this subsection is not effective unless written notice of cancellation has been delivered or mailed to the license holder and to the Commissioner not less than 30 days before the proposed effective date of cancellation. The notice must be given or mailed by certified mail to the license holder at its last known address. The notice must state the reason for cancellation. Cancellation for nonpayment of premium is not effective if the amount due is paid before the effective date set forth in the notice of cancellation. Cancellation of the surety shall not affect any liability incurred or accrued prior to the termination of the 30-day notice period.

(g) A corporate surety may refuse to renew a surety bond furnished pursuant to this section by giving or mailing written notice of nonrenewal to the license holder and to the Commissioner not less than 30 days prior to the premium anniversary date of the surety bond. The notice must be given or mailed by certified mail to the license holder at its last known address. Nonrenewal of the surety bond shall not affect any liability incurred or accrued prior to the premium anniversary date of the surety bond.

History.
1955, c. 1243, s. 4; 1975, c. 716, s. 5; 1977, c. 560, s. 2; 1979, c. 254; 1981, c. 952, s. 3; 1985, c. 262; 1991, c. 495, s. 1; c. 662, s. 3; 1993, c. 440, s. 3; 1997-429, s. 1; 2001-345, s. 2; 2001-492, s. 4; 2003-254, s. 2; 2004-167, s. 9; 2004-199, s. 59; 2005-99, s. 2; 2006-105, s. 2.3; 2006-191, s. 1; 2006-259, s. 12; 2011-290, ss. 1, 2; 2017-148, s. 1; 2019-125, s. 11; 2020-77, s. 5(a)

§ 20-289. License fees

(a) The license fee for each fiscal year, or part thereof, shall be as follows:

(1) For motor vehicle dealers, distributors, distributor branches, and wholesalers, ninety dollars ($ 90.00) for each place of business.

(2) For manufacturers, one hundred ninety-five dollars ($ 195.00) and for each factory branch in this State, one hundred thirty dollars ($ 130.00).

(3) For motor vehicle sales representatives, twenty dollars ($ 20.00).

(4) For factory representatives, or distributor representatives, twenty dollars ($ 20.00).

(5) Repealed by Session Laws 1991, c. 662, s. 4.

(b) The fees collected under this section shall be credited to the Highway Fund. These fees are in addition to all other taxes and fees.

History.
1955, c. 1243, s. 5; 1969, c. 593; 1977, c. 802, s. 8; 1981, c. 690, s. 16; 1991, c. 662, s. 4; c. 689, s. 335; 2005-276, s. 44.1(o); 2015-241, s. 29.30(p)

§ 20-290. Licenses to specify places of business; display of license and list of salesmen; advertising

(a) The license of a motor vehicle dealer shall list each of the dealer's established salesrooms in this State. A license of a manufacturer, factory branch, distributor, distributor branch, or wholesaler shall list each of the license holder's places of business in this State. A license shall be conspicuously displayed at each place of business. In the event the location of a business changes, the Division shall endorse the change of location on the license, without charge.

(b) Each dealer shall keep a current list of his licensed salesmen, showing the name of each licensed salesman, posted in a conspicuous place in each place of business.

(c) Whenever any licensee places an advertisement in any newspaper or publication, the licensee's name shall appear in the advertisement.

History.
1955, c. 1243, s. 6; 1975, c. 716, s. 5; 1991, c. 662, s. 5; 2005-99, s. 3

§ 20-291. Representatives to carry license and display it on request; license to name employer

Every person to whom a sales representative, factory representative, or distributor representative license is issued shall carry the license when engaged in business, and shall display it upon request. The license shall state the name of the representative's employer. If the representative changes employers, the representative shall immediately apply to the Division for a license that states the name of the representative's new employer. The fee for issuing a license stating the name of a new employer is ten dollars ($ 10.00).

History.
1955, c. 1243, s. 7; 1975, c. 716, s. 5; 1991, c. 662, s. 6; c. 689, s. 336; 2005-99, s. 4; 2005-276, s. 44.1(r)

§ 20-292. Dealers may display motor vehicles for sale at retail only at established salesrooms

(a) A new or used motor vehicle dealer may display a motor vehicle for sale at retail only at the dealer's established salesroom, unless the display is of a motor vehicle that meets any of the following descriptions:

(1) Contains the dealer's name or other sales information and is used by the dealer as a "demonstrator" for transportation purposes.

(2) Is displayed at a trade show or exhibit at which no selling activities relating to the vehicle take place and contains the dealer's name and business location.

(3) Is displayed at the home or place of business of a customer at the request or with the permission or consent of the customer.

(b) Nothing contained in this section or in any other provision contained in Article 12 of this Chapter shall be deemed to prohibit or restrict a new or used motor vehicle dealer or an employee, agent, or contractee of a new or used motor vehicle dealer from doing any of the following:

(1) Delivering a motor vehicle purchased or leased by a customer to the customer's home or place of business or having a customer execute forms and other documents relating to vehicle purchase, lease, titling, registration, financing, insurance, and other products and services provided to the customer by or through the dealer that are presented to a customer at the customer's home or place of business by any employee or authorized agent of the dealer; provided, however, that all such forms and other documents have been fully agreed to and were fully completed in advance of their presentation to the customer, no additional negotiations or modifications related to the content of any of these forms or other documents take place, and no modifications are made to the content of any of these forms and other documents other than the correction of clerical or typographical errors.

(2) Having any employee or authorized agent of the dealer explain vehicle operation, features, care, and warranties to the customer at the time the customer's vehicle is delivered.

(3) Retrieving from the customer's home or place of business a motor vehicle that has been sold by the customer to the dealer.

(c) This section does not apply to recreational vehicles, house trailers, or boat, animal, camping, or other utility trailers.

History.
1955, c. 1243, s. 8; 1991, c. 662, s. 7; 2021-147, s. 15

§ 20-292.1. Supplemental temporary license for sale of antique and specialty vehicles

Any dealer licensed as a motor vehicle dealer under this Article may apply to the Commissioner and receive, at no additional charge, a supplemental temporary license authorizing the off-premises sales of antique motor vehicles and specialty motor vehicles for a period not to exceed 10 consecutive calendar days. To obtain a temporary supplemental license for the off-premises sale of antique motor vehicles and specialty motor vehicles, the applicant shall:

(1) Be licensed as a motor vehicle dealer under this Article.

(2) Notify the applicable local office of the Division of the specific dates and location for which the license is requested.

(3) Display a sign at the licensed location clearly identifying the dealer.

(4) Keep and maintain the records required for the sale of motor vehicles under this Article.

(5) Provide staff to work at the temporary location for the duration of the off-premises sale.

(6) Meet any local government permitting requirements.

(7) Have written permission from the property owner to sell at the location.

For purposes of this section, the term "antique motor vehicle" shall mean any motor vehicle for private use manufactured at least 25 years prior to the current model year, and the term "specialty motor vehicle" shall mean any model or series of motor vehicle for private use manufactured at least three years prior to the current model year of which no more than 5,000 vehicles were sold within the United States during the model year the vehicle was manufactured.

This section does not apply to a nonselling motor vehicle show or public display of new motor vehicles.

History.
2003-113, s. 1

N.C. Gen. Stat. § 20-293

Repealed by Session Laws 1993, c. 440, s. 10.

§ 20-294. Grounds for denying, suspending, placing on probation, or revoking licenses

The Division may deny, suspend, place on probation, or revoke a license issued under this Article for any one or more of the following grounds:

(1) Making a material misstatement in an application for a license.

(2) Willfully and intentionally failing to comply with this Article, Article 15 of this Chapter, or G.S. 20-52.1, 20-75, 20-79.1, 20-79.2, 20-108, 20-109, 20-109.3, or a rule adopted by the Division under this Article. It shall be an affirmative defense, exclusive to the dealer licensee, if the violation is a result of fraud, theft, or embezzlement against the licensee. Responsible persons, including officers, directors, and sales representative licensees, may be charged individually if they actively and knowingly participated in the unlawful activity. This affirmative defense is waived if any violation charged creates an unrecoverable loss for a citizen or another licensed motor vehicle dealer of this State.

(3) Failing to have an established salesroom, if the license holder is a motor vehicle dealer, or failing to have an established office, if the license holder is a wholesaler.

(4) Willfully defrauding any retail or wholesale buyer, to the buyer's damage, or any other person in the conduct of the licensee's business.

(5) Employing fraudulent devices, methods or practices in connection with compliance with the requirements under the laws of this State with respect to the retaking of motor vehicles under retail installment contracts and the redemption and resale of such motor vehicles.

(6) Using unfair methods of competition or unfair or deceptive acts or practices that cause actual damages to the buyer.

(7) Knowingly advertising by any means, any assertion, representation or statement of fact which is untrue, misleading or deceptive in any particular relating to the conduct of the business licensed or for which a license is sought.

(8) Knowingly advertising a used motor vehicle for sale as a new motor vehicle.

(9) Being convicted of an offense set forth under G.S. 14-71.2, 20-106.1, 20-107, or 20-112 while holding such a license or within five years next preceding the date of filing the application; or being convicted of a felony involving moral turpitude under the laws of this State, another state, or the United States. It shall be an affirmative defense, and will operate as a stay of this violation, if the person charged is determined to qualify and obtains expunction, certificate of relief, or pardon, or, if the violative conviction is vacated. If relief is granted, this violation is dismissed. If relief is denied, the stay is lifted.

(10) Submitting a bad check to the Division of Motor Vehicles in payment of highway use taxes collected by the licensee.

(11) Knowingly giving an incorrect certificate of title, or failing to give a certificate of title to a purchaser, a lienholder, or the Division, as appropriate, after a vehicle is sold. It shall be an affirmative defense, exclusive to the dealer licensee, if it is found the violation is a result of fraud, theft, or embezzlement against the licensee. Responsible persons, including officers, directors, and sales representative licensees, may be charged individually if they actively and knowingly participated in the unlawful activity. This affirmative defense is waived if any violation charged creates an unrecoverable loss for a citizen or another licensed motor vehicle dealer of this State.

(12) Making a material misstatement in an application for a dealer license plate.

(13) Failure to pay a civil penalty imposed under G.S. 20-287.

History.
1955, c. 1243, s. 10; 1963, c. 1102; 1967, c. 1126, s. 2; 1975, c. 716, s. 5; 1977, c. 560, s. 3; 1983, c. 704, s. 4; 1985, c. 687; ss. 1, 2; 1991, c. 193, s. 2; 1993, c. 440, s. 11; 2001-345, ss. 3, 4; 2010-132, s. 16; 2014-108, s. 5(a); 2018-43, s. 4; 2021-134, s. 1.2(a)

§ 20-295. Action on application; grace period while application for license renewal is pending

(a) **Division Action.** -- The Division shall either grant or deny an application for a license or license renewal within 30 days after receiving it. Any applicant denied a license shall, upon filing a written request within 30 days, be given a hearing at the time and place determined by the Commissioner or a person designated by the Commissioner. A hearing shall be public and shall be held with reasonable promptness.

(b) **Pending License Renewal Grace Period.** -- When an application for license renewal has been timely submitted prior to expiration of the license, the license shall remain valid for up to 30 days after the expiration date until the Division grants or denies the application. The Division shall (i) ensure that any database maintained by the Division that indicates the status of a license issued under this Article reflects that the license continues to be valid during this period and (ii) send a temporary license to the applicant for display while the Division reviews the application.

History.
1955, c. 1243, s. 11; 1975, c. 716, s. 5; 1993, c. 440, s. 1; 2020-77, s. 6(a); 2021-134, s. 5

§ 20-296. Notice and hearing upon denial, suspension, revocation, placing on probation, or refusal to renew license

No license shall be suspended, revoked, denied, placed on probation, or renewal thereof refused, until a written notice of the complaint made has been furnished to the licensee against whom the same is directed, and a hearing thereon has been had before the Commissioner, or a person designated by him. At least 10 days' written notice of the time and place of such hearing shall be given to the licensee by certified mail with return receipt requested to his last known address as shown on his license or other record of information in possession of the Division. At any such hearing, the licensee shall have the right to be heard personally or by counsel. After hearing, the Division shall have power to suspend, revoke, place on probation, or refuse to renew the license in question. Immediate notice of any such action shall be given to the licensee in accordance with G.S. 1A-1, Rule 4(j) of the Rules of Civil Procedure.

History.
1955, c. 1243, s. 12; 1975, c. 716, s. 5; 1981, c. 108; 2014-108, s. 6(a)

§ 20-297. Retention and inspection of certain records

(a) **Vehicles.** -- A dealer must keep a record of all vehicles received by the dealer and all vehicles sold by the dealer. The records must contain the information that the Division requires and be made available for inspection by the Division within a reasonable period of time after being requested by the Division. A dealer may satisfy the record-keeping requirements contained in this subsection either by (i) keeping and maintaining written or paper records at the dealership facility where the vehicles were sold or at another site within this State provided that the location and the name of a designated contact agent are provided to the Division or (ii) maintaining electronic copies of the records required by this subsection, provided that the Division shall have access to these electronic records from a location within this State. For purposes of this section, the location where dealership written or electronic records are kept and maintained may be owned and operated by a party other than the dealer.

(b) **Inspection.** -- The Division may inspect the pertinent books, records, letters, and contracts of a licensee relating to any written complaint made to the Division against the licensee.

(c) **Records Format.** -- Any record required to be kept and maintained under this section may be converted to electronic form and retained by a dealer in electronic form without retention of the original or any copies of the record in paper or other nonelectronic form.

History.
1955, c. 1243, s. 13; 1975, c. 716, s. 5; 1995, c. 163, s. 5; 2007-481, s. 3; 2016-74, s. 1

§ 20-297.1. Franchise-related form agreements

(a) All franchise-related form agreements, as defined in this subsection, offered to a motor vehicle dealer in this State shall provide that all terms and conditions in the agreement inconsistent with any of the laws or rules of this State are of no force and effect. For purposes of this section, the term "franchise-related form agreements" means one or more contracts between a franchised motor vehicle dealer and a manufacturer, factory branch, distributor, or distributor branch, including a written communication from a manufacturer or distributor in which a duty is imposed on the franchised motor vehicle dealer under which:

(1) The franchised motor vehicle dealer is granted the right to sell and service new motor vehicles manufactured or distributed by the manufacturer or distributor or only to service motor vehicles under the contract and a manufacturer's warranty;

(2) The franchised motor vehicle dealer is a component of the manufacturer or distributor's distribution system as an independent business;

(3) The franchised motor vehicle dealer is substantially associated with the manufacturer or distributor's trademark, trade name, and commercial symbol;

(4) The franchised motor vehicle dealer's business substantially relies on the manufacturer or distributor for a continued supply of motor vehicles, parts, and accessories; or

(5) Any right, duty, or obligation granted or imposed by this Chapter is affected.

(b) Notwithstanding the terms of any franchise or agreement, it shall be unlawful for any manufacturer, factory branch, distributor, or distributor branch to offer to a dealer, revise, modify, or replace a franchise-related form agreement, as defined above in this section, which agreement, modification, or replacement may adversely affect or alter the rights, obligations, or liability of a motor vehicle dealer or may adversely impair the sales, service obligations, investment, or profitability of any motor vehicle dealer located in this State, unless:

(1) The manufacturer, factory branch, distributor, or distributor branch provides prior written notice by registered or certified mail to each affected dealer, the Commissioner, and the North Carolina Automobile Dealers Association, Inc., of the modification or replacement in the form and within the time frame set forth within this section and in subsection (c) of this section; and

(2) If a protest is filed under this section, the Commissioner approves the modification or replacement.

(c) The notice required by subdivision (b)(1) of this section shall:

(1) Be given not later than the 60th day before the effective date of the modification or replacement;

(2) Contain on its first page a conspicuous statement that reads: "NOTICE TO DEALER: YOU MAY BE ENTITLED TO FILE A PROTEST WITH THE COMMISSIONER OF THE NORTH CAROLINA DIVISION OF MOTOR VEHICLES AND HAVE A HEARING IN WHICH YOU MAY PROTEST THE PROPOSED INITIAL OFFERING, MODIFICATION, OR REPLACEMENT OF CERTAIN FRANCHISE-RELATED FORM AGREEMENTS UNDER THE TERMS OF THE MOTOR VEHICLE DEALERS AND MANUFACTURERS LICENSING LAW, IF YOU OPPOSE THIS ACTION"; and

(3) Contain a separate letter or statement that identifies all substantive modifications or revisions and the principal reasons for each such modification or revision.

(d) A franchised dealer may file a protest with the Commissioner of the offering, modification, or replacement pursuant to this section not later than the latter of:

(1) The 60th day after the date of the receipt of the notice; or

(2) The time specified in the notice.

(e) After a protest is filed, the Commissioner shall determine whether the manufacturer, factory branch, distributor, or distributor branch has established by a preponderance of the evidence that there is good cause for the proposed offering, modification, or replacement. The prior franchise-related form agreement, if any, continues in effect until the Commissioner resolves the protest.

(f) The Commissioner is authorized and directed to investigate and prevent violations of this section, including inconsistencies of any franchise-related form agreement with the provisions of this Article.

(g) Nothing contained in this section shall in any way limit a dealer's rights under any other provision of this Article or other applicable law.

History.
1997-319, s. 1; 2005-409, s. 1

§ 20-298. Insurance

It shall be unlawful for any dealer or salesman or any employee of any dealer, to coerce or offer anything of value to any purchaser of a motor vehicle to provide any type of insurance coverage on said motor vehicle. No dealer, salesman or representative of either shall accept any policy as collateral on any vehicle sold by him to secure an interest in such vehicle in any company not qualified under the insurance laws of this State: Provided, nothing in this Article shall prevent a dealer or his representative from requiring adequate insurance coverage on a motor vehicle which is the subject of an installment sale.

History.
1955, c. 1243, s. 14

§ 20-298.1. Provision of certain products and services to those covered under the Military Lending Act

A motor vehicle dealer that does not market or extend to a covered borrower a loan or credit transaction covered by Section 987 of Title 10 of the United States Code, or any subsequent amendments thereto, and Part 232 (commencing with Section 232.1) of Subchapter M of Chapter I of Subtitle A of Title 32 of the Code of Federal Regulations, or any subsequent amendments thereto, shall not be in violation of G.S. 127B-11 or otherwise under the law with respect to all transactions entered into on or after October 3, 2016, regardless of whether the motor vehicle dealer markets or extends the loan or credit transaction to other persons who are not covered borrowers. For purposes of this section, "covered borrower" has the same meaning as provided in Part 232 (commencing with Section 232.1) of Subchapter M of Chapter I of Subtitle A of Title 32 of the Code of Federal Regulations and any subsequent amendments thereto.

History.
2019-181, s. 4

§ 20-299. Acts of officers, directors, partners, salesmen and other representatives

(a) The Division may deny, suspend, place on probation, or revoke a license issued to a corporation, limited liability company, limited liability partnership, or any other business entity that is a licensee under this Article if more than fifty percent (50%) of the business entity ownership engaged in conduct prohibited by G.S. 20-294. A license issued to a business entity under this Article may also be revoked if any damages suffered due to a violation of this Article are not satisfied, including damages caused by a sales representative while acting as an agent of the business entity. An owner of a business entity that did not engage personally in a violation of G.S. 20-294 and did not knowingly omit any duty may not be penalized for the acts of a business entity found to have violated this section.

(b) Every licensee who is a manufacturer or a factory branch shall be responsible for the acts of any or all of its agents and representatives while acting in the conduct of said licensee's business whether or not such licensee approved, authorized, or had knowledge of such acts.

History.
1955, c. 1243, s. 15; 1973, c. 559; 2021-134, s. 1.3

§ 20-300. Appeals from actions of Commissioner

Appeals from actions of the Commissioner shall be governed by the provisions of Chapter 150B of the General Statutes.

History.
1955, c. 1243, s. 16; 1973, c. 1331, s. 3; 1987, c. 827, s. 1

§ 20-301. Powers of Commissioner

(a) The Commissioner shall promote the interests of the retail buyer of motor vehicles.

(b) The Commissioner shall have power to prevent unfair methods of competition and unfair or deceptive acts or practices and other violations of this Article. Any franchised new motor vehicle dealer who believes that a manufacturer, factory branch, distributor, or distributor branch with whom the dealer holds a currently valid franchise has violated or is currently violating any provision of this Article may file a petition before the Commissioner setting forth the factual and legal basis for such violations. The Commissioner shall promptly forward a copy of the petition to the named manufacturer, factory branch, distributor, or distributor branch requesting a reply to the petition within 30 days. Allowing for sufficient time for the parties to conduct discovery, the Commissioner or his designee shall then hold an evidentiary hearing and render findings of fact and conclusions of law based on the evidence presented. Any parties to a hearing by the Commissioner concerning the establishment or relocating of a new motor vehicle dealer shall have a right of review of the decision in a court of competent jurisdiction pursuant to Chapter 150B of the General Statutes.

(c) The Commissioner shall have the power in hearings arising under this Article to enter scheduling orders and limit the time and scope of discovery; to determine the date, time, and place where hearings are to be held; to subpoena witnesses; to take depositions of witnesses; and to administer oaths.

(d) The Commissioner may, whenever he shall believe from evidence submitted to him that any person has been or is violating any provision of this Article, in addition to any other remedy, bring an action in the name of the State against that person and any other persons concerned or in any way participating in, or about to participate in practices or acts so in violation, to enjoin any persons from continuing the violations.

(e) The Commissioner may issue rules and regulations to implement the provisions of this section and to establish procedures related to administrative proceedings commenced under this section.

(f) In the event that a dealer, who is permitted or required to file a notice, protest, or petition before the Commissioner within a certain period of time in order to adjudicate, enforce, or protect rights afforded the dealer under this Article, voluntarily elects to appeal a policy, determination, or decision of the manufacturer through an appeals board or internal grievance procedure of the manufacturer, or to participate in or refer the matter to mediation, arbitration, or other alternative dispute resolution procedure or process established or endorsed by the manufacturer, the applicable period of time for the dealer to file the notice, protest, or petition

Chapter 20

before the Commissioner under this Article shall not commence until the manufacturer's appeal board or internal grievance procedure, mediation, arbitration, or appeals process of the manufacturer has been completed and the dealer has received notice in writing of the final decision or result of the procedure or process. Nothing, however, contained in this subsection shall be deemed to require that any dealer exhaust any internal grievance or other alternative dispute process required or established by the manufacturer before seeking redress from the Commissioner as provided in this Article.

(g) Notwithstanding any other statute, regulation, or rule or the existence of a pending legal or administrative proceeding in any other forum any franchised new motor vehicle dealer or any manufacturer, factory branch, distributor, or distributor branch may elect to file a petition before the Commissioner for resolution of any dispute that may arise with respect to any of the rights or obligations of the dealer or of the manufacturer, factory branch, distributor, or distributor branch related to a franchise or franchise-related form agreement. The Commissioner shall have the authority to apply principles of law, equity, and good faith in determining such matters. The filing of a petition by a dealer or a manufacturer, factory branch, distributor, or distributor branch pursuant to this section shall not preclude the party filing the petition from pursuing any other form of recourse it may have, either before the Commissioner or in another form, including any damages and injunctive relief. The Commissioner shall have the authority to receive and evaluate the facts in the matter of controversy and render a decision by entering an order which shall thereafter become binding and enforceable with respect to the parties, subject to the right of review of the decision in a court of competent jurisdiction pursuant to Chapter 150B of the General Statutes.

History.
1955, c. 1243, s. 17; 1983, c. 704, s. 23; 1991, c. 510, s. 1; 1997-319, s. 2; 1999-335, s. 1; 2011-290, s. 3

§ 20-301.1. Notice of additional charges against dealer's account; informal appeals procedure

(a) Notwithstanding the terms of any contract, franchise, novation, or agreement, it shall be unlawful for any manufacturer, factory branch, distributor, or distributor branch to charge or assess one of its franchised motor vehicle dealers located in this State, or to charge or debit the account of the franchised motor vehicle dealer for merchandise, tools, or equipment, or other charges or amounts which total more [than] five thousand dollars ($ 5,000),

other than the published cost of new motor vehicles, and merchandise, tools, or equipment specifically ordered by the franchised motor vehicle dealer, unless the franchised motor vehicle dealer receives a detailed itemized description of the nature and amount of each charge in writing at least 10 days prior to the date the charge or account debit is to become effective or due. For purposes of this subsection, the prior written notice required pursuant to this subsection includes, but is not limited to, all charges or debits to a dealer's account for advertising or advertising materials; advertising or showroom displays; customer informational materials; computer or communications hardware or software; special tools; equipment; dealership operation guides; Internet programs; and any additional charges or surcharges made or proposed for merchandise, tools, or equipment previously charged to the dealer; and any other charges or amounts which total more than five thousand dollars ($ 5,000). If the franchised new motor vehicle dealer disputes all or any portion of an actual or proposed charge or debit to the dealer's account, the dealer may proceed as provided in G.S. 20-301(b) and G.S. 20-308.1. Upon the filing of a petition pursuant to G.S. 20-301(b) or a civil action pursuant to G.S. 20-308.1, the affected manufacturer, factory branch, distributor, or distributor branch shall not require payment from the dealer, or debit or charge the dealer's account, unless and until a final judgment supporting the payment or charge has been rendered by the Commissioner or court.

(b) Any franchised new motor vehicle dealer who seeks to challenge an actual or proposed charge, debit, payment, reimbursement, or credit to the franchised new motor vehicle dealer or to the franchised new motor vehicle dealer's account in an amount less than or equal to ten thousand dollars ($ 10,000) and that is in violation of this Article or contrary to the terms of the franchise may, prior to filing a formal petition before the Commissioner as provided in G.S. 20-301(b) or a civil action in any court of competent jurisdiction under G.S. 20-308.1, request and obtain a mediated settlement conference as provided in this subsection. Unless objection to the timeliness of the franchised new motor vehicle dealer's request for mediation under this subsection is waived in writing by the affected manufacturer, factory branch, distributor, or distributor branch, a franchised new motor vehicle dealer's request to mediate must be sent to the Commissioner within 75 days after the franchised new motor vehicle dealer's receipt of written notice from a manufacturer, factory branch, distributor, or distributor branch of the charges, debits, payments, reimbursements, or credits challenged by the franchised new motor vehicle dealer. If the franchised new motor vehicle dealer has requested in writing that the manufacturer, factory branch, distributor, or distributor branch review the questioned charges, debits, payments, reimbursements, or credits, a franchised new motor vehicle dealer's request to mediate must be sent to the Commissioner within 30 days after the franchised new motor vehicle dealer's receipt of the final written determination on the issue from the manufacturer, factory branch, distributor, or distributor branch.

(1) It is the policy and purpose of this subsection to implement a system of settlement events that are designed to reduce the cost of litigation under this Article to the general public and the parties, to focus the parties' attention on settlement rather than on trial preparation, and to provide a structured opportunity for settlement negotiations to take place.

(2) The franchised new motor vehicle dealer shall send a letter to the Commissioner by certified or registered mail, return receipt requested, identifying the actual or proposed charges the franchised new motor vehicle dealer seeks to challenge and the reason or basis for the challenge. The charges, debits, payments, reimbursements, or credits challenged by the franchised new motor vehicle dealer need not be related, and multiple issues may be resolved in a single proceeding. The franchised new motor vehicle dealer shall send a copy of the letter to the affected manufacturer, factory branch, distributor, or distributor branch, addressed to the current district, zone, or regional manager in charge of overseeing the dealer's operations, or the registered agent for acceptance of legal process in this State. Upon the mailing of a letter to the Commissioner and the manufacturer, factory branch, distributor, or distributor branch pursuant to this subsection, any chargeback to or any payment required of a franchised new motor vehicle dealer by a manufacturer, factory branch, distributor, or distributor branch shall be stayed during the pendency of the mediation. Upon the mailing of a letter to the Commissioner and manufacturer, factory branch, distributor, or distributor branch pursuant to this subsection, any statute of limitation or other time limitation for filing a petition before the Commissioner or civil action shall be tolled during the pendency of the mediation.

(3) Upon receipt of the written request of the franchised new motor vehicle dealer, the Commissioner shall appoint a mediator and send notice of that appointment to the parties. A person is qualified to serve as mediator as provided by this subdivision if the person is certified to serve as a mediator under Rule 8 of the North Carolina Rules Implementing Statewide Mediated Settlement Conferences in Superior Court Civil Actions and does not represent motor vehicle dealers or manufacturers, factory branches, distributors, or distributor branches. A mediator acting pursuant to this subdivision shall have judicial immunity in the same manner and to the same extent as a judge of the General Court of Justice.

(4) The parties shall by written agreement select a venue and schedule for the mediated settlement conference conducted under this subsection. If the parties are unable to agree on a venue and schedule, the mediator shall select a venue and schedule. Except by written agreement of all parties, a mediation proceeding and mediated settlement conference under this subsection shall be held in North Carolina.

(5) In this subsection, "mediation" means a nonbinding forum in which an impartial person, the mediator, facilitates communication between parties to promote reconciliation, settlement, or understanding among them. A mediator may not impose his or her own judgment on the issues for that of the parties.

(6) At least 10 days prior to the mediated settlement conference, the affected manufacturer, factory branch, distributor, or distributor branch shall, by certified or registered mail, return receipt requested, send the mediator and the franchised new motor vehicle dealer a detailed response to the allegations raised in the franchised new motor vehicle dealer's written request. The mediation may be conducted by officers or employees of the parties themselves without the appearance of legal counsel. However, at least 10 days prior to the mediated settlement conference, either party may give notice to the other and to the mediator of its intention to appear at the mediation with legal counsel, in which event either party may appear at the mediation with legal counsel.

(7) A mediation proceeding conducted pursuant to this subsection shall be complete not later than the sixtieth day after the date of the Commissioner's notice of the appointment of the mediator; this deadline may be extended by written agreement of the parties. The parties shall be solely responsible for the compensation and expenses of the mediator on a 50/50 basis. The Commissioner is not liable for the compensation paid or to be paid a mediator employed pursuant to this subsection.

(8) A party may attend a mediated settlement conference telephonically in lieu of

Chapter 20

personal appearance. If a party or other person required to attend a mediated settlement conference fails to attend without good cause, the Commissioner may impose upon the party or person any appropriate monetary sanction, including the payment of fines, attorneys' fees, mediator fees, expenses, and loss of earnings incurred by persons attending the conference.

(9) If the mediation fails to result in a resolution of the dispute, the franchised new motor vehicle dealer may proceed as provided in G.S. 20-301(b) and G.S. 20-308.1. Upon the filing of a petition pursuant to G.S. 20-301(b) or a civil action pursuant to G.S. 20-308.1, the affected manufacturer, factory branch, distributor, or distributor branch shall not require payment from the dealer, or debit or charge the dealer's account, unless and until a final judgment supporting the payment or charge has been rendered by the Commissioner or court. All communications made during a mediation proceeding, including, but not limited to, those communications made during a mediated settlement conference are presumed to be made in compromise negotiation and shall be governed by Rule 408 of the North Carolina Rules of Evidence.

History.
2001-510, s. 1; 2011-290, s. 4

§ 20-302. Rules and regulations

The Commissioner may make such rules and regulations, not inconsistent with the provisions of this Article, as he shall deem necessary or proper for the effective administration and enforcement of this Article, provided that the Commissioner shall make a copy of such rules and regulations available on a Web site maintained by the Division or the Department of Transportation 30 days prior to the effective date of such rules and regulations.

History.
1955, c. 1243, s. 18; 2018-74, s. 8

§ 20-303. Installment sales to be evidenced by written instrument; statement to be delivered to buyer

(a) Every retail installment sale shall be evidenced by one or more instruments in writing, which shall contain all the agreements of the parties and shall be signed by the buyer.

(b) For every retail installment sale, prior to or about the time of the delivery of the motor vehicle, the seller shall deliver to the buyer a written statement describing clearly the motor vehicle sold to the buyer, the cash sale price

thereof, the cash paid down by the buyer, the amount credited the buyer for any trade-in and a description of the motor vehicle traded, the amount of the finance charge, the amount of any other charge specifying its purpose, the net balance due from the buyer, the terms of the payment of such net balance and a summary of any insurance protection to be effected. The written statement shall be signed by the buyer.

History.
1955, c. 1243, s. 19; 2007-513, s. 1

§ 20-304. Coercion of retail dealer by manufacturer or distributor in connection with installment sales contract prohibited

(a) It shall be unlawful for any manufacturer, wholesaler or distributor, or any officer, agent or representative of either, to coerce, or attempt to coerce, any retail motor vehicle dealer or prospective retail motor vehicle dealer in this State to sell, assign or transfer any retail installment sales contract, obtained by such dealer in connection with the sale by him in this State of motor vehicles manufactured or sold by such manufacturer, wholesaler, or distributor, to a specified finance company or class of such companies, or to any other specified persons, by any of the acts or means hereinafter set forth, namely:

(1) By any statement, suggestion, promise or threat that such manufacturer, wholesaler, or distributor will in any manner benefit or injure such dealer, whether such statement, suggestion, threat or promise is expressed or implied, or made directly or indirectly,

(2) By any act that will benefit or injure such dealer,

(3) By any contract, or any expressed or implied offer of contract, made directly or indirectly to such dealer, for handling motor vehicles, on the condition that such dealer sell, assign or transfer his retail installment sales contract thereon, in this State, to a specified finance company or class of such companies, or to any other specified person,

(4) By any expressed or implied statement or representation, made directly or indirectly, that such dealer is under any obligation whatsoever to sell, assign or transfer any of his retail sales contracts, in this State, on motor vehicles manufactured or sold by such manufacturer, wholesaler, or distributor to such finance company, or class of companies, or other specified person, because of any relationship or affiliation between such manufacturer, wholesaler, or distributor and such finance

company or companies or such other specified person or persons.

(b) Any such statements, threats, promises, acts, contracts, or offers of contracts, when the effect thereof may be to lessen or eliminate competition, or tend to create a monopoly, are declared unfair trade practices and unfair methods of competition and against the public policy of this State, are unlawful and are hereby prohibited.

History.
1955, c. 1243, s. 20

§ 20-305. Coercing dealer to accept commodities not ordered; threatening to cancel franchise; preventing transfer of ownership; granting additional franchises; terminating franchises without good cause; preventing family succession

It shall be unlawful for any manufacturer, factory branch, distributor, or distributor branch, or any field representative, officer, agent, or any representative whatsoever of any of them:

(1) To require, coerce, or attempt to coerce any dealer to accept delivery of any motor vehicle or vehicles, parts or accessories therefor, or any other commodities, which shall not have been ordered by that dealer, or to accept delivery of any motor vehicle or vehicles which have been equipped in a manner other than as specified by the dealer.

(2) To require, coerce, or attempt to coerce any dealer to enter into any agreement with such manufacturer, factory branch, distributor, or distributor branch, or representative thereof, or do any other act unfair to such dealer, by threatening to cancel any franchise existing between such manufacturer, factory branch, distributor, distributor branch, or representative thereof, and such dealer;

(3) *(See Editor's note for applicability)* Unfairly without due regard to the equities of the dealer, and without just provocation, to cancel the franchise of such dealer;

(4) Notwithstanding the terms of any franchise agreement, to prevent or refuse to approve the sale or transfer of the ownership of a dealership by the sale of the business, stock transfer, or otherwise, or the transfer, sale or assignment of a dealer franchise, or a change in the executive management or principal operator of the dealership, change in use of an existing facility to provide for the sales or service of one or more additional line-makes of new motor vehicles, or relocation of the dealership to another site within the dealership's relevant market area, if the Commissioner has determined, if requested in writing by the dealer within 30 days after receipt of an objection to the proposed transfer, sale, assignment, relocation, or change, and after a hearing on the matter, that the failure to permit or honor the transfer, sale, assignment, relocation, or change is unreasonable under the circumstances.

a. No franchise may be transferred, sold, assigned, relocated, or the executive management or principal operators changed, or the use of an existing facility changed, unless the franchisor has been given at least 30 days' prior written notice of all of the following:

1. The proposed transferee's name and address, financial ability, and qualifications of the proposed transferee, a copy of the purchase agreement between the dealership and the proposed transferee.

2. The identity and qualifications of the persons proposed to be involved in executive management or as principal operators.

3. The location and site plans of any proposed relocation or change in use of a dealership facility.

b. If the franchisor objects to the proposed transfer, sale, assignment, relocation, or change, the franchisor shall send the dealership and the proposed transferee notice of objection, by registered or certified mail, return receipt requested, to the proposed transfer, sale, assignment, relocation, or change within 30 days after receipt of notice from the dealer, as provided in this section. The notice of objection shall state in detail all factual and legal bases for the objection on the part of the franchisor to the proposed transfer, sale, assignment, relocation, or change that is specifically referenced in this subdivision. An objection to a proposed transfer, sale, assignment, relocation, or change in the executive management or principal operator of the dealership or change in the use of the facility may only be premised upon the factual and legal bases specifically referenced in this subdivision or G.S. 20-305(11), as it relates to change in the use of a facility. A manufacturer's notice of objection which is based upon factual or legal issues that are not specifically referenced in this subdivision or G.S. 20-305(11) with respect to a change in the use of an existing facility as being issues upon which the Commissioner shall base his determination shall not be effective to preserve the franchisor's right to object to the proposed transfer sale, assignment, relocation, or change, provided the dealership or proposed transferee has submitted written notice, as required above, as to the proposed transferee's name and address, financial ability, and qualifications of the proposed transferee, a copy of the purchase agreement between the dealership and the proposed transferee, the identity and qualifications of the persons proposed to be involved in the executive management or as principal operators, and the location and site plans of any proposed relocation or change in the use of an existing facility.

c. Failure by the franchisor to send notice of objection within 30 days shall constitute waiver by the franchisor of any right to object to the proposed transfer, sale, assignment, relocation, or change. If the franchisor requires additional information to complete its review, the franchisor shall notify the dealership within 15 days after receipt of the notice to franchisor under sub-subdivision a. of this subdivision. If the franchisor fails to request additional information from the dealer or proposed transferee within 15 days of receipt of this initial information, the 30-day time period within which the franchisor may provide notice of objection shall be deemed to run from the initial receipt date. Otherwise, the 30-day time period within which the franchisor may provide notice of objection shall run from the date the franchisor has received the supplemental information requested from the dealer or proposed transferee; provided, however, that failure by the franchisor to send notice of objection within 60 days of the franchisor's receipt of the initial information from the dealer shall constitute waiver by the franchisor of any right to object to the proposed transfer, sale, assignment, relocation, or change.

d. With respect to a proposed transfer of ownership, sale, or assignment, the sole issue for determination by the Commissioner and the sole issue upon which the Commissioner shall hear or consider evidence is whether, by reason of lack of good moral character, lack of general business experience, or lack of financial ability, the proposed transferee is unfit to own the dealership. For purposes of this subdivision, the

refusal by the manufacturer to accept a proposed transferee who is of good moral character and who otherwise meets the written, reasonable, and uniformly applied business experience and financial requirements, if any, required by the manufacturer of owners of its franchised automobile dealerships is presumed to demonstrate the manufacturer's failure to prove that the proposed transferee is unfit to own the dealership.

e. With respect to a proposed change in the executive management or principal operator of the dealership, the sole issue for determination by the Commissioner and the sole issue on which the Commissioner shall hear or consider evidence shall be whether, by reason of lack of training, lack of prior experience, poor past performance, or poor character, the proposed candidate for a position within the executive management or as principal operator of the dealership is unfit for the position. For purposes of this subdivision, the refusal by the manufacturer to accept a proposed candidate for executive management or as principal operator who is of good moral character and who otherwise meets the written, reasonable, and uniformly applied standards or qualifications, if any, of the manufacturer relating to the business experience and prior performance of executive management required by the manufacturers of its dealers is presumed to demonstrate the manufacturer's failure to prove the proposed candidate for executive management or as principal operator is unfit to serve the capacity.

f. With respect to a proposed change in use of a dealership facility to provide for the sales or service of one or more additional line-makes of new motor vehicles, the sole issue for determination by the Commissioner is whether the new motor vehicle dealer has a reasonable line of credit for each make or line of motor vehicle and remains in compliance with any reasonable capital standards and facilities requirements of the manufacturer or distributor. The reasonable facilities requirements of the manufacturer or distributor shall not include any requirement that a new motor vehicle dealer establish or maintain exclusive facilities, personnel, or display space.

g. With respect to a proposed relocation or other proposed change, the issue for determination by the Commissioner is whether the proposed relocation or other change is unreasonable under the circumstances. For purposes of this subdivision, the refusal by the manufacturer to agree to a proposed relocation which meets the written, reasonable, and uniformly applied standards or criteria, if any, of the manufacturer relating to dealer relocations is presumed to demonstrate that the manufacturer's failure to prove the proposed relocation is unreasonable under the circumstances.

h. The manufacturer shall have the burden of proof before the Commissioner under this subdivision.

i. It is unlawful for a manufacturer to, in any way, do any of the following:

1. Condition its approval of a proposed transfer, sale, assignment, change in the dealer's executive management, principal operator, or appointment of a designated successor, on the existing or proposed dealer's willingness to construct a new facility, renovate the existing facility, acquire or refrain from acquiring one or more line-makes of vehicles, separate or divest one or more line-makes of vehicle, or establish or maintain exclusive facilities, personnel, or display space.

2. Condition its approval of a proposed relocation on the existing or proposed dealer's willingness to acquire or refrain from acquiring one or more line-makes of vehicles, separate or divest one or more line-makes of vehicle, or establish or maintain exclusive facilities, personnel, or display space. The opinion or determination of a franchisor that the continued existence of one of its franchised dealers situated in this State is not viable, or that the dealer holds or fails to hold licensing rights for the sale of other line-makes of vehicles in a manner consistent with the franchisor's existing or future distribution or marketing plans, shall not constitute a lawful basis for the franchisor to fail or refuse to approve a dealer's proposed change in use of a dealership facility or relocation: provided, however, that nothing contained in this subdivision shall be deemed to prevent or prohibit a franchisor from failing to approve a dealer's proposed relocation on grounds that the specific site or facility proposed by the dealer is otherwise unreasonable under the circumstances. Approval of a relocation pursuant to this subdivision shall not in itself constitute the franchisor's representation or assurance of the dealer's viability at that location.

3. Condition, directly or indirectly, the approval of the sale or transfer of the ownership of a dealership by the sale of the business, stock transfer, or otherwise, or the transfer, sale, succession, or assignment of a dealer's franchise, or a change in the executive management or principal operator of the dealership upon the existing or proposed dealer's willingness to renovate, construct, or relocate the dealership facility, or to enroll in a facility program; provided, however, that this provision shall not apply to or affect the validity of an ownership transfer or change in executive management or principal operator of the dealership that occurred prior to July 1, 2021. This sub-sub-subdivision shall not be construed to annul or impair an existing agreement regarding the renovation, construction, or relocation of a dealership facility that existed prior to the transfer, sale, succession, assignment of the dealer's franchise, change in executive management or change in principal operator. This sub-sub-subdivision does not prevent a manufacturer or distributor from requiring changes to a facility that are necessary in order to sell or service a motor vehicle.

4. Condition, directly or indirectly, the approval of the sale or transfer of the ownership of a dealership by the sale of the business, stock transfer, or otherwise, or the transfer, sale, succession, or assignment of a dealer's franchise, or a change in the executive management or principal operator of the dealership, or a dealer's proposed relocation of the dealership facility, or a dealer's satisfaction of the terms of any incentive program or contest, upon the existing or proposed dealer's willingness to enter into a right of first refusal in favor of the manufacturer.

(5) To enter into a franchise establishing an additional new motor vehicle dealer or

relocating an existing new motor vehicle dealer into a relevant market area where the same line make is then represented without first notifying in writing the Commissioner and each new motor vehicle dealer in that line make in the relevant market area of the intention to establish an additional dealer or to relocate an existing dealer within or into that market area. Within 30 days of receiving such notice or within 30 days after the end of any appeal procedure provided by the manufacturer, any new motor vehicle dealer may file with the Commissioner a protest to the establishing or relocating of the new motor vehicle dealer. When a protest is filed, the Commissioner shall promptly inform the manufacturer that a timely protest has been filed, and that the manufacturer shall not establish or relocate the proposed new motor vehicle dealer until the Commissioner has held a hearing and has determined that there is good cause for permitting the addition or relocation of such new motor vehicle dealer.

a. This section does not apply:

1. To the relocation of an existing new motor vehicle dealer within that dealer's relevant market area, provided that the relocation not be at a site within 10 miles of a licensed new motor vehicle dealer for the same line make of motor vehicle. If this sub-subdivision is applicable, only dealers trading in the same line-make of vehicle that are located within the 10-mile radius shall be entitled to notice from the manufacturer and have the protest rights afforded under this section.

2. If the proposed additional new motor vehicle dealer is to be established at or within two miles of a location at which a former licensed new motor vehicle dealer for the same line make of new vehicle had ceased operating within the previous two years.

3. To the relocation of an existing new motor vehicle dealer within two miles of the existing site of the new motor vehicle dealership if the franchise has been operating on a regular basis from the existing site for a minimum of three years immediately preceding the relocation.

4. To the relocation of an existing new motor vehicle dealer if the proposed site of the relocated new motor vehicle dealership is further away from all other new motor vehicle dealers of the same line make in that relevant market area.

5. Repealed by Session Laws 2008-156, s. 3, effective August 3, 2008.

b. In determining whether good cause has been established for not entering into or relocating an additional new motor vehicle dealer for the same line make, the Commissioner shall take into consideration the existing circumstances, including, but not limited to:

1. The permanency of the investment of both the existing and proposed additional new motor vehicle dealers;

2. Growth or decline in population, density of population, and new car registrations in the relevant market area;

3. Effect on the consuming public in the relevant market area;

4. Whether it is injurious or beneficial to the public welfare for an additional new motor vehicle dealer to be established;

5. Whether the new motor vehicle dealers of the same line make in that relevant market area are providing adequate competition and convenient customer care for the motor vehicles of the same line make in the market area which shall include the adequacy of motor vehicle sales and service facilities, equipment, supply of motor vehicle parts, and qualified service personnel;

6. Whether the establishment of an additional new motor vehicle dealer or relocation of an existing new motor vehicle dealer in the relevant market area would increase competition in a manner such as to be in the long-term public interest; and

7. The effect on the relocating dealer of a denial of its relocation into the relevant market area.

c. The Commissioner shall try to conduct the hearing and render his final determination if possible, within 180 days after a protest is filed.

d. Any parties to a hearing by the Commissioner concerning the establishment or relocating of a new motor vehicle dealer shall have a right of review of the decision in a court of competent jurisdiction pursuant to Chapter 150B of the General Statutes.

e. In a hearing involving a proposed additional dealership, the manufacturer or distributor has the burden of proof under this section. In a proceeding involving the relocation of an existing dealership, the dealer seeking to relocate has the burden of proof under this section.

f. If the Commissioner determines, following a hearing, that good cause exists for permitting the proposed additional or relocated motor vehicle dealership, the dealer seeking the proposed additional or relocated motor vehicle dealership must, within two years, obtain a license from the Commissioner for the sale of vehicles at the relevant site, and actually commence operations at the site selling new motor vehicles of all line makes, as permitted by the Commissioner. Failure to obtain a permit and commence sales within two years shall constitute waiver by the dealer of the dealer's right to the additional or relocated dealership, requiring renotification, a new hearing, and a new determination as provided in this section. If the Commissioner fails to determine that good cause exists for permitting the proposed additional or relocated motor vehicle dealership, the manufacturer seeking the proposed additional dealership or dealer seeking to relocate may not again provide notice of its intention or otherwise attempt to establish an additional dealership or relocate to any location within 10 miles of the site of the original proposed additional dealership or relocation site for a minimum of three years from the date of the Commissioner's determination.

g. *(See Editor's note for applicability)* For purposes of this subdivision, the addition, creation, or operation of a "satellite" or other facility, not physically part of or contiguous to an existing licensed new motor vehicle dealer, whether or not owned or operated by a person or other entity holding a franchise as defined by G.S. 20-286(8a), at which warranty service work authorized or reimbursed by a manufacturer is performed or at which new motor vehicles are offered for sale to the public, shall be considered an additional new motor vehicle dealer requiring a showing of good cause, prior notification to existing new motor vehicle dealers of the same line make of vehicle within the relevant market area by the manufacturer and the opportunity for a hearing before the Commissioner as provided in this subdivision.

(6) Notwithstanding the terms, provisions or conditions of any franchise or notwithstanding the terms or provisions of any waiver, to terminate, cancel or fail to renew any franchise with a licensed new motor vehicle dealer unless the manufacturer has satisfied the notice requirements of sub-subdivision c. of this subdivision and the Commissioner has determined, if requested in writing by the dealer within (i) the time period specified in G.S. 20-305(6) c.1.II., III., or IV., as applicable, or (ii) the effective date of the franchise termination specified or proposed by the manufacturer in the notice of termination, whichever period of time is longer, and after a hearing on the matter, that there is good cause for the termination, cancellation, or nonrenewal of the franchise and that the manufacturer has acted in good faith as defined in this act regarding the termination, cancellation or nonrenewal. When such a petition is made to the Commissioner by a dealer for determination as to the existence of good cause and good faith for the termination, cancellation or nonrenewal of a franchise, the Commissioner shall promptly inform the manufacturer that a timely petition has been filed, and the franchise in question shall continue in effect pending the Commissioner's decision. The Commissioner shall try to conduct the hearing and render a final determination within 180 days after a petition has been filed. If the termination, cancellation or nonrenewal is pursuant to G.S. 20-305(6)c.1.III. then the Commissioner shall give the proceeding priority consideration and shall try to render his final determination no later than 90 days after the petition has been filed. Any parties to a hearing by the Commissioner under this section shall have a right of review of the decision in a court of competent jurisdiction pursuant to Chapter 150B of the General Statutes. Any determination of the Commissioner under this section finding that good cause exists for the nonrenewal, cancellation, or termination of any franchise shall automatically be stayed during any period that the affected dealer shall have the right to judicial review or appeal of the determination before the superior court or any other appellate court and during the pendency of any appeal; provided, however, that within 30 days of entry of the Commissioner's order, the affected dealer provide such security as the reviewing court, in its discretion, may deem appropriate for payment of such costs and damages as may be incurred or sustained by the manufacturer

by reason of and during the pendency of the stay. Although the right of the affected dealer to such stay is automatic, the procedure for providing such security and for the award of damages, if any, to the manufacturer upon dissolution of the stay shall be in accordance with G.S. 1A-1, Rule 65(d) and (e). No such security provided by or on behalf of any affected dealer shall be forfeited or damages awarded against a dealer who obtains a stay under this subdivision in the event the ownership of the affected dealership is subsequently transferred, sold, or assigned to a third party in accordance with this subdivision or subdivision (4) of this section and the closing on such transfer, sale, or assignment occurs no later than 180 days after the date of entry of the Commissioner's order. Furthermore, unless and until the termination, cancellation, or nonrenewal of a dealer's franchise shall finally become effective, in light of any stay or any order of the Commissioner determining that good cause exists for the termination, cancellation, or nonrenewal of a dealer's franchise as provided in this subdivision, a dealer who receives a notice of termination, cancellation, or nonrenewal from a manufacturer as provided in this subdivision shall continue to have the same rights to assign, sell, or transfer the franchise to a third party under the franchise and as permitted under G.S. 20-305(4) as if notice of the termination had not been given by the manufacturer. Any franchise under notice or threat of termination, cancellation, or nonrenewal by the manufacturer which is duly transferred in accordance with G.S. 20-305(4) shall not be subject to termination by reason of failure of performance or breaches of the franchise on the part of the transferor.

a. Notwithstanding the terms, provisions or conditions of any franchise or the terms or provisions of any waiver, good cause shall exist for the purposes of a termination, cancellation or nonrenewal when:

1. There is a failure by the new motor vehicle dealer to comply with a provision of the franchise which provision is both reasonable and of material significance to the franchise relationship provided that the dealer has been notified in writing of the failure within 180 days after the manufacturer first acquired knowledge of such failure;

2. If the failure by the new motor vehicle dealer relates to the performance of the new motor vehicle dealer in sales or service, then good cause shall be defined as the failure of the new motor vehicle dealer to comply with reasonable performance criteria established by the manufacturer if the new motor vehicle dealer was apprised by the manufacturer in writing of the failure; and

I. The notification stated that notice was provided of failure of performance pursuant to this section;

II. The new motor vehicle dealer was afforded a reasonable opportunity, for a period of not less than 180 days, to comply with the criteria; and

III. The new motor vehicle dealer failed to demonstrate substantial progress towards compliance with the manufacturer's performance criteria during such period and the new motor vehicle dealer's failure was not primarily due to economic or market factors within the dealer's relevant market area which were beyond the dealer's control.

b. The manufacturer shall have the burden of proof under this section.

c. **Notification of Termination, Cancellation and Nonrenewal. --**

1. Notwithstanding the terms, provisions or conditions of any franchise prior to the termination, cancellation or nonrenewal of any franchise, the manufacturer shall furnish notification of termination, cancellation or nonrenewal to the new motor vehicle dealer as follows:

I. In the manner described in G.S. 20-305(6)c2 below; and

II. Not less than 90 days prior to the effective date of such termination, cancellation or nonrenewal; or

III. Not less than 15 days prior to the effective date of such termination, cancellation or nonrenewal with respect to any of the following:

A. Insolvency of the new motor vehicle dealer, or filing of any petition by or against the new motor vehicle dealer under any bankruptcy or receivership law;

B. Failure of the new motor vehicle dealer to conduct its

customary sales and service operations during its customary business hours for seven consecutive business days, except for acts of God or circumstances beyond the direct control of the new motor vehicle dealer;

C. Revocation of any license which the new motor vehicle dealer is required to have to operate a dealership;

D. Conviction of a felony involving moral turpitude, under the laws of this State or any other state, or territory, or the District of Columbia.

IV. Not less than 180 days prior to the effective date of such termination, cancellation, or nonrenewal which occurs as a result of any change in ownership, operation, or control of all or any part of the business of the manufacturer, factory branch, distributor, or distributor branch whether by sale or transfer of assets, corporate stock or other equity interest, assignment, merger, consolidation, combination, joint venture, redemption, operation of law or otherwise; or the termination, suspension, or cessation of a part or all of the business operations of the manufacturers, factory branch, distributor, or distributor branch; or discontinuance of the sale of the line-make or brand, or a change in distribution system by the manufacturer whether through a change in distributors or the manufacturer's decision to cease conducting business through a distributor altogether.

V. Unless the failure by the new motor vehicle dealer relates to the performance of the new motor vehicle dealer in sales or service, not more than one year after the manufacturer first acquired knowledge of the basic facts comprising the failure.

2. Notification under this section shall be in writing; shall be by certified mail or personally delivered to the new motor vehicle dealer; and shall contain:

I. A statement of intention to terminate, cancel or not to renew the franchise;

II. A detailed statement of all of the material reasons for the termination, cancellation or nonrenewal; and

III. The date on which the termination, cancellation or nonrenewal takes effect.

3. Notification provided in G.S. 20-305(6)c1II of 90 days prior to the effective date of such termination, cancellation or renewal may run concurrent with the 180 days designated in G.S. 20-305(6)a2II provided the notification is clearly designated by a separate written document mailed by certified mail or personally delivered to the new motor vehicle dealer.

d. Payments.

1. Notwithstanding the terms of any franchise, agreement, or waiver, upon the termination, nonrenewal or cancellation of any franchise by the manufacturer or distributor, the cessation of business or the termination, nonrenewal, or cancellation of any franchise by any new motor vehicle dealer located in this State, or upon any of the occurrences set forth in G.S. 20-305(6)c.1.IV., the manufacturer or distributor shall purchase from and compensate the new motor vehicle dealer for all of the following:

I. Each new and unsold motor vehicle within the new motor vehicle dealer's inventory that has been acquired within 24 months of the effective date of the termination from the manufacturer or distributor or another same line-make dealer in the ordinary course of business, and which has not been substantially altered or damaged to the prejudice of the manufacturer or distributor while in the new motor vehicle dealer's possession, and which has been driven less than 1,000 miles or, for purposes of a recreational vehicle motor home as defined in G.S. 20-4.01(32b) c., less than 1,500 miles following the original date of delivery to the dealer, and for which no certificate of title

Chapter 20

has been issued. For purposes of this sub-subdivision, the term "ordinary course of business" shall include inventory transfers of all new, same line-make vehicles between affiliated dealerships, or otherwise between dealerships having common or interrelated ownership, provided that the transfer is not intended solely for the purpose of benefiting from the termination assistance described in this sub-subdivision.

II. Unused, undamaged and unsold supplies and parts purchased from the manufacturer or distributor or sources approved by the manufacturer or distributor, at a price not to exceed the original manufacturer's price to the dealer, provided such supplies and parts are currently offered for sale by the manufacturer or distributor in its current parts catalogs and are in salable condition.

III. Equipment, signs, and furnishings that have not been substantially altered or damaged and that have been required by the manufacturer or distributor to be purchased by the new motor vehicle dealer from the manufacturer or distributor, or their approved sources.

IV. Special tools that have not been altered or damaged, normal wear and tear excepted, and that have been required by the manufacturer or distributor to be purchased by the new motor vehicle dealer from the manufacturer or distributor, or their approved sources within five years immediately preceding the termination, nonrenewal or cancellation of the franchise. The amount of compensation which shall be paid to the new motor vehicle dealer by the manufacturer or distributor shall be the net acquisition price if the item was acquired in the 12 months preceding the date of receipt of the dealer's request for compensation; seventy-five percent (75%) of

the net acquisition price if the item was acquired between 13 and 24 months preceding the dealer's request for compensation; fifty percent (50%) of the net acquisition price if the item was acquired between 25 and 36 months preceding the dealer's request for compensation; twenty-five percent (25%) of the net acquisition price if the item was acquired between 37 and 60 months preceding the dealer's request for compensation.

2. The compensation provided above shall be paid by the manufacturer or distributor not later than 90 days after the manufacturer or distributor has received notice in writing from or on behalf of the new motor vehicle dealer specifying the elements of compensation requested by the dealer; provided the new motor vehicle dealer has, or can obtain, clear title to the inventory and has conveyed, or can convey, title and possession of the same to the manufacturer or distributor. Within 15 days after receipt of the dealer's written request for compensation, the manufacturer or distributor shall send the dealer detailed written instructions and forms required by the manufacturer or distributor to effectuate the receipt of the compensation requested by the dealer. The manufacturer or distributor shall be obligated to pay or reimburse the dealer for any transportation charges associated with the repurchase obligations of the manufacturer or distributor under this sub-subdivision. The manufacturer or distributor shall also compensate the dealer for any handling, packing, or similar payments contemplated in the franchise. In no event may the manufacturer or distributor charge the dealer any handling, restocking, or other similar costs or fees associated with items repurchased by the manufacturer under this sub-subdivision.

3. In addition to the other payments set forth in this section, if a termination, cancellation, or nonrenewal is premised upon any of the occurrences set forth in G.S. 20-305(6)c.1.IV., then

the manufacturer or distributor shall be liable to the dealer for an amount at least equivalent to the fair market value of the franchise on (i) the date the franchisor announces the action which results in termination, cancellation, or nonrenewal; or (ii) the date the action which results in termination, cancellation, or nonrenewal first became general knowledge; or (iii) the day 18 months prior to the date on which the notice of termination, cancellation, or nonrenewal is issued, whichever amount is higher. Payment is due not later than 90 days after the manufacturer or distributor has received notice in writing from, or on behalf of, the new motor vehicle dealer specifying the elements of compensation requested by the dealer. Any contract, agreement, or release entered into between any manufacturer and any dealer in which the dealer waives the dealer's right to receive monetary compensation in any sum or amount not less than the fair market value of the franchise as provided in this subdivision, including any contract, agreement, or release in which the dealer would accept the right to continue to offer and be compensated for service, parts, or both service and parts provided by the dealer in lieu of receiving all or a portion of the fair market value of the franchise, shall be voidable at the election of the dealer within 90 days of the effective date of the agreement. If the termination, cancellation, or nonrenewal is due to a manufacturer's change in distributors, but the line-make or brand in this State would continue to be sold through the new distributor, the manufacturer may avoid paying fair market value to the dealer if the new distributor or the manufacturer offers the dealer a franchise agreement with terms acceptable to the dealer.

e. Dealership Facilities Assistance upon Termination, Cancellation or Nonrenewal.

In the event of the occurrence of any of the events specified in G.S. 20-305(6)d.1. above, except termination, cancellation or nonrenewal for license revocation, conviction of a crime involving moral turpitude, or fraud by a dealer-owner:

1. Subject to sub-sub-subdivision 3. of this sub-subdivision, if the new motor vehicle dealer is leasing the dealership facilities from a lessor other than the manufacturer or distributor, the manufacturer or distributor shall pay the new motor vehicle dealer a sum equivalent to the rent for the unexpired term of the lease or three year's rent, whichever is less, or such longer term as is provided in the franchise agreement between the dealer and manufacturer; except that, in the case of motorcycle dealerships, the manufacturer shall pay the new motor vehicle dealer the sum equivalent to the rent for the unexpired term of the lease or one year's rent, whichever is less, or such longer term as provided in the franchise agreement between the dealer and manufacturer; or

2. Subject to sub-sub-subdivision 3. of this sub-subdivision, if the new motor vehicle dealer owns the dealership facilities, the manufacturer or distributor shall pay the new motor vehicle dealer a sum equivalent to the reasonable rental value of the dealership facilities for three years, or for one year in the case of motorcycle dealerships.

3. In order to be entitled to facilities assistance from the manufacturer or distributor, as provided in this sub-subdivision, the dealer, owner, or lessee, as the case may be, shall have the obligation to mitigate damages by listing the demised premises for lease or sublease with a licensed real estate agent within 30 days after the effective date of the termination of the franchise and thereafter by reasonably cooperating with said real estate agent in the performance of the agent's duties and responsibilities. In the event that the dealer, owner, or lessee is able to lease or sublease the demised premises, the dealer shall be obligated to pay the manufacturer the net revenue received from such mitigation up to the total amount of facilities assistance which the dealer has received from the manufacturer pursuant to sub-subdivisions 1. and 2. To the extent and for such uses and purposes as may be consistent with the terms of the lease, a manufacturer who pays facilities assistance to a dealer under this sub-subdivision shall be entitled to occupy and use the dealership facilities during the years for which the manufacturer shall have paid rent under sub-subdivisions 1. and 2.

4. In the event the termination relates to fewer than all of the franchises operated by the dealer at a single location, the amount of facilities assistance which the manufacturer or distributor is required to pay the dealer under this sub-subdivision

Chapter 20

shall be based on the proportion of gross revenue received from the sale and lease of new vehicles by the dealer and from the dealer's parts and service operations during the three years immediately preceding the effective date of the termination (or any shorter period that the dealer may have held these franchises) of the line-makes being terminated, in relation to the gross revenue received from the sale and lease of all line-makes of new vehicles by the dealer and from the total of the dealer's and parts and service operations from this location during the same three-year period.

5. The compensation required for facilities assistance under this sub-subdivision shall be paid by the manufacturer or distributor within 90 days after the manufacturer or distributor has received notice in writing from, or on behalf of, a new motor vehicle dealer specifying the elements of compensation requested by the dealer.

f. The provisions of sub-subdivision e. above shall not be applicable when the termination, nonrenewal, or cancellation of the franchise agreement by a new motor vehicle dealer is the result of the sale of assets or stock of the motor vehicle dealership. The provisions of sub-subdivisions d. and e. above shall not be applicable when the termination, nonrenewal, or cancellation of the franchise agreement is at the initiation of a new motor vehicle dealer of recreational vehicle motor homes, as defined in G.S. 20-4.01(32b) c., provided that at the time of the termination, nonrenewal, or cancellation, the recreational vehicle manufacturer or distributor has paid to the dealer all claims for warranty or recall work, including payments for labor, parts, and other expenses, which were submitted by the dealer 30 days or more prior to the date of termination, nonrenewal, or cancellation.

g. A franchise shall continue in full force and operation notwithstanding a change, in whole or in part, of an established plan or system of distribution of the motor vehicles offered for sale under the franchise. The appointment of a new manufacturer, factory branch, distributor, or distributor branch for motor vehicles offered for sale under the franchise agreement shall be deemed to be a change of an established plan or system of distribution.

Upon the occurrence of the change, the Division shall deny an application of a manufacturer, factory branch, distributor, or distributor branch for a license or license renewal unless the applicant for a license as a manufacturer, factory branch, distributor, or distributor branch offers to each motor vehicle dealer who is a party to a franchise for that line make, without any separate or additional fee or charge, a new franchise agreement containing substantially the same provisions which were contained in the previous franchise agreement or files an affidavit with the Division acknowledging its undertaking to assume and fulfill, without any separate or additional fee or charge to its dealers, the rights, duties, and obligations of its predecessor under the previous franchise agreement. Should the Division fail to deny an application following the change, as required by this subsection, the Division shall then deny any subsequent renewal of such license until such time as the manufacturer, factory branch, distributor, or distributor branch offers to each motor vehicle dealer who is a party to a franchise for that line make a new franchise agreement on substantially the same provisions which were contained in the previous franchise agreement.

(7) Notwithstanding the terms of any contract or agreement, to prevent or refuse to honor the succession to a dealership, including the franchise, by a motor vehicle dealer's designated successor as provided for under this subsection.

a. Any owner of a new motor vehicle dealership may appoint by will, or any other written instrument, a designated successor to succeed in the respective ownership interest or interest as principal operator of the owner in the new motor vehicle dealership, including the franchise, upon the death or incapacity of the owner or principal operator. In order for succession to the position of principal operator to occur by operation of law in accordance with sub-subdivision c. below, the owner's choice of a successor must be approved by the dealer, in accordance with the dealer's bylaws, if applicable, either prior or subsequent to the death or incapacity of the existing principal operator.

b. Any objections by a manufacturer or distributor to an

owner's appointment of a designated successor shall be asserted in accordance with the following procedure:

1. Within 30 days after receiving written notice of the identity of the owner's designated successor and general information as to the financial ability and qualifications of the designated successor, the franchisor shall send the owner and designated successor notice of objection, by registered or certified mail, return receipt requested, to the appointment of the designated successor. The notice of objection shall state in detail all facts which constitute the basis for the contention on the part of the manufacturer or distributor that good cause, as defined in this sub-subdivision below, exists for rejection of the designated successor. Failure by the franchisor to send notice of objection within 30 days and otherwise as provided in this sub-subdivision shall constitute waiver by the franchisor of any right to object to the appointment of the designated successor.

2. Any time within 30 days of receipt of the manufacturer's notice of objection the owner or the designated successor may file a request in writing with the Commissioner that the Commissioner hold an evidentiary hearing and determine whether good cause exists for rejection of the designated successor. When such a request is filed, the Commissioner shall promptly inform the affected manufacturer or distributor that a timely request has been filed.

3. The Commissioner shall endeavor to hold the evidentiary hearing required under this sub-subdivision and render a determination within 180 days after receipt of the written request from the owner or designated successor. In determining whether good cause exists for rejection of the owner's appointed designated

successor, the manufacturer or distributor has the burden of proving that the designated successor is a person who is not of good moral character or does not meet the franchisor's existing written and reasonable standards and, considering the volume of sales and service of the new motor vehicle dealer, uniformly applied minimum business experience standards in the market area for the proposed principal operator of the dealership.

4. Any parties to a hearing by the Commissioner concerning whether good cause exists for the rejection of the dealer's designated successor shall have a right of review of the decision in a court of competent jurisdiction pursuant to Chapter 150B of the General Statutes.

5. Nothing in this subsubdivision shall preclude a manufacturer or distributor from, upon its receipt of written notice from an owner of the identity of the owner's designated successor, requiring that the designated successor promptly provide personal and financial data that is reasonably necessary to determine the financial ability and qualifications of the designated successor; provided, however, that such a request for additional information shall not delay any of the time periods or constraints contained herein.

6. In the event death or incapacity of the owner or principal operator occurs prior to the time a manufacturer or distributor receives notice of the owner's appointment of a designated successor or before the Commissioner has rendered a determination as provided above, the existing franchise shall remain in effect and the designated successor shall be deemed to have succeeded to all of the owner's or principal operator's rights and obligations in the dealership and under the franchise until a determination

is made by the Commissioner or the rights of the parties have otherwise become fixed in accordance with this sub-subdivision.

c. Except as otherwise provided in sub-subdivision d. of this subdivision, any designated successor of a deceased or incapacitated owner or principal operator of a new motor vehicle dealership appointed by such owner in substantial compliance with this section shall, by operation of law, succeed at the time of such death or incapacity to all of the rights and obligations of the owner or principal operator in the new motor vehicle dealership and under either the existing franchise or any other successor, renewal, or replacement franchise.

d. Within 60 days after the death or incapacity of the owner or principal operator, a designated successor appointed in substantial compliance with this section shall give the affected manufacturer or distributor written notice of his or her succession to the position of owner or principal operator of the new motor vehicle dealership; provided, however, that the failure of the designated successor to give the manufacturer or distributor written notice as provided above within 60 days of the death or incapacity of the owner or principal operator shall not result in the waiver or termination of the designated successor's right to succeed to the ownership of the new motor vehicle dealership unless the manufacturer or distributor gives written notice of this provision to either the designated successor or the deceased or incapacitated owner's executor, administrator, guardian or other fiduciary by certified or registered mail, return receipt requested, and said written notice grants not less than 30 days within which the designated successor may give the notice required hereunder,

provided the designated successor or the deceased or incapacitated owner's executor, administrator, guardian or other fiduciary has given the manufacturer reasonable notice of death or incapacity. Within 30 days of receipt of the notice by the manufacturer or distributor from the designated successor provided in this sub-subdivision, the manufacturer or distributor may request that the designated successor complete the application forms generally utilized by the manufacturer or distributor to review the designated successor's qualifications to establish a successor dealership. Within 30 days of receipt of the completed forms, the manufacturer or distributor shall send a letter by certified or registered mail, return receipt requested, advising the designated successor of facts and circumstances which have changed since the manufacturer's or distributor's original approval of the designated successor, and which have caused the manufacturer or distributor to object to the designated successor. Upon receipt of such notice, the designated successor may either designate an alternative successor or may file a request for evidentiary hearing in accordance with the procedures provided in sub-subdivisions b.2.-5. of this subdivision. In any such hearing, the manufacturer or distributor shall be limited to facts and circumstances which did not exist at the time the designated successor was originally approved or evidence which was originally requested to be produced by the designated successor at the time of the original request and was fraudulent.

e. The designated successor shall agree to be bound by all terms and conditions of the franchise in effect between the manufacturer or distributor and the owner at the time of the owner's or principal operator's death or incapacity, if so requested in writing by the manufacturer or distributor subsequent to the owner's or principal operator's death or incapacity.

f. This section does not preclude an owner of a new motor vehicle dealership from designating any person as his or her successor by written instrument filed with the manufacturer or distributor, and, in the event there is an inconsistency between the successor named in such written instrument and the designated successor otherwise appointed by the owner consistent with the provisions of this section, and that written instrument has not been revoked by the owner of the new motor vehicle dealership in writing to the manufacturer or distributor, then the written instrument filed with the manufacturer or distributor shall govern as to the appointment of the successor.

(8) To require, coerce, or attempt to coerce any new motor vehicle dealer in this State to order or accept delivery of any new motor vehicle with special features, accessories or equipment not included in the list price of those motor vehicles as publicly advertised by the manufacturer or distributor.

(9) To require, coerce, or attempt to coerce any new motor vehicle dealer in this State to purchase or lease a specific dealer management computer system for communication with the manufacturer, factory branch, distributor, or distributor branch or any computer hardware or software used for any purpose other than the maintenance or repair of motor vehicles, to participate monetarily in an advertising campaign or contest, to purchase off-lease or other preowned vehicles, or to purchase unnecessary or unreasonable quantities of any promotional materials, training materials, training programs, showroom or other display decorations, materials, computer equipment or programs, charging stations, or special tools at the expense of the new motor vehicle dealer, provided that nothing in this subsection shall preclude a manufacturer or distributor from including an unitemized uniform charge in the base price of the new motor vehicle charged to the dealer where such charge is attributable to advertising costs incurred or to be incurred by the manufacturer or distributor in the ordinary courses of its business.

Notwithstanding the terms or conditions of any franchise or other agreement, policy, or incentive program, it is unlawful for any manufacturer or distributor to require, coerce, or attempt to coerce any of its franchised dealers in this State to purchase or lease any electric vehicle charging stations at the dealer's expense unless the dealer has notified the manufacturer or distributor of the dealer's intention to begin selling and servicing electric vehicles manufactured or distributed by that manufacturer or distributor. If the dealer is actually offering for sale to the public or providing warranty service on electric vehicles manufactured or distributed by that manufacturer or distributor, the dealer may not be required to purchase or lease, at the dealer's expense, (a) more than the number of electric vehicle charging stations for use by service technicians and customer education than would reasonably be necessary for the dealer to perform these functions based on the dealer's estimated sales and service volume during the following three-year period or (b) to make electric vehicle charging stations located at the dealership available for use by the general public. Nothing in this subdivision shall prohibit a manufacturer or distributor from establishing an incentive program for its dealers within this State that provides financial assistance to dealers that purchase or install electric charging stations; provided, however, that the incentive compensation paid to the dealer for the dealer's purchase or lease and installation of all charging stations is reasonable and the amount paid separately reflects incentive compensation related to the charging stations.

Notwithstanding the terms or conditions of any franchise or other agreement, policy, or incentive program, it is unlawful for any manufacturer or distributor to require that any of its franchised dealers in this State purchase or lease any diagnostic equipment or tool for the maintenance, servicing, or repair of electric vehicles if the dealer has other diagnostic equipment or tools available for servicing another brand or line make of vehicle manufactured or distributed by that manufacturer or distributor that can perform the work to the standards required by and which have been approved by the applicable manufacturer or distributor; provided that approval by the manufacturer or distributor shall not be unreasonably withheld.

Chapter 20

Notwithstanding the terms or conditions of any franchise or other agreement, a franchised dealer that sells fewer than 250 new motor vehicles per year may request approval from the manufacturer to enter into a tool loaner agreement with another dealer, in lieu of purchasing or leasing any special tools required by any manufacturer, factory branch, distributor, or distributor branch, provided, however, that all of the following conditions are satisfied:

a. The manufacturer does not offer its dealers a special tool loaner/sharing program in which the dealer would be eligible to participate.

b. Eligible special tools exceed a cost of two thousand dollars ($ 2,000) per special tool, are easily and readily transportable, and would be utilized for service on less than 10 vehicles per month at the requesting dealer's dealership.

c. The dealers participating in a special tools loaner agreement do so pursuant to a written agreement, including designation of the dealer responsible for purchasing the specified tools.

d. All participating dealers are of the same line-make franchise with the manufacturer.

e. All participating dealers are located within a 40-mile radius of the dealer responsible for purchasing the specified special tools.

f. No more than five dealers participate in a special tool loaner agreement.

g. The manufacturer has approved the special tool loaner agreement, including the list of participating dealers and the list of eligible special tools to be included, which approval shall not be unreasonably withheld, conditioned, or delayed.

h. The manufacturer, factory branch, distributor, or distributor branch shall have the right to disapprove or terminate, upon 30 days written notice to all of the affected dealers, any special tool loaner agreement, if it determines that the agreement has resulted or is likely to result in a warranty repair delay of more than 48 hours, excessive warranty expense, or significant customer dissatisfaction.

(10) To require, coerce, or attempt to coerce any new motor vehicle dealer in this State to change the capital structure of the new motor vehicle dealer or the means by or through which the new motor vehicle dealer finances the operation of the dealership provided that the new motor vehicle dealer at all times meets any reasonable capital standards determined by the manufacturer in accordance with uniformly applied criteria; and also provided that no change in the capital structure shall cause a change in the principal management or have the effect of a sale of the franchise without the consent of the manufacturer or distributor, provided that said consent shall not be unreasonably withheld.

(11) To require, coerce, or attempt to coerce any new motor vehicle dealer in this State to refrain from participation in the management of, investment in, or the acquisition of any other line of new motor vehicle or related products; Provided, however, that this subsection does not apply unless the new motor vehicle dealer maintains a reasonable line of credit for each make or line of new motor vehicle, and the new motor vehicle dealer remains in compliance with any reasonable capital standards and facilities requirements of the manufacturer. The reasonable facilities requirements shall not include any requirement that a new motor vehicle dealer establish or maintain exclusive facilities, personnel, or display space.

(12) To require, coerce, or attempt to coerce any new motor vehicle dealer in this State to change location of the dealership, or to make any substantial alterations to the dealership premises or facilities, when to do so would be unreasonable, or without written assurance of a sufficient supply of new motor vehicles so as to justify such expense, in light of the current market and economic conditions. If a dealer is required by the manufacturer or distributor to change the location of the dealership and has not sold its existing dealership facility and real estate within the later of 180 days of listing the property for sale or 90 days after the facility relocation, then, upon the written request of the dealer, the manufacturer or distributor shall purchase the dealer's existing dealership facility and real estate at its fair market value as determined by an independent appraiser agreed upon by the dealer and the manufacturer or distributor. If a manufacturer or distributor purchases a dealership facility and real estate, then it shall be entitled to sole ownership, possession, use, and control of any items, buildings, or property that were included in the contract to purchase.

(13) To require, coerce, or attempt to coerce any new motor vehicle dealer in this State to prospectively assent to a release, assignment, novation, waiver or estoppel which would relieve any

person from liability to be imposed by this law or to require any controversy between a new motor vehicle dealer and a manufacturer, distributor, or representative, to be referred to any person other than the duly constituted courts of the State or the United States of America, or to the Commissioner, if such referral would be binding upon the new motor vehicle dealer.

(14) To delay, refuse, or fail to deliver motor vehicles or motor vehicle parts or accessories in reasonable quantities relative to the new motor vehicle dealer's facilities and sales potential in the new motor vehicle dealer's market area as determined in accordance with reasonably applied economic principles, or within a reasonable time, after receipt of an order from a dealer having a franchise for the retail sale of any new motor vehicle sold or distributed by the manufacturer or distributor, any new vehicle, parts or accessories to new vehicles as are covered by such franchise, and such vehicles, parts or accessories as are publicly advertised as being available or actually being delivered. The delivery to another dealer of a motor vehicle of the same model and similarly equipped as the vehicle ordered by a motor vehicle dealer who has not received delivery thereof, but who has placed his written order for the vehicle prior to the order of the dealer receiving the vehicle, shall be evidence of a delayed delivery of, or refusal to deliver, a new motor vehicle to a motor vehicle dealer within a reasonable time, without cause. Additionally, except as may be required by any consent decree of the Commissioner or other order of the Commissioner or court of competent jurisdiction, any sales objectives which a manufacturer, factory branch, distributor, or distributor branch establishes for any of its franchised dealers in this State must be reasonable, and every manufacturer, factory branch, distributor, or distributor branch must allocate its products within this State in a manner that does all of the following:

a. Provides each of its franchised dealers in this State an adequate supply of vehicles by series, product line, and model in a fair, reasonable, and equitable manner based on each dealer's historical selling pattern and reasonable sales standards as compared to other same line-make dealers in the State.

b. Allocates an adequate supply of vehicles to each of its dealers by series, product line, and model so as to allow the dealer to achieve any performance standards established by the manufacturer and distributor.

c. Is fair and equitable to all of its franchised dealers in this State.

d. Makes available to each of its franchised dealers in this State a minimum of one of each vehicle series, model, or product line that the manufacturer makes available to any dealer in this State and advertises in the State as being available for purchase.

e. Does not unfairly discriminate among its franchised dealers in its allocation process.

f. Provides each of its franchised dealers in this State a process for a dealer to appeal the dealer's vehicle allocation should the dealer believe it was not allocated or did not receive vehicle inventory in a manner that complies with both this subdivision and the manufacturer's or distributor's uniformly applied allocation formula. Participation in the appeal process does not waive or impair any rights, claims, or defenses available to the dealer, manufacturer, or distributor under applicable law. All in-person meetings, mediations, or other proceedings related to the appeal process shall be conducted in this State unless otherwise agreed to by the parties.

This subdivision is not violated, however, if such failure is caused solely by the occurrence of temporary international, national, or regional product shortages resulting from natural disasters, unavailability of parts, labor strikes, product recalls, and other factors and events beyond the control of the manufacturer that temporarily reduce a manufacturer's product supply. The willful or malicious maintenance, creation, or alteration of a vehicle allocation process or formula by a manufacturer, factory branch, distributor, or distributor branch that is in any part designed or intended to force or coerce a dealer in this State to close or sell the dealer's franchise, cause the dealer financial distress, or to relocate, update, or renovate the dealer's existing dealership facility shall constitute an unfair and deceptive trade practice under G.S. 75-1.1.

(15) To refuse to disclose to any new motor vehicle dealer, handling the same line make, the manner and mode of distribution of that line make within the State.

(16) To award money, goods, services, or any other benefit to any new motor vehicle dealership employee, either directly or indirectly, unless such benefit is promptly accounted for, and transmitted to, or approved by, the new motor vehicle dealer.

(17) To increase prices of new motor vehicles which the new motor vehicle dealer had ordered and which the manufacturer or distributor has accepted for immediate delivery for private retail consumers prior to the new motor vehicle dealer's receipt of the written official price increase notification. A sales contract signed by a private retail consumer shall constitute evidence of each such order provided that the vehicle is in fact delivered to that customer. Price differences applicable to new model or series shall not be considered a price increase or price decrease. Price changes caused by either: (i) the addition to a new motor vehicle of required or optional equipment; or (ii) revaluation of the United States dollar, in the case of foreign-make vehicles or components; or (iii) an increase in transportation charges due to increased rates imposed by carriers; or (iv) new tariffs or duties imposed by the United States of America or any other governmental authority, shall not be subject to the provisions of this subsection.

(18) To prevent or attempt to prevent a dealer from receiving fair and reasonable compensation for the value of the franchised business transferred in accordance with G.S. 20-305(4) above, or to prevent or attempt to prevent, through the exercise of any contractual right of first refusal, option to purchase, or otherwise, a dealer located in this State from transferring the franchised business to such persons or other entities as the dealer shall designate in accordance with G.S. 20-305(4). The opinion or determination of a manufacturer that the existence or location of one of its franchised dealers situated in this State is not viable or is not consistent with the manufacturer's distribution or marketing forecast or plans shall not constitute a lawful basis for the manufacturer to fail or refuse to approve a dealer's proposed transfer of ownership submitted in accordance with G.S. 20-305(4), or "good cause" for the termination, cancellation, or nonrenewal of the franchise under G.S. 20-305(6) or grounds for the objection to an owner's designated successor appointed pursuant to G.S. 20-305(7).

(19) To offer any refunds or other types of inducements to any person for the purchase of new motor vehicles of a certain line make to be sold to the State or any political subdivision thereof without making the same offer available upon request to all other new motor vehicle dealers in the same line make within the State.

(20) To release to any outside party, except under subpoena or as otherwise required by law or in an administrative, judicial or arbitration proceeding involving the manufacturer or new motor vehicle dealer, any confidential business, financial, or personal information which may be from time to time provided by the new motor vehicle dealer to the manufacturer, without the express written consent of the new motor vehicle dealer. A manufacturer shall not require, or include in any incentive program, a requirement that any of its motor vehicle dealers in this State provide an exclusive financial statement for a franchise or line make when the dealer company operates more than one franchise or sells more than one line make.

(21) To deny any new motor vehicle dealer the right of free association with any other new motor vehicle dealer for any lawful purpose.

(22) To unfairly discriminate among its new motor vehicle dealers with respect to warranty reimbursements or authority granted its new motor vehicle dealers to make warranty adjustments with retail customers.

(23) To engage in any predatory practice against or unfairly compete with a new motor vehicle dealer located in this State.

(24) To terminate any franchise solely because of the death or incapacity of an owner who is not listed in the franchise as one on whose expertise and abilities the manufacturer relied in the granting of the franchise.

(25) To require, coerce, or attempt to coerce a new motor vehicle dealer in

this State to either establish or maintain exclusive facilities, personnel, or display space.

(26) To resort to or to use any false or misleading advertisement in the conducting of its business as a manufacturer or distributor in this State.

(27) To knowingly make, either directly or through any agent or employee, any material statement which is false or misleading or conceal any material facts which induce any new motor vehicle dealer to enter into any agreement or franchise or to take any action which is materially prejudicial to that new motor vehicle dealer or his business.

(28) To require, coerce, or attempt to coerce any new motor vehicle dealer to purchase, order, or accept any preowned or new motor vehicle as a precondition to purchasing, ordering, or receiving any other new motor vehicle or vehicles. Nothing herein shall prevent a manufacturer from requiring that a new motor vehicle dealer fairly represent and inventory the full line of current model year new motor vehicles which are covered by the franchise agreement, provided that such inventory representation requirements are not unreasonable under the circumstances.

(29) To require, coerce, or attempt to coerce any new motor vehicle dealer to sell, transfer, or otherwise issue stock or other ownership interest in the dealership corporation to a general manager or any other person involved in the management of the dealership other than the dealer principal or dealer operator named in the franchise, unless the dealer principal or dealer operator is an absentee owner who is not involved in the operation of the dealership on a regular basis.

(30) To vary the price charged to any of its franchised new motor vehicle dealers located in this State for new motor vehicles based on the dealer's purchase of new facilities, supplies, tools, equipment, or other merchandise from the manufacturer, the dealer's relocation, remodeling, repair, or renovation of existing dealerships or construction of a new facility, the dealer's participation in training programs sponsored, endorsed, or recommended by the manufacturer, whether or not the dealer is dualed with one or more other line makes of new motor vehicles, or the dealer's sales penetration.

Except as provided in this subdivision, it shall be unlawful for any manufacturer, factory branch, distributor, or distributor branch, or any field representative, officer, agent, or any representative whatsoever of any of them to vary the price charged to any of its franchised new motor vehicle dealers located in this State for new motor vehicles based on the dealer's sales volume, the dealer's level of sales or customer service satisfaction, the dealer's purchase of advertising materials, signage, nondiagnostic computer hardware or software, communications devices, or furnishings, or the dealer's participation in used motor vehicle inspection or certification programs sponsored or endorsed by the manufacturer.

The price of the vehicle, for purposes of this subdivision shall include the manufacturer's use of rebates, credits, or other consideration that has the effect of causing a variance in the price of new motor vehicles offered to its franchised dealers located in the State.

Notwithstanding the foregoing, nothing in this subdivision shall be deemed to preclude a manufacturer from establishing sales contests or promotions that provide or award dealers or consumers rebates or incentives; provided, however, that the manufacturer complies with all of the following conditions:

a. With respect to manufacturer to consumer rebates and incentives, the manufacturer's criteria for determining eligibility shall:

1. Permit all of the manufacturer's franchised new motor vehicle dealers in this State to offer the rebate or incentive; and

2. Be uniformly applied and administered to all eligible consumers.

b. With respect to manufacturer to dealer rebates and incentives, the rebate or incentive program shall:

1. Be based solely on the dealer's actual or reasonably anticipated sales volume or on a uniform per vehicle sold or leased basis;

2. Be uniformly available, applied, and administered to all of the manufacturer's franchised new motor vehicle dealers in this State; and

3. Provide that any of the manufacturer's franchised new motor vehicle dealers in this State may, upon written request, obtain the method or formula used by the manufacturer in establishing the sales volumes for receiving the rebates or incentives and the specific calculations for determining the

Chapter 20

required sales volumes of the inquiring dealer and any of the manufacturer's other franchised new motor vehicle dealers located within 75 miles of the inquiring dealer.

Nothing contained in this subdivision shall prohibit a manufacturer from providing assistance or encouragement to a franchised dealer to remodel, renovate, recondition, or relocate the dealer's existing facilities, provided that this assistance, encouragement, or rewards are not determined on a per vehicle basis.

It is unlawful for any manufacturer to charge or include the cost of any program or policy prohibited under this subdivision in the price of new motor vehicles that the manufacturer sells to its franchised dealers or purchasers located in this State.

In the event that as of October 1, 1999, a manufacturer was operating a program that varied the price charged to its franchised dealers in this State in a manner that would violate this subdivision, or had in effect a documented policy that had been conveyed to its franchised dealers in this State and that varied the price charged to its franchised dealers in this State in a manner that would violate this subdivision, it shall be lawful for that program or policy, including amendments to that program or policy that are consistent with the purpose and provisions of the existing program or policy, or a program or policy similar thereto implemented after October 1, 1999, to continue in effect as to the manufacturer's franchised dealers located in this State until June 30, 2025.

In the event that as of June 30, 2001, a manufacturer was operating a program that varied the price charged to its franchised dealers in this State in a manner that would violate this subdivision, or had in effect a documented policy that had been conveyed to its franchised dealers in this State and that varied the price charged to its franchised dealers in this State in a manner that would violate this subdivision, and the program or policy was implemented in this State subsequent to October 1, 1999, and prior to June 30, 2001, and provided that the program or policy is in compliance with this subdivision as it existed as of June 30, 2001, it shall be lawful for that program or policy, including amendments to that program or policy

that comply with this subdivision as it existed as of June 30, 2001, to continue in effect as to the manufacturer's franchised dealers located in this State until June 30, 2025.

Any manufacturer shall be required to pay or otherwise compensate any franchise dealer who has earned the right to receive payment or other compensation under a program in accordance with the manufacturer's program or policy.

The provisions of this subdivision shall not be applicable to multiple or repeated sales of new motor vehicles made by a new motor vehicle dealer to a single purchaser under a bona fide fleet sales policy of a manufacturer, factory branch, distributor, or distributor branch.

(31) Notwithstanding the terms of any contract, franchise, agreement, release, or waiver, to require that in any civil or administrative proceeding in which a new motor vehicle dealer asserts any claims, rights, or defenses arising under this Article or under the franchise, that the dealer or any nonprevailing party compensate the manufacturer or prevailing party for any court costs, attorneys' fees, or other expenses incurred in the litigation.

(32) To require that any of its franchised new motor vehicle dealers located in this State pay any extra fee, purchase unreasonable or unnecessary quantities of advertising displays or other materials, or remodel, renovate, or recondition the dealers' existing facilities in order to receive any particular model or series of vehicles manufactured or distributed by the manufacturer for which the dealers have a valid franchise. Notwithstanding the foregoing, nothing contained in this subdivision shall be deemed to prohibit or prevent a manufacturer from requiring that its franchised dealers located in this State purchase special tools or equipment, stock reasonable quantities of certain parts, or participate in training programs which are reasonably necessary for those dealers to sell or service any model or series of vehicles.

(33) To fail to reimburse a dealer located in this State in full for the

actual cost, including applicable taxes and third-party fees, of providing a loaner or rental vehicle to any customer who is having a vehicle serviced at the dealership if the provision of such a loaner or rental vehicle is required by the manufacturer. It is unlawful for a manufacturer to fail to reimburse the dealer in full as provided above (i) whether or not the dealer provides the customer with a model vehicle similar to the vehicle the customer brought in for service, in the event the dealer does not have a similar model loaner or rental vehicle available, or (ii) if the provision of a rental or loaner vehicle to a customer is required or approved by the manufacturer or distributor and further provided that all or any portion of the time the dealer has provided the customer with a loaner or rental vehicle is due to the unavailability of one or more parts sold or distributed by the manufacturer or through a supplier designated or approved by the manufacturer.

(34) To require, coerce, or attempt to coerce any new motor vehicle dealer in this State to participate monetarily in any training program whose subject matter is not expressly limited to specific information necessary to sell or service the models of vehicles the dealer is authorized to sell or service under the dealer's franchise with that manufacturer. Examples of training programs with respect to which a manufacturer is prohibited from requiring the dealer's monetary participation include, but are not limited to, those which purport to teach morale-boosting employee motivation, teamwork, or general principles of customer relations. A manufacturer is further prohibited from requiring the personal attendance of an owner or dealer principal of any dealership located in this State at any meeting or training program at which it is reasonably possible for another member of the dealer's management to attend and later relate the subject matter of the meeting or training program to the dealership's owners or principal operator.

(35) Notwithstanding the terms of any franchise, agreement,

waiver or novation, to limit the number of franchises of the same line make of vehicle that any franchised motor vehicle dealer, including its parent(s), subsidiaries, and affiliates, if any, may own or operate or attach any restrictions or conditions on the ownership or operation of multiple franchises of the same line make of motor vehicle without making the same limitations, conditions, and restrictions applicable to all of its other franchisees.

(36) With regard to any manufacturer, factory branch, distributor, distributor branch, or subsidiary thereof that owns and operates a new motor vehicle dealership, directly or indirectly through any subsidiary or affiliated entity as provided in G.S. 20-305.2, to unreasonably discriminate against any other new motor vehicle dealer in the same line make in any matter governed by the motor vehicle franchise, including the sale or allocation of vehicles or other manufacturer or distributor products, or the execution of dealer programs for benefits.

(37) Subdivisions (11) and (25) of this section shall not apply to any manufacturer, manufacturer branch, distributor, distributor branch, or any affiliate or subsidiary thereof of new motor vehicles which manufactures or distributes exclusively new motor vehicles with a gross weight rating of 8,500 pounds or more, provided that the following conditions are met: (i) the manufacturer has, as of November 1, 1996, an agreement in effect with at least three of its franchised dealers within the State, and which agreement was, in fact, being enforced by the manufacturer, requiring the dealers to maintain separate and exclusive facilities for the vehicles it manufactures or distributes; and (ii) there existed at least seven dealerships (locations) of that manufacturer within the State as of January 1, 1999.

(38) Notwithstanding the terms, provisions, or conditions of any agreement, franchise, novation, waiver, or other written instrument, to assign or change a franchised new motor vehicle dealer's

area of responsibility under the franchise arbitrarily or without due regard to the present or projected future pattern of motor vehicle sales and registrations within the dealer's market and without having provided the affected dealer with written notice of the change in the dealer's area of responsibility and a detailed description of the change in writing by registered or certified mail, return receipt requested. A franchised new motor vehicle dealer who believes that a manufacturer, factory branch, distributor, or distributor branch with whom the dealer has entered into a franchise has assigned or changed the dealer's area of responsibility, is proposing to assign or change the dealer's area of responsibility arbitrarily or without due regard to the present or projected future pattern of motor vehicle sales and registrations within the dealer's market, or failed to provide the dealer with the notice required under this subdivision may file a petition within 60 days of receiving notice of a manufacturer, factory branch, distributor, or distributor branch's proposed assignment or change to the dealer's area of responsibility and have an evidentiary hearing before the Commissioner as provided in G.S. 20-301(b) contesting the franchised new motor vehicle dealer's assigned area of responsibility. Provided that the dealer has not previously filed a petition pursuant to this subdivision within the preceding 48 months regarding the dealer's currently assigned area of responsibility, a franchised new motor vehicle dealer who believes that it is unreasonable for a manufacturer, factory branch, distributor, or distributor branch with whom that dealer has entered into a franchise to include one or more portions of the dealer's existing area of responsibility previously assigned to that dealer by the manufacturer, factory branch, distributor, or distributor branch may request the elimination of the contested territory from the dealer's area of responsibility by submitting the request in writing via U.S. registered or certified mail, return receipt requested, to

the manufacturer, factory branch, distributor, or distributor branch. The dealer shall state in its request that the request is being made pursuant to this subdivision, describe the territory the dealer seeks to remove from its area of responsibility, and provide a general statement as to the factual basis for the dealer's contention of the changed factors warranting modification of the dealer's area of responsibility. The dealer's request shall be deemed accepted by the manufacturer, factory branch, distributor, or distributor branch if the manufacturer, factory branch, distributor, or distributor branch has not sent the dealer notice of objection to the dealer's request via U.S. registered or certified mail, return receipt requested, within 90 days after receipt of the dealer's request. Within 30 days of the dealer's receipt of notice from the manufacturer, factory branch, distributor, or distributor branch of the manufacturer's rejection, in whole or in part, of the dealer's request for the elimination of the contested territory from the dealer's area of responsibility, either party may request mediation under the manufacturer's internal mediation program, if any. Any such mediation shall commence within 60 days after the request for mediation is made and be concluded within 120 days after the date the manufacturer, factory branch, distributor, or distributor branch objected to the dealer's proposed change in its area of responsibility. Within 60 days of the conclusion of a requested mediation process, or, if a mediation process has not been timely requested under this subdivision, within 60 days of receiving notice from the manufacturer, factory branch, distributor, or distributor branch of the manufacturer's rejection, in whole or in part, of the dealer's request for the elimination of the contested territory from the dealer's area of responsibility, a dealer may file a petition and have an evidentiary hearing before the Commissioner as provided in G.S. 20-301(b) contesting the manufacturer's rejection, in whole or in part, of the dealer's request for the

Chapter 20

elimination of the contested territory from the franchised new motor vehicle dealer's assigned area of responsibility. In determining at an evidentiary hearing requested under this subdivision whether all or any portion of the existing or proposed area of responsibility assigned to the dealer is unreasonable or has been assigned arbitrarily or without due regard to the present or projected future pattern of motor vehicle sales and registrations within the dealer's market, the Commissioner may take into consideration the relevant circumstances, including, but not limited to:

a. The investment of time, money, or other resources made for the purpose of developing the market for the vehicles of the same line-make in the existing or proposed area of responsibility by the petitioning dealer, other same line-make dealers who would be affected by the change in the area of responsibility, or by the manufacturer, factory branch, distributor, distributor branch, or any dealer or regional advertising association.

b. The present and future projected traffic patterns and drive times between consumers and the same line-make franchised dealers of the affected manufacturer, factory branch, distributor, or distributor branch who are located within the market.

c. The historical and projected future pattern of new vehicle sales and registrations of the affected manufacturer, factory branch, distributor, or distributor branch within various portions of the area of responsibility and within the market as a whole.

d. The growth or decline in population, density of population, and new car registrations in the market.

e. If the affected manufacturer, factory branch, distributor, or distributor branch has removed territory from a dealer's area of responsibility or is proposing to remove territory from a dealer's area of responsibility, the projected economic effects, if any, that these changes in the dealer's area of responsibility will have on the petitioning dealer, other same line-make dealers, the public, and the manufacturer, factory branch, distributor, or distributor branch.

f. The projected effects that the changes in the petitioning dealer's area of responsibility that have been made or proposed by the affected manufacturer, manufacturer branch, distributor, or distributor branch will have on the consuming public within the market.

g. The presence or absence of natural geographical obstacles or boundaries, such as mountains and rivers.

h. The proximity of census tracts or other geographic units used by the affected manufacturer, factory branch, distributor, or distributor branch in determining same line-make dealers' respective areas of responsibility.

i. The public interest, consumer welfare, and customer convenience.

j. The reasonableness of the change or proposed change to the dealer's area of responsibility considering the benefits and harm to the petitioning dealer, other same line-make dealers, and the manufacturer, factory branch, distributor, or distributor branch.

At the evidentiary hearing before the Commissioner, following the filing of a petition by a dealer contesting the proposed assignment or change to the dealer's area of responsibility by a manufacturer, factory branch, distributor, or distributor branch, the affected manufacturer, factory branch, distributor, or distributor branch shall have the burden of proving that all portions of its current or proposed area of responsibility for the petitioning franchised new motor vehicle dealer are reasonable in light of the present or projected future pattern of motor vehicle sales and registrations within the franchised new motor vehicle dealer's market. At an evidentiary hearing before the Commissioner held pursuant to a franchised new motor vehicle dealer's petition to eliminate contested territory from the dealer's existing area of responsibility previously assigned to the dealer by the manufacturer, factory branch, distributor, or distributor branch, the franchised new motor vehicle dealer shall have the burden of proving that it would be unreasonable to continue to include the contested territory in the dealer's area of responsibility due to changes in circumstances under sub-subdivisions a. through j. of this subdivision that are beyond the control of the dealer. A policy or protocol of a manufacturer, factory branch, distributor, or distributor branch that determines a dealer's area of responsibility based solely on the proximity of census tracts or other geographic units to its franchised dealers and the existence of natural boundaries fails to satisfy the burden of proof on the affected manufacturer, factory branch, distributor, or distributor branch under this subdivision. Upon the filing of a petition before the Commissioner under this subdivision, any changes in the petitioning franchised new motor vehicle dealer's area of responsibility that have been proposed by the affected manufacturer, factory branch, distributor, or distributor branch shall be stayed during the pendency of the determination by the Commissioner. If a protest is or has been filed under G.S. 20-305(5) and the franchised new motor vehicle dealer's area of responsibility is included in the relevant market area under the protest, any protest filed under this subdivision shall be consolidated with that protest for

hearing and joint disposition of all of the protests. Nothing in this subdivision shall apply to the determination of whether good cause exists for the establishment by a manufacturer, factory branch, distributor, or distributor branch of an additional new motor vehicle dealer or relocation of an existing new motor vehicle dealer, which shall be governed in accordance with the requirements and criteria contained in G.S. 20-305(5) and not this subdivision.

(39) Notwithstanding the terms, provisions, or conditions of any agreement, franchise, novation, waiver, or other written instrument, to require, coerce, or attempt to coerce any of its franchised motor vehicle dealers in this State to purchase, lease, erect, or relocate one or more signs displaying the name of the manufacturer or franchised motor vehicle dealer upon unreasonable or onerous terms or conditions or if installation of the additional signage would violate local signage or zoning laws to which the franchised motor vehicle dealer is subject. Any term, provision, or condition of any agreement, franchise, waiver, novation, or any other written instrument which is in violation of this subdivision shall be deemed null and void and without force and effect.

(40) Notwithstanding the terms, provisions, or conditions of any agreement or franchise, to require any dealer to floor plan any of the dealer's inventory or finance the acquisition, construction, or renovation of any of the dealer's property or facilities by or through any financial source or sources designated by the manufacturer, factory branch, distributor, or distributor branch, including any financial source or sources that is or are directly or indirectly owned, operated, or controlled by the manufacturer, factory branch, distributor, or distributor branch.

(41) Notwithstanding the terms, provisions, or conditions of any agreement or franchise, to use or consider the performance of any of its franchised new motor vehicle dealers located in this State

relating to the sale of the manufacturer's new motor vehicles or ability to satisfy any minimum sales or market share quota or responsibility relating to the sale of the manufacturer's new motor vehicles in determining:

a. The dealer's eligibility to purchase program, certified, or other used motor vehicles from the manufacturer;

b. The volume, type, or model of program, certified, or other used motor vehicles the dealer shall be eligible to purchase from the manufacturer;

c. The price or prices of any program, certified, or other used motor vehicles that the dealer shall be eligible to purchase from the manufacturer; or

d. The availability or amount of any discount, credit, rebate, or sales incentive the dealer shall be eligible to receive from the manufacturer for the purchase of any program, certified, or other used motor vehicles offered for sale by the manufacturer.

(42) Notwithstanding the terms, provisions, or conditions of any agreement or waiver, to directly or indirectly condition the awarding of a franchise to a prospective new motor vehicle dealer, the addition of a line make or franchise to an existing dealer, the renewal of a franchise of an existing dealer, the approval of the relocation of an existing dealer's facility, or the approval of the sale or transfer of the ownership of a franchise on the willingness of a dealer, proposed new dealer, or owner of an interest in the dealership facility to enter into a site control agreement or exclusive use agreement. For purposes of this subdivision, the terms "site control agreement" and "exclusive use agreement" include any agreement that has the effect of either: (i) requiring that the dealer establish or maintain exclusive dealership facilities; or (ii) restricting the ability of the dealer, or the ability of the dealer's lessor in the event the dealership facility is being leased, to transfer, sell, lease, or change the use of the dealership premises, whether by sublease, lease, collateral pledge of lease, right of first refusal to purchase or lease, option to purchase, option to lease, or other similar agreement, regardless of the parties to such agreement. Any provision contained in any agreement entered into on or after August 26, 2009, that is inconsistent with the provisions of this subdivision shall be voidable at the election of the affected dealer, prospective dealer, or owner of an interest in the dealership facility.

(43) Notwithstanding the terms, provisions, or conditions of any agreement, franchise, novation, waiver, or other written instrument, to require, coerce, or attempt to coerce any of its franchised motor vehicle dealers in this State to change the principal operator, general manager, or any other manager or supervisor employed by the dealer. Any term, provision, or condition of any agreement, franchise, waiver, novation, or any other written instrument that is inconsistent with this subdivision shall be deemed null and void and without force and effect.

(44) Notwithstanding the terms, provisions, or conditions of any agreement or franchise, to require, coerce, or attempt to coerce any new motor vehicle dealer located in this State to refrain from displaying in the dealer's showroom or elsewhere within the dealership facility any sports-related honors, awards, photographs, displays, or other artifacts or memorabilia; provided, however, that such sports-related honors, awards, photographs, displays, or other artifacts or memorabilia (i) pertain to an owner, investor, or executive manager of the dealership; (ii) relate to professional sports; (iii) do not reference or advertise a competing brand of motor vehicles; and (iv) do not conceal or disparage any of the required branding elements that are part of the dealership facility.

(45) Notwithstanding the terms, provisions, or conditions of any agreement or franchise, to discriminate against a new motor vehicle dealer located in this State for selling or offering for sale a service contract, debt cancellation

agreement, maintenance agreement, or similar product not approved, endorsed, sponsored, or offered by the manufacturer, distributor, affiliate, or captive finance source. For purposes of this subdivision, discrimination includes any of the following:

a. Requiring or coercing a dealer to exclusively sell or offer for sale service contracts, debt cancellation agreements, or similar products approved, endorsed, sponsored, or offered by the manufacturer, distributor, affiliate, or captive finance source.

b. Taking or threatening to take any adverse action against a dealer (i) because the dealer sells or offers for sale any service contracts, debt cancellation agreements, maintenance agreements, or similar products that have not been approved, endorsed, sponsored, or offered by the manufacturer, distributor, affiliate, or captive finance source or (ii) because the dealer fails to sell or offer for sale service contracts, debt cancellation agreements, maintenance agreements, or similar products approved, endorsed, sponsored, or offered by the manufacturer, distributor, their affiliate, or captive finance source.

c. Measuring a dealer's performance under a franchise in any part based upon the dealer's sale of service contracts, debt cancellation agreements, or similar products approved, endorsed, sponsored, or offered by the manufacturer, distributor, affiliate, or captive finance source.

d. Requiring a dealer to exclusively promote the sale of service contracts, debt cancellation agreements, or similar products approved, endorsed, sponsored, or offered by the manufacturer, distributor, affiliate, or captive finance source.

e. Considering the dealer's sale of service contracts, debt cancellation agreements, or similar products approved,

endorsed, sponsored, or offered by the manufacturer, distributor, affiliate, or captive finance source in determining any of the following:

1. The dealer's eligibility to purchase any vehicles, parts, or other products or services from the manufacturer or distributor.

2. The volume of vehicles or other parts or services the dealer shall be eligible to purchase from the manufacturer or distributor.

3. The price or prices of any vehicles, parts, or other products or services that the dealer shall be eligible to purchase from the manufacturer or distributor.

4. The availability or amount of any vehicle discount, credit, special pricing, rebate, or sales or service incentive the dealer shall be eligible to receive from the manufacturer, distributor, affiliate, or captive finance source in which the incentives are calculated or paid on a per-vehicle basis or any vehicle discount, credit, special pricing, or rebate that are calculated or paid on a per-vehicle basis.

For purposes of this subdivision, discrimination does not include, and nothing shall prohibit a manufacturer, distributor, affiliate, or captive finance source from, offering discounts, rebates, or other incentives to dealers who voluntarily sell or offer for sale service contracts, debt cancellation agreements, or similar products approved, endorsed, sponsored, or offered by the manufacturer, distributor, affiliate, or captive finance source; provided, however, that such discounts, rebates, or other incentives are based solely on the sales volume of the service contracts, debt cancellation agreements, or similar products sold by the dealer and do not provide vehicle sales or service incentives.

For purposes of this subdivision, a service contract

provider or its representative shall not complete any sale or transaction of an extended service contract, extended maintenance plan, or similar product using contract forms that do not disclose the identity of the service contract provider.

(46) To require, coerce, or attempt to coerce a dealer located in this State to purchase goods or services of any nature from a vendor selected, identified, or designated by a manufacturer, distributor, affiliate, or captive finance source when the dealer may obtain goods or services of substantially similar quality and design from a vendor selected by the dealer, provided the dealer obtains prior approval from the manufacturer, distributor, affiliate, or captive finance source, for the use of the dealer's selected vendor. Such approval by the manufacturer, distributor, affiliate, or captive finance source may not be unreasonably withheld. For purposes of this subdivision, the term "goods" does not include moveable displays, brochures, and promotional materials containing material subject to the intellectual property rights of a manufacturer or distributor, or special tools or parts as reasonably required by the manufacturer to be used in repairs under warranty obligations of a manufacturer or distributor. If the manufacturer, distributor, affiliate, or captive finance source claims that a vendor chosen by the dealer cannot supply goods and services of substantially similar quality and design, the dealer may file a protest with the Commissioner. When a protest is filed, the Commissioner shall promptly inform the manufacturer, distributor, affiliate, or captive finance source that a protest has been filed. The Commissioner shall conduct a hearing on the merits of the protest within 90 days following the filing of a response to the protest. The manufacturer, distributor, affiliate, or captive finance source shall bear the burden of proving that the goods or services chosen by the dealer are not of substantially similar quality and design to those required by the

manufacturer, distributor, affiliate, or captive finance source.

(47) To fail to provide to a dealer, if the goods or services to be supplied to the dealer by a vendor selected, identified, or designated by the manufacturer or distributor are signs or other franchisor image elements to be purchased or leased to the dealer, the right to purchase or lease the signs or other franchisor image elements of similar quality and design from a vendor selected by the dealer. This subdivision and subdivision (46) of this section shall not be construed to allow a dealer or vendor to violate directly or indirectly the intellectual property rights of the manufacturer or distributor, including, but not limited to, the manufacturer's or distributor's intellectual property rights in any trademarks or trade dress, or other intellectual property interests owned or controlled by the manufacturer or distributor, or to permit a dealer to erect or maintain signs that do not conform to the reasonable intellectual property right or trademark and trade dress usage guidelines of the manufacturer or distributor.

(48) To unreasonably interfere with a dealer's independence in staffing the dealership by engaging in any of the following conduct: (i) requiring, coercing, or attempting to coerce a dealer located in this State to employ, appoint, or designate an individual to serve full-time or exclusively in any specific capacity, role, or job function at the dealership, other than the employment or appointment of a full-time general manager; (ii) requiring a dealer to employ, appoint, or designate an individual to serve full-time or exclusively in any specific capacity, role, or job function at the dealership, other than the employment or appointment of a full-time general manager, in order to participate in or qualify for any incentive program offered or sponsored by the manufacturer or distributor or to otherwise receive any discounts, credits, rebates, or incentives of any kind that are calculated or paid on a per-vehicle basis; or (iii) requiring that the dealer obtain the approval of the manufacturer or

distributor prior to employing or appointing any individual in any capacity, role, or job function at the dealership, other than the employment or appointment of a full-time general manager. Except as expressly provided above, nothing contained in this subdivision shall be deemed to prevent or prohibit a manufacturer or distributor from requiring that a dealer employ a reasonable number of trained employees to sell and service the factory's vehicles.

(49) A manufacturer or distributor may not charge a dealer more than a reasonable cost for any tool that the manufacturer or distributor sells to a dealer and designates as a special or essential tool. A manufacturer or distributor that collects tool fees as a convenience for the dealer and passes the payment through to a tool manufacturer or supplier which is not owned, operated, or controlled by the manufacturer, distributor, or affiliate shall not be considered to be selling the tool provided that the manufacturer or distributor's involvement does not increase the cost of the special tool or essential tool. Nothing in this subdivision shall prohibit a manufacturer or distributor from charging a reasonable nominal fee in addition to the cost of the special or essential tool that includes manufacturer or distributor handling costs. For any special or essential tool that the manufacturer or distributor sells to the dealer at a price exceeding two hundred fifty dollars ($ 250.00), the manufacturer or distributor shall disclose on an invoice or similar billing statement submitted to the dealer for the tool, the actual cost of the special or essential tool paid by the manufacturer or distributor.

(50) To require, coerce, or attempt to coerce any new motor vehicle dealer located in this State to change location of its dealership, or to make any substantial alterations to its dealership premises or facilities, if the dealer (i) has changed the location of its dealership or made substantial alterations to its dealership premises or facilities within the preceding 10 years at a cost of more than

two hundred fifty thousand dollars ($ 250,000), indexed to the Consumer Price Index, over this 10-year period, and (ii) the change in location or alteration was made toward compliance with a facility initiative or facility program that was sponsored or supported by the manufacturer, factory branch, distributor, or distributor branch, with the approval of the manufacturer, factory branch, distributor, or distributor branch. If a manufacturer, factory branch, distributor, or distributor branch offers incentives, or other payments under a program that are in any part conditioned on a dealer's construction of a new facility, facility improvements, or installation of signs or other image elements, a dealer that constructed a new facility, made facility improvements, or installed signs or other image elements required by or approved by the manufacturer that were completed at a cost of more than two hundred fifty thousand dollars ($ 250,000), indexed to the Consumer Price Index, within the preceding 10 years shall be deemed to be in compliance with any applicable facility requirements included in the manufacturer's program, and the dealer shall be entitled to receive all such incentives or other payments awardable under the program. If, during the 10-year period, the manufacturer revises or discontinues an existing program, standard, or policy or establishes a new program, standard, or policy or other benefit relating to construction or substantial alteration of a dealership, a motor vehicle dealer that completed construction or alteration of a dealership at a cost of more than two hundred fifty thousand dollars ($ 250,000) as part of a prior program, standard, or policy and elects not to participate in the new or revised program, standard, or policy shall not be entitled to the benefits under the new or revised program but shall remain entitled to all benefits under the prior program, standard, or policy according to the terms of the prior program, standard, or policy. If the prior program, standard, or policy under which the dealer completed a construction or alteration does not contain a specific period of time during which the manufacturer or distributor must provide payments or benefits to a dealer, then the manufacturer or distributor may not deny the dealer payment or benefits under the terms of that prior program, as it existed when the dealer began to perform under the prior program, for the balance of the 10-year term, regardless of whether the manufacturer's or distributor's program, standard, or policy has been revised or discontinued. For any dealer that did not change the location of its dealership or make substantial alterations to its dealership premises or facilities within the preceding 10 years at a cost of more than two hundred fifty thousand dollars ($ 250,000), indexed to the Consumer Price Index, the dealer's obligation to make any substantial alteration to its dealership premises or facilities, at the request of a manufacturer, factory branch, distributor, or distributor branch, or to satisfy a requirement or condition of an incentive program sponsored by a manufacturer, factory branch, distributor, or distributor branch, shall be governed by the applicable provisions of subdivisions (4), (11), (12), (25), (30), (32), and (42) of this section. This section shall not apply to any facility or premises improvement or alteration that is voluntarily agreed to by the new motor vehicle dealer and for which the dealer receives facilities-related compensation from the manufacturer or distributor for the facility improvement or alteration equivalent to at least a majority of the cost incurred by the dealer for the facility improvement or alteration.

(51) To establish, implement, or enforce criteria for measuring the sales or service performance of any of its franchised new motor vehicle dealers in this State for any of the purposes in subsubdivisions a. through c. of this subdivision that (i) are unfair, unreasonable, arbitrary, or inequitable; (ii) do not consider available relevant and material State and regional criteria, data, and facts. Relevant and material criteria,

data, or facts include those of motor vehicle dealerships of comparable size in comparable markets; and (iii) if such performance measurement criteria are based, in whole or in part, on a survey, such survey must be based on a statistically significant and valid random sample. In any proceeding under this subdivision, the applicable manufacturer or distributor shall bear the burden of proof (i) with regard to all issues raised in the proceeding and (ii) that the dealer performance measurements comply with all of the provisions hereof and are, and have been, implemented and enforced uniformly by the manufacturer or distributor among its franchised dealers in this State. Prior to taking a final action on an event described in sub-subdivisions a. through c. of this subdivision, if the dealer's current or past sales or service performance constitute any part of the basis for the final action, a manufacturer or distributor shall allow a dealer to present relevant local criteria, data, and facts beyond the control of the dealer, which the manufacturer or distributor shall consider. In the event it is determined that the performance criteria employed by a manufacturer or distributor for measuring the sales, service, or customer satisfaction performance of any of its franchised motor vehicle dealers in this State are unfair, unreasonable, arbitrary, or inequitable, or that the performance criteria does not consider available State and regional criteria, data, and facts required in this subsection, or that the performance criteria have not been implemented and enforced uniformly by the manufacturer or distributor among its franchised dealers in this State, or that the performance criteria do not consider relevant local criteria, data, and facts presented by the dealer in accordance with this subdivision, the performance criteria of the manufacturer or distributor may not constitute any part of the basis for a determination in any franchise-related decision pertaining to any of the following:

a. Whether to allow a dealer's proposed transfer of

ownership pursuant to subdivision (4) of this section.

b. Whether good cause exists for the termination of a dealer's franchise pursuant to subdivision (6) of this section.

c. Whether to allow appointment of a designated successor to a franchise pursuant to subdivision (7) of this section.

If a dealer's current or past performance in sales or service constitutes any part of the basis for the decision of the manufacturer, factory branch, distributor, or distributor branch pertaining to sub-subdivisions a. through c. of this subdivision, the dealer and the applicable manufacturer, factory branch, distributor, or distributor branch shall have the right to present local criteria, data, and facts in any petition or hearing before the Commissioner requested by the dealer pursuant to subdivision (4), (6), or (7) of this section.

(52) To prohibit or to in any way unreasonably limit or restrict a dealer from offering for sale over the Internet, including online e-commerce marketplaces, parts and accessories obtained by the dealer from the manufacturer, factory branch, distributor, or distributor branch, or from any source recommended or approved by the manufacturer, factory branch, distributor, or distributor branch. Nothing in this subdivision shall eliminate or impair the intellectual property rights of a manufacturer, factory branch, distributor, or distributor branch.

(53) Notwithstanding the terms of any franchise or agreement, or the terms of any program or policy, to do any of the following if it has any franchised dealers in this State and if it permits retail customers the option of reserving or requesting to purchase or lease a vehicle directly from such manufacturer or distributor:

a. Fail to assign any retail vehicle reservation or request to purchase or lease received by the manufacturer or distributor from a resident of this State to the franchised dealer

authorized to sell that make and model which is designated by the customer, or if none is designated, to its franchised dealer authorized to sell that make and model located in closest proximity to the customer's location, provided that if the customer does not purchase or lease the vehicle from that dealer within 10 days of the vehicle being assigned to the dealer, or if the customer requests that the transaction be assigned to another dealer, then the manufacturer or distributor may assign the transaction to another franchised dealer authorized to sell that make and model.

b. Prohibit a retail customer that has reserved or requested to purchase or lease a vehicle directly from the manufacturer or distributor from negotiating the final purchase price of the vehicle directly with the dealer if the dealer is authorized to sell that make and model and to agree on a final price for a new motor vehicle which varies from the MSRP established by the manufacturer or distributor.

c. Prohibit a retail customer that has reserved or requested to purchase or lease a vehicle directly from the manufacturer or distributor from using any vehicle financing or leasing source available from or through the dealer to whom the customer's vehicle reservation or request to purchase or lease has been assigned or to prohibit a franchised dealer in this State from offering and negotiating directly with the customer the terms of vehicle financing or leasing through all sources available to the dealer.

d. Prohibit a retail customer that has reserved or requested to purchase or lease a vehicle directly from the manufacturer or distributor from purchasing on terms negotiated or agreed to directly between the customer and the dealer to whom the customer's reservation or request to purchase or lease has been assigned, any service contract, extended warranty, vehicle maintenance contract, or guaranteed asset protection (GAP) agreement, or any other vehicle-related products and services offered by the dealer, provided that a manufacturer, distributor, or captive finance source shall not be required to finance any such product or service that is not offered or supported by the manufacturer or distributor.

e. Prohibit a retail customer that has reserved or requested to purchase or lease a vehicle directly from the manufacturer or distributor and the dealer to whom the customer's reservation or request to purchase or lease has been assigned from directly negotiating the trade-in value the customer will receive, or to prohibit the dealer from conducting an on-site inspection of the condition of a trade-in vehicle before the dealer becomes contractually obligated to accept the trade-in value negotiated.

f. Use a third party to accomplish what would otherwise be prohibited by this subdivision.

Nothing contained in this subdivision shall (i) require that a manufacturer or distributor allocate or supply additional or supplemental inventory to a franchised dealer located in this State in order to satisfy a retail customer's vehicle reservation or request submitted directly to the manufacturer or distributor as provided in this section, (ii) apply to the generation of sales leads; provided, however, that for purposes of this subdivision the term "sales leads" shall not include any reservation or request to purchase or lease a vehicle submitted directly by a customer or potential customer to a manufacturer or distributor, or (iii) apply to a reservation or request to purchase or lease a vehicle directly from the

manufacturer or distributor received from customer that is a resident of this State if the customer designates a dealer outside of this State to be assigned the reservation or request to purchase or lease, or if the dealer located in closest proximity to the customer's location is in another state and the manufacturer or distributor assigns the reservation or request to purchase or lease to that dealer.

(54) To prohibit or to in any way unreasonably limit or restrict a dealer from using electronic signature technology that conforms to Article 40 of Chapter 66 of the General Statutes to facilitate or execute loaner, demonstrator, rental, and test drive agreements and forms.

History.

1955, c. 1243, s. 21; 1973, c. 88, ss. 1, 2; 1983, c. 704, ss. 5-10; 1987, c. 827, s. 1; 1991, c. 510, ss. 2 -4; 1993, c. 123, s. 1; c. 331, s. 2; 1995, c. 163, s. 13; c. 480, s. 3; 1997-319, s. 3; 1999-335, s. 2; 1999-336, s. 1; 2001-510, ss. 2, 6; 2003-113, ss. 2, 3, 4; 2005-409, s. 2; 2005-463, s. 2; 2007-513, ss. 2 -4, 9, 12; 2008-156, s. 3; 2008-187, s. 50; 2009-338, ss. 1, 2, 5; 2009-496, s. 1; 2011-290, ss. 5 -9; 2013-302, s. 7; 2014-58, s. 10(e), (f); 2015-209, ss. 2, 3, 4, 5; 2017-102, s. 5.2(b); 2017-148, s. 2; 2018-27, ss. 1, 4; 2019-125, ss. 2 -5; 2021-147, ss. 1(a) -(c), 2(a), (b), 3(a), (b), 4-8, 11-13

§ 20-305.1. Automobile dealer warranty and recall obligations

(a) Each motor vehicle manufacturer, factory branch, distributor or distributor branch, shall specify in writing to each of its motor vehicle dealers licensed in this State the dealer's obligations for preparation, delivery, warranty, manufacturer-sponsored maintenance programs, manufacturer extended warranty, parts exchange programs, and recall service on its products. The disclosure required under this subsection shall include the schedule of compensation to be paid the dealers for parts, work, and service in connection with preparation, delivery, warranty, and recall service, and the time allowances for the performance of the work and service. In no event shall the schedule of compensation fail to include reasonable compensation for diagnostic work, shipping, if required by the manufacturer or distributor, and for battery disposal or other disposal charges and all other associated fees that were actually incurred by the dealer, and associated administrative requirements as well as repair service and labor.

Chapter 20

Time allowances for the performance of preparation, delivery, warranty, and recall work and service shall be reasonable and adequate for the work to be performed. The compensation paid under this section shall be reasonable, provided, however, that under no circumstances shall the reasonable compensation under this section for warranty and recall service be in an amount less than the dealer's current retail labor rate and the amount charged to retail customers for the manufacturer's or distributor's original parts for nonwarranty work of like kind, provided the amount is competitive with the retail rates charged for parts and labor by other franchised dealers of the same line-make located within the dealer's market. If there is no other same line-make dealer located in the dealer's market or if all other same line-make dealers in the dealer's market are owned or operated by the same entities or individuals as the dealership being compared, the retail rates charged for parts and labor by other franchised dealers located in the dealer's market that sell competing line-make motor vehicles as the dealer may be considered when determining whether the dealer's rates are competitive.

(a1) The retail rate customarily charged by the dealer for parts and labor may be established at the election of the dealer by the dealer submitting to the manufacturer or distributor 100 sequential nonwarranty customer-paid service repair orders which contain warranty-like parts, or 60 consecutive days of nonwarranty customer-paid service repair orders which contain warranty-like parts, whichever is less, covering repairs made no more than 180 days before the submission and declaring the average percentage markup. The average of the parts markup rate and the average labor rate shall both be presumed to be reasonable, however, a manufacturer or distributor may, not later than 30 days after submission, rebut that presumption by reasonably substantiating that the rate is unfair and unreasonable in light of the retail rates charged for parts and labor by all other franchised motor vehicle dealers located in the dealer's relevant market area offering the same line-make vehicles. In the event there are no other franchised dealers offering the same line-make of vehicle in the dealer's relevant market area, the manufacturer or distributor may compare the dealer's retail rate for parts and labor with the retail rates charged for parts and labor by other same segment franchised dealers who are selling competing line-makes of vehicles within the dealer's relevant market area. In the event there is also no other same segment franchised dealer who is selling a competing line-make of vehicle within the dealer's relevant market area, the manufacturer or distributor may then compare the dealer's retail rate for parts and labor with the retail rates charged for parts and labor by other same line-make dealers or same segment franchised dealers who are selling competing line-makes of vehicles that are located within the relevant market area of the franchised dealer who is located in closest proximity, measured by straight-line distance, to the dealer, provided they are not all owned, operated, or controlled by the subject dealer. For the purposes of this section, the term "relevant market area" shall have the same meaning as set forth in G.S. 20-286(13b). The retail rate and the average labor rate shall go into effect 30 days following the manufacturer's approval, but in no event later than 60 days following the declaration, subject to audit of the submitted repair orders by the manufacturer or distributor and a rebuttal of the declared rate as described above. If the declared rate is rebutted, the manufacturer or distributor shall propose an adjustment of the average percentage markup based on that rebuttal not later than 30 days after such audit, but in no event later than 60 days after submission. If the dealer does not agree with the proposed average percentage markup, the dealer may file a protest with the Commissioner not later than 30 days after receipt of that proposal by the manufacturer or distributor. If such a protest is filed, the Commissioner shall inform the manufacturer or distributor that a timely protest has been filed and that a hearing will be held on such protest. In any hearing held pursuant to this subsection, the manufacturer or distributor shall have the burden of proving by a preponderance of the evidence that the rate declared by the dealer was unreasonable as described in this subsection and that the proposed adjustment of the average percentage markup is reasonable pursuant to the provisions of this subsection. If the dealer prevails at a protest hearing, the dealer's proposed rate, affirmed at the hearing, shall be effective as of 60 days after the date of the dealer's initial submission of the customer-paid service orders to the manufacturer or distributor. If the manufacturer or distributor prevails at a protest hearing, the rate proposed by the manufacturer or distributor, that was affirmed at the hearing, shall be effective beginning 30 days following issuance of the final order.

(a2) In calculating the retail rate customarily charged by the dealer for parts and labor, the following work shall not be included in the calculation:

(1) Repairs for manufacturer or distributor special events, specials, coupons, or other promotional discounts for retail customer repairs.

(2) Parts sold at wholesale or at reduced or specially negotiated rates for insurance repairs.

(3) Engine assemblies.

(4) Routine maintenance, including fluids, filters, alignments, flushes, oil changes, belts, and brake drums/rotors and shoes/pads not provided in the course of repairs.

(5) Nuts, bolts, fasteners, and similar items that do not have an individual part number.

(6) Tires and vehicle alignments.

(7) Vehicle reconditioning.

(8) Batteries and light bulbs.

(a3) If a manufacturer or distributor furnishes a part or component to a dealer, at reduced or no cost, to use in performing repairs under a recall, campaign service action, or warranty repair, the manufacturer or distributor shall compensate the dealer for the part or component in the same manner as warranty parts compensation under this section by compensating the dealer on the basis of the dealer's average markup on the cost for the part or component as listed in the manufacturer's or distributor's price schedule less the cost for the part or component.

(a4) A manufacturer or distributor may not require a dealer to establish the retail rate customarily charged by the dealer for parts and labor by an unduly burdensome or time-consuming method or by requiring information that is unduly burdensome or time consuming to provide, including, but not limited to, part-by-part or transaction-by-transaction calculations.

(b) Notwithstanding the terms of any franchise agreement, it is unlawful for any motor vehicle manufacturer, factory branch, distributor, or distributor branch to fail to perform any of its warranty or recall obligations with respect to a motor vehicle, to fail to fully compensate its motor vehicle dealers licensed in this State for a qualifying used motor vehicle pursuant to subsections (i) and (j) of this section or warranty and recall parts other than parts used to repair the living facilities of recreational vehicles, including motor homes, travel trailers, fifth-wheel trailers, camping trailers, and truck campers as defined in G.S. 20-4.01(32b), at the prevailing retail rate according to the factors in subsection (a) of this section, or, in service in accordance with the schedule of compensation provided the dealer pursuant to subsection (a) of this section, or to otherwise recover all or any portion of its costs for compensating its motor vehicle dealers licensed in this State for warranty or recall parts and service or for payments for a qualifying used motor vehicle pursuant to subsections (i) and (j) of this section either by reduction in the amount due to the dealer, or by separate charge, surcharge, or other imposition, and to fail to indemnify and hold harmless its franchised dealers licensed in this State against any judgment for damages or settlements agreed to by the manufacturer, including, but not limited to, court costs and reasonable attorneys' fees of the motor vehicle dealer, arising out of complaints, claims or lawsuits including, but not limited to, strict liability, negligence, misrepresentation, express or implied warranty, or recision or revocation of acceptance of the sale of a motor vehicle as defined in G.S. 25-2-608, to the extent that the judgment or settlement relates to the alleged defective or negligent manufacture, assembly or design of new motor vehicles, parts or accessories or other functions by the manufacturer, factory branch, distributor or distributor branch, beyond the control of the dealer. Any audit, other than an audit conducted for cause, for warranty or recall parts or service compensation, or compensation for a qualifying used motor vehicle in accordance with subsections (i) and (j) of this section may only be conducted one time within any 12-month period and shall only be for the 12-month period immediately following the date of the payment of the claim by the manufacturer, factory branch, distributor, or distributor branch. Any audit, other than an audit conducted for cause, for sales incentives, service incentives, rebates, or other forms of incentive compensation may only be conducted one time within any 12-month period and shall only be for the 12-month period immediately following the date of the payment of the claim by the manufacturer, factory branch, distributor, or distributor branch pursuant to a sales incentives program, service incentives program, rebate program, or other form of incentive compensation program. Provided, however, these limitations shall not be effective in the case of fraudulent claims. For purposes of this subsection, the term "audit conducted for cause" is defined as an audit based on any of the following: (i) statistical evidence that the dealer's claims are unreasonably high in comparison to other dealers similarly situated or the dealer's claim history, (ii) that the dealer's claims submissions violate reasonable claims documentation or other requirements of the applicable manufacturer, factory branch, distributor, or distributor branch, (iii) a follow up to an earlier audit in which the dealer was notified of a claim documentation procedure violation that occurred within the prior 12-month period, provided the audit and any chargeback are in compliance with subdivision (b1) or (b2) of this section and are limited in scope to just the specific violation determined previously, or (iv) reasonable evidence of malfeasance or fraud. In the event a manufacturer, factory branch, distributor, or distributor branch elects to perform an audit conducted for cause, the manufacturer, factory branch, distributor, or distributor branch, simultaneously with providing the affected dealer with written notice of the audit, shall further be required to explain in detail in the notice the data or other foundation upon which the cause is based.

(b1) All claims made by motor vehicle dealers pursuant to this section for compensation for delivery, preparation, warranty, and recall work, including compensation for a qualifying used motor vehicle in accordance with subsection (i) of this section, labor, parts, and other expenses, shall be paid by the manufacturer within 30 days after receipt of claim from the dealer. When any claim is disapproved, the dealer shall be notified in writing of the grounds for disapproval. Any claim not specifically disapproved in writing within 30 days after receipt shall be considered approved and payment is due immediately. No claim which has been approved and paid may be charged back to the dealer unless it can be shown that the claim was false or fraudulent, that the repairs were not properly made or were unnecessary to correct the defective condition, or the dealer failed to reasonably substantiate the claim either in accordance with the manufacturer's reasonable written procedures or by other reasonable means. A manufacturer or distributor shall not deny a claim or reduce the amount to be reimbursed to the dealer as long as the dealer has provided reasonably sufficient documentation that the dealer:

(1) Made a good faith attempt to perform the work in compliance with the written policies and procedures of the manufacturer; and

(2) Actually performed the work.

Notwithstanding the foregoing, a manufacturer shall not fail to fully compensate a dealer for warranty or recall work or make any chargeback to the dealer's account based on the dealer's failure to comply with the manufacturer's claim documentation procedure or procedures unless both of the following requirements have been met:

(1) The dealer has, within the previous 12 months, failed to comply with the same specific claim documentation procedure or procedures; and

(2) The manufacturer has, within the previous 12 months, provided a written warning to the dealer by certified United States mail, return receipt requested, identifying the specific claim documentation procedure or procedures violated by the dealer.

Nothing contained in this subdivision shall be deemed to prevent or prohibit a manufacturer from adopting or implementing a policy or procedure which provides or allows for the self-audit of dealers, provided, however, that if any such self-audit procedure contains provisions relating to claim documentation, such claim documentation policies or procedures shall be subject to the prohibitions and requirements contained in this subdivision.

Notices sent by a manufacturer under a bona fide self-audit procedure shall be deemed sufficient notice to meet the requirements of this subsection provided that the dealer is given reasonable opportunity through self-audit to identify and correct any out-of-line procedures for a period of at least 60 days before the manufacturer conducts its own audit of the dealer warranty operations and procedures. A manufacturer may further not charge a dealer back subsequent to the payment of the claim unless a representative of the manufacturer has met in person at the dealership, or by telephone, with an officer or employee of the dealer designated by the dealer and explained in detail the basis for each of the proposed charge-backs and thereafter given the dealer's representative a reasonable opportunity at the meeting, or during the telephone call, to explain the dealer's position relating to each of the proposed charge-backs. In the event the dealer was selected for audit or review on the basis that some or all of the dealer's claims were viewed as excessive in comparison to average, mean, or aggregate data accumulated by the manufacturer, or in relation to claims submitted by a group of other franchisees of the manufacturer, the manufacturer shall, at or prior to the meeting or telephone call with the dealer's representative, provide the dealer with a written statement containing the basis or methodology upon which the dealer was selected for audit or review.

(b2) A manufacturer may not deny a motor vehicle dealer's claim for sales incentives, service incentives, rebates, or other forms of incentive compensation, reduce the amount to be paid to the dealer, or charge a dealer back subsequent to the payment of the claim unless it can be shown that the claim was false or fraudulent or that the dealer failed to reasonably substantiate the claim either in accordance with the manufacturer's reasonable written procedures or by other reasonable means.

(b3) (1) For purposes of this subsection, the term "manufacturer" shall include the terms "manufacturer," "manufacturer branch," "distributor," and "distributor branch," as those terms are defined in G.S. 20-286.

(2) Notwithstanding the terms of any franchise or other agreement, or the terms of any program, policy, or procedure of any manufacturer, it shall be unlawful for any manufacturer to take or threaten to take any adverse action against a dealer located in this State, or to otherwise discriminate

Chapter 20

against any dealer located in this State when:

a. The dealer failed to ensure that the purchaser or lessee paid personal property tax on the vehicle purchased or leased from the dealer;

b. The dealer failed to ensure that the vehicle being purchased or leased had been permanently registered in this State or in any other state in which the dealer was not required to ensure that the vehicle's permanent registration was processed or submitted at the time of the vehicle's purchase or lease;

c. The manufacturer extrapolated the imposition of any adverse action based on a certain number or percentage of the vehicles sold or leased by a dealer over a specified period of time having been exported or brokered; or

d. The dealer sold or leased a motor vehicle to a customer who either exported the vehicle to a foreign country or who resold the vehicle to a third party, unless:

1. The dealer reasonably should have known that the customer intended to export or resell the motor vehicle prior to the customer's purchase or lease of the vehicle from the dealer;

2. The vehicle sold or leased by the dealer was exported to a foreign country within 180 days after the date of sale or lease by the dealer; and

3. The affected manufacturer provided written notification to the affected motor vehicle dealer of the resale or export within 12 months from the date of sale or lease.

Notwithstanding the provisions of sub-subdivision d. of this subdivision, a manufacturer may take adverse action against a dealer located in this State if the dealer sold or leased a motor vehicle to a customer who either exported the vehicle to a foreign country or who resold the vehicle to a third party and the dealer, prior to the customer's purchase or lease of the vehicle from the dealer, had actual knowledge that the customer intended to export or resell the motor vehicle.

(3) The adverse action and discrimination prohibited under this subsection includes, but is not limited to, a manufacturer's actual or threatened:

a. Failure or refusal to allocate, sell, or deliver motor vehicles to the dealer;

b. Discrimination against any dealer in the allocation of vehicles;

c. Charging back or withholding payments or other compensation or consideration that a dealer is otherwise entitled to receive and that is not otherwise the subject of a dispute for warranty reimbursement or under a sales promotion, incentive program, contest, or other program or policy that would provide any compensation or support for the dealer;

d. Disqualification of a dealer from participating in, or discrimination against any dealer relating to, any sales promotion, incentive program, contest, or other program or policy that would provide any compensation or support for the dealer;

e. Termination of a franchise; or

f. The imposition of any fine, penalty, chargeback, or other disciplinary or punitive measure.

(4) In any proceeding brought pursuant to this subsection, the affected manufacturer shall have the burden of proving that the dealer knew or reasonably should have known that the customer intended to export or resell the motor vehicle prior to the customer's purchase or lease of the vehicle from the dealer, subject to the following provisions:

a. There shall be a rebuttable presumption that the dealer, prior to the customer's purchase or lease of the vehicle, did not know nor should have reasonably known that the customer intended to export or resell the motor vehicle, if:

1. Following the sale or lease, the dealer submitted the requisite documentation to the appropriate governmental entity to enable the vehicle to be titled, registered and, where applicable, sales or highway use tax paid in any state or territory within the United States in the name of a customer who was physically present at the dealership at or prior to the time of sale or lease; and

2. The customer's identifying information was not included on a list of known or suspected exporters or resellers identified and made readily accessible to the dealer by the applicable manufacturer at the time of the sale or lease.

b. There shall be a rebuttable presumption that the dealer, prior to the customer's purchase or lease of the vehicle, knew or reasonably should have known that the customer intended to export or resell the motor vehicle if the customer's identifying information was included on a list of known or suspected exporters or resellers identified and made readily accessible to the dealer by the applicable manufacturer at the time of the sale or lease.

c. Nothing contained in subdivision (2) of this subsection shall be deemed to prevent or prohibit the Commissioner or the affected manufacturer from considering one or more of the factors delineated in sub-subdivisions a. through c. of subdivision (2) of this subsection in determining whether the dealer knew or reasonably should have known that the customer intended to export or resell the motor vehicle prior to the customer's purchase or lease of the vehicle from the dealer.

(5) Any audit of a dealer by a manufacturer for sales or leases made to known exporters or brokers may only be conducted one time within any 12-month period and shall only be for the 12-month period immediately preceding the audit, provided, however, that nothing in this subsection shall prohibit or limit the ability of a manufacturer, factory branch, distributor, or distributor branch to conduct any audit of sales or leases made by one of its franchised dealers to known exporters or brokers for cause at any time during the permitted time period. For purposes of this subdivision, the term "for cause" means the dealer's sale or lease of motor vehicles to individuals identified on a list of known motor vehicle exporters or brokers previously provided by or posted on a Web site made accessible to the dealer by the manufacturer, factory branch, distributor, or distributor branch or reasonable evidence that the dealer knew or reasonably should have known that the customer intended to export or resell the motor vehicle.

(b4) Any person or other entity employed or contracted by a manufacturer, factory branch, distributor, or distributor branch to conduct an audit of a motor vehicle dealer regulated by this section shall comply with all the requirements of this section. It shall be unlawful for any manufacturer, factory branch, distributor, or distributor branch to contract with or employ any person or other entity to conduct an audit of any motor vehicle dealer located in this State regulated under this section for which the person or other entity conducting the audit of the dealer would be in any part compensated on the basis of the dollar amount, volume, or number of chargebacks that would result to the dealer from the audit.

(c) In the event there is a dispute between the manufacturer, factory branch, distributor, or distributor branch, and the dealer with respect to any matter referred to in subsection (a), (b), (b1), (b2), (b3), (b4), (d), or (i) of this section, either party may petition the Commissioner in writing, within 30 days after either party has given written notice of the dispute to the other, for a hearing on the subject and the decision of the Commissioner shall be binding on the parties, subject to rights of judicial review and appeal as provided in Chapter 150B of the General Statutes; provided, however, that nothing contained herein shall give the Commissioner any authority as to the content of any manufacturer's or distributor's warranty. Upon the filing of a petition before the Commissioner under this subsection, any chargeback to or any payment required of a dealer by a manufacturer relating to warranty or recall parts or service compensation, or to sales incentives, service incentives, rebates, other forms of incentive compensation, or the withholding or chargeback of other compensation or support that a dealer would otherwise be eligible to receive, shall be stayed during the pendency of the determination by the Commissioner.

(d) **Transportation damages. --**

(1) Notwithstanding the terms, provisions or conditions of any agreement or franchise, the manufacturer is liable for all damages to motor vehicles before delivery to a carrier or transporter.

(2) If a new motor vehicle dealer determines the method of transportation, the risk of loss passes to the dealer upon delivery of the vehicle to the carrier.

(3) In every other instance, the risk of loss remains with the manufacturer until such time as the new motor vehicle dealer or his designee accepts the vehicle from the carrier.

(4) Whenever a motor vehicle is damaged while in transit when the carrier or the means of transportation is designated by the manufacturer or distributor, or whenever a motor vehicle is otherwise damaged prior to delivery to the dealer, the dealer must:

a. Notify the manufacturer or distributor of such damage within three working days or within such additional time as authorized by the franchise agreement of the occurrence of the delivery of the motor vehicle as defined in subsection (1) of this section; and

b. Must request from the manufacturer or distributor authorization to repair the damages sustained or to replace the parts or accessories damaged.

(5) In the event the manufacturer or distributor refuses or fails to authorize repair or replacement of any such damage within ten working days after receipt of notification of damage by the dealer, ownership of the motor vehicle shall revert to the manufacturer or distributor, and the dealer shall incur no obligation, financial or otherwise, for such damage to the motor vehicle.

(5a) No manufacturer shall fail to disclose in writing to a new motor vehicle dealer, at the time of delivery of a new motor vehicle, the nature and extent of any and all damage and post-manufacturing repairs made to such motor vehicle while in the possession or under the control of the manufacturer if the cost of such post-manufacturing repairs exceeds three percent (3%) of the manufacturer's suggested retail price. A manufacturer is not required to disclose to a new motor vehicle dealer that any glass, tires or bumper of a new motor vehicle was damaged at any time if the damaged item has been replaced with original or comparable equipment.

(6) Nothing in this subsection (d) shall relieve the dealer of the obligation to cooperate with the manufacturer as necessary in filing any transportation damage claim with the carrier.

(e) **Damage/Repair Disclosure.** -- Notwithstanding the provisions of subdivision (d)(4) of this section and in supplementation thereof, a new motor vehicle dealer shall disclose in writing to a purchaser of the new motor vehicle prior to entering into a sales contract any damage and repair to the new motor vehicle if the damage exceeds five percent (5%) of the manufacturer's suggested retail price as calculated at the rate of the dealer's authorized warranty rate for labor and parts.

(1) A new motor vehicle dealer is not required to disclose to a purchaser that any damage of any nature occurred to a new motor vehicle at any time if the total cost of all repairs fails to exceed five percent (5%) of the manufacturer's suggested retail price as calculated at the time the repairs were made based upon the dealer's authorized warranty rate for labor and parts and the damaged item has been replaced with original or comparable equipment.

(2) If disclosure is not required under this section, a purchaser may not revoke or rescind a sales contract or have or file any cause of action or claim against the dealer or manufacturer for breach of contract, breach of warranty, fraud, concealment, unfair and deceptive acts or practices, or otherwise due solely to the fact that the new motor vehicle was damaged and repaired prior to completion of the sale.

(3) For purposes of this section, "manufacturer's suggested retail price" means the retail price of the new motor vehicle suggested by the manufacturer including the retail delivered price suggested by the manufacturer for each accessory or item of optional equipment physically attached to the new motor vehicle at the time of delivery to the new motor vehicle dealer which is not included within the retail price suggested by the manufacturer for the new motor vehicle.

(f) The provisions of subsections (a), (b), (b1), (d) and (e) shall not apply to manufacturers and dealers of "motorcycles" as defined in G.S. 20-4.01(27).

(f1) The provisions of subsections (a), (b), (b1), (b2), and (c) of this section applicable to a motor vehicle manufacturer shall also apply to a component parts manufacturer. For purposes of this section, a component parts manufacturer means a person, resident, or nonresident of this State who manufactures or assembles new motor vehicle "component parts" and directly warrants the component parts to the consumer. For purposes of this section, component parts means an engine, power train, rear axle, or other part of a motor vehicle that is not warranted by the final manufacturer of the motor vehicle.

(f2) The provisions of subsections (d) and (e) of this section shall not apply to a State agency that assists the United States Department of Defense with purchasing, transferring, or titling a vehicle to another State agency, a unit of local government, a volunteer fire department, or a volunteer rescue squad.

(g) **Truck Dealer Cost Reimbursement.** -- Every manufacturer, manufacturer branch, distributor, or distributor branch of new motor vehicles, or any affiliate or subsidiary thereof, which manufactures or distributes new motor vehicles with a gross vehicle weight rating of 16,000 pounds or more shall compensate its new motor vehicle dealers located in this State for the cost of special tools, equipment, and training for which its dealers are liable when the applicable manufacturer, manufacturer branch, distributor, or distributor branch sells a portion of its vehicle inventory to converters and other nondealer retailers. The purpose of this reimbursement is to compensate truck dealers for special additional costs these dealers are required to pay for servicing these vehicles when the dealers are excluded from compensation for these expenses at the point of sale. The compensation which shall be paid pursuant to this subsection shall be applicable only with respect to new motor vehicles with a gross vehicle weight rating of 16,000 pounds or more which are registered to end users within this State and that are sold by a manufacturer, manufacturer branch, distributor, or distributor branch to either of the following:

(1) Persons or entities other than new motor vehicle dealers with whom the manufacturer, manufacturer branch, distributor, or distributor branch has entered into franchises.

(2) Persons or entities that install custom bodies on truck chassis, including, but not limited to, mounted equipment or specialized bodies for concrete distribution, firefighting equipment, waste disposal, recycling, garbage disposal, buses, utility service, street sweepers, wreckers, and rollback bodies for vehicle recovery; provided, however, that no compensation shall be required to be paid pursuant to this subdivision with respect to vehicles sold for purposes of manufacturing or assembling school buses. Additionally, no compensation shall be required to be paid pursuant to this subdivision with respect to any vehicles that were sold to the end user by a franchised new motor vehicle dealer.

The amount of compensation that shall be payable by the applicable manufacturer, manufacturer branch, distributor, or distributor branch shall be one thousand five hundred dollars ($ 1,500) per new motor vehicle registered in this State whose chassis has a gross vehicle weight rating of 16,000 pounds or more. The compensation required pursuant to this subsection shall be paid by the applicable manufacturer, manufacturer branch, distributor, or distributor branch to its franchised new motor vehicle dealer in closest proximity to the registered address of the end user to whom the motor vehicle has been registered within 30 days after registration of the vehicle. Upon receiving a request in writing from one of its franchised dealers located in this State, a manufacturer, manufacturer branch, distributor, or distributor branch shall promptly make available to the dealer its records relating to the registered addresses of its new motor vehicles registered in this State for the previous 12 months and its payment of compensation to dealers as provided in this subsection.

(h) **Right to Return Unnecessary Parts or Accessories.** -- Notwithstanding the terms of any franchise agreement, it is unlawful for any motor vehicle manufacturer, factory branch, distributor, or distributor branch to deny a franchised new motor vehicle dealer the right to return any part or accessory that the dealer has not sold after 15 months where the part or accessory was not obtained through a specific order initiated by the franchised new motor vehicle dealer, but instead was specified for, sold

to, and shipped to the dealer pursuant to an automated ordering system, provided that the part or accessory is in the condition required for return to the manufacturer, factory branch, distributor, or distributor branch and the dealer returns the part within 60 days of it becoming eligible under this subsection. For purposes of this subsection, an "automated ordering system" shall be a computerized system required by the manufacturer that automatically specifies parts and accessories for sale and shipment to the dealer without specific order thereof initiated by the dealer. The manufacturer, factory branch, distributor, or distributor branch shall not charge a restocking or handling fee for any part or accessory being returned under this subsection.

(i) **Compensation for Used Motor Vehicle Recall.** -- Notwithstanding the terms of any franchise or other agreement other than an agreement permitted by this subsection (i) of this section, it is unlawful for any motor vehicle manufacturer, factory branch, distributor, or distributor branch to fail to compensate a franchised motor vehicle dealer for any qualifying used motor vehicle in the inventory of a dealer authorized to sell new motor vehicles of the same line-make or by a dealer authorized to perform recall repairs on vehicles of the same line-make in the manner specified in this subsection. The manufacturer, factory branch, distributor, or distributor branch shall compensate the dealer for any qualifying used motor vehicle in the inventory of the dealer at the prorated rate of at least one and one-half percent (1.5%) per month of the average trade-in value of the qualifying used motor vehicle beginning on the date the vehicle becomes a qualifying used motor vehicle and ending on and including the date the vehicle ceases to be a qualifying used motor vehicle pursuant to subsection (j) of this section. Any claim by a dealer for compensation owed under this subsection may be submitted by the dealer on a monthly basis, and the manufacturer, factory branch, distributor, or distributor branch shall approve or disapprove the claim within 30 days of receipt of the claim and shall process and pay the claim within 60 days after the approval of the claim. Every manufacturer, manufacturer branch, distributor, and distributor branch licensed by the Commissioner under this Article shall establish a simple, convenient, and efficient process for its franchised dealers to submit claims for compensation under this subsection on a monthly basis. Such process shall provide for a manner and method for a dealer to demonstrate the inventory status of a qualifying used motor vehicle, provided the manner and method is reasonable and does not require information that is unduly burdensome. Nothing in this subsection shall prohibit a manufacturer, factory branch, distributor, or distributor branch from compensating a dealer for a qualifying used motor vehicle under a national recall compensation program instead of the basis established in this section, provided that the compensation paid to dealers under the program is equal to or exceeds the level of compensation required by this subsection on a monthly basis and the compensation payments are made within the time periods required by this section. Nothing in this subsection shall prohibit a dealer and a manufacturer, factory branch, distributor, or distributor branch from voluntarily entering an agreement the sole subject matter of which is compensation for a dealer for a used motor vehicle subject to a recall and which provides a compensation amount or other related terms that differ from the compensation amount and other requirements specified in subsection (j) of this section provided that the dealer's ability to participate in or qualify for any incentive program offered or sponsored by the manufacturer or distributor or to otherwise receive any discounts, credits, rebates, or incentives of any kind is not conditioned upon the dealer's willingness to enter such an agreement. Nothing in this subsection shall require a manufacturer, factory branch, distributor, or distributor branch to provide total compensation in excess of the total average trade-in value of the qualifying used motor vehicle.

(j) Definitions -- The following definitions apply in this section:

(1) "Average trade-in value" means the value of a used motor vehicle as determined by reference to a generally accepted, nationally published, third-party used vehicle valuation guide book.

(2) "Qualifying used motor vehicle" means a motor vehicle that meets all of the following: (i) a used motor vehicle of a line-make for which the dealer holds an active franchise with the manufacturer to sell and service new motor vehicles; (ii) a used motor vehicle of a model subject to a recall notice and subject to or covered under a stop-sale or do-not-drive order issued by the manufacturer of the motor vehicle or issued by the National Highway Traffic Safety Administration; (iii) parts or other remedy sufficient to fully repair the underlying defect that resulted in the recall of the motor vehicle to the extent that the motor vehicle is no longer subject to or covered by a stop-sale or do-not-drive order issued by the manufacturer of the motor vehicle were not made available to the dealer within 30 days of the date of the notice of recall by the manufacturer; (iv) a motor vehicle in the dealer's inventory or otherwise owned by the dealer at the time a stop-sale or do-not-drive order is issued or taken into the used motor vehicle inventory of the dealer as a consumer trade-in incident to the purchase of a motor vehicle from the dealer after the stop-sale or do-not-drive order is issued. A motor vehicle meeting the definition of a "qualifying used motor vehicle" pursuant to this subdivision shall cease to be a "qualifying used motor vehicle" on the earlier of the following: (i) the date the remedy or parts to fully repair the underlying defect that resulted in the recall of the motor vehicle to an extent that the motor vehicle is no longer subject to or covered by a stop-sale or do-not-drive order issued by the manufacturer of the motor vehicle are made available to the dealer; (ii) the date the dealer sells, trades, or otherwise disposes of the qualifying used motor vehicle; or (iii) the date the manufacturer provides notice to the dealer that the stop-sale or do-not-drive order is no longer in effect.

(3) "Stop-sale or do-not-drive order" means a notification, directive, or order issued by a manufacturer, factory branch, distributor, or distributor branch to its franchised dealers or issued by the National Highway Traffic Safety Administration stating that motor vehicle models of certain used vehicles in inventory shall not be sold or leased, at either retail or wholesale, due to a federal safety recall for a defect or a noncompliance recall, or a federal emissions recall.

Nothing in this subsection shall be construed as excluding from the definition of a qualifying used motor vehicle a motor vehicle on which a previously issued notice of recall or a stop-sale or do-not-drive order remains in effect as of the effective date of this subsection, or a motor vehicle that becomes subject to a notice of recall or a stop-sale or do-not drive order on or after the effective date of this subsection, provided that the motor vehicle otherwise meets the criteria for a qualifying used motor vehicle. Subsections (i) and (j) of this section shall not be applicable to any manufacturer, factory branch, distributor, or distributor branch that manufactures or distributes recreational vehicles.

(k) Any compensation provided to the dealer that meets the minimum requirements of subsection (i) of this section is exclusive and may not be combined with any other state or federal recall compensation civil remedy for used motor vehicles subject to recall.

History.
1973, c. 88, s. 3; c. 1331, s. 3; 1983, c. 704, ss. 11-13; 1987, c. 827, s. 1; 1989, c. 614, ss. 1, 2; 1991, c. 561, ss. 1 -4; 1993, c. 116, ss. 1, 2; 1995, c. 156, s. 1; 1997-319, s. 4; 1999-335, ss. 3, 3.1, 4; 2003-113, s. 5; 2003-258, s. 4; 2007-513, ss. 5 -7, 11; 2009-338, ss. 3, 4; 2009-550,

Chapter 20

s. 2(c); 2011-290, s. 10; 2013-302, s. 10; 2015-209, ss. 6, 7, 8, 9; 2017-148, s. 3; 2018-27, s. 2; 2019-125, ss. 6, 9; 2021-147, s. 9

§ 20-305.2. Unfair methods of competition; protection of car-buying public

(a) It is unlawful for any motor vehicle manufacturer, factory branch, distributor, distributor branch, or subsidiary thereof, to directly or indirectly through any parent, subsidiary, or affiliated entity, whether or not such motor vehicle manufacturer, factory branch, distributor, distributor branch, or subsidiary thereof has entered into a franchise, within the meaning of G.S. 20-286(8a), with any person or entity in this State, own any ownership interest in, operate, or control any motor vehicle dealer in this State or any entity in this State that provides warranty service or repairs at retail, to file a motor vehicle dealer application with the Division pursuant to G.S. 20-288, or to be licensed by the Division as a motor vehicle dealer, provided that this section shall not be construed to prohibit any of the following:

(1) The operation by a manufacturer, factory branch, distributor, distributor branch, or subsidiary thereof, of a dealership for a temporary period (not to exceed one year) during the transition from one owner or operator to another.

(2) The ownership or control of a dealership by a manufacturer, factory branch, distributor, distributor branch, or subsidiary thereof, while in a bona fide relationship with an economically disadvantaged or other independent person, other than a manufacturer, factory branch, distributor, distributor branch, or an agent or affiliate thereof, who has made a bona fide, unencumbered initial investment of at least six percent (6%) of the total sales price that is subject to loss in the dealership and who can reasonably expect to acquire full ownership of the dealership within a reasonable period of time, not to exceed 12 years, and on reasonable terms and conditions.

(3) The ownership, operation or control of a dealership by a manufacturer, factory branch, distributor, distributor branch, or subsidiary thereof, if such manufacturer, factory branch, distributor, distributor branch, or subsidiary has been engaged in the retail sale of motor vehicles through such dealership for a continuous period of three years prior to March 16, 1973, and if the Commissioner determines, after a hearing on the matter at the request of any party, that there is no independent dealer available in the relevant market area to own and operate the franchise in a manner consistent with the public interest.

(4) Repealed by Session Laws 2019-125, s. 10, effective July 19, 2019.

(4a) The ownership, operation, or control of a maximum total number of five motor vehicle dealership locations within this State prior to December 31, 2020, or a maximum total number of six motor vehicle dealership locations within this State on or after January 1, 2021, by a manufacturer that manufactures and sells only motor vehicles that are plug-in electric vehicles that do not rely on any nonelectric source of power in all modes of operation; provided, however, that this subdivision shall be applicable only to a manufacturer that had at least one motor vehicle dealership licensed in this State by the Division as of March 1, 2019. The Division shall deny any motor vehicle dealer application that, if granted by the Division, would allow said manufacturer, or any parent, subsidiary, or other person or entity affiliated with the manufacturer, to own, operate, or control any more than the maximum total number of motor vehicle dealership locations in this State permitted by this subdivision. Provided further, that the Commissioner shall promptly revoke any motor vehicle dealer license granted under this section upon discovery of the occurrence of any of the following events:

a. The manufacturer ceases to manufacturer or distribute only motor vehicles that are electric vehicles that do not rely on any nonelectric source of power in all modes of operation.

b. The manufacturer enters into a franchise with any dealer located in this State.

c. The manufacturer acquires a substantial affiliation with any motor vehicle manufacturer or distributor that currently has or at any point in the past has ever entered into a franchise with a dealer located in this State. For purposes of this sub-subdivision, the term "substantial affiliation" means either of the following:

1. The ownership by the manufacturer of a direct or indirect interest of greater than thirty percent (30%) of the shareholder voting control of an entity that is a motor vehicle manufacturer, factory branch, distributor, or distributor branch, as these terms are defined in G.S. 20-286.

2. The combined direct or indirect ownership by one or more motor vehicle manufacturers, factory branches, distributors, or distributor branches, as these terms

Chapter 20

are defined in G.S. 20-286, or one of their affiliates, of greater than thirty percent (30%) of the shareholder voting control of the manufacturer.

d. The manufacturer sells or offers for sale any new motor vehicles identified as, or bearing the logo or brand of, a motor vehicle manufacturer or distributor which has any franchised dealers within this State, provided, however, that this provision shall not be deemed to be violated if any component parts of a motor vehicle are branded with the name of or logo of another motor vehicle manufacturer as long as the vehicle as a whole is clearly identified as, and branded exclusively with the brand of the electric vehicle manufacturer that holds the motor vehicle dealer license.

(5) The ownership, operation, or control of any facility (location) of a new motor vehicle dealer in this State at which the dealer sells only new and used motor vehicles with a gross weight rating of 8,500 pounds or more, provided that both of the following conditions have been met:

a. The facility is located within 35 miles of manufacturing or assembling facilities existing as of January 1, 1999, and is owned or operated by the manufacturer, manufacturing branch, distributor, distributor branch, or any affiliate or subsidiary thereof which assembles, manufactures, or distributes new motor vehicles with a gross weight rating of 8,500 pounds or more by such dealer at said location; and

b. The facility is located in the largest Standard Metropolitan Statistical Area (SMSA) in the State.

(6) As to any line make of motor vehicle for which there is in aggregate no more than 13 franchised new motor vehicle dealers (locations) licensed and in operation within the State as of January 1, 1999, the ownership, operation, or control of one or more new motor vehicle dealership trading solely in such line make of vehicle by the manufacturer, factory branch, distributor, distributor branch, or subsidiary or affiliate thereof, provided however, that all of the following conditions are met:

a. The manufacturer, factory branch, distributor, distributor branch, or subsidiary or affiliate thereof does not own directly or indirectly, in aggregate, in excess of forty-five percent (45%) interest in the dealership;

b. At the time the manufacturer, factory branch, distributor, distributor branch, or subsidiary or affiliate

thereof first acquires ownership or assumes operation or control with respect to any such dealership, the distance between the dealership thus owned, operated, or controlled and the nearest other new motor vehicle dealership trading in the same line make of vehicle, is no less than 35 miles;

c. All the manufacturer's franchise agreements confer rights on the dealer of the line make to develop and operate within a defined geographic territory or area, as many dealership facilities as the dealer and manufacturer shall agree are appropriate; and

d. That as of July 1, 1999, not fewer than half of the dealers of the line make within the State own and operate two or more dealership facilities in the geographic territory or area covered by the franchise agreement with the manufacturer.

(7) The ownership, operation, or control of a dealership that sells primarily recreational vehicles as defined in G.S. 20-4.01 by a manufacturer, factory branch, distributor, or distributor branch, or subsidiary thereof, if the manufacturer, factory branch, distributor, or distributor branch, or subsidiary thereof, owned, operated, or controlled the dealership as of October 1, 2001.

(8) A manufacturer that manufactures and distributes only low-speed vehicles that meet the applicable NHTSA standards for low-speed vehicles; provided, however, that this subdivision is applicable only to a manufacturer that had at least one motor vehicle dealership licensed in this State by the Division as of March 1, 2019.

(b) Subsection (a) of this section does not apply to manufacturers or distributors of trailers or semitrailers that are not recreational vehicles as defined in G.S. 20-4.01.

(c) For purposes of subsection (d) of this section, the following definitions apply:

(1) **Former Franchisee.** -- A new motor vehicle dealer, as defined in G.S. 20-286(13), that has entered into a franchise, as defined in G.S. 20-286(8a) with a predecessor manufacturer and that has either:

a. Entered into a termination agreement or deferred termination agreement with a predecessor or successor manufacturer related to such franchise; or

b. Has had such franchise canceled, terminated, nonrenewed, noncontinued, rejected, nonassumed, or otherwise ended.

(2) **Relevant market area.** -- The area within a 10-, 15-, or 20-mile radius around

1701

the site of the previous franchisee's dealership facility, as determined in the same manner that the relevant market area is determined under G.S. 20-286(13b) when a manufacturer is seeking to establish an additional new motor vehicle dealer.

(3) **Successor manufacturer.** -- Any motor vehicle manufacturer, as defined in G.S. 20-286(8e), that, on or after January 1, 2009, acquires, succeeds to, or assumes any part of the business of another manufacturer, referred to as the "predecessor manufacturer," as the result of any of the following:

    a. A change in ownership, operation, or control of the predecessor manufacturer by sale or transfer of assets, corporate stock or other equity interest, assignment, merger, consolidation, combination, joint venture, redemption, court-approved sale, operation of law or otherwise.

    b. The termination, suspension, or cessation of a part or all of the business operations of the predecessor manufacturer.

    c. The discontinuance of the sale of the product line.

    d. A change in distribution system by the predecessor manufacturer, whether through a change in distributor or the predecessor manufacturer's decision to cease conducting business through a distributor altogether.

(d) For a period of four years from the date that a successor manufacturer acquires, succeeds to, or assumes any part of the business of a predecessor manufacturer, it shall be unlawful for such successor manufacturer to enter into a same line make franchise with any person, as defined in G.S. 20-4.01(28), or to permit the relocation of any existing same line make franchise, for a line make of the predecessor manufacturer that would be located or relocated within the relevant market area of a former franchisee who owned or leased a dealership facility in that relevant market area without first offering the additional or relocated franchise to the former franchisee, or the designated successor of such former franchisee in the event the former franchisee is deceased or disabled, at no cost and without any requirements or restrictions other than those imposed generally on the manufacturer's other franchisees at that time, unless one of the following applies:

(1) As a result of the former franchisee's cancellation, termination, noncontinuance, or nonrenewal of the franchise, the predecessor manufacturer had consolidated the line make with another of its line makes for which the predecessor manufacturer had a franchisee with a then-existing dealership facility located within that relevant market area.

(2) The successor manufacturer has paid the former franchisee, or the designated successor of such former franchisee in the event the former franchisee is deceased or disabled, the fair market value of the former franchisee's franchise calculated as prescribed in G.S. 20-305(6)d.3.

(3) The successor manufacturer proves that the former franchisee, or the designated successor of such former franchisee in the event the former franchisee is deceased or disabled, by reason of lack of training, lack of prior experience, poor past performance, lack of financial ability, or poor character, is unfit to own or manage the dealership. A successor manufacturer who seeks to assert that a former franchisee is unfit to own or manage the dealership must file a petition seeking a hearing on this issue before the Commissioner and shall have the burden of proving lack of fitness at such hearing. The Commissioner shall try to conduct the hearing and render a final determination within 120 days after the manufacturer's petition has been filed. No successor dealer, other than the former franchisee, may be appointed or franchised by the successor manufacturer within the relevant market area until the Commissioner has held a hearing and rendered a determination on the issue of the fitness of the previous franchisee to own or manage the dealership.

(e) For purposes of this section, an unfair method of competition includes any physical or mechanical warranty repair made or provided directly by a manufacturer or distributor to any motor vehicle located within this State requiring the direct participation of a dealer franchised by the manufacturer or distributor and without such dealer receiving reasonable compensation, equal to an amount no less than the amount provided in G.S. 20-305.1.

(f) No claim or cause of action may be brought against a dealer in this State arising out of any warranty repair, fix, repair, or update that was provided by the manufacturer or distributor without the direct involvement and participation of the dealer. Any manufacturer or distributor that provides or attempts to provide a warranty repair, fix, repair, update, or adjustment directly to any motor vehicle located within this State without the direct participation of a dealer franchised by the manufacturer or distributor shall fully indemnify and hold harmless any dealer located in this State for all claims, demands, judgments, damages, attorneys' fees, litigation expenses, and all other costs and expenses incurred by the dealer arising out of the actual or attempted warranty repair, fix, repair, update, or adjustment.

Chapter 20

History.

1973, c. 88, s. 3; 1983, c. 704, ss. 14, 15; 1999-335, s. 5; 2001-510, s. 3; 2002-72, ss. 19(d), 19(e); 2003-416, s. 11; 2009-496, s. 2; 2013-302, s. 8; 2019-125, s. 10

§ 20-305.3. Hearing notice

In every case of a hearing before the Commissioner authorized under this Article, the Commissioner shall give reasonable notice of each such hearing to all interested parties, and the Commissioner's decision shall be binding on the parties, subject to the rights of judicial review and appeal as provided in Chapter 150B of the General Statutes. The costs of such hearings shall be assessed by the Commissioner.

History.

1973, c. 88, s. 3; c. 1331, s. 3; 1987, c. 827, s. 1

§ 20-305.4. Motor Vehicle Dealers' Advisory Board (Repealed effective June 20, 2023)

(a) The Motor Vehicle Dealers' Advisory Board shall consist of six members; three of which shall be appointed by the Speaker of the House of Representatives, and three of which shall be appointed by the President Pro Tempore of the Senate to consult with and advise the Commissioner with respect to matters brought before the Commissioner under the provisions of G.S. 20-304 through 20-305.4.

(b) Each member of the Motor Vehicle Dealers' Advisory Board shall be a resident of North Carolina. Three members of the Board shall be franchised dealers in new automobiles or trucks, duly licensed and engaged in business as such in North Carolina, provided that no two of such dealers may be franchised to sell automobiles or trucks manufactured or distributed by the same person or a subsidiary or affiliate of the same person. Three members of the Board shall not be motor vehicle dealers or employees of a motor vehicle dealer.

(c) The Speaker shall appoint two of the dealer members and one of the public members and shall fill any vacancy in said positions and the President Pro Tempore of the Senate shall appoint one of the dealer members and two of the public members and shall fill any vacancy in said positions. In making the initial appointments the Speaker shall designate that the two dealer members shall serve for one and three years respectively and the public member shall serve for two years, and in making the initial appointments the Lieutenant Governor shall designate that the dealer member shall serve for two years and the two public members shall serve for one and three years respectively.

(d) Two members of the first Board appointed shall serve for a period of three years, two members of the first Board shall serve for a period of two years, and two members of the first Board shall serve for a period of one year. Subsequent appointments shall be for terms of three years, except appointments to fill vacancies which shall be for the unexpired terms. Members of the Board shall meet at the call of the Commissioner and shall receive as compensation for their services seven dollars ($ 7.00) for each day actually engaged in the exercise of the duties of the Board and such travel expenses and subsistence allowances as are generally allowed other State commissions and boards.

History.

1973, c. 88, s. 3; 1995, c. 490, s. 36

DELAYED REPEAL OF SECTION. -- Session Laws 2021-90, s. 16(a), repealed this section effective June 30, 2023.

§ 20-305.5. Recreational vehicle manufacturer warranty recall obligations

(a) It is unlawful for any manufacturer, factory branch, distributor, or distributor branch that manufactures or distributes recreational vehicles to fail to fully compensate its dealers located in this State in accordance with this section for warranty or recall work performed by the dealers related to the living facilities of the vehicle, including all labor and parts used to repair such living facilities and any equipment, plumbing, appliances, and other options included by the manufacturer, factory branch, distributor, or distributor branch in the purchase price paid by the dealer for the vehicle. For purposes of this section, the term "recreational vehicle" includes motor homes, travel trailers, fifth-wheel trailers, camping trailers, and truck campers as defined by G.S. 20-4.01(32b). With respect to those portions of the living facilities of recreational vehicles and any equipment, plumbing, appliances, and other options that are part of such living facilities and that are included by the recreational vehicle manufacturer, factory branch, distributor, or distributor branch in the purchase price paid by the dealer for the vehicle, the term "warrantor" shall mean any manufacturer or distributor of such living facilities or any equipment, plumbing, appliances, and other options that are part of such living facilities that offers a warranty in writing to either the recreational vehicle dealer or to the ultimate purchaser of the recreational vehicle. The term "warrantor" does not include a person that provides a service contract, mechanical or other insurance, or an extended warranty sold for separate consideration by a dealer or other person not controlled by a warrantor. Notwithstanding the terms or conditions of any contract or agreement, it is unlawful for any recreational vehicle manufacturer, factory branch, distributor, or distributor branch to fail to fully and timely compensate any of its franchised recreational vehicle dealers located in this State in accordance with this section for all parts and labor used by such franchised dealers in making warranty or recall repairs to such living facilities of recreational vehicles, including any equipment, plumbing, appliances, and other options included by the recreational vehicle manufacturer, factory branch, distributor, or distributor branch in the purchase price paid by the dealer for the vehicle, to the extent that the individual components of such living facilities are not separately warranted by the manufacturers or distributors of such components. Notwithstanding the terms or conditions of any warranty, contract, or agreement, it is unlawful for any warrantor, as defined in this subdivision, to fail to fully and timely compensate any franchised recreational vehicle dealer located in this State in accordance with this section for all parts and labor used by such franchised recreational vehicle dealer in making warranty or recall repairs to any component parts of the living facilities of recreational vehicles manufactured or distributed by such warrantor, including any equipment, plumbing, appliances, and other options included by a recreational vehicle manufacturer, factory branch, distributor, or distributor branch in the purchase price paid by the dealer for the vehicle.

(b) Each warrantor as defined in this subdivision and each recreational vehicle manufacturer, factory branch, distributor, and distributor branch that sells or distributes recreational vehicles in this State shall specify in writing to each recreational vehicle dealer licensed in this State who sells products manufactured or distributed by such warrantor or such recreational vehicle manufacturer, factory branch, distributor, or distributor branch, the recreational vehicle dealer's obligations for preparation, delivery, and warranty and recall service on its products, the schedule of compensation to be paid such dealers for parts, work, and service in connection with warranty or recall service, and the time allowances for the performance of such work and service. In no event shall such schedule of compensation fail to include reasonable compensation for diagnostic work and associated administrative requirements as well as repair service, labor, and transportation provided by the dealer to transport a recreational vehicle to and from a location at which the repairs can be made. Provided, however, that with respect to reimbursement for a recreational vehicle dealer's transportation expenses, the dealer is required to obtain the prior written authorization of the affected warrantor before incurring any transportation expenses, which authorization shall not be unreasonably denied by the warrantor, and provided further that any such request for transportation reimbursement must be denied by the warrantor within 5 business days of the warrantor's receipt of the dealer's request for reimbursement or the request shall be deemed authorized and allowed. Time allowances for the performance of warranty work and service shall be reasonable and adequate for the work to be performed. The compensation which must be paid under this section must be reasonable; provided, however, that under no circumstances may the reasonable compensation under this section be in an amount less than the recreational vehicle dealer's current retail labor rate for nonwarranty work of like kind, provided such amount is competitive with the retail rates charged for parts and labor by other franchised recreational dealers within the dealer's market.

(c) A warrantor may not require a dealer to establish the rate customarily charged by the recreational vehicle dealer for labor by an unduly burdensome or time-consuming method or by requiring information that is unduly burdensome or time-consuming to provide, including, but not limited to, part-by-part or transaction-by-transaction calculations.

(d) For any part, equipment, plumbing system or device, or appliance or option, a warrantor shall reimburse the dealer the cost of the part, equipment, plumbing system or device, appliance or option, plus a minimum of a thirty percent (30%) handling charge and pay the cost, if any, of freight to return the part, equipment, appliance, or option to the warrantor.

(e) If a warrantor furnishes a part or component to a dealer, at reduced or no cost, to use in performing repairs under a warranty or recall repair, the warrantor shall compensate the dealer for the part or component in the same manner as warranty parts compensation under this section, by compensating the dealer on the basis of a thirty percent (30%) handling charge for the part or component as listed in the warrantor's price schedule less the cost for the part or component.

(f) Notwithstanding the terms of any warranty, contract, or agreement, all claims made by recreational dealers pursuant to this section for compensation for delivery, preparation, warranty and recall work, and transportation costs, including labor, parts, and other expenses, shall be paid by the affected warrantor within 30 days after receipt of claim from the dealer. When any claim is disapproved, the dealer shall be notified in writing of the grounds for disapproval. Any claim not specifically disapproved in writing within 30 days after receipt shall be considered approved and payment is due immediately. No claim which has been approved and paid may be charged back to the dealer unless it can be shown that the claim was false or fraudulent, that the repairs were not properly made or were unnecessary to correct the defective condition, or the dealer failed to reasonably substantiate the claim either in accordance with the manufacturer's reasonable written procedures or by other reasonable means. A warrantor shall not deny a claim or reduce the amount to be reimbursed to the dealer as long as the dealer has provided reasonably sufficient documentation that the dealer (i) made a good-faith attempt to perform the work in compliance with the written policies and procedures of the warrantor and (ii) actually performed the work.

Notwithstanding the foregoing, a warrantor shall not fail to fully compensate a dealer for warranty or recall work or make any chargeback to the dealer's account based on the dealer's failure to comply with the warrantor's claim documentation procedure or procedures unless both of the following requirements have been met:

(1) The dealer has, within the previous 12 months, failed to comply with the same specific claim documentation procedure or procedures.

(2) The warrantor has, within the previous 12 months, provided a written warning to the dealer by certified United States mail, return receipt requested, identifying the specific claim documentation procedure or procedures violated by the dealer.

(g) Every recreational vehicle manufacturer, factory branch, distributor, or distributor branch that manufactures or distributes recreational vehicles for sale in this State shall designate at least one of its employees knowledgeable in warranty administration who shall be the designated warranty contact person with whom its franchised dealers licensed in this State can communicate to assist them in filing and getting paid on warranty claims related to all component parts of all recreational vehicles such recreational vehicle manufacturer, factory branch, distributor, or distributor branch sells or distributes in this State. Each recreational vehicle manufacturer, factory branch, distributor, or distributor branch shall promptly notify, in writing, all of its franchised recreational vehicle dealers licensed in this State, the Commissioner, and the North Carolina Automobile Dealers Association, Incorporated, of the identity and contact information of the designated warranty contact person and any changes in this information. A recreational vehicle manufacturer or distributor that represents multiple suppliers or multiple line-makes of vehicles shall be permitted to designate a single individual as the designated warranty contact person for all such suppliers and line-makes of vehicles represented by such recreational vehicle manufacturer or distributor.

(h) It shall be unlawful for any warrantor or for any recreational vehicle manufacturer,

factory branch, distributor, or distributor branch to recover or attempt to recover all or any portion of its costs for compensating recreational vehicle dealers licensed in this State for warranty or recall parts and service either by reduction in the amount due to the dealer or by separate charge, surcharge, or other imposition.

(i) It shall be unlawful for any recreational vehicle manufacturer, factory branch, distributor, or distributor branch to fail to indemnify and hold harmless its franchised dealers licensed in this State against any judgment for damages or settlements agreed to by the manufacturer, including, but not limited to, court costs and reasonable attorneys' fees of the recreational vehicle dealer, arising out of complaints, claims, or lawsuits, including, but not limited to, strict liability, negligence, misrepresentation, express or implied warranty, or rescission or revocation of acceptance of the sale of a vehicle as defined in G.S. 25-2-608, to the extent that the judgment or settlement relates to the alleged defective or negligent manufacture, assembly, or design of new recreational vehicles, parts, or accessories or other functions by the manufacturer, factory branch, distributor, or distributor branch beyond the control of the dealer. It shall be unlawful for any warrantor to fail to indemnify and hold harmless any recreational vehicle dealer located in this State who sold one or more products warranted by such warrantor against any judgment for damages or settlements agreed to by the warrantor, including, but not limited to, court costs and reasonable attorneys' fees of the recreational vehicle dealer, arising out of complaints, claims, or lawsuits, including, but not limited to, strict liability, negligence, misrepresentation, express or implied warranty, or rescission or revocation of acceptance of the sale of a vehicle or vehicle part, component, or accessory, as defined in G.S. 25-2-608, to the extent that the judgment or settlement relates to the alleged defective or negligent manufacture, assembly, or design of a product warranted by the warrantor or other functions of the warrantor beyond the control of the dealer. Any audit for warranty or recall parts or service compensation shall only be for the 12-month period immediately following the date of the payment of the claim by the manufacturer, factory branch, distributor, distributor branch, or warrantor. Any audit for sales incentives, service incentives, rebates, or other forms of incentive compensation shall only be for the 12-month period immediately following the date of the payment of the claim by the manufacturer, factory branch, distributor, distributor branch, or warrantor. Provided, however, these limitations shall not be effective in the case of fraudulent claims.

(j) It shall be unlawful for any warrantor or for any recreational vehicle manufacturer, factory branch, distributor, or distributor branch to direct or encourage any owner or purchaser of a recreational vehicle to have warranty or recall service work or other repairs on a recreational vehicle made by a repair facility other than either the franchised dealer that sold the vehicle owner the recreational vehicle or the franchised dealer closest in proximity to such recreational vehicle owner or purchaser, provided that the recreational vehicle dealer who sold the vehicle to the owner or purchaser or who is located in closest proximity to such recreational vehicle owner or purchaser has sufficiently trained personnel and the necessary tools and equipment to make the required repairs to the vehicle, has not expressly stated in writing its desire to have the repairs made elsewhere, and is willing to make the repairs within a reasonable period of time after the necessary parts have been supplied to the dealer.

(k) In the event there is a dispute between a recreational vehicle dealer and a warrantor or a recreational vehicle manufacturer, factory branch, distributor, or distributor branch, with relating to any matter referred to in this section, either party may petition the Commissioner in writing, within 30 days after either party has given written notice of the dispute to the other, for a hearing on the subject and the decision of the Commissioner shall be binding on the parties, subject to rights of judicial review and appeal as provided in Chapter 150B of the General Statutes; provided, however, that nothing contained herein shall give the Commissioner any authority as to the content of any warrantor's warranty. Upon the filing of a petition before the Commissioner under this subsection, any chargeback to or any payment required of a recreational vehicle dealer by a warrantor or by a recreational vehicle manufacturer, factory branch, distributor, or distributor branch relating to warranty or recall parts or service compensation, or to sales incentives, service incentives, rebates, other forms of incentive compensation, or the withholding or chargeback of other compensation or support that a dealer would otherwise be eligible to receive, shall be stayed during the pendency of the determination by the Commissioner.

(l) *(Effective until June 30, 2023)* The provisions of G.S. 20-305(4) through G.S. 20-305(28) and G.S. 20-305.2 to G.S. 20-305.4 shall not apply to manufacturers of or dealers in mobile or manufactured type housing or who sell or distribute only nonmotorized recreational trailers; provided, however, that unless specifically exempted, each of these provisions shall be applicable to all recreational vehicle manufacturers, factory branches, distributors, and distributor branches who sell or distribute any motorized recreational vehicles in this State. The provisions of G.S. 20-305.1 shall not apply

to manufacturers of or dealers in mobile or manufactured type housing.

(l) *(Effective June 30, 2023)* The provisions of G.S. 20-305(4) through G.S. 20-305(28) and G.S. 20-305.2 to G.S. 20-305.3 shall not apply to manufacturers of or dealers in mobile or manufactured type housing or who sell or distribute only nonmotorized recreational trailers; provided, however, that unless specifically exempted, each of these provisions shall be applicable to all recreational vehicle manufacturers, factory branches, distributors, and distributor branches who sell or distribute any motorized recreational vehicles in this State. The provisions of G.S. 20-305.1 shall not apply to manufacturers of or dealers in mobile or manufactured type housing.

(m) To the extent not expressly inconsistent with the provisions of this section, all of the terms and provisions of G.S. 20-305.1 shall be applicable to recreational vehicle dealers and to recreational vehicle manufacturers, factory branches, distributors, and distributor branches under this section. For purposes of this section and Article 12 of Chapter 20 of the General Statutes of North Carolina, the relationship between a recreational vehicle manufacturer or recreational vehicle distributor, on the one part, and a recreational vehicle dealer that is located within this State, on the other part, pursuant to which the recreational vehicle dealer purchases and resells new recreational vehicles from the recreational vehicle manufacturer or recreational vehicle distributor, shall be considered a "franchise", as this term is defined in G.S. 20-286(8a), whether or not the rights and responsibilities of the parties have been delineated in a written agreement or contract.

History.
1973, c. 88, s. 4; 1983, c. 704, s. 18; 2017-148, s. 4; 2021-90, s. 16(b)

§ 20-305.6. Unlawful for manufacturers to unfairly discriminate among dealers

Notwithstanding the terms of any contract, franchise, novation, or agreement, it shall be unlawful for any manufacturer, factory branch, distributor, or distributor branch to do any of the following:

(1) Discriminate against any similarly situated franchised new motor vehicle dealers in this State.

(2) Unfairly discriminate against franchised new motor vehicle dealers located in this State who have dualed facilities at which the vehicles distributed by the manufacturer, factory branch, distributor, or distributor branch are sold or serviced with one or more other line makes of vehicles.

(3) Unfairly discriminate against one of its franchised new motor vehicle dealers in this State with respect to any aspect of the franchise agreement.

(4) Use any financial services company or leasing company owned or controlled by the manufacturer or distributor to accomplish what would otherwise be illegal conduct on the part of the manufacturer or distributor pursuant to this section. This section shall not limit the right of the financial services or leasing company to engage in business practices in accordance with the trade.

History.
2001-510, s. 4

§ 20-305.7. Protecting dealership data and consent to access dealership information

(a) Except as expressly authorized in this section, no manufacturer, factory branch, distributor, or distributor branch shall require a new motor vehicle dealer to provide its customer lists, customer information, consumer contact information, transaction data, or service files. Any requirement by a manufacturer, factory branch, distributor, or distributor branch that a new motor vehicle dealer provide its customer lists, customer information, consumer contact information, transaction data, or service files to the manufacturer, factory branch, distributor, or distributor branch, or to any third party as a condition to the dealer's participation in any incentive program or contest, for a customer or dealer to receive any incentive payments otherwise earned under an incentive program or contest, for the dealer to obtain consumer or customer leads, or for the dealer to receive any other benefits, rights, merchandise, or services for which the dealer would otherwise be entitled to obtain under the franchise or any other contract or agreement, or which shall customarily be provided to dealers, shall be voidable at the option of the dealer, and the dealer shall automatically be entitled to all benefits earned under the applicable incentive program or contest or any other contract or agreement, unless all of the following conditions are satisfied: (i) the customer information requested relates solely to the specific program requirements or goals associated with such manufacturer's or distributor's own vehicle makes and does not require that the dealer provide general customer information or other information related to the dealer; (ii) such requirement is lawful and would also not require the dealer to allow any customer the right to opt out under the federal Gramm-Leach-Bliley Act, 15 U.S.C., Subchapter I, § 1608, et seq.; and (iii) the dealer is either permitted to restrict the data fields that may be accessed in the dealer's dealer management

computer system, or the dealer is permitted to provide the same dealer, consumer, or customer data or information specified by the manufacturer or distributor by timely obtaining and pushing or otherwise furnishing the required data in a widely accepted file format such as comma delimited in accordance with subsection (g1) of this section. Nothing contained in this section shall limit the ability of the manufacturer, factory branch, distributor, or distributor branch to require that the dealer provide, or use in accordance with the law, such customer information related solely to such manufacturer's or distributor's own vehicle makes to the extent necessary to do any of the following:

(1) Satisfy any safety or recall notice obligations.

(2) Complete the sale and delivery of a new motor vehicle to a customer.

(3) Validate and pay customer or dealer incentives.

(4) Submit to the manufacturer, factory branch, distributor, or distributor branch claims for any services supplied by the dealer for any claim for warranty parts or repairs.

At the request of a manufacturer or distributor or of a third party acting on behalf of a manufacturer or distributor, a dealer may only be required to provide customer information related solely to such manufacturer's or distributor's own vehicle makes for reasonable marketing purposes, market research, consumer surveys, market analysis, and dealership performance analysis, but the dealer is only required to provide such customer information to the extent lawfully permissible; to the extent the requested information relates solely to specific program requirements or goals associated with such manufacturer's or distributor's own vehicle makes and does not require the dealer to provide general customer information or other information related to the dealer; and to the extent the requested information can be provided without requiring that the dealer allow any customer the right to opt out under the federal Gramm-Leach-Bliley Act, 15 U.S.C., Subchapter I, § 6801, et seq.

No manufacturer, factory branch, distributor, or distributor branch shall access or obtain dealer or customer data from or write dealer or customer data to a dealer management computer system utilized by a motor vehicle dealer located in this State, or require or coerce a motor vehicle dealer located in this State to utilize a particular dealer management computer system, unless the dealer management computer system allows the dealer to reasonably maintain the security, integrity, and confidentiality of the data maintained in the system. No manufacturer, factory branch, distributor, distributor branch, dealer management computer system vendor, or any third party acting on behalf of any manufacturer, factory branch, distributor, distributor branch, or dealer management computer system vendor shall prohibit a dealer from providing a means to regularly and continually monitor the specific data accessed from or written to the dealer's computer system and from complying with applicable State and federal laws and any rules or regulations promulgated thereunder. These provisions shall not be deemed to impose an obligation on a manufacturer, factory branch, distributor, distributor branch, dealer management computer system vendor, or any third party acting on behalf of any manufacturer, factory branch, distributor, distributor branch, or dealer management computer system vendor to provide such capability. Notwithstanding the terms or conditions of any incentive program or contest that is either required or voluntary on the part of the dealer, or the terms or conditions of any other contract or agreement, it shall be unlawful for any manufacturer, factory branch, distributor, or distributor branch to fail or refuse to provide dealer notice, in a standalone written document, at least 30 days prior to making any changes in any of the dealer or customer data the dealer is requested or required to share with a manufacturer, factory branch, distributor, or distributor branch, or any third party. The changes in any of the dealer or customer data the dealer is required or requested to provide shall be void unless the applicable manufacturer, factory branch, distributor, or distributor branch complies with the notice requirements contained in this paragraph.

(b) No manufacturer, factory branch, distributor, distributor branch, dealer management computer system vendor, or any third party acting on behalf of any manufacturer, factory branch, distributor, distributor branch, or dealer management computer system vendor may access or utilize customer or prospect information maintained in a dealer management computer system utilized by a motor vehicle dealer located in this State for purposes of soliciting any such customer or prospect on behalf of, or directing the customer or prospect to, any other dealer. The limitations in this subsection do not apply to any of the following:

(1) A customer that requests a reference to another dealership.

(2) A customer that moves more than 60 miles away from the dealer whose data was accessed.

(3) Customer or prospect information that was provided to the dealer by the manufacturer, factory branch, distributor, or distributor branch.

(4) Customer or prospect information obtained by the manufacturer, factory branch, distributor, or distributor branch where the dealer agrees to allow the manufacturer, factory branch, distributor, distributor branch, dealer management computer system vendor, or any third party acting on behalf of any manufacturer, factory branch, distributor, distributor branch, or dealer management computer system vendor the right to access and utilize the customer or prospect information maintained in the dealer's dealer management computer system for purposes of soliciting any customer or prospect of the dealer on behalf of, or directing the customer or prospect to, any other dealer in a separate, stand-alone written instrument dedicated solely to the authorization.

No manufacturer, factory branch, distributor, distributor branch, dealer management computer system vendor, or any third party acting on behalf of any manufacturer, factory branch, distributor, distributor branch, or dealer management computer system vendor may provide access to customer or dealership information maintained in a dealer management computer system utilized by a motor vehicle dealer located in this State, without first obtaining the dealer's prior express written consent, revocable by the dealer upon five business days written notice, to provide the access. Prior to obtaining this consent and prior to entering into an initial contract or renewal of a contract with a dealer located in this State, the manufacturer, factory branch, distributor, distributor branch, dealer management computer system vendor, or any third party acting on behalf of, or through any manufacturer, factory branch, distributor, distributor branch, or dealer management computer system vendor shall provide to the dealer a written list of all specific third parties to whom any data obtained from the dealer has actually been provided within the 12-month period ending November 1 of the prior year. The list shall further describe the scope and specific fields of the data provided. In addition to the initial list, a dealer management computer system vendor or any third party acting on behalf of or through a dealer management computer system vendor shall provide to the dealer an annual list of each and every third party to whom the data is actually being provided on November 1 of each year and each and every third party to whom the data was actually provided in the preceding 12 months and for each and every third party identified, the scope and specific fields of the data provided to the third party during the 12-month period. This list shall be provided to the dealer by January 1 of each year. The lists required in this subsection of the third parties to whom any data obtained from the dealer has actually been provided shall be specific to each affected dealer. It is insufficient and unlawful for the provider of this information to furnish any dealer a list of third parties who could or may have received any of the affected dealer's data, as the information required to be provided in this subsection requires the provider of this information to state the identity and other specified information of each and every third party to whom the data was actually provided during the relevant period of time. Any dealer management computer system vendor's contract that directly relates to the transfer or accessing of dealer or dealer customer information must conspicuously state, "NOTICE TO DEALER: THIS AGREEMENT RELATES TO THE TRANSFER AND ACCESSING OF CONFIDENTIAL INFORMATION AND CONSUMER RELATED DATA". This consent does not change any such person's obligations to comply with the terms of this section and any additional State or federal laws (and any rules or regulations adopted under these laws) applicable to the person with respect to the access. In addition, no dealer management computer system vendor shall refuse to provide a dealer management computer system to a motor vehicle dealer located in this State if the dealer refuses to provide any consent under this subsection.

(b1) Notwithstanding the terms of any contract or agreement with a dealer management computer system vendor or third party, for purposes of this subsection, the dealer's data contained in or on a dealer management computer system owned, leased, or licensed by a dealer located in this State is the property of the dealer. For purposes of this section, the terms "dealer data" and "dealer's data" shall be defined as any information or other data that has been entered, by direct entry or otherwise, or stored on the dealer's dealer management computer system by an officer or employee of the dealer or third party contracted by the dealer, whether stored or hosted on-site at a dealer location or on the cloud or at any other remote location, that contains data or other information about any of the following: (i) the dealer's sales, service, or parts customers or the dealer's customer transactions, (ii) customer leads generated by or

provided to the dealer, (iii) the tracking, history, or performance of the dealer's internal processing of customer orders and work, (iv) customer deal files, (v) customer recommendations or complaints communicated by any means to the dealer, (vi) the tracking of dealer or customer incentive payments sought or received from any manufacturer or distributor, (vii) business plans, goals, objectives, or strategies created by any officer, employer, or contractee of the dealer; (viii) the dealer's internal bank, financial, or business records, (ix) email, voice, and other communications between or among the dealer's officers or employees, (x) email, voice, and other communications between the dealer's officers or employees and third parties, (xi) contracts and agreements with third parties and all records related to the performance of such contracts and agreements, (xii) employee performance, (xiii) dealer personnel records, and (xiv) dealer inventory data. The terms "dealer data" and "dealer's data" specifically exclude the proprietary software, intellectual property, data, or information of a dealer management computer system vendor, manufacturer, factory branch, distributor, or distributor branch, data specifically licensed from a third party by a dealer management computer system vendor, manufacturer, factory branch, distributor, or distributor branch, and data provided to a dealer by a manufacturer, factory branch, distributor, distributor branch, subsidiary, or affiliate.

Notwithstanding the terms of any contract or agreement, it shall be unlawful for any dealer management computer system vendor, or any third party having access to any dealer management computer system, to:

(1) Unreasonably interfere with a dealer's ability to protect, store, copy, share, or use any dealer data downloaded from a dealer management computer system utilized by a new motor vehicle dealer located in this State. Unlawful conduct prohibited by this section includes, but is not limited to:

a. Imposing any unreasonable fees or other restrictions on the dealer or any third party for access to or sharing of dealer data. For purposes of this section, the term "unreasonable fees" means charges for access to customer or dealer data beyond any direct costs incurred by any dealer management computer system vendor in providing access to the dealer's customer or dealer data to a third party that the dealer has authorized to access its dealer management computer system or allowing any third party that the dealer has authorized to access its dealer management computer system to write data to its dealer management

Chapter 20

computer system. Nothing contained in this subdivision shall be deemed to prohibit the charging of a fee, which includes the ability of the service provider to recoup development costs incurred to provide the services involved and to make a reasonable profit on the services provided. Any charges must be both (i) reasonable in amount and (ii) disclosed to the dealer in reasonably sufficient detail prior to the fees being charged to the dealer, or they will be deemed prohibited, unreasonable fees.

b. Imposing unreasonable restrictions on secure integration by any third party that the dealer has explicitly authorized to access its dealer management computer system for the purpose of accessing dealer data. Examples of unreasonable restrictions include, but are not limited to, any of the following:

1. Unreasonable restrictions on the scope or nature of the dealer's data shared with a third party authorized by the dealer to access the dealer's dealer management computer system.

2. Unreasonable restrictions on the ability of a third party authorized by the dealer to securely access the dealer's dealer management computer system to share dealer data or securely write dealer data to a dealer management computer system.

3. Requiring unreasonable access to sensitive, competitive, or other confidential business information of a third party as a condition for access dealer data.

4. It shall not be an unreasonable restriction to condition a third party's access to the dealer management computer system on that third party's compliance with reasonable security standards or operational protocols that the dealer management computer system vendor specifies.

c. Sharing dealer data with any third party, if sharing the data is not authorized by the dealer.

d. Prohibiting or unreasonably limiting a dealer's ability to store, copy, securely share, or use dealer data outside the dealer's dealer management computer system in any manner and for any reason once it has been downloaded from the dealer management computer system.

e. Permitting access to or accessing dealer data without first obtaining the dealer's express written consent in a standalone document or contractual provision that is conspicuous in appearance, contained in a separate page or screen from any other written material, and requires an independent mark or affirmation from a dealer principal, general manager, or other management level employee of the dealership expressly authorized in writing by the dealer principal or general manager.

f. Upon receipt of a written request from a dealer, failing or refusing to block specific data fields containing dealer data from being shared with one or more third parties. Where blocking hinders, blocks, diminishes, or otherwise interferes with the functionality of a third party's service or product or the dealer's ability to participate in an incentive or other program of a manufacturer, factory branch, distributor, or distributor branch, or other third party authorized by the dealer, the dealer management computer system vendor shall be held harmless from the dealer's decision to block specified data fields, so long as the dealer management computer system vendor was acting at the direction of the dealer.

(2) Access, use, store, or share any dealer data from a dealer management computer system in any manner other than as expressly permitted in its written agreement with the dealer.

(3) Fail to provide the dealer with the option and ability to securely obtain and push or otherwise distribute specified dealer data within the dealer's dealer management computer system to any third party instead of the third party receiving the dealer data directly from the dealer's dealer management computer system vendor or providing the third party direct access to the dealer's dealer management computer system. A dealer management computer system vendor shall be held harmless for any errors, breach, misuse, or any harms directly or indirectly caused by a dealer sharing data with any third party beyond the control of the dealer management computer system vendor. In the event a dealer sharing data with a third party outside of the control of the dealer computer management system vendor causes damage to the dealer management computer system or any third party, the party or parties that caused the damage shall be liable for the damage.

(4) Fail to provide the dealer, within seven days of receiving a dealer's written request, access to any SOC 2 audit conducted on behalf of the dealer management

computer system vendor and related to the services licensed by the dealer.

(5) Fail to promptly provide a dealer, upon the dealer's written request, a written listing of all entities with whom it is currently sharing any data from the dealer's dealer management computer system and with whom it has, within the immediately 12 preceding months, shared any data from the dealer's dealer management computer system, the specific data fields shared with each entity identified, and the dates any data was shared, to the extent that information can reasonably be stored by the dealership management computer system vendor.

(6) Upon receipt of a dealer's written request to terminate any contract or agreement for the provision of hardware or software related to the dealer's dealer management computer system, to fail to promptly provide a copy of the dealer's data maintained on its dealership management computer system to the dealer in a secure, usable format.

Nothing in this section prevents the charging of a fee, which includes the ability of the dealer management computer system vendor to recoup costs incurred to provide the services involved and to make a reasonable profit on the services provided. Charges must be disclosed to and approved by the dealer prior to the time the dealer incurs the charges.

Nothing in this section prevents any dealer or third party from discharging its obligations as a service provider under federal, State, or local law to protect and secure protected dealer data.

Nothing in this section shall be deemed to prohibit a dealer management computer system vendor from conditioning a party's access to, or integration with, a dealer's dealer management computer system on that party's compliance with reasonable security standards or other operational protocols that the dealer's computer management system vendor specifies.

For purposes of this subsection, the term "third party" shall not be applicable to any manufacturer, factory branch, distributor, distributor branch, or subsidiary or affiliate thereof.

(b2) The rights conferred on dealers in this section are not waivable and may not be reduced or otherwise modified by any contract or agreement.

(c) No dealer management computer system vendor, or third party acting on behalf of or through any dealer management computer system vendor, may access or obtain data from or write data to a dealer management computer system utilized by a motor vehicle dealer located in this State, unless the dealer management computer system allows the dealer to reasonably maintain the security, integrity, and confidentiality of the customer and dealership information maintained in the system. No dealer management computer system vendor, or third party acting on behalf of or through any dealer management computer system vendor, shall prohibit a dealer from providing a means to regularly and continually monitor the specific data accessed from or written to the dealer's computer system and from complying with applicable State and federal laws and any rules or regulations adopted under these laws. This section does not impose an obligation on a manufacturer, factory branch, distributor, distributor branch, dealer management computer system vendor, or any third party acting on behalf of any manufacturer, factory branch, distributor, distributor branch, or dealer management computer system vendor to provide this capability.

(d) Any manufacturer, factory branch, distributor, distributor branch, dealer management computer system vendor, or any third party acting on behalf of or through any dealer management computer system vendor, having electronic access to customer or motor vehicle dealership data in a dealership management computer system utilized by a motor vehicle dealer located in this State shall provide notice to the dealer of any security breach of dealership or customer data obtained through the access, which at the time of the breach was in the possession or custody of the manufacturer, factory branch, distributor, distributor branch, dealer management computer system vendor, or third party. The disclosure notification shall be made without unreasonable delay by the manufacturer, factory branch, distributor, distributor branch, dealer management computer system vendor, or third party following discovery by the person, or notification to the person, of the breach. The disclosure notification shall describe measures reasonably necessary to determine the scope of the breach and corrective actions that may be taken in an effort to restore the integrity, security, and confidentiality of the data. These measures and corrective actions shall be implemented as soon as practicable by all persons responsible for the breach.

(e) Nothing in this section precludes, prohibits, or denies the right of the manufacturer, factory branch, distributor, or distributor branch to receive customer or dealership information from a motor vehicle dealer located in this State for the purposes of complying with federal or State safety requirements or implementing steps related to manufacturer recalls at such times as necessary in order to comply with federal and State requirements or manufacturer recalls so long as receiving this information from the dealer does not impair, alter, or reduce the security, integrity, and confidentiality of the customer and dealership information collected or generated by the dealer.

(f) The following definitions apply to this section:

(1) **Dealer management computer system.** -- A computer hardware and software system that is owned or leased by the dealer, including a dealer's use of Web applications, software, or hardware, whether located at the dealership or provided at a remote location and that provides access to customer records and transactions by a motor vehicle dealer located in this State and that allows the motor vehicle dealer timely information in order to sell vehicles, parts, or services through the motor vehicle dealership.

(2) **Dealer management computer system vendor.** -- A seller or reseller of dealer management computer systems, a person that sells computer software for use on dealer management computer systems, or a person that services or maintains dealer management computer systems, but only to the extent that each of the sellers, resellers, or other persons listed in this subdivision are engaged in these activities.

(3) **Security breach.** -- An incident of unauthorized access to and acquisition of records or data containing dealership or dealership customer information where unauthorized use of the dealership or dealership customer information has occurred or is reasonably likely to occur or that creates a material risk of harm to a dealership or a dealership's customer. Any incident of unauthorized access to and acquisition of records or data containing dealership or dealership customer information or any incident of disclosure of dealership customer information to one or more third parties that has not been specifically authorized by the dealer or customer constitutes a security breach.

(g) G.S. 20-308.1(d) does not apply to an action brought under this section against a dealer management computer system vendor.

(g1) Notwithstanding any of the terms or provisions contained in this section or in any consent, authorization, release, novation, franchise, or other contract or agreement, whenever any manufacturer, factory branch, distributor, distributor branch, dealer management computer system vendor, or any third party acting on behalf of or through, or approved, referred, endorsed, authorized, certified, granted preferred status, or recommended by, any manufacturer, factory branch, distributor, distributor branch, or dealer management computer system vendor requires that a new motor vehicle dealer

provide any dealer, consumer, or customer data or information through direct access to a dealer's computer system, the dealer is not required to provide, and shall not be required to consent to provide in any written agreement, such direct access to its computer system. The dealer may instead provide the same dealer, consumer, or customer data or information specified by the requesting party by timely obtaining and pushing or otherwise furnishing the requested data to the requesting party in a widely accepted file format such as comma delimited. When a dealer would otherwise be required to provide direct access to its computer system under the terms of a consent, authorization, release, novation, franchise, or other contract or agreement, a dealer that elects to provide data or information through other means may be charged a reasonable initial set-up fee and a reasonable processing fee based on the actual incremental costs incurred by the party requesting the data for establishing and implementing the process for the dealer. Any term or provision contained in any consent, authorization, release, novation, franchise, or other contract or agreement that is inconsistent with any term or provision contained in this subsection is voidable at the option of the dealer.

(g2) Notwithstanding the terms or conditions of any consent, authorization, release, novation, franchise, or other contract or agreement, every manufacturer, factory branch, distributor, distributor branch, dealer management computer system vendor, or any third party acting on behalf of or through any manufacturer, factory branch, distributor, distributor branch, or dealer management computer system vendor, having electronic access to consumer or customer data or other information in a computer system utilized by a new motor vehicle dealer, or who has otherwise been provided consumer or customer data or information by the dealer, shall fully indemnify and hold harmless any dealer from whom it has acquired the consumer or customer data or other information from all damages, costs, and expenses incurred by the dealer. This indemnification by the manufacturer, factory branch, distributor, distributor branch, dealer management computer system vendor, or third party acting on behalf of these entities includes, but is not limited to, judgments, settlements, fines, penalties, litigation costs, defense costs, court costs, costs related to the disclosure of security breaches, and attorneys' fees arising out of complaints, claims, civil or administrative actions, and, to the fullest extent allowable under the law, governmental investigations and prosecutions to the extent caused by a security breach; the access, storage, maintenance, use, sharing, disclosure, or retention of the dealer's consumer or customer data or other information; or maintenance or services provided to any computer system utilized by a new motor vehicle dealer.

(h) This section applies to contracts entered into on or after November 1, 2005.

History.
2005-409, s. 4; 2007-513, s. 10; 2011-290, s. 11; 2013-302, s. 9; 2018-27, s. 3; 2019-125, s. 7; 2019-177, s. 4.2; 2020-51, s. 2

§ 20-306. Unlawful for salesman to sell except for his employer; multiple employment; persons who arrange transactions involving the sale of new motor vehicles

It shall be unlawful for any motor vehicle salesman licensed under this Article or an individual who has submitted an application for a license as required in G.S. 20-288 and who is engaging in activities as a supervised sales representative applicant while the application is pending pursuant to G.S. 20-287(a) to sell or exchange or offer or attempt to sell or exchange any motor vehicle other than his own except for the licensed motor vehicle dealer or dealers by whom he is employed, or to offer, transfer or assign, any sale or exchange, that he may have negotiated, to any other dealer or salesman. A salesman may be employed by more than one dealer provided such multiple employment is clearly indicated on his license. It shall be unlawful for any person to, for a fee, commission, or other valuable consideration, arrange or offer to arrange a transaction involving the sale of a new motor vehicle; provided, however, this prohibition shall not be applicable to:

(1) A franchised motor vehicle dealer as defined in G.S. 20-286(8b) who is licensed under this Article or a sales representative who is licensed under this Article when acting on behalf of the dealer;

(2) A manufacturer who is licensed under this Article or bona fide employee of such manufacturer when acting on behalf of the manufacturer;

(3) A distributor who is licensed under this Article or a bona fide employee of such distributor when acting on behalf of the distributor; or

(4) At any point in the transaction the bona fide owner of the vehicle involved in the transaction.

(5) A motor vehicle dealer, as defined in G.S. 20-286(11), who offers valuable consideration to a person not licensed under this Article, or a person who is offered or receives valuable consideration from a motor vehicle dealer for the referral of a customer to the dealer, provided that the consideration paid by the motor vehicle dealer does not exceed two hundred fifty dollars

($ 250.00) in value per referral and the person receiving the consideration has received no more than five referral payments from that motor vehicle dealer in the same calendar year.

History.
1955, c. 1243, s. 22; 1993, c. 331, s. 3; 2019-181, s. 3

§ 20-307. Article applicable to existing and future franchises and contracts

The provisions of this Article shall be applicable to all franchises and contracts existing between dealers and manufacturers, factory branches, and distributors at the time of its ratification, and to all such future franchises and contracts.

History.
1955, c. 1243, s. 23

§ 20-307.1. Jurisdiction

A franchisee who is substantially and primarily engaged in the sale of motor vehicles or parts, materials, or components of motor vehicles, including batteries, tires, transmissions, mufflers, painting, lubrication or tune-ups may bring suit against any franchisor, engaged in commerce, in the General Court of Justice in the State of North Carolina that has proper venue.

History.
1983, c. 704, s. 24

§ 20-308. Penalties

Any person violating any of the provisions of this Article, except for G.S. 20-305.7, shall be guilty of a Class 1 misdemeanor.

History.
1955, c. 1243, s. 24; 1993, c. 539, s. 386; 1994, Ex. Sess., c. 24, s. 14(c); 2005-409, s. 5

§ 20-308.1. Civil actions for violations

(a) Notwithstanding the terms, provisions or conditions of any agreement or franchise or other terms or provisions of any novation, waiver or other written instrument, any motor vehicle dealer who is or may be injured by a violation of a provision of this Article, or any party to a franchise who is so injured in his business or property by a violation of a provision of this Article relating to that franchise, or an arrangement which, if consummated, would be in violation of this Article may, notwithstanding the initiation or pendency of, or failure to initiate an administrative proceeding before

Chapter 20

the Commissioner concerning the same parties or subject matter, bring an action for damages and equitable relief, including injunctive relief, in any court of competent jurisdiction with regard to any matter not within the jurisdiction of the Commissioner or that seeks relief wholly outside the authority or jurisdiction of the Commissioner to award.

(b) Where the violation of a provision of this Article can be shown to be willful, malicious, or wanton, or if continued multiple violations of a provision or provisions of this Article occur, the court may award punitive damages, attorneys' fees and costs in addition to any other damages under this Article.

(c) A new motor vehicle dealer, if he has not suffered any loss of money or property, may obtain final equitable relief if it can be shown that the violation of a provision of this Article by a manufacturer or distributor may have the effect of causing a loss of money or property.

(d) In order to prevent injury or harm to all or a substantial number of its members or to prevent injury or harm to the franchise distribution system of new motor vehicles within this State, any association that is comprised of a minimum of 400 new motor vehicle dealers, or a minimum of 10 motorcycle dealers or recreational vehicle dealers, substantially all of whom are new motor vehicle dealers located within North Carolina, and which represents the collective interests of its members, shall have standing to intervene as a party in any civil or administrative proceeding in any of the courts or administrative agencies of this State, or to file a petition before the Commissioner or a civil action or cause of action in any court of competent jurisdiction for itself, or on behalf of any or all of its members, seeking declaratory and injunctive relief. An action brought pursuant to this subsection may seek a determination whether one or more manufacturers, factory branches, distributors, or distributor branches doing business in this State have violated any of the provisions of this Article, or for the determination of any rights created or defined by this Article, so long as the association alleges an injury to the collective interest of its members cognizable under this section. A cognizable injury to the collective interest of the members of the association shall be deemed to occur if a manufacturer, factory branch, distributor, or distributor branch doing business in this State, or seeking to be licensed by the Division in any capacity or to otherwise engage in business in this State, applies for licensure to own, operate, or control a motor vehicle dealership in this State in violation of this Article or engages in any conduct or takes any action that either: (i) has harmed or would harm or which has adversely affected or would adversely affect a majority of its franchised new

motor vehicle dealers in this State or a majority of all franchised new motor vehicle dealers in this State, or (ii) would erode or cause any other damage or injury to the franchise system of distribution of new motor vehicles within this State, whether or not the manufacturer, factory branch, distributor, or distributor branch currently has or proposes to have any franchised dealer in this State. Notwithstanding the foregoing, nothing in this subsection shall be construed to convey standing for an association to intervene in the denial of a renewal license or revocation of existing licenses issued by the Division pursuant to this Chapter or other enforcement actions taken against individual dealers or other individual licensees that may be initiated by the Division pursuant to G.S. 20-294 or other statute. Intervention by the association shall be limited to seeking declaratory relief, injunctive relief, or both declaratory and injunctive relief. With respect to any administrative or civil action filed by an association pursuant to this subsection, the relief granted shall be limited to declaratory and injunctive relief and in no event shall the Commissioner or court enter an award of monetary damages. In the event that, in any civil action before a court of this State in which an association has exercised standing in accordance with this subsection and becomes a party to the action, the court enters a declaratory ruling as to the facial applicability of any of the provisions contained in this Article, or interpreting the rights and obligations of one or more manufacturers or distributors or the rights and obligations of one or more dealers, the court's determination shall be collateral estoppel in any subsequent civil action or administrative proceeding involving the same manufacturer or manufacturers, or the same distributor or distributors, or the same dealer or dealers on all issues of fact and law decided in the original civil action in which the association was a party, provided the same decision or specific portion of the decision qualifies for application of collateral estoppel under North Carolina law. Notwithstanding anything contained herein, this subsection shall not be applicable to motor vehicle dealer licenses issued by the Division to a manufacturer pursuant to G.S. 20-305.2(a)(4a), provided that this exclusion from association standing shall not be applicable in the event the manufacturer applies for or is issued more than the maximum total number of motor vehicle dealer licenses permitted in G.S. 20-305.2(a)(4a) or upon the occurrence of any of the events listed in sub-subdivisions a. through d. of G.S. 20-305.2(a)(4a).

History.
1983, c. 704, s. 16; 1991, c. 510, s. 5; 2001-510, s. 5; 2007-513, s. 8; 2019-125, s. 8

§ 20-308.2. Applicability of this Article

(a) Any person who engages directly or indirectly in purposeful contacts within this State in connection with the offering or advertising for sale, or has business dealings, with respect to a new motor vehicle sale within this State, shall be subject to the provisions of this Article and shall be subject to the jurisdiction of the courts of this State.

(b) The applicability of this Article shall not be affected by a choice of law clause in any franchise, agreement, waiver, novation, or any other written instrument.

(c) Any provision of any agreement, franchise, waiver, novation or any other written instrument which is in violation of any section of this Article shall be deemed null and void and without force and effect.

(d) It shall be unlawful for a manufacturer or distributor to use any subsidiary corporation, affiliated corporation, or any other controlled corporation, partnership, association or person to accomplish what would otherwise be illegal conduct under this Article on the part of the manufacturer or distributor.

(e) The provisions of this Article shall apply to all written agreements between a manufacturer, wholesaler, or distributor with a motor vehicle dealer including, but not limited to, the franchise offering, the franchise agreement, sales of goods, services or advertising, leases or deeds of trust of real or personal property, promises to pay, security interests, pledges, insurance contracts, advertising contracts, construction or installation contracts, servicing contracts, and all other such agreements between a motor vehicle dealer and a manufacturer, wholesaler, or distributor.

History.
1983, c. 704, s. 17; 2005-409, s. 6

§§ 20-308.3 through 20-308.12

Reserved for future codification purposes.

ARTICLE 12A
MOTOR VEHICLE CAPTIVE FINANCE SOURCE LAW

§ 20-308.13. Regulation of motor vehicle captive finance sources

The General Assembly finds and declares that the distribution of motor vehicles in the State of North Carolina vitally affects the general economy of the State and the public interest and public welfare, and in the exercise of its police power, it is necessary to regulate motor vehicle captive finance sources doing business in North Carolina to protect and preserve the investments and properties of the citizens of this State.

History.
2005-409, s. 3

§ 20-308.14. Definitions

The definitions contained in G.S. 20-286 shall be applicable to the provisions of this Article.

History.
2005-409, s. 3

§ 20-308.15. Prohibited contractual requirements imposed by manufacturer, distributor, or captive finance source

It shall be unlawful for any manufacturer, factory branch, captive finance source, distributor, or distributor branch, or any field representative, officer, agent, or any representative of them, notwithstanding the terms, provisions, or conditions of any agreement or franchise, to require any of its franchised dealers located in this State to agree to any terms, conditions, or requirements that are set forth in subdivisions (1) through (8) below in order for any such dealer to sell to any captive finance source (defined below) any retail installment contract, loan, or lease of any motor vehicles purchased or leased by any of the dealer's customers ("contract for sale or lease"), or to be able to participate in, or otherwise, directly or indirectly, obtain the benefits of any consumer transaction incentive program payable to the consumer or the dealer and offered by or through any financial source that provides automotive-related loans or purchases retail installment contracts or lease contracts for motor vehicles in North Carolina and is, directly or indirectly, owned, operated, or controlled by such manufacturer, factory branch, distributor, or distributor branch ("captive finance source"):

(1) Require a dealer to grant such captive finance source a power of attorney to do anything on behalf of the dealer other than sign the dealer's name on any check, draft, or other instrument received in payment or proceeds under any contract for the sale or lease of a motor vehicle that is made payable to the dealer but which is properly payable to the captive finance source, is for the purpose of correcting an error in a customer's finance application or title processing document, or is for the purpose of processing regular titling of the vehicle.

(2) Require a dealer to warrant or guarantee the accuracy and completeness of any personal, financial, or credit information provided by the customer on the credit

application and/or in the course of applying for credit other than to require that the dealer make reasonable inquiry regarding the accuracy and completeness of such information and represent that such information is true and correct to the best of the dealer's knowledge.

(3) Require a dealer to repurchase, pay off, or guaranty any contract for the sale or lease of a motor vehicle or to require a dealer to indemnify, defend, or hold harmless the captive finance source for settlements, judgments, damages, litigation expenses, or other costs or expenses incurred by such captive finance source unless the obligation to repurchase, pay off, guaranty, indemnify, or hold harmless resulted directly from (i) the subject dealer's material breach of the terms of a written agreement with the captive finance source or the terms for the purchase of an individual contract for sale or lease that the captive finance source communicates to the dealer before each such purchase, except to the extent the breached terms are otherwise prohibited under subdivisions (1) through (8) of this section, or (ii) the subject dealer's violation of applicable law. For purposes of this section, the dealer may, however, contractually obligate itself to warrant the accuracy of the information provided on the finance contact, but such warranty can only be enforced if the captive finance source gives the dealer a reasonable opportunity to cure or correct any errors on the finance contract where cure or correction is possible. For purposes of this section, any allegation by a third party that would constitute a breach of the terms of a written agreement between the dealer and a captive finance source shall be considered a material breach.

(4) Notwithstanding the terms of any contract or agreement, treat a dealer's breach of an agreement between the dealer and a captive finance source with respect to the captive finance source's purchase of individual contracts for the sale or lease of a motor vehicle as a breach of such agreement with respect to purchase of other such contracts, nor shall such a breach, in and of itself, constitute a breach of any other agreement between the dealer and the captive finance source, or between the dealer and any affiliate of such captive finance source.

(5) Require a dealer to waive any defenses that may be available to it under its agreements with the captive finance source or under any applicable laws.

(6) Require a dealer to settle or contribute any of its own funds or financial resources toward the settlement of any multiparty or class action litigation without obtaining the dealer's voluntary and written consent subsequent to the filing of such litigation.

(7) Require a dealer to contribute to any reserve or contingency account established or maintained by the captive finance source, for the financing of the sale or lease of any motor vehicles purchased or leased by any of the dealer's customers, in any amount or on any basis other than the reasonable expected amount of future finance reserve chargebacks to the dealer's account. This section shall not apply to or limit (i) reasonable amounts reserved and maintained related to the sale or financing of any products ancillary to the sale, lease, or financing of the motor vehicle itself; (ii) a delay or reduction in the payment of dealer's portion of the finance income pursuant to an agreement between the dealer and a captive finance source under which the dealer agrees to such delay or reduction in exchange for the limitation, reduction, or elimination of the dealer's responsibility for finance reserve chargebacks; or (iii) a chargeback to a dealer (or offset of any amounts otherwise payable to a dealer by the captive finance source) for any indebtedness properly owing from a dealer to the captive finance source as part of a specific program covered by this section, the terms of which have been agreed to by the dealer in advance, except to the extent such chargeback would otherwise be prohibited under subdivisions (1) through (8) of this section.

(8) Require a dealer to repossess or otherwise gain possession of a motor vehicle at the request of or on behalf of the captive finance source. This section shall not apply to any requirements contained in any agreement between the dealer and the captive finance source wherein the dealer agrees to receive and process vehicles that are voluntarily returned by the customer or returned to the lessor at the end of the lease term.

Any clause or provision in any franchise or agreement between a dealer and a manufacturer, factory branch, distributor, or distributor branch, or between a dealer and any captive finance source, that is in violation of or that is inconsistent with any of the provisions of this section shall be voidable, to the extent that it violates this section, at any time at the election of the dealer.

History.
2005-409, s. 3

§ 20-308.16. Powers of Commissioner

(a) The Commissioner shall promote the interests of the retail buyer of motor vehicles.

(b) The Commissioner shall have power to prevent unfair or deceptive acts or practices and other violations of this Article. Any franchised new motor vehicle dealer who believes that a captive finance source with whom the dealer does business in North Carolina has violated or is currently violating any provision of this Article may file a petition before the Commissioner setting forth the factual and legal basis for such violations. The Commissioner shall promptly forward a copy of the petition to the named captive finance source requesting a reply to the petition within 30 days. Allowing for sufficient time for the parties to conduct discovery, the Commissioner or his designee shall then hold an evidentiary hearing and render findings of fact and conclusions of law based on the evidence presented.

(c) The Commissioner shall have the power in hearings arising under this Article to enter scheduling orders and limit the time and scope of discovery; to determine the date, time, and place where hearings are to be held; to subpoena witnesses; to take depositions of witnesses; and to administer oaths.

(d) The Commissioner may, whenever he shall believe from evidence submitted to him that any person has been or is violating any provision of this Article, in addition to any other remedy, bring an action in the name of the State against that person and any other persons concerned or in any way participating in, or about to participate in, practices or acts so in violation, to enjoin any persons from continuing the violations.

(e) The Commissioner may issue rules and regulations to implement the provisions of this section and to establish procedures related to administrative proceedings commenced under this section.

(f) In the event that a dealer, who is permitted or required to file a notice, protest, or petition before the Commissioner within a certain period of time in order to adjudicate, enforce, or protect rights afforded the dealer under this Article, voluntarily elects to appeal a policy, determination, or decision of the captive finance source through an appeals board or internal grievance procedure of the captive finance source, or to participate in or refer the matter to mediation, arbitration, or other alternative dispute resolution procedure or process established or endorsed by the captive finance source, the applicable period of time for the dealer to file the notice, protest, or petition before the Commissioner under this Article shall not commence until the captive finance source's appeal board or internal grievance procedure, mediation, arbitration, or appeals process of the captive finance source has been completed and the dealer has received notice in writing of the final decision or result of the procedure or process. Nothing, however, contained in this subsection shall be deemed to require that any dealer exhaust any internal grievance or other alternative dispute process required or established by the captive finance source before seeking redress from the Commissioner as provided in this Article.

History.
2005-409, s. 3

§ 20-308.17. Rules and regulations

The Commissioner may make such rules and regulations, not inconsistent with the provisions of this Article, as he shall deem necessary or proper for the effective administration and enforcement of this Article, provided that a copy of such rules and regulations shall be mailed to each motor vehicle dealer licensee and captive finance source 30 days prior to the effective date of such rules and regulations.

History.
2005-409, s. 3

§ 20-308.18. Hearing notice

In every case of a hearing before the Commissioner authorized under this Article, the Commissioner shall give reasonable notice of each such hearing to all interested parties, and the Commissioner's decision shall be binding on the parties, subject to the rights of judicial review and appeal as provided in Chapter 150B of the General Statutes. The costs of such hearings shall be assessed by the Commissioner.

History.
2005-409, s. 3

§ 20-308.19. Article applicable to existing and future agreements

The provisions of this Article shall be applicable to all contracts and agreements existing between dealers and captive finance sources at the time of its ratification and to all such future contracts and agreements.

History.
2005-409, s. 3

§ 20-308.20. Jurisdiction

A new motor vehicle dealer located in this State may bring suit against any captive finance source engaged in commerce in this State

Chapter 20

in the General Court of Justice in the State of North Carolina that has proper venue.

History.
2005-409, s. 3

§ 20-308.21. Civil actions for violations

(a) Notwithstanding the terms, provisions, or conditions of any agreement or other terms or provisions of any novation, waiver, arbitration agreement, or other written instrument, any person who is or may be injured by a violation of a provision of this Article, or any party to an agreement who is so injured in his business or property by a violation of a provision of this Article relating to that agreement, or an arrangement which, if consummated, would be in violation of this Article may, notwithstanding the initiation or pendency of, or failure to initiate an administrative proceeding before the Commissioner concerning the same parties or subject matter, bring an action for damages and equitable relief, including injunctive relief, in any court of competent jurisdiction with regard to any matter not within the jurisdiction of the Commissioner or that seeks relief wholly outside the authority or jurisdiction of the Commissioner to award.

(b) Where the violation of a provision of this Article can be shown to be willful, malicious, or wanton, or if continued multiple violations of a provision or provisions of this Article occur, the court may award punitive damages, attorneys' fees and costs in addition to any other damages under this Article.

(c) A new motor vehicle dealer, if he has not suffered any loss of money or property, may obtain final equitable relief if it can be shown that the violation of a provision of this Article by a captive finance source may have the effect of causing a loss of money or property.

(d) Any association that is comprised of a minimum of 400 new motor vehicle dealers, or a minimum of 10 motorcycle dealers, substantially all of whom are new motor vehicle dealers located within North Carolina, and which represents the collective interests of its members, shall have standing to file a petition before the Commissioner or a cause of action in any court of competent jurisdiction for itself, or on behalf of any or all of its members, seeking declaratory and injunctive relief. Prior to bringing an action, the association and captive finance source shall initiate mediation as set forth in G.S. 20-301.1(b). An action brought pursuant to this subsection may seek a determination whether one or more captive finance sources doing business in this State have violated any of the provisions of this Article, or for the determination of any rights created or defined by this Article, so long as the association alleges

an injury to the collective interest of its members cognizable under this section. A cognizable injury to the collective interest of the members of the association shall be deemed to occur if a captive finance source doing business in this State has engaged in any conduct or taken any action which actually harms or affects all of the franchised new motor vehicle dealers holding agreements with that captive finance source in this State. With respect to any administrative or civil action filed by an association pursuant to this subsection, the relief granted shall be limited to declaratory and injunctive relief and in no event shall the Commissioner or court enter an award of monetary damages.

History.
2005-409, s. 3

§ 20-308.22. Applicability of this Article

(a) Any captive finance source who engages directly or indirectly in purposeful contacts within this State in connection with the offering or advertising the availability of financing for the sale or lease of motor vehicles within this State, or who has business dealings within this State, shall be subject to the provisions of this Article and shall be subject to the jurisdiction of the courts of this State.

(b) The applicability of this Article shall not be affected by a choice of law clause in any agreement, waiver, novation, or any other written instrument.

(c) Any provision of any agreement, waiver, novation, or any other written instrument which is in violation of any section of this Article shall be deemed null and void and without force and effect to the extent it violates this section.

(d) It shall be unlawful for a captive finance source to use any subsidiary corporation, affiliated corporation, or any other controlled corporation, partnership, association, or person to accomplish what would otherwise be illegal conduct under this Article on the part of the captive finance source.

History.
2005-409, s. 3

ARTICLE 13
THE VEHICLE FINANCIAL RESPONSIBILITY ACT OF 1957

§ 20-309. Financial responsibility prerequisite to registration; must be

maintained throughout registration period

(a) No motor vehicle shall be registered in this State unless the owner at the time of registration provides proof of financial responsibility for the operation of such motor vehicle, as provided in this Article. The owner of each motor vehicle registered in this State shall maintain financial responsibility continuously throughout the period of registration. For purposes of this Article, the term "motor vehicle" includes mopeds, as that term is defined in G.S. 20-4.01.

(a1) An owner of a commercial motor vehicle, as defined in G.S. 20-4.01(3d), shall have financial responsibility for the operation of the motor vehicle in an amount equal to that required for for-hire carriers transporting nonhazardous property in interstate or foreign commerce in 49 C.F.R. § 387.9.

(a2) Notwithstanding any other provision of this Chapter, an owner's policy of liability insurance issued to a foster parent or parents, which policy includes an endorsement excluding coverage for one or more foster children residing in the foster parent's or parents' household, may be certified as proof of financial responsibility, provided that each foster child for whom coverage is excluded is insured in an amount equal to or greater than the minimum limits required by G.S. 20-279.21 under some other owner's policy of liability insurance or a named nonowner's policy of liability insurance. The North Carolina Rate Bureau shall establish, with the approval of the Commissioner of Insurance, a named driver exclusion endorsement or endorsements for foster children as described herein.

(b) Financial responsibility shall be a liability insurance policy or a financial security bond or a financial security deposit or by qualification as a self-insurer, as these terms are defined and described in Article 9A, Chapter 20 of the General Statutes of North Carolina, as amended.

(c) When it is certified that financial responsibility is a liability insurance policy, the Commissioner of Motor Vehicles may require that the owner produce records to prove the fact of such insurance, and failure to produce such records shall be prima facie evidence that no financial responsibility exists with regard to the vehicle concerned. It shall be the duty of insurance companies, upon request of the Division, to verify the accuracy of any owner's certification.

(c1) The proof of insurance required to demonstrate financial responsibility under subsection (c) of this section may be satisfied by producing records of insurance in either physical or electronic format. Acceptable electronic formats include display of electronic images on a mobile phone or other portable electronic device produced through an application or Web site of the insurer.

(d) When liability insurance with regard to any motor vehicle is terminated by cancellation or failure to renew, or the owner's financial responsibility for the operation of any motor vehicle is otherwise terminated, the owner shall forthwith surrender the registration certificate and plates of the vehicle to the Division of Motor Vehicles unless financial responsibility is maintained in some other manner in compliance with this Article.

(e) Repealed by Session Laws 2006-213, s. 5, effective July 1, 2008, and applicable to lapses occurring on or after that date.

(f) The Commissioner shall administer and enforce the provisions of this Article and may make rules and regulations necessary for its administration and shall provide for hearings upon request of persons aggrieved by orders or acts of the Commissioner under the provisions of this Article.

(g) Repealed by Session Laws 2007-484, s. 7(a), effective July 1, 2008, and applicable to lapses occurring on or after that date.

(h) Recodified as G.S. 20-311(g) by Session Laws 2007-484, s. 7(d), effective July 1, 2008, and applicable to lapses occurring on or after that date.

History.

1957, c. 1393, s. 1; 1959, c. 1277, s. 1; 1963, c. 964, s. 1; 1965, c. 272; c. 1136, ss. 1, 2; 1967, c. 822, ss. 1, 2; c. 857, ss. 1, 2; 1971, c. 477, ss. 1, 2; c. 924; 1975, c. 302; c. 348, ss. 1-3; c. 716, s. 5; 1979, 2nd Sess., c. 1279, s. 1; 1981, c. 690, s. 25; 1983, c. 761, s. 146; 1983 (Reg. Sess., 1984), c. 1069, ss. 1, 2; 1985, c. 666, s. 84; 1991, c. 402, s. 1; 1999-330, s. 4; 1999-452, s. 20; 2000-140, s. 100(a); 2000-155, s. 20; 2005-276, s. 6.37(p); 2006-213, s. 5; 2006-264, s. 38; 2007-484, ss. 7(a), (d); 2009-550, s. 4; 2015-125, s. 3; 2015-135, s. 4.3; 2015-146, s. 4

N.C. Gen. Stat. § 20-309.1

Repealed by Session Laws 1993 (Reg. Sess., 1994), c. 761, s. 28.

§ 20-309.2. Insurer shall notify Division of actions on insurance policies

(a) **Notice Required.** -- An insurer shall notify the Division upon any of the following with regard to a motor vehicle liability policy:

(1) Issues a new or replacement policy.

(2) Terminates a policy, either by cancellation or failure to renew, unless the same insurer issues a replacement policy complying with this Article at the same time the insurer terminates the old policy and no lapse in coverage results.

(3) Reinstates a policy after the insurer has notified the Division of a cancellation or termination.

(b) **Time Period.** -- An insurer shall notify the Division as required by subsection (a) of this section within 20 business days.

(c) **Form of Notice.** -- Any insurer with twenty-five million dollars ($ 25,000,000) or more in annual vehicle insurance premium volume shall submit the notices required under this section by electronic means. All other insurers may submit the notices required under this section by either paper or electronic means.

(d) **Trade Secret Protection.** -- The names of insureds and the beginning date and termination date of insurance coverage provided to the Division by an insurer under this section constitutes a designated trade secret under G.S. 132-1.2.

(e) **Civil Penalty.** -- The Commissioner of Insurance may assess a civil penalty of two hundred dollars ($ 200.00) against an insurer that fails to notify the Division as required by this section. The Commissioner may waive the penalty if the insurer establishes good cause for the failure.

(f) **Clear Proceeds of Penalties.** -- The clear proceeds of all civil penalties, civil forfeitures, and civil fines that are collected by the Department of Transportation pursuant to this section shall be remitted to the Civil Penalty and Forfeiture Fund in accordance with G.S. 115C-457.2.

History.
2006-213, s. 1; 2007-484, s. 7(b)

N.C. Gen. Stat. § 20-310

Repealed by Session Laws 1993 (Reg. Sess., 1994), c. 761, s. 29.

N.C. Gen. Stat. § 20-310.1

Repealed by Session Laws 1963, c. 964, s. 3.

N.C. Gen. Stat. § 20-310.2

Repealed by Session Laws 1993 (Reg. Sess., 1994), c. 761, s. 31.

§ 20-311. Action by the Division when notified of a lapse in financial responsibility

(a) **Action.** -- When the Division receives evidence, by a notice of termination of a motor vehicle liability policy or otherwise, that the owner of a motor vehicle registered or required to be registered in this State does not have financial responsibility for the operation of the vehicle, the Division shall send the owner a letter. The letter shall notify the owner of the evidence and inform the owner that the owner shall respond to the letter within 10 days of the date on the

letter and explain how the owner has met the duty to have continuous financial responsibility for the vehicle. Based on the owner's response, the Division shall take the appropriate action listed:

(1) **Division correction.** -- If the owner responds within the required time and the response establishes that the owner has not had a lapse in financial responsibility, the Division shall correct its records.

(2) **Penalty only.** -- If the owner responds within the required time and the response establishes all of the following, the Division shall assess the owner a penalty in the amount set in subsection (b) of this section:

    a. The owner had a lapse in financial responsibility, but the owner now has financial responsibility.

    b. The vehicle was not involved in an accident during the lapse in financial responsibility.

    c. The owner did not operate the vehicle or allow the vehicle to be operated during the lapse with knowledge that the owner had no financial responsibility for the vehicle.

(3) **Penalty and revocation.** -- If the owner responds within the required time and the response establishes either of the following, the Division shall assess the owner a penalty in the amount set in subsection (b) of this section and revoke the registration of the owner's vehicle for the period set in subsection (c) of this section:

    a. The owner had a lapse in financial responsibility and still does not have financial responsibility.

    b. The owner now has financial responsibility even though the owner had a lapse, but the response also establishes any of the following:

        1. The vehicle was involved in an accident during the lapse.

        2. The owner operated the vehicle during the lapse with knowledge that the owner had no financial responsibility for the vehicle.

        3. The owner allowed the vehicle to be operated during the lapse with knowledge that the owner had no financial responsibility for the vehicle.

(4) **Penalty and revocation for failure to respond.** -- Except as otherwise provided in this subdivision, if the owner does not respond within the required time, the Division shall assess a penalty in the applicable amount set forth in subsection (b) of this section and shall revoke the registration of the owner's vehicle for the period set in subsection (c) of this section. If

Chapter 20

the owner does not respond within the required time, but later responds and establishes that the owner has not had a lapse in financial responsibility, the Division shall correct its records, rescind any revocation under this subdivision of the registration of the owner's vehicle, and the owner shall not be responsible for any fee or penalty arising under this section from the owner's failure to timely respond.

(b) **Penalty Amount.** -- The following table determines the amount of a penalty payable under this section by an owner who has had a lapse in financial responsibility; the amount is based on the number of times the owner has been assessed a penalty under this section during the three-year period before the date the owner's current lapse began:

Number of Lapses in Previous Three Years	Penalty Amount
None	$ 50.00
One	$ 100.00
Two or More	$ 150.00

(c) **Revocation Period.** -- The revocation period for a revocation based on a response that establishes that a vehicle owner does not have financial responsibility is indefinite and ends when the owner obtains financial responsibility or transfers the vehicle to an owner who has financial responsibility. The revocation period for a revocation based on a response that establishes the occurrence of an accident during a lapse in financial responsibility or the knowing operation of a vehicle without financial responsibility is 30 days. The revocation period for a revocation based on failure of a vehicle owner to respond is indefinite and ends when the owner (i) establishes that the owner has not had a lapse in financial responsibility, (ii) obtains financial responsibility, or (iii) transfers the vehicle to an owner who has financial responsibility, whichever occurs first.

(d) **Revocation Notice.** -- When the Division revokes the registration of an owner's vehicle, it shall notify the owner of the revocation. The notice shall inform the owner of the following:

(1) That the owner shall return the vehicle's registration plate and registration card to the Division, if the owner has not done so already, and that failure to do so is a Class 2 misdemeanor under G.S. 20-45.

(2) That the vehicle's registration plate and registration card are subject to seizure by a law enforcement officer.

(3) That the registration of the vehicle cannot be renewed while the registration is revoked.

(4) That the owner shall pay any penalties assessed within 30 days of the date of the notice, a restoration fee, and the fee for a registration plate when the owner applies

to the Division to register a vehicle whose registration was revoked.

(5) That failure of an owner to pay any penalty or fee assessed pursuant to this section shall result in the Division withholding the registration renewal of any motor vehicle registered in that owner's name.

(e) **Registration After Revocation.** -- A vehicle whose registration has been revoked may not be registered during the revocation period in the name of the owner, a child of the owner, the owner's spouse, or a child of the owner's spouse. This restriction does not apply to a spouse who is living separate and apart from the owner. At the end of a revocation period, a vehicle owner who has financial responsibility may apply to register a vehicle whose registration was revoked. The owner shall provide proof of current financial responsibility and pay any penalty assessed, a restoration fee of fifty dollars ($ 50.00), and the fee for a registration plate. Pursuant to G.S. 20-54, failure of an owner to pay any penalty or fee assessed pursuant to this section shall result in the Division withholding the registration renewal of any motor vehicle registered in that owner's name.

(f) **Clear Proceeds of Penalties.** -- The clear proceeds of all civil penalties, civil forfeitures, and civil fines that are collected by the Department of Transportation pursuant to this section shall be remitted to the Civil Penalty and Forfeiture Fund in accordance with G.S. 115C-457.2.

(g) **Military Waiver.** -- Notwithstanding the penalty and restoration fee provisions of this section, any monetary penalty or restoration fee shall be waived for any person who, at the time of notification of a lapse in financial responsibility, was deployed as a member of the Armed Forces of the United States outside of the continental United States for a total of 45 or more days. In addition, no insurance points under the Safe Driver Incentive Plan shall be assessed for any violation for which a monetary penalty or restoration fee is waived pursuant to this subsection. All of the following apply to a person qualifying under this subsection:

(1) The person shall have an affirmative defense to any criminal charge based upon the failure to return any registration card or registration plate to the Division.

(2) Upon reregistration, the person shall receive without cost from the Division all necessary registration cards or plates.

(3) Upon notice of revocation, the person shall be permitted to transfer the vehicle's registration immediately to his or her spouse, child, or spouse's child, notwithstanding the provisions of subsection (e) of this section.

(g1) **Out-of-State Waiver.** -- Notwithstanding the penalty and restoration fee provisions

Chapter 20

of this section, any monetary penalty or restoration fee shall be waived for any person who meets all of the following requirements:

(1) The owner has become a resident of another state and has registered the owner's vehicle in that state within 30 days of the cancellation or expiration of the owner's North Carolina motor vehicle liability policy.

(2) The owner has submitted a copy of their current out-of-state registration card to the Division.

(3) The owner has returned the North Carolina registration plate or has submitted an affidavit indicating that the North Carolina registration plate has been lost, stolen, or destroyed.

(h) **Applicability.** -- The penalty and revocation imposed under this section do not apply when the sole owner of a vehicle dies and that owner had financial responsibility for the vehicle as of the date of the owner's death.

History.
1957, c. 1393, s. 3; 1959, c. 1277, s. 2; 1963, c. 964, s. 4; 1965, c. 205; c. 1136, s. 3; 1967, c. 822, s. 3; c. 857, s. 4; 1971, c. 477, s. 3; 1975, c. 348, s. 4; c. 716, s. 5; 1979, 2nd Sess., c. 1279, s. 2; 1983, c. 761, s. 147; 1983 (Reg. Sess., 1984), c. 1069, s. 2; 2006-213, s. 2; 2006-264, s. 38; 2007-484, ss. 7(c), (d); 2011-183, s. 24; 2015-241, s. 29.31(a); 2019-227, s. 4

N.C. Gen. Stat. § 20-312

Repealed by Session Laws 2006-213, s. 5, effective July 1, 2008, and applicable to lapses occurring on or after that date.

§ 20-313. Operation of motor vehicle without financial responsibility a misdemeanor

(a) On or after July 1, 1963, any owner of a motor vehicle registered or required to be registered in this State who shall operate or permit such motor vehicle to be operated in this State without having in full force and effect the financial responsibility required by this Article shall be guilty of a Class 3 misdemeanor.

(b) Evidence that the owner of a motor vehicle registered or required to be registered in this State has operated or permitted such motor vehicle to be operated in this State, coupled with proof of records of the Division of Motor Vehicles indicating that the owner did not have financial responsibility applicable to the operation of the motor vehicle in the manner certified by him for purposes of G.S. 20-309, shall be prima facie evidence that such owner did at the time and place alleged operate or permit such motor vehicle to be operated without having in full force and effect the financial

responsibility required by the provisions of this Article.

History.
1957, c. 1393, s. 5; 1959, c. 1277, s. 3; 1963, c. 964, s. 5; 1975, c. 716, s. 5; 1993, c. 539, s. 388; 1994, Ex. Sess., c. 24, s. 14(c); 2013-360, s. 18B.14 (*l*)

§ 20-313.1. Making false certification or giving false information a misdemeanor

(a) Any owner of a motor vehicle registered or required to be registered in this State who shall make a false certification concerning his financial responsibility for the operation of such motor vehicle shall be guilty of a Class 1 misdemeanor.

(b) Any person, firm, or corporation giving false information to the Division concerning another's financial responsibility for the operation of a motor vehicle registered or required to be registered in this State, knowing or having reason to believe that such information is false, shall be guilty of a Class 1 misdemeanor.

History.
1963, c. 964, s. 6; 1975, c. 716, s. 5; 1993, c. 539, s. 389; 1994, Ex. Sess., c. 24, s. 14(c)

§ 20-314. Applicability of Article 9A; its provisions continued

The provisions of Article 9A, Chapter 20 of the General Statutes, as amended, which pertain to the method of giving and maintaining proof of financial responsibility and which govern and define "motor vehicle liability policy" and assigned risk plans shall apply to filing and maintaining proof of financial responsibility required by this Article. It is intended that the provisions of Article 9A, Chapter 20 of the General Statutes, as amended, relating to proof of financial responsibility required of each operator and each owner of a motor vehicle involved in an accident, and relating to nonpayment of a judgment as defined in G.S. 20-279.1, shall continue in full force and effect.

History.
1957, c. 1393, s. 6; 1963, c. 964, s. 7

§ 20-315. Commissioner to administer Article; rules and regulations

The Commissioner of Motor Vehicles shall administer and enforce the provisions of this Article relating to registration of motor vehicles and may make necessary rules and regulations for its administration.

History.
1957, c. 1393, s. 7

§ 20-316. Divisional hearings upon lapse of liability insurance coverage

Any person whose registration plate has been revoked under G.S. 20-311 may request a hearing. Upon receipt of such request, the Division shall, as early as practical, afford an opportunity for hearing. At the hearing the duly authorized agents of the Division may administer oaths and issue subpoenas for the attendance of witnesses and the production of relevant books and documents. If it appears that continuous financial responsibility existed for the vehicle involved, or if it appears the lapse of financial responsibility is not reasonably attributable to the neglect or fault of the person whose registration plate was revoked, the Division shall withdraw its order of revocation and such person may retain the registration plate. Otherwise, the order of revocation shall be affirmed and the registration plate surrendered.

History.
1971, c. 1218, s. 1; 1973, c. 1144, ss. 1, 2; 1975, c. 716, s. 5; 2006-213, s. 3

N.C. Gen. Stat. § 20-316.1

Repealed by Session Laws 2006-213, s. 5, effective July 1, 2008, and applicable to lapses occurring on or after that date.

§ 20-317. Insurance required by any other law; certain operators not affected

This Article shall not be held to apply to or affect policies of automobile insurance against liability which may now or hereafter be required by any other law of this State, and such policies, if they contain an agreement or are endorsed to conform to the requirements of this Article, may be certified as proof of financial responsibility under this Article. This Article applies to vehicles of motor carriers required to register with the Division under G.S. 20-382 or G.S. 20-382.1 only to the extent that the amount of financial responsibility required by this Article exceeds the amount required by the United States Department of Transportation.

History.
1957, c. 1393, s. 9; 1959, c. 1252, s. 1; 1975, c. 716, s. 5; 1995 (Reg. Sess., 1996), c. 756, s. 19

§ 20-318. Federal, State and political subdivision vehicles excepted

This Article does not apply to any motor vehicle owned by the State of North Carolina or by a political subdivision of the State, nor to any motor vehicle owned by the federal government.

History.
1957, c. 1393, s. 10

§ 20-319. Effective date

This Article shall be effective from and after January 1, 1958.

History.
1957, c. 1393, s. 12; 1961, c. 276

ARTICLE 13A
CERTIFICATION OF AUTOMOBILE INSURANCE COVERAGE BY INSURANCE COMPANIES

§ 20-319.1. Company to forward certification within seven days after receipt of request

Upon the receipt by an insurance company at its home office of a registered letter from an insured requesting that it certify to the North Carolina Division of Motor Vehicles whether or not a previously issued policy of automobile liability insurance was in full force and effect on a designated day, it shall be the duty of such insurance company to forward such certification within seven days.

History.
1967, c. 908, s. 1; 1975, c. 716, s. 5

§ 20-319.2. Penalty for failure to forward certification

If any insurance company shall without good cause fail to forward said certification within seven days after its receipt of such registered letter, the North Carolina Commissioner of Insurance shall be authorized in his discretion to impose a civil penalty upon said company in the amount of two hundred dollars ($ 200.00) for such violation.

History.
1967, c. 908, s. 2

ARTICLE 14
DRIVER TRAINING SCHOOL LICENSING LAW

§ 20-320. Definitions

As used in this Article:

(1) "Commercial driver training school" or "school" means a business enterprise conducted by an individual, association,

partnership or corporation which educates or trains persons to operate or drive motor vehicles or which furnishes educational materials to prepare an applicant for an examination given by the State for a driver's license or learner's permit, and charges a consideration or tuition for such service or materials.

(2) "Commissioner" means the Commissioner of Motor Vehicles.

(3) "Instructor" means any person who operates a commercial driver training school or who teaches, conducts classes, gives demonstrations, or supervises practical training of persons learning to operate or drive motor vehicles in connection with operation of a commercial driver training school.

History.
1965, c. 873; 1979, c. 667, s. 39

§ 20-321. Enforcement of Article by Commissioner

(a) The Commissioner shall adopt and prescribe such regulations concerning the administration and enforcement of this Article as are necessary to protect the public. The Commissioner or his authorized representative shall have the duty of examining applicants for commercial driver training schools and instructor's licenses, licensing successful applicants, and inspecting school facilities, records, and equipment.

(b) The Commissioner shall administer and enforce the provisions of this Article, and may call upon the State Superintendent of Public Instruction for assistance in developing and formulating appropriate regulations.

History.
1965, c. 873; 1973, c. 1331, s. 3; 1987, c. 69; c. 827, § 3

§ 20-322. Licenses for schools necessary; regulations as to requirements

(a) No commercial driver training school shall be established nor any such existing school be continued on or after July 1, 1965, unless such school applies for and obtains from the Commissioner a license in the manner and form prescribed by the Commissioner.

(b) Regulations adopted by the Commissioner shall state the requirements for a school license, including requirements concerning location, equipment, courses of instruction, instructors, financial statements, schedule of fees and charges, character and reputation of the operators, insurance, bond or other security in such sum and with such provisions as the Commissioner deems necessary to protect adequately

the interests of the public, and such other matters as the Commissioner may prescribe. A driver education course offered to prepare an individual for a limited learner's permit or another provisional license must meet the requirements set in G.S. 115C-215 for the program of driver education offered in the public schools.

History.
1965, c. 873; 1997-16, s. 4; 1997-443, s. 32.20; 2011-145, s. 28.37(e)

§ 20-323. Licenses for instructors necessary; regulations as to requirements

(a) No person shall act as an instructor on or after July 1, 1965, unless such person applies for and obtains from the Commissioner a license in the manner and form prescribed by the Commissioner.

(b) Regulations adopted by the Commissioner shall state the requirements for an instructor's license, including requirements concerning moral character, physical condition, knowledge of the courses of instruction, knowledge of the motor vehicle laws and safety principles, previous personal and employment records, and such other matters as the Commissioner may prescribe, for the protection of the public.

History.
1965, c. 873

§ 20-324. Expiration and renewal of licenses; fees

(a) **Renewal.** -- A license issued under this Article expires two years after the date the license is issued. To renew a license, the license holder must file an application for renewal with the Division.

(b) **Fees.** -- An application for an initial license or the renewal of a license must be accompanied by the application fee for the license. The application fee for a school license is eighty dollars ($ 80.00). The application fee for an instructor license is sixteen dollars ($ 16.00). The application fee for a license is not refundable. Fees collected under this section must be credited to the Highway Fund.

History.
1965, c. 873; 1977, c. 802, s. 9; 1981, c. 690, s. 15; 1997-33, s. 1

§ 20-325. Cancellation, suspension, revocation, and refusal to issue or renew licenses

The Commissioner may cancel, suspend, revoke, or refuse to issue or renew a school or instructor's license in any case where he finds the licensee or applicant has not complied with, or has violated any of the provisions of this Article or any regulation adopted by the Commissioner hereunder. A suspended or revoked license shall be returned to the Commissioner by the licensee, and its holder shall not be eligible to apply for a license under this Article until 12 months have elapsed since the date of such suspension or revocation.

History.
1965, c. 873

§ 20-326. Exemptions from Article

The provisions of this Article shall not apply to any person giving driver training lessons without charge, to employers maintaining driver training schools without charge for their employees only, or to schools or classes conducted by colleges, universities and high schools.

History.
1965, c. 873

§ 20-327. Penalties for violating Article or regulations

Violation of any provision of this Article or any regulation promulgated pursuant hereto, shall constitute a Class 3 misdemeanor.

History.
1965, c. 873; 1993, c. 539, s. 390; 1994, Ex. Sess., c. 24, s. 14(c)

§ 20-328. Administration of Article

This Article shall be administered by the Division of Motor Vehicles with no additional appropriations.

History.
1965, c. 873; 1973, c. 440; 1975, c. 716, s. 5

§§ 20-329 through 20-339

Reserved for future codification purposes.

ARTICLE 15
VEHICLE MILEAGE ACT

§ 20-340. Purpose

This Article shall provide State remedies for persons injured by motor vehicle odometer alteration, and to provide purchasers of motor vehicles with information to assist them in determining the condition and value of such vehicles. Such remedies shall be in addition to remedies provided by the federal odometer law (Motor Vehicle Information and Cost Savings Act, Public Law 92-513, 86 Stat. 947, enacted October 20, 1972).

History.
1973, c. 679, s. 1

§ 20-341. Definitions

As used in this Article:
(1) The term "odometer" means an instrument for measuring and recording the actual distance a motor vehicle travels while in operation; but shall not include any auxiliary odometer designed to be reset by the operator of the motor vehicle for the purpose of recording mileage on trips.
(2) The term "repair and replacement" means to restore to a sound working condition by replacing the odometer or any part thereof or by correcting what is inoperative.
(3) The term "transfer" means to change ownership by purchase, gift, or any other means.
(4) The term "transferee" means any person to whom the ownership in a motor vehicle is transferred or any person who, as agent, accepts transfer of ownership in a motor vehicle for another by purchase, gift, or any means other than by creation of a security interest.
(5) The term "transferor" means any person who or any person who, as agent, transfers his ownership in a motor vehicle by sale, gift or any means other than by creation of a security interest.
(6) The term "lessee" means any person, or the agent for any person, to whom a motor vehicle has been leased for a term of at least four months.
(7) The term "lessor" means any person, or the agent for any person, who has leased five or more vehicles in the past 12 months.
(8) The term "mileage" means the actual distance that a vehicle has traveled.

History.
1973, c. 679, s. 1; 1989, c. 482, s. 1

§ 20-342. Unlawful devices

It is unlawful for any person knowingly to advertise for sale, to sell, to use, or to install or to have installed, any device which causes an odometer to register any mileage other than the true mileage driven. For the purposes of this section, the true mileage driven is that mileage driven by the vehicle as registered by the odometer within the manufacturer's designed tolerance.

Chapter 20

History.
1973, c. 679, s. 1

§ 20-343. Unlawful change of mileage

It is unlawful for any person or his agent to disconnect, reset, or alter the odometer of any motor vehicle with the intent to change the number of miles indicated thereon. Whenever evidence shall be presented in any court of the fact that an odometer has been reset or altered to change the number of miles indicated thereon, it shall be prima facie evidence in any court in the State of North Carolina that the resetting or alteration was made by the person, firm or corporation who held title or by law was required to hold title to the vehicle in which the reset or altered odometer was installed at the time of such resetting or alteration or if such person has more than 20 employees and has specifically and in writing delegated responsibility for the motor vehicle to an agent, that the resetting or alteration was made by the agent.

History.
1973, c. 679, s. 1; 1979, c. 696

§ 20-344. Operation of vehicle with intent to defraud

It is unlawful for any person with the intent to defraud to operate a motor vehicle on any street or highway knowing that the odometer of such vehicle is disconnected or nonfunctional.

History.
1973, c. 679, s. 1

§ 20-345. Conspiracy

No person shall conspire with any other person to violate G.S. 20-342, 20-343, 20-344, 20-346, 20-347, or 20-347.1.

History.
1973, c. 679, s. 1; 1989, c. 482, s. 7

§ 20-346. Lawful service, repair, or replacement of odometer

Nothing in this Article shall prevent the service, repair, or replacement of an odometer, provided the mileage indicated thereon remains the same as before the service, repair, or replacement. Where the odometer is incapable of registering the same mileage as before such service, repair, or replacement, the odometer shall be adjusted to read zero and a notice in writing shall be attached to the left door frame of the vehicle by the owner or his agent specifying the mileage prior to repair or replacement of the odometer and the date on which it was repaired

or replaced. Any removal or alteration of such notice so affixed shall be unlawful.

History.
1973, c. 679, s. 1

§ 20-347. Disclosure requirements

(a) In connection with the transfer of a motor vehicle, the transferor shall disclose the mileage to the transferee in writing on the title or on the document used to reassign the title. This written disclosure must be signed by the transferor, including the printed name, and shall contain the following information:

(1) The odometer reading at the time of the transfer (not to include tenths of miles);

(2) The date of the transfer;

(3) The transferor's name and current address;

(3a) The transferee's printed name, signature and current address;

(4) The identity of the vehicle, including its make, model, body type, and vehicle identification number, and the license plate number most recently used on the vehicle; and

(5) Certification by the transferor that to the best of his knowledge the odometer reading

a. Reflects the actual mileage; or

b. Reflects the amount of mileage in excess of the designed mechanical odometer limit; or

c. Does not reflect the actual mileage and should not be relied on.

(6), (7) Repealed by Session Laws 1989, c. 482, s. 2.

(a1) Before executing any transfer of ownership document, each lessor of a leased motor vehicle shall notify the lessee in writing that the lessee is required to provide written disclosure to the lessor regarding mileage. In connection with the transfer of ownership of the leased motor vehicle, the lessee shall furnish to the lessor a written statement signed by the lessee containing the following information:

(1) The printed name of the person making the disclosure;

(2) The current odometer reading (not to include tenths of miles);

(3) The date of the statement;

(4) The lessee's printed name and current address;

(5) The lessor's printed name, signature, and current address;

(6) The identity of the vehicle, including its make, model, year, body type, and vehicle identification number;

(7) The date that the lessor notified the lessee of the disclosure requirements and the date the lessor received the completed disclosure statement; and

(8) Certification by the lessee that to the best of his knowledge the odometer reading:

a. Reflects the actual mileage;

b. Reflects the amount of mileage in excess of the designed mechanical odometer limit; or

c. Does not reflect the actual mileage and should not be relied on.

If the lessor transfers the leased vehicle without obtaining possession of it, the lessor may indicate on the title the mileage disclosed by the lessee under this subsection, unless the lessor has reason to believe that the disclosure by the lessee does not reflect the actual mileage of the vehicle.

(b) Repealed by Session Laws 1973, c. 1088.

(c) It shall be unlawful for any transferor to violate any rules under this section or to knowingly give a false statement to a transferee in making any disclosure required by such rules.

(d) The provisions of this disclosure statement section shall not apply to the following transfers:

(1) A vehicle having a gross vehicle weight rating of more than 16,000 pounds.

(2) A vehicle that is not self-propelled.

(2a) A vehicle sold directly by the manufacturer to any agency of the United States in conformity with contractual specifications.

(3) A vehicle that is 10 years old or older.

(4) A new vehicle prior to its first transfer for purposes other than resale.

(5) A vehicle that is transferred by a State agency that assists the United States Department of Defense with purchasing, transferring, or titling a vehicle to another State agency, a unit of local government, a volunteer fire department, or a volunteer rescue squad.

History.
1973, c. 679, s. 1; c. 1088; 1983, c. 387; 1989, c. 482, ss. 2 -5; 1993, c. 553, s. 11; 2009-550, s. 2(d)

§ 20-347.1. Odometer disclosure record retention

(a) Dealers and distributors of motor vehicles who are required by this Part to execute an odometer disclosure statement shall retain, for five years, a photostat, carbon, or other facsimile copy of each odometer mileage statement which they issue or receive. They shall retain all odometer disclosure statements at their primary place of business in an order that is appropriate to business requirements and that permits systematic retrieval.

(b) Lessors shall retain, for five years following the date they transfer ownership of the leased vehicle, each odometer disclosure statement which they receive from a lessee. They shall retain all odometer disclosure statements at their primary place of business in an order that is appropriate to business requirements and that permits systematic retrieval.

(c) Each auction company shall establish and retain at its primary place of business in an order that is appropriate to business requirements and that permits systematic retrieval, for five years following the date of sale of each motor vehicle, the following records:

(1) The name of the most recent owner (other than the auction company);

(2) The name of the buyer;

(3) The vehicle identification number; and

(4) The odometer reading on the date which the auction company took possession of the motor vehicle.

(d) Records required to be kept under this section shall be open to inspection and copying by law enforcement officers of the Division in order to determine compliance with this Article.

History.
1989, c. 482, s. 6

§ 20-348. Private civil action

(a) Any person who, with intent to defraud, violates any requirement imposed under this Article shall be liable in an amount equal to the sum of:

(1) Three times the amount of actual damages sustained or one thousand five hundred dollars ($ 1,500), whichever is the greater; and

(2) In the case of any successful action to enforce the foregoing liability, the costs of the action together with reasonable attorney fees as determined by the court.

(b) An action to enforce any liability created under subsection (a) of this section may be brought in any court of the trial division of the General Court of Justice of the State of North Carolina within four years from the date on which the liability arises.

History.
1973, c. 679, s. 1; 1981 (Reg. Sess., 1982), c. 1280, s. 1

§ 20-349. Injunctive enforcement

Upon petition by the Attorney General of North Carolina, a violation of this Article may be enjoined as an unfair and deceptive trade practice, as prohibited by G.S. 75-1.1.

History.
1973, c. 679, s. 1

§ 20-350. Criminal offense

Any person, firm or corporation violating G.S. 20-343 shall be guilty of a Class I felony. A violation of any remaining provision of this Article shall be a Class 1 misdemeanor.

History.

1973, c. 679, s. 1; 1989, c. 482, s. 7.1; 1993, c. 539, ss. 391, 1262; 1994, Ex. Sess., c. 24, s. 14(c)

ARTICLE 15A
NEW MOTOR VEHICLES WARRANTIES ACT

§ 20-351. Purpose

This Article shall provide State and private remedies against motor vehicle manufacturers for persons injured by new motor vehicles failing to conform to express warranties.

History.
1987, c. 385, s. 1

§ 20-351.1. Definitions

As used in this Article:

(1) "Consumer" means the purchaser, other than for purposes of resale, or lessee from a commercial lender, lessor, or from a manufacturer or dealer, of a motor vehicle, and any other person entitled by the terms of an express warranty to enforce the obligations of that warranty.

(2) "Manufacturer" means any person or corporation, resident or nonresident, who manufactures or assembles or imports or distributes new motor vehicles which are sold in the State of North Carolina.

(3) "Motor vehicle" includes a motor vehicle as defined in G.S. 20-4.01 that is sold or leased in this State, but does not include "house trailer" as defined in G.S. 20-4.01 or any motor vehicle that weighs more than 10,000 pounds.

(4) "New motor vehicle" means a motor vehicle for which a certificate of origin, as required by G.S. 20-52.1 or a similar requirement in another state, has never been supplied to a consumer, or which a manufacturer, its agent, or its authorized dealer states in writing is being sold as a new motor vehicle.

History.
1987, c. 385, s. 1; 1989, c. 43, s. 2; c. 519, s. 2; 2005-436, s. 1

§ 20-351.2. Require repairs; when mileage warranty begins to accrue

(a) Express warranties for a new motor vehicle shall remain in effect at least one year or 12,000 miles. If a new motor vehicle does not conform to all applicable express warranties for a period of one year, or the term of the express warranties, whichever is greater, following the date of original delivery of the motor vehicle to the consumer, and the consumer reports the nonconformity to the manufacturer, its agent, or its authorized dealer during such period, the manufacturer shall make, or arrange to have made, repairs necessary to conform the vehicle to the express warranties, whether or not these repairs are made after the expiration of the applicable warranty period.

(b) Any express warranty for a new motor vehicle expressed in terms of a certain number of miles shall begin to accrue from the mileage on the odometer at the date of original delivery to the consumer.

History.
1987, c. 385, s. 1; 1989, c. 14

§ 20-351.3. Replacement or refund; disclosure requirement

(a) When the consumer is the purchaser or a person entitled by the terms of the express warranty to enforce the obligations of the warranty, if the manufacturer is unable, after a reasonable number of attempts, to conform the motor vehicle to any express warranty by repairing or correcting, or arranging for the repair or correction of, any defect or condition or series of defects or conditions which substantially impair the value of the motor vehicle to the consumer, and which occurred no later than 24 months or 24,000 miles following original delivery of the vehicle, the manufacturer shall, at the option of the consumer, replace the vehicle with a comparable new motor vehicle or accept return of the vehicle from the consumer and refund to the consumer the following:

(1) The full contract price including, but not limited to, charges for undercoating, dealer preparation and transportation, and installed options, plus the non-refundable portions of extended warranties and service contracts;

(2) All collateral charges, including but not limited to, sales tax, license and registration fees, and similar government charges;

(3) All finance charges incurred by the consumer after he first reports the nonconformity to the manufacturer, its agent, or its authorized dealer; and

(4) Any incidental damages and monetary consequential damages.

(b) When consumer is a lessee, if the manufacturer is unable, after a reasonable number of attempts, to conform the motor vehicle to any express warranty by repairing or correcting, or arranging for the repair or correction of, any defect or condition or series of defects or conditions which substantially impair the value of the motor vehicle to the consumer, and which occurred no later than 24 months or 24,000 miles following original delivery of the vehicle, the manufacturer shall, at the option of the consumer, replace the vehicle with a comparable new motor vehicle or accept return of the vehicle from the consumer and refund the following:

(1) To the consumer:

a. All sums previously paid by the consumer under the terms of the lease;

b. All sums previously paid by the consumer in connection with entering into the lease agreement, including, but not limited to, any capitalized cost reduction, sales tax, license and registration fees, and similar government charges; and

c. Any incidental and monetary consequential damages.

(2) To the lessor, a full refund of the lease price, plus an additional amount equal to five percent (5%) of the lease price, less eighty-five percent (85%) of the amount actually paid by the consumer to the lessor pursuant to the lease. The lease price means the actual purchase cost of the vehicle to the lessor.

In the case of a refund, the leased vehicle shall be returned to the manufacturer and the consumer's written lease shall be terminated by the lessor without any penalty to the consumer. The lessor shall transfer title of the motor vehicle to the manufacturer as necessary to effectuate the consumer's rights pursuant to this Article, whether the consumer chooses vehicle replacement or refund.

(c) Refunds shall be made to the consumer, lessor, and any lienholders as their interests may appear. The refund to the consumer shall be reduced by a reasonable allowance for the consumer's use of the vehicle. A reasonable allowance for use is calculated from the number of miles used by the consumer up to the date of the third attempt to repair the same nonconformity which is the subject of the claim, or the twentieth cumulative business day when the vehicle is out of service by reason of repair of one or more nonconformities, whichever occurs first. The number of miles used by the consumer is multiplied by the purchase price of the vehicle or the lessor's actual lease price, and divided by 120,000.

(d) If a manufacturer, its agent, or its authorized dealer resells a motor vehicle that was returned pursuant to this Article or any other State's applicable law, regardless of whether there was any judicial determination that the motor vehicle had any defect or that it failed to conform to all express warranties, the manufacturer, its agent, or its authorized dealer shall disclose to the subsequent purchaser prior to the sale:

(1) That the motor vehicle was returned pursuant to this Article or pursuant to the applicable law of any other State; and

(2) The defect or condition or series of defects or conditions which substantially impaired the value of the motor vehicle to the consumer.

Any subsequent purchaser who purchases the motor vehicle for resale with notice of the return, shall make the required disclosures to any person to whom he resells the motor vehicle.

History.
1987, c. 385, s. 1; 1989, c. 43, s. 1; c. 519, s. 1; 2005-436, s. 2

§ 20-351.4. Affirmative defenses

It is an affirmative defense to any claim under this Article that an alleged nonconformity or series of nonconformities are the result of abuse, neglect, odometer tampering by the consumer or unauthorized modifications or alterations of a motor vehicle.

History.
1987, c. 385, s. 1

§ 20-351.5. Presumption

(a) It is presumed that a reasonable number of attempts have been undertaken to conform a motor vehicle to the applicable express warranties if:

(1) The same nonconformity has been presented for repair to the manufacturer, its agent, or its authorized dealer four or more times but the same nonconformity continues to exist; or

(2) The vehicle was out of service to the consumer during or while awaiting repair of the nonconformity or a series of nonconformities for a cumulative total of 20 or more business days during any 12-month period of the warranty,

provided that the consumer has notified the manufacturer directly in writing of the existence of the nonconformity or series of nonconformities and allowed the manufacturer a reasonable period, not to exceed 15 calendar days, in which to correct the nonconformity or series of nonconformities. The manufacturer must clearly and conspicuously disclose to the consumer in the warranty or owners manual that written notification of a nonconformity is required before a consumer may be eligible for a refund or replacement of the vehicle and the manufacturer shall include in the warranty or owners manual the name and address where the written notification may be sent. Provided, further, that notice to the manufacturer shall not be required if the manufacturer fails to make the disclosures provided herein.

(b) The consumer may prove that a defect or condition substantially impairs the value of the motor vehicle to the consumer in a manner other than that set forth in subsection (a) of this section.

(c) The term of an express warranty, the one-year period, and the 20-day period shall be extended by any period of time during which repair services are not available to the consumer because of war, strike, or natural disaster.

History.
1987, c. 385, s. 1

§ 20-351.6. Civil action by the Attorney General

Whenever, in his opinion, the interests of the public require it, it shall be the duty of the Attorney General upon his ascertaining that any of the provisions of this Article have been violated by the manufacturer to bring a civil action in the name of the State, or any officer or department thereof as provided by law, or in the name of the State on relation of the Attorney General.

History.
1987, c. 385, s. 1

§ 20-351.7. Civil action by the consumer

A consumer injured by reason of any violation of the provisions of this Article may bring a civil action against the manufacturer; provided, however, the consumer has given the manufacturer written notice of his intent to bring an action against the manufacturer at least 10 days prior to filing such suit. Nothing in this section shall prevent a manufacturer from requiring a consumer to utilize an informal settlement procedure prior to litigation if that procedure substantially complies in design and operation with the Magnuson-Moss Warranty Act, 15 USC § 2301 et seq., and regulations promulgated thereunder, and that requirement is written clearly and conspicuously, in the written warranty and any warranty instructions provided to the consumer.

History.
1987, c. 385, s. 1

§ 20-351.8. Remedies

In any action brought under this Article, the court may grant as relief:

(1) A permanent or temporary injunction or other equitable relief as the court deems just;

(2) Monetary damages to the injured consumer in the amount fixed by the verdict. Such damages shall be trebled upon a finding that the manufacturer unreasonably refused to comply with G.S. 20-351.2 or G.S. 20-351.3. The jury may consider as damages all items listed for refund under G.S. 20-351.3;

(3) A reasonable attorney's fee for the attorney of the prevailing party, payable by the losing party, upon a finding by the court that:

a. The manufacturer unreasonably failed or refused to fully resolve the matter which constitutes the basis of such action; or

b. The party instituting the action knew, or should have known, the action was frivolous and malicious.

History.
1987, c. 385, s. 1

§ 20-351.9. Dealership liability

No authorized dealer shall be held liable by the manufacturer for any refunds or vehicle replacements in the absence of evidence indicating that dealership repairs have been carried out in a manner substantially inconsistent with the manufacturers' instructions. This Article does not create any cause of action by a consumer against an authorized dealer.

History.
1987, c. 385, s. 1

§ 20-351.10. Preservation of other remedies

This Article does not limit the rights or remedies which are otherwise available to a consumer under any other law.

History.
1987, c. 385, s. 1

§ 20-351.11. Manufacturer's warranty for State motor vehicles that operate on diesel fuel

Every new motor vehicle purchased by the State that is designed to operate on diesel fuel shall be covered by an express manufacturer's warranty that allows the use of B-20 fuel, as defined in G.S. 143-58.4. This section does not apply if the intended use, as determined by the agency, of the new motor vehicle requires a type of vehicle for which an express manufacturer's warranty allows the use of B-20 fuel is not available.

History.
2007-420, s. 1

§§ 20-352, 20-353

Reserved for future codification purposes.

ARTICLE 15B
NORTH CAROLINA MOTOR VEHICLE REPAIR ACT

§ 20-354. Short title

This act shall be known and may be cited as the "North Carolina Motor Vehicle Repair Act."

History.
1999-437, s. 1

§ 20-354.1. Scope and application

This act shall apply to all motor vehicle repair shops in North Carolina, except:

(1) Any motor vehicle repair shop of a municipal, county, State, or federal government when carrying out the functions of the government.

(2) Any person who engages solely in the repair of any of the following:

a. Motor vehicles that are owned, maintained, and operated exclusively by that person for that person's own use.

b. For-hire vehicles which are rented for periods of 30 days or less.

(3) Any person who repairs only motor vehicles which are operated principally for agricultural or horticultural pursuits on farms, groves, or orchards and which are operated on the highways of this State only incidentally en route to or from the farms, groves, or orchards.

(4) Motor vehicle auctions or persons in the performance of motor vehicle repairs solely for motor vehicle auctions.

(5) Any motor vehicle repair shop in the performance of a motor vehicle repair if the cost of the repair does not exceed three hundred fifty dollars ($ 350.00).

(6) Any person or motor vehicle repair shop in the performance of repairs on commercial construction equipment or motor vehicles that have a GVWR of at least 26,001 pounds.

(7) When a third party has waived in writing the right to receive written estimates from the motor vehicle repair shop; the third party indicates to the motor vehicle repair shop that the repairs will be paid for by the third party under an insurance policy, service contract, mechanical breakdown contract, or manufacturer's warranty; and the third party further indicates that the customer's share of the cost of repairs, if any, will not exceed three hundred fifty dollars ($ 350.00).

History.
1999-437, s. 1; 2001-298, s. 1

§ 20-354.2. Definitions

As used in this act:

(1) "Customer" means the person who signs the written repair estimate or any other person whom that person designates as a person who may authorize repair work.

(2) "Employee" means an individual who is employed full time or part time by a motor vehicle repair shop and performs motor vehicle repairs.

(3) "Motor vehicle" means any automobile, truck, bus, recreational vehicle, motorcycle, motor scooter, or other motor-powered vehicle, but does not include trailers, mobile homes, travel trailers, or trailer coaches without independent motive power, or watercraft or aircraft.

(4) "Motor vehicle repair" means all maintenance of and modification and repairs to motor vehicles and the diagnostic work incident to those repairs, including, but not limited to, the rebuilding or restoring of rebuilt vehicles, body work, painting, warranty work, shop supply fees, hazardous material disposal fees incident to a repair, and other work customarily undertaken by motor vehicle repair shops. Motor vehicle repair does not include the sale or installation of tires when authorized by the customer.

(5) "Motor vehicle repair shop" means any person who, for compensation, engages or attempts to engage in the repair of motor vehicles owned by other persons and includes, but is not limited to:

a. Mobile motor vehicle repair shops.

b. Motor vehicle and recreational vehicle dealers.

c. Garages.

d. Service stations.

e. Self-employed individuals.

f. Truck stops.

g. Paint and body shops.

h. Brake, muffler, or transmission shops.

i. Shops doing glasswork.

Any person who engages solely in the maintenance or repair of the coach portion of a recreational vehicle is not a motor vehicle repair shop.

History.
1999-437, s. 1; 2005-463, s. 1

§ 20-354.3. Written motor vehicle repair estimate and disclosure statement required

(a) When any customer requests a motor vehicle repair shop to perform repair work on a motor vehicle, the cost of which repair work will exceed three hundred fifty dollars ($ 350.00) to the customer, the shop shall prepare a written repair estimate, which is a form setting forth the estimated cost of repair work, including diagnostic work, before effecting any diagnostic work or repair. In determining under this section whether the cost of the repair work exceeds three hundred fifty dollars ($ 350.00), the cost of the repair work shall consist of the cost of parts and labor necessary for the repair work and any charges for necessary diagnostic work and teardown, if any, and shall include any taxes, any other repair shop supplies or overhead, and any other extra services that are incidental to the repair work. The written repair estimate shall also include a statement allowing the customer to indicate whether replaced parts should be saved for inspection or return and a statement indicating the daily charge for storing the customer's motor vehicle after the customer has been notified that the repair work has been completed.

(b) The information required by subsection (a) of this section need not be provided if the customer waives in writing his or her right to receive a written estimate. A customer may waive his or her right to receive any written estimates from a motor vehicle repair shop for a period of time specified by the customer in the waiver.

(c) Except as provided in subsection (e) of this section, a copy of the written repair estimate required by subsection (a) of this section shall be given to the customer before repair work is begun.

(d) If the customer leaves his or her motor vehicle at a motor vehicle repair shop during hours when the shop is not open, or if the motor vehicle repair shop reasonably believes that an accurate estimate of the cost of repairs cannot be made until after the diagnostic work has been completed, or if the customer permits the shop or another person to deliver the motor vehicle to the shop, there shall be an implied partial waiver of the written estimate; however, upon completion of the diagnostic work

necessary to estimate the cost of repair, the shop shall notify the customer as required by G.S. 20-354.5(a).

(e) Nothing in this section shall be construed to require a motor vehicle repair shop to give a written estimate price if the motor vehicle repair shop does not agree to perform the requested repair.

History.
1999-437, s. 1; 2001-298, s. 2; 2005-304, s. 1

§ 20-354.4. Charges for motor vehicle repair estimate; requirement of waiver of rights prohibited

(a) Before proceeding with preparing an estimate, the shop shall do both of the following:

(1) Disclose to the customer the amount, if any, of the charge for preparing the estimate.

(2) Obtain a written authorization to prepare an estimate if there is a charge for that estimate.

(b) It is a violation of this Article for any motor vehicle repair shop to require that any person waive his or her rights provided in this Article as a precondition to the repair of his or her vehicle by the shop or to impose or threaten to impose any charge which is clearly excessive in relation to the work involved in making the price estimate for the purpose of inducing the customer to waive his or her rights provided in this Article.

History.
1999-437, s. 1

§ 20-354.5. Notification of charges in excess of repair estimate; prohibited charges; refusal to return vehicle prohibited; inspection of parts

(a) In the event that any of the following applies, the customer shall be promptly notified by telephone, telegraph, mail, or other means of the additional repair work and estimated cost of the additional repair work:

(1) The written repair estimate contains only an estimate for diagnostic work necessary to estimate the cost of repair and such diagnostic work has been completed.

(2) A determination is made by a motor vehicle repair shop that the actual charges for the repair work will exceed the written estimate by more than ten percent (10%).

(3) An implied partial waiver exists for diagnostic work, and the diagnostic work has been completed.

When a customer is notified, he or she shall, orally or in writing, authorize, modify, or cancel the order for repair.

(b) If a customer cancels the order for repair or, after diagnostic work is performed, decides not to have the repairs performed, and if the customer authorizes the motor vehicle repair shop to reassemble the motor vehicle, the shop shall expeditiously reassemble the motor vehicle in a condition reasonably similar to the condition in which it was received.

After cancellation of the repair order or a decision by the customer not to have repairs made after diagnostic work has been performed, the shop may charge for and the customer is obligated to pay the cost of repairs actually completed that were authorized by the written repair estimate as well as the cost of diagnostic work and teardown, the cost of parts and labor to replace items that were destroyed by teardown, and the cost to reassemble the component or the vehicle, provided the customer was notified of these possible costs in the written repair estimate or at the time the customer authorized the motor vehicle repair shop to reassemble the motor vehicle.

(c) It is a violation of this Article for a motor vehicle repair shop to charge more than the written estimate and the amount by which the motor vehicle repair shop has obtained authorization to exceed the written estimate in accordance with subsections (a) or (b) of this section, plus ten percent (10%).

(d) It is a violation of this Article for any motor vehicle repair shop to refuse to return any customer's motor vehicle because the customer refused to pay for repair charges that exceed a written estimate and any amounts authorized by the customer in accordance with subsection (a) or (b) of this section by more than ten percent (10%), provided that the customer has paid the motor vehicle repair shop the amount of the estimate and the amounts authorized by the customer in accordance with subsections (a) and (b) of this section, plus ten percent (10%).

(e) Upon request made at the time the repair work is authorized by the customer, the customer is entitled to inspect parts removed from his or her vehicle or, if the shop has no warranty arrangement or exchange parts program with a manufacturer, supplier, or distributor, have them returned to him or her. A motor vehicle repair shop may discard parts removed from a customer's vehicle or sell them and retain the proceeds for the shop's own account if the customer fails to take possession of the parts at the shop within two business days after taking delivery of the repaired vehicle.

History.
1999-437, s. 1; 2001-298, ss. 3, 4

§ 20-354.6. Invoice required of motor vehicle repair shop

The motor vehicle repair shop shall provide each customer, upon completion of any repair, with a legible copy of an invoice for such repair. The invoice shall include the following information:

(1) A statement indicating what was done to correct the problem or a description of the service provided.

(2) An itemized description of all labor, parts, and merchandise supplied and the costs of all labor, parts, and merchandise supplied. No itemized description is required to be provided to the customer for labor, parts, and merchandise supplied when a third party has indicated to the motor vehicle repair shop that the repairs will be paid for under a service contract, under a mechanical breakdown contract, or under a manufacturer's warranty, without charge to the customer.

(3) A statement identifying any replacement part as being used, rebuilt, or reconditioned, as the case may be.

History.
1999-437, s. 1; 2001-298, s. 5; 2002-159, s. 32

§ 20-354.7. Required disclosure; signs; notice to customers

A sign, at least 24 inches on each side, shall be posted in a manner conspicuous to the public. The sign shall contain:

(1) That the consumer has a right to receive a written estimate or to waive receipt of that estimate if the cost of repairs will exceed three hundred fifty dollars ($ 350.00).

(2) That the consumer may request, at the time the work order is taken, the return or inspection of all parts that have been replaced during the motor vehicle repair.

History.
1999-437, s. 1

§ 20-354.8. Prohibited acts and practices

It shall be a violation of this Article for any motor vehicle repair shop or employee of a motor vehicle repair shop to do any of the following:

(1) Charge for repairs which have not been expressly or impliedly authorized by the customer.

(2) Misrepresent that repairs have been made to a motor vehicle.

(3) Misrepresent that certain parts and repairs are necessary to repair a vehicle.

(4) Misrepresent that the vehicle being inspected or diagnosed is in a dangerous condition or that the customer's continued use of the vehicle may be harmful or cause great damage to the vehicle.

Chapter 20

(5) Fraudulently alter any customer contract, estimate, invoice, or other document.

(6) Fraudulently misuse any customer's credit card.

(7) Make or authorize in any manner or by any means whatever any written or oral statement which is untrue, deceptive, or misleading, and which is known, or which by the exercise of reasonable care should be known, to be untrue, deceptive, or misleading, related to this Article.

(8) Make fraudulent promises of a character likely to influence, persuade, or induce a customer to authorize the repair, service, or maintenance of a motor vehicle.

(9) Substitute used, rebuilt, salvaged, or straightened parts for new replacement parts without notice to the motor vehicle owner and to his or her insurer if the cost of repair is to be paid pursuant to an insurance policy and the identity of the insurer or its claims adjuster is disclosed to the motor vehicle repair shop.

(10) Cause or allow a customer to sign any work order that does not state the repairs requested by the customer.

(11) Refuse to give to a customer a copy of any document requiring the customer's signature upon completion or cancellation of the repair work.

(12) Rebuild or restore a rebuilt vehicle without the knowledge of the owner in a manner that does not conform to the original vehicle manufacturer's established repair procedures or specifications and allowable tolerances for the particular model and year.

(13) Perform any other act that is a violation of this Article or that constitutes fraud or misrepresentation under this Article.

History.
1999-437, s. 1

§ 20-354.9. Remedies

Any customer injured by a violation of this Article may bring an action in the appropriate court for relief. The prevailing party in that action may be entitled to damages plus court costs and reasonable attorneys' fees. The customer may also bring an action for injunctive relief in the appropriate court. A violation of this Article is not punishable as a crime; however, this Article does not limit the rights or remedies which are otherwise available to a consumer under any other law.

History.
1999-437, s. 1

§§ 20-354.10 through 20-355

Reserved for future codification purposes.

ARTICLE 16
PROFESSIONAL HOUSEMOVING

§ 20-356. Definitions

As used in this Article, the following terms mean:

(1) **Department.** -- The Department of Transportation.

(2) **House.** -- A dwelling, building, or other structure in excess of 15 feet in width. Mobile homes, manufactured homes, or modular homes, or portions thereof, are not within this definition when being transported from the manufacturer or from a licensed retail dealer location to the first set-up site.

(3) **Housemover.** -- A person licensed under this Article.

(4) **Person.** -- An individual, corporation, partnership, association, or any other business entity.

(5) **Secretary.** -- The Secretary of the Department of Transportation.

(6) **Unsafe practices.** -- Any act that is determined by a final agency decision of an enforcing agency or by a court of competent jurisdiction to create a hazard to the motoring public, or any citations under the Occupational Safety and Health Act that have become a final order within the last three years for willful serious violations or for failing to abate serious violations, as defined in G.S. 95-127.

History.
1977, c. 720, s. 1; 1979, c. 475, s. 2; 2001-424, s. 27.17(a); 2005-354, s. 1; 2008-89, s. 1

§ 20-357. Housemovers to be licensed

All persons who engage in the profession of housemoving on roads and highways on the State Highway System shall be licensed by the Department.

History.
1977, c. 720, s. 2

§ 20-358. Qualifications to become licensed

The Department shall issue annual printed licenses to applicants meeting the following conditions:

(1) The applicant must be at least 21 years of age; present acceptable evidence

of good character and show sufficient housemoving experience on the application form furnished by the Department. Proof of creditable housemoving experience must be furnished at the time of application for those applicants not previously licensed by the Department. Creditable housemoving experience means extensive and responsible training gained by the applicant while engaged actively and directly on a full-time basis in the moving of houses and structures on public roads and highways with at least five years of experience. Examples of the capacity in which a person may work in gaining experience include the following in building moving operations:

 a. Moving superintendent,

 b. Moving foreman, and

 c. General mechanic and helper in the housemoving profession or trade.

To comply with the requirement of proof of creditable housemoving experience, each applicant not previously licensed under this Article shall submit to the Department an affidavit from a certified public accountant that the applicant has documented employment records for a period of five continuous years from a person or persons licensed by this State or another state for housemoving. Each applicant not previously licensed under this Article shall also submit to the Department affidavits from a person or persons licensed in this State or another state in housemoving, who have employed the applicant in housemoving, providing in detail the applicant's full-time experience, including any supervisory duties and experience, in housemoving.

(2) Repealed by Session Laws 1981, c. 818, s. 3.

(3) The applicant must furnish proof that all of the vehicles, excluding "beams and dollies" and "hauling units," to be used in the movement of buildings, structures, or other extraordinary objects wider than 15 feet have met the requirements of G.S. 20-183.2 pertaining to the equipment inspection of motor vehicles; provided that the "beams and dollies" and "hauling units" are excluded from inspection under G.S. 20-183.2 and, further, are not required to be equipped with brakes.

(4) The applicant must exhibit his federal employer's identification number.

(5) The applicant must pay an annual license fee of one hundred dollars ($ 100.00).

History.

1977, c. 720, s. 3; 1981, c. 818, s. 3; 1991 (Reg. Sess., 1992), c. 813, s. 2; 2005-354, s. 2; 2008-89, s. 2

§ 20-359. Effective period of license

A license issued hereunder shall be effective from date of issuance and expire on July 31 of each year and shall be renewable on an annual basis.

History.

1977, c. 720, s. 4; 2005-354, s. 3

§ 20-359.1. Insurance requirements

(a) No license shall be issued or renewed pursuant to this Article unless the applicant files with the Department a certificate or certificates of insurance, from an insurance company or companies authorized to do business in this State, providing:

 (1) Motor vehicle insurance for bodily injury to or death of one or more persons in any one accident and for injury to or destruction of property of others in any one accident with minimum coverage of three hundred fifty thousand dollars ($ 350,000) combined single limit of liability;

 (2) Comprehensive general liability insurance with a minimum coverage of three hundred fifty thousand dollars ($ 350,000) combined single limit of liability, including coverage of operations on North Carolina streets and highways that are not covered by motor vehicle insurance; and

 (3) Workers' compensation insurance that complies with Chapter 97 for all employees if the person is licensed as a professional housemover. The exemptions in G.S. 97-13 from the provisions of Chapter 97 shall not apply to licensed professional housemovers.

(b) The certificate or certificates shall provide for continuous coverage during the effective period of the license issued pursuant to this Article. At the time the certificate is filed, the applicant shall also file with the Department a current list of all motor vehicles covered by the certificate. The applicant shall file amendments to the list within 15 days of any changes.

(c) An insurance company issuing any insurance policy required by subsection (a) of this section shall notify the Department of any of the following events at least 30 days before its occurrence: (i) cancellation of the policy, (ii) non-renewal of the policy, or (iii) any change in the policy.

(d) In addition to all coverages required by this section, the applicant shall file with the Department a copy of either: (i) a bond or other acceptable surety providing coverage in the amount of twenty-five thousand dollars ($ 25,000) for the benefit of a person contracting with the housemover to move that person's structure for all claims for property damage arising from the movement of a structure pursuant to this Article, or (ii) a policy of cargo

Chapter 20

insurance in the amount of fifty thousand dollars ($ 50,000).

History.
1981, c. 818, s. 1; 1991 (Reg. Sess., 1992), c. 813, s. 1

§ 20-360. Requirements for permit

(a) Persons licensed as professional housemovers shall also be required to secure a permit from the Department for every move undertaken on the State Highway System of roads; that permit shall be issued by the Department after determining that the applicant is (i) properly licensed, (ii) furnished special surety bonds as required by the Department, and (iii) complying with such other regulations as required by the Department.

(b) It shall be the duty of the applicant to see that the "beams and dollies" and "hauling units" used shall be constructed with proper material in a suitable manner and utilized so as to provide for the safety of the general public and the structure being relocated. Any violation of this duty may result in suspension or revocation of his license by the Department.

(c) A license shall not be required for an individual owner of a towing vehicle moving their own buildings from or to property owned individually by those persons; however, a permit will be required for all moves.

(d) Licensed housemovers shall furnish front and rear certified escort vehicles on all moves, one or both of which may be a marked police, sheriff or State Highway Patrol vehicle as determined by the issuing agent, or one or two properly equipped certified escort vehicles depending on the number of law-enforcement vehicles escorting the move; escort vehicles shall operate where possible at a distance of 300 feet from the structure being moved; that this interval will be closed in cities and other congested areas to protect other traffic from the swing of the load at corners and turns, and the certified escort vehicles shall comply with all restrictions as provided on the permit secured for movement of the structure.

History.
1977, c. 720, s. 5; 1981, c. 818, s. 2; 2005-354, s. 4

§ 20-361. Application for permit and permit fee

Application for a permit to move a structure must be made to the division or district engineer having jurisdiction at least two days prior to the date of the move. For good cause shown, this time may be waived by the district or division engineer. A travel plan and a permit application fee of twenty dollars ($ 20.00) shall accompany the application. Division or district engineers

are authorized to issue permits for individual moves of a structure or building whose width does not exceed 36 feet. The travel plan will show the proposed route, the time estimated for each segment of the move, a plan to handle traffic so that no one delay to other highway users shall exceed 20 minutes. The division or district engineers shall review the travel plan and if the route cannot accommodate the move due to roadway weight limits, bridge size or weight limits, or will cause undue interruption of traffic flow, the permit shall not be issued. The applicant may submit alternate plans if desired until an acceptable route is determined. If the width of the building or structure to be relocated is more than 36 feet, or if no acceptable travel plan has been filed, and the denial of the permit would cause a hardship, the application and travel plan may be submitted to the Department on appeal. After reviewing the route and travel plan, the Department may in its discretion issue the permit after considering the practical physical limitations of the route, the nature and purpose of the move, the size and weight of the structure, the distance the structure is to be moved, and the safety and convenience of the traveling public. A surety bond in an amount to cover the cost of any damage to the pavement, structures, bridges, roadway or other damages that may occur can be required if deemed necessary by the Department.

History.
1977, c. 720, s. 6; 1991 (Reg. Sess., 1992), c. 813, s. 3

§ 20-362. Liability of housemovers

The permittee assumes all responsibility for injury to persons or damage to property of any kind and agrees to hold the Department harmless for any claims arising out of his conduct or actions.

History.
1977, c. 720, s. 7

§ 20-363. Removal and replacement of obstructions

All obstructions, including mailboxes, traffic signals, signs, and utility lines will be removed immediately prior to and replaced immediately after the move at the expense of the mover. Any property, real or personal, to be removed, which is not located in the right-of-way, shall not be removed until the owner is notified and arrangements for and approval from the owner are obtained.

History.
1977, c. 720, s. 8; 2008-89, s. 3

§ 20-364. Route changes

Irrespective of the route shown on the permit, an alternate route will be followed:

(1) If directed by a peace officer.

(2) If directed by a uniformed officer assigned to a weigh station to follow a route to a weighing device.

(3) If the specified route is officially detoured. Should a detour be encountered, the driver shall check with the office issuing permit on which he is traveling prior to proceeding.

History.
1977, c. 720, s. 9; 2004-124, s. 18.3(d)

§ 20-365. Loading or parking on right-of-way

The object to be transported will not be loaded, unloaded, nor parked, day or night, on highway right-of-way without specific permission from the district or division engineer.

History.
1977, c. 720, s. 10

§ 20-366. Effect of weather

No move will be made when atmospheric conditions render visibility lower than safe for travel. Moves will not be made when highway is covered with snow or ice, or at any time travel conditions are considered unsafe by the Department or Highway Patrol or other law-enforcement officers having jurisdiction.

History.
1977, c. 720, s. 11

§ 20-367. Obtaining license or permit by fraud

The permit may be voided if any conditions of the permit are violated. Upon any violation, the permit must be surrendered and a new permit obtained before proceeding. Misrepresentation of information on application to obtain a license, fraudulently obtaining a permit, alteration of a permit, or unauthorized use of a permit will render the permit void.

History.
1977, c. 720, s. 12

§ 20-368. Municipal regulations

All moves on streets on the municipal system of streets shall comply with local regulations.

History.
1977, c. 720, s. 13

§ 20-369. Out-of-state licenses and permits

An out-of-state person, partnership, or corporation engaging in the structural moving business may apply to the Department for a license to engage in the housemoving profession in North Carolina, and obtain permits for moves by complying with the provisions of this Article and the regulations of the Department in the same manner as is required of North Carolina residents and by showing that the state in which the housemover operates his business extends similar privileges to housemovers licensed in North Carolina.

History.
1977, c. 720, s. 14; 1979, c. 475, s. 1

§ 20-370. Speed limits

The speed of moves will be that which is reasonable and prudent for the load, considering weight and bulk, under conditions existing at the time.

History.
1977, c. 720, s. 15

§ 20-371. Penalties

(a) Any person violating the provisions of this Article or the regulations of the Department governing housemoving shall be guilty of a Class 1 misdemeanor.

(b) The Department is hereby authorized in the name of the State to apply for relief by injunction, in the established manner provided in cases of civil procedure, without bond, to enforce the provisions of this Article, or to restrain any violation thereof. In such proceedings, it shall not be necessary to allege or prove either that an adequate remedy at law does not exist, or that substantial or irreparable damage would result from the continued violation thereof.

History.
1977, c. 720, s. 16; 1993, c. 539, s. 392; 1994, Ex. Sess., c. 24, s. 14(c); 2008-89, s. 4

§ 20-372. Invalid section; severability

If any of the provisions of this Article, or if the application of such provisions to any person or circumstance shall be held invalid, the remainder of this Article and the application of such provision of this Article other than those as to which it is held valid, shall not be affected thereby.

Chapter 20

History.

1977, c. 720, s. 17

N.C. Gen. Stat. § 20-373

Reserved for future codification purposes.

§ 20-374. Unsafe practices

(a) If the Department determines that a housemover has engaged in unsafe practices, all licenses, permits, and authorizations issued to the person pursuant to this Article shall be revoked for a period of six months.

(b) Any person whose license, permit, or authorization issued under this Article is revoked pursuant to this section may request a hearing to be held before the Secretary or a person designated by the Secretary. The licensee shall be notified in writing no less than 10 days prior to the hearing of the time and place of the hearing. At the hearing, the parties shall be given an opportunity to present evidence on issues of fact, examine and cross-examine witnesses, and present arguments on issues of law. The decision of the Secretary or of the person designated by the Secretary shall be final. Any person aggrieved by the final decision may seek judicial review of the decision in accordance with the provisions of Article 4 of Chapter 150B of the General Statutes.

History.

2008-89, s. 5

N.C. Gen. Stat. § 20-375

Reserved for future codification purposes.

ARTICLE 17
MOTOR CARRIER SAFETY REGULATION UNIT

PART 1
GENERAL PROVISIONS

§ 20-376. Definitions

The following definitions apply in this Article:

(1) **Federal safety and hazardous materials regulations.** -- The federal motor carrier safety regulations contained in 49 C.F.R. Parts 171 through 180, 382, and 390 through 398.

(2) **Foreign commerce.** -- Commerce between any of the following:

a. A place in the United States and a place in a foreign country.

b. Places in the United States through any foreign country.

(3) **Interstate commerce.** -- As defined in 49 C.F.R. Part 390.5.

(3a) **Interstate motor carrier.** -- Any person, firm, or corporation that operates or controls a commercial motor vehicle as defined in 49 C.F.R. § 390.5 in interstate commerce.

(4) **Intrastate commerce.** -- As defined in 49 C.F.R. Part 390.5.

(5) **Intrastate motor carrier.** -- Any person, firm, or corporation that operates or controls a motor vehicle in intrastate commerce when the vehicle:

a. Is a vehicle having a gross vehicle weight rating (GVWR) or gross combination weight rating (GCWR) or gross vehicle weight (GVW) or gross combination weight (GCW) of 26,001 pounds or more, whichever is greater.

b. Is designed or used to transport 16 or more passengers, including the driver.

c. Is used in transporting a hazardous material in a quantity requiring placarding pursuant to 49 C.F.R. Parts 170 through 185.

History.

1985, c. 454, s. 1; 1993 (Reg. Sess., 1994), c. 621, s. 5; 1995 (Reg. Sess., 1996), c. 756, s. 20; 1997-456, s. 36; 1998-149, s. 11; 1999-452, s. 21; 2002-152, s. 3; 2010-129, s. 5

PART 2
AUTHORITY AND POWERS OF DEPARTMENT OF PUBLIC SAFETY

§ 20-377. General powers of Department of Public Safety

The Department of Public Safety shall have and exercise such general power and authority to supervise and control the motor carriers of the State as may be necessary to carry out the laws providing for their regulation, and all such other powers and duties as may be necessary or incident to the proper discharge of its duties.

History.

1985, c. 454, s. 1; 2002-159, s. 31.5(b); 2002-190, s. 2; 2011-145, s. 19.1(g)

N.C. Gen. Stat. § 20-378

Repealed by Session Laws 1995 (Regular Session, 1996), c. 756, s. 21.

Chapter 20

§ 20-379. Department of Public Safety to audit motor carriers for compliance

The Department of Public Safety must periodically audit each motor carrier to determine if the carrier is complying with this Article and, if the motor carrier is subject to regulation by the North Carolina Utilities Commission, with Chapter 62 of the General Statutes. In conducting the audit, the Department of Public Safety may examine a person under oath, compel the production of papers and the attendance of witnesses, and copy a paper for use in the audit. An employee of the Department of Public Safety may enter the premises of a motor carrier during reasonable hours to enforce this Article. When on the premises of a motor carrier, an employee of the Department of Public Safety may set up and use equipment needed to make the tests required by this Article.

History.
1985, c. 454, s. 1; 1995 (Reg. Sess., 1996), c. 756, s. 22; 2002-159, s. 31.5(b); 2002-190, s. 2; 2011-145, s. 19.1(g)

§ 20-380. Department of Public Safety may investigate accidents involving motor carriers and promote general safety program

The Department of Public Safety may conduct a program of accident prevention and public safety covering all motor carriers with special emphasis on highway safety and transport safety and may investigate the causes of any accident on a highway involving a motor carrier. Any information obtained in an investigation shall be reduced to writing and a report thereof filed in the office of the Department of Public Safety, which shall be subject to public inspection but such report shall not be admissible in evidence in any civil or criminal proceeding arising from such accident. The Department of Public Safety may adopt rules for the safety of the public as affected by motor carriers and the safety of motor carrier employees. The Department of Public Safety shall cooperate with and coordinate its activities for motor carriers with other agencies and organizations engaged in the promotion of highway safety and employee safety.

History.
1985, c. 454, s. 1; 1995 (Reg. Sess., 1996), c. 756, s. 23; 2002-159, s. 31,5(b); 2002-190, s. 2; 2011-145, s. 19.1(g)

§ 20-381. Specific powers and duties of Department of Public Safety applicable to motor carriers; agricultural exemption

(a) The Department of Public Safety has the following powers and duties concerning motor carriers:

(1) To prescribe qualifications and maximum hours of service of drivers and their helpers.

(1a) To set safety standards for vehicles of motor carriers engaged in foreign, interstate, or intrastate commerce over the highways of this State and for the safe operation of these vehicles. The Department of Public Safety may stop, enter upon, and perform inspections of motor carriers' vehicles in operation to determine compliance with these standards and may conduct any investigations and tests it finds necessary to promote the safety of equipment and the safe operation on the highway of these vehicles.

(1b) To enforce this Article, rules adopted under this Article, and the federal safety and hazardous materials regulations.

(2) To enter the premises of a motor carrier to inspect a motor vehicle or any equipment used by the motor carrier in transporting passengers or property.

(2a) To prohibit the use by a motor carrier of any motor vehicle or motor vehicle equipment the Department of Public Safety finds, by reason of its mechanical condition or loading, would be likely to cause a crash or breakdown in the transportation of passengers or property on a highway. If an agent of the Department of Public Safety finds a motor vehicle of a motor carrier in actual use upon the highways in the transportation of passengers or property that, by reason of its mechanical condition or loading, would be likely to cause a crash or breakdown, the agent shall declare the vehicle "Out of Service." The agent shall require the operator thereof to discontinue its use and to substitute therefor a safe vehicle, parts or equipment at the earliest possible time and place, having regard for both the convenience and the safety of the passengers or property. When an inspector or agent stops a motor vehicle on the highway, under authority of this section, and the motor vehicle is declared "Out of Service," no motor carrier operator shall require, or permit, any person to operate, nor shall any person operate, any motor vehicle equipment declared "Out of Service" until all repairs required by the "Out of Service" notice have been satisfactorily completed. Such agents or inspectors shall also have the right to stop any motor vehicle which is being used upon the public highways for the transportation of passengers or property by a motor carrier subject to the provisions of this Article and to eject therefrom any driver or operator who shall be operating or be in charge of such motor vehicle while under the influence of alcoholic beverages or impairing substances. It shall be the duty of all inspectors and agents of the Department of Public Safety to make a written report, upon a form prescribed by the Department of Public Safety, of inspections of all motor equipment and a copy of each such written report, disclosing defects in such equipment, shall be served promptly upon the motor carrier operating the same, either in person by the inspector or agent or by mail. Such agents and inspectors shall also make and serve a similar written report in cases where a motor vehicle is operated in violation of this Chapter or, if the motor vehicle is subject to regulation by the North Carolina Utilities Commission, of Chapter 62 of the General Statutes.

(3) To relieve the highways of all undue burdens and safeguard traffic thereon by adopting and enforcing rules and orders designed and calculated to minimize the dangers attending transportation on the highways of all hazardous materials and other commodities.

(4) To determine the safety fitness of intrastate motor carriers, to assign safety ratings to intrastate motor carriers as defined in 49 C.F.R. § 385.3, to direct intrastate motor carriers to take remedial action when required, to prohibit the operation of intrastate motor carriers when subject to an out-of-service order issued by the Federal Motor Carrier Safety Administration or the Department.

(5) To enforce any order issued by the Federal Motor Carrier Safety Administration including the authority to seize registration plates pursuant to the provisions of G.S. 20-45 from motor carriers whose registration was rescinded and cancelled pursuant to G.S. 20-110(m) or G.S. 20-110(n).

(b) The definitions set out in 49 Code of Federal Regulations § 171.8 apply to this subsection. The transportation of an agricultural product, other than a Class 2 material, over local roads between fields of the same farm by a farmer operating as an intrastate private motor carrier is exempt from the requirements of Parts 171 through 180 of 49 CFR as provided in 49 CFR § 173.5(a). The transportation of an agricultural product to or from a farm within 150 miles of the farm by a farmer operating as an intrastate private motor carrier is exempt from the requirements of Subparts G and H of Part 172 of 49 CFR as provided in 49 CFR § 173.5(b).

(c) For purposes of 49 C.F.R. § 395.1(k) and any other federal law or regulation relating to hours-of-service rules for drivers engaged in the transportation of agricultural commodities and farm supplies for agricultural purposes, the terms "planting and harvesting season" and "planting and harvesting period" refer to the period from January 1 through December 31 of each year.

(d) The definitions set out in 49 C.F.R. § 390.5 apply to this subsection. A covered farm vehicle engaged in intrastate commerce is exempt from the requirements of 49 C.F.R. § 390.21.

History.

1985, c. 454, s. 1; 1995 (Reg. Sess., 1996), c. 756, s. 24; 1997-456, ss. 37, 38; 1998-149, s. 12; 1998-165, s. 1; 1999-452, s. 22; 2002-152, ss. 4, 5; 2002-159, s. 31.5(b); 2002-190, s. 2; 2009-376, s. 9; 2011-145, s. 19.1(g); 2014-103, s. 5; 2017-108, s. 17; 2019-196, s. 4

§ 20-382. For-hire motor carrier registration, insurance verification, and temporary trip permit authority

(a) **UCRA.** -- The Commissioner may enter into the Unified Carrier Registration Agreement (UCRA), established pursuant to Section 4305 of Public Law 109-73, and into agreements with jurisdictions participating in the UCRA to exchange information for any audit or enforcement activity required by the UCRA. Upon entry into the UCRA, the requirements set under the UCRA apply to the Division. If a requirement set under the UCRA conflicts with this section, the UCRA controls. Rules adopted to implement this section must ensure compliance with mandates of the Federal Motor Carrier Safety Administration and the United States Department of Transportation.

(a1) **Carrier Registration.** -- A motor carrier may not operate a for-hire motor vehicle in interstate commerce in this State unless the motor carrier has complied with all of the following requirements:

(1) Registered its operations with its base state.

(1a) Done one of the following:

a. Filed a copy of the certificate of authority issued to it by the United States Department of Transportation allowing it to transport regulated items in this State and any amendments to that authority.

b. Certified to the Division that it carries only items that are not regulated by the United States Department of Transportation.

(2) Verified, in accordance with subsection (b) of this section, that it has insurance for each for-hire motor vehicle it operates.

(3) Paid the fees set in G.S. 20-385.

(b) **Insurance Verification.** -- A motor carrier that operates a for-hire motor vehicle in interstate commerce in this State and is regulated by the United States Department of Transportation must verify to the Division that each for-hire motor vehicle the motor carrier operates in this State is insured in accordance with the requirements set by the United States Department of Transportation. A motor carrier that operates a for-hire motor vehicle in interstate commerce in this State and is exempt from regulation by the United States Department of Transportation must verify to the Division that each for-hire motor vehicle the motor carrier operates in this State is insured in accordance with the requirements set by the North Carolina Utilities Commission.

(c) **Trip Permit.** -- A motor carrier that is not registered as required by this section may obtain an emergency trip permit. An emergency trip permit allows the motor carrier to operate a for-hire motor vehicle in this State for a period not to exceed 10 days.

History.
1985, c. 454, s. 1; 1993 (Reg. Sess., 1994), c. 621, s. 1; 1995 (Reg. Sess., 1996), c. 756, s. 25; 2007-492, s. 3; 2010-97, s. 4

§ 20-382.1. Registration of for-hire intrastate motor carriers and verification that their vehicles are insured

(a) **Registration.** -- A for-hire motor carrier may not operate a for-hire motor vehicle in intrastate commerce in this State unless the motor carrier has complied with all of the following requirements:

(1) For a motor carrier that hauls household goods, registered its operations with the State by doing one of the following:

a. Obtaining a certificate of authority from the North Carolina Utilities Commission.

b. Obtaining a certificate of exemption from the Division.

(1a) For a motor carrier that does not haul household goods, registered its operations with the Division.

(2) Verified, in accordance with subsection (b) of this section, that it has insurance for each for-hire motor vehicle it operates in this State.

(3) Paid the fees set in G.S. 20-385.

(b) **Insurance Verification.** -- A for-hire motor carrier that operates a for-hire vehicle in intrastate commerce in this State must verify to the Division that each for-hire motor vehicle it operates in this State is insured. To do this, the motor carrier must submit an insurance verification form to the Division and must file annually with the Division a list of the for-hire vehicles it operates in this State.

History.
1993 (Reg. Sess., 1994), c. 621, s. 2; 1995 (Reg. Sess., 1996), c. 756, s. 26

§ 20-382.2. Penalty for failure to comply with registration or insurance verification requirements

(a) **Acts.** -- A motor carrier who does any of the following is subject to a civil penalty of one thousand dollars ($ 1,000):

(1) Operates a for-hire motor vehicle in this State without registering its operations, as required by this Part.

(2) Repealed by Session Laws 2007-492, s. 4, effective August 30, 2007.

(3) Operates a for-hire motor vehicle in intrastate commerce in this State for which it has not verified it has insurance, as required by G.S. 20-382.1.

(b) **Payment and Review.** -- When the Department of Public Safety finds that a for-hire motor vehicle is operated in this State in violation of the registration and insurance verification requirements of this Part, the Department must place the motor vehicle out of service until the motor carrier is in compliance and the penalty imposed under this section is paid unless the officer that imposes the penalty determines that operation of the motor vehicle will not jeopardize collection of the penalty. A motor carrier that denies liability for a penalty imposed under this section may pay the penalty under protest and follow the procedure in G.S. 20-178.1 for a departmental review of the penalty.

(c) **Judicial Restriction.** -- A court of this State may not issue a restraining order or an injunction to restrain or enjoin the collection of a penalty imposed under this section or to permit the operation of a vehicle placed out of service under this section without payment of the penalty.

(d) **Proceeds.** -- A penalty imposed under this section is payable to the Department of Transportation, Fiscal Section. The clear proceeds of all civil penalties assessed by the Department pursuant to this section, minus any fees paid as interest, filing fees, attorneys' fees, or other necessary costs of court associated with the defense of penalties imposed pursuant to this section shall be remitted to the Civil Penalty and Forfeiture Fund in accordance with G.S. 115C-457.2.

History.
1993 (Reg. Sess., 1994), c. 621, s. 3; 1997-466, s. 3; 2002-159, s. 31.5(b); 2002-190, ss. 2, 3; 2005-64, s. 1; 2007-492, s. 4; 2009-376, ss. 2(b), 14; 2011-145, s. 19.1(g)

§ 20-383. Inspectors and officers given enforcement authority

Only designated inspectors, officers, and personnel of the Department of Public Safety shall have the authority to enforce the provisions of this Article and provisions of Chapter 62 applicable to motor transportation, and they are empowered to make complaint for the issue of appropriate warrants, information, presentments or other lawful process for the enforcement and prosecution of violations of the transportation laws against all offenders, whether they be regulated motor carriers or not, and to appear in court or before the North Carolina Utilities Commission and offer evidence at the trial pursuant to such processes.

History.

1985, c. 454, s. 1; 2002-159, s. 31.5(b); 2002-190, s. 2; 2011-145, s. 19.1(g); 2012-78, s. 10

§ 20-384. Penalty for certain violations

A motor carrier who fails to conduct a safety inspection of a vehicle as required by Part 396 of the federal safety regulations or who fails to mark a vehicle that has been inspected as required by that Part commits an infraction and, if found responsible, is liable for a penalty of up to fifty dollars ($ 50.00).

History.

1985, c. 454, s. 1; c. 757, s. 164(b); 1985 (Reg. Sess., 1986), c. 1018, s. 13; 1993 (Reg. Sess., 1994), c. 754, s. 6; 1995 (Reg. Sess., 1996), c. 756, s. 27

PART 3
FEES AND CHARGES

§ 20-385. Fee schedule

(a) The fees listed in this section apply to a motor carrier. These fees are in addition to any fees required under the Unified Carrier Registration Agreement.

(1) Repealed by Session Laws 2007-492, s. 5, effective August 30, 2007.

(2) Application by an intrastate motor carrier for a certificate of exemption ....$ 60.00

(3) Certification by an interstate motor carrier that it is not regulated by the United States Department of Transportation..60.00

(4) Application by an interstate motor carrier for an emergency trip permit 23.00

(b) Repealed by Session Laws 2007-492, s. 5, effective August 30, 2007.

History.

1985, c. 454, s. 1; 1993 (Reg. Sess., 1994), c. 621, s. 4; 1995 (Reg. Sess., 1996), c. 756, s. 28; 2005-276, s. 44.1(p); 2007-492, s. 5; 2015-241, s. 29.30(q)

§ 20-386. Fees, charges and penalties; disposition

All fees and charges received by the Division under G.S. 20-385 shall be in addition to any other tax or fee provided by law and shall be placed in the Highway Fund.

History.

1985, c. 454, s. 1

PART 4
PENALTIES AND ACTIONS

§ 20-387. Motor carrier violating any provision of Article, rules or orders; penalty

Any motor carrier which violates any of the provisions of this Article or refuses to conform to or obey any rule, order or regulation of the Division or Department of Public Safety shall, in addition to the other penalties prescribed in this Article forfeit and pay a sum up to one thousand dollars ($ 1,000) for each offense, to be recovered in an action to be instituted in the Superior Court of Wake County, in the name of the State of North Carolina on the relation of the Department of Public Safety; and each day such motor carrier continues to violate any provision of this Article or continues to refuse to obey or perform any rule, order or regulation prescribed by the Division or Department of Public Safety shall be a separate offense.

History.

1985, c. 454, s. 1; 2002-159, s. 31.5(b); 2002-159, s. 31.5(b); 2002-190, s. 10; 2011-145, s. 19.1(g)

§ 20-388. Willful acts of employees deemed those of motor carrier

The willful act of any officer, agent, or employee of a motor carrier, acting within the scope of his official duties of employment, shall, for the purpose of this Article, be deemed to be the willful act of the motor carrier.

History.

1985, c. 454, s. 1

§ 20-389. Actions to recover penalties

Except as otherwise provided in this Article, an action for the recovery of any penalty under this Article shall be instituted in Wake County, and shall be instituted in the name of the State of North Carolina on the relation of the Department of Public Safety against the person incurring such penalty; or whenever such action is upon the complaint of any injured person, it shall be instituted in the name of the State of North Carolina on the relation of the Department of Public Safety upon the complaint of such injured person against the person incurring such penalty. Such action may be instituted and prosecuted by the Attorney General, the District Attorney of the Wake County Superior Court, or the injured person. The procedure in such actions, the right of appeal and the rules regulating appeals shall be the same as provided by law in other civil actions.

History.

1985, c. 454, s. 1; 2002-159, s. 31.5(b); 2002-190, s. 2; 2011-145, s. 19.1(g)

§ 20-390. Refusal to permit Department of Public Safety to inspect records made misdemeanor

Any motor carrier, its officers or agents in charge thereof, that fails or refuses upon the written demand of the Department of Public Safety to permit its authorized representatives or employees to examine and inspect its books, records, accounts and documents, or its plant, property, or facilities, as provided for by law, shall be guilty of a Class 3 misdemeanor. Each day of such failure or refusal shall constitute a separate offense and each such offense shall be punishable only by a fine of not less than five hundred dollars ($ 500.00) and not more than five thousand dollars ($ 5,000).

History.

1985, c. 454, s. 1; 1993, c. 539, s. 393; 1994, Ex. Sess., c. 24, s. 14(c); 2002-159, s. 31.5(b); 2002-190, s. 2; 2011-145, s. 19.1(g)

§ 20-391. Violating rules, with injury to others

If any motor carrier doing business in this State by its agents or employees shall be guilty of the violations of the rules and regulations provided and prescribed by the Division or the Department of Public Safety, and if after due notice of such violation given to the principal officer thereof, if residing in the State, or, if not, to the manager or superintendent or secretary or treasurer if residing in the State, or, if not, then to any local agent thereof, ample and full recompense for the wrong or injury done thereby to any person as may be directed by the Division or Department of Public Safety shall not be made within 30 days from the time of such notice, such motor carrier shall incur a penalty for each offense of five hundred dollars ($ 500.00).

History.

1985, c. 454, s. 1; 2002-159, s. 31.5(b); 2002-190, s. 11; 2011-145, s. 19.1(g)

§ 20-392. Failure to make report; obstructing Division or Department of Public Safety

Every officer, agent or employee of any motor carrier, who shall willfully neglect or refuse to make and furnish any report required by the Division or Department of Public Safety for the purposes of this Article, or who shall willfully or unlawfully hinder, delay or obstruct the Division or Department of Public Safety in the discharge of the duties hereby imposed upon it, shall forfeit and pay five hundred dollars ($ 500.00) for each offense, to be recovered in an action in the name of the State. A delay of 10 days to make and furnish such report shall raise the presumption that the same was willful.

History.

1985, c. 454, s. 1; 2002-159, s. 31.5(b); 2002-190, s. 12; 2011-145, s. 19.1(g)

§ 20-393. Disclosure of information by employee of Department of Public Safety unlawful

It shall be unlawful for any agent or employee of the Department of Public Safety knowingly and willfully to divulge any fact or information which may come to his knowledge during the course of any examination or inspection made under authority of this Article, except to the Department of Public Safety or as may be directed by the Department of Public Safety or upon approval of a request to the Department of Public Safety by the Utilities Commission or by a court or judge thereof.

History.

1985, c. 454, s. 1; 2002-159, s. 31.5(b); 2002-190, s. 2; 2011-145, s. 19.1(g)

§ 20-394. Remedies for injuries cumulative

The remedies given by this Article to persons injured shall be regarded as cumulative to the remedies otherwise provided by law against motor carriers.

History.

1985, c. 454, s. 1

§ 20-395. Willful injury to property of motor carrier a misdemeanor

If any person shall willfully do or cause to be done any act or acts whatever whereby any building, construction or work of any motor carrier, or any engine, machine or structure of any matter or thing appertaining to the same shall be stopped, obstructed, impaired, weakened, injured or destroyed, he shall be guilty of a Class 1 misdemeanor.

History.

1985, c. 454, s. 1; 1993, c. 539, s. 394; 1994, Ex. Sess., c. 24, s. 14(c)

§ 20-396. Unlawful motor carrier operations

(a) Any person, whether carrier, shipper, consignee, or any officer, employee, agent, or representative thereof, who by means of any false statement or representation, or by the use of any false or fictitious bill, bill of lading, receipt, voucher, roll, account, claim, certificate, affidavit, deposition, lease, or bill of sale, or by any other means or device, shall knowingly and willfully seek to evade or defeat regulations as in this Article provided for motor carriers, shall be deemed guilty of a Class 3 misdemeanor and only punished by a fine of not more than five hundred dollars ($ 500.00) for the first offense and not more than two thousand dollars ($ 2,000) for any subsequent offense.

(b) Any motor carrier, or other person, or any officer, agent, employee, or representative thereof, who shall willfully fail or refuse to make a report to the Division or Department of Public Safety as required by this Article, or other applicable law, or to make specific and full, true, and correct answer to any question within 30 days from the time it is lawfully required by the Division or Department of Public Safety so to do, or to keep accounts, records, and memoranda in the form and manner prescribed by the Division or Department of Public Safety or shall knowingly and willfully falsify, destroy, mutilate, or alter any such report, account, record, or memorandum, or shall knowingly and willfully neglect or fail to make true and correct entries in such accounts, records, or memoranda of all facts and transactions appertaining to the business of the carrier, or person required under this Article to keep the same, or shall knowingly and willfully keep any accounts, records, or memoranda contrary to the rules, regulations, or orders of the Division or Department of Public Safety with respect thereto, shall be deemed guilty of a Class 3 misdemeanor and be punished for each offense only by a fine of not more than five thousand dollars ($ 5,000). As used in this subsection the words "kept" and "keep" shall be construed to mean made, prepared or compiled as well as retained.

History.

1985, c. 454, s. 1; 1993, c. 539, s. 395; 1994, Ex. Sess., c. 24, s. 14(c); 2002-159, s. 31.5(b); 2002-190, s. 13; 2011-145, s. 19.1(g)

§ 20-397. Furnishing false information to the Department of Public Safety; withholding information from the Department of Public Safety

(a) Every person, firm or corporation operating under the jurisdiction of the Department of Public Safety or who is required by law to file reports with the Department of Public Safety who shall knowingly or willfully file or give false information to the Department of Public Safety in any report, reply, response, or other statement or document furnished to the Department of Public Safety shall be guilty of a Class 1 misdemeanor.

(b) Every person, firm, or corporation operating under the jurisdiction of the Department of Public Safety or who is required by law to file reports with the Department of Public Safety who shall willfully withhold clearly specified and reasonably obtainable information from the Department of Public Safety in any report, response, reply or statement filed with the Department of Public Safety in the performance of the duties of the Department of Public Safety or who shall fail or refuse to file any report, response, reply or statement required by the Department of Public Safety in the performance of the duties of the Department of Public Safety shall be guilty of a Class 1 misdemeanor.

History.

1985, c. 454, s. 1; 1993, c. 539, s. 396; 1994, Ex. Sess., c. 24, s. 14(c); 2002-159, s. 31.5(b); 2002-190, s. 2; 2011-145, s. 19.1(g)

§ 20-398. Household goods carrier; marking or identification of vehicles

(a) No carrier shall operate or attempt to operate any motor vehicle upon a highway, public street, or public vehicular area within the State in the transportation of household goods for compensation unless the name or trade name and the North Carolina number assigned to the carrier by the North Carolina Utilities Commission appear on each side of the vehicle in letters and figures not less than three inches high. The North Carolina number assigned to the carrier shall also be placed on the rear left upper quadrant of the vehicle in letters and figures not less than three inches high. In case of a tractor-trailer unit, the side markings must be on the tractor and the rear markings must be on the trailer. The markings required may be printed on the vehicle or on durable placards securely fastened on the vehicle.

(b) Except as provided in subsection (b) of this section, the provisions of this section shall apply to every vehicle used by the carrier in his or her operation whether owned, rented, leased, or otherwise. However, if a vehicle is rented or leased, the words "Operated By" shall also appear above or preceding the name of the carrier, unless the vehicles are under permanent lease, in which case the name of the lessor and the words "Operated By" need not appear.

(c) The provisions of this section do not apply to carriers engaged only in interstate commerce. If the carrier is engaged in both interstate and intrastate commerce and is marked as required by the Federal Motor Carrier Safety Administration, then in that case, it will only be necessary for the carrier to print his or her North Carolina number in a conspicuous place near his or her name in letters and figures corresponding in size with Federal Motor Carrier Safety Administration regulations.

(d) Any person, whether carrier or any officer, employee, agent, or representative thereof, who violates this section shall be guilty of a Class 3 misdemeanor and punished only by a fine of not more than five hundred dollars ($ 500.00) for the first offense and not more than two thousand dollars ($ 2,000) for any subsequent offense.

(e) Notwithstanding the provisions of G.S. 20-383 to the contrary, any law enforcement officer with territorial jurisdiction is authorized to enforce the provisions of this section.

History.
2011-244, s. 1; 2021-23, s. 1

ARTICLE 18
REGULATION OF FULLY AUTONOMOUS VEHICLES

§ 20-400. Definitions

The following definitions apply in this Article:

(1) **Automated driving system.** -- The hardware and software that are collectively capable of performing the entire dynamic driving task on a sustained basis, regardless of whether it is operating within a limited or unlimited operational design domain.

(2) **Dynamic driving task.** -- All of the real-time operational and tactical control functions required to operate a motor vehicle in motion or which has the engine running, such as:

a. Lateral vehicle motion control via steering.

b. Longitudinal motion control via acceleration and deceleration.

c. Monitoring the driving environment via object and event detection, recognition, classification, and response preparation.

d. Object and event response execution.

e. Maneuver planning.

f. Enhancing conspicuity via lighting, signaling, and gesturing.

(3) **Fully autonomous vehicle.** -- A motor vehicle equipped with an automated driving system that will not at any time require an occupant to perform any portion of the dynamic driving task when the automated driving system is engaged. If equipment that allows an occupant to perform any portion of the dynamic driving task is installed, it must be stowed or made unusable in such a manner that an occupant cannot assume control of the vehicle when the automated driving system is engaged.

(4) **Minimal risk condition.** -- An operating mode in which a fully autonomous vehicle engaged with the automated driving system engaged achieves a reasonably safe state, bringing the vehicle to a complete stop, upon experiencing a failure of the automatic driving system that renders the vehicle unable to perform any portion of the dynamic driving task.

(5) **Operator.** -- For the purposes of this Article, is a person as defined in G.S. 20-4.01. An operator does not include an occupant within a fully autonomous vehicle performing solely strategic driving functions.

(6) **Operational design domain.** -- Specific conditions under which an automated driving system is limited to effectively operate, such as geographical limitations, roadway types, speed range, and environmental conditions.

(7) **Strategic driving functions.** -- Control of navigational parameters such as trip scheduling or the selection of destinations and waypoints but does not include any portion of the dynamic driving task.

History.
2017-166, s. 1

§ 20-401. Regulation of fully autonomous vehicles

(a) **Driver's License Not Required.** -- Notwithstanding the provisions of G.S. 20-7 and this Chapter, the operator of a fully autonomous vehicle with the automated driving system engaged is not required to be licensed to operate a motor vehicle.

(b) **Vehicle Registration Card in Vehicle.** -- For a fully autonomous vehicle, the provisions of G.S. 20-49(4) and G.S. 20-57(c) are satisfied if the vehicle registration card is in the vehicle, physically or electronically, and readily available to be inspected by an officer or inspector.

(c) **Parent or Legal Guardian Responsible for Certain Violations.** -- The parent or legal guardian of a minor is responsible for a violation of G.S. 20-135.2B, the prohibition on children in an open bed of a pickup, or G.S. 20-137.1, the child restraint law, if the violation occurs in a fully autonomous vehicle.

(d) **Minimum Age for Unsupervised Minors in Fully Autonomous Vehicles.** -- It is unlawful for any parent or legal guardian of a person less than 12 years of age to knowingly permit that person to occupy a fully autonomous vehicle in motion or which has the engine running unless the person is under the supervision of a person 18 years of age or older.

(e) **Registered Owner Responsible for Moving Violations.** -- The person in whose name the fully autonomous vehicle is registered is responsible for a violation of this Chapter that is considered a moving violation, if the violation involves a fully autonomous vehicle.

(f) **Unattended Vehicle.** -- A vehicle shall not be considered unattended pursuant to G.S. 20-163 or any other provision of Chapter 20 of the General Statutes merely because it is a fully autonomous vehicle with the automated driving system engaged.

(g) **Duty to Stop in the Event of a Crash.** -- If all of the following conditions are met when a fully autonomous vehicle is involved in a crash, then the provisions of subsections (a) through (c2) and subsection (e) of G.S. 20-166 and subsections (a) and (c) of G.S. 20-166.1 shall be considered satisfied, and no violation of those provisions shall be charged:

(1) The vehicle or the operator of the vehicle promptly contacts the appropriate law enforcement agency to report the crash.

(2) The vehicle or operator of the vehicle promptly calls for medical assistance, if appropriate.

(3) For a reportable crash, the vehicle remains at the scene of the crash until vehicle registration and insurance information is provided to the parties affected by the crash and a law enforcement officer authorizes the vehicle to be removed.

(4) For a nonreportable crash, the vehicle remains at the scene or in the immediate vicinity of the crash until vehicle registration and insurance information is provided to the parties affected by the crash.

(h) **Operation.** -- A person may operate a fully autonomous vehicle if the vehicle meets all of the following requirements:

(1) Unless an exception or exemption has been granted under applicable State or federal law, the vehicle:

    a. Is capable of being operated in compliance with Articles 3, 3A, 7, 11, and 13 of this Chapter;

    b. Complies with applicable federal law and regulations; and

    c. Has been certified in accordance with federal regulations in 49 C.F.R. Part 567 as being in compliance with applicable federal motor vehicle safety standards and bears the required certification label or labels.

(2) The vehicle has the capability to meet the requirements of subsection (g) of this section.

(3) The vehicle can achieve a minimal risk condition.

(4) The vehicle is covered by a motor vehicle liability policy meeting the applicable requirements of G.S. 20-279.21.

(5) The vehicle is registered in accordance with Part 3 of Article 3 of this Chapter, and, if registered in this State, the vehicle shall be identified on the registration and registration card as a fully autonomous vehicle.

(i) **Preemption.** -- No local government shall enact any local law or ordinance related to the regulation or operation of fully autonomous vehicles or vehicles equipped with an automated driving system, other than regulation specifically authorized in Chapter 153A and Chapter 160A of the General Statutes that is not specifically related to those types of motor vehicles.

History.
2017-166, s. 1

§ 20-402. Applicability to vehicles other than fully autonomous vehicles

(a) **Definitions.** -- As used in this section, a "request to intervene" means notification by a vehicle to the human operator that the operator should promptly begin or resume performance of part or all of the dynamic driving task.

(b) **Applicability.** -- Operation of a motor vehicle equipped with an automated driving system capable of performing the entire dynamic driving task with the expectation that a human operator will respond appropriately to a request to intervene is lawful under this Chapter and subject to the provisions of this Chapter.

History.
2017-166, s. 1

§ 20-403. Fully Autonomous Vehicle Committee

(a) **Committee Established.** -- There is hereby created a Fully Autonomous Vehicle Committee within the Department of Transportation.

(b) **Membership.** -- The following persons shall serve on the Committee:

(1) Secretary of Transportation, or the Secretary's designee.

(2) The Secretary of Commerce, or the Secretary's designee.

(3) The Commissioner of Insurance, or the Commissioner's designee.

(4) A representative of the Highway Patrol, designated by the Commander.

(5) A representative of the North Carolina Association of Chiefs of Police, designated by its Executive Director.

(6) A representative of the North Carolina Sheriffs' Association, designated by its President.

(7) A representative of the University of North Carolina Highway Safety Research Center, designated by the Director.

(8) At least two representatives from the autonomous vehicle industry, designated by the Secretary of Transportation.

(9) A representative of the Attorney General's Office, designated by the Attorney General, who is familiar with motor vehicle law.

(10) A representative of local law enforcement, designated by the Secretary of Transportation.

(11) A representative of the trucking industry, designated by the North Carolina Trucking Association.

(12) A planner from an urban area, designated by the North Carolina League of Municipalities.

(13) A planner from a rural area, designated by the North Carolina Association of County Commissioners.

(14) Two members of the North Carolina Senate, designated by the President Pro Tempore of the Senate.

(15) Two members of the North Carolina House of Representatives, designated by the Speaker of the House.

(c) **Duties.** -- The Committee shall meet regularly, and at a minimum four times a year, to consider matters relevant to fully autonomous vehicle technology, review State motor vehicle law as they relate to the deployment of fully autonomous vehicles onto the State highway system and municipal streets, make recommendations concerning the testing of fully autonomous vehicles, identify and make recommendations for Department of Transportation traffic rules and ordinances, and make recommendations to the General Assembly on any needed changes to State law.

(d) **Staff.** -- The Department of Transportation shall provide staff and meeting space, from reasonably available resources, to the Committee.

History.
2017-166, s. 1

CHAPTER 42
LANDLORD AND TENANT

ARTICLE 1
GENERAL PROVISIONS

§ 42-11. Willful destruction by tenant misdemeanor

If any tenant shall, during his term or after its expiration, willfully and unlawfully demolish, destroy, deface, injure or damage any tenement house, uninhabited house or other outhouse, belonging to his landlord or upon his premises by removing parts thereof or by burning, or in any other manner, or shall unlawfully and willfully burn, destroy, pull down, injure or remove any fence, wall or other inclosure or any part thereof, built or standing upon the premises of such landlord, or shall willfully and unlawfully cut down or destroy any timber, fruit, shade or ornamental tree belonging to said landlord, he shall be guilty of a Class 1 misdemeanor.

History.
1883, c. 224; Code, s. 1761; Rev., s. 3686; C.S., s. 2351; 1993, c. 539, s. 402; 1994, Ex. Sess., c. 24, s. 14(c)

§ 42-13. Wrongful surrender to other than landlord misdemeanor

Any tenant or lessee of lands who shall willfully, wrongfully and with intent to defraud the landlord or lessor, give up the possession of the rented or leased premises to any person other than his landlord or lessor, shall be guilty of a Class 1 misdemeanor.

History.
1883, c. 138; Code, s. 1760; Rev., s. 3682; C.S., s. 2353; 1993, c. 539, s. 403; 1994, Ex. Sess., c. 24, s. 14(c)

ARTICLE 2
AGRICULTURAL TENANCIES

§ 42-22. Unlawful seizure by landlord or removal by tenant misdemeanor

If any landlord shall unlawfully, willfully, knowingly and without process of law, and unjustly seize the crop of his tenant when there is nothing due him, he shall be guilty of a Class 1 misdemeanor. If any lessee or cropper, or the assigns of either, or any other person, shall remove a crop, or any part thereof, from land without the consent of the lessor or his assigns, and without giving him or his agent five days' notice of such intended removal, and before satisfying all the liens held by the lessor or his assigns, on said crop, he shall be guilty of a Class 1 misdemeanor.

History.
1876-7, c. 283, s. 6; 1883, c. 83; Code, s. 1759; Rev., ss. 3664, 3665; C.S., s. 2362; 1993, c. 539, s. 404; 1994, Ex. Sess., c. 24, s. 14(c)

CHAPTER 49
CHILDREN BORN OUT OF WEDLOCK

ARTICLE 1
SUPPORT OF CHILDREN BORN OUT OF WEDLOCK

§ 49-1. Title

This Article shall be referred to as "An act concerning the support of children of parents not married to each other."

History.
1933, c. 228, s. 11

§ 49-2. Nonsupport of child born out of wedlock by parents made misdemeanor

Any parent who willfully neglects or who refuses to provide adequate support and maintain his or her child born out of wedlock shall be guilty of a Class 2 misdemeanor. A child within the meaning of this Article shall be any person less than 18 years of age and any person whom either parent might be required under the laws of North Carolina to support and maintain if the child were the legitimate child of the parent.

History.
1933, c. 228, s. 1; 1937, c. 432, s. 1; 1939, c. 217, ss. 1, 2; 1951, c. 154, s. 1; 1977, c. 3, s. 1; 1993, c. 539, s. 414; 1994, Ex. Sess., c. 24, s. 14(c); 2013-198, s. 17

§ 49-3. Place of birth of child no consideration

The provisions of this Article shall apply whether such child shall have been begotten or shall have been born within or without the State of North Carolina: Provided, that the child to be supported is a bona fide resident of this State at the time of the institution of any proceedings under this Article.

History.
1933, c. 228, s. 2

§ 49-4. When prosecution may be commenced

The prosecution of the reputed father of a child born out of wedlock may be instituted under this Chapter within any of the following periods, and not thereafter:

(1) Three years next after the birth of the child; or

(2) Where the paternity of the child has been judicially determined within three years next after its birth, at any time before the child attains the age of 18 years; or

(3) Where the reputed father has acknowledged paternity of the child by payments for the support thereof within three years next after the birth of the child, three years from the date of the last payment whether the last payment was made within three years of the birth of the child or thereafter: Provided, the action is instituted before the child attains the age of 18 years.

The prosecution of the mother of a child born out of wedlock may be instituted under this Chapter at any time before the child attains the age of 18 years.

History.
1933, c. 228, s. 3; 1939, c. 217, s. 3; 1945, c. 1053; 1951, c. 154, s. 2; 2013-198, s. 18

§ 49-5. Prosecution; death of mother no bar; determination of fatherhood

Proceedings under this Article may be brought by the mother or her personal representative or, if the child is likely to become a public charge, the director of social services or such person as by law performs the duties of such official in said county where the mother resides or the child is found. Proceedings under this Article may be brought in the county where the mother resides or is found, or in the county where the putative father resides or is found, or in the county where the child is found. The fact that the child was born outside of the State of North Carolina shall not be a bar to proceedings against the putative father in any county where he resides or is found, or in the county where the mother resides or the child is found. The death of the mother shall in no wise affect any proceedings under this Article. Preliminary proceedings under this Article to determine the paternity of the child may be instituted prior to the birth of the child but when the judge or court trying the issue of paternity deems it proper, he may continue the case until the woman is delivered of the child. When a continuance is granted, the courts shall recognize the person accused of being the father of the child with surety for his appearance, either at the next session of the court or at a time to be fixed by the judge or court granting a continuance, which shall be after the delivery of the child.

History.
1933, c. 228, s. 4; 1961, c. 186; 1969, c. 982; 1971, c. 1185, s. 18; 1981, c. 599, s. 13

Chapter 49

§ 49-6. Mother not excused on ground of self-incrimination; not subject to penalty

No mother of a child born out of wedlock shall be excused, on the ground that it may tend to incriminate her or subject her to a penalty or a forfeiture, from attending and testifying, in obedience to a subpoena of any court, in any suit or proceeding based upon or growing out of the provisions of this Article, but no such mother shall be prosecuted or subjected to any penalty or forfeiture for or on account of any transaction, matter, or thing as to which, in obedience to a subpoena and under oath, she may so testify.

History.

1933, c. 228, s. 5; 1939, c. 217, s. 5; 2013-198, s. 19

§ 49-7. Issues and orders

The court before which the matter may be brought shall determine whether or not the defendant is a parent of the child on whose behalf the proceeding is instituted. After this matter has been determined in the affirmative, the court shall proceed to determine the issue as to whether or not the defendant has neglected or refused to provide adequate support and maintain the child who is the subject of the proceeding. After this matter has been determined in the affirmative, the court shall fix by order, subject to modification or increase from time to time, a specific sum of money necessary for the support and maintenance of the child, subject to the limitations of G.S. 50-13.10. The amount of child support shall be determined as provided in G.S. 50-13.4(c). The order fixing the sum shall require the defendant to pay it either as a lump sum or in periodic payments as the circumstances of the case may appear to the court. The social security number, if known, of the minor child's parents shall be placed in the record of the proceeding. Compliance by the defendant with any or all of the further provisions of this Article or the order or orders of the court requiring additional acts to be performed by the defendant shall not be construed to relieve the defendant of his or her responsibility to pay the sum fixed or any modification or increase thereof.

The court before whom the matter may be brought, on motion of the State or the defendant, shall order that the alleged-parent defendant, the known natural parent, and the child submit to any blood tests and comparisons which have been developed and adapted for purposes of establishing or disproving parentage and which are reasonably accessible to the alleged-parent defendant, the known natural parent, and the child. The results of those blood tests and comparisons, including the statistical likelihood of the alleged parent's parentage, if available, shall be admitted in evidence when offered by a duly qualified, licensed practicing physician, duly qualified immunologist, duly qualified geneticist or other duly qualified person. The evidentiary effect of those blood tests and comparisons and the manner in which the expenses therefor are to be taxed as costs shall be as prescribed in G.S. 8-50.1. In addition, if a jury tries the issue of parentage, they shall be instructed as set out in G.S. 8-50.1. From a finding on the issue of parentage against the alleged-parent defendant, the alleged-parent defendant has the same right of appeal as though he or she had been found guilty of the crime of willful failure to support a child born out of wedlock.

History.

1933, c. 228, s. 6; 1937, c. 432, s. 2; 1939, c. 217, ss. 1, 4; 1944, c. 40; 1947, c. 1014; 1971, c. 1185, s. 19; 1975, c. 449, s. 3; 1977, c. 3, s. 2; 1979, c. 576, s. 2; 1987, c. 739, s. 1; 1989, c. 529, s. 6; 1997-433, s. 4.1; 1998-17, s. 1; 2013-198, s. 20

§ 49-8. Power of court to modify orders, suspend sentence, etc

Upon the determination of the issues set out in G.S. 49-7 and for the purpose of enforcing the payment of the sum fixed, the court is hereby given discretion, having regard for the circumstances of the case and the financial ability and earning capacity of the defendant and his or her willingness to cooperate, to make an order or orders upon the defendant and to modify such order or orders from time to time as the circumstances of the case may in the judgment of the court require subject to the limitations of G.S. 50-13.10. The order or orders made in this regard may include any or all of the following alternatives:

(1) Repealed by Session Laws 1994, Extra Session, c. 14, s. 35.

(2) Suspend sentence and continue the case from term to term;

(3) Release the defendant from custody on probation conditioned upon the defendant's compliance with the terms of the probation and the payment of the sum fixed for the support and maintenance of the child;

(4) Order the defendant to pay to the mother of the said child the necessary expenses of birth of the child and suitable medical attention for her;

(5) Require the defendant to sign a recognizance with good and sufficient security, for compliance with any order which the court may make in proceedings under this Article.

History.

1933, c. 228, s. 7; 1939, c. 217, s. 6; 1987, c. 739, s. 2; 1994, Ex. Sess., c. 14, s. 35

§ 49-9. Bond for future appearance of defendant

At the preliminary hearing of any case arising under this Article it shall be the duty of the court, if it finds reasonable cause for holding the accused for a further hearing, to require a bond in the sum of not less than one hundred dollars ($ 100.00), conditioned upon the reappearance of the accused at the further hearing under this Article. This bond and all other bonds provided for in this Article shall be justified before, and approved by, the court or the clerk thereof.

History.
1933, c. 228, s. 8

CHAPTER 50B
DOMESTIC VIOLENCE

§ 50B-1. Domestic violence; definition

(a) Domestic violence means the commission of one or more of the following acts upon an aggrieved party or upon a minor child residing with or in the custody of the aggrieved party by a person with whom the aggrieved party has or has had a personal relationship, but does not include acts of self-defense:

    (1) Attempting to cause bodily injury, or intentionally causing bodily injury; or

    (2) Placing the aggrieved party or a member of the aggrieved party's family or household in fear of imminent serious bodily injury or continued harassment, as defined in G.S. 14-277.3A, that rises to such a level as to inflict substantial emotional distress; or

    (3) Committing any act defined in G.S. 14-27.21 through G.S. 14-27.33.

(b) For purposes of this section, the term "personal relationship" means a relationship wherein the parties involved:

    (1) Are current or former spouses;

    (2) Are persons of opposite sex who live together or have lived together;

    (3) Are related as parents and children, including others acting in loco parentis to a minor child, or as grandparents and grandchildren. For purposes of this subdivision, an aggrieved party may not obtain an order of protection against a child or grandchild under the age of 16;

    (4) Have a child in common;

    (5) Are current or former household members;

    (6) Are persons of the opposite sex who are in a dating relationship or have been in a dating relationship. For purposes of this subdivision, a dating relationship is one wherein the parties are romantically involved over time and on a continuous basis during the course of the relationship. A casual acquaintance or ordinary fraternization between persons in a business or social context is not a dating relationship.

(c) As used in this Chapter, the term "protective order" includes any order entered pursuant to this Chapter upon hearing by the court or consent of the parties.

History.
1979, c. 561, s. 1; 1985, c. 113, s. 1; 1987, c. 828; 1987 (Reg. Sess., 1988), c. 893, ss. 1, 3; 1995 (Reg. Sess., 1996), c. 591, s. 1; 1997-471, s. 1; 2001-518, s. 3; 2003-107, s. 1; 2009-58, s. 5; 2015-181, s. 36

§ 50B-2. Institution of civil action; motion for emergency relief; temporary orders; temporary custody

(a) Any person residing in this State may seek relief under this Chapter by filing a civil action or by filing a motion in any existing action filed under Chapter 50 of the General Statutes alleging acts of domestic violence against himself or herself or a minor child who resides with or is in the custody of such person. Any aggrieved party entitled to relief under this Chapter may file a civil action and proceed pro se, without the assistance of legal counsel. The district court division of the General Court of Justice shall have original jurisdiction over actions instituted under this Chapter. Any action for a domestic violence protective order requires that a summons be issued and served. The summons issued pursuant to this Chapter shall require the defendant to answer within 10 days of the date of service. Attachments to the summons shall include the complaint, notice of hearing, any temporary or ex parte order that has been issued, and other papers through the appropriate law enforcement agency where the defendant is to be served. In compliance with the federal Violence Against Women Act, no court costs or attorneys' fees shall be assessed for the filing, issuance, registration, or service of a protective order or petition for a protective order or witness subpoena, except as provided in G.S. 1A-1, Rule 11.

(b) **Emergency Relief. --** A party may move the court for emergency relief if he or she believes there is a danger of serious and immediate injury to himself or herself or a minor child. A hearing on a motion for emergency relief, where no ex parte order is entered, shall be held after five days' notice of the hearing to the other party or after five days from the date of service of process on the other party, whichever occurs first, provided, however, that no hearing shall be required if the service of process is not completed on the other party. If the party is proceeding pro se and does not request an ex parte hearing, the clerk shall set a date for hearing and issue a notice of hearing within the time periods provided in this subsection, and shall effect service of the summons, complaint, notice, and other papers through the appropriate law enforcement agency where the defendant is to be served.

(c) **Ex Parte Orders. --**

    (1) Prior to the hearing, if it clearly appears to the court from specific facts shown, that there is a danger of acts of domestic violence against the aggrieved party or a minor child, the court may enter orders as it deems necessary to protect the aggrieved party or minor children from those acts.

    (2) A temporary order for custody ex parte and prior to service of process and

notice shall not be entered unless the court finds that the child is exposed to a substantial risk of physical or emotional injury or sexual abuse.

(3) If the court finds that the child is exposed to a substantial risk of physical or emotional injury or sexual abuse, upon request of the aggrieved party, the court shall consider and may order the other party to (i) stay away from a minor child, or (ii) return a minor child to, or not remove a minor child from, the physical care of a parent or person in loco parentis, if the court finds that the order is in the best interest of the minor child and is necessary for the safety of the minor child.

(4) If the court determines that it is in the best interest of the minor child for the other party to have contact with the minor child or children, the court shall issue an order designed to protect the safety and well-being of the minor child and the aggrieved party. The order shall specify the terms of contact between the other party and the minor child and may include a specific schedule of time and location of exchange of the minor child, supervision by a third party or supervised visitation center, and any other conditions that will ensure both the well-being of the minor child and the aggrieved party.

(5) Upon the issuance of an ex parte order under this subsection, a hearing shall be held within 10 days from the date of issuance of the order or within seven days from the date of service of process on the other party, whichever occurs later. A continuance shall be limited to one extension of no more than 10 days unless all parties consent or good cause is shown. The hearing shall have priority on the court calendar.

(6) If an aggrieved party acting pro se requests ex parte relief, the clerk of superior court shall schedule an ex parte hearing with the district court division of the General Court of Justice within 72 hours of the filing for said relief, or by the end of the next day on which the district court is in session in the county in which the action was filed, whichever shall first occur. If the district court is not in session in said county, the aggrieved party may contact the clerk of superior court in any other county within the same judicial district who shall schedule an ex parte hearing with the district court division of the General Court of Justice by the end of the next day on which said court division is in session in that county.

(7) Upon the issuance of an ex parte order under this subsection, if the party is proceeding pro se, the Clerk shall set a date for hearing and issue a notice of hearing within the time periods provided in this subsection, and shall effect service of the summons, complaint, notice, order and other papers through the appropriate law enforcement agency where the defendant is to be served.

(c1) **Ex Parte Orders by Authorized Magistrate. --** The chief district court judge may authorize a magistrate or magistrates to hear any motions for emergency relief ex parte. Prior to the hearing, if the magistrate determines that at the time the party is seeking emergency relief ex parte the district court is not in session and a district court judge is not and will not be available to hear the motion for a period of four or more hours, the motion may be heard by the magistrate. If it clearly appears to the magistrate from specific facts shown that there is a danger of acts of domestic violence against the aggrieved party or a minor child, the magistrate may enter orders as it deems necessary to protect the aggrieved party or minor children from those acts, except that a temporary order for custody ex parte and prior to service of process and notice shall not be entered unless the magistrate finds that the child is exposed to a substantial risk of physical or emotional injury or sexual abuse. If the magistrate finds that the child is exposed to a substantial risk of physical or emotional injury or sexual abuse, upon request of the aggrieved party, the magistrate shall consider and may order the other party to stay away from a minor child, or to return a minor child to, or not remove a minor child from, the physical care of a parent or person in loco parentis, if the magistrate finds that the order is in the best interest of the minor child and is necessary for the safety of the minor child. If the magistrate determines that it is in the best interest of the minor child for the other party to have contact with the minor child or children, the magistrate shall issue an order designed to protect the safety and well-being of the minor child and the aggrieved party. The order shall specify the terms of contact between the other party and the minor child and may include a specific schedule of time and location of exchange of the minor child, supervision by a third party or supervised visitation center, and any other conditions that will ensure both the well-being of the minor child and the aggrieved party. An ex parte order entered under this subsection shall expire and the magistrate shall schedule an ex parte hearing before a district court judge by the end of the next day on which the district court is in session in the county in which the action was filed. Ex parte orders entered by the district court judge pursuant to this subsection shall be entered and scheduled in accordance with subsection (c) of this section.

(c2) The authority granted to authorized magistrates to award temporary child custody pursuant to subsection (c1) of this section and pursuant to G.S. 50B-3(a)(4) is granted subject to custody rules to be established by the supervising chief district judge of each judicial district.

(d) **Pro Se Forms.** -- The clerk of superior court of each county shall provide to pro se complainants all forms that are necessary or appropriate to enable them to proceed pro se pursuant to this section. The clerk shall, whenever feasible, provide a private area for complainants to fill out forms and make inquiries. The clerk shall provide a supply of pro se forms to authorized magistrates who shall make the forms available to complainants seeking relief under subsection (c1) of this section.

(e) All documents filed, issued, registered, or served in an action under this Chapter relating to an ex parte, emergency, or permanent domestic violence protective order may be filed electronically.

History.

1979, c. 561, s. 1; 1985, c. 113, ss. 2, 3; 1987 (Reg. Sess., 1988), c. 893, s. 2; 1989, c. 461, s. 1; 1994, Ex. Sess., c. 4, s. 1; 1997-471, s. 2; 2001-518, s. 4; 2002-126, s. 29A.6(a); 2004-186, ss. 17.2, 19.1; 2009-342, s. 2; 2012-20, s. 1; 2013-390, s. 1; 2015-62, s. 3(b); 2021-47, s. 10(i)

§ 50B-3. Relief

(a) If the court, including magistrates as authorized under G.S. 50B-2(c1), finds that an act of domestic violence has occurred, the court shall grant a protective order restraining the defendant from further acts of domestic violence. A protective order may include any of the following types of relief:

(1) Direct a party to refrain from such acts.

(2) Grant to a party possession of the residence or household of the parties and exclude the other party from the residence or household.

(3) Require a party to provide a spouse and his or her children suitable alternate housing.

(4) Award temporary custody of minor children and establish temporary visitation rights pursuant to G.S. 50B-2 if the order is granted ex parte, and pursuant to subsection (a1) of this section if the order is granted after notice or service of process.

(5) Order the eviction of a party from the residence or household and assistance to the victim in returning to it.

(6) Order either party to make payments for the support of a minor child as required by law.

(7) Order either party to make payments for the support of a spouse as required by law.

(8) Provide for possession of personal property of the parties, including the care, custody, and control of any animal owned, possessed, kept, or held as a pet by either party or minor child residing in the household.

(9) Order a party to refrain from doing any or all of the following:

　a. Threatening, abusing, or following the other party.

　b. Harassing the other party, including by telephone, visiting the home or workplace, or other means.

　b1. Cruelly treating or abusing an animal owned, possessed, kept, or held as a pet by either party or minor child residing in the household.

　c. Otherwise interfering with the other party.

(10) Award attorney's fees to either party.

(11) Prohibit a party from purchasing a firearm for a time fixed in the order.

(12) Order any party the court finds is responsible for acts of domestic violence to attend and complete an abuser treatment program if the program is approved by the Domestic Violence Commission.

(13) Include any additional prohibitions or requirements the court deems necessary to protect any party or any minor child.

(a1) Upon the request of either party at a hearing after notice or service of process, the court shall consider and may award temporary custody of minor children and establish temporary visitation rights as follows:

(1) In awarding custody or visitation rights, the court shall base its decision on the best interest of the minor child with particular consideration given to the safety of the minor child.

(2) For purposes of determining custody and visitation issues, the court shall consider:

　a. Whether the minor child was exposed to a substantial risk of physical or emotional injury or sexual abuse.

　b. Whether the minor child was present during acts of domestic violence.

　c. Whether a weapon was used or threatened to be used during any act of domestic violence.

　d. Whether a party caused or attempted to cause serious bodily injury to the aggrieved party or the minor child.

　e. Whether a party placed the aggrieved party or the minor child in reasonable fear of imminent serious bodily injury.

f. Whether a party caused an aggrieved party to engage involuntarily in sexual relations by force, threat, or duress.

g. Whether there is a pattern of abuse against an aggrieved party or the minor child.

h. Whether a party has abused or endangered the minor child during visitation.

i. Whether a party has used visitation as an opportunity to abuse or harass the aggrieved party.

j. Whether a party has improperly concealed or detained the minor child.

k. Whether a party has otherwise acted in a manner that is not in the best interest of the minor child.

(3) If the court awards custody, the court shall also consider whether visitation is in the best interest of the minor child. If ordering visitation, the court shall provide for the safety and well-being of the minor child and the safety of the aggrieved party. The court may consider any of the following:

a. Ordering an exchange of the minor child to occur in a protected setting or in the presence of an appropriate third party.

b. Ordering visitation supervised by an appropriate third party, or at a supervised visitation center or other approved agency.

c. Ordering the noncustodial parent to attend and complete, to the satisfaction of the court, an abuser treatment program as a condition of visitation.

d. Ordering either or both parents to abstain from possession or consumption of alcohol or controlled substances during the visitation or for 24 hours preceding an exchange of the minor child.

e. Ordering the noncustodial parent to pay the costs of supervised visitation.

f. Prohibiting overnight visitation.

g. Requiring a bond from the noncustodial parent for the return and safety of the minor child.

h. Ordering an investigation or appointment of a guardian ad litem or attorney for the minor child.

i. Imposing any other condition that is deemed necessary to provide for the safety and well-being of the minor child and the safety of the aggrieved party.

If the court grants visitation, the order shall specify dates and times for the visitation to take place or other specific parameters or conditions that are appropriate. A person, supervised visitation center, or other agency may be approved to supervise visitation after appearing in court or filing an affidavit accepting that responsibility and acknowledging accountability to the court.

(4) A temporary custody order entered pursuant to this Chapter shall be without prejudice and shall be for a fixed period of time not to exceed one year. Nothing in this section shall be construed to affect the right of the parties to a de novo hearing under Chapter 50 of the General Statutes.

(a2) If the court orders that the defendant attend an abuser treatment program pursuant to G.S. 50B-3(a)(12), the defendant shall begin regular attendance of the program within 60 days of the entry of the order. When ordering a defendant to attend an abuser treatment program, the court shall also specify a date and time for a review hearing with the court to assess whether the defendant has complied with that part of the order. The review hearing shall be held as soon as practicable after 60 days from the entry of the original order. The date of the review shall be set at the same time as the entry of the original order, and the clerk shall issue a Notice of Hearing for the compliance review to be given to the defendant and filed with the court on the same day as the entry of the order. If a defendant is not present in court at the time the order to attend an abuser treatment program is entered and the Notice of Hearing for review is filed, the clerk shall serve a copy of the Notice of Hearing together with the service of the order. The plaintiff may, but is not required to, attend the 60-day review hearing.

(a3) At any time prior to the 60-day review hearing set forth in subsection (a2) of this section, a defendant who is ordered to attend an abuser treatment program may present to the clerk a written statement from an abuser treatment program showing that the defendant has enrolled in and begun regular attendance in an abuser treatment program. Upon receipt of the written statement, the clerk shall remove the 60-day review hearing from the court docket, and the defendant shall not be required to appear for the 60-day review hearing. The clerk shall also notify the plaintiff that the defendant has complied with the order and that no 60-day review hearing will occur.

(b) Protective orders entered pursuant to this Chapter shall be for a fixed period of time not to exceed one year. The court may renew a protective order for a fixed period of time not to exceed two years, including an order that previously has been renewed, upon a motion by the aggrieved party filed before the expiration of the current order; provided, however, that a temporary award of custody entered as part of a protective order may not be renewed to extend a temporary award of custody beyond the maximum one-year period. The court may renew a protective order for good cause. The commission of an act as defined in G.S. 50B-1(a) by the defendant after entry of the current order is not required for an order to be renewed. Protective orders entered, including consent orders, shall not be mutual in nature except where both parties file a claim and the court makes detailed findings of fact indicating that both parties acted as aggressors, that neither party acted primarily in self-defense, and that the right of each party to due process is preserved. Protective orders entered pursuant to this Chapter expire at 11:59 P.M. on the indicated expiration date, unless specifically stated otherwise in the order.

(b1) A consent protective order may be entered pursuant to this Chapter without findings of fact and conclusions of law if the parties agree in writing that no findings of fact and conclusions of law will be included in the consent protective order. The consent protective order shall be valid and enforceable and shall have the same force and effect as a protective order entered with findings of fact and conclusions of law.

(b2) Upon the written request of either party at a hearing after notice or service of process, the court may modify any protective order entered pursuant to this Chapter after a finding of good cause.

(c) A copy of any order entered and filed under this Article shall be issued to each party. Law enforcement agencies shall accept receipt of copies of the order issued by the clerk of court by electronic or facsimile transmission for service on defendants. In addition, a copy of the order shall be issued promptly to and retained by the police department of the city of the victim's residence. If the victim does not reside in a city or resides in a city with no police department, copies shall be issued promptly to and retained by the sheriff, and the county police department, if any, of the county in which the victim resides. If the defendant is ordered to stay away from the child's school, a copy of the order shall be delivered promptly by the sheriff to the principal or, in the principal's absence, the assistant principal or the principal's designee of each school named in the order.

(c1) When a protective order issued under this Chapter is filed with the Clerk of Superior Court, the clerk shall provide to the applicant an informational sheet developed by the Administrative Office of the Courts that includes:

(1) Domestic violence agencies and services.

(2) Sexual assault agencies and services.

(3) Victims' compensation services.

(4) Legal aid services.

(5) Address confidentiality services.

(6) An explanation of the plaintiff's right to apply for a permit under G.S. 14-415.15.

(d) The sheriff of the county where a domestic violence order is entered shall provide for prompt entry of the order into the National Crime Information Center registry and shall provide for access of such orders to magistrates on a 24-hour-a-day basis. Modifications, terminations, renewals, and dismissals of the order shall also be promptly entered.

History.

1979, c. 561, s. 1; 1985, c. 463; 1994, Ex. Sess., c. 4, s. 2; 1995, c. 527, s. 1; 1995 (Reg. Sess., 1996), c. 591, s. 2; c. 742, s. 42.1.; 1999-23, s. 1; 2000-125, s. 9; 2002-105, s. 2; 2002-126, s. 29A.6(b); 2003-107, s. 2; 2004-186, ss. 17.3 -17.5; 2005-343, s. 2; 2005-423, s. 1; 2007-116, s. 3; 2009-425, s. 1; 2013-237, s. 1; 2015-176, s. 1; 2017-92, s. 2; 2019-168, ss. 1, 2(b)

§ 50B-3.1. Surrender and disposal of firearms; violations; exemptions

(a) **Required Surrender of Firearms.** -- Upon issuance of an emergency or ex parte order pursuant to this Chapter, the court shall order the defendant to surrender to the sheriff all firearms, machine guns, ammunition, permits to purchase firearms, and permits to carry concealed firearms that are in the care, custody, possession, ownership, or control of the defendant if the court finds any of the following factors:

(1) The use or threatened use of a deadly weapon by the defendant or a pattern of prior conduct involving the use or threatened use of violence with a firearm against persons.

(2) Threats to seriously injure or kill the aggrieved party or minor child by the defendant.

(3) Threats to commit suicide by the defendant.

(4) Serious injuries inflicted upon the aggrieved party or minor child by the defendant.

(b) **Ex Parte or Emergency Hearing.** -- The court shall inquire of the plaintiff, at the ex parte or emergency hearing, the presence of, ownership of, or otherwise access to firearms by the defendant, as well as ammunition, permits to purchase firearms, and permits to carry concealed firearms, and include, whenever possible, identifying information regarding the description, number, and location of firearms, ammunition, and permits in the order.

(c) **Ten-Day Hearing.** -- The court, at the 10-day hearing, shall inquire of the defendant the presence of, ownership of, or otherwise access to firearms by the defendant, as well as ammunition, permits to purchase firearms, and permits to carry concealed firearms, and include, whenever possible, identifying information regarding the description, number, and location of firearms, ammunition, and permits in the order.

(d) **Surrender.** -- Upon service of the order, the defendant shall immediately surrender to the sheriff possession of all firearms, machine guns, ammunition, permits to purchase firearms, and permits to carry concealed firearms that are in the care, custody, possession, ownership, or control of the defendant. In the event that weapons cannot be surrendered at the time the order is served, the defendant shall surrender the firearms, ammunitions, and permits to the sheriff within 24 hours of service at a time and place specified by the sheriff. The sheriff shall store the firearms or contract with a licensed firearms dealer to provide storage.

(1) If the court orders the defendant to surrender firearms, ammunition, and permits, the court shall inform the plaintiff and the defendant of the terms of the protective order and include these terms on the face of the order, including that the defendant is prohibited from possessing, purchasing, or receiving or attempting to possess, purchase, or receive a firearm for so long as the protective order or any successive protective order is in effect. The terms of the order shall include instructions as to how the defendant may request retrieval of any firearms, ammunition, and permits surrendered to the sheriff when the protective order is no longer in effect. The terms shall also include notice of the penalty for violation of G.S. 14-269.8.

(2) The sheriff may charge the defendant a reasonable fee for the storage of any firearms and ammunition taken pursuant to a protective order. The fees are payable to the sheriff. The sheriff shall transmit the proceeds of these fees to the county finance officer. The fees shall be used by the sheriff to pay the costs of administering this section and for other law enforcement purposes. The county shall expend the restricted funds for these purposes only. The sheriff shall not release firearms, ammunition, or permits without a court order granting the release. The defendant must remit all fees owed prior to the authorized return of any firearms, ammunition, or permits. The sheriff shall not incur any civil or criminal liability for alleged damage or deterioration due to storage or transportation of any firearms or ammunition held pursuant to this section.

(e) **Retrieval.** -- If the court does not enter a protective order when the ex parte or emergency order expires, the defendant may retrieve any weapons surrendered to the sheriff unless the court finds that the defendant is precluded from owning or possessing a firearm pursuant to State or federal law or final disposition of any pending criminal charges committed against the person that is the subject of the current protective order.

(f) **Motion for Return.** -- The defendant may request the return of any firearms, ammunition, or permits surrendered by filing a motion with the court at the expiration of the current order or final disposition of any pending criminal charges committed against the person that is the subject of the current protective order and not later than 90 days after the expiration of the current order or final disposition of any pending criminal charges committed against the person that is the subject of the current protective order. Upon receipt of the motion, the court shall schedule a hearing and provide written notice to the plaintiff who shall have the right to appear and be heard and to the sheriff who has control of the firearms, ammunition, or permits. The court shall determine whether the defendant is subject to any State or federal law or court order that precludes the defendant from owning or possessing a firearm. The inquiry shall include:

(1) Whether the protective order has been renewed.

(2) Whether the defendant is subject to any other protective orders.

(3) Whether the defendant is disqualified from owning or possessing a firearm pursuant to 18 U.S.C. § 922 or any State law.

(4) Whether the defendant has any pending criminal charges, in either State or federal court, committed against the person that is the subject of the current protective order.

The court shall deny the return of firearms, ammunition, or permits if the court finds that the defendant is precluded from owning or possessing a firearm pursuant to State or federal law or if the defendant has any pending criminal charges, in either State or federal court, committed against the person that is the subject of the current protective order until the final disposition of those charges.

(g) **Motion for Return by Third-Party Owner.** -- A third-party owner of firearms, ammunition, or permits who is otherwise eligible to possess such items may file a motion requesting the return to said third party of any such items in the possession of the sheriff seized as a result of the entry of a domestic violence protective order. The motion must be filed not later than 30 days after the seizure of the items by the sheriff. Upon receipt of the third party's motion, the court shall schedule a hearing and provide written notice to all parties and the sheriff. The court shall order return of the items to the third party unless the court determines that the third party is disqualified from owning or possessing said items pursuant to State or federal law. If the court denies the return of said items to the third party, the items shall be disposed of by the sheriff as provided in subsection (h) of this section.

(h) **Disposal of Firearms.** -- If the defendant does not file a motion requesting the return of any firearms, ammunition, or permits surrendered within the time period prescribed by this section, if the court determines that the defendant is precluded from regaining possession of any firearms, ammunition, or permits surrendered, or if the defendant or third-party owner fails to remit all fees owed for the storage of the firearms or ammunition within 30 days of the entry of the order granting the return of the firearms, ammunition, or permits, the sheriff who has control of the firearms, ammunition, or permits shall give notice to the defendant, and the sheriff shall apply to the court for an order of disposition of the firearms, ammunition, or permits. The judge, after a hearing, may order the disposition of the firearms, ammunition, or permits in one or more of the ways authorized by law, including subdivision (4), (4b), (5), or (6) of G.S. 14-269.1. If a sale by the sheriff does occur, any proceeds from the sale after deducting any costs associated with the sale, and in accordance with all applicable State and federal law, shall be provided to the defendant, if requested by the defendant by motion made before the hearing or at the hearing and if ordered by the judge.

(i) It is unlawful for any person subject to a protective order prohibiting the possession or purchase of firearms to:

    (1) Fail to surrender all firearms, ammunition, permits to purchase firearms, and permits to carry concealed firearms to the sheriff as ordered by the court;

    (2) Fail to disclose all information pertaining to the possession of firearms, ammunition, and permits to purchase and permits to carry concealed firearms as requested by the court; or

    (3) Provide false information to the court pertaining to any of these items.

(j) **Violations.** -- In accordance with G.S. 14-269.8, it is unlawful for any person to possess, purchase, or receive or attempt to possess, purchase, or receive a firearm, as defined in G.S. 14-409.39(2), machine gun, ammunition, or permits to purchase or carry concealed firearms if ordered by the court for so long as that protective order or any successive protective order entered against that person pursuant to this Chapter is in effect. Any defendant violating the provisions of this section shall be guilty of a Class H felony.

(k) **Official Use Exemption.** -- This section shall not prohibit law enforcement officers and members of any branch of the Armed Forces of the United States, not otherwise prohibited under federal law, from possessing or using firearms for official use only.

(l) Nothing in this section is intended to limit the discretion of the court in granting additional relief as provided in other sections of this Chapter.

History.
2003-410, s. 1; 2004-203, s. 34(a); 2005-287, s. 4; 2005-423, ss. 2, 3; 2011-183, s. 40; 2011-268, ss. 23, 24

§ 50B-4. Enforcement of orders

(a) A party may file a motion for contempt for violation of any order entered pursuant to this Chapter. This party may file and proceed with that motion pro se, using forms provided by the clerk of superior court or a magistrate authorized under G.S. 50B-2(c1). Upon the filing pro se of a motion for contempt under this subsection, the clerk, or the authorized magistrate, if the facts show clearly that there is danger of acts of domestic violence against the aggrieved party or a minor child and the motion is made at a time when the clerk is not available, shall schedule and issue notice of a show cause hearing with the district court division of the General Court of Justice at the earliest possible date pursuant to G.S. 5A-23. The Clerk, or the magistrate in the case of notice issued by the magistrate pursuant to this subsection, shall effect service of the motion, notice, and other papers through the appropriate law enforcement agency where the defendant is to be served.

(b) Repealed by Session Laws 1999-23, s. 2, effective February 1, 2000.

(c) A valid protective order entered pursuant to this Chapter shall be enforced by all North Carolina law enforcement agencies without further order of the court.

(d) A valid protective order entered by the courts of another state or the courts of an Indian tribe shall be accorded full faith and credit by the courts of North Carolina whether or not the order has been registered and shall be enforced by the courts and the law enforcement agencies of North Carolina as if it were an order issued by a North Carolina court. In determining the validity of an out-of-state order for purposes of enforcement, a law enforcement officer may rely upon a copy of the protective order issued by another state or the courts of an Indian tribe that is provided to the officer and on the statement of a person protected by the order that the order remains in effect. Even though registration is not required, a copy of a protective order may be registered in North Carolina by filing with the clerk of superior court in any county a copy of the order and an affidavit by a person protected by the order that to the best of that person's knowledge the order is presently in effect as written. Notice of the registration shall not be given to the defendant. Upon registration of the order, the clerk shall promptly forward a copy to the sheriff of that county. Unless the issuing state has already entered the order, the sheriff shall provide for prompt entry of the order into the National Crime Information Center registry pursuant to G.S. 50B-3(d).

(e) Upon application or motion by a party to the court, the court shall determine whether an out-of-state order remains in full force and effect.

(f) The term "valid protective order," as used in subsections (c) and (d) of this section, shall include an emergency or ex parte order entered under this Chapter.

(g) Notwithstanding the provisions of G.S. 1-294, a valid protective order entered pursuant to this Chapter which has been appealed to the appellate division is enforceable in the trial court during the pendency of the appeal. Upon motion by the aggrieved party, the court of the appellate division in which the appeal is pending may stay an order of the trial court until the appeal is decided, if justice so requires.

History.

1979, c. 561, s. 1; 1985, c. 113, s. 4; 1987, c. 739, s. 6; 1989, c. 461, s. 2; 1994, Ex. Sess., c. 4, s. 3; 1995 (Reg. Sess., 1996), c. 591, s. 3; 1999-23, s. 2; 2002-126, s. 29A.6(c); 2003-107, s. 3; 2009-342, s. 4; 2017-92, s. 1

§ 50B-4.1. Violation of valid protective order

(a) Except as otherwise provided by law, a person who knowingly violates a valid protective order entered pursuant to this Chapter or who knowingly violates a valid protective order entered by the courts of another state or the courts of an Indian tribe shall be guilty of a Class A1 misdemeanor.

(b) A law enforcement officer shall arrest and take a person into custody, with or without a warrant or other process, if the officer has probable cause to believe that the person knowingly has violated a valid protective order excluding the person from the residence or household occupied by a victim of domestic violence or directing the person to refrain from doing any or all of the acts specified in G.S. 50B-3(a)(9).

(c) When a law enforcement officer makes an arrest under this section without a warrant, and the party arrested contests that the out-of-state order or the order issued by an Indian court remains in full force and effect, the party arrested shall be promptly provided with a copy of the information applicable to the party which appears on the National Crime Information Center registry by the sheriff of the county in which the arrest occurs.

(d) Unless covered under some other provision of law providing greater punishment, a person who commits a felony at a time when the person knows the behavior is prohibited by a valid protective order as provided in subsection (a) of this section shall be guilty of a felony one class higher than the principal felony described in the charging document. This subsection shall not apply to convictions of a Class A or B1 felony or to convictions of the offenses set forth in subsection (f) or subsection (g) of this section.

(e) An indictment or information that charges a person with committing felonious conduct as described in subsection (d) of this section shall also allege that the person knowingly violated a valid protective order as described in subsection (a) of this section in the course of the conduct constituting the underlying felony. In order for a person to be punished as described in subsection (d) of this section, a finding shall be made that the person knowingly violated the protective order in the course of conduct constituting the underlying felony.

(f) Unless covered under some other provision of law providing greater punishment, any person who knowingly violates a valid protective order as provided in subsection (a) of this section, after having been previously convicted of two offenses under this Chapter, shall be guilty of a Class H felony.

(g) Unless covered under some other provision of law providing greater punishment, any person who, while in possession of a deadly weapon on or about his or her person or within close proximity to his or her person, knowingly violates a valid protective order as provided in subsection (a) of this section by failing to stay away from a place, or a person, as so directed under the terms of the order, shall be guilty of a Class H felony.

(g1) Unless covered under some other provision of law providing greater punishment, any person who is subject to a valid protective order, as provided in subsection (a) of this section, who enters property operated as a safe house or haven for victims of domestic violence, where a person protected under the order is residing, shall be guilty of a Class H felony. A person violates this subsection regardless of whether the person protected under the order is present on the property.

(h) For the purposes of this section, the term "valid protective order" shall include an emergency or ex parte order entered under this Chapter.

History.

1997-471, s. 3; 1997-456, s. 27; 1999-23, s. 4; 2001-518, s. 5; 2007-190, s. 1; 2008-93, s. 1; 2009-342, s. 5; 2009-389, s. 2; 2010-5, s. 1; 2015-91, s. 3

§ 50B-4.2. False statement regarding protective order a misdemeanor

A person who knowingly makes a false statement to a law enforcement agency or officer that a protective order entered pursuant to this Chapter or by the courts of another state or Indian tribe remains in effect shall be guilty of a Class 2 misdemeanor.

History.
1999-23, s. 5

§ 50B-5. Emergency assistance

(a) A person who alleges that he or she or a minor child has been the victim of domestic violence may request the assistance of a local law enforcement agency. The local law enforcement agency shall respond to the request for assistance as soon as practicable. The local law enforcement officer responding to the request for assistance may take whatever steps are reasonably necessary to protect the complainant from harm and may advise the complainant of sources of shelter, medical care, counseling and other services. Upon request by the complainant and where feasible, the law enforcement officer may transport the complainant to appropriate facilities such as hospitals, magistrates' offices, or public or private facilities for shelter and accompany the complainant to his or her residence, within the jurisdiction in which the request for assistance was made, so that the complainant may remove food, clothing, medication and such other personal property as is reasonably necessary to enable the complainant and any minor children who are presently in the care of the complainant to remain elsewhere pending further proceedings.

(b) In providing the assistance authorized by subsection (a), no officer may be held criminally or civilly liable on account of reasonable measures taken under authority of subsection (a).

History.
1979, c. 561, s. 1; 1985, c. 113, s. 5; 1999-23, s. 6

§ 50B-5.5. Employment discrimination unlawful

(a) No employer shall discharge, demote, deny a promotion, or discipline an employee because the employee took reasonable time off from work to obtain or attempt to obtain relief under this Chapter. An employee who is absent from the workplace shall follow the employer's usual time-off policy or procedure, including advance notice to the employer, when required by the employer's usual procedures, unless an emergency prevents the employee from doing so. An employer may require documentation of any emergency that prevented the employee from complying in advance with the employer's usual time-off policy or procedure, or any other information available to the employee which supports the employee's reason for being absent from the workplace.

(b) The Commissioner of Labor shall enforce the provisions of this section according to Article 21 of Chapter 95 of the General Statutes, including the rules and regulations issued pursuant to the Article.

History.
2004-186, s. 18.1

§ 50B-6. Construction of Chapter

This Chapter shall not be construed as granting a status to any person for any purpose other than those expressly stated herein. This Chapter shall not be construed as relieving any person or institution of the duty to report to the department of social services, as required by G.S. 7B-301, if the person or institution has cause to suspect that a juvenile is abused or neglected.

History.
1979, c. 561, s. 1; 1985, c. 113, s. 6; 1998-202, s. 13(r)

§ 50B-7. Remedies not exclusive

(a) The remedies provided by this Chapter are not exclusive but are additional to remedies provided under Chapter 50 and elsewhere in the General Statutes.

(b) Any subsequent court order entered supersedes similar provisions in protective orders issued pursuant to this Chapter.

History.
1979, c. 561, s. 1; 2019-168, s. 2(a)

§ 50B-8. Effect upon prosecution for violation of § 14-184 or other offense against public morals

The granting of a protective order, prosecution for violation of this Chapter, or the granting of any other relief or the institution of any other enforcement proceedings under this Chapter shall not be construed to afford a defense to any person or persons charged with fornication and adultery under G.S. 14-184 or charged with any other offense against the public morals; and prosecution, conviction, or prosecution and conviction for violation of any provision of this Chapter shall not be a bar to prosecution for violation of G.S. 14-184 or of any other statute defining an offense or offenses against the public morals.

History.
1979, c. 561, s. 1; 2003-107, s. 4

§ 50B-9. Domestic Violence Center Fund

(a) The Domestic Violence Center Fund is established within the State Treasury. The fund shall be administered by the Department of Administration, North Carolina Council for Women, and shall be used to make grants to centers for victims of domestic violence and to The North Carolina Coalition Against Domestic Violence, Inc. This fund shall be administered in accordance with the provisions of the Executive Budget Act. The Department of Administration shall make quarterly grants to each eligible domestic violence center and to The North Carolina Coalition Against Domestic Violence, Inc. Effective July 1, 2017, and each fiscal year thereafter, the Department of Administration shall send the contracts to grantees within 10 business days of the date the Current Operations Appropriations Act, as defined in G.S. 143C-1-1, is certified for that fiscal year.

(b) Each grant recipient shall receive the same amount. To be eligible to receive funds under this section, a domestic violence center must meet the following requirements:

(1) It shall have been in operation on the preceding July 1 and shall continue to be in operation.

(2) It shall offer all of the following services: a hotline, transportation services, community education programs, daytime services, and call forwarding during the night and it shall fulfill other criteria established by the Department of Administration.

(3) It shall be a nonprofit corporation or a local governmental entity.

(c) The North Carolina Council for Women shall report on the quarterly distributions of the grants from the Domestic Violence Center Fund to the House and Senate chairs of the General Government Appropriations Committee within five business days of distribution. The report shall include the date, amount, and recipients of the fund disbursements. The report shall also include any eligible programs which are ineligible to receive funding during the relative reporting cycle as well as the reason of the ineligibility for that relative reporting cycle.

History.
1991, c. 693, s. 3; 1991 (Reg. Sess., 1992), c. 988, s. 1; 2017-57, s. 31.2(a)

Chapter 50B

CHAPTER 50D
PERMANENT CIVIL
NO-CONTACT ORDER
AGAINST SEX OFFENDER
ON BEHALF OF CRIME
VICTIM

§ 50D-1. Definitions

The following definitions apply in this Chapter:

(1) **Permanent civil no-contact order.** -- A permanent injunction that prohibits any contact by a respondent with the victim of a sex offense for which the respondent is convicted.

(2) **Respondent.** -- The person who committed the sex offense.

(3) **Sex offense.** -- Any criminal offense that requires registration under Article 27A of Chapter 14 of the General Statutes.

(4) **Victim.** -- The person against whom the sex offense was committed.

History.
2015-91, s. 1

§ 50D-2. Commencement of action; filing fees not permitted; assistance

(a) An action is commenced under this Chapter by filing a verified complaint for a permanent civil no-contact order in district court or by filing a motion in any existing civil action, by any of the following:

(1) A person who is the victim of a sex offense that occurs in this State.

(2) A competent adult who resides in this State on behalf of a minor child who is the victim of a sex offense that occurs in this State.

(3) A competent adult who resides in this State on behalf of an incompetent adult who is the victim of a sex offense that occurs in this State.

(b) No court costs or attorneys' fees shall be assessed for the filing or service of the complaint, or the service of any orders, except as provided in G.S. 1A-1, Rule 11.

(c) An action commenced under this Chapter may be filed in any county permitted under G.S. 1-82 or where the respondent was convicted of the sex offense.

(d) If the victim states that disclosure of the victim's address would place the victim or any member of the victim's family or household at risk for further unlawful conduct, the victim's address may be omitted from all documents filed with the court. If the victim has not disclosed an address under this subsection, the victim shall designate an alternative address to receive notice of any motions or pleadings from the opposing party.

History.
2015-91, s. 1

§ 50D-3. Process for action for permanent civil no-contact order

(a) Any action for a permanent civil no-contact order requires that a summons be issued and served. The summons issued pursuant to this Chapter shall require the respondent to answer within 10 days of the date of service. Attachments to the summons shall include the complaint for the permanent civil no-contact order.

(b) Service of the summons and attachments shall be by the sheriff by personal delivery in accordance with Rule 4 of the Rules of Civil Procedure, and if the respondent cannot with due diligence be served by the sheriff by personal delivery, the respondent may be served by publication by the complainant in accordance with Rule 4(j1) of the Rules of Civil Procedure.

(c) The court may enter a permanent civil no-contact order by default for the remedy sought in the complaint if the respondent has been served in accordance with this section and fails to answer as directed, or fails to appear on any subsequent appearance or hearing date agreed to by the parties or set by the court.

History.
2015-91, s. 1

§ 50D-4. Hearsay exception

In proceedings for an order or prosecutions for violation of an order under this Chapter, the prior sexual activity or the reputation of the victim is inadmissible except when it would be admissible in a criminal prosecution under G.S. 8C, Rule 412.

History.
2015-91, s. 1

§ 50D-5. Remedy

(a) If the court finds all of the following, the court may issue a permanent civil no-contact order:

(1) The respondent was convicted of committing a sex offense against the victim.

(2) The victim did not seek a permanent no-contact order under G.S. 15A-1340.50.

(3) Reasonable grounds exist for the victim to fear future contact with the respondent.

(4) Process was properly served on the respondent.

(5) The respondent answered the complaint and notice of hearing was given or the respondent failed to answer the complaint and is in default.

(b) The court may grant one or more of the following forms of relief in a permanent civil no-contact order under this Chapter:

(1) Order the respondent not to threaten, visit, assault, molest, or otherwise interfere with the victim.

(2) Order the respondent not to follow the victim, including at the victim's workplace.

(3) Order the respondent not to harass the victim.

(4) Order the respondent not to abuse or injure the victim.

(5) Order the respondent not to contact the victim by telephone, written communication, or electronic means.

(6) Order the respondent to refrain from entering or remaining present at the victim's residence, school, place of employment, or other specified places at times when the victim is present.

(7) Order other relief deemed necessary and appropriate by the court.

(c) No permanent civil no-contact order shall be issued under this Chapter without notice to the respondent.

History.
2015-91, s. 1

§ 50D-6. Duration

A permanent civil no-contact order issued pursuant to this Chapter remains effective for the lifetime of the respondent.

History.
2015-91, s. 1

§ 50D-7. Notice of orders

(a) The clerk of court shall deliver, on the same day that a permanent civil no-contact order is issued, a certified copy of that order to the sheriff.

(b) If the respondent was not present in court when the order was issued, the respondent may be served in the manner provided for service of process in civil proceedings in accordance with Rule 4(j) of the Rules of Civil Procedure. If the summons has not yet been served upon the respondent, it shall be served with the order.

(c) A copy of the order shall be issued promptly to and retained by the police department of the municipality of the victim's residence. If the victim's residence is not located in a municipality or is located in a municipality with no police department, copies shall be issued promptly to and retained by the sheriff and the county police department, if any, of the county in which the victim's residence is located.

(d) Any order modifying or revoking any permanent civil no-contact order shall be promptly delivered to the sheriff by the clerk of court and served in a manner provided for service of process in accordance with the provisions of this section.

History.
2015-91, s. 1

§ 50D-8. Enforcement

A victim may file a motion for contempt for violation of an order entered pursuant to this Chapter.

History.
2015-91, s. 1

§ 50D-9. Rescission

At any time after the issuance of the order, the victim may make a motion to rescind the permanent no-contact order. If the court determines that reasonable grounds for the victim to fear any future contact with the respondent no longer exist, the court may rescind the permanent no-contact order.

History.
2015-91, s. 1

§ 50D-10. Violation

(a) A person who knowingly violates an order entered pursuant to this Chapter is guilty of a Class A1 misdemeanor.

(b) A permanent civil no-contact order entered pursuant to this Chapter shall be enforced by all North Carolina law enforcement agencies without further order of the court. A law enforcement officer shall arrest and take a person into custody, with or without a warrant or other process, if the officer has probable cause to believe that the person knowingly has violated a permanent civil no-contact order.

History.
2015-91, s. 1

§ 50D-11. Remedies not exclusive

The remedies provided by this Chapter are not exclusive but are additional to other remedies provided under law.

History.
2015-91, s. 1

CHAPTER 51
MARRIAGE

ARTICLE 2
MARRIAGE LICENSES

§ 51-7. Penalty for solemnizing without license

Every minister, officer, or any other person authorized to solemnize a marriage under the laws of this State, who marries any couple without a license being first delivered to that person, as required by law, or after the expiration of such license, or who fails to return such license to the register of deeds within 10 days after any marriage celebrated by virtue thereof, with the certificate appended thereto duly filled up and signed, shall forfeit and pay two hundred dollars ($ 200.00) to any person who sues therefore, and shall also be guilty of a Class 1 misdemeanor.

History.
R.C., c. 68, ss. 6, 13; 1871-2, c. 193, s. 8; Code, s. 1817; Rev., ss. 2087, 3372; C.S., s. 2499; 1953, c. 638, s. 1; 1967, c. 957, s. 5; 1993, c. 539, s. 415; 1994, Ex. Sess., c. 24, s. 14(c); 2001-62, s. 7

§ 51-15. Obtaining license by false representation misdemeanor

If any person shall obtain, or aid and abet in obtaining, a marriage license by misrepresentation or false pretenses, that person shall be guilty of a Class 1 misdemeanor.

History.
1885, c. 346; Rev., s. 3371; C.S., s. 2501; 1967, c. 957, s. 4; 1993, c. 539, s. 417; 1994, Ex. Sess., c. 24, s. 14(c); 2001-62, s. 10

§ 51-17. Penalty for issuing license unlawfully

Every register of deeds who knowingly or without reasonable inquiry, personally or by deputy, issues a license for the marriage of any two persons to which there is any lawful impediment, or where either of the persons is under the age of 18 years, without the consent required by law, shall forfeit and pay two hundred dollars ($ 200.00) to any parent, guardian, or other person standing in loco parentis, who sues for the same: Provided, that requiring a party to a proposed marriage to present a certified copy of his or her birth certificate, or a certified copy of his or her birth record in the form of a birth registration card as provided in G.S. 130-102, in accordance with the provisions of G.S. 51-8, shall be considered a reasonable inquiry into the matter of the age of such party.

History.
R.C., c. 68, s. 13; 1871-2, c. 193, s. 7; Code, s. 1816; 1895, c. 387; 1901, c. 722; Rev., s. 2090; C.S., s. 2503; 1957, c. 506, s. 2

CHAPTER 52C
UNIFORM INTERSTATE FAMILY SUPPORT ACT

ARTICLE 1
GENERAL PROVISIONS

§ 52C-1-100. Short title

This Chapter may be cited as the Uniform Interstate Family Support Act.

History.
1995, c. 538, s. 7(c)

§ 52C-1-101. Definitions

As used in this Chapter:

(1) "Child" means an individual, whether over or under the age of majority, who is or is alleged to be owed a duty of support by the individual's parent or who is or is alleged to be the beneficiary of a support order directed to the parent.

(2) "Child support order" means a support order for a child, including a child who has attained the age of majority under the law of the issuing state or foreign country.

(2a) "Convention" means the Convention on the International Recovery of Child Support and Other Forms of Family Maintenance, concluded at The Hague on November 23, 2007.

(2b) "Department" means the North Carolina Department of Health and Human Services, Division of Social Services.

(3) "Duty of support" means an obligation imposed or imposable by law to provide support for a child, spouse, or former spouse, including an unsatisfied obligation to provide support.

(3a) "Foreign country" means a country, including a political subdivision thereof, other than the United States, that authorizes the issuance of support orders and:

a. Which has been declared under the law of the United States to be a foreign reciprocating country;

b. Which has established a reciprocal arrangement for child support with this State as provided in G.S. 52C-3-308;

c. Which has enacted a law or established procedures for the issuance and enforcement of support orders which are substantially similar to the procedures under this Chapter; or

d. In which the Convention is in force with respect to the United States.

(3b) "Foreign support order" means a support order of a foreign tribunal.

(3c) "Foreign tribunal" means a court, administrative agency, or quasi-judicial entity of a foreign country which is authorized to establish, enforce, or modify support orders or to determine parentage of a child. The term includes a competent authority under the Convention.

(4) "Home state" means the state or foreign country in which a child lived with a parent or a person acting as parent for at least six consecutive months immediately preceding the time of filing of a petition or comparable pleading for support and, if a child is less than six-months old, the state or foreign country in which the child lived from birth with any of them. A period of temporary absence of any of them is counted as part of the six-month or other period.

(5) "Income" includes earnings or other periodic entitlements to money from any source and any other property subject to withholding for support under the law of this State.

(6) "Income-withholding order" means an order or other legal process directed to an obligor's employer, other debtor, or payor as defined under Chapter 110 of the General Statutes, to withhold support from the income of the obligor.

(7) Repealed by Session Laws 2015-117, s. 1, effective June 24, 2015.

(8) "Initiating tribunal" means the tribunal of a state or foreign country from which a petition or comparable pleading is forwarded or in which a petition or comparable pleading is filed for forwarding to another state or foreign country.

(8a) "Issuing foreign country" means the foreign country in which a tribunal issues a support order or a judgment determining parentage of a child.

(9) "Issuing state" means the state in which a tribunal issues a support order or a judgment determining parentage of a child.

(10) "Issuing tribunal" means the tribunal of a state or foreign country that issues a support order or a judgment determining parentage of a child.

(11) "Law" includes decisional and statutory law and rules and regulations having the force of law.

(12) "Obligee" means:

a. An individual to whom a duty of support is or is alleged to be owed or in whose favor a support order or a judgment determining parentage of a child has been issued;

b. A foreign country, state, or political subdivision of a state to which the rights under a duty of support or support order have been assigned or which has independent claims based on financial assistance provided to an individual obligee in place of child support;

c. An individual seeking a judgment determining parentage of the individual's child; or

d. A person that is a creditor in a proceeding under Article 7 of this Chapter.

(13) "Obligor" means an individual who, or the estate of a decedent that:

a. Owes or is alleged to owe a duty of support;

b. Is alleged but has not been adjudicated to be a parent of a child;

c. Is liable under a support order; or

d. Is a debtor in a proceeding under Article 7 of this Chapter.

(13a) "Outside this State" means a location in another state or country other than the United States, whether or not the country is a foreign country.

(13b) "Person" means an individual, corporation, business trust, estate, trust, partnership, limited liability company, association, joint venture, public corporation, government or governmental subdivision, agency, or instrumentality, or any other legal or commercial entity.

(13c) "Record" means information that is inscribed on a tangible medium or that is stored in an electronic or other medium and is retrievable in perceivable form.

(14) "Register" means to file in a tribunal of this State a support order or judgment determining parentage of a child issued in another state or a foreign country.

(15) "Registering tribunal" means a tribunal in which a support order or judgment determining parentage of a child is registered.

(16) "Responding state" means a state in which a petition or comparable pleading for support or to determine parentage of a child is filed or to which a petition or comparable pleading is forwarded for filing from another state or a foreign country.

(17) "Responding tribunal" means the authorized tribunal in a responding state or a foreign country.

(18) "Spousal-support order" means a support order for a spouse or former spouse of the obligor.

(19) "State" means a state of the United States, the District of Columbia, Puerto Rico, the United States Virgin Islands, or any territory or insular possession under the jurisdiction of the United States. The term includes an Indian nation or tribe.

(20) "Support enforcement agency" means a public official, governmental entity, or private agency authorized to:

a. Seek enforcement of support orders or duties of support;

b. Seek establishment or modification of child support;

c. Request determination of parentage of a child;

d. Attempt to locate obligors or their assets; or

e. Request determination of the controlling child support order.

(21) "Support order" means a judgment, decree, order, decision, or directive, whether temporary, final, or subject to modification, issued in a state or a foreign country for the benefit of a child, a spouse, or a former spouse, which provides for monetary support, health care, arrearages, retroactive support, or reimbursement for financial assistance provided to an individual obligee in place of child support. The term may include related costs and fees, interest, income withholding, automatic adjustment, reasonable attorneys' fees, and other relief.

(22) "Tribunal" means a court, administrative agency, or quasi-judicial entity authorized to establish, enforce, or modify support orders or to determine parentage of a child.

History.
1995, c. 538, s. 7(c); 1997-433, s. 10; 1997-456, s. 27; 1998-17, s. 1; 2015-117, s. 1

§ 52C-1-102. State tribunal and support enforcement agency

(a) The General Court of Justice, District Court Division, is the tribunal of this State.

(b) The Department and the county child support agencies under G.S. 110-141 are the support enforcement agencies of this State.

History.
1995, c. 538, s. 7(c); 2015-117, s. 1

§ 52C-1-103. Remedies cumulative

(a) Remedies provided by this Chapter are cumulative and do not affect the availability of remedies under other law or the recognition of a foreign support order on the basis of comity.

(b) This Chapter does not:

(1) Provide the exclusive method of establishing or enforcing a support order under the law of this State; or

(2) Grant a tribunal of this State jurisdiction to render judgment or issue an order relating to child custody or visitation in a proceeding under this Chapter.

History.

1995, c. 538, s. 7(c); 2015-117, s. 1

§ 52C-1-104. Application of Chapter to resident of foreign country and foreign support proceeding

(a) A tribunal of this State shall apply Articles 1 through 6 and, as applicable, Article 7 of this Chapter, to a support proceeding involving:

(1) A foreign support order;

(2) A foreign tribunal; or

(3) An obligee, obligor, or child residing in a foreign country.

(b) A tribunal of this State that is requested to recognize and enforce a support order on the basis of comity may apply the procedural and substantive provisions of Articles 1 through 6 of this Chapter.

(c) Article 7 of this Chapter applies only to a support proceeding under the Convention. In such a proceeding, if a provision of Article 7 is inconsistent with Articles 1 through 6 of this Chapter, Article 7 controls.

History.

2015-117, s. 1

ARTICLE 2
JURISDICTION

§ 52C-2-201. Bases for jurisdiction over nonresident

(a) In a proceeding to establish or enforce a support order or to determine parentage of a child, a tribunal of this State may exercise personal jurisdiction over a nonresident individual or the individual's guardian or conservator if:

(1) The individual is personally served with a summons and complaint within this State;

(2) The individual submits to the jurisdiction of this State by consent in a record, by entering a general appearance, or by filing a responsive document having the effect of waiving any contest to personal jurisdiction;

(3) The individual resided with the child in this State;

(4) The individual resided in this State and provided prenatal expenses or support for the child;

(5) The child resides in this State as a result of the acts or directives of the individual;

(6) The individual engaged in sexual intercourse in this State and the child may have been conceived by that act of intercourse; or

(7) Repealed by Session Laws 2015-117, s. 1, effective June 24, 2015.

(8) There is any other basis consistent with the constitutions of this State and the United States for the exercise of personal jurisdiction.

(b) The bases of personal jurisdiction set forth in subsection (a) of this section or in any other law of this State may not be used to acquire personal jurisdiction for a tribunal of the State to modify a child support order of another state unless the requirements of G.S. 52C-6-611 are met, or, in the case of a foreign support order, unless the requirements of G.S. 52C-6-615 are met.

History.

1995, c. 538, s. 7(c); 2015-117, s. 1

§ 52C-2-202. Duration of personal jurisdiction

Personal jurisdiction acquired by a tribunal of this State in a proceeding under this Chapter or other law of this State relating to a support order continues as long as a tribunal of this State has continuing, exclusive jurisdiction to modify its order or continuing jurisdiction to enforce its order as provided by G.S. 52C-2-205, 52C-2-206, and 52C-2-211.

History.

1995, c. 538, s. 7(c); 2015-117, s. 1

§ 52C-2-203. Initiating and responding tribunal of state

Under this Chapter, a tribunal of this State may serve as an initiating tribunal to forward proceedings to a tribunal of another state and as a responding tribunal for proceedings initiated in another state or foreign country.

History.

1995, c. 538, s. 7(c); 1997-433, s. 10.1; 1998-17, s. 1; 2015-117, s. 1

§ 52C-2-204. Simultaneous proceedings

(a) A tribunal of this State may exercise jurisdiction to establish a support order if the petition or comparable pleading is filed after a petition or comparable pleading is filed in another state or foreign country only if:

(1) The petition or comparable pleading in this State is filed before the expiration of the time allowed in the other state or the foreign country for filing a responsive pleading challenging the exercise of jurisdiction by the other state or the foreign country;

Chapter 52C

(2) The contesting party timely challenges the exercise of jurisdiction in the other state or the foreign country; and

(3) If relevant, this State is the home state of the child.

(b) A tribunal of this State may not exercise jurisdiction to establish a support order if the petition or comparable pleading is filed before a petition or comparable pleading is filed in another state or a foreign country if:

(1) The petition or comparable pleading in the other state or foreign country is filed before the expiration of the time allowed in this State for filing a responsive pleading challenging the exercise of jurisdiction by this State;

(2) The contesting party timely challenges the exercise of jurisdiction in this State; and

(3) If relevant, the other state or foreign country is the home state of the child.

History.
1995, c. 538, s. 7(c); 2015-117, s. 1

§ 52C-2-205. Continuing, exclusive jurisdiction to modify child support order

(a) A tribunal of this State that has issued a child support order consistent with the law of this State has and shall exercise continuing, exclusive jurisdiction to modify its child support order if the order is the controlling order and:

(1) At the time of the filing of a request for modification, this State is the residence of the obligor, the individual obligee, or the child for whose benefit the support order is issued; or

(2) Even if this State is not the residence of the obligor, the individual obligee, or the child for whose benefit the support order is issued, the parties consent in a record or in open court that the tribunal of this State may continue to exercise jurisdiction to modify its order.

(b) A tribunal of this State that has issued a child support order consistent with the law of this State may not exercise continuing, exclusive jurisdiction to modify the order if:

(1) All of the parties who are individuals file consent in a record with the tribunal of this State that a tribunal of another state that has jurisdiction over at least one of the parties who is an individual or that is located in the state of residence of the child may modify that order and assume continuing, exclusive jurisdiction; or

(2) Its order is not the controlling order.

(c) Repealed by Session Laws 2015-117, s. 1, effective June 24, 2015.

(d) If a tribunal of another state has issued a child support order pursuant to the Uniform

Interstate Family Support Act or a law substantially similar to that Act that modifies a child support order of a tribunal of this State, tribunals of this State shall recognize the continuing, exclusive jurisdiction of the tribunal of the other state.

(d1) A tribunal of this State that lacks continuing, exclusive jurisdiction to modify a child support order may serve as an initiating tribunal to request a tribunal of another state to modify a support order issued in that state.

(e) A temporary support order issued ex parte or pending resolution of a jurisdictional conflict does not create continuing, exclusive jurisdiction in the issuing tribunal.

(f) Repealed by Session Laws 2015-117, s. 1, effective June 24, 2015.

History.
1995, c. 538, s. 7(c); 1997-433, s. 10.2; 1998-17, s. 1; 2015-117, s. 1

§ 52C-2-206. Continuing jurisdiction to enforce child support order

(a) A tribunal of this State that has issued a child support order consistent with the law of this State may serve as an initiating tribunal to request a tribunal of another state to enforce:

(1) The order if the order is the controlling order and has not been modified by a tribunal of another state that assumed jurisdiction pursuant to the Uniform Interstate Family Support Act; or

(2) A money judgment for arrears of support and interest on the order accrued before a determination that an order of a tribunal of another state is the controlling order.

(b) A tribunal of this State having continuing jurisdiction over a support order may act as a responding tribunal to enforce the order.

(c) Repealed by Session Laws 2015-117, s. 1, effective June 24, 2015.

History.
1995, c. 538, s. 7(c); 2015-117, s. 1

§ 52C-2-207. Determination of controlling child support order

(a) If a proceeding is brought under this Chapter and only one tribunal has issued a child support order, the order of that tribunal controls and must be recognized.

(b) If a proceeding is brought under this Chapter, and two or more child support orders have been issued by tribunals of this State, another state, or a foreign country with regard to the same obligor and same child, a tribunal of this State having personal jurisdiction over both the obligor and individual obligee shall apply the

Chapter 52C

following rules and by order shall determine which order controls and must be recognized:

(1) If only one of the tribunals would have continuing, exclusive jurisdiction under this Chapter, the order of that tribunal controls.

(2) If more than one of the tribunals would have continuing, exclusive jurisdiction under this Chapter:

a. An order issued by a tribunal in the current home state of the child controls; or

b. If an order has not been issued in the current home state of the child, the order most recently issued controls.

(3) If none of the tribunals would have continuing, exclusive jurisdiction under this Chapter, the tribunal of this State shall issue a child support order, which controls.

(c) If two or more child support orders have been issued for the same obligor and same child, upon request of a party who is an individual or that is a support enforcement agency, a tribunal of this State having personal jurisdiction over both the obligor and the obligee who is an individual shall determine which order controls under subsection (b) of this section. The request may be filed with a registration for enforcement or registration for modification pursuant to Article 6 of this Chapter or may be filed as a separate proceeding.

(c1) A request to determine which is the controlling order must be accompanied by a copy of every child support order in effect and the applicable record of payments. The requesting party shall give notice of the request to each party whose rights may be affected by the determination.

(d) The tribunal that issued the controlling order under subsection (a), (b), or (c) of this section has continuing jurisdiction to the extent provided in G.S. 52C-2-205 or G.S. 52C-2-206.

(e) A tribunal of this State that determines by order which is the controlling order under subdivision (b)(1) or (2) or subsection (c) of this section, or that issues a new controlling order under subdivision (b)(3) of this section, shall state in that order:

(1) The basis upon which the tribunal made its determination;

(2) The amount of the prospective support, if any; and

(3) The total amount of consolidated arrears and accrued interest, if any, under all of the orders after all payments made are credited as provided by G.S. 52C-2-209.

(f) Within 30 days after issuance of an order determining which is the controlling order, the party obtaining the order shall file a certified copy of the order in each tribunal that issued or registered an earlier order of child support. A party or support enforcement agency obtaining the order that fails to file a certified copy is subject to appropriate sanctions by a tribunal in which the issue of failure to file arises. The failure to file does not affect the validity or enforceability of the controlling order.

(g) An order that has been determined to be the controlling order, or a judgment for consolidated arrears of support and interest, if any, made pursuant to this section must be recognized in proceedings under this Chapter.

History.
1995, c. 538, s. 7(c); 1997-433, s. 10.3(b); 1998-17, s. 1; 2015-117, s. 1

§ 52C-2-208. Child support orders for two or more obligees

In responding to registrations or petitions for enforcement of two or more child support orders in effect at the same time with regard to the same obligor and different individual obligees, at least one of which was issued by a tribunal of another state or a foreign country, a tribunal of this State shall enforce those orders in the same manner as if the orders had been issued by a tribunal of this State.

History.
1995, c. 538, s. 7(c); 2015-117, s. 1

§ 52C-2-209. Credit for payments

A tribunal of this State shall credit amounts collected for a particular period pursuant to any child support order against the amounts owed for the same period under any other child support order for support of the same child issued by a tribunal of this State, another state, or a foreign country.

History.
1995, c. 538, s. 7(c); 2015-117, s. 1

§ 52C-2-210. Application of this Chapter to nonresident subject to personal jurisdiction

A tribunal of this State exercising personal jurisdiction over a nonresident in a proceeding under this Chapter, under other law of this State relating to a support order, or recognizing a foreign support order may receive evidence from outside this State pursuant to G.S. 52C-3-316 [G.S. 52C-3-315], communicate with a tribunal outside this State pursuant to G.S. 52C-3-317 [G.S. 52C-3-316], and obtain discovery through a tribunal outside this State pursuant to G.S. 52C-3-318 [G.S. 52C-3-317]. In all other respects, Articles 3 through 6 of this Chapter do not apply and the tribunal shall apply the procedural and substantive law of this State.

Chapter 52C

History.
2015-117, s. 1

§ 52C-2-211. Continuing, exclusive jurisdiction to modify spousal support order

(a) A tribunal of this State issuing a spousal support order consistent with the law of this State has continuing, exclusive jurisdiction to modify the spousal support order throughout the existence of the support obligation.

(b) A tribunal of this State may not modify a spousal support order issued by a tribunal of another state or a foreign country having continuing, exclusive jurisdiction over that order under the law of that state or foreign country.

(c) A tribunal of this State that has continuing, exclusive jurisdiction over a spousal support order may serve as:

(1) An initiating tribunal to request a tribunal of another state to enforce the spousal support order issued in this State; or

(2) A responding tribunal to enforce or modify its own spousal support order.

History.
2015-117, s. 1

ARTICLE 3
CIVIL PROVISIONS OF GENERAL APPLICATION

§ 52C-3-301. Proceedings under this Chapter

(a) Except as otherwise provided in this Chapter, this Article applies to all proceedings under this Chapter.

(b) Repealed by Session Laws 2015-117, s. 1, effective June 24, 2015.

(c) An individual petitioner or a support enforcement agency may initiate a proceeding authorized under this Chapter by filing a petition in an initiating tribunal for forwarding to a responding tribunal or by filing a petition or a comparable pleading directly in a tribunal of another state or a foreign country which has or can obtain personal jurisdiction over the respondent.

History.
1995, c. 538, s. 7(c); 2015-117, s. 1

§ 52C-3-302. Proceeding by minor parent

A minor parent, or a guardian or other legal representative of a minor parent, may maintain a proceeding on behalf of or for the benefit of the minor's child.

History.
1995, c. 538, s. 7(c); 2015-117, s. 1

§ 52C-3-303. Application of law of this State

Except as otherwise provided in this Chapter, a responding tribunal of this State shall:

(1) Apply the procedural and substantive law generally applicable to similar proceedings originating in this State and may exercise all powers and provide all remedies available in those proceedings; and

(2) Determine the duty of support and the amount payable in accordance with the law and support guidelines of this State.

History.
1995, c. 538, s. 7(c); 2015-117, s. 1

§ 52C-3-304. Duties of initiating tribunal

(a) Upon the filing of a petition authorized by this Chapter, an initiating tribunal of this State shall forward the petition and its accompanying documents:

(1) To the responding tribunal or appropriate support enforcement agency in the responding state; or

(2) If the identity of the responding tribunal is unknown, to the state information agency of the responding state with a request that they be forwarded to the appropriate tribunal and that receipt be acknowledged.

(b) If requested by the responding tribunal, a tribunal of this State shall issue a certificate or other document and make findings required by the law of the responding state. If the responding tribunal is in a foreign country, upon request, the tribunal of this State shall specify the amount of support sought, convert that amount into the equivalent amount in the foreign currency under applicable official or market exchange rate as publicly reported, and provide any other documents necessary to satisfy the requirements of the responding foreign tribunal.

History.
1995, c. 538, s. 7(c); 1997-433, s. 10.4; 1998-17, s. 1; 2015-117, s. 1

§ 52C-3-305. Duties and powers of responding tribunal

(a) When a responding tribunal of this State receives a petition or comparable pleading from an initiating tribunal or directly pursuant to G.S. 52C-3-301(c) it shall cause the petition or pleading to be filed and notify the petitioner where and when it was filed.

(b) A responding tribunal of this State, to the extent not prohibited by law, may do one or more of the following:

(1) Establish or enforce a support order, modify a child support order, determine the controlling child support order, or determine parentage of a child;

(2) Order an obligor to comply with a support order, specifying the amount and the manner of compliance;

(3) Order income withholding;

(4) Determine the amount of any arrears, and specify a method of payment;

(5) Enforce orders by civil or criminal contempt, or both;

(6) Set aside property for satisfaction of the support order;

(7) Place liens and order execution on the obligor's property;

(8) Order an obligor to keep the tribunal informed of the obligor's current residential address, electronic-mail address, telephone number, employer, address of employment, and telephone number at the place of employment;

(9) Issue an order for arrest for an obligor who has failed after proper notice to appear at a hearing ordered by the tribunal and enter the order for arrest in any local and State computer systems for criminal warrants;

(10) Order the obligor to seek appropriate employment by specified methods;

(11) Award reasonable attorneys' fees and other fees and costs; and

(12) Grant any other available remedy.

(c) A responding tribunal of this State shall include in a support order issued under this Chapter, or in the documents accompanying the order, the calculations on which the support order is based.

(d) A responding tribunal of this State may not condition the payment of a support order issued under this Chapter upon compliance by a party with provisions for visitation.

(e) If a responding tribunal of this State issues an order under this Chapter, the tribunal shall send a copy of the order to the petitioner and the respondent and to the initiating tribunal, if any.

(f) If requested to enforce a support order, arrears, or judgment or modify a support order stated in a foreign currency, a responding tribunal of this State shall convert the amount stated in the foreign currency to the equivalent amount in dollars under the applicable official or market exchange rate as publicly reported.

History.
1995, c. 538, s. 7(c); 1997-433, s. 10.5; 1998-17, s. 1; 2015-117, s. 1

§ 52C-3-306. Inappropriate tribunal

If a petition or comparable pleading is received by an inappropriate tribunal of this State, the tribunal shall forward the pleading and accompanying documents to an appropriate tribunal of this State or another state and notify the petitioner where and when the pleading was sent.

History.
1995, c. 538, s. 7(c); 1997-433, s. 10.6; 1998-17, s. 1; 2015-117, s. 1

§ 52C-3-307. Duties of support enforcement agency

(a) In a proceeding under this Chapter, a support enforcement agency of this State, upon request, shall provide the following:

(1) Services to a petitioner residing in a state.

(2) Services to a petitioner requesting services through a central authority of a foreign country as described in G.S. 52C-1-102(3a)a. or d [G.S. 52C-1-101(3a)a. or d.].

A support enforcement agency of this State may provide services to a petitioner who is an individual not residing in a state.

(b) A support enforcement agency of this State that is providing services to the petitioner shall:

(1) Take all steps necessary to enable an appropriate tribunal of this State, another state, or a foreign country to obtain jurisdiction over the respondent;

(2) Request an appropriate tribunal to set a date, time, and place for a hearing;

(3) Make a reasonable effort to obtain all relevant information, including information as to income and property of the parties;

(4) Within two days, exclusive of Saturdays, Sundays, and legal holidays, after receipt of notice in a record from an initiating, responding, or registering tribunal, send a copy of the notice to the petitioner;

(5) Within two days, exclusive of Saturdays, Sundays, and legal holidays, after receipt of communication in a record from the respondent or the respondent's attorney, send a copy of the communication to the petitioner; and

(6) Notify the petitioner if jurisdiction over the respondent cannot be obtained.

(b1) A support enforcement agency of this State that requests registration of a child support order in this State for enforcement or for modification shall make reasonable efforts to:

(1) Ensure that the order to be registered is the controlling order; or

(2) If two or more child support orders exist and the identity of the controlling order has not been determined, ensure that a request for such a determination is made in a tribunal having jurisdiction to do so.

(b2) A support enforcement agency of this State that requests registration and enforcement of a support order, arrears, or judgment stated in a foreign currency shall convert the amounts stated in the foreign currency into the equivalent amounts in dollars under the applicable official or market exchange rate as publicly reported.

(b3) A support enforcement agency of this State shall issue or request a tribunal of this State to issue a child support order and an income-withholding order that redirect payment of current support, arrears, and interest if requested to do so by a support enforcement agency of another state pursuant to G.S. 52C-3-318.

(c) This Chapter does not create or negate a relationship of attorney and client or other fiduciary relationship between a support enforcement agency or the attorney for the agency and the individual being assisted by the agency.

History.
1995, c. 538, s. 7(c); 1997-433, s. 10.7; 1998-17, s. 1; 2015-117, s. 1

§ 52C-3-308. Duty of Department

(a) If the Department determines that the support enforcement agency is neglecting or refusing to provide services to an individual, the Department may order the agency to perform its duties under this Chapter or may provide those services directly to the individual.

(b) The Department may determine that a foreign country has established a reciprocal arrangement for child support with this State and take appropriate action for notification of the determination.

History.
1995, c. 538, s. 7(c); 2015-117, s. 1

§ 52C-3-308.1. Private counsel

An individual may employ private counsel to represent the individual in proceedings authorized by this Chapter.

History.
2015-117, s. 1

§ 52C-3-309. Duties of State information agency

(a) The Department is the State information agency under this Chapter.

(b) The State information agency shall:

(1) Compile and maintain a current list, including addresses, of the tribunals in this State which have jurisdiction under this Chapter and any support enforcement agencies in this State and transmit a copy to the state information agency of every other state;

(2) Maintain a register of names and addresses of tribunals and support enforcement agencies received from other states;

(3) Forward to the appropriate tribunal in the county in this State in which the obligee who is an individual or the obligor resides, or in which the obligor's property is believed to be located, all documents concerning a proceeding under this Chapter received from another state or a foreign country; and

(4) Obtain information concerning the location of the obligor and the obligor's property within this State not exempt from execution, by such means as postal verification and federal or state locator services, examination of telephone directories, requests for the obligor's address from employers, and examination of governmental records, including, to the extent not prohibited by other law, those relating to real property, vital statistics, law enforcement, taxation, motor vehicles, drivers licenses, and social security.

History.
1995, c. 538, s. 7(c); 1997-443, s. 11A.118(a); 2015-117, s. 1

§ 52C-3-310. Pleadings and accompanying documents

(a) In a proceeding under this Chapter, a petitioner seeking to establish a support order, to determine parentage of a child, or to register and modify a support order of a tribunal of another state or a foreign country must file a petition. Unless otherwise ordered under G.S. 52C-3-311, the petition or accompanying documents must provide, so far as known, the name, residential address, and social security numbers of the obligor and the obligee or the parent and alleged parent, and the name, sex, residential address, social security number, and date of birth of each child for whose benefit support is sought or whose parentage is to be determined. Unless filed at the time of registration, the petition must be accompanied by a copy of any support order known to have been issued by another tribunal. The petition may include any other information that may assist in locating or identifying the respondent.

(b) The petition must specify the relief sought. The petition and accompanying documents must conform substantially with the requirements imposed by the forms mandated by federal law for use in cases filed by a support enforcement agency.

History.
1995, c. 538, s. 7(c); 2015-117, s. 1

§ 52C-3-311. Nondisclosure of information in exceptional circumstances

If a party alleges in an affidavit or a pleading under oath that the health, safety, or liberty of a party or child would be jeopardized by disclosure of specific identifying information, that information must be sealed and may not be disclosed to the other party or the public. After a hearing in which a tribunal takes into consideration the health, safety, or liberty of the party or child, the tribunal may order disclosure of information that the tribunal determines to be in the interest of justice.

History.
1995, c. 538, s. 7(c); 2015-117, s. 1

§ 52C-3-312. Costs and fees

(a) The petitioner shall not be required to pay a filing fee or other costs.

(b) If an obligee prevails, a responding tribunal of this State may assess against an obligor filing fees, reasonable attorneys' fees, other costs, and necessary travel and other reasonable expenses incurred by the obligee and the obligee's witnesses. The tribunal may not assess fees, costs, or expenses against the obligee or the support enforcement agency of either the initiating or the responding state or foreign country, except as provided by other law. Attorneys' fees may be taxed as costs, and may be ordered paid directly to the attorney, who may enforce the order in the attorney's own name. Payment of support owed to the obligee has priority over fees, costs, and expenses.

(c) The tribunal shall order the payment of costs and reasonable attorneys' fees if it determines that a hearing was requested primarily for delay. In a proceeding under Article 6 of this Chapter, a hearing is presumed to have been requested primarily for delay if a registered support order is confirmed or enforced without change.

History.
1995, c. 538, s. 7(c); 2015-117, s. 1

§ 52C-3-313. Limited immunity of petitioner

(a) Participation by a petitioner in a proceeding under this Chapter before a responding tribunal, whether in person, by private attorney, or through services provided by the support enforcement agency, does not confer personal jurisdiction over the petitioner in another proceeding.

(b) A petitioner is not amenable to service of civil process while physically present in this State to participate in a proceeding under this Chapter.

(c) The immunity granted by this section does not extend to civil litigation based on acts unrelated to a proceeding under this Chapter committed by a party while present in this State to participate in the proceeding.

History.
1995, c. 538, s. 7(c); 2015-117, s. 1

§ 52C-3-314. Nonparentage as defense

A party whose parentage of a child has been previously determined by or pursuant to law may not plead nonparentage as a defense to a proceeding under this Chapter.

History.
1995, c. 538, s. 7(c)

§ 52C-3-315. Special rules of evidence and procedure

(a) The physical presence of a nonresident party who is an individual in a tribunal of this State is not required for the establishment, enforcement, or modification of a support order or the rendition of a judgment determining parentage of a child.

(b) An affidavit, a document substantially complying with federally mandated forms, or a document incorporated by reference in any of them, which would not be excluded under the hearsay rule if given in person, is admissible in evidence if given under penalty of perjury by a party or witness residing outside this State.

(c) A copy of the record of child support payments certified as a true copy of the original by the custodian of the record may be forwarded to a responding tribunal. The copy is evidence of facts asserted in it and is admissible to show whether payments were made.

(d) Copies of bills for testing for parentage of a child, and for prenatal and postnatal health care of the mother and child, furnished to the adverse party at least 10 days before trial, are admissible in evidence to prove the amount of the charges billed and that the charges were reasonable, necessary, and customary.

(e) Documentary evidence transmitted from outside this State to a tribunal of this State by telephone, telecopier, or other electronic means that do not provide an original record may not be excluded from evidence on an objection based on the means of transmission.

(f) In a proceeding under this Chapter, a tribunal of this State shall permit a party or witness residing outside this State to be deposed or to testify under penalty of perjury by telephone, audiovisual means, or other electronic means at a designated tribunal or other location. A tribunal of this State shall cooperate with other tribunals in designating an appropriate location for the deposition or testimony.

(g) If a party called to testify at a civil hearing refuses to answer on the ground that the testimony may be self-incriminating, the trier of fact may draw an adverse inference from the refusal.

(h) A privilege against disclosure of communication between spouses does not apply in a proceeding under this Chapter.

(i) The defense of immunity based on the relationship of marital partners or parent and child does not apply in a proceeding under this Chapter.

(j) A voluntary acknowledgement of paternity, certified as a true copy, is admissible to establish parentage of the child.

History.
1995, c. 538, s. 7(c); 2015-117, s. 1

§ 52C-3-316. Communications between tribunals

A tribunal of this State may communicate with a tribunal outside this State in a record or by telephone, electronic mail, or other means, to obtain information concerning the laws, the legal effect of a judgment, decree, or order of that tribunal, and the status of a proceeding. A tribunal of this State may furnish similar information by similar means to a tribunal outside this State.

History.
1995, c. 538, s. 7(c); 2015-117, s. 1

§ 52C-3-317. Assistance with discovery

A tribunal of this State may:

(1) Request a tribunal outside this State to assist in obtaining discovery; and

(2) Upon request, may compel a person over whom it has jurisdiction to respond to a discovery order issued by a tribunal outside this State.

History.
1995, c. 538, s. 7(c); 2015-117, s. 1

§ 52C-3-318. Receipt and disbursement of payments

(a) A support enforcement agency or tribunal of this State shall disburse promptly any amounts received pursuant to a support order, as directed by the order. The agency or tribunal shall furnish to a requesting party or tribunal of another state or a foreign country a certified statement by the custodian of the record of the amounts and dates of all payments received.

(b) If neither the obligor, nor the obligee who is an individual, nor the child resides in this State, upon request from the support enforcement agency of this State or another state, the support enforcement agency of this State or a tribunal of this State shall:

(1) Direct that the support payment be made to the support enforcement agency in the state in which the obligee is receiving services; and

(2) Issue and send to the obligor's employer a conforming income-withholding order or an administrative notice of change of payee, reflecting the redirected payments.

(c) The support enforcement agency of this State receiving redirected payments from another state pursuant to a law similar to subsection (b) of this section shall furnish to a requesting party or tribunal of the other state a certified statement by the custodian of the record of the amount and dates of all payments received.

History.
1995, c. 538, s. 7(c); 2015-117, s. 1

ARTICLE 4
ESTABLISHMENT OF SUPPORT ORDER OR DETERMINATION OF PARENTAGE

§ 52C-4-401. Establishment of support order

(a) If a support order entitled to recognition under this Chapter has not been issued, a responding tribunal of this State with personal jurisdiction over the parties may issue a support order if:

(1) The individual seeking the order resides outside this State; or

(2) The support enforcement agency seeking the order is located outside this State.

(b) The tribunal may issue a temporary child support order if the tribunal determines that such an order is appropriate and the individual ordered to pay is any of the following:

(1) A presumed father of the child.

(2) Petitioning to have his paternity adjudicated.

(3) Identified as the father of the child through genetic testing.

(4) An alleged father who has declined to submit to genetic testing.

(5) Shown by clear and convincing evidence to be the father of the child.

(6) An acknowledged father as provided by Chapter 110 of the General Statutes.

(7) The mother of the child.

(8) An individual who has been ordered to pay child support in a previous proceeding and the order has not been reversed or vacated.

(c) Upon finding, after notice and opportunity to be heard, that an obligor owes a duty of support, the tribunal shall issue a support order directed to the obligor and may issue other orders pursuant to G.S. 52C-3-305.

History.

1995, c. 538, s. 7(c); 2015-117, s. 1

§ 52C-4-402. Proceeding to determine parentage

A tribunal of this State authorized to determine parentage of a child may serve as a responding tribunal in a proceeding to determine parentage of a child brought under this Chapter or a law or procedure substantially similar to this Chapter.

History.

2015-117, s. 1

ARTICLE 5
ENFORCEMENT OF ORDER OF ANOTHER STATE WITHOUT REGISTRATION

§ 52C-5-501. Employer's receipt of income-withholding order of another state

(a) An income-withholding order issued in another state may be sent by or on behalf of the obligee, or by the support enforcement agency, to the person defined or identified as the obligor's employer or payor under the income-withholding provisions of Chapter 50 or Chapter 110 of the General Statutes, as applicable, without first filing a petition or comparable pleading or registering the order with a tribunal of this State.

(b) Repealed by Session Laws 1997-433, s. 10.8.

History.

1995, c. 538, s. 7(c); 1997-433, s. 10.8; 1998-17, s. 1; 1999-293, s. 5; 2011-401, s. 3.3; 2015-117, s. 1

§ 52C-5-502. Employer's compliance with income-withholding order of another state

(a) Upon receipt of an income-withholding order, the obligor's employer shall immediately provide a copy of the order to the obligor.

(b) The employer shall treat an income-withholding order issued in another state which appears regular on its face as if it had been issued by a tribunal of this State.

(c) Except as otherwise provided in subsection (d) of this section and G.S. 52C-5-503, the employer shall withhold and distribute the funds as directed in the income-withholding order by complying with terms of the order which specify:

(1) The duration and amount of periodic payments of current child support, stated as a sum certain;

(2) The person designated to receive payments and the address to which the payments are to be forwarded;

(3) Medical support, whether in the form of periodic cash payment, stated as a sum certain, or ordering the obligor to provide health insurance coverage for the child under a policy available through the obligor's employment;

(4) The amount of periodic payments of fees and costs for a support enforcement agency, the issuing tribunal, and the obligee's attorney, stated as sums certain; and

(5) The amount of periodic payments of arrearages and interest on arrearages, stated as sums certain.

(d) An employer shall comply with the law of the state of the obligor's principal place of employment for withholding from income with respect to:

(1) The employer's fee for processing an income-withholding order;

(2) The maximum amount permitted to be withheld from the obligor's income; and

(3) The times within which the employer must implement the income-withholding order and forward the child support payment.

History.

1995, c. 538, s. 7(c); 1997-433, s. 10.8; 1998-17, s. 1; 2015-117, s. 1

§ 52C-5-503. Employer's compliance with two or more income-withholding orders

If an obligor's employer receives two or more income-withholding orders with respect to the earnings of the same obligor, the employer satisfies the terms of the orders if the employer complies with the law of the state of the obligor's principal place of employment to establish the priorities for withholding and allocating income withheld for two or more child support obligees.

History.
1997-433, s. 10.8; 1998-17, s. 1; 2015-117, s. 1

§ 52C-5-504. Immunity from civil liability

An employer that complies with an income-withholding order issued in another state in accordance with this Article is not subject to civil liability to an individual or agency with regard to the employer's withholding of child support from the obligor's income.

History.
1997-433, s. 10.8; 1998-17, s. 1; 2015-117, s. 1

§ 52C-5-505. Penalties for noncompliance

An employer that willfully fails to comply with an income-withholding order issued in another state and received for enforcement is subject to the same penalties that may be imposed for noncompliance with an order issued by a tribunal of this State.

History.
1997-433, s. 10.8; 1998-17, s. 1; 2015-117, s. 1

§ 52C-5-506. Contest by obligor

(a) An obligor may contest the validity or enforcement of an income-withholding order issued in another state and received directly by an employer in this State by registering the order in a tribunal of this State and filing a contest to that order as provided in Article 6 of this Chapter, or otherwise contesting the order in the same manner as if the order had been issued by a tribunal of this State.

(b) The obligor shall give notice of the contest to:

(1) A support enforcement agency providing services to the obligee;

(2) Each employer that has directly received an income-withholding order relating to the obligor; and

(3) The person designated to receive payments in the income-withholding order or, if no person is designated, to the obligee.

History.
1997-433, s. 10.8; 1998-17, s. 1; 2015-117, s. 1

§ 52C-5-507. Administrative enforcement of orders

(a) A party or support enforcement agency seeking to enforce a support order or an income-withholding order, or both, issued in another state or a foreign support order may send the documents required for registering the order to a support enforcement agency of this State.

(b) Upon receipt of the documents, the support enforcement agency, without initially seeking to register the order, shall consider and, if appropriate, use any administrative procedure authorized by the law of this State to enforce a support order or an income-withholding order, or both. If the obligor does not contest administrative enforcement, the order need not be registered. If the obligor contests the validity or administrative enforcement of the order, the support enforcement agency shall register the order pursuant to this Chapter.

History.
1997-433, s. 10.8; 1998-17, s. 1; 2015-117, s. 1

ARTICLE 6
REGISTRATION, ENFORCEMENT, AND MODIFICATION OF SUPPORT ORDER

PART 1
REGISTRATION FOR ENFORCEMENT OF SUPPORT ORDER

§ 52C-6-601. Registration of order for enforcement

A support order or income-withholding order issued in another state or a foreign support order may be registered in this State for enforcement.

History.
1995, c. 538, s. 7(c); 1997-433, s. 10.9; 1998-17, s. 1; 2015-117, s. 1

§ 52C-6-602. Procedure to register order for enforcement

(a) Except as otherwise provided in G.S. 52C-7-706, a support order or income-withholding order of another state or a foreign support order may be registered in this State by sending the following records to the appropriate tribunal in this State:

(1) A letter of transmittal to the tribunal requesting registration and enforcement;

(2) Two copies, including one certified copy, of the order to be registered, including any modification of the order;

(3) A sworn statement by the person requesting registration or a certified

statement by the custodian of the records showing the amount of any arrearage;

(4) The name of the obligor and, if known:

a. The obligor's address and social security number;

b. The name and address of the obligor's employer and any other source of income of the obligor; and

c. A description and the location of property of the obligor in this State not exempt from execution; and

(5) Except as otherwise provided in G.S. 52C-3-311, the name and address of the obligee and, if applicable, the person to whom support payments are to be remitted.

(b) On receipt of a request for registration, the registering tribunal shall cause the order to be filed as an order of another state or a foreign support order, together with one copy of the documents and information, regardless of their form.

(c) A petition or comparable pleading seeking a remedy that must be affirmatively sought under other law of this State may be filed at the same time as the request for registration or later. The pleading must specify the grounds for the remedy sought.

(d) If two or more orders are in effect, the person requesting registration shall do each of the following:

(1) Furnish to the tribunal a copy of every support order asserted to be in effect in addition to the documents specified in this section.

(2) Specify the order alleged to be the controlling order, if any.

(3) Specify the amount of consolidated arrears, if any.

(e) A request for a determination of which is the controlling order may be filed separately or with a request for registration and enforcement or for registration and modification. The person requesting registration shall give notice of the request to each party whose rights may be affected by the determination.

History.

1995, c. 538, s. 7(c); 1997-456, s. 27; 2015-117, s. 1

§ 52C-6-603. Effect of registration for enforcement

(a) A support order or income-withholding order issued in another state or a foreign support order is registered when the order is filed in the registering tribunal of this State.

(b) A registered support order issued in another state or a foreign country is enforceable in the same manner and is subject to the same procedures as an order issued by a tribunal of this State.

(c) Except as otherwise provided in this Chapter, a tribunal of this State shall recognize and enforce, but may not modify, a registered support order if the issuing tribunal had jurisdiction.

History.

1995, c. 538, s. 7(c); 2015-117, s. 1

§ 52C-6-604. Choice of law

(a) Except as otherwise provided in subsection (d) of this section, the law of the issuing state or foreign country governs all of the following:

(1) The nature, extent, amount, and duration of current payments under a registered support order.

(2) The computation and payment of arrearages and accrual of interest on the arrearages under the support order.

(3) The existence and satisfaction of other obligations under the support order.

(b) In a proceeding for arrears under a registered support order, the statute of limitations of this State, or of the issuing state or foreign country, whichever is longer, applies.

(c) A responding tribunal of this State shall apply the procedures and remedies of this State to enforce current support and collect arrears and interest due on a support order of another state or a foreign country registered in this State.

(d) After a tribunal of this State or another state determines which is the controlling order and issues an order consolidating arrears, if any, a tribunal of this State shall prospectively apply the law of the state or foreign country issuing the controlling order, including its law on interest on arrears, on current and future support, and on consolidated arrears.

History.

1995, c. 538, s. 7(c); 2015-117, s. 1

PART 2
CONTEST OF VALIDITY OR ENFORCEMENT

§ 52C-6-605. Notice of registration of order

(a) When a support order or income-withholding order issued in another state or a foreign support order is registered, the registering tribunal of this State shall notify the nonregistering party. The notice must be accompanied by a copy of the registered order and the documents and relevant information accompanying the order.

(b) A notice must inform the nonregistering party:

(1) That a registered order is enforceable as of the date of registration in the same

manner as an order issued by a tribunal of this State.

(2) That a hearing to contest the validity or enforcement of the registered order must be requested within 20 days after notice, unless the registered order is under G.S. 52C-7-707;

(3) That failure to contest the validity or enforcement of the registered order in a timely manner will result in confirmation of the order and enforcement of the order and the alleged arrearages; and

(4) Of the amount of any alleged arrearages.

(b1) If the registering party asserts that two or more orders are in effect, a notice must also do each of the following:

(1) Identify the two or more orders and the order alleged by the registering party to be the controlling order and the consolidated arrears, if any.

(2) Notify the nonregistering party of the right to a determination of which is the controlling order.

(3) State that the procedures provided in subsection (b) of this section apply to the determination of which is the controlling order.

(4) State that failure to contest the validity or enforcement of the order alleged to be the controlling order in a timely manner may result in confirmation that the order is the controlling order.

(c) Upon registration of an income-withholding order for enforcement, the support enforcement agency or the registering tribunal shall notify the obligor's employer pursuant to the income-withholding provisions of Chapter 50 or Chapter 110 of the General Statutes, as applicable.

History.
1995, c. 538, s. 7(c); 1997-433, s. 10.10; 1998-17, s. 1; 2015-117, s. 1

§ 52C-6-606. Procedure to contest validity or enforcement of registered support order

(a) A nonregistering party seeking to contest the validity or enforcement of a registered order in this State shall request a hearing within the time required by G.S. 52C-6-605. The nonregistering party may seek to vacate the registration, to assert any defense to an allegation of noncompliance with the registered order, or to contest the remedies being sought or the amount of any alleged arrears pursuant to G.S. 52C-6-607.

(b) If the nonregistering party fails to contest the validity or enforcement of the registered support order in a timely manner, the order is confirmed by operation of law.

(c) If a nonregistering party requests a hearing to contest the validity or enforcement of the registered support order, the registering tribunal shall schedule the matter for hearing and give notice to the parties of the date, time, and place of the hearing.

History.
1995, c. 538, s. 7(c); 1997-433, s. 10.11; 1998-17, s. 1; 2015-117, s. 1

§ 52C-6-607. Contest of registration or enforcement

(a) A party contesting the validity or enforcement of a registered support order or seeking to vacate the registration has the burden of proving one or more of the following defenses:

(1) The issuing tribunal lacked personal jurisdiction over the contesting party;

(2) The order was obtained by fraud;

(3) The order has been vacated, suspended, or modified by a later order;

(4) The issuing tribunal has stayed the order pending appeal;

(5) There is a defense under the law of this State to the remedy sought;

(6) Full or partial payment has been made;

(7) The statute of limitations under G.S. 52C-6-604 precludes enforcement of some or all of the alleged arrearages; or

(8) The alleged controlling order is not the controlling order.

(b) If a party presents evidence establishing a full or partial defense under subsection (a) of this section, a tribunal may stay enforcement of a registered support order, continue the proceeding to permit production of additional relevant evidence, and issue other appropriate orders. An uncontested portion of the registered order may be enforced by all remedies available under the law of this State.

(c) If the contesting party does not establish a defense under subsection (a) of this section to the validity or enforcement of a registered support order, the registering tribunal shall issue an order confirming the order.

History.
1995, c. 538, s. 7(c); 2015-117, s. 1

§ 52C-6-608. Confirmed order

Confirmation of a registered support order, whether by operation of law or after notice and hearing, precludes further contest of the order with respect to any matter that could have been asserted at the time of registration.

History.
1995, c. 538, s. 7(c); 2015-117, s. 1

PART 3
REGISTRATION AND MODIFICATION OF CHILD SUPPORT ORDER OF ANOTHER STATE.

§ 52C-6-609. Procedure to register child support order of another state for modification

A party or support enforcement agency seeking to modify, or to modify and enforce, a child support order issued in another state shall register that order in this State in the same manner provided in G.S. 52C-6-601 through G.S. 52C-6-608 if the order has not been registered. A petition for modification may be filed at the same time as a request for registration, or later. The pleading must specify the grounds for modification.

History.
1995, c. 538, s. 7(c); 2015-117, s. 1

§ 52C-6-610. Effect of registration for modification

A tribunal of this State may enforce a child support order of another state registered for purposes of modification, in the same manner as if the order had been issued by a tribunal of this State, but the registered support order may be modified only if the requirements of G.S. 52C-6-611 or G.S. 52C-6-613 have been met.

History.
1995, c. 538, s. 7(c); 2015-117, s. 1

§ 52C-6-611. Modification of child support order of another state

(a) If G.S. 52C-6-613 does not apply, upon petition, a tribunal of this State may modify a child support order issued in another state which is registered in this State if, after notice and hearing, the tribunal finds that:

(1) The following requirements are met:

a. Neither the child, nor the obligee who is an individual, nor the obligor resides in the issuing state;

b. A petitioner who is a nonresident of this State seeks modification; and

c. The respondent is subject to the personal jurisdiction of the tribunal of this State; or

(2) This State is the residence of the child, or a party who is an individual, is subject to the personal jurisdiction of the tribunal of this State and all of the parties who are individuals have filed consents in a record in the issuing tribunal for a tribunal of this

State to modify the support order and assume continuing, exclusive jurisdiction.

(b) Modification of a registered child support order is subject to the same requirements, procedures, and defenses that apply to the modification of an order issued by a tribunal of this State, and the order may be enforced and satisfied in the same manner.

(c) A tribunal of this State may not modify any aspect of a child support order that may not be modified under the law of the issuing state, including the duration of the obligation of support. If two or more tribunals have issued child support orders for the same obligor and same child, the order that controls and must be so recognized under G.S. 52C-2-207 establishes the aspects of the support order which are nonmodifiable.

(c1) In a proceeding to modify a child support order, the law of the state that is determined to have issued the initial controlling order governs the duration of the obligation of support. The obligor's fulfillment of the duty of support established by that order precludes imposition of a further obligation of support by a tribunal of this State.

(d) On the issuance of an order by a tribunal of this State modifying a child support order issued in another state, the tribunal of this State becomes the tribunal of continuing, exclusive jurisdiction.

(d1) Notwithstanding subsections (a) through (d) of this section and G.S. 52C-2-201(b), a tribunal of this State retains jurisdiction to modify an order issued by a tribunal of this State if:

(1) One party resides in another state; and

(2) The other party resides outside the United States.

(e) Repealed by Session Laws 1997-443, s. 10.12.

History.
1995, c. 538, s. 7(c); 1997-433, s. 10.12; 1997-456, s. 27; 1998-17, s. 1; 2015-117, s. 1

§ 52C-6-612. Recognition of order modified in another state

If a child support order issued by a tribunal of this State is modified by a tribunal of another state which assumed jurisdiction pursuant to the Uniform Interstate Family Support Act, a tribunal of this State:

(1) May enforce its order that was modified only as to arrears and interest accruing before the modification;

(2) Repealed by Session Laws 2015-117, s. 1, effective June 24, 2015.

(3) May provide other appropriate relief for violations of its order which occurred

before the effective date of the modification; and

(4) Shall recognize the modifying order of the other state, upon registration, for the purpose of enforcement.

History.
1995, c. 538, s. 7(c); 2015-117, s. 1

§ 52C-6-613. Jurisdiction to modify child support order of another state when individual parties reside in this State

(a) If all of the parties who are individuals reside in this State and the child does not reside in the issuing state, a tribunal of this State has jurisdiction to enforce and to modify the issuing state's child support order in a proceeding to register that order.

(b) A tribunal of this State exercising jurisdiction under this section shall apply the provisions of Articles 1 and 2 of this Chapter, this Article, and the procedural and substantive law of this State to the proceeding for enforcement or modification. Articles 3, 4, 5, 7, and 8 of this Chapter do not apply.

History.
1997-433, s. 10.13; 1998-17, s. 1

§ 52C-6-614. Notice to issuing tribunal of modification

Within 30 days after issuance of a modified child support order, the party obtaining the modification shall file a certified copy of the order with the issuing tribunal that had continuing, exclusive jurisdiction over the earlier order, and in each tribunal in which the party knows the earlier order has been registered. A party who obtains the order and fails to file a certified copy is subject to appropriate sanctions by a tribunal in which the issue of failure to file arises. The failure to file does not affect the validity or enforceability of the modified order of the new tribunal having continuing, exclusive jurisdiction.

History.
1997-433, s. 10.13; 1998-17, s. 1

PART 4
REGISTRATION AND MODIFICATION OF FOREIGN CHILD SUPPORT ORDER

§ 52C-6-615. Jurisdiction to modify child support order of foreign country

(a) Except as otherwise provided in G.S. 52C-7-711, if a foreign country lacks or refuses to exercise jurisdiction to modify its child support order pursuant to its laws, a tribunal of this State may assume jurisdiction to modify the child support order and bind all individuals subject to the personal jurisdiction of the tribunal whether the consent to modification of a child support order otherwise required of the individual pursuant to G.S. 52C-6-611 has been given or whether the individual seeking modification is a resident of this State or of the foreign country.

(b) An order issued by a tribunal of this State modifying a foreign child support order pursuant to this section is the controlling order.

History.
2015-117, s. 1

§ 52C-6-616. Procedure to register child support order of foreign country for modification

A party or support enforcement agency seeking to modify, or to modify and enforce, a foreign child support order not under the Convention may register that order in this State under G.S. 52C-6-601 through G.S. 52C-6-608 if the order has not been registered. A petition for modification may be filed at the same time as a request for registration, or at another time. The petition must specify the grounds for modification.

History.
2015-117, s. 1

ARTICLE 7
SUPPORT PROCEEDING UNDER CONVENTION

§ 52C-7-701. Definitions

As used in this Article:

(1) "Application" means a request under the Convention by an obligee or obligor, or on behalf of a child, made through a central authority for assistance from another central authority.

(2) "Central authority" means the entity designated by the United States or a foreign country described in G.S. 52C-1-101(3a)d. to perform the functions specified in the Convention.

(3) "Convention support order" means a support order of a tribunal of a foreign country described in G.S. 52C-1-101(3a)d.

(4) "Direct request" means a petition filed by an individual in a tribunal of this State in a proceeding involving an obligee, obligor, or child residing outside the United States.

(5) "Foreign central authority" means the entity designated by a foreign country described in G.S. 52C-1-101(3a)d. to perform the functions specified in the Convention.

(6) "Foreign support agreement" means an agreement for support in a record that:

a. Is enforceable as a support order in the country of origin;

b. Has been (i) formally drawn up or registered as an authentic instrument by a foreign tribunal or (ii) authenticated by or concluded, registered, or filed with a foreign tribunal; and

c. May be reviewed and modified by a foreign tribunal.

The term includes a maintenance arrangement or authentic instrument under the Convention.

(7) "United States central authority" means the Secretary of the United States Department of Health and Human Services.

History.
1995, c. 538, s. 7(c); 2015-117, s. 1

§ 52C-7-702. Applicability

This Article applies only to a support proceeding under the Convention. In such a proceeding, if a provision of this Article is inconsistent with Articles 1 through 6 of this Chapter, this Article controls.

History.
2015-117, s. 1

§ 52C-7-703. Relationship of Department to United States central authority

The Department is recognized as the agency designated by the United States central authority to perform specific functions under the Convention.

History.
2015-117, s. 1

§ 52C-7-704. Initiation by Department of support proceeding under Convention

(a) In a support proceeding under this Article, the Department shall do the following:

(1) Transmit and receive applications.

(2) Initiate or facilitate the institution of a proceeding regarding an application in a tribunal of this State.

(b) The following support proceedings are available to an obligee under the Convention:

(1) Recognition or recognition and enforcement of a foreign support order.

(2) Enforcement of a support order issued or recognized in this State.

(3) Establishment of a support order if there is no existing order, including, if necessary, determination of parentage of a child.

(4) Establishment of a support order if recognition of a foreign support order is refused under G.S. 52C-7-708(b)(2), (4), or (9).

(5) Modification of a support order of a tribunal of this State.

(6) Modification of a support order of a tribunal of another state or foreign country.

(c) The following support proceedings are available under the Convention to an obligor against which there is an existing support order:

(1) Recognition of an order suspending or limiting enforcement of an existing support order of a tribunal of this State.

(2) Modification of a support order of a tribunal of this State.

(3) Modification of a support order of a tribunal of another state or a foreign country.

(d) A tribunal of this State may not require security, bond, or deposit, however described, to guarantee the payment of costs and expenses in proceedings under the Convention.

History.
2015-117, s. 1

§ 52C-7-705. Direct request

(a) A petitioner may file a direct request seeking establishment or modification of a support order or determination of parentage of a child. In the proceeding, the law of this State applies.

(b) A petitioner may file a direct request seeking recognition and enforcement of a support order or support agreement. In the proceeding, G.S. 52C-7-706 through G.S. 52C-7-713 apply.

(c) In a direct request for recognition and enforcement of a Convention support order or foreign support agreement:

(1) A security, bond, or deposit is not required to guarantee the payment of costs and expenses; and

(2) An obligee or obligor that in the issuing country has benefited from free legal assistance is entitled to benefit, at least to the same extent, from any free legal assistance provided for by the law of this State under the same circumstances.

(d) A petitioner filing a direct request is not entitled to assistance from the Department or the county child support agency.

Chapter 52C

(e) This Article does not prevent the application of laws of this State that provide simplified, more expeditious rules regarding a direct request for recognition and enforcement of a foreign support order or foreign support agreement.

History.
2015-117, s. 1

§ 52C-7-706. Registration of Convention support order

(a) Except as otherwise provided in this Article, a party who is an individual or a support enforcement agency seeking recognition of a Convention support order shall register the order in this State as provided in Article 6 of this Chapter.

(b) Notwithstanding G.S. 52C-3-310 and G.S. 52C-6-602(a), a request for registration of a Convention support order must be accompanied by:

(1) A complete text of the support order or an abstract or extract of the support order drawn up by the issuing foreign tribunal, which may be in the form recommended by the Hague Conference on Private International Law;

(2) A record stating that the support order is enforceable in the issuing country;

(3) If the respondent did not appear and was not represented in the proceedings in the issuing country, a record attesting, as appropriate, either that the respondent had proper notice of the proceedings and an opportunity to be heard or that the respondent had proper notice of the support order and an opportunity to be heard in a challenge or appeal on fact or law before a tribunal;

(4) A record showing the amount of arrears, if any, and the date the amount was calculated;

(5) A record showing a requirement for automatic adjustment of the amount of support, if any, and the information necessary to make the appropriate calculations; and

(6) If necessary, a record showing the extent to which the applicant received free legal assistance in the issuing country.

(c) A request for registration of a Convention support order may seek recognition and partial enforcement of the order.

(d) A tribunal of this State may vacate the registration of a Convention support order without the filing of a contest under G.S. 52C-7-707 only if, acting on its own motion, the tribunal finds that recognition and enforcement of the order would be manifestly incompatible with public policy.

(e) The tribunal shall promptly notify the parties of the registration or the order vacating the registration of a Convention support order.

History.
2015-117, s. 1

§ 52C-7-707. Contest of registered Convention support order

(a) Except as otherwise provided in this Article, G.S. 52C-6-605 through G.S. 52C-6-608 apply to a contest of a registered Convention support order.

(b) A party contesting a registered Convention support order shall file a contest not later than 30 days after notice of the registration, but if the contesting party does not reside in the United States, the contest must be filed not later than 60 days after notice of the registration.

(c) If the nonregistering party fails to contest the registered Convention support order by the time specified in subsection (b) of this section, the order is enforceable.

(d) A contest of a registered Convention support order may be based only on grounds set forth in G.S. 52C-7-708. The contesting party bears the burden of proof.

(e) In a contest of a registered Convention support order, a tribunal of this State:

(1) Is bound by the findings of fact on which the foreign tribunal based its jurisdiction; and

(2) May not review the merits of the order.

(f) A tribunal of this State deciding a contest of a registered Convention support order shall promptly notify the parties of its decision.

(g) A challenge or appeal, if any, does not stay the enforcement of a Convention support order unless there are exceptional circumstances.

History.
2015-117, s. 1

§ 52C-7-708. Recognition and enforcement of registered Convention support order

(a) Except as otherwise provided in subsection (b) of this section, a tribunal of this State shall recognize and enforce a registered Convention support order.

(b) The following grounds are the only grounds on which a tribunal of this State may refuse recognition and enforcement of a registered Convention support order:

(1) Recognition and enforcement of the order is manifestly incompatible with public policy, including the failure of the issuing tribunal to observe minimum standards

of due process, which include notice and an opportunity to be heard.

(2) The issuing tribunal lacked personal jurisdiction consistent with G.S. 52C-2-201.

(3) The order is not enforceable in the issuing country.

(4) The order was obtained by fraud in connection with a matter of procedure.

(5) A record transmitted in accordance with G.S. 52C-7-706 lacks authenticity or integrity.

(6) A proceeding between the same parties and having the same purpose is pending before a tribunal of this State and that proceeding was the first to be filed.

(7) The order is incompatible with a more recent support order involving the same parties and having the same purpose if the more recent support order is entitled to recognition and enforcement under this Chapter in this State.

(8) Payment, to the extent alleged arrears have been paid in whole or in part.

(9) In a case in which the respondent neither appeared nor was represented in the proceeding in the issuing foreign country:

a. If the law of that country provides for prior notice of proceedings, the respondent did not have proper notice of the proceedings and an opportunity to be heard; or

b. If the law of that country does not provide for prior notice of the proceedings, the respondent did not have proper notice of the order and an opportunity to be heard in a challenge or appeal on fact or law before a tribunal.

(10) The order was made in violation of G.S. 52C-7-711.

(c) If a tribunal of this State does not recognize a Convention support order under subdivision (b)(2), (4), or (9) of this section, then:

(1) The tribunal may not dismiss the proceeding without allowing a reasonable time for a party to request the establishment of a new Convention support order; and

(2) The Department and the county child support agency shall take all appropriate measures to request a child support order for the obligee if the application for recognition and enforcement was received under G.S. 52C-7-704.

History.
2015-117, s. 1

§ 52C-7-709. Partial enforcement

If a tribunal of this State does not recognize and enforce a Convention support order in its entirety, it shall enforce any severable part of the order. An application or direct request may seek recognition and partial enforcement of a Convention support order.

History.
2015-117, s. 1

§ 52C-7-710. Foreign support agreement

(a) Except as otherwise provided in subsections (c) and (d) of this section, a tribunal of this State shall recognize and enforce a foreign support agreement registered in this State.

(b) An application or direct request for recognition and enforcement of a foreign support agreement must be accompanied by each of the following:

(1) A complete text of the foreign support agreement.

(2) A record stating that the foreign support agreement is enforceable as an order of support in the issuing country.

(c) A tribunal of this State may vacate the registration of a foreign support agreement only if, acting on its own motion, the tribunal finds that recognition and enforcement would be manifestly incompatible with public policy.

(d) In a contest of a foreign support agreement, a tribunal of this State may refuse recognition and enforcement of the agreement if it finds any of the following:

(1) Recognition and enforcement of the agreement is manifestly incompatible with public policy.

(2) The agreement was obtained by fraud or falsification.

(3) The agreement is incompatible with a support order involving the same parties and having the same purpose in this State, another state, or a foreign country if the support order is entitled to recognition and enforcement under this Chapter in this State.

(4) The record submitted under subsection (b) of this section lacks authenticity or integrity.

(e) A proceeding for recognition and enforcement of a foreign support agreement must be suspended during the pendency of a challenge to or appeal of the agreement before a tribunal of another state or a foreign country.

History.
2015-117, s. 1

§ 52C-7-711. Modification of Convention child support order

(a) A tribunal of this State may not modify a Convention child support order if the obligee remains a resident of the foreign country where the support order was issued unless:

(1) The obligee submits to the jurisdiction of a tribunal of this State, either expressly or by defending on the merits of the case without objecting to the jurisdiction at the first available opportunity; or

(2) The foreign tribunal lacks or refuses to exercise jurisdiction to modify its support order or issue a new support order.

(b) If a tribunal of this State does not modify a Convention child support order because the order is not recognized in this State, G.S. 52C-7-708(c) applies.

History.
2015-117, s. 1

§ 52C-7-712. Personal information; limit on use

Personal information gathered or transmitted under this Article may be used only for the purposes for which it was gathered or transmitted.

History.
2015-117, s. 1

§ 52C-7-713. Record in original language; English translation

A record filed with a tribunal of this State under this Article must be in the original language and, if not in English, must be accompanied by an English translation.

History.
2015-117, s. 1

ARTICLE 8
INTERSTATE RENDITION

§ 52C-8-801. Grounds for rendition

(a) For purposes of this Article, "governor" includes an individual performing the functions of governor or the executive authority of a state covered by this Chapter.

(b) The Governor of this State may:

(1) Demand that the governor of another state surrender an individual found in the other state who is charged criminally in this State with having failed to provide for the support of an obligee; or

(2) On the demand of the governor of another state, surrender an individual found in this State who is charged criminally in the other state with having failed to provide for the support of an obligee.

(c) A provision for extradition of individuals not inconsistent with this Chapter applies to the demand even if the individual whose surrender is demanded was not in the demanding state when the crime was allegedly committed and has not fled therefrom.

History.
1995, c. 538, s. 7(c); 2015-117, s. 1

§ 52C-8-802. Conditions of rendition

(a) Before making demand that the governor of another state surrender an individual charged criminally in this State with having failed to provide for the support of an obligee, the Governor of this State may require a prosecutor of this State to demonstrate that at least 60 days previously the obligee has initiated proceedings for support pursuant to this Chapter or that the proceeding would be of no avail.

(b) If, under this Chapter or a law substantially similar to this Chapter, the governor of another state makes a demand that the Governor of this State surrender an individual charged criminally in that state with having failed to provide for the support of a child or other individual to whom a duty of support is owed, the governor may require a prosecutor to investigate the demand and report whether a proceeding for support has been initiated or would be effective. If it appears that a proceeding would be effective but has not been initiated, the governor may delay honoring the demand for a reasonable time to permit the initiation of a proceeding.

(c) If a proceeding for support has been initiated and the individual whose rendition is demanded prevails, the governor may decline to honor the demand. If the petitioner prevails and the individual whose rendition is demanded is subject to a support order, the governor may decline to honor the demand if the individual is complying with the support order.

History.
1995, c. 538, s. 7(c); 2015-117, s. 1

ARTICLE 9
MISCELLANEOUS PROVISIONS

§ 52C-9-901. Uniformity of application and construction

In applying and construing this uniform act, consideration must be given to the need to promote uniformity of the law with respect to its subject matter among states that enact it.

History.
1995, c. 538, s. 7(c); 2015-117, s. 1

§ 52C-9-901.1. Transitional provision

This Chapter applies to proceedings begun on or after the effective date of this Chapter to establish a support order or determine parentage of a child or to register, recognize, enforce, or modify a prior support order, determination, or agreement, whenever issued or entered.

History.
2015-117, s. 1

§ 52C-9-902. Severability clause

If any provision of this Chapter or its application to any person or circumstance is held invalid, the invalidity does not affect other provisions or applications of this Chapter which can be given effect without the invalid provision or application, and to this end the provisions of this Chapter are severable.

History.
1995, c. 538, s. 7(c)

CHAPTER 58
INSURANCE

ARTICLE 2
COMMISSIONER OF INSURANCE

§ 58-2-161. False statement to procure or deny benefit of insurance policy or certificate

(a) For the purposes of this section:

(1) "Insurer" has the same meaning as in G.S. 58-1-5(3) and also includes:

a. Any hull insurance and protection and indemnity club operating under Article 20 of this Chapter.

b. Any surplus lines insurer operating under Article 21 of this Chapter.

c. Any risk retention group or purchasing group operating under Article 22 of this Chapter.

d. Any local government risk pool operating under Article 23 of this Chapter.

e. Any risk-sharing plan operating under Article 42 of this Chapter.

f. The North Carolina Insurance Underwriting Association operating under Article 45 of this Chapter.

g. The North Carolina Joint Insurance Underwriting Association operating under Article 46 of this Chapter.

h. The North Carolina Insurance Guaranty Association operating under Article 48 of this Chapter.

i. Any multiple employer welfare arrangement operating under Article 50A of this Chapter.

j. The North Carolina Life and Health Insurance Guaranty Association operating under Article 62 of this Chapter.

k. Any service corporation operating under Article 65 of this Chapter.

l. Any health maintenance organization operating under Article 67 of this Chapter.

m. The State Health Plan for Teachers and State Employees and any optional plans or programs operating under Part 2 of Article 3 of Chapter 135 of the General Statutes.

n. A group of employers self-insuring their workers' compensation liabilities under Article 47 of this Chapter.

o. An employer self-insuring its workers' compensation liabilities under Article 5 of Chapter 97 of the General Statutes.

p. The North Carolina Self-Insurance Security Association under Article 4 of Chapter 97 of the General Statutes.

q. Any reinsurer licensed or accredited under this Chapter.

(2) "Statement" includes any application, notice, statement, proof of loss, bill of lading, receipt for payment, invoice, account, estimate of property damages, bill for services, diagnosis, prescription, hospital or doctor records, X rays, test result, or other evidence of loss, injury, or expense.

(b) Any person who, with the intent to injure, defraud, or deceive an insurer or insurance claimant:

(1) Presents or causes to be presented a written or oral statement, including computer-generated documents as part of, in support of, or in opposition to, a claim for payment or other benefit pursuant to an insurance policy, knowing that the statement contains false or misleading information concerning any fact or matter material to the claim, or

(2) Assists, abets, solicits, or conspires with another person to prepare or make any written or oral statement that is intended to be presented to an insurer or insurance claimant in connection with, in support of, or in opposition to, a claim for payment or other benefit pursuant to an insurance policy, knowing that the statement contains false or misleading information concerning a fact or matter material to the claim

is guilty of a Class H felony. Each claim shall be considered a separate count. Upon conviction, if the court imposes probation, the court may order the defendant to pay restitution as a condition of probation. In determination of the amount of restitution pursuant to G.S. 15A-1343(d), the reasonable costs and attorneys' fees incurred by the victim in the investigation of, and efforts to recover damages arising from, the claim, may be considered part of the damage caused by the defendant arising out of the offense.

In a civil cause of action for recovery based upon a claim for which a defendant has been convicted under this section, the conviction may be entered into evidence against the defendant. The court may award the prevailing party compensatory damages, attorneys' fees, costs, and reasonable investigative costs. If the prevailing party can demonstrate that the defendant has engaged in a pattern of violations of this section, the court may award treble damages.

History.

1899, c. 54, s. 60; Rev., s. 3487; 1913, c. 89, s. 28; C.S., s. 4369; 1937, c. 248; 1967, c. 1088, s. 1; 1979, c. 760, s. 5; 1989 (Reg. Sess., 1990), c. 1054, s. 2; 1995, c. 43, s. 1; 1999-294, s. 3; 2005-400, s. 17; 2007-298, s. 8.1; 2007-323, s. 28.22A(o); 2007-345, s. 12; 2019-202, s. 8

§ 58-2-162. Embezzlement by insurance agents, brokers, or administrators

If any insurance agent, broker, or administrator embezzles or fraudulently converts to his own use, or, with intent to use or embezzle, takes, secretes, or otherwise disposes of, or fraudulently withholds, appropriates, lends, invests, or otherwise uses or applies any money, negotiable instrument, or other consideration received by him in his performance as an agent, broker, or administrator, he shall be guilty of a felony. If the value of the money, negotiable instrument, or other consideration is one hundred thousand dollars ($ 100,000) or more, violation of this section is a Class C felony. If the value of the money, negotiable instrument, or other consideration is less than one hundred thousand dollars ($ 100,000), violation of this section is a Class H felony.

History.

1889, c. 54, s. 103; Rev., s. 3489; 1911, c. 196, s. 8; C.S., s. 4274; 1989 (Reg. Sess., 1990), c. 1054, s. 2; 1997-443, s. 19.25(n)

§ 58-2-163. Report to Commissioner

Whenever any insurance company, or employee or representative of such company, or any other person licensed or registered under Articles 1 through 67 of this Chapter knows or has reasonable cause to believe that any other person has violated G.S. 58-2-161, 58-2-162, 58-2-164, 58-2-180, 58-8-1, 58-24-180(e), or whenever any insurance company, or employee or representative of such company, or any other person licensed or registered under Articles 1 through 67 of this Chapter knows or has reasonable cause to believe that any entity licensed by the Commissioner is financially impaired, it is the duty of such person, upon acquiring such knowledge, to notify the Commissioner and provide the Commissioner with a complete statement of all of the relevant facts and circumstances. Such report is a privileged communication, and when made without actual malice does not subject the person making the same to any liability whatsoever. The Commissioner may suspend, revoke, or refuse to renew the license of any licensee who willfully fails to comply with this section.

History.

1945, c. 382; 1987, c. 752, s. 2; 1989 (Reg. Sess., 1990), c. 1054, s. 2; 2007-443, s. 4

§ 58-2-180. Punishment for making false statement

If any person in any financial or other statement required by this Chapter willfully misstates information, that person making oath to or subscribing the statement is guilty of a Class I felony; and the entity on whose behalf the person made the oath or subscribed the statement is subject to a fine imposed by the court of not less than two thousand dollars ($ 2,000) nor more than ten thousand dollars ($ 10,000).

History.

1899, c. 54, s. 97; Rev., s. 3493; C.S., s. 6281; 1985, c. 666, s. 13; 1989 (Reg. Sess., 1990), c. 1054, s. 5; 1993 (Reg. Sess., 1994), c. 767, s. 23

ARTICLE 24
FRATERNAL BENEFIT SOCIETIES

§ 58-24-180. Penalties

(a) Any person, officer, member, or examining physician of any society authorized to do business under this Article who shall knowingly or willfully make any false or fraudulent statement or representation in or with reference to any application for membership, or for the purpose of obtaining money from or benefit in any society transacting business under this Article, shall be guilty of a Class 1 misdemeanor.

(b) Any person who shall solicit membership for, or in any manner assist in procuring membership in any fraternal benefit society not licensed to do business in this State, or who shall solicit membership for, or in any manner assist in procuring membership in any such society not authorized as herein provided to do business as herein defined in this State, shall be guilty of a Class 3 misdemeanor and upon conviction thereof shall be punished only by a fine of not less than one thousand dollars ($ 1,000) nor more than five thousand dollars ($ 5,000).

(c) Any society, or any officer, agent, or employee thereof, neglecting or refusing to comply with, or violating, any of the provisions of this Article, the penalty for which neglect, refusal, or violation is not specified in this section, shall be guilty of a Class 3 misdemeanor, and upon conviction shall be punished only by a fine not to exceed five thousand dollars ($ 5,000).

(d) Any person violating the provisions of G.S. 58-24-65 shall be guilty of a Class I felony.

(e) Any person who willfully makes any false statement under oath in any verified report or declaration that is required by law from fraternal benefit societies, is guilty of a Class I felony.

History.
1987, c. 483, s. 2; 1989 (Reg. Sess., 1990), c. 1054, s. 3; 1993, c. 539, ss. 451, 1273; 1994, Ex. Sess., c. 24, s. 14(c); 1993 (Reg. Sess., 1994), c. 767, s. 25

ARTICLE 36
NORTH CAROLINA RATE BUREAU

§ 58-36-75. At-fault accidents and certain moving traffic violations under the Safe Driver Incentive Plan

(a) The subclassification plan promulgated pursuant to G.S. 58-36-65(b) may provide for separate surcharges for major, intermediate, and minor accidents. A "major accident" is an at-fault accident that results in either (i) bodily injury or death or (ii) only property damage of three thousand eight hundred fifty dollars ($ 3,850) or more. An "intermediate accident" is an at-fault accident that results in only property damage of more than two thousand three hundred dollars ($ 2,300) but less than three thousand eight hundred fifty dollars ($ 3,850). A "minor accident" is an at-fault accident that results in only property damage of two thousand three hundred dollars ($ 2,300) or less. The subclassification plan may also exempt certain minor accidents from the Facility recoupment surcharge. The Bureau shall assign varying Safe Driver Incentive Plan point values and surcharges for bodily injury in at-fault accidents that are commensurate with the severity of the injury, provided that the point value and surcharge assigned for the most severe bodily injury shall not exceed the point value and surcharge assigned to a major accident involving only property damage.

(a1) The subclassification plan shall provide that there shall be no premium surcharge, increase in premium on account of cession to the Reinsurance Facility, or assessment of points against an insured where: (i) the insured is involved and is at fault in a "minor accident," as defined in subsection (a) of this section; (ii) the insured is not convicted of a moving traffic violation in connection with the accident; (iii) neither the vehicle owner, principal operator, nor any licensed operator in the owner's household has a driving record consisting of one or more convictions for a moving traffic violation or one or more at-fault accidents during the three-year period immediately preceding the date of the application for a policy or the date of the preparation of the renewal of a policy; and (iv) the insured has been covered by liability insurance with the same company or company group continuously for at least the six months immediately preceding the accident. Notwithstanding

(iv) of this subsection, if the insured has been covered by liability insurance with the same company or company group for at least six continuous months, some or all of which were after the accident, the insurance company shall remove any premium surcharge or assessment of points against the insured if requirements (i), (ii), and (iii) of this subsection are met. Also notwithstanding (iv) of this subsection, an insurance company may choose not to assess a premium surcharge or points against an insured who has been covered by liability insurance with that company or with the company's group for less than six months immediately preceding the accident, if requirements (i), (ii), and (iii) are met.

(a2) The subclassification plan shall provide that there shall be no premium surcharge or assessment of points against an insured where (i) the insured's driver's license has been revoked under G.S. 20-16.5; and (ii) the insured is subsequently acquitted of the offense involving impaired driving, as defined in G.S. 20-4.01(24a), that is related to the revocation, or the charge for that offense is dismissed. In addition, no insurer shall use, for rating, underwriting, or classification purposes, including ceding any risk to the Facility or writing any kind of coverage subject to this Article, any license revocation under G.S. 20-16.5 if the insured is acquitted or the charge is dismissed as described in this subsection.

(b) Repealed by Session Laws 1999-294, s. 12(a), effective July 14, 1999.

(c) Repealed by Session Laws 1999-132, s. 8.1, effective June 4, 1999.

(d) There shall be no Safe Driver Incentive Plan surcharges under G.S. 58-36-65 for accidents occurring when only operating a firefighting, rescue squad, or law enforcement vehicle in accordance with G.S. 20-125(b) and in response to an emergency if the operator of the vehicle at the time of the accident was a paid or volunteer member of any fire department, rescue squad, or any law enforcement agency. This exception does not include an accident occurring after the vehicle ceases to be used in response to the emergency and the emergency ceases to exist.

(e) Repealed by Session Laws 1999-294, s. 12(a), effective July 14, 1999.

(f) The subclassification plan shall provide that with respect to a conviction for a "violation of speeding 10 miles per hour or less over the speed limit" there shall be no premium surcharge nor any assessment of points unless there is a driving record consisting of a conviction or convictions for a moving traffic violation or violations, except for a prayer for judgment continued for any moving traffic violation, during the three years immediately preceding the date of application or the preparation of the renewal. The subclassification plan shall also provide that with respect to a prayer for judgment continued for any moving traffic violation, there shall be no premium surcharge nor any assessment of points unless the vehicle owner, principal operator, or any licensed operator in the owner's household has a driving record consisting of a prayer or prayers for judgment continued for any moving traffic violation or violations during the three years immediately preceding the date of application or the preparation of the renewal. For the purpose of this subsection, a "prayer for judgment continued" means a determination of guilt by a jury or a court though no sentence has been imposed. For the purpose of this subsection, a "violation of speeding 10 miles per hour or less over the speed limit" does not include the offense of speeding in a school zone in excess of the posted school zone speed limit.

(f1) The subclassification plan shall provide that in the event an insured is at fault in an accident and is convicted of a moving traffic violation in connection with the accident, only the higher plan premium surcharge between the accident and the conviction shall be assessed on the policy.

(g) As used in this section "conviction" means a conviction as defined in G.S. 20-279.1 and means an infraction as defined in G.S. 14-3.1.

(h) The North Carolina Rate Bureau shall assign one insurance point under the Safe Driver Incentive Plan for persons who fail to yield to a pedestrian under G.S. 20-158(b)(2)b.

History.
1987, c. 869, s. 6; 1991, c. 101, s. 1; c. 713, s. 1; c. 720, s. 90; 1991 (Reg. Sess., 1992), c. 837, s. 11; c. 997, s. 1; 1993, c. 285, s. 11; 1995 (Reg. Sess., 1996), c. 730, s. 3; 1997-332, s. 1; 1997-443, s. 19.26(d); 1999-132, s. 8.1; 1999-294, s. 12(a), (b); 2003-137, s. 1; 2004-172, s. 4; 2015-241, s. 20.3(a); 2015-268, s. 7.1; 2016-78, s. 1.1

ARTICLE 39
CONSUMER AND CUSTOMER INFORMATION PRIVACY

PART 2
ENFORCEMENT, SANCTIONS, REMEDIES, AND RIGHTS

§ 58-39-115. Obtaining information under false pretenses

Any person who knowingly and willfully obtains information about an individual from an insurance institution, agent, or insurance-support organization under false pretenses shall, upon conviction, be guilty of a Class 1 misdemeanor.

History.
1981, c. 846, s. 1; 1985, c. 666, s. 33; 1993, c. 539, s. 465; 1994, Ex. Sess., c. 24, s. 14(c); 2003-262, s. 2(2)

ARTICLE 71
BAIL BONDSMEN AND RUNNERS

§ 58-71-1. Definitions

The following definitions apply in this Article:

(1) **Accommodation bondsman.** -- A person who shall not charge a fee or receive any consideration for action as surety and who endorses the bail bond after providing satisfactory evidences of ownership, value, and marketability of real or personal property to the extent necessary to reasonably satisfy the official taking bond that the real or personal property will in all respects be sufficient to assure that the full principal sum of the bond will be realized if there is a breach of the conditions of the bond. "Consideration" as used in this subdivision does not include the legal rights of a surety against a principal by reason of breach of the conditions of a bail bond nor does it include collateral furnished to and securing the surety as long as the value of the surety's rights in the collateral do not exceed the principal's liability to the surety by reason of a breach in the conditions of the bail bond.

(1a) **Approved provider.** -- A person or entity whose certificate of authority issued by the Commissioner to provide either bail bond continuing education or prelicensing courses in this state in accordance with G.S. 58-71-72 was in effect on May 15, 2015, and remains in effect. The certificate of authority issued by the Commissioner to any such person or entity is not transferable or assignable to any other person or entity nor are the benefits or any part thereof transferable or assignable to any other person or entity.

(2) **Bail bond.** -- An undertaking by the principal to appear in court as required upon penalty of forfeiting bail to the State in a stated amount; and may include an unsecured appearance bond, a premium-secured appearance bond, an appearance bond secured by a cash deposit of the full amount of the bond, an appearance bond secured by a mortgage pursuant to G.S. 58-74-5, and an appearance bond secured by at least one surety. A bail bond may also include a bond securing the return of a motor vehicle subject to forfeiture in accordance with G.S. 20-28.3(e).

(3) **Bail bondsman.** -- A surety bondsman, professional bondsman or an accommodation bondsman as defined in this section.

(4) **Commissioner.** -- The North Carolina Commissioner of Insurance.

(4a) **First-year licensee.** -- Any person who has been licensed as a bail bondsman or runner under this Article and who has held the license for a period of less than 12 months.

(5) **Insurer.** -- Any domestic, foreign, or alien surety company which has qualified generally to transact surety business and specifically to transact bail bond business in this State.

(6) **Obligor.** -- A principal or a surety on a bail bond.

(6a) **Premium.** -- An amount of money paid in exchange for a bail bondsman's services in writing a bail bond.

(7) **Principal.** -- A defendant or witness obligated to appear in court as required upon penalty of forfeiting bail under a bail bond or a person obligated to return a motor vehicle subject to forfeiture in accordance with G.S. 20-28.3(e).

(8) **Professional bondsman.** -- Any person who is approved and licensed by the Commissioner and who pledges cash or approved securities with the Commissioner as security for bail bonds written in connection with a judicial proceeding and who receives or is promised money or other things of value in exchange for writing the bail bonds.

(8a) **Resident.** -- A person who lives in this State for at least six consecutive months immediately before applying for a license under this Article.

(9) **Runner.** -- A person employed by a bail bondsman for the purpose of assisting the bail bondsman in presenting the defendant in court when required, assisting in the apprehension and surrender of defendant to the court, keeping the defendant under necessary surveillance, or executing bonds on behalf of the licensed bondsman when the power of attorney has been duly recorded. "Runner" does not include a duly licensed attorney-at-law or a law-enforcement officer assisting a bondsman.

(9a) **Supervising bail bondsman.** -- Any person licensed by the Commissioner as a professional bondsman or surety bondsman who employs or contracts with any new licensee under this Article.

(10) **Surety.** -- One who, with the principal, is liable for the amount of the bail bond upon forfeiture of bail.

(11) **Surety bondsman.** -- Any person who is licensed by the Commissioner as a surety bondsman under this Article, is appointed by an insurer by power of attorney to execute or countersign bail bonds for the insurer in connection with judicial proceedings, and who receives or is promised consideration for doing so.

History.
1963, c. 1225, s. 1; 1975, c. 619, s. 1; 1995 (Reg. Sess., 1996), c. 726, s. 1; 1998-182, s. 16; 2000-180, ss. 1, 2; 2001-269, s. 2.1; 2007-228, s. 1; 2015-247, s. 13(a); 2019-179, s. 7(a)

§ 58-71-5. Commissioner of Insurance to administer Article; rules and regulations; employees; evidence of Commissioner's actions

(a) The Commissioner shall have full power and authority to administer the provisions of this Article, which regulates bail bondsmen and runners and to that end to adopt and promulgate rules and regulations to enforce the purposes and provisions of this Article. Subject to the provisions of the North Carolina Human Resources Act, the Commissioner may employ and discharge such employees, examiners, investigators and such other assistants as shall be deemed necessary, and he shall prescribe their duties.

(b) Any written instrument purporting to be a copy of any action, proceeding, or finding of fact by the Commissioner, or any record of the Commissioner authenticated under the head of the Commissioner by the seal of his office shall be accepted by all the courts of this State as prima facie evidence of the contents thereof.

History.
1963, c. 1225, s. 2; 1975, c. 619, s. 1; 2013-382, s. 9.1(c)

§ 58-71-10. Defects not to invalidate undertakings; liability not affected by agreement or lack of qualifications

(a) No undertaking shall be invalid because of any defect of form, omission or recital or of condition, failure to note or record the default of any principal or surety, or because of any other irregularity, if it appears from the tenor of the undertaking before what magistrate or at what court the principal was bound to appear, and that the official before whom it was entered into was legally authorized to take it and the amount of bail is stated.

(b) The liability of a person on an undertaking shall not be affected by reason of the lack of any qualifications, sufficiency or competency provided in the criminal procedure law, or by reason of any other agreement whether or not the agreement is expressed in the undertaking, or because the defendant has not joined in the undertaking.

History.

1963, c. 1225, s. 3; 1975, c. 619, s. 1; 2001-269, s. 2.2

§ 58-71-15. Qualifications of sureties on bail

Each and every surety for the release of a person on bail shall be qualified as:

(1) An insurer and represented by a surety bondsman or bondsmen; or

(2) A professional bondsman; or

(3) An accommodation bondsman.

History.

1963, c. 1225, s. 4; 1971, c. 1231, s. 1; 1975, c. 619, s. 1

§ 58-71-16. No return of premium; bond reduction

Notwithstanding any other provision of law or rules adopted by the Commissioner under this Article, if, after an agreement has been entered into between a defendant and a surety, the defendant's bond is reduced, the surety shall not be required to return any portion of the premium to the defendant.

History.

2011-377, s. 1

§ 58-71-20. Surrender of defendant by surety; when premium need not be returned

At any time before there has been a breach of the undertaking in any type of bail or fine and cash bond the surety may surrender the defendant to the sheriff of the county in which the defendant is bonded to appear or to the sheriff where the defendant was bonded; in such case the full premium shall be returned within 72 hours after the surrender. The defendant may be surrendered without the return of premium for the bond if the defendant does any of the following:

(1) Willfully fails to pay the premium to the surety or willfully fails to make a premium payment under the agreement specified in G.S. 58-71-167.

(2) Changes his or her address without notifying the surety before the address change.

(3) Physically hides from the surety.

(4) Leaves the State without the permission of the surety.

(5) Violates any order of the court.

(6) Fails to disclose information or provides false information regarding any failure to appear in court, any previous felony convictions within the past 10 years, or any charges pending in any State or federal court.

(7) Knowingly provides the surety with incorrect personal identification, or uses a false name or alias.

History.

1963, c. 1225, s. 5; 1975, c. 619, s. 1; 1998-211, s. 30; 2001-269, s. 2.3; 2007-399, s. 1

§ 58-71-25. Procedure for surrender.

After there has been a breach of the undertaking in a bail bond, the surety may surrender the defendant as provided in G.S. 15A-540.

History.

1963, c. 1225, s. 6; 1975, c. 619, s. 1; 2000-133, s. 7

§ 58-71-30. Arrest of defendant for purpose of surrender

For the purpose of surrendering the defendant, the surety may arrest him before the forfeiture of the undertaking, or by his written authority endorsed on a certified copy of the undertaking, may request any judicial officer to order arrest of the defendant.

History.

1963, c. 1225, s. 7; 1975, c. 619, s. 1

§ 58-71-35. Forfeiture of bail

(a) Except for bonds issued to secure the return of a motor vehicle subject to forfeiture in accordance with G.S. 20-28.3(e), the procedure for forfeiture of bail shall be that provided in Article 26 of Chapter 15A of the General Statutes and all provisions of that Article shall continue in full force and effect.

(b) At any time before execution is issued on a judgment of forfeiture against a principal or his surety, the court may direct that the judgment be remitted in whole or in part, upon such conditions as the court may impose, if it appears that justice requires the remission of part or all of the judgment.

History.

1963, c. 1225, s. 8; 1975, c. 619, s. 1; 1998-182, s. 17

§ 58-71-40. Bail bondsmen and runners to be qualified and licensed; license applications generally

(a) No person shall act in the capacity of a professional bondsman, surety bondsman, or runner or perform any of the functions, duties, or powers prescribed for professional bondsmen, surety bondsmen, or runners under this Article unless that person is qualified and licensed under this Article. No license shall be issued under this Article except to an individual natural person.

(b) The applicant shall apply for a license on forms prepared and supplied by the Commissioner. The Commissioner may propound any reasonable interrogatories to an applicant for a license under this Article about the applicant's qualifications, residence, prospective place of business, and any other matters that the Commissioner considers necessary to protect the public and ascertain the qualifications of the applicant. The Commissioner may also conduct any reasonable inquiry or investigation relative to the determination of the applicant's fitness to be licensed or to continue to be licensed.

(c) A person whose application is denied may reapply, but the Commissioner shall not consider more than one application submitted by the same person within any one-year period.

(d) When a license is issued under this section, the Commissioner shall issue a picture identification card, of design, size, and content approved by the Commissioner, to the licensee. Each licensee must carry this card at all times when working in the scope of the licensee's employment. A licensee whose license terminates or is terminated shall surrender the identification card to the Commissioner within 10 working days after the termination. The Commissioner may contract directly with persons for the processing and issuance of picture identification cards required by this section and may charge a reasonable fee in addition to the license fee charged under G.S. 58-71-55 in an amount that offsets the cost of the service, including the costs associated with the contract authorized by this subsection. Contracts entered into pursuant to this subsection shall not be subject to Article 3 of Chapter 143 of the General Statutes. However, the Commissioner shall: (i) submit all proposed contracts for supplies, materials, printing, equipment, and contractual services that exceed one million dollars ($ 1,000,000) authorized by this subsection to the Attorney General or the Attorney General's designee for review as provided in G.S. 114-8.3; and (ii) include in all contracts to be awarded by the Commissioner under this subsection a standard clause which provides that the State Auditor and internal auditors of the Commissioner may audit the records of the contractor during and after the term of the contract to verify accounts and data affecting fees and performance. The Commissioner shall not award a cost plus percentage of cost agreement or contract for any purpose.

(d1) While engaged in official duties, a licensee is authorized to carry, possess, and display a shield as described in this subsection. The shield shall fulfill all of the following requirements:

(1) Be an exact duplicate in size, shape, color, and design of the shield approved

under G.S. 74C-5(12) and pictured in 12 NCAC 07D. 0405 on May 1, 2013, except that the design may be altered by stamping, inlaying, embossing, enameling, or engraving to accommodate the license number. With respect to size of the shield, the shield shall be 1.88 inches wide and 2.36 inches high.

(2) Include the licensee's last name and corresponding license number in the same locations as the shield referenced in subdivision (1) of this subsection.

(3) With reference to the shield described in subdivision (1) of this subsection, in lieu of the word "Private," the shield shall have the words "North Carolina," and in lieu of the word "Investigator," the shield shall have the words "Bail Agent."

Any shield that deviates from the design requirements as specified in this section shall be an unauthorized shield and its possession by a licensee shall constitute a violation of the statute by the licensee.

(e) This section does not prohibit the hiring of personnel by a bail bondsman to perform only normal office duties. As used in this subsection, "normal office duties" do not include acting as a bail bondsman or runner.

History.
1963, c. 1225, s. 9; 1975, c. 619, s. 1; 1995 (Reg. Sess., 1996), c. 726, s. 2; 2001-269, s. 2.4; 2007-507, s. 11; 2010-194, s. 10; 2011-326, s. 15(j); 2013-209, s. 1; 2014-120, s. 12(a)

§ 58-71-41. First-year licensees; limitations

(a) Except as provided in this section, a first-year licensee shall have the same authority as other persons licensed as bail bondsmen or runners under this Article. Except as provided in subsection (d) of this section, a first-year licensee shall operate only under the supervision of and from the official business address of a licensed supervising bail bondsman for the first 12 months of licensure. A first-year licensee may only be employed by or contract with one supervising bail bondsman.

(b) When a first-year licensee has completed 12 months of supervision, six of which shall be uninterrupted, the supervising bail bondsman shall give notice of that fact to the Commissioner in writing. If the licensee will continue to be employed by or contract with the supervising bail bondsman beyond the initial 12-month period, the supervising bail bondsman shall continue to supervise and be responsible for the licensee's acts.

(c) If the employment of or contract with a first-year licensee is terminated, the supervising bail bondsman shall notify the Commissioner in writing and shall specify the reason for the termination.

(d) If, after exercising due diligence, a first-year licensed bail bondsman is unable to become employed by or to contract with a supervising bail bondsman, the first-year licensed bail bondsman must submit to the Department a sworn affidavit stating the relevant facts and circumstances regarding the first-year licensed bail bondman's inability to become employed by or contract with a supervising bail bondsman. The Department shall review the affidavit and determine whether the first-year licensed bail bondsman will be allowed to operate as an unsupervised bail bondsman. A first-year licensed bail bondsman is prohibited from becoming a supervising bail bondsman during the first two years of licensure.

(e) Provided all other licensing requirements are met, an applicant for a bail bondsman or runner's license who has previously been licensed with the Commissioner for a period of at least 18 consecutive months and who has been inactive or unlicensed for a period of not more than three consecutive years shall not be deemed a new licensee for purposes of this section.

History.
2000-180, s. 3

§ 58-71-45. Terms of licenses

A license issued to a bail bondsman or to a runner authorizes the licensee to act in that capacity until the license is lapsed, suspended or revoked. The licensee shall return the license to the Commissioner within 10 working days of the lapse, suspension, or revocation of the license. A license of a bail bondsman and a license of a runner shall be renewed in accordance with G.S. 58-71-75. After notifying the Commissioner in writing, a professional bondsman who employs a runner may cancel the runner's authority to act for the professional bondsman.

History.
1963, c. 1225, s. 10; 1975, c. 619, s. 1; 1995 (Reg. Sess., 1996), c. 726, s. 3; 2009-536, ss. 1, 6; 2009-566, s. 14; 2019-179, s. 7(b)

§ 58-71-50. Qualification for bail bondsmen and runners

(a) **Criminal History Record Check. --** Upon receipt of an application for a license as a bail bondsman or runner, the Commissioner shall conduct a criminal history record check in accordance with G.S. 58-71-51 to determine whether the applicant meets the requirements for a license as provided in this section.

(b) **Qualifications. --** Every applicant for a license under this Article as a bail bondsman or runner must meet all of the following qualifications:

(1) Be 21 years of age or over.

(1a) Have obtained a high school diploma or its equivalent.

(2) Be a resident of this State.

(3) Repealed by Session Laws 1998-211, s. 23, effective November 1, 1998.

(4) Have knowledge, training, or experience of sufficient duration and extent to provide the competence necessary to fulfill the responsibilities of a licensee.

(5) Have no outstanding bail bond obligations.

(6) Have no current or prior violations of any provision of this Article or of Article 26 of Chapter 15A of the General Statutes or of any similar provision of law of any other state.

(7) Not have been in any manner disqualified under the laws of this State or any other state to engage in the bail bond business.

(8) Hold a valid and current North Carolina drivers license or valid North Carolina identification card issued by the Division of Motor Vehicles.

(c) **Proof of Residency. --** An applicant for a license as a bail bondsman or runner shall provide to the Commissioner at least two of the documents listed in this subsection as proof of residency in this State. Subject to rules adopted by the Commissioner, an applicant may be required to provide additional documentation. The permissible documents are:

(1) A pay stub showing the applicant's residential address in this State.

(2) A utility bill showing the applicant's residential address in this State.

(3) A written lease agreement or contract for purchase and sale signed by the applicant and for a residence located in this State.

(4) A receipt for personal property taxes paid by the applicant to a North Carolina unit of local government.

(5) A receipt for real property taxes paid by the applicant to a North Carolina unit of local government.

(6) A monthly or quarterly statement showing the applicant's residential address in this State and issued by a financial institution for an account held by the applicant.

History.
1963, c. 1225, s. 11; 1971, c. 1231, s. 1; 1975, c. 619, s. 1; 1987, c. 728, s. 1; 1989, c. 485, s. 39; 1991, c. 720, s. 41; 1995 (Reg. Sess., 1996), c. 726, s. 4; 1998-211, s. 23; 2007-228, ss. 2, 3; 2009-536, ss. 2, 6; 2009-566, s. 12; 2015-180, s. 1

§ 58-71-51. Criminal history record checks

(a) **Authorization.** -- The Department of Public Safety may provide a criminal history record check to the Commissioner for a person who has applied to the Commissioner for a new or renewal license as a bail bondsman or runner. The Commissioner shall provide to the Department of Public Safety, along with the request, the fingerprints of the new or renewal applicant. The applicant shall furnish the Commissioner with a complete set of the applicant's fingerprints in a manner prescribed by the Commissioner. The Department of Public Safety shall provide a criminal history record check based upon the new or renewal applicant's fingerprints. The Commissioner shall provide any additional information required by the Department of Public Safety and a form signed by the applicant consenting to the check of the criminal record and to the use of the fingerprints and other identifying information required by the State or national repositories. The new or renewal applicant's fingerprints shall be forwarded to the State Bureau of Investigation for a search of the State's criminal history record file, and the State Bureau of Investigation shall forward a set of the fingerprints to the Federal Bureau of Investigation for a national criminal history check. The Department of Public Safety may charge each new or renewal applicant a fee for conducting the checks of criminal history records authorized by this subsection.

(b) **Confidentiality.** -- The Commissioner shall keep all information obtained pursuant to this section confidential in accordance with applicable State law and federal guidelines, and the information shall not be a public record under Chapter 132 of the General Statutes.

History.
2009-536, s. 3; 2014-100, s. 17.1(o)

§ 58-71-55. License fees

A nonrefundable license fee of two hundred dollars ($ 200.00) shall be paid to the Commissioner with each application for license as a bail bondsman and a license fee of one hundred twenty dollars ($ 120.00) shall be paid to the Commissioner with each application for license as a runner.

History.
1963, c. 1225, s. 12; 1975, c. 619, s. 1; 1983, c. 790, s. 11; 1991, c. 721, s. 4; 1995 (Reg. Sess., 1996), c. 726, s. 5; 2009-451, s. 21.7(a)

N.C. Gen. Stat. § 58-71-60

Repealed by Session Laws 1995 (Regular Session, 1996), c. 726, s. 6.

§ 58-71-65. Contents of application for runner's license; endorsement by professional bondsman

In addition to the other requirements of this Article, an applicant for a license to be a runner must affirmatively show:

(1) That the applicant will be employed by only one professional bondsman, who will supervise the work of the applicant and be responsible for the runner's conduct in the bail bond business.

(2) That the application is endorsed by the appointing professional bondsman, who must agree in the application to supervise the runner's activities.

(3) Whether or not the applicant has ever been licensed as a bail bondsman or runner. An applicant who has been licensed as a bail bondsman must list all outstanding bail bond obligations. An applicant who has been licensed as a runner must list all prior employment as such, indicating the name of each supervising professional bondsman and the reasons for the termination of the employment.

History.
1963, c. 1225, s. 14; 1975, c. 619, s. 1; 1987, c. 728, s. 2; 1995 (Reg. Sess., 1996), c. 726, s. 7

§ 58-71-70. Examination; fees

Each applicant for a license as a professional bondsman, surety bondsman, or runner shall appear in person and take an examination prepared by the Commissioner testing the applicant's ability and qualifications. Each applicant is eligible for examination 30 days after the date the application is received by the Commissioner. If an applicant is unable to complete the examination requirement within 30 days after notification from the Commissioner of the applicant's eligibility to take the examination, the applicant shall again be subject to the criminal history record check prescribed by G.S. 58-71-50(a) so that current information is available for review with the application. Each examination shall be held at a time and place as designated by the Commissioner. Each applicant shall be given notice of the designated time and place no sooner than 15 days before the examination. The Commissioner may contract with a person to process applications for the examination and administer and grade the examination in the same manner as for agent examinations under Article 33 of this Chapter.

The fee for each examination is twenty-five dollars ($ 25.00) plus an amount that offsets the cost of any contract for examination services. This examination fee is nonrefundable.

An applicant who fails an examination may take a subsequent examination, but at least one year must intervene between examinations.

History.
1963, c. 1225, s. 15; 1975, c. 619, s. 1; 1991, c. 721, s. 5; 1995 (Reg. Sess., 1996), c. 726, s. 8; 2009-566, s. 13

§ 58-71-71. Examination; educational requirements; penalties

(a) In order to be eligible to take the examination required to be licensed as a runner or bail bondsman under G.S. 58-71-70, each person shall complete at least 12 hours of education as provided by an approved provider in subjects pertinent to the duties and responsibilities of a runner or bail bondsman, including all laws and regulations related to being a runner or bail bondsman.

(b) Each year by June 30 every licensee shall complete at least three hours of continuing education as provided by an approved provider in subjects related to the duties and responsibilities of a runner or bail bondsman. This continuing education shall not include a written or oral examination. A person who receives his or her first license on or after January 1 of any year does not have to comply with this subsection until June 30 of the following year.

(c) Any person licensed as a runner or bail bondsman before January 1, 1994, is not subject to the prelicensing education requirement of this section, but is subject to the continuing education requirement of this section. A licensed runner or bail bondsman who is 65 years of age or older and who has been licensed as a runner or bail bondsman for 15 years or more is exempt from both the prelicensing education and continuing education requirements of this section.

(d) Educational courses offered by an approved provider under this section must be approved by the Commissioner before they may be offered. Before approving a course, the Commissioner must be satisfied that the course will enhance the professional competence and professional responsibility of bail bondsmen and runners. Approved providers shall not offer, sponsor, or conduct any course under this section unless the Commissioner has given authorization to do so. The Commissioner shall not authorize educational courses to be offered solely online.

(e) The license of any person who fails to comply with the continuing education requirements under this section shall lapse. The Commissioner may, for good cause shown, grant extensions of time to licensees to comply with these requirements. Any licensee who, after obtaining an extension under this subsection, offers evidence satisfactory to the Commissioner that the licensee has satisfactorily completed the required continuing professional education courses is in compliance with this section.

(f) The Commissioner may adopt rules for the effective administration of this section.

History.
1993, c. 409, s. 22; 1993 (Reg. Sess., 1994), c. 678, s. 32; 1995 (Reg. Sess., 1996), c. 726, s. 9; 1998-211, ss. 25, 26, 28; 2004-124, s. 21.3; 2012-183, s. 1; 2015-247, s. 13(b); 2018-120, s. 4.7

§ 58-71-72. Qualifications of instructors

(a) A person who provides, presents, or instructs a prelicensing course or continuing education course under G.S. 58-71-71 must have a certificate of authority issued by the Commissioner. The Commissioner may establish requirements for the issuance or renewal of a certificate of authority and grounds for the summary suspension or termination of a certificate of authority.

(b) The Commissioner may summarily suspend or terminate a certificate of authority to provide, present, or instruct a course if the Commissioner finds that the course is inaccurate or it received a poor evaluation from both a Department monitor and a majority of those who attended the course and responded to a Department questionnaire about the course.

History.
1995 (Reg. Sess., 1996), c. 726, s. 10

§ 58-71-75. License renewal; criminal history record checks; renewal fees

(a) **Biennial Renewal.** -- A license of a bail bondsman and a license of a runner shall be renewed on July 1 of each even year upon payment of the applicable biennial renewal fee. In addition to paying the biennial renewal fee, an applicant seeking renewal must submit an application for renewal in accordance with this section. The Commissioner is not required to print renewal licenses.

(b) **Renewal Application.** -- In even-numbered years, a bail bondsman or runner seeking to renew a license shall provide the Commissioner prior to the expiration date of the bail bondsman's or runner's current license, all of the following:

(1) A renewal application containing all of the following:

    a. Proof that the applicant is a resident of this State as required by G.S. 58-71-50(c).

    b. Proof that the applicant meets the qualifications set out in G.S. 58-71-50(b)(5) through G.S. 58-71-50(b)(7).

c. The information required by G.S. 58-2-69.

(2) The biennial renewal fee as provided in subsection (d) of this section.

(3) Repealed by Session Laws 2016-107, s. 4, effective July 22, 2016.

(c) **Criminal History Record Check.** -- For every other biennial license renewal cycle, the Commissioner shall conduct a criminal history record check of the applicant seeking renewal in accordance with G.S. 58-71-51. Along with the renewal application requirements provided in subsection (b) of this section, a bail bondsman or runner seeking to renew a license every other biennial license renewal cycle shall provide the Commissioner with a complete set of fingerprints of the bail bondsman or runner and a fee to cover the cost of conducting the criminal history record check. The fingerprints shall be submitted in the manner prescribed by the Commissioner and shall be certified by an authorized law enforcement officer.

(d) **Fee.** -- The renewal fee for a runner's license is one hundred twenty dollars ($ 120.00). The renewal fee for a bail bondsman's license is two hundred dollars ($ 200.00). A renewed license continues in effect until suspended or revoked for cause.

History.

1963, c. 1225, s. 16; 1975, c. 619, s. 1; 1991, c. 721, s. 6; 1995 (Reg. Sess., 1996), c. 726, s. 11; 2009-536, s. 4; 2010-96, s. 10; 2016-107, s. 4

§ 58-71-80. Grounds for denial, suspension, probation, revocation, or nonrenewal of licenses

(a) The Commissioner may deny, place on probation, suspend, revoke, or refuse to renew any license issued under this Article, in accordance with the provisions of Article 3A of Chapter 150B of the General Statutes, for any one or more of the following causes:

(1) For any cause sufficient to deny, suspend, or revoke the license under any other provision of this Article.

(2) A conviction of any misdemeanor committed in the course of dealings under the license issued by the Commissioner.

(3) Material misstatement, misrepresentation or fraud in obtaining the license.

(4) Misappropriation, conversion or unlawful withholding of moneys belonging to insurers or others and received in the conduct of business under the license.

(5) Fraudulent, coercive, or dishonest practices in the conduct of business or demonstrating incompetence, untrustworthiness, or financial irresponsibility in the conduct of business in this State or any other jurisdiction.

(6) Conviction of a crime involving dishonesty, breach of trust, or moral turpitude.

(7) Failure to comply with or violation of the provisions of this Article or of any order, subpoena, rule or regulation of the Commissioner or person with similar regulatory authority in another jurisdiction.

(8) When in the judgment of the Commissioner, the licensee has in the conduct of the licensee's affairs under the license, demonstrated incompetency, financial irresponsibility, or untrustworthiness; or that the licensee is no longer in good faith carrying on the bail bond business; or that the licensee is guilty of rebating, or offering to rebate, or offering to divide the premiums received for the bond.

(9) For failing to pay any judgment or decree rendered on any forfeited undertaking in any court of competent jurisdiction.

(10) For charging or receiving, as premium or compensation for the making of any deposit or bail bond, any sum in excess of that permitted by this Article.

(11) For requiring, as a condition of executing a bail bond, that the principal agree to engage the services of a specified attorney.

(12) For cheating on an examination for a license under this Article.

(13) For entering into any business association or agreement with any person who is at that time found by the Commissioner to be in violation of any of the bail bond laws of this State, or who has been in any manner disqualified under the bail bond laws of this State or any other state, whereby the person has any direct or indirect financial interest in the bail bond business of the licensee or applicant.

(14) For knowingly aiding or abetting others to evade or violate the provisions of this Article.

(14a) Having any professional license denied, suspended, or revoked in this State or any other jurisdiction for causes substantially similar to those listed in this subsection.

(14b) Violation of (i) any law governing bail bonding or insurance in this State or any other jurisdiction or (ii) any rule of the Financial Industry Regulatory Authority (FINRA).

(14c) Failure to comply with an administrative order or court order imposing a child support obligation after entry of a final judgment or order finding the violation to have been willful.

(14d) Failure to pay State or federal income tax or any liens that result from such failure to comply with any administrative or court order directing payment of State or federal income tax after entry of a final judgment or order.

(14e) Forging another's name to any document related to a bail bond transaction.

(15) Any cause for which issuance of the license could have been refused had it then existed and been known to the Commissioner at the time of issuance.

(b) The Commissioner shall deny, revoke, or refuse to renew any license under this Article if the applicant or licensee is or has ever been convicted of a felony.

(b1) The Commissioner shall revoke or refuse to renew any license under this Article if the licensee has been convicted on or after October 1, 2009, of a misdemeanor drug violation under Article 5 of Chapter 90 of the General Statutes.

(b2) The Commissioner shall deny any license under this Article if the applicant has been convicted of a misdemeanor drug violation under Article 5 of Chapter 90 of the General Statutes within the previous 24 months of the date of the application for the license.

(c) In the case of a first-year licensee whose employment or contract is terminated prior to the end of the 12-month supervisory period, the Commissioner may consider all information provided in writing by the supervising bail bondsman in determining whether sufficient cause exists to suspend, revoke, or refuse to renew the license or to warrant criminal prosecution of the first-year licensee. If the Commissioner determines there is not sufficient cause for adverse administrative action or criminal prosecution, the termination shall not be deemed an interruption and the period of time the licensee was employed by or contracted with the terminating supervising bail bondsman will be credited toward the licensee's completion of the required 12 months of supervision with a subsequent supervising bail bondsman.

(d) The Commissioner shall retain the authority to enforce the provisions of, and impose any penalty or remedy authorized by, this Chapter against any person who is under investigation for or charged with a violation of this Chapter even if the person's license or registration has been surrendered or has lapsed.

(e) Notwithstanding the notice and hearing requirements of subsection (a) of this section or G.S. 58-71-85, and in addition to the authority granted to the Commissioner under G.S. 150B-3, the Commissioner may order summary suspension of a license upon a written finding of good cause to believe that emergency action is required to protect the public health, safety, or welfare or to avoid a significant risk of unsatisfied bond forfeitures. The order shall be effective on the date specified in the order or upon service of the certified copy of the order at the last known address of the licensee, whichever is later, and shall remain effective during the

proceedings to suspend, revoke, or refuse renewal provided for in this section. Those proceedings shall be promptly commenced and determined.

History.
1963, c. 1225, s. 17; 1975, c. 619, s. 1; 1989, c. 485, s. 40; 1991, c. 644, s. 17; 1993, c. 409, s. 16; 1998-211, s. 24; 2000-180, s. 4; 2009-536, s. 5; 2011-377, s. 2; 2016-107, s. 3

§ 58-71-81. Notice of receivership

Upon the filing for protection under the United States Bankruptcy Code or any state receivership law by any bail bondsman licensed under this Article or by any bail bond business in which the bondsman holds a position of management or ownership, the bondsman shall notify the Commissioner of the filing for protection within three business days after the filing. Upon the appointment of a receiver by a State or federal court for any professional bondsman licensed under this Article, or for any bail bond business in which the bondsman holds a position of management or ownership, the bondsman shall notify the Commissioner of the filing for protection within three business days after the filing. The failure to notify the Commissioner within three business days after the filing for bankruptcy protection shall, after hearing, cause the license of any person failing to make the required notification to be suspended for a period of not less than 60 days nor more than three years, in the discretion of the Commissioner.

History.
1993, c. 409, s. 17; 1995 (Reg. Sess., 1996), c. 726, s. 12

§ 58-71-82. Dual license holding

If an individual holds a professional bondsman's license or a runner's license and a surety bondsman's license simultaneously, they are considered one license for the purpose of disciplinary actions involving suspension, revocation, or nonrenewal under this Article. Separate renewal fees must be paid for each license, however. Nothing in this Article shall be construed to prohibit a person from simultaneously holding a professional bondsman's license and a runner's license.

History.
1995 (Reg. Sess., 1996), c. 726, ss. 13, 15; 1999-132, s. 5; 2011-377, s. 3

§ 58-71-85. License sanction and denial procedures

(a) The suspension or revocation of, or refusal to renew, any license under G.S. 58-71-80 shall be in accordance with the provisions of Chapter 150B of the General Statutes.

(b) Whenever the Commissioner denies an initial application for a license or an application for a reissuance of a license, the Commissioner shall notify the applicant and advise, in writing, the applicant of the reasons for the denial of the license. The application may also be denied for any reason for which a license may be suspended or revoked or not renewed under G.S. 58-71-80(a). In order for an applicant to be entitled to a review of the Commissioner's action to determine the reasonableness of the action, the applicant must make a written demand upon the Commissioner for a review no later than 30 days after service of the notification upon the applicant. The review shall be completed without undue delay, and the applicant shall be notified promptly in writing of the outcome of the review. In order for an applicant who disagrees with the outcome of the review to be entitled to a hearing under Article 3A of Chapter 150B of the General Statutes, the applicant must make a written demand upon the Commissioner for a hearing no later than 30 days after service upon the applicant of the notification of the outcome.

History.

1963, c. 1225, s. 18; 1975, c. 619, s. 1; 1989, c. 485, s. 33; 1993, c. 504, s. 33; 1998-211, s. 29; 2005-240, s. 2

N.C. Gen. Stat. § 58-71-90

Repealed by Session Laws 1999-132, s. 1.1.

§ 58-71-95. Prohibited practices

No bail bondsman or runner shall:

(1) Pay a fee or rebate or give or promise anything of value, directly or indirectly, to a jailer, law-enforcement officer, committing magistrate, or any other person who has power to arrest or hold in custody, or to any public official or public employee in order to secure a settlement, compromise, remission or reduction of the amount of any bail bond or the forfeiture thereof, including the payment to law-enforcement officers, directly or indirectly, for the arrest or apprehension of a principal or principals who have caused or will cause a forfeiture.

(2) Pay a fee or rebate or give anything of value to an attorney in bail bond matters, except in defense of any action on a bond.

(3) Pay a fee or rebate or give or promise anything of value to the principal or anyone in his behalf.

(4) Participate in the capacity of an attorney at a trial or hearing of one on whose bond he is surety, nor suggest or advise the employment of, or name for employment any particular attorney to represent his principal.

(5) Accept anything of value from a principal or from anyone on behalf of a principal except the premium, which shall not exceed fifteen percent (15%) of the face amount of the bond; provided that the bondsman shall be permitted to accept collateral security or other indemnity from a principal or from anyone on behalf of a principal. Such collateral security or other indemnity required by the bondsman must be reasonable in relation to the amount of the bond and shall be returned within 15 days after final termination of liability on the bond. Any bail bondsman who knowingly and willfully fails to return any collateral security, the value of which exceeds one thousand five hundred dollars ($ 1,500), is guilty of a Class I felony. All collateral security, such as personal and real property, subject to be returned must be done so under the same conditions as requested and received by the bail bondsman.

(6) Solicit business in any of the courts or on the premises of any of the courts of this State, in the office of any magistrate and in or about any place where prisoners are confined. Loitering in or about a magistrate's office or any place where prisoners are confined shall be prima facie evidence of soliciting.

(7) Advise or assist the principal for the purpose of forfeiting bond.

(8) Impersonate a law-enforcement officer.

(9) Falsely represent that the bail bondsman or runner is in any way connected with an agency of the federal government or of a state or local government.

History.

1963, c. 1225, s. 20; 1975, c. 619, s. 1; 1993, c. 409, s. 18; 1995 (Reg. Sess., 1996), c. 726, s. 16; 1998-211, s. 31; 2000-180, s. 5; 2015-180, s. 2

§ 58-71-100. Receipts for collateral; trust accounts

(a) When a bail bondsman accepts collateral he shall give a written receipt for the collateral. The receipt shall give in detail a full description of the collateral received. Collateral security shall be held and maintained in trust. When collateral security is received in the form of cash or check or other negotiable instrument, the licensee shall deposit the cash or instrument within two banking days after receipt, in an established, separate noninterest-bearing trust account in any bank located in North Carolina.

The trust account funds under this section shall not be commingled with other operating funds.

(b) With the approval of the Commissioner, bail bondsmen operating out of the same business office or location may establish a shared trust account for collateral security received by them. The Commissioner may require the bondsmen desiring to establish the shared trust account to furnish the Commissioner information about their business that the Commissioner considers necessary to administer this Article effectively.

History.
1963, c. 1225, s. 21; 1975, c. 619, s. 1; 2000-180, s. 6; 2001-269, s. 2.5

§ 58-71-105. Persons prohibited from becoming surety or runners

No sheriff, deputy sheriff, other law-enforcement officer, judicial official, attorney, parole officer, probation officer, jailer, assistant jailer, employee of the General Court of Justice, nor other public employee assigned to duties relating to the administration of criminal justice, nor the spouse of any such person, may in any case become surety on a bail bond for any person. In addition, no person covered by this section may act as an agent for any bonding company or bail bondsman. No such person may have an interest, directly or indirectly, in the financial affairs of any firm or corporation whose principal business is acting as a bail bondsman. However, nothing in this section prohibits any such person from being surety upon the bond of his or her spouse, parent, brother, sister, child, or descendant.

History.
1963, c. 1225, s. 22; 1973, c. 108, s. 39; 1975, c. 619, s. 1; 1991, c. 644, s. 18; 1995 (Reg. Sess., 1996), c. 726, s. 17

§ 58-71-110. Bonds not to be signed in blank; authority to countersign only given to licensed employee

A bail bondsman shall not sign nor countersign in blank bail bonds, nor shall he give a power of attorney to, or otherwise authorize, anyone to countersign his name to bonds unless the person so authorized is a licensed bondsman or runner directly employed by the bondsman giving such power of attorney. Copies of all such powers of attorney and revocations of such powers of attorney must be filed immediately with the Commissioner and the clerk of superior court of any county in the State where said bondsman giving the power of attorney is currently writing or is obligated on bail bonds.

History.
1963, c. 1225, s. 23; 1975, c. 619, s. 1

§ 58-71-115. Insurers to annually report surety bondsmen; notices of appointments and terminations; information confidential

(a) Before July 1 of each year, every insurer shall furnish the Commissioner a list of all surety bondsmen appointed by the insurer to write bail bonds on the insurer's behalf. An insurer who appoints a surety bondsman in the State on or after July 1 of each year shall notify the Commissioner of the appointment. All appointments are subject to the issuance of the proper license to the appointee under this Article.

(b) An insurer terminating the appointment of a surety bondsman shall file a written notice of the termination with the Commissioner, together with a statement that the insurer has given or mailed notice of the termination to the surety bondsman. The notice to the Commissioner shall state the reasons, if any, for the termination. Information furnished in the notice to the Commissioner shall be privileged and shall not be used as evidence in or basis for any action against the insurer or any of its representatives.

(c) Notwithstanding any other provision of this Article, any documents, materials, or other information in the control or possession of the Commissioner or any organization of which the Commissioner is a member and (i) furnished by an insurer or an employee or agent thereof acting on behalf of the insurer under this section or (ii) obtained by the Commissioner in an investigation under this section shall be confidential by law and privileged, shall not be considered public records under G.S. 58-2-100 or Chapter 132 of the General Statutes, shall not be subject to subpoena, and shall not be subject to discovery in any civil action other than a proceeding brought by the Commissioner against a person to whom the documents, materials, or other information relate. However, the Commissioner may use the documents, materials, or other information in the furtherance of any regulatory or legal action brought as a part of the Commissioner's duties. Neither the Commissioner nor any person who receives documents, materials, or other information while acting under the authority of the Commissioner shall be permitted or required to testify in any civil action other than a proceeding brought by the Commissioner against a person to whom the documents, materials, or other information relate.

History.
1963, c. 1225, s. 24; 1975, c. 619, s. 1; 1995 (Reg. Sess., 1996), c. 726, s. 18; 2007-507, s. 12; 2011-377, s. 4

§ 58-71-120. Bail bondsman to give notice of discontinuance of business; cancellation of license

Any bail bondsman who discontinues writing bail bonds during the period for which the bail bondsman is licensed shall return the license to the Commissioner for cancellation within 30 days after the discontinuance.

History.
1963, c. 1225, s. 25; 1975, c. 619, s. 1; 2009-566, s. 15

§ 58-71-121. Death, incapacitation, or incompetence of a bail bondsman

In the case of death, incapacitation, or incompetence of a licensed bail bondsman, the spouse or surviving spouse, next of kin, person or persons holding a power of attorney, guardian, executor, or administrator of the licensed bail bondsman may contract with another licensed bail bondsman to perform those duties to have the licensee's outstanding bail bond obligations resolved to the satisfaction of the courts. The contract must be filed with the Commissioner and every clerk of superior court where it can be determined the licensee has pending outstanding bail bond obligations. The licensed bail bondsman who has agreed to perform these duties shall not, at the time of the execution of the contract, have any administrative or criminal actions pending against him or her.

History.
2000-180, s. 7

§ 58-71-122. Transfer of business by bail bondsman

A licensed professional bondsman may contract to transfer, convey, or assign the professional bondsman's business to another professional bondsman licensed under this Article. The contract shall include a list of the transferring professional bondsman's pending outstanding bail bond obligations and shall be filed with the Commissioner. The contract shall allow for the transferring professional bondsman to transfer, convey, or assign assets to the purchasing professional bondsman that include, but are not limited to, any pledged cash or any pledged approved securities with the Commissioner as security for bail bonds. Notwithstanding the filing of the contract with the Commissioner, the transferor remains responsible for all outstanding bond obligations until relieved from an individual obligation pursuant to G.S. 15A-534(h), by a substitution of surety pursuant to G.S. 15A-538, or satisfaction of any final judgment of forfeiture entered thereon.

History.
2011-377, s. 5

§ 58-71-125. Persons eligible as runners; bail bondsmen to annually report runners; notices of appointments and terminations; information confidential

Every person duly licensed as a bail bondsman may appoint as runner any person who has been issued runner's license. Each bail bondsman must, on or before July 1 of each year, furnish to the Commissioner a list of all runners appointed by him. Each such bail bondsman who shall, subsequent to the filing of this list, appoint additional persons as runners shall file written notice with the Commissioner of such appointment.

A bail bondsman terminating the appointment of a runner shall file written notice thereof with the Commissioner, together with a statement that he has given or mailed notice to the runner. Such notice filed with the Commissioner shall state the reasons, if any, for such termination. Information so furnished the Commissioner shall be privileged and shall not be used as evidence in any action against the bail bondsman.

History.
1963, c. 1225, s. 26; 1975, c. 619, s. 1

§ 58-71-130. Substituting bail by sureties for deposit

If money or bonds have been deposited, bail by sureties may be substituted therefor at any time before a breach of the undertaking, and the official taking the new bail shall make an order that the money or bonds be refunded to the person depositing the same and they shall be refunded accordingly, and the original undertakings shall be canceled.

History.
1963, c. 1225, s. 27; 1975, c. 619, s. 1

§ 58-71-135. Deposit for defendant admitted to bail authorizes release and cancellation of undertaking

When the defendant has been admitted to bail, he, or another in his behalf, may deposit with an official authorized to take bail, a sum of money, or nonregistered bonds of the United States, or of the State, or of any county, city or town within the State, equal in market value to the amount of such bail, together with his personal undertaking, and an undertaking of such other person, if the money or bonds are deposited by another. Upon delivery to the official in whose custody the defendant is of a certificate

Chapter 58

of such deposit, he shall be discharged from custody in the cause.

When bail other than a deposit of money or bonds has been given, the defendant or the surety may, at any time before a breach of the undertaking, deposit the sum mentioned in the undertaking, and upon such deposit being made, accompanied by a new undertaking, the original undertaking shall be canceled.

History.
1963, c. 1225, s. 28; 1975, c. 619, s. 1

§ 58-71-140. Registration of licenses and power of appointments by insurers

(a) Before the date of the notice provided for in subsection (e) of this section, no professional bail bondsman shall become a surety on an undertaking unless he or she has registered his or her current license in the office of the clerk of superior court in the county in which he or she resides and a certified copy of the same with the clerk of superior court in any other county in which he or she shall write bail bonds.

(b) Before the date of the notice provided for in subsection (e) of this section, a surety bondsman shall register his or her current surety bondsman's license and a certified copy of his or her power of appointment with the clerk of superior court in the county in which the surety bondsman resides and with the clerk of superior court in any other county in which the surety bondsman writes bail bonds on behalf of an insurer.

(c) Before the date of the notice provided for in subsection (e) of this section, no runner shall become surety on an undertaking on behalf of a professional bondsman unless that runner has registered his or her current license and a certified copy of his or her power of attorney in the office of the clerk of superior court in the county in which the runner resides and with the clerk of superior court in any other county in which the runner writes bail bonds on behalf of the professional bondsman.

(c1) On or after the date of the notice provided for in subsection (e) of this section, all licensed professional bail bondsmen, surety bondsmen, and runners shall register in the statewide Electronic Bondsmen Registry in accordance with subsection (e) of this section.

(d) Professional bondsmen, surety bondsmen, and runners shall file with the clerk of court having jurisdiction over the principal an affidavit on a form furnished by the Administrative Office of the Courts. The affidavit shall include, but not be limited to:

(1) If applicable, a statement that the bondsman has not, nor has anyone for the bondsman's use, been promised or received any collateral, security, or premium for executing this appearance bond.

(2) If promised a premium, the amount of the premium promised and the due date.

(3) If the bondsman has received a premium, the amount of premium received.

(4) If given collateral security, the name of the person from whom it is received and the nature and amount of the collateral security listed in detail.

(e) On or before October 1, 2006, the Administrative Office of the Courts shall establish a statewide Electronic Bondsmen Registry (Registry) for all licenses, powers of appointment, and powers of attorney requiring registration under this section. When the Registry is established, the Administrative Office of the Courts shall notify the Commissioner and the Commissioner shall notify all licensed professional bondsmen, surety bondsmen, runners, and qualified insurance companies of the Registry. On or after the date of that notice, a person may register as required under this section by maintaining a record of each required license, power of appointment, or power of attorney in the Registry. After a bondsman, surety bondsman, or runner has completed registration in the Registry, he or she is authorized to execute bail bonds pursuant to his or her registered license, power of appointment, or power of attorney in all counties so long as the registered license, power of appointment, or power of attorney remains in effect.

History.
1963, c. 1225, s. 31; 1975, c. 619, s. 1; 1995 (Reg. Sess., 1996), c. 726, s. 19; 2001-269, s. 2.6; 2006-188, s. 1

§ 58-71-141. Appointment of bail bondsmen; affidavit required

(a) Before receiving an appointment, a surety bondsman shall submit to the Commissioner an affidavit, signed under oath, by the surety bondsman and by any former insurer, stating that the surety bondsman does not owe any premium or unsatisfied judgment to any insurer and that the bondsman agrees to discharge all outstanding forfeitures and judgments on bonds previously written. The affidavit shall be in a form prescribed by the Commissioner and shall be submitted by the surety bondsman to the former insurer. If the surety bondsman does not satisfy or discharge all forfeitures or judgments, the former insurer shall submit a notice, with supporting documents, to the appointing insurer, the surety bondsman, and the Commissioner, which states, under oath, that the surety bondsman has failed to satisfy, in a timely manner, the forfeitures and judgments on bonds written by the surety bondsman and that the former insurer has satisfied the forfeiture or judgment from its own funds. The former insurer shall submit the notice and supporting documents to the appointing insurer, the surety bondsman, and the Commissioner within 30 days after the former insurer receives the affidavit from the surety bondsman. Upon receipt of the notice and supporting documents, the appointing insurer shall immediately cancel the surety bondsman's appointment. The surety bondsman may be reappointed only upon certification by the former insurer that all forfeitures and judgments on bonds written by the surety bondsman have been discharged. The appointing insurer or surety bondsman may, within 10 days after receiving the notice and supporting documents from the former insurer, appeal to the Commissioner.

(b) The Commissioner shall adopt rules, including rules regarding the procedures for appeals and stays of the requirements of this section, to implement this section.

(c) As used in this section, "former insurer" means the insurer with whom the surety bondsman had a prior appointment and who is responsible for any outstanding bonds written by the surety bondsman.

History.
2003-148, s. 1; 2007-507, s. 13

§ 58-71-145. Financial responsibility of professional bondsmen

Each professional bondsman acting as surety on bail bonds in this State shall maintain a deposit of securities with and satisfactory to the Commissioner of a fair market value of at least one-twelfth the amount of all bonds or undertakings written in this State on which he is absolutely or conditionally liable as of the first day of the current month. The amount of this deposit must be reconciled with the bondsman's liabilities as of the first day of the month on or before the fifteenth day of said month and the value of said deposit shall in no event be less than fifteen thousand dollars ($ 15,000).

History.
1963, c. 1225, s. 29; 1975, c. 619, s. 1; 2000-180, s. 8; 2018-38, s. 3

N.C. Gen. Stat. § 58-71-150

Repealed by Session Laws 2005-240, s. 4, effective October 1, 2005, and applicable to all notices of applications denied by the Commissioner served on or after that date and to all notices of review outcomes served on or after that date.

§ 58-71-151. Securities held in trust by Commissioner; authority to dispose of same

The securities deposited by a professional bondsman with the Commissioner shall be held in trust for the protection and benefit of the holder of bail bonds executed by or on behalf of the undersigned bondsman in this State. Notwithstanding any other provision of law, the Commissioner is authorized to select a bank or trust company as master trustee to hold cash securities to be pledged to the State when deposited with the Commissioner pursuant to statute. Securities may be held by the master trustee in any form that in fact perfects the security interest of the State in the securities. The Commissioner shall by rule establish the manner in which the master trust shall operate. The master trustee may charge the person making the deposit reasonable fees for services rendered in connection with the operation of the trust, and the assets of the account may be used to pay such charges.

A pro rata portion of the securities shall be returned to the bondsman when the Commissioner is satisfied that the deposit of securities is in excess of the amount required to be maintained with the Commissioner by said bondsman; and all the securities shall be returned if the Commissioner is satisfied that the bondsman has satisfied, or satisfactory arrangements have been made to satisfy, the obligations of the bondsman on all the bondsman's bail bonds written in the State.

If a bondsman discontinues writing bonds due to death, permanent incapacitation, or some other circumstance that results in the bondsman returning the license issued under this Article to the Commissioner and the Commissioner is satisfied that no more bonds can be written against the bondsman's security deposit, the Commissioner shall return the portion of the security deposit in excess of that required to secure the bondsman's outstanding bond liability.

The Commissioner may sell or transfer any and all of said securities or utilize the proceeds thereof for the purpose of satisfying the liabilities of the professional bondsman on bail bonds given in this State on which the bondsman is liable.

History.
2005-240, s. 3; 2015-180, s. 3

§ 58-71-155. Bondsman to furnish power of attorney with securities

With the securities deposited with the Commissioner, the professional bondsman shall at the same time deliver to the Commissioner of Insurance a power of attorney, on a form supplied by the Commissioner, executed and acknowledged by the professional bondsman authorizing the sale or transfer of said securities or any part thereof. The power of attorney shall read as follows:

POWER OF ATTORNEY

AUTHORIZING THE COMMISSIONER OF INSURANCE TO SELL, OR TRANSFER SECURITIES DEPOSITED BY PROFESSIONAL BONDSMEN IN NORTH CAROLINA.

KNOW ALL MEN BY THESE PRESENTS, That _____, a professional bondsman, located in the County of _____, in the State of _____, has authorized and appointed for himself, his successors, heirs and assigns, the Commissioner of Insurance of the State of North Carolina, in the name and in behalf of said professional bondsman, his true and lawful attorney to sell or transfer any securities deposited or that may be deposited, by said professional bondsman with said Commissioner, under the laws and regulations requiring a deposit of securities to be made by professional bondsmen doing business in the State of North Carolina, insofar as the sale or transfer is deemed necessary by the Commissioner of Insurance to pay any liability arising under a bond which purports to be given by the undersigned bondsman in any county in this State and execution has been issued against said bondsman pursuant to a judgment on the bond and the same has not been satisfied. The securities so deposited are to be held in trust by the Commissioner for the sole protection and benefit of the holder of bail bonds executed by, or on behalf of, the undersigned bondsman. IN WITNESS WHEREOF, I have hereunto set my hand and affixed my seal this _____ day of _____, _____. _____ Professional Bondsman Before me, a Notary Public in and for the State of _____ personally appeared _____, a professional bondsman who acknowledged that he executed the foregoing power of attorney. WITNESS my hand and Notarial Seal, this _____ day of _____, _____. _____ Notary Public My Commission Expires:

History.
1975, c. 619, s. 1; 1999-456, s. 59

§ 58-71-160. Security deposit to be maintained

(a) Any professional bondsman, whose security deposits with the Commissioner are, for any reason, reduced in value below the requirements of this Article, shall immediately upon receipt of a notice of deficiency from the Commissioner deposit such additional securities as are necessary to comply with the law. No professional bondsman shall sign, endorse, execute, or become surety on any additional bail bonds, or pledge or deposit any cash, check, or other security of any nature in lieu of a bail

bond in any county in North Carolina until the professional bondsman has made such additional deposit of securities as required by the notice of deficiency.

(b) The Commissioner may deny the renewal of any license held by a professional bondsman under this Chapter or may deny the issuance of any license applied for by a professional bondsman under this Chapter if, at the time of the renewal application or license application, the professional bondsman has not complied with a notice of deficiency under subsection (a) of this section. The Commissioner may issue the renewal license or the new license upon compliance by the professional bondsman with the notice of deficiency.

History.
1975, c. 619, s. 1; 2001-269, s. 2.7

§ 58-71-165. Report required

(a) Each professional bail bondsman shall file with the Commissioner a written report in a form prescribed by the Commissioner regarding all bail bonds on which the bondsman is liable as of the first day of each month showing (i) each individual bonded, (ii) the date the bond was given, (iii) the principal sum of the bond, (iv) the court file or docket number for the principal's court obligation, (v) the fee charged for the bonding service in each instance, and (vi) the certificate seal number for each bond issued.

(b) Each insurer that appoints surety bondsmen in this State shall file with the Commissioner a written report in a form adopted by the Commissioner regarding all bail bonds on which the insurer is liable as of the last day of each calendar quarter showing the total dollar amount for which the insurer is liable. The report shall be filed on or before the fifteenth day following the end of each calendar quarter.

(c) The reports required by subsection (a) of this section shall be filed on or before the fifteenth day of each month.

(d) Any person who knowingly and willfully falsifies a report required by this section is guilty of a Class I felony.

History.
1975, c. 619, s. 1; 1989, c. 485, s. 43; 1991, c. 644, s. 20; 1993, c. 539, s. 1276; 1994, Ex. Sess., c. 24, s. 14(c); 1998-211, s. 27; 2007-484, s. 44.5; 2007-507, s. 14; 2019-179, s. 7(c)

§ 58-71-167. Portion of bond premium payments deferred

(a) In any case where the agreement between principal and surety calls for some portion of the bond premium payments to be deferred or paid after the defendant has been released from

Chapter 58

custody, a written memorandum of agreement between the principal and surety shall be kept on file by the surety with a copy provided to the principal. The memorandum shall contain the following information:

    (1) The amount of the premium payment deferred or not yet paid at the time the defendant is released from jail.

    (2) The method and schedule of payment to be made by the defendant to the bondsman, which shall include the dates of payment and amount to be paid on each date.

    (3) That the principal is entitled to a copy of the memorandum.

(b) The memorandum must be signed by the defendant and the bondsman, or one of the bondsman's agents, and dated at the time the agreement is made. Any subsequent modifications of the memorandum must be in writing, signed, dated, and kept on file by the surety, with a copy provided to the principal.

History.
1991, c. 644, s. 22; 2019-179, s. 7(d)

§ 58-71-168. Records to be maintained

All records related to executing bail bonds, including bail bond registers, monthly reports, receipts, collateral security agreements, and memoranda of agreements, shall be kept separate from records of any other business and must be maintained for not less than three years after the final entry has been made.

History.
1991, c. 644, s. 22

§ 58-71-170. Examinations

(a) Whenever the Commissioner considers it prudent, the Commissioner shall visit and examine or cause to be visited and examined by a competent person appointed by the Commissioner for that purpose any professional bail bondsman, surety bondsman, or runner subject to this Article. For this purpose the Commissioner or person making the examination shall have free access to all records of the licensee that relate to the licensee's business and to the records kept by any of the licensee's agents.

(b) The Commissioner may conduct examinations of surety bondsmen under G.S. 58-2-195 as well as under subsection (a) of this section.

History.
1975, c. 619, s. 1; 1991, c. 644, s. 21; 2001-269, s. 2.8

§ 58-71-175. Limit on principal amount of bond to be written by professional bondsman

No professional bondsman shall become liable on any bond or multiple of bonds for any one individual that totals more than one-fourth of the value of the securities deposited with the Commissioner at that time, until final termination of liability on such bond or multiple of bonds.

History.
1975, c. 619, s. 1; 1987, c. 728, s. 3; 1989, c. 485, s. 42

§ 58-71-180. Disposition of fees

Fees collected by the Commissioner pursuant to this Article shall be credited to the Insurance Regulatory Fund created under G.S. 58-6-25.

History.
1963, c. 1225, s. 32; 1975, c. 619, s. 1; 1991, c. 689, s. 294; 2003-221, s. 9

§ 58-71-185. Penalties for violations

Except as otherwise provided in this Article, any person who violates any of the provisions of this Article is guilty of a Class 1 misdemeanor.

History.
1963, c. 1225, s. 33; 1975, c. 619, s. 1; 1991, c. 644, s. 19; 1993, c. 539, s. 473; 1994, Ex. Sess., c. 24, s. 14(c); 2000-180, s. 9

§ 58-71-190. Duplication of regulation forbidden

No county, city or town in this State shall license or levy a license tax on bail bondsmen nor require such bondsmen to deposit collateral security as a condition for continuing to write bail bonds.

History.
1975, c. 619, s. 1

§ 58-71-195. Conflicting laws

Section 41.1 of Chapter 105 of the General Statutes of North Carolina and all laws and clauses of laws in conflict with the provisions of the Chapter are hereby repealed. Provided, however, that in the event of any conflict between the provisions of this Chapter and those of Chapter 15A of the General Statutes of North Carolina, the provisions of Chapter 15A shall control and continue in full force and effect.

History.
1975, c. 619, s. 2

§ 58-71-200. Bondsman access to criminal and civil records

(a) In order to assist licensed sureties and their agents in evaluating potential and current clients for the purposes of bail, the Administrative Office of the Courts shall provide any individual with a current license to act as professional bondsman, surety bondsman, or runner with access to search criminal records in the Administrative Office of the Courts' real-time criminal and civil information systems.

(b) Access granted under subsection (a) of this section shall be limited to information systems containing general criminal and civil case information, as maintained by the clerks of superior court. Access shall not include systems for the production of criminal process by law enforcement officials and judicial officials under G.S. 15A-301.1 or other information not subject to public disclosure.

(c) Access provided pursuant to subsection (a) of this section shall be without charge for individual searches of the Administrative Office of the Courts' criminal and civil information systems. In order to defray the costs of establishing access, the Administrative Office of the Courts shall charge initial setup fees equivalent to its fees for governmental agencies granted access to its systems to each individual granted access pursuant to subsection (a) of this section.

(d) All hardware, software, telecommunications charges, or other expenditures required for such access shall be the sole responsibility of the individual bondsman or runner. No State funds may be expended for any such expenses.

(e) The Commissioner shall coordinate the access granted under subsection (a) of this section by providing all information requested by the Administrative Office of the Courts for the establishment of access. The Administrative Office of the Courts shall not provide access to any bondsman or runner who fails to provide all information requested by the Commissioner.

(f) The Commissioner shall notify the Administrative Office of the Courts within 24 hours of any action to suspend or revoke a bondsman's or runner's license or authority to act as a bondsman or runner. The Administrative Office of the Courts shall immediately revoke access of the suspended or revoked bondsman or runner to its criminal information systems.

(g) The Administrative Office of the Courts shall provide to the Commissioner copies of its current policies for access to court information systems for users outside the Judicial Branch. Any bondsman or runner granted access pursuant to subsection (a) of this section shall adhere to all such policies. The Administrative Office of the Courts shall revoke access of any bondsman or runner who violates such policies.

(h) It is unlawful for any person to willfully do any of the following:

(1) For any person to access information systems of the Administrative Office of the Courts by means of an online identifier, as defined in G.S. 14-208.6(1n), that was assigned to another individual by the Administrative Office of the Courts pursuant to subsection (a) of this section.

(2) For any bondsman or runner granted access pursuant to subsection (a) of this section to allow any other person, directly or indirectly, to make use of access granted to the bondsman or runner pursuant to subsection (a) of this section.

(3) For any bondsman or runner granted access pursuant to subsection (a) of this section to make use of that access at any time when the bondsman or runner knows or has reason to know that his or her license issued under this Article is in a state of suspension or revocation.

(4) For any bondsman or runner granted access pursuant to subsection (a) of this section to distribute, in any medium or manner, information obtained from the information systems of the Administrative Office of the Courts to any person for any reason not directly related to the evaluation of the individual to whom the information pertains for the purposes of bail.

Unless the conduct is covered under some other provision of law providing for a greater punishment, any violation of this subsection shall be a Class H felony.

History.
2011-412, s. 4.1; 2015-180, s. 4

ARTICLE 74
MORTGAGE IN LIEU OF BOND

§ 58-74-1. Mortgage in lieu of required bond

An administrator, executor, guardian, collector or receiver, or an officer required to give an official bond, or the agent or surety of such person or officer, may execute a mortgage on real estate, of the value of the bond required to be given by him to the State of North Carolina, conditioned to the same effect as the bond should be, were the same given, with a power of sale, which power of sale may be executed by the clerk of the superior court, with whom said mortgage shall be deposited, upon a breach of any of the conditions of said mortgage, after advertisement for 30 days.

History.
1874-5, c. 103, s. 2; Code, s. 118; Rev., s. 265; C.S., s. 346

§ 58-74-5. Mortgage in lieu of security for appearance, costs, or fine

Any person required to give a bond or undertaking, or required to enter into a recognizance for his appearance at any court, in any criminal proceeding, or for the security of any costs or fine in any criminal action, may also execute a mortgage on real or personal property of the value of such bond or recognizance, payable to the State of North Carolina, conditioned as such bond or recognizance would be required, with power of sale, which power shall be executed by the clerk in whose court said mortgage is executed, upon a breach of any of the conditions of said mortgage.

No such mortgage on real property executed for the security for costs or fine shall allow a longer time for payment of said costs or fine than six months from the execution thereof, and no mortgage on personal property a longer time than three months, except in cases of appeal, when the time allowed shall be counted from the date of the final decision in the cause.

All legitimate expenses of sale, which shall only be made after due advertisement according to law, shall be paid out of the proceeds of the sale.

History.
1874-5, c. 103, s. 3; Code, s. 120; 1891, c. 425, ss. 1, 2, 3; Rev., s. 266; C.S., s. 347; 1973, c. 108, s. 57

§ 58-74-10. Cancellation of mortgage in such proceedings

Any mortgage given by any person in lieu of bond as administrator, executor, guardian, collector, receiver or as an officer required to give an official bond, or as agent or surety of such person or officer, or in lieu of bond or undertaking or recognizance for his appearance at any court in any criminal proceeding, or for the security of any cost or fine in a criminal action which has been registered, when such party as administrator, executor, guardian, collector, or receiver has filed his final account and when the time required by statute for the bond given by any administrator, executor, guardian, collector, or receiver to remain in force for the purpose of action thereon has expired, or when the officer required to give an official bond has fully complied with the conditions of such bond and the time within which suit is allowed by law to be brought thereon has expired, or when the person giving such mortgage in lieu of bond has made his appearance at the court to which he was bound and did not depart the court without leave, or paid the cost or fine required, may be canceled or discharged by the clerk of the superior court of the county where such action was pending or where the mortgage in lieu of bond is recorded by recording a satisfaction

document pursuant to G.S. 45-37(a)(7), and such satisfaction document shall have the effect to discharge and release all the right, title and interest of the State of North Carolina in and to the property described in such mortgage.

History.
1905, c. 106; Rev., s. 267; C.S., s. 348; 1921, c. 29, ss. 1, 2; 1925, c. 252, s. 1; 2011-246, s. 9

§ 58-74-15. Validating statute

All acts heretofore done by the several superior court clerks, cancelling or satisfying any mortgage, or other instruments, herein mentioned and specified are hereby validated.

History.
1925, c. 252, s. 2

§ 58-74-20. Clerk of court may give surety by mortgage deposited with register

In all cases where the clerk of the superior court may be required to give surety, he may deposit a mortgage with the register of deeds, payable to the State, and conditioned, as the bond would have been required, with power of sale. The power of sale shall be executed by the register of deeds, upon a breach of any of the conditions of said mortgage; and the register of deeds shall in all cases immediately register the same, at the expense of the said clerk.

History.
1874-5, c. 103, s. 6; Code, s. 122; Rev., s. 268; C.S., s. 349

§ 58-74-25. Mortgage in lieu of bond to prosecute or defend in civil case

It is lawful for any person desiring to commence any civil action or special proceeding, or to defend the same, his agent or surety, to execute a mortgage on real estate of the value of the bond or undertaking required to be given, at the beginning of said action, or at any stage thereof, to the party to whom the bond or undertaking would be required to be made, conditioned to the same effect as such bond or undertaking, with power of sale, which power of sale may be executed upon a breach of any of the conditions of the said mortgage after advertisement for 30 days.

History.
1874-5, c. 103, s. 1; Code, s. 117; Rev., s. 269; C.S., s. 35

§ 58-74-30. Affidavit of value of property required

In all cases where a mortgage is executed, as hereinbefore permitted, it is the duty of the clerk of the court in which it is executed to require an affidavit of the value of the property mortgaged to be made by at least one witness not interested in the matter, action or proceeding in which the mortgage is given.

History.
1874-5, c. 103, s. 4; Code, s. 121; Rev., s. 270; C.S., s. 351; 1973, c. 108, s. 58

§ 58-74-35. When additional security required

If, from any cause, the property mortgaged in lieu of a bond becomes of less value than the amount of the bond in lieu of which the mortgage is given, and it so appears upon affidavit of any person having any interest in the matter as a security for which the mortgage was given, it is the duty of the mortgagor to give additional security by a deposit of money, or the execution of a mortgage on more property, or justify as required in cases where bond or undertaking is given.

History.
1874-5, c. 103, s. 5; Code, s. 119; Rev., s. 271; C.S., s. 352

ARTICLE 75
DEPOSIT IN LIEU OF BOND

§ 58-75-1. Deposit of cash or securities in lieu of bond; conditions and requirements

In lieu of any written undertaking or bond required by law in any matter, before any court of the State, the party required to make such undertaking or bond may make a deposit in cash or securities of the State of North Carolina or of the United States of America, of the amount required by law or, in the case of fiduciaries, of the amount of the trust, in lieu of the said undertaking or bond and such deposit shall be subject to all of the same conditions and requirements as are provided for in written undertakings or bonds, in lieu of which such deposit is made.

History.
1923, c. 58; C.S., s. 352(a); 1947, c. 936

ARTICLE 77
GUARANTEED ARREST
BOND CERTIFICATES
OF AUTOMOBILE CLUBS

AND ASSOCIATIONS IN
LIEU OF BOND

§§ 58-77-1, 58-77-5

Repealed by Session Laws 1999-132, s. 12.1, effective June 4, 1999.

ARTICLE 79
INVESTIGATION OF FIRES
AND INSPECTION OF
PREMISES

§ 58-79-1. Fires investigated; reports; records

The Director of the State Bureau of Investigation, through the State Bureau of Investigation, the Office of the State Fire Marshal, and the chief of the fire department, or chief of police where there is no chief of the fire department, in municipalities and towns, and the county fire marshal and the sheriff of the county and the chief of the rural fire department where such fire occurs outside of a municipality, are hereby authorized to investigate the cause, origin, and circumstances of every fire occurring in such municipalities or counties in which property has been destroyed or damaged, and shall specially make investigation whether the fire was the result of carelessness or design. A preliminary investigation shall be made by the chief of fire department or chief of police, where there is no chief of fire department in municipalities, and by the county fire marshal and the sheriff of the county or the chief of the rural fire department where such fire occurs outside of a municipality, and must be begun within three days, exclusive of Sunday, of the occurrence of the fire, and the Director of the State Bureau of Investigation, through the State Bureau of Investigation, shall have the right to supervise and direct the investigation when he deems it expedient or necessary.

The officer making the investigation of fires shall forthwith notify the Director of the State Bureau of Investigation, and must within one week of the occurrence of the fire furnish to the Director of the State Bureau of Investigation a written statement of all facts relating to the cause and origin of the fire, the kind, value and ownership of the property destroyed, and such other information as is called for by the forms provided by the Director of the State Bureau of Investigation. Departments capable of submitting the required information by the utilization of computers and related equipment, by means of an approved format of standard punch cards, magnetic tapes or an approved telecommunications system, may do so in lieu of the submission of the written statement as provided for in this section. The Director of the State Bureau of Investigation shall keep in his office a record of all reports submitted pursuant to this section. These reports shall at all times be open to public inspection.

History.

1899, c. 58; 1901, c. 387; 1903, c. 719; Rev., s. 4818; C.S., s. 6074; 1943, c. 170; 1969, c. 894; 1977, c. 596, s. 1; 2014-100, s. 17.1(p); 2017-57, s. 22.4(a); 2018-31, s. 3

§ 58-79-5. Director of the State Bureau of Investigation to make examination; arrests and prosecution

It is the duty of the Director of the State Bureau of Investigation to examine, or cause examination to be made, into the cause, circumstances, and origin of all fires occurring within the State to which his attention has been called in accordance with the provisions of G.S. 58-79-1, or by interested parties, by which property is accidentally or unlawfully burned, destroyed, or damaged, whenever in his judgment the evidence is sufficient, and to specially examine and decide whether the fire was the result of carelessness or the act of an incendiary. The Director of the State Bureau of Investigation shall, in person, by deputy or otherwise, fully investigate all circumstances surrounding such fire, and, when in his opinion such proceedings are necessary, take or cause to be taken the testimony on oath of all persons supposed to be cognizant of any facts or to have means of knowledge in relation to the matters as to which an examination is herein required to be made, and shall cause the same to be reduced in writing. If the Director of the State Bureau of Investigation or any deputy appointed to conduct such investigations, is of the opinion that there is evidence to charge any person or persons with the crime of arson, or other willful burning, or fraud in connection with the crime of arson or other willful burning, he may arrest with warrant or cause such person or persons to be arrested, charged with such offense, and prosecuted, and shall furnish to the district attorney of the district all such evidence, together with the names of witnesses and all other information obtained by him, including a copy of all pertinent and material testimony taken in the case.

History.

1899, c. 58, s. 2; 1901, c. 387, s. 2; 1903, c. 719; Rev., s. 4819; C.S., s. 6075; 1943, c. 170; 1955, c. 642, s. 1; 1959, c. 1183; 1973, c. 47, s. 2; 1977, c. 596, s. 2; 2014-100, s. 17.1(p)

§ 58-79-10. Powers of Director of the State Bureau of Investigation in investigations

The Director of the State Bureau of Investigation, or his deputy appointed to conduct such examination, has the powers of a trial justice for the purpose of summoning and compelling the attendance of witnesses to testify in relation to any matter which is by provisions of this Article a subject of inquiry and investigation, and may administer oaths and affirmations to persons appearing as witnesses before them. False swearing in any such matter or proceeding is perjury and shall be punished as such. The Director of the State Bureau of Investigation or his deputy has authority at all times of the day or night, in performance of the duties imposed by the provisions of this Article, to enter upon and examine any building or premises where any fire has occurred, and other buildings and premises adjoining or near the same. All investigations held by or under the direction of the Director of the State Bureau of Investigation or his deputy may, in their discretion, be private, and persons other than those required to be present by the provisions of this Article may be excluded from the place where the investigation is held, and witnesses may be kept apart from each other and not allowed to communicate with each other until they have been examined.

History.

1899, c. 58, s. 3; 1901, c. 387, s. 3; Rev., s. 4820; C.S., s. 6076; 1943, c. 170; 1977, c. 596, s. 2; 2014-100, s. 17.1(p)

§ 58-79-15. Failure to comply with summons or subpoena

The failure of a person to comply with a summons or subpoena of the Director of the State Bureau of Investigation or his deputy under G.S. 58-79-10 shall be brought before a court of record and punished as for contempt in the same manner as if he had failed to appear and testify before said court of record.

History.

1955, c. 642, s. 2; 1977, c. 596, s. 2; 2014-100, s. 17.1(p)

§ 58-79-20. Inspection of premises; dangerous material removed

The Commissioner of Insurance, or the chief of fire department or chief of police where there is no chief of fire department, or the city or county building inspector, electrical inspector, heating inspector, or fire prevention inspector has the right at all reasonable hours, for the purpose of examination, to enter into and upon all buildings and premises in their jurisdiction. When any of such officers find in any building or upon any premises overcrowding in violation of occupancy limits established pursuant to the

North Carolina State Building Code, combustible material or inflammable conditions dangerous to the safety of such building or premises they shall order the same to be removed or remedied, and this order shall be forthwith complied with by the owner or occupant of such buildings or premises. The owner or occupant may, within twenty-four hours, appeal to the Commissioner of Insurance from the order, and the cause of the complaint shall be at once investigated by his direction, and unless by his authority the order of the officer above named is revoked it remains in force and must be forthwith complied with by the owner or occupant. The Commissioner of Insurance, fire chief, or building inspector, electrical inspector, heating inspector, or fire prevention inspector shall make an immediate investigation as to the presence of combustible material or the existence of inflammable conditions in any building or upon any premises under their jurisdiction upon complaint of any person having an interest in such building or premises or property adjacent thereto. The Commissioner may, in person or by deputy, visit any municipality or county and make such inspections alone or in company with the local officer. The Commissioner shall submit annually, as early as consistent with full and accurate preparation, and not later than the first day of June, a detailed report of his official action under this Article, and it shall be embodied in his report to the General Assembly.'

History.
1899, c. 58, s. 4; 1901, c. 387, s. 4; 1903, c. 719; Rev., s. 4821; C.S., s. 6077; 1943, c. 170; 1969, c. 1063, s. 3; 1977, c. 596, s. 4; 1985, c. 576, s. 2

§ 58-79-22. Door lock exemption permit

Any business entity licensed to sell automatic weapons as a federal firearms dealer that is in the business of selling firearms or ammunition and that operates a firing range which rents firearms and sells ammunition that desires to be exempt from the door lock requirements of Chapter 10 of Volume 1 of the North Carolina State Building Code may apply for a permit to do so with the Department in accordance with G.S. 143-143.4 and rules adopted by the Department. The Department shall charge a permit fee of five hundred dollars ($ 500.00) for the issuance of a permit issued pursuant to G.S. 143-143.4.

History.
2001-324, s. 2

§ 58-79-25. Deputy investigators

It shall be the duty of the Director of the State Bureau of Investigation to appoint two or more persons as deputies, whose particular duty it shall be to investigate forest fires and endeavor to ascertain the persons guilty of setting such fires and cause prosecution to be instituted against those who, as a result of such investigation, are deemed guilty.

History.
1899, c. 58, s. 6; 1901, c. 387, s. 6; 1903, c. 719, s. 2; Rev., s. 4823; 1915, c. 109, s. 2; 1919, c. 186, s. 7; C.S., s. 6078; Ex. Sess. 1924, c. 119; 1943, c. 170; 1977, c. 596, s. 2; 2014-100, s. 17.1(p)

N.C. Gen. Stat. § 58-79-30

Repealed by Session Laws 1999-456, s. 66.

§ 58-79-35. Fire prevention and Fire Prevention Day

It is the duty of the Commissioner of Insurance, the Superintendent of Public Instruction and the State Board of Education to provide a pamphlet containing printed instructions for properly conducting fire drills in all schools and auxiliary school buildings and the principal of every public and private school shall conduct at least one fire drill every month during the regular school session in each building in his charge where children are assembled. The fire drills shall include all children and teachers and the use of various ways of egress to assimilate evacuation of said buildings under various conditions, and such other regulations as prescribed by the Commissioner of Insurance, Superintendent of Public Instruction and State Board of Education.

The Commissioner of Insurance and Superintendent of Public Instruction shall further provide for the teaching of "Fire Prevention" in the colleges and schools of the State, and to arrange for a textbook adapted to such use. The ninth day of October of every year shall be set aside and designated as "Fire Prevention Day," and the Governor shall issue a proclamation urging the people to a proper observance of the day, and the Commissioner of Insurance shall bring the day and its observance to the attention of the officials of all organized fire departments of the State, whose duty it shall be to disseminate the materials and to arrange suitable programs to be followed in its observance.

History.
1915, c. 166, s. 5; C.S., s. 6080; 1925, c. 130; 1943, c. 170; 1947, c. 781; 1957, c. 845

§ 58-79-40. Insurance company to furnish information

(a) The chief of any municipal fire or police department, county fire marshal or sheriff, or special agent of the State Bureau of Investigation may request any insurance company investigating a fire loss of real or personal property to release any information in its possession relative to that loss. The company shall release the information and cooperate with any official authorized to request such information pursuant to this section. The information shall include, but is not limited to:

    (1) Any insurance policy relevant to a fire loss under investigation and any application for such a policy;

    (2) Policy premium payment records;

    (3) History of previous claims made by the insured for fire loss;

    (4) Material relating to the investigation of the loss, including statements of any person, proof of loss, and any other relevant evidence.

(b) If an insurance company (or insurance agency) has reason to suspect that a fire loss to its insured's real or personal property was caused by incendiary means, the company shall furnish the State Bureau of Investigation with all relevant material acquired during its investigation of the fire loss, cooperate with and take such action as may be requested of it by any law-enforcement agency, and permit any person ordered by a court to inspect any of its records pertaining to the policy and the loss.

(c) In the absence of fraud or malice, no insurance company (or insurance agency), or person who furnishes information on its behalf, shall be liable for damages in a civil action or subject to criminal prosecution for any oral or written statement made or any other action that is necessary to supply information required pursuant to this section.

(d) The officials and departmental and agency personnel receiving any information furnished pursuant to this section shall hold the information in confidence until such time as its release is required pursuant to a criminal or civil proceeding.

(e) Any official referred to in subsection (a) of this section may be required to testify as to any information in his possession regarding the fire loss of real or personal property in any civil action in which any person seeks recovery under a policy against an insurance company for the fire loss.

History.
1977, c. 520, s. 1

§ 58-79-45. Fire incident reports

(a) Whenever a fire department responds to a fire, the chief of that department shall complete or cause to be completed a fire incident report, which report shall be on a form prescribed by the Department of Insurance. When such report is made without fraud, bad faith, or actual malice, the person making the report is not subject to liability for libel or slander.

(b) The fire department shall forward a copy of the completed form to the fire marshal of the county in which the fire occurred. If there is no fire marshal in that county, the fire department shall forward a copy of the report to the county commissioners. The fire department shall retain the original of the report. The fire department and the fire marshal or county commissioners to whom reports are sent shall retain the reports for a period of five years.

(c) At the request of any person, the county fire marshal or county commissioners shall provide such person, for a reasonable copying charge, a certified copy of the report.

History.
1989 (Reg. Sess., 1990), c. 1054, s. 7

ARTICLE 81
HOTELS; SAFETY PROVISIONS

§ 58-81-5. Careless or negligent setting of fires

Any person who in any fashion or manner negligently or carelessly sets fire to any bedding, furniture, draperies, house or household furnishings or other equipment or appurtenances in or to any hotel or other building of like occupancy shall be guilty of a Class 1 misdemeanor.

History.
1947, c. 1066; 1993, c. 539, s. 474; 1994, Ex. Sess., c. 24, s. 14(c)

§ 58-81-10. Penalty for noncompliance

Any owner, owners, proprietor or keeper of any hotel or other building of like occupancy who fails to comply with any of the foregoing provisions of this Article shall be guilty of a Class 3 misdemeanor and punished only by a fine of not less than ten dollars ($ 10.00) nor more than fifty dollars ($ 50.00). Each day of noncompliance herewith shall constitute a separate offense.

History.
1947, c. 1066; 1993, c. 539, s. 475; 1994, Ex. Sess., c. 24, s. 14(c)

ARTICLE 82
AUTHORITY AND LIABILITY OF FIREMEN

§ 58-82-1. Authority of firemen; penalty for willful interference with firemen

Members and employees of county, municipal corporation, fire protection district, sanitary district or privately incorporated fire departments shall have authority to do all acts reasonably necessary to extinguish fires and protect life and property from fire. Any person, including the owner of property which is burning, who shall willfully interfere in any manner with firemen engaged in the performance of their duties shall be guilty of a Class 1 misdemeanor.

History.
1965, c. 648; 1993, c. 539, s. 476; 1994, Ex. Sess., c. 24, s. 14(c)

§ 58-82-5. Liability limited

(a) For the purpose of this section, a "rural fire department" means a bona fide fire department incorporated as a nonprofit corporation which under schedules filed with or approved by the Commissioner of Insurance, is classified as not less than Class "9" in accordance with rating methods, schedules, classifications, underwriting rules, bylaws, or regulations effective or applied with respect to the establishment of rates or premiums used or charged pursuant to Article 36 or Article 40 of this Chapter and which operates fire apparatus of the value of five thousand dollars ($ 5,000) or more.

(b) A rural fire department or a fireman who belongs to the department shall not be liable for damages to persons or property alleged to have been sustained and alleged to have occurred by reason of an act or omission, either of the rural fire department or of the fireman at the scene of a reported fire, when that act or omission relates to the suppression of the reported fire or to the direction of traffic or enforcement of traffic laws or ordinances at the scene of or in connection with a fire, accident, or other hazard by the department or the fireman unless it is established that the damage occurred because of gross negligence, wanton conduct or intentional wrongdoing of the rural fire department or the fireman.

(c) Any member of a volunteer fire department or rescue squad who receives no compensation for his services as a fire fighter or emergency medical care provider, who renders first aid or emergency health care treatment at the scene of a fire to a person who is unconscious, ill, or injured as a result of the fire shall not be liable in civil damages for any acts or omissions relating to such services rendered, unless such acts or omissions amount to gross negligence, wanton conduct or intentional wrongdoing.

History.
1983, c. 520, s. 1; 1985, c. 611, s. 1; 1987, c. 146, s. 2

ARTICLE 82A
PYROTECHNICS TRAINING AND PERMITTING

§ 58-82A-1. State Fire Marshal establish pyrotechnic safety guidelines

(a) **Guidelines.** -- The Commissioner of Insurance through the Office of the State Fire Marshal, in consultation with the State Fire and Rescue Commission, must establish guidelines, testing, and training requirements for the following:

(1) Individuals who assist a display operator with the exhibition, use, handling, or discharge of pyrotechnics in connection with a concert or public exhibition authorized under Article 54 of Chapter 14 of the General Statutes.

(2) Individuals seeking to obtain a display operator license, proximate audience display operator license, or assistant display operator license under this Article.

(b) **Definitions.** -- The definitions in G.S. 14-410 apply in this Article.

(c) **Rule making.** -- The Commissioner may adopt rules to implement this Article.

History.
2009-507, s. 3; 2010-22, s. 1

§ 58-82A-1.1. Definitions

The following definitions apply in this Article:

(1) **Assistant display operator.** -- An individual who, under the supervision of the display operator, assists with the safety, setup, and discharge of a pyrotechnic display and who is licensed pursuant to this Article.

(2) **Event employee.** -- An individual who works under the supervision of the display operator and who assists with the safety, setup, and discharge of a pyrotechnic display but does not handle the pyrotechnic materials.

(3) **Outdoor pyrotechnics display.** -- A pyrotechnic display that is outdoors and uses 1.4G, 1.3G, 1.2G, and 1.1G pyrotechnics and is a minimum of 75 feet from the audience in accordance with NFPA 1123.

(4) **Proximate audience display.** -- A display of pyrotechnics that occurs within a building or structure or that occurs outside before an audience within 75 feet of the pyrotechnics in accordance with NFPA 1126.

(5) **Proximate audience display operator.** -- An individual who is responsible for the safety, setup, and discharge of the proximate audience display and who is licensed under this Article.

(6) **Pyrotechnics.** -- All fireworks not exempted by G.S. 14-414 and that are used for professional outdoor displays and classified as fireworks by UN0333 (1.1G), UN0334 (1.2G), UN0335 (1.3G), or UN0336 (1.4G) by the United States Department of Transportation under 49 C.F.R. § 172.101.

(7) **Pyrotechnics display operator.** -- An individual who is responsible for the safety, setup, and discharge of the pyrotechnic display, who is responsible for the supervision of personnel at the pyrotechnic display, and who is licensed under this Article.

(8) **Supervision.** -- The direction and management of the activities of personnel in the safety, setup, handling, and display of an outdoor pyrotechnic display, a proximate audience display, or a flame effect display.

History.
2010-22, s. 2

§ 58-82A-1.5. Commissioner of Insurance to administer Article; rules; employees; evidence of Commissioner's action

(a) The Commissioner shall have full power and authority to administer the provisions of this Article, which establishes guidelines for the use, handling, exhibiting, or discharge of pyrotechnics in connection with a concert or public exhibition, as allowed under Article 54 of Chapter 14 of the General Statutes, and to license and regulate pyrotechnic operators. The Commissioner shall adopt any rules necessary to enforce the purposes and provisions of this Article.

(b) Any written instrument purporting to be a copy of any action, proceeding, or finding of fact by the Commissioner, or any record of the Commissioner authenticated under the head of the Commissioner by the seal of the Commissioner's office, shall be accepted by all courts of this State as prima facie evidence of the contents thereof.

History.
2010-22, s. 3

§ 58-82A-2. Individual training requirements

An individual may not use, handle, exhibit, or discharge pyrotechnics in connection with a concert or public exhibition, as allowed under Article 54 of Chapter 14 of the General Statutes, unless the individual successfully completes the training approved or offered by the Commissioner of Insurance through the Office of State Fire Marshal or meets all of the following conditions:

(1) Is an active member in good standing with a local fire or rescue department and has experience in pyrotechnics or explosives, as verified by the State Fire Marshal.

(2) Possesses the professional qualifications required by the State Fire Marshal or the professional qualifications required by the jurisdiction where permitting is being sought, whichever is greater. The professional qualifications set by the State Fire Marshal may not be less than the voluntary minimum professional qualifications for all levels of fire service and rescue service personnel established by the State Fire and Rescue Commission under G.S. 58-78-5.

History.
2009-507, s. 3

§ 58-82A-2.1. Require licenses

(a) No person shall obtain a pyrotechnics permit under Article 54 of Chapter 14 of the General Statutes unless the person possesses the appropriate license, as provided by this Article.

(b) An applicant for a license authorized by this Article shall apply on forms supplied by the Commissioner. The Commissioner shall inquire as to the applicant's qualifications and other matters relative to the applicant's fitness to be licensed or to continue to be licensed.

(c) When a license is issued under this section, the Commissioner shall issue to the licensee an identification card approved by the Commissioner. Each licensee must carry this card at all times when working in the scope of the licensee's employment. A licensee whose license terminates or is terminated shall surrender the identification card to the Commissioner, when requested by the Commissioner. The Commissioner may contract directly with persons for the processing and issuance of identification cards required by this section and may charge a reasonable fee in addition to the license fee in an amount that offsets the cost of the service, including the costs associated with the contract authorized by this subsection. Contracts entered into under this subsection shall not be subject to Article 3 of Chapter 143 of the General Statutes.

History.
2010-22, s. 4

§ 58-82A-2.5. Terms of licenses

A license issued to a pyrotechnics display operator, a proximate audience display operator, or an assistant display operator under this Article authorizes the licensee to act in that capacity until the license is suspended, revoked, or not renewed. Upon the suspension or revocation of a license, or the failure to renew a license, the licensee shall return the license to the Commissioner. A pyrotechnics display operator's license, a proximate audience display operator's license, and an assistant display operator's license is valid for three years unless suspended or revoked and may be renewed every three years from the date of issuance upon payment of the applicable renewal fee.

History.
2010-22, s. 5

§ 58-82A-3. Pyrotechnics display operator license

(a) **License Required.** -- A display operator license issued by the Commissioner is required for an individual to obtain the necessary authorization under Article 54 of Chapter 14 of the General Statutes to exhibit, use, handle, manufacture, or discharge pyrotechnics at a concert or public exhibition in this State. A license issued under this section is valid for three years unless it is revoked by the Commissioner.

(b) **Requirements.** -- The Commissioner may issue a display operator license to an individual if all of the following conditions are met:

(1) The individual is at least 21 years of age.

(2) The individual has assisted a display operator as an assistant display operator in the exhibition, use, or display of pyrotechnics at a concert or public exhibition, as allowed under Article 54 of Chapter 14 of the General Statutes, on at least three occasions.

(3) The individual successfully completes the minimum training requirements established by the State Fire Marshal.

(4) The individual successfully passes an examination approved by the State Fire Marshal that demonstrates the individual has the knowledge to safely handle, store, and exhibit Class 1.4g, 1.3g, 1.2g, and 1.1g pyrotechnics or provides satisfactory evidence of current certification by a third party acceptable to the State Fire Marshal.

(5) Repealed by Session Laws 2010-22, s. 6, effective October 1, 2010.

(6) The individual has no violations of any provision of this Article or of any similar provision of any other state and submits an "Employer Possessor Letter of Clearance" issued to the individual by the Bureau of Alcohol, Tobacco and Firearms pursuant to 18 U.S.C. Chapter 40.

(b1) The Commissioner may issue a Limited Pyrotechnic Operator license to an individual meeting all the requirements of subsection (b) of this section with the exception of the "Employer Possessor Letter of Clearance" required by subdivision (6) of subsection (b) of this section if the individual signs a statement provided by the Commissioner affirming that the individual has not been convicted of violating 18 U.S.C. Chapter 40, Section 842(i), and is not otherwise prohibited from possessing pyrotechnic materials by any provision of 18 U.S.C. Chapter 40, Section 842(i).

(c), (d) Repealed by Session Laws 2010-22, s. 6, effective October 1, 2010.

(e) Public exhibitions consisting of materials exempted by G.S. 14-414 are exempt from the operator license requirements.

History.
2009-507, s. 3; 2010-22, s. 6; 2013-275, s. 3

CHAPTER 62
PUBLIC UTILITIES

ARTICLE 11
RAILROADS

§§ 62-223 through 62-226

Recodified as G.S. 136-191 through 136-194 by Session Laws 1998-128, s. 14.

ARTICLE 12
MOTOR CARRIERS

§ 62-273. Embezzlement of C.O.D. shipments

Household goods received by any motor carrier to be transported in intrastate commerce and delivered upon collection on such delivery and remittance to the shipper of the sum of money stated in the shipping instructions to be collected and remitted to the shipper, and the money collected upon delivery of such party, are hereby declared to be held in trust by any carrier having possession thereof or the carrier making the delivery or collection, and upon failure of any such carrier to account for the household goods so received, either to the shipper to whom the collection is payable or the carrier making delivery to any carrier handling the household goods or making the collection, within 15 days after demand in writing by the shipper, or carrier, or upon failure of the delivering carrier to remit the sum so directed to be collected and remitted to the shipper, within 15 days after collection is made, shall be prima facie evidence that the household goods so received, or the funds so received, have been wilfully converted by such carrier to its own use, and the carrier so offending shall be guilty of a Class H felony and such carrier may be indicted, tried, and punished in the county in which such shipment was delivered to the carrier or in any other county into or through which such shipment was transported by such carrier.

History.
1947, c. 1008, s. 33; 1963, c. 1165, s. 1; 1993, c. 539, s. 1277; 1994, Ex. Sess., c. 24, s. 14(c); 1995, c. 523, s. 26

§ 62-278. Revocation of license plates by Utilities Commission

(a) The license plates of any carrier of persons or household goods by motor vehicle for compensation may be revoked and removed from the vehicles of any such carrier for wilful violation of any provision of this Chapter, or for the wilful violation of any lawful rule or regulation made and promulgated by the Utilities Commission. To that end the Commission shall have power upon complaint or upon its own motion, after notice and hearing, to order the license plates of any such offending carrier revoked and removed from the vehicles of such carrier for a period not exceeding 30 days, and it shall be the duty of the Department of Motor Vehicles to execute such orders made by the Utilities Commission upon receipt of a certified copy of the same.

(b) This section shall be in addition to and independent of other provisions of law for the enforcement of the motor carrier laws of this State.

History.
1951, c. 1120; 1963, c. 1165, s. 1; 1995, c. 523, s. 27

ARTICLE 15
PENALTIES AND ACTIONS

§ 62-319. Riding on train unlawfully; venue

If any person, with the intention of being transported free in violation of law, rides or attempts to ride on top of any car, coach, engine or tender, on any railroad in this State, or on the drawheads between cars, or under cars, on truss rods, or trucks, or in any freight car, or on a platform of any baggage car, express car or mail car on any train, he shall be guilty of a Class 3 misdemeanor. Any person charged with a violation of this section may be tried in any county in this State through which such train may pass carrying such person, or in any county in which such violation may have occurred or may be discovered.

History.
1899, c. 625; 1905, c. 32; Rev., s. 3748; C.S., s. 3508; 1963, c. 1165, s. 1; 1993, c. 539, s. 485; 1994, Ex. Sess., c. 24, s. 14(c)

N.C. Gen. Stat. § 62-320

Repealed by Session Laws 1995, c. 523, s. 30.

§ 62-323. Willful injury to property of public utility a misdemeanor

If any person shall willfully do or cause to be done any act or acts whatever whereby any building, construction or work of any public utility, or any engine, machine or structure or any matter or thing appertaining to the same shall be stopped, obstructed, impaired, weakened, injured or destroyed, he shall be guilty of a Class 1 misdemeanor.

History.
1871-2, c. 138, s. 39; Code, s. 1974; Rev., s. 3756; C.S., s. 3478; 1963, c. 1165, s. 1; 1993, c. 539, s. 488; 1994, Ex. Sess., c. 24, s. 14(c)

CHAPTER 62A
PUBLIC SAFETY TELEPHONE SERVICE AND WIRELESS TELEPHONE SERVICE

ARTICLE 1
PUBLIC SAFETY TELEPHONE SERVICE

§§ 62A-1 through 62A-12

Repealed by Session Laws 2007-383, s. 2(a), effective January 1, 2008.

ARTICLE 2
WIRELESS TELEPHONE SERVICE

§§ 62A-21 through 62A-32

Repealed by Session Laws 2007-383, s. 3(a), effective January 1, 2008.

ARTICLE 3
EMERGENCY TELEPHONE SERVICE

§§ 62A-40 through 62A-56

Recodified as G.S. 143B-1400 through 143B-1416 by Session Laws 2015-241, s. 7A.3(2), effective September 18, 2015.

CHAPTER 63
AERONAUTICS

ARTICLE 2
STATE REGULATION

§ 63-11. Sovereignty in space

Sovereignty in space above the lands and waters of this State is declared to rest in the State, except where granted to and assumed by the United States.

History.
1929, c. 190, s. 2

§ 63-12. Ownership of space

The ownership of the space above the lands and waters of this State is declared to be vested in the several owners of the surface beneath, subject to the right of flight described in G.S. 63-13.

History.
1929, c. 190, s. 3

§ 63-13. Lawfulness of flight

Flight in aircraft over the lands and waters of this State is lawful, unless at such a low altitude as to interfere with the then existing use to which the land or water, or the space over the land or water, is put by the owner, or unless so conducted as to be injurious to the health and happiness, or imminently dangerous to persons or property lawfully on the land or water beneath. The landing of an aircraft on the lands or waters of another, without his consent, is unlawful, except in the case of a forced landing. For damages caused by a forced landing, however, the owner or lessee of the aircraft or the aeronaut shall be liable as provided in G.S. 63-14.

History.
1929, c. 190, s. 4; 1947, c. 1001, s. 1

N.C. Gen. Stat. § 63-14

Repealed by Session Laws 1947, c. 1069, s. 3.

§ 63-15. Collision of aircraft

The liability of the owners of one aircraft to the owner of another aircraft, or to aeronauts or passengers on either aircraft, for damages caused by collision on land or in the air shall be determined by the rules of law applicable to torts on land.

History.
1929, c. 190, s. 6

§ 63-16. Jurisdiction over crimes and torts

All crimes, torts, and other wrongs committed by or against an airman or passenger while in flight over this State shall be governed by the laws of this State; and the question whether damage occasioned by or to an aircraft while in flight over this State constitutes a tort, crime or other wrong by or against the owner of such aircraft shall be determined by the laws of this State.

History.
1929, c. 190, s. 7; 1971, c. 936, s. 3

§ 63-17. Jurisdiction over contracts

All contractual and other legal relations entered into by airmen or passengers while in flight over this State shall have the same effect as if entered into on the land or water beneath.

History.
1929, c. 190, s. 8; 1971, c. 936, s. 3

§ 63-18. Dangerous flying a misdemeanor

Any airman or passenger who, while in flight over a thickly inhabited area or over a public gathering within this State, shall engage in trick or acrobatic flying, or in any acrobatic feat, or shall except while in landing or taking off, fly at such a low level as to disturb the public peace or the rights of private persons in the enjoyment of their homes, or injure the health, or endanger the persons or property on the surface beneath, or drop any object except loose water or loose sand ballast, shall be guilty of a Class 1 misdemeanor.

History.
1929, c. 190, s. 9; 1947, c. 1001, s. 2; 1971, c. 936, s. 3; 1993, c. 539, s. 493; 1994, Ex. Sess., c. 24, s. 14(c)

N.C. Gen. Stat. § 63-19

Repealed by Session Laws 1943, c. 543.

§ 63-20. Qualifications of operator; federal license

The public safety requiring, and the advantages of uniform regulation making it desirable, in the interest of aeronautical progress, that a person engaging within this State in operating aircraft, in any form of aerial navigation for which a license to operate aircraft issued by the United States government would then be required if such aerial navigation were interstate, should have the qualifications necessary for obtaining and holding such a license, it shall be unlawful for any person to engage in operating aircraft within the State, in any such form of aerial navigation, unless he have such federal license.

History.
1929, c. 190, s. 11

§ 63-21. Possession and exhibition of license certificate

The certificate of the license, herein required, shall be kept in the personal possession of the licensee when he is operating aircraft within this State and must be presented for inspection upon the demand of any passenger, any peace officer of this State, or any official, manager or person in charge of any airport or landing field in this State upon which he shall land.

History.
1929, c. 190, s. 12

§ 63-22. Aircraft; construction, design and airworthiness; federal registration

The public safety requiring, and the advantages of uniform regulation making it desirable, in the interest of aeronautical progress, that aircraft to be operated within this State should conform, with respect to design, construction and airworthiness, to standards then prescribed by the United States government with respect to aerial navigation of aircraft subject to its jurisdiction, it shall be unlawful for any person to operate an aircraft within this State unless it is registered pursuant to the lawful rules and regulations of the United States government then in force, if the circumstances of such aerial navigation are of a character that such registration would be required in the case of interstate aerial navigation.

History.
1929, c. 190, s. 13

§ 63-23. Penalties

A person who violates any provision of G.S. 63-20, 63-21 or 63-22 of this Article shall be guilty of a Class 2 misdemeanor; provided, however, that acts or omissions made unlawful by G.S. 63-20, 63-21 or 63-22 of this Article shall not be deemed to include any act or omission which violates the laws or lawful regulations of the United States.

History.
1929, c. 190, s. 14; 1993, c. 539, s. 494; 1994, Ex. Sess., c. 24, s. 14(c)

§ 63-24. Jurisdiction of State over crimes and torts retained

Provided that this Article shall not be construed as a waiver of jurisdiction of the courts of the State of North Carolina over any crime or tort committed within the State of North Carolina, and provided, further, that the General Assembly of North Carolina may at any time amend, regulate or control any of the powers which may be assumed by the United States Department of Commerce under this Article.

History.
1929, c. 190, s. 15

ARTICLE 3
STEALING, TAMPERING WITH, OR OPERATING AIRCRAFT WHILE INTOXICATED

§ 63-25. Taking of aircraft made crime of larceny

Any person who, under circumstances not constituting larceny shall, without the consent of the owner, take, use or operate or cause to be taken, used or operated, an airplane or other aircraft or its equipment, for his own profit, purpose or pleasure, steals the same, is guilty of a Class H felony.

History.
1929, c. 90, s. 1; 1993, c. 539, s. 1278; 1994, Ex. Sess., c. 24, s. 14(c)

§ 63-26. Tampering with aircraft made crime

Any person who shall, without the consent of the owner, go upon or enter, tamper with or in any way damage or injure any airplane or other aircraft, or any personal property under the control of or being used by any public or private airport or aircraft landing facility shall be guilty of a Class 1 misdemeanor, and the showing of willful or malicious intent shall not be necessary to sustain a conviction hereunder.

History.
1929, c. 90, s. 2; 1987, c. 818, s. 3; 1993, c. 539, s. 495; 1994, Ex. Sess., c. 24, s. 14(c)

§ 63-26.1. Trespass upon airport property made a crime

(a) It shall be unlawful for any person to trespass upon airport property. For purposes of this section "airport property" means property that is under the control of or is being used by any public or private airport or aircraft landing facility.

(b) A person commits the offense of trespass upon airport property if, without authorization, he enters or remains on airport property that is so enclosed or posted or secured as to demonstrate clearly an intent to keep out intruders. Violation of this section is a Class 2 misdemeanor.

History.
1987, c. 818, s. 4; 1993, c. 539, s. 496; 1994, Ex. Sess., c. 24, s. 14(c)

§ 63-27. Operation of aircraft while impaired

(a) **Offense.** -- A person commits the offense of operation of an aircraft while impaired if he operates an aircraft, whether on the ground or in the air or on water, within this State:

(1) While under the influence of an impairing substance; or

(2) After having consumed sufficient alcohol that he has, at any relevant time after the operating of an aircraft, an alcohol concentration of 0.04 or more.

The relevant definitions contained in G.S. 20-4.01 shall apply to this section.

(b) **Defense precluded.** -- The fact that a person charged with violating this section is or has been legally entitled to use alcohol or a drug is not a defense to a charge under this section.

(c) **Pleading.** -- In any prosecution for operating an aircraft while impaired, the pleading is sufficient if it states the time and place of the alleged offense in the usual form and charges that the defendant operated the aircraft within this State while subject to an impairing substance.

(d) **Chemical Analysis.** -- Any person who operates an airplane or other aircraft, whether on the ground or in the air or on the water within the territorial limits of this State gives consent to chemical analysis if he is charged with the offense of operating an aircraft while impaired. The charging officer must designate the type of chemical analysis to be administered, and it may be administered when he has reasonable grounds to believe that the person charged has committed the specified crime. The chemical analysis shall be performed pursuant to the procedures established under Chapter 20 of the General Statutes applying to motor vehicle violations with the exception that if the person charged refuses to be tested, the charging officer shall, in writing, notify the local office of the Federal Aviation Administration of the individual's refusal. The results of any chemical tests administered pursuant to this section will be admissible into evidence at trial on the offense charged and a written report of the test results shall be made available to the local office of the Federal Aviation Administration.

(e) **Punishment.** -- A person violating this section shall be guilty of a Class 1 misdemeanor. Provided, however, for a second and all subsequent convictions of this section, a person shall be guilty of a Class I felony.

History.
1929, c. 90, s. 3; 1953, c. 675, s. 8; 1987, c. 818, s. 1; 1993, c. 539, ss. 497, 1279; 1994, Ex. Sess., c. 24, s. 14(c)

§ 63-28. Infliction of serious bodily injury by operation of an aircraft while impaired

(a) **Offense.** -- A person commits the offense of infliction of serious bodily injury by operation of an aircraft while impaired if, while in violation of G.S. 63-27, he does serious bodily injury to another.

(b) **Defense precluded.** -- The fact that a person charged with violating this section is or has been legally entitled to use alcohol or a drug is not a defense to a charge under this section.

(c) **Pleading.** -- In any prosecution for infliction of serious bodily injury by operation of an aircraft while impaired, the pleading is sufficient if it states the time and place of the alleged offense in the usual form and charges that the defendant did serious bodily injury to another while operating an aircraft within this State while subject to an impairing substance.

(d) **Punishment.** -- Violation of this section is a Class F felony.

History.
1929, c. 90, s. 4; 1953, c. 675, s. 9; 1987, c. 818, s. 2; 1993, c. 539, s. 1280; 1994, Ex. Sess., c. 24, s. 14(c)

ARTICLE 4
MODEL AIRPORT ZONING ACT

§ 63-37.1. Airport obstructions illegal

Any person, other than the owner or operator of an airport, who intentionally obstructs the lawful takeoff and landing operations and patterns of aircraft at an existing public or private airport shall be guilty of a Class 1 misdemeanor.

History.
1995, c. 507, s. 19.5(m)

Chapter 63

ARTICLE 10
OPERATION OF UNMANNED AIRCRAFT SYSTEMS

§ 63-94. Applicability of Article

(a) **Applicability.** -- This Article does not apply to model aircraft, as defined in subsection (b) of this section.

(b) **Model aircraft.** -- An aircraft, as defined in G.S. 63-1, that is mechanically driven or launched into flight and that meets all of the following requirements:

(1) Is flown solely for hobby or recreational purposes.

(2) Is not used for payment, consideration, gratuity, or benefit, directly or indirectly charged, demanded, received, or collected, by any person for the use of the aircraft or any photographic or video image produced by the aircraft.

History.
2017-160, s. 5

§ 63-95. Training required for operation of unmanned aircraft systems

(a) As used in this Article, the term "Division" means the Division of Aviation of the Department of Transportation.

(b) The Division shall develop a knowledge test for operating an unmanned aircraft system that complies with all applicable State and federal regulations and shall provide for administration of the test. The test shall ensure that the operator of an unmanned aircraft system is knowledgeable of the State statutes and regulations regarding the operation of unmanned aircraft systems. The Division may permit a person, including an agency of this State, an agency of a political subdivision of this State, an employer, or a private training facility, to administer the test developed pursuant to this subsection, provided the test is the same as that administered by the Division and complies with all applicable State and federal regulations.

(c) No agent or agency of the State, or agent or agency of a political subdivision of the State, may operate an unmanned aircraft system within the State without completion of the test set forth in subsection (b) of this section.

History.
2014-100, s. 34.30(g); 2015-232, s. 2.3

§ 63-96. Permit required for commercial operation of unmanned aircraft systems

(a) No person shall operate an unmanned aircraft system, as defined in G.S. 15A-300.1, in this State for commercial purposes unless the person is in possession of a permit issued by the Division valid for the unmanned aircraft system being operated. Application for the permit shall be made in the manner provided by the Division. Unless suspended or revoked, the permit shall be effective for a period to be established by the Division not exceeding eight years.

(b) No person shall be issued a permit under this section unless all of the following apply:

(1) The person is at least the minimum age required by federal regulation for operation of an unmanned aircraft system.

(2) The person possesses a valid government-issued photographic identification acceptable to the Federal Aviation Administration for issuing authorization to operate an unmanned aircraft system.

(3) The person has passed the knowledge test for operating an unmanned aircraft system as prescribed in G.S. 63-95(b).

(4) The person has satisfied all other applicable requirements of this Article or federal regulation.

(c) A permit to operate an unmanned aircraft system for commercial purposes shall not be issued to a person while the person's license or permit to operate an unmanned aircraft system is suspended, revoked, or cancelled in any state.

(d) The Division shall develop and administer a program that complies with all applicable federal regulations to issue permits to operators of unmanned aircraft systems for commercial purposes, including a fee structure for permits. Criteria and requirements established under the subdivisions set forth in this subsection shall be no more restrictive than the rules or regulations adopted by the Federal Aviation Administration setting forth the criteria and requirements under which a person may operate an unmanned aircraft system for commercial purposes. The program must include the following components:

(1) A system for classifying unmanned aircraft systems based on characteristics determined to be appropriate by the Division.

(2) Repealed by Session Laws 2017-160, s. 4, effective July 21, 2017.

(3) A permit application process, which shall include a requirement that the Division provide notice to an applicant of the Division's decision on issuance of a permit no later than 10 days from the date the Division receives the applicant's application.

(4) Technical guidance for complying with program requirements.

(5) Criteria under which the Division may suspend or revoke a permit.

(6) Criteria under which the Division may waive permitting requirements for applicants currently holding a valid license or

permit to operate unmanned aircraft systems issued by another state or territory of the United States, the District of Columbia, or the United States.

(7) A designation of the geographic area within which a permittee shall be authorized to operate an unmanned aircraft system.

(8) Requirements pertaining to the collection, use, and retention of data by permittees obtained through the operation of unmanned aircraft systems, to be established in consultation with the State Chief Information Officer.

(9) Requirements for the marking of each unmanned aircraft system operated pursuant to a permit issued under this section sufficient to allow identification of the owner of the system and the person issued a permit to operate it.

(10) A system for providing agencies that conduct other operations within regulated airspace with the identity and contact information of permittees and the geographic areas within which the permittee is authorized to operate an unmanned aircraft system.

(e) A person who operates an unmanned aircraft system for commercial purposes other than as authorized under this section shall be guilty of a Class 1 misdemeanor.

(f) Subject to the limitations set forth in subsection (d) of this section, the Division may issue rules and regulations to implement the provisions of this section.

History.
2014-100, s. 34.30(g); 2015-232, s. 2.4; 2016-90, s. 14.5; 2017-160, s. 4

CHAPTER 65
CEMETERIES

ARTICLE 9
NORTH CAROLINA
CEMETERY ACT

§ 65-72. Burial without regard to race or color

(a) It shall be the public policy of the State that all cemetery companies or other legal entities conducting or maintaining public or private cemeteries shall sell to all applicants and bury all deceased human beings on equal terms without regard to race or color. Anything contrary hereto is void and of no legal effect. Bylaws, rules and regulations, contracts, deeds, etc., may permit designation of parts of cemeteries or burial grounds for the specific use of persons whose religious code required isolation. Any program offering free burial rights to veterans or any other person or group of persons shall not be conditioned by any requirement to purchase additional burial rights or merchandise.

(b) Any cemetery company or other legal entity violating the provisions of this section shall be guilty of a Class 1 misdemeanor, and each violation of this section shall constitute a separate offense.

History.
1975, c. 768, s. 1; 1993, c. 539, s. 502; 1994, Ex. Sess., c. 24, s. 14(c)

CHAPTER 66
COMMERCE AND BUSINESS

ARTICLE 1
REGULATION AND INSPECTION

§ 66-10. Failure of dealers of scrap, salvage, or surplus to keep record of purchases of certain items misdemeanor

(a) Every person, firm, or corporation buying rubber or leather, rubber belts, and belting, as scrap, salvage, or surplus shall keep a register containing a true and accurate record of each purchase, including the description of the article purchased, the name from whom purchased, the amount paid for the article purchased, the date of the purchase, and any and all marks or brands upon the rubber or leather, rubber belts, and belting. This register and the rubber, leather, rubber belts, and belting purchased shall be at all times open to the inspection of the public. A failure to comply with these requirements or the making of a false entry concerning the rubber or leather, rubber belts, or belting shall constitute a Class 1 misdemeanor.

(b) Every person, firm, or corporation engaged in the business of buying or dealing in scrap, salvage, or surplus, including glass, waste paper, burlap, cloth, cordage, rubber, leather, or belting of every kind, in addition to the above requirements under subsection (a) of this section, shall make and keep a record of the name and address of the person from whom this scrap, salvage, or surplus is purchased and the license number, if any, and if there is no license, a description of the vehicle in which this scrap, salvage, or surplus is delivered. Any person, firm, or corporation which fails to comply with the requirements of this subsection shall be guilty of a Class 3 misdemeanor and upon conviction shall only be fined not in excess of fifty dollars ($ 50.00) in the discretion of the court.

History.
1917, c. 46; C.S., s. 5090; 1957, c. 791; 1993, c. 295, s. 1; 1993, c. 539, s. 504; 1994, Ex. Sess., c. 24, s. 14(c)

§§ 66-11, 66-11.1

Repealed by Session Laws 2012-46, s. 26, effective October 1, 2012, and applicable to offenses committed on or after that date.

History.
§ 66-11: 1907, c. 464; 1909, c. 855, s. 1; C.S., s. 5091; 1967, c. 792; 1971, c. 1231, s. 1; 1975, c. 182, s. 2; 1993,

c. 295, s. 2; c. 539, s. 505; 1994, Ex. Sess., c. 14, s. 40; c. 24, s. 14(c); 2007-301, s. 1; 2009-200, s. 1; repealed by 2012-46, s. 26, effective October 1, 2012. § 66-11: 1975, c. 182, s. 1; 1993, c. 539, s. 506; 1994, Ex. Sess., c. 24, s. 14(c); repealed by 2012-46, s. 26, effective October 1, 2012

N.C. Gen. Stat. § 66-11.2

Recodified as G.S. 66-426 by Session Laws 2012-46, s. 27, effective October 1, 2012, and applicable to offenses committed on or after that date.

ARTICLE 25
REGULATION OF PRECIOUS METAL BUSINESSES

§§ 66-163 through 66-173

Recodified as Part 2 of Article 45 of Chapter 66, G.S. 66-405 through 66-414, by Session Laws 2012-46, s. 15, effective October 1, 2012, and applicable to offenses committed on or after that date.

ARTICLE 42
STATE FRANCHISE FOR CABLE TELEVISION SERVICE

§ 66-350. Definitions

The following definitions apply in this Article:

(1) **Cable service.** -- Defined in G.S. 105-164.3.

(2) **Cable system.** -- Defined in 47 U.S.C. § 522.

(3) **Channel.** -- A portion of the electromagnetic frequency spectrum that is used in a cable system and is capable of delivering a television channel.

(4) **Existing agreement.** -- A local franchise agreement that was awarded under G.S. 153A-137 or G.S. 160A-319 and meets either of the following:

a. Is in effect on January 1, 2007.

b. Expired before January 1, 2007, and the cable service provider under the agreement provides cable service to subscribers in the franchise area on January 1, 2007.

(5) **Pass a household.** -- Make service available to a household, regardless of whether the household subscribes to the service.

(6) **PEG channel.** -- A public, educational, or governmental access channel provided to a county or city.

(7) **Secretary.** -- The Secretary of State.

(8) **Video programming.** -- Defined in G.S. 105-164.3.

History.
2006-151, s. 1

§ 66-351. State franchising authority

(a) **Authority.** -- The Secretary of State is designated the exclusive franchising authority in this State for cable service provided over a cable system. This designation replaces the authorization to counties and cities in former G.S. 153A-137 and G.S. 160A-319 to award a franchise for cable service. This designation is effective January 1, 2007. After this date, a county or city may not award or renew a franchise for cable service.

(b) **Award and Scope.** -- The Secretary is considered to have awarded a franchise to a person who files a notice of franchise under G.S. 66-352. A franchise for cable service authorizes the holder of the franchise to construct and operate a cable system over public rights-of-way within the area to be served. Chapter 160A of the General Statutes governs the regulation of public rights-of-way by a city.

History.
2006-151, s. 1

§ 66-355. Effect on existing local franchise agreement

(a) **Existing Agreement.** -- This Article does not affect an existing agreement except as follows:

(1) Effective January 1, 2007, gross revenue used to calculate the payment of the franchise tax imposed by G.S. 153A-154 or G.S. 160A-214 does not include gross receipts from cable service subject to sales tax under G.S. 105-164.4. This exclusion does not otherwise affect the calculation of gross revenue and the payment to counties and cities of franchise tax revenue under existing agreements that have not been terminated under subsection (b) of this section.

(2) A cable service provider under an existing agreement that is in effect on January 1, 2007, may terminate the agreement in accordance with subsection (b) of this section in any of the following circumstances:

a. A notice of service filed under G.S. 66-352 indicates that one or more households in the franchise area of the existing agreement are passed by both the cable service provider under the existing agreement and the holder of a State-issued franchise.

b. As of January 1, 2007, a county or city has an existing agreement with more than one cable service provider for substantially the same franchise area and at least twenty-five percent (25%) of the households in the franchise areas of the existing agreements are passed by more than one cable service provider.

c. A person provides wireline competition in the franchise area of the existing agreement by offering video programming over wireline facilities to single family households by a method that does not require a franchise under this Article. A notice of termination filed on the basis of wireline competition must include evidence of the competition in providing video programming service, such as an advertisement announcing the availability of the service, the acceptance of an order for the service, and information on the provider's Web site about the availability of the service. A county or city is allowed 60 days to review the evidence. The effective date of the termination is tolled during this review period. At the end of this period, the termination proceeds unless the county or city has obtained an order enjoining the termination based on the cable service provider's failure to establish the existence of wireline competition in its franchise area.

(3) A cable service provider under an existing agreement that expired before January 1, 2007, may obtain a State-issued franchise. The provider does not have to terminate the agreement in accordance with subsection (b) of this section because the agreement has expired.

(b) **Termination.** -- To terminate an existing agreement, a cable service provider must file a notice of termination with the affected county or city and file a notice of franchise with the Secretary. A termination of an existing agreement becomes effective at the end of the month in which the notice of termination is filed with the affected county or city. A termination of an existing agreement ends the obligations under the agreement and under any local cable regulatory ordinance that specifically authorizes the agreement as of the effective date of the termination but does not affect the rights or liabilities of the county or city, a taxpayer, or another person arising under the existing agreement or local ordinance before the effective date of the termination.

History.
2006-151, s. 1

§ 66-356. Service standards and requirements

(a) **Discrimination Prohibited.** -- A person who provides cable service over a cable system may not deny access to the service to any group of potential residential subscribers within the filed service area because of the race or income of the residents. A violation of this subsection is an unfair or deceptive act or practice under G.S. 75-1.1.

In determining whether a cable service provider has violated this subsection with respect to a group of potential residential subscribers in a service area, the following factors must be considered:

(1) The length of time since the provider filed the notice of service for the area. If less than a year has elapsed since the notice of service was filed, it is conclusively presumed that a violation has not occurred.

(2) The cost of providing service to the affected group due to distance from facilities, density, or other factors.

(3) Technological impediments to providing service to the affected group.

(4) Inability to obtain access to property required to provide service to the affected group.

(5) Competitive pressure to respond to service offered by another cable service provider or other provider of video programming.

(b) **FCC Standards.** -- A person who provides cable service over a cable system must comply with the customer service requirements in 47 C.F.R. Part 76 and emergency alert requirements established by the Federal Communications Commission.

(c) **Complaints.** -- The Consumer Protection Division of the Attorney General's Office is designated as the State agency to receive and respond to customer complaints concerning cable services. Persistent or repeated violations of the federal customer service requirements or the terms and conditions of the cable service provider's agreement with customers are unfair or deceptive acts or practices under G.S. 75-1.1.

To facilitate the resolution of customer complaints, the cable service provider must include the following statement on the customer's bill: "If you have a complaint about your cable service, you should first contact customer service at the following telephone number: (insert the cable service provider's customer service telephone number). If the cable service provider does not satisfactorily resolve your complaint, contact the Consumer Protection Division of the Attorney General's Office of the State of North Carolina (insert information on how to contact the Consumer Protection Division of the Attorney General's Office).

(d) **No Build-Out.** -- No build-out requirements apply to a person who provides cable service under a State-issued franchise.

(e) [**Report to Revenue Laws Study Committee.** --] The Consumer Protection Division of the Attorney General's Office must report to the Revenue Laws Study Committee on or before April 1 of each year, beginning April 1, 2008, on the following information concerning cable service complaints the Division has received from cable customers under this section:

(1) The number of customer complaints.

(2) The types of customer complaints.

(3) The different means of resolving customer complaints.

History.
2006-151, ss. 1, 18

§ 66-357. Availability and use of PEG channels

(a) **Application.** -- This section applies to a person who provides cable service under a State-issued franchise. It does not apply to a person who provides cable service under an existing agreement.

(b) **Local Request.** -- A county or city must make a written request to a cable service provider for PEG channel capacity. The request must include a statement describing the county's or city's plan to operate and program each channel requested. The cable service provider must provide the requested PEG channel capacity within the later of the following:

(1) 120 days after the cable service provider receives the written request.

(2) 30 days after any interconnection requested under G.S. 66-358(a)(1) is accomplished.

(c) **Initial PEG Channels.** -- A city with a population of at least 50,000 is allowed a minimum of three initial PEG channels plus any channels in excess of this minimum that are activated, as of July 1, 2006, under the terms of an existing franchise agreement whose franchise area includes the city. A city with a population of less than 50,000 is allowed a minimum of two initial PEG channels plus any channels in excess of this minimum that are activated, as of July 1, 2006, under the terms of an existing franchise agreement whose franchise area includes the city. For a city included in the franchise area of an existing agreement, the agreement determines the service tier placement and transmission quality of the initial PEG channels. For a city that is not included in the franchise area of an existing agreement, the initial PEG channels must be on a basic service tier, and the transmission quality of the channels must be equivalent to those of the closest city covered by an existing agreement.

A county is allowed a minimum of two initial PEG channels plus any channels in excess of this minimum that are activated, as of July 1, 2006, under the terms of an existing franchise agreement whose franchise area includes the county. For a county included in the franchise area of an existing agreement, the agreement determines the service tier placement and transmission quality of the initial PEG channels. For a county that is not included in the franchise area of an existing agreement, the initial PEG channels must be on a basic service tier and the transmission quality of the channels must be equivalent to those of any city with PEG channels in the county.

The cable service provider must maintain the same channel designation for a PEG channel unless the service area of the State-issued franchise includes PEG channels that are operated by different counties or cities and those PEG channels have the same channel designation. Each county and city whose PEG channels are served by the same cable system headend must cooperate with each other and with the cable system provider in sharing the capacity needed to provide the PEG channels.

(d) **Additional PEG Channels.** -- A county or city that does not have seven PEG channels, including the initial PEG channels, is eligible for an additional PEG channel if it meets the programming requirements in this subsection. A county or city that has seven PEG channels is not eligible for an additional channel.

A county or city that meets the programming requirements in this subsection may make a written request under subsection (b) of this section for an additional channel. The additional channel may be provided on any service tier. The transmission quality of the additional channel must be at least equivalent to the transmission quality of the other channels provided.

The PEG channels operated by a county or city must meet the following programming requirements for at least 120 continuous days in order for the county or city to obtain an additional channel:

    (1) All of the PEG channels must have scheduled programming for at least eight hours a day.

    (2) The programming content of each of the PEG channels must not repeat more than fifteen percent (15%) of the programming content on any of the other PEG channels.

    (3) No more than fifteen percent (15%) of the programming content on any of the PEG channels may be character-generated programming.

(e) **Use of Channels.** -- If a county or city no longer provides any programming for transmission over a PEG channel it has activated, the channel may be reprogrammed at the cable service provider's discretion. A cable service provider must give at least a 60-day notice to a county or city before it reprograms a PEG channel that is not used. The cable service provider must restore a previously lost PEG channel within 120 days of the date a county or city certifies to the provider a schedule that demonstrates the channel will be used.

(f) **Operation of Channels.** -- A cable service provider is responsible only for the transmission of a PEG channel. The county or city to which the PEG channel is provided is responsible for the operation and content of the channel. A county or city that provides content to a cable service provider for transmission on a PEG channel is considered to have authorized the provider to transmit the content throughout the provider's service area, regardless of whether part of the service area is outside the boundaries of the county or city.

All programming on a PEG channel must be noncommercial. A cable service provider may not brand content on a PEG channel with its logo, name, or other identifying marks. A cable service provider is not required to transmit content on a PEG channel that is branded with the logo, name, or other identifying marks of another cable service provider.

(g) **Compliance.** -- A county or city that has not received PEG channel capacity as required by this section may bring an action to compel a cable service provider to comply with this section.

History.
2006-151, s. 1

ARTICLE 45
PAWNBROKERS, METAL DEALERS, AND SCRAP DEALERS

PART 1
PAWNBROKERS AND CASH CONVERTERS

§ 66-385. Short title

This Part shall be known and may be cited as the Pawnbrokers and Cash Converters Modernization Act.

History.
1989, c. 638, s. 2; 2011-325, s. 2; 2012-46, ss. 2, 4

§ 66-386. Purpose

The making of pawn loans and the acquisition and disposition of tangible personal property by and through pawnshops and cash converters vitally affects the general economy of this State and the public interest and welfare of its citizens. In recognition of these facts, it is the policy of this State and the purpose of the Pawnbrokers and Cash Converters Modernization Act to do all of the following:

(1) Ensure a sound system of making loans and acquiring and disposing of tangible personal property by and through pawnshops, and to prevent unlawful property transactions, particularly in stolen property, through licensing and regulating pawnbrokers.

(2) Ensure a sound system of acquiring and disposing of tangible personal property by and through cash converters and to prevent unlawful property transactions, particularly in stolen property, by requiring record keeping by cash converters.

(3) Provide for pawnbroker licensing fees and investigation fees of licensees.

(4) Ensure financial responsibility to the State and the general public.

(5) Ensure compliance with federal and State laws.

(6) Assist local governments in the exercise of their police authority.

History.

1989, c. 638, s. 2; 2011-325, s. 3; 2012-46, ss. 2, 5

§ 66-387. Definitions

The following definitions apply in this Part:

(1) **Cash.** -- Lawful currency of the United States.

(2) **Currency converter.** -- Either (i) a person engaged in the business of purchasing goods from the public for cash at a permanently located retail store or (ii) an itinerant merchant as defined in G.S. 66-250(1) who holds himself or herself out to the public by signs, advertising, or other methods as engaging in that business. The term does not include any of the following:

a. Pawnbrokers, except with regard to the purchase of a gift card or merchandise card.

b. Persons whose goods purchases are made directly from manufacturers or wholesalers for their inventories.

c. Precious metals dealers, to the extent that their transactions are regulated under Part 2 of this Article.

d. Purchases by persons primarily in the business of obtaining from the public, either by purchase or exchange, used clothing, children's furniture, and children's products, provided (i) the amount paid for the individual item purchased is less than fifty dollars

($ 50.00) and (ii) the individual item purchased is not a gift card or merchandise card of any value.

e. Purchases by persons primarily in the business of obtaining from the public, either by purchase or exchange, sporting goods and sporting equipment, provided (i) the amount paid for the individual item purchased is less than fifty dollars ($ 50.00) and (ii) the individual item purchased is not a gift card or merchandise card of any value.

(2a) **E-buyer.** -- A currency converter engaged in the business of purchasing gift cards or merchandise cards online.

(3) **Pawn or pawn transaction.** -- A written bailment of personal property as security for a debt, redeemable on certain terms within 180 days, unless renewed, and with an implied power of sale on default.

(4) **Pawnbroker.** -- A person engaged in the business of lending money on the security of pledged goods and who may also purchase merchandise for resale from dealers and traders.

(5) **Pawnshop.** -- The location at which, or premises in which, a pawnbroker regularly conducts business.

(6) **Person.** -- Any individual, corporation, joint venture, association, or any other legal entity, however organized.

(7) **Pledged goods.** -- Tangible personal property which is deposited with, or otherwise actually delivered into, the possession of a pawnbroker in the course of his business in connection with a pawn transaction.

(8) **Purchase.** -- An item purchased from an individual for the purpose of resale whereby the seller no longer has a vested interest in the item.

History.

1989, c. 638, s. 2; 2011-325, s. 4; 2012-46, ss. 2, 6; 2013-410, s. 26; 2017-162, s. 3

§ 66-388. Pawnbroker authority

A pawnbroker licensee is authorized to: (i) make loans on pledges of tangible personal property, (ii) deal in bullion stocks, (iii) purchase merchandise for resale from dealers, traders, and wholesale suppliers and (iv) use its capital and funds in any lawful manner within the general scope and purpose of its creation. Notwithstanding the provisions of this section, no pawnbroker has the authority enumerated in this section unless he has fully complied with the laws regulating the particular transactions involved.

History.

1989, c. 638, s. 2; 2012-46, s. 2

§ 66-389. License required

It is unlawful for any person, firm, or corporation to establish or conduct a business of pawnbroker unless such person, firm, or corporation has procured a license to conduct business in compliance with the requirements of this Part.

History.
1989, c. 638, s. 2; 2012-46, ss. 2, 7.

§ 66-390. Requirements for licensure

(a) To be eligible for a pawnbroker's license, an applicant must:

(1) Be of good moral character; and

(2) Not have been convicted of a felony within the last 10 years.

(b) Every person, firm or corporation desiring to engage in the business of pawnbroker shall petition the appropriate city or county agency in the area in which the pawnshop is to be operated for a license to conduct such business. Such petitions shall provide:

(1) The name and address of the person, and, in case of a firm or corporation, the names and addresses of the persons composing such firm or of the officers, directors, and stockholders of such corporation, excluding shareholders of publicly traded companies;

(2) The name of the business and the street and mailing address where the business is to be operated;

(3) A statement indicating the amount of net assets or capital proposed to be used by the petitioner in operation of the business; this statement shall be accompanied by an unaudited statement from an accountant or certified public accountant verifying the information contained in the accompanying statement;

(4) An affidavit by the petitioner that he has not been convicted of a felony; and

(5) A certificate from the chief of police, or sheriff of the county, or the State Bureau of Investigation that the petitioner has not been convicted of a felony.

(c) Licenses shall be granted under this Part by the city if the pawnshop is to be operated within the corporate limits of a city as defined by G.S. 160A-1, and by a county if it is to be operated outside the corporate limits of any city as defined by G.S. 160A-1.

(d) Any license granted under this Part may be revoked by the county or city issuing it, after a hearing, for substantial abuses of this Part by the licensee.

History.
1989, c. 638, s. 2; 2012-46, ss. 2, 8.

§ 66-391. Record-keeping requirements for pawnbrokers

(a) Every pawnbroker shall keep consecutively numbered records of each and every pawn transaction, which shall correspond in all essential particulars to a detachable pawn ticket or copy thereof attached to the record.

(b) The pawnbroker shall, at the time of making the pawn or purchase transaction, enter upon the pawn ticket a record of the following information which shall be typed or written in ink and in the English language:

(1) A clear and accurate description of the property, including model and serial number if indicated on the property;

(2) The name, residence address, phone number, and date of birth of pledgor;

(3) Date of the pawn transaction;

(4) Type of identification and the identification number accepted from pledgor;

(5) Description of the pledgor including approximate height, weight, sex, and race;

(6) Amount of money advanced;

(7) The date due and the amount due;

(8) All monthly pawn charges, including interest, annual percentage rate on interest, and total recovery fee; and

(9) Agreed upon "stated value" between pledgor and pawnbroker in case of loss or destruction of pledged item; unless otherwise noted, "stated value" is the same as the loan value.

(c) The following shall be printed on all pawn tickets:

(1) The statement that "ANY PERSONAL PROPERTY PLEDGED TO A PAWNBROKER WITHIN THIS STATE IS SUBJECT TO SALE OR DISPOSAL WHEN THERE HAS BEEN NO PAYMENT MADE ON THE ACCOUNT FOR A PERIOD OF 60 DAYS PAST MATURITY DATE OF THE ORIGINAL CONTRACT. NO FURTHER NOTICE IS NECESSARY.";

(2) The statement that "THE PLEDGOR OF THIS ITEM ATTESTS THAT IT IS NOT STOLEN, HAS NO LIENS OR ENCUMBRANCES, AND IS THE PLEDGOR'S TO SELL OR PAWN.";

(3) The statement that "THE ITEM PAWNED IS REDEEMABLE ONLY BY THE BEARER OF THIS TICKET OR BY IDENTIFICATION OF THE PERSON MAKING THE PAWN."; and

(4) A blank line for the pledgor's signature and the pawnbroker's signature or initials.

(d) The pledgor shall sign the pawn ticket and shall receive an exact copy of the pawn ticket which shall be signed or initialed by the pawnbroker or any employee of the pawnbroker. These records shall be available for inspection and pickup each regular workday by the sheriff of the county, or the sheriff's designee or the chief of police, or the chief's designee of the municipality in which the pawnshop is located. These records may be electronically reported to the sheriff of the county or the chief of police of the municipality in which the pawnshop is located by transmission over the Internet or by facsimile transmission in a manner authorized by the applicable sheriff or chief of police. These records shall be a correct copy of the entries made of the pawn or purchase transaction and shall be carefully preserved without alteration, and shall be available during regular business hours.

(e) Except as otherwise provided in this Part, any person presenting a pawn ticket to a pawnbroker is presumed to be entitled to redeem the pledged goods described on the ticket.

History.
1989, c. 638, s. 2; 2007-415, s. 2; 2011-325, s. 5; 2012-46, ss. 2, 9

§ 66-392. Record-keeping requirements for currency converters and e-buyers

(a) Every currency converter shall keep consecutively numbered records of each cash purchase. The currency converter shall, at the time of making the purchase, enter upon each record all of the following information, which shall be typed or written in ink and in the English language:

(1) A clear and accurate description of the property purchased by the currency converter from the seller, including model and serial number if indicated on the property.

(2) The name, residence address, phone number, and date of birth of the seller.

(3) The date of the purchase.

(4) The type of identification and the identification number accepted from the seller.

(5) A description of the seller, including approximate height, weight, sex, and race.

(6) The purchase price.

(7) The statement that "THE SELLER OF THIS ITEM ATTESTS THAT IT IS NOT STOLEN, HAS NO LIENS OR ENCUMBRANCES, AND IS THE SELLER'S TO SELL."

(b) The seller shall sign the record and shall receive an exact copy of the record, which shall be signed or initialed by the currency converter or any employee of the currency converter. These records shall be available for inspection and pickup each regular workday by the sheriff of the county or the sheriff's designee or the chief of police or the chief's designee of the municipality in which the currency converter is located. These records may be electronically reported to the sheriff of the county or the chief of police of the municipality in which the currency converter is located by transmission over the Internet or by facsimile transmission in a manner authorized by the applicable sheriff or chief of police. These records shall be a correct copy of the entries made of the purchase transaction, shall be carefully preserved without alteration, and shall be available during regular business hours.

(c) This section does not apply to purchases directly from a manufacturer or wholesaler for a currency converter's inventory.

(d) Notwithstanding subsection (a) of this section, an e-buyer shall record all of the following information, which shall be typed or written in ink and in the English language:

(1) A clear and accurate description of the goods purchased by the currency converter from the seller, including the brand of the gift card or merchandise card and the last four digits of the card number.

(2) The name, address, and phone number or e-mail address of the seller.

(3) The date of the purchase.

(4) If identification is captured by the e-buyer, the type of identification and the identification number provided to the e-buyer, including any photograph of the seller, if obtained.

(5) The IP address utilized by the seller if captured by the e-buyer.

(6) The purchase price and value of the gift card or merchandise card.

(7) A statement to the effect that "THE SELLER OF THIS ITEM ATTESTS THAT IT IS NOT STOLEN, HAS NO LIENS OR ENCUMBRANCES, AND IS THE SELLER'S TO SELL."

Unless subject to an active investigation by law enforcement, an e-buyer shall make the records described in this subsection available electronically via a secure connection upon a reasonable request to the law enforcement officials described in subsection (b) of this section, but no more frequently than on a monthly basis. If the request for information is related to an active investigation, an e-buyer shall make the record available to the investigating law enforcement agency electronically via a secure connection within one business day of the request.

History.
2011-325, s. 6; 2012-46, s. 2; 2013-410, s. 26; 2017-162, s. 4

§ 66-393. Pawnbroker fees; interest rates

No pawnbroker shall demand or receive an effective rate of interest greater than two percent

Chapter 66

(2%) per month, and no other charge of any description or for any purpose shall be made by the pawnbroker, except that the pawnbroker may charge, contract for, and recover an additional monthly fee for the following services, including but not limited to:

(1) Title investigation;

(2) Handling, appraisal, and storage;

(3) Insuring a security;

(4) Application fee;

(5) Making daily reports to local law enforcement officers; and

(6) For other expenses, including losses of every nature, and all other services.

In no event may the total of the above listed monthly fees on a pawn transaction exceed twenty percent (20%) of the principal up to a maximum of the following:

First month.................... $ 100.00
Second month..................... 75.00
Third month...................... 75.00
Fourth month and thereafter....... 50.00

In addition, pawnbrokers may charge fees for returned checks as allowed by G.S. 25-3-506.

History.
1989, c. 638, s. 2; 1995 (Reg. Sess., 1996), c. 742, s. 37; 2012-46, s. 2

§ 66-394. Pawnbroker transactions

In every pawn transaction:

(1) The original pawn contract shall have a maturity date of not less than 30 days, provided that nothing herein shall prevent the pledgor from redeeming the property before the maturity date;

(2) Any personal property pledged to a pawnbroker in this State is subject to sale or disposal when there has been no payment made on the account for a period of 60 days past maturity date of the original contract; provided that the contract between the pledgor and the pawnbroker is renewable if renewal is agreed upon by both the parties;

(3) Every pawn ticket or receipt for such pawn shall have printed thereon the provisions of subdivision (1) of this section which shall constitute: (i) notice of such sale or disposal, (ii) notice of intention to sell or dispose of the property without further notice, and (iii) consent to such sale or disposal. The pledgor thereby forfeits all right, title and interest of, in, and to such pawned property to the pawnbroker who thereby acquires absolute title to the same, whereupon the debt is satisfied and the pawnbroker may sell or dispose of the unredeemed pledges as his own property. Any sale or disposal of property under this

section terminates all liability of the pawnbroker and vests in the purchaser the right, title, and interest of the borrower and the pawnbroker;

(4) If the borrower loses his pawn ticket he shall not thereby forfeit his right to redeem, but may, before the lapse of the redemption period, make an affidavit with indemnification for such loss. The affidavit shall describe the property pawned and shall take the place of the lost pawn ticket unless the pawned property has already been redeemed with the original pawn ticket; and

(5) A pledgor is not obligated to redeem pledged goods or make any payment on a pawn transaction.

History.
1989, c. 638, s. 2; 2012-46, s. 2

§ 66-395. Prohibitions

(a) A pawnbroker shall not:

(1) Accept a pledge from a person under the age of 18 years.

(2) Make any agreement requiring the personal liability of a pledgor in connection with a pawn transaction.

(3) Accept any waiver, in writing or otherwise, of any right or protection accorded a pledgor under this Part.

(4) Fail to exercise reasonable care to protect pledged goods from loss or damage.

(5) Fail to return pledged goods to a pledgor upon payment of the full amount due the pawnbroker on the pawn transaction. In the event such pledged goods are lost or damaged while in the possession of the pawnbroker, it shall be the responsibility of the pawnbroker to replace the lost or damaged goods with merchandise of like kind and equivalent value. In the event the pledgor and pawnbroker cannot agree as to replacement, the pawnbroker shall reimburse the pledgor in the amount of the value agreed upon pursuant to G.S. 66-391(b).

(6) Take any article in pawn, pledge, or as security from any person, which is known to such pawnbroker to be stolen, unless there is a written agreement with local or State law enforcement.

(7) Sell, exchange, barter, or remove from the pawnshop any goods pledged, pawned, or purchased before the earlier of seven days after the date the pawn ticket record is electronically reported in accordance with G.S. 66-391(d) or 30 days after the transaction, except in case of redemption

by pledgor or items purchased for resale from wholesalers.

　(8) Operate more than one pawnshop under one license, and such shop must be at a permanent place of business.

　(9) Take as pledged goods any manufactured mobile home, recreational vehicle, or motor vehicle other than a motorcycle.

(b) A currency converter shall not purchase from any person property which is known to the currency converter to be stolen, unless there is a written agreement with local or State law enforcement.

History.

1989, c. 638, s. 2; 2007-415, s. 1; 2011-325, s. 7; 2012-46, ss. 2, 10; 2013-410, s. 26

§ 66-396. Penalties

(a) Every person, firm, or corporation, their guests or employees, who shall knowingly violate any of the provisions of this Part, shall, on conviction thereof, be deemed guilty of a Class 2 misdemeanor. If the violation is by an owner or major stockholder or managing partner of the pawnshop and the violation is knowingly committed by the owner, major stockholder, or managing partner of the pawnshop, then the license of the pawnshop may be suspended at the discretion of the court.

(b) The provision of subsection (a) of this section shall not apply to violations of G.S. 66-395(a) (6) or G.S. 66-395(b) which shall be prosecuted under the North Carolina criminal statutes.

(c) Any contract of pawn the making or collecting of which violates any provision of this Part, except as a result of accidental or bona fide error of computation, shall be void, and the licensee shall have no right to collect, receive or retain any interest or fee whatsoever with respect to such pawn.

History.

1989, c. 638, s. 2; 1993, c. 539, s. 655; 1994, Ex. Sess., c. 24, s. 14(c); 2011-325, s. 8; 2012-46, ss. 2, 11

§ 66-397. Municipal or county authority

All of the counties and cities as defined by G.S. 160A-1 may by ordinance adopt the provisions of this Part and may adopt such further rules and regulations as the governing bodies of the counties and cities deem appropriate; provided, however, no county or city may regulate:

　(1) Interest, fees, or recovery charges;

　(2) Hours of operation, unless such regulation applies to businesses generally;

　(3) The nature of the business or type of pawn transaction; or

　(4) License fees in excess of rates set by the State.

History.

1989, c. 638, s. 2; 1993, c. 539, s. 655; 1994, Ex. Sess., c. 24, s. 14(c); 2011-325, s. 8; 2012-46, ss. 2, 12

§ 66-398. License renewal

Notwithstanding any provision of this Part to the contrary, any person, firm, or corporation licensed as a pawnbroker on or before October 1, 1989, shall continue in force until the natural expiration thereof and all other provisions of this Part shall apply to such license. Such pawnbroker shall be eligible for renewal of his license upon its expiration or subsequent renewals, provided such license complies with the requirements for renewal that were in effect immediately prior to October 1, 1989.

History.

1989, c. 638, s. 2; 2012-46, ss. 2, 13

§ 66-399. Bond

Every person, firm, or corporation licensed under this Part shall, at the time of receiving the license, file with the city or county issuing the license a bond payable to such city or county in the sum of five thousand dollars ($ 5,000), to be executed by the licensee, and by two responsible sureties or a surety company licensed to do such business in this State, to be approved by the city or county, which shall be for the faithful performance of the requirements and obligations pertaining to the business so licensed. The city or county may sue for forfeiture of the bond upon a breach thereof. Any person who obtains a judgment against a pawnbroker and upon which judgment execution is returned unsatisfied may maintain an action in his own name upon the bond, to satisfy the judgment.

History.

1989, c. 638, s. 2; 2012-46, ss. 2, 14

PART 2
PRECIOUS METAL BUSINESS

§ 66-405. Legislative finding

The General Assembly finds and declares that precious metal businesses in North Carolina vitally affect the general economy of the State and the public interest and public welfare, and in the exercise of its police power, it is necessary to regulate such businesses, in order to prevent thefts, disposal of stolen property, and other abuses upon its citizens.

History.

1981, c. 956, s. 1; 2012-46, s. 15

§ 66-406. Definitions

The following definitions apply in this Part:

(1) **Dealer.** -- A person who purchases precious metals from the public, other than by an exempted transaction, in the form of jewelry, flatware, silver services, or other forms and holds himself or herself out to the public by signs, advertising, or other methods as engaging in such purchases, including any independent contractor purchasing precious metals under any arrangement in any department store. An exempted transaction is one that is (i) not considered in determining whether a person is a dealer under this Part and (ii) not subject to the requirements of this Part, even if it is entered into by a person otherwise defined and regulated as a dealer. Exempted transactions are:

a. Purchases directly from manufacturers or wholesalers of precious metals by permanently located retail merchants for their inventories.

b. Pawns, pledges, or purchases of items made of precious metals, if the transaction is entered into by a licensed pawnbroker and the transaction is regulated under the provisions of Part 1 of this Article.

c. The acquisition of precious metals by a permanently located retail merchant through barter or exchange for other items sold in the ordinary course of the merchant's business, provided that the seller does not receive, as part of the transaction, any sum of money or any gift card or stored-value card, unless the card is redeemable only at that merchant's business.

(2) **Local law enforcement agency.** -- The term means the following, as applicable:

a. The county police force, if the dealer's business is located within a county with a county police force and outside the corporate limits of a municipality.

b. The municipal police force, if the dealer's business is located within the corporate limits of a municipality having a police force.

c. The county sheriff's office of the county in which the dealer's business is located, if neither sub-subdivision a. nor b. of this subdivision applies.

(3) **Precious metal.** -- Gold, silver, platinum, or palladium, as defined below, but excluding coins, medals, medallions, tokens, numismatic items, art ingots, or art bars.

a. **Gold.** -- Any item or article containing 10 karats of gold or more which may be in combination or alloy with any other metal.

b. **Silver.** -- Any item or article containing 925 parts per thousand of silver which may be in combination or alloy with any nonprecious metal or which is marked "sterling".

c. **Platinum.** -- Any item or article containing 900 parts per thousand or more of platinum which may be in combination or alloy with any other metal.

d. **Palladium.** -- Any item or article containing 950 parts per thousand or more of palladium which may be in combination or alloy with any other metal.

History.

1981, c. 956, s. 1; c. 1001, s. 3; 1989 (Reg. Sess., 1990), c. 1024, s. 10(b); 2009-482, s. 1; 2012-46, ss. 15, 17

§ 66-407. Permits

(a) **Dealer Permit.** -- Except as provided in subsection (c) of this section, it is unlawful for any person to engage as a dealer in the business of purchasing precious metals either as a separate business or in connection with other business operations without first obtaining a permit for the business from the local law enforcement agency. The Department of Public Safety shall approve the forms for both the application and the permit. The application shall be given under oath and shall be notarized. A 30-day waiting period from the date of filing of the application is required prior to initial issuance of a permit. A separate permit shall be issued for each location, place, or premises within the jurisdiction of the local law enforcement agency which is used for conducting a precious metals business, and each permit shall designate the location, place or premises to which it applies. No business shall be conducted in a place other than that designated in the permit, or in a mobile home, trailer, camper, or other vehicle, or structure not permanently affixed to the ground or in any room customarily used for lodging in any hotel, motel, tourist court, or tourist home. The permit shall be posted in a prominent place on the designated premises. Permits shall be valid for a period of 12 months from the date issued and may be renewed without a waiting period upon filing of an application and payment of the annual fee. The annual fee for a permit within each jurisdiction is one hundred eighty dollars ($ 180.00) to provide for the administrative costs of the local law enforcement agency, including the purchase of required forms and the cost of conducting the criminal history record check of the applicant. The fee is not refundable even if the permits are denied or later suspended or revoked. A permit issued under this section is in addition to and not in lieu of other business licenses and is not transferable.

No person other than the dealer named on the permit and that dealer's employees may engage in the business of purchasing precious metals under the authority of the permit.

Any dealer applying to the local law enforcement agency for a permit shall furnish the local law enforcement agency with the following information:

(1) The applicant's full name, and any other names used by the applicant during the preceding five years. In the case of a partnership, association, or corporation, the applicant shall list any partnership, association, or corporate names used during the preceding five years.

(2) Current address, and all addresses used by the applicant during the preceding five years.

(3) Physical description.

(4) Age.

(5) Driver's license number, if any, and state of issuance.

(6) Recent photograph.

(7) Record of felony convictions.

(8) Record of other convictions during the preceding five years.

(9) A full set of fingerprints of the applicant.

If the applicant for a dealer's permit is a partnership or association, all persons owning a ten percent (10%) or more interest in the partnership or association shall comply with the provisions of this subsection. These permits shall be issued in the name of the partnership or association.

If the applicant for a dealer's permit is a corporation, each officer, director and stockholder owning ten percent (10%) or more of the corporation's stock, of any class, shall comply with the provisions of this subsection. These permits shall be issued in the name of the corporation.

No permit shall be issued to an applicant who has been convicted of a felony involving a crime of moral turpitude, or larceny, or receiving stolen goods or of similar charges in any federal court or a court of this or any other state, unless the applicant has had his or her rights of citizenship restored pursuant to Chapter 13 of the General Statutes for five years or longer immediately preceding the date of application. In the case of a partnership, association, or corporation, no permit shall be issued to any applicant with an officer, partner, or director who has been convicted of a felony involving a crime of moral turpitude, or larceny, or receiving stolen goods or of similar charges in any federal court or a court of this or any other state, unless that person has had his or her rights of citizenship restored pursuant to Chapter 13 of the General Statutes for five years or longer immediately preceding the date of application.

The Department of Public Safety may provide a criminal history record check to the local law enforcement agency for a person who has applied for a permit through the agency. The agency shall provide to the Department of Public Safety, along with the request, the fingerprints of the applicant, any additional information required by the Department of Public Safety, and a form signed by the applicant consenting to the check of the criminal record and to the use of the fingerprints and other identifying information required by the State or national repositories. The applicant's fingerprints shall be forwarded to the State Bureau of Investigation for a search of the State's criminal history record file, and the State Bureau of Investigation shall forward a set of the fingerprints to the Federal Bureau of Investigation for a national criminal history record check. The agency shall keep all information pursuant to this subsection privileged, in accordance with applicable State law and federal guidelines, and the information shall be confidential and shall not be a public record under Chapter 132 of the General Statutes.

The Department of Public Safety may charge each applicant a fee for conducting the checks of criminal history records authorized by this subsection.

(b) **Employee Requirements.** -- Every employee engaged in the precious metals purchasing business shall, within two business days of being so engaged, register his or her name and address with the local law enforcement agency and have his or her photograph taken by the agency. The employee also shall consent to a criminal history record check, which shall be performed by the local law enforcement agency. A person who refuses to consent to a criminal history record check shall not be employed by a dealer required to be licensed under this section. A person who has been convicted of a felony involving a crime of moral turpitude, larceny, receiving stolen goods, or of similar charges shall not be employed by a dealer required to be licensed under this section, unless the person has had his or her rights of citizenship restored pursuant to Chapter 13 of the General Statutes for five years or longer immediately preceding the date of registration. The agency shall issue to the employee a certificate of compliance with this section upon the applicant's payment of the sum of ten dollars ($ 10.00) to the agency. The certificate shall be renewed annually for a three-dollar ($ 3.00) fee and shall be posted in the work area of the registered employee. An employee is not subject to the requirements of this subsection if the employee is engaged in the precious metals purchasing business only incidentally to his or her main job responsibilities, and each precious metals transaction with which the employee is involved is overseen by a licensed dealer or registered employee. All records of transactions must be signed by the licensed dealer or registered employee at the time of the transaction, as required under G.S. 66-410(a).

The Department of Public Safety may provide a criminal history record check to the local law enforcement agency for an employee engaged in the precious metals business. The agency shall provide to the Department of Public Safety, along with the request, the fingerprints of the employee, any additional information required by the Department of Public Safety, and a form signed by the employee consenting to the check of the criminal record and to the use of the fingerprints and other identifying information required by the State or national repositories. The employee's fingerprints shall be forwarded to the State Bureau of Investigation for a search of the State's criminal history record file, and the State Bureau of Investigation shall forward a set of the fingerprints to the Federal Bureau of Investigation for a national criminal history record check. The agency shall keep all information pursuant to this subsection privileged, in accordance with applicable State law and federal guidelines, and the information shall be confidential and shall not be a public record under Chapter 132 of the General Statutes.

The Department of Public Safety may charge each employee a fee for conducting the checks of criminal history records authorized by this subsection.

(c) **Special Occasion Permit. --** A special occasion permit authorizes the permittee to purchase precious metals as a dealer participating in any trade shows, antique shows, and crafts shows conducted within the State. A special occasion permit shall be issued by any local law enforcement agency; provided, however, that a permittee under subsection (a) of this section shall apply for a special occasion permit with the local law enforcement agency that issued the dealer's permit. The Department of Public Safety shall approve the forms for both the application and the permit. The application shall be given under oath and notarized. A 30-day waiting period from the date of filing of the application is required prior to initial issuance of a permit.

Any dealer applying to a local law enforcement agency for a special occasion permit shall furnish the local law enforcement agency with the information required in an application for a dealer's permit as set forth in subsection (a) of this section. In addition, the applicant shall provide a physical address where any item included in a dealer purchase will be held for the period required under G.S. 66-411. The physical address shall be the location where the purchase was made, unless another physical address within the law enforcement jurisdiction where the purchase was made is approved by the law enforcement agency that issues the permit. The items shall be available at all reasonable times for inspection on the premises by law enforcement agencies.

If the applicant for a special occasion permit is a partnership or association, all persons owning a ten percent (10%) or more interest in the partnership or association shall comply with the provisions of this subsection. Any such permits shall be issued in the name of the partnership or association.

If the applicant for a special occasion permit is a corporation, each officer, director and stockholder owning ten percent (10%) or more of the corporation's stock, of any class, shall comply with the provisions of this subsection. Any such permits shall be issued in the name of the corporation.

No permit shall be issued to an applicant who has been convicted of a felony involving a crime of moral turpitude, or larceny, or receiving stolen goods or of similar charges in any federal court or a court of this or any other state, unless the applicant has had his or her rights of citizenship restored pursuant to Chapter 13 of the General Statutes for five years or longer immediately preceding the date of application. In the case of a partnership, association, or corporation, no permit shall be issued to any applicant with an officer, partner, or director who has been convicted of a felony involving a crime of moral turpitude, or larceny, or receiving stolen goods or of similar charges in any federal court or a court of this or any other state, unless that person has had his or her rights of citizenship restored pursuant to Chapter 13 of the General Statutes for five years or longer immediately preceding the date of application.

The Department of Public Safety may provide a criminal history record check to the local law enforcement agency for a person who has applied for a permit through the agency. The agency shall provide to the Department of Public Safety, along with the request, the fingerprints of the applicant, any additional information required by the Department of Public Safety, and a form signed by the applicant consenting to the check of the criminal record and to the use of the fingerprints and other identifying information required by the State or national repositories. The applicant's fingerprints shall be forwarded to the State Bureau of Investigation for a search of the State's criminal history record file, and the State Bureau of Investigation shall forward a set of the fingerprints to the Federal Bureau of Investigation for a national criminal history record check.

The agency shall keep all information pursuant to this subsection privileged, in accordance with applicable State law and federal guidelines, and the information shall be confidential and shall not be a public record under Chapter 132 of the General Statutes.

The Department of Public Safety may charge each applicant a fee for conducting the checks of criminal history records authorized by this subsection.

The filing fee for a special occasion permit application is one hundred eighty dollars ($ 180.00) to provide for the administrative cost of the local law enforcement agency including purchase of required forms and the cost of conducting the criminal history record check of the applicant. The fee is not refundable even if the permit is denied or is later suspended or revoked. A special occasion permit is in addition to and not in lieu of other business licenses and is not transferable. No person other than the dealer named on the permit and that dealer's employees may engage in the business of purchasing precious metals under the authority of the permit.

A special occasion permit is valid for 12 months from the date issued, unless earlier surrendered, suspended, or revoked. Application for renewal of a permit for an additional 12 months shall be on a form approved by the Department of Public Safety and shall be accompanied by a nonrefundable renewal fee of one hundred eighty dollars ($ 180.00).

Each special occasion permit shall be posted in a prominent place on the premises of any show at which the permittee purchases precious metals.

History.
1981, c. 956, s. 1; 2002-147, s. 2; 2009-482, s. 2; 2011-145, s. 19.1(g); 2012-46, ss. 15, 18; 2014-100, s. 17.1(o)

§ 66-408. Perjury; punishment

Any person who shall willfully commit perjury in any application for a permit or exemption filed pursuant to this Part shall be guilty of a Class 2 misdemeanor.

History.
1981, c. 956, s. 1; 1993, c. 539, s. 525; 1994, Ex. Sess., c. 24, s. 14(c); 2012-46, ss. 15, 19

§ 66-409. Bond or trust account required

Before any permit shall be issued to a dealer pursuant to G.S. 66-407, the dealer shall execute a satisfactory cash or surety bond or establish a trust account with a licensed and insured bank or savings institution located in the State of North Carolina in the sum of ten thousand dollars ($ 10,000). The bond or trust account shall be in favor of the State of North Carolina. A surety bond is to be executed by the dealer and by two responsible sureties or a surety company licensed to do business in the State of North Carolina and shall be on a form approved by the Department of Public Safety. Any bond shall be kept in full force and effect and shall be delivered to the law-enforcement agency which first issued a current permit to the dealer. A bond or trust account shall be for the faithful performance of the requirements and obligations of the dealer's business in conformity with this Part. Any law-enforcement agency shall have full power and authority to revoke the permit and sue for forfeiture of the bond or trust account upon a breach thereof. Any person who shall have suffered any loss or damage by any act of the permittee that constitutes a violation of this Part shall have the right to institute an action to recover against such permittee and the surety or trust account. Upon termination of the bond or trust account the permit shall become void.

History.
1981, c. 956, s. 1; c. 1001, s. 4; 2011-145, s. 19.1(g); 2012-46, ss. 15, 20

§ 66-410. Records to be kept

(a) Every dealer to whom a permit has been issued pursuant to G.S. 66-407 shall maintain consecutively numbered records of each precious metals transaction. Each consecutively numbered record shall be made at the time of the transaction and shall contain a clear and accurate description of the transaction. A valid description shall include each of the following applicable and available items of information: the manufacturer's name, the model, the model number, the serial number, and any engraved numbers or initials found on the items; the date of the transaction; the name, sex, race, residence, telephone number and driver's license number of the person selling the items purchased; and the signature of both the dealer or registered employee and the seller. In the event the seller cannot furnish valid, unexpired photographic identification in the form of a drivers license, State-issued identification card, passport, or military identification card, the dealer shall require two forms of positive identification.

(b) The consecutively numbered records required by this section shall be kept either (i) in a paginated, bound book or set of books with pages numbered in sequence or (ii) in an electronic database that prevents record deletion, tracks all modifications to records, and provides for electronic signatures.

(c) The records shall be open at all reasonable times to inspection on the premises by law

Chapter 66

enforcement agencies, and an individual record shall be retained for at least two years after a transaction. If a dealer maintains a record book rather than an electronic database, the book shall be retained until at least two years following the last recorded transaction.

(d) A copy of each consecutively numbered record entry shall be filed within 48 hours of the transaction in the office of the local law enforcement agency. Records shall be filed in the manner authorized by the local law enforcement agency, which may include reporting electronically by transmission over a computer network, by facsimile machine, or by hand delivering hard copies to the local law enforcement agency. In any case where a technological failure prevents a dealer from reporting electronically or by facsimile, the dealer shall have the option of hand delivering a hard copy of the record to the local law enforcement agency. Regardless of the manner in which the local law enforcement agency allows reporting, a dealer shall provide a hard copy of records upon the request of a law enforcement agency.

(e) The files of local law enforcement agencies that contain copies of records shall not be subject to inspection and examination as authorized by G.S. 132-6. Any public official or employee who shall knowingly and willfully permit any person to have access to or custody or possession of any portion of such files, unless the person is one specifically authorized by the local law enforcement agency to have access for purposes of law enforcement investigation or civil or criminal proceedings, shall be guilty of a Class 3 misdemeanor and upon conviction shall only be fined up to five hundred dollars ($ 500.00) in the discretion of the court.

History.
1981, c. 956, s. 1; 1993, c. 539, s. 526; 1994, Ex. Sess., c. 24, s. 14(c); 2009-482, s. 4; 2012-46, ss. 15, 21

§ 66-411. Items not to be modified

No item included in a dealer purchase shall be sold, traded or otherwise disposed of, melted, cut or otherwise changed in form nor shall any item be removed from the licensed premises, or other location specified on the application for a special occasion permit, for a period of seven days from the date the transaction was reported in accordance with G.S. 66-410.

History.
1981, c. 956, s. 1; 2009-482, s. 5; 2012-46, ss. 15, 22

§ 66-412. Purchasing from juvenile

No dealer or employee or agent thereof shall purchase from any juvenile under 18 years of age any article made, in whole or in part, of precious metal.

History.
1981, c. 956, s. 1; 2012-46, s. 15

§ 66-413. Penalties

Any dealer who violates the provisions of this Part shall be deemed guilty of a Class 2 misdemeanor. In addition any dealer so convicted shall be ineligible for a dealer's permit for a period of three years from the date of conviction. Each and every violation shall constitute a separate and distinct offense.

History.
1981, c. 956, s. 1; 1993, c. 539, s. 527; 1994, Ex. Sess., c. 24, s. 14(c); 2012-46, ss. 15, 23

§ 66-414. Portable smelters prohibited

It shall be unlawful for any person to possess or operate a smelter in any mobile home, trailer, camper, or other vehicle or structure not permanently affixed to the ground, for the purpose of refining precious metals. Violation of the provisions of this section shall constitute a Class 2 misdemeanor.

History.
1981, c. 956, s. 1; 1993, c. 539, s. 528; 1994, Ex. Sess., c. 24, s. 14(c); 2012-46, s. 15

PART 3
REGULATION OF SALES AND PURCHASES OF METALS

§ 66-420. Definitions

The following definitions apply in this Part:

(1) **Cash card system.** -- A system of payment that provides payment in cash or in a form other than cash and that when providing payment in the form of cash (i) captures a photograph of the seller at the time payment is received and (ii) uses an automated cash dispenser, including, but not limited to, an automated teller machine.

(1a) **Copper.** -- Nonferrous metals, including, but not limited to, copper wire, copper clad steel wire, copper pipe, copper bars, copper sheeting, copper tubing and pipe fittings, and insulated copper wire. The term shall not include brass alloys, bronze alloys, lead, nickel, zinc, or items not containing a significant quantity of copper.

(2) **Fixed site.** -- A site occupied by a secondary metals recycler as the owner of the site or as a lessee of the site under a

lease or other rental agreement providing for occupation of the site by a nonferrous metals purchaser for a total duration of not less than 364 days.

(3) **Law enforcement officer.** -- Any duly constituted law enforcement officer of the State or of any municipality or county.

(4) **Nonferrous metals.** -- Metals not containing significant quantities of iron or steel, including, but not limited to, copper, aluminum other than aluminum cans, a product that is a mixture of aluminum and copper, catalytic converters, lead-acid batteries, and stainless steel beer kegs or containers. The term shall not include precious metals as defined and regulated in Part 2 of this Article.

(5) **Nonferrous metals purchaser.** -- A secondary metals recycler who purchases, gathers, or obtains nonferrous metals.

(6) **Permit.** -- A permit issued pursuant to G.S. 66-426(a).

(7) **Regulated metals property.** -- All ferrous and nonferrous metals.

(8) **Secondary metals recycler.** -- Any person, firm, or corporation in the State:

a. That is engaged in the business of gathering or obtaining ferrous or nonferrous metals that have served their original economic purpose or is in the business of performing the manufacturing process by which ferrous metals or nonferrous metals are converted into raw material products consisting of prepared grades and having an existing or potential economic value; or

b. That has facilities for performing the manufacturing process by which ferrous metals or nonferrous metals are converted into raw material products consisting of prepared grades and having an existing or potential economic value, by methods including, but not limited to, the processing, sorting, cutting, classifying, cleaning, baling, wrapping, shredding, shearing, or changing the physical form or chemical content of the metals, but not including the exclusive use of hand tools.

History.
2012-46, s. 28; 2013-169, s. 1

§ 66-420.1. Applicability

This Chapter shall not apply to a salvage yard regulated pursuant to Chapter 20 of the General Statutes, unless the salvage yard is engaged in the business of gathering or obtaining ferrous or nonferrous metals that have served their original economic purpose and is in the business of performing the manufacturing

process by which ferrous metals or nonferrous metals are converted into raw material products consisting of prepared grades and having an existing or potential economic value.

History.
2013-410, s. 30.5

§ 66-421. Required records and receipts for regulated metals transactions

(a) **Receipt Required.** -- A secondary metals recycler shall issue a receipt for all purchase transactions in which the secondary metals recycler purchases regulated metals property. This receipt shall be issued to and signed by the person delivering the property, and the secondary metals recycler shall be able to provide documentation regarding the employee who completed the transaction.

(b) **Records Required.** -- A secondary metals recycler shall maintain an electronic record of all purchase transactions in which the secondary metals recycler purchases regulated metals property. The record of each transaction shall contain the following information:

(1) The name and address of the secondary metals recycler.

(2) The name, initials, or other identification of the individual entering the information.

(3) The date of the transaction.

(4) The weight of the regulated metals property purchased.

(5) The description made in accordance with the custom of the trade of the type of regulated metals property purchased and the physical address where the regulated metals were obtained by the seller and the date when purchased, and a statement signed by the seller or the seller's agent certifying that the seller or the seller's agent has the lawful right to sell and dispose of the property.

(6) The amount of consideration given for the regulated metals property.

(7) The name and address of the vendor of the regulated metals property and the license plate number, make, model, and color of the vehicle used to deliver the regulated metals.

(8) A photocopy or electronic scan of the unexpired drivers license or state or federally issued photo identification card of the person delivering the regulated metals property to the secondary metals recycler. If the secondary metals recycler has a copy of the valid photo identification of the person delivering the regulated metals property on file, the secondary metals recycler must examine the photo identification and verify that it has not expired, but

may reference the photo identification that is on file without making a separate photocopy or electronic scan for each subsequent transaction. If the person delivering the regulated metals property does not have an unexpired drivers license or an unexpired state or federally issued photo identification card, the secondary metals recycler shall not complete the transaction.

(9) A copy of the receipt required under subsection (a) of this section when all the information required under subsection (a) of this section is clear and legible or, in the event the copy of the receipt is not clear or not legible, the original receipt.

(10) A video or digital photograph of the seller together with the regulated metals property being delivered by the seller. The video or photograph required by this section shall be of a quality that is sufficient to allow a person of ordinary faculties to identify the person recorded or photographed.

(11) In transactions involving catalytic converters that are not attached to a vehicle, and central air conditioner evaporator coils or condensers, the person delivering the materials shall place next to that person's signature on the receipt required under subsection (a) of this section, a clear impression of that person's index finger that is in ink and free of any smearing. A secondary metals recycler may elect to obtain the fingerprint electronically. If the secondary metals recycler has a copy of the fingerprint of the person delivering the nonferrous metal on file, the secondary metals recycler must examine the photo identification, but may reference the fingerprint that is on file without making a separate fingerprint for each subsequent transaction. If a secondary metals recycler purchases a catalytic converter pursuant to G.S. 66-424(a)(3a), then the secondary metals recycler shall make and retain a copy of all documentation provided to and relied upon by the secondary metals recycler in determining the status of the seller of the catalytic converter.

History.
2012-46, s. 28; 2021-154, s. 2

§ 66-422. Inspection of regulated metals property and records

(a) **Retention of Records.** -- A secondary metals recycler shall keep and maintain the information required under G.S. 66-421(b) for not less than two years from the date of the purchase of the regulated metals property. Records shall be securely maintained at all times and shall be destroyed in a manner that protects the identity of the owner of the property, the seller of the property, and the purchaser of the property.

(b) **Inspection of Regulated Metals Property and Records.** -- During the usual and customary business hours of a secondary metals recycler, a law enforcement officer shall have the right to inspect all of the following:

(1) Any and all purchased regulated metals property in the possession of the secondary metals recycler.

(2) Any and all records required to be maintained under G.S. 66-421(b).

(c) **Making Receipts Available for Inspection by Law Enforcement.** -- A secondary metals recycler shall make receipts for the purchase of regulated metals property available for pickup each regular workday if requested by the sheriff or chief of police of the county or the chief of police of the municipality in which the secondary metals recycler is located. The sheriff or the chief of police may request these receipts to be electronically transferred directly to the law enforcement agency. Records retained by a law enforcement agency shall be securely retained as required by law and destroyed in a manner that protects the identity of the owner of the property, the seller of the property, and the purchaser of the property.

(d) **Records Are Not Public.** -- Records submitted to any public law enforcement agency pursuant to this section are records of criminal investigations or records of criminal intelligence information as defined in G.S. 132-1.4 and are not public records as defined by G.S. 132-1.

History.
2012-46, s. 28

§ 66-423. Hold notices for nonferrous metals; retention of nonferrous metals

(a) **Hold Notices.** -- When a law enforcement officer has reasonable suspicion to believe that any item of nonferrous metal in the possession of a nonferrous metals purchaser has been stolen, the law enforcement officer may issue a hold notice to the nonferrous metals purchaser. The hold notice must be in writing, be delivered to the nonferrous metals purchaser, specifically identify those items of nonferrous metal that are believed to have been stolen and that are subject to the notice, and inform the nonferrous metals purchaser of the information contained in this section. Upon receipt of the notice, the nonferrous metals purchaser must not process or remove the items of nonferrous metal identified in the notice, or any portion thereof, from the secondary metal recycler's fixed site for 15 calendar days after receipt of the notice unless released prior to the 15-day period by the law enforcement officer. A hold notice may be renewed for an additional 30 days by the law enforcement officer. A renewal must satisfy the same requirements as an initial hold notice in order to be valid.

(b) **Retention of Nonferrous Metals. --** Any secondary metals recycler owner convicted of a felonious violation of this Article, G.S. 14-71, 14-71.1, or 14-72 shall hold and retain nonferrous metals for seven days from the date of purchase before selling, dismantling, crushing, defacing, or in any manner altering or disposing of the regulated metals property.

History.
2012-46, s. 28

§ 66-424. Prohibited activities and transactions

(a) A secondary metals recycler shall not do any of the following:

(1) Operate any business that cashes checks at a fixed site at which the secondary metals recycler purchases regulated metals property.

(2) Purchase nonferrous metals for the purpose of recycling the nonferrous metals, unless the nonferrous metals purchaser possesses a valid permit.

(3) Purchase any central air conditioner evaporator coils or condensers, except that a secondary metals recycler may purchase these items from a company, contractor, or individual that is in the business of installing, replacing, maintaining, or removing these items.

(3a) Purchase any catalytic converters that are not attached to a vehicle, except that a secondary metals recycler may purchase these items from a person listed in G.S. 14-72.8(b).

(4) Purchase any regulated metals property that the secondary metals recycler knows or reasonably should know to be stolen.

(b) It shall be unlawful to transport or possess on highways of this State an amount of copper weighing in the aggregate more than 25 pounds, unless at least one of the following is true:

(1) The vehicle is used in the ordinary course of business for the purpose of transporting nonferrous metals. This term includes vehicles used by gas, electric, communications, water, plumbing, electrical, and climate conditioning service providers, and their employees, agents, and contractors, in the course of providing these services.

(2) The person transporting or possessing the copper possesses, and presents when requested, a valid bill of sale for the copper.

(3) A law enforcement officer determines that the copper is not stolen and is in the rightful possession of the person.

(c) A secondary metals recycler shall not purchase any of the following:

(1) Any regulated metal marked with the initials or other identification of a telephone, cable, electric, water, or other public utility, or any brewer.

(2) Any utility access cover.

(3) Any street light pole or fixture.

(4) Any road or bridge guard rail.

(5) Any highway or street sign.

(6) Any water meter cover.

(7) Any metal beer keg, including any made of stainless steel that is clearly marked as being the property of the beer manufacturer.

(8) Any traffic directional or control sign.

(9) Any traffic light signal.

(10) Any regulated metal marked with the name of a government entity.

(11) Any spikes, plates, or other railroad track components or signs, and any property owned by a railroad and marked and otherwise identified as such.

(12) Any historical marker or any grave marker or burial vase.

(d) It shall be unlawful for any person that is not a secondary metals recycler to purchase a used catalytic converter not attached to a vehicle.

(e) The provisions of this section do not apply to a used and detached catalytic converter that has been tested, certified, and labeled, or otherwise approved for reuse, and being bought or sold for purposes of reuse, in accordance with the federal Clean Air Act (42 U.S.C. § 7401 et seq.) and regulations under the Clean Air Act, as they may, from time to time, be amended.

History.
2012-46, s. 28; 2021-154, s. 4

§ 66-425. Permissible payment methods for nonferrous metals purchasers

Limitation on Cash Purchases. No nonferrous metals purchaser shall enter into a cash transaction for the purchase of copper, and no nonferrous metals purchaser shall purchase any nonferrous metal property for any cash consideration greater than one hundred dollars ($ 100.00) per transaction. Any payment in excess of one hundred dollars ($ 100.00) per transaction shall be made by check, money order or cash card system. A nonferrous metals purchaser shall not make more than one cash purchase per day from any individual, business, corporation or partnership.

History.
2012-46, s. 28

§ 66-426. Issuance of nonferrous metals purchase permits by Sheriff; form; fees; recordkeeping

(a) **Issuance of Permits. --** The sheriff of each county shall issue a nonferrous metals purchase permit to an applicant if the applicant (i) has a fixed site in the sheriff's county; (ii) declares on a form provided by the sheriff that the applicant is informed of and will comply with the provisions of this Part; (iii) does not have a permit that has been revoked pursuant to G.S. 66-429(b) at the time of the application; and (iv) has not been convicted of more than three violations of this Part. A permit shall be valid for 12 months and shall be valid only for fixed sites in the county of issuance. A permit shall be obtained for each fixed site at which nonferrous metals are purchased.

(b) **Form. --** The Attorney General shall prescribe a standard application form and a standard permit form to be used by sheriffs. The permit form shall contain, at a minimum, the date of issuance and the name and address of the permit holder.

(c) **Fees; Record-Keeping Requirements. --** The sheriff shall not charge a fee for a permit, and shall retain a copy of any permit issued.

History.
2012-46, s. 28; 2012-194, s. 46(a)

§ 66-427. Exemptions

This Part does not apply to:

(1) Purchases of regulated metals property from a manufacturing, industrial, government, or other commercial vendor that generates or sells regulated metals property in the ordinary course of its business.

(2) Purchases of regulated metals property that involve only beverage containers, except that G.S. 66-423 shall apply in that case.

History.
2012-46, s. 28

§ 66-428. Preemption

A county or municipality shall not enact any local law, ordinance, or regulation regulating secondary metals recyclers or regulated metals property that conflicts with this Part, and this Part preempts all existing laws, ordinances, or regulations that conflict with it.

History.
2012-46, s. 28

§ 66-429. Violations

(a) **Punishment Generally. --** Unless the conduct is covered by some other provision of law providing greater punishment, any person knowingly and willfully violating any of the provisions of this Part shall be guilty of a Class 1 misdemeanor for a first offense. A second or subsequent violation of this Part is a Class I felony. In addition to any other punishment imposed for a violation of this Part, any person knowingly and willfully violating any of the provisions of this Part involving the purchase of a catalytic converter shall be punished by a fine of one thousand dollars ($ 1,000) for each violation.

(b) **Revocation of Permits. --** If the owner or the employees of a fixed site are convicted of an aggregate of three or more violations of this Part within a 10 year period, the permit associated with that fixed site shall be immediately revoked by the sheriff for a period of six months. Any attempt to circumvent this subsection by procuring a permit through a family member shall result in extension of the revocation period for an additional 18 months.

History.
2012-46, s. 28; 2021-154, s. 3

§ 66-430. Restitution

The court may order a defendant to make restitution to the secondary metals recycler or property owner, as appropriate, for any damage or loss caused by the defendant and arising out of a violation of G.S. 14-71, G.S. 14-71.1, G.S. 14-72, G.S.14-159.4, G.S. 66-424(a)(3), G.S. 66-424(a)(3a), or G.S. 66-424(a)(4) committed by the defendant.

History.
2012-46, s. 28; 2021-154, s. 5

§ 66-431. Forfeiture of vehicles used to transport unlawfully obtained regulated metals property

(a) Vehicles which are used or intended for use to convey or transport, or in any manner to facilitate the conveyance or transportation of unlawfully obtained regulated metals property, as defined by this Part, are subject to forfeiture, except that:

(1) No conveyance shall be forfeited under the provisions of this section by reason of any act or omission, committed or omitted while such conveyance was unlawfully in the possession of a person other than the owner in violation of the criminal laws of the United States, or of any state;

(2) No conveyance shall be forfeited unless the violation involved is a felony;

(3) A forfeiture of a vehicle encumbered by a bona fide security interest is subject to the interest of the secured party who had no knowledge of or consented to the act or omission;

(4) No conveyance shall be forfeited under the provisions of this section unless the owner knew or had reason to believe the vehicle was being used in the commission of any violation that may subject the conveyance to forfeiture under this section.

(b) Any vehicle subject to forfeiture under this section may be seized by any law enforcement officer upon process issued by any district or superior court having jurisdiction over the vehicle except that seizure without such process may be made when:

(1) The seizure is incident to an arrest or a search under a search warrant;

(2) The vehicle subject to seizure has been the subject of a prior judgment in favor of the State in a criminal injunction or forfeiture proceeding under this section.

(c) Vehicles taken or detained under this section shall not be repleviable, but shall be deemed to be in custody of the law enforcement agency seizing it, which may:

(1) Place the vehicle under seal; or

(2) Remove the vehicle to a place designated by it; or

(3) Request that the North Carolina Department of Justice take custody of the vehicle and remove it to an appropriate location for disposition in accordance with law.

Any vehicle seized by a State, local, or county law enforcement officer shall be held in safekeeping as provided in this subsection until an order of disposition is properly entered by the judge.

(d) Whenever a vehicle is forfeited under this section, the law enforcement agency having custody of it may:

(1) Retain the vehicle for official use; or

(2) Sell any forfeited vehicle, provided that the proceeds be disposed of for payment of all proper expenses of the proceedings for forfeiture and sale, including expense of seizure, maintenance of custody, advertising, and court costs; or

(3) Transfer any vehicles which are forfeited under the provisions of this section to the North Carolina Department of Justice when, in the discretion of the presiding judge and upon application of the North Carolina Department of Justice, said vehicle may be of official use to the North Carolina Department of Justice;

(4) Upon determination by the director of any law enforcement agency that a vehicle transferred pursuant to the provisions of this section is of no further use to said agency for use in official investigations, such vehicle may be sold as surplus property in the same manner as other vehicles owned by the law enforcement agency, and the proceeds from such sale after deducting the cost of sale shall be paid to the treasurer or proper officer authorized to receive fines and forfeitures to be used for the school fund of the county in the county in which said vehicle was seized; provided, that any vehicle transferred to any law enforcement agency under the provisions of this section which has been modified to increase speed shall be used in the performance of official duties only and not for resale, transfer, or disposition other than as junk.

History.
2007-301, s. 3; 2012-46, ss. 27, 29

CHAPTER 67
DOGS

ARTICLE 1
OWNER'S LIABILITY

§ 67-1. Liability for injury to livestock or fowls

If any dog, not being at the time on the premises of the owner or person having charge thereof, shall kill or injure any livestock or fowls, the owner or person having such dog in charge shall be liable for damages sustained by the injury, killing, or maiming of any livestock, and costs of suit.

History.

1911, c. 3, s. 1; C.S., s. 1669

§ 67-2. Permitting bitch at large

If any person owning or having any bitch shall knowingly permit her to run at large during the erotic stage of copulation he shall be guilty of a Class 3 misdemeanor.

History.

1862-3, c. 41, s. 2; Code, s. 2501; Rev., s. 3303; C.S., s. 1670; 1993, c. 539, s. 529; 1994, Ex. Sess., c. 24, s. 14(c)

§ 67-3. Sheep-killing dogs to be killed

If any person owning or having any dog that kills sheep or other domestic animals, or that kills a human being, upon satisfactory evidence of the same being made before any judge of the district court in the county, and the owner duly notified thereof, shall refuse to kill it, and shall permit such dog to go at liberty, he shall be guilty of a Class 3 misdemeanor, and the dog may be killed by anyone if found going at large.

History.

1862-3, c. 41, s. 1; 1874-5, c. 108, s. 2; Code, s. 2500; Rev., s. 3304; C.S., s. 1671; 1973, c. 108, s. 24; 1977, c. 597; 1993, c. 539, s. 530; 1994, Ex. Sess., c. 24, s. 14(c)

§ 67-4. Failing to kill mad dog

If the owner of any dog shall know, or have good reason to believe, that his dog, or any dog belonging to any person under his control, has been bitten by a mad dog, and shall neglect or refuse immediately to kill the same, he shall forfeit and pay the sum of fifty dollars ($ 50.00) to him who will sue therefor; and the offender shall be liable to pay all damages which may be sustained by anyone, in his property or person, by the bite of any such dog, and shall be guilty of a Class 3 misdemeanor.

History.

R.C., c. 67; Code, s. 2499; Rev., s. 3305; C.S., s. 1672; 1993, c. 539, s. 531; 1994, Ex. Sess., c. 24, s. 14(c)

ARTICLE 1A
DANGEROUS DOGS

§ 67-4.1. Definitions and procedures

(a) As used in this Article, unless the context clearly requires otherwise and except as modified in subsection (b) of this section, the term:

  (1) "Dangerous dog" means

    a. A dog that:

      1. Without provocation has killed or inflicted severe injury on a person; or

      2. Is determined by the person or Board designated by the county or municipal authority responsible for animal control to be potentially dangerous because the dog has engaged in one or more of the behaviors listed in subdivision (2) of this subsection.

    b. Any dog owned or harbored primarily or in part for the purpose of dog fighting, or any dog trained for dog fighting.

  (2) "Potentially dangerous dog" means a dog that the person or Board designated by the county or municipal authority responsible for animal control determines to have:

    a. Inflicted a bite on a person that resulted in broken bones or disfiguring lacerations or required cosmetic surgery or hospitalization; or

    b. Killed or inflicted severe injury upon a domestic animal when not on the owner's real property; or

    c. Approached a person when not on the owner's property in a vicious or terrorizing manner in an apparent attitude of attack.

  (3) "Owner" means any person or legal entity that has a possessory property right in a dog.

  (4) "Owner's real property" means any real property owned or leased by the owner of the dog, but does not include any public right-of-way or a common area of a condominium, apartment complex, or townhouse development.

  (5) "Severe injury" means any physical injury that results in broken bones or disfiguring lacerations or required cosmetic surgery or hospitalization.

(b) The provisions of this Article do not apply to:

(1) A dog being used by a law enforcement officer to carry out the law enforcement officer's official duties;

(2) A dog being used in a lawful hunt;

(3) A dog where the injury or damage inflicted by the dog was sustained by a domestic animal while the dog was working as a hunting dog, herding dog, or predator control dog on the property of, or under the control of, its owner or keeper, and the damage or injury was to a species or type of domestic animal appropriate to the work of the dog; or

(4) A dog where the injury inflicted by the dog was sustained by a person who, at the time of the injury, was committing a willful trespass or other tort, was tormenting, abusing, or assaulting the dog, had tormented, abused, or assaulted the dog, or was committing or attempting to commit a crime.

(c) The county or municipal authority responsible for animal control shall designate a person or a Board to be responsible for determining when a dog is a "potentially dangerous dog" and shall designate a separate Board to hear any appeal. The person or Board making the determination that a dog is a "potentially dangerous dog" must notify the owner in writing, giving the reasons for the determination, before the dog may be considered potentially dangerous under this Article. The owner may appeal the determination by filing written objections with the appellate Board within three days. The appellate Board shall schedule a hearing within 10 days of the filing of the objections. Any appeal from the final decision of such appellate Board shall be taken to the superior court by filing notice of appeal and a petition for review within 10 days of the final decision of the appellate Board. Appeals from rulings of the appellate Board shall be heard in the superior court division. The appeal shall be heard de novo before a superior court judge sitting in the county in which the appellate Board whose ruling is being appealed is located.

History.
1989 (Reg. Sess., 1990), c. 1023, s. 1

§ 67-4.2. Precautions against attacks by dangerous dogs

(a) It is unlawful for an owner to:

(1) Leave a dangerous dog unattended on the owner's real property unless the dog is confined indoors, in a securely enclosed and locked pen, or in another structure designed to restrain the dog;

(2) Permit a dangerous dog to go beyond the owner's real property unless the dog is leashed and muzzled or is otherwise securely restrained and muzzled.

(b) If the owner of a dangerous dog transfers ownership or possession of the dog to another person (as defined in G.S. 12-3(6)), the owner shall provide written notice to:

(1) The authority that made the determination under this Article, stating the name and address of the new owner or possessor of the dog; and

(2) The person taking ownership or possession of the dog, specifying the dog's dangerous behavior and the authority's determination.

(c) Violation of this section is a Class 3 misdemeanor.

History.
1989 (Reg. Sess., 1990), c. 1023, s. 1; 1993, c. 539, s. 532; 1994, Ex. Sess., c. 24, s. 14(c)

§ 67-4.3. Penalty for attacks by dangerous dogs

The owner of a dangerous dog that attacks a person and causes physical injuries requiring medical treatment in excess of one hundred dollars ($ 100.00) shall be guilty of a Class 1 misdemeanor.

History.
1989 (Reg. Sess., 1990), c. 1023, s. 1; 1993, c. 539, s. 533; 1994, Ex. Sess., c. 24, s. 14(c)

§ 67-4.4. Strict liability

The owner of a dangerous dog shall be strictly liable in civil damages for any injuries or property damage the dog inflicts upon a person, his property, or another animal.

History.
1989 (Reg. Sess., 1990), c. 1023, s. 1

§ 67-4.5. Local ordinances

Nothing in this Article shall be construed to prevent a city or county from adopting or enforcing its own program for control of dangerous dogs.

History.
1989 (Reg. Sess., 1990), c. 1023, s. 1

ARTICLE 2
LICENSE TAXES ON DOGS

§ 67-12. Permitting dogs to run at large at night; penalty; liability for damage

No person shall allow his dog over six months old to run at large in the nighttime unaccompanied by the owner or by some member of the owner's family, or some other person by the owner's permission. Any person intentionally, knowingly, and willfully violating this section shall be guilty of a Class 3 misdemeanor, and shall also be liable in damages to any person injured or suffering loss to his property or chattels.

History.

1919, c. 116, s. 5; C.S., s. 1680; 1993, c. 539, s. 534; 1994, Ex. Sess., c. 24, s. 14(c).

§ 67-14. Mad dogs, dogs killing sheep, etc., may be killed

Any person may kill any mad dog, and also any dog if he is killing sheep, cattle, hogs, goats, or poultry.

History.

1919, c. 116, s. 8; C.S., s. 1682

§ 67-14.1. Dogs injuring deer or bear on wildlife management area may be killed; impounding unmuzzled dogs running at large

(a) Any dog which trails, runs, injures or kills any deer or bear on any wildlife refuge, sanctuary or management area, now or hereafter so designated and managed by the Wildlife Resources Commission, during the closed season for hunting with dogs on such refuge or management area, is hereby declared to be a public nuisance, and any wildlife protector or other duly authorized agent or employee of the Wildlife Resources Commission may destroy, by humane method, any dog discovered trailing, running, injuring or killing any deer or bear in any such area during the closed season therein for hunting such game with dogs, without incurring liability by reason of his act in conformity with this section.

(b) Any unmuzzled dog running at large upon any wildlife refuge, sanctuary, or management area, when unaccompanied by any person having such dog in charge, shall be seized and impounded by any wildlife protector, or other duly authorized agent or employee of the Wildlife Resources Commission.

(c) The person impounding such dog shall cause a notice to be published at least once a week for two successive weeks in some newspaper published in the county wherein the dog was taken, or if none is published therein, in some newspaper having general circulation in the county. Such notice shall set forth a description of the dog, the place where it is impounded, and that the dog will be destroyed if not claimed and payment made for the advertisement, a catch fee of one dollar ($ 1.00) and the boarding, computed at the rate of fifty cents (50 cent(s)) per day, while impounded, by a certain date

which date shall be not less than 15 days after the publication of the first notice. A similar notice shall be posted at the courthouse door.

(d) The owner of the dog, or his agent, may recover such dog upon payment of the cost of the publication of the notices hereinbefore described together with a catch fee of one dollar ($ 1.00) and the expense, computed at the rate of fifty cents (50 cent(s)) per day, incurred while impounding and boarding the dog.

(e) If any impounded dog is not recovered by the owner within 15 days after the publication of the first notice of the impounding, the dog may be destroyed in a humane manner by any wildlife protector or other duly authorized agent or employee of the North Carolina Wildlife Resources Commission, and no liability shall attach to any person acting in accordance with this section.

History.

1951, c. 1021, s. 1

§ 67-16. Failure to discharge duties imposed under this Article

Any person failing to discharge any duty imposed upon him under this Article shall be guilty of a Class 3 misdemeanor.

History.

1919, c. 116, s. 10; C.S., s. 1684; 1993, c. 539, s. 535; 1994, Ex. Sess., c. 24, s. 14(c)

§ 67-18. Application of Article

This Article, G.S. 67-5 to 67-18, inclusive, is hereby made applicable to every county in the State of North Carolina, notwithstanding any provisions in local, special or private acts exempting any county or any township or municipality from the provisions of the same enacted at any General Assembly commencing at the General Assembly of 1919 and going through the General Assembly of 1929.

History.

1929, c. 318

ARTICLE 5
PROTECTION OF LIVESTOCK AND POULTRY FROM RANGING DOGS

§ 67-30. Appointment of animal control officers authorized; salary, etc

A county may appoint one or more animal control officers and may fix their salaries, allowances, and expenses.

History.
1951, c. 931, s. 1; 1955, c. 1333, s. 1; 1957, cc. 81, 840; 1973, c. 822, s. 6

§ 67-31. Powers and duties of dog warden

The powers and duties of the county dog warden shall be as follows:

(1) He shall have the power of arrest and be responsible for the enforcement within his county of all public and public-local laws pertaining to the ownership and control of dogs, and shall cooperate with all other law-enforcement officers operating within the county in fulfilling this responsibility.

(2) In those counties having a rabies control officer, the county dog warden shall act as assistant to the rabies control officer, working under the supervision of the county health department, to collect the dog tax. In those counties having no rabies control officer, the county dog warden shall serve as rabies control officer.

History.
1951, c. 931, s. 2

§ 67-36. Article supplements existing laws

The provisions of this Article are to be construed as supplementing and not repealing existing State laws pertaining to the ownership, taxation, and control of dogs.

History.
1951, c. 931, s. 7

CHAPTER 68
FENCES AND STOCK LAW

ARTICLE 3
LIVESTOCK LAW

§ 68-15. Term "livestock" defined

The word "livestock" in this Chapter shall include, but shall not be limited to, equine animals, bovine animals, sheep, goats, llamas, and swine.

History.
Code, s. 2822; Rev., s. 1681; C.S., s. 1841; 1971, c. 741, s. 1; 1997-84, s. 2

§ 68-16. Allowing livestock to run at large forbidden

If any person shall allow his livestock to run at large, he shall be guilty of a Class 3 misdemeanor.

History.
Code, s. 2811; 1889, c. 504; Rev., s. 3319; C.S., s. 1849; 1971, c. 741, s. 1; 1993, c. 539, s. 536; 1994, Ex. Sess., c. 24, s. 14(c)

§ 68-17. Impounding livestock at large; right to recover costs and damages; abandoned livestock

(a) Any person may take up any livestock running at large or straying and impound the same; and such impounder may recover from the owner the reasonable costs of impounding and maintaining the livestock as well as damages to the impounder caused by such livestock, and may retain the livestock, with the right to use with proper care until such recovery is had. Reasonable costs of impounding shall include any fees paid pursuant to G.S. 68-18.1 in order to locate the owner.

(b) Livestock is deemed to be abandoned when (i) it is placed in the custody of any other person for treatment, boarding, or care; (ii) the owner of the livestock does not retake custody of the animal within two months after the last day the owner paid a fee to the custodian for the treatment, boarding, or care of the livestock; and (iii) the custodian has made reasonable attempts to collect any past-due fees during the two-month period. If, after the end of the two-month period, the custodian of the abandoned livestock has been unsuccessful in collecting the past-due fees and the owner of the livestock has not retaken custody of the livestock, the custodian may sell or transfer the livestock by executing an affidavit that identifies the buyer or transferee of the livestock and certifies compliance with the criteria and requirements of this subsection. If the custodian is unable to sell or transfer the livestock, the custodian may, but shall not be required to, otherwise humanely dispose of the abandoned livestock. A custodian shall provide written notice of the provisions of this subsection in conspicuous type to the owner of livestock at the time the livestock is delivered for treatment, boarding, or care as follows: "Pursuant to N.C. General Statutes § 68-17(b), the owner of this facility is entitled to sell, transfer, or otherwise humanely dispose of any livestock abandoned at this facility."

History.
Code, s. 2186; Rev., s. 1679; C.S., s. 1850; 1951, c. 569; 1971, c. 741, s. 1; 1991, c. 472, s. 3; 2017-108, s. 4

§ 68-18. Notice and demand when owner known

If the owner of impounded livestock is or becomes known to the impounder, actual notice of the whereabouts of the impounded livestock must be immediately given to the owner and the impounder must then make demand upon the owner of the livestock for the costs of impoundment and the damages to the impounder, if any, caused by such livestock.

History.
Code, s. 2817; Rev., s. 1680; C.S., s. 1851; 1971, c. 741, s. 1

§ 68-18.1. Notice when owner not known

If the owner of the impounded livestock is not known or cannot be found, the impounder shall inform the sheriff of the county in which the livestock was found of the impoundment, giving a full description of the livestock impounded, including all marks or brands on the livestock, and shall state when and where the animal was taken up.

History.
1874-5, c. 258, s. 2; Code, s. 3768; Rev., s. 2833; C.S., s. 3951; 1991, c. 472, s. 2; 2012-18, s. 1.10

§ 68-19. Determination of damages by selected landowners or by referee

If the owner and impounder cannot agree as to the cost of impounding and maintaining such livestock, as well as damages to the impounder caused by such livestock running at large, then such costs and damages shall be determined by three disinterested landowners, one to be selected by the owner of the livestock, one to be selected by the impounder and a third to

Chapter 68

be selected by the first two. If within 10 days a majority of the landowners so selected cannot agree, or if the owner of the livestock or the impounder fails to make his selection, or if the two selected fail to select a third, then the clerk of superior court of the county where the livestock is impounded shall select a referee. The determination of such costs and damages by the landowners or by the referee shall be final.

History.
Code, s. 2186; Rev., s. 1679; C.S., s. 1850; 1951, c. 569; 1971, c. 741, s. 1

§ 68-20. Notice of sale and sale where owner fails to redeem or is unknown; application of proceeds

If the owner fails to redeem his livestock within three days after the notice and demand as provided in G.S. 68-18 is received or within three days after the determination of the costs and damages as provided in G.S. 68-19, the impounder shall notify the local Sheriff's office and the Sheriff shall post a notice fully describing the livestock and stating the place, date, and hour of sale on the Web site of the Sheriff's department. After 10 days from such posting, the impounder shall sell the livestock at public auction. If the owner of the livestock remains unknown to the impounder, then, three days after publication of the notice required by G.S. 68-18.1, the impounder shall notify the local Sheriff's office and the Sheriff shall post a notice fully describing the livestock and stating the place, date, and hour of sale on the Web site of the Sheriff's department. After 10 days from such posting, the impounder shall sell the livestock at public auction. The proceeds of any such public sale shall be applied to pay the reasonable costs of impounding and maintaining the livestock and the damages to the impounder caused by the livestock. Reasonable costs of impounding shall include any fees paid pursuant to G.S. 68-18.1 in an attempt to locate the owner of the livestock. The balance, if any, shall be paid to the owner of the livestock, if known, or, if the owner is not known, then to the school fund of the county where the livestock was impounded.

History.
Code, s. 2817; Rev., s. 1680; C.S., s. 1851; 1971, c. 741, s. 1; 1991, c. 472, s. 4; 2015-263, s. 24(a)

§ 68-21. Illegally releasing or receiving impounded livestock misdemeanor

If any person willfully releases any lawfully impounded livestock without the permission of the impounder or receives such livestock knowing that it was unlawfully released, he shall be guilty of a Class 3 misdemeanor.

History.
Code, s. 2819; 1889, c. 504; Rev., s. 3310; C.S., s. 1853; 1971, c. 741, s. 1; 1993, c. 539, s. 537; 1994, Ex. Sess., c. 24, s. 14(c)

§ 68-22. Impounded livestock to be fed and watered

If any person shall impound or cause to be impounded any livestock and shall fail to supply to the livestock during the confinement a reasonably adequate quantity of good and wholesome feed and water, he shall be guilty of a Class 3 misdemeanor.

History.
1881, c. 368, s. 3; Code, s. 2484; 1891, c. 65; Rev., s. 3311; C.S., s. 1854; 1971, c. 741, s. 1; 1993, c. 539, s. 538; 1994, Ex. Sess., c. 24, s. 14(c)

§ 68-23. Right to feed impounded livestock; owner liable

When any livestock is impounded under the provisions of this Chapter and remains without reasonably adequate feed and water for more than 24 hours, any person may lawfully enter the area of impoundment to supply the livestock with feed and water. Such person shall not be liable in trespass for such entry and may recover of the owner or, if the owner is unknown, of the impounder of the livestock, the reasonable costs of the feed and water.

History.
1881, c. 368, s. 4; Code, s. 2485; Rev., s. 1682; C.S., s. 1855; 1971, c. 741, s. 1

§ 68-24. Penalties for violation of this Article

A violation of G.S. 68-16, 68-21 or 68-22 is a Class 3 misdemeanor.

History.
1971, c. 741, s. 1; 1993, c. 539, s. 539; 1994, Ex. Sess., c. 24, s. 14(c)

§ 68-25. Domestic fowls running at large after notice

(a) If any person shall permit any turkeys, geese, chickens, ducks or other domestic fowls to run at large on the lands of any other person while such lands are under cultivation in any kind of grain or feedstuff or while being used for gardens or ornamental purposes, after having received actual or constructive notice of such running at large, the person is guilty of a Class 3 misdemeanor.

(b) If any person permits any domestic fowls to run at large on the lands of a commercial poultry operation of any other person after

Chapter 68

having received actual or constructive notice of such running at large, the person is guilty of a Class 3 misdemeanor. For purposes of this subsection, a commercial poultry operation means any premises or operation where domestic poultry are fed, caged, housed, or otherwise kept for meat or egg production until sold or marketed.

(b1) Repealed by Session Laws 2011-412, s. 3.1, effective October 15, 2011.

(c) If it shall appear to any magistrate that after three days' notice any person persists in allowing his fowls to run at large in violation of this section and fails or refuses to keep them upon his own premises, then the said magistrate may, in his discretion, order any sheriff or other officer to kill the fowls when they are running at large as herein provided.

History.
C.S., s. 1864; 1971, c. 741, s. 1; 1993, c. 539, s. 540; 1994, Ex. Sess., c. 24, s. 14(c); 2011-313, s. 1; 2011-412, s. 3.1

CHAPTER 72
INNS, HOTELS AND RESTAURANTS

ARTICLE 3
IMMORAL PRACTICES OF GUESTS OF HOTELS AND LODGING HOUSES

§ 72-30. Registration to be in true name; addresses; peace officers

No person shall write, or cause to be written, or if in charge of a register knowingly permit to be written, in any register in any lodging house or hotel any other or different name or designation than the true name or names in ordinary use of the person registering or causing himself to be registered therein. Any person occupying any room or rooms in any lodging house or hotel shall register or cause himself to be registered where registration is required by such lodging house or hotel. Any person registering or causing himself to be registered at any lodging house or hotel, shall write, or cause to be written, in the register of such lodging house or hotel the correct address of the person registering, or causing himself to be registered. Any person violating any provision of this section shall be guilty of a Class 3 misdemeanor, and upon conviction shall only be punished by a fine not exceeding two hundred dollars ($ 200.00). This section shall not apply to any peace officer of this State who shall privately give his true name to the clerk or proprietor of such hotel or lodging house.

History.
1921, c. 111; C.S., s. 2283(v); 1993, c. 539, s. 546; 1994, Ex. Sess., c. 24, s. 14(c)

ARTICLE 4
LICENSING AND REGULATION OF TOURIST CAMPS AND HOMES, CABIN CAMPS, ROADHOUSES AND PUBLIC DANCE HALLS

§§ 72-31 through 72-38

Repealed by Session Laws 2004-203, s. 38, effective August 17, 2004.

§§ 72-40 through 72-45

Repealed by Session Laws 2004-203, s. 38, effective August 17, 2004.

CHAPTER 74C
PRIVATE PROTECTIVE SERVICES

ARTICLE 1
PRIVATE PROTECTIVE SERVICES BOARD

§ 74C-1. Title

This Chapter may be cited as the Private Protective Services Act. The purpose of this act is to increase the level of integrity, competency, and performance of Private Protective Service Professions in order to safeguard the public health, safety, and welfare.

History.
1979, c. 818, s. 2; 1989, c. 759, s. 1

§ 74C-2. Licenses required

(a) No private person, firm, association, or corporation shall engage in, perform any services as, or in any way represent or hold itself out as engaging in a private protective services profession or activity in this State without having first complied with the provisions of this Chapter. Compliance with the licensing requirements of this Chapter shall not relieve any person, firm, association or corporation from compliance with any other licensing law.

(b) An individual in possession of a valid private protective services license or private detective trainee permit issued prior to October 1, 1989, shall not be subject to forfeiture of such license by virtue of this Chapter. Such license shall, however, remain subject to suspension, denial, or revocation in the same manner in which all other licenses issued pursuant to this Chapter are subject to suspension, denial, or revocation.

(c) In its discretion, the Private Protective Services Board may issue a trainee permit in lieu of a private investigator license provided that the applicant works under the direct supervision of a licensee.

History.
1973, c. 528, s. 1; 1979, c. 818, s. 1; 1989, c. 759, s. 2

§ 74C-3. Private protective services profession defined

(a) As used in this Chapter, the term "private protective services profession" means and includes the following:

(1) **Armored car profession. --** Any person, firm, association, or corporation which for a fee or other valuable consideration provides secured transportation and protection from one place or point to another place or point of money, currency, coins, bullion, securities, checks, documents, stocks, bonds, jewelry, paintings, and other valuables. This definition does not include a person operating an armored car business pursuant to a motor carrier certificate or permit issued by the North Carolina Utilities Commission which grants operating rights for such business; however, armed armored car service guards shall be subject to the provisions of G.S. 74C-13.

(2) Repealed by Session Laws 1983, c. 786, s. 2.

(3) Redesignated as subdivision (a)(5a) by the Revisor of Statutes. See Editor's notes.

(4) **Courier service profession. --** Any person, firm, association, or corporation which for a fee or other valuable consideration transports or offers to transport from one place or point to another place or point documents, papers, maps, stocks, bonds, checks, or other small items of value which require expeditious services. Armed courier service guards shall be subject to the provisions of G.S. 74C-13.

(5) **Detection of deception examiner.** -- Any person, firm, association, or corporation which uses any device or instrument, regardless of its name or design, for the purpose of the detection of deception or any person who reviews the work product of an examiner including charts, tapes or other methods of record keeping for the purpose of detecting deception or determining accuracy.

(5a) **Electronic countermeasures profession. --** Any person, firm, association, or corporation which for a fee or other valuable consideration discovers, locates, or disengages by electronic, electrical, or mechanical means any listening or other monitoring equipment surreptitiously placed to gather information concerning any individual, firm, association, or corporation.

(6) **Security guard and patrol profession. --** Any person, firm, association, or corporation that provides a security guard on a contractual basis for another person, firm, association, or corporation for a fee or other valuable consideration and performs one or more of the following functions:

a. Prevention or detection of intrusion, entry, larceny, vandalism, abuse, fire, or trespass on private property.

b. Prevention, observation, or detection of any unauthorized activity on private property.

c. Protection of patrons and persons lawfully authorized to be on the premises or being escorted between premises of the person, firm, association, or corporation that entered into the contract for security services.

d. Control, regulation, or direction of the flow or movement of the public, whether by vehicle or otherwise, only to the extent and for the time directly and specifically required to assure the protection of properties.

e. *(Delayed expiration -- see note)* Security services related to entry and exit, direction and movement of individuals at entry and exit, security working towers, and perimeter security patrols at State prison facilities.

(7) **Guard dog service profession. --** Any person, firm, association, or corporation which for a fee or other valuable consideration contracts with another person, firm, association, or corporation to place, lease, rent, or sell a trained dog for the purpose of protecting lives or property.

(8) **Private detective or private investigator. --** Any person who engages in the profession of or accepts employment to furnish, agrees to make, or makes inquiries or investigations concerning any of the following on a contractual basis:

a. Crimes or wrongs done or threatened against the United States or any state or territory of the United States.

b. The identity, habits, conduct, business, occupation, honesty, integrity, credibility, knowledge, trustworthiness, efficiency, loyalty, activity, movement, whereabouts, affiliations, associations, transactions, acts, reputation, or character of any person.

c. The location, disposition, or recovery of lost or stolen property.

d. The cause or responsibility for fires, libels, losses, accidents, damages, or injuries to persons or to properties.

e. Securing evidence to be used before any court, board, officer, or investigative committee.

f. Protection of individuals from serious bodily harm or death.

(9) **Special limited guard and patrol profession. --** Any person who is licensed under Chapter 74D of the General Statutes of North Carolina and provides armed alarm responders pursuant to G.S. 74C-13. Applicants for this limited license shall not be required to meet the experience requirements for a security guard and patrol license. Any experience gained under this limited license shall not be counted as experience for a security guard and patrol license.

(b) "Private protective services" shall not include any of the following:

(1) Licensed insurance adjusters legally employed as such and who engage in no other investigative activities unconnected with adjustment or claims against an insurance company.

(2) An officer or employee of the United States, this State, or any political subdivision of either while the officer or employee is engaged in the performance of his or her official duties within the course and scope of his or her employment with the United States, this State, or any political subdivision of either.

(3) A person engaged exclusively in the business of obtaining and furnishing information as to the financial rating or credit worthiness of persons; and a person who provides consumer reports in connection with:

a. Credit transactions involving the consumer on whom the information is to be furnished and involving the extensions of credit to the consumer,

b. Information for employment purposes,

c. Information for the underwriting of insurance involving the consumer,

d. Information in connection with a determination of the consumer's eligibility for a license or other benefit granted by a governmental instrumentality required by law to consider an applicant's financial responsibility, or

e. A legitimate business need for the information in connection with a business transaction involving the consumer.

(4) An attorney at law licensed to practice in North Carolina while engaged in the practice of law and the attorney's agent, provided the agent is performing duties only in connection with his or her principal's practice of law.

(5) The legal owner or lien holder, and his or her agents and employees, of personal property which has been sold in a transaction wherein a security interest in personal property has been created to secure the sales transaction, who engage in repossession of the personal property.

(6) Repealed by Session Laws 1989, c. 759, s. 3.

(7) Repealed by Session Laws 1981, c. 807, s. 1.

(8) Employees of a licensee who are employed exclusively as undercover agents; provided that for purposes of this section, undercover agent means an individual hired by another person, firm, association, or corporation to perform a job for that

person, firm, association, or corporation and, while performing the job, to act as an undercover operative, employee, or independent contractor of a licensee, but under the supervision of a licensee.

(9) A person who is engaged in an alarm systems business subject to the provisions of Chapter 74D of the General Statutes.

(10) A person who obtains or verifies information regarding applicants for employment, with the knowledge and consent of the applicant, and is (i) engaged in business as a private personnel service as defined in G.S. 95-47.1 or engaged in business as a private employer fee pay personnel service, (ii) engaged in the business of obtaining or verifying information regarding applicants for employment, or (iii) an employer with whom the applicant has applied for employment.

(11) A person who conducts efficiency studies. An efficiency study is an analysis of an employer's business, made at the request of the employer, to determine one or more of the following:

a. The most efficient procedures by which an employee of the business can perform the employee's assigned duties.

b. The adequacy of an employee's performance of the employee's assigned duties that require interaction with a client or customer of the business.

If a person making an efficiency study observes an instance of theft or another illegal act committed by an employee of the business, the person may report the instance to the employer without violating G.S. 74C-3(a)(8).

(12) Research laboratories and consultants who analyze, test, or in any way apply their expertise to interpreting, evaluating, or analyzing facts or evidence submitted by another in order to determine the cause or effect of physical or psychological occurrences, and give their opinions and findings to the requesting source or to a designee of the requestor.

(13) A person who works regularly and exclusively as an employee of an employer in connection with the business affairs of that employer. If the employee is an armed security guard and wears, carries, or possesses a firearm in the performance of the employee's duties, the provisions of G.S. 74C-13 apply.

(14) An employee of a security department of a private business or other employee whose primary duty involves loss prevention or that conducts investigations on matters internal to the business affairs of the business or related to the location,

disposition, or recovery of lost or stolen property reasonably believed to be owned by the business.

(15) Representatives of nonprofit organizations funded all or in part by business improvement districts who provide information and directions to local tourists and residents, engage in street cleaning and beautification services within the business improvement districts, and notify local law enforcement of any illegal activity observed by the representatives within the business improvement districts.

(16) Emergency medical services personnel credentialed under Article 7 of Chapter 131E of the General Statutes who engage in search and rescue activities at the request of either the State, a political subdivision of the State, or one of the following types of facilities: an adult care home licensed under Chapter 131D of the General Statutes, a health care facility or agency licensed under Chapter 131E of the General Statutes, or a facility licensed to offer mental health, developmental disabilities, or substance abuse services under Chapter 122C of the General Statutes. For the purposes of this subdivision, "search and rescue" means activities and documents relating to efforts to locate an individual following the individual's disappearance. This exemption shall not apply if the emergency medical services provider provides services beyond emergency search and rescue and said activities meet the definition of private protective services as defined in G.S. 74C-3.

(17) A person engaged in (i) computer or digital forensic services or in the acquisition, review, or analysis of digital or computer-based information, whether for the purposes of obtaining or furnishing information for evidentiary or other purposes, or for providing expert testimony before a court; or (ii) network or system vulnerability testing, including network scans and risk assessment and analysis of computers connected to a network.

History.

1973, c. 528, s. 1; 1977, c. 481; 1979, c. 818, s. 2; 1981, c. 807, ss. 1-3; 1983, c. 259; c. 786, ss. 2, 3; c. 794, s. 1; 1987, c. 284; c. 657, s. 1; 1989, c. 759, s. 3; 2001-487, s. 64(a); 2006-264, s. 46; 2007-469, s. 6; 2007-511, s. 1; 2009-328, s. 1; 2019-193, s. 1(a); 2020-3, s. 4.15(a); 2020-15, s. 2

§ 74C-4. Private Protective Services Board established; members; terms; vacancies; compensation; meetings

(a) The Private Protective Services Board is hereby established in the Department of Public

Safety to administer the licensing and set educational and training requirements for persons, firms, associations, and corporations engaged in a private protective services profession within this State.

(b) The Board shall consist of 14 members: the Secretary of Public Safety or the Secretary's designated representative, seven persons appointed by the Governor, three persons appointed by the General Assembly upon the recommendation of the President Pro Tempore of the Senate, and three persons appointed by the General Assembly upon the recommendation of the Speaker of the House of Representatives. All appointments by the General Assembly shall be subject to the provisions of G.S. 120-121, and vacancies in the positions filled by those appointments shall be filled pursuant to G.S. 120-122. One of those persons appointed by the General Assembly upon the recommendation of the President Pro Tempore of the Senate, three of the members appointed by the Governor, and all three persons appointed by the General Assembly upon the recommendation of the Speaker of the House of Representatives shall be licensees under this Chapter; all other appointees may not be licensees of the Board nor licensed by the Board while serving as Board members. All persons appointed shall serve terms of three years. With the exception of the Secretary of Public Safety or the Secretary's designated representative, no person shall serve more than eight consecutive years on the Board. Board members may continue to serve until their successors have been appointed. The initial terms of three of the members appointed by the Governor shall expire July 1, 2020. The initial terms of one member appointed by each authority making an appointment pursuant to this subsection shall expire July 1, 2021. All other initial terms of members appointed pursuant to this subsection shall expire July 1, 2022.

(c) Vacancies on the Board occurring for any reason shall be filled by the authority making the original appointment of the person causing the vacancy.

(d) Each member of the Board, before assuming the duties of his office, shall take an oath for the faithful performance of his duties. A Board member may be removed at the pleasure of the authority making the original appointment or by the Board for misconduct, incompetence, or neglect of duty.

(e) Members of the Board who are State officers or employees shall receive no per diem compensation for serving on the Board, but shall be reimbursed for their expenses in accordance with G.S. 138-6. Members of the Board who are full-time salaried public officers or employees other than State officers or employees shall receive no per diem compensation for

serving on the Board, but shall be reimbursed for their expenses in accordance with G.S. 138-6 in the same manner as State officers or employees. All other Board members shall receive per diem compensation and reimbursement in accordance with G.S. 93B-5.

(f) The Board shall elect a Chair, vice-chair, and other officers and committee Chairs from among its members as the Board deems necessary and desirable at the first meeting after July 1 of each year. The Chair and vice-chair shall be selected by the members of the Board for a term of one year and shall be eligible for reelection. The Board shall meet at the call of the Chair or a majority of the members of the Board at such time, date, and location as may be decided upon by a majority of the Board.

(g) All decisions heretofore made by the Private Protective Services Board, established pursuant to Chapter 74B, shall remain in full force and effect unless and until repealed or suspended by action of the Private Protective Services Board established herein.

(h) The Board shall pay the appropriate State agency for the use of physical facilities and services provided to it by the State.

History.
1973, c. 528, s. 1; 1975, c. 592, ss. 8, 9; 1977, c. 535; 1979, c. 818, s. 2; 1981, c. 148, s. 1; c. 807, s. 7; 1983, c. 794, s. 7; 1985, c. 597, s. 12; 1989, c. 759, s. 4; 1995, c. 490, s. 39; 2000-181, s. 2.3; 2011-145, s. 16.3(a); 2014-100, s. 17.5(c); 2019-32, s. 4

§ 74C-5. Powers of the Board

In addition to the powers conferred upon the Board elsewhere in this Chapter, the Board shall have the power to do all of the following:

(1) Adopt rules necessary to carry out and administer the provisions of this Chapter including the authority to require the submission of reports and information by licensees under this Chapter.

(2) Determine minimum qualifications, establish and require written or oral examinations, and establish minimum education, experience, and training standards for applicants and licensees under this Chapter.

(3) Conduct investigations regarding alleged violations and to make evaluations as may be necessary to determine if licensees and trainees under this Chapter are complying with the provisions of this Chapter.

(4) Adopt and amend bylaws, consistent with law, for its internal management and control.

(5) Approve individual applicants to be licensed or registered according to this Chapter.

(6) Deny, suspend, or revoke any license or trainee permit issued or to be issued

under this Chapter to any applicant, licensee, or permit holder who fails to satisfy the requirements of this Chapter or the rules established by the Board. The denial, suspension, or revocation shall be in accordance with Chapter 150B of the General Statutes of North Carolina.

(7) Issue subpoenas to compel the attendance of witnesses and the production of pertinent books, accounts, records, and documents. The district court shall have the power to impose punishment pursuant to G.S. Chapter 5A, Article 2, for acts occurring in matters pending before the Private Protective Services Board which would constitute civil contempt if the acts occurred in an action pending in court.

(8) Repealed by Session Laws 1989, c. 759, s. 5.

(9) Adopt rules governing detection of deception schools, and charge fees for reimbursement of costs incurred pursuant to approval of the schools.

(10) Contract for services as necessary to carry out the functions of the Board.

(11) Approve training schools, instructors, and course materials for any person, firm, association, or corporation wishing to provide training described in this Chapter.

(12) Approve a design for a badge or shield that indicates a person is licensed or registered to engage in private protective services. The badge or shield shall be approved by the North Carolina Sheriffs' Association and the North Carolina Association of Chiefs of Police.

History.
1973, c. 528, s. 1; c. 1331, s. 3; 1979, c. 818, s. 2; 1981 (Reg. Sess., 1982), c. 1359, s. 3; 1983, c. 794, s. 2; c. 810; 1989, c. 759, s. 5; 1999-456, s. 19; 2007-511, s. 2

§ 74C-6. Position of Director created

The position of Director of the Private Protective Services Board is hereby created within the Department of Public Safety. The Secretary of Public Safety shall appoint a person to fill this full-time position. The Director's duties shall be to administer the directives contained in this Chapter and the rules promulgated by the Board to implement this Chapter and to carry out the administrative duties incident to the functioning of the Board in order to actively police the private protective services industry to ensure compliance with the law in all aspects.

History.
1973, c. 528, s. 1; 1979, c. 818, s. 2; 1999-456, s. 20; 2001-487, s. 64(b); 2014-100, s. 17.5(b), (d)

§ 74C-7. Investigative powers of the Secretary of Public Safety

The Secretary of Public Safety for the State of North Carolina shall have the power to investigate or cause to be investigated any complaints, allegations, or suspicions of wrongdoing or violations of this Chapter involving individuals licensed, or to be licensed, under this Chapter. Any investigation conducted pursuant to this section is confidential and is not subject to review under G.S. 132-1 until the investigation is complete and a report is presented to the Board. However, the report may be released to the licensee after the investigation is complete but before the report is presented to the Board.

History.
1973, c. 528, s. 1; 1979, c. 818, s. 2; 2009-328, s. 2; 2014-100, s. 17.5(b)

§ 74C-8. License requirements

(a) **License Required.** -- Any person, firm, association, or corporation desiring to carry on or engage in the private protective services profession in this State shall be licensed in accordance with this Chapter.

(b) **Application.** -- To apply for a license, an applicant must submit a verified application in writing to the Board that includes all of the following:

(1) Full name, home address, post office box, and the actual street address of the applicant's business.

(2) The name under which the applicant intends to do business.

(3) A statement as to the general nature of the business in which the applicant intends to engage.

(4) The full name and address of any partners in the business and the principal officers, directors and business manager, if any.

(5) The names of not less than three unrelated and disinterested persons as references of whom inquiry can be made as to the character, standing, and reputation of the persons making the application.

(6) Such other information, evidence, statements, or documents as may be required by the Board.

(7) Accompanying trainee permit applications only, a notarized statement signed by the applicant and his employer stating that the trainee applicant will at all times work with and under the direct supervision of a licensed private detective.

(c) **Qualifying Agent.** -- A business entity, other than a sole proprietorship, that engages in private protective services is subject to all of the requirements listed in this subsection with respect to a qualifying agent. For purposes of this Chapter, a "qualifying agent" is an individual in a management position who is licensed under this Chapter and whose name and address have been registered with the Director. The requirements are:

(1) The business entity shall employ a designated resident qualifying agent who meets the requirements for a license issued under this Chapter and who is, in fact, licensed under the provisions of this Chapter, unless otherwise approved by the Board. Provided however, that this approval shall not be given unless the business entity has and continuously maintains in this State a registered agent who shall be an individual resident in this State. Service upon the registered agent appointed by the business entity of any process, notice, or demand required by or permitted to be served upon the business entity by the Private Protective Services Board shall be binding upon the business entity and the licensee. Nothing herein contained shall limit or affect the right to serve any process, notice, or demand required or permitted by law to be served upon a business entity in any other manner now or hereafter permitted by law.

(2) Repealed by Session Laws 2009-328, s. 3, effective October 1, 2009.

(3) In the event that the qualifying agent upon whom the business entity relies in order to do business ceases to perform his duties as qualifying agent, the business entity shall notify the Director within 10 working days. The business entity must obtain a substitute qualifying agent within 30 days after the original qualifying agent ceases to serve as qualifying agent unless the Board, in its discretion, extends this period, for good cause, for a period of time not to exceed three months.

(4) The certificate authorizing the business entity to engage in a private protective services profession shall list the name of at least one designated qualifying agent. No licensee shall serve as the qualifying agent for more than one business entity without prior approval of the Director, subject to the approval of the Board.

(5) Repealed by Session Laws 2009-328, s. 3, effective October 1, 2009.

(d) **Criminal Record Check.** -- An applicant must meet all of the following requirements and qualifications determined by a background investigation conducted by the Board in accordance with G.S. 74C-8.1 and upon receipt of an application:

(1) That the applicant is at least 18 years of age.

(2) That the applicant is of good moral character and temperate habits. The following shall be prima facie evidence that the applicant does not have good moral character or temperate habits: conviction by any local, State, federal, or military court of any crime involving the illegal use, carrying, or possession of a firearm; conviction of any crime involving the illegal use, possession, sale, manufacture, distribution, or transportation of a controlled substance, drug, narcotic, or alcoholic beverage; conviction of a crime involving felonious assault or an act of violence; conviction of a crime involving unlawful breaking or entering, burglary, larceny, or any offense involving moral turpitude; or a history of addiction to alcohol or a narcotic drug; provided that, for purposes of this subsection, "conviction" means and includes the entry of a plea of guilty or no contest or a verdict rendered in open court by a judge or jury.

(3) Repealed by Session Laws 1989, c. 759, s. 6.

(4) That the applicant has the necessary training, qualifications, and experience in order to determine the applicant's competency and fitness as the Board may determine by rule for all licenses to be issued by the Board.

(e) **Examination.** -- The Board may require the applicant to demonstrate the applicant's qualifications by oral or written examination or by successful completion of a Board-approved training program, or all three.

(f) **Issuance.** -- Upon a finding that the application is in proper form, the completion of the background investigation, and the completion of an examination required by the Board, the Director shall submit to the Board the application and the Director's recommendations. Upon completion of the background investigation, the Director may issue a temporary license pending approval of the application by the Board at the next regularly scheduled meeting. The Board shall determine whether to approve or deny the application for a license. Upon approval by the Board, a license will be issued to the applicant upon payment by the applicant of the initial license fee and the required contribution to the Private Protective Services Education Fund, and certificate of liability insurance.

(1) through (5) Repealed by Session Laws 1989, c. 759, s. 6.

(g) **Confidentiality.** -- Except for purposes of administering the provisions of this section and for law enforcement purposes, the home address or telephone number of an applicant, licensee, or the spouse, children, or parents of an applicant or licensee is confidential under G.S. 132-1.2, and the Board shall not disclose this information unless the applicant or licensee consents to the disclosure. The provisions of this subsection shall not apply when a licensee's home address or telephone number is also the licensee's business address and telephone number. Violation of this subsection shall constitute a Class 3 misdemeanor.

History.
1973, c. 47, s. 2; c. 528, s. 1; 1975, c. 592, s. 1; 1977, c. 570, s. 2; 1979, c. 818, s. 2; 1983, c. 673, s. 3; c. 794, ss. 3, 11; 1985, c. 560; 1987, c. 657, ss. 2, 2.1; 1989, c. 759, s. 6; 1999-446, s. 1; 2001-487, s. 64(c); 2002-147, s. 3; 2009-328, s. 3

§ 74C-8.1. Criminal background checks

(a) **Authorization.** -- Upon receipt of an application for a license, registration, certification, or permit, the Board shall conduct a background investigation to determine whether the applicant meets the requirements for a license, registration, certification, or permit set out in G.S. 74C-8(d). The Department of Public Safety may provide a criminal record check to the Board for a person who has applied for a new or renewal license, registration, certification, or permit through the Board. The Board shall provide to the Department of Public Safety, along with the request, the fingerprints of a new applicant, and the Department of Public Safety shall provide a criminal record check based upon the applicant's fingerprints. The Board may request a criminal record check from the Department of Public Safety for a renewal applicant based upon the applicant's fingerprints in accordance with policy adopted by the Board. The Board shall provide any additional information required by the Department of Public Safety and a form signed by the applicant consenting to the check of the criminal record and to the use of the fingerprints and other identifying information required by the State or national repositories. The applicant's fingerprints shall be forwarded to the State Bureau of Investigation for a search of the State's criminal history record file, and the State Bureau of Investigation shall forward a set of the fingerprints to the Federal Bureau of Investigation for a national criminal history check. The Department of Public Safety may charge each applicant a fee for conducting the checks of criminal history records authorized by this subsection.

The Board may require a new or renewal applicant to obtain a criminal record report from one or more reporting services designated by the Board to provide criminal record reports. Applicants are required to pay the designated reporting service for the cost of these reports.

(b) **Confidentiality.** -- The Board shall keep all information obtained pursuant to this section confidential in accordance with applicable State law and federal guidelines, and the information shall not be a public record under Chapter 132 of the General Statutes.

History.
2009-328, s. 4; 2014-100, s. 17.1(o)

§ 74C-9. Form of license; term; renewal; posting; branch offices; not assignable; late renewal fee

(a) The license when issued shall be in such form as may be determined by the Board and shall state:

(1) The name of the licensee,

(2) The name under which the licensee is to operate, and

(3) The number and expiration date of the license.

(b) The license shall be issued for a term of two years. A trainee permit shall be issued for a term of two years. All licenses must be renewed prior to the expiration of the term of the license. Following issuance, the license shall at all times be posted in a conspicuous place in the licensee's principal place of business, in North Carolina, unless for good cause exempted by the Director. A license issued under this Chapter is not assignable. The Board may require all licensees to complete continuing education courses approved by the Board before renewal of their licenses.

(c) Repealed by Session Laws 1989, c. 759, s. 7.

(d) The operator or manager of any branch office shall be properly licensed or registered. The license shall be posted at all times in a conspicuous place in the branch office. This license shall be issued for a term of two years. Every business covered under the provisions of this Chapter shall file in writing with the Board the addresses of each of its branch offices, if any, within 10 working days after the establishment, closing, or changing of the location of any branch office. The Director may, upon the successful completion of an investigation of the application, issue a temporary branch office license pending approval of the application by the Board.

(e) The Board is authorized to charge reasonable application and license fees as follows:

(1) A nonrefundable initial application fee in an amount not to exceed one hundred fifty dollars ($ 150.00).

(2) A new or renewal license fee in an amount not to exceed two hundred fifty dollars ($ 250.00) per year of the license term.

(3) A new or renewal trainee permit fee in an amount not to exceed two hundred fifty dollars ($ 250.00) per year of the license term.

(4) A new or renewal fee for each license or duplicate license in addition to the basic license referred to in subsection (2) in an amount not to exceed fifty dollars ($ 50.00) per year of the license term.

(5) A late renewal fee to be paid within 90 days from the date the license, registration, permit, or certification expires in addition to the renewal fee due in an amount not to exceed one hundred dollars ($ 100.00), if the license, registration, permit, or certification has not been renewed on or before the expiration date of the license, registration, permit, or certification.

(6) A new, renewal, replacement or reissuance fee for an unarmed registration identification card in an amount not to exceed thirty dollars ($ 30.00).

(7) An application fee for a firearm registration permit not to exceed fifty dollars ($ 50.00).

(8) A new, renewal, replacement, or reissuance fee for a firearm registration permit not to exceed thirty dollars ($ 30.00).

(9) An application fee for certification as a certified trainer not to exceed fifty dollars ($ 50.00).

(10) A renewal or replacement fee for certified trainer certification not to exceed twenty-five dollars ($ 25.00).

(11) A new nonresident temporary permit fee not to exceed one hundred dollars ($ 100.00).

(12) An unarmed registration transfer fee not to exceed fifteen dollars ($ 15.00).

(13) A branch office license fee not to exceed fifty dollars ($ 50.00) per year of the license term.

(14) A special limited guard and patrol license fee not to exceed one hundred dollars ($ 100.00) per year of the license term.

(15) A correctable error fee not to exceed one hundred dollars ($ 100.00) for each subsequent filing of an application following review and rejection of the initial application.

Except as provided in G.S. 74C-13(k), all fees collected pursuant to this section shall be expended, under the direction of the Board, for the purpose of defraying the expenses of administering this Chapter.

(f) A license or trainee permit granted under the provisions of this Chapter may be renewed by the Private Protective Services Board upon notification by the licensee or permit holder to the Director of intended renewal, the payment of the proper fee, and evidence of a policy of liability insurance as prescribed in G.S. 74C-10(e). The renewal shall be finalized before the expiration date of the license. In no event will renewal be granted more than three months after the date of expiration of a license or trainee permit.

(g) Upon notification of approval of the application by the Board, an applicant must furnish evidence that the applicant has obtained the necessary liability insurance required by G.S. 74C-10 and obtain the license applied for or the application shall lapse.

(h) Trainee permits shall not be issued to applicants that qualify for a private detective license. A licensed private detective may supervise no more than five trainees at any given time.

History.

1973, c. 528, s. 1; c. 1428; 1975, c. 592, ss. 2-4; 1979, c. 818, s. 2; 1983, c. 67, s. 1; c. 794, s. 8; 1985, c. 597, ss. 1-7; 1987, c. 657, s. 3; 1989, c. 759, s. 7; 2001-487, s. 64(d); 2007-511, s. 3; 2009-328, ss. 5, 6

§ 74C-10. Certificate of liability insurance required; form and approval; suspension for noncompliance

(a) through (d) Repealed by Session Laws 1983, c. 673, s. 4.

(e) No security guard and patrol, armored car, or special limited guard and patrol license shall be issued under this Chapter unless the applicant files with the Board evidence of a policy of liability insurance. The policy must provide for the following minimum coverage: fifty thousand dollars ($ 50,000) because of bodily injury or death of one person as a result of the negligent act or acts of the principal insured or his agents operating in the course and scope of his employment; subject to said limit for one person, one hundred thousand dollars ($ 100,000) because of bodily injury or death of two or more persons as the result of the negligent act or acts of the principal insured or his agents operating in the course and scope of his or her agency; twenty thousand dollars ($ 20,000) because of injury to or destruction of property of others as the result of the negligent act or acts of the principal insured or his agents operating in the course and scope of his or her agency. If the licensee, other than a security guard and patrol, armored car, or special limited guard and patrol licensee, carries a firearm while engaged in private protective services activities, the licensee shall obtain a policy of liability insurance with a minimum coverage as specified above. A licensee is deemed to be "carrying a firearm" for purposes of this section while engaged in private protective services if the licensee has a firearm on the licensee's person or in the automobile the licensee is using to perform private protective services.

(f) An insurance carrier shall have the right to cancel such policy of liability insurance upon giving a 30-day notice to the Board. Provided, however, that such cancellation shall not affect any liability on the policy which accrued prior thereto. The policy of liability shall be approved by the Board as to form, execution, and terms thereon.

(g) The holder of any trainee permit and persons registered pursuant to G.S. 74C-11 shall not be required to obtain a certificate of liability insurance.

(h) Every security guard and patrol licensee, armored car licensee, special limited guard and patrol licensee, or licensee carrying a firearm while engaged in private protective services shall at all times maintain on file with the Board the certificate of insurance required by this Chapter in full force and effect and upon failure to do so, the license of such licensee shall be automatically suspended and shall not be reinstated until an application therefor, in the form prescribed by the Board, is filed together with a proper insurance certificate.

No cancellation or refusal to renew by an insurer of a licensee under this Chapter shall be effective unless the insurer has given the insured licensee notice of the cancellation or refusal to renew. Upon termination of insurance coverage for said licensee, the insurer shall give notice to the Director of the Board.

(i) The Board may deny the application notwithstanding the applicant's compliance with this section:

(1) For any reason which would justify refusal to issue or a suspension or revocation of a license; or

(2) Because the applicant engaged in a private protective services profession while the applicant's license was suspended for failure to keep the required liability insurance policy in force.

History.

1973, c. 528, s. 1; 1979, c. 818, s. 2; 1981, c. 807, ss. 4, 5; 1983, c. 673, ss. 4-6, 8; c. 794, s. 4; 1989, c. 759, s. 8; 2001-487, s. 64(e); 2007-511, ss. 4, 5

§ 74C-11. Probationary employees and registration of regular employees; unarmed security guard required to have registration card

(a) All licensees may employ unarmed security guards as probationary employees for 20 consecutive calendar days. Upon completion of the probationary period and the desire of the licensee to hire an unarmed security guard as a regular employee, the licensee shall register the employee who will be engaged in providing private protective services covered by this Chapter with the Board within 30 days after the probationary employment period ends, unless the Director, in the Director's discretion, extends the time period, for good cause. Before a probationary employee engages in private protective services, the employee shall complete any training requirements, and the licensee shall conduct a criminal record check on the employee, as the Board deems appropriate. The licensee shall submit a list of the probationary employees to the Director on a monthly basis. The list shall include the name, address, social security number, and dates of employment of the employees.

To register an employee after the probationary period ends, a licensee must give the Board the following:

(1) Set(s) of classifiable fingerprints on standard F.B.I. applicant cards; recent photograph(s) of acceptable quality for identification; and

(2) Statements of any criminal records obtained from the appropriate authority in each area where the employee has resided within the immediately preceding 48 months.

(b) A security guard and patrol company may not employ an unarmed security guard in a regular position unless the guard has a registration card issued under subsection (d) of this section. A person engaged in a private protective services profession may not employ an armed security guard unless the guard has a firearm registration permit issued under G.S. 74C-13.

(c) The Director shall be notified in writing of the termination of any regular employee registered under subsection (a) of this section within 10 days after the termination.

(d) An unarmed security guard shall make application to the Director for an unarmed registration card which the Director shall issue to the applicant after receipt of the information required to be submitted by the applicant's employer pursuant to subsection (a) of this section, and after meeting any additional requirements which the Board, in its discretion, deems to be necessary. The unarmed security guard registration card shall be in the form of a pocket card designed by the Board, shall be issued in the name of the applicant, and may have the applicant's photograph affixed to the card. The unarmed security guard registration card shall expire one year after its date of issuance and shall be renewed every year. The Board may require all registration holders to complete continuing education courses approved by the Board before renewal of their registrations. If an unarmed registered security guard is terminated by a licensee and changes employment to another security guard and patrol company, the security guard's registration card shall remain valid, provided the security guard pays the unarmed guard registration transfer fee to the Board and a new unarmed security guard registration card is issued. An unarmed security guard whose transfer registration application and transfer fee have been sent to the Board may work with a copy of the transfer application until the registration card is issued.

(e) Notwithstanding the provisions of this section, a licensee may employ a person properly registered or licensed as an unarmed security guard in another state for a period not to exceed 10 days in any given month; provided the licensee, prior to employing the unarmed security guard, submits to the Director the name, address, and social security number of the unarmed guard and the name of the state of current registration or licensing, and the Director approves the employment of the unarmed guard in this State.

(f) Repealed by Session Laws 2005-211, s. 1, effective July 20, 2005.

History.
1979, c. 818, s. 2; 1983, c. 67, s. 2; 1985, c. 597, ss. 8, 9; 1987, c. 657, ss. 4, 5; 1989, c. 759, s. 9; 2001-487, s. 64(f); 2005-211, s. 1; 2007-511, s. 6; 2009-328, s. 7

§ 74C-12. Denial, suspension, or revocation of license, registration, or permit; duty to report criminal arrests

(a) The Board may, after compliance with Chapter 150B of the General Statutes, deny, suspend or revoke a license, registration, or permit issued under this Chapter if it is determined that the applicant, licensee, registrant, or permit holder has done any of the following acts:

(1) Made any false statement or given any false information in connection with any application for a license, registration, or permit or for the renewal or reinstatement of a license, registration, or permit.

(2) Violated any provision of this Chapter.

(3) Violated any rule adopted by the Board pursuant to the authority contained in this Chapter.

(4) Repealed by Session Laws 1989, c. 759, s. 10.

(5) Impersonated or permitted or aided and abetted any other person to impersonate a law enforcement officer of the United States, this State, any other state, or any political subdivision of a state.

(6) Engaged in or permitted any employee to engage in a private protective services profession when not lawfully in possession of a valid license issued under the provisions of this Chapter.

(7) Willfully failed or refused to render to a client service as agreed between the parties and for which compensation has been paid or tendered in accordance with the agreement of the parties.

(8) Knowingly made any false report to the employer or client for whom information is being obtained.

(9) Committed an unlawful breaking or entering, assault, battery, or kidnapping.

(10) Knowingly violated or advised, encouraged, or assisted the violation of any court order or injunction in the course of business as a licensee.

(11) Repealed by Session Laws 1989, c. 759, s. 10.

(12) Undertaken to give legal advice or counsel or to in any way falsely represent that he or she is representing any attorney or he or she is appearing or will appear as an attorney in any legal proceeding.

(13) Issued, delivered, or uttered any simulation of process of any nature which might lead a person to believe that such simulation -- written, printed, or typed -- may be a summons, warrant, writ or court process, or any pleading in any court proceeding.

(14) Failed to make the required contribution to the Private Protective Services Education Fund or failed to maintain the certificate of liability insurance required by this Chapter.

(15) Violated the firearm provisions set forth in this Chapter.

(16) Repealed by Session Laws 1989, c. 759, s. 10.

(17) Failed to notify the Director by a business entity other than a sole proprietorship licensed pursuant to this Chapter of the cessation of employment of the business entity's qualifying agent within the time set forth in this Chapter.

(18) Failed to obtain a substitute qualifying agent by a business entity within 30 days after its qualifying agent has ceased to serve as the business entity's qualifying agent.

(19) Been judged incompetent by a court having jurisdiction under Chapter 35A or former Chapter 35 of the General Statutes or committed to a mental health facility for treatment of mental illness, as defined in G.S. 122C-3, by a court under G.S. 122C-271.

(20) Failed or refused to offer a report to a client within 30 days of the client's written request after the client has paid for services rendered.

(21) Been previously denied a license, registration, or permit under this Chapter or previously had a license, registration, or permit revoked for cause. The denial or revocation shall include a principal in the applicant's business.

(22) Engaged in a private protective services profession under a name other than the name under which the license was obtained under the provisions of this Chapter.

(23) Divulged to any person, except as required by law, any information acquired by the license holder except at the direction of the employer or client for whom the information was obtained. A licensee may divulge to any law enforcement officer or district attorney or district attorney's

representative any information the law enforcement officer may require to investigate a criminal offense with the prior approval and consent of the client.

(24) Fraudulently held himself or herself out as employed by or licensed by the State Bureau of Investigation or any other governmental authority.

(25) Demonstrated intemperate habits or a lack of good moral character. The acts that are prima facie evidence of intemperate habits or lack of good moral character under G.S. 74C-8(d)(2) are prima facie evidence of the same under this subdivision.

(26) Advertised or solicited business using a name other than that in which the license was issued.

(27) Worn, carried, or accepted any badge or shield purporting to indicate that the person is a law enforcement officer while licensed under the provisions of this Chapter as a private investigator.

(28) Possessed or displayed a badge or shield while providing private protective services that was not designed and approved by the Board pursuant to G.S. 74C-5(12).

(29) Failed or refused to reasonably cooperate with the Board or its agents during an investigation of any complaint, allegation, suspicion of wrongdoing, or violation of this Chapter.

(30) Failed to properly make any disclosure to the Board or provide documents or information required by this Chapter or rules adopted by the Board.

(31) Engaged in conduct constituting dereliction of duty or otherwise deceived, defrauded, or harmed the public in the course of professional activities or services.

(32) Demonstrated a lack of financial responsibility.

(b) The denial, revocation, or suspension of a license, registration, or permit by the Board shall be in writing, be signed by the Director of the Board, and state the grounds upon which the Board decision is based. The aggrieved person shall have the right to appeal from this decision as provided in Chapter 150B of the General Statutes. The aggrieved person shall file the appeal within 60 days of receipt of the Board's decision.

(c) The following persons may not be issued a license under this Chapter:

(1) A sworn court official.

(2) A holder of a company police commission under Chapter 74E of the General Statutes.

(d) A licensee shall report to the Board in writing within 30 days any charge, arrest for, or conviction of a misdemeanor or felony for any of the following:

(1) Crimes that have as an essential element dishonesty, deceit, fraud, or misrepresentation.

(2) Illegal use, possession, sale, manufacture, distribution, or transportation of a controlled substance, drug, narcotic, or alcoholic beverage.

(3) Illegal use, carrying, or possession of a firearm.

(4) Acts involving assault.

(5) Acts involving unlawful breaking or entering, burglary, or larceny.

(6) Any offense involving moral turpitude.

For purposes of this section, the term "conviction" includes the entry of a plea of guilty, a plea of nolo contendere, prayer for judgment continued, or a finding of guilt by a court of competent jurisdiction. The licensee's failure to report a charge, arrest for, or conviction of a misdemeanor or felony is grounds for revocation of the license.

History.
1979, c. 818, s. 2; 1981, c. 807, s. 6; 1987, c. 550, s. 20; c. 657, s. 6; 1989, c. 759, s. 10; 1991 (Reg. Sess., 1992), c. 1043, s. 5; 2001-487, s. 64(g); 2007-511, s. 7; 2009-328, ss. 8, 9

§ 74C-13. Armed licensee or registered employee required to have firearm registration permit; firearms training

(a) It shall be unlawful for any person performing private protective services duties to carry a firearm in the performance of those duties without first having met the qualifications of this section and having been issued a firearm registration permit by the Board. A licensee shall register any individual carrying a firearm within 30 days of employment. Before engaging in any private protective services activity, the individual shall receive any required training prescribed by the Board.

(a1) The following definitions apply in this section:

(1) **Armed private investigator.** -- A licensed private investigator who, at any time, wears, carries, or possesses a firearm in the performance of duty.

(1a) **Armed security guard.** -- An individual employed by a contract security company or a proprietary security organization whose principal duty is that of an armed security watchman; armed armored car service guard; armed alarm system company responder; or armed courier service who at any time wears, carries, or possesses a firearm in the performance of duty.

(2) **Contract security company.** -- Any person, firm, association, or corporation engaging in a private protective services

profession that provides services on a contractual basis for a fee or other valuable consideration to any other person, firm, association, or corporation.

(3) **Proprietary security organization.** -- Any person, firm, association, or corporation or department thereof which employs security guards, alarm responders, armored car personnel, or couriers who are employed regularly and exclusively as an employee by an employer in connection with the business affairs of the employer.

(b) It shall be unlawful for any person, firm, association, or corporation and its agents and employees to employ an armed security guard or an armed private investigator and knowingly authorize or permit the armed security guard or armed private investigator to carry a firearm during the course of performing his or her duties as an armed security guard or an armed private investigator if the Board has not issued him or her a firearm registration permit under this section or if the person, firm, association, or corporation permits an armed security guard or an armed private investigator to carry a firearm during the course of performing his or her duties whose firearm registration permit has been suspended, revoked, or has otherwise expired:

(1) A firearm registration permit grants authority to the armed security guard, or armed private investigator, while in the performance of his or her duties or traveling directly to and from work, to carry any firearm approved by the Board and not otherwise prohibited by law. The use of any firearm not approved by the Board is prohibited.

(2) All firearms carried by authorized armed security guards in the performance of their duties shall be owned or leased by the employer. Personally owned firearms shall not be carried by an armed security guard in the performance of his or her duties.

(c) The applicant for a firearm registration permit shall submit an application to the Board on a form provided by the Board.

(d) Each firearm registration permit issued under this section to an armed security guard shall be in the form of a pocket card designed by the Board and shall identify the contract security company or proprietary security organization by whom the holder of the firearm registration permit is employed. A firearm registration permit issued to an armed security guard expires one year after the date of its issuance and must be renewed annually unless the permit holder's employment terminates before the expiration of the permit. The Board may require all permit holders to complete continuing education courses approved by the Board before renewal of their permits.

(d1) Each firearm registration permit issued under this section to an armed private investigator shall be in the form of a pocket card designed by the Board and shall identify the name of the armed private investigator. While carrying a firearm and engaged in private protective services, the armed private investigator shall carry the firearms registration permit issued by the Board, together with valid identification, and shall disclose to any law enforcement officer that the person holds a valid permit and is carrying a firearm, whether concealed or in plain view, when approached or addressed by the law enforcement officer, and shall display both the permit and the proper identification upon the request of a law enforcement officer. A private investigator firearm registration permit expires one year from the date of issuance and shall be renewed annually. The Board may require all permit holders to complete continuing education courses approved by the Board before renewal of their permits.

(e) If an armed security guard terminates his or her employment with the contract security company or proprietary security organization, the firearm registration permit expires and must be returned to the Board within 15 working days of the date of termination of the employee.

(f) A contract security company or proprietary security organization shall be allowed to employ an individual for 30 days as an armed security guard pending completion of the firearms training required by this Chapter, if the contract security company or proprietary security organization obtains prior approval from the Director. The Board and the Secretary of Public Safety shall provide by rule the procedure by which an armed private investigator, a contract security company, or a proprietary security organization applicant may be issued a temporary firearm registration permit by the Director of the Board pending a determination by the Board of whether to grant or deny an applicant a firearm registration permit.

(g) The Board may suspend, revoke, or deny a firearm registration permit if the holder or applicant has been convicted of any crime involving moral turpitude or any crime involving the illegal use, carrying, or possession of a deadly weapon or for violation of this section or rules promulgated by the Board to implement this section. The Director may summarily suspend a firearm registration permit pending resolution of charges involving the illegal use, carrying, or possession of a firearm lodged against the holder of the permit.

(h) The Board and the Secretary of Public Safety shall establish a firearms training program for licensees and registered employees to be conducted by agencies and institutions approved by the Board and the Secretary of Public

Safety. The Board and the Secretary of Public Safety may approve training programs conducted by a contract security company and the security department of a proprietary security organization, if the contract security company or security department of a proprietary security organization offers the courses listed in subdivision (1) of this subsection and if the instructors of the training program are certified trainers approved by the Board and the Secretary of Public Safety:

(1) The basic training course approved by the Board and the Secretary of Public Safety shall consist of a minimum of four hours of classroom training which shall include all of the following:

a. Legal limitations on the use of hand guns and on the powers and authority of an armed security guard.

b. Familiarity with this section.

c. Range firing and procedure and hand gun safety and maintenance.

d. Any other topics of armed security guard training curriculum which the Board deems necessary.

(2) An applicant for a firearm registration permit must fire a minimum qualifying score to be determined by the Board and the Secretary of Public Safety on any approved target course approved by the Board and the Secretary of Public Safety.

(3) A firearms registrant must complete a refresher course and shall requalify on the prescribed target course prior to the renewal of his or her firearm registration permit.

(4) The Board and the Secretary of Public Safety shall have the authority to promulgate all rules necessary to administer the provisions of this section concerning the training requirements of this section.

(i) The Board may not issue a firearm registration permit to an applicant until the applicant's employer submits evidence satisfactory to the Board that the applicant:

(1) Has satisfactorily completed an approved training course.

(2) Meets all the qualifications established by this section and by the rules promulgated to implement this section.

(3) Is mentally and physically capable of handling a firearm within the guidelines set forth by the Board and the Secretary of Public Safety.

(j) The Board and the Secretary of Public Safety are authorized to prescribe reasonable rules to implement this section, including rules for periodic requalification with the firearm and for the maintenance of records relating to persons issued a firearm registration permit by the Board.

(k) All fees collected pursuant to G.S. 74C-9(e)(7) and (8) shall be expended, under the direction of the Board, for the purpose of defraying the expense of administering the firearms provisions of this Chapter.

(l) The Board and the Secretary of Public Safety shall establish a training program for certified trainers to be conducted by agencies and institutions approved by the Board and the Secretary of Public Safety. The Board or the Secretary of Public Safety shall have the authority to promulgate all rules necessary to administer the provisions of this subsection.

(1) The Board and the Secretary of Public Safety shall also establish renewal requirements for certified trainers. The Board may require all certified trainers to complete continuing education courses approved by the Board before renewal of their certifications.

(2) No certified firearms trainer shall certify a licensee or registrant unless the licensee or registrant has successfully completed the firearms training requirements set out above in subsection (h) of this section.

(m) The Board and the Secretary of Public Safety shall establish a training program for unarmed security guards to be conducted by agencies and institutions approved by the Board and the Secretary of Public Safety. The Board and the Secretary of Public Safety shall have the authority to promulgate all rules necessary to administer the provisions of this subsection.

(n) A private investigator shall be permitted to carry a concealed weapon during the performance of his or her duties as a private investigator upon: (i) obtaining a concealed weapon permit issued pursuant to G.S. 14-415.11; (ii) successfully completing the firearms training course approved by the Board and the Secretary of Public Safety; and (iii) having a notation affixed to the face of the firearms registration card designating that the armed private investigator is allowed to carry a concealed weapon. A private investigator who does not carry a weapon during the course of his or her duties as a private investigator but who wishes to carry a concealed weapon while not engaged in private investigative duties shall be permitted to do so upon completion of the requirements set forth in Article 54B of Chapter 14 of the General Statutes.

History.
1979, c. 818, s. 2; 1983, c. 67, s. 3; 1989, c. 759, s. 11; 2001-487, s. 64(h); 2007-511, s. 8; 2009-328, s. 10; 2014-100, s. 17.5(b)

N.C. Gen. Stat. § 74C-14

Repealed by Session Laws 2009-328, s. 11, effective October 1, 2009.

§ 74C-15. Pocket identification cards issued to licensees and trainees

(a) Upon the issuance of a license or trainee permit, a pocket identification card of design, size, and content approved by the Board shall be issued by the Board without charge to each licensee or trainee. The holder must have this card in his possession at all times when he is on duty and working within the scope of his employment. When a licensee or trainee to whom a card has been issued terminates his position as a licensee or trainee, the card must be surrendered to the Director of the Board within 10 working days thereafter.

(b) Repealed by Session Laws 1989, c. 759, s. 12.

History.
1979, c. 818, s. 2; 1989, c. 759, s. 12; 2001-487, s. 64(i)

§ 74C-16. Prohibited acts

(a), (b) Repealed by Session Laws 1989, c. 759, s. 13.

(c) It shall be unlawful for anyone not licensed or registered as required under this Chapter to:
  (1) Advertise or to hold himself out to be a licensee;
  (2) Advertise or to hold himself out to perform services for which a license is required when, in fact, the individual is not licensed or registered in accordance with this Chapter.
  (3) Repealed by Session Laws 1989, c. 759, s. 13.

(d) through (f) Repealed by Session Laws 1989, c. 759, s. 13.

History.
1979, c. 818, s. 2; 1983, c. 794, s. 5; 1987, c. 657, ss. 7, 8; 1989, c. 759, s. 13

§ 74C-17. Enforcement

(a) The Board may apply in its own name to any judge of the superior court of the General Court of Justice for an injunction in order to prevent any violation or threatened violation of the provisions of this Chapter.

(b) Any person, firm, association, or corporation or their agents and employees violating any of the provisions of this Chapter is guilty of a Class 1 misdemeanor. The Attorney General, or the Attorney General's representative, has concurrent jurisdiction with the district attorneys of this State to prosecute violations of this Chapter.

(c) In lieu of revocation or suspension of a license or permit under G.S. 74C-12, a civil penalty of not more than two thousand dollars ($ 2,000) may be assessed by the Board against any person or business that violates any provision of this Chapter or any rule of the Board adopted pursuant to this Chapter. In determining the amount of any penalty, the Board shall consider the degree and extent of harm caused by the violation. The clear proceeds of civil penalties provided for in this subsection shall be remitted to the Civil Penalty and Forfeiture Fund in accordance with G.S. 115C-457.2.

(d) Proceedings for the assessment of civil penalties under this section are governed by Chapter 150B of the General Statutes. If the person assessed a civil penalty fails to pay the penalty to the Board, the Board may institute an action in the superior court of the county in which the person resides or has a principal place of business to recover the unpaid amount of the penalty. An action to recover a civil penalty under this section does not relieve any party from any other penalty prescribed by law.

History.
1979, c. 818, s. 2; 1983, c. 794, s. 6; 1989, c. 759, s. 14; 1993, c. 539, s. 557; 1994, Ex. Sess., c. 24, s. 14(c); 1998-215, s. 98; 2021-84, s. 3

§ 74C-18. Reciprocity; temporary permit

(a) To the extent that other states which provide for licensing of any private protective services profession provide for similar action for citizens of this State, the Board, in its discretion, may grant a private protective services license to a nonresident who holds a valid private protective services license of the same type from another state upon satisfactory proof furnished to the Board that the standards of licensure in such other states are at least substantially equivalent to those prevailing in this State. Applicants shall make application to the Board on the form prescribed by the Board for all applicants, shall comply with the provisions of G.S. 74C-10, and shall pay the fees required of all applicants.

(b) The Director, in his discretion and subject to the approval of the Board, may issue a temporary permit to a nonresident who has complied with the provisions of G.S. 74C-10 and who is validly licensed in another state to engage in a private protective service activity incidental to a specific case originating in another state. A temporary permit may be issued for a period of no more than 30 days and may be renewed. A temporary permit may contain such restrictions which the Board, in its discretion, deems appropriate.

History.
1979, c. 818, s. 2; 1983, c. 67, s. 4; 1989, c. 759, s. 15; 2001-487, s. 64(j)

§ 74C-19. Severability

If any provision of this Chapter or the application thereof to any person or circumstance is for any reason held invalid, such invalidity shall not affect other provisions or applications of the Article which can be given effect without the invalid provision or application, and to this end the provisions of this Chapter are declared to be severable.

History.
1979, c. 818, s. 2

N.C. Gen. Stat. § 74C-20

Repealed by Session Laws 1983, c. 673, s. 9.

§ 74C-21. Law enforcement officer provisions

(a) No law enforcement officer of the United States, this State, any other state, or any political subdivision of a state shall be licensed as a private detective or security guard and patrol licensee under this Chapter.

(b) An off-duty law enforcement officer may be employed during his off-duty hours by a licensed security guard and patrol company on an employer-employee basis. An off-duty law enforcement officer shall not wear his police officer's uniform or use the police equipment while working for a security guard and patrol company.

(c) A law enforcement officer may provide security guard and patrol services on an individual employer-employee basis to a person, firm, association, or corporation that is not engaged in a security guard and patrol profession.

History.
1989, c. 759, s. 16

§ 74C-22. Continuing education

The Board may require individuals holding a license, registration, certificate, or permit to complete continuing education courses approved by the Board before renewal. The Board shall establish, by rule, the number of hours of continuing education necessary for renewal and any other requirements for completion of continuing education courses. The Board shall have the authority to approve continuing education courses and shall consider the continuing education course criteria, including the course curriculum, the qualifications of the instructor, the potential benefit to the industry, and any other criteria the Board deems appropriate.

History.
2007-511, s. 9

§ 74C-23. Acquisition or change of ownership or control of licensed firm, association, or corporation

In the event a company, firm, or corporation licensed under this Chapter transfers ownership, control, or a majority of assets to another person, firm, association, or corporation, the person, firm, association, or corporation acquiring control or ownership shall have the following responsibilities:

(1) Notify the Director of the acquisition or change of ownership or control by registered mail within five business days from the date of the transaction.

(2) Describe the transaction that has occurred by providing the following information:

a. The name and address of the registered agent of the party acquiring control or ownership or otherwise succeeding the licensee.

b. The name and address of the acquiring party, including each individual owner of any interest in the party or, if the party is a corporation, the name and address of each officer of the corporation and member of the board of directors.

c. Any change in location of any branch office.

d. Any change in insurance or bonding limits.

(3) Return to the Director all licenses held by the licensee within five business days from the date of the transaction if the acquiring party does not continue to operate the business under its previous name and license.

(4) Provide to the Director within 60 calendar days from the date of the transaction the following:

a. A list of all registrants or licensees affected by the transaction.

b. Written confirmation of completion of any changes necessary for the acquiring party to comply with the requirements of this Chapter or any applicable rules adopted by the Board on a form approved by the Director.

History.
2009-328, s. 12

§§ 74C-24 through 74C-29

Reserved for future codification purposes.

CHAPTER 74E
COMPANY POLICE ACT

§ 74E-1. Title

This Chapter is the "Company Police Act" and may be cited by that name.

History.
1991 (Reg. Sess., 1992), c. 1043, s. 1

§ 74E-2. Policy and scope

(a) The purpose of this Chapter is to ensure a minimum level of integrity, proficiency, and competence among company police agencies and company police officers. To achieve this purpose, the General Assembly finds that a Company Police Program needs to be established. As part of the Company Police Program, the Attorney General is given the authority to certify an agency as a company police agency and to commission an individual as a company police officer.

(b) A hospital, a State institution, or a corporation engaged in providing on-site police security personnel services for persons or property may apply to the Attorney General to be certified as a company police agency. A company police agency may apply to the Attorney General to commission an individual designated by the agency to act as a company police officer for the agency.

History.
1991 (Reg. Sess., 1992), c. 1043, s. 1; 2005-231, s. 2

§ 74E-3. Liability insurance policy or certificate of self-insurance required; suspension of company police agency certification for failure to comply

(a) An applicant for certification as a company police agency must file with the Attorney General either a copy of a liability insurance policy that meets the requirements of this section or a certificate of self-insurance designating assets sufficient to satisfy the coverage requirements of this section if the applicant is a nonpublic entity. The policy or certificate of self-insurance must provide not less than one million dollars ($ 1,000,000) of coverage per incident for personal injury or property damage resulting from a negligent act of the applicant or an agent or employee of the applicant operating in the course and scope of employment or under color of law. The form, execution, and terms of a liability insurance policy must meet the requirements of the Attorney General.

(b) An insurance carrier that issues a liability insurance policy required by this section may cancel the policy upon giving 30 days' written notice to both the company police agency and the Attorney General. The written notice must be given by certified mail, return receipt requested. Cancellation of a liability insurance policy does not affect any liability on the policy that accrued prior to the effective cancellation date.

(c) A company police agency that is a nonpublic entity must maintain the liability insurance policy or certificate of self-insurance required by this section in effect at all times. The Attorney General shall suspend the certification of a company police agency that fails to maintain a liability insurance policy or certificate of self-insurance when required to do so by this section. A certification suspended for this reason may not be reinstated until the person whose certification was suspended files with the Attorney General an application for reinstatement and either the required liability insurance policy or certificate of self-insurance.

History.
1991 (Reg. Sess., 1992), c. 1043, s. 1

§ 74E-4. Powers of Attorney General

The Attorney General has the following powers in addition to those conferred elsewhere in this Chapter:

(1) To establish minimum education, experience, and training standards and establish and require written or oral examinations for an applicant for certification as a company police agency, a certified company police agency, an applicant for commission as a company police officer, or a commissioned company police officer.

(2) To require a company police agency or a company police officer to submit reports or other information.

(3) To inspect records maintained by a company police agency.

(4) To conduct investigations regarding alleged violations of this Chapter or a rule adopted under this Chapter and to make evaluations as may be necessary to determine if a company police agency or a company police officer is complying with this Chapter or a rule adopted under this Chapter.

(5) To deny, suspend, or revoke a certification as a company police agency or a commission as a company police officer for failure to meet the requirements of or comply with this Chapter or a rule adopted under this Chapter, in accordance with Article 3 of Chapter 150B of the General Statutes.

(6) To appear in the name of the Company Police Program and apply to the courts having jurisdiction for injunctions to

Chapter 74E

prevent a violation of this Chapter or a rule adopted under this Chapter.

(7) To delegate the authority to administer this Chapter.

(8) To require that the Criminal Justice Standards Division provide administrative support staff for the Company Police Program.

(9) To adopt rules needed to implement this Chapter, in accordance with Chapter 150B of the General Statutes.

(10) To monitor compliance with G.S. 20-185.1(d).

History.
1871-2, c. 138, ss. 51, 52; Code, ss. 1988, 1989; Rev., ss. 2605, 2606; 1907, c. 128, s. 1; C.S., s. 3484; 1923, c. 23; 1933, c. 61; 1943, c. 676, ss. 1, 4; 1947, c. 390; 1963, c. 1165, s. 2; 1965, cc. 297, 581; 1977, c. 148, s. 4; 1991 (Reg. Sess., 1992), c. 1043, s. 1; 2018-5, s. 35.25(f)

§ 74E-5. Records

(a) The Attorney General is the legal custodian of all books, papers, documents, or other records and property of the Company Police Program.

(b) Any papers, documents, or other records that become the property of the Company Police Program and are placed in a company police officer's personnel file maintained by the Attorney General are subject to the same restrictions concerning disclosure as set forth in Chapters 126, 153A, and 160A of the General Statutes for other personnel records.

(c) Notwithstanding the provisions of subsection (b), the Attorney General may disclose the contents of any records maintained under the authority of this Chapter to the Criminal Justice Education and Training Standards Commission, the Sheriff's Education and Training Standards Commission, or any other criminal justice agency for certification or employment purposes.

History.
1991 (Reg. Sess., 1992), c. 1043, s. 1

§ 74E-6. Oaths, powers, and authority of company police officers

(a) **Requirements.** -- An individual who is commissioned as a company police officer must take the oath of office required of a law enforcement officer before the individual assumes the duties of a company police officer. The person in each company police agency who is responsible for the agency's company police officers must be commissioned as a company police officer.

(b) **Categories.** -- The following three distinct classifications of company police officers are established:

(1) Campus Police Officers -- Only those company police officers who are employed by any college or university that is a constituent institution of The University of North Carolina or any private college or university that is licensed or exempted from licensure as prescribed by G.S. 116-15, and who are employed by a campus police agency that was licensed pursuant to this Chapter prior to the enactment of Chapter 74G of the General Statutes.

(2) Railroad Police Officers -- Those company police officers who are employed by a certified rail carrier and commissioned as company police officers under this Chapter.

(3) Special Police Officers -- All company police officers not designated as a campus police officer or railroad police officer.

(c) **All Company Police.** -- Company police officers, while in the performance of their duties of employment, have the same powers as municipal and county police officers to make arrests for both felonies and misdemeanors and to charge for infractions on any of the following:

(1) Real property owned by or in the possession and control of their employer.

(2) Real property owned by or in the possession and control of a person who has contracted with the employer to provide on-site company police security personnel services for the property.

(3) Any other real property while in continuous and immediate pursuit of a person for an offense committed upon property described in subdivisions (1) or (2) of this subsection.

Company police officers shall have, if duly authorized by the superior officer in charge, the authority to carry concealed weapons pursuant to and in conformity with G.S. 14-269(b)(4) and (5).

(d) **Campus Police.** -- Campus police officers have the powers contained in subsection (c) of this section and also have the powers in that subsection upon that portion of any public road or highway passing through or immediately adjoining the property described in that subsection, wherever located. The board of trustees of any college or university that qualifies as a campus police agency pursuant to this Chapter may enter into a mutual aid agreement with the governing board of a municipality or, with the consent of the county sheriff, a county to the same extent as a municipal police department pursuant to Chapter 160A.

(e) **Railroad Police.** -- Railroad police officers have the powers contained in subsection (c) and also have the powers and authority granted by federal law or by a regulation promulgated by the United States Secretary of Transportation. Notwithstanding any of the provisions of this Chapter, the limitations on the power to make arrests contained in subsection (c) above, shall not be applicable to railroad police officers commissioned by the Attorney General pursuant to the authority of this Chapter.

(f) Repealed by Session Laws 2005-231, s. 3, effective July 28, 2005.

(g) **Exclusive Authority.** -- Notwithstanding any other provision of law, the authority granted to company police officers shall be limited to the provisions of this Chapter.

(h) **Mutual Aid Agreements.** -- All company police agencies that qualify pursuant to this Chapter may enter into mutual aid agreements with the governing board of a municipality or, with the consent of the county sheriff, a county to the same extent as a municipal police department pursuant to Chapter 160A of the General Statutes.

(i) **As-Needed Assistance.** -- All company police may provide temporary assistance to a law enforcement agency at the request of the head of that agency, or the head of that agency's designee, such as the sheriff or chief of police, regardless of whether there is an agreement in place under subsection (h) of this section. While acting pursuant to this section, a company police officer shall have the same powers vested in law enforcement officers of the agency asking for temporary assistance, but shall not be considered an officer, employee, or agent of the law enforcement agency asking for temporary assistance. Nothing in this subsection shall be construed to expand company police officers' authority to initiate or conduct an independent investigation into violations of criminal laws outside the scope of their subject matter or territorial jurisdiction.

History.
1871-2, c. 138, s. 53; Code, s. 1990; Rev., s. 2607; 1907, c. 128, s. 2; c. 462; c. 470, ss.3, 4; C.S., ss. 3483, 3485; 1933, c. 134, s. 8; 1941, c. 97, s. 5; 1943, c. 676, s. 2; 1959, c. 124, s. 1; 1963, c. 1165, s. 2; 1965, c. 872; 1969, c. 844, s. 8; 1977, c. 148, s. 4; 1981, c. 884, s. 4; 1987, c. 469; 1989, c. 518, s. 1; 1991 (Reg. Sess., 1992), c. 1043, s. 1; 1997-441, s. 1; 1999-68, s. 3; 2005-231, s. 3; 2006-259, s. 5(b); 2017-57, s. 17.2(a)

§ 74E-7. Badges, uniforms, weapons, and vehicles

Company police agencies shall be responsible for ensuring that all employees, whether or not commissioned, comply with the provisions of this Chapter and the rules adopted under this Chapter, including those provisions pertaining to the wearing of badges and uniforms, the carrying of weapons, and the operation of vehicles.

History.
1871-2, c. 138, s. 54; Code, s. 1991; Rev., s. 2608; C.S., s. 3486; 1963, c. 1165, s. 2; 1991 (Reg. Sess., 1992), c. 1043, s. 1

§ 74E-8. Minimum standards for company police officers

Applicants for commission as a company police officer and a commissioned company police officer must meet and maintain the same minimum preemployment and in-service standards as are required for State law enforcement officers by the North Carolina Criminal Justice Education and Training Standards Commission, and must meet and maintain any other preemployment and in-service requirements set by the Attorney General.

History.
1991 (Reg. Sess., 1992), c. 1043, s. 1

§ 74E-9. Compensation of company police officers

The compensation of a company police officer shall be paid by the company police agency for which the officer is commissioned, as may be agreed on between them.

History.
1871-2, c. 138, s. 55; Code, s. 1992; Rev., s. 2609; C.S., s. 3487; 1963, c. 1165, s. 2; 1991 (Reg. Sess., 1992), c. 1043, s. 1

§ 74E-10. Expiration, renewal, and termination of agency certification or officer commission

(a) **Agency.** -- Unless sooner suspended or revoked by the Attorney General, a company police agency's certification expires on June 30 following the date it is issued. A company police agency may renew the certification upon payment of the appropriate fee and compliance with this Chapter and the rules adopted under this Chapter. An entity whose company police agency's certification was denied or revoked for a violation of this Chapter or a rule adopted under this Chapter is not eligible to apply again for that certification for three years.

(b) **Officer.** -- Unless sooner suspended or revoked by the Attorney General, a company police officer's commission expires on June 30 following the date it is issued. A company police officer may renew a commission upon payment of the appropriate fee and compliance with this Chapter and the rules adopted under this Chapter. The Attorney General shall immediately revoke the commission of a company police officer when any of the following occurs:

(1) Termination of employment with the company police agency for which the officer is commissioned.

(2) Termination, suspension, or revocation of the certification of the company

police agency for which the officer is commissioned.

(3) Failure to meet in-service training requirements as required by this Chapter or the rules adopted under this Chapter.

(4) Violation of this Chapter or a rule adopted under this Chapter.

An individual whose company police officer's commission was denied or revoked for a violation of this Chapter or a rule adopted under this Chapter is not eligible to apply again for a commission for three years.

History.
1871-2, c. 138, s. 56; Code, s. 1993; Rev., s. 2610; C.S., s. 3488; 1943, c. 676, s. 3; 1959, c. 124, s. 2; 1963, c. 1165, s. 2; 1977, c. 148, s. 5; 1991 (Reg. Sess., 1992), c. 1043, s. 1

§ 74E-11. Immunity

Neither the Attorney General nor any of the Attorney General's employees may be held criminally or civilly liable for any acts or omissions in carrying out the provisions of this Chapter or for the acts or omissions of agencies or officers certified or commissioned under this Chapter.

History.
1991 (Reg. Sess., 1992), c. 1043, s. 1

§ 74E-12. Fees

The Attorney General may charge fees for the items listed in the following table, not to exceed the amounts listed in the table:

Item	Maximum Fee
Application for certification as a company police agency	$ 250
Annual renewal of certification as a company police agency	$ 200
Application for reinstatement of certification as a company police agency	$ 1,000
Application for commission as a company police officer	$ 100

Item	Maximum Fee
Annual renewal of commission as a company police officer	$ 50
Application for reinstatement of commission as a company police officer	$ 150

The fees imposed under this section are not refundable. Fees collected under this section shall be applied to the cost of administering this Chapter.

History.
1991 (Reg. Sess., 1992), c. 1043, s. 1

§ 74E-13. Penalties and enforcement

(a) No private person, firm, association, or corporation, and no public institution, agency, or other entity shall engage in, perform any services as, or in any way hold itself out as a company police agency or engage in the recruitment or hiring of company police officers without having first complied with the provisions of this Chapter. Any person, firm, association, or corporation, or their agents and employees violating any of the provisions of this Chapter shall be guilty of a Class 1 misdemeanor.

(b) The Company Police Program may apply in its own name to the superior court for an injunction to prevent any violation or threatened violation of this Chapter or a rule adopted under this Chapter, and the superior courts have jurisdiction to grant the requested relief, irrespective of whether or not criminal prosecution has been instituted or administrative sanctions imposed because of the violation. The venue for an action brought under this subsection shall be in any county selected by the Attorney General.

(c) This section does not relieve a company police agency from any civil liability for the acts of its company police officers in exercising or attempting to exercise the powers conferred by this Chapter.

History.
1991 (Reg. Sess., 1992), c. 1043, s. 1; 1993 (Reg. Sess., 1994), c. 767, s. 26

CHAPTER 74G
CAMPUS POLICE ACT

§ 74G-1. Title

This Chapter is the "Campus Police Act" and may be cited by that name.

History.
2005-231, s. 1

§ 74G-2. Policy and scope

(a) The purpose of this Chapter is to protect the safety and welfare of students, faculty, and staff in institutions of higher education by fostering integrity, proficiency, and competence among campus police agencies and campus police officers. To achieve this purpose, the General Assembly finds that a Campus Police Program needs to be established. As part of the Campus Police Program, the Attorney General is given the authority to certify a private, nonprofit institution of higher education, other than those described by G.S. 116-15(d), as a campus police agency and to commission an individual as a campus police officer.

(b) The purpose of this Chapter is also to assure, to the extent consistent with the State and federal constitutions, that this protection is not denied to students, faculty, and staff at private, nonprofit institutions of higher education originally established by or affiliated with religious denominations. To achieve this purpose, the General Assembly finds that:

(1) Most of the State's private, nonprofit institutions of higher education were originally established by or affiliated with religious denominations;

(2) These institutions have made and continue to make significant contributions in education to the State and the nation;

(3) These institutions admit students regardless of their spiritual or religious beliefs;

(4) These institutions' principal mission is educational;

(5) All of these institutions are accredited by the Commission on Colleges of the Southern Association of Colleges and Schools and as such have independent governing boards of trustees;

(6) The principal State power conferred on campus police by this Chapter is the power of arrest;

(7) This power is important to protect the safety and welfare of students, faculty, and staff at these institutions;

(8) In exercising the power of arrest, these officers apply standards established by State and federal law only; and

(9) The exercise of this power is reviewable by the General Court of Justice and the federal courts.

(c) Public educational institutions operating under the authority of the Board of Governors of The University of North Carolina or the State Board of Community Colleges and private educational institutions that are licensed by the Board of Governors of The University of North Carolina pursuant to G.S. 116-15 or that are exempt from licensure by the Board of Governors pursuant to G.S. 116-15(c) may apply to the Attorney General to be certified as a campus police agency. A campus police agency may apply to the Attorney General to commission an individual designated by the agency to act as a campus police officer for the agency.

History.
2005-231, s. 1

§ 74G-3. Liability insurance policy or certificate of self-insurance required; suspension of campus police agency certification for failure to comply

(a) An applicant for certification as a campus police agency must file with the Attorney General either a copy of a liability insurance policy that meets the requirements of this section or a certificate of self-insurance designating assets sufficient to satisfy the coverage requirements of this section if the applicant is a nonpublic entity. The policy or certificate of self-insurance must provide not less than one million dollars ($ 1,000,000) of coverage per incident for personal injury or property damage resulting from a negligent act of the applicant or an agent or employee of the applicant operating in the course and scope of employment or under color of law. The form, execution, and terms of a liability insurance policy must meet the requirements of the Attorney General.

(b) An insurance carrier that issues a liability insurance policy required by this section may cancel the policy upon giving 30 days' written notice to both the campus police agency and the Attorney General. The written notice must be given by certified mail, return receipt requested. Cancellation of a liability insurance policy does not affect any liability on the policy that accrued prior to the effective cancellation date.

(c) A campus police agency that is a nonpublic entity must maintain the liability insurance policy or certificate of self-insurance required by this section in effect at all times. The Attorney General shall suspend the certification of a campus police agency that fails to maintain a liability insurance policy or certificate of self-insurance when required to do so by this section. A certification suspended for this reason may not be reinstated until the person whose

Chapter 74G

certification was suspended files with the Attorney General an application for reinstatement and either the required liability insurance policy or certificate of self-insurance.

History.
2005-231, s. 1

§ 74G-4. Powers of Attorney General

The Attorney General has the following powers in addition to those conferred elsewhere in this Chapter:

(1) To establish minimum education, experience, and training standards and establish and require written or oral examinations for an applicant for certification as a campus police agency, a certified campus police agency, an applicant for commission as a campus police officer, or a commissioned campus police officer.

(2) To require a campus police agency or a campus police officer to submit reports or other information.

(3) To inspect records maintained by a campus police agency.

(4) To conduct investigations regarding alleged violations of this Chapter or a rule adopted under this Chapter and to make evaluations as may be necessary to determine if a campus police agency or a campus police officer is complying with this Chapter or a rule adopted under this Chapter.

(5) To deny, suspend, or revoke a certification as a campus police agency or a commission as a campus police officer for failure to meet the requirements of or comply with this Chapter or a rule adopted under this Chapter, in accordance with Article 3 of Chapter 150B of the General Statutes.

(6) To appear in the name of the Campus Police Program and apply to the courts having jurisdiction for injunctions to prevent a violation of this Chapter or a rule adopted under this Chapter.

(7) To delegate the authority to administer this Chapter.

(8) To require that the Criminal Justice Standards Division provide administrative support staff for the Campus Police Program.

(9) To adopt rules needed to implement this Chapter, in accordance with Chapter 150B of the General Statutes.

History.
2005-231, s. 1

§ 74G-5. Campus police program records

(a) The Attorney General is the legal custodian of all books, papers, documents, or other records and property of the Campus Police Program.

(b) Any papers, documents, or other records that become the property of the Campus Police Program and are placed in a campus police officer's personnel file maintained by the Attorney General are subject to the same restrictions concerning disclosure as set forth in Chapters 126, 153A, and 160A of the General Statutes for other personnel records.

(c) Notwithstanding the provisions of subsection (b) of this section, the Attorney General may disclose the contents of any records maintained under the authority of this Chapter to the Criminal Justice Education and Training Standards Commission, the Sheriff's Education and Training Standards Commission, or any other criminal justice agency for certification or employment purposes.

History.
2005-231, s. 1; 2013-97, s. 1

§ 74G-5.1. Campus police agency records

(a) Each campus police agency is the legal custodian of all books, papers, documents, records of criminal investigations or of criminal intelligence information, or other records and property maintained by the campus police agency. Books, papers, documents, records of criminal investigations or of criminal intelligence information, or other records maintained by a campus police agency that is affiliated with a private, nonprofit institution of higher education shall not be public records as that term is defined in G.S. 132-1.

(b) As used in this section:

(1) "Complaining witness" means an alleged victim or other person who reports a violation or apparent violation of the law to a campus police agency.

(2) "Violation of the law" means crimes and offenses that are prosecutable as misdemeanors or felonies in the criminal courts in this State or the United States.

(c) Notwithstanding the provisions of subsection (a) of this section, as a condition of certification, a campus police agency affiliated with a private, nonprofit institution of higher education shall, upon request by any person and subject to the provisions and implementing regulations of the federal Jeanne Clery Disclosure of Campus Security Policy and Campus Crime Statistics Act, 20 U.S.C. § 1092(f), and the federal Family Educational Rights and Privacy Act, 20 U.S.C. § 1232g, permit the following information maintained by the campus police agency to be inspected at reasonable times and under reasonable supervision:

(1) The time, date, location, and nature of a violation or apparent violation of the law reported to the campus police agency.

(2) The name, sex, age, address, employment, and alleged violation of law of a person arrested or formally charged or indicted for an alleged violation of law in a court of competent jurisdiction.

(3) The circumstances surrounding an arrest, including the time and place of the arrest, whether the arrest involved resistance, possession or use of weapons, or pursuit, and a description of any items seized in connection with the arrest.

(4) The contents of emergency telephone calls received by or on behalf of the campus police agency, except for such contents that reveal the natural voice, name, address, telephone number, or other information that may identify the caller, victim, or witness. In order to protect the identity of the complaining witness, the contents of emergency telephone calls may be released pursuant to this section in the form of a written transcript or altered voice reproduction; provided that the original shall be provided under process to be used as evidence in any relevant civil or criminal proceeding.

(5) The contents of communications between or among employees of the campus police agency pertaining to the information described in subdivisions (1) through (4) of this subsection that are broadcast over the public airways.

(6) The name, sex, age, and address of a complaining witness.

(7) The daily log of crimes reported to the campus police agency that is maintained pursuant to the federal Jeanne Clery Disclosure of Campus Security Policy and Campus Crime Statistics Act and implementing regulations.

(d) The campus police agency shall furnish copies of the information requested in subsection (c) of this section upon payment of the actual cost of reproducing the information. Any person denied access to or copies of the information listed in subsection (c) of this section may apply to a court of competent jurisdiction for an order compelling disclosure of the information.

(e) A campus police agency shall temporarily withhold the name or address of a complaining witness if release of the information is reasonably likely to pose a threat to the mental health, physical health, or personal safety of the complaining witness or materially compromise an ongoing or future criminal investigation or criminal intelligence operation. Information temporarily withheld under this subsection shall be made available for inspection or copying as soon as the circumstances that justify withholding it cease to exist. Any person denied access to information withheld under this subsection may apply to a court of competent jurisdiction for an order compelling disclosure of

the information. In such action, the court shall balance the interests of the requesting individual in disclosure against the interests of the campus police agency and the alleged victim in withholding the information.

(f) If a campus police agency believes that the release of information listed in subsection (c) of this section will jeopardize the right of the State to prosecute a defendant or the right of a defendant to receive a fair trial, will undermine an ongoing or future investigation, or will violate the provisions and implementing regulations of the federal Jeanne Clery Disclosure of Campus Security Policy and Campus Crime Statistics Act or the federal Family Educational Rights and Privacy Act, it may seek an order from a court of competent jurisdiction to prevent disclosure of the information.

(g) Actions brought pursuant to subsection (d), (e), or (f) of this section shall be set down for immediate hearing, and subsequent proceedings in such actions shall be accorded priority by the trial and appellate courts.

(h) Nothing in this section shall be construed as requiring campus police agencies to disclose the following:

(1) Information that would not be required to be disclosed under Chapter 15A of the General Statutes.

(2) Information that is reasonably likely to identify a confidential informant.

(i) Campus police agencies shall not be required to maintain any recordings of emergency telephone calls for more than 30 days from the time of the call, unless a court of competent jurisdiction orders a portion sealed.

History.
2013-97, s. 2

§ 74G-6. Oaths, powers, and authority of campus police officers

(a) **Requirements.** -- An individual who is commissioned as a campus police officer must take the oath of office required of a law enforcement officer before the individual assumes the duties of a campus police officer. The person in each campus police agency who is responsible for the agency's campus police officers must be commissioned as a campus police officer.

(b) **Powers and Authority of Officers.** -- Campus police officers, while in the performance of their duties of employment, have the same powers as municipal and county police officers to make arrests for both felonies and misdemeanors and to charge for infractions on any of the following:

(1) Real property owned by or in the possession and control of the institution employing the officer.

(2) Any portion of any public road or highway passing through the real property described in subdivision (1) of this subsection or immediately adjoining it, wherever located.

(3) Any other real property while in continuous and immediate pursuit of a person for an offense committed upon property described in subdivision (1) or (2) of this subsection.

In exercising the powers conferred by this subsection, campus police officers shall apply the standards established by the law of this State and the United States.

(c) **Powers and Authority of Institutions.** -- The governing body of any private educational institution that has a campus police agency may:

(1) Enter into joint agreements with the governing board of any municipality to extend the law enforcement authority of campus police officers into any or all of the municipality's jurisdiction and to determine the circumstances in which this extension of authority may be granted;

(2) Enter into joint agreements with the governing board of any county and, with the consent of the sheriff, to extend the law enforcement authority of campus police officers into any or all of the county's jurisdiction and to determine the circumstances in which this extension of authority may be granted; and

(3) Enter into joint agreements with the governing board of any other public or private educational institution that has a campus police agency pursuant to this Chapter or pursuant to G.S. 116-40.5 to extend the law enforcement authority of its campus police officers into any or all of the other institution's jurisdiction and to determine the circumstances as to which its extension of authority may be granted.

(d) **Concealed Weapons.** -- Campus police officers shall have, if duly authorized by their campus police agency and by the sheriff of the county in which the campus police agency is located, the authority to carry concealed weapons pursuant to and in conformity with G.S. 14-269(b)(5).

(e) **Public Institutions Option.** -- Notwithstanding any of the provisions of this Chapter, the board of trustees of any constituent institution of The University of North Carolina may elect to have its officers certified under Article 1 of Chapter 17C and Chapter 116 of the General Statutes, and the board of trustees of any community college may elect to have its officers certified under Article 1 of Chapter 17C and Chapter 115D of the General Statutes rather than requesting certification as a campus police

agency and campus police commission pursuant to the provisions of this Chapter.

(f) **Exclusive Authority.** -- Notwithstanding any other provision of law, the authority granted to campus police officers certified under this Chapter shall be limited to the provisions of this Chapter.

History.
2005-231, s. 1

§ 74G-7. Badges, uniforms, weapons, and vehicles

Campus police agencies shall be responsible for ensuring that all employees, whether or not commissioned, comply with the provisions of this Chapter and the rules adopted under this Chapter, including those provisions pertaining to the wearing of badges and uniforms, the carrying of weapons, and the operation of vehicles.

History.
2005-231, s. 1

§ 74G-8. Minimum standards for campus police officers

Applicants for commission as a campus police officer and a commissioned campus police officer must meet and maintain the same minimum preemployment and in-service standards as are required for State law enforcement officers by the North Carolina Criminal Justice Education and Training Standards Commission and must meet and maintain any other preemployment and in-service requirements set by the Attorney General.

History.
2005-231, s. 1

§ 74G-9. Compensation of campus police officers

The compensation of a campus police officer shall be paid by the campus police agency for which the officer is commissioned, as may be agreed on between them.

History.
2005-231, s. 1

§ 74G-10. Expiration, renewal, and termination of agency certification or officer commission

(a) **Agency.** -- Unless sooner suspended or revoked by the Attorney General, a campus police agency's certification expires on June 30 of the calendar year following the date it is issued. A campus police agency may renew the certification upon payment of the appropriate fee and compliance with this Chapter and the rules adopted under this Chapter. An entity whose campus police agency's certification was denied or revoked for a violation of this Chapter or a rule adopted under this Chapter is not eligible to apply again for that certification for three years.

(b) **Officer.** -- Unless sooner suspended or revoked by the Attorney General, a campus police officer's commission expires on June 30 of the calendar year following the date it is issued. A campus police officer may renew a commission upon payment of the appropriate fee and compliance with this Chapter and the rules adopted under this Chapter. The Attorney General shall immediately revoke the commission of a campus police officer when any of the following occurs:

(1) Termination of employment with the campus police agency for which the officer is commissioned.

(2) Termination, suspension, or revocation of the certification of the campus police agency for which the officer is commissioned.

(3) Failure to meet in-service training requirements as required by this Chapter or the rules adopted under this Chapter.

(4) Violation of this Chapter or a rule adopted under this Chapter.

An individual whose campus police officer's commission was denied or revoked for a violation of this Chapter or a rule adopted under this Chapter is not eligible to apply again for a commission for three years.

History.
2005-231, s. 1

§ 74G-11. Immunity

Neither the Attorney General nor any of the Attorney General's employees may be held criminally or civilly liable for any acts or omissions in carrying out the provisions of this Chapter or for the acts or omissions of agencies or officers certified or commissioned under this Chapter.

History.
2005-231, s. 1

§ 74G-12. Fees

The Attorney General may charge fees for the items listed in the following table, not to exceed the amounts listed in the table:

Item	Maximum Fee:
Application for certification as a campus police agency	$ 250.00
Annual renewal of certification as a campus police agency	$ 200.00
Application for reinstatement of certification as a campus police agency	$ 1,000
Application for commission as a campus police officer	$ 100.00
Annual renewal of commission as a campus police officer	$ 50.00
Application for reinstatement of commission as a campus police officer	$ 150.00

The fees imposed under this section are not refundable. Fees collected under this section shall be applied to the cost of administering this Chapter.

History.
2005-231, s. 1

§ 74G-13. Penalties and enforcement

(a) No private person, firm, association, or corporation, and no public institution, agency, or other entity shall engage in, perform any services as, or in any way hold itself out as a campus police agency or engage in the recruitment or hiring of campus police officers without having first complied with the provisions of this Chapter. Any person, firm, association, or corporation or their agents and employees violating any of the provisions of this Chapter shall be guilty of a Class 1 misdemeanor.

(b) The Campus Police Program may apply in its own name to the superior court for an injunction to prevent any violation or threatened violation of this Chapter or a rule adopted under this Chapter, and the superior courts have jurisdiction to grant the requested relief, irrespective of whether or not criminal prosecution has been instituted or administrative sanctions imposed because of the violation. The venue for an action brought under this subsection shall be in any county selected by the Attorney General.

(c) This section does not relieve a campus police agency from any civil liability for the acts of its campus police officers in exercising or attempting to exercise the powers conferred by this Chapter.

History.
2005-231, s. 1

Chapter 74G

CHAPTER 75A
BOATING AND WATER SAFETY

ARTICLE 1
BOATING SAFETY ACT

§ 75A-10. Operating vessel or manipulating water skis, etc., in reckless manner; operating, etc., while intoxicated, etc.; depositing or discharging litter, etc

(a) No person shall operate any motorboat or vessel, or manipulate any water skis, surfboard, or similar device on the waters of this State in a reckless or negligent manner so as to endanger the life, limb, or property of any person.

(b) No person shall manipulate any water skis, surfboard, nonmotorized vessel, or similar device on the waters of this State while under the influence of an impairing substance.

(b1) No person shall operate any vessel while underway on the waters of this State:

(1) While under the influence of an impairing substance, or

(2) After having consumed sufficient alcohol that the person has, at any relevant time after the boating, an alcohol concentration of 0.08 or more.

(b2) The fact that a person charged with violating this subsection is or has been legally entitled to use alcohol or a drug is not a defense to a charge under subsections (b) and (b1) of this section. The relevant definitions contained in G.S. 20-4.01 shall apply to subsections (b), (b1), and (b2) of this section.

(b3) A person who violates a provision of subsection (a) or (b) of this section is guilty of a Class 2 misdemeanor.

(b4) A person who violates subsection (b1) of this section is guilty of a Class 2 misdemeanor, and upon conviction, in addition to any other penalty imposed, shall be fined not less than two hundred fifty dollars ($ 250.00).

(c) No person shall place, throw, deposit, or discharge or cause to be placed, thrown, deposited, or discharged on the waters of this State or into the inland lake waters of this State, any litter, raw sewage, bottles, cans, papers, or other liquid or solid materials which render the waters unsightly, noxious, or otherwise unwholesome so as to be detrimental to the public health or welfare or to the enjoyment and safety of the water for recreational purposes.

(d) No person shall place, throw, deposit, or discharge or cause to be placed, thrown, deposited, or discharged on the waters of this State or into the inland lake waters of this State any medical waste as defined by G.S. 130A-290 which renders the waters unsightly, noxious, or otherwise unwholesome so as to be detrimental to the public health or welfare or to the enjoyment and safety of the water for recreational purposes.

(e) A person who willfully violates subsection (d) of this section is guilty of a Class 1 misdemeanor. A person who willfully violates subsection (d) of this section and in so doing releases medical waste that creates a substantial risk of physical injury to any person who is not a participant in the offense is guilty of a Class F felony which may include a fine not to exceed fifty thousand dollars ($ 50,000) per day of violation.

History.

1959, c. 1064, s. 10; 1965, c. 634, s. 3; 1985, c. 615, ss. 1-5; 1989, c. 742, s. 1; 1995, c. 506, s. 14; 2006-185, s. 1; 2013-380, s. 5; 2016-34, s. 3

§ 75A-10.3. Death or serious injury by impaired boating; repeat offenses

(a) **Death by Impaired Boating.** -- A person commits the offense of death by impaired boating if all of the following apply:

(1) The person unintentionally causes the death of another person.

(2) The person was engaged in the offense of impaired boating under G.S. 75A-10(b1).

(3) The commission of the offense in subdivision (2) of this subsection is the proximate cause of the death.

(b) **Serious Injury by Impaired Boating.** -- A person commits the offense of serious injury by impaired boating if all of the following apply:

(1) The person unintentionally causes serious injury to another person.

(2) The person was engaged in the offense of impaired boating under G.S. 75A-10(b1).

(3) The commission of the offense in subdivision (2) of this subsection is the proximate cause of the serious injury.

(c) **Aggravated Serious Injury by Impaired Boating.** -- A person commits the offense of aggravated serious injury by impaired boating if all of the following apply:

(1) The person unintentionally causes serious injury to another person.

(2) The person was engaged in the offense of impaired boating under G.S. 75A-10(b1).

(3) The commission of the offense in subdivision (2) of this subsection is the proximate cause of the serious injury.

(4) The person has a previous conviction of impaired boating under G.S. 75A-10(b1) within seven years of the date of the offense.

(d) **Aggravated Death by Impaired Boating.** -- A person commits the offense of aggravated death by impaired boating if all of the following apply:

(1) The person unintentionally causes the death of another person.

(2) The person was engaged in the offense of impaired boating under G.S. 75A-10(b1).

(3) The commission of the offense in subdivision (2) of this subsection is the proximate cause of the death.

(4) The person has a previous conviction of impaired boating under G.S. 75A-10(b1) within seven years of the date of the offense.

(e) **Repeat Death by Impaired Boating.** -- A person commits the offense of repeat death by impaired boating if all of the following apply:

(1) The person commits an offense under subsection (a) or subsection (d) of this section.

(2) The person has a previous conviction under at least one of the following:

a. Subsection (a) of this section.

b. Subsection (d) of this section.

c. G.S. 14-17 or G.S. 14-18, and the basis of the conviction was the unintentional death of another person while engaged in the offense of impaired boating under G.S. 75A-10(b1).

The pleading and proof of previous convictions shall be in accordance with the provisions of G.S. 15A-928.

(f) **Punishments.** -- Unless the conduct is covered under some other provision of law providing greater punishment, the following classifications apply to the offenses set forth in this section:

(1) Repeat death by impaired boating is a Class B2 felony.

(2) Aggravated death by impaired boating is a Class D felony. Notwithstanding the provisions of G.S. 15A-1340.17, the court shall sentence the defendant in the aggravated range of the appropriate Prior Record Level.

(3) Death by impaired boating is a Class D felony. Notwithstanding the provisions of G.S. 15A-1340.17, intermediate punishment is authorized for a defendant who is a Prior Record Level I offender.

(4) Aggravated serious injury by impaired boating is a Class E felony.

(5) Serious injury by impaired boating is a Class F felony.

(g) **No Double Prosecutions.** -- No person who has been placed in jeopardy upon a charge of death by impaired boating may be prosecuted for the offense of manslaughter arising out of the same death; and no person who has been placed in jeopardy upon a charge of manslaughter may be prosecuted for death by impaired boating arising out of the same death.

History.
2016-34, s. 2

§ 75A-11. Duty of operator involved in collision, accident, casualty, or other occurrence

(a) For the purposes of this section, the term "occurrence" means a collision, accident, casualty, or other similar occurrence involving a vessel. The operator of a vessel involved in an occurrence, so far as the operator is able to do so without serious danger to the operator's vessel, crew, and passengers (if any), shall render persons affected by the occurrence any assistance as may be practicable and necessary in order to save them from or minimize any danger caused by the occurrence, and also to give the operator's name, address, and identification of the operator's vessel in writing to any person injured and to the owner of any property damaged in the occurrence.

(b) If an occurrence results in the death, injury, or disappearance indicating death or injury of a person or damage to a vessel or other property of two thousand dollars ($ 2,000) or more, or if there is complete loss of any vessel, the operator of the vessel shall file with the Commission a full description of the occurrence, including any information the agency may, by rule, require. If an occurrence results in death, disappearance, or injury, the operator of the vessel shall file the report with the Commission within 48 hours of the occurrence. If the occurrence results in vessel or property damage, or complete loss of any vessel, the operator of the vessel shall file the report with the Commission within 10 days of the occurrence. When the operator of the vessel cannot submit the report, the owner of the vessel shall submit the report. Reports filed pursuant to this subsection shall not be admissible as evidence.

(c) When, as a result of an occurrence that involves a vessel or its equipment, a person dies or disappears from a vessel, the operator of the vessel shall, without delay and by the most expeditious means available, notify the nearest law enforcement agency of all of the following:

(1) The date, time, and exact location of the occurrence.

(2) The name of each person who died or disappeared.

(3) The certificate of number and name of the vessel.

(4) The name and address of the vessel owner or owners and the vessel operator.

(d) If the operator of the vessel cannot give notice required by this section, each person on board the vessel shall notify the law enforcement agency or determine that notice has been given. Upon receiving notice under this section, a law enforcement agency shall immediately provide the Commission and the United States Coast Guard with the information required by this section.

Chapter 75A

History.
1959, c. 1064, s. 11; 1999-248, s. 3; 2006-185, s. 1

§ 75A-13. Water skis, surfboards, etc

(a) No person shall operate a vessel on any water of this State for towing a person or persons on water skis, a surfboard, or similar device unless at least one of the following conditions is met:

(1) There is in the vessel a person, in addition to the operator, in a position to observe the progress of the person or persons being towed.

(2) The persons being towed wear a personal flotation device.

(3) The vessel is equipped with a rear view mirror.

(b) No person shall operate a vessel on any water of this State towing a person or persons on water skis, a surfboard, or similar device, nor shall any person engage in water skiing, surfboarding, or similar activity at any time between the hours from one hour after sunset to one hour before sunrise.

(c) The provisions of subsections (a) and (b) of this section do not apply to a performer engaged in a professional exhibition.

(d) No person shall operate or manipulate any vessel, tow rope, or other device by which the direction or location of water skis, a surfboard, or similar device may be affected or controlled in such a way as to cause the water skis, surfboard, or similar device, or any person thereon to collide with any object or person.

History.
1959, c. 1064, s. 13; 2006-185, s. 1

§ 75A-13.1. Skin and scuba divers

(a) No person shall engage in skin diving or scuba diving in the waters of this State that are open to boating, or assist in such diving, without displaying a diver's flag from a mast, buoy, or other structure at the place of diving; and no person shall display such flag except when diving operations are under way or in preparation.

(b) The diver's flag shall be square, not less than 12 inches on a side, and shall be of red background with a diagonal white stripe, of a width equal to one fifth of the flag's height, running from the upper corner adjacent to the mast downward to the opposite outside corner.

(c) No operator of a vessel under way in the waters of this State shall permit the vessel to approach closer than 50 feet to any structure from which a diver's flag is then being displayed, except where the flag is so positioned as to constitute an unreasonable obstruction to navigation; and no person shall engage in skin diving or scuba diving or display a diver's flag

in any locality that will unreasonably obstruct vessels from making legitimate navigational use of the water.

(d) A person who violates a provision of this section is responsible for an infraction as provided in G.S. 14-3.1.

History.
1969, c. 97, s. 1; 2006-185, s. 1; 2013-360, s. 18B.15(b); 2013-380, s. 6

N.C. Gen. Stat. § 75A-13.2

Repealed by Session Laws 1999-447, s. 3.

§ 75A-13.3. Personal watercraft

(a) No person shall operate a personal watercraft on the waters of this State at any time between sunset and sunrise. For purposes of this section, "personal watercraft" means a small vessel that uses an outboard or propeller-driven motor, or an inboard motor powering a water jet pump, as its primary source of motive power and which is designed to be operated by a person sitting, standing, or kneeling on, or being towed behind the vessel, rather than in the conventional manner of sitting or standing inside the vessel.

(a1) No person shall operate a personal watercraft on the waters of this State at greater than no-wake speed within 100 feet of an anchored or moored vessel, a dock, pier, swim float, marked swimming area, swimmers, surfers, persons engaged in angling, or any manually operated propelled vessel, unless the personal watercraft is operating in a narrow channel. No person shall operate a personal watercraft in a narrow channel at greater than no-wake speed within 50 feet of an anchored or moored vessel, a dock, pier, swim float, marked swimming area, swimmers, surfers, persons engaged in angling, or any manually operated propelled vessel.

(b) Except as otherwise provided in this subsection, no person under 16 years of age shall operate a personal watercraft on the waters of this State, and it is unlawful for the owner of a personal watercraft or a person who has temporary or permanent responsibility for a person under the age of 16 to knowingly allow that person to operate a personal watercraft. A person of at least 14 years of age but under 16 years of age may operate a personal watercraft on the waters of this State if:

(1) The person is accompanied by a person of at least 18 years of age who physically occupies the watercraft and who is in compliance with G.S. 75A-16.2; or

(2) The person (i) possesses on his or her person while operating the watercraft, identification showing proof of age and a boating safety certification card issued by

the Commission, proof of other satisfactory completion of a boating safety education course approved by the National Association of State Boating Law Administrators (NASBLA), or proof of other boating safety education in compliance with G.S. 75A-16.2; and (ii) produces that identification and proof upon the request of an officer of the Commission or local law enforcement agency.

(b1) A person who is the lawful owner of a personal watercraft or a person having control of a personal watercraft who knowingly allows a person under 16 years of age to operate a personal watercraft in violation of the provisions of subsection (b) of this section is responsible for an infraction as provided in G.S. 14-3.1.

(c) No livery shall lease, hire, or rent a personal watercraft to or for operation by a person under 16 years of age, except as provided in subsection (b) of this section.

(c1) No person, firm, or corporation shall engage in the business of renting personal watercraft to the public for operation by the rentee unless the person, firm, or corporation has secured insurance for the liability of the person, firm, or corporation and that of the rentee, in such an amount as is hereinafter provided, from an insurance company duly authorized to sell liability insurance in this State. Each personal watercraft rented must be covered by a policy of liability insurance insuring the owner and rentee and their agents and employees while in the performance of their duties against loss from any liability imposed by law for damages including damages for care and loss of services because of bodily injury to or death of any person and injury to or destruction of property caused by accident arising out of the operation of such personal watercraft, subject to the following minimum limits: three hundred thousand dollars ($ 300,000) per occurrence.

(c2) A vessel livery that fails to carry liability insurance in violation of subsection (c1) of this section is guilty of a Class 2 misdemeanor and shall only be subject to a fine not to exceed one thousand dollars ($ 1,000).

(c3) A vessel livery shall provide the operator of a leased personal watercraft with basic safety instruction prior to allowing the operation of the leased personal watercraft. "Basic safety instruction" shall include direction on how to safely operate the personal watercraft and a review of the safety provisions of this section. A vessel livery that fails to provide basic safety instruction is responsible for an infraction as provided in G.S. 14-3.1.

(d) No person shall operate a personal watercraft on the waters of this State, nor shall the owner of a personal watercraft knowingly allow another person to operate that personal watercraft on the waters of this State, unless:

(1) Each person riding on or being towed behind the vessel is wearing a type I, type II, type III, or type V personal flotation device approved by the United States Coast Guard. Inflatable personal flotation devices do not satisfy this requirement; and

(2) In the case of a personal watercraft equipped by the manufacturer with a lanyard-type engine cut-off switch, the lanyard is securely attached to the person, clothing, or flotation device of the operator at all times while the personal watercraft is being operated in such a manner to turn off the engine if the operator dismounts while the watercraft is in operation.

(d1) No person shall operate a personal watercraft towing another person on water skis, a surfboard, or similar device unless:

(1) The personal watercraft has on board, in addition to the operator, an observer who shall monitor the progress of the person or persons being towed, or the personal watercraft is equipped with a rearview mirror; and

(2) The total number of persons operating, observing, and being towed does not exceed the number of passengers identified by the manufacturer as the maximum safe load for the vessel.

(e) A personal watercraft must at all times be operated in a reasonable and prudent manner. Maneuvers that endanger life, limb, or property shall constitute reckless operation of a vessel as provided in G.S. 75A-10, and include any of the following:

(1) Unreasonably or unnecessarily weaving through congested vessel traffic.

(2) Jumping the wake of another vessel within 100 feet of the other vessel or when visibility around the other vessel is obstructed.

(3) Intentionally approaching another vessel in order to swerve at the last possible moment to avoid collision.

(4) Repealed by Session Laws 2000-52, s. 2.

(5) Operating contrary to the "rules of the road" or following too closely to another vessel, including another personal watercraft. For purposes of this subdivision, "following too closely" means proceeding in the same direction and operating at a speed in excess of 10 miles per hour when approaching within 100 feet to the rear or 50 feet to the side of another vessel that is underway unless that vessel is operating in a narrow channel, in which case a personal watercraft may operate at the speed and flow of other vessel traffic.

(f) The provisions of this section do not apply to a performer engaged in a professional exhibition, a person or persons engaged in an activity authorized under G.S. 75A-14, or a person attempting to rescue another person who is in danger of losing life or limb.

(f1) For purposes of this section, "narrow channel" means a segment of the waters of the State 300 feet or less in width.

(g) Repealed by Session Laws 1999-447, s. 1.

(h) Nothing in this section prohibits units of local government, marine commissions, or local lake authorities from regulating personal watercraft pursuant to the provisions of G.S. 160A-176.2 or any other law authorizing such regulation, provided that the regulations are more restrictive than the provisions of this section or regulate aspects of personal watercraft operation that are not covered by this section. Whenever a unit of local government, marine commission, or local lake authority regulates personal watercraft pursuant to this subsection, it shall conspicuously post signs that are reasonably calculated to provide notice to personal watercraft users of the stricter regulations.

History.

1997-129, s. 1; 1999-447, s. 1; 2000-52, ss. 1 -4; 2005-161, s. 1; 2006-185, s. 1; 2009-282, s. 2; 2013-360, s. 18B.15(c); 2013-380, ss. 7, 8

§ 75A-15. Rules on water safety; adoption of the United States Aids to Navigation System

(a) In accordance with subsection (b) of this section, the Commission is empowered to adopt rules, for the local water in question, as to:

(1) Operation of vessels, including restrictions concerning speed zones, and type of activity conducted.

(2) Promotion of boating and water safety generally by occupants of vessels, swimmers, fishermen, and others using the water.

(3) Placement and maintenance of navigation aids and markers, in conformity with governing provisions of law.

Prior to the adoption of any rules, the Commission shall investigate the water recreation and safety needs of the local water in question. In conducting the investigation, the Commission in its discretion may hold public hearings on the rules proposed and the general needs of the local water in question. After completion of the investigation and application of standards, the Commission may in its discretion adopt the rules requested, adopt them in an amended form, or refuse to adopt them. After adoption, the Commission may amend or repeal the rules after first holding a public hearing.

(b) Any subdivision of this State may, but only after public notice, make formal application to the Commission for rules on waters within the subdivision's territorial limits as to the matters listed in subsection (a) of this section. The Commission may adopt rules applicable to local areas of water defined by the Commission that are found to be heavily used for water recreation purposes by persons from other areas of the State and as to which there is not coordinated local interest in regulation.

(b1) The Commission may adopt rules to prohibit entry of vessels into public swimming areas and to establish speed zones at public vessel launching ramps, marinas, or vessel service areas and on other congested water areas where there are demonstrated water safety hazards. Enforcement of rules adopted pursuant to this subsection shall be dependent upon placement and maintenance of regulatory markers in accordance with the United States Aids to Navigation System by the Commission or an agency designated by the Commission.

(c) The United States Aids to Navigation System, as established by 33 Code of Federal Regulations Part 62 (July 1, 2005 edition), is hereby adopted for use on the waters of North Carolina. The Commission is authorized to adopt rules implementing the marking system and may:

(1) Modify provisions as necessary to meet the special water recreational and safety needs of this State, provided that the modifications do not depart in any essential manner from the uniform standards being adopted in other states.

(2) Modify provisions as necessary to conform with amendments to the marking system that may be proposed for adoption by the states.

(3) Enact supplementary standards regarding design, construction, placement, and maintenance of markers.

(4) Enact clarifying rules as to matters not covered with precision in the United States Aids to Navigation System.

(5) Enact implementing rules as to matters left to State discretion in the United States Aids to Navigation System.

(6) Enact rules forbidding or restricting the placement of markers either throughout the State or in certain classes or areas of waters without prior permission having been obtained from the Commission or some agency or official designated by the Commission.

(c1) It is unlawful to place or maintain any marker of the sort covered by the marking system in the waters of North Carolina that does not conform to or is in violation of the marking system and the implementing rules of the Commission.

(d) Rules enacted under the authority of subsections (a), (b), and (b1) of this section shall supersede all local rules in conflict or incompatible with such rules. As used in this subsection, "local rules" shall include provisions relating to boating, water safety, or other recreational use of local waters in special local, or private acts, in ordinances or rules of local governing bodies, or in ordinances or rules of local water authorities. Except as may be authorized in subsections (a), (b), and (b1) of this section, no local rules may be made respecting the United States Aids to Navigation System and its implementation or respecting supplemental safety equipment on vessels.

(e) The Commission may adopt rules prohibiting entry or use by vessels or swimmers of waters of the State immediately surrounding impoundment structures and powerhouses associated with electric generating facilities that are found to pose a hazard to water safety. This subsection shall not apply to the Person-Caswell Lake Authority, Carolina Power and Light Company Lake (Hyco).

History.
1959, c. 1064, s. 15; 1965, c. 394; 1969, c. 1093, s. 4; 1977, c. 424; 1983 (Reg. Sess., 1984), c. 1082, ss. 4, 5; 1987, c. 827, s. 5; 1993 (Reg. Sess., 1994), c. 753, s. 3; 2006-185, s. 1

§ 75A-16.1. Boating safety course

(a) The Commission shall institute and coordinate a statewide course of instruction in boating safety, and in so doing may cooperate with any political subdivision of the State or with any reputable organization having as one of its objectives the promotion of boating safety.

(b) The Commission shall designate those persons or agencies authorized to conduct the course of instruction, and this designation shall be valid until revoked by the Commission. Within 30 days of completion of a course of instruction, a designated person or agency shall submit to the Commission a list of the names of all persons who successfully completed the course of instruction conducted by the designated person or agency.

(c) The Commission may conduct the course in boating safety using Commission personnel or other persons at times or in areas in which competent agencies are unable or unwilling to meet the demand for instruction.

(d) The Commission shall issue a boating safety certification card to each person who successfully completes the course of instruction.

(e) The Commission shall adopt rules to provide for the course of instruction and the issuance of boating safety certification cards consistent with the purposes of this section.

(f) Any person who presents a fictitious boating safety certification card or who attempts to obtain a boating safety certification card through fraud is guilty of a Class 2 misdemeanor.

History.
2006-185, s. 1

§ 75A-16.2. Boating safety education required

(a) No person shall operate a vessel with a motor of 10 horsepower or greater on the public waters of this State unless the operator has met the requirements for boating safety education.

(b) A person shall be considered in compliance with the requirements of boating safety education if the person does one of the following:

(1) Completes and passes the boating safety course instituted by the Wildlife Resources Commission under G.S. 75A-16.1 or another boating safety course that is approved by the National Association of State Boating Law Administrators (NASBLA) and accepted by the Wildlife Resources Commission;

(2) Passes a proctored equivalency examination that tests the knowledge of information included in the curriculum of an approved course;

(3) Possesses a valid or expired license to operate a vessel issued to maritime personnel by the United States Coast Guard;

(4) Possesses a State-approved nonrenewable temporary operator's certificate to operate a vessel for 90 days that was issued with the certificate of number for the vessel, if the boat was new or was sold with a transfer of ownership;

(5) Possesses a rental or lease agreement from a vessel rental or leasing business that lists the person as the authorized operator of the vessel;

(6) Properly displays Commission-issued dealer registration numbers during the demonstration of the vessel;

(7) Operates the vessel under onboard direct supervision of a person who is at least 18 years of age and who meets the requirements of this section;

(8) Demonstrates that he or she is not a resident, is temporarily using the waters of this State for a period not to exceed 90 days, and meets any applicable boating safety education requirements of the state or nation of residency;

(9) Has assumed operation of the vessel due to the illness or physical impairment of the initial operator, and is returning the vessel to shore in order to provide assistance or care for the operator;

(10) Is registered as a commercial fisherman or a person who is under the onboard direct supervision of a commercial fisherman while operating the commercial fisherman's boat; or

(11) Provides proof that he or she was born before January 1, 1988.

Any person who operates a vessel with a motor of 10 horsepower or greater on the waters of this State shall, upon the request of a law enforcement officer, present to the officer a certification card or proof that the person has complied with the provisions of this section.

(c) Any person who violates a provision of this section or a rule adopted pursuant to this section is responsible for an infraction, as provided in G.S. 14-3.1, and shall pay a fine of fifty dollars ($ 50.00). A person may not be responsible for violating this section if the person produces in court at the adjudicatory hearing a certification card or proof that the person has completed and passed a boating safety course in compliance with subdivision (b)(1) of this section.

(d) No unit of local government shall enact any ordinance or rule relating to boating safety education, and this law preempts all existing ordinances or rules.

(e) An operator of a personal watercraft on the public waters of this State remains subject to any more specific provision of law found in G.S. 75A-13.3.

History.

2009-282, s. 1; 2013-380, s. 9

§ 75A-18. Penalties

(a) Except as otherwise provided, a person who violates a provision of this Article is responsible for an infraction as provided in G.S. 14-3.1. This limitation shall not apply in a case where a more severe penalty is prescribed in this Chapter.

(b) through (e) Repealed by Session Laws 2006-185, s. 1.

(f) Except as otherwise provided in this Chapter, a person who violates a rule adopted by the Commission under the authority of this Chapter is responsible for an infraction as provided in G.S. 14-3.1 and shall pay a fine of fifty dollars ($ 50.00). A person responsible for an infraction under this Chapter shall not be assessed court costs.

History.

1959, c. 1064, s. 18; 1965, c. 634, s. 3; c. 793; 1969, c. 97, s. 2; 1979, c. 761, s. 8; 1985, c. 615, ss. 6, 7; 1989, c. 742, s. 2; 1993, c. 539, ss. 566, 1285; 1994, Ex. Sess., c. 24, s. 14(c); 1997-129, s. 3; 1999-447, s. 2; 2006-185, s. 1; 2013-360, s. 18B.15(e); 2013-380, s. 10

CHAPTER 75D RACKETEER INFLUENCED AND CORRUPT ORGANIZATIONS

§ 75D-1. Short title

This Chapter shall be known and may be cited as the North Carolina Racketeer Influenced and Corrupt Organizations Act (RICO).

History.
1985 (Reg. Sess., 1986), c. 999, s. 1; 1989, c. 489, s. 1

§ 75D-2. Findings and intent of General Assembly

(a) The General Assembly finds that a severe problem is posed in this State by the increasing organization among certain unlawful elements and the increasing extent to which organized unlawful activities and funds acquired as a result of organized unlawful activity are being directed to and against the legitimate economy of the State.

(b) The General Assembly declares that the purpose and intent of this Chapter is: to deter organized unlawful activity by imposing civil equitable sanctions against this subversion of the economy by organized unlawful elements; to prevent the unjust enrichment of those engaged in organized unlawful activity; to restore the general economy of the State all of the proceeds, money, profits, and property, both real and personal of every kind and description which is owned, used or acquired through organized unlawful activity by any person or association of persons whether natural, incorporated or unincorporated in this State; and to provide compensation to private persons injured by organized unlawful activity. It is not the intent of the General Assembly to in any way interfere with the attorney-client relationship.

(c) It is not the intent of the General Assembly that this Chapter apply to isolated and unrelated incidents of unlawful conduct but only to an interrelated pattern of organized unlawful activity, the purpose or effect of which is to derive pecuniary gain. Further, it is not the intent of the General Assembly that legitimate business organizations doing business in this State, having no connection to, or any relationship or involvement with organized unlawful elements, groups or activities be subject to suit under the provisions of this Chapter.

History.
1985 (Reg. Sess., 1986), c. 999, s. 1; 1989, c. 489, s. 1

§ 75D-3. Definitions

As used in this Chapter, the term:

(a) "Enterprise" means any person, sole proprietorship, partnership, corporation, business trust, union chartered under the laws of this State, or other legal entity; or any unchartered union, association, or group of individuals associated in fact although not a legal entity; and it includes illicit as well as licit enterprises and governmental as well as other entities.

(b) "Pattern of racketeering activity" means engaging in at least two incidents of racketeering activity that have the same or similar purposes, results, accomplices, victims, or methods of commission or otherwise are interrelated by distinguishing characteristics and are not isolated and unrelated incidents, provided at least one of such incidents occurred after October 1, 1986, and that at least one other of such incidents occurred within a four-year period of time of the other, excluding any periods of imprisonment, after the commission of a prior incident of racketeering activity.

(c) (1) "Racketeering activity" means to commit, to attempt to commit, or to solicit, coerce, or intimidate another person to commit an act or acts which would be chargeable by indictment if such act or acts were accompanied by the necessary mens rea or criminal intent under the following laws of this State:

a. Article 5 of Chapter 90 of the General Statutes of North Carolina relating to controlled substances and counterfeit controlled substances;

b. Chapter 14 of the General Statutes of North Carolina except Articles 9, 22A, 38, 40, 43, 46, 47, 59 thereof; and further excepting G.S. Sections 14-78.1, 14-82, 14-86, 14-145, 14-146, 14-147, 14-177, 14-178, 14-179, 14-183, 14-184, 14-186, 14-190.9, 14-195, 14-197, 14-201, 14-202, 14-247, 14-248, 14-313 thereof.

c. Any conduct involved in a "money laundering" activity; and

(2) "Racketeering activity" also includes the description in Title 18, United States Code, Section 1961(1).

(d) "Documentary material" means any book, paper, document, writing, drawing, graph, chart, photograph, phonocord, magnetic tape, computer printout, other data compilation from which information can be obtained or from which information can be translated into useable form, or other tangible item.

(e) "RICO lien notice" means the notice described in G.S. 75D-13.

(f) "Attorney General" means the Attorney General of North Carolina or any employee of the Department of Justice designated by him in writing. Any district attorney of this State, with his consent, may be designated in writing by the Attorney General to enforce the provisions of this Chapter.

(g) (1) "Beneficial interest" means either of the following:

    a. The interest of a person as a beneficiary under any other trust arrangement pursuant to which a trustee holds legal or record title to real property for the benefit of such person; or

    b. The interest of a person under any other form of express fiduciary arrangement pursuant to which any other person holds legal or record title to real property for the benefit of such person.

    (2) "Beneficial interest" does not include the interest of a stockholder in a corporation or the interest of a partner in either a general partnership or limited partnership. A beneficial interest shall be deemed to be located where the real property owned by the trustee is located.

(h) "Real property" means any real property situated in this State or any interest in such real property, including, but not limited to, any lease of or mortgage upon such real property.

(i) (1) "Trustee" means either of the following:

    a. Any person who holds legal or record title to real property for which any other person has a beneficial interest; or

    b. Any successor trustee or trustees to any of the foregoing persons.

    (2) "Trustee" does not include the following:

      a. Any person appointed or acting as a personal representative under Chapter 35A of the General Statutes relating to guardian and ward, or under Chapter 28A of the General Statutes relating to the administration of estates; or

      b. Any person appointed or acting as a trustee of any testamentary trust or as trustee of any indenture of trust under which any bonds are to be issued.

(j) "Criminal proceeding" means any criminal action commenced by the State for a violation of any provision of those criminal laws referred to in G.S. 75D-3(c).

(k) "Civil proceeding" means any civil proceeding commenced by the Attorney General or an injured person under any provision of this Chapter.

History.
1985 (Reg. Sess., 1986), c. 999, s. 1; 1987, ch. 550, s. 22; 1989, c. 489, s. 1

§ 75D-4. Prohibited activities

(a) No person shall:

    (1) Engage in a pattern of racketeering activity or, through a pattern of racketeering activities or through proceeds derived therefrom, acquire or maintain, directly or indirectly, any interest in or control of any enterprise, real property, or personal property of any nature, including money; or

    (2) Conduct or participate in, directly or indirectly, any enterprise through a pattern of racketeering activity whether indirectly, or employed by or associated with such enterprise; or

    (3) Conspire with another or attempt to violate any of the provisions of subdivision (1) or (2) of this subsection.

(b) Violation of this section is inequitable and constitutes a civil offense only and is not a crime, therefore a mens rea or criminal intent is not an essential element of any of the civil offenses set forth in this section.

History.
1985 (Reg. Sess., 1986), c. 999, s. 1; 1989, c. 489, s. 1

§ 75D-5. RICO civil forfeiture proceedings

(a) All property of every kind used or intended for use in the course of, derived from, or realized through a racketeering activity or pattern of racketeering activity is subject to forfeiture to the State. Forfeiture shall be had by a civil procedure known as a RICO forfeiture proceeding.

(b) A RICO forfeiture proceeding shall be governed by Chapter 1A of the General Statutes of North Carolina except to the extent that special rules of procedure are stated in this Chapter.

(c) A RICO forfeiture proceeding shall be an in rem proceeding against the property.

(d) A RICO forfeiture proceeding shall be instituted by complaint and prosecuted only by the Attorney General of North Carolina or his designated representative. The proceeding may be commenced and a final judgment rendered thereon before or after seizure of the property and before or after any criminal conviction of any person for violation of those laws set forth in G.S. 75D-3(c).

(e) If the complaint is filed before seizure, it shall state what property is sought to be forfeited, that the property is within the jurisdiction of the court, the grounds for forfeiture, and the names of all persons known to have or claim an interest in the property. The court shall determine ex parte whether there is reasonable ground to believe that the property is subject to forfeiture and, if the State so alleges, whether notice to those persons having or claiming an interest in the property prior to seizure would cause the loss or destruction of the property. If the court finds:

(1) That reasonable ground does not exist to believe that the property is subject to forfeiture, it shall dismiss the complaint; or

(2) That reasonable ground does exist to believe the property is subject to forfeiture but there is not reasonable ground to believe that prior notice would result in loss or destruction, it shall order service on all persons known to have or claim an interest in the property prior to a further hearing on whether a writ of seizure should issue; or

(3) That there is reasonable ground to believe that the property is subject to forfeiture and to believe that prior notice would cause loss or destruction, it shall without any further hearing or notice, issue a writ of seizure directing the sheriff of or any other law enforcement officer in the county where the property is found to seize it.

(f) Seizure may be effected by a law enforcement officer authorized to enforce the penal laws of this State prior to the filing of the complaint and without a writ of seizure if the seizure is incident to a lawful arrest, search, or inspection and the officer has probable cause to believe the property is subject to forfeiture and will be lost or destroyed if not seized. Within 24 hours of the time of seizure, the seizure shall be reported by the officer to the district attorney of the prosecutorial district as defined in G.S. 7A-60 in which the seizure is effected who shall immediately report such seizure to the Attorney General. The Attorney General shall, within 30 days after receiving notice of seizure, examine the evidence surrounding such seizure, and if he believes reasonable ground exists for forfeiture under this Chapter, shall file a complaint for forfeiture. The complaint shall state, in addition to the information required in subsection (e) of this section, the date and place of seizure.

(g) After the complaint is filed or the seizure effected, whichever is later, every person known to have or claim an interest in the property, or in the property or enterprise of which the subject property is a part or represents any interest, shall be served, if not previously served, with a copy of the complaint and a notice of seizure in the manner provided by Chapter 1A of the General Statutes of North Carolina. Service by publication may be ordered upon any party whose whereabouts cannot be determined with reasonable diligence within 30 days of filing of the complaint.

(h) (1) Any person claiming an interest in the property, may become a party to the action at any time prior to judgment whether named in the complaint or not. Any party claiming a substantial interest in the property, upon motion may be allowed by the court to take possession of the property upon posting bond with good and sufficient security in double the amount of the property's value conditioned to pay the value of any interest in the property found to be subject to forfeiture or the value of any interest of another not subject to forfeiture.

(2) The court, upon such terms and conditions as it may prescribe, may order that the property be sold by an innocent party who holds a lien on or security interest in the property at anytime during the proceedings. Any proceeds from such sale over and above the amount necessary to satisfy the lien or security interest shall be paid into court pending final judgment in the forfeiture proceeding. No such sale shall be ordered, however, unless the obligation upon which the lien or security interest is based is in default.

(3) Pending final judgment in the forfeiture proceeding, the court may make any other disposition of the property necessary to protect it or in the interest of substantial justice, and which adequately protects the interests of innocent parties.

(i) The interest of an innocent party in the property shall not be subject to forfeiture. An innocent party is one who did not have actual or constructive knowledge that the property was subject to forfeiture. An attorney who is paid a fee for representing any person subject to this act, shall be rebuttably presumed to be an innocent party as to that fee transaction.

(j) Subject to the requirement of protecting the interest of all innocent parties, the court may, after judgment of forfeiture, make any of the following orders for disposition of the property:

(1) Destruction of the property or contraband, the possession of, or use of, which is illegal;

(2) Retention for official use by a law enforcement agency, the State or any political subdivision thereof. When such agency or political subdivision no longer has use for such property, it shall be disposed of by judicial sale as provided in Article 29A of Chapter 1 of the General Statutes of North Carolina, and the proceeds shall be paid to the State Treasurer;

(3) Transfer to the Department of Natural and Cultural Resources of property

useful for historical or instructional purposes;

(4) Retention of the property by any innocent party having an interest therein, including the right to restrict sale of an interest to outsiders, such as a right of first refusal, upon payment or approval of a plan for payment into court of the value of any forfeited interest in the property. The plan may include, in the case of an innocent party who holds an interest in the property through an estate by the entirety, or an undivided interest in the property, or a lien on or security interest in the property, the sale of the property by the innocent party under such terms and conditions as may be prescribed by the court and the payment into court of any proceeds from such sale over and above the amount necessary to satisfy the divided ownership value of the innocent party's interest or the lien or security interest. Proceeds paid into the court must then be paid to the State Treasurer;

(5) Judicial sale of the property as provided in Article 29A of Chapter 1 of the General Statutes of North Carolina, with the proceeds being paid to the State Treasurer;

(6) Transfer of the property to any innocent party having an interest therein equal to or greater than the value of the property; or

(7) Any other disposition of the property which is in the interest of substantial justice and adequately protects innocent parties, with any proceeds being paid to the State Treasurer.

(k) In addition to the provisions of subsections (c) through (g) relating to in rem actions, the State may bring an in personam action for the forfeiture of any property subject to forfeiture under subsection (a) of this section.

(l) Upon the entry of a final civil judgment of forfeiture in favor of the State:

(1) The title of the State to the forfeited property shall:

a. In the case of real property or beneficial interest, relate back to the date of filing of the RICO lien notice in the official record of the county where the real property or beneficial interest is located and, if no RICO lien notice is filed, then to the date of the filing of any notice of lis pendens in the official records of the county where the real property or beneficial interest is located and, if no RICO lien notice or notice of lis pendens is so filed, then to the date of recording of the final judgment of forfeiture in the official records of the county where the real property or beneficial interest is located; and

b. In the case of personal property, relate back to the date the personal property was seized pursuant to the provisions of this Chapter.

(2) If property subject to forfeiture is conveyed, alienated, disposed of, or otherwise rendered unavailable for forfeiture after the filing of a RICO lien notice or after the filing of a RICO civil proceeding whichever is earlier, the Attorney General may, on behalf of the State, institute in action in an appropriate court against the person named in the RICO lien notice or the defendant in the civil proceeding and the court shall enter final judgment against the person named in the RICO lien notice or the defendant in the civil proceeding in an amount equal to the fair market value of the property, together with investigative costs and attorney's fees incurred by the Attorney General in the action.

History.

1985 (Reg. Sess., 1986), c. 999, s. 1; 1987 (Reg. Sess., 1988), c. 1037, ss. 98, 99; 1989, c. 489, s. 1; 2015-241, s. 14.30(s)

§ 75D-6. Power to compel examination

Whenever the Attorney General has reason to believe that any person or enterprise may have information or may be in possession, custody or control of any documentary materials relevant to an activity prohibited under G.S. 75D-4, he may issue in writing, and cause to be served upon such person or upon the appropriate officers, agents, and employees of any such enterprise (other than one employed as an attorney by such person or enterprise), a notice requiring such person or enterprise to submit themselves to examination by him, and produce for his inspection any documentary material relevant to an investigation of activities prohibited by G.S. 75D-4.

The notice shall be served either personally or by registered or certified mail return receipt requested. The notice shall specify the general purpose of the examination, a general description of the documentary material to be produced, and the time and place where such examination will take place. The witness shall be placed under oath or affirmation to testify truthfully. The examination shall be recorded and the witness has the right to a copy upon payment of its cost. The witness has the right to have legal counsel present during the examination.

The Attorney General shall also have the right to apply to any judge of the superior court division, after five days' prior notice of such application served in the same manner as the notice of examination described in this section, for an order requiring such person or enterprise to appear and subject himself or itself to examination, and disobedience of such order shall constitute contempt, and shall be punishable as in other cases of disobedience of a proper order of such court.

No such demand or order of a court shall contain any requirement which would be held to be unreasonable if contained in a civil discovery request or court order issued pursuant to G.S. 1A-1, Rules of Civil Procedure 26-36. Any person or enterprise upon whom a demand is served and who objects to complying with such demand in whole or in part, shall, within five days of service of the demand, serve a written reply upon the Attorney General specifying the nature of the objection.

Such examination shall be held in camera and no one, except the person or enterprise being examined, may release information obtained from the examination prior to a proceeding being instituted under this Chapter by the Attorney General. Such information may be used in any proceeding instituted under this Chapter by the Attorney General. Any person violating the provisions of this paragraph shall be guilty of a Class 1 misdemeanor. If such offending person is a public officer or employee, he shall also be dismissed from such office or employment and shall not hold any public office or employment in this State for a period of five years after conviction. This paragraph does not prohibit disclosure of this information to other employees of the Department of Justice, or to district attorneys designated in writing by the Attorney General as authorized to receive this information.

History.
1985 (Reg. Sess., 1986), c. 999, s. 1; 1989, c. 489, s. 1; 1993, c. 539, s. 569; 1994, Ex. Sess., c. 24, s. 14(c)

§ 75D-7. False testimony

False testimony as to any material fact by any person examined under the provisions of this Chapter shall constitute perjury and a conviction shall be punishable as in other cases of perjury as a Class F felony.

History.
1985 (Reg. Sess., 1986), c. 999, s. 1; 1993, c. 539, s. 1286; 1994, Ex. Sess., c. 24, s. 14(c)

§ 75D-8. Available RICO civil remedies

(a) As part of a final judgment of forfeiture, any judge of the superior court may, after giving reasonable notice to potential innocent claimants, enjoin violations of G.S. 75D-4, by issuing appropriate orders and judgments:

(1) Ordering any defendant to divest himself of any interest in any enterprise, real property, or personal property including property held by the entirety. Where property is held by the entirety and one of the spouses is an innocent person as defined in G.S. 75D-5(i), upon entry of a final judgment of forfeiture of entirety property, the judgment operates, to convert the entirety to a tenancy in common, and only the one-half undivided interest of the offending spouse shall be forfeited according to the provisions of this Chapter;

(2) Imposing reasonable restrictions upon the future activities or investments of any defendant in the same or similar type of endeavor as the enterprise in which he was engaged in violation of G.S. 75D-4;

(3) Ordering the dissolution or reorganization of any enterprise;

(4) Ordering the suspension or revocation of any license, permit, or prior approval granted to any enterprise by any agency of the State;

(5) Ordering the forfeiture of the charter of a corporation organized under the laws of this State or the revocation of a certificate authorizing a foreign corporation to conduct business within this State upon a finding that the board of directors or a managerial agent acting on behalf of the corporation, in conducting affairs of the corporation, has authorized or engaged in conduct in violation of G.S. 75D-4, and that, for the prevention of future unlawful activity, the public interest requires that the charter of the corporation be dissolved or the certificate be revoked;

(6) Appointment of a receiver pursuant to the provisions of Article 38 of Chapter 1 of the General Statutes of North Carolina, to collect, conserve and dispose of all the proceeds, money, profits and property, both real and personal, subject to the provisions of this Chapter in accordance with the provisions hereof as directed by the final judgment of the superior court having jurisdiction over the parties or subject matter of the action; or

(7) Any other equitable remedy appropriate to effect complete forfeiture of property subject to forfeiture, or to prevent future violations of this Chapter.

(b) The State through the Attorney General may institute a proceeding under G.S. 75D-5. In such proceeding, relief shall be granted in conformity with the principles that govern the granting of injunctive relief from threatened loss or damage in other civil cases, provided that no showing of special or irreparable damage to the person shall have to be made and provided further that the State shall not be required to execute any bond before or after obtaining temporary restraining orders or preliminary injunctions.

(c) Any innocent person who is injured or damaged in his business or property by reason of any violation of G.S. 75D-4 involving a pattern of racketeering activity shall have a cause of action for three times the actual damages sustained and reasonable attorneys fees. For purposes of this subsection, "pattern of racketeering activity" shall require that at least one act of racketeering activity be an act of racketeering activity other than (i) an act indictable under 18 U.S.C. § 1341 or U.S.C. § 1343, or (ii) an act which is an offense involving fraud in the sale of securities. Any person filing a private action under this subsection must concurrently notify the Attorney General in writing of the commencement of the action. Thereafter, the Attorney General may file a motion for a protective order in the court where the private action is pending and shall be granted a stay of the private action for a reasonable time if the court finds either:

(1) The bringing of a private action is likely to materially interfere with or impair a public forfeiture action; or

(2) The public interest is so great as to require the Attorney General to investigate and bring a forfeiture action.

(d) Any injured innocent person shall have a right or claim to forfeited property or to the proceeds derived therefrom superior to any right or claim the State has in the same property or proceeds. To enforce such a claim the injured innocent person must intervene in the forfeiture proceeding prior to its final disposition.

(e) A final conviction in any criminal proceeding for a violation of those laws set forth in G.S. 75D-3(c), shall estop the defendant in any subsequent civil action or proceeding under this Chapter as to all matters proved in the criminal proceeding.

(f) A defendant in an action commenced by the State pursuant to this Chapter whose convictions of two or more criminal offenses of those criminal statutes as set forth in G.S. 75D-3(c) have become final, which offenses have occurred within a four-year period of each other as set forth in G.S. 75D-3(b) shall be deemed to have, per se violated the provisions of G.S. 75D-4(a)(1) or (2) as of the date of the second conviction.

(g) Any party is entitled to a jury trial in any action brought under this Chapter.

History.
1985 (Reg. Sess., 1986), c. 999, s. 1; 1989, c. 489, s. 1

§ 75D-9. Period of limitations as to civil proceedings under this Chapter

Notwithstanding any other provision of law, a civil action or proceeding under this Chapter may be commenced within five years after the conduct in violation of a provision of this Chapter terminates or the claim for relief accrues, whichever is later. If a civil action is brought by the State for forfeiture or to prevent any violation of the Chapter, then the running of this period of limitations with respect to any innocent person's claim for relief which is based upon any matter complained of in such action by the State, shall be suspended during the pendency of the action by the State and for two years thereafter.

History.
1985 (Reg. Sess., 1986), c. 999, s. 1; 1989, c. 489, s. 1

§ 75D-10. Civil remedies are supplemental and not mutually exclusive

The application of one civil remedy under this Chapter shall not preclude the application of any other remedy under this Chapter or any other provision of law. Civil remedies under this Chapter are cumulative, supplemental and not exclusive, and are in addition to the fines, penalties and forfeitures set forth in a final judgment of conviction of a violation of the criminal laws of this State as punishment for violation of the penal laws of this State.

History.
1985 (Reg. Sess., 1986), c. 999, s. 1; 1989, c. 489, s. 1

§ 75D-11. Reciprocal agreements with other states

The Attorney General is authorized to enter into reciprocal agreements with any United States attorney or the attorney general or chief prosecuting attorney of any other state having a civil forfeiture law substantially similar to this Chapter so as to further the purpose of this Chapter.

History.
1985 (Reg. Sess., 1986), c. 999, s. 1; 1989, c. 489, s. 1

§ 75D-12. Venue

In any forfeiture action brought pursuant to this Chapter, the claim for relief shall be considered to have arisen in any county in which an incident of racketeering occurred or in which an interest or control of an enterprise or real or personal property is acquired or maintained. Venue in any private action shall be as provided in Article 7, Chapter 1, of the General Statutes of North Carolina.

History.
1985 (Reg. Sess., 1986), c. 999, s. 1; 1989, c. 489, s. 1

§ 75D-13. Filing and attachment of RICO lien notice

(a) Upon the institution of any proceeding under this Chapter, the Attorney General then or at any time during the pendency of the proceeding may file in the official records of any one or more counties a RICO lien notice. No filing fee or other charge shall be required as a condition for filing the RICO lien notice. The clerk of the superior court shall, upon the presentation of a RICO lien notice, immediately record it in the official records.

(b) The RICO lien shall be signed by the Attorney General or his designee or by a designated district attorney. The notice shall be in such form as the Attorney General prescribes and, in addition to a description of the particular property sought to be forfeited, shall set forth the following information:

(1) If brought in the name of a person, the name of the person against whom the civil proceeding has been brought. In his discretion, the Attorney General may also name in the RICO lien notice any other aliases, names or fictitious names under which the person may be known;

(2) If known to the Attorney General the present residence and business addresses of the person named in the RICO lien notice and of the other names set forth in the RICO lien notice;

(3) A reference to the civil proceeding stating that a proceeding under this Chapter has been brought against the person named in the RICO lien notice, the name of the county or counties where the proceeding has been brought, and, if known to the Attorney General at the time of filing the RICO lien notice, the case number of the proceeding;

(4) A statement that the notice is being filed pursuant to this Chapter; and

(5) The name and address of the person in the Attorney General's office filing the RICO lien notice and the name of the individual signing the RICO lien notice.

(c) A RICO lien notice shall apply only to one person and, to the extent applicable, any aliases, fictitious names, or other names, including names of corporations, partnerships, or other entities, to the extent permitted in paragraph (1) of subsection (b) of this section. A separate RICO lien notice shall be filed for any other person against whom the Attorney General desires to file a RICO lien notice under this section.

(d) The Attorney General shall, as soon as practicable after the filing of each RICO lien notice, serve, by any method provided for by G.S. 1A-1, Rule 4, upon the person named in the notice and any other person who holds an interest of record, either a copy of the recorded notice or a copy of the notice with a notation thereon of the county or counties in which the notice has been recorded.

(e) The filing of a RICO lien notice creates, from the time of its filing, a lien in favor of the State on the following property of the person named in the notice and against any other names sets forth in the notice:

(1) Any real property situated in the county where the notice is filed then or thereafter owned by the person or under any of the names; and

(2) Any beneficial interest situated in the county where the notice is filed then or thereafter owned by the person or under any of the names.

(f) The lien shall commence and attach as of the time of filing of the RICO lien notice and shall continue thereafter until expiration, termination, or release pursuant to G.S. 75D-14. The lien created in favor of the State shall be superior and prior to the interest of any other person in the real property or beneficial interests if the interest is acquired subsequent to the filing of the notice.

(g) In conjunction with any proceedings pursuant to this Chapter:

(1) The Attorney General may file without prior court order in any county a lis pendens and, in such case, any person acquiring an interest in the subject real property or beneficial interest subsequent to the filing of lis pendens, shall take the interest subject to the civil proceeding and any subsequent judgment of forfeiture; and

(2) If a RICO lien notice has been filed, the Attorney General may name as defendants, in addition to the person named in the notice, any persons acquiring an interest in the real property or beneficial interest subsequent to the filing of the notice. If a judgment of forfeiture is entered in the proceeding in favor of the State, the interest of any person in the property that was acquired subsequent to the filing of the notice shall be subject to the notice and judgment of forfeiture.

(h) (1) A trustee upon whom a RICO lien notice or a RICO civil proceeding has been served shall immediately furnish to the Attorney General the following:

a. The name and addresses, as known to the trustee, of all persons for whose benefit the trustee holds title to the real property; and

b. If requested by the Attorney General's office, a copy of the trust agreement or other instrument pursuant to which the trustee holds legal or record title to the real property.

(2) Any trustee who fails to comply with the provisions of this subsection

shall be removed by court order and a substitute trustee shall be named in lieu of the trustee so removed.

(i) The filing of a RICO lien notice shall not affect the use to which real property or a beneficial interest owned by the person named in the RICO lien notice may be put or in the right of the person to receive any avails, rents, or other proceeds resulting from the use and ownership, but not the sale, of the property until a judgment of forfeiture is entered.

(j) All forfeitures or dispositions under this section shall be made with due provision for the rights of innocent persons.

History.

1985 (Reg. Sess., 1986), c. 999, s. 1; 1989, c. 489, s. 1

§ 75D-14. Release of lien notice

The Attorney General filing the RICO lien notice, or the court for good cause shown at anytime, may release in whole or in part any RICO lien notice or may release any specific property or beneficial interest from the RICO lien notice upon such terms and conditions as he may determine. Any release of a RICO lien notice executed by the Attorney General or ordered by the court may be filed in the official records of any county. No charge or fee shall be imposed for the filing of any release of a RICO lien notice.

History.

1985 (Reg. Sess., 1986), c. 999, s. 1; 1989, c. 489, s. 1

CHAPTER 77
RIVERS, CREEKS, AND COASTAL WATERS

ARTICLE 2
OBSTRUCTIONS IN STREAMS

§ 77-12. Obstructing passage of boats

If any person shall obstruct the free passage of boats along any river or creek, by felling trees, or by any other means whatever, he shall be guilty of a Class 1 misdemeanor.

History.
1796, c. 460, s. 2; R.C., c. 100, s. 6; Code, s. 3711; Rev., s. 3561; C.S., s. 7376; 1993, c. 539, s. 580; 1994, Ex. Sess., c. 24, s. 14(c)

§ 77-13. Obstructing streams a misdemeanor

If any person, firm, or corporation shall fell any tree, or put any obstruction, except for the purposes of utilizing water as a motive power, in any branch, creek, stream, or other natural passage for water, whereby the natural flow of water through such passage is lessened or retarded, or whereby the navigation of such stream may be impeded, delayed, or prevented, the person, firm, or corporation so offending shall be guilty of a Class 2 misdemeanor. In addition to any fine or imprisonment imposed, the court may, in its discretion, order the person, firm, or corporation so offending to remove the obstruction and restore the affected waterway to an undisturbed condition, or allow authorized employees of the enforcing agency to enter upon the property and accomplish the removal of the obstruction and the restoration of the waterway to an undisturbed condition, in which case the costs of the removal and restoration shall be paid to the enforcing agency by the offending party. Nothing in this section shall prevent the erection of fish dams or hedges across any stream which do not extend across more than two thirds of its width at the point of obstruction. If the fish dams or hedges extend more than two thirds of the width of any stream, the said penalties shall attach. This section may be enforced by marine fisheries inspectors and wildlife protectors. Within the bounds of any county or municipality, this section may also be enforced by any law enforcement officer having territorial jurisdiction, or by the county engineer. This section may also be enforced by specially commissioned forest law-enforcement officers of the Department of Agriculture and Consumer Services for offenses occurring in woodlands. For purposes of this section, the term "woodlands" means all forested areas, including swamp and timber lands, cutover lands, and second-growth stands in previously cultivated sites.

History.
1872-3, c. 107, ss. 1, 2; Code, s. 1123; Rev., s. 3559; C.S., s. 7377; 1975, c. 509; 1977, c. 771, s. 4; 1979, c. 493, s. 1; 1987, c. 641, s. 12; 1989, c. 727, s. 218(19); 1991, c. 152, s. 1; 1993, c. 539, s. 581; 1994, Ex. Sess., c. 24, s. 14(c); 1997-443, s. 11A.119(a); 2013-155, s. 3

§ 77-14. Obstructions in streams and drainage ditches

If any person, firm or corporation shall fell any tree or put any slabs, stumpage, sawdust, shavings, lime, refuse or any other substances in any creek, stream, river or natural or artificial drainage ravine or ditch, or in any other outlet which serves to remove water from any land whatsoever whereby the drainage of said land is impeded, delayed or prevented, the person, firm or corporation so offending shall be guilty of a Class 2 misdemeanor: Provided, however, nothing herein shall prevent the construction of any dam or weir not otherwise prohibited by any valid local or State statute or regulation. In addition to any fine or imprisonment imposed, the court may, in its discretion, order the person, firm, or corporation so offending to remove the obstruction and restore the affected waterway to an undisturbed condition, or allow authorized employees of the enforcing agency to enter upon the property and accomplish the removal of the obstruction and the restoration of the waterway to an undisturbed condition, in which case the costs of the removal and restoration shall be paid to the enforcing agency by the offending party. This section may be enforced by marine fisheries inspectors and wildlife protectors. Within the boundaries of any county or municipality this section may also be enforced by any law enforcement officer having territorial jurisdiction, or by the county engineer. This section may also be enforced by specially commissioned forest law-enforcement officers of the Department of Agriculture and Consumer Services for offenses occurring in woodlands. For purposes of this section, the term "woodlands" means all forested areas, including swamp and timber lands, cutover lands and second-growth stands on previously cultivated sites.

History.
1953, c. 1242; 1957, c. 524; 1959, cc. 160, 1125; 1961, c. 507; 1969, c. 790, s. 1; 1975, c. 509; 1977, c. 771, s. 4; 1979, c. 493, s. 1; 1987, c. 641, s. 13; 1989, c. 727, s. 218(20); 1991, c. 152, s. 2; 1993, c. 539, s. 582; 1994, Ex. Sess., c. 24, s. 14(c); 1997-443, s. 11A.119(a); 2013-155, s. 4

Chapter 77

CHAPTER 84
ATTORNEYS-AT-LAW

ARTICLE 1
QUALIFICATIONS OF ATTORNEY; UNAUTHORIZED PRACTICE OF LAW

§ 84-1. Oaths taken in open court

Attorneys before they shall be admitted to practice law shall, in open court before a justice or judge of the General Court of Justice, personally appear and take the oath prescribed for attorneys by G.S. 11-11, and also the oaths of allegiance to the State, and to support the Constitution of the United States, prescribed for all public officers by Article VI, Sec. 7 of the North Carolina Constitution and G.S. 11-7, and the same shall be entered on the records of the court; and, upon such qualification had, and oath taken may act as attorneys during their good behavior.

History.

1777, c. 115, s. 8; R.C., c. 9, s. 3; Code, s. 19; Rev., s. 209; C.S., s. 197; 1969, c. 44, s. 58; 1973, c. 108, s. 35; 1995, c. 431, s. 1

§ 84-2. Persons disqualified

No justice, judge, magistrate, full-time district attorney, full-time assistant district attorney, full-time public defender, full-time assistant public defender, clerk, deputy or assistant clerk of the General Court of Justice, register of deeds, deputy or assistant register of deeds, sheriff or deputy sheriff shall engage in the private practice of law. As used in this section, the private practice of law shall not include the performance of pro bono legal services by a lawyer, other than a justice or judge of the general court of justice, who is otherwise disqualified by this section if the pro bono services are sponsored or organized by a professional association of lawyers or a nonprofit corporation rendering legal services pursuant to G.S. 84-5.1. Persons violating this provision shall be guilty of a Class 3 misdemeanor and only fined not less than two hundred dollars ($ 200.00).

History.

C.C.P., s. 424; 1870-1, c. 90; 1871-2, c. 120; 1880, c. 43; 1883, c. 406; Code, ss. 27, 28, 110; Rev., ss. 210, 3641; 1919, c. 205; C.S., s. 198; 1933, c. 15; 1941, c. 177; 1943, c. 543; 1965, c. 418, s. 1; 1969, c. 44, s. 59; 1973, c. 47, s. 2; c. 108, s. 36; 1981, c. 788, s. 1; 1993, c. 539, s. 596; 1994, Ex. Sess., c. 24, s. 14(c); 1995, c. 431, s. 2; 2007-484, s. 28(a); 2017-158, s. 26

§ 84-2.1. "Practice law" defined

(a) The phrase "practice law" as used in this Chapter is defined to be performing any legal service for any other person, firm or corporation, with or without compensation, specifically including the preparation or aiding in the preparation of deeds, mortgages, wills, trust instruments, inventories, accounts or reports of guardians, trustees, administrators or executors, or preparing or aiding in the preparation of any petitions or orders in any probate or court proceeding; abstracting or passing upon titles, the preparation and filing of petitions for use in any court, including administrative tribunals and other judicial or quasi-judicial bodies, or assisting by advice, counsel, or otherwise in any legal work; and to advise or give opinion upon the legal rights of any person, firm or corporation: Provided, that the above reference to particular acts which are specifically included within the definition of the phrase "practice law" shall not be construed to limit the foregoing general definition of the term, but shall be construed to include the foregoing particular acts, as well as all other acts within the general definition.

(b) The phrase "practice law" does not encompass:

(1) The drafting or writing of memoranda of understanding or other mediation summaries by mediators at community mediation centers authorized by G.S. 7A-38.5 or by mediators of employment-related matters for The University of North Carolina or a constituent institution, or for an agency, commission, or board of the State of North Carolina.

(2) The selection or completion of a preprinted form by a real estate broker licensed under Chapter 93A of the General Statutes, when the broker is acting as an agent in a real estate transaction and in accordance with rules adopted by the North Carolina Real Estate Commission, or the selection or completion of a preprinted residential lease agreement by any person or Web site provider. Nothing in this subdivision or in G.S. 84-2.2 shall be construed to permit any person or Web site provider who is not licensed to practice law in accordance with this Chapter to prepare for any third person any contract or deed conveying any interest in real property, or to abstract or pass upon title to any real property, which is located in this State.

(3) The completion of or assisting a consumer in the completion of various agreements, contracts, forms, and other documents related to the sale or lease of a motor

vehicle as defined in G.S. 20-286(10), or of products or services ancillary or related to the sale or lease of a motor vehicle, by a motor vehicle dealer licensed under Article 12 of Chapter 20 of the General Statutes.

History.

C.C.P., s. 424; 1870-1, c. 90; 1871-2, c. 120; 1880, c. 43; 1883, c. 406; Code, ss. 27, 28, 110; Rev., ss. 210, 3641; 1919, c. 205; C.S., s. 198; 1933, c. 15; 1941, c. 177; 1943, c. 543; 1945, c. 468; 1995, c. 431, s. 3; 1999-354, s. 2; 2004-154, s, 2; 2013-410, s. 32; 2016-60, s. 1

§ 84-2.2. Exemption and additional requirements for Web site providers

(a) The practice of law, including the giving of legal advice, as defined by G.S. 84-2.1 does not include the operation of a Web site by a provider that offers consumers access to interactive software that generates a legal document based on the consumer's answers to questions presented by the software, provided that all of the following are satisfied:

(1) The consumer is provided a means to see the blank template or the final, completed document before finalizing a purchase of that document.

(2) An attorney licensed to practice law in the State of North Carolina has reviewed each blank template offered to North Carolina consumers, including each and every potential part thereof that may appear in the completed document. The name and address of each reviewing attorney must be kept on file by the provider and provided to the consumer upon written request.

(3) The provider must communicate to the consumer that the forms or templates are not a substitute for the advice or services of an attorney.

(4) The provider discloses its legal name and physical location and address to the consumer.

(5) The provider does not disclaim any warranties or liability and does not limit the recovery of damages or other remedies by the consumer.

(6) The provider does not require the consumer to agree to jurisdiction or venue in any state other than North Carolina for the resolution of disputes between the provider and the consumer.

(7) The provider must have a consumer satisfaction process. All consumer concerns involving the unauthorized practice of law made to the provider shall be referred to the North Carolina State Bar. The consumer satisfaction process must be conspicuously displayed on the provider's Web site.

(b) A Web site provider subject to this section shall register with the North Carolina State Bar prior to commencing operation in the State and shall renew its registration with the State Bar annually. The State Bar may not refuse registration.

(c) Each Web site provider subject to this section shall pay an initial registration fee in an amount not to exceed one hundred dollars ($ 100.00) and an annual renewal fee in an amount not to exceed fifty dollars ($ 50.00).

History.

2016-60, s. 2

N.C. Gen. Stat. § 84-3

Repealed by Session Laws 1973, c. 108, s. 37.

§ 84-4. Persons other than members of State Bar prohibited from practicing law

Except as otherwise permitted by law, it shall be unlawful for any person or association of persons, except active members of the Bar of the State of North Carolina admitted and licensed to practice as attorneys-at-law, to appear as attorney or counselor at law in any action or proceeding before any judicial body, including the North Carolina Industrial Commission, or the Utilities Commission; to maintain, conduct, or defend the same, except in his own behalf as a party thereto; or, by word, sign, letter, or advertisement, to hold out himself, or themselves, as competent or qualified to give legal advice or counsel, or to prepare legal documents, or as being engaged in advising or counseling in law or acting as attorney or counselor-at-law, or in furnishing the services of a lawyer or lawyers; and it shall be unlawful for any person or association of persons except active members of the Bar, for or without a fee or consideration, to give legal advice or counsel, perform for or furnish to another legal services, or to prepare directly or through another for another person, firm or corporation, any will or testamentary disposition, or instrument of trust, or to organize corporations or prepare for another person, firm or corporation, any other legal document. Provided, that nothing herein shall prohibit any person from drawing a will for another in an emergency wherein the imminence of death leaves insufficient time to have the same drawn and its execution supervised by a licensed attorney-at-law. The provisions of this section shall be in addition to and not in lieu of any other provisions of this Chapter. Provided, however, this section shall not apply to corporations authorized to practice law under the provisions of Chapter 55B of the General Statutes of North Carolina.

History.

1931, c. 157, s. 1; 1937, c. 155, s. 1; 1955, c. 526, s. 1; 1969, c. 718, s. 19; 1981, c. 762, s. 3; 1995, c. 431, s. 4

Chapter 84

§ 84-4.1. Limited practice of out-of-state attorneys

Any attorney domiciled in another state, and regularly admitted to practice in the courts of record of and in good standing in that state, having been retained as attorney for a party to any civil or criminal legal proceeding pending in the General Court of Justice of North Carolina, the North Carolina Utilities Commission, the North Carolina Industrial Commission, the Office of Administrative Hearings of North Carolina, or any administrative agency, may, on motion to the relevant forum, be admitted to practice in that forum for the sole purpose of appearing for a client in the proceeding. The motion required under this section shall be signed by the attorney and shall contain or be accompanied by:

(1) The attorney's full name, post-office address, bar membership number, and status as a practicing attorney in another state.

(2) A statement, signed by the client, setting forth the client's address and declaring that the client has retained the attorney to represent the client in the proceeding.

(3) A statement that unless permitted to withdraw sooner by order of the court, the attorney will continue to represent the client in the proceeding until its final determination, and that with reference to all matters incident to the proceeding, the attorney agrees to be subject to the orders and amenable to the disciplinary action and the civil jurisdiction of the General Court of Justice and the North Carolina State Bar in all respects as if the attorney were a regularly admitted and licensed member of the Bar of North Carolina in good standing.

(4) A statement that the state in which the attorney is regularly admitted to practice grants like privileges to members of the Bar of North Carolina in good standing.

(5) A statement to the effect that the attorney has associated and is personally appearing in the proceeding, with an attorney who is a resident of this State, has agreed to be responsible for filing a registration statement with the North Carolina State Bar, and is duly and legally admitted to practice in the General Court of Justice of North Carolina, upon whom service may be had in all matters connected with the legal proceedings, or any disciplinary matter, with the same effect as if personally made on the foreign attorney within this State.

(6) A statement accurately disclosing a record of all that attorney's disciplinary history. Discipline shall include (i) public discipline by any court or lawyer regulatory organization, and (ii) revocation of any pro hac vice admission.

(7) A fee in the amount of two hundred twenty-five dollars ($ 225.00) submitted and made payable to one of the following: (i) for judicial proceedings, the presiding clerk of court and (ii) for administrative proceedings, the presiding administrative agency. The clerk of court or administrative agency shall: (i) remit two hundred dollars ($ 200.00) of the fee collected to the State Treasurer for support of the General Court of Justice, and (ii) transmit twenty-five dollars ($ 25.00) of the fee collected to the North Carolina State Bar to regulate the practice of out-of-state attorneys as provided in this section.

Compliance with the foregoing requirements does not deprive the court of the discretionary power to allow or reject the application.

History.
1967, c. 1199, s. 1; 1971, c. 550, s. 1; 1975, c. 582, ss. 1, 2; 1977, c. 430; 1985 (Reg. Sess., 1986), c. 1022, s. 8; 1991, c. 210, s. 2; 1995, c. 431, s. 5; 2003-116, s. 1; 2004-186, s. 4.2; 2005-396, s. 1; 2007-200, s. 4; 2007-323, s. 30.8(k); 2021-60, s. 1.1

§ 84-4.2. Summary revocation of permission granted out-of-state attorneys to practice

Permission granted under G.S. 84-4.1 may be summarily revoked by the General Court of Justice or any agency, including the North Carolina Utilities Commission, on its own motion and in its discretion.

History.
1967, c. 1199, s. 2; 1971, c. 550, s. 2; 1995, c. 431, s. 6

§ 84-5. Prohibition as to practice of law by corporation

(a) It shall be unlawful for any corporation to practice law or appear as an attorney for any person in any court in this State, or before any judicial body or the North Carolina Industrial Commission, Utilities Commission, or the Department of Commerce, Division of Employment Security, or hold itself out to the public or advertise as being entitled to practice law; and no corporation shall organize corporations, or draw agreements, or other legal documents, or draw wills, or practice law, or give legal advice, or hold itself out in any manner as being entitled to do any of the foregoing acts, by or through any person orally or by advertisement, letter or circular. The provisions of this section shall be in addition to and not in lieu of any other provisions of Chapter 84. Provided, that nothing in this section shall be construed to prohibit a banking corporation authorized and licensed to act in a fiduciary capacity from performing any clerical, accounting, financial or business acts required of it in the performance of its duties as a fiduciary or from performing ministerial and clerical acts in the preparation and filing of such tax returns as are so required, or from discussing the business and financial aspects of fiduciary relationships. Provided, however, this section shall not apply to corporations authorized to practice law under the provisions of Chapter 55B of the General Statutes of North Carolina.

To further clarify the foregoing provisions of this section as they apply to corporations which are authorized and licensed to act in a fiduciary capacity:

(1) A corporation authorized and licensed to act in a fiduciary capacity shall not:

a. Draw wills or trust instruments; provided that this shall not be construed to prohibit an employee of such corporation from conferring and cooperating with an attorney who is not a salaried employee of the corporation, at the request of such attorney, in connection with the attorney's performance of services for a client who desires to appoint the corporation executor or trustee or otherwise to utilize the fiduciary services of the corporation.

b. Give legal advice or legal counsel, orally or written, to any customer or prospective customer or to any person who is considering renunciation of the right to qualify as executor or administrator or who proposes to resign as guardian or trustee, or to any other person, firm or corporation.

c. Advertise to perform any of the acts prohibited herein; solicit to perform any of the acts prohibited herein; or offer to perform any of the acts prohibited herein.

(2) Except as provided in subsection (b) of this section, when any of the following acts are to be performed in connection with the fiduciary activities of such a corporation, said acts shall be performed for the corporation by a duly licensed attorney, not a salaried employee of the corporation, retained to perform legal services required in connection with the particular estate, trust or other fiduciary matter:

a. Offering wills for probate.

b. Preparing and publishing notice of administration to creditors.

c. Handling formal court proceedings.

d. Drafting legal papers or giving legal advice to spouses concerning rights to an elective share under Article 1A of Chapter 30 of the General Statutes.

e. Resolving questions of domicile and residence of a decedent.

f. Handling proceedings involving year's allowances of widows and children.

g. Drafting deeds, notes, deeds of trust, leases, options and other contracts.

h. Drafting instruments releasing deeds of trust.

i. Drafting assignments of rent.

j. Drafting any formal legal document to be used in the discharge of the corporate fiduciary's duty.

k. In matters involving estate and inheritance taxes, gift taxes, and federal and State income taxes:

1. Preparing and filing protests or claims for refund, except requests for a refund based on mathematical or clerical errors in tax returns filed by it as a fiduciary.

2. Conferring with tax authorities regarding protests or claims for refund, except those based on mathematical or clerical errors in tax returns filed by it as a fiduciary.

3. Handling petitions to the tax court.

l. Performing legal services in insolvency proceedings or before a referee in bankruptcy or in court.

m. In connection with the administration of an estate or trust:

1. Making application for letters testamentary or letters of administration.

2. Abstracting or passing upon title to property.

3. Handling litigation relating to claims by or against the estate or trust.

4. Handling foreclosure proceedings of deeds of trust or other security instruments which are in default.

(3) When any of the following acts are to be performed in connection with the fiduciary activities of such a corporation, the corporation shall comply with the following:

a. The initial opening and inventorying of safe deposit boxes in connection with the administration of an estate for which the corporation is executor or administrator shall be handled by, or with the advice of, an attorney, not a salaried employee of the corporation, retained by the corporation to perform legal services required in connection with that particular estate.

b. The furnishing of a beneficiary with applicable portions of a testator's will relating to such beneficiary shall, if accompanied by any legal advice or opinion, be handled by, or with the advice of, an attorney, not a salaried employee of the corporation, retained by the corporation to perform legal services required in connection with that particular estate or matter.

c. In matters involving estate and inheritance taxes and federal and State income taxes, the corporation shall not execute waivers of statutes of limitations without the advice of an attorney, not a salaried employee of the corporation, retained by the corporation to perform legal services in connection with that particular estate or matter.

d. An attorney, not a salaried employee of the corporation, retained by the corporation to perform legal services required in connection with an estate or trust shall be furnished copies of inventories and accounts proposed for filing with any court and proposed federal estate and North Carolina inheritance tax returns and, on request, copies of proposed income and intangibles tax returns, and shall be afforded an opportunity to advise and counsel the corporate fiduciary concerning them prior to filing.

(b) Nothing in this section shall prohibit an attorney retained by a corporation, whether or not the attorney is also a salaried employee of the corporation, from representing the corporation or an affiliate, or from representing an officer, director, or employee of the corporation or an affiliate in any matter arising in connection with the course and scope of the employment of the officer, director, or employee. Notwithstanding the provisions of this subsection, the attorney providing such representation shall be governed by and subject to all of the Rules of Professional Conduct of the North Carolina State Bar to the same extent as all other attorneys licensed by this State.

History.
1931, c. 157, s. 2; 1937, c. 155, s. 2; 1955, c. 526, s. 2; 1969, c. 718, s. 20; 1971, c. 747; 1997-203, s. 1; 2000-178, s. 8; 2011-401, s. 3.5

§ 84-5.1. Rendering of legal services by certain nonprofit corporations

(a) Subject to the rules and regulations of the North Carolina State Bar, as approved by the Supreme Court of North Carolina, a nonprofit corporation, tax exempt under 26 U.S.C. § 501(c)(3), organized or authorized under Chapter 55A of the General Statutes of North Carolina and operating as a public interest law firm as defined by the applicable Internal Revenue Service guidelines or for the primary purpose of rendering indigent legal services, may render such services provided by attorneys duly licensed to practice law in North Carolina, for the purposes for which the nonprofit corporation was organized. The nonprofit corporation must have a governing structure that does not permit an individual or group of individuals other than an attorney duly licensed to practice law in North Carolina to control the manner or course of the legal services rendered and must continually satisfy the criteria established by the Internal Revenue Service for 26 U.S.C. § 501(c)(3) status, whether or not any action has been taken to revoke that status.

(b) In no instance may legal services rendered by a nonprofit corporation under subsection (a) of this section be conditioned upon the purchase or payment for any product, good, or service other than the legal service rendered.

History.
1977, c. 841, s. 1; 2009-231, s. 1

§ 84-6. Exacting fee for conducting foreclosures prohibited to all except licensed attorneys

It shall be unlawful to exact, charge, or receive any attorney's fee for the foreclosure of any mortgage under power of sale, unless the foreclosure is conducted by licensed attorney-at-law of North Carolina, and unless the full amount charged as attorney's fee is actually paid to and received and retained by such attorney, without being directly or indirectly shared with or rebated to anyone else, and it shall be unlawful for any such attorney to make any showing that he has received such a fee unless he has received the same, or to share with or rebate to any other person, firm, or corporation such fee or any part thereof received by him; but such attorney may divide such fee with another licensed attorney-at-law maintaining his own place of business and not an officer or employee of the foreclosing party, if such attorney has assisted in performing the services for which the fee is paid, or resides in a place other than that where the foreclosure proceedings are conducted, and has forwarded the case to the attorney conducting such foreclosure.

History.
1931, c. 157, s. 3

§ 84-7. District attorneys, upon application, to bring injunction or criminal proceedings

The district attorney of any of the superior courts shall, upon the application of any member of the Bar, or of any bar association, of the State of North Carolina, bring such action in the name of the State as may be proper to enjoin any such person, corporation, or association of persons who it is alleged are violating the provisions of G.S. 84-4 to 84-8, and it shall be the duty of the district attorneys of this State to indict any person, corporation, or association of persons upon the receipt of information of the violation of the provisions of G.S. 84-4 to 84-8.

History.

1931, c. 157, s. 4; 1973, c. 47, s. 2

§ 84-7.1. Legal clinics of law schools and certain law students and lawyers excepted

The provisions of G.S. 84-4 through G.S. 84-6 shall not apply to any of the following:

(1) Any law school conducting a legal clinic and receiving as its clientage only those persons unable financially to compensate for legal advice or services rendered and any law student permitted by the North Carolina State Bar to act as a legal intern in such a legal clinic.

(2) Any law student permitted by the North Carolina State Bar to act as a legal intern for a federal, State, or local government agency.

(3) Any lawyer licensed by another state and permitted by the North Carolina State Bar to represent indigent clients on a pro bono basis under the supervision of active members employed by nonprofit corporations qualified to render legal services pursuant to G.S. 84-5.1. This provision does not apply to a lawyer whose license has been suspended or revoked in any state.

History.

2011-336, s. 5

§ 84-8. Punishment for violations

(a) Any person, corporation, or association of persons violating any of the provisions of G.S. 84-4 through G.S. 84-6 or G.S. 84-9 shall be guilty of a Class 1 misdemeanor.

(b) No person shall be entitled to collect any fee for services performed in violation of G.S. 84-4 through G.S. 84-6, G.S. 84-9, or G.S. 84-10.1.

History.

1931, c. 157, s. 5; c. 347; 1993, c. 539, s. 597; 1994, Ex. Sess., c. 24, s. 14(c); 2007-200, s. 3; 2011-336, s. 4

§ 84-9. Unlawful for anyone except attorney to appear for creditor in insolvency and certain other proceedings

It shall be unlawful for any corporation, or any firm or other association of persons other than a law firm, or for any individual other than an attorney duly licensed to practice law, to appear for another in any bankruptcy or insolvency proceeding, or in any action or proceeding for or growing out of the appointment of a receiver, or in any matter involving an assignment for the benefit of creditors, or to present or vote any claim of another, whether under an assignment or transfer of such claim or in any other manner, in any of the actions, proceedings or matters hereinabove set out.

History.

1931, c. 208, s. 2

N.C. Gen. Stat. § 84-10

Repealed by Session Laws 2011-336, s. 6, effective December 1, 2011, and applicable to offenses committed on or after December 1, 2011.

History.

1931, c. 208, s. 3; 1993, c. 539, s. 598; 1994, Ex. Sess., c. 24, s. 14(c); repealed by 2011-336, s. 6, effective December 1, 2011

§ 84-10.1. Private cause of action for the unauthorized practice of law

If any person knowingly violates any of the provisions of G.S. 84-4 through G.S. 84-6 or G.S. 84-9, fraudulently holds himself or herself out as a North Carolina certified paralegal by use of the designations set forth in G.S. 84-37(a), or knowingly aids and abets another person to commit the unauthorized practice of law, in addition to any other liability imposed pursuant to this Chapter or any other applicable law, any person who is damaged by the unlawful acts set out in this section shall be entitled to maintain a private cause of action to recover damages and reasonable attorneys' fees and other injunctive relief as ordered by court. No order or judgment under this section shall have any effect upon the ability of the North Carolina State Bar to take any action authorized by this Chapter.

History.

2011-336, s. 7; 2016-60, s. 3

CHAPTER 90
MEDICINE AND ALLIED OCCUPATIONS

ARTICLE 1
PRACTICE OF MEDICINE

N.C. Gen. Stat. § 90-12.2

Recodified as G.S. 90-12.5, by Session Laws 2007-346, s. 7, effective October 1, 2007.

§ 90-12.5. Disasters and emergencies

In the event of an occurrence which the Governor of the State of North Carolina has declared a state of emergency, or in the event of an occurrence for which a county or municipality has enacted an ordinance to deal with states of emergency under G.S. 166A-19.31, or to protect the public health, safety, or welfare of its citizens under Article 22 of Chapter 130A of the General Statutes, G.S. 160A-174(a) or G.S. 153A-121(a), as applicable, the Board may waive the requirements of this Article in order to permit the provision of emergency health services to the public.

History.

2002-179, s. 20(a); 2007-346, s. 7; 2012-12, s. 2(ff)

§ 90-12.7. Treatment of overdose with opioid antagonist; immunity

(a) As used in this section, "opioid antagonist" means naloxone hydrochloride that is approved by the federal Food and Drug Administration for the treatment of a drug overdose.

(b) The following individuals may prescribe an opioid antagonist in the manner prescribed by this subsection:

(1) A practitioner acting in good faith and exercising reasonable care may directly or by standing order prescribe an opioid antagonist to (i) a person at risk of experiencing an opiate-related overdose or (ii) a family member, friend, or other person in a position to assist a person at risk of experiencing an opiate-related overdose. As an indicator of good faith, the practitioner, prior to prescribing an opioid under this subsection, may require receipt of a written communication that provides a factual basis for a reasonable conclusion as to either of the following:

a. The person seeking the opioid antagonist is at risk of experiencing an opiate-related overdose.

b. The person other than the person who is at risk of experiencing an opiate-related overdose, and who is seeking the opioid antagonist, is in relation to the person at risk of experiencing an opiate-related overdose:

1. A family member, friend, or other person.

2. In the position to assist a person at risk of experiencing an opiate-related overdose.

(2) The State Health Director or a designee may prescribe an opioid antagonist pursuant to subdivision (1) of this subsection by means of a statewide standing order.

(3) A practitioner acting in good faith and exercising reasonable care may directly or by standing order prescribe an opioid antagonist to any governmental or nongovernmental organization, including a local health department, a law enforcement agency, or an organization that promotes scientifically proven ways of mitigating health risks associated with substance use disorders and other high-risk behaviors, for the purpose of distributing, through its agents, the opioid antagonist to (i) a person at risk of experiencing an opiate-related overdose or (ii) a family member, friend, or other person in a position to assist a person at risk of experiencing an opiate-related overdose.

(c) A pharmacist may dispense an opioid antagonist to a person or organization pursuant to a prescription issued in accordance with subsection (b) of this section. For purposes of this section, the term "pharmacist" is as defined in G.S. 90-85.3.

(c1) A governmental or nongovernmental organization, including a local health department, a law enforcement agency, or an organization that promotes scientifically proven ways of mitigating health risks associated with substance use disorders and other high-risk behaviors may, through its agents, distribute an opioid antagonist obtained pursuant to a prescription issued in accordance with subdivision (3) of subsection (b) of this section to (i) a person at risk of experiencing an opiate-related overdose or (ii) a family member, friend, or other person in a position to assist a person at risk of experiencing an opiate-related overdose. An organization, through its agents, shall include with any distribution of an opioid antagonist pursuant to this subsection basic instruction and information on how to administer the opioid antagonist.

(d) A person who receives an opioid antagonist that was prescribed pursuant to subsection (b) of this section or distributed pursuant to subsection (c1) of this section may administer an opioid antagonist to another person if (i) the person has a good faith belief that the other person is experiencing a drug-related overdose and (ii) the person exercises reasonable care in administering the drug to the other person. Evidence of the use of reasonable care in administering the drug shall include the receipt of basic instruction and information on how to administer the opioid antagonist.

(e) All of the following individuals are immune from any civil or criminal liability for actions authorized by this section:

(1) Any practitioner who prescribes an opioid antagonist pursuant to subsection (b) of this section.

(2) Any pharmacist who dispenses an opioid antagonist pursuant to subsection (c) of this section.

(3) Any person who administers an opioid antagonist pursuant to subsection (d) of this section.

(4) The State Health Director acting pursuant to subsection (b) of this section.

(5) Any organization, or agent of the organization, that distributes an opioid antagonist pursuant to subsection (c1) of this section.

History.
2013-23, s. 2; 2015-94, s. 3; 2016-17, s. 2; 2017-74, s. 2; 2017-102, s. 37(a), (b).

ARTICLE 1C
PHYSICIANS AND HOSPITAL REPORTS

§ 90-21.20. Reporting by physicians and hospitals of wounds, injuries and illnesses

(a) Such cases of wounds, injuries or illnesses as are enumerated in subsection (b) shall be reported as soon as it becomes practicable before, during or after completion of treatment of a person suffering such wounds, injuries, or illnesses. If such case is treated in a hospital, sanitarium or other medical institution or facility, such report shall be made by the Director, Administrator, or other person designated by the Director or Administrator, or if such case is treated elsewhere, such report shall be made by the physician or surgeon treating the case, to the chief of police or the police authorities of the city or town of this State in which the hospital or other institution, or place of treatment is located. If such hospital or other institution or place of treatment is located outside the corporate limits of a city or town, then the report shall be made by the proper person in the manner set forth above to the sheriff of the respective county or to one of his deputies.

(b) Cases of wounds, injuries or illnesses which shall be reported by physicians, and hospitals include every case of a bullet wound, gunshot wound, powder burn or any other injury arising from or caused by, or appearing to arise from or be caused by, the discharge of a gun or firearm, every case of illness apparently caused by poisoning, every case of a wound or injury caused, or apparently caused, by a knife or sharp or pointed instrument if it appears to the physician or surgeon treating the case that a criminal act was involved, and every case of a wound, injury or illness in which there is grave bodily harm or grave illness if it appears to the physician or surgeon treating the case that the wound, injury or illness resulted from a criminal act of violence.

(c) Each report made pursuant to subsections (a) and (b) above shall state the name of the wounded, ill or injured person, if known, and the age, sex, race, residence or present location, if known, and the character and extent of his injuries.

(c1) In addition to the reporting requirements of subsection (b) of this section, cases involving recurrent illness or serious physical injury to any child under the age of 18 years where the illness or injury appears, in the physician's professional judgment, to be the result of non-accidental trauma shall be reported by the physician as soon as it becomes practicable before, during, or after completion of treatment. If the case is treated in a hospital, sanitarium, or other medical institution or facility, the report shall be made by the Director, Administrator, or other person designated by the Director or Administrator of the medical institution or facility, or if the case is treated elsewhere, the report shall be made by the physician or surgeon treating the case to the chief of police or the police authorities of the city or town in this State in which the hospital or other institution or place of treatment is located. If the hospital or other institution or place of treatment is located outside the corporate limits of a city or town, then the report shall be made by the proper person in the manner set forth above to the sheriff of the respective county or to one of the sheriff's deputies. This reporting requirement is in addition to the duty set forth in G.S. 7B-301 to report child abuse, neglect, dependence, or the death of any juvenile as the result of maltreatment to the director of the department of social services in the county where the juvenile resides or is found.

(d) Any hospital, sanitarium, or other like institution or Director, Administrator, or other designated person, or physician or surgeon participating in good faith in the making of a report pursuant to this section shall have immunity from any liability, civil or criminal, that might otherwise be incurred or imposed as the result of the making of such report.

History.
1971, c. 4; 1977, c. 31; c. 843, s. 2; 2008-179, s. 1

§ 90-21.20A. Reporting by physicians of pilots' mental or physical disabilities or infirmities

(a) A physician who reports to a government agency responsible for pilots' licenses or certificates or a government agency responsible for air safety that a pilot or an applicant for a pilot's license or certificate suffers from or probably suffers from a physical disability or infirmity that the physician believes will or reasonably could affect the person's ability to safely operate an aircraft shall have immunity, civil or criminal, that might otherwise be incurred or imposed as the result of making such a report.

(b) A physician who gives testimony about a pilot's or an applicant's mental or physical disability or infirmity in any administrative hearing or other proceeding held to consider the issuance, renewal, revocation, or suspension of a pilot's license or certificate shall have immunity from any liability, civil or criminal, that might otherwise be incurred or imposed as the result of such testimony.

History.
1997-464, s. 2

§ 90-21.20B. Access to and disclosure of medical information for certain purposes

(a) Notwithstanding G.S. 8-53 or any other provision of law, a health care provider may disclose to a law enforcement officer protected health information only to the extent that the information may be disclosed under the federal Standards for Privacy of Individually Identifiable Health Information, 45 C.F.R. § 164.512(f) and is not specifically prohibited from disclosure by other state or federal law.

(a1) Notwithstanding any other provision of law, if a person is involved in a vehicle crash:

(1) Any health care provider who is providing medical treatment to the person shall, upon request, disclose to any law enforcement officer investigating the crash the following information about the person: name, current location, and whether the person appears to be impaired by alcohol, drugs, or another substance.

(2) Law enforcement officers shall be provided access to visit and interview the person upon request, except when the health care provider requests temporary privacy for medical reasons.

(3) A health care provider shall disclose a certified copy of all identifiable health information related to that person as specified

in a search warrant or an order issued by a judicial official.

(b) A prosecutor or law enforcement officer receiving identifiable health information under this section shall not disclose this information to others except as necessary to the investigation or otherwise allowed by law.

(c) A certified copy of identifiable health information, if relevant, shall be admissible in any hearing or trial without further authentication.

(d) As used in this section, "health care provider" has the same meaning as in G.S. 90-21.11.

(e) Notwithstanding G.S. 8-53 or any other provision of law, a health care provider may disclose protected health information for purposes of treatment, payment, or health care operations to the extent that disclosure is permitted under 45 C.F.R. § 164.506 and is not specifically prohibited by other state or federal law. As used in this subsection, "treatment, payment, or health care operations" are as defined in the Standards for Privacy of Individually Identifiable Health Information.

History.
2006-253, s. 17; 2007-115, s. 3

ARTICLE 4A
NORTH CAROLINA PHARMACY PRACTICE ACT

PART 1
NORTH CAROLINA PHARMACY PRACTICE ACT

§ 90-85.40. Violations

(a) It shall be unlawful for any owner or manager of a pharmacy or other place to allow or cause anyone other than a pharmacist to dispense or compound any prescription drug unless that person is a pharmacy technician or a pharmacy student who is enrolled in a school of pharmacy approved by the Board and is working under the supervision of a pharmacist.

(b) Every person lawfully authorized to compound or dispense prescription drugs shall comply with all the laws and regulations governing the labeling and packaging of such drugs by pharmacists.

(c) It shall be unlawful for any person not licensed as a pharmacist to compound or dispense any prescription drug, unless that person is a pharmacy technician or a pharmacy student who is enrolled in a school of pharmacy approved by the Board and is working under the supervision of a pharmacist.

(d) It shall be unlawful for any person to manage any place of business where devices are dispensed or sold at retail without a permit as required by this Article.

(d1) It is unlawful for a person to own or manage a place of business from which medical equipment is delivered without a permit as required by this Article.

(e) It shall be unlawful for any person without legal authorization to dispose of an article that has been embargoed under this Article.

(f) It shall be unlawful to violate any provision of this Article or of any rules or regulations enacted pursuant to it.

(g) This Article shall not be construed to prohibit any person from performing an act that person is authorized to perform pursuant to North Carolina law. Health care providers who are authorized to prescribe drugs without supervision are authorized to dispense drugs without supervision.

(h) A violation of this Article shall be a Class 1 misdemeanor.

History.
1905, c. 108, ss. 4, 23, 24; Rev., ss. 3649, 3650, 4487; C.S., ss. 6667, 6668, 6669; 1921, c. 68, ss. 6, 7; Ex. Sess. 1924, c. 116; 1953, c. 1051; 1957, c. 617; 1959, c. 1222; 1981 (Reg. Sess., 1982), c. 1188, s. 1; 1993, c. 539, s. 621; 1994, Ex. Sess., c. 24, s. 14(c); 1993 (Reg. Sess., 1994), c. 692, s. 4; 2001-375, ss. 6, 7

ARTICLE 5
NORTH CAROLINA CONTROLLED SUBSTANCES ACT

§ 90-86. Title of Article

This Article shall be known and may be cited as the "North Carolina Controlled Substances Act."

History.
1971, c. 919, s. 1

§ 90-87. Definitions

As used in this Article:

(1) "Administer" means the direct application of a controlled substance, whether by injection, inhalation, ingestion, or any other means to the body of a patient or research subject by:

    a. A practitioner (or, in his presence, by his authorized agent), or

    b. The patient or research subject at the direction and in the presence of the practitioner.

(2) "Agent" means an authorized person who acts on behalf of or at the direction of a manufacturer, distributor, or dispenser but does not include a common or contract carrier, public warehouseman, or employee thereof.

(3) "Bureau" means the Bureau of Narcotics and Dangerous Drugs, United States Department of Justice or its successor agency.

(3a) "Commission" means the Commission for Mental Health, Developmental Disabilities, and Substance Abuse Services established under Part 4 of Article 3 of Chapter 143B of the General Statutes.

(4) "Control" means to add, remove, or change the placement of a drug, substance, or immediate precursor included in Schedules I through VI of this Article.

(5) "Controlled substance" means a drug, substance, or immediate precursor included in Schedules I through VI of this Article.

(5a) "Controlled substance analogue" means a substance (i) the chemical structure of which is substantially similar to the chemical structure of a controlled substance in Schedule I or II; (ii) which has a stimulant, depressant, or hallucinogenic effect on the central nervous system that is substantially similar to or greater than the stimulant, depressant, or hallucinogenic effect on the central nervous system of a controlled substance in Schedule I or II; or (iii) with respect to a particular person, which such person represents or intends to have a stimulant, depressant, or hallucinogenic effect on the central nervous system that is substantially similar to or greater than the stimulant, depressant, or hallucinogenic effect on the central nervous system of a controlled substance in Schedule I or II; and does not include (i) a controlled substance; (ii) any substance for which there is an approved new drug application; (iii) with respect to a particular person any substance, if an exemption is in effect for investigational use, for that person, under § 355 of Title 21 of the United States Code to the extent conduct with respect to such substance is pursuant to such exemption; or (iv) any substance to the extent not intended for human consumption before such an exemption takes effect with respect to that substance. The designation of gamma butyrolactone or any other chemical as a listed chemical pursuant to subdivision 802(34) or 802(35) of Title 21 of the United States Code does not preclude a finding pursuant to this subdivision that the chemical is a controlled substance analogue.

(6) "Counterfeit controlled substance" means:

a. A controlled substance which, or the container or labeling of which, without authorization, bears the trademark, trade name, or other identifying mark, imprint, number, or device, or any likeness thereof, of a manufacturer, distributor, or dispenser other than the person or persons who in fact manufactured, distributed, or dispensed such substance and which thereby falsely purports, or is represented to be the product of, or to have been distributed by, such other manufacturer, distributor, or dispenser; or

b. Any substance which is by any means intentionally represented as a controlled substance. It is evidence that the substance has been intentionally misrepresented as a controlled substance if the following factors are established:

1. The substance was packaged or delivered in a manner normally used for the illegal delivery of controlled substances.

2. Money or other valuable property has been exchanged or requested for the substance, and the amount of that consideration was substantially in excess of the reasonable value of the substance.

3. The physical appearance of the tablets, capsules or other finished product containing the substance is substantially identical to a specified controlled substance.

(7) "Deliver" or "delivery" means the actual constructive, or attempted transfer from one person to another of a controlled substance, whether or not there is an agency relationship.

(8) "Dispense" means to deliver a controlled substance to an ultimate user or research subject by or pursuant to the lawful order of a practitioner, including the prescribing, administering, packaging, labeling, or compounding necessary to prepare the substance for that delivery.

(9) "Dispenser" means a practitioner who dispenses.

(10) "Distribute" means to deliver other than by administering or dispensing a controlled substance.

(11) "Distributor" means a person who distributes.

(12) "Drug" means a. substances recognized in the official United States Pharmacopoeia, official Homeopathic Pharmacopoeia of the United States, or official National Formulary, or any supplement to any of them; b. substances intended for use in the diagnosis, cure, mitigation,

treatment, or prevention of disease in man or other animals; c. substances (other than food) intended to affect the structure or any function of the body of man or other animals; and d. substances intended for use as a component of any article specified in a, b, or c of this subdivision; but does not include devices or their components, parts, or accessories.

(13) "Drug dependent person" means a person who is using a controlled substance and who is in a state of psychic or physical dependence, or both, arising from use of that controlled substance on a continuous basis. Drug dependence is characterized by behavioral and other responses which include a strong compulsion to take the substance on a continuous basis in order to experience its psychic effects, or to avoid the discomfort of its absence.

(14) "Immediate precursor" means a substance which the Commission has found to be and by regulation designates as being the principal compound commonly used or produced primarily for use, and which is an immediate chemical intermediary used or likely to be used in the manufacture of a controlled substance, the control of which is necessary to prevent, curtail, or limit such manufacture.

(14a) The term "isomer" means the optical isomer, unless otherwise specified.

(15) "Manufacture" means the production, preparation, propagation, compounding, conversion, or processing of a controlled substance by any means, whether directly or indirectly, artificially or naturally, or by extraction from substances of a natural origin, or independently by means of chemical synthesis, or by a combination of extraction and chemical synthesis; and "manufacture" further includes any packaging or repackaging of the substance or labeling or relabeling of its container except that this term does not include the preparation or compounding of a controlled substance by an individual for his own use or the preparation, compounding, packaging, or labeling of a controlled substance:

a. By a practitioner as an incident to his administering or dispensing of a controlled substance in the course of his professional practice, or

b. By a practitioner, or by his authorized agent under his supervision, for the purpose of, or as an incident to research, teaching, or chemical analysis and not for sale.

(16) *(See editor's note for expiration of last sentence)* "Marijuana" means all parts of the plant of the genus Cannabis, whether growing or not; the seeds thereof; the resin

extracted from any part of such plant; and every compound, manufacture, salt, derivative, mixture, or preparation of such plant, its seeds or resin, but shall not include the mature stalks of such plant, fiber produced from such stalks, oil, or cake made from the seeds of such plant, any other compound, manufacture, salt, derivative, mixture, or preparation of such mature stalks (except the resin extracted therefrom), fiber, oil, or cake, or the sterilized seed of such plant which is incapable of germination. The term does not include industrial hemp as defined in G.S. 106-568.51, when the industrial hemp is produced and used in compliance with rules issued by the North Carolina Industrial Hemp Commission.

(17) "Narcotic drug" means any of the following, whether produced directly or indirectly by extraction from substances of vegetable origin, or independently by means of chemical synthesis, or by a combination of extraction and chemical synthesis:

a. Opium, opiate and opioid, and any salt, compound, derivative, or preparation of opium, opiate, or opioid.

b. Any salt, compound, isomer, derivative, or preparation thereof which is chemically equivalent or identical with any of the substances referred to in clause a, but not including the isoquinoline alkaloids of opium.

c. Opium poppy and poppy straw.

d. Cocaine and any salt, isomer (whether optical or geometric), salts of isomers, compound, derivative, or preparation thereof, or coca leaves and any salt, isomer, salts of isomers, compound, derivative or preparation of coca leaves, or any salt, isomer, salts of isomers, compound, derivative, or preparation thereof which is chemically equivalent or identical with any of these substances, except that the substances shall not include decocainized coca leaves or extraction of coca leaves, which extractions do not contain cocaine or ecgonine.

(18) "Opiate" means any substance having an addiction-forming or addiction-sustaining liability similar to morphine or being capable of conversion into a drug having addiction-forming or addiction-sustaining liability. It does not include, unless specifically designated as controlled under G.S. 90-88, the dextrorotatory isomer of 3-methoxy-n-methyl-morphinan and its salts (dextromethorphan). It does include its racemic and levorotatory forms.

(18a) "Opioid" means any synthetic narcotic drug having opiate-like activities but is not derived from opium.

(19) "Opium poppy" means the plant of the species Papaver somniferum L., except its seeds.

(20) "Person" means individual, corporation, government or governmental subdivision or agency, business trust, estate, trust, partnership or association, or any other legal entity.

(21) "Poppy straw" means all parts, except the seeds, of the opium poppy, after mowing.

(22) "Practitioner" means:

a. A physician, dentist, optometrist, veterinarian, scientific investigator, or other person licensed, registered or otherwise permitted to distribute, dispense, conduct research with respect to or to administer a controlled substance so long as such activity is within the normal course of professional practice or research in this State.

b. A pharmacy, hospital or other institution licensed, registered, or otherwise permitted to distribute, dispense, conduct research with respect to or to administer a controlled substance so long as such activity is within the normal course of professional practice or research in this State.

(23) "Prescription" means:

a. A written order or other order which is promptly reduced to writing for a controlled substance as defined in this Article, or for a preparation, combination, or mixture thereof, issued by a practitioner who is licensed in this State to administer or prescribe drugs in the course of his professional practice; or issued by a practitioner serving on active duty with the Armed Forces of the United States or the United States Veterans Administration who is licensed in this or another state or Puerto Rico, provided the order is written for the benefit of eligible beneficiaries of armed services medical care; a prescription does not include an order entered in a chart or other medical record of a patient by a practitioner for the administration of a drug; or

b. A drug or preparation, or combination, or mixture thereof furnished pursuant to a prescription order.

(24) "Production" includes the manufacture, planting, cultivation, growing, or harvesting of a controlled substance.

(25) "Registrant" means a person registered by the Commission to manufacture, distribute, or dispense any controlled substance as required by this Article.

(26) "State" means the State of North Carolina.

(26a) "Targeted controlled substance" means any controlled substance included in G.S. 90-90(1) or (2) or G.S. 90-91(d).

(27) "Ultimate user" means a person who lawfully possesses a controlled substance for his own use, or for the use of a member of his household, or for administration to an animal owned by him or by a member of his household.

History.

1971, c. 919, s. 1; 1973, c. 476, s. 128; c. 540, ss. 2-4; c. 1358, ss. 1, 15; 1977, c. 482, s. 6; 1981, c. 51, ss. 8, 9; c. 75, s. 1; c. 732; 1985, c. 491; 1987, c. 105, ss. 1, 2; 1991 (Reg. Sess., 1992), c. 1030, s. 21; 1997-456, s. 27; 2003-249, s. 2; 2011-183, s. 60; 2015-299, s. 2; 2016-93, s. 6; 2017-74, s. 3; 2017-115, s. 2; 2021-155, s. 1

§ 90-88. Authority to control

(a) The Commission may add, delete, or reschedule substances within Schedules I through VI of this Article on the petition of any interested party, or its own motion. In every case the Commission shall give notice of and hold a public hearing pursuant to Chapter 150B of the General Statutes prior to adding, deleting or rescheduling a controlled substance within Schedules I through VI of this Article, except as provided in subsection (d) of this section. A petition by the Commission, the North Carolina Department of Justice, or the North Carolina Board of Pharmacy to add, delete, or reschedule a controlled substance within Schedules I through VI of this Article shall be placed on the agenda, for consideration, at the next regularly scheduled meeting of the Commission, as a matter of right.

(a1) In making a determination regarding a substance, the Commission shall consider the following:

(1) The actual or relative potential for abuse;

(2) The scientific evidence of its pharmacological effect, if known;

(3) The state of current scientific knowledge regarding the substance;

(4) The history and current pattern of abuse;

(5) The scope, duration, and significance of abuse;

(6) The risk to the public health;

(7) The potential of the substance to produce psychic or physiological dependence liability; and

(8) Whether the substance is an immediate precursor of a substance already controlled under this Article.

(b) After considering the required factors, the Commission shall make findings with respect thereto and shall issue an order adding, deleting or rescheduling the substance within Schedules I through VI of this Article.

(c) If the Commission designates a substance as an immediate precursor, substances which are precursors of the controlled precursor shall not be subject to control solely because they are precursors of the controlled precursor.

(d) If any substance is designated, rescheduled or deleted as a controlled substance under federal law, the Commission shall similarly control or cease control of, the substance under this Article unless the Commission objects to such inclusion. The Commission, at its next regularly scheduled meeting that takes place 30 days after publication in the Federal Register of a final order scheduling a substance, shall determine either to adopt a rule to similarly control the substance under this Article or to object to such action. No rule-making notice or hearing as specified by Chapter 150B of the General Statutes is required if the Commission makes a decision to similarly control a substance. However, if the Commission makes a decision to object to adoption of the federal action, it shall initiate rule-making procedures pursuant to Chapter 150B of the General Statutes within 180 days of its decision to object.

(e) The Commission shall exclude any non-narcotic substance from the provisions of this Article if such substance may, under the federal Food, Drug and Cosmetic Act, lawfully be sold over-the-counter without prescription.

(f) Authority to control under this Article does not include distilled spirits, wine, malt beverages, or tobacco.

(g) The Commission shall similarly exempt from the provisions of this Article any chemical agents and diagnostic reagents not intended for administration to humans or other animals, containing controlled substances which either (i) contain additional adulterant or denaturing agents so that the resulting mixture has no significant abuse potential, or (ii) are packaged in such a form or concentration that the particular form as packaged has no significant abuse potential, where such substance was exempted by the Federal Bureau of Narcotics and Dangerous Drugs.

(h) Repealed by Session Laws 1987, c. 413, s. 4.

(i) The North Carolina Department of Health and Human Services shall maintain a list of all preparations, compounds, or mixtures which are excluded, exempted and excepted from control under any schedule of this Article by the United States Drug Enforcement Administration and/or the Commission. This list and any changes to this list shall be mailed to the North Carolina Board of Pharmacy, the State Bureau of Investigation and each district attorney of this State.

History.

1971, c. 919, s. 1; 1973, c. 476, s. 128; cc. 524, 541; c. 1358, ss. 2, 3, 15; 1977, c. 667, s. 3; 1981, c. 51, s. 9; 1987, c. 413, ss. 1-4; 1989, c. 770, s. 16; 1997-443, s. 11A.118(a); 2000-189, s. 4; 2001-487, s. 22

§ 90-89. Schedule I controlled substances

This schedule includes the controlled substances listed or to be listed by whatever official name, common or usual name, chemical name, or trade name designated. In determining that a substance comes within this schedule, the Commission shall find: a high potential for abuse, no currently accepted medical use in the United States, or a lack of accepted safety for use in treatment under medical supervision. The following controlled substances are included in this schedule:

(1) **Opiates.** -- Any of the following opiates or opioids, including the isomers, esters, ethers, salts and salts of isomers, esters, and ethers, unless specifically excepted, or listed in another schedule, whenever the existence of such isomers, esters, ethers, and salts is possible within the specific chemical designation:

a. Acetyl-alpha-methylfentanyl (N[1-(1-methyl-2-phenethyl)-4-piperidinyl]-N-phenylacet amide).

b. Acetylmethadol.

c. Repealed by Session Laws 1987, c. 412, s. 2.

d. Alpha-methylthiofentanyl (N-[1-methyl-2-(2-thienyl)ethyl/-4-piperidinyl]-N-phenylpro panamide).

e. Allylprodine.

f. Alphacetylmethadol (except levo-alphacetylmethadol, also known as levomethadyl acetate and LAAM).

g. Alphameprodine.

h. Alphamethadol.

i. Alpha-methylfentanyl (N-(1-(alpha-methyl-beta-phenyl) ethyl-4-piperidyl) propionalilide; 1(1-methyl-2-phenyl-ethyl)-4-(N-propanilido) piperidine).

j. Benzethidine.

k. Betacetylmethadol.

l. Beta-hydroxfentanyl (N-[1-(2-hydroxy-2-phenethyl)-4-piperidinyl]-N-phenylpropanamide).

m. Beta-hydroxy-3-methylfentanyl (N-[1-(2-hydroxy-2-phenethyl)-3-methyl-4-piperidinyl]-N-phenylpropanamide).

n. Betameprodine.

o. Betamethadol.

p. Betaprodine.

q. Clonitazene.

r. Dextromoramide.

s. Diampromide.

t. Diethylthiambutene.

u. Difenoxin.

v. Dimenoxadol.

w. Dimepheptanol.

x. Dimethylthiambutene.

y. Dioxaphetyl butyrate.

z. Dipipanone.

aa. Ethylmethylthiambutene.

bb. Etonitazene.

cc. Etoxeridine.

dd. Furethidine.

ee. Hydroxypethidine.

ff. Ketobemidone.

gg. Levomoramide.

hh. Levophenacylmorphan. For purposes of this sub-subdivision only, the term "isomer" includes the optical and geometric isomers.

ii. 1-methyl-4-phenyl-4-propionoxypiperidine (MPPP).

jj. 3-Methylfentanyl (N-[3-methyl-1-(2-Phenylethyl)-4-Pi- peridyl]-N-Phenylpropanamide).

kk. 3-Methylthiofentanyl (N-[(3-methyl-1-(2-thienyl)ethyl-4-piperidinyl]-N-phenylpropanamide).

ll. Morpheridine.

mm. Noracymethadol.

nn. Norlevorphanol.

oo. Normethadone.

pp. Norpipanone.

qq. Para-fluorofentanyl (N-(4-fluorophenyl)-N-[1-(2-phen-ethyl)-4-piperidinyl]-propanamide.

rr. Phenadoxone.

ss. Phenampromide.

tt. 1-(2-phenethyl)-4-phenyl-4-acetoxypiperidine (PEPAP).

uu. Phenomorphan.

vv. Phenoperidine.

ww. Piritramide.

xx. Proheptazine.

yy. Properidine.

zz. Propiram.

aaa. Racemoramide.

bbb. Thiofentanyl (N-phenyl-N-[1-(2-thienyl)ethyl-4-piperidinyl]-propanamide.

ccc. Tilidine.

ddd. Trimeperidine.

eee. Acetyl Fentanyl.

fff. Trans-3,4-dichloro-N-(2(dimethy lamino)cyclohexyl)-N-methyl-benzamide (U47700).

ggg. 3,4-dichloro-N-([1(dimethylamino)cyclohexyl]methyl)benzamide; 1-(3,4-dichlorobenzamidomethyl) cyclohexyldimethylamine) (also known as AH-7921).

hhh. 3,4-dichloro-N-([diethylamino) cyclohexyl]-N-methylbenzamide (also known as U-49900).

iii. U-77891.

jjj. 1-phenylethylpiperidylidene-2-(4-chlorphenyl)sulfonamide; 1-(4-nitrophenylethyl)piperidylidene-2-(4-chlorophenyl)sulfonamide; 4-chloro-N-[1-[2-(4-nitrophenyl)ethyl]-2-piperidinylidene]-benzenesulfonamide (also known as W-18).

kkk. 1-phenylethylpiperidylidene-2-(4-chlorphenyl)sulfonamide; 4-chloro-N-[1-(2-phenylethyl)-2-piperidinylidene]-benzenesulfonamide (also known as W-15).

lll. 1-cyclohexyl-4-(1,2-diphenylethyl) piperazine (also known as MT-45).

mmm. 3,4-dichloro-N-[2-(dimethylamino)cyclohexyl]-N-isopropylbenzami de (also known as Isopropyl-U-47700).

nnn. 2-(3,4-dichlorophenyl)-N-[2-(dimethylamino)cyclohexyl]-N-methyl acetamide (also known as U-51754).

ooo. 2-(2,4-dichlorophenyl)-N-[2-(dimethylamino)cyclohexyl]-N-methyl acetamide (also known as U-48800).

ppp. Isotonitazene.

qqq. Metonitazene.

rrr. Brorphine.

(1a) **Fentanyl derivatives.** -- Unless specifically excepted, listed in another schedule, or contained within a pharmaceutical product approved by the United States Food and Drug Administration, any compound structurally derived from N-[1-(2-phenylethyl)-4-piperidinyl]-N-phenylpropanamide (Fentanyl) by any substitution on or replacement of the phenethyl group, any substitution on the piperidine ring, any substitution on or replacement of the propanamide group, any substitution on the anilido phenyl group, or any combination of the above unless specifically excepted or listed in another schedule to include their salts, isomers, and salts of isomers. Fentanyl derivatives include, but are not limited to, the following:

a. N-(1-phenylethylpiperidin-4-yl)-N-phenylfuran-2-carboxamide (also known as Furanyl Fentanyl).

b. N-(1-phenethylpiperidin-4-yl)-N-phenylbutyramide; N-(1-phenethyl piperidin-4-yl)-N-phenylbutanamide (also known as Butyryl Fentanyl).

c. N-[1-[2-hydroxy-2-(thiophen-2-yl) ethyl]piperidin-4-yl]-N-phenylpropionamide; N-[1-[2-hydroxy-2-(2-thienyl)ethyl]-4-piperidinyl]-N-phenyl propanamide (also known as Beta-Hydroxythiofentanyl).

d. N-phenyl-N-[1-(2-phenylethyl) piperidin-4-yl]-2propenamide (also known as Acrylfentanyl).

e. N-phenyl-N-[1-(2-phenylethyl)-4-piperidinyl]-pentanamide (also known as Valeryl Fentanyl).

f. N-(2-fluorophenyl)-N-[1-(2-phenylethyl)-4-piperidinyl]-propanamide (also known as 2-fluorofentanyl).

g. N-(3-fluorophenyl)-N-[1-(2-pheny lethyl)-4-piperidinyl]-propanamide (also known as 3-fluorofentanyl).

h. N-(1-phenethylpiperidin-4-yl)-N-phenyltetrahydrofuran-2-carboxamide (also known as tetrahydrofuran fentanyl).

i. N-(4-fluorophenyl)-2-methyl-N-[1-(2-phenylethyl)-4-piperidinyl]-propanamide (also known as 4-fluoroisobutyryl fentanyl, 4-FIBF).

j. N-(4-fluorophenyl)-N-[1-(2-pheny lethyl)-4-piperidinyl]-butanamide (also known as 4-fluorobutyryl fentanyl, 4-FBF).

(2) **Opium derivatives.** -- Any of the following opium derivatives, including their salts, isomers (whether optical, positional, or geometric), and salts of isomers, unless specifically excepted, or listed in another schedule, whenever the existence of such salts, isomers, and salts of isomers is possible within the specific chemical designation:

a. Acetorphine.

b. Acetyldihydrocodeine.

c. Benzylmorphine.

d. Codeine methylbromide.

e. Codeine-N-Oxide.

f. Cyprenorphine.

g. Desomorphine.

h. Dihydromorphine.

i. Etorphine (except hydrochloride salt).

j. Heroin.

k. Hydromorphinol.

l. Methyldesorphine.

m. Methyldihydromorphine.

n. Morphine methylbromide.

o. Morphine methylsulfonate.

p. Morphine-N-Oxide.

q. Myrophine.

r. Nicocodeine.

s. Nicomorphine.

t. Normorphine.

u. Pholcodine.

v. Thebacon.

w. Drotebanol.

(3) **Hallucinogenic substances.** -- Any material, compound, mixture, or preparation which contains any quantity of the following hallucinogenic substances, including their salts, isomers, and salts of isomers, unless specifically excepted, or listed in another schedule, whenever the

existence of such salts, isomers (whether optical, positional, or geometric), and salts of isomers is possible within the specific chemical designation:

a. 3, 4-methylenedioxyamphetamine.

b. 5-methoxy-3, 4-methylenedioxyam phetamine.

c. 3, 4-Methylenedioxy methamphetamine (MDMA).

d. 3,4-methylenedioxy-N-ethylamphetamine (also known as N-ethyl-alpha-methyl-3,4-(methylenedioxy) phenethylamine, N-ethyl MDA, MDE, and MDEA).

e. N-hydroxy-3,4-methylenedioxy amphetamine (also known as N-hydroxy-alpha-methyl-3,4-(methylenedioxy) phenethylamine, and N-hydroxy MDA).

f. 3, 4, 5-trimethoxyamphetamine.

g. Alpha-ethyltryptamine. Some trade or other names: etryptamine, Monase, alpha-ethyl-1H-indole-3-ethanamine, 3-(2-aminobutyl) indole, alpha-ET, and AET.

h. Bufotenine.

i. Diethyltryptamine.

j. Dimethyltryptamine.

k. 4-methyl-2, 5-dimethoxyamphetamine.

l. Ibogaine.

m. Lysergic acid diethylamide.

n. Mescaline.

o. Peyote, meaning all parts of the plant presently classified botanically as Lophophora Williamsii Lemaire, whether growing or not; the seeds thereof; any extract from any part of such plant; and every compound, manufacture, salt, derivative, mixture or preparation of such plant, its seed or extracts.

p. N-ethyl-3-piperidyl benzilate.

q. N-methyl-3-piperidyl benzilate.

r. Psilocybin.

s. Psilocin.

t. 2, 5-dimethoxyamphetamine.

u. 2, 5-dimethoxy-4-ethylamphetamine. Some trade or other names: DOET.

v. v. 4-bromo-2, 5-dimethoxyam phetamine.

w. 4-methoxyamphetamine.

x. Ethylamine analog of phencyclidine. Some trade or other names: N-ethyl-1-phenylcyclohexylamine, (1-phenylcyclohexyl) ethylamine, N-(1-phenylcyclohexyl) ethylamine, cyclohexamine, PCE.

y. Pyrrolidine analog of phencyclidine. Some trade or other

names: 1-(1-phenylcyclohexyl)-pyrrolidine, PCPy, PHP.

z. Thiophene analog of phencyclidine. Some trade or other names: 1-[1-(2-thienyl)-cyclohexyl]-piperidine, 2-thienyl analog of phencyclidine, TPCP, TCP.

aa. 1-[1-(2-thienyl)cyclohexyl] pyrrolidine; Some other names: TCPy.

bb. Parahexyl.

cc. 4-Bromo-2, 5-Dimethoxyphenethylamine.

dd. Alpha-Methyltryptamine.

ee. 5-Methoxy-N,N-diisopropyltryptamine.

ff. Methoxetamine (other names: MXE, 3-MeO-2-Oxo-PCE).

gg. BTCP (Benzothiophenylcy clohexylpiperidine).

hh. Deschloroketamine.

jj. 3-MeO-PCP (3-methoxyphencyclidine).

kk. 4-hydroxy-MET.

ll. 4-OH-MiPT (4-hydroxy-N-methyl-N-isopropyltryptamine).

mm. 5-methoxy-N-methyl-N-propyltryptamine (5-MeO-MiPT).

nn. **Substituted tryptamines. --** Any compound, unless specifically excepted, specifically named in this schedule, or listed under a different schedule, structurally derived from 2-(1H-indol-3-yl) ethanamine (i.e., tryptamine) by mono- or di-substitution of the amine nitrogen with alkyl or alkenyl groups or by inclusion of the amino nitrogen atom in a cyclic structure whether or not the compound is further substituted at the alpha position with an alkyl group or whether or not further substituted on the indole ring to any extent with any alkyl, alkoxy, halo, hydroxyl, or acetoxy groups. Substances in this class include, but are not limited to: 4-AcO-DiPT (4-acetoxy-N,N-diisopropyltryptamine), 4-HO-MPMI ((R)-3-(N-methylpyrrolidin-2-ylmethyl)-4-hydoxyindole), and DALT (N,N-diallyltryptamine).

oo. **Substituted phenylcyclohexylamines. --** Any compound, unless specifically excepted or unless listed in another schedule, or contained within a pharmaceutical product approved by the United States Food and Drug Administration, any material, compound, mixture, or preparation containing a phenylcyclohexylamine structure, with or without any substitution on the phenyl ring, any substitution on the cyclohexyl ring, any replacement of the phenyl ring with a thiophenyl or benzothiophenyl ring, with or without substitution on the amine with alkyl, dialkyl, or alkoxy substituents, inclusion of the nitrogen in a cyclic structure, or any combination of the above. Substances in this class include, but are not limited to: BCP (benocyclidine), PCMPA ((phenylcyclohexyl(methoxyropylamine)), and Hydroxy-PCP ((hydroxyphenyl)cyclohexylpiperidine).

(4) **Systemic depressants.** -- Any material compound, mixture, or preparation which contains any quantity of the following substances having a depressant effect on the central nervous system, including its salts, isomers, and salts of isomers whenever the existence of such salts, isomers, and salts of isomers is possible within the specific chemical designation, unless specifically excepted or unless listed in another schedule:

a. Mecloqualone.

b. Methaqualone.

c. Gamma hydroxybutyric acid; Some other names: GHB, gamma-hydroxybutyrate, 4-hydroxybutyrate, 4-hydroxybutanoic acid; sodium oxybate; sodium oxybutyrate.

d. Etizolam.

e. Flubromazepam.

f. Phenazepam.

g. Clonazolam.

h. Flualprazolam.

i. Flubromazolam.

(5) **Stimulants.** -- Unless specifically excepted or unless listed in another schedule, any material, compound, mixture, or preparation that contains any quantity of the following substances having a stimulant effect on the central nervous system, including its salts, isomers, and salts of isomers:

a. Aminorex. Some trade or other names: aminoxaphen; 2-amino-5-phenyl-2-oxazoline; or 4,5-dihydro-5-phenyl-2-oxazolamine.

b. Cathinone. Some trade or other names: 2-amino-1-phenyl-1-propanone, alpha-aminopropiophenone, 2-aminopropiophenone, and norephedrone.

c. Fenethylline.

d. Methcathinone. Some trade or other names: 2-(methylamino)-propiophenone, alpha-(methylamino) propiophenone, 2-(methy- lamino)-1-phenylpropan-1-one, alpha-N-methylamino- propiophenone, monomethylproprion, ephedrone, N-methylcathinone, methylcathinone, AL-464, AL-422, AL-463, and UR1432.

e. (+-)cis-4-methylaminorex [(+-) cis-4,5-dihydro-4-methyl-5-phenyl-2-oxazolamine] (also known as 2-amino-4-methyl-5-phenyl-2-oxazoline).

f. N,N-dimethylamphetamine. Some other names: N,N,alpha-tri- methylbenzeneethaneamine; N,N,alpha-trimethylphenethylamine.

g. N-ethylamphetamine.

h. 4-methylmethcathinone (also known as mephedrone). For this compound, the term "isomer" includes the optical, positional, or geometric isomer.

i. 3,4-Methylenedioxypyrovalerone (also known as MDPV). For this compound, the term "isomer" includes the optical, positional, or geometric isomer.

j. Substituted cathinones. A compound, other than bupropion, that is structurally derived from 2-amino-1-phenyl-1-propanone by modification in any of the following ways: (i) by substitution in the phenyl ring to any extent with alkyl, alkoxy, alkylenedioxy, haloalkyl, or halide substituents, whether or not further substituted in the phenyl ring by one or more other univalent substituents; (ii) by substitution at the 3-position to any extent; or (iii) by substitution at the nitrogen atom with alkyl, dialkyl, benzyl, or methoxybenzyl groups or by inclusion of the nitrogen atom in a cyclic structure. For the purpose of this paragraph, the term "isomer" includes the optical, positional, or geometric isomer.

k. N-Benzylpiperazine.

l. 2,5 -- Dimethoxy-4-(n)-propylthiophenethylamine.

(6) **NBOMe compounds.** -- Any material compound, mixture, or preparation which contains any quantity of the following substances, including its salts, isomers (whether optical, positional, or geometric), and salts of isomers whenever the existence of such salts, isomers, and salts of isomers is possible within the specific chemical designation unless specifically excepted or unless listed in another schedule:

a. 25B-NBOMe (2C-B-NBOMe) 2-(4-Bromo-2,5-dimethoxyphenyl)-N-(2-methoxybenzyl)ethanamine.

b. 25C-NBOMe (2C-C-NBOMe) 2-(4-Chloro-2,5-dimethoxyphenyl)-N-(2-methoxybenzyl)ethanamine.

c. 25D-NBOMe (2C-D-NBOMe) 2-(2,5-dimethoxy-4-methylphenyl)-N-(2-methoxybenzyl)ethanamine.

d. 25E-NBOMe (2C-E-NBOMe) 2-(4-Ethyl-2,5-dimethoxyphenyl)-N-(2-methoxybenzyl)ethanamine.

e. 25G-NBOMe (2C-G-NBOMe) 2-(2,5-dimethoxy-3,4-dimethylphenyl)-N-(2-methoxybenzyl)ethanamine.

f. 25H-NBOMe (2C-H-NBOMe) 2-(2,5-dimethoxyphenyl)-N-(2-methoxybenzyl)ethanamine.

g. 25I-NBOMe (2C-I-NBOMe) 2-(4-Iodo-2,5-dimethoxyphenyl)-N-(2-methoxybenzyl) ethanamine.

h. 25N-NBOMe (2C-N-NBOMe) 2-(2,5-dimethoxy-4-nitrophenyl)-N-(2-methoxybenzyl)ethanamine.

i. 25P-NBOMe (2C-P-NBOMe) 2-(4-Propyl-2,5-dimethoxyphenyl)-N-(2-methoxybenzyl)ethanamine.

j. 25T2-NBOMe (2C-T2-NBOMe) 2,5-dimethoxy-N-[(2-methoxyphenyl) methyl]-4-(methylthio)-benzeneethanamine.

k. 25T4-NBOMe (2C-T4-NBOMe) 2,5-dimethoxy-N-[(2-methoxyphenyl) methyl]-4-[(1-methylethyl)thio]-benzeneethanamine.

l. 25T7-NBOMe (2C-T7-NBOMe) 2,5-dimethoxy-N-[(2-methoxyphenyl) methyl]-4-(propylthio)-benzeneethanamine.

(7) **Synthetic cannabinoids.** -- Any quantity of any synthetic chemical compound that (i) is a cannabinoid receptor agonist and mimics the pharmacological effect of naturally occurring substances or (ii) has a stimulant, depressant, or hallucinogenic effect on the central nervous system that is not listed as a controlled substance in Schedules I through V, and is not an FDA-approved drug. Synthetic cannabinoids include, but are not limited to, the substances listed in sub-subdivisions a. through p. of this subdivision and any substance that contains any quantity of their salts, isomers (whether optical, positional, or geometric), homologues, and salts of isomers and homologues, unless specifically excepted, whenever the existence of these salts, isomers, homologues, and salts of isomers and homologues is possible within the specific chemical designation. The following substances are examples of synthetic cannabinoids and are not intended to be inclusive of the substances included in this Schedule:

a. Naphthoylindoles. Any compound containing a 3-(1-naphthoyl) indole structure with substitution at the nitrogen atom of the indole ring by an alkyl, haloalkyl, alkenyl, cycloalkylmethyl, cycloalkylethyl, 1-(N-methyl-2-piperidinyl)methyl, or 2-(4-morpholinyl)ethyl group, whether or not further substituted in the indole ring to any extent and whether or not substituted in the naphthyl ring to any extent. Some trade or other names: JWH-015, JWH-018, JWH-019,

JWH-073, JWH-081, JWH-122, JWH-200, JWH-210, JWH-398, AM-2201, and WIN 55-212.

b. Naphthylmethylindoles. Any compound containing a 1H-indol-3-yl-(1-naphthyl)methane structure with substitution at the nitrogen atom of the indole ring by an alkyl, haloalkyl, alkenyl, cycloalkylmethyl, cycloalkylethyl, 1-(N-methyl-2-piperidinyl)methyl, or 2-(4-morpholinyl)ethyl group, whether or not further substituted in the indole ring to any extent and whether or not substituted in the naphthyl ring to any extent.

c. Naphthoylpyrroles. Any compound containing a 3-(1-naphthoyl)pyrrole structure with substitution at the nitrogen atom of the pyrrole ring by an alkyl, haloalkyl, alkenyl, cycloalkylmethyl, cycloalkylethyl, 1-(N-methyl-2-piperidinyl) methyl, or 2-(4-morpholinyl)ethyl group, whether or not further substituted in the pyrrole ring to any extent and whether or not substituted in the naphthyl ring to any extent. Another name: JWH-307.

d. Naphthylmethylindenes. Any compound containing a naphthylideneindene structure with substitution at the 3-position of the indene ring by an alkyl, haloalkyl, alkenyl, cycloalkylmethyl, cycloalkylethyl, 1-(N-methyl-2-piperidinyl)methyl, or 2-(4-morpholinyl)ethyl group, whether or not further substituted in the indene ring to any extent and whether or not substituted in the naphthyl ring to any extent.

e. Phenylacetylindoles. Any compound containing a 3-phenylacetylindole structure with substitution at the nitrogen atom of the indole ring by an alkyl, haloalkyl, alkenyl, cycloalkylmethyl, cycloalkylethyl, 1-(N-methyl-2-piperidinyl) methyl, or 2-(4-morpholinyl)ethyl group, whether or not further substituted in the indole ring to any extent and whether or not substituted in the phenyl ring to any extent. Some trade or other names: SR-18, RCS-8, JWH-250, and JWH-203.

f. Cyclohexylphenols. Any compound containing a 2-(3-hydroxycyclohexyl) phenol structure with substitution at the 5-position of the phenolic ring by an alkyl, haloalkyl, alkenyl, cycloalkylmethyl, cycloalkylethyl, 1-(N-methyl-2-piperidinyl)methyl, or 2-(4-morpholinyl)ethyl group, whether or not substituted in the cyclohexyl ring to any extent. Some trade or other names: CP 47,497 (and homologues), cannabicyclohexanol.

g. Benzoylindoles. Any compound containing a 3-(benzoyl)indole structure with substitution at the nitrogen atom of the indole ring by an alkyl, haloalkyl, alkenyl, cycloalkylmethyl, cycloalkylethyl, 1-(N-methyl-2-piperidinyl)methyl, or 2-(4-morpholinyl) ethyl group, whether or not further substituted in the indole ring to any extent and whether or not substituted in the phenyl ring to any extent. Some trade or other names: AM-694, Pravadoline (WIN 48,098), and RCS-4.

h. 2,3-Dihydro-5-methyl-3-(4-morpholinylmethyl)pyrrolo[1,2,3-de]-1, 4-benzoxazin-6-yl]-1-napthalenylmethanone. Some trade or other name: WIN 55,212-2.

i. (6aR,10aR)-9-(hydroxymethyl)-6, 6-dimethyl-3-(2-methyloctan-2-yl)-6a,7,10,10a-tetrahydrobenzo[c] chromen-1-ol 7370. Some trade or other name: HU-210.

j. 3-(cyclopropylmethanone) indole or 3-(cyclobutylmethanone) indole or 3-(cyclopentylmethanone) indole by substitution at the nitrogen atom of the indole ring, whether or not further substituted in the indole ring to any extent, whether or not further substituted on the cyclopropyl, cyclobutyl, or cyclopentyl rings to any extent. Substances in this class include, but are not limited to: UR-144, fluoro-UR-144, XLR-11, A-796,260, and A-834,735.

k. Indole carboxaldehydes. Any compound structurally derived from 1H-indole-3-carboxaldehyde or 1H-indole-2-carboxaldehyde substituted in both of the following ways:

1. At the nitrogen atom of the indole ring by an alkyl, haloalkyl, cyanoalkyl, alkenyl, cycloalkyl methyl, cycloalkylethyl, 1-(N-methyl-2-piperidinyl)methyl, 2-(4-morpholinyl)ethyl, 1-(N-methyl-2-pyrrolidinyl)methyl, 1-(N-methyl-3-morpholinyl)methyl, tetrahydropyranylmethyl, benzyl, or halo benzyl group; and

2. At the carbon of the carboxaldehyde by a phenyl, benzyl, naphthyl, adamantyl, cyclopropyl, or propionaldehyde group;

whether or not the compound is further modified to any extent in the following ways: (i) substitution to the indole ring to any extent, (ii) substitution to the phenyl, benzyl, naphthyl, adamantyl, cyclopropyl, or propionaldehyde group to any extent, (iii) a nitrogen heterocyclic

analog of the indole ring, or (iv) a nitrogen heterocyclic analog of the phenyl, benzyl, naphthyl, adamantyl, or cyclopropyl ring. Substances in this class include, but are not limited to: AB-001.

l. Indole carboxamides. Any compound structurally derived from 1H-indole-3-carboxamide or 1H-indole-2-carboxamide substituted in both of the following ways:

1. At the nitrogen atom of the indole ring by an alkyl, haloalkyl, cyanoalkyl, alkenyl, cycloalkylmethyl, cycloalkylethyl, 1-(N-methyl-2-piperidinyl)methyl, 2-(4-morpholinyl)ethyl, 1-(N-methyl-2-pyrrolidinyl)methyl, 1-(N-methyl-3-morpholinyl)methyl, tetrahydropyranylmethyl, benzyl, or halo benzyl group; and

2. At the nitrogen of the carboxamide by a phenyl, benzyl, naphthyl, adamantyl, cyclopropyl, or propionaldehyde group;

whether or not the compound is further modified to any extent in the following ways: (i) substitution to the indole ring to any extent, (ii) substitution to the phenyl, benzyl, naphthyl, adamantyl, cyclopropyl, or propionaldehyde group to any extent, (iii) a nitrogen heterocyclic analog of the indole ring, or (iv) a nitrogen heterocyclic analog of the phenyl, benzyl, naphthyl, adamantyl, or cyclopropyl ring. Substances in this class include, but are not limited to: SDB-001 and STS-135.

m. Indole carboxylic acids. Any compound structurally derived from 1H-indole-3-carboxylic acid or 1H-indole-2-carboxylic acid substituted in both of the following ways:

1. At the nitrogen atom of the indole ring by an alkyl, haloalkyl, cyanoalkyl, alkenyl, cycloalkylmethyl, cycloalkylethyl, 1-(N-methyl-2-piperidinyl)methyl, 2-(4-morpholinyl)ethyl, 1-(N-methyl-2-pyrrolidinyl)methyl, 1-(N-methyl-3-morpholinyl)methyl, tetrahydropyranylmethyl, benzyl, or halo benzyl group; and

2. At the nitrogen of the carboxamide by a phenyl, benzyl, naphthyl, adamantyl, cyclopropyl, or propionaldehyde group;

whether or not the compound is further modified to any extent in the following ways: (i) substitution to the indole ring to any extent, (ii) substitution to the phenyl, benzyl, naphthyl, adamantyl, cyclopropyl, or propionaldehyde group to any extent, (iii) a nitrogen heterocyclic analog of the indole ring, or (iv) a nitrogen heterocyclic analog of the phenyl, benzyl, naphthyl, adamantyl, or cyclopropyl ring. Substances in this class include, but are not limited to: SDB-001 and STS-135.

whether or not the compound is further modified to any extent in the following ways: (i) substitution to the indole ring to any extent, (ii) substitution to the phenyl, benzyl, naphthyl, adamantyl, cyclopropyl, or propionaldehyde group to any extent, (iii) a nitrogen heterocyclic analog of the indole ring, or (iv) a nitrogen heterocyclic analog of the phenyl, benzyl, naphthyl, adamantyl, or cyclopropyl ring. Substances in this class include, but are not limited to: PB-22 and fluoro-PB-22.

n. Indazole carboxaldehydes. Any compound structurally derived from 1H-indazole-3-carboxaldehyde or 1H-indazole-2-carboxaldehyde substituted in both of the following ways:

1. At the nitrogen atom of the indazole ring by an alkyl, haloalkyl, cyanoalkyl, alkenyl, cycloalkyl methyl, cycloalkylethyl, 1-(N-methyl-2-piperidinyl)methyl, 2-(4-morpholinyl)ethyl, 1-(N-methyl-2-pyrrolidinyl)methyl, 1-(N-methyl-3-morpholinyl)methyl, tetrahydropyranylmethyl, benzyl, or halo benzyl group; and

2. At the carbon of the carboxaldehyde by a phenyl, benzyl,

whether or not the compound is further modified to any extent in the following ways: (i) substitution to the indazole ring to any extent, (ii) substitution to the phenyl, benzyl, naphthyl, adamantyl, cyclopropyl, or propionaldehyde group to any extent, (iii) a nitrogen heterocyclic analog of the indazole ring, or (iv) a nitrogen heterocyclic analog of the phenyl, benzyl, naphthyl, adamantyl, or cyclopropyl ring.

o. Indazole carboxamides. Any compound structurally derived from 1H-indazole-3-carboxamide or 1H-indazole-2-carboxamide substituted in both of the following ways:

1. At the nitrogen atom of the indazole ring by an alkyl, haloalkyl, cyanoalkyl, alkenyl,

cycloalkylmethyl, cycloalkylethyl, 1-(N-methyl-2-piperidinyl)methyl, 2-(4-morpholinyl)ethyl, 1-(N-methyl-2-pyrrolidinyl)methyl, 1-(N-methyl-3-morpholinyl)methyl, tetrahydropyranylmethyl, benzyl, or halo benzyl group; and

2. At the nitrogen of the carboxamide by a phenyl, benzyl, naphthyl, adamantyl, cyclopropyl, or propionaldehyde group;

whether or not the compound is further modified to any extent in the following ways: (i) substitution to the indazole ring to any extent, (ii) substitution to the phenyl, benzyl, naphthyl, adamantyl, cyclopropyl, or propionaldehyde group to any extent, (iii) a nitrogen heterocyclic analog of the indazole ring, or (iv) a nitrogen heterocyclic analog of the phenyl, benzyl, naphthyl, adamantyl, or cyclopropyl ring. Substances in this class include, but are not limited to: AKB-48, fluoro-AKB-48, APINCACA, AB-PINACA, AB-FUBINACA, ADB-FUBINACA, and ADB-PINACA.

p. Indazole carboxylic acids. Any compound structurally derived from 1H-indazole-3-carboxylic acid or 1H-indazole-2-carboxylic acid substituted in both of the following ways:

1. At the nitrogen atom of the indazole ring by an alkyl, haloalkyl, cyanoalkyl, alkenyl, cycloalkylmethyl, cycloalkylethyl, 1-(N-methyl-2-piperidinyl)methyl, 2-(4-morpholinyl)ethyl, 1-(N-methyl-2-pyrrolidinyl)methyl, 1-(N-methyl-3-morpholinyl)methyl, tetrahydropyranylmethyl, benzyl, or halo benzyl group; and

2. At the hydroxyl group of the carboxylic acid by a phenyl, benzyl, naphthyl, adamantyl, cyclopropyl, or propionaldehyde group; whether or not the compound is further modified to any extent in the following ways: (i) substitution to the indazole ring to any extent, (ii) substitution to the phenyl, benzyl, naphthyl, adamantyl, cyclopropyl, or propionaldehyde group to any extent, (iii) a nitrogen heterocyclic analog of the indazole ring, or (iv) a nitrogen heterocyclic analog of the phenyl, benzyl, naphthyl, adamantyl, or cyclopropyl ring.

q. Carbazoles. Any compound containing a carbazole ring system with a substituent on the nitrogen atom and bearing an additional substituent at the 1, 2, or 3 position of the carbazole ring system, with a linkage connecting the ring system to the substituent:

1. Where the linkage connecting the carbazole ring system to the substituent if its 1, 2, or 3 position is any of the following: Alkyl, Carbonyl, Ester, Thione, Thioester, Amino, Alkylamino, Amido, or Alkylamido.

2. Where the substituent at the 1, 2, or 3 position of the carbazole ring system, disregarding the linkage, is any of the following groups: Naphthyl, Quinolinyl, Adamantyl, Phenyl, Cycloalkyl (limited to cyclopropyl, cyclobutyl, cyclopentyl, or cyclohexyl), Biphenyl, Alkylamido (limited to ethylamido, propylamido, butanamido, pentamido), Benzyl, Carboxylic acid, Ester, Ether, Phenylpropylamido, or Phenylpropylamino; whether or not further substituted in either of the following ways: (i) the substituent at the 1, 2, or 3 position of the carbazole ring system, disregarding the linkage, is further substituted to any extent (ii) further substitution on the carbazole ring system to any extent. This class includes, but is not limited to, the following: MDMB CHMCZCA, EG-018, and EG-2201.

r. Naphthoylnaphthalenes. Any compound structurally derived from naphthalene-1-yl-(naphthalene-1-yl) methanone with substitutions on either of the naphthalene rings to any extent. Substances in this class include, but are not limited to: CB-13.

(8) **Substituted phenethylamines.** -- This includes any compound, unless specifically excepted, specifically named or included in another subset in this schedule, or listed under a different schedule, structurally derived from phenylethan-2-amine by substitution on the phenyl ring in any of the following ways, that is to say, by substitution with a fused methylenedioxy ring, fused furan ring, or fused tetrahydrofuran ring; by substitution with two alkoxy groups; by substitution with one alkoxy and either one fused furan, tetrahydrofuran, or tetrahydropyran ring system; or by substitution with two fused ring systems from any combination of the furan, tetrahydrofuran, or tetrahydropyran ring systems. Whether or not the compound is further modified in any of the following ways, that is to say: (i) by substitution of phenyl ring by any halo, hydroxyl, alkyl, trifluoromethyl, alkoxy, or alylthio groups, (ii) by substitution at the 2-position by any alkyl groups, or (iii) by substitution at the 2-amino nitrogen atom with alkyl, dialkyl, benzyl, hydroxybenzyl, methylenedioxybenzyl, or methoxybenzyl groups. Substances in this class include, but are not limited to: 2C-I (4-Iodo-2,5-dimethoxyphenethylamine), APDB ((2-aminopropyl)-2,3-dihydrobenzofuran), MBDB (3,4-methylenedioxy-N-methylbutanamine), and 2C-I-NBOH (N-(2-hydroxybenzyl)-4-iodo-2,5-dimethoxyphenethylamine).

(9) **N-Benzyl phenethylamines.** -- Unless specifically excepted or listed in another schedule, or contained within a pharmaceutical product approved by the United States Food and Drug Administration, any material, compound, mixture, or preparation, including its salts, isomers (whether optical, geometric, or positional), esters, or ethers, and salts of isomers, esters, or ethers, whenever the existence of such salts is possible within any of the following specific chemical designations, any compound containing a phenethylamine structure without a beta-keto group, with substitution on the nitrogen atom of the amino group with a benzyl substituent, with or without substitution on the phenyl or benzyl ring to any extent with alkyl, alkoxy, thio, alkylthio, halide, fused alkylenedioxy, fused furan, fused benzofuran, or fused tetrahydropyran substituents, whether or not further substituted on a ring to any extent, with or without substitution at the alpha position by any alkyl substituent. Substances in this class include, but are not limited to: 25B-NBOH (4-bromo-2,5-dimethoxy-[N-(2-hydroxybenzyl)]phenethylamine), 25I-NBF (4-iodo-2,5-dimethoxy-[N-(2-fluorobenzyl)]phenethylamine), and 25C-NBMD (4-chloro-2,5-dimethoxy-[N-(2,3-methylenedioxybenzyl)]phenethyl amine).

History.
1971, c. 919, s. 1; 1973, c. 476, s. 128; c. 844; c. 1358, ss. 4, 5, 15; 1975, c. 443, s. 1; c. 790; 1977, c. 667, s. 3; c. 891, s. 1; 1979, c. 434, s. 1; 1981, c. 51, s. 9; 1983, c. 695, s. 1; 1985, c. 172, ss. 1-3; 1987, c. 412, ss. 1-5; 1989 (Reg. Sess., 1990), c. 1040, s. 1; 1993, c. 319, ss. 1, 2; 1995, c. 186, ss. 1 -3; c. 509, s. 135.1(c); 1997-456, ss. 12, 27; 1999-165, s. 1; 2000-140, s. 92.2(a); 2011-12, s. 1; 2011-326, s. 14(a), (b); 2015-162, s. 1; 2015-264, s. 13; 2017-115, s. 3; 2018-44, ss. 2, 3; 2021-155, s. 2

§ 90-89.1. Treatment of controlled substance analogues

A controlled substance analogue shall, to the extent intended for human consumption, be

Chapter 90

treated for the purposes of any State law as a controlled substance in Schedule I.

History.
2003-249, s. 1

§ 90-90. Schedule II controlled substances

This schedule includes the controlled substances listed or to be listed by whatever official name, common or usual name, chemical name, or trade name designated. In determining that a substance comes within this schedule, the Commission shall find: a high potential for abuse; currently accepted medical use in the United States, or currently accepted medical use with severe restrictions; and the abuse of the substance may lead to severe psychic or physical dependence. The following controlled substances are included in this schedule:

(1) Any of the following substances whether produced directly or indirectly by extraction from substances of vegetable origin, or independently by means of chemical synthesis, or by a combination of extraction and chemical synthesis, unless specifically excepted or unless listed in another schedule:

a. Opium, opiate, or opioid and any salt, compound, derivative, or preparation of opium and opiate, excluding apomorphine, nalbuphine, dextrorphan, naloxone, naltrexone and nalmefene, and their respective salts, but including the following:

1. Raw opium.
2. Opium extracts.
3. Opium fluid extracts.
4. Powdered opium.
5. Granulated opium.
6. Tincture of opium.
7. Codeine.
8. Ethylmorphine.
9. Etorphine hydrochloride.
10. Any material, compound, mixture, or preparation which contains any quantity of hydrocodone.
11. Hydromorphone.
12. Metopon.
13. Morphine.
14. Oxycodone.
15. Oxymorphone.
16. Thebaine.
17. Dihydroetorphine.

b. Any salt, compound, derivative, or preparation thereof which is chemically equivalent or identical with any of the substances referred to in paragraph 1 of this subdivision, except that these substances shall not include the isoquinoline alkaloids of opium.

c. Opium poppy and poppy straw.

d. Cocaine and any salt, isomer (whether optical or geometric), salts of isomers, compound, derivative, or preparation thereof, or coca leaves and any salt, isomer, salts of isomers, compound, derivative, or preparation of coca leaves, or any salt, isomer, salts of isomers, compound, derivative, or preparation thereof which is chemically equivalent or identical with any of these substances, except that the substances shall not include decocainized coca leaves or extraction of coca leaves, which extractions do not contain cocaine or ecgonine.

e. Concentrate of poppy straw (the crude extract of poppy straw in either liquid, solid or powder form which contains the phenanthrine alkaloids of the opium poppy).

(2) Any of the following opiates or opioids, including their isomers, esters, ethers, salts, and salts of isomers, whenever the existence of such isomers, esters, ethers, and salts is possible within the specific chemical designation unless specifically exempted or listed in other schedules:

a. Alfentanil.
b. Alphaprodine.
c. Anileridine.
d. Bezitramide.
e. Carfentanil.
f. Dihydrocodeine.
g. Diphenoxylate.
h. Fentanyl.
h1. Fentanyl immediate precursor chemical, 4-anilino-N-phenethyl-4-piperidine (ANPP).
h2. Norfentanyl (N-phenyl-N-(piperidin-4-yl) propionamide).
i. Isomethadone.
j. Levo-alphacetylmethadol. Some trade or other names: levo-alpha-acetylmethadol, levomethadyl acetate, or LAAM.
k. Levomethorphan.
l. Levorphanol.
m. Metazocine.
n. Methadone.
o. Methadone -- Intermediate, 4-cyano-2-dimethylamino-4, 4-diphenyl butane.
p. Moramide -- Intermediate, 2-methyl-3-morpholino-1, 1-diphenyl-propane-carboxylic acid.
q. Pethidine.
r. Pethidine -- Intermediate -- A, 4-cyano-1-methyl-4/y-phenylpiperidine.
s. Pethidine -- Intermediate -- B, ethyl-4-phenylpiperidine-4-carboxylate.

t. Pethidine -- Intermediate -- C, 1-m ethyl-4-phenylpiperidine-4-carboxylic acid.

u. Phenazocine.

v. Piminodine.

w. Racemethorphan.

x. Racemorphan.

y. Remifentanil.

z. Sufentanil.

aa. Tapentadol.

(3) Any material, compound, mixture, or preparation which contains any quantity of the following substances having a potential for abuse associated with a stimulant effect on the central nervous system unless specifically exempted or listed in another schedule:

a. Amphetamine, its salts, optical isomers, and salts of its optical isomers.

b. Phenmetrazine and its salts.

c. Methamphetamine, including its salts, isomers, and salts of isomers.

d. Methylphenidate, including its salts, isomers, and salts of its isomers.

e. Phenylacetone. Some trade or other names: Phenyl-2-propanone; P2P; benzyl methyl ketone; methyl benzyl ketone.

f. Lisdexamfetamine, including its salts, isomers, and salts of isomers.

(4) Any material, compound, mixture, or preparation which contains any quantity of the following substances having a depressant effect on the central nervous system, including its salts, isomers, and salts of isomers whenever the existence of such salts, isomers, and salts of isomers is possible within the specific chemical designation, unless specifically exempted by the Commission or listed in another schedule:

a. Amobarbital

b. Glutethimide

c. Repealed by Session Laws 1983, c. 695, s. 2.

d. Pentobarbital

e. Phencyclidine

f. Phencyclidine immediate precursors:

1. 1-Phenylcyclohexylamine

2. 1-Piperidinocyclohexanecarbo nitrile (PCC)

g. Secobarbital.

(5) Any material, compound, mixture, or preparation which contains any quantity of the following hallucinogenic substances, including their salts, isomers, and salts of isomers, unless specifically excepted, or listed in another schedule, whenever the existence of such salts, isomers, and salts of isomers is possible within the specific chemical designation:

a. Repealed by Session Laws 2001-233, s. 2(a), effective June 21, 2001.

b. Nabilone [Another name for nabilone: (+/-)-trans-3-(1,1-dimethylheptyl)-6,6a,7,8,10,10a-hexahyd ro-1-hydroxy-6,6-dimethyl-9H-dibenzo[b,d]pyran-9-one].

History.

1971, c. 919, s. 1; 1973, c. 476, s. 128; c. 540, s. 6; c. 1358, ss. 6, 15; 1975, c. 443, s. 2; 1977, c. 667, s. 3; c. 891, s. 2; 1979, c. 434, s. 2; 1981, c. 51, s. 9; 1983, c. 695, s. 2; 1985, c. 172, ss. 4, 5; 1987, c. 105, s. 3; c. 412, ss. 5A-7; 1989 (Reg. Sess., 1990), c. 1040, s. 2; 1993, c. 319, ss. 3, 4; 1995, c. 186, s. 4; 1997-385, s. 1; 1997-456, s. 27; 1999-165, s. 2; 2001-233, ss. 1, 2(a); 2011-326, s. 14(c), (d); 2015-162, s. 2; 2017-115, s. 4; 2018-44, s. 4; 2021-155, ss. 3, 4

§ 90-91. Schedule III controlled substances

This schedule includes the controlled substances listed or to be listed by whatever official name, common or usual name, chemical name, or trade name designated. In determining that a substance comes within this schedule, the Commission shall find: a potential for abuse less than the substances listed in Schedules I and II; currently accepted medical use in the United States; and abuse may lead to moderate or low physical dependence or high psychological dependence. The following controlled substances are included in this schedule:

(a) Repealed by Session Laws 1973, c. 540, s. 5.

(b) Any material, compound, mixture, or preparation which contains any quantity of the following substances having a depressant effect on the central nervous system unless specifically exempted or listed in another schedule:

1. Any substance which contains any quantity of a derivative of barbituric acid, or any salt of a derivative of barbituric acid.

2. Chlorhexadol.

3. Repealed by Session Laws 1993, c. 319, s. 5.

4. Lysergic acid.

5. Lysergic acid amide.

6. Methyprylon.

7. Sulfondiethylmethane.

8. Sulfonethylmethane.

9. Sulfonmethane.

9a. Tiletamine and zolazepam or any salt thereof. Some trade or other names for tiletamine-zolazepam combination product: Telazol. Some trade or other names for tiletamine:

2-(ethylamino)-2-(2-thienyl)-cyclohexanone. Some trade or

other names for zolazepam:
4-(2-fluorophenyl)-6,8-dihydro-
1,3,8-trimethylpyrazolo-[3,4-e]
[1,4]-diazepin-7(1H)-one.
flupyrazapon.

10. Any compound, mixture or preparation containing

    (i) Amobarbital.

    (ii) Secobarbital.

    (iii) Pentobarbital.

    or any salt thereof and one or more active ingredients which are not included in any other schedule.

11. Any suppository dosage form containing

    (i) Amobarbital.

    (ii) Secobarbital.

    (iii) Pentobarbital.

    or any salt of any of these drugs and approved by the federal Food and Drug Administration for marketing as a suppository.

12. Ketamine.

(c) Nalorphine.

(d) Any material, compound, mixture, or preparation containing limited quantities of any of the following narcotic drugs, or any salts thereof unless specifically exempted or listed in another schedule:

1. Not more than 1.80 grams of codeine per 100 milliliters or not more than 90 milligrams per dosage unit with an equal or greater quantity of an isoquinoline alkaloid of opium.

2. Not more than 1.80 grams of codeine per 100 milliliters or not more than 90 milligrams per dosage unit, with one or more active, nonnarcotic ingredients in recognized therapeutic amounts.

3., 4. Repealed by Session Laws 2017-115, s. 5, effective December 1, 2017, and applicable to offenses committed on or after that date.

5. Not more than 1.80 grams of dihydrocodeine per 100 milliliters or not more than 90 milligrams per dosage unit, with one or more active, nonnarcotic ingredients in recognized therapeutic amounts.

6. Not more than 300 milligrams of ethylmorphine per 100 milliliters or not more than 15 milligrams per dosage unit, with one or more active, nonnarcotic ingredients in recognized therapeutic amounts.

7. Not more than 500 milligrams of opium per 100 milliliters or per 100 grams, or not more than 25 milligrams per dosage unit, with one or more active, nonnarcotic ingredients in recognized therapeutic amounts.

8. Not more than 50 milligrams of morphine per 100 milliliters or per 100 grams with one or more active, nonnarcotic ingredients in recognized therapeutic amounts.

9. Buprenorphine.

(e) Any compound, mixture or preparation containing limited quantities of the following narcotic drugs, which shall include one or more active, nonnarcotic, medicinal ingredients in sufficient proportion to confer upon the compound, mixture, or preparation, valuable medicinal qualities other than those possessed by the narcotic drug alone:

1. Paregoric, U.S.P.; provided, that no person shall purchase or receive by any means whatsoever more than one fluid ounce of paregoric within a consecutive 24-hour period, except on prescription issued by a duly licensed physician.

(f) Paregoric, U.S.P., may be dispensed at retail as permitted by federal law or administrative regulation without a prescription only by a registered pharmacist and no other person, agency or employee may dispense paregoric, U.S.P., even if under the direct supervision of a pharmacist.

(g) Notwithstanding the provisions of G.S. 90-91(f), after the pharmacist has fulfilled his professional responsibilities and legal responsibilities required of him in this Article, the actual cash transaction, credit transaction, or delivery of paregoric, U.S.P., may be completed by a nonpharmacist. A pharmacist may refuse to dispense a paregoric, U.S.P., substance until he is satisfied that the product is being obtained for medicinal purposes only.

(h) Paregoric, U.S.P., may only be sold at retail without a prescription to a person at least 18 years of age. A pharmacist must require every retail purchaser of a paregoric, U.S.P., substance to furnish suitable identification, including proof of age when appropriate, in order to purchase paregoric, U.S.P. The name and address obtained from such identification shall be entered in the record of disposition to consumers.

(i) The Commission may by regulation except any compound, mixture, or preparation containing any stimulant or depressant substance listed in paragraphs (a)1 and (a)2 of this schedule from the application of all or any part of this Article if the compound, mixture, or preparation contains one or more active medicinal ingredients not having a stimulant or depressant effect on the central nervous system; and if the ingredients are included therein in such combinations, quantity, proportion, or concentration that vitiate the potential for abuse of the substances which have a stimulant or depressant effect on the central nervous system.

(j) Any material, compound, mixture, or preparation which contains any quantity of the following substances having a stimulant effect on the central nervous system, including its salts, isomers (whether optical, positional, or geometric), and salts of said isomers whenever the existence of such salts, isomers, and salts of isomers is possible within the specific chemical designation, unless specifically excluded or listed in some other schedule.

1. Benzphetamine.

2. Chlorphentermine.

3. Clortermine.

4. Repealed by Session Laws 1987, c. 412, s. 10.

5. Phendimetrazine.

(k) Anabolic steroids. The term "anabolic steroid" means any drug or hormonal substance, chemically and pharmacologically related to testosterone (other than estrogens, progestins, and corticosteroids) that promotes muscle growth, including, but not limited to, the following:

1. Methandrostenolone,

2. Stanozolol,

3. Ethylestrenol,

4. Nandrolone phenpropionate,

5. Nandrolone decanoate,

6. Testosterone propionate,

7. Chorionic gonadotropin,

8. Boldenone,

8a. Boldione,

9. Chlorotestosterone (4-chlorotestosterone),

10. Clostebol,

11. Dehydrochlormethyltestosterone,

11a. Desoxymethyltesterone (17[alpha]-methyl-5[alpha]-androst-2-en-17[beta]-ol) (also known as madol),

12. Dibydrostestosterone (4-dihydrotestosterone),

13. Drostanolone,

14. Fluoxymesterone,

15. Formebulone (formebolone),

16. Mesterolene,

17. Methandienone,

18. Methandranone,

19. Methandriol,

19a. Methasterone,

20. Methenolene,

21. Methyltestosterone,

22. Mibolerone,

23. Nandrolene,

24. Norethandrolene,

25. Oxandrolone,

26. Oxymesterone,

27. Oxymetholone,

28. Stanolone,

29. Testolactone,

30. Testosterone,

31. Trenbolone,

31a. 19-nor-4,9(10)-androstadienedione (estra-4,9(10)-diene-3,17-dione), and

32. Any salt, ester, or isomer of a drug or substance described or listed in this subsection, if that salt, ester, or isomer promotes muscle growth. Except such term does not include (i) an anabolic steroid which is expressly intended for administration through implants to cattle or other nonhuman species and which has been approved by the Secretary of Health and Human Services for such administration or (ii) chorionic gonadotropin when administered by injection for veterinary use by a licensed veterinarian or the veterinarian's designated agent. If any person prescribes, dispenses, or distributes such steroid for human use, such person shall be considered to have prescribed, dispensed, or distributed an anabolic steroid within the meaning of this subsection.

(l) Repealed by Session Laws 2001-233, s. 3(a), effective June 21, 2001.

(m) Any drug product containing gamma hydroxybutyric acid, including its salts, isomers, and salts of isomers, for which an application is approved under section 505 of the Federal Food, Drug, and Cosmetic Act.

(n) Dronabinol (synthetic) in sesame oil and encapsulated in a soft gelatin capsule in a U.S. Food and Drug Administration approved drug product. [Some other names: (6aR-trans), -6a,7,8,10a-tetrahydro-6,6,9-tri methyl-3-pentyl-6H-dibenzo [b,d]pyran-1-o1 or (-)-delta-9-(trans)-tetrahydrocannabinol].

History.

1971, c. 919, s. 1; 1973, c. 476, s. 128; c. 540, s. 5; c. 1358, ss. 7, 15; 1975, c. 442; 1977, c. 667, s. 3; 1979, c. 434, s. 3; 1981, c. 51, s. 9; 1987, c. 412, ss. 8-10; 1987 (Reg. Sess., 1988), c. 1055; 1991, c. 413, s. 1; 1993, c. 319, s. 5; 1999-370, s. 3; 2000-140, s. 92.2(b); 2001-233, ss. 2(b), 3(a), 3(b); 2011-326, s. 14(e); 2016-113, s. 9; 2017-115, s. 5; 2021-155, s. 5

§ 90-92. Schedule IV controlled substances

(a) This schedule includes the controlled substances listed or to be listed by whatever official name, common or usual name, chemical name, or trade name designated. In determining that a substance comes within this schedule, the Commission shall find: a low potential for abuse relative to the substances listed in Schedule III of this Article; currently accepted medical use in the United States; and limited physical or pyschological dependence relative to the substances listed in Schedule III of this Article. The following controlled substances are included in this schedule:

(1) **Depressants.** -- Unless specifically excepted or unless listed in another schedule, any material, compound, mixture, or preparation which contains any quantity of the following substances, including its salts, isomers, and salts of isomers whenever the existence of such salts, isomers, and salts of isomers is possible within the specific chemical designation:

a. Alprazolam.
b. Barbital.
c. Bromazepam.
d. Camazepam.
d1. Carisoprodol.
e. Chloral betaine.
f. Chloral hydrate.
g. Chlordiazepoxide.
h. Clobazam.
i. Clonazepam.
j. Clorazepate.
k. Clotiazepam.
l. Cloxazolam.
m. Delorazepam.
m1. Desalkylflurazepam.
n. Diazepam.
n1. Dichloralphenazone.
n2. Diclazepam.
o. Estazolam.
p. Ethchlorvynol.
q. Ethinamate.
r. Ethyl loflazepate.
s. Fludiazepam.
t. Flunitrazepam.
u. Flurazepam.
u1. Fospropol.
v. Repealed by Session Laws 2000, c. 140, s. 92.2(c), effective December 1, 2000.
w. Halazepam.
x. Haloxazolam.
y. Ketazolam.
z. Loprazolam.
aa. Lorazepam.
bb. Lormetazepam.
cc. Mebutamate.
dd. Medazepam.
ee. Meprobamate.
ff. Methohexital.
gg. Methylphenobarbital (mephobarbital).
hh. Midazolam.
ii. Nimetazepam.
jj. Nitrazepam.
kk. Nordiazepam.
ll. Oxazepam.
mm. Oxazolam.
nn. Paraldehyde.
oo. Petrichloral.
pp. Phenobarbital.

qq. Pinazepam.
rr. Prazepam.
ss. Quazepam.
tt. Temazepam.
uu. Tetrazepam.
vv. Triazolam.
ww. Zolpidem.
xx. Zaleplon.
yy. Zopiclone.
zz. **Designer benzodiazepines.** -- Unless specifically excepted or listed in another schedule, or contained within a pharmaceutical product approved by the United States Food and Drug Administration, any material, compound, derivative, mixture, or preparation, including its salts, isomers, salts of isomers, halogen analogues, or homologues, whenever the existence of such salts, isomers, or salts of isomers, halogen analogues, or homologues is possible within the specific chemical designation, structurally derived from 1,4 benzodiazepine by substitution at the 5 position with a phenyl ring system (which may be further substituted), whether or not the compound is further modified in any of the following ways:

1. By substitution at the 2 position with a ketone;
2. By substitution at the 3 position with a hydroxyl group or ester group, which itself may be further substituted;
3. By a fused triazole ring at the 1,2 position, which itself may be further substituted;
4. By a fused imidazole ring at the 1,2 position, which itself may be further substituted;
5. By a fused oxazolidine ring at the 4,5 position, which itself may be further substituted;
6. By a fused oxazine ring at the 4,5 position, which itself may be further substituted;
7. By substitution at the 7 position with a nitro group;
8. By substitution at the 7 position with a halogen group; or
9. By substitution at the 1 position with an alkyl group, which itself may be further substituted.

(2) Any material, compound, mixture, or preparation which contains any of the following substances, including its salts, or isomers and salts of such isomers, whenever the existence of such salts, isomers, and salts of isomers is possible:

a. Fenfluramine. For this compound, the term "isomer" includes the optical, positional, or geometric isomer.

b. Pentazocine.

(3) **Stimulants.** -- Unless specifically excepted or unless listed in another schedule, any material, compound, mixture, or preparation which contains any quantity of the following substances having a stimulant effect on the central nervous system, including its salts, isomers (whether optical, position, or geometric), and salts of such isomers whenever the existence of such salts, isomers, and salts of isomers is possible within the specific chemical designation:

a. Diethylpropion.

b. Mazindol.

c. Pemoline (including organometallic complexes and chelates thereof).

d. Phentermine.

e. Cathine.

f. Fencamfamin.

g. Fenproporex.

h. Mefenorex.

i. Sibutramine.

j. Modafinil.

(4) **Other Substances.** -- Unless specifically excepted or unless listed in another schedule, any material, compound, mixture or preparation which contains any quantity of the following substances, including its salts:

a. Dextropropoxyphene (Alpha-(plus)-4-dimethylamino-1, 2-diphenyl-3-methyl-2-propionoxybutane).

b. Pipradrol.

c. SPA ((-)-1-dimethylamino-1, 2-diphenylethane).

d. Butorphanol.

(5) **Narcotic Drugs.** -- Unless specifically excepted or unless listed in another schedule, any material, compound, mixture, or preparation containing limited quantities of any of the following narcotic drugs, or any salts thereof:

a. Not more than 1 milligram of difenoxin and not less than 25 micrograms of atropine sulfate per dosage unit.

b. Repealed by Session Laws 2017-115, s. 6, effective December 1, 2017, and applicable to offenses committed on or after that date.

c. 2-[(dimethylamino)methyl]-1-(3-methoxyphenyl)cyclohexanol, its salts, optical and geometric isomers, and salts of these isomers (including tramadol).

(b) The Commission may by regulation except any compound, mixture, or preparation containing any stimulant or depressant substance listed in this schedule from the application of all or any part of this Article if the compound, mixture, or preparation contains one or more active, nonnarcotic, medicinal ingredients not

having a stimulant or depressant effect on the central nervous system; provided, that such admixtures shall be included therein in such combinations, quantity, proportion, or concentration as to vitiate the potential for abuse of the substances which do have a stimulant or depressant effect on the central nervous system.

History.

1971, c. 919, s. 1; 1973, c. 476, s. 128; c. 1358, ss. 8, 15; c. 1446, s. 5; 1975, cc. 401, 819; 1977, c. 667, s. 3; c. 891, s. 3; 1979, c. 434, ss. 4-6; 1981, c. 51, s. 9; 1985, c. 172, ss. 6-8; c. 439, s. 1; 1987, c. 412, ss. 11, 12; 1993, c. 319, s. 6; 1995, c. 509, s. 38; 1997-456, s. 27; 1997-501, s. 1; 1999-165, s. 3; 2000-140, s. 92.2(c); 2001-233, s. 4; 2017-115, s. 6; 2017-212, s. 8.8(a), (b); 2021-155, s. 6

§ 90-93. Schedule V controlled substances

(a) This schedule includes the controlled substances listed or to be listed by whatever official name, common or usual name, chemical name, or trade name designated. In determining that a substance comes within this schedule, the Commission shall find: a low potential for abuse relative to the substances listed in Schedule IV of this Article; currently accepted medical use in the United States; and limited physical or psychological dependence relative to the substances listed in Schedule IV of this Article. The following controlled substances are included in this schedule:

(1) Any compound, mixture or preparation containing any of the following limited quantities of narcotic drugs or salts thereof, which shall include one or more nonnarcotic active medicinal ingredients in sufficient proportion to confer upon the compound, mixture, or preparation valuable medicinal qualities other than those possessed by the narcotic alone:

a. Not more than 200 milligrams of codeine or any of its salts per 100 milliliters or per 100 grams.

b. Not more than 100 milligrams of dihydrocodeine or any of its salts per 100 milliliters or per 100 grams.

c. Not more than 100 milligrams of ethylmorphine or any of its salts per 100 milliliters or per 100 grams.

d. Not more than 2.5 milligrams of diphenoxylate and not less than 25 micrograms of atropine sulfate per dosage unit.

e. Not more than 100 milligrams of opium per 100 milliliters or per 100 grams.

f. Not more than 0.5 milligram of difenoxin and not less than 25 micrograms of atropine sulfate per dosage unit.

(2) Repealed by Session Laws 1985, c. 172, s. 9.

(3) **Stimulants.** -- Unless specifically exempted or excluded or unless listed in another schedule, any material, compound, mixture, or preparation which contains any quantity of the following substances having a stimulant effect on the central nervous system, including its salts, isomers and salts of isomers:

    a. Repealed by Session Laws 1993, c. 319, s. 7.

    b. Pyrovalerone.

(4) **Anticonvulsants.** -- Unless specifically exempted or excluded or unless listed in another schedule, any material, compound, mixture, or preparation which contains any quantity of the following substances having a stimulant effect on the central nervous system, including its salts, isomers, and salts of isomers:

    a. Ezogabine.

    b. Lacosamide.

    c. Brivaracetam.

    d. Pregabalin.

    e. Cenobamate.

    f. Lasmiditan.

(b) A Schedule V substance may be sold at retail without a prescription only by a registered pharmacist and no other person, agent or employee may sell a Schedule V substance even if under the direct supervision of a pharmacist.

(c) Notwithstanding the provisions of G.S. 90-93(b), after the pharmacist has fulfilled the responsibilities required of him in this Article, the actual cash transaction, credit transaction, or delivery of a Schedule V substance, may be completed by a nonpharmacist. A pharmacist may refuse to sell a Schedule V substance until he is satisfied that the product is being obtained for medicinal purposes only.

(d) A Schedule V substance may be sold at retail without a prescription only to a person at least 18 years of age. The pharmacist must require every retail purchaser of a Schedule V substance to furnish suitable identification, including proof of age when appropriate, in order to purchase a Schedule V substance. The name and address obtained from such identification shall be entered in the record of disposition to consumers.

History.

1971, c. 919, s. 1; 1973, c. 476, s. 128; c. 1358, ss. 9, 15; 1977, c. 667, s. 3; 1979, c. 434, ss. 7, 8; 1981, c. 51, s. 9; 1985, c. 172, s. 9; 1989 (Reg. Sess., 1990), c. 1040, s. 3; 1993, c. 319, s. 7; 1997-456, s. 27; 2017-115, s. 7; 2021-155, s. 8.5

§ 90-94. Schedule VI controlled substances

This schedule includes the controlled substances listed or to be listed by whatever official name, common or usual name, chemical name, or trade name designated. In determining that such substance comes within this schedule, the Commission shall find: no currently accepted medical use in the United States, or a relatively low potential for abuse in terms of risk to public health and potential to produce psychic or physiological dependence liability based upon present medical knowledge, or a need for further and continuing study to develop scientific evidence of its pharmacological effects.

The following controlled substances are included in this schedule:

(1) Marijuana.

(2) Tetrahydrocannabinols.

(3) Repealed by Session Laws 2017-115, s. 8, effective December 1, 2017, and applicable to offenses committed on or after that date.

History.

1971, c. 919, s. 1; 1973, c. 476, s. 128; c. 1358, s. 15; 1977, c. 667, s. 3; 1981, c. 51, s. 9; 1997-456, s. 27; 2011-12, s. 5; 2013-109, s. 1; 2015-162, s. 3; 2015-264, s. 48(a); 2017-115, s. 8

§ 90-94.1. Exemption for use or possession of hemp extract

(a) As used in this section, "hemp extract" means an extract from a cannabis plant, or a mixture or preparation containing cannabis plant material, that has all of the following characteristics:

(1) Is composed of less than nine-tenths of one percent (0.9%) tetrahydrocannabinol by weight.

(2) Is composed of at least five percent (5%) cannabidiol by weight.

(3) Contains no other psychoactive substance.

(b) Notwithstanding any other provision of this Chapter, an individual may possess or use hemp extract, and is not subject to the penalties described in this Chapter, if the individual satisfies all of the following criteria:

(1) Possesses or uses the hemp extract only to treat intractable epilepsy, as defined in G.S. 90-113.101.

(2) Possesses, in close proximity to the hemp extract, a certificate of analysis that indicates the hemp extract's ingredients, including its percentages of tetrahydrocannabinol and cannabidiol by weight.

(3) Is a caregiver, as defined in G.S. 90-113.101.

(c) Notwithstanding any other provision of this Chapter, an individual who possesses hemp extract lawfully under this section may administer hemp extract to another person under the individual's care and is not subject to the penalties described in this Chapter for administering the hemp extract to the person if the individual is the person's caregiver, as defined in G.S. 90-113.101.

(d) Any individual who possesses or uses hemp extract, as defined under this section, shall dispose of all residual oil from the extract at a secure collection box managed by a law enforcement agency. No criminal penalty shall attach for any violation of this subsection.

History.
2014-53, s. 3; 2015-154, s. 1; 2018-36, s. 1

§ 90-95. Violations; penalties

(a) Except as authorized by this Article, it is unlawful for any person:

   (1) To manufacture, sell or deliver, or possess with intent to manufacture, sell or deliver, a controlled substance;

   (2) To create, sell or deliver, or possess with intent to sell or deliver, a counterfeit controlled substance;

   (3) To possess a controlled substance.

(b) Except as provided in subsections (h) and (i) of this section, any person who violates G.S. 90-95(a)(1) with respect to:

   (1) A controlled substance classified in Schedule I or II shall be punished as a Class H felon, except as follows: (i) the sale of a controlled substance classified in Schedule I or II shall be punished as a Class G felony, and (ii) the manufacture of methamphetamine shall be punished as provided by subdivision (1a) of this subsection.

   (1a) The manufacture of methamphetamine shall be punished as a Class C felony unless the offense was one of the following: packaging or repackaging methamphetamine, or labeling or relabeling the methamphetamine container. The offense of packaging or repackaging methamphetamine, or labeling or relabeling the methamphetamine container shall be punished as a Class H felony.

   (2) A controlled substance classified in Schedule III, IV, V, or VI shall be punished as a Class I felon, except that the sale of a controlled substance classified in Schedule III, IV, V, or VI shall be punished as a Class H felon. The transfer of less than 5 grams of marijuana for no remuneration shall not constitute a delivery in violation of G.S. 90-95(a)(1).

(c) Any person who violates G.S. 90-95(a)(2) shall be punished as a Class I felon.

(d) Except as provided in subsections (h) and (i) of this section, any person who violates G.S. 90-95(a)(3) with respect to:

   (1) A controlled substance classified in Schedule I shall be punished as a Class I felon. However, if the controlled substance is MDPV and the quantity of the MDPV is 1 gram or less, the violation shall be punishable as a Class 1 misdemeanor.

   (2) A controlled substance classified in Schedule II, III, or IV shall be guilty of a Class 1 misdemeanor. If the controlled substance exceeds four tablets, capsules, or other dosage units or equivalent quantity of hydromorphone or if the quantity of the controlled substance, or combination of the controlled substances, exceeds one hundred tablets, capsules or other dosage units, or equivalent quantity, the violation shall be punishable as a Class I felony. If the controlled substance is methamphetamine, amphetamine, phencyclidine, cocaine, fentanyl, or carfentanil and any salt, isomer, salts of isomers, compound, derivative, or preparation thereof, or coca leaves and any salt, isomer, salts of isomers, compound, derivative, or preparation of coca leaves, or any salt, isomer, salts of isomers, compound, derivative or preparation thereof which is chemically equivalent or identical with any of these substances (except decocanized coca leaves or any extraction of coca leaves which does not contain cocaine or ecgonine), the violation shall be punishable as a Class I felony.

   (3) A controlled substance classified in Schedule V shall be guilty of a Class 2 misdemeanor;

   (4) A controlled substance classified in Schedule VI shall be guilty of a Class 3 misdemeanor, but any sentence of imprisonment imposed must be suspended and the judge may not require at the time of sentencing that the defendant serve a period of imprisonment as a special condition of probation. If the quantity of the controlled substance exceeds one-half of an ounce (avoirdupois) of marijuana or one-twentieth of an ounce (avoirdupois) of the extracted resin of marijuana, commonly known as hashish, the violation shall be punishable as a Class 1 misdemeanor. If the quantity of the controlled substance exceeds one and one-half ounces (avoirdupois) of marijuana, or three-twentieths of an ounce (avoirdupois) of the extracted resin of marijuana, commonly known as hashish, or if the controlled substance consists of any quantity of synthetic tetrahydrocannabinols or tetrahydrocannabinols isolated from the resin of marijuana, the violation shall be punishable as a Class I felony.

(d1) (1) Except as authorized by this Article, it is unlawful for any person to:

   a. Possess an immediate precursor chemical with intent to manufacture a controlled substance; or

   b. Possess or distribute an immediate precursor chemical knowing, or having reasonable cause to believe, that the immediate precursor chemical will be used to manufacture a controlled substance; or

c. Possess a pseudoephedrine product if the person has a prior conviction for the possession of methamphetamine, possession with the intent to sell or deliver methamphetamine, sell or deliver methamphetamine, trafficking methamphetamine, possession of an immediate precursor chemical, or manufacture of methamphetamine. The prior conviction may be from any jurisdiction within the United States.

Except where the conduct is covered under subdivision (2) of this subsection, any person who violates this subdivision shall be punished as a Class H felon.

(2) Except as authorized by this Article, it is unlawful for any person to:

a. Possess an immediate precursor chemical with intent to manufacture methamphetamine; or

b. Possess or distribute an immediate precursor chemical knowing, or having reasonable cause to believe, that the immediate precursor chemical will be used to manufacture methamphetamine.

Any person who violates this subdivision shall be punished as a Class F felon.

(d2) The immediate precursor chemicals to which subsection (d1) of this section applies are those immediate precursor chemicals designated by the Commission pursuant to its authority under G.S. 90-88, and the following (until otherwise specified by the Commission):

(1) Acetic anhydride.
(2) Acetone.
(2a) Ammonium nitrate.
(2b) Ammonium sulfate.
(3) Anhydrous ammonia.
(4) Anthranilic acid.
(5) Benzyl chloride.
(6) Benzyl cyanide.
(7) 2-Butanone (Methyl Ethyl Ketone).
(8) Chloroephedrine.
(9) Chloropseudoephedrine.
(10) D-lysergic acid.
(11) Ephedrine.
(12) Ergonovine maleate.
(13) Ergotamine tartrate.
(13a) Ether based starting fluids.
(14) Ethyl ether.
(15) Ethyl Malonate.
(16) Ethylamine.
(17) Gamma-butyrolactone.
(18) Hydrochloric Acid. (Muriatic Acid).
(19) Iodine.
(20) Isosafrole.
(21) Sources of lithium metal.
(22) Malonic acid.
(23) Methylamine.
(24) Methyl Isobutyl Ketone.
(25) N-acetylanthranilic acid.
(26) N-ethylephedrine.
(27) N-ethylpseudoephedrine.
(28) N-methylephedrine.
(29) N-methylpseudoephedrine.
(29a) N-phenethyl-4-piperidinone (NPP).
(30) Norpseudoephedrine.
(30a) Petroleum based organic solvents such as camping fuels and lighter fluids.
(31) Phenyl-2-propanone.
(32) Phenylacetic acid.
(33) Phenylpropanolamine.
(34) Piperidine.
(35) Piperonal.
(36) Propionic anhydride.
(37) Pseudoephedrine.
(38) Pyrrolidine.
(39) Red phosphorous.
(40) Safrole.
(40a) Sodium hydroxide (Lye).
(41) Sources of sodium metal.
(42) Sulfuric Acid.
(43) Tetrachloroethylene.
(44) Thionylchloride.
(45) Toluene.

(e) The prescribed punishment and degree of any offense under this Article shall be subject to the following conditions, but the punishment for an offense may be increased only by the maximum authorized under any one of the applicable conditions:

(1), (2) Repealed by Session Laws 1979, c. 760, s. 5.

(3) If any person commits a Class 1 misdemeanor under this Article and if he has previously been convicted for one or more offenses under any law of North Carolina or any law of the United States or any other state, which offenses are punishable under any provision of this Article, he shall be punished as a Class I felon. The prior conviction used to raise the current offense to a Class I felony shall not be used to calculate the prior record level.

(4) If any person commits a Class 2 misdemeanor, and if he has previously been convicted for one or more offenses under any law of North Carolina or any law of the United States or any other state, which offenses are punishable under any provision of this Article, he shall be guilty of a Class 1 misdemeanor. The prior conviction used to raise the current offense to a Class 1 misdemeanor shall not be used to calculate the prior conviction level.

(5) Any person 18 years of age or over who violates G.S. 90-95(a)(1) by selling or delivering a controlled substance to a person under 16 years of age but more than 13 years of age or a pregnant female shall be punished as a Class D felon. Any person 18 years of age or over who violates G.S. 90-95(a)(1) by selling or delivering a controlled

Chapter 90

substance to a person who is 13 years of age or younger shall be punished as a Class C felon. Mistake of age is not a defense to a prosecution under this section. It shall not be a defense that the defendant did not know that the recipient was pregnant.

(6) For the purpose of increasing punishment under G.S. 90-95(e)(3) and (e)(4), previous convictions for offenses shall be counted by the number of separate trials at which final convictions were obtained and not by the number of charges at a single trial.

(7) If any person commits an offense under this Article for which the prescribed punishment requires that any sentence of imprisonment be suspended, and if he has previously been convicted for one or more offenses under any law of North Carolina or any law of the United States or any other state, which offenses are punishable under any provision of this Article, he shall be guilty of a Class 2 misdemeanor.

(8) Any person 21 years of age or older who commits an offense under G.S. 90-95(a)(1) on property used for a child care center, or for an elementary or secondary school or within 1,000 feet of the boundary of real property used for a child care center, or for an elementary or secondary school shall be punished as a Class E felon. For purposes of this subdivision, the transfer of less than five grams of marijuana for no remuneration shall not constitute a delivery in violation of G.S. 90-95(a)(1). For purposes of this subdivision, a child care center is as defined in G.S. 110-86(3)a., and that is licensed by the Secretary of the Department of Health and Human Services.

(9) Any person who violates G.S. 90-95(a)(3) on the premises of a penal institution or local confinement facility shall be guilty of a Class H felony.

(10) Any person 21 years of age or older who commits an offense under G.S. 90-95(a)(1) on property that is a public park or within 1,000 feet of the boundary of real property that is a public park shall be punished as a Class E felon. For purposes of this subdivision, the transfer of less than five grams of marijuana for no remuneration shall not constitute a delivery in violation of G.S. 90-95(a)(1).

(f) Any person convicted of an offense or offenses under this Article who is sentenced to an active term of imprisonment that is less than the maximum active term that could have been imposed may, in addition, be sentenced to a term of special probation. Except as indicated in this subsection, the administration of special probation shall be the same as probation. The conditions of special probation shall be fixed in the same manner as probation, and the conditions

may include requirements for rehabilitation treatment. Special probation shall follow the active sentence. No term of special probation shall exceed five years. Special probation may be revoked in the same manner as probation; upon revocation, the original term of imprisonment may be increased by no more than the difference between the active term of imprisonment actually served and the maximum active term that could have been imposed at trial for the offense or offenses for which the person was convicted, and the resulting term of imprisonment need not be diminished by the time spent on special probation.

(g) Whenever matter is submitted to the North Carolina State Crime Laboratory, the Charlotte, North Carolina, Police Department Laboratory or to the Toxicology Laboratory, Reynolds Health Center, Winston-Salem for chemical analysis to determine if the matter is or contains a controlled substance, the report of that analysis certified to upon a form approved by the Attorney General by the person performing the analysis shall be admissible without further authentication and without the testimony of the analyst in all proceedings in the district court and superior court divisions of the General Court of Justice as evidence of the identity, nature, and quantity of the matter analyzed. Provided, however, the provisions of this subsection may be utilized by the State only if:

(1) The State notifies the defendant at least 15 business days before the proceeding at which the report would be used of its intention to introduce the report into evidence under this subsection and provides a copy of the report to the defendant, and

(2) The defendant fails to file a written objection with the court, with a copy to the State, at least five business days before the proceeding that the defendant objects to the introduction of the report into evidence.

If the defendant's attorney of record, or the defendant if that person has no attorney, fails to file a written objection as provided in this subsection, then the objection shall be deemed waived and the report shall be admitted into evidence without the testimony of the analyst. Upon filing a timely objection, the admissibility of the report shall be determined and governed by the appropriate rules of evidence.

Nothing in this subsection precludes the right of any party to call any witness or to introduce any evidence supporting or contradicting the evidence contained in the report.

(g1) **Procedure for establishing chain of custody without calling unnecessary witnesses. --**

(1) For the purpose of establishing the chain of physical custody or control of

evidence consisting of or containing a substance tested or analyzed to determine whether it is a controlled substance, a statement signed by each successive person in the chain of custody that the person delivered it to the other person indicated on or about the date stated is prima facie evidence that the person had custody and made the delivery as stated, without the necessity of a personal appearance in court by the person signing the statement.

(2) The statement shall contain a sufficient description of the material or its container so as to distinguish it as the particular item in question and shall state that the material was delivered in essentially the same condition as received. The statement may be placed on the same document as the report provided for in subsection (g) of this section.

(3) The provisions of this subsection may be utilized by the State only if:

a. The State notifies the defendant at least 15 days before trial of its intention to introduce the statement into evidence under this subsection and provides the defendant with a copy of the statement, and

b. The defendant fails to notify the State at least five days before trial that the defendant objects to the introduction of the statement into evidence.

If the defendant's attorney of record, or the defendant if that person has no attorney, fails to file a written objection as provided in this subsection, then the objection shall be deemed waived and the statement shall be admitted into evidence without the necessity of a personal appearance by the person signing the statement. Upon filing a timely objection, the admissibility of the report shall be determined and governed by the appropriate rules of evidence.

(4) Nothing in this subsection precludes the right of any party to call any witness or to introduce any evidence supporting or contradicting the evidence contained in the statement.

(h) Notwithstanding any other provision of law, the following provisions apply except as otherwise provided in this Article:

(1) Any person who sells, manufactures, delivers, transports, or possesses in excess of 10 pounds (avoirdupois) of marijuana shall be guilty of a felony which felony shall be known as "trafficking in marijuana" and if the quantity of such substance involved:

a. Is in excess of 10 pounds, but less than 50 pounds, such person shall be punished as a Class H felon and shall be sentenced to a minimum term of 25

months and a maximum term of 39 months in the State's prison and shall be fined not less than five thousand dollars ($ 5,000);

b. Is 50 pounds or more, but less than 2,000 pounds, such person shall be punished as a Class G felon and shall be sentenced to a minimum term of 35 months and a maximum term of 51 months in the State's prison and shall be fined not less than twenty-five thousand dollars ($ 25,000);

c. Is 2,000 pounds or more, but less than 10,000 pounds, such person shall be punished as a Class F felon and shall be sentenced to a minimum term of 70 months and a maximum term of 93 months in the State's prison and shall be fined not less than fifty thousand dollars ($ 50,000);

d. Is 10,000 pounds or more, such person shall be punished as a Class D felon and shall be sentenced to a minimum term of 175 months and a maximum term of 222 months in the State's prison and shall be fined not less than two hundred thousand dollars ($ 200,000).

(1a) For the purpose of this subsection, a "dosage unit" shall consist of 3 grams of synthetic cannabinoid or any mixture containing such substance. Any person who sells, manufactures, delivers, transports, or possesses in excess of 50 dosage units of a synthetic cannabinoid or any mixture containing such substance, shall be guilty of a felony, which felony shall be known as "trafficking in synthetic cannabinoids," and if the quantity of such substance involved:

a. Is in excess of 50 dosage units, but less than 250 dosage units, such person shall be punished as a Class H felon and shall be sentenced to a minimum term of 25 months and a maximum term of 39 months in the State's prison and shall be fined not less than five thousand dollars ($ 5,000);

b. Is 250 dosage units or more, but less than 1250 dosage units, such person shall be punished as a Class G felon and shall be sentenced to a minimum term of 35 months and a maximum term of 51 months in the State's prison and shall be fined not less than twenty-five thousand dollars ($ 25,000);

c. Is 1250 dosage units or more, but less than 3750 dosage units, such person shall be punished as a Class F felon and shall be sentenced to a minimum term of 70 months and a maximum term of 93 months in the State's prison and shall be fined not less than fifty thousand dollars ($ 50,000);

d. Is 3750 dosage units or more, such person shall be punished as a Class D felon and shall be sentenced to a minimum term of 175 months and a maximum term of 222 months in the State's prison and shall be fined not less than two hundred thousand dollars ($ 200,000).

(2) Any person who sells, manufactures, delivers, transports, or possesses 1,000 tablets, capsules or other dosage units, or the equivalent quantity, or more of methaqualone, or any mixture containing such substance, shall be guilty of a felony which felony shall be known as "trafficking in methaqualone" and if the quantity of such substance or mixture involved:

a. Is 1,000 or more dosage units, or equivalent quantity, but less than 5,000 dosage units, or equivalent quantity, such person shall be punished as a Class G felon and shall be sentenced to a minimum term of 35 months and a maximum term of 51 months in the State's prison and shall be fined not less than twenty-five thousand dollars ($ 25,000);

b. Is 5,000 or more dosage units, or equivalent quantity, but less than 10,000 dosage units, or equivalent quantity, such person shall be punished as a Class F felon and shall be sentenced to a minimum term of 70 months and a maximum term of 93 months in the State's prison and shall be fined not less than fifty thousand dollars ($ 50,000);

c. Is 10,000 or more dosage units, or equivalent quantity, such person shall be punished as a Class D felon and shall be sentenced to a minimum term of 175 months and a maximum term of 222 months in the State's prison and shall be fined not less than two hundred thousand dollars ($ 200,000).

(3) Any person who sells, manufactures, delivers, transports, or possesses 28 grams or more of cocaine and any salt, isomer (whether optical or geometric), salts of isomers, compound, derivative, or preparation thereof, or any coca leaves and any salt, isomer, salts of isomers, compound, derivative, or preparation of coca leaves, and any salt, isomer, salts of isomers, compound, derivative or preparation thereof which is chemically equivalent or identical with any of these substances (except decocainized coca leaves or any extraction of coca leaves which does not contain cocaine) or any mixture containing such substances, shall be guilty of a felony, which felony shall be known as "trafficking in cocaine" and if the quantity of such substance or mixture involved:

a. Is 28 grams or more, but less than 200 grams, such person shall be punished as a Class G felon and shall be sentenced to a minimum term of 35 months and a maximum term of 51 months in the State's prison and shall be fined not less than fifty thousand dollars ($ 50,000);

b. Is 200 grams or more, but less than 400 grams, such person shall be punished as a Class F felon and shall be sentenced to a minimum term of 70 months and a maximum term of 93 months in the State's prison and shall be fined not less than one hundred thousand dollars ($ 100,000);

c. Is 400 grams or more, such person shall be punished as a Class D felon and shall be sentenced to a minimum term of 175 months and a maximum term of 222 months in the State's prison and shall be fined at least two hundred fifty thousand dollars ($ 250,000).

(3a) Repealed by Session Laws 1999-370, s. 1, effective December 1, 1999.

(3b) Any person who sells, manufactures, delivers, transports, or possesses 28 grams or more of methamphetamine or any mixture containing such substance shall be guilty of a felony which felony shall be known as "trafficking in methamphetamine" and if the quantity of such substance or mixture involved:

a. Is 28 grams or more, but less than 200 grams, such person shall be punished as a Class F felon and shall be sentenced to a minimum term of 70 months and a maximum term of 93 months in the State's prison and shall be fined not less than fifty thousand dollars ($ 50,000);

b. Is 200 grams or more, but less than 400 grams, such person shall be punished as a Class E felon and shall be sentenced to a minimum term of 90 months and a maximum term of 120 months in the State's prison and shall be fined not less than one hundred thousand dollars ($ 100,000);

c. Is 400 grams or more, such person shall be punished as a Class C felon and shall be sentenced to a minimum term of 225 months and a maximum term of 282 months in the State's prison and shall be fined at least two hundred fifty thousand dollars ($ 250,000).

(3c) Any person who sells, manufactures, delivers, transports, or possesses 28 grams or more of amphetamine or any mixture containing such substance shall be guilty of a felony, which felony shall be known as "trafficking in amphetamine", and if the quantity of such substance or mixture involved:

a. Is 28 grams or more, but less than 200 grams, such person shall be punished as a Class H felon and shall be sentenced to a minimum term of 25 months and a maximum term of 39 months in the State's prison and shall be fined not less than five thousand dollars ($ 5,000);

b. Is 200 grams or more, but less than 400 grams, such person shall be punished as a Class G felon and shall be sentenced to a minimum term of 35 months and a maximum term of 51 months in the State's prison and shall be fined not less than twenty-five thousand dollars ($ 25,000);

c. Is 400 grams or more, such person shall be punished as a Class E felon and shall be sentenced to a minimum term of 90 months and a maximum term of 120 months in the State's prison and shall be fined at least one hundred thousand dollars ($ 100,000).

(3d) Any person who sells, manufactures, delivers, transports, or possesses 28 grams or more of any substituted cathinone, as defined in G.S. 90-89(5)(j), or any mixture containing such substance shall be guilty of a felony, which felony shall be known as "trafficking in substituted cathinones," and if the quantity of such substance or mixture involved:

a. Is 28 grams or more, but less than 200 grams, such person shall be punished as a Class F felon and shall be sentenced to a minimum term of 70 months and a maximum term of 93 months in the State's prison and shall be fined not less than fifty thousand dollars ($ 50,000);

b. Is 200 grams or more, but less than 400 grams, such person shall be punished as a Class E felon and shall be sentenced to a minimum term of 90 months and a maximum term of 120 months in the State's prison and shall be fined not less than one hundred thousand dollars ($ 100,000);

c. Is 400 grams or more, such person shall be punished as a Class C felon and shall be sentenced to a minimum term of 225 months and a maximum term of 282 months in the State's prison and shall be fined at least two hundred fifty thousand dollars ($ 250,000).

(3e) Repealed by Session Laws 2018-44, s. 7, effective December 1, 2018.

(4) Any person who sells, manufactures, delivers, transports, or possesses four grams or more of opium, opiate, or opioid, or any salt, compound, derivative, or preparation of opium, opiate, or opioid (except apomorphine, nalbuphine, analoxone and naltrexone and their respective salts), including heroin, or any mixture containing such substance, shall be guilty of a felony which felony shall be known as "trafficking in opium, opiate, opioid, or heroin" and if the quantity of such controlled substance or mixture involved:

a. Is four grams or more, but less than 14 grams, such person shall be punished as a Class F felon and shall be sentenced to a minimum term of 70 months and a maximum term of 93 months in the State's prison and shall be fined not less than fifty thousand dollars ($ 50,000);

b. Is 14 grams or more, but less than 28 grams, such person shall be punished as a Class E felon and shall be sentenced to a minimum term of 90 months and a maximum term of 120 months in the State's prison and shall be fined not less than one hundred thousand dollars ($ 100,000);

c. Is 28 grams or more, such person shall be punished as a Class C felon and shall be sentenced to a minimum term of 225 months and a maximum term of 282 months in the State's prison and shall be fined not less than five hundred thousand dollars ($ 500,000).

(4a) Any person who sells, manufactures, delivers, transports, or possesses 100 tablets, capsules, or other dosage units, or the equivalent quantity, or more, of Lysergic Acid Diethylamide, or any mixture containing such substance, shall be guilty of a felony, which felony shall be known as "trafficking in Lysergic Acid Diethylamide". If the quantity of such substance or mixture involved:

a. Is 100 or more dosage units, or equivalent quantity, but less than 500 dosage units, or equivalent quantity, such person shall be punished as a Class G felon and shall be sentenced to a minimum term of 35 months and a maximum term of 51 months in the State's prison and shall be fined not less than twenty-five thousand dollars ($ 25,000);

b. Is 500 or more dosage units, or equivalent quantity, but less than 1,000 dosage units, or equivalent quantity, such person shall be punished as a Class F felon and shall be sentenced to a minimum term of 70 months and a maximum term of 93 months in the State's prison and shall be fined not less than fifty thousand dollars ($ 50,000);

    c. Is 1,000 or more dosage units, or equivalent quantity, such person shall be punished as a Class D felon and shall be sentenced to a minimum term of 175 months and a maximum term of 222 months in the State's prison and shall be fined not less than two hundred thousand dollars ($ 200,000).

  (4b) Any person who sells, manufactures, delivers, transports, or possesses 100 or more tablets, capsules, or other dosage units, or 28 grams or more of 3,4-methylenedioxyamphetamine (MDA), including its salts, isomers, and salts of isomers, or 3,4-methylenedioxymethamphetamine (MDMA), including its salts, isomers, and salts of isomers, or any mixture containing such substances, shall be guilty of a felony, which felony shall be known as "trafficking in MDA/MDMA." If the quantity of the substance or mixture involved:

    a. Is 100 or more tablets, capsules, or other dosage units, but less than 500 tablets, capsules, or other dosage units, or 28 grams or more, but less than 200 grams, the person shall be punished as a Class G felon and shall be sentenced to a minimum term of 35 months and a maximum term of 51 months in the State's prison and shall be fined not less than twenty-five thousand dollars ($ 25,000);

    b. Is 500 or more tablets, capsules, or other dosage units, but less than 1,000 tablets, capsules, or other dosage units, or 200 grams or more, but less than 400 grams, the person shall be punished as a Class F felon and shall be sentenced to a minimum term of 70 months and a maximum term of 93 months in the State's prison and shall be fined not less than fifty thousand dollars ($ 50,000);

    c. Is 1,000 or more tablets, capsules, or other dosage units, or 400 grams or more, the person shall be punished as a Class D felon and shall be sentenced to a minimum term of 175 months and a maximum term of 222 months in the State's prison and shall be fined not less than two hundred fifty thousand dollars ($ 250,000).

  (5) Except as provided in this subdivision or subdivision (5a) of this subsection, a person being sentenced under this subsection may not receive a suspended sentence or be placed on probation. The sentencing judge may reduce the fine, or impose a prison term less than the applicable minimum prison term provided by this subsection, or suspend the prison term imposed and place a person on probation when such person has, to the best of the person's knowledge, provided substantial assistance in the identification, arrest, or conviction of any accomplices, accessories, co-conspirators, or principals if the sentencing judge enters in the record a finding that the person to be sentenced has rendered such substantial assistance.

  (5a) A judge sentencing a person for a conviction pursuant to G.S. 90-95(h) or G.S. 90-95(i) for conspiracy to commit a violation of G.S. 90-95(h) shall impose the applicable minimum prison term provided by this subsection. The sentencing judge may reduce the fine and sentence the person consistent with the applicable offense classification and prior record level provided in G.S. 15A-1340.17, if after a hearing and an opportunity for the district attorney to present evidence, including evidence from the investigating law enforcement officer, other law enforcement officers, or witnesses with knowledge of the defendant's conduct at any time prior to sentencing, the judge enters into the record specific findings that all of the following are met:

    a. The defendant has accepted responsibility for the defendant's criminal conduct.

    b. The defendant has not previously been convicted of a felony under G.S. 90-95.

    c. The defendant did not use violence or a credible threat of violence, or possess a firearm or other dangerous weapon, in the commission of the offense for which the defendant is being sentenced.

    d. The defendant did not use violence or a credible threat of violence, or possess a firearm or other dangerous weapon, in the commission of any other violation of law.

    e. The defendant has admitted that he or she has a substance abuse disorder involving a controlled substance and has successfully completed a treatment program approved by the Court to address the substance abuse disorder.

    f. Imposition of the mandatory minimum prison term would result in substantial injustice.

    g. Imposition of the mandatory minimum prison sentence is not necessary for the protection of the public.

    h. The defendant is being sentenced solely for trafficking, or conspiracy to commit trafficking, as a result of possession of a controlled substance.

i. There is no substantial evidence that the defendant has ever engaged in the transport for purpose of sale, sale, manufacture, or delivery of a controlled substance or the intent to transport for purpose of sale, sell, manufacture, or deliver a controlled substance.

j. The defendant, to the best of his or her knowledge, has provided all reasonable assistance in the identification, arrest, or conviction of any accomplices, accessories, co-conspirators, or principals.

k. The defendant is being sentenced for trafficking, or conspiracy to commit trafficking, for possession of an amount of a controlled substance that is not of a quantity greater than the lowest category for which a defendant may be convicted for trafficking of that controlled substance under G.S. 90-95(h).

(6) Sentences imposed pursuant to this subsection shall run consecutively with and shall commence at the expiration of any sentence being served by the person sentenced hereunder.

(i) The penalties provided in subsection (h) of this section shall also apply to any person who is convicted of conspiracy to commit any of the offenses described in subsection (h) of this section.

(j) Beginning December 1, 2021, and annually thereafter, the Administrative Office of the Courts shall publish on its Web site a report on the number of sentences modified under G.S. 90-95(h)(5a) in the prior calendar year.

History.
1971, c. 919, s. 1; 1973, c. 654, s. 1; c. 1078; c. 1358, s. 10; 1975, c. 360, s. 2; 1977, c. 862, ss. 1, 2; 1979, c. 760, s. 5; 1979, 2nd Sess., c. 1251, ss. 4-7; 1983, c. 18; c. 294, s. 6; c. 414; 1985, c. 569, s. 1; c. 675, ss. 1, 2; 1987, c. 90; c. 105, ss. 4, 5; c. 640, ss. 1, 2; c. 783, s. 4; 1989, c. 641; c. 672; c. 690; c. 770, s. 68; 1989 (Reg. Sess., 1990), c. 1024, s. 17; c. 1039, s. 5; c. 1081, s. 2; 1991, c. 484, s. 1; 1993, c. 538, s. 30; c. 539, s. 1358.1; 1994, Ex. Sess., c. 11, s. 1; c. 14, ss. 46, 47; c. 24, s. 14(b); 1996, 2nd Ex. Sess., c. 18, s. 20.13(c); 1997-304, ss. 1, 2; 1997-443, s. 19.25(b), (u), (ii); 1998-212, s. 17.16(e); 1999-165, s. 4; 1999-370, s. 1; 2000-140, s. 92.2(d); 2001-307, s. 1; 2001-332, s. 1; 2004-178, ss. 3, 4, 5, 6; 2007-375, s. 1; 2009-463, ss. 1, 2; 2009-473, s. 7; 2011-12, ss. 2 -4, 6-8; 2011-19, s. 5; 2012-188, s. 5; 2013-124, s. 1; 2013-171, ss. 7, 8; 2014-115, s. 41(a); 2015-32, s. 1; 2015-173, s. 4; 2017-115, s. 11; 2018-44, ss. 5 -7; 2020-47, ss. 2(a), 3; 2021-155, ss. 7, 8

§ 90-95.1. Continuing criminal enterprise

(a) Any person who engages in a continuing criminal enterprise shall be punished as a Class C felon and in addition shall be subject to the forfeiture prescribed in subsection (b) of this section.

(b) Any person who is convicted under subsection (a) of engaging in a continuing criminal enterprise shall forfeit to the State of North Carolina:

(1) The profits obtained by him in such enterprise, and

(2) Any of his interest in, claim against, or property or contractual rights of any kind affording a source of influence over, such enterprise.

(c) For purposes of this section, a person is engaged in a continuing criminal enterprise if:

(1) He violates any provision of this Article, the punishment of which is a felony; and

(2) Such violation is a part of a continuing series of violations of this Article;

a. Which are undertaken by such person in concert with five or more other persons with respect to whom such person occupies a position of organizer, a supervisory position, or any other position of management; and

b. From which such person obtains substantial income or resources.

(d) Repealed by Session Laws 1979, c. 760, s. 5.

History.
1971, s. 919, s. 1; 1979, c. 760, s. 5

§ 90-95.2. Cooperation between law-enforcement agencies

(a) The head of any law-enforcement agency may temporarily provide assistance to another agency in enforcing the provisions of this Article if so requested in writing by the head of the other agency. The assistance may comprise allowing officers of the agency to work temporarily with officers of the other agency (including in an undercover capacity) and lending equipment and supplies. While working with another agency under the authority of this section, an officer shall have the same jurisdiction, powers, rights, privileges, and immunities (including those relating to the defense of civil actions and payment of judgments) as the officers of the requesting agency in addition to those he normally possesses. While on duty with the other agency, he shall be subject to the lawful operational commands of his superior officers in the other agency, but he shall for personnel and administrative purposes remain under the control of his own agency, including for purposes of pay. He shall furthermore be entitled to workers' compensation when acting pursuant to this section to the same extent as though he were functioning within the normal scope of his duties.

Chapter 90

(b) As used in this section:

(1) "Head" means any director or chief officer of a law-enforcement agency, including the chief of police of a local police department and the sheriff of a county, or an officer of the agency to whom the head of the agency has delegated authority to make or grant requests under this section, but only one officer in the agency shall have this delegated authority at any time.

(2) "Law-enforcement agency" means any State or local agency, force, department, or unit responsible for enforcing criminal laws in this State, including any local police department or sheriff's department.

(c) This section in no way reduces the jurisdiction or authority of State law-enforcement officers.

History.
1975, c. 782, s. 1; 1981, c. 93, s. 1; 1991, c. 636, s. 3

§ 90-95.3. Restitution to law-enforcement agencies for undercover purchases; restitution for drug analyses; restitution for seizure and cleanup of clandestine laboratories

(a) When any person is convicted of an offense under this Article, the court may order him to make restitution to any law-enforcement agency for reasonable expenditures made in purchasing controlled substances from him or his agent as part of an investigation leading to his conviction.

(b) *(See Editor's Note)* Repealed by Session Laws 2002-126, s. 29A.8(b), effective October 1, 2002.

(c) When any person is convicted of an offense under this Article involving the manufacture of controlled substances, the court must order the person to make restitution for the actual cost of cleanup to the law enforcement agency that cleaned up any clandestine laboratory used to manufacture the controlled substances, including personnel overtime, equipment, and supplies.

History.
1975, c. 782, s. 2; 1989 (Reg. Sess., 1990), c. 1039, s. 3; 1999-370, s. 2; 2002-126, s. 29A.8(b)

§ 90-95.4. Employing or intentionally using minor to commit a drug law violation

(a) A person who is at least 18 years old but less than 21 years old who hires or intentionally uses a minor to violate G.S. 90-95(a)(1) shall be guilty of a felony. An offense under this subsection shall be punishable as follows:

(1) If the minor was more than 13 years of age, then as a felony that is one class more severe than the violation of G.S. 90-95(a)(1) for which the minor was hired or intentionally used.

(2) If the minor was 13 years of age or younger, then as a felony that is two classes more severe than the violation of G.S. 90-95(a)(1) for which the minor was hired or intentionally used.

(b) A person 21 years of age or older who hires or intentionally uses a minor to violate G.S. 90-95(a)(1) shall be guilty of a felony. An offense under this subsection shall be punishable as follows:

(1) If the minor was more than 13 years of age, then as a felony that is three classes more severe than the violation of G.S. 90-95(a)(1) for which the minor was hired or intentionally used.

(2) If the minor was 13 years of age or younger, then as a felony that is four classes more severe than the violation of G.S. 90-95(a)(1) for which the minor was hired or intentionally used.

(c) **Mistake of Age.** -- Mistake of age is not a defense to a prosecution under this section.

(d) The term "minor" as used in this section is defined as an individual who is less than 18 years of age.

History.
1989 (Reg. Sess., 1990), c. 1081, s. 1; 1998-212, s. 17.16(f)

§ 90-95.5. Civil liability -- employing a minor to commit a drug offense

A person 21 years of age or older, who hires, employs, or intentionally uses a person under 18 years of age to commit a violation of G.S. 90-95 is liable in a civil action for damages for drug addiction proximately caused by the violation. The doctrines of contributory negligence and assumption of risk are no defense to liability under this section.

History.
1989 (Reg. Sess., 1990), c. 1081, s. 3; 1998-212, s. 17.16(g)

§ 90-95.6. Promoting drug sales by a minor

(a) A person who is 21 years of age or older is guilty of promoting drug sales by a minor if the person knowingly:

(1) Entices, forces, encourages, or otherwise facilitates a minor in violating G.S. 90-95(a)(1).

(2) Supervises, supports, advises, or protects the minor in violating G.S. 90-95(a)(1).

(b) Mistake of age is not a defense to a prosecution under this section.

(c) A violation of this section is a Class D felony.

History.
1998-212, s. 17.16(h)

§ 90-95.7. Participating in a drug violation by a minor

(a) A person 21 years of age or older who purchases or receives a controlled substance from a minor 13 years of age or younger who possesses, sells, or delivers the controlled substance in violation of G.S. 90-95(a)(1) is guilty of participating in a drug violation of a minor.

(b) Mistake of age is not a defense to a prosecution under this section.

(c) A violation of this section is a Class G felony.

History.
1998-212, s. 17.16(h)

§ 90-96. Conditional discharge for first offense

(a) Whenever any person who has not previously been convicted of (i) any felony offense under any state or federal laws; (ii) any offense under this Article; or (iii) an offense under any statute of the United States or any state relating to those substances included in Article 5 or 5A of Chapter 90 or to that paraphernalia included in Article 5B of Chapter 90 of the General Statutes pleads guilty to or is found guilty of (i) a misdemeanor under this Article by possessing a controlled substance included within Schedules I through VI of this Article or by possessing drug paraphernalia as prohibited by G.S. 90-113.22 or G.S. 90-113.22A or (ii) a felony under G.S. 90-95(a)(3), the court shall, without entering a judgment of guilt and with the consent of the person, defer further proceedings and place the person on probation upon such reasonable terms and conditions as it may require, unless the court determines with a written finding, and with the agreement of the District Attorney, that the offender is inappropriate for a conditional discharge for factors related to the offense. Notwithstanding the provisions of G.S. 15A-1342(c) or any other statute or law, probation may be imposed under this section for an offense under this Article for which the prescribed punishment includes only a fine. To fulfill the terms and conditions of probation the court may allow the defendant to participate in a drug education program approved for this purpose by the Department of Health and Human Services or in the Treatment for Effective Community

Supervision Program under Subpart B of Part 6 of Article 13 of Chapter 143B of the General Statutes. Upon violation of a term or condition, the court may enter an adjudication of guilt and proceed as otherwise provided. Upon fulfillment of the terms and conditions, the court shall discharge the person and dismiss the proceedings. Discharge and dismissal under this section shall be without court adjudication of guilt and shall not be deemed a conviction for purposes of this section or for purposes of disqualifications or disabilities imposed by law upon conviction of a crime including the additional penalties imposed for second or subsequent convictions under this Article. Discharge and dismissal under this section or G.S. 90-113.14 may occur only once with respect to any person. Disposition of a case to determine discharge and dismissal under this section at the district court division of the General Court of Justice shall be final for the purpose of appeal. Prior to taking any action to discharge and dismiss under this section the court shall make a finding that the defendant has no record of previous convictions as provided in this subsection.

(a1) Upon the first conviction only of any offense which qualifies under the provisions of subsection (a) of this section, and the provisions of this subsection, the court may place defendant on probation under this section for an offense under this Article including an offense for which the prescribed punishment includes only a fine. The probation, if imposed, shall be for not less than one year and shall contain a minimum condition that the defendant who was found guilty or pleads guilty enroll in and successfully complete, within 150 days of the date of the imposition of said probation, the program of instruction at the drug education school approved by the Department of Health and Human Services pursuant to G.S. 90-96.01. The court may impose probation that does not contain a condition that defendant successfully complete the program of instruction at a drug education school if:

(1) There is no drug education school within a reasonable distance of the defendant's residence; or

(2) There are specific, extenuating circumstances which make it likely that defendant will not benefit from the program of instruction.

The court shall enter such specific findings in the record; provided that in the case of subdivision (2) above, such findings shall include the specific, extenuating circumstances which make it likely that the defendant will not benefit from the program of instruction.

Upon fulfillment of the terms and conditions of the probation, the court shall discharge such person and dismiss the proceedings against the person.

For the purposes of determining whether the conviction is a first conviction or whether a person has already had discharge and dismissal, no prior offense occurring more than seven years before the date of the current offense shall be considered. In addition, convictions for violations of a provision of G.S. 90-95(a)(1) or 90-95(a)(2) or 90-95(a)(3), or 90-113.10, or 90-113.11, or 90-113.12, or 90-113.22, or 90-113.22A shall be considered previous convictions.

Failure to complete successfully an approved program of instruction at a drug education school shall constitute grounds to revoke probation pursuant to this subsection and deny application for expunction of all recordation of defendant's arrest, indictment, or information, trial, finding of guilty, and dismissal and discharge pursuant to G.S. 15A-145.2. For purposes of this subsection, the phrase "failure to complete successfully the prescribed program of instruction at a drug education school" includes failure to attend scheduled classes without a valid excuse, failure to complete the course within 150 days of imposition of probation, willful failure to pay the required fee for the course as provided in G.S. 90-96.01(b), or any other manner in which the person fails to complete the course successfully. The instructor of the course to which a person is assigned shall report any failure of a person to complete successfully the program of instruction to the court which imposed probation. Upon receipt of the instructor's report that the person failed to complete the program successfully, the court shall revoke probation, shall not discharge such person, shall not dismiss the proceedings against the person, and shall deny application for expunction of all recordation of defendant's arrest, indictment, or information, trial, finding of guilty, and dismissal and discharge pursuant to G.S. 15A-145.2. A person may obtain a hearing before the court of original jurisdiction prior to revocation of probation or denial of application for expunction.

This subsection is supplemental and in addition to existing law and shall not be construed so as to repeal any existing provision contained in the General Statutes of North Carolina.

(b) Upon the discharge of such person, and dismissal of the proceedings against the person under subsection (a) or (a1) of this section, such person, if he or she was not over 21 years of age at the time of the offense, may be eligible to apply for expunction of certain records relating to the offense pursuant to G.S. 15A-145.2(a).

(c) Repealed by Session Laws 2009-510, s. 8(b), effective October 1, 2010.

(d) Whenever any person is charged with a misdemeanor under this Article by possessing a controlled substance included within Schedules I through VI of this Article or a felony under G.S. 90-95(a)(3), upon dismissal by the State of the charges against such person, upon entry of a nolle prosequi, or upon a finding of not guilty or other adjudication of innocence, the person may be eligible to apply for expunction of certain records relating to the offense pursuant to G.S. 15A-145.2(b).

(e) Whenever any person who has not previously been convicted of (i) any felony offense under any state or federal laws; (ii) any offense under this Article; or (iii) an offense under any statute of the United States or any state relating to controlled substances included in any schedule of this Article or to that paraphernalia included in Article 5B of Chapter 90 of the General Statutes pleads guilty to or has been found guilty of (i) a misdemeanor under this Article by possessing a controlled substance included within Schedules I through VI of this Article, or by possessing drug paraphernalia as prohibited by G.S. 90-113.22 or G.S. 90-113.22A, or (ii) a felony under G.S. 90-95(a)(3), the person may be eligible to apply for cancellation of the judgment and expunction of certain records related to the offense pursuant to G.S. 15A-145.2(c).

(f) Repealed by Session Laws 2009-577, s. 6, effective December 1, 2009, and applicable to petitions for expunctions filed on or after that date.

History.
1971, c. 919, s. 1; 1973, c. 654, s. 2; c. 1066; 1977, 2nd Sess., c. 1147, s. 11B; 1979, c. 431, ss. 3, 4; c. 550; 1981, c. 922, ss. 1-4; 1994, Ex. Sess., c. 11, s. 1.1; 1997-443, s. 11A.118(a); 2002-126, s. 29A.5(d); 2009-510, s. 8(a) -(d); 2009-577, s. 6; 2010-174, ss. 10 -12; 2011-192, s. 5(a); 2013-210, s. 1; 2017-102, s. 38

§ 90-96.01. Drug education schools; responsibilities of the Department of Health and Human Services; fees

(a) The Commission for Mental Health, Developmental Disabilities, and Substance Abuse Services shall establish standards and guidelines for the curriculum and operation of local drug education programs. The Department of Health and Human Services shall oversee the development of a statewide system of schools and shall insure that schools are available in all localities of the State as soon as is practicable.

(1) A fee of one hundred fifty dollars ($ 150.00) shall be paid by all persons enrolling in an accredited drug education school established pursuant to this section. That fee must be paid to an official

designated for that purpose and at a time and place specified by the area mental health, developmental disabilities, and substance abuse authority providing the course of instruction in which the person is enrolled. If the clerk of court in the county in which the person is convicted agrees to collect the fees, the clerk shall collect all fees for persons convicted in that county. The clerk shall pay the fees collected to the area mental health, developmental disabilities, and substance abuse authority for the catchment area where the clerk is located regardless of the location where the defendant attends the drug education school and that authority shall distribute the funds in accordance with the rules and regulations of the Department. The fee must be paid in full within two weeks of the date the person is convicted and before he attends any classes, unless the court, upon a showing of reasonable hardship, allows the person additional time to pay the fee or allows him to begin the course of instruction without paying the fee. If the person enrolling in the school demonstrates to the satisfaction of the court that ordered him to enroll in the school that he is unable to pay and his inability to pay is not willful, the court may excuse him from paying the fee. Parents or guardians of persons attending drug education school shall be allowed to audit the drug education school along with their children or wards at no extra expense.

(2) The Department of Health and Human Services shall have the authority to approve programs to be implemented by area mental health, developmental disabilities, and substance abuse authorities. Area mental health, developmental disabilities, and substance abuse authorities may subcontract for the delivery of drug education program services. The Department shall have the authority to approve budgets and contracts with public and private governmental and nongovernmental bodies for the operation of such schools.

(3) Fees collected under this section and retained by the area mental health, developmental disabilities, and substance abuse authority shall be placed in a nonreverting fund. That fund must be used, as necessary, for the operation, evaluation and administration of the drug educational schools; excess funds may only be used to fund other drug or alcohol programs. The area mental health, developmental disabilities, and substance abuse authority shall remit five percent (5%) of each fee collected to the Department of Health and Human Services on a monthly basis. Fees received by the Department as required by this section

may only be used in supporting, evaluating, and administering drug education schools, and any excess funds will revert to the General Fund.

(4) All fees collected by any area mental health, developmental disabilities, and substance abuse authority under the authority of this section may not be used in any manner to match other State funds or be included in any computation for State formula-funded allocations.

(b) Willful failure to pay the fee is one ground for a finding that a person placed on probation or who may make application for expunction of all recordation of his arrest or conviction has not successfully completed the course. If the court determines the person is unable to pay, he shall not be deemed guilty of a willful failure to pay the fee.

History.
1981, c. 922, s. 8; 1991, c. 636, s. 19(b), (c); 1993, c. 395, s. 1; 1997-443, s. 11A.118(a)

§ 90-96.1. Immunity from prosecution for minors

Whenever any person who is not more than 18 years of age, who has not previously been convicted of any offense under this Article or under any statute of the United States of any state relating to controlled substances included in any schedule of this Article, is accused with possessing or distributing a controlled substance in violation of G.S. 90-95(a)(1) or 90-95(a)(2) or 90-95(a)(3), the court may, upon recommendation of the district attorney, grant said person immunity from prosecution for said violation(s) if said person shall disclose the identity of the person or persons from whom he obtained the controlled substance(s) for which said person is being accused of possessing or distributing.

History.
1973, c. 47, s. 2; c. 654, s. 3

§ 90-96.2. Drug-related overdose treatment; limited immunity

(a) As used in this section, "drug-related overdose" means an acute condition, including mania, hysteria, extreme physical illness, coma, or death resulting from the consumption or use of a controlled substance, or another substance with which a controlled substance was combined, and that a layperson would reasonably believe to be a drug overdose that requires medical assistance.

(b) **Limited Immunity for Samaritan. --** A person shall not be prosecuted for any of the offenses listed in subsection (c3) of this section if all of the following requirements and conditions are met:

    (1) The person sought medical assistance for an individual experiencing a drug-related overdose by contacting the 911 system, a law enforcement officer, or emergency medical services personnel.

    (2) The person acted in good faith when seeking medical assistance, upon a reasonable belief that he or she was the first to call for assistance.

    (3) The person provided his or her own name to the 911 system or to a law enforcement officer upon arrival.

    (4) The person did not seek the medical assistance during the course of the execution of an arrest warrant, search warrant, or other lawful search.

    (5) The evidence for prosecution of the offenses listed in subsection (c3) of this section was obtained as a result of the person seeking medical assistance for the drug-related overdose.

    (c) **Limited Immunity for Overdose Victim.** -- The immunity described in subsection (b) of this section shall extend to the person who experienced the drug-related overdose if all of the requirements and conditions listed in subdivisions (1), (2), (4), and (5) of subsection (b) of this section are satisfied.

    (c1) **Probation or Release.** -- A person shall not be subject to arrest or revocation of pretrial release, probation, parole, or post-release if the arrest or revocation is based on an offense for which the person is immune from prosecution under subsection (b) or (c) of this section. The arrest of a person for an offense for which subsection (b) or (c) of this section may provide the person with immunity will not itself be deemed to be a commission of a new criminal offense in violation of a condition of the person's pretrial release, condition of probation, or condition of parole or post-release.

    (c2) **Civil Liability for Arrest or Charges.** -- In addition to any other applicable immunity or limitation on civil liability, a law enforcement officer who, acting in good faith, arrests or charges a person who is thereafter determined to be entitled to immunity under this section shall not be subject to civil liability for the arrest or filing of charges.

    (c3) **Covered Offenses.** -- A person shall have limited immunity from prosecution under subsections (b) and (c) of this section for only the following offenses:

    (1) A misdemeanor violation of G.S. 90-95(a)(3).

    (2) A felony violation of G.S. 90-95(a)(3) for possession of less than one gram of cocaine.

    (3) A felony violation of G.S. 90-95(a)(3) for possession of less than one gram of heroin.

    (4) A violation of G.S. 90-113.22.

    (d) **Construction.** -- Nothing in this section shall be construed to do any of the following:

    (1) Bar the admissibility of any evidence obtained in connection with the investigation and prosecution of (i) other crimes committed by a person who otherwise qualifies for limited immunity under this section or (ii) any crimes committed by a person who does not qualify for limited immunity under this section.

    (2) Limit any seizure of evidence or contraband otherwise permitted by law.

    (3) Limit or abridge the authority of a law enforcement officer to detain or take into custody a person in the course of an investigation of, or to effectuate an arrest for, any offense other than an offense listed in subsection (c3) of this section.

    (4) Limit or abridge the authority of a probation officer to conduct drug testing of persons on pretrial release, probation, or parole.

History.
2013-23, s. 1; 2015-94, s. 1

§ 90-97. Other penalties

Any penalty imposed for violation of this Article shall be in addition to, and not in lieu of, any civil or administrative penalty or sanction authorized by law. If a violation of this Article is a violation of a federal law or the law of another state, a conviction or acquittal under federal law or the law of another state for the same act is a bar to prosecution in this State.

History.
1971, c. 919, s. 1

§ 90-98. Attempt and conspiracy; penalties

Except as otherwise provided in this Article, any person who attempts or conspires to commit any offense defined in this Article is guilty of an offense that is the same class as the offense which was the object of the attempt or conspiracy and is punishable as specified for that class of offense and prior record or conviction level in Article 81B of Chapter 15A of the General Statutes.

History.
1971, c. 919, s. 1; 1979, c. 760, s. 5; 1997-80, s. 9

§ 90-99. Republishing of schedules

The North Carolina Department of Health and Human Services shall update and republish the schedules established by this Article on a semiannual basis for two years from January 1, 1972, and thereafter on an annual basis.

History.
1971, c. 919, s. 1; 1977, c. 667, s. 3; 1997-443, s. 11A.118(a)

§ 90-100. Rules

The Commission may adopt rules relating to the registration and control of the manufacture, distribution, security, and dispensing of controlled substances within this State.

History.
1971, c. 919, s. 1; 1977, c. 667, s. 3; 1981, c. 51, s. 9; 1991, c. 309, s. 2; 1993, c. 384, s. 1

§ 90-101. Annual registration and fee to engage in listed activities with controlled substances; effect of registration; exceptions; waiver; inspection

(a) Every person who manufactures, distributes, dispenses, or conducts research with any controlled substance within this State or who proposes to engage in any of these activities shall annually register with the North Carolina Department of Health and Human Services, in accordance with rules adopted by the Commission, and shall pay the registration fee set by the Commission for the category to which the applicant belongs. An applicant for registration shall file an application for registration with the Department of Health and Human Services and submit the required fee with the application. The categories of applicants and the maximum fee for each category are as follows:

CATEGORY	MAXIMUM FEE
Clinic	$ 150.00
Animal Shelter	150.00
Hospital	350.00
Nursing Home	150.00
Teaching Institution	150.00
Researcher	150.00
Analytical Laboratory	150.00
Dog Handler	150.00
Distributor	600.00
Manufacturer	700.00

(a1) Repealed by Session Laws 2019-159, s. 1.1, effective July 22, 2019.

(a2) An animal shelter may register under this section for the limited purpose of obtaining, possessing, and using sodium pentobarbital and other drugs approved by the Department in consultation with the North Carolina Veterinary Medical Association for the euthanasia of animals lawfully held by the animal shelter. An animal shelter registered under this section shall also register with the federal Drug Enforcement Agency under the federal Controlled Substances Act. An animal shelter's acquisition of sodium pentobarbital and other approved drugs for use in the euthanizing of animals shall be made only by the shelter's manager or chief operating officer or by a licensed veterinarian.

A person certified by the Department of Agriculture and Consumer Services to administer euthanasia by injection is authorized to possess and administer sodium pentobarbital and other approved euthanasia drugs for the purposes of euthanizing domestic dogs (Canis familiaris) and cats (Felis domestica) lawfully held by an animal shelter. Possession and administration of sodium pentobarbital and other approved drugs for use in the euthanizing of dogs and cats by a certified euthanasia technician shall be limited to the premises of the animal shelter.

For purposes of this section, "animal shelter" means an animal shelter registered under Article 3 of Chapter 19A of the General Statutes and owned, operated, or maintained by a unit of local government or under contract with a unit of local government for the purpose of housing or containing seized, stray, homeless, quarantined, abandoned, or unwanted animals.

(b) Persons registered by the North Carolina Department of Health and Human Services under this Article (including research facilities) to manufacture, distribute, dispense or conduct research with controlled substances may possess, manufacture, distribute, dispense or conduct research with those substances to the extent authorized by their registration and in conformity with the other provisions of this Article.

(c) The following persons shall not be required to register and may lawfully possess controlled substances under the provisions of this Article:

(1) An agent, or an employee thereof, of any registered manufacturer, distributor, or dispenser of any controlled substance if such agent is acting in the usual course of his business or employment;

(2) The State courier service operated by the Department of Administration, a common or contract carrier, or a public warehouseman, or an employee thereof, whose possession of any controlled substance is in the usual course of his business or employment;

(3) An ultimate user or a person in possession of any controlled substance pursuant to a lawful order of a practitioner;

(4) Repealed by Session Laws 1977, c. 891, s. 4.

(5) Any law-enforcement officer acting within the course and scope of official duties, or any person employed in an official capacity by, or acting as an agent of, any law-enforcement agency or other agency charged with enforcing the provisions of this Article when acting within the course and scope of official duties; and

Chapter 90

(6) A practitioner, as defined in G.S. 90-87(22)a., who is required to be licensed in North Carolina by his respective licensing board.

(d) The Commission may, by rule, waive the requirement for registration of certain classes of manufacturers, distributors, or dispensers if it finds it consistent with the public health and safety.

(e) A separate registration shall be required at each principal place of business, research or professional practice where the registrant manufactures, distributes, dispenses or uses controlled substances.

(f) The North Carolina Department of Health and Human Services is authorized to inspect the establishment of a registrant, applicant for registration, or practitioner in accordance with rules adopted by the Commission.

(g) Practitioners licensed in North Carolina by their respective licensing boards may possess, dispense or administer controlled substances to the extent authorized by law and by their boards.

(h) A physician licensed by the North Carolina Medical Board pursuant to Article 1 of this Chapter may possess, dispense or administer tetrahydrocannabinols in duly constituted pharmaceutical form for human administration for treatment purposes pursuant to rules adopted by the Commission.

(i) A physician licensed by the North Carolina Medical Board pursuant to Article 1 of this Chapter may dispense or administer Dronabinol or Nabilone as scheduled in G.S. 90-90(5) only as an antiemetic agent in cancer chemotherapy.

History.
1971, c. 919, s. 1; 1973, c. 1358, s. 12; 1977, c. 667, s. 3; c. 891, s. 4; 1979, c. 781; 1981, c. 51, s. 9; 1983, c. 375, s. 2; 1985, c. 439, s. 2; 1987, c. 412, s. 13; 1989 (Reg. Sess., 1990), c. 1040, s. 4; 1993, c. 384, s. 2; 1995, c. 94, ss. 26, 27; 1997-443, s. 11A.118(a); 1997-456, s. 27; 2003-335, s. 1; 2003-398, s. 1; 2010-127, s. 1; 2019-159, s. 1.1

§ 90-102. Additional provisions as to registration

(a) The North Carolina Department of Health and Human Services shall register an applicant to manufacture or distribute controlled substances included in Schedules I through VI of this Article unless it determines that the issuance of such registration is inconsistent with the public interest. In determining the public interest, the following factors shall be considered:

(1) Maintenance of effective controls against diversion of any controlled substances and any substance compounded therefrom into other than legitimate medical, scientific, or industrial channels;

(2) Compliance with applicable federal, State and local law;

(3) Prior conviction record of applicant, its agents or employees under federal and State laws relating to the manufacture, distribution, or dispensing of such substances;

(4) Past experience in the manufacture of controlled substances, and the existence in the establishment or facility of effective controls against diversion; and

(5) Any factor relating to revocation, suspension, or denial of past registrations, licenses, or applications under this or any other State or federal law;

(6) Such other factors as may be relevant to and consistent with the public health and safety.

(b) Registration granted under subsection (a) of this section shall not entitle a registrant to manufacture and distribute controlled substances included in Schedule I or II other than those specified in the registration.

(c) Individual practitioners licensed to dispense and authorized to conduct research under federal law with Schedules II through V substances must be registered with the North Carolina Department of Health and Human Services to conduct such research.

(d) Manufacturers and distributors registered or licensed under federal law to manufacture or distribute controlled substances included in Schedules I through VI of this Article are entitled to registration under this Article, but this registration is expressly made subject to the provisions of G.S. 90-103.

(e) The North Carolina Department of Health and Human Services shall initially permit persons to register who own or operate any establishment engaged in the manufacture, distribution, or dispensing of any substances prior to January 1, 1972, and who are registered or licensed by the State.

History.
1971, c. 919, s. 1; 1973, c. 1358, s. 14; 1977, c. 667, s. 3; 1985, c. 439, ss. 3, 4; 1997-443, s. 11A.118(a)

§ 90-102.1. Registration of persons requiring limited use of controlled substances for training purposes in certain businesses

(a) **Definitions. --** As used in this Article:

(1) "Commercial detection service" means any person, firm, association, or corporation contracting with another person, firm, association, or corporation for a fee or other valuable consideration to place, lease, or rent a trained drug detection dog with a dog handler.

(2) "Dog handler" means a person trained in the handling of drug detection dogs, including the care, feeding, and maintenance of drug detection dogs and the procedures necessary to train and control the behavior of drug detection dogs.

(3) "Drug detection dog" means a dog trained to locate controlled substances by scent.

(b) **Registration.** -- A dog handler who is not exempt from registration under G.S. 90-101 who intends to use any controlled substance included in Schedules I through VI for the limited purpose of the initial training and maintenance training of drug detection dogs shall file an application for registration with the Department of Health and Human Services and pay the applicable fee as provided in G.S. 90-101.

(c) **Prerequisites for Registration.** -- Upon receipt of an application, the Department of Health and Human Services shall conduct a background investigation, during the course of which the applicant shall be required to show that the applicant meets all the following requirements and qualifications:

(1) That the applicant is at least 21 years of age.

(2) That the applicant is of good moral character and temperate habits. The following shall be prima facie evidence that the applicant does not have good moral character or temperate habits:

a. Conviction of any crime involving the illegal use, possession, sale, manufacture, distribution, or transportation of a controlled substance, drug, narcotic, or alcoholic beverage;

b. Conviction of a felony or a crime involving an act of violence;

c. Conviction of a crime involving unlawful breaking or entering, burglary, larceny, or any offense involving moral turpitude; or

d. A history of addiction to alcohol or a narcotic drug;

provided that, for purposes of this subsection, conviction means and includes the entry of a plea of guilty or no contest or a verdict rendered in open court by a judge or jury.

(3) That the applicant has not been convicted of any felony involving the illegal use, possession, sale, manufacture, distribution, or transportation of a controlled substance, drug, narcotic, or alcoholic beverage.

(4) That the applicant has the necessary training, qualifications, and experience to demonstrate competency and fitness as a dog handler as the Department of Health and Human Services may determine by rule for all registrations to be approved by the Department.

(5) That the applicant affirms in writing that if the application for registration is approved, the applicant shall report all dog alerts to, or finds of, any controlled substance to a law enforcement agency having jurisdiction in the area where the dog alert occurs or where the controlled substance is found.

(d) **Criminal Record Check.** -- The Department of Public Safety may provide a criminal record check to the Department of Health and Human Services for a person who has applied for a new or renewal registration. The Department of Health and Human Services shall provide to the Department of Public Safety, along with the request, the fingerprints of the applicant, any additional information required by the Department of Public Safety, and a form signed by the applicant consenting to the check of the criminal record and to the use of the fingerprints and other identifying information required by the State or national repositories. The applicant's fingerprints shall be forwarded to the State Bureau of Investigation for a search of the State's criminal history record file, and the State Bureau of Investigation shall forward a set of the fingerprints to the Federal Bureau of Investigation for a national criminal history check. The Department of Health and Human Services shall keep all information pursuant to this subsection privileged, in accordance with applicable State law and federal guidelines, and the information shall be confidential and shall not be a public record under Chapter 132 of the General Statutes. The Department of Public Safety may charge each applicant a fee for conducting the checks of criminal history records authorized by this subsection.

(e) **Acquisition of Controlled Substances.** -- If the application for registration is approved, the registrant may lawfully obtain and possess controlled substances in the manner and to the extent authorized by the registration, in conformity with G.S. 90-105, other provisions of this Article, and rules promulgated by the Commission pursuant to G.S. 90-100.

(f) **Record Keeping; Physical Security.** -- Each registrant shall keep records and maintain inventories in the manner specified in G.S. 90-104. Registrants shall provide effective controls and procedures to guard against theft and diversion of controlled substances. Controlled substances shall be stored in a securely locked, substantially constructed cabinet, and the storage area shall be protected by an alarm system that is continuously monitored by an alarm company central station.

(g) **Disclosure of Discovery of Controlled Substances.** -- A dog handler shall, upon a dog alert or finding of a controlled substance, notify the State or local law enforcement agency having jurisdiction over the area where the dog alert occurs or the controlled substance is found. Before leaving the premises where the dog alert occurs or where the controlled substance is found, the dog handler shall inform law enforcement of the dog alert or the finding of a controlled substance and shall provide all relevant information concerning the dog alert or the discovery of the controlled substance.

(h) **Commercial Detection Services; Dog Certification and Client Confidentiality.** -- Any drug detection dog utilized in a commercial detection service in this State shall first be certified by a canine certification association approved by the Department of Health and Human Services. Any person, including a nonresident, engaged in providing a commercial detection service in this State shall comply with the requirements of subsection (g) of this section regarding disclosure of the discovery of controlled substances. Client records of a dog handler who provides a commercial detection service for controlled substances shall be confidential unless the dog handler is required to report a dog alert or finding of a controlled substance in the course of a search, the records are lawfully subpoenaed, or the records are obtained by a law enforcement officer pursuant to a court order, a search warrant, or an exception to the search warrant requirement.

(i) **Notice of Disclosure Requirement.** -- A dog handler shall provide conspicuous written notice to clients at the dog handler's place of business and in the contract for services stating that the dog handler is required by law to notify law enforcement of any dog alert or finding of a controlled substance.

Any person who contracts with a dog handler to provide commercial drug detection services shall provide conspicuous written notice to any person whose person or property may be subject to search stating that the premises is subject to search and that the dog handler is required by law to notify law enforcement of any dog alert or finding of a controlled substance.

(j) The Department of Health and Human Services shall have the power to investigate or cause to be investigated any complaints, allegations, or suspicions of wrongdoing or violations of this section involving individuals registered or applying to be registered under this section. The Department or the Commission may deny, suspend, or revoke a registration issued under this section if it is determined that the applicant or registrant has:

(1) Made any false statement or given any false information in connection with any application for a registration or for the renewal or reinstatement of a registration.

(2) Violated any provision of this Article.

(3) Violated any rule promulgated by the Department of Health and Human Services or the Commission for Mental Health, Developmental Disabilities, and Substance Abuse Services pursuant to the authority contained in this Article.

(k) This section does not apply to law enforcement agencies, to dog handlers and drug detection dogs that are employed or under contract to law enforcement agencies, or to other persons who are exempt from registration under G.S. 90- 101(c)(5).

History.
2003-398, s. 2; 2014-100, s. 17.1(o)

§ 90-103. Revocation or suspension of registration

(a) A registration under G.S. 90-102 to manufacture, distribute, or dispense a controlled substance, may be suspended or revoked by the Commission upon a finding that the registrant:

(1) Has furnished false or fraudulent material information in any application filed under this Article;

(2) Has been convicted of a felony under any State or federal law relating to any controlled substance; or

(3) Has had his federal registration suspended or revoked to manufacture, distribute, or dispense controlled substances.

(b) The Commission may limit revocation or suspension of a registration to the particular controlled substance with respect to which grounds for revocation or suspension exist.

(c) Before denying, suspending, or revoking a registration or refusing a renewal of registration, the Commission shall serve upon the applicant or registrant an order to show cause why registration should not be denied, revoked, or suspended, or why the renewal should not be refused. The order to show cause shall contain a statement of the basis therefor and shall call upon the applicant or registrant to appear before the Commission at a time and place not less than 30 days after the date of service of the order, but in the case of a denial or renewal of registration, the show cause order shall be served not later than 30 days before the expiration of the registration. These proceedings shall be conducted in accordance with rules and regulations of the Commission required by Chapter 150B of the General Statutes, and subject to judicial review as provided in Chapter 150B of the General Statutes. Such proceedings shall be independent of, and not in lieu of, criminal prosecutions or other proceedings under this Article or any law of the State.

(d) The Commission may suspend, without an order to show cause, any registration simultaneously with the institutions of proceedings under this section, or where renewal of registration is refused if it finds that there is an imminent danger to the public health or safety which warrants this action. The suspension shall continue in effect until the conclusion of the proceedings, including judicial review thereof, unless sooner withdrawn by the Commission or dissolved by a court of competent jurisdiction.

(e) In the event the Commission suspends or revokes a registration granted under G.S. 90-102, all controlled substances owned or possessed by the registrant pursuant to such registration at the time of suspension or the effective date of the revocation order, as the case may be, may in the discretion of the Commission be placed under seal. No disposition may be made of substances under seal until the time for taking an appeal has elapsed or until all appeals have been concluded unless a court, upon application therefor, orders the sale of perishable substances and the deposit of the proceeds of the sale with the court. Upon a revocation order becoming final, all such controlled substances may be ordered forfeited to the State.

(f) The Bureau shall promptly be notified of all orders suspending or revoking registration.

History.
1971, c. 919, s. 1; 1973, c. 1331, s. 3; 1977, c. 667, s. 3; 1981, c. 51, s. 9; 1987, c. 827, s. 1

§ 90-104. Records of registrants or practitioners

Each registrant or practitioner manufacturing, distributing, or dispensing controlled substances under this Article shall keep records and maintain inventories in conformance with the record-keeping and the inventory requirements of the federal law and shall conform to such rules and regulations as may be promulgated by the Commission.

History.
1971, c. 919, s. 1; 1977, c. 667, s. 3; 1981, c. 51, s. 9

§ 90-105. Order forms

Controlled substances included in Schedules I and II of this Article shall be distributed only by a registrant or practitioner, pursuant to an order form. Compliance with the provisions of the Federal Controlled Substances Act or its successor respecting order forms shall be deemed compliance with this section.

History.
1971, c. 919, s. 1

§ 90-106. Prescriptions and labeling

(a) **Definitions.** -- As used in this section, the following terms have the following meanings:

(1) **Acute pain.** -- Pain, whether resulting from disease, accident, intentional trauma, or other cause, that the practitioner reasonably expects to last for three months or less. The term does not include chronic pain or pain being treated as part of cancer care, hospice care, palliative care, or medication-assisted treatment for a substance use disorder. The term does not include pain being treated as part of cancer care, hospice care, or palliative care provided by a person licensed to practice veterinary medicine pursuant to Article 11 of this Chapter.

(2) **Chronic pain.** -- Pain that typically lasts for longer than three months or that lasts beyond the time of normal tissue healing.

(3) **Surgical procedure.** -- A procedure that is performed for the purpose of structurally altering the human body by incision or destruction of tissues as part of the practice of medicine or a procedure that is performed for the purpose of structurally altering the animal body by incision or destruction of tissues as part of the practice of veterinary medicine. This term includes the diagnostic or therapeutic treatment of conditions or disease processes by use of instruments such as lasers, ultrasound, ionizing, radiation, scalpels, probes, or needles that cause localized alteration or transportation of live human tissue, or live animal tissue in the practice of veterinary medicine, by cutting, burning, vaporizing, freezing, suturing, probing, or manipulating by closed reduction for major dislocations and fractures, or otherwise altering by any mechanical, thermal, light-based, electromagnetic, or chemical means.

(a1) **Electronic Prescription Required; Exceptions.** -- Unless otherwise exempted by this subsection, a practitioner shall electronically prescribe all targeted controlled substances. This subsection does not apply to prescriptions for targeted controlled substances issued by any of the following:

(1) A practitioner, other than a pharmacist, who dispenses directly to an ultimate user.

(2) A practitioner who orders a controlled substance to be administered in a hospital, nursing home, hospice facility, outpatient dialysis facility, or residential care facility, as defined in G.S. 14-32.2(i).

(3) A practitioner who experiences temporary technological or electrical failure or other extenuating circumstance that prevents the prescription from being transmitted electronically. The practitioner, however, shall document the reason for this exception in the patient's medical record.

(4) A practitioner who writes a prescription to be dispensed by a pharmacy located on federal property. The practitioner, however, shall document the reason for this exception in the patient's medical record.

(5) A person licensed to practice veterinary medicine pursuant to Article 11 of this Chapter. A person licensed to practice veterinary medicine pursuant to Article 11 of this Chapter may continue to prescribe targeted controlled substances from valid written, oral, or facsimile prescriptions that are otherwise consistent with applicable laws.

(a2) **Verification by Dispenser Not Required.** -- A dispenser is not required to verify that a practitioner properly falls under one of the exceptions specified in subsection (a1) of this section prior to dispensing a targeted controlled substance. A dispenser may continue to dispense targeted controlled substances from valid written, oral, or facsimile prescriptions that are otherwise consistent with applicable laws.

(a3) **Limitation on Prescriptions Upon Initial Consultation for Acute Pain.** -- A practitioner shall not prescribe more than a five-day supply of any targeted controlled substance upon the initial consultation and treatment of a patient for acute pain, unless the prescription is for post-operative acute pain relief for use immediately following a surgical procedure. A practitioner shall not prescribe more than a seven-day supply of any targeted controlled substance for post-operative acute pain relief immediately following a surgical procedure. Upon any subsequent consultation for the same pain, the practitioner may issue any appropriate renewal, refill, or new prescription for a targeted controlled substance. This subsection does not apply to prescriptions for controlled substances issued by a practitioner who orders a controlled substance to be wholly administered in a hospital, nursing home licensed under Chapter 131E of the General Statutes, hospice facility, or residential care facility, as defined in G.S. 14-32.2(i). This subsection does not apply to prescriptions for controlled substances issued by a practitioner who orders a controlled substance to be wholly administered in an emergency facility, veterinary hospital, or animal hospital, as defined in G.S. 90-181.1. A practitioner who acts in accordance with the limitation on prescriptions as set forth in this subsection is immune from any civil liability or disciplinary action from the practitioner's occupational licensing agency for acting in accordance with this subsection.

(a4) Repealed by Session Laws 2019-76, s. 12(b) effective January 1, 2020, and applicable to offenses committed on or after that date.

(a5) **Dispenser Immunity.** -- A dispenser is immune from any civil or criminal liability or

disciplinary action from the Board of Pharmacy for dispensing a prescription written by a prescriber in violation of this section.

(b) **Dispensing of Schedule II Controlled Substances.** -- No Schedule II substance shall be dispensed pursuant to a written or electronic prescription more than six months after the date it was prescribed. In emergency situations, as defined by rule of the Commission, Schedule II controlled substances may be dispensed upon oral prescription of a practitioner, reduced promptly to writing and filed by the dispensing agent. Prescriptions shall be retained in conformity with the requirements of G.S. 90-104. No prescription for a Schedule II substance shall be refilled.

(c) **Dispensing of Schedule III and IV Controlled Substances.** -- Except when dispensed directly by a practitioner, other than a pharmacist, to an ultimate user, no controlled substance included in Schedules III or IV, except paregoric, U.S.P., as provided in G.S. 90-91(e)1., shall be dispensed without a prescription, and oral prescriptions shall be promptly reduced to writing and filed with the dispensing agent. The prescription shall not be filled or refilled more than six months after the date of the prescription or be refilled more than five times after the date of the prescription.

(d) **Dispensing of Schedule V Controlled Substances.** -- No controlled substance included in Schedule V of this Article or paregoric, U.S.P., shall be distributed or dispensed other than for a medical purpose.

(e) **Dispensing of Schedule VI Controlled Substances.** -- No controlled substance included in Schedule VI of this Article shall be distributed or dispensed other than for scientific or research purposes by persons registered under, or permitted by, this Article to engage in scientific or research projects.

(f) **Labeling Requirements.** -- No controlled substance shall be dispensed or distributed in this State unless the substance is in a container clearly labeled in accord with regulations lawfully adopted and published by the federal government or the Commission.

(g) **Copies.** -- When a copy of a prescription for a controlled substance under this Article is given as required by G.S. 90-70, the copy shall be plainly marked: "Copy -- for information only." Copies of prescriptions for controlled substances shall not be filled or refilled.

(h) **Fill Date.** -- A pharmacist dispensing a controlled substance under this Article shall enter the date of dispensing on the prescription order pursuant to which the controlled substance was dispensed.

(i) **Distribution of Complimentary Samples.** -- A manufacturer's sales representative may distribute a controlled substance as a complimentary sample only upon the written request of a practitioner. The request must be made on each distribution and must contain the names and addresses of the supplier and the requester and the name and quantity of the specific controlled substance requested. The manufacturer shall maintain a record of each request for a period of two years.

History.
1971, c. 919, s. 1; 1973, c. 476, s. 128; c. 1358, s. 15; 1975, c. 572; 1977, c. 667, s. 3; 1981, c. 51, s. 9; 2007-248, s. 2; 2013-379, s. 5; 2017-74, s. 6; 2018-76, ss. 5, 7; 2019-76, s. 12(b)

§ 90-106.1. Photo ID requirement for Schedule II controlled substances

(a) Immediately prior to dispensing a Schedule II controlled substance, or any of the Schedule III controlled substances listed in subdivisions 1. through 8. of G.S. 90-91(d), each pharmacy holding a valid permit pursuant to G.S. 90-85.21 shall require the person seeking the dispensation to present one of the following valid, unexpired forms of government-issued photographic identification: (i) a drivers license, (ii) a special identification card issued under G.S. 20-37.7, (iii) a military identification card, or (iv) a passport. Upon presentation of the required photographic identification, the pharmacy shall document the name of the person seeking the dispensation, the type of photographic identification presented by the person seeking the dispensation, and the photographic identification number. The pharmacy shall retain this identifying information on the premises or at a central location apart from the premises as part of its business records for a period of three years following dispensation.

(b) The pharmacy shall make the identifying information available to any person authorized under G.S. 90-113.74 to receive prescription information data in the controlled substances reporting system within 72 hours after a request for the identifying information. A pharmacy that submits the identifying information required under this section to the controlled substances reporting system established and maintained pursuant to G.S. 90-113.73 is deemed in compliance with this subsection.

(c) Nothing in this section shall be deemed to require that the person seeking the dispensation and the person to whom the prescription is issued be the same person, and nothing in this section shall apply to the dispensation of controlled substances to employees of "health care facilities", as that term is defined in G.S. 131E-256(b), when the controlled substances are delivered to the health care facilities for the benefit of residents or patients of such health care facilities.

History.
2011-349, s. 1

§ 90-106.2. Treatment of overdose with opioid antagonist; immunity

(a) As used in this section, "opioid antagonist" means naloxone hydrochloride that is approved by the federal Food and Drug Administration for the treatment of a drug overdose.

(b) A practitioner acting in good faith and exercising reasonable care may directly or by standing order prescribe an opioid antagonist to (i) a person at risk of experiencing an opiate-related overdose or (ii) a family member, friend, or other person in a position to assist a person at risk of experiencing an opiate-related overdose. As an indicator of good faith, the practitioner, prior to prescribing an opioid under this subsection, may require receipt of a written communication that provides a factual basis for a reasonable conclusion as to either of the following:

(1) The person seeking the opioid antagonist is at risk of experiencing an opiate-related overdose.

(2) The person other than the person who is at risk of experiencing an opiate-related overdose, and who is seeking the opioid antagonist, is in relation to the person at risk of experiencing an opiate-related overdose:

a. A family member, friend, or other person.

b. In the position to assist a person at risk of experiencing an opiate-related overdose.

(b1) A pharmacist may dispense an opioid antagonist to a person described in subsection (b) of this section pursuant to a prescription issued in accordance with subsection (b) of this section. For purposes of this section, the term "pharmacist" is as defined in G.S. 90-85.3.

(c) A person who receives an opioid antagonist that was prescribed pursuant to subsection (b) of this section may administer an opioid antagonist to another person if (i) the person has a good faith belief that the other person is experiencing a drug-related overdose and (ii) the person exercises reasonable care in administering the drug to the other person. Evidence of the use of reasonable care in administering the drug shall include the receipt of basic instruction and information on how to administer the opioid antagonist.

(d) All of the following individuals are immune from any civil or criminal liability for actions authorized by this section:

(1) Any practitioner who prescribes an opioid antagonist pursuant to subsection (b) of this section.

(1a) Any pharmacist who dispenses an opioid antagonist pursuant to subsection (b1) of this section.

(2) Any person who administers an opioid antagonist pursuant to subsection (c) of this section.

History.
2013-23, s. 2; 2015-94, s. 3.

§ 90-106.3. Disposal of residual pain prescriptions following death of hospice or palliative care patient

Any hospice or palliative care provider who prescribes a targeted controlled substance to be administered to a patient in his or her home for the treatment of pain as part of in-home hospice or palliative care shall, at the commencement of treatment, provide oral and written information to the patient and his or her family regarding the proper disposal of such targeted controlled substances. This information shall include the availability of permanent drop boxes or periodic "drug take-back" events that allow for the safe disposal of controlled substances such as those permanent drop boxes and events that may be identified through North Carolina Operation Medicine Drop.

History.
2017-74, s. 7.

§ 90-107. Prescriptions, stocks, etc., open to inspection by officials

Prescriptions, order forms and records, required by this Article, and stocks of controlled substances included in Schedules I through VI of this Article shall be open for inspection only to federal and State officers, whose duty it is to enforce the laws of this State or of the United States relating to controlled substances included in Schedules I through VI of this Article, and to authorized employees of the North Carolina Department of Health and Human Services. No officer having knowledge by virtue of his office of any such prescription, order, or record shall divulge such knowledge other than to other law-enforcement officials or agencies, except in connection with a prosecution or proceeding in court or before a licensing board or officer to which prosecution or proceeding the person to whom such prescriptions, orders, or records relate is a party.

History.
1971, c. 919, s. 1; 1973, c. 1358, s. 13; 1977, c. 667, s. 3; 1997-443, s. 11A.118(a).

§ 90-107.1. Certified diversion investigator access to prescription records

(a) A certified diversion investigator associated with a qualified law enforcement agency,

as those terms are defined in G.S. 90-113.74(i), shall request and receive from a pharmacy copies of prescriptions and records related to prescriptions in connection with a bona fide active investigation related to the enforcement of laws governing licit or illicit drugs by providing in writing or electronically all of the following:

(1) The certified diversion investigator's name and certification number.

(2) The name of the qualified law enforcement agency for whom the investigator works.

(3) The case number associated with the request.

(4) A description of the nature and purpose of the request.

(5) The first name, last name, and date of birth of each individual whose prescription and records related to the prescription the investigator seeks, including, when appropriate, any alternative name, spelling, or date of birth associated with each such individual.

(b) When a certified diversion investigator transmits such a request to a pharmacy, the certified diversion investigator shall also transmit a copy of the request to the North Carolina State Bureau of Investigation, Diversion and Environmental Crimes Unit. The North Carolina State Bureau of Investigation shall conduct periodic audits of a random sample of these requests.

(c) A pharmacy shall provide copies of requested prescriptions and records related to prescriptions as soon as practicable and no later than two business days after receipt of the request from the certified diversion investigator.

(d) No certified diversion investigator having knowledge by virtue of his office of any such prescription or record related to prescriptions shall divulge such knowledge other than to other law enforcement officials or agencies involved in the bona fide active investigation, except in connection with a prosecution or proceeding in court or before a licensing board or officer to which prosecution or proceeding the person to whom such prescriptions, orders, or records relate is a party, or as provided in G.S. 90-113.74 (i)(4), or as otherwise allowed by law.

(e) A pharmacy or pharmacist that in good faith complies with this section and provides copies of prescriptions and records related to prescriptions to a certified diversion investigator shall have no liability for improper use of information divulged to the certified diversion investigator.

History.
2018-44, s. 8.

§ 90-108. Prohibited acts; penalties

(a) It shall be unlawful for any person:

(1) Other than practitioners licensed under Articles 1, 2, 4, 6, 11, 12A of this Chapter to represent to any registrant or practitioner who manufactures, distributes, or dispenses a controlled substance under the provision of this Article that he or she is a licensed practitioner in order to secure or attempt to secure any controlled substance as defined in this Article or to in any way impersonate a practitioner for the purpose of securing or attempting to secure any drug requiring a prescription from a practitioner as listed above and who is licensed by this State.

(2) Who is subject to the requirements of G.S. 90-101 or a practitioner to distribute or dispense a controlled substance in violation of G.S. 90-105 or G.S. 90-106.

(3) Who is a registrant to manufacture, distribute, or dispense a controlled substance not authorized by his or her registration to another registrant or other authorized person.

(4) To omit, remove, alter, or obliterate a symbol required by the Federal Controlled Substances Act or its successor.

(5) To refuse or fail to make, keep, or furnish any record, notification, order form, statement, invoice or information required under this Article.

(6) To refuse any entry into any premises or inspection authorized by this Article.

(7) To knowingly keep or maintain any store, shop, warehouse, dwelling house, building, vehicle, boat, aircraft, or any place whatever, which is resorted to by persons using controlled substances in violation of this Article for the purpose of using such substances, or which is used for the keeping or selling of the same in violation of this Article.

(8) Who is a registrant or a practitioner to distribute a controlled substance included in Schedule I or II of this Article in the course of his or her legitimate business, except pursuant to an order form as required by G.S. 90-105.

(9) To use in the course of the manufacture or distribution of a controlled substance a registration number which is fictitious, revoked, suspended, or issued to another person.

(10) To acquire or obtain possession of a controlled substance by misrepresentation, fraud, forgery, deception, or subterfuge.

(11) To furnish false or fraudulent material information in, or omit any material information from, any application, report, or other document required to be kept or filed under this Article, or any record required to be kept by this Article.

(12) To make, distribute, or possess any punch, die, plate, stone, or other thing designed to print, imprint, or reproduce the trademark, trade name, or other identifying mark, imprint, or device of another or any likeness of any of the foregoing upon any drug or container or labeling thereof so as to render such drug a counterfeit controlled substance.

(13) To obtain controlled substances through the use of legal prescriptions which have been obtained by the knowing and willful misrepresentation to or by the intentional withholding of information from one or more practitioners.

(14) Who is a registrant or practitioner or an employee of a registrant or practitioner and who is authorized to possess controlled substances or has access to controlled substances by virtue of employment, to embezzle or fraudulently or knowingly and willfully misapply or divert to his or her own use or other unauthorized or illegal use or to take, make away with or secrete, with intent to embezzle or fraudulently or knowingly and willfully misapply or divert to his or her own use or other unauthorized or illegal use any controlled substance which shall have come into his or her possession or under his or her care.

(15) Who is not a registrant or practitioner nor an employee of a registrant or practitioner and who, by virtue of his or her occupation or profession, administers or provides medical care, aid, emergency treatment, or any combination of these to a person who is prescribed a controlled substance, to embezzle or fraudulently or knowingly and willfully misapply or divert to his or her own use or other unauthorized or illegal use or to take, make away with, or secrete, with intent to embezzle or fraudulently or knowingly and willfully misapply or divert to his or her own use or other unauthorized or illegal use any controlled substance that is prescribed to another.

(b) Any person who violates this section shall be guilty of a Class 1 misdemeanor. Provided, that if the criminal pleading alleges that the violation was committed intentionally, and upon trial it is specifically found that the violation was committed intentionally, such violations shall be a Class I felony unless one of the following applies:

(1) A person who violates subdivision (7) of subsection (a) of this section and also fortifies the structure, with the intent to impede law enforcement entry, (by barricading windows and doors) shall be punished as a Class I felon.

(2) A person who violates subdivision (14) or (15) of subsection (a) of this section shall be punished as a Class G felon.

(3) A person who violates subdivision (14) or (15) of subsection (a) of this section and intentionally diverts any controlled substance by means of dilution or substitution or both shall be punished as a Class E felon. As used in this subdivision, the following terms have the following meanings:

    a. **Dilution.** -- The act of diluting or the state of being diluted; the act of reducing the concentration of a mixture or solution.

    b. **Substitution.** -- To take the place of or replace.

History.

1971, c. 919, s. 1; 1973, c. 1358, s. 11; 1979, c. 760, ss. 5, 6; 1979, 2nd Sess., c. 1316, s. 47; 1981, c. 63, s. 1; c. 179, s. 14; 1983, c. 294, s. 7; c. 773; 1991 (Reg. Sess., 1992), c. 1041, s. 1; 1993, c. 539, s. 622; 1994, Ex. Sess., c. 24, s. 14(c); 2013-90, s. 1; 2018-44, s. 9

§ 90-109. Licensing required

A facility for drug treatment as defined in G.S. 122C-3(14)b. shall obtain the license required by Article 2 of Chapter 122C of the General Statutes permitting operation. Subject to rules governing the operation and licensing of these facilities set by the Commission for Mental Health, Developmental Disabilities, and Substance Abuse Services, the Department of Health and Human Services shall be responsible for issuing licenses. These licensing rules shall be consistent with the licensing rules adopted under Article 2 of Chapter 122C of the General Statutes.

History.

1971, c. 919, s. 1; 1973, c. 1361; 1977, c. 667, s. 3; 1981, c. 51, s. 9; 1983, c. 718, s. 2; 1985, c. 589, s. 32; 1995, c. 509, s. 39; 1997-443, s. 11A.118(a)

§ 90-109.1. Treatment

(a) A person may request treatment and rehabilitation for drug dependence from a practitioner, and such practitioner or employees thereof shall not disclose the name of such person to any law-enforcement officer or agency; nor shall such information be admissible as evidence in any court, grand jury, or administrative proceeding unless authorized by the person seeking treatment. A practitioner may undertake the treatment and rehabilitation of such person or refer such person to another practitioner for such purpose and under the same requirement of confidentiality.

(b) An individual who requests treatment or rehabilitation for drug dependence in a program where medical services are to be an integral component of his treatment shall be examined and evaluated by a practitioner before receiving treatment and rehabilitation services.

If a practitioner performs an initial examination and evaluation, the practitioner shall prescribe a proper course of treatment and medication, if needed. That practitioner may authorize another practitioner to provide the prescribed treatment and rehabilitation services.

(c) Every practitioner that provides treatment or rehabilitation services to a person dependent upon drugs shall periodically as required by the Secretary of the North Carolina Department of Health and Human Services commencing January 1, 1972, make a statistical report to the Secretary of the North Carolina Department of Health and Human Services in such form and manner as the Secretary shall prescribe for each such person treated or to whom rehabilitation services were provided. The form of the report prescribed shall be furnished by the Secretary of the North Carolina Department of Health and Human Services. Such report shall include the number of persons treated or to whom rehabilitation services were provided; the county of such person's legal residence; the age of such person; the number of such persons treated as inpatients and the number treated as outpatients; the number treated who had received previous treatment or rehabilitation services; and any other data required by the Secretary. If treatment or rehabilitation services are provided to a person by a hospital, public agency, or drug treatment facility, such hospital, public agency, or drug treatment facility shall coordinate with the treating medical practitioner so that statistical reports required in this section shall not duplicate one another. The Secretary shall cause all such reports to be compiled into periodical reports which shall be a public record.

History.

1971, c. 919, s. 1; 1977, c. 667, s. 3; 1985, c. 439, s. 5; 1997-443, s. 11A.118(a)

§ 90-110. Injunctions

(a) The superior court of North Carolina shall have jurisdiction in proceedings in accordance with the rules of those courts to enjoin violations of this Article.

(b) In case of an alleged violation of an injunction or restraining order issued under this section, trial shall, upon demand of the accused, be by a jury in accordance with the rules of the superior courts of North Carolina.

History.

1971, c. 919, s. 1

§ 90-111. Cooperative arrangements

The North Carolina Department of Health and Human Services and the Attorney General of North Carolina shall cooperate with federal and other State agencies in discharging their responsibilities concerning traffic in controlled substances and in suppressing the abuse of controlled substances. To this end, they are authorized to:

(1) Arrange for the exchange of information between governmental officials concerning the use and abuse of controlled substances;

(2) Coordinate and cooperate in training programs on controlled substances for law enforcement at the local and State levels;

(3) Cooperate with the Bureau by establishing a centralized unit which will accept, catalogue, file, and collect statistics, including records of drug-dependent persons and other controlled substance law offenders within the State, and make such information available for federal, State, and local law-enforcement purposes. Provided that neither the Attorney General of North Carolina, the North Carolina Department of Health and Human Services nor any other State officer or agency shall be authorized to accept or file, or give out the names or other form of personal identification of drug-dependent persons who voluntarily seek treatment or assistance related to their drug dependency.

History.
1971, c. 919, s. 1; 1977, c. 667, s. 3; 1997-443, s. 11A.118(a)

§ 90-112. Forfeitures

(a) The following shall be subject to forfeiture:

(1) All controlled substances which have been manufactured, distributed, dispensed, or acquired in violation of the provisions of this Article;

(2) All money, raw material, products, and equipment of any kind which are acquired, used, or intended for use, in selling, purchasing, manufacturing, compounding, processing, delivering, importing, or exporting a controlled substance in violation of the provisions of this Article;

(3) All property which is used, or intended for use, as a container for property described in subdivisions (1) and (2);

(4) All conveyances, including vehicles, vessels, or aircraft, which are used or intended for use to unlawfully conceal, convey, or transport, or in any manner to facilitate the unlawful concealment, conveyance, or transportation of property described in (1) or (2), except that

a. No conveyance used by any person as a common carrier in the transaction of business as a common carrier shall be forfeited under the provisions of this Article unless it shall appear that the owner or other person in charge of such conveyance was a consenting party or privy to a violation of this Article;

b. No conveyance shall be forfeited under the provisions of this section by reason of any act or omission, committed or omitted while such conveyance was unlawfully in the possession of a person other than the owner in violation of the criminal laws of the United States, or of any state;

c. No conveyance shall be forfeited unless the violation involved is a felony under this Article;

d. A forfeiture of a conveyance encumbered by a bona fide security interest is subject to the interest of the secured party who had no knowledge of or consented to the act or omission.

(5) All books, records, and research, including formulas, microfilm, tapes, and data which are used, or intended for use, in violation of this Article.

(b) Any property subject to forfeiture under this Article may be seized by any law-enforcement officer upon process issued by any district or superior court having jurisdiction over the property except that seizure without such process may be made when:

(1) The seizure is incident to an arrest or a search under a search warrant;

(2) The property subject to seizure has been the subject of a prior judgment in favor of the State in a criminal injunction or forfeiture proceeding under this Article.

(c) Property taken or detained under this section shall not be repleviable, but shall be deemed to be in custody of the law-enforcement agency seizing it, which may:

(1) Place the property under seal; or,

(2) Remove the property to a place designated by it; or,

(3) Request that the North Carolina Department of Justice take custody of the property and remove it to an appropriate location for disposition in accordance with law.

Any property seized by a State, local, or county law enforcement officer shall be held in safekeeping as provided in this subsection until an order of disposition is properly entered by the judge.

(d) Whenever property is forfeited under this Article, the law-enforcement agency having custody of it may:

(1) Retain the property for official use; or

(2) Sell any forfeited property which is not required to be destroyed by law and which is not harmful to the public, provided that the proceeds be disposed of for payment of all proper expenses of the proceedings for

forfeiture and sale including expense of seizure, maintenance of custody, advertising, and court costs; or

(3) Transfer any conveyance including vehicles, vessels, or aircraft which are forfeited under the provisions of this Article to the North Carolina Department of Justice when, in the discretion of the presiding judge and upon application of the North Carolina Department of Justice, said conveyance may be of official use to the North Carolina Department of Justice;

(4) Upon determination by the director of any law-enforcement agency that a vehicle, vessel or aircraft transferred pursuant to the provisions of this Article is of no further use to said agency for use in official investigations, such vehicle, vessel or aircraft may be sold as surplus property in the same manner as other vehicles owned by the law-enforcement agency and the proceeds from such sale after deducting the cost of sale shall be paid to the treasurer or proper officer authorized to receive fines and forfeitures to be used for the school fund of the county in the county in which said vehicle, vessel or aircraft was seized; provided, that any vehicle transferred to any law-enforcement agency under the provisions of this Article which has been modified to increase speed shall be used in the performance of official duties only and not for resale, transfer or disposition other than as junk.

(d1) Notwithstanding the provisions of subsection (d), the law-enforcement agency having custody of money that is forfeited pursuant to this section shall pay it to the treasurer or proper officer authorized to receive fines and forfeitures to be used for the school fund of the county in which the money was seized.

(e) All substances included in Schedules I through VI that are possessed, transferred, sold, or offered for sale in violation of the provisions of this Article shall be deemed contraband and seized and summarily forfeited to the State. All substances included in Schedules I through VI of this Article which are seized or come into the possession of the State, the owners of which are unknown, shall be deemed contraband and summarily forfeited to the State according to rules and regulations of the North Carolina Department of Justice.

All species of plants from which controlled substances included in Schedules I, II and VI of this Article may be derived, which have been planted or cultivated in violation of this Article, or of which the owners or cultivators are unknown, or which are wild growths, may be seized and summarily forfeited to the State.

The failure, upon demand by the Attorney General of North Carolina, or his duly authorized agent, of the person in occupancy or in control of land or premises upon which such species of plants are growing or being stored, to produce an appropriate registration, or proof that he is the holder thereof, shall constitute authority for the seizure and forfeiture.

(f) All other property subject to forfeiture under the provisions of this Article shall be forfeited as in the case of conveyances used to conceal, convey, or transport intoxicating beverages.

History.
1971, c. 919, s. 1; 1973, cc. 447, 542; c. 1446, s. 6; 1983, c. 528; ss. 1-3; 1989, c. 772, s. 4

§ 90-112.1. Remission or mitigation of forfeitures; possession pending trial

(a) Whenever, in any proceeding in court for a forfeiture, under G.S. 90-112 of any conveyance seized for a violation of this Article the court shall have exclusive jurisdiction to continue, remit or mitigate the forfeiture.

(b) In any such proceeding the court shall not allow the claim of any claimant for remission or mitigation unless and until he proves (i) that he has an interest in such conveyance, as owner or otherwise, which he acquired in good faith; (ii) that he had no knowledge, or reason to believe, that it was being or would be used in the violation of laws of this State relating to controlled substances; (iii) that his interest is in an amount in excess or equal to the fair market value of such conveyance.

(c) If the court, in its discretion, allows the remission or mitigation the conveyance shall be returned to the claimant; and should there be joint request of any two or more claimants, whose claims are allowed, the court shall order the return of the conveyance to such of the joint requesting claimants as have the prior claim on lien. Such return shall be made only upon payment of all expenses incident to the seizure and forfeiture incurred by the State. In all other cases the court shall order disposition of such conveyance as provided in G.S. 90-112, and after satisfaction of the expenses of the sale, and such claims as may be approved by the court, the funds shall be paid to the treasurer or proper officer authorized to receive fines and forfeitures to be used for the school fund of the county in which said vehicle was seized.

(d) If the court should determine that the conveyance should be held for purposes of evidence, then it may order the vehicle to be held until the case is heard.

History.
1975, c. 601

N.C. Gen. Stat. § 90-113

Repealed by Session Laws 1973, c. 540, s. 7.

§ 90-113.1. Burden of proof; liabilities

(a) It shall not be necessary for the State to negate any exemption or exception set forth in this Article in any complaint, information, indictment, or other pleading or in any trial, hearing, or other proceeding under this Article, and the burden of proof of any such exemption or exception shall be upon the person claiming its benefit.

(b) In the absence of proof that a person is the duly authorized holder of an appropriate registration or order form issued under this Article, he shall be presumed not to be the holder of such registration or form, and the burden of proof shall be upon him to rebut such presumption.

(c) No liability shall be imposed by virtue of this Article upon any duly authorized officer, engaged in the lawful enforcement of this Article.

History.
1971, c. 919, s. 1

§ 90-113.2. Judicial review

All final determinations, findings, and conclusions of the Commission under this Article shall be final and conclusive decisions of the matters involved, except that any person aggrieved by such decision may obtain review of the decision as provided in Chapter 150B of the General Statutes. Findings of fact by the Commission, if supported by substantial evidence, shall be conclusive.

History.
1971, c. 919, s. 1; 1973, c. 476, s. 128; c. 1331, s. 3; 1977, c. 667, s. 3; c. 891, s. 5; 1981, c. 51, s. 9; 1987, c. 827, s. 1

§ 90-113.3. Education and research

(a) The North Carolina Department of Public Instruction and the Board of Governors of the University of North Carolina are authorized and directed to carry out educational programs designed to prevent and deter misuse and abuse of controlled substances. In connection with such programs, they are authorized to:

(1) Promote better recognition of the problems of misuse and abuse of controlled substances within the regulated industry and among interested groups and organizations;

(2) Assist the regulated industry and interested groups and organizations in contributing to the reduction of misuse and abuse of controlled substances; and

(3) Disseminate the results of research on misuse and abuse of controlled substances to promote a better public understanding of what problems exist and what can be done to combat them.

(b) The North Carolina Department of Public Instruction and the Board of Governors of the University of North Carolina or either of them may enter into contracts for educational activities related to controlled substances.

(c) The North Carolina Department of Health and Human Services is authorized and directed to encourage research on misuse and abuse of controlled substances. In connection with such research and in furtherance of the enforcement of this Article, it is authorized to:

(1) Establish methods to assess accurately the effects of controlled substances and to identify and characterize controlled substances with potential for abuse;

(2) Make studies and undertake programs of research to:

a. Develop new or improved approaches, techniques, systems, equipment, and devices to strengthen the enforcement of this Article;

b. Determine patterns of misuse and abuse of controlled substances and the social effect thereof; and

c. Improve methods for preventing, predicting, understanding, and dealing with the misuse and abuse of controlled substances.

(3) Enter into contracts with other public agencies, any district attorney, institutions of higher education, and private organizations or individuals for the purpose of conducting research, demonstrations, or special projects which bear directly on misuse and abuse of controlled substances.

(d) The North Carolina Department of Health and Human Services may enter into contracts for research activities related to controlled substances, and the North Carolina Department of Public Instruction and the Board of Governors of the University of North Carolina or either of them may enter into contracts for educational activities related to controlled substances, without performance bonds.

(e) The North Carolina Department of Health and Human Services may authorize persons engaged in research on the use and effects of controlled substances to withhold the names and other identifying characteristics of persons who are the subjects of such research. Persons who obtain this authorization may not be compelled in any State civil, criminal, administrative, legislative, or other proceeding to identify the subjects of research for which such authorization was obtained.

(f) The North Carolina Department of Health and Human Services may authorize persons engaged in research to possess and distribute controlled substances in accordance with such restrictions as the authorization may impose.

Persons who obtain this authorization shall be exempt from State prosecution for possession and distribution of controlled substances to the extent authorized by the North Carolina Department of Health and Human Services.

History.

1971, c. 919, s. 1; c. 1244, s. 14; 1973, c. 476, s. 128; 1977, c. 667, s. 3; 1981, c. 218; 1997-443, s. 11A.118(a)

N.C. Gen. Stat. § 90-113.4

Repealed by Session Laws 1981, c. 500, s. 2.

N.C. Gen. Stat. § 90-113.4A

Repealed by Session Laws 1989, c. 784, s. 4, effective with respect to acts committed on or after October 1, 1989.

§ 90-113.5. State Board of Pharmacy, State Bureau of Investigation and peace officers to enforce Article

It is hereby made the duty of the State Board of Pharmacy, its officers, agents, inspectors, and representatives, and all peace officers within the State, including agents of the State Bureau of Investigation, and all State's attorneys, to enforce all provisions of this Article, except those specifically delegated, and to cooperate with all agencies charged with the enforcement of the laws of the United States, of this State, and of all other states, relating to controlled substances. The State Bureau of Investigation is hereby authorized to make initial investigation of all violations of this Article, and is given original but not exclusive jurisdiction in respect thereto with all other law-enforcement officers of the State.

History.

1971, c. 919, s. 1; 2014-100, s. 17.1(hh)

§ 90-113.6. Payments and advances

(a) The Attorney General is authorized to pay any person, from funds appropriated for the North Carolina Department of Justice, for information concerning a violation of this Article, such sum or sums of money as he may find appropriate, without reference to any rewards to which such persons may otherwise be entitled by law.

(b) Moneys expended from appropriations of the North Carolina Department of Justice for the purchase of controlled substances or other substances proscribed by this Article which is subsequently recovered shall be reimbursed to the current appropriation for the Department.

(c) The Attorney General is authorized to direct the advance of funds by the State Treasurer

in connection with the enforcement of this Article.

History.

1971, c. 919, s. 1

§ 90-113.7. Pending proceedings

(a) Prosecutions for any violation of law occurring prior to January 1, 1972, shall not be affected by these repealers, or amendments, or abated by reason, thereof.

(b) Civil seizures or forfeitures and injunctive proceedings commenced prior to January 1, 1972, shall not be affected by these repealers, or amendments, or abated by reason, thereof.

(c) All administrative proceedings pending on January 1, 1972, shall be continued and brought to final determination in accord with laws and regulations in effect prior to January 1, 1972. Such drugs placed under control prior to January 1, 1972, which are not included within Schedules I through VI of this Article shall automatically be controlled and listed in the appropriate schedule.

(d) The provisions of this Article shall be applicable to violations of law, seizures and forfeiture, injunctive proceedings, administrative proceedings, and investigations which occur following January 1, 1972.

History.

1971, c. 919, s. 1

§ 90-113.8. Continuation of regulations

Any orders, rules, and regulations which have been promulgated under any law affected by this act [c. 919 of the 1971 Session Laws] and which are in effect on the day preceding January 1, 1972, shall continue in effect until modified, superseded, or repealed by proper authority.

History.

1971, c. 919, s. 2

ARTICLE 5A
NORTH CAROLINA TOXIC VAPORS ACT

§ 90-113.8A. Title

This Article shall be known and may be cited as the "North Carolina Toxic Vapors Act."

History.

1971, c. 1208, s. 1

§ 90-113.9. Definitions

For purposes of this Article, unless the context requires otherwise,

(1) "Intoxication" means drunkenness, stupefaction, depression, giddiness, paralysis, irrational behavior, or other change, distortion, or disturbance of the auditory, visual, or mental processes.

(2) "Commission" means the Commission for Mental Health, Developmental Disabilities, and Substance Abuse Services, established under Part 4 of Article 3 of Chapter 143B of the General Statutes.

History.
1971, c. 1208, s. 1; 1979, c. 671, s. 1; 1981, c. 51, s. 10; 1995, c. 509, s. 40

§ 90-113.10. Inhaling fumes for purpose of causing intoxication

It is unlawful for any person to knowingly breathe or inhale any compound, liquid, or chemical containing toluol, hexane, trichloroethane, isopropanol, methyl isobutyl ketone, methyl cellosolve acetate, cyclohexanone, ethyl alcohol, or any other substance for the purpose of inducing a condition of intoxication. This section does not apply to any person using as an inhalant any chemical substance pursuant to the direction of a licensed medical provider authorized by law to prescribe the inhalant or chemical substance possessed.

History.
1971, c. 1208, s. 1; 1979, c. 671, s. 2; 2007-134, s. 1

§ 90-113.10A. Alcohol vaporizing devices prohibited

It shall be unlawful for any person to knowingly manufacture, sell, give, deliver, possess, or use an alcohol vaporizing device. As used in this section, "alcohol vaporizing device" or "AVD" means a device, machine, apparatus, or appliance that is designed or marketed for the purpose of mixing ethyl alcohol with pure or diluted oxygen, or another gas, to produce an alcoholic vapor that an individual can inhale or snort. An AVD does not include an inhaler, nebulizer, atomizer, or other device that is designed and intended by the manufacturer to dispense either a substance prescribed by a licensed medical provider authorized by law to prescribe the inhalant or chemical substance possessed, or an over-the-counter medication approved by monograph or new drug application under the Federal Food, Drug, and Cosmetic Act (21 U.S.C. § 301, et seq.), provided the instrument is not used for the purpose of inducing a condition of intoxication through inhalation. Violation of

this section is not a lesser included offense of G.S. 90-113.22.

History.
2007-134, s. 2

§ 90-113.11. Possession of substances

It is unlawful for any person to possess any compound, liquid, or chemical containing toluol, hexane, trichloroethane, isopropanol, methyl isobutyl ketone, methyl cellosolve acetate, cyclohexanone, ethyl alcohol, or any other substance which will induce a condition of intoxication through inhalation for the purpose of violating G.S. 90-113.10.

History.
1971, c. 1208, s. 1; 1979, c. 671, s. 3; 2007-134, s. 3

§ 90-113.12. Sale of substance

It is unlawful for any person to sell, offer to sell, deliver, give, or possess with the intent to sell, deliver, or give any other person any compound, liquid, or chemical containing toluol, hexane, trichloroethane, isopropanol, methyl isobutyl ketone, methyl cellosolve acetate, cyclohexanone, ethyl alcohol, or any other substance which will induce a condition of intoxication through inhalation if he has reasonable cause to suspect that the product sold, offered for sale, given, delivered, or possessed with the intent to sell, give, or deliver, will be used for the purpose of violating G.S. 90-113.10.

History.
1971, c. 1208, s. 1; 1979, c. 671, s. 4; 2007-134, s. 4

§ 90-113.13. Violation a misdemeanor

Violation of this Article is a Class 1 misdemeanor.

History.
1979, c. 671, s. 5; 1993, c. 539, s. 623; 1994, Ex. Sess., c. 24, s. 14(c)

§ 90-113.14. Conditional discharge for first offenses

(a) Whenever any person who has not previously been convicted of any offense under this Article or under any statute of the United States or any state relating to those substances included in Article 5 or 5A or 5B of Chapter 90 pleads guilty to or is found guilty of inhaling or possessing any substance having the property of releasing toxic vapors or fumes in violation of Article 5A of Chapter 90, the court may, without entering a judgment of guilt and with the consent of such person, defer further proceedings and place him on probation upon such reasonable terms and conditions as it may require. Notwithstanding the provisions of G.S. 15A-1342(c) or any other statute or law, probation may be imposed under this section for an offense under this Article for which the prescribed punishment includes only a fine. To fulfill the terms and conditions of probation the court may allow the defendant to participate in a drug education program approved for this purpose by the Department of Health and Human Services. Upon violation of a term or condition, the court may enter an adjudication of guilt and proceed as otherwise provided. Upon fulfillment of the terms and conditions, the court shall discharge such person and dismiss the proceedings against him. Discharge and dismissal under this section shall be without court adjudication of guilt and shall not be deemed a conviction for purposes of this section or for purposes of disqualifications or disabilities imposed by law upon conviction of a crime including the additional penalties imposed for second or subsequent convictions. Discharge and dismissal under this section or G.S. 90-96 may occur only once with respect to any person. Disposition of a case to determine discharge and dismissal under this section at the district court division of the General Court of Justice shall be final for the purpose of appeal. Prior to taking any action to discharge or dismiss under this section the court shall make a finding that the defendant has no record of previous convictions under the "North Carolina Toxic Vapors Act", Article 5A, Chapter 90, the "North Carolina Controlled Substances Act", Article 5, Chapter 90, or the "Drug Paraphernalia Act", Article 5B, Chapter 90.

(a1) Upon the first conviction only of any offense included in G.S. 90-113.10 or 90-113.11 and subject to the provisions of this subsection (a1), the court may place defendant on probation under this section for an offense under this Article including an offense for which the prescribed punishment includes only a fine. The probation, if imposed, shall be for not less than one year and shall contain a minimum condition that the defendant who was found guilty or pleads guilty enroll in and successfully complete, within 150 days of the date of the imposition of said probation, the program of instruction at the drug education school approved by the Department of Health and Human Services pursuant to G.S. 90-96.01. The court may impose probation that does not contain a condition that defendant successfully complete the program of instruction at a drug education school if:

(1) There is no drug education school within a reasonable distance of the defendant's residence; or

(2) There are specific, extenuating circumstances which make it likely that

defendant will not benefit from the program of instruction.

The court shall enter such specific findings in the record; provided that in the case of subsection (2) above, such findings shall include the specific, extenuating circumstances which make it likely that the defendant will not benefit from the program of instruction.

Upon fulfillment of the terms and conditions of the probation, the court shall discharge such person and dismiss the proceedings against the person.

For the purpose of determining whether the conviction is a first conviction or whether a person has already had discharge and dismissal, no prior offense occurring more than seven years before the date of the current offense shall be considered. In addition, convictions for violations of a provision of G.S. 90-95(a)(1) or 90-95(a)(2) or 90-95(a)(3), or 90-113.10, or 90-113.11, or 90-113.12, or 90-113.22 shall be considered previous convictions.

Failure to complete successfully an approved program of instruction at a drug education school shall constitute grounds to revoke probation pursuant to this subsection and deny application for expunction of all recordation of defendant's arrest, indictment, or information, trial, finding of guilty, and dismissal and discharge pursuant to G.S. 15A-145.3. For purposes of this subsection, the phrase "failure to complete successfully the prescribed program of instruction at a drug education school" includes failure to attend scheduled classes without a valid excuse, failure to complete the course within 150 days of imposition of probation, willful failure to pay the required fee for the course as provided in G.S. 90-96.01(b), or any other manner in which the person fails to complete the course successfully. The instructor of the course to which a person is assigned shall report any failure of a person to complete successfully the program of instruction to the court which imposed probation. Upon receipt of the instructor's report that the person failed to complete the program successfully, the court shall revoke probation, shall not discharge such person, shall not dismiss the proceedings against the person, and shall deny application for expunction of all recordation of defendant's arrest, indictment, or information, trial, finding of guilty, and dismissal and discharge pursuant to G.S. 15A-145.3. A person may obtain a hearing before the court of original jurisdiction prior to revocation of probation or denial of application for expunction.

This subsection is supplemental and in addition to existing law and shall not be construed so as to repeal any existing provision contained in the General Statutes of North Carolina.

(b) Upon the dismissal of such person, and discharge of the proceedings against the person under subsection (a) or (a1) of this section, such person, if he or she was not over 21 years of age at the time of the offense, may be eligible to apply for expunction of certain records relating to the offense pursuant to G.S. 15A-145.3(a).

(c) The clerk of superior court in each county in North Carolina shall, as soon as practicable after each term of court in the clerk's county, file with the Commission, the names of all persons convicted under such Articles, together with the offense or offenses of which such persons were convicted.

(d) Whenever any person is charged with a misdemeanor under this Article or possessing drug paraphernalia as prohibited by G.S. 90-113.22 upon dismissal by the State of the charges against him or her or upon entry of a nolle prosequi or upon a finding of not guilty or other adjudication of innocence, the person may be eligible to apply for expunction of certain records relating to the offense pursuant to G.S. 15A-145.3(b).

(e) Whenever any person who has not previously been convicted of an offense under this Article or under any statute of the United States or any state relating to controlled substances included in any schedule of Article 5 of Chapter 90 of the General Statutes or to that paraphernalia included in Article 5B of Chapter 90 of the General Statutes pleads guilty to or has been found guilty of a misdemeanor under this Article, the person may be eligible to apply for cancellation of the judgment and expunction of certain records related to the offense pursuant to G.S. 15A-145.3(c).

History.
1971, c. 1078; 1975, c. 650, ss. 3, 4; 1977, c. 642, s. 3; 1979, c. 431, ss. 3, 4; 1981, c. 51, s. 11; c. 922, ss. 5-7; 1997-443, s. 11A.118(a); 2009-510, s. 9(a) -(d); 2009-577, s. 7; 2010-174, ss. 13 -15

ARTICLE 5B
DRUG PARAPHERNALIA

§ 90-113.20. Title

This Article shall be known and may be cited as the "North Carolina Drug Paraphernalia Act."

History.
1981, c. 500, s. 1

§ 90-113.21. General provisions

(a) As used in this Article, "drug paraphernalia" means all equipment, products and materials of any kind that are used to facilitate, or intended or designed to facilitate, violations of the Controlled Substances Act, including planting, propagating, cultivating, growing, harvesting, manufacturing, compounding, converting, producing, processing, preparing, testing, analyzing, packaging, repackaging, storing, containing, and concealing controlled substances and injecting, ingesting, inhaling, or otherwise introducing controlled substances into the human body. "Drug paraphernalia" includes, but is not limited to, the following:

(1) Kits for planting, propagating, cultivating, growing, or harvesting any species of plant which is a controlled substance or from which a controlled substance can be derived;

(2) Kits for manufacturing, compounding, converting, producing, processing, or preparing controlled substances;

(3) Isomerization devices for increasing the potency of any species of plant which is a controlled substance;

(4) Testing equipment for identifying, or analyzing the strength, effectiveness, or purity of controlled substances;

(5) Scales and balances for weighing or measuring controlled substances;

(6) Diluents and adulterants, such as quinine, hydrochloride, mannitol, mannite, dextrose, and lactose for mixing with controlled substances;

(7) Separation gins and sifters for removing twigs and seeds from, or otherwise cleaning or refining, marijuana;

(8) Blenders, bowls, containers, spoons, and mixing devices for compounding controlled substances;

(9) Capsules, balloons, envelopes and other containers for packaging small quantities of controlled substances;

(10) Containers and other objects for storing or concealing controlled substances;

(11) Hypodermic syringes, needles, and other objects for parenterally injecting controlled substances into the body;

(12) Objects for ingesting, inhaling, or otherwise introducing marijuana, cocaine, hashish, or hashish oil into the body, such as:

a. Metal, wooden, acrylic, glass, stone, plastic, or ceramic pipes with or without screens, permanent screens, hashish heads, or punctured metal bowls;

b. Water pipes;

c. Carburetion tubes and devices;

d. Smoking and carburetion masks;

e. Objects, commonly called roach clips, for holding burning material, such as a marijuana cigarette, that has become too small or too short to be held in the hand;

f. Miniature cocaine spoons and cocaine vials;

g. Chamber pipes;

h. Carburetor pipes;

i. Electric pipes;

j. Air-driven pipes;

k. Chillums;

l. Bongs;

m. Ice pipes or chillers.

(b) The following, along with all other relevant evidence, may be considered in determining whether an object is drug paraphernalia:

(1) Statements by the owner or anyone in control of the object concerning its use;

(2) Prior convictions of the owner or other person in control of the object for violations of controlled substances law;

(3) The proximity of the object to a violation of the Controlled Substances Act;

(4) The proximity of the object to a controlled substance;

(5) The existence of any residue of a controlled substance on the object;

(6) The proximity of the object to other drug paraphernalia;

(7) Instructions provided with the object concerning its use;

(8) Descriptive materials accompanying the object explaining or depicting its use;

(9) Advertising concerning its use;

(10) The manner in which the object is displayed for sale;

(11) Whether the owner, or anyone in control of the object, is a legitimate supplier of like or related items to the community, such as a seller of tobacco products or agricultural supplies;

(12) Possible legitimate uses of the object in the community;

(13) Expert testimony concerning its use;

(14) The intent of the owner or other person in control of the object to deliver it to persons whom he knows or reasonably should know intend to use the object to facilitate violations of the Controlled Substances Act.

History.
1981, c. 500, s. 1

§ 90-113.22. Possession of drug paraphernalia

(a) It is unlawful for any person to knowingly use, or to possess with intent to use, drug paraphernalia to plant, propagate, cultivate, grow, harvest, manufacture, compound, convert, produce, process, prepare, test, analyze, package, repackage, store, contain, or conceal a controlled substance other than marijuana which it would be unlawful to possess, or to inject, ingest, inhale, or otherwise introduce into the body a controlled substance other than marijuana which it would be unlawful to possess.

(b) Violation of this section is a Class 1 misdemeanor.

(c) Prior to searching a person, a person's premises, or a person's vehicle, an officer may ask the person whether the person is in possession of a hypodermic needle or other sharp object that may cut or puncture the officer or whether such a hypodermic needle or other sharp object is on the premises or in the vehicle to be searched. If there is a hypodermic needle or other sharp object on the person, on the person's premises, or in the person's vehicle and the person alerts the officer of that fact prior to the search, the person shall not be charged with or prosecuted for possession of drug paraphernalia for the needle or sharp object, or for residual amounts of a controlled substance contained in the needle or sharp object. The exemption under this subsection does not apply to any other drug paraphernalia that may be present and found during the search. For purposes of this subsection, the term "officer" includes "criminal justice officers" as defined in G.S. 17C-2(3) and a "justice officer" as defined in G.S. 17E-2(3).

(d) Notwithstanding the provisions of subsection (a) of this section, it is not unlawful for (i) a person who introduces a controlled substance into his or her body, or intends to introduce a controlled substance into his or her body, to knowingly use, or to possess with intent to use, testing equipment for identifying or analyzing the strength, effectiveness, or purity of that controlled substance or (ii) a governmental or nongovernmental organization that promotes scientifically proven ways of mitigating health risks associated with drug use and other high-risk behaviors to possess such testing equipment or distribute such testing equipment to a person who intends to introduce a controlled substance into his or her body.

History.
1981, c. 500, s. 1; 1993, c. 539, s. 624; 1994, Ex. Sess., c. 24, s. 14(c); 2013-147, s. 1; 2014-119, s. 3(a); 2015-284, s. 2; 2019-159, s. 2.1

§ 90-113.22A. Possession of marijuana drug paraphernalia

(a) It is unlawful for any person to knowingly use, or to possess with intent to use, drug paraphernalia to plant, propagate, cultivate, grow, harvest, manufacture, compound, convert, produce, process, prepare, test, analyze, package, repackage, store, contain, or conceal marijuana or to inject, ingest, inhale, or otherwise introduce marijuana into the body.

(b) A violation of this section is a Class 3 misdemeanor. A violation of this section shall be a lesser included offense of G.S. 90-113.22.

(c) Notwithstanding the provisions of subsection (a) of this section, it is not unlawful for (i) a person who introduces a controlled substance into his or her body, or intends to introduce a controlled substance into his or her body, to knowingly use, or to possess with intent to use, testing equipment for identifying or analyzing the strength, effectiveness, or purity of that controlled substance or (ii) a governmental or nongovernmental organization that promotes scientifically proven ways of mitigating health risks associated with drug use and other high-risk behaviors to possess such testing equipment or distribute such testing equipment to a person who intends to introduce a controlled substance into his or her body.

History.
2014-119, s. 3(b); 2019-159, s. 2.2

§ 90-113.23. Manufacture or delivery of drug paraphernalia

(a) It is unlawful for any person to deliver, possess with intent to deliver, or manufacture with intent to deliver, drug paraphernalia knowing that it will be used to plant, propagate, cultivate, grow, harvest, manufacture, compound, convert, produce, process, prepare, test, analyze, package, repackage, store, contain, or conceal a controlled substance which it would be unlawful to possess, or that it will be used to inject, ingest, inhale, or otherwise introduce into the body a controlled substance which it would be unlawful to possess.

(b) Delivery, possession with intent to deliver, or manufacture with intent to deliver, of each separate and distinct item of drug paraphernalia is a separate offense.

(c) Violation of this section is a Class 1 misdemeanor. However, delivery of drug paraphernalia by a person over 18 years of age to someone under 18 years of age who is at least three years younger than the defendant shall be punishable as a Class I felony.

History.
1981, c. 500, s. 1; c. 903, s. 1; 1993, c. 539, s. 625; 1994, Ex. Sess., c. 24, s. 14(c)

§ 90-113.24. Advertisement of drug paraphernalia

(a) It is unlawful for any person to purchase or otherwise procure an advertisement in any newspaper, magazine, handbill, or other publication, or purchase or otherwise procure an advertisement on a billboard, sign, or other outdoor display, when he knows that the purpose of the advertisement, in whole or in part, is to promote the sale of objects designed or intended for use as drug paraphernalia described in this Article.

(b) Violation of this section is a Class 2 misdemeanor.

History.
1981, c. 500, s. 1; c. 903, s. 1; 1993, c. 539, s. 626; 1994, Ex. Sess., c. 24, s. 14(c)

§ 90-113.27. Needle and hypodermic syringe exchange programs authorized; limited immunity

(a) Any governmental or nongovernmental organization, including a local or district health department or an organization that promotes scientifically proven ways of mitigating health risks associated with drug use and other high-risk behaviors, may establish and operate a needle and hypodermic syringe exchange program. The objectives of the program shall be to do all of the following:

(1) Reduce the spread of HIV, AIDS, viral hepatitis, and other bloodborne diseases in this State.

(2) Reduce needle stick injuries to law enforcement officers and other emergency personnel.

(3) Encourage individuals who use drugs illicitly to enroll in evidence-based treatment.

(4) Reduce the number of drug overdoses in this State.

(b) Programs established pursuant to this section shall offer all of the following:

(1) Disposal of used needles and hypodermic syringes.

(2) Needles, hypodermic syringes, and other injection supplies at no cost and in quantities sufficient to ensure that needles, hypodermic syringes, and other injection supplies are not shared or reused.

(3) Reasonable and adequate security of program sites, equipment, and personnel. Written plans for security shall be provided to the police and sheriff's offices with jurisdiction in the program location and shall be updated annually.

(4) Educational materials on all of the following:

a. Overdose prevention.

b. The prevention of HIV, AIDS, and viral hepatitis transmission.

c. Drug abuse prevention.

d. Treatment for mental illness, including treatment referrals.

e. Treatment for substance abuse, including referrals for medication assisted treatment.

(5) Access to naloxone kits that contain naloxone hydrochloride that is approved by the federal Food and Drug Administration for the treatment of a drug overdose, or referrals to programs that provide access to naloxone hydrochloride that is approved by the federal Food and Drug Administration for the treatment of a drug overdose.

(6) For each individual requesting services, personal consultations from a program employee or volunteer concerning mental health or addiction treatment as appropriate.

(c) Notwithstanding any provision of the Controlled Substances Act in Article 5 of Chapter 90 of the General Statutes or any other law, no employee, volunteer, or participant of a program established pursuant to this section shall be charged with or prosecuted for possession of any of the following:

(1) Needles, hypodermic syringes, or other injection supplies obtained from or returned to a program established pursuant to this section.

(2) Residual amounts of a controlled substance contained in a used needle, used hypodermic syringe, or used injection supplies obtained from or returned to a program established pursuant to this section.

The limited immunity provided in this subsection shall apply only if the person claiming immunity provides written verification that a needle, syringe, or other injection supplies were obtained from a needle and hypodermic syringe exchange program established pursuant to this section. In addition to any other applicable immunity or limitation on civil liability, a law enforcement officer who, acting on good faith, arrests or charges a person who is thereafter determined to be entitled to immunity from prosecution under this section shall not be subject to civil liability for the arrest or filing of charges.

(d) Prior to commencing operations of a program established pursuant to this section, the governmental or nongovernmental organization shall report to the North Carolina Department of Health and Human Services, Division of Public Health, all of the following information:

(1) The legal name of the organization or agency operating the program.

(2) The areas and populations to be served by the program.

(3) The methods by which the program will meet the requirements of subsection (b) of this section.

(e) Not later than one year after commencing operations of a program established pursuant to this section, and every 12 months thereafter, each organization operating such a program shall report the following information to the North Carolina Department of Health and Human Services, Division of Public Health:

(1) The number of individuals served by the program.

(2) The number of needles, hypodermic syringes, and needle injection supplies dispensed by the program and returned to the program.

(3) The number of naloxone kits distributed by the program.

(4) The number and type of treatment referrals provided to individuals served by the program, including a separate report of the number of individuals referred to programs that provide access to naloxone hydrochloride that is approved by the federal Food and Drug Administration for the treatment of a drug overdose.

History.
2016-88, s. 4; 2017-74, s. 8; 2019-159, s. 3.1

ARTICLE 5D
CONTROL OF METHAMPHETAMINE PRECURSORS

§ 90-113.51. Definitions

(a) For purposes of this Article, "pseudoephedrine product" means a product containing any detectable quantity of pseudoephedrine or ephedrine base, their salts or isomers, or salts of their isomers.

(b) For purposes of this Article, a "retailer" means an individual or entity that is the general owner of an establishment where pseudoephedrine products are available for sale.

(c) For purposes of this Article, the "Commission" means the Commission for Mental Health, Developmental Disabilities, and Substance Abuse Services.

History.
2005-434, s. 1

§ 90-113.52. Pseudoephedrine: restrictions on sales

(a) A pseudoephedrine product in the form of a tablet, caplet, or gel cap shall not be offered for retail sale loose in bottles but shall be sold only in blister packages.

(b) Pseudoephedrine products shall not be offered for retail sale by self-service, but shall be stored and sold in the following manner: Any pseudoephedrine product in the form of a tablet or caplet containing pseudoephedrine as the sole active ingredient or in combination with other active ingredients shall be stored and sold behind a pharmacy counter.

(c) A pseudoephedrine product may be sold at retail without a prescription only to a person at least 18 years of age. The retailer shall require every retail purchaser of a pseudoephedrine product to furnish a valid, unexpired, government-issued photo identification and to provide, in print or orally, a current valid personal residential address. If the retailer has reasonable grounds to believe that the prospective purchaser is under 18 years of age, the retailer shall require the prospective purchaser to furnish photo identification showing the date of birth of the person. The name and address of every purchaser shall be entered in a record of disposition of pseudoephedrine products to the consumer on a form approved by the Commission. The record of disposition shall also identify each pseudoephedrine product purchased, including the number of grams the product contains and the purchase date of the transaction. The retailer shall require that every purchaser sign the form attesting to the validity of the information. The form approved by the Commission shall be constructed so that it allows for entry of information in electronic format, including electronic signature. The form shall also be constructed and maintained so as to minimize disclosure of personal information to unauthorized persons.

(d) A retailer shall maintain a record of disposition of pseudoephedrine products to the consumer for a period of two years from the date of each transaction. A record shall be readily available within 48 hours of the time of the transaction for inspection by an authorized official of a federal, State, or local law enforcement agency. The records maintained by a retailer are privileged information and are not public records but are for the exclusive use of the retailer and law enforcement. The retailer may destroy the information after two years from the date of the transactions.

(e) This section does not apply to any pseudoephedrine product that is in the form of a liquid, liquid capsule, gel capsule, or pediatric product labeled pursuant to federal regulation primarily intended for administration to children under 12 years of age according to label instruction, except as to those specific products for which the Commission issues an order pursuant to G.S. 90-113.58 subjecting the product to requirements under this Article.

History.
2005-434, s. 1; 2006-186, s. 1; 2012-35, s. 2

§ 90-113.52A. Electronic record keeping

(a) A retailer shall, before completing a sale of a product containing a pseudoephedrine product, electronically submit the required information to the National Precursor Log Exchange (NPLEx) administered by the National Association of Drug Diversion Investigators (NADDI), provided that the NPLEx system is available to retailers in the State without a charge for accessing the system and the retailer has Internet access. The seller shall not complete the sale if the system generates a stop alert. Absent negligence, wantoness, recklessness, or deliberate misconduct, any retailer utilizing the electronic sales tracking system in accordance with this subsection shall not be civilly liable as a result of any act or omission in carrying out the duties required by this subsection and shall be immune from liability to any third party unless the retailer has violated any provision of this subsection in relation to a claim brought for such violation.

(b) If a pharmacy selling a product containing a pseudoephedrine product experiences mechanical or electronic failure of the electronic sales tracking system and is unable to comply with the electronic sales tracking requirement, the pharmacy or retail establishment shall record that the sale was made without submission to the NPLEx system in the record of disposition required under G.S. 90-113.52.

(c) The NADDI shall forward North Carolina transaction records in NPLEx to the State Bureau of Investigation weekly and provide real-time access to NPLEx information through the NPLEx online portal to law enforcement in the State as authorized by the SBI, provided that the SBI executes a memorandum of understanding with NADDI governing access.

(d) This system shall be capable of generating a stop sale alert, which shall be a notification that completion of the sale would result in the seller or purchaser violating the quantity limits set forth in G.S. 90-113.52. The system shall contain an override function that may be used by a dispenser of a pseudoephedrine product who has a reasonable fear of imminent bodily harm if the dispenser does not complete a sale. Each instance in which the override function is utilized shall be logged by the system.

History.
2011-240, s. 2

§ 90-113.53. Pseudoephedrine transaction limits

(a) No person shall deliver to any one person, attempt to deliver to any one person, purchase, or attempt to purchase at retail more than 3.6 grams of any pseudoephedrine products per calendar day. This limit does not apply if the product is dispensed under a valid prescription.

(b) No person shall purchase at retail more than 9 grams of pseudoephedrine products within any 30-day period. This limit does not apply if the product is dispensed under a valid prescription.

(c) This section does not apply to any pseudoephedrine products that are in the form of liquids, liquid capsules, gel capsules, or pediatric products labeled pursuant to federal regulation primarily intended for administration to children under 12 years of age according to label instruction, except as to those specific products for which the Commission issues an order pursuant to G.S. 90-113.58 subjecting the product to requirements under this Article.

History.
2005-434, s. 1; 2006-186, s. 2; 2012-35, s. 1

§ 90-113.56. Penalties

(a) If a retailer willfully and knowingly violates the provisions of G.S. 90-113.52, 90-113.52A, 90-113.53, or 90-113.54, the retailer shall be guilty of a Class A1 misdemeanor for the first offense and a Class I felony for a second or subsequent offense. A retailer convicted of a third offense occurring on the premises of a single establishment shall be prohibited from making pseudoephedrine products available for sale at that establishment.

(b) Any purchaser or employee who willfully and knowingly violates G.S. 90-113.52A, G.S. 90-113.52(c) or G.S. 90-113.53 shall be guilty of a Class 1 misdemeanor for the first offense, a Class A1 misdemeanor for a second offense, and a Class I felony for a third or subsequent offense. This subsection shall not be construed to apply to bona fide innocent purchasers.

(c) A retailer who fails to train employees in accordance with G.S. 90-113.55, adequately supervise employees in transactions involving pseudoephedrine products, or reasonably discipline employees for violations of this Article shall be fined up to five hundred dollars ($ 500.00) for the first violation, up to seven hundred fifty dollars ($ 750.00) for the second violation, and up to one thousand dollars ($ 1,000) for a third or subsequent violation of this section.

History.
2005-434, s. 1; 2011-240, s. 3

§ 90-113.57. Immunity

A retailer or an employee of the retailer who, reasonably and in good faith, reports to any law enforcement agency any alleged criminal activity related to the sale or purchase of pseudoephedrine products, or who refuses to sell a pseudoephedrine product to a person reasonably believed to be ineligible to purchase a pseudoephedrine product pursuant to

this Article, is immune from civil liability for that conduct except in cases of willful misconduct. No retailer shall retaliate in any manner against any employee of the establishment for a report made in good faith to any law enforcement agency concerning alleged criminal activity related to the sale or purchase of pseudoephedrine products.

History.
2005-434, s. 1

ARTICLE 5F
CONTROL OF POTENTIAL DRUG PARAPHERNALIA PRODUCTS

§ 90-113.80. Title

This Article shall be known and may be cited as the "Drug Paraphernalia Control Act of 2009."

History.
2009-205, s. 1

§ 90-113.81. Definitions

For the purposes of this Article:

(a) "Glass tube" means an object which meets all of the following requirements:

(1) A hollow glass cylinder, either open or closed at either end.

(2) No less than two or more than seven inches in length.

(3) No less than one-eighth inch or more than three-fourths inch in diameter.

(4) May be used to facilitate, or intended or designed to facilitate, violations of the Controlled Substances Act, including, but not limited to, processing, preparing, testing, analyzing, packaging, repackaging, storing, containing, and concealing controlled substances and injecting, ingesting, inhaling, or otherwise introducing controlled substances into the human body.

(5) Sold individually, or in connection with another object such as a novelty holder, flower vase, or pen. The foregoing descriptions are intended to be illustrative and not exclusive.

(b) "Retailer" means an individual or entity that is the general owner of an establishment where glass tubes or splitters are available for sale.

(c) "Splitter" means a ring-shaped device that does both of the following:

(1) Allows the insertion of a wrapped tobacco product, such as a cigar, so that it can be pulled through the device.

(2) Cuts or slices the wrapping of the tobacco product along the product's length as it is drawn through the device.

History.
2009-205, s. 1

§ 90-113.82. Glass tubes or splitters; restrictions on sales

(a) Glass tubes or splitters shall not be offered for retail sale by self-service, but shall be stored and sold from behind a counter where the general public cannot access them without the assistance of a retailer's agent or employee.

(b) The retailer shall require any member of the public to whom it transfers a glass tube or splitter, with or without consideration, to do all of the following:

(1) Present identification that includes a photograph that is an accurate depiction of the person and that also includes the person's name and current address.

(2) Enter his or her name and current address on a record that the retailer shall maintain solely for the purposes of this section.

(3) Sign his or her name, verifying by signature the glass tube or splitter will not be used as drug paraphernalia in violation of the criminal laws of the State of North Carolina.

(c) The retailer shall maintain the record described in subsection (b) of this section for a period of two years from the date of each transaction, after which it may be destroyed.

(d) The record shall be readily available within 48 hours of the time of the transaction for inspection by an authorized official of a federal, State, or local law enforcement agency.

(e) The retailer shall train its agents and employees on the requirements of this section.

History.
2009-205, s. 1

§ 90-113.83. Penalties

(a) A retailer, or an employee of the retailer, who willfully and knowingly violates any one of the subsections of G.S. 90-113.82 shall be guilty of a Class 2 misdemeanor.

(b) Any person who knowingly makes a false statement or representation in fulfilling the requirements in G.S. 90-113.82(b) shall be guilty of a Class 1 misdemeanor.

History.
2009-205, s. 1

§ 90-113.84. Immunity

A retailer, or an employee of the retailer, who, reasonably and in good faith, (i) reports to any law enforcement agency any alleged criminal activity related to the sale or purchase of glass tubes or splitters or (ii) refuses to sell a glass tube or splitter to a person reasonably believed to be purchasing it for use as drug paraphernalia is immune from civil liability for that conduct, except in cases of willful misconduct.

History.
2009-205, s. 1

ARTICLE 20
NURSING HOME ADMINISTRATOR ACT

§ 90-288. Misdemeanor

It is unlawful and constitutes a Class 1 misdemeanor for a person to do any of the following:

(1) Act or serve in the capacity as, or hold oneself out to be, a nursing home administrator, or use any title, sign, or other indication that the person is a nursing home administrator, unless the person is the holder of a valid license as a nursing home administrator, issued in accordance with the provisions of this Article.

(2) Violate any of the provisions of this Article.

History.
1969, c. 843, s. 1; 1993, c. 539, s. 649; 1994, Ex. Sess., c. 24, s. 14(c); 2021-84, s. 8

ARTICLE 23
RIGHT TO NATURAL DEATH; BRAIN DEATH

§ 90-320. General purpose of Article

(a) The General Assembly recognizes as a matter of public policy that an individual's rights include the right to a peaceful and natural death and that a patient or the patient's representative has the fundamental right to control the decisions relating to the rendering of the patient's own medical care, including the decision to have life-prolonging measures withheld or withdrawn in instances of a terminal condition. This Article is to establish an optional and nonexclusive procedure by which a patient or the patient's representative may exercise these rights. A military advanced medical directive executed in accordance with 10 U.S.C. § 1044 or other applicable law is valid in this State.

(b) Nothing in this Article shall be construed to authorize any affirmative or deliberate act or omission to end life other than to permit the natural process of dying. Nothing in this Article shall impair or supersede any legal right or legal responsibility which any person may have to effect the withholding or withdrawal of life-prolonging measures in any lawful manner. In such respect the provisions of this Article are cumulative.

History.
1977, c. 815; 1979, c. 715, s. 1; 1983, c. 313, s. 1; 2007-502, s. 10

§ 90-321. Right to a natural death.

(a) The following definitions apply in this Article:

(1) **Declarant.** -- A person who has signed a declaration in accordance with subsection (c) of this section.

(1a) **Declaration.** -- Except as provided in G.S. 90-321.1, any signed, witnessed, dated, and proved document meeting the requirements of subsection (c) of this section.

(2) Repealed by Session Laws 2007-502, s. 11(a), effective October 1, 2007.

(2a) **Life-prolonging measures.** -- As defined in G.S. 32A-16(4).

(3) **Physician.** -- Any person licensed to practice medicine under Article 1 of Chapter 90 of the laws of the State of North Carolina.

(4) Repealed by Session Laws 2007-502, s. 11(a), effective October 1, 2007.

(b) If a person has expressed through a declaration, in accordance with subsection (c) of this section, a desire that the person's life not be prolonged by life-prolonging measures, and the declaration has not been revoked in accordance with subsection (e) of this section; and

(1) It is determined by the attending physician that the declarant's present condition is a condition described in subsection (c) of this section and specified in the declaration for applying the declarant's directives, and

(2) There is confirmation of the declarant's present condition as set out in subdivision (b)(1) of this section by a physician other than the attending physician;

then the life-prolonging measures identified by the declarant shall or may, as specified by the declarant, be withheld or discontinued upon the direction and under the supervision of the attending physician.

(c) The attending physician shall follow, subject to subsections (b), (e), and (k) of this section, a declaration:

(1) That expresses a desire of the declarant that life-prolonging measures not be used to prolong the declarant's life if, as specified in the declaration as to any or all of the following:

a. The declarant has an incurable or irreversible condition that will result in the declarant's death within a relatively short period of time; or

b. The declarant becomes unconscious and, to a high degree of medical certainty, will never regain consciousness; or

c. The declarant suffers from advanced dementia or any other condition resulting in the substantial loss of cognitive ability and that loss, to a high degree of medical certainty, is not reversible.

(2) That states that the declarant is aware that the declaration authorizes a physician to withhold or discontinue the life-prolonging measures; and

(3) Except as provided in G.S. 90-321.1, that has been signed by the declarant in the presence of two witnesses who believe the declarant to be of sound mind and who state that they (i) are not related within the third degree to the declarant or to the declarant's spouse, (ii) do not know or have a reasonable expectation that they would be entitled to any portion of the estate of the declarant upon the declarant's death under any will of the declarant or codicil thereto then existing or under the Intestate Succession Act as it then provides, (iii) are not the attending physician, licensed health care providers who are paid employees of the attending physician, paid employees of a health facility in which the declarant is a patient, or paid employees of a nursing home or any adult care home in which the declarant resides, and (iv) do not have a claim against any portion of the estate of the declarant at the time of the declaration; and

(4) That has been proved before a clerk or assistant clerk of superior court, or a notary public who certifies substantially as set out in subsection (d1) of this section. A notary who takes the acknowledgement may but is not required to be a paid employee of the attending physician, a paid employee of a health facility in which the declarant is a patient, or a paid employee of a nursing home or any adult care home in which the declarant resides.

(d) Repealed by Session Laws 2007-502, s. 11(b), effective October 1, 2007.

(d1) The following form is specifically determined to meet the requirements of subsection (c) of this section:

ADVANCE DIRECTIVE FOR A NATURAL DEATH ("LIVING WILL")

NOTE: YOU SHOULD USE THIS DOCUMENT TO GIVE YOUR HEALTH CARE PROVIDERS INSTRUCTIONS TO WITHHOLD OR WITHDRAW LIFE-PROLONGING MEASURES IN CERTAIN SITUATIONS. THERE IS NO LEGAL REQUIREMENT THAT ANYONE EXECUTE A LIVING WILL.

GENERAL INSTRUCTIONS: You can use this Advance Directive ("Living Will") form to give instructions for the future if you want your health care providers to withhold or withdraw life-prolonging measures in certain situations. You should talk to your doctor about what these terms mean. The Living Will states what choices you would have made for yourself if you were able to communicate. Talk to your family members, friends, and others you trust about your choices. Also, it is a good idea to talk with professionals such as your doctors, clergypersons, and lawyers before you complete and sign this Living Will.

You do not have to use this form to give those instructions, but if you create your own Advance Directive you need to be very careful to ensure that it is consistent with North Carolina law.

This Living Will form is intended to be valid in any jurisdiction in which it is presented, but places outside North Carolina may impose requirements that this form does not meet.

If you want to use this form, you must complete it, sign it, and have your signature witnessed by two qualified witnesses and proved by a notary public. Follow the instructions about which choices you can initial very carefully. Do not sign this form until two witnesses and a notary public are present to watch you sign it. You then should consider giving a copy to your primary physician and/or a trusted relative, and should consider filing it with the Advanced Health Care Directive Registry maintained by the North Carolina Secretary of State: http://www.nclifelinks.org/ahcdr/

My Desire for a Natural Death

I,_____, *being of sound mind, desire that, as specified below, my life not be prolonged by life-prolonging measures:*

1. My directions about prolonging my life shall apply IF my attending physician determines that I lack capacity to make or communicate health care decisions and:

NOTE: YOU MAY INITIAL ANY AND ALL OF THESE CHOICES.

_____ *(Initial)*   *I have an incurable or irreversible condition that will result in my death within a relatively short period of time.*

_____ *(Initial)*   *I become unconscious and my health care providers determine that, to a high degree of medical certainty, I will never regain my consciousness.*

_____ *(Initial)*   *I suffer from advanced dementia or any other condition which results in the substantial loss of my cognitive ability and my health care providers determine that, to a high degree of medical certainty, this loss is not reversible.*

2. In those situations I have initialed in Section 1, I direct that my health care providers:

NOTE: INITIAL ONLY IN ONE PLACE.

_____ *(Initial)*   *may withhold or withdraw life-prolonging measures.*

_____ *(Initial)*   *shall withhold or withdraw life-prolonging measures.*

3. NOTE: INITIAL ONLY IF YOU WANT TO MAKE EXCEPTIONS TO YOUR INSTRUCTIONS IN PARAGRAPH 2.

EVEN THOUGH I do not want my life prolonged in those situations I have initialed in Section 1:

_____ *(Initial)*   *I DO want to receive BOTH artificial hydration AND artificial nutrition (for example, through tubes) in those situations.*
NOTE: DO NOT INITIAL THIS BLOCK IF ONE OF THE BLOCKS BELOW IS INITIALED.

_____ *(Initial)*   *I DO want to receive ONLY artificial hydration (for example, through tubes) in those situations.*

NOTE: DO NOT INITIAL THE BLOCK ABOVE OR BELOW IF THIS BLOCK IS INITIALED.

_____
(Initial)

I DO want to receive ONLY artificial nutrition (for example, through tubes) in those situations.
NOTE: DO NOT INITIAL EITHER OF THE TWO BLOCKS ABOVE IF THIS BLOCK IS INITIALED.

4. *I direct that my health care providers take reasonable steps to keep me as clean, comfortable, and free of pain as possible so that my dignity is maintained, even though this care may hasten my death.*

5. *I am aware and understand that this document directs certain life-prolonging measures to be withheld or discontinued in accordance with my advance instructions.*

6. *If I have appointed a health care agent by executing a health care power of attorney or similar instrument, and that health care agent is acting and available and gives instructions that differ from this Advance Directive, then I direct that:*

_____
(Initial)

Follow Advance Directive: This Advance Directive will override instructions my health care agent gives about prolonging my life.

_____
(Initial)

Follow Health Care Agent: My health care agent has authority to override this Advance Directive.
NOTE:

7. *My Health Care Providers May Rely on this Directive My health care providers shall not be liable to me or to my family, my estate, my heirs, or my personal representative for following the instructions I give in this instrument. Following my directions shall not be considered suicide, or the cause of my death, or malpractice or unprofessional conduct. If I have revoked this instrument but my health care providers do not know that I have done so, and they follow the instructions in this instrument in good faith, they shall be entitled to the same protections to which they would have been entitled if the instrument had not been revoked.*

8. *I Want this Directive to be Effective Anywhere I intend that this Advance Directive be followed by any health care provider in any place.*

9. *I have the Right to Revoke this Advance Directive I understand that at any time I may revoke this Advance Directive in a writing I sign or by communicating in any clear and consistent manner my intent to revoke it to my attending physician. I understand that if I revoke this instrument I should try to destroy all copies of it.*

This the _____ day of _____, _____.

_____
Print Name _____

I hereby state that the declarant, _____, being of sound mind, signed (or directed another to sign on declarant's behalf) the foregoing Advance Directive for a Natural Death in my presence, and that I am not related to the declarant by blood or marriage, and I would not be entitled to any portion of the estate of the declarant under any existing will or codicil of the declarant or as an heir under the Intestate Succession Act, if the declarant died on this date without a will. I also state that I am not the declarant's attending physician, nor a licensed health care provider who is (1) an employee of the declarant's attending physician, (2) nor an employee of the health facility in which the declarant is a patient, or (3) an employee of a nursing home or any adult care home where the declarant resides. I further state that I do not have any claim against the declarant or the estate of the declarant.

Date: _____   Witness: _____
Date: _____   Witness: _____
_____ COUNTY, _____ STATE
Sworn to (or affirmed) and subscribed before me this day by

_____
(type/print name of declarant)

_____
(type/print name of declarant)

(type / print name of witness)

(type / print name of witness)

(type / print name of witness)

(type / print name of witness)

Date _____

(Official Seal)   Signature of Notary Public

_____, Notary Public

Printed or typed name

My commission expires: _____

(e) A declaration may be revoked by the declarant, in writing or in any manner by which the declarant is able to communicate the declarant's intent to revoke in a clear and consistent manner, without regard to the declarant's mental or physical condition. A health care provider shall have no liability for acting in accordance with a revoked declaration unless the provider has actual notice of the revocation. A health care agent may not revoke a declaration unless the health care power of attorney explicitly authorizes that revocation; however, a health care agent may exercise any authority explicitly given to the health care agent in a declaration. A guardian of the person of the declarant or general guardian may not revoke a declaration.

(f) The execution and consummation of declarations made in accordance with subsection (c) shall not constitute suicide for any purpose.

(g) No person shall be required to sign a declaration in accordance with subsection (c) as a condition for becoming insured under any insurance contract or for receiving any medical treatment.

(h) The withholding or discontinuance of life prolonging measures in accordance with this section shall not be considered the cause of death for any civil or criminal purposes nor shall it be considered unprofessional conduct or a lack of professional competence. Any person, institution or facility against whom criminal or civil liability is asserted because of conduct in compliance with this section may interpose this section as a defense. The protections of this section extend to any valid declaration, including a document valid under subsection (l) of

this section; these protections are not limited to declarations prepared in accordance with the statutory form provided in subsection (d1) of this section, or to declarations filed with the Advance Health Care Directive Registry maintained by the Secretary of State. A health care provider may rely in good faith on an oral or written statement by legal counsel that a document appears to meet the statutory requirements for a declaration.

(i) Use of the statutory form prescribed in subsection (d1) of this section is an optional and nonexclusive method for creating a declaration and does not affect the use of other forms of a declaration, including previous statutory forms.

(j) The form provided by this section may be combined with or incorporated into a health care power of attorney form meeting the requirements of Article 3 of Chapter 32A of the General Statutes; provided, however, that the resulting form shall be signed, witnessed, and proved in accordance with the provisions of this section.

(k) Notwithstanding subsection (c) of this section:

(1) An attending physician may decline to honor a declaration that expresses a desire of the declarant that life-prolonging measures not be used if doing so would violate that physician's conscience or the conscience-based policy of the facility at which the declarant is being treated; provided, an attending physician who declines to honor a declaration on these grounds must not interfere, and must cooperate reasonably, with efforts to substitute an attending physician whose conscience would not be violated by

honoring the declaration, or transfer the declarant to a facility that does not have policies in force that prohibit honoring the declaration.

(2) An attending physician may decline to honor a declaration if after reasonable inquiry there are reasonable grounds to question the genuineness or validity of a declaration. The subsection imposes no duty on the attending physician to verify a declaration's genuineness or validity.

(l) Notwithstanding subsection (c) of this section, a declaration or similar document executed in a jurisdiction other than North Carolina shall be valid in this State if it appears to have been executed in accordance with the applicable requirements of that jurisdiction or this State.

History.
1977, c. 815; 1979, c. 112, ss. 1-6; 1981, c. 848, ss. 1-3; 1991, c. 639, s. 3; 1993, c. 553, s. 28; 2001-455, s. 4; 2001-513, s. 30(b); 2007-502, ss. 11(a) -(e); 2020-3, s. 4.10(c).

§ 90-321.1. Advanced directive for a natural death executed during a state of emergency.

(a) The requirement of G.S. 90-321 that an advanced directive for a natural death declaration be executed in the presence of two qualified witnesses shall be waived for all instruments executed on or after the effective date of this section and prior to termination of the state of emergency declared by Governor Roy Cooper in Executive Order No. 116, on March 10, 2020, as the same may be extended by any subsequent executive order, such that an instrument that is signed by the declarant, properly acknowledged before a notary public, and otherwise executed in compliance with the provisions of this Article, shall not be invalidated by the declarant's failure to execute the advanced directive for a natural death declaration in the presence of two qualified witnesses.

(b) Advanced directives for a natural death declaration executed without two qualified witnesses during the time period defined in subsection (a) of this section shall contain a short and plain statement indicating that the instrument was executed in accordance with the procedures of this section, which may but need not be cited by title or section number.

(c) This section shall expire at 12:01 A.M. on August 1, 2020; provided, however, all instruments made in accordance with this section and while this section is in effect shall remain effective and shall not need to be reaffirmed.

History.
2020-3, s. 4.10(d)

§ 90-322. Procedures for natural death in the absence of a declaration

(a) If the attending physician determines, to a high degree of medical certainty, that a person lacks capacity to make or communicate health care decisions and the person will never regain that capacity, and:

(1) Repealed by Session Laws 2007-502, s. 12, effective October 1, 2007.

(1a) That the person:

a. Has an incurable or irreversible condition that will result in the person's death within a relatively short period of time; or

b. Is unconscious and, to a high degree of medical certainty, will never regain consciousness; and

(2) There is confirmation of the person's present condition as set out above in this subsection, in writing by a physician other than the attending physician; and

(3) A vital bodily function of the person could be restored or is being sustained by life-prolonging measures;

(4) Repealed by Session Laws 2007-502, s. 12, effective October 1, 2007.

then, life-prolonging measures may be withheld or discontinued in accordance with subsection (b) of this section.

(b) If a person's condition has been determined to meet the conditions set forth in subsection (a) of this section and no instrument has been executed as provided in G.S. 90-321, then life-prolonging measures may be withheld or discontinued upon the direction and under the supervision of the attending physician with the concurrence of the following persons, in the order indicated:

(1) A guardian of the patient's person, or a general guardian with powers over the patient's person, appointed by a court of competent jurisdiction pursuant to Article 5 of Chapter 35A of the General Statutes; provided that, if the patient has a health care agent appointed pursuant to a valid health care power of attorney, the health care agent shall have the right to exercise the authority to the extent granted in the health care power of attorney and to the extent provided in G.S. 32A-19(b) unless the Clerk has suspended the authority of that health care agent in accordance with G.S. 35A-1208(a).

(2) A health care agent appointed pursuant to a valid health care power of attorney, to the extent of the authority granted.

(3) An agent, with powers to make health care decisions for the patient, appointed by

the patient, to the extent of the authority granted.

(4) The patient's spouse.

(5) A majority of the patient's reasonably available parents and children who are at least 18 years of age.

(6) A majority of the patient's reasonably available siblings who are at least 18 years of age.

(7) An individual who has an established relationship with the patient, who is acting in good faith on behalf of the patient, and who can reliably convey the patient's wishes.

If none of the above is reasonably available then at the discretion of the attending physician the life-prolonging measures may be withheld or discontinued upon the direction and under the supervision of the attending physician.

(c) Repealed by Session Laws 1979, c. 715, s. 2.

(d) The withholding or discontinuance of such life-prolonging measures shall not be considered the cause of death for any civil or criminal purpose nor shall it be considered unprofessional conduct. Any person, institution or facility against whom criminal or civil liability is asserted because of conduct in compliance with this section may interpose this section as a defense.

History.
1977, c. 815; 1979, c. 715, s. 2; 1981, c. 848, s. 5; 1983, c. 313, ss. 2-4; c. 768, s. 5.1; 1991, c. 639, s. 4; 1993, c. 553, s. 29; 2007-502, s. 12; 2017-153, s. 2.6; 2018-142, s. 35(b)

§ 90-323. Death; determination by physician

The determination that a person is dead shall be made by a physician licensed to practice medicine applying ordinary and accepted standards of medical practice. Brain death, defined as irreversible cessation of total brain function, may be used as a sole basis for the determination that a person has died, particularly when brain death occurs in the presence of artificially maintained respiratory and circulatory functions. This specific recognition of brain death as a criterion of death of the person shall not preclude the use of other medically recognized criteria for determining whether and when a person has died.

History.
1979, c. 715, s. 3

CHAPTER 91A
PAWNBROKERS AND CASH CONVERTERS MODERNIZATION ACT

§§ 91A-1 through 91A-14

Recodified as Part 1 of Article 45 of Chapter 66, G.S. 66-385 through 66-399, by Session Laws 2012-46, s. 2, effective October 1, 2012.

Editor's Note. -- This Chapter was recodified as Part 1 of Article 45 of Chapter 66 by Session Laws 2012-46, s. 2, effective October 1, 2012, and applicable to offenses committed on or after that date.

The following table shows G.S. sections from former Chapter 91A, and their comparable, new Chapter 66, Article 45, Part 1 numbers.

CHAPTER 95
DEPARTMENT OF LABOR AND LABOR REGULATIONS

ARTICLE 15
PASSENGER TRAMWAY SAFETY

§ 95-125.1. Operation of unsafe device

No person shall operate, permit to be operated, or use any device subject to the provisions of this Article if the person knows or reasonably should know that the operation or use of the device will expose the public to an unsafe condition which is likely to result in personal injury or property damage.

History.
2017-211, s. 14(c)

§ 95-125.2. Reports required

(a) The owner of any device regulated under the provisions of this Article, or the owner's authorized agent, shall, within 24 hours, notify the Commissioner of each and every occurrence involving the device when either of the following occurs:

(1) Death or injury requiring medical treatment, other than first aid, by a physician. For the purposes of this section, "first aid" means (i) the one-time treatment or observation of scratches, cuts not requiring stitches, burns, splinters, or contusions or (ii) performing a diagnostic procedure, including examination and X rays, which does not ordinarily require medical treatment even though provided by a physician or other licensed personnel.

(2) Damage to the device indicating a substantial defect in design, mechanics, structure, or equipment that affects the future safe operation of the device. No reporting is required in the case of normal wear and tear.

(b) The Commissioner, without delay, after notification and determination that an occurrence involving injury or damage as specified in subsection (a) of this section has occurred, shall make a complete and thorough investigation of the occurrence. The report of the investigation shall be placed on file in the office of the division and shall give in detail all facts and information available. The owner may submit for inclusion in the file results of investigations independent of the department's investigation.

(c) No person, after an occurrence specified in subsection (a) of this section, shall do either of the following:

(1) Operate, attempt to operate, use, or move or attempt to move such device or part thereof without the approval of the Commissioner, unless so as to prevent injury to any person or persons.

(2) Remove or attempt to remove from the premises any damaged or undamaged part of such device or repair or attempt to repair any damaged part necessary to a complete and thorough investigation. The Department must initiate its investigation within 24 hours of being notified.

History.
2017-211, s. 14(c)

§ 95-125.3. Violations; civil penalties; appeal; criminal penalties

(a) Any person who violates G.S. 95-118 (Registration required; application procedures) is subject to a civil penalty not to exceed one thousand two hundred fifty dollars ($ 1,250) for each day each device is so operated or used.

(b) Any person who violates G.S. 95-120.1 (Liability insurance) or G.S. 95-125.2 (Reports required) is subject to a civil penalty not to exceed two thousand five hundred dollars ($ 2,500) for each day each device is so operated and used.

(c) Any person who violates G.S. 95-125.1 (Operation of unsafe device) is subject to a civil penalty not to exceed five thousand dollars ($ 5,000) for each day each device is so operated and used.

(d) In determining the amount of any penalty ordered under authority of this section, the Commissioner shall give due consideration to the appropriateness of the penalty with respect to the annual gross volume of the person being charged, the gravity of the violation, the good faith of the person, and the record of previous violations.

(e) The Commissioner's determination of the amount of the penalty is final, unless within 15 days after receipt of notice thereof by certified mail with return receipt, by signature confirmation as provided by the U.S. Postal Service, by a designated delivery service authorized pursuant to 26 U.S.C. § 7502(f)(2) with delivery receipt, or via hand delivery, the person charged with the violation takes exception to the determination, in which event final determination of the penalty shall be made in an administrative proceeding pursuant to Chapter 150B of the General Statutes, the Administrative Procedures Act.

(f) The Commissioner may file in the office of the clerk of the superior court of the county wherein the person, against whom a civil penalty has been ordered, resides or, if a corporation is involved, in the county wherein the violation occurred, a certified copy of a final order of the Commissioner unappealed form, or of a final order of the Commissioner affirmed upon appeal. Upon such filing, the clerk of said court shall enter judgment in accordance with the final order and notify the parties. The judgment shall have the same effect, and all proceedings in relation to the judgment shall thereafter be the same, as though the judgment had been rendered in a suit duly heard and determined by the superior court of the General Court of Justice.

(g) Any person who willfully violates any provision of this Article and that violation causes the serious injury or death of any person, then the person is guilty of a Class E felony, which shall include a fine.

(h) Nothing in this section prevents any prosecuting officer of the State of North Carolina from proceeding against a person who violates this Article on a prosecution charging any degree of willful or culpable homicide.

History.
2017-211, s. 14(c)

CHAPTER 97
WORKERS' COMPENSATION ACT

ARTICLE 1
WORKERS' COMPENSATION ACT

§ 97-29. Rates and duration of compensation for total incapacity

(a) When an employee qualifies for total disability, the employer shall pay or cause to be paid, as hereinafter provided by subsections (b) through (d) of this section, to the injured employee a weekly compensation equal to sixty-six and two-thirds percent (662/3%) of his average weekly wages, but not more than the amount established annually to be effective January 1 as provided herein, nor less than thirty dollars ($ 30.00) per week.

(b) When a claim is compensable pursuant to G.S. 97-18(b), paid without prejudice pursuant to G.S. 97-18(d), agreed by the parties pursuant to G.S. 97-82, or when a claim has been deemed compensable following a hearing pursuant to G.S. 97-84, the employee qualifies for temporary total disability subject to the limitations noted herein. The employee shall not be entitled to compensation pursuant to this subsection greater than 500 weeks from the date of first disability unless the employee qualifies for extended compensation under subsection (c) of this section.

(c) An employee may qualify for extended compensation in excess of the 500-week limitation on temporary total disability as described in subsection (b) of this section only if (i) at the time the employee makes application to the Commission to exceed the 500-week limitation on temporary total disability as described in subsection (b) of this section, 425 weeks have passed since the date of first disability and (ii) pursuant to the provisions of G.S. 97-84, unless agreed to by the parties, the employee shall prove by a preponderance of the evidence that the employee has sustained a total loss of wage-earning capacity. If an employee makes application for extended compensation pursuant to this subsection and is awarded extended compensation by the Commission, the award shall not be stayed pursuant to G.S. 97-85 or G.S. 97-86 until the full Commission or an appellate court determines otherwise. Upon its own motion or upon the application of any party in interest, the Industrial Commission may review an award for extended compensation in excess of the 500-week limitation on temporary total disability described in subsection (b) of this section, and, on such review, may make an award ending or continuing extended compensation. When reviewing a prior award to determine if the employee remains entitled to extended compensation, the Commission shall determine if the employer has proven by a preponderance of the evidence that the employee no longer has a total loss of wage-earning capacity. When an employee is receiving full retirement benefits under section 202(a) of the Social Security Act, after attainment of retirement age, as defined in section 216(*l*) of the Social Security Act, the employer may reduce the extended compensation by one hundred percent (100%) of the employee's retirement benefit. The reduction shall consist of the employee's primary benefit paid pursuant to section 202(a) of the Social Security Act but shall not include any dependent or auxiliary benefits paid pursuant to any other section of the Social Security Act, if any, or any cost-of-living increases in benefits made pursuant to section 215(i) of the Social Security Act.

(d) An injured employee may qualify for permanent total disability only if the employee has one or more of the following physical or mental limitations resulting from the injury:

(1) The loss of both hands, both arms, both feet, both legs, both eyes, or any two thereof, as provided by G.S. 97-31(17).

(2) Spinal injury involving severe paralysis of both arms, both legs, or the trunk.

(3) Severe brain or closed head injury as evidenced by severe and permanent:

    a. Sensory or motor disturbances;

    b. Communication disturbances;

    c. Complex integrated disturbances of cerebral function; or

    d. Neurological disorders.

(4) Second-degree or third-degree burns to thirty-three percent (33%) or more of the total body surface.

An employee who qualifies for permanent total disability pursuant to this subsection shall be entitled to compensation, including medical compensation, during the lifetime of the injured employee, unless the employer shows by a preponderance of the evidence that the employee is capable of returning to suitable employment as defined in G.S. 97-2(22). Provided, however, the termination or suspension of compensation because the employee is capable of returning to suitable employment as defined in G.S. 97-2(22) does not affect the employee's entitlement to medical compensation. An employee who qualifies for permanent total disability under subdivision (1) of this subsection is entitled to lifetime compensation, including medical compensation, regardless of whether or not the employee has returned to work in any capacity. In no other case shall an employee be eligible for lifetime compensation for permanent total disability.

(e) An employee shall not be entitled to benefits under this section or G.S. 97-30 and G.S. 97-31 at the same time.

(f) Where an employee can show entitlement to compensation pursuant to this section or G.S. 97-30 and a specific physical impairment pursuant to G.S. 97-31, the employee shall not collect benefits concurrently pursuant to both this section or G.S. 97-30 and G.S. 97-31, but rather is entitled to select the statutory compensation which provides the more favorable remedy.

(g) The weekly compensation payment for members of the North Carolina National Guard and the North Carolina State Defense Militia shall be the maximum amount established annually in accordance with subsection (i) of this section per week as fixed herein. The weekly compensation payment for deputy sheriffs, or those acting in the capacity of deputy sheriffs, who serve upon a fee basis, shall be thirty dollars ($ 30.00) a week as fixed herein.

(h) An officer or member of the State Highway Patrol shall not be awarded any weekly compensation under the provisions of this section for the first two years of any incapacity resulting from an injury by accident arising out of and in the course of the performance by him of his official duties if, during such incapacity, he continues to be an officer or member of the State Highway Patrol, but he shall be awarded any other benefits to which he may be entitled under the provisions of this Article.

(i) Notwithstanding any other provision of this Article, on July 1 of each year, a maximum weekly benefit amount shall be computed. The amount of this maximum weekly benefit shall be derived by obtaining the average weekly insured wage, as defined in G.S. 96-1, by multiplying such average weekly insured wage by 1.10, and by rounding such figure to its nearest multiple of two dollars ($ 2.00), and this said maximum weekly benefit shall be applicable to all injuries and claims arising on and after January 1 following such computation. Such maximum weekly benefit shall apply to all provisions of this Chapter and shall be adjusted July 1 and effective January 1 of each year as herein provided.

(j) If death results from the injury or occupational disease, then the employer shall pay compensation in accordance with the provisions of G.S. 97-38.

History.
1929, c. 120, s. 29; 1939, c. 277, s. 1; 1943, c. 502, s. 3; c. 543; c. 672, s. 2; 1945, c. 766; 1947, c. 823; 1949,

c. 1017; 1951, c. 70, s. 1; 1953, c. 1135, s. 1; c. 1195, s. 2; 1955, c. 1026, s. 5; 1957, c. 1217; 1963, c. 604, s. 1; 1967, c. 84, s. 1; 1969, c. 143, s. 1; 1971, c. 281, s. 1; c. 321, s. 1; 1973, c. 515, s. 1; c. 759, s. 1; c. 1103, s. 1; c. 1308, ss. 1, 2; 1975, c. 284, s. 4; 1979, c. 244; 1981, c. 276, s. 2; c. 378, s. 1; c. 421, s. 3; c. 521, s. 2; c. 920, s. 1; 1987, c. 729, s. 6; 1991, c. 703, s. 4; 1999-456, s. 33(d); 2009-281, s. 1; 2011-287, s. 10; 2012-135, s. 6; 2013-2, s. 9(e); 2013-224, s. 19; 2013-410, s. 19

§ 97-29.1. Increase in payments in cases for total and permanent disability occurring prior to July 1, 1973

In all cases of total and permanent disability occurring prior to July 1, 1973, weekly compensation payments shall be increased effective July 1, 1977, to an amount computed by multiplying the number of calendar years prior to July 1, 1973, that the case arose by five percent (5%). Payments made by the employer or its insurance carrier by reason of such increase in weekly benefits may be deducted by such employer or insurance carrier from the tax levied on such employer or carrier pursuant to G.S. 105-228.5 or G.S. 97-100. Every employer or insurance carrier claiming such deduction or credit shall verify such claim to the Secretary of Revenue or the Industrial Commission by affidavit or by such other method as may be prescribed by the Secretary of Revenue or the Industrial Commission.

History.
1977, c. 651

§ 97-30. Partial incapacity

Except as otherwise provided in G.S. 97-31, where the incapacity for work resulting from the injury is partial, the employer shall pay, or cause to be paid, as hereinafter provided, to the injured employee during such disability, a weekly compensation equal to sixty-six and two-thirds percent (662/3%) of the difference between his average weekly wages before the injury and the average weekly wages which he is able to earn thereafter, but not more than the amount established annually to be effective January 1 as provided in G.S. 97-29 a week, and in no case shall the employee receive more than 500 weeks of payments under this section. Any weeks of payments made pursuant to G.S. 97-29 shall be deducted from the 500 weeks of payments available under this section. An officer or member of the State Highway Patrol shall not be awarded any weekly compensation under the provisions of this section for the first two years of any incapacity resulting from an injury by accident arising out of and in the course of the performance by him of his official duties if, during such incapacity, he continues to be an officer or member of the State Highway Patrol, but he shall be awarded any other benefits to which he may be entitled under the provisions of this Article.

History.
1929, c. 120, s. 30; 1943, c. 502, s. 4; 1947, c. 823; 1951, c. 70, s. 2; 1953, c. 1195, s. 3; 1955, c. 1026, s. 6; 1957, c. 1217; 1963, c. 604, s. 2; 1967, c. 84, s. 2; 1969, c. 143, s. 2; 1971, c. 281, s. 2; 1973, c. 515, s. 2; c. 759, s. 2; 1981, c. 276, s. 1; 2011-287, s. 11

CHAPTER 99A
CIVIL REMEDIES FOR INTERFERENCE WITH PROPERTY

§ 99A-1. Recovery of damages for interference with property rights

Notwithstanding any other provisions of the General Statutes of North Carolina, when personal property is wrongfully taken and carried away from the owner or person in lawful possession of such property without his consent and with the intent to permanently deprive him of the use, possession and enjoyment of said property, a right of action arises for recovery of actual and punitive damages from any person who has or has had, possession of said property knowing the property to be stolen.

An agent having possession, actual or constructive, of property lawfully owned by his principal, shall have a right of action in behalf of his principal for any unlawful interference with that possession by a third person.

In cases of bailments where the possession is in the bailee, a trespass committed during the existence of the bailment shall give a right of action to the bailee for the interference with his special property and a concurrent right of action to the bailor for the interference with his general property.

Any abuse of, or damage done to, the personal property of another or one who is in possession thereof, unlawfully, is a trespass for which damages may be recovered.

History.
1973, c. 809

§ 99A-2. Recovery of damages for exceeding the scope of authorized access to property

(a) Any person who intentionally gains access to the nonpublic areas of another's premises and engages in an act that exceeds the person's authority to enter those areas is liable to the owner or operator of the premises for any damages sustained. For the purposes of this section, "nonpublic areas" shall mean those areas not accessible to or not intended to be accessed by the general public.

(b) For the purposes of this section, an act that exceeds a person's authority to enter the nonpublic areas of another's premises is any of the following:

(1) An employee who enters the nonpublic areas of an employer's premises for a reason other than a bona fide intent of seeking or holding employment or doing business with the employer and thereafter without authorization captures or removes the employer's data, paper, records, or any other documents and uses the information to breach the person's duty of loyalty to the employer.

(2) An employee who intentionally enters the nonpublic areas of an employer's premises for a reason other than a bona fide intent of seeking or holding employment or doing business with the employer and thereafter without authorization records images or sound occurring within an employer's premises and uses the recording to breach the person's duty of loyalty to the employer.

(3) Knowingly or intentionally placing on the employer's premises an unattended camera or electronic surveillance device and using that device to record images or data.

(4) Conspiring in organized retail theft, as defined in Article 16A of Chapter 14 of the General Statutes.

(5) An act that substantially interferes with the ownership or possession of real property.

(c) Any person who intentionally directs, assists, compensates, or induces another person to violate this section shall be jointly liable.

(d) A court may award to a party who prevails in an action brought pursuant to this section one or more of the following remedies:

(1) Equitable relief.

(2) Compensatory damages as otherwise allowed by State or federal law.

(3) Costs and fees, including reasonable attorneys' fees.

(4) Exemplary damages as otherwise allowed by State or federal law in the amount of five thousand dollars ($ 5,000) for each day, or portion thereof, that a defendant has acted in violation of subsection (a) of this section.

(e) Nothing in this section shall be construed to diminish the protections provided to employees under Article 21 of Chapter 95 or Article 14 of Chapter 126 of the General Statutes, nor may any party who is covered by these Articles be liable under this section.

(f) This section shall not apply to any governmental agency or law enforcement officer engaged in a lawful investigation of the premises or the owner or operator of the premises.

(g) Nothing in this section shall be construed to limit any other remedy available at common law or provided by the General Statutes.

History.
2015-50, s. 1

CHAPTER 103
SUNDAYS, HOLIDAYS AND SPECIAL DAYS

§ 103-2. Method of take when hunting on Sunday

(a) Any landowner or member of the landowner's family, or any person with written permission from the landowner, may, subject to rules established by the Wildlife Resources Commission, hunt wild animals and upland game birds with the use of firearms on Sunday on the landowner's property, except that all of the following limitations apply:

(1) Hunting on Sunday between 9:30 A.M. and 12:30 P.M. is prohibited, except on controlled hunting preserves licensed pursuant to G.S. 113-273(g).

(2) Repealed by Session Laws 2017-182, s. 1, effective July 25, 2017.

(3) The use of a firearm to take deer that are run or chased by dogs on Sunday is prohibited.

(4) Hunting on Sunday within 500 yards of a place of religious worship, as defined by G.S. 14-54.1(b), or any accessory structure thereof, is prohibited.

(5) Repealed by Session Laws 2017-182, s. 1, effective July 25, 2017.

(a1) Any person may, subject to rules established by the Wildlife Resources Commission, hunt wild animals and upland game birds with the use of firearms on Sunday on public lands of the State managed for hunting, except that the following limitations apply:

(1) Hunting on Sunday between 9:30 A.M. and 12:30 P.M. is prohibited.

(2) The use of a firearm to take deer that are run or chased by dogs on Sunday is prohibited.

(3) Hunting on Sunday within 500 yards of a place of religious worship, as defined by G.S. 14-54.1(b), or any accessory structure thereof, is prohibited.

(a2) The hunting of migratory birds on Sunday is prohibited unless authorized by proclamation or rules of the Wildlife Resources Commission, subject to the following limitations:

(1) Hunting on Sunday between 9:30 A.M. and 12:30 P.M. is prohibited, except on controlled hunting preserves licensed pursuant to G.S. 113-273(g).

(2) Hunting on Sunday within 500 yards of a place of religious worship, as defined by G.S. 14-54.1(b), or any accessory structure thereof, is prohibited.

(3) The Wildlife Resources Commission shall not authorize hunting of migratory birds on Sunday prior to March 1, 2018.

(b) A person who hunts on Sunday in a manner prohibited under this section or rules adopted by the Wildlife Resources Commission shall be guilty of a Class 3 misdemeanor. Provided, that the provisions of this section are not applicable to military reservations, the jurisdiction of which is exclusively in the federal government, to field trials authorized by the Wildlife Resources Commission, or to actions taken in defense of a person's property. Wildlife protectors are granted authority to enforce the provisions of this section.

History.
1868-9, c. 18, ss. 1, 2; Code, s. 3783; Rev., s. 3842; C.S., s. 3956; 1945, c. 1047; 1967, c. 1003; 1979, c. 830, s. 13; 1989, c. 642, s. 3; 1993, c. 539, s. 684; 1994, Ex. Sess., c. 24, s. 14(c); 2015-144, s. 5(a); 2017-182, s. 1

§ 103-3. Execution of process on Sunday

It shall be lawful for any sheriff or other lawful officer to execute any summons, capias, or other process on Sunday.

History.
1957, c. 1052; 1973, c. 108, s. 47

CHAPTER 105
TAXATION

SUBCHAPTER 01.
LEVY OF TAXES

ARTICLE 2A
TOBACCO PRODUCTS TAX

PART 1
GENERAL PROVISIONS

§ 105-113.4G. Records to be kept

Every person required to be licensed under this Article and every person required to make reports under this Article shall keep complete and accurate records of all purchases, inventories, sales, shipments, and deliveries of tobacco products, and other information as required under this Article. The records shall be in the form prescribed by the Secretary and shall be open at all times for inspection by the Secretary or an authorized representative of the Secretary.

These records shall be safely preserved for a period of three years in a manner to ensure their security and accessibility for inspection by the Department.

History.
2020-58, s. 2.5(a)

PART 2
CIGARETTE TAX

§ 105-113.17. Identification of dispensers

Each vending machine that dispenses cigarettes must be marked to identify its owner in the manner required by the Secretary.

History.
1969, c. 1075, s. 2; 1973, c. 476, s. 193; 1991 (Reg. Sess., 1992), c. 955, s. 8

§ 105-113.27. Non-tax-paid cigarettes

(a) Except as otherwise provided in this Article, licensed distributors shall not sell, borrow, loan, or exchange non-tax-paid cigarettes to, from, or with other licensed distributors.

(b) Except as otherwise provided in this Article, no person shall sell or offer for sale non-tax-paid cigarettes.

(c) The possession of more than six hundred cigarettes on which tax has been paid to another state or country, by any person other than a licensed distributor, is prima facie evidence that the cigarettes are possessed in violation of this Part.

History.
1969, c. 1075, s. 2; 1993, c. 442, s. 11; 1999-337, s. 18; 2020-58, s. 2.7

§ 105-113.29. Unlicensed place of business

It is unlawful for a person to maintain a place of business within this State required by this Article to be licensed to engage in the business of selling, offering for sale, or possessing with the intent to sell cigarettes or other tobacco products without first obtaining the licenses.

History.
1969, c. 1075, s. 2; 2017-39, s. 10; 2019-169, s. 4.14(a)

§ 105-113.32. Non-tax-paid cigarettes subject to confiscation

All non-tax-paid cigarettes subject to the tax imposed by this Part, together with any container in which they are stored or displayed for sale (including but not limited to vending machines), are declared to be contraband goods and may be seized by any officer of the law. The officer shall arrest any person in charge of the contraband goods and shall at once proceed against the person arrested, under the provisions of this Part, in any court having competent jurisdiction. The disposition of the seized cigarettes and container shall be governed by the provisions of G.S. 105-113.31.

History.
1969, c. 1075, s. 2; 1993, c. 442, s. 13

§ 105-113.33. Criminal penalties

Any person who violates any of the provisions of this Article for which no other punishment is specifically prescribed shall be guilty of a Class 1 misdemeanor.

History.
1969, c. 1075, s. 2; 1993, c. 539, s. 700; 1994, Ex. Sess., c. 24, s. 14(c)

ARTICLE 2D
UNAUTHORIZED
SUBSTANCES TAXES

§ 105-113.105. Purpose

The purpose of this Article is to levy an excise tax to generate revenue for State and local law enforcement agencies and for the General Fund. Nothing in this Article may in any manner provide immunity from criminal prosecution for a person who possesses an illegal substance.

History.
1989, c. 772, s. 1; 1995, c. 340, s. 1; 1997-292, s. 1; 1998-98, s. 59

§ 105-113.106. Definitions

The following definitions apply in this Article:

(1) **Controlled Substance.** -- Defined in G.S. 90-87.

(2) Repealed by Session Laws 1995, c. 340, s. 1 .

(3) **Dealer.** -- Any of the following:

a. A person who actually or constructively possesses more than 42.5 grams of marijuana, seven or more grams of any other controlled substance that is sold by weight, or 10 or more dosage units of any other controlled substance that is not sold by weight.

b. A person who in violation of Chapter 18B of the General Statutes possesses illicit spirituous liquor for sale.

c. A person who in violation of Chapter 18B of the General Statutes possesses mash.

d. A person who in violation of Chapter 18B of the General Statutes possesses an illicit mixed beverage for sale.

(4) Repealed by Session Laws 1995, c. 340, s. 1.

(4a) **Illicit mixed beverage.** -- A mixed beverage, as defined in G.S. 18B-101, composed in whole or in part from spirituous liquor on which the charge imposed by G.S. 18B-804(b)(8) has not been paid, but not including a premixed cocktail served from a closed package containing only one serving.

(4b) **Illicit spirituous liquor.** -- Spirituous liquor, as defined in G.S. 105-113.68, not authorized by the North Carolina Alcoholic Beverage Control Commission. Some examples of illicit spirituous liquor are the products known as "bootleg liquor", "moonshine", "non-tax-paid liquor", and "white liquor".

(4c) **Local law enforcement agency.** -- A municipal police department, a county police department, or a sheriff's office.

(4d) **Low-street-value drug.** -- Any of the following controlled substances:

a. An anabolic steroid as defined in G.S. 90-91(k).

b. A depressant described in G.S. 90-89(4), 90-90(4), 90-91(b), or 90-92(a).

c. A hallucinogenic substance described in G.S. 90-89(3) or G.S. 90-90(5).

d. A stimulant described in G.S. 90-89(5), 90-90(3), 90-91(j), 90-92(a)(3), or 90-93(a)(3).

e. A controlled substance described in G.S. 90-91(c), (d), or (e), 90-92(a)(3), or (a)(5), or 90-93(a)1.

(5) Repealed by Session Laws 1995, c. 340, s. 1.

(6) **Marijuana.** -- All parts of the plant of the genus Cannabis, whether growing or not; the seeds of this plant; the resin extracted from any part of this plant; and every compound, salt, derivative, mixture, or preparation of this plant, its seeds, or its resin.

(6a) **Mash.** -- The fermentable starchy mixture from which spirituous liquor can be distilled.

(7) **Person.** -- Defined in G.S. 105-228.90.

(8) **Secretary.** -- Defined in G.S. 105-228.90.

(8a) **State law enforcement agency.** -- Any State agency, force, department, or unit responsible for enforcing criminal laws.

(9) **Unauthorized substance.** -- A controlled substance, an illicit mixed beverage, illicit spirituous liquor, or mash.

History.
1989, c. 772, s. 1; 1993, c. 354, s. 10; 1995, c. 340, s. 1; 1997-292, s. 1; 1999-337, s. 19; 2000-119, ss. 3, 4

§ 105-113.107. Excise tax on unauthorized substances

(a) **Controlled Substances.** -- An excise tax is levied on controlled substances possessed, either actually or constructively, by dealers at the following rates:

(1) At the rate of forty cents (40 cent(s)) for each gram, or fraction thereof, of harvested marijuana stems and stalks that have been separated from and are not mixed with any other parts of the marijuana plant.

(1a) At the rate of three dollars and fifty cents ($ 3.50) for each gram, or fraction thereof, of marijuana, other than separated stems and stalks taxed under subdivision (1) of this [sub]section, or synthetic cannabinoids.

(1b) At the rate of fifty dollars ($ 50.00) for each gram, or fraction thereof, of cocaine.

(1c) At the rate of fifty dollars ($ 50.00) for each gram, or fraction thereof, of any low-street-value drug that is sold by weight.

(2) At the rate of two hundred dollars ($ 200.00) for each gram, or fraction thereof, of any other controlled substance that is sold by weight.

(2a) At the rate of fifty dollars ($ 50.00) for each 10 dosage units, or fraction thereof, of any low-street-value drug that is not sold by weight.

(3) At the rate of two hundred dollars ($ 200.00) for each 10 dosage units, or fraction thereof, of any other controlled substance that is not sold by weight.

(a1) **Weight.** -- A quantity of marijuana or other controlled substance is measured by the weight of the substance whether pure or impure or dilute, or by dosage units when the substance is not sold by weight, in the dealer's possession. A quantity of a controlled substance is dilute if it consists of a detectable quantity of pure controlled substance and any excipients or fillers.

(b) **Illicit Spirituous Liquor.** -- An excise tax is levied on illicit spirituous liquor possessed by a dealer at the following rates:

(1) At the rate of thirty-one dollars and seventy cents ($ 31.70) for each gallon, or fraction thereof, of illicit spirituous liquor sold by the drink.

(2) At the rate of twelve dollars and eighty cents ($ 12.80) for each gallon, or fraction thereof, of illicit spirituous liquor not sold by the drink.

(c) **Mash.** -- An excise tax is levied on mash possessed by a dealer at the rate of one dollar and twenty-eight cents ($ 1.28) for each gallon or fraction thereof.

(d) **Illicit Mixed Beverages.** -- A tax is levied on illicit mixed beverages sold by a dealer at the rate of twenty dollars ($ 20.00) on each four liters and a proportional sum on lesser quantities.

History.
1989, c. 772, s. 1; 1995, c. 340, s. 1; 1997-292, s. 1; 1998-218, s. 1; 2012-79, s. 2.2(a); 2014-3, s. 14.25

§ 105-113.107A. Exemptions

(a) **Authorized Possession.** -- The tax levied in this Article does not apply to a substance in the possession of a dealer who is authorized by law to possess the substance. This exemption applies only during the time the dealer's possession of the substance is authorized by law.

(b) **Certain Marijuana Parts.** -- The tax levied in this Article does not apply to the following marijuana:

(1) Harvested mature marijuana stalks when separated from and not mixed with any other parts of the marijuana plant.

(2) Fiber or any other product of marijuana stalks described in subdivision (1) of this subsection, except resin extracted from the stalks.

(3) Marijuana seeds that have been sterilized and are incapable of germination.

(4) Roots of the marijuana plant.

History.
1995, c. 340, s. 1; 1997-292, s. 1

§ 105-113.108. Reports; revenue stamps

(a) **Revenue Stamps.** -- The Secretary shall issue stamps to affix to unauthorized substances to indicate payment of the tax required by this Article. Dealers shall report the taxes payable under this Article at the time and on the return prescribed by the Secretary. Notwithstanding any other provision of law, dealers are not required to give their name, address, social security number, or other identifying information on the return, and the return is not required to be verified by oath or affirmation. Upon payment of the tax, the Secretary shall issue stamps in an amount equal to the amount of the tax paid. Taxes may be paid and stamps may be issued either by mail or in person.

(b) **Reports.** -- Every local law enforcement agency and every State law enforcement agency must report to the Department within 48 hours after seizing an unauthorized substance, or making an arrest of an individual in possession of an unauthorized substance, listed in this subsection upon which a stamp has not been affixed. The report must be in the form prescribed by the Secretary and it must include the time and place of the arrest or seizure, the amount, location, and kind of substance, the identification of an individual in possession of the substance and that individual's social security number, and any other information prescribed by the Secretary. The report must be made when the arrest or seizure involves any of the following unauthorized substances upon which a stamp has not been affixed as required by this Article:

(1) More than 42.5 grams of marijuana.

(2) Seven or more grams of any other controlled substance that is sold by weight.

(3) Ten or more dosage units of any other controlled substance that is not sold by weight.

(4) Any illicit mixed beverage.

(5) Any illicit spirituous liquor.

(6) Mash.

History.
1989, c. 772, s. 1; 1995, c. 340, s. 1; 1997-292, s. 1; 2000-119, s. 5; 2004-170, s. 8

§ 105-113.109. When tax payable

The tax imposed by this Article is payable by any dealer who actually or constructively possesses an unauthorized substance in this State upon which the tax has not been paid, as evidenced by a stamp. The tax is payable within 48 hours after the dealer acquires actual or constructive possession of a non-tax-paid unauthorized substance, exclusive of Saturdays, Sundays, and legal holidays of this State, in which case the tax is payable on the next working day. Upon payment of the tax, the dealer shall permanently affix the appropriate stamps to the unauthorized substance. Once the tax due on an unauthorized substance has been paid, no additional tax is due under this Article even though the unauthorized substance may be handled by other dealers.

History.

1989, c. 772, s. 1; 1995, c. 340, s. 1; 1997-292, s. 1

N.C. Gen. Stat. § 105-113.110

Repealed by Session Laws 1995, c. 340, s. 1.

§ 105-113.110A. Administration

Article 9 of this Chapter applies to this Article.

History.

1989 (Reg. Sess., 1990), c. 814, s. 7; 1995, c. 340, s. 1; 1997, c. 292, s. 1; 1998-218, s. 2

§ 105-113.111. Assessments

Notwithstanding any other provision of law, an assessment against a dealer who possesses an unauthorized substance to which a stamp has not been affixed as required by this Article shall be made as provided in this section. The Secretary shall assess a tax, applicable penalties, and interest based on personal knowledge or information available to the Secretary. The Secretary shall notify the dealer in writing of the amount of the tax, penalty, and interest due, and demand its immediate payment. The notice and demand shall be either mailed to the dealer at the dealer's last known address or served on the dealer in person. If the dealer does not pay the tax, penalty, and interest immediately upon receipt of the notice and demand, the Secretary shall collect the tax, penalty, and interest pursuant to the jeopardy collection procedures in G.S. 105-241.23 or the general collection procedures in G.S. 105-242, including causing execution to be issued immediately against the personal property of the dealer, unless the dealer files with the Secretary a bond in the amount of the asserted liability for the tax, penalty, and interest. The Secretary shall use all means available to collect the tax, penalty, and interest from any property in which the dealer has a legal, equitable, or beneficial interest. The dealer may seek review of the assessment as provided in Article 9 of this Chapter.

History.

1989, c. 772, s. 1; 1989 (Reg. Sess., 1990), c. 1039, s. 2; 1991 (Reg. Sess., 1992), c. 900, s. 20(d); 1995, c. 340, s. 1; 1997-292, s. 1; 2007-491, s. 8

§ 105-113.112. Confidentiality of information

(a) Information obtained by the Department in the course of administering the tax imposed by this Article, including information on whether the Department has issued a revenue stamp to a person, is confidential tax information and is subject to the provisions of G.S. 105-259.

(b) Information obtained by the Department from the taxpayer in the course of administering the tax imposed by this Article, including information on whether the Department has issued a revenue stamp to a person, may not be used as evidence, as defined in G.S. 15A-971, by a prosecutor in a criminal prosecution of the taxpayer for an offense related to the manufacturing, possession, transportation, distribution, or sale of the unauthorized substance. Under this prohibition, no officer, employee, or agent of the Department may testify about this information in a criminal prosecution of the taxpayer for an offense related to the manufacturing, possession, transportation, distribution, or sale of the unauthorized substance. This subsection implements the protections against double jeopardy and self-incrimination set out in Amendment V of the United States Constitution and the restrictions in it apply regardless of whether information may be disclosed under G.S. 105-259. An officer, employee, or agent of the Department who provides evidence or testifies in violation of this subdivision is guilty of a Class 1 misdemeanor.

History.

1989, c. 772, s. 1; 1993, c. 539, s. 702; 1994, Ex. Sess., c. 24, s. 14(c); 1997, c. 292, s. 1; 2005-435, s. 27; 2008-134, s. 68(a); 2013-414, s. 21

§ 105-113.113. Use of tax proceeds

(a) **Special Account.** -- The Unauthorized Substances Tax Account is established as a special nonreverting account. The Secretary shall credit the proceeds of the tax levied by this Article to the Account.

(b) **Distribution.** -- The Secretary shall distribute unencumbered tax proceeds in the Unauthorized Substances Tax Account on a quarterly or more frequent basis. Tax proceeds in the Account are unencumbered when they are collectible under G.S. 105-241.22. The Secretary shall distribute seventy-five percent (75%) of the unencumbered tax proceeds in the Account that were collected by assessment to the State or local law enforcement agency that conducted the investigation of a dealer that led to the assessment. If more than one State or local law enforcement agency conducted the investigation, the Secretary shall determine the equitable share for each agency based on the contribution each agency made to the investigation. The Secretary shall credit the remaining unencumbered tax proceeds in the Account to the General Fund.

(c) **Refunds.** -- The refund of a tax that has already been distributed shall be drawn initially from the Unauthorized Substances Tax Account. The amount of refunded taxes that were distributed to a law enforcement agency under this section and any interest shall be subtracted from succeeding distributions from the Account to that law enforcement agency. The amount of refunded taxes that were credited to the General Fund under this section and any interest shall be subtracted from succeeding credits to the General Fund from the Account.

History.
1991 (Reg. Sess., 1992), c. 900, s. 20(c); 1995, c. 340, s. 1; 1997-292, s. 1; 2007-491, s. 9

ARTICLE 5A
NORTH CAROLINA HIGHWAY USE TAX

§ 105-187.1. Definitions

(a) The following definitions and the definitions in G.S. 105-164.3 apply to this Article:

(1) **Commissioner.** -- The Commissioner of Motor Vehicles.

(2) **Division.** -- The Division of Motor Vehicles, Department of Transportation.

(2a) **Limited possession commitment.** -- Long-term lease or rental, short-term lease or rental, and vehicle subscriptions.

(3) **Long-term lease or rental.** -- A lease or rental made under a written agreement to lease or rent one or more vehicles to the same person for a period of at least 365 continuous days and that is not a vehicle subscription.

(3a) **Park model RV.** -- A vehicle that meets all of the following conditions:

a. Is designed and marketed as temporary living quarters for recreational, camping, travel, or seasonal use.

b. Is certified by the manufacturer as complying with ANSI A119.5.

c. Is built on a single chassis mounted on wheels with a gross trailer area not exceeding 400 square feet in the setup mode.

(4) **Recreational vehicle.** -- Defined in G.S. 20-4.01. The term also includes a park model RV.

(5) **Rescue squad.** -- An organization that provides rescue services, emergency medical services, or both.

(6) **Retailer.** -- A retailer as defined in G.S. 105-164.3 who is engaged in the business of selling, leasing, renting, or offering vehicle subscriptions for motor vehicles.

(7) **Short-term lease or rental.** -- A lease or rental of a motor vehicle or motor vehicles, including a vehicle sharing service, that is not a long-term lease or rental or a vehicle subscription.

(8) **Vehicle sharing service.** -- A service for which a person pays a membership fee for the right to use a motor vehicle or motor vehicles upon payment of an additional time-based or mileage-based fee.

(9) **Vehicle subscription.** -- A written agreement that grants a person the right to use and exchange motor vehicles owned, directly or indirectly, by the person offering the agreement upon payment of a subscription fee, but it does not include a vehicle sharing service. The subscription fee must provide a person exclusive use of an agreed-upon number of motor vehicles at any given time during the full term of the subscription.

(b) This section does not apply to Chapter 20 of the General Statutes, including the licensing requirements, restrictions, limitations, and prohibitions on unfair methods of competition contained in Article 12 of that Chapter.

History.
1989, c. 692, s. 4.1; 1991, c. 79, s. 4; 2000-173, s. 10(a); 2001-424, s. 34.24(e); 2001-497, s. 2(b); 2002-72, s. 19(a); 2016-5, s. 3.19(a); 2019-69, s. 1

§ 105-187.2. Highway use tax imposed

A tax is imposed on the privilege of using the highways of this State. This tax is in addition to all other taxes and fees imposed.

History.
1989, c. 692, s. 4.1

§ 105-187.3. Rate of tax

(a) **Tax Base.** -- The tax imposed by this Article is applied to the sum of the retail value of a motor vehicle for which a certificate of title is issued and any fee regulated by G.S. 20-101.1. The tax does not apply to the sales price of a service contract, provided the charge is separately stated on the bill of sale or other similar document given to the purchaser at the time of the sale.

(a1) **Tax Rate. --** The tax rate is three percent (3%). The maximum tax is two thousand dollars ($ 2,000) for each certificate of title issued for a Class A or Class B motor vehicle that is a commercial motor vehicle, as defined in G.S. 20-4.01, and for each certificate of title issued for a recreational vehicle. The tax is payable as provided in G.S. 105-187.4.

(b) **Retail Value. --** The retail value of a motor vehicle for which a certificate of title is issued because of a sale of the motor vehicle by a retailer is the sales price of the motor vehicle, including all accessories attached to the vehicle when it is delivered to the purchaser, less the amount of any allowance given by the retailer for a motor vehicle taken in trade as a full or partial payment for the purchased motor vehicle.

The retail value of a motor vehicle for which a certificate of title is issued because of a sale of the motor vehicle by a seller who is not a retailer is the market value of the vehicle, less the amount of any allowance given by the seller for a motor vehicle taken in trade as a full or partial payment for the purchased motor vehicle. A transaction in which two parties exchange motor vehicles is considered a sale regardless of whether either party gives additional consideration as part of the transaction.

The retail value of a motor vehicle for which a certificate of title is issued because of a reason other than the sale of the motor vehicle is the market value of the vehicle. The market value of a vehicle is presumed to be the value of the vehicle set in a schedule of values adopted by the Commissioner.

The retail value of a vehicle for which a certificate of title is issued because of a transfer by a State agency that assists the United States Department of Defense with purchasing, transferring, or titling a vehicle to another State agency, a unit of local government, a volunteer fire department, or a volunteer rescue squad is the sales price paid by the State agency, unit of local government, volunteer fire department, or volunteer rescue squad.

(c) **Schedules. --** In adopting a schedule of values for motor vehicles, the Commissioner shall adopt a schedule whose values do not exceed the wholesale values of motor vehicles as published in a recognized automotive reference manual.

History.
1989, c. 692, ss. 4.1, 4.2; c. 770, s. 74.13; 1993, c. 467, s. 3; 1995, c. 349, s. 1; c. 390, s. 30; 2001-424, s. 34.24(a); 2001-497, s. 2(a); 2009-550, s. 2(e); 2010-95, s. 5; 2013-360, s. 34.29(a); 2013-363, s. 8.1; 2014-3, s. 6.1(g); 2014-39, s. 3; 2015-241, s. 29.34A(a); 2015-259, s. 5(d); 2015-268, s. 10.1(d)

§ 105-187.4. Payment of tax

(a) **Method. --** The tax imposed by this Article must be paid to the Commissioner when applying for a certificate of title for a motor vehicle. The Commissioner may not issue a certificate of title for a vehicle until the tax imposed by this Article has been paid. The tax may be paid in cash or by check.

(b) **Sale by Retailer. --** When a certificate of title for a motor vehicle is issued because of a sale of the motor vehicle by a retailer, the applicant for the certificate of title must attach a copy of the bill of sale for the motor vehicle to the application. A retailer who sells a motor vehicle may collect from the purchaser of the vehicle the tax payable upon the issuance of a certificate of title for the vehicle, apply for a certificate of title on behalf of the purchaser, and remit the tax due on behalf of the purchaser. If a check submitted by a retailer in payment of taxes collected under this section is not honored by the financial institution upon which it is drawn because the retailer's account did not have sufficient funds to pay the check or the retailer did not have an account at the institution, the Division may suspend or revoke the license issued to the retailer under Article 12 of Chapter 20 of the General Statutes.

History.
1989, c. 692, s. 4.1; 1991, c. 193, s. 1

§ 105-187.5. Alternate tax for a limited possession commitment

(a) **Election. --** A retailer may elect not to pay the tax imposed by this Article at the rate set in G.S. 105-187.3 when applying for a certificate of title for a motor vehicle purchased by the retailer for a limited possession commitment. A retailer who makes this election shall pay a tax on the gross receipts of the limited possession commitment of the vehicle. The portion of a limited possession commitment billing or payment that represents any amount applicable to the sales price of a service contract as defined in G.S. 105-164.3 should not be included in the gross receipts subject to the tax imposed by this Article. The charge must be separately stated on documentation given to the purchaser at the time the limited possession commitment goes into effect, or on the monthly billing statement or other documentation given to the purchaser. When a limited possession commitment is sold to another retailer, the seller of the limited possession commitment should provide to the purchaser of the limited possession commitment the documentation showing that the service contract and applicable sales taxes were separately stated at the time the limited possession commitment went into effect and the new retailer must retain the information to support an allocation for tax computed on the gross receipts subject to highway use tax. Like the tax imposed by G.S. 105-187.3, this alternate tax is a tax on the privilege of using the highways of this State. The tax is imposed on a retailer, but is to be added to the limited possession commitment of a motor vehicle and thereby be paid by the person who enters into a limited possession commitment with a retailer.

(b) **Rate.** -- The applicable tax rates on the gross receipts from a limited possession commitment are as listed in this subsection. Gross receipts does not include the amount of any allowance given for a motor vehicle taken in trade as a partial payment on the limited possession commitment. The maximum tax in G.S. 105-187.3(a1) on certain motor vehicles applies to a continuous limited possession commitment of such a motor vehicle to the same person. The applicable tax rates are as follows:

Type of Limited Possession Commitment	Tax Rate
Short-term lease or rental	8%
Vehicle subscription	5%
Long-term lease or rental	3%

(c) **Method.** -- A retailer who elects to pay tax on the gross receipts of the limited possession commitment of a motor vehicle shall make this election when applying for a certificate of title for the vehicle. To make the election, the retailer shall complete a form provided by the Division giving information needed to collect the alternate tax based on gross receipts. Once made, an election is irrevocable.

(d) **Administration.** -- The Division shall notify the Secretary of Revenue of a retailer who makes the election under this section. A retailer who makes this election shall report and remit to the Secretary the tax on the gross receipts of the limited possession commitment of the motor vehicle. The Secretary shall administer the tax imposed by this section on gross receipts in the same manner as the tax levied under G.S. 105-164.4(a)(2). The administrative provisions and powers of the Secretary that apply to the tax levied under G.S. 105-164.4(a)(2) apply to the tax imposed by this section. In addition, the Division may request the Secretary to audit a retailer who elects to pay tax on gross receipts under this section. When the Secretary conducts an audit at the request of the Division, the Division shall reimburse the Secretary for the cost of the audit, as determined by the Secretary. In conducting an audit of a retailer under this section, the Secretary may audit any sales of motor vehicles made by the retailer.

History.
1989, c. 692, s. 4.1; 1991, c. 79, s. 5; c. 193, s. 3; 1995, c. 410, s. 1; 2000-173, s. 10(b); 2001-424, s. 34.24(b); 2001-497, s. 2(c); 2014-3, s. 6.1(h); 2015-259, s. 5(e); 2016-92, s. 2.7; 2016-94, s. 38.5(k); 2019-69, s. 2

§ 105-187.6. Exemptions from highway use tax

(a) **Full Exemptions.** -- The tax imposed by this Article does not apply when a certificate of title is issued as the result of a transfer of a motor vehicle:

(1) To (i) the insurer of the motor vehicle under G.S. 20-109.1 because the vehicle is a salvage vehicle or (ii) a used motor vehicle dealer under G.S. 20-109.1 because the vehicle is a salvage vehicle that was abandoned.

(2) To either a manufacturer, as defined in G.S. 20-286, or a motor vehicle retailer for the purpose of resale.

(3) To the same owner to reflect a change or correction in the owner's name.

(3a) To one or more of the same co-owners to reflect the removal of one or more other co-owners, when there is no consideration for the transfer.

(4) By will or intestacy.

(5) By a gift between a husband and wife, a parent and child, or a stepparent and a stepchild.

(6) By a distribution of marital or divisible property incident to a marital separation or divorce.

(7) Repealed by Session Laws 2009-445, s. 16, effective August 7, 2009.

(8) To a local board of education for use in the driver education program of a public school when the motor vehicle is transferred:

    a. By a retailer and is to be transferred back to the retailer within 300 days after the transfer to the local board.

    b. By a local board of education.

(9) To a volunteer fire department or volunteer rescue squad that is not part of a unit of local government, has no more than two paid employees, and is exempt from State income tax under G.S. 105-130.11, when the motor vehicle is one of the following:

    a. A fire truck, a pump truck, a tanker truck, or a ladder truck used to suppress fire.

    b. A four-wheel drive vehicle intended to be mounted with a water tank and hose and used for forest fire fighting.

    c. An emergency services vehicle.

(10) To a State agency from a unit of local government, volunteer fire department, or volunteer rescue squad to enable the State agency to transfer the vehicle to another unit of local government, volunteer fire department, or volunteer rescue squad.

(11) To a revocable trust from an owner who is the sole beneficiary of the trust.

(12) To a charitable organization operating under section 501(c)(3) of the Internal Revenue Code (26 U.S.C. § 501(c)(3)) where the vehicle was donated to the charitable organization solely for purposes of resale by the charitable organization.

(b) **Partial Exemptions.** -- A maximum tax of forty dollars ($ 40.00) applies when a certificate of title is issued as the result of a transfer of a motor vehicle:

(1) To a secured party who has a perfected security interest in the motor vehicle.

(2) To a partnership, limited liability company, corporation, trust, or other person where no gain or loss arises on the transfer of the motor vehicle under section 351 or section 721 of the Code, or because the transfer is treated under the Code as being to an entity that is not a separate entity from its owner or whose separate existence is otherwise disregarded, or to a partnership, limited liability company, or corporation by merger, conversion, or consolidation in accordance with applicable law.

(c) **Out-of-state Vehicles.** -- A maximum tax of two hundred fifty dollars ($ 250.00) applies when a certificate of title is issued for a motor vehicle that, at the time of applying for a certificate of title, is and has been titled in the name of the owner of the motor vehicle in another state for at least 90 days prior to the date of application for a certificate of title in this State.

(d) **Exemption Limitation.** -- The full exemptions set out in subsection (a) of this section, except for those set out in subdivisions (1), (2), (9), and (10) of subsection (a) of this section, do not apply to a certificate of title issued for a motor vehicle titled in another state at the time of the transfer. The partial exemptions set out in subsection (b) of this section do not apply to a certificate of title issued for a motor vehicle titled in another state at the time of the transfer.

History.
1989, c. 692, s. 4.1; c. 770, ss. 74.9, 74.10; 1991, c. 193, s. 4; c. 689, s. 323; 1993, c. 467, s. 1; 1995, c. 390, s. 31; 1997-443, s. 11A.118(a); 1998-98, s. 15.1; 1999-369, s. 5.9; 2000-140, s. 68; 2001-387, s. 151; 2001-424, s. 34.24(d); 2001-487, s. 68; 2009-81, s. 2; 2009-445, s. 16; 2010-95, s. 6; 2013-400, s. 6; 2015-241, ss. 29.34(a), 29.34A(b); 2015-268, s. 10.1(d); 2017-69, s. 1; 2018-43, s. 5.

§ 105-187.7. Credits

(a) **Tax Paid in Another State.** -- A person who, within 90 days before applying for a certificate of title for a motor vehicle on which the tax imposed by this Article is due, has paid a sales tax, an excise tax, or a tax substantially equivalent to the tax imposed by this Article on the vehicle to a taxing jurisdiction outside this State is allowed a credit against the tax due under this Article for the amount of tax paid to the other jurisdiction.

(b) **Tax Paid Within One Year.** -- A person who applies for a certificate of title for a motor vehicle that is titled in another state but was formerly titled in this State is allowed a credit against the tax due under this Article for the amount of tax paid under this Article by that person on the same vehicle within one year before the application for a certificate of title.

History.
1989, c. 692, s. 4.1; 1995, c. 390, s. 32; c. 512, s. 1

§ 105-187.8. Refund for return of purchased motor vehicle

When a purchaser of a motor vehicle returns the motor vehicle to the seller of the motor vehicle within 90 days after the purchase and receives a vehicle replacement for the returned vehicle or a refund of the price paid the seller, whether from the seller or the manufacturer of the vehicle, the purchaser may obtain a refund of the privilege tax paid on the certificate of title issued for the returned motor vehicle.

To obtain a refund, the purchaser must apply to the Division for a refund within 30 days after receiving the replacement vehicle or refund of the purchase price. The application must be made on a form prescribed by the Commission and must be supported by documentation from the seller of the returned vehicle.

History.
1989, c. 692, s. 4.1; 1995, c. 390, s. 33

§ 105-187.9. Disposition of tax proceeds

(a) **Distribution.** -- Of the taxes collected under this Article at the rate of five percent (5%) and eight percent (8%), the sum of ten million dollars ($ 10,000,000) shall be credited annually to the Highway Fund, and the remainder shall be credited to the General Fund. Taxes collected under this Article at the rate of three percent (3%) shall be credited to the North Carolina Highway Trust Fund.

(b) Repealed by Session Laws 2010-31, s. 28.7(i), and Session Laws 2013-183, s. 4.1, effective July 1, 2013.

(c) Repealed by Session Laws 2013-183, s. 4.1, effective July 1, 2013.

History.
1989, c. 692, s. 4.1; c. 799, s. 33; 1993, c. 321, s. 164(a); 2001-424, s. 34.24(c); 2001-513, s. 15; 2008-107, s. 25.5(a), (c), (e); 2010-31, s. 28.7(f), (h)-(j); 2011-145,

ss. 28.33(c), (d); 2011-391, s. 57; 2012-142, s. 24.8(b); 2013-183, s. 4.1; 2017-57, s. 2.2(f); 2019-69, s. 3

§ 105-187.10. Penalties and remedies

(a) **Penalties.** -- The penalty for bad checks in G.S. 105-236(1) applies to a check offered in payment of the tax imposed by this Article. In addition, if a check offered to the Division in payment of the tax imposed by this Article is returned unpaid and the tax for which the check was offered, plus the penalty imposed under G.S. 105-236(1), is not paid within 30 days after the Commissioner demands its payment, the Commissioner may revoke the registration plate of the vehicle for which a certificate of title was issued when the check was offered.

(b) **Unpaid Taxes.** -- The remedies for collection of taxes in Article 9 of this Chapter apply to the taxes levied by this Article and collected by the Commissioner. In applying these remedies, the Commissioner has the same authority as the Secretary.

(c) **Appeals.** -- A taxpayer who disagrees with the presumed value of a motor vehicle must pay the tax based on the presumed value, but may appeal the value to the Commissioner. A taxpayer who appeals the value must provide two estimates of the value of the vehicle to the Commissioner. If the Commissioner finds that the value of the vehicle is less than the presumed value of the vehicle, the Commissioner shall refund any overpayment of tax made by the taxpayer with interest at the rate specified in G.S. 105-241.21 from the date of the overpayment.

History.

1989, c. 692, s. 4.1; c. 770, s. 74.8; 2007-491, ss. 21, 44(1)b

N.C. Gen. Stat. § 105-187.11

Repealed by Session Laws 2007-527, s. 30, effective August 31, 2007.

ARTICLE 9
GENERAL ADMINISTRATION; PENALTIES AND REMEDIES

§ 105-236. Penalties; situs of violations; penalty disposition

(a) **Penalties.** -- The following civil penalties and criminal offenses apply:

(1) **Penalty for Bad Checks.** -- When the bank upon which any uncertified check tendered to the Department of Revenue in payment of any obligation due to the Department returns the check because of insufficient funds or the nonexistence of an account of the drawer, the Secretary shall assess a penalty equal to ten percent (10%) of the check, subject to a minimum of one dollar ($ 1.00) and a maximum of one thousand dollars ($ 1,000). This penalty does not apply if the Secretary finds that, when the check was presented for payment, the drawer of the check had sufficient funds in an account at a financial institution to pay the check and, by inadvertence, the drawer of the check failed to draw the check on the account that had sufficient funds.

(1a) **Penalty for Bad Electronic Funds Transfer.** -- When an electronic funds transfer cannot be completed due to insufficient funds or the nonexistence of an account of the transferor, the Secretary shall assess a penalty equal to ten percent (10%) of the amount of the transfer, subject to a minimum of one dollar ($ 1.00) and a maximum of one thousand dollars ($ 1,000). This penalty may be waived by the Secretary in accordance with G.S. 105-237.

(1b) **Making Payment in Wrong Form.** -- For making a payment of tax in a form other than the form required by the Secretary pursuant to G.S. 105-241(a), the Secretary shall assess a penalty equal to five percent (5%) of the amount of the tax, subject to a minimum of one dollar ($ 1.00) and a maximum of one thousand dollars ($ 1,000). This penalty may be waived by the Secretary in accordance with G.S. 105-237.

(2) **Failure to Obtain a License.** -- For failure to obtain a license before engaging in a business, trade or profession for which a license is required, the Secretary shall assess a penalty equal to five percent (5%) of the amount prescribed for the license per month or fraction thereof until paid, not to exceed twenty-five percent (25%) of the amount so prescribed, but in any event shall not be less than five dollars ($ 5.00). In cases in which the taxpayer, after written notification by the Department, fails to obtain a license as required under G.S. 105-449.65 or G.S. 105-449.131, the Secretary may assess a penalty of one thousand dollars ($ 1,000).

(3) **Failure to File Return.** -- In case of failure to file any return on the date it is due, determined with regard to any extension of time for filing, the Secretary shall assess a penalty equal to five percent (5%) of the amount of the tax if the failure is for not more than one month, with an additional five percent (5%) for each additional month, or fraction thereof, during which the failure continues, not exceeding twenty-five percent (25%) in aggregate.

(4) **Failure to Pay Tax When Due.** -- In the case of failure to pay any tax when due, without intent to evade the tax, the

Secretary shall assess a penalty equal to ten percent (10%) of the tax. This penalty does not apply in any of the following circumstances:

a. When the amount of tax shown as due on an amended return is paid when the return is filed.

b. When the Secretary proposes an assessment for tax due but not shown on a return and the tax due is paid within 45 days after the later of the following:

1. The date of the notice of proposed assessment of the tax, if the taxpayer does not file a timely request for a Departmental review of the proposed assessment.

2. The date the proposed assessment becomes collectible under one of the circumstances listed in G.S. 105-241.22(3) through (6), if the taxpayer files a timely request for a Departmental review of the proposed assessment.

c. When a taxpayer timely files a consolidated or combined return at the request of the Secretary under Part 1 of Article 4 of this Chapter and the tax due is paid within 45 days after the latest of the following:

1. The date the return is filed.

2. The date of a notice of proposed assessment based on the return, if the taxpayer does not file a timely request for a Departmental review of the proposed assessment.

3. The date the Departmental review of the proposed assessment ends as a result of the occurrence of one of the actions listed in G.S. 105-241.22(3) through (6), if the taxpayer files a timely request for a Departmental review.

(5) **Negligence.** --

a. **Finding of negligence.** -- For negligent failure to comply with any of the provisions to which this Article applies, or rules issued pursuant thereto, without intent to defraud, the Secretary shall assess a penalty equal to ten percent (10%) of the deficiency due to the negligence.

b. **Large individual income tax deficiency.** -- In the case of individual income tax, if a taxpayer understates taxable income, by any means, by an amount equal to twenty-five percent (25%) or more of gross income, the Secretary shall assess a penalty equal to twenty-five percent (25%) of the deficiency. For purposes of this subdivision, "gross income" means gross income as defined in section 61 of the Code.

c. **Other large tax deficiency.** -- In the case of a tax other than individual income tax, if a taxpayer understates tax liability by twenty-five percent (25%) or more, the Secretary shall assess a penalty equal to twenty-five percent (25%) of the deficiency.

d. **No double penalty.** -- If a penalty is assessed under subdivision (6) of this section, no additional penalty for negligence shall be assessed with respect to the same deficiency.

e. Repealed by Session Laws 2013-316, s. 7(c), effective January 1, 2013, and applicable to estates of decedents dying on or after that date.

f. **Consolidated or combined return.** -- The amount of tax shown as due on a consolidated or combined return filed at the request of the Secretary under Part 1 of Article 4 of this Chapter is not considered a deficiency and is not subject to this subdivision unless one or more of the following applies:

1. The return is an amended consolidated or combined return that includes the same corporations as the initial consolidated or combined return filed at the request of the Secretary. In this case the deficiency is the extent to which the amount shown as due on the amended return exceeds the amount shown as due on the initial return.

2. Repealed by Session Laws 2011-390, s. 5, effective January 1, 2012.

3. Pursuant to a written request from a taxpayer, the Secretary has provided written advice to that taxpayer stating that the Secretary will require a consolidated or combined return under the facts and circumstances set out in the request, and the Secretary requires a taxpayer to file a consolidated or combined return under G.S. 105-130.5A because the taxpayer's facts and circumstances meet those described in the written advice.

(5a) **Misuse of Exemption Certificate.** -- For misuse of an exemption certificate by a purchaser, the Secretary shall assess a penalty equal to two hundred fifty dollars ($ 250.00). An exemption certificate is a certificate issued by the Secretary that authorizes a retailer to sell tangible personal property to the holder of the certificate and either collect tax at a preferential rate or not collect tax on the sale. Examples of an exemption certificate include a certificate of exemption, a direct pay certificate, and a conditional exemption certificate.

(5b) **Road Tax Understatement.** -- If a motor carrier understates its liability for the road tax imposed by Article 36B of this Chapter by twenty-five percent (25%) or more, the Secretary shall assess the motor carrier a penalty in an amount equal to two times the amount of the deficiency.

(6) **Fraud.** -- If there is a deficiency or delinquency in payment of any tax because of fraud with intent to evade the tax, the Secretary shall assess a penalty equal to fifty percent (50%) of the total deficiency.

(7) **Attempt to Evade or Defeat Tax.** -- Any person who willfully attempts, or any person who aids or abets any person to attempt in any manner to evade or defeat a tax or its payment, shall, in addition to other penalties provided by law, be guilty of a Class H felony.

(8) **Willful Failure to Collect, Withhold, or Pay Over Tax.** -- Any person required to collect, withhold, account for, and pay over any tax who willfully fails to collect or truthfully account for and pay over the tax shall, in addition to other penalties provided by law, be guilty of a Class 1 misdemeanor. Notwithstanding any other provision of law, no prosecution for a violation brought under this subdivision shall be barred before the expiration of six years after the date of the violation.

(9) **Willful Failure to File Return, Supply Information, or Pay Tax.** -- Any person required to pay any tax, to file a return, to keep any records, or to supply any information, who willfully fails to pay the tax, file the return, keep the records, or supply the information, at the time or times required by law, or rules issued pursuant thereto, is, in addition to other penalties provided by law, guilty of a Class 1 misdemeanor. Notwithstanding any other provision of law, no prosecution for a violation brought under this subdivision is barred before the expiration of six years after the date of the violation.

(9a) **Aid or Assistance.** -- Any person, pursuant to or in connection with the revenue laws, who willfully aids, assists in, procures, counsels, or advises the preparation, presentation, or filing of a return, affidavit, claim, or any other document that the person knows is fraudulent or false as to any material matter, whether or not the falsity or fraud is with the knowledge or consent of the person authorized or required to present

or file the return, affidavit, claim, or other document, is guilty of a felony as follows:

a. If the person who commits an offense under this subdivision is an income tax return preparer and the amount of all taxes fraudulently evaded on returns filed in one taxable year is one hundred thousand dollars ($ 100,000) or more, the person is guilty of a Class C felony.

b. If the person who commits an offense under this subdivision is an income tax return preparer and the amount of all taxes fraudulently evaded on returns filed in one taxable year is less than one hundred thousand dollars ($ 100,000), the person is guilty of a Class F felony.

c. If the person who commits an offense under this subdivision is not covered under sub-subdivision a. or b. of this subdivision, the person is guilty of a Class H felony.

(9b) **Identity Theft.** -- A person who knowingly obtains, possesses, or uses identifying information of another person, living or dead, with the intent to fraudulently utilize that information in a submission to the Department to obtain anything of value, benefit, or advantage for themselves or another is guilty of a Class G felony. If the person whose identifying information is obtained, possessed, or used by another in this manner suffers any adverse financial impact as a proximate result of the offense, then the person who obtained, possessed, or used the identifying information is guilty of a Class F felony. Each person's identity obtained, possessed, or used in this manner shall count as a separate offense. The term "identifying information" as used in this subdivision includes the following:

a. Legal name.

b. Date of birth.

c. Social Security Number.

d. Taxpayer Identification Number.

e. Federal Identification Number.

f. Bank account numbers.

g. Federal or State tax or tax return information.

(10) **Penalties Regarding Informational Returns.** -- The following penalties apply with regard to an informational return required by Article 2A, 2C, 4, 4A, 5, 9, 36C, or 36D of this Chapter:

a. Repealed by Session Laws 1998-212, s. 29A.14(m), effective January 1, 1999.

b. Repealed by Session Laws 2018-5, s. 38.10(p), effective June 12, 2018.

c. For failure to file with the Secretary by the date the return is due, the

Secretary shall assess a penalty of fifty dollars ($ 50.00) per day, up to a maximum penalty of one thousand dollars ($ 1,000).

d. For failure to file in the format prescribed by the Secretary, the Secretary shall assess a penalty of two hundred dollars ($ 200.00).

(10a) **Filing a Frivolous Return.** -- If a taxpayer files a frivolous return under Part 2 of Article 4 of this Chapter, the Secretary shall assess a penalty in the amount of up to five hundred dollars ($ 500.00). A frivolous return is a return that meets both of the following requirements:

a. It fails to provide sufficient information to permit a determination that the return is correct or contains information which positively indicates the return is incorrect, and

b. It evidences an intention to delay, impede or negate the revenue laws of this State or purports to adopt a position that is lacking in seriousness.

(10b) **Misrepresentation Concerning Payment.** -- A person who receives money from a taxpayer with the understanding that the money is to be remitted to the Secretary for application to the taxpayer's tax liability and who willfully fails to remit the money to the Secretary is guilty of a Class F felony.

(11) Repealed by Session Laws 2006-162, s. 12(b), effective July 24, 2006.

(12) Repealed by Session Laws 1991, c. 45, s. 27.

(b) **Situs.** -- A violation of a tax law is considered an act committed in part at the office of the Secretary in Raleigh. The certificate of the Secretary that a tax has not been paid, a return has not been filed, or information has not been supplied, as required by law, is prima facie evidence that the tax has not been paid, the return has not been filed, or the information has not been supplied.

(c) **Penalty Disposition.** -- Civil penalties assessed by the Secretary are assessed as an additional tax. The clear proceeds of civil penalties assessed by the Secretary must be credited to the Civil Penalty and Forfeiture Fund established in G.S. 115C-457.1.

History.
1939, c. 158, s. 907; 1953, c. 1302, s. 7; 1959, c. 1259, s. 8; 1963, c. 1169, s. 6; 1967, c. 1110, s. 9; 1973, c. 476, s. 193; c. 1287, s. 13; 1979, c. 156, s. 2; 1985, c. 114, s. 11; 1985 (Reg. Sess., 1986), c. 983; 1987 (Reg. Sess., 1988), c. 1076; 1989, c. 557, ss. 7 to 10; 1989 (Reg. Sess., 1990), c. 1005, s. 9; 1991, c. 45, s. 27; 1991 (Reg. Sess., 1992), c. 914, s. 2; c. 1007, s. 10; 1993, c. 354, s. 22; c. 450, s. 10; c. 539, ss. 709, 710, 1292, 1293; 1994, Ex. Sess., c. 24, s. 14(c); 1995, c. 390, s. 36; 1995 (Reg.

Sess., 1996), c. 646, s. 10; c. 647, s. 51; c. 696, s. 1; 1997-6, s. 8; 1997-109, s. 3; 1998-178, ss. 1, 2; 1998-212, s. 29A.14(m); 1999-415, ss. 2, 3; 1999-438, ss. 15, 16; 2000-119, s. 2; 2000-120, s. 7; 2000-140, s. 70; 2002-106, ss. 2, 4; 2005-276, s. 6.37(n); 2005-435, s. 1; 2006-162, s. 12(b); 2007-491, s. 26; 2008-107, s. 28.18(b); 2010-31, s. 31.10(a), (b); 2011-330, s. 32; 2011-390, s. 5; 2011-411, s. 8(b); 2012-79, s. 2.18(a); 2013-316, s. 7(c); 2013-414, s. 1(h); 2014-3, s. 3.1(c); 2015-259, s. 7.1(b); 2017-204, s. 3.1(a); 2018-5, s. 38.10(p); 2018-98, s. 2(a); 2019-169, ss. 5.2(a), 6.8

§ 105-269.3. Enforcement of Subchapter V and fuel inspection tax

The State Highway Patrol and law enforcement officers and other appropriate personnel in the Department of Public Safety may assist the Department of Revenue in enforcing Subchapter V of this Chapter and Article 3 of Chapter 119 of the General Statutes. The State Highway Patrol and law enforcement officers of the Department of Public Safety have the power of peace officers in matters concerning the enforcement of Subchapter V of this Chapter and Article 3 of Chapter 119 of the General Statutes.

History.
1963, c. 1169, s. 6; 1991, c. 42, s. 16; 1991 (Reg. Sess., 1992), c. 1007, s. 17; 1993, c. 485, s. 15; 1993 (Reg. Sess., 1994), c. 745, s. 19; 2002-159, s. 31.5(b); 2002-190, s. 2; 2011-145, s. 19.1(g)

SUBCHAPTER 02.
LISTING, APPRAISAL, AND ASSESSMENT OF PROPERTY AND COLLECTION OF TAXES ON PROPERTY

ARTICLE 22A
MOTOR VEHICLES

§ 105-330. Definitions

The following definitions apply in this Article:

(1) **Classified motor vehicle.** -- A motor vehicle classified under this Article.

(1a) **Collecting authority.** -- The Division of Motor Vehicles or an agent contracting with the Division of Motor Vehicles.

(2) **Motor vehicle.** -- Defined in G.S. 20-4.01(23).

(2a) **Municipal corporation.** -- Defined in G.S. 105-273(11).

(3) **Public service company.** -- Defined in G.S. 105-333(14).

(4) **Registered classified motor vehicle.** -- Any of the following:

a. A classified motor vehicle that has a registration plate issued under Article 3 of Chapter 20 of the General Statutes and whose registration is current.

b. A classified motor vehicle transferred to an owner who has applied for a registration plate for the motor vehicle.

(5) **Registration fees.** -- Fees set out in G.S. 20-87 and G.S. 20-88.

(6) **Unregistered classified motor vehicle.** -- A classified motor vehicle that is not a registered classified motor vehicle.

History.

1991, c. 624, s. 1; 2005-294, s. 1; 2006-259, s. 31.5; 2007-527, s. 22(b); 2008-134, s. 65; 2009-445, s. 24(a); 2010-95, s. 22(c); 2011-330, s. 42(a); 2012-79, s. 3.6; 2013-414, s. 70(b), (d)

§ 105-330.1. Classification of motor vehicles

(a) **Classification.** -- All motor vehicles other than the motor vehicles listed in subsection (b) of this section are designated a special class of property under Article V, Sec. 2(2) of the North Carolina Constitution and are considered classified motor vehicles. Classified motor vehicles must be listed and assessed as provided in this Article and taxes on classified motor vehicles must be collected as provided in this Article.

(b) **Exceptions.** -- The following motor vehicles are not classified under subsection (a) of this section:

(1) Motor vehicles exempt from registration pursuant to G.S. 20-51.

(2) Manufactured homes, mobile classrooms, and mobile offices.

(3) Semitrailers or trailers registered on a multiyear basis.

(4) Motor vehicles owned or leased by a public service company and appraised under G.S. 105-335.

(5) Repealed by Session Laws 2000, c. 140, s. 75(a), effective July 1, 2000.

(6) Motor vehicles registered under the International Registration Plan.

(7) Motor vehicles issued permanent registration plates under G.S. 20-84.

(8) Self-propelled property-carrying vehicles issued three-month registration plates at the farmer rate under G.S. 20-88.

(9) Motor vehicles owned by participants in the Address Confidentiality Program authorized under Chapter 15C of the General Statutes.

History.

1991, c. 624, s. 1; 1991 (Reg. Sess., 1992), c. 961, s. 3; 1993, c. 485, s. 18; c. 543, s. 4; 1993 (Reg. Sess., 1994), c. 745, s. 1; 2000-140, s. 75(a); 2007-471, s. 6; 2009-445,

ss. 24(a), 25(a); 2010-95, s. 22(c), (d); 2013-414, ss. 70(b), (c), 72

§ 105-330.2. Appraisal, ownership, and situs

(a) **Determination Date for Registered Vehicle.** -- The ownership, situs, and taxability of a registered classified motor vehicle is determined annually as of the date on which the vehicle's current registration is renewed, regardless of whether the registration is renewed after it has expired, or on the date an application for a new registration is submitted. The situs of a registered classified motor vehicle may not be changed until the next registration date. The value of a registered classified motor vehicle is determined as follows:

(1) For a registration expiring or an application for a new registration during the period January 1 through August 31, the value is determined as of January 1 of the current year.

(2) For a registration expiring or an application for a new registration during the period September 1 through December 31, the value is determined as of January 1 of the following year.

(3) For a new motor vehicle whose value cannot be determined as of January 1 of the year specified in subdivision (1) or (2) of this subsection, the value is determined as of the date that model of motor vehicle is first offered for sale at retail in this State.

(4) For a motor vehicle whose value cannot be determined as of the date set under any other subdivision in this subsection, the value is determined using the most currently available January 1 retail value of the vehicle.

(a1) **Determination Date for Unregistered Vehicle.** -- The ownership, situs, and taxability of an unregistered classified motor vehicle is determined as of January 1 of the year in which the registration of the motor vehicle expires and is not renewed or the motor vehicle is acquired and the owner does not submit an application for registration. The value of an unregistered classified motor vehicle is determined as of January 1 of the year the vehicle is required to be listed.

(b) **Value.** -- An assessor must appraise a classified motor vehicle at its true value in money as prescribed by G.S. 105-283. The sales price of a classified motor vehicle purchased from a dealer, including all accessories attached to the vehicle when it is delivered to the purchaser, is considered the true value of the vehicle, and the assessor must appraise the vehicle at this value. The sales price excludes the tax imposed under Article 5A of this Chapter. The Property Tax Division of the Department of Revenue must annually adopt a schedule of values, standards, and rules to be used in the valuation of all other classified motor vehicles to ensure equitable statewide valuations, taking into account local market conditions and allowing adjustments for mileage and the condition of the vehicles.

(b1) **Valuation Appeal.** -- The owner of a classified motor vehicle may appeal the appraised value of the vehicle by filing a request for appeal with the assessor within 30 days of the date taxes are due on the vehicle under G.S. 105-330.4. An owner who appeals the appraised value of a classified motor vehicle must pay the tax on the vehicle when due, subject to a full or partial refund if the appeal is decided in the owner's favor.

The combined tax and registration notice or tax receipt for a classified motor vehicle must explain the right to appeal the appraised value of the vehicle. A lessee of a vehicle that is required by the terms of the lease to pay the tax on the vehicle is considered the owner of the vehicle for purposes of filing an appeal under this subsection. Appeals filed under this subsection shall proceed in the manner provided in G.S. 105-312(d).

(b2) **Exemption or Exclusion Appeal.** -- The owner of a classified motor vehicle may appeal the vehicle's eligibility for an exemption or exclusion by filing a request for appeal with the assessor within 30 days of the assessor's initial decision on the exemption or exclusion application filed by the owner pursuant to G.S. 105-330.3(b). Appeals filed under this subsection shall proceed in the manner provided in G.S. 105-312(d).

(c) Repealed by Session Laws 2008-134, s. 61, effective July 28, 2008.

History.
1991, c. 624, s. 1; 1991 (Reg. Sess., 1992), c. 961, s. 4; 1995, c. 510, s. 1; 1995 (Reg. Sess., 1996), c. 646, s. 24; 1997-6, s. 10; 1999-353, s. 1; 2005-294, s. 2; 2005-303, s. 1; 2006-259, s. 31.5; 2007-527, s. 22(b); 2008-134, ss. 61, 65; 2009-445, s. 24(a); 2010-95, s. 22(c); 2011-330, s. 42(a); 2012-79, ss. 3.2, 3.6; 2013-414, ss. 70(b), (d), 71(a), (b)

§ 105-330.3. Listing requirements for classified motor vehicles; application for exempt status

(a) **Registered Vehicles.** -- The assessor must list a registered classified motor vehicle each year for each taxing unit in the name of the record owner as of the day on which the current vehicle registration is renewed or the day on which an owner to whom the vehicle is transferred applies for a new registration. The owner of a classified motor vehicle listed pursuant to this subsection need not list the vehicle as provided in G.S. 105-306. G.S. 105-312 does not apply to a classified motor vehicle listed pursuant to this subsection.

(a1) **Unregistered Vehicles.** -- The owner of an unregistered classified motor vehicle must list the vehicle for taxes by filing an abstract with the assessor of the county in which the vehicle is located on or before January 31 following the date the owner acquired the unregistered vehicle or, in the case of a registration that is not renewed, January 31 following the date the registration expires, and on or before January 31 of each succeeding year that the vehicle is unregistered. If a classified motor vehicle required to be listed pursuant to this subsection is registered before the end of the fiscal year for which it was required to be listed, the following applies:

(1) The vehicle is taxed as a registered vehicle, and the tax assessed pursuant to this subsection for the fiscal year in which the vehicle was required to be listed shall be released and/or refunded.

(2) *(**Effective for taxes imposed for taxable years beginning before July 1, 2017**)* For any months for which the vehicle was not taxed between the date the registration expired and the start of the current registered vehicle tax year, the vehicle is taxed as an unregistered vehicle as follows:

a. The value of the motor vehicle is determined as of January 1 of the year in which the registration of the motor vehicle expires.

b. In computing the taxes, the assessor must use the tax rates and any additional motor vehicle taxes of the various taxing units in effect on the date the taxes are computed.

c. The tax on the motor vehicle is the product of a fraction and the number of months for which the vehicle was not taxed between the date the registration expires and the start of the current registered vehicle tax year. The numerator of the fraction is the product of the appraised value of the motor vehicle and the tax rate of the various taxing units. The denominator of the fraction is 12.

d. The taxes are due on the first day of the second month following the month the notice was prepared.

e. Interest accrues on unpaid taxes for these unregistered classified motor vehicles at the rate of five percent (5%) for the remainder of the month following the month the taxes are due. Interest accrues at the rate of three-fourths percent (3/4%) for each following month until the taxes are paid, unless the notice is prepared after the date the taxes are due. In that circumstance, the

Chapter 105

interest accrues beginning the second month following the date of the notice until the taxes are paid.

(2) *(Effective for taxes imposed for taxable years beginning on or after July 1, 2017)* For any months for which the vehicle was not taxed between the date the registration expired and the start of the current registered vehicle tax year, the vehicle is taxed as an unregistered vehicle as follows:

    a. The value of the motor vehicle is determined as of January 1 of the year in which the taxes are computed.

    b. In computing the taxes, the assessor must use the tax rates and any additional motor vehicle taxes of the various taxing units in effect on the date the taxes are computed.

    c. The tax on the motor vehicle is the product of a fraction and the number of months for which the vehicle was not taxed between the date the registration expires and the start of the current registered vehicle tax year. The numerator of the fraction is the product of the appraised value of the motor vehicle and the tax rate of the various taxing units. The denominator of the fraction is 12.

    d. The taxes are due on September 1 following the date the notice was prepared. Taxes are payable at par or face amount if paid before January 6 following the due date. Taxes paid on or after January 6 following the due date are subject to interest charges. Interest accrues on taxes paid on or after January 6 pursuant to G.S. 105-360.

    e. Repealed by Session Laws 2017-204, s. 5.1(a), effective for taxable years beginning on or after July 1, 2017.

(3) A vehicle required to be listed pursuant to this subsection that is not listed by January 31 and is not registered before the end of the fiscal year for which it was required to be listed is subject to discovery pursuant to G.S. 105-312.

(b) **Exemption or Exclusion.** -- The owner of a classified motor vehicle who claims an exemption or exclusion from tax under this Subchapter has the burden of establishing that the vehicle is entitled to the exemption or exclusion. The owner may establish prima facie entitlement to exemption or exclusion of the classified motor vehicle by filing an application for exempt status with the assessor within 30 days of the date taxes on the vehicle are due. When an approved application is on file, the assessor must omit from the tax records the classified motor vehicles described in the application. An application is not required for vehicles qualifying

for the exemptions or exclusions listed in G.S. 105-282.1(a)(1). The remaining provisions of G.S. 105-282.1 do not apply to classified motor vehicles.

(c) **Duty to report changes.** -- The owner of a classified motor vehicle that has been omitted from the tax records as provided in subsection (b) of this section must report to the assessor any classified motor vehicle registered in the owner's name or owned by that person but not registered in the person's name that does not qualify for exemption or exclusion for the current year. This report must be made within 30 days after the renewal of registration or initial registration of the vehicle or, for an unregistered vehicle, on or before January 31 of the year in which the vehicle is required to be listed by subsection (a1) of this section. A classified motor vehicle that does not qualify for exemption or exclusion but has been omitted from the tax records as provided in subsection (b) is subject to discovery under the provisions of G.S. 105-312, except that in lieu of the penalties prescribed by G.S. 105-312(h) a penalty of one hundred dollars ($ 100.00) is assessed for each registration period that elapsed before the disqualification was discovered.

(d) **Criminal Sanction.** -- A person who willfully attempts, or who willfully aids or abets another person to attempt, in any manner to evade or defeat the taxes subject to this Article, whether by removal or concealment of property or otherwise, is guilty of a Class 2 misdemeanor.

History.
1991, c. 624, s. 1; 2008-134, s. 62; 2009-445, s. 24(a); 2010-95, s. 22(c); 2012-79, s. 3.3; 2013-414, ss. 70(b), 71(a), (c); 2017-204, s. 5.1(a)

§ 105-330.4. Due date, interest, and enforcement remedies

(a) **Due Date.** -- The registration of a classified motor vehicle may not be issued unless a temporary registration plate is issued for the motor vehicle under G.S. 20-79.1A or the taxes for the motor vehicle's tax year that begins after the issuance of the registration are paid upon registration. A registration of a classified motor vehicle may not be renewed unless the taxes for the motor vehicle's tax year that begins after the registration expires are paid upon registration. If the registration of a classified motor vehicle is renewed earlier than the date the taxes are due, the taxes must be paid as if they were due. Taxes on a classified motor vehicle are due as follows:

    (1) For an unregistered classified motor vehicle, the taxes are due on September 1 following the date by which the vehicle was required to be listed.

(2) For a registered classified motor vehicle that is registered under the staggered system, the taxes are due each year on the date the owner applies for a new registration or the fifteenth day of the month following the month in which the registration renewal sticker expires pursuant to G.S. 20-66(g).

(3) For a registered classified motor vehicle that is registered under the annual system, taxes are due on the date the owner applies for a new registration or 45 days after the registration expires.

(4) For a registered classified motor vehicle that has a temporary registration plate issued under G.S. 20-79.1 or a limited registration plate issued under G.S. 20-79.1A, the taxes are due on the last day of the second month following the date the owner applied for the plate.

(a1) Repealed by Session Laws 2009-445, s. 24(a), effective July 1, 2013, and applicable to combined tax and registration notices issued on or after that date.

(b) **Interest.** -- Interest accrues on unpaid taxes and unpaid registration fees for registered classified motor vehicles at the rate of five percent (5%) for the remainder of the month the taxes are due under subsection (a) of this section. Interest does not accrue for the first month following the due date. Interest accrues at the rate of three-fourths percent (3/4%) beginning the second month following the due date and for each following month until the taxes and fees are paid. Subject to the provisions of G.S. 105-395.1, interest accrues on delinquent taxes on unregistered classified motor vehicles as provided in G.S. 105-360(a) and the discounts allowed in G.S. 105-360(a) apply to the payment of the taxes.

(c) **Remedies.** -- The enforcement remedies in this Subchapter apply to unpaid taxes on an unregistered classified motor vehicle and to unpaid taxes on a registered classified motor vehicle for which the tax year begins before October 1, 2013.

(d) **Payments.** -- Tax payments submitted by mail are deemed to be received as of the date shown on the postmark affixed by the United States Postal Service. If no date is shown on the postmark or if the postmark is not affixed by the United States Postal Service, the tax payment is deemed to be received when the payment is received by the collecting authority. In any dispute arising under this subsection, the burden of proof is on the taxpayer to show that the payment was timely made.

(e) **Waiver.** -- Notwithstanding G.S. 105-380, the governing board of a county may adopt a resolution to create a uniform policy to allow the reduction or waiver of interest or penalties on delinquent motor vehicle taxes for registered classified motor vehicles for tax years prior to July 1, 2013.

History.
1991, c. 624, s. 1; 1991 (Reg. Sess., 1992), c. 961, s. 5; 1995, c. 510, s. 2; 2001-139, s. 8; 2005-294, ss. 3, 4, 5; 2006-259, s. 31.5; 2007-471, s. 3; 2007-527, s. 22(b); 2008-134, s. 65; 2009-445, ss. 24(a), 25(a); 2010-95, s. 22(c), (d); 2011-330, ss. 40, 42(a); 2012-79, ss. 3.4, 3.6; 2013-414, ss. 70(b) -(d), 71(a), (d); 2015-204, s. 1

§ 105-330.5. Notice required; distribution and collection fees

(a) **Notice for Registered Vehicle.** -- The Property Tax Division of the Department of Revenue or a third-party contractor selected by the Property Tax Division must prepare a combined tax and registration notice for each registered classified motor vehicle. The combined tax and registration notice must contain all county and municipal corporation taxes and fees due on the motor vehicle as computed by the assessor in the county of registration. If the motor vehicle has a temporary or limited registration plate issued under G.S. 20-79.1 or G.S. 20-79.1A, the combined tax and registration notice must state that the vehicle registration fees for the plate have been paid and that the vehicle's registration becomes valid for the remainder of the year upon payment of the county and municipal corporation taxes and fees that are due. A combined tax and registration notice that sets out the required information on a vehicle issued a limited registration plate constitutes the registration certificate for that vehicle.

In computing the taxes, the assessor must appraise the motor vehicle in accordance with G.S. 105-330.2 and must use the tax rates and any additional motor vehicle taxes of the various taxing units in effect on the date the taxes are computed. The tax on the motor vehicle is the product of a fraction and the number of months in the motor vehicle tax year. The numerator of the fraction is the product of the appraised value of the motor vehicle and the tax rate of the various taxing units. The denominator of the fraction is 12. This procedure constitutes the listing and assessment of each classified motor vehicle for taxation.

The combined tax and registration notice must contain the following:

(1) The appraised value of the motor vehicle.

(2) The tax rate of each taxing unit.

(3) A statement that the appraised value and the taxability of the motor vehicle may be appealed to the assessor in writing within 30 days of the due date.

(4) The registration fee imposed by the Division of Motor Vehicles and any other information required by the Division of

Chapter 105

Motor Vehicles to comply with the provisions of Chapter 20 of the General Statutes.

(5) Instructions for payment.

(a1) **Proration. --** When a new registration is obtained for a registered classified motor vehicle that is registered under the annual system, the taxes are prorated for the remainder of the calendar year. The amount of prorated taxes due is the product of the proration fraction and the taxes computed according to subsection (a) of this section. The numerator of the proration fraction is the number of full months remaining in the calendar year following the registration application date and the denominator of the fraction is 12.

(a2) Repealed by Session Laws 2009-445, s. 24(a), effective July 1, 2011, and applicable to combined tax and registration notices issued on or after that date, or when the Division of motor vehicles and the Department of Revenue certify that the integrated computer system or registration renewal and property tax collection for motor vehicles is in operation, whichever occurs first.

(b) **Distribution and Collection Fees. --** The Property Tax Division of the Department of Revenue or a third-party contractor selected by the Property Tax Division must send a copy of the combined tax and registration notice for a registered classified motor vehicle to the motor vehicle owner, as defined in G.S. 20-4.01. Upon receiving written consent from the motor vehicle owner, the notice required under this subsection may be sent electronically to an e-mail address provided by the motor vehicle owner. The Department must establish a fee equal to the actual cost of preparing, printing, and sending the notice. The Department may receive a fee for each notice generated for a vehicle registered in a county or municipal corporation from the taxes and fees remitted to the county or municipal corporation in which the vehicle is registered. The collecting authority is responsible for collecting county and municipal taxes and fees assessed under this Article and may receive a fee for collecting these taxes and fees. The amount of this fee for an agent contracting with the Division of Motor Vehicles must equal at least the applicable amount set under G.S. 20-63(h). The amount of this fee for the Division of Motor Vehicles is the amount set by the memorandum of understanding entered into under G.S. 105-330.11 but shall not exceed the amount set under G.S. 20-63. The Property Tax Division must establish procedures to ensure that tax payments and fees received pursuant to this Article and Chapter 20 of the General Statutes are properly accounted for and taxes and fees due other taxing units and the Division of Motor Vehicles are remitted at least once each month.

(b1) Repealed by Session Laws 1995, c. 329, s. 2.

(c) **Notice for Unregistered Vehicle. --** The assessor must prepare and send a tax notice for each unregistered classified motor vehicle before September 1 following the January 31 listing date. The notice must include all county and special district taxes due on the motor vehicle. In computing the taxes, the assessor must use the tax rates of the taxing units in effect for the fiscal year that begins on July 1 following the January 31 listing date. Municipalities must list, assess, and tax unregistered classified motor vehicles as provided in G.S. 105-326, 105-327, and 105-328.

(d) **Scope of Levy. --** A county must include taxes on registered classified motor vehicles in the tax levy for the fiscal year in which the taxes are collected.

(e) Repealed by Session Laws 2012-79, s. 3.5, effective June 26, 2012.

History.
1991, c. 624, s. 1; 1991 (Reg. Sess., 1992), c. 961, s. 6; 1995, c. 24, s. 1; c. 329, s. 2; c. 510, s. 3; 2005-294, s. 6; 2005-313, s. 8; 2006-259, s. 31.5; 2007-471, ss. 4, 5; 2007-527, s. 22(b); 2008-134, s. 65; 2009-445, ss. 24(a), 25(a); 2010-95, s. 22(c), (d); 2011-330, s. 42(a); 2012-79, ss. 3.5, 3.6; 2013-372, s. 2(b); 2013-414, s. 70(b) -(d); 2014-3, s. 13.3; 2015-108, s. 1

§ 105-330.6. Motor vehicle tax year; transfer of plates; surrender of plates

(a) **Tax Year. --** The tax year for a classified motor vehicle listed pursuant to G.S. 105-330.3(a)(1) and registered under the staggered system begins on the first day of the first month following the date on which the former registration expires or the new registration is applied for and ends on the last day of the month in which the current registration expires. The tax year for a classified motor vehicle listed pursuant to G.S. 105-330.3(a)(1) and registered under the annual system begins on the first day of the first month following the date on which the registration expires or the new registration is applied for and ends the following December 31. The tax year for a classified motor vehicle listed pursuant to G.S. 105-330.3(a)(2) is the fiscal year that opens in the calendar year in which the vehicle is required to be listed.

(a1) **Change in Tax Year. --** If the tax year for a classified motor vehicle changes because of a change in its registration for a reason other than the transfer of its registration plates to another classified motor vehicle pursuant to G.S. 20-64, and the new tax year begins before the expiration of the vehicle's original tax year, the taxpayer may receive a credit, in the form of a release, against the taxes on the vehicle for the new tax year. The amount of the credit is equal to a proportion of the taxes paid on the vehicle for the original tax year. The proportion is the number of full calendar months remaining in the original tax year as of the first day of the new tax year, divided by the number of months in the original tax year. To obtain the credit allowed in this subsection, the taxpayer must apply within 30 days after the taxes for the new tax year are due and must provide the county tax collector information establishing the original tax year of the vehicle, the amount of taxes paid on the vehicle for that year, and the reason for the change in registration.

(b) **Transfer of Plates.** -- If the owner of a classified motor vehicle listed pursuant to G.S. 105-330.3(a)(1) transfers the registration plates from the listed vehicle to another classified motor vehicle pursuant to G.S. 20-64 during the listed vehicle's tax year, the vehicle to which the plates are transferred is not required to be listed or taxed until the current registration expires or is renewed.

(c) **Surrender of Plates.** -- If the owner of a classified motor vehicle, who pays the tax as required by G.S. 105-330.4(a), either transfers the motor vehicle to a new owner or moves out-of-state and registers the vehicle in another jurisdiction, and the owner surrenders the registration plates from the listed vehicle to the Division of Motor Vehicles, then the owner may apply for a release or refund of taxes on the vehicle for any full calendar months remaining in the vehicle's tax year after the date of surrender. To apply for a release or refund, the owner must present to the county tax collector within one year after surrendering the plates the receipt received from the Division of Motor Vehicles accepting surrender of the registration plates. The county tax collector shall then multiply the amount of the taxes for the tax year on the vehicle by a fraction, the denominator of which is the number of months in the tax year and the numerator of which is the number of full calendar months remaining in the vehicle's tax year after the date of surrender of the registration plates. The product of the multiplication is the amount of taxes to be released or refunded. If the taxes have not been paid at the date of application, the county tax collector shall make a release of the prorated taxes and credit the owner's tax notice with the amount of the release. If the taxes have been paid at the date of application, the county tax collector shall direct an order for a refund of the prorated taxes to the county finance officer, and the finance officer shall issue a refund to the vehicle owner.

History.
1991, c. 624, s. 1; 1991 (Reg. Sess., 1992), c. 961, s. 7; 1995, c. 510, s. 4; 1998-139, s. 3; 2001-406, s. 1; 2001-497, s. 1(a); 2005-313, s. 9; 2017-204, s. 5.2

N.C. Gen. Stat. § 105-330.7

Repealed by Session Laws 2005-294, s. 7, effective July 1, 2013, and applicable to combined tax and registration notices issued on or after that date.

History.
1991, c. 624, s. 1; 1991 (Reg. Sess., 1992), c. 961, s. 8; 2005-294, s. 13; 2006-259, s. 31.5; 2007-527, s. 22; 2008-134, s. 65; 2005-294, s. 7; 2011-330, s. 42(a); 2012-79, s. 3.6; 2013-414, s. 70(d); repealed by 2005-294, s. 7, effective July 1, 2013

§ 105-330.8. Deadlines not extended

Except as otherwise provided in this Article, the following sections of the General Statutes do not apply:

(1) G.S. 105-395.1 and G.S. 103-5.
(2) G.S. 105-321(f).
(3) G.S. 105-360.

History.
1991, c. 624, s. 1; 2009-445, s. 24(a); 2010-95, s. 22(c); 2013-414, s. 70(b)

§ 105-330.9. Antique automobiles

(a) **Definition.** -- For the purpose of this section, the term "antique automobile" means a motor vehicle that meets all of the following conditions:

(1) It is registered with the Division of Motor Vehicles and has an historic vehicle special license plate under G.S. 20-79.4.
(2) It is maintained primarily for use in exhibitions, club activities, parades, and other public interest functions.
(3) It is used only occasionally for other purposes.
(4) It is owned by an individual, or owned directly or indirectly through one or more pass-through entities, by an individual.
(5) It is used by the owner for a purpose other than the production of income and is not used in connection with a business.

(b) **Classification.** -- Antique automobiles are designated a special class of property under Article V, Sec. 2(2) of the North Carolina Constitution and must be assessed for taxation in accordance with this section. An antique automobile must be assessed at the lower of its true value or five hundred dollars ($ 500.00).

History.
1995, c 512, s 2; 2009-445, s. 24(a); 2013-414, s. 70(b); 2017-10, s. 2.8

§ 105-330.10. Disposition of interest

The interest collected on unpaid registration fees pursuant to G.S. 105-330.4 shall be transferred on a monthly basis to the North Carolina Highway Fund.

History.

2005-294, ss. 8, 9; 2006-30, s. 3; 2006-259, s. 31.5; 2007-471, s. 7(a); 2007-527, s. 22(a) -(c); 2008-134, ss. 63, 65, 66, 79; 2009-445, s. 25(b); 2010-95, s. 22(a), (b), (e); 2011-330, s. 42(a) -(c); 2013-414, s. 70(a), (c), (d); 2015-241, s. 29.30(n)

§ 105-330.11. Memorandum of understanding

The Department of Revenue, acting through the Property Tax Division, and the Department of Transportation, acting through the Division of Motor Vehicles are directed to enter into a memorandum of understanding concerning the administration of this Article. The memorandum of understanding must include the following:

(1) A procedure for the administration of the listing, appraisal, and assessment of classified motor vehicles.

(2) Information concerning vehicle identification, the name and address of a vehicle's owner, and other information that will be required on a motor vehicle registration form to implement the tax listing and collection provisions of this Article.

(3) A procedure for the business practices, accounting, and costs of carrying out the integrated computer system for registration renewal and property tax collection for motor vehicles once the system has been certified to be in operation by the Department of Revenue and the Department of Transportation. The Departments must consult with the North Carolina Association of County Commissioners, acting on behalf of the counties, and the North Carolina League of Municipalities, acting on behalf of the municipalities, in developing the procedures under this subdivision and obtain their signed endorsements before any part of this procedure is implemented.

History.

2008-134, s. 64; 2009-445, s. 24(a); 2013-414, s. 70(b)

SUBCHAPTER 05. MOTOR FUEL TAXES

ARTICLE 36B TAX ON MOTOR CARRIERS

§ 105-449.37. Definitions; tax liability; application

(a) **Definitions.** -- The following definitions apply in this Article:

(1) **International Fuel Tax Agreement.** -- The Articles of Agreement adopted by the International Fuel Tax Association, Inc., as amended as of December 1, 2018.

(2) **Motor carrier.** -- A person who operates or causes to be operated on any highway in this State a motor vehicle that is a qualified motor vehicle. The term does not include the United States, a state, or a political subdivision of a state.

(3) **Motor vehicle.** -- Defined in G.S. 20-4.01.

(4) **Operations.** -- The movement of a qualified motor vehicle by a motor carrier, whether loaded or empty and whether or not operated for compensation.

(5) **Person.** -- Defined in G.S. 105-228.90.

(6) **Qualified motor vehicle.** -- Defined in the International Fuel Tax Agreement.

(7) **Secretary.** -- Defined in G.S. 105-228.90.

(b) **Liability.** -- A motor carrier who operates on one or more days of a reporting period is liable for the tax imposed by this Article for that reporting period and is entitled to the credits allowed for that reporting period.

(c) **Application.** -- A motor carrier who operates a qualified motor vehicle in this State must submit an application, as provided in this Article, and obtain the appropriate license and decals for the vehicle. The Article applies to both an interstate motor carrier subject to the International Fuel Tax Agreement and to an intrastate motor carrier.

History.

1955, c. 823, s. 1; 1973, c. 476, s. 193; 1983, c. 713, s. 55; 1989, c. 7, s. 1; 1991, c. 182, s. 2; c. 487, s. 2; 1991 (Reg. Sess., 1992), c. 913, s. 8; 1993, c. 354, s. 28; 1999-337, s. 36; 2000-140, s. 74; 2008-134, s. 16; 2010-95, s. 27; 2014-3, s. 9.5(b); 2017-39, s. 11; 2020-58, s. 2.9

§ 105-449.38. Tax levied

A road tax for the privilege of using the streets and highways of this State is imposed upon every motor carrier on the amount of motor fuel or alternative fuel used by the carrier in its operations within this State. The tax shall be at the rate established by the Secretary pursuant to G.S. 105-449.80 or G.S. 105-449.136, as appropriate. This tax is in addition to any other taxes imposed on motor carriers.

History.

1955, c. 823, s. 2; 1969, c. 600, s. 22; 1981, c. 690, s. 3; 1985 (Reg. Sess., 1986), c. 982, s. 16; 1995, c. 390, s. 16; 2001-205, s. 2; 2008-134, s. 17

§ 105-449.39. Credit for payment of motor fuel tax

Every motor carrier subject to the tax levied by this Article is entitled to a credit on its quarterly return for tax paid by the carrier on fuel purchased in the State. The amount of the credit is determined using the tax rate in effect under G.S. 105-449.80 for the time period covered by the return. To obtain a credit, the motor carrier must furnish evidence satisfactory to the Secretary that the tax for which the credit is claimed has been paid.

If the amount of a credit to which a motor carrier is entitled for a quarter exceeds the motor carrier's liability for that quarter, the excess is refundable in accordance with G.S. 105-241.7.

History.
1955, c. 823, s. 3; 1969, c. 600, s. 22; c. 1098; 1973, c. 476, s. 193; 1979, 2nd Sess., c. 1098; 1981, c. 690, s. 3; 1985 (Reg. Sess., 1986), c. 982, s. 17; 1987, c. 315; 1989, c. 692, s. 5.7; 1991, c. 182, s. 3; c. 487, s. 3; 1998-146, s. 1; 1999-337, s. 37; 2005-435, s. 3; 2007-491, s. 40; 2010-95, s. 26(a); 2016-5, s. 4.10(a)

§ 105-449.40. Secretary may require bond

(a) **Authority.** -- The Secretary may require a motor carrier to furnish a bond when any of the following occurs:

(1) The motor carrier fails to file a return within the time required by this Article.

(2) The motor carrier fails to pay a tax when due under this Article.

(3) After auditing the motor carrier's records, the Secretary determines that a bond is needed to protect the State from loss in collecting the tax due under this Article.

(b) **Amount.** -- A bond required of a motor carrier under this section may not be more than the larger of the following amounts:

(1) Five hundred dollars ($ 500.00).

(2) Four times the motor carrier's average tax liability or refund for a reporting period.

A bond must be in the form required by the Secretary.

History.
1955, c. 823, s. 4; 1967, c. 1110, s. 15; 1973, c. 476, s. 193; 1991, c. 487, s. 4; 2010-95, s. 26(b).

N.C. Gen. Stat. § 105-449.41

Repealed by Session Laws 2002-108, s. 2, effective January 1, 2003.

§ 105-449.42. Payment of tax

The tax levied by this Article is due when a motor carrier files a quarterly return under G.S. 105-449.45. The amount of tax due is calculated on the amount of motor fuel or alternative fuel used by the motor carrier in its operations within this State during the quarter covered by the return.

History.
1955, c. 823, s. 6; 1973, c. 476, s. 193; 1979, 2nd Sess., c. 1086, s. 2; 1983, c. 29, s. 2; 1991, c. 182, s. 4; 1999-337, s. 38; 2010-95, s. 26(c)

§ 105-449.42A. Leased motor vehicles

(a) **Lessor in Leasing Business.** -- A lessor who is regularly engaged in the business of leasing or renting motor vehicles without drivers for compensation is the motor carrier for a leased or rented motor vehicle unless the lessee of the leased or rented motor vehicle gives the Secretary written notice, by filing a return or otherwise, that the lessee is the motor carrier. In that circumstance, the lessee is the motor carrier for the leased or rented motor vehicle.

Before a lessee gives the Secretary written notice under this subsection that the lessee is the motor carrier, the lessee and lessor must make a written agreement for the lessee to be the motor carrier. Upon request of the Secretary, the lessee must give the Secretary a copy of the agreement.

(b) **Independent Contractor.** -- The lessee of a motor vehicle that is leased from an independent contractor is the motor carrier for the leased motor vehicle unless one of the circumstances listed in this subsection applies. If either of these circumstances applies, the lessor is the motor carrier for the leased motor vehicle.

(1) The motor vehicle is leased for fewer than 30 days.

(2) The motor vehicle is leased for at least 30 days and the lessor gives the Secretary written notice, by filing a return or otherwise, that the lessor is the motor carrier. Before a lessor gives the Secretary written notice that the lessor is the motor carrier, the lessor and lessee must make a written agreement for the lessor to be the motor carrier. Upon request of the Secretary, the lessor must give the Secretary a copy of the agreement.

(c) **Liability.** -- An independent contractor who leases a motor vehicle to another for fewer than 30 days is liable for compliance with this Article and the person to whom the motor vehicle is leased is not liable. Otherwise, both the lessor and lessee of a motor vehicle are jointly and severally liable for compliance with this Article.

History.
1983, c. 29, s. 3; 1985 (Reg. Sess., 1986), c. 826, s. 11; 1991, c. 487, s. 5; 1991 (Reg. Sess., 1992), c. 913, s. 9; 2010-95, s. 26(d)

§ 105-449.43. Application of tax proceeds

Tax revenue collected under this Article and tax refunds or credits allowed under this Article shall be allocated among and charged to the funds and accounts listed in G.S. 105-449.125 in accordance with that section.

History.
1955, c. 823, s. 7; 1981 (Reg. Sess., 1982), c. 1211, s. 3; 1989, c. 692, s. 1.16; 1995, c. 390, s. 17

§ 105-449.44. How to determine the amount of fuel used in the State; presumption of amount used

(a) **Calculation.** -- The amount of motor fuel or alternative fuel a motor carrier uses in its operations in this State for a reporting period is the number of miles the motor carrier travels in this State during that period divided by the calculated miles per gallon for the motor carrier for all qualified motor vehicles during that period.

(b) **Presumption.** -- The Secretary must check returns filed under this Article against the weigh station records and other records of the Division of Motor Vehicles of the Department of Transportation and the State Highway Patrol of the Department of Public Safety concerning motor carriers to determine if motor carriers that are operating in this State are filing the returns required by this Article. If the records indicate that a motor carrier operated in this State in a quarter and either did not file a return for that quarter or understated its mileage in this State on a return filed for that quarter by at least twenty-five percent (25%), the Secretary may assess the motor carrier for an amount based on the motor carrier's presumed operations. The motor carrier is presumed to have mileage in this State equal to 10 trips of 450 miles each for each of the motor carrier's qualified motor vehicles and to have fuel usage of four miles per gallon.

(c) **Vehicles.** -- The number of qualified motor vehicles of a motor carrier that is licensed under this Article is the number of sets of decals issued to the carrier. The number of qualified motor vehicles of a carrier that is not licensed under this Article is the number of qualified motor vehicles licensed or registered by the motor carrier in the carrier's base state under the International Registration Plan.

History.
1955, c. 823, s. 8; 1995, c. 390, s. 35; 1999-337, s. 39; 2000-173, s. 12; 2005-435, s. 4; 2008-134, s. 18; 2010-95, s. 26(e); 2011-145, s. 19.1(g); 2017-204, s. 4.4(a)

§ 105-449.45. Returns of carriers

(a) **Return.** -- A motor carrier must report its operations to the Secretary on a quarterly basis unless subsection (b) of this section exempts the motor carrier from this requirement.

A quarterly return covers a calendar quarter and is due by the last day in April, July, October, and January. A return must be filed in the form required by the Secretary.

(b) **Exemptions.** -- A motor carrier is not required to file a quarterly return if any of the following applies:

(1) All the motor carrier's operations during the quarter were made under a temporary permit issued under G.S. 105-449.49.

(2) The motor carrier is an intrastate motor carrier, as indicated on the motor carrier's application for licensure with the Secretary.

(c) **Informational Returns.** -- A motor carrier must file with the Secretary any informational returns concerning its operations that the Secretary requires.

(d) **Penalties.** -- A motor carrier that fails to file a return under this section by the required date is subject to a penalty of fifty dollars ($ 50.00).

(e) **Interest.** -- Interest on overpayments and underpayments of tax imposed on motor carriers under this Article is subject to the interest rate adopted in the International Fuel Tax Agreement.

History.
1955, c. 823, s. 9; 1973, c. 476, s. 193; 1979, 2nd Sess., c. 1086, s. 2; 1981 (Reg. Sess., 1982), c. 1254, s. 2; 1989 (Reg. Sess., 1990), c. 1050, s. 1; 1991, c. 182, s. 5; 1995, c. 17, s. 13.1; 1998-212, s. 29A.14(q); 1999-337, s. 40; 2009-445, s. 31(a); 2010-95, s. 26(f); 2016-5, s. 4.8; 2017-204, s. 4.4(b)

§ 105-449.46. Inspection of books and records

The Secretary and his authorized agents and representatives shall have the right at any reasonable time to inspect the books and records of any motor carrier subject to the tax imposed by this Article or to the registration fee imposed by Article 3 of Chapter 20 of the General Statutes.

History.
1955, c. 823, s. 10; 1973, c. 476, s. 193; 2005-435, s. 5

§ 105-449.47. Licensure of vehicles

(a) **Requirement.** -- A motor carrier may not operate or cause to be operated in this State a qualified motor vehicle unless both the motor carrier and at least one qualified motor vehicle are licensed as provided in this subsection. This subsection applies to a motor carrier that operates a recreational vehicle that is used in connection with any business endeavor. A motor carrier that is subject to the International Fuel Tax Agreement must be licensed with the motor carrier's base state jurisdiction. A motor carrier that is not subject to the International Fuel Tax Agreement must be licensed with the Secretary for purposes of the tax imposed by this Article.

(a1) **License and Decal.** -- When the Secretary licenses a motor carrier, the Secretary must issue a license for the motor carrier and a set of decals for each qualified motor vehicle. A motor carrier must keep records of decals issued to it and must be able to account for all decals it receives from the Secretary. Licenses and decals issued by the Secretary are for a calendar year. All decals issued by the Secretary remain the property of the State. The Secretary may revoke a license or a decal when a motor carrier fails to comply with this Article or Article 36C or 36D of this Subchapter.

A motor carrier must carry a copy of its license in each motor vehicle operated by the motor carrier when the vehicle is in this State. Unless operating under a temporary permit under G.S. 105-449.49, a motor vehicle must clearly display one decal on each side of the vehicle at all times. A decal must be affixed to the qualified motor vehicle for which it was issued in the place and manner designated by the authority that issued it.

(b) **Exemption.** -- This section does not apply to the operation of a qualified motor vehicle that is licensed in another state and is operated temporarily in this State by a public utility, a governmental or cooperative provider of utility services, or a contractor for one of these entities for the purpose of restoring utility services in an emergency outage.

History.
1955, c. 823, s. 11; 1973, c. 746, s. 193; 1983, c. 713, s. 56; 1985 (Reg. Sess., 1986), c. 937, s. 20; 1989, c. 692, s. 6.2; 1991, c. 487, s. 6; 1995, c. 50, s. 5; c. 390, s. 18; 1999-337, s. 41; 2002-108, s. 3; 2004-170, s. 24; 2005-435, s. 6; 2008-134, s. 19; 2014-3, s. 9.5(c); 2017-204, s. 4.4(c); 2020-58, s. 2.10(a)

§ 105-449.47A. Denial of license application and decal issuance

The Secretary may refuse to license and issue a decal to an applicant that does not meet the requirements set out in G.S. 105-449.69(b) or that has done any of the following:

(1) Had a license issued under Chapter 105 or Chapter 119 of the General Statutes revoked by the Secretary.

(2) Had a license issued by another jurisdiction, pursuant to the International Fuel Tax Agreement, revoked.

(3) Been convicted of fraud or misrepresentation.

(4) Been convicted of any other offense that indicates that the applicant may not comply with this Article if licensed and issued a decal.

(5) Failed to remit payment for a tax debt under Chapter 105 or Chapter 119 of the General Statutes. The term "tax debt" has the same meaning as defined in G.S. 105-243.1.

(6) Failed to file a return due under Chapter 105 or Chapter 119 of the General Statutes.

(7) Failed to maintain motor vehicle registration on the qualified motor vehicle.

History.
2005-435, s. 7; 2008-134, s. 20; 2009-445, s. 32; 2010-95, s. 28; 2017-204, s. 4.4(d); 2019-169, s. 4.10

N.C. Gen. Stat. § 105-449.48

Repealed by Session Laws 2006-162, s. 12(c), effective July 24, 2006.

§ 105-449.49. Temporary permits

(a) **Permitting Service.** -- Upon application to the Secretary and payment of a fee of fifty dollars ($ 50.00), a permitting service may obtain a temporary permit authorizing a motor carrier to operate a vehicle in the State for three days without licensing the vehicle in accordance with G.S. 105-449.47. The permitting service may sell the temporary permit to a motor carrier. A motor carrier to whom a temporary permit has been issued may elect not to report its operation of the vehicle during the three-day period. Fees collected under this subsection are credited to the Highway Fund.

(b) Repealed by Session Laws 2016-5, s. 4.6, effective May 11, 2016.

(c) **Licensed Motor Carrier.** -- A licensed motor carrier in North Carolina, who is subject to the International Fuel Tax Agreement, may apply for a temporary permit authorizing the motor carrier to operate a qualified motor vehicle in the State for 30 days without a decal. The licensed motor carrier must be in compliance with this Article, and the application must be on a form prescribed by the Secretary and contain information required by the Secretary.

(d) **Permit.** -- A motor carrier operating under a temporary permit issued pursuant to this section must keep a copy of the permit in the motor vehicle.

History.
1955, c. 823, s. 13; 1973, c. 476, s. 193; 1979, c. 11; 1981 (Reg. Sess., 1982), c. 1254, s. 1; 1983, c. 713, s. 58; 1991, c. 182, s. 6; c. 487, s. 7; 1991 (Reg. Sess., 1992), c. 913, s. 10; 2003-349, s. 10.1; 2006-162, s. 12(d); 2016-5, s. 4.6; 2017-204, s. 4.4(e); 2020-58, s. 2.10(b)

N.C. Gen. Stat. § 105-449.50

Repealed by Session Laws 2008-134, s. 21, effective January 1, 2009.

§ 105-449.51. Violations declared to be misdemeanors

A person who operates or causes to be operated on a highway in this State a qualified motor vehicle that does not carry a license as required by this Article, does not properly display a decal as required by this Article, or is not licensed in accordance with this Article commits a Class 3 misdemeanor and is punishable by a fine of two hundred dollars ($ 200.00). Each day's operation in violation of this section constitutes a separate offense.

History.

1955, c. 823, s. 15; 1973, c. 476, s. 193; 1983, c. 713, s. 59; 1993, c. 539, s. 734; 1994, Ex. Sess., c. 24, s. 14(c); 2005-435, s. 8; 2008-134, s. 22; 2017-204, s. 4.4(f)

§ 105-449.52. Civil penalties applicable to motor carriers

(a) **Penalty.** -- A motor carrier who does any of the following is subject to a civil penalty:

(1) Operates in this State or causes to be operated in this State a qualified motor vehicle that either fails to carry the license required by this Article or fails to display a decal in accordance with this Article. The amount of the penalty is one hundred dollars ($ 100.00).

(2) Is unable to account for a decal the Secretary issues the motor carrier, as required by G.S. 105-449.47. The amount of the penalty is one hundred dollars ($ 100.00) for each decal for which the carrier is unable to account.

(3) Displays a decal on a qualified motor vehicle operated by a motor carrier that was not issued to the carrier by the Secretary under G.S. 105-449.47. The amount of the penalty is one thousand dollars ($ 1,000) for each decal unlawfully obtained. Both the licensed motor carrier to whom the Secretary issued the decal and the motor carrier displaying the unlawfully obtained decal are jointly and severally liable for the penalty under this subdivision.

(a1) **Payment.** -- A penalty imposed under this section is payable to the agency that assessed the penalty. When a qualified motor vehicle is found to be operating without a license or a decal or with a decal the Secretary did not issue for the vehicle, the qualified motor vehicle may not be driven for a purpose other than to park it until the penalty imposed under this section is paid unless the officer that imposes the penalty determines that operating it will not jeopardize collection of the penalty.

(b) **Penalty Reduction.** -- The Secretary may reduce or waive the penalty as provided under G.S. 105-449.119.

History.

1955, c. 823, s. 16; 1957, c. 948; 1973, c. 476, s. 193; 1975, c. 716, s. 5; 1981, c. 690, s. 18; 1983, c. 713, s. 60; 1991, c. 42, s. 14; 1991 (Reg. Sess., 1992), c. 913, s. 11; 1998-146, s. 2; 1999-337, s. 43; 2002-108, s. 4; 2004-170, s. 25; 2007-527, s. 16(a); 2008-134, ss. 8, 23; 2014-3, s. 9.8(a); 2017-204, s. 4.4(g)

N.C. Gen. Stat. § 105-449.53

Repealed by Session Laws 1963, c. 1169, s. 6.

§ 105-449.54. Commissioner of Motor Vehicles made process agent of nonresident motor carriers

By operating a motor vehicle on the highways of this State, a nonresident motor carrier consents to the appointment of the Commissioner of Motor Vehicles as its attorney in fact and process agent for all summonses or other lawful process or notice in any action, assessment, or other proceeding under this Chapter.

History.

1955, c. 823, s. 18; 2004-170, s. 26

§§ 105-449.55, 105-449.56

Repealed by Session Laws 1991, c. 42, s. 17.

§ 105-449.57. Cooperative agreements between jurisdictions

(a) **Authority.** -- The Secretary may enter into cooperative agreements with other jurisdictions for exchange of information in administering the tax imposed by this Article. No agreement, arrangement, declaration, or amendment to an agreement is effective until stated in writing and approved by the Secretary or the Secretary's designee.

(b) **Content.** -- An agreement may provide for determining the base state for motor carriers, records requirements, audit procedures, exchange of information, persons eligible for tax licensing, defining qualified motor vehicles, determining if bonding is required, specifying reporting requirements and periods, including defining uniform penalty and interest rates for late reporting, determining methods for collecting and forwarding of motor carrier taxes and penalties to another jurisdiction, and any other provisions that will facilitate the administration of the agreement.

(c) **Disclosure.** -- In accordance with G.S. 105-259, the Secretary may, as required by the terms of an agreement, forward to officials of another jurisdiction any information in the Department's possession relative to the administration and collection of a tax imposed on the use of motor fuel or alternative fuel by any motor carrier. The Secretary may disclose to officials of another jurisdiction the location of offices, motor vehicles, and other real and personal property of motor carriers.

(d) **Audits.** -- An agreement may provide for each jurisdiction to audit the records of motor carriers based in the jurisdiction to determine if the taxes due each jurisdiction are properly reported and paid. Each jurisdiction must forward the findings of the audits performed on motor carriers based in the jurisdiction to each jurisdiction in which the carrier has taxable use of motor fuel or alternative fuel. For motor carriers not based in this State, the Secretary may utilize the audit findings received from another jurisdiction as the basis upon which to propose assessments of taxes against the carrier as though the audit had been conducted by the Secretary. Penalties and interest must be assessed at the rates provided in the agreement.

No agreement entered into pursuant to this section may preclude the Department from auditing the records of any motor carrier covered by this Chapter.

The provisions of Article 9 of this Chapter apply to any assessment or order made under this section.

(e) **Restriction.** -- The Secretary or the Secretary's designee may not enter into any agreement that would increase or decrease taxes

and fees imposed under Subchapter V of Chapter 105 of the General Statutes. Any provision to the contrary is void.

History.
1989, c. 667, s. 1; 1993, c. 485, s. 36; 1995 (Reg. Sess., 1996), c. 647, s. 50; 1999-337, s. 42; 2016-5, ss. 4.5(b), 4.7(a), (b)

ARTICLE 36C
GASOLINE, DIESEL, AND BLENDS

PART 6
ENFORCEMENT AND ADMINISTRATION

§ 105-449.118A. Civil penalty for refusing to allow the taking of a motor fuel sample

A person who refuses to allow the taking of a motor fuel sample is subject to a civil penalty of one thousand dollars ($ 1,000). The penalty is payable to the agency that assessed the penalty. If the refusal is for a sample to be taken from a vehicle, the penalty is payable by the person in whose name the vehicle is registered. If the refusal is for a sample to be taken from any other storage tank or container, the penalty is payable by the owner of the container.

History.
1995 (Reg. Sess., 1996), c. 647, s. 41; 2007-527, s. 16(f)

CHAPTER 106
AGRICULTURE

ARTICLE 75
PROTECTION AND DEVELOPMENT OF FORESTS; FIRE CONTROL

§ 106-899. Powers of forest rangers and deputy rangers to prevent and extinguish fires; authority to issue citations and warning tickets

(a) Forest rangers or deputy rangers shall prevent and extinguish forest fires and shall have control and direction of all persons and equipment while engaged in the extinguishing of forest fires. During a season of drought, the Commissioner or his designate may establish a fire patrol in any district, and in case of fire in or threatening any forest or woodland, the forest ranger or deputy ranger shall attend forthwith and use all necessary means to confine and extinguish such fire. The forest ranger may summon any resident between the ages of 18 and 45 years, inclusive, to assist in extinguishing fires and may require the use of crawler tractors and other property needed for such purposes; any person so summoned and who is physically able who refuses or neglects to assist or to allow the use of equipment and such other property required shall be guilty of a Class 3 misdemeanor and upon conviction shall only be subject to a fine of not less than fifty dollars ($ 50.00) nor more than one hundred dollars ($ 100.00). No action for trespass shall lie against any forest ranger, deputy ranger, or person summoned by a forest ranger for crossing lands, backfiring, burning out or performing his duties as a forest ranger or deputy ranger.

(b) Forest rangers are authorized to issue and serve citations under the terms of G.S. 15A-302 and warning tickets under the terms of G.S. 106-901 for offenses under the forest laws. This subsection may not be interpreted to confer the power of arrest on forest rangers, and does not make them criminal justice officers within the meaning of G.S. 17C-2.

History.
1915, c. 243, s. 6; C.S., s. 6137; 1925, c. 106, ss. 1, 2; c. 240; 1927, c. 150, s. 4; 1951, c. 575; 1963, c. 312, s. 2; 1973, c. 108, s. 65; c. 1262, s. 86; 1975, c. 620, s. 2; 1977, c. 771, s. 4; 1983, c. 327, s. 3; 1989, c. 727, s. 63; 1993, c. 539, s. 832; 1994, Ex. Sess., c. 24, s. 14(c); 2011-145, s. 13.25(p), (q); 2017-108, s. 12(b)

§ 106-900. Powers of Department of Agriculture and Consumer Services law-enforcement officers

The Commissioner is authorized to appoint as many Department of Agriculture and Consumer Services law enforcement officers as he or she deems necessary to investigate and enforce any violation of the laws within the authority of the Department or which occur on Department property. Such officers shall meet the requirements of Article 1 of Chapter 17C of the General Statutes and shall take the oath of office prescribed by Section 7 of Article VI of the North Carolina Constitution. Of these officers, the Commissioner may designate certain officers to also have the powers and the duties of a forest ranger enumerated in G.S. 106-898 and G.S. 106-899 and the power to enforce the forest laws. A Department law enforcement officer may arrest, without warrant, any person or persons committing any crime in the officer's presence or who such officer has probable cause for believing has committed a crime in the officer's presence and bring such person or persons forthwith before a district court or other officer having jurisdiction. Department law enforcement officers shall also have authority to obtain and serve warrants including warrants for violation of any duly promulgated rule of the Department.

History.
1975, c. 620, s. 3; 1977, c. 771, s. 4; 1983, c. 327, s. 5; 1989, c. 727, s. 64; 2011-145, s. 13.25(p), (q); 2014-103, s. 7

§ 106-901. Warning tickets for violations of the forest laws

(a) To encourage the cooperation of the public in achieving the objectives of the forest laws, the Commissioner may provide for the issuance of warning tickets instead of the initiation of criminal prosecution by forest rangers and forest law-enforcement officers. Issuance of the warning tickets shall be in accordance with criteria administratively promulgated by the Commissioner within the requirements of this section. These criteria are exempt from Article 2A of Chapter 150B of the General Statutes.

(b) No warning ticket may be issued unless all of the following conditions are met:

(1) The forest ranger or the forest law-enforcement officer must be convinced that the offense was not committed intentionally.

(2) The offense is not one, or a type of offense, for which the Commissioner has prohibited the issuance of warning tickets.

(3) At the time of the violation it was not reasonably foreseeable that the conduct of the offender could result in any significant

destruction of forests or woodlands or constitute a hazard to the public.

(c) A warning ticket may not be issued if the offender has previously been charged with, or issued a warning ticket for, the same or a similar offense within the preceding three years. A list of persons who have been issued warning tickets under this section within the preceding three years shall be maintained and periodically updated by the Commissioner.

(d) This section does not entitle any person who has committed an offense to the right to be issued a warning ticket, and the issuance of a warning ticket does not prohibit the later initiation of criminal prosecution for the same offense for which the warning ticket was issued.

History.
1983, c. 327, s. 6; 1987, c. 827, s. 6; 2000-189, s. 8; 2011-145, s. 13.25(p), (q).

§ 106-910. Violation of proclamation a misdemeanor

Any person, firm or corporation who enters upon any woodlands or inland waters of the State for the purpose of hunting, fishing or trapping, or who builds a campfire or burns brush, grass or other debris within 500 feet of any woodland, after a proclamation has been issued by the Governor forbidding such activities, or who violates any other provisions of the Governor's proclamation with regard to permissible activities in closed woodlands shall be guilty of a Class 1 misdemeanor.

History.
1953, c. 305; 1993, c. 539, s. 834; 1994, Ex. Sess., c. 24, s. 14(c); 2011-145, s. 13.25(p)

ARTICLE 78
REGULATION OF OPEN FIRES

§ 106-940. Purpose and findings

The purpose of this Article is to regulate certain open burning in order to protect the public from the hazards of forest fires and air pollution and to adapt such regulation to the needs and circumstances of the different areas of North Carolina. The General Assembly finds that open burning in proximity to woodlands must be regulated in all counties to protect against forest fires and air pollution. The General Assembly further finds that in certain counties a high percentage of the land area contains organic soils or forest types which may pose greater problems of forest fire and air pollution controls, and that in counties in which a great amount of land-clearing operations is taking place on

these organic soils or these forest types, additional control of open burning is required. The counties subject to the need for additional control are classified as high hazard counties for purpose of this Article.

History.
1981, c. 1100, s. 2; 1981 (Reg. Sess., 1982), c. 1385, s. 1; 2011-145, s. 13.25(w)

§ 106-941. Definitions

As used in this Article:

(1) "Department" means the Department of Agriculture and Consumer Services.

(2) "Forest ranger" means a forest ranger designated under G.S. 106-896(3).

(3) "Person" means any individual, firm, partnership, corporation, association, public or private institution, political subdivision, or government agency.

(4) "Woodland" means woodland as defined in G.S. 106-904.

History.
1981, c. 1100, s. 2; 1989, c. 727, s. 218(53); 1991 (Reg. Sess., 1992), c. 890, s. 3; 1997-443, s. 11A.119(a); 2011-145, s. 13.25(w), (x); 2017-108, s. 12(e)

§ 106-942. High hazard counties; permits required; standards

(a) The provisions of this section apply only to the counties of Beaufort, Bladen, Brunswick, Camden, Carteret, Chowan, Craven, Currituck, Dare, Duplin, Gates, Hyde, Jones, Onslow, Pamlico, Pasquotank, Perquimans, Tyrrell, and Washington which are classified as high hazard counties in accordance with G.S. 106-940.

(b) It is unlawful for any person to willfully start or cause to be started any fire in any woodland under the protection of the Department or within 500 feet of any such woodland without first having obtained a permit from the Department. Permits for starting fires may be obtained from forest rangers or other agents authorized by the forest ranger to issue such permits in the county in which the fire is to be started. Such permits shall be issued by the ranger or other agent unless permits for the area in question have been prohibited or cancelled in accordance with G.S. 106-944 or G.S. 106-946.

(c) It is unlawful for any person to willfully burn any debris, stumps, brush or other flammable materials resulting from ground clearing activities and involving more than five contiguous acres, regardless of the proximity of the burning to woodland and on which such materials are placed in piles or windrows without first having obtained a special permit from the Department. Areas less than five acres in size will require a regular permit in accordance with G.S. 106-942(b).

(1) Prevailing winds at the time of ignition must be away from any city, town, development, major highway, or other populated area, the ambient air of which may be significantly affected by smoke, fly ash, or other air contaminates from the burning.

(2) The location of the burning must be at least 500 feet from any dwelling or structure located in a predominately residential area other than a dwelling or structure located on the property on which the burning is conducted unless permission is granted by the occupants.

(3) The amount of dirt or organic soil on or in the material to be burned must be minimized and the material arranged in a way suitable to facilitate rapid burning.

(4) Burning may not be initiated when it is determined by a forest ranger, based on information supplied by a competent authority that stagnant air conditions or inversions exist or that such conditions may occur during the duration of the burn.

(5) Heavy oils, asphaltic material, or items containing natural or synthetic rubber may not be used to ignite the material to be burned or to promote the burning of such material.

(6) Initial burning may be commenced only between the hours of 8:00 A.M. and 4:00 P.M. and no combustible material may be added to the fire between 4:00 P.M. on one day and 8:00 A.M. on the following day, except that when favorable meteorological conditions exist, any forest ranger authorized to issue the permit may authorize in writing a deviation from the restrictions.

History.
1981, c. 1100, s. 2; 1981 (Reg. Sess., 1982), c. 1165; c. 1385, s. 2; 2002-132, s. 1; 2011-145, s. 13.25(w), (x); 2013-265, s. 15; 2017-108, s. 12(f)

§ 106-943. Open burning in non-high hazard counties; permits required; standards

(a) The provisions of this section apply only to the counties not designated as high hazard counties in G.S. 106-942(a).

(b) It shall be unlawful for any person to start or cause to be started any fire or ignite any material in any woodland under the protection of the Department or within 500 feet of any such woodland during the hours starting at midnight and ending at 4:00 P.M. without first obtaining a permit from the Department. Permits may be obtained from forest rangers or other agents authorized by the forest ranger to issue such permits in the county in which the fire is to be started. Such permits shall be issued by the ranger or other agent unless permits for the area in question have been prohibited or cancelled under G.S. 106-944 or G.S. 106-946.

History.
1981, c. 1100, s. 2; 2011-145, s. 13.25(w), (x)

§ 106-944. Open burning prohibited statewide

During periods of hazardous forest fire conditions or during air pollution episodes declared pursuant to Article 21B of Chapter 143 of the General Statutes, the Commissioner is authorized to prohibit all open burning regardless of whether a permit is required under G.S. 106-942 or G.S. 106-943. The Commissioner shall issue a press release containing relevant details of the prohibition to news media serving the area affected.

History.
1981, c. 1100, s. 2; 2011-145, s. 13.25(w), (x)

§ 106-945. Permit conditions

Permits issued under this Article shall be issued in the name of the person undertaking the burning and shall specify the specific area in which the burning is to occur, the type and amount of material to be burned, the duration of the permit, and such other factors as are necessary to identify the burning which is allowed under the permit.

History.
1981, c. 1100, s. 2; 2011-145, s. 13.25(w)

§ 106-946. Permit suspension and cancellation

Upon a determination that hazardous forest fire conditions exist the Commissioner is authorized to cancel any permit issued under this Article and suspend the issuance of any new permits. Upon a determination by the Environmental Management Commission or its agent that open burning permitted under this Article is causing significant contravention of ambient air quality standards or that an air pollution episode exists pursuant to Article 21B of Chapter 143 of the General Statutes, the Commissioner shall cancel any permits issued under authority of this Article and shall suspend the issuance of any new permits.

History.
1981, c. 1100, s. 2; 2011-145, s. 13.25(w), (x)

§ 106-947. Control of existing fires

(a) If a fire is set without a permit required by G.S. 106-942, 106-943, or 106-944, and is set in an area in which permits are prohibited or cancelled at the time the fire is set, the person responsible for setting the fire or causing the fire to be set shall immediately extinguish the fire or take such other action as directed by any forest ranger authorized to issue permits under G.S. 106-942(c). In the event that the person responsible does not immediately undertake efforts to extinguish the fire or take such other action as directed by the forest ranger, the Department may enter the property and take reasonable steps to extinguish or control the fire and the person responsible for setting the fire shall reimburse the Department for the expenses incurred by the Department. A showing that a fire is associated with land-clearing activities is prima facie evidence that the person undertaking the land clearing is responsible for setting the fire or causing the fire to be set.

(b) If a fire requiring a permit under G.S. 106-942(c) is set without a permit and a forest ranger authorized to issue such permits determines that a permit would not have been issued for the fire at the time it was set, the person responsible for setting the fire or causing the fire to be set shall immediately take such action as the forest ranger directs to extinguish or control the fire. In the event the person responsible does not immediately undertake efforts to extinguish the fire or take such other action as directed by the forest ranger, the Department may enter the property and take reasonable steps to extinguish or control the fire and the person responsible for setting the fire shall reimburse the Department for the expenses incurred by the Department. A showing that a fire is associated with land-clearing activities is prima facie evidence that the person undertaking the land clearing is responsible for setting the fire or causing the fire to be set.

(c) If a fire is set in accordance with a permit but the burning is taking place contrary to the conditions of the permit, any forest ranger with authority to issue permits in the area in question may order the permittee in writing to undertake the steps necessary to comply with the conditions of his permit. If the permittee is not making a reasonable effort to comply with the order, the forest ranger may enter the property and take reasonable steps to extinguish or control the fire and the permittee shall reimburse the Department for the expenses incurred by the Department.

History.
1981, c. 1100, s. 2; 2011-145, s. 13.25(w), (x)

§ 106-948. Penalties

Any person violating the provisions of this Article or of any permit issued under the authority of this Article shall be guilty of a Class 3 misdemeanor. It is not a violation of this Article or any permit issued under the authority of this Article if a person unintentionally fails to comply with a setback requirement so long as the difference between the required setback and the actual setback is no more than five percent (5%) of the required setback. The penalties imposed by this section shall be separate and apart and not in lieu of any civil or criminal penalties which may be imposed by G.S. 143-215.114A or G.S. 143-215.114B. The penalties imposed are also in addition to any liability the violator incurs as a result of actions taken by the Department under G.S. 106-947.

History.
1981, c. 1100, s. 2; 1989 (Reg. Sess., 1990), c. 1045, s. 11; 1993, c. 539, s. 835; 1994, Ex. Sess., c. 24, s. 14(c); 2011-145, s. 13.25(w), (x); 2011-394, s. 2(h)

§ 106-949. Effect on other laws

This Article shall not be construed as affecting or abridging the lawful authority of local governments to pass ordinances relating to open burning within their boundaries. Nothing in this Article shall relieve any person from compliance with the provisions of Article 21B of Chapter 143 of the General Statutes and regulations adopted thereunder. In the event that permits are required for open burning associated with land clearing under the authority of Article 21B of Chapter 143 of the General Statutes, the authority to issue such permits shall be delegated to forest rangers who are authorized to issue permits under G.S. 106-942(c).

History.
1981, c. 1100, s. 2; 2011-145, s. 13.25(w), (x)

§ 106-950. Exempt fires; no permit fees

This section has more than one version with varying effective dates. To view a complete list of the versions of this section see Table of Contents.

(a) This Article does not apply to any fires started, or caused to be started, within 100 feet of an occupied dwelling house if the fire is confined (i) within an enclosure from which burning material may not escape or (ii) within a protected area upon which a watch is being maintained and which is provided with adequate fire protection equipment.

(a1) Except in cases where the Commissioner has prohibited all open burning during periods of hazardous forest fire conditions or during air pollution episodes declared pursuant to Article 21B of Chapter 143 of the General Statutes, this Article does not apply to, and no air quality permit shall be required for, the burning of poly-ethylene agricultural plastic used in connection with agricultural operations related to the growing, harvesting, or maintenance of crops, when all of the following conditions apply:

(1) The burning does not violate any State or federal ambient air quality standards.

(2) The burning is conducted between an hour after sunrise and an hour before sunset.

(3) The fire is set back at least 250 feet from any paved public roadway and at least 500 feet from any dwelling, group of dwellings, commercial or institutional establishment, or other occupied structure not located on the property on which the burning is conducted.

(4) The burning is conducted in a manner such that it does not constitute a public nuisance.

(5) The burning is conducted by any of the following means:

a. By professionally manufactured equipment solely for the purpose of plastic mulch burning or incineration and approved by the Commissioner.

b. By a fire that is enclosed in a non-combustible container.

c. By a fire that is restricted to a pile no greater than eight feet in diameter built upon ground cleared of all combustible material.

(a2) Except in cases where the Commissioner has prohibited all open burning during periods of hazardous forest fire conditions or during air pollution episodes declared pursuant to Article 21B of Chapter 143 of the General Statutes, this Article does not apply to any fires started, or caused to be started, for cooking, warming, or ceremonial events, if the fire is confined (i) within an enclosure from which burning material may not escape or (ii) within a protected area upon which a watch is being maintained and which is provided with adequate fire protection equipment.

(b) No charge shall be made for the granting of any permit required by this Article.

History.
1981, c. 1100, s. 2; 2011-145, s. 13.25(w); 2015-286, s. 4.39(a); 2017-102, s. 15.2; 2021-78, s. 3(a)

CHAPTER 108A
SOCIAL SERVICES

ARTICLE 2
PROGRAMS OF PUBLIC ASSISTANCE

PART 2
WORK FIRST PROGRAM

§ 108A-39. Fraudulent misrepresentation

(a) Any person whether provider or recipient, or person representing himself as such, who willfully and knowingly and with intent to deceive makes a false statement or representation or who fails to disclose a material fact and as a result of making a false statement or representation or failing to disclose a material fact obtains, for himself or another person, attempts to obtain for himself or another person, or continues to receive or enables another person to continue to receive public assistance in the amount of not more than four hundred dollars ($ 400.00) is guilty of a Class 1 misdemeanor.

(b) Any person, whether provider or recipient, or person representing himself as such who willfully and knowingly with the intent to deceive makes a false statement or representation or fails to disclose a material fact and as a result of making a false statement or representation or failing to disclose a material fact, obtains for himself or another person, attempts to obtain for himself or another person, or continues to receive or enables another person to continue to receive public assistance in an amount of more than four hundred dollars ($ 400.00) is guilty of a Class I felony.

(c) As used in this section the word "person" means person, association, consortium, corporation, body politic, partnership, or other group, entity, or organization.

History.
1937, c. 288, ss. 27, 57; 1963, cc. 1013, 1024, 1062; 1969, c. 546, s. 1; 1977, c. 604, s. 1; 1979, c. 510, s. 2; c. 907; 1981, c. 275, s. 1; 1993, c. 539, s. 813; 1994, Ex. Sess., c. 24, s. 14(c)

PART 5
FOOD AND NUTRITION SERVICES

§ 108A-53. Fraudulent misrepresentation

(a) Any person, whether provider or recipient or person representing himself as such, who knowingly obtains or attempts to obtain, or aids or abets any person to obtain by means of making a willfully false statement or representation or by impersonation or by failing to disclose material facts or in any manner not authorized by this Part or the regulations issued pursuant thereto, transfers with intent to defraud any electronic food and nutrition benefit to which that person is not entitled in the amount of four hundred dollars ($ 400.00) or less shall be guilty of a Class 1 misdemeanor. Whoever knowingly obtains or attempts to obtain, or aids or abets any person to obtain by means of making a willfully false statement or representation or by impersonation or by failing to disclose material facts or in any manner not authorized by this Part or the regulations issued pursuant thereto, transfers with intent to defraud any electronic food and nutrition benefit to which he is not entitled in an amount more than four hundred dollars ($ 400.00) shall be guilty of a Class I felony.

(b) Whoever presents, or causes to be presented, electronic food and nutrition benefits for payment or redemption, knowing the same to have been received, transferred, or used in any manner in violation of the provisions of this Part or the regulations issued pursuant to this Part shall be guilty of a Class 1 misdemeanor.

(c) Whoever receives any electronic food and nutrition benefits for any consumable item knowing that such benefits were procured fraudulently under subsections (a) and/or (b) of this section shall be guilty of a Class 1 misdemeanor.

(d) Whoever receives any electronic food and nutrition benefits for any consumable item whose exchange is prohibited by the United States Department of Agriculture shall be guilty of a Class 1 misdemeanor.

History.
1981, c. 275, s. 1; 1991, c. 523, s. 5; 1993, c. 539, ss. 814, 1299; 1994, Ex. Sess., c. 24, s. 14(c); 1995, c. 507, s. 19.5(n); 1996, 2nd Ex. Sess., c. 18, s. 24.31(a); 2007-97, s. 11; 2008-187, s. 18

§ 108A-53.1. Illegal possession or use of electronic food and nutrition benefits

(a) Any person who knowingly buys, sells, distributes, or possesses with the intent to sell, or distribute electronic food and nutrition benefits or access devices in any manner contrary to that authorized by this Part or the regulations issued pursuant thereto shall be guilty of a Class H felony.

(b) Any person who knowingly uses, transfers, acquires, alters, or possesses electronic food and nutrition benefits or access devices in any manner contrary to that authorized by this Part or the regulations issued pursuant thereto, other than as set forth in subsection (a) of this section, shall be guilty of a Class 1 misdemeanor if the value of such electronic food and nutrition benefits or access devices is less than one hundred dollars ($ 100.00), or a Class A1 misdemeanor if the value of such electronic food and nutrition benefits or access devices is equal to at least one hundred dollars ($ 100.00) but less than five hundred dollars ($ 500.00), or a Class I felony if the value of such electronic food and nutrition benefits or access devices is equal to at least five hundred dollars ($ 500.00) but less than one thousand dollars ($ 1,000), or a Class H felony if the value of such electronic food and nutrition benefits or access devices equals or exceeds one thousand dollars ($ 1,000).

History.
1997-497, s. 2; 2007-97, s. 12

PART 6
MEDICAL ASSISTANCE PROGRAM

§ 108A-60. Protection of patient property

(a) It shall be unlawful for any person:

(1) To willfully commingle or cause or solicit the commingling of the personal funds or moneys of a recipient resident of a provider health care facility with the funds or moneys of such facility; or

(2) To willfully embezzle, convert, or appropriate or cause or solicit the embezzlement, conversion or appropriation of recipient personal funds or property to his own use or to the use of any provider or other person or entity.

(b) A violation of subdivision (a)(1) of this section shall be a Class 1 misdemeanor. A violation of subdivision (a)(2) of this section shall be a Class H felony.

(c) For purposes of this section:

(1) "Health care facility" shall include skilled nursing facilities, intermediate care facilities, rest homes, or any other residential health care facility; and

(2) "Person" includes any natural person, association, consortium, corporation, body politic, partnership, or other group, entity or organization; and

(3) "Recipient" shall include current resident recipients, deceased recipients and recipients who no longer reside at such facility.

History.
1979, c. 510, s. 1; 1981, c. 275, s. 1; 1993, c. 539, ss. 816, 1300; 1994, Ex. Sess., c. 24, s. 14(c)

§ 108A-63. Medical assistance provider fraud

(a) It shall be unlawful for any provider of medical assistance under this Part to knowingly and willfully make or cause to be made any false statement or representation of a material fact:

(1) In any application for payment under this Part, or for use in determining entitlement to such payment; or

(2) With respect to the conditions or operation of a provider or facility in order that such provider or facility may qualify or remain qualified to provide assistance under this Part.

(b) It shall be unlawful for any provider of medical assistance to knowingly and willfully conceal or fail to disclose any fact or event affecting:

(1) His initial or continued entitlement to payment under this Part; or

(2) The amount of payment to which such person is or may be entitled.

(c) Except as otherwise provided in subsection (e) of this section, any person who violates a provision of this section shall be guilty of a Class I felony.

(d) "Provider" shall include any person who provides goods or services under this Part and any other person acting as an employee, representative or agent of such person.

(e) In connection with the delivery of or payment for benefits, items, or services under this Part, it shall be unlawful for any provider of medical assistance under this Part to knowingly and willfully execute, or attempt to execute, a scheme or artifice to:

(1) Defraud the Medical Assistance Program.

(2) Obtain, by means of false or fraudulent pretenses, representations, or promises of material fact, any of the money or property owned by, or under the custody or control of, the Medical Assistance Program.

A violation of this subsection is a Class H felony. A conspiracy to violate this subsection is a Class I felony.

(f) It shall be unlawful for any provider, with the intent to obstruct, delay, or mislead an investigation of a violation of this section by the Attorney General's office, to knowingly and willfully make or cause to be made a false entry in, alter, destroy, or conceal, or make a false statement about a financial, medical, or other record related to the provision of a benefit, item, or service under this Part.

(g) It shall be unlawful for any person to knowingly and willfully solicit or receive any remuneration (including any kickback, bribe, or rebate) directly or indirectly, overtly or covertly, in cash or in-kind:

(1) In return for referring an individual to a person for the furnishing or arranging for the furnishing of any item or service for which payment may be made in whole or in part under this Part.

(2) In return for purchasing, leasing, ordering, or arranging for or recommending purchasing, leasing, or ordering any good, facility, service, or item for which payment may be made in whole or in part under this Part.

(h) It shall be unlawful for any person to knowingly and willfully offer or pay any remuneration (including any kickback, bribe, or rebate) directly or indirectly, overtly or covertly, in cash or in-kind to any person to induce such person:

(1) To refer an individual to a person for the furnishing or arranging for the furnishing of any item or service for which payment may be made in whole or in part under this Part.

(2) To purchase, lease, order, or arrange for or recommend purchasing, leasing, or ordering any good, facility, service, or item for which payment may be made in whole or in part under this Part.

(i) Subsections (g) and (h) of this section shall not apply to:

(1) Contracts between the State and a public or private agency where part of the agency's responsibility is referral of a person to a provider.

(2) Any conduct or activity that is specified in 42 U.S.C. § 1320a-7b(b)(3), as amended, or any federal regulations adopted pursuant thereto.

(j) Nothing in subsections (g) and (h) of this section shall be interpreted or construed to conflict with 42 U.S.C. § 1320a-7b(b), as amended, or with federal common law or federal agency interpretations of the statute.

History.
1979, c. 510, s. 1; 1981, c. 275, s. 1; 2009-554, s. 3; 2010-185, s. 1

§ 108A-63.1. Health care fraud subpoena to produce documents

(a) The Attorney General, acting through the Medicaid Investigations Unit of the Department of Justice, may, when engaged in an investigation of an alleged violation of G.S. 108A-63 and prior to the arrest of a suspect, issue in writing and cause to be served a subpoena to produce documents upon any corporation or governmental entity requiring the production of any records, books, papers, electronic media, objects, or other documents which may be relevant to a criminal investigation of a violation of G.S. 108A-63.

(b) A subpoena under this section may require the custodian of records of the corporation or governmental entity to produce an affidavit certifying that the custodian made a thorough and diligent search for the documents requested and that the documents produced constitute all the records requested to the best of the custodian's knowledge, information, and belief.

(c) A subpoena under this section shall describe the documents required to be produced and prescribe a return date within a reasonable period of time, of no less than 20 days from the date of service, within which the documents can be assembled and made available.

(d) A corporation or governmental entity may comply with a subpoena issued under this section by delivering the documents to the Medicaid Investigations Unit by any of the following methods:

(1) By hand delivery.

(2) By mailing the documents by certified mail.

(3) By making the documents reasonably available for transfer to an agent of the Medicaid Investigations Unit at a place of business of the corporation or governmental entity.

(4) If agreed to by the Medicaid Investigations Unit and the corporation or governmental entity, by any other means.

(e) A corporation or governmental entity may move to quash or modify a subpoena issued under this section if it is oppressive or unreasonable or does not comply with the requirements of this section. The motion must be made before the time specified in the subpoena for production and may be made before a judge of the superior court.

(f) In the case of failure by any corporation or governmental entity without adequate excuse to obey a subpoena issued under this section, the Attorney General may invoke the aid of a judge of the superior court. The court may issue an order requiring the subpoenaed corporation or governmental entity to appear before the Attorney General to produce records. Failure to obey the order of the court may be punished as contempt of court.

History.
2009-554, s. 2

§ 108A-64. Medical assistance recipient fraud

(a) It shall be unlawful for any person to knowingly and willfully and with intent to defraud make or cause to be made a false statement or representation of a material fact in an application for assistance under this Part, or intended for use in determining entitlement to such assistance.

(b) It shall be unlawful for any applicant, recipient or person acting on behalf of such applicant or recipient to knowingly and willfully and with intent to defraud, conceal or fail to disclose any condition, fact or event affecting such applicant's or recipient's initial or continued entitlement to receive assistance under this Part.

(b1) It is unlawful for any person knowingly, willingly, and with intent to defraud, to obtain or attempt to obtain, or to assist, aid, or abet another person, either directly or indirectly, to obtain money, services, or any other thing of value to which the person is not entitled as a recipient under this Part, or otherwise to deliberately misuse a Medicaid identification card. This misuse includes the sale, alteration, or lending of the Medicaid identification card to others for services and the use of the card by someone other than the recipient to receive or attempt to receive Medicaid program coverage for services rendered to that individual.

Proof of intent to defraud does not require proof of intent to defraud any particular person.

(c) (1) A person who violates a provision of this section shall be guilty of a Class I felony if the value of the assistance wrongfully obtained is more than four hundred dollars ($ 400.00).

(2) A person who violates a provision of this section shall be guilty of a Class 1 misdemeanor if the value of the assistance wrongfully obtained is four hundred dollars ($ 400.00) or less.

(d) For purposes of this section the word "person" includes any natural person, association, consortium, corporation, body politic, partnership, or other group, entity or organization.

History.
1981, c. 275, s. 1; 1993, c. 539, s. 817; 1994, Ex. Sess., c. 24, s. 14(c); 1995, c. 317, s. 1

§ 108A-64.1. Incentives to counties to recover fraudulent Medicaid expenditures

The Department of Health and Human Services, Division of Health Benefits, shall provide incentives to counties that successfully recover fraudulently spent Medicaid funds by sharing State savings with counties responsible for the recovery of the fraudulently spent funds.

History.
2013-360, s. 12H.5; 2019-81, s. 15(a)

§ 108A-65. Conflict of interest

(a) It shall be unlawful for any person who is or has been an officer or employee of State or county government, and as such is or has been responsible for the expenditure of substantial amounts of federal, State or county money under the State medical assistance plan, or any person who is the partner of the present or former officer or employee, to engage in any of the following activities relating to the State medical assistance program:

(1) Knowingly to act as agent or attorney for, or otherwise knowingly to represent, any person other than the United States, the State or a county, in any formal or informal appearance before, or with the intent to influence, make any oral or written communication on behalf of any other person other than the United States, the State or a county to:

a. Any department, agency, court, board, commission, legislature or committee of the United States, the State or a county, or any officer or employee thereof,

b. In connection with any of the following matters in which the United States, the State, or a county is a party or has a direct and substantial interest, such as any judicial or other proceeding, legislation, application, request for a ruling or other determination, contract, claim, controversy, investigation, charge, accusation, arrest, or other particular matter involving a specific party or parties,

c. In which he participated personally and substantially as an officer or an employee through decision, approval, recommendation, the rendering of advice, investigation or otherwise.

(2) Within two years after his employment has ceased, knowingly to act as agent or attorney for, or otherwise knowingly to represent, any other person other than the United States, the State or a county, in any formal or informal appearance before, or, with the intent to influence, make any oral or written communication on behalf of any other person other than the United States, the State or a county to:

a. Any department, agency, court, board, commission, legislature or committee of the United States, the State, or a county, or any officer or employee thereof,

b. In connection with any of the following matters in which the United States, the State, or a county is a party or has a direct and substantial interest, such as, any judicial or other proceeding, legislation, application, request for a ruling or other determination, contract, claim, controversy, investigation, charge, accusation, arrest, or other particular matter involving a specific party or parties,

c. Which was actually pending under his official responsibility as an officer or employee within a period of one year prior to the termination of responsibility.

(3) Within two years after his employment has ceased, knowingly to aid, counsel, advise, consult or by personal presence represent any other person other than the United States, the State or a county in any formal or informal appearance before:

a. Any department, agency, court, board, commission, legislature or committee of the United States, the State, or the county, or any officer or employee thereof,

b. In connection with any of the following matters in which the United States, the State, or a county is a party or has a direct and substantial interest, such as, any judicial or other proceeding, legislation, application, request for a ruling or other determination, contract, claim, controversy, investigation, charge, accusation, arrest, or other particular matter involving a specific party or parties,

c. Which was actually pending under his official responsibility as an officer or employee within the period of one year prior to the termination of such responsibility.

(4) To participate personally and substantially as an officer or employee, through decision, approval, disapproval, recommendation, rendering of advice, investigation or otherwise, in a judicial or other proceeding legislation, application, request for a ruling or other determination, contract, claim, controversy, charge, accusation, arrest or other particular matter in which, to his knowledge, he, his spouse, minor child, partner, organization in which he is serving as an officer, director, trustee, partner or employee, or any person or organization with whom he is negotiating or has any arrangement concerning prospective employment, has a financial interest.

(b) Violation of this statute is a Class 1 misdemeanor.

(c) The Department of Health and Human Services shall annually identify and designate by rule or regulation those positions which are filled by State or county officers or employees who are responsible for the expenditure of substantial amounts of moneys under the State medical assistance plan.

History.
1981, c. 679, s. 1; 1993, c. 539, s. 818; 1994, Ex. Sess., c. 24, s. 14(c); 1997-443, s. 11A.118(a)

ARTICLE 6
PROTECTION OF THE ABUSED, NEGLECTED OR EXPLOITED DISABLED ADULT ACT

§ 108A-99. Short title

This Article may be cited as the "Protection of the Abused, Neglected, or Exploited Disabled Adult Act."

History.
1973, c. 1378; s. 1; 1975, c. 797; 1981, c. 275, s. 1

§ 108A-100. Legislative intent and purpose

Determined to protect the increasing number of disabled adults in North Carolina who are abused, neglected, or exploited, the General Assembly enacts this Article to provide protective services for such persons.

History.
1973, c. 1378, s. 1; 1975, c. 797; 1981, c. 275, s. 1

§ 108A-101. Definitions

(a) The word "abuse" means the willful infliction of physical pain, injury or mental anguish, unreasonable confinement, or the willful deprivation by a caretaker of services which are necessary to maintain mental and physical health.

(b) The word "caretaker" shall mean an individual who has the responsibility for the care of the disabled adult as a result of family relationship or who has assumed the responsibility for the care of the disabled adult voluntarily or by contract.

(c) The word "director" shall mean the director of the county department of social services in the county in which the person resides or is present, or his representative as authorized in G.S. 108A-14.

(d) The words "disabled adult" shall mean any person 18 years of age or over or any lawfully emancipated minor who is present in the State of North Carolina and who is physically or mentally incapacitated due to an intellectual disability, cerebral palsy, epilepsy or autism; organic brain damage caused by advanced age or other physical degeneration in connection therewith; or due to conditions incurred at any age which are the result of accident, organic brain damage, mental or physical illness, or continued consumption or absorption of substances.

(e) A "disabled adult" shall be "in need of protective services" if that person, due to his physical or mental incapacity, is unable to perform or obtain for himself essential services and if that person is without able, responsible, and willing persons to perform or obtain for his essential services.

(f) The words "district court" shall mean the judge of that court.

(g) The word "emergency" refers to a situation where (i) the disabled adult is in substantial danger of death or irreparable harm if protective services are not provided immediately, (ii) the disabled adult is unable to consent to services, (iii) no responsible, able, or willing caretaker is available to consent to emergency services, and (iv) there is insufficient time to utilize procedure provided in G.S. 108A-105.

(h) The words "emergency services" refer to those services necessary to maintain the person's vital functions and without which there is reasonable belief that the person would suffer irreparable harm or death. This may include taking physical custody of the disabled person.

(i) The words "essential services" shall refer to those social, medical, psychiatric, psychological or legal services necessary to safeguard the disabled adult's rights and resources and to maintain the physical or mental well-being of the individual. These services shall include, but not be limited to, the provision of medical care for physical and mental health needs, assistance in personal hygiene, food, clothing, adequately heated and ventilated shelter, protection from health and safety hazards, protection from physical mistreatment, and protection from exploitation. The words "essential services" shall not include taking the person into physical custody without his consent except as provided for in G.S. 108A-106 and in Chapter 122C of the General Statutes.

(j) The word "exploitation" means the illegal or improper use of a disabled adult or his resources for another's profit or advantage.

(k) The word "indigent" shall mean indigent as defined in G.S. 7A-450.

(l) The words "lacks the capacity to consent" shall mean lacks sufficient understanding or capacity to make or communicate responsible decisions concerning his person, including but not limited to provisions for health or mental health care, food, clothing, or shelter, because of physical or mental incapacity. This may be reasonably determined by the director or he may seek a physician's or psychologist's assistance in making this determination.

(m) The word "neglect" refers to a disabled adult who is either living alone and not able to provide for himself or herself the services which are necessary to maintain the person's mental or physical health or is not receiving services from the person's caretaker. A person is not receiving services from his caretaker if, among other things and not by way of limitation, the person is a resident of one of the State-owned

psychiatric hospitals listed in G.S. 122C-181(a)(1), the State-owned Developmental Centers listed in G.S. 122C-181(a)(2), or the State-owned Neuro-Medical Treatment Centers listed in G.S. 122C-181(a)(3), the person is, in the opinion of the professional staff of that State-owned facility, mentally incompetent to give consent to medical treatment, the person has no legal guardian appointed pursuant to Chapter 35A, or guardian as defined in G.S. 122C-3(15), and the person needs medical treatment.

(n) The words "protective services" shall mean services provided by the State or other government or private organizations or individuals which are necessary to protect the disabled adult from abuse, neglect, or exploitation. They shall consist of evaluation of the need for service and mobilization of essential services on behalf of the disabled adult.

History.
1973, c. 1378, s. 1; 1975, c. 797; 1979, c. 1044, ss. 1-4; 1981, c. 275, s. 1; 1985, c. 589, s. 34; 1987, c. 550, s. 24; 1989, c. 770, s. 29; 1991, c. 258, s. 2; 2007-177, s. 4; 2019-76, s. 14

§ 108A-102. Duty to report; content of report; immunity

(a) Any person having reasonable cause to believe that a disabled adult is in need of protective services shall report such information to the director.

(b) The report may be made orally or in writing. The report shall include the name and address of the disabled adult; the name and address of the disabled adult's caretaker; the age of the disabled adult; the nature and extent of the disabled adult's injury or condition resulting from abuse or neglect; and other pertinent information.

(c) Anyone who makes a report pursuant to this statute, who testifies in any judicial proceeding arising from the report, or who participates in a required evaluation shall be immune from any civil or criminal liability on account of such report or testimony or participation, unless such person acted in bad faith or with a malicious purpose.

History.
1973, c. 1378, s. 1; 1975, c. 797; 1981, c. 275, s. 1

§ 108A-103. Duty of director upon receiving report

(a) Any director receiving a report that a disabled adult is in need of protective services shall make a prompt and thorough evaluation to determine whether the disabled adult is in need of protective services and what services are needed. The evaluation shall include a visit to the person and consultation with others having knowledge of the facts of the particular case. When necessary for a complete evaluation of the report, the director shall have the authority to review and copy any and all records, or any part of such records, related to the care and treatment of the disabled adult that have been maintained by any individual, facility or agency acting as a caretaker for the disabled adult. This shall include but not be limited to records maintained by facilities licensed by the North Carolina Department of Health and Human Services. Use of information so obtained shall be subject to and governed by the provisions of G.S. 108A-80 and Article 3 of Chapter 122C of the General Statutes. The director shall have the authority to conduct an interview with the disabled adult with no other persons present. After completing the evaluation the director shall make a written report of the case indicating whether he believes protective services are needed and shall notify the individual making the report of his determination as to whether the disabled adult needs protective services.

(b) The staff and physicians of local health departments, area mental health, developmental disabilities, and substance abuse authorities, and other public or private agencies shall cooperate fully with the director in the performance of his duties. These duties include immediate accessible evaluations and in-home evaluations where the director deems this necessary.

(c) The director may contract with an agency or private physician for the purpose of providing immediate accessible medical evaluations in the location that the director deems most appropriate.

(d) The director shall initiate the evaluation described in subsection (a) of this section as follows:

(1) Immediately upon receipt of the complaint if the complaint alleges a danger of death in an emergency as defined in G.S. 108A-101(g).

(2) Within 24 hours if the complaint alleges danger of irreparable harm in an emergency as defined by G.S. 108A-101(g).

(3) Within 72 hours if the complaint does not allege danger of death or irreparable harm in an emergency as defined by G.S. 108A-101(g).

(4) Repealed by Session Laws 2000, c. 131, s. 1, effective July 14, 2000.

The evaluation shall be completed within 30 days for allegations of abuse or neglect and within 45 days for allegations of exploitation.

History.
1973, c. 1378, s. 1; 1975, c. 797; 1981, c. 275, s. 1; 1985, c. 589, s. 35; c. 658, s. 1; 1985 (Reg. Sess., 1986), c. 863,

s. 6; 1991, c. 636, s. 19(c); 1997-443, s. 11A.118(a); 1999-334, s. 1.10; 2000-131, s. 1

§ 108A-104. Provision of protective services with the consent of the person; withdrawal of consent; caretaker refusal

(a) If the director determines that a disabled adult is in need of protective services, he shall immediately provide or arrange for the provision of protective services, provided that the disabled adult consents.

(b) When a caretaker of a disabled adult who consents to the receipt of protective services refuses to allow the provision of such services to the disabled adult, the director may petition the district court for an order enjoining the caretaker from interfering with the provision of protective services to the disabled adult. The petition must allege specific facts sufficient to show that the disabled adult is in need of protective services and consents to the receipt of protective services and that the caretaker refuses to allow the provision of such services. If the judge finds by clear, cogent, and convincing evidence that the disabled adult is in need of protective services and consents to the receipt of protective services and that the caretaker refuses to allow the provision of such services, he may issue an order enjoining the caretaker from interfering with the provision of protective services to the disabled adult.

(c) If a disabled adult does not consent to the receipt of protective services, or if he withdraws his consent, the services shall not be provided.

History.
1973, c. 1378, s. 1; 1975, c. 797; 1981, c. 275, s. 1

§ 108A-105. Provision of protective services to disabled adults who lack the capacity to consent; hearing, findings, etc

(a) If the director reasonably determines that a disabled adult is being abused, neglected, or exploited and lacks capacity to consent to protective services, then the director may petition the district court for an order authorizing the provision of protective services. The petition must allege specific facts sufficient to show that the disabled adult is in need of protective services and lacks capacity to consent to them.

(b) The court shall set the case for hearing within 14 days after the filing of the petition. The disabled adult must receive at least five days' notice of the hearing. He has the right to be present and represented by counsel at the hearing. If the person, in the determination of the judge, lacks the capacity to waive the right to counsel, then a guardian ad litem shall be appointed pursuant to G.S. 1A-1, Rule 17, and rules adopted by the Office of Indigent Defense

Chapter 108A

Services. If the person is indigent, the cost of representation shall be borne by the State.

(c) If, at the hearing, the judge finds by clear, cogent, and convincing evidence that the disabled adult is in need of protective services and lacks capacity to consent to protective services, he may issue an order authorizing the provision of protective services. This order may include the designation of an individual or organization to be responsible for the performing or obtaining of essential services on behalf of the disabled adult or otherwise consenting to protective services in his behalf. Within 60 days from the appointment of such an individual or organization, the court will conduct a review to determine if a petition should be initiated in accordance with Chapter 35A; for good cause shown, the court may extend the 60 day period for an additional 60 days, at the end of which it shall conduct a review to determine if a petition should be initiated in accordance with Chapter 35A. No disabled adult may be committed to a mental health facility under this Article.

(d) A determination by the court that a person lacks the capacity to consent to protective services under the provisions of this Chapter shall in no way affect incompetency proceedings as set forth in Chapters 33, 35 or 122 of the General Statutes of North Carolina, or any other proceedings, and incompetency proceedings as set forth in Chapters 33, 35, or 122 shall have no conclusive effect upon the question of capacity to consent to protective services as set forth in this Chapter.

History.
1973, c. 1378, s. 1; 1975, c. 797; 1977, c. 725, s. 3, 1979, c. 1044, s. 5; 1981, c. 275, s. 1; 1985, c. 658, s. 2; 1987, c. 550, s. 25; 2000-144, s. 36

§ 108A-106. Emergency intervention; findings by court; limitations; contents of petition; notice of petition; court authorized entry of premises; immunity of petitioner

(a) Upon petition by the director, a court may order the provision of emergency services to a disabled adult after finding that there is reasonable cause to believe that:

(1) A disabled adult lacks capacity to consent and that he is in need of protective service;

(2) An emergency exists; and

(3) No other person authorized by law or order to give consent for the person is available and willing to arrange for emergency services.

(b) The court shall order only such emergency services as are necessary to remove the conditions creating the emergency. In the event that such services will be needed for more than 14 days, the director shall petition the court in accordance with G.S. 108A-105.

(c) The petition for emergency services shall set forth the name, address, and authority of the petitioner; the name, age and residence of the disabled adult; the nature of the emergency; the nature of the disability if determinable; the proposed emergency services; the petitioner's reasonable belief as to the existence of the conditions set forth in subsection (a) above; and facts showing petitioner's attempts to obtain the disabled adult's consent to the services.

(d) Notice of the filing of such petition and other relevant information, including the factual basis of the belief that emergency services are needed and a description of the exact services to be rendered shall be given to the person, to his spouse, or if none, to his adult children or next of kin, to his guardian, if any. Such notice shall be given at least 24 hours prior to the hearing of the petition for emergency intervention; provided, however, that the court may issue immediate emergency order ex parte upon finding as fact (i) that the conditions specified in G.S. 108A-106(a) exist; (ii) that there is likelihood that the disabled adult may suffer irreparable injury or death if such order be delayed; and (iii) that reasonable attempts have been made to locate interested parties and secure from them such services or their consent to petitioner's provision of such service; and such order shall contain a show-cause notice to each person upon whom served directing such person to appear immediately or at any time up to and including the time for the hearing of the petition for emergency services and show cause, if any exists, for the dissolution or modification of the said order. Copies of the said order together with such other appropriate notices as the court may direct shall be issued and served upon all of the interested parties designated in the first sentence of this subsection. Unless dissolved by the court for good cause shown, the emergency order ex parte shall be in effect until the hearing is held on the petition for emergency services. At such hearing, if the court determines that the emergency continues to exist, the court may order the provision of emergency services in accordance with subsections (a) and (b) of this section.

(e) Where it is necessary to enter a premises without the disabled adult's consent after obtaining a court order in compliance with subsection (a) above, the representative of the petitioner shall do so.

(f) (1) Upon petition by the director, a court may order that:

a. The disabled adult's financial records be made available at a certain day and time for inspection by the director or his designated agent; and

b. The disabled adult's financial assets be frozen and not withdrawn, spent or transferred without prior order of the court.

(2) Such an order shall not issue unless the court first finds that there is reasonable cause to believe that:

a. A disabled adult lacks the capacity to consent and that he is in need of protective services;

b. The disabled adult is being financially exploited by his caretaker; and

c. No other person is able or willing to arrange for protective services.

(3) Provided, before any such inspection is done, the caretaker and every financial institution involved shall be given notice and a reasonable opportunity to appear and show good cause why this inspection should not be done. And, provided further, that any order freezing assets shall expire ten days after such inspection is completed, unless the court for good cause shown, extends it.

(g) No petitioner shall be held liable in any action brought by the disabled adult if the petitioner acted in good faith.

History.
1975, c. 797; 1981, c. 275, s. 1; 1985, c. 658, s. 3

§ 108A-107. Motion in the cause

Notwithstanding any finding by the court of lack of capacity of the disabled adult to consent, the disabled adult or the individual or organization designated to be responsible for the disabled adult shall have the right to bring a motion in the cause for review of any order issued pursuant to this Article.

History.
1973, c. 1378, s. 1; 1975, c. 797; 1981, c. 275, s. 1

§ 108A-108. Payment for essential services

At the time the director, in accordance with the provisions of G.S. 108A-103 makes an evaluation of the case reported, then it shall be determined, according to regulations set by the Social Services Commission, whether the individual is financially capable of paying for the essential services. If he is, he shall make reimbursement for the costs of providing the needed essential services. If it is determined that he is not financially capable of paying for such essential services, they shall be provided at no cost to the recipient of the services.

History.
1975, c. 797; 1981, c. 275, s. 1

§ 108A-109. Reporting abuse

Upon finding evidence indicating that a person has abused, neglected, or exploited a disabled adult, the director shall notify the district attorney.

History.
1975, c. 797; 1981, c. 275, s. 1

§ 108A-110. Funding of protective services

Any funds appropriated by counties for home health care, boarding home, nursing home, emergency assistance, medical or psychiatric evaluations, and other protective services and for the development and improvement of a system of protective services, including additional staff, may be matched by State and federal funds. Such funds shall be utilized by the county department of social services for the benefit of disabled adults in need of protective services.

History.
1975, c. 797; 1981, c. 275, s. 1

§ 108A-111. Adoption of standards

The Department and the administrative office of the court shall adopt standards and other procedures and guidelines with forms to insure the effective implementation of the provisions of this Article.

History.
1975, c. 797; 1981, c. 275, s. 1

ARTICLE 6A
PROTECTION OF DISABLED AND OLDER ADULTS FROM FINANCIAL EXPLOITATION

§ 108A-112. Legislative intent and purpose

Determined to fight the growing problem of fraud and financial exploitation targeting disabled and older adults in North Carolina, the General Assembly enacts this Article to facilitate the collection of records needed to investigate and prosecute such incidents.

History.
2013-337, s. 4

§ 108A-113. Definitions

As used in this Article, the following definitions apply:

Chapter 108A

(1) **Customer.** -- A person who is a present or former holder of an account with a financial institution.

(2) **Disabled adult.** -- An individual 18 years of age or older or a lawfully emancipated minor who is present in the State of North Carolina and who is physically or mentally incapacitated as defined in G.S. 108A-101(d).

(3) **Financial exploitation.** -- The illegal or improper use of a disabled adult's or older adult's financial resources for another's profit or pecuniary advantage.

(4) **Financial institution.** -- A banking corporation, trust company, savings and loan association, credit union, or other entity principally engaged in lending money or receiving or soliciting money on deposit.

(5) **Financial record.** -- An original of, a copy of, or information derived from a record held by a financial institution pertaining to a customer's relationship with the financial institution and identified with or identifiable with the customer.

(6) **Investigating entity.** -- A law enforcement agency investigating alleged financial exploitation of a disabled adult or an older adult, or a county department of social services investigating alleged financial exploitation of a disabled adult.

(7) **Law enforcement agency.** -- Any duly accredited State or local government agency possessing authority to enforce the criminal statutes of North Carolina.

(8) **Older adult.** -- An individual 65 years of age or older.

(9) **Promptly.** -- As soon as practicable, with reasonable allowance to be made for the time required to retrieve older data or records that are not readily or immediately retrievable due to their current storage media.

History.
2013-337, s. 4

§ 108A-114. Financial institutions encouraged to offer disabled adult and older adult customers the opportunity to submit a list of trusted persons to be contacted in case of financial exploitation

All financial institutions are encouraged, but not required, to offer to disabled adult and older adult customers the opportunity to submit, and periodically update, a list of persons that the disabled adult or older adult customer would like the financial institution to contact in case of suspected financial exploitation of the disabled adult or older adult customer. No financial institution, or officer or employee thereof, who acts in good faith in offering to its customer

the opportunity to submit and update a list of such contact persons may be held liable in any action for doing so.

History.
2013-337, s. 4

§ 108A-115. Duty to report suspected fraud; content of report; immunity for reporting

(a) Any financial institution, or officer or employee thereof, having reasonable cause to believe that a disabled adult or older adult is the victim or target of financial exploitation shall report such information to the following:

(1) Persons on the list provided by the customer under G.S. 108A-114, if such a list has been provided by the customer. The financial institution may choose not to contact persons on the provided list if the financial institution suspects that those persons are financially exploiting the disabled adult or older adult.

(2) The appropriate local law enforcement agency.

(3) The appropriate county department of social services, if the customer is a disabled adult.

(b) The report may be made orally or in writing. The report shall include the name and address of the disabled adult or older adult, the nature of the suspected financial exploitation, and any other pertinent information.

(c) No financial institution, or officer or employee thereof, who acts in good faith in making a report under this section may be held liable in any action for doing so.

History.
2013-337, s. 4

§ 108A-116. Production of customers' financial records in cases of suspected financial exploitation; immunity; records may not be used against account owner

(a) An investigating entity may, under the conditions specified in this section, petition the district court to issue a subpoena directing a financial institution to provide to the investigating entity the financial records of a disabled adult or older adult customer. The petition shall be filed in the county of residence of the disabled adult or older adult customer whose financial records are being subpoenaed. The court shall hear the case within two business days after the filing of the petition. The court shall issue the subpoena upon finding that all of the following conditions are met:

(1) The investigating entity is investigating, pursuant to the investigating entity's

statutory authority, a credible report that the disabled adult or older adult is being or has been financially exploited.

(2) The disabled adult's or older adult's financial records are needed in order to substantiate or evaluate the report.

(3) Time is of the essence in order to prevent further exploitation of that disabled adult or older adult.

(b) Delivery of the subpoena may be effected by hand, via certified mail, return receipt requested, or through a designated delivery service authorized pursuant to 26 U.S.C. § 7502(f)(2) and may be addressed to the financial institution's local branch or office vice president, its local branch or office manager or assistant branch or office manager, or the agent for service of process listed by the financial institution with the North Carolina Secretary of State or, if there is none, with the agent for service of process listed by the financial institution in any state in which it is domiciled.

(b1) A financial institution may challenge the subpoena by filing a motion to quash or modify the subpoena within ten days after receipt of delivery of the subpoena pursuant to subsection (b) of this section. The subpoena may be challenged only for the following reasons:

(1) There is a procedural defect with the subpoena.

(2) The subpoena contains insufficient information to identify the records subject to the subpoena.

(3) The financial institution is otherwise prevented from promptly complying with the subpoena.

(4) The petition was filed or subpoena requested for an improper purpose or based upon insufficient grounds.

(5) The subpoena subjects the financial institution to an undue burden or is otherwise unreasonable or oppressive.

Within two business days after the motion is filed, the court shall hear the motion and issue an order upholding, modifying, or quashing the subpoena.

(c) Upon receipt of a subpoena delivered pursuant to subsection (b) of this section identifying the disabled adult or older adult customer or, if the subpoena is challenged pursuant to subsection (b1) of this section, entry of a court order upholding or modifying a subpoena, a financial institution shall promptly provide to the head of an investigating entity, or his or her designated agent, the financial records of a disabled adult or older adult customer.

(d) All produced copies of the disabled adult's or older adult's financial records, as well as any information obtained pursuant to the duty to report found in G.S. 108A-115, shall be kept confidential by the investigating entity unless required by court order to be disclosed to a party

to a court proceeding or introduced and admitted into evidence in an open court proceeding.

(e) No financial institution or investigating entity, or officer or employee thereof, who acts in good faith in providing, seeking, or obtaining financial records or any other information in accordance with this section, or in providing testimony in any judicial proceeding based upon the contents thereof, may be held liable in any action for doing so.

(f) No customer may be subject to indictment, criminal prosecution, criminal punishment, or criminal penalty by reason of or on account of anything disclosed by a financial institution pursuant to this section, nor may any information obtained through such disclosure be used as evidence against the customer in any criminal or civil proceeding. Notwithstanding the foregoing, information obtained may be used against a person who is a joint account owner accused of financial exploitation of a disabled adult or older adult joint account holder, but solely for criminal or civil proceedings directly related to the alleged financial exploitation of the disabled adult or older adult joint account holder.

(g) The petition and the court's entire record of the proceedings under this section is not a matter of public record. Records qualifying under this subsection shall be maintained separately from other records, shall be withheld from public inspection, and may be examined only by order of the court.

History.
2013-337, s. 4; 2014-115, s. 44(a)

§ 108A-117. Notice to customer; delayed notice

(a) Upon the issuance of a subpoena pursuant to G.S. 108A-116, the investigating entity shall immediately provide the customer with written notice of its action by first-class mail to the customer's last known address, unless an order for delayed notice is obtained pursuant to subsection (b) of this section. The notice shall be sufficient to inform the customer of the name of the investigating entity that has obtained the subpoena, the financial records subject to production pursuant to the subpoena, and the purpose of the investigation.

(b) An investigating entity may include in its application for a subpoena pursuant to G.S. 108A-116 a request for an order delaying the customer notice required pursuant to subsection (a) of this section. The court issuing the subpoena may order a delayed notice in accordance with subsection (c) of this section if it finds, based on affidavit or oral testimony under oath or affirmation before the issuing court, that all of the following conditions are met:

Chapter 108A

(1) The investigating entity is investigating a credible report that the adult is being or has been financially exploited.

(2) There is reason to believe that the notice will result in at least one of the following:

    a. Endangering the life or physical safety of any person.

    b. Flight from prosecution.

    c. Destruction of or tampering with evidence.

    d. Intimidation of potential witnesses.

    e. Serious jeopardy to an investigation or official proceeding.

    f. Undue delay of a trial or official proceeding.

(c) Upon making the findings required in subsection (b) of this section, the court shall enter an ex parte order granting the requested delay for a period not to exceed 30 days. If the court finds there is reason to believe that the notice may endanger the life or physical safety of any person, the court may order that the delay be for a period not to exceed 180 days. An order delaying notice shall direct that:

(1) The financial institution not disclose to any person the existence of the investigation, of the subpoena, or of the fact that the customer's financial records have been provided to the investigating entity for the duration of the period of delay authorized in the order;

(2) The investigating entity deliver a copy of the order to the financial institution along with the subpoena that is delivered pursuant to G.S. 108-116(b); and

(3) The order be sealed until otherwise ordered by the court.

(d) Upon application by the investigating entity, further extensions of the delay of notice may be granted by order of a court in the county of residence of the disabled adult or older adult customer whose financial records are being subpoenaed, upon a finding of the continued existence of the conditions set forth in subdivisions (1) and (2) of subsection (b) of this section, and subject to the requirements of subsection (c) of this section. If the initial delay was granted for a period not to exceed 30 days, the delay may be extended by additional periods of up to 30 days each and the total delay in notice granted under this section shall not exceed 90 days. If the initial delay was granted for a period not to exceed 180 days, the delay may be extended by additional periods of up to 180 days each and may continue to be extended until the court finds the notice would no longer endanger the life or physical safety of any person.

(e) Upon the expiration of the period of delay of notice granted under this section, including any extensions thereof, the customer shall be served with a copy of the notice required by subsection (a) of this section.

History.
2013-337, s. 4; 2014-115, s. 44(b)

§§ 108A-118, 108A-119

Reserved for future codification purposes.

CHAPTER 110
CHILD WELFARE

ARTICLE 1A
EXHIBITION OF CHILDREN

§ 110-20.1. Exhibition of certain children prohibited

(a) Except to the extent otherwise provided in subsection (d) of this section, it is unlawful to exhibit publicly for any purpose, or to exhibit privately for the purpose of entertainment, or solely or primarily for the satisfaction of the curiosity of any observer, any child under the age of 18 years who has a mental illness or intellectual disability or who presents the appearance of having any deformity or unnatural physical formation or development, whether or not the exhibiting of the child is in return for a monetary or other consideration.

(b) It is unlawful to employ, use, have custody of, or in any way be associated with any child described in subsection (a) of this section for the purpose of an exhibition prohibited by subsection (a) of this section, or for one who has the care, custody, or control of the child as a parent, relative, guardian, employer, or otherwise, to neglect or refuse to restrain the child from participating in the exhibition.

(c) It is unlawful to procure or arrange for, or participate in procuring or arranging for, anything made unlawful by subsections (a) and (b) of this section.

(d) This section does not apply to the transmission of an image by television by a duly licensed television station, or to any exhibition by a federal, State, county, or municipal government, or political subdivision or agency thereof, or to any exhibition by any corporation, unincorporated association, or other organization organized and operated exclusively for religious, charitable, or educational purposes, no part of the net earnings of which inures to the benefit of any private shareholder or individual.

(e) Any violation of this Article is a Class 3 misdemeanor. Each day during which any violation of this Article continues after notice to the violator, from any county social services director, to cease and desist from any violation of this section is a separate and distinct offense. Any act or omission prohibited by this Article is, with respect to each child, a separate and distinct offense.

History.
1969, c. 457, s. 1; c. 982; 1993, c. 539, s. 821; 1994, Ex. Sess., c. 24, s. 14(c); 2018-47, s. 8

ARTICLE 2
JUVENILE SERVICES

N.C. Gen. Stat. § 110-23

Repealed by Session Laws 1998-202, s. 1(a), effective January 1, 1999.

ARTICLE 7
CHILD CARE FACILITIES

N.C. Gen. Stat. § 110-101

Repealed by Session Laws 1997-506, s. 16 .

§ 110-102.1. Reporting of missing or deceased children

(a) Notwithstanding G.S. 14-318.5, operators and staff, as defined in G.S. 110-86(7), and G.S. 110-91(8), or any adult present with the approval of the care provider in a child care facility as defined in G.S. 110-86(3) and G.S. 110-106, upon learning that a child which has been placed in their care or presence is missing, shall immediately report the missing child to law enforcement. For purposes of this Article, a child is anyone under the age of 16.

(b) If a child dies while in child care, or of injuries sustained in child care, a report of the death must be made by the child care operator to the Secretary within 24 hours of the child's death or on the next working day.

History.
1985, c. 392; 1987, c. 788, s. 12; 1997-506, s. 19; 2013-52, s. 4

§ 110-102.1A. Unauthorized administration of medication

(a) It is unlawful for an employee, owner, household member, volunteer, or operator of a licensed or unlicensed child care facility as defined in G.S. 110-86, including child care facilities operated by public schools and nonpublic schools as defined in G.S. 110-86(2)(f), to willfully administer, without written authorization, prescription or over-the-counter medication to a child attending the child care facility. For the purposes of this section, written authorization shall include the child's name, date or dates for which the authorization is applicable, dosage instructions, and signature of the child's parent or guardian. For the purposes of this section, a child care facility operated by a public school does not include kindergarten through twelfth grade classes.

(b) In the event of an emergency medical condition and the child's parent or guardian is unavailable, it shall not be unlawful to administer medication to a child attending the child care facility without written authorization as required under subsection (a) of this section if the medication is administered with the authorization and in accordance with instructions from a bona fide medical care provider. For purposes of this subsection, the following definitions apply:

(1) A bona fide medical care provider means an individual who is licensed, certified, or otherwise authorized to prescribe the medication.

(2) An emergency medical condition means circumstances where a prudent layperson acting reasonably would have believed that an emergency medical condition existed.

(c) A violation of this section that results in serious injury to the child shall be punished as a Class F felony.

(d) Any other violation of this section where medication is administered willfully shall be punished as a Class A1 misdemeanor.

History.
2003-406, s. 2

§ 110-102.2. Administrative penalties

For failure to comply with this Article, the Secretary may:

(1) Issue a written warning and a request for compliance;

(2) Issue an official written reprimand;

(3) Place a licensee upon probation until his compliance with this Article has been verified by the Commission or its agent;

(4) Order suspension of a license for a specified length of time not to exceed one year;

(5) Permanently revoke a license issued under this Article.

The issuance of an administrative penalty may be appealed as provided in G.S. 110-90(5) and G.S. 110-90(9).

History.
1985, c. 757, s. 156(ff); 1987, c. 788, s. 13; c. 827, s. 235

N.C. Gen. Stat. § 110-105.2

Repealed by Session Laws 2015-123, s. 7, effective January 1, 2016.

History.
1985, c. 757, s. 156(w); 1987, c. 788, s. 19; 1997-506, s. 25; 1998-202, s. 13(x); 2003-407, s. 2; repealed by 2015-123, s. 7, effective January 1, 2016

§ 110-105.3. Child maltreatment

(a) The purpose of this section is to assign the authority to investigate instances of child maltreatment in child care facilities to the Department of Health and Human Services, Division of Child Development and Early Education. The General Assembly recognizes that the ability to properly investigate child maltreatment in licensed child care facilities is dependent upon the cooperation of State and local law enforcement agencies, as well as county departments of social services.

(b) The following definitions shall apply in this Article:

(1) **Caregiver. --** The operator of a licensed child care facility or religious-sponsored child care facility, a child care provider, as defined in G.S. 110-90.2(a)(2), a volunteer, or any person who has the approval of the provider to assume responsibility for children under the care of the provider.

(2) **Child care facilities. --** Any of the following:

a. All facilities required to be licensed under this Article.

b. All religious-sponsored facilities operating pursuant to G.S. 110-106.

c. All locations where children are being cared for by someone other than their parent or legal guardian that require a license under this Article but have not been issued a license by the Department.

(3) **Child maltreatment. --** Any act or series of acts of commission or omission by a caregiver that results in harm, potential for harm, or threat of harm to a child. Acts of commission include, but are not limited to, physical, sexual, and psychological abuse. Acts of omission include, but are not limited to, failure to provide for the physical, emotional, or medical well-being of a child, and failure to properly supervise children, which results in exposure to potentially harmful environments.

(c) The Department, local departments of social services, and local law enforcement personnel shall cooperate with the medical community to ensure that reports of child maltreatment in child care facilities are properly investigated.

(d) When a report of child maltreatment is received, the Department shall make a prompt and thorough assessment to ascertain the facts of the case, the extent of the maltreatment, and the risk of harm to children enrolled at the child care facility. When the report alleges maltreatment meeting the definition of abuse or neglect as defined in G.S. 14-318.2 and G.S. 14-318.4, the Department shall contact local law enforcement officials to investigate the report.

(e) During the pendency of an investigation, the Department may issue a protection plan restricting an individual alleged to have maltreated a child from being on the premises of the facility while children are in care. The Department may also suspend activities at a facility under investigation, including, but not limited to, transportation, aquatic activities, and field trips.

(f) At any time during the pendency of a child maltreatment investigation, the Department may order immediate corrective action as required to protect the health, safety, or welfare of children in care. If the corrective action does not occur within the period specified in the corrective action order, the Department may take administrative action to protect the health, safety, or welfare of the children at the child care facility.

(g) The Department may, in accordance with G.S. 150B-3(c), summarily suspend the license of a child care facility if the Department determines that emergency action is required to protect the health, safety, or welfare of the children in a child care facility regulated by the Department.

(h) In the event the Department determines child maltreatment did not occur in a child care facility, nothing in this section shall prevent the Department from citing a violation or issuing an administrative action based upon violations of child care licensure law or rules based upon its investigation. Citations of violations or administrative actions issued pursuant to this subsection shall not be confidential.

(i) During the pendency of an investigation, all matters regarding the investigation, including, but not limited to, any complaint, allegation, or documentation regarding inspections or the identity of the reporter, shall be held in strictest confidence as provided by subsection (j) of this section. Following a determination that maltreatment has occurred, the investigation findings shall be made public, as well as the date of any visits made pursuant to the investigation, and any corrective action taken, if applicable. DCDEE shall not post on its Internet Web site that a maltreatment investigation occurred if the allegation of maltreatment was unsubstantiated.

(j) Regardless of the Department's final determination regarding child maltreatment, all information received by the Department during the course of its investigation shall be held in the strictest confidence by the Department, except for the following:

(1) The Department shall disclose confidential information, other than the identity of the reporter, to any federal, State, or local government entity or its agent in order to protect a juvenile from child maltreatment, abuse, or neglect. Any confidential information disclosed to any federal, State, or local government entity or its agent pursuant to this subdivision shall remain confidential with the other government entity or its agent and shall only be redisclosed for purposes directly connected with carrying out that entity's mandated responsibilities.

(2) The Department shall only disclose information identifying the reporter pursuant to a court order, except that the Department may disclose information identifying the reporter without a court order only to a federal, State, or local government entity that demonstrates a need for the reporter's name to carry out the entity's mandated responsibilities.

(3) A district court, superior court, or administrative law judge of this State presiding over a civil matter in which the Department is not a party may order the Department to release confidential information. The court may order the release of confidential information after providing the Department with reasonable notice and an opportunity to be heard and then determining that the information is relevant, necessary to the trial of the matter before the court, and unavailable from any other source.

(k) When a report of child maltreatment alleges facts that indicate that a report is required under G.S. 7B-301, the Department shall contact the local department of social services in the county where the juvenile resides or is found and make the necessary report.

(l) In performing any duties related to the assessment of a report of child maltreatment, the Department may consult with any public or private agencies or individuals, including the available State or local law enforcement officers, probation and parole officers, and the director of any county department of social services who shall assist in the assessment and evaluation of the seriousness of any report of child maltreatment when requested by the Department. The Department or the Department's representatives may make a written demand for any information or reports, whether or not confidential, that may in the Department's opinion be relevant to the assessment of the report. Upon the Department or the Department's representative's request and unless protected by attorney-client privilege, any public or private agency or individual shall provide access to and copies of this confidential information and the records required by this subsection, to the extent permitted by federal law and regulations.

(m) The North Carolina Child Care Commission shall adopt, amend, and repeal all rules necessary for the implementation of this section. Rules promulgated subject to this section shall be exempt from the provisions of G.S. 150B-19.1(e) and (f).

Chapter 110

History.
2015-123, s. 8

§ 110-105.4. Duty to report child maltreatment

(a) Any person who has cause to suspect that a child in a child care facility has been maltreated, as defined by G.S. 110-105.3, or has died as the result of maltreatment occurring in a child care facility, shall report the case of that child to the Department. The report may be made orally, by telephone, or in writing. The report shall include information as is known to the person making the report, including (i) the name and address of the child care facility where the child was allegedly maltreated, (ii) the name and address of the child's parent, guardian, or caretaker, (iii) the age of the child, (iv) the present whereabouts of the child if not at the home address, (v) the nature and extent of any injury or condition resulting from maltreatment, and (vi) any other information the person making the report believes might assist in the investigation of the report. If the report is made orally or by telephone, the person making the report shall give the person's name, address, and telephone number. Refusal of the person making the report to give a name shall not preclude the Department's assessment of the alleged maltreatment.

(b) Upon receipt of any report of maltreatment involving sexual abuse of the child in a child care facility, the Department shall notify the State Bureau of Investigation within 24 hours or on the next workday. If sexual abuse in a child care facility is not alleged in the initial report, but during the course of the assessment there is reason to suspect that sexual abuse has occurred, the Department shall immediately notify the State Bureau of Investigation. Upon notification that sexual abuse may have occurred in a child care facility, the State Bureau of Investigation may form a task force to investigate the report.

History.
2015-123, s. 8

§ 110-105.5. Child maltreatment registry

(a) The Department shall establish and maintain a registry containing the names of all caregivers who have been confirmed by the Department of having maltreated a child pursuant to G.S. 110-105.3.

(b) Individuals who wish to contest findings under subsection (a) of this section are entitled to an administrative hearing as provided by the Administrative Procedure Act under Chapter 150B of the General Statutes. A petition for a contested case shall be filed within 30 days of the mailing of the written notice of the Department's intent to place its findings about the person in the Child Maltreatment Registry.

(c) Individuals whose names are listed on the Registry shall not be a caregiver as defined in G.S. 110-105.3(b)(1) at any licensed child care facility or religious-sponsored child care facility.

(d) No person shall be liable for providing any information for the Child Maltreatment Registry if the information is provided in good faith. Neither an employer, potential employer, nor the Department shall be liable for using any information from the Child Maltreatment Registry if the information is used in good faith for the purpose of screening prospective applicants for employment or reviewing the employment status of an employee. The immunity established by this subsection does not extend to malicious conduct or intentional wrongdoing.

(e) Upon request, a child care facility, as defined in G.S. 110-105.3, is permitted to provide confidential or other identifying information to the Department, including social security numbers, taxpayer identification numbers, parent's legal surname prior to marriage, and dates of birth, for the purpose of verifying the identity of the accused caregiver.

(f) With the exception of the names of individuals listed on the Child Maltreatment Registry, all other information received by or pertaining to the Child Maltreatment Registry shall be confidential and is not a public record under Chapter 132 of the General Statutes.

(g) In order to determine an individual's fitness to care for or adopt a child, information from the Child Maltreatment Registry may be used by any of the Department's divisions responsible for licensing homes or facilities that care for children, and the Department may provide information from this list to child-caring institutions, child-placing agencies, group home facilities, and other providers of foster care, child care, or adoption services.

(h) The North Carolina Child Care Commission shall adopt, amend, and repeal all rules necessary for the implementation of this section.

History.
2015-123, s. 8; 2015-264, s. 56(a)

§ 110-105.6. Penalties for child maltreatment

(a) For purposes of this Article, child maltreatment occurring in child care facilities is a violation of this Article, licensure standards, and licensure laws.

(b) Pursuant to G.S. 110-105.3, when an investigation confirms that child maltreatment did occur in a child care facility, the Department may issue an administrative action up to and including summary suspension and revocation of the facility's child care license.

(c) If the facility is permitted to remain open after an administrative action has been issued, the administrative action shall specify any corrective action to be taken by the operator.

(d) The Department shall make unannounced visits to determine whether the corrective action has occurred. If the corrective action has not occurred, then the Department may take further action against the facility as necessary to protect the health, safety, or welfare of the children at the child care facility.

(e) Administrative actions issued shall include a statement of the reasons for the action and shall specify corrective action that shall be taken by the operator.

(f) Under the terms of the administrative action, the Department may limit enrollment of new children until satisfied the situation giving rise to the confirmation of child maltreatment no longer exists.

(g) Specific corrective action required by an administrative action authorized by this Article may include the removal of the individual responsible for child maltreatment from child care pending a final determination or appeal of the individual's placement on the Child Maltreatment Registry.

(h) Nothing in this section shall restrict the Department from using any other statutory or administrative remedies available.

History.
2015-123, s. 8

§ 110-107. Fraudulent misrepresentation

(a) A person, whether a provider or recipient of child care subsidies or someone claiming to be a provider or recipient of child care subsidies, commits the offense of fraudulent misrepresentation when both of the following occur:

(1) With the intent to deceive, that person makes a false statement or representation regarding a material fact, or fails to disclose a material fact.

(2) As a result of the false statement or representation or the omission, that person obtains, attempts to obtain, or continues to receive a child care subsidy for himself or herself or for another person.

(b) If the child care subsidy is not more than one thousand dollars ($ 1,000), the person is guilty of a Class 1 misdemeanor. If the child care subsidy is more than one thousand dollars ($ 1,000), the person is guilty of a Class I felony.

(c) As used in this section:

(1) "Child care subsidy" means the use of public funds to pay for day care services for children.

(2) "Person" means an individual, association, consortium, corporation, body politic, partnership, or other group, entity, or organization.

History.
1999-279, s. 1

N.C. Gen. Stat. § 110-108

Repealed by Session Laws 2002-126, s. 10.58, effective July 1, 2002.

ARTICLE 9
CHILD SUPPORT

§ 110-128. Purposes

The purposes of this Article are to provide for the financial support of dependent children; to enforce spousal support when a child support order is being enforced; to provide that public assistance paid to dependent children is a supplement to the support required to be provided by the responsible parent; to provide that the payment of public assistance creates a debt to the State; to provide that the acceptance of public assistance operates as an assignment of the right to child support; to provide for the location of absent parents; to provide for a determination that a responsible parent is able to support his children; and to provide for enforcement of the responsible parent's obligation to furnish support and to provide for the establishment and administration of a program of child support enforcement in North Carolina.

History.
1975, c. 827, s. 1; 1977, 2nd Sess., c. 1186, s. 1; 1985, c. 506, s. 2

§ 110-129. Definitions

As used in this Article:

(1) "Court order" means any judgment or order of the courts of this State or of another state.

(2) "Dependent child" means any person under the age of 18 who is not otherwise emancipated, married or a member of the Armed Forces of the United States, or any person over the age of 18 for whom a court orders that support payments continue as provided in G.S. 50-13.4(c).

(3) "Responsible parent" means the natural or adoptive parent of a dependent child who has the legal duty to support said child and includes the father of a child born out-of-wedlock and the parents of a dependent child who is the custodial or noncustodial parent of the dependent child requiring

support. If both the parents of the child requiring support were unemancipated minors at the time of the child's conception, the parents of both minor parents share primary liability for their grandchild's support until both minor parents reach the age of 18 or become emancipated. If only one parent of the child requiring support was an unemancipated minor at the time of the child's conception, the parents of both parents are liable for any arrearages in child support owed by the adult or emancipated parent until the other parent reaches the age of 18 or becomes emancipated.

(4) "Program" means the Child Support Enforcement Program established and administered pursuant to the provisions of this Article and Title IV-D of the Social Security Act.

(5) "Designated representative" means any person or agency designated by a board of county commissioners or the Department of Health and Human Services to administer a program of child support enforcement for a county or region of the State.

(6) "Disposable income" means any form of periodic payment to an individual, regardless of sources, including but not limited to wages, salary, commission, self-employment income, bonus pay, severance pay, sick pay, incentive pay, vacation pay, compensation as an independent contractor, worker's compensation, unemployment compensation benefits, disability, annuity, survivor's benefits, pension and retirement benefits, interest, dividends, rents, royalties, trust income and other similar payments, which remain after the deduction of amounts for federal, State, and local taxes, Social Security, and involuntary retirement contributions. However, Supplemental Security Income, Work First Family Assistance, and other public assistance payments shall be excluded from disposable income. For employers, disposable income means "wage" as it is defined by G.S. 95-25.2(16). Unemployment compensation benefits shall be treated as disposable income only for the purposes of income withholding under the provisions of G.S. 110-136.4, and the amount withheld shall not exceed twenty-five percent (25%) of the unemployment compensation benefits.

(7) "IV-D case" means a case in which services have been applied for or are being provided by a child support enforcement agency established pursuant to Title IV-D of the Social Security Act as amended and this Article.

(8) "Non-IV-D case" means any case, other than a IV-D case, in which child support is legally obligated to be paid.

(9) "Initiating party" means the party, the attorney for a party, a child support enforcement agency who initiates an action, proceeding, or procedure as allowed or required by law for the establishment or enforcement of a child support obligation.

(10) "Mistake of fact" means that the obligor:

    a. Is not in arrears in an amount equal to the support payable for one month; or

    b. Did not request that withholding begin, if withholding is pursuant to a purported request by the obligor for withholding; or

    c. Is not the person subject to the court order of support for the child named in the advance notice of withholding; or

    d. Does not owe the amount of current support or arrearages specified in the advance notice or motion of withholding; or

    e. Has a rate of withholding which exceeds the amount of support specified in the court order.

(11) "Obligee", in a IV-D case, means the child support enforcement agency, and in a non-IV-D case means the individual to whom a duty of support, whether child support, alimony, or postseparation support, is owed or the individual's legal representative.

(12) "Obligor" means the individual who owes a duty to make child support payments or payments of alimony or postseparation support under a court order.

(13) "Payor" means any payor, including any federal, State, or local governmental unit, of disposable income to an obligor. When the payor is an employer, payor means employer as is defined at 29 USC § 203(d) in the Fair Labor Standards Act.

History.
1975, c. 827, s. 1; 1977, 2nd Sess., c. 1186, ss. 2, 3; 1985, c. 592; 1985 (Reg. Sess., 1986), c. 949, s. 1; 1987, c. 764, s. 3; 1989, c. 601, s. 1; 1991, c. 541, s. 3; 1995, c. 518, s. 2; 1997-443, ss. 11A.118(a), 12.27; 1997-465, s. 27; 1998-176, ss. 9, 10; 2010-96, s. 30; 2011-183, s. 75

§ 110-129.1. Additional powers and duties of the Department

(a) In addition to other powers and duties conferred upon the Department of Health and Human Services, Child Support Enforcement Program, by this Chapter or other State law, the Department shall have the following powers and duties:

(1) Upon authorization of the Secretary, to issue a subpoena for the production of

books, papers, correspondence, memoranda, agreements, or other information, documents, or records relevant to a child support establishment or enforcement proceeding or paternity establishment proceeding. The subpoena shall be signed by the Secretary and shall state the name of the person or entity required to produce the information authorized under this section, and a description of the information compelled to be produced. The subpoena may be served in the manner provided for service of subpoenas under the North Carolina Rules of Civil Procedure. The form of subpoena shall generally follow the practice in the General Court of Justice in North Carolina. Return of the subpoena shall be to the person who issued the subpoena. Upon the refusal of any person to comply with the subpoena, it shall be the duty of any judge of the district court, upon application by the person who issued the subpoena, to order the person subpoenaed to show cause why he should not comply with the requirements, if in the discretion of the judge the requirements are reasonable and proper. Refusal to comply with the subpoena or with the order shall be dealt with as for contempt of court and as otherwise provided by law. Information obtained as a result of a subpoena issued pursuant to this subdivision is confidential and may be used only by the Child Support Enforcement Program in conjunction with a child support establishment or enforcement proceeding or paternity establishment proceeding.

(2) For the purposes of locating persons, establishing paternity, or enforcing child support orders, the Program shall have access to any information or data storage and retrieval system maintained and used by the Department of Transportation for drivers license issuance or motor vehicle registration, or by a law enforcement agency in this State for law enforcement purposes, as permitted pursuant to G.S. 132-1.4, except that the Program shall have access to information available to the law enforcement agency pertaining to drivers licenses and motor vehicle registrations issued in other states.

(3) Establish and implement procedures under which in IV-D cases either parent or, in the case of an assignment of support, the State may request that a child support order enforced under this Chapter be reviewed and, if appropriate, adjusted in accordance with the most recently adopted uniform statewide child support guidelines prescribed by the Conference of Chief District Court Judges.

(4) Develop procedures for entering into agreements with financial institutions to develop and operate a data match system as provided under G.S. 110-139.2.

(5) Develop procedures for ensuring that when a noncustodial parent providing health care coverage pursuant to a court order changes employers and is eligible for health care coverage from the new employer, the new employer, upon receipt of notice of the order from the Department, enrolls the child in the employer's health care plan.

(6) Develop and implement an administrative process for paternity establishment in accordance with G.S. 110-132.2.

(7) Establish and implement administrative procedures to change the child support payee to ensure that child support payments are made to the appropriate caretaker when custody of the child has changed, in accordance with G.S. 50-13.4(d).

(8) Establish and implement expedited procedures to take the following actions relating to the establishment of paternity or to establishment of support orders, without obtaining an order from a judicial tribunal:

    a. Subpoena the parties to undergo genetic testing as provided under G.S. 110-132.2;

    b. Implement income withholding in accordance with this Chapter;

    c. For the purpose of securing overdue support, increase the amount of monthly support payments by implementation of income withholding procedures established under G.S. 110-136.4, or by notice and opportunity to contest to an obligor who is not subject to income withholding. Increases under this subdivision are subject to the limitations of G.S. 110-136.6;

    d. For purposes of exerting and retaining jurisdiction in IV-D cases, transfer cases between jurisdictions in this State without the necessity for additional filing by the petitioner or service of process upon the respondent.

(9) Implement and maintain performance standards for each of the State and county child support enforcement offices across the State. The performance standards shall include the following:

    a. Cost per collections.

    b. Consumer satisfaction.

    c. Paternity establishments.

    d. Administrative costs.

    e. Orders established.

    f. Collections on arrearages.

    g. Location of absent parents.

    h. Other related performance measures.

The Department shall monitor the performance of each office and shall implement a system of reporting that allows each local office to review its performance as well as the performance of other local offices. The Department shall publish an annual performance report that includes the statewide and local office performance of each child support office.

(b) As used in this section, the term "Secretary" means the Secretary of Health and Human Services, the Secretary's designee, or a designated representative as defined under G.S. 110-129(5).

History.
1997-433, s. 2; 1997-443, s. 11A.122; 1998-17, s. 1; 2009-451, s. 10.46

§ 110-129.2. State Directory of New Hires established; employers required to report; civil penalties for noncompliance; definitions

(a) **Directory Established.** -- There is established the State Directory of New Hires. The Directory shall be developed and maintained by the Department. The Directory shall be a central repository for employment information to assist in the location of persons owing child support, and in the establishment and enforcement of child support orders.

(b) **Employer Reporting.** -- Every employer in this State shall report to the Directory the hiring of every employee for whom a federal W-4 form is required to be completed by the employee at the time of hiring. The employer shall report the information required under this section not later than 20 days from the date of hire, or, in the case of an employer who transmits new hire reports magnetically or electronically by two monthly transmissions, not less than 12 nor more than 16 days apart. The Department shall notify employers of the information they must report under this section and of the penalties for not reporting the required information. The required forms must be provided by the Department to employers.

(c) **Report Contents.** -- Each report required by this section shall contain the name, address, social security number of the newly hired employee, the date services for remuneration were first performed by the newly hired employee, and the name and address of the employer and the employer's identifying number assigned under section 6109 of the Internal Revenue Code of 1986 and the employer's State employer identification number. Reports shall be made on the W-4 form or, at the option of the employer, an equivalent form, and may be transmitted magnetically, electronically, or by first-class mail.

(d) **Penalties for Failure to Report.** -- Upon a finding that an employer has failed to comply with the reporting requirements of this section, the district court shall impose a civil penalty in an amount not to exceed twenty-five dollars ($ 25.00). If the court finds that an employer's failure to comply with the reporting requirements is the result of a conspiracy between the employer and the employee to not supply the required report or to supply a false or incomplete report, then the court shall impose upon the employer a civil penalty in an amount not to exceed five hundred dollars ($ 500.00). Penalties collected under this subsection shall be deposited to the General Fund.

(e) **Entry of Report Data Into Directory.** -- Within five business days of receipt of the report from the employer, the Department shall enter the information from the report into the Directory.

(f) **Notice to Employer to Withhold.** -- Within two business days of the date the information was entered into the Directory, the Department or its designated representative as defined under G.S. 110-129(5) shall transmit notice to the employer of the newly hired employee directing the employer to withhold from the income of the employee an amount equal to the monthly or other periodic child support obligation, including any past-due support obligation of the employee and subject to the limitations of G.S. 110-136.6, unless the employee's income is not subject to withholding.

(g) **Other Uses of Directory Information.** -- The following agencies may access information entered into the Directory from employer reports for the purposes stated:

(1) The Division of Employment Security for the purpose of administering employment security programs.

(2) The North Carolina Industrial Commission for the purpose of administering workers' compensation programs.

(3) The Department of Revenue for the purpose of administering the taxes it has a duty to collect under Chapter 105 of the General Statutes.

(h) **Department May Contract for Services.** -- The Department may contract with other State or private entities to perform the services necessary to implement this section.

(i) **Information Confidential.** -- Except as otherwise provided in this section, information contained in the Directory is confidential and may be used only by the State Child Support Enforcement Program.

(j) **Definitions.** -- As used in this section, unless the context clearly requires otherwise, the term:

(1) "Business day" means a day on which State offices are open for business.

(2) "Department" means the Department of Health and Human Services.

(3) "Employee" means an individual who is an employee within the meaning of Chapter 24 of the Internal Revenue Code of 1986. The term "employee" does not include an employee of a federal or State agency performing intelligence or counterintelligence functions, if the head of the agency has determined that reporting information as required under this section could endanger the safety of the employee or compromise an ongoing investigation or intelligence mission.

(4) "Employer" has the meaning given the term in section 3401(d) of the Internal Revenue Code of 1986 and includes persons who are governmental entities and labor organizations. The term "labor organization" shall have the meaning given that term in section 2(5) of the National Labor Relations Act, and includes any entity which is used by the organization and an employer to carry out requirements described in section 8(f)(3) of the National Labor Relations Act of an agreement between the organization and the employer.

(5) "Newly hired employee" means (i) an employee who has not previously been employed by the employer and (ii) an employee who was previously employed by the employer but has been separated from such prior employment for at least 60 consecutive days.

History.
1997-433, s. 1; 1997-443, s. 11A.122; 1998-17, s. 1; 1999-438, s. 30; 2011-401, s. 3.13; 2012-134, s. 3(a), (b)

§ 110-130. Action by the designated representatives of the county commissioners

Any county interested in the paternity and/or support of a dependent child may institute civil or criminal proceedings against the responsible parent of the child, or may take up and pursue any paternity and/or support action commenced by the mother, custodian or guardian of the child. Such action shall be undertaken by the designated representative in the county where the mother of the child resides or is found, in the county where the father resides or is found, or in the county where the child resides or is found. Any legal proceeding instituted under this section may be based upon information or belief. The parent of the child may be subpoenaed for testimony at the trial of the action to establish the paternity of and/or to obtain support for the child either instituted or taken up by the designated representative of the county commissioners. The husband-wife privilege shall not be grounds for excusing the mother or father from testifying at the trial nor shall said

privilege be grounds for the exclusion of confidential communications between husband and wife. If a parent called for examination declines to answer upon the grounds that his testimony may tend to incriminate him, the court may require him to answer in which event he shall not thereafter be prosecuted for any criminal act involved in the conception of the child whose paternity is in issue and/or for whom support is sought, except for perjury committed in this testimony.

History.
1975, c. 827, s. 1; 1977, 2nd Sess., c. 1186, s. 4; 1985, c. 410

§ 110-130.1. Non-Work First services

(a) All child support collection and paternity determination services provided under this Article to recipients of public assistance shall be made available to any individual not receiving public assistance in accordance with federal law and as contractually authorized by the non-recipient, upon proper application and payment of a nonrefundable application fee of twenty-five dollars ($ 25.00). The fee shall be reduced to ten dollars ($ 10.00) if the individual applying for the services is indigent. An indigent individual is an individual whose gross income does not exceed one hundred percent (100%) of the federal poverty guidelines issued each year in the Federal Register by the U.S. Department of Health and Human Services. For the purposes of this subsection, the term "gross income" has the same meaning as defined in G.S. 105-153.3.

In the case of an individual who has never received assistance under a State program funded pursuant to Title IV-A of the Social Security Act and for whom the State has collected and disbursed to the family in a federal fiscal year at least five hundred fifty dollars ($ 550.00) of support, the State shall impose an annual fee of thirty-five dollars ($ 35.00) for each case in which services are furnished. The child support agency shall retain the fee from support collected on behalf of the individual. However, the child support agency shall not retain the fee from the first five hundred fifty dollars ($ 550.00) collected. The child support agency shall use the fee to support the ongoing operation of the program.

(b) Repealed by Session Laws 1989, c. 490.

(b1) In cases in which a public assistance debt which accrued pursuant to G.S. 110-135 remains unrecovered, support payments shall be transmitted to the Department of Health and Human Services for appropriate distribution. When services are terminated and all costs and any public assistance debts have been satisfied, the support payment shall be redirected to the client.

(c) Actions or proceedings to establish, enforce, or modify a duty of support or establish paternity as initiated under this Article shall be brought in the name of the county or State agency on behalf of the public assistance recipient or nonrecipient client. Collateral disputes between a custodial parent and noncustodial parent, involving visitation, custody and similar issues, shall be considered only in separate proceedings from actions initiated under this Article. The attorney representing the designated representative of programs under Title IV-D of the Social Security Act shall be deemed attorney of record only for proceedings under this Article, and not for the separate proceedings. No attorney/client relationship shall be considered to have been created between the attorney who represents the child support enforcement agency and any person by virtue of the action of the attorney in providing the services required.

(c1) The Department is hereby authorized to use the electronic and print media in attempting to locate absent and deserting parents. Due diligence must be taken to ensure that the information used is accurate or has been verified. Print media shall be under no obligation or duty, except that of good faith, to anyone to verify the correctness of any information furnished to it by the Department or county departments of social services.

(d) Any fee imposed by the North Carolina Department of Revenue or the Secretary of the Treasury to cover their costs of withholding for non-Work First arrearages certified for the collection of past due support from State or federal income tax refunds or administrative offsets, as defined by 31 C.F.R. § 285.1(a), shall be borne by the client by deducting the fee from the amount collected.

Any income tax refund offset amounts or administrative offsets, as defined by 31 C.F.R. § 285.1(a), which are subsequently determined to have been incorrectly withheld and distributed to a client, and which must be refunded by the State to a responsible parent or the nondebtor spouse, shall constitute a debt to the State owed by the client.

History.
1983, c. 527, s. 1; 1985, c. 781, ss. 1-5; 1985 (Reg. Sess., 1986), c. 931, ss. 1-3; 1989, c. 490; 1995, c. 538, s. 3; 1997-223, s. 2; 1997-443, ss. 11A.118(a), 12.28; 2007-460, s. 1; 2015-62, s. 2(a); 2015-117, s. 3; 2018-5, s. 11C.3; 2018-97, s. 3.4

§ 110-130.2. Collection of spousal support

Spousal support shall be collected for a spouse or former spouse with whom the absent parent's child is living when a child support order is being enforced under this Article. However, the spousal support shall be collected: (i)

only if there is an order establishing the support obligation with respect to such spouse; and (ii) only if an order establishing the support obligation with respect to the child is being enforced under this Article. The Child Support Enforcement Program is not authorized to assist in the establishment of a spousal support obligation.

History.
1985, c. 506, s. 1

§ 110-131. Compelling disclosure of information respecting the nonsupporting responsible parent of a child receiving public assistance

(a) If a parent of any dependent child receiving public assistance fails or refuses to cooperate with the county in locating and securing support from a nonsupporting responsible parent, this parent may be cited to appear before any judge of the district court and compelled to disclose such information under oath and/or may be declared ineligible for public assistance by the county department of social services for as long as he fails to cooperate.

(b) Any parent who, having been cited to appear before a judge of the district court pursuant to subsection (a), fails or refuses to appear or fails or refuses to provide the information requested may be found to be in contempt of said court and may be fined not more than one hundred dollars ($ 100.00) or imprisoned not more than six months or both.

(c) Any parent who is declared ineligible for public assistance by the county department of social services shall have his needs excluded from consideration in determining the amount of the grant, and the needs of the remaining family members shall be met in the form of a protective payment in accordance with G.S. 108-50.

History.
1975, c. 827, s. 1

§ 110-131.1. Notice; due process requirements met

In any child support enforcement proceeding the trial court may deem State due process requirements for notice and service of process to be met with respect to the nonmoving party, upon delivery of written notice in accordance with the notice requirements of Chapter 1A-1, Rule 5(b) of the Rules of Civil Procedure with respect to all pleadings subsequent to the original complaint.

History.
1997-433, s. 2.3; 1998-17, s. 1

§ 110-132. Affidavit of parentage and agreement to motion to set aside affidavit of parentage

(a) In lieu of or in conclusion of any legal proceeding instituted to establish paternity, the written affidavits of parentage executed by the putative father and the mother of the dependent child shall constitute an admission of paternity and shall have the same legal effect as a judgment of paternity for the purpose of establishing a child support obligation, subject to the right of either signatory to rescind within the earlier of:

(1) 60 days of the date the document is executed, or

(2) The date of entry of an order establishing paternity or an order for the payment of child support.

In order to rescind, a challenger must request the district court to order the rescission and to include in the order specific findings of fact that the request for rescission was filed with the clerk of court within 60 days of the signing of the document. The court must also find that all parties, including the child support enforcement agency, if appropriate, have been served in accordance with Rule 4 of the North Carolina Rules of Civil Procedure. In the event the court orders rescission and the putative father is thereafter found not to be the father of the child, then the clerk of court shall send a copy of the order of rescission to the State Registrar of Vital Statistics. Upon receipt of an order of rescission, the State Registrar shall remove the putative father's name from the birth certificate. In the event that the putative father defaults or fails to present or prosecute the issue of paternity, the trial court shall find the putative father to be the biological father as a matter of law.

(a1) Paternity established under subsection (a) of this section may be set aside in accordance with subsection (a2) of this section or in accordance with G.S. 50-13.13.

(a2) Notwithstanding the time limitations of G.S. 1A-1, Rule 60 of the North Carolina Rules of Civil Procedure, or any other provision of law, an affidavit of parentage may be set aside by a trial court after 60 days have elapsed if each of the following applies:

(1) The affidavit of parentage was entered as the result of fraud, duress, mutual mistake, or excusable neglect.

(2) Genetic tests establish that the putative father is not the biological father of the child.

The burden of proof in any motion to set aside an affidavit of parentage after 60 days allowed for rescission shall be on the moving party. Upon proper motion alleging fraud, duress, mutual mistake, or excusable neglect, the court shall order the child's mother, the child whose parentage is at issue, and the putative father to submit to genetic paternity testing pursuant to G.S. 8-50.1(b1). If the court determines, as a result of genetic testing, the putative father is not the biological father of the child and the affidavit of parentage was entered as a result of fraud, duress, mutual mistake, or excusable neglect, the court may set aside the affidavit of parentage. Nothing in this subsection shall be construed to affect the presumption of legitimacy where a child is born to a mother and the putative father during the course of a marriage.

(a3) A written agreement to support the child by periodic payments, which may include provision for reimbursement for medical expenses incident to the pregnancy and the birth of the child, accrued maintenance and reasonable expense of prosecution of the paternity action, when acknowledged as provided herein, filed with, and approved by a judge of the district court at any time, shall have the same force and effect as an order of support entered by that court, and shall be enforceable and subject to modification in the same manner as is provided by law for orders of the court in such cases. The written affidavit shall contain the social security number of the person executing the affidavit. Voluntary agreements to support shall contain the social security number of each of the parties to the agreement. The written affidavits and agreements to support shall be sworn to before a certifying officer or notary public or the equivalent or corresponding person of the state, territory, or foreign country where the affirmation, acknowledgment, or agreement is made, and shall be binding on the person executing the same whether the person is an adult or a minor. The child support enforcement agency shall ensure that the mother and putative father are given oral and written notice of the legal consequences and responsibilities arising from the signing of an affidavit of parentage and of any alternatives to the execution of an affidavit of parentage. The mother shall not be excused from making the affidavit on the grounds that it may tend to disgrace or incriminate her; nor shall she thereafter be prosecuted for any criminal act involved in the conception of the child as to whose paternity she attests.

(b) At any time after the filing with the district court of an affidavit of parentage, upon the application of any interested party, the court or any judge thereof shall cause a summons signed by him or by the clerk or assistant clerk of superior court, to be issued, requiring the putative father to appear in court at a time and place named therein, to show cause, if any he has, why the court should not enter an order for the support of the child by periodic payments, which order may include provision for reimbursement for medical expenses incident to the pregnancy and the birth of the child, accrued maintenance and reasonable expense of the action under this subsection on the affidavit of parentage previously filed with said court. The court may order the responsible parents in a IV-D establishment case to perform a job search, if the responsible parent is not incapacitated. This includes IV-D cases in which the responsible parent is a noncustodial mother or a noncustodial father whose affidavit of parentage has been filed with the court or when paternity is not at issue for the child. The court may further order the responsible parent to participate in the work activities, as defined in 42 U.S.C. § 607, as the court deems appropriate. The amount of child support payments so ordered shall be determined as provided in G.S. 50-13.4(c). The prior judgment as to paternity shall be res judicata as to that issue and shall not be reconsidered by the court.

History.
1975, c. 827, s. 1; 1977, 2nd Sess., c. 1186, ss. 5, 6; 1981, c. 275, s. 8; 1989, c. 529, s. 8; 1997-433, s. 4.7; 1998-17, s. 1; 1999-293, s. 1; 2001-237, s. 2; 2011-328, s. 2

§ 110-132.1. Paternity determination by another state entitled to full faith and credit

A paternity determination made by another state:

    (1) In accordance with the laws of that state, and

    (2) By any means that is recognized in that state as establishing paternity

shall be entitled to full faith and credit in this State.

History.
1993 (Reg. Sess., 1994), c. 733, s. 2

§ 110-132.2. Expedited procedures to establish paternity in IV-D cases

(a) In a IV-D court action, a local child support enforcement office may, without obtaining a court order, subpoena a minor child, the minor child's mother, and the putative father of the minor child (including the mother's husband, if different from the putative father) to appear for the purpose of undergoing blood or genetic testing to establish paternity. A subpoena issued pursuant to this section must be served in accordance with Rule 4 of the North Carolina Rules of Civil Procedure. Refusal to comply with a subpoena may be dealt with as for contempt

of court, and as otherwise provided under law. A party may contest the results of the genetic or blood test. If the results are contested, the agency shall, upon request and advance payment by the contestant, obtain additional testing.

(b) A person subpoenaed to submit to testing pursuant to subsection (a) of this section may contest the subpoena. To contest the subpoena, a person must, within 15 days of receipt of the subpoena, request a hearing in the county where the local child support enforcement office that issued the subpoena is located. The hearing shall be before the district court and notice of the hearing must be served by the petitioner on all parties to the proceeding. Service shall be in accordance with Rule 4 of the North Carolina Rules of Civil Procedure. The hearing shall be held and a determination made within 30 days of the petitioner's request for hearing as to whether the petitioner must comply with the subpoena to undergo testing. If the trial court determines that the petitioner must comply with the subpoena, the determination shall not prejudice any defenses the petitioner may present at any future paternity litigation.

History.
1997-433, s. 4.11; 1998-17, s. 1

§ 110-133. Agreements of support

In lieu of or in conclusion of any legal proceeding instituted to obtain support from a responsible parent for a dependent child born of the marriage, a written agreement to support the child by periodic payments executed by the responsible parent when acknowledged before a certifying officer or notary public or the equivalent or corresponding person of the state, territory, or foreign country where the acknowledgment is made and filed with and approved by a judge of the district court in the county where the custodial parent of the child resides or is found, or in the county where the noncustodial parent resides or is found, or in the county where the child resides or is found shall have the same force and effect, retroactively and prospectively, in accordance with the terms of the agreement, as an order of support entered by the court, and shall be enforceable and subject to modification in the same manner as is provided by law for orders of the court in such cases. A responsible parent executing a written agreement under this section shall provide on the agreement the responsible parent's social security number.

History.
1975, c. 827, s. 1; 1977, 2nd Sess., c. 1186, s. 7; 1995, c. 538, s. 5; 1997-433, s. 4.8; 1998-17, s. 1

§ 110-134. Filing of affidavits, agreements, and orders; fees

All affidavits, agreements, and resulting orders entered into under the provisions of G.S. 110-132 and G.S. 110-133 shall be filed by the clerk of superior court in the county in which they are entered. The filing fee for the institution of an action through the entry of an order under either of these provisions shall be in an amount equal to that provided in G.S. 7A-308(a) (18).

History.
1975, c. 827, s. 1; 1977, 2nd Sess., c. 1186, s. 8; 2001-237, s. 3; 2010-31, s. 15.6

§ 110-135. Debt to State created

Acceptance of public assistance by or on behalf of a dependent child creates a debt, in the amount of public assistance paid, due and owing the State by the responsible parent or parents of the child. Provided, however, that in those cases in which child support was required to be paid incident to a court order during the time of receipt of public assistance, the debt shall be limited to the amount specified in such court order. This liability shall attach only to public assistance granted subsequent to June 30, 1975, and only with respect to the period of time during which public assistance is granted, and only if the responsible parent or parents were financially able to furnish support during this period.

The United States, the State of North Carolina, and any county within the State which has provided public assistance to or on behalf of a dependent child shall be entitled to share in any sum collected under this section, and their proportionate parts of such sum shall be determined in accordance with the matching formulas in use during the period for which assistance was paid.

No action to collect such debt shall be commenced after the expiration of five years subsequent to the receipt of the last grant of public assistance. The county attorney or an attorney retained by the county and/or State shall represent the State in all proceedings brought under this section.

A past-due public assistance debt as described in this section may be deemed negotiable and subject to reduction if the public assistance debt is not less than fifteen thousand dollars ($ 15,000) and the responsible parent continues to be obligated to pay current child support. Upon agreement between the State and the responsible parent, and upon approval of the court upon an inquiry into the financial status of the obligor, the responsible parent shall pay all child support payments, including payments due on child support arrears, entered by a valid court order for a 24-month period of time. Upon the timely payment of each court-ordered child support obligation during the full 24-month period, including payments due on child support arrears, the State shall reduce the responsible parent's public assistance debt by two-thirds. If the responsible parent is late or defaults on any single payment during the 24-month period, no portion of the public assistance debt shall be reduced. The responsible parent may attempt to achieve 24 consecutive months of child support payments as often as possible in order to reduce his or her public assistance debt. However, once the responsible parent's public assistance debt has been reduced by two-thirds because of the successful completion of this agreement, the responsible parent shall no longer be eligible for this program. The reduction of public assistance debt as set forth in this section shall be in addition to all other remedies available to the State for the retirement of the debt. This program shall not prevent the State from taking any and all other measures available by law.

Upon the termination of a child support obligation due to the death of the obligor, the Department shall determine whether the obligor's estate contains sufficient assets to satisfy any child support arrearages. If sufficient assets are available, the Department shall attempt to collect the arrearage.

History.
1975, c. 827, s. 1; 1977, 2nd Sess., c. 1186, ss. 9, 10; 2003-288, s. 1.1; 2005-389, s. 2

§ 110-136. Garnishment for enforcement of child-support obligation

(a) Notwithstanding any other provision of the law, in any case in which a responsible parent is under a court order or has entered into a written agreement pursuant to G.S. 110-132 or 110-133 to provide child support, a judge of the district court in the county where the mother of the child resides or is found, or in the county where the father resides or is found, or in the county where the child resides or is found may enter an order of garnishment whereby no more than forty percent (40%) of the responsible parent's monthly disposable earnings shall be garnished for the support of his minor child. For purposes of this section, "disposable earnings" is defined as that part of the compensation paid or payable to the responsible parent for personal services, whether denominated as wages, salary, commission, bonus, or otherwise (including periodic payments pursuant to a pension, retirement, or other deferred compensation program) which remains after the deduction of any amounts required by law to be withheld. The garnishee is the person, firm, association, or corporation by whom the responsible parent is employed.

(b) The mother, father, custodian, or guardian of the child or any designated representative interested in the support of a dependent child may move the court for an order of garnishment. The motion shall be verified and shall state that the responsible parent is under court order or has entered into a written agreement pursuant to G.S. 110-132 or 110-133 to provide child support, that said parent is delinquent in such child support or has been erratic in making child-support payments, the name and address of the employer of the responsible parent, the responsible parent's monthly disposable earnings from said employer (which may be based upon information and belief), and the amount sought to be garnished, not to exceed forty percent (40%) of the responsible parent's monthly disposable earnings. The motion for the wage garnishment order along with a motion to join the alleged employer as a third-party garnishee defendant shall be served on both the responsible parent and the alleged employer in accordance with the provisions of G.S. 1A-1, Rules of Civil Procedure. The time period for answering or otherwise responding to pleadings, motions and other papers issued pursuant to this section shall be in accordance with the time periods set forth in G.S. 1A-1, Rules of Civil Procedure, except that the alleged employer third-party garnishee shall have 10 days from the date of service of process to answer both the motion to join him as a defendant garnishee and the motion for the wage garnishment order.

(b1) In addition to the foregoing method for instituting a continuing wage garnishment proceeding for child support through motion, the mother, father, custodian, or guardian of the child or any designated representative interested in the support of a dependent child may in an independent proceeding petition the court for an order of continuing wage garnishment. The petition shall be verified and shall state that the responsible parent is under court order or has entered into a written agreement pursuant to G.S. 110-132 or 110-133 to provide child support, that said parent is delinquent in such child support or has been erratic in making child-support payments, the name and address of the alleged-employer garnishee of the responsible parent, the responsible parent's monthly disposable earnings from said employer (which may be based on information and belief), and the amount sought to be garnished, not to exceed forty percent (40%) of the responsible parent's monthly disposable earnings. The petition shall be served on both the responsible parent and his alleged employer in accordance with the provisions of G.S. 1A-1, Rule 4. The time period for answering or otherwise responding to process issued pursuant to this section shall be

in accordance with the time periods set forth in G.S. 1A-1, Rules of Civil Procedure.

(c) Following the hearing held pursuant to this section, the court may enter an order of garnishment not to exceed forty percent (40%) of the responsible parent's monthly disposable earnings. If an order of garnishment is entered, a copy of same shall be served on the responsible parent and the garnishee either personally or by certified or registered mail, return receipt requested. The order shall set forth sufficient findings of fact to support the action by the court and the amount to be garnished for each pay period. The amount garnished shall be increased by an additional one dollar ($ 1.00) processing fee to be assessed and retained by the employer for each payment under the order. The order shall be subject to review for modification and dissolution upon the filing of a motion in the cause.

(d) Upon receipt of an order of garnishment, the garnishee shall transmit without delay to the State Child Support Collection and Disbursement Unit the amount ordered by the court to be garnished. These funds shall be disbursed to the party designated by the court which in those cases of dependent children receiving public assistance shall be the North Carolina Department of Health and Human Services.

(e) Any garnishee violating the terms of an order of garnishment shall be subject to punishment as for contempt.

History.
1975, c. 827, s. 1; 1977, 2nd Sess., c. 1186, ss. 11, 12; 1979, c. 386, ss. 1-8; 1983 (Reg. Sess., 1984), c. 1047, s. 1; 1985, c. 660, s. 2; 1997-443, s. 11A.118(a); 1999-293, s. 17

§ 110-136.1. Assignment of wages for child support

Pursuant to G.S. 50-13.4(f) (1), the court may require the responsible parent to execute an assignment of wages, salary, or other income due or to become due whenever his employer's voluntary written acceptance of the wage assignment under G.S. 95-31 is filed with the court. Such acceptance remains effective until the employer files an express written revocation with the court. The amount assigned shall be increased by an additional one dollar ($ 1.00) processing fee to be assessed and retained by the employer for each payment under the order.

History.
1981, c. 275, s. 7; 1983 (Reg. Sess., 1984), c. 1047, s. 2

§ 110-136.2. Use of unemployment compensation benefits for child support

(a) A responsible parent may voluntarily assign unemployment compensation benefits to a child support agency to satisfy a child support obligation or a child support enforcement agency may request a responsible parent to voluntarily assign unemployment benefits to satisfy a child support obligation. An assignment of less than the full amount of the support obligation shall not relieve the responsible parent of liability for the remaining amount.

(b) Upon notification of a voluntary assignment by the Department of Health and Human Services, the Division of Employment Security shall deduct and withhold the amount assigned by the responsible parent as provided in G.S. 96-17.

(c) Any amount deducted and withheld shall be paid by the Division of Employment Security to the Department of Health and Human Services for distribution as required by federal law.

(d) Voluntary assignment of unemployment compensation benefits shall remain effective until the Division of Employment Security receives notification from the Department of Health and Human Services of an express written revocation by the responsible parent.

(e) The Department of Health and Human Services shall ensure that payments received under this section are properly credited against the responsible parent's child support obligation.

(f) In the absence of a voluntary assignment of unemployment compensation benefits, the Department of Health and Human Services shall implement income withholding as provided in this Article for IV-D cases. The amount withheld shall not exceed twenty-five percent (25%) of the unemployment compensation benefits. Notice of the requirement to withhold shall be served upon the Division and payment shall be made by the Division directly to the Department of Health and Human Services pursuant to G.S. 96-17 or to another state under G.S. 52C-5-501. Except for the requirement to withhold from unemployment compensation benefits and the forwarding of withheld funds to the Department of Health and Human Services or to another state under G.S. 52C-5-501, the Division is exempt from the provisions of G.S. 110-136.8.

History.
1983, c. 33, s. 1; 1987, c. 764, ss. 1, 2; 1997-443, s. 11A.118(a); 1999-293, s. 6; 2011-401, s. 3.14

§ 110-136.3. Income withholding procedures; applicability

(a) Required Contents of Support Orders. Required Contents of Support Orders. All child support orders, civil or criminal, entered or modified in the State in IV-D cases shall include a provision ordering income withholding to take effect immediately. All child support orders, civil or criminal, initially entered in the State

in non-IV-D cases on or after January 1, 1994, shall include a provision ordering income withholding to take effect immediately as provided in G.S. 110-136.5(c1), unless one of the exceptions specified in G.S. 110-136.5(c1) applies. A non-IV-D child support order that contains an income withholding requirement and a IV-D child support order shall comply with each of the following:

(1) Require the obligor to keep the clerk of court or IV-D agency informed of the obligor's current residence and mailing address.

(2), (2a) Repealed by Session Laws 1993, c. 517, s. 1 .

(3) Require the obligor to cooperate fully with the initiating party in the verification of the amount of the obligor's disposable income.

(4) Require the custodial party to keep the obligor informed of the custodial party's disposable income and the amount and effective date of any substantial change in this disposable income.

(4a) Include the current residence and mailing address of the custodial parent, or the address of the child if the address of the custodial parent and the address of the child are different. However, there is no requirement that the child support order contain the address of the custodial parent or the child if (i) there is an existing order prohibiting disclosure of the custodial parent's or child's address to the obligor or (ii) the court has determined that notice to the obligor is inappropriate because the obligor has made verbal or physical threats that constitute domestic violence under Chapter 50B of the General Statutes.

(5) Require the obligor to keep the initiating party informed of the name and address of any payor of the obligor's disposable income and of the amount and effective date of any substantial change in this disposable income.

(a1) Payment Plan/Work Requirement for Past-Due Support. In any IV-D case in which an obligor owes past-due support and income withholding has been ordered but cannot be implemented against the obligor, the court may order the obligor to pay the support in accordance with a payment plan approved by the court and, if the obligor is subject to the payment plan and is not incapacitated, the court may order the obligor to participate in such work activities, as defined under 42 U.S.C. § 607, as the court deems appropriate.

(b) When obligor subject to withholding.

(1) In IV-D cases in which a new or modified child support order is entered on or after October 1, 1989, an obligor is subject to income withholding immediately upon

entry of the order. In IV-D cases in which the child support order was entered prior to October 1, 1989, an obligor shall become subject to income withholding on the date on which the obligor fails to make legally obligated child support payments in an amount equal to the support payable for one month, or the date on which the obligor or obligee requests withholding.

(2) In non-IV-D cases in which the child support order was entered prior to January 1, 1994, an obligor shall be subject to income withholding on the earliest of:

a. The date on which the obligor fails to make legally obligated child support payments in an amount equal to the support payable for one month;

b. The date on which the obligor requests withholding; or

c. The date on which the court determines, pursuant to a motion or independent action filed by the obligee under G.S. 110-136.5(a), that the obligor is or has been delinquent in making child support payments or has been erratic in making child support payments.

(3) In IV-D child support cases in which an order was issued or modified in this State prior to October 1, 1996, and in which the obligor is not otherwise subject to withholding, the obligor shall become subject to withholding if the obligor fails to make legally obligated child support payments in an amount equal to the support payable for one month.

(4) In the enforcement of alimony or postseparation support orders pursuant to G.S. 110-130.2, an obligor shall become subject to income withholding on the earlier of:

a. The date on which the obligor fails to make legally obligated alimony or postseparation payments; or

b. The date on which the obligor or obligee requests withholding.

(c) Repealed by Session Laws 1993, c. 517, s. 1.

(d) Interstate cases. An interstate case is one in which a child support order of one state is to be enforced in another state.

(1) In interstate cases withholding provisions shall apply to a child support order of this or any other state. A petition addressed to this State to enforce a child support order of another state or a petition from an initiating party in this State addressed to another state to enforce a child support order entered in this State shall include:

a. A certified copy of the support order with all modifications, including any income withholding notice or order still in effect;

b. A copy of the income withholding law of the jurisdiction which issued the support order, provided that this jurisdiction has a withholding law;

c. A sworn statement of arrearages;

d. The name, address, and social security number of the obligor, if known;

e. The name and address of the obligor's employer or of any other source of income of the obligor derived in the state in which withholding is sought; and

f. The name and address of the agency or person to whom support payments collected by income withholding shall be transmitted.

(2) The law of the state in which the support order was entered shall apply in determining when withholding shall be implemented and interpreting the child support order. The law and procedures of the state where the obligor is employed shall apply in all other respects.

(3) Except as otherwise provided by subdivision (2), income withholding initiated under this subsection is subject to all of the notice, hearing and other provisions of Chapter 110.

(4) In all interstate cases notices and orders to withhold shall be served upon the payor by a North Carolina agency or judicial officer. In all interstate non-IV-D cases, the advance notice to the obligor shall be served pursuant to G.S. 1A-1, Rule 4, Rules of Civil Procedure.

(5) For purposes of enforcing a petition under this subsection, jurisdiction is limited to the purposes of income withholding and Chapter 52A of the General Statutes shall not apply. Nothing in this subsection precludes any remedy otherwise available in a proceeding under Chapter 52A of the General Statutes.

(d1) Recodified as § 110-139(c1) by Session Laws 2001-237, s. 5, effective June 23, 2001.

(e) Procedures and regulations. Procedures, rules, regulations, forms, and instructions necessary to effect the income withholding provisions of this Article shall be established by the Secretary of the Department of Health and Human Services or the Secretary's designee and the Administrative Office of the Courts. Forms and instructions shall be sent with each order or notice of withholding.

History.
1985 (Reg. Sess., 1986), c. 949, s. 2; 1987, c. 589, s. 1; 1989, c. 601, s. 2; 1993, c. 517, s. 1; 1997-433, ss. 3, 6.1; 1997-443, s. 11A.118(a); 1998-17, s. 1; 1998-176, s. 4; 2000-140, s. 20(b); 2001-237, s. 5; 2014-115, s. 44.5

§ 110-136.4. Implementation of withholding in IV-D cases

(a) Withholding based on arrearages or obligor's request.

(1) Advance notice of withholding. When an obligor in a IV-D case becomes subject to income withholding, the obligee shall, after verifying the obligor's current employer or other payor, wages or other disposable income, and mailing address, serve the obligor with advance notice of withholding in accordance with G.S. 1A-1, Rule 4, Rules of Civil Procedure.

(2) Contents of advance notice. The advance notice to the obligor shall contain, at a minimum, the following information:

a. Whether the proposed withholding is based on the obligor's failure to make legally obligated child support, alimony or postseparation support payments on the obligor's request for withholding, on the obligee's request for withholding, or on the obligor's eligibility for withholding under G.S. 110-136.3(b)(3);

b. The amount of overdue child support, overdue alimony or postseparation support payments, the total amount to be withheld, and when the withholding will occur;

c. The name of each child or person for whose benefit the child support, alimony or postseparation support payments are due and information sufficient to identify the court order under which the obligor has a duty to support the child, spouse, or former spouse;

d. The amount and sources of disposable income;

e. That the withholding will apply to the obligor's wages or other sources of disposable income from current payors and all subsequent payors once the procedures under this section are invoked;

f. An explanation of the obligor's rights and responsibilities pursuant to this section;

g. That withholding will be continued until terminated pursuant to G.S. 110-136.10.

(3) Contested withholding. The obligor may contest the withholding only on the basis of a mistake of fact, except that G.S. 110-129(10)(a) is not applicable if withholding is based on the obligor's or obligee's request for withholding. To contest the withholding, the obligor must, within 10 days of receipt of the advance notice of withholding, request a hearing in the county where the support order was entered before the district court and give notice to the obligee specifying the mistake of fact upon which the hearing request is based. If the asserted mistake of fact can be resolved by agreement between the obligee and the obligor, no hearing shall occur. Otherwise, a hearing shall be held and a determination made, within 30 days of the obligor's receipt of the advance notice of withholding, as to whether the asserted mistake of fact is valid. No withholding shall occur pending the hearing decision. The failure to hold a hearing within 30 days shall not invalidate an otherwise properly entered order. If it is determined that a mistake of fact exists, no withholding shall occur. Otherwise, within 45 days of the obligor's receipt of the advance notice of withholding, the obligee shall serve the payor, pursuant to G.S. 1A-1, Rule 5, Rules of Civil Procedure, or by electronic transmission in compliance with the federal Office of Child Support Enforcement (OCSE) electronic income withholding (e-IWO) procedures, with notice of his obligation to withhold, and shall mail a copy of such notice to the obligor and file a copy with the clerk. In the event of appeal, withholding shall not be stayed. If the appeal is concluded in favor of the obligor, the obligee shall promptly repay sums wrongfully withheld and notify the payor to cease withholding.

(4) Uncontested withholding. If the obligor does not contest the withholding within the 10-day response period, the obligee shall serve the payor, pursuant to G.S. 1A-1, Rule 5, Rules of Civil Procedure, or by electronic transmission in compliance with the federal Office of Child Support Enforcement (OCSE) electronic income withholding (e-IWO) procedures, with notice of his obligation to withhold, and shall mail a copy of such notice to the obligor and file a copy with the clerk.

(5) Payment not a defense to withholding. The payment of overdue support shall not be a basis for terminating or not implementing withholding.

(6) Inability to implement withholding. When an obligor is subject to withholding, but withholding under this section cannot be implemented because the obligor's location is unknown, because the extent and source of his disposable income cannot be determined, or for any other reason, the obligee shall either request the clerk of superior court to initiate enforcement proceedings under G.S. 15A-1344.1(d) or G.S. 50-13.9(d) or take other appropriate available measures to enforce the support obligation.

(b) Immediate income withholding. When a new or modified child support order is entered, the district court judge shall, after hearing evidence regarding the obligor's disposable income, place the obligor under an order for immediate income withholding. The IV-D agency shall serve the payor pursuant to G.S. 1A-1, Rule 5, Rules of Civil Procedure, or by electronic transmission in compliance with the federal Office of Child Support Enforcement (OCSE) electronic income withholding (e-IWO) procedures, with a notice of his obligation to withhold, and shall mail a copy of such notice to the obligor and file a copy with the clerk. If information is unavailable regarding an obligor's disposable income, or the obligor is unemployed, or an agreement is reached between both parties which provides for an alternative arrangement, immediate income withholding shall not apply. The obligor, however, is subject to income withholding pursuant to G.S. 110-136.4(a).

(c) Subsequent payors. If the obligor changes employment or source of disposable income, notice to subsequent payors of their obligation to withhold shall be served as required by G.S. 1A-1, Rule 5, Rules of Civil Procedure or by electronic transmission in compliance with the federal Office of Child Support Enforcement (OCSE) electronic income withholding (e-IWO) procedures. Copies of such notice shall be filed with the clerk of court and served upon the obligor by first class mail.

(d) Multiple withholdings. The obligor must notify the obligee if the obligor is currently subject to another withholding for child support. In the case of two or more withholdings against one obligor, the obligee or obligees shall attempt to resolve any conflict between the orders in a manner that is fair and equitable to all parties and within the limits specified by G.S. 110-136.6. If the conflict cannot be so resolved, an injured party, upon request, shall be granted a hearing in accordance with the procedure specified in G.S. 110-136.4(c). The conflict between the withholding orders shall be resolved in accordance with G.S. 110-136.7.

(e) Modification of withholding. When an order for withholding has been entered under this section, the obligee may modify the withholding based on changed circumstances. The obligee shall proceed as is provided in this section.

(f) Applicability of section. The provisions of this section apply to IV-D cases only.

History.
1985 (Reg. Sess., 1986), c. 949, s. 2; 1989, c. 601, s. 3; 1997-433, s. 6.2; 1998-17, s. 1; 1998-176, s. 5; 2001-237, s. 4; 2015-62, s. 2(b); 2015-117, s. 4

§ 110-136.5. Implementation of withholding in non-IV-D cases

(a) Withholding based on delinquent or erratic payments. Notwithstanding any other provision of law, when an obligor is delinquent in making child support payments or has been erratic in making child support payments, the obligee may apply to the court, by motion or in an independent action, for an order for income withholding.

(1) The motion or complaint shall be verified and state, to the extent known:
    a. Whether the obligor is under a court order to provide child support and, if so, information sufficient to identify the order;
    b. Either:
        1. That the obligor is currently delinquent in making child support payments; or
        2. That the obligor has been erratic in making child support payments;
    c. The amount of overdue support and the total amount sought to be withheld;
    d. The name of each child for whose benefit support is payable; and
    e. The name, location, and mailing address of the payor or payors from whom withholding is sought and the amount of the obligor's monthly disposable income from each payor.

(2) The motion or complaint shall include or be accompanied by a notice to the obligor, stating:
    a. That withholding, if implemented, will apply to the obligor's current payors and all subsequent payors; and
    b. That withholding, if implemented, will be continued until terminated pursuant to G.S. 110-136.10.
    At any time the parties may agree to income withholding by consent order.

(b) Withholding Based on Obligor's Request. The obligor may request at any time that income withholding be implemented. The request may be made either verbally in open court or by written request.

(1) A written request for withholding shall state:
    a. That the obligor is under a court order to provide child support, and information sufficient to identify the order;
    b. Whether the obligor is delinquent and the amount of any overdue support;
    c. The name of each child for whose benefit support is payable;
    d. The name, location, and mailing address of the payor or payors from whom the obligor receives disposable income and the amount of the obligor's monthly disposable income from each payor;

e. That the obligor understands that withholding, if implemented, will apply to the obligor's current payors and all subsequent payors and will be continued until terminated pursuant to G.S. 110-136.10; and

f. That the obligor understands that the amount withheld will include an amount sufficient to pay current child support, an additional amount toward liquidation of any arrearages, and a two dollar ($ 2.00) processing fee to be retained by the employer for each withholding, but that the total amount withheld may not exceed the following percent of disposable income:

1. Forty percent (40%) if there is only one order for withholding;

2. Forty-five percent (45%) if there is more than one order for withholding and the obligor is supporting other dependent children or his or her spouse; or

3. Fifty percent (50%) if there is more than one order for withholding and the obligor is not supporting other dependent children or a spouse.

(2) A written request for withholding shall be filed in the office of the clerk of superior court of the court that entered the order for child support. If the request states and the clerk verifies that the obligor is not delinquent, the court may enter an order for withholding without further notice or hearing. If the request states or the clerk finds that the obligor is delinquent, the matter shall be scheduled for hearing unless the obligor in writing waives his right to a hearing and consents to the entry of an order for withholding of an amount the court determines to be appropriate. The court may require a hearing in any case. Notice of any hearing under this subdivision shall be sent to the obligee.

(c) Order for withholding. If the district court judge finds after hearing evidence that the obligor, at the time of the filing of the motion or complaint was, or at the time of the hearing is, delinquent in child support payments or that the obligor has been erratic in making child support payments in accordance with G.S. 110-136.5(a), or that the obligor has requested that income withholding begin in accordance with G.S. 110-136.5(b), the court shall enter an order for income withholding, unless:

(1) The obligor proves a mistake of fact, except that G.S. 110-129(10)(a) is not applicable if withholding is based on the obligee's motion or independent action alleging that the obligor is delinquent or has been erratic in making child support payments; or

(2) The court finds that the child support obligation can be enforced and the child's right to receive support can be ensured without entry of an order for income withholding; or

(3) The court finds that the obligor has no disposable income subject to withholding or that withholding is not feasible for any other reason.

If the obligor fails to respond or appear, the court shall hear evidence and enter an order as provided herein.

(c1) Immediate income withholding. In non-IV-D cases in which a child support order is initially entered on or after January 1, 1994, an obligor is subject to income withholding immediately upon entry of the order, unless either of the following applies:

a. One of the parties demonstrates, and the court finds, that there is good cause not to require immediate income withholding.

b. A written agreement is reached between the parties that provides for an alternative arrangement.

The term "good cause" as used in this subsection includes a reasonable and workable plan for consistent and timely payments by some means other than income withholding. In considering whether a plan is reasonable, the court may consider the obligor's employment history and record of meeting financial obligations in a timely manner.

In entering an order for immediate income withholding under this subsection, the court shall follow the requirements and procedures as specified in other sections of this Article, including amount to be withheld, multiple withholdings, notice to payor, and termination of withholding.

(d) Notice to payor and obligor. If an order for income withholding is entered, a notice of obligation to withhold shall be served on the payor as required by G.S. 1A-1, Rule 5, Rules of Civil Procedure. Copies of such notice shall be filed with the clerk of court and served upon the obligor by first class mail.

(e) Modification of withholding. When an order for withholding has been entered under this section, any party may file a motion seeking modification of the withholding based on changed circumstances. The clerk or the court on its own motion may initiate a hearing for modification when it appears that modification of the withholding is required or appropriate.

History.
1985 (Reg. Sess., 1986), c. 949, s. 2; 1987, c. 60; 1989, c. 601, s. 4; 1993, c. 517, s. 2; 1999-293, s. 18; 2001-487, s. 72

§ 110-136.6. Amount to be withheld

(a) Computation of amount. When income withholding is implemented pursuant to this Article, the amount to be withheld shall include:

(1) An amount sufficient to pay current child support; and

(2) An additional amount toward liquidation of arrearages; and

(3) A processing fee of two dollars ($ 2.00) to cover the cost of withholding, to be retained by the payor for each withholding unless waived by the payor.

The amount withheld may also include court costs and attorneys fees as may be awarded by the court in non-IV-D cases and as may be awarded by the court in IV-D cases pursuant to G.S. 110-130.1.

(b) Limits on amount withheld. Withholding for current support, arrearages, processing fees, court costs, and attorneys fees shall not exceed forty percent (40%) of the obligor's disposable income for one pay period from the payor when there is one order of withholding. The sum of multiple withholdings, for current support, arrearages, processing fees, court costs, and attorneys fees shall not exceed:

(1) Forty-five percent (45%) of disposable income for one pay period from the payor in the case of an obligor who is supporting his spouse or other dependent children; or

(2) Fifty percent (50%) of disposable income for one pay period from the payor in the case of an obligor who is not supporting a spouse or other dependent children.

(b1) When there is an order of income withholding for current or delinquent payments of alimony or postseparation support or for any portion of the payments, the total amount withheld under this Article and under G.S. 50-16.7 shall not exceed the amounts allowed under section 303(b) of the Consumer Credit Protection Act, 15 U.S.C. § 1673(b).

(c) Contents of order and notice. An order or advance notice for withholding and any notice to a payor of his obligation to withhold shall state a specific monetary amount to be withheld and the amount of disposable income from the applicable payor on which the amount to be withheld was determined. The notice shall clearly indicate that in no event shall the amount withheld exceed the appropriate percentage of disposable income paid by a payor as provided in subsection (b).

History.
1985 (Reg. Sess., 1986), c. 949, s. 2; 1998-176, s. 6

§ 110-136.7. Multiple withholding

When an obligor is subject to more than one withholding for child support, withholding for current child support shall have priority over past-due support. Where two or more orders for current support exist, each family shall receive a pro rata share of the total amount withheld based on the respective child support orders being enforced.

History.
1985 (Reg. Sess., 1986), c. 949, s. 2

§ 110-136.8. Notice to payor; payor's responsibilities

(a) Contents of notice. Notice to a payor of his obligation to withhold shall include information regarding the payor's rights and responsibilities, the amount of disposable income attributable to that payor on which that withholding is based, the penalties under this section, and the maximum percentages of disposable income that may be withheld as provided in G.S. 110-136.6.

(b) Payor's responsibilities. A payor who has been properly served with a notice to withhold is required to:

(1) Withhold from the obligor's disposable income and, within 7 business days of the date the obligor is paid, send to the State Child Support Collection and Disbursement Unit the amount specified in the notice and the date the amount was withheld, but in no event more than the amount allowed by G.S. 110-136.6; however, if a lesser amount of disposable income is available for any pay period, the payor shall either:

a. Compute, and send the appropriate amount to the State Child Support Collection and Disbursement Unit, using the percentages as provided in G.S. 110-136.6; or

b. Request the initiating party to inform the payor of the proper amount to be withheld for that period;

(2) Continue withholding until further notice from the IV-D agency, the clerk of superior court, or the State Child Support Collection and Disbursement Unit;

(3) Withhold for child support before withholding pursuant to any other legal process under State law against the same disposable income;

(4) Begin withholding from the first payment due the obligor in the first pay period that occurs 14 days following the date the notice of the obligation to withhold was served on the payor;

(5) Promptly notify the obligee in a IV-D case, or the clerk of superior court or the State Child Support Collection and Disbursement Unit in a non-IV-D case, in writing:

a. If there are one or more orders of child support withholding for the obligor;

a1. If there are one or more orders of alimony or postseparation support withholding for the obligor;

b. When the obligor terminates employment or otherwise ceases to be entitled to disposable income from the payor, and provide the obligor's last known address, and the name and address of his new employer, if known;

c. Of the payor's inability to comply with the withholding for any reason; and

(6) Cooperate fully with the initiating party in the verification of the amount of the obligor's disposable income.

(c) Change in obligor's employment. If the obligor changes employment within the State when withholding is in effect, the requirement for withholding shall continue, and

(1) In a IV-D case, the IV-D obligee shall make any necessary adjustments to the withholding, notify the obligor and his new employer in accordance with this section, and file a copy of the adjusted withholding with the clerk of superior court;

(2) In a non-IV-D case, the clerk shall serve a notice of obligation to withhold according to the terms of the withholding order on the new employer and on the obligor; if the obligor or payor gives notice that an adjustment to the withholding order, other than the change in payor, is needed, the matter shall be scheduled for hearing before a child support hearing officer or district court judge who shall make any necessary adjustments to the withholding.

(d) The payor may combine amounts withheld from obligors' disposable incomes in a single payment to the State Child Support Collection and Disbursement Unit if the payor separately identifies by name and case number the portion of the single payment attributable to each individual obligor and the date that each payment was withheld from the obligor's disposable income.

(e) Prohibited conduct by payor; civil penalty. Notwithstanding any other provision of law, when a court finds, pursuant to a motion in the cause filed by the initiating party joining the payor as a third party defendant, with 30 days notice to answer the motion, that a payor has willfully refused to comply with the provisions of this section, such payor shall be ordered to commence withholding and shall be held liable to the initiating party for any amount which such payor should have withheld, except that such payor shall not be required to vary the normal pay or disbursement cycles in order to comply with these provisions.

A payor shall not discharge from employment, refuse to employ, or otherwise take disciplinary action against any obligor solely because of the withholding. When a court finds that a payor has taken any of these actions, the payor shall be liable for a civil penalty. For a first offense, the civil penalty shall be one hundred dollars ($ 100.00). For second and third offenses, the civil penalty shall be five hundred dollars ($ 500.00) and one thousand dollars ($ 1,000), respectively. Any payor who violates any provision of this paragraph shall be liable in a civil action for reasonable damages suffered by an obligor as a result of the violation, and an obligor discharged or demoted in violation of this paragraph shall be entitled to be reinstated to his former position. The statute of limitations for actions under this subsection shall be one year pursuant to G.S. 1-54.

The clear proceeds of civil penalties provided for in this subsection shall be remitted to the Civil Penalty and Forfeiture Fund in accordance with G.S. 115C-457.2.

(f) Any payor who withholds the sum provided in any notice or order to the payor shall not be liable for any penalties under this section.

History.
1985 (Reg. Sess., 1986), c. 949, s. 2; 1987, c. 589, s. 2; 1991, c. 541, ss. 1, 2; 1997-433, s. 6; 1997-465, s. 27; 1998-17, s. 1; 1998-176, s. 7; 1998-215, s. 76; 1999-293, ss. 19, 20

§ 110-136.9. Payment of withheld funds

In all cases, the State Child Support Collection and Disbursement Unit shall distribute payments received from payors to the appropriate recipient.

History.
1985 (Reg. Sess., 1986), c. 949, s. 2; 1997-443, s. 11A.118(a); 1999-293, s. 21

§ 110-136.10. Termination of withholding

A requirement that income be withheld for child support shall promptly terminate as to prospective payments when the payor receives notice from the court or IV-D agency that:

(1) The child support order has expired or become invalid; or

(2) The initiating party, the obligor, and the district court judge agree to termination because there is another adequate means to collect child support or arrearages; or

(3) The whereabouts of the child and obligee are unknown, except that withholding shall not be terminated until all valid arrearages to the State are paid in full.

History.
1985 (Reg. Sess., 1986), c. 949, s. 2

§ 110-136.11. National Medical Support Notice required

(a) **Notice Required. --** The National Medical Support Notice shall be used to notify employers and health insurers or health care plan administrators of an order entered pursuant to G.S. 50-13.11 for dependent health benefit plan coverage in a IV-D case. For purposes of this section and G.S. 110-136.12 through G.S. 110-136.14, the terms "health benefit plan" and "health insurer" are as defined in G.S. 108A-69(a).

(b) **Exception. --** The National Medical Support Notice shall not be used in cases where the court has ordered nonemployment-based health benefit plan coverage or where the parties have stipulated to nonemployment-based health benefit plan coverage.

History.
2001-237, s. 8

§ 110-136.12. IV-D agency responsibilities

(a) Within five business days after the order for dependent health benefit plan coverage has been filed in a IV-D case, the IV-D agency shall serve, pursuant to G.S. 1A-1, Rule 5, Rules of Civil Procedure, the National Medical Support Notice on the employer, if known to the agency, of the noncustodial parent.

(b) In cases where the obligor is a newly hired employee, the agency shall serve, pursuant to G.S. 1A-1, Rule 5, Rules of Civil Procedure, the National Medical Support Notice, along with the income withholding notice pursuant to G.S. 110-136.8, on the employer within two business days after the date of entry of an obligor in the State Directory of New Hires.

(c) The IV-D agency shall notify the employer within 10 business days when there is no longer a current order for medical support for which the agency is responsible.

(d) In cases where the health insurer or health care plan administrator reports that there is more than one health care option available under the health benefit plan, the IV-D agency, in consultation with the custodian, may within 20 business days of the date the insurer or administrator informed the agency of the option, select an option and inform the health insurer or health care plan administrator of the option selected.

History.
2001-237, s. 9

§ 110-136.13. Employer responsibilities

(a) For purposes of this section, G.S. 110-136.11, 110-136.12, and 110-136.14, the term "employer" means employer as is defined at 29 U.S.C. § 203(d) in the Fair Labor Standards Act.

(b) Within 20 business days after the date of the National Medical Support Notice, the employer shall transfer the Notice to the health insurer or health care plan administrator that provides health benefit plan coverage for which the child is eligible unless one of following applies:

(1) The employer does not maintain or contribute to plans providing dependent or family health insurance.

(2) The employee is among a class of employees that are not eligible for family health benefit plan coverage under any group health plan maintained by the employer or to which the employer contributes.

(3) Health benefit plan coverage is not available because the employee is no longer employed by this employer.

(4) State or federal withholding limitations prevent the withholding from the obligor's income of the amount required to obtain insurance under the terms of the plan.

(c) If the employer is not required to transfer the Notice under subsection (b) of this section, then the employer shall, within the 20 business days after the date of the Notice, inform the agency in writing of the reason or reasons the Notice was not transferred.

(d) Upon receipt from the health insurer or health care plan administrator of the cost of dependent coverage, the employer shall withhold this amount from the obligor's wages and transfer this amount directly to the insurer or plan administrator.

(e) In the event the health insurer or health care plan administrator informs the employer that the Notice is not a "qualified medical child support order" (QMCSO), the employer shall notify the agency in writing.

(f) In the event the health insurer or health care plan administrator informs the employer of a waiting period for enrollment, the employer shall inform the insurer or administrator when the employee is eligible to be enrolled in the plan.

(g) An employer obligated to provide health benefit plan coverage pursuant to this section shall inform the IV-D agency upon termination of the noncustodial parent's employment within 10 business days. The notice shall be in writing to the agency and shall include the obligor's last known address and the name and address of the new employer, if known.

(h) In the event the employee contests the withholding order, the employer shall initiate and continue the withholding until the employer receives notice that the contested case is resolved.

(i) An employer shall not discharge from employment, refuse to employ, or otherwise take disciplinary action against any obligor solely because of the withholding.

(j) If a court finds that an employer has failed to comply with this section, the employer is liable as a payor pursuant to G.S. 110-136.8(e). Additionally, an employer who violates this section is liable in a civil action for reasonable damages.

History.
2001-237, s. 10; 2004-203, s. 9

§110-136.14. Health insurer or health care plan administrator responsibilities

(a) Upon receipt of the National Medical Support Notice from the employer, and within 40 business days after the date of the Notice, a health care plan administrator shall determine if the Notice is a "qualified medical child support order" (QMCSO), as defined under the Employee Retirement Income Security Act (ERISA) or the Child Support Performance and Incentive Act (CSPIA). If the Notice is not a qualified medical support order, the plan administrator shall inform the employer within the time set forth in this subsection.

(b) Upon receipt of the Notice in a nonqualified ERISA plan, or upon a finding that the Notice constitutes a qualified medical child support order, the health insurer or plan administrator shall enroll the dependent child or children in a health benefit plan, determine the cost of the coverage, and inform the employer of the amount of the employee contribution to be withheld from the obligor's wages, if appropriate. If the child or children are already enrolled in a health benefit plan, the employer shall be so notified. The employer shall also be notified of any applicable enrollment waiting periods.

(c) If there is more than one health benefit plan in which the dependent child or children may be enrolled, the insurer or plan administrator shall so inform the custodian within the time specified in this subsection. If no plan has been selected within 20 days from the date the insurer or administrator informed the agency of the option, the insurer or administrator may enroll the child or children in the insurer's or administrator's default option.

(d) If the obligor is subject to a waiting period for enrollment, the insurer or administrator shall inform the agency, the employer, the obligor, and the custodial parent. Upon the completion of the waiting period, the enrollment shall be instituted.

(e) When a court finds that a health insurer or health care plan administrator has failed to comply with this section, the employer is liable as a payor pursuant to G.S. 110-136.10(e). Additionally, a health insurer or health care plan administrator who violates this section is liable in a civil action for reasonable damages.

History.
2001-237, s. 11

§110-137. Acceptance of public assistance constitutes assignment of support rights to the State or county

By accepting public assistance for or on behalf of a dependent child or children, the recipient shall be deemed to have made an assignment to the State or to the county from which such assistance was received of the right to any child support owed for the child or children up to the amount of public assistance paid. The State or county shall be subrogated to the right of the child or children or the person having custody to initiate a support action under this Article and to recover any payments ordered by the court of this or any other state.

History.
1975, c. 827, s. 1; 1977, 2nd Sess., c. 1186, s. 13

§110-138. Duty of county to obtain support

Whenever a county department of social services receives an application for public assistance on behalf of a dependent child, and it shall appear to the satisfaction of the county department that the child has been abandoned by one or both responsible parents, or that the responsible parent(s) has failed to provide support for the child, the county department shall without delay notify the designated representative who shall take appropriate action under this Article to provide that the parent(s) responsible supports the child.

History.
1975, c. 827, s. 1; 1977, 2nd Sess., c. 1186, s. 14

§110-138.1. Duty of judicial officials to assist in obtaining support

Any party to whom child support has been ordered to be paid, and who has failed to receive the ordered support payments for two consecutive months, may make application to a magistrate for issuance of criminal process against the responsible parent for violation of G.S. 14-322. If the magistrate determines that the applicant has failed to receive the ordered support for two consecutive months, and that the responsible parent has willfully neglected or refused to make such payments, he shall make

Chapter 110

a finding of probable cause and issue criminal process for violation of G.S. 14-322. It shall be the duty of the District Attorney to prosecute such charges according to law. It shall be the duty of the Clerk of Superior Court to assist the applicant in making such application to the magistrate for the issuance of criminal process, and to supply such necessary child support records as are in his possession to the magistrate, District Attorney, and the Court.

History.
1981, c. 613, s. 4

§ 110-139. Location of absent parents

(a) The Department of Health and Human Services shall attempt to locate absent parents for the purpose of establishing paternity of and/or securing support for dependent children. The Department is to serve as a registry for the receipt of information which directly relates to the identity or location of absent parents, to assist any governmental agency or department in locating an absent parent, to answer interstate inquiries concerning deserting parents, and to develop guidelines for coordinating activities with any governmental department, board, commission, bureau or agency in providing information necessary for the location of absent parents.

(b) In order to carry out the responsibilities imposed under this Article, the Department may request from any governmental department, board, commission, bureau or agency information and assistance. All State, county and city agencies, officers and employees shall cooperate with the Department in the location of parents who have abandoned and deserted children with all pertinent information relative to the location, income and property of such parents, notwithstanding any provision of law making such information confidential. Except as otherwise stated in this subsection, all non-judicial records maintained by the Department pertaining to child-support enforcement shall be confidential, and only duly authorized representatives of social service agencies, public officials with child-support enforcement and related duties, and members of legislative committees shall have access to these records. The payment history of an obligor pursuant to a support order may be examined by or released to the court, the obligor, or the person on whose behalf enforcement actions are being taken or that person's designee. Income and expense information of either parent may be released to the other parent for the purpose of establishing or modifying a support order.

(c) Notwithstanding any other provision of law making such information confidential, an employer doing business in this State or incorporated under the laws of this State shall provide the Department with the following information upon certification by the Department that the information is needed to locate a parent for the purpose of collecting child support or to enforce an order for child support: full name, social security account number, date of birth, home address, wages, existing or available medical, hospital, and dental insurance coverage, and number of dependents listed for tax purposes.

(c1) **Employment verifications.** -- For the purpose of establishing, enforcing, or modifying a child support order, the amount of the obligor's gross income may be established by a written statement signed by the obligor's employer or the employer's designee or an Employee Verification form produced by the Automated Collections Tracking System that has been completed and signed by the obligor's employer or the employer's designee. A written statement signed by the employer of the obligor or the employer's designee that sets forth an obligor's gross income, as well as an Employee Verification form signed by the obligor's employer or the employer's designee, shall be admissible evidence in any action establishing, enforcing, or modifying a child support order.

(d) Notwithstanding any other provision of law making this information confidential, including Chapter 53B of the General Statutes, any utility company, cable television company, electronic communications or Internet service provider, or financial institution, including federal, State, commercial, or savings banks, savings and loan associations and cooperative banks, federal or State chartered credit unions, benefit associations, insurance companies, safe deposit companies, money market mutual funds, and investment companies doing business in this State or incorporated under the laws of this State, shall provide the Department of Health and Human Services with the following information upon certification by the Department that the information is needed to locate a parent for the purpose of collecting child support or to establish or enforce an order for child support: full name, social security number, address, telephone number, account numbers, and other identifying data for any person who maintains an account at the utility company, cable television company, electronic communications or Internet service provider, or financial institution. A utility company, cable television company, electronic communications or Internet service provider, or financial institution that discloses information pursuant to this subsection in good faith reliance upon certification by the Department is not liable for damages resulting from the disclosure.

(e) Repealed by Session Laws 2019-240, s. 13, effective November 6, 2019.

(f) There is established the State Child Support Collection and Disbursement Unit. The duties of the Unit shall be the collection and disbursement of payments under support orders for all cases. The Department may administer and operate the Unit or may contract with another State or private entity for the administration and operation of the Unit.

History.

1975, c. 827, s. 1; 1977, 2nd Sess., c. 1186, s. 15; 1987, c. 591; 1991, c. 419, s. 1; 1995, c. 538, s. 4; 1997-433, ss. 8.1, 9.1; 1997-443, s. 11A.118(a); 1998-17, s. 1; 1999-293, s. 22; 2000-140, s. 20(b); 2001-237, ss. 5, 6; 2003-288, s. 3.1; 2019-240, s. 13

§ 110-139.1. Access to federal parent locator service; parental kidnapping and child custody cases

(a) Except as otherwise provided in this section, the parent locator service of the Department of Health and Human Services shall transmit, upon payment of the fee prescribed by federal law, requests for information as to the whereabouts of any parent or child to the federal parental locator service when such requests are made by judges, clerks of superior court, district attorneys, or United States attorneys, and when the information is to be used to locate the parent or child for the purpose of enforcing State or federal law with respect to:

(1) The unlawful taking or restraint of a child;

(2) Making or enforcing a child custody determination, including visitation orders;

(3) Establishing paternity; or

(4) Establishing, setting or modifying the amount of, or enforcing child support obligations.

The Department shall not disclose any information from or through the parent locator service if there is reasonable evidence of domestic violence or child abuse and the disclosure of the information could be harmful to the custodial parent or the child of the custodial parent.

(b) For the purpose of this section, custody determination means a judgment, decree, or other order of the court providing for the custody or visitation of a child and includes permanent or temporary orders, and initial orders and modifications.

(c) All nonjudicial records maintained by the Department pertaining to the unlawful taking or restraint of a child or child custody determinations shall be confidential, and only individuals directly connected with the administration of the child support enforcement program and those authorized herein shall have access to these records.

History.

1983, c. 15, s. 1; 1997-433, s. 8.2; 1997-443, s. 11A.118(a); 1998-17, s. 1

§ 110-139.2. Data match system; agreements with financial institutions

(a) The Department of Health and Human Services and financial institutions doing business in this State shall enter into mutual agreements for the purpose of facilitating the enforcement of child support obligations. The agreements shall provide for the development and operation of a data match system that will enable the financial institutions to provide to the Department on a quarterly basis the information required under G.S. 110-139(d). Financial institutions shall provide the information upon certification by the Department that the person about whom the information is requested is subject to a child support order and the information is necessary to enforce the order. The Department may pay a reasonable fee to the financial institution for conducting the data match required under this section provided that the fee shall not exceed the actual costs incurred by the financial institution to conduct the match.

(b) A financial institution shall not be liable under any State law, including but not limited to Chapter 53B of the General Statutes, for disclosure of information to the State child support agency under this section, and for any other action taken by the financial institution in good faith to comply with this section or with G.S. 110-139.

(b1) The Department of Health and Human Services Child Support Enforcement Agency may notify any financial institution doing business in this State that an obligor who maintains an identified account with the financial institution has a child support obligation that may be eligible for levy on the account in an amount that satisfies some or all of the amount of unpaid support owed. In order to be able to attach a lien on and levy an obligor's account, the amount of unpaid support owed shall be an amount not less than the amount of support owed for six months or one thousand dollars ($ 1,000), whichever is less.

Upon certification of the amount of unpaid support owed in accordance with G.S. 44-86(c), the Child Support Agency shall serve or cause to be served upon the obligor, and when the matched account is owned jointly, any other nonliable owner of the account, and the financial institution a notice as provided by this subsection. The notice shall include the name of the obligor, the financial institution where the account is located, the account number of the account to be levied to satisfy the lien, the certified amount of unpaid support, information for the obligor or account owner on how to remove the lien or contest the lien in order to avoid the levy, and a reference to the applicable law, G.S. 110-139.2. The notice shall be served on the obligor, and any nonliable account owner, in any manner provided in Rule 4 of the North Carolina Rules of Civil Procedure. The financial institution shall be served notice in accordance with Rule 5 of the North Carolina Rules of Civil Procedure. Upon service of the notice, the financial institution shall proceed in the following manner:

(1) Immediately attach a lien to the identified account.

(2) Notify the Child Support Agency of the balance of the account and date of the lien or that the account does not meet the requirement for levy under this subsection.

In order for an obligor or account owner to contest the lien, within 10 days after the obligor or account owner is served with the notice, the obligor or account owner shall send written notice of the basis of the contest to the Child Support Agency and shall request a hearing before the district court in the county where the support order was entered. The obligor account holder may contest the lien only on the basis that the amount owed is an amount less than the amount of support owed for six months, or is less than one thousand dollars ($ 1,000), whichever is less, or the contesting party is not the person subject to the court order of support. The district court may assess court costs against the nonprevailing party. If no response is received from the obligor or account owner within 10 days of the service of the notice, the Child Support Agency shall notify the financial institution to submit payment, up to the total amount of the child support arrears, if available. This amount is to be applied to the debt of the obligor.

A financial institution shall not be liable to any person for complying in good faith with this subsection. The remedy set forth in this section shall be in addition to all other remedies available to the State for the reduction of the obligor's child support arrears. This remedy shall not prevent the State from taking any and all other concurrent measures available by law.

This levy procedure is to be available for direct use by all states' child support programs to financial institutions in this State without involvement of the Department.

(c) As used in this subdivision, a financial institution includes federal, State, commercial, or savings banks, savings and loan associations and cooperative banks, federal or State chartered credit unions, benefit associations, insurance companies, safe deposit companies, money

market mutual funds, and investment companies doing business in this State or incorporated under the laws of this State.

History.
1997-433, s. 9; 1997-443, s. 11A.122; 1998-17, s. 1; 2003-288, s. 4; 2004-203, s. 42; 2005-389, s. 5; 2015-62, s. 2(c); 2015-117, s. 5

§ 110-139.3. High-volume, automated administrative enforcement in interstate cases (AEI)

Upon request of another state, the Department of Health and Human Services shall use automated data processing to search State databases and determine if information is available regarding a parent who owes a child support obligation and shall seize identified assets using the same techniques as used in intrastate cases. Any request by another state to enforce support orders shall certify the amount of each obligor's debt and that appropriate due process requirements have been met by the requesting state with respect to each obligor. The Department of Health and Human Services shall likewise transmit to other states requests for assistance in enforcing support orders through high-volume, automated administrative enforcement where appropriate.

History.
1999-293, s. 7

§ 110-140. Conformity with federal requirements; restriction on options without federal funding

(a) Nothing in this Article is intended to conflict with any provision of federal law or to result in the loss of federal funds.

(b) Effective July 24, 1997, the Department of Health and Human Services shall not elect any child support distribution option for families receiving cash assistance under the State Plan for the Temporary Assistance for Needy Families (TANF) Block Grant Program for which the federal government does not provide funding to the State to exercise the option.

History.
1975, c. 827, s. 1; 1997-223, s. 1; 1997-443, s. 11A.122

§ 110-141. Effectuation of intent of Article

The North Carolina Department of Health and Human Services shall supervise the administration of the program in accordance with federal law and shall cause the provisions of this Article to be effectuated and to secure child support from absent, deserting, abandoning and nonsupporting parents.

Effective July 1, 2010, each child support enforcement program being administered by the Department of Health and Human Services on behalf of counties shall be administered, or the administration provided for, by the board of county commissioners of those counties. Until July 1, 2010, it shall be the responsibility of the Department of Health and Human Services to administer or provide for the administration of the program in those counties.

A county may negotiate alternative arrangements to the procedure outlined in G.S. 110-130 for designating a local person or agency to administer the provisions of this Article in that county.

History.
1975, c. 827, s. 1; 1977, 2nd Sess., c. 1186, s. 16; 1979, c. 488; 1983 (Reg. Sess., 1984), c. 1034, s. 76; 1985, c. 244; c. 479, s. 103; 1985 (Reg. Sess., 1986), c. 1014, s. 129; 1997-443, s. 11A.118(a); 2009-451, s. 10.46A(a)

§ 110-142. Definitions; suspension and revocation of occupational, professional, or business licenses of obligors who are delinquent in court-ordered child support, or who are not in compliance with subpoenas issued pursuant to child support or paternity establishment proceedings

The definitions in G.S. 110-129 and G.S. 147-54.12 apply to this section and G.S. 110-142.1, and G.S. 110-142.2. In addition, to these sections the following definitions apply:

(1) "Applicant" means any person applying for issuance or renewal of a license.

(2) "Board" means any department, division, agency, officer, board, or other unit of State government that issues licenses.

(3) "Certified list" means a list provided by the designated representative to the Department of Health and Human Services that verifies, under penalty of perjury, that the names contained therein are obligors who have been found to be out of compliance with a judgment or order for support in a IV-D case.

(4) "Compliance with an order for support" means that, as set forth in a judgment or order for child support or family support, the obligor is no more than 90 calendar days in arrears in making payments for current support, in making periodic payments on a support arrearage, or in making periodic payments on a reimbursement for public assistance, has obtained a judicial finding that precludes enforcement of the order, or has entered into a payment schedule, including G.S. 110-142.1(h), for the child support arrearage with the approval of the obligee in a IV-D case.

(5) "License" means (i) for the purposes of G.S. 110-142.1, a license, certificate, permit, registration, or any other authorization issued by a board that allows a person to engage in a business, occupation, or profession or (ii) for the purposes of G.S. 110-142.2, a license to operate a regular or commercial motor vehicle, or to participate in hunting, fishing, or trapping.

(6) "Licensee" means any person holding a license.

(7) "Obligor" means the individual who owes a duty to make child support payments under a court order.

History.
1995, c. 538, s. 1.4; 1997-433, s. 5; 1997-443, s. 11A.118(a); 1998-17, s. 1

§ 110-142.1. IV-D notified suspension, revocation, and issuance of occupational, professional, or business licenses of obligors who are delinquent in court-ordered child support or who are not in compliance with subpoenas issued pursuant to child support or paternity establishment proceedings

(a) Effective July 1, 1996, the Department of Health and Human Services may notify any board that a person licensed by that board is not in compliance with an order for child support or has been found by the court not to be in compliance with a subpoena issued pursuant to child support or paternity establishment proceedings.

(b) The designated representative shall submit a certified list with the names, social security numbers, and last known address of individuals who are not in compliance with a child support order or with a subpoena issued pursuant to a child support or paternity establishment proceeding. The designated representative shall verify, under penalty of perjury, that the individuals listed are subject to an order for the payment of support and are not in compliance with the order, or have been found by the court to be not in compliance with a subpoena issued pursuant to a child support or paternity establishment proceeding. The verification shall include the name, address, and telephone number of the designated representative who certified the list. An updated certified list shall be submitted to the Department on a monthly basis.

The Department of Health and Human Services, Division of Social Services, Child Support Enforcement Office, shall consolidate the certified lists received from the designated representatives and, within 30 calendar days of receipt, shall furnish each board with a certified list of the individuals, as specified in this section.

(c) Each board shall coordinate with the Department of Health and Human Services, Division of Social Services, Child Support Enforcement Office, in the development of forms and procedures to implement this section.

(d) Promptly after receiving the certified list of individuals from the Department of Health and Human Services, each board shall determine whether its applicant or licensee is an individual on the list. If the applicant or licensee is on the list, the board shall immediately send notice as specified in this subsection to the applicant or licensee of the board's intent to revoke or suspend the licensee's license in 20 days from the date of the notice, or that the board is withholding issuance or renewal of an applicant's license, until the designated representative certifies that the applicant or licensee is entitled to be licensed or reinstated. The notice shall be made personally or by certified mail to the individual's last known mailing address on file with the board.

(e) Unless notified by the designated representative as provided in subsection (h) of this section, the board shall revoke or suspend the individual's license 20 days from the date of the notice to the individual of the board's intent to revoke or suspend the license. In the event that a license is revoked or application is denied pursuant to this section, the board is not required to refund fees paid by the individual.

(f) Notices shall be developed by each board in accordance with guidelines provided by the Department of Health and Human Services and shall be subject to the approval of the Department of Health and Human Services. The notice shall include the address and telephone number of the designated representative who submitted the name on the certified list, and shall emphasize the necessity of obtaining a certification of compliance from the designated representative or the child support enforcement agency as a condition of issuance, renewal, or reinstatement of the license. The notice shall inform the individual that if a license is revoked or application is denied pursuant to this subsection, the board is not required to refund fees paid by the individual. The Department of Health and Human Services shall also develop a form that the individual shall use to request a review by the designated representative. A copy of this form shall be included with every notice sent pursuant to subsection (d) of this section.

(g) The Department of Health and Human Services shall establish review procedures consistent with this section to allow an individual to have the underlying arrearage and any relevant defenses investigated, to provide an individual information on the process of obtaining a modification of a support order, or, if the circumstances so warrant, to provide an individual assistance in the establishment of a payment schedule on arrears.

(h) If the individual wishes to challenge the submission of the individual's name on the certified list, or if the individual wishes to negotiate a payment schedule, the individual shall within 14 days of the date of notice from the board request a review from the designated representative. The designated representative shall within six days of the date of the request for review notify the appropriate board of the request for review and direct the board to stay any action revoking or suspending the individual's license until further notice from the designated representative. The designated representative shall review the case and inform the individual in writing of the representative's findings and decision upon completion of the review. If the findings so warrant, the designated representative shall immediately send a notice to the appropriate board certifying the individual's compliance with this section. The agreement shall also provide for the maintenance of current support obligations and shall be incorporated into a consent order to be entered by the court. If the individual fails to meet the conditions of this subsection, the designated representative shall notify the appropriate board to immediately revoke or suspend the individual's license. Upon receipt of notice from the designated representative, the board shall immediately revoke or suspend the individual's license.

(i) The designated representative shall notify the individual in writing that the individual may, by filing a motion, request any or all of the following:

(1) Judicial review of the designated representative's decision.

(2) A judicial determination of compliance.

(3) A modification of the support order.

The notice shall also contain the name and address of the court in which the individual shall file the motion and inform the individual that the individual's name shall remain on the certified list unless the judicial review results in a finding by the court that the individual is in compliance with this section. The notice shall also inform the individual that the individual must comply with all statutes and rules of court regarding motions and notices of hearing and that any motion filed under this section is subject to the limitations of G.S. 50-13.10.

(j) The motion for judicial review of the designated representative's decision shall state the grounds for which review is requested and judicial review shall be limited to those stated grounds. After service of the request for review, the court shall hold an evidentiary hearing at the next regularly scheduled session for the hearing of child support matters in civil district court. The request for judicial review shall be served by the individual upon the designated representative who submitted the individual's name on the certified list within seven calendar days of the filing of the motion.

(k) If the judicial review results in a finding by the court that the individual is no longer in arrears or that the individual's license should be reinstated to allow the individual an opportunity to comply with a payment schedule on arrears or reimbursement and current support obligations, the designated representative shall immediately send a notice to the appropriate board certifying the individual's compliance with this section. If the judicial review results in a finding that the individual has complied with or is no longer subject to the subpoena that was the basis for the revocation, then the designated representative shall immediately send a notice to the appropriate board certifying the individual's compliance with this section. In the event of an appeal from judicial review, the license revocation shall not be stayed unless the court specifically provides otherwise.

(l) The Department of Health and Human Services shall prescribe forms for use by the designated representative. When the individual is no longer in arrears or negotiates an agreement with the designated representative for a payment schedule on arrears or reimbursement, the designated representative shall mail to the individual and the appropriate board a notice certifying that the individual is in compliance. The receipt of certification shall serve to notify the individual and the board that, for the purposes of this section, the individual is in compliance with the order for support. When the individual has complied with or is no longer subject to a subpoena issued pursuant to a child support or paternity establishment proceeding, the designated representative shall mail to the individual and the appropriate board a notice certifying that the individual is in compliance. The receipt of certification shall serve to notify the individual and the board that the individual is in compliance with this section.

(m) The Department of Health and Human Services may enter into interagency agreements with the boards necessary to implement this section.

(n) The procedures specified in Articles 3 and 3A of Chapter 150B of the General Statutes, the Administrative Procedure Act, shall not apply to the denial or failure to issue or renew a license pursuant to this section.

(o) Any board receiving an inquiry as to the licensed status of an applicant or licensee who has had a license denied or revoked under this section shall respond only that the license was denied or revoked pursuant to this section. Information collected pursuant to this section shall be confidential and shall not be disclosed except in accordance with the laws of this State.

(p) If any provision of this section or its application to any person or circumstance is held invalid, that invalidity shall not affect other provisions or applications of this section that can be given effect without the invalid provision or application, and to this end the provisions of this section are severable.

History.
1995, c. 538, s. 1.4; 1997-433, s. 5.1; 1997-443, ss. 11A.118(a), 122; 1998-17, s. 1; 2007-484, ss. 12(a), (b)

§ 110-142.2. Suspension, revocation, restriction of license to operate a motor vehicle or hunting, fishing, or trapping licenses; refusal of registration of motor vehicle

(a) Effective December 1, 1996, notwithstanding any other provision of law, when an individual is at least 90 days in arrears in making child support payments, or has been found by the court to be not in compliance with a subpoena issued pursuant to child support or paternity establishment proceedings, the child support enforcement agency may apply to the court, pursuant to the regular show cause and contempt provisions of G.S. 50-13.9(d), for an order doing any of the following:

(1) Revoking the individual's regular or commercial license to operate a motor vehicle;

(2) Revoking the individual's hunting, fishing, or trapping licenses;

(3) Directing the Department of Transportation, Division of Motor Vehicles, to refuse, pursuant to G.S. 20-50.4, to register the individual's motor vehicle.

(b) Upon finding that the individual has willfully failed to comply with the child support order or with a subpoena issued pursuant to child support proceedings, and that the obligor is at least 90 days in arrears, or upon a finding that an individual subject to a subpoena issued pursuant to child support or paternity establishment proceedings has failed to comply with the subpoena, the court may enter an order instituting the sanctions as provided in subsection (a) of this section. If an individual is adjudicated to be in civil or criminal contempt for a third or subsequent time for failure to comply with a child support order, the court shall enter an order instituting any one or more of the sanctions, if applicable, as provided in subsection (a) of this section. The court may stay the effectiveness of the sanctions upon conditions requiring the obligor to make full payment of the delinquency over time. Any court-ordered payment plan under this subsection shall require the individual to extinguish the delinquency within a reasonable period of time. In determining the amount to be applied to the delinquency, the court shall consider the amount of the debt and the individual's financial ability to pay. The payment shall not exceed the limits under G.S. 110-136.6(b). The individual shall make an immediate initial payment representing at least five percent (5%) of the total delinquency or five hundred dollars ($ 500.00), whichever is less. Any stay of an order under this subsection shall also be conditioned upon the obligor's maintenance of current child support. The court may stay the effectiveness of the sanctions against an individual subject to a subpoena issued pursuant to child support or paternity establishment proceedings upon a finding that the individual has complied with or is no longer subject to the subpoena. Upon entry of an order pursuant to this section that is not stayed, the individual shall surrender any licenses revoked by the court's order to the child support enforcement agency and the agency shall forward a report to the appropriate licensing authority within 30 days of the order.

(c) If the individual's regular or commercial drivers license is revoked under this section and the court, after the hearing, makes a finding that a license to operate a motor vehicle is necessary to the individual's livelihood, the court may issue a limited driving privilege, with those terms and conditions applying as the court shall prescribe. An individual whose license has been revoked for reasons not related to this section and whose license remains revoked at the time of the hearing shall not be eligible and may not be issued a limited driving privilege. The court may modify or revoke the limited driving privilege pursuant to G.S. 20-179.3(i).

(d) An individual may file a request with the child support enforcement agency for certification that the individual is no longer delinquent in child support payments upon submission of proof satisfactory to the child support enforcement agency that the individual has paid the delinquent amount in full. An individual subject to a subpoena issued pursuant to a child support or paternity establishment proceeding may file a request with the child support enforcement agency for certification that the individual has complied with or is no longer subject to the subpoena. The child support enforcement agency shall provide a form to be used by the individual for a request for certification. If the child support enforcement agency finds that the individual has met the requirements for reinstatement under this subsection, then the child support enforcement agency shall certify that the individual is no longer delinquent or that the individual has complied with or is no longer subject to a subpoena issued pursuant to child support or paternity establishment proceedings

and shall provide a copy of the certification to the individual.

(e) If licensing privileges are revoked under this section, the individual may petition the district court for a reinstatement of such privileges. The court may order the privileges reinstated conditioned upon full payment of the delinquency over time, or. as applicable, may order the reinstatement if the court finds that the individual has complied with or is no longer subject to the subpoena issued pursuant to paternity establishment proceedings. Any order allowing license reinstatement shall additionally require the obligor's maintenance of current child support. Upon reinstatement under this subsection, the child support enforcement agency shall certify that the individual is no longer delinquent, or, as applicable, that the individual has complied with or is no longer subject to the subpoena issued pursuant to child support or paternity establishment proceedings and shall provide a copy of the certification to the individual, as applicable.

(f) Upon receipt of certification under subsection (d) or (e) of this section, the Division of Motor Vehicles shall reinstate the license to operate a motor vehicle in accordance with G.S. 20-24.1, and remove any restriction of the individual's motor vehicle registration.

(g) Upon receipt of certification under subsection (d) or (e) of this section, the licensing board having jurisdiction over the individual's hunting, fishing, or trapping license shall reinstate the license.

(h) If the court imposes sanctions under subdivision (3) of subsection (a) of this section and the sanctions are stayed upon conditions as provided in subsection (b) of this section, the child support enforcement agency may, without any further application to the court, notify the Division of Motor Vehicles if the individual violates the terms and conditions of the stay. The Division shall then take such action as provided in subdivision (3) of subsection (a) of this section. The Division shall not remove any restriction of the individual's motor vehicle registration, until receipt of certification pursuant to subsection (d) or (e) of this section.

(i) The Department of Health and Human Services, the Administrative Office of the Courts, the Division of Motor Vehicles, and the Department of Environmental Quality shall work together to develop the forms and procedures necessary for the implementation of this process.

History.
1995, c. 538, s. 1.4; 1997-433, s. 5.2; 1997-443, ss. 11A.118(a), 11A.119(a); 1998-17, s. 1; 1999-293, s. 2; 2015-241, s. 14.30(u)

CHAPTER 113
CONSERVATION AND DEVELOPMENT

SUBCHAPTER 01.
GENERAL PROVISIONS

ARTICLE 1A
SPECIAL PEACE OFFICERS

§ 113-28.2. Powers of arrest

Any employee of either the Department of Natural and Cultural Resources or the Department of Environmental Quality commissioned as a special peace officer shall have the right to arrest with warrant any person violating any law or rule on or relating to the State parks, lakes, reservations and other lands or waters under the control or supervision of the employee's respective Department, and shall have the power to pursue and arrest without warrant any person violating in his presence any law or rule on or relating to said parks, lakes, reservations and other lands or waters under the control or supervision of the employee's respective Department.

History.
1947, c. 577; 1973, c. 1262, s. 86; 1977, c. 771, s. 4; 1989, c. 727, s. 47; 1997-443, s. 11A.119(a); 2015-241, s. 14.30(pp)

§ 113-28.2A. Cooperation between law enforcement agencies

Special peace officers employed by either the Department of Natural and Cultural Resources or the Department of Environmental Quality are officers of a "law enforcement agency" for purposes of G.S. 160A-288, and each Department shall have the same authority as a city or county governing body to approve cooperation between law enforcement agencies under that section.

History.
2002-111, s. 1; 2015-241, s. 14.30(qq)

SUBCHAPTER 02.
STATE PARKS

ARTICLE 4
PROTECTION AND DEVELOPMENT OF FORESTS; FIRE CONTROL

§§ 113-51 through 113-60.3

Recodified as Article 75 of Chapter 106, G.S. 106-895 through G.S. 106-910, by Session Laws 2011-145, s. 13.25(p), effective July 1, 2011.

ARTICLE 4C
REGULATION OF OPEN FIRES

§§ 113-60.21 through 113-60.31

Recodified as Article 78 of Chapter 106, G.S. 106-940 through G.S. 106-950, by Session Laws 2011-145, s. 13.25(w), effective July 1, 2011.

SUBCHAPTER 04.
CONSERVATION OF MARINE AND ESTUARINE AND WILDLIFE RESOURCES

ARTICLE 13
JURISDICTION OF CONSERVATION AGENCIES

§ 113-138. Enforcement jurisdiction of special conservation officers

(a) The Wildlife Resources Commission by rule may confer law-enforcement powers over matters within its jurisdiction with respect to wildlife resources conservation laws and rules within its jurisdiction upon the employees of the United States Fish and Wildlife Service, and the Marine Fisheries Commission may confer law-enforcement powers over matters within its jurisdiction with respect to marine and estuarine resources conservation laws and rules upon the employees of the National Marine Fisheries Service, who:

(1) Possess special law-enforcement jurisdiction that would not otherwise extend to the subject matter of this Subchapter;

(2) Are assigned during the duration of such appointment to duty stations within North Carolina; and

(3) Take the oath required of public officers before an officer authorized to administer oaths.

These conferred powers do not constitute an appointment of any officer to an additional office.

(b) The Marine Fisheries Commission and Wildlife Resources Commission shall limit the exercise of this authority to situations when:

(1) The best interests of the conservation of marine and estuarine and wildlife resources managed by the respective State

Chapter 113

and federal agencies are being adversely affected by restrictions upon jurisdictional subject matter that limit law-enforcement authority; and

(2) The best interests of the conservation of marine and estuarine and wildlife resources managed by the adopting Commission will benefit by conferring law-enforcement authority on the employees of the United States Fish and Wildlife Service or the National Marine Fisheries Service.

(c) The enabling rule shall specify the particular officers or class of officers upon whom the law-enforcement powers are conferred and the geographic areas within which the special enforcement officers can exercise the law-enforcement powers over matters within the jurisdiction of the adopting Commission. The conferred powers may be used only during the scope of employment of the special conservation officers.

(d) Unless otherwise provided by the enabling rule, such special enforcement officers shall have the same jurisdiction and powers with respect to resource conservation and the same rights, privileges and immunities (including those relating to the defense of civil actions and payment of judgments) as the State officers in addition to those the federal officer normally possesses.

History.
1965, c. 957, s. 2; 1973, c. 1262, ss. 18, 28; 1977, c. 771, s. 4; 1983, c. 484; 1987, c. 827, s. 98; 1991 (Reg. Sess., 1992), c. 890, s. 5

CHAPTER 114
DEPARTMENT OF JUSTICE

ARTICLE 1
ATTORNEY GENERAL

§ 114-8.6. Designation of State Crime Laboratory as Internet Crimes Against Children affiliated agency

The Attorney General shall designate the North Carolina State Crime Laboratory as a North Carolina Internet Crimes Against Children (ICAC) affiliated agency.

History.
2013-360, s. 17.6(p)

§ 114-8.7. Reports of animal cruelty and animal welfare violations

(a) The Attorney General shall establish a hotline to receive reports of allegations of animal cruelty or violations of the Animal Welfare Act, Article 3 of Chapter 19A of the General Statutes, against animals under private ownership, by means including telephone, electronic mail, and Internet Web site. The Attorney General shall periodically publicize the hotline telephone number, electronic mail address, Internet Web site address, and any other means by which the Attorney General may receive reports of allegations of animal cruelty or violations of the Animal Welfare Act. Any individual who makes a report under this section shall disclose his or her name and telephone number and any other information the Attorney General may require.

(b) When the Attorney General receives allegations involving activity that the Attorney General determines may involve cruelty to animals under private ownership in violation of Article 47 of Chapter 14 of the General Statutes, the allegations shall be referred to the appropriate local animal control authority for the unit or units of local government within which the violations are alleged to have occurred. When the Attorney General receives allegations involving activity that the Attorney General determines may involve violations of the Animal Welfare Act, the allegations shall be referred to the Department of Agriculture and Consumer Services. The Attorney General shall record the total number of reports received on the hotline and the number of reports received against any individual on the hotline.

(c) Notwithstanding other provisions of law, the Department of Justice is authorized to spend any federal, State, local, or private funds available for this purpose to administer the provisions of this section.

(d) Notwithstanding G.S. 147-33.72C and related provisions of law, in order to expedite the timely implementation of technology systems to record and manage public allegations and complaints received pursuant to this section, the Department of Justice is exempted from external agency project approval standards.

History.
2015-286, s. 4.36(a)

ARTICLE 3
DIVISION OF CRIMINAL INFORMATION

§§ 114-10 through 114-10.1

Recodified as G.S. 143B-902 through 143B-905 by Session Laws 2014-100, s. 17.1(h), effective July 1, 2014.

ARTICLE 3A
SPECIAL PROSECUTION DIVISION

§ 114-11.6. Division established; duties

There is hereby established in the office of the Attorney General of North Carolina, a Special Prosecution Division. The attorneys assigned to this Division shall be available to prosecute or assist in the prosecution of criminal cases when requested to do so by a district attorney and the Attorney General approves. In addition, these attorneys assigned to this Division shall serve as legal advisers to the State Bureau of Investigation and the Police Information Network and perform any other duties assigned to them by the Attorney General.

History.
1973, c. 47, s. 2; c. 813

ARTICLE 4
STATE BUREAU OF INVESTIGATION

PART 1
GENERAL POWERS AND DUTIES OF THE STATE BUREAU OF INVESTIGATION

N.C. Gen. Stat. § 114-12

Recodified as G.S. 143B-915 by Session Laws 2014-100, s. 17.1(j), effective July 1, 2014.

§ 114-12.1. Minority sensitivity training for law enforcement personnel

(a) The Department of Justice shall develop guidelines for minority sensitivity training for all law enforcement personnel throughout the State. The Department shall ensure that all persons who work with minority juveniles in the juvenile justice system are taught how to communicate effectively with minority juveniles and how to recognize and address the needs of those juveniles. The Department shall also advise all law enforcement and professionals who work within the juvenile justice system of ways to improve the treatment of minority juveniles so that all juveniles receive equal treatment. Except where local law enforcement has existing minority sensitivity training that meets the Department guidelines, the Department shall conduct the minority sensitivity training annually. Prior to the training each year, the Department shall assess whether minorities are receiving fair and equal treatment in the juvenile justice system with regard to the administration of predisposition procedures, of diversion methods, of dispositional alternatives, and of treatment and post-release supervision plans.

(b) The Juvenile Justice Section of the Division of Adult Correction and Juvenile Justice of the Department of Public Safety shall ensure that all juvenile court counselors and other Division personnel receive the minority sensitivity training specified in subsection (a) of this section.

History.

1998-202, s. 17; 2000-137, s. 4(i); 2003-214, s. 1; 2011-145, s. 19.1 (*l*); 2017-186, s. 2 (wwww)

N.C. Gen. Stat. § 114-13

Repealed by Session Laws 2014-100, s. 17.1(f), effective July 1, 2014.

History.

1937, c. 349, s. 4; 1939, c. 315, s. 6; 1955, c. 1185, s. 1; 1957, c. 269, s. 1; 1979, 2nd Sess., c. 1272, s. 3; 2003-214, s. 1(1); 2011-145, s. 19.1(q1); 2011-391, s. 43(g); repealed by Session Laws 2014-100, s. 17.1(f), effective July 1, 2014

N.C. Gen. Stat. § 114-14

Recodified as G.S. 143B-917 by Session Laws 2014-100, s. 17.1(j), effective July 1, 2014.

N.C. Gen. Stat. § 114-14.1

Recodified as G.S. 143B-918 by Session Laws 2014-100, s. 17.1(j), effective July 1, 2014.

§§ 114-15 through 114-15.3

Recodified as G.S. 143B-919 through 143B-922 by Session Laws 2014-100, s. 17.1(j), effective July 1, 2014.

§§ 114-16 through 114-16.2

Recodified as Article 9 of Chapter 114, G.S. 114-60 through 114-62, by Session Laws 2013-360, s. 17.6(d), effective July 1, 2013.

N.C. Gen. Stat. § 114-17

Recodified as G.S. 143B-923 by Session Laws 2014-100, s. 17.1(j), effective July 1, 2014.

N.C. Gen. Stat. § 114-17.1

Repealed by Session Laws 1995, c. 507, s. 6 .

N.C. Gen. Stat. § 114-18

Recodified as G.S. 143B-924 by Session Laws 2014-100, s. 17.1(j), effective July 1, 2014.

N.C. Gen. Stat. § 114-18.1

Repealed by Session Laws 2000-119, s. 6, effective December 1, 2000.

N.C. Gen. Stat. § 114-19

Recodified as G.S. 143B-906 by Session Laws 2014-100, s. 17.1(k), effective July 1, 2014.

PART 2
CRIMINAL HISTORY RECORD CHECKS

N.C. Gen. Stat. § 114-19.01

This section has more than one version with varying effective dates. To view a complete list of the versions of this section see Table of Contents.

Recodified as G.S. 143B-925 by Session Laws 2014-100, s. 17.1 (*l*), effective July 1, 2014.

§§ 114-19.2 through 114-19.34

Recodified as G.S. 143B-931 through 143B-965 by Session Laws 2014-100, s. 17.1(m), effective July 1, 2014.

§§ 114-19.35 through 114-19.49

Recodified as G.S. 143B-966 through 143B-980 by Session Laws 2014-100, s. 17.1(m), effective July 1, 2014.

N.C. Gen. Stat. § 114-19.50

Recodified as G.S. 143B-981 by Session Laws 2014-100, s. 17.1(m), effective July 1, 2014.

PART 3
PROTECTION OF PUBLIC OFFICIALS

§§ 114-20, 114-20.1

Recodified as Subpart E of Part 4 of Article 13 of Chapter 143B, G.S. 143B-986 and G.S. 143B-987, by Session Laws 2014-100, s. 17.1(n), effective July 1, 2014.

N.C. Gen. Stat. § 114-21

Recodified as G.S. 114-12.1 by Session Laws 2003-214, s. 1(4), effective June 19, 2003.

ARTICLE 6
OFFICE OF THE INSPECTOR GENERAL

§§ 114-40 through 114-42

Repealed by Session Laws 2001-424, s. 23.10, effective January 1, 2002.

ARTICLE 7
METHAMPHETAMINE WATCH PROGRAM

§§ 114-44 through 114-49

Reserved for future codification purposes.

ARTICLE 9
NORTH CAROLINA STATE CRIME LABORATORY

§ 114-60. Laboratory and clinical facilities; employment of criminologists; services of scientists, etc., employed by State; radio system

In the Department of Justice there shall be provided laboratory facilities for the analysis of evidences of crime, including the determination of presence, quantity and character of poisons, the character of bloodstains, microscopic and other examination material associated with the commission of crime, examination and analysis of projectiles of ballistic imprints and records which might lead to the determination or identification of criminals, the examination and identification of fingerprints, and other evidence leading to the identification, apprehension, or conviction of criminals. A sufficient number of persons skilled in such matters shall be employed to render a reasonable service to the public through the criminal justice system and to the criminal justice system in the discharge of their duties.

The laboratory and clinical facilities of the institutions of the State, both educational and departmental, shall be made available to the Laboratory, and scientists and doctors now working for the State through its institutions and departments may be called upon by the Governor to aid the Laboratory in the evaluation, preparation, and preservation of evidence in which scientific methods are employed, and a reasonable fee may be allowed by the Governor for such service.

History.
1937, c. 349, s. 7; 2003-214, s. 1(1); 2011-19, s. 10; 2013-360, s. 17.6(d), (m).

§ 114-61. Forensic Science Advisory Board

(a) **Creation and Membership.** -- The North Carolina Forensic Science Advisory Board (Board) is hereby established as an advisory board within the Department of Justice. The Board shall consist of 15 members, consisting of the State Crime Laboratory Director, and 14 members appointed by the Attorney General as follows:

(1) A forensic scientist or any other person with an advanced degree who has received substantial education, training, or experience in the subject of laboratory standards or quality assurance regulation and monitoring.

(2) The Chief Medical Examiner of the State.

(3) A forensic scientist with an advanced degree who has education, training, or experience in the discipline of molecular biology.

(4) A forensic scientist with an advanced degree who has experience in the discipline of population genetics.

(5) A scientist with an advanced degree who has experience in the discipline of forensic chemistry.

(6) A scientist with an advanced degree who has experience in the discipline of forensic biology.

(7) A forensic scientist or any other person with an advanced degree who has education, training, or experience in the discipline of trace evidence.

(8) A scientist with an advanced degree who has experience in the discipline of forensic toxicology.

(9) A member of the International Association for Identification.

(10) A member of the Association of Firearms and Tool Mark Examiners.

(11) A member of the International Association for Chemical Testing.

(12) Repealed by Session Laws 2014-115, s. 46, effective August 11, 2014.

(13) A member of the American Society of Crime Laboratory Directors.

(14) A member of the Academy of Forensic Sciences.

(15) A member of the American Statistical Association.

A chairman shall be elected from among the members appointed, and staff shall be provided by the Department of Justice.

(b) **Meetings.** -- The Board shall meet biannually and at such other times and places as it determines. Members of the Board cannot designate a proxy to vote in their absence.

(c) **Terms.** -- Members of the Board initially appointed shall serve the following terms: five members shall serve a term of two years; five members shall serve a term of three years; and five members shall serve a term of four years. Thereafter, all appointments shall be for a term of four years. A vacancy other than by expiration of term shall be filled by the Attorney General for the unexpired term. Members of the Board cannot designate a proxy to vote in their absence.

(d) **Expenses.** -- Members of the Board shall be paid reasonable and necessary expenses incurred in the performance of their duties. Members of the Board who are State officers or employees shall receive no compensation for serving on the Board but may be reimbursed for their expenses in accordance with G.S. 138-6. Members of the Board who are full-time salaried public officers or employees other than State officers or employees shall receive no compensation for serving on the Board but may be reimbursed for their expenses in accordance with G.S. 138-5(b). All other members of the Board may receive compensation and reimbursement for expenses in accordance with G.S. 138-5.

(e) **Functions.** -- The Board may review State Crime Laboratory operations and make recommendations concerning the services furnished to user agencies. The Board shall review and make recommendations as necessary to the Laboratory Director concerning any of the following:

(1) New scientific programs, protocols, and methods of testing.

(2) Plans for the implementation of new programs; sustaining existing programs and improving upon them where possible; and the elimination of programs which are no longer needed.

(3) Protocols for testing and examination methods and guidelines for the presentation of results in court.

(4) Qualification standards for the various forensic scientists of the Laboratory.

(f) **Review Process.** -- Upon request of the Laboratory Director, the Board shall review analytical work, reports, and conclusions of scientists employed by the Laboratory. Records reviewed by this Board retain their confidential status and continue to be considered records of a criminal investigation as defined in G.S. 132-1.4. These records shall be reviewed only in a closed session meeting pursuant to G.S. 143-318.11 of the Board, and each member of the Board shall, prior to receiving any documents to review, sign a confidentiality agreement agreeing to maintain the confidentiality of and not to disclose the documents nor the contents of the documents reviewed. The Board shall recommend to the Laboratory a review process to use when there is a request that the Laboratory retest or reexamine evidence that has been previously examined by the Laboratory.

History.
2011-19, s. 2; 2013-360, s. 17.6(d); 2014-115, s. 46

§ 114-62. North Carolina State Crime Laboratory Ombudsman

The position of ombudsman is created in the North Carolina State Crime Laboratory within the North Carolina Department of Justice. The primary purpose of this position shall be to work with defense counsel, prosecutorial agencies, criminal justice system stakeholders, law enforcement officials, and the general public to ensure all processes, procedures, practices, and protocols at the State Crime Laboratory are consistent with State and federal law, best forensic law practices, and in the best interests of justice in this State. The ombudsman shall mediate complaints brought to the attention of the ombudsman between the Crime Laboratory and defense counsel, prosecutorial agencies, law enforcement agencies, and the general public. The ombudsman shall ensure all criminal justice stakeholders and the general public are aware of the availability, responsibilities, and role of the ombudsman and shall regularly attend meetings of the Conferences of the District Attorneys, District and Superior Court Judges, Public Defenders, the Advocates for Justice, and Bar Criminal Law Sections. The ombudsman shall make recommendations on a regular basis to the Director of the State Crime Laboratory and the Attorney General of North Carolina as to policies, procedures, practices, and training of employees needed at the Laboratory to ensure compliance with State and federal law, best forensic law practices, and to resolve any meritorious systemic complaints received by the ombudsman.

History.
2011-19, s. 6(a); 2013-360, s. 17.6(d), (n)

§ 114-63. Transfer of personnel

The Director of the North Carolina State Crime Laboratory shall have authority to transfer employees of the Crime Laboratory from one Crime Laboratory location in the State to another, or between Sections of the Laboratory, as the Director may deem necessary. When any member of the Crime Laboratory is transferred from one location to another for the convenience of the Crime Laboratory, or otherwise than

upon the request of the employee, the Crime Laboratory shall be responsible for transporting the household goods, furniture, and personal effects of the employee and members of his or her household.

History.
2013-360, s. 17.6(q); 2014-100, s. 17.7(b)

§ 114-64. SBI and State Crime Laboratory access to view and analyze recordings

Any State or local law enforcement agency that uses the services of the State Bureau of Investigation or the North Carolina State Crime Laboratory to analyze a recording covered by G.S. 132-1.4A shall, at no cost, provide access to a method to view and analyze the recording upon request of the State Bureau of Investigation or the North Carolina State Crime Laboratory.

History.
2016-88, s. 2(c)

CHAPTER 115C
ELEMENTARY AND SECONDARY EDUCATION

SUBCHAPTER 02.
ADMINISTRATIVE ORGANIZATION OF STATE AND LOCAL EDUCATION AGENCIES

ARTICLE 5
LOCAL BOARDS OF EDUCATION

§ 115C-46.2. Probation officer visits at school; limitations

(a) Except as provided in this section, probation officers are not authorized to visit students during school hours on school property.

(b) Probation officers of the Section of Community Corrections of the Division of Adult Correction and Juvenile Justice, when working as a part of the Section's School Partnership Program, may visit students during school hours on school property with prior authorization by school administrators. For purposes of this section, "authorization" includes requests for assistance from guidance counselors or school resource officers.

(c) Each local board of education shall develop policies and guidelines for coordinating with probation officers of the Section of Community Corrections of the Division of Adult Correction and Juvenile Justice in the planning and scheduling of school visits as provided in this section, utilizing existing administrative capacity to manage scheduling. Visits shall be conducted in a private area designated for such use and located away from contact with the general student population. The probation officer shall not initiate direct contact with a student while the student is in class or between classes. Initial contact with the student shall be made by a school administrator or other designated school employee, who shall direct the student to a private area to meet with the probation officer.

History.
2011-145, s. 19.1(k); 2012-149, s. 6; 2017-186, s. 2 (xxxx)

SUBCHAPTER 04.
EDUCATION PROGRAM

ARTICLE 8C
LOCAL PLANS FOR ALTERNATIVE SCHOOLS/ ALTERNATIVE LEARNING PROGRAMS AND MAINTAINING SAFE AND ORDERLY SCHOOLS

§ 115C-105.49. School safety exercises

(a) At least once annually, each local school administrative unit shall require each school under its control to hold a full school-wide tabletop exercise and drill based on the procedures documented in its School Risk Management Plan (SRMP). The drill shall include a practice school lockdown due to an intruder on school grounds. Each school is encouraged to hold a tabletop exercise and drill for multiple hazards included in its SRMP. Schools are strongly encouraged to include local law enforcement agencies and emergency management agencies in their tabletop exercises and drills. The purpose of the tabletop exercises and drills shall be to permit participants to (i) discuss simulated emergency situations in a low-stress environment, (ii) clarify their roles and responsibilities and the overall logistics of dealing with an emergency, and (iii) identify areas in which the SRMP needs to be modified.

(b) For the purposes of this section, a tabletop exercise is an exercise involving key personnel conducting simulated scenarios related to emergency planning.

(c) For the purposes of this section, a drill is a school-wide practice exercise in which simulated scenarios related to emergency planning are conducted.

(d) The Department of Public Safety, Division of Emergency Management, and the Center for Safer Schools shall provide guidance and recommendations to local school administrative units on the types of multiple hazards to plan and respond to, including intruders on school grounds.

History.
2013-360, s. 8.38; 2015-241, s. 8.26(b)

§ 115C-105.49A. School Risk and Response Management System

(a) The Department of Public Safety, Division of Emergency Management, and the Center for Safer Schools shall construct and maintain a statewide School Risk and Response Management System (SRRMS). The system shall fully integrate and leverage existing data and applications that support school risk planning, exercises, monitoring, and emergency response via 911 dispatch.

(b) In constructing the SRRMS, the Division of Emergency Management and the Center for Safer Schools, in collaboration with the Department of Public Instruction, Division of School Operations, shall leverage the existing enterprise risk management database, the School Risk Management Planning tool managed by the Division of Emergency Management. The Division of Emergency Management shall also leverage the local school administrative unit schematic diagrams of school facilities. Where technically feasible, the SRRMS shall integrate any anonymous tip lines established pursuant to G.S. 115C-105.51 and any 911-initiated panic alarm systems authorized as part of a SRMP pursuant to G.S. 115C-47(40). The Division of Emergency Management and the Center for Safer Schools shall collaborate with the Department of Public Instruction, Division of School Operations, and the North Carolina 911 Board in the design, implementation, and maintenance of the SRRMS.

(c) All data and information acquired and stored in the SRRMS as provided in subsections (a) and (b) of this section are not considered public records as the term "public record" is defined under G.S. 132-1 and shall not be subject to inspection and examination under G.S. 132-6.

History.
2015-241, s. 8.26(c); 2018-97, s. 2.4(b)

§ 115C-105.51. Anonymous tip lines and monitoring and response applications

(a) The governing body of each public secondary school shall develop and operate an anonymous tip line, in coordination with local law enforcement and social services agencies, to receive anonymous information on internal or external risks to the school population, school buildings, and school-related activities. The Department of Public Instruction, in consultation with the Department of Public Safety, may develop standards and guidelines for the development, operation, and staffing of tip lines. The governing body of each public secondary school may use the anonymous safety tip line application developed pursuant to subsection (b) of this section, or another application that meets standards and guidelines developed by the Department of Public Instruction, to achieve the purposes of this subsection.

(b) The Department of Public Instruction and the Center for Safer Schools, in collaboration with the Department of Public Safety, Division of Emergency Management, shall implement and maintain an anonymous safety tip line application available statewide for purposes of receiving anonymous student information on internal or external risks to the school population, school buildings, and school-related activities. Public secondary schools shall inform students about the application and provide opportunities for students to learn about its purpose and function. The governing body of each public secondary school shall work with the Department of Public Instruction, Division of School Operations, and the Center for Safer Schools to ensure that employees of the public secondary schools receive adequate training in its operation.

(c) The Department of Public Safety, Division of Emergency Management, and the North Carolina 911 Board, in collaboration with the Department of Public Instruction, Division of School Operations, and the Center for Safer Schools, shall implement and maintain a statewide panic alarm system for the purposes of launching real-time 911 messaging to public safety answering points of internal and external risks to the school population, school buildings, and school-related activities. The Department of Public Safety, in consultation with the Department of Public Instruction and the North Carolina 911 Board, may develop standards and guidelines for the operations and use of the panic alarm tool.

(d) The Department of Public Instruction and the Department of Public Safety shall ensure that the anonymous safety tip line application is integrated with and supports the statewide School Risk and Response Management System (SRRMS) as provided in G.S. 115C-105.49A. Where technically feasible and cost efficient, the Department of Public Instruction and the Department of Public Safety are encouraged to implement a single solution supporting both the anonymous safety tip line application and panic alarm system.

(e) All data and information acquired and stored by the anonymous safety tip line application are not considered public records as the term "public record" is defined under G.S. 132-1 and shall not be subject to inspection and examination under G.S. 132-6.

(f) Notwithstanding subsection (e) of this section, the Department of Public Instruction, Division of School Operations, may collect the annual aggregate number and type of tips sent to the anonymous tip line. The collection of this aggregate data shall not have any identifying information on the reporter of the tip, including, but not limited to, the school where the incident was reported and the date the tip was reported.

(g) For the purposes of this section, a "public secondary school" is any of the following types of public school serving grades six or higher:

(1) A school under the control of a local school administrative unit.

(2) A school under the control of the State Board of Education, including schools

operated under Article 7A and Article 9C of this Chapter.

(3) A school under the control of The University of North Carolina.

(4) A charter school.

(5) A regional school.

History.
2013-360, s. 8.40; 2015-241, s. 8.26(d); 2017-102, s. 41.5; 2018-5, s. 7.26(a)

§ 115C-105.52. School crisis kits

The Center for Safer Schools, in consultation with the Department of Public Safety and the Department of Public Instruction, Division of School Operations, may develop and adopt policies on the placement of school crisis kits in schools and on the contents of those kits. The kits should include, at a minimum, basic first-aid supplies, communications devices, and other items recommended by the International Association of Chiefs of Police.

The principal of each school, in coordination with the law enforcement agencies that are part of the local board of education's School Risk Management Plan, may place one or more crisis kits at appropriate locations in the school.

History.
2013-360, s. 8.42; 2015-241, s. 8.26(e); 2018-97, s. 2.4(c)

§ 115C-105.53. Schematic diagrams and emergency access to school buildings for local law enforcement agencies

(a) Each local school administrative unit shall provide the following to local law enforcement agencies: (i) schematic diagrams, including digital schematic diagrams, and (ii) either keys to the main entrance of all school buildings or emergency access to key storage devices such as KNOX(R) boxes for all school buildings. Local school administrative units shall provide updates of the schematic diagrams to local law enforcement agencies when substantial modifications such as new facilities or modifications to doors and windows are made to school buildings. Local school administrative units shall also be responsible for providing local law enforcement agencies with updated access to school buildings when changes are made to the locks of the main entrances or to key storage devices such as KNOX(R) boxes.

(b) The Department of Public Instruction, in consultation with the Department of Public Safety, shall develop standards and guidelines for the preparation and content of schematic diagrams and necessary updates. Local school administrative units may use these standards and guidelines to assist in the preparation of their schematic diagrams.

(c) Schematic diagrams are not considered a public record as the term "public record" is defined under G.S. 132-1 and shall not be subject to inspection and examination under G.S. 132-6.

History.
2014-100, s. 8.20(b); 2015-241, s. 8.26(f)

§ 115C-105.54. Schematic diagrams and emergency response information provided to Division of Emergency Management

(a) Each local school administrative unit shall provide the following to the Division of Emergency Management (Division) at the Department of Public Safety: (i) schematic diagrams, including digital schematic diagrams, and (ii) emergency response information requested by the Division for the School Risk Management Plan (SRMP). Local school administrative units shall also provide updated schematic diagrams and emergency response information to the Division when such updates are made. The Division shall ensure that the diagrams and emergency response information are securely stored and distributed as provided in the SRMP to first responders, emergency personnel, and school personnel and approved by the Department of Public Instruction.

(b) The schematic diagrams and emergency response information are not considered a public record as the term "public record" is defined under G.S. 132-1 and shall not be subject to inspection and examination under G.S. 132-6.

History.
2014-100, s. 8.20(b); 2015-241, s. 8.26(g)

ARTICLE 14
DRIVER EDUCATION

§ 115C-215. Administration of driver education program by the Department of Public Instruction

(a) In accordance with criteria and standards approved by the State Board of Education, the State Superintendent of Public Instruction shall organize and administer a standardized program of driver education to be offered at the public high schools of this State for all physically and mentally qualified persons who (i) are older than 14 years and six months, (ii) are approved by the principal of the school, pursuant to rules adopted by the State Board of Education, (iii) are enrolled in a public or private high school within the State or are receiving instruction through a home school as provided by Part 3 of Article 39 of Chapter 115C of the General Statutes, and (iv) have not previously enrolled in the program. The driver education program shall be for the purpose of making available public education to all students on driver safety and training. The State Board of Education shall use for this purpose all funds appropriated pursuant to subsection (f) of this section to the Department of Public Instruction and may use all other funds that become available for its use for this purpose.

(b) The driver education curriculum shall include the following:

(1) Instruction on the rights and privileges of the handicapped and the signs and symbols used to assist the handicapped relative to motor vehicles, including the "international symbol of accessibility" and other symbols and devices as provided in Article 2A of Chapter 20 of the General Statutes.

(2) At least six hours of instruction on the offense of driving while impaired and related subjects.

(3) At least six hours of actual driving experience. To the extent practicable, this experience may include at least one hour of instruction on the techniques of defensive driving.

(4) At least one hour of motorcycle safety awareness training.

(5) Instruction on law enforcement procedures for traffic stops that is developed in consultation with the State Highway Patrol, the North Carolina Sheriff's Association, and the North Carolina Association of Chiefs of Police. The instruction shall provide a description of the actions that a motorist should take during a traffic stop, including appropriate interactions with law enforcement officers.

(c) The State Board of Education shall establish and implement a strategic plan for the driver education program. At a minimum, the strategic plan shall consist of goals and performance indicators, including the number of program participants as compared to the number of persons projected to be eligible to participate in the program, the implementation of a standard curriculum for the program, expenditures for the program, and the success rate of program participants in receiving a drivers license as reported by the Division of Motor Vehicles. The strategic plan shall also outline specific roles and duties of an advisory committee consisting of employees of the Division of Motor Vehicles and the Department of Public Instruction, and other stakeholders in driver education.

(c1) If a local school administrative unit does not comply with any reporting requirements imposed on the unit for the purposes of implementing the strategic plan established by the State Board of Education pursuant to subsection (c) of this section, the Department of Public Instruction may withhold up to five percent (5%) of the State funds allocated to a local school administrative unit for driver education until the unit reports the information required by the Department.

(d) The State Board of Education shall adopt a salary range for the delivery of driver education courses by driver education instructors who are public school employees. The salary range shall be based on the driver education instructor's qualifications, certification, and licensure specific to driver education.

(e) The State Board of Education shall adopt rules to permit local boards of education to enter contracts with public or private entities to provide a program of driver education at public high schools. All driver education instructors shall meet the requirements established by the State Board of Education; provided, however, driver education instructors shall not be required to hold teacher certificates.

(f) The clear proceeds of the newly established motor vehicle registration late fee charged pursuant to G.S. 20-88.03, as enacted by S.L. 2015-241, shall be used to provide a dedicated source of revenue for the drivers education program administered by the Department of Public Instruction in accordance with this section and shall be appropriated by the General Assembly for this purpose for the 2016-2017 fiscal year and subsequent fiscal years thereafter.

(g) The Department of Public Instruction shall have a full-time director and other professional, administrative, technical, and clerical personnel as may be necessary for the statewide administration of the driver education program. Of the funds appropriated to the Department each fiscal year pursuant to subsection (f) of this section, the Department may use up to two percent (2%) of those funds for the direct costs for the statewide administration of the program, including any necessary positions.

History.
1953, c. 1196; 1955, c. 1372, art. 23, s. 4; 1959, c. 573, s. 16; 1981, c. 423, s. 1; 1991, c. 689, s. 32(b); 2011-145, s. 28.37(a); 2011-334, s. 1; 2015-241, ss. 5.3(c), 8.39(a); 2016-94, ss. 5.2, 8.5; 2017-95, s. 2; 2018-5, s. 7.11(b)

§ 115C-216. Boards of education required to provide courses in operation of motor vehicles

(a) **Course of Training and Instruction Required in Public High Schools.** -- Local boards of education shall offer noncredit driver education courses in high schools using the standardized curriculum provided by the Department of Public Instruction.

(b) **Inclusion of Expense in Budget.** -- The local boards of education shall include as an item of instructional service and as a part of the current expense fund of the budget of the high schools under their supervision, the expense necessary to offer the driver education course.

(c) through (f) Repealed by Session Laws 1991, c. 689, s. 32(c) .

(g) **Fee for Instruction.** -- The local boards of education shall fund driver education courses from funds available to them and may charge each student participating in a driver education course a fee of up to sixty-five dollars ($ 65.00) to offset the costs of providing the training and instruction. If a local board of education charges a fee for participation in a driver education course, the local board shall provide a process for reduction or waiver of that fee for students unable to pay the fee due to economic hardship.

History.

1955, c. 817; 1965, c. 397; 1981, c. 423, s. 1; 1991, c. 689, s. 32(c); 2011-145, ss. 28.37(b), 31.1; 2013-360, s. 34.20(a); 2014-100, s. 8.15(c); 2015-241, s. 8.39(b); 2016-94, s. 8.5

ARTICLE 17
SUPPORTING SERVICES

PART 1
TRANSPORTATION

§ 115C-240. Authority and duties of State Board of Education

(a) The State Board of Education shall promulgate rules and regulations for the operation of a public school transportation system.

(b) The State Board of Education shall be under no duty to supply transportation to any pupil or employee enrolled or employed in any school. Neither the State nor the State Board of Education shall in any manner be liable for the failure or refusal of any local board of education to furnish transportation, by school bus or otherwise, to any pupil or employee of any school, or for any neglect or action of any county or city board of education, or any employee of any such board, in the operation or maintenance of any school bus.

(c) The State Board of Education shall from time to time adopt such rules and regulations with reference to the construction, equipment, color, and maintenance of school buses, the number of pupils who may be permitted to ride at the same time upon any bus, and the age and qualifications of drivers of school buses as it shall deem to be desirable for the purpose of promoting safety in the operation of school buses. Every school bus that is capable of operating on diesel fuel shall be capable of operating on diesel fuel with a minimum biodiesel concentration of B-20, as defined in G.S. 143-58.4. No

school bus shall be operated for the transportation of pupils unless such bus is constructed and maintained as prescribed in such regulations and is equipped with adequate heating facilities, a standard signaling device for giving due notice that the bus is about to make a turn, an alternating flashing stoplight on the front of the bus, an alternating flashing stoplight on the rear of the bus, and such other warning devices, fire protective equipment and first aid supplies as may be prescribed for installation upon such buses by the regulation of the State Board of Education.

(d) The State Board of Education shall assist local boards of education by establishing guidelines and a framework through which local boards may establish, review and amend school bus routes prepared pursuant to G.S. 115C-246. The State Board shall also require local boards to implement the Transportation Information Management System or an equivalent system approved by the State Board of Education, no later than September 1, 1992. The State Board of Education shall also assist local boards of education with reference to the acquisition and maintenance of school buses or any other question which may arise in connection with the organization and operation of school bus transportation systems of local boards.

(e) The State Board of Education shall allocate to the respective local boards of education funds appropriated from time to time by the General Assembly for the purpose of providing transportation to the pupils enrolled in the public schools within this State. Such funds shall be allocated by the State Board of Education in accordance with the number of pupils to be transported, the length of bus routes, road conditions and all other circumstances affecting the cost of the transportation of pupils by school bus to the end that the funds so appropriated may be allocated on a fair and equitable basis, according to the needs of the respective local school administrative units and so as to provide the most efficient use of such funds. Such allocation shall be made by the State Board of Education at the beginning of each fiscal year, except that the State Board may reserve for future allocation from time to time within such fiscal year as the need therefor shall be found to exist, a reasonable amount not to exceed ten percent (10%) of the total funds available for transportation in such fiscal year from such appropriation. If there is evidence of inequitable or inefficient use of funds, the State Board of Education shall be empowered to review school bus routes established by local boards pursuant to G.S. 115C-246 as well as other factors affecting the cost of the transportation of pupils by school bus.

(f) The respective local boards shall use such funds for the purposes of replacing, maintaining, insuring, and operating public school buses and service vehicles in accordance with the provisions of G.S. 115C-239 to 115C-246, 115C-248 to 115C-254 and 115C-256 to 115C-259 and for no other purpose, but in the making of expenditures for such purposes shall be subject to rules and regulations promulgated by the State Board of Education.

History.

1955, c. 1372, art. 21, p. 2; 1981, c. 423, s. 1; 1983, c. 630, ss. 3-6; 1989 (Reg. Sess., 1990), c. 1066, s. 96(a); 1991 (Reg. Sess., 1992), c. 900, s. 77(a); 2007-423, s. 1

§ 115C-242.1. Installation and operation of automated school bus safety camera

(a) **Definition.** -- An "automated school bus safety camera" is a device that is affixed to a school bus, as that term is used in G.S. 20-217, that is synchronized to automatically record photographs or video of a vehicle at the time the vehicle is detected for a violation of (i) G.S. 20-217 or (ii) an ordinance adopted under G.S. 153A-246.

(b) **Installation and Operation.** -- Automated school bus safety cameras may be installed and operated on any school bus operated by a local board of education within a county that has adopted an ordinance under G.S. 153A-246 as follows:

(1) A local board of education may install and operate automated school bus safety cameras without contracting with a private vendor.

(2) A local board of education may enter into a service contract to install and operate automated school bus safety cameras with a private vendor. Contracts shall be let in accordance with the provisions of G.S. 143-129 applicable to purchases of apparatus, supplies, materials, or equipment. The maximum length of any contract entered into under this subdivision shall be three years. A contract entered into under this subdivision may contain an option to renew or extend the contract for only one additional term not to exceed three years.

(3) Upon request by one or more local boards of education, the State Board of Education shall enter into a contract for a statewide service or contracts for regional services to install and operate automated school bus safety cameras with a private vendor. These contracts shall be let in accordance with the provisions of Article 3 of Chapter 143 of the General Statutes.

(c) **Interlocal Agreements.** -- Any local board of education, board of county commissioners, and law enforcement agency may enter into an interlocal agreement pursuant to Part 1 of Article 20 of Chapter 160A of the General Statutes that is necessary and proper to effectuate the purpose and intent of this section and G.S. 153A-246. Any agreement entered into pursuant to this subsection may include provisions on cost-sharing and reimbursement to which the local board of education, board of county commissioners, or law enforcement agency freely and voluntarily agree for the purposes of effectuating this section and G.S. 153A-246.

(d) **Evidence in Criminal Proceeding.** -- Any photographs or videos recorded by an automated school bus safety camera that capture a violation of G.S. 20-217 shall also be provided to the investigating law enforcement agency for use as evidence in any proceeding alleging a violation of G.S. 20-217.

History.

2017-188, s. 2

SUBCHAPTER 06.
STUDENTS

ARTICLE 26
ATTENDANCE

PART 1
COMPULSORY ATTENDANCE

§ 115C-378. Children required to attend

(a) Every parent, guardian or custodian in this State having charge or control of a child between the ages of seven and 16 years shall cause the child to attend school continuously for a period equal to the time which the public school to which the child is assigned shall be in session. Every parent, guardian, or custodian in this State having charge or control of a child under age seven who is enrolled in a public school in grades kindergarten through two shall also cause the child to attend school continuously for a period equal to the time which the public school to which the child is assigned shall be in session unless the child has withdrawn from school.

(b) No person shall encourage, entice or counsel any child of compulsory school age to be unlawfully absent from school. The parent, guardian, or custodian of a child shall notify the school of the reason for each known absence of the child, in accordance with local school board policy.

(c) The principal, superintendent, or a designee of the principal or superintendent shall have the right to excuse a child temporarily from attendance on account of sickness or other unavoidable cause that does not constitute unlawful absence as defined by the State Board of Education. The term "school" as used in this section includes all public schools and any non-public schools which have teachers and curricula that are approved by the State Board of Education.

(d) All nonpublic schools receiving and instructing children of compulsory school age shall be required to make, maintain, and render attendance records of those children and maintain the minimum curriculum standards required of public schools. If a nonpublic school refuses or neglects to make, maintain, and render required attendance records, attendance at that school shall not be accepted in lieu of attendance at the public school of the district to which the child shall be assigned. Instruction in a nonpublic school shall not be regarded as meeting the requirements of the law unless the courses of instruction run concurrently with the term of the public school in the district and extend for at least as long a term.

(e) The principal or the principal's designee shall notify the parent, guardian, or custodian of his or her child's excessive absences after the child has accumulated three unexcused absences in a school year. After not more than six unexcused absences, the principal or the principal's designee shall notify the parent, guardian, or custodian by mail that he or she may be in violation of the Compulsory Attendance Law and may be prosecuted if the absences cannot be justified under the established attendance policies of the State and local boards of education. Once the parents are notified, the school attendance counselor shall work with the child and the child's family to analyze the causes of the absences and determine steps, including adjustment of the school program or obtaining supplemental services, to eliminate the problem. The attendance counselor may request that a law enforcement officer accompany him or her if the attendance counselor believes that a home visit is necessary.

(f) After 10 accumulated unexcused absences in a school year, the principal or the principal's designee shall review any report or investigation prepared under G.S. 115C-381 and shall confer with the student and the student's parent, guardian, or custodian, if possible, to determine whether the parent, guardian, or custodian has received notification pursuant to this section and made a good faith effort to comply with the law. If the principal or the principal's designee determines that the parent, guardian, or custodian has not made a good faith effort to comply with the law, the principal shall notify the district attorney and the director of social services of the county where the child resides. If the principal or the principal's designee determines that the parent, guardian, or custodian has made a good faith effort to comply with the law, the principal may file a complaint with

the juvenile court counselor pursuant to Chapter 7B of the General Statutes that the child is habitually absent from school without a valid excuse. Upon receiving notification by the principal or the principal's designee, the director of social services shall determine whether to undertake an investigation under G.S. 7B-302.

(g) Documentation that demonstrates that the parents, guardian, or custodian were notified and that the child has accumulated 10 absences which cannot be justified under the established attendance policies of the local board shall constitute prima facie evidence that the child's parent, guardian, or custodian is responsible for the absences.

History.

1955, c. 1372, art. 20, s. 1; 1956, Ex. Sess., c. 5; 1963, c. 1223, s. 6; 1969, c. 339; c. 799, s. 1; 1971, c. 846; 1975, c. 678, s. 2; c. 731, s. 3; 1979, c. 847; 1981, c. 423, s. 1; 1985, c. 297; 1991 (Reg. Sess., 1992), c. 769, s. 2; 1998-202, s. 13(aa); 2001-490, s. 2.38; 2003-304, s. 3; 2009-404, s. 1

§ 115C-380. Penalty for violation

Except as otherwise provided in G.S. 115C-379, any parent, guardian or other person violating the provisions of this Part shall be guilty of a Class 1 misdemeanor.

History.

1955, c. 1372, art. 20, s. 4; 1969, c. 799, s. 2; 1981, c. 423, s. 1; 1993, c. 539, s. 888; 1994, Ex. Sess., c. 24, s. 14(c); 2005-318, s. 1

ARTICLE 27
DISCIPLINE

§ 115C-390.1. State policy and definitions

(a) In order to create and maintain a safe and orderly school environment conducive to learning, school officials and teachers need adequate tools to maintain good discipline in schools. However, the General Assembly also recognizes that removal of students from school, while sometimes necessary, can exacerbate behavioral problems, diminish academic achievement, and hasten school dropout. School discipline must balance these interests to provide a safe and productive learning environment, to continually teach students to respect themselves, others, and property, and to conduct themselves in a manner that fosters their own learning and the learning of those around them.

(b) The following definitions apply in this Article:

(1) **Alternative education services. --** Part or full-time programs, wherever situated, providing direct or computer-based

instruction that allow a student to progress in one or more core academic courses. Alternative education services include programs established by the local board of education in conformity with G.S. 115C-105.47A and local board of education policies.

(2) **Corporal punishment.** -- The intentional infliction of physical pain upon the body of a student as a disciplinary measure.

(3) **Destructive device.** -- An explosive, incendiary, or poison gas:

a. Bomb.

b. Grenade.

c. Rocket having a propellant charge of more than four ounces.

d. Missile having an explosive or incendiary charge of more than one-quarter ounce.

e. Mine.

f. Device similar to any of the devices listed in this subdivision.

(4) **Educational property.** -- Any school building or bus, school campus, grounds, recreational area, athletic field, or other property under the control of any local board of education or charter school.

(5) **Expulsion.** -- The indefinite exclusion of a student from school enrollment for disciplinary purposes.

(6) **Firearm.** -- Any of the following:

a. A weapon, including a starter gun, which will or is designed to or may readily be converted to expel a projectile by the action of an explosive.

b. The frame or receiver of any such weapon.

c. Any firearm muffler or firearm silencer.

The term shall not include an inoperable antique firearm, a BB gun, stun gun, air rifle, or air pistol.

(7) **Long-term suspension.** -- The exclusion for more than 10 school days of a student from school attendance for disciplinary purposes from the school to which the student was assigned at the time of the disciplinary action. If the offense leading to the long-term suspension occurs before the final quarter of the school year, the exclusion shall be no longer than the remainder of the school year in which the offense was committed. If the offense leading to the long-term suspension occurs during the final quarter of the school year, the exclusion may include a period up to the remainder of the school year in which the offense was committed and the first semester of the following school year.

(8) **Parent.** -- Includes a parent, legal guardian, legal custodian, or other caregiver adult who is acting in the place of a parent and is entitled to enroll the student in school under Article 25 of this Chapter.

(9) **Principal.** -- Includes the principal and the principal's designee.

(10) School official. A superintendent or any other central office administrator to whom the superintendent has delegated duties under this Article and any principal or assistant principal.

(11) School personnel. Any of the following:

a. An employee of a local board of education.

b. Any person working on school grounds or at a school function under a contract or written agreement with the public school system to provide educational or related services to students.

c. Any person working on school grounds or at a school function for another agency providing educational or related services to students.

(12) **Short-term suspension.** -- The exclusion of a student from school attendance for disciplinary purposes for up to 10 school days from the school to which the student was assigned at the time of the disciplinary action.

(13) **Substantial evidence.** -- Such relevant evidence as a reasonable person might accept as adequate to support a conclusion; it is more than a scintilla or permissible inference.

(14) **Superintendent.** -- Includes the superintendent and the superintendent's designee.

(c) Notwithstanding the provisions of this Article, the policies and procedures for the discipline of students shall be consistent with the requirements of the Gun Free Schools Act, 20 U.S.C. § 7151, the Individuals with Disabilities Education Act (IDEA), 29 U.S.C. § 1400, et seq., section 504 of the Rehabilitation Act of 1973, 29 U.S.C. § 701, et seq., and with other federal laws and regulations.

History.
2011-270, s. 1; 2011-282, s. 16; 2011-282, s. 2

§ 115C-390.2. Discipline policies

(a) Local boards of education shall adopt policies to govern the conduct of students and establish procedures to be followed by school officials in disciplining students. These policies must be consistent with the provisions of this Article and the constitutions, statutes, and regulations of the United States and the State of North Carolina.

(b) Board policies shall include or provide for the development of a Code of Student Conduct that notifies students of the standards of behavior expected of them, conduct that may subject them to discipline, and the range of disciplinary measures that may be used by school officials.

(c) Board policies may authorize suspension for conduct not occurring on educational property, but only if the student's conduct otherwise violates the Code of Student Conduct and the conduct has or is reasonably expected to have a direct and immediate impact on the orderly and efficient operation of the schools or the safety of individuals in the school environment.

(d) Board policies shall not allow students to be long-term suspended or expelled from school solely for truancy or tardiness offenses and shall not allow short-term suspension of more than two days for such offenses.

(e) Board policies shall not impose mandatory long-term suspensions or expulsions for specific violations unless otherwise provided in State or federal law.

(f) Board policies shall minimize the use of long-term suspension and expulsion by restricting the availability of long-term suspension or expulsion to those violations deemed to be serious violations of the board's Code of Student Conduct that either threaten the safety of students, staff, or school visitors or threaten to substantially disrupt the educational environment. Examples of conduct that would not be deemed to be a serious violation include the use of inappropriate or disrespectful language, noncompliance with a staff directive, dress code violations, and minor physical altercations that do not involve weapons or injury. The principal may, however, in his or her discretion, determine that aggravating circumstances justify treating a minor violation as a serious violation.

(g) Board policies shall not prohibit the superintendent and principals from considering the student's intent, disciplinary and academic history, the potential benefits to the student of alternatives to suspension, and other mitigating or aggravating factors when deciding whether to recommend or impose long-term suspension.

(h) Board policies shall include the procedures to be followed by school officials in suspending, expelling, or administering corporal punishment to any student, which shall be consistent with this Article.

(i) Each local board shall publish all policies, administrative procedures, or school rules mandated by this section and make them available to each student and his or her parent at the beginning of each school year and upon request.

(j) Local boards of education are encouraged to include in their safe schools plans, adopted pursuant to G.S. 115C-105.47, research-based behavior management programs that take positive approaches to improving student behaviors.

(k) School officials are encouraged to use a full range of responses to violations of disciplinary rules, such as conferences, counseling, peer mediation, behavior contracts, instruction in conflict resolution and anger management, detention, academic interventions, community service, and other similar tools that do not remove a student from the classroom or school building.

(l) *(Applicable to children enrolling in the public schools for the first time beginning with the 2016-2017 school year)* Board policies shall state that absences under G.S. 130A-440 shall not be suspensions. A student subject to an absence under G.S. 130A-440 shall be provided the following:

(1) The opportunity to take textbooks and school-furnished digital devices home for the duration of the absence.

(2) Upon request, the right to receive all missed assignments and, to the extent practicable, the materials distributed to students in connection with the assignment.

(3) The opportunity to take any quarterly, semester, or grading period examinations missed during the absence period.

History.
2011-282, s. 2; 2015-222, s. 4.5

§ 115C-390.3. Reasonable force

(a) School personnel may use physical restraint only in accordance with G.S. 115C-391.1.

(b) School personnel may use reasonable force to control behavior or to remove a person from the scene in those situations when necessary for any of the following reasons:

(1) To correct students.

(2) To quell a disturbance threatening injury to others.

(3) To obtain possession of weapons or other dangerous objects on the person, or within the control, of a student.

(4) For self-defense.

(5) For the protection of persons or property.

(6) To maintain order on educational property, in the classroom, or at a school-related activity on or off educational property.

(c) Notwithstanding any other law, no officer, member, or employee of the State Board of Education, the Superintendent of Public Instruction, or of a local board of education, individually or collectively, shall be civilly liable for using reasonable force in conformity with State law, State or local rules, or State or local policies regarding the control, discipline, suspension, and expulsion of students. Furthermore, the burden of proof is on the claimant to show that the amount of force used was not reasonable.

(d) No school employee shall be reprimanded or dismissed for acting or failing to act to stop or intervene in an altercation between students if the employee's actions are consistent with local board policies. Local boards of education shall adopt policies, pursuant to their authority under G.S. 115C-47(18), which provide guidelines for an employee's response if the employee has personal knowledge or actual notice of an altercation between students.

History.
2011-282, s. 2; 2012-149, s. 10; 2016-126, 4th Ex. Sess., s. 23

§ 115C-390.4. Corporal punishment

(a) Each local board of education shall determine whether corporal punishment will be permitted in its school administrative unit. Notwithstanding a local board of education's prohibition on the use of corporal punishment, school personnel may use physical restraint in accordance with federal law and G.S. 115C-391.1 and reasonable force pursuant to G.S. 115C-390.3.

(b) To the extent that corporal punishment is permitted, the policies adopted for the administration of corporal punishment shall include at a minimum the following:

(1) Corporal punishment shall not be administered in a classroom with other students present.

(2) Only a teacher, principal, or assistant principal may administer corporal punishment and may do so only in the presence of a principal, assistant principal, or teacher who shall be informed beforehand and in the student's presence of the reason for the punishment.

(3) A school person shall provide the student's parent with notification that corporal punishment has been administered, and the person who administered the corporal punishment shall provide the student's parent a written explanation of the reasons and the name of the second person who was present.

(4) The school shall maintain records of each administration of corporal punishment and the reasons for its administration.

(5) In no event shall excessive force be used in the administration of corporal punishment. Excessive force includes force that results in injury to the child that requires medical attention beyond simple first aid.

(6) Corporal punishment shall not be administered on a student whose parent or guardian has stated in writing that corporal punishment shall not be administered to that student. Parents and guardians shall be given a form to make such an election at the beginning of the school year or when the student first enters the school during the year. The form shall advise the parent or guardian that the student may be subject to suspension, among other possible punishments, for offenses that would otherwise not require suspension if corporal punishment were available. If the parent or guardian does not return the form, corporal punishment may be administered on the student.

(c) Each local board of education shall report annually to the State Board of Education, in a manner prescribed by the State Board of Education, on the number of times that corporal punishment was administered. The report shall be in compliance with the federal Family Educational Rights and Privacy Act, 20 U.S.C. § 1232g, and shall include the following:

(1) The number of students who received corporal punishment.

(2) The number of students who received corporal punishment who were also students with disabilities and were eligible to receive special education and related services under the federal Individuals with Disabilities Education Act, 20 U.S.C. § 1400, et seq.

(3) The grade level of the students who received corporal punishment.

(4) The race, gender, and ethnicity of the students who received corporal punishment.

(5) The reason for the administration of the corporal punishment for each student who received corporal punishment.

History.
2011-282, s. 2

§ 115C-390.5. Short-term suspension

(a) The principal shall have authority to impose short-term suspension on a student who willfully engages in conduct that violates a provision of the Code of Student Conduct authorizing short-term suspension.

(b) If a student's short-term suspensions accumulate to more than 10 days in a semester, to the extent the principal has not already done so, he or she shall invoke the mechanisms provided for in the applicable safe schools plan adopted pursuant to G.S. 115C-105.47(b)(5) and (b)(6).

(c) A student subject to short-term suspension shall be provided the following:

(1) The opportunity to take textbooks home for the duration of the suspension.

(2) Upon request, the right to receive all missed assignments and, to the extent practicable, the materials distributed to students in connection with the assignment.

(3) The opportunity to take any quarterly, semester, or grading period examinations missed during the suspension period.

History.
2011-282, s. 2

§ 115C-390.6. Short-term suspension procedures

(a) Except as authorized in this section, no short-term suspension shall be imposed upon a student without first providing the student an opportunity for an informal hearing with the principal. The notice to the student of the charges may be oral or written, and the hearing may be held immediately after the notice is given. The student has the right to be present, to be informed of the charges and the basis for the accusations, and to make statements in defense or mitigation of the charges.

(b) The principal may impose a short-term suspension without providing the student an opportunity for a hearing if the presence of the student creates a direct and immediate threat to the safety of other students or staff, or substantially disrupts or interferes with the education of other students or the maintenance of discipline at the school. In such cases, the notice of the charges and informal hearing described in subsection (a) of this section shall occur as soon as practicable.

(c) The principal shall provide notice to the student's parent of any short-term suspension, including the reason for the suspension and a description of the alleged student conduct upon which the suspension is based. The notice shall be given by the end of the workday during which the suspension is imposed when reasonably possible, but in no event more than two days after the suspension is imposed. The notice shall be given by certified mail, telephone, facsimile, e-mail, or any other method reasonably designed to achieve actual notice.

(d) If English is the second language of the parent, the notice shall be provided in the parent's primary language, when the appropriate foreign language resources are readily available, and in English, and both versions shall be in plain language and shall be easily understandable.

(e) A student is not entitled to appeal the principal's decision to impose a short-term suspension to the superintendent or local board of education. Further, such a decision is not subject to judicial review. Notwithstanding this subsection, the local board of education, in its discretion, may provide students an opportunity for a review or appeal of a short-term suspension to the superintendent or local board of education.

History.
2011-282, s. 2

§ 115C-390.7. Long-term suspension

(a) A principal may recommend to the superintendent the long-term suspension of any student who willfully engages in conduct that violates a provision of the Code of Student Conduct that authorizes long-term suspension. Only the superintendent has the authority to long-term suspend a student.

(b) Before the superintendent's imposition of a long-term suspension, the student must be provided an opportunity for a hearing consistent with G.S. 115C-390.8.

(c) If the student recommended for long-term suspension declines the opportunity for a hearing, the superintendent shall review the circumstances of the recommended long-term suspension. Following such review, the superintendent (i) may impose the suspension if is it consistent with board policies and appropriate under the circumstances, (ii) may impose another appropriate penalty authorized by board policy, or (iii) may decline to impose any penalty.

(d) If a teacher is assaulted or injured by a student and as a result the student is long-term suspended or reassigned to alternative education services, the student shall not be returned to that teacher's classroom unless the teacher consents.

(e) Disciplinary reassignment of a student to a full-time educational program that meets the academic requirements of the standard course of study established by the State Board of Education as provided in G.S. 115C-12 and provides the student with the opportunity to make timely progress towards graduation and grade promotion is not a long-term suspension requiring the due process procedures described in G.S. 115C-390.8.

History.
2011-282, s. 2

§ 115C-390.8. Long-term suspension procedures

(a) When a student is recommended by the principal for long-term suspension, the principal shall give written notice to the student's parent. The notice shall be provided to the student's parent by the end of the workday during which the suspension was recommended when reasonably possible or as soon thereafter as practicable. The written notice shall provide at least the following information:

(1) A description of the incident and the student's conduct that led to the long-term suspension recommendation.

Chapter 115C

(2) A reference to the provisions of the Code of Student Conduct that the student is alleged to have violated.

(3) The specific process by which the parent may request a hearing to contest the decision, including the number of days within which the hearing must be requested.

(4) The process by which a hearing will be held, including, at a minimum, the procedures described in subsection (e) of this section.

(5) Notice that the parent is permitted to retain an attorney to represent the student in the hearing process.

(6) The extent to which the local board policy permits the parent to have an advocate, instead of an attorney, accompany the student to assist in the presentation of his or her appeal.

(7) Notice that the parent has the right to review and obtain copies of the student's educational records before the hearing.

(8) A reference to the local board policy on the expungement of discipline records as required by G.S. 115C-402.

(b) Written notice may be provided by certified mail, fax, e-mail, or any other written method reasonably designed to achieve actual notice of the recommendation for long-term suspension. When school personnel are aware that English is not the primary language of the parent or guardian, the notice shall be written in both English and in the primary language of the parent or guardian when the appropriate foreign language resources are readily available. All notices described in this section shall be written in plain English, and shall include the following information translated into the dominant non-English language used by residents within the local school administrative unit:

(1) The nature of the document, i.e., that it is a long-term suspension notice.

(2) The process by which the parent may request a hearing to contest the long-term suspension.

(3) The identity and phone number of a school employee that the parent may call to obtain assistance in understanding the English language information included in the document.

(c) No long-term suspension shall be imposed on a student until an opportunity for a formal hearing is provided to the student. If a hearing is timely requested, it shall be held and a decision issued before a long-term suspension is imposed, except as otherwise provided in this subsection. The student and parent shall be given reasonable notice of the time and place of the hearing.

(1) If no hearing is timely requested, the superintendent shall follow the procedures described in G.S. 115C-390.7(c).

(2) If the student or parent requests a postponement of the hearing, or if the hearing is requested beyond the time set for such request, the hearing shall be scheduled, but the student shall not have the right to return to school pending the hearing.

(3) If neither the student nor parent appears for the scheduled hearing, after having been given reasonable notice of the time and place of the hearing, the parent and student are deemed to have waived the right to a hearing and the superintendent shall conduct the review required by G.S. 115C-390.7(c).

(d) The formal hearing may be conducted by the local board of education, by the superintendent, or by a person or group of persons appointed by the local board or superintendent to serve as a hearing officer or hearing panel. Neither the board nor the superintendent shall appoint any individual to serve as a hearing officer or on a hearing panel who is under the direct supervision of the principal recommending suspension. If the hearing is conducted by an appointed hearing officer or hearing panel, such officer or panel shall determine the relevant facts and credibility of witnesses based on the evidence presented at the hearing. Following the hearing, the superintendent or local board shall make a final decision regarding the suspension. The superintendent or board shall adopt the hearing officer's or panel's factual determinations unless they are not supported by substantial evidence in the record.

(e) Long-term suspension hearings shall be conducted in accordance with policies adopted by the board of education. Such policies shall offer the student procedural due process including, but not limited to, the following:

(1) The right to be represented at the hearing by counsel or, in the discretion of the local board, a non-attorney advocate.

(2) The right to be present at the hearing, accompanied by his or her parents.

(3) The right of the student, parent, and the student's representative to review before the hearing any audio or video recordings of the incident and, consistent with federal and State student records laws and regulations, the information supporting the suspension that may be presented as evidence at the hearing, including statements made by witnesses related to the charges consistent with subsection (h) of this section.

(4) The right of the student, parent, or the student's representative to question witnesses appearing at the hearing.

(5) The right to present evidence on his or her own behalf, which may include

written statements or oral testimony, relating to the incident leading to the suspension, as well as any of the factors listed in G.S. 115C-390.2(g).

(6) The right to have a record made of the hearing.

(7) The right to make his or her own audio recording of the hearing.

(8) The right to a written decision, based on substantial evidence presented at the hearing, either upholding, modifying, or rejecting the principal's recommendation of suspension and containing at least the following information:

    a. The basis for the decision, including a reference to any policy or rule that the student is determined to have violated.

    b. Notice of what information will be included in the student's official record pursuant to G.S. 115C-402.

    c. The student's right to appeal the decision and notice of the procedures for such appeal.

(f) Following the issuance of the decision, the superintendent shall implement the decision by authorizing the student's return to school or by imposing the suspension reflected in the decision.

(g) Unless the decision was made by the local board, the student may appeal the decision to the local board in accordance with G.S. 115C-45(c) and policies adopted by the board. Notwithstanding the provisions of G.S. 115C-45(c), a student's appeal to the board of a decision upholding a long-term suspension shall be heard and a final written decision issued in not more than 30 calendar days following the request for such appeal.

(h) Nothing in this section shall compel school officials to release names or other information that could allow the student or his or her representative to identify witnesses when such identification could create a safety risk for the witness.

(i) A decision of the local board to uphold the long-term suspension of a student is subject to judicial review in accordance with Article 4 of Chapter 150B of the General Statutes. The action must be brought within 30 days of the local board's decision. A person seeking judicial review shall file a petition in the superior court of the county where the local board made its decision. Local rules notwithstanding, petitions for judicial review of a long-term suspension shall be set for hearing in the first succeeding term of superior court in the county following the filing of the certified copy of the official record.

History.
2011-282, s. 2

§ 115C-390.9. Alternative education services

(a) Students who are long-term suspended shall be offered alternative education services unless the superintendent provides a significant or important reason for declining to offer such services. The following may be significant or important reasons, depending on the circumstances and the nature and setting of the alternative education services:

(1) The student exhibits violent behavior.

(2) The student poses a threat to staff or other students.

(3) The student substantially disrupts the learning process.

(4) The student otherwise engaged in serious misconduct that makes the provision of alternative educational services not feasible.

(5) Educationally appropriate alternative education services are not available in the local school administrative unit due to limited resources.

(6) The student failed to comply with reasonable conditions for admittance into an alternative education program.

(b) If the superintendent declines to provide alternative education services to the suspended student, the student may seek review of such decision by the local board of education as permitted by G.S. 115C-45(c)(2). If the student seeks such review, the superintendent shall provide to the student and the local board, in advance of the board's review, a written explanation for the denial of services together with any documents or other information supporting the decision.

History.
2011-282, s. 2

§ 115C-390.10. 365-day suspension for gun possession

(a) All local boards of education shall develop and implement written policies and procedures, as required by the federal Gun Free Schools Act, 20 U.S.C. § 7151, requiring suspension for 365 calendar days of any student who is determined to have brought or been in possession of a firearm or destructive device on educational property, or to a school-sponsored event off of educational property. A principal shall recommend to the superintendent the 365-day suspension of any student believed to have violated board policies regarding weapons. The superintendent has the authority to suspend for 365 days a student who has been recommended for such suspension by the principal when such recommendation is consistent with board policies. Notwithstanding the foregoing, the superintendent may modify, in writing, the required

365-day suspension for an individual student on a case-by-case basis. The superintendent shall not impose a 365-day suspension if the superintendent determines that the student took or received the firearm or destructive device from another person at school or found the firearm or destructive device at school, provided that the student delivered or reported the firearm or destructive device as soon as practicable to a law enforcement officer or a school employee and had no intent to use such firearm or destructive device in a harmful or threatening way.

(b) The principal must report all incidents of firearms or destructive devices on educational property or at a school-sponsored event as required by G.S. 115C-288(g) and State Board of Education policy.

(c) Nothing in this provision shall apply to a firearm that was brought onto educational property for activities approved and authorized by the local board of education, provided that the local board of education has adopted appropriate safeguards to protect student safety.

(d) At the time the student and parent receive notice that the student is suspended for 365 days under this section, the superintendent shall provide notice to the student and the student's parent of the right to petition the local board of education for readmission pursuant to G.S. 115C-390.12.

(e) The procedures described in G.S. 115C-390.8 apply to students facing a 365-day suspension pursuant to this section.

(f) Students who are suspended for 365 days pursuant to this section shall be considered for alternative educational services consistent with the provisions of G.S. 115C-390.9.

History.
2011-282, s. 2

§ 115C-390.11. Expulsion

(a) Upon recommendation of the superintendent, a local board of education may expel any student 14 years of age or older whose continued presence in school constitutes a clear threat to the safety of other students or school staff. Prior to the expulsion of any student, the local board shall conduct a hearing to determine whether the student's continued presence in school constitutes a clear threat to the safety of other students or school staff. The student shall be given reasonable notice of the recommendation in accordance with G.S. 115C-390.8(a) and (b), as well as reasonable notice of the time and place of the scheduled hearing.

(1) The procedures described in G.S. 115C-390.8(e)(1)-(8) apply to students facing expulsion pursuant to this section, except that the decision to expel a student by the local board of education shall be based

on clear and convincing evidence that the student's continued presence in school constitutes a clear threat to the safety of other students and school staff.

(2) A local board of education may expel any student subject to G.S. 14-208.18 in accordance with the procedures of this section. Prior to ordering the expulsion of a student, the local board of education shall consider whether there are alternative education services that may be offered to the student. As provided by G.S. 14-208.18(f), if the local board of education determines that the student shall be provided educational services on school property, the student shall be under the supervision of school personnel at all times.

(3) At the time a student is expelled under this section, the student shall be provided notice of the right to petition for readmission pursuant to G.S. 115C-390.12.

(b) During the expulsion, the student is not entitled to be present on any property of the local school administrative unit and is not considered a student of the local board of education. Nothing in this section shall prevent a local board of education from offering access to some type of alternative educational services that can be provided to the student in a manner that does not create safety risks to other students and school staff.

History.
2011-282, s. 2

§ 115C-390.12. Request for readmission

(a) All students suspended for 365 days or expelled may, after 180 calendar days from the date of the beginning of the student's suspension or expulsion, request in writing readmission to the local school administrative unit. The local board of education shall develop and publish written policies and procedures for the readmission of all students who have been expelled or suspended for 365 days, which shall provide, at a minimum, the following process:

(1) The process for 365-day suspended students.

a. At the local board's discretion, either the superintendent or the local board itself shall consider and decide on petitions for readmission. If the decision maker is the superintendent, the superintendent shall offer the student an opportunity for an in-person meeting. If the decision maker is the local board of education, the board may offer the student an in-person meeting or may make a determination based on the records submitted by the student and the superintendent.

b. The student shall be readmitted if the student demonstrates to the satisfaction of the board or superintendent that the student's presence in school no longer constitutes a threat to the safety of other students or staff.

c. A superintendent's decision not to readmit the student may be appealed to the local board of education pursuant to G.S. 115C-45(c). The superintendent shall notify the parents of the right to appeal.

d. There is no right to judicial review of the board's decision not to readmit a 365-day suspended student.

e. A decision on readmission under this subsection shall be issued within 30 days of the petition.

(2) The process for expelled students.

a. The board of education shall consider all petitions for readmission of expelled students, together with the recommendation of the superintendent on the matter, and shall rule on the request for readmission. The board shall consider the petition based on the records submitted by the student and the response by the administration and shall allow the parties to be heard in the same manner as provided by G.S. 115C-45(c).

b. The student shall be readmitted if the student demonstrates to the satisfaction of the board or superintendent that his or her presence in a school no longer constitutes a clear threat to the safety of other students or staff.

c. A decision by a board of education to deny readmission of an expelled student is not subject to judicial review.

d. An expelled student may subsequently request readmission not more often than every six months. The local board of education is not required to consider subsequent readmission petitions filed sooner than six months after the previous petition was filed.

e. A decision on readmission under this section shall be issued within 30 days of the petition.

(b) If a student is readmitted under this section, the board and the superintendent have the right to assign the student to any program within the school system and to place reasonable conditions on the readmission.

(c) If a teacher was assaulted or injured by a student, and as a result the student was expelled, the student shall not be returned to that teacher's classroom following readmission unless the teacher consents.

History.
2011-282, s. 2

§ 115C-391.1. Permissible use of seclusion and restraint

(a) It is the policy of the State of North Carolina to:

(1) Promote safety and prevent harm to all students, staff, and visitors in the public schools.

(2) Treat all public school students with dignity and respect in the delivery of discipline, use of physical restraints or seclusion, and use of reasonable force as permitted by law.

(3) Provide school staff with clear guidelines about what constitutes use of reasonable force permissible in North Carolina public schools.

(4) Improve student achievement, attendance, promotion, and graduation rates by employing positive behavioral interventions to address student behavior in a positive and safe manner.

(5) Promote retention of valuable teachers and other school personnel by providing appropriate training in prescribed procedures, which address student behavior in a positive and safe manner.

(b) The following definitions apply in this section:

(1) "Assistive technology device" means any item, piece of equipment, or product system that is used to increase, maintain, or improve the functional capacities of a child with a disability.

(2) "Aversive procedure" means a systematic physical or sensory intervention program for modifying the behavior of a student with a disability which causes or reasonably may be expected to cause one or more of the following:

a. Significant physical harm, such as tissue damage, physical illness, or death.

b. Serious, foreseeable long-term psychological impairment.

c. Obvious repulsion on the part of observers who cannot reconcile extreme procedures with acceptable, standard practice, for example: electric shock applied to the body; extremely loud auditory stimuli; forcible introduction of foul substances to the mouth, eyes, ears, nose, or skin; placement in a tub of cold water or shower; slapping, pinching, hitting, or pulling hair; blindfolding or other forms of visual blocking; unreasonable withholding of meals; eating one's own vomit; or denial of reasonable access to toileting facilities.

(3) "Behavioral intervention" means the implementation of strategies to address

behavior that is dangerous, disruptive, or otherwise impedes the learning of a student or others.

(4) "IEP" means a student's Individualized Education Plan.

(5) "Isolation" means a behavior management technique in which a student is placed alone in an enclosed space from which the student is not prevented from leaving.

(6) "Law enforcement officer" means a sworn law enforcement officer with the power to arrest.

(7) "Mechanical restraint" means the use of any device or material attached or adjacent to a student's body that restricts freedom of movement or normal access to any portion of the student's body and that the student cannot easily remove.

(8) "Physical restraint" means the use of physical force to restrict the free movement of all or a portion of a student's body.

(9) "School personnel" means:

    a. Employees of a local board of education.

    b. Any person working on school grounds or at a school function under a contract or written agreement with the public school system to provide educational or related services to students.

    c. Any person working on school grounds or at a school function for another agency providing educational or related services to students.

(10) "Seclusion" means the confinement of a student alone in an enclosed space from which the student is:

    a. Physically prevented from leaving by locking hardware or other means.

    b. Not capable of leaving due to physical or intellectual incapacity.

(11) "Time-out" means a behavior management technique in which a student is separated from other students for a limited period of time in a monitored setting.

(c) Physical Restraint:

(1) Physical restraint of students by school personnel shall be considered a reasonable use of force when used in the following circumstances:

    a. As reasonably needed to obtain possession of a weapon or other dangerous objects on a person or within the control of a person.

    b. As reasonably needed to maintain order or prevent or break up a fight.

    c. As reasonably needed for self-defense.

    d. As reasonably needed to ensure the safety of any student, school employee, volunteer, or other person present, to teach a skill, to calm or comfort

a student, or to prevent self-injurious behavior.

    e. As reasonably needed to escort a student safely from one area to another.

    f. If used as provided for in a student's IEP or Section 504 plan or behavior intervention plan.

    g. As reasonably needed to prevent imminent destruction to school or another person's property.

(2) Except as set forth in subdivision (1) of this subsection, physical restraint of students shall not be considered a reasonable use of force, and its use is prohibited.

(3) Physical restraint shall not be considered a reasonable use of force when used solely as a disciplinary consequence.

(4) Nothing in this subsection shall be construed to prevent the use of force by law enforcement officers in the lawful exercise of their law enforcement duties.

(d) Mechanical Restraint:

(1) Mechanical restraint of students by school personnel is permissible only in the following circumstances:

    a. When properly used as an assistive technology device included in the student's IEP or Section 504 plan or behavior intervention plan or as otherwise prescribed for the student by a medical or related service provider.

    b. When using seat belts or other safety restraints to secure students during transportation.

    c. As reasonably needed to obtain possession of a weapon or other dangerous objects on a person or within the control of a person.

    d. As reasonably needed for self-defense.

    e. As reasonably needed to ensure the safety of any student, school employee, volunteer, or other person present.

(2) Except as set forth in subdivision (1) of this subsection, mechanical restraint, including the tying, taping, or strapping down of a student, shall not be considered a reasonable use of force, and its use is prohibited.

(3) Nothing in this subsection shall be construed to prevent the use of mechanical restraint devices such as handcuffs by law enforcement officers in the lawful exercise of their law enforcement duties.

(e) Seclusion:

(1) Seclusion of students by school personnel may be used in the following circumstances:

    a. As reasonably needed to respond to a person in control of a weapon or other dangerous object.

Chapter 115C

b. As reasonably needed to maintain order or prevent or break up a fight.

c. As reasonably needed for self-defense.

d. As reasonably needed when a student's behavior poses a threat of imminent physical harm to self or others or imminent substantial destruction of school or another person's property.

e. When used as specified in the student's IEP, Section 504 plan, or behavior intervention plan; and

1. The student is monitored while in seclusion by an adult in close proximity who is able to see and hear the student at all times.

2. The student is released from seclusion upon cessation of the behaviors that led to the seclusion or as otherwise specified in the student's IEP or Section 504 plan.

3. The space in which the student is confined has been approved for such use by the local education agency.

4. The space is appropriately lighted.

5. The space is appropriately ventilated and heated or cooled.

6. The space is free of objects that unreasonably expose the student or others to harm.

(2) Except as set forth in subdivision (1) of this subsection, the use of seclusion is not considered reasonable force, and its use is not permitted.

(3) Seclusion shall not be considered a reasonable use of force when used solely as a disciplinary consequence.

(4) Nothing in this subsection shall be construed to prevent the use of seclusion by law enforcement officers in the lawful exercise of their law enforcement duties.

(f) **Isolation. --** Isolation is permitted as a behavior management technique provided that:

(1) The space used for isolation is appropriately lighted, ventilated, and heated or cooled.

(2) The duration of the isolation is reasonable in light of the purpose of the isolation.

(3) The student is reasonably monitored while in isolation.

(4) The isolation space is free of objects that unreasonably expose the student or others to harm.

(g) **Time-Out. --** Nothing in this section is intended to prohibit or regulate the use of time-out as defined in this section.

(h) **Aversive Procedures. --** The use of aversive procedures as defined in this section is prohibited in public schools.

(i) Nothing in this section modifies the rights of school personnel to use reasonable force as permitted under G.S. 115C-390.3 or modifies the rules and procedures governing discipline under G.S. 115C-390.1 through G.S. 115C-390.12.

(j) Notice, Reporting, and Documentation.

(1) **Notice of procedures. --** Each local board of education shall provide copies of this section and all local board policies developed to implement this section to school personnel and parents or guardians at the beginning of each school year.

(2) Notice of specified incidents:

a. School personnel shall promptly notify the principal or principal's designee of:

1. Any use of aversive procedures.

2. Any prohibited use of mechanical restraint.

3. Any use of physical restraint resulting in observable physical injury to a student.

4. Any prohibited use of seclusion or seclusion that exceeds 10 minutes or the amount of time specified on a student's behavior intervention plan.

b. When a principal or principal's designee has personal knowledge or actual notice of any of the events described in this subdivision, the principal or principal's designee shall promptly notify the student's parent or guardian and will provide the name of a school employee the parent or guardian can contact regarding the incident.

(3) As used in subdivision (2) of this subsection, "promptly notify" means by the end of the workday during which the incident occurred when reasonably possible, but in no event later than the end of following workday.

(4) The parent or guardian of the student shall be provided with a written incident report for any incident reported under this section within a reasonable period of time, but in no event later than 30 days after the incident. The written incident report shall include:

a. The date, time of day, location, duration, and description of the incident and interventions.

b. The events or events that led up to the incident.

c. The nature and extent of any injury to the student.

d. The name of a school employee the parent or guardian can contact regarding the incident.

(5) No local board of education or employee of a local board of education shall discharge, threaten, or otherwise retaliate against

another employee of the board regarding that employee's compensation, terms, conditions, location, or privileges of employment because the employee makes a report alleging a prohibited use of physical restraint, mechanical restraint, aversive procedure, or seclusion, unless the employee knew or should have known that the report was false.

(k) Nothing in this section shall be construed to create a private cause of action against any local board of education, its agents or employees, or any institutions of teacher education or their agents or employees or to create a criminal offense.

History.
2005-205, s. 2; 2006-264, s. 58; 2011-282, s. 3

ARTICLE 28
STUDENT LIABILITY

§ 115C-399. Trespass on or damage to school bus

Any person who willfully trespasses upon or damages a school bus may be liable pursuant to the provisions of G.S. 14-132.2.

History.
1981, c. 423, s. 1

ARTICLE 29
PROTECTIVE PROVISIONS AND MAINTENANCE OF STUDENT RECORDS

§ 115C-400. School personnel to report child abuse

Any person who has cause to suspect child abuse or neglect has a duty to report the case of the child to the Director of Social Services of the county, as provided in Article 3 of Chapter 7B of the General Statutes.

History.
1981, c. 423, s. 1; 1998-202, s. 13(bb)

CHAPTER 115D
COMMUNITY COLLEGES

ARTICLE 2
LOCAL ADMINISTRATION

§ 115D-21. Traffic regulations; fines and penalties

(a) All of the provisions of Chapter 20 of the General Statutes relating to the use of highways of the State of North Carolina and the operation of motor vehicles thereon shall apply to the streets, roads, alleys and driveways on the campuses of all institutions in the North Carolina Community College System. Any person violating any of the provisions of Chapter 20 of the General Statutes in or on the streets, roads, alleys and driveways on the campuses of institutions in the North Carolina Community College System shall, upon conviction thereof, be punished as prescribed in this section and as provided by Chapter 20 of the General Statutes relating to motor vehicles. Nothing contained in this section shall be construed as in any way interfering with the ownership and control of the streets, roads, alleys and driveways on the campuses of institutions in the system as is now vested by law in the trustees of each individual institution in the North Carolina Community College System.

(b) The trustees are authorized and empowered to make additional rules and regulations and to adopt additional ordinances with respect to the use of the streets, roads, alleys and driveways and to establish parking areas on or off the campuses not inconsistent with the provisions of Chapter 20 of the General Statutes of North Carolina. Upon investigation, the trustees may determine and fix speed limits on streets, roads, alleys, and driveways subject to such rules, regulations, and ordinances, lower than those provided in G.S. 20-141. The trustees may make reasonable provisions for the towing or removal of unattended vehicles found to be in violation of rules, regulations and ordinances. All rules, regulations and ordinances adopted pursuant to the authority of this section shall be recorded in the proceedings of the trustees; shall be printed; and copies of such rules, regulations and ordinances shall be filed in the office of the Secretary of State of North Carolina. Violation of any such rules, regulations, or ordinances, is an infraction punishable by a penalty of not more than one hundred dollars ($ 100.00).

Regardless of whether an institution does its own removal and disposal of motor vehicles or contracts with another person to do so, the institution shall provide a hearing procedure for the owner. For purposes of this subsection, the definitions in G.S. 20-219.9 apply:

(1) If the institution operates in such a way that the person who tows the vehicle is responsible for collecting towing fees, all provisions of Article 7A, Chapter 20, apply.

(2) If the institution operates in such a way that it is responsible for collecting towing fees, it shall:

   a. Provide by contract or ordinance for a schedule of reasonable towing fees,

   b. Provide a procedure for a prompt fair hearing to contest the towing,

   c. Provide for an appeal to district court from that hearing,

   d. Authorize release of the vehicle at any time after towing by the posting of a bond or paying of the fees due, and

   e. If the institution chooses to enforce its authority by sale of the vehicle, provide a sale procedure similar to that provided in G.S. 44A-4, 44A-5, and 44A-6, except that no hearing in addition to the probable cause hearing is required. If no one purchases the vehicle at the sale and if the value of the vehicle is less than the amount of the lien, the institution may destroy it.

(c) The trustees may by rules, regulations, or ordinances provide for a system of registration of all motor vehicles where the owner or operator does park on the campus or keeps said vehicle on the campus. The trustees shall cause to be posted at appropriate places on campus notice to the public of applicable parking and traffic rules, regulations, and ordinances governing the campus over which it has jurisdiction. The trustees may by rules, regulations, or ordinances establish or cause to have established a system of citations that may be issued to owners or operators of motor vehicles who violate established rules, regulations, or ordinances. The trustees shall provide for the administration of said system of citations; establish or cause to be established a system of fines to be levied for the violation of established rules, regulations and ordinances; and enforce or cause to be enforced the collection of said fines. The fine for each offense shall not exceed twenty-five dollars ($ 25.00). The trustees shall be empowered to exercise the right to prohibit repeated violators of such rules, regulations, or ordinances from parking on the campus.

(d) The clear proceeds of all civil penalties collected pursuant to this section shall be remitted to the Civil Penalty and Forfeiture Fund in accordance with G.S. 115C-457.2.

History.
1971, c. 795, ss. 1-3; 1979, c. 462, s. 2; 1983, c. 420, s. 4; 1985, c. 764, s. 38; 2012-142, s. 8.9

§ 115D-21.1. Campus law enforcement agencies

(a) The board of trustees of any community college may establish a campus law enforcement agency and employ campus police officers. These officers shall meet the requirements of Article 1 of Chapter 17C of the General Statutes, shall take the oath of office prescribed by Article VI, Section 7 of the Constitution, and shall have all the powers of law enforcement officers generally. The territorial jurisdiction of a campus police officer shall include all property owned or leased to the community college employing the officer and that portion of any public road or highway passing through the property and immediately adjoining it, wherever located.

(b) The board of trustees of any community college that establishes a campus law enforcement agency under subsection (a) of this section may enter into joint agreements with the governing board of any municipality to extend the law enforcement authority of campus police officers into the municipality's jurisdiction and to determine the circumstances under which this extension of authority may be granted.

(c) The board of trustees of any community college that establishes a campus law enforcement agency under subsection (a) of this section may enter into joint agreements with the governing board of any county, with the consent of the sheriff, to extend the law enforcement authority of campus police officers into the county's jurisdiction and to determine the circumstances under which this extension of authority may be granted.

History.
1999-68, s. 1

CHAPTER 116
HIGHER EDUCATION

ARTICLE 1
THE UNIVERSITY OF NORTH CAROLINA

PART 6
TRAFFIC AND PARKING

§ 116-44.3. Definitions

Unless the context clearly requires another meaning, the following words and phrases have the meanings indicated when used in this Part:

(1) "Board of trustees" and "constituent institution" have the meanings assigned in G.S. 116-2.

(2) "Campus" means that University property, without regard to location, which is used wholly or partly for the purposes of a particular constituent institution of the University of North Carolina.

(3) "University" means a constituent institution as defined in G.S. 116-2.

(4) "University property" means property that is owned or leased in whole or in part by the State of North Carolina and which is subject to the general management and control of the Board of Governors of the University of North Carolina.

History.
1973, c. 495, s. 1

§ 116-44.4. Regulation of traffic and parking and registration of motor vehicles

(a) Except as otherwise provided in this Part, all of the provisions of Chapter 20 of the General Statutes relating to the use of highways of the State and the operation of motor vehicles thereon are applicable to all streets, alleys, driveways, parking lots, and parking structures on University property. Nothing in this section modifies any rights of ownership or control of University property, now or hereafter vested in the Board of Governors of the University of North Carolina or the State of North Carolina.

(b) Each board of trustees may by ordinance prohibit, regulate, divert, control, and limit pedestrian or vehicular traffic and the parking of motor vehicles and other modes of conveyance on the campus. In fixing speed limits, the board of trustees is not subject to G.S. 20-141(f1) or (g2), but may fix any speed limit reasonable and safe under the

circumstances as conclusively determined by the board of trustees. The board of trustees may not regulate traffic on streets open to the public as of right, except as specifically provided in this Part.

(c) Each board of trustees may by ordinance provide for the registration of motor vehicles maintained or operated on the campus by any student, faculty member, or employee of the University, and may fix fees for such registration. The ordinance may make it unlawful for any person to operate an unregistered motor vehicle on the campus when the vehicle is required by the ordinance to be registered.

(d) Each board of trustees may by ordinance set aside parking lots and other parking facilities on the campus for use by students, faculty, and employees of the University and members of the general public attending schools, conferences, or meetings at the University, visiting or making use of any University facilities, or attending to official business with the University. The board of trustees may issue permits to park in these lots and garages and may charge a fee therefor. The board of trustees may also by ordinance make it unlawful for any person to park a motor vehicle in any lot or other parking facility without procuring the requisite permit and displaying it on the vehicle. No permit to park shall be issued until the student requesting the permit provides the name of the insurer, the policy number under which the student has financial responsibility, and the student certifies that the motor vehicle is insured at the levels set in G.S. 20-279.1(11) or higher. This subsection applies to motor vehicles that are registered in other states as well as motor vehicles that are registered in this State pursuant to Chapter 20 of the General Statutes.

(e) Each board of trustees may by ordinance set aside spaces in designated parking areas or facilities in which motor vehicles may be parked for specified periods of time. To regulate parking in such spaces, the board of trustees may install a system of parking meters and make it unlawful for any person to park a motor vehicle in a metered space without activating the meter for the entire time that the vehicle is parked, up to the maximum length of time allowed for that space. The meters may be activated by coins of the United States. The board of trustees may also install automatic gates, employ attendants, and use any other device or procedure to control access to and collect the fees for using its parking areas and facilities.

(f) The board of trustees may by ordinance provide for the issuance of stickers, decals, permits, or other indicia representing the registration status of vehicles or the eligibility of vehicles to park on the campus and may by ordinance prohibit the forgery, counterfeiting, unauthorized transfer, or unauthorized use of them.

(g) Violation of an ordinance adopted under any portion of this Part is an infraction as defined in G.S. 14-3.1 and is punishable by a penalty of not more than fifty dollars ($ 50.00). An ordinance may provide that certain prohibited acts shall not be infractions and in such cases the provisions of subsection (h) may be used to enforce the ordinance.

(h) An ordinance adopted under any portion of this Part may provide that violation subjects the offender to a civil penalty. Penalties may be graduated according to the seriousness of the offense or the number of prior offenses by the person charged. Each board of trustees may establish procedures for the collection of these penalties and they may be enforced by civil action in the nature of debt. The board of trustees may also provide for appropriate administrative sanctions if an offender does not pay a validly due penalty or upon repeated offenses. Appropriate administrative sanctions include, but are not limited to, revocation of parking permits, termination of vehicle registration, and termination or suspension of enrollment in or employment by the University.

(i) An ordinance adopted under any portion of this Part may provide that any vehicle illegally parked may be removed to a storage area. Regardless of whether a constituent institution does its own removal and disposal of motor vehicles or contracts with another person to do so, the institution shall provide a hearing procedure for the owner. For purposes of this subsection, the definitions in G.S. 20-219.9 apply.

(1) If the institution operates in such a way that the person who tows the vehicle is responsible for collecting towing fees, all provisions of Article 7A, Chapter 20, apply.

(2) If the institution operates in such a way that it is responsible for collecting towing fees, it shall:

    a. Provide by contract or ordinance for a schedule of reasonable towing fees,

    b. Provide a procedure for a prompt fair hearing to contest the towing,

    c. Provide for an appeal to district court from that hearing,

    d. Authorize release of the vehicle at any time after towing by the posting of a bond or paying of the fees due, and

    e. If the institution chooses to enforce its authority by sale of the vehicle, provide a sale procedure similar to that provided in G.S. 44A-4, 44A-5, and 44A-6, except that no hearing in addition to the probable cause hearing is required. If no one purchases the vehicle at the sale and if the value of the vehicle is less than the amount of the lien, the institution may destroy it.

(j) Evidence that a motor vehicle was found parked or unattended in violation of an ordinance of the board of trustees is prima facie evidence that the vehicle was parked by:

(1) The person holding a University parking permit for the vehicle, or

(2) If no University parking permit has been issued for the vehicle, the person in whose name the vehicle is registered with the University pursuant to subsection (c), or

(3) If no University parking permit has been issued for the vehicle and the vehicle is not registered with the University, the person in whose name it is registered with the North Carolina Division of Motor Vehicles or the corresponding agency of another state or nation.

The rule of evidence established by this subsection applies only in civil, criminal, or administrative actions or proceedings concerning violations of ordinances of the board of trustees. G.S. 20-162.1 does not apply to such actions or proceedings.

(k) Each board of trustees shall cause to be posted appropriate notice to the public of applicable traffic and parking restrictions.

(*l*) All ordinances adopted under this Part shall be recorded in the minutes of the board of trustees and copies thereof shall be filed in the offices of the President of the University of North Carolina and the Secretary of State. Each board of trustees shall provide for printing and distributing copies of its traffic and parking ordinances.

(m) All moneys received pursuant to this Part, except for the clear proceeds of all civil penalties collected pursuant to subsection (h) of this section, shall be placed in a trust account in each constituent institution, are appropriated, and may be used for any of the following purposes:

(1) To defray the cost of administering and enforcing ordinances adopted under this Part;

(2) To develop, maintain, and supervise parking areas and facilities;

(3) To provide bus service or other transportation systems and facilities, including payments to any public or private transportation system serving University students, faculty, or employees;

(4) As a pledge to secure revenue bonds for parking facilities issued under Article 21 of this Chapter;

(5) Other purposes related to parking, traffic, and transportation on the campus.

The clear proceeds of all civil penalties collected pursuant to subsection (h) of this section shall be remitted to the Civil Penalty and Forfeiture Fund in accordance with G.S. 115C-457.2.

History.
1973, c. 495, s. 1; 1975, c. 716, s. 5; 1981 (Reg. Sess., 1982), c. 1239, s. 3; 1983, c. 420, s. 5; 1985, c. 764, s. 36; 2001-336, s. 1; 2005-276, s. 6.37(r); 2006-203, s. 51

CHAPTER 120
GENERAL ASSEMBLY

ARTICLE 14
LEGISLATIVE ETHICS ACT

PART 1
CODE OF LEGISLATIVE ETHICS

§ 120-86. Bribery, economic threats made to influence legislation; violations

(a) No person shall offer or give to a legislator or a member of a legislator's immediate family, or to a business with which the legislator is associated, and no legislator shall solicit or receive, anything of monetary value, including a gift, favor or service or a promise of future employment, based on any understanding that the legislator's vote, official actions or judgment would be influenced thereby, or where it could reasonably be inferred that the thing of value would influence the legislator in the discharge of the legislator's duties.

(b) It shall be unlawful for the partner, client, customer, or employer of a legislator or the agent of that partner, client, customer, or employer, directly or indirectly, to threaten economically that legislator with the intent to influence the legislator in the discharge of the legislator's duties.

(b1) It shall be unlawful for any person, directly or indirectly, to threaten economically another person in order to compel the threatened person to attempt to influence a legislator in the discharge of the legislator's duties.

(c) It shall be unethical for a legislator to contact the partner, client, customer, or employer of another legislator if the purpose of the contact is to cause the partner, client, customer, or employer, directly or indirectly, to threaten economically that legislator with the intent to influence that legislator in the discharge of the legislator's duties.

(d) Repealed by Session Laws 2006-201, s. 6, effective January 1, 2007.

(e) Violation of subsection (a), (b), or (b1) is a Class F felony. Violation of subsection (c) is not a crime but is punishable under G.S. 120-103.1.

History.
1975, c. 564, s. 1; 1983, c. 780, s. 2; 1993, c. 539, s. 1302; 1994, Ex. Sess., c. 24, s. 14(c); 1997-443, s. 19.27(a); 2006-201, s. 6

§ 120-86.1. Personnel-related action unethical

It shall be unethical for a legislator to take, promise, or threaten any legislative action, as defined in G.S. 120C-100(9), for the purpose of influencing or in retaliation for any action regarding State employee hirings, promotions, grievances, or disciplinary actions subject to Chapter 126 of the General Statutes.

History.
1997-520, s. 7; 2006-201, s. 20(a); 2017-6, s. 3; 2018-146, ss. 3.1(a), (b), 6.1

CHAPTER 122C
MENTAL HEALTH, DEVELOPMENTAL DISABILITIES, AND SUBSTANCE ABUSE ACT OF 1985

ARTICLE 1
GENERAL PROVISIONS

§ 122C-3. Definitions

The following definitions apply in this Chapter:

(1) **Area authority.** -- The area mental health, developmental disabilities, and substance abuse authority.

(2) **Area board.** -- The area mental health, developmental disabilities, and substance abuse board.

(2a) **Area director.** -- The administrative head of the area authority program appointed pursuant to G.S. 122C-121.

(2b) "Behavioral health and intellectual/developmental disabilities tailored plan" or "BH IDD tailored plan" has the same meaning as in G.S. 108D-1.

(2c) **Board of county commissioners.** -- Includes the participating boards of county commissioners for multicounty area authorities and multicounty programs.

(3) **Camp Butner reservation.** -- The original Camp Butner reservation as may be designated by the Secretary as having been acquired by the State and includes not only areas which are owned and occupied by the State but also those which may have been leased or otherwise disposed of by the State, and also includes those areas within the municipal boundaries of the Town of Butner and that portion of the extraterritorial jurisdiction of the Town of Butner consisting of lands not owned by the State of North Carolina.

(4) **Catchment area.** -- The geographic part of the State served by a specific area authority or county program.

(5) **City.** -- As defined in G.S. 153A-1(1).

(6) **Client.** -- An individual who is admitted to and receiving service from, or who in the past had been admitted to and received services from, a facility.

(7) **Client advocate.** -- A person whose role is to monitor the protection of client rights or to act as an individual advocate on behalf of a particular client in a facility.

(8) **Commission.** -- The Commission for Mental Health, Developmental Disabilities, and Substance Abuse Services, established under Part 4 of Article 3 of Chapter 143B of the General Statutes.

(8a) **Commitment examiner.** -- A physician, an eligible psychologist, or any health professional or mental health professional who is certified under G.S. 122C-263.1 to perform the first examination for involuntary commitment described in G.S. 122C-263(c) or G.S. 122C-283(c) as required by Parts 7 and 8 of this Article.

(9) **Confidential information.** -- Any information, whether recorded or not, relating to an individual served by a facility that was received in connection with the performance of any function of the facility. "Confidential information" does not include statistical information from reports and records or information regarding treatment or services which is shared for training, treatment, habilitation, or monitoring purposes that does not identify clients either directly or by reference to publicly known or available information.

(9a) **Core services.** -- Services that are necessary for the basic foundation of any service delivery system. Core services are of two types: front-end service capacity such as screening, assessment, and emergency triage, and indirect services such as prevention, education, and consultation at a community level.

(10) **County of residence.** -- The county of a client's domicile at the time of his or her admission or commitment to a facility. A county of residence is not changed because an individual is temporarily out of his or her county in a facility or otherwise.

(10a) **County program.** -- A mental health, developmental disabilities, and substance abuse services program established, operated, and governed by a county pursuant to G.S. 122C-115.1.

(11) Dangerous to self or others.

a. **Dangerous to self.** -- Within the relevant past, the individual has done any of the following:

1. The individual has acted in such a way as to show all of the following:

I. The individual would be unable, without care, supervision, and the continued assistance of others not otherwise available, to exercise self-control, judgment, and discretion in the conduct of the individual's daily responsibilities and social relations, or to satisfy the individual's need for nourishment, personal or medical care, shelter, or self-protection and safety.

II. There is a reasonable probability of the individual's suffering serious physical debilitation within the near future unless adequate treatment is given pursuant to this Chapter. A showing of behavior that is grossly irrational, of actions that the individual is unable to control, of behavior that is grossly inappropriate to the situation, or of other evidence of severely impaired insight and judgment shall create a prima facie inference that the individual is unable to care for himself or herself.

2. The individual has attempted suicide or threatened suicide and that there is a reasonable probability of suicide unless adequate treatment is given pursuant to this Chapter.

3. The individual has mutilated himself or herself or has attempted to mutilate himself or herself and that there is a reasonable probability of serious self-mutilation unless adequate treatment is given pursuant to this Chapter.

Previous episodes of dangerousness to self, when applicable, may be considered when determining reasonable probability of physical debilitation, suicide, or self-mutilation.

b. **Dangerous to others.** -- Within the relevant past, the individual has inflicted or attempted to inflict or threatened to inflict serious bodily harm on another, or has acted in such a way as to create a substantial risk of serious bodily harm to another, or has engaged in extreme destruction of property; and that there is a reasonable probability that this conduct will be repeated. Previous episodes of dangerousness to others, when applicable, may be considered when determining reasonable probability of future dangerous conduct. Clear, cogent, and convincing evidence that an individual has committed a homicide in the relevant past is prima facie evidence of dangerousness to others.

(11a) **Day/night service.** -- A service provided on a regular basis, in a structured environment that is offered to the same individual for a period of three or more hours within a 24-hour period.

(12) **Department.** -- The North Carolina Department of Health and Human Services.

(12a) **Developmental disability.** -- A severe, chronic disability of a person that satisfies all of the following:

a. Is attributable to a mental or physical impairment or combination of mental and physical impairments.

b. Is manifested before the person attains age 22, unless the disability is caused by a traumatic brain injury, in which case the disability may be manifested after attaining age 22.

c. Is likely to continue indefinitely.

d. Results in substantial functional limitations in three or more of the following areas of major life activity: self-care, receptive and expressive language, capacity for independent living, learning, mobility, self-direction, and economic self-sufficiency.

e. Reflects the person's need for a combination and sequence of special interdisciplinary, or generic care, treatment, or other services that are of a lifelong or extended duration and are individually planned and coordinated; or when applied to children from birth through age four, may be evidenced as a developmental delay.

f. Repealed by Session Laws 2019-76, s. 1, effective October 1, 2019, and applicable to proceedings commenced or services rendered on or after that date.

(13) **Division.** -- The Division of Mental Health, Developmental Disabilities, and Substance Abuse Services of the Department.

(13a) Repealed by Session Laws 2000-67, s. 11.21(c), effective July 1, 2000.

(13a1) Recodified as subdivision (13c).

(13b) Recodified as subdivision (13d).

(13c) **Eligible infants and toddlers.** -- Children with or at risk for developmental delays or atypical development until all of the following have occurred:

a. They have reached their third birthday.

b. Their parents have requested to have them receive services in the preschool program for children with disabilities established under Article 9 of Chapter 115C of the General Statutes.

c. They have been placed in the program by the local educational agency.

In no event shall a child be considered an eligible toddler after the beginning of the school year immediately following the child's third birthday, unless the Secretary and the State Board enter into an agreement under G.S. 115C-107.1(c).

The early intervention services that may be provided for these children and their families include early identification and screening, multidisciplinary evaluations, case management services, family training, counseling and home visits, psychological services, speech pathology and audiology, and occupational and physical therapy. All evaluations performed as part of early intervention services shall be appropriate to the individual child's age and development.

(13d) **Eligible psychologist.** -- A licensed psychologist who has at least two years' clinical experience. After January 1, 1995, "eligible psychologist" means a licensed psychologist who holds permanent licensure and certification as a health services provider psychologist issued by the North Carolina Psychology Board.

(14) **Facility.** -- Any person at one location whose primary purpose is to provide services for the care, treatment, habilitation, or rehabilitation of individuals with mental illnesses or intellectual or other developmental disabilities or substance abusers, and includes all of the following:

a. An "area facility," which is a facility that is operated by or under contract with the area authority or county program. For the purposes of this subparagraph, a contract is a contract, memorandum of understanding, or other written agreement whereby the facility agrees to provide services to one or more clients of the area authority or county program. Area facilities may also be licensable facilities in accordance with Article 2 of this Chapter. A State facility is not an area facility.

b. A "licensable facility," which is a facility for one or more minors or for two or more adults that provides services to individuals who have mental illnesses or intellectual or other developmental disabilities or are substance abusers. These services shall be day services offered to the same individual for a period of three hours or more during a 24-hour period, or residential services provided for 24 consecutive hours or more. Facilities for individuals who are substance abusers include chemical dependency facilities.

c. A "private facility," which is a facility that is either a licensable facility or a special unit of a general hospital or a part of either in which the specific service provided is not covered under the terms of a contract with an area authority.

d. The psychiatric service of the University of North Carolina Hospitals at Chapel Hill.

e. A "residential facility," which is a 24-hour facility that is not a hospital, including a group home.

f. A "State facility", which is a facility that is operated by the Secretary.

g. A "24-hour facility," which is a facility that provides a structured living environment and services for a period of 24 consecutive hours or more and includes hospitals that are facilities under this Chapter.

h. A Veterans Administration facility or part thereof that provides services for the care, treatment, habilitation, or rehabilitation of individuals with mental illnesses or intellectual or other developmental disabilities or substance abusers.

(15) **Guardian.** -- A person appointed as a guardian of the person or general guardian by the court under Chapters 7A or 35A or former Chapters 33 or 35 of the General Statutes.

(16) **Habilitation.** -- Training, care, and specialized therapies undertaken to assist a client in maintaining his current level of functioning or in achieving progress in developmental skills areas.

(16a) **Health screening.** -- An appropriate screening suitable for the symptoms presented and within the capability of the entity, including ancillary services routinely available to the entity, to determine whether or not an emergency medical condition exists. An emergency medical condition exists if an individual has acute symptoms of sufficient severity, including severe pain, such that the absence of immediate medical attention could reasonably be expected to result in placing the individual's health in serious jeopardy, serious impairment to bodily functions, or serious dysfunction of any bodily organ or part.

(16b) **Incapable.** -- With respect to an individual, as defined in G.S. 122C-72(4). An adult individual who is incapable is not the same as an incompetent adult unless the adult individual has been adjudicated incompetent under Chapter 35A of the General Statutes.

(17) **Incompetent adult.** -- An adult individual who has been adjudicated incompetent under Chapter 35A of the General Statutes.

Chapter 122C

(17a) **Intellectual disability.** -- A developmental disability characterized by significantly subaverage general intellectual functioning existing concurrently with deficits in adaptive behavior and manifested before age 22.

(18) **Intoxicated.** -- The condition of an individual whose mental or physical functioning is presently substantially impaired as a result of the use of alcohol or other substance.

(19) **Law enforcement officer.** -- Sheriff, deputy sheriff, police officer, State highway patrolman, or an officer employed by a city or county under G.S. 122C-302.

(20) "Legally responsible person" means: (i) when applied to an adult, who has been adjudicated incompetent, a guardian, subject to the limitations of G.S. 35A-1241(3); (ii) when applied to a minor, a parent, guardian, a person standing in loco parentis, or a legal custodian other than a parent who has been granted specific authority by law or in a custody order to consent for medical care, including psychiatric treatment; or (iii) when applied to an adult who has a health care power of attorney and who is incapable as defined in G.S. 122C-72(4) a health care agent named pursuant to a valid health care power of attorney unless the adult is adjudicated incompetent following the execution of the health care power of attorney and the health care agent's authority is suspended pursuant to G.S. 32A-22 and G.S. 35A-1208; provided that if an incapable adult does not have a health care agent or guardian, "legally responsible person" means one of the persons specified in subdivisions (3) through (7) of subsection (c) of G.S. 90-21.13, to be selected based on the priority indicated in said subdivisions (3) through (7).

(20a) **Local funds.** -- Fees from services, including client payments, Medicare and the local and federal share of Medicaid receipts, fees from agencies under contract, gifts and donations, and county and municipal funds, and any other funds not administered by the Division.

(20b) **Local management entity (LME).** -- An area authority.

(20c) **Local management entity/managed care organization (LME/MCO).** -- A local management entity that is under contract with the Department to operate the combined Medicaid Waiver program authorized under Section 1915(b) and Section 1915(c) of the Social Security Act or to operate a BH IDD tailored plan.

(21) **Mental illness.** -- The following:
a. When applied to an adult, an illness which so lessens the capacity of the individual to use self-control, judgment, and discretion in the conduct of the individual's affairs and social relations as to make it necessary or advisable for the individual to be under treatment, care, supervision, guidance, or control.

b. When applied to a minor, a mental condition, other than an intellectual disability alone, that so impairs the minor's capacity to exercise age adequate self-control or judgment in the conduct of the minor's activities and social relationships so that the minor is in need of treatment.

(22), (23) Repealed by Session Laws 2019-76, s. 1, effective October 1, 2019, and applicable to proceedings commenced or services rendered on or after that date.

(23a) **Minimally adequate services.** -- A level of service required for compliance with all applicable State and federal laws, rules, regulations, and policies and with generally accepted professional standards and principles.

(24) **Next of kin.** -- The individual designated in writing by the client or the client's legally responsible person upon the client's acceptance at a facility. If no such designation has been made, "next of kin" means the client's spouse or nearest blood relation in accordance with G.S. 104A-1.

(25) **Operating costs.** -- Expenditures made by an area authority in the delivery of services for mental health, developmental disabilities, and substance abuse as provided in this Chapter and includes the employment of legal counsel on a temporary basis to represent the interests of the area authority.

(26) Repealed by Session Laws 1987, c. 345, s. 1.

(26a) **Other recipient.** -- An individual who is not admitted to a facility but who receives a service other than care, treatment, or rehabilitation services. The services that the "other recipient" may receive include consultative, preventative, educational, and assessment services.

(27) **Outpatient treatment.** -- As used in Part 7 of Article 5 of this Chapter, means treatment in an outpatient setting and may include medication, individual or group therapy, day or partial day programming activities, services and training including educational and vocational activities, supervision of living arrangements, and any other services prescribed either to alleviate the individual's illness or disability, to maintain semi-independent functioning, or to prevent further deterioration that may reasonably be predicted to result in the

need for inpatient commitment to a 24-hour facility.

(27a) **Outpatient treatment physician or center.** -- As used in Part 7 of Article 5 of this Chapter, a physician or center that provides treatment services directly to the outpatient commitment respondent. An LME/MCO that contracts with an outpatient treatment physician or center to provide outpatient treatment services to a respondent is not an outpatient treatment physician or center. Every LME/MCO is responsible for contracting with qualified providers of services in accordance with G.S. 122C-141, 122C-142(a), 122C-115.2(b)(1)b., and 122C-115.4(b)(2) to ensure the availability of qualified providers of outpatient commitment services to clients of LME/MCOs who are respondents to outpatient commitment proceedings and meet the criteria for outpatient commitment. A contracted provider with an LME/MCO shall not be designated as an outpatient treatment physician or center on an outpatient commitment order unless the respondent enrolled with an LME/MCO or is eligible for services through an LME/MCO, or the respondent otherwise qualifies for the provision of services offered by the provider.

(28) **Person.** -- Any individual, firm, partnership, corporation, company, association, joint stock association, agency, or area authority.

(29) **Physician.** -- An individual licensed to practice medicine in North Carolina under Chapter 90 of the General Statutes or a licensed medical doctor employed by the Veterans Administration.

(29a) Repealed by Session Laws 2018-33, s. 1, effective October 1, 2019.

(29b) "Prepaid health plan" has the same meaning as in G.S. 108D-1.

(30) **Provider of support services.** -- A person that provides to a facility support services such as data processing, dosage preparation, laboratory analyses, or legal, medical, accounting, or other professional services, including human services.

(30a) **Psychologist.** -- An individual licensed to practice psychology under Chapter 90 of the General Statutes. The term "eligible psychologist" is defined in subdivision (13d) of this section.

(30b) **Public services.** -- Publicly funded mental health, developmental disabilities, and substance abuse services, whether provided by public or private providers.

(31) **Qualified professional.** -- Any individual with appropriate training or experience as specified by the General Statutes or by rule of the Commission in the fields of mental health or developmental disabilities or substance abuse treatment or habilitation, including physicians, psychologists, psychological associates, educators, social workers, registered nurses, certified fee-based practicing pastoral counselors, and certified counselors.

(32) **Responsible professional.** -- An individual within a facility who is designated by the facility director to be responsible for the care, treatment, habilitation, or rehabilitation of a specific client and who is eligible to provide care, treatment, habilitation, or rehabilitation relative to the client's disability.

(32a) **Secretary.** -- The Secretary of the Department of Health and Human Services.

(32b) **Security recordings.** -- Any films, videos, or electronic or other media recordings of a common area in a State facility that are produced for the purpose of maintaining or enhancing the health and safety of clients, residents, staff, or visitors of that State facility. The term does not include recordings of a client's clinical sessions or any other recordings that are part of a client's confidential records or information.

(33) Renumbered as subdivision (32a).

(33a) **Severe and persistent mental illness.** -- A mental disorder suffered by persons of 18 years of age or older that leads these persons to exhibit emotional or behavioral functioning that is so impaired as to interfere substantially with their capacity to remain in the community without supportive treatment or services of a long term or indefinite duration. This disorder is a severe and persistent mental disability, resulting in a long-term limitation of functional capacities for the primary activities of daily living, such as interpersonal relations, homemaking, self-care, employment, and recreation.

(34) Repealed by Session Laws 2001-437, s. 1.2(c), effective July 1, 2002.

(35) Repealed by Session Laws 2001-437, s. 1.2(c), effective July 1, 2002.

(35a) Renumbered as subdivision (35e).

(35b) **Specialty services.** -- Services that are provided to consumers from low-incidence populations.

(35c) **State or Local Consumer Advocate.** -- The individual carrying out the duties of the State or Local Consumer Advocacy Program Office in accordance with Article 1A of this Chapter.

(35d) **State Plan.** -- The State Plan for Mental Health, Developmental Disabilities, and Substance Abuse Services.

(35e) **State resources.** -- State and federal funds and other receipts administered by the Division.

Chapter 122C

(36) **Substance abuse.** -- The pathological use or abuse of alcohol or other drugs in a way or to a degree that produces an impairment in personal, social, or occupational functioning. "Substance abuse" may include a pattern of tolerance and withdrawal.

(37) **Substance abuser.** -- An individual who engages in substance abuse.

(38) **Targeted population.** -- Those individuals who are given service priority under the State Plan.

(38a) **Traumatic brain injury.** -- An injury to the brain caused by an external physical force resulting in total or partial functional disability, psychosocial impairment, or both, and meets all of the following criteria:

a. Involves an open or closed head injury.

b. Resulted from a single event, or resulted from a series of events which may include multiple concussions.

c. Occurs with or without a loss of consciousness at the time of injury.

d. Results in impairments in one or more areas of the following functions: cognition; language; memory; attention; reasoning; abstract thinking; judgment; problem-solving; sensory, perceptual, and motor abilities; psychosocial behavior; physical functions; information processing; and speech.

e. Does not include brain injuries that are congenital or degenerative.

(39) **Uniform portal process.** -- A standardized process and procedures used to ensure consumer access to, and exit from, public services in accordance with the State Plan.

History.
1899, c. 1, s. 28; Rev., s. 4574; C.S., s. 6189; 1945, c. 952, s. 18; 1947, c. 537, s. 12; 1949, c. 71, s. 3; 1955, c. 887, s. 1; 1957, c. 1232, s. 13; 1959, c. 1028, s. 4; 1963, c. 1166, ss. 2, 10; c. 1184, s. 1; 1965, c. 933; 1973, c. 475, s. 2; c. 476, s. 133; c. 726, s. 1; c. 1408, ss. 1, 3; 1977, c. 400, ss. 2, 12; c. 568, s. 1; c. 679, s. 7; 1977, 2nd Sess., c. 1134, s. 2; 1979, c. 164, ss. 3, 4; c. 171, s. 2; c. 358, ss. 2, 26; c. 915, s. 1; c. 751, s. 28; 1981, c. 51, ss. 2-4; c. 539, s. 1; 1983, c. 280; c. 383, s. 2; c. 638, s. 2; c. 718, s. 1; c. 864, s. 4; 1983 (Reg. Sess., 1984), c. 1110, s. 4; 1985, c. 589, s. 2; c. 695, s. 1; c. 777, s. 2; 1985 (Reg. Sess., 1986), c. 863, s. 7; 1987, c. 345, s. 1; c. 830, ss. 47(a), (b); 1989, c. 141, s. 8; c. 223; c. 486, s. 2; c. 625, s. 2; 1989 (Reg. Sess., 1990), c. 823, s. 11; c. 1003, s. 2; c. 1024, s. 26(a); 1993, c. 321, s. 220(a) -(c); c. 375, s. 6; c. 396, ss. 1, 2; 1995, c. 249, s. 1; c. 406, s. 5; 1997-443, s. 11A.118(a); 1997-456, s. 27; 1998-198, s. 3; 1998-202, s. 4(r); 1999-186, s. 1; 2000-67, s. 11.21(c); 2001-437, ss. 1.2(b), 1.2(c); 2001-437, s. 1.2(a); 2003-313, s. 1; 2006-69, s. 3(n); 2006-142, ss. 4(a), 7; 2007-269, s. 3.1;

2007-502, s. 15(a); 2008-107, s. 10.15(dd); 2013-85, s. 1; 2018-33, s. 1; 2019-76, s. 1; 2019-81, s. 9; 2019-240, ss. 20(a), 22, 26(a); 2021-77, s.1

ARTICLE 2
LICENSURE OF FACILITIES FOR INDIVIDUALS WITH MENTAL HEALTH DISORDERS, DEVELOPMENTAL DISABILITIES, AND SUBSTANCE USE DISORDERS.

§ 122C-24.1. Penalties; remedies

(a) **Violation Classification and Penalties.** -- The Department of Health and Human Services shall impose an administrative penalty in accordance with provisions of this Article on any facility licensed under this Article which is found to be in violation of Article 2 or 3 of this Chapter or applicable State and federal laws and regulations. Citations for violations shall be classified and penalties assessed according to the nature of the violation as follows:

(1) "Type A1 Violation" means a violation by a facility of the regulations, standards, and requirements set forth in Article 2 or 3 of this Chapter or applicable State or federal laws and regulations governing the licensure or certification of a facility which results in death or serious physical harm, abuse, neglect, or exploitation. The person making the findings shall do the following:

a. Orally and immediately inform the facility of the Type A1 Violation and the specific findings.

a1. Require a written plan of protection regarding how the facility will immediately abate the Type A1 Violation in order to protect clients from further risk or additional harm.

b. Within 15 working days of the investigation, send a report of the findings to the facility.

c. Require a plan of correction to be submitted to the Department, based on a written report of the findings, that describes steps the facility will take to achieve and maintain compliance.

The Department shall impose a civil penalty in an amount not less than five hundred dollars ($ 500.00) nor more than ten thousand dollars ($ 10,000) for each Type A1 Violation in facilities or programs that serve six or fewer persons. The Department shall impose a civil penalty in an amount not less than one thousand dollars ($ 1,000) nor more than twenty thousand dollars ($ 20,000) for each Type A1 Violation in facilities or programs that serve seven or more persons. Where a facility has failed to correct a Type A1 Violation, the Department shall access the facility a civil penalty in the amount of up to one thousand dollars ($ 1,000) for each day that the violation continues beyond the time specified for correction. The Department or its authorized representative shall determine whether the violation has been corrected.

(1a) "Type A2 Violation" means a violation by a facility of the regulations, standards, and requirements set forth in Article 2 or 3 of this Chapter or applicable State or federal laws and regulations governing the licensure or certification of a facility which results in substantial risk that death or serious physical harm, abuse, neglect, or exploitation will occur. The person making the findings shall do the following:

    a. Orally and immediately inform the facility of the Type A2 Violation and the specific findings.

    b. Require a written plan of protection regarding how the facility will immediately abate the Type A2 Violation in order to protect clients or residents from further risk or additional harm.

    c. Within 15 working days of the investigation, send a report of the findings to the facility.

    d. Require a plan of correction to be submitted to the Department, based on the written report of the findings, that describes steps the facility will take to achieve and maintain compliance.

The violation or violations shall be corrected within the time specified for correction by the Department or its authorized representative. The Department may or may not assess a penalty taking into consideration the compliance history, preventative measures, and response to previous violations by the facility. Where a facility has failed to correct a Type A2 Violation, the Department shall assess the facility a civil penalty in the amount of up to one thousand dollars ($ 1,000) for each day that the deficiency continues beyond the time specified for correction by the Department or its authorized representative. The Department or its authorized representative shall determine whether the violation has been corrected.

(1b) Repealed by Session Laws 2016-50, s. 1, effective June 30, 2016.

(2) "Type B Violation" means a violation by a facility of the regulations, standards, and requirements set forth in Article 2 or 3 of this Chapter or applicable State or federal laws and regulations governing the licensure or certification of a facility which is detrimental to the health, safety, or welfare of any client or patient, but which does not result in substantial risk that death or serious physical harm, abuse, neglect, or exploitation will occur. The person making the findings shall do the following:

    a. Orally and immediately inform the facility of the Type B Violation and the specific findings.

    b. Require a written plan of protection regarding how the facility will immediately abate the Type B Violation in order to protect clients or residents from further risk or additional harm.

    c. Within 15 working days of the investigation, send a report of the findings to the facility.

    d. Require a plan of correction to be submitted to the Department, based on the written report of the findings, that describes steps the facility will take to achieve and maintain compliance.

Where a facility has failed to correct a Type B Violation within the time specified for correction by the Department or its authorized representative, the Department shall assess the facility a civil penalty in the amount of up to four hundred dollars ($ 400.00) for each day that the violation continues beyond the date specified for correction without just reason for the failure. The Department or its authorized representative shall ensure that the violation has been corrected.

(2a) A Type A1, Type A2, or Type B Violation as defined above shall not include a violation by a facility of the regulations, standards, and requirements set forth in Article 2 or 3 of this Chapter or applicable State or federal laws and regulations governing the licensure or certification of a facility if all of the following criteria are met:

    a. The violation was discovered by the facility.

    b. The Department determines that the violation was abated immediately.

    c. The violation was corrected prior to inspection by the Department.

    d. The Department determines that reasonable preventative measures were in place prior to the violation.

    e. The Department determines that subsequent to the violation, the facility implemented corrective measures to achieve and maintain compliance.

(2b) As used in this section, "substantial risk" shall mean the risk of an outcome

Chapter 122C

that is substantially certain to materialize if immediate action is not taken.

(3) **Repeat Violations. --** The Department shall impose a civil penalty which is treble the amount assessed under this subsection when a facility under the same management or ownership has received a citation during the previous 12 months for which the appeal rights are exhausted and penalty payment is expected or has occurred, and the current violation is for the same specific provision of a statute or regulation for which it received a violation during the previous 12 months.

(b) Repealed by Session Laws 2011-249, s. 1, effective June 23, 2011.

(c) **Factors to Be Considered in Determining Amount of Initial Penalty. --** In determining the amount of the initial penalty to be imposed under this section, the Department shall consider the following factors:

(1) There is substantial risk that serious physical harm, abuse, neglect, or exploitation will occur, and this has not been corrected within the time specified by the Department or its authorized representative;

(2) Serious physical harm, abuse, neglect, or exploitation, without substantial risk for client death, did occur;

(3) Serious physical harm, abuse, neglect, or exploitation, with substantial risk for client death, did occur;

(3a) A client died;

(3b) A client died and there is substantial risk to others for serious physical harm, abuse, neglect, or exploitation;

(3c) A client died and there is substantial risk for further client death;

(4) The reasonable diligence exercised by the licensee to comply with G.S. 131E-256 and other applicable State and federal laws and regulations;

(5) Efforts by the licensee to correct violations;

(6) The number and type of previous violations committed by the licensee within the past 36 months; and

(7) Repealed by Session Laws 2011-249, s. 1, effective June 23, 2011.

(8) The number of clients or patients put at risk by the violation.

(d) The facts found to support the factors in subsection (c) of this section shall be the basis in determining the amount of the penalty. The Department shall document the findings in written record and shall make the written record available to all affected parties including:

(1) The licensee involved;

(2) The clients or patients affected; and

(3) The family members or guardians of the clients or patients affected.

(e) The Department shall impose a civil penalty of fifty dollars ($ 50.00) per day on any facility which refuses to allow an authorized representative of the Department to inspect the premises and records of the facility.

(f) Any facility wishing to contest a penalty shall be entitled to an administrative hearing as provided in Chapter 150B of the General Statutes. A petition for a contested case shall be filed within 30 days after the Department mails a notice of penalty to a licensee. At least the following specific issues shall be addressed at the administrative hearing:

(1) The reasonableness of the amount of any civil penalty assessed, and

(2) The degree to which each factor has been evaluated pursuant to subsection (c) of this section to be considered in determining the amount of an initial penalty.

If a civil penalty is found to be unreasonable or if the evaluation of each factor is found to be incomplete, the hearing officer may recommend that the penalty be adjusted accordingly.

(g) Any penalty imposed by the Department of Health and Human Services under this section shall commence on the date of the letter of notification of the penalty amount.

(h) The Secretary may bring a civil action in the superior court of the county wherein the violation occurred to recover the amount of the administrative penalty whenever a facility:

(1) Which has not requested an administrative hearing fails to pay the penalty within 60 days after being notified of the penalty, or

(2) Which has requested an administrative hearing fails to pay the penalty within 60 days after receipt of a written copy of the decision as provided in G.S. 150B-37.

(i) In lieu of assessing all or some of the administrative penalty, the Secretary may order a facility to provide staff training, or consider the approval of training completed by the facility after the violation, if all of the following criteria are met:

(1) The training is determined by the Department to be specific to the violation.

(2) The training is approved by the Department.

(3) The training is taught by someone approved by the Department.

(4) The facility has corrected the violation and continues to remain in compliance with the regulation.

(j) The clear proceeds of civil penalties provided for in this section shall be remitted to the State Treasurer for deposit in accordance with State law.

(k) In considering renewal of a license, the Department shall not renew a license if outstanding fines and penalties imposed by the Department against the facility or program have not been paid. Fines and penalties for which an appeal is pending are exempt from consideration for nonrenewal under this subsection.

History.
2000-55, s. 4; 2005-276, ss. 10.40A(e), 10.40A(f); 2011-249, s. 1; 2011-398, s. 39; 2016-50, s. 1

§ 122C-28. Penalties

This section has more than one version with varying effective dates. To view a complete list of the versions of this section see Table of Contents.

Operating a licensable facility without a license is a Class H felony, including a fine of one thousand dollars ($ 1,000) per day that the facility is in operation in violation of this Article.

History.
1983, c. 718, s. 1; 1985, c. 589, s. 2; 1993, c. 539, s. 919; 1994, Ex. Sess., c. 24, s. 14(c); 2021-77, s. 7.2(a)

§ 122C-28.1. Facilities in violation of this Article

(a) If the Department has directed a facility not licensed under this Article that is providing services requiring a license under this Article to cease and desist from engaging in any act or practice in violation of this Article, then the Department shall conduct a follow-up visit to determine if the Secretary may issue a cease and desist order pursuant to G.S. 122C-27, unless a cease and desist order has already been issued.

(b) The district attorney's office with jurisdiction over the facility shall collect information on the total amount of fines collected pursuant to G.S. 122C-28 and report that information to the Department.

History.
2021-77, s. 7.1(a)

ARTICLE 3
CLIENTS' RIGHTS AND ADVANCE INSTRUCTION

PART 1
CLIENT'S RIGHTS

§ 122C-51. Declaration of policy on clients' rights

It is the policy of the State to assure basic human rights to each client of a facility. These rights include the right to dignity, privacy, humane care, and freedom from mental and physical abuse, neglect, and exploitation. Each facility shall assure to each client the right to live as normally as possible while receiving care and treatment.

It is further the policy of this State that each client who is admitted to and is receiving services from a facility has the right to treatment, including access to medical care and habilitation, regardless of age or degree of mental illness, developmental disabilities, or substance abuse. Each client has the right to an individualized written treatment or habilitation plan setting forth a program to maximize the development or restoration of his capabilities.

History.
1973, c. 475, s. 1; c. 1436, ss. 1, 8; 1985, c. 589, s. 2; 1989, c. 625, s. 7; 1997-442, s. 1

§ 122C-52. Right to confidentiality

(a) Except as provided in G.S. 132-5 and G.S. 122C-31(h), confidential information acquired in attending or treating a client is not a public record under Chapter 132 of the General Statutes.

(b) Except as authorized by G.S. 122C-53 through G.S. 122C-56, no individual having access to confidential information may disclose this information, provided, however, a HIPAA covered entity or business associate receiving confidential information that has been disclosed pursuant to G.S. 122C-53 through G.S. 122C-56 may use and disclose such information as permitted or required under 45 Code of Federal Regulations Part 164, Subpart E.

(c) Except as provided by G.S. 122C-53 through G.S. 122C-56, each client has the right that no confidential information acquired be disclosed by the facility.

(d) No provision of G.S. 122C-205 and G.S. 122C-53 through G.S. 122C-56 permitting disclosure of confidential information may apply to the records of a client when federal statutes or regulations applicable to that client prohibit the disclosure of this information.

(e) Except as required or permitted by law, disclosure of confidential information to someone not authorized to receive the information is a Class 3 misdemeanor and is punishable only by a fine, not to exceed five hundred dollars ($ 500.00).

History.
1955, c. 887, s. 12; 1963, c. 1166, s. 10; 1965, c. 800, s. 4; 1973, c. 47, s. 2; c. 476, s. 133; c. 673, s. 5; c. 1408, s. 2; 1979, c. 147; 1983, c. 383, s. 10; c. 491; c. 638, s. 22; c. 864, s. 4; 1985, c. 589, s. 2; 1985 (Reg. Sess., 1986), c. 863, s. 11; 1987, c. 749, s. 2; 1993, c. 539, s. 920; 1994, Ex. Sess., c. 24, s. 14(c); 2009-299, s. 5; 2011-314, s. 2(a)

§ 122C-53. Exceptions; client

(a) A facility may disclose confidential information if the client or the legally responsible person consents in writing to the release of the information to a specified person. This release is valid for a specified length of time and is subject to revocation by the consenting individual.

(b) A facility may disclose (i) the fact of admission or discharge of a client and (ii) the time and location of admission or discharge to the client's next of kin whenever the responsible professional determines that the disclosure is in the best interest of the client.

(c) Upon request a client shall have access to confidential information in the client's record except information that would be injurious to the client's physical or mental well-being as determined by the attending physician or, if there is none, by the facility director or the facility director's designee. If the attending physician or, if there is none, the facility director or the facility director's designee has refused to provide confidential information to a client, the client may request that the information be sent to a physician or psychologist of the client's choice, and in this event the information shall be so provided.

(d) Except as provided by G.S. 90-21.4(b), upon request the legally responsible person of a client shall have access to confidential information in the client's record; except information that would be injurious to the client's physical or mental well-being as determined by the attending physician or, if there is none, by the facility director or the facility director's designee. If the attending physician or, if there is none, the facility director or the facility director's designee has refused to provide confidential information to the legally responsible person, the legally responsible person may request that the information be sent to a physician or psychologist of the legally responsible person's choice, and in this event the information shall be so provided.

(e) A client advocate's access to confidential information and the client's responsibility for safeguarding this information are as provided by subsection (g) of this section.

(f) As used in subsection (g) of this section, the following terms have the meanings specified:

(1) "Internal client advocate" means a client advocate who is employed by the facility or has a written contractual agreement with the Department or with the facility to provide monitoring and advocacy services to clients in the facility in which the client is receiving services.

(2) "External client advocate" means a client advocate acting on behalf of a particular client with the written consent and authorization under either of the following circumstances:

a. In the case of a client who is an adult and who has not been adjudicated incompetent under Chapter 35A or former Chapters 33 or 35 of the General Statutes, of the client.

b. In the case of any other client, of the client and the legally responsible person.

(g) An internal client advocate shall be granted, without the consent of the client or the legally responsible person, access to routine reports and other confidential information necessary to fulfill monitoring and advocacy functions. In this role, the internal client advocate may disclose confidential information received to the client involved, to the legally responsible person, to the director of the facility or the director's designee, to other individuals within the facility who are involved in the treatment or habilitation of the client, or to the Secretary in accordance with the rules of the Commission. Any further disclosure shall require the written consent of the client and the legally responsible person. An external client advocate shall have access to confidential information only upon the written consent of the client and his legally responsible person. In this role, the external client advocate may use the information only as authorized by the client and his legally responsible person.

(h) In accordance with G.S. 122C-205, the facility shall notify the appropriate individuals upon the escape from and subsequent return of clients to a 24-hour facility.

(i) Upon the request of (i) a client who is an adult and who has not been adjudicated incompetent under Chapter 35A or former Chapters 33 or 35 of the General Statutes, or (ii) the legally responsible person for any other client, a facility shall disclose to an attorney confidential information relating to that client.

History.

1973, c. 475, s. 1; c. 1436, ss. 2-5; 1985, c. 589, s. 2; 1989 (Reg. Sess., 1990), c. 1024, s. 26(d); 1995, c. 507, s. 23.4; 2018-33, s. 3

§ 122C-54. Exceptions; abuse reports and court proceedings

(a) A facility shall disclose confidential information if a court of competent jurisdiction issues an order compelling disclosure.

(a1) Upon a determination by the facility director or the facility director's designee that disclosure is in the best interests of the client, a facility may disclose confidential information for purposes of filing a petition for involuntary commitment of a client pursuant to Article 5 of this Chapter or for purposes of filing a petition for the adjudication of incompetency of the client and the appointment of a guardian or an interim guardian under Chapter 35A of the General Statutes.

(b) If an individual is a defendant in a criminal case and a mental examination of the defendant has been ordered by the court as provided in G.S. 15A-1002, the facility shall send the results or the report of the mental examination to the clerk of court, to the district attorney or prosecuting officer, and to the attorney of record for the defendant as provided in G.S. 15A-1002(d). The report shall contain a treatment recommendation, if any, and an opinion as to whether there is a likelihood that the defendant will gain the capacity to proceed.

(c) When an individual is held at a facility under involuntary commitment or voluntary admission proceedings that require district court hearings or rehearings pursuant to Article 5 of this Chapter, certified copies of written results of examinations, gathered during the course of the current commitment or admission, shall be furnished by the facility to the client's counsel, the attorney representing the State's interest, and the court. Upon request, the facility shall disclose to respondent's counsel, the attorney representing the State's interest, and the court confidential information collected, maintained, or used in attending or treating the respondent during the proceeding for voluntary admission or involuntary commitment. Other medical records shall be furnished only upon court order. The confidentiality of client information shall be preserved in all matters except those pertaining to the necessity for admission or continued stay in the facility or commitment under review.

(d) Any individual seeking confidential information contained in the court files or the court records of a proceeding made pursuant to Article 5 of this Chapter may file a written motion in the cause setting out why the information is needed. A district court judge may issue an order to disclose the confidential information sought if he finds the order is appropriate under the circumstances and if he finds that it is in the best interest of the individual admitted or committed or of the public to have the information disclosed.

(d1) Repealed by Session Laws 2015-195, s. 11(a), effective January 1, 2016.

(d2) The record of involuntary commitment for inpatient or outpatient mental health treatment or for substance abuse treatment required to be reported to the National Instant Criminal Background Check System (NICS) by G.S. 14-409.43 shall be accessible only by the sheriff or the sheriff's designee for the purposes of conducting background checks under G.S. 14-404 and shall remain otherwise confidential as provided by this Article.

(e) Upon the request of the legally responsible person or the minor admitted or committed, and after that minor has both been released and reached adulthood, the court records of that minor made in proceedings pursuant to Article 5 of this Chapter may be expunged from the files of the court. The minor and the minor's legally responsible person shall be informed in writing by the court of the right provided by this subsection at the time that the application for admission is filed with the court.

(f) A State facility and the psychiatric service of the University of North Carolina Hospitals at Chapel Hill may disclose confidential information to staff attorneys of the Attorney General's office whenever the information is necessary to the performance of the statutory responsibilities of the Attorney General's office or to its performance when acting as attorney for a State facility or the psychiatric service of the University of North Carolina Hospitals at Chapel Hill.

(g) A facility may disclose confidential information to an attorney who represents either the facility or an employee of the facility, if such information is relevant to litigation, to the operations of the facility, or to the provision of services by the facility. An employee may discuss confidential information with the employee's attorney or with an attorney representing the facility in which the employee is employed.

(h) A facility shall disclose confidential information for purposes of complying with Article 3 of Chapter 7B of the General Statutes and Article 6 of Chapter 108A of the General Statutes, or as required by other State or federal law.

(i) G.S. 132-1.4 shall apply to the records of criminal investigations conducted by any law enforcement unit of a State facility, and information described in G.S. 132-1.4(c) that is collected by the State facility law enforcement unit shall be public records within the meaning of G.S. 132-1.

(j) Notwithstanding any other provision of this Chapter, the Secretary may inform any person of any incident or event involving the welfare of a client or former client when the Secretary determines that the release of the information is essential to maintaining the integrity of the Department. However, the release shall not include information that identifies the client directly, or information for which disclosure is prohibited by State or federal law or requirements, or information for which, in the Secretary's judgment, by reference to publicly known or available information, there is a reasonable basis to believe the client will be identified.

History.
1955, c. 887, s. 12; 1963, c. 1166, s. 10; 1973, c. 47, s. 2; c. 476, s. 133; c. 673, s. 5; c. 1408, s. 2; 1977, c. 696, s. 1; 1979, c. 147; c. 915, s. 20; 1983, c. 383, s. 10; c. 491;

c. 638, s. 22; c. 864, s. 4; 1985, c. 589, s. 2; 1987, c. 638, ss. 1, 3.1; 1989, c. 141, s. 9; 1993, c. 516, s. 12; 1998-202, s. 13(dd); 2003-313, s. 2; 2008-210, s. 1; 2009-299, s. 6; 2013-18, s. 7; 2013-369, ss. 7, 8; 2015-195, s. 11(a), (e); 2018-33, s. 4

N.C. Gen. Stat. § 122C-54.1

Recodified as G.S. 14-409.42 by Session Laws 2015-195, s. 11(b), effective August 5, 2015.

§ 122C-55. Exceptions; care and treatment

(a) Any facility may share confidential information regarding any client of that facility with any other facility when necessary to coordinate appropriate and effective care, treatment, or habilitation of the client. For the purposes of this section, the following definitions apply:

(1) "Client" includes an enrollee as defined in G.S. 108D-1.

(1a) **Coordinate.** -- The provision, coordination, or management of mental health, developmental disabilities, and substance abuse services and other health or related services by one or more facilities and includes the referral of a client from one facility to another.

(2) **Facility or area facility.** -- Include[s] an area authority or a prepaid health plan.

(3) **Secretary.** -- Includes any primary care case management programs that contract with the Department to provide a primary care case management program for recipients of publicly funded health and related services.

(a1) Any facility may share confidential information regarding any client of that facility with the Secretary, and the Secretary may share confidential information regarding any client with a facility when necessary to conduct quality assessment and improvement activities or to coordinate appropriate and effective care, treatment, or habilitation of the client. For purposes of this subsection, subsection (a6), and subsection (a7) of this section, the purposes or activities for which confidential information may be disclosed include, but are not limited to, case management and care coordination, disease management, outcomes evaluation, the development of clinical guidelines and protocols, the development of care management plans and systems, population-based activities relating to improving or reducing health care costs, and the provision, coordination, or management of mental health, developmental disabilities, and substance abuse services and other health or related services.

(a2) Any facility or the psychiatric service of the University of North Carolina Hospitals at Chapel Hill may share confidential information regarding any client of that facility with any other area facility or State facility or the psychiatric service of the University of North Carolina Hospitals at Chapel Hill when necessary to conduct payment activities relating to an individual served by the facility. Payment activities are activities undertaken by a facility to obtain payment or receive reimbursement for the provision of services and may include, but are not limited to, determinations of eligibility or coverage, coordination of benefits, determinations of cost-sharing amounts, claims management, claims processing, claims adjudication, claims appeals, billing and collection activities, medical necessity reviews, utilization management and review, precertification and preauthorization of services, concurrent and retrospective review of services, and appeals related to utilization management and review.

(a3) Whenever there is reason to believe that a client is eligible for benefits through a Department program, any facility or the psychiatric service of the University of North Carolina Hospitals at Chapel Hill may share confidential information regarding any client of that facility with the Secretary, and the Secretary may share confidential information regarding any client with an area facility or State facility or the psychiatric services of the University of North Carolina Hospitals at Chapel Hill. Disclosure is limited to that information necessary to establish initial eligibility for benefits, determine continued eligibility over time, and obtain reimbursement for the costs of services provided to the client.

(a4) An area authority or prepaid health plan may share confidential information regarding any client with any area facility, and any area facility may share confidential information regarding any client of that facility with the area authority or prepaid health plan, when the area authority or prepaid health plan determines the disclosure is necessary to develop, manage, monitor, or evaluate the area authority's or prepaid health plan's network of qualified providers as provided in G.S. 122C-115.2(b)(1)b., G.S. 122C-141(a), Article 3 of Chapter 108D of the General Statutes, the State Plan, rules of the Secretary, and contracts between the facility and the Department. For the purposes of this subsection, the purposes or activities for which confidential information may be disclosed include, but are not limited to, quality assessment and improvement activities, provider accreditation and staff credentialing, developing contracts and negotiating rates, investigating and responding to client grievances and complaints, evaluating practitioner and provider performance, auditing functions, on-site monitoring, conducting consumer satisfaction studies, and collecting and analyzing performance data.

(a5) Any area facility may share confidential information with any other area facility regarding an applicant when necessary to determine whether the applicant is eligible for area facility services. For the purpose of this subsection, the term "applicant" means an individual who contacts an area facility for services.

(a6) When necessary to conduct quality assessment and improvement activities or to coordinate appropriate and effective care, treatment, or habilitation of the client, the Department's Community Care of North Carolina Program, or other primary care case management program, may disclose confidential information acquired pursuant to subsection (a1) of this section to a health care provider or other entity that has entered into a written agreement with the Community Care of North Carolina Program, or other primary care case management program, to participate in the care management support network and systems developed and maintained by the primary care case manager for the purpose of coordinating and improving the quality of care for recipients of publicly funded health and related services. Health care providers and other entities receiving confidential information that has been disclosed pursuant to this subsection may use and disclose the information as permitted or required under 45 Code of Federal Regulations Part 164, Subpart E.

(a7) A facility may share confidential information with one or more HIPAA covered entities or business associates for the same purposes set forth in subsection (a1) of this section. Before making disclosures under this subsection, the facility shall inform the client or the client's legally responsible person that the facility may make the disclosures unless the client or the client's legally responsible person objects in writing or signs a non-disclosure form that shall be supplied by the facility. If the client or the client's legally responsible person objects in writing or signs a non-disclosure form, the disclosures otherwise permitted by this subsection are prohibited. A covered entity or business associate receiving confidential information that has been disclosed by a facility pursuant to this subsection may use and disclose the information as permitted or required under 45 Code of Federal Regulations Part 164, Subpart E. This confidential information, however, shall not be used or disclosed for discriminatory purposes including, without limitation, employment discrimination, medical insurance coverage or rate discrimination, or discrimination by law enforcement officers.

(b) A facility, physician, or other individual responsible for evaluation, management, supervision, or treatment of respondents examined or committed for outpatient treatment under the provisions of Article 5 of this Chapter may request, receive, and disclose confidential information to the extent necessary to fulfill the facility's, physician's, or individual's responsibilities.

(c) A facility may furnish confidential information in its possession to the Division of Adult Correction and Juvenile Justice of the Department of Public Safety when requested by that department regarding any client of that facility when the inmate has been determined by the Division of Adult Correction and Juvenile Justice of the Department of Public Safety to be in need of treatment for mental illness, developmental disabilities, or substance abuse. The Division of Adult Correction and Juvenile Justice of the Department of Public Safety may furnish to a facility confidential information in its possession about treatment for mental illness, developmental disabilities, or substance abuse that the Division of Adult Correction and Juvenile Justice of the Department of Public Safety has provided to any present or former inmate if the inmate is presently seeking treatment from the requesting facility or if the inmate has been involuntarily committed to the requesting facility for inpatient or outpatient treatment. Under the circumstances described in this subsection, the consent of the client or inmate is not required in order for this information to be furnished, and the information shall be furnished despite objection by the client or inmate. Confidential information disclosed pursuant to this subsection is restricted from further disclosure.

(c1) *(See editor's note for effective date information)* A facility may furnish confidential information in its possession to the sheriff of any county when requested by the sheriff regarding any client of that facility who is confined in the county's jail or jail annex when the inmate has been determined by the county jail medical unit to be in need of treatment for mental illness, developmental disabilities, or substance abuse. The sheriff may furnish to a facility confidential information in its possession about treatment for mental illness, developmental disabilities, or substance abuse that the county jail medical unit has provided to any present or former inmate if the inmate is presently seeking treatment from the requesting facility or if the inmate has been involuntarily committed to the requesting facility for inpatient or outpatient treatment. Under the circumstances described in this subsection, the consent of the client or inmate is not required in order for this information to be furnished, and the information shall be furnished despite objection by the client or inmate. Confidential information disclosed pursuant to this subsection is restricted from further disclosure.

(d) A responsible professional may disclose confidential information when in the responsible professional's opinion there is an imminent danger to the health or safety of the client or another individual or there is a likelihood of the commission of a felony or violent misdemeanor.

(e) A responsible professional may exchange confidential information with a physician or other health care provider that is providing emergency medical services to a client. Disclosure of the information is limited to that necessary to meet the emergency as determined by the responsible professional.

(e1) A State facility may furnish client identifying information to the Department for the purpose of maintaining an index of clients served in State facilities that may be used by State facilities only if that information is necessary for the appropriate and effective evaluation, care, and treatment of the client.

(e2) A responsible professional may disclose an advance instruction for mental health treatment or confidential information from an advance instruction to a physician, psychologist, or other qualified professional when the responsible professional determines that disclosure is necessary to give effect to or provide treatment in accordance with the advance instruction.

(f) A facility may disclose confidential information to a provider of support services whenever the facility has entered into a written agreement with a person to provide support services and the agreement includes a provision in which the provider of support services acknowledges that in receiving, storing, processing, or otherwise dealing with any confidential information, the provider of support services will safeguard and not further disclose the information.

(g) Whenever there is reason to believe that the client is eligible for financial benefits through a governmental agency, a facility may disclose confidential information to State, local, or federal government agencies. Except as provided in subsections (a3) and (g1) of this section, disclosure is limited to that confidential information necessary to establish financial benefits for a client. Except as provided in subsection (g1) of this section, after establishment of these benefits, the consent of the client or the client's legally responsible person is required for further release of confidential information under this subsection.

(g1) A State facility operated under the authority of G.S. 122C-181 may disclose confidential information for the purpose of collecting payment due the facility for the cost of care, treatment, or habilitation.

(g2) Whenever there is reason to believe that the client is eligible for educational services through a governmental agency, a facility shall disclose client identifying information to the Department of Public Instruction. Disclosure is limited to that information necessary to establish, coordinate, or maintain educational services. The Department of Public Instruction may further disclose client identifying information to a local school administrative unit as necessary.

(h) Within a facility, employees, students, consultants, or volunteers involved in the care, treatment, or habilitation of a client may exchange confidential information as needed for the purpose of carrying out their responsibility in serving the client.

(i) Upon specific request, a responsible professional may release confidential information to a physician or psychologist who referred the client to the facility.

(j) Upon request of the next of kin or other family member who has a legitimate role in the therapeutic services offered, or other person designated by the client or the client's legally responsible person, the responsible professional shall provide the next of kin or other family member or the designee with notification of the client's diagnosis, the prognosis, the medications prescribed, the dosage of the medications prescribed, the side effects of the medications prescribed, if any, and the progress of the client, if the client or the client's legally responsible person has consented in writing, or the client has consented orally in the presence of a witness selected by the client, prior to the release of this information. Both the client's or the legally responsible person's consent and the release of this information shall be documented in the client's medical record. This consent shall be valid for a specified length of time only and is subject to revocation by the consenting individual.

(k) Notwithstanding G.S. 122C-53(b) or G.S. 122C-206, upon request of the next of kin or other family member who has a legitimate role in the therapeutic services offered, or other person designated by the client or the client's legally responsible person, the responsible professional shall provide the next of kin, the family member, or the designee, notification of the client's admission to the facility, transfer to another facility, decision to leave the facility against medical advice, discharge from the facility, and referrals and appointment information for treatment after discharge, after notification to the client that this information has been requested.

(l) In response to a written request of the next of kin or other family member who has a legitimate role in the therapeutic services offered, or other person designated by the client, for additional information not provided for in subsections (j) and (k) of this section, and when the written request identifies the intended use for this information, the responsible professional shall, in a timely manner, do one or more of the following:

(1) Provide the information requested based upon the responsible professional's determination that providing this information will be to the client's therapeutic benefit, if the client or the client's legally

responsible person has consented in writing to the release of the information requested.

(2) Refuse to provide the information requested based upon the responsible professional's determination that providing this information will be detrimental to the therapeutic relationship between client and professional.

(3) Refuse to provide the information requested based upon the responsible professional's determination that the next of kin or family member or designee does not have a legitimate need for the information requested.

(m) The Commission for Mental Health, Developmental Disabilities, and Substance Abuse Services shall adopt rules specifically to define the legitimate role referred to in subsections (j), (k), and (l) of this section.

History.
1955, c. 887, s. 12; 1963, c. 1166, s. 10; 1973, c. 47, s. 2; c. 476, s. 133; c. 673, s. 5; c. 1408, s. 2; 1979, c. 147; 1983, c. 383, s. 10; c. 491; c. 638, s. 22; c. 864, s. 4; 1985, c. 589, s. 2; c. 695, s. 15; 1987, c. 638, ss. 2, 3; 1989, c. 141, s. 10; c. 438; c. 625, s. 8; 1989 (Reg. Sess., 1990), c. 1024, s. 27; 1991, c. 359, s. 1; c. 544, s. 1; 1998-198, s. 4; 2003-313, s. 3; 2009-65, s. 1(a), (b); 2009-487, s. 5; 2009-570, s. 43; 2011-102, ss. 3, 4; 2011-145, ss. 10.14, 19.1(h); 2011-314, s. 2(b); 2011-391, s. 23; 2014-100, s. 8.39(d); 2017-186, s. 2 (kkkkk); 2018-33, s. 5; 2019-81, s. 9A; 2019-177, s. 6.1(a), (b); 2019-240, s. 26(c)

§ 122C-56. Exceptions; research and planning

(a) The Secretary may require information that does not identify clients from State and area facilities for purposes of preparing statistical reports of activities and services and for planning and study. The Secretary may also receive confidential information from State and area facilities when specifically required by other State or federal law.

(b) The Secretary may have access to confidential information from private or public agencies or agents for purposes of research and evaluation in the areas of mental health, developmental disabilities, and substance abuse. No confidential information shall be further disclosed.

(c) A facility may disclose confidential information to persons responsible for conducting general research or clinical, financial, or administrative audits if there is a justifiable documented need for this information. A person receiving the information may not directly or indirectly identify any client in any report of the research or audit or otherwise disclose client identity in any way.

History.
1965, c. 800, s. 4; 1973, c. 476, s. 133; 1985, c. 589, s. 2; 1989, c. 625, s. 9

§ 122C-56.1. Exceptions; security recordings

(a) Security recordings are not a public record under Chapter 132 of the General Statutes and are confidential information under this Chapter.

(b) A State facility is not required to disclose its security recordings unless required under federal law or compelled by a court of competent jurisdiction.

(c) A State facility shall allow viewing of security recordings by an internal client advocate.

(d) A State facility may allow viewing of a security recording by a client or their legally responsible person if, in the opinion of the responsible professional, it is determined to be in the best interest of the client.

History.
2019-240, s. 20(b)

§ 122C-57. Right to treatment and consent to treatment

(a) Each client who is admitted to and is receiving services from a facility has the right to receive age-appropriate treatment for a mental illness, an intellectual or other developmental disability, substance abuse, or a combination thereof. Each client within 30 days of admission to a facility shall have an individual written treatment or habilitation plan implemented by the facility. The client and the client's legally responsible person shall be informed in advance of the potential risks and alleged benefits of the treatment choices.

(b) Each client has the right to be free from unnecessary or excessive medication. Medication shall not be used for punishment, discipline, or staff convenience.

(c) Medication shall be administered in accordance with accepted medical standards and only upon the order of a physician as documented in the client's record.

(d) Each voluntarily admitted client or the client's legally responsible person (including a health care agent named pursuant to a valid health care power of attorney) has the right to consent to or refuse any treatment offered by the facility. Consent may be withdrawn at any time by the person who gave the consent. If treatment is refused, the qualified professional shall determine whether treatment in some other modality is possible. If all appropriate treatment modalities are refused, the voluntarily admitted client may be discharged. In an emergency, a voluntarily admitted client may be administered treatment or medication, other than those specified in subsection (f) of this section, despite the refusal of the client or the client's legally responsible person, even if the client's refusal is expressed in a valid advance instruction for mental health treatment. The Commission may adopt rules to provide a procedure to be followed when a voluntarily admitted client refuses treatment.

(d1) Except as provided in G.S. 90-21.4, discharge of a voluntarily admitted minor from treatment shall include notice to and consultation with the minor's legally responsible person and in no event shall a minor be discharged from treatment upon the minor's request alone.

(e) In the case of an involuntarily committed client, treatment measures other than those requiring express written consent as specified in subsection (f) of this section may be given despite the refusal of the client, the client's legally responsible person, a health care agent named pursuant to a valid health care power of attorney, or the client's refusal expressed in a valid advance instruction for mental health treatment in the event of an emergency or when consideration of side effects related to the specific treatment measure is given and in the professional judgment, as documented in the client's record, of the treating physician and a second physician, who is either the director of clinical services of the facility, or the director's designee, that any of the following is true:

(1) The client, without the benefit of the specific treatment measure, is incapable of participating in any available treatment plan which will give the client a realistic opportunity of improving the client's condition.

(2) There is, without the benefit of the specific treatment measure, a significant possibility that the client will harm self or others before improvement of the client's condition is realized.

(f) Treatment involving electroshock therapy, the use of experimental drugs or procedures, or surgery other than emergency surgery may not be given without the express and informed written consent of the client, the client's legally responsible person, a health care agent named pursuant to a valid health care power of attorney, or the client's consent expressed in a valid advance instruction for mental health treatment. This consent may be withdrawn at any time by the person who gave the consent. The Commission may adopt rules specifying other therapeutic and diagnostic procedures that require the express and informed written consent of the client, the client's legally responsible person, or a health care agent named pursuant to a valid health care power of attorney.

History.
1973, c. 475, s. 1; c. 1436, ss. 6, 7; 1981, c. 328, ss. 1, 2; 1985, c. 589, s. 2; 1995, c. 336, s. 1; 1997-442, s. 3; 1998-198, s. 5; 1998-217, s. 53(a)(4); 1999-456, s. 4; 2007-502, s. 15(b); 2019-76, s. 2

§ 122C-58. Civil rights and civil remedies

Except as otherwise provided in this Chapter, each adult client of a facility keeps the same right as any other citizen of North Carolina to exercise all civil rights, including the right to dispose of property, execute instruments, make purchases, enter into contractual relationships, register and vote, bring civil actions, and marry and get a divorce, unless the exercise of a civil right has been precluded by an unrevoked adjudication of incompetency. This section shall not be construed as validating the act of any client who was in fact incompetent at the time he performed the act.

History.
1973, c. 475, s. 1; c. 1436, ss. 2-5; 1985, c. 589, s. 2

§ 122C-59. Use of corporal punishment

Corporal punishment may not be inflicted upon any client.

History.
1973, c. 475, s. 1; 1985, c. 589, s. 2

§ 122C-60. Use of physical restraints or seclusion

(a) Physical restraint or seclusion of a client shall be employed only when there is imminent danger of abuse or injury to the client or others, when substantial property damage is occurring, or when the restraint or seclusion is necessary as a measure of therapeutic treatment. For purposes of this section, a technique to reenact the birthing process as defined by G.S. 14-401.21 is not a measure of therapeutic treatment. All instances of restraint or seclusion and the detailed reasons for such action shall be documented in the client's record. Each client who is restrained or secluded shall be observed frequently, and a written notation of the observation shall be made in the client's record.

(a1) A facility that employs physical restraint or seclusion of a client shall collect data on the use of the restraints and seclusion. The data shall reflect for each incidence, the type of procedure used, the length of time employed, alternatives considered or employed, and the effectiveness of the procedure or alternative employed. The facility shall analyze the data on at least a quarterly basis to monitor effectiveness, determine trends, and take corrective action where necessary. The facility shall make the data available to the Secretary upon request. Nothing in this subsection abrogates State or federal law or requirements pertaining to the confidentiality, privilege, or other prohibition against disclosure of information provided to the Secretary under this subsection. In reviewing data requested under this subsection, the Secretary shall adhere to State and federal requirements of confidentiality, privilege, and other prohibitions against disclosure and release applicable to the information received under this subsection.

(a2) Facilities shall implement policies and practices that emphasize the use of alternatives to physical restraint and seclusion. Physical restraint and seclusion may be employed only by staff who have been trained and have demonstrated competence in the proper use of and alternatives to these procedures. Facilities shall ensure that staff authorized to employ and terminate these procedures are retrained and have demonstrated competence at least annually.

(b) The Commission shall adopt rules to implement this section. In adopting rules, the Commission shall take into consideration federal regulations and national accreditation standards. Rules adopted by the Commission shall include:

(1) Staff training and competence in:

a. The use of positive behavioral supports.

b. Communication strategies for defusing and deescalating potentially dangerous behavior.

c. Monitoring vital indicators.

d. Administration of CPR.

e. Debriefing with client and staff.

f. Methods for determining staff competence, including qualifications of trainers and training curricula.

g. Other areas to ensure the safe and appropriate use of restraints and seclusion.

(2) Other matters relating to the use of physical restraint or seclusion of clients necessary to ensure the safety of clients and others.

The Department may investigate complaints and inspect a facility at any time to ensure compliance with this section.

History.
1973, c. 475, s. 1; 1985, c. 589, s. 2; 2000-129, s. 1; 2003-205, s. 2

§ 122C-61. Treatment rights in 24-hour facilities

In addition to the rights set forth in G.S. 122C-57, each client who is receiving services at a 24-hour facility has the following rights:

(1) The right to receive necessary treatment for and prevention of physical ailments based upon the client's condition and projected length of stay. The facility may seek to collect appropriate reimbursement for its costs in providing the treatment and prevention; and

(2) The right to have, as soon as practical during treatment or habilation but not later than the time of discharge, an individualized written discharge plan containing recommendations for further services designed to enable the client to live as normally as possible. A discharge plan may not be required when it is not feasible because of an unanticipated discontinuation of a client's treatment. With the consent of the client or his legally responsible person, the professionals responsible for the plans shall contact appropriate agencies at the client's destination or in his home community before formulating the recommendations. A copy of the plan shall be furnished to the client or to his legally responsible person and, with the consent of the client, to the client's next of kin.

History.
1973, c. 475, s. 1; c. 1436, ss. 6, 7; 1981, c. 328, ss. 1, 2; 1985, c. 589, s. 2

§ 122C-62. Additional rights in 24-hour facilities

(a) In addition to the rights enumerated in G.S. 122C-51 through G.S. 122C-61, each adult client who is receiving treatment or habilation in a 24-hour facility keeps the right to:

(1) Send and receive sealed mail and have access to writing material, postage, and staff assistance when necessary;

(2) Contact and consult with, at his own expense and at no cost to the facility, legal counsel, private physicians, and private mental health, developmental disabilities, or substance abuse professionals of his choice; and

(3) Contact and consult with a client advocate if there is a client advocate.

The rights specified in this subsection may not be restricted by the facility and each adult client may exercise these rights at all reasonable times.

(b) Except as provided in subsections (e) and (h) of this section, each adult client who is receiving treatment or habilation in a 24-hour facility at all times keeps the right to:

(1) Make and receive confidential telephone calls. All long distance calls shall be paid for by the client at the time of making the call or made collect to the receiving party;

(2) Receive visitors between the hours of 8:00 a.m. and 9:00 p.m. for a period of at least six hours daily, two hours of which shall be after 6:00 p.m.; however visiting shall not take precedence over therapies;

(3) Communicate and meet under appropriate supervision with individuals of his own choice upon the consent of the individuals;

(4) Make visits outside the custody of the facility unless:

a. Commitment proceedings were initiated as the result of the client's being charged with a violent crime, including a crime involving an assault with a deadly weapon, and the respondent was found not guilty by reason of insanity or incapable of proceeding;

b. The client was voluntarily admitted or committed to the facility while under order of commitment to a correctional facility of the Division of Adult Correction and Juvenile Justice of the Department of Public Safety; or

c. The client is being held to determine capacity to proceed pursuant to G.S. 15A-1002;

A court order may expressly authorize visits otherwise prohibited by the existence of the conditions prescribed by this subdivision;

(5) Be out of doors daily and have access to facilities and equipment for physical exercise several times a week;

(6) Except as prohibited by law, keep and use personal clothing and possessions, unless the client is being held to determine capacity to proceed pursuant to G.S. 15A-1002;

(7) Participate in religious worship;

(8) Keep and spend a reasonable sum of his own money;

(9) Retain a driver's license, unless otherwise prohibited by Chapter 20 of the General Statutes; and

(10) Have access to individual storage space for his private use.

(c) In addition to the rights enumerated in G.S. 122C-51 through G.S. 122C-57 and G.S. 122C-59 through G.S. 122C-61, each minor client who is receiving treatment or habilitation in a 24-hour facility has the right to have access to proper adult supervision and guidance. In recognition of the minor's status as a developing individual, the minor shall be provided opportunities to enable him to mature physically, emotionally, intellectually, socially, and vocationally. In view of the physical, emotional, and intellectual immaturity of the minor, the 24-hour facility shall provide appropriate structure, supervision and control consistent with the rights given to the minor pursuant to this Part. The facility shall also, where practical, make reasonable efforts to ensure that each minor client receives treatment apart and separate from adult clients unless the treatment needs of the minor client dictate otherwise.

Each minor client who is receiving treatment or habilitation from a 24-hour facility has the right to:

(1) Communicate and consult with his parents or guardian or the agency or individual having legal custody of him;

(2) Contact and consult with, at his own expense or that of his legally responsible person and at no cost to the facility, legal counsel, private physicians, private mental health, developmental disabilities, or substance abuse professionals, of his or his legally responsible person's choice; and

(3) Contact and consult with a client advocate, if there is a client advocate.

The rights specified in this subsection may not be restricted by the facility and each minor client may exercise these rights at all reasonable times.

(d) Except as provided in subsections (e) and (h) of this section, each minor client who is receiving treatment or habilitation in a 24-hour facility has the right to:

(1) Make and receive telephone calls. All long distance calls shall be paid for by the client at the time of making the call or made collect to the receiving party;

(2) Send and receive mail and have access to writing materials, postage, and staff assistance when necessary;

(3) Under appropriate supervision, receive visitors between the hours of 8:00 a.m. and 9:00 p.m. for a period of at least six hours daily, two hours of which shall be after 6:00 p.m.; however visiting shall not take precedence over school or therapies;

(4) Receive special education and vocational training in accordance with federal and State law;

(5) Be out of doors daily and participate in play, recreation, and physical exercise on a regular basis in accordance with his needs;

(6) Except as prohibited by law, keep and use personal clothing and possessions under appropriate supervision, unless the client is being held to determine capacity to proceed pursuant to G.S. 15A-1002;

(7) Participate in religious worship;

(8) Have access to individual storage space for the safekeeping of personal belongings;

(9) Have access to and spend a reasonable sum of his own money; and

(10) Retain a driver's license, unless otherwise prohibited by Chapter 20 of the General Statutes.

(e) No right enumerated in subsections (b) or (d) of this section may be limited or restricted except by the qualified professional responsible for the formulation of the client's treatment or habilitation plan. A written statement shall be placed in the client's record that indicates the detailed reason for the restriction. The restriction shall be reasonable and related to the client's treatment or habilitation needs. A restriction is effective for a period not to exceed 30 days. An evaluation of each restriction shall be conducted by the qualified professional at least every seven days, at which time the restriction may be removed. Each evaluation of a restriction shall be documented in the client's record. Restrictions on rights may be renewed only by a written statement entered by the qualified professional in the client's record that states the reason for the renewal of the restriction. In the case of an adult client who has not been adjudicated incompetent, in each instance of an initial restriction or renewal of a restriction of rights, an individual designated by the client shall, upon the consent of the client, be notified of the restriction and of the reason for it. In the case of a minor client or an incompetent adult client, the legally responsible person shall be notified of each instance of an initial restriction or renewal of a restriction of rights and of the reason for it. Notification of the designated individual or legally responsible person shall be documented in writing in the client's record.

(f) The Commission may adopt rules to implement subsection (e) of this section.

(g) With regard to clients being held to determine capacity to proceed pursuant to G.S. 15A-1002 or clients in a facility for substance abuse, and notwithstanding the prior provisions of this section, the Commission may adopt rules restricting the rights set forth under (b)(2), (b)(3), and (d)(3) of this section if restrictions are necessary and reasonable in order to protect the health, safety, and welfare of the client involved or other clients.

(h) The rights stated in subdivisions (b)(2), (b)(4), (b)(5), (b)(10), (d)(3), (d)(5) and (d)(8) may be modified in a general hospital by that hospital to be the same as for other patients in that hospital; provided that any restriction of a specific client's rights shall be done in accordance with the provisions of subsection (e) of this section.

History.

1973, c. 475, s. 1; c. 1436, ss. 2-5, 8; 1985, c. 589, s. 2; 1989, c. 625, s. 10; 1995, c. 299, s. 2; 1997-456, s. 27; 2011-145, s. 19.1(h); 2017-186, s. 2 (*lllll*)

§ 122C-63. Assurance for continuity of care for individuals with intellectual disabilities

(a) Any individual with an intellectual disability admitted for residential care or treatment for other than respite or emergency care to any residential facility operated under the authority of this Chapter and supported all or in part by State-appropriated funds has the right to residential placement in an alternative facility if the client is in need of placement and if the original facility can no longer provide the necessary care or treatment.

(b) The operator of a residential facility providing residential care or treatment, for other than respite or emergency care, for individuals with intellectual disabilities shall notify the area authority serving the client's county of residence of the operator's intent to close a facility or to discharge a client who may be in need of continuing care at least 60 days prior to the closing or discharge.

The operator's notification to the area authority of intent to close a facility or to discharge a client who may be in need of continuing care constitutes the operator's acknowledgement of the obligation to continue to serve the client until whichever of the following occurs first:

(1) The area authority determines that the client is not in need of continuing care.

(2) The client is moved to an alternative residential placement.

(3) Sixty days have elapsed.

In cases in which the safety of the client who may be in need of continuing care, of other clients, of the staff of the residential facility, or of the general public, is concerned, this 60-day notification period may be waived by securing an emergency placement in a more secure and safe facility. The operator of the residential facility shall notify the area authority that an emergency placement has been arranged within 24 hours of the placement. The area authority and the Secretary shall retain their respective responsibilities upon receipt of this notice.

(c) An individual who may be in need of continuing care may be discharged from a residential facility without further claim for continuing care against the area authority or the State if any of the following is true:

(1) After the parent or guardian, if the client is a minor or an adjudicated incompetent adult, or the client, if an adult not adjudicated incompetent, has entered into a contract with the operator upon the client's admission to the original residential facility, the parent, guardian, or client who entered into the contract refuses to carry out the contract.

Chapter 122C

(2) After an alternative placement for a client in need of continuing care is located, the parent or guardian who admitted the client to the residential facility, if the client is a minor or an adjudicated incompetent adult, or the client, if the client is an adult not adjudicated incompetent, refuses the alternative placement.

(d) Decisions made by the area authority regarding the need for continued placement or regarding the availability of an alternative placement of a client may be appealed pursuant to the appeals process of the area authority and subsequently to the Secretary or the Commission under their rules. If the appeal process extends beyond the operator's 60-day obligation to continue to serve the client, the Secretary shall arrange a temporary placement in a State developmental center pending the outcome of the appeal.

(e) The area authority that serves the county of residence of the client is responsible for assessing the need for continuity of care and for the coordination of the placement among available public and private facilities whenever the authority is notified that a client may be in need of continuing care. If an alternative placement is not available beyond the operator's 60-day obligation to continue to serve the client, the Secretary shall arrange for a temporary placement in a State developmental center. The area authority shall retain responsibility for coordination of placement during a temporary placement in a State developmental center.

(f) The Secretary is responsible for coordinative and financial assistance to the area authority in the performing of its duties to coordinate placement so as to assure continuity of care and for assuring a continuity of care placement beyond the operator's 60-day obligation period.

(g) The area authority's financial responsibility, through local and allocated State resources, is limited to the following:

(1) Costs relating to the identification and coordination of alternative placements.

(2) If the original facility is an area facility, maintenance of the client in the original facility for up to 60 days.

(3) Release of allocated categorical State funds used to support the care or treatment of the specific client at the time of alternative placement if the Secretary requires the release.

(h) In accordance with G.S. 143B-147(a)(1) the Commission shall develop programmatic rules to implement this section, and, in accordance with G.S. 122C-112(a)(6), the Secretary shall adopt budgetary rules to implement this section.

History.
1981, c. 1012; 1985, c. 589, s. 2; 2019-76, s. 3

§ 122C-64. Client rights and human rights committees

Client rights and human rights committees responsible for protecting the rights of clients shall be established at each State facility, for each local management entity, and provider agency. The Commission shall adopt rules for the establishment, composition, and duties of the committees and procedures for appointment and coordination with the State and Local Consumer Advocacy programs. The membership of the client rights and human rights committee for a multicounty program or local management entity shall include a representative from each of the participating counties.

History.
1985-589, s. 2; 2001-437, s. 1.3; 2009-190, s. 1

§ 122C-65. Offenses relating to clients

(a) For the protection of clients receiving treatment or habilitation in a 24-hour facility, it is unlawful for any individual who is not a developmentally disabled client in a facility:

(1) To assist, advise, or solicit, or to offer to assist, advise, or solicit a client of a facility to leave without authority;

(2) To transport or to offer to transport a client of a facility to or from any place without the facility's authority;

(3) To receive or to offer to receive a minor client of a facility into any place, structure, building, or conveyance for the purpose of engaging in any act that would constitute a sex offense, or to solicit a minor client of a facility to engage in any act that would constitute a sex offense;

(4) To hide an individual who has left a facility without authority; or

(5) To engage in, or offer to engage in an act with a client of a facility that would constitute a sex offense.

(b) Violation of this section is a Class 1 misdemeanor.

History.
1899, c. 1, s. 53; Rev., s. 3694; C.S., s. 6171; 1963, c. 1184, ss. 1, 6; 1985, c. 589, s. 2; 1989, c. 625, s. 11; 1993, c. 539, s. 921; 1994, Ex. Sess., c. 24, s. 14(c)

§ 122C-66. Protection from abuse and exploitation; reporting

(a) An employee of or a volunteer at a facility who, other than as a part of generally accepted medical or therapeutic procedure, knowingly causes pain or injury to a client is guilty of a Class A1 misdemeanor. Any employee or volunteer who uses reasonable force to carry out the provisions of G.S. 122C-60 or to protect himself or others from a violent client does not violate this subsection.

(a1) An employee of or a volunteer at a facility who borrows or takes personal property from a client is guilty of a Class 1 misdemeanor. Any employee or volunteer who uses reasonable force to carry out the provisions of G.S. 122C-60 or to protect himself or others from a violent client does not violate this subsection.

(b) An employee of or a volunteer at a facility who witnesses or has knowledge of a violation of subsection (a), subsection (a1), or of an accidental injury to a client shall report the violation or accidental injury to authorized personnel designated by the facility. No employee making a report may be threatened or harassed by any other employee or volunteer on account of the report. Violation of this subsection is a Class 1 misdemeanor.

(b1) The employee of or a volunteer at a facility who witnesses a client become a victim of a violation of Article 7A or Article 26 of Chapter 14 of the General Statutes shall report the allegations within 24 hours after witnessing the violation to one of the following: (i) the department of social services in the county where the facility serves the client; (ii) the district attorney in the district where the facility serves the client; or (iii) the appropriate local law enforcement agency in the city or county where the facility serves the client. A violation of this section is a Class A1 misdemeanor. No employee making a report may be threatened or harassed by any other employee or volunteer on account of the report.

(c) The identity of an individual who makes a report under this section or who cooperates in an ensuing investigation may not be disclosed without the reporting individual's consent, except to persons authorized by the facility or by State or federal law to investigate or prosecute these incidents, or in a grievance or personnel hearing or civil or criminal action in which the reporting individual is testifying, or when disclosure is legally compelled or authorized by judicial discovery. This subsection shall not be interpreted to require the disclosure of the identity of an individual where it is otherwise prohibited by law.

(d) An employee who makes a report in good faith under this section is immune from any civil liability that might otherwise occur for the report. In any case involving liability, making of a report under this section is prima facie evidence that the maker acted in good faith.

(e) The duty imposed by this section is in addition to any duty imposed by G.S. 7B-301 or G.S. 108A-102.

(f) Except for reports made pursuant to subsection (b1) of this section, the facility shall investigate or provide for the investigation of all reports made under the provisions of this section.

(g) The county department of social services and the district attorney to whom a report is made under subsection (b1) of this section shall investigate or provide for the investigation of each such report.

History.
1985, c. 589, s. 2; 1993, c. 539, ss. 922, 923; 1994, Ex. Sess., c. 24, s. 14(c); 1998-202, s. 13(ee); 2015-36, s. 2

§ 122C-67. Other rules regarding abuse, exploitation, neglect not prohibited

G.S. 122C-66 does not prohibit the Commission from adopting rules for State and area facilities and does not prohibit other facilities from issuing policies regarding other forms of prohibited abuse, exploitation, or neglect.

History.
1985, c. 589, s. 2

PART 2
ADVANCE INSTRUCTION FOR MENTAL HEALTH TREATMENT

§ 122C-71. Purpose

(a) The General Assembly recognizes as a matter of public policy the fundamental right of an individual to control the decisions relating to the individual's mental health care.

(b) The purpose of this Part is to establish an additional, nonexclusive method for an individual to exercise the right to consent to or refuse mental health treatment when the individual lacks sufficient understanding or capacity to make or communicate mental health treatment decisions.

(c) This Part is intended and shall be construed to be consistent with the provisions of Article 3 of Chapter 32A of the General Statutes, provided that in the event of a conflict between the provisions of this Part and Article 3 of Chapter 32A, the provisions of this Part control.

History.
1997-442, s. 2; 1998-198, s. 2

§ 122C-72. Definitions

As used in this Part, unless the context clearly requires otherwise, the following terms have the meanings specified:

(1) "Advance instruction for mental health treatment" or "advance instruction" means a written instrument, signed in the presence of two qualified witnesses who believe the principal to be of sound mind at

the time of the signing, and acknowledged before a notary public, pursuant to which the principal makes a declaration of instructions, information, and preferences regarding the principal's mental health treatment and states that the principal is aware that the advance instruction authorizes a mental health treatment provider to act according to the instruction. It may also state the principal's instructions regarding, but not limited to, consent to or refusal of mental health treatment when the principal is incapable.

(2) "Attending physician" means the physician who has primary responsibility for the care and treatment of the principal.

(3) Repealed by Session Laws 1998-198, s. 2, effective October 1, 1998.

(4) "Incapable" means that, in the opinion of a physician or eligible psychologist, the person currently lacks sufficient understanding or capacity to make and communicate mental health treatment decisions. As used in this Part, the term "eligible psychologist" has the meaning given in G.S. 122C-3(13d).

(5) "Mental health treatment" means the process of providing for the physical, emotional, psychological, and social needs of the principal for the principal's mental illness. "Mental health treatment" includes, but is not limited to, electroconvulsive treatment (ECT), commonly referred to as "shock treatment", treatment of mental illness with psychotropic medication, and admission to and retention in a facility for care or treatment of mental illness.

(6) "Principal" means the person making the advance instruction.

(7) "Qualified witness" means a witness who affirms that the principal is personally known to the witness, that the principal signed or acknowledged the principal's signature on the advance instruction in the presence of the witness, that the witness believes the principal to be of sound mind and not to be under duress, fraud, or undue influence, and that the witness is not:

　　a. The attending physician or mental health service provider or an employee of the physician or mental health treatment provider;

　　b. An owner, operator, or employee of an owner or operator of a health care facility in which the principal is a patient or resident; or

　　c. Related within the third degree to the principal or to the principal's spouse.

History.
1997-442, s. 2; 1998-198, s. 2

§ 122C-73. Scope, use, and authority of advance instruction for mental health treatment

(a) Any adult of sound mind may make an advance instruction regarding mental health treatment. The advance instruction may include consent to or refusal of mental health treatment.

(b) An advance instruction may include, but is not limited to, the names and telephone numbers of individuals to be contacted in case of a mental health crisis, situations that may cause the principal to experience a mental health crisis, responses that may assist the principal to remain in the principal's home during a mental health crisis, the types of assistance that may help stabilize the principal if it becomes necessary to enter a facility, and medications that the principal is taking or has taken in the past and the effects of those medications.

(c) An individual shall not be required to execute or to refrain from executing an advance instruction as a condition for insurance coverage, as a condition for receiving mental or physical health services, as a condition for receiving privileges while in a facility, or as a condition of discharge from a facility.

(c1) A principal, through an advance instruction, may grant or withhold authority for mental health treatment, including, but not limited to, the use of psychotropic medication, electroconvulsive treatment, and admission to and retention in a facility for the care or treatment of mental illness.

(d) A principal may nominate, by advance instruction for mental health treatment, the guardian of the person of the principal if a guardianship proceeding is thereafter commenced. The court shall make its appointment in accordance with the principal's most recent nomination in an unrevoked advance instruction for mental health treatment, except for good cause shown.

(e) If, following the execution of an advance instruction for mental health treatment, a court of competent jurisdiction appoints a guardian of the person of the principal, or a general guardian with powers over the person of the principal, the guardian shall follow the advance instruction consistent with G.S. 35A-1201(a)(5).

(f) An advance instruction for mental health treatment may be combined with a health care power of attorney or general power of attorney that is executed in accordance with the requirements of Chapter 32A or Chapter 32C of the General Statutes so long as each form shall be executed in accordance with its own statute.

History.
1997-442, s. 2; 1998-198, s. 2; 2017-153, s. 2.7

§ 122C-74. Effectiveness and duration; revocation

(a) A validly executed advance instruction becomes effective upon its proper execution and remains valid unless revoked.

(b) The attending physician or other mental health treatment provider may consider valid and rely upon an advance instruction, or a copy of that advance instruction that is obtained from the Advance Health Care Directive Registry maintained by the Secretary of State pursuant to Article 21 of Chapter 130A of the General Statutes, in the absence of actual knowledge of its revocation or invalidity.

(c) An attending physician or other mental health treatment provider may presume that a person who executed an advance instruction in accordance with this Part was of sound mind and acted voluntarily when he or she executed the advance instruction.

(d) An attending physician or other mental health treatment provider shall act in accordance with an advance instruction when the principal has been determined to be incapable. If a patient is incapable, an advance instruction executed in accordance with this Article is presumed to be valid.

(e) The attending physician or mental health treatment provider shall continue to obtain the principal's informed consent to all mental health treatment decisions when the principal is capable of providing informed consent or refusal, as required by G.S. 122C-57. Unless the principal is deemed incapable by the attending physician or eligible psychologist, the instructions of the principal at the time of treatment shall supersede the declarations expressed in the principal's advance instruction.

(f) The fact of a principal's having executed an advance instruction shall not be considered an indication of a principal's capacity to make or communicate mental health treatment decisions at such times as those decisions are required.

(g) Upon being presented with an advance instruction, an attending physician or other mental health treatment provider shall make the advance instruction a part of the principal's medical record. When acting under authority of an advance instruction, an attending physician or other mental health treatment provider shall comply with the advance instruction unless:

(1) Compliance, in the opinion of the attending physician or other mental health treatment provider, is not consistent with generally accepted community practice standards of treatment to benefit the principal;

(2) Compliance is not consistent with the availability of treatments requested;

(3) Compliance is not consistent with applicable law;

(4) The principal is committed to a 24-hour facility pursuant to Article 5 of Chapter 122C of the General Statutes, and treatment is authorized in compliance with G.S. 122C-57 and rules adopted pursuant to it; or

(5) Compliance, in the opinion of the attending physician or other mental health treatment provider, is not consistent with appropriate treatment in case of an emergency endangering life or health.

In the event that one part of the advance instruction is unable to be followed because of one or more of the above, all other parts of the advance instruction shall nonetheless be followed.

(h) If the attending physician or other mental health treatment provider is unwilling at any time to comply with any part or parts of an advance instruction for one or more of the reasons set out in subdivisions (1) through (5) of subsection (g), the attending physician or other mental health care treatment provider shall promptly notify the principal and, if applicable, the health care agent and shall document the reason for not complying with the advance instruction and shall document the notification in the principal's medical record.

(i) An advance instruction does not limit any authority provided in Article 5 of G.S. 122C either to take a person into custody, or to admit, retain, or treat a person in a facility.

(j) An advance instruction may be revoked at any time by the principal so long as the principal is not incapable. The principal may exercise this right of revocation in any manner by which the principal is able to communicate an intent to revoke and by notifying the revocation to the treating physician or other mental health treatment provider. The attending physician or other mental health treatment provider shall note the revocation as part of the principal's medical record.

History.
1997-442, s. 2; 1998-198, s. 2; 2001-455, s. 5; 2001-513, s. 30(b)

§ 122C-75. Reliance on advance instruction for mental health treatment

(a) An attending physician or eligible psychologist who in good faith determines that the principal is or is not incapable for the purpose of deciding whether to proceed or not to proceed according to an advance instruction, is not subject to criminal prosecution, civil liability, or professional disciplinary action for making and acting upon that determination.

(b) In the absence of actual knowledge of the revocation of an advance instruction, no attending physician or other mental health treatment provider shall be subject to criminal prosecution or civil liability or be deemed to have engaged in unprofessional conduct as a result of the provision of treatment to a principal in accordance with this Part unless the absence of actual knowledge resulted from the negligence of the attending physician or mental health treatment provider.

(c) An attending physician or mental health treatment provider who administers or does not administer mental health treatment according to and in good faith reliance upon the validity of an advance instruction is not subject to criminal prosecution, civil liability, or professional disciplinary action resulting from a subsequent finding of an advance instruction's invalidity.

(d) No attending physician or mental health treatment provider who administers or does not administer treatment under authorization obtained pursuant to this Part shall incur liability arising out of a claim to the extent that the claim is based on lack of informed consent or authorization for this action.

(e) This section shall not be construed as affecting or limiting any liability that arises out of a negligent act or omission in connection with the medical diagnosis, care, or treatment of a principal under an advance instruction or that arises out of any deviation from reasonable medical standards.

History.
1997-442, s. 2; 1998-198, s. 2

§ 122C-76. Penalty

It is a Class 2 misdemeanor for a person, without authorization of the principal, willfully to alter, forge, conceal, or destroy an instrument, the reinstatement or revocation of an instrument, or any other evidence or document reflecting the principal's desires and interests, with the intent or effect of affecting a mental health treatment decision.

History.
1997-442, s. 2

§ 122C-77. Statutory form for advance instruction for mental health treatment

(a) This Part shall not be construed to invalidate an advance instruction for mental health treatment that was executed and was otherwise valid.

(b) The use of the following or similar form after the effective date of this Part in the creation of an advance instruction for mental health treatment is lawful, and, when used, it shall specifically meet the requirements and be construed in accordance with the provisions of this Part.

"ADVANCE INSTRUCTION FOR MENTAL HEALTH TREATMENT

I, _____, being an adult of sound mind, willfully and voluntarily make this advance instruction for mental health treatment to be followed if it is determined by a physician or eligible psychologist that my ability to receive and evaluate information effectively or communicate decisions is impaired to such an extent that I lack the capacity to refuse or consent to mental health treatment. "Mental health treatment" means the process of providing for the physical, emotional, psychological, and social needs of the principal. "Mental health treatment" includes electroconvulsive treatment (ECT), commonly referred to as "shock treatment", treatment of mental illness with psychotropic medication, and admission to and retention in a facility for care or treatment of mental illness. I understand that under G.S. 122C-57, other than for specific exceptions stated there, mental health treatment may not be administered without my express and informed written consent or, if I am incapable of giving my informed consent, the express and informed consent of my legally responsible person, my health care agent named pursuant to a valid health care power of attorney, or my consent expressed in this advance instruction for mental health treatment. I understand that I may become incapable of giving or withholding informed consent for mental health treatment due to the symptoms of a diagnosed mental disorder. These symptoms may include:

PSYCHOACTIVE MEDICATIONS

If I become incapable of giving or withholding informed consent for mental health treatment, my instructions regarding psychoactive medications are as follows: (Place initials beside choice.)

_____ I consent to the administration of the following medications:

_____
_____

_____ I do not consent to the administration of the following medications:

_____
_____

Conditions or limitations: _____

ADMISSION TO AND RETENTION IN FACILITY

If I become incapable of giving or withholding informed consent for mental health treatment, my instructions regarding admission to and retention in a health care facility for mental health treatment are as follows: (Place initials beside choice.)

_____ I consent to being admitted to a health care facility for mental health treatment.

My facility preference is _____

_____ I do not consent to being admitted to a health care facility for mental health treatment.

This advance instruction cannot, by law, provide consent to retain me in a facility for more than 15 days.

Conditions or limitations _____

_____

ADDITIONAL INSTRUCTIONS

These instructions shall apply during the entire length of my incapacity.

In case of mental health crisis, please contact:

1. Name: _____
   Home Address: _____
   Home Telephone Number: Work
   Telephone _____
   Number: _____
   Relationship to Me: _____
2. Name: _____
   Home Address: _____
   Home Telephone Number: Work
   Telephone _____
   Number: _____
   Relationship to Me: _____
3. My Physician: _____
   Name: _____
   Telephone Number: _____
4. My Therapist: _____
   Name: _____
   Telephone Number: _____

The following may cause me to experience a mental health crisis:

_____

_____

The following may help me avoid a hospitalization:_____

_____

I generally react to being hospitalized as follows:

_____

_____

Staff of the hospital or crisis unit can help me by doing the following:

_____

_____

I give permission for the following person or people to visit me:

_____

_____

Instructions concerning any other medical interventions, such as electroconvulsive (ECT) treatment (commonly referred to as "shock treatment"):

_____

_____

_____

_____

Other instructions:_____

_____

_____

_____

_____

_____ I have attached an additional sheet of instructions to be followed

and considered part of this advance instruction.

SHARING OF INFORMATION BY PROVIDERS

I understand that the information in this document may be shared by my mental health treatment provider with any other mental health treatment provider who may serve me when necessary to provide treatment in accordance with this advance instruction.

Other instructions about sharing of information:

_____

_____

SIGNATURE OF PRINCIPAL

By signing here, I indicate that I am mentally alert and competent, fully informed as to the contents of this document, and understand the full impact of having made this advance instruction for mental health treatment. _____

Signature of Principal   Date

NATURE OF WITNESSES

I hereby state that the principal is personally known to me, that the principal signed or acknowledged the principal's signature on this advance instruction for mental health treatment in my presence, that the principal appears to be of sound mind and not under duress, fraud, or undue influence, and that I am not:

   a. The attending physician or mental health service provider or an
   employee of the physician or mental health treatment provider;

   b. An owner, operator, or employee of an owner or operator of a health
   care facility in which the principal is a patient or resident; or

   c. Related within the third degree to the principal or to the
   principal's spouse.

AFFIRMATION OF WITNESSES

We affirm that the principal is personally known to us, that the principal signed or acknowledged the principal's signature on this advance instruction for mental health treatment in our presence, that the principal appears to be of sound mind and not under duress, fraud, or undue influence, and that neither of us is:

A person appointed as an attorney-in-fact by this document;

The principal's attending physician or mental health service provider or a relative of the physician or provider;

The owner, operator, or relative of an owner or operator of a facility in which the principal is a patient or resident; or

A person related to the principal by blood, marriage, or adoption.

Witnessed by:

Witness: _____ Date: _____

Witness: _____ Date: _____

STATE OF NORTH CAROLINA COUNTY OF_____

CERTIFICATION OF NOTARY PUBLIC

STATE OF NORTH CAROLINA
COUNTY OF

I, _____, a Notary Public for the County cited above in the State of North Carolina, hereby certify that appeared before me and swore or affirmed to me and to the witnesses in my presence that this instrument is an advance instruction for mental health treatment, and that he/she willingly and voluntarily made and executed it as his/her free act and deed for the purposes expressed in it. I further certify that _____ and _____, witnesses, appeared before me and swore or affirmed that they witnessed sign the attached advance instruction for mental health treatment, believing him/her to be of sound mind; and also swore that at the time they witnessed the signing they were not (i) the attending physician or mental health treatment provider or an employee of the physician or mental health treatment provider and (ii) they were not an owner, operator, or employee of an owner or operator of a health care facility in which the principal is a patient or resident, and (iii) they were not related within the third degree to the principal or to the principal's spouse. I further certify that I am satisfied as to the genuineness and due execution of the instrument.

This is the _____ day of, _____
_____

Notary Public
My Commission expires:

NOTICE TO PERSON MAKING AN INSTRUCTION FOR MENTAL HEALTH TREATMENT

This is an important legal document. It creates an instruction for mental health treatment. Before signing this document you should know these important facts: This document allows you to make decisions in advance about certain types of mental health treatment. The instructions you include in this declaration will be followed if a physician or eligible psychologist determines that you are incapable of making and communicating treatment decisions. Otherwise you will be considered capable to give or withhold consent for the treatments. Your instructions may be overridden if you are being held in accordance with civil commitment law. Under the Health Care Power of Attorney you may also appoint a person as your health care agent to make treatment decisions for you if you become incapable. You have the right to revoke this document at any time you have not been determined to be incapable. YOU MAY NOT REVOKE THIS ADVANCE INSTRUCTION WHEN YOU ARE FOUND INCAPABLE BY A PHYSICIAN OR OTHER AUTHORIZED MENTAL HEALTH TREATMENT PROVIDER. A revocation is effective when it is communicated to your attending physician or other provider. The physician or other provider shall note the revocation in your medical record. To be valid, this advance instruction must be signed by two qualified witnesses, personally known to you, who are present when you sign or acknowledge your signature. It must also be acknowledged before a notary public.

NOTICE TO PHYSICIAN OR OTHER MENTAL HEALTH TREATMENT PROVIDER Under North Carolina law, a person may use this advance instruction to provide consent for future mental health treatment if the person later becomes incapable of making those decisions. Under the Health Care Power of Attorney the person may also appoint a health care agent to make mental health treatment decisions for the person when incapable. A person is "incapable" when in the opinion of a physician or eligible psychologist the person currently lacks sufficient understanding or capacity to make and communicate mental health treatment decisions. This document becomes effective upon its proper execution and remains valid unless revoked. Upon being presented with this advance instruction, the physician or other provider must make it a part of the person's medical record. The attending physician or other mental health treatment provider must act in accordance with the statements expressed in the advance instruction when the person is determined to be incapable, unless compliance is not consistent with G.S. 122C-74(g). The physician or other mental health treatment provider shall promptly notify the principal and, if applicable, the health care agent, and document noncompliance with any part of an advance instruction in the principal's medical record. The physician or other mental health treatment provider may rely upon the authority of a signed, witnessed, dated, and notarized advance instruction, as provided in G.S. 122C-75."

History.
1997-442, s. 2; 1998-198, s. 2; 1998-217, s. 53(a)(5); 2019-240, s. 26(d)

ARTICLE 3A
MISCELLANEOUS PROVISIONS

§ 122C-80. Criminal history record check required for certain applicants for employment

(a) **Definition.** -- As used in this section, the term "provider" applies to an area authority/county program and any provider of mental health, developmental disability, and substance abuse services that is licensable under Article 2 of this Chapter.

(b) **Requirement.** -- An offer of employment by a provider licensed under this Chapter to an applicant to fill a position that does not require the applicant to have an occupational license is conditioned on consent to a State and national criminal history record check of the applicant. If the applicant has been a resident of this State for less than five years, then the offer of employment is conditioned on consent to a State and national criminal history record check of the applicant. The national criminal history record check shall include a check of the applicant's fingerprints. If the applicant has been a resident of this State for five years or more, then the offer is conditioned on consent to a State criminal history record check of the applicant. A provider shall not employ an applicant who refuses to consent to a criminal history record check required by this section. Except as otherwise provided in this subsection, within five business days of making the conditional offer of employment, a provider shall submit a request to the Department of Public Safety under G.S. 143B-939 to conduct a criminal history record check required by this section or shall submit a request to a private entity to conduct a State criminal history record check required by this section. Notwithstanding G.S. 143B-939, the Department of Public Safety shall return the results of national criminal history record checks for employment positions not covered by Public Law 105-277 to the Department of Health and Human Services, Criminal Records Check Unit. Within five business days of receipt of the national criminal history of the person, the Department of Health and Human Services, Criminal Records Check Unit, shall notify the provider as to whether the information received may affect the employability of the applicant. In no case shall the results of the national criminal history record check be shared with the provider. Providers shall make available upon request verification that a criminal history check has been completed on any staff covered by this section. A county that has adopted an appropriate local ordinance and has access to the Department of Public Safety data bank may conduct on behalf of a provider a State criminal history record check required by this section without the provider having to submit a request to the Department of Justice. In such a case, the county shall commence with the State criminal history record check required by this section within five business days of the conditional offer of employment by the provider. All criminal history information received by the provider is confidential and may not be disclosed, except to the applicant as provided in subsection (c) of this section. For purposes of this subsection, the term "private entity" means a business regularly engaged in conducting criminal history record checks utilizing public records obtained from a State agency.

(c) **Action.** -- If an applicant's criminal history record check reveals one or more convictions of a relevant offense, the provider shall consider all of the following factors in determining whether to hire the applicant:

(1) The level and seriousness of the crime.

(2) The date of the crime.

(3) The age of the person at the time of the conviction.

(4) The circumstances surrounding the commission of the crime, if known.

(5) The nexus between the criminal conduct of the person and the job duties of the position to be filled.

(6) The prison, jail, probation, parole, rehabilitation, and employment records of the person since the date the crime was committed.

(7) The subsequent commission by the person of a relevant offense.

The fact of conviction of a relevant offense alone shall not be a bar to employment; however, the listed factors shall be considered by the provider. If the provider disqualifies an applicant after consideration of the relevant factors, then the provider may disclose information contained in the criminal history record check that is relevant to the disqualification, but may not provide a copy of the criminal history record check to the applicant.

(d) **Limited Immunity.** -- A provider and an officer or employee of a provider that, in good faith, complies with this section shall be immune from civil liability for:

(1) The failure of the provider to employ an individual on the basis of information provided in the criminal history record check of the individual.

(2) Failure to check an employee's history of criminal offenses if the employee's criminal history record check is requested and received in compliance with this section.

(e) **Relevant Offense.** -- As used in this section, "relevant offense" means a county, state, or federal criminal history of conviction or pending indictment of a crime, whether a misdemeanor or felony, that bears upon an individual's fitness to have responsibility for the safety and well-being of persons needing mental health, developmental disabilities, or substance abuse services. These crimes include the criminal offenses set forth in any of the following Articles of Chapter 14 of the General Statutes: Article 5, Counterfeiting and Issuing Monetary Substitutes; Article 5A, Endangering Executive and Legislative Officers; Article 6, Homicide; Article 7B, Rape and Other Sex Offenses; Article 8, Assaults; Article 10, Kidnapping and Abduction; Article 13, Malicious Injury or Damage by Use of Explosive or Incendiary Device or Material; Article 14, Burglary and Other Housebreakings; Article 15, Arson and Other Burnings; Article 16, Larceny; Article 17, Robbery; Article 18, Embezzlement; Article 19, False Pretenses and Cheats; Article 19A, Obtaining Property or Services by False or Fraudulent Use of Credit Device or Other Means; Article 19B, Financial Transaction Card Crime Act; Article 20, Frauds; Article 21, Forgery; Article 26, Offenses Against Public Morality and Decency; Article 26A, Adult Establishments; Article 27, Prostitution; Article 28, Perjury; Article 29, Bribery; Article 31, Misconduct in Public Office; Article 35, Offenses Against the Public Peace; Article 36A, Riots, Civil Disorders, and Emergencies; Article 39, Protection of Minors; Article 40, Protection of the Family; Article 59, Public Intoxication; and Article 60, Computer-Related Crime. These crimes also include possession or sale of drugs in violation of the North Carolina Controlled Substances Act, Article 5 of Chapter 90 of the General Statutes, and alcohol-related offenses such as sale to underage persons in violation of G.S. 18B-302 or driving while impaired in violation of G.S. 20-138.1 through G.S. 20-138.5.

(f) **Penalty for Furnishing False Information.** -- Any applicant for employment who willfully furnishes, supplies, or otherwise gives false information on an employment application that is the basis for a criminal history record check under this section shall be guilty of a Class A1 misdemeanor.

(g) **Conditional Employment.** -- A provider may employ an applicant conditionally prior to obtaining the results of a criminal history record check regarding the applicant if both of the following requirements are met:

(1) The provider shall not employ an applicant prior to obtaining the applicant's consent for criminal history record check as required in subsection (b) of this section or the completed fingerprint cards as required in G.S. 143B-939.

(2) The provider shall submit the request for a criminal history record check not later than five business days after the individual begins conditional employment.

History.
2000-154, s. 4; 2001-155, s. 1; 2004-124, ss. 10.19D(c), (h); 2005-4, ss. 1, 2, 3, 4, 5(a); 2007-444, s. 3; 2012-12, s. 2(tt); 2014-100, s. 17.1(q), (ddd); 2015-181, s. 47

ARTICLE 4

ORGANIZATION AND SYSTEM FOR DELIVERY OF MENTAL HEALTH, DEVELOPMENTAL DISABILITIES, AND SUBSTANCE ABUSE SERVICES

PART 7

CONTESTED CASE HEARINGS FOR ELIGIBLE ASSAULTIVE AND VIOLENT CHILDREN

§§ 122C-194 through 122C-200

Repealed by Session Laws 2000-67, s. 11.21(e), effective July 1, 2000.

ARTICLE 5

PROCEDURES FOR ADMISSION AND DISCHARGE OF CLIENTS

PART 1

GENERAL PROVISIONS

§ 122C-201. Declaration of policy

It is State policy to encourage voluntary admissions to facilities. It is further State policy that no individual shall be involuntarily committed to a 24-hour facility unless that individual is mentally ill or a substance abuser and dangerous to self or others. All admissions and commitments shall be accomplished under conditions that protect the dignity and constitutional rights of the individual.

It is further State policy that, except as provided in G.S. 122C-212(b), individuals who have been voluntarily admitted shall be discharged upon application and that involuntarily committed individuals shall be discharged as soon as a less restrictive mode of treatment is appropriate.

History.

1973, c. 723, s. 1; c. 726, s. 1; c. 1084; c. 1408, s. 1; 1977, c. 400, s. 1; 1979, c. 915, ss. 2, 11; 1983, c. 638, s. 1; c. 864, s. 4; 1985, c. 589, s. 2; 1995 (Reg. Sess., 1996), c. 739, s. 2

§ 122C-202. Applicability of Article

This Article applies to all facilities unless expressly provided otherwise. Specific provisions that are delineated by the disability of the client, whether the client has a mental illness, has an intellectual or other developmental disability, or is a substance abuser, also apply to all facilities for that client's disability. Provisions that refer to a specific facility or type of facility apply only to the designated facility or facilities.

History.

1985, c. 589, s. 2; 1989, c. 625, s. 20; 2019-76, s. 4

§ 122C-202.1. Hospital privileges

Nothing in this Article related to admission, commitment, or treatment shall be deemed to mandate hospitals to grant or deny to any individuals privileges to practice in hospitals.

History.

1985, c. 589, s. 2

§ 122C-202.2. LME/MCO community crisis services plan; commitment examiners; transporting agencies; training; collaboration

(a) Every LME/MCO shall adopt a community crisis services plan in accordance with this section to facilitate first examination in conjunction with a health screening at the same location required pursuant to Parts 7 and 8 of this Article within its catchment area. The community crisis services plan for the LME/MCO's catchment area shall be comprised of separate plans, known as "local area crisis services plans" for each of the local areas or regions within the catchment area that the LME/MCO identifies as an appropriate local planning area, taking into consideration the available resources and interested stakeholders within a particular geographic area or region of the catchment area. Each LME/MCO may determine the number and geographic boundaries of the local planning areas within its catchment area. Each local area crisis services plan shall, for the local area covered by the local plan, do at least all of the following:

(1) Incorporate the involuntary commitment transportation agreement adopted pursuant to G.S. 122C-251(g) for the cities and counties within the local planning areas which identifies the law enforcement officers, designees under G.S. 122C-251(g), or individuals or entities otherwise required to provide custody and transportation of a respondent for a first examination in conjunction with a health screening at the same location required by G.S. 122C-263(a) and G.S. 122C-283. Notwithstanding the foregoing, counties and cities shall retain the responsibilities for custody and transportation set forth in this Article, except as otherwise set forth in a plan developed, agreed upon, and adopted in compliance with this section and G.S. 122C-251(g).

(2) Identify one or more area facilities or other locations in accordance with G.S. 122C-263 and G.S. 122C-283. Each LME/MCO shall contract with one or more facilities or other locations described in G.S. 122C-263 and G.S. 122C-283 for the provision of health screenings and first examinations required by G.S. 122C-263 and G.S. 122C-283 for the provision of first examination in conjunction with a health screening required by G.S. 122C-263 and G.S. 122C-283, to meet the needs of its local planning area.

(3) Identify available training for law enforcement personnel and other persons designated or required under G.S. 122C-251(g) to provide transportation and custody of involuntary commitment respondents. Law enforcement officers may request to participate in the training program identified by the LME/MCO. Persons who are designated in compliance with G.S. 122C-251(g) to provide all or part of the transportation and custody required for involuntary commitment proceedings under this Article and who are not law enforcement officers shall participate in the training. To the extent feasible, the identified training shall address the use of de-escalation strategies and techniques, the safe use of force and restraint, respondent rights relevant to custody and transportation, the location of any area facilities identified by the LME/MCO pursuant to subdivision (1) of this subsection, and the completion and return of the custody order to the clerk of superior court. The training identified by the LME/MCO may be comprised of one or more programs and may include a Crisis Intervention Team program or other mental health training program or a combination of these programs.

(b) Law enforcement agencies, acute care hospitals, magistrates, area facilities with identified commitment examiners, and other affected agencies shall participate with the LME/MCO in the development of the local area crisis services plans described in this section. Other stakeholders and community partners identified by the LME/MCO may be invited to participate in the planning. No local area crisis services plan developed under this section shall be adopted or thereafter be effective or implemented unless such plan first has been mutually agreed upon in writing by all entities identified in the plan pursuant to subsection (a) of this section. If any member of the Crisis Planning Committee fails to agree to the plan in writing, the Secretary shall develop a procedure to attempt to resolve the conflict in order to achieve approval of the Plan.

(c) The plans adopted under this section may, by mutual agreement of all entities identified in the plan, address any other matters necessary to facilitate the custody, transportation, examination, and treatment of respondents to commitment proceedings under Parts 7 and 8 of this Article.

History.
2018-33, s. 8

§ 122C-203. Admission or commitment and incompetency proceedings to have no effect on one another

The admission or commitment to a facility of an individual who allegedly has a mental illness, an alleged substance abuser, or an individual who allegedly has an intellectual or other developmental disability under the provisions of this Article shall in no way affect incompetency proceedings as set forth in Chapter 35A or former Chapters 33 or 35 of the General Statutes and incompetency proceedings under those Chapters shall have no effect upon admission or commitment proceedings under this Article.

History.
1963, c. 1184, s. 1; 1985, c. 589, s. 2; 1989, c. 625, s. 21; 1989 (Reg. Sess., 1990), c. 1024, s. 26(b); 2019-76, s. 5

§ 122C-204. Civil liability for corruptly attempting admission or commitment

Nothing in this Article relieves from liability in any suit instituted in the courts of this State any individual who unlawfully, maliciously, and corruptly attempts to admit or commit any individual to any facility under this Article.

History.
1963, c. 1184, s. 1; 1985, c. 589, s. 2

§ 122C-205. Return of clients to 24-hour facilities

(a) When a client of a 24-hour facility who:
(1) Has been involuntarily committed;
(2) Is being detained pending a judicial hearing;

(3) Has been voluntarily admitted but is a minor or incompetent adult;
(4) Has been placed on conditional release from the facility; or
(5) Has been involuntarily committed or voluntarily admitted and is the subject of a detainer placed with the 24-hour facility by an appropriate official

escapes or breaches a condition of his release, if applicable, the responsible professional shall notify or cause to be notified immediately the appropriate law enforcement agency in the county of residence of the client, the appropriate law enforcement agency in the county where the facility is located, and the appropriate law enforcement agency in any county where there are reasonable grounds to believe that the client may be found. The responsible professional shall determine the amount of personal identifying and background information reasonably necessary to divulge to the law enforcement agency or agencies under the particular circumstances involved in order to assure the expeditious return of the client to the 24-hour facility involved and protect the general public.

(b) When a competent adult who has been voluntarily admitted to a 24-hour facility escapes or breaches a condition of his release, the responsible professional, in the exercise of accepted professional judgment, practice, and standards, will determine if it is reasonably foreseeable that:
(1) The client may cause physical harm to others or himself;
(2) The client may cause damage to property;
(3) The client may commit a felony or a violent misdemeanor; or
(4) That the health or safety of the client may be endangered

unless he is immediately returned to the facility. If the responsible professional finds that any or all of these occurrences are reasonably foreseeable, he will follow the same procedures as those set forth in subsection (a) of this section.

(c) Upon receipt of notice of an escape or breach of a condition of release as described in subsections (a) and (b) of this section, an appropriate law enforcement officer shall take the client into custody and have the client returned to the 24-hour facility from which the client has escaped or has been conditionally released. Transportation of the client back to the 24-hour facility shall be provided in the same manner as described in G.S. 122C-251 and G.S. 122C-408(b). Law enforcement agencies who are notified of a client's escape or breach of conditional release shall be notified of the client's return by the responsible 24-hour facility. Under the circumstances described in this section, the initial notification by the 24-hour facility of the client's escape or breach of conditional release shall be given by telephone communication to the appropriate law enforcement agency or agencies and, if available and appropriate, by Department of Public Safety message to any law enforcement agency in or out of state and by entry into the National Crime Information Center (NCIC) telecommunications system. As soon as reasonably possible following notification, written authorization to take the client into custody shall also be issued by the 24-hour facility. Under this section, law enforcement officers shall have the authority to take a client into custody upon receipt of the telephone notification or Department of Public Safety message prior to receiving written authorization. The notification of a law enforcement agency does not, in and of itself, render this information public information within the purview of Chapter 132 of the General Statutes. However, the responsible law enforcement agency shall determine the extent of disclosure of personal identifying and background information reasonably necessary, under the circumstances, in order to assure the expeditious return of a client to the 24-hour facility involved and to protect the general public and is authorized to make such disclosure. The responsible law enforcement agency may also place any appropriate message or entry into either the Department of Public Safety's Criminal Information System or National Crime Information System, or both, as appropriate.

(d) In the situations described in subsections (a) and (b) of this section, the responsible professional shall also notify or cause to be notified as soon as practicable:

(1) The next of kin of the client or legally responsible person for the client;

(2) The clerk of superior court of the county of commitment of the client;

(3) The area authority of the county of residence of the client, if appropriate;

(4) The physician or eligible psychologist who performed the first examination for a commitment of the client, if appropriate; and

(5) Any official who has placed a detainer on a client as described in subdivision (a)(5) of this section

of the escape or breach of condition of the client's release upon occurrence of either action and of his subsequent return to the facility.

History.
1899, c. 1, s. 27; Rev., s. 4563; C.S., s. 6175; 1927, c. 114; 1945, c. 952, s. 12; 1953, c. 256, s. 1; 1955, c. 887, s. 3; 1973, c. 673, s. 11; 1983, c. 548; 1985, c. 589, s. 2; c. 695, s. 2; 1985 (Reg. Sess., 1986), c. 863, ss. 12-14; 1987, c. 749, s. 1; 2014-100, s. 17.1(eee)

§ 122C-205.1. Discharge of clients who escape or breach the condition of release

(a) As described in G.S. 122C-205(a), when a client of a 24-hour facility escapes or breaches the condition of his release and does not return to the facility, the facility shall:

(1) If the client was admitted under Part 2 of this Article or under Parts 3 or 4 of this Article to a nonrestrictive facility, discharge the client based on the professional judgment of the responsible professional;

(2) If the client was admitted under Part 3 or Part 4 of this Article to a restrictive facility, discharge the client when the period for continued treatment, as specified by the court, expires;

(3) If the client was admitted pending a district court hearing under Part 7 of this Article, request that the court consider dismissal or continuance of the case at the initial district court hearing; or

(4) If the client was committed under Part 7 of this Article, discharge the client when the commitment expires.

(b) As described in G.S. 122C-205(a), when a client of a 24-hour facility who was admitted under Part 8 of this Article escapes or breaches the conditions of his release and does not return to the facility, the facility may discharge the client from the facility based on the professional judgment of the responsible professional and following consultation with the appropriate area authority or physician.

(c) Upon discharge of the client, the 24-hour facility shall notify all the persons directed to be notified of the client's escape or breach of conditional release under 122C-205(a), (b) and (d) that the client has been discharged.

(d) If the client is returned to the 24-hour facility subsequent to discharge from the facility, applicable admission or commitment procedures shall be followed, when appropriate.

History.
1987, c. 674, s. 1

§ 122C-206. Transfers of clients between 24-hour facilities; transfer of clients from 24-hour facilities to acute care hospitals

(a) Before transferring a voluntary adult client from one 24-hour facility to another, the responsible professional at the original facility shall: (i) get authorization from the receiving facility that the facility will admit the client; (ii) get consent from the client; and (iii) if consent to share information is granted by the client, or if the disclosure of information is permitted under G.S. 122C-53(b), notify the next of kin of the time and location of the transfer. The preceding requirements of this paragraph may be waived if the client has been admitted under emergency procedures to a State facility not serving the client's region of the State. Following an emergency admission, the client may be transferred to the appropriate State facility without consent according to the rules of the Commission.

(b) Before transferring a respondent held for a district court hearing or a committed respondent from one 24-hour facility to another, the responsible professional at the original facility shall:

(1) Obtain authorization from the receiving facility that the facility will admit the respondent; and

(2) Provide reasonable notice to the respondent or the legally responsible person, and to the respondent's counsel, of the reason for the transfer and document the notice in the client's record.

No later than 24 hours after the transfer, the responsible professional at the original facility shall notify the petitioner, the clerk of court, the respondent's counsel, and, if consent is granted by the respondent, or if the disclosure of the information is permitted under G.S. 122C-53 or other applicable law, the next of kin, that the transfer is complete. If the transfer is completed before the judicial commitment hearing, these proceedings shall be initiated by the receiving facility. If the respondent is a minor, an incompetent adult, or is deemed incapable, then the responsible professional at the original facility shall, not later than 24 hours after the transfer, notify the respondent's legally responsible person of the location of the transfer and that the transfer is complete.

(c) Minors and incompetent adults, admitted pursuant to Parts 3 and 4 of this Article, may be transferred from one 24-hour facility to another following the same procedures specified in subsection (b) of this section. In addition, the legally responsible person shall be consulted before the proposed transfer and notified, within 24 hours after the transfer is complete, of the location of the transfer and that the transfer is complete. If the transfer is completed before the judicial determination required in G.S. 122C-223 or G.S. 122C-232, these proceedings shall be initiated by the receiving facility.

(c1) If a client described in subsections (b) or (c) of this section is to be transferred from one 24-hour facility to another, or to an acute care hospital pursuant to subsection (e) of this section, and transportation is needed, the responsible professional at the original facility shall notify the clerk of court or magistrate, and the clerk of court or magistrate shall issue a custody order for transportation of the client as provided by G.S. 122C-251.

(d) Minors and incompetent adults, admitted pursuant to Part 5 of this Article and incapable adults admitted pursuant to Part 2A of this Article, may be transferred from one 24-hour facility to another provided that prior to transfer the responsible professional at the original facility shall:

(1) Obtain authorization from the receiving facility that the facility will admit the client; and

(2) Provide reasonable notice to the client regarding the reason for transfer and document the notice in the client's record; and

(3) Provide reasonable notice to and consult with the legally responsible person regarding the reason for the transfer and document the notice and consultation in the client's record.

No later than 24 hours after the transfer, the responsible professional at the original facility shall notify the legally responsible person that the transfer is completed.

(e) The responsible professional may transfer a client from one 24-hour facility to another or to an acute care hospital for emergency medical treatment, emergency medical evaluation, or emergency surgery without notice to or consent from the client. Within a reasonable period of time the responsible professional shall notify the next of kin or the legally responsible person of the client of the transfer.

(f) When a client is transferred from one 24-hour facility to another solely for medical reasons, the client shall be returned to the original facility when the medical care is completed unless the responsible professionals at both facilities concur that discharge of the client who is not subject to G.S. 122C-266(b) is appropriate.

(f1) When a client is transferred from a 24-hour facility to an acute care hospital solely for medical reasons, the hospital shall return the client to the original facility as soon as the next client space becomes available at the original facility after completion of the client's medical care. With the exception of facility-based crisis centers, the original facility must allow at least 12 hours for the client's return before assigning the client's room or bed to another patient, unless both facilities agree that return of the client in this time period is not feasible. The original facility must accept the return of the client in priority over other clients seeking admission, except in the cases of patients designated incapable to proceed to trial by court order. If the responsible professionals at both facilities concur that discharge of a client who is not subject to G.S. 122C-266(b) is appropriate, the client may be discharged. If, at the time of the transfer, a client is being held under a custody order pending a second commitment examination or a district court hearing under involuntary commitment proceedings, the custody order shall remain valid throughout the period of time necessary to complete the client's medical care and transport the client between the 24-hour facility and the acute care hospital; provided, however, that the requirement for a timely hearing under G.S. 122C-268(a) applies. Any decision to terminate the proceedings because the respondent no longer meets the criteria for commitment or because a hearing cannot be held within the time required by G.S. 122C-268(a) shall be documented and reported to the clerk of superior court in accordance with G.S. 122C-266(c).

(g) The Commission may adopt rules to implement this section.

History.
1919, c. 330; C.S., s. 6163; 1925, c. 51, s. 1; 1945, c. 925, s. 5; 1947, c. 537, s. 9; c. 623, s. 1; 1953, c. 675, s. 15; 1955, c. 1274, s. 1; 1959, c. 1002, s. 11; 1963, c. 1166, ss. 10, 12; 1973, c. 475, s. 1; c. 476, s. 133; c. 673, ss. 7, 8; c. 1436, ss. 6, 7; 1977, c. 679, s. 7; 1981, c. 51, s. 3; c. 328, ss. 1, 2; 1985, c. 589, s. 2; 1985 (Reg. Sess., 1986), c. 863, s. 15; 1991, c. 704, s. 1; 2018-33, s. 9

§ 122C-207. Confidentiality

Court records made in all proceedings pursuant to this Article are confidential, and are not open to the general public except as provided for by G.S. 122C-54(d).

History.
1977, c. 696, s. 1; 1979, c. 164, s. 2; c. 915, s. 20; 1985, c. 589, s. 2

§ 122C-208. Voluntary admission not admissible in involuntary proceeding

Except when considering treatment history as it pertains to an involuntary outpatient commitment, the fact that an individual has been voluntarily admitted for treatment shall not be competent evidence in an involuntary commitment proceeding.

History.
1985, c. 589, s. 2

§ 122C-209. Voluntary admissions acceptance

Nothing contained in Parts 2 through 5 of this Article requires a private physician or private facility to accept an individual as a client for examination or treatment. Examination or treatment at a private facility or by a private physician is at the expense of the individual to the extent that charges are not disposed of by contract between the area authority and private facility.

History.
1985, c. 589, s. 2

§ 122C-210. Guardian to pay expenses out of estate

It is the duty of the guardian who has legal custody of the estate of an incompetent individual held pursuant to the provisions of this Article in a facility to supply funds for his support in the facility during the stay as long as there are sufficient funds for that purpose over and beyond maintaining and supporting those individuals who may be legally dependent on the estate.

History.
1985, c. 589, s. 2

§ 122C-210.1. Immunity from liability

No facility, person, or entity, including an area facility, a facility licensed under this Chapter, an acute care hospital, a general hospital, an area authority, a law enforcement officer, an LME, or an LME/MCO, or any of their officials, staff, or employees, or any other physician or individual who is responsible for the custody, transportation, examination, admission, management, supervision, treatment, or release of a respondent or client and who is not grossly negligent, is civilly or criminally liable, personally or otherwise, for that person's or entity's actions or omissions arising from these responsibilities or for the actions or omissions of a respondent or client. This immunity is in addition to any other legal immunity from liability to which these persons, entities, facilities, agencies, or individuals may be entitled and applies to actions performed in connection with, or arising out of, the custody, transportation, examination, commitment, admission, management, supervision, treatment, or release of any individual pursuant to or under the authority of this Article or otherwise.

History.
1899, c. 1, s. 31; Rev., s. 4560; C.S., s. 6172; 1961, c. 511, s. 1; 1973, c. 673, s. 10; 1983, c. 638, s. 15; c. 864, s. 4; 1985, c. 589, s. 2; 1995 (Reg. Sess., 1996), c. 739, s. 3; 2018-33, s. 10

§ 122C-210.2. Research at State facilities for the mentally ill

(a) For research purposes, State facilities for the mentally ill may be designated by the Secretary as facilities for the voluntary admission of adults who are not admissible as clients otherwise. Designation of these facilities shall be made in accordance with rules of the Secretary that assure the protection of those admitted for research purposes.

(b) Individuals may be admitted to such designated facilities on either an outpatient or inpatient basis.

(c) The Human Rights Committee of the designated facility shall monitor the care of individuals admitted for research during their participation in any research program.

(d) For these individuals admitted to such designated facilities for research purposes only, the following provisions shall apply:

(1) A written application for admission pursuant to G.S. 122C-211(a) and an examination by a physician within 24 hours of admission shall be provided to each of these individuals;

(2) They shall be exempt from the provisions of G.S. 122C-57(a) governing the rights to treatment and to a treatment plan; the requirements of G.S. 122C-61(2) and G.S. 122C-212(b); and the requirements of any single portal of entry and exit plan; however, nothing in this section shall take away the individual's right to be informed of the potential risks and alleged benefits of their participation in any research program;

(3) The Secretary shall exempt these individuals from the provisions of Article 7 of Chapter 143 of the General Statutes requiring payment for treatment in a State institution. The Secretary may also authorize reasonable compensation to be paid to individuals participating in research projects for their services; provided, that the compensation is paid from research grant funds; and

(4) The Commission shall adopt rules regarding the admission, care and discharge of those individuals admitted for research purposes only.

History.
1987, c. 358, s. 1

§ 122C-210.3. Electronic and facsimile transmission of custody orders

A custody order entered by the clerk or magistrate pursuant to this Chapter may be delivered to the law enforcement officer or other person designated or required to provide transportation and custody pursuant to G.S. 122C-251 by electronic or facsimile transmission.

History.
2015-176, s. 2.5(b); 2018-33, s. 11

PART 2
VOLUNTARY ADMISSIONS AND DISCHARGES, COMPETENT ADULTS, FACILITIES FOR THE MENTALLY ILL AND SUBSTANCE ABUSERS

§ 122C-211. Admissions

(a) Except as provided in subsections (b) through (f) of this section, any individual, including a parent in a family unit, in need of treatment for mental illness or substance abuse may seek voluntary admission at any facility by presenting himself or herself for evaluation to the facility. No physician's statement is necessary, but a written application for evaluation or admission, signed by the individual seeking admission, or the individual's legally responsible person, is required. The application form shall be available at all times at all facilities. However, no one shall be denied admission because application forms are not available. An evaluation shall determine whether the individual is in need of care, treatment, habilitation or rehabilitation for mental illness or substance abuse or further evaluation by the facility. Information provided by family members regarding the individual's need for treatment shall be reviewed in the evaluation. If applicable, information provided in an advance instruction for mental health treatment by the client or the client's legally responsible person shall be reviewed in the evaluation. An individual may not be accepted as a client if the facility determines that the individual does not need or cannot benefit from the care, treatment, habilitation, or rehabilitation available and that the individual is not in need of further evaluation by the facility. The facility shall give to an individual who is denied admission a referral to another facility or facilities that may be able to provide the treatment needed by the client.

(b) In 24-hour facilities the application shall acknowledge that the applicant may be held by the facility for a period of 72 hours after any written request for release that the applicant may make, and shall acknowledge that the 24-hour facility may have the legal right to petition for involuntary commitment of the applicant during that period. At the time of application, the facility shall tell the applicant about procedures for discharge.

(c) Any individual who voluntarily seeks admission to a 24-hour facility in which medical care is an integral component of the treatment shall be examined and evaluated by a physician of the facility within 24 hours of admission. The evaluation shall determine whether the individual is in need of treatment for mental illness or substance abuse or further evaluation by the facility. If the evaluating physician determines that the individual will not benefit from the treatment available, the individual shall not be accepted as a client.

(d) Any individual who voluntarily seeks admission to any 24-hour facility, other than one in which medical care is an integral component of the treatment, shall have a medical examination within 30 days before or after admission if it is reasonably expected that the individual will receive treatment for more than 30 days or shall produce a current, valid physical examination report, signed by a physician, completed within 12 months prior to the current admission. When applicable, this examination may be included in an examination conducted to meet the requirements of G.S. 122C-223 or G.S. 122C-232.

(e) Repealed by Session Laws 2018-33, s. 12, effective October 1, 2019, and applicable to proceedings initiated on or after that date.

(f) A family unit may voluntarily seek admission to a 24-hour substance abuse facility that is able to provide, directly or by contract, treatment, habilitation, or rehabilitation services that will specifically address the family unit's needs. These services shall include gender-specific substance abuse treatment, habilitation, or rehabilitation for the parent as well as assessment, well-child care, and, as needed, early intervention services for the child. A family unit that voluntarily seeks admission to a 24-hour substance abuse facility shall be evaluated by the facility to determine whether the family unit would benefit from the services of the facility. A facility shall not accept a family unit as a client if the facility determines that the family unit does not need or cannot benefit from the care, habilitation, or rehabilitation available at the facility. The facility shall give to a family unit that is denied admission a referral to another facility or facilities that may be able to provide treatment needed by the family unit. Except as otherwise provided, this section applies to a parent in a family unit seeking admission under this section.

(f1) Repealed by Session Laws 2018-33, s. 12, effective October 1, 2019, and applicable to proceedings initiated on or after that date.

(g) As used in this Part, the term "family unit" means a parent and the parent's dependent children under the age of three years.

History.
1945, c. 952, s. 47 1/2; 1963, c. 1184, s. 22; 1973, c. 723, s. 1; c. 1084; 1983, c. 383, s. 4; 1985, c. 589, s. 2; 1985 (Reg. Sess., 1986), c. 863, s. 16; 1989, c. 287; 1998-47, s. 1(a); 1998-198, s. 6; 1998-217, s. 53(a)(1), (2); 1999-456, s. 5; 2018-33, s. 12

§ 122C-212. Discharges

(a) Except as provided in subsection (b) of this section, an individual who has been voluntarily admitted to a facility shall be discharged upon the individual's own request. A request for discharge from a 24-hour facility shall be in writing.

(b) An individual who has been voluntarily admitted to a 24-hour facility may be held for 72 hours after the individual's written application for discharge is submitted.

History.
1973, c. 723, s. 1; c. 1084; 1983, c. 383, s. 4; 1985, c. 589, s. 2; 2018-33, s. 13

PART 2A
VOLUNTARY ADMISSIONS AND DISCHARGES; INCAPABLE ADULTS; FACILITIES FOR INDIVIDUALS WITH MENTAL ILLNESS AND SUBSTANCE USE DISORDER

§ 122C-216. Voluntary admission of individuals determined to be incapable

(a) An individual in need of treatment for mental illness and who is incapable, as defined in G.S. 122C-3 and G.S. 122C-72, may be admitted to and treated in a facility pursuant to an advance instruction for mental health treatment executed in accordance with Part 2 of Article 3 of this Chapter or pursuant to the authority of a health care agent named in a valid health care power of attorney executed in accordance with Article 3 of Chapter 32A of the General Statutes.

(b) Except as otherwise provided in this Part, G.S. 122C-211 applies to admissions of incapable adults under this Part.

(c) An advance instruction for mental health treatment shall be governed by Part 2 of Article 3 of this Chapter.

(d) When a health care power of attorney authorizes a health care agent pursuant to G.S. 32A-19 to make mental health treatment decisions for an incapable individual, the health care agent shall act for the individual in applying for admission and consenting to treatment at a facility, consistent with the extent and limitations of authority granted in the health care power of attorney for as long as the individual remains incapable.

(e) A 24-hour facility may not hold an individual under a voluntary admission who is determined to be incapable at the time of admission and who is admitted pursuant to an advance instruction for mental health treatment for more than 15 days, except as provided in G.S. 122C-211(b); provided, however, that an individual who regains sufficient understanding and capacity to make and communicate mental health treatment decisions may elect to continue his or her admission and treatment pursuant to the individual's informed consent in accordance with G.S. 122C-211. A 24-hour facility may file a petition for involuntary commitment pursuant to Article 5 of this Chapter if an individual meets applicable criteria at the conclusion of this 15-day period.

(f) For purposes of this section, if an incapable adult in need of treatment has no health care power of attorney or advance instruction for mental health treatment that addresses the needed treatment, and the incapable adult has not been adjudicated incompetent under Chapter 35A of the General Statutes, the legally responsible person for the incapable adult shall be one of the persons listed in subdivisions (3) through (7) of subsection (c) of G.S. 90-21.13, to be selected based on the priority order indicated in said subdivisions (3) through (7); provided that the persons listed in subdivisions (4) through (7) of subsection (c) of G.S. 90-21.13 shall not have the authority to admit an incapable adult to a 24-hour facility where the adult will be subject to the same or similar restrictions on freedom of movement present in the State facilities for the mentally ill.

History.
2018-33, s. 14; 2019-240, s. 26(e)

§ 122C-217. Discharge of individuals determined to be incapable

(a) The responsible professional shall unconditionally discharge an individual admitted to a facility pursuant to this Part at any time it is determined the individual is no longer mentally ill or in need of treatment at the facility.

(b) An individual who has been voluntarily admitted to a facility pursuant to this Part and who is no longer deemed incapable shall be discharged upon his or her own request. An individual's request for discharge from a 24-hour facility shall be in writing. A facility may hold an individual who has been voluntarily admitted to a 24-hour facility pursuant to this Part for up to 72 hours after the individual submits a written request for discharge, but the facility shall release the individual upon the expiration of 72 hours following submission of the written request for discharge unless the responsible professional obtains an order under Part 7 or 8 of this Article to hold the client.

(c) A health care agent named in a valid health care power of attorney or the legally responsible person may submit on behalf of an individual

admitted to a facility under this Part a written request to have the individual discharged from the facility, provided (i) the individual remains incapable at the time of the request and (ii) the request is not inconsistent with the authority expressed in the health care power of attorney or other controlling document. A facility may hold an individual for up to 72 hours after a health care agent submits a written request for the individual's discharge but shall release the individual upon the expiration of 72 hours following submission of the written request for discharge unless the responsible professional obtains an order under Part 7 or 8 of this Article to hold the client.

(d) If, in the opinion of a physician or eligible psychologist, an individual admitted to a facility under this Part regains sufficient understanding and capacity to make and communicate mental health treatment decisions while in treatment, and the individual refuses to sign an authorization for continued treatment within 72 hours after regaining decisional capacity, the facility shall discharge the individual unless the responsible professional obtains an order under Part 7 or 8 of this Article to hold the client.

(e) In any case in which an order is issued authorizing the involuntary commitment of an individual admitted to a facility under this Part, the facility's further treatment and holding of the individual shall be in accordance with Part 7 or 8 of this Article, whichever is applicable.

History.
2018-33, s. 14

PART 3
VOLUNTARY ADMISSIONS AND DISCHARGES, MINORS, FACILITIES FOR THE MENTALLY ILL AND SUBSTANCE ABUSERS

§ 122C-221. Admissions

(a) Except as otherwise provided in this Part, a minor may be admitted to a facility if the minor is mentally ill or a substance abuser and in need of treatment. Except as otherwise provided in this Part, the provisions of G.S. 122C-211 shall apply to admissions of minors under this Part. Except as provided in G.S. 90-21.5, in applying for admission to a facility, in consenting to medical treatment when consent is required, and in any other legal procedure under this Article, the legally responsible person shall act for the minor. The application of the minor shall be in writing and signed by the legally responsible person. If a minor reaches the age of 18 while in treatment under this Part, further treatment is authorized only on the written authorization of the client or under the provisions of Part 7 or Part 8 of Article 5 of this Chapter.

(b) The Commission shall adopt rules governing procedures for admission to 24-hour facilities not falling within the category of facilities where freedom of movement is restricted. These rules shall be designed to ensure that no minor is improperly admitted to or improperly remains in a 24-hour facility.

History.
1973, c. 1084; 1983, c. 302, s. 1; 1985, c. 589, s. 2; 1987, c. 370, s. 1; 2018-33, s. 15

§ 122C-222. Admissions to State facilities

Admission of a minor who is a resident of a county that is not in a single portal area shall be made to a State facility following screening and upon referral by an area authority, a physician, or an eligible psychologist. Further planning of treatment and discharge for the minor is the joint responsibility of the State facility and the person making the referral.

History.
1987, c. 370, s. 1

§ 122C-223. Emergency admission to a 24-hour facility

(a) In an emergency situation, when the legally responsible person does not appear with the minor to apply for admission, a minor who is mentally ill or a substance abuser and in need of treatment may be admitted to a 24-hour facility upon his own written application. The application shall serve as the initiating document for the hearing required by G.S. 122C-224.

(b) Within 24 hours of admission, the facility shall notify the legally responsible person of the admission unless notification is impossible due to an inability to identify, to locate, or to contact him after all reasonable means to establish contact have been attempted.

(c) If the legally responsible person cannot be located within 72 hours of admission, the responsible professional shall initiate proceedings for juvenile protective services as described in Article 3 of Chapter 7B of the General Statutes in either the minor's county of residence or in the county in which the facility is located.

(d) Within 24 hours of an emergency admission to a State facility, the State facility shall notify the area authority and, as appropriate, the minor's physician or eligible psychologist. Further planning of treatment and discharge for the minor is the joint responsibility of the State facility and the appropriate person in the community.

History.
1973, c. 1084; 1983, c. 302, s. 1; 1985, c. 589, s. 2; 1987, c. 370, s. 1; 1998-202, s. 13(ff)

§ 122C-224. Judicial review of voluntary admission

(a) When a minor is admitted to a 24-hour facility where the minor will be subjected to the same restrictions on his freedom of movement present in the State facilities for the mentally ill, or to similar restrictions, a hearing shall be held by the district court in the county in which the 24-hour facility is located within 15 days of the day that the minor is admitted to the facility. A continuance of not more than five days may be granted.

(b) Before the admission, the facility shall provide the minor and his legally responsible person with written information describing the procedures for court review of the admission and informing them about the discharge procedures. They shall also be informed that, after a written request for discharge, the facility may hold the minor for 72 hours during which time the facility may apply for a petition for involuntary commitment.

(c) Within 24 hours after admission, the facility shall notify the clerk of court in the county where the facility is located that the minor has been admitted and that a hearing for concurrence in the admission must be scheduled. At the time notice is given to schedule a hearing, the facility shall (i) notify the clerk of the names and addresses of the legally responsible person and the responsible professional and (ii) provide the clerk with a copy of the legally responsible person's written application for admission of the minor and the facility's written evaluation of the minor, both of which are required under G.S. 122C-211(a).

History.
1975, c. 839; 1977, c. 756; 1979, c. 171, s. 1; 1983, c. 889, ss. 1, 2; 1985, c. 589, s. 2; 1987, c. 370, s. 1; 2018-33, s. 16

§ 122C-224.1. Duties of clerk of court

(a) Within 48 hours of receipt of notice that a minor has been admitted to a 24-hour facility wherein his freedom of movement will be restricted, an attorney shall be appointed for the minor in accordance with rules adopted by the Office of Indigent Defense Services. When a minor has been admitted to a State facility for the mentally ill, the attorney appointed shall be the attorney employed in accordance with G.S. 122C-270(a) through (c). All minors shall be conclusively presumed to be indigent, and it shall not be necessary for the court to receive from any minor an affidavit of indigency. The

Chapter 122C

attorney shall be paid a reasonable fee in accordance with rules adopted by the Office of Indigent Defense Services. The judge may require payment of the attorney's fee from a person other than the minor as provided in G.S. 7A-450.1 through G.S. 7A-450.4.

(b) Upon receipt of notice that a minor has been admitted to a 24-hour facility wherein his freedom of movement will be restricted, the clerk shall calendar a hearing to be held within 15 days of admission for the purpose of review of the minor's admission. Notice of the time and place of the hearing shall be given as provided in G.S. 1A-1, Rule 4(j) to the attorney in lieu of the minor, as soon as possible but not later than 72 hours before the scheduled hearing. Notice of the hearing shall be sent to the legally responsible person and the responsible professional as soon as possible but not later than 72 hours before the hearing by first-class mail postage prepaid to the individual's last known address.

(c) The clerk shall schedule all hearings and rehearings and send all notices as required by this Part.

History.
1987, c. 370, s. 1; 2000-144, s. 37

§ 122C-224.2. Duties of the attorney for the minor

(a) The attorney shall meet with the minor within 10 days of his appointment but not later than 48 hours before the hearing. In addition, the attorney shall inform the minor of the scheduled hearing and shall give the minor a copy of the notice of the time and place of the hearing no later than 48 hours before the hearing.

(b) The attorney shall counsel the minor concerning the hearing procedure and the potential effects of the hearing proceeding on the minor. If the minor does not wish to appear, the attorney shall file a motion with the court before the scheduled hearing to waive the minor's right to be present at the hearing procedure except during the minor's own testimony. If the attorney determines that the minor does not wish to appear before the judge to provide his own testimony, the attorney shall file a separate motion with the court before the hearing to waive the minor's right to testify.

(c) In all actions on behalf of the minor, the attorney shall represent the minor until formally relieved of the responsibility by the judge.

History.
1987, c. 370, s. 1

§ 122C-224.3. Hearing for review of admission

(a) Hearings shall be held at the 24-hour facility in which the minor is being treated, if it is located within the judge's district court district as defined in G.S. 7A-133, unless the judge determines that the court calendar will be disrupted by such scheduling. In cases where the hearing cannot be held in the 24-hour facility, the judge may schedule the hearing in another location, including the judge's chambers. The hearing may not be held in a regular courtroom, over objection of the minor's attorney, if in the discretion of the judge a more suitable place is available.

(b) The minor shall have the right to be present at the hearing unless the judge rules favorably on the motion of the attorney to waive the minor's appearance. However, the minor shall retain the right to appear before the judge to provide his own testimony and to respond to the judge's questions unless the judge makes a separate finding that the minor does not wish to appear upon motion of the attorney.

(c) Certified copies of reports and findings of physicians, psychologists and other responsible professionals as well as previous and current medical records are admissible in evidence, but the minor's right, through his attorney, to confront and cross-examine witnesses may not be denied.

(d) Hearings shall be closed to the public unless the attorney requests otherwise.

(e) A copy of all documents admitted into evidence and a transcript of the proceedings shall be furnished to the attorney, on request, by the clerk upon the direction of a district court judge. The copies shall be provided at State expense.

(f) For an admission to be authorized beyond the hearing, the minor must be (1) mentally ill or a substance abuser and (2) in need of further treatment at the 24-hour facility to which he has been admitted. Further treatment at the admitting facility should be undertaken only when lesser measures will be insufficient. It is not necessary that the judge make a finding of dangerousness in order to support a concurrence in the admission.

(g) The court shall make one of the following dispositions:

(1) If the court finds by clear, cogent, and convincing evidence that the requirements of subsection (f) have been met, the court shall concur with the voluntary admission and set the length of the authorized admission of the minor for a period not to exceed 90 days; or

(2) If the court determines that there exist reasonable grounds to believe that the

requirements of subsection (f) have been met but that additional diagnosis and evaluation is needed before the court can concur in the admission, the court may make a one time authorization of up to an additional 15 days of stay, during which time further diagnosis and evaluation shall be conducted; or

(3) If the court determines that the conditions for concurrence or continued diagnosis and evaluation have not been met, the judge shall order that the minor be released.

(h) The decision of the District Court in all hearings and rehearings is final. Appeal may be had to the Court of Appeals by the State or by any party on the record as in civil cases. The minor may be retained and treated in accordance with this Part, pending the outcome of the appeal, unless otherwise ordered by the District Court or the Court of Appeals.

History.
1987, c. 370, s. 1; 1987 (Reg. Sess., 1988), c. 1037, s. 113

§ 122C-224.4. Rehearings

(a) A minor admitted to a 24-hour facility upon order of the court for further diagnosis and evaluation shall have the right to a rehearing if the responsible professional determines that the minor is in need of further treatment beyond the time authorized by the court for diagnosis and evaluation.

(b) A minor admitted to a 24-hour facility upon the concurrence of the court shall have the right to a rehearing for further concurrence in continued treatment before the end of the period authorized by the court. The court shall review the continued admission in accordance with the hearing procedures in this Part. The court may order discharge of the minor if the minor no longer meets the criteria for admission. If the minor continues to meet the criteria for admission the court shall concur with the continued admission of the minor and set the length of the authorized admission for a period not to exceed 180 days. Subsequent rehearings shall be scheduled at the end of each subsequent authorized treatment period, but no longer than every 180 days.

(c) The responsible professional shall notify the clerk, no later than 15 days before the end of the authorized admission, that continued stay beyond the authorized admission is recommended for the minor. The clerk shall calendar the rehearing to be held before the end of the current authorized admission.

History.
1987, c. 370, s. 1

§ 122C-224.5. Transportation

When it is necessary for a minor to be transported to a location other than the treating facility for the purpose of a hearing, transportation shall be provided under the provisions of G.S. 122C-251. However, the 24-hour facility may obtain permission from the court to routinely provide transportation of minors to and from hearings.

History.
1987, c. 370, s. 1

§ 122C-224.6. Treatment pending hearing and after authorization for or concurrence in admission

(a) Pending the initial hearing and after authorization for further diagnosis and evaluation, or concurrence in admission, the responsible professional may administer to the minor reasonable and appropriate medication and treatment that is consistent with accepted medical standards and consistent with Article 3 of this Chapter.

(b) The responsible professional may release the minor conditionally for periods not in excess of 30 days on specified appropriate conditions. Violation of the conditions is grounds for return of the minor to the 24-hour facility. A law enforcement officer, on request of the responsible professional, shall take the minor into custody and return him to the facility in accordance with G.S. 122C-205.

History.
1987, c. 370, s. 1

§ 122C-224.7. Discharge

(a) The responsible professional shall unconditionally discharge a minor from treatment at any time that it is determined that the minor is no longer mentally ill or a substance abuser, or no longer in need of treatment at the facility.

(b) The legally responsible person may file a written request for discharge from the facility at any time. The facility may hold the minor in the facility for 72 hours after receipt of the request for discharge. If the responsible professional believes that the minor is mentally ill and dangerous to himself or others, he may file a petition for involuntary commitment under the provisions of Part 7 of this Article. If the responsible professional believes that the minor is a substance abuser and dangerous to himself or others, he may file a petition for involuntary commitment under the provisions of Part 8 of this Article. If an order authorizing the holding of the minor under involuntary commitment procedures is issued, further treatment and holding shall follow the provisions of Part 7 or

Part 8 whichever is applicable. If an order authorizing the holding of the minor under involuntary commitment procedures is not issued, the minor shall be discharged.

(c) If a client reaches age 18 while in treatment, and the client refuses to sign an authorization for continued treatment within 72 hours of reaching 18, he shall be discharged unless the responsible professional obtains an order to hold the client under the provisions of Part 7 or Part 8 of this Article pursuant to an involuntary commitment.

History.
1975, c. 839; 1977, c. 756; 1979, c. 171, s. 1; 1983, c. 889, ss. 1, 2; 1985, c. 589, s. 2; 1987, c. 370, s. 1

PART 4
VOLUNTARY ADMISSIONS AND DISCHARGES, INCOMPETENT ADULTS, FACILITIES FOR THE MENTALLY ILL AND SUBSTANCE ABUSERS

§ 122C-230. Applicability of Part 4

This Part applies to adults who are adjudicated incompetent by a court of competent jurisdiction. This Part does not apply to the admission of adults who are deemed incapable but who have not been adjudicated incompetent.

History.
2018-33, s. 17

§ 122C-231. Admissions

Except as otherwise provided in this Part an incompetent adult may be admitted to a facility when the individual is mentally ill or a substance abuser and in need of treatment. The provisions of G.S. 122C-211 shall apply to admissions of an incompetent adult under this Part except that the legally responsible person shall act for the individual, in applying for admission to a facility, in consenting to medical treatment when consent is required, in giving or receiving any legal notice, and in any other legal procedure under this Article.

History.
1973, c. 1084; 1983, c. 302, s. 1; 1985, c. 589, s. 2

§ 122C-232. Judicial determination

(a) When an incompetent adult is admitted to a 24-hour facility where the incompetent adult will be subjected to the same restrictions on freedom of movement present in the State facilities for the mentally ill, or to similar restrictions, a hearing shall be held in the district court in the county in which the 24-hour facility is located within 10 days after the day the incompetent adult is admitted to the facility. A continuance of not more than five days may be granted upon motion [of] any of the following:

(1) The court.
(2) Respondent's counsel.
(3) The responsible professional.

The Commission shall adopt rules governing procedures for admission to other 24-hour facilities not falling within the category of facilities where freedom of movement is restricted; these rules shall be designed to ensure that no incompetent adult is improperly admitted to or remains in a facility.

(a1) Prior to admission, the facility shall provide the incompetent adult and the legally responsible person with written information describing the procedures for court review of the admission and the procedures for discharge.

(a2) Within 24 hours after admission, the facility shall notify the clerk of court of the county in which the facility is located that the incompetent adult has been admitted and that a hearing for concurrence in the admission must be scheduled. At the time the facility provides notice to the court to schedule a hearing for concurrence, the facility shall notify the clerk of the names and addresses of the legally responsible person and the responsible professional and provide a copy of the legally responsible person's written application for evaluation or admission of the incompetent adult and the facility's evaluation of the incompetent adult.

(b) In any case requiring the hearing described in subsection (a) of this section, no petition is necessary; the written application for voluntary admission shall serve as the initiating document for the hearing. The court shall determine whether the incompetent adult is mentally ill or a substance abuser and is in need of further treatment at the facility. Further treatment at the facility should be undertaken only when lesser measures will be insufficient. If the court finds by clear, cogent, and convincing evidence that these requirements have been met, the court shall concur with the voluntary admission of the incompetent adult and set the length of the authorized admission for a period not to exceed 90 days. If the court finds that these requirements have not been met, it shall order that the incompetent adult be released. A finding of dangerousness to self or others is not necessary to support the determination that further treatment should be undertaken.

(c) Unless otherwise provided in this Part, the hearing specified in subsection (a) of this section, including the provisions for representation of indigent incompetent adults, all subsequent proceedings, and conditional release are governed by the involuntary commitment procedures of Part 7 of this Article.

(d) In addition to the notice of hearings and rehearings to the incompetent adult and his or her counsel required under Part 7 of this Article, notice shall be given by the clerk to the legally responsible person or a successor to the legally responsible person. The legally responsible person or a successor to the legally responsible person may also file with the clerk of court a written waiver of the right to receive notice.

History.
1975, c. 839; 1977, c. 756; 1979, c. 171, s. 1; 1983, c. 889, ss. 1, 2; 1985, c. 589, s. 2; 2018-33, s. 18

§ 122C-233. Discharges

(a) Except as provided in subsection (b) of this section, an incompetent adult shall be discharged upon the request of the legally responsible person as provided in G.S. 122C-212.

(b) After the court has concurred in the admission of an incompetent adult to a 24-hour facility as provided in G.S. 122C-232, only the facility or the court may release the incompetent adult at any time when either determines that the incompetent adult does not need further treatment at the facility. If the legally responsible person believes that release is in the best interest of the incompetent adult, and the facility refuses release, the legally responsible person may apply to the court for a hearing for discharge.

History.
1975, c. 839; 1977, c. 756; 1979, c. 171, s. 1; 1983, c. 889, ss. 1, 2; 1985, c. 589, s. 2

PART 5
VOLUNTARY ADMISSIONS AND DISCHARGES, MINORS AND ADULTS, FACILITIES FOR INDIVIDUALS WITH DEVELOPMENTAL DISABILITIES

§ 122C-241. Admissions

(a) Except as provided in subsection (c) of this section, an individual with intellectual or other developmental disabilities may be admitted to a facility for individuals with intellectual or other developmental disabilities to receive care, habilitation, rehabilitation, training, or treatment. Application for admission is made as follows:

(1) A minor with intellectual or other developmental disabilities may be admitted upon application by both the father and the mother if they are living together and, if not, by the parent or parents having custody or by the legally responsible person.

(2) An adult with intellectual or other developmental disabilities who has been adjudicated incompetent under Chapter 35A or former Chapters 33 or 35 of the General Statutes may be admitted upon application by the adult's guardian.

(3) An adult with intellectual or other developmental disabilities who has not been adjudicated incompetent under Chapter 35A or former Chapters 33 or 35 of the General Statutes may be admitted upon the adult's own application.

(b) Prior to admission to a 24-hour facility, the individual shall be examined and evaluated by a physician or psychologist to determine whether the individual has a developmental disability. In addition, the individual shall be examined and evaluated by a qualified developmental disabilities professional no sooner than 31 days prior to admission or within 72 hours after admission to determine whether the individual is in need of care, habilitation, rehabilitation, training, or treatment by the facility. If the evaluating professional determines that the individual will not benefit from an admission, the individual shall not be admitted as a client.

(c) An admission to an area or State 24-hour facility of an individual from a single portal area shall follow the procedures as prescribed in the area plan. When an individual from a single portal area presents himself or herself or is presented for admission directly to a State developmental center and is in need of an emergency admission, he or she may be accepted for admission. The State developmental center shall notify the area authority within 24 hours of the admission and further planning of treatment for the individual is the joint responsibility of the area authority and the State developmental center as prescribed in the area plan.

History.
1963, c. 1184, s. 6; 1965, c. 800, s. 12; 1973, c. 476, s. 133; 1977, c. 679, s. 7; 1981, c. 51, s. 3; 1983, c. 383, s. 7; 1985, c. 589, s. 2; c. 695, s. 14; 1989, c. 625, s. 22; 1989 (Reg. Sess., 1990), c. 1024, s. 26(d); 2019-76, s. 6

§ 122C-242. Discharges

(a) Except as provided in subsections (b) through (d) of this section, discharges from facilities for individuals with developmental disabilities are made upon request of the individual authorized in G.S. 122C-241(a) to make application for admission or by the director of the facility.

Chapter 122C

(b) Any adult who has not been declared incompetent and who is admitted to a 24-hour facility shall be discharged upon his own request, unless the director of the facility has reason to believe that the adult is endangering himself by the discharge. In this case the individual may be held for a period not to exceed five days while the director petitions for the adjudication of incompetency of the individual and the appointment of an interim guardian under Chapter 35A of the General Statutes.

(c) Any individual admitted to a 24-hour facility may be discharged when in the judgment of the director of the facility the individual is no longer in need of care, treatment, habilitation or rehabilitation by the facility or the individual will no longer benefit from the service available. In the case of an area or State facility rules adopted by the Commission or by the Secretary in accordance with G.S. 122C-63 shall be followed.

(d) When the individual to be discharged from an area or State 24-hour facility is a resident of a single portal area, the discharge shall follow the procedures described in the area plan.

History.
1963, c. 1184, s. 6; 1973, c. 476, s. 133; 1983, c. 383, s. 8; 1985, c. 589, s. 2; 1989, c. 625, s. 22; 1989 (Reg. Sess., 1990), c. 1024, s. 26(c)

PART 6
INVOLUNTARY COMMITMENT -- GENERAL PROVISIONS

§ 122C-251. Custody and transportation

(a) Except as provided in subsections (c), (f), and (g) [of this section], transportation of a respondent within a county under the involuntary commitment proceedings of this Article, including admission and discharge, shall be provided by the city or county. The city has the duty to provide transportation of a respondent who is a resident of the city or who is physically taken into custody in the city limits. The county has the duty to provide transportation for a respondent who resides in the county outside city limits or who is physically taken into custody outside of city limits. However, cities and counties may contract with each other to provide transportation.

(b) Except as provided in subsections (c), (f), and (g) [of this section] or in G.S. 122C-408(b), transportation between counties under the involuntary commitment proceedings of this Article for a first examination as described in G.S. 122C-263(a) and G.S. 122C-283(a) and for admission to a 24-hour facility shall be provided by the county where the respondent is taken into custody. Transportation between counties

under the involuntary commitment proceedings of this Article for respondents held in 24-hour facilities who have requested a change of venue for the district court hearing shall be provided by the county where the petition for involuntary commitment was initiated. Transportation between counties under the involuntary commitment proceedings of this Article for discharge of a respondent from a 24-hour facility shall be provided by the county of residence of the respondent. However, a respondent being discharged from a facility may use his own transportation at his own expense.

(c) Transportation of a respondent may be (i) by city- or county-owned vehicles, (ii) by private vehicle by contract with the city or county, or (iii) as provided in an agreement developed and adopted under subsection (g) of this section and G.S. 122C-202.2. To the extent feasible, law enforcement officers transporting respondents shall dress in plain clothes and shall travel in unmarked vehicles. Further, law enforcement officers, to the extent possible, shall advise respondents when taking them into custody that they are not under arrest and have not committed a crime, but are being taken into custody and transported to receive treatment and for their own safety and that of others.

(d) To the extent feasible, in providing transportation of a respondent, a city or county shall provide a driver or attendant who is the same sex as the respondent, unless the law enforcement officer allows a family member of the respondent to accompany the respondent in lieu of an attendant of the same sex as the respondent.

(e) In taking custody and providing transportation as required by this section, the law enforcement officer may use reasonable force to restrain the respondent if it appears necessary to protect the law enforcement officer, the respondent, or others. Any use of restraints shall be as reasonably determined by the officer to be necessary under the circumstances for the safety of the respondent, the law enforcement officer, and other persons. Every effort to avoid restraint of a child under the age of 10 shall be made by the transporting officer unless the child's behavior or other circumstances dictate that restraint is necessary. The law enforcement officer shall respond to all inquiries from the facility concerning the respondent's behavior and the use of any restraints related to the custody and transportation of the respondent, except in circumstances where providing that information is confidential or would otherwise compromise a law enforcement investigation. No law enforcement officer or other person designated or required to provide custody or transport of a client under G.S. 122C-251 may be held criminally or civilly liable for assault, false imprisonment, or other torts or crimes on account of reasonable measures taken under the authority of this Article.

(f) Notwithstanding the provisions of subsections (a), (b), and (c) of this section, a clerk, a magistrate, or a district court judge, where applicable, may authorize either a health care provider of the respondent or the family or immediate friends of the respondent, if they so request, to transport the respondent in accordance with the procedures of this Article. This authorization shall only be granted in cases where the danger to the public, the health care provider of the respondent, the family or friends of the respondent, or the respondent himself or herself is not substantial. The health care provider of the respondent or the family or immediate friends of the respondent shall bear the costs of providing this transportation.

(g) The governing body of a city or county shall adopt a plan known as an "involuntary commitment transportation agreement" or "transportation agreement" for the custody and transportation of respondents in involuntary commitment proceedings under this Article as follows:

(1) Law enforcement and other affected agencies, including local acute care hospitals and other mental health providers, shall participate in developing the transportation agreement. The area authority may participate in developing the transportation agreement.

(2) The transportation agreement may designate law enforcement officers, volunteers, or other public or private personnel who have agreed pursuant to subsection (g) of this section to provide all or parts of the custody and transportation required by involuntary commitment proceedings. Persons so designated or otherwise required to provide all or parts of the custody and transportation required by involuntary commitment proceedings shall be trained as set forth in G.S. 122C-202.2(a)(3), and the plan shall assure adequate safety and protections for both the public and the respondent. Any person or agency designated or required to provide all or parts of the custody and transportation required by involuntary commitment proceedings shall follow the procedures in this Article. References in this Article to a law enforcement officer apply to any person or entity designated to provide custody or transportation. The transportation agreement may provide that private personnel or agencies may contract for transportation services to transport respondents under involuntary commitment from one entity to another.

(3) A person shall not be designated under subsection (g) of this section without that person's written consent and the written consent of his or her employer, if applicable. An agency, corporation, or entity shall not be designated without the written consent of that agency, corporation, or entity. Any person, agency, corporation, or other entity shall be designated to provide only the services which the person, agency, corporation, or other entity has previously consented in writing to provide and shall be permitted to withdraw from or discontinue providing services, in whole or in part, upon written notice to the designating governing body. The transportation agreement shall be submitted to the magistrates in the city or county's judicial district, to the county clerks of court, to the LME/MCO that serves the city or county, and to the Division of Mental Health, Developmental Disabilities, and Substance Abuse Services on or before January 1, 2019. If the city or county modifies the transportation agreement, it will submit the modified agreement to their magistrates in their judicial district, county clerks of court, the LME/MCO that serves the city or county, and the Division of Mental Health, Developmental Disabilities, and Substance Abuse Services at least 10 days prior to the effective date of the new plan.

(4) Counties and cities shall retain and be required to perform the responsibilities set forth in this Article, except as set forth in a plan developed, agreed upon, and adopted in compliance with this subsection.

(h) The cost and expenses of custody and transportation of a respondent as required by the involuntary commitment procedures of this Article, to the extent they are not reimbursed by a third-party insurer, are the responsibility of the county of residence of the respondent. The State (when providing transportation under G.S. 122C-408(b)), a city, or a county is entitled to recover the reasonable cost of transportation from the county of residence of the respondent. The county of residence of the respondent shall reimburse the State, another county, or a city the reasonable transportation costs incurred as authorized by this subsection. The county of residence of the respondent is entitled to recover the reasonable cost of transportation it has paid to the State, a city, or a county. Provided that the county of residence provides the respondent or other individual liable for the respondent's support a reasonable notice and opportunity to object to the reimbursement, the county of residence of the respondent may recover that cost from:

(1) The respondent, if the respondent is not indigent;

(2) Any person or entity that is legally liable for the resident's support and

Chapter 122C

maintenance provided there is sufficient property to pay the cost;

(3) Any person or entity that is contractually responsible for the cost; or

(4) Any person or entity that otherwise is liable under federal, State, or local law for the cost.

History.

1899, c. 1, s. 32; Rev., s. 4555; 1919, c. 326, s. 4; C.S., ss. 6201, 6202; 1945, c. 952, ss. 29, 30; 1953, c. 256, s. 6; 1961, c. 186; 1963, c. 1184, s. 1; 1969, c. 982; 1973, c. 1408, s. 1; 1979, c. 915, ss. 21, 22; 1983, c. 138, ss. 1, 2; 1985, c. 589, s. 2; 1987, c. 268; 1995 (Reg. Sess., 1996), c. 739, s. 4; 1999-201, s. 1; 1999-456, s. 36; 2015-176, s. 2.5(a); 2018-33, s. 19; 2019-240, s. 26(f); 2021-138, s. 6(a)

§ 122C-252. Twenty-four hour facilities for custody and treatment of involuntary clients

State facilities, 24-hour facilities licensed under this Chapter or hospitals licensed under Chapter 131E may be designated by the Secretary as facilities for the custody and treatment of involuntary clients. Designation of these facilities shall be made in accordance with rules of the Secretary that assure the protection of the client and the general public. Facilities so designated may detain a client under the procedures of Parts 7 and 8 of this Article both before a district court hearing and after commitment of the respondent.

History.

1973, c. 726, s. 1; c. 1408, s. 1; 1977, c. 400, s. 4; c. 679, s. 8; c. 739, s. 1; 1979, c. 358, s. 27; c. 915, s. 4; 1983, c. 380, ss. 4, 10; c. 638, ss. 6, 7, 25.1; c. 864, s. 4; 1985, c. 589, s. 2

§ 122C-253. Fees under commitment order

Nothing contained in Parts 6, 7, or 8 of this Article requires a private physician, private psychologist, commitment examiner, or private facility to accept a respondent as a client either before or after commitment. Treatment at a private facility or by a private physician, psychologist, or commitment examiner is at the expense of the respondent to the extent that the charges are not disposed of by contract between the area authority and the private facility. An area authority and its contract agencies shall set and recover fees for inpatient or outpatient treatment services provided under a commitment order in accordance with G.S. 122C-146.

History.

1973, c. 726, s. 1; c. 1408, s. 1; 1977, c. 400, s. 8; c. 739, s. 2; 1979, c. 358, s. 26; c. 915, ss. 8, 15, 16; 1981, c. 537,

s. 1; 1983, c. 380, s. 8; c. 638, s. 14; c. 864, s. 4; 1985, c. 589, s. 2; c. 695, s. 3; 2018-33, s. 20

§ 122C-254. Housing responsibility for certain clients in or escapees from involuntary commitment

(a) Any individual who has been involuntarily committed under the provisions of this Article to a 24-hour facility:

(1) Who escapes from or is absent without authorization from the facility before being discharged; and

(2) Who is charged with a criminal offense committed after the escape or during the unauthorized absence; and

(3) Whose involuntary commitment is determined to be still valid by the judge or judicial officer who would make the pretrial release determination regarding the criminal offense under the provisions of G.S. 15A-533 and G.S. 15A-534; or

(4) Who is charged with committing a crime while still residing in the facility and whose commitment is still valid as prescribed by subdivision (3) of this section;

shall be denied pretrial release pursuant to G.S. 15A-533 and G.S. 15A-534. In lieu of pretrial release, and pending the additional proceedings on the criminal offense, the individual shall be returned to the 24-hour facility in which he was residing at the time of the alleged crime or from which he escaped or absented himself for continuation of his commitment.

(b) Absent findings of lack of mental responsibility for his criminal offense or lack of competency to stand trial for the criminal offense, the involuntary commitment of an individual as described in subsection (a) of this section shall not be utilized in lieu of nor shall it constitute a bar to proceeding to trial for the criminal offense. At any time that the district court or the responsible professional of the 24-hour facility finds that the individual should be unconditionally discharged, committed for outpatient treatment, or conditionally released, the facility shall notify the clerk of superior court in the county in which the criminal charge is pending before making the change in status. At this time, a pretrial release determination pursuant to the provisions of G.S. 15A-533 and G.S. 15A-534 shall be made. In this event, arrangements for returning the individual for the pretrial release determination shall be the responsibility of the clerk of superior court.

(c) An individual who has been processed in accordance with subsections (a) and (b) of this section may not later be returned to a 24-hour facility before trial except pursuant to involuntary commitment proceedings by the district court in accordance with Parts 7 and 8 of this

Article or after proceedings in accordance with the provisions of G.S. 15A-1002 or G.S. 15A-1321.

(d) Other involuntarily committed respondents who escape, but do not meet the additional criteria specified in subsection (a) of this section, are handled in accordance with the provisions of G.S. 122C-205.

History.
1981, c. 936, s. 1; 1985, c. 589, s. 2

§ 122C-255. Report required

Each 24-hour facility that (i) falls under the category of nonhospital medical detoxification, facility-based crisis service, or inpatient hospital treatment, (ii) is not a State facility under the jurisdiction of the Secretary of Health and Human Services, and (iii) is designated by the Secretary of Health and Human Services as a facility for the custody and treatment of individuals under a petition of involuntary commitment pursuant to G.S. 122C-252 and 10A NCAC 26C.0101 shall submit a written report on involuntary commitments each January 1 and each July 1 to the Department of Health and Human Services, Division of Mental Health, Developmental Disabilities, and Substance Abuse Services. The report shall include all of the following:

(1) The number and primary presenting conditions of individuals receiving treatment from the facility under a petition of involuntary commitment.

(1a) The transportation method utilized by individuals admitted under a petition of involuntary commitment to the 24-hour facility.

(1b) The number of individuals moved to voluntary status at any time between arrival at the 24-hour facility and completion of the required 24-hour examination.

(2) The number of individuals for whom an involuntary commitment proceeding was initiated at the facility, who were referred to a different facility or program.

(3) The reason for referring the individuals described in subdivision (2) of this section to a different facility or program, including the need for more intensive medical supervision.

History.
2011-346, s. 2; 2018-33, s. 21; 2021-77, s. 5

PART 7
INVOLUNTARY COMMITMENT OF THE MENTALLY ILL; FACILITIES FOR THE MENTALLY ILL

§ 122C-261. Affidavit and petition before clerk or magistrate when immediate hospitalization is not necessary; custody order

(a) Anyone who has knowledge of an individual who has a mental illness and is either (i) dangerous to self, as defined in G.S. 122C-3(11) a., or dangerous to others, as defined in G.S. 122C-3(11)b., or (ii) in need of treatment in order to prevent further disability or deterioration that would predictably result in dangerousness, may appear before a clerk or assistant or deputy clerk of superior court or a magistrate and execute an affidavit to this effect, and petition the clerk or magistrate for issuance of an order to take the respondent into custody for examination by a commitment examiner. The affidavit shall include the facts on which the affiant's opinion is based. If the affiant has knowledge or reasonably believes that the respondent, in addition to having a mental illness, also has an intellectual disability, this fact shall be stated in the affidavit. Jurisdiction under this subsection is in the clerk or magistrate in the county where the respondent resides or is found.

(b) If the clerk or magistrate finds reasonable grounds to believe that the facts alleged in the affidavit are true and that the respondent probably has a mental illness and is either (i) dangerous to self, as defined in G.S. 122C-3(11)a., or dangerous to others, as defined in G.S. 122C-3(11)b., or (ii) in need of treatment in order to prevent further disability or deterioration that would predictably result in dangerousness, the clerk or magistrate shall issue an order to a law enforcement officer or any other designated person under G.S. 122C-251(g) to take the respondent into custody for examination by a commitment examiner. If the clerk or magistrate finds that, in addition to probably having a mental illness, the respondent also probably has an intellectual disability, the clerk or magistrate shall contact the area authority before issuing a custody order and the area authority shall designate the facility to which the respondent is to be taken for examination by a commitment examiner. The clerk or magistrate shall provide the petitioner and the respondent, if present, with specific information regarding the next steps that will occur for the respondent.

(c) If the clerk or magistrate issues a custody order, the clerk or magistrate shall also make inquiry in any reliable way as to whether the respondent is indigent within the meaning of G.S. 7A-450. A magistrate shall report the result of this inquiry to the clerk.

(d) If the affiant is a commitment examiner, all of the following apply:

(1) If the affiant has examined the respondent, the affiant may execute the affidavit before any official authorized to administer

Chapter 122C

oaths. This affiant is not required to appear before the clerk or magistrate for this purpose. This affiant shall file the affidavit with the clerk or magistrate by delivering to the clerk or magistrate the original affidavit, by transmitting a copy in paper form that is printed through the facsimile transmission of the affidavit, or by delivering the affidavit through electronic transmission. If the affidavit is filed through electronic or facsimile transmission, the affiant shall mail the original affidavit no later than five days after the facsimile transmission of the affidavit to the clerk or magistrate to be filed by the clerk or magistrate with the facsimile copy of the affidavit.

(2) This affiant's examination shall comply with the requirements of the initial examination as provided in G.S. 122C-263(c). The affiant shall document in writing and file the examination findings with the affidavit delivered to the clerk or magistrate in accordance with subdivision (1) of subsection (d) of this section.

(3) If the commitment examiner recommends outpatient commitment according to the criteria for outpatient commitment set forth in G.S. 122C-263(d)(1) and the clerk or magistrate finds probable cause to believe that the respondent meets the criteria for outpatient commitment, the clerk or magistrate shall issue an order that a hearing before a district court judge be held to determine whether the respondent will be involuntarily committed. The commitment examiner shall contact the LME/MCO that serves the county where the respondent resides or the LME/MCO that coordinated services for the respondent to inform the LME/MCO that the respondent has been scheduled for an appointment with an outpatient treatment physician or center. The commitment examiner shall provide the respondent with written notice of any scheduled appointment and the name, address, and telephone number of the proposed outpatient treatment physician or center.

(4) If the commitment examiner recommends inpatient commitment based on the criteria for inpatient commitment set forth in G.S. 122C-263(d)(2) and the clerk or magistrate finds probable cause to believe that the respondent meets the criteria for inpatient commitment, the clerk or magistrate shall issue an order to a law enforcement officer to take the respondent into custody for transportation to a 24-hour facility described in G.S. 122C-252, provided that if a 24-hour facility is not immediately available or appropriate to the respondent's medical condition, the respondent may be temporarily detained under

appropriate supervision and, upon further examination, released in accordance with G.S. 122C-263(d)(2).

(5) If the affiant is a physician or eligible psychologist at a 24-hour facility described in G.S. 122C-252 who recommends inpatient commitment; the respondent is physically present on the premises of the same 24-hour facility; and the clerk or magistrate finds probable cause to believe that the respondent meets the criteria for inpatient commitment, then the clerk or magistrate may issue an order by facsimile transmission or may issue an electronically scanned order by electronic transmission to the physician or eligible psychologist at the 24-hour facility, or a designee, to take the respondent into custody at the 24-hour facility and proceed according to G.S. 122C-266. Upon receipt of the custody order, the physician or eligible psychologist at the 24-hour facility, or a designee, shall immediately (i) notify the respondent that the respondent is not under arrest and has not committed a crime but is being taken into custody to receive treatment and for the respondent's own safety and the safety of others, (ii) take the respondent into custody, and (iii) complete and sign the appropriate portion of the custody order and return the order to the clerk or magistrate either by facsimile transmission or by scanning it and sending it by electronic transmission. The physician or eligible psychologist, or a designee, shall mail the original custody order no later than five days after returning it by means of facsimile or electronic transmission to the clerk or magistrate. The clerk or magistrate shall file the original custody order with the copy of the custody order that was electronically returned.

Notwithstanding the provisions of this subdivision, a clerk or magistrate shall not issue a custody order to a physician or eligible psychologist at a 24-hour facility, or a designee, if the physician or eligible psychologist, or a designee, has not completed training in proper service and return of service. As used in this subdivision, the term "designee" includes the 24-hour facility's on-site police security personnel.

The Department of Health and Human Services shall cooperate and collaborate with the Administrative Office of the Courts and the UNC School of Government to develop protocols to implement this section, including a procedure for notifying clerks and magistrates of the names of the physicians, psychologists, and designees who have completed the training. The Secretary of the Department shall oversee implementation of these protocols.

Chapter 122C

(6) If the clerk or magistrate finds probable cause to believe that the respondent, in addition to having a mental illness, also has an intellectual disability, the clerk or magistrate shall contact the area authority before issuing the order and the area authority shall designate the facility to which the respondent is to be transported.

(7) If a commitment examiner executes an affidavit for inpatient commitment of a respondent, a physician who is not the commitment examiner who performed the examination under this section shall be required to perform the examination required by G.S. 122C-266.

(8) No commitment examiner, area facility, acute care hospital, general hospital, or other site of first examination, or its officials, staff, employees, or other individuals responsible for the custody, examination, detention, management, supervision, treatment, or release of an individual examined for commitment, who is not grossly negligent, shall be held liable in any civil or criminal action for taking measures to temporarily detain an individual for the period of time necessary to complete a commitment examination, submit an affidavit to the magistrate or clerk of court, and await the issuance of a custody order as authorized by this section.

(e) Except as provided in subdivision (5) of subsection (d) of this section, upon receipt of the custody order of the clerk or magistrate or a custody order issued by the court pursuant to G.S. 15A-1003, a law enforcement officer, person designated under G.S. 122C-251(g), or other person identified in the order shall take the respondent into custody within 24 hours after the order is signed, and proceed according to G.S. 122C-263. The custody order is valid throughout the State.

Notwithstanding the provisions of this section, in no event shall an individual known or reasonably believed to have an intellectual disability be admitted to a State psychiatric hospital, except the following:

(1) Persons described in G.S. 122C-266(b).

(2) Persons admitted pursuant to G.S. 15A-1321.

(3) Respondents who are so extremely dangerous as to pose a serious threat to the community and to other patients committed to non-State hospital psychiatric inpatient units, as determined by the Director of the Division of Mental Health, Developmental Disabilities, and Substance Abuse Services or the Director's designee.

(4) Respondents who are so gravely disabled by both multiple disorders and medical fragility or multiple disorders and deafness that alternative care is inappropriate, as determined by the Director of the Division of Mental Health, Developmental Disabilities, and Substance Abuse Services or the Director's designee.

Individuals transported to a State facility for individuals with mental illnesses who are not admitted by the facility may be transported by appropriate law enforcement officers or designated staff of the State facility in State-owned vehicles to an appropriate 24-hour facility that provides psychiatric inpatient care.

No later than 24 hours after the transfer, the responsible professional at the original facility shall notify the petitioner, the clerk of court, and, if consent is granted by the respondent, the next of kin, that the transfer has been completed.

(f) Repealed by Session Laws 2018-33, s. 46, effective October 1, 2019.

History.
1973, c. 726, s. 1; c. 1408, s. 1; 1977, c. 400, s. 3; 1979, c. 164, s. 2; c. 915, ss. 3, 18; 1983, c. 383, s. 5; c. 638, ss. 3-5; c. 864, s. 4; 1985, c. 589, s. 2; c. 695, ss. 2, 4; 1985 (Reg. Sess., 1986), c. 863, s. 17; 1989 (Reg. Sess., 1990), c. 823, ss. 1, 2; c. 1024, s. 27.1; 1991, c. 37, s. 7; 1995 (Reg. Sess., 1996), c. 739, s. 6; 1997-456, s. 47; 2004-23, s. 1(a); 2005-135, s. 1; 2009-315, s. 1; 2009-340, s. 1; 2013-308, ss. 1, 2; 2018-33, s. 22; 2019-76, s. 7; 2019-240, s. 26(g)

§ 122C-262. Special emergency procedure for individuals needing immediate hospitalization

(a) Anyone, including a law enforcement officer, who has knowledge of an individual who is subject to inpatient commitment according to the criteria of G.S. 122C-263(d)(2) and who requires immediate hospitalization to prevent harm to self or others, may transport the individual directly to an area facility or other place, including a State facility for individuals with mental illnesses, for examination by a commitment examiner in accordance with G.S. 122C-263(c).

(b) Upon examination by the commitment examiner, if the individual meets the inpatient commitment criteria specified in G.S. 122C-263(d)(2) and requires immediate hospitalization to prevent harm to self or others, the commitment examiner shall so certify in writing before any official authorized to administer oaths. The certificate shall also state the reason that the individual requires immediate hospitalization. If the commitment examiner knows or has reason to believe that the individual has an intellectual disability, the certificate shall so state.

(c) If the commitment examiner executes the oath, appearance before a magistrate shall be waived. The commitment examiner shall send a copy of the certificate to the clerk of superior court by the most reliable and expeditious means. If it cannot be reasonably anticipated that the clerk will receive the copy within 24 hours, excluding Saturday, Sunday, and holidays, of the time that it was signed, the physician or eligible psychologist shall also communicate the findings to the clerk by telephone.

(d) Anyone, including a law enforcement officer if necessary, may transport the individual to a 24-hour facility described in G.S. 122C-252 for examination and treatment pending a district court hearing. If there is no area 24-hour facility and if the respondent is indigent and unable to pay for care at a private 24-hour facility, the law enforcement officer or other designated person providing transportation shall take the respondent to a State facility for individuals with mental illnesses designated by the Commission in accordance with G.S. 143B-147(a)(1)a. and immediately notify the clerk of superior court of this action. The commitment examiner's certificate shall serve as the custody order and the law enforcement officer or other designated person shall provide transportation in accordance with G.S. 122C-251. If a 24-hour facility is not immediately available or appropriate to the respondent's medical condition, the respondent may be temporarily detained under appropriate supervision in accordance with G.S. 122C-263(d)(2) and released in accordance with G.S. 122C-263(d)(2).

In the event an individual known or reasonably believed to have an intellectual disability is transported to a State facility for individuals with mental illnesses, in no event shall that individual be admitted to that facility unless the individual is in one or more of the following categories:

(1) Persons described in G.S. 122C-266(b).

(2) Persons admitted pursuant to G.S. 15A-1321.

(3) Respondents who are so extremely dangerous as to pose a serious threat to the community and to other patients committed to non-State hospital psychiatric inpatient units, as determined by the Director of the Division of Mental Health, Developmental Disabilities, and Substance Abuse Services or the Director's designee.

(4) Respondents who are so gravely disabled by both multiple disorders and medical fragility or multiple disorders and deafness that alternative care is inappropriate, as determined by the Director of the Division of Mental Health, Developmental Disabilities, and Substance Abuse Services or the Director's designee.

Individuals transported to a State facility for individuals with mental illnesses

who are not admitted by the facility may be transported by law enforcement officers or designated staff of the State facility in State-owned vehicles to an appropriate 24-hour facility that provides psychiatric inpatient care.

No later than 24 hours after the transfer, the responsible professional at the original facility shall notify the petitioner, the clerk of court, and, if consent is granted by the respondent, the next of kin, that the transfer has been completed.

(e) Respondents received at a 24-hour facility under this section shall be examined by a second physician in accordance with G.S. 122C-266. After receipt of notification that the district court has determined reasonable grounds for the commitment, further proceedings shall be carried out in the same way as for all other respondents under this Part.

(f) If, upon examination of a respondent presented in accordance with subsection (a) of this section, the commitment examiner finds that the individual meets the criteria for inpatient commitment specified in G.S. 122C-263(d)(2) but does not require immediate hospitalization to prevent harm to self or others, the commitment examiner may petition the clerk or magistrate in accordance with G.S. 122C-261(d) for an order to take the individual into custody for transport to a 24-hour facility described in G.S. 122C-252. If the commitment examiner recommends inpatient commitment and the clerk or magistrate finds probable cause to believe that the respondent meets the criteria for inpatient commitment, the clerk or magistrate shall issue an order for transport to or custody at a 24-hour facility described in G.S. 122C-252. If, however, a 24-hour facility is not immediately available or appropriate to the respondent's medical condition, the respondent may be temporarily detained under appropriate supervision in accordance with G.S. 122C-263(d)(2) and released in accordance with G.S. 122C-263(d)(2).

(g) This section applies exclusively to an individual who is transported to an area facility or other place for an examination by a commitment examiner in accordance with subsection (a) of this section.

History.
1973, c. 726, s. 1; c. 1408, s. 1; 1985, c. 589, s. 2; c. 695, s. 2; 1987, c. 596, s. 1; 1995 (Reg. Sess., 1996), c. 739, s. 7; 2018-33, s. 23; 2019-76, s. 8

§ 122C-263. Duties of law enforcement officer; first examination

(a) Without unnecessary delay after assuming custody, the law enforcement officer or the individual designated or required to provide transportation pursuant to G.S. 122C-251(g) shall take the respondent to a facility or other location identified by the LME/MCO in the community crisis services plan adopted pursuant to G.S. 122C-202.2 that has an available commitment examiner and is capable of performing a first examination in conjunction with a health screening at the same location, unless circumstances indicate the respondent appears to be suffering a medical emergency in which case the law enforcement officer will seek immediate medical assistance for the respondent. If a commitment examiner is not available, whether on-site, on-call, or via telehealth, at any facility or location, or if a plan has not been adopted, the person designated to provide transportation shall take the respondent to an alternative non-hospital provider or facility-based crisis center for a first examination in conjunction with a health screening at the same location. If no non-hospital provider or facility-based crisis center for a first examination in conjunction with a health screening at the same location for health screening and first examination exists, the person designated to provide transportation shall take the respondent to a private hospital or clinic, a general hospital, an acute care hospital, or a State facility for individuals with mental illnesses. If a commitment examiner is not immediately available, the respondent may be temporarily detained in an area facility, if one is available; if an area facility is not available, the respondent may be detained under appropriate supervision in the respondent's home, in a private hospital or a clinic, in a general hospital, or in a State facility for individuals with mental illnesses, but not in a jail or other penal facility. For the purposes of this section, "non-hospital provider" means an outpatient provider that provides either behavioral health or medical services.

(a1) A facility or other location to which a respondent is transported under subsection (a) of this section shall provide a health screening of the respondent. The health screening shall be conducted by a commitment examiner or other individual who is determined by the area facility, contracted facility, or other location to be qualified to perform the health screening. The Department will work with commitment examiner professionals to develop a screening tool for this purpose. The respondent may either be in the physical face-to-face presence of the person conducting the screen or may be examined utilizing telehealth equipment and procedures. Documentation of the health screening required under this subsection that is completed prior to transporting the patient to any general hospital, acute care hospital, or designated facility shall accompany the patient or otherwise be made available at the time of transportation to the receiving facility.

(b) The examination set forth in subsection (a) of this section is not required under any of the following circumstances:

(1) The affiant who obtained the custody order is a commitment examiner who recommends inpatient commitment.

(2) The custody order states that the respondent was charged with a violent crime, including a crime involving assault with a deadly weapon, and the respondent was found incapable of proceeding.

(3) Repealed by Session Laws 1987, c. 596, s. 3.

In any of these cases, the law enforcement officer or person designated under G.S. 122C-251(g) shall take the respondent directly to a 24-hour facility described in G.S. 122C-252.

(c) The commitment examiner described in subsection (a) of this section shall examine the respondent as soon as possible, and in any event within 24 hours after the respondent is presented for examination. When the examination set forth in subsection (a) of this section is performed by a commitment examiner, the respondent may either be in the physical face-to-face presence of the commitment examiner or may be examined utilizing telehealth equipment and procedures. A commitment examiner who examines a respondent by means of telehealth must be satisfied to a reasonable medical certainty that the determinations made in accordance with subsection (d) of this section would not be different if the examination had been done in the physical presence of the commitment examiner. A commitment examiner who is not so satisfied must note that the examination was not satisfactorily accomplished, and the respondent must be taken for a face-to-face examination in the physical presence of a person authorized to perform examinations under this section. As used in this section, "telehealth" means the use of two-way, real-time interactive audio and video where the respondent and commitment examiner can hear and see each other. A recipient is referred by one provider to receive the services of another provider via telehealth.

The examination shall include an assessment of at least all of the following with respect to the respondent:

(1) Current and previous mental illness and intellectual disability including, if available, previous treatment history.

(2) Dangerousness to self, as defined in G.S. 122C-3(11)a. or others, as defined in G.S. 122C-3(11)b.

(3) Ability to survive safely without inpatient commitment, including the availability of supervision from family, friends, or others.

(4) Capacity to make an informed decision concerning treatment.

(d) After the conclusion of the examination the commitment examiner shall make the following determinations:

(1) If the commitment examiner finds all of the following, the commitment examiner shall so show on the examination report and shall recommend outpatient commitment:

a. The respondent has a mental illness.

b. The respondent is capable of surviving safely in the community with available supervision from family, friends, or others.

c. Based on the respondent's psychiatric history, the respondent is in need of treatment in order to prevent further disability or deterioration that would predictably result in dangerousness as defined by G.S. 122C-3(11).

d. The respondent's current mental status or the nature of the respondent's illness limits or negates the respondent's ability to make an informed decision to seek voluntarily or comply with recommended treatment.

In addition, the commitment examiner shall show the name, address, and telephone number of the proposed outpatient treatment physician or center in accordance with subsection (f) of this section. The person designated in the order to provide transportation shall return the respondent to the respondent's regular residence or, with the respondent's consent, to the home of a consenting individual located in the originating county, and the respondent shall be released from custody.

(2) If the commitment examiner finds that the respondent has a mental illness and is dangerous to self, as defined in G.S. 122C-3(11)a., or others, as defined in G.S. 122C-3(11)b., the commitment examiner shall recommend inpatient commitment, and shall so show on the examination report. If, in addition to mental illness and dangerousness, the commitment examiner also finds that the respondent is known or reasonably believed to have an intellectual disability, this finding shall be shown on the report. Upon notification, the law enforcement officer or other designated person shall take the respondent to a 24-hour facility described in G.S. 122C-252 pending a district court hearing. To the extent feasible, in providing the transportation of the respondent, the law enforcement officer shall act within six hours of notification. The other designated person shall take the respondent to a 24-hour facility described in G.S. 122C-252 pending a district court

hearing within six hours of notification. If there is no area 24-hour facility and if the respondent is indigent and unable to pay for care at a private 24-hour facility, the law enforcement officer or other designated person shall take the respondent to a State facility for individuals with mental illnesses designated by the Commission in accordance with G.S. 143B-147(a)(1)a. for custody, observation, and treatment and immediately notify the clerk of superior court of this action. If a 24-hour facility is not immediately available or appropriate to the respondent's medical condition, the respondent may be temporarily detained under appropriate supervision at the site of the first examination. Upon the commitment examiner's determination that a 24-hour facility is available and medically appropriate, the law enforcement officer or other designated person shall transport the respondent after receiving a request for transportation by the facility of the commitment examiner. To the extent feasible, in providing the transportation of the respondent, the law enforcement officer shall act within six hours of notification. The other designated person shall transport the respondent without unnecessary delay and within six hours after receiving a request for transportation by the facility of the commitment examiner. At any time during the respondent's temporary detention under appropriate supervision, if a commitment examiner determines that the respondent is no longer in need of inpatient commitment, the proceedings shall be terminated and the respondent transported and released in accordance with subdivision (3) of this subsection. However, if the commitment examiner determines that the respondent meets the criteria for outpatient commitment, as defined in subdivision (1) of this subsection, the commitment examiner may recommend outpatient commitment, and the respondent shall be transported and released in accordance with subdivision (1) of this subsection. Any decision to terminate the proceedings or to recommend outpatient commitment after an initial recommendation of inpatient commitment shall be documented and reported to the clerk of superior court in accordance with subsection (e) of this section. If the respondent is temporarily detained and a 24-hour facility is not available or medically appropriate seven days after the issuance of the custody order, a commitment examiner shall report this fact to the clerk of superior court and the proceedings shall be terminated. Termination of proceedings pursuant to this subdivision shall not prohibit or prevent the initiation of new involuntary commitment proceedings when appropriate. A commitment examiner may initiate a new involuntary commitment proceeding prior to the expiration of this seven-day period, as long as the respondent continues to meet applicable criteria. Affidavits filed in support of proceedings terminated pursuant to this subdivision shall not be submitted in support of any subsequent petitions for involuntary commitment. If the affiant initiating new commitment proceedings is a commitment examiner, the affiant shall conduct a new examination and shall not rely upon examinations conducted as part of proceedings terminated pursuant to this subdivision.

In the event an individual known or reasonably believed to have an intellectual disability is transported to a State facility for individuals with mental illnesses, in no event shall that individual be admitted to that facility unless the individual is in one or more of the following categories:

a. Persons described in G.S. 122C-266(b).

b. Persons admitted pursuant to G.S. 15A-1321.

c. Respondents who are so extremely dangerous as to pose a serious threat to the community and to other patients committed to non-State hospital psychiatric inpatient units, as determined by the Director of the Division of Mental Health, Developmental Disabilities, and Substance Abuse Services or the Director's designee.

d. Respondents who are so gravely disabled by both multiple disorders and medical fragility or multiple disorders and deafness that alternative care is inappropriate, as determined by the Director of the Division of Mental Health, Developmental Disabilities, and Substance Abuse Services or the Director's designee.

Individuals transported to a State facility for individuals with mental illnesses who are not admitted by the facility may be transported by law enforcement officers or designated staff of the State facility in State-owned vehicles to an appropriate 24-hour facility that provides psychiatric inpatient care.

No later than 24 hours after the transfer, the responsible professional at the original facility shall notify the petitioner, the clerk of court, and, if consent is granted by the respondent, the next of kin, that the transfer has been completed.

(3) If the commitment examiner finds that neither condition described in subdivisions (1) or (2) of this subsection exists, the proceedings shall be terminated. The person designated in the order to provide transportation shall return the respondent to the respondent's regular residence or, with the respondent's consent, to the home of a consenting individual located in the originating county and the respondent shall be released from custody.

(e) The findings of the commitment examiner and the facts on which they are based shall be in writing in all cases. The commitment examiner shall send a copy of the findings to the clerk of superior court by the most reliable and expeditious means. If it cannot be reasonably anticipated that the clerk will receive the copy within 48 hours of the time that it was signed, the physician or eligible psychologist shall also communicate his findings to the clerk by telephone.

(f) When outpatient commitment is recommended, the commitment examiner, if different from the proposed outpatient treatment physician or center, shall contact the LME/MCO that serves the county where the respondent resides or the LME/MCO that coordinated services for the respondent to inform the LME/MCO that the respondent is being recommended for outpatient commitment. The commitment examiner shall give the respondent a written notice listing the name, address, and telephone number of the proposed outpatient treatment physician or center.

(g) The commitment examiner, at the completion of the examination, shall provide the respondent with specific information regarding the next steps that will occur.

History.

1973, c. 726, s. 1; c. 1408, s. 1; 1977, c. 400, s. 4; c. 679, s. 8; c. 739, s. 1; 1979, c. 358, s. 27; c. 915, s. 4; 1983, c. 380, ss. 4, 10; c. 638, ss. 6, 7, 25.1; c. 864, s. 4; 1985, c. 589, s. 2; c. 695, ss. 2, 5, 6; 1985 (Reg. Sess., 1986), c. 863, s. 18; 1987, c. 596, s. 3; 1989, c. 225, s. 2; c. 770, s. 74; 1989 (Reg. Sess., 1990), c. 823, ss. 3, 4; 1991, c. 37, s. 8; c. 636, s. 2(1); c. 761, s. 49; 1995 (Reg. Sess., 1996), c. 739, s. 8(a)-(d); 2009-315, s. 2; 2009-340, s. 2; 2018-33, s. 24; 2018-76, s. 3.2(a); 2019-76, s. 9; 2019-177, s. 7(a); 2021-77, s. 6(a)

§ 122C-263.1. Secretary's authority to certify commitment examiners; training of certified commitment examiners performing first examinations

(a) Physicians and eligible psychologists are qualified to perform the commitment examinations required under G.S. 122C-263(c) and G.S. 122C-283(c). The Secretary of Health and Human Services may individually certify to

Chapter 122C

perform the first commitment examinations required by G.S. 122C-261 through G.S. 122C-263 and G.S. 122C-281 through G.S. 122C-283 other health, mental health, and substance abuse professionals whose scope of practice includes diagnosing and documenting psychiatric or substance use disorders and conducting mental status examinations to determine capacity to give informed consent to treatment as follows:

(1) The Secretary has received a request:

    a. To certify a licensed clinical social worker, a master's or higher level degree nurse practitioner, a licensed clinical mental health counselor, a licensed marriage and family therapist, or a physician assistant to conduct the first examinations described in G.S. 122C-263(c) and G.S. 122C-283(c).

    b. To certify a master's level licensed clinical addictions specialist to conduct the first examination described in G.S. 122C-283(c).

(2) The Secretary shall review the request and may approve it upon finding all of the following:

    a. The request meets the requirements of this section.

    b., c. Repealed by Session Laws 2018-33, s. 25, effective October 1, 2019.

    d. The Department determines that the applicant possesses the professional licensure, registration, or certification to qualify the applicant as a professional whose scope of practice includes diagnosing and documenting psychiatric or substance use disorders and conducting mental status examinations to determine capacity to give informed consent to treatment.

    e. The applicant for certification has successfully completed the Department's standardized training program for involuntary commitment and has successfully passed the examination for that program.

(3) Repealed by Session Laws 2018-33, s. 25, effective October 1, 2019.

(4) A certification granted by the Secretary under this section shall be in effect for a period of up to three years and may be rescinded at any time within this period if the Secretary finds the certified individual has failed to meet the requirements of this section. Certification may be renewed every three years upon completion of a refresher training program approved by the Department.

(5) In no event shall the certification of a licensed clinical social worker, master's or higher level degree nurse practitioner, licensed clinical mental health counselor, a licensed marriage and family therapist,

physician assistant, or master's level certified clinical addictions specialist under this section be construed as authorization to expand the scope of practice of the licensed clinical social worker, the master's level nurse practitioner, licensed clinical mental health counselor, a licensed marriage and family therapist, physician assistant, or the master's level certified clinical addictions specialist.

(6) The Department shall require that individuals certified to perform initial examinations under this section have successfully completed the Department's standardized involuntary commitment training program and examination. The Department shall maintain a list of these individuals on its Internet Web site.

(7) Repealed by Session Laws 2018-33, s. 25, effective October 1, 2019.

(7a) No less than annually, the Department shall submit a list of certified first commitment examiners to the Chief District Court Judge of each judicial district in North Carolina and maintain a current list of certified first commitment examiners on its Internet Web site.

(8) A master's level licensed clinical addiction specialist shall only be authorized to conduct the initial examination of individuals meeting the criteria of G.S. 122C-281(a).

(9) A licensed marriage and family therapist shall not be authorized to conduct the initial examination of an individual married to a patient of the licensed marriage and family therapist.

(b) The Department shall expand its standardized certification training program to include refresher training for all certified providers performing initial examinations pursuant to subsection (a) of this section.

History.
2011-346, s. 1; 2018-33, s. 25; 2019-240, ss. 3(i), 26(h); 2020-82, s. 2(a)

§ 122C-263.2. Mental health crisis management: reasonable safety and containment measures

An acute care hospital licensed under Chapter 131E, a department thereof, or other site of first examination that that uses reasonable safety or containment measures and precautions to manage the population of patients being held under appropriate supervision pending involuntary commitment placement and that does not otherwise operate as a licensable mental health facility shall not be deemed to be acting as a 24-hour facility; operating a psychiatric, substance abuse, or special care unit; offering psychiatric or substance abuse services; or acting as a licensed or unlicensed mental health facility. Actions considered to be reasonable safety or containment measures and precautions shall include the following: (i) altering rooms or removing items to prevent injury; (ii) placing patients in a consolidated location of the hospital; (iii) improvements to security and protection of staff; and (iv) any other reasonable measures that do not violate applicable law.

Reasonable safety or containment measures and precautions shall not be considered a violation of rules regulating acute care hospitals or mental health facilities. Placing patients in a consolidated location of the hospital pursuant to this subsection shall not constitute a special care unit. Nothing in this subsection relieves an acute care hospital or other site of first examination from complying with all other applicable laws or rules.

History.
2012-128, s. 1

§ 122C-264. Duties of clerk of superior court and the district attorney

(a) Upon receipt of a commitment examiner's finding that the respondent meets the criteria of G.S. 122C-263(d)(1) and that outpatient commitment is recommended, the clerk of superior court of the county where the petition was initiated, upon direction of a district court judge, shall calendar the matter for hearing and shall notify the respondent, the proposed outpatient treatment physician or center, and the petitioner of the time and place of the hearing. The petitioner may file a written waiver of his right to notice under this subsection with the clerk of court.

(b) Upon receipt by the clerk of superior court pursuant to G.S. 122C-266(c) of a commitment examiner's finding that a respondent meets the criteria of G.S. 122C-263(d)(2) and that inpatient commitment is recommended, the clerk of superior court of the county where the 24-hour facility is located shall, after determination required by G.S. 122C-261(c) and upon direction of a district court judge, assign counsel if necessary, calendar the matter for hearing, and notify the respondent, his counsel, and the petitioner of the time and place of the hearing. The petitioner or respondent, directly or through counsel, may file a written waiver of the right to notice under this subsection with the clerk of court.

(b1) Upon receipt of a commitment examiner's certificate that a respondent meets the criteria of G.S. 122C-261(a) and that immediate hospitalization is needed pursuant to G.S. 122C-262, the clerk of superior court of the

county where the treatment facility is located shall submit the certificate to the Chief District Court Judge. The court shall review the certificate within 24 hours, excluding Saturday, Sunday, and holidays, for a finding of reasonable grounds in accordance with [G.S.] 122C-261(b). The clerk shall notify the treatment facility of the court's findings by telephone and shall proceed as set forth in subsections (b), (c), and (f) of this section.

(c) Notice to the respondent, required by subsections (a) and (b) of this section, shall be given as provided in G.S. 1A-1, Rule 4(j) at least 72 hours before the hearing. Notice to other individuals shall be sent at least 72 hours before the hearing by first-class mail postage prepaid to the individual's last known address. G.S. 1A-1, Rule 6 shall not apply.

(d) In cases described in G.S. 122C-266(b) in addition to notice required in subsections (a) and (b) of this section, the clerk of superior court shall notify the chief district judge and the district attorney in the county in which the defendant was found incapable of proceeding. The notice shall be given in the same way as the notice required by subsection (c) of this section. The judge or the district attorney may file a written waiver of his right to notice under this subsection with the clerk of court.

(d1) For hearings and rehearings pursuant to G.S. 122C-268.1 and G.S. 122C-276.1, the clerk of superior court shall calendar the hearing or rehearing and shall notify the respondent, his counsel, counsel for the State, and the district attorney involved in the original trial. The notice shall be given in the same manner as the notice required by subsection (c) of this section. Upon receipt of the notice, the district attorney shall notify any persons he deems appropriate, including anyone who has filed with his office a written request for notification of any hearing or rehearing concerning discharge or conditional release of a respondent. Notice sent by the district attorney shall be by first-class mail to the person's last known address.

(e) Repealed by Session Laws 2017-158, s. 21, effective July 21, 2017.

(f) The clerk of superior court of the county where inpatient commitment hearings and rehearings are held shall provide all notices, send all records and maintain a record of all proceedings as required by this Part; provided that if the respondent has been committed to a 24-hour facility in a county other than his county of residence and the district court hearing is held in the county of the facility, the clerk of superior court in the county of the facility shall forward the record of the proceedings to the clerk of superior court in the county of respondent's residence, where they shall be maintained by receiving clerk.

History.

1973, c. 1408, s. 1; 1977, c. 400, s. 5; c. 414, s. 1; 1979, c. 915, s. 5; 1983, c. 380, s. 9; c. 638, ss. 8, 16; c. 864, s. 4; 1985, c. 589, s. 2; c. 695, s. 7; 1985 (Reg. Sess., 1986), c. 863, s. 19; 1987, c. 596, s. 2; 1991, c. 37, s. 4; 1995 (Reg. Sess., 1996), c. 739, s. 9; 2017-158, s. 21; 2018-33, s. 26

§ 122C-265. Outpatient commitment; examination and treatment pending hearing

(a) If a respondent, who has been recommended for outpatient commitment by [a] commitment examiner different from the proposed outpatient treatment physician or center, fails to appear for examination by the proposed outpatient treatment physician or center at the designated time, the physician or center shall notify the clerk of superior court who shall issue an order to a law enforcement officer to take the respondent into custody and take him immediately to the outpatient treatment physician or center for evaluation. The custody order is valid throughout the State. The law-enforcement officer may wait during the examination and return the respondent to his home after the examination.

(b) The examining commitment examiner or the proposed outpatient treatment physician or center may prescribe to the respondent reasonable and appropriate medication and treatment that are consistent with accepted medical standards pending the district court hearing.

(c) In no event may a respondent released on a recommendation that he or she meets the outpatient commitment criteria be physically forced to take medication or forcibly detained for treatment pending a district court hearing.

(d) If at any time pending the district court hearing the outpatient treatment physician or center determines that the respondent does not meet the criteria of G.S. 122C-263(d)(1), the physician shall release the respondent and notify the clerk of court and the proceedings shall be terminated.

(e) If a respondent becomes dangerous to self as defined in G.S. 122C-3(11)a., or others, as defined in G.S. 122C-3(11)b., pending a district court hearing on outpatient commitment, new proceedings for involuntary inpatient commitment may be initiated.

(f) If an inpatient commitment proceeding is initiated pending the hearing for outpatient commitment and the respondent is admitted to a 24-hour facility to be held for an inpatient commitment hearing, notice shall be sent by the clerk of court in the county where the respondent is being held to the clerk of court of the county where the outpatient commitment was initiated and the outpatient commitment proceeding shall be terminated.

History.

1983, c. 638, s. 11; c. 864, s. 4; 1985, c. 589, s. 2; c. 695, s. 6; 1989 (Reg. Sess., 1990), c. 823, s. 5; 1991, c. 636, s. 2(2); c. 761, s. 49; 2004-23, s. 2(a); 2018-33, s. 27

§ 122C-266. Inpatient commitment; second examination and treatment pending hearing

(a) Except as provided in subsections (b) and (e), within 24 hours of arrival at a 24-hour facility described in G.S. 122C-252, the respondent shall be examined by a physician. This physician shall not be the same physician who completed the certificate or examination under the provisions of G.S. 122C-262 or G.S. 122C-263. The examination shall include but is not limited to the assessment specified in G.S. 122C-263(c).

(1) If the physician finds that the respondent is mentally ill and is dangerous to self, as defined by G.S. 122C-3(11)a., or others, as defined by G.S. 122C-3(11)b., the physician shall hold the respondent at the facility pending the district court hearing.

(2) If the physician finds that the respondent meets the criteria for outpatient commitment under G.S. 122C-263(d)(1), the physician shall show these findings on the physician's examination report, release the respondent pending the district court hearing, and notify the clerk of superior court of the county where the petition was initiated of these findings. In addition, the examining physician shall show on the examination report the name, address, and telephone number of the proposed outpatient treatment physician or center. The physician shall give the respondent a written notice listing the name, address, and telephone number of the proposed outpatient treatment physician or center and directing the respondent to appear at that address at a specified date and time. The examining physician before the appointment shall notify by telephone and shall send a copy of the notice and the examination report to the proposed outpatient treatment physician or center.

(3) If the physician finds that the respondent does not meet the criteria for commitment under either G.S. 122C-263(d)(1) or G.S. 122C-263(d)(2), the physician shall release the respondent and the proceedings shall be terminated.

(4) If the respondent is released under subdivisions (2) or (3) of this subsection, the law enforcement officer or other person designated to provide transportation shall return the respondent to the respondent's residence in the originating county or, if requested by the respondent, to another location in the originating county.

(a1) The second examination of a respondent required by subsection (a) of this section to determine whether the respondent will be involuntarily committed due to mental illness may be conducted either in the physical face-to-face presence of a physician or utilizing telehealth equipment and procedures, provided that the physician who examines the respondent by means of telehealth is satisfied to a reasonable medical certainty that the determinations made in accordance with subdivisions (a)(1) through (a)(3) of this section would not be different if the examination had been done in the physical presence of the examining physician. An examining physician who is not so satisfied shall note that the examination was not satisfactorily accomplished, and the respondent shall be taken for a face-to-face examination in the physical presence of a physician. As used in this section, "telehealth" means the use of two-way, real-time interactive audio and video where the respondent and commitment examiner can hear and see each other.

(b) If the custody order states that the respondent was charged with a violent crime, including a crime involving assault with a deadly weapon, and that he was found incapable of proceeding, the physician shall examine him as set forth in subsection (a) of this section. However, the physician may not release him from the facility until ordered to do so following the district court hearing.

(c) The findings of the physician and the facts on which they are based shall be in writing, in all cases. A copy of the findings shall be sent to the clerk of superior court by reliable and expeditious means.

(d) Pending the district court hearing, the physician attending the respondent may administer to the respondent reasonable and appropriate medication and treatment that is consistent with accepted medical standards. Except as provided in subsection (b) of this section, if at any time pending the district court hearing, the attending physician determines that the respondent no longer meets the criteria of either G.S. 122C-263(d)(1) or (d)(2), he shall release the respondent and notify the clerk of court and the proceedings shall be terminated.

(e) If the 24-hour facility described in G.S. 122C-252 or G.S. 122C-262 is the facility in which the first examination by a physician or eligible psychologist occurred and is the same facility in which the respondent is held, the second examination shall occur not later than the following regular working day.

History.

1973, c. 726, s. 1; c. 1408, s. 1; 1977, c. 400, s. 6; 1979, c. 915, s. 6; 1983, c. 380, s. 5; c. 638, ss. 9, 10; c. 864, s. 4; 1985, c. 589, s. 2; c. 695, s. 2; 1987, c. 596, s. 4; 1989

(Reg. Sess., 1990), c. 823, s. 6; 1991, c. 37, s. 9; 1995 (Reg. Sess., 1996), c. 739, s. 10(a), (b); 2021-77, s. 6(b)

§ 122C-267. Outpatient commitment; district court hearing

(a) A hearing shall be held in district court within 10 days of the day the respondent is taken into custody pursuant to G.S. 122C-261(e). Upon its own motion or upon motion of the proposed outpatient treatment physician or the respondent, the court may grant a continuance of not more than five days.

(b) The respondent shall be present at the hearing. A subpoena may be issued to compel the respondent's presence at a hearing. The petitioner and the proposed outpatient treatment physician or his designee may be present and may provide testimony.

(c) Certified copies of reports and findings of commitment examiners and medical records of previous and current treatment are admissible in evidence.

(d) At the hearing to determine the necessity and appropriateness of outpatient commitment, the respondent need not, but may, be represented by counsel. However, if the court determines that the legal or factual issues raised are of such complexity that the assistance of counsel is necessary for an adequate presentation of the merits or that the respondent is unable to speak for himself, the court may continue the case for not more than five days and order the appointment of counsel for an indigent respondent. Appointment of counsel shall be in accordance with rules adopted by the Office of Indigent Defense Services.

(e) Hearings may be held at the area facility in which the respondent is being treated, if it is located within the judge's district court district as defined in G.S. 7A-133, or in the judge's chambers. A hearing may not be held in a regular courtroom, over objection of the respondent, if in the discretion of a judge a more suitable place is available.

(f) The hearing shall be closed to the public unless the respondent requests otherwise.

(g) A copy of all documents admitted into evidence and a transcript of the proceedings shall be furnished to the respondent on request by the clerk upon the direction of a district court judge. If the client is indigent, the copies shall be provided at State expense.

(h) To support an outpatient commitment order, the court is required to find by clear, cogent, and convincing evidence that the respondent meets the criteria specified in G.S. 122C-263(d) (1). The court shall record the facts which support its findings and shall show on the order the center or physician who is responsible for the management and supervision of the respondent's outpatient commitment.

History.

1973, c. 726, s. 1; c. 1408, s. 1; 1975, cc. 322, 459; 1977, c. 400, s. 7; c. 1126, s. 1; 1979, c. 915, ss. 7, 13; 1983, c. 380, s. 6; c. 638, ss. 12, 13; c. 864, s. 4; 1985, c. 589, s. 2; c. 695, s. 8; 1987, c. 282, s. 18; 1987 (Reg. Sess., 1988), c. 1037, s. 113.1; 2000-144, s. 38; 2018-33, s. 28

§ 122C-268. Inpatient commitment; district court hearing

(a) A hearing shall be held in district court within 10 days of the day the respondent is taken into law enforcement custody pursuant to G.S. 122C-261(e) or G.S. 122C-262. If a respondent temporarily detained under G.S. 122C-263(d)(2) is subject to a series of successive custody orders issued pursuant to G.S. 122C-263(d)(2), the hearing shall be held within 10 days after the day that the respondent is taken into custody under the most recent custody order. A continuance of not more than five days may be granted upon motion of any of the following:

(1) The court.

(2) Respondent's counsel.

(3) The State, sufficiently in advance to avoid movement of the respondent.

(b) The attorney, who is a member of the staff of the Attorney General assigned to one of the State's facilities for the mentally ill or the psychiatric service of the University of North Carolina Hospitals at Chapel Hill, shall represent the State's interest at commitment hearings, rehearings, and supplemental hearings held for respondents admitted pursuant to this Part or G.S. 15A-1321 at the facility to which he is assigned.

In addition, the Attorney General may, in his discretion, designate an attorney who is a member of his staff to represent the State's interest at any commitment hearing, rehearing, or supplemental hearing held in a place other than at one of the State's facilities for the mentally ill or the psychiatric service of the University of North Carolina Hospitals at Chapel Hill.

(c) If the respondent's custody order indicates that he was charged with a violent crime, including a crime involving an assault with a deadly weapon, and that he was found incapable of proceeding, the clerk shall give notice of the time and place of the hearing as provided in G.S. 122C-264(d). The district attorney in the county in which the respondent was found incapable of proceeding may represent the State's interest at the hearing.

(d) The respondent shall be represented by counsel of his choice; or if he is indigent within the meaning of G.S. 7A-450 or refuses to retain counsel if financially able to do so, he shall be represented by counsel appointed in accordance with rules adopted by the Office of Indigent Defense Services.

(e) With the consent of the court, counsel may in writing waive the presence of the respondent.

(f) Certified copies of reports and findings of commitment examiners and previous and current medical records are admissible in evidence, but the respondent's right to confront and cross-examine witnesses may not be denied.

(g) To the extent feasible, hearings shall be held in an appropriate room at the facility in which the respondent is being treated in a manner approved by the chief district court judge if the facility is located within the presiding judge's district court district as defined in G.S. 7A-133. Hearings may be held in the judge's chambers. A hearing may not be held in a regular courtroom, over objection of the respondent, if in the discretion of a judge a more suitable place is available. Regardless of the manner and location for hearings, hearings shall be held in a manner that complies with any applicable federal and State laws governing the confidentiality and security of confidential information. If the respondent has counsel, the respondent shall be allowed to communicate fully and confidentially with his attorney during the proceeding.

(h) The hearing shall be closed to the public unless the respondent requests otherwise.

(i) A copy of all documents admitted into evidence and a transcript of the proceedings shall be furnished to the respondent on request by the clerk upon the direction of a district court judge. If the respondent is indigent, the copies shall be provided at State expense.

(j) To support an inpatient commitment order, the court shall find by clear, cogent, and convincing evidence that the respondent is mentally ill and dangerous to self, as defined in G.S. 122C-3(11)a., or dangerous to others, as defined in G.S. 122C-3(11)b. The court shall record the facts that support its findings.

History.

1985, c. 589, s. 2; c. 695, s. 8; 1985 (Reg. Sess., 1986), c. 1014, s. 195(b); 1987 (Reg. Sess., 1988), c. 1037, s. 114; 1989, c. 141, s. 11; 1989 (Reg. Sess., 1990), c. 823, s. 7; 1991, c. 37, s. 10; c. 257, s. 2; 1995 (Reg. Sess., 1996), c. 739, s. 11(a), (b); 2000-144, s. 39; 2014-107, s. 6.1; 2017-158, s. 16; 2018-33, s. 29; 2021-47, s. 10 (*l*)

§ 122C-268.1. Inpatient commitment; hearing following automatic commitment

(a) A respondent who is committed pursuant to G.S. 15A-1321 shall be provided a hearing, unless waived, before the expiration of 50 days from the date of his commitment.

(b) The district attorney in the county in which the respondent was found not guilty by reason of insanity may represent the State's interest at the hearing, rehearings, and supplemental rehearings. Notwithstanding the provisions of G.S. 122C-269, if the district attorney elects to represent the State's interest, upon

Chapter 122C

motion of the district attorney, the venue for the hearing, rehearings, and supplemental rehearings shall be the county in which the respondent was found not guilty by reason of insanity. If the district attorney declines to represent the State's interest, then the representation shall be determined as follows. An attorney, who is a member of the staff of the Attorney General assigned to one of the State's facilities for the mentally ill or the psychiatric service of the University of North Carolina Hospitals at Chapel Hill, may represent the State's interest at commitment hearings, rehearings, and supplemental hearings. Alternatively, the Attorney General may, in his discretion, designate an attorney who is a member of his staff to represent the State's interest at any commitment hearing, rehearing, or supplemental hearing.

(c) The clerk shall give notice of the time and place of the hearing as provided in G.S. 122C-264(d1).

(d) The respondent shall be represented by counsel of his choice, or if he is indigent within the meaning of G.S. 7A-450 or refuses to retain counsel if financially able to do so, he shall be represented by counsel appointed in accordance with rules adopted by the Office of Indigent Defense Services.

(e) With the consent of the court, counsel may in writing waive the presence of the respondent.

(f) Certified copies of reports and findings of physicians and psychologists and previous and current medical records are admissible in evidence, but the respondent's right to confront and cross-examine witnesses may not be denied.

(g) The hearing shall take place in the trial division in which the original trial was held. The hearing shall be open to the public. For purposes of this subsection, "trial division" means either the superior court division or the district court division of the General Court of Justice.

(h) A copy of all documents admitted into evidence and a transcript of the proceedings shall be furnished to the respondent on request by the clerk upon the direction of the presiding judge. If the respondent is indigent, the copies shall be provided at State expense.

(i) The respondent shall bear the burden to prove by a preponderance of the evidence that he (i) no longer has a mental illness as defined in G.S. 122C-3(21), or (ii) is no longer dangerous to others as defined in G.S. 122C-3(11)b. If the court is so satisfied, then the court shall order the respondent discharged and released. If the court finds that the respondent has not met his burden of proof, then the court shall order that inpatient commitment continue at a 24-hour facility designated pursuant to G.S. 122C-252 for a period not to exceed 90 days. The court shall make a written record of the facts that support its findings.

(j) Nothing in this section shall limit the respondent's right to habeas corpus relief.

History.
1991, c. 37, s. 2; 1991 (Reg. Sess., 1992), c. 1034, ss. 2, 3; 1995, c. 140, s. 1; 2000-144, s. 40

§ 122C-269. Venue of hearing when respondent held at a 24-hour facility pending hearing

(a) In all cases where the respondent is held at a 24-hour facility pending hearing as provided in G.S. 122C-268, G.S. 122C-268.1, 122C-276.1, or 122C-277(b1), unless the respondent through counsel objects to the venue, the hearing shall be held in the county in which the facility is located. Upon objection to venue, the hearing shall be held in the county where the petition was initiated, except as otherwise provided in subsection (c) of this section.

(b) An official of the facility shall immediately notify the clerk of superior court of the county in which the facility is located of a determination to hold the respondent pending hearing. That clerk shall request transmittal of all documents pertinent to the proceedings from the clerk of superior court where the proceedings were initiated. The requesting clerk shall assume all duties set forth in G.S. 122C-264. The counsel provided for in G.S. 122C-268(d) shall be appointed in accordance with rules adopted by the Office of Indigent Defense Services.

(c) Upon motion of any interested person, the venue of an initial hearing described in G.S. 122C-268(c) or G.S. 122C-268.1 or a rehearing required by G.S. 122C-276(b), G.S. 122C-276.1, or subsections (b) or (b1) of G.S. 122C-277 shall be moved to the county in which the respondent was found not guilty by reason of insanity or incapable of proceeding when the convenience of witnesses and the ends of justice would be promoted by the change.

History.
1975, 2nd Sess., c. 983, s. 133; 1981, c. 537, s. 6; 1983, c. 380, s. 7; 1985, c. 589, s. 2; 1991, c. 37, ss. 11, 12; 1995, c. 140, s. 2; 2000-144, s. 41; 2001-487, s. 29

§ 122C-270. Attorneys to represent the respondent and the State

(a) In a superior court district or set of districts as defined in G.S. 7A-41.1 in which a State facility for the mentally ill is located, the Commission on Indigent Defense Services shall appoint an attorney licensed to practice in North Carolina as special counsel for indigent respondents who are mentally ill. These special counsel shall serve at the pleasure of the Commission, may not privately practice law, and shall receive annual compensation within the

Chapter 122C

salary range for assistant public defenders as fixed by the Office of Indigent Defense Services. The special counsel shall represent all indigent respondents at all hearings, rehearings, and supplemental hearings held at the State facility. Special counsel shall determine indigency in accordance with G.S. 7A-450(a). Indigency is subject to redetermination by the presiding judge. If the respondent appeals, counsel for the appeal shall be appointed in accordance with rules adopted by the Office of Indigent Defense Services.

(b) The State facility shall provide suitable office space for the counsel to meet privately with respondents. The Office of Indigent Defense Services shall provide secretarial and clerical service and necessary equipment and supplies for the office.

(c) In the event of a vacancy in the office of special counsel, counsel's incapacity, or a conflict of interest, counsel for indigents at hearings or rehearings may be assigned in accordance with rules adopted by the Office of Indigent Defense Services. No mileage or compensation for travel time is paid to a counsel appointed pursuant to this subsection. Counsel may also be so assigned when, in the opinion of the Director of the Office of Indigent Defense Services, the volume of cases warrants.

(d) At hearings held in counties other than those designated in subsection (a) of this section, counsel for indigent respondents shall be appointed in accordance with rules adopted by the Office of Indigent Defense Services.

(e) If the respondent is committed to a non-State 24-hour facility, assigned counsel remains responsible for the respondent's representation at the trial level until discharged by order of district court, until the respondent is unconditionally discharged from the facility, or until the respondent voluntarily admits himself or herself to the facility. If the respondent is transferred to a State facility for the mentally ill, assigned counsel is discharged. If the respondent appeals, counsel for the appeal shall be appointed in accordance with rules adopted by the Office of Indigent Defense Services.

(f) The Attorney General may employ four attorneys, one to be assigned by him full-time to each of the State facilities for the mentally ill, to represent the State's interest at commitment hearings, rehearings and supplemental hearings held under this Article at the State facilities for respondents admitted to those facilities pursuant to Part 3, 4, 7, or 8 of this Article or G.S. 15A-1321 and to provide liaison and consultation services concerning these matters. These attorneys are subject to Chapter 126 of the General Statutes and shall also perform additional duties as may be assigned by the Attorney General. The attorney employed by the Attorney General in accordance with G.S.

114-4.2B shall represent the State's interest at commitment hearings, rehearings and supplemental hearings held for respondents admitted to the University of North Carolina Hospitals at Chapel Hill pursuant to Part 3, 4, 7, or 8 of this Article or G.S. 15A-1321.

History.

1973, c. 47, s. 2; c. 1408, s. 1; 1977, c. 400, s. 11; 1979, c. 915, s. 12; 1983, c. 275, ss. 1, 2; 1985, c. 589, s. 2; 1987 (Reg. Sess., 1988), c. 1037, s. 115; 1989, c. 141, s. 12; 1991, c. 257, s. 1; 1995 (Reg. Sess., 1996), c. 739, s. 12(a); 2000-144, s. 42; 2006-264, s. 61(a)

§ 122C-271. Disposition

(a) If a commitment examiner has recommended outpatient commitment and the respondent has been released pending the district court hearing, the court may make one of the following dispositions:

(1) If the court finds by clear, cogent, and convincing evidence that the respondent has a mental illness; that the respondent is capable of surviving safely in the community with available supervision from family, friends, or others; that based on respondent's treatment history, the respondent is in need of treatment in order to prevent further disability or deterioration that would predictably result in dangerousness as defined in G.S. 122C-3(11); and that the respondent's current mental status or the nature of the respondent's illness limits or negates the respondent's ability to make an informed decision to seek voluntarily or comply with recommended treatment, it may order outpatient commitment for a period not in excess of 90 days.

(2) If the court does not find that the respondent meets the criteria of commitment set out in subdivision (1) of this subsection, the respondent shall be discharged and the proposed outpatient physician center shall be so notified.

(3) Before ordering any outpatient commitment under this subsection, the court shall make findings of fact as to the availability of outpatient treatment from an outpatient treatment physician or center that has agreed to accept the respondent as a client of outpatient treatment services. The court shall show on the order the outpatient treatment physician or center that is to be responsible for the management and supervision of the respondent's outpatient commitment. If the designated outpatient treatment physician or center will be monitoring and supervising the respondent's outpatient commitment pursuant to a contract for services with an LME/MCO, the court shall show on the order the identity of

the LME/MCO. The clerk of court shall send a copy of the outpatient commitment order to the designated outpatient treatment physician or center and to the respondent client or the legally responsible person. The clerk of court shall also send a copy of the order to that LME/MCO. Copies of outpatient commitment orders sent by the clerk of court to an outpatient treatment center or physician under this section, including orders sent to an LME/MCO, shall be sent by the most reliable and expeditious means, but in no event less than 48 hours after the hearing.

(b) If the respondent has been held in a 24-hour facility pending the district court hearing pursuant to G.S. 122C-268, the court may make one of the following dispositions:

(1) If the court finds by clear, cogent, and convincing evidence that the respondent has a mental illness; that the respondent is capable of surviving safely in the community with available supervision from family, friends, or others; that based on respondent's psychiatric history, the respondent is in need of treatment in order to prevent further disability or deterioration that would predictably result in dangerousness as defined by G.S. 122C-3(11); and that the respondent's current mental status or the nature of the respondent's illness limits or negates the respondent's ability to make an informed decision voluntarily to seek or comply with recommended treatment, it may order outpatient commitment for a period not in excess of 90 days. If the commitment proceedings were initiated as the result of the respondent's being charged with a violent crime, including a crime involving an assault with a deadly weapon, and the respondent was found incapable of proceeding, the commitment order shall so show.

(2) If the court finds by clear, cogent, and convincing evidence that the respondent has a mental illness and is dangerous to self, as defined in G.S. 122C-3(11)a., or others, as defined in G.S. 122C-3(11)b., it may order inpatient commitment at a 24-hour facility described in G.S. 122C-252 for a period not in excess of 90 days. However, no respondent found to have both an intellectual disability and a mental illness may be committed to a State, area, or private facility for individuals with intellectual disabilities. An individual who has a mental illness and is dangerous to self, as defined in G.S. 122C-3(11)a., or others, as defined in G.S. 122C-3(11)b., may also be committed to a combination of inpatient and outpatient commitment at both a 24-hour facility and an outpatient treatment physician or center for a period not in excess of 90 days.

If the commitment proceedings were initiated as the result of the respondent's being charged with a violent crime, including a crime involving an assault with a deadly weapon, and the respondent was found incapable of proceeding, the commitment order shall so show. If the court orders inpatient commitment for a respondent who is under an outpatient commitment order, the outpatient commitment is terminated; and the clerk of the superior court of the county where the district court hearing is held shall send a notice of the inpatient commitment to the clerk of superior court where the outpatient commitment was being supervised.

(3) If the court does not find that the respondent meets either of the commitment criteria set out in subdivisions (1) and (2) of this subsection, the respondent shall be discharged, and the facility in which the respondent was last a client shall be so notified.

(4) Before ordering any outpatient commitment, the court shall make findings of fact as to the availability of outpatient treatment from an outpatient treatment physician or center that has agreed to accept the respondent as a client of outpatient treatment services. The court shall also show on the order the outpatient treatment physician or center who is to be responsible for the management and supervision of the respondent's outpatient commitment. When an outpatient commitment order is issued for a respondent held in a 24-hour facility, the court may order the respondent held at the facility for no more than 72 hours in order for the facility to notify the designated outpatient treatment physician or center of the treatment needs of the respondent. The clerk of court in the county where the facility is located shall send a copy of the outpatient commitment order to the designated outpatient treatment physician or center and to the respondent or the legally responsible person. If the designated outpatient treatment physician or center shall be monitoring and supervising the respondent's outpatient commitment pursuant to a contract for services with an LME/MCO, the clerk of court shall show on the order the identity of the LME/MCO. The clerk of court shall send a copy of the order to the LME/MCO. Copies of outpatient commitment orders sent by the clerk of court to an outpatient treatment center or physician pursuant to this subdivision, including orders sent to an LME/MCO, shall be sent by the most reliable and expeditious means, but in no event less than 48 hours after the hearing. If the

Chapter 122C

outpatient commitment will be supervised in a county other than the county where the commitment originated, the court shall order venue for further court proceedings to be transferred to the county where the outpatient commitment will be supervised. Upon an order changing venue, the clerk of superior court in the county where the commitment originated shall transfer the file to the clerk of superior court in the county where the outpatient commitment is to be supervised.

(c) If the respondent was found not guilty by reason of insanity and has been held in a 24-hour facility pending the court hearing held pursuant to G.S. 122C-268.1, the court may make one of the following dispositions:

(1) If the court finds that the respondent has not proved by a preponderance of the evidence that the respondent no longer has a mental illness or that the respondent is no longer dangerous to others, it shall order inpatient treatment at a 24-hour facility for a period not to exceed 90 days.

(2) If the court finds that the respondent has proven by a preponderance of the evidence that the respondent no longer has a mental illness or that the respondent is no longer dangerous to others, the court shall order the respondent discharged and released.

History.
1973, c. 726, s. 1; c. 1408, s. 1; 1977, c. 400, s. 8; c. 739, s. 2; 1979, c. 358, s. 26; c. 915, ss. 8, 15, 16; 1981, c. 537, s. 1; 1983, c. 380, s. 8; c. 638, s. 14; c. 864, s. 4; 1985, c. 589, s. 2; c. 695, s. 2; 1985 (Reg. Sess., 1986), c. 863, ss. 20-22; 1989, c. 225, s. 1; c. 770, s. 73; 1989 (Reg. Sess., 1990), c. 823, s. 8; 1991, c. 37, s. 13; 1991 (Reg. Sess., 1992), c. 1034, s. 5; 1995 (Reg. Sess., 1996), c. 739, s. 13; 2018-33, s. 30; 2019-76, s. 10

§ 122C-272. Appeal

Judgment of the district court is final. Appeal may be had to the Court of Appeals by the State or by any party on the record as in civil cases. Appeal does not stay the commitment unless so ordered by the Court of Appeals. The Attorney General represents the State's interest on appeal. The district court retains limited jurisdiction for the purpose of hearing all reviews, rehearings, or supplemental hearings allowed or required under this Part.

History.
1973, c. 726, s. 1; c. 1408, s. 1; 1979, c. 915, s. 19; 1985, c. 589, s. 2; 2009-570, s. 27

§ 122C-273. Duties for follow-up on commitment order

(a) Unless prohibited by Chapter 90 of the General Statutes, if the commitment order directs outpatient treatment, the outpatient treatment physician may prescribe or administer, or the center may administer, to the respondent reasonable and appropriate medication and treatment that are consistent with accepted medical standards.

(1) If the respondent fails to comply or clearly refuses to comply with all or part of the prescribed treatment, the physician, the physician's designee, or the center shall make all reasonable effort to solicit the respondent's compliance. These efforts shall be documented and reported to the court with a request for a supplemental hearing.

(2) If the respondent fails to comply, but does not clearly refuse to comply, with all or part of the prescribed treatment after reasonable effort to solicit the respondent's compliance, the physician, the physician's designee, or the center may request the court to order the respondent taken into custody for the purpose of examination. Upon receipt of this request, the clerk shall issue an order to a law-enforcement officer to take the respondent into custody and to take him immediately to the designated outpatient treatment physician or center for examination. The custody order is valid throughout the State. The law-enforcement officer shall turn the respondent over to the custody of the physician or center who shall conduct the examination and then release the respondent. The law-enforcement officer may wait during the examination and return the respondent to his home after the examination. An examination conducted under this subsection in which a physician or eligible psychologist determines that the respondent meets the criteria for inpatient commitment may be substituted for the first examination required by G.S. 122C-263 if the clerk or magistrate issues a custody order within six hours after the examination was performed.

(3) In no case may the respondent be physically forced to take medication or forcibly detained for treatment unless he poses an immediate danger to himself or others. In such cases inpatient commitment proceedings shall be initiated.

(4) At any time that the outpatient treatment physician or center finds that the respondent no longer meets the criteria set out in G.S. 122C-263(d)(1), the physician or center shall so notify the court and the case shall be terminated; provided, however, if the respondent was initially committed as a result of conduct resulting in his being charged with a violent crime, including a crime involving an assault with

a deadly weapon, and the respondent was found incapable of proceeding, the designated outpatient treatment physician or center shall notify the clerk that discharge is recommended. The clerk shall calendar a supplemental hearing as provided in G.S. 122C-274 to determine whether the respondent meets the criteria for outpatient commitment.

(5) Any individual who has knowledge that a respondent on outpatient commitment has become dangerous to himself, as defined by G.S. 122C-3(11)a., and others, as defined in G.S. 122C-3(11)b., may initiate a new petition for inpatient commitment as provided in this Part. If the respondent is committed as an inpatient, the outpatient commitment shall be terminated and notice sent by the clerk of court in the county where the respondent is committed as an inpatient to the clerk of court of the county where the outpatient commitment is being supervised.

(b) If the respondent on outpatient commitment intends to move or moves to another county within the State, the designated outpatient treatment physician or center shall request that the clerk of court in the county where the outpatient commitment is being supervised calendar a supplemental hearing.

(c) If the respondent moves to another state or to an unknown location, the designated outpatient treatment physician or center shall notify the clerk of superior court of the county where the outpatient commitment is supervised and the outpatient commitment shall be terminated.

(d) If the commitment order directs inpatient treatment, the physician attending the respondent may administer to the respondent reasonable and appropriate medication and treatment that are consistent with accepted medical standards. The attending physician shall release or discharge the respondent in accordance with G.S. 122C-277.

History.
1983, c. 638, s. 16; c. 864, s. 4; 1985, c. 589, s. 2; 1985 (Reg. Sess., 1986), c. 863, ss. 23-26; 1989 (Reg. Sess., 1990), c. 823, s. 9; 1991, c. 37, s. 14; 2004-23, s. 2(b)

§ 122C-274. Supplemental hearings

(a) Upon receipt of a request for a supplemental hearing, the clerk shall calendar a hearing to be held within 14 days and notify, at least 72 hours before the hearing, the petitioner, the respondent, his attorney, if any, and the designated outpatient treatment physician or center. The respondent shall be notified at least 72 hours before the hearing by personally serving on him an order to appear. Other persons shall be notified as provided in G.S. 122C-264(c).

(b) The procedures for the hearing shall follow G.S. 122C-267.

(c) In supplemental hearings for alleged noncompliance, the court shall determine whether the respondent has failed to comply and, if so, the causes for noncompliance. If the court determines that the respondent has failed or refused to comply it may:

(1) Upon finding probable cause to believe that the respondent is mentally ill and dangerous to himself, as defined in G.S. 122C-3(11)a., or others, as defined in G.S. 122C-3(11)b., order an examination by the same or different physician or eligible psychologist as provided in G.S. 122C-263(c) in order to determine the necessity for continued outpatient or inpatient commitment;

(2) Reissue or change the outpatient commitment order in accordance with G.S. 122C-271; or

(3) Discharge the respondent from the order and dismiss the case.

(d) At the supplemental hearing for a respondent who has moved or intends to move to another county, the court shall determine if the respondent meets the criteria for outpatient commitment set out in G.S. 122C-263(d)(1). If the court determines that the respondent no longer meets the criteria for outpatient commitment, it shall discharge the respondent from the order and dismiss the case. If the court determines that the respondent continues to meet the criteria for outpatient commitment, it shall continue the outpatient commitment but shall designate a physician or center at the respondent's new residence to be responsible for the management or supervision of the respondent's outpatient commitment. The court shall order the respondent to appear for treatment at the address of the newly designated outpatient treatment physician or center and shall order venue for further court proceedings under the outpatient commitment to be transferred to the new county of supervision. Upon an order changing venue, the clerk of court in the county where the outpatient commitment has been supervised shall transfer the records regarding the outpatient commitment to the clerk of court in the county where the commitment will be supervised. Also, the clerk of court in the county where the outpatient commitment has been supervised shall send a copy of the court's order directing the continuation of outpatient treatment under new supervision to the newly designated outpatient treatment physician or center.

(e) At any time during the term of an outpatient commitment order, a respondent may apply to the court for a supplemental hearing for the purpose of discharge from the order. The application shall be made in writing by the respondent to the clerk of superior court of the county where the outpatient commitment is being supervised. At the supplemental hearing the court shall determine whether the respondent continues to meet the criteria specified in G.S. 122C-263(d)(1). The court may either re-issue or change the commitment order or discharge the respondent and dismiss the case.

(f) At supplemental hearings requested pursuant to G.S. 122C-277(a) for transfer from inpatient to outpatient commitment, the court shall determine whether the respondent meets the criteria for either inpatient or outpatient commitment. If the court determines that the respondent continues to meet the criteria for inpatient commitment, it shall order the continuation of the original commitment order. If the court determines that the respondent meets the criteria for outpatient commitment, it shall order outpatient commitment for a period of time not in excess of 90 days. If the court finds that the respondent does not meet either criteria, the respondent shall be discharged and the case dismissed.

History.

1983, c. 638, s. 17; c. 864, s. 4; 1985, c. 589, s. 2; c. 695, s. 2; 1989 (Reg. Sess., 1990), c. 823, s. 10

§ 122C-275. Outpatient commitment; rehearings

(a) Fifteen days before the end of the initial or subsequent periods of outpatient commitment if the outpatient treatment physician or center determines that the respondent continues to meet the criteria specified in G.S. 122C-263(d)(1), he shall so notify the clerk of superior court of the county where the outpatient commitment is supervised. If the respondent no longer meets the criteria, the physician shall so notify the clerk who shall dismiss the case; provided, however, if the respondent was initially committed as a result of conduct resulting in his being charged with a violent crime, including a crime involving an assault with a deadly weapon, and the respondent was found incapable of proceeding, the physician or center shall notify the clerk that discharge is recommended. The clerk, at least 10 days before the end of the commitment period, on order of the district court, shall calendar the rehearing.

(b) Notice and procedures of rehearings are governed by the same procedures as initial hearings, and the respondent has the same rights he had at the initial hearing including the right to appeal.

(c) If the court finds that the respondent no longer meets the criteria of G.S. 122C-263(d)(1), it shall unconditionally discharge him. A copy of the discharge order shall be furnished by the clerk to the designated outpatient treatment physician or center. If the respondent continues to meet the criteria of G.S. 122C-263(d)(1), the court may order outpatient commitment for an additional period not in excess of 180 days.

History.

1983, c. 638, s. 20; c. 864, s. 4; 1985, c. 589, s. 2; 1991, c. 37, s. 15

§ 122C-276. Inpatient commitment; rehearings for respondents other than insanity acquittees

(a) Fifteen days before the end of the initial inpatient commitment period if the attending physician determines that commitment of a respondent beyond the initial period will be necessary, he shall so notify the clerk of superior court of the county in which the facility is located. The clerk, at least 10 days before the end of the initial period, on order of a district court judge of the district court district as defined in G.S. 7A-133 in which the facility is located, shall calendar the rehearing. If the respondent was initially committed as the result of conduct resulting in his being charged with a violent crime, including a crime involving an assault with a deadly weapon, and respondent was found incapable of proceeding, the clerk shall also notify the chief district court judge, the clerk of superior court, and the district attorney in the county in which the respondent was found incapable of proceeding of the time and place of the hearing.

(b) Fifteen days before the end of the initial treatment period of a respondent who was initially committed as a result of conduct resulting in his being charged with a violent crime, including a crime involving an assault with a deadly weapon, having been found incapable of proceeding, if the attending physician determines that commitment of the respondent beyond the initial period will not be necessary, he shall so notify the clerk of superior court who shall schedule a rehearing as provided in subsection (a) of this section.

(c) Subject to the provisions of G.S. 122C-269(c), rehearings shall be held as authorized in G.S. 122C-268(g). The judge is a judge of the district court of the district court district as defined in G.S. 7A-133 in which the facility is located or a district court judge temporarily assigned to that district.

(d) Notice and proceedings of rehearings are governed by the same procedures as initial hearings and the respondent has the same rights he had at the initial hearing including the right to appeal.

(e) At rehearings the court may make the same dispositions authorized in G.S. 122C-271(b) except a second commitment order may be for an additional period not in excess of 180 days.

(f) Fifteen days before the end of the second commitment period and annually thereafter, the attending physician shall review and evaluate the condition of each respondent; and if he determines that a respondent is in continued need of inpatient commitment or, in the alternative, in need of outpatient commitment, or a combination of both, he shall so notify the respondent, his counsel, and the clerk of superior court of the county, in which the facility is located. Unless the respondent through his counsel files with the clerk a written waiver of his right to a rehearing, the clerk, on order of a district court judge of the district in which the facility is located, shall calendar a rehearing for not later than the end of the current commitment period. The procedures and standards for the rehearing are the same as for the first rehearing. No third or subsequent inpatient recommitment order shall be for a period longer than one year.

(g) At any rehearings the court has the option to order outpatient commitment for a period not in excess of 180 days in accordance with the criteria specified in G.S. 122C-263(d)(1) and following the procedures as specified in this Article.

History.
1973, c. 726, s. 1; c. 1408, s. 1; 1977, c. 400, s. 9; 1979, c. 915, ss. 9, 17; 1981, c. 537, ss. 2-4; 1983, c. 638, ss. 18, 19; c. 864, s. 4; 1985, c. 589, s. 2; 1987 (Reg. Sess., 1988), c. 1037, s. 116; 1991, c. 37, s. 5; 2018-33, s. 31

§ 122C-276.1. Inpatient commitment; rehearings for respondents who are insanity acquittees

(a) At least 15 days before the end of any inpatient commitment period ordered pursuant to G.S. 122C-268.1, the clerk shall calendar the hearing and notify the parties as specified in G.S. 122C-264(d1), unless the hearing is waived by the respondent.

(b) The proceedings of the rehearing shall be governed by the same procedures provided by G.S. 122C-268.1.

(c) The respondent shall bear the burden to prove by a preponderance of the evidence that he (i) no longer has a mental illness as defined in G.S. 122C-3(21), or (ii) is no longer dangerous to others as defined in G.S. 122C-3(11)b. If the court is so satisfied, then the court shall order the respondent discharged and released. If the court finds that the respondent has not met his burden of proof, then the court shall order inpatient commitment be continued for a period not to exceed 180 days. The court shall make a written record of the facts that support its findings.

(d) At least 15 days before the end of any commitment period ordered pursuant to subsection (c) of this section and annually thereafter, the clerk shall calendar the hearing and notify the parties as specified in G.S. 122C-264(d1). The procedures and standards for the rehearing are

the same as under this section. No third or subsequent inpatient recommitment order shall be for a period longer than one year.

History.
1991, c. 37, s. 3; 1991 (Reg. Sess., 1992), c. 1034, s. 4

§ 122C-277. Release and conditional release; judicial review

(a) Except as provided in subsections (b) and (b1) of this section, the attending physician shall discharge a committed respondent unconditionally at any time he determines that the respondent is no longer in need of inpatient commitment. However, if the attending physician determines that the respondent meets the criteria for outpatient commitment as defined in G.S. 122C-263(d)(1), he may request the clerk to calendar a supplemental hearing to determine whether an outpatient commitment order shall be issued. Except as provided in subsections (b) and (b1) of this section, the attending physician may also release a respondent conditionally for periods not in excess of 30 days on specified medically appropriate conditions. Violation of the conditions is grounds for return of the respondent to the releasing facility. A law-enforcement officer, on request of the attending physician, shall take a conditional releasee into custody and return him to the facility in accordance with G.S. 122C-205. Notice of discharge and of conditional release shall be furnished to the clerk of superior court of the county of commitment and of the county in which the facility is located.

(b) If the respondent was initially committed as the result of conduct resulting in his being charged with a violent crime, including a crime involving an assault with a deadly weapon, and respondent was found incapable of proceeding, 15 days before the respondent's discharge or conditional release the attending physician shall notify the clerk of superior court of the county in which the facility is located of his determination regarding the proposed discharge or conditional release. The clerk shall then schedule a rehearing to determine the appropriateness of respondent's release under the standards of commitment set forth in G.S. 122C-271(b). The clerk shall give notice as provided in G.S. 122C-264(d). The district attorney of the district where respondent was found incapable of proceeding may represent the State's interest at the hearing.

(b1) If the respondent was initially committed pursuant to G.S. 15A-1321, 15 days before the respondent's discharge or conditional release the attending physician shall notify the clerk of superior court. The clerk shall calendar a hearing and shall give notice as provided by G.S. 122C-264(d1). The district attorney for the original trial may represent the State's interest at the hearing. The hearing shall be conducted under the standards and procedures set forth in G.S. 122C-268.1. Provided, that in no event shall discharge or conditional release under this section be allowed for a respondent during the period from automatic commitment to hearing under G.S. 122C-268.1.

(c) If a committed respondent under subsections (a), (b), or (b1) of this section is from a single portal area, the attending physician shall plan jointly with the area authority as prescribed in the area plan before discharging or releasing the respondent.

History.

1973, c. 726, s. 1; c. 1408, s. 1; 1981, c. 537, s. 5; 1983, c. 383, s. 6; c. 638, s. 21; c. 864, s. 4; 1985, c. 589, s. 2; 1991, c. 37, s. 6

§ 122C-278. Reexamination for capacity to proceed prior to discharge

Whenever a respondent has been committed to either inpatient or outpatient treatment pursuant to this Chapter after having been found incapable of proceeding and referred by the court for civil commitment proceedings, the respondent shall not be discharged from the custody of the hospital or institution or the outpatient commitment case terminated until the respondent has been examined for capacity to proceed and a report filed with the clerk of court pursuant to G.S. 15A-1002.

History.

2013-18, s. 8

PART 8
INVOLUNTARY COMMITMENT OF SUBSTANCE ABUSERS, FACILITIES FOR SUBSTANCE ABUSERS

§ 122C-281. Affidavit and petition before clerk or magistrate; custody order

(a) Any individual who has knowledge of a substance abuser who is dangerous to self or others may appear before a clerk or assistant or deputy clerk of superior court or a magistrate, execute an affidavit to this effect, and petition the clerk or magistrate for issuance of an order to take the respondent into custody for examination by a commitment examiner. The affidavit shall include the facts on which the affiant's opinion is based. Jurisdiction under this subsection is in the clerk or magistrate in the county where the respondent resides or is found.

(b) If the clerk or magistrate finds reasonable grounds to believe that the facts alleged in the affidavit are true and that the respondent is probably a substance abuser and dangerous to self or others, the clerk or magistrate shall issue an order to a law enforcement officer or any other person designated under G.S.122C-251(g) to take the respondent into custody for examination by a commitment examiner.

(c) If the clerk or magistrate issues a custody order, the clerk or magistrate shall also make inquiry in any reliable way as to whether the respondent is indigent within the meaning of G.S. 7A-450. A magistrate shall report the result of this inquiry to the clerk.

(d) If the affiant is a commitment examiner who has examined the respondent, he or she may execute the affidavit before any official authorized to administer oaths. The commitment examiner is not required to appear before the clerk or magistrate for this purpose. The commitment examiner's examination shall comply with the requirements of the initial examination as provided in G.S. 122C-283(c). The affiant shall file the affidavit and examination findings with the clerk of court in the manner described in G.S. 122C-261(d)(1). If the commitment examiner recommends commitment and the clerk or magistrate finds probable cause to believe that the respondent meets the criteria for commitment, the clerk or magistrate shall issue an order to a law enforcement officer to take the respondent into custody for transportation to a 24-hour facility, or, if the respondent is released pending hearing, as described in G.S. 122C-283(d)(1), order that a hearing be held as provided in G.S. 122C-284(a). If a physician or eligible psychologist executes an affidavit for commitment of a respondent, a second qualified professional shall perform the examination required by G.S. 122C-285. Any person or entity who or which has been designated in compliance with G.S. 122C-251(g) shall be permitted to complete all or part of the duties of a law enforcement officer, in accord with the designation.

(e) Upon receipt of the custody order of the clerk or magistrate, a law enforcement officer or other designated person identified in the order shall take the respondent into custody within 24 hours after the order is signed. The custody order is valid throughout the State.

(e1) No commitment examiner, area facility, acute care hospital, general hospital, or other site of first examination, or their officials, staff, employees, or other individuals responsible for the custody, examination, detention, management, supervision, treatment, or release of an individual examined for commitment, who is not grossly negligent, shall be held liable in any civil or criminal action for taking measures to temporarily detain an individual for the period of time necessary to complete a commitment examination, submit an affidavit to the magistrate or clerk of court, and await the issuance of a custody order as authorized by subsection (d) of this section.

(f) Repealed by Session Laws 2018-33, s. 32, effective October 1, 2019.

History.
1973, c. 726, s. 1; c. 1408, s. 1; 1977, c. 400, s. 3; 1979, c. 164, s. 2; c. 915, ss. 3, 18; 1983, c. 383, s. 5; c. 638, ss. 3-5; c. 864, s. 4; 1985, c. 589, s. 2; c. 695, ss. 2, 4; 2004-23, s. 1(b); 2018-33, s. 32

§ 122C-282. Special emergency procedure for violent individuals

When an individual subject to commitment under the provisions of this Part is also violent and requires restraint and when delay in taking the individual to a commitment examiner for examination would likely endanger life or property, a law enforcement officer may take the person into custody and take him or her immediately before a magistrate or clerk. The law enforcement officer shall execute the affidavit required by G.S. 122C-281 and in addition shall swear that the respondent is violent and requires restraint and that delay in taking the respondent to a commitment examiner for an examination would endanger life or property.

If the clerk or magistrate finds by clear, cogent, and convincing evidence that the facts stated in the affidavit are true, that the respondent is in fact violent and requires restraint, and that delay in taking the respondent to a commitment examiner for an examination would endanger life or property, the clerk or magistrate shall order the law enforcement officer to take the respondent directly to a 24-hour facility described in G.S. 122C-252.

Respondents received at a 24-hour facility under the provisions of this section shall be examined and processed thereafter in the same way as all other respondents under this Part.

History.
1973, c. 726, s. 1; c. 1408, s. 1; 1985, c. 589, s. 2; c. 695, s. 2; 2018-33, s. 33

§ 122C-283. Duties of law enforcement officer; first examination by commitment examiner

(a) Without unnecessary delay after assuming custody, the law enforcement officer or the individual designated or required to provide transportation under G.S. 122C-251(g) shall take the respondent to a facility or other location identified by the LME/MCO in the community crisis services plan adopted pursuant to G.S. 122C-202.2 that has an available commitment examiner and is capable of performing a first examination in conjunction with a health screening in the same location, unless circumstances indicate the respondent appears to be suffering a medical emergency in which case the law enforcement officer will seek immediate medical assistance for the respondent. If a commitment examiner is not available, whether on-site, on-call, or via telehealth, at any facility or location, or if a plan has not been adopted, the person designated to provide transportation shall take the respondent to an alternative non-hospital provider or facility-based crisis center for a first examination in conjunction with a health screening at the same location. If no non-hospital provider or facility-based crisis center for a first examination in conjunction with a health screening at the same location, the person designated to provide transportations shall take the respondent to a private hospital or clinic, a general hospital, an acute care hospital, or a State facility for individuals with mental illnesses. If a commitment examiner is not immediately available, the respondent may be temporarily detained in an area facility if one is available; if an area facility is not available, the respondent may be detained under appropriate supervision, in the respondent's home, in a private hospital or a clinic, or in a general hospital, but not in a jail or other penal facility. For the purposes of this section, "non-hospital provider" means an outpatient provider that provides either behavioral health or medical services.

(b) The examination set forth in subsection (a) of this section is not required if:

(1) The affiant who obtained the custody order is a physician or eligible psychologist; or

(2) The respondent is in custody under the special emergency procedure described in G.S. 122C-282.

In these cases when it is recommended that the respondent be detained in a 24-hour facility, the law-enforcement officer shall take the respondent directly to a 24-hour facility described in G.S. 122C-252.

(c) The commitment examiner described in subsection (a) of this section shall examine the respondent as soon as possible, and in any event within 24 hours, after the respondent is presented for examination. The examination performed by a commitment examiner pursuant to subsection (a) of this section may be performed either in the physical face-to-face presence of the commitment examiner or utilizing telehealth equipment and procedures. A commitment examiner who examines a respondent by means of telehealth must be satisfied to a reasonable medical certainty that the determinations made in accordance with subsection (d) of this section would not be different if the examination had been conducted in the physical presence of the commitment examiner. A commitment examiner who is not so satisfied shall note that the examination was not satisfactorily accomplished, and the respondent shall be taken for a face-to-face examination in the physical presence of a person authorized to perform examinations under this section. As used in this section, "telehealth" is the use of two-way, real-time interactive audio and video where the respondent and commitment examiner can hear and see each other. A recipient is referred by one provider to receive the services of another provider via telehealth. The examination shall include but is not limited to an assessment of all of the following:

(1) The respondent's current and previous substance abuse including, if available, previous treatment history.

(2) The respondent's dangerousness to self or others as defined in G.S. 122C-3(11).

(d) After the conclusion of the examination the physician or eligible psychologist shall make the following determinations:

(1) If the physician or eligible psychologist finds that the respondent is a substance abuser and is dangerous to himself or others, he shall recommend commitment and whether the respondent should be released or be held at a 24-hour facility pending hearing and shall so show on [the] his examination report. Based on the physician's or eligible psychologist's recommendation the law-enforcement officer or other designated individual shall take the respondent to a 24-hour facility described in G.S. 122C-252 or release the respondent.

(2) If the physician or eligible psychologist finds that the condition described in subdivision (1) of this subsection does not exist, the respondent shall be released and the proceedings terminated.

(e) The findings of the physician or eligible psychologist and the facts on which they are based shall be in writing in all cases. A copy of the findings shall be sent to the clerk of superior court by the most reliable and expeditious means. If it cannot be reasonably anticipated that the clerk will receive the copy within 48 hours of the time that it was signed, the physician or eligible psychologist shall also communicate his findings to the clerk by telephone.

History.
1973, c. 726, s. 1; c. 1408, s. 1; 1977, c. 400, s. 4; c. 679, s. 8; c. 739, s. 1; 1979, c. 358, s. 27; c. 915, s. 4; 1983, c. 380, ss. 4, 10; c. 638, ss. 6, 7, 25.1; c. 864, s. 4; 1985, c. 589, s. 2; c. 695, ss. 2, 9; 2018-33, s. 34; 2018-76, s. 3.2(b); 2019-177, s. 7(b); 2021-77, s. 6(c)

§ 122C-284. Duties of clerk of superior court

(a) Upon receipt by the clerk of superior court of a finding made by a commitment examiner or other qualified professional pursuant to G.S. 122C-285(c) that a respondent is a substance abuser and dangerous to self or others and that commitment is recommended, the clerk of superior court of the county where the facility is located, if the respondent is held in a 24-hour facility, or the clerk of superior court where the petition was initiated shall upon direction of a district court judge assign counsel, calendar the matter for hearing, and notify the respondent, the respondent's counsel, and the petitioner of the time and place of the hearing. The petitioner or respondent, directly, or through counsel, may file a written waiver of the right to notice under this subsection with the clerk of court.

(b) Notice to the respondent required by subsection (a) of this section shall be given as provided in G.S. 1A-1, Rule 4(j) at least 72 hours before the hearing. Notice to other individuals shall be given by mailing at least 72 hours before the hearing a copy by first-class mail postage prepaid to the individual at his or her last known address. G.S. 1A-1, Rule 6 shall not apply.

(c) Upon receipt of notice that transportation is necessary to take a committed respondent to a 24-hour facility pursuant to G.S. 122C-290(b), the clerk shall issue a custody order for the respondent.

(d) The clerk of superior court shall upon the direction of a district court judge calendar all hearings, supplemental hearings, and rehearings and provide all notices required by this Part.

History.
1973, c. 1408, s. 1; 1977, c. 400, s. 5; c. 414, s. 1; 1979, c. 915, s. 5; 1983, c. 380, s. 9; c. 638, s. 8; c. 864, s. 4; 1985, c. 589, s. 2; c. 695, s. 10; 1985 (Reg. Sess., 1986), c. 863, s. 27; 2018-33, s. 35

§ 122C-285. Commitment; second examination and treatment pending hearing

(a) Within 24 hours of arrival at a 24-hour facility described in G.S. 122C-252, the respondent shall be examined by a qualified professional. This professional shall be a physician if the initial commitment evaluation was conducted by a commitment examiner who is not a physician. The examination shall include the assessment specified in G.S. 122C-283(c). If the physician or qualified professional finds that the respondent is a substance abuser and is dangerous to self or others, the physician or qualified professional shall hold and treat the respondent at the facility or designate other treatment pending the district court hearing. If the physician or qualified professional finds that the respondent does not meet the criteria for commitment under G.S. 122C-283(d)(1), the physician or qualified professional shall release the respondent and the proceeding shall be terminated. In this case the reasons for the release shall be reported in writing to the clerk of superior court of the county in which the custody order originated. If the respondent is released, the law enforcement officer or other person designated or required under G.S. 122C-251(g) to provide transportation shall return the respondent to the originating county.

(a1) The second examination of a respondent required by subsection (a) of this section to determine whether the respondent will be involuntarily committed due to substance abuse may be conducted either in the physical face-to-face presence of a physician or utilizing telehealth equipment and procedures, provided that the physician who examines the respondent by means of telehealth is satisfied to a reasonable medical certainty that the determinations made in accordance with subsection (a) of this section would not be different if the examination had been done in the physical presence of the commitment examiner. An examining physician who is not so satisfied shall note that the examination was not satisfactorily accomplished, and the respondent shall be taken for a face-to-face examination in the physical presence of a qualified professional; provided, however, that if the initial commitment examination was performed by a qualified professional, then this face-to-face examination shall be in the presence of a physician. As used in this section, "telehealth" means the use of two-way, real-time interactive audio and video where the respondent and commitment examiner can hear and see each other.

(b) If the 24-hour facility described in G.S. 122C-252 is the facility in which the first examination by a commitment examiner occurred and is the same facility in which the respondent is held, the second examination must occur not later than the following regular working day.

(c) The findings of the physician or qualified professional along with a summary of the facts on which they are based shall be made in writing in all cases. A copy of the written findings shall be sent to the clerk of superior court by reliable and expeditious means.

History.

1973, c. 726, s. 1; c. 1408, s. 1; 1977, c. 400, s. 6; 1979, c. 915, s. 6; 1983, c. 380, s. 5; c. 638, ss. 9, 10; c. 864, s. 4; 1985, c. 589, s. 2; c. 695, s. 11; 1985 (Reg. Sess., 1986), c. 863, s. 28; 2018-33, s. 36; 2021-77, s. 6(d)

§ 122C-286. Commitment; district court hearing

(a) A hearing shall be held in district court within 10 days of the day the respondent is taken into custody. If a respondent temporarily detained under G.S. 122C-263(d)(2) is subject to a series of successive custody orders issued pursuant to G.S. 122C-263(d)(2), the hearing shall be held within 10 days after the day the respondent is taken into custody under the most recent custody order. Upon its own motion or upon motion of the responsible professional, the respondent, or the State, the court may grant a continuance of not more than five days.

(b) The respondent shall be present at the hearing unless the respondent, through counsel, submits a written waiver of personal appearance. A subpoena may be issued to compel the respondent's presence at a hearing. The petitioner and the responsible professional of the area facility or the proposed treating physician or a designee of the proposed treating physician may be present and may provide testimony.

(c) Certified copies of reports and findings of physicians, psychologists, and other commitment examiners and medical records of previous and current treatment are admissible in evidence, but the respondent's right to confront and cross-examine witnesses shall not be denied.

(d) The respondent may be represented by counsel of choice. If the respondent is indigent within the meaning of G.S. 7A-450, counsel shall be appointed to represent the respondent in accordance with rules adopted by the Office of Indigent Defense Services.

(e) Hearings may be held at a facility if it is located within the judge's district court district as defined in G.S. 7A-133 or in the judge's chambers. A hearing may not be held in a regular courtroom, over objection of the respondent, if in the discretion of a judge a more suitable place is available.

(f) The hearing shall be closed to the public unless the respondent requests otherwise. The hearing for a respondent being held at a 24-hour facility shall be held in a location and in the manner provided in G.S. 122C-268(g).

(g) A copy of all documents admitted into evidence and a transcript of the proceedings shall be furnished to the respondent on request by the clerk upon the direction of a district court judge. If the respondent is indigent, the copies shall be provided at State expense.

(h) To support a commitment order, the court shall find by clear, cogent, and convincing evidence that the respondent meets the criteria specified in G.S. 122C-283(d)(1). The court shall record the facts that support its findings and shall show on the order the area facility or physician who is responsible for the management and supervision of the respondent's treatment.

History.

1985, c. 589, s. 2; c. 695, s. 8; 1985 (Reg. Sess., 1986), c. 863, ss. 29, 30; 1987 (Reg. Sess., 1988), c. 1037, s. 117; 2000-144, s. 43; 2018-33, s. 37

§ 122C-286.1. Venue of district court hearing when respondent held at a 24-hour facility pending hearing

(a) In all cases where the respondent is held at a 24-hour facility pending the district court hearing as provided in G.S. 122C-286, unless the respondent through counsel objects to the venue, the hearing shall be held in the county in which the facility is located. Upon objection to venue, the hearing shall be held in the county where the petition was initiated.

(b) An official of the facility shall immediately notify the clerk of superior court of the county in which the facility is located of a determination to hold the respondent pending hearing. That clerk shall request transmittal of all documents pertinent to the proceedings from the clerk of superior court where the proceedings were initiated. The requesting clerk shall assume all duties set forth in G.S. 122C-284. The counsel provided for in G.S. 122C-286(d) shall be appointed in accordance with rules adopted by the Office of Indigent Defense Services.

History.

1985 (Reg. Sess., 1986), c. 863, s. 31; 2000-144, s. 44

§ 122C-287. Disposition

The court may make one of the following dispositions:

(1) If the court finds by clear, cogent, and convincing evidence that the respondent is a substance abuser and is dangerous to self or others, it shall order for a period not in excess of 180 days commitment to and treatment by an area facility or physician who is responsible for the management and supervision of the respondent's commitment and treatment. Before ordering commitment to and treatment by an area facility or a physician who is not a physician at an inpatient facility, the court shall follow the procedures specified in G.S. 122C-271(a)(3) and G.S. 122C-271(b)(4), as applicable.

(2) If the court finds that the respondent does not meet the commitment criteria set out in subdivision (1) of this subsection, the respondent shall be discharged and the facility in which he was last treated so notified.

History.

1973, c. 726, s. 1; c. 1408, s. 1; 1977, c. 400, s. 8; c. 739, s. 2; 1979, c. 358, s. 26; c. 915, ss. 8, 15, 16; 1981, c. 537, s. 1; 1983, c. 380, s. 8; c. 638, s. 14; c. 864, s. 4; 1985, c. 589, s. 2; 2018-33, s. 38

§ 122C-288. Appeal

Judgment of the district court is final. Appeal may be had to the Court of Appeals by the State or by any party on the record as in civil cases.

Appeal does not stay the commitment unless so ordered by the Court of Appeals. The Attorney General shall represent the State's interest on appeal. The district court retains limited jurisdiction for the purpose of hearing all reviews, rehearings, or supplemental hearings allowed or required under this Part.

History.

1973, c. 726, s. 1; c. 1408, s. 1; 1979, c. 915, s. 19; 1985, c. 589, s. 2

§ 122C-289. Duty of assigned counsel; discharge

If the respondent is committed, assigned counsel remains responsible for the respondent's representation at the trial level until discharged by order of district court or until the respondent is otherwise unconditionally discharged. If the respondent appeals, counsel for the appeal shall be appointed in accordance with rules adopted by the Office of Indigent Defense Services.

History.

1973, c. 1408, s. 1; 1985, c. 589, s. 2; 2006-264, s. 61(b)

§ 122C-290. Duties for follow-up on commitment order

(a) The area facility or physician responsible for management and supervision of the respondent's commitment and treatment may prescribe or administer to the respondent reasonable and appropriate treatment either on an outpatient basis or in a 24-hour facility.

(b) If the respondent whose treatment is provided on an outpatient basis fails to comply with all or part of the prescribed treatment after reasonable effort to solicit the respondent's compliance or whose treatment is provided on an inpatient basis is discharged in accordance with G.S. 122C-205.1(b), the area facility or physician may request the clerk or magistrate to order the respondent taken into custody for the purpose of examination. Upon receipt of this request, the clerk or magistrate shall issue an order to a law enforcement officer to take the respondent into custody and to take him immediately to the designated area facility or physician for examination. The custody order is valid throughout the State. The law enforcement officer shall turn the respondent over to the custody of the physician or area facility who shall conduct the examination and release the respondent or have the respondent taken to a 24-hour facility upon a determination that treatment in the facility will benefit the respondent. Transportation to the 24-hour facility shall be provided as specified in G.S. 122C-251, upon notice to the clerk or magistrate that transportation is necessary, or as provided in G.S.

122C-408(b). If placement in a 24-hour facility is to exceed 45 consecutive days, the area facility or physician shall notify the clerk of court by the 30th day and request a supplemental hearing as specified in G.S. 122C-291.

(c) If the respondent intends to move or moves to another county within the State, the area facility or physician shall notify the clerk of court in the county where the commitment is being supervised and request that a supplemental hearing be calendared.

(d) If the respondent moves to another state or to an unknown location, the designated area facility or physician shall notify the clerk of superior court of the county where the commitment is supervised and the commitment shall be terminated.

History.
1983, c. 638, s. 16; c. 864, s. 4; 1985, c. 589, s. 2; 1985 (Reg. Sess., 1986), c. 863, s. 32; 1987, c. 674, s. 2; c. 750; 2004-23, s. 2(c); 2018-33, s. 39

§ 122C-291. Supplemental hearings

(a) Upon receipt of a request for a supplemental hearing, the clerk shall calendar a hearing to be held within 14 days and notify, at least 72 hours before the hearing, the petitioner, the respondent, his attorney, if any, and the designated area facility or physician. Notice shall be provided in accordance with G.S. 122C-284(b). The procedures for the hearing shall follow G.S. 122C-286.

(b) At the supplemental hearing for a respondent who has moved or may move to another county, the court shall determine if the respondent meets the criteria for commitment set out in G.S. 122C-283(d)(1). If the court determines that the respondent no longer meets the criteria for commitment, it shall discharge the respondent from the order and dismiss the case. If the court determines that the respondent continues to meet the criteria for commitment, it shall continue the commitment but shall designate an area facility or physician at the respondent's new residence to be responsible for the management or supervision of the respondent's commitment. The court shall order the respondent to appear for treatment at the address of the newly designated area facility or physician and shall order venue for further court proceedings under the commitment to be transferred to the new county of supervision. Upon an order changing venue, the clerk of court in the county where the commitment has been supervised shall transfer the records regarding the commitment to the clerk of court in the county where the commitment will be supervised. Also, the clerk of court in the county where the commitment has been supervised shall send a copy of the court's order directing the continuation of treatment under new supervision to the newly designated area facility or physician.

(c) At a supplemental hearing for a respondent to be held longer than 45 consecutive days in a 24-hour facility, the court shall determine if the respondent meets the criteria for commitment set out in G.S. 122C-283(d)(1). If the court determines that the respondent continues to meet the criteria and that further treatment in the 24-hour facility is necessary, the court may authorize continued care in the facility for not more than 90 days, after which a rehearing for the purpose of determining the need for continued care in the 24-hour facility shall be held, or the court may order the respondent released from the 24-hour facility and continued on the commitment on an outpatient basis. If the court determines that the respondent no longer meets the criteria for commitment the respondent shall be released and his case dismissed.

(d) At any time during the term of commitment order, a respondent may apply to the court for a supplemental hearing for the purpose of discharge from the order. The application shall be made in writing to the clerk of superior court. At the supplemental hearing the court shall determine whether the respondent continues to meet the criteria for commitment. The court may reissue or change the commitment order or discharge the respondent and dismiss the case.

History.
1985, c. 589, s. 2; 2018-33, s. 40

§ 122C-292. Rehearings

(a) Fifteen days before the end of the initial or subsequent periods of commitment if the area facility or physician determines that the respondent continues to meet the criteria specified in G.S. 122C-283(d)(1), the clerk of superior court of the county where commitment is supervised shall be notified. The clerk, at least 10 days before the end of the commitment period, on order of the district court, shall calendar the rehearing. If the respondent no longer meets the criteria, the area facility or physician shall so notify the clerk who shall dismiss the case.

(b) Rehearings are governed by the same notice and procedures as initial hearings, and the respondent has the same rights that were available to the respondent at the initial hearing including the right to appeal.

(c) If the court finds that the respondent no longer meets the criteria of G.S. 122C-283(d)(1), it shall unconditionally discharge him. A copy of the discharge order shall be furnished by the clerk to the designated area facility or physician. If the respondent continues to meet the criteria of G.S. 122C-283(d)(1), the court may order commitment for additional periods not in excess of 365 days each.

History.

1973, c. 726, s. 1; c. 1408, s. 1; 1977, c. 400, s. 9; 1979, c. 915, ss. 9, 17; 1981, c. 537, ss. 2-4; 1983, c. 638, ss. 18-19; 864, s. 4; 1985, c. 589, s. 2; 2018-33, s. 41

§ 122C-293. Release by area facility or physician

The area facility or physician as designated in the order shall discharge a committed respondent unconditionally at any time the physician determines that the respondent no longer meets the criteria of G.S. 122C-283(d)(1). Notice of discharge and the reasons for the release shall be reported in writing to the clerk of superior court of the county in which the commitment was ordered.

History.

1973, c. 726, s. 1; c. 1408, s. 1; 1981, c. 537, s. 5; 1983, c. 383, s. 6; c. 638, s. 21; c. 864, s. 4; 1985, c. 589, s. 2; 2018-33, s. 42

§ 122C-294. Local plan and data submission

(a) The "local area crisis services plans" adopted in accordance with G.S. 122C-202.2 and G.S. 122C-251(g) shall be submitted to the Division of Mental Health, Developmental Disabilities, and Substance Abuse Services beginning October 1, 2019, but no later than August 1, 2020. If the area authority modifies any plan, the modified plan shall be submitted to the Division of Mental Health, Developmental Disabilities, and Substance Abuse Services at least 10 days prior to the effective date of the new plan.

(b) The Department shall provide the data collected by the Division of Mental Health, Developmental Disabilities, and Substance Abuse Services concerning the number of respondents receiving treatment under involuntary commitment in designated facilities to the Fiscal Research Division and the Joint Legislative Oversight Committee for Health and Human Services on October 1 of each year beginning in 2019 and any other time upon request.

History.

1973, c. 1408, s. 1; 1977, c. 679, s. 8; 1979, c. 358, ss. 26, 27; 1985, c. 589, s. 2; 2018-33, s. 43; 2019-240, s. 26(i)

PART 9
PUBLIC INTOXICATION

§ 122C-301. Assistance to an individual who is intoxicated in public; procedure for commitment to shelter or facility

(a) An officer may assist an individual found intoxicated in a public place by taking any of the following actions:

(1) The officer may direct or transport the intoxicated individual home;

(2) The officer may direct or transport the intoxicated individual to the residence of another individual willing to accept him;

(3) If the intoxicated individual is apparently in need of and apparently unable to provide for himself food, clothing, or shelter but is not apparently in need of immediate medical care, the officer may direct or transport him to an appropriate public or private shelter facility;

(4) If the intoxicated individual is apparently in need of but apparently unable to provide for himself immediate medical care, the officer may direct or transport him to an area facility, hospital, or physician's office; or the officer may direct or transport the individual to any other appropriate health care facility; or

(5) If the intoxicated individual is apparently a substance abuser and is apparently dangerous to himself or others, the officer may proceed as provided in Part 8 of this Article.

(b) In providing the assistance authorized by subsection (a) of this section, the officer may use reasonable force to restrain the intoxicated individual if it appears necessary to protect himself, the intoxicated individual, or others. No officer may be held criminally or civilly liable for assault, false imprisonment, or other torts or crimes on account of reasonable measures taken under authority of this Part.

(c) If the officer takes the action described in either subdivision (a)(3) or (a)(4) of this section, the facility to which the intoxicated individual is taken may detain him only until he becomes sober or a maximum of 24 hours. The individual may stay a longer period if he wishes to do so and the facility is able to accommodate him.

(d) Any individual who has knowledge that a person assisted to a shelter or other facility under subdivisions (a)(3) or (a)(4) of this section is a substance abuser and is dangerous to himself or others may proceed as provided in Part 8 of this Article.

History.

1977, 2nd Sess., c. 1134, s. 2; 1981, c. 519, s. 5; 1985, c. 589, s. 2

§ 122C-302. Cities and counties may employ officers to assist intoxicated individuals

A city or county may employ officers to assist individuals who are intoxicated in public. Officers employed for this purpose shall be trained to give assistance to those who are intoxicated in public including the administration of first aid. An officer employed by a city or county to assist intoxicated individuals has the powers and duties set out in G.S. 122C-301 within the same territory in which criminal laws are enforced by law-enforcement officers of that city or county.

History.
1977, 2nd Sess., c. 1134, s. 2; 1985, c. 589, s. 2

§ 122C-303. Use of jail for care for intoxicated individual

In addition to the actions authorized by G.S. 122C-301(a), an officer may assist an individual found intoxicated in a public place by directing or transporting that individual to a city or county jail. That action may be taken only if the intoxicated individual is apparently in need of and apparently unable to provide for himself food, clothing, or shelter but is not apparently in need of immediate medical care and if no other facility is readily available to receive him. The officer and employees of the jail are exempt from liability as provided in G.S. 122C-301(b). The intoxicated individual may be detained at the jail only until he becomes sober or a maximum of 24 hours and may be released at any time to a relative or other individual willing to be responsible for his care.

History.
1977, 2nd Sess., c. 1134, s. 3; 1985, c. 589, s. 2

PART 10
VOLUNTARY ADMISSIONS, INVOLUNTARY COMMITMENTS AND DISCHARGES, INMATES AND PAROLEES, DIVISION OF ADULT CORRECTION AND JUVENILE JUSTICE OF THE DEPARTMENT OF PUBLIC SAFETY

§ 122C-311. Individuals on parole

Any individual who has been released from any correctional facility on parole is admitted, committed and discharged from facilities in accordance with the procedures specified in this Article for other individuals.

History.
1959, c. 1002, s. 24; 1963, c. 1184, s. 28; 1973, c. 253, s. 4; 1985, c. 589, s. 2

§ 122C-312. Voluntary admissions and discharges of inmates of the Division of Adult Correction and Juvenile Justice of the Department of Public Safety

Inmates in the custody of the Division of Adult Correction and Juvenile Justice of the Department of Public Safety may seek voluntary admission to State facilities for the mentally ill or substance abusers. The provisions of Part 2 of this Article shall apply except that an admission may be accomplished only when the Secretary and the Secretary of Public Safety jointly agree to the inmate's request. When an inmate is admitted he shall be discharged in accordance with the provisions of Part 2 of this Article except that an inmate who is ready for discharge, but still under a term of incarceration, shall be discharged only to an official of the Division of Adult Correction and Juvenile Justice of the Department of Public Safety. The Division of Adult Correction and Juvenile Justice of the Department of Public Safety is responsible for the security and cost of transporting inmates to and from facilities under the provisions of this section.

History.
1979, c. 547; 1985, c. 589, s. 2; 2011-145, s. 19.1(h), (i); 2017-186, s. 2 (ppppp)

§ 122C-313. Inmate becoming mentally ill and dangerous to himself or others

(a) An inmate who becomes mentally ill and dangerous to himself or others after incarceration in any facility operated by the Division of Adult Correction and Juvenile Justice of the Department of Public Safety in the State is processed in accordance with Part 7 of this Article, as modified by this section, except when the provisions of Part 7 are manifestly inappropriate. A staff psychiatrist or eligible psychologist of the correctional facility shall execute the affidavit required by G.S. 122C-261 and send it to the clerk of superior court of the county in which the correctional facility is located. Upon receipt of the affidavit, the clerk shall calendar a district court hearing and notify the respondent and his counsel as required by G.S. 122C-284(a). The hearing is conducted in a district courtroom. If the judge finds by clear, cogent, and convincing evidence that the respondent is mentally ill and dangerous to himself or others, he shall order him transferred for treatment to a State facility designated by the Secretary. The judge shall not order outpatient commitment for an inmate-respondent.

(b) If the sentence of an inmate-respondent expires while he is committed to a State facility, he is considered in all respects as if he had been initially committed under Part 7 of this Article.

(c) If the sentence of an inmate-respondent has not expired, and if in the opinion of the attending physician of the State facility an inmate-respondent ceases to be mentally ill and dangerous to himself or others, he shall notify the Division of Adult Correction and Juvenile Justice of the Department of Public Safety which shall arrange for the inmate-respondent's return to a correctional facility.

(d) Special counsel at a State facility shall represent any inmate who becomes mentally ill and dangerous to himself or others while confined in a correctional facility in the same county, otherwise counsel is assigned in accordance with G.S. 122C-270(d).

(e) The Division of Adult Correction and Juvenile Justice of the Department of Public Safety is responsible for the security and cost of transporting inmates to and from State facilities under the provisions of this section.

History.
1899, c. 1, s. 66; Rev., s. 4619; C.S., s. 6238; 1923, c. 165, s. 55; 1945, c. 952, s. 55; 1955, c. 887, s. 14; 1957, c. 1232, s. 26; 1963, c. 1184, s. 27; 1965, c. 800, s. 13; 1973, c. 253, s. 3; c. 1433; 1977, c. 679, s. 8; 1979, c. 358, s. 27; c. 915, s. 11; 1985, c. 589, s. 2; c. 695, s. 2; 2011-145, s. 19.1(h); 2017-186, s. 2 (ppppp)

PART 11
VOLUNTARY ADMISSIONS, INVOLUNTARY COMMITMENTS AND DISCHARGES, THE PSYCHIATRIC SERVICE OF THE UNIVERSITY OF NORTH CAROLINA HOSPITALS AT CHAPEL HILL

§ 122C-321. Voluntary admissions and discharges

Any individual in need of treatment for mental illness or substance abuse may seek voluntary admission to the psychiatric service of the University of North Carolina Hospitals at Chapel Hill. Procedures for admission and discharge shall be made in accordance with Parts 2 through 4 of this Article. The applicant may be admitted only upon the approval of the director of the psychiatric service or his designee.

History.
1955, c. 1274, s. 2; 1963, c. 1184, s. 2; 1973, c. 723, s. 3; c. 1084; 1985, c. 589, s. 2; 1989, c. 141, s. 14

§ 122C-322. Involuntary commitments

(a) Except as otherwise specifically provided in this section references in Parts 6 through 8 of this Article to 24-hour facilities, outpatient treatment centers, or area authorities, or private facilities shall include the psychiatric service of the University of North Carolina Hospitals at Chapel Hill. The psychiatric service may be used for temporary detention pending a district court hearing, for commitment of the respondent after the hearing, or as the manager and supervisor of outpatient commitment. However, no individual may be held at or committed to the psychiatric service without the prior approval of the director of the psychiatric service or his designee.

(b) Initial hearings, supplemental hearings, and rehearings may be held at the psychiatric service facility or at any place in Orange County where district court can be held under G.S. 7A-133. Legal counsel for the respondent at all hearings and rehearings shall be assigned from among the members of the bar of the same county in accordance with G.S. 122C-270(d).

History.
1977, c. 738, s. 1; 1981, c. 442; 1985, c. 589, s. 2; 1989, c. 141, s. 15

PART 12
VOLUNTARY ADMISSIONS, INVOLUNTARY COMMITMENTS AND DISCHARGES, VETERANS ADMINISTRATION FACILITIES

§ 122C-331. Voluntary admissions and discharges

Veterans in need of treatment for mental illness or substance abuse may seek voluntary admission to a facility operated by the Veterans Administration. Procedures for admission and discharge shall be made in accordance with Parts 2 and 4 of this Article. The Veterans Administration may require additional procedures not inconsistent with these Parts.

History.
1973, c. 1408, s. 1; 1985, c. 589, s. 2

§ 122C-332. Involuntary commitments

(a) Except as otherwise specifically provided in this section, references in Parts 6 through 8 of this Article to 24-hour facilities, outpatient treatment centers, or area authorities, or private facilities shall include the facilities operated by the Veterans Administration. Veterans Administration facilities may be used for temporary detention pending a district court hearing, for commitment of the respondent after the hearing, or as the manager and supervisor of outpatient commitment. Eligibility of the veteran-respondent for treatment at a Veterans Administration facility and the availability of space shall be determined by the Veterans Administration in all cases before sending or committing a veteran-respondent.

(b) Initial hearings, supplemental hearings, and rehearings for veteran-respondents may be held at the facility or at the county courthouse in the county in which the facility is located, and counsel shall be assigned from among the members of the bar of the same county in accordance with G.S. 122C-270(d).

History.
1985, c. 589, s. 2

§ 122C-333. Order of another state

The judgment or order of commitment by a court of competent jurisdiction of another state, committing a person to the Veterans Administration or another federal agency that is located in this State shall have the same force and effect on the committed person while in this State as in the jurisdiction of the court entering the judgment or making the order. The courts of the committing state shall retain jurisdiction of the person so committed for the purpose of inquiring into the mental condition of the person, and for determining the necessity for continuance of his restraint. Consent is given to the application of the law of the committing state on the authority of the chief officer of any facility of the Veterans Administration or of any institution operated in this State by any other federal agency to retain custody, transfer, parole, or discharge the committed person.

History.
1985, c. 589, s. 2

PART 13
VOLUNTARY ADMISSIONS, INVOLUNTARY COMMITMENT AND DISCHARGE OF NON-STATE RESIDENTS AND THE RETURN OF NORTH CAROLINA RESIDENT CLIENTS

§ 122C-341. Determination of residence

It is the responsibility of the facility to determine if a client is not a resident of the State.

History.
1899, c. 1, s. 18; Rev., ss. 3591, 4587, 4588; C.S., ss. 6187, 6188; 1945, c. 952, ss. 16, 17; 1947, c. 537, s.

11; 1953, c. 256, s. 3; 1957, c. 1386; 1963, c. 1184, s. 1; 1973, c. 673, s. 13; 1985, c. 589, s. 2

§ 122C-342. Voluntary admissions and discharges

A non-State resident may be admitted to and discharged from a facility on a voluntary basis in accordance with Parts 2 through 5 of this Article at his own expense. If the facility determines that the client should be returned to his own state the provisions of G.S. 122C-345 or G.S. 122C-361, as appropriate, shall apply.

History.
1899, c. 1, s. 16; Rev., s. 4584; C.S., s. 6210; 1945, c. 952, s. 33; 1947, c. 537, s. 18; 1963, c. 1184, s. 1; 1971, c. 1140; 1973, c. 476, s. 133; c. 673, s. 13; 1985, c. 589, s. 2

§ 122C-343. Involuntary commitments

Involuntary commitments of non-State residents are made under the provisions of Parts 6 through 8 of this Article. If after commitment to a 24-hour facility the facility determines that the respondent needs long-term care and should be returned to his state of residence, the provisions of G.S. 122C-345 or G.S. 122C-361, as appropriate, shall apply.

History.
1899, c. 1, s. 16; Rev., s. 4584; C.S., s. 6210; 1945, c. 952, s. 33; 1947, c. 537, s. 18; 1963, c. 1184, s. 1; 1971, c. 1140; 1973, c. 476, s. 133; c. 673, s. 13; 1985, c. 589, s. 2

§ 122C-344. Citizens of other countries

In addition to the provisions of G.S. 122C-341 through G.S. 122C-343, if a 24-hour facility determines that a client is not a citizen of the United States, the facility shall notify the Governor of this State of the name of the client, the country and place of his residence in the country and other facts in the case as can be obtained, together with a copy of pertinent medical records. The Governor shall send the information to the nearest consular office of the committed foreign national, with the request that the consular office tell the minister resident or plenipotentiary of the country of which the client is alleged to be a citizen.

History.
1899, c. 1, s. 16; Rev., s. 4585; C.S., s. 6211; 1963, c. 1184, s. 1; 1985, c. 589, s. 2; 1993, c. 561, s. 86(a)

§ 122C-345. Return of a non-State resident client to his resident state

(a) Except as provided in subsection (c) of this section, it is the responsibility of the director of a facility to arrange for the transfer of a client to his resident state. The cost of returning the client to his resident state is the responsibility of the client or his family.

(b) A non-State resident client of an area 24-hour facility may be transferred to a State facility in accordance with G.S. 122C-206 in order for the client to be returned to his resident state.

(c) A non-State resident client of a State facility may be returned to his resident state under procedures established under G.S. 122C-346 or G.S. 122C-361. The cost of returning a client to his resident state under this subsection shall be the responsibility of the State.

History.
1899, c. 1, s. 16; Rev., s. 4584; C.S., s. 6210; 1945, c. 952, s. 33; 1947, c. 537, ss. 18, 20; 1955, c. 887, s. 13; 1959, c. 1002, s. 22; 1963, c. 1184, s. 1; 1971, c. 1140; 1973, c. 476, s. 133; c. 673, s. 13; 1977, c. 679, s. 7; 1981, c. 51, s. 3; 1985, c. 589, s. 2

§ 122C-346. Authority of the Secretary to enter reciprocal agreements

The Secretary may enter agreements with other states for the return of non-State resident clients to their resident state and for the return of North Carolina residents to North Carolina when under treatment in another state.

History.
1947, c. 537, s. 20; 1955, c. 887, s. 13; 1959, c. 1002, s. 22; 1963, c. 1184, s. 1; 1973, c. 476, s. 133; 1977, c. 679, s. 7; 1981, c. 51, s. 3; 1985, c. 589, s. 2

§ 122C-347. Return of North Carolina resident clients from other states

North Carolina residents who are in treatment in another state may be returned to North Carolina either under an agreement authorized in G.S. 122C-346 or under the provisions of G.S. 122C-361. The cost of returning a North Carolina resident to this State is the responsibility of the sending state. Within 72 hours after admission in a State facility, a returned resident shall be evaluated. The returned resident may agree to a voluntary admission or may be released, or proceedings for an involuntary commitment under this Article may be initiated as necessary by the responsible professional in the facility.

History.
1945, c. 952, s. 34; 1947, c. 537, s. 19; 1959, c. 1002, ss. 20, 21; 1963, c. 1184, s. 1; 1965, c. 800, s. 9; 1969, c. 982; 1973, c. 476, ss. 133, 138; c. 673, s. 13; 1985, c. 589, s. 2

§ 122C-348. Residency not affected

(a) A nonresident of this State who is under care in a 24-hour facility in this State is not considered a resident. No length of time spent in this State while a client in a 24-hour facility is sufficient to make a nonresident a resident or entitled to care or treatment.

(b) A North Carolina resident who is under care and treatment in a 24-hour facility in another state shall retain his residency in North Carolina.

History.
1899, c. 1, s. 18; Rev., ss. 3591, 4587, 4588; C.S., ss. 6187, 6188; 1945, c. 952, ss. 16, 17; 1947, c. 537, ss. 11, 20; 1953, c. 256, s. 3; 1955, c. 887, s. 13; 1957, c. 1386; 1959, c. 1002, s. 22; 1963, c. 1184, s. 1; 1973, c. 476, s. 133; c. 673, s. 13; 1977, c. 679, s. 7; 1981, c. 51, s. 3; 1985, c. 589, s. 2

PART 14
INTERSTATE COMPACT ON MENTAL HEALTH

§ 122C-361. Compact entered into; form of Compact

The Interstate Compact on Mental Health is hereby enacted into law and entered into by this State with all other states legally joining therein in the form substantially as follows: The contracting states solemnly agree that:

ARTICLE I.

The party states find that the proper and expeditious treatment of the mentally ill and mentally deficient can be facilitated by cooperative action, to the benefit of the patients, their families, and society as a whole. Further, the party states find that the necessity of and desirability for furnishing such care and treatment bears no primary relation to the residence or citizenship of the patient but, that, on the contrary, the controlling factors of community safety and humanitarianism require that facilities and services be made available for all who are in need of them. Consequently, it is the purpose of this Compact and of the party states to provide the necessary legal basis for the institutionalization or other appropriate care and treatment of the mentally ill and mentally deficient under a system that recognizes the paramount importance of patient welfare and to establish the responsibilities of the party states in term of such welfare.

ARTICLE II.

As used in this Compact:

(a) "Sending state" shall mean a party state from which a patient is transported pursuant to the provisions of the Compact or from which it is contemplated that a patient may be so sent.

(b) "Receiving state" shall mean a party state to which a patient is transported pursuant to the provisions of the Compact or to which it is contemplated that a patient may be so sent.

(c) "Institution" shall mean any hospital or other facility maintained by a party state or political subdivision thereof for the care and treatment of mental illness or mental deficiency.

(d) "Patient" shall mean any person subject to or eligible as determined by the laws of the sending state, for institutionalization or other care, treatment, or supervision pursuant to the provisions of this Compact.

(e) "Aftercare" shall mean care, treatment and services provided a patient, as defined herein, on convalescent status or conditional release.

(f) "Mental illness" shall mean mental disease to such extent that a person so afflicted requires care and treatment for his own welfare, or the welfare of others, or of the community.

(g) "Mental deficiency" shall mean mental deficiency as defined by appropriate clinical authorities to such extent that a person so afflicted is incapable of managing himself and his affairs, but shall not include mental illness as defined herein.

(h) "State" shall mean any state, territory or possession of the United States, the District of Columbia, and the Commonwealth of Puerto Rico.

ARTICLE III.

(a) Whenever a person physically present in any party state shall be in need of institutionalization by reason of mental illness or mental deficiency, he shall be eligible for care and treatment in an institution in that state irrespective of his residence, settlement or citizenship qualifications.

(b) The provisions of paragraph (a) of this Article to the contrary notwithstanding, any patient may be transferred to an institution in another state whenever there are factors based upon clinical determinations indicating that the care and treatment of said patient would be facilitated or improved thereby. Any such institutionalization may be for the entire period of care and treatment or for any portion or portions thereof. The factors referred to in this paragraph shall include the patient's full record with due regard for the location of the patient's family, character of the illness and probable duration thereof, and such other factors as shall be considered appropriate.

(c) No state shall be obliged to receive any patient pursuant to the provisions of paragraph (b) of this Article unless the sending state has given advance notice of its intention to send the patient; furnished all available medical and other pertinent records concerning the patient; given the qualified medical or other appropriate clinical authorities of the receiving state an opportunity to examine the patient if said authorities so wish; and unless the receiving state shall agree to accept the patient.

(d) In the event that the laws of the receiving state establish a system of priorities for the admission of patients, an interstate patient under this Compact shall receive the same priority as a local patient and shall be taken in the same order and at the same time that it would be taken if he were a local patient.

(e) Pursuant to this Compact, the determination as to the suitable place of institutionalization for a patient may be reviewed at any time and such further transfer of the patient may be made as seems likely to be in the best interest of the patient.

ARTICLE IV.

(a) Whenever, pursuant to the laws of the state in which a patient is physically present, it shall be determined that the patient should receive aftercare or supervision, such care or supervision may be provided in a receiving state. If the medical or other appropriate clinical authorities have responsibility for the care and treatment of the patient in the sending state shall have reason to believe that aftercare in another state would be in the best interest of the patient and would not jeopardize the public safety, they shall request the appropriate authorities in the receiving state to investigate the desirability of affording the patient such aftercare in said receiving state, and such investigation shall be made with all reasonable speed. The request for investigation shall be accompanied by complete information concerning the patient's intended place of residence and the identity of the person in whose charge it is proposed to place the patient, the complete medical history of the patient, and such other documents as may be pertinent.

(b) If the medical or other appropriate clinical authorities having responsibility for the care and treatment of the patient in the sending state and the appropriate authorities in the receiving state find that the best interest of the patient would be served thereby, and if the public safety would not be jeopardized thereby, the patient may receive aftercare or supervision in the receiving state.

(c) In supervising, treating, or caring for a patient on aftercare pursuant to the terms of this

Article, a receiving state shall employ the same standards of visitation, examination, care, and treatment that it employs for similar local patients.

ARTICLE V.

Whenever a dangerous or potentially dangerous patient escapes from an institution in any party state, that state shall promptly notify all appropriate authorities within and without the jurisdiction of the escape in a way reasonably calculated to facilitate the speedy apprehension of the escapee. Immediately upon the apprehension and identification of any such dangerous or potentially dangerous patient, he shall be detained in the state where found pending disposition in accordance with law.

ARTICLE VI.

The duly accredited officers of any state party to this Compact, upon the establishment of their authority and the identity of the patient, shall be permitted to transport any patient being moved pursuant to this Compact through any and all states party to this Compact, without interference.

ARTICLE VII.

(a) No person shall be deemed a patient of more than one institution at any given time. Completion of transfer of any patient to an institution in a receiving state shall have the effect of making the person a patient of the institution in the receiving state.

(b) The sending state shall pay all costs of and incidental to the transportation of any patient pursuant to this Compact, but any two or more party states may, by making a specific agreement for that purpose, arrange for a different allocation of costs as among themselves.

(c) No provision of this Compact shall be construed to alter or affect any internal relationships among the departments, agencies and officers of and in the government of a party state, or between a party state and its subdivisions, as to the payment of costs, or responsibilities therefor.

(d) Nothing in this Compact shall be construed to prevent any party state or subdivision thereof from asserting any right against any person, agency or other entity in regard to costs for which such party state or subdivision thereof may be responsible pursuant to any provision of this Compact.

(e) Nothing in this Compact shall be construed to invalidate any reciprocal agreement between a party state and a nonparty state relating to institutionalization, care or treatment of the mentally ill or mentally deficient, or any statutory authority pursuant to which such agreements may be made.

ARTICLE VIII.

(a) Nothing in this Compact shall be construed to abridge, diminish, or in any way impair the rights, duties, and responsibilities of any patient's guardian on his own behalf or in respect of any patient for whom he may serve, except that where the transfer of any patient to another jurisdiction makes advisable the appointment of a supplemental or substitute guardian, any court of competent jurisdiction in the receiving state may make such supplemental or substitute appointment and the court which appointed the previous guardian shall upon being duly advised of the new appointment, and upon the satisfactory completion of such accounting and other acts as such court may by law require, relieve the previous guardian of power and responsibility to whatever extent shall be appropriate in the circumstances; provided, however, that in the case of any patient having settlement in the sending state, the court of competent jurisdiction in the sending state shall have the sole discretion to relieve a guardian appointed by it or continue his power and responsibility, whichever it shall deem advisable. The court in the receiving state may, in its discretion, confirm or reappoint the person or persons previously serving as guardian in the sending state in lieu of making a supplemental or substitute appointment.

(b) The term "guardian" as used in paragraph (a) of this Article shall include any guardian, trustee, legal committee, conservator, or other person or agency however denominated who is charged by law with power to act for or responsibility for the person or property of a patient.

ARTICLE IX.

(a) No provision of this Compact except Article V shall apply to any person institutionalized while under sentence in a penal or correctional institution or while subject to trial on a criminal charge, or whose institutionalization is due to the commission of an offense for which, in the absence of mental illness or mental deficiency, said person would be subject to incarceration in a penal or correctional institution.

(b) To every extent possible, it shall be the policy of states party to this Compact that no patient shall be placed or detained in any prison, jail or lockup, but such patient shall, with all expedition, be taken to a suitable institutional facility for mental illness or mental deficiency.

ARTICLE X.

(a) Each party state shall appoint a "Compact Administrator" who, on behalf of his state, shall act as general coordinator of activities under the Compact in his state and who shall receive copies of all reports, correspondence, and other documents relating to any patient processed under the Compact by his state either in the capacity of sending or receiving state. The Compact Administrator or his duly designated representative shall be the official with whom other party states shall deal in any matter relating to the Compact or any patient processed thereunder.

(b) The Compact Administrators of the respective party states shall have power to promulgate reasonable rules and regulations to carry out more effectively the terms and provisions of this Compact.

ARTICLE XI.

The duly constituted administrative authorities of any two or more party states may enter into supplementary agreements for the provision of any service or facility or for the maintenance of any institution on a joint or cooperative basis whenever the states concerned shall find that such agreements will improve services, facilities, or institutional care and treatment in the fields of mental illness or mental deficiency. No such supplementary agreement shall be construed so as to relieve any party state of any obligation which it otherwise would have under other provisions of this Compact.

ARTICLE XII.

This Compact shall enter into full force and effect as to any state when enacted by it into law and such state shall thereafter be a party thereto with any and all states legally joining therein.

ARTICLE XIII.

(a) A state party to this Compact may withdraw therefrom by enacting a statute repealing the same. Such withdrawal shall take effect one year after notice thereof has been communicated officially and in writing to the governors and Compact administrators of all other party states. However, the withdrawal of any state shall not change the status of any patient who has been sent to said state or sent out of said state pursuant to the provisions of the Compact.

(b) Withdrawal from any agreement permitted by Article VII(b) as to costs or from any supplementary agreement made pursuant to Article XI shall be in accordance with the terms of such agreement.

ARTICLE XIV.

This Compact shall be liberally construed so as to effectuate the purposes thereof. The provisions of this Compact shall be severable and if any phrase, clause, sentence or provision of this Compact is declared to be contrary to the constitution of any party state or of the United States or the applicability thereof to any government, agency, person or circumstance is held invalid, the validity of the remainder of this Compact and the applicability thereof to any government, agency, person or circumstance shall not be affected thereby. If this Compact shall be held contrary to the constitution of any state party thereto, the Compact shall remain in full force and effect as to the remaining states and in full force and effect as to the state affected as to all severable matters.

History.
1959, c. 1003, s. 1; 1963, c. 1184, s. 12; 1985, c. 589, s. 2

§ 122C-362. Compact Administrator

Pursuant to the Compact, the Secretary is the Compact Administrator and, acting jointly with like officers of other party states, may adopt rules to carry out more effectively the terms of the Compact. The Compact Administrator shall cooperate with all departments, agencies and officers of and in the government of this State and its subdivisions in facilitating the proper administration of the Compact, of any supplementary agreement, or agreements entered into by this State.

History.
1959, c. 1003, s. 2; 1963, c. 1184, s. 12; 1973, c. 476, s. 133; 1985, c. 589, s. 2

§ 122C-363. Supplementary agreements

The Compact Administrator may enter into supplementary agreements with appropriate officials of other states pursuant to Articles VII and XI of the Compact. In the event that these supplementary agreements shall require or contemplate the use of any institution or facility of this State or require or contemplate the provision of any service by this State, no such agreement shall be effective until approved by the head of the department or agency under whose jurisdiction the institution or facility is operated or whose department or agency will be charged with the rendering of this service.

History.
1959, c. 1003, s. 3; 1963, c. 1184, s. 12; 1985, c. 589, s. 2

§ 122C-364. Financial arrangements

The Compact Administrator, with the approval of the Director of the Budget, may make or arrange for any payments necessary to discharge any financial obligations imposed upon this State by the Compact or by any supplementary agreement entered into under it.

Chapter 122C

History.

1959, c. 1003, s. 4; 1963, c. 1184, s. 12; 1985, c. 589, s. 2

§ 122C-365. Transfer of clients

The Compact Administrator is directed to consult with the immediate family or legally responsible person of any proposed transferee.

History.

1959, c. 1003, s. 5; 1963, c. 1184, ss. 12, 38; 1985, c. 589, s. 2

§ 122C-366. Transmittal of copies of Part

Copies of this Part shall, upon its approval, be transmitted by the Compact Administrator to the governor of each state, the attorney general of each state, the Administrator of General Services of the United States, and the Council of State Governments.

History.

1959, c. 1003, s. 6; 1963, c. 1184, s. 12; 1985, c. 589, s. 2

CHAPTER 125
LIBRARIES

ARTICLE 1
STATE LIBRARY AGENCY

§ 125-11. Failure to return books

Any person who shall fail to return any book, periodical, or other material withdrawn by him from the Library shall be guilty of a Class 3 misdemeanor if he shall fail to return the borrowed material within 30 days after receiving a notice from the State Librarian that the material is overdue. The provisions of this section shall not be in effect unless a copy of this section is attached to the overdue notice by the State Librarian.

History.
1955, c. 505, s. 3; 1993, c. 539, s. 929; 1994, Ex. Sess., c. 24, s. 14(c)

CHAPTER 126
NORTH CAROLINA
HUMAN RESOURCES ACT

ARTICLE 2
SALARIES, PROMOTIONS, AND LEAVE OF STATE EMPLOYEES

§ 126-8.2. Replacement of law-enforcement officer on final sick leave

When a sworn law-enforcement officer employed by the State is on sick leave, and the head of the department employing the officer has obtained a certification from a physician that the officer will not recover and return to duty, a replacement for the officer may be hired even though the resulting number of employees in the department exceeds the number for which an appropriation was made in the Current Operations Appropriations Act, if sufficient funds are available from appropriations to the department for salaries to pay the salary of both the new employee and the officer on sick leave until the officer's accumulated leave is exhausted or his employment is terminated.

History.
1983 (Reg. Sess., 1984), c. 1034, s. 105

ARTICLE 7
THE PRIVACY OF STATE EMPLOYEE PERSONNEL RECORDS

§ 126-27. Penalty for permitting access to confidential file by unauthorized person

Any public official or employee who shall knowingly and willfully permit any person to have access to or custody or possession of any portion of a personnel file designated as confidential by this Article, unless such person is one specifically authorized by G.S. 126-24 to have access thereto for inspection and examination, shall be guilty of a Class 3 misdemeanor and upon conviction shall only be fined in the discretion of the court but not in excess of five hundred dollars ($ 500.00).

History.
1975, c. 257, s. 1; 1993, c. 539, s. 934; 1994, Ex. Sess., c. 24, s. 14(c)

§ 126-28. Penalty for examining, copying, etc., confidential file without authority

Any person, not specifically authorized by G.S. 126-24 to have access to a personnel file designated as confidential by this Article, who shall knowingly and willfully examine in its official filing place, remove or copy any portion of a confidential personnel file shall be guilty of a Class 3 misdemeanor and upon conviction shall only be fined in the discretion of the court but not in excess of five hundred dollars ($ 500.00).

History.
1975, c. 257, s. 1; 1993, c. 539, s. 935; 1994, Ex. Sess., c. 24, s. 14(c)

CHAPTER 128
OFFICES AND PUBLIC OFFICERS

ARTICLE 1
GENERAL PROVISIONS

§ 128-3. Bargains for office void

All bargains, bonds and assurances made or given for the purchase or sale of any office whatsoever, the sale of which is contrary to law, shall be void.

History.
5 and 6 Edw. VI, c. 16, s. 3; R.C., c. 77, s. 2; Code, s. 1871; Rev., s. 2366; C.S., s. 3202

§ 128-4. Receiving compensation of subordinates for appointment or retention; removal

Any official or employee of this State or any political subdivision thereof, in whose office or under whose supervision are employed one or more subordinate officials or employees who shall, directly or indirectly, receive or demand, for himself or another, any part of the compensation of any such subordinate, as the price of appointment or retention of such subordinate, shall be guilty of a Class 1 misdemeanor: Provided, that this section shall not apply in cases in which an official or employee is given an allowance for the conduct of his office from which he is to compensate himself and his subordinates in such manner as he sees fit. Any person convicted of violating this section, in addition to the criminal penalties, shall be subject to removal from office. The procedure for removal shall be the same as that provided for removal of certain local officials from office by G.S. 128-16 to 128-20, inclusive.

History.
1937, c. 32, ss. 1, 2; 1993, c. 539, s. 942; 1994, Ex. Sess., c. 24, s. 14(c)

ARTICLE 2
REMOVAL OF UNFIT OFFICERS

§ 128-16. Officers subject to removal; for what offenses

Any sheriff or police officer shall be removed from office by the judge of the superior court,

resident in or holding the courts of the district where said officer is resident upon charges made in writing, and hearing thereunder, for the following causes:

(1) For willful or habitual neglect or refusal to perform the duties of his office.

(2) For willful misconduct or maladministration in office.

(3) For corruption.

(4) For extortion.

(5) Upon conviction of a felony.

(6) For intoxication, or upon conviction of being intoxicated.

History.
P.L. 1913, c. 761, s. 20; 1919, c. 288; C.S., s. 3208; 1959, c. 1286; 1961, c. 991; 1973, c. 108, s. 82

§ 128-17. Petition for removal; county attorney to prosecute

The complaint or petition shall be entitled in the name of the State of North Carolina, and may be filed upon the relation of any five qualified electors of the county in which the person charged is an officer, upon the approval of the county attorney of such county, or the district attorney of the district, or by any such officer upon his own motion. It shall be the duty of the county attorney or district attorney to appear and prosecute this proceeding.

History.
P.L. 1913, c. 761, s. 21; 1919, c. 288; C.S., s. 3209; 1973, c. 47, s. 2

§ 128-18. Petition filed with clerk; what it shall contain; answer

The accused shall be named as defendant, and the petition shall be signed by some elector, or by such officer. The petition shall state the charges against the accused, and may be amended, and shall be filed in the office of the clerk of the superior court of the county in which the person charged is an officer. The accused may at any time prior to the time fixed for hearing file in the office of the clerk of the superior court his answer, which shall be verified.

History.
P.L. 1913, c. 761, s. 22; 1919, c. 288; C.S., s. 3210

§ 128-19. Suspension pending hearing; how vacancy filled

Upon the filing of the petition in the office of the clerk of the superior court, and the presentation of the same to the judge, the judge may suspend the accused from office if in his judgment sufficient cause appear from the petition and affidavit, or affidavits, which may be presented in support of the charges contained therein. In case of suspension, as herein provided, the temporary vacancy shall be filled in the manner provided by law for filling of the vacancies in such office.

History.
P.L. 1913, c. 761, s. 23; 1919, c. 288; C.S., s. 3211

§ 128-20. Precedence on calendar; costs

In the trial of the cause in the superior court the cause shall be advanced and take precedence over all other causes upon the court calendar, and shall be heard at the next session after the petition is filed, provided the proceedings are filed in said court in time for said

action to be heard. The superior court shall fix the time of hearing. If the final termination of such proceedings be favorable to any accused officer, said officer shall be allowed the reasonable and necessary expense, including a reasonable attorney fee, to be fixed by the judge, he has incurred in making his defense, by the county, if he be a county officer, or by the city or town in which he holds office, if he be a city officer. If the action is instituted upon the complaint of citizens as herein provided, and it appears to the court that there was no reasonable cause for filing the complaint, the costs may be taxed against the complaining parties.

History.
P.L. 1913, c. 761, s. 24; 1919, c. 288; C.S., s. 3212; 1973, c. 108, s. 83

CHAPTER 130A
PUBLIC HEALTH

ARTICLE 16
POSTMORTEM INVESTIGATION AND DISPOSITION

PART 1
POSTMORTEM MEDICOLEGAL EXAMINATIONS AND SERVICES

§ 130A-383. Medical examiner jurisdiction

(a) Upon the death of any person resulting from violence, poisoning, accident, suicide or homicide; occurring suddenly when the deceased had been in apparent good health or when unattended by a physician; occurring in a jail, prison, correctional institution or in police custody; occurring in State facilities operated in accordance with Part 5 of Article 4 of Chapter 122C of the General Statutes; occurring pursuant to Article 19 of Chapter 15 of the General Statutes; or occurring under any suspicious, unusual or unnatural circumstance, the medical examiner of the county in which the body of the deceased is found shall be notified by a physician in attendance, hospital employee, law-enforcement officer, funeral home employee, emergency medical technician, relative or by any other person having suspicion of such a death. No person shall disturb the body at the scene of such a death until authorized by the medical examiner unless in the unavailability of the medical examiner it is determined by the appropriate law enforcement agency that the presence of the body at the scene would risk the integrity of the body or provide a hazard to the safety of others. For the limited purposes of this Part, expression of opinion that death has occurred may be made by a nurse, an emergency medical technician or any other competent person in the absence of a physician.

(b) The discovery of anatomical material suspected of being part of a human body shall be reported to the medical examiner of the county in which the material is found.

(c) Upon completion of the investigation and in accordance with the rules of the Commission, the medical examiner shall release the body to the next of kin or other interested person who will assume responsibility for final disposition.

History.
1955, c. 972, s. 1; 1957, c. 1357, s. 1; 1963, c. 492, s. 4; 1967, c. 1154, s. 1; 1983, c. 891, s. 2; 1989, c. 353, s. 1; 2008-131, s. 2

§ 130A-384. Notification concerning out-of-state body

When a body is brought into this State for disposal and there is reason to believe either that the death was not investigated properly or that there is not an adequate certificate of death, the body shall be reported to a medical examiner in the county where the body resides or to the Chief Medical Examiner. These deaths may be investigated by the same procedure as deaths occurring in this State under G.S. 130A-383.

History.
1983, c. 891, s. 2

§ 130A-385. Duties of medical examiner upon receipt of notice; reports; copies

(a) Upon receipt of a notification under G.S. 130A-383, the medical examiner shall take charge of the body, make inquiries regarding the cause and manner of death, reduce the findings to writing and promptly make a full report to the Chief Medical Examiner on forms prescribed for that purpose.

The Chief Medical Examiner or the county medical examiner is authorized to inspect and copy the medical records of the decedent whose death is under investigation. In addition, in an investigation conducted pursuant to this Article, the Chief Medical Examiner or the county medical examiner is authorized to inspect all physical evidence and documents which may be relevant to determining the cause and manner of death of the person whose death is under investigation, including decedent's personal possessions associated with the death, clothing, weapons, tissue and blood samples, cultures, medical equipment, X rays and other medical images. The Chief Medical Examiner or county medical examiner is further authorized to seek an administrative search warrant pursuant to G.S. 15-27.2 for the purpose of carrying out the duties imposed under this Article. In addition to the requirements of G.S. 15-27.2, no administrative search warrant shall be issued pursuant to this section unless the Chief Medical Examiner or county medical examiner submits an affidavit from the office of the district attorney in the district in which death occurred stating that the death in question is not under criminal investigation.

The Chief Medical Examiner shall provide directions as to the nature, character and extent of an investigation and appropriate forms for the required reports. The facilities of the central and district offices and their staff services shall be available to the medical examiners and designated pathologists in their investigations.

(b) The medical examiner shall complete a certificate of death, stating the name of the disease which in his opinion caused death. If the death was from external causes, the medical examiner shall state on the certificate of death the means of death, and whether, in the medical examiner's opinion, the manner of death was accident, suicide, homicide, execution by the State, or undetermined. The medical examiner shall also furnish any information as may be required by the State Registrar of Vital Statistics in order to properly classify the death.

(c) The Chief Medical Examiner shall have authority to amend a medical examiner death certificate.

(d) A copy of the report of the medical examiner investigation may be forwarded to the appropriate district attorney.

(e) In cases where death occurred due to an injury received in the course of the decedent's employment, the Chief Medical Examiner shall forward to the Commissioner of Labor a copy of the medical examiner's report of the investigation, including the location of the fatal injury and the name and address of the decedent's employer at the time of the fatal injury. The Chief Medical Examiner shall forward this report within 30 days of receipt of the information from the medical examiner.

(f) If a death occurred in a facility licensed subject to Article 2 or Article 3 of Chapter 122C of the General Statutes, or Articles 1 or 1A of Chapter 131D of the General Statutes, and the deceased was a client or resident of the facility or a recipient of facility services at the time of death, then the Chief Medical Examiner shall forward a copy of the medical examiner's report to the Secretary of Health and Human Services within 30 days of receipt of the report from the medical examiner.

History.
1955, c. 972, s. 1; 1957, c. 1357, s. 1; 1967, c. 1154, s. 1; 1973, c. 476, s. 128; 1977, 2nd Sess., c. 1145; 1983, c. 891, s. 2; 1989, c. 353, s. 2; c. 797; 1991 (Reg. Sess., 1992), c. 894, s. 6; 2000-129, s. 4

§ 130A-386. Subpoena authority

The Chief Medical Examiner and the county medical examiners are authorized to issue subpoenas for the attendance of persons and for the production of documents as may be required by their investigation.

History.
1983, c. 891, s. 2

§ 130A-387. Fees

For each investigation and prompt filing of the required report, the medical examiner shall receive a fee paid by the State. However, if the deceased is a resident of the county in which the death or fatal injury occurred, that county shall pay the fee. The fee shall be two hundred dollars ($ 200.00).

History.
1983, c. 891, s. 2; 1991, c. 463, s. 1; 2005-368, s. 1; 2015-241, s. 12E.6(a)

§ 130A-388. Medical examiner's permission necessary before embalming, burial and cremation

(a) No person knowing or having reason to know that a death may be under the jurisdiction of the medical examiner pursuant to G.S. 130A-383 or 130A-384, shall embalm, bury or cremate the body without the permission of the medical examiner.

(b) A dead body shall not be cremated or buried at sea unless a medical examiner certifies that he has inquired into the cause and the manner of death and has the opinion that no further examination is necessary. This subsection shall not apply to deaths occurring less than 24 hours after birth or to deaths of patients resulting only from natural disease and occurring in a licensed hospital unless the death falls within the jurisdiction of the medical examiner under G.S. 130A-383 or 130A-384. The Commission is authorized to adopt rules creating additional exceptions to this subsection. For making this certification, the medical examiner shall be entitled to a fee in an amount determined reasonable and appropriate by the Secretary, not to exceed fifty dollars ($ 50.00), to be paid by the applicant.

History.
1955, c. 972, s. 1; 1957, c. 1357, s. 1; 1963, c. 492, s. 4; 1967, c. 1154, s. 1; 1971, c. 444, s. 7; 1973, c. 873, s. 7; 1983, c. 891, s. 2

§ 130A-389. Autopsies

(a) If, in the opinion of the medical examiner investigating the case or of the Chief Medical Examiner, it is advisable and in the public interest that an autopsy or other study be made; or, if an autopsy or other study is requested by the district attorney of the county or by any superior court judge, an autopsy or other study shall be made by the Chief Medical Examiner or by a competent pathologist designated by the Chief Medical Examiner. A complete autopsy report of findings and interpretations, prepared on forms designated for the purpose, shall be submitted promptly to the Chief Medical Examiner.

Subject to the limitations of G.S. 130A-389.1 relating to photographs and video or audio recordings of an autopsy, a copy of the report shall be furnished to any person upon request. The fee for the autopsy or other study shall be two thousand eight hundred dollars ($ 2,800) to be paid as follows:

(1) Except as provided in subdivision (2) of this subsection, the county in which the deceased resided shall pay a fee of one thousand seven hundred fifty dollars ($ 1,750) and the State shall pay the remaining balance of one thousand fifty dollars ($ 1,050).

(2) If the death or fatal injury occurred outside the county in which the deceased resided, the State shall pay the entire fee in the amount of two thousand eight hundred dollars ($ 2,800).

(b) In deaths where the Chief Medical Examiner and the medical examiner investigating the case do not deem it advisable and in the public interest that an autopsy be performed, but the next-of-kin of the deceased requests that an autopsy be performed, the Chief Medical Examiner or a designated pathologist may perform the autopsy, unless the deceased's health care power of attorney granted authority for such decisions to the health care agent. If the Chief Medical Examiner or a designated pathologist performs the autopsy at the request of the next of kin, the cost shall be paid by the next of kin.

(c) When the next-of-kin of a decedent whose death does not fall under G.S. 130A-383 or 130A-384 requests that an autopsy be performed, the Chief Medical Examiner or a designated pathologist may perform that autopsy and the cost shall be paid by the next-of-kin.

(d) The report of autopsies performed pursuant to subsections (b) and (c) shall be a part of the decedents' medical records and therefore not public records open to inspection.

History.
1955, c. 972, s. 1; 1957, c. 1357, s. 1; 1967, c. 1154, s. 1; 1973, c. 47, s. 2; c. 476, s. 128; 1975, c. 9; 1981, c. 187, s. 7; c. 562, p. 5; 1983, c. 891, s. 2; 1991, c. 463, s. 2; 1998-212, s. 29A.10(a); 2005-351, s. 4; 2005-393, s. 2; 2006-226, s. 32; 2013-360, s. 12E.8(a); 2015-241, s. 12E.5(a)

§ 130A-389.1. Photographs and video or audio recordings made pursuant to autopsy

(a) Except as otherwise provided by law, any person may inspect and examine original photographs or video or audio recordings of an autopsy performed pursuant to G.S. 130A-389(a) at reasonable times and under reasonable supervision of the custodian of the photographs or recordings. Except as otherwise provided by this section, no custodian of the original recorded images shall furnish copies of photographs or video or audio recordings of an autopsy to the public. For purposes of this section, the Chief Medical Examiner shall be the custodian of all autopsy photographs or video or audio recordings unless the photographs or recordings were taken by or at the direction of an investigating medical examiner and the investigating medical examiner retains the original photographs or recordings. If the investigating medical examiner has retained the original photographs or recordings, then the investigating medical examiner is the custodian of the photographs or video or audio recordings and must allow the public to inspect and examine them in accordance with this subsection.

(b) The following public officials may obtain copies of autopsy photographs or video or audio recordings for official use only. These public officials shall not disclose the photographs or video or audio recordings to the public except as provided by law:

(1) The Chief Medical Examiner or a pathologist designated by the Chief Medical Examiner.

(2) Investigating Medical Examiner.

(3) District attorney.

(4) Superior court judge.

(5) Law enforcement officials conducting an investigation relating to the death.

A public official authorized by this subsection to obtain copies may provide a copy of the photograph or videotape to another person for the sole purpose of aiding in the identification of the deceased through publication of the photograph or videotape.

(c) The following persons may obtain copies of autopsy photographs or video or audio recordings but may not disclose the photographs or video or audio recordings to the public unless otherwise authorized by law:

(1) The personal representative of the estate of the deceased.

(2) A person authorized by an order issued in a special proceeding pursuant to subsection (d) of this section.

(3) A physician licensed to practice in North Carolina who uses a copy of the photographs or video or audio recording to confer with attorneys or others with a bona fide professional need to use or understand forensic science, provided that the physician promptly returns the copy to the custodian.

(4) After redacting all information identifying the decedent, including name, address, and social security number, and after anonymizing any physical recognition, a medical examiner, coroner, physician, or their designee who uses such material for:

a. Medical or scientific teaching or training purposes;

b. Teaching or training of law enforcement personnel;

c. Teaching or training of attorneys or others with a bona fide professional need to use or understand forensic science;

d. Conferring with medical or scientific experts in the field of forensic science; or

e. Publication in a scientific or medical journal or textbook.

A medical examiner, coroner, or physician who has in good faith complied with this subsection shall not be subject to any penalty under this section.

Any person who lawfully obtains a copy of a photograph or video or audio recording pursuant to this subsection shall be required to sign a statement acknowledging that they have received notice that any unauthorized disclosure of the photograph or video or audio recording is a Class 2 misdemeanor.

(d) A person who is denied access to copies of photographs or video or audio recordings, or who is restricted in the use the person may make of the photographs or video or audio recordings under this section, may commence a special proceeding in accordance with Article 33 of Chapter 1 of the General Statutes. Upon a showing of good cause, the clerk may issue an order authorizing the person to copy or disclose a photograph or video or audio recording of an autopsy and may prescribe any restrictions or stipulations that the clerk deems appropriate. In determining good cause, the clerk shall consider whether the disclosure is necessary for the public evaluation of governmental performance; the seriousness of the intrusion into the family's right to privacy and whether the disclosure is the least intrusive means available; and the availability of similar information in other public records, regardless of form. In all cases, the viewing, copying, listening to, or other handling of a photograph or video or audio recording of an autopsy shall be under the direct supervision of the Chief Medical Examiner or the Chief Medical Examiner's designee. A party aggrieved by an order of the clerk may appeal to the appropriate court in accordance with Article 27A of Chapter 1 of the General Statutes.

(e) The petitioner shall provide reasonable notice of the commencement of a special proceeding, as authorized by subsection (d) of this section, and reasonable notice of the opportunity to be present and heard at any hearing on the matter in accordance with Rule 5 of the Rules of Civil Procedure. The notice shall be provided to the personal representative of the estate of the deceased, if any, and to the surviving spouse of the deceased. If there is no surviving spouse, then the notice shall be provided to the deceased's parents, and if the deceased has no living parent, then to the adult child of the

deceased or to the guardian or custodian of a minor child of the deceased.

(f) This section does not apply to the use of autopsy photographs or video or audio recordings in a criminal, civil, or administrative proceeding except that nothing in this section prohibits a court or presiding officer, upon good cause shown, from restricting or otherwise controlling the disclosure to persons other than the parties and attorneys to the proceeding of an autopsy, crime scene, or similar photograph or video or audio recordings in the manner provided under this section.

(g) Any person who willfully and knowingly violates this section is guilty of a Class 2 misdemeanor, provided that more than one disclosure of the same item by the same person is not a separate offense.

(h) Any person not authorized by this section to obtain a copy of an autopsy photograph or video or audio recording, who knowingly and willfully removes, copies, or otherwise creates an image of an autopsy photograph or video or audio recording with intent to steal the same, is guilty of a Class 1 misdemeanor.

History.
2005-393, s. 3

§ 130A-390. Exhumations

(a) In any case of death described in G.S. 130A-383 or 130A-384 where the body is buried without investigation by a medical examiner as to the cause and manner of death or where sufficient cause develops for further investigation after a body is buried as determined by a county medical examiner or the Chief Medical Examiner, the Chief Medical Examiner shall authorize an investigation and send a report of the investigation with recommendations to the appropriate district attorney. The district attorney may forward the report to the superior court judge and petition for disinterment. The judge may order that the body be exhumed and that an autopsy be performed by the Chief Medical Examiner. A report of the autopsy and other pathological studies shall be delivered to the judge. The cost of the exhumation, autopsy, transportation and disposition of the body shall be paid by the State. However, if the deceased is a resident of the county in which death or fatal injury occurred, that county shall pay the cost.

(b) Any person may petition a judge of the superior court for an order of exhumation. Upon showing of sufficient cause, the judge may order the body exhumed. The cost incurred shall be assigned to the petitioner.

(c) Without applying for a judicial exhumation order, the next-of-kin of a deceased person may have the remains exhumed, examined by the Chief Medical Examiner and redisposed. The cost shall be paid by the next-of-kin.

History.
1983, c. 891, s. 2; 1991, c. 463, s. 3

N.C. Gen. Stat. § 130A-391

Repealed by Session Laws 2008-153, s. 3, effective August 2, 2008.

§ 130A-392. Reports and records as evidence

Reports of investigations made by a county medical examiner or by the Chief Medical Examiner and toxicology and autopsy reports made pursuant to this Part may be received as evidence in any court or other proceeding. Copies of records, photographs, laboratory findings and records in the Office of the Chief Medical Examiner, any county medical examiner or designated pathologist, when duly certified, shall have the same evidentiary value as the original.

History.
1967, c. 1154, s. 1; 1973, c. 476, s. 128; 1981, c. 187, s. 8; 1983, c. 891, s. 2

§ 130A-393. Rules

The Commission shall adopt rules to carry out the intent and purpose of this Part.

History.
1967, c. 1154, s. 1; 1973, c. 476, s. 128; 1981, c. 614, s. 15; 1983, c. 891, s. 2

§ 130A-394. Coroner to hold inquests

In every case requiring the medical examiner to be notified, as provided by G.S. 130A-383, the coroner shall be notified by the medical examiner, and the coroner shall hold an inquest and preliminary hearing in those instances as required in G.S. 152-7. The coroner shall file a written report of his investigation with the district attorney of the superior court and the medical examiner. The body shall remain in the custody and control of the medical examiner. However, if a county has abolished the office of coroner pursuant to the provisions of Chapter 152A at a time when Chapter 152A was in effect in the county: (i) The provisions of this Article relating to coroner shall not be applicable to the county, (ii) the provisions of G.S. 152A-9 shall remain in full force and effect in the county, and (iii) Chapter 152 of the General Statutes shall not be applicable in the county.

History.
1955, c. 972, s. 1; 1957, c. 1357, s. 1; 1967, c. 1154, s. 1; 1969, c. 299; 1973, c. 47, s. 2; 1983, c. 891, s. 2; 1985, c. 462, s. 1

§ 130A-395. Handling and transportation of bodies

(a) It shall be the duty of the physician licensed to practice medicine under Chapter 90 attending any person who dies and is known to have smallpox, plague, HIV infection, hepatitis B infection, rabies, or Jakob-Creutzfeldt to provide written notification to all individuals handling the body of the proper precautions to prevent infection. This written notification shall be provided to funeral service personnel at the time the body is removed from any hospital, nursing home, or other health care facility. When the patient dies in a location other than a health care facility, the attending physician shall notify the funeral service personnel verbally of the precautions required in subsections (b) and (c) as soon as the physician becomes aware of the death.

(b) The body of a person who died from smallpox or plague shall not be embalmed. The body shall be enclosed in a strong, tightly sealed outer case which will prevent leakage or escape of odors as soon as possible after death and before the body is removed from the hospital room, home, building, or other premises where the death occurred. This case shall not be reopened except with the consent of the local health director.

(c) Persons handling bodies of persons who died and were known to have HIV infection, hepatitis B infection, Jakob-Creutzfeldt, or rabies shall be provided written notification to observe blood and body fluid precautions.

History.
1989, c. 698, s. 4

PART 2
AUTOPSIES

§ 130A-398. Limitation on right to perform autopsy

The right to perform an autopsy shall be limited to those cases in which:

(1) The Chief Medical Examiner or a county medical examiner, acting pursuant to G.S. 130A-389, directs that an autopsy be performed;

(2) The Commission of Anatomy, acting pursuant to G.S. 130A-415, has given written consent for an autopsy to be performed on an unclaimed body;

(3) A prosecuting officer or district attorney, acting pursuant to G.S. 15-7 in case of homicide, directs that an autopsy be performed;

(4) The decedent directs in writing prior to death that an autopsy be performed upon the occurrence of the decedent's death;

(4a) The health care agent under a health care power of attorney with authority to make decisions with respect to autopsies requests that an autopsy be performed upon the deceased principal;

(5) The personal representative of the estate of the decedent requests that an autopsy be performed upon the decedent; or

(6) Any of the following persons, in order of priority, when persons in prior classes are not available at the time of death, and in the absence of actual notice of contrary indications by the decedent or actual opposition by a member of the same or prior class, authorizes an autopsy to be performed:

    a. The spouse;

    b. Any adult child or stepchild;

    c. Any parent or stepparents;

    d. Any adult sibling;

    e. A guardian of the person of the decedent at the time of the decedent's death;

    f. Any relative or person who accepts responsibility for final disposition of the body by other customary and lawful procedures;

    g. Any person under obligation to dispose of the body.

History.

1931, c. 152; 1933, c. 209; 1967, c. 1154, s. 4; 1969, c. 444; 1973, c. 47, s. 2; 1983, c. 891, s. 2; 2005-351, s. 5; 2006-226, s. 32

§ 130A-399. Postmortem examination of inmates of certain public institutions

Upon the death of any inmate of an institution maintained by the State, or a city, county, or other political subdivision of the State, for the care of individuals with a sickness, mental illness, or intellectual disability, the administrator of the institution in which the death occurs may authorize a postmortem examination of the deceased person. The examination shall be of a scope and nature necessary to promote knowledge of the human organism and its disorders.

History.

1943, c. 87, s. 1; 1983, c. 891, s. 2; 2018-47, s. 10(a)

§ 130A-400. Written consent for postmortem examinations required

An administrator of an institution shall not authorize a postmortem examination described in G.S. 130A-399 without first securing the written consent of the deceased person's spouse, one of the next-of-kin or nearest known relative, or other person charged by law with the duty of burial, in the order named and as known. A copy of the written consent shall be filed in the office of the administrator of the institution where the inmate died.

History.

1943, c. 87, s. 3; 1983, c. 891, s. 2

§ 130A-401. Postmortem examinations in certain medical schools

The postmortem examinations and studies authorized by G.S. 130A-399 may be made in the laboratories of medical schools of colleges and universities on conditions established by the administrator.

History.

1943, c. 87, s. 2; 1983, c. 891, s. 2

ARTICLE 22
A TERRORIST INCIDENT USING NUCLEAR, BIOLOGICAL, OR CHEMICAL AGENTS

§ 130A-475. Suspected terrorist attack

(a) If the State Health Director reasonably suspects that a public health threat may exist and that the threat may have been caused by a terrorist incident using nuclear, biological, or chemical agents, the State Health Director is authorized to order any of the following:

(1) Require any person or animal to submit to examinations and tests to determine possible exposure to the nuclear, biological, or chemical agents.

(2) Test any real or personal property necessary to determine the presence of nuclear, biological, or chemical agents.

(3) Evacuate or close any real property, including any building, structure, or land when necessary to investigate suspected contamination of the property. The period of closure during an investigation shall not exceed 10 calendar days. If the State Health Director determines that a longer period of closure is necessary to complete the investigation, the Director may institute an action in superior court to order the property to remain closed until the investigation is completed.

(4) Limit the freedom of movement or action of a person or animal that is contaminated with, or reasonably suspected of being contaminated with, a biological, chemical or nuclear agent that may be conveyed to other persons or animals.

(5) Limit access by any person or animal to an area or facility that is housing persons or animals whose movement or action has been limited under subdivision (4) of this subsection or to an area or facility that is contaminated with, or reasonably suspected of being contaminated with, a biological, chemical or nuclear agent that may be conveyed to other persons or animals. Nothing in this subdivision shall be construed to restrict the access of authorized health care, law enforcement, or emergency medical services personnel to quarantine or isolation premises as necessary in conducting their duties.

(b) The authority under subsection (a) of this section shall be exercised only when and so long as a public health threat may exist, all other reasonable means for correcting the problem have been exhausted, and no less restrictive alternative exists. Before applying the authority under subdivision (4) or (5) of subsection (a) of this section to livestock or poultry for the purpose of preventing the direct or indirect conveyance of a biological, chemical or nuclear agent to persons, the State Health Director shall consult with the State Veterinarian in the Department of Agriculture and Consumer Services.

The period of limited freedom of movement or access under subdivisions (4) and (5) of subsection (a) of this section shall not exceed 30 calendar days. Any person substantially affected by that limitation may institute, in superior court in Wake County or in the county in which the limitation is imposed, an action to review the limitation. The State Health Director shall give the persons known by the State Health Director to be substantially affected by the limitation reasonable notice under the circumstances of the right to institute an action to review the limitation. If a person or a person's representative requests a hearing, the hearing shall be held within 72 hours of the filing of the request, excluding Saturdays and Sundays. The person substantially affected by that limitation is entitled to be represented by counsel of the person's own choice or if the person is indigent, the person shall be represented by counsel appointed in accordance with Article 36 of Chapter 7A of the General Statutes and the rules adopted by the Office of Indigent Defense Services. The court shall reduce or terminate the limitation unless it determines, by the preponderance of the evidence, that the limitation is reasonably necessary to prevent or limit the conveyance of biological, chemical or nuclear agents to others, and may apply such conditions to the limitation as the court deems reasonable and necessary.

If the State Health Director determines that a 30-calendar-day limitation on freedom of movement or access is not adequate to protect the public health, the State Health Director must institute in superior court in the county in which the limitation is imposed, an action to obtain an order extending the period limiting the freedom of movement or access. If the person substantially affected by the limitation has already instituted an action in superior court in Wake County, the State Health Director must institute the action in superior court in Wake County or as a counterclaim in the pending case. The court shall continue the limitation for a period not to exceed 30 days, subject to conditions it deems reasonable and necessary, if it determines by the preponderance of the evidence, that additional limitation is reasonably necessary to prevent or limit the conveyance of biological, chemical, or nuclear agents to others. The court order shall specify the period of time the limitation is to be continued and shall provide for automatic termination of the order upon written determination by the State Health Director or local health director that the limitation on freedom of movement or access is no longer necessary to protect the public health. In addition, where the petitioner can prove by a preponderance of the evidence that the limitation on freedom of movement or access was not or is no longer needed for protection of the public health, the person so limited may move the trial court to reconsider its order extending the limitation on freedom of movement or access before the time for the order otherwise expires and may seek immediate or expedited termination of the order. Before the expiration of an order issued under this section, the State Health Director may move to continue the order for additional periods not to exceed 30 days each.

(c) If the State Health Director reasonably suspects that there exists a public health threat that may have been caused by a terrorist incident using nuclear, biological, or chemical agents, the State Health Director shall notify the Governor and the Secretary of Public Safety. If the Secretary of Public Safety reasonably suspects that a public health threat may exist and that the threat may have been caused by a terrorist incident using nuclear, biological, or chemical agents, the Secretary shall notify the Governor and the State Health Director.

(d) For the purpose of this Article, the term "public health threat" means a situation that is likely to cause an immediate risk to human life, an immediate risk of serious physical injury or illness, or an immediate risk of serious adverse health effects.

(e) Nothing in this section shall limit any authority otherwise granted to local or State public health officials under this Chapter.

History.
2002-179, s. 1; 2004-80, s. 3; 2004-199, s. 33; 2011-145, s. 19.1(g)

§ 130A-476. Access to health information

(a) Notwithstanding any other provision of law, a health care provider, a person in charge of a health care facility, or a unit of State or local government may report to the State Health Director or a local health director any events that may indicate the existence of a case or outbreak of an illness, condition, or health hazard that may have been caused by a terrorist incident using nuclear, biological, or chemical agents. Events that may be reported include unusual types or numbers of symptoms or illnesses presented to the provider, unusual trends in health care visits, or unusual trends in prescriptions or purchases of over-the-counter pharmaceuticals. To the extent practicable, a person who makes a report under this subsection shall not disclose personally identifiable information. A person disclosing or not disclosing information pursuant to this subsection is immune from any civil or criminal liability that might otherwise be incurred or imposed based on the disclosure or lack of disclosure provided that the health care provider was acting in good faith and without malice. In any proceeding involving liability, good faith and lack of malice are presumed. Notwithstanding the foregoing, if a health care provider or unit of State or local government willfully does not disclose information pursuant to this subsection, the immunity from civil or criminal liability provided under this subsection shall not be available if the person had actual knowledge that a condition or illness was caused by use of a nuclear, biological, or chemical weapon of mass destruction as defined in G.S. 14-288.21(c).

(b) The State Health Director may issue a temporary order requiring health care providers to report symptoms, diseases, conditions, trends in use of health care services, or other health-related information when necessary to conduct a public health investigation or surveillance of an illness, condition, or health hazard that may have been caused by a terrorist incident using nuclear, biological, or chemical agents. The order shall specify which health care providers must report, what information is to be reported, and the period of time for which reporting is required. The period of time for which reporting is required pursuant to a temporary order shall not exceed 90 days. The Commission may adopt rules to continue the reporting requirement when necessary to protect the public health.

(c) Health care providers and persons in charge of health care facilities or laboratories shall, upon request and proper identification, permit the State Health Director or a local health director to examine, review, and obtain a copy of records containing confidential or protected health information, or a summary of pertinent portions of those records, (i) that pertain to a report authorized by subsection (a) or required by subsection (b) of this section, or (ii) that, in the opinion of the State Health Director or local health director, are necessary for an investigation of a case or outbreak of an illness, condition, or health hazard that may have been caused by a terrorist incident using nuclear, biological, or chemical agents.

(d) A person who makes a report pursuant to subsection (b) of this section or permits examination, review, or copying of medical records pursuant to subsection (c) of this section is immune from any civil or criminal liability that otherwise might be incurred or imposed as a result of complying with those subsections.

(e) Confidential or protected health information received by the State Health Director or a local health director pursuant to this section shall be confidential and shall not be released, except when the release is:

(1) Made pursuant to any other provision of law;

(2) To another federal, state, or local public health agency for the purpose of preventing or controlling a public health threat; or

(3) To a court or law enforcement official or law enforcement officer for the purpose of enforcing the provisions of this Chapter or for the purpose of investigating a terrorist incident using nuclear, biological, or chemical agents. A court or law enforcement official or law enforcement officer who receives the information shall not disclose it further, except (i) when necessary to conduct an investigation of a terrorist incident using nuclear, biological, or chemical agents, or (ii) when the State Health Director or a local health director seeks the assistance of the court or law enforcement official or law enforcement officer in preventing or controlling the public health threat and expressly authorizes the disclosure as necessary for that purpose.

(f) Repealed by Session Laws 2004-124, s. 10.34(a), effective January 1, 2005.

(g) In this section the following terms shall include:

(1) "Health care provider" includes a physician licensed to practice medicine in North Carolina or a person who is licensed, certified, or credentialed to practice or provide health care services, including, but not limited to, pharmacists, dentists, physician assistants, registered nurses, licensed

practical nurses, advanced practice nurses, chiropractors, respiratory care therapists, and emergency medical technicians; and

(2) "Health care facility" includes hospitals, skilled nursing facilities, intermediate care facilities, psychiatric facilities, rehabilitation facilities, home health agencies, ambulatory surgical facilities, or any other health care related facility, whether publicly or privately owned.

History.
2002-179, s. 1; 2004-80, s. 7; 2004-124, s. 10.34(a)

§ 130A-477. Abatement of public health threat

If it is determined that a public health threat may exist because of the contamination of property caused by a terrorist incident using nuclear, biological, or chemical agents, the State Health Director may order any action to abate that public health threat. To the extent that any owner, lessee, operator, or other person in control of the property is innocent of culpability in the creation of the public health threat, that person shall not be responsible for the costs of abating the public health threat.

History.
2002-179, s. 1

§ 130A-478. Tort liability

Article 31 of Chapter 143 applies to negligent acts committed by any officer, employee, involuntary servant or agent of the State acting pursuant to this Article.

History.
2002-179, s. 1

§ 130A-479. Biological agents registry; rules; penalties

(a) The Department shall establish and administer a program for the registration of biological agents. The biological agents registry shall identify the biological agents possessed and maintained by any person in this State and shall contain other information required under rules adopted by the Commission.

(b) The following definitions apply in this section:

(1) "Biological agent" means:

a. Any select agent that is a microorganism, virus, bacterium, fungus, rickettsia, or toxin listed in Appendix A of Part 72 of Title 42 of the Code of Federal Regulations.

b. Any genetically modified microorganisms or genetic elements from an organism on Appendix A of Part 72 of Title 42 of the Code of Federal Regulations, shown to produce or encode for a factor associated with a disease.

c. Any genetically modified microorganisms or genetic elements that contain nucleic acid sequences coding for any of the toxins listed on Appendix A of Part 72 of Title 42 of the Code of Federal Regulations, or their toxic submits.

(2) "Person" means any association, business, corporation, facility, firm, individual, institution of higher education, organization, partnership, society, State agency, or other legal entity.

(c) The Commission shall adopt rules for the implementation of the registry program, as follows:

(1) Determining and listing the biological agents required to be reported under this section.

(2) Designating persons required to make reports and specific information required to be reported including time limits for reporting, form of reports, and to whom reports shall be submitted.

(3) Providing for the release of information in the registry to State and federal law enforcement agencies and the United States Centers for Disease Control and Prevention pursuant to a communicable disease investigation commenced or conducted by the Department, the Commission, or other state or federal law enforcement agency having investigatory authority, or in connection with any investigation involving release, theft, or loss of biological agents.

(4) Establishing a system of safeguards that requires persons possessing and maintaining biological agents subject to this section to comply with the same federal standards that apply to persons registered to possess the same agents under federal law.

(5) Establishing a process for persons that possess and maintain biological agents to alert appropriate authorities of unauthorized possession or attempted possession of biological agents. The rules shall designate appropriate authorities for receipt of alerts from these persons.

(d) Any person that possesses and maintains any biological agent required to be reported under this section shall report to the Department the information required by the Commission for inclusion in the biological agent registry.

(e) Except as otherwise provided in this section, information prepared for or maintained in the registry under this section shall be confidential and shall not be a public record under G.S. 132-1. The Department may, in accordance with rules adopted by the Commission, release information contained in the biological agent registry for the purpose of conducting or aiding in a communicable disease investigation. The Department shall cooperate with and may share information contained in the biological agent registry with the United States Centers for Disease Control and Prevention, and state and federal law enforcement agencies in any investigation involving the release, theft, or loss of a biological agent required to be reported under this section. Release of information from the registry as authorized under this subsection shall not render the information released a public record under G.S. 132-1. Release of information from the registry as authorized under this subsection also shall not render the information prepared for or maintained in the registry a public record under G.S. 132-1.

(f) The Department shall impose a civil penalty for a willful or knowing violation of this section in the amount of up to one thousand dollars ($ 1,000). Each day of a continuing violation shall be a separate offense. Any person wishing to contest a penalty shall be entitled to an administrative hearing in accordance with Chapter 150B of the General Statutes.

History.
2001-469, s. 1; 2002-179, s. 2(a)

CHAPTER 132
PUBLIC RECORDS

§ 132-1.4. Criminal investigations; intelligence information records; Innocence Inquiry Commission records

(a) Records of criminal investigations conducted by public law enforcement agencies, records of criminal intelligence information compiled by public law enforcement agencies, and records of investigations conducted by the North Carolina Innocence Inquiry Commission, are not public records as defined by G.S. 132-1. Records of criminal investigations conducted by public law enforcement agencies or records of criminal intelligence information may be released by order of a court of competent jurisdiction.

(b) As used in this section:

(1) "Records of criminal investigations" means all records or any information that pertains to a person or group of persons that is compiled by public law enforcement agencies for the purpose of attempting to prevent or solve violations of the law, including information derived from witnesses, laboratory tests, surveillance, investigators, confidential informants, photographs, and measurements. The term also includes any records, worksheets, reports, or analyses prepared or conducted by the North Carolina State Crime Laboratory at the request of any public law enforcement agency in connection with a criminal investigation.

(2) "Records of criminal intelligence information" means records or information that pertain to a person or group of persons that is compiled by a public law enforcement agency in an effort to anticipate, prevent, or monitor possible violations of the law.

(3) "Public law enforcement agency" means a municipal police department, a county police department, a sheriff's department, a company police agency commissioned by the Attorney General pursuant to G.S. 74E-1, et seq., and any State or local agency, force, department, or unit responsible for investigating, preventing, or solving violations of the law.

(4) "Violations of the law" means crimes and offenses that are prosecutable in the criminal courts in this State or the United States and infractions as defined in G.S. 14-3.1.

(5) "Complaining witness" means an alleged victim or other person who reports a violation or apparent violation of the law to a public law enforcement agency.

(c) Notwithstanding the provisions of this section, and unless otherwise prohibited by law, the following information shall be public records within the meaning of G.S. 132-1.

(1) The time, date, location, and nature of a violation or apparent violation of the law reported to a public law enforcement agency.

(2) The name, sex, age, address, employment, and alleged violation of law of a person arrested, charged, or indicted.

(3) The circumstances surrounding an arrest, including the time and place of the arrest, whether the arrest involved resistance, possession or use of weapons, or pursuit, and a description of any items seized in connection with the arrest.

(4) The contents of "911" and other emergency telephone calls received by or on behalf of public law enforcement agencies, except for such contents that reveal the natural voice, name, address, telephone number, or other information that may identify the caller, victim, or witness. In order to protect the identity of the complaining witness, the contents of "911" and other emergency telephone calls may be released pursuant to this section in the form of a written transcript or altered voice reproduction; provided that the original shall be provided under process to be used as evidence in any relevant civil or criminal proceeding.

(5) The contents of communications between or among employees of public law enforcement agencies that are broadcast over the public airways.

(6) The name, sex, age, and address of a complaining witness.

(d) A public law enforcement agency shall temporarily withhold the name or address of a complaining witness if release of the information is reasonably likely to pose a threat to the mental health, physical health, or personal safety of the complaining witness or materially compromise a continuing or future criminal investigation or criminal intelligence operation. Information temporarily withheld under this subsection shall be made available for release to the public in accordance with G.S. 132-6 as soon as the circumstances that justify withholding it cease to exist. Any person denied access to information withheld under this subsection may apply to a court of competent jurisdiction for an order compelling disclosure of the information. In such action, the court shall balance the interests of the public in disclosure against the interests of the law enforcement agency and the alleged victim in withholding the information. Actions brought pursuant to this subsection shall be set down for immediate hearing, and subsequent proceedings in such actions shall be accorded priority by the trial and appellate courts.

(e) If a public law enforcement agency believes that release of information that is a public record under subdivisions (c)(1) through (c)(5) of this section will jeopardize the right of the State to prosecute a defendant or the right of a defendant to receive a fair trial or will undermine an ongoing or future investigation, it may seek an order from a court of competent jurisdiction to prevent disclosure of the information. In such action the law enforcement agency shall have the burden of showing by a preponderance of the evidence that disclosure of the information in question will jeopardize the right of the State to prosecute a defendant or the right of a defendant to receive a fair trial or will undermine an ongoing or future investigation. Actions brought pursuant to this subsection shall be set down for immediate hearing, and subsequent proceedings in such actions shall be accorded priority by the trial and appellate courts.

(f) Nothing in this section shall be construed as authorizing any public law enforcement agency to prohibit or prevent another public agency having custody of a public record from permitting the inspection, examination, or copying of such public record in compliance with G.S. 132-6. The use of a public record in connection with a criminal investigation or the gathering of criminal intelligence shall not affect its status as a public record.

(g) Disclosure of records of criminal investigations and criminal intelligence information that have been transmitted to a district attorney or other attorney authorized to prosecute a violation of law shall be governed by this section and Chapter 15A of the General Statutes.

(h) Nothing in this section shall be construed as requiring law enforcement agencies to disclose the following:

(1) Information that would not be required to be disclosed under Chapter 15A of the General Statutes; or

(2) Information that is reasonably likely to identify a confidential informant.

(i) Law enforcement agencies shall not be required to maintain any tape recordings of "911" or other communications for more than 30 days from the time of the call, unless a court of competent jurisdiction orders a portion sealed.

(j) When information that is not a public record under the provisions of this section is deleted from a document, tape recording, or other record, the law enforcement agency shall make clear that a deletion has been made. Nothing in this subsection shall authorize the destruction of the original record.

(k) The following court records are public records and may be withheld only when sealed by court order: arrest and search warrants that have been returned by law enforcement

agencies, indictments, criminal summons, and nontestimonial identification orders.

(*l*) Records of investigations of alleged child abuse shall be governed by Article 29 of Chapter 7B of the General Statutes.

History.
1993, c. 461, s. 1; 1998-202, s. 13(jj); 2006-184, s. 7; 2010-171, s. 5; 2011-321, s. 1; 2013-360, s. 17.6(o)

§ 132-1.4A. Law enforcement agency recordings

(a) **Definitions.** -- The following definitions apply in this section:

(1) **Body-worn camera.** -- An operational video or digital camera or other electronic device, including a microphone or other mechanism for allowing audio capture, affixed to the uniform or person of law enforcement agency personnel and positioned in a way that allows the camera or device to capture interactions the law enforcement agency personnel has with others.

(2) **Custodial law enforcement agency.** -- The law enforcement agency that owns or leases or whose personnel operates the equipment that created the recording at the time the recording was made.

(3) **Dashboard camera.** -- A device or system installed or used in a law enforcement agency vehicle that electronically records images or audio depicting interaction with others by law enforcement agency personnel. This term does not include body-worn cameras.

(4) **Disclose or disclosure.** -- To make a recording available for viewing or listening to by the person requesting disclosure, at a time and location chosen by the custodial law enforcement agency. This term does not include the release of a recording.

(5) **Personal representative.** -- A parent, court-appointed guardian, spouse, or attorney licensed in North Carolina of a person whose image or voice is in the recording. If a person whose image or voice is in the recording is deceased, the term also means the personal representative of the estate of the deceased person; the deceased person's surviving spouse, parent, or adult child; the deceased person's attorney licensed in North Carolina; or the parent or guardian of a surviving minor child of the deceased.

(6) **Recording.** -- A visual, audio, or visual and audio recording captured by a body-worn camera, a dashboard camera, or any other video or audio recording device operated by or on behalf of a law enforcement agency or law enforcement agency

personnel when carrying out law enforcement responsibilities. This term does not include any video or audio recordings of interviews regarding agency internal investigations or interviews or interrogations of suspects or witnesses.

(7) **Release.** -- To provide a copy of a recording.

(8) **Serious bodily injury.** -- A bodily injury that creates a substantial risk of death, or that causes serious permanent disfigurement, coma, a permanent or protracted condition that causes extreme pain, or permanent or protracted loss or impairment of the function of any bodily member or organ, or that results in prolonged hospitalization.

(b) **Public Record and Personnel Record Classification.** -- Recordings are not public records as defined by G.S. 132-1. Recordings are not personnel records as defined in Part 7 of Chapter 126 of the General Statutes, G.S. 160A-168, or G.S. 153A-98.

(b1) **Immediate Disclosure.** -- When requested by submission of the notarized form described in subsection (b2) of this section to the head of a law enforcement agency, any portion of a recording in the custody of a law enforcement agency which depicts a death or serious bodily injury shall, upon order of the court pursuant to subsection (b3) of this section, be disclosed to a personal representative of the deceased, the injured individual, or a personal representative on behalf of the injured individual. Any disclosure ordered by the court pursuant to subsection (b3) of this section shall be done by the agency in a private setting. A person who receives disclosure as ordered by the court pursuant to subsection (b3) of this section shall not record or copy the recording. Except as provided in subsection (b3) of this section, the portion of the recording relevant to the death or serious bodily injury shall not be edited or redacted.

(b2) **Notarized Form.** -- A person requesting disclosure pursuant to subsection (b1) of this section must submit a signed and notarized form provided by the law enforcement agency. The form shall be developed by the Administrative Office of the Courts and shall include notice that, if disclosed, the recording may not be recorded or copied, or if unlawfully recorded or copied may not be knowingly disseminated, and notice of the criminal penalties provided in subsection (b4) of this section.

(b3) **Immediate Disclosure Review.** -- No later than three business days from receipt of the notarized form requesting immediate disclosure pursuant to subsection (b1) of this section, a law enforcement agency shall file a petition in the superior court in any county where any portion of the recording was made for issuance of a court order regarding disclosure of the recording requested pursuant to subsection (b1) of this section and shall also deliver a copy of the petition and a copy of the recording, which shall remain confidential unless the court issues an order of disclosure pursuant to this section, to the senior resident superior court judge for that superior court district or their designee. There shall be no fee for filing the petition. The court shall conduct an in-camera review of the recording and shall enter an order within seven business days of the filing of the petition instructing that the recording be (i) immediately disclosed without editing or redaction; (ii) immediately disclosed with editing or redaction; (iii) disclosed at a later date, with or without editing or redaction; or (iv) not disclosed to the person or persons seeking disclosure. In determining whether the recording may be disclosed pursuant to this section, the court shall consider the following factors:

(1) If the person requesting disclosure of the recording is a person authorized to receive disclosure pursuant to subsection (c) of this section.

(2) If the recording contains information that is otherwise confidential or exempt from disclosure or release under State or federal law.

(3) If disclosure would reveal information regarding a person that is of a highly sensitive and personal nature.

(4) If disclosure may harm the reputation or jeopardize the safety of a person.

(5) If disclosure would create a serious threat to the fair, impartial, and orderly administration of justice.

(6) If confidentiality is necessary to protect either an active or inactive internal or criminal investigation or potential internal or criminal investigation.

In any proceeding pursuant to this subsection, the following persons shall be notified and those persons, or their designated representative, shall be given an opportunity to be heard at any proceeding: (i) the head of the custodial law enforcement agency, (ii) any law enforcement agency personnel whose image or voice is in the portion of the recording requested to be disclosed and the head of that person's employing law enforcement agency, (iii) the District Attorney, (iv) the investigating law enforcement agency, and (v) the party requesting the disclosure. The court may order any conditions or restrictions on the disclosure that the court deems appropriate.

Petitions filed pursuant to this subsection shall be scheduled for hearing as soon as practicable, and the court shall issue an order pursuant to the provisions of this subsection no later than seven business days after the filing of the petition. Any subsequent proceedings in such actions shall be accorded priority by the trial and appellate courts.

If disclosure of a recording is denied based on subdivision (6) of this subsection, the court shall schedule a subsequent hearing, to be held no more than 20 business days after the issuance of the order, to reconsider whether the recording should be disclosed.

(b4) Any person who willfully records, copies, or attempts to record or copy a recording disclosed pursuant to subsection (b1) of this section shall be guilty of a Class 1 misdemeanor. Any person who knowingly disseminates a recording or a copy of a recording disclosed pursuant to subsection (b1) of this section is guilty of a Class I felony.

(c) **Disclosure; General.** -- Recordings in the custody of a law enforcement agency shall be disclosed only as provided by this section. Recordings depicting a death or serious bodily injury shall only be disclosed as provided in subsections (b1) through (b3) of this section.

A person requesting disclosure of a recording must make a written request to the head of the custodial law enforcement agency that states the date and approximate time of the activity captured in the recording or otherwise identifies the activity with reasonable particularity sufficient to identify the recording to which the request refers.

The head of the custodial law enforcement agency may only disclose a recording to the following:

(1) A person whose image or voice is in the recording.

(2) A personal representative of an adult person whose image or voice is in the recording, if the adult person has consented to the disclosure.

(3) A personal representative of a minor or of an adult person under lawful guardianship whose image or voice is in the recording.

(4) A personal representative of a deceased person whose image or voice is in the recording.

(5) A personal representative of an adult person who is incapacitated and unable to provide consent to disclosure.

When disclosing the recording, the law enforcement agency shall disclose only those portions of the recording that are relevant to the person's request. A person who receives disclosure pursuant to this subsection shall not record or copy the recording.

(d) **Disclosure; Factors for Consideration.** -- Upon receipt of the written request for disclosure, as promptly as possible, the custodial law enforcement agency must either

disclose the portion of the recording relevant to the person's request or notify the requestor of the custodial law enforcement agency's decision not to disclose the recording to the requestor.

The custodial law enforcement agency may consider any of the following factors in determining if a recording is disclosed:

(1) If the person requesting disclosure of the recording is a person authorized to receive disclosure pursuant to subsection (c) of this section.

(2) If the recording contains information that is otherwise confidential or exempt from disclosure or release under State or federal law.

(3) If disclosure would reveal information regarding a person that is of a highly sensitive personal nature.

(4) If disclosure may harm the reputation or jeopardize the safety of a person.

(5) If disclosure would create a serious threat to the fair, impartial, and orderly administration of justice.

(6) If confidentiality is necessary to protect either an active or inactive internal or criminal investigation or potential internal or criminal investigation.

(e) **Appeal of Disclosure Denial.** -- If a law enforcement agency denies disclosure pursuant to subsection (d) of this section, or has failed to provide disclosure more than three business days after the request for disclosure, the person seeking disclosure may apply to the superior court in any county where any portion of the recording was made for a review of the denial of disclosure. The court may conduct an in-camera review of the recording. The court may order the disclosure of the recording only if the court finds that the law enforcement agency abused its discretion in denying the request for disclosure. The court may only order disclosure of those portions of the recording that are relevant to the person's request. A person who receives disclosure pursuant to this subsection shall not record or copy the recording. An order issued pursuant to this subsection may not order the release of the recording.

In any proceeding pursuant to this subsection, the following persons shall be notified and those persons, or their designated representative, shall be given an opportunity to be heard at any proceeding: (i) the head of the custodial law enforcement agency, (ii) any law enforcement agency personnel whose image or voice is in the recording and the head of that person's employing law enforcement agency, and (iii) the District Attorney. Actions brought pursuant to this subsection shall be set down for hearing as soon as practicable, and subsequent proceedings in such actions shall be accorded priority by the trial and appellate courts.

(f) **Release of Recordings to Certain Persons; Expedited Process.** -- Notwithstanding the provisions of subsection (g) of this section, a person authorized to receive disclosure pursuant to subsection (c) of this section, or the custodial law enforcement agency, may petition the superior court in any county where any portion of the recording was made for an order releasing the recording to a person authorized to receive disclosure. There shall be no fee for filing the petition which shall be filed on a form approved by the Administrative Office of the Courts and shall state the date and approximate time of the activity captured in the recording, or otherwise identify the activity with reasonable particularity sufficient to identify the recording. If the petitioner is a person authorized to receive disclosure, notice and an opportunity to be heard shall be given to the head of the custodial law enforcement agency. Petitions filed pursuant to this subsection shall be set down for hearing as soon as practicable and shall be accorded priority by the court.

The court shall first determine if the person to whom release of the recording is requested is a person authorized to receive disclosure pursuant to subsection (c) of this section. In making this determination, the court may conduct an in-camera review of the recording and may, in its discretion, allow the petitioner to be present to assist in identifying the image or voice in the recording that authorizes disclosure to the person to whom release is requested. If the court determines that the person is not authorized to receive disclosure pursuant to subsection (c) of this section, there shall be no right of appeal and the petitioner may file an action for release pursuant to subsection (g) of this section.

If the court determines that the person to whom release of the recording is requested is a person authorized to receive disclosure pursuant to subsection (c) of this section, the court shall consider the standards set out in subsection (g) of this section and any other standards the court deems relevant in determining whether to order the release of all or a portion of the recording. The court may conduct an in-camera review of the recording. The court shall release only those portions of the recording that are relevant to the person's request and may place any conditions or restrictions on the release of the recording that the court, in its discretion, deems appropriate.

(g) **Release of Recordings; General; Court Order Required.** -- Recordings in the custody of a law enforcement agency shall only be released pursuant to court order. Any custodial law enforcement agency or any person requesting release of a recording may file an action in the superior court in any county where any portion of the recording was made for an

order releasing the recording. The request for release must state the date and approximate time of the activity captured in the recording, or otherwise identify the activity with reasonable particularity sufficient to identify the recording to which the action refers. The court may conduct an in-camera review of the recording. In determining whether to order the release of all or a portion of the recording, in addition to any other standards the court deems relevant, the court shall consider the applicability of all of the following standards:

(1) Release is necessary to advance a compelling public interest.

(2) The recording contains information that is otherwise confidential or exempt from disclosure or release under State or federal law.

(3) The person requesting release is seeking to obtain evidence to determine legal issues in a current or potential court proceeding.

(4) Release would reveal information regarding a person that is of a highly sensitive personal nature.

(5) Release may harm the reputation or jeopardize the safety of a person.

(6) Release would create a serious threat to the fair, impartial, and orderly administration of justice.

(7) Confidentiality is necessary to protect either an active or inactive internal or criminal investigation or potential internal or criminal investigation.

(8) There is good cause shown to release all portions of a recording.

The court shall release only those portions of the recording that are relevant to the person's request, and may place any conditions or restrictions on the release of the recording that the court, in its discretion, deems appropriate.

In any proceeding pursuant to this subsection, the following persons shall be notified and those persons, or their designated representative, shall be given an opportunity to be heard at any proceeding: (i) the head of the custodial law enforcement agency, (ii) any law enforcement agency personnel whose image or voice is in the recording and the head of that person's employing law enforcement agency, and (iii) the District Attorney. Actions brought pursuant to this subsection shall be set down for hearing as soon as practicable, and subsequent proceedings in such actions shall be accorded priority by the trial and appellate courts.

(h) **Release of Recordings; Law Enforcement Purposes.** -- Notwithstanding the requirements of subsections (c), (f), and (g) of this section, a custodial law enforcement agency

Chapter 132

shall disclose or release a recording to a district attorney (i) for review of potential criminal charges, (ii) in order to comply with discovery requirements in a criminal prosecution, (iii) for use in criminal proceedings in district court, or (iv) for any other law enforcement purpose, and may disclose or release a recording for any of the following purposes:

(1) For law enforcement training purposes.

(2) Within the custodial law enforcement agency for any administrative, training, or law enforcement purpose.

(3) To another law enforcement agency for law enforcement purposes.

(4) For suspect identification or apprehension.

(5) To locate a missing or abducted person.

(i) **Retention of Recordings. --** Any recording subject to the provisions of this section shall be retained for at least the period of time required by the applicable records retention and disposition schedule developed by the Department of Natural and Cultural Resources, Division of Archives and Records.

(j) **Agency Policy Required. --** Each law enforcement agency that uses body-worn cameras or dashboard cameras shall adopt a policy applicable to the use of those cameras.

(k) No civil liability shall arise from compliance with the provisions of this section, provided that the acts or omissions are made in good faith and do not constitute gross negligence, willful or wanton misconduct, or intentional wrongdoing.

(l) **Fee for Copies. --** A law enforcement agency may charge a fee to offset the cost incurred by it to make a copy of a recording for

release. The fee shall not exceed the actual cost of making the copy.

(m) **Attorneys' Fees. --** The court may not award attorneys' fees to any party in any action brought pursuant to this section.

History.
2016-88, s. 1; 2019-48, s. 1; 2021-138, s. 21(a)

§ 132-1.5. 911 database

Automatic number identification and automatic location identification information that consists of the name, address, and telephone numbers of telephone subscribers, or the e-mail addresses of subscribers to an electronic emergency notification or reverse 911 system, that is contained in a county or municipal 911 database, or in a county or municipal telephonic or electronic emergency notification or reverse 911 system, is confidential and is not a public record as defined by Chapter 132 of the General Statutes if that information is required to be confidential by the agreement with the telephone company by which the information was obtained. Dissemination of the information contained in the 911, electronic emergency notification or reverse 911 system, or automatic number and automatic location database is prohibited except on a call-by-call basis only for the purpose of handling emergency calls or for training, and any permanent record of the information shall be secured by the public safety answering points and disposed of in a manner which will retain that security except as otherwise required by applicable law.

History.
1997-287, s. 1; 2007-107, s. 3.2(a)

CHAPTER 134A
YOUTH SERVICES
[REPEALED]

§§ 134A-1 through 134A-39

Repealed by Session Laws 1998-202, s. 1(a), effective January 1, 1999.

CHAPTER 136
TRANSPORTATION

ARTICLE 1
ORGANIZATION OF DEPARTMENT OF TRANSPORTATION

§ 136-13. Malfeasance of officers and employees of Department of Transportation, members of Board of Transportation, contractors, and others

(a) It is unlawful for any person, firm, or corporation to directly or indirectly corruptly give, offer, or promise anything of value to any officer or employee of the Department of Transportation or member of the Board of Transportation, or to promise any officer or employee of the Department of Transportation or any member of the Board of Transportation to give anything of value to any other person with intent:

(1) To influence any official act of any officer or employee of the Department of Transportation or member of the Board of Transportation;

(2) To influence such member of the Board of Transportation, or any officer or employee of the Department of Transportation to commit or aid in committing, or collude in, or allow, any fraud, or to make opportunity for the commission of any fraud on the State of North Carolina; and

(3) To induce a member of the Board of Transportation, or any officer or employee of the Department of Transportation to do or omit to do any act in violation of his lawful duty.

(b) It shall be unlawful for any member of the Board of Transportation, or any officer or employee of the Department of Transportation, directly or indirectly, to corruptly ask, demand, exact, solicit, accept, receive, or agree to receive anything of value for himself or any other person or entity in return for:

(1) Being influenced in his performance of any official act;

(2) Being influenced to commit or aid in committing, or to collude in, or allow, any fraud, or to make opportunity for the commission of any fraud on the State of North Carolina; and

(3) Being induced to do or omit to do any act in violation of his official duty.

(c) The violation of any of the provisions of this section shall be cause for forfeiture of public office and shall be a Class H felony which may include a fine of not more than twenty thousand dollars ($ 20,000) or three times the monetary equivalent of the thing of value whichever is greater.

History.

1921, c. 2, s. 49; C.S., s. 3846(cc); 1933, c. 172, s. 17; 1957, c. 65, s. 11; 1965, c. 55, s. 7; 1973, c. 507, s. 6; 1975, c. 716, s. 7; 1977, c. 464, ss. 7.1, 10, 10.1; 1979, c. 298, ss. 3, 4; 1993, c. 539, s. 1308; 1994, Ex. Sess., c. 24, s. 14(c)

ARTICLE 2
POWERS AND DUTIES OF DEPARTMENT AND BOARD OF TRANSPORTATION

§ 136-26. Closing of State transportation infrastructure during construction or for dangerous conditions; driving through, removal, injury to barriers, warning signs, etc

(a) If it shall appear necessary to the Department of Transportation, its officers, or appropriate employees, to close any transportation infrastructure coming under its jurisdiction so as to permit proper completion of construction work which is being performed, or to prohibit traffic on transportation infrastructure due to damage posing a danger to public safety, the Department of Transportation, its officers or employees, may close, or cause to be closed, the whole or any portion of transportation infrastructure deemed necessary to be excluded from public travel. While any transportation infrastructure, or portion thereof, is so closed, or while any transportation infrastructure, or portion thereof, is in process of construction or maintenance, the Department of Transportation, its officers or appropriate employees, or its contractor, under authority from the Department of Transportation, may erect, or cause to be erected, suitable barriers or obstruction thereon; may post, or cause to be posted, conspicuous notices to the effect that the transportation infrastructure, or portion thereof, is closed; and may place warning signs, lights and lanterns on transportation infrastructure, or portions thereof.

(b) When infrastructure is closed to the public as provided herein, any person who willfully drives onto transportation infrastructure closed pursuant to this section or removes, injures or destroys any such barrier or barriers or obstructions on the road closed or being constructed, or tears down, removes or destroys any such notices, or extinguishes, removes, injures or destroys any such warning signs, lights, or lanterns so erected, posted, or placed pursuant to this section, shall be guilty of a Class 1 misdemeanor.

(c) This prohibition [in this section] does not apply to law enforcement, first responders, personnel of emergency management agencies, or Department of Transportation personnel acting in the course of, and within the scope of, their official duties; or personnel acting in the course of, and within the scope of, installation, restoration or maintenance of utility services in coordination with the Department of Transportation.

History.
1921, c. 2, s. 12; C.S., s. 3846(t); 1933, c. 172, s. 17; 1957, c. 65, s. 11; 1973, c. 507, s. 5; 1977, c. 464, s. 7.1; 1993, c. 539, s. 980; 2009-266, s. 10; 2019-84, s. 1

§ 136-32.2. Placing blinding, deceptive or distracting lights unlawful

(a) If any person, firm or corporation shall place or cause to be placed any lights, which are flashing, moving, rotating, intermittent or steady spotlights, in such a manner and place and of such intensity:

(1) Which, by the use of flashing or blinding lights, blinds, tends to blind and effectively hampers the vision of the operator of any motor vehicle passing on a public highway; or

(2) Which involves red, green or amber lights or reflectorized material and which resembles traffic signal lights or traffic control signs; or

(3) Which, by the use of lights, reasonably causes the operator of any motor vehicle passing upon a public highway to mistakenly believe that there is approaching or situated in his lane of travel some other motor vehicle or obstacle, device or barricade, which would impede his traveling in such lane;

[he or it] shall be guilty of a Class 3 misdemeanor.

(b) Each 10 days during which a violation of the provisions of this section is continued after conviction therefor shall be deemed a separate offense.

(c) The provisions of this section shall not apply to any lights or lighting devices erected or maintained by the Department of Transportation or other properly constituted State or local authorities and intended to effect or implement traffic control and safety. Nothing contained in this section shall be deemed to prohibit the otherwise reasonable use of lights or lighting devices for advertising or other lawful purpose when the same do not fall within the provisions of subdivisions (1) through (3) of subsection (a) of this section.

(d) The enforcement of this section shall be the specific responsibility and duty of the State Highway Patrol in addition to all other law-enforcement agencies and officers within this State; provided, however, no warrant shall issue charging a violation of this section unless the violation has continued for 10 days after notice of the same has been given to the person, firm or corporation maintaining or owning such device or devices alleged to be in violation of this section.

History.
1959, c. 560; 1973, c. 507, s. 5; 1975, c. 716, s. 5; 1977, c. 464, ss. 7.1, 17; 1993, c. 539, s. 983; 1994, Ex. Sess., c. 24, s. 14(c)

§ 136-32.3. Litter enforcement signs

The Department of Transportation shall place signs on the Interstate Highway System notifying motorists of the penalties for littering. The signs shall include the amount of the maximum penalty for littering. The Department of Transportation shall determine the locations of and distance between the signs.

History.
2001-512, s. 4

N.C. Gen. Stat. § 136-33.2

Repealed by Session Laws 2007-164, s. 2, effective July 1, 2007.

§ 136-33.2A. Signs marking beginning of reduced speed zones

If a need to reduce speed in a speed zone is determined to exist by an engineer of the Department, there shall be a sign erected, of adequate size, at least 600 feet in advance of the beginning of any speed zone established by any agency of the State authorized to establish the same, which shall indicate a change in the speed limit.

History.
2007-164, s. 3

ARTICLE 6D
CONTROLLED-ACCESS FACILITIES

§ 136-89.58. Unlawful use of National System of Interstate and Defense Highways and other controlled-access facilities

On those sections of highways which are or become a part of the National System of Interstate and Defense Highways and other controlled-access facilities it shall be unlawful for any person:

(1) To drive a vehicle over, upon or across any curb, central dividing section or other separation or dividing line on said highways.

(2) To make a left turn or a semicircular or U-turn except through an opening provided for that purpose in the dividing curb section, separation, or line on said highways.

(3) To drive any vehicle except in the proper lane provided for that purpose and in the proper direction and to the right of the central dividing curb, separation section, or line on said highways.

(4) To drive any vehicle into the main travel lanes or lanes of connecting ramps or interchanges except through an opening or connection provided for that purpose by the Department of Transportation.

(5) To stop, park, or leave standing any vehicle, whether attended or unattended, on any part or portion of the right-of-way of said highways, except in the case of an emergency or as directed by a peace officer, or as designated parking areas.

(6) To willfully damage, remove, climb, cross or breach any fence erected within the rights-of-way of said highways.

(7) Repealed by Session Laws 1999-330, s. 6, effective December 1, 1999.

Any person who violates any of the provisions of this section shall be guilty of a Class 2 misdemeanor.

History.
1959, c. 647; 1965, c. 474, s. 2; 1973, c. 507, s. 5; 1977, c. 464, s. 7.1; c. 731, s. 2; 1993, c. 539, s. 988; 1994, Ex. Sess., c. 24, s. 14(c); 1999-330, s. 6

ARTICLE 6H
PUBLIC TOLL ROADS AND BRIDGES

PART 1
TURNPIKE AUTHORITY AND TOLL PROJECTS

§ 136-89.198. Authority to toll existing interstate highways

(a) **General.** -- Notwithstanding any other provision of this Article, the Authority may collect tolls on any existing interstate highway for which the United States Department of Transportation has granted permission by permit, or any other lawful means, to do so. The revenue generated from the collected tolls shall be used by the Authority to repair and maintain the interstate on which the tolls were collected. These revenues shall not be used to repair, maintain, or upgrade any State primary or secondary road adjacent to or connected with the interstate highways.

(b) **Method.** -- The Authority shall establish toll locations on the permitted interstate highway in accordance with federal guidelines. Toll locations shall be erected at or near the borders of the State and at such other locations that are not impracticable, unfeasible, or that would result in an unsafe or hazardous condition.

(c) **Severability.** -- If any provision of this section or its application is held invalid, the invalidity does not affect other provisions or applications of this section that can be given effect without the invalid provisions or application, and to this end the provisions of this section are severable.

History.
2005-276, s. 28.21(b)

§ 136-89.199. Designation of high-occupancy toll and managed lanes

(a) **Authority.** -- Notwithstanding any other provision of this Article, the Authority may designate one or more lanes of any highway, or portion thereof, within the State, including lanes that may previously have been designated as HOV lanes under G.S. 20-146.2, as high-occupancy toll (HOT) or other type of managed lanes; provided, however, that such designation shall not reduce the number of existing non-toll general purpose lanes. In making such designations, the Authority shall specify the high-occupancy requirement or other conditions for use of such lanes, which may include restricting vehicle types, access controls, or the payment of tolls for vehicles that do not meet the high-occupancy requirements or conditions for use.

(b) **Reporting.** -- At least 90 days prior to the letting of a contract for the designation of a HOT lane or other type of managed lane under subsection (a) of this section, the Authority shall submit a report to the Joint Legislative Transportation Oversight Committee detailing (i) the reasoning for the designation of the HOT lane or other type of managed lane and (ii) the terms of the contract that will be let. The reporting requirement in this subsection does not apply to any project proposed by the Authority that is subject to the reporting requirement set forth in G.S. 136-89.183(a)(2).

History.
2013-183, s. 5.5; 2013-360, s. 34.30; 2013-410, s. 38(e); 2018-5, s. 34.5(b)

Reserved for future codification purposes.

ARTICLE 7
MISCELLANEOUS PROVISIONS

§ 136-90. Obstructing highways and roads misdemeanor

If any person shall willfully alter, change or obstruct any highway, cartway, mill road or road leading to and from any church or other place of public worship, whether the right-of-way thereto be secured in the manner provided for by law or by purchase, donation or otherwise, such person shall be guilty of a Class 1 misdemeanor. If any person shall hinder or in any manner interfere with the making of any road or cartway laid off according to law, he shall be guilty of a Class 1 misdemeanor.

History.
1872-3, c. 189, s. 6; 1883, c. 383; Code, s. 2065; Rev., s. 3784; C.S., s. 3789; 1993, c. 539, s. 989; 1994, Ex. Sess., c. 24, s. 14(c)

§ 136-91. Placing glass, etc., or injurious obstructions in road

(a) No person shall throw, place, or deposit any glass or other sharp or cutting substance or any injurious obstruction in or upon any highway or public vehicular area.

(b) As used in this section:

(1) "Highway" shall be defined as it is in G.S. 20-4.01; and

(2) "Public vehicular area" shall be defined as it is in G.S. 20-4.01.

(c) Any person violating the provisions of this section shall be guilty of a Class 3 misdemeanor.

History.
1917, c. 140, ss. 18, 21; C.S., ss. 2599, 2619; 1971, c. 200; 1993, c. 539, s. 990; 1994, Ex. Sess., c. 24, s. 14(c); 2001-441, s. 3

§ 136-102. Billboard obstructing view at entrance to school, church or public institution on public highway

(a) It shall be unlawful for any person, firm, or corporation to construct or maintain outside the limits of any city or town in this State any billboard larger than six square feet at or nearer than 200 feet to the point where any walk or drive from any school, church, or public institution located along any highway enters such highway except under the following conditions:

(1) Such billboard is attached to the side of a building or buildings which are or may be erected within 200 feet of any such walk or drive and the attachment thereto causes no additional obstruction of view.

(2) A building or other structure is located so as to obstruct the view between such walk or drive and such billboard.

(3) Such billboard is located on the opposite side of the highway from the entrance to said walk or drive.

(b) Any person, firm, or corporation convicted of violating the provisions of this section shall be guilty of a Class 3 misdemeanor and punished only by a fine of ten dollars ($ 10.00), and each day that such violation continues shall be considered a separate offense.

History.
1947, c. 304, ss. 1, 2; 1993, c. 539, s. 994; 1994, Ex. Sess., c. 24, s. 14(c)

§ 136-102.7. Hurricane evacuation standard

Evacuation Standard. -- The hurricane evacuation standard to be used for any bridge or highway construction project pursuant to this Chapter shall be no more than 18 hours, as recommended by the State Emergency Management officials.

History.
2005-275, s. 5

§ 136-102.8. Subdivision streets; traffic calming devices

The Department shall establish policies and procedures for the installation or utilization of traffic tables or traffic calming devices erected on State-maintained subdivision streets adopted by the Department, pursuant to G.S. 136-102.6, if all of the following requirements are met:

(1) A traffic engineering study has been approved by the Department detailing types and locations of traffic calming devices.

(2) Installation and utilization of traffic tables or traffic calming devices is within one of the following areas:

a. A subdivision with a homeowners association.

b. A neighborhood in which the property owners have established a contractual agreement outlining responsibility for traffic calming devices installed in the neighborhood.

(3) The traffic tables or traffic calming devices are paid for and maintained by the subdivision homeowners association, or its

successor, or pursuant to a neighborhood agreement.

(4) The homeowners association has the written support, for the installation of each traffic table or traffic calming device approved by the Department pursuant to this section, of at least sixty percent (60%) of the member property owners, or the neighborhood agreement is signed by at least sixty percent (60%) of the neighborhood property owners.

(5) The homeowners association, or neighborhood pursuant to its agreement, posts a performance bond with the Department sufficient to fund maintenance or removal of the traffic tables or calming devices, if the homeowners association, or neighborhood pursuant to its agreement, fails to maintain them, or is dissolved. The bond shall remain in place for a period of three years from the date of installation.

History.
2009-310, s. 1; 2015-217, s. 2

ARTICLE 12
JUNKYARD CONTROL ACT

§ 136-144. Restrictions as to location of junkyards

No junkyard shall be established, operated or maintained, any portion of which is within 1,000 feet of the nearest edge of the right-of-way of any interstate or primary highway, or a North Carolina route in a county that has no interstate or federal aid primary highways, except the following:

(1) Those which are screened by natural objects, plantings, fences or other appropriate means so as not to be visible from the main-traveled way of the highway at any season of the year or otherwise removed from sight or screened in accordance with the rules and regulations promulgated by the Department of Transportation.

(2) Those located within areas which are zoned for industrial use under authority of law.

(3) Those located within unzoned industrial areas, which areas shall be determined from actual land uses and defined by regulations to be promulgated by the Department of Transportation.

(4) Those which are not visible from the main-traveled way of an interstate or primary highway or a North Carolina route in a county that does not have an interstate or

federal aid primary highway at any season of the year.

History.
1967, c. 1198, s. 4; 1973, c. 507, s. 5; 1977, c. 464, s. 7.1; 1993, c. 493, s. 2

§ 136-145. Enforcement provisions

Any person, firm, corporation or association that establishes, operates or maintains a junkyard within 1,000 feet of the nearest edge of the right-of-way of any interstate or primary highway, after the effective date of this Article as determined by G.S. 136-155, that does not come within one or more of the exceptions contained in G.S. 136-144 hereof, shall be guilty of a Class 1 misdemeanor, and each day that the junkyard remains within the prohibited distance shall constitute a separate offense. In addition thereto, said junkyard is declared to be a public nuisance and the Department of Transportation may seek injunctive relief in the superior court of the county in which the offense is committed to abate the said nuisance and to require the removal of all junk from the prohibited area.

History.
1967, c. 1198, s. 5; 1973, c. 507, s. 5; c. 1439, s. 6; 1977, c. 464, s. 7.1; 1993, c. 539, s. 999; 1994, Ex. Sess., c. 24, s. 14(c)

ARTICLE 15
RAILROADS

§ 136-192. Obstructing highways; defective crossings; notice; failure to repair after notice misdemeanor

(a) Whenever, in their construction, the works of any railroad corporation shall cross established roads or ways, the corporation shall so construct its works as not to impede the passage or transportation of persons or property along the same. If any railroad corporation shall so construct its crossings with public streets, thoroughfares or highways, or keep, allow or permit the same at any time to remain in such condition as to impede, obstruct or endanger the passage or transportation of persons or property along, over or across the same, the governing body of the county, city or town, or other public road authority having charge, control or oversight of such roads, streets or thoroughfares may give to such railroad notice, in writing, directing it to place any such crossing in good condition, so that persons may cross and property be safely transported across the same.

(b) The notice may be served upon the agent of the offending railroad located nearest to the defective or dangerous crossing about which the notice is given, or it may be served upon the section master whose section includes such crossing. Such notice may be served by delivering a copy to such agent or section master, or by registered or certified mail addressed to either of such persons.

(c) If the railroad corporation shall fail to put such crossing in a safe condition for the passage of persons and property within 30 days from and after the service of the notice, it shall be guilty of a Class 1 misdemeanor. Each calendar month which shall elapse after the giving of the notice and before the placing of such crossing in repair shall be a separate offense.

(d) This section shall in nowise be construed to abrogate, repeal or otherwise affect any existing law now applicable to railroad corporations with respect to highway and street crossings; but the duty imposed and the remedy given by this section shall be in addition to other duties and remedies now prescribed by law.

History.
R.C., c. 61, s. 30; 1874-5, c. 83; Code, s. 1710; Rev., s. 2569; 1915, c. 250, ss. 1, 2; C.S., ss. 3449, 3450; 1963, c. 1165, s. 1; 1993, c. 539, s. 480; 1994, Ex. Sess., c. 24, s. 14(c); 1998-128, s. 14

§ 136-194. Cattle guards and private crossings; failure to erect and maintain misdemeanor

Every company owning, operating or constructing any railroad passing through and over the enclosed land of any person shall, at its own expense, construct and constantly maintain, in good and safe condition, good and sufficient cattle guards at the points of entrance upon and exit from such enclosed land and shall also make and keep in constant repair crossings to any private road thereupon. Every railroad corporation which shall fail to erect and constantly maintain the cattle guards and crossings provided for by this section shall be liable to an action for damages to any party aggrieved, and shall be guilty of a Class 3 misdemeanor and only fined in the discretion of the court. Any cattle guard approved by the Commission shall be deemed a good and sufficient guard under this section.

History.
1883, c. 394, ss. 1, 2, 3; Code, s. 1975; Rev., ss. 2601, 3753; 1915, c. 127; C.S., s. 3454; 1933, c. 134, s. 8; 1941, c. 97, s. 5; 1963, c. 1165, s. 1; 1993, c. 539, s. 481; 1994, Ex. Sess., c. 24, s. 14(c); 1998-128, s. 14

CHAPTER 143
STATE DEPARTMENTS, INSTITUTIONS, AND COMMISSIONS

ARTICLE 69
CRIMINAL JUSTICE INFORMATION NETWORK GOVERNING BOARD

§§ 143-660 through 143-664

Recodified as Part 9 of Article 15 of Chapter 143B (G.S. 143B-1390 through 143B-1394) by Session Laws 2015-241, s. 7A.3(1), effective September 18, 2015.

CHAPTER 143B
EXECUTIVE ORGANIZATION ACT OF 1973

ARTICLE 6A
NORTH CAROLINA STATE-COUNTY CRIMINAL JUSTICE PARTNERSHIP ACT

§§ 143B-273 through 143B-273.19

Repealed by Session Laws 2011-192, s. 6(a), effective July 1, 2011.

History.
G.S. 143B-273: 1993, c. 534, s. 1; repealed by 2011-192, s. 6(a), effective July 1, 2011; G.S. 143B-273.1: 1993, c. 534, s. 1; repealed by 2011-192, s. 6(a), effective July 1, 2011; G.S. 143B-273.2: 1993, c. 534, s. 1; repealed by 2011-192, s. 6(a), effective July 1, 2011; G.S. 143B-273.3: 1993, c. 534, s. 1; repealed by 2011-192, s. 6(a), effective July 1, 2011; G.S. 143B-273.4: 1993, c. 534, s. 1; 1997-443, s. 19.8(b); 2005-276, s. 17.23(f); 2009-349, s. 1; repealed by 2011-192, s. 6(a), effective July 1, 2011; G.S. 143B-273.5: 1993, c. 534, s. 1; repealed by 2011-192, s. 6(a), effective July 1, 2011; G.S. 143B-273.6: 1993, c. 534, s. 1; 1998-170, s. 2; repealed by 2011-192, s. 6(a), effective July 1, 2011; G.S. 143B-273.7: 1993, c. 534, s. 1; repealed by 2011-192, s. 6(a), effective July 1, 2011; G.S. 143B-273.8: 1993, c. 534, s. 1; 1999-237, s. 18(d); 2000-67, s. 16; 2001-138, s. 2; 2009-349, s. 2.1; repealed by 2011-192, s. 6(a), effective July 1, 2011; G.S. 143B-273.9: 1993, c. 534, s. 1; repealed by 2011-192, s. 6(a), effective July 1, 2011; G.S. 143B-273.10: 1993, c. 534, s. 1; 2009-372, s. 18; repealed by 2011-192, s. 6(a), effective July 1, 2011; G.S. 143B-273.11: 1993, c. 534, s. 1; repealed by 2011-192, s. 6(a), effective July 1, 2011; G.S. 143B-273.12: 1993, c. 534, s. 1; 1997-443, s. 19.8(c); repealed by 2011-192, s. 6(a), effective July 1, 2011; G.S. 143B-273.13: 1993, c. 534, s. 1; repealed by 2011-192, s. 6(a), effective July 1, 2011; G.S. 143B-273.14: 1993, c. 534, s. 1; 2005-276, s. 17.23(e), (i); 2009-349, s. 2; 2010-31, s. 19.9; repealed by 2011-192, s. 6(a), effective July 1, 2011; G.S. 143B-273.15: 1993, c. 534, s. 1; 1995, c. 324, s. 19; 2001-424, s. 25.16(a); 2005-276, s. 17.23(g); 2008-107, s. 17.7(a); repealed by 2011-192, s. 6(a), effective July 1, 2011; G.S. 143B-273.15A: 2008-107, s. 17.7(b); repealed by 2011-192, s. 6(a), effective July 1, 2011; G.S. 143B-273.16: 1993, c. 534, s. 1; repealed by 2011-192, s. 6(a), effective July 1, 2011; G.S. 143B-273.17: 1993, c. 534, s. 1; repealed by 2011-192, s. 6(a), effective July 1, 2011; G.S. 143B-273.18: 1993, c. 534, s. 1; repealed by 2011-192, s. 6(a), effective July 1, 2011; G.S. 143B-273.19: 1993, c. 534, s. 1; repealed by 2011-192, s. 6(a), effective July 1, 2011

ARTICLE 11
DEPARTMENT OF CRIME CONTROL AND PUBLIC SAFETY

PART 1
GENERAL PROVISIONS

§§ 143B-473 through 143B-475

Repealed by Session Laws 2011-145, s. 19.1(u), as amended by Session Laws 2011-391, s. 43(h), effective January 1, 2012.

History.
G.S. 143B-473: 1977, c. 70, s. 1; repealed by 2011-145, s. 19.1(u), effective January 1, 2012; G.S. 143B-474: 1977, c. 70, s. 1; 2009-281, s. 1; 2011-183, s. 127(c); repealed by 2011-145, s. 19.1(u), effective January 1, 2012; G.S. 143B-475: 1977, c. 70, s. 1; 1981, c. 929; 1983, c. 832, s. 3; 1983 (Reg. Sess., 1984), c. 1034, s. 103; 1989, c. 751, s. 7(42); 1991, c. 301, s. 1; 1991 (Reg. Sess., 1992), c. 959, s. 73; 2002-159, s. 31.5(b); 2002-190, s. 14; 2009-397, s. 1; 2009-451, s. 17.3(d); repealed by 2011-145, s. 19.1(u), effective January 1, 2012

N.C. Gen. Stat. § 143B-475.1

Recodified as G.S. 143B-262.4 by Session Laws 2001-487, s. 91(a), effective December 16, 2001.

N.C. Gen. Stat. § 143B-475.2

Repealed by Session Laws 2010-31, s. 17.1(b), effective July 1, 2010.

History.
§ 143B-475.2: 2009-451, s. 17.5; repealed by 2010-31, s. 17.1(b), effective July 1, 2010

N.C. Gen. Stat. § 143B-476

Repealed by Session Laws 2011-145, s. 19.1(u), as amended by Session Laws 2011-391, s. 43(h), effective January 1, 2012.

History.
G.S. 143B-476: 1977, c. 70, s. 1; 1979, 2nd Sess., c. 1310, s. 1; 1981 (Reg. Sess., 1982), c. 1191, s. 17; 1985, c. 757, s. 164(c); 1985 (Reg. Sess., 1986), c. 1018, s. 13; 1998-212, s. 19.5(a); 2002-159, s. 31.5(b); 2002-190, s. 15; 2008-142, s. 1; 2009-451, s. 17.3(e); 2011-284, s. 102; repealed by 2011-145, s. 19.1(u), effective January 1, 2012

PART 2
CRIME CONTROL DIVISION

Chapter 143B

N.C. Gen. Stat. § 143B-477

Recodified as G.S. 143B-1103, effective January 1, 2012.

PART 3
GOVERNOR'S CRIME COMMISSION

§§ 143B-478 through 143B-480

Recodified as G.S. 143B-1100 through G.S. 143B-1102, effective January 1, 2012.

PART 3A
ASSISTANCE PROGRAM FOR VICTIMS OF RAPE AND SEX OFFENSES

N.C. Gen. Stat. § 143B-480.1

Recodified as G.S. 143B-1200, effective January 1, 2012.

N.C. Gen. Stat. § 143B-480.2

Repealed by Session Laws 2009-354, s. 1(a), effective July 27, 2009.

N.C. Gen. Stat. § 143B-480.3

Recodified as G.S. 143B-1201, effective January 1, 2012.

PART 5A
NORTH CAROLINA CENTER FOR MISSING PERSONS

§§ 143B-495 through 143B-499.8

Recodified as G.S. 143B-1010 through G.S. 143B-1022, effective January 1, 2012.

PART 6
COMMUNITY PENALTIES PROGRAM

§§ 143B-500 through 143B-507

Recodified as Article 61 of Subchapter XIII of Chapter 7A, G.S. 7A-770 through 7A-777, by Session Laws 1991, c. 566, s. 2.

PART 7
LAW ENFORCEMENT SUPPORT SERVICES DIVISION

§§ 143B-508, 143B-508.1

Repealed by Session Laws 2011-145, s. 19.1(u), as amended by Session Laws 2011-391, s. 43(h), effective January 1, 2012.

History.
G.S. 143B-508: 2009-81, s. 3; repealed by 2011-145, s. 19.1(u), as amended by 2011-391, s. 43(h), effective January 1, 2012; G.S. 143B-508.1: 2010-31, s. 17.1(c); repealed by 2011-145, s. 19.1(u), as amended by 2011-391, s. 43(h), effective January 1, 2012

PART 8
EMERGENCY MANAGEMENT DIVISION

N.C. Gen. Stat. § 143B-509

Recodified as G.S. 143B-1000, effective January 1, 2012.

PART 9
STATE CAPITOL POLICE DIVISION

N.C. Gen. Stat. § 143B-509.1

Recodified as G.S. 143B-900, effective January 1, 2012.

N.C. Gen. Stat. § 143B-510

Reserved for future codification purposes.

ARTICLE 12
DEPARTMENT OF JUVENILE JUSTICE AND DELINQUENCY PREVENTION

§§ 143B-511 through 143B-549

Recodified as G.S. 143B-800 through 143B-851 by Session Laws 2011-145, s. 19.1(t), effective January 1, 2012.

N.C. Gen. Stat. § 143B-550

Recodified as G.S. 143B-1104 by Session Laws 2011-145, s. 19.1(s), effective January 1, 2012.

§§ 143B-551 through 143B-555

Reserved for future codification purposes.

§§ 143B-556, 143B-557

Repealed by Laws 2008-118, s. 3.12(a), effective July 1, 2008.

ARTICLE 13
DEPARTMENT OF PUBLIC SAFETY

PART 3
JUVENILE JUSTICE SECTION

SUBPART A
CREATION OF DIVISION

§ 143B-800. Creation of Juvenile Justice Section of the Division of Adult Correction and Juvenile Justice of the Department of Public Safety

There is hereby created and constituted a section to be known as the " Juvenile Justice Section of the Division of Adult Correction and Juvenile Justice of the Department of Public Safety", with the organization, powers, and duties as set forth in this Article or as prescribed by the Director of the Division of Adult Correction and Juvenile Justice.

History.
1998-202, s. 1(b); 2000-137, s. 1(b); 2011-145, s. 19.1 (*l*), (t); 2017-186, s. 1(p)

§ 143B-801. Transfer of Office of Juvenile Justice authority to the Juvenile Justice Section of the Division of Adult Correction and Juvenile Justice of the Department of Public Safety

(a) All (i) statutory authority, powers, duties, and functions, including directives of S.L. 1998-202, rule making, budgeting, and purchasing, (ii) records, (iii) personnel, personnel positions, and salaries, (iv) property, and (v) unexpended balances of appropriations, allocations, reserves, support costs, and other funds of the Office of Juvenile Justice under the Office of the Governor are transferred to and vested in the Juvenile Justice Section of the Division of Adult Correction and Juvenile Justice of the Department of Public Safety. This transfer has all of the elements of a Type I transfer as defined in G.S. 143A-6.

(b) The Section shall be considered a continuation of the Office of Juvenile Justice for the purpose of succession to all rights, powers, duties, and obligations of the Office and of those rights, powers, duties, and obligations exercised by the Office of the Governor on behalf of the Office of Juvenile Justice. Where the Office of Juvenile Justice or the Division of Juvenile Justice of the Department of Public Safety is referred to by law, contract, or other document, that reference shall apply to the Juvenile Justice Section of the Division of Adult Correction and Juvenile Justice. Where the Office of the Governor is referred to by contract or other document, where the Office of the Governor is acting on behalf of the Office of Juvenile Justice, that reference shall apply to the Section.

(c) All institutions previously operated by the Office of Juvenile Justice and the present central office of the Office of Juvenile Justice, including land, buildings, equipment, supplies, personnel, or other properties rented or controlled by the Office or by the Office of the Governor for the Office of Juvenile Justice, shall be administered by the Juvenile Justice Section of the Division of Adult Correction and Juvenile Justice of the Department of Public Safety.

History.
1998-202, s. 1(b); 2000-137, s. 1(b); 2011-145, s. 19.1 (*l*), (t); 2017-186, s. 1(q)

§§ 143B-802 through 143B-804

Reserved for future codification purposes.

SUBPART B
GENERAL PROVISIONS

§ 143B-805. Definitions

In this Part, unless the context clearly requires otherwise, the following words have the listed meanings:

(1) **Chief court counselor.** -- The person responsible for administration and supervision of juvenile intake, probation, and post-release supervision in each judicial district, operating under the supervision of the Juvenile Justice Section of the Division of Adult Correction and Juvenile Justice of the Department of Public Safety.

(1a) **Juvenile consultation.** -- The provision of services to a vulnerable juvenile and to the parent, guardian, or custodian of a vulnerable juvenile pursuant to G.S. 7B-1706.1. Juvenile consultation cases are subject to confidentiality laws provided in Subchapter III of Chapter 7B of the General Statutes.

(2) **Community-based program.** -- A program providing nonresidential or residential treatment to a juvenile under the jurisdiction of the juvenile court in the community where the juvenile's family lives. A community-based program may include specialized foster care, family counseling, shelter care, and other appropriate treatment.

(3) **County Councils.** -- Juvenile Crime Prevention Councils created under G.S. 143B-846.

(4) **Court.** -- The district court division of the General Court of Justice.

(5) **Custodian.** -- The person or agency that has been awarded legal custody of a juvenile by a court.

(6) **Delinquent juvenile.** --

a. Any juvenile who, while less than 16 years of age but at least 10 years of age, commits a crime or infraction under State law or under an ordinance of local government, including violation of the motor vehicle laws, or who commits indirect contempt by a juvenile as defined in G.S. 5A-31.

b. Any juvenile who, while less than 18 years of age but at least 16 years of age, commits a crime or an infraction under State law or under an ordinance of local government, excluding all violations of the motor vehicle laws under Chapter 20 of the General Statutes, or who commits indirect contempt by a juvenile as defined in G.S. 5A-31.

c. Any juvenile who, while less than 10 years of age but at least 8 years of age, commits a Class A, B1, B2, C, D, E, F, or G felony under State law.

d. Any juvenile who, while less than 10 years of age but at least 8 years of age, commits a crime or an infraction under State law or under an ordinance of local government, including violation of the motor vehicle laws, and has been previously adjudicated delinquent.

(7) **Detention.** -- The secure confinement of a juvenile under a court order.

(8) **Detention facility.** -- A facility approved to provide secure confinement and care for juveniles. Detention facilities include both State and locally administered detention homes, centers, and facilities.

(9) **District.** -- Any district court district as established by G.S. 7A-133.

(10) Repealed by Session Laws 2017-186, s. 1(r), effective December 1, 2017.

(11) **Judge.** -- Any district court judge.

(12) **Judicial district.** -- Any district court district as established by G.S. 7A-133.

(13) **Juvenile.** -- Except as provided in subdivisions (6) and (20) of this section, any person who has not reached the person's eighteenth birthday and is not married, emancipated, or a member of the Armed Forces of the United States. Wherever the term "juvenile" is used with reference to rights and privileges, that term encompasses the attorney for the juvenile as well.

(14) **Juvenile court.** -- Any district court exercising jurisdiction under this Chapter.

(15) **Juvenile court counselor.** -- A person responsible for intake services and court supervision services to juveniles under the supervision of the chief court counselor.

(16) **Post-release supervision.** -- The supervision of a juvenile who has been returned to the community after having been committed to the Division for placement in a training school.

(17) **Probation.** -- The status of a juvenile who has been adjudicated delinquent, is subject to specified conditions under the supervision of a juvenile court counselor, and may be returned to the court for violation of those conditions during the period of probation.

(18) **Protective supervision.** -- The status of a juvenile who has been adjudicated undisciplined and is under the supervision of a juvenile court counselor.

(19) **Secretary.** -- The Secretary of Public Safety.

(19a) **Section.** -- The Juvenile Justice Section of the Division of Adult Correction and Juvenile Justice of the Department of Public Safety.

(20) **Undisciplined juvenile.** --

a. A juvenile who, while less than 16 years of age but at least 10 years of age, is unlawfully absent from school; or is regularly disobedient to and beyond the disciplinary control of the juvenile's parent, guardian, or custodian; or is regularly found in places where it is unlawful for a juvenile to be; or has run away from home for a period of more than 24 hours; or

b. A juvenile who is 16 or 17 years of age and who is regularly disobedient to and beyond the disciplinary control of the juvenile's parent, guardian, or custodian; or is regularly found in places where it is unlawful for a juvenile to be; or has run away from home for a period of more than 24 hours.

(20a) **Vulnerable juvenile.** -- Any juvenile who, while less than 10 years of age but at least 6 years of age, commits a crime or infraction under State law or under an ordinance of local government, including violation of the motor vehicle laws, and is not a delinquent juvenile.

(21) **Youth development center.** -- A secure residential facility authorized to provide long-term treatment, education, and rehabilitative services for delinquent juveniles committed by the court to the Division.

History.
1998-202, ss. 1(b), 2(a); 2000-137, s. 1(b); 2001-95, ss. 3, 4; 2001-490, s. 2.39; 2008-118, s. 3.12(b); 2011-145, s. 19.1 (*l*), (m), (t), (ccc); 2011-183, s. 105; 2017-57, s. 16D.4(r); 2017-186, s. 1(r); 2018-142, s. 23(b); 2019-186, s. 1(b); 2021-123, s. 6(a)

§ 143B-806. Duties and powers of the Juvenile Justice Section of the Division of Adult Correction and Juvenile Justice of the Department of Public Safety

(a) Repealed by Session Laws 2013-289, s. 5, effective July 18, 2013.

(b) In addition to its other duties, the Juvenile Justice Section of the Division of Adult Correction and Juvenile Justice shall have the following powers and duties:

(1) Give leadership to the implementation as appropriate of State policy that requires that youth development centers be phased out as populations diminish.

(2) Close a State youth development center when its operation is no longer justified and transfer State funds appropriated for the operation of that youth development center to fund community-based programs, to purchase care or services for predelinquents, delinquents, or status offenders in community-based or other appropriate programs, or to improve the efficiency of existing youth development centers, after consultation with the Joint Legislative Commission on Governmental Operations.

(3) Administer a sound admission or intake program for juvenile facilities, including the requirement of a careful evaluation of the needs of each juvenile prior to acceptance and placement.

(4) Operate juvenile facilities and implement programs that meet the needs of juveniles receiving services and that assist them to become productive, responsible citizens.

(5) Adopt rules to implement this Part and the responsibilities of the Secretary and the Division under Chapter 7B of the General Statutes. The Secretary may adopt rules applicable to local human services agencies providing juvenile court and delinquency prevention services for the purpose of program evaluation, fiscal audits, and collection of third-party payments.

(6) Ensure a statewide and uniform system of juvenile intake, protective supervision, probation, and post-release supervision services in all district court districts of the State. The system shall provide appropriate, adequate, and uniform services to all juveniles who are alleged or found to be undisciplined or delinquent.

(7) Establish procedures for substance abuse testing for juveniles adjudicated delinquent for substance abuse offenses.

(8) Plan, develop, and coordinate comprehensive multidisciplinary services and programs statewide for the prevention of juvenile delinquency, early intervention, and rehabilitation of juveniles, including services for vulnerable juveniles receiving juvenile consultation services.

(9) Develop standards, approve yearly program evaluations, and make recommendations based on the evaluations to the General Assembly concerning continuation funding.

(10) Collect expense data for every program operated and contracted by the Division.

(11) Develop a formula for funding, on a matching basis, juvenile court and delinquency prevention services as provided for in this Part. This formula shall be based upon the county's or counties' relative ability to fund community-based programs for juveniles.

Local governments receiving State matching funds for programs under this Part must maintain the same overall level of effort that existed at the time of the filing of the county assessment of juvenile needs with the Division.

(12) Assist local governments and private service agencies in the development of juvenile court services and delinquency prevention services and provide information on the availability of potential funding sources and assistance in making application for needed funding.

(13) Develop and administer a comprehensive juvenile justice information system to collect data and information about delinquent juveniles for the purpose of developing treatment and intervention plans and allowing reliable assessment and evaluation of the effectiveness of rehabilitative and preventive services provided to delinquent juveniles.

(14) Coordinate State-level services in relation to delinquency prevention and juvenile court services so that any citizen may go to one place in State government to receive information about available juvenile services.

(14a) Develop and administer a system to provide information to victims and complainants regarding the status of pending complaints and the right of a complainant and victim to request review under G.S. 7B-1704 of a decision to not file a petition.

(15) Appoint the chief court counselor in each district.

(16) Develop a statewide plan for training and professional development of chief court counselors, court counselors, and other personnel responsible for the care, supervision, and treatment of juveniles. The plan shall include attendance at appropriate professional meetings and opportunities for educational leave for academic study.

(17) Study issues related to qualifications, salary ranges, appointment of personnel on a merit basis, including chief court counselors, court counselors, secretaries, and other appropriate personnel, at the State and district levels in order to adopt appropriate policies and procedures governing personnel.

(18) Set, in consultation with the Office of State Human Resources, the salary supplement paid to teachers, instructional support personnel, and school-based administrators who are employed at juvenile facilities and are licensed by the State Board of Education. The salary supplement shall be at least five percent (5%), but not more than the percentage supplement they would receive if they were employed in the local school administrative unit where the job site is located. These salary supplements shall not be paid to central office staff. Nothing in this subdivision shall be construed to include "merit pay" under the term "salary supplement".

(19) Designate persons, as necessary, as State juvenile justice officers, to provide for the care and supervision of juveniles placed in the physical custody of the Division.

(20) Provide for the transportation to and from any State or local juvenile facility of any person under the jurisdiction of the juvenile court for any purpose required by Chapter 7B of the General Statutes or upon order of the court.

(c) Repealed by Session Laws 2017-186, s. 1(s), effective December 1, 2017.

(d) Where Division statistics indicate the presence of minority youth in juvenile facilities disproportionate to their presence in the general population, the Division shall develop and recommend appropriate strategies designed to ensure fair and equal treatment in the juvenile justice system.

(e) The Division may provide consulting services and technical assistance to courts, law enforcement agencies, and other agencies, local governments, and public and private organizations. The Division may develop or assist Juvenile Crime Prevention Councils in developing community needs, assessments, and programs relating to the prevention and treatment of delinquent and undisciplined behavior.

(f) The Division shall develop a cost-benefit model for each State-funded program. Program commitment and recidivism rates shall be components of the model.

History.

1998-202, ss. 1(b), 2(b), 2(f); 1998-217, ss. 57(2), 57(3); 2000-137, s. 1(b); 2001-95, s. 5; 2001-490, s. 2.40; 2003-284, s. 17.2(a); 2005-276, s. 29.19(b); 2006-203, s. 111; 2008-118, s. 3.12(c); 2011-145, s. 19.1 (*l*), (t); 2012-83, s. 12; 2013-289, s. 5; 2013-360, s. 16D.7(b); 2013-382, s. 9.1(c); 2017-57, s. 16D.4(s), (w); 2017-186, s. 1(s); 2018-142, s. 23(b); 2021-123, s. 6(b)

§ 143B-807. Authority to contract with other entities

(a) The Section may contract with any governmental agency, person, or association for the accomplishment of its duties and responsibilities. The expenditure of funds under these contracts shall be for the purposes for which the funds were appropriated and not otherwise prohibited by law.

(b) The Section may enter into contracts with, and act as intermediary between, any federal government agency and any county of this State for the purpose of assisting the county to recover monies expended by a county-funded financial assistance program. As a condition of assistance, the county shall agree to hold and save harmless the Section against any claims, loss, or expense which the Section might incur under the contracts by reason of any erroneous, unlawful, or tortious act or omission of the county or its officials, agents, or employees.

(c) The Section and any other appropriate State or local agency may purchase services from public or private agencies providing delinquency prevention programs or juvenile court services, including parenting responsibility classes. The programs shall meet State standards. As institutional populations are reduced, the Section may divert State funds appropriated for institutional programs to purchase the services under the State Budget Act.

(d) Each programmatic, residential, and service contract or agreement entered into by the Section shall include a cooperation clause to ensure compliance with the Section's quality assurance requirements and cost-accounting requirements.

History.

1998-202, s. 1(b); 2000-137, s. 1(b); 2011-145, s. 19.1 (*l*), (t); 2017-186, s. 1(s1)

§ 143B-808. Authority to assist private nonprofit foundations

The Section may provide appropriate services or allow employees of the Section to assist any private nonprofit foundation that works directly with the Section's services or programs and whose sole purpose is to support these services and programs. A Section employee shall be allowed to work with a foundation no more than 20 hours in any one month. These services are not subject to Chapter 150B of the General Statutes.

The board of directors of each private, nonprofit foundation shall secure and pay for the services of the Department of State Auditor or employ a certified public accountant to conduct an annual audit of the financial accounts of the foundation. The board of directors shall transmit to the Section a copy of the annual financial audit report of the private nonprofit foundation.

History.
1998-202, s. 1(b); 2000-137, s. 1(b); 2011-145, s. 19.1 (*l*), (t); 2017-186, s. 1(s2)

§ 143B-809. Teen court programs

(a) All teen court programs administered by the Juvenile Justice Section of the Division of Adult Correction and Juvenile Justice of the Department of Public Safety shall operate as community resources for the diversion of juveniles pursuant to G.S. 7B-1706(c). A juvenile diverted to a teen court program shall be tried by a jury of other juveniles, and, if the jury finds the juvenile has committed the delinquent act, the jury may assign the juvenile to a rehabilitative measure or sanction, including counseling, restitution, curfews, and community service.

Teen court programs may also operate as resources to the local school administrative units to handle problems that develop at school but that have not been turned over to the juvenile authorities.

(b) Every teen court program that receives funds from Juvenile Crime Prevention Councils shall comply with rules and reporting requirements of the Juvenile Justice Section of the Division of Adult Correction and Juvenile Justice of the Department of Public Safety.

History.
2001-424, s. 24.8; 2002-126, s. 16.2(b); 2011-145, s. 19.1 (*l*), (t); 2017-186, s. 1(t)

§ 143B-810. Youth Development Center annual report

The Department of Public Safety shall report by October 1 of each year to the Chairs of the House of Representatives and Senate Appropriations Subcommittees on Justice and Public Safety, the Chairs of the Joint Legislative Oversight Committee on Justice and Public Safety, and the Fiscal Research Division of the Legislative Services Commission on the Youth Development Center (YDC) population, staffing, and capacity in the preceding fiscal year. Specifically, the report shall include all of the following:

(1) The on-campus population of each YDC, including the county the juveniles are from.

(2) The housing capacity of each YDC.

(3) A breakdown of staffing for each YDC, including number, type of position, position title, and position description.

(4) The per-bed and average daily population cost for each facility.

(5) The operating cost for each facility, including personnel and nonpersonnel items.

(6) A brief summary of the treatment model, education, services, and plans for reintegration into the community offered at each facility.

(7) The average length of stay in the YDCs.

(8) The number of incidents of assaults and attacks on staff at each facility.

History.
2013-360, s. 16D.3

§ 143B-811. Annual evaluation of intensive intervention services

The Department of Public Safety shall conduct an annual evaluation of intensive intervention services. Intensive intervention services are evidence-based or research-supported community-based or residential services that are necessary for a juvenile in order to (i) prevent the juvenile's commitment to a youth development center or detention facility, (ii) facilitate the juvenile's successful return to the community following commitment, or (iii) prevent further involvement in the juvenile justice system. In conducting the evaluation, the Department shall consider whether participation in intensive intervention services results in a diversion from or reduction of court involvement among juveniles. The Department shall also determine whether the programs are achieving the goals and objectives of the Juvenile Justice Reform Act, S.L. 1998-202.

The Department shall report the results of the evaluation to the Chairs of the Joint Legislative Oversight Committee on Justice and Public Safety and the Chairs of the Senate and House of Representatives Appropriations Subcommittees on Justice and Public Safety by March 1 of each year.

Chapter 143B

History.

2013-360, s. 16D.1; 2020-83, s. 1; 2021-123, s. 6(c)

§§ 143B-812 through 143B-814

Reserved for future codification purposes.

SUBPART C
JUVENILE FACILITIES

§ 143B-815. Juvenile facilities

In order to provide any juvenile in a juvenile facility with appropriate treatment according to that juvenile's need, the Section shall be responsible for the administration of statewide educational, clinical, psychological, psychiatric, social, medical, vocational, and recreational services or programs.

History.

1998-202, s. 1(b); 2000-137, s. 1(b); 2011-145, s. 19.1 (*l*), (t); 2017-186, s. 1(t1)

§ 143B-816. Authority to provide necessary medical or surgical care

The Section may provide any medical and surgical treatment necessary to preserve the life and health of juveniles committed to the custody of the Section; however, no surgical operation may be performed except as authorized in G.S. 148-22.2.

History.

1998-202, s. 1(b); 2000-137, s. 1(b); 2011-145, s. 19.1 (*l*), (t); 2017-186, s. 1(t2)

§ 143B-817. Compensation to juveniles in care

A juvenile who has been committed to the Section may be compensated for work or participation in training programs at rates approved by the Secretary within available funds. The Secretary may provide for a reasonable allowance to the juvenile for incidental personal expenses, and any balance of the juvenile's earnings remaining at the time the juvenile is released shall be paid to the juvenile or the juvenile's parent or guardian. The Section may accept grants or funds from any source to compensate juveniles under this section.

History.

1998-202, s. 1(b); 2000-137, s. 1(b); 2011-145, s. 19.1 (*l*), (t); 2017-186, s. 1(t3)

§ 143B-818. Visits and community activities

(a) The Section shall encourage visits by parents or guardians and responsible relatives of juveniles committed to the custody of the Section.

(b) The Section shall develop a program of home visits for juveniles in the custody of the Section. The visits shall begin after the juvenile has been in the custody of the Section for a period of at least six months. In developing the program, the Section shall adopt criteria that promote the protection of the public and the best interests of the juvenile.

History.

1998-202, ss. 1(b), (2c); 2000-137, s. 1(b); 2011-145, s. 19.1 (*l*), (t); 2017-186, s. 1(t4)

§ 143B-819. Regional detention services

The Section is responsible for juvenile detention services, including the development of a statewide plan for regional juvenile detention services that offer juvenile detention care of sufficient quality to meet State standards to any juvenile requiring juvenile detention care within the State in a detention facility as follows:

(1) The Section shall plan with the counties operating a county detention facility to provide regional juvenile detention services to surrounding counties. The Section has discretion in defining the geographical boundaries of the regions based on negotiations with affected counties, distances, availability of juvenile detention care that meets State standards, and other appropriate factors.

(2) The Section may plan with any county that has space within its county jail system to use the existing space for a county detention facility when needed, if the space meets the State standards for a detention facility and meets all of the requirements of G.S. 153A-221. The use of space within the county jail system shall be constructed to ensure that juveniles are not able to converse with, see, or be seen by the adult population, and juveniles housed in a space within a county jail shall be supervised closely.

(3) The Section shall plan for and administer regional detention facilities. The Section shall carefully plan the location, architectural design, construction, and administration of a program to meet the needs of juveniles in juvenile detention care. The physical facility of a regional detention facility shall comply with all applicable State and federal standards. The programs of a regional detention facility shall comply with the standards established by the Section.

History.
1998-202, ss. 1(b), 2(f); 1998-217, s. 57(3); 2000-137, s. 1(b); 2011-145, s. 19.1 (*l*), (t); 2017-186, s. 1(t5)

§ 143B-820. State subsidy to county detention facilities

The Section shall administer a State subsidy program to pay a county that provides juvenile detention services and meets State standards a certain per diem per juvenile. In general, this per diem should be fifty percent (50%) of the total cost of caring for a juvenile from within the county and one hundred percent (100%) of the total cost of caring for a juvenile from another county. Any county placing a juvenile in a detention facility in another county shall pay fifty percent (50%) of the total cost of caring for the juvenile to the Section. The Section may vary the exact funding formulas to operate within existing State appropriations or other funds that may be available to pay for juvenile detention care.

History.
1998-202, ss. 1(b), 2(f); 1998-217, s. 57(3); 2000-137, s. 1(b); 2011-145, s. 19.1 (*l*), (t); 2017-186, s. 1(t6)

§ 143B-821. Authority for implementation

In order to allow for effective implementation of a statewide regional approach to juvenile detention, the Section may:

(1) Release or transfer a juvenile from one detention facility to another when necessary to administer the juvenile's detention appropriately.

(2) Plan with counties that operate county detention facilities to provide regional services and to upgrade physical facilities to contract with counties for services and care, and to pay State subsidies to counties providing regional juvenile detention services that meet State standards.

(3) Allow the State to reimburse law enforcement officers or other appropriate employees of local government for the costs of transportation of a juvenile to and from any juvenile detention facility.

(4) Seek funding for juvenile detention services from federal sources, and accept gifts of funds from public or private sources.

History.
1998-202, ss. 1(b), 2(f); 1998-217, s. 57(3); 2000-137, s. 1(b); 2011-145, s. 19.1 (*l*), (t); 2017-186, s. 1(t7)

§ 143B-822. Juvenile facility monthly commitment report

The Department of Public Safety shall report electronically on the first day of each month to the Fiscal Research Division regarding each juvenile correctional facility and the average daily population for the previous month. The report shall include (i) the average daily population for each detention center and (ii) the monthly summary of the Committed Youth Report.

History.
2013-360, s. 16D.4

§§ 143B-823 through 143B-829

Reserved for future codification purposes.

SUBPART D
JUVENILE COURT SERVICES

§ 143B-830. Duties and powers of chief court counselors

The chief court counselor in each district appointed under G.S. 143B-806(b)(15) may:

(1) Appoint juvenile court counselors, secretaries, and other personnel authorized by the Section in accordance with the personnel policies adopted by the Section.

(2) Supervise and direct the program of juvenile intake, protective supervision, probation, and post-release supervision within the district.

(3) Provide in-service training for staff as required by the Section.

(4) Keep any records and make any reports requested by the Secretary in order to provide statewide data and information about juvenile needs and services.

(5) Delegate to a juvenile court counselor or supervisor the authority to carry out specified responsibilities of the chief court counselor to facilitate the effective operation of the district.

(6) Designate a juvenile court counselor in the district as acting chief court counselor, to act during the absence or disability of the chief court counselor.

History.
1998-202, ss. 1(b), 2(f); 1998-217, s. 57(3); 2000-137, s. 1(b); 2009-320, s. 1; 2011-145, s. 19.1 (*l*), (t), (ddd); 2017-186, s. 1(t8)

§ 143B-831. Duties and powers of juvenile court counselors

As the court or the chief court counselor may direct or require, all juvenile court counselors shall have the following powers and duties:

(1) Secure or arrange for any information concerning a case that the court may require before, during, or after the hearing.

(2) Prepare written reports for the use of the court.

(3) Appear and testify at court hearings.

(4) Assume custody of a juvenile as authorized by G.S. 7B-1900, or when directed by court order.

(5) Furnish each juvenile on probation or protective supervision and that juvenile's parents, guardian, or custodian with a written statement of the juvenile's conditions of probation or protective supervision, and consult with the juvenile's parents, guardian, or custodian so that they may help the juvenile comply with the conditions.

(6) Keep informed concerning the conduct and progress of any juvenile on probation or under protective supervision through home visits or conferences with the parents or guardian and in other ways.

(7) See that the juvenile complies with the conditions of probation or bring to the attention of the court any juvenile who violates the juvenile's probation.

(8) Make periodic reports to the court concerning the adjustment of any juvenile on probation or under court supervision.

(9) Keep any records of the juvenile's work as the court may require.

(10) Account for all funds collected from juveniles.

(11) Serve necessary court documents pertaining to delinquent and undisciplined juvenile matters.

(12) Assume custody of juveniles under the jurisdiction of the court when necessary for the protection of the public or the juvenile, and when necessary to carry out the responsibilities of juvenile court counselors under this section and under Chapter 7B of the General Statutes.

(13) Use reasonable force and restraint necessary to secure custody assumed under subdivision (12) of this section.

(14) Provide supervision for a juvenile transferred to the counselor's supervision from another court or another state, and provide supervision for any juvenile released from an institution operated by the Section when requested by the Section to do so.

(15) Assist in the implementation of any order entered pursuant to G.S. 5A-32 as directed by a judicial official exercising jurisdiction under that section.

(16) Assist in the development of post-release supervision and the supervision of juveniles.

(17) Screen and evaluate a complaint alleging that a juvenile is delinquent or undisciplined to determine whether the complaint should be filed as a petition.

(17a) Provide and coordinate multidisciplinary service referrals for the prevention of juvenile delinquency and early intervention for juveniles, including vulnerable juveniles who are in receipt of juvenile consultation services. If the juvenile court counselor has cause to suspect that a juvenile who is receiving services pursuant to this subdivision is abused, neglected, or dependent, the juvenile court counselor shall make a report to the director of social services as required by G.S. 7B-1700.1.

(18) Have any other duties as the court may direct.

(19) Have any other duties as the Section may direct.

History.

1998-202, ss. 1(b), 2(d), 2(e), 2(f); 1998-217, s. 57(3); 2000-137, s. 1(b); 2001-490, s. 2.41; 2007-168, s. 7; 2011-145, s. 19.1 (*l*), (t); 2017-186, s. 1(t9); 2021-123, s. 6(d)

§§ 143B-832 through 143B-839

Reserved for future codification purposes.

SUBPART E
COMPREHENSIVE JUVENILE DELINQUENCY AND SUBSTANCE ABUSE PREVENTION PLAN

§ 143B-840. Comprehensive Juvenile Delinquency and Substance Abuse Prevention Plan

(a) The Section shall develop and implement a comprehensive juvenile delinquency and substance abuse prevention plan and shall coordinate with County Councils for implementation of a continuum of services and programs at the community level.

The Section shall ensure that localities are informed about best practices in juvenile delinquency and substance abuse prevention.

(b) The plan shall contain the following:

(1) Identification of the risk factors at the developmental stages of a juvenile's life that may result in delinquent behavior.

(2) Identification of the protective factors that families, schools, communities, and the State must support to reduce the risk of juvenile delinquency.

(3) Programmatic concepts that are effective in preventing juvenile delinquency and substance abuse and that should be made available as basic services in the communities, including:

　　a. Early intervention programs and services.

b. In-home training and community-based family counseling and parent training.

c. Adolescent and family substance abuse prevention services, including alcohol abuse prevention services, and substance abuse education.

d. Programs and activities offered before and after school hours.

e. Life and social skills training programs.

f. Classes or seminars that teach conflict resolution, problem solving, and anger management.

g. Services that provide personal advocacy, including mentoring relationships, tutors, or other caring adult programs.

(c) The Section shall cooperate with all other affected State agencies and entities in implementing this section.

History.
1998-202, s. 1(b); 2000-137, s. 1(b); 2011-145, s. 19.1 (*l*), (t); 2012-83, s. 13; 2017-186, s. 1(t10)

§§ 143B-841 through 143B-844

Reserved for future codification purposes.

SUBPART F
JUVENILE CRIME
PREVENTION COUNCILS

§ 143B-845. Legislative intent

It is the intent of the General Assembly to prevent juveniles who are at risk from becoming delinquent. The primary intent of this Subpart is to develop community-based alternatives to youth development centers and to provide community-based delinquency, substance abuse, and gang prevention strategies and programs. Additionally, it is the intent of the General Assembly to provide noninstitutional dispositional alternatives that will protect the community and the juveniles.

These programs and services shall be planned and organized at the community level and developed in partnership with the State. These planning efforts shall include appropriate representation from local government, local public and private agencies serving juveniles and their families, local business leaders, citizens with an interest in youth problems, youth representatives, and others as may be appropriate in a particular community. The planning bodies at the local level shall be the Juvenile Crime Prevention Councils.

History.
1998-202, s. 1(b); 2000-137, s. 1(b); 2001-95, s. 5; 2008-56, s. 2; 2011-145, s. 19.1(t), (eee)

§ 143B-846. Creation; method of appointment; membership; chair and vice-chair

(a) As a prerequisite for a county receiving funding for juvenile court services and delinquency prevention programs, the board of commissioners of a county shall appoint a Juvenile Crime Prevention Council. The County Council shall consist of not more than 26 members and should include, if possible, the following:

(1) The local school superintendent, or that person's designee.

(2) A chief of police in the county, or the appointed chief's designee.

(3) The local sheriff, or that person's designee.

(4) The district attorney, or that person's designee.

(5) The chief court counselor, or that person's designee.

(6) The director of the area local management entity/managed care organization (LME/MCO) or that person's designee.

(7) The director of the county department of social services, or consolidated human services agency, or that person's designee.

(8) The county manager, or that person's designee.

(9) A substance abuse professional.

(10) A member of the faith community.

(11) A county commissioner.

(12) Two persons under the age of 21 years, or one person under the age of 21 years and one member of the public representing the interests of families of at-risk juveniles.

(13) A juvenile defense attorney.

(14) The chief district court judge, or a judge designated by the chief district court judge.

(15) A member of the business community.

(16) The local health director, or that person's designee.

(17) A representative from the United Way or other nonprofit agency.

(18) A representative of a local parks and recreation program.

(19) Up to seven members of the public to be appointed by the board of commissioners of a county.

The board of commissioners of a county shall modify the County Council's membership as necessary to ensure that the members reflect the racial and socioeconomic diversity of the community and to minimize potential conflicts of interest by members.

(b) Two or more counties may establish a multicounty Juvenile Crime Prevention Council under subsection (a) of this section. The membership shall be representative of each participating county.

(c) The members of the County Council shall elect annually the chair and vice-chair.

History.
1998-202, s. 1(b); 2000-137, s. 1(b); 2001-199, s. 1; 2011-145, s. 19.1(t); 2020-83, s. 2

§ 143B-847. Terms of appointment

Each member of a County Council shall serve for a term of two years, except for initial terms as provided in this section. Each member's term is a continuation of that member's term under G.S. 147-33.62. Members may be reappointed. The initial terms of appointment began January 1, 1999. In order to provide for staggered terms, persons appointed for the positions designated in subdivisions (9), (10), (12), (15), (17), and (18) of G.S. 143B-846(a) were appointed for an initial term ending on June 30, 2000. The initial term of the second member added to each County Council pursuant to G.S. 143B-846(a) (12) shall begin on July 1, 2001, and end on June 30, 2002. After the initial terms, persons appointed for the positions designated in subdivisions (9), (10), (12), (15), (17), and (18) of G.S. 143B-846(a) shall be appointed for two-year terms, beginning on July 1. All other persons appointed to the Council were appointed for an initial term ending on June 30, 2001, and, after those initial terms, persons shall be appointed for two-year terms beginning on July 1.

History.
1998-202, s. 1(b); 1999-423, s. 15; 2000-137, s. 1(b); 2001-199, s. 2; 2011-145, s. 19.1(t), (fff)

§ 143B-848. Vacancies; removal

Appointments to fill vacancies shall be for the remainder of the former member's term.

Members shall be removed only for malfeasance or nonfeasance as determined by the board of county commissioners.

History.
1998-202, s. 1(b); 2000-137, s. 1(b); 2011-145, s. 19.1(t)

§ 143B-849. Meetings; quorum

County Councils shall meet at least six times per year, or more often if a meeting is called by the chair.

A majority of members constitutes a quorum.

History.
1998-202, s. 1(b); 1999-423, s. 16; 2000-137, s. 1(b); 2011-145, s. 19.1(t); 2020-83, s. 3

§ 143B-850. Compensation of members

Members of County Councils shall receive no compensation but may receive a per diem in an amount established by the board of county commissioners.

History.
1998-202, s. 1(b); 2000-137, s. 1(b); 2011-145, s. 19.1(t)

§ 143B-851. Powers and duties

(a) Each County Council shall review biennially the needs of juveniles in the county who are at risk of delinquency or who have been adjudicated undisciplined or delinquent and the resources available to address those needs. In particular, each County Council shall assess the needs of juveniles in the county who are at risk or who have been associated with gangs or gang activity, and the local resources that are established to address those needs. The Council shall develop and advertise a request for proposal process and submit a written plan of action for the expenditure of juvenile sanction and prevention funds to the board of county commissioners for its approval. Upon the county's authorization, the plan shall be submitted to the Section for final approval and subsequent implementation.

(b) Each County Council shall ensure that appropriate intermediate dispositional options are available and shall prioritize funding for dispositions of intermediate and community-level sanctions for court-adjudicated juveniles under minimum standards adopted by the Section.

(c) On an ongoing basis, each County Council shall:

(1) Assess the needs of juveniles in the community, evaluate the adequacy of resources available to meet those needs, and develop or propose ways to address unmet needs.

(2) Evaluate the performance of juvenile services and programs in the community. The Council shall evaluate each funded program as a condition of continued funding.

(3) Increase public awareness of the causes of delinquency and of strategies to reduce the problem.

(4) Develop strategies to intervene and appropriately respond to and treat the needs of juveniles at risk of delinquency through appropriate risk assessment instruments.

(5) Provide funds for services for treatment, counseling, or rehabilitation for juveniles and their families. These services may

include court-ordered parenting responsibility classes.

(6) Plan for the establishment of a permanent funding stream for delinquency prevention services.

(7) Develop strategies to intervene and appropriately respond to the needs of juveniles who have been associated with gang activity or who are at risk of becoming associated with gang activity.

(d) The Councils may examine the benefits of joint program development between counties and judicial districts.

History.
1998-202, s. 1(b); 2000-137, s. 1(b); 2008-56, s. 3; 2011-145, s. 19.1 (*l*), (t); 2017-186, s. 1(t11); 2020-83, s. 4

§ 143B-852. Department of Public Safety to report on Juvenile Crime Prevention Council grants

(a) On or before February 1 of each year, the Department of Public Safety shall submit to the Chairs of the Joint Legislative Oversight Committee on Justice and Public Safety and the Chairs of the House of Representatives Appropriations Committee on Justice and Public Safety and the Senate Appropriations Committee on Justice and Public Safety a list of the recipients of the grants awarded, or preapproved for award, from funds appropriated to the Department for local Juvenile Crime Prevention Council (JCPC) grants, including the following information:

(1) The amount of the grant awarded.

(2) The membership of the local committee or council administering the award funds on the local level.

(3) The type of program funded.

(4) A short description of the local services, programs, or projects that will receive funds.

(5) Identification of any programs that received grant funds at one time but for which funding has been eliminated by the Department.

(6) The number of at-risk, diverted, and adjudicated juveniles served by each county.

(7) The Department's actions to ensure that county JCPCs prioritize funding for dispositions of intermediate and community-level sanctions for court-adjudicated juveniles under minimum standards adopted by the Department.

(8) The total cost for each funded program, including the cost per juvenile and the essential elements of the program.

(b) On or before February 1 of each year, the Department of Public Safety shall send to the Fiscal Research Division of the Legislative Services Commission an electronic copy of the list and information required under subsection (a) of this section.

History.
2013-360, s. 16D.2(a); 2017-57, s. 16D.3

§ 143B-853. Funding for programs

(a) Annually, the Division of Adult Correction and Juvenile Justice shall develop and implement a funding mechanism for programs that meet the standards developed under this Subpart. The Division shall ensure that the guidelines for the State and local partnership's funding process include the following requirements:

(1) **Fund effective programs. --** The Division shall fund programs that it determines to be effective in preventing delinquency and recidivism. Programs that have proven to be ineffective shall not be funded.

(2) **Use a formula for the distribution of funds. --** A funding formula shall be developed that ensures that even the smallest counties will be able to provide the basic prevention and alternative services to juveniles in their communities.

(3) **Allow and encourage local flexibility. --** A vital component of the State and local partnership established by this section is local flexibility to determine how best to allocate prevention and alternative funds.

(4) **Combine resources. --** Counties shall be allowed and encouraged to combine resources and services.

(5) **Allow for a two-year funding cycle. --** In the discretion of the Division, awards may be provided in amounts that fund two years of services for programs that meet the requirements of this section and have been awarded funds in a prior funding cycle.

(b) The Division shall adopt rules to implement this section. The Division shall provide technical assistance to County Councils and shall require them to evaluate all State-funded programs and services on an ongoing and regular basis.

(c) The Juvenile Justice Section of the Division of Adult Correction and Juvenile Justice of the Department of Public Safety shall report to the Senate and House of Representatives Appropriations Subcommittees on Justice and Public Safety no later than March 1, 2006, and annually thereafter, on the results of intensive intervention services. Intensive intervention services are evidence-based or research-supported community-based or residential services that are necessary for a juvenile in order to (i) prevent the juvenile's commitment to a youth development center or detention

Chapter 143B

facility, (ii) facilitate the juvenile's successful return to the community following commitment, or (iii) prevent further involvement in the juvenile justice system. Specifically, the report shall provide a detailed description of each intensive intervention service, including the numbers of juveniles served, their adjudication status at the time of service, the services and treatments provided, the length of service, the total cost per juvenile, and the six- and 12-month recidivism rates for the juveniles after the termination of program services.

History.
1998-202, s. 1(b); 2000-137, s. 1(b); 2005-276, s. 16.11(c); 2011-145, s. 19.1 (*l*), (x), (ggg); 2017-186, s. 2 (*lllll*); 2020-83, s. 5; 2021-123, s. 6(e)

§§ 143B-853 through 143B-899

Reserved for future codification purposes.

PART 4
LAW ENFORCEMENT

SUBPART A
GENERAL PROVISIONS

N.C. Gen. Stat. § 143B-900

Recodified as G.S. 143B-911 by Session Laws 2014-100, s. 17.1(i), effective July 1, 2014.

§ 143B-901. Reporting system and database on certain domestic-violence-related homicides; reports by law enforcement agencies required; annual report to the General Assembly

The Department of Public Safety, in consultation with the North Carolina Council for Women/Domestic Violence Commission, the North Carolina Sheriffs' Association, and the North Carolina Association of Chiefs of Police, shall develop a reporting system and database that reflects the number of homicides in the State where the offender and the victim had a personal relationship, as defined by G.S. 50B-1(b). The information in the database shall also include the type of personal relationship that existed between the offender and the victim, whether the victim had obtained an order pursuant to G.S. 50B-3, and whether there was a pending charge for which the offender was on pretrial release pursuant to G.S. 15A-534.1. All State and local law enforcement agencies shall report information to the Department of Public Safety upon making a determination that a homicide meets the reporting system's criteria. The report shall be made in the format adopted

by the Department of Public Safety. The Department of Public Safety shall report to the chairs of the Joint Legislative Oversight Committee on Justice and Public Safety, no later than April 1 of each year, with the data collected for the previous calendar year.

History.
2007-14, s. 2; 2014-100, s. 17.1(g), (rr); 2016-94, s. 17B.2

§ 143B-902. Division of Criminal Information

In addition to its other duties, it shall be the duty of the Department of Public Safety to do all of the following:

(1) To collect and correlate information in criminal law administration, including crimes committed, arrests made, dispositions on preliminary hearings, prosecutions, convictions, acquittals, punishment, appeals, together with the age, race, and sex of the offender, the necessary data to make a trace regarding all firearms seized, forfeited, found, or otherwise coming into the possession of any State or local law enforcement agency of the State that are believed to have been used in the commission of a crime, and such other information concerning crime and criminals as may appear significant or helpful. To correlate such information with the operations of agencies and institutions charged with the supervision of offenders on probation, in penal and correctional institutions, on parole and pardon, so as to show the volume, variety and tendencies of crime and criminals and the workings of successive links in the machinery set up for the administration of the criminal law in connection with the arrests, trial, punishment, probation, prison parole and pardon of all criminals in North Carolina.

(2) To collect, correlate, and maintain access to information that will assist in the performance of duties required in the administration of criminal justice throughout the State. This information may include, but is not limited to, motor vehicle registration, drivers' licenses, wanted and missing persons, stolen property, warrants, stolen vehicles, firearms registration, sexual offender registration as provided under Article 27A of Chapter 14 of the General Statutes, drugs, drug users and parole and probation histories. In performing this function, the Division may arrange to use information available in other agencies and units of State, local and federal government, but shall provide security measures to insure that such information shall be

made available only to those whose duties, relating to the administration of justice, require such information.

(3) To make scientific study, analysis and comparison from the information so collected and correlated with similar information gathered by federal agencies, and to provide the Governor and the General Assembly with the information so collected biennially, or more often if required by the Governor.

(4) To perform all the duties heretofore imposed by law upon the Attorney General with respect to criminal statistics.

(5) To perform such other duties as may be from time to time prescribed by the Attorney General.

(6) To promulgate rules and regulations for the administration of this Article.

History.

1939, c. 315, s. 2; 1955, c. 1257, ss. 1, 2; 1969, c. 1267, s. 1; 1995, c. 545, s. 2; 1999-26, s. 1; 1999-225, s. 1; 2000-67, s. 17.2(a); 2001-424, s. 23.7(a); 2002-159, s. 18(a); 2012-182, s. 1; 2014-100, ss. 17.1(h), (ss)

§ 143B-903. Collection of traffic law enforcement statistics

(a) In addition to its other duties, the Department of Public Safety shall collect, correlate, and maintain the following information regarding traffic law enforcement by law enforcement officers:

(1) The number of drivers stopped for routine traffic enforcement by law enforcement officers, the officer making each stop, the date each stop was made, the agency of the officer making each stop, and whether or not a citation or warning was issued.

(2) Identifying characteristics of the drivers stopped, including the race or ethnicity, approximate age, and sex.

(3) The alleged traffic violation that led to the stop.

(4) Whether a search was instituted as a result of the stop.

(5) Whether the vehicle, personal effects, driver, or passenger or passengers were searched, and the race or ethnicity, approximate age, and sex of each person searched.

(6) Whether the search was conducted pursuant to consent, probable cause, or reasonable suspicion to suspect a crime, including the basis for the request for consent, or the circumstances establishing probable cause or reasonable suspicion.

(7) Whether any contraband was found and the type and amount of any such contraband.

(8) Whether any written citation or any oral or written warning was issued as a result of the stop.

(9) Whether an arrest was made as a result of either the stop or the search.

(10) Whether any property was seized, with a description of that property.

(11) Whether the officers making the stop encountered any physical resistance from the driver or passenger or passengers.

(12) Whether the officers making the stop engaged in the use of force against the driver, passenger, or passengers for any reason.

(13) Whether any injuries resulted from the stop.

(14) Whether the circumstances surrounding the stop were the subject of any investigation, and the results of that investigation.

(15) The geographic location of the stop; if the officer making the stop is a member of the State Highway Patrol, the location shall be the Highway Patrol District in which the stop was made; for all other law enforcement officers, the location shall be the city or county in which the stop was made.

(b) For purposes of this section, "law enforcement officer" means any of the following:

(1) All State law enforcement officers.

(2) Law enforcement officers employed by county sheriffs or county police departments.

(3) Law enforcement officers employed by police departments in municipalities with a population of 10,000 or more persons.

(4) Law enforcement officers employed by police departments in municipalities employing five or more full-time sworn officers for every 1,000 in population, as calculated by the Department for the calendar year in which the stop was made.

(c) The information required by this section need not be collected in connection with impaired driving checks under G.S. 20-16.3A or other types of roadblocks, vehicle checks, or checkpoints that are consistent with the laws of this State and with the State and federal constitutions, except when those stops result in a warning, search, seizure, arrest, or any of the other activity described in subdivisions (4) through (14) of subsection (a) of this section.

(d) Each law enforcement officer making a stop covered by subdivision (1) of subsection (a) of this section shall be assigned an anonymous identification number by the officer's employing agency. The anonymous identifying number shall be public record and shall be reported to the Department to be correlated along with the data collected under subsection (a) of this section. The correlation between the identification numbers and the names of the officers shall not be a public record, and shall not be disclosed by the agency except when required by order

Chapter 143B

of a court of competent jurisdiction to resolve a claim or defense properly before the court.

(e) Any agency subject to the requirements of this section shall submit information collected under subsection (a) of this section to the Department within 60 days of the close of each month. Any agency that does not submit the information as required by this subsection shall be ineligible to receive any law enforcement grants available by or through the State until the information which is reasonably available is submitted.

(f) The Department shall publish and distribute by December 1 of each year a list indicating the law enforcement officers that will be subject to the provisions of this section during the calendar year commencing on the following January 1.

History.
1939, c. 315, s. 2; 1955, c. 1257, ss. 1, 2; 1969, c. 1267, s. 1; 1995, c. 545, s. 2; 1999-26, s. 1; 1999-225, s. 1; 2000-67, s. 17.2(a); 2001-424, s. 23.7(a); 2002-159, s. 18(a), (b); 2009-544, s. 1; 2012-182, s. 1; 2014-100, s. 17.1(h), (tt)

§ 143B-904. Collection of statistics on the use of deadly force by law enforcement officers

(a) In addition to its other duties, the Department of Public Safety shall collect, maintain, and annually publish the number of deaths, by law enforcement agency, resulting from the use of deadly force by law enforcement officers in the course and scope of their official duties.

(b) For purposes of this section, "law enforcement officer" means sworn law enforcement officers with the power of arrest, both State and local.

History.
2009-106, s. 1; 2012-182, s. 1; 2014-100, s. 17.1(h), (uu)

§ 143B-905. Criminal Information Network

(a) The Department of Public Safety is authorized to establish, devise, maintain and operate a system for receiving and disseminating to participating agencies information collected, maintained and correlated under authority of G.S. 143B-902. The system shall be known as the Criminal Information Network.

(b) The Department of Public Safety is authorized to cooperate with the Division of Motor Vehicles, Department of Administration, and other State, local and federal agencies and organizations in carrying out the purpose and intent of this section, and to utilize, in cooperation with other State agencies and to the extent as may be practical, computers and related equipment as may be operated by other State agencies.

(c) The Department of Public Safety, after consultation with participating agencies, shall adopt rules and regulations governing the organization and administration of the Criminal Information Network, including rules and regulations governing the types of information relating to the administration of criminal justice to be entered into the system, and who shall have access to such information. The rules and regulations governing access to the Criminal Information Network shall not prohibit an attorney who has entered a criminal proceeding in accordance with G.S. 15A-141 from obtaining information relevant to that criminal proceeding. The rules and regulations governing access to the Criminal Information Network shall not prohibit an attorney who represents a person in adjudicatory or dispositional proceedings for an infraction from obtaining the person's driving record or criminal history.

(d) The Department may impose monthly fees on participating agencies. The monthly fees collected under this subsection shall be used to offset the cost of operating and maintaining the Criminal Information Network.

(1) The Department may impose a monthly circuit fee on agencies that access the Criminal Information Network through a circuit maintained and operated by the Department of Public Safety. The amount of the monthly fee is three hundred dollars ($ 300.00) plus an additional fee amount for each device linked to the Network. The additional fee amount varies depending upon the type of device. For a desktop device after the first seven desktop devices, the additional monthly fee is twenty-five dollars ($ 25.00) per device. For a mobile device, the additional monthly fee is twelve dollars ($ 12.00) per device.

(2) The Department may impose a monthly device fee on agencies that access the Criminal Information Network through some other approved means. The amount of the monthly device fee varies depending upon the type of device. For a desktop device, the monthly fee is twenty-five dollars ($ 25.00) per device. For a mobile device, the fee is twelve dollars ($ 12.00) per device.

History.
1969, c. 1267, s. 2; 1975, c. 716, s. 5; 1977, c. 836; 1993, c. 39, s. 1; 2005-276, ss. 43.4(a), 43.4(b); 2011-145, s. 19.1(h); 2012-83, s. 36; 2012-182, s. 1; 2014-100, s. 17.1(h), (vv)

§ 143B-906. Criminal statistics

It shall be the duty of the State Bureau of Investigation to receive and collect criminal information, to assist in locating, identifying, and keeping records of criminals in this State, and from other states, and to compare, classify, compile, publish, make available and disseminate any and all such information to the sheriffs, constables, police authorities, courts or any other officials of the State requiring such criminal identification, crime statistics and other information respecting crimes local and national, and to conduct surveys and studies for the purpose of determining so far as is possible the source of any criminal conspiracy, crime wave, movement or cooperative action on the part of the criminals, reporting such conditions, and to cooperate with all officials in detecting and preventing.

History.
1965, c. 1049, s. 1; 1973, c. 1286, s. 19; 1989, c. 772, s. 3; 1989 (Reg. Sess., 1990), c. 814, s. 9; 2000-119, s. 7; 2003-214, s. 1(1); 2014-100, s. 17.1(k), (zzz)

§§ 143B-907 through 143B-910

Reserved for future codification purposes.

SUBPART B
STATE CAPITOL POLICE DIVISION

§ 143B-911. Creation of State Capitol Police Division; powers and duties

(a) **Division Established. --** There is created the State Capitol Police Division of the Department of Public Safety with the organization, powers, and duties defined in Article 1 of this Chapter, except as modified in this Part.

(b) **Purpose. --** The State Capitol Police Division shall serve as a special police agency of the Department of Public Safety. The Chief of the State Capitol Police, appointed by the Secretary pursuant to G.S. 143B-602, with the approval of the Governor, may appoint as special police officers such reliable persons as the Chief may deem necessary.

(c) **Appointment of Officers. --** Special police officers appointed pursuant to this section may not exercise the power of arrest until they shall take an oath, to be administered by any person authorized to administer oaths, as required by law.

(d) **Jurisdiction of Officers. --** Each special police officer of the State Capitol Police shall have the same power of arrest as the police officers of the City of Raleigh. Such authority may be exercised within the same territorial jurisdiction as exercised by the police officers of the City of Raleigh, and in addition thereto the authority of a deputy sheriff may be exercised on property owned, leased, or maintained by the State located in the County of Wake.

(e) **Public Safety. --** The Chief of the State Capitol Police, or the Chief's designee, shall exercise at all times those means that, in the opinion of the Chief or the designee, may be effective in protecting all State buildings and grounds, except for the State legislative buildings and grounds as defined in G.S. 120-32.1(d), and the persons within those buildings and grounds from fire, bombs, bomb threats, or any other emergency or potentially hazardous conditions, including both the ordering and control of the evacuation of those buildings and grounds. The Chief, or the Chief's designee, may employ the assistance of other available law enforcement agencies and emergency agencies to aid and assist in evacuations of those buildings and grounds.

History.
2009-451, s. 17.3(f); 2011-145, s. 19.1(g), (u), (y); 2014-100, s. 17.1(i); 2015-241, s. 16A.7(f); 2015-267, s. 3; 2017-57, s. 16B.10(c)

§§ 143B-912 through 143B-914

Reserved for future codification purposes.

SUBPART C
STATE BUREAU OF INVESTIGATION

§ 143B-915. Bureau of Investigation created; powers and duties

In order to secure a more effective administration of the criminal laws of the State, to prevent crime, and to procure the speedy apprehension of criminals, there is established the State Bureau of Investigation, which shall be administratively located in the Department of Public Safety. The Bureau shall be an independent agency under the direction and supervision of the Director, who shall serve as chief executive officer of the Bureau and shall be solely responsible for all management functions. Notwithstanding any provisions to the contrary, the Director shall have such authority as is necessary to direct and oversee the Bureau, and may delegate any duties and responsibilities necessary to ensure the proper management of the Bureau. The Department of Public Safety shall provide administrative support to the Bureau. The State Bureau of Investigation shall have charge of and administer the agencies and activities herein set up for the identification of criminals, for their apprehension, and investigation and preparation of evidence to be used in criminal courts; and the said Bureau shall have charge of investigation of criminal matters herein especially mentioned, and of such other crimes and criminal procedure as the Governor may direct.

Chapter 143B

In the personnel of the Bureau shall be included a sufficient number of persons of training and skill in the investigation of crime and in the preparation of evidence as to be of service to local enforcement officers, under the direction of the Governor, in criminal matters of major importance.

History.

1937, c. 349, s. 1; 1939, c. 315, s. 6; 2003-214, s. 1(1); 2013-360, s. 17.6 (*l*); 2014-100, s. 17.1(j), (ww); 2015-241, s. 16A.7(a)

§ 143B-916. SBI liaison

The State Bureau of Investigation may designate liaison personnel to lobby for legislative action in accordance with Article 5C of Chapter 120C of the General Statutes.

History.

2015-241, s. 16A.7(c); 2017-6, s. 3; 2018-146, ss. 3.1(a), (b), 6.1

§ 143B-917. General powers and duties of Director and law enforcement officers of the State Bureau of Investigation

The Director of the Bureau and other sworn law enforcement officers of the State Bureau of Investigation are given the same power of arrest as is now vested in the sheriffs of the several counties, and their jurisdiction shall be statewide. The Director of the Bureau and other sworn law enforcement officers of the Bureau may give assistance to sheriffs, police officers, district attorneys, and judges when called upon by them and so directed. They shall also give assistance, when requested, to the Department of Public Safety in the investigation of cases pending before the parole office and of complaints lodged against parolees, when so directed by the Governor.

History.

1937, c. 349, s. 5; 1973, c. 47, s. 2; c. 1262, s. 10; 2003-214, s. 1(1); 2011-145, s. 19.1(h), (q1); 2011-391, s. 43(g); 2012-83, s. 37; 2014-100, s. 17.1(j), (xx)

§ 143B-918. Transfer of personnel

The Director of the State Bureau of Investigation shall have authority to transfer members of the Bureau from one locality in the State to another as he may deem necessary. When any member of the State Bureau of Investigation is transferred from one point to another for the convenience of the State, or otherwise than upon the request of the employee, the Bureau shall be responsible for transporting the household goods, furniture, and personal effects of the employee and members of his household.

History.

1955, c. 1185, s. 2; 2003-214, s. 1(1); 2011-145, s. 19.1(q1); 2011-391, s. 43(g); 2014-100, s. 17.1(j)

§ 143B-919. Investigations of lynchings, election frauds, etc.; services subject to call of Governor; witness fees and mileage for employees

(a) The Bureau shall, upon request of the Governor, investigate and prepare evidence in the event of any lynching or mob violence in the State; shall investigate all cases arising from frauds in connection with elections when requested to do so by the Board of Elections, and when so directed by the Governor. Such investigation, however, shall in nowise interfere with the power of the Attorney General to make such investigation as the Attorney General is authorized to make under the laws of the State. The Bureau is authorized further, at the request of the Governor, to investigate cases of frauds arising under the Social Security Laws of the State, of violations of the gaming laws, and lottery laws, and matters of similar kind when called upon by the Governor so to do. In all such cases it shall be the duty of the Department to keep such records as may be necessary and to prepare evidence in the cases investigated, for the use of enforcement officers and for the trial of causes. The services of employees of the Bureau may be required by the Governor in connection with the investigation of any crime committed anywhere in the State when called upon by the enforcement officers of the State, and when, in the judgment of the Governor, such services may be rendered with advantage to the enforcement of the criminal law. The State Bureau of Investigation is hereby authorized to investigate without request the attempted arson of, or arson of, damage of, theft from, or theft of, or misuse of, any State-owned personal property, buildings, or other real property or any assault upon or threats against any legislative officer named in G.S. 147-2(1), (2), or (3), any executive officer named in G.S. 147-3(c), or any court officer as defined in G.S. 14-16.10(1).

(b) The Bureau also is authorized at the request of the Governor to conduct a background investigation on a person that the Governor plans to nominate for a position that must be confirmed by the General Assembly, the Senate, or the House of Representatives. The background investigation of the proposed nominee shall be limited to an investigation of the person's criminal record, educational background, employment record, records concerning the listing and payment of taxes, and credit record, and to a requirement that the person provide the information contained in the statements of economic interest required to be filed by persons subject to Chapter 138A of the General

Statutes. The Governor must give the person being investigated written notice that the Governor intends to request a background investigation at least 10 days prior to the date that the Governor requests the State Bureau of Investigation to conduct the background investigation. The written notice shall be sent by regular mail, and there is created a rebuttable presumption that the person received the notice if the Governor has a copy of the notice.

(b1) The Bureau shall, upon request of the Governor or a sheriff, chief of police, head of a State law enforcement agency, district attorney, or the Commissioner of Prisons, investigate and prepare evidence in the event of any of the following:

(1) A sworn law enforcement officer with the power to arrest uses force against an individual in the performance of the officer's duties that results in the death of the individual.

(2) An individual in the custody of the Department of Public Safety, a State prison, a county jail, or a local confinement facility, regardless of the physical location of the individual, dies.

(c) The State Bureau of Investigation is further authorized, upon request of the Governor or the Attorney General, to investigate the commission or attempted commission of the crimes defined in the following statutes:

(1) Article 4A of Chapter 14 of the General Statutes;

(1a) G.S. 14-43.11;

(2) G.S. 14-277.1;

(3) G.S. 14-277.2;

(4) G.S. 14-283;

(5) G.S. 14-284;

(6) G.S. 14-284.1;

(7) G.S. 14-288.2;

(8) G.S. 14-288.7;

(9) G.S. 14-288.8;

(10) G.S. 14-288.20;

(10a) G.S. 14-288.21;

(10b) G.S. 14-288.22;

(10c) G.S. 14-288.23;

(10d) G.S. 14-288.24;

(11) G.S. 14-284.2;

(12) G.S. 14-399(e);

(12a) G.S. 15A-287 and G.S. 15A-288;

(13) G.S. 130A-26.1;

(14) G.S. 143-215.6B;

(15) G.S. 143-215.88B; and

(16) G.S. 143-215.114B.

(d) The State Bureau of Investigation is further authorized, upon request of the Governor or Attorney General, to investigate the solicitation, commission, or attempted commission, by means of a computer, computer network, computer system, electronic mail service provider, or the Internet, of the crimes defined in the following statutes:

(1) G.S. 14-190.6;

(2) G.S. 14-190.7;

(3) G.S. 14-190.8;

(4) G.S. 14-190.14;

(5) G.S. 14-190.15;

(6) G.S. 14-190.16;

(7) G.S. 14-190.17;

(8) G.S. 14-190.17A;

(9) G.S. 14-190.18;

(10) G.S. 14-190.19;

(11) G.S. 14-202.3;

Upon determining the location of the criminal violation, the State Bureau of Investigation shall promptly notify the sheriff and local law enforcement of its investigation.

(e) All records and evidence collected and compiled by employees of the Bureau shall, upon request, be made available to the district attorney of any district if the same concerns persons or investigations in his district.

(f) In all cases where the cost is assessed against the defendant and paid by him, there shall be assessed in the bill of cost, mileage and witness fees to any employees of the Bureau who are witnesses in cases arising in courts of this State. The fees so assessed, charged and collected shall be forwarded by the clerks of the court to the Treasurer of the State of North Carolina, and there credited to the Bureau of Identification and Investigation Fund.

History.

1937, c. 349, s. 6; 1947, c. 280; 1965, c. 772; 1973, c. 47, s. 2; 1981, c. 822, s. 2; 1987, c. 858, s. 1; c. 867, s. 3; 1991, c. 725, s. 2; 1993, c. 461, s. 2; 1995, c. 407, s. 2; 1999-398, s. 2; 2003-214, s. 1(1); 2005-121, s. 3; 2008-213, s. 88; 2011-145, s. 19.1(q1); 2011-391, s. 43(g); 2014-100, s. 17.1(j), (yy); 2017-57, s. 16B.10(a); 2017-6, s. 3; 2018-146, ss. 3.1(a), (b), 6.1; 2021-138, s. 10(a)

§ 143B-920. Department heads to report possible violations of criminal statutes involving misuse of State property to State Bureau of Investigation

Any person employed by the State of North Carolina, its agencies or institutions, who receives any information or evidence of an attempted arson, or arson, damage of, theft from, or theft of, or embezzlement from, or embezzlement of, or misuse of, any state-owned personal property, buildings or other real property, shall as soon as possible, but not later than three days from receipt of the information or evidence, report such information or evidence to his immediate supervisor, who shall in turn report such information or evidence to the head of the respective department, agency, or institution. The head of any department, agency, or institution receiving such information or evidence shall, within a reasonable time but no later than 10 days from receipt thereof, report such information, excluding damage or loss resulting from motor vehicle accidents or unintentional loss of property, in writing to the Director of the State Bureau of Investigation.

Upon receipt of notification and information as provided for in this section, the State Bureau of Investigation shall, if appropriate, conduct an investigation.

The employees of all State departments, agencies and institutions are hereby required to cooperate with the State Bureau of Investigation, its officers and agents, as far as may be possible, in aid of such investigation.

If such investigation reveals a possible violation of the criminal laws, the results thereof shall be reported by the State Bureau of Investigation to the district attorney of any district if the same concerns persons or offenses in his district.

History.
1977, c. 763; 2003-214, s. 1(1); 2011-145, s. 19.1(q1); 2011-391, s. 43(g); 2014-100, s. 17.1(j); 2014-115, s. 45(a)

§ 143B-921. Use of private investigators limited

No State executive officer, department, agency, institution, commission, bureau, or other organized activity of the State that receives support in whole or in part from the State except for counties, cities, towns, other municipal corporations or political subdivisions of the State or any agencies of these subdivisions, or county or city boards of education may employ a private investigator without the consent of the Director of the State Bureau of Investigation. If the Director of the State Bureau of Investigation determines that it is impracticable for the Bureau to conduct the investigation, the Director of the State Bureau of Investigation shall employ a private investigator and shall fix the compensation for his services. The cost of the private investigator shall be paid from funds credited to the entity requesting the investigation or from the Contingency and Emergency Fund.

History.
1985, c. 479, s. 138; 2003-214, s. 1(1); 2014-100, s. 17.1(p), (j)

§ 143B-922. Investigations of child sexual abuse in child care

The Director of the Bureau may form a task force to investigate and gather evidence following a notification by the director of a county department of social services, pursuant to G.S. 7B-301, that child sexual abuse may have occurred in a child care facility.

History.
1991, c. 593, s. 3; 1991 (Reg. Sess., 1992), c. 923, s. 5; 1997-506, s. 37; 1998-202, s. 13(z); 2003-214, s. 1(1); 2011-145, s. 19.1(q1); 2011-391, s. 43(g); 2014-100, s. 17.1(j)

§ 143B-923. Cooperation of local enforcement officers

All local enforcement officers are hereby required to cooperate with the said Bureau, its officers and agents, as far as may be possible, in aid of such investigations and arrest and apprehension of criminals as the outcome thereof.

History.
1937, c. 349, s. 8; 2003-214, s. 1(1); 2014-100, s. 17.1(j)

§ 143B-924. Governor authorized to transfer activities of Central Prison Identification Bureau to the new Bureau; photographing and fingerprinting records

The records and equipment of the Identification Bureau now established at Central Prison shall be made available to the said Bureau of Investigation, and the activities of the Identification Bureau now established at Central Prison may, in the future, if the Governor deem advisable, be carried on by the Bureau hereby established; except that the Bureau established by this Article shall have authority to make rules and regulations whereby the photographing and fingerprinting of persons confined in the Central Prison, or clearing through the Central Prison, or sentenced by any of the courts of this State to service upon the roads, may be taken and filed with the Bureau.

History.
1937, c. 349, s. 2; 1939, c. 315, s. 6; 2003-214, s. 1(1); 2014-100, s. 17.1(j)

§ 143B-925. Study and report on use of pseudoephedrine products to make methamphetamine

The State Bureau of Investigation shall study issues regarding the use of pseudoephedrine products to make methamphetamine, including any data on the use of particular pseudoephedrine products in that regard, pertinent law enforcement statistics, trends observed, and other relevant information, and report annually to the Commission for Mental Health, Developmental Disabilities, and Substance Abuse Services and the Joint Governmental Operations Subcommittee on Justice and Public Safety.

History.
2005-434, s. 8; 2014-100, s. 17.1 (*l*); 2021-90, s. 8(c)

§ 143B-926. Appointment and term of the Director of the State Bureau of Investigation

(a) The Director of the State Bureau of Investigation shall be appointed by the Governor for a term of eight years subject to confirmation by the General Assembly by joint resolution. The term of office of the Director of the State Bureau of Investigation shall be for eight years; the first full term shall begin July 1, 2015. The name of the person to be appointed by the Governor shall be submitted by the Governor to the General Assembly for confirmation by the General Assembly on or before May 1 of the year in which the term for which the appointment is to be made expires. Upon failure of the Governor to submit a name as herein provided, the President Pro Tempore of the Senate and the Speaker of the House of Representatives jointly shall submit a name of an appointee to the General Assembly on or before May 15 of the same year. The appointment shall then be made by enactment of a bill. The bill shall state the name of the person being appointed, the office to which the appointment is being made, the effective date of the appointment, the date of expiration of the term, the residence of the appointee, and that the appointment is made upon the joint recommendation of the Speaker of the House of Representatives and the President Pro Tempore of the Senate. Nothing precludes any member of the General Assembly from proposing an amendment to any bill making such an appointment. If there is no vacancy in the office of the Director of the State Bureau of Investigation, and a bill that would confirm the appointment of the person as Director fails a reading in either chamber of the General Assembly, then the Governor shall submit a new name within 30 days.

(b) The Director may be removed from office only by the Governor and solely for the grounds set forth in G.S. 143B-13(b), (c), and (d). In case of a vacancy in the office of the Director of the State Bureau of Investigation for any reason prior to the expiration of the Director's term of office, the name of the Director's successor shall be submitted by the Governor to the General Assembly not later than 60 days after the vacancy arises. If a vacancy arises in the office when the General Assembly is not in session, an acting Director shall be appointed by the Governor to serve pending confirmation by the General Assembly. However, in no event shall an acting Director serve (i) for more than 12 months without General Assembly confirmation or (ii) after a bill that would confirm the appointment of the person as Director fails a reading in either chamber of the General Assembly.

History.
2014-100, s. 17.1(ppp)

§ 143B-927. Personnel of the State Bureau of Investigation

The Director of the State Bureau of Investigation may appoint a sufficient number of assistants who shall be competent and qualified to do the work of the Bureau. The Director shall be responsible for making all hiring and personnel decisions of the Bureau. Notwithstanding the provisions of this Chapter or Chapter 143A of the General Statutes, the Director may hire or fire personnel and transfer personnel within the Bureau.

History.
2014-100, s. 17.1(ttt); 2015-264, s. 20

§ 143B-928. Alcohol Law Enforcement Branch to remain separate and discrete component of the State Bureau of Investigation; retention of funds; youth access to tobacco products

(a) Notwithstanding any overlap between the duties and jurisdiction of the Alcohol Law Enforcement Branch and the remainder of the State Bureau of Investigation, the Alcohol Law Enforcement Branch is a separate and discrete branch of the State Bureau of Investigation and alcohol law enforcement officers are separate and discrete from other sworn law enforcement officers of the Bureau. No funds or positions shall be transferred from budget code 14550, fund code 1401, to any other fund code or budget code except by act of the General Assembly.

(b) Where the General Statutes confer narrower authority on the State Bureau of Investigation than on the Alcohol Law Enforcement Branch, the narrower authority shall not be construed to limit the authority of the Alcohol Law Enforcement Division.

(c) Any funds or property distributed to the Alcohol Law Enforcement Branch as a result of any federal forfeiture proceeding shall only be expended for purposes related to the Alcohol Law Enforcement Branch.

(d) The Alcohol Law Enforcement branch has jurisdiction and primary responsibility to enforce G.S. 14-313 regarding youth access to tobacco products.

History.
2014-100, s. 17.1(vvv); 2017-57, s. 16B.11; 2018-5, s. 16B.3(a).

§ 143B-929. Operation and management of Information Sharing and Analysis Center

The State Bureau of Investigation shall operate and manage the Information Sharing and Analysis Center, and its operation and

Chapter 143B

management shall be under the sole direction and control of the Director of the State Bureau of Investigation. The Information Sharing and Analysis Center is authorized to analyze information related to any threat of violence to the safety of any individual associated with (i) an educational property as defined in G.S. 14-269.2 or (ii) a place of worship as defined in G.S. 14-54.1. The Information Sharing and Analysis Center shall promptly notify the sheriff and local law enforcement agency with jurisdiction if (i) a threat is determined to be credible and (ii) the location of the educational property or place of worship associated with the threat, or the location of any individual suspected of creating the threat, is ascertained. The Director of the State Bureau of Investigation and other sworn law enforcement officers of the State Bureau of Investigation may give assistance to sheriffs and police officers when called upon by them and so directed, as provided in G.S. 143B-917.

History.
2015-241, s. 16A.7(d); 2018-67, s. 4

SUBPART D
CRIMINAL HISTORY RECORD CHECKS

§ 143B-930. Criminal history background investigations; fees

(a) When the Department of Public Safety determines that any person is entitled by law to receive information, including criminal records, from the State Bureau of Investigation, for any purpose other than the administration of criminal justice, the State Bureau of Investigation shall charge the recipient of such information a reasonable fee for retrieving such information. The fee authorized by this section shall not exceed the actual cost of storing, maintaining, locating, editing, researching and retrieving the information, and may be budgeted for the support of the State Bureau of Investigation.

(b) As used in this section, "administration of criminal justice" means the performance of any of the following activities: the detection, apprehension, detention, pretrial release, post-trial release, prosecution, adjudication, correctional supervision, or rehabilitation of persons suspected of, accused of or convicted of a criminal offense. The term also includes screening for suitability for employment, appointment or retention of a person as a law enforcement or criminal justice officer or for suitability for appointment of a person who must be appointed or confirmed by the General Assembly, the Senate, or the House of Representatives.

(c) In providing criminal history record checks, the Department of Public Safety shall process requests in the following priority order:
(1) Administration of criminal justice record checks,
(2) Mandatory noncriminal justice criminal history record checks,
(3) Voluntary noncriminal justice criminal history record checks.

(d) Nothing in this section shall be construed as enlarging any right to receive any record of the State Bureau of Investigation. Such rights are and shall be controlled by G.S. 143B-919, 143B-906, 120-19.4A, and other applicable statutes.

History.
1979, c. 816; 1981, c. 832, s. 1; 1987, c. 867, s. 1; 1995 (Reg. Sess., 1996), c. 606, s. 4; 2002-126, s. 29A.12(a); 2003-214, s. 1(2); 2014-100, s. 17.1(m), (o), (zz); 2015-267, s. 1(b)

§ 143B-931. Criminal record checks of school personnel

(a) The Department of Public Safety may provide a criminal record check to the local board of education of a person who is employed in a public school in that local school district or of a person who has applied for employment in a public school in that local school district, if the employee or applicant consents to the record check. The Department may also provide a criminal record check of school personnel as defined in G.S. 115C-332 by fingerprint card to the local board of education from National Repositories of Criminal Histories, in accordance with G.S. 115C-332. The information shall be kept confidential by the local board of education as provided in Article 21A of Chapter 115C of the General Statutes.

(b) The Department of Public Safety may provide a criminal history record check to the board of directors of a regional school of a person who is employed at a regional school or of a person who has applied for employment at a regional school if the employee or applicant consents to the record check. The Department may also provide a criminal history record check of school personnel as defined in G.S. 115C-238.73 by fingerprint card to the board of directors of the regional school from the National Repositories of Criminal Histories, in accordance with G.S. 115C-238.73. The information shall be kept confidential by the board of directors of the regional school as provided in G.S. 115C-238.73.

(b1) The Department of Public Safety may provide a criminal history record check to the chancellor operating a University of North Carolina laboratory school of a person who is employed at a laboratory school or of a person who has applied for employment at a laboratory school if the employee or applicant consents to the record check. The Department may also provide a criminal history record check of school personnel, as defined in G.S. 116-239.12, by fingerprint card to the chancellor operating the laboratory school from the National Repositories of Criminal Histories, in accordance with G.S. 116-239.12. The information shall be kept confidential by the chancellor operating the laboratory school as provided in G.S. 116-239.12.

(c) The Department of Public Safety may provide a criminal record check to the employer of a person who is employed in a nonpublic school or of a person who has applied for employment in a nonpublic school, if the employee or applicant consents to the record check. For purposes of this subsection, the term nonpublic school is one that is subject to the provisions of Article 39 of Chapter 115C of the General Statutes, but does not include a home school as defined in that Article.

(d) The Department of Public Safety shall charge a reasonable fee for conducting a criminal record check under this section. The fee shall not exceed the actual cost of locating, editing, researching, and retrieving the information.

(e) The Department of Public Safety may provide a criminal record check to the schools within the Department of Health and Human Services of a person who is employed, applies for employment, or applies to be selected as a volunteer, if the employee or applicant consents to the record check. The Department of Health and Human Services shall keep all information pursuant to this subsection confidential, as provided in Article 7 of Chapter 126 of the General Statutes.

(f) The Department of Public Safety shall adopt rules to implement this section.

History.
1991, c. 705, s. 1; 1993, c. 350, s. 1; 1995, c. 373, s. 2; 1997-443, s. 11A.118(a); 2003-214, s. 1(2); 2011-241, s. 2; 2014-100, s. 17.1(m), (o); 2017-102, s. 25; 2017-117, s. 3

§ 143B-932. Criminal record checks of providers of treatment for or services to children, the elderly, mental health patients, the sick, and the disabled

(a) **Authority.** -- The Department of Public Safety may provide to any of the following entities a criminal record check of an individual who is employed by that entity, has applied for employment with that entity, or has volunteered to provide direct care on behalf of that entity:

(1) Hospitals licensed under Chapter 131E of the General Statutes.

(2) Hospices licensed under Chapter 131E of the General Statutes.

(3) Child placing agencies licensed under Chapter 131D of the General Statutes.

(4) Residential child care facilities licensed under Chapter 131D of the General Statutes.

(5) Hospitals licensed under Chapter 122C of the General Statutes.

(6) Licensed child care facilities and non-licensed child care homes regulated by the State.

(7) Any other organization or corporation, whether for profit or nonprofit, that provides direct care or services to children, the sick, the disabled, or the elderly.

(b) **Procedure.** -- A criminal record check may be conducted by using an individual's fingerprint or any information required by the Department of Public Safety to identify that individual. A criminal record check shall be provided only if the individual whose record is checked consents to the record check. The information shall be kept confidential by the entity that receives the information. Upon the disclosure of confidential information under this section by the entity, the Department may refuse to provide further criminal record checks to that entity.

(c) **Foster or Adoptive Parent.** -- The Department of Public Safety, at the request of a child placing agency licensed under Chapter 131D of the General Statutes or a local department of social services, may provide a criminal record check of a prospective foster care or adoptive parent if the prospective parent consents to the record check. The information shall be kept confidential and upon the disclosure of confidential information under this section by the agency or department, the Department may refuse to provide further criminal record checks to that agency or department.

(d) **Fee.** -- The Department may charge a fee to offset the cost incurred by it to conduct a criminal record check under this section. The fee may not exceed fourteen dollars ($ 14.00).

History.
1993, c. 403, s. 1; 1995, c. 453, s. 1; 1995 (Reg. Sess., 1996), c. 606, s. 1; 1997-506, s. 38; 2000-154, s. 5; 2003-214, s. 1(2); 2014-100, s. 17.1(m), (o)

§ 143B-933. Criminal record checks for foster care

The Department of Public Safety may provide to the Division of Social Services, Department of Health and Human Services, the criminal history from the State and National Repositories of Criminal Histories as defined in G.S. 131D-10.2(6a). The Division shall provide to the Department of Public Safety, along with the request, the fingerprints of the individual to be checked, any additional information required by the Department of Public Safety, and a form consenting to the check of the criminal record and to the use of fingerprints and other identifying information required by the State or National Repositories signed by the individual to be checked. The fingerprints of the individual shall be forwarded to the State Bureau of Investigation for a search of the State's criminal history record file, and the State Bureau of Investigation shall forward a set of fingerprints to the Federal Bureau of Investigation for a national criminal history record check. The Division shall keep all information pursuant to this section privileged, as provided in G.S. 131D-10.3A(g). The Department of Public Safety shall charge a reasonable fee only for conducting the checks of the national criminal history records authorized by this section.

History.
1995, c. 507, s. 23.26(c); 1997-140, s. 3; 1997-443, s. 11A.118(a); 2003-214, s. 1(2); 2014-100, s. 17.1(m), (o)

§ 143B-934. Criminal record checks of child care providers

The Department of Public Safety may provide to the Division of Child Development, Department of Health and Human Services, the criminal history from the State and National Repositories of Criminal Histories in accordance with G.S. 110-90.2, of any child care provider, as defined in G.S. 110-90.2. The Division shall provide to the Department of Public Safety, along with the request, the fingerprints of the provider to be checked, any additional information required by the Department of Public Safety, and a form consenting to the check of the criminal record and to the use of fingerprints and other identifying information required by the State or National Repositories signed by the child care provider to be checked. The Division shall keep all information pursuant to this section privileged, as provided in G.S. 110-90.2(e). The Department of Public Safety shall charge a reasonable fee only for conducting the checks of the national criminal history records authorized by this section.

History.
1995, c. 507, s. 23.25(b); 1997-443, s. 11A.118(a); 1997-506, s. 39; 2003-214, s. 1(2); 2014-100, s. 17.1(m), (o)

§ 143B-935. Criminal history record checks of employees of and applicants for employment with the Department of Health and Human Services, and the Juvenile Justice Section of the Division of

Adult Correction and Juvenile Justice of the Department of Public Safety

(a) **Definitions.** -- As used in this section, the term:

(1) "Covered person" means any of the following:

a. An applicant for employment or a current employee in a position in the Juvenile Justice Section of the Division of Adult Correction and Juvenile Justice of the Department of Public Safety who provides direct care for a client, patient, student, resident or ward of the Division.

b. A person who supervises positions in the Juvenile Justice Section of the Division of Adult Correction and Juvenile Justice of the Department of Public Safety providing direct care for a client, patient, student, resident or ward of the Division.

c. An applicant for employment or a current employee in a position in the Department of Health and Human Services.

d. An independent contractor or an employee of an independent contractor that has contracted to provide services to the Department of Health and Human Services.

e. A person who has been approved to perform volunteer services for the Department of Health and Human Services.

f. An independent contractor or an employee of an independent contractor who has contracted with the Juvenile Justice Section of the Division of Adult Correction and Juvenile Justice of the Department of Public Safety to provide direct care for a client, patient, student, resident, or ward of the Division.

g. A person who has been approved to perform volunteer services in or for the Juvenile Justice Section of the Division of Adult Correction and Juvenile Justice of the Department of Public Safety to provide direct care for a client, patient, student, resident, or ward of the Division.

(2) "Criminal history" means a State or federal history of conviction of a crime, whether a misdemeanor or felony, that bears upon a covered person's fitness for employment in the Department of Health and Human Services or the Juvenile Justice Section of the Division of Adult Correction and Juvenile Justice of the Department of Public Safety. The crimes include, but are not limited to, criminal offenses as set forth in any of the following Articles of

Chapter 14 of the General Statutes: Article 5, Counterfeiting and Issuing Monetary Substitutes; Article 5A, Endangering Executive and Legislative Officers; Article 6, Homicide; Article 7B, Rape and Other Sex Offenses; Article 8, Assaults; Article 10, Kidnapping and Abduction; Article 13, Malicious Injury or Damage by Use of Explosive or Incendiary Device or Material; Article 14, Burglary and Other House-breakings; Article 15, Arson and Other Burnings; Article 16, Larceny; Article 17, Robbery; Article 18, Embezzlement; Article 19, False Pretenses and Cheats; Article 19A, Obtaining Property or Services by False or Fraudulent Use of Credit Device or Other Means; Article 19B, Financial Transaction Card Crime Act; Article 20, Frauds; Article 21, Forgery; Article 26, Offenses Against Public Morality and Decency; Article 26A, Adult Establishments; Article 27, Prostitution; Article 28, Perjury; Article 29, Bribery; Article 31, Misconduct in Public Office; Article 35, Offenses Against the Public Peace; Article 36A, Riots, Civil Disorders, and Emergencies; Article 39, Protection of Minors; Article 40, Protection of the Family; Article 59, Public Intoxication; and Article 60, Computer-Related Crime. The crimes also include possession or sale of drugs in violation of the North Carolina Controlled Substances Act, Article 5 of Chapter 90 of the General Statutes, and alcohol-related offenses such as sale to underage persons in violation of G.S. 18B-302, or driving while impaired in violation of G.S. 20-138.1 through G.S. 20-138.5.

(b) When requested by the Department of Health and Human Services or the Juvenile Justice Section of the Division of Adult Correction and Juvenile Justice of the Department of Public Safety, the North Carolina Department of Public Safety may provide to the requesting department or division a covered person's criminal history from the State Repository of Criminal Histories. Such requests shall not be due to a person's age, sex, race, color, national origin, religion, creed, political affiliation, or handicapping condition as defined by G.S. 168A-3. For requests for a State criminal history record check only, the requesting department or division shall provide to the Department of Public Safety a form consenting to the check signed by the covered person to be checked and any additional information required by the Department of Public Safety. National criminal record checks are authorized for covered applicants who have not resided in the State of North Carolina during the past five years. For national checks the Department of Health and Human Services or the Juvenile Justice Section of the Division of Adult Correction and Juvenile Justice of

the Department of Public Safety shall provide to the North Carolina Department of Public Safety the fingerprints of the covered person to be checked, any additional information required by the Department of Public Safety, and a form signed by the covered person to be checked consenting to the check of the criminal record and to the use of fingerprints and other identifying information required by the State or National Repositories. The fingerprints of the individual shall be forwarded to the State Bureau of Investigation for a search of the State criminal history record file and the State Bureau of Investigation shall forward a set of fingerprints to the Federal Bureau of Investigation for a national criminal history record check. The Department of Health and Human Services and the Juvenile Justice Section of the Division of Adult Correction and Juvenile Justice of the Department of Public Safety shall keep all information pursuant to this section confidential. The Department of Public Safety shall charge a reasonable fee for conducting the checks of the criminal history records authorized by this section.

(c) All releases of criminal history information to the Department of Health and Human Services or the Juvenile Justice Section of the Division of Adult Correction and Juvenile Justice of the Department of Public Safety shall be subject to, and in compliance with, rules governing the dissemination of criminal history record checks as adopted by the North Carolina Department of Public Safety. All of the information either department receives through the checking of the criminal history is privileged information and for the exclusive use of that department.

(d) If the covered person's verified criminal history record check reveals one or more convictions covered under subsection (a) of this section, then the conviction shall constitute just cause for not selecting the person for employment, or for dismissing the person from current employment with the Department of Health and Human Services or the Juvenile Justice Section of the Division of Adult Correction and Juvenile Justice of the Department of Public Safety. The conviction shall not automatically prohibit employment; however, the following factors shall be considered by the Department of Health and Human Services or the Juvenile Justice Section of the Division of Adult Correction and Juvenile Justice of the Department of Public Safety in determining whether employment shall be denied:

(1) The level and seriousness of the crime;

(2) The date of the crime;

(3) The age of the person at the time of the conviction;

(4) The circumstances surrounding the commission of the crime, if known;

(5) The nexus between the criminal conduct of the person and job duties of the person;

(6) The prison, jail, probation, parole, rehabilitation, and employment records of the person since the date the crime was committed; and

(7) The subsequent commission by the person of a crime listed in subsection (a) of this section.

(e) The Department of Health and Human Services and the Juvenile Justice Section of the Division of Adult Correction and Juvenile Justice of the Department of Public Safety may deny employment to or dismiss a covered person who refuses to consent to a criminal history record check or use of fingerprints or other identifying information required by the State or National Repositories of Criminal Histories. Any such refusal shall constitute just cause for the employment denial or the dismissal from employment.

(f) The Department of Health and Human Services and the Juvenile Justice Section of the Division of Adult Correction and Juvenile Justice of the Department of Public Safety may extend a conditional offer of employment pending the results of a criminal history record check authorized by this section.

History.
1997-260, s. 1; 1997-443, s. 11A.118(b); 1998-202, s. 4(f); 2000-137, s. 4(h); 2003-214, s. 1(2); 2005-114, s. 4; 2011-145, s. 19.1 (*l*); 2012-12, s. 2(nn); 2012-83, s. 5; 2014-100, s. 17.1(m), (o), (q), (aaa); 2015-181, s. 47; 2017-186, ss. 2 (jjjjjj), 3(b)

§ 143B-935.1. Criminal record checks of applicants and current employees who access federal tax information

(a) The Department of Public Safety may, upon request, provide to the Division of Social Services or Division of Health Benefits within the Department of Health and Human Services or a county agency the criminal history from the State and National Repositories of Criminal Histories of the following individuals if the individual is permitted, or will be permitted, to access federal tax information:

(1) An applicant for employment.

(2) A current employee.

(3) A contractual employee or applicant.

(4) An employee of a contractor.

(b) Along with the request, the requesting agency shall provide the following to the Department of Public Safety:

(1) The fingerprints of the person who is the subject of the record check.

(2) A form signed by the person who is the subject of the record check consenting to:

a. The criminal record check.

b. The use of fingerprints.

c. Any other identifying information required by the State and National Repositories.

d. Any additional information required by the Department of Public Safety.

(c) The fingerprints shall be forwarded to the State Bureau of Investigation for a search of the State's criminal history record file, and the State Bureau of Investigation shall forward a set of fingerprints to the Federal Bureau of Investigation for a national criminal history record check.

(d) The requesting agency shall keep all information obtained pursuant to this section confidential.

(e) The Department of Public Safety may charge a fee to offset the cost incurred by it to conduct a criminal record check under this section. The fee shall not exceed the actual cost of locating, editing, researching, and retrieving the information.

History.
2018-5, s. 11C.4; 2019-81, s. 15(a)

§ 143B-936. Criminal record checks required prior to placement for adoption of a minor who is in the custody or placement responsibility of a county department of social services

The Department of Public Safety may provide to the Division of Social Services, Department of Health and Human Services, the criminal history from the State and National Repositories of Criminal Histories as defined in G.S. 48-1-101(5a). The Division shall provide to the Department of Public Safety, along with the request, the fingerprints of any individual to be checked, any additional information required by the Department of Public Safety, and a form consenting to the check of the criminal record and to the use of fingerprints and other identifying information required by the State or National Repositories signed by the individual to be checked. The fingerprints of the individual shall be forwarded to the State Bureau of Investigation for a search of the State's criminal history record file, and the State Bureau of Investigation shall forward a set of fingerprints to the Federal Bureau of Investigation for a national criminal history record check. The Division shall keep all information pursuant to this section privileged, as provided in G.S. 48-3-309(f). The Department of Public Safety shall charge a reasonable fee only for conducting the checks of the national criminal history records authorized by this section.

History.
1998-229, s. 16; 2003-214, s. 1(2); 2005-114, s. 3; 2014-100, s. 17.1(m), (o)

§ 143B-937. Criminal record checks of applicants for auctioneer, apprentice auctioneer, or auction firm license

The Department of Public Safety may provide to the North Carolina Auctioneers Commission from the State and National Repositories of Criminal Histories the criminal history of any applicant for an auctioneer's license under Chapter 85B of the General Statutes. Along with the request, the Commission shall provide to the Department of Public Safety the fingerprints of the applicant, a form signed by the applicant consenting to the criminal record check and the use of fingerprints and other identifying information required by the State or National Repositories, and any additional information required by the Department of Public Safety. The applicant's fingerprints shall be forwarded to the State Bureau of Investigation for a check of the State's criminal history record file, and the State Bureau of Investigation shall forward a set of fingerprints to the Federal Bureau of Investigation for a national criminal history record check. The Commission shall keep all information obtained pursuant to this section confidential. Department of Public Safety may charge a fee to offset the cost incurred by it to conduct a criminal record check under this section. The fee shall not exceed the actual cost of locating, editing, researching, and retrieving the information.

History.
1999-142, s. 9; 2000-140, s. 59(c); 2003-214, s. 1(2); 2014-100, s. 17.1(m), (o)

§ 143B-938. Criminal record checks of McGruff House Program volunteers

(a) **Authority.** -- The Department of Public Safety and the Federal Bureau of Investigation may provide to any local law enforcement agency a criminal record check of any individual who applies as a volunteer for the McGruff House Program in that community and a criminal record check of all persons 18 years of age or older who live in the applying household. The North Carolina criminal record check may also be done by a certified DCI operator within the local law enforcement agency.

(b) **Procedure.** -- A criminal record check must be conducted by using an individual's fingerprints and all identification information required by the Department of Public Safety

to identify that individual. A criminal record check shall be provided only if: (i) the individual whose record is checked consents to the record check, and (ii) every individual who is 18 years of age or older who lives in the household also consents to the record check. Refusal to give consent is considered withdrawal of the application. The information shall be kept confidential by the local law enforcement agency that receives the information. If the confidential information is disclosed under this section, the Department may refuse to provide further criminal record checks to that local law enforcement agency.

History.
1999-214, s. 1; 2003-214, s. 1(2); 2014-100, s. 17.1(m), (o)

§ 143B-939. Criminal record checks for adult care homes, nursing homes, home care agencies, and providers of mental health, developmentaldisabilities, and substance abuse services

The Department of Public Safety may provide to the following entities the criminal history from the State and National Repositories of Criminal Histories:

(1) Nursing homes or combination homes licensed under Chapter 131E of the General Statutes.

(2) Adult care homes licensed under Chapter 131D of the General Statutes.

(3) Home care agencies licensed under Chapter 131E of the General Statutes.

(4) Providers licensed under Chapter 122C of the General Statutes, including a contract agency of a provider that is subject to the provisions of Article 4 of that Chapter.

The criminal history shall be provided to nursing homes and home care agencies in accordance with G.S. 131E-265, to adult care homes in accordance with G.S. 131D-40, and to a provider in accordance with G.S. 122C-80. The requesting entity shall provide to the Department of Public Safety, along with the request, the fingerprints of the individual to be checked if a national criminal history record check is required, any additional information required by the Department of Public Safety, and a form signed by the individual to be checked consenting to the check of the criminal record and to the use of fingerprints and other identifying information required by the State or National Repositories of Criminal Histories. If a national criminal history record check is required, the fingerprints of the individual shall be forwarded to the State Bureau of Investigation for a search of the State's criminal history record file, and the State Bureau of Investigation shall forward a set of

Chapter 143B

fingerprints to the Federal Bureau of Investigation for a national criminal history record check. All information received by the entity shall be kept confidential in accordance with G.S. 131E-265, 131D-40, and 122C-80, as applicable. The Department of Public Safety shall charge a reasonable fee for conducting the checks authorized by this section. The fee for the State check may not exceed fourteen dollars ($ 14.00).

History.
2000-154, s. 1; 2003-214, s. 1(2); 2005-4, s. 5(b); 2014-100, s. 17.1(m), (o)

§ 143B-940. Criminal record checks of applicants for licensure as registered nurses or licensed practical nurses

The Department of Public Safety may provide to the North Carolina Board of Nursing from the State and National Repositories of Criminal Histories the criminal history of any applicant for licensure as a registered nurse or licensed practical nurse under Article 9A of Chapter 90 of the General Statutes. Along with the request, the Board shall provide to the Department of Public Safety the fingerprints of the applicant, a form signed by the applicant consenting to the criminal record check and use of fingerprints and other identifying information required by the State and National Repositories, and any additional information required by the Department of Public Safety. The applicant's fingerprints shall be forwarded to the State Bureau of Investigation for a search of the State's criminal history record file and the State Bureau of Investigation shall forward a set of fingerprints to the Federal Bureau of Investigation for a national criminal history record check. The Board shall keep all information obtained pursuant to this section confidential. The Department of Public Safety may charge a fee to offset the cost incurred by it to conduct a criminal record check under this section. The fee shall not exceed the actual cost of locating, editing, researching, and retrieving the information.

History.
2001-371, s. 1; 2003-214, s. 1(2); 2014-100, s. 17.1(m), (o)

§ 143B-941. Criminal record checks of applicants for registration, certification, or licensure as a substance abuse professional

The Department of Public Safety may provide to the North Carolina Substance Abuse Professional Practice Board from the State and National Repositories of Criminal Histories the criminal history of any applicant for registration, certification, or licensure pursuant to

Article 5C of Chapter 90 of the General Statutes. Along with the request, the Board shall provide to the Department of Public Safety the fingerprints of the applicant, a form signed by the applicant consenting to the criminal record check and use of fingerprints and other identifying information required by the State and National Repositories, and any additional information required by the Department of Public Safety. The applicant's fingerprints shall be forwarded to the State Bureau of Investigation for a search of the State's criminal history record file, and the State Bureau of Investigation shall forward a set of fingerprints to the Federal Bureau of Investigation for a national criminal history record check. The Board shall keep all information obtained pursuant to this section confidential. The Department of Public Safety may charge a fee to offset the cost incurred by it to conduct a criminal record check under this section. The fee shall not exceed the actual cost of locating, editing, researching, and retrieving the information.

History.
2005-431, s. 2; 2014-100, s. 17.1(m), (o)

§ 143B-942. Criminal record checks of applicants for licensure as massage and bodywork therapists

The Department of Public Safety may provide to the North Carolina Board of Massage and Bodywork Therapy from the State and National Repositories of Criminal Histories the criminal history of any applicant for licensure pursuant to Article 36 of Chapter 90 of the General Statutes. Along with the request, the Board shall provide to the Department of Public Safety the fingerprints of the applicant, a form signed by the applicant consenting to the criminal record check and use of fingerprints and other identifying information required by the State and National Repositories, and any additional information required by the Department of Public Safety. The applicant's fingerprints shall be forwarded to the State Bureau of Investigation for a search of the State's criminal history record file, and the State Bureau of Investigation shall forward a set of fingerprints to the Federal Bureau of Investigation for a national criminal history record check. The Board shall keep all information obtained pursuant to this section confidential. Department of Public Safety may charge a fee to offset the cost incurred by it to conduct a criminal record check under this section. The fee shall not exceed the actual cost of locating, editing, researching, and retrieving the information.

History.
2008-224, s. 20; 2014-100, s. 17.1(m), (o)

§ 143B-943. Criminal history record checks of applicants to and current members of fire departments and emergency medical services

(a) **Definitions.** -- The following definitions apply in this section:

(1) **Applicant.** -- A person who applies for a paid or volunteer position with a fire department or an emergency medical service.

(2) **Criminal history.** -- A State or federal history of conviction of a crime, whether a misdemeanor or felony, that bears upon a covered person's fitness for holding a paid or volunteer position with a fire department. The crimes include, but are not limited to, criminal offenses as set forth in any of the following Articles of Chapter 14 of the General Statutes: Article 5, Counterfeiting and Issuing Monetary Substitutes; Article 5A, Endangering Executive and Legislative Officers; Article 6, Homicide; Article 7B, Rape and Other Sex Offenses; Article 8, Assaults; Article 10, Kidnapping and Abduction; Article 13, Malicious Injury or Damage by Use of Explosive or Incendiary Device or Material; Article 14, Burglary and Other Housebreakings; Article 15, Arson and Other Burnings; Article 16, Larceny; Article 17, Robbery; Article 18, Embezzlement; Article 19, False Pretenses and Cheats; Article 19A, Obtaining Property or Services by False or Fraudulent Use of Credit Device or Other Means; Article 19B, Financial Transaction Card Crime Act; Article 20, Frauds; Article 21, Forgery; Article 26, Offenses Against Public Morality and Decency; Article 26A, Adult Establishments; Article 27, Prostitution; Article 28, Perjury; Article 29, Bribery; Article 31, Misconduct in Public Office; Article 35, Offenses Against the Public Peace; Article 36A, Riots, Civil Disorders, and Emergencies; Article 39, Protection of Minors; Article 40, Protection of the Family; Article 59, Public Intoxication; and Article 60, Computer-Related Crime. The crimes also include possession or sale of drugs in violation of the North Carolina Controlled Substances Act, Article 5 of Chapter 90 of the General Statutes, and alcohol-related offenses such as sale to underage persons in violation of G.S. 18B-302, or driving while impaired in violation of G.S. 20-138.1 through G.S. 20-138.5.

(3) **Current member.** -- A person who serves in a paid or volunteer position with a fire department or an emergency medical service.

(b) When requested by a designated local Homeland Security director, a local fire chief of a rated fire department, a county fire marshal, an emergency services director, or if there is no designated local Homeland Security director, local fire chief of a rated fire department, county fire marshal, or emergency services director, when requested by a local law enforcement agency, the North Carolina Department of Public Safety may provide to the requesting director, chief, marshal, director, or agency an applicant's or current member's criminal history from the State and National Repositories of Criminal Histories. The local Homeland Security director, local fire chief, marshal, director, or local law enforcement agency shall provide to the North Carolina Department of Public Safety the fingerprints of the applicant to be checked, any additional information required by the Department of Public Safety, and a form signed by the applicant to be checked consenting to the check of the criminal record and to the use of fingerprints and other identifying information required by the State or National Repositories. The fingerprints of the individual shall be forwarded to the State Bureau of Investigation for a search of the State criminal history record file, and the State Bureau of Investigation shall forward a set of fingerprints to the Federal Bureau of Investigation for a national criminal history record check. The local Homeland Security director, local fire chief, county fire marshal, emergency services director, or local law enforcement agency shall keep all information pursuant to this section confidential. Department of Public Safety shall charge a reasonable fee for conducting the checks of the criminal history records authorized by this section.

(c) All releases of criminal history information to the local Homeland Security director, local fire chief, county fire marshal, emergency services director, or local law enforcement agency shall be subject to, and in compliance with, rules governing the dissemination of criminal history record checks as adopted by the North Carolina Department of Public Safety. All of the information the local Homeland Security director, local fire chief, county fire marshal, emergency services director, or local law enforcement agency receives through the checking of the criminal history is privileged information and for the exclusive use of that director, chief, marshal, or agency.

(d) If the applicant's or current member's verified criminal history record check reveals one or more convictions covered under subdivision (a)(2) of this section, then the conviction shall constitute just cause for not selecting the applicant for the position or for dismissing the current member from a current position with the local fire department or emergency medical services. The conviction shall not automatically prohibit volunteering or employment; however, the following factors shall be considered by the local Homeland Security director, local fire chief, county fire marshal, emergency services director, or local law enforcement agency in determining whether the position shall be denied or the current member dismissed from a current position:

    (1) The level and seriousness of the crime;

    (2) The date of the crime;

    (3) The age of the person at the time of the conviction;

    (4) The circumstances surrounding the commission of the crime, if known;

    (5) The nexus between the criminal conduct of the person and the duties of the person;

    (6) The prison, jail, probation, parole, rehabilitation, and employment records of the person since the date the crime was committed; and

    (7) The subsequent commission by the person of a crime listed in subsection (a) of this section.

(e) The local fire department or emergency medical services may deny the applicant or current member the position or dismiss an applicant or current member who refuses to consent to a criminal history record check or use of fingerprints or other identifying information required by the State or National Repositories of Criminal Histories. This refusal constitutes just cause for the denial of the position or the dismissal from a current position.

(f) The local fire department or emergency medical services may extend a conditional offer of the position pending the results of a criminal history record check authorized by this section.

(g) For purposes of this section, "local fire chief" shall include the fire chief of any bona fide fire department certified to the Commissioner of Insurance with at least a Class 9S rating for insurance grading purposes; "county fire marshal" shall include only fire marshals who are paid employees of a county; and "emergency services director" shall include only emergency services directors who are paid employees of a city or county.

History.
2003-182, s. 1; 2007-479, s. 1; 2012-12, s. 2(oo); 2014-27, s. 1; 2014-100, s. 17.1(m), (o), (q); 2015-181, s. 47

§ 143B-944. Criminal record checks of applicants for manufactured home manufacturer, dealer, salesperson, or set-up contractor licensure

The Department of Public Safety may provide to the North Carolina Manufactured Housing Board from the State and National Repositories of Criminal Histories the criminal history of any applicant for licensure as a manufactured home manufacturer, dealer, salesperson, or set-up contractor under Article 9A of Chapter 143 of the General Statutes. Along with the request,

the Board shall provide to the Department of Public Safety the fingerprints of the applicant, a form signed by the applicant consenting to the criminal record check, and use of fingerprints and other identifying information required by the State and National Repositories, and any additional information required by the Department of Public Safety. The applicant's fingerprints shall be forwarded to the State Bureau of Investigation for a search of the State's criminal history record file, and the State Bureau of Investigation shall forward a set of fingerprints to the Federal Bureau of Investigation for a national criminal history record check. The Board shall keep all information obtained pursuant to this section confidential. The Department of Public Safety may charge a fee to offset the cost incurred by it to conduct a criminal record check under this section. The fee shall not exceed the actual cost of locating, editing, researching, and retrieving the information.

History.
2003-400, s. 12; 2014-100, s. 17.1(m), (o)

§ 143B-945. Criminal record checks for municipalities and county governments

The Department of Public Safety may provide to a city or county from the State and National Repositories of Criminal Histories the criminal history of any person who applies for employment with the city or county. The city or county shall provide to the Department of Public Safety, along with the request, the fingerprints of the applicant, a form signed by the applicant consenting to the criminal record check and use of fingerprints and other identifying information required by the State and National Repositories, and any additional information required by the Department of Public Safety. The applicant's fingerprints shall be forwarded to the State Bureau of Investigation for a search of the State's criminal history record file, and the State Bureau of Investigation shall forward a set of fingerprints to the Federal Bureau of Investigation for a national criminal history record check. The city or county shall keep all information obtained pursuant to this section confidential. The Department of Public Safety may charge a fee to offset the cost incurred by it to conduct a criminal record check under this section. The fee shall not exceed the actual cost of locating, editing, researching, and retrieving the information.

History.
2003-214, s. 4; 2005-358, s. 1; 2014-100, s. 17.1(m), (o)

§ 143B-946. Criminal record checks of applicants for locksmith licensure or apprentice designation

The Department of Public Safety may provide to the North Carolina Locksmith Licensing Board from the State and National Repositories of Criminal Histories the criminal history of any applicant for licensure as a locksmith or an apprentice under Chapter 74F of the General Statutes. Along with the request, the Board shall provide to the Department of Public Safety the fingerprints of the applicant, a form signed by the applicant consenting to the criminal record check and use of fingerprints and other identifying information required by the State and National Repositories, and any additional information required by the Department of Public Safety. The applicant's fingerprints shall be forwarded to the State Bureau of Investigation for a search of the State's criminal history record file, and the State Bureau of Investigation shall forward a set of fingerprints to the Federal Bureau of Investigation for a national criminal history record check. The Board shall keep all information obtained pursuant to this section confidential. The Department of Public Safety may charge a fee to offset the cost incurred by it to conduct a criminal record check under this section. The fee shall not exceed the actual cost of locating, editing, researching, and retrieving the information.

History.
2003-350, s. 12; 2014-100, s. 17.1(m).

§ 143B-947. Criminal record checks for the North Carolina State Lottery Commission and its Director

The Department of Public Safety may provide to the North Carolina State Lottery Commission and to its Director from the State and National Repositories of Criminal Histories the criminal history of any prospective employee of the Commission and any potential contractor. The North Carolina State Lottery Commission or its Director shall provide to the Department of Public Safety, along with the request, the fingerprints of the prospective employee of the Commission, or of the potential contractor, a form signed by the prospective employee of the Commission, or of the potential contractor consenting to the criminal record check and use of fingerprints and other identifying information required by the State and National Repositories, and any additional information required by the Department of Public Safety. The fingerprints of the prospective employee of the Commission, or potential contractor, shall be forwarded to the State Bureau of Investigation for a search of the State's criminal history record file, and the State Bureau of Investigation shall forward a set of fingerprints to the Federal Bureau of Investigation for a national criminal history record check. The North Carolina State Lottery Commission and its Director shall remit any

fingerprint information retained by the Commission to alcohol law enforcement agents appointed under Article 5 of Chapter 18B of the General Statutes and shall keep all information obtained pursuant to this section confidential. The Department of Public Safety shall charge a reasonable fee only for conducting the checks of the criminal history records authorized by this section.

History.
2005-344, s. 6; 2005-276, s. 31.1(w); 2006-259, s. 8(g); 2006-264, s. 91(c); 2009-570, s. 32(e); 2014-100, s. 17.1(m), (o)

§ 143B-948. Criminal record checks of applicants for permit or license to conduct exploration, recovery, or salvage operations and archaeological investigations

The Department of Public Safety may provide to the Department of Natural and Cultural Resources from the State and National Repositories of Criminal Histories the criminal history of any applicant for a permit or license under Article 3 of Chapter 121 of the General Statutes or Article 2 of Chapter 70 of the General Statutes. Along with the request, the Department of Natural and Cultural Resources shall provide to the Department of Public Safety the fingerprints of the applicant, a form signed by the applicant consenting to the criminal history record check and use of fingerprints and other identifying information required by the State and National Repositories, and any additional information required by the Department of Public Safety. The applicant's fingerprints shall be forwarded to the State Bureau of Investigation for a search of the State's criminal history record file, and the State Bureau of Investigation shall forward a set of fingerprints to the Federal Bureau of Investigation for a national criminal history record check. The Department of Natural and Cultural Resources shall keep all information obtained under this section confidential. The Department of Public Safety may charge a fee to offset the cost incurred by it to conduct a criminal record check under this section. The fee shall not exceed the actual cost of locating, editing, researching, and retrieving the information.

History.
2005-367, s. 1; 2014-100, s. 17.1(m), (o); 2015-241, s. 14.30(s)

§ 143B-949. Criminal record checks of applicants for licensure and licensees

The Department of Public Safety may provide to the North Carolina Psychology Board from the State and National Repositories of Criminal Histories the criminal history of any applicant for licensure or reinstatement of a license to practice psychology or a licensed psychologist or psychological associate under Article 18A of Chapter 90 of the General Statutes. Along with the request, the Board shall provide to the Department of Public Safety the fingerprints of the applicant or licensee; a form signed by the applicant or licensee consenting to the criminal record check and use of fingerprints and other identifying information required by the State and National Repositories, and any additional information required by the Department of Public Safety. The applicant's or licensee's fingerprints shall be forwarded to the State Bureau of Investigation for a search of the State's criminal history record file, and the State Bureau of Investigation shall forward a set of fingerprints to the Federal Bureau of Investigation for a national criminal history record check. The Board shall keep all information obtained pursuant to this section confidential. The Department of Public Safety may charge each applicant or licensee a fee to offset the cost incurred by it to conduct a criminal record check under this section. The fee shall not exceed the actual cost of locating, editing, researching, and retrieving the information.

History.
2006-175, s. 3; 2006-259, s. 42; 2014-100, s. 17.1(m), (o)

§ 143B-950. Criminal record checks for the Judicial Department

(a) The Department of Public Safety may provide to the Judicial Department from the State and National Repositories of Criminal Histories the criminal history of any current or prospective employee, volunteer, or contractor of the Judicial Department. The Judicial Department shall provide to the Department of Public Safety, along with the request, the fingerprints of the current or prospective employee, volunteer, or contractor, a form signed by the current or prospective employee, volunteer, or contractor consenting to the criminal record check and use of fingerprints and other identifying information required by the State and National Repositories, and any additional information required by the Department of Public Safety. The fingerprints of the current or prospective employee, volunteer, or contractor shall be forwarded to the State Bureau of Investigation for a search of the State's criminal history record file, and the State Bureau of Investigation shall forward a set of fingerprints to the Federal Bureau of Investigation for a national criminal history record check. The Judicial Department

shall keep all information obtained pursuant to this section confidential.

(b) The Department of Public Safety may charge a fee to offset the cost incurred by it to conduct a criminal record check under this section. The fee shall not exceed the actual cost of locating, editing, researching, and retrieving the information.

History.
2006-187, s. 3(a); 2006-259, s. 42; 2014-100, s. 17.1(m), (o)

§ 143B-951. Criminal record checks for the Department of Information Technology

(a) The Department of Public Safety may provide to the Department of Information Technology from the State and National Repositories of Criminal Histories the criminal history of any current or prospective employee, volunteer, or contractor of the Department of Information Technology. The Department of Information Technology shall provide to the Department of Public Safety, along with the request, the fingerprints of the current or prospective employee, volunteer, or contractor, a form signed by the current or prospective employee, volunteer, or contractor consenting to the criminal record check and use of fingerprints and other identifying information required by the State and National Repositories, and any additional information required by the Department of Public Safety. The fingerprints of the current or prospective employee, volunteer, or contractor shall be forwarded to the State Bureau of Investigation for a search of the State's criminal history record file, and the State Bureau of Investigation shall forward a set of fingerprints to the Federal Bureau of Investigation for a national criminal history record check. The Department of Information Technology shall keep all information obtained pursuant to this section confidential.

(b) The Department of Public Safety may charge a fee to offset the cost incurred by it to conduct a criminal record check under this section. The fee shall not exceed the actual cost of locating, editing, researching, and retrieving the information.

History.
2007-155, s. 3; 2007-189, ss. 3, 5.1; 2014-100, s. 17.1(m), (o); 2015-241, s. 7A.4(y)

§ 143B-952. Criminal record checks of EMS personnel

The Department of Public Safety may provide to the Department of Health and Human Services the criminal history from the State and National Repositories of Criminal Histories of an individual who applies for EMS credentials, seeks to renew EMS credentials, or holds EMS credentials, when the criminal history is requested by the Department. The Department of Health and Human Services shall provide to the Department of Public Safety the request for the criminal history, the fingerprints of the individual to be checked, any additional information required by the Department of Public Safety, and a form consenting to the check of the criminal record and to the use of fingerprints and other identifying information required by the State or National Repositories signed by the individual to be checked. The Department of Health and Human Services and Emergency Medical Services Disciplinary Committee, established by G.S. 143-519, shall keep all information obtained pursuant to this section confidential. The Department of Public Safety shall charge a reasonable fee to offset the costs incurred by it to conduct the checks of criminal history records authorized by this section.

History.
2007-411, s. 2; 2014-100, s. 17.1(m), (o).

§ 143B-953. Criminal record checks of applicants for licensure as chiropractic physicians

The Department of Public Safety may provide to the State Board of Chiropractic Examiners from the State and National Repositories of Criminal Histories the criminal history of any applicant for licensure pursuant to Article 8 of Chapter 90 of the General Statutes. Along with the request, the Board shall provide to the Department of Public Safety the fingerprints of the applicant, a form signed by the applicant consenting to the criminal record check and use of fingerprints and other identifying information required by the State and National Repositories, and any additional information required by the Department of Public Safety. The applicant's fingerprints shall be forwarded to the State Bureau of Investigation for a search of the State's criminal history record file, and the State Bureau of Investigation shall forward a set of fingerprints to the Federal Bureau of Investigation for a national criminal history record check. The Board shall keep all information obtained pursuant to this section confidential. The Department of Public Safety may charge a fee to offset the cost incurred by it to conduct a criminal record check under this section. The fee shall not exceed the actual cost of locating, editing, researching, and retrieving the information.

History.
2007-525, s. 2; 2014-100, s. 17.1(m), (o)

§ 143B-954. Criminal history record checks of employees of and applicants for employment with the Department of Public Instruction

(a) **Definitions.** -- As used in this section, the term:

(1) "Covered person" means any of the following:

a. An applicant for employment or a current employee in a position in the Department of Public Instruction.

b. An independent contractor or an employee of an independent contractor that has contracted to provide services to the Department of Public Instruction.

(2) "Criminal history" means a State or federal history of conviction of a crime, whether a misdemeanor or felony, that bears upon a covered person's fitness for employment in the Department of Public Instruction. The crimes include, but are not limited to, criminal offenses as set forth in any of the following Articles of Chapter 14 of the General Statutes: Article 5, Counterfeiting and Issuing Monetary Substitutes; Article 5A, Endangering Executive and Legislative Officers; Article 6, Homicide; Article 7B, Rape and Other Sex Offenses; Article 8, Assaults; Article 10, Kidnapping and Abduction; Article 13, Malicious Injury or Damage by Use of Explosive or Incendiary Device or Material; Article 14, Burglary and Other Housebreakings; Article 15, Arson and Other Burnings; Article 16, Larceny; Article 17, Robbery; Article 18, Embezzlement; Article 19, False Pretenses and Cheats; Article 19A, Obtaining Property or Services by False or Fraudulent Use of Credit Device or Other Means; Article 19B, Financial Transaction Card Crime Act; Article 20, Frauds; Article 21, Forgery; Article 26, Offenses Against Public Morality and Decency; Article 26A, Adult Establishments; Article 27, Prostitution; Article 28, Perjury; Article 29, Bribery; Article 31, Misconduct in Public Office; Article 35, Offenses Against the Public Peace; Article 36A, Riots, Civil Disorders, and Emergencies; Article 39, Protection of Minors; Article 40, Protection of the Family; Article 59, Public Intoxication; and Article 60, Computer-Related Crime. The crimes also include possession or sale of drugs in violation of the North Carolina Controlled Substances Act, Article 5 of Chapter 90 of the General Statutes, and alcohol-related offenses such as sale to underage persons in violation of G.S. 18B-302, or driving while impaired violation of G.S. 20-138.1 through G.S. 20-138.5.

(b) When requested by the Department of Public Instruction, the North Carolina Department of Public Safety may provide to the requesting department a covered person's criminal history from the State Repository of Criminal Histories. Such request shall not be due to a person's age, sex, race, color, national origin, religion, creed, political affiliation, or handicapping condition as defined by G.S. 168A-3. For requests for a State criminal history record check only, the requesting department shall provide to the Department of Public Safety a form consenting to the check, signed by the covered person to be checked and any additional information required by the Department of Public Safety. National criminal record checks are authorized for covered applicants who have not resided in the State of North Carolina during the past five years. For national checks the Department of Public Instruction shall provide to the North Carolina Department of Public Safety the fingerprints of the covered person to be checked, any additional information required by the Department of Public Safety, and a form signed by the covered person to be checked, consenting to the check of the criminal record and to the use of fingerprints and other identifying information required by the State or National Repositories. The fingerprints of the individual shall be forwarded to the State Bureau of Investigation for a search of the State criminal history record file and the Federal Bureau of Investigation for a national criminal history record check. The Department of Public Instruction shall keep all information pursuant to this section confidential. The Department of Public Safety shall charge a reasonable fee for conducting the checks of the criminal history records authorized by this section.

(c) All releases of criminal history information to the Department of Public Instruction shall be subject to, and in compliance with, rules governing the dissemination of criminal history record checks as adopted by the North Carolina Department of Public Safety. All of the information the department receives through the checking of the criminal history is privileged information and for the exclusive use of the department.

(d) If the covered person's verified criminal history record check reveals one or more convictions covered under subsection (a) of this section, then the conviction shall constitute just cause for not selecting the person for employment, or for dismissing the person from current employment with the Department of Public Instruction. The conviction shall not automatically prohibit employment; however, the following factors shall be considered by the Department of Public Instruction in determining whether employment shall be denied:

(1) The level and seriousness of the crime;

(2) The date of the crime;

(3) The age of the person at the time of the conviction;

(4) The circumstances surrounding the commission of the crime, if known;

(5) The nexus between the criminal conduct of the person and job duties of the person;

(6) The prison, jail, probation, parole, rehabilitation, and employment records of the person since the date the crime was committed; and

(7) The subsequent commission by the person of a crime listed in subsection (a) of this section.

(e) The Department of Public Instruction may deny employment to or dismiss a covered person who refuses to consent to a criminal history record check or use of fingerprints or other identifying information required by the State or National Repositories of Criminal Histories. Any such refusal shall constitute just cause for the employment denial or the dismissal from employment.

(f) The Department of Public Instruction may extend a conditional offer of employment pending the results of a criminal history record check authorized by this section.

History.
2007-516, s. 1; 2012-12, s. 2(pp); 2014-100, s. 17.1(m), (o), (q); 2015-181, s. 47

§ 143B-955. Criminal record checks of applicants and of current employees who are involved in the manufacture or production of drivers licenses and identification cards

(a) The Department of Public Safety may, upon request, provide to the Department of Transportation, Division of Motor Vehicles, the criminal history from the State and National Repositories of Criminal Histories of the following individuals if the individual (i) is or will be involved in the manufacture or production of drivers licenses and identification cards, or (ii) has or will have the ability to affect the identity information that appears on drivers licenses or identification cards:

(1) An applicant for employment.

(2) A current employee.

(3) A contractual employee or applicant.

(4) An employee of a contractor.

(b) Along with the request, the Division of Motor Vehicles shall provide the following to the Department of Public Safety:

(1) The fingerprints of the person who is the subject of the record check.

(2) A form signed by the person who is the subject of the record check consenting to:

a. The criminal record check.

b. The use of fingerprints.

c. Any other identifying information required by the State and National Repositories.

d. Any additional information required by the Department of Public Safety.

(c) The fingerprints shall be forwarded to the State Bureau of Investigation for a search of the State's criminal history record file, and the State Bureau of Investigation shall forward a set of fingerprints to the Federal Bureau of Investigation for a national criminal history record check.

(d) The Division of Motor Vehicles shall keep all information obtained pursuant to this section confidential.

(e) The Department of Public Safety may charge a fee to offset the cost incurred by it to conduct a criminal record check under this section. The fee shall not exceed the actual cost of locating, editing, researching, and retrieving the information.

History.
2008-202, s. 1; 2014-100, s. 17.1(m), (o)

§ 143B-956. Criminal history record checks of applicants for licensure as nursing home administrators

(a) The Department of Public Safety may provide to the North Carolina State Board of Examiners for Nursing Home Administrators from the State and National Repositories of Criminal Histories the criminal history of any applicant for licensure as a nursing home administrator under Article 20 of Chapter 90 of the General Statutes. Along with the request, the Board shall provide to the Department of Public Safety the fingerprints of the applicant, a form signed by the applicant consenting to the criminal history record check and use of fingerprints and other identifying information required by the State and National Repositories, and any additional information required by the Department of Public Safety. The applicant's fingerprints shall be forwarded to the State Bureau of Investigation for a search of the State's criminal history record file, and the State Bureau of Investigation shall forward a set of fingerprints to the Federal Bureau of Investigation for a national criminal history record check. The Board shall keep all information obtained pursuant to this section confidential.

(b) The Department of Public Safety may charge a fee to offset the cost incurred by it to conduct a criminal history record check under this section. The fee shall not exceed the actual cost of locating, editing, researching, and retrieving the information.

History.
2008-183, s. 2; 2014-100, s. 17.1(m), (o)

§ 143B-957. Criminal record checks of applicants for licensure as clinical mental health counselors

The Department of Public Safety may provide to the North Carolina Board of Licensed Clinical Mental Health Counselors from the State and National Repositories of Criminal Histories the criminal history of any applicant for licensure or reinstatement of a license or licensee under Article 24 of Chapter 90 of the General Statutes. Along with the request, the Board shall provide to the Department of Public Safety the fingerprints of the applicant or licensee, a form signed by the applicant or licensee consenting to the criminal record check and use of fingerprints and other identifying information required by the State and National Repositories, and any additional information required by the Department of Public Safety. The applicant or licensee's fingerprints shall be forwarded to the State Bureau of Investigation for a search of the State's criminal history record file, and the State Bureau of Investigation shall forward a set of fingerprints to the Federal Bureau of Investigation for a national criminal history record check. The Board shall keep all information obtained pursuant to this section confidential. The Department of Public Safety may charge a fee to offset the cost incurred by it to conduct a criminal record check under this section. The fee shall not exceed the actual cost of locating, editing, researching, and retrieving the information.

History.
2009-367, s. 10; 2014-100, s. 17.1(m), (o); 2019-240, s. 3(j)

§ 143B-958. Criminal history record checks of applicants for licensure as marriage and family therapists and marriage and family therapy associates

The Department of Public Safety may provide to the North Carolina Marriage and Family Therapy Licensure Board from the State and National Repositories of Criminal Histories the criminal history of any applicant for licensure or reinstatement of a license or licensee under Article 18C of Chapter 90 of the General Statutes. Along with the request, the Board shall provide to the Department of Public Safety the fingerprints of the applicant or licensee, a form signed by the applicant or licensee consenting to the criminal history record check and use of fingerprints and other identifying information required by the State and National Repositories, and any additional information required by the Department of Public Safety. The applicant's or licensee's fingerprints shall be forwarded to the State Bureau of Investigation for a search of the State's criminal history record file, and the State Bureau of Investigation shall forward a set of fingerprints to the Federal Bureau of Investigation for a national criminal history record check. The Board shall keep all information obtained pursuant to this section confidential. The Department of Public Safety may charge a fee to offset the cost incurred by the Department to conduct a criminal history record check under this section. The fee shall not exceed the actual cost of locating, editing, researching, and retrieving the information.

History.
2009-393, s. 18; 2014-100, s. 17.1(m), (o)

§ 143B-959. Criminal record checks of petitioners for restoration of firearms rights

(a) A person who petitions the court to have the person's firearms rights restored shall submit a full set of the petitioner's fingerprints, to be administered by the sheriff. The petitioner shall also submit to the sheriff a form signed by the petitioner consenting to the criminal record check and use of fingerprints and other identifying information required by the State and National Repositories, and any additional information required by the State Bureau of Investigation or the Federal Bureau of Investigation. The sheriff shall forward the set of fingerprints and the signed consent form to the State Bureau of Investigation for a records check of State and national databases.

(b) Upon receipt of the fingerprints and consent form forwarded by the sheriff pursuant to subsection (a) of this section, the State Bureau of Investigation shall conduct a search of the State criminal history record file and shall forward a set of the fingerprints and a copy of the signed consent form to the Federal Bureau of Investigation for a national criminal history record check.

(c) The State Bureau of Investigation shall provide a copy of the information obtained pursuant to this section to the clerk of superior court, which shall be kept confidential in the court file for the petition for restoration of firearms rights.

(d) The Department of Public Safety may charge a fee to offset the cost incurred by it to conduct a criminal record check under this section. The fee shall not exceed the actual cost of locating, editing, researching, and retrieving the information.

History.
2010-108, s. 2; 2011-2, ss. 1, 2; 2014-100, s. 17.1(m), (o)

§ 143B-960. Criminal record checks of applicants for certification by the Department of Agriculture and Consumer Services as euthanasia technicians

The Department of Public Safety may provide a criminal record check to the Department of Agriculture and Consumer Services for a person who has applied for a new or renewal certification as a euthanasia technician. The Department of Agriculture and Consumer Services shall provide the Department of Public Safety a request for the criminal record check, the fingerprints of the individual to be checked, any additional information required by the Department of Public Safety, and a form signed by the person seeking certification consenting to the check of the criminal record. The fingerprints shall be forwarded to the State Bureau of Investigation for a search of the State's criminal history record file, and the State Bureau of Investigation shall forward a set of fingerprints to the Federal Bureau of Investigation for a national criminal history record check. The Department of Agriculture and Consumer Services shall keep all information pursuant to this section privileged, in accordance with applicable State law and federal guidelines, and the information shall be confidential and shall not be a public record under Chapter 132 of the General Statutes. The Department of Public Safety may charge each applicant a fee for conducting the checks of criminal history records authorized by this section.

History.
2010-127, s. 4; 2014-100, s. 17.1(m), (o)

§ 143B-961. Criminal history record checks of applicants for trainee registration, appraiser licensure, appraiser certification, or registrants for registration as real estate appraisal management companies

The Department of Public Safety may provide to the North Carolina Appraisal Board from the State and National Repositories of Criminal Histories the criminal history of any applicant or registrant for registration under Article 1 and Article 2 of Chapter 93E of the General Statutes. Along with the request, the Board shall provide to the Department of Public Safety the fingerprints of the applicant or registrant, a form signed by the applicant or registrant consenting to the criminal history record check and use of fingerprints and other identifying information required by the State and National Repositories, and any additional information required by the Department of Public Safety. The applicant's or registrant's fingerprints shall be forwarded to the State Bureau of Investigation for a search of the State's criminal history record file, and the State Bureau of Investigation shall forward a set of fingerprints to the Federal Bureau of Investigation for a national criminal history record check. The Board shall keep all information obtained pursuant to this section confidential. The Department of Public Safety may charge a fee to offset the cost incurred by the Department to conduct a criminal history record check under this section. The fee shall not exceed the actual cost of locating, editing, researching, and retrieving the information.

History.
2010-141, s. 2; 2013-403, s. 8; 2014-100, s. 17.1(m), (o)

§ 143B-962. Criminal history record checks of applicants for a restoration of a revoked drivers license

The Department of Public Safety may provide to the Division of Motor Vehicles, from the State and National Repositories of Criminal Histories, the criminal history record of any applicant for a restoration of a revoked drivers license. Along with the request, the Division shall provide to the Department of Public Safety the fingerprints of the applicant, a form signed by the applicant consenting to the criminal history record check and use of fingerprints, other identifying information required by the State and National Repositories, and any additional information required by the Department of Public Safety. The applicant's fingerprints shall be forwarded to the State Bureau of Investigation for a search of the State's criminal history record file, and the State Bureau of Investigation shall forward a set of fingerprints to the Federal Bureau of Investigation for a national criminal history record check. The Division shall keep all information obtained pursuant to this section confidential. The Department of Public Safety may charge a fee to offset the cost incurred by it to conduct a criminal history record check under this section. The fee shall not exceed the actual cost of locating, editing, researching, and retrieving the information. Fees and other costs incurred by the Division under this statute may be charged to the applicant.

History.
2011-381, s. 5; 2014-100, s. 17.1(m), (o)

§ 143B-963. Criminal history record checks of applicants for and current

holders of certificate to transport household goods

(a) The Department of Public Safety may provide to the Utilities Commission from the State and National Repositories of Criminal Histories the criminal history of any applicant for or current holder of a certificate to transport household goods. Along with the request, the Commission shall provide to the Department of Public Safety the fingerprints of the applicant or current holder, a form signed by the applicant or current holder consenting to the criminal history record check and use of fingerprints and other identifying information required by the State and National Repositories of Criminal Histories, and any additional information required by the Department of Public Safety. The applicant's or current holder's fingerprints shall be forwarded to the State Bureau of Investigation for a search of the State's criminal history record file, and the State Bureau of Investigation shall forward a set of fingerprints to the Federal Bureau of Investigation for a national criminal history record check. The Utilities Commission shall keep all information obtained pursuant to this section confidential. The Department of Public Safety may charge a fee to offset the cost incurred by it to conduct a criminal history record check under this section. The fee shall not exceed the actual cost of locating, editing, researching, and retrieving the information. The Department of Public Safety shall send a copy of the results of the criminal history record checks directly to the Utilities Commission Chief Clerk.

(b) The Utilities Commission may provide the information obtained pursuant to subsection (a) of this section to the Public Staff for use in proceedings before the Commission. The Public Staff shall keep all information obtained pursuant to subsection (a) of this section confidential.

History.
2012-9, s. 2; 2014-100, s. 17.1(m), (o); 2021-23, s. 22

§ 143B-964. Criminal history record checks of applicants for licensure as physical therapists or physical therapist assistants

The Department of Public Safety may provide to the North Carolina Board of Physical Therapy Examiners a criminal history record from the State and National Repositories of Criminal Histories for applicants for licensure by the Board. Along with a request for criminal history records, the Board shall provide to the Department of Public Safety the fingerprints of the applicant or subject, a form signed by the applicant consenting to the criminal history record check and use of the fingerprints and other identifying information required by the

Repositories, and any additional information required by the Department. The fingerprints shall be forwarded to the State Bureau of Investigation for a search of the State's criminal history record file, and the State Bureau of Investigation shall forward a set of fingerprints to the Federal Bureau of Investigation for a national criminal history record check. The Board shall keep all information obtained pursuant to this section confidential. The Department of Public Safety may charge a fee to offset the cost incurred by the Department of Public Safety to conduct a criminal history record check under this section, but the fee shall not exceed the actual cost of locating, editing, researching, and retrieving the information.

History.
2013-312, s. 6; 2014-100, s. 17.1(m), (o)

§ 143B-965. Criminal record checks of applicants and recipients of programs of public assistance

(a) Upon receipt of a request from a county department of social services pursuant to G.S. 108A-26.1, the Department of Public Safety shall, to the extent allowed by federal law, provide to the county department of social services the criminal history from the State or National Repositories of Criminal Histories of an applicant for, or recipient of, program assistance under Part 2 or Part 5 of Article 2 of Chapter 108A of the General Statutes.

(b) The county department of social services shall provide to the Department of Public Safety, along with the request, any information required by the Department of Public Safety and a form signed by the individual to be checked consenting to the check of the criminal record and to the use of any necessary identifying information required by the State or National Repositories. The county department of social services shall keep all information pursuant to this section confidential and privileged, except as provided in G.S. 108A-26.1.

(c) The Department of Public Safety may charge a reasonable fee only for conducting the checks of the criminal history records authorized by this section.

History.
2013-417, s. 3; 2014-100, s. 17.1(m), (o)

§ 143B-966. Criminal record checks for the Office of State Controller

The Department of Public Safety may provide to the Office of State Controller from the State and National Repositories of Criminal Histories the criminal history of any current or prospective employee, volunteer, or contractor of the Office of State Controller. The Office of State Controller shall provide to the Department of Public Safety, along with the request, the fingerprints of the current or prospective employee, volunteer, or contractor, a form signed by the current or prospective employee, volunteer, or contractor consenting to the criminal record check and use of fingerprints and other identifying information required by the State and National Repositories, and any additional information required by the Department of Public Safety. The fingerprints of the current or prospective employee, volunteer, or contractor shall be forwarded to the State Bureau of Investigation for a search of the State's criminal history record file, and the State Bureau of Investigation shall forward a set of fingerprints to the Federal Bureau of Investigation for a national criminal history record check. The Office of State Controller shall keep all information obtained pursuant to this section confidential. The Department of Public Safety may charge a fee to offset the cost incurred by it to conduct a criminal record check under this section. The fee shall not exceed the actual cost of locating, editing, researching, and retrieving the information.

History.
2016-28, s. 2

§ 143B-967. Criminal record checks for the Department of Revenue

(a) The Department of Public Safety shall, upon request, provide to the Department of Revenue from the State and National Repositories of Criminal Histories the criminal history of any of the following individuals:

(1) A current or prospective permanent or temporary employee.

(2) A contractor with the Department.

(3) An employee or agent of a contractor with the Department.

(4) Any other individual otherwise engaged by the Department who will have access to federal tax information.

(b) Along with the request, the Department of Revenue shall provide to the Department of Public Safety the fingerprints of the individual whose record is being sought, a form signed by the individual consenting to the criminal record check and use of fingerprints and other identifying information required by the State and National Repositories, and any additional information required by the Department of Public Safety. The individual's fingerprints shall be forwarded to the State Bureau of Investigation for a search of the State's criminal history record file, and the State Bureau of Investigation shall forward a set of fingerprints to the Federal Bureau of Investigation for a national criminal history record check. The Department of Revenue shall keep all information obtained pursuant to this section confidential.

(c) The Department of Public Safety may charge a fee to offset the cost incurred by it to conduct a criminal record check under this section. The fee shall not exceed the actual cost of locating, editing, researching, and retrieving the information.

History.
2017-57, s. 32.1

§ 143B-968. Criminal record checks for the Office of State Human Resources

(a) The Department of Public Safety may provide to the Office of State Human Resources from the State and National Repositories of Criminal Histories the criminal history of any prospective temporary employee of a State agency or department if a criminal record check is a requirement for employment by the agency or department with which the individual would be temporarily assigned. The Office of State Human Resources shall provide to the Department of Public Safety, along with the request, the fingerprints of the prospective temporary employee, a form signed by the prospective temporary employee consenting to the criminal record check and use of fingerprints and other identifying information required by the State and National Repositories, and any additional information required by the Department of Public Safety. The fingerprints of the prospective employee shall be forwarded to the State Bureau of Investigation for a search of the State's criminal history record file, and the State Bureau of Investigation shall forward a set of fingerprints to the Federal Bureau of Investigation for a national criminal history record check. The Office of State Human Resources shall keep all information obtained pursuant to this section confidential.

(b) The Department of Public Safety may charge a fee to offset the cost incurred by it to conduct a criminal record check under this section. The fee shall not exceed the actual cost of locating, editing, researching, and retrieving the information. If the Department of Public Safety charges the Office of State Human Resources a fee for conducting the criminal record check, the agency or department with which the individual would be temporarily assigned shall reimburse the Office of State Human Resources for the fee charged.

History.
2018-5, s. 26A.1

§ 143B-969. Criminal record checks for employees and contractors of the State

Board of Elections and county directors of elections

(a) As used in this section, the term:

(1) "Current or prospective employee" means any of the following:

    a. A current or prospective permanent or temporary employee of the State Board or a current or prospective county director of elections.

    b. A current or prospective contractor with the State Board.

    c. An employee or agent of a current or prospective contractor with the State Board.

    d. Any other individual otherwise engaged by the State Board who has or will have the capability to update, modify, or change elections systems or confidential elections or ethics data.

(2) "State Board" means the State Board of Elections.

(b) The Department of Public Safety may provide to the Executive Director of the State Board a current or prospective employee's criminal history from the State and National Repositories of Criminal Histories. The Executive Director shall provide to the Department of Public Safety, along with the request, the fingerprints of the current or prospective employee, a form signed by the current or prospective employee consenting to the criminal record check and use of fingerprints and other identifying information required by the State and National Repositories, and any additional information required by the Department of Public Safety. The fingerprints of the current or prospective employee shall be forwarded to the State Bureau of Investigation for a search of the State's criminal history record file, and the State Bureau of Investigation shall forward a set of fingerprints to the Federal Bureau of Investigation for a national criminal history record check.

(c) The Department of Public Safety may charge a fee to offset the cost incurred by it to conduct a criminal record check under this section. The fee shall not exceed the actual cost of locating, editing, researching, and retrieving the information.

(d) The criminal history report shall be provided to the Executive Director of the State Board, who shall keep all information obtained pursuant to this section confidential to the State Board. A criminal history report obtained as provided in this section is not a public record under Chapter 132 of the General Statutes.

History.
2018-13, s. 1(a); 2018-146, s. 6.1

§ 143B-970. Criminal record checks for employees of county boards of elections

(a) As used in this section, the term:

(1) "Current or prospective employee" means a current or prospective permanent or temporary employee of a county board of elections.

(2) "State Board" means the State Board of Elections.

(b) The Department of Public Safety may provide to a county board of elections a current or prospective employee's criminal history from the State and National Repositories of Criminal Histories. The county board of elections shall provide to the Department of Public Safety, along with the request, the fingerprints of the current or prospective employee, a form signed by the current or prospective employee consenting to the criminal record check and use of fingerprints and other identifying information required by the State and National Repositories, and any additional information required by the Department of Public Safety. The fingerprints of the current or prospective employee shall be forwarded to the State Bureau of Investigation for a search of the State's criminal history record file, and the State Bureau of Investigation shall forward a set of fingerprints to the Federal Bureau of Investigation for a national criminal history record check.

(c) The Department of Public Safety may charge a fee to offset the cost incurred by it to conduct a criminal record check under this section. The fee shall not exceed the actual cost of locating, editing, researching, and retrieving the information.

(d) The criminal history report shall be provided to the county board of elections, who shall keep all information obtained pursuant to this section confidential to the county board of elections, the county director of elections, the State Board, and the Executive Director of the State Board. A criminal history report obtained as provided in this section is not a public record under Chapter 132 of the General Statutes.

History.
2018-13, s. 1(b); 2018-146, s. 1

§ 143B-971. Criminal record checks of applicants for licensure as dietitian/ nutritionists or nutritionists

The Department of Public Safety may provide to the North Carolina Board of Dietetics/Nutrition a criminal history record from the State and National Repositories of Criminal Histories for applicants for licensure by the Board. Along with a request for criminal history records, the Board shall provide to the Department of Public Safety the fingerprints of the applicant or subject, a form signed by the applicant consenting to the criminal history record check and use of

the fingerprints and other identifying information required by the Repositories, and any additional information required by the Department. The fingerprints shall be forwarded to the State Bureau of Investigation for a search of the State's criminal history record file, and the State Bureau of Investigation shall forward a set of fingerprints to the Federal Bureau of Investigation for a national criminal history record check. The Board shall keep all information obtained pursuant to this section confidential. The Department of Public Safety may charge a fee to offset the cost incurred by the Department of Public Safety to conduct a criminal history record check under this section, but the fee shall not exceed the actual cost of locating, editing, researching, and retrieving the information.

History.
2018-91, s. 15

§ 143B-972. National criminal record checks for child care institutions

The Department of Public Safety shall provide to the Department of Health and Human Services, Criminal Records Check Unit, in accordance with G.S. 108A-150, the criminal history of any current or prospective employee or volunteer in a child care institution as defined by Title IV-E of the Social Security Act, including individuals working with a contract agency in a child care institution. The Department of Health and Human Services, Criminal Records Check Unit, shall provide to the Department of Public Safety, along with the request, the fingerprints of the individual to be checked, any additional information required by the Department of Public Safety, and a form signed by the individual to be checked consenting to the check of the criminal record and to the use of fingerprints and other identifying information required by the State or National Repositories of Criminal Histories. The fingerprints of the individual shall be forwarded to the State Bureau of Investigation for a search of the State's criminal history record file, and the State Bureau of Investigation shall forward a set of fingerprints to the Federal Bureau of Investigation for a national criminal history record check. All information received by the Department of Health and Human Services, Criminal Records Check Unit, shall be kept confidential in accordance with G.S. 108A-150. The Department of Public Safety may charge a reasonable fee to conduct a criminal record check under this section.

History.
2019-240, s. 25(c)

§ 143B-972.1. (Effective January 1, 2023) Criminal record checks for North Carolina Criminal Justice Education and Training Standards Commission and North Carolina Sheriffs' Education and Training Standards Commission; fingerprints sent to Federal Bureau of Investigation

(a) The State Bureau of Investigation (SBI) shall provide to the North Carolina Criminal Justice Education and Training Standards Commission and the North Carolina Sheriffs' Education and Training Standards Commission the criminal history of any person who applies for certification or is certified, as a criminal justice officer or justice officer, from the State and National Repositories of Criminal Histories. Each agency employing certified criminal justice officers or justice officers shall provide to the SBI, the fingerprints of any person who applies for certification and certified officers, other identifying information required by the State and National Repositories, and any additional information required by the SBI.

(b) The SBI shall conduct a criminal history records check using the fingerprints of the applicants and certified officers, in accordance with 12 NCAC 09B. 0103 and 12 NCAC 10B. 0302, and enroll the fingerprints in the State-wide Automated Fingerprint Identification System (SAFIS).

(c) In addition to searching the State's criminal history record file, the SBI shall forward a set of fingerprints to the Federal Bureau of Investigation (FBI) for a national criminal history record check. The SBI shall enroll each individual whose fingerprints are received under this section in the Federal Bureau of Investigation's Next Generation Identification (NGI) System and Criminal Justice Record of Arrest and Prosecution Background (Rap Back) Service. The SBI will also notify the certifying Commission of any subsequent arrest of an individual identified through the Rap Back Service.

(d) Within 15 business days of receiving notification by either Commission that the individual whose fingerprints have been stored in the State Automated Fingerprint Identification System (SAFIS) pursuant to subsection (b) of this section has withdrawn the application or separated from employment and an Affidavit of Separation has been filed with either Commission, the SBI shall remove the individual's fingerprints from SAFIS and forward a request to the FBI to remove the fingerprints from the NGI System and the Criminal Justice Rap Back Service.

(e) The Commissions shall keep all information obtained pursuant to this section confidential.

History.
2021-138, s. 2(a)

§ 143B-973. Criminal record checks for the Legislative Services Commission.

The Department of Public Safety may provide to the Legislative Services Officer from the State and National Repositories of Criminal Histories the criminal history of any prospective employee, volunteer, or contractor of the General Assembly. The Legislative Services Officer shall provide to the Department of Public Safety, along with the request, the fingerprints of the prospective employee, volunteer, or contractor, a form signed by the prospective employee, volunteer, or contractor consenting to the criminal record check and use of fingerprints and other identifying information required by the State and National Repositories and any additional information required by the Department of Public Safety. The fingerprints of the prospective employee, volunteer, or contractor shall be forwarded to the State Bureau of Investigation for a search of the State's criminal history record file, and the State Bureau of Investigation shall forward a set of fingerprints to the Federal Bureau of Investigation for a national criminal history record check. The Legislative Services Officer shall keep all information obtained pursuant to this section confidential. The Department of Public Safety may charge a fee to offset the cost incurred by it to conduct a criminal record check under this section. The fee shall not exceed the actual cost of locating, editing, researching, and retrieving the information.

History.
2020-29, s. 12(a)

§ 143B-974. Criminal record checks for sheriffs

(a) The Department of Public Safety may provide to the North Carolina Sheriffs' Education and Training Standards Commission a criminal history from the State and National Repositories of Criminal Histories for any person filing a notice of candidacy, or any potential appointee to fill a vacancy, to the office of sheriff. The North Carolina Sheriffs' Education and Training Standards Commission shall provide to the Department of Public Safety, along with the request, the fingerprints of the person filing a notice of candidacy, or any potential appointee to fill a vacancy, to the office of sheriff; a form signed by the individual consenting to the criminal record check and use of fingerprints and other identifying information required by the State and National Repositories; and any additional information required by the Department of Public Safety. The fingerprints of the individual shall be forwarded to the State Bureau of Investigation for a search of the State's criminal history record file, and the State Bureau of Investigation shall forward a set of fingerprints to the Federal Bureau of Investigation for a national criminal history record check.

(b) The criminal history report shall be provided to the North Carolina Sheriffs' Education and Training Standards Commission, who shall keep all information obtained pursuant to this section confidential to the North Carolina Sheriffs' Education and Training Standards Commission. A criminal history report obtained as provided in this section is not a public record under Chapter 132 of the General Statutes.

History.
2021-107, s. 9

§§ 143B-975 through 143B-980

Reserved for future codification purposes.

§ 143B-981. The National Crime Prevention and Privacy Compact

The National Crime Prevention and Privacy Compact is enacted into law and entered into with all jurisdictions legally joining in the compact in the form substantially as set forth in this section, as follows:

Preamble.

Whereas, it is in the interest of the State to facilitate the dissemination of criminal history records from other states for use in North Carolina as authorized by State law; and

Whereas, the National Crime Prevention and Privacy Compact creates a legal framework for the cooperative exchange of criminal history records for noncriminal justice purposes; and

Whereas, the compact provides for the organization of an electronic information-sharing system among the federal government and the states to exchange criminal history records for noncriminal justice purposes authorized by federal or state law, such as background checks for governmental licensing and employment; and

Whereas, under the compact, the FBI and the party states agree to maintain detailed databases of their respective criminal history records, including arrests and dispositions, and to make them available to the federal government and party states for authorized purposes; and

Whereas, the FBI shall manage the federal data facilities that provide a significant part of the infrastructure for the system; and

Whereas, entering into the compact would facilitate the interstate and federal-state exchange of criminal history information to streamline the processing of background checks for noncriminal justice purposes; and

Whereas, release and use of information obtained through the system for noncriminal justice purposes would be governed by the laws of the receiving state; and

Whereas, entering into the compact will provide a mechanism for establishing and enforcing uniform standards for record accuracy and for the confidentiality and privacy interests of record subjects.

Article I.

Definitions.

As used in this compact, the following definitions apply:

(1) "Attorney General" means the Attorney General of the United States.

(2) "Compact officer" means:

a. With respect to the federal government, an official so designated by the director of the FBI; and

b. With respect to a party state, the chief administrator of the state's criminal history record repository or a designee of the chief administrator who is a regular, full-time employee of the repository.

(3) "Council" means the compact council established under Article VI.

(4) "Criminal history record repository" means the Department of Public Safety.

(5) "Criminal history records" means information collected by criminal justice agencies on individuals consisting of identifiable descriptions and notations of arrests, detentions, indictments, or other formal criminal charges and any disposition arising therefrom, including acquittal, sentencing, correctional supervision, or release. The term does not include identification information such as fingerprint records if the information does not indicate involvement of the individual with the criminal justice system.

(6) "Criminal justice" includes activities relating to the detection, apprehension, detention, pretrial release, posttrial release, prosecution, adjudication, correctional supervision, or rehabilitation of accused persons or criminal offenders. The administration of criminal justice includes criminal identification activities and the collection, storage, and dissemination of criminal history records.

(7) "Criminal justice agency" means: (i) courts; and (ii) a governmental agency or any subunit of an agency that performs the

administration of criminal justice pursuant to a statute or executive order and allocates a substantial part of its annual budget to the administration of criminal justice. The term includes federal and state inspector general offices.

(8) "Criminal justice services" means services provided by the FBI to criminal justice agencies in response to a request for information about a particular individual or as an update to information previously provided for criminal justice purposes.

(9) "Direct access" means access to the national identification index by computer terminal or other automated means not requiring the assistance of or intervention by any other party or agency.

(10) "Executive order" means an order of the President of the United States or the chief executive officer of a state that has the force of law and that is promulgated in accordance with applicable law.

(11) "FBI" means the Federal Bureau of Investigation.

(12) "III system" means the interstate identification index system, which is the cooperative federal-state system for the exchange of criminal history records. The term includes the national identification index, the national fingerprint file, and, to the extent of their participation in the system, the criminal history record repositories of the states and the FBI.

(13) "National fingerprint file" means a database of fingerprints or of other uniquely personal identifying information that relates to an arrested or charged individual and that is maintained by the FBI to provide positive identification of record subjects indexed in the III system.

(14) "National identification index" means an index maintained by the FBI consisting of names, identifying numbers, and other descriptive information relating to record subjects about whom there are criminal history records in the III system.

(15) "National indices" means the national identification index and the national fingerprint file.

(16) "Noncriminal justice purposes" means uses of criminal history records for purposes authorized by federal or state law other than purposes relating to criminal justice activities, including employment suitability, licensing determinations, immigration and naturalization matters, and national security clearances.

(17) "Nonparty state" means a state that has not ratified this compact.

(18) "Party state" means a state that has ratified this compact.

(19) "Positive identification" means a determination, based upon a comparison of fingerprints or other equally reliable biometric identification techniques, that the subject of a record search is the same person as the subject of a criminal history record or records indexed in the III system. Identifications based solely upon a comparison of subjects' names or other nonunique identification characteristics or numbers, or combinations thereof, does not constitute positive identification.

(20) "Sealed record information" means:

  a. With respect to adults, that portion of a record that is:

    1. Not available for criminal justice uses;

    2. Not supported by fingerprints or other accepted means of positive identification; or

    3. Subject to restrictions on dissemination for noncriminal justice purposes pursuant to a court order related to a particular subject or pursuant to a federal or state statute that requires action on a sealing petition filed by a particular record subject; and

  b. With respect to juveniles, whatever each state determines is a sealed record under its own law and procedure.

(21) "State" means any state, territory, or possession of the United States, the District of Columbia, and the Commonwealth of Puerto Rico.

Article II.

Purposes.

The purposes of this compact are to:

(1) Provide a legal framework for the establishment of a cooperative federal-state system for the interstate and federal-state exchange of criminal history records for noncriminal justice uses;

(2) Require the FBI to permit use of the national identification index and the national fingerprint file by each party state and to provide, in a timely fashion, federal and state criminal history records to requesting states, in accordance with the terms of this compact and with rules, procedures, and standards established by the council under Article VI;

(3) Require party states to provide information and records for the national identification index and the national fingerprint file and to provide criminal history records, in a timely fashion, to criminal history record repositories of other states and the federal government for noncriminal justice purposes, in accordance with the terms of this compact and with rules, procedures,

Chapter 143B

and standards established by the council under Article VI;

(4) Provide for the establishment of a council to monitor III system operations and to prescribe system rules and procedures for the effective and proper operation of the III system for noncriminal justice purposes; and

(5) Require the FBI and each party state to adhere to III system standards concerning record dissemination and use, response times, system security, data quality, and other duly established standards, including those that enhance the accuracy and privacy of such records.

Article III.

Responsibilities of Compact Parties.
(a) The director of the FBI shall:

(1) Appoint an FBI compact officer who shall:

a. Administer this compact within the Department of Public Safety and among federal agencies and other agencies and organizations that submit search requests to the FBI pursuant to Article V(c);

b. Ensure that compact provisions and rules, procedures, and standards prescribed by the council under Article VI are complied with by the Department of Public Safety and federal agencies and other agencies and organizations referred to in sub-subdivision (a)(1)a. of this Article III; and

c. Regulate the use of records received by means of the III system from party states when such records are supplied by the FBI directly to other federal agencies;

(2) Provide to federal agencies and to state criminal history record repositories criminal history records maintained in its database for the noncriminal justice purposes described in Article IV, including:

a. Information from nonparty states; and

b. Information from party states that is available from the FBI through the III system but is not available from the party states through the III system;

(3) Provide a telecommunications network and maintain centralized facilities for the exchange of criminal history records for both criminal justice purposes and the noncriminal justice purposes described in Article IV and ensure that the exchange of records for criminal justice purposes has priority over exchange for noncriminal justice purposes; and

(4) Modify or enter into user agreements with nonparty state criminal history record repositories to require them to establish record request procedures conforming to those prescribed in Article V.

(b) Each party state shall:

(1) Appoint a compact officer who shall:

a. Administer this compact within that state;

b. Ensure that compact provisions and rules, procedures, and standards established by the council under Article VI are complied with in the state; and

c. Regulate the in-state use of records received by means of the III system from the FBI or from other party states;

(2) Establish and maintain a criminal history record repository, which shall provide:

a. Information and records for the national identification index and the national fingerprint file; and

b. The state's III system-indexed criminal history records for noncriminal justice purposes described in Article IV;

(3) Participate in the national fingerprint file; and

(4) Provide and maintain telecommunications links and related equipment necessary to support the criminal justice services set forth in this compact.

(c) In carrying out their responsibilities under this compact, the FBI and each party state shall comply with III system rules, procedures, and standards duly established by the council concerning record dissemination and use, response times, data quality, system security, accuracy, privacy protection, and other aspects of III system operation.

(d) Use of the III system for noncriminal justice purposes authorized in this compact must be managed so as not to diminish the level of services provided in support of criminal justice purposes. Administration of compact provisions may not reduce the level of service available to authorized noncriminal justice users on the effective date of this compact.

Article IV.

Authorized Record Disclosures.
(a) To the extent authorized by section 552a of Title 5, United States Code (commonly known as the Privacy Act of 1974), the FBI shall provide on request criminal history records, excluding sealed record information, to state criminal history record repositories for noncriminal justice purposes allowed by federal statute, federal executive order, or a state statute that has been approved by the Attorney General to ensure that the state statute explicitly authorizes national indices checks.

(b) The FBI, to the extent authorized by section 552a of Title 5, United States Code (commonly known as the Privacy Act of 1974), and state criminal history record repositories shall provide criminal history records, excluding sealed record information, to criminal justice agencies and other governmental or nongovernmental agencies for noncriminal justice purposes allowed by federal statute, federal executive order, or a state statute that has been approved by the Attorney General to ensure that the state statute explicitly authorizes national indices checks.

(c) Any record obtained under this compact may be used only for the official purposes for which the record was requested. Each compact officer shall establish procedures consistent with this compact and with rules, procedures, and standards established by the council under Article VI, which procedures shall protect the accuracy and privacy of the records and shall:

(1) Ensure that records obtained under this compact are used only by authorized officials for authorized purposes;

(2) Require that subsequent record checks are requested to obtain current information whenever a new need arises; and

(3) Ensure that record entries that may not legally be used for a particular noncriminal justice purpose are deleted from the response and, if no information authorized for release remains, that an appropriate "no record" response is communicated to the requesting official.

Article V.

Record Request Procedures.

(a) Subject fingerprints or other approved forms of positive identification must be submitted with all requests for criminal history record checks for noncriminal justice purposes.

(b) Each request for a criminal history record check utilizing the national indices made under any approved state statute must be submitted through that state's criminal history record repository. A state criminal history record repository shall process an interstate request for noncriminal justice purposes through the national indices only if the request is transmitted through another state criminal history record repository or the FBI.

(c) Each request for criminal history record checks utilizing the national indices made under federal authority must be submitted through the FBI or, if the state criminal history record repository consents to process fingerprint submissions, through the criminal history record repository in the state in which the request originated. Direct access to the national identification index by entities other than the FBI and state criminal history record

repositories may not be permitted for noncriminal justice purposes.

(d) A state criminal history record repository or the FBI:

(1) May charge a fee, in accordance with applicable law, for handling a request involving fingerprint processing for noncriminal justice purposes; and

(2) May not charge a fee for providing criminal history records in response to an electronic request for a record that does not involve a request to process fingerprints.

(e) (1) If a state criminal history record repository cannot positively identify the subject of a record request made for noncriminal justice purposes, the request, together with fingerprints or other approved identifying information, must be forwarded to the FBI for a search of the national indices.

(2) If, with respect to a request forwarded by a state criminal history record repository under subdivision (e)(1) of this Article V, the FBI positively identifies the subject as having a III system-indexed record or records:

a. The FBI shall so advise the state criminal history record repository; and

b. The state criminal history record repository is entitled to obtain the additional criminal history record information from the FBI or other state criminal history record repositories.

Article VI.

Establishment of Compact Council.

(a) There is established a council to be known as the compact council which has the authority to promulgate rules and procedures governing the use of the III system for noncriminal justice purposes, not to conflict with FBI administration of the III system for criminal justice purposes. The council shall:

(1) Continue in existence as long as this compact remains in effect;

(2) Be located, for administrative purposes, within the FBI; and

(3) Be organized and hold its first meeting as soon as practicable after the effective date of this compact.

(b) The council must be composed of 15 members, each of whom must be appointed by the Attorney General, as follows:

(1) Nine members, each of whom shall serve a two-year term, who must be selected from among the compact officers of party states based on the recommendation of the compact officers of all party states, except that in the absence of the requisite number of compact officers available to serve, the chief administrators of the criminal history record repositories of nonparty states must be eligible to serve on an interim basis;

(2) Two at-large members, nominated by the director of the FBI, each of whom shall serve a three-year term, of whom:

    a. One must be a representative of the criminal justice agencies of the federal government and may not be an employee of the FBI; and

    b. One must be a representative of the noncriminal justice agencies of the federal government;

(3) Two at-large members, nominated by the chair of the council once the chair is elected pursuant to subsection (c) of this Article VI, each of whom shall serve a three-year term, of whom:

    a. One must be a representative of state or local criminal justice agencies; and

    b. One must be a representative of state or local noncriminal justice agencies;

(4) One member who shall serve a three-year term and who shall simultaneously be a member of the FBI's advisory policy board on criminal justice information services, nominated by the membership of that policy board; and

(5) One member, nominated by the director of the FBI, who shall serve a three-year term and who must be an employee of the FBI.

(c) From its membership, the council shall elect a chair and a vice-chair of the council. Both the chair and vice-chair of the council: (i) must be a compact officer, unless there is no compact officer on the council who is willing to serve, in which case the chair may be an at-large member and (ii) shall serve two-year terms and may be reelected to only one additional two-year term. The vice-chair of the council shall serve as the chair of the council in the absence of the chair.

(d) The council shall meet at least once each year at the call of the chair. Each meeting of the council must be open to the public. The council shall provide prior public notice in the federal register of each meeting of the council, including the matters to be addressed at the meeting. A majority of the council or any committee of the council shall constitute a quorum of the council or of a committee, respectively, for the conduct of business. A lesser number may meet to hold hearings, take testimony, or conduct any business not requiring a vote.

(e) The council shall make available for public inspection and copying at the council office within the FBI and shall publish in the federal register any rules, procedures, or standards established by the council.

(f) The council may request from the FBI reports, studies, statistics, or other information or materials that the council determines to be necessary to enable the council to perform its duties under this compact. The FBI, to the extent authorized by law, may provide assistance or information upon a request.

(g) The chair may establish committees as necessary to carry out this compact and may prescribe their membership, responsibilities, and duration.

Article VII.

Ratification of Compact.

This compact takes effect upon being entered into by two or more states as between those states and the federal government. When additional states subsequently enter into this compact, it becomes effective among those states and the federal government and each party state that has previously ratified it. When ratified, this compact has the full force and effect of law within the ratifying jurisdictions. The form of ratification must be in accordance with the laws of the executing state.

Article VIII.

Miscellaneous Provisions.

(a) Administration of this compact may not interfere with the management and control of the director of the FBI over the FBI's collection and dissemination of criminal history records and the advisory function of the FBI's advisory policy board chartered under the Federal Advisory Committee Act (5 U.S.C. App.) for all purposes other than noncriminal justice.

(b) Nothing in this compact may require the FBI to obligate or expend funds beyond those appropriated to the FBI.

(c) Nothing in this compact may diminish or lessen the obligations, responsibilities, and authorities of any state, whether a party state or a nonparty state, or of any criminal history record repository or other subdivision or component thereof under the Departments of State, Justice, and Commerce, the Judiciary, and Related Agencies Appropriation Act, 1973 (Public Law 92-544) or regulations and guidelines promulgated thereunder, including the rules and procedures promulgated by the council under Article VI(a), regarding the use and dissemination of criminal history records and information.

Article IX.

Renunciation.

(a) This compact shall bind each party state until renounced by the party state.

(b) Any renunciation of this compact by a party state must:

    (1) Be effected in the same manner by which the party state ratified this compact; and

    (2) Become effective 180 days after written notice of renunciation is provided by

the party state to each other party state and to the federal government.

Article X.

Severability.

The provisions of this compact must be severable. If any phrase, clause, sentence, or provision of this compact is declared to be contrary to the constitution of any participating state or to the Constitution of the United States or if the applicability of any phrase, clause, sentence, or provision of this compact to any government, agency, person, or circumstance is held invalid, the validity of the remainder of this compact and the applicability of the remainder of the compact to any government, agency, person, or circumstance may not be affected by the severability. If a portion of this compact is held contrary to the constitution of any party state, all other portions of this compact must remain in full force and effect as to the remaining party states and in full force and effect as to the party state affected, as to all other provisions.

Article XI.

Adjudication of Disputes.

(a) The council:

    (1) Has initial authority to make determinations with respect to any dispute regarding:

        a. Interpretation of this compact;

        b. Any rule or standard established by the council pursuant to Article VI; and

        c. Any dispute or controversy between any parties to this compact; and

    (2) Shall hold a hearing concerning any dispute described in subdivision (a)(1) of this Article XI at a regularly scheduled meeting of the council and only render a decision based upon a majority vote of the members of the council. The decision must be published pursuant to the requirements of Article VI(e).

(b) The FBI shall exercise immediate and necessary action to preserve the integrity of the III system, to maintain system policy and standards, to protect the accuracy and privacy of records, and to prevent abuses until the council holds a hearing on the matters.

(c) The FBI or a party state may appeal any decision of the council to the Attorney General and after that appeal may file suit in the appropriate district court of the United States that has original jurisdiction of all cases or controversies arising under this compact. Any suit arising under this compact and initiated in a state court must be removed to the appropriate district court of the United States in the manner provided by section 1446 of Title 28, United States Code, or other statutory authority.

History.

2003-214, s. 2; 2004-199, s. 28; 2014-100, s. 17.1(m), (o), (q)

§§ 143B-982 through 143B-985

Reserved for future codification purposes.

SUBPART E
PROTECTION OF PUBLIC OFFICIALS

§ 143B-986. Authority to provide protection to certain public officials

The North Carolina State Bureau of Investigation is authorized to provide protection to public officials who request it, and who, in the discretion of the Director of the Bureau demonstrate a need for such protection. The Director of the Bureau shall notify the Governor whenever the State Bureau of Investigation provides protection to public officials pursuant to this section. The bureau shall not provide protection for any individual other than the Governor for a period greater than 30 days without review and approval by the Governor. This review and reapproval shall be required at the end of each 30-day period.

History.

1977, c. 571; 2003-214, s. 1(3); 2011-145, s. 19.1(q1); 2011-391, s. 43(g); 2014-100, s. 17.1(bbb)

§ 143B-987. Authority to designate areas for protection of public officials

(a) The Director of the State Bureau of Investigation is authorized to designate buildings and grounds which constitute temporary residences or temporary offices of any public official being protected under authority of G.S. 143B-986, or any area that will be visited by any such official, a public building or facility during the time of such use.

(b) The Director of the State Bureau of Investigation may, with the consent of the official to be protected, make rules governing ingress to or egress from such buildings, grounds or areas designated under this section.

History.

1981, c. 499, s. 1; 2003-214, s. 1(3); 2011-145, s. 19.1(q1); 2011-391, s. 43(g); 2014-100, s. 17.1(n), (ccc)

SUBPART F
ALCOHOL LAW ENFORCEMENT DIVISION

Chapter 143B

§ 143B-990. Creation of Alcohol Law Enforcement Division of the Department of Public Safety

There is created and established a division to be known as the Alcohol Law Enforcement Division of the Department of Public Safety with the organization, powers, and duties defined in Article 1 of this Chapter and G.S. 18B-500, except as modified in this Part.

History.
2019-203, s. 2

Sections 143B-988 through 143B-999

Reserved for future codification purposes.

PART 5
DIVISION OF EMERGENCY MANAGEMENT

SUBPART A
EMERGENCY MANAGEMENT DIVISION

§ 143B-1000. Division of Emergency Management of the Department of Public Safety

(a) There is established, within the Department of Public Safety, the Division of Emergency Management, which shall be organized and staffed in accordance with applicable laws and regulations and within the limits of authorized appropriations.

(b) The Division of Emergency Management shall have the following powers and duties:

(1) Repealed by Session Laws 2011-145, s. 19.1(aa), effective January 1, 2012.

(2) To exercise the powers and duties conferred on it by Chapter 166A of the General Statutes.

(3) To exercise any other powers vested by law.

History.
2009-397, s. 3; 2011-145, s. 19.1(g), (w), (aa)

§§ 143B-1001 through 143B-1009

Reserved for future codification purposes.

SUBPART B
NORTH CAROLINA CENTER FOR MISSING PERSONS

§ 143B-1010. North Carolina Center for Missing Persons established

There is established within the Department of Public Safety the North Carolina Center for Missing Persons, which shall be organized and staffed in accordance with applicable laws. The purpose of the Center is to serve as a central repository for information regarding missing persons and missing children, with special emphasis on missing children. The Center may utilize the Federal Bureau of Investigation/National Crime Information Center's missing person computerized file (hereinafter referred to as FBI/NCIC) through the use of the Police Information Network in the North Carolina Department of Justice.

History.
1985, c. 765, s. 1; 1985 (Reg. Sess., 1986), c. 1000, s. 1; 2011-145, s. 19.1(g), (w)

§ 143B-1011. Definitions

For the purpose of this Part:

(1) **Missing child.** -- A juvenile as defined in G.S. 7B-101 whose location has not been determined, who has been reported as missing to a law-enforcement agency, and whose parent's, spouse's, guardian's or legal custodian's temporary or permanent residence is in North Carolina or is believed to be in North Carolina.

(2) **Missing person.** -- Any individual who is 18 years of age or older, whose temporary or permanent residence is in North Carolina, or is believed to be in North Carolina, whose location has not been determined, and who has been reported as missing to a law-enforcement agency.

(3) **Missing person report.** -- A report prepared on a prescribed form for transmitting information about a missing person or a missing child to an appropriate law-enforcement agency.

(4) **NamUs.** -- The National Missing and Unidentified Persons System created by the United States Department of Justice's National Institute of Justice.

History.
1985 (Reg. Sess., 1986), c. 1000, s. 1; 1998-202, s. 13(mm); 2011-145, s. 19.1(w); 2019-90, s. 1

§ 143B-1012. Control of the Center

The Center is under the direction of the Secretary of the Department of Public Safety and may be organized and structured in a manner as the Secretary deems appropriate to ensure that the objectives of the Center are achieved. The Secretary may employ those Center personnel as the General Assembly may authorize and provide funding for.

History.
1985 (Reg. Sess., 1986), c. 1000, s. 1; 2011-145, s. 19.1(g), (w)

§ 143B-1013. Secretary to adopt rules

The Secretary shall adopt rules prescribing all of the following:

(1) Procedures for accepting and disseminating information maintained at the Center.

(2) The confidentiality of the data and information, including the missing person report, maintained by the Center.

(3) The proper disposition of all obsolete data, including the missing person report; provided, data for an individual who has reached the age of 18 and remains missing must be preserved.

(4) Procedures allowing a communication link with the Police Information Network and the FBI/NCIC's missing person file to ensure compliance with FBI/NCIC policies.

(5) Forms, including but not limited to a missing person report, considered necessary for the efficient and proper operation of the Center.

History.
1985 (Reg. Sess., 1986), c. 1000, s. 1; 2011-145, s. 19.1(w); 2019-90, s. 1

§ 143B-1014. Submission of missing person reports to the Center

Any parent, spouse, guardian, legal custodian, or person responsible for the supervision of the missing individual may submit a missing person report to the Center of any missing child or missing person, regardless of the circumstances, after having first submitted a missing person report on the individual to the law-enforcement agency having jurisdiction of the area in which the individual became or is believed to have become missing, regardless of the circumstances.

History.
1985 (Reg. Sess., 1986), c. 1000, s. 1; 2007-469, s. 1; 2011-145, s. 19.1(w)

§ 143B-1015. Dissemination of missing persons data by law-enforcement agencies

(a) A law-enforcement agency, upon receipt of a missing person report by a parent, spouse, guardian, legal custodian, or person responsible for the supervision of the missing individual

shall immediately make arrangements for the entry of data about the missing person or missing child into the national missing persons file in accordance with criteria set forth by the FBI/NCIC, immediately inform all of its on-duty law-enforcement officers of the missing person report, initiate a statewide broadcast to all appropriate law-enforcement agencies to be on the lookout for the individual, and transmit a copy of the report to the Center. No law enforcement agency shall establish or maintain any policy which requires the observance of any waiting period before accepting a missing person report.

If the report involves a missing child and the report meets the criteria established in G.S. 143B-1021(b), as soon as practicable after receipt of the report, the law enforcement agency shall notify the Center and the National Center for Missing and Exploited Children of the relevant data about the missing child.

(b) A law-enforcement agency may enter information from a missing person report or about an unidentified person into NamUs at any time.

(c) A law-enforcement agency shall enter information from a missing person report or about an unidentified person into NamUs in any of the following circumstances:

(1) A missing person has been missing for more than 30 days.

(2) An unidentified person has not been identified for more than 30 days following the person's death.

(3) A missing child has been missing for more than 30 days.

(d) If a law-enforcement agency enters information into NamUs pursuant to subsection (b) or (c) of this section, the law-enforcement agency shall do all of the following:

(1) Include all information regarding the missing child or person, or unidentified person, including medical records, DNA records, and dental records.

(2) Enter into NamUs the fact that (i) a missing child or person has been found or (ii) an unidentified person has been identified, if either of these circumstances occurs following the original entry of the person's information into NamUs.

History.
1985 (Reg. Sess., 1986), c. 1000, s. 1; 2002-126, s. 18.7(a); 2003-191, s. 1; 2007-469, s. 2; 2011-145, s. 19.1(w), (yy); 2019-90, s. 1

§ 143B-1016. Responsibilities of Center

The Center shall do all of the following:

(1) Assist local law-enforcement agencies with entering data about missing persons or missing children into the national missing persons file, ensure that proper entry criteria have been met as set forth by the

FBI/NCIC, and confirm entry of the data about the missing persons or missing children.

(2) Gather and distribute information and data on missing children and missing persons.

(3) Encourage research and study of missing children and missing persons, including the prevention of child abduction and the prevention of the exploitation of missing children.

(4) Serve as a statewide resource center to assist local communities in programs and initiatives to prevent child abduction and the exploitation of missing children.

(5) Continue increasing public awareness of the reasons why children are missing and vulnerability of missing children.

(6) Achieve maximum cooperation with other agencies of the State, with agencies of other states and the federal government and with the National Center for Missing and Exploited Children in rendering assistance to missing children and missing persons and their parents, guardians, spouses, or legal custodians.

(6a) Cooperate with interstate and federal efforts to identify deceased individuals.

(7) Develop and maintain the AMBER Alert System as created by G.S. 143B-1021.

(8) Forward the appropriate information to the Police Information Network to assist it in maintaining and publishing a bulletin of currently missing children and missing persons.

(9) Maintain a directory of existing public and private agencies, groups, and individuals that provide effective assistance to families in the areas of prevention of child abduction, location of missing children and missing persons, and follow-up services to the child or person and family, as determined by the Secretary of Public Safety.

(10) Annually compile and publish reports on the actual number of children and persons missing each year, listing the categories and causes, when known, for the disappearances.

(11) Provide follow-up referrals for services to missing children or persons and their families.

(12) Maintain a toll-free 1-800 telephone service that will be in service at all times.

(13) Perform such other activities that the Secretary of Public Safety considers necessary to carry out the intent of its mandate.

History.
1985 (Reg. Sess., 1986), c. 1000, s. 1; 2002-126, s. 18.7(b); 2003-191, s. 2; 2011-145, s. 19.1(g), (w), (zz); 2019-90, s. 1

§ 143B-1017. Duty of individuals to notify Center and law-enforcement agency when missing person has been located

Any parent, spouse, guardian, legal custodian, or person responsible for the supervision of the missing individual who submits a missing person report to a law-enforcement agency or to the Center, shall immediately notify the law-enforcement agency and the Center of any individual whose location has been determined. The Center shall confirm the deletion of the individual's records from the FBI/NCIC's missing person file, as long as there are no grounds for criminal prosecution, and follow up with the local law-enforcement agency having jurisdiction of the records.

History.
1985 (Reg. Sess., 1986), c. 1000, s. 1; 2007-469, s. 3; 2011-145, s. 19.1(w)

§ 143B-1018. Release of information by Center

The following may make inquiries of, and receive data or information from, the Center:

(1) Any police, law-enforcement, or criminal justice agency investigating a report of a missing or unidentified person or child, whether living or deceased.

(2) A court, upon a finding by the court that access to the data, information, or records of the Center may be necessary for the determination of an issue before the court.

(3) Any district attorney of a prosecutorial district as defined in G.S. 7A-60 in this State or the district attorney's designee or representative.

(4) Any person engaged in bona fide research when approved by the Secretary; provided, no names or addresses may be supplied to this person.

(5) Any other person authorized by the Secretary of the Department of Public Safety pursuant to G.S. 143B-1013.

History.
1985 (Reg. Sess., 1986), c. 1000, s. 1; 1987, c. 282, s. 28; 1987 (Reg. Sess., 1988), c. 1037, s. 119; 2011-145, s. 19.1(g), (w), (aaa)

§ 143B-1019. Provision of toll-free service; instructions to callers; communication with law-enforcement agencies

The Center shall provide a toll-free telephone line for anyone to report the disappearance of any individual or the sighting of any missing child or missing person. The Center personnel shall instruct the caller, in the case of a report concerning the disappearance of an individual, of the requirements contained in G.S. 143B-1014 of first having to submit a missing person report on the individual to the law-enforcement agency having jurisdiction of the area in which the individual became or is believed to have become missing. Any law-enforcement agency may retrieve information imparted to the Center by means of this phone line. The Center shall directly communicate any report of a sighting of a missing person or a missing child to the law-enforcement agency having jurisdiction in the area of disappearance or sighting.

History.
1985 (Reg. Sess., 1986), c. 1000, s. 1; 2007-469, s. 4; 2011-145, s. 19.1(w), (bbb)

§ 143B-1020. Improper release of information; penalty

Any person working under the supervision of the Director of Victims and Justice Services who knowingly and willfully releases, or authorizes the release of, any data, information, or records maintained or possessed by the Center to any agency, entity, or person other than as specifically permitted by Subpart B or in violation of any rule adopted by the Secretary is guilty of a Class 2 misdemeanor.

History.
1985 (Reg. Sess., 1986), c. 1000, s. 1; 1993, c. 539, s. 1050; 1994, Ex. Sess., c. 24, s. 14(c); 2011-145, s. 19.1(w)

§ 143B-1021. North Carolina AMBER Alert System established

(a) There is established within the North Carolina Center for Missing Persons the AMBER Alert System. The purpose of AMBER Alert is to provide a statewide system for the rapid dissemination of information regarding abducted children.

(b) The AMBER Alert System shall make every effort to disseminate information on missing children as quickly as possible when the following criteria are met:

(1) The child is 17 years of age or younger;

(2) The abduction is not known or suspected to be by a parent of the child, unless the child's life is suspected to be in danger of injury or death;

(3) The child is believed:

    a. To have been abducted, or

    b. To be in danger of injury or death;

(4) The child is not a runaway or voluntarily missing; and

(5) The abduction has been reported to and investigated by a law enforcement agency.

If the abduction of the child is known or suspected to be by a parent of the child, the Center, in its discretion, may disseminate information through the AMBER Alert System if the child is believed to be in danger of injury or death.

(c) The Center shall adopt guidelines and develop procedures for the statewide implementation of the AMBER Alert System and shall provide education and training to encourage radio and television broadcasters to participate in the System. The Center shall work with the Department of Justice in developing training material regarding the AMBER Alert System for law enforcement, broadcasters, and community interest groups.

(d) The Center shall consult with the Department of Transportation and develop a procedure for the use of overhead permanent changeable message signs to provide information on the abduction of a child meeting the criteria established in subsection (b) of this section, when information is available that would enable motorists to assist law enforcement in the recovery of the missing child. The Center and the Department of Transportation shall develop guidelines for the content, length, and frequency of any message to be placed on an overhead permanent changeable message sign.

(e) The Center shall consult with the Division of Emergency Management, in the Department of Public Safety, to develop a procedure for the use of the Emergency Alert System to provide information on the abduction of a child meeting the criteria established in subsection (b) of this section.

(f) The Department of Public Safety, on behalf of the Center, may accept grants, contributions, devises, and gifts, which shall be kept in a separate fund, which shall be nonreverting, and shall be used to fund the operations of the Center and the AMBER Alert System.

History.
2002-126, s. 18.7(c); 2003-191, s. 3; 2011-145, s. 19.1(g), (w); 2011-284, s. 103

§ 143B-1022. North Carolina Silver Alert System established

(a) There is established within the North Carolina Center for Missing Persons the Silver Alert System. The purpose of the Silver Alert System is to provide a statewide system for the rapid dissemination of information regarding a missing person or missing child who is believed to be suffering from dementia, Alzheimer's disease, or a disability that requires them to be protected from potential abuse or other physical harm, neglect, or exploitation.

(b) If the Center receives a request that involves a missing person or missing child as described in subsection (a) of this section, the Center shall issue an alert providing for rapid dissemination of information statewide regarding the missing person or missing child. The Center shall make every effort to disseminate the information as quickly as possible when the person's or child's status as missing has been reported to a law enforcement agency.

(c) The Center shall adopt guidelines and develop procedures for issuing an alert for missing persons and missing children as described in subsection (a) of this section and shall provide education and training to encourage radio and television broadcasters to participate in the alert. The guidelines and procedures shall ensure that specific health information about the missing person or missing child is not made public through the alert or otherwise.

(d) The Center shall consult with the Department of Transportation and develop a procedure for the use of overhead permanent changeable message signs to provide information on the missing person or missing child meeting the criteria of this section when information is available that would enable motorists to assist in the recovery of the missing person or missing child. The Center and the Department of Transportation shall develop guidelines for the content, length, and frequency of any message to be placed on an overhead permanent changeable message sign.

History.
2007-469, s. 5; 2008-83, s. 1; 2009-143, s. 1; 2010-96, s. 16; 2011-145, s. 19.1(w); 2016-87, s. 3

§ 143B-1023. North Carolina Blue Alert System established

(a) There is established within the North Carolina Center for Missing Persons the Blue Alert System. The purpose of the Blue Alert System is to aid in the apprehension of a suspect who kills or inflicts serious bodily injury on a law enforcement officer by providing a statewide system for the rapid dissemination of information regarding the suspect. The term "serious bodily injury" is as defined in G.S. 14-32.4(a).

(b) The Center shall make every effort to rapidly disseminate information on a suspect when the following criteria are met:

(1) A law enforcement officer is killed or suffers serious bodily injury.

(2) A law enforcement agency with jurisdiction (i) determines that the suspect poses a threat to the public and other law enforcement personnel and (ii) possesses information that may assist in locating the suspect, including information regarding the suspect's vehicle, complete or partial license plate information, and a detailed description of the suspect, or that a law enforcement officer is missing while on duty

under circumstances warranting concern for the law enforcement officer's safety.

(3) The head of a law enforcement agency with jurisdiction recommends the issuance of a blue alert to the Center.

(c) The Center shall adopt guidelines and develop procedures for the statewide implementation of the Blue Alert System and shall provide education and training to encourage radio and television broadcasters to participate in the alert.

(d) The Center shall consult with the Department of Transportation and develop a procedure for the use of overhead permanent changeable message signs to provide information on a suspect when the criteria established in subsection (b) of this section are met. The Center and the Department of Transportation shall develop guidelines for the content, length, and frequency of any message to be placed on the overhead permanent changeable message sign pursuant to the issuance of a blue alert.

(e) The Center shall consult with the Division of Emergency Management in the Department of Public Safety to develop a procedure for the use of the Blue Alert System to provide information on a suspect when the criteria established in subsection (b) of this section are met.

History.
2016-87, s. 1

§§ 143B-1024 through 143B-1029

Reserved for future codification purposes.

PART 6
DIVISION OF ADMINISTRATION

SUBPART A
GOVERNOR'S CRIME COMMISSION

§ 143B-1100. Governor's Crime Commission -- creation; composition; terms; meetings, etc

(a) There is hereby created the Governor's Crime Commission of the Department of Public Safety. The Commission shall consist of 37 voting members and five nonvoting members. The composition of the Commission shall be as follows:

(1) The voting members shall be:

a. The Governor, the Chief Justice of the Supreme Court of North Carolina (or the Chief Justice's designee), the Attorney General, the Director of the

Administrative Office of the Courts, the Secretary of the Department of Health and Human Services, the Secretary of Public Safety (or the Secretary's designee), and the Superintendent of Public Instruction;

b. A judge of superior court, a judge of district court specializing in juvenile matters, a chief district court judge, a clerk of superior court, and a district attorney;

c. A defense attorney, three sheriffs (one of whom shall be from a "high crime area"), three police executives (one of whom shall be from a "high crime area"), eight citizens (two with knowledge of juvenile delinquency and the public school system, two of whom shall be under the age of 21 at the time of their appointment, one advocate for victims of all crimes, one representative from a domestic violence or sexual assault program, one representative of a "private juvenile delinquency program," and one in the discretion of the Governor), three county commissioners or county officials, and three mayors or municipal officials;

d. Four public members.

(2) The nonvoting members shall be the Director of the State Bureau of Investigation, the Deputy Chief of the Juvenile Justice Section of the Division of Adult Correction and Juvenile Justice of the Department of Public Safety who is responsible for Intervention/Prevention programs, the Deputy Chief of the Juvenile Justice Section of the Division of Adult Correction and Juvenile Justice of the Department of Public Safety who is responsible for Youth Development programs, the Section Chief of the Section of Prisons of the Division of Adult Correction and Juvenile Justice and the Section Chief of the Section of Community Corrections of the Division of Adult Correction and Juvenile Justice.

(b) The membership of the Commission shall be selected as follows:

(1) The following members shall serve by virtue of their office: the Governor, the Chief Justice of the Supreme Court, the Attorney General, the Director of the Administrative Office of the Courts, the Secretary of the Department of Health and Human Services, the Secretary of Public Safety, the Director of the State Bureau of Investigation, the Section Chief of the Section of Prisons of the Division of Adult Correction and Juvenile Justice, the Section Chief of the Section of Community Corrections of the Division of Adult Correction and Juvenile Justice, the Deputy Chief who is

responsible for Intervention/Prevention of the Juvenile Justice Section of the Division of Adult Correction and Juvenile Justice of the Department of Public Safety, the Deputy Chief who is responsible for Youth Development of the Juvenile Justice Section of the Division of Adult Correction and Juvenile Justice of the Department of Public Safety, and the Superintendent of Public Instruction. Should the Chief Justice of the Supreme Court choose not to serve, his alternate shall be selected by the Governor from a list submitted by the Chief Justice which list must contain no less than three nominees from the membership of the Supreme Court.

(2) The following members shall be appointed by the Governor: the district attorney, the defense attorney, the three sheriffs, the three police executives, the eight citizens, the three county commissioners or county officials, the three mayors or municipal officials.

(3) The following members shall be appointed by the Governor from a list submitted by the Chief Justice of the Supreme Court, which list shall contain no less than three nominees for each position and which list must be submitted within 30 days after the occurrence of any vacancy in the judicial membership: the judge of superior court, the clerk of superior court, the judge of district court specializing in juvenile matters, and the chief district court judge.

(4) Two public members provided by subsubdivision (a)(1)d. of this section shall be appointed by the General Assembly upon recommendation of the Speaker of the House of Representatives and two public members provided by sub-subdivision (a)(1)d. of this section shall be appointed by the General Assembly upon recommendation of the President Pro Tempore of the Senate.

(5) The Governor may serve as chairman, designating a vice-chairman to serve at his pleasure, or he may designate a chairman and vice-chairman both of whom shall serve at his pleasure.

(c) The initial members of the Commission shall be those appointed under subsection (b) above, which appointments shall be made by March 1, 1977. The terms of the present members of the Governor's Commission on Law and Order shall expire on February 28, 1977. Effective March 1, 1977, the Governor shall appoint members, other than those serving by virtue of their office, to serve staggered terms; seven shall be appointed for one-year terms, seven for two-year terms, and seven for three-year terms. At the end of their respective terms of office their successors shall be appointed for terms of three years and until their successors are appointed and qualified. The public members appointed pursuant to subdivision (4) of subsection (b) of this section shall serve two-year terms effective March 1, of each odd-numbered year. Any Commission member no longer serving in the office from which the member qualified for appointment shall be disqualified from serving on the Commission. Any appointment to fill a vacancy on the Commission created by the resignation, dismissal, death, disability, or disqualification of a member shall be for the balance of the unexpired term.

(d) The Governor shall have the power to remove any member from the Commission for misfeasance, malfeasance or nonfeasance.

(e) The Commission shall meet quarterly and at other times at the call of the chairman or upon written request of at least eight of the members. A majority of the voting members shall constitute a quorum for the transaction of business.

(f) The Commission shall be treated as a board for purposes of Chapter 138A of the General Statutes.

History.
1965, c. 663; 1977, c. 11, s. 1; 1981, c. 467, ss. 1-5; 1981 (Reg. Sess., 1982), c. 1189, s. 4; 1991, c. 739, s. 32; 1997-443, s. 11A.118(a); 1998-170, s. 3; 1998-202, s. 4(aa); 1999-423, s. 11; 2000-137, s. 4(ee); 2001-95, s. 6; 2001-487, s. 47(g); 2007-454, s. 1; 2010-169, s. 11; 2011-145, s. 19.1(g), (i)-(l), (x); 2012-83, s. 54; 2013-410, s. 13; 2015-9, s. 2.3(a), (b); 2015-264, s. 79(a), (b); 2017-6, s. 3; 2017-186, s. 2 (kkkkkk); 2018-146, ss. 3.1(a), (b), 6.1

§ 143B-1101. Governor's Crime Commission -- powers and duties

(a) The Governor's Crime Commission shall have the following powers and duties:

(1) To serve, along with its adjunct committees, as the chief advisory board to the Governor and to the Secretary of the Department of Public Safety on matters pertaining to the criminal justice system.

(2) To recommend a comprehensive statewide plan for the improvement of criminal justice throughout the State which is consistent with and serves to foster the following established goals of the criminal justice system:

a. To reduce crime,
b. To protect individual rights,
c. To achieve justice,
d. To increase efficiency in the criminal justice system,
e. To promote public safety,
f. To provide for the administration of a fair and humane system which offers reasonable opportunities for

adjudicated offenders to develop progressively responsible behavior, and

g. To increase professional skills of criminal justice officers.

(3) To advise State and local law-enforcement agencies in improving law enforcement and the administration of criminal justice;

(4) To make studies and recommendations for the improvement of law enforcement and the administration of criminal justice;

(5) To encourage public support and respect for the criminal justice system in North Carolina;

(6) To seek ways to continue to make North Carolina a safe and secure State for its citizens;

(7) To recommend objectives and priorities for the improvement of law enforcement and criminal justice throughout the State;

(8) To recommend recipients of grants for use in pursuing its objectives, under such conditions as are deemed to be necessary;

(9) To serve as a coordinating committee and forum for discussion of recommendations from its adjunct committees formed pursuant to G.S. 143B-1102; and

(10) To serve as the primary channel through which local law-enforcement departments and citizens can lend their advice, and state their needs, to the Department of Public Safety.

(b) The Governor's Crime Commission shall review the level of gang activity throughout the State and assess the progress and accomplishments of the State, and of local governments, in preventing the proliferation of gangs and addressing the needs of juveniles who have been identified as being associated with gang activity.

(c) All directives of the Governor's Crime Commission shall be administered by the Director, Crime Control Division of the Department of Public Safety.

History.
1975, c. 663; 1977, c. 11, s. 2; 1979, c. 107, s. 11; 1981, c. 931, s. 3; 1981 (Reg. Sess., 1982), c. 1191, s. 15; 2008-56, s.7; 2008-187, s. 44.5(b); 2011-145, s. 19.1(g), (x), (xx); 2014-100, s. 16A.2; 2015-241, s. 16B.3(b)

§ 143B-1102. Adjunct committees of the Governor's Crime Commission -- creation; purpose; powers and duties

(a) There are hereby created by way of extension and not limitation, the following adjunct committees of the Governor's Crime Commission: the Judicial Planning Committee, the Juvenile Justice Planning Committee, the Law

Enforcement Planning Committee, the Corrections Planning Committee, and the Juvenile Code Revision Committee.

(b) The composition of the adjunct committees shall be as designated by the Governor by executive order, except for the Judicial Planning Committee, the composition of which shall be designated by the Supreme Court. The Governor's appointees shall serve two-year terms beginning March 1, of each odd-numbered year, and members of the Judicial Planning Committee shall serve at the pleasure of the Supreme Court.

(c) The adjunct committees created herein shall report directly to the Governor's Crime Commission and shall have the following powers and duties:

(1) The Law Enforcement Planning Committee shall advise the Governor's Crime Commission on all matters which are referred to it relevant to law enforcement, including detention; shall participate in the development of the law-enforcement component of the State's comprehensive plan; shall consider and recommend priorities for the improvement of law-enforcement services; and shall offer technical assistance to State and local agencies in the planning and implementation of programs contemplated by the comprehensive plan for the improvement of law-enforcement services.

The Law Enforcement Planning Committee shall maintain contact with the National Commission on Accreditation for Law Enforcement Agencies, assist the National Commission in the furtherance of its efforts, adapt the work of the National Commission by an analysis of law-enforcement agencies in North Carolina, develop standards for the accreditation of law-enforcement agencies in North Carolina, make these standards available to those law-enforcement agencies which desire to participate voluntarily in the accreditation program, and assist participants to achieve voluntary compliance with the standards.

(2) The Judicial Planning Committee (which shall be appointed by the Supreme Court) shall establish court improvement priorities, define court improvement programs and projects, and develop an annual judicial plan in accordance with the Crime Control Act of 1976 (Public Law 94-503); shall advise the Governor's Crime Commission on all matters which are referred to it relevant to the courts; shall consider and recommend priorities for the improvement of judicial services; and shall offer technical assistance to State agencies in the planning and implementation of programs contemplated by the comprehensive plan for the improvement of judicial services.

(3) The Corrections Planning Committee shall advise the Governor's Crime Commission on all matters which are referred to it relevant to corrections; shall participate in the development of the adult corrections component of the State's comprehensive plan; shall consider and recommend priorities for the improvement of correction services; and shall offer technical assistance to State agencies in the planning and implementation of programs contemplated by the comprehensive plan for the improvement of corrections.

(4) The Juvenile Justice Planning Committee shall advise the Governor's Crime Commission on all matters which are referred to it relevant to juvenile justice; shall participate in the development of the juvenile justice component of the State's comprehensive plan; shall consider and recommend priorities for the improvement of juvenile justice services; and shall offer technical assistance to State and local agencies in the planning and implementation of programs contemplated by the comprehensive plan for the improvement of juvenile justice.

(5) The Juvenile Code Revision Committee shall study problems relating to young people who come within the juvenile jurisdiction of the district court as defined by Article 23 of Chapter 7A of the General Statutes and develop a legislative plan which will best serve the needs of young people and protect the interests of the State; shall study the existing laws, services, agencies and commissions and recommend whether they should be continued, amended, abolished or merged; and shall take steps to insure that all agencies, organizations, and private citizens in the State of North Carolina have an opportunity to lend advice and suggestions to the development of a revised juvenile code. If practical, the Committee shall submit a preliminary report to the General Assembly prior to its adjournment in 1977. It shall make a full and complete report to the General Assembly by March 1, 1979. This adjunct committee shall terminate on February 28, 1979.

(d) The Governor shall have the power to remove any member of any adjunct committee from the Committee for misfeasance, malfeasance or nonfeasance. Each Committee shall meet at the call of the chairman or upon written request of one third of its membership. A majority of a committee shall constitute a quorum for the transaction of business.

(e) The actions and recommendations of each adjunct committee shall be subject to the final approval of the Governor's Crime Commission.

Chapter 143B

History.
1975, c. 663; 1977, c. 11, s. 3; 1981, c. 605, s. 1; 1983 (Reg. Sess., 1984), c. 995, s. 8; 2011-145, s. 19.1(x)

§ 143B-1103. Additional duties of the Grants Management Section

(a) Repealed by Session Laws 2011-145, s. 19.1(ww), effective January 1, 2012.

(b) The Grants Management Section shall administer the State Law Enforcement Assistance Program and such additional related programs as may be established by or assigned to the Section. It shall serve as the single State planning agency for purposes of the Crime Control Act of 1976 (Public Laws 94-503). Administrative responsibilities shall include, but are not limited to, the following:

(1) Compiling data, establishing needs and setting priorities for funding and policy recommendations for the Governor's Crime Commission;

(2) Preparing and revising statewide plans for adoption by the Governor's Crime Commission which are designed to improve the administration of criminal justice and to reduce crime in North Carolina;

(3) Advising State and local interests of opportunities for securing federal assistance for crime reduction and for improving criminal justice administration and planning within the State of North Carolina;

(4) Stimulating and seeking financial support from federal, State, and local government and private sources for programs and projects which implement adopted criminal justice administration improvement and crime reduction plans;

(5) Assisting State agencies and units of general local government and combinations thereof in the preparation and processing of applications for financial aid to support improved criminal justice administration, planning and crime reduction;

(6) Encouraging and assisting coordination at the federal, State, and local government levels in the preparation and implementation of criminal justice administration improvements and crime reduction plans;

(7) Applying for, receiving, disbursing, and auditing the use of funds received for the program from any public and private agencies and instrumentalities for criminal justice administration, planning, and crime reduction purposes;

(8) Entering into, monitoring, and evaluating the results of contracts and agreements necessary or incidental to the discharge of its assigned responsibilities;

(9) Providing technical assistance to State and local law-enforcement agencies in developing programs for improvement of the law-enforcement and criminal justice system; and

(10) Taking such other actions as may be deemed necessary or appropriate to carry out its assigned duties and responsibilities.

(c) Repealed by Session Laws 2011-145, s. 19.1(ww), effective January 1, 2012.

History.
1977, c. 11, s. 4; 2011-145, s. 19.1(x), (ww).

N.C. Gen. Stat. § 143B-1104

Recodified as G.S. 143B-853 by Session Laws 2020-83, s. 5, effective July 1, 2020.

§ 143B-1105. Grants reporting

(a) **State Grants.** -- Beginning August 1, 2018, and annually thereafter, the Governor's Crime Commission (Commission) shall report to the chairs of the Joint Legislative Oversight Committee on Justice and Public Safety (Committee) on all grant awards made by the Commission from State funds during the prior fiscal year. The report shall contain all of the following information:

(1) The name of the unit of local government receiving the grant.

(2) The purpose of the grant.

(3) The economic tier of the county where the unit of local government receiving the grant is located.

(4) Any recommended changes to State-funded grant programs to benefit local law enforcement agencies.

(b) **Federal Grants.** -- Beginning December 1, 2018, and annually thereafter, the Commission shall report to the chairs of the Committee on Justice and Public Safety on all grant awards made by the Commission from federal funds during the prior federal fiscal year. The report shall contain all of the following information:

(1) A list of all federal grants administered in the prior federal fiscal year.

(2) The names of all entities receiving federal grants.

(3) The amount, the purpose, and the terms of each grant.

(4) Whether there are any terms, conditions, or other contingencies that may arise as a result of a freeze on federal funds or result in compliance issues.

(5) A list of any penalties that have been assessed. The list shall include the entity against which the penalty was assessed, the reason for the assessment, and the source of funds used to pay any penalty.

(c) **Reporting Notice of Penalty.** -- The Commission shall notify the chairs of the

Committee of the receipt of any notice of assessment or notice of penalty. The Commission must notify the chairs in writing, within 30 days of the receipt of the notice, and must include a copy of the notice and any subsequent correspondence by the Commission with the agency assessing the penalty.

History.
2018-5, s. 16.2(a)

§§ 143B-1106 through 143B-1149

Reserved for future codification purposes.

PART 7
OFFICE OF EXTERNAL AFFAIRS

§ 143B-1200. Assistance Program for Victims of Rape and Sex Offenses

(a) **Establishment of Program.** -- There is established an Assistance Program for Victims of Rape and Sex Offenses, hereinafter referred to as the "Program." The Secretary shall administer and implement the Program and shall have authority over all assistance awarded through the Program. The Secretary shall promulgate rules and guidelines for the Program.

(b) **Victims to Be Provided Free Forensic Medical Examinations.** -- It is the policy of this State to arrange for victims to obtain forensic medical examinations free of charge. Whenever a forensic medical examination is conducted as a result of a sexual assault or an attempted sexual assault that occurred in this State, the Program shall pay for the cost of the examination. A medical facility or medical professional that performs a forensic medical examination on the victim of a sexual assault or attempted sexual assault shall not seek payment for the examination except from the Program.

(c) **No Billing of Victim.** -- A medical facility or medical professional that performs a forensic medical examination shall accept payment made under this section as payment in full of the amount owed for the cost of the examination and other eligible expenses and shall not bill victims, their personal insurance, Medicaid, Medicare, or any other collateral source for the examination. Furthermore, a medical facility or medical professional shall not seek reimbursement from the Program after one year from the date of the examination.

(d) **Eligible Expenses.** -- Medical facilities and medical professionals who perform forensic medical examinations shall do so using a Sexual Assault Evidence Collection Kit. Payments by the Program for the forensic medical examination shall be limited to the following:

Service	Maximum Amount Paid by Program
Physician or SANE Nurse	$ 350.00
Hospital/Facility Fee	$ 250.00
Other Expenses Deemed Eligible by the Program	$ 200.00
Total:	$ 800.00

(e) **Payment Directly to Provider.** -- The Program shall make payment directly to the medical facility or medical professional. Bills submitted to the Program for payment shall specify under which categories of expense set forth in subsection (d) of this section the billed services fall.

(f) **Additional Victim Notification Requirements.** -- A medical facility or medical professional who performs a forensic medical examination shall encourage victims to submit an application for reimbursement of medical expenses beyond the forensic examination to the Crime Victims Compensation Commission for consideration of those expenses. Medical facilities and medical professionals shall not seek reimbursement from the Program after one year from the date of the exam.

(g) **Judicial Review.** -- Upon an adverse determination by the Secretary on a claim for assistance under this Part, a victim is entitled to judicial review of that decision. The person seeking review shall file a petition in the Superior Court of Wake County.

(h) The Secretary shall adopt rules to encourage, whenever practical, the use of licensed registered nurses trained under G.S. 90-171.38(b) to conduct medical examinations and procedures.

(i) **Definitions.** -- The following definitions apply in this section:

(1) **Forensic medical examination.** -- An examination provided to a sexual assault victim by medical personnel trained to gather evidence of a sexual assault in a manner suitable for use in a court of law. The examination should include at a minimum an examination of physical trauma, a patient interview, a determination of penetration or force, and a collection and evaluation of evidence. This definition shall be interpreted consistently with 28 C.F.R. § 90.2(b) and other relevant federal law.

(2) **SANE nurse.** -- A Sexual Assault Nurse Examiner that is a licensed registered nurse trained pursuant to G.S. 90-171.38(b) who obtains preliminary histories, conducts in-depth interviews, and conducts medical examinations of rape victims or victims of related sexual offenses.

Chapter 143B

(3) **Sexual assault.** -- Any of the following crimes:

 a. First-degree forcible rape as defined in G.S. 14-27.21.

 b. Second-degree forcible rape as defined in G.S. 14-27.22.

 c. First-degree statutory rape as defined in G.S. 14-27.24.

 d. Statutory rape of a person who is 15 years of age or younger as defined in G.S. 14-27.25.

 e. First-degree forcible sexual offense as defined in G.S. 14-27.26.

 f. Second-degree forcible sexual offense as defined in G.S. 14-27.27.

 g. First-degree statutory sexual offense as defined in G.S. 14-27.29.

 h. Statutory sexual offense with a person who is 15 years of age or younger as defined in G.S. 14-27.30.

(4) **Sexual Assault Evidence Collection Kit.** -- The kit assembled and paid for by the Program and used to conduct forensic medical examinations in this State.

History.
1981, c. 931, s. 2; 1981 (Reg. Sess., 1982), c. 1191, s. 16; 2009-354, s. 1(b); 2011-145, s. 19.1(x1); 2011-391, s. 43(i); 2015-181, s. 38

§ 143B-1201. Restitution; actions

(a) The Program shall be an eligible recipient for restitution or reparation under G.S. 15A-1021, 15A-1343, 148-33.1, 148-33.2, 148-57.1, and any other applicable statutes.

(b) When any victim who:

(1) Has received assistance under this Part;

(2) Brings an action for damages arising out of the rape, attempted rape, sexual offense, or attempted sexual offense for which she received that assistance; and

(3) Recovers damages including the expenses for which she was awarded assistance, the court shall make as part of its judgment an order for reimbursement to the Program of the amount of any assistance awarded less reasonable expenses allocated by the court to that recovery.

(c) Funds appropriated to the Department of Public Safety for this program may be used to purchase and distribute sexual assault evidence collection kits approved by the Director of the State Crime Laboratory.

(d) The Secretary, in consultation with the Director of the State Crime Laboratory, shall require that all sexual assault evidence collection kits purchased or distributed on or after October 1, 2018, are compatible with the Statewide Sexual Assault Evidence Collection Kit Tracking System established under G.S. 114-65.

History.
1981, c. 931, s. 2; 1983, c. 715, s. 3; 2008-107, s. 18.2(b); 2009-354, s. 2; 2011-145, s. 19.1(g), (x1); 2018-70, s. 2

ARTICLE 15
DEPARTMENT OF INFORMATION TECHNOLOGY

PART 9
CRIMINAL JUSTICE INFORMATION

§ 143B-1390. Definitions

As used in this Part:

(1) "Board" means the Criminal Justice Information Network Governing Board established by G.S. 143B-1391.

(2) "Local government user" means a unit of local government of this State having authorized access to the Network.

(3) "Network" means the Criminal Justice Information Network established by the Board pursuant to this Part.

(4) "Network user" or "user" means any person having authorized access to the Network.

(5) "State agency" means any State department, agency, institution, board, commission, or other unit of State government.

History.
1996, 2nd Ex. Sess., c. 18, s. 23.3(a); 2015-241, s. 7A.3(1)

§ 143B-1391. Criminal Justice Information Network Governing Board -- creation; purpose; membership; conflicts of interest

(a) The Criminal Justice Information Network Governing Board is established within the Department of Information Technology, as a Type II transfer, to operate the State's Criminal Justice Information Network, the purpose of which shall be to provide the governmental and technical information systems infrastructure necessary for accomplishing State and local governmental public safety and justice functions in the most effective manner by appropriately and efficiently sharing criminal justice and juvenile justice information among law enforcement, judicial, and corrections agencies. The Board is established within the Office of the State Chief Information Officer, for organizational and budgetary purposes only and the Board shall exercise all of its statutory powers in this Part independent of control by the Office of the State Chief Information Officer.

(b) The Board shall consist of 21 members, appointed as follows:

(1) Five members appointed by the Governor, including one member who is a director or employee of a State correction agency for a term to begin September 1, 1996 and to expire on June 30, 1997, one member who is an employee of the North Carolina Department of Public Safety for a term beginning September 1, 1996 and to expire on June 30, 1997, one member selected from the North Carolina Association of Chiefs of Police for a term to begin September 1, 1996 and to expire on June 30, 1999, one member who is an employee of the Juvenile Justice Section of the Division of Adult Correction and Juvenile Justice of the Department of Public Safety, and one member who represents the Division of Motor Vehicles.

(2) Six members appointed by the General Assembly in accordance with G.S. 120-121, as follows:

a. Three members recommended by the President Pro Tempore of the Senate, including two members of the general public for terms to begin on September 1, 1996 and to expire on June 30, 1997, and one member selected from the North Carolina League of Municipalities who is a member of, or an employee working directly for, the governing board of a North Carolina municipality for a term to begin on September 1, 1996 and to expire on June 30, 1999; and

b. Three members recommended by the Speaker of the House of Representatives, including two members of the general public for terms to begin on September 1, 1996 and to expire on June 30, 1999, and one member selected from the North Carolina Association of County Commissioners who is a member of, or an employee working directly for, the governing board of a North Carolina county for a term to begin on September 1, 1996 and to expire on June 30, 1997.

(3) Two members appointed by the Attorney General, including one member who is an employee of the Attorney General for a term to begin on September 1, 1996 and to expire on June 30, 1997, and one member from the North Carolina Sheriffs' Association for a term to begin on September 1, 1996 and to expire on June 30, 1999.

(4) Six members appointed by the Chief Justice of the North Carolina Supreme Court, as follows:

a. The Director of the Administrative Office of the Courts, or an employee of the Administrative Office of the Courts, for a term beginning July 1, 1997, and expiring June 30, 2001.

b. One member who is a district attorney or an assistant district attorney upon the recommendation of the Conference of District Attorneys of North Carolina, for a term beginning July 1, 1998, and expiring June 30, 1999.

c. Two members who are superior court or district court judges for terms beginning July 1, 1998, and expiring June 30, 2001.

d. One member who is a magistrate upon the recommendation of the North Carolina Magistrates' Association, for a term beginning July 1, 1998, and expiring June 30, 1999.

e. One member who is a clerk of superior court upon the recommendation of the North Carolina Association of Clerks of Superior Court, for a term beginning July 1, 1998, and expiring June 30, 1999.

(5) One member appointed by the State Chief Information Officer.

(6) One member appointed by the President of the North Carolina Chapter of the Association of Public Communications Officials International, who is an active member of the Association, for a term to begin on September 1, 1996 and to expire on June 30, 1999.

The respective appointing authorities are encouraged to appoint persons having a background in and familiarity with criminal information systems and networks generally and with the criminal information needs and capacities of the constituency from which the member is appointed.

As the initial terms expire, subsequent members of the Board shall be appointed to serve four-year terms. At the end of a term, a member shall continue to serve on the Board until a successor is appointed. A member who is appointed after a term is begun serves only for the remainder of the term and until a successor is appointed. Any vacancy in the membership of the Board shall be filled by the same appointing authority that made the appointment, except that vacancies among members appointed by the General Assembly shall be filled in accordance with G.S. 120-122.

(c) Members of the Board shall not be employed by or serve on the board of directors or other corporate governing body of any information systems, computer hardware, computer software, or telecommunications vendor of goods and services to the State or to any unit of local government in the State. No member of the Board shall vote on an action affecting solely the member's own State agency or local governmental unit or specific judicial office.

History.

1996, 2nd Ex. Sess., c. 18, s. 23.3(a); 1998-202, s. 9; 1998-212, s. 18.2(b); 2001-424, s. 23.6(b); 2001-487, s. 90; 2003-284, s. 17.1(a); 2004-129, s. 42; 2011-145, ss. 6A.11(b), 19.1(g), (*l*); 2015-241, ss. 7A.2(d), 7A.3(1); 2017-186, s. 2 (fffff), (qqqqqq)

§ 143B-1392. Compensation and expenses of Board members; travel reimbursements

Members of the Board shall serve without compensation but may receive travel and subsistence as follows:

(1) Board members who are officials or employees of a State agency or unit of local government, in accordance with G.S. 138-6.

(2) All other Board members, at the rate established in G.S. 138-5.

History.

1996, 2nd Ex. Sess., c. 18, s. 23.3(a); 2015-241, s. 7A.3(1)

§ 143B-1393. Powers and duties

(a) The Board shall have the following powers and duties:

(1) To establish and operate the Network as an integrated system of State and local government components for effectively and efficiently storing, communicating, and using criminal justice information at the State and local levels throughout North Carolina's law enforcement, judicial, juvenile justice, and corrections agencies, with the components of the Network to include electronic devices, programs, data, and governance and to set the Network's policies and procedures.

(2) To develop and adopt uniform standards and cost-effective information technology, after thorough evaluation of the capacity of information technology to meet the present and future needs of the State and, in consultation with the Department of Information Technology, to develop and adopt standards for entering, storing, and transmitting information in criminal justice databases and for achieving maximum compatibility among user technologies.

(3) To identify the funds needed to establish and maintain the Network, identify public and private sources of funding, and secure funding to:

a. Create the Network and facilitate the sharing of information among users of the Network; and

b. Make grants to local government users to enable them to acquire or improve elements of the Network that lie within the responsibility of their agencies or State agencies; provided that the elements developed with the funds must be available for use by the State or by local governments without cost and the applicable State agencies join in the request for funding.

(4) To provide assistance to local governments for the financial and systems planning for Network-related automation and to coordinate and assist the Network users of this State in soliciting bids for information technology hardware, software, and services in order to assure compliance with the Board's technical standards, to gain the most advantageous contracts for the Network users of this State, and to assure financial accountability where State funds are used.

(5) To provide a liaison among local government users and to advocate on behalf of the Network and its users in connection with legislation affecting the Network.

(6) To facilitate the sharing of knowledge about information technologies among users of the Network.

(7) To take any other appropriate actions to foster the development of the Network.

(b) All grants or other uses of funds appropriated or granted to the Board shall be conditioned on compliance with the Board's technical and other standards.

History.

1996, 2nd Ex. Sess., c. 18, s. 23.3(a); 2003-284, s. 17.2(b); 2004-129, s. 43; 2015-241, ss. 7A.2(e), 7A.3(1), 7A.4(w)

§ 143B-1394. Election of officers; meetings; staff, etc

(a) The Governor shall call the first meeting of the Board. At the first meeting, the Board shall elect a chair and a vice-chair, each to serve a one-year term, with subsequent officers to be elected for one-year terms. The Board shall hold at least two regular meetings each year, as provided by policies and procedures adopted by the Board. The Board may hold additional meetings upon the call of the chair or any three Board members. A majority of the Board membership constitutes a quorum.

(b) The staff of the Criminal Justice Information Network shall provide the Board with professional and clerical support and any additional support the Board needs to fulfill its mandate. The Board's staff shall use space provided by the Department of Information Technology.

History.

1996, 2nd Ex. Sess., c. 18, s. 23.3(a); 2003-284, s. 17.1(b); 2011-145, ss. 6A.11(c), 19.1(g); 2015-241, ss. 7A.2(f), 7A.3(1)

PART 10
EMERGENCY TELEPHONE SERVICE

§ 143B-1401. 911 Board

(a) **Membership.** -- The 911 Board is established in the Department of Information Technology. Neither a local government unit that receives a distribution from the fund under G.S. 143B-1406 nor a telecommunication service provider may have more than one representative on the 911 Board. The 911 Board consists of 17 members as follows:

(1) Four members appointed by the Governor as follows:

    a. An individual who represents a municipality where a primary PSAP is located, appointed upon the recommendation of the North Carolina League of Municipalities.

    b. An individual who represents a county where a primary PSAP is located, appointed upon the recommendation of the North Carolina Association of County Commissioners.

    c. An individual who represents a VoIP provider.

    d. An individual who represents the North Carolina chapter of the National Emergency Number Association (NENA).

(2) Six members appointed by the General Assembly upon the recommendation of the Speaker of the House of Representatives as follows:

    a. An individual who is a sheriff, appointed upon the recommendation of the North Carolina Sheriffs' Association, Inc.

    b. An individual who represents CMRS providers operating in North Carolina.

    c. An individual who represents the North Carolina chapter of the Association of Public Safety Communications Officials (APCO).

    d. Two individuals who represent local exchange carriers operating in North Carolina, one of whom represents a local exchange carrier with less than 50,000 access lines.

    e. A fire chief with experience operating or supervising a PSAP or a director/manager of a fire-based PSAP, appointed upon the recommendation of the North Carolina State Firefighters' Association.

(3) Six members appointed by the General Assembly upon the recommendation of the President Pro Tempore of the Senate as follows:

    a. An individual who is a chief of police, appointed upon the recommendation of the North Carolina Association of Chiefs of Police.

    b. Two individuals who represent CMRS providers operating in North Carolina.

    c. A Rescue or Emergency Medical Services Chief with experience operating or supervising a PSAP, appointed upon the recommendation of the North Carolina Association of Rescue and Emergency Medical Services.

    d. Two individuals who represent local exchange carriers operating in North Carolina, one of whom represents a local exchange carrier with less than 200,000 access lines.

(4) The State Chief Information Officer or the State Chief Information Officer's designee, who serves as the chair.

(b) **Term.** -- A member's term is four years. No member may serve more than two terms. Members remain in office until their successors are appointed and qualified. Vacancies are filled in the same manner as the original appointment. The Governor may remove any member for misfeasance, malfeasance, or nonfeasance in accordance with G.S. 143B-13(d).

(c) **Meetings.** -- Members of the 911 Board serve without compensation. Members receive per diem, subsistence, and travel allowances at the rate established in G.S. 138-5. A quorum of the 911 Board is nine members. The 911 Board meets upon the call of the chair.

(d) **Public Servants.** -- The members of the 911 Board are public servants under G.S. 138A-3 and are subject to the provisions of Chapter 138A of the General Statutes.

History.
2007-383, s. 1(a); 2010-158, s. 2(a); 2013-286, s. 2; 2015-241, ss. 7A.3(2), 7A.4(f); 2015-264, s. 46; 2016-51, s. 6; 2017-6, s. 3; 2018-146, ss. 3.1(a), (b), 6.1

CHAPTER 147
STATE OFFICERS

ARTICLE 3
THE GOVERNOR

§ 147-21. Form and contents of applications for pardon

Every application for pardon must be made to the Governor in writing, signed by the party convicted, or by some person in his behalf. And every such application shall contain the grounds and reasons upon which the executive pardon is asked, and shall be in every case accompanied by a certified copy of the indictment, and the verdict and judgment of the court thereon.

History.
1869-70, c. 171; 1870-1, c. 61; Code, s. 3336; Rev., s. 5334; C.S., s. 7642

§ 147-23. Conditional pardons may be granted

In any case in which the Governor is authorized by the Constitution to grant a pardon he may, upon the petition of the prisoner, grant it, subject to such conditions, restrictions, and limitations as he considers proper and necessary, and he may issue his warrant to all proper officers to carry such pardon into effect in such manner as he thinks proper.

History.
1905, c. 356; Rev., s. 5335; C.S., s. 7643

§ 147-24. Governor's duties when conditions of pardon violated

If a prisoner who has been pardoned upon conditions to be observed and performed by him violates such conditions, or any of them, the Governor, upon receiving information of such violation, shall forthwith cause him to be arrested and detained until the case can be examined by him. The Governor shall examine the case of such prisoner, and if it appears by his own admission or by such evidence as the Governor may require that he has violated the conditions of his pardon, the Governor shall order him remanded and confined for the unexpired term of his sentence; said confinement, if the prisoner is under any other sentence of imprisonment at the time of said order, to begin upon expiration of such sentence. In computing the period of his confinement the time between the conditional pardon and subsequent arrest shall not be taken to be a part of the time of his sentence. If it appears to the Governor that

he has not broken the conditions of his conditional pardon he shall be released and his conditional pardon shall remain in force.

History.
1905, c. 356, ss. 2, 3; Rev., s. 5336; C.S., s. 7644

§ 147-25. Duty of sheriff and clerk on pardon granted

If a prisoner is pardoned conditionally or unconditionally, or his punishment is commuted, the officer to whom the warrant for such purpose is issued shall, as soon as may be after executing it, make return thereof, signed by him, with his doing thereon, to the Governor's office, and shall file in the office of the clerk of the court in which the offender was convicted an attested copy of the warrant and return, and the clerk shall file the same in his office and subjoin a brief abstract thereof to the record of the conviction and sentence, and at the next regular term of said court said warrant shall be entered upon the minutes of the court.

History.
1905, c. 356, s. 4; Rev., s. 5337; C.S., s. 7645

ARTICLE 3A
EMERGENCY WAR POWERS OF GOVERNOR

§ 147-33.3. Orders, rules and regulations

All orders, rules and regulations promulgated by the Governor pursuant to this Article shall have the full force and effect of law from and after the date of the filing of a duly authenticated copy thereof in the office of the Secretary of State. All laws, ordinances, rules and regulations, insofar as they are inconsistent with the provisions of this Article or of any rule, order or regulation made pursuant to this Article, shall be suspended during the period of time and to the extent that such conflict exists. A violation of any such order, rule or regulation, unless otherwise provided therein, shall be deemed a Class 1 misdemeanor.

History.
1943, c. 706, s. 3; 1959, c. 337, s. 6; 1993, c. 539, s. 1054; 1994, Ex. Sess., c. 24, s. 14(c)

ARTICLE 3C
OFFICE OF JUVENILE JUSTICE

§§ 147-33.30 through 147-33.71

Repealed by Session Laws 2000-137, s. 1(a), effective July 20, 2000.

CHAPTER 148
STATE PRISON SYSTEM

ARTICLE 2
PRISON REGULATIONS

§ 148-19.2. Mandatory HIV testing

Each person sentenced to imprisonment and committed to the custody of the Division of Adult Correction and Juvenile Justice of the Department of Public Safety shall be tested to determine whether the person is HIV positive.

Each inmate who has not previously tested positive for HIV shall also be tested:

 (1) Not less than once every four years from the date of that inmate's initial testing.

 (2) Prior to the inmate's release from the custody of the Division of Adult Correction and Juvenile Justice, except that testing is not mandatory prior to the release of an inmate who has been tested within one year of the inmate's release date.

In each case, the results of the test shall be reported to the inmate. If an inmate tests positive for HIV, that inmate shall be referred to public health officials for counseling.

History.
2013-360, s. 16C.15(a); 2017-186, s. 2 (kkkkkkk)

§ 148-23.1. Tobacco products prohibited on State correctional facilities premises

(a) The General Assembly finds that in order to protect the health, welfare, and comfort of inmates in the custody of the Division of Adult Correction and Juvenile Justice of the Department of Public Safety and to reduce the costs of inmate health care, it is necessary to prohibit inmates from using tobacco products on the premises of State correctional facilities and to ensure that employees and visitors do not use tobacco products on the premises of those facilities.

(b) No person may use tobacco products on the premises of a State correctional facility, except for authorized religious purposes. Notwithstanding any other provision of law, inmates in the custody of the Division of Adult Correction and Juvenile Justice of the Department of Public Safety and persons facilitating religious observances may use and possess tobacco products for religious purposes consistent with the policies of the Division.

(b1) Except as provided in subsection (b) of this section, no person may possess tobacco products on the premises of a State correctional facility. Notwithstanding the provisions of this subsection, an employee or visitor may possess tobacco products within the confines of a motor vehicle located in a designated parking area of a correctional facility's premises if the tobacco product remains in the vehicle and the vehicle is locked when the employee or visitor has exited the vehicle.

(c) The Division of Adult Correction and Juvenile Justice of the Department of Public Safety may adopt rules to implement the provisions of this section. Inmates in violation of this section are subject to disciplinary measures to be determined by the Division, including the potential loss of sentence credits earned prior to that violation. Employees in violation of this section are subject to disciplinary action by the Division. Visitors in violation of this section are subject to removal from the facility and loss of visitation privileges.

(d) As used in this section, the following terms mean:

 (1) **State correctional facility.** -- All buildings and grounds of a State correctional institution operated by the Division of Adult Correction and Juvenile Justice of the Department of Public Safety.

 (2) **Tobacco products.** -- Cigars, cigarettes, snuff, loose tobacco, or similar goods made with any part of the tobacco plant that are prepared or used for smoking, chewing, dipping, or other personal use. The term includes vapor products.

 (3) **Vapor products.** -- Nonlighted, noncombustible products that employ a mechanical heating element, battery, or electronic circuit regardless of shape or size and that can be used to heat a liquid nicotine solution contained in a vapor cartridge. The term includes electronic cigarettes, electronic cigars, electronic cigarillos, and electronic pipes. The term does not include any product regulated by the United States Food and Drug Administration under Chapter V of the federal Food, Drug, and Cosmetic Act.

History.
2005-372, s. 2; 2009-560, s. 1; 2011-145, s. 19.1(h); 2014-3, s. 15.2(a); 2017-186, s. 2 (ooooooo)

§ 148-23.2. Mobile phones prohibited on State correctional facilities premises

Except as authorized by Division of Adult Correction and Juvenile Justice of the Department of Public Safety policy, no person shall possess a mobile telephone or other wireless communications device on the premises of a State correctional facility. Notwithstanding the provisions of this section, an employee or visitor may possess a mobile telephone or other wireless communications device within the confines of a motor vehicle located in a designated parking area of a correctional facility's premises if the mobile telephone or other wireless communications device remains in the vehicle and the vehicle is locked when the employee or visitor has exited the vehicle.

History.
2009-560, s. 2; 2011-145, s. 19.1(h); 2017-186, s. 2 (ppppppp)

ARTICLE 3
LABOR OF PRISONERS

§ 148-45. Escaping or attempting escape from State prison system; failure of conditionally and temporarily released prisoners and certainyouthful offenders to return to custody of Division of Adult Correction and Juvenile Justice of the Department of Public Safety

(a) Any person in the custody of the Division of Adult Correction and Juvenile Justice of the Department of Public Safety in any of the classifications hereinafter set forth who shall escape from the State prison system, shall for the first such offense, except as provided in subsection (g) of this section, be guilty of a Class 1 misdemeanor:

(1) A prisoner serving a sentence imposed upon conviction of a misdemeanor;

(2) A person who has been charged with a misdemeanor and who has been committed to the custody of the Division of Adult Correction and Juvenile Justice of the Department of Public Safety under the provisions of G.S. 162-39;

(3) Repealed by Session Laws 1985, c. 226, s. 4.

(4) A person who shall have been convicted of a misdemeanor and who shall have been committed to the Division of Adult Correction and Juvenile Justice of the Department of Public Safety for presentence diagnostic study under the provisions of G.S. 15A-1332(c).

(b) Any person in the custody of the Division of Adult Correction and Juvenile Justice of the Department of Public Safety, in any of the classifications hereinafter set forth, who shall escape from the State prison system, shall, except as provided in subsection (g) of this section, be punished as a Class H felon:

(1) A prisoner serving a sentence imposed upon conviction of a felony;

(2) A person who has been charged with a felony and who has been committed to the custody of the Division of Adult Correction

and Juvenile Justice of the Department of Public Safety under the provisions of G.S. 162-39;

(3) Repealed by Session Laws 1985, c. 226, s. 5.

(4) A person who shall have been convicted of a felony and who shall have been committed to the Division of Adult Correction and Juvenile Justice of the Department of Public Safety for presentence diagnostic study under the provisions of G.S. 15A-1332(c); or

(5) Any person previously convicted of escaping or attempting to escape from the State prison system.

(c) Repealed by Session Laws 1979, c. 760, s. 5.

(d) Any person who aids or assists other persons to escape or attempt to escape from the State prison system shall be guilty of a Class 1 misdemeanor.

(e) Repealed by Session Laws 1983, c. 465, s. 5.

(f) Any person convicted of an escape or attempt to escape classified as a felony by this section shall be immediately classified and treated as a convicted felon even if such person has time remaining to be served in the State prison system on a sentence or sentences imposed upon conviction of a misdemeanor or misdemeanors.

(g) (1) Any person convicted and in the custody of the Division of Adult Correction and Juvenile Justice of the Department of Public Safety and ordered or otherwise assigned to work under the work-release program, G.S. 148-33.1, or any convicted person in the custody of the Division of Adult Correction and Juvenile Justice of the Department of Public Safety and temporarily allowed to leave a place of confinement by the Secretary of Public Safety or his designee or other authority of law, who shall fail to return to the custody of the Division of Adult Correction and Juvenile Justice of the Department of Public Safety, shall be guilty of the crime of escape and subject to the applicable provisions of this section and shall be deemed an escapee. For the purpose of this subsection, escape is defined to include, but is not restricted to, willful failure to return to an appointed place and at an appointed time as ordered.

(2) If a person, who would otherwise be guilty of a first violation of G.S. 148-45(g) (1), voluntarily returns to his place of confinement within 24 hours of the time at which he was ordered to return, such person shall not be charged with an escape as provided in this section but shall be subject to such administrative action as may be deemed appropriate for an escapee by the Division of Adult Correction and Juvenile Justice of the Department of Public Safety; said escapee shall not be allowed to be placed on work release for a four-month

period or for the balance of his term if less than four months; provided, however, that if such person commits a subsequent violation of this section then such person shall be charged with that offense and, if convicted, punished under the provisions of this section.

History.
1933, c. 172, s. 26; 1955, c. 279, s. 2; 1963, c. 681; 1965, c. 283; 1967, c. 996, s. 13; 1973, c. 1120; c. 1262, s. 10; 1975, cc. 170, 241, 705; c. 770, ss. 1, 2; 1977, c. 732, ss. 3, 4; c. 745; 1979, c. 760, s. 5; 1979, 2nd Sess., c. 1316, s. 47; 1981, c. 63, s. 1; c. 179, s. 14; 1983, c. 465, ss. 1-5; 1985, c. 226, ss. 3(4)-6; 1993, c. 539, ss. 1058, 1321, 1322; 1994, Ex. Sess., c. 24, s. 14(c); 1997-443, s. 19.25(t); 2011-145, s. 19.1(h), (i); 2012-83, s. 61; 2017-186, s. 2 (eeeeeeee)

§ 148-46. Degree of protection against violence allowed

(a) When any prisoner, or several combined shall offer violence to any officer, overseer, or correctional officer, or to any fellow prisoner, or attempt to do any injury to the prison building, or to any workshop, or other equipment, or shall attempt to escape, or shall resist, or disobey any lawful command, the officer, overseer, or correctional officer shall use any means necessary to defend himself, or to enforce the observance of discipline, or to secure the person of the offender, and to prevent an escape.

(b) A misdemeanor prisoner classified and treated as a convicted felon as the result of a consecutive felony sentence or sentences, or a convicted felon placed in the custody of the Secretary of Public Safety pending the outcome of an appeal, or a defendant charged with a felony or felonies and placed in the custody of the Secretary of Public Safety pending trial, shall be considered as a convicted felon in the custody of the Secretary of Public Safety against whom any means reasonably necessary, including deadly force, may be used to prevent an escape.

History.
1933, c. 172, s. 27; 1975, c. 230; 2011-145, s. 19.1(i); 2016-77, s. 8(d)

§ 148-46.1. Inflicting or assisting in infliction of self injury to prisoner resulting in incapacity to perform assigned duties

Any person serving a sentence or sentences within the State prison system who, during the term of such imprisonment, willfully and intentionally inflicts upon himself any injury resulting in a permanent or temporary incapacity to perform work or duties assigned to him by the Division of Adult Correction and Juvenile Justice of the Department of Public Safety, or any prisoner who aids or abets any other prisoner in the commission of such offense, shall be punished as a Class H felon.

History.
1959, c. 1197; 1967, c. 996, s. 13; 1979, c. 760, s. 5; 1979, 2nd Sess., c. 1316, s. 47; 1981, c. 63, s. 1; c. 179, s. 14; 1993, c. 539, s. 1323; 1994, Ex. Sess., c. 24, s. 14(c); 1997-443, s. 19.25(v); 2011-145, s. 19.1(h); 2012-83, s. 61; 2017-186, s. 2 (ffffffff)

ARTICLE 4
PAROLES

§ 148-63. Arrest powers of police officers

Any officer who is authorized to make arrests of fugitives from justice shall have full authority and power to arrest any parolee whose parole has been revoked or any post-release supervisee who has been revoked.

History.
1935, c. 414, s. 13; 1993, c. 538, s. 53; 1994, Ex. Sess., c. 24, s. 14(b)

ARTICLE 12
INTERSTATE CORRECTIONS COMPACT

§ 148-119. Short title

This Article shall be known and may be cited as the Interstate Corrections Compact.

History.
1979, c. 623

§ 148-120. Governor to execute; form of compact

The Governor of North Carolina is hereby authorized and requested to execute, on behalf of the State of North Carolina, with any other state or states legally joining therein a compact which shall be in form substantially as follows:

The contracting states solemnly agree that:

(1) The party states, desiring by common action to fully utilize and improve their institutional facilities and provide adequate programs for the confinement, treatment and rehabilitation of various types of offenders, declare that it is the policy of each of the party states to provide such facilities and programs on a basis of cooperation

with one another, and with the federal government, thereby serving the best interest of such offenders and of society and effecting economies in capital expenditures and operational costs. The purpose of this compact is to provide for the mutual development and execution of such programs of cooperation for the confinement, treatment and rehabilitation of offenders with the most economical use of human and material resources.

(2) As used in this compact, unless the context clearly requires otherwise:

a. "State" means a state of the United States; the United States of America; a territory or possession of the United States; the District of Columbia; the Commonwealth of Puerto Rico.

b. "Sending state" means a state party to this compact in which conviction or court commitment was had.

c. "Receiving state" means a state party to this compact to which an inmate is sent for confinement other than a state in which conviction or court commitment was had.

d. "Inmate" means a male or female offender who is committed, under sentence to or confined in a penal or correctional institution.

e. "Institution" means any penal or correctional facility, including but not limited to a facility for the mentally ill or mentally defective, in which inmates as defined in (2) d. above may lawfully be confined.

(3) a. Each party state may make one or more contracts with any one or more of the other party states, or with the federal government, for the confinement of inmates on behalf of a sending state in institutions situated within receiving states. Any such contract shall provide for:

1. Its duration;

2. Payments to be made to the receiving state or to the federal government, by the sending state for inmate maintenance, extraordinary medical and dental expenses, and any participation in or receipt by inmates of rehabilitative or correctional services, facilities, programs or treatment not reasonably included as part of normal maintenance;

3. Participation in programs of inmate employment, if any; the disposition or crediting of any payments received by inmates on account thereof; and the crediting of proceeds from or disposal of any products resulting therefrom;

4. Delivery and retaking of inmates;

5. Such other matters as may be necessary and appropriate to fix the obligations, responsibilities and rights of the sending and receiving states.

b. The terms and provisions of this compact shall be a part of any contract entered into by the authority of or pursuant thereto and nothing in any such contract shall be inconsistent therewith.

(4) a. Whenever the duly constituted authorities in a state party to this compact, and which has entered into a contract pursuant to Article III, Subsection (1) [paragraph a. of subdivision (3)] shall decide that confinement in, or transfer of an inmate to, an institution within the territory of another party state is necessary or desirable in order to provide adequate quarters and care or an appropriate program of rehabilitation or treatment, said officials may direct that the confinement be within an institution within the territory of said other party state, the receiving state to act in that regard solely as agent for the sending state.

b. The appropriate officials of any state party to this compact shall have access, at all reasonable times, to any institution in which it has a contractual right to confine inmates for the purpose of inspecting the facilities thereof and visiting such of its inmates as may be confined in the institution.

c. Inmates confined in an institution pursuant to the terms of this compact shall at all times be subject to the jurisdiction of the sending state and may at any time be removed therefrom for transfer to a prison or other institution within the sending state, for transfer to another institution in which the sending state may have a contractual or other right to confine inmates, for release on probation or parole, for discharge, or for any other purpose permitted by the laws of the sending state, provided that the sending state shall continue to be obligated to such payments as may be required pursuant to the terms of any contract entered into under the terms of Article III, Subsection (1) [paragraph a. of subdivision (3)].

d. Each receiving state shall provide regular reports to each sending state on the inmates of that sending state in institutions pursuant to this compact including a conduct record of each inmate and certify said record to the official designated by the sending state, in order that each inmate may have official review of his or her record in determining and altering the disposition of said inmate in accordance with the law which may obtain in the sending state and in order that the same may be a source of information for the sending state.

e. All inmates who may be confined in an institution pursuant to the provisions of this compact shall be treated in a reasonable and humane manner and shall be treated equally with such similar inmates of the receiving state as may be confined in the same institution. The fact of confinement in a receiving state shall not deprive any inmate so confined of any legal rights which said inmate would have had if confined in an appropriate institution of the sending state.

f. Any hearing or hearings to which an inmate confined pursuant to this compact may be entitled by the laws of the sending state may be had before the appropriate authorities of the sending state, or of the receiving state if authorized by the sending state. The receiving state shall provide adequate facilities for such hearings as may be conducted by the appropriate officials of a sending state. In the event such hearing or hearings are had before officials of the receiving state, the governing law shall be that of the sending state and a record of the hearing or hearings as prescribed by the sending state shall be made. Said record, together with any recommendations of the hearing officials, shall be transmitted forthwith to the official or officials before whom the hearing would

have been had if it had taken place in the sending state. In any and all proceedings had pursuant to the provisions of this subdivision, the officials of the receiving state shall act solely as agents of the sending state and no final determination shall be made in any matter except by the appropriate officials of the sending state.

g. Any inmate confined pursuant to this compact shall be released within the territory of the sending state unless the inmate, and the sending and receiving states, shall agree upon release in some other place. The sending state shall bear the cost of such return to its territory.

h. Any inmate confined pursuant to the terms of this compact shall have any and all rights to participate in and derive any benefits or incur or be relieved of any obligations or have such obligations modified or his status changed on account of any action or proceeding in which he could have participated if confined in any appropriate institution of the sending state located within such state.

i. The parents, guardian, trustee, or other person or persons entitled under the laws of the sending state to act for, advise or otherwise function with respect to any inmate shall not be deprived of or restricted in his exercise of any power in respect of any inmate confined pursuant to the terms of this compact.

(5) a. Any decision of the sending state in respect to any matter over which it retains jurisdiction pursuant to this compact shall be conclusive upon and not reviewable within the receiving state, but if at the time the sending state seeks to remove an inmate from an institution in the receiving state there is pending against the inmate within such state any criminal charge or if the inmate is formally accused of having committed within such state a criminal offense, the inmate shall not be returned without the consent of the receiving state until discharge from prosecution or other form of proceeding, imprisonment or detention for such offense. The duly accredited officers of the sending state shall be permitted to transport inmates pursuant to this compact through any and

all states party to this compact without interference.

    b. An inmate who escapes from an institution in which he is confined pursuant to this compact shall be deemed a fugitive from the sending state and from the state in which the institution is situated. In the case of an escape to a jurisdiction other than the sending or receiving state, the responsibility for institution of extradition or rendition proceedings shall be that of the sending state, but nothing contained herein shall be construed to prevent or affect the activities of officers and agencies of any jurisdiction directed toward the apprehension and return of an escapee.

  (6) Any state party to this compact may accept federal aid for use in connection with any institution or program, the use of which is or may be affected by this compact or any contract pursuant hereto; and any inmate in a receiving state pursuant to this compact may participate in any such federally-aided program or activity for which the sending and receiving states have made contractual provision, provided that if such program or activity is not part of the customary correctional regimen, the express consent of the appropriate official of the sending state shall be required therefor.

  (7) This compact shall enter into force and become effective and binding upon the states so acting when it has been enacted into law by any two states. Thereafter, this compact shall enter into force and become effective and binding as to any other of said states upon similar action by such state.

  (8) This compact shall continue in force and remain binding upon a party state until it shall have enacted a statute repealing the same and providing for the sending of formal written notice of withdrawal from the compact to the appropriate official of all other party states. An actual withdrawal shall not take effect until one year after the notice provided in said statute has been sent. Such withdrawal shall not relieve the withdrawing state from its obligations assumed hereunder prior to the effective date of withdrawal. Before effective date of withdrawal, a withdrawing state shall remove to its territory,

at its own expense, such inmates as it may have confined pursuant to the provisions of this compact.

  (9) Nothing contained in this compact shall be construed to abrogate or impair any agreement or other arrangement which a party state may have with a nonparty state for the confinement, rehabilitation or treatment of inmates nor to repeal any other laws of a party state authorizing the making of cooperative institutional arrangements.

  (10) The provisions of this compact shall be liberally construed and shall be severable. If any phrase, clause, sentence or provision of this compact is declared to be contrary to the constitution of any participating state or of the United States or the applicability thereof to any government, agency, person or circumstance is held invalid, the validity of the remainder of this compact and the applicability thereof to any government, agency, person or circumstance shall not be affected thereby. If this compact shall be held contrary to the constitution of any state participating therein, the compact shall remain in full force and effect as to the remaining states and in full force and effect as to the state affected as to all severable matters.

History.
1979, c. 623

§ 148-121. Proceedings to be open; all documents public records; exception

  (a) Except as provided in subsection (c) of this section, at least 30 days before a transfer of a North Carolina inmate to another state system pursuant to this Article is approved, the Secretary of Public Safety shall give notice that the transfer is being considered. The Secretary shall give notice of the proposed transfer by:

    (1) Notifying the district attorney of the district where the prisoner was convicted, the judge who presided at the prisoner's trial, the law-enforcement agency that arrested the prisoner, and the victim of the prisoner's crime;

    (2) Posting notice at the courthouse in the county in which the prisoner was convicted; and

    (3) Notifying any other person who has made a written request to receive notice of a transfer of the prisoner.

  (b) Except as provided in subsection (c) of this section, all written comments regarding a transfer are public records under General Statutes Chapter 132.

(c) If, in the discretion of the Secretary, such notice or disclosure requirements provided for in this section would jeopardize the safety of persons or property, the provisions of this section do not apply.

History.
1983, c. 874, s. 1; 2011-145, s. 19.1(i)

ARTICLE 13
TRANSFER OF CONVICTED FOREIGN CITIZENS UNDER FEDERAL TREATY

§ 148-122. Transfer of convicted foreign citizens under treaty; consent by Governor

If a treaty in effect between the United States and a foreign country provides for the transfer or exchange of convicted offenders to the country of which the offenders are citizens or nationals, the Governor may, on behalf of the State and subject to the terms of the treaty, authorize the Secretary of Public Safety to consent to the transfer or exchange of offenders and take any other action necessary to initiate the participation of the State in the treaty.

History.
2002-166, s. 4; 2011-145, s. 19.1(i)

CHAPTER 152
CORONERS

§ 152-1. Election; vacancies in office; appointment by clerk in special cases

In each county a coroner shall be elected by the qualified voters thereof in the same manner and at the same time as the election of members of the General Assembly, and shall hold office for a term of four years, or until his successor is elected and qualified.

A vacancy in the office of coroner shall be filled by the county commissioners, and the person so appointed shall, upon qualification, hold office until his successor is elected and qualified. If the coroner were elected as the nominee of a political party, then the county commissioners shall consult with the county executive committee of that political party before filling the vacancy, and shall appoint the person recommended by that committee if the party makes a recommendation within 30 days of the occurrence of the vacancy; this sentence shall apply only to the counties of Alamance, Alleghany, Avery, Beaufort, Brunswick, Buncombe, Burke, Cabarrus, Caldwell, Cherokee, Clay, Cleveland, Davidson, Davie, Graham, Guilford, Haywood, Henderson, Jackson, Madison, McDowell, Mecklenburg, Moore, New Hanover, Polk, Randolph, Rockingham, Rutherford, Stanly, Stokes, Transylvania, Wake, and Yancey.

When the coroner shall be out of the county, or shall for any reason be unable to hold the necessary inquest as provided by law, or there is a vacancy existing in the office of coroner which has not been filled by the county commissioners and it is made to appear to the clerk of the superior court by satisfactory evidence that a deceased person whose body has been found within the county probably came to his death by the criminal act or default of some person, it is the duty of the clerk to appoint some suitable person to act as coroner in such special case.

History.

Const., art. 4, s. 24; 1903, c. 661; Rev., ss. 1047, 1049; C.S., ss. 1014, 1018; Ex. Sess. 1924, c. 65; 1935, c. 376; 1981, c. 504, s. 8; c. 763, s. 5; c. 830

§ 152-2. Oaths to be taken

Every coroner, before entering upon the duties of his office, shall take and subscribe to the oaths prescribed for public officers, and an oath of office.

History.

Code, s. 661; Rev., s. 1048; C.S., s. 1015; Ex. Sess. 1924, c. 65

§ 152-3. Coroner's bond

Every coroner shall execute an undertaking conditioned upon the faithful discharge of the duties of his office with good and sufficient surety in the penal sum of two thousand dollars ($ 2,000), payable to the State of North Carolina, and approved by the board of county commissioners.

History.

1791, c. 342, ss. 1, 2, P. R.; 1820, c. 1047, ss. 1, 2, P. R.; R. C., c. 25, s. 2; Code, s. 661; 1899, c. 54, s. 52; Rev., s. 299; C.S., s. 1016; Ex. Sess. 1924, c. 65

§ 152-4. Coroners' bonds registered; certified copies evidence

All official bonds of coroners shall be duly approved, certified, registered, and filed as sheriffs' bonds are required to be; and certified copies of the same duly certified by the register of deeds, with official seal attached, shall be received and read in evidence in the like cases and in like manner as such copies of sheriffs' bonds are now allowed to be read in evidence.

History.

1860-1, c. 18; Code, s. 662; Rev., s. 300; C.S., s. 1017; Ex. Sess. 1924, c. 65

§ 152-5. Fees of coroners

Fees of coroners shall be the same as are or may be allowed sheriffs in similar cases:

For holding an inquest over a dead body, five dollars ($ 5.00); if necessarily engaged more than one day, for each additional day, five dollars ($ 5.00).

For burying a pauper over whom an inquest has been held, all necessary and actual expenses, to be approved by the board of county commissioners, and paid by the county.

History.

Code, s. 3743; 1903, c. 781; Rev., s. 2775; C.S., s. 3905; 1967, c. 1154, s. 6

§ 152-6. Powers, penalties, and liabilities of special coroner

The special coroner appointed under the provisions of G.S. 152-1 shall be invested with all the powers and duties conferred upon the several coroners in respect to holding inquests over deceased bodies, and shall be subject to the penalties and liabilities imposed on the said coroners.

History.

1903, c. 661, s. 2; Rev., s. 1050; C.S., s. 1019; Ex. Sess. 1924, c. 65

§ 152-7. Duties of coroners with respect to inquests and preliminary hearings

The duties of the several coroners with respect to inquests and preliminary hearings shall be as follows:

(1) Whenever it appears that the deceased probably came to his death by the criminal act or default of some person, he shall go to the place where the body of such deceased person is and make a careful investigation and inquiry as to when and by what means such deceased person came to his death and the name of the deceased, if to be found out, together with all the material circumstances attending his death, and shall make a complete record of such personal investigation: Provided, however, that the coroner shall not proceed to summon a jury as is hereinafter provided if he shall be satisfied from his personal investigation that the death of the said deceased was from natural causes, or that no person is blamable in any respect in connection with such death, and shall so find and make such finding in writing as a part of his report, giving the reason for such finding; unless an affidavit be filed with the coroner indicating blame in connection with the death of the deceased. A written report of said investigation shall be filed by the coroner with the medical examiner and the district attorney of the superior court.

(2) To empanel a jury of six persons, under oath, to make further inquiry as to the circumstances of death and to call witnesses as necessary to determine the circumstances. The coroner shall order that the names of at least 15 persons be drawn from the jury box in accordance with the procedure in G.S. 9-5. The coroner shall examine the jurors appearing in obedience to the summons, and may excuse jurors for whom service would be an extreme hardship, who would be unable to remain impartial in determining the issues, or are otherwise disqualified to serve as jurors. If the remaining jurors are less than six in number, the coroner shall cause sufficient additional names to be drawn from the jury box and have them summoned, so as to obtain the immediate attendance of at least six qualified jurors. The first six qualified jurors constitute the inquest jury.

(3) If it appears that the deceased was slain, or came to his death in such manner as to indicate any person or persons guilty of the crime in connection with the said death, then the said inquiry shall ascertain who was guilty, either as principal or accessory, or otherwise, if known; and the cause and manner of his death.

(4) Whenever in such investigations, whether preliminary or before his jury, it shall appear to the coroner or to the jury that any person or persons are culpable in the matter of such death, he shall forthwith issue his warrant for such persons and cause the same to be brought before him and the inquiry shall proceed as in the case of preliminary hearings in the district court, and in case it appears to the said coroner and the jury that such persons are probably guilty of any crime in connection with the death of the deceased, then the said coroner shall commit such persons to jail, if it appears that such persons are probably guilty of a capital crime, and in case it appears that such persons are not probably guilty of a capital crime, but are probably guilty of a lesser crime, then such coroner is to have the power and authority to fix bail for such person or persons. All such persons as are found probably guilty in such hearing shall be delivered to the keeper of the common jail for such county by the sheriff or such other officer as may perform his duties at such hearings and committed to jail unless such persons have been allowed and given the bail fixed by such coroner.

(5) As many persons as are found to be material witnesses in the matters involved in such inquiry and hearings, and are not culpable themselves shall be bound in recognizance with sufficient surety to appear at the next superior court to give evidence, and such as may default in giving such recognizance may be by such coroner committed to jail as is provided for State witnesses in other cases.

(6) Immediately upon information of the death of a person within his county, under such circumstances as call for an investigation as provided in G.S. 130A-383, the coroner shall notify the district attorney of the superior court and the medical examiner.

(7) If an inquest or preliminary hearing be ordered, to arrange for the examination of any and all witnesses including those who may be offered by the county medical examiner.

(8) To permit counsel for the family of the deceased, the solicitor of his district, or anyone designated by him, and counsel for any accused person to be present and participate in such hearing and examine and cross-examine witnesses and, whenever a warrant shall have been issued for any accused person, such accused person shall be entitled to counsel and to a full and complete hearing.

(9) To hold his inquiry where the body of the deceased shall be or at any other place in the county, and the body of the deceased need not be present at such hearing. The hearing may be adjourned to other times and places.

(10) To reduce to writing all of the testimony of all witnesses, and to have each witness to sign his testimony in the presence of the coroner, who shall attest the same, and, upon direction of the district attorney of the district, all of the testimony heard by the coroner and his jury shall be taken stenographically, and expense of such taking, when approved by the coroner and the district attorney of the district, shall be paid by the county. When the testimony is taken by a stenographer, the witness shall be caused to sign the same after it has been written out, and the coroner shall attest such signature. The attestation of all the signatures of witnesses who shall testify before the coroner shall include attaching his seal, and such statements, when so signed and attested, shall be received as competent evidence in all courts either for the purpose of contradiction or corroboration of witnesses who make the same, under the same rules as other evidence to contradict or corroborate may be now admitted. The coroner shall file a copy of all written testimony given at the hearing with the county medical examiner and with the district attorney of the superior court.

History.
Code, s. 657; 1899, c. 478; 1905, c. 628; Rev., s. 1051; 1909, c. 707, s. 1; C.S., s. 1020; Ex. Sess. 1924, c. 65; 1955, c. 972, s. 2; 1957, c. 503, ss. 1, 2; 1967, c. 1154, s. 6; 1973, c. 47, s. 2; c. 108, s. 92; c. 558; 2007-484, s. 11(d)

§ 152-8. Acts as sheriff in certain cases; special coroner

If at any time there is no person properly qualified to act as sheriff in any county, the coroner of such county is hereby required to execute all process and in all other things to act as sheriff, until some person is appointed sheriff in said county; and he shall be under the same rules and regulations, and subject to the same forfeitures, fines, and penalties as sheriffs are by law for neglect or disobedience of the same duties. If at any time the sheriff of any county is interested in or a party to any proceeding in any court, and there is no coroner in such county, or if the coroner is interested in any such proceeding, then the clerk of the court from which such process issues shall appoint some suitable person to act as special

coroner to execute such process, and such special coroner shall be under the same rules, regulations, and penalties as hereinabove provided for.

History.
Code, s. 658; 1891, c. 173; Rev., s. 1052; C.S., s. 1021; Ex. Sess. 1924, c. 65

§ 152-9. Compensation of jurors at inquest

All persons who may be summoned to act as jurors in any inquest held by a coroner over dead bodies, and who, in obedience thereto, appear and act as such jurors, shall be entitled to the same compensation in per diem and mileage as is allowed by law to jurors acting in the superior courts. The coroners of the respective counties are authorized and empowered to take proof of the number of days of service of each juror so acting, and also of the number of miles traveled by such juror in going to and returning from such place of inquest, and shall file with the board of commissioners of the county a correct account of the same, which shall be, by such commissioners, audited and paid in the manner provided for the pay of jurors acting in the superior courts.

History.
Code, ss. 659, 660; Rev., s. 1053; C.S., s. 1022; Ex. Sess. 1924, c. 65

§ 152-10. Hearing by coroner in lieu of other preliminary hearing; habeas corpus

All hearings by a coroner and his jury, as provided herein, when the accused has been arrested and has participated in such hearing, shall be in lieu of any other preliminary hearing, and such cases shall be immediately sent to the clerk of the superior court of such county and docketed by him in the same manner as warrants from magistrates. Any accused person who shall be so committed by a coroner shall have the right, upon habeas corpus, to have a judge of the superior or district court review the action of the coroner in fixing bail or declining the same.

History.
Ex. Sess. 1924, c. 65; 1973, c. 108, s. 93

§ 152-11. Service of process issued by coroner

All process, both subpoenas and warrants for the arrest of any person or persons, and orders for the summoning of a jury, in case it may appear necessary for such coroner to issue such order, shall be served by the sheriff or other lawful officer of the county in which such dead body is found, and in case it is necessary to subpoena witnesses or to arrest persons in a county other than such county in which the body of the deceased is found, then such coroner may issue his process to any other county in the State, with his official seal attached, and such process shall be served by the sheriff or other lawful officer of the county to which it is directed, but such process shall not be served outside of the county in which such dead body is found unless attested by the official seal of such coroner.

History.
Ex. Sess. 1924, c. 65

CHAPTER 153A
COUNTIES

ARTICLE 4
FORM OF GOVERNMENT

PART 3
ORGANIZATION AND PROCEDURES OF THE BOARD OF COMMISSIONERS

§ 153A-48. Ordinance book

The clerk shall maintain an ordinance book, separate from the minute book of the board of commissioners. The ordinance book shall be indexed and shall be available for public inspection in the office of the clerk. Except as provided in this section and in G.S. 153A-47, each county ordinance shall be filed and indexed in the ordinance book.

The budget ordinance and any amendments thereto, any bond order, and any other ordinance of limited interest or transitory nature may be omitted from the ordinance book. However, the ordinance book shall contain a section showing the caption of each omitted ordinance and the page in the commissioners' minute book at which the ordinance may be found.

If a county adopts and issues a code of its ordinances, county ordinances need be recorded and indexed in the ordinance book only until they are placed in the codification.

History.
1963, c. 1060, ss. 1, 11/2; 1965, cc. 388, 567, 1083, 1158; 1967, c. 495, s. 2; 1969, c. 36, s. 1; 1971, c. 702, ss. 1-3; 1973, c. 822, s. 1

§ 153A-49. Code of ordinances

A county may adopt and issue a code of its ordinances. The code may be reproduced by any method that gives legible and permanent copies, and may be issued as a securely bound book or books with periodic separately bound supplements, or as a loose-leaf book maintained by replacement pages. Supplements or replacement pages should be adopted and issued at least annually, unless there have been no additions to or modifications of the code during the year.

A code may consist of two parts, the "General Ordinances" and the "Technical Ordinances." The technical ordinances may be published as separate books or pamphlets, and may include ordinances regarding the construction of buildings, the installation of plumbing and electric wiring, and the installation of cooling and heating equipment; ordinances regarding the use of public utilities, buildings, or facilities operated by the county; the zoning ordinance; the subdivision control ordinance; and other similar ordinances designated as technical ordinances by the board of commissioners. The board may omit from the code the budget ordinance, any bond orders, and other designated classes of ordinances of limited interest or transitory nature, but the code shall clearly describe the classes of ordinances omitted from it.

The board of commissioners may provide that ordinances (i) establishing or amending the boundaries of county zoning areas or (ii) establishing or amending the boundaries of zoning districts shall be codified by appropriate entries upon official map books to be retained permanently in the office of the clerk or some other county office generally accessible to the public.

History.
1973, c. 822, s. 1; 2014-3, s. 12.3(e)

§ 153A-50. Pleading and proving county ordinances

County ordinances shall be pleaded and proved under the rules and procedures of G.S. 160A-79. References to G.S. 160A-77 and G.S. 160A-78 appearing in G.S. 160A-79 are deemed, for purposes of this section, to refer to G.S. 153A-49 and G.S. 153A-48, respectively.

History.
1973, c. 822, s. 1

ARTICLE 5
ADMINISTRATION

PART 4
PERSONNEL

§ 153A-94.2. Criminal history record checks of employees permitted

The board of commissioners may adopt or provide for rules and regulations or ordinances concerning a requirement that any applicant for employment be subject to a criminal history record check of State and National Repositories of Criminal Histories conducted by the Department of Public Safety in accordance with G.S. 143B-945. The local or regional public employer may consider the results of these criminal history record checks in its hiring decisions.

History.
2005-358, s. 2; 2014-100, s. 17.1(mmm)

ARTICLE 6
DELEGATION AND EXERCISE OF THE GENERAL POLICE POWER

§ 153A-121. General ordinance-making power

(a) A county may by ordinance define, regulate, prohibit, or abate acts, omissions, or conditions detrimental to the health, safety, or welfare of its citizens and the peace and dignity of the county; and may define and abate nuisances.

(b) This section does not authorize a county to regulate or control vehicular or pedestrian traffic on a street or highway under the control of the Board of Transportation, nor to regulate or control any right-of-way or right-of-passage belonging to a public utility, electric or telephone membership corporation, or public agency of the State. In addition, no county ordinance may regulate or control a highway right-of-way in a manner inconsistent with State law or an ordinance of the Board of Transportation.

(c) This section does not impair the authority of local boards of health to adopt rules and regulations to protect and promote public health.

History.
1963, c. 1060, ss. 1, 11/2; 1965, cc. 388, 567, 1083, 1158; 1967, c. 495, s. 2; 1969, c. 36, s. 1; 1971, c. 702, ss. 1-3; 1973, c. 507, s. 5; c. 822, s. 1

§ 153A-122. Territorial jurisdiction of county ordinances

(a) Except as otherwise provided in this Article, the board of commissioners may make any ordinance adopted pursuant to this Article applicable to any part of the county not within a city.

(b) The governing board of a city may by resolution permit a county ordinance adopted pursuant to this Article to be applicable within the city. In the resolution permitting the county ordinance to be applicable within the city, the governing board of the city may specify that any signage required by the county ordinance be in compliance with city ordinances. The city may by resolution withdraw its permission to such an ordinance. If it does so, the city shall give written notice to the county of its withdrawal of permission; 30 days after the day the county receives this notice the county ordinance ceases to be applicable within the city.

History.
1963, c. 1060, ss. 1, 1 1/2; 1965, cc. 388, 567, 1083, 1158; 1967, c. 495, s. 2; 1969, c. 36, s. 1; 1971, c. 702, ss. 1-3; 1973, c. 822, s. 1; 2015-166, s. 1

§ 153A-123. Enforcement of ordinances

(a) A county may provide for fines and penalties for violation of its ordinances and may secure injunctions and abatement orders to further insure compliance with its ordinances, as provided by this section.

(b) Unless the board of commissioners has provided otherwise, violation of a county ordinance is a misdemeanor or infraction as provided by G.S. 14-4. An ordinance may provide by express statement that the maximum fine, term of imprisonment, or infraction penalty to be imposed for a violation is some amount of money or number of days less than the maximum imposed by G.S. 14-4.

(b) Except for the types of ordinances listed in subsection (b1) of this section, violation of a county ordinance may be a misdemeanor or infraction as provided by G.S. 14-4 only if the county specifies such in the ordinance. An ordinance may provide by express statement that the maximum fine, term of imprisonment, or infraction penalty to be imposed for a violation is some amount of money or number of days less than the maximum imposed by G.S. 14-4. Notwithstanding G.S. 153A-45, no ordinance specifying a criminal penalty may be enacted at the meeting in which it is first introduced.

(b1) No ordinance of the following types may impose a criminal penalty:

(1) Any ordinance adopted under Article 18 of this Chapter, Planning and Regulation of Development or, its successor, Chapter 160D of the General Statutes, except for those ordinances related to unsafe buildings.

(2) Any ordinance adopted pursuant to G.S. 153A-134, Regulating and licensing businesses, trades, etc.

(3) Any ordinance adopted pursuant to G.S. 153A-138, Registration of mobile homes, house trailers, etc.

(4) Any ordinance adopted pursuant to G.S. 153A-140.1, Stream-clearing programs.

(5) Any ordinance adopted pursuant to G.S. 153A-143, Regulation of outdoor advertising or, its successor, G.S. 160D-912, Outdoor advertising.

(6) Any ordinance adopted pursuant to G.S. 153A-144, Limitations on regulating solar collectors or, its successor, G.S. 160D-914, Solar collectors.

(7) Any ordinance adopted pursuant to G.S. 153A-145, Limitations on regulating cisterns and rain barrels.

(8) Any ordinance regulating trees.

(c) An ordinance may provide that violation subjects the offender to a civil penalty to be recovered by the county in a civil action in the nature of debt if the offender does not pay the

Chapter 153A

penalty within a prescribed period of time after he has been cited for violation of the ordinance.

(c1) An ordinance may provide for the recovery of a civil penalty by the county for violation of the fire prevention code of the State Building Code as authorized under G.S. 143-139.

(d) An ordinance may provide that it may be enforced by an appropriate equitable remedy issuing from a court of competent jurisdiction. In such a case, the General Court of Justice has jurisdiction to issue any order that may be appropriate, and it is not a defense to the county's application for equitable relief that there is an adequate remedy at law.

(e) An ordinance that makes unlawful a condition existing upon or use made of real property may provide that it may be enforced by injunction and order of abatement, and the General Court of Justice has jurisdiction to issue such an order. When a violation of such an ordinance occurs, the county may apply to the appropriate division of the General Court of Justice for a mandatory or prohibitory injunction and order of abatement commanding the defendant to correct the unlawful condition upon or cease the unlawful use of the property. The action shall be governed in all respects by the laws and rules governing civil proceedings, including the Rules of Civil Procedure in general and Rule 65 in particular.

In addition to an injunction, the court may enter an order of abatement as a part of the judgment in the cause. An order of abatement may direct that buildings or other structures on the property be closed, demolished, or removed; that fixtures, furniture, or other movable property be removed from buildings on the property; that grass and weeds be cut; that improvements or repairs be made; or that any other action be taken that is necessary to bring the property into compliance with the ordinance. If the defendant fails or refuses to comply with an injunction or with an order of abatement within the time allowed by the court, he may be cited for contempt and the county may execute the order of abatement. If the county executes the order, it has a lien on the property, in the nature of a mechanic's and materialman's lien, for the costs of executing the order. The defendant may secure cancellation of an order of abatement by paying all costs of the proceedings and posting a bond for compliance with the order. The bond shall be given with sureties approved by the clerk of superior court in an amount approved by the judge before whom the matter was heard and shall be conditioned on the defendant's full compliance with the terms of the order of abatement within the time fixed by the judge. Cancellation of an order of abatement does not suspend or cancel an injunction issued in conjunction with the order.

(f) Subject to the express terms of the ordinance, a county ordinance may be enforced by any one or more of the remedies authorized by this section.

(g) A county ordinance may provide, when appropriate, that each day's continuing violation is a separate and distinct offense.

(h) Notwithstanding any authority under this Article or any local act of the General Assembly, no ordinance regulating trees may be enforced on land owned or operated by a public airport authority.

History.
1973, c. 822, s. 1; 1985, c. 764, s. 34; 1985 (Reg. Sess., 1986), c. 852, s. 17; 1993, c. 329, s. 5; 2013-331, s. 1; 2021-138, s. 13(a)

§ 153A-124. Enumeration not exclusive

The enumeration in this Article or other portions of this Chapter of specific powers to define, regulate, prohibit, or abate acts, omissions, or conditions is not exclusive, nor is it a limit on the general authority to adopt ordinances conferred on counties by G.S. 153A-121.

History.
1973, c. 822, s. 1

§ 153A-125. Regulation of solicitation campaigns, flea markets and itinerant merchants

A county may by ordinance regulate, restrict, or prohibit the solicitation of contributions from the public for charitable or eleemosynary purposes, and also the business activities of itinerant merchants, salesmen, promoters, drummers, peddlers, flea market operators and flea market vendors and hawkers. These ordinances may include, but are not limited to, requirements that an application be made and a permit issued, that an investigation be made, that activities be reasonably limited as to time and place, that proper credentials and proof of financial stability be submitted, that not more than a stated percentage of contributions to solicitation campaigns be retained for administrative expenses, and that an adequate bond be posted to protect the public from fraud. A county may charge a fee for a permit issued pursuant to such an ordinance.

History.
1967, c. 80, ss. 1-2 1/2; 1973, c. 822, s. 1; 1987, c. 708, s. 7

§ 153A-126. Regulation of begging

A county may by ordinance prohibit or regulate begging or otherwise canvassing the public for contributions for the private benefit of the solicitor or any other person.

History.
1973, c. 822, s. 1

§ 153A-127. Abuse of animals

A county may by ordinance define and prohibit the abuse of animals.

History.
1973, c. 822, s. 1

§ 153A-128. Regulation of explosive, corrosive, inflammable, or radioactive substances

A county may by ordinance regulate, restrict, or prohibit the sale, possession, storage, use or conveyance of any explosive, corrosive, inflammable, or radioactive substance or of any weapon or instrumentality of mass death and destruction.

History.
1973, c. 822, s. 1

§ 153A-129. Firearms

(a) Except as provided in this section, a county may by ordinance regulate, restrict, or prohibit the discharge of firearms at any time or place except in any of the following instances:

(1) When used to take birds or animals pursuant to Chapter 113, Subchapter IV.

(2) When used in defense of person or property.

(3) When used pursuant to lawful directions of law-enforcement officers.

(b) A county may by ordinance prohibit hunting on Sunday as allowed under G.S. 103-2, provided the ordinance complies with all of the following:

(1) The ordinance shall be applicable from January 1 until December 31 of any year of effectiveness.

(2) The ordinance shall allow for individuals hunting in an adjacent county with no restriction on Sunday hunting to retrieve any animal lawfully shot from the adjacent county.

(3) The ordinance shall be applicable to the entire county.

(4) The ordinance shall not be effective unless approved by a majority of those voting in a county-wide referendum held as provided in G.S. 163-287. Such special election shall only be held at the time provided by G.S. 163-287(a)(1).

(c) A county may regulate the display of firearms on the public roads, sidewalks, alleys, or other public property.

(d) This section does not limit a county's authority to take action under Article 1A of Chapter 166A of the General Statutes.

History.
1973, c. 822, s. 1; 2006-264, s. 16; 2012-12, s. 2(yy); 2015-144, s. 5(b); 2017-6, s. 3; 2017-182, s. 3(a); 2018-146, ss. 3.1(a), (b), 6.1

§ 153A-130. Pellet guns

A county may by ordinance regulate, restrict, or prohibit the sale, possession, or use of pellet guns or any other mechanism or device designed or used to project a missile by compressed air or mechanical action with less than deadly force.

History.
1973, c. 822, s. 1

§ 153A-131. Possession or harboring of dangerous animals

A county may by ordinance regulate, restrict, or prohibit the possession or harboring of animals which are dangerous to persons or property. No such ordinance shall have the effect of permitting any activity or condition with respect to a wild animal which is prohibited or more severely restricted by regulations of the Wildlife Resources Commission.

History.
1973, c. 822, s. 1; 1977, c. 407, s. 1

§ 153A-132. Removal and disposal of abandoned and junked motor vehicles; abandoned vessels

(a) **Grant of Power.** -- A county may by ordinance prohibit the abandonment of motor vehicles on public grounds and private property within the county's ordinance-making jurisdiction and on county-owned property wherever located. The county may enforce the ordinance by removing and disposing of abandoned or junked motor vehicles according to the procedures prescribed in this section.

(b) **Definitions.** -- "Motor vehicle" includes any machine designed or intended to travel over land or water by self-propulsion or while attached to self-propelled vehicle.

(1) An "abandoned motor vehicle" is one that:

a. Is left on public grounds or county-owned property in violation of a law or ordinance prohibiting parking; or

b. Is left for longer than 24 hours on property owned or operated by the county; or

c. Is left for longer than two hours on private property without the consent of the owner, occupant, or lessee of the property; or

d. Is left for longer than seven days on public grounds.

(2) A "junked motor vehicle" is an abandoned motor vehicle that also:

a. Is partially dismantled or wrecked; or

b. Cannot be self-propelled or moved in the manner in which it originally was intended to move; or

c. Is more than five years old and appears to be worth less than one hundred dollars ($ 100.00); or

d. Does not display a current license plate.

(c) **Removal of Vehicles.** -- A county may remove to a storage garage or area an abandoned or junked motor vehicle found to be in violation of an ordinance adopted pursuant to this section. A vehicle may not be removed from private property, however, without the written request of the owner, lessee, or occupant of the premises unless the board of commissioners or a duly authorized county official or employee has declared the vehicle to be a health or safety hazard. Appropriate county officers and employees have a right, upon presentation of proper credentials, to enter on any premises within the county ordinance-making jurisdiction at any reasonable hour in order to determine if any vehicles are health or safety hazards. The county may require a person requesting the removal from private property of an abandoned or junked motor vehicle to indemnify the county against any loss, expense, or liability incurred because of the vehicle's removal, storage, or sale.

When an abandoned or junked motor vehicle is removed, the county shall give notice to the owner as required by G.S. 20-219.11(a) and (b).

(d) **Hearing Procedure.** -- Regardless of whether a county does its own removal and disposal of motor vehicles or contracts with another person to do so, the county shall provide a hearing procedure for the owner. For purposes of this subsection, the definitions in G.S. 20-219.9 apply.

(1) If the county operates in such a way that the person who tows the vehicle is responsible for collecting towing fees, all provisions of Article 7A, Chapter 20, apply.

(2) If the county operates in such a way that it is responsible for collecting towing fees, it shall:

a. Provide by contract or ordinance for a schedule of reasonable towing fees,

b. Provide a procedure for a prompt fair hearing to contest the towing,

c. Provide for an appeal to district court from that hearing,

d. Authorize release of the vehicle at any time after towing by the posting of a bond or paying of the fees due, and

e. Provide a sale procedure similar to that provided in G.S. 44A-4, 44A-5, and 44A-6, except that no hearing in addition to the probable cause hearing is required. If no one purchases the vehicle at the sale and if the value of the vehicle is less than the amount of the lien, the county may destroy it.

(e), (f) Repealed by Session Laws 1983, c. 420, s. 10.

(g) **No Liability.** -- No person nor any county may be held to answer in a civil or criminal action to any owner or other person legally entitled to the possession of an abandoned, junked, lost, or stolen motor vehicle for disposing of the vehicle as provided in this section.

(h) **Exceptions.** -- This section does not apply to any vehicle in an enclosed building, to any vehicle on the premises of a business enterprise being operated in a lawful place and manner if the vehicle is necessary to the operation of the enterprise, or to any vehicle in an appropriate storage place or depository maintained in a lawful place and manner by the county.

(i) A county may by ordinance prohibit the abandonment of vessels in navigable waters within the county's ordinance-making jurisdiction, subject to the provisions of this subsection. The provisions of this section shall apply to abandoned vessels in the same manner that they apply to abandoned or junked motor vehicles to the extent that the provisions may apply to abandoned vessels. For purposes of this subsection, an "abandoned vessel" is one that meets any of the following:

(1) A vessel that is moored, anchored, or otherwise located for more than 30 consecutive days in any 180 consecutive-day period without permission of the dock owner.

(2) A vessel that is in danger of sinking, has sunk, is resting on the bottom, or is located such that it is a hazard to navigation or is an immediate danger to other vessels.

Shipwrecks, vessels, cargoes, tackle, and other underwater archeological remains that have been in place for more than 10 years shall not be considered abandoned vessels and shall not be removed under the provisions of this section without the approval of the Department of Natural and Cultural Resources, which is the legal custodian of these properties pursuant to G.S. 121-22 and G.S. 121-23. This subsection applies only to the counties set out in G.S. 113A-103(2).

History.
1971, c. 489; 1973, c. 822, s. 1; 1975, c. 716, s. 5; 1983, c. 420, ss. 8-10; 1997-456, s. 27; 2013-182, s. 2; 2015-241, ss. 14.6(n), (o), 14.30(s)

§ 153A-132.1. To provide for the removal and disposal of trash, garbage, etc

The board of county commissioners of any county is hereby authorized to enact ordinances governing the removal, method or manner of disposal, depositing or dumping of any trash, debris, garbage, litter, discarded cans or receptacles or any waste matter whatsoever within the rural areas of the county and outside and beyond the corporate limits of any municipality of said county. An ordinance adopted pursuant hereto may make it unlawful to place, discard, dispose, leave or dump any trash, debris, garbage, litter, discarded cans or receptacles or any waste matter whatsoever upon a street or highway located within that county or upon property owned or operated by the county unless such trash, debris, garbage, litter, discarded cans or receptacles or any waste matter is placed in a designated location or container for removal by a specific garbage or trash service collector.

Boards of county commissioners may also provide by ordinance enacted pursuant to this section, that the placing, discarding, disposing, leaving or dumping of the articles forbidden by this section shall, for each day or portion thereof the articles or matter are left, constitute a separate offense, and that a person in violation of the ordinance may be punished by a fine not exceeding fifty dollars ($ 50.00) or imprisoned not exceeding 30 days, or both, for each offense.

History.
1973, c. 952

§ 153A-132.2. Regulation, restraint and prohibition of abandonment of junked motor vehicles

(a) A county may by ordinance regulate, restrain or prohibit the abandonment of junked motor vehicles on public grounds and on private property within the county's ordinance-making jurisdiction upon a finding that such regulation, restraint or prohibition is necessary and desirable to promote or enhance community, neighborhood or area appearance, and may enforce any such ordinance by removing and disposing of junked motor vehicles subject to the ordinance according to the procedures prescribed in this section. The authority granted by this section shall be supplemental to any other authority conferred upon counties. Nothing in this section shall be construed to authorize a county to require the removal or disposal of a motor vehicle kept or stored at a bona fide "automobile graveyard" or "junkyard" as defined in G.S. 136-143.

For purposes of this section, the term "junked motor vehicle" means a vehicle that does not display a current license plate and that:

(1) Is partially dismantled or wrecked; or

(2) Cannot be self-propelled or moved in the manner in which it originally was intended to move; or

(3) Is more than five years old and appears to be worth less than one hundred dollars ($ 100.00).

(a1) Any junked motor vehicle found to be in violation of an ordinance adopted pursuant to this section may be removed to a storage garage or area, but no such vehicle shall be removed from private property without the written request of the owner, lessee, or occupant of the premises unless the board of commissioners or a duly authorized county official or employee finds in writing that the aesthetic benefits of removing the vehicle outweigh the burdens imposed on the private property owner. Such finding shall be based on a balancing of the monetary loss of the apparent owner against the corresponding gain to the public by promoting or enhancing community, neighborhood or area appearance. The following, among other relevant factors, may be considered:

(1) Protection of property values;

(2) Promotion of tourism and other economic development opportunities;

(3) Indirect protection of public health and safety;

(4) Preservation of the character and integrity of the community; and

(5) Promotion of the comfort, happiness, and emotional stability of area residents.

(a2) The county may require any person requesting the removal of a junked or abandoned motor vehicle from private property to indemnify the county against any loss, expense, or liability incurred because of the removal, storage, or sale thereof. When an abandoned or junked motor vehicle is removed, the county shall give notice to the owner as required by G.S. 20-219.11(a) and (b).

(a3) **Hearing Procedure. --** Regardless of whether a county does its own removal and disposal of motor vehicles or contracts with another person to do so, the county shall provide a prior hearing procedure for the owner. For purposes of this subsection, the definitions in G.S. 20-219.9 apply.

(1) If the county operates in such a way that the person who tows the vehicle is responsible for collecting towing fees, all provisions of Article 7A, Chapter 20, apply.

(2) If the county operates in such a way that it is responsible for collecting towing fees, it shall:

a. Provide by contract or ordinance for a schedule of reasonable towing fees,

b. Provide a procedure for a prompt fair hearing to contest the towing,

c. Provide for an appeal to district court from that hearing,

d. Authorize release of the vehicle at any time after towing by the posting of a bond or paying of the fees due, and

e. Provide a sale procedure similar to that provided in G.S. 44A-4, 44A-5, and 44A-6, except that no hearing in addition to the probable cause hearing is required. If no one purchases the vehicle at the sale and if the value of the vehicle is less than the amount of the lien, the city may destroy it.

(a4) Any person who removes a vehicle pursuant to this section shall not be held liable for damages for the removal of the vehicle to the owner, lienholder or other person legally entitled to the possession of the vehicle removed; however, any person who intentionally or negligently damages a vehicle in the removal of such vehicle, or intentionally or negligently inflicts injury upon any person in the removal of such vehicle, may be held liable for damages.

(b) Any ordinance adopted pursuant to this section shall include a prohibition against removing or disposing of any motor vehicle that is used on a regular basis for business or personal use.

History.
1983, c. 841, s. 1; 1985, c. 737, s. 1; 1987, c. 42, s. 1; c. 451, s. 1; 1987 (Reg. Sess., 1988), c. 902, s. 1; 1989, c. 743, s. 1

§ 153A-133. Noise regulation

A county may by ordinance regulate, restrict, or prohibit the production or emission of noises or amplified speech, music, or other sounds that tend to annoy, disturb, or frighten its citizens.

History.
1973, c. 822, s. 1

§ 153A-134. Regulating and licensing businesses, trades, etc

(a) A county may by ordinance, subject to the general law of the State, regulate and license occupations, businesses, trades, professions, and forms of amusement or entertainment and prohibit those that may be inimical to the public health, welfare, safety, order, or convenience. In licensing trades, occupations, and professions, the county may, consistent with the general law of the State, require applicants for licenses to be examined and charge a reasonable fee therefor.

This section does not authorize a county to examine or license a person holding a license issued by an occupational licensing board of this State as to the profession or trade that he has been licensed to practice or pursue by the State.

(b) Repealed by Session Laws 2015-237, s. 4, effective October 1, 2015.

(c) Nothing in this section shall authorize a county to regulate and license a TNC service regulated under Article 10A of Chapter 20 of the General Statutes.

History.
1868, c. 20, s. 8; Code, s. 707; Rev., s. 1318; C.S., s. 1297; 1973, c. 822, s. 1; 2013-413, s. 12.1(c); 2015-237, s. 4

§ 153A-135. Regulation of places of amusement

A county may by ordinance regulate places of amusement and entertainment, and may regulate, restrict, or prohibit the operation of pool and billiard halls, dance halls, carnivals, circuses, or itinerant shows or exhibitions of any kind. Places of amusement and entertainment include coffeehouses, cocktail lounges, nightclubs, beer halls, and similar establishments, but any regulation of such places shall be consistent with any permit or license issued by the North Carolina Alcoholic Beverage Control Commission.

History.
1963, c. 1060, ss. 1, 1 1/2; 1965, cc. 388, 567, 1083, 1158; 1967, c. 495, s. 2; 1969, c. 36, s. 1; 1971, c. 702, ss. 1-3; 1973, c. 822, s. 1; 1981, c. 412, ss. 4, 5

§ 153A-136. Regulation of solid wastes

(a) A county may by ordinance regulate the storage, collection, transportation, use, disposal, and other disposition of solid wastes. Such an ordinance may:

(1) Regulate the activities of persons, firms, and corporations, both public and private.

(2) Require each person wishing to commercially collect or dispose of solid wastes to secure a license from the county and prohibit any person from commercially collecting or disposing of solid wastes without a license. A fee may be charged for a license.

(3) Grant a franchise to one or more persons for the exclusive right to commercially collect or dispose of solid wastes within all or a defined portion of the county and prohibit any other person from commercially collecting or disposing of solid wastes in that area. The board of commissioners may set the terms of any franchise; provided, however, no franchise shall be granted for a period of more than 30 years, except for

a franchise granted to a sanitary landfill for the life-of-site of the landfill pursuant to G.S. 130A-294(b1), which may not exceed 60 years. A franchise granted for a sanitary landfill shall be subject to all requirements pertaining thereto under G.S. 130A-294. No franchise by its terms may impair the authority of the board of commissioners to regulate fees as authorized by this section.

(4) Regulate the fees, if any, that may be charged by licensed or franchised persons for collecting or disposing of solid wastes.

(5) Require the source separation of materials prior to collection of solid waste for disposal.

(6) Require participation in a recycling program by requiring separation of designated materials by the owner or occupant of the property prior to disposal. An owner of recovered materials as defined by G.S. 130A-290(a)(24) retains ownership of the recovered materials until the owner conveys, sells, donates, or otherwise transfers the recovered materials to a person, firm, company, corporation, or unit of local government. A county may not require an owner to convey, sell, donate, or otherwise transfer recovered materials to the county or its designee. If an owner places recovered materials in receptacles or delivers recovered materials to specific locations, receptacles, and facilities that are owned or operated by the county or its designee, then ownership of these materials is transferred to the county or its designee.

(6a) Regulate the illegal disposal of solid waste, including littering on public and private property, provide for enforcement by civil penalties as well as other remedies, and provide that such regulations may be enforced by county employees specially appointed as environmental enforcement officers.

(7) Include any other proper matter.

(b) Any ordinance adopted pursuant to this section shall be consistent with and supplementary to any rules adopted by the Commission for Public Health or the Department of Environmental Quality.

(c) The board of commissioners of a county shall consider alternative sites and socioeconomic and demographic data and shall hold a public hearing prior to selecting or approving a site for a new sanitary landfill that receives residential solid waste that is located within one mile of an existing sanitary landfill within the State. The distance between an existing and a proposed site shall be determined by measurement between the closest points on the outer boundary of each site. The definitions set out in G.S. 130A-290 apply to this subsection. As used in this subsection:

(1) "Approving a site" refers to prior approval of a site under G.S. 130A-294(a)(4).

(2) "Existing sanitary landfill" means a sanitary landfill that is in operation or that has been in operation within the five-year period immediately prior to the date on which an application for a permit is submitted.

(3) "New sanitary landfill" means a sanitary landfill that includes areas not within the legal description of an existing sanitary landfill as set out in the permit for the existing sanitary landfill.

(4) "Socioeconomic and demographic data" means the most recent socioeconomic and demographic data compiled by the United States Bureau of the Census and any additional socioeconomic and demographic data submitted at the public hearing.

(d) As used in this section, "solid waste" means nonhazardous solid waste, that is, solid waste as defined in G.S. 130A-290 but not including hazardous waste.

(e) A county that has planning jurisdiction over any portion of the site of a sanitary landfill may employ a local government landfill liaison. No person who is responsible for any aspect of the management or operation of the landfill may serve as a local government landfill liaison. A local government landfill liaison shall have a right to enter public or private lands on which the landfill facility is located at reasonable times to inspect the landfill operation in order to:

(1) Ensure that the facility meets all local requirements.

(2) Identify and notify the Department of suspected violations of applicable federal or State laws, regulations, or rules.

(3) Identify and notify the Department of potentially hazardous conditions at the facility.

(f) Entry pursuant to subsection (e) of this section shall not constitute a trespass or taking of property.

History.
1955, c. 1050; 1957, cc. 120, 376; 1961, c. 40; c. 514, s. 1; cc. 711, 803; c. 806, s. 1; 1965, c. 452; 1967, cc. 34, 90; c. 183, s. 1; cc. 304, 339; c. 495, s. 4; 1969, cc. 79, 155, 176; c. 234, s. 1; c. 452; c. 1003, s. 4; 1973, c. 476, s. 128; c. 822, s. 1; 1989 (Reg. Sess., 1990), c. 1009, s. 1; 1991 (Reg. Sess., 1992), c. 1013, s. 1; 1993, c. 165, s. 1; 1997-443, s. 11A.123; 2001-512, s. 5; 2007-182, s. 2; 2007-550, s. 11(a); 2015-241, s. 14.30(u); 2017-10, s. 3.2(d); 2018-114, s. 21(c)

N.C. Gen. Stat. § 153A-137

Repealed by Session Laws 2006-151, s. 10, effective January 1, 2007.

§ 153A-138. Registration of mobile homes, house trailers, etc

A county may by ordinance provide for the annual registration of mobile homes, house trailers and similar vehicular equipment designed for use as living or business quarters and for the display of a sticker or other device thereon as evidence of such registration. No fee shall be charged for such registration.

History.
1975, c. 693

§ 153A-139. Regulation of traffic at parking areas and driveways

The governing body of any county may, by ordinance, regulate the stopping, standing, or parking of vehicles in specified areas of any parking areas or driveways of a hospital, shopping center, apartment house, condominium complex, or commercial office complex or any other privately owned public vehicular area, or prohibit such stopping, standing, or parking during any specified hours, provided the owner or person in general charge of the operation and control of that area requests in writing that such an ordinance be adopted. The owner of a vehicle parked in violation of an ordinance adopted pursuant to this subsection shall be deemed to have appointed any appropriate law-enforcement officer as his agent for the purpose of arranging for the transportation and safe storage of such vehicle.

History.
1979, c. 745, s. 1

§ 153A-140. Abatement of public health nuisances

A county shall have authority, subject to the provisions of Article 57 of Chapter 106 of the General Statutes, to remove, abate, or remedy everything that is dangerous or prejudicial to the public health or safety. Pursuant to this section, a board of commissioners may order the removal of a swimming pool and its appurtenances upon a finding that the swimming pool or its appurtenances is dangerous or prejudicial to public health or safety. The expense of the action shall be paid by the person in default, and, if not paid, shall be a lien upon the land or premises where the nuisance arose, and shall be collected as unpaid taxes. The authority granted by this section may only be exercised upon adequate notice, the right to a hearing, and the right to appeal to the General Court of Justice. Nothing in this section shall be deemed to restrict or repeal the authority of any municipality to abate or remedy health nuisances pursuant to G.S. 160A-174, 160A-193, or any other

general or local law. This section shall not affect bona fide farms, but any use of farm property for nonfarm purposes is subject to this section.

History.
1981 (Reg. Sess., 1982), c. 1314, s. 1; 2002-116, s. 2

§ 153A-140.1. Stream-clearing programs

(a) A county shall have the authority to remove natural and man-made obstructions in stream channels and in the floodway of streams that may impede the passage of water during rain events.

(b) The actions of a county to clear obstructions from a stream shall not create or increase the responsibility of the county for the clearing or maintenance of the stream, or for flooding of the stream. In addition, actions by a county to clear obstructions from a stream shall not create in the county any ownership in the stream, obligation to control the stream, or affect any otherwise existing private property right, responsibility, or entitlement regarding the stream. These provisions shall not relieve a county for negligence that might be found under otherwise applicable law.

(c) Nothing in this section shall be construed to affect existing rights of the State to control or regulate streams or activities within streams. In implementing a stream-clearing program, the county shall comply with all requirements in State or federal statutes and rules.

History.
2005-441, s. 1

§ 153A-140.2. Annual notice to chronic violators of public nuisance ordinance

A county may notify a chronic violator of the county's public nuisance ordinance that, if the violator's property is found to be in violation of the ordinance, the county shall, without further notice in the calendar year in which notice is given, take action to remedy the violation, and the expense of the action shall become a lien upon the property and shall be collected as unpaid taxes. The notice shall be sent by certified mail. A chronic violator is a person who owns property whereupon, in the previous calendar year, the county gave notice of violation at least three times under any provision of the public nuisance ordinance.

History.
2009-287, s. 2

N.C. Gen. Stat. § 153A-141

Repealed by Session Laws 1995, c. 501, s. 3 .

§ 153A-142. Curfews

A county may by an appropriate ordinance impose a curfew on persons of any age less than 18.

History.
1997-189, s. 2

§ 153A-143. (Repealed effective August 1, 2021)

History.
2004-152, s. 1; 2019-111, s. 2.6(d); 2020-3, s. 4.33(a).

§ 153A-144. (Repealed effective August 1, 2021)

§ 153A-145. Limitations on regulating cisterns and rain barrels

No county ordinance may prohibit or have the effect of prohibiting the installation and maintenance of cisterns and rain barrel collection systems used to collect water for irrigation purposes. A county may regulate the installation and maintenance of those cisterns and rain barrel collection systems for the purpose of protecting the public health and safety and for the purpose of preventing them from becoming a public nuisance.

History.
2011-394, s. 12(d)

§ 153A-145.1. Transportation impact mitigation ordinances prohibited

No county may enact or enforce an ordinance, rule, or regulation that requires an employer to assume financial, legal, or other responsibility for the mitigation of the impact of his or her employees' commute or transportation to or from the employer's workplace, which may result in the employer being subject to a fine, fee, or other monetary, legal, or negative consequences.

History.
2013-413, s. 10.1(b)

§ 153A-145.2. Limitations on regulating soft drink sizes

No county ordinance may prohibit the sale of soft drinks above a particular size. This section does not prohibit any ordinance regulating the sanitation or other operational aspect of a device for the dispensing of soft drinks. For purposes of this section, "soft drink" shall have the meaning set forth in G.S. 105-164.3.

History.
2013-309, s. 3

§ 153A-145.3. Counties enforce ordinances within public trust areas

(a) Notwithstanding the provisions of G.S. 113-131 or any other provision of law, a county may, by ordinance, define, prohibit, regulate, or abate acts, omissions, or conditions upon the State's ocean beaches and prevent or abate any unreasonable restriction of the public's rights to use the State's ocean beaches. In addition, a county may, in the interest of promoting the health, safety, and welfare of the public, regulate, restrict, or prohibit the placement, maintenance, location, or use of equipment, personal property, or debris upon the State's ocean beaches. A county may enforce any ordinance adopted pursuant to this section or any other provision of law upon the State's ocean beaches located within the county's jurisdictional boundaries to the same extent that a county may enforce ordinances within the county's jurisdictional boundaries. A county may enforce an ordinance adopted pursuant to this section by any remedy provided for in G.S. 153A-123. For purposes of this section, the term "ocean beaches" has the same meaning as in G.S. 77-20(e).

(b) Nothing in this section shall be construed to (i) limit the authority of the State or any State agency to regulate the State's ocean beaches as authorized by G.S. 113-131, or common law as interpreted and applied by the courts of this State; (ii) limit any other authority granted to counties by the State to regulate the State's ocean beaches; (iii) deny the existence of the authority recognized in this section prior to the date this section becomes effective; (iv) impair the right of the people of this State to the customary free use and enjoyment of the State's ocean beaches, which rights remain reserved to the people of this State as provided in G.S. 77-20(d); (v) change or modify the riparian, littoral, or other ownership rights of owners of property bounded by the Atlantic Ocean; or (vi) apply to the removal of permanent residential or commercial structures and appurtenances thereto from the State's ocean beaches.

History.
2015-70, s. 1

§ 153A-145.4. Limitations on standards of care for farm animals

Notwithstanding any other provision of law, no county ordinance may regulate standards of care for farm animals. For purposes of this section, "standards of care for farm animals" includes the following: the construction, repair, or improvement of farm animal shelter or housing; restrictions on the types of feed or medicines that may be administered to farm animals; and exercise and social interaction requirements. For purposes of this section, the term "farm animals" includes the following domesticated animals: cattle, oxen, bison, sheep, swine, goats, horses, ponies, mules, donkeys, hinnies, llamas, alpacas, lagomorphs, ratites, and poultry.

History.
2015-192, s. 1

§ 153A-145.5. Adoption of sanctuary ordinance prohibited

(a) No county may have in effect any policy, ordinance, or procedure that limits or restricts the enforcement of federal immigration laws to less than the full extent permitted by federal law.

(b) No county shall do any of the following related to information regarding the citizenship or immigration status, lawful or unlawful, of any individual:

(1) Prohibit law enforcement officials or agencies from gathering such information.

(2) Direct law enforcement officials or agencies not to gather such information.

(3) Prohibit the communication of such information to federal law enforcement agencies.

History.
2015-294, s. 15(a)

§ 153A-145.6. Requiring compliance with voluntary State regulations and rules prohibited

(a) If a State department or agency declares a regulation or rule to be voluntary or the General Assembly delays the effective date of a regulation or rule proposed or adopted by the Environmental Management Commission, or any other board or commission, a county shall not require or enforce compliance with the applicable regulation or rule, including any regulation or rule previously or hereafter incorporated as a condition or contractual obligation imposed by, agreed upon, or accepted by the county in any zoning, land use, subdivision, or other developmental approval, including, without limitation, a development permit issuance, development agreement, site-specific development plan, or phased development plan.

(b) This section shall apply to the following regulations and rules:

(1) Those currently in effect.

(2) Those repealed or otherwise expired.

(3) Those temporarily or permanently held in abeyance.

(4) Those adopted but not yet effective.

(c) This section shall not apply to any water usage restrictions during either extreme or exceptional drought conditions as determined by the Drought Management Advisory Council pursuant to G.S. 143-355.1.

History.
2015-246, s. 2(a)

§ 153A-145.7. Hours of certain alcohol sales

In accordance with G.S. 18B-1004(c), a county may adopt an ordinance allowing for the sale of malt beverages, unfortified wine, fortified wine, and mixed beverages beginning at 10:00 A.M. on Sunday pursuant to the licensed premises' permit issued under G.S. 18B-1001.

History.
2017-87, s. 4(b)

§ 153A-145.8. Limitations on regulation of catering by bona fide farms

Notwithstanding any other provision of law, no county may require a business located on a property used for bona fide farm purposes, as provided in G.S. 160D-903(a), that provides on- and off-site catering services, to obtain a permit to provide catering services within the county. This section shall not be construed to exempt the business from any health and safety rules adopted by a local health department, the Department of Health and Human Services, or the Commission for Public Health.

History.
2020-18, s. 5(c); 2020-74, s. 21(a)

§ 153A-145.9. Authorization of social district

A county may adopt an ordinance designating a social district for use in accordance with G.S. 18B-904.1.

History.
2021-150, s. 20.1

§ 153A-145.10. Authorization of expanded area for ABC licensed premises

In accordance with G.S. 18B-904(h), a county may adopt an ordinance authorizing permittees holding a permit under Article 10 or 11 of Chapter 18B of the General Statutes to utilize an area that is not part of the permittee's licensed premises for the outdoor possession and consumption of alcoholic beverages sold by the permittee.

History.
2021-150, s. 21.1

ARTICLE 10
LAW ENFORCEMENT AND CONFINEMENT FACILITIES

PART 1
LAW ENFORCEMENT

§ 153A-211. Training and development programs for law enforcement

A county may plan and execute training and development programs for law-enforcement agencies, and for that purpose may:

(1) Contract with other counties, cities, and the State and federal governments and their agencies;

(2) Accept, receive, and disburse funds, grants, and services;

(3) Pursuant to the procedures and provisions of Chapter 160A, Article 20, Part 1, create joint agencies to act for and on behalf of the participating counties and cities;

(4) Apply for, receive, administer, and expend federal grant funds;

(5) Appropriate funds not otherwise limited as to use by law.

History.
1969, c. 1145, s. 2; 1973, c. 822, s. 1

§ 153A-212. Cooperation in law-enforcement matters

A county may cooperate with the State and other local governments in law-enforcement matters, as permitted by G.S. 160A-283 (joint auxiliary police), by G.S. 160A-288 (emergency aid), G.S. 160A-288.1 (assistance by State law-enforcement officers), and by Chapter 160A, Article 20, Part 1.

History.
1973, c. 822, s. 1; 1979, c. 639, s. 2

§ 153A-212.1. Resources to protect the public

Subject to the requirements of G.S. 7A-41, 7A-44.1, 7A-64, 7A-102, 7A-133, and 7A-498.7, a county may appropriate funds under contract with the State for the provision of services for the speedy disposition of cases involving drug offenses, domestic violence, or other offenses involving threats to public safety. Nothing in this section shall be construed to obligate the General Assembly to make any appropriation to implement the provisions of this section. Further, nothing in this section shall be construed to obligate the Administrative Office of the Courts or the Office of Indigent Defense Services to maintain positions or services initially provided for under this section.

History.
1999-237, s. 17.17(b); 2000-67, s. 15.4(e); 2001-424, s. 22.11(e)

§ 153A-212.2. Neighborhood crime watch programs

A county may establish neighborhood crime watch programs within the county to encourage residents and business owners to promote citizen involvement in securing homes, businesses, and personal property against criminal activity and to report suspicious activities to law enforcement officials.

History.
2006-181, s. 1

PART 2
LOCAL CONFINEMENT FACILITIES

§ 153A-216. Legislative policy

The policy of the General Assembly with respect to local confinement facilities is:

(1) Local confinement facilities should provide secure custody of persons confined therein in order to protect the community and should be operated so as to protect the health and welfare of prisoners and provide for their humane treatment.

(2) Minimum statewide standards should be provided to guide and assist local governments in planning, constructing, and maintaining confinement facilities and in developing programs that provide for humane treatment of prisoners and contribute to the rehabilitation of offenders.

(3) The State should provide services to local governments to help improve the quality of administration and local confinement facilities. These services should include inspection, consultation, technical assistance, and other appropriate services.

(4) Adequate qualifications and training of the personnel of local confinement facilities are essential to improving the quality of these facilities. The State shall establish entry level employment standards for jailers and supervisory and administrative personnel of local confinement facilities to include training as a condition of employment in a local confinement

facility pursuant to the provisions of Article 1 of Chapter 17C and Chapter 17E and the rules promulgated thereunder.

History.
1967, c. 581, s. 2; 1973, c. 822, s. 1; 1983, c. 745, s. 4

§ 153A-217. Definitions

Unless otherwise clearly required by the context, the words and phrases defined in this section have the meanings indicated when used in this Part:

(1) "Commission" means the Social Services Commission.

(2) "Secretary" means the Secretary of Health and Human Services.

(3) "Department" means the Department of Health and Human Services.

(4) "Governing body" means the governing body of a county or city or the policy-making body for a district or regional confinement facility.

(5) "Local confinement facility" includes a county or city jail, a local lockup, a regional or district jail, a juvenile detention facility, a detention facility for adults operated by a local government, and any other facility operated by a local government for confinement of persons awaiting trial or serving sentences except that it shall not include a county satellite jail/work release unit governed by Part 3 of Article 10 of Chapter 153A.

(6) "Prisoner" includes any person, adult or juvenile, confined or detained in a confinement facility.

(7) "Unit," "unit of local government," or "local government" means a county or city.

History.
1967, c. 581, s. 2; 1969, c. 981, s. 1; 1973, c. 476, s. 138; c. 822, s. 1; 1987, c. 207, s. 2; 1997-443, s. 11A.118(a); 1998-202, s. 4(cc)

§ 153A-218. County confinement facilities

A county may establish, acquire, erect, repair, maintain, and operate local confinement facilities and may for these purposes appropriate funds not otherwise limited as to use by law. Subject to the holdover provisions in G.S. 7B-2204, no person under the age of 18 may be held in a county confinement facility unless there is an agreement between the county confinement facility and the Division of Adult Correction and Juvenile Justice allowing the housing of persons under the age of 18 at the facility or a portion of the facility that has been approved as a juvenile detention facility by the Juvenile Justice Section. A juvenile detention facility may be located in the same facility as a county jail provided that the juvenile detention facility meets the requirements of this Article and G.S. 147-33.40.

History.
1868, c. 20, s. 8; Code, s. 707; Rev., s. 1318; 1915, c. 140; C.S., s. 1297; 1973, c. 822, s. 1; 1998-202, s. 4(dd); 2020-83, s. 8(n)

§ 153A-219. District confinement facilities

(a) Two or more units of local government may enter into and carry out an agreement to establish, finance, and operate a district confinement facility. The units may construct such a facility or may designate an existing facility as a district confinement facility. In addition, two or more units of local government may enter into and carry out agreements under which one unit may use the local confinement facility owned and operated by another. In exercising the powers granted by this section, the units shall proceed according to the procedures and provisions of Chapter 160A, Article 20, Part 1.

(b) If a district confinement facility is established, the units involved shall provide for a jail administrator for the facility. The administrator need not be the sheriff or any other official of a participating unit. The administrator and the other custodial personnel of a district confinement facility have the authority of law-enforcement officers for the purposes of receiving, maintaining custody of, and transporting prisoners.

(c) If a district confinement facility is established, or if one unit contracts to use the local confinement facility of another, the law-enforcement officers of the contracting units and the custodial personnel of the facility may transport prisoners to and from the facility.

(d) The Department shall provide technical and other assistance to units wishing to exercise any of the powers granted by this section.

History.
1933, c. 201; 1967, c. 581, s. 2; 1969, c. 743; 1971, c. 341, s. 1; 1973, c. 822, s. 1

§ 153A-220. Jail and detention services

The Commission has policy responsibility for providing and coordinating State services to local government with respect to local confinement facilities. The Department shall:

(1) Consult with and provide technical assistance to units of local government with respect to local confinement facilities.

(2) Develop minimum standards for the construction and operation of local confinement facilities.

(3) Visit and inspect local confinement facilities; advise the sheriff, jailer, governing

board, and other appropriate officials as to deficiencies and recommend improvements; and submit written reports on the inspections to appropriate local officials.

(4) Review and approve plans for the construction and major modification of local confinement facilities.

(5) Repealed by Session Laws 1983, c. 745, s. 5.

(6) Perform any other duties that may be necessary to carry out the State's responsibilities concerning local confinement facilities.

History.
1967, c. 581, s. 2; 1973, c. 476, s. 138; c. 822, s. 1; 1983, c. 745, s. 5

§ 153A-221. Minimum standards

(a) The Secretary shall develop and publish minimum standards for the operation of local confinement facilities and may from time to time develop and publish amendments to the standards. The standards shall be developed with a view to providing secure custody of prisoners and to protecting their health and welfare and providing for their humane treatment. The standards shall provide for all of the following:

(1) Secure and safe physical facilities.

(2) Jail design.

(3) Adequacy of space per prisoner.

(4) Heat, light, and ventilation.

(5) Supervision of prisoners.

(6) Personal hygiene and comfort of prisoners.

(7) Medical care for prisoners, including mental health, behavioral health, intellectual and other developmental disability, and substance abuse services.

(8) Sanitation.

(9) Food allowances, food preparation, and food handling.

(10) Any other provisions that may be necessary for the safekeeping, privacy, care, protection, and welfare of prisoners.

(b) In developing the standards and any amendments thereto, the Secretary shall consult with organizations representing local government and local law enforcement, including the North Carolina Association of County Commissioners, the North Carolina League of Municipalities, the North Carolina Sheriffs' Association, and the North Carolina Police Executives' Association. The Secretary shall also consult with interested State departments and agencies, including the Division of Adult Correction and Juvenile Justice of the Department of Public Safety, the Department of Health and Human Services, the Department of Insurance, and the North Carolina Criminal Justice Education and Training Standards Commission, and the North Carolina Sheriffs' Education and Training Standards Commission.

(c) Before the standards or any amendments thereto may become effective, they must be approved by the Commission and the Governor. Upon becoming effective, they have the force and effect of law.

(d) Notwithstanding any law or rule to the contrary, each dormitory in a county detention facility may house up to 64 inmates as long as the dormitory provides all of the following:

(1) A minimum floor space of 70 square feet per inmate, including both the sleeping and dayroom areas.

(2) One shower per eight inmates, one toilet per eight inmates, one sink with a security mirror per eight inmates, and one water fountain.

(3) A telephone jack or other telephone arrangement provided within the dormitory.

(4) Space designed to allow a variety of activities.

(5) Sufficient seating and tables for all inmates.

(6) A way for officers to observe the entire area from the entrance.

(e) A local confinement facility shall be subject to the requirements of Part 2B of Article 10 of Chapter 153A of the General Statutes.

History.
1967, c. 581, s. 2; 1973, c. 476, ss. 128, 133, 138; c. 822, s. 1; 1983, c. 745, s. 6; c. 768, s. 20; 1991, c. 237, s. 1; 1997-443, s. 11A.118(a); 2008-194, s. 10(a), (b); 2011-145, s. 19.1(h); 2011-324, s. 1; 2014-22, s. 1; 2017-186, s. 2 (eeeeeeeee); 2019-76, s. 30; 2021-143, s. 3(b)

§ 153A-221.1. Standards and inspections

The legal responsibility of the Juvenile Justice Section of the Division of Adult Correction and Juvenile Justice of the Department of Public Safety for State services to county juvenile detention homes under this Article is hereby confirmed and shall include the following: development of State standards under the prescribed procedures; inspection; consultation; technical assistance; and training.

The Secretary of Health and Human Services, in consultation with the Secretary of Public Safety, shall also develop standards under which a local jail may be approved as a holdover facility for not more than five calendar days pending placement in a juvenile detention home which meets State standards, providing the local jail is so arranged that any child placed in the holdover facility cannot converse with, see, or be seen by the adult population of the jail while in the holdover facility. The personnel responsible for the administration of a jail with an approved holdover facility shall provide close supervision of any child placed in the holdover facility for the protection of the child.

History.

1973, c. 1230, s. 2; c. 1262, s. 10; 1975, c. 426, s. 2; 1983, c. 768, s. 21; 1997-443, s. 11A.118(a); 1998-202, s. 13(nn); 1999-423, s. 12; 2000-137, s. 4(hh); 2012-172, s. 2; 2013-360, s. 16D.7(c); 2017-186, s. 2 (ffffffff)

§ 153A-222. Inspections of local confinement facilities

Department personnel shall visit and inspect each local confinement facility at least semi-annually. The purpose of the inspections is to investigate the conditions of confinement, the treatment of prisoners, the maintenance of entry level employment standards for jailers and supervisory and administrative personnel of local confinement facilities as provided for in G.S. 153A-216(4), and to determine whether the facilities meet the minimum standards published pursuant to G.S. 153A-221. The inspector shall make a written report of each inspection and submit it within 30 days after the day the inspection is completed to the governing body and other local officials responsible for the facility. The report shall specify each way in which the facility does not meet the minimum standards. The governing body shall consider the report at its first regular meeting after receipt of the report and shall promptly initiate any action necessary to bring the facility into conformity with the standards. Notwithstanding the provisions of G.S. 8-53 or any other provision of law relating to the confidentiality of communications between physician and patient, the representatives of the Department of Health and Human Services who make these inspections may review any writing or other record in any recording medium which pertains to the admission, discharge, medication, treatment, medical condition, or history of persons who are or have been inmates of the facility being inspected. Physicians, psychologists, psychiatrists, nurses, and anyone else involved in giving treatment at or through a facility who may be interviewed by representatives of the Department may disclose to these representatives information related to an inquiry, notwithstanding the existence of the physician-patient privilege in G.S. 8-53 or any other rule of law; provided the patient, resident or client has not made written objection to such disclosure. The facility, its employees, and any person interviewed during these inspections shall be immune from liability for damages resulting from the disclosure of any information to the Department. Any confidential or privileged information received from review of records or interviews shall be kept confidential by the Department and not disclosed without written authorization of the inmate or legal representative, or unless disclosure is ordered by a court of competent jurisdiction. The Department shall institute appropriate policies and procedures to ensure that this information shall not be disclosed without authorization or court order. The Department shall not disclose the name of anyone who has furnished information concerning a facility without the consent of that person. Neither the names of persons furnishing information nor any confidential or privileged information obtained from records or interviews shall be considered "public records" within the meaning of G.S. 132-1. Prior to releasing any information or allowing any inspections referred to in this section the patient, resident or client must be advised in writing that he has the right to object in writing to such release of information or review of his records and that by an objection in writing he may prohibit the inspection or release of his records.

History.

1947, c. 915; 1967, c. 581, s. 2; 1973, c. 822, s. 1; 1981, c. 586, s. 6; 1983, c. 745, s. 7; 1997-443, s. 11A.118(a)

§ 153A-223. Enforcement of minimum standards

If an inspection conducted pursuant to G.S. 153A-222 discloses that the jailers and supervisory and administrative personnel of a local confinement facility do not meet the entry level employment standards established pursuant to Article 1 of Chapter 17C or Chapter 17E or that a local confinement facility does not meet the minimum standards published pursuant to G.S. 153A-221 and, in addition, if the Secretary determines that conditions in the facility jeopardize the safe custody, safety, health, or welfare of persons confined in the facility, the Secretary may order corrective action or close the facility, as provided in this section:

(1) The Secretary shall give notice of his determination to the governing body and each other local official responsible for the facility. The Secretary shall also send a copy of this notice, along with a copy of the inspector's report, to the senior resident superior court judge of the superior court district or set of districts as defined in G.S. 7A-41.1 in which the facility is located. Upon receipt of the Secretary's notice, the governing body shall call a public hearing to consider the report. The hearing shall be held within 20 days after the day the Secretary's notice is received. The inspector shall appear at this hearing to advise and consult with the governing body concerning any corrective action necessary to bring the facility into conformity with the standards.

(2) The governing body shall, within 30 days after the day the Secretary's notice is

received, request a contested case hearing, initiate appropriate corrective action or close the facility. The corrective action must be completed within a reasonable time.

(3) A contested case hearing, if requested, shall be conducted pursuant to G.S. 150B, Article 3. The issues shall be: (i) whether the facility meets the minimum standards; (ii) whether the conditions in the facility jeopardize the safe custody, safety, health, or welfare of persons confined therein; and (iii) the appropriate corrective action to be taken and a reasonable time to complete that action.

(4) If the governing body does not, within 30 days after the day the Secretary's notice is received, or within 30 days after service of the final decision if a contested case hearing is held, either initiate corrective action or close the facility, or does not complete the action within a reasonable time, the Secretary may order that the facility be closed.

(5) The governing body may appeal an order of the Secretary or a final decision to the senior resident superior court judge. The governing body shall initiate the appeal by giving by registered mail to the judge and to the Secretary notice of its intention to appeal. The notice must be given within 15 days after the day the Secretary's order or the final decision is received. If notice is not given within the 15-day period, the right to appeal is terminated.

(6) The senior resident superior court judge shall hear the appeal. He shall cause notice of the date, time, and place of the hearing to be given to each interested party, including the Secretary, the governing body, and each other local official involved. The Office of Administrative Hearings, if a contested case hearing has been held, shall file the official record, as defined in G.S. 150B-37, with the senior resident superior court judge and shall serve a copy on each person who has been given notice of the hearing. The judge shall conduct the hearing without a jury. He shall consider the official record, if any, and may accept evidence from the Secretary, the governing body, and each other local official which he finds appropriate. The issue before the court shall be whether the facility continues to jeopardize the safe custody, safety, health, or welfare of persons confined therein. The court may affirm, modify, or reverse the Secretary's order.

History.
1947, c. 915; 1967, c. 581, s. 2; 1973, c. 476, s. 138; c. 822, s. 1; 1981, c. 614, ss. 20, 21; 1983, c. 745, s. 8; 1987, c. 827, s. 1; 1987 (Reg. Sess., 1988), c. 1037, s. 123; 2011-398, s. 55

§ 153A-224. Supervision of local confinement facilities

(a) No person may be confined in a local confinement facility unless custodial personnel are present and available to provide continuous supervision in order that custody will be secure and that, in event of emergency, such as fire, illness, assaults by other prisoners, or otherwise, the prisoners can be protected. These personnel shall supervise prisoners closely enough to maintain safe custody and control and to be at all times informed of the prisoners' general health and emergency medical needs.

(b) In a medical emergency, the custodial personnel shall secure emergency medical care from a licensed physician according to the unit's plan for medical care. If a physician designated in the plan is not available, the personnel shall secure medical services from any licensed physician who is available. The unit operating the facility shall pay the cost of emergency medical services unless the inmate has third-party insurance, in which case the third-party insurer shall be the initial payor and the medical provider shall bill the third-party insurer. The county shall only be liable for costs not reimbursed by the third-party insurer, in which event the county may recover from the inmate the cost of the non-reimbursed medical services.

(c) If a person violates any provision of this section, he is guilty of a Class 1 misdemeanor.

History.
1967, c. 581, s. 2; 1973, c. 822, s. 1; 1993, c. 510, s. 1; c. 539, s. 1061; 1994, Ex. Sess., c. 24, s. 14(c)

§ 153A-225. Medical care of prisoners

(a) Each unit that operates a local confinement facility shall develop a plan for providing medical care for prisoners in the facility. The plan:

(1) Shall be designed to protect the health and welfare of the prisoners and to avoid the spread of contagious disease;

(2) Shall provide for medical supervision of prisoners and emergency medical care for prisoners to the extent necessary for their health and welfare;

(3) Shall provide for the detection, examination and treatment of prisoners who are infected with tuberculosis or venereal diseases; and

(4) May utilize Medicaid coverage for inpatient hospitalization or for any other Medicaid services allowable for eligible prisoners, provided that the plan includes a reimbursement process which pays to the State the State portion of the costs, including the costs of the services provided and any administrative costs directly related to

Chapter 153A

the services to be reimbursed, to the State's Medicaid program.

The unit shall develop the plan in consultation with appropriate local officials and organizations, including the sheriff, the county physician, the local or district health director, and the local medical society. The plan must be approved by the local or district health director after consultation with the area mental health, developmental disabilities, and substance abuse authority, if it is adequate to protect the health and welfare of the prisoners. Upon a determination that the plan is adequate to protect the health and welfare of the prisoners, the plan must be adopted by the governing body.

As a part of its plan, each unit may establish fees of not more than twenty dollars ($ 20.00) per incident for the provision of nonemergency medical care to prisoners and a fee of not more than ten dollars ($ 10.00) for a 30-day supply or less of a prescription drug. In establishing fees pursuant to this section, each unit shall establish a procedure for waiving fees for indigent prisoners.

(b) If a prisoner in the custody of a local confinement facility dies, the medical examiner and the coroner shall be notified immediately, regardless of the physical location of the prisoner at the time of death. Within five days after the day of the death, the administrator of the facility shall make a written report to the local or district health director and to the Secretary of Health and Human Services. The report shall be made on forms developed and distributed by the Department of Health and Human Services.

(b1) Whenever a local confinement facility transfers a prisoner from that facility to another local confinement facility, the transferring facility shall provide the receiving facility with any health information or medical records the transferring facility has in its possession pertaining to the transferred prisoner.

(c) If a person violates any provision of this section (including the requirements regarding G.S. 130-97 and 130-121), he is guilty of a Class 1 misdemeanor.

History.
1967, c. 581, s. 2; 1973, c. 476, ss. 128, 138; c. 822, s. 1; 1973, c. 1140, s. 3; 1989, c. 727, s. 204; 1991, c. 237, s. 2; 1993, c. 539, s. 1062; 1994, Ex. Sess., c. 24, s. 14(c); 1995, c. 385, s. 1; 1997-443, s. 11A.112; 2003-392, s. 1; 2004-199, s. 46(a); 2011-145, s. 31.26(f); 2011-192, s. 7(n); 2013-387, s. 2; 2013-389, s. 1; 2018-76, s. 1

§ 153A-225.1. Duty of custodial personnel when prisoners are unconscious or semiconscious

(a) Whenever a custodial officer of a local confinement facility takes custody of a prisoner who is unconscious, semiconscious, or otherwise apparently suffering from some disabling condition and unable to provide information on the causes of the condition, the officer should make a reasonable effort to determine if the prisoner is wearing a bracelet or necklace containing the Medic Alert Foundation's emergency alert symbol to indicate that the prisoner suffers from diabetes, epilepsy, a cardiac condition or any other form of illness which would cause a loss of consciousness. If such a symbol is found indicating that the prisoner suffers from one of those conditions, the officer must make a reasonable effort to have appropriate medical care provided.

(b) Failure of a custodial officer of a local confinement facility to make a reasonable effort to discover an emergency alert symbol as required by this section does not by itself establish negligence of the officer but may be considered along with other evidence to determine if the officer took reasonable precautions to ascertain the emergency medical needs of the prisoner in his custody.

(c) A prisoner who is provided medical care under the provisions of this section is liable for the reasonable costs of that care unless he is indigent.

(d) Repealed by Session Laws 1975, c. 818, s. 2.

History.
1975, c. 306, s. 2; c. 818, s. 2

§ 153A-225.2. Payment of medical care of prisoners

(a) Counties shall reimburse those providers and facilities providing requested or emergency medical care outside of the local confinement facility the lesser amount of either a rate of seventy percent (70%) of the provider's then-current prevailing charge or two times the then-current Medicaid rate for any given service. Each county shall have the right to audit any provider from whom the county has received a bill for services under this section but only to the extent necessary to determine the actual prevailing charge to ensure compliance with this section.

(b) Nothing in this section shall preclude a county from contracting with a provider for services at rates that provide greater documentable cost avoidance for the county than do the rates contained in subsection (a) of this subsection or at rates that are less favorable to the county but that will ensure the continued access to care.

(c) The county shall make reasonable efforts to equitably distribute prisoners among all hospitals or other appropriate health care facilities located within the same county and shall do so based upon the licensed acute care bed capacity at each of the hospitals located within the same county. Counties with more than one hospital or other appropriate health care facility shall provide semiannual reports conspicuously posted on the county's Web site that detail compliance with this section, including information on the distribution of prisoner health care services among different hospitals and health care facilities.

(d) For the purposes of this section, "requested or emergency medical care" shall include all medically necessary and appropriate care provided to an individual from the time that individual presents to the provider or facility in the custody of county law enforcement officers until the time that the individual is safely transferred back to the care of county law enforcement officers or medically discharged to another community setting, as appropriate.

History.
2013-387, s. 1

§ 153A-226. Sanitation and food

(a) The Commission for Public Health shall adopt rules governing the sanitation of local confinement facilities, including the kitchens and other places where food is prepared for prisoners. The rules shall address, but not be limited to, the cleanliness of floors, walls, ceilings, storage spaces, utensils, ventilation equipment, and other facilities; adequacy of lighting, water, lavatory facilities, bedding, food protection facilities, treatment of eating and drinking utensils, and waste disposal; methods of food preparation, handling, storage, and serving; and any other item necessary to the health of the prisoners or the public.

(b) The Commission for Public Health shall prepare a score sheet to be used by local health departments in inspecting local confinement facilities. The local health departments shall inspect local confinement facilities as often as may be required by the Commission for Public Health. If an inspector of the Department finds conditions that reflect hazards or deficiencies in the sanitation or food service of a local confinement facility, he shall immediately notify the local health department. The health department shall promptly inspect the facility. After making its inspection, the local health department shall forward a copy of its report to the Department of Health and Human Services and to the unit operating the facility, on forms prepared by the Department of Environmental Quality. The report shall indicate whether the facility and its kitchen or other place for preparing food is approved or disapproved for public health purposes. If the facility is disapproved, the situation shall

be rectified according to the procedures of G.S. 153A-223.

History.
1967, c. 581, s. 2; 1973, c. 476, s. 128; c. 822, s. 1; 1989, c. 727, s. 205; 1993, c. 262, s. 5; 1997-443, ss. 11A.113, 11A.118(a); 2007-182, s. 2; 2015-241, s. 14.30(u)

N.C. Gen. Stat. § 153A-227

Repealed by Session Laws 1983, c. 745, s. 9.

§ 153A-228. Separation of sexes

Male and female prisoners shall be confined in separate facilities or in separate quarters in local confinement facilities.

History.
1967, c. 581, s. 2; 1973, c. 822, s. 1

§ 153A-229. Jailers' report of jailed defendants

The person having administrative control of a local confinement facility must furnish to the clerk of superior court a report listing such information reasonably at his disposal as is necessary to enable said clerk of superior court to comply with the provisions of G.S. 7A-109.1.

History.
1973, c. 1286, s. 23; 1981, c. 522

PART 2B
DIGNITY FOR WOMEN INCARCERATED IN LOCAL CONFINEMENT FACILITIES

§ 153A-229.1. Definitions

As used in this Article, the following definitions apply:

(1) **Body cavity searches.** -- The probing of body orifices in search of contraband.

(2) **Escape risk.** -- An incarcerated person who is determined to be at high risk for escape based on an individualized risk assessment.

(3) **Facility employee.** -- Any person who is employed by the local government and who works at or in a local confinement facility.

(4) **Important circumstance.** -- There has been an individualized determination that there are reasonable grounds to believe that the female incarcerated person presents a threat of harming herself, the fetus, or any other person, or an escape risk that cannot be reasonably contained

by other means, including the use of additional personnel.

(5) **Incarcerated person.** -- Any person incarcerated or detained in a local confinement facility who is accused of, convicted of, sentenced for, or adjudicated delinquent for violations of criminal law or the terms and conditions of parole, probation, pretrial release, or a diversionary program.

(6) **Local confinement facility.** -- "Local confinement facility" includes a county or city jail, a local lockup, a regional or district jail, a juvenile detention facility, a detention facility for adults operated by a local government, and any other facility operated by a local government for confinement of persons awaiting trial or serving sentences except that it shall not include a county satellite jail/work release unit governed by Part 3 of Article 10 of Chapter 153A of the General Statutes.

(7) **Menstrual products.** -- Products that women use during their menstrual cycle. These include tampons and sanitary napkins.

(8) **Postpartum recovery.** -- The six-week period following delivery, or longer, as determined by the health care professional responsible for the health and safety of the female incarcerated person.

(9) **Restraints.** -- Any physical or mechanical device used to restrict or control the movement of an incarcerated person's body, limbs, or both.

(10) **Restrictive housing.** -- Any type of detention that involves removal from general population and an inability to leave a room or cell for the vast majority of the day. This term shall not include any of the following:

    a. Single-cell accommodations in facilities that provide those accommodations to all incarcerated persons.

    b. Single-cell accommodations in facilities that provide those accommodations to all persons of a certain sex or gender.

    c. Single-cell accommodations provided for medical reasons, except when pregnancy, alone, is the medical reason for the single-cell accommodations.

    d. Single-cell accommodations provided when an individualized determination has been made that there are reasonable grounds to believe that there exists a threat of harm to the female incarcerated person or the fetus.

    e. Single-cell accommodations provided at the request of the incarcerated person.

(11) **State of undress.** -- A situation when an incarcerated person is partially or fully naked, either in the shower, toilet areas, a medical examination room, or while having a body cavity search conducted.

History.
2021-143, s. 3(a)

§ 153A-229.2. Care for female incarcerated persons related to pregnancy, childbirth, and postpartum recovery

(a) **Limitation on Use of Restraints.** -- Except as otherwise provided in this subsection, facility employees shall not apply restraints on a pregnant female incarcerated person during the second and third trimester of pregnancy, during labor and delivery, and during the postpartum recovery period.

A female incarcerated person who is in the postpartum recovery period may only be restrained if a facility employee makes an individualized determination that an important circumstance exists. In this case, only wrist handcuffs held in front of the female incarcerated person's body may be used and only when she is ambulatory. The facility employee ordering use of restraints on any female incarcerated person while in the postpartum recovery period shall submit a written report to the sheriff or administrator of the local confinement facility within five days following the use of restraints. The report shall contain the justification for restraining the female incarcerated person during postpartum recovery.

Nothing in this subsection shall prohibit the use of handcuffs or wrist restraints held in front of the female incarcerated person's body when in transport outside of the local confinement facility, except that these restraints shall not be used in transport when the female incarcerated person is in labor or is suspected to be in labor.

Nothing in this subsection shall prohibit the use of medical restraints by a licensed health care professional to ensure the medical safety of a pregnant female incarcerated person.

(b) **Body Cavity Searches.** -- No facility employee, other than a certified health care professional, shall conduct body cavity searches of a female incarcerated person who is pregnant or in the postpartum recovery period unless the facility employee has probable cause to believe that the female incarcerated person is concealing contraband that presents an immediate threat of harm to the female incarcerated person, the fetus, or another person. In this case, the facility employee shall submit a written report to the sheriff or administrator of the local confinement facility within five days following the body cavity search, containing the justification for the body cavity search and the presence or absence of any contraband.

(c) **Nutrition.** -- The sheriff or the administrator of the local confinement facility shall ensure that pregnant female incarcerated persons are provided sufficient food and dietary supplements and are provided access to food at appropriate times of day, as ordered by a physician, a physician staff member, or a local confinement facility nutritionist to meet generally accepted prenatal nutritional guidelines for pregnant female incarcerated persons. While in the hospital, pregnant female incarcerated persons and female incarcerated persons in the postpartum recovery period shall have access to the full range of meal options provided by the hospital to ensure that each meal meets the female incarcerated person's nutritional needs.

(d) **Restrictive Housing.** -- The sheriff or the administrator of the local confinement facility shall not place any pregnant female incarcerated person, or any female incarcerated person who is in the postpartum recovery period, in restrictive housing unless a local confinement facility employee makes an individualized determination that an important circumstance exists. In this case, the facility employee authorizing the placement of the female incarcerated person in restrictive housing shall submit a written report to the sheriff or administrator of the local confinement facility within five days following the transfer. The report shall contain the justification for confining the female incarcerated person in restrictive housing.

(e) **Bed Assignments.** -- The sheriff or the administrator of the local confinement facility shall not assign any female incarcerated person who is pregnant or in postpartum recovery to any bed that is elevated more than 3 feet from the floor of the local confinement facility.

(f) **Cost of Care.** -- While a pregnant female incarcerated person is incarcerated, the pregnant female incarcerated person shall be provided necessary prenatal, labor, and delivery care as needed at no cost to the pregnant female incarcerated person.

(g) **Bonding Period.** -- Following the delivery of a newborn by a female incarcerated person, the administrator of the local confinement facility shall permit the newborn to remain with the female incarcerated person while the female incarcerated person is in the hospital, unless the medical provider has a reasonable belief that remaining with the female incarcerated person poses a health or safety risk to the newborn.

(h) **Nutritional and Hygiene Products During the Postpartum Period.** -- During the period of postpartum recovery, the sheriff or administrator of the local confinement facility shall make available the necessary nutritional and hygiene products, including sanitary napkins, underwear, and hygiene products for the postpartum female incarcerated person. The products shall be provided at no cost to the female incarcerated person.

(i) **Reporting.** -- The sheriff or administrator of the local confinement facility shall compile a monthly summary of all written reports received pursuant to this section and G.S. 148-25.3.

History.
2021-143, s. 3(a)

§ 153A-229.3. Inspection by facility employees

(a) **Inspections When a Female Incarcerated Person is in the State of Undress.** -- To the greatest extent practicable and consistent with safety and order in a local confinement facility, there shall be a limitation on inspections by male facility employees when a female incarcerated person is in a state of undress. Nothing in this section shall limit the ability of a male facility employee from conducting inspections when a female incarcerated person may be in a state of undress if no female facility employees are available within a reasonable period of time.

(b) **Documentation Requirement.** -- If a male facility employee deems it is appropriate to conduct an inspection or search while a female incarcerated person is in a clear state of undress in an area such as the shower, the medical examination room, toilet areas, or while a female incarcerated person is having a body cavity search, the male local confinement facility employee shall submit a written report to the sheriff or administrator of the local confinement facility within five days following the inspection or search, containing the justification for a male facility employee to inspect the female incarcerated person while in a state of undress.

History.
2021-143, s. 3(a)

§ 153A-229.4. Access to menstrual products

Access to Menstrual Products. -- The sheriff or the administrator of the local confinement facility shall ensure that sufficient menstrual products are available at the local confinement facility for all female incarcerated persons who have an active menstrual cycle. Female incarcerated persons who menstruate shall be provided menstrual products as needed at no cost to the female incarcerated person.

History.
2021-143, s. 3(a)

PART 3
SATELLITE JAIL/WORK RELEASE UNITS

§ 153A-230. Legislative policy

The policy of the General Assembly with respect to satellite jail/work release units is:

(1) To encourage counties to accept responsibility for incarcerated misdemeanants thereby relieving the State prison system of its misdemeanant population;

(2) To assist counties in providing suitable facilities for certain misdemeanants who receive active sentences;

(3) To allow more misdemeanants who are employed at the time of sentencing to retain their jobs by eliminating the time involved in processing persons through the State system;

(4) To enable misdemeanants to pay for their upkeep while serving time, to pay restitution, to continue to support their dependents, and to remain near the communities and families to which they will return after serving their time;

(5) To provide more appropriate, cost effective housing for certain minimum custody misdemeanants and to utilize vacant buildings where possible and suitable for renovation;

(6) To provide a rehabilitative atmosphere for non-violent misdemeanants who otherwise would face a substantial threat of imprisonment; and

(7) To encourage the use of alternative to incarceration programs.

History.
1987, c. 207, s. 1

§ 153A-230.1. Definitions

Unless otherwise clearly required by the context, the words and phrases defined in this section have the meanings indicated when used in this Part:

(1) "Office" means the Office of State Budget and Management.

(2) "Satellite Jail/Work Release Unit" means a building or designated portion of a building primarily designed, staffed, and used for the housing of misdemeanants participating in a work release program. These units shall house misdemeanants only, except that, if he so chooses, the Sheriff may accept responsibility from the Division of Adult Correction and Juvenile Justice of the Department of Public Safety for the housing of felons who do not present security risks, who have achieved work release

status, and who will be employed on work release, or for felons committed directly to his custody pursuant to G.S. 15A-1352(b). These units shall be operated on a full time basis, i.e., seven days/nights a week.

History.
1987, c. 207, s. 1; 1987, (Reg. Sess., 1988), c. 1106, s. 1; 2000-140, s. 93.1(a); 2001-424, s. 12.2(b); 2011-145, s. 19.1(h); 2017-186, s. 2 (gggggggggg)

§ 153A-230.2. Creation of Satellite Jail/Work Release Unit Fund

(a) There is created in the Office of State Budget and Management the County Satellite Jail/Work Release Unit Fund to provide State grant funds for counties or groups of counties for construction of satellite jail/work release units for certain misdemeanants who receive active sentences. A county or group of counties may apply to the Office for a grant under this section. The application shall be in a form established by the Office. The Office shall:

(1) Develop application and grant criteria based on the basic requirements listed in this Part,

(2) Provide all Boards of County Commissioners and Sheriffs with the criteria and appropriate application forms, technical assistance, if requested, and a proposed written agreement,

(3) Review all applications,

(4) Select grantees and award grants,

(5) Award no more than seven hundred fifty thousand dollars ($ 750,000) for any one county or group of counties except that if a group of counties agrees to jointly operate one unit for males and one unit for females, the maximum amount may be awarded for each unit,

(6) Take into consideration the potential number of misdemeanants and the percentage of the county's or counties' misdemeanant population to be diverted from the State prison system,

(7) Take into consideration the utilization of existing buildings suitable for renovation where appropriate,

(8) Take into consideration the timeliness with which a county proposes to complete and occupy the unit,

(9) Take into consideration the appropriateness and cost effectiveness of the proposal,

(10) Take into consideration the plan with which the county intends to coordinate the unit with other community service programs such as intensive supervision, community penalties, and community service.

When considering the items listed in subdivisions (6) through (10), the Office shall determine the appropriate weight to be given each item.

(b) A county or group of counties is eligible for a grant under this section if it agrees to abide by the basic requirements for satellite jail/work release units established in G.S. 153A-230.3. In order to receive a grant under this section, there must be a written agreement to abide by the basic requirements for satellite jail/work release units set forth in G.S. 153A-230.3. The written agreement shall be signed by the Chairman of the Board of County Commissioners, with approval of the Board of County Commissioners and after consultation with the Sheriff, and a representative of the Office of State Budget and Management. If a group of counties applies for the grant, then the agreement must be signed by the Chairman of the Board of County Commissioners of each county. Any variation from, including termination of, the original signed agreement must be approved by both the Office of State Budget and Management and by a vote of the Board of County Commissioners of the county or counties.

When the county or group of counties receives a grant under this section, the county or group of counties accepts ownership of the satellite jail/work release unit and full financial responsibility for maintaining and operating the unit, and for the upkeep of its occupants who comply with the eligibility criteria in G.S. 153A-230.3(a)(1). The county shall receive from the Division of Adult Correction and Juvenile Justice of the Department of Public Safety the amount paid to local confinement facilities under G.S. 148-32.1 for prisoners which are in the unit, but do not meet the eligibility of requirements under G.S. 153A-230.3(a)(1).

History.
1987, c. 207, s. 1; 1987 (Reg. Sess., 1988), c. 1106, ss. 2, 3; 1989, c. 761, s. 2; 2000-140, s. 93.1(a); 2001-424, s. 12.2(b); 2009-372, s. 7; 2011-145, s. 19.1(h); 2017-186, s. 2 (hhhhhhhh)

§ 153A-230.3. Basic requirements for satellite jail/work release units

(a) **Eligibility for Unit.** -- The following rules shall govern which misdemeanants are housed in a satellite jail/work release unit:

(1) Any convicted misdemeanant who:

a. Receives an active sentence in the county or group of counties operating the unit,

b. Is employed in the area or can otherwise earn his keep by working at the unit on maintenance and other jobs related to upkeep and operation of the

unit or by assignment to community service work, and

c. Consents to placement in the unit under these conditions,

shall not be sent to the State prison system except by written findings of the sentencing judge that the misdemeanant is violent or otherwise a threat to the public and therefore unsuitable for confinement in the unit.

(2) The County shall offer work release programs to both male and female misdemeanants, through local facilities for both, or through a contractual agreement with another entity for either, provided that such arrangement is in reasonable proximity to the misdemeanant's workplace.

(3) The sentencing judge shall make a finding of fact as to whether the misdemeanant is qualified for occupancy in the unit pursuant to G.S. 15A-1352(a). If the sentencing judge determines that the misdemeanant is qualified for occupancy in the unit and the misdemeanant meets the requirements of subdivision (1), then the custodian of the local confinement facility may transfer the misdemeanant to the unit. If at any time either prior to or after placement of an inmate into the unit the Sheriff determines that there is an indication of violence, unsuitable behavior, or other threat to the public that could make the prisoner unsuitable for the unit, the Sheriff may place the prisoner in the county jail.

(4) The Sheriff may accept work release misdemeanants from other counties provided that those inmates agree to pay for their upkeep, that space is available, and that the Sheriff is willing to accept responsibility for the prisoner after screening.

(5) The Sheriff may accept work release misdemeanants or felons from the Division of Adult Correction and Juvenile Justice of the Department of Public Safety provided that those inmates agree to pay for their upkeep, that space is available, and that the Sheriff is willing to accept responsibility for the prisoner after screening.

(a1) **Non-eligible for unit.** -- If the sentencing judge finds that the misdemeanant does not meet the eligibility criteria set forth in G.S. 135A-230.3(a)(1)b, but is otherwise eligible for placement in the unit, then the Sheriff may transfer the misdemeanant from the local confinement facility to the unit if the misdemeanant meets the eligibility criteria at a later date. The Sheriff may also transfer prisoners who were placed in the unit pursuant to G.S. 148-32.1(b) to the local confinement facility when space becomes available.

(b) **Operation of Satellite Jail/Work Release Unit.** -- A county or group of counties

Chapter 153A

operating a satellite jail/work release unit shall comply with the following requirements concerning operation of the unit:

(1) The county shall make every effort to ensure that at least eighty percent (80%) of the unit occupants shall be employed and on work release, and that the remainder shall earn their keep by working at the unit on maintenance and other jobs related to the upkeep and operation of the unit or by assignment to community service work, and that alcohol and drug rehabilitation be available through community resources.

(2) The county shall require the occupants to give their earnings, less standard payroll deduction required by law and premiums for group health insurance coverage, to the Sheriff. The county may charge a per day charge from those occupants who are employed or otherwise able to pay from other resources available to the occupants. The per day charge shall be calculated based on the following formula: The charge shall be either the amount that the Division of Adult Correction and Juvenile Justice of the Department of Public Safety deducts from a prisoner's work-release earnings to pay for the cost of the prisoner's keep or fifty percent (50%) of the occupant's net weekly income, whichever is greater, but in no event may the per day charge exceed an amount that is twice the amount that the Division of Adult Correction and Juvenile Justice of the Department of Public Safety pays each local confinement facility for the cost of providing food, clothing, personal items, supervision, and necessary ordinary medical expenses. The per day charge may be adjusted on an individual basis where restitution and/or child support has been ordered, or where the occupant's salary or resources are insufficient to pay the charge.

The county also shall accumulate a reasonable sum from the earnings of the occupant to be returned to him when he is released from the unit. The county also shall follow the guidelines established for the Division of Adult Correction and Juvenile Justice of the Department of Public Safety in G.S. 148-33.1(f) for determining the amount and order of disbursements from the occupant's earnings.

(3) Any and all proceeds from daily fees shall belong to the county's General Fund to aid in offsetting the operation and maintenance of the satellite unit.

(4) The unit shall be operated on a full-time basis, i.e., seven days/nights a week, but weekend leave may be granted by the Sheriff. In granting weekend leave, the Sheriff shall follow the policies and procedures of the Division of Adult Correction and Juvenile Justice of the Department of Public Safety for granting weekend leave for Level 3 minimum custody inmates.

(5) Earned time shall be applied to these county prisoners in the same manner as prescribed in G.S. 15A-1340.20 and G.S. 148-13 for State prisoners.

(6) The Sheriff shall maintain complete and accurate records on each inmate. These records shall contain the same information as required for State prisoners that are housed in county local confinement facilities.

History.
1987, c. 207, s. 1; 1987 (Reg. Sess., 1988), c. 1106, ss. 4, 5; 1989, c. 761, ss. 4, 7; 1993 (Reg. Sess., 1994), c. 767, s. 3; 2011-145, s. 19.1(h); 2017-186, s. 2 (iiiiiiiii)

§ 153A-230.4. Standards

The county satellite jail/work release units for misdemeanants shall not be subject to the standards promulgated for local confinement facilities pursuant to G.S. 153A-221. The Secretary of Health and Human Services shall develop and enforce standards for satellite/work release units. The Secretary shall take into consideration that they are to house only screened misdemeanants most of whom are on work release and therefore occupy the premises only in their off-work hours. After consultation with the North Carolina Sheriff's Association, the North Carolina Association of County Commissioners, and the Joint Legislative Commission on Governmental Operations, the Secretary of Health and Human Services shall promulgate standards suitable for these units by January 1, 1988, and shall include these units in the Division's monitoring and inspection responsibilities. Further, the North Carolina Sheriffs' Education and Training Standards Commission shall include appropriate training for Sheriffs and other county law enforcement personnel in regard to the operation, management and guidelines for county work release centers pursuant to its authority under G.S. 17E-4.

History.
1987, c. 207, s. 1; 1987 (Reg. Sess., 1988), c. 1106, s. 6; 1997-443, s. 11A.118(a); 2011-145, s. 19.1(h)

§ 153A-230.5. Satellite jails/work release units built with non-State funds

(a) If a county is operating a satellite jail/work release unit prior to the enactment of this act, the county may apply to the Office of State Budget and Management for grant funds to recover any verifiable construction or renovation costs for those units and for improvement funds except that the total for reimbursement and improvement shall not exceed seven hundred fifty thousand dollars ($ 750,000). Any county accepting such a grant or any other State monies for county satellite jails must agree to all of the basic requirements listed in G.S. 153A-230.2 and G.S. 153A-230.3.

(b) If a county operates a non-State funded satellite jail/work release unit that does not comply with the basic requirements listed in G.S. 153A-230.2 and G.S. 153A-230.3, then the satellite jail shall be subject to the standards, rules, and regulations to be promulgated by the Secretary of Health and Human Services pursuant to Part 2 of Article 10 of Chapter 153A. If a county is reimbursed for the cost of a prisoner's keep from an inmate's work release earnings in an amount equal to or greater than that paid by the Division of Adult Correction and Juvenile Justice of the Department of Public Safety to local confinement facilities under G.S. 148-32.1, the county may not receive additional payments from the Division for the cost of a prisoner's keep. However, if reimbursement to the county for the cost of a prisoner's keep is less than the amount allowed under G.S. 148-32.1, the county may receive from the Division of Adult Correction and Juvenile Justice of the Department of Public Safety the difference in the amount received from work release earnings and the amount paid by the Division to local confinement facilities. The Division may promulgate rules regarding such payment arrangements.

History.
1987, c. 207, s. 1; 1987 (Reg. Sess., 1988), c. 1106, s. 7; 1989, c. 761, s. 5; 1997-443, s. 11A.118(a); 2000-140, s. 93.1(a); 2001-424, s. 12.2(b); 2011-145, s. 19.1(h); 2017-186, s. 2 (jjjjjjjj)

ARTICLE 12
ROADS AND BRIDGES

§ 153A-246. Use of photographs or videos recorded by automated school bus safety cameras

(a) **Definitions.** -- The following definitions apply in this section:

(1) **Automated school bus safety camera.** -- As defined in G.S. 115C-242.1.

(2) **Officials or agents.** -- This term includes a local board of education located within the county or a private vendor contracted with under G.S. 115C-242.1.

(3) **School bus.** -- As used in G.S. 20-217.

(b) **Civil Enforcement.** -- A county may adopt an ordinance for the civil enforcement of G.S. 20-217 by means of an automated school bus safety camera installed and operated on any school bus located within that county. An ordinance adopted pursuant to this section shall not apply to any violation of G.S. 20-217 that results in injury or death. Notwithstanding the provisions of G.S. 14-4, in the event that a county adopts an ordinance pursuant to this section, a violation of the ordinance shall not be an infraction. An ordinance authorized by this subsection shall provide all of the following:

(1) The notice of the violation shall be given in the form of a citation and shall be received by the registered owner of the vehicle no more than 60 days after the date of the violation.

(2) The registered owner of a vehicle shall be responsible for a violation unless the vehicle was, at the time of the violation, in the care, custody, or control of another person or unless the citation was not received by the registered owner within 60 days after the date of the violation.

(3) A person wishing to contest a citation shall, within 30 days after receiving the citation, deliver to the officials or agents of the county that issued the citation a written request for a hearing accompanied by an affidavit stating the basis for contesting the citation, including, as applicable:

a. The name and address of the person other than the registered owner who had the care, custody, or control of the vehicle.

b. A statement that the vehicle involved was stolen at the time of the violation, with a copy of any insurance report or police report supporting this statement.

c. A statement that the citation was not received within 60 days after the date of the violation, and a statement of the date on which the citation was received.

d. A copy of a criminal pleading charging the person with a violation of G.S. 20-217 arising out of the same facts as those for which the citation was issued.

(4) The citation shall include all of the following:

a. The date and time of the violation, the location of the violation, the amount of the civil monetary penalty imposed, and the date by which the civil monetary penalty shall be paid or contested.

b. An image taken from the recorded image showing the vehicle involved in the violation.

c. A copy of a statement or electronically generated affirmation of a law enforcement officer employed by a law enforcement agency with whom an agreement has been reached pursuant to G.S. 115C-242.1(c) stating that, based upon inspection of the recorded images, the owner's motor vehicle was operated in violation of the ordinance adopted pursuant to this subsection.

d. Instructions explaining the manner in which, and the time within which, liability under the citation may be contested pursuant to subdivision (3) of this subsection.

e. A warning that failure to pay the civil monetary penalty or to contest liability in a timely manner shall waive any right to contest liability and shall result in a late penalty of one hundred dollars ($ 100.00), in addition to the civil monetary penalty.

f. In citations issued to the registered owner of the vehicle, a warning that failure to pay the civil monetary penalty or to contest liability in a timely manner shall result in refusal by the Division of Motor Vehicles to register the motor vehicle, in addition to imposition of the civil monetary penalty and late penalty.

(5) Violations of the ordinance shall be deemed a noncriminal violation for which a civil penalty shall be assessed and for which no points authorized by G.S. 20-16(c) and no insurance points authorized by G.S. 58-36-65 shall be assigned to the registered owner or driver of the vehicle. The amount of such penalty shall be four hundred dollars ($ 400.00) for the first offense, seven hundred fifty dollars ($ 750.00) for the second violation, and one thousand dollars ($ 1,000) for each subsequent violation of the ordinance.

(6) If a registered owner provides an affidavit that the vehicle was, at the time of the violation, in the care, custody, or control of another person or company, the identified person or company may be issued a citation complying with the requirements of subdivision (4) of this subsection.

(7) The citation shall be processed by officials or agents of the county and shall be served by any method permitted for service of process pursuant to G.S. 1A-1, Rule 4 of the North Carolina Rules of Civil Procedure, or by first-class mail to the address of the registered owner of the vehicle provided on the motor vehicle registration or, as applicable, to the address of the person identified in an affidavit submitted by the registered owner of the vehicle.

(8) If the person to whom a citation is issued makes a timely request for a hearing pursuant to subdivision (3) of this subsection, a summons shall be issued by any

method permitted for service of process pursuant to G.S. 1A-1, Rule 4 of the North Carolina Rules of Civil Procedure, directing the person to appear at the place and time specified in the summons in order to contest the citation at an administrative hearing.

(9) A citation recipient who, within 30 days after receiving the citation, fails either to pay the civil penalty or to request a hearing to contest the citation shall have waived the right to contest responsibility for the violation and shall be subject to a late penalty of one hundred dollars ($ 100.00) in addition to the civil penalty assessed under this subsection.

(10) The county shall institute a nonjudicial administrative hearing to hear contested citations or penalties issued or assessed under this section. The decision on a contested citation shall be rendered in writing within five days after the hearing and shall be served upon the person contesting the citation by any method permitted for service of process pursuant to G.S. 1A-1, Rule 4 of the North Carolina Rules of Civil Procedure. If the decision is adverse to the person contesting the citation, the decision shall contain instructions explaining the manner and the time within which the decision may be appealed pursuant to subdivision (11) of this subsection.

(11) A person may appeal to the district court division of the General Court of Justice from any adverse decision on a contested citation by filing notice of appeal in the office of the clerk of superior court. Enforcement of an adverse decision shall be stayed pending the outcome of a timely appeal. Except as otherwise provided in this subdivision, appeal shall be in accordance with the procedure set forth in Article 19 of Chapter 7A of the General Statutes applicable to appeals from the magistrate to the district court. For purposes of calculating the time within which any action must be taken to meet procedural requirements of the appeal, the date upon which the person contesting the citation is served with the adverse decision shall be deemed to be the date of entry of judgment.

(12) In the event a person is charged in a criminal pleading with a violation of G.S. 20-217, all of the following shall apply:

a. The charging law enforcement agency shall provide written notice to the county office responsible for processing civil citations pursuant to subdivision (7) of subsection (b) of this section containing the name and address of the person charged with violation of G.S. 20-217 and the date of the violation.

b. After receiving notice pursuant to this subdivision that a person has been charged in a criminal pleading with a violation of G.S. 20-217, the county shall not impose a civil penalty against that person arising out of the same facts as those for which the person was charged in the criminal pleading.

c. The county shall issue a full refund of any civil penalty payment received from a person who was charged in a criminal pleading with a violation of G.S. 20-217 if the civil penalty arose out of the same facts as those for which that person was charged in the criminal pleading, together with interest at the legal rate as provided by G.S. 24-1 from the date the penalty was paid until the date of refund.

(13) If a citation is not contested pursuant to subdivision (3) of this subsection, payment of the civil penalty is due within 30 days after receipt of the citation. If the citation is contested, and the result of the administrative hearing held pursuant to subdivision (10) of this subsection is a decision adverse to the citation recipient, then payment is due within 30 days after receipt of the adverse decision, unless the citation recipient appeals the adverse decision pursuant to subdivision (11) of this subsection. If the adverse decision is appealed, and if the final decision on appeal is adverse to the citation recipient, then payment of the civil penalty is due within 30 days after the citation recipient receives notice of the final adverse decision on appeal.

(14) If the registered owner of a motor vehicle who receives a citation fails to pay the civil penalty when due, the Division of Motor Vehicles shall refuse to register the motor vehicle for the owner in accordance with G.S. 20-54(11). The county may establish procedures for providing notice to the Division of Motor Vehicles and for the collection of these penalties and may enforce the penalties by civil action in the nature of debt.

(15) The county shall provide each law enforcement agency within its jurisdiction with the name and address of the county official to whom written notice of persons charged with violation of G.S. 20-217 should be given pursuant to subdivision (12) of this subsection.

(c) **Notice.** -- An automated school bus safety camera installed on a school bus must be identified by appropriate warning signs conspicuously posted on the school bus. All warning signs shall be consistent with a statewide standard adopted by the State Board of Education in conjunction with local boards of education that install and operate automated school bus safety cameras on their school buses.

(d) **Application.** -- Nothing in this section shall be construed to do any of the following:

(1) Require the installation and operation of automated school bus safety cameras on a school bus.

(2) Prohibit the use and admissibility of any photograph or video recorded by an automated school bus safety camera in any criminal proceeding alleging a violation of G.S. 20-217.

(3) Prohibit the imposition of penalties, including the assignment of points authorized by G.S. 20-16(c) and insurance points authorized by G.S. 58-36-65, on any registered owner or driver of the vehicle convicted of a misdemeanor or felony violation of G.S. 20-217.

(e) **Criminal Prosecution Encouraged.** -- The General Assembly of North Carolina encourages criminal prosecution for violation of G.S. 20-217 whenever photographs or videos recorded by an automated school bus safety camera provide evidence sufficient to support such prosecution.

(f) A county that adopts an ordinance as provided in this section, shall maintain records of all violations of that ordinance for which a civil penalty is assessed. Upon request, the county shall provide at least five years of those records to the North Carolina Child Fatality Task Force and the North Carolina General Assembly.

History.
2017-188, ss. 1, 5

ARTICLE 18
PLANNING AND REGULATION OF DEVELOPMENT

PART 4
BUILDING INSPECTION

§ 153A-356. (Repealed effective August 1, 2021) Failure to perform duties

(a) If a member of an inspection department willfully fails to perform the duties required of him by law, or willfully improperly issues a permit, or gives a certificate of compliance without first making the inspections required by law, or willfully improperly gives a certificate of compliance, he is guilty of a Class 1 misdemeanor.

(b) A member of the inspection department shall not be in violation of this section when the county, its inspection department, or one of the inspectors accepted a signed written document of compliance with the North Carolina State Building Code or the North Carolina Residential Code for One- and Two-Family Dwellings from a licensed architect or licensed engineer in accordance with G.S. 153A-352(c).

History.

1969, c. 1066, s. 1; 1973, c. 822, s. 1; 1993, c. 539, s. 1064; 1994, Ex. Sess., c. 24, s. 14(c); 2015-145, s. 9(b); 2019-111, s. 2.2; 2020-3, s. 4.33(a).

§ 153A-367. (Repealed effective August 1, 2021) Removing notice from condemned building

If a person removes a notice that has been affixed to a building by a local inspector and that states the dangerous character of the building, he is guilty of a Class 1 misdemeanor.

History.

1969, c. 1066, s. 1; 1973, c. 822, s. 1; 1993, c. 539, s. 1068; 1994, Ex. Sess., c. 24, s. 14(c); 2019-111, s. 2.2; 2020-3, s. 4.33(a).

ARTICLE 23
MISCELLANEOUS PROVISIONS

§ 153A-436.1. SBI and State Crime Laboratory access to view and analyze recordings

The local law enforcement agency of any county that uses the services of the State Bureau of Investigation or the North Carolina State Crime Laboratory to analyze a recording covered by G.S. 132-1.4A shall, at no cost, provide access to a method to view and analyze the recording upon request of the State Bureau of Investigation or the North Carolina State Crime Laboratory.

History.

2016-88, s. 2(a)

CHAPTER 160A
CITIES AND TOWNS

ARTICLE 5
FORM OF GOVERNMENT

PART 3
ORGANIZATION AND PROCEDURES OF THE COUNCIL

§ 160A-77. Code of ordinances

(a) Not later than July 1, 1974, each city having a population of 5,000 or more shall adopt and issue a code of its ordinances. The code may be reproduced by any method that gives legible and permanent copies, and may be issued as a securely bound book or books with periodic separately bound supplements, or as a loose-leaf book maintained by replacement pages. Supplements or replacement pages should be adopted and issued annually at least, unless no additions to or modifications of the code have been adopted by the council during the year. The code may consist of two separate parts, the "General Ordinances" and the "Technical Ordinances." The technical ordinances may be published as separate books or pamphlets, and may include ordinances regarding the construction of buildings, the installation of plumbing and electric wiring, the installation of cooling and heating equipment, the use of public utilities, buildings, or facilities operated by the city, the zoning ordinance, the subdivision control ordinance, the privilege license tax ordinance, and other similar technical ordinances designated as such by the council. The council may omit from the code designated classes of ordinances of limited interest or transitory nature, but the code should clearly describe the classes of ordinances omitted therefrom.

(b) The council may provide that one or more of the following classes of ordinances shall be codified by appropriate entries upon official map books to be retained permanently in the office of the city clerk or some other city office generally accessible to the public:

(1) Establishing or amending the boundaries of zoning districts;

(2) Designating the location of traffic control devices;

(3) Designating areas or zones where regulations are applied to parking, loading, bus stops, or taxicab stands;

(4) Establishing speed limits;

(4a) Restricting or regulating traffic at certain times on certain streets, or to certain types, weights or sizes of vehicles;

(5) Designating the location of through streets, stop intersections, yield-right-of-way intersections, waiting lanes, one-way streets, or truck traffic routes; and

(6) Establishing regulations upon vehicle turns at designated locations.

(b1) The council may provide that the classes of ordinances described in paragraphs (2) through (6) of subsection (b) above, and ordinances establishing rates for utility or other public enterprise services, or ordinances establishing fees of any nature, shall be codified by entry upon official lists or schedules of the regulations established by such ordinances, or schedules of such rates or fees, to be maintained in the office of the city clerk.

(c) It is the intent of this section to make uniform the law concerning the adoption of city codes. To this end, all charter provisions in conflict with this section in effect as of January 1, 1972, are expressly repealed, except to the extent that the charter makes adoption of a code mandatory, and no local act taking effect on or after January 1, 1972, shall be construed to repeal or amend this section in whole or in part unless it shall expressly so provide by specific reference.

History.
1971, c. 698, s. 1; 1979, 2nd Sess., c. 1247, ss. 8, 9

§ 160A-78. Ordinance book

Effective January 1, 1972, each city shall file a true copy of each ordinance adopted on or after January 1, 1972, in an ordinance book separate and apart from the council's minute book. The ordinance book shall be appropriately indexed and maintained for public inspection in the office of the city clerk. Effective July 1, 1973, true copies of all ordinances that were adopted before January 1, 1972, and are still in effect shall be filed and indexed in the ordinance book. If the city has adopted and issued a code of ordinances in compliance with G.S. 160A-77, its ordinances shall be filed and indexed in the ordinance book until they are codified.

History.
1971, c. 698, s. 1

§ 160A-79. Pleading and proving city ordinances

(a) In all civil and criminal cases a city ordinance that has been codified in a code of ordinances adopted and issued in compliance with G.S. 160A-77 must be pleaded by both section number and caption. In all civil and criminal cases a city ordinance that has not been codified in a code of ordinances adopted and issued in compliance with G.S. 160A-77 must be pleaded by its caption. In both instances, it is not necessary to plead or allege the substance or effect of the ordinance unless the ordinance has no caption and has not been codified.

(b) Any of the following shall be admitted in evidence in all actions or proceedings before courts or administrative bodies and shall have the same force and effect as would an original ordinance:

    (1) A city code adopted and issued in compliance with G.S. 160A-77, containing a statement that the code is published by order of the council.

    (2) Copies of any part of an official map book maintained in accordance with G.S. 160A-77 and certified under seal by the city clerk as having been adopted by the council and maintained in accordance with its directions (the clerk's certificate need not be authenticated).

    (3) A copy of an ordinance as set out in the minutes, code, or ordinance book of the council, certified under seal by the city clerk as a true copy (the clerk's certificate need not be authenticated).

    (4) Copies of any official lists or schedules maintained in accordance with G.S. 160A-77 and certified under seal by the city clerk as having been adopted by the council and maintained in accordance with its directions (the clerk's certificate need not be authenticated).

(c) The burden of pleading and proving the existence of any modification or repeal of an ordinance, map, or code, a copy of which has been duly pleaded or admitted in evidence in accordance with this section, shall be upon the party asserting such modification or repeal. It shall be presumed that any portion of a city code that is admitted in evidence in accordance with this section has been codified in compliance with G.S. 160A-77, and the burden of pleading and proving to the contrary shall be upon the party seeking to obtain an advantage thereby.

(d) From and after the respective effective dates of G.S. 160A-77 and 160A-78, no city ordinance shall be enforced or admitted into evidence in any court unless it has been codified or filed and indexed in accordance with G.S. 160A-77 or 160A-78. It shall be presumed that an ordinance which has been properly pleaded and proved in accordance with this section has been codified or filed and indexed in accordance with G.S. 160A-77 or 160A-78, and the burden of pleading and proving to the contrary shall be upon the party seeking to obtain an advantage thereby.

(e) It is the intent of this section to make uniform the law concerning the pleading and

proving of city ordinances. To this end, all charter provisions in conflict with this section in effect as of January 1, 1972, are expressly repealed, and no local act taking effect on or after January 1, 1972, shall be construed to repeal or amend this section in whole or in part unless it shall expressly so provide by specific reference.

History.
1917, c. 136, subch. 13, s. 14; C.S., s. 2825; 1959, c. 631; 1971, c. 698, s. 1; 1973, c. 426, s. 18; 1979, 2nd Sess., c. 1247, s. 10

§ 160A-80. Power of investigation; subpoena power

(a) The council shall have power to investigate the affairs of the city, and for that purpose may subpoena witnesses, administer oaths, and compel the production of evidence.

(b) If a person fails or refuses to obey a subpoena issued pursuant to this section, the council may apply to the General Court of Justice for an order requiring that its order be obeyed, and the court shall have jurisdiction to issue these orders after notice to all proper parties. No testimony of any witness before the council pursuant to a subpoena issued in exercise of the power conferred by this section may be used against him on the trial of any civil or criminal action other than a prosecution for false swearing committed on the examination. If any person, while under oath at an investigation by the council, willfully swears falsely, he is guilty of a Class 1 misdemeanor.

(c) Repealed by Session Laws 1991, c. 512, s. 1, effective July 2, 1991.

History.
1971, c. 698, s. 1; 1991, c. 512, s. 1; 1993, c. 539, s. 1083; 1994, Ex. Sess., c. 24, s. 14(c)

ARTICLE 8
DELEGATION AND EXERCISE OF THE GENERAL POLICE POWER

§ 160A-174. General ordinance-making power

(a) A city may by ordinance define, prohibit, regulate, or abate acts, omissions, or conditions, detrimental to the health, safety, or welfare of its citizens and the peace and dignity of the city, and may define and abate nuisances.

(b) A city ordinance shall be consistent with the Constitution and laws of North Carolina and of the United States. An ordinance is not consistent with State or federal law when:

(1) The ordinance infringes a liberty guaranteed to the people by the State or federal Constitution;

(2) The ordinance makes unlawful an act, omission or condition which is expressly made lawful by State or federal law;

(3) The ordinance makes lawful an act, omission, or condition which is expressly made unlawful by State or federal law;

(4) The ordinance purports to regulate a subject that cities are expressly forbidden to regulate by State or federal law;

(5) The ordinance purports to regulate a field for which a State or federal statute clearly shows a legislative intent to provide a complete and integrated regulatory scheme to the exclusion of local regulation;

(6) The elements of an offense defined by a city ordinance are identical to the elements of an offense defined by State or federal law.

The fact that a State or federal law, standing alone, makes a given act, omission, or condition unlawful shall not preclude city ordinances requiring a higher standard of conduct or condition.

History.
1971, c. 698, s. 1

§ 160A-175. Enforcement of ordinances

(a) A city shall have power to impose fines and penalties for violation of its ordinances, and may secure injunctions and abatement orders to further insure compliance with its ordinances as provided by this section.

(b) Except for the types of ordinances listed in subsection (b1) of this section, violation of a city ordinance may be a misdemeanor or infraction as provided by G.S. 14-4 only if the city specifies such in the ordinance. An ordinance may provide by express statement that the maximum fine, term of imprisonment, or infraction penalty to be imposed for a violation is some amount of money or number of days less than the maximum imposed by G.S. 14-4. Notwithstanding G.S. 160A-75, no ordinance specifying a criminal penalty may be enacted at the meeting in which it is first introduced.

(b1) No ordinance of the following types may impose a criminal penalty:

(1) Any ordinance adopted under Article 19 of this Chapter, Planning and Regulation of Development, or its successor, Chapter 160D of the General Statutes, except for those ordinances related to unsafe buildings.

(2) Any ordinance adopted pursuant to G.S. 160A-193.1, Stream-clearing programs.

(3) Any ordinance adopted pursuant to G.S. 160A-194, Regulating and licensing businesses, trades, etc.

(4) Any ordinance adopted pursuant to G.S. 160A-199, Regulation of outdoor advertising or, its successor, G.S. 160D-912, Outdoor advertising.

(5) Any ordinance adopted pursuant to G.S. 160A-201, Limitations on regulating solar collectors or, its successor, G.S. 160D-914, Solar collectors.

(6) Any ordinance adopted pursuant to G.S. 160A-202, Limitations on regulating cisterns and rain barrels.

(7) Any ordinance adopted pursuant to G.S. 160A-304, Regulation of taxis.

(8) Any ordinance adopted pursuant to G.S. 160A-306, Building setback lines.

(9) Any ordinance adopted pursuant to G.S. 160A-307, Curb cut regulations.

(10) Any ordinance regulating trees.

(c) An ordinance may provide that violation shall subject the offender to a civil penalty to be recovered by the city in a civil action in the nature of debt if the offender does not pay the penalty within a prescribed period of time after he has been cited for violation of the ordinance.

(c1) An ordinance may provide for the recovery of a civil penalty by the city for violation of the fire prevention code of the State Building Code as authorized under G.S. 143-139.

(d) An ordinance may provide that it may be enforced by an appropriate equitable remedy issuing from a court of competent jurisdiction. In such case, the General Court of Justice shall have jurisdiction to issue such orders as may be appropriate, and it shall not be a defense to the application of the city for equitable relief that there is an adequate remedy at law.

(e) An ordinance that makes unlawful a condition existing upon or use made of real property may be enforced by injunction and order of abatement, and the General Court of Justice shall have jurisdiction to issue such orders. When a violation of such an ordinance occurs the city may apply to the appropriate division of the General Court of Justice for a mandatory or prohibitory injunction and order of abatement commanding the defendant to correct the unlawful condition upon or cease the unlawful use of the property. The action shall be governed in all respects by the laws and rules governing civil proceedings, including the Rules of Civil Procedure in general and Rule 65 in particular.

In addition to an injunction, the court may enter an order of abatement as a part of the judgment in the cause. An order of abatement may direct that buildings or other structures on the property be closed, demolished, or removed; that fixtures, furniture, or other movable property be removed from buildings on the property; that grass and weeds be cut; that improvements or repairs be made; or that any other action be taken that is necessary to bring the property into compliance with the ordinance. If the defendant fails or refuses to comply with an injunction or with an order of abatement within the time allowed by the court, he may be cited for contempt, and the city may execute the order of abatement. The city shall have a lien on the property for the cost of executing an order of abatement in the nature of a mechanic's and materialman's lien. The defendant may secure cancellation of an order of abatement by paying all costs of the proceedings and posting a bond for compliance with the order. The bond shall be given with sureties approved by the clerk of superior court in an amount approved by the judge before whom the matter is heard and shall be conditioned on the defendant's full compliance with the terms of the order of abatement within a time fixed by the judge. Cancellation of an order of abatement shall not suspend or cancel an injunction issued in conjunction therewith.

(f) Subject to the express terms of the ordinance, a city ordinance may be enforced by any one, all, or a combination of the remedies authorized and prescribed by this section.

(g) A city ordinance may provide, when appropriate, that each day's continuing violation shall be a separate and distinct offense.

(h) Notwithstanding any authority under this Article or any local act of the General Assembly, no ordinance regulating trees may be enforced on land owned or operated by a public airport authority.

History.
1971, c. 698, s. 1; 1985, c. 764, s. 35; 1993, c. 329, s. 4; 2013-331, s. 2; 2021-138, s. 13(b)

§ 160A-176. Ordinances effective on city property outside limits

Any city ordinance may be made effective on and to property and rights-of-way belonging to the city and located outside the corporate limits.

History.
1917, c. 136, subch. 5, s. 2; C.S., s. 2790; 1971, c. 698, s. 1; 1973, c. 426, s. 24

§ 160A-176.1. Ordinances effective in Atlantic Ocean

(a) A city may adopt ordinances to regulate and control swimming, surfing and littering in the Atlantic Ocean adjacent to that portion of the city within its boundaries or within its extraterritorial jurisdiction; provided, however, nothing contained herein shall be construed to permit any city to prohibit altogether swimming and surfing or to make these activities unlawful.

(b) This section shall apply only to cities in the counties of Brunswick, Carteret, Currituck, Dare, Hyde, New Hanover, Onslow, and Pender.

History.
1973, c. 539, s. 1

§ 160A-176.2. Ordinances effective in Atlantic Ocean

(a) A city may adopt ordinances to regulate and control swimming, personal watercraft operation, surfing and littering in the Atlantic Ocean and other waterways adjacent to that portion of the city within its boundaries or within its extraterritorial jurisdiction; provided, however, nothing contained herein shall be construed to permit any city to prohibit altogether swimming or surfing or to make these activities unlawful.

(b) Subsection (a) of this section applies to the Towns of Atlantic Beach, Calabash, Cape Carteret, Carolina Beach, Caswell Beach, Duck, Emerald Isle, Holden Beach, Kill Devil Hills, Kitty Hawk, Manteo, Nags Head, Oak Island, Ocean Isle Beach, Southern Shores, Sunset Beach, Topsail Beach, and Wrightsville Beach, and the City of Southport only.

History.
1991, c. 494, ss. 1, 2; 1991 (Reg. Sess., 1992), c. 801; 1993, c. 67, s. 5; c. 125, s. 2; 1993 (Reg. Sess., 1994), c. 625, s. 1; 1997-48, s. 1; 2002-141, s. 1; 2004-203, s. 55

§ 160A-177. Enumeration not exclusive

The enumeration in this Article or other portions of this Chapter of specific powers to regulate, restrict or prohibit acts, omissions, and conditions shall not be deemed to be exclusive or a limiting factor upon the general authority to adopt ordinances conferred on cities by G.S. 160A-174.

History.
1971, c. 698, s. 1

§ 160A-178. Regulation of solicitation campaigns, flea markets and itinerant merchants

A city may by ordinance regulate, restrict or prohibit the solicitation of contributions from the public for any charitable or eleemosynary purpose, and also the business activities of itinerant merchants, salesmen, promoters, drummers, peddlers, flea market operators and flea market vendors or hawkers. These ordinances may include, but shall not be limited to, requirements that an application be made and a permit issued, that an investigation be made, that activities be reasonably limited as to time and place, that proper credentials and proof of financial stability be submitted, that not more than a stated percentage of contributions to solicitation campaigns be retained for administrative expenses, and that an adequate bond be posted to protect the public from fraud.

History.
1963, c. 789; 1971, c. 698, s. 1; 1987, c. 708, s. 8

§ 160A-179. Regulation of begging

A city may by ordinance prohibit or regulate begging or otherwise canvassing the public for contributions for the private benefit of the solicitor or any other person.

History.
1971, c. 698, s. 1

§ 160A-180. Regulation of aircraft overflights

A city may by ordinance regulate the operation of aircraft over the city.

History.
1971, c. 698, s. 1

§ 160A-181. Regulation of places of amusement

A city may by ordinance regulate places of amusement and entertainment, and may regulate, restrict or prohibit the operation of pool and billiard halls, dance halls, carnivals, circuses, or any itinerant show or exhibition of any kind. Places of amusement and entertainment shall include coffee houses, cocktail lounges, night clubs, beer halls, and similar establishments, but any regulations thereof shall be consistent with any permits or licenses issued by the North Carolina Alcoholic Beverage Control Commission.

History.
1917, c. 136, subch. 5, s. 1; 1919, cc. 136, 237; C.S., s. 2787; 1971, c. 698, s. 1; 1981, c. 412, ss. 4, 5

N.C. Gen. Stat. § 160A-181.1

Repealed by Session Laws 2019-111, s. 2.6(c), as amended by Session Laws 2020-3, s. 4.33(a), and Session Laws 2020-25, s. 51(a), (b), (d), effective June 19, 2020.

History.
1998-46, s. 1; repealed by 2019-111, s. 2.6(c), as amended by 2020-3, s. 4.33(a), and 2020-25, s. 51(a), (b), (d), effective June 19, 2020

§ 160A-182. Abuse of animals

A city may by ordinance define and prohibit the abuse of animals.

History.
1917, c. 136, subch. 5, s. 1; 1919, cc. 136, 237; C.S., s. 2787; 1971, c. 698, s. 1

§ 160A-183. Regulation of explosive, corrosive, inflammable, or radioactive substances

A city may by ordinance restrict, regulate or prohibit the sale, possession, storage, use, or conveyance of any explosive, corrosive, inflammable, or radioactive substances, or any weapons or instrumentalities of mass death and destruction within the city.

History.
1917, c. 136, subch. 5, s. 1; 1919, cc. 136, 237; C.S., s. 2787; 1971, c. 698, s. 1

§ 160A-184. Noise regulation

A city may by ordinance regulate, restrict, or prohibit the production or emission of noises or amplified speech, music, or other sounds that tend to annoy, disturb, or frighten its citizens.

History.
1971, c. 698, s. 1; 1973, c. 426, s. 25

§ 160A-185. Emission of pollutants or contaminants

A city may by ordinance regulate, restrict, or prohibit the emission or disposal of substances or effluents that tend to pollute or contaminate land, water, or air, rendering or tending to render it injurious to human health or welfare, to animal or plant life or to property, or interfering or tending to interfere with the enjoyment of life or property. A city may by ordinance regulate the illegal disposal of solid waste, including littering on public and private property, provide for enforcement by civil penalties as well as other remedies, and provide that such regulations may be enforced by city employees specially appointed as environmental enforcement officers. Any such ordinance shall be consistent with and supplementary to State and federal laws and regulations.

History.
1917, c. 136, subch. 5, s. 1; 1919, cc. 136, 237; C.S., s. 2787; 1949, c. 594, s. 2; 1971, c. 698, s. 1; 1973, c. 426, s. 26; 2001-512, s. 6

§ 160A-186. Regulation of domestic animals

A city may by ordinance regulate, restrict, or prohibit the keeping, running, or going at large of any domestic animals, including dogs and cats. The ordinance may provide that animals allowed to run at large in violation of the ordinance may be seized and sold or destroyed after reasonable efforts to notify their owner.

History.

1917, c. 136, subch. 5, s. 1; 1919, cc. 136, 237; C.S., s. 2787; 1971, c. 698, s. 1

§ 160A-187. Possession or harboring of dangerous animals

A city may by ordinance regulate, restrict, or prohibit the possession or harboring within the city of animals which are dangerous to persons or property. No such ordinance shall have the effect of permitting any activity or condition with respect to a wild animal which is prohibited or more severely restricted by regulations of the Wildlife Resources Commission.

History.

1971, c. 698, s. 1; 1977, c. 407, s. 2

§ 160A-188. Bird sanctuaries

A city may by ordinance create and establish a bird sanctuary within the city limits. The ordinance may not protect any birds classed as a pest under Article 22A of Chapter 113 of the General Statutes and the Structural Pest Control Act of North Carolina of 1955 or the North Carolina Pesticide Law of 1971. When a bird sanctuary has been established, it shall be unlawful for any person to hunt, kill, trap, or otherwise take any protected birds within the city limits except pursuant to a permit issued by the North Carolina Wildlife Resources Commission under G.S. 113-274(c) (1a) or under any other license or permit of the Wildlife Resources Commission specifically made valid for use in taking birds within city limits.

History.

1951, c. 411, ss. 1, 2; 1971, c. 698, s. 1; 1979, c. 830, s. 3

§ 160A-189. Firearms

A city may by ordinance regulate, restrict, or prohibit the discharge of firearms at any time or place within the city except when used in defense of person or property or pursuant to lawful directions of law-enforcement officers, and may regulate the display of firearms on the streets, sidewalks, alleys, or other public property. Nothing in this section shall be construed to limit a city's authority to take action under Article 1A of Chapter 166A of the General Statutes.

History.

1971, c. 698, s. 1; 2012-12, s. 2(zz)

§ 160A-190. Pellet guns

A city may by ordinance regulate, restrict, or prohibit the sale, possession or use within the city of pellet guns or any other mechanism or device designed or used to project a missile by compressed air or mechanical action with less than deadly force.

History.

1971, c. 698, s. 1

§ 160A-191. Limitations on enactment of Sunday-closing ordinances

No ordinance regulating or prohibiting business activity on Sundays shall be enacted unless the council shall hold a public hearing on the proposed ordinance. Notice of the hearing shall be published once each week for four successive weeks before the date of the hearing. The notice shall fix the date, hour and place of the public hearing, and shall contain a statement of the council's intent to consider a Sunday-closing ordinance, the purpose for such an ordinance, and one or more reasons for its enactment. No ordinance shall be held invalid for failure to observe the procedural requirements for enactment imposed by this section unless the issue is joined in an appropriate proceeding initiated within 90 days after the date of final enactment. This section shall not apply to ordinances enacted pursuant to G.S. 18B-1004(d).

History.

1967, c. 1156, s. 1; 1971, c. 698, s. 1; 1973, c. 426, s. 27; 1983, c. 768, s. 22

N.C. Gen. Stat. § 160A-192

Repealed by Session Laws 1991, c. 698, s. 1 .

§ 160A-193. Abatement of public health nuisances

(a) A city shall have authority to summarily remove, abate, or remedy everything in the city limits, or within one mile thereof, that is dangerous or prejudicial to the public health or public safety. Pursuant to this section, the governing board of a city may order the removal of a swimming pool and its appurtenances upon a finding that the swimming pool or its appurtenances is dangerous or prejudicial to public health or safety. The expense of the action shall be paid by the person in default. If the expense is not paid, it is a lien on the land or premises where the nuisance occurred. A lien established pursuant to this subsection shall have the same priority and be collected as unpaid ad valorem taxes.

(b) The expense of the action is also a lien on any other real property owned by the person in default within the city limits or within one mile of the city limits, except for the person's primary residence. A lien established pursuant to this subsection is inferior to all prior liens and shall be collected as a money judgment. This subsection shall not apply if the person in default can show that the nuisance was created solely by the actions of another.

(c) The authority granted by this section does not authorize the application of a city ordinance banning or otherwise limiting outdoor burning to persons living within one mile of the city, unless the city provides those persons with either (i) trash and yard waste collection services or (ii) access to solid waste dropoff sites on the same basis as city residents.

History.
1917, c. 136, subch. 7, s. 4; C.S., s. 2800; 1971, c. 698, s. 1; 1979, 2nd Sess., c. 1247, s. 20; 2001-448, s. 1; 2002-116, s. 3; 2014-120, s. 24(h).

§ 160A-193.1. Stream-clearing programs

(a) A city shall have the authority to remove natural and man-made obstructions in stream channels and in the floodway of streams that may impede the passage of water during rain events.

(b) The actions of a city to clear obstructions from a stream shall not create or increase the responsibility of the city for the clearing or maintenance of the stream, or for flooding of the stream. In addition, actions by a city to clear obstructions from a stream shall not create in the city any ownership in the stream, obligation to control the stream, or affect any otherwise existing private property right, responsibility, or entitlement regarding the stream. These provisions shall not relieve a city for negligence that might be found under otherwise applicable law.

(c) Nothing in this section shall be construed to affect otherwise existing rights of the State to control or regulate streams or activities within streams. In implementing a stream-clearing program, the city shall comply with all requirements in State or federal statutes and rules.

History.
2005-441, s. 2

§ 160A-194. Regulating and licensing businesses, trades, etc

(a) A city may by ordinance, subject to the general law of the State, regulate and license occupations, businesses, trades, professions, and forms of amusement or entertainment and prohibit those that may be inimical to the public health, welfare, safety, order, or convenience. In licensing trades, occupations, and professions, the city may, consistent with the general law of the State, require applicants for licenses to be examined and charge a reasonable fee therefor.

(b) Nothing in this section shall authorize a city to examine or license a person holding a license issued by an occupational licensing board of this State as to the profession or trade that he has been licensed to practice or pursue by the State.

(c) Nothing in this section shall authorize a city to regulate and license a TNC service regulated under Article 10A of Chapter 20 of the General Statutes.

History.
1971, c. 698, s. 1; 2013-413, s. 12.1(a); 2014-3, s. 12.3(c); 2014-115, s. 17; 2015-237, s. 5

N.C. Gen. Stat. § 160A-195

Repealed by Session Laws 1998-128, s. 11, effective September 4, 1998.

§ 160A-196. Sewage tie-ons

Cities that (in whole or in part) are adjacent to, adjoining, intersected by or bounded by the Atlantic Ocean and Roanoke, Albemarle, Currituck, or Pamlico Sound may by ordinance regulate the tie-ons to sewage systems within their corporate limits.

History.
1985, c. 525, s. 1; 1987, c. 303

N.C. Gen. Stat. § 160A-197

Repealed by Session Laws 1995, c. 501, s. 4 .

§ 160A-198. Curfews

A city may by an appropriate ordinance impose a curfew on persons of any age less than 18.

History.
1997-189, s. 1

N.C. Gen. Stat. § 160A-199

Repealed by Session Laws 2019-111, s. 2.6(e), as amended by Session Laws 2020-3, s. 4.33(a), and Session Laws 2020-25, s. 51(a), (b), (d) effective June 19, 2020.

History.
2004-152, s. 2; repealed by 2019-111, s. 2.6(e), as amended by 2020-3, s. 4.33(a), and 2020-25, s. 51(a), (b), (d), effective June 19, 2020

Chapter 160A

N.C. Gen. Stat. § 160A-200

Repealed by Session Laws 2015-246, s. 1(a), effective September 23, 2015.

History.

1999-58, s. 2; 2000-33, s. 1; 2000-38, s. 1; 2001-107, s. 1; 2003-77, s. 1; 2003-80, s. 1; 2005-81, s. 1; 2005-202, s. 1; 2007-31, s. 1; 2007-258, s. 1; 2008-6, s. 1; 2008-25, s. 1; 2009-3, s. 1; 2009-19, s. 1; 2009-570, s. 46; repealed by 2015-246, s. 1(a), effective September 23, 2015

§ 160A-200.1. Annual notice to chronic violators of public nuisance or overgrown vegetation ordinance

(a) A city may notify a chronic violator of the city's public nuisance ordinance that, if the violator's property is found to be in violation of the ordinance, the city shall, without further notice in the calendar year in which notice is given, take action to remedy the violation, and the expense of the action shall become a lien upon the property and shall be collected as unpaid taxes.

(b) The notice shall be sent by registered or certified mail. When service is attempted by registered or certified mail, a copy of the notice may also be sent by regular mail. Service shall be deemed sufficient if the registered or certified mail is unclaimed or refused, but the regular mail is not returned by the post office within 10 days after the mailing. If service by regular mail is used, a copy of the notice shall be posted in a conspicuous place on the premises affected.

(c) A city may also give notice to a chronic violator of the city's overgrown vegetation ordinance in accordance with this section.

(d) For purposes of this section, a chronic violator is a person who owns property whereupon, in the previous calendar year, the city gave notice of violation at least three times under any provision of the public nuisance ordinance.

History.

2009-287, s. 1; 2013-151, s. 1; 2015-246, s. 1(b)

§ 160A-201. (Repealed effective August 1, 2021)

History.

2007-279, s. 1; 2009-553, s. 1; 2019-111, s. 2.6(g); 2020-3, s. 4.33(a).

§ 160A-202. Limitations on regulating cisterns and rain barrels

No city ordinance may prohibit or have the effect of prohibiting the installation and maintenance of cisterns and rain barrel collection systems used to collect water for irrigation purposes. A city may regulate the installation and maintenance of those cisterns and rain barrel

collection systems for the purpose of protecting the public health and safety and for the purpose of preventing them from becoming a public nuisance.

History.

2011-394, s. 12(e)

§ 160A-203. Limitations on regulating soft drink sizes

No city ordinance may prohibit the sale of soft drinks above a particular size. This section does not prohibit any ordinance regulating the sanitation or other operational aspect of a device for the dispensing of soft drinks. For purposes of this section, "soft drink" shall have the meaning set forth in G.S. 105-164.3.

History.

2013-309, s. 2

§ 160A-203.1. Limitations on standards of care for farm animals

Notwithstanding any other provision of law, no city ordinance may regulate standards of care for farm animals. For purposes of this section, "standards of care for farm animals" includes the following: the construction, repair, or improvement of farm animal shelter or housing; restrictions on the types of feed or medicines that may be administered to farm animals; and exercise and social interaction requirements. For purposes of this section, the term "farm animals" includes the following domesticated animals: cattle, oxen, bison, sheep, swine, goats, horses, ponies, mules, donkeys, hinnies, llamas, alpacas, lagomorphs, ratites, and poultry flocks of greater than 20 birds.

History.

2015-192, s. 2

§ 160A-203.2. Limitations on regulation of catering by bona fide farms

Notwithstanding any other provision of law, no city may require a business located on a property used for bona fide farm purposes, as provided in G.S. 160D-903(a), that provides on- and off-site catering services, to obtain a permit to provide catering services within the city. This section shall not be construed to exempt the business from any health and safety rules adopted by a local health department, the Department of Health and Human Services, or the Commission for Public Health.

History.

2020-18, s. 5(d); 2020-74, s. 21(b)

§ 160A-204. Transportation impact mitigation ordinances prohibited

No city may enact or enforce an ordinance, rule, or regulation that requires an employer to assume financial, legal, or other responsibility for the mitigation of the impact of his or her employees' commute or transportation to or from the employer's workplace, which may result in the employer being subject to a fine, fee, or other monetary, legal, or negative consequences.

History.
2013-413, s. 10.1(a); 2014-115, s. 17

§ 160A-205. Cities enforce ordinances within public trust areas

(a) Notwithstanding the provisions of G.S. 113-131 or any other provision of law, a city may, by ordinance, define, prohibit, regulate, or abate acts, omissions, or conditions upon the State's ocean beaches and prevent or abate any unreasonable restriction of the public's rights to use the State's ocean beaches. In addition, a city may, in the interest of promoting the health, safety, and welfare of the public, regulate, restrict, or prohibit the placement, maintenance, location, or use of structures that are uninhabitable and without water and sewer services for more than 120 days, as determined by the city with notice provided to the owner of record of the determination by certified mail at the time of the determination, equipment, personal property, or debris upon the State's ocean beaches. A city may enforce any ordinance adopted pursuant to this section or any other provision of law upon the State's ocean beaches located within or adjacent to the city's jurisdictional boundaries to the same extent that a city may enforce ordinances within the city's jurisdictional boundaries. A city may enforce an ordinance adopted pursuant to this section by any remedy provided for in G.S. 160A-175. For purposes of this section, the term "ocean beaches" has the same meaning as in G.S. 77-20(e).

(b) Nothing in this section shall be construed to (i) limit the authority of the State or any State agency to regulate the State's ocean beaches as authorized by G.S. 113-131, or common law as interpreted and applied by the courts of this State; (ii) limit any other authority granted to cities by the State to regulate the State's ocean beaches; (iii) deny the existence of the authority recognized in this section prior to the date this section becomes effective; (iv) impair the right of the people of this State to the customary free use and enjoyment of the State's ocean beaches, which rights remain reserved to the people of this State as provided in G.S. 77-20(d); (v) change or modify the riparian, littoral, or other ownership rights of owners of property bounded by the Atlantic Ocean; or (vi) apply to the removal of permanent residential or commercial structures and appurtenances thereto from the State's ocean beaches, except as provided in subsection (a) of this section.

History.
2013-384, s. 4(a); 2015-246, s. 1.5

§ 160A-205.1. Requiring compliance with voluntary State regulations and rules prohibited

(a) If a State department or agency declares a regulation or rule to be voluntary or the General Assembly delays the effective date of a regulation or rule proposed or adopted by the Environmental Management Commission, or any other board or commission, a city shall not require or enforce compliance with the applicable regulation or rule, including any regulation or rule previously or hereafter incorporated as a condition or contractual obligation imposed by, agreed upon, or accepted by the city in any zoning, land use, subdivision, or other developmental approval, including, without limitation, a development permit issuance, development agreement, site-specific development plan, or phased development plan.

(b) This section shall apply to the following regulations and rules:
(1) Those currently in effect.
(2) Those repealed or otherwise expired.
(3) Those temporarily or permanently held in abeyance.
(4) Those adopted but not yet effective.

(c) This section shall not apply to any water usage restrictions during either extreme or exceptional drought conditions as determined by the Drought Management Advisory Council pursuant to G.S. 143-355.1.

History.
2015-246, s. 2(b)

§ 160A-205.2. Adoption of sanctuary ordinances prohibited

(a) No city may have in effect any policy, ordinance, or procedure that limits or restricts the enforcement of federal immigration laws to less than the full extent permitted by federal law.

(b) No city shall do any of the following related to information regarding the citizenship or immigration status, lawful or unlawful, of any individual:
(1) Prohibit law enforcement officials or agencies from gathering such information.
(2) Direct law enforcement officials or agencies not to gather such information.

Chapter 160A

(3) Prohibit the communication of such information to federal law enforcement agencies.

History.
2015-294, s. 15(b)

§ 160A-205.3. Hours of certain alcohol sales

In accordance with G.S. 18B-1004(c), a city may adopt an ordinance allowing for the sale of malt beverages, unfortified wine, fortified wine, and mixed beverages beginning at 10:00 A.M. on Sunday pursuant to the licensed premises' permit issued under G.S. 18B-1001.

History.
2017-87, s. 4(c)

§ 160A-205.4. Authorization of social district

A city may adopt an ordinance designating a social district for use in accordance with G.S. 18B-904.1.

History.
2021-150, s. 20.2

§ 160A-205.5. Authorization of expanded area for ABC licensed premises

In accordance with G.S. 18B-904(h), a city may adopt an ordinance authorizing permittees holding a permit under Article 10 or 11 of Chapter 18B of the General Statutes to utilize an area that is not part of the permittee's licensed premises for the outdoor possession and consumption of alcoholic beverages sold by the permittee.

History.
2021-150, s. 21.2

ARTICLE 13
LAW ENFORCEMENT

§ 160A-281. Policemen appointed

A city is authorized to appoint a chief of police and to employ other police officers who may reside outside the corporate limits of the city unless the council provides otherwise.

History.
R.C., c. 111, s. 16; Code, c. 3803; Rev., s. 2926; C.S., s. 2641; 1969, c. 23, s. 1; 1971, c. 698, s. 1; 1973, c. 426, s. 45

§ 160A-282. Auxiliary law-enforcement personnel; workers' compensation benefits

(a) A city may by ordinance provide for the organization of an auxiliary police department made up of volunteer members.

(b) A city, by enactment of an ordinance, may provide that, while undergoing official training and while performing duties on behalf of the city pursuant to orders or instructions of the chief of police of the city, auxiliary law-enforcement personnel shall be entitled to benefits under the North Carolina Workers' Compensation Act and to any fringe benefits for which such volunteer personnel qualify.

(c) The board of commissioners of any county may provide that persons who are deputized by the sheriff of the county as special deputy sheriffs or persons who are serving as volunteer law-enforcement officers at the request of the sheriff and under his authority, while undergoing official training and while performing duties on behalf of the county pursuant to orders or instructions of the sheriff, shall be entitled to benefits under the North Carolina Workers' Compensation Act and to any fringe benefits for which such persons qualify.

This subsection shall not apply to volunteer school safety resource officers as described in G.S. 162-26.

History.
1969, c. 206, s. 1; 1971, c. 698, s. 1; 1973, c. 1263, s. 1; 1979, c. 714, s. 2; 1979, 2nd Sess., c. 1247, s. 28; 2013-360, s. 8.45(d)

§ 160A-283. Joint county and city auxiliary police

The governing body of any city, town, or county is hereby authorized to create and establish a joint law-enforcement officers' auxiliary force with one or more cities, towns, or counties. Each participating city, town, or county shall, by resolution or ordinance, establish the joint auxiliary police force. The resolution or ordinance shall specify whether the members of the joint auxiliary police force shall be volunteers or shall be paid. Members shall be appointed by the respective governmental units and shall take the oath required for regular police officers. The joint auxiliary force may be called into active service at any time by the mayor or chief of police of the participating town or city or the chairman of the board of commissioners or sheriff of a participating county. Members of the joint auxiliary force, while undergoing official training and while on active duty shall be members of the unit which called the auxiliary force into active duty and shall be entitled to all powers, privileges and immunities afforded by law to regularly employed law-enforcement officers of that unit including benefits under the Workers' Compensation Act. Members of the joint auxiliary force shall not be considered as public officers within the meaning of the North Carolina Constitution. Such members shall be dressed in the uniform prescribed by such auxiliary force at any time such members or member exercises any of the duties or authority herein provided for.

History.

1971, c. 607; c. 896, s. 4; 1979, c. 714, s. 2

§ 160A-284. Oath of office; holding other offices

(a) Each person appointed or employed as chief of police, policeman, or auxiliary policeman shall take and subscribe before some person authorized by law to administer oaths the oath of office required by Article VI, Sec. 7, of the Constitution. The oath shall be filed with the city clerk.

(b) The offices of policeman and chief of police are hereby declared to be offices that may be held concurrently with any other appointive office pursuant to Article VI, Sec. 9, of the Constitution. The offices of policeman and chief of police are hereby declared to be offices that may be held concurrently with any elective office, other than elective office in the municipality employing the policeman or chief of police, pursuant to Section 9 of Article VI of the Constitution.

(c) The office of auxiliary policeman is hereby declared to be an office that may be held concurrently with any elective office or appointive office pursuant to Article VI, Sec. 9, of the Constitution.

History.

1971, c. 698, s. 1; c. 896, s. 4; 1975, c. 664, s. 10; 2018-13, s. 4(a)

§ 160A-285. Powers and duties of policemen

As a peace officer, a policeman shall have within the corporate limits of the city all of the powers invested in law-enforcement officers by statute or common law. He shall also have power to serve all civil and criminal process that may be directed to him by any officer of the General Court of Justice and may enforce the ordinances and regulations of the city as the council may direct.

History.

Code, s. 3811; Rev., s. 2927; C.S., s. 2642; 1971, c. 698, s. 1; c. 896, s. 4

§ 160A-286. Extraterritorial jurisdiction of policemen

In addition to their authority within the corporate limits, city policemen shall have all the powers invested in law-enforcement officers by statute or common law within one mile of the corporate limits of the city, and on all property owned by or leased to the city wherever located.

Any officer pursuing an offender outside the corporate limits or extraterritorial jurisdiction of the city shall be entitled to all of the privileges, immunities, and benefits to which he would be entitled if acting within the city, including coverage under the workers' compensation laws.

History.

1971, c. 698, s. 1; c. 896, s. 4; 1973, c. 426, s. 46; c. 1286, s. 24; 1991, c. 636, s. 3

§ 160A-287. City lockups

A city shall have authority to establish, erect, repair, maintain and operate a lockup for the temporary detention of prisoners pending their transferal to the county or district jail or the State Division of Adult Correction and Juvenile Justice.

History.

Code, ss. 704, 3117; 1901, c. 283; 1905, c. 526; Rev., s. 2916; 1907, c. 978; P.L. 1917, c. 223; C.S., s. 2623; Ex. Sess. 1921, c. 58; 1927, c. 14; 1933, c. 69; 1949, c. 938; 1955, c. 77; 1959, c. 391; 1961, c. 308; 1967, c. 100, s. 2; c. 1122, s. 1; 1969, c. 944; 1971, c. 698, s. 1; c. 896, s. 4; 2011-145, s. 19.1(h); 2017-186, s. 3(a)

§ 160A-288. Cooperation between law enforcement agencies

(a) Unless specifically prohibited or limited by an ordinance officially adopted by the governing body of the city or county by which the person is employed, appointed, or elected to serve, the head of any law enforcement agency may temporarily provide assistance to another agency if so requested in writing by the head of the requesting agency. The assistance may comprise allowing officers of the agency to work temporarily with officers of the requesting agency (including in an undercover capacity) and lending equipment and supplies. While working with the requesting agency under the authority of this section, an officer shall have the same jurisdiction, powers, rights, privileges and immunities (including those relating to the defense of civil actions and payment of judgments) as the officers of the requesting agency in addition to those the officer normally possesses. While on duty with the requesting agency, the officer shall be subject to the lawful operational commands of the officer's superior officers in the requesting agency, but the officer shall for personnel and administrative purposes, remain under the control of the officer's own agency, including for purposes of pay. The officer shall furthermore be entitled to workers' compensation and the same benefits when acting pursuant to this section to the same extent as though the officer were functioning within the normal scope of the officer's duties.

(b) As used in this section:

(1) "Head" means any director or chief officer of a law enforcement agency including the chief of police of a local department, chief of police of county police department, and the sheriff of a county, or an officer of one of the above named agencies to whom the head of that agency has delegated authority to make or grant requests under this section, but only one officer in the agency shall have this delegated authority at any time.

(2) "Law enforcement agency" or "agency" means a municipal police department, a county police department, or a sheriff's office of this State. Subject to G.S. 15A-403, it also includes a municipal police department, a county police department, or a sheriff's office of another state if the laws of the other state allow for the provision of mutual aid with out-of-state law enforcement officers. All other State and local agencies are exempted from the provisions of this section.

(c) This section in no way reduces the jurisdiction or authority of State law enforcement officers.

(d) For purposes of this section, the following shall be considered the equivalent of a municipal police department:

(1) Campus law enforcement agencies established pursuant to G.S. 115D-21.1(a) or G.S. 116-40.5(a).

(2) Colleges or universities which are licensed, or exempted from licensure, by G.S. 116-15 and which employ company police officers commissioned by the Attorney General pursuant to Chapter 74E or Chapter 74G of the General Statutes.

(3) Law enforcement agencies operated or eligible to be operated by a municipality pursuant to G.S. 63-53(2).

(4) Repealed by Session Laws 2013-360, s. 16B.4(d), effective July 1, 2013.

(5) A Company Police agency of the Department of Agriculture and Consumer Services commissioned by the Attorney General pursuant to Chapter 74E of the General Statutes.

History.
1967, c. 846; 1971, c. 698, s.1; c. 896, s.4; 1977, c. 534; 1981, c. 93, s. 2; 1987, c. 671, s. 4; 1989, c. 518, s. 2;

1991, c. 636, s. 3; 1991 (Reg. Sess., 1992), c. 1043, s. 6; 1997-143, s. 1; 1999-68, s. 4; 2005-231, s. 8; 2006-159, s. 4; 2009-94, s. 1; 2011-260, s. 4; 2013-360, s. 16B.4(d); 2018-87, s. 1; 2019-130, s. 1

§ 160A-288.1. Assistance by State law-enforcement officers; rules; cost

(a) The governing body of any city or county may request the Governor to assign temporarily State law-enforcement officers with state-wide authority to provide law-enforcement protection when local law-enforcement officers: (i) are engaged in a strike; (ii) are engaged in a slowdown; (iii) otherwise refuse to fulfill their law-enforcement responsibilities; or (iv) submit mass resignations. The request from the governing body of the city or county shall be in writing. The request from a county governing board shall be upon the advice of the sheriff of the county.

(b) The Governor shall formulate such rules, policies or guidelines as may be necessary to establish a plan under which temporary State law-enforcement assistance will be provided to cities and counties. The Governor may delegate the responsibility for developing appropriate rules, policies or guidelines to the head of any State department. The Governor may also delegate to a department head the authority to determine the number of officers to be assigned in a particular case, if any, and the length of time they are to be assigned.

(c) While providing assistance to a city or county, a State law-enforcement officer shall be considered an employee of the State for all purposes, including compensation and fringe benefits.

(d) While providing assistance to the city or county, a State officer shall be subject to the lawful operational commands of his State superior officers. The ranking representative of each State law-enforcement agency providing assistance shall consult with the appropriate city or county officials prior to deployment of the State officers under his command.

History.
1979, c. 639, s. 1

§ 160A-288.2. Assistance to State law-enforcement agencies

(a) Unless specifically prohibited or limited by an ordinance officially adopted by the governing body of the city or county by which the officer is employed, appointed, or elected to serve, the head of any local law-enforcement agency may temporarily provide assistance to a State law-enforcement agency in enforcing the laws of North Carolina if so requested in writing by the head of the State agency. The assistance may comprise allowing officers of the local agency to work temporarily with officers of the State agency (including in an undercover capacity) and lending equipment and supplies. While working with the State agency under the authority of this section, an officer shall have the same jurisdiction, powers, rights, privileges and immunities (including those relating to the defense of civil actions and the payment of judgments) as the officers of the State agency in addition to those the officer normally possesses. While on duty with the State agency, the officer shall be subject to the lawful operational commands of the officer's superior officers in the State agency, but the officer shall for personnel and administrative purposes, remain under the control of the local agency, including for purposes of pay. The officer shall furthermore be entitled to workers' compensation and the same benefits when acting pursuant to this section to the same extent as though the officer were functioning within the normal scope of the officer's duties.

(b) As used in this section:

(1) "Head" means any director or chief officer of any State or local law-enforcement agency including the chief of police of a local department, chief of police of a county police department, and the sheriff of a county, or an officer of the agency to whom the head of that agency has delegated authority to make or grant requests under this section, but only one officer in the agency shall have this delegated authority at any time.

(2) "Local law-enforcement agency" means any municipal police department, a county police department, or a sheriff's office.

(3) "State law-enforcement agency" means any State agency, force, department, or unit responsible for enforcing criminal laws.

(c) This section in no way reduces the jurisdiction or authority of State law-enforcement officers.

(d) For the purposes of this section, the following shall be considered the equivalent of a municipal police department:

(1) Campus law-enforcement agencies established pursuant to G.S. 116-40.5(a).

(2) Colleges or universities which are licensed, or exempted from licensure, by G.S. 116-15 and which employ company police officers commissioned by the Attorney General pursuant to Chapter 74E or Chapter 74G of the General Statutes.

(3) Repealed by Session Laws 2013-360, s. 16B.4(e), effective July 1, 2013.

History.
1981, c. 878; 1989, c. 518, s. 3; 1991, c. 636, s. 3; 1991 (Reg. Sess., 1992), c. 1043, s. 7; 2005-231, s. 9;

2006-159, s. 5; 2011-260, s. 5; 2011-326, s. 10; 2013-360, s. 16B.4(e); 2018-87, s. 2

§ 160A-288.3. (Expires October 1, 2020)

History.
2019-109, s. 1

§ 160A-288.4. Police chief may establish volunteer school safety resource officer program

(a) The chief of police of a local police department or of a county police department may establish a volunteer school safety resource officer program to provide nonsalaried special law enforcement officers to serve as school safety resource officers in public schools. To be a volunteer in the program, a person must have prior experience as either (i) a sworn law enforcement officer or (ii) a military police officer with a minimum of two years' service. If a person with experience as a military police officer is no longer in the armed services, the person must also have an honorable discharge. A program volunteer must receive training on research into the social and cognitive development of elementary, middle, and high school children and must also meet the selection standards and any additional criteria established by the chief of police.

(b) Each volunteer shall report to the chief of police and shall work under the direction and supervision of the chief of police or the chief's designee when carrying out the volunteer's duties as a school safety resource officer. No volunteer may be assigned to a school as a school safety resource officer until the volunteer has updated or renewed the volunteer's law enforcement training and has been certified by the North Carolina Criminal Justice Education and Training Standards Commission as meeting the educational and firearms proficiency standards required of persons serving as criminal justice officers. A volunteer is not required to meet the physical standards required by the North Carolina Criminal Justice Education and Training Standards Commission but must have a standard medical exam to ensure the volunteer is in good health. A person selected by the chief of police to serve as a volunteer under this section shall have the power of arrest while performing official duties as a volunteer school safety resource officer.

(c) The chief of police may enter into an agreement with the local board of education to provide volunteer school safety resource officers who meet both the criteria established by this section and the selection and training requirements set by the chief of police of the municipality or county in which the schools are located.

The chief of police shall be responsible for the assignment of any volunteer school safety resource officer assigned to a public school and for the supervision of the officer.

(d) There shall be no liability on the part of and no cause of action shall arise against a volunteer school safety resource officer, the chief of police or employees of the local law enforcement agency supervising a volunteer school safety officer, or the public school system or its employees for any good-faith action taken by them in the performance of their duties with regard to the volunteer school safety resource officer program established pursuant to this section.

History.
2013-360, s. 8.45(f)

§ 160A-289. Training and development programs for law enforcement

A city shall have authority to plan and execute training and development programs for law-enforcement agencies, and for that purpose may

(1) Contract with other cities, counties, and the State and federal governments and their agencies;

(2) Accept, receive, and disburse funds, grants and services;

(3) Create joint agencies to act for and on behalf of participating counties and cities;

(4) Make applications for, receive, administer, and expend federal grant funds; and

(5) Appropriate and expend available tax or nontax funds.

History.
1969, c. 1145, s. 3; 1971, c. 698, s. 1; c. 896, s. 4

§ 160A-289.1. Resources to protect the public

Subject to the requirements of G.S. 7A-41, 7A-44.1, 7A-64, 7A-102, 7A-133, and 7A-498.7, a city may appropriate funds under contract with the State for the provision of services for the speedy disposition of cases involving drug offenses, domestic violence, or other offenses

involving threats to public safety. Nothing in this section shall be construed to obligate the General Assembly to make any appropriation to implement the provisions of this section. Further, nothing in this section shall be construed to obligate the Administrative Office of the Courts or the Office of Indigent Defense Services to maintain positions or services initially provided for under this section.

History.
1999-237, s. 17.17(c); 2000-67, s. 15.4(f); 2001-424, s. 22.11(f)

§ 160A-289.2. Neighborhood crime watch programs

A city may establish neighborhood crime watch programs within the city to encourage residents and business owners to promote citizen involvement in securing homes, businesses, and personal property against criminal activity and to report suspicious activities to law enforcement officials.

History.
2006-181, s. 2

ARTICLE 21
MISCELLANEOUS

§ 160A-490.1. SBI and State Crime Laboratory access to view and analyze recordings

The local law enforcement agency of any city that uses the services of the State Bureau of Investigation or the North Carolina State Crime Laboratory to analyze a recording covered by G.S. 132-1.4A shall, at no cost, provide access to a method to view and analyze the recording upon request of the State Bureau of Investigation or the North Carolina State Crime Laboratory.

History.
2016-88, s. 2(b)

CHAPTER 162
SHERIFF

ARTICLE 1
THE OFFICE

§ 162-1. Election and term of office

In each county a sheriff shall be elected by the qualified voters thereof, as is prescribed for members of the General Assembly, and shall hold his office for four years.

History.
Const., art. 4, s. 24; Rev., s. 2808; C.S., s. 3925

§ 162-2. Disqualifications for the office

(a) No person shall be eligible for the office of sheriff if any of the following apply:

(1) The person is not of the age of 21 years.

(2) The person has been convicted of a felony in this State, the United States, or any other state, whether or not that person has been restored to the rights of citizenship or granted an expunction. This subdivision shall not include an unconditional pardon of innocence.

(3) The person is not a qualified voter in the county in which the candidate is chosen.

(b) Notwithstanding Article 5 of Chapter 15A of the General Statutes, any person filing a notice of candidacy, or any appointee selected to fill a vacancy, to the office of sheriff shall provide a statement of disclosure prepared by the North Carolina Sheriffs' Education and Training Standards Commission in accordance with Article 3 of Chapter 17E of the General Statutes.

(c) No person shall engage in the practice of law or serve as a member of the General Assembly while serving as sheriff.

History.
1777, c. 118, ss. 2, 4, P.R.; 1806, c. 699, s. 2, P.R.; 1829, c. 5, s. 6; 1830, c. 25, ss. 2, 3; R.C., c. 105, ss. 5, 6, 7; Code, ss. 2067, 2068, 2069; Rev., s. 2809; C.S., s. 3926; 1971, c. 1231, s. 1; 1983, c. 670, s. 1; 2021-107, s. 1

§ 162-3. Sheriff may resign

Every sheriff may vacate his office by resigning the same to the board of county commissioners of his county; and thereupon the board may proceed to elect another sheriff.

History.
1777, c. 118, s. 1, P.R.; 1808, c. 752, P.R.; R.C., c. 105, s. 15; Code, s. 2077; Rev., s. 2810; C.S., s. 3927

N.C. Gen. Stat. § 162-4

Repealed by Session Laws 1979, c. 518.

§ 162-5. Vacancy filled; duties performed by coroner or chief deputy

(a) If any vacancy occurs in the office of sheriff, the coroner of the county shall execute all process directed to the sheriff until the first meeting of the board of county commissioners next succeeding such vacancy, when the board of county commissioners shall appoint a sheriff to supply the vacancy for the residue of the term, who shall possess the same qualifications, enter into the same bond, and be subject to removal, as the sheriff regularly elected.

(b) If the board of county commissioners should fail to fill such vacancy, the coroner shall continue to discharge the duties of sheriff until it shall be filled. In those counties where the office of coroner has been abolished, the chief deputy sheriff, or if there is no chief deputy, then the senior deputy in years of service, shall perform all the duties of the sheriff until the board of county commissioners appoint some person to fill the unexpired term. In all counties the regular deputy sheriffs shall, during the interim of the vacancy, continue to perform their duties with full authority.

(c) The board of county commissioners shall not make any appointment under this section without first being presented with a valid disclosure statement of no felony convictions or expungements, issued within 90 days prior to the appointment, prepared by the North Carolina Sheriffs' Education and Training Standards Commission pursuant to Article 3 of Chapter 17E of the General Statutes with respect to the individual being appointed.

History.
1829, c. 5, s. 8; R.S., c. 109, s. 11; R.C., c. 105, s. 11; Code, s. 2071; Rev., s. 2811; C.S., s. 3929; 1973, c. 74; 1983, c. 670, s. 2; 2021-107, s. 8(a)

§ 162-5.1. Vacancy filled in certain counties; duties performed by coroner or chief deputy

(a) If any vacancy occurs in the office of sheriff, the coroner of the county shall execute all process directed to the sheriff until the board of county commissioners shall appoint a sheriff to supply the vacancy for the residue of the term, who shall possess the same qualifications, enter into the same bond, and be subject to removal, as the sheriff regularly elected.

Chapter 162

(b) If the sheriff were elected as a nominee of a political party, the board of county commissioners shall consult the county executive committee of that political party before filling the vacancy, and shall appoint the person recommended by the county executive committee of that party, if the party makes a recommendation within 30 days of the occurrence of the vacancy.

(c) If the board should fail to fill such vacancy, the coroner shall continue to discharge the duties of sheriff until it shall be filled. In those counties where the office of coroner has been abolished, the chief deputy sheriff, or if there is no chief deputy, then the senior deputy in years of service, shall perform all the duties of the sheriff until the board of county commissioners appoint some person to fill the unexpired term. In all counties the regular deputy sheriffs shall, during the interim of the vacancy, continue to perform their duties with full authority.

(d) The board of county commissioners shall not make any appointment under this section without first being presented with a valid disclosure statement of no felony convictions or expungements, issued within 90 days prior to the appointment, prepared by the North Carolina Sheriffs' Education and Training Standards Commission pursuant to Article 3 of Chapter 17E of the General Statutes with respect to the individual being appointed.

(e) This section shall apply only in the following counties: Alamance, Alleghany, Avery, Beaufort, Brunswick, Buncombe, Cabarrus, Caldwell, Carteret, Cherokee, Clay, Davidson, Davie, Edgecombe, Forsyth, Gaston, Graham, Guilford, Haywood, Henderson, Hyde, Jackson, Lee, Lincoln, Madison, McDowell, Mecklenburg, Moore, New Hanover, Onslow, Pender, Polk, Randolph, Richmond, Rockingham, Rutherford, Sampson, Stokes, Surry, Swain, Transylvania, Wake, Washington, Wayne, and Yancey.

History.
1981, c. 763, ss. 10, 14; c. 830; 1983, c. 670, s. 2; 1987, c. 196, s. 3; 1989, c. 83; c. 497, s. 1; 1991, c. 15, s. 1; c. 558, s. 2; 2001-257, s. 2; 2003-39, s. 1; 2003-90, s. 1; 2009-32, s. 2; 2011-175, s. 4(a); 2012-25, s. 1; 2015-251, s. 1; 2019-5, s. 1; 2019-206, s. 1; 2021-107, s. 8(b); 2021-141, s. 1

§§ 162-6, 162-7

Repealed by Session Laws 1973, c. 108, s. 99.

ARTICLE 2
SHERIFF'S BOND

§ 162-8. Bond required

The sheriff shall furnish a bond payable to the State of North Carolina for the due execution and return of process, the payment of fees and moneys collected, and the faithful execution of his office as sheriff, which shall be conditioned as follows:

The condition of the above obligation is such that, whereas the above bounden is elected and appointed sheriff of County; if therefore, he shall well and truly execute and due return make of all process and precepts to him directed, and pay and satisfy all fees and sums of money by him received or levied by virtue of any process into the proper office into which the same, by the tenor thereof, ought to be paid, or to the person to whom the same shall be due, his executors, administrators, attorneys, or agents; and in all other things well and truly and faithfully execute the said office of sheriff during his continuance therein, then above obligation to be void; otherwise to remain in full force and effect.

The amount of the bond shall be determined by the board of county commissioners, but shall not exceed twenty-five thousand dollars ($ 25,000).

History.
1777, c. 118, s. 1, P.R.; 1823, c. 1223, P.R.; R.C., c. 105, s. 13; 1879, c. 109; Code, s. 2073; 1895, c. 270, ss. 1, 2; 1899, c. 54, s. 52; c. 207, s. 2; 1903, c. 12; Rev., s. 298; C.S., s. 3930; 1943, c. 543; 1983, c. 670, s. 4

§ 162-9. County commissioners to take and approve bonds

The board of county commissioners in every county shall take and approve the official bond of the sheriffs, which they shall cause to be registered and the original deposited with the clerk of superior court for safekeeping. The bond shall be taken on the first Monday of December next after the election.

History.
1806, c. 699, s. 2, P.R.; 1830, c. 5, s. 5; R.C., c. 105, s. 6; 1868, c. 20, s. 32; 1876-7, c. 276, s. 5; Code, ss. 2066, 2068; Rev., s. 2812; C.S., s. 3931; 1983, c. 670, s. 5

§ 162-10. Duty of commissioners when bond insufficient

Whenever the board of county commissioners finds that the sheriff has been unable to provide the bond prescribed by the board, the board shall give written notice to the sheriff to appear before the board within 10 days and provide a sufficient bond. If the sheriff fails to appear or provide a sufficient bond, the sheriff shall forfeit his office, and the commissioners shall elect a suitable person in the county as sheriff for the unexpired term, pursuant to G.S. 162-5 or G.S. 162-5.1, as appropriate.

History.

1879, c. 109, s. 2; Code, s. 2074; Rev., s. 2813; C.S., s. 3932; 1983, c. 670, s. 6

N.C. Gen. Stat. § 162-11

Repealed by Session Laws 1983, c. 670, s. 7.

§ 162-12. Liability of sureties

The sureties to a sheriff's bond shall be liable for all fines and amercements imposed on him, in the same manner as they are liable for other defaults in his official duty.

History.

1829, c. 33; R.C., c. 105, s. 14; Code, s. 2076; Rev., s. 2815; C.S., s. 3934

ARTICLE 3
DUTIES OF SHERIFF

§ 162-13. To receipt for process

Every sheriff or coroner shall, when requested, give his receipt for all original and mesne process placed in his hands for execution, to the party suing out the same, his agent or attorney; and such receipt shall be admissible as evidence of the facts therein stated, against such officer and his sureties, in any suit between the party taking the receipt and such officer and his sureties.

History.

1848, c. 97; R.C., c. 105, s. 18; Code, s. 2081; Rev., s. 2816; C.S., s. 3935; 1995, c. 379, s. 14(d)

§ 162-14. Duty to execute process

Every sheriff, by himself or his lawful deputies, shall execute and make due return of all writs and other process to him legally issued and directed, within his county or upon any river, bay or creek adjoining thereto, or in any other place where he may lawfully execute the same.

History.

1777, c. 218, s. 5, P.R.; 1821, c. 1110, P.R.; R.C., c. 105, s. 17; 1874, c. 33; Code, s. 2079; 1899, c. 25; Rev., s. 2817; C.S., s. 3936; 1973, c. 108, s. 98; 1983, c. 670, s. 8

§ 162-15. Imposition of penalty; procedure

In any case in which a person aggrieved seeks the imposition of penalties against a sheriff for failure or neglect to perform any duty of office or for any default in office as provided in G.S. 162-12, he may proceed by motion in the cause, supported by an affidavit, in a pending action.

Upon the filing of a motion in the cause the clerk shall deliver a copy of the motion and affidavit and an order to show cause to the sheriff.

History.

1871-2, c. 74, s. 4; Code, s. 446; Rev., s. 2818; C.S., s. 3937; 1983, c. 670, s. 9

§ 162-16. Execute summons, order or judgment

Whenever the sheriff may be required to serve or execute any summons, order or judgment, or to do any other act, he shall be bound to do so in like manner as upon process issued to him, and shall be equally liable in all respects for neglect of duty; and if the sheriff be a party, the coroner shall be bound to perform the service, as he is now bound to execute process where the sheriff is a party; and this Chapter relating to sheriffs shall apply to coroners when the sheriff is a party. Sheriffs and coroners may return process by mail. Their liabilities in respect to the execution of process shall be as prescribed by law.

In those counties where the office of coroner has been abolished, or is vacant, and in which process is required to be served or executed on the sheriff, the authority to serve or execute such process shall be vested in the clerk of court; however, the clerk of court is hereby empowered to designate and direct by appropriate order some person to act in his stead to serve or execute the same.

History.

C.C.P., s. 354; Code, s. 598; Rev., s. 2819; C.S., s. 3938; 1971, c. 653, s. 1

§ 162-17. Duties of outgoing sheriff for unexecuted process

It shall be the duty of any sheriff who shall have received a precept, and shall go out of office before the return day thereof, without having executed the same, to deliver same to the succeeding sheriff with sufficient time allowed for it to be executed by him.

History.

R.C., c. 105, s. 25; Code, s. 2088; Rev., s. 2820; C.S., s. 3939; 1983, c. 670, s. 10

§ 162-18. Payment of money collected on execution.

In all cases where a sheriff has collected money upon an execution placed in his hands, if there be no bona fide contest over the application thereof, he shall immediately pay the same into the office of the clerk of the court from which the execution issued.

History.

Code, s. 2080; Rev., s. 2821; C.S., s. 3940; 1983, c. 670, s. 11; 2021-47, s. 14(d)

N.C. Gen. Stat. § 162-19

Repealed by Session Laws 1953, c. 973, s. 3.

§§ 162-20, 162-21

Repealed by Session Laws 1983, c. 670, ss. 12, 13.

§ 162-22. Custody of jail

The sheriff shall have the care and custody of the jail in his county; and shall be, or appoint, the keeper thereof.

No law-enforcement officer or jailer who shall have the care and custody of any jail shall receive any portion of any jail fee or charge paid by or for any person confined in such jail, nor shall the compensation or remuneration of such officer be affected to any extent by the costs of goods or services furnished to any person confined in such jail.

History.

R.C., c. 105, s. 22; Code, s. 2085; Rev., s. 2824; C.S., s. 3944; 1967, c. 581, s. 3; 1969, c. 1090; 1983, c. 670, s. 14

§ 162-23. Prevent entering jail for lynching; county liable

When the sheriff of any county has good reason to believe that the jail of his county is in danger of being broken or entered for the purpose of killing or injuring a prisoner placed by the law in his custody, it shall be his duty at once to call on the commissioners of the county, or some one of them, for a sufficient guard for the jail, and in such case, if the commissioner or commissioners fail to authorize the employment of necessary guards to protect the jail, and by reason of such failure the jail is entered and a prisoner killed, the county in whose jail the prisoner is confined shall be responsible in damages, to be recovered by the personal representatives of the prisoner thus killed, by action begun and prosecuted before the superior court of any county in this State.

History.

1893, c. 461, s. 7; Rev., s. 2825; C.S., s. 3945

§ 162-24. Delegation of official duties

The sheriff may not delegate to another person the final responsibility for discharging his official duties, but he may appoint a deputy or employ others to assist him in performing his official duties.

History.

23 Hen. VI, c. 10; R.C., c. 105, s. 21; Code, s. 2084; Rev., s. 2828; C.S., s. 3946; 1983, c. 670, s. 15

§ 162-25. Obligations taken by sheriff payable to himself

The sheriff or his deputy shall take no obligation of or from any person in his custody for or concerning any matter or thing relating to his office otherwise payable than to himself as sheriff and dischargeable upon the prisoner's appearance and rendering himself at the day and place required in the writ (whereupon he was or shall be taken or arrested), and his sureties discharging themselves therefrom as special bail of such prisoner or such person keeping within the limits and rules of any prison; and every other obligation taken by any sheriff in any other manner or form, by color of his office, shall be void, except in any special case and other obligation shall be, by law, particularly and expressly directed; and no sheriff shall demand, exact, take or receive any greater fee or reward whatsoever, nor shall have any allowance, reward or satisfaction from the public, for any service by him done, other than such sum as the court shall allow for ex officio services and the allowance given and provided by law.

History.

1777, c. 118, s. 8, P.R.; R.C., c. 105, s. 19; Code, s. 2082; Rev., s. 2829; C.S., s. 3947

§ 162-26. Sheriff may establish volunteer school safety resource officer program

(a) The sheriff may establish a volunteer school safety resource officer program to provide nonsalaried special deputies to serve as school safety resource officers in public schools. To be a volunteer in the program, a person must have prior experience as either (i) a sworn law enforcement officer or (ii) a military police officer with a minimum of two years' service. If a person with experience as a military police officer is no longer in the armed services, the person must also have an honorable discharge. A program volunteer must receive training on research into the social and cognitive development of elementary, middle, and high school children and must also meet the selection standards and any additional criteria established by the sheriff.

(b) Each volunteer shall report to the sheriff and shall work under the direction and supervision of the sheriff or the sheriff's designee when carrying out the volunteer's duties as a school safety resource officer. No volunteer may be assigned to a school as a school safety resource officer until the volunteer has updated or renewed the volunteer's law enforcement training and has been certified by the North Carolina Sheriff's Education and Training Standards Commission as meeting the educational and firearms proficiency standards required of persons serving as special deputy sheriffs. A volunteer is not required to meet the physical standards required by the North Carolina Sheriff's Education and Training Standards Commission but must have a standard medical exam to ensure the volunteer is in good health. A person selected by the sheriff to serve as a volunteer under this section shall have the power of arrest while performing official duties as a volunteer school safety resource officer.

(c) The sheriff may enter into an agreement with the local board of education to provide volunteer school safety resource officers who meet both the criteria established by this section and the selection and training requirements set by the sheriff of the county for the schools. The sheriff shall be responsible for the assignment of any volunteer school safety resource officer assigned to a public school and for the supervision of the officer.

(d) There shall be no liability on the part of and no cause of action shall arise against a volunteer school safety resource officer, the Sheriff or employees of the sheriff supervising a volunteer school safety officer, or the public school system or its employees for any good-faith action taken by them in the performance of their duties with regard to the volunteer school safety resource officer program established pursuant to this section.

History.
2013-360, s. 8.45(e)

§§ 162-27 through 162-30

Reserved for future codification purposes.

ARTICLE 4
COUNTY PRISONERS

N.C. Gen. Stat. § 162-31

Repealed by Session Laws 1975, c. 166, s. 26.

§ 162-32. Bond of prisoner committed on capias in civil action

Every bond given by any person committed in arrest and bail, or in custody after final judgment, shall be assigned by the sheriff to the party at whose instance such person was committed to jail, and shall be returned to the office of the clerk of the court where the judgment was rendered, and shall have the force of a judgment. If any person who obtains the rules of any prison, as aforesaid, escapes out of the

same before he has paid the debt or damages and costs according to the condition of his bond, the court where the bond is filed, upon motion of the assignee thereof, shall award execution against such person and his sureties for the debt or damages and costs, with interest from the time of escape till payment, and no person committed to jail on such execution shall be allowed the rules of prison: Provided, the obligors have ten days' previous notice of such motion, in writing; but they shall not be admitted to deny the making of the bond in their answer, unless by affidavit they prove the truth of the plea.

History.
1759, c. 65, ss. 2, 3, P.R.; R.C., c. 87, s. 14; Code, s. 3469; Rev., s. 1341; C.S., s. 1345; 1973, c. 822, s. 3

§ 162-33. Prisoner may furnish necessaries

With the sheriff's approval, prisoners shall be allowed to purchase and procure such necessaries, in addition to the diet furnished by the jailer, as they may think proper.

History.
1795, c. 433, s. 6, P.R.; R.C., c. 87, s. 8; Code, s. 3463; Rev., s. 1344; C.S., s. 1348; 1973, c. 822, s. 3; 2001-487, s. 95

§ 162-34. United States prisoners

When a prisoner is delivered to the keeper of the county jail by the authority of the United States, such keeper shall receive and commit such prisoner if the jail has adequate and available housing space. The keeper of the county jail shall not be subject to any pains or penalties for refusal to receive and commit a federal prisoner. The United States shall reimburse the county for the incarceration of any federal prisoner at such rate as may be agreed upon between the county and the United States.

History.
1790, c. 322, ss. 1, 2, P.R.; R.C., c. 87, s. 1; Code, s. 3456; Rev., s. 1342; C.S., s. 1349; 1973, c. 822, s. 3; 1983, c. 219

§ 162-35. Arrest of escaped persons from penal institutions

Upon information received from the superintendent of any correctional or any penal institution, established by the laws of the State, that any person confined in such institution or assigned thereto by juvenile or other court under authority of law, has escaped therefrom and is still at large, it shall be the duty of sheriffs of the respective counties of the State, and of any peace officer in whose jurisdiction such person may be found, to take into his custody such escaped person, if to be found in his county, and to cause his return to the custody of the proper officer of the institution from which he has escaped.

History.
1933, c. 105, s. 1; 1973, c. 822, s. 3

§ 162-36. Transfer of prisoners to succeeding sheriff

The delivery of prisoners, by indenture between the late and present sheriff, or the entering on record in court the names of the several prisoners, and the causes of their commitment, delivered over to the present sheriff, shall be sufficient to discharge the late sheriff from all liability for any escape that shall happen.

History.
1777, c. 118, s. 12, P.R.; R.C., c. 87, s. 15; Code, s. 3470; Rev., s. 1348; C.S., s. 1352; 1973, c. 822, s. 3

N.C. Gen. Stat. § 162-37

Repealed by Session Laws 1983, c. 670, s. 16.

§ 162-38. Where jail unfit or insecure, courts may commit to jail of adjoining county

Whenever there is an unfit or insecure jail in any county, the judicial officers of such county may commit any persons brought before them, whether in a criminal or civil proceeding, to the jail of any adjoining county, for the same causes and under the like regulations that they might have ordered commitments to the usual jail; and the sheriffs and other officers of such county in which there is an unfit or insecure jail, and the sheriffs or keepers of the jails of the adjoining counties, shall obey any order of commitment so made.

History.
1835, c. 2, s. 2; R.C., c. 87, s. 3; Code, s. 3458; Rev., s. 1350; C.S., s. 1354; 1973, c. 57, s. 2; c. 822, s. 3; 1983, c. 670, s. 17

§ 162-39. Transfer of prisoners when necessary for safety and security; application of section to municipalities

(a) Whenever necessary for the safety of a prisoner held in any county jail or to avoid a breach of the peace in any county or whenever prisoners are arrested in such numbers that county jail facilities are insufficient and inadequate for the housing of such prisoners, the resident judge of the superior court or any judge holding superior court in the district or any district court judge may order the prisoner

transferred to a fit and secure jail in some other county where the prisoner shall be held for such length of time as the judge may direct.

(b) Whenever necessary to avoid a security risk in any county jail, or whenever prisoners are arrested in such numbers that county jail facilities are insufficient and inadequate for the housing of such prisoners, the resident judge of the superior court or any judge holding superior court in the district or any district court judge may order the prisoner transferred to a unit of the State prison system designated by the Secretary of Public Safety or his authorized representative. For purposes of this subsection, a prisoner poses a security risk if the prisoner:

(1) Poses a serious escape risk;

(2) Exhibits violently aggressive behavior that cannot be contained and warrants a higher level of supervision;

(3) Needs to be protected from other inmates, and the county jail facility cannot provide such protection;

(4) Is a female or a person 18 years of age or younger, and the county jail facility does not have adequate housing for such prisoners;

(5) Is in custody at a time when a fire or other catastrophic event has caused the county jail facility to cease or curtail operations; or

(6) Otherwise poses an imminent danger to the staff of the county jail facility or to other prisoners in the facility.

(b1) The Department of Public Safety, Health Services Section, shall maintain records of prisoners transferred to a unit of the State prison system pursuant to subsection (b) of this section. The records shall utilize unique identifiers for each transferred prisoner and shall include all of the following information:

(1) The date the transfer order was received.

(2) The statutory basis upon which the order was granted.

(3) The date the prisoner was transferred to State custody.

(4) The State prison facility where the prisoner was transferred.

(5) The county where the prisoner was removed.

(6) The dates the prisoner received health services from the Department.

(7) A list of health services provided to the prisoner and the corresponding charges.

(8) The date the Department determined that the prisoner no longer needs health services to be provided by the State prison system.

(9) The date and method used by the Department to notify the county that the prisoner should be transferred back to the custody of the county.

Chapter 162

(10) The date that the prisoner is returned to the custody of the county.

(c) The sheriff of the county from which the prisoner is removed shall be responsible for conveying the prisoner to the jail or prison unit where the prisoner is to be held, and for returning the prisoner to the common jail of the county from which the prisoner was transferred. The return shall be made at the expiration of the time designated in the court order directing the transfer unless the judge, by appropriate order, directs otherwise. The sheriff or keeper of the jail of the county designated in the court order, or the officer in charge of the prison unit designated by the Secretary of Public Safety, shall receive and release custody of the prisoner in accordance with the terms of the court order. If a prisoner is transferred to a unit of the State prison system, the county from which the prisoner is transferred shall pay the Division of Adult Correction and Juvenile Justice of the Department of Public Safety for maintaining the prisoner for the time designated by the court at the per day, per inmate rate at which the Division of Adult Correction and Juvenile Justice of the Department of Public Safety pays a local jail for maintaining a prisoner. The county shall also pay the Division of Adult Correction and Juvenile Justice of the Department of Public Safety for the costs of medical care incurred while the prisoner was in the custody of the Division of Adult Correction and Juvenile Justice of the Department of Public Safety, defined as follows:

(1) Medical expenses incurred as a result of providing health care to a prisoner as an inpatient (hospitalized).

(2) Other medical expenses when the total cost exceeds thirty-five dollars ($ 35.00) per occurrence or illness as a result of providing health care to a prisoner as an outpatient (nonhospitalized).

(3) Cost of replacement of eyeglasses and dental prosthetic devices if those eyeglasses or devices are broken while the prisoner is incarcerated, provided the prisoner was using the eyeglasses or devices at the time of his commitment and then only if prior written consent of the county is obtained by the Division.

(4) Transportation and custody costs associated with the transfer of prisoners receiving health care outside of the prison facility. The county shall reimburse the State for services provided to the prisoner at the same mileage reimbursement rate and hourly custody rate that are reimbursed pursuant to the Statewide Misdemeanant Confinement Program.

(5) Cost of sick call encounters at the rate charged to State prison inmates.

(c1) If the prisoner is transferred to a jail in some other county, the county from which the prisoner is transferred shall pay to the county receiving the prisoner in its jail the actual cost of maintaining the prisoner for the time designated by the court. Counties are authorized to enter into contractual agreements with other counties to provide jail facilities to which prisoners may be transferred as deemed necessary under this section.

(c2) Whenever prisoners are arrested in such numbers that county jail facilities are insufficient and inadequate for the safekeeping of such prisoners, the resident judge of the superior court or any superior or district court judge holding court in the district may order the prisoners transferred to a unit of the Division of Adult Correction and Juvenile Justice of the Department of Public Safety designated by the Secretary of Public Safety or the Secretary's authorized representative, where the prisoners may be held for such length of time as the judge may direct, such detention to be in cells separate from those used for imprisonment of persons already convicted of crimes, except when admission to an inpatient prison medical or mental health unit is required to provide services deemed necessary by a prison health care clinician. The sheriff of the county from which the prisoners are removed shall be responsible for conveying the prisoners to the prison unit or units where they are to be held, and for returning them to the common jail of the county from which they were transferred. However, if due to the number of prisoners to be conveyed the sheriff is unable to provide adequate transportation, the sheriff may request the assistance of the Division of Adult Correction and Juvenile Justice of the Department of Public Safety, and the Division of Adult Correction and Juvenile Justice of the Department of Public Safety is hereby authorized and directed to cooperate with the sheriff and provide whatever assistance is available, both in vehicles and manpower, to accomplish the conveying of the prisoners to and from the county to the designated prison unit or units. The officer in charge of the prison unit designated by the Secretary of Public Safety or the Secretary's authorized representative shall receive and release the custody of the prisoners in accordance with the terms of the court order. The county from which the prisoners are transferred shall pay to the Division of Adult Correction and Juvenile Justice of the Department of Public Safety the actual cost of transporting the prisoners and the cost of maintaining the prisoners at the per day, per inmate rate at which the Division of Adult Correction and Juvenile Justice of the Department of Public Safety pays a local jail for maintaining a prisoner, provided, however, that a county is not required to reimburse the State for transporting or maintaining a prisoner who was a resident of another state or county at the time the prisoner was arrested. However, if the county commissioners shall certify to the Governor that the county is unable to pay the bill submitted by the Division of Adult Correction and Juvenile Justice of the Department of Public Safety to the county for the services rendered, either in whole or in part, the Governor may recommend to the Council of State that the State of North Carolina assume and pay, in whole or in part, the obligation of the county to the Division of Adult Correction and Juvenile Justice of the Department of Public Safety, and upon approval of the Council of State the amount so approved shall be paid from the Contingency and Emergency Fund to the Division of Adult Correction and Juvenile Justice of the Department of Public Safety.

(c3) When, due to an emergency, it is not feasible to obtain from a judge of the superior or district court a prior order of transfer, the sheriff of the county and the Division of Adult Correction and Juvenile Justice of the Department of Public Safety may exercise the authority hereinafter conferred; provided, however, that the sheriff shall, as soon as possible after the emergency, obtain an order from the judge authorizing the prisoners to be held in the designated place of confinement for such period as the judge may direct. All provisions of this section shall be applicable to municipalities whenever prisoners are arrested in such numbers that the municipal jail facilities and the county jail facilities are insufficient and inadequate for the safekeeping of the prisoners. The chief of police is hereby authorized to exercise the authority herein conferred upon the sheriff, and the municipality shall be liable for the cost of transporting and maintaining the prisoners to the same extent as a county would be unless action is taken by the Governor and Council of State as herein provided for counties which are unable to pay such costs.

(d) Whenever a prisoner held in a county jail requires medical or mental health treatment that the county decides can best be provided by the Division of Adult Correction and Juvenile Justice of the Department of Public Safety, the resident judge of the superior court or any judge holding superior court in the district or any district court judge may order the prisoner transferred to a unit of the State prison system designated by the Secretary of Public Safety or the Secretary's authorized representative for an initial period not to exceed 30 days. The sheriff of the county from which the prisoner is removed shall be responsible for conveying the prisoner to the prison unit where the prisoner is to be held, and for returning the prisoner to the jail of the county from which the prisoner was transferred. The officer in charge of the prison unit designated by the Secretary of Public

Safety shall receive custody of the prisoner in accordance with the terms of the order. Prior to the conclusion of the 30-day period, the Division of Adult Correction and Juvenile Justice shall conduct an assessment of treatment and venue needs. The assessment shall be conducted by the attending medical or mental health professional and shall assess the medical and mental health needs of the prisoner and make a recommendation on whether the prisoner should remain in the custody of the Division of Adult Correction and Juvenile Justice of the Department of Public Safety or if the prisoner should be returned to the custody of the county. To extend the order beyond the initial 30-day period, the sheriff shall provide the Division of Adult Correction and Juvenile Justice assessment and any other relevant information to the resident judge of the superior court or any judge holding superior court in the district or any district court judge who shall determine whether to extend the transfer of the prisoner to a unit of the State prison system beyond the initial 30-day period. If the judge determines that the prisoner should remain in the custody of the Division of Adult Correction and Juvenile Justice, the judge shall renew the order and include a date certain for review by the court. Prior to the date of review, the Division shall conduct a reassessment of treatment and venue needs and the sheriff shall provide the reassessment and any other relevant information to the court, as described in this subsection. If the judge determines that the prisoner should not remain in the custody of the Division of Adult Correction and Juvenile Justice, the officer in charge of the prison unit designated by the Secretary of Public Safety shall release custody of the prisoner in accordance with the court order and the instructions of the attending medical or mental health professional. The county from which the prisoner is transferred shall pay the Division of Adult Correction and Juvenile Justice of the Department of Public Safety for maintaining the prisoner for the period of treatment at the per day, per inmate rate at which the Division of Adult Correction and Juvenile Justice of the Department of Public Safety pays a local jail for maintaining a prisoner, and for extraordinary medical expenses as set forth in subsection (c) of this section.

(e) The number of county prisoners incarcerated in the State prison system pursuant to safekeeping orders from the various counties pursuant to subsection (b) of this section or for medical or mental health treatment pursuant to subsection (d) of this section may not exceed 200 at any given time unless authorized by the Secretary of Public Safety. The Secretary may refuse to accept any safekeeper and may return any safekeeper transferred under a safekeeping order when this capacity limit is reached.

The Secretary shall not refuse to accept a safe-keeper because a county has failed to pay the Department of Public Safety for services rendered pursuant to this section.

(f) If, after 10 days of receiving notification and request for transfer from the Department of Public Safety pursuant to G.S. 148-19.3(a), the sheriff fails to assume custody of the county prisoner from the State prison facility to which the prisoner was assigned, then, in addition to the actual cost of transporting the prisoner and the cost of maintaining the prisoner at the per day, per inmate rate at which the Division of Adult Correction and Juvenile Justice of the Department of Public Safety pays a local jail for maintaining a prisoner, the county shall be liable to the State for an additional per day, per inmate rate not to exceed twenty dollars ($ 20.00) for each day the sheriff fails to assume custody of the prisoner, unless the sheriff has obtained an extension of the order because the inmate cannot be safely housed in the local jail. The section chief of the Health Services Section may waive up to 10 days of the additional per day rate if the sheriff provides documentation of extenuating circumstances.

History.
1957, c. 1265; 1967, c. 996, ss. 13, 15; 1969, cc. 462, 1130; 1973, c. 822, s. 3; c. 1262, s. 10; 1983, c. 165, ss. 1-4; 1985 (Reg. Sess., 1986), c. 1014, s. 198(a)-(c); 1989, c. 1, s. 7; 1991, c. 535, s. 1; 1991 (Reg. Sess., 1992), c. 983, s. 1; 2002-126, s. 17.1; 2011-145, s. 19.1(h), (i); 2012-83, s. 60; 2017-186, s. 2 (kkkkkkkk); 2019-171, s. 1

§ 162-40. When jail destroyed, transfer of prisoners provided for

When the jail of any county is destroyed by fire or other accident, any judicial officer of such county may cause all prisoners then confined therein to be brought before him. Upon the production of the process under which any prisoner was confined, such judicial officer shall order his commitment to the jail of any adjacent county. The sheriff or other officer of the county deputized for that purpose shall obey the order; and the sheriff or keeper of the common jail of such adjacent county shall receive such prisoners consistent with those provisions of G.S. 162-38.

History.
1835, c. 2, s. 1; R.C., c. 87, s. 2; Code, s. 3457; Rev., s. 1351; C.S., s. 1355; 1973, c. 57, s. 3; c. 822, s. 3; 1983, c. 670, s. 18.

§ 162-40.1. Reimbursement for transfer of prisoners

The county receiving prisoners pursuant to G.S. 162-38, 162-39 and 162-40 shall be reimbursed at the usual jail fee rate for each 24 hours of confinement or part thereof by the county from which the prisoner is transferred.

History.
1983, c. 670, s. 19

N.C. Gen. Stat. § 162-41

Repealed by Session Laws 1977, c. 711, s. 33.

§§ 162-42 through 162-44

Repealed by Session Laws 1983, c. 670, s. 20.

N.C. Gen. Stat. § 162-45

Repealed by Session Laws 1977, c. 711, s. 33.

N.C. Gen. Stat. § 162-46

Repealed by Session Laws 1979, c. 760, s. 4.

N.C. Gen. Stat. § 162-47

Repealed by Session Laws 1977, c. 711, s. 33.

N.C. Gen. Stat. § 162-48

Repealed by Session Laws 1983, c. 670, s. 20.

N.C. Gen. Stat. § 162-49

Repealed by Session Laws 1977, c. 711, s. 33.

§ 162-50. Penalties

Upon a finding that the sheriff, personally or through his lawful deputies, has willfully failed or neglected to perform any duty imposed by this Chapter, or has made any false return, he shall be subject to damages of not more than five hundred dollars ($ 500.00), and such damages recovered shall be paid to the person aggrieved. Nothing in this section bars an independent action for damages by the person aggrieved.

History.
1983, c. 670, s. 21

§§ 162-51 through 162-54

Reserved for future codification purposes.

§ 162-55. Injury to prisoner by jailer

If the keeper of a jail shall do, or cause to be done, any wrong or injury to the prisoners committed to his custody, contrary to law, he shall not only pay treble damages to the person injured, but shall be guilty of a Class 1 misdemeanor.

History.

1795, c. 433, s. 6, P.R.; R.C., c. 87, s. 8; Code, s. 3463; Rev., s. 3661; C.S., s. 4407; 1983, c. 631, s. 1; 1993, c. 539, s. 1098; 1994, Ex. Sess., c. 24, s. 14(c)

§ 162-56. Place of confinement

Persons committed to the custody of a sheriff shall be confined in the facilities designated by law for such confinement, and shall not be confined in any other place. Nothing herein shall be construed to prohibit or limit the authority of a sheriff to house prisoners committed to his custody in quarters, approved by the Department of Health and Human Services, other than the county jail.

History.

1795, c. 433, s. 4; R.C., c. 87, s. 16; Code, s. 3471; Rev., s. 3660; C.S., s. 4408; 1983, c. 631, s. 2; 1997-443, s. 11A.118(a)

§ 162-57. Record to be kept; items of record

The superintendent or other person having charge of prisoners shall keep a record showing, the name, age, date of sentence, length of sentence, crime for which convicted, home address, next of kin, and the conduct of each prisoner received.

History.

1927, c. 178, s. 2; 1983, c. 631, s. 3

§ 162-58. Counties may work prisoners

The board of commissioners of the several counties may enact by resolution all necessary rules and regulations for work on projects to benefit units of State or local government by persons convicted of misdemeanors or felonies and imprisoned in the local confinement facilities or satellite jail/work release units of their respective counties. The sheriff shall approve rules and regulations enacted by the board. Prisoners working under this section shall be supervised by county employees or by the sheriff. The rules enacted by the board of county commissioners and approved by the sheriff shall specify a procedure for ensuring that county employees supervising prisoners pursuant to this section be provided with notice that the persons placed under their supervision are inmates from a local confinement facility or a satellite jail/work release unit.

History.

1991 (Reg. Sess., 1992), c. 841, s. 1; 2002-159, s. 54

§ 162-59. Person having custody to approve prisoners for work

No prisoner shall perform work pursuant to G.S. 162-58 unless the prisoner has been approved for the work by the person having custody of the prisoner. The decision to approve a prisoner for work shall be based on the prisoner's history of violence, if any, past criminal convictions, and current sentence. For purposes of this section, the person having custody of the prisoner is the sheriff, except that when the prisoner is confined in a district confinement facility the person having custody of the prisoner is the jail administrator. The person having custody of the prisoner may use his discretion to revoke his approval at any time and to return the prisoner to the local confinement facility or satellite jail/work release unit. Neither the person having custody of the prisoner nor any jailer may be held liable for the actions of any prisoner, including those actions committed during and after the escape of a prisoner, while the prisoner is outside their supervision pursuant to this section.

History.

1991 (Reg. Sess., 1992), c. 841, s. 1

§ 162-59.1. Person having custody to approve prisoners for participation in education and other programs

The person having custody of a prisoner convicted of a misdemeanor offense may approve that prisoner's participation in an adult high school equivalency diploma program or in any other education, rehabilitation, or training program. The person having custody of the prisoner may revoke this approval at any time. For purposes of this section, the person having custody of the prisoner is the sheriff, except that when the prisoner is confined in a district confinement facility the person having custody of the prisoner is the jail administrator.

History.

2001-200, s. 1; 2014-115, s. 28(h)

§ 162-60. Reduction in sentence allowed for work, education, and other programs

(a) A prisoner who has faithfully performed the duties assigned to the prisoner under G.S. 162-58 is entitled to a reduction in the prisoner's sentence of four days for each 30 days of work performed.

(b) A prisoner who is convicted of a misdemeanor offense and housed in a local confinement facility or a person under the age of 18 convicted of a misdemeanor offense and housed in a detention facility approved by the Juvenile Justice Section of the Division of Adult

Correction and Juvenile Justice who faithfully participates in an adult high school equivalency diploma program or in any other education, rehabilitation, or training program is entitled to a reduction in the prisoner's sentence of four days for each 30 days of classes attended, up to the maximum credit allowed under G.S. 15A-1340.20(d).

(c) The person having custody of the prisoner, as defined in G.S. 162-59, is the sole judge as to whether the prisoner has faithfully performed the assigned duties under G.S. 162-58 or has faithfully participated in an adult high school equivalency diploma program or other education, rehabilitation, or training program under subsection (b) of this section. A prisoner who escapes or attempts to escape while performing work pursuant to G.S. 162-58 or while participating in an adult high school equivalency diploma program or other education, rehabilitation, or training program shall forfeit any reduction in sentence that the prisoner would have been entitled to under this section.

History.
1991 (Reg. Sess., 1992), c. 841, s. 1; 1993, c. 538, s. 36; 1994, Ex. Sess., c. 24, s. 14(b); 1993 (Reg. Sess., 1994), c. 767, s. 2; 2001-200, s. 2; 2014-115, s. 28(i); 2020-83, s. 8(o)

§ 162-61. Liability of county

The county working prisoners pursuant to G.S. 162-58 shall remain liable for emergency medical services for those prisoners pursuant to G.S. 153A-224 while the prisoners are working. The county working the prisoners shall be liable to third parties for injuries incurred by the third parties through the negligence of the working prisoners to the same extent as the county is liable for the actions of its employees. Chapters 96 and 97 of the General Statutes shall have no application to prisoners working pursuant to G.S. 162-58.

History.
1991 (Reg. Sess., 1992), c. 841, s. 1

§ 162-62. Legal status of prisoners

(a) When any person charged with a felony or an impaired driving offense is confined for any period in a county jail, local confinement facility, district confinement facility, or satellite jail/work release unit, the administrator or other person in charge of the facility shall attempt to determine if the prisoner is a legal resident of the United States by an inquiry of the prisoner, or by examination of any relevant documents, or both.

(b) If the administrator or other person in charge of the facility is unable to determine if that prisoner is a legal resident or citizen of the United States or its territories, the administrator or other person in charge of the facility holding the prisoner, where possible, shall make a query of Immigration and Customs Enforcement of the United States Department of Homeland Security. If the prisoner has not been lawfully admitted to the United States, the United States Department of Homeland Security will have been notified of the prisoner's status and confinement at the facility by its receipt of the query from the facility.

(c) Nothing in this section shall be construed to deny bond to a prisoner or to prevent a prisoner from being released from confinement when that prisoner is otherwise eligible for release.

(d) Repealed by Session Laws 2010-97, s. 12, effective July 20, 2010.

History.
2007-494, s. 1; 2010-97, s. 12

CHAPTER 163
ELECTIONS AND ELECTION LAWS

DIVISION 02.
ELECTION OFFICERS

ARTICLE 3
STATE BOARD OF ELECTIONS

§ 163-27.1. Emergency powers

(a) The Executive Director, as chief State elections official, may exercise emergency powers to conduct an election in a district where the normal schedule for the election is disrupted by any of the following:

    (1) A natural disaster.

    (2) Extremely inclement weather.

    (3) An armed conflict involving Armed Forces of the United States, or mobilization of those forces, including North Carolina National Guard and reserve components of the Armed Forces of the United States.

    In exercising those emergency powers, the Executive Director shall avoid unnecessary conflict with the provisions of this Chapter. The Executive Director shall adopt rules describing the emergency powers and the situations in which the emergency powers will be exercised.

(b) Nothing in this Chapter shall grant authority to the State Board of Elections to alter, amend, correct, impose, or substitute any plan apportioning or redistricting State legislative or congressional districts other than a plan imposed by a court under G.S. 120-2.4 or a plan enacted by the General Assembly.

(c) Nothing in this Chapter shall grant authority to the State Board of Elections to alter, amend, correct, impose, or substitute any plan apportioning or redistricting districts for a unit of local government other than a plan imposed by a court, a plan enacted by the General Assembly, or a plan adopted by the appropriate unit of local government under statutory or local act authority.

(d) Under no circumstances shall the Executive Director or the State Board of Elections have the authority to do any of the following:

    (1) Deliver absentee ballots to an eligible voter who did not submit a valid written request form for absentee ballots as provided in G.S. 163-230.1 and G.S. 163-230.2.

    (2) Order an election to be conducted using all mail-in absentee ballots.

History.
1999-455, s. 23; 2001-319, s. 11; 2011-183, s. 110; 2016-125, 4th Ex. Sess., s. 20(d); 2017-6, s. 3; 2018-146, s. 3.1(a), (b); 2020-17, s. 6

DIVISION 05.
NOMINATION OF CANDIDATES

ARTICLE 10
PRIMARY ELECTIONS

§ 163-105. Payment of expense of conducting primary elections

The expense of printing and distributing the poll and registration books and blanks to be furnished by the State, and the per diem and expenses of the State Board of Elections while engaged in the discharge of primary election duties imposed by law upon that Board, shall be paid by the State.

The expenses of printing and distributing ballots pursuant to G.S. 163-165.3 and the per diem (or salary) and expenses of the county board of elections and the chief judges and judges of election, while engaged in the discharge of primary election duties imposed by law upon them, shall be paid by the counties.

History.
1915, c. 101, s. 7; 1917, c. 218; C.S., s. 6026; 1927, c. 260, s. 21; 1933, c. 165, s. 14; 1967, c. 775, s. 1; 1985, c. 563, s. 1; 1993 (Reg. Sess., 1994), c. 762, s. 30; 2017-6, s. 3; 2018-146, s. 3.1(a), (b); 2020-69, s. 5.5

DIVISION 06.
CONDUCT OF PRIMARIES AND ELECTIONS

ARTICLE 12A
PRECINCT BOUNDARIES

§ 163-132.5G. Voting data maintained by precinct

(a) Each county board of elections shall maintain voting data by voting precinct so that precinct returns for each item on the ballot shall include the votes cast by all residents of that voting precinct who voted, regardless of where the voter voted. The county board shall not be required to report returns by voting precinct for voters who voted other than at the voting precinct associated with that voter's voter registration until 30 days after the election. In reporting returns, the county board shall not compromise the secrecy of an individual's ballot. In reporting returns, the county board shall report, by precinct for each item on the ballot, the number of voters who did not select a choice for that item on the ballot and the number of voters who selected more choices than available for that item on the ballot.

(b) The 30-day deadline for reporting returns by voting precinct does not relieve the county board of the duty to report all returns as soon as practicable after the election according to other categories specified by the State Board.

(c) The State Board shall adopt rules for the enforcement of this section.

(d) If a county board of elections does not comply with the requirements of this section, the State Board shall direct the chair of the county board of elections to appear and explain the delay at the next official meeting of the State Board.

History.
2001-466, s. 2; 2003-183, s. 1; 2005-323, s. 1(e); 2007-391, s. 6(c); 2008-187, s. 33(b); 2016-109, s. 9(a); 2017-6, s. 3; 2018-146, s. 3.1(a), (b); 2020-17, s. 10.5

ARTICLE 14A
VOTING

PART 2
BALLOTS AND VOTING SYSTEMS

§ 163-165.9A. Voting systems: requirements for voting systems vendors; penalties

(a) **Duties of Vendor.** -- Every vendor that has a contract to provide a voting system in North Carolina shall do all of the following:

(1) The vendor shall place in escrow with an independent escrow agent approved by the State Board of Elections all software that is relevant to functionality, setup, configuration, and operation of the voting system, including, but not limited to, a complete copy of the source and executable code, build scripts, object libraries, application program interfaces, and complete documentation of all aspects of the system including, but not limited to, compiling instructions, design documentation, technical documentation, user documentation, hardware and software specifications, drawings, records, and data. The State Board of Elections may require in its request for proposal that additional items be escrowed, and if any vendor that agrees in a contract to escrow additional

items, those items shall be subject to the provisions of this section. The documentation shall include a list of programmers responsible for creating the software and a sworn affidavit that the source code includes all relevant program statements in low-level and high-level languages.

(2) The vendor shall notify the State Board of Elections of any change in any item required to be escrowed by subdivision (1) of this subsection.

(3) The chief executive officer of the vendor shall sign a sworn affidavit that the source code and other material in escrow is the same being used in its voting systems in this State. The chief executive officer shall ensure that the statement is true on a continuing basis.

(4) The vendor shall promptly notify the State Board of Elections and the county board of elections of any county using its voting system of any decertification of the same system in any state, of any defect in the same system known to have occurred anywhere, and of any relevant defect known to have occurred in similar systems.

(5) The vendor shall maintain an office in North Carolina with staff to service the contract.

(b) **Penalties.** -- Willful violation of any of the duties in subsection (a) of this section is a Class G felony. Substitution of source code into an operating voting system without notification as provided by subdivision (a)(2) of this section is a Class I felony. In addition to any other applicable penalties, violations of this section are subject to a civil penalty to be assessed by the State Board of Elections in its discretion in an amount of up to one hundred thousand dollars ($ 100,000) per violation. A civil penalty assessed under this section shall be subject to the provisions of G.S. 163-278.34(e).

(c) **Definitions.** -- For the purposes of this section, the term "voting system" shall include an electronic poll book or a ballot duplication system.

History.
2005-323, s. 2(a); 2017-6, s. 3; 2018-13, s. 3.7(b); 2018-146, s. 3.1(a), (b)

PART 3
PROCEDURES AT THE VOTING PLACE

§ 163-166.11. Provisional voting requirements

If an individual seeking to vote claims to be a registered voter in a jurisdiction as provided in G.S. 163-82.1 and though eligible to vote in the election does not appear on the official list of eligible registered voters in the voting place, that individual may cast a provisional official ballot as follows:

(1) An election official at the voting place shall notify the individual that the individual may cast a provisional official ballot in that election.

(2) The individual may cast a provisional official ballot at that voting place upon executing a written affirmation before an election official at the voting place, stating that the individual is a registered voter in the jurisdiction as provided in G.S. 163-82.1 in which the individual seeks to vote and is eligible to vote in that election.

(3) A voter who has moved within the county more than 30 days before election day but has not reported the move to the board of elections shall not be required on that account to vote a provisional ballot at the one-stop site, as long as the one-stop site has available all the information necessary to determine whether a voter is registered to vote in the county and which ballot the voter is eligible to vote based on the voter's proper residence address. The voter with that kind of unreported move shall be allowed to vote the same kind of absentee ballot as other one-stop voters as provided in G.S. 163-227.2.

(4) At the time the individual casts the provisional official ballot, the election officials shall provide the individual written information stating that anyone casting a provisional official ballot can ascertain whether and to what extent the ballot was counted and, if the ballot was not counted in whole or in part, the reason it was not counted. The State Board of Elections or the county board of elections shall establish a system for so informing a provisional voter. It shall make the system available to every provisional voter without charge, and it shall build into it reasonable procedures to protect the security, confidentiality, and integrity of the voter's personal information and vote.

(5) The cast provisional official ballot and the written affirmation shall be secured by election officials at the voting place according to guidelines and procedures adopted by the State Board of Elections. At the close of the polls, election officials shall transmit the provisional official ballots cast at that voting place to the county board of elections for prompt verification according to guidelines and procedures adopted by the State Board of Elections. No later than 12:00 P.M. two days after the close of the polls, the county board of elections shall publish the number of provisional ballots

cast on election day, cast by one-stop absentee voting, cast by mail-in absentee ballots received as of election day, and cast by military and overseas absentee ballots cast under Article 21A of this Chapter and received as of election day.

History.
2003-226, s. 15; 2005-2, s. 4; 2005-428, s. 6(b); 2013-381, s. 49.3; 2014-111, s. 12(b); 2017-6, s. 3; 2018-146, s. 3.1(a), (b); 2020-17, s. 4.5(b)

§ 163-166.16. Requirement for photo identification to vote in person

(a) **Photo Identification Required to Vote.** -- When a registered voter presents to vote in person, the registered voter shall produce any of the following forms of identification that contain a photograph of the registered voter:

(1) Any of the following that is valid and unexpired, or has been expired for one year or less:

a. A North Carolina drivers license.

b. A special identification card for nonoperators issued under G.S. 20-37.7 or other form of nontemporary identification issued by the Division of Motor Vehicles of the Department of Transportation.

c. A United States passport.

d. A North Carolina voter photo identification card of the registered voter issued pursuant to G.S. 163-82.8A.

e. Recodified as sub-subdivision (a)(2)c. of this section by Session Laws 2019-22, s. 1, effective June 3, 2019.

f. Reserved.

g. A student identification card issued by a constituent institution of The University of North Carolina, a community college, as defined in G.S. 115D-2(2), or eligible private postsecondary institution as defined in G.S. 116-280(3), provided that card is issued in accordance with G.S. 163-166.17.

h. An employee identification card issued by a state or local government entity, including a charter school, provided that card is issued in accordance with G.S. 163-166.18.

i. A drivers license or special identification card for nonoperators issued by another state, the District of Columbia, or a territory or commonwealth of the United States, but only if the voter's voter registration was within 90 days of the election.

(2) Any of the following, regardless of whether the identification contains a printed expiration or issuance date:

a. A military identification card issued by the United States government.

b. A Veterans Identification Card issued by the United States Department of Veterans Affairs for use at Veterans Administration medical facilities.

c. A tribal enrollment card issued by a State or federal recognized tribe.

d. An identification card issued by a department, agency, or entity of the United States government or this State for a government program of public assistance.

(3) Any expired form of identification allowed in this subsection presented by a registered voter having attained the age of 65 years at the time of presentation at the voting place, provided that the identification was unexpired on the registered voter's sixty-fifth birthday.

(b) **Verification of Photo Identification.** -- After presentation of the required identification described in subsection (a) of this section, the precinct officials assigned to check registration shall compare the photograph contained on the required identification with the person presenting to vote. The precinct official shall verify that the photograph is that of the person seeking to vote. If the precinct official disputes that the photograph contained on the required identification is the person presenting to vote, a challenge shall be conducted in accordance with the procedures of G.S. 163-88. A voter shall be permitted to vote unless the judges of election present unanimously agree that the photo identification presented does not bear a reasonable resemblance to that voter.

(c) **Provisional Ballot Required Without Photo Identification.** -- If the registered voter cannot produce the identification as required in subsection (a) of this section, the registered voter may cast a provisional ballot that is counted only if the registered voter brings an acceptable form of photograph identification listed in subsection (a) of this section to the county board of elections no later than the end of business on the business day prior to the canvass by the county board of elections as provided in G.S. 163-182.5. The State Board shall provide the registered voter casting a provisional ballot due to failure to provide photo identification an information sheet on the deadline to return to the county board of elections to present photo identification, and what forms of photo identification are acceptable, in order for the voter's provisional ballot to be counted.

(d) **Exceptions.** -- The following exceptions are provided for a registered voter who does not produce an acceptable form of identification as required in subsection (a):

(1) **Religious Objection.** -- If a registered voter does not produce an acceptable form of photograph identification due to a religious objection to being photographed, the registered voter may complete an affidavit under penalty of perjury at the voting place and affirm that the registered voter: (i) is the same individual who personally appears at the voting place; (ii) will cast the provisional ballot while voting in person; and (iii) has a religious objection to being photographed. Upon completion of the affidavit, the registered voter may cast a provisional ballot.

(2) **Reasonable Impediment.** -- If a registered voter does not produce an acceptable form of photograph identification because the registered voter suffers from a reasonable impediment that prevents the registered voter from presenting photograph identification, the registered voter may complete an affidavit under the penalty of perjury at the voting place and affirm that the registered voter: (i) is the same individual who personally appears at the voting place; (ii) will cast the provisional ballot while voting in person; and (iii) suffers from a reasonable impediment that prevents the registered voter from presenting photograph identification. The registered voter also shall complete a reasonable impediment declaration form provided in subsection (e) of this section, unless otherwise prohibited by state or federal law. Upon completion of the affidavit, the registered voter may cast a provisional ballot.

(3) **Natural Disaster.** -- If a registered voter does not produce an acceptable form of photograph identification due to being a victim of a natural disaster occurring within 100 days before election day that resulted in a disaster declaration by the President of the United States or the Governor of this State, the registered voter may complete an affidavit under penalty of perjury at the voting place and affirm that the registered voter: (i) is the same individual who personally appears at the voting place; (ii) will cast the provisional ballot while voting in person; and (iii) was a victim of a natural disaster occurring within 100 days before election day that resulted in a disaster declaration by the President of the United States or the Governor of this State. Upon completion of the affidavit, the registered voter may cast a provisional ballot.

(e) **Reasonable Impediment Declaration Form.** -- The State Board shall adopt a reasonable impediment declaration form that, at a minimum, includes the following as separate boxes that a registered voter may check to identify the registered voter's reasonable impediment:

(1) Inability to obtain photo identification due to:

Chapter 163

2303

a. Lack of transportation.

b. Disability or illness.

c. Lack of birth certificate or other underlying documents required.

d. Work schedule.

e. Family responsibilities.

(2) Lost or stolen photo identification.

(3) Photo identification applied for but not yet received by the registered voter voting in person.

(4) Other reasonable impediment. If the registered voter checks the "other reasonable impediment" box, a further brief written identification of the reasonable impediment shall be required, including the option to indicate that State or federal law prohibits listing the impediment.

(f) **County Board Review of Exceptions. --** If the county board of elections determines that the registered voter voted a provisional ballot only due to the inability to provide proof of identification and the required affidavit required in subsection (d) of this section is submitted, the county board of elections shall find that the provisional ballot is valid unless the county board has grounds to believe the affidavit is false.

(g) **Purpose. --** The purpose of the identification required pursuant to subsection (a) of this section is to confirm the person presenting to vote is the registered voter on the voter registration records. Any address listed on the identification is not determinative of a registered voter's residence for the purpose of voting. A registered voter's residence for the purpose of voting is determined pursuant to G.S. 163-57.

History.
2018-144, s. 1.2(a); 2018-146, s. 3.1(a); 2019-22, s. 1; 2020-17, s. 10

ARTICLE 15A
COUNTING BALLOTS, CANVASSING VOTES, HEARING PROTESTS, AND CERTIFYING RESULTS

§ 163-182.2. Initial counting of official ballots

(a) The initial counting of official ballots shall be conducted according to the following principles:

(1) Vote counting at the precinct shall occur immediately after the polls close and shall be continuous until completed.

(2) Vote counting at the precinct shall be conducted with the participation of precinct officials of all political parties then present. Vote counting at the county board of elections shall be conducted in the presence or under the supervision of board members of all political parties then present.

(3) Any member of the public wishing to witness the vote count at any level shall be allowed to do so. No witness shall interfere with the orderly counting of the official ballots. Witnesses shall not participate in the official counting of official ballots.

(4) If the county board of elections finds that an individual voting a provisional official ballot (i) was registered in the county as provided in 163-82.1, (ii) voted in the proper precinct under G.S. 163-55 and G.S. 163-57, and (iii) was otherwise eligible to vote, the provisional official ballots shall be counted by the county board of elections before the canvass. Except as provided in G.S. 163-82.15(e), if the county board finds that an individual voting a provisional official ballot (i) did not vote in the proper precinct under G.S. 163-55 and G.S. 163-57, (ii) is not registered in the county as provided in G.S. 163-82.1, or (iii) is otherwise not eligible to vote, the ballot shall not be counted. If a voter was properly registered to vote in the election by the county board, no mistake of an election official in giving the voter a ballot or in failing to comply with G.S. 163-82.15 or G.S. 163-166.11 shall serve to prevent the counting of the vote on any ballot item the voter was eligible by registration and qualified by residency to vote.

(5) Precinct officials shall provide a preliminary report of the vote counting on election day to the county board of elections as quickly as possible. The preliminary report shall be unofficial, has no binding effect upon the official county canvass to follow, and shall include the number of provisional ballots cast in that precinct.

(6) In counties that use any certified mechanical or electronic voting system, subject to the sample counts under G.S. 163-182.1 and subdivision (2) of subsection (b) of this section, and of a hand-to-eye recount under G.S. 163-182.7 and G.S. 163-182.7A, a board of elections shall rely in its canvass on the mechanical or electronic count of the vote rather than the full hand-to-eye count of the paper ballots or records. In the event of a material discrepancy between the electronic or mechanical count and a hand-to-eye count or recount, the hand-to-eye count or recount shall control, except where paper ballots or records have been lost or destroyed or where there is another reasonable basis to conclude that the hand-to-eye count is not the true count.

(b) The State Board of Elections shall promulgate rules for the initial counting of official ballots. All election officials shall be governed by those rules. In promulgating those rules, the

State Board shall adhere to the following guidelines:

(1) For each voting system used, the rules shall specify the role of precinct officials and of the county board of elections in the initial counting of official ballots.

(2) For optical scan and direct record electronic voting systems, and for any other voting systems in which ballots are counted other than on paper by hand and eye, those rules shall provide for a sample hand-to-eye count of the paper ballots of a sampling of a statewide ballot item in every county. The presidential ballot item shall be the subject of the sampling in a presidential election. If there is no statewide ballot item, the State Board shall provide a process for selecting district or local ballot items to adequately sample the electorate. The State Board shall approve in an open meeting the procedure for randomly selecting the sample precincts for each election. The random selection of precincts for any county shall be done publicly after the initial count of election returns for that county is publicly released or 24 hours after the polls close on election day, whichever is earlier. The sample chosen by the State Board shall be of one or more full precincts, full counts of mailed absentee ballots, and full counts of one or more one-stop early voting sites. The size of the sample of each category shall be chosen to produce a statistically significant result and shall be chosen after consultation with a statistician. The actual units shall be chosen at random. In the event of a material discrepancy between the electronic or mechanical count and a hand-to-eye count, the hand-to-eye count shall control, except where paper ballots have been lost or destroyed or where there is another reasonable basis to conclude that the hand-to-eye count is not the true count. If the discrepancy between the hand-to-eye count and the mechanical or electronic count is significant, a complete hand-to-eye count shall be conducted. The sample count need not be done on election night.

(3) The rules shall provide for accurate unofficial reporting of the results from the precinct to the county board of elections with reasonable speed on the night of the election.

(4) The rules shall provide for the prompt and secure transmission of official ballots from the voting place to the county board of elections.

The State Board shall direct the county boards of elections in the application of the principles and rules in individual circumstances.

History.
2001-398, s. 3; 2005-2, s. 5; 2005-323, s. 5(b); 2006-192, s. 7(b); 2006-264, s. 76(c); 2013-381, ss. 30.6, 49.4; 2014-111, s. 12(c); 2015-103, s. 6(b); 2017-6, s. 3; 2018-13, s. 3.11(b); 2018-146, s. 3.1(a), (b); 2020-17, s. 4.5(a)

DIVISION 07.
ABSENTEE VOTING

ARTICLE 20
ABSENTEE BALLOT

§ 163-226.3. Certain acts declared felonies

(a) Any person who shall, in connection with absentee voting in any election held in this State, do any of the acts or things declared in this section to be unlawful, shall be guilty of a Class I felony. It shall be unlawful:

(1) For any person except the voter's near relative or the voter's verifiable legal guardian to assist the voter to vote an absentee ballot when the voter is voting an absentee ballot other than under the procedure described in G.S. 163-227.2, 163-227.5, and 163-227.6; provided that if there is not a near relative or legal guardian available to assist the voter, the voter may request some other person to give assistance.

(2) For any person to assist a voter to vote an absentee ballot under the absentee voting procedure authorized by G.S. 163-227.2, 163-227.5, and 163-227.6 except as provided in that section.

(3) For a voter who votes an absentee ballot under the procedures authorized by G.S. 163-227.2, 163-227.5, and 163-227.6 to vote that voter's absentee ballot outside of the voting booth or private room provided to the voter for that purpose in or adjacent to the office of the county board of elections or at the additional site provided by G.S. 163-227.2, or to receive assistance except as provided in G.S. 163-227.2, 163-227.5, and 163-227.6.

(4) For any owner, manager, director, employee, or other person, other than the voter's near relative or verifiable legal guardian, to (i) make a written request pursuant to G.S. 163-230.1 or (ii) sign an application or certificate as a witness, on behalf of a registered voter, who is a patient in any hospital, clinic, nursing home or rest home in this State or for any owner, manager, director, employee, or other person other than the voter's near relative or verifiable legal guardian, to mark the voter's absentee ballot or assist such a voter in marking an absentee ballot. This subdivision does not

apply to members, employees, or volunteers of the county board of elections, if those members, employees, or volunteers are working as part of a multipartisan team trained and authorized by the county board of elections to assist voters with absentee ballots. Each county board of elections shall train and authorize such teams, pursuant to procedures which shall be adopted by the State Board of Elections. If neither the voter's near relative nor a verifiable legal guardian is available to assist the voter, and a multipartisan team is not available to assist the voter within seven calendar days of a telephonic request to the county board of elections, the voter may obtain such assistance from any person other than (i) an owner, manager, director, employee of the hospital, clinic, nursing home, or rest home in which the voter is a patient or resident; (ii) an individual who holds any elective office under the United States, this State, or any political subdivision of this State; (iii) an individual who is a candidate for nomination or election to such office; or (iv) an individual who holds any office in a State, congressional district, county, or precinct political party or organization, or who is a campaign manager or treasurer for any candidate or political party; provided that a delegate to a convention shall not be considered a party office. None of the persons listed in (i) through (iv) of this subdivision may sign the application or certificate as a witness for the patient.

(5) For any person to take into that person's possession for delivery to a voter or for return to a county board of elections the absentee ballot of any voter, provided, however, that this prohibition shall not apply to a voter's near relative or the voter's verifiable legal guardian.

(6) Except as provided in subsections (1), (2), (3) and (4) of this section, G.S. 163-231(a), and G.S. 163-227.2(e), for any voter to permit another person to assist the voter in marking that voter's absentee ballot, to be in the voter's presence when a voter votes an absentee ballot, or to observe the voter mark that voter's absentee ballot.

(b) The State Board of Elections or a county board of elections, upon receipt of a sworn affidavit from any qualified voter of the State or the county, as the case may be, attesting to first-person knowledge of any violation of subsection (a) of this section, shall transmit that affidavit to the appropriate district attorney, who shall investigate and prosecute any person violating subsection (a).

(c) For the purposes of this section, a "multipartisan team" shall consist of at least two registered voters of the county. The two political parties having the highest number of affiliated voters in the State, as reflected by the registration statistics published by the State Board on January 1 of the current year, shall each be represented by at least one team member of the party's affiliation, as recommended by the members of that political party serving on the county board of elections. If the team consists of more than two members, voters who are unaffiliated or affiliated with other political parties recognized by the State may be team members. If a county board of elections finds an insufficient number of voters available to meet this requirement, the county board of elections, upon a unanimous vote of all of its sworn members, may appoint an unaffiliated team member to serve instead of a team member representing one of the two political parties having the highest number of affiliated voters in the State.

History.
1979, c. 799, s. 4; 1983, c. 331, s. 2; 1985, c. 563, s. 4; 1987, c. 565, s. 7; c. 583, ss. 8, 10; 1995, c. 243, s. 1; 1999-455, s. 3; 2005-428, s. 5(b); 2007-391, s. 29(a); 2013-381, s. 4.6(a); 2014-111, s. 15(a); 2017-6, s. 3; 2018-144, s. 3.4(d); 2018-146, s. 3.1(a), (b); 2020-17, s. 2.5(a)

§ 163-229. Absentee ballots, applications on container-return envelopes, and instruction sheets

(a) **Absentee Ballot Form. --** In accordance with the provisions of G.S. 163-230.1, persons entitled to vote by absentee ballot shall be furnished with official ballots.

(b) **Application on Container-Return Envelope. --** In time for use not later than 60 days before a statewide general election in an even-numbered year, and not later than 50 days before a statewide primary, other general election or county bond election, the county board of elections shall print a sufficient number of envelopes in which persons casting absentee ballots may transmit their marked ballots to the county board of elections. However, in the case of municipal elections, sufficient container-return envelopes shall be made available no later than 30 days before an election. Each container-return envelope shall have printed on it an application which shall be designed and prescribed by the State Board, providing for all of the following:

(1) The voter's certification of eligibility to vote the enclosed ballot and of having voted the enclosed ballot in accordance with this Part.

(2) A space for identification of the envelope with the voter and the voter's signature.

(3) A space for the identification of the two persons witnessing the casting of the absentee ballot in accordance with G.S.

Chapter 163

163-231, those persons' signatures, and those persons' addresses.

(4) A space for the name and address of any person who, as permitted under G.S. 163-226.3(a), assisted the voter if the voter is unable to complete and sign the certification and that individual's signature.

(5) A space for approval by the county board of elections.

(6) A space to allow reporting of a change of name as provided by G.S. 163-82.16.

(7) A prominent display of the unlawful acts under G.S. 163-226.3 and G.S. 163-275, except if there is not room on the envelope, the State Board may provide for that disclosure to be made on a separate piece of paper to be included along with the container-return envelope.

(8) An area to attach additional documentation necessary to comply with the identification requirements in accordance with State Board rules, as provided in G.S. 163-230.1.

(9) A bar code or other unique identifier to allow both the county board of elections and the voter to track the ballot following return of the voted ballot to the county board of elections by the voter.

The container-return envelope shall be printed in accordance with the instructions of the State Board, which shall prohibit the display of the voter's party affiliation on the outside of the container-return envelope.

(c) **Instruction Sheets.** -- In time for use not later than 60 days before a statewide general election in an even-numbered year, and not later than 50 days before a statewide primary, other general or county bond election, the county board of elections shall prepare and print a sufficient number of sheets of instructions on how voters are to prepare absentee ballots and return them to the county board of elections. However, in the case of municipal elections, instruction sheets shall be made available no later than 30 days before an election.

History.
1929, c. 164, s. 39; 1939, c. 159, ss. 3, 4; 1943, c. 751, s. 2; 1963, c. 457, ss. 3, 4; 1965, c. 1208; 1967, c. 775, s. 1; c. 851, s. 1; c. 952, s. 5; 1973, c. 536, s. 1; 1975, c. 844, s. 13; 1977, c. 469, s. 1; 1985, c. 562, ss. 3, 4; 1985 (Reg. Sess., 1986), c. 986, s. 2; 1987, c. 485, ss. 2, 5; c. 509, s. 9; c. 583, s. 3; 1989, c. 635, s. 5; 1995 (Reg. Sess., 1996), c. 561, s. 5; 1999-455, s. 8; 2009-537, s. 4; 2013-381, s. 4.1; 2017-6, s. 3; 2018-144, s. 1.2(d); 2018-146, s. 3.1(a), (b); 2019-239, s. 1.4; 2020-17, s. 3(a)

§ 163-230.1. Simultaneous issuance of absentee ballots with application

(a) **Written Request.** -- A qualified voter who is eligible to vote by absentee ballot under G.S. 163-226, or that voter's near relative or verifiable legal guardian, shall complete a request form for an absentee application and absentee ballots so that the county board of elections receives that completed request form not later than 5:00 P.M. on the Tuesday before the election. That completed written request form shall be in compliance with G.S. 163-230.2. The county board of elections shall enter in the register of absentee requests, applications, and ballots issued the information required in G.S. 163-228 as soon as each item of that information becomes available. Upon receiving the completed request form, the county board of elections shall cause to be mailed to that voter a single package that includes all of the following:

(1) The official ballots the voter is entitled to vote.

(2) A container-return envelope for the ballots, printed in accordance with G.S. 163-229.

(3) An instruction sheet.

(4) A clear statement of the requirement for a photocopy of identification described in G.S. 163-166.16(a) or an affidavit as described in G.S. 163-166.16(d)(1), (d)(2), or (d)(3) with the returned ballot.

(a1) **Mailing of Application and Ballots.** -- The ballots, envelope, and instructions shall be mailed to the voter by the county board's chair, member, officer, or employee as determined by the board and entered in the register as provided by this Article.

(b) **Absence for Sickness or Physical Disability.** -- Notwithstanding the provisions of subsection (a) of this section, if a voter expects to be unable to go to the voting place to vote in person on election day because of that voter's sickness or other physical disability, that voter or that voter's near relative or verifiable legal guardian may make the request for absentee ballots in person to the board of elections of the county in which the voter is registered after 5:00 p.m. on the Tuesday before the election but not later than 5:00 p.m. on the day before the election. The county board of elections shall treat that completed request form in the same manner as a request under subsection (a) of this section but may personally deliver the application and ballots to the voter or that voter's near relative or verifiable legal guardian, and shall enter in the register of absentee requests, applications, and ballots issued the information required in G.S. 163-228 as soon as each item of that information becomes available. The county board of elections shall personally deliver to the requester in a single package:

(1) The official ballots the voter is entitled to vote.

(2) A container-return envelope for the ballots, printed in accordance with G.S. 163-229.

(3) An instruction sheet.

(4) A clear statement of the requirement for a photocopy of identification described in G.S. 163-166.16(a) or an affidavit as described in G.S. 163-166.16(d)(1), (d)(2), or (d)(3) with the returned application and voted ballots.

(c) **Delivery of Absentee Ballots and Container-Return Envelope to Applicant.** -- When the county board of elections receives a completed request form for applications and absentee ballots from the voter, or the near relative or the verifiable legal guardian of that voter, the county board shall promptly issue and transmit them to the voter in accordance with the following instructions:

(1) On the top margin of each ballot the applicant is entitled to vote, the chair, a member, officer, or employee of the board of elections shall write or type the words "Absentee Ballot No. " or an abbreviation approved by the State Board and insert in the blank space the number assigned the applicant's application in the register of absentee requests, applications, and ballots issued. That person shall not write, type, or print any other matter upon the ballots transmitted to the absentee voter. Alternatively, the board of elections may cause to be barcoded on the ballot the voter's application number, if that barcoding system is approved by the State Board.

(2) The chair, member, officer, or employee of the board of elections shall fold and place the ballots (identified in accordance with the preceding instruction) in a container-return envelope and write or type in the appropriate blanks thereon, in accordance with the terms of G.S. 163-229(b), the absentee voter's name, the absentee voter's application number, and the designation of the precinct in which the voter is registered. If the ballot is barcoded under this section, the envelope may be barcoded rather than having the actual number appear. The person placing the ballots in the envelopes shall leave the container-return envelope holding the ballots unsealed.

(3) The chair, member, officer, or employee of the board of elections shall then place the unsealed container-return envelope holding the ballots together with printed instructions for voting and returning the ballots, in an envelope addressed to the voter at the post office address stated in the request, seal the envelope, and mail it at the expense of the county board of elections: Provided, that in case of a request received after 5:00 p.m. on the Tuesday before the election under the provisions of subsection (b) of this section, in lieu of transmitting the ballots to the voter in person or by mail, the chair, member, officer, or employee of the board of elections may deliver the sealed envelope containing the instruction sheet and the container-return envelope holding the ballots to a near relative or verifiable legal guardian of the voter.

The county board of elections may receive completed written request forms for applications at any time prior to the election but shall not mail applications and ballots to the voter or issue applications and ballots in person earlier than 60 days prior to the statewide general election in an even-numbered year, or earlier than 50 days prior to any other election, except as provided in G.S. 163-227.2, 163-227.5, and 163-227.6. No election official shall issue applications for absentee ballots except in compliance with this Article.

(d) **Voter to Complete.** -- The application shall be completed and signed by the voter personally, the ballots marked, the ballots sealed in the container-return envelope, and the certificate completed as provided in G.S. 163-231.

(e) **Approval of Applications.** -- At its next official meeting after return of the completed container-return envelope with the voter's ballots, the county board of elections shall determine whether the container-return envelope has been properly executed. If the board determines that the container-return envelope has been properly executed, it shall approve the application and deposit the container-return envelope with other container-return envelopes for the envelope to be opened and the ballots counted at the same time as all other container-return envelopes and absentee ballots.

(f) **Required Meeting of County Board of Elections.** -- During the period commencing on the fifth Tuesday before an election, in which absentee ballots are authorized, the county board of elections shall hold one or more public meetings each Tuesday at 5:00 p.m. for the purpose of action on applications for absentee ballots. At these meetings, the county board of elections shall pass upon applications for absentee ballots.

If the county board of elections changes the time of holding its meetings or provides for additional meetings in accordance with the terms of this subsection, notice of the change in hour and notice of the schedule of additional meetings, if any, shall be published in a newspaper circulated in the county at least 30 days prior to the election.

At the time the county board of elections makes its decision on an application for absentee ballots, the board shall enter in the appropriate column in the register of absentee requests, applications, and ballots issued opposite the name of the applicant a notation of whether the applicant's application was "Approved" or "Disapproved".

The decision of the board on the validity of an application for absentee ballots shall be final subject only to such review as may be necessary in the event of an election contest. The county board of elections shall constitute the proper official body to pass upon the validity of all applications for absentee ballots received in the county; this function shall not be performed by the chair or any other member of the board individually.

(f1) Each container-return envelope returned to the county board with application and voted ballots under this section shall be accompanied by a photocopy of identification described in G.S. 163-166.16(a) or an affidavit as described in G.S. 163-166.16(d)(1), (d)(2), or (d)(3).

(g) **Rules.** -- The State Board, by rule or by instruction to the county board of elections, shall establish procedures to provide appropriate safeguards in the implementation of this section. The State Board shall adopt rules to provide for the forms of identification that shall be included with returned application and voted ballots. At a minimum, the rules shall include the following:

(1) Acceptable photocopies of forms of readable identification, as described in G.S. 163-166.16(a).

(2) A process for a voter without acceptable photocopies of forms of readable identification under subdivision (1) of this subsection to complete an alternative affidavit in accordance with G.S. 163-166.16(d)(1), (d)(2), or (d)(3) that includes inability to attach a physical copy of the voter's identification with the written request as a reasonable impediment to compliance with the identification requirement. If a reasonable impediment under this subdivision states inability to attach a physical copy of the voter's identification with the written request, the reasonable impediment shall include one of the following:

a. The number of the voter's North Carolina drivers license issued under Article 2 of Chapter 20 of the General Statutes, including a learner's permit or a provisional license.

b. The number of the voter's special identification card for nonoperators issued under G.S. 20-37.7.

c. The last four digits of the voter's social security number.

(h) Recodified as G.S. 163-226(f) by Session Laws 2019-239, s. 1.2(a), effective January 1, 2020, and applicable to elections conducted on or after that date.

History.
1983, c. 304, s. 1; 1985, c. 759, ss. 5.1-5.5; 1991, c. 727, s. 6.3; 1993, c. 553, s. 67; 1995, c. 243, s. 1; 1999-455, s. 10; 2001-337, s. 3; 2002-159, s. 55(m); 2009-537, s. 5; 2013-381, s. 4.2; 2017-6, s. 3; 2018-144, s. 3.4(i); 2018-146, s. 3.1(a), (b); 2019-239, s. 1.2(a), (b); 2020-17, s. 4

§ 163-230.2. Method of requesting absentee ballots

(a) **Valid Types of Written Requests.** -- A completed written request form for absentee ballots as required by G.S. 163-230.1 is valid only if it is on a form created by the State Board and signed by the voter requesting absentee ballots or that voter's near relative or verifiable legal guardian. The State Board shall make the blank request form available at its offices, online, and in each county board of elections office, and that blank request form may be reproduced. A voter may call the State Board of Elections or a county board of elections office and request that the blank request form be sent to the voter by mail, e-mail, or fax. The request form created by the State Board shall require at least the following information:

(1) The name and address of the residence of the voter.

(2) The name and address of the voter's near relative or verifiable legal guardian if that individual is making the request.

(3) The address of the voter to which the application and absentee ballots are to be mailed if different from the residence address of the voter.

(4) One of the following:

a. The number of the applicant's North Carolina drivers license issued under Article 2 of Chapter 20 of the General Statutes, including a learner's permit or a provisional license.

b. The number of the applicant's special identification card for nonoperators issued under G.S. 20-37.7.

c. The last four digits of the applicant's social security number.

(5) The voter's date of birth.

(6) The signature of the voter or of the voter's near relative or verifiable legal guardian if that individual is making the request.

(7) A clear indicator of the date the election generating the request is to be held, except for annual calendar year requests in accordance with G.S. 163-226(b).

(b) **Request to Update Voter Registration.** -- A completed request form for absentee ballots shall be deemed a request to update the official record of voter registration for that voter and shall be confirmed in writing in accordance with G.S. 163-82.14(d).

(c) **Return of Request.** -- The completed request form for absentee ballots shall be delivered to the county board of elections only by any of the following:

(1) The voter.

(2) The voter's near relative or verifiable legal guardian.

(3) A member of a multipartisan team trained and authorized by the county board of elections pursuant to G.S. 163-226.3.

(d) **Confirmation of Voter Registration.** -- Upon receiving a completed request form for absentee ballots, the county board shall confirm that voter's registration. If that voter is confirmed as a registered voter of the county, the absentee ballots and certification form shall be mailed to the voter, unless personally delivered in accordance with G.S. 163-230.1(b). If the voter's official record of voter registration conflicts with the completed request form for absentee ballots or cannot be confirmed, the voter shall be so notified. If the county board cannot resolve the differences, no application or absentee ballots shall be issued.

(e) **Invalid Types of Written Requests.** -- If a county board of elections receives a request for absentee ballots that does not comply with this subsection or subsection (a) of this section, the board shall not issue an application and ballots under G.S. 163-230.1. A request for absentee ballots is not valid if any of the following apply:

(1) The completed written request is not on a form created by the State Board.

(2) The completed written request is completed, partially or in whole, or signed by anyone other than the voter, or the voter's near relative or verifiable legal guardian. A member of a multipartisan team trained and authorized by the county board of elections pursuant to G.S. 163-226.3 may assist in completion of the request.

(3) The written request does not contain all of the information required by subsection (a) of this section.

(4) The completed written request is returned to the county board by someone other than a person listed in subsection (c) of this section, the United States Postal Service, or a designated delivery service authorized pursuant to 26 U.S.C. § 7502(f)(2).

(e1) **Assistance by Others.** -- If a voter is in need of assistance completing the written request form due to blindness, disability, or inability to read or write and there is not a near relative or legal guardian available to assist that voter, the voter may request some other person to give assistance, notwithstanding any other provision of this section. If another person gives assistance in completing the written request form, that person's name and address shall be disclosed on the written request form in addition to the information listed in subsection (a) of this section.

(f) **Rules by State Board.** -- The State Board shall adopt rules for the enforcement of this section.

History.
2002-159, s. 57(a); 2013-381, s. 4.3; 2017-6, s. 3; 2018-144, s. 1.2(e); 2018-146, s. 3.1(a), (b); 2019-239, s. 1.3(a); 2020-17, s. 5

§ 163-230.3. Online request for absentee ballots

(a) Notwithstanding G.S. 163-230.1 and G.S. 163-230.2, a qualified voter who is eligible to vote by absentee ballot under G.S. 163-226, or that voter's near relative or verifiable legal guardian, may submit a request for absentee ballots online using the procedures set forth in this section in lieu of the completed written request on a form established by the State Board. All other provisions in G.S. 163-230.1 and G.S. 163-230.2 shall apply.

(b) The State Board shall establish a secure Internet Web site to permit individuals described in subsection (a) of this section to submit an online request for absentee ballots. The Internet Web site must be able to track the IP address of anyone who accesses the Web site. The Web site must require that the voter or the voter's near relative or verifiable legal guardian provide all of the following information:

(1) All information required for a valid written request for absentee ballots in G.S. 163-230.2.

(2) An electronic signature, as defined in G.S. 66-312 of the Uniform Electronic Transaction Act, of the voter, or the voter's near relative or verifiable legal guardian, if requesting on the voter's behalf.

(c) Upon receipt of an online request for absentee ballots, the State Board shall submit the request to the county board of elections in which the voter resides. The county board of elections shall process the online request in the same manner as processing a completed written request for absentee ballots submitted under G.S. 163-230.1.

History.
2020-17, s. 7(a)

§ 163-234. Counting absentee ballots by county board of elections

All absentee ballots returned to the county board of elections in the container-return envelopes shall be retained by the board to be counted by the county board of elections as follows:

(1) Only those absentee ballots returned to the county board of elections no later than 5:00 p.m. on the day before election day in a properly executed container-return envelope or absentee ballots received pursuant to G.S. 163-231(b)(2)b. or c. shall be

counted, except to the extent federal law requires otherwise.

(2) The county board of elections shall meet at 5:00 p.m. on election day in the board office or other public location in the county courthouse for the purpose of counting all absentee ballots except those which have been challenged before 5:00 p.m. on election day and those received pursuant to G.S. 163-231(b)(2)b. or c. Any elector of the county shall be permitted to attend the meeting and allowed to observe the counting process, so long as the elector does not in any manner interfere with the election officials in the discharge of their duties.

The county board of elections may begin counting absentee ballots issued under Article 21A of this Chapter between the hours of 9:00 a.m. and 5:00 p.m. and may begin counting all absentee ballots between the hours of 2:00 p.m. and 5:00 p.m. upon the adoption of a resolution at least two weeks prior to the election in which the hour and place of counting absentee ballots shall be stated. The resolution also may provide for an additional meeting following the day of the election and prior to the day of canvass to count absentee ballots received pursuant to G.S. 163-231(b)(2)b. or c. as provided in subdivision (11) of this section. A copy of the resolution shall be published once a week for two weeks prior to the election, in a newspaper having general circulation in the county. Notice may additionally be made on a radio or television station or both, but the notice shall be in addition to the newspaper and other required notice. The count shall be continuous until completed and the members shall not separate or leave the counting place except for unavoidable necessity, except that if the count has been completed prior to the time the polls close, it shall be suspended until that time pending receipt of any additional ballots. Nothing in this section prohibits a county board of elections from taking preparatory steps for the count earlier than the times specified in this section, as long as the preparatory steps do not reveal to any individual not engaged in the actual count election results before the times specified in this subdivision for the count to begin. By way of illustration and not limitation, a preparatory step for the count would be the entry of tally cards from direct record electronic voting units into a computer for processing. The board shall not announce the result of the count before 7:30 p.m.

(3) Notwithstanding subdivision (2) of this section, a county board of elections may, at each meeting at which it approves absentee ballot applications pursuant to G.S. 163-230.1(e) and (f), remove those ballots from their envelopes and have them read by an optical scanning machine, without printing the totals on the scanner. The board shall complete the counting of these ballots at the times provided in subdivision (2) of this section. The State Board of Elections shall provide instructions to county boards of elections for executing this procedure, and the instructions shall be designed to ensure the accuracy of the count, the participation of board members of both parties, and the secrecy of the results before election day. This subdivision applies only in counties that use optical scan devices to count absentee ballots.

(4) The counting of absentee ballots shall not commence until a majority and at least one board member of each political party represented on the board is present and that fact is publicly declared and entered in the official minutes of the county board.

(5) The county board of elections may employ such assistants as deemed necessary to count the absentee ballots, but each board member present shall be responsible for and observe and supervise the opening and tallying of the ballots.

(6) As each ballot envelope is opened, the board shall cause to be entered into a pollbook designated "Pollbook of Absentee Voters" the name of the absentee voter, or if the pollbook is computer-generated, the board shall check off the name. Preserving secrecy, the ballots shall be placed in the appropriate ballot boxes, at least one of which shall be provided for each type of ballot. The "Pollbook of Absentee Voters" shall also contain the names of all persons who voted under G.S. 163-227.2, 163-227.5, and 163-227.6, but those names may be printed by computer for inclusion in the pollbook.

After all ballots have been placed in the boxes, the counting process shall begin.

If one-stop ballots under G.S. 163-227.2, 163-227.5, and 163-227.6 are counted electronically, that count shall commence at the time the polls close. If one-stop ballots are paper ballots counted manually, that count shall commence at the same time as other absentee ballots are counted.

If a challenge transmitted to the board on canvass day by a chief judge is sustained, the ballots challenged and sustained shall be withdrawn from the appropriate boxes, as provided in G.S. 163-89(e).

As soon as the absentee ballots have been counted and the names of the absentee voters entered in the pollbook as required in this subdivision, the board members and assistants employed to count the absentee ballots shall each sign the pollbook immediately beneath the last absentee voter's name entered in the pollbook. The county board of elections is responsible for the safekeeping of the pollbook of absentee voters.

(7) Upon completion of the counting process the board members shall cause the results of the tally to be entered on the absentee abstract prescribed by the State Board of Elections. The abstract shall be signed by the members of the board in attendance and the original mailed immediately to the State Board of Elections. The county board of elections may have a separate count on the abstract for one-stop absentee ballots under G.S. 163-227.2, 163-227.5, and 163-227.6.

(8) One copy of the absentee abstract shall be retained by the county board of elections and the totals appearing on the absentee abstract shall be added to the final totals of all votes cast in the county for each office as determined on the official canvass.

(9) In the event a political party does not have a member of the county board of elections present at the meeting to count absentee ballots due to illness or other cause of the member, the counting shall not commence until the county party chairman of the absent member, or a member of the party's county executive committee, is in attendance. The person shall act as an official witness to the counting and shall sign the absentee ballot abstract as an "observer".

(10) The county board of elections shall retain all container-return envelopes and absentee ballots, in a safe place, for at least four months, and longer if any contest is pending concerning the validity of any ballot.

(11) The county board of elections shall meet after election day and prior to the date of canvass to determine whether the container-return envelopes for absentee ballots received pursuant to G.S. 163-231(b)(2)b. or c. have been properly executed. The county board of elections shall comply with the requirements of G.S. 163-230.1 for approval of applications. Any absentee ballots received pursuant to G.S. 163-231(b)(2)b. or c. shall be counted by the county board of elections on the day of canvass. The county board of elections may also meet following the day of the election and prior to the day of canvass to count absentee ballots received pursuant to G.S. 163-231(b)(2)b. or c. upon the adoption of a resolution pursuant to subdivision (2) of this section. The county board of elections shall comply with all other requirements of this section for the counting of these absentee ballots.

History.
1939, c. 159, ss. 8, 9; 1945, c. 758, s. 8; 1953, c. 1114; 1963, c. 547, s. 8; 1967, c. 775, s. 1; c. 851, s. 2; 1973, c. 536, s. 1; 1975, c. 798, s. 3; 1977, c. 469, s. 1; c. 626, s. 1; 1989, c. 93, s. 7; 1993 (Reg. Sess., 1994), c. 762, s. 55; 1995, c. 243, s. 1; 1999-455, s. 14; 2005-159, s. 1; 2006-262, s. 1; 2009-537, s. 8(d); 2011-182, s. 7; 2017-6, s. 3; 2018-144, s. 3.4(k); 2018-146, s. 3.1(a), (b); 2020-69, s. 5.6

§ 163-237. Certain violations of absentee ballot law made criminal offenses

(a) **False Statements under Oath Made Class 1 Misdemeanor.** -- If any person shall willfully and falsely make any affidavit or statement, under oath, which affidavit or statement under oath, is required to be made by the provisions of this Article, that person shall be guilty of a Class 1 misdemeanor.

(b) **False Statements Not under Oath Made Class 1 Misdemeanor.** -- Except as provided by G.S. 163-275(16), if any person, for the purpose of obtaining or voting any official ballot under the provisions of this Article, shall willfully sign any printed or written false statement which does not purport to be under oath, or which, if it purports to be under oath, was not duly sworn to, that person shall be guilty of a Class 1 misdemeanor.

(c) **Candidate Witnessing Absentee Ballots of Nonrelative Made Class 1 Misdemeanor.** -- A person is guilty of a Class 1 misdemeanor if that person acts as a witness under G.S. 163-231(a) in any primary or election in which the person is a candidate for nomination or election, unless the voter is the candidate's near relative as defined in G.S. 163-226(f).

(d) **Fraud in Connection with Absentee Vote; Forgery.** -- Any person attempting to aid and abet fraud in connection with any absentee vote cast or to be cast, under the provisions of this Article, shall be guilty of a misdemeanor. Attempting to vote by fraudulently signing the name of a regularly qualified voter is a Class G felony.

(d1) **Sell or Attempt to Sell Completed Absentee Ballot.** -- Any person who sells or attempts to sell, or purchases or agrees to purchase, a completed written request, a completed application for absentee ballots, or voted absentee ballots, shall be guilty of a Class I felony.

(d2) **Destruction of Absentee Ballot.** -- Any person who intentionally, with the intent of obstructing a vote by a registered voter, fails to deliver or intentionally destroys a completed written request, a completed application for absentee ballots, or voted absentee ballots, shall be guilty of a Class G felony.

(d3) **Copies or Retention of Identifying Information.** -- Any person, other than the voter or near relative or verifiable legal guardian of that voter, who copies or otherwise retains the request for absentee ballots, a completed application for absentee ballots, or any identifying information, as defined in G.S. 14-113.20, disclosed in a request or application, shall be guilty of a Class G felony.

(d4) **Compensation Based on Requests.** -- Any person who compensates another, or who accepts compensation, based on the number of returned written requests for absentee ballots under G.S. 163-230.2, shall be guilty of a Class I felony.

(d5) **Intent to Unlawfully Influence.** -- Any person who commits, attempts to commit, or conspires to commit a crime identified in G.S. 163-82.6(b), 163-226.3(a), 163-274, 163-275, or this section with the intent to unlawfully influence or interfere with a primary or election, or to otherwise unlawfully gain, shall be guilty of a Class F felony.

(d6) **Disclosure of Register of Absentee Ballot Requests.** -- Notwithstanding G.S. 132-3(a), any person who steals, releases, or possesses the official register of absentee requests for mail-in absentee ballots as provided in G.S. 163-228 prior to the opening of the voting place in accordance with G.S. 163-166.01, for a purpose other than the conduct of business at the county board of elections, shall be guilty of a Class G felony.

(d7) **Sending of Unrequested Absentee Ballot.** -- Any member serving on the State Board or on any county board of elections, or any employee of the State Board or a county board of elections, who knowingly sends or delivers an absentee ballot to any person who has not requested an absentee ballot in accordance with the requirements of Chapter 163 of the General Statutes shall be guilty of a Class I felony.

(e) **Violations Not Otherwise Provided for Made Class 1 Misdemeanors.** -- If any person shall willfully violate any of the provisions of this Article, or willfully fail to comply with any of the provisions thereof, for which no other punishment is herein provided, that person shall be guilty of a Class 1 misdemeanor.

History.
1929, c. 164, s. 40; 1939, c. 159, ss. 12, 13, 15; 1967, c. 775, s. 1; 1977, c. 469, s. 1, 1985, c. 562, s. 6; 1987, c. 565, s. 8; 1993, c. 539, ss. 1106, 1324; 1994, Ex. Sess., c. 24, s. 14(c); 1999-455, s. 22; 2014-111, s. 15(b); 2017-6, s. 3; 2018-146, s. 3.1(a), (b); 2019-239, s. 1.5(a); 2020-17, s. 8(a)

DIVISION 08.
REGULATION OF ELECTION CAMPAIGNS

ARTICLE 22
CORRUPT PRACTICES AND OTHER OFFENSES AGAINST THE ELECTIVE FRANCHISE

§ 163-273. Offenses of voters; interference with voters; penalty

(a) Any person who shall, in connection with any primary or election in this State, do any of the acts and things declared in this section to be unlawful, shall be guilty of a Class 2 misdemeanor. It shall be unlawful:

(1) For a voter, except as otherwise provided in this Chapter, to allow his ballot to be seen by any person.

(2) For a voter to take or remove, or attempt to take or remove, any ballot from the voting enclosure.

(3) For any person to interfere with, or attempt to interfere with, any voter when inside the voting enclosure.

(4) For any person to interfere with, or attempt to interfere with, any voter when marking his ballots.

(5) For any voter to remain longer than the specified time allowed by this Chapter in a voting booth, after being notified that his time has expired.

(6) For any person to endeavor to induce any voter, while within the voting enclosure, before depositing his ballots, to show how he marks or has marked his ballots.

(7) For any person to aid, or attempt to aid, any voter by means of any mechanical device, or any other means whatever, while within the voting enclosure, in marking his ballots.

(b) Election officers shall cause any person committing any of the offenses set forth in subsection (a) of this section to be arrested and shall cause charges to be preferred against the person so offending in a court of competent jurisdiction.

History.
1929, c. 164, s. 29; 1967, c. 775, s. 1; 1987, c. 565, s. 12; 1993, c. 539, s. 1111; 1994, Ex. Sess., c. 24, s. 14(c); 2017-6, s. 3; 2018-146, s. 3.1(a), (b)

ARTICLE 22A
REGULATING CONTRIBUTIONS AND EXPENDITURES IN POLITICAL CAMPAIGNS

PART 1
IN GENERAL

§ 163-278.8A. Campaign sales by political party executive committees

(a) Exempt Purchase Price Not Treated as "Contribution." -- Notwithstanding the provisions of G.S. 163-278.6(13), the purchase price of goods or services sold by a political party executive committee or affiliated party committee as provided in subsection (b) of this section shall not be treated as a "contribution" for purposes of account-keeping under G.S. 163-278.8, for purposes of the reporting of contributions under G.S. 163-278.11, or for the purpose of the limit on contributions under G.S. 163-278.13. The treasurer is not required to obtain, maintain, or report the name or other identifying information of the purchaser of the goods or services, as long as the requirements of subsection (b) of this section are satisfied. However, the proceeds from the sales of those goods and services shall be treated as contributions for other purposes, and expenditures of those proceeds shall be reported as expenditures under this Article.

(b) **Exempt Purchase Price.** -- A purchase price for goods or services sold by a political party executive committee or affiliated party committee qualifies for the exemption provided in subsection (a) of this section as long as the sale of the goods or services adheres to a plan that the treasurer has submitted to and that has been approved in writing by the Executive Director of the State Board of Elections. The Executive Director shall approve the treasurer's plan upon and only upon finding that all the following requirements are satisfied:

(1) That the price to be charged for the goods or services is reasonably close to the market price for the goods or services.

(2) That the total amount to be raised from sales under all plans by the committee does not exceed twenty thousand dollars ($ 20,000) per election cycle.

(3) That no purchaser makes total purchases under the plan that exceed fifty dollars ($ 50.00).

(4) That the treasurer include in the report under G.S. 163-278.11, covering the relevant time period, all of the following:

a. A description of the plan.

b. The amount raised from sales under the plan.

c. The number of purchases made.

(5) That the treasurer shall include in the appropriate report under G.S. 163-278.11 any in-kind contribution made to the political party in providing the goods or services sold under the plan and that no

in-kind contribution accepted as part of the plan violates any provision of this Article.

The Executive Director may require a format for submission of a plan, but that format shall not place undue paperwork burdens upon the treasurer. As used in this subdivision, the term "election cycle" has the same meaning as in G.S. 163-278.6(32).

History.
2008-150, s. 8(a); 2015-258, s. 3(d); 2017-6, s. 3; 2018-146, s. 3.1(a), (b); 2020-84, s. 1(a)

DIVISION 09.
MUNICIPAL ELECTIONS

ARTICLE 24
CONDUCT OF MUNICIPAL ELECTIONS

§ 163-302. Absentee voting

(a) In any municipal election, including a primary or general election or referendum, absentee voting may, upon resolution of the municipal governing body, be permitted. Such resolution must be adopted no later than 60 days prior to an election in order to be effective for that election. Any such resolution shall remain effective for all future elections unless repealed no later than 60 days before an election. A copy of all resolutions adopted under this section shall be filed with the State Board of Elections and the county board of elections conducting the election within 10 days of passage in order to be effective. In addition, absentee voting shall be allowed in any referendum on incorporation of a municipality.

(b) *(Effective until March 9, 2022)* The provisions of Articles 20 and 21 of this Chapter shall apply to absentee voting in municipal elections, special district elections, and other elections for an area less than an entire county other than elections for the General Assembly, except that the earliest date by which absentee ballots shall be required to be available for absentee voting in such elections shall be 30 days prior to the primary or election or as quickly following the filing deadline specified in G.S. 163-291(2) or G.S. 163-294(c) as the county board of elections is able to secure the official ballots. In elections on incorporation of a municipality not held at the same time as another election in the same area, the county board of elections shall adopt a special schedule of meetings of the county board of elections to approve absentee ballot applications so as to reduce the cost of the process, and to further implement the last paragraph of G.S. 163-230(2)a. If no application has been received since the last meeting, no meeting shall be held of the county board of elections under such schedule unless the meeting is scheduled for another purpose. If another election is being held in the same area on the same day, or elsewhere in the county, the cost of per diem for meetings of the county board of elections to approve absentee ballots shall not be considered a cost of the election to be billed to the municipality being created.

(b) *(Effective March 9, 2022 until June 1, 2022)* The provisions of Articles 20 and 21 of this Chapter shall apply to absentee voting in municipal elections, special district elections, and other elections for an area less than an entire county other than elections for the General Assembly, except that the earliest date by which absentee ballots shall be required to be available for absentee voting in such elections shall be 30 days prior to the primary or election or as quickly following the filing deadline as the county board of elections is able to secure the official ballots. In elections on incorporation of a municipality not held at the same time as another election in the same area, the county board of elections shall adopt a special schedule of meetings of the county board of elections to approve absentee ballot applications so as to reduce the cost of the process, and to further implement the last paragraph of G.S. 163-230(2)a. If no application has been received since the last meeting, no meeting shall be held of the county board of elections under such schedule unless the meeting is scheduled for another purpose. If another election is being held in the same area on the same day, or elsewhere in the county, the cost of per diem for meetings of the county board of elections to approve absentee ballots shall not be considered a cost of the election to be billed to the municipality being created.

(b) *(Effective June 1, 2022)* The provisions of Articles 20 and 21 of this Chapter shall apply to absentee voting in municipal elections, special district elections, and other elections for an area less than an entire county other than elections for the General Assembly, except that the earliest date by which absentee ballots shall be required to be available for absentee voting in such elections shall be 30 days prior to the primary or election or as quickly following the filing deadline specified in G.S. 163-291(2) or G.S. 163-294(c) as the county board of elections is able to secure the official ballots. In elections on incorporation of a municipality not held at the same time as another election in the same area, the county board of elections shall adopt a special schedule of meetings of the county board of elections to approve absentee ballot applications so as to reduce the cost of the process, and to further implement the last paragraph of G.S. 163-230(2) a. If no application has been received since the last meeting, no meeting shall be held of the county board of elections under such schedule unless the meeting is scheduled for another purpose. If another election is being held in the same area on the same day, or elsewhere in the county, the cost of per diem for meetings of the county board of elections to approve absentee ballots shall not be considered a cost of the election to be billed to the municipality being created.

History.

1971, c. 835, s. 1; 1975, c. 370, s. 1; c. 836; 1977, c. 475, s. 1; 1983, c. 324, s. 6; 1991 (Reg. Sess., 1992), c. 933, s. 1; 2014-111, s. 10; 2017-6, s. 3; 2018-146, s. 3.1(a), (b); 2021-56, s. 1.5(c)

§§ 163-1 through 163-335

Recodified as Subchapter III of Chapter 163A, by Session Laws 2017-6, s. 3, effective May 1, 2017.

CHAPTER 163A
ELECTIONS AND ETHICS ENFORCEMENT ACT

DIVISION 03.
ELECTION AND ELECTION LAWS

ARTICLE 20
CONDUCT OF PRIMARIES AND ELECTIONS

PART 3
VOTING

SUBPART 2
BALLOTS AND VOTING SYSTEMS

§ 163A-1118. Voting systems: requirements for voting systems vendors; penalties

(a) **Duties of Vendor.** -- Every vendor that has a contract to provide a voting system in North Carolina shall do all of the following:

(1) The vendor shall place in escrow with an independent escrow agent approved by the State Board all software that is relevant to functionality, setup, configuration, and operation of the voting system, including, but not limited to, a complete copy of the source and executable code, build scripts, object libraries, application program interfaces, and complete documentation of all aspects of the system including, but not limited to, compiling instructions, design documentation, technical documentation, user documentation, hardware and software specifications, drawings, records, and data. The State Board may require in its request for proposal that additional items be escrowed, and if any vendor that agrees in a contract to escrow additional items, those items shall be subject to the provisions of this section. The documentation shall include a list of programmers responsible for creating the software and a sworn affidavit that the source code includes all relevant program statements in low-level and high-level languages.

(2) The vendor shall notify the State Board of any change in any item required to be escrowed by subdivision (1) of this subsection.

(3) The chief executive officer of the vendor shall sign a sworn affidavit that the source code and other material in escrow is the same being used in its voting systems in this State. The chief executive officer shall ensure that the statement is true on a continuing basis.

(4) The vendor shall promptly notify the State Board and the county board of elections of any county using its voting system of any decertification of the same system in any state, of any defect in the same system known to have occurred anywhere, and of any relevant defect known to have occurred in similar systems.

(5) The vendor shall maintain an office in North Carolina with staff to service the contract.

(b) **Penalties.** -- Willful violation of any of the duties in subsection (a) of this section is a Class G felony. Substitution of source code into an operating voting system without notification as provided by subdivision (a)(2) of this section is a Class I felony. In addition to any other applicable penalties, violations of this section are subject to a civil penalty to be assessed by the State Board in its discretion in an amount of up to one hundred thousand dollars ($ 100,000) per violation. A civil penalty assessed under this section shall be subject to the provisions of G.S. 163A-1451(e).

(c) **Definitions.** -- For the purposes of this section, the term "voting system" shall include an electronic poll book or a ballot duplication system.

History.
2005-323, s. 2(a); 2017-6, s. 3; 2018-13, s. 3.7(b).

ARTICLE 21
ABSENTEE VOTING

PART 1
ABSENTEE BALLOT

§ 163A-1317. Certain violations of absentee ballot law made criminal offenses

(a) **False Statements under Oath Made Class 2 Misdemeanor.** -- If any person shall willfully and falsely make any affidavit or statement, under oath, which affidavit or statement under oath, is required to be made by the provisions of this Part, he shall be guilty of a Class 2 misdemeanor.

(b) **False Statements Not under Oath Made Class 2 Misdemeanor.** -- Except as provided by G.S. 163A-1389(16), if any person, for the purpose of obtaining or voting any official ballot under the provisions of this Part, shall willfully sign any printed or written false statement which does not purport to be under oath, or which, if it purports to be under oath, was not duly sworn to, he shall be guilty of a Class 2 misdemeanor.

(c) **Candidate Witnessing Absentee Ballots of Nonrelative Made Class 2 Misdemeanor.** -- A person is guilty of a Class 2 misdemeanor if that person acts as a witness under G.S. 163A-1310(a) in any primary or election in which the person is a candidate for nomination or election, unless the voter is the candidate's near relative as defined in G.S. 163A-1308(h).

(d) **Fraud in Connection with Absentee Vote; Forgery.** -- Any person attempting to aid and abet fraud in connection with any absentee vote cast or to be cast, under the provisions of this Part, shall be guilty of a misdemeanor. Attempting to vote by fraudulently signing the name of a regularly qualified voter is a Class I felony.

(e) **Violations Not Otherwise Provided for Made Class 2 Misdemeanors.** -- If any person shall willfully violate any of the provisions of this Part, or willfully fail to comply with any of the provisions thereof, for which no other punishment is herein provided, he shall be guilty of a Class 2 misdemeanor.

History.
1929, c. 164, s. 40; 1939, c. 159, ss. 12, 13, 15; 1967, c. 775, s. 1; 1977, c. 469, s. 1, 1985, c. 562, s. 6; 1987, c. 565, s. 8; 1993, c. 539, ss. 1106, 1324; 1994, Ex. Sess., c. 24, s. 14(c); 1999-455, s. 22; 2014-111, s. 15(b); 2017-6, s. 3.

CHAPTER 166A
NORTH CAROLINA EMERGENCY MANAGEMENT ACT

ARTICLE 1A
NORTH CAROLINA EMERGENCY MANAGEMENT ACT

PART 5
ADDITIONAL POWERS DURING STATES OF EMERGENCY

§ 166A-19.30. Additional powers of the Governor during state of emergency

(a) In addition to any other powers conferred upon the Governor by law, during a gubernatorially or legislatively declared state of emergency, the Governor shall have the following powers:

(1) To utilize all available State resources as reasonably necessary to cope with an emergency, including the transfer and direction of personnel or functions of State agencies or units thereof for the purpose of performing or facilitating emergency services.

(2) To take such action and give such directions to State and local law enforcement officers and agencies as may be reasonable and necessary for the purpose of securing compliance with the provisions of this Article and with the orders, rules, and regulations made pursuant thereto.

(3) To take steps to assure that measures, including the installation of public utilities, are taken when necessary to qualify for temporary housing assistance from the federal government when that assistance is required to protect the public health, welfare, and safety.

(4) Subject to the provisions of the State Constitution to relieve any public official having administrative responsibilities under this Article of such responsibilities for willful failure to obey an order, rule, or regulation adopted pursuant to this Article.

(5) Through issuance of an executive order to waive requirements for an environmental document or permit issued under Articles 1, 4, and 7 of Chapter 113A of the General Statutes for the repair, protection, safety enhancement, or replacement of a component of the State highway system that provides the sole road access to an incorporated municipality or an unincorporated inhabited area bordering the Atlantic Ocean or any coastal sound where bridge or road conditions as a result of the events leading to the declaration of the state of emergency pose a substantial risk to public health, safety, or welfare. The executive order shall list the duration of the waiver and the activities to which the waiver applies. For purposes of this subdivision, "coastal sound" shall have the definition set forth in G.S. 113A-103, and "replacement" shall not be interpreted to exclude a replacement that increases size or capacity or that is located in a different location than the component that is replaced.

(b) During a gubernatorially or legislatively declared state of emergency, with the concurrence of the Council of State, the Governor has the following powers:

(1) To direct and compel the evacuation of all or part of the population from any stricken or threatened area within the State, to prescribe routes, modes of transportation, and destinations in connection with evacuation; and to control ingress and egress of an emergency area, the movement of persons within the area, and the occupancy of premises therein.

(2) To establish a system of economic controls over all resources, materials, and services to include food, clothing, shelter, fuel, rents, and wages, including the administration and enforcement of any rationing, price freezing, or similar federal order or regulation.

(3) To regulate and control the flow of vehicular and pedestrian traffic, the congregation of persons in public places or buildings, lights and noises of all kinds, and the maintenance, extension, and operation of public utility and transportation services and facilities.

(4) To waive a provision of any regulation or ordinance of a State agency or a political subdivision which restricts the immediate relief of human suffering.

(5) To perform and exercise such other functions, powers, and duties as are necessary to promote and secure the safety and protection of the civilian population.

(6) To appoint or remove an executive head of any State agency or institution, the executive head of which is regularly selected by a State board or commission.

a. Such an acting executive head will serve during the following:

1. The physical or mental incapacity of the regular office holder, as determined by the Governor

after such inquiry as the Governor deems appropriate.

2. The continued absence of the regular holder of the office.

3. A vacancy in the office pending selection of a new executive head.

b. An acting executive head of a State agency or institution appointed in accordance with this subdivision may perform any act and exercise any power which a regularly selected holder of such office could lawfully perform and exercise.

c. All powers granted to an acting executive head of a State agency or institution under this section shall expire immediately:

1. Upon the termination of the incapacity as determined by the Governor of the officer in whose stead the Governor acts;

2. Upon the return of the officer in whose stead the Governor acts; or

3. Upon the selection and qualification of a person to serve for the unexpired term, or the selection of an acting executive head of the agency or commission authorized to make such selection, and the person's qualification.

(7) To procure, by purchase, condemnation, seizure, or by other means to construct, lease, transport, store, maintain, renovate, or distribute materials and facilities for emergency management without regard to the limitation of any existing law.

(c) In addition to any other powers conferred upon the Governor by law, during a gubernatorially or legislatively declared state of emergency, if the Governor determines that local control of the emergency is insufficient to assure adequate protection for lives and property because (i) needed control cannot be imposed locally because local authorities responsible for preservation of the public peace have not enacted appropriate ordinances or issued appropriate declarations as authorized by G.S. 166A-19.31; (ii) local authorities have not taken implementing steps under such ordinances or declarations, if enacted or declared, for effectual control of the emergency that has arisen; (iii) the area in which the emergency exists has spread across local jurisdictional boundaries, and the legal control measures of the jurisdictions are conflicting or uncoordinated to the extent that efforts to protect life and property are, or unquestionably will be, severely hampered; or (iv) the scale of the emergency is so great

that it exceeds the capability of local authorities to cope with it, the Governor has the following powers:

(1) To impose by declaration prohibitions and restrictions in the emergency area. These prohibitions and restrictions may, in the Governor's discretion, as appropriate to deal with the emergency, impose any of the types of prohibitions and restrictions enumerated in G.S. 166A-19.31(b), and may amend or rescind any prohibitions and restrictions imposed by local authorities. Prohibitions and restrictions imposed pursuant to this subdivision shall take effect in accordance with the provisions of G.S. 166A-19.31(d) and shall expire upon the earliest occurrence of either of the following: (i) the prohibition or restriction is terminated by the Governor or (ii) the state of emergency is terminated.

(2) Give to all participating State and local agencies and officers such directions as may be necessary to assure coordination among them. These directions may include the designation of the officer or agency responsible for directing and controlling the participation of all public agencies and officers in the emergency. The Governor may make this designation in any manner which, in the Governor's discretion, seems most likely to be effective. Any law enforcement officer participating in the control of a state of emergency in which the Governor is exercising control under this section shall have the same power and authority as a sheriff throughout the territory to which the law enforcement officer is assigned.

(d) **Violation.** -- Any person who violates any provision of a declaration or executive order issued pursuant to this section shall be guilty of a Class 2 misdemeanor in accordance with G.S. 14-288.20A.

History.
Former G.S. 14-288.15: 1969, c. 869, s. 1; 1993, c. 539, s. 197; 1994, Ex. Sess., c. 24, s. 14(c) . Former G.S. 166A-6: 1951, c. 1016, s. 4; 1955, c. 387, s. 4; 1959, c. 284, s. 2; c. 337, s. 4; 1975, c. 734, ss. 11, 14; 1977, c. 848, s. 2; 1979, 2nd Sess., c. 1310, s. 2; 1993, c. 321, s. 181(a); 1995, c. 509, s. 125; 2001-214, s. 3; 2011-145, s. 19.1(g); 2011-183, s. 127(c); 2012-90, s. 1; 2012-12, s. 1(b); 2014-100, s. 14.7(i)

§ 166A-19.31. Power of municipalities and counties to enact ordinances to deal with states of emergency

(a) **Authority to Enact Prohibitions and Restrictions.** -- The governing body of any municipality or county may enact ordinances designed to permit the imposition of prohibitions and restrictions within the emergency area during a state of emergency declared pursuant to G.S. 166A-19.22. Authority to impose by declaration prohibitions and restrictions under this section, and to impose those prohibitions and restrictions at a particular time as appropriate, may be delegated by ordinance to the mayor of a municipality or to the chair of the board of county commissioners of a county.

(b) **Type of Prohibitions and Restrictions Authorized.** -- The ordinances authorized by this section may permit prohibitions and restrictions:

(1) Of movements of people in public places, including any of the following:

a. Imposing a curfew.

b. Directing and compelling the voluntary or mandatory evacuation of all or part of the population from any stricken or threatened area within the governing body's jurisdiction.

c. Prescribing routes, modes of transportation, and destinations in connection with evacuation.

d. Controlling ingress and egress of an emergency area, and the movement of persons within that area.

e. Providing for the closure, within the emergency area, of streets, roads, highways, bridges, public vehicular areas, or other areas ordinarily used for vehicular travel, except to the movement of emergency responders and other persons necessary for recovery from the emergency. In addition to any other notice or dissemination of information, notification of any closure of a road or public vehicular area under the authority of this sub-subdivision shall be given to the Department of Transportation as soon as practicable. The ordinance may designate the sheriff to exercise the authority granted by this sub-subdivision. G.S. 166A-19.70(c) and (d) shall apply to this sub-subdivision.

(2) Of the operation of offices, business establishments, and other places to or from which people may travel or at which they may congregate.

(3) Upon the possession, transportation, sale, purchase, and consumption of alcoholic beverages.

(4) Upon the possession, transportation, sale, purchase, storage, and use of gasoline, and dangerous weapons and substances, except that this subdivision does not authorize prohibitions or restrictions on lawfully possessed firearms or ammunition. As used in this subdivision, the term "dangerous weapons and substances" has the same meaning as it does under G.S. 14-288.1. As used in this subdivision, the term "firearm"

has the same meaning as it does under G.S. 14-409.39(2).

(5) Upon other activities or conditions the control of which may be reasonably necessary to maintain order and protect lives or property during the state of emergency.

The ordinances authorized by this section need not require or provide for the imposition of all of the types of prohibitions or restrictions, or any particular prohibition or restriction, authorized by this section during an emergency but may instead authorize the official or officials who impose those prohibitions or restrictions to determine and impose the prohibitions or restrictions deemed necessary or suitable to a particular state of emergency.

(c) **When Ordinances Take Effect.** -- Notwithstanding any other provision of law, whether general or special, relating to the promulgation or publication of ordinances by any municipality or county, upon the declaration of a state of emergency by the mayor or chair of the board of county commissioners within the municipality or the county, any ordinance enacted under the authority of this section shall take effect immediately unless the ordinance sets a later time. If the effect of this section is to cause an ordinance to go into effect sooner than it otherwise could under the law applicable to the municipality or county, the mayor or chair of the board of county commissioners, as the case may be, shall take steps to cause reports of the substance of the ordinance to be disseminated in a fashion that its substance will likely be communicated to the public in general, or to those who may be particularly affected by the ordinance if it does not affect the public generally. As soon as practicable thereafter, appropriate distribution or publication of the full text of any such ordinance shall be made.

(d) **When Prohibitions and Restrictions Take Effect.** -- All prohibitions and restrictions imposed by declaration pursuant to ordinances adopted under this section shall take effect in the emergency area immediately upon publication of the declaration unless the declaration sets a later time. Publication shall include at least (i) posting of a signed copy of the declaration conspicuously posted on the Web site of the municipality or county, if the municipality or county has a Web site, and (ii) submittal of notice and a signed copy of the declaration to the Department of Public Safety WebEOC critical incident management system. Publication may also consist of reports of the substance of the prohibitions and restrictions in the mass communications media serving the emergency area or other effective methods of disseminating the necessary information quickly. As soon as practicable, however, appropriate distribution of the full text of any declaration shall be made. This subsection shall not be governed by the provisions of G.S. 1-597.

(e) **Expiration of Prohibitions and Restrictions.** -- Prohibitions and restrictions imposed pursuant to this section shall expire upon the earliest occurrence of any of the following:

(1) The prohibition or restriction is terminated by the official or entity that imposed the prohibition or restriction.

(2) The state of emergency terminates.

(f) **Intent to Supplement Other Authority.** -- This section is intended to supplement and confirm the powers conferred by G.S. 153A-121(a), G.S. 160A-174(a), and all other general and local laws authorizing municipalities and counties to enact ordinances for the protection of the public health and safety in times of riot or other grave civil disturbance or emergency.

(g) **Previously Enacted Ordinances Remain in Effect.** -- Any ordinance of a type authorized by this section promulgated prior to October 1, 2012, if otherwise valid, continue in full force and effect without reenactment.

(h) **Violation.** -- Any person who violates any provision of an ordinance or a declaration enacted or declared pursuant to this section shall be guilty of a Class 2 misdemeanor in accordance with G.S. 14-288.20A.

History.
Former G.S. 14-288.12: 1969, c. 869, s. 1; 1981, c. 412, s. 4(4); c. 747, s. 66; 1989, c. 770, s. 2; 1993, c. 539, s. 194; 1994, Ex. Sess., c. 24, s. 14(c); 2009-146, s. 1 . Former G.S. 14-288.13: 1969, c. 869, s. 1; 1993, c. 539, s. 195; 1994, Ex. Sess., c. 24, s. 14(c) . Former G.S. 14-288.16: 1969, c. 869, s. 1. Former G.S. 14-288.17: 1969, c. 869, s. 1. 2012-12, s. 1(b); 2019-89, s. 1; 2020-83, s. 11.7

CONSTITUTION OF NORTH CAROLINA

ARTICLE I.
DECLARATION OF RIGHTS

Section 1. The equality and rights of persons

We hold it to be self-evident that all persons are created equal; that they are endowed by their Creator with certain inalienable rights; that among these are life, liberty, the enjoyment of the fruits of their own labor, and the pursuit of happiness.

History.
1969, c. 1258, s. 1

Sec. 2. Sovereignty of the people

All political power is vested in and derived from the people; all government of right originates from the people, is founded upon their will only, and is instituted solely for the good of the whole.

History.
1969, c. 1258, s. 1

Sec. 3. Internal government of the State

The people of this State have the inherent, sole, and exclusive right of regulating the internal government and police thereof, and of altering or abolishing their Constitution and form of government whenever it may be necessary to their safety and happiness; but every such right shall be exercised in pursuance of law and consistently with the Constitution of the United States.

History.
1969, c. 1258, s. 1

Sec. 4. Secession prohibited

This State shall ever remain a member of the American Union; the people thereof are part of the American Nation; there is no right on the part of this State to secede; and all attempts, from whatever source or upon whatever pretext, to dissolve this Union or to sever this Nation, shall be resisted with the whole power of the State.

History.
1969, c. 1258, s. 1

Sec. 5. Allegiance to the United States

Every citizen of this State owes paramount allegiance to the Constitution and government of the United States, and no law or ordinance of the State in contravention or subversion thereof can have any binding force.

History.
1969, c. 1258, s. 1

Sec. 6. Separation of powers

The legislative, executive, and supreme judicial powers of the State government shall be forever separate and distinct from each other.

History.
1969, c. 1258, s. 1

Sec. 7. Suspending laws

All power of suspending laws or the execution of laws by any authority, without the consent of the representatives of the people, is injurious to their rights and shall not be exercised.

History.
1969, c. 1258, s. 1

Sec. 8. Representation and taxation

The people of this State shall not be taxed or made subject to the payment of any impost or duty without the consent of themselves or their representatives in the General Assembly, freely given.

History.
1969, c. 1258, s. 1

Sec. 9. Frequent elections

For redress of grievances and for amending and strengthening the laws, elections shall be often held.

History.
1969, c. 1258, s. 1

Sec. 10. Free elections

All elections shall be free.

History.
1969, c. 1258, s. 1

Sec. 11. Property qualifications

As political rights and privileges are not dependent upon or modified by property, no property qualification shall affect the right to vote or hold office.

History.
1969, c. 1258, s. 1

Sec. 12. Right of assembly and petition

The people have a right to assemble together to consult for their common good, to instruct their representatives, and to apply to the General Assembly for redress of grievances; but secret political societies are dangerous to the liberties of a free people and shall not be tolerated.

History.
1969, c. 1258, s. 1

Sec. 13. Religious liberty

All persons have a natural and inalienable right to worship Almighty God according to the dictates of their own consciences, and no human authority shall, in any case whatever, control or interfere with the rights of conscience.

History.
1969, c. 1258, s. 1

Sec. 14. Freedom of speech and press

Freedom of speech and of the press are two of the great bulwarks of liberty and therefore shall never be restrained, but every person shall be held responsible for their abuse.

History.
1969, c. 1258, s. 1

Sec. 15. Education

The people have a right to the privilege of education, and it is the duty of the State to guard and maintain that right.

History.
1969, c. 1258, s. 1

Sec. 16. Ex post facto laws

Retrospective laws, punishing acts committed before the existence of such laws and by them only declared criminal, are oppressive, unjust, and incompatible with liberty, and therefore no ex post facto law shall be enacted. No law taxing retrospectively sales, purchases, or other acts previously done shall be enacted.

History.
1969, c. 1258, s. 1

Sec. 17. Slavery and involuntary servitude

Slavery is forever prohibited. Involuntary servitude, except as a punishment for crime whereof the parties have been adjudged guilty, is forever prohibited.

History.
1969, c. 1258, s. 1

Sec. 18. Courts shall be open

All courts shall be open; every person for an injury done him in his lands, goods, person, or reputation shall have remedy by due course of law; and right and justice shall be administered without favor, denial, or delay.

History.
1969, c. 1258, s. 1

Sec. 19. Law of the land; equal protection of the laws

No person shall be taken, imprisoned, or disseized of his freehold, liberties, or privileges, or outlawed, or exiled, or in any manner deprived of his life, liberty, or property, but by the law of the land. No person shall be denied the equal protection of the laws; nor shall any person be subjected to discrimination by the State because of race, color, religion, or national origin.

History.
1969, c. 1258, s. 1

Sec. 20. General warrants

General warrants, whereby any officer or other person may be commanded to search suspected places without evidence of the act committed, or to seize any person or persons not named, whose offense is not particularly described and supported by evidence, are dangerous to liberty and shall not be granted.

History.
1969, c. 1258, s. 1

Sec. 21. Inquiry into restraints on liberty

Every person restrained of his liberty is entitled to a remedy to inquire into the lawfulness thereof, and to remove the restraint if unlawful, and that remedy shall not be denied or delayed. The privilege of the writ of habeas corpus shall not be suspended.

History.
1969, c. 1258, s. 1

Sec. 22. Modes of prosecution

Except in misdemeanor cases initiated in the District Court Division, no person shall be put to answer any criminal charge but by indictment, presentment, or impeachment. But any person, when represented by counsel, may, under such regulations as the General Assembly shall prescribe, waive indictment in noncapital cases.

History.

1969, c. 1258, s. 1

Sec. 23. Rights of accused

In all criminal prosecutions, every person charged with crime has the right to be informed of the accusation and to confront the accusers and witnesses with other testimony, and to have counsel for defense, and not be compelled to give self-incriminating evidence, or to pay costs, jail fees, or necessary witness fees of the defense, unless found guilty.

History.

1969, c. 1258, s. 1

Sec. 24. Right of jury trial in criminal cases

No person shall be convicted of any crime but by the unanimous verdict of a jury in open court, except that a person accused of any criminal offense for which the State is not seeking a sentence of death in superior court may, in writing or on the record in the court and with the consent of the trial judge, waive jury trial, subject to procedures prescribed by the General Assembly. The General Assembly may, however, provide for other means of trial for misdemeanors, with the right of appeal for trial de novo.

History.

1969, c. 1258, s. 1; 2013-300, s. 1

Sec. 25. Right of jury trial in civil cases

In all controversies at law respecting property, the ancient mode of trial by jury is one of the best securities of the rights of the people, and shall remain sacred and inviolable.

History.

1969, c. 1258, s. 1

Sec. 26. Jury service

No person shall be excluded from jury service on account of sex, race, color, religion, or national origin.

History.

1969, c. 1258, s. 1

Sec. 27. Bail, fines, and punishments

Excessive bail shall not be required, nor excessive fines imposed, nor cruel or unusual punishments inflicted.

History.

1969, c. 1258, s. 1

Sec. 28. Imprisonment for debt

There shall be no imprisonment for debt in this State, except in cases of fraud.

History.

1969, c. 1258, s. 1

Sec. 29. Treason against the State

Treason against the State shall consist only of levying war against it or adhering to its enemies by giving them aid and comfort. No person shall be convicted of treason unless on the testimony of two witnesses to the same overt act, or on confession in open court. No conviction of treason or attainder shall work corruption of blood or forfeiture.

History.

1969, c. 1258, s. 1

Sec. 30. Militia and the right to bear arms

A well regulated militia being necessary to the security of a free State, the right of the people to keep and bear arms shall not be infringed; and, as standing armies in time of peace are dangerous to liberty, they shall not be maintained, and the military shall be kept under strict subordination to, and governed by, the civil power. Nothing herein shall justify the practice of carrying concealed weapons, or prevent the General Assembly from enacting penal statutes against that practice.

History.

1969, c. 1258, s. 1

Sec. 31. Quartering of soldiers

No soldier shall in time of peace be quartered in any house without the consent of the owner, nor in time of war but in a manner prescribed by law.

History.

1969, c. 1258, s. 1

Constitution of North Carolina

Sec. 32. Exclusive emoluments

No person or set of persons is entitled to exclusive or separate emoluments or privileges from the community but in consideration of public services.

History.
1969, c. 1258, s. 1

Sec. 33. Hereditary emoluments and honors

No hereditary emoluments, privileges, or honors shall be granted or conferred in this State.

History.
1969, c. 1258, s. 1

Sec. 34. Perpetuities and monopolies

Perpetuities and monopolies are contrary to the genius of a free state and shall not be allowed.

History.
1969, c. 1258, s. 1

Sec. 35. Recurrence to fundamental principles

A frequent recurrence to fundamental principles is absolutely necessary to preserve the blessings of liberty.

History.
1969, c. 1258, s. 1

Sec. 36. Other rights of the people

The enumeration of rights in this Article shall not be construed to impair or deny others retained by the people.

History.
1969, c. 1258, s. 1

Sec. 37. Rights of victims of crime

(1) **Basic rights.** Victims of crime or acts of delinquency shall be treated with dignity and respect by the criminal justice system.

(1a) **Enumerated rights.** When the crime or act of delinquency is one against or involving the person of the victim or is equivalent to a felony property crime, the victim is entitled to the following rights:

(a) The right upon request to reasonable, accurate, and timely notice of court proceedings of the accused.

(a1) The right upon request to be present at court proceedings of the accused.

(b) The right to be reasonably heard at any court proceeding involving the plea, conviction, adjudication, sentencing, or release of the accused.

(c) The right to receive restitution in a reasonably timely manner, when ordered by the court.

(d) The right to be given information about the crime or act of delinquency, how the criminal justice system works, the rights of victims, and the availability of services for victims.

(e) The right upon request to receive information about the conviction, adjudication, or final disposition and sentence of the accused.

(f) The right upon request to receive notification of escape, release, proposed parole or pardon of the accused, or notice of a reprieve or commutation of the accused's sentence.

(g) The right to present the victim's views and concerns to the Governor or agency considering any action that could result in the release of the accused, prior to such action becoming effective.

(h) The right to reasonably confer with the prosecution.

(1b) **Enforcement of rights.** Except as otherwise provided herein, the General Assembly shall further provide, by general law, the procedure whereby a victim may assert the rights provided in this section. The victim or, if the victim is a minor, is legally incapacitated, or deceased, a family member, guardian, or legal custodian may assert the rights provided in this section. The procedure shall be by motion to the court of jurisdiction within the same criminal or juvenile proceeding giving rise to the rights. The victim, family member, guardian, or legal custodian have the right to counsel at this hearing but do not have the right to counsel provided by the State. If the matter involves an allegation that the district attorney failed to comply with the rights of a victim when obligated to so do by law, the victim must first afford the district attorney with jurisdiction over the criminal action an opportunity to resolve any issue in a timely manner.

(2) **No money damages; other claims.** Nothing in this section shall be construed as creating a claim for money damages, or any cause of action, against the State, a county, a municipality, or any of the agencies, instrumentalities, or officers and employees thereof.

(3) **No ground for relief in criminal case.** The failure or inability of any person to provide a right or service provided under this section may not be used by a defendant in a criminal case, an inmate, or any other accused as a ground for relief in any trial, appeal, postconviction litigation, habeas corpus, civil action, or

any similar criminal or civil proceeding. Nothing in this section shall be construed to provide grounds for a victim (i) to appeal any decision made in a criminal or juvenile proceeding; (ii) to challenge any verdict, sentence, or adjudication; (iii) to participate as a party in any proceeding; or (iv) to obtain confidential juvenile records.

(4) *No restriction of authority.* Nothing in this section shall be construed to restrict the power of the district attorney, or the inherent authority of the court.

(5) Implementation. The General Assembly may prescribe general laws to further define and implement this section.

History.
1995, c. 438, s. 1; 2018-110, s. 1

ARTICLE IV.
JUDICIAL

Sec. 2. General Court of Justice

The General Court of Justice shall constitute a unified judicial system for purposes of jurisdiction, operation, and administration, and shall consist of an Appellate Division, a Superior Court Division, and a District Court Division.

History.
1969, c. 1258, s. 1

Sec. 3. Judicial powers of administrative agencies

The General Assembly may vest in administrative agencies established pursuant to law such judicial powers as may be reasonably necessary as an incident to the accomplishment of the purposes for which the agencies were created. Appeals from administrative agencies shall be to the General Court of Justice.

History.
1969, c. 1258, s. 1

Sec. 4. Court for the Trial of Impeachments

The House of Representatives solely shall have the power of impeaching. The Court for the Trial of Impeachments shall be the Senate. When the Governor or Lieutenant Governor is impeached, the Chief Justice shall preside over the Court. A majority of the members shall be necessary to a quorum, and no person shall be convicted without the concurrence of two-thirds of the Senators present. Judgment upon conviction shall not extend beyond removal from and disqualification to hold office in this State, but

the party shall be liable to indictment and punishment according to law.

History.
1969, c. 1258, s. 1

Sec. 5. Appellate division

The Appellate Division of the General Court of Justice shall consist of the Supreme Court and the Court of Appeals.

History.
1969, c. 1258, s. 1

Sec. 6. Supreme Court

(1) *Membership.* The Supreme Court shall consist of a Chief Justice and six Associate Justices, but the General Assembly may increase the number of Associate Justices to not more than eight. In the event the Chief Justice is unable, on account of absence or temporary incapacity, to perform any of the duties placed upon him, the senior Associate Justice available may discharge those duties.

(2) *Sessions of the Supreme Court.* The sessions of the Supreme Court shall be held in the City of Raleigh unless otherwise provided by the General Assembly.

History.
1969, c. 1258, s. 1

Sec. 7. Court of Appeals

The structure, organization, and composition of the Court of Appeals shall be determined by the General Assembly. The Court shall have not less than five members, and may be authorized to sit in divisions, or other than en banc. Sessions of the Court shall be held at such times and places as the General Assembly may prescribe.

History.
1969, c. 1258, s. 1

Sec. 8. Retirement of Justices and Judges

The General Assembly shall provide by general law for the retirement of Justices and Judges of the General Court of Justice, and may provide for the temporary recall of any retired Justice or Judge to serve on the court or courts of the division from which he was retired. The General Assembly shall also prescribe maximum age limits for service as a Justice or Judge.

History.
1969, c. 1258, s. 1; 1971, c. 451, s. 1; 1981, c. 513, s. 1

Sec. 9. Superior Courts

(1) **Superior Court districts.** The General Assembly shall, from time to time, divide the State into a convenient number of Superior Court judicial districts and shall provide for the election of one or more Superior Court Judges for each district. Each regular Superior Court Judge shall reside in the district for which he is elected. The General Assembly may provide by general law for the selection or appointment of special or emergency Superior Court Judges not selected for a particular judicial district.

(2) **Open at all times; sessions for trial of cases.** The Superior Courts shall be open at all times for the transaction of all business except the trial of issues of fact requiring a jury. Regular trial sessions of the Superior Court shall be held at times fixed pursuant to a calendar of courts promulgated by the Supreme Court. At least two sessions for the trial of jury cases shall be held annually in each county.

(3) **Clerks.** A Clerk of the Superior Court for each county shall be elected for a term of four years by the qualified voters thereof, at the same time and places as members of the General Assembly are elected. If the office of Clerk of the Superior Court becomes vacant otherwise than by the expiration of the term, or if the people fail to elect, the senior regular resident Judge of the Superior Court serving the county shall appoint to fill the vacancy until an election can be regularly held.

History.
1969, c. 1258, s. 1

Sec. 10. District Courts

The General Assembly shall, from time to time, divide the State into a convenient number of local court districts and shall prescribe where the District Courts shall sit, but a District Court must sit in at least one place in each county. District Judges shall be elected for each district for a term of four years, in a manner prescribed by law. When more than one District Judge is authorized and elected for a district, the Chief Justice of the Supreme Court shall designate one of the judges as Chief District Judge. Every District Judge shall reside in the district for which he is elected. For each county, the senior regular resident Judge of the Superior Court serving the county shall appoint from nominations submitted by the Clerk of the Superior Court of the county, one or more Magistrates who shall be officers of the District Court. The initial term of appointment for a magistrate shall be for two years and subsequent terms shall be for four years. The number of District Judges and Magistrates shall, from time to time, be determined by the General Assembly. Vacancies in the office of District Judge shall be filled for the unexpired term in a manner prescribed by law. Vacancies in the office of Magistrate shall be filled for the unexpired term in the manner provided for original appointment to the office, unless otherwise provided by the General Assembly.

History.
1969, c. 1258, s. 1; 2004-128, s. 16

Sec. 11. Assignment of Judges

The Chief Justice of the Supreme Court, acting in accordance with rules of the Supreme Court, shall make assignments of Judges of the Superior Court and may transfer District Judges from one district to another for temporary or specialized duty. The principle of rotating Superior Court Judges among the various districts of a division is a salutary one and shall be observed. For this purpose the General Assembly may divide the State into a number of judicial divisions. Subject to the general supervision of the Chief Justice of the Supreme Court, assignment of District Judges within each local court district shall be made by the Chief District Judge.

History.
1969, c. 1258, s. 1

Sec. 12. Jurisdiction of the General Court of Justice

(1) **Supreme Court.** The Supreme Court shall have jurisdiction to review upon appeal any decision of the courts below, upon any matter of law or legal inference. The jurisdiction of the Supreme Court over "issues of fact" and "questions of fact" shall be the same exercised by it prior to the adoption of this Article, and the Court may issue any remedial writs necessary to give it general supervision and control over the proceedings of the other courts. The Supreme Court also has jurisdiction to review, when authorized by law, direct appeals from a final order or decision of the North Carolina Utilities Commission.

(2) **Court of Appeals.** The Court of Appeals shall have such appellate jurisdiction as the General Assembly may prescribe.

(3) **Superior Court.** Except as otherwise provided by the General Assembly, the Superior Court shall have original general jurisdiction throughout the State. The Clerks of the Superior Court shall have such jurisdiction and powers as the General Assembly shall prescribe by general law uniformly applicable in every county of the State.

(4) **District Courts; Magistrates.** The General Assembly shall, by general law uniformly applicable in every local court district of the

State, prescribe the jurisdiction and powers of the District Courts and Magistrates.

(5) **Waiver.** The General Assembly may by general law provide that the jurisdictional limits may be waived in civil cases.

(6) **Appeals.** The General Assembly shall by general law provide a proper system of appeals. Appeals from Magistrates shall be heard de novo, with the right of trial by jury as defined in this Constitution and the laws of this State.

History.
1969, c. 1258, s. 1; 1981, c. 803, s. 1

Sec. 13. Forms of action; rules of procedure

(1) **Forms of Action.** There shall be in this State but one form of action for the enforcement or protection of private rights or the redress of private wrongs, which shall be denominated a civil action, and in which there shall be a right to have issues of fact tried before a jury. Every action prosecuted by the people of the State as a party against a person charged with a public offense, for the punishment thereof, shall be termed a criminal action.

(2) **Rules of Procedure.** The Supreme Court shall have exclusive authority to make rules of procedure and practice for the Appellate Division. The General Assembly may make rules of procedure and practice for the Superior Court and District Court Divisions, and the General Assembly may delegate this authority to the Supreme Court. No rule of procedure or practice shall abridge substantive rights or abrogate or limit the right of trial by jury. If the General Assembly should delegate to the Supreme Court the rule-making power, the General Assembly may, nevertheless, alter, amend, or repeal any rule of procedure or practice adopted by the Supreme Court for the Superior Court or District Court Divisions.

History.
1969, c. 1258, s. 1

Sec. 14. Waiver of jury trial

In all issues of fact joined in any court, the parties in any civil case may waive the right to have the issues determined by a jury, in which case the finding of the judge upon the facts shall have the force and effect of a verdict by a jury.

History.
1969, c. 1258, s. 1

Sec. 15. Administration

The General Assembly shall provide for an administrative office of the courts to carry out the provisions of this Article.

History.
1969, c. 1258, s. 1

Sec. 16. Terms of office and election of Justices of the Supreme Court, Judges of the Court of Appeals, and Judges of the Superior Court

Justices of the Supreme Court, Judges of the Court of Appeals, and regular Judges of the Superior Court shall be elected by the qualified voters and shall hold office for terms of eight years and until their successors are elected and qualified. Justices of the Supreme Court and Judges of the Court of Appeals shall be elected by the qualified voters of the State. Regular Judges of the Superior Court may be elected by the qualified voters of the State or by the voters of their respective districts, as the General Assembly may prescribe.

History.
1969, c. 1258, s. 1

Sec. 17. Removal of Judges, Magistrates and Clerks

(1) **Removal of Judges by the General Assembly.** Any Justice or Judge of the General Court of Justice may be removed from office for mental or physical incapacity by joint resolution of two-thirds of all the members of each house of the General Assembly. Any Justice or Judge against whom the General Assembly may be about to proceed shall receive notice thereof, accompanied by a copy of the causes alleged for his removal, at least 20 days before the day on which either house of the General Assembly shall act thereon. Removal from office by the General Assembly for any other cause shall be by impeachment.

(2) **Additional method of removal of Judges.** The General Assembly shall prescribe a procedure, in addition to impeachment and address set forth in this section, for the removal of a Justice or Judge of the General Court of Justice for mental or physical incapacity interfering with the performance of his duties which is, or is likely to become, permanent, and for the censure and removal of a Justice or Judge of the General Court of Justice for wilful misconduct in office, wilful and persistent failure to perform his duties, habitual intemperance, conviction of a crime involving moral turpitude, or conduct prejudicial to the administration of justice that brings the judicial office into disrepute.

(3) **Removal of Magistrates.** The General Assembly shall provide by general law for the removal of Magistrates for misconduct or mental or physical incapacity.

(4) **Removal of Clerks.** Any Clerk of the Superior Court may be removed from office for

misconduct or mental or physical incapacity by the senior regular resident Superior Court Judge serving the county. Any Clerk against whom proceedings are instituted shall receive written notice of the charges against him at least 10 days before the hearing upon the charges. Any Clerk so removed from office shall be entitled to an appeal as provided by law.

History.

1969, c. 1258, s. 1; 1971, c. 560, s. 1

Sec. 18. District Attorney and prosecutorial districts

(1) *District Attorneys.* The General Assembly shall, from time to time, divide the State into a convenient number of prosecutorial districts, for each of which a District Attorney shall be chosen for a term of four years by the qualified voters thereof, at the same time and places as members of the General Assembly are elected. Only persons duly authorized to practice law in the courts of this State shall be eligible for election or appointment as a District Attorney. The District Attorney shall advise the officers of justice in his district, be responsible for the prosecution on behalf of the State of all criminal actions in the Superior Courts of his district, perform such duties related to appeals therefrom as the Attorney General may require, and perform such other duties as the General Assembly may prescribe.

(2) *Prosecution in District Court Division.* Criminal actions in the District Court Division shall be prosecuted in such manner as the General Assembly may prescribe by general law uniformly applicable in every local court district of the State.

History.

1969, c. 1258, s. 1; 1973, c. 394, s. 1; 1983, c. 298, s. 2

Sec. 19. Vacancies

Unless otherwise provided in this Article, all vacancies occurring in the offices provided for by this Article shall be filled by appointment of the Governor, and the appointees shall hold their places until the next election for members of the General Assembly that is held more than 60 days after the vacancy occurs, when elections shall be held to fill the offices. When the unexpired term of any of the offices named in this Article of the Constitution in which a vacancy has occurred, and in which it is herein provided that the Governor shall fill the vacancy, expires on the first day of January succeeding the next election for members of the General Assembly, the Governor shall appoint to fill that vacancy for the unexpired term of the office. If any person elected or appointed to any of these offices

shall fail to qualify, the office shall be appointed to, held, and filled as provided in case of vacancies occurring therein. All incumbents of these offices shall hold until their successors are qualified.

History.

1969, c. 1258, s. 1; 1985 (Reg. Sess., 1986), c. 920, s. 2

Sec. 20. Revenues and expenses of the judicial department

The General Assembly shall provide for the establishment of a schedule of court fees and costs which shall be uniform throughout the State within each division of the General Court of Justice. The operating expenses of the judicial department, other than compensation to process servers and other locally paid nonjudicial officers, shall be paid from State funds.

History.

1969, c. 1258, s. 1

Sec. 21. Fees, salaries, and emoluments

The General Assembly shall prescribe and regulate the fees, salaries, and emoluments of all officers provided for in this Article, but the salaries of Judges shall not be diminished during their continuance in office. In no case shall the compensation of any Judge or Magistrate be dependent upon his decision or upon the collection of costs.

History.

1969, c. 1258, s. 1

Sec. 22. Qualification of Justices and Judges

Only persons duly authorized to practice law in the courts of this State shall be eligible for election or appointment as a Justice of the Supreme Court, Judge of the Court of Appeals, Judge of the Superior Court, or Judge of District Court. This section shall not apply to persons elected to or serving in such capacities on or before January 1, 1981.

History.

1969, c. 1258, s. 1; 1979, c. 638, s. 1

ARTICLE IX. EDUCATION

Sec. 7. County school fund; State fund for certain moneys

(a) Except as provided in subsection (b) of this section, all moneys, stocks, bonds, and other property belonging to a county school fund, and the clear proceeds of all penalties and forfeitures and of all fines collected in the several counties for any breach of the penal laws of the State, shall belong to and remain in the several counties, and shall be faithfully appropriated and used exclusively for maintaining free public schools.

(b) The General Assembly may place in a State fund the clear proceeds of all civil penalties, forfeitures, and fines which are collected by State agencies and which belong to the public schools pursuant to subsection (a) of this section. Moneys in such State fund shall be faithfully appropriated by the General Assembly, on a per pupil basis, to the counties, to be used exclusively for maintaining free public schools.

History.
1969, c. 1258, s. 1; 2003-423, s. 1

ARTICLE XI.
PUNISHMENTS,
CORRECTIONS, AND
CHARITIES

Sec. 2. Death punishment

The object of punishments being not only to satisfy justice, but also to reform the offender and thus prevent crime, murder, arson, burglary, and rape, and these only, may be punishable with death, if the General Assembly shall so enact.

History.
1969, c. 1258, s. 1

Sec. 3. Charitable and correctional institutions and agencies

Such charitable, benevolent, penal, and correctional institutions and agencies as the needs of humanity and the public good may require shall be established and operated by the State under such organization and in such manner as the General Assembly may prescribe.

History.
1969, c. 1258, s. 1

Sec. 4. Welfare policy; board of public welfare

Beneficent provision for the poor, the unfortunate, and the orphan is one of the first duties of a civilized and a Christian state. Therefore the General Assembly shall provide for and define the duties of a board of public welfare.

History.
1969, c. 1258, s. 1

Constitution of North Carolina

Index

INDEX

SAFE HAVEN FOR INFANTS.
Child abuse or neglect.
Exceptions, §§14-318.2, 14-318.4.
Infants under seven days of age.
Voluntary delivery to individual by infant's parents.
Abandonment of child or nonsupport.
Not prosecuted for, §14-322.3.
Temporary custody, §7B-500.
Termination of parental rights.
Grounds, §7B-1111.

SAFETY ZONES.
Driving through prohibited, §20-160.

SAGE OF THE SEERS.
Salvia divinorum.
Manufacture, sale, delivery, possession.
Unlawful, §14-401.23.

SALIVA SAMPLES.
Criminal identification, §§15A-271 to 15A-282.

SALLY D.
Salvia divinorum.
Manufacture, sale, delivery, possession.
Unlawful, §14-401.23.

SALVAGE.
Abandoned shipwrecks and other underwater sites.
Criminal record checks of applicants for permit or license, §143B-948.

SALVIA DIVINORUM.
Possession.
Unlawful, §14-401.23.

SANCTIONS.
Citations, §15A-302.
Infractions, §14-3.1.
Pretrial motions.
Failure to file, §15A-952.
Punitive damages actions.
Frivolous or malicious actions, §1D-45.
Sentencing generally. See SENTENCING.
Subpoenas.
Failure to obey subpoena, §1A-1 Rule 45.

SANCTUARY ORDINANCES.
City adoption prohibited, §160A-205.2.
County adoption prohibited, §153A-145.5.

SANITARY DISTRICTS.
Motor vehicles, special license plates, §20-84.

SATELLITE-BASED MONITORING.
Electronic monitoring of sex offenders, §§14-208.40 to 14-208.45.
Parole.
Mandatory conditions, §15A-1374.
Post-release supervision.
Special conditions, §15A-1368.4.
Probation, §15A-1343.
Electronic technology in criminal process and procedure.
Definitions, §15A-101.1.

SAWED-OFF SHOTGUN.
Weapon of mass death and destruction, §14-288.8.

SBI, §§143B-915 to 143B-987.

SCALES.
Drug paraphernalia, §§90-113.20 to 90-113.24.

SCALPING TICKETS.
Sale of tickets in excess of printed price, §14-344.
Internet resale, §14-344.1.
Software to interfere with operation of ticket seller, §14-344.2.
Train tickets, §14-343.

SCHOOL BUSES.
Authority of state board of education, §115C-240.
Automated camera or video recording system.
Installation and operation of automated school bus safety camera, §115C-242.1.
Person failing to stop for bus receiving or discharging passengers.
Use in detecting and prosecuting violations, §20-217.
Disorderly conduct, §14-288.4.
Drivers.
Standard qualifications, §20-218.
Inspections.
Exception, §20-183.2.
Railroad grade crossings.
Stopping required, §20-142.3.
Red lights, use, §20-130.1.
Stopping for properly marked school buses, §20-217.
Student liability for trespass or vandalism, §115C-399.
Trespass, §14-132.2.
Vandalism, §§14-132.2, 115C-399.

SCHOOL COUNSELOR PRIVILEGE, §8-53.4.

SCHOOL PERSONNEL.
Altercations between students.
Discipline of employee acting in accordance with local board policies, prohibition, §115C-390.3.
Criminal history records checks, §143B-931.
Employees and applicants for department of public instruction, §143B-954.
Cyber-bullying by student, §14-458.2.
Misdemeanor assault on employee or volunteer, §14-33.
Taking indecent liberties with a student, §14-202.4.

SCHOOLS.
Altercations or fights between students.
School employee taking actions to end, §14-33.
Arson, §14-60.
Compulsory school attendance, §§115C-378, 115C-380.
County school fund.
Composition, NC Const Art IX §7.
Criminal record checks of school personnel, §143B-931.
Criminal records checks for department of public instruction employees and applicants, §143B-954.
Crisis kits, §115C-105.52.
Discipline of students, §§115C-390.1 to 115C-391.1.
Driver education, §§115C-215, 115C-216.
Emergencies.
Anonymous tip lines for internal or external risks to buildings and activities, §115C-105.51.
Lockdown exercises for schools, §115C-105.49.
Schematic diagrams of school buildings.
Not considered public records, §§115C-105.53, 115C-105.54.
Provision to emergency management division of department of public safety, §115C-105.54.
Provision to local law enforcement agencies, §115C-105.53.
Standards for preparation and content of diagrams, §115C-105.53.
School crisis kits, §115C-105.52.
School risk and response management system, §115C-105.49A.

Hotlines.
Anonymous tip lines for internal or external risks to buildings and activities, §115C-105.51.
Lockdown exercises for schools, §115C-105.49.
Probation officers, visiting students at school, §115C-46.2.
Safe and orderly schools.
Anonymous tip lines for internal or external risks to buildings and activities, §115C-105.51.
Sex offenders.
Residence restrictions, §14-208.16.
Unlawful presence on premises, §14-208.18.
School personnel, email notifications, §14-208.19.
Speed limits in school zones, §20-141.1.
State's duty to guard and maintain, NC Const Art I §15.
Taking indecent liberties with a student, §14-202.4.
Threat of mass violence.
Conditional discharge if under age 20, §14-277.8.
Educational property, §14-277.6.
False report of, §14-277.5.
Weapons.
Possession or carrying, §14-269.2.

SCOTLAND COUNTY.
Ambulance services.
Obtaining without intending to pay, §14-111.2.

SCRAP AND SALVAGE DEALERS.
Failure to keep records of certain items purchased, §66-10.
Purchase of vehicle for scrap or parts only, §20-62.1.
Secondary metals recyclers, §§66-420 to 66-431.

SCUBA DIVING.
Safety violation, §§75A-13.1, 75A-18.

SEA OATS.
Unlawful to take, §14-129.2.

SEARCH AND RESCUE ANIMALS.
Disposition of retired service animals, §20-187.4.
Self defense.
Defense to killing, assaulting, §14-163.1.

SEARCHES AND SEIZURES.
Consent searches, §§15A-221 to 15A-223.
Criminal gangs.
Seizure and forfeiture of property, §14-50.23.
Parole.
Warrantless searches, conditions, §15A-1374.
Post-release supervision.
Warrantless searches, conditions, §15A-1368.4.
Probation.
Warrantless searches, conditions, §15A-1343.
Warrants, §§15A-241 to 15A-259.

SEARCH WARRANTS, §§15A-241 to 15A-259.
Administrative search and inspection warrants, §15-27.2.
Amendment to show ownership to property, §15-24.1.
General warrants, NC Const Art I §20.
Obscenity offenses, §14-190.20.
Public record, §132-1.4.
Quashing for informality, §15-153.
Riot areas.
Warrants to inspect vehicles, §14-288.11.

SEASHORE.
Displaying false lights on seashore, §14-282.